THE EUROPA WORLD YEAR BOOK 2014

VOLUME 1

PART ONE: INTERNATIONAL ORGANIZATIONS
PART TWO: AFGHANISTAN–JORDAN

Routledge
Taylor & Francis Group
LONDON AND NEW YORK

55th edition published 2014
by Routledge
2 Park Square, Milton Park, Abingdon, Oxon, OX14 4RN

and by Routledge
711 Third Avenue, New York, NY 10017

Routledge is an imprint of the Taylor & Francis Group, an Informa business

First published 1926

ISBN: 978-1-85743-714-0 (The Set)
978-1-85743-715-7 (Vol. 1)
ISSN: 0956-2273

Senior Editor: Juliet Love

Senior Editor, Statistics: Philip McIntyre

Senior Editor, Directory: Iain Frame

Regional Editors: Imogen Gladman, Cathy Hartley, Dominic Heaney, Neil Higgins, Christopher Matthews, Jacqueline West

International Organizations Editor: Helen Canton

Contributing Editors: Catriona Holman, Jillian O'Brien

Editorial Assistant: Lydia de Cruz

Statistics Researchers: Varun Wadhawan *(Team Manager)*, Mohd Khalid Ansari *(Senior Research and Training Associate)*, Meghal Arora, Swati Gambhir, Suchi Kedia, Nirbachita Sarkar

Directory Editorial Researchers: Arijit Khasnobis *(Team Manager)*, Rima Kar *(Deputy Team Leader)*, Birendra Pratap Nayak, Thoithoi Pukhrambam, C. Sandhya *(Senior Editorial Researchers)*, Shubha Banerjee *(Editorial Research Associate)*, Bhawna Chauhan, Swati Chopra, Anveshi Gupta, Sneha Malik, Rituparna Sengupta, Surabhi Srivastava

Contributors: Christopher Bell, Rebecca Bomford, Camilla Chew, Katie Dawson, Lucy Dean, Driss Fatih, Kirstie Hughes, Joanne Maher, Catriona Marcham, Elizabeth Salzman

Editorial Director: Paul Kelly

Typeset in New Century Schoolbook
by Data Standards Limited, Frome, Somerset

FSC
www.fsc.org
MIX
Paper from responsible sources
FSC® C020872

FOREWORD

THE EUROPA WORLD YEAR BOOK was first published in 1926. Since 1960 it has appeared in annual two-volume editions, and has become established as an authoritative reference work, providing a wealth of detailed information on the political, economic and commercial institutions of the world.

Volume 1 contains a comprehensive listing of more than 2,000 international organizations, commissions and specialized bodies, and the first part of the alphabetical survey of countries of the world, from Afghanistan to Jordan. Volume 2 contains countries from Kazakhstan to Zimbabwe. An Index of Territories covered in both volumes is to be found at the end of Volume 2.

The International Organizations section gives extensive coverage to the United Nations and its related agencies and bodies. There are also detailed articles concerning other major international and regional organizations; entries for many affiliated organizations appear within these articles. In addition, the section includes briefer details of some 1,300 other international organizations. A comprehensive Index of International Organizations is included at the end of Volume 1.

Each country is covered by an individual chapter, containing: an introductory survey including contemporary political history, economic affairs, constitution and government, regional and international co-operation, and public holidays; a statistical survey presenting the latest available figures on demographics, labour force, health and welfare, agriculture, forestry, fishing, mining, industry, currency and exchange rates, government finance, international reserves and the monetary sector, cost of living, national accounts, balance of payments, external trade, railways, roads, shipping, civil aviation, tourism, media and telecommunications, and education; and a directory section listing names, addresses and other useful facts about organizations in the fields of government, election commissions, political parties, diplomatic representation, judiciary, religions, the media, telecommunications, banking, insurance, trade and industry, development organizations, chambers of commerce, industrial and trade associations, utilities, trade unions, transport, tourism, defence, and education.

The entire content of the print edition of THE EUROPA WORLD YEAR BOOK is available online at www.europaworld.com. This prestigious resource incorporates sophisticated search and browse functions as well as specially commissioned visual and statistical content. An ongoing programme of updates of key areas of information ensures currency of content, and enhances the richness of the coverage for which THE EUROPA WORLD YEAR BOOK is renowned.

Readers are referred to the nine titles in the Europa Regional Surveys of the World series: AFRICA SOUTH OF THE SAHARA, CENTRAL AND SOUTH-EASTERN EUROPE, EASTERN EUROPE, RUSSIA AND CENTRAL ASIA, THE FAR EAST AND AUSTRALASIA, THE MIDDLE EAST AND NORTH AFRICA, SOUTH AMERICA, CENTRAL AMERICA AND THE CARIBBEAN, SOUTH ASIA, THE USA AND CANADA, and WESTERN EUROPE, available both in print and online, offer comprehensive analysis at regional, sub-regional and country level. More detailed coverage of international organizations is to be found in THE EUROPA DIRECTORY OF INTERNATIONAL ORGANIZATIONS.

The content of THE EUROPA WORLD YEAR BOOK is extensively revised and updated by a variety of methods, including direct contact with organizations covered. Many other sources are used, such as national statistical offices, government departments and diplomatic missions. The editors thank the innumerable individuals and organizations worldwide whose generous co-operation in providing current information for this edition is invaluable in presenting the most accurate and up-to-date material available.

May 2014

ACKNOWLEDGEMENTS

The editors gratefully acknowledge particular indebtedness for permission to reproduce material from the following sources: the United Nations' statistical databases and *Demographic Yearbook*, *Statistical Yearbook*, *Monthly Bulletin of Statistics*, *Industrial Commodity Statistics Yearbook* and *International Trade Statistics Yearbook*; the United Nations Educational, Scientific and Cultural Organization's *Statistical Yearbook* and Institute for Statistics database; the *Human Development Report* of the United Nations Development Programme; the Food and Agriculture Organization of the United Nations' statistical database; the statistical databases of the World Health Organization; the statistical databases of the UNCTAD/WTO International Trade Centre; the International Labour Office's statistical database and *Yearbook of Labour Statistics*; the World Bank's *World Bank Atlas*, *Global Development Finance*, *World Development Report* and *World Development Indicators*; the International Monetary Fund's statistical database, *International Financial Statistics* and *Government Finance Statistics Yearbook*; the World Tourism Organization's *Compendium* and *Yearbook of Tourism Statistics*; the US Geological Survey; the International Telecommunication Union; the International Road Federation's *World Road Statistics*; Lloyd's List; and *The Military Balance 2014*, a publication of the International Institute for Strategic Studies, Arundel House, 13–15 Arundel Street, London WC2R 3DX. Statistics Canada information is used with the permission of Statistics Canada. Users are forbidden to copy this material and/or redisseminate the data, in an original or modified form, for commercial purposes, without the expressed permission of Statistics Canada. Information on the availability of the wide range of data from Statistics Canada can be obtained from Statistics Canada's Regional Offices, its website at www.statcan.ca, and its toll-free access number 1-800-263-1136.

HEALTH AND WELFARE STATISTICS: SOURCES AND DEFINITIONS

Total fertility rate Source: WHO Statistical Information System (part of the Global Health Observatory). The number of children that would be born per woman, assuming no female mortality at child-bearing ages and the age-specific fertility rates of a specified country and reference period.

Under-5 mortality rate Source: WHO Statistical Information System. Defined by WHO as the probability of a child born in a specific year or period dying before reaching the age of five, if subject to the age-specific mortality rates of that year or period.

HIV/AIDS Source: UNAIDS. Estimated percentage of adults aged 15 to 49 years living with HIV/AIDS. < indicates 'fewer than'.

Health expenditure Source: WHO Statistical Information System.
US $ per head (PPP)
International dollar estimates, derived by dividing local currency units by an estimate of their purchasing-power parity (PPP) compared with the US dollar. PPPs are the rates of currency conversion that equalize the purchasing power of different currencies by eliminating the differences in price levels between countries.
% of GDP
GDP levels for OECD countries follow the most recent UN System of National Accounts. For non-OECD countries a value was estimated by utilizing existing UN, IMF and World Bank data.
Public expenditure
Government health-related outlays plus expenditure by social schemes compulsorily affiliated with a sizeable share of the population, and extrabudgetary funds allocated to health services. Figures include grants or loans provided by international agencies, other national authorities, and sometimes commercial banks.

Access to water and sanitation Source: WHO/UNICEF Joint Monitoring Programme on Water Supply and Sanitation (JMP) (Progress on Drinking Water and Sanitation, 2013 Update). Defined in terms of the percentage of the population using improved facilities in terms of the type of technology and levels of service afforded. For water, this includes house connections, public standpipes, boreholes with handpumps, protected dug wells, protected spring and rainwater collection; allowance is also made for other locally defined technologies. Sanitation is defined to include connection to a sewer or septic tank system, pour-flush latrine, simple pit or ventilated improved pit latrine, again with allowance for acceptable local technologies. Access to water and sanitation does not imply that the level of service or quality of water is 'adequate' or 'safe'.

Carbon dioxide emissions Source: World Bank, World Development Indicators database, citing the Carbon Dioxide Information Analysis Center (sponsored by the US Department of Energy). Emissions comprise those resulting from the burning of fossil fuels (including those produced during consumption of solid, liquid and gas fuels and from gas flaring) and from the manufacture of cement.

Human Development Index (HDI) Source: UNDP, *Human Development Report* (2012). A summary of human development measured by three basic dimensions: prospects for a long and healthy life, measured by life expectancy at birth; access to knowledge, measured by a combination of mean years of schooling and expected years of schooling; and standard of living, measured by GNI per head (PPP US $). The index value obtained lies between zero and one. A value above 0.796 indicates very high human development, between 0.710 and 0.796 high human development, between 0.534 and 0.710 medium human development and below 0.534 low human development. A centralized data source for all three dimensions was not available for all countries. In some cases other data sources were used to calculate a substitute value; however, this was excluded from the ranking. Other countries, including non-UNDP members, were excluded from the HDI altogether. In total, 187 countries were ranked for 2012.

CONTENTS

* A complete Index of International Organizations is to be found at the end of this volume.

PART TWO

Afghanistan–Jordan

An Index of Territories is to be found at the end of Volume 2.

ABBREVIATIONS

AB	Aktiebolag (Joint-Stock Company); Alberta
Abog.	Abogado (Lawyer)
Acad.	Academician; Academy
ACP	African, Caribbean and Pacific (countries)
ACT	Australian Capital Territory
AD	anno Domini
ADB	African Development Bank; Asian Development Bank
ADC	aide-de-camp
ADIZ	air defence identification zone
Adm.	Admiral
admin.	administration
AEC	African Economic Community; African Economic Conference
AfDB	African Development Bank
AG	Aktiengesellschaft (Joint-Stock Company)
AGOA	Africa Growth and Opportunity Act
AH	anno Hegirae
a.i.	ad interim
AID	(US) Agency for International Development
AIDS	acquired immunodeficiency syndrome
AK	Alaska
Al.	Aleja (Alley, Avenue)
AL	Alabama
ALADI	Asociación Latinoamericana de Integración
Alt.	Alternate
AM	Amplitude Modulation
a.m.	ante meridiem (before noon)
amalg.	amalgamated
Apdo	Apartado (Post Box)
APEC	Asia-Pacific Economic Cooperation
approx.	approximately
Apt	Apartment
AR	Arkansas
ARV	advanced retroviral
AŞ	Anonim Şirketi (Joint-Stock Company)
A/S	Aktieselskab (Joint-Stock Company)
ASEAN	Association of South East Asian Nations
asscn	association
assoc.	associate
ASSR	Autonomous Soviet Socialist Republic
asst	assistant
AU	African Union
Aug.	August
auth.	authorized
av., Ave	Avenija, Avenue
Av., Avda	Avenida (Avenue)
Avv.	Avvocato (Lawyer)
AZ	Arizona
b.b.	bez broja (without number)
BC	British Columbia
BC	before Christ
Bd	Board
Bd, Bld, Blv., Blvd	Boulevard
b/d	barrels per day
BFPO	British Forces' Post Office
Bhd	Berhad (Public Limited Company)
Bldg	Building
blk	block
Blvr	Bulevar
BP	Boîte postale (Post Box)
br.(s)	branch(es)
Brig.	Brigadier
BSE	bovine spongiform encephalopathy
BSEC	(Organization of the) Black Sea Economic Cooperation
bte	boîte (box)
Bul.	Bulvar (boulevard)
bulv.	bulvaris (boulevard)
C	Centigrade
c.	circa; cuadra(s) (block(s))
CA	California
CACM	Central American Common Market
Cad.	Caddesi (Street)
CAP	Common Agricultural Policy
cap.	capital
Capt.	Captain
CAR	Central African Republic
CARICOM	Caribbean Community and Common Market
CBSS	Council of Baltic Sea States
CCL	Caribbean Congress of Labour
CDMA	Code Division Multiple Access
Cdre	Commodore
CEMAC	Communauté Economique et Monétaire de l'Afrique Centrale
Cen.	Central
CEO	Chief Executive Officer
CET	common external tariff
CFA	Communauté Financière Africaine; Coopération Financière en Afrique centrale
CFE	Treaty on Conventional Armed Forces in Europe
CFP	Common Fisheries Policy; Communauté française du Pacifique; Comptoirs français du Pacifique
Chair.	Chairman/person/woman
Chih.	Chihuahua
CI	Channel Islands
Cia	Companhia
Cía	Compañía
Cie	Compagnie
c.i.f.	cost, insurance and freight
C-in-C	Commander-in-Chief
circ.	circulation
CIS	Commonwealth of Independent States
CJD	Creutzfeldt-Jakob disease
cm	centimetre(s)
cnr	corner
CO	Colorado
Co	Company; County
c/o	care of
Coah.	Coahuila
Col	Colonel
Col.	Colima; Colonia
COMESA	Common Market for Eastern and Southern Africa
Comm.	Commission; Commendatore
Commdr	Commander
Commdt	Commandant
Commr	Commissioner
Cond.	Condiminio
Conf	Confederation
confs	conferences
Cont.	Contador (Accountant)
COO	Chief Operating Officer
COP	Conference of (the) Parties
Corp.	Corporate
Corpn	Corporation
CP	Case Postale, Caixa Postal, Casella Postale (Post Box); Communist Party
C por A	Compañía por Acciones (Joint Stock Company)
CPOB	Central Post Office Box
CPSU	Communist Party of the Soviet Union
Cres.	Crescent
CSCE	Conference on Security and Cooperation in Europe
CSTAL	Confederación Sindical de los Trabajadores de América Latina
CT	Connecticut
CTCA	Confederación de Trabajadores Centro-americanos
Cttee	Committee
cu	cubic
cwt	hundredweight
DC	District of Columbia; Distrito Capital; Distrito Central
d.d.	delniška družba, dioničko društvo (joint stock company)
DE	Delaware; Departamento Estatal
Dec.	December
Del.	Delegación
Dem.	Democrat; Democratic
Dep.	Deputy
dep.	deposits
Dept	Department
devt	development
DF	Distrito Federal
Dgo	Durango
Diag.	Diagonal
Dir	Director
Div.	Division(al)
DM	Deutsche Mark
DMZ	demilitarized zone
DNA	deoxyribonucleic acid
DN	Distrito Nacional
Doc.	Docent
Dott.	Dottore/essa
DPRK	Democratic People's Republic of Korea
Dr	Doctor
Dr.	Drive
Dra	Doctora
Dr Hab.	Doktor Habilitowany (Assistant Professor)
DRC	Democratic Republic of the Congo
DR-CAFTA	Dominican Republic-Central American Free Trade Agreement
Drs	Doctorandus
DU	depleted uranium
dwt	dead weight tons
E	East; Eastern
EAC	East African Community
EBRD	European Bank for Reconstruction and Development
EC	European Community
ECA	(United Nations) Economic Commission for Africa
ECE	(United Nations) Economic Commission for Europe
ECF	Extended Credit Facility
ECLAC	(United Nations) Economic Commission for Latin America and the Caribbean
ECO	Economic Cooperation Organization
Econ.	Economics; Economist
ECOSOC	(United Nations) Economic and Social Council

ABBREVIATIONS

ECOWAS Economic Community of West African States
ECU European Currency Unit
Edif. Edificio (Building)
edn edition
EEA European Economic Area
EFTA European Free Trade Association
e.g. exempli gratia (for example)
EIB European Investment Bank
EMS European Monetary System
EMU Economic and Monetary Union
eMv electron megavolt
Eng. Engineer; Engineering
EP Empresa Pública
ERM Exchange Rate Mechanism
ESACA Emisora de Capital Abierto Sociedad Anónima
Esc. Escuela; Escudos; Escritorio
ESCAP (United Nations) Economic and Social Commission for Asia and the Pacific
ESCWA (United Nations) Economic and Social Commission for Western Asia
esq. esquina (corner)
est. established; estimate; estimated
etc. et cetera
EU European Union
eV eingetragener Verein
excl. excluding
exec. executive
Ext. Extension

F Fahrenheit
f. founded
FAO Food and Agriculture Organization
f.a.s. free alongside ship
FDI foreign direct investment
Feb. February
Fed. Federal; Federation
feds federations
FL Florida
FM frequency modulation
fmr(ly) former(ly)
f.o.b. free on board
Fr Father
Fr. Franc
Fri. Friday
FRY Federal Republic of Yugoslavia
ft foot (feet)
FTA free trade agreement/area
FYRM former Yugoslav republic of Macedonia

g gram(s)
g. gatve (street)
GA Georgia
GATT General Agreement on Tariffs and Trade
GCC Gulf Cooperation Council
Gdns Gardens
GDP gross domestic product
GEF Gobal Environment Facility
Gen. General
GeV giga electron volts
GM genetically modified
GmbH Gesellschaft mit beschränkter Haftung (Limited Liability Company)
GMO(s) genetically modified organism(s)
GMT Greenwich Mean Time
GNI gross national income
GNP gross national product
Gov. Governor
Govt Government
GPOB General Post Office Box
Gro Guerrero
grt gross registered tons
GSM Global System for Mobile Communications
Gto Guanajuato
GWh gigawatt hour(s)

ha hectares
HD high-definition
HDI Human Development Index
HDTV high-definition television
HE His/Her Eminence; His/Her Excellency
hf hlutafelag (Limited Company)
HI Hawaii
HIPC heavily indebted poor country
HIV human immunodeficiency virus
hl hectolitre(s)
HLTF High Level Task Force
HM His/Her Majesty
Hon. Honorary, Honourable
HPAI highly pathogenic avian influenza
HQ Headquarters
HRH His/Her Royal Highness
HS Harmonized System
HSH His/Her Serene Highness
Hwy Highway

IA Iowa
IBRD International Bank for Reconstruction and Development
ICC International Chamber of Commerce; International Criminal Court
ICRC International Committee of the Red Cross
ICT information and communication technology
ICTR International Criminal Tribunal for Rwanda
ICTY International Criminal Tribunal for the former Yugoslavia
ID Idaho
IDA International Development Association
IDB Inter-American Development Bank
IDPs internally displaced persons
i.e. id est (that is to say)
IFC International Finance Corporation
IGAD Intergovernmental Authority on Development
IHL International Humanitarian Law
IL Illinois
ILO International Labour Organization/Office
IMF International Monetary Fund
IML International Migration Law
in (ins) inch (inches)
IN Indiana
Inc, Incorp. Incd Incorporated
incl. including
Ind. Independent
INF Intermediate-Range Nuclear Forces
Ing. Engineer
Insp. Inspector
Int. International
Inzå. Engineer
IP intellectual property
IPU Inter-Parliamentary Union
Ir Engineer
IRF International Road Federation
irreg. irregular
Is Islands
ISIC International Standard Industrial Classification
IT information technology
ITU International Telecommunication Union
ITUC International Trade Union Confederation
Iur. Lawyer
IUU illegal, unreported and unregulated

Jal. Jalisco
Jan. January
Jnr Junior
Jr Jonkheer (Esquire); Junior
Jt Joint

Kav. Kaveling (Plot)
kg kilogram(s)
KG Kommandit Gesellschaft (Limited Partnership)
kHz kilohertz
KK Kaien Kaisha (Limited Company)
km kilometre(s)
kom. komnata (room)
kor. korpus (block)
k'och. k'ochasi (street)
KS Kansas
küç küçasi (street)
kv. kvartal (apartment block); kvartira (apartment)
kW kilowatt(s)
kWh kilowatt hour(s)
KY Kentucky

LA Louisiana
lauk laukums (square)
lb pound(s)
LDCs Least Developed Countries
Lic. Licenciado
Licda Licenciada
LLC Limited Liability Company
LNG liquefied natural gas
LPG liquefied petroleum gas
Lt, Lieut Lieutenant
Ltd Limited

m metre(s)
m. million
MA Massachusetts
Maj. Major
Man. Manager; managing
MB Manitoba
mbH mit beschränkter Haftung (with limited liability)
MD Maryland
MDG Millennium Development Goal
MDRI multilateral debt relief initiative
ME Maine
Me Maître
mem.(s) member(s)
MEP Member of the European Parliament
Mercosul Mercado Comum do Sul (Southern Common Market)
Mercosur Mercado Común del Sur (Southern Common Market)
MERS Middle East respiratory syndrome coronavirus
Méx. México
MFN most favoured nation
mfrs manufacturers
Mgr Monseigneur; Monsignor
MHz megahertz
MI Michigan
MIA missing in action
Mich. Michoacán
MIGA Multilateral Investment Guarantee Agency
Mil. Military
Mlle Mademoiselle
mm millimetre(s)
Mme Madame
MN Minnesota
mnt. mante (road)
MO Missouri
Mon. Monday
Mor. Morelos
MOU Memorandum of Understanding
movt movement
MP Member of Parliament
MS Mississippi
MSS Manuscripts

MT	Montana
MW	megawatt(s); medium wave
MWh	megawatt hour(s)
N	North; Northern
n.a.	not available
nab.	naberezhnaya (embankment, quai)
NAFTA	North American Free Trade Agreement
nám.	náměstí (square)
Nat.	National
NATO	North Atlantic Treaty Organization
Nay.	Nayarit
NB	New Brunswick
NC	North Carolina
NCD	National Capital District
NCO	non-commissioned officer
ND	North Dakota
NE	Nebraska; North-East
NEPAD	New Partnership for Africa's Development
NGO	non-governmental organization
NH	New Hampshire
NJ	New Jersey
NL	Newfoundland and Labrador, Nuevo León
NM	New Mexico
NMP	net material product
no	numéro, número (number)
no.	number
Nov.	November
NPT	Non-Proliferation Treaty
nr	near
nrt	net registered tons
NS	Nova Scotia
NSW	New South Wales
NT	Northwest Territories
NU	Nunavut Territory
NV	Naamloze Vennootschap (Limited Company); Nevada
NW	North-West
NY	New York
NZ	New Zealand
OAPEC	Organization of Arab Petroleum Exporting Countries
OAS	Organization of American States
OAU	Organization of African Unity
Oax.	Oaxaca
Oct.	October
OECD	Organisation for Economic Co-operation and Development
OECS	Organisation of Eastern Caribbean States
Of.	Oficina (Office)
OH	Ohio
OIC	Organization of Islamic Cooperation
OK	Oklahoma
ON	Ontario
OPEC	Organization of the Petroleum Exporting Countries
opp.	opposite
OR	Oregon
ORB	OPEC Reference Basket
Org.	Organization
ORIT	Organización Regional Interamericana de Trabajadores
OSCE	Organization for Security and Co-operation in Europe
p.	page
p.a.	per annum
PA	Palestinian Authority; Pennsylvania
Parl.	Parliament(ary)
per.	pereulok (lane, alley)
PE	Prince Edward Island
Perm. Rep.	Permanent Representative
PF	Postfach (Post Box)
PICTs	Pacific Island countries and territories
PK	Posta Kutusu (Post Box)
Pl.	Plac, Plads (square)
pl.	platz; place; ploshchad (square)
PLC	Public Limited Company
PLO	Palestine Liberation Organization
p.m.	post meridiem (after noon)
PMB	Private Mail Bag
PNA	Palestinian National Authority
POB	Post Office Box
pp.	pages
PPP	purchasing-power parity
PQ	Québec
PR	Puerto Rico
pr.	prospekt, prospekti (avenue)
Pres.	President
PRGF	Poverty Reduction and Growth Facility
Prin.	Principal
Prof.	Professor
Propr	Proprietor
Prov.	Province; Provincial; Provinciale (Dutch)
prov.	provulok (lane)
PRSP	Poverty Reduction Strategy Paper
PSI	Policy Support Instrument, Poverty Strategies Initiative
pst.	puistotie (avenue)
PT	Perseroan Terbatas (Limited Company)
Pte	Private; Puente (Bridge)
Pty	Proprietary
p.u.	paid up
publ.	publication; published
Publr	Publisher
Pue.	Puebla
Pvt	Private
QC	Québec
QIP	Quick Impact Project
Qld	Queensland
Qro	Querétaro
Q. Roo	Quintana Roo
q.v.	quod vide (to which refer)
Rag.	Ragioniere (Accountant)
Rd	Road
R(s)	rand; rupee(s)
REC	regional economic communities
reg., regd	register; registered
reorg.	reorganized
Rep.	Republic; Republican; Representative
Repub.	Republic
res	reserve(s)
retd	retired
Rev.	Reverend
RI	Rhode Island
RJ	Rio de Janeiro
Rm	Room
RN	Royal Navy
ro-ro	roll-on roll-off
RP	Recette principale
Rp.(s)	rupiah(s)
Rpto	Reparto (Estate)
RSFSR	Russian Soviet Federative Socialist Republic
Rt	Right
S	South; Southern; San
SA	Société Anonyme, Sociedad Anónima (Limited Company); South Australia
SAARC	South Asian Association for Regional Cooperation
SACN	South American Community of Nations
SADC	Southern African Development Community
SA de CV	Sociedad Anónima de Capital Variable (Variable Capital Company)
SAECA	Sociedad Anónima Emisora de Capital Abierto
SAR	Special Administrative Region
SARL	Sociedade Anônima de Responsabilidade Limitada (Joint-Stock Company of Limited Liability)
SARS	Severe Acute Respiratory Syndrome
Sat.	Saturday
SC	South Carolina
SD	South Dakota
Sdn Bhd	Sendirian Berhad (Private Limited Company)
SDR(s)	Special Drawing Right(s)
SE	South-East
Sec.	Secretary
Secr.	Secretariat
Sen.	Senior; Senator
Sept.	September
SER	Sua Eccellenza Reverendissima (His Eminence)
SFRY	Socialist Federal Republic of Yugoslavia
SGP	Stability and Growth Pact
Sin.	Sinaloa
SIS	Small(er) Island States
SITC	Standard International Trade Classification
SJ	Society of Jesus
SK	Saskatchewan
Skt	Sankt (Saint)
SLP	San Luis Potosí
SMEs	small and medium-sized enterprises
s/n	sin número (without number)
Soc.	Society
Sok.	Sokak (Street)
Son.	Sonora
Şos.	Şosea (Road)
SP	São Paulo
SpA	Società per Azioni (Joint-Stock Company)
Sq.	Square
sq	square (in measurements)
Sr	Senior; Señor
Sra	Señora
Srl	Società a Responsabilità Limitata (Limited Company)
SRSG	Special Representative of the UN Secretary-General
SSR	Soviet Socialist Republic
St	Saint, Sint; Street
Sta	Santa
Ste	Sainte
STI(s)	sexually transmitted infection(s)
Str., str.	Strasse, strada, stradă, strasse (street)
str-la	stradelă (street)
subs.	subscribed; subscriptions
Sun.	Sunday
Supt	Superintendent
SUV	sports utility vehicle
sv.	Saint
SW	South-West
Tab.	Tabasco
Tamps	Tamaulipas
TAŞ	Turkiye Anonim Şirketi (Turkish Joint-Stock Company)
Tas	Tasmania
TD	Teachta Dàla (Member of Parliament)
tech., techn.	technical
tel.	telephone
TEU	20-ft equivalent unit
Thur.	Thursday
TN	Tennessee
tř	třída (avenue)

Treas.	Treasurer
Tue.	Tuesday
TV	television
TWh	terawatt hour(s)
TX	Texas
u.	utca (street)
u/a	unit of account
UAE	United Arab Emirates
UEE	Unidade Económica Estatal
UEMOA	Union Economique et Monétaire Ouest-Africaine
UK	United Kingdom
ul.	ulica, ulitsa (street)
UM	ouguiya
UN	United Nations
UNAIDS	United Nations Joint Programme on HIV/AIDS
UNCTAD	United Nations Conference on Trade and Development
UNDP	United Nations Development Programme
UNEP	United Nations Environment Programme
UNESCO	United Nations Educational, Scientific and Cultural Organization
UNHCHR	UN High Commissioner for Human Rights
UNHCR	United Nations High Commissioner for Refugees
UNICEF	United Nations Children's Fund
Univ.	University
UNODC	United Nations Office on Drugs and Crime
UNRWA	United Nations Relief and Works Agency for Palestine Refugees in the Near East
UNWTO	World Tourism Organization
Urb.	Urbanización (District)
US	United States
USA	United States of America
USAID	United States Agency for International Development
USSR	Union of Soviet Socialist Republics
UT	Utah
VA	Virginia
VAT	value-added tax
VEB	Volkseigener Betrieb (Public Company)
v-CJD	new variant Creutzfeldt-Jakob disease
Ven.	Venerable
Ver.	Veracruz
VHF	Very High Frequency
VI	(US) Virgin Islands
Vic	Victoria
Vn	Veien (Street)
vol.(s)	volume(s)
VT	Vermont
vul.	vulitsa, vulytsa (street)
W	West; Western
WA	Washington (State); Western Australia
Wed.	Wednesday
WEU	Western European Union
WFP	World Food Programme
WFTU	World Federation of Trade Unions
WHO	World Health Organization
WI	Wisconsin
WSSD	World Summit on Sustainable Development
WTO	World Trade Organization
WV	West Virginia
WY	Wyoming
yr	year
YT	Yukon Territory
Yuc.	Yucatán

INTERNATIONAL TELEPHONE CODES

To make international calls to telephone and fax numbers listed in *The Europa World Year Book*, dial the international access code of the country from which you are calling, followed by the appropriate country code for the organization you wish to call (listed below), followed by the area code (if applicable) and telephone or fax number listed in the entry.

	Country code	+ or – GMT*
Abkhazia	7	+4
Afghanistan	93	+4½
Åland Islands	358	+2
Albania	355	+1
Algeria	213	+1
American Samoa	1 684	–11
Andorra	376	+1
Angola	244	+1
Anguilla	1 264	–4
Antigua and Barbuda	1 268	–4
Argentina	54	–3
Armenia	374	+4
Aruba	297	–4
Ascension Island	247	0
Australia	61	+8 to +10
Austria	43	+1
Azerbaijan	994	+5
Bahamas	1 242	–5
Bahrain	973	+3
Bangladesh	880	+6
Barbados	1 246	–4
Belarus	375	+2
Belgium	32	+1
Belize	501	–6
Benin	229	+1
Bermuda	1 441	–4
Bhutan	975	+6
Bolivia	591	–4
Bonaire	599	–4
Bosnia and Herzegovina	387	+1
Botswana	267	+2
Brazil	55	–3 to –4
British Indian Ocean Territory (Diego Garcia)	246	+5
British Virgin Islands	1 284	–4
Brunei	673	+8
Bulgaria	359	+2
Burkina Faso	226	0
Burundi	257	+2
Cambodia	855	+7
Cameroon	237	+1
Canada	1	–3 to –8
Cape Verde	238	–1
Cayman Islands	1 345	–5
Central African Republic	236	+1
Ceuta	34	+1
Chad	235	+1
Chile	56	–4
China, People's Republic	86	+8
Christmas Island	61	+7
Cocos (Keeling) Islands	61	+6½
Colombia	57	–5
Comoros	269	+3
Congo, Democratic Republic	243	+1
Congo, Republic	242	+1
Cook Islands	682	–10
Costa Rica	506	–6
Côte d'Ivoire	225	0
Croatia	385	+1
Cuba	53	–5
Curaçao	599	–4
Cyprus	357	+2
Czech Republic	420	+1
Denmark	45	+1

	Country code	+ or – GMT*
Djibouti	253	+3
Dominica	1 767	–4
Dominican Republic	1 809	–4
Ecuador	593	–5
Egypt	20	+2
El Salvador	503	–6
Equatorial Guinea	240	+1
Eritrea	291	+3
Estonia	372	+2
Ethiopia	251	+3
Falkland Islands	500	–4
Faroe Islands	298	0
Fiji	679	+12
Finland	358	+2
France	33	+1
French Guiana	594	–3
French Polynesia	689	–9 to –10
Gabon	241	+1
Gambia	220	0
Georgia	995	+4
Germany	49	+1
Ghana	233	0
Gibraltar	350	+1
Greece	30	+2
Greenland	299	–1 to –4
Grenada	1 473	–4
Guadeloupe	590	–4
Guam	1 671	+10
Guatemala	502	–6
Guernsey	44	0
Guinea	224	0
Guinea-Bissau	245	0
Guyana	592	–4
Haiti	509	–5
Honduras	504	–6
Hong Kong	852	+8
Hungary	36	+1
Iceland	354	0
India	91	+5½
Indonesia	62	+7 to +9
Iran	98	+3½
Iraq	964	+3
Ireland	353	0
Isle of Man	44	0
Israel	972	+2
Italy	39	+1
Jamaica	1 876	–5
Japan	81	+9
Jersey	44	0
Jordan	962	+2
Kazakhstan	7	+6
Kenya	254	+3
Kiribati	686	+12 to +13
Korea, Democratic People's Republic (North Korea)	850	+9
Korea, Republic (South Korea)	82	+9
Kosovo	381†	+3
Kuwait	965	+3
Kyrgyzstan	996	+5
Laos	856	+7
Latvia	371	+2
Lebanon	961	+2
Lesotho	266	+2
Liberia	231	0

	Country code	+ or – GMT*
Libya	218	+1
Liechtenstein	423	+1
Lithuania	370	+2
Luxembourg	352	+1
Macao	853	+8
Macedonia, former Yugoslav republic	389	+1
Madagascar	261	+3
Malawi	265	+2
Malaysia	60	+8
Maldives	960	+5
Mali	223	0
Malta	356	+1
Marshall Islands	692	+12
Martinique	596	–4
Mauritania	222	0
Mauritius	230	+4
Mayotte	262	+3
Melilla	34	+1
Mexico	52	–6 to –7
Micronesia, Federated States	691	+10 to +11
Moldova	373	+2
Monaco	377	+1
Mongolia	976	+7 to +9
Montenegro	382	+1
Montserrat	1 664	–4
Morocco	212	0
Mozambique	258	+2
Myanmar	95	+6½
Nagornyi Karabakh	374	+4
Namibia	264	+2
Nauru	674	+12
Nepal	977	+5¾
Netherlands	31	+1
New Caledonia	687	+11
New Zealand	64	+12
Nicaragua	505	–6
Niger	227	+1
Nigeria	234	+1
Niue	683	–11
Norfolk Island	672	+11½
Northern Mariana Islands	1 670	+10
Norway	47	+1
Oman	968	+4
Pakistan	92	+5
Palau	680	+9
Palestinian Territories	970 or 972	+2
Panama	507	–5
Papua New Guinea	675	+10
Paraguay	595	–4
Peru	51	–5
Philippines	63	+8
Pitcairn Islands	872	–8
Poland	48	+1
Portugal	351	0
Puerto Rico	1 787	–4
Qatar	974	+3
Réunion	262	+4
Romania	40	+2
Russian Federation	7	+3 to +12
Rwanda	250	+2
Saba	599	–4
Saint-Barthélemy	590	–4
Saint Christopher and Nevis	1 869	–4
Saint Helena	290	0
Saint Lucia	1 758	–4
Saint-Martin	590	–4
Saint Pierre and Miquelon	508	–3
Saint Vincent and the Grenadines	1 784	–4
Samoa	685	+13
San Marino	378	+1
São Tomé and Príncipe	239	0
Saudi Arabia	966	+3

	Country code	+ or – GMT*
Senegal	221	0
Serbia	381	+1
Seychelles	248	+4
Sierra Leone	232	0
Singapore	65	+8
Sint Eustatius	1721	–4
Sint Maarten	1721	–4
Slovakia	421	+1
Slovenia	386	+1
Solomon Islands	677	+11
Somalia	252	+3
South Africa	27	+2
South Ossetia	7	+4
South Sudan	211	+2
Spain	34	+1
Sri Lanka	94	+5½
Sudan	249	+2
Suriname	597	–3
Svalbard	47	+1
Swaziland	268	+2
Sweden	46	+1
Switzerland	41	+1
Syria	963	+2
Taiwan	886	+8
Tajikistan	992	+5
Tanzania	255	+3
Thailand	66	+7
Timor-Leste	670	+9
Togo	228	0
Tokelau	690	+15
Tonga	676	+13
Transnistria	373	+2
Trinidad and Tobago	1 868	–4
Tristan da Cunha	290	0
Tunisia	216	+1
Turkey	90	+2
'Turkish Republic of Northern Cyprus'	90 392	+2
Turkmenistan	993	+5
Turks and Caicos Islands	1 649	–5
Tuvalu	688	+12
Uganda	256	+3
Ukraine‡	380	+2
United Arab Emirates	971	+4
United Kingdom	44	0
United States of America	1	–5 to –10
United States Virgin Islands	1 340	–4
Uruguay	598	–3
Uzbekistan	998	+5
Vanuatu	678	+11
Vatican City	39	+1
Venezuela	58	–4½
Viet Nam	84	+7
Wallis and Futuna Islands	681	+12
Yemen	967	+3
Zambia	260	+2
Zimbabwe	263	+2

* The times listed compare the standard (winter) times in the various countries. Some countries adopt Summer (Daylight Saving) Time—i.e. +1 hour—for part of the year.

† Mobile telephone numbers for Kosovo use either the country code for Monaco (377) or the country code for Slovenia (386).

‡ The Republic of Crimea and the city of Sevastopol were placed in the time zone GMT+4 following their annexation by Russia in 2014.

Note: Telephone and fax numbers using the Inmarsat ocean region code 870 are listed in full. No country or area code is required, but it is necessary to precede the number with the international access code of the country from which the call is made.

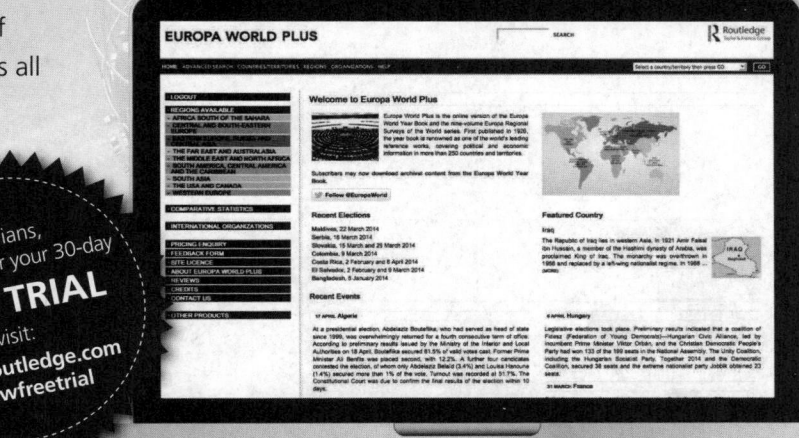

PART ONE
International Organizations

UNITED NATIONS

Address: United Nations, New York, NY 10017, USA.

Telephone: (212) 963-1234; **fax:** (212) 963-4879; **internet:** www.un.org.

The United Nations (UN) was founded in 1945 to maintain international peace and security and to develop international co-operation in addressing economic, social, cultural and humanitarian problems.

The 'United Nations' was a name devised by President Franklin D. Roosevelt of the USA. It was first used in the Declaration by United Nations of 1 January 1942, when representatives of 26 nations pledged their governments to continue fighting together against the Axis powers.

The UN Charter was drawn up by the representatives of 50 countries at the UN Conference on International Organization, which met in San Francisco, USA, from 25 April to 26 June 1945. The representatives deliberated on the basis of proposals put forward by representatives of China, the USSR, the United Kingdom and the USA at Dumbarton Oaks in August–October 1944. The Charter was signed on 26 June 1945. Poland, not represented at the Conference, signed it at a later date but nevertheless became one of the original 51 members.

The UN officially came into existence on 24 October 1945, when the Charter had been ratified by China, France, the USSR, the United Kingdom and the USA, and by a majority of other signatories. United Nations Day is celebrated annually on 24 October.

The UN's chief administrative officer is the Secretary-General, elected for a five-year term by the General Assembly on the recommendation of the Security Council. He acts in that capacity at all meetings of the General Assembly, the Security Council, the Economic and Social Council, and the Trusteeship Council, and performs such other functions as are entrusted to him by those organs. He is required to submit an annual report to the General Assembly and may bring to the attention of the Security Council any matter which, in his opinion, may threaten international peace.

Secretary-General: BAN KI-MOON (Republic of Korea) (2007–16).

Membership

MEMBERS OF THE UNITED NATIONS

(with assessments for percentage contributions to the UN budget during 2013–15, and year of admission)

Afghanistan	0.005	1946
Albania	0.010	1955
Algeria	0.137	1962
Andorra	0.008	1993
Angola	0.010	1976
Antigua and Barbuda	0.002	1981
Argentina	0.432	1945
Armenia	0.007	1992
Australia	2.074	1945
Austria	0.798	1955
Azerbaijan	0.040	1992
Bahamas	0.017	1973
Bahrain	0.039	1971
Bangladesh	0.010	1974
Barbados	0.008	1966
Belarus[1]	0.056	1945
Belgium	0.998	1945
Belize	0.001	1981
Benin	0.003	1960
Bhutan	0.001	1971
Bolivia	0.009	1945
Bosnia and Herzegovina	0.017	1992
Botswana	0.017	1966
Brazil	2.984	1945
Brunei	0.026	1984
Bulgaria	0.047	1955
Burkina Faso	0.003	1960
Burundi	0.001	1962
Cambodia	0.004	1955
Cameroon	0.012	1960
Canada	2.984	1945
Cape Verde	0.001	1975
Central African Republic	0.001	1960
Chad	0.002	1960
Chile	0.334	1945
China, People's Republic	5.148	1945
Colombia	0.259	1945
Comoros	0.001	1975
Congo, Democratic Republic	0.003	1960
Congo, Republic	0.005	1960
Costa Rica	0.038	1945
Côte d'Ivoire	0.011	1960
Croatia	0.126	1992
Cuba	0.069	1945
Cyprus	0.047	1960
Czech Republic[2]	0.386	1993
Denmark	0.675	1945
Djibouti	0.001	1977
Dominica	0.001	1978
Dominican Republic	0.045	1945
Ecuador	0.044	1945
Egypt	0.134	1945
El Salvador	0.016	1945
Equatorial Guinea	0.010	1968
Eritrea	0.001	1993
Estonia	0.040	1991
Ethiopia	0.010	1945
Fiji	0.003	1970
Finland	0.519	1955
France	5.593	1945
Gabon	0.020	1960
The Gambia	0.001	1965
Georgia	0.007	1992
Germany	7.141	1973
Ghana	0.014	1957
Greece	0.638	1945
Grenada	0.001	1974
Guatemala	0.027	1945
Guinea	0.001	1958
Guinea-Bissau	0.001	1974
Guyana	0.001	1966
Haiti	0.003	1945
Honduras	0.008	1945
Hungary	0.266	1955
Iceland	0.027	1946
India	0.666	1945
Indonesia	0.346	1950
Iran	0.356	1945
Iraq	0.068	1945
Ireland	0.418	1955
Israel	0.396	1949
Italy	4.448	1955
Jamaica	0.014	1962
Japan	10.833	1956
Jordan	0.022	1955
Kazakhstan	0.121	1992
Kenya	0.013	1963
Kiribati	0.001	1999
Korea, Democratic People's Republic	0.006	1991
Korea, Republic	1.994	1991
Kuwait	0.273	1963
Kyrgyzstan	0.002	1992
Laos	0.002	1955
Latvia	0.047	1991
Lebanon	0.042	1945
Lesotho	0.001	1966
Liberia	0.001	1945
Libya	0.142	1955
Liechtenstein	0.009	1990
Lithuania	0.073	1991
Luxembourg	0.081	1945
Macedonia, former Yugoslav republic	0.003	1993
Madagascar	0.003	1960
Malawi	0.002	1964
Malaysia	0.281	1957
Maldives	0.001	1965
Mali	0.004	1960
Malta	0.016	1964
Marshall Islands	0.001	1991
Mauritania	0.002	1961
Mauritius	0.013	1968
Mexico	1.842	1945
Micronesia, Federated States	0.001	1991
Moldova	0.003	1992
Monaco	0.012	1993
Mongolia	0.003	1961
Montenegro[3]	0.005	2006

Morocco	0.062	1956
Mozambique	0.003	1975
Myanmar	0.010	1948
Namibia	0.010	1990
Nauru	0.001	1999
Nepal	0.006	1955
Netherlands	1.654	1945
New Zealand	0.253	1945
Nicaragua	0.003	1945
Niger	0.002	1960
Nigeria	0.090	1960
Norway	0.851	1945
Oman	0.102	1971
Pakistan	0.085	1947
Palau	0.001	1994
Panama	0.026	1945
Papua New Guinea	0.004	1975
Paraguay	0.010	1945
Peru	0.117	1945
Philippines	0.154	1945
Poland	0.921	1945
Portugal	0.474	1955
Qatar	0.209	1971
Romania	0.226	1955
Russia[4]	2.438	1945
Rwanda	0.002	1962
Saint Christopher and Nevis	0.001	1983
Saint Lucia	0.001	1979
Saint Vincent and the Grenadines	0.001	1980
Samoa	0.001	1976
San Marino	0.003	1992
São Tomé and Príncipe	0.001	1975
Saudi Arabia	0.864	1945
Senegal	0.006	1960
Serbia[3]	0.040	2000
Seychelles	0.001	1976
Sierra Leone	0.001	1961
Singapore	0.384	1965
Slovakia[2]	0.171	1993
Slovenia	0.100	1992
Solomon Islands	0.001	1978
Somalia	0.001	1960
South Africa	0.372	1945
South Sudan[5]	0.004	2011
Spain	2.973	1955
Sri Lanka	0.025	1955
Sudan	0.010	1956
Suriname	0.004	1975
Swaziland	0.003	1968
Sweden	0.960	1946
Switzerland	1.047	2002
Syria	0.036	1945
Tajikistan	0.003	1992
Tanzania	0.008	1961
Thailand	0.239	1946
Timor-Leste	0.002	2002
Togo	0.001	1960
Tonga	0.001	1999
Trinidad and Tobago	0.044	1962
Tunisia	0.036	1956
Turkey	1.328	1945
Turkmenistan	0.019	1992
Tuvalu	0.001	2000
Uganda	0.006	1962
Ukraine[1]	0.099	1945
United Arab Emirates	0.595	1971
United Kingdom	5.179	1945
USA	22.000	1945
Uruguay	0.052	1945
Uzbekistan	0.015	1992
Vanuatu	0.001	1981
Venezuela	0.627	1945
Viet Nam	0.042	1977
Yemen[6]	0.010	1947/67
Zambia	0.006	1964
Zimbabwe	0.002	1980

Total Membership: 193 (April 2014)

[1] Until December 1991 both Belarus and Ukraine were integral parts of the USSR and not independent countries, but had separate UN membership.

[2] Czechoslovakia, which had been a member of the UN since 1945, ceased to exist as a single state on 31 December 1992. In January 1993, as Czechoslovakia's legal successors, the Czech Republic and Slovakia were granted UN membership, and seats on subsidiary bodies that had previously been held by Czechoslovakia were divided between the two successor states.

[3] Montenegro was admitted as a member of the UN on 28 June 2006, following its declaration of independence on 3 June; Serbia retained the seat formerly held by Serbia and Montenegro.

[4] Russia assumed the USSR's seat in the General Assembly and its permanent seat on the Security Council in December 1991, following the USSR's dissolution.

[5] South Sudan was admitted to the UN on 14 July 2011, having achieved independence on 9 July.

[6] The Yemen Arab Republic (admitted to the UN as Yemen in 1947) and the People's Democratic Republic of Yemen (admitted as Southern Yemen in 1967) merged to form the Republic of Yemen in May 1990.

SOVEREIGN STATES NOT IN THE UNITED NATIONS

(April 2014)

Palestine   Taiwan (Republic of China)   Vatican City (Holy See)

Note: Palestine and Vatican City have non-member observer state status at the UN, granted in 2012 and 1964, respectively.

Diplomatic Representation

PERMANENT MISSIONS TO THE UNITED NATIONS

(April 2014)

Afghanistan: 633 Third Ave, 27th Floor New York, NY 10017; tel. (212) 972-1212; fax (212) 972-1216; e-mail info@afghanistan-un.org; Permanent Representative Dr ZAHIR TANIN.

Albania: 320 East 79th St, New York, NY 10075; tel. (212) 249-2059; fax (212) 535-2917; e-mail albania.un@albania-un.org; Permanent Representative FERIT HOXHA.

Algeria: 326 East 48th St, New York, NY 10017; tel. (212) 750-1960; fax (212) 759-5274; e-mail mission@algeria-un.org; internet www.algeria-un.org; Permanent Representative SABRI BOUKADOUM.

Andorra: Two United Nations Plaza, 27th Floor, New York, NY 10017; tel. (212) 750-8064; fax (212) 750-6630; e-mail contact@andorraun.org; internet www.mae.ad; Permanent Representative NARCIS CASAL DE FONSDEVIELA.

Angola: 820 Second Ave, 12th Floor, New York, NY 10017; tel. (212) 861-5656; fax (212) 861-9295; e-mail themission@angolaun.org; internet www.angolamissionun.org; Permanent Representative ISMAEL ABRAÃO GASPAR MARTINS.

Antigua and Barbuda: 305 East 47th St, 6th Floor, New York, NY 10017; tel. (212) 541-4117; fax (212) 757-1607; e-mail unmission@abgov.org; internet www.abgov.org; Permanent Representative Dr JOHN W. ASHE.

Argentina: One United Nations Plaza, 25th Floor, New York, NY 10017; tel. (212) 688-6300; fax (212) 980-8395; e-mail enaun@mrecic.gov.ar; internet enaun.mrecic.gov.ar; Permanent Representative MARÍA CRISTINA PERCEVAL.

Armenia: 119 East 36th St, New York, NY 10016; tel. (212) 686-9079; fax (212) 686-3934; e-mail armenia@un.int; internet www.un.mfa.am; Permanent Representative GAREN A. NAZARIAN.

Australia: 150 East 42nd St, 33rd Floor, New York, NY 10017; tel. (212) 351-6600; fax (212) 351-6610; e-mail australia@un.int; Permanent Representative GARY QUINLAN.

Austria: 600 Third Ave, 31st Floor, New York, NY 10016; tel. (212) 542-8400; fax (212) 949-1840; e-mail new-york-ov@bmeia.gv.at; internet www.un.int/austria; Permanent Representative MARTIN SAJDIK.

Azerbaijan: 866 United Nations Plaza, Suite 560, New York, NY 10017; tel. (212) 371-2559; fax (212) 371-2784; e-mail azerbaijan@un.int; Permanent Representative AGSHIN MEHDIYEV.

Bahamas: 231 East 46th St, New York, NY 10017; tel. (212) 421-6925; fax (212) 759-2135; e-mail mission@bahamasny.com; Permanent Representative ELLISTON RAHMING.

Bahrain: 866 Second Ave, 14th/15th Floor, New York, NY 10017; tel. (212) 223-6200; fax (212) 319-0687; e-mail bahrain1@un.int; Permanent Representative JAMAL FARES ALROWAIEI.

Bangladesh: 820 Second Ave, 4th Floor, New York, NY 10017; tel. (212) 867-3434; fax (212) 972-4038; e-mail bdpmny@gmail.com; internet www.un.int/bangladesh; Permanent Representative ABULKALAM ABDUL MOMEN.

Barbados: 820 Second Ave, 9th Floor, New York, NY 10017; tel. (212) 551-4300; fax (212) 986-1030; e-mail prun@foreign.gov.bb; Permanent Representative JOSEPH E. GODDARD.

Belarus: 136 East 67th St, 4th Floor, New York, NY 10065; tel. (212) 535-3420; fax (212) 734-4810; e-mail usa.un@mfa.gov.by; internet www.un.int/belarus; Permanent Representative ANDREI DAPKIUNAS.

Belgium: One Dag Hammarskjöld Plaza, 885 Second Ave, 41st Floor, New York, NY 10017; tel. (212) 378-6300; fax (212) 681-7618; e-mail newyorkun@diplobel.fed.be; internet www.diplomatie.be/newyorkun; Permanent Representative Bénédicte Frankinet.

Belize: 675 Third Ave, Suite 1911, New York, NY 10017; tel. (212) 986-1240; fax (212) 593-0932; e-mail blzun@aol.com; Permanent Representative Lois Michele Young.

Benin: 125 East 38th St, New York, NY 10016; tel. (212) 684-1339; fax (212) 684-2058; e-mail beninewyork@gmail.com; Permanent Representative Jean-Francis Régis Zinsou.

Bhutan: 343 43rd St, New York, NY 10017; tel. (212) 682-2268; fax (212) 661-0551; e-mail chadorpmb@yahoo.com; Permanent Representative Kunzang Choden Namgyel.

Bolivia: 801 Second Ave, 4th Floor, Suite 402, New York, NY 10017; tel. (212) 682-8132; fax (212) 687-4642; e-mail delgaliviaonu@hotmail.com; Permanent Representative Sacha Sergio Llorentty Solíz.

Bosnia and Herzegovina: 420 Lexington Ave, Suites 607–608, New York, NY 10170; tel. (212) 751-9015; fax (212) 751-9019; e-mail bihun@mfa.gov.ba; internet www.bhmisijaun.org; Permanent Representative Mirsada Čolaković.

Botswana: 154 East 46th St, New York, NY 10017; tel. (212) 889-2277; fax (212) 725-5061; e-mail botswana@un.int; Permanent Representative Charles Thembani Ntwaagae.

Brazil: 747 Third Ave, 9th Floor, New York, NY 10017; tel. (212) 372-2600; fax (212) 371-5716; e-mail delbrasonu@delbrasonu.org; internet www.un.int/brazil; Permanent Representative Antonio de Aguiar Patriota.

Brunei: 771 United Nations Plaza, New York, NY 10017; tel. (212) 697-3465; fax (212) 697-9889; e-mail brunei@un.int; Permanent Representative Dato' Abdul Ghafar Ismail.

Bulgaria: 11 East 84th St, New York, NY 10028; tel. (212) 737-4790; fax (212) 472-9865; e-mail mission.newyork@mfa.bg; internet www.mfa.bg/embassies/usapr; Permanent Representative Stephan Tafrov.

Burkina Faso: 866 United Nations Plaza, Suite 326, New York, NY 10017; tel. (212) 308-4720; fax (212) 308-4690; e-mail bfapm@un.int; internet www.burkina-onu.org; Permanent Representative Der Kogda.

Burundi: 336 East 45th St, 12th Floor, New York, NY 10017; tel. (212) 499-0001; fax (212) 499-0006; e-mail burundi@un.int; Permanent Representative Herménégilde Niyonzima.

Cambodia: 327 East 58th St, New York, NY 10022; tel. (212) 336-0777; fax (212) 759-7672; e-mail cambodia@un.int; internet www.un.int/cambodia; Permanent Representative Ry Tuy.

Cameroon: 22 East 73rd St, New York, NY 10021; tel. (212) 794-2295; fax (212) 249-0533; e-mail cameroon.mission@yahoo.com; Permanent Representative Tommo Monthe.

Canada: One Dag Hammarskjöld Plaza, 885 Second Ave, 14th Floor, New York, NY 10017; tel. (212) 848-1100; fax (212) 848-1195; e-mail canada.un@international.gc.ca; internet www.un.int/canada; Permanent Representative Guillermo E. Rishchynski.

Cape Verde: 27 East 69th St, New York, NY 10021; tel. (212) 472-0333; fax (212) 794-1398; e-mail capeverde@un.int; Permanent Representative Fernando Jorge Wahnon Ferreira.

Central African Republic: 866 United Nations Plaza, Suite 444, New York, NY 10017; tel. (646) 415-9122; fax (646) 415-9149; e-mail repercaf.ny@gmail.com; internet www.pmcar.org; Permanent Representative Charles-Armel Doubane.

Chad: 129 East 36th St, New York, NY 10017; tel. (212) 986-0980; fax (212) 986-0152; e-mail chadmission@gmail.com; Permanent Representative Mahamat Zene Cherif.

Chile: One Dag Hammarskjöld Plaza, 885 Second Ave, 40th Floor, New York, NY 10017; tel. (917) 322-6800; fax (917) 322-6890; e-mail chile.un@minrel.gov.cl; internet chileabroad.gov.cl/onu/en; Permanent Representative Cristián Barros Melet.

China, People's Republic: 350 East 35th St, New York, NY 10016; tel. (212) 655-6100; fax (212) 634-7626; e-mail chinesemission@yahoo.com; internet www.china-un.org; Permanent Representative Liu Jieyi.

Colombia: 140 East 57th St, 5th Floor, New York, NY 10022; tel. (212) 355-7776; fax (212) 371-2813; e-mail colombia@colombiaun.org; internet www.colombia.un.org; Permanent Representative María Emma Mejía Vélez.

Comoros: 866 United Nations Plaza, Suite 418, New York, NY 10017; tel. (212) 750-1637; fax (212) 750-1657; e-mail comoros@un.int; Permanent Representative Roubani Kaambi.

Congo, Democratic Republic: 866 United Nations Plaza, Suite 511, New York, NY 10017; tel. (212) 319-8061; fax (212) 319-8232; e-mail missiondrc@gmail.com; Permanent Representative Ignace Gata Mavita wa Lufuta.

Congo, Republic: 14 East 65th St, New York, NY 10065; tel. (212) 744-7840; fax (212) 744-7975; e-mail congo@un.int; Permanent Representative Raymond Serge Balé.

Costa Rica: 211 East 43rd St, Rm 903, New York, NY 10017; tel. (212) 986-6373; fax (212) 986-6842; e-mail contact@missioncrun.org; Permanent Representative Eduardo Ulibarri-Bilbao.

Côte d'Ivoire: 800 Second Ave, 5th Floor, New York, NY 10017; tel. (646) 649-5061; fax (646) 781-9974; e-mail cotedivoiremission@yahoo.com; Permanent Representative Youssoufou Bamba.

Croatia: 820 Second Ave, 19th Floor, New York, NY 10017; tel. (212) 986-1585; fax (212) 986-2011; e-mail cromiss.un@mvp.hr; internet www.un.mfa.hr; Permanent Representative Vladimir Drobnjak.

Cuba: 315 Lexington Ave and 38th St, New York, NY 10016; tel. (212) 689-7215; fax (212) 779-1697; e-mail cuba_onu@cubanmission.com; Permanent Representative Rodolfo Reyes Rodríguez.

Cyprus: 13 East 40th St, New York, NY 10016; tel. (212) 481-6023; fax (212) 685-7316; e-mail mission@cyprusun.org; internet www.un.int/cyprus; Permanent Representative Nicholas Emiliou.

Czech Republic: 1109–1111 Madison Ave, New York, NY 10028; tel. (646) 981-4001; fax (646) 981-4099; e-mail un.newyork@embassy.mzv.cz; internet www.mfa.cz; Permanent Representative Edita Hrdá.

Denmark: One Dag Hammarskjöld Plaza, 885 Second Ave, 18th Floor, New York, NY 10017; tel. (212) 308-7009; fax (212) 308-3384; e-mail nycmis@um.dk; internet www.missionfnnewyork.um.dk/en/; Permanent Representative Ib Petersen.

Djibouti: 866 United Nations Plaza, Suite 4011, New York, NY 10017; tel. (212) 753-3163; fax (212) 223-1276; e-mail djibouti@nyct.net; Permanent Representative Roble Olhaye.

Dominica: 800 Second Ave, Suite 400H, New York, NY 10017; tel. (212) 949-0853; fax (212) 808-4975; e-mail dominicaun@gmail.com; Permanent Representative Vince Henderson.

Dominican Republic: 144 East 44th St, 4th Floor, New York, NY 10017; tel. (212) 867-0833; fax (212) 986-4694; e-mail drun@un.int; internet www.un.int/dr; Chargé d'affaires a.i. Marcos Montilla.

Ecuador: 866 United Nations Plaza, Rm 516, New York, NY 10017; tel. (212) 935-1680; fax (212) 935-1835; e-mail ecuador@un.int; internet www.ecuadoronu.com; Permanent Representative Xavier Lasso Mendoza.

Egypt: 304 East 44th St, New York, NY 10017; tel. (212) 503-0300; fax (212) 949-5999; e-mail egypt@un.int; Permanent Representative Mootaz Ahmadein Khalil.

El Salvador: 46 Park Ave, New York, NY 10016; tel. (212) 679-1616; fax (212) 725-3467; e-mail elsalvadormissiontoun@outlook.com; Permanent Representative Carlos Enrique García González.

Equatorial Guinea: 800 Second Ave, Suite 305, New York, NY 10017; tel. (212) 223-2324; fax (212) 223-2366; e-mail equatorialguineamission@yahoo.com; Permanent Representative Anatolio Ndong Mba.

Eritrea: 800 Second Ave, 18th Floor, New York, NY 10017; tel. (212) 687-3390; fax (212) 687-3138; e-mail general@eritrea-unmission.org; internet www.eritrea-unmission.org; Permanent Representative Girma Asmerom Tesfay (designate).

Estonia: 3 Dag Hammarskjöld Plaza, 305 East 47th St, Unit 6B, New York, NY 10017; tel. (212) 883-0640; fax (646) 514-0099; e-mail mission.newyork@mfa.ee; Permanent Representative Margus Kolga.

Ethiopia: 866 Second Ave, 3rd Floor, New York, NY 10017; tel. (212) 421-1830; fax (212) 756-4690; e-mail ethiopia@un.int; Permanent Representative Tekeda Alemu.

Fiji: 801 Second Ave, 10th Floor, New York, NY 10017; tel. (212) 687-4130; fax (212) 687-3963; e-mail mission@fijiprun.org; Permanent Representative Peter Thomson.

Finland: 866 United Nations Plaza, Suite 222, New York, NY 10017; tel. (212) 355-2100; fax (212) 759-6156; e-mail sanomat.yke@formin.fi; internet www.finlandun.org; Permanent Representative Jarmo Viinanen.

France: One Dag Hammarskjöld Plaza, 245 East 47th St, 44th Floor, New York, NY 10017; tel. (212) 702-4900; fax (212) 421-6889; e-mail france@franceonu.org; Permanent Representative Gérard Araud.

Gabon: 18 East 41st St, 9th Floor, New York, NY 10017; tel. (212) 686-9720; fax (212) 689-5769; e-mail info@gabon-un.org; Permanent Representative Nelson Messone.

The Gambia: 800 Second Ave, Suite 400F, New York, NY 10017; tel. (212) 949-6640; fax (212) 856-9820; e-mail gambia_un@hotmail.com; internet gambia.un.int; Permanent Representative Mamadou Tangara.

Georgia: One United Nations Plaza, 26th Floor, New York, NY 10021; tel. (212) 759-1949; fax (212) 759-1832; e-mail geomission.un@mfa.gov.ge; internet www.un.int/georgia; Permanent Representative Kaha Imnadze.

Germany: 871 United Nations Plaza, New York, NY 10017; tel. (212) 940-0400; fax (212) 940-0402; e-mail info@new-york-un.diplo.de; internet www.germany-info.org/un; Permanent Representative HANS PETER WITTIG.

Ghana: 19 East 47th St, New York, NY 10017; tel. (212) 832-1300; fax (212) 751-6743; e-mail ghanaperm@aol.com; Permanent Representative KEN KANDA.

Greece: 866 Second Ave, 13th Floor, New York, NY 10017; tel. (212) 888-6900; fax (212) 888-4440; e-mail grdel.un@mfa.gr; internet www.greeceun.org; Permanent Representative MICHEL SPINELLIS.

Grenada: 800 Second Ave, Suite 400K, New York, NY 10017; tel. (212) 599-0301; fax (212) 599-1540; e-mail grenada@un.int; Permanent Representative DENIS G. ANTOINE.

Guatemala: 57 Park Ave, New York, NY 10016; tel. (212) 679-4760; fax (212) 685-8741; e-mail guatemala@un.int; internet www.guatemalaun.org; Permanent Representative GERT ROSENTHAL.

Guinea: 140 East 39th St, New York, NY 10016; tel. (212) 687-8115; fax (212) 687-8248; e-mail missionofguinea@aol.com; Permanent Representative MAMADI TOURÉ.

Guinea-Bissau: 866 United Nations Plaza, Suite 481, New York, NY 10017; tel. (212) 896-8311; fax (212) 896-8313; e-mail guinebissauonu@gmail.com; Permanent Representative JOÃO SOARES DA GAMA.

Guyana: 801 Second Ave, 5th Floor, New York, NY 10017; tel. (212) 573-5828; fax (212) 573-6225; e-mail guyana@un.int; Permanent Representative GEORGE WILFRIED TALBOT.

Haiti: 815 Second Ave, 6th Floor, New York, NY 10017; tel. (212) 370-4840; fax (212) 661-8698; e-mail mphonu.newyork@diplomatie.ht; Permanent Representative DENIS REGIS.

Honduras: 866 United Nations Plaza, Suite 417, New York, NY 10017; tel. (212) 752-3370; fax (212) 223-0498; e-mail honduras_un@hotmail.com; internet www.un.int/honduras; Permanent Representative MARY ELIZABETH FLORES FLAKE.

Hungary: 227 East 52nd St, New York, NY 10022; tel. (212) 752-0209; fax (212) 755-5395; e-mail hungary@un.int; Permanent Representative CSABA KŐRÖSI.

Iceland: 800 Third Ave, 36th Floor, New York, NY 10022; tel. (212) 593-2700; fax (212) 593-6269; e-mail unmission@mfa.is; Permanent Representative GRÉTA GUNNARSDÓTTIR.

India: 235 East 43rd St, New York, NY 10017; tel. (212) 490-9660; fax (212) 490-9656; e-mail india@un.int; internet www.un.int/india; Permanent Representative ASOKE KUMAR MUKERJI.

Indonesia: 325 East 38th St, New York, NY 10016; tel. (212) 972-8333; fax (212) 972-9780; e-mail ptri@indonesiamission-ny.org; internet www.indonesiamission-ny.org; Permanent Representative DESRA PERCAYA.

Iran: 622 Third Ave, 34th Floor, New York, NY 10017; tel. (212) 687-2020; fax (212) 867-7086; e-mail iran@un.int; internet www.iran-un.org; Permanent Representative HAMID ABUTALEBI (designate).

Iraq: 14 East 79th St, New York, NY 10075; tel. (212) 737-4433; fax (212) 772-1794; e-mail iraqny@un.int; Permanent Representative MOHAMED ALI ALHAKIM.

Ireland: 885 Second Ave, 19th Floor, New York, NY 10017; tel. (212) 421-6934; fax (212) 752-4726; e-mail newyorkpmun@dfa.ie; internet www.irelandunnewyork.org; Permanent Representative DAVID DONOGHUE.

Israel: 800 Second Ave, New York, NY 10017; tel. (212) 499-5510; fax (212) 499-5515; e-mail info-un@newyork.mfa.gov.il; internet www.israel-un.org; Permanent Representative RON PROSOR.

Italy: One Dag Hammarskjöld Plaza, 885 Second Ave, 49th Floor, New York, NY 10017; tel. (212) 486-9191; fax (212) 486-1036; e-mail info.italyun@esteri.it; internet www.italyun.esteri.it; Permanent Representative SEBASTIANO CARDI.

Jamaica: 767 Third Ave, 9th Floor, New York, NY 10017; tel. (212) 935-7509; fax (212) 935-7607; e-mail jamaica@un.int; internet www.un.int/jamaica; Permanent Representative COURTENEY RATTRAY.

Japan: 866 United Nations Plaza, 2nd Floor, New York, NY 10017; tel. (212) 223-4300; fax (212) 751-1966; e-mail p-m-j@dn.mofa.go.jp; Permanent Representative MOTOHIDE YOSHIKAWA.

Jordan: 866 Second Ave, 4th Floor, New York, NY 10017; tel. (212) 832-9553; fax (212) 832-5346; e-mail missionun@jordanmissionun.com; Permanent Representative Prince ZEID RA'AD ZEID AL-HUSSEIN.

Kazakhstan: 3 Dag Hammarskjöld Plaza, 305 East 47th St, 3rd Floor, New York, NY 10017; tel. (212) 230-1900; fax (212) 230-1172; e-mail kazakhstan@un.int; internet www.kazakhstanun.org; Permanent Representative KAIRAT ABDRAKHMANOV.

Kenya: 866 United Nations Plaza, Rm 304, New York, NY 10017; tel. (212) 421-4740; fax (212) 486-1985; e-mail info@kenyaun.org; Permanent Representative MACHARIA KAMAU.

Kiribati: 800 Second Ave, Suite 400A, New York, NY 10017; tel. (212) 867-3310; fax (212) 867-3320; Permanent Representative MAKURITA BAARO.

Korea, Democratic People's Republic: 820 Second Ave, 13th Floor, New York, NY 10017; tel. (212) 972-3105; fax (212) 972-3154; e-mail dpr.korea@verizon.net; Permanent Representative JA SONG-NAM.

Korea, Republic: 335 East 45th St, New York, NY 10017; tel. (212) 439-4000; fax (212) 986-1083; e-mail korea.un@mofa.go.kr; internet un.mofat.go.kr; Permanent Representative OH JOON.

Kuwait: 321 East 44th St, New York, NY 10017; tel. (212) 973-4300; fax (212) 370-1733; e-mail contact@kuwaitmission.org; internet www.kuwaitmission.com; Permanent Representative MANSOUR AYYAD AL-OTAIBI.

Kyrgyzstan: 866 United Nations Plaza, Suite 477, New York, NY 10017; tel. (212) 486-4214; fax (212) 486-5259; e-mail kyrgyzstan@un.int; internet www.un.int/kyrgyzstan; Permanent Representative TALAIBEK KYDYROV.

Laos: 317 East 51st St, New York, NY 10022; tel. (212) 832-2734; fax (212) 750-0039; e-mail lao@un.int; internet www.un.int/lao; Chargé d'affaires a.i. KHAM-INH KHITCHADETH.

Latvia: 333 East 50th St, New York, NY 10022; tel. (212) 838-8877; fax (212) 838-8920; e-mail mission.un-ny@mfa.gov.lv; Permanent Representative JĀNIS MAŽEIKS.

Lebanon: 866 United Nations Plaza, Rm 531–533, New York, NY 10017; tel. (212) 355-5460; fax (212) 838-2819; e-mail contact@lebanonun.org; internet www.un.int/lebanon; Permanent Representative NAWAF A. SALAM.

Lesotho: 204 East 39th St, New York, NY 10016; tel. (212) 661-1690; fax (212) 682-4388; e-mail lesotho@un.int; Permanent Representative KELEBONE MAOPE.

Liberia: 866 United Nations Plaza, Suite 480, New York, NY 10017; tel. (212) 687-1033; fax (212) 687-1035; e-mail liberia@un.int; Permanent Representative MARJON V. KAMARA.

Libya: 309–315 East 48th St, New York, NY 10017; tel. (212) 752-5775; fax (212) 593-4787; e-mail info@libyanmission-un.org; internet www.libyanmission-un.org; Permanent Representative IBRAHMIN O. A. DABBASHI.

Liechtenstein: 633 Third Ave, 27th Floor, New York, NY 10017; tel. (212) 599-0220; fax (212) 599-0064; e-mail mission@nyc.llv.li; internet www.un.int/liechtenstein; Permanent Representative CHRISTIAN WENAWESER.

Lithuania: 708 Third Ave, 10th Floor, New York, NY 10018; tel. (212) 983-9474; fax (212) 983-9473; e-mail lithuania@un.int; internet mission-un-ny.mfa.lt; Permanent Representative RAIMONDA MURMOKAITĖ.

Luxembourg: 17 Beekman Pl., New York, NY 10022; tel. (212) 935-3589; fax (212) 935-5896; e-mail newyork.rp@mae.etat.lu; internet www.un.int/luxembourg; Permanent Representative SYLVIE LUCAS.

Macedonia, former Yugoslav republic: 866 United Nations Plaza, Suite 517, New York, NY 10017; tel. (212) 308-8504; fax (212) 308-8724; e-mail newyork@mfa.gov.mk; Permanent Representative VASILE ANDONOSKI.

Madagascar: 820 Second Ave, Suite 800, New York, NY 10017; tel. (212) 986-9491; fax (212) 986-6271; e-mail repermad@verizon.net; Permanent Representative ZINA ANDRIANARIVELO-RAZAFY.

Malawi: 866 United Nations Plaza, Suite 486, New York, NY 10017; tel. (212) 317-8738; fax (212) 317-8729; e-mail malawinewyork@aol.com; Permanent Representative CHARLES PETER MSOSA.

Malaysia: 313 East 43rd St, New York, NY 10017; tel. (212) 986-6310; fax (212) 490-8576; e-mail malnyun@kln.gov.my; internet www.un.int/malaysia; Permanent Representative HANIFF HUSSEIN.

Maldives: 800 Second Ave, Suite 400E, New York, NY 10017; tel. (212) 599-6195; fax (212) 661-6405; e-mail info@maldivesmission.com; internet www.maldivesmission.com; Permanent Representative AHMED SAREER.

Mali: 111 East 69th St, New York, NY 10021; tel. (212) 737-4150; fax (212) 472-3778; e-mail malionu@aol.com; internet www.un.int/mali; Permanent Representative SÉKOU KASSÉ.

Malta: 249 East 35th St, New York, NY 10016; tel. (212) 725-2345; fax (212) 779-7097; e-mail malta-un.newyork@gov.mt; Permanent Representative CHRISTOPHER GRIMA.

Marshall Islands: 800 Second Ave, 18th Floor, New York, NY 10017; tel. (212) 983-3040; fax (212) 983-3202; e-mail marshallislands@un.int; internet marshallislands.un.int; Permanent Representative AMATLAIN ELIZABETH KABUA.

Mauritania: 116 East 38th St, New York, NY 10016; tel. (212) 252-0113; fax (212) 252-0175; e-mail mauritaniamission@gmail.com; Chargé d'affaires a.i. JIDDOU JIDDOU.

Mauritius: 211 East 43rd St, 15th Floor, Suite 1502, New York, NY 10017; tel. (212) 949-0190; fax (212) 697-3829; e-mail mauritius@un

.int; Permanent Representative MILAN JAYA NYAMRAJSINGH MEETARBHAN.

Mexico: Two United Nations Plaza, 28th Floor, New York, NY 10017; tel. (212) 752-0220; fax (212) 688-8862; e-mail onuusr1@sre.gob.mx; internet www.sre.gob.mx/onu; Permanent Representative JORGE MARIO MONTAÑO Y MARTÍNEZ.

Micronesia, Federated States: 300 East 42nd St, Suite 1600, New York, NY 10017; tel. (212) 697-8370; fax (212) 697-8295; e-mail fsmun@fsmgov.org; internet www.fsmgov.org/fsmun; Permanent Representative JANE JIMMY CHIGIYAL.

Moldova: 35 East 29th St, New York, NY 10016; tel. (212) 447-1867; fax (212) 447-4067; e-mail unmoldova@aol.com; internet www.onu.mfa.md; Permanent Representative VLADIMIR LUPAN.

Monaco: 866 United Nations Plaza, Suite 520, New York, NY 10017; tel. (212) 832-0721; fax (212) 832-5358; e-mail monaco@un.int; Permanent Representative ISABELLE F. PICCO.

Mongolia: 6 East 77th St, New York, NY 10075; tel. (212) 737-3874; fax (212) 861-9464; e-mail mongolianmission@twcmetrobiz.com; internet www.un.int/mongolia; Permanent Representative ODYN OCH.

Montenegro: 801 Second Ave, 7th Floor, New York, NY 10017; tel. (212) 661-3700; fax (212) 661-3755; e-mail un.newyork@mfa.gov.me; Permanent Representative MILORAD ŠĆEPANOVIĆ.

Morocco: 866 Second Ave, 6th and 7th Floors, New York, NY 10017; tel. (212) 421-1580; fax (212) 980-1512; e-mail info@morocco-un.org; Permanent Representative OMAR HILALE.

Mozambique: 420 East 50th St, New York, NY 10022; tel. (212) 644-5965; fax (212) 644-5972; e-mail mozambique@un.int; Permanent Representative ANTÓNIO GUMENDE.

Myanmar: 10 East 77th St, New York, NY 10075; tel. (212) 744-1271; fax (212) 744-1290; e-mail myanmarmission@verizon.net; Permanent Representative KYAW TIN.

Namibia: 360 Lexington Ave, Suite 1502, New York, NY 10017; tel. (212) 685-2003; fax (212) 685-1561; e-mail namibia@un.int; Permanent Representative WILFRIED INOTIRA EMVULA.

Nauru: 801 Second Ave, Third Floor, New York, NY 10017; tel. (212) 937-0074; fax (212) 937-0079; e-mail nauru@un.int; internet www.un.int/nauru; Permanent Representative MARLENE INEMWIN MOSES.

Nepal: 820 Second Ave, Suite 17B, New York, NY 10017; tel. (212) 370-3988; fax (212) 953-2038; e-mail nepal@un.int; internet www.un.int/nepal; Permanent Representative DURGA PRASAD BHATTARAI.

Netherlands: 666 Third Ave, 19th Floor, New York, NY 10017; tel. (212) 519-9500; fax (212) 370-1954; e-mail nyv@minbuza.nl; internet www.netherlandsmission.org; Permanent Representative KAREL JAN GUSTAAF VAN OOSTEROM.

New Zealand: 600 Third Ave, 14th Floor, New York, NY 10016; tel. (212) 826-1960; fax (212) 758-0827; e-mail nzpmun@gmail.com; internet www.nzmissionny.org; Permanent Representative JIM MCLAY.

Nicaragua: 820 Second Ave, 8th Floor, New York, NY 10017; tel. (212) 490-7997; fax (212) 286-0815; e-mail nicaragua@un.int; internet www.un.int/nicaragua; Permanent Representative MARÍA RUBIALES DE CHAMORRO.

Niger: 417 East 50th St, New York, NY 10022; tel. (212) 421-3260; fax (212) 753-6931; e-mail nigermission@ymail.com; Permanent Representative BOUBACAR BOUREIMA.

Nigeria: 828 Second Ave, New York, NY 10017; tel. (212) 953-9130; fax (212) 697-1970; e-mail permny@nigeriaunmission.org; internet nigeriaunmission.org; Permanent Representative U. JOY OGWU.

Norway: 825 Third Ave, 39th Floor, New York, NY 10022; tel. (646) 430-7510; fax (646) 430-7591; e-mail delun@mfa.no; internet www.un.norway-un.org; Permanent Representative GEIR O. PEDERSON.

Oman: 3 Dag Hammarskjöld Plaza, 305 East 47th St, 12th Floor, New York, NY 10017; tel. (212) 355-3505; fax (212) 644-0070; e-mail oman@un.int; Permanent Representative LYUTHA S. AL-MUGHAIRY.

Pakistan: 8 East 65th St, New York, NY 10021; tel. (212) 879-8600; fax (212) 744-7348; e-mail pakistan@un.int; internet www.pakun.org; Permanent Representative MASOOD KHAN.

Palau: 866 United Nations Plaza, Suite 575, New York, NY 10017; tel. (212) 813-0310; fax (212) 813-0317; e-mail mission@palauun.org; internet www.palauun.org; Permanent Representative Dr CALEB OTTO.

Panama: 866 United Nations Plaza, Suite 4030, New York, NY 10017; tel. (212) 421-5420; fax (212) 421-2694; e-mail emb@panama-un.org; internet www.panama-un.org; Permanent Representative PABLO ANTONIO THALASSINÓS.

Papua New Guinea: 201 East 42nd St, Suite 405, New York, NY 10017; tel. (212) 557-5001; fax (212) 557-5009; e-mail pngmission@pngun.org; Permanent Representative ROBERT GUBA AISI.

Paraguay: 801 Second Ave, Suite 702, New York, NY 10017; tel. (212) 687-3490; fax (212) 818-1282; e-mail paraguay@un.int; Permanent Representative JOSÉ ANTONIO DOS SANTOS.

Peru: 820 Second Ave, Suite 1600, New York, NY 10017; tel. (212) 687-3336; fax (212) 972-6975; e-mail onuper@unperu.org; internet www.un.int/peru; Permanent Representative GUSTAVO MEZA-CUADRA VELÁSQUEZ.

Philippines: 556 Fifth Ave, 5th Floor, New York, NY 10036; tel. (212) 764-1300; fax (212) 840-8602; e-mail newyorkpm@gmail.com; internet www.un.int/philippines; Permanent Representative LIBRAN N. CABACTULAN.

Poland: 750 Third Ave, 30th Floor, New York, NY 10017; tel. (212) 744-2506; fax (212) 517-6771; e-mail nowyjork.onz.sekretariat@msz.gov.pl; internet www.nowyjorkonz.msz.gov.pl; Permanent Representative RYSZARD STANISLAW SARCOWICZ.

Portugal: 866 Second Ave, 9th Floor, New York, NY 10017; tel. (212) 759-9444; fax (212) 355-1124; e-mail portugal@missionofportugal.org; internet www.un.int/portugal; Permanent Representative ÁLVARO JOSÉ COSTA DE MENDONÇA E MOURA.

Qatar: 809 United Nations Plaza, 4th Floor, New York, NY 10017; tel. (212) 486-9335; fax (212) 758-4952; e-mail pmun@mofa.gov.qa; Permanent Representative ALYA AHMED SEIF AL-THANI.

Romania: 573–577 Third Ave, New York, NY 10016; tel. (212) 682-3273; fax (212) 682-9746; e-mail misiune@romaniaun.org; internet www.mpnewyork.mae.ro; Permanent Representative SIMONA MIRELA MICULESCU.

Russia: 136 East 67th St, New York, NY 10065; tel. (212) 861-4900; fax (212) 628-0252; e-mail mission@russiaun.ru; internet www.russiaun.ru; Permanent Representative VITALII I. CHURKIN.

Rwanda: 370 Lexington Ave, Suite 401, New York, NY 10017; tel. (212) 679-9010; fax (212) 679-9133; e-mail ambanewyork@minaffet.gov.rw; Permanent Representative EUGÈNE-RICHARD GASANA.

Saint Christopher and Nevis: 414 East 75th St, 5th Floor, New York, NY 10021; tel. (212) 535-1234; fax (212) 535-6854; e-mail sknmission@aol.com; Permanent Representative DELANO FRANK BART.

Saint Lucia: 800 Second Ave, 9th Floor, New York, NY 10017; tel. (212) 697-9360; fax (212) 697-4993; e-mail info@stluciamission.org; Permanent Representative MENISSA RAMBALLY.

Saint Vincent and the Grenadines: 800 Second Ave, Suite 400G, New York, NY 10017; tel. (212) 599-0950; fax (212) 599-1020; e-mail mission@svg-un.org; Permanent Representative INGA RHONDA KING.

Samoa: 800 Second Ave, Suite 400J, New York, NY 10017; tel. (212) 599-6196; fax (212) 599-0797; e-mail www.samoa@un.int; internet www.samoa.un.int; Permanent Representative ALI'IOAIGA FETURI ELISAIA.

San Marino: 327 East 50th St, New York, NY 10022; tel. (212) 751-1234; fax (212) 751-1436; e-mail sanmarinoun@hotmail.com; Permanent Representative DANIELE BODINI.

São Tomé and Príncipe: 675 Third Ave, Suite 1807, New York, NY 10017; tel. (347) 905-5703; fax (347) 201-4834; e-mail pmstpun@gmail.com; Permanent Representative CARLOS FILOMENO AGOSTINHO DAS NEVES.

Saudi Arabia: 809 United Nations Plaza, 10th and 11th Floors, New York, NY 10017; tel. (212) 557-1525; fax (212) 983-4895; e-mail saudi-mission@un.int; Permanent Representative ABDULLAH YAHYA AL-MOUALLIMI.

Senegal: 747 Third Ave, 21st Floor (46th & 47th St), New York, NY 10017; tel. (212) 517-9030; fax (212) 517-3032; e-mail senegal.mission@yahoo.fr; Permanent Representative ABDOU SALAM DIALLO.

Serbia: 854 Fifth Ave, New York, NY 10065; tel. (212) 879-8700; fax (212) 879-8705; e-mail info@serbiamissionun.org; internet www.un.int/serbia; Permanent Representative MILAN MILANOVIĆ.

Seychelles: 800 Second Ave, Suite 400C, New York, NY 10017; tel. (212) 972-1785; fax (212) 972-1786; e-mail seychelles@un.int; Permanent Representative MARIE-LOUISE POTTER.

Sierra Leone: 245 East 49th St, New York, NY 10017; tel. (212) 688-1656; fax (212) 688-4924; e-mail sierraleone@un.int; Permanent Representative VANDI CHIDI MINAH.

Singapore: 231 East 51st St, New York, NY 10022; tel. (212) 826-0840; fax (212) 826-2964; e-mail singapore@un.int; internet www.mfa.gov.sg/newyork; Permanent Representative KAREN TAN.

Slovakia: 801 Second Ave, 12th Floor, New York, NY 10017; tel. (212) 286-8418; fax (212) 286-8419; e-mail un.newyork@mzv.sk; internet www.msv.sk/unnewyork; Permanent Representative FRANTIŠEK RUŽIČKA.

Slovenia: 630 Third Ave, 20th Floor, New York, NY 10016; tel. (212) 370-3007; fax (212) 370-1824; e-mail slovenia@un.int; internet www.un.int/slovenia; Permanent Representative ANDREJ LOGAR.

Solomon Islands: 800 Second Ave, Suite 400L, New York, NY 10017; tel. (212) 599-6193; fax (212) 661-8925; e-mail simun@solomons.com; Permanent Representative COLLIN D. BECK.

Somalia: 425 East 61st St, Suite 702, New York, NY 10065; tel. (212) 688-9410; fax (212) 759-0651; e-mail somalia@un.int; Permanent Representative ELMI AHMED DUALE.

South Africa: 333 East 38th St, 9th Floor, New York, NY 10016; tel. (212) 213-5583; fax (212) 692-2498; e-mail pmun.newyork@dirco.gov.za; Permanent Representative JEREMIAH NYAMANE KINGSLEY MAMABOLO.

South Sudan: 336 East 45th St, 5th Floor, New York, NY 10017; tel. (212) 937-7977; fax (212) 867-9242; e-mail info@rssun-nyc.org; Permanent Representative FRANCIS MADING DENG.

Spain: One Dag Hammarskjöld Plaza, 245 East 47th St, 36th Floor, New York, NY 10017; tel. (212) 661-1050; fax (212) 949-7247; e-mail rep.nuevayorkonu@maec.es; internet www.spainun.org; Permanent Representative ROMÁN OYARZUN MARCHESI.

Sri Lanka: 820 Second Ave, 2nd Floor, New York, NY 10017; tel. (212) 986-7040; fax (212) 986-1838; e-mail mail@slmission.com; internet www.slmission.com; Permanent Representative PALITHA T. B. KOHONA.

Sudan: 305 East 47th St, 3 Dag Hammarskjöld Plaza, 4th Floor, New York, NY 10017; tel. (212) 573-6033; fax (212) 573-6160; e-mail sudan@sudanmission.org; Permanent Representative RAHAMTALLA MOHAMED OSMAN.

Suriname: 866 United Nations Plaza, Suite 320, New York, NY 10017; tel. (212) 826-0660; fax (212) 980-7029; e-mail suriname@un.int; Permanent Representative HENRY LEONARD MACDONALD.

Swaziland: 408 East 50th St, New York, NY 10022; tel. (212) 371-8910; fax (212) 754-2755; e-mail swazinymission@yahoo.com; Permanent Representative ZWELETHU MNISI.

Sweden: One Dag Hammarskjöld Plaza, 885 Second Ave, 46th Floor, New York, NY 10017; tel. (212) 583-2500; fax (212) 583-2549; e-mail sweden@un.int; internet www.un.int/sweden; Permanent Representative MÅRTEN GRUNDITZ.

Switzerland: 633 Third Ave, 29th Floor, New York, NY 10017; tel. (212) 286-1540; fax (212) 286-1555; e-mail vertretung-un@nyc.rep.admin.ch; internet www.eda.admin.ch/missny; Permanent Representative PAUL R. SEGER.

Syria: 820 Second Ave, 15th Floor, New York, NY 10017; tel. (212) 661-1313; fax (212) 983-4439; e-mail exesec.syria@gmail.com; internet www.syria-un.org; Permanent Representative BASHAR JA'AFARI.

Tajikistan: 216 East 49th St, 4th Floor, New York, NY 10017; tel. (212) 207-3315; fax (212) 207-3855; e-mail tajikistan@un.int; Permanent Representative MAHMADAMIN MAHMADAMINOV.

Tanzania: 201 East 42nd St, Suite 425, New York, NY 10017; tel. (212) 697-3612; fax (212) 697-3618; e-mail tzrepny@aol.com; Permanent Representative TUVAKO NATHANIEL MANONGI.

Thailand: 351 East 52nd St, New York, NY 10022; tel. (212) 754-2230; fax (212) 688-3029; e-mail thailand@un.int; Permanent Representative NORACHIT SINHASENI.

Timor-Leste: 866 Second Ave, Suite 441, New York, NY 10017; tel. (212) 759-3675; fax (212) 759-4196; e-mail timor-leste@un.int; Permanent Representative SOFIA MESQUÍTA BORGES.

Togo: 336 East 45th St, New York, NY 10017; tel. (212) 490-3455; fax (212) 983-6684; e-mail togo@un.int; Permanent Representative KODJO MENAN.

Tonga: 250 East 51st St, New York, NY 10022; tel. (917) 369-1025; fax (917) 369-1024; e-mail tongaunmission@gmail.com; Permanent Representative MAHE 'ULI'ULI SANDHURST TUPOUNIUA.

Trinidad and Tobago: 633 Third Ave, 12th Floor, New York, NY 10017; tel. (212) 697-7620; fax (212) 682-3580; e-mail tto@un.int; internet www.un.int/trinidadandtobago; Permanent Representative RODNEY CHARLES.

Tunisia: 31 Beekman Pl., New York, NY 10022; tel. (212) 751-7503; fax (212) 751-0569; e-mail tunisnyc@nyc.rr.com; Permanent Representative MOHAMED KHALED KHIARI.

Turkey: 821 United Nations Plaza, 10th Floor, New York, NY 10017; tel. (212) 949-0150; fax (212) 949-0086; e-mail tr-delegation.newyork@mfa.gov.tr; internet www.turkuno.dt.mfa.gov.tr; Permanent Representative YAŞAR HALIT ÇEVIK.

Turkmenistan: 866 United Nations Plaza, Suite 424, New York, NY 10017; tel. (212) 486-8908; fax (212) 486-2521; e-mail turkmenistan@un.int; Permanent Representative Dr AKSOLTAN T. ATAYEVA.

Tuvalu: 800 Second Ave, Suite 400D, New York, NY 10017; tel. (212) 490-0534; fax (212) 808-4975; e-mail tuvalu@onecommonwealth.org; Permanent Representative AUNESE MAKOI SIMATI.

Uganda: 336 East 45th St, New York, NY 10017; tel. (212) 949-0110; fax (212) 687-4517; e-mail ugandaunny@un.int; internet ugandamissionunny.net; Permanent Representative RICHARD NDUHUURA.

Ukraine: 220 East 51st St, New York, NY 10022; tel. (212) 759-7003; fax (212) 355-9455; e-mail uno_us@mfa.gov.ua; internet www.un.mfa.gov.ua; Permanent Representative YURIY A. SERGEYEV.

United Arab Emirates: 3 Dag Hammarskjöld Plaza, 305 East 47th St, 7th Floor, New York, NY 10017; tel. (212) 371-0480; fax (212) 371-4923; e-mail uae@uaemission.org; Permanent Representative LANA ZAKI NUSSEIBEH.

United Kingdom: One Dag Hammarskjöld Plaza, 885 Second Ave, New York, NY 10017; tel. (212) 745-9200; fax (212) 745-9316; e-mail uk@un.int; internet ukun.fco.gov.uk/en; Permanent Representative Sir MARK LYALL GRANT.

United States of America: 799 United Nations Plaza, New York, NY 10017; tel. (212) 415-4000; fax (212) 415-4443; e-mail usunpolfax@state.gov; internet www.usunnewyork.usmission.gov; Permanent Representative SAMANTHA POWER.

Uruguay: 866 United Nations Plaza, Suite 322, New York, NY 10017; tel. (212) 752-8240; fax (212) 593-0935; e-mail uruguay@un.int; internet www.un.int/uruguay; Permanent Representative GONZALO KONCKE PIZZORNO.

Uzbekistan: 801 Second Ave, 20th Floor, New York, NY 10017; tel. (212) 486-4242; fax (212) 486-7998; e-mail uzbekistan.un@gmail.com; Chargé d'affaires a.i. ILDAR SHIGABUTDINOV.

Vanuatu: 800 Second Ave, Suite 400B, New York, NY 10017; tel. (212) 661-4303; fax (212) 661-5544; e-mail vanunmis@aol.com; Chargé d'affaires a.i. ERIC BELLEAY KALOTITI.

Venezuela: 335 East 46th St, New York, NY 10017; tel. (212) 557-2055; fax (212) 557-3528; e-mail missionvene@venezuela.gob.ve; Permanent Representative JORGE SAMUEL MONCADA.

Viet Nam: 866 United Nations Plaza, Suite 435, New York, NY 10017; tel. (212) 644-0594; fax (212) 644-5732; e-mail info@vietnam-un.org; internet www.un.int/vietnam; Permanent Representative LE HOAI TRUNG.

Yemen: 413 East 51st St, New York, NY 10022; tel. (212) 355-1730; fax (212) 750-9613; e-mail ymiss-newyork@mofa.gov.ye; Permanent Representative JAMAL ABDULLAH AL-SALLAL.

Zambia: 237 East 52nd St, New York, NY 10022; tel. (212) 888-5770; fax (212) 888-5213; e-mail zambia@un.int; Permanent Representative MWABA PATRICIA KASESE-BOTA.

Zimbabwe: 128 East 56th St, New York, NY 10022; tel. (212) 980-9511; fax (212) 308-6705; e-mail zimnewyork@gmail.com; Permanent Representative CHITSAKA CHIPAZIWA.

OBSERVERS

Intergovernmental organizations, etc., which have received an invitation to participate in the sessions and the work of the General Assembly as Observers, maintaining permanent offices at the UN:

African Union: 305 East 47th St, 5th Floor, 3 Dag Hammarskjöld Plaza, New York, NY 10017; tel. (212) 319-5490; fax (212) 319-7135; e-mail aumission_ny@yahoo.com; internet www.africa-union.org; Permanent Observer TÉTE ANTÓNIO.

Asian-African Legal Consultative Organization: 188 East 76th St, Apt 26B, New York, NY 10021; tel. (917) 623-2861; fax (206) 426-5442; e-mail aalco@un.int; Permanent Observer ROY LEE.

Caribbean Community: 88 Burnett Ave, Maplewood, NJ 07040; tel. (973) 378-9333; fax (973) 327-2671; e-mail caripoun@gmail.com; Permanent Observer NOEL SINCLAIR.

Central American Integration System: 320 West 75th St, Suite 1A, New York, NY 10023; tel. (212) 682-1550; fax (212) 877-9021; e-mail ccampos@sgsica-ny.org; Permanent Observer CARLOS CAMPOS.

Commonwealth Secretariat: 800 Second Ave, 4th Floor, New York, NY 10017; tel. (212) 599-6190; fax (212) 808-4975; e-mail comsec@onecommonwealth.org.

Cooperation Council for the Arab States of the Gulf: One Dag Hammarskjöld Plaza, 885 Second Ave, 40th Floor, New York, NY 10017; tel. (212) 319-3088; fax (212) 319-3434; Permanent Observer ADNAN AHMED ABDULLAH AL-ANSARI.

European Union: 666 Third Ave, 26th Floor, New York, NY 10017; tel. (212) 292-8600; fax (212) 292-8680; e-mail delegation-new-york@eeas.europa.eu; internet www.eu-un.europa.eu; the Observer is the Permanent Representative to the UN of the country currently exercising the Presidency of the Council of Ministers of the European Union; Head of Delegation THOMAS MAYR-HARTING.

Holy See: 25 East 39th St, New York, NY 10016; tel. (212) 370-7885; fax (212) 370-9622; e-mail office@holyseemission.org; internet www.holyseemission.org; Permanent Observer Most Rev. FRANCIS ASSISI CHULLIKATT (Titular Archbishop of Ostra).

International Committee of the Red Cross: 801 Second Ave, 18th Floor, New York, NY 10017; tel. (212) 599-6021; fax (212) 599-

6009; e-mail newyork@icrc.org; Head of Delegation WALTER A. FÜLLEMANN.

International Criminal Court: 866 United Nations Plaza, Suite 476, New York, NY 10017; tel. (212) 486-1362; fax (212) 486-1361; e-mail liaisonofficeny@icc-cpi.int; Head of Liaison Office KAREN ODABA MOSOTI.

International Criminal Police Organization (INTERPOL): One United Nations Plaza, Suite 2610, New York, NY 10017; tel. (917) 367-3463; fax (917) 367-3476; e-mail nyoffice@interpol.int; internet www.interpol.int; Special Representative WILLIAM J. S. ELLIOTT (Canada).

International Development Law Organization: 336 East 45th St, 11th Floor, New York, NY 10017; tel. (212) 867-9707; fax (212) 867-9719; e-mail pcivili@idlo.int; internet www.idlo.int; Permanent Observer PATRIZIO M. CIVILI.

International Federation of Red Cross and Red Crescent Societies: 420 Lexington Ave, Suite 2811, New York, NY 10017; tel. (212) 338-0161; fax (212) 338-9832; e-mail ifrcny@un.int; Head of Delegation and Permanent Observer MARWAN JILANI.

International Institute for Democracy and Electoral Assistance: 336 East 45th St, 14th Floor, New York, NY 10017; tel. (212) 286-1084; fax (212) 286-0260; e-mail unobserver@idea.int; Permanent Observer MASSIMO TOMMASOLI.

International Olympic Committee: 708 Third Ave, 6th Floor, New York, NY 10017; tel. (212) 209-3952; fax (212) 209-7100; e-mail IOC-UNObserver@olympic.org; Permanent Observer MARIO PESCANTE.

International Organization for Migration: 122 East 42nd St, Suite 1610, New York, NY 10168; tel. (212) 681-7000; fax (212) 867-5887; e-mail unobserver@iom.int; internet www.un.int/iom; Permanent Observer MICHELE KLEIN SOLOMON.

International Organization of La Francophonie (Organisation Internationale de la Francophonie): 801 Second Ave, Suite 605, New York, NY 10017; tel. (212) 867-6771; fax (212) 867-3840; e-mail francophonie@un.int; Permanent Observer FILIPE SAVADOGO.

International Renewable Energy Agency: 336 East 45th St, 11th Floor, New York, NY 10017; tel. (646) 738-2014; fax (646) 738-5582; internet www.irena.org.

International Seabed Authority: One United Nations Plaza, Rm 1140, New York, NY 10017; tel. (212) 963-6470; fax (212) 963-0908; e-mail seaun@un.org; Permanent Observer NII ALLOTEY ODUNTON.

International Tribunal for the Law of the Sea: Two United Nations Plaza, Rm 438, New York, NY 10017; tel. (212) 963-6140; fax (212) 963-5847; Permanent Observer SHUNJI YANAI (Pres. of the Tribunal).

Inter-Parliamentary Union: 336 East 45th St, 10th Floor, New York, NY 10017; tel. (212) 557-5880; fax (212) 557-3954; e-mail ny-office@mail.ipu.org; internet www.ipu.org/Un-e/un-opo.htm; Permanent Observer PATRICIA ANN TORSNEY.

International Union for Conservation of Nature (IUCN): 551 Fifth Ave, Suites 800 A-B, New York, NY 10176; tel. (212) 346-1163; fax (212) 346-1046; e-mail iucn@un.int; internet www.iucn.org; Permanent Observer NARINDER KAKAR (India).

League of Arab States: 866 United Nations Plaza, Suite 494, New York, NY 10017; tel. (212) 838-8700; fax (212) 355-3909; e-mail las.mail@un.int; Permanent Observer AHMED FATHALLA.

Organization of Islamic Cooperation: 320 East 51st St, New York, NY 10022; tel. (212) 883-0140; fax (212) 883-0143; e-mail oicny@un.int; internet www.oicun.org; Permanent Observer UFUK GOKCEN.

Palestine: 115 East 65th St, New York, NY 10065; tel. (212) 288-8500; fax (212) 517-2377; e-mail palestine@un.int; internet www.palestineun.org; Permanent Observer RIYAD H. MANSOUR.

Partners in Population and Development: 336 East 45th St, 14th Floor, New York, NY 10017; tel. (212) 286-1082; fax (212) 286-0260; e-mail nalam@ppdsec.org; internet www.partners-popdev.org; Permanent Observer MOHAMMAD NURUL ALAM.

Sovereign Military Order of Malta: 216 East 47th St, 8th Floor, New York, NY 10017; tel. (212) 355-6213; fax (212) 355-4014; e-mail orderofmalta@un.int; Permanent Observer ROBERT L. SHAFER.

University for Peace: 551 Fifth Ave, Suites 800 A-B, New York, NY 10176; tel. (212) 346-1163; fax (212) 346-1046; e-mail nyinfo@upeace.org; internet www.upeace.org; Permanent Observer NARINDER KAKAR (India).

The following intergovernmental organizations have a standing invitation to participate as Observers, but do not maintain permanent offices at the UN: African, Caribbean and Pacific Group of States; African Development Bank; Agency for the Prohibition of Nuclear Weapons in Latin America and the Caribbean; Andean Community; Asian Development Bank; Association of Caribbean States; Association of Southeast Asian Nations; Central European Initiative; Collective Security Treaty Organization; Common Fund for Commodities; Commonwealth of Independent States; Communauté économique des états de l'Afrique centrale; Community of Sahel-Saharan States; Comunidade dos Países de Língua Portuguesa; Conference on Interaction and Confidence-building Measures in Asia; Council of Europe; East African Community; Economic Community of West African States; Economic Cooperation Organization; Energy Charter Conference; Eurasian Development Bank; Eurasian Economic Community; Global fund to Fight AIDS, Tuberculosis and Malaria; Indian Ocean Commission; GUAM: Organization for Democracy and Economic Development; Hague Conference on Private International Law; Ibero-American General Secretariat; Inter-American Development Bank; Intergovernmental Authority on Development; International Centre for Migration Policy Development; International Conference on the Great Lakes Region of Africa; International Fund for Saving the Aral Sea; International Humanitarian Fact-Finding Commission; International Hydrographic Organization; International Trade Union Confederation, Islamic Development Bank; Italian-Latin American Institute; Latin American Economic System; Latin American Integration Association; Latin American Parliament; OPEC Fund for International Development; Organisation for Economic Co-operation and Development; Organisation of Eastern Caribbean States; Organization for Security and Co-operation in Europe; Organization of American States; Organization of the Black Sea Economic Cooperation; Pacific Islands Forum; Parliamentary Assembly of the Mediterranean; Permanent Court of Arbitration; Regional Centre on Small Arms and Light Weapons in the Great Lakes Region, the Horn of Africa and Bordering States; Shanghai Cooperation Organization; South Asian Association for Regional Cooperation; South Centre; Southern African Development Community; Union of South American Nations; World Customs Organization.

United Nations Information Centres/Services

Algeria: POB 444, Hydre, Algiers; tel. and fax (21) 92 54 42; e-mail unic.dz@undp.org; internet algiers.unic.org.

Argentina: Junín 1940, 1°, 1113 Buenos Aires; tel. (11) 4803-7671; fax (11) 4804-7545; e-mail unic.buenosaires@unic.org; internet www.unic.org.ar; also covers Uruguay.

Armenia: 375010 Yerevan, 14 Petros Adamian St; tel. (10) 56-02-12; fax (10) 56-14-06; e-mail uno.yerevan@unic.org; internet www.un.am.

Australia: POB 5366, Kingston, ACT 2604; tel. (2) 6270-9200; fax (2) 6273-8206; e-mail unic.canberra@unic.org; internet www.un.org.au; also covers Fiji, Kiribati, Nauru, New Zealand, Samoa, Tonga, Tuvalu and Vanuatu.

Austria: POB 500, Vienna International Centre, Wagramerstr. 5, 1400 Vienna; tel. (1) 26060-3325; fax (1) 26060-5899; e-mail unis@unvienna.org; internet www.unis.unvienna.org; also covers Hungary, Slovakia and Slovenia.

Azerbaijan: 1001 Baku, UN 50th Anniversary St 3; tel. (12) 498-98-88; fax (12) 498-32-35; e-mail un-dpi@un-az.org; internet www.baku.sites.unicnetwork.org.

Bahrain: POB 26814, UN House, Bldg 69, Rd 1901, Manama 319; tel. 17311676; fax 17311600; e-mail unic.manama@unic.org; internet www.manama.unic.org; also covers Qatar and the United Arab Emirates.

Bangladesh: IDB Bhahan, 8th Floor, Rokeya Sharani Sher-e-Bangla Nagar, Dhaka 1207; tel. (2) 9183086; fax (2) 9183106; e-mail unic.dhaka@undp.org; internet www.unicdhaka.org.

Belarus: 220050 Minsk, vul. Kirova 17, 6th Floor; tel. (17) 327-48-76; fax (17) 226-03-40; e-mail dpi.staff.by@undp.org; internet www.un.by.

Bolivia: Calle 14 esq. Sánchez Bustamante, Ed. Metrobol II, Calacoto, La Paz; tel. (2) 2795544; fax (2) 2795820; e-mail unic.lapaz@unic.org; internet www.nu.org.bo.

Brazil: Palacio Itamaraty, Avda Marechal Floriano 196, 20080-002 Rio de Janeiro; tel. (21) 2253-2211; fax (21) 2233-5753; e-mail unic.brazil@unic.org; internet unicrio.org.br.

Burkina Faso: BP 135, 14 ave de la Grande Chancellerie, Secteur 4, Ouagadougou; tel. 50-30-60-76; fax 50-31-13-22; e-mail unic.ouagadougou@unic.org; internet ouagadougou.unic.org; also covers Chad, Mali and Niger.

Burundi: BP 2160, ave de la Révolution 117, Bujumbura; tel. (2) 225018; fax (2) 241798; e-mail unic.bujumbura@unic.org; internet bujumbura.unic.org.

Cameroon: PB 836, Immeuble Tchinda, rue 2044, Yaoundé; tel. 221-23-67; fax 221-23-68; e-mail unic.yaounde@unic.org; internet yaounde.unic.org; also covers the Central African Republic and Gabon.

Colombia: Calle 100, No. 8A-55, 10°, Edificio World Trade Center, Torre C, Bogotá 2; tel. (1) 257-6044; fax (1) 257-6244; e-mail unic.bogota@unic.org; internet www.nacionesunidas.org.co; also covers Ecuador and Venezuela.

Congo, Republic: POB 13210, ave Foch, Case ORTF 15, Brazzaville; tel. 661-20-68; e-mail unic.brazzaville@unic.org; internet brazzaville.unic.org.

Czech Republic: Železná 24, 110 00 Prague 1; tel. 255711645; fax 257316761; e-mail info@osn.cz; internet www.osn.cz.

Egypt: 1 Osiris St, Garden City, Cairo; tel. (2) 7900022; fax (2) 7953705; e-mail info@unic-eg.org; internet www.unic-eg.org; also covers Saudi Arabia.

Eritrea: Hiday St, Airport Rd, Asmara; tel. (1) 151166; fax (1) 151081; e-mail dpi.er@undp.org; internet asmara.unic.org.

Georgia: 0179 Tbilisi, Eristavi St 9; tel. (32) 25-11-26; fax (32) 25-02-71; e-mail uno.tbilisi@unic.org; internet www.ungeorgia.ge.

Ghana: POB GP 2339, Gamel Abdul Nassar/Liberia Rds, Accra; tel. (2) 785385; fax (2) 773899; e-mail unic.accra@unic.org; internet accra.unic.org; also covers Sierra Leone.

India: 55 Lodi Estate, New Delhi 110 003; tel. (11) 46532242; fax (11) 24620293; e-mail unicindia@unicindia.org; internet www.unic.org.in; also covers Bhutan.

Indonesia: Gedung Surya, 14th Floor, 9 Jalan M. H. Thamrin Kavling, Jakarta 10350; tel. (21) 3983-1011; fax (21) 3983-1014; e-mail unic-jakarta@unic.org; internet www.unic-jakarta.org.

Iran: POB 15875-4557; 8 Shahrzad Blvd, Darrous, Tehran; tel. (21) 2287-3837; fax (21) 2287-3395; e-mail unic.tehrani@unic.org; internet www.unic-ir.org.

Japan: UNU Bldg, 8th Floor, 53–70 Jingumae 5-chome, Shibuya-ku, Tokyo 150 0001; tel. (3) 5467-4451; fax (3) 5467-4455; e-mail unic.tokyo@unic.org; internet www.unic.or.jp.

Kazakhstan: 67 Tole Bi Street, 050000 Almatı; tel. (727) 258-26-43; fax (727) 258-26-45; e-mail kazakhstan@unic.org; internet kazakhstan.unic.org.

Kenya: POB 30552, United Nations Office, Gigiri, Nairobi; tel. (20) 76225421; fax (20) 7624349; e-mail nairobi.unic@unon.org; internet www.unicnairobi.org; also covers Seychelles and Uganda.

Lebanon: UN House, Riad es-Solh Sq., POB 11-8575, Beirut; tel. (1) 981301; fax (1) 970424; e-mail unic-beirut@un.org; internet www.unicbeirut.org; also covers Jordan, Kuwait and Syria.

Lesotho: POB 301, Maseru 100; tel. (22) 313790; fax (22) 310042; e-mail unic.maseru@unic.org; internet maseru.unic.org.

Libya: POB 286, Khair Aldeen Baybers St, Hay al-Andalous, Tripoli; tel. (21) 4770251; fax (21) 4777343; e-mail tripoli@un.org; internet tripoli.unic.org.

Madagascar: 159 rue Damantsoa Ankorahotra, Antananarivo; tel. (20) 2233050; fax (20) 2236794; e-mail unic.antananarivo@unic.org; internet antananarivo.unic.org.

Mexico: Montes Urales 440, 3°, Col. Chapultepec Morales, México 11 000, DF; tel. (55) 4000-9725; fax (55) 5203-8638; e-mail unicmex@un.org.mx; internet www.cinu.mx; also covers Cuba and the Dominican Republic.

Morocco: BP 601; rue Tarik ibn Zyad 6, Rabat; tel. (3) 7750393; fax (3) 7750383; e-mail cinu.rabat@unic.org; internet www.unicmor.ma.

Myanmar: 6 Natmauk Rd, Tamwe P.O., Yangon; tel. (1) 546933; fax (1) 542634; e-mail unic.yangon@unic.org; internet yangon.unic.org.

Namibia: Private Bag 13351, 38-44 Stein St, Windhoek; tel. (61) 2046111; fax (61) 2046521; e-mail unic.windhoek@unic.org; internet windhoek.unic.org.

Nepal: POB 107, UN House, Kathmandu; tel. (1) 5523200; fax (1) 5543723; e-mail kathmandu.unic@unic.org; internet kathmandu.unic.org.

Nigeria: 17 Alfred Rewane (formerly Kingsway) Rd, Ikoyi, Lagos; tel. (1) 7755989; fax (1) 4630915; e-mail lagos@unic.org; internet lagos.unic.org.

Pakistan: POB 1107, Serena Business Complex, G-5/1, Islamabad; tel. (51) 8355719; fax (51) 2271856; e-mail unic.islamabad@unic.org; internet www.unic.org.pk.

Panama: UN House Bldg 128, Ciudad del Saber, Clayton, Panama City; tel. (7) 301-0035; fax (7) 301-0037; e-mail unic.panama@unic.org; internet www.cinup.org.

Paraguay: Casilla de Correo 1107; Edif. Naciones Unidas, Avda Mariscal López, Asunción; tel. (21) 614443; fax (21) 611988; e-mail unic.py@undp.org; internet asuncion.unic.org.

Peru: POB 14-0199, Av. Perez Aranibar 750, Magdalena, Lima 17; tel. (1) 625-9140; fax (1) 625-9100; e-mail unic.lima@unic.org; internet www.uniclima.org.pe.

Philippines: 5/F GC Corporate Plaza, 150 Legaspi St, Legazpi Village, Makati City 1229; tel. (2) 336-7720; fax (2) 336-7177; e-mail unic.manila@unic.org; internet www.unicmanila.org; also covers Papua New Guinea and Solomon Islands.

Poland: Al. Niepodległości 186; 00-608 Warsaw; tel. (22) 8255784; fax (22) 8257706; e-mail unic.poland@unic.org; internet www.unic.un.org.pl.

Romania: 011975 Bucharest, Bd. Primaverii 48A; tel. (21) 201-78-72; fax (21) 201-78-28; e-mail unic.romania@unic.org; internet www.onuinfo.ro.

Russia: 119002 Moscow, per. Glazovskii 4/16; tel. (499) 241-28-94; fax (495) 695-21-38; e-mail unic.moscow@unic.org; internet www.unic.ru.

Senegal: Immeuble SOUMEX, 3rd Floor, Mamelles, Almadies, Dakar; tel. 869-99-11; fax 860-51-48; e-mail unic.dakar@unic.org; internet dakar.unic.org; also covers Cape Verde, Côte d'Ivoire, The Gambia, Guinea-Bissau and Mauritania.

South Africa: Metro Park Bldg, 351 Schoeman St, POB 12677, Pretoria 0126; tel. (12) 354-8506; fax (12) 354-8501; e-mail info.pretoria@unic.org; internet pretoria.unic.org.

Sri Lanka: POB 1505, 202/204 Bauddhaloka Mawatha, Colombo 7; tel. (11) 2580691; fax (11) 2501396; e-mail unic.colombo@unic.org; internet colombo.unic.org.

Sudan: POB 1992, UN Compound, House No. 7, Blk 5, Gamma'a Ave, Khartoum; tel. (183) 783755; fax (183) 773772; e-mail unic.sd@undp.org; internet khartoum.unic.org; also covers Somalia.

Switzerland: Palais des Nations, 1211 Geneva 10; tel. 229171234; fax 229170123; e-mail webmaster@unog.ch; internet www.unog.ch.

Tanzania: POB 9224, International House, 6th Floor, Garden Ave/Shaaban Robert St, Dar es Salaam; tel. (22) 2199326; fax (22) 2667633; e-mail unic.daressalaam@unic.org; internet daressalaam.unic.org.

Thailand: ESCAP, United Nations Bldg, Rajadamnern Nok Ave, Bangkok 10200; tel. (2) 288-1864; fax (2) 288-1052; e-mail unisbkk.unescap@un.org; internet www.unescap.org/unis; also covers Cambodia, Laos, Malaysia, Singapore and Viet Nam.

Togo: 486 angle rue Atimé et ave de la Libération, Lomé; tel. and fax 221-23-06; e-mail cinutogo@gmail.com; internet lome.unic.org; also covers Benin.

Trinidad and Tobago: 2nd Floor, Bretton Hall, 16 Victoria Ave, Port of Spain; tel. 623-4813; fax 623-4332; e-mail unic.portofspain@unic.org; internet portofspain.unic.org; also covers Antigua and Barbuda, Aruba, the Bahamas, Barbados, Belize, Dominica, Grenada, Guyana, Jamaica, the Netherlands Antilles, Saint Christopher and Nevis, Saint Lucia, Saint Vincent and the Grenadines, and Suriname.

Tunisia: BP 863, 41 ave Louis Braille, Tunis; tel. (71) 902-203; fax (71) 906-811; e-mail unic.tunis@unic.org; internet www.unictunis.org.tn.

Turkey: PK 415, Birlik Mahallesi, 2 Cad. No. 11, 06610 Cankaya, Ankara; tel. (312) 4541052; fax (312) 4961499; e-mail unic.ankara@unic.org; internet www.unicankara.org.tr.

Ukraine: 01021 Kyiv, Klovsky uzviz, 1; tel. (44) 253-93-63; fax (44) 253-26-07; e-mail registry@un.org.ua; internet www.un.org.ua.

USA: 1775 K St, NW, Suite 400, Washington, DC 20006; tel. (202) 331-8670; fax (202) 331-9191; e-mail unicdc@unicwash.org; internet www.unicwash.org.

Uzbekistan: 100029 Tashkent, Shevchenko ko'ch 4; tel. (71) 120-34-50; fax (71) 120-34-85; e-mail registry@undp.org; internet www.un.uz.

Western Europe: United Nations Regional Information Centre, Residence Palace, Bloc C, Level 7, 155 rue de la Loi/Wetstraat, 1040 Brussels, Belgium; tel. (2) 788-84-84; fax (2) 788-84-85; e-mail info@unric.org; internet www.unric.org; serves Belgium, Cyprus, Denmark, Finland, France, Germany, Greece, the Holy See, Iceland, Ireland, Italy, Luxembourg, Malta, Monaco, the Netherlands, Norway, Portugal, San Marino, Spain, Sweden, United Kingdom; also provides liaison with the institutions of the European Union.

Yemen: POB 237; St 5, off Al-Boniya St, Handhal Zone, San'a; tel. (1) 274000; fax (1) 274043; e-mail unicyem@y.net.ye; internet www.unicyemen.org.

Zambia: POB 32905, Revenue House, Ground Floor, Cairo Rd (Northend), Lusaka; tel. (21) 1228487; fax (21) 1222958; e-mail unic.lusaka@unic.org; internet lusaka.unic.org; also covers Botswana, Malawi and Swaziland.

Zimbabwe: POB 4408, Sanders House, 2nd Floor, First St/Jason Moyo Ave, Harare; tel. (4) 777060; fax (4) 750476; e-mail unic.harare@unic.org; internet harare.unic.org.

Conferences

Global conferences are convened regularly by the United Nations. Special sessions of the General Assembly assess progress achieved in the implementation of conference action plans. The following global conferences were scheduled for 2014:

Conference on Disarmament (Jan.–March, May–June, July–Sept.: Geneva, Switzerland);

High-level Dialogue on Financing for Development (April: New York);

Development Co-operation Forum (July: New York);

Third International Conference on Small Island Developing States (Sept.: Apia, Samoa);

UNESCO World Conference on Education for Sustainable Development (Nov.: Okayama, Japan);

Second International Conference on Nutrition (Nov.: Rome, Italy).

System-wide Coherence

The Senior Management Group, a committee of senior UN personnel established in 1997, acts as the Secretary-General's cabinet and as the central policy-planning body of the UN. The 28-member UN System Chief Executives Board for Co-ordination (CEB) convenes at least twice a year under the chairmanship of the Secretary-General to co-ordinate UN system-wide policies, activities and management issues. The UN Development Group (UNDG) unites, under the chairmanship of the Administrator of the UN Development Programme (UNDP), the heads of some 32 UN funds, programmes and departments concerned with sustainable development, in order to promote coherent policy at country level. The UNDG is supported by the UN Development Operations Coordination Office. Several inter-agency mechanisms, including UN-Energy, UN-Oceans and UN-Water, facilitate UN system-wide inter-agency co-operation and coherence. Project management services are provided throughout the UN system of entities and organizations, as well as to certain bilateral donors, international financial institutions and governments, by the UN Office for Project Services. The Inter-Agency Standing Committee comprises the executive heads of 17 leading UN and other agencies and non-governmental organization consortia, who convene at least twice a year under the leadership of the Emergency Relief Co-ordinator (see OCHA). It co-ordinates and administers the international response to complex and major humanitarian disasters, and the development of relevant policies.

In February 2005 the Secretary-General appointed a High-level Panel on UN System-wide Coherence in the Areas of Development, Humanitarian Assistance and the Environment, to study means of strengthening UN performance; in November the Panel published a report entitled *Ten ways for the UN to 'deliver as one'*, outlining the following 10 recommendations for future inter-agency co-operation: (i) the UN should 'deliver as one' at country level, with one leader, one programme, one budget and, where appropriate, one office; (ii) a UN Sustainable Development Board should be established to oversee the One UN Country Programme; (iii) a Global Leaders' Forum should be established within the Economic and Social Council (ECOSOC) to upgrade its policy co-ordination role in economic, social and related issues; (iv) the UN Secretary-General, the President of the World Bank and the Managing Director of the IMF should initiate a process to review, update and conclude formal agreements on their respective roles and relations at the global and country levels; (v) a Millennium Development Goal funding mechanism should be established to provide multi-year funding for the One UN Country Programme; (vi) the UN's leading role in humanitarian disasters and transition from relief to development should be enhanced; (vii) international environmental governance should be strengthened and made more coherent in order to improve effectiveness and targeted action of environmental activities in the UN system; (viii) a dynamic UN entity focused on gender equality and women's empowerment should be established; (ix) a UN common evaluation system should be established, while other business practices, such as human resource policies, planning and results-based management, should be upgraded and harmonized across the UN system to stimulate improved performance; and (x) the Secretary-General should establish an independent task force to eliminate further duplication within the UN system and, where necessary, to consolidate UN entities. In 2007 a *Delivering as One* pilot initiative was launched to test enhanced co-ordination in the provision of development assistance, based on the principles of one leader, one budget, one programme, and one office, in eight volunteer countries: Albania, Cape Verde, Mozambique, Pakistan, Rwanda, Tanzania, Uruguay, and Viet Nam. The CEB has established an action framework for co-ordinating system-wide activities to address climate change under the *Delivering as One* commitment. In January 2012 the Secretary-General announced a second generation of inter-agency *Delivering as One* co-operation, with a focus on enhanced monitoring of results and accountability.

CO-ORDINATING AND INTER-AGENCY BODIES

UN Collaborative Programme on Reducing Emissions from Deforestation and Forest Degradation in Developing Countries (UN-REDD): UN-REDD Inter-agency Secretariat, International Environment House, 11–13 Chemin des Anémones, 1219 Châtelaine, Geneva, Switzerland; tel. 229178946; e-mail rosa.andolfato@un-redd.org; internet www.un-redd.org; f. 2008 to support developing countries in preparing and implementing national REDD+ strategies, involving investment in low-carbon routes to sustainable development, reversal of deforestation and the promotion of conservation, sustainable management of forests, and enhancement of forest carbon stocks; provides assistance to 46 partner countries in Africa, Asia, the Pacific, and Latin America; extends support to national programme activities aimed at developing and implementing REDD+ strategies in 16 of the partner countries, having (by June 2013) approved funding totalling US $172.4m. in this respect, channelled through a Multi-Partner Trust Fund; governed by a Policy Board comprising representatives from UNEP, UNDP and FAO and from partner countries, donors to the MPTF, civil society, and indigenous peoples; Head of the Secretariat MARIO BOCCUCCI (Italy).

UN-Energy: UN Energy Secretariat, c/o UN Department of Economic and Social Affairs, Two United Nations Plaza, New York, NY 10017, USA; internet www.un-energy.org; f. 2002; established following the 2002 World Summit on Sustainable Development, held in Johannesburg, South Africa, as a mechanism to promote coherence among UN agencies in energy matters, and to develop increased collective engagement between UN agencies and key external stakeholders; focal areas of activity include energy access, renewable energy and energy efficiency; the sub-programme UN-Energy Africa, established in May 2004 by a meeting of African ministers responsible for energy affairs, is the principal inter-agency mechanism in the field of energy within Africa; in 2013 UN-Energy, with UNIDO and other agencies, co-led global consultations on advancing a post-2015 development framework in the thematic area of energy; Chair. KANDEH K. YUMKELLA (Sierra Leone).

UN-Oceans: UN-Oceans Secretariat, c/o UNDP Water and Ocean Governance Programme, One United Nations Plaza, New York, NY 10017, USA; tel. (212) 906-5300; e-mail Andrew.Hudson@undp.org; internet www.unoceans.org; f. 2003; has task forces on Marine Biodiversity beyond National Jurisdiction; on Establishing a Regular Process for Global Assessment of the Marine Environment; on Global Partnership for Climate, Fisheries and Aquaculture; and on Marine Protected Areas and Other Area-Based Management Tools; inter-agency activities include updating the *UN Atlas of the Oceans*, an internet-based information system for policy-makers and scientists; implementing the Programme of Action for the Protection of the Marine Environment; undertaking the International Coral Reef Initiative (ICRI); the Joint Group of Experts on the Scientific Aspects of Marine Environmental Protection (GESAMP); the Global Ocean Observing System (led by UNESCO/IOC); the Global Climate Observing System (led by WMO); organizing World Oceans Day, held annually on 8 June; and developing the International Waters focal area under the Global Environment Facility; Co-ordinator Dr ANDREW HUDSON.

UN-Water: UN-Water Secretariat, Rm 2250, c/o UN Department of Economic and Social Affairs, Two United Nations Plaza, New York, NY 10017, USA; fax (212) 963-4340; e-mail unwater@un.org; internet www.unwater.org; f. 2003 as an inter-agency mechanism to foster greater co-operation and information sharing among UN agencies and other partners on water-related issues, with a focus on all aspects of freshwater and sanitation, including surface and groundwater resources, the interface between freshwater and seawater, and water-related disasters; appoints task forces, including on transboundary waters, and climate change and water; specific agencies host activities and programmes on behalf of UN-Water, which is not itself an implementing body; Exec. Head MICHEL JARRAUD (France) (Sec.-Gen. of WMO).

Finance

UN member states pay mandatory assessed contributions towards the regular budget, towards peacekeeping operations, to international tribunals, and to the Capital Master Plan (which manages renovation works at UN headquarters in New York, USA). Ability to pay assessed contributions to the regular budget is determined by a

10-year average of national gross domestic product figures, adjusted to take into account high levels of foreign debt or very low per caput income (the minimum assessment is 0.001% of the budget). From 2001 the upper level of contributions to the UN's regular budget was capped at 22.0%, while annual contributions were raised for several nations with rapidly developing economies. The most recent scale of assessments calculation for the regular budget, valid for the period 2013–15, was adopted in December 2012; the three largest contributors were the USA (22.0%), Japan (10.8%) and Germany (7.1%). At 1 October 2013 outstanding unpaid assessments to the regular budget stood at US $945m.

Since the 1990s the UN has suffered financial difficulties, owing to an expansion of the organization's political and humanitarian activities, delay on the part of some member states in paying their assessed contributions, and reductions in donations paid to agencies' voluntary funding mechanisms. In December 1997 a UN Development Account was established to channel administrative savings achieved as a result of reforms to the UN's administrative structure towards financing development projects. In 1997 a US business executive, Ted Turner, announced a donation of US $1,000m. to finance UN humanitarian and environmental causes. The donation has been paid in instalments and administered through his 'UN Foundation', and a UN Fund for International Partnerships was established by the UN Secretary-General in 1998 to facilitate relations between the UN system and the UN Foundation. The Foundation, which is also sustained by resources from other partners and by grass-roots donors, supports the UN through advocacy, grant-making, and the implementation of public-private partnerships. In July 2005 the UN Secretary-General established a UN Democracy Fund, which promotes human rights, supports democratic institutions, and aims to broaden participation in the democratic process.

In December 2013 the UN General Assembly approved a proposed regular budget of US $5,530.3m. for the two-year period 2014–15.

PROPOSED TWO-YEAR BUDGET OF THE UNITED NATIONS
(US $'000)

	2014–15
Overall policy-making, direction and co-ordination	790,612.2
Political affairs	1,344,301.8
International justice and law	100,154.0
International co-operation for development	496,111.1
Regional co-operation for development	572,413.4
Human rights and humanitarian affairs	353,091.3
Public information	188,443.9
Common support services	657,782.4
Internal oversight	40,552.3
Jointly financed activities and special expenses	155,018.0
Capital expenditures	75,268.7
Safety and security	241,370.1
Development Account	28,398.8
Staff Assessment	486,831.8
Total	5,530,349.8

United Nations Publications

Demographic Yearbook.
Index to Proceedings (of the General Assembly; the Security Council; the Economic and Social Council; the Trusteeship Council).
International Law Catalogue.
Monthly Bulletin of Statistics.
Population and Vital Statistics Report (quarterly).
Statement of Treaties and International Agreements (monthly).
Statistical Yearbook.
UN Chronicle (quarterly).
United Nations Disarmament Yearbook.
United Nations Juridical Yearbook.
World Economic and Social Survey.
World Situation and Prospects.
World Statistics Pocketbook.
Yearbook of the United Nations.

Other UN publications are listed in the chapters dealing with the agencies concerned. The official languages of the UN are Arabic, Chinese, English, French, Russian and Spanish; publications may be presented in all or some of these, and, where relevant, in other national languages. UN Information Centres in member states produce information materials in local languages, and also translate some UN publications into these.

Secretariat

The Secretary-General is the chief administrative officer of the UN, and he/she may appoint further staff as required. In December 2007 a new post of Deputy Secretary-General was created to assist in the management of Secretariat operations, and represent the Secretary-General as required. The chief administrative staff of the UN Regional Commissions and of all the subsidiary organs of the UN are also members of the Secretariat staff and are listed in the appropriate chapters. The Secretariat staff also includes high-level envoys and special appointments. The Secretariat comprises about 15,000 permanent staff, excluding staff working for the UN specialized agencies and subsidiary organs. The working languages at the Secretariat are English and French.

The Secretary-General chairs the Senior Management Group, a committee of senior UN personnel that acts as a cabinet and as the central policy-planning body of the UN.

In February 2005 the Secretary-General appointed a High-Level Panel on United Nations System-wide Coherence in the Areas of Development, Humanitarian Assistance and the Environment. In November, the Panel published a report entitled *Ten ways for the UN to 'deliver as one'*, outlining 10 recommendations for future inter-agency co-operation. In February 2011 the Secretary-General appointed an Evaluation Management Group to assess lessons learnt from the *Delivering as One* initiative.

In 2007 the UN Secretary-General established a Millennium Development Goal Gap Task Force, which tracks, systematically and at both international and country level, international commitments in the areas of official development assistance, market access, debt relief, access to essential medicines and technology. The Task Force, led by the UN Department of Economic and Social Affairs and by the UN Development Programme, includes more than 20 UN agencies, the Organisation for Economic Co-operation and Development and the World Trade Organization.

In April 2008 the Secretary-General announced that he was to chair a new High Level Task Force (HLTF) on the Global Food Security Crisis, comprising the heads of UN bodies and experts from the UN and the wider international community. The HLTF was to address the impact of soaring global levels of food and fuel prices and formulate a comprehensive framework for action, with a view to preventing the escalation of widespread hunger, malnutrition and related social unrest. The Department of Economic and Social Affairs, with the IMF, leads an initiative to strengthen monitoring and analysis surveillance, and to implement an effective warning system, one of nine Joint Crisis Initiatives that were endorsed in April 2009 by the UN System Chief Executives Board for Co-ordination, with the aim of alleviating the impact of the global economic and financial crisis on poor and vulnerable populations.

In May 2011 the UN Secretary-General established a Change Management Team (CMT), with a mandate to guide an agenda for further reform of the UN. The initial task of the CMT was to formulate a comprehensive plan to streamline processes, increase accountability and improve the efficiency of the delivery of its mandates.

In September 2011 the UN Secretary-General launched a new initiative, Sustainable Energy for All by 2030, and a high-level group responsible for its implementation. The initiative aimed to meet three interlinked global targets: universal access to modern energy services; doubling energy efficiency; and doubling the share of renewable energy in the world's energy supply.

In January 2012, at the commencement of his second term of office, covering the period 2012–16, Ban Ki-Moon announced a five-year agenda for action with the following priority areas of activity: sustainable development; prevention in the areas of natural disaster risk reduction, violent conflict, and human rights abuses; building a more secure world; supporting nations in transition; working with and for women and young people; enhancing system-wide partnerships; and strengthening the UN. The agenda envisaged a second generation of inter-agency *Delivering as One* co-operation, with enhanced monitoring of results and accountability.

In January 2012 the UN Secretary-General established a UN System Task Team—led jointly by the UNDP Administrator-General and the UN Under-Secretary-General for Economic and Social Affairs—which has subsequently supported system-wide consultations, in 11 thematic areas, on the advancement of a post-2015 global development agenda. The Secretary-General appointed a Special Adviser on Post-2015 Development Planning in June 2012. In May and July, respectively, the Co-Chairs and membership were announced of a new High-level Panel to Advise on the Global Development Agenda Beyond 2015, and in September 2012 the Panel's Executive Secretary was appointed and the Panel's inaugural meeting was held, on the sidelines of the UN General Assembly. In May 2013 the Panel presented to the Secretary-General a draft document entitled 'A New Global Partnership: Eradicate Poverty and Transform Economies through Sustainable Development', which set out a universal agenda to eradicate extreme poverty globally by 2030, and to pursue and deliver sustainable development. The Panel has consulted closely with a working group of experts tasked by the UN Conference on Sustainable Development (convened in June 2012) to formulate a series of Sustainable Development Goals.

Secretary-General: BAN KI-MOON (Republic of Korea).

Deputy Secretary-General: JAN ELIASSON (Sweden).

OFFICES AND DEPARTMENTS OF THE SECRETARIAT

Executive Office of the Secretary-General

Under-Secretary-General, Chef de Cabinet: SUSANA MALCORRA (Argentina).

Spokesperson for the Secretary-General: STÉPHANE DUJARRIC DE LA RIVIÈRE (France).

Executive Director of the Global Compact: GEORG KELL (Germany).

Assistant Secretary-General for Policy Co-ordination and Strategic Planning: DR ROBERT C. ORR (USA).

Assistant Secretary-General, Chief Information Technology Officer: ATEFEH RIAZI (USA).

Department for Safety and Security

Under-Secretary-General: KEVIN KENNEDY (Ireland/USA).

Assistant Under-Secretary-General: MBARANGA GASARABWE (Rwanda).

Department of Economic and Social Affairs

Under-Secretary-General: WU HONGBO (People's Republic of China).

Under-Secretary-General for Gender Equality and the Advancement of Women: PHUMZILE MLAMBO-NGCUKA (South Africa).

Assistant Secretary-General for Intergovernmental Support and Strategic Partnerships at UN Women: LAKSHMI PURI (India).

Assistant Secretary-General for Policy and Programmes at UN Women: JOHN HENDRA (Canada).

Assistant Secretary-General, Senior Adviser on Economic Development and Finance: (vacant).

Assistant Secretary-General, Policy Co-ordination and Inter-Agency Affairs: THOMAS GASS (Switzerland).

Department of Field Support

Under-Secretary-General: AMEERAH HAQ (Bangladesh).

Assistant Secretary-General: ANTHONY BANBURY (USA).

Department of General Assembly and Conference Management

Under-Secretary-General: TEGEGNEWORK GETTU (Ethiopia).

Assistant Secretary-General for General Assembly Affairs and Conference Management: FRANZ BAUMANN (Germany).

Department of Management

Under-Secretary-General: YUKIO TAKASU (Japan).

Assistant Secretary-General, Central Support Services: STEPHEN JOHN CUTTS (United Kingdom).

Assistant Secretary-General for Programme Planning, Budget and Accounts: MARIA EUGENIA CASAR PEREZ (Mexico).

Assistant Secretary-General, Enterprise Resource Planning Project: ERNESTO ENRIQUE BACA (Argentina).

Assistant Secretary-General, Human Resources Management: CATHERINE POLLARD (Guyana).

Department of Peacekeeping Operations

Under-Secretary-General: HERVÉ LADSOUS (France).

Assistant Secretary-General: EDMOND MULET (Guatemala).

Assistant Secretary-General, Military Adviser for Peacekeeping Operations: Lt-Gen. MAQSOOD AHMED (Pakistan).

Assistant Secretary-General, Rule of Law and Security Institutions: DMITRY TITOV (Russia).

Department of Political Affairs

Under-Secretary-General: JEFFREY D. FELTMAN (USA).

Assistant Secretary-General, Mediator-in-Residence: Mediator Debriefing and Lessons Learned Programme: MARGARET VOGT (Nigeria).

Assistant Secretary-General: TAYÉ-BROOK ZERIHOUN (Ethiopia).

Assistant Secretary-General: OSCAR FERNANDEZ-TARANCO (Argentina).

Department of Communications and Public Information

Under-Secretary-General and Co-ordinator for Multilingualism: PETER LAUNSKY-TIEFFENTHAL (Austria).

Office for Disarmament Affairs

Under-Secretary-General, High Representative for Disarmament Affairs: ANGELA KANE (Germany).

Office for the Co-ordination of Humanitarian Affairs

Under-Secretary-General for Humanitarian Affairs and Emergency Relief Co-ordinator: VALERIE AMOS (United Kingdom).

Deputy Emergency Relief Co-ordinator and Assistant Secretary-General for Humanitarian Affairs: FLAVIA PANSIERI (Italy).

Office of Internal Oversight Services

Under-Secretary-General: CARMEN L. LAPOINTE (Canada).

Assistant Secretary-General: DAVID MUCHOKI KANJA (Kenya).

Office of Legal Affairs

Under-Secretary-General, The Legal Counsel: MIGUEL DE SERPA SOARES (Portugal).

Assistant Secretary-General, Legal Affairs: D. STEPHEN MATHIAS (USA).

Office of the Capital Master Plan

Assistant Secretary-General, Executive Director of the Office of the Capital Master Plan: MICHAEL ADLERSTEIN (USA).

Office of the High Representative for the Least Developed Countries, Landlocked Developing Countries and Small Island Developing States

Under-Secretary-General and High Representative: GYAN CHANDRA ACHARYA (Nepal).

Office of the Special Representative of the Secretary-General for Children and Armed Conflict

Under-Secretary-General and Special Representative: LEILA ZERROUGUI (Algeria).

Office of the United Nations High Commissioner for Human Rights

Palais des Nations, 1211 Geneva 10, Switzerland; tel. 229179000; fax 229179010; internet www.unhchr.ch.

High Commissioner: NAVANETHEM PILLAY (South Africa).

Deputy High Commissioner: KYUNG-WHA KANG (Republic of Korea).

Assistant Secretary-General: IVAN ŠIMONOVIC (Croatia).

Office on Drugs and Crime

Under-Secretary-General: YURI FEDOTOV (Russia).

Peacebuilding Support Office

Assistant Secretary-General: JUDY CHENG-HOPKINS (Malaysia).

UN Ombudsperson and Mediation Services

Assistant Secretary-General, UN Ombudsman: JOHNSTONE BARKAT (USA).

Geneva Office

Palais des Nations, 1211 Geneva 10, Switzerland; tel. 2291071234; fax 229170123; internet www.unog.ch.

Director-General: MICHAEL MØLLER (Denmark) (acting).

Nairobi Office

POB 30552, Nairobi, Kenya; tel. (20) 7621234.

Director-General and Under-Secretary-General: SAHLE-WORK ZEWDE (Ethiopia).

Vienna Office

Vienna International Centre, POB 500, 1400 Vienna, Austria; tel. (1) 26060; fax (1) 263-3389; internet www.unvienna.org.

Director-General: YURI FEDOTOV (Russia).

SPECIAL HIGH LEVEL APPOINTMENTS OF THE UN SECRETARY-GENERAL

Special Advisers

Special Adviser: JOSEPH V. REED (USA).

Special Adviser: RIZA IQBAL (Pakistan).

Special Adviser and Mediator in the Border Dispute between Equatorial Guinea and Gabon: NICOLAS MICHEL (Switzerland).

Special Adviser for Community Based Medicine and Lessons From Haiti: DR PAUL FARMER (USA).

Special Adviser for Relocation of Camp Hurriya Residents Outside of Iraq: JANE HOLL LUTE (USA).

Special Adviser for Timor-Leste: NOELEEN HEYZER (Singapore).

Special Adviser on Africa: MAGED ABDELAZIZ (Egypt).

Special Adviser on Change Implementation: KIM WON-SOO (Republic of Korea).

Special Adviser on Cyprus: ALEXANDER DOWNER (Australia).

Special Adviser on Human Security: YUKIO TAKASU (Japan).

Special Adviser on Innovative Financing for Development: PHILIPPE DOUSTE-BLAZY (France).

Special Adviser on Inter-regional Policy Co-operation: JUAN SOMAVÍA (Chile).

Special Adviser on Myanmar: VIJAY K. NAMBIAR (India).

Special Adviser on Sport for Development and Peace: WIFRIED LEMKE (Germany).

Special Adviser on the Global Compact: KLAUS M. LEISINGER (Germany).

Special Adviser on the Millennium Development Goals: JEFFREY D. SACHS (USA).

Special Adviser on Post-2015 Development Planning: AMINA J. MOHAMMED (Nigeria).

Special Adviser on the Prevention of Genocide: ADAMA DIENG (Senegal).

Special Adviser on the Responsibility to Protect: JENNIFER WELSH (Canada).

Special Adviser on Yemen: JAMAL BENOMAR (Morocco).

Special Adviser to the Special Envoy on the Great Lakes Region: MODIBO TOURÉ (Mali).

Special Envoys

Envoy on Youth: AHMAD ALHINDAWI (Jordan).

Joint Special Representative of the UN and the League of Arab States on Syria: LAKHDAR BRAHIMI (Algeria).

Special Envoy for Global Education: GORDON BROWN (United Kingdom).

Special Envoy for the Implementation of UN Security Council Resolution 1559 (on Lebanon): TERJE ROED-LARSEN (Norway).

Special Envoy for HIV/AIDS in Africa: SPECIOSA WANDIRA-KASIBWE (Uganda).

Special Envoy for HIV/AIDS in Asia and in the Pacific: J. V. R. PRASADA RAO (India).

Special Envoy for HIV/AIDS in the Caribbean Region: DR EDWARD GREENE (Guyana).

Special Envoy for HIV/AIDS in Eastern Europe and Central Asia: DR MICHEL KAZATCHKINE (France).

Special Envoy for Malaria and for the Financing of the Health-Related Millennium Development Goals: RAY CHAMBERS (USA).

Special Envoy for Sudan and South Sudan: HAILE MENKERIOS (South Africa).

Special Envoy for the Sahel Region: ROMANO PRODI (Italy).

Special Envoy on Cities and Climate Change: MICHAEL BLOOMBERG (USA).

Special Envoy on Disability and Accessibility: LENÍN VOLTAIRE MORENO GARCES (Ecuador).

Special Envoy on Disaster Risk Reduction and Water: HAN SEUNG-SOO (Republic of Korea).

Special Envoy on the Great Lakes Region of Africa: MARY ROBINSON (Ireland).

Special Envoys on Climate Change: JOHN KUFUOR (Ghana), JENS STOLTENBERG (Norway).

Special Representatives

UN Representative to the Geneva International Discussions on Georgia and the Georgia Joint Incident Prevention and Response Mechanisms: ANTTI TURUNEN (Finland).

Special Representative to the African Union: HAILE MENKERIOS (South Africa).

Special Representative for Migration: PETER SUTHERLAND (Ireland).

Special Representative for the Implementation of the International Strategy for Disaster Reduction: MARGARETA WAHLSTRÖM (Sweden).

Special Representative for Sustainable Energy for All: KANDEH YUMKELLA (Sierra Leone).

Special Representative for the United Nations International School: MICHAEL ADLERSTEIN (USA).

Special Representative on Food Security and Nutrition; and on Avian and Human Influenza: DR DAVID NABARRO (United Kingdom).

Special Representative on Sexual Violence in Conflict: ZAINAB HAWA BANGURA (Sierra Leone).

Special Representative on Violence against Children: MARTA SANTOS PAIS (Portugal).

Other Special High Level Appointments

Head of the International Commission against Impunity in Guatemala: IVÁN VELÁSQUEZ GÓMEZ (Colombia).

High Representative for the Alliance of Civilizations: NASSIR ABDULAZIZ AL-NASSER (Qatar).

Humanitarian Envoy for Kuwait: ABDULLAH AL-MATOUQ (Kuwait).

Personal Envoy for Haiti: BILL (WILLIAM JEFFERSON) CLINTON (USA).

Personal Envoy for the Greece-FYRM Talks: MATTHEW NIMETZ (USA).

Personal Envoy for Western Sahara: CHRISTOPHER ROSS (USA).

Personal Representative on the Border Controversy between Guyana and Venezuela: (vacant).

Representative for Human Rights of IDPs: WALTER KÄLIN (Switzerland).

Special Co-ordinator for Lebanon: DEREK PLUMBLY (United Kingdom).

Special Co-ordinator for the Middle East Peace Process, Personal Representative to the Palestine Liberation Organization and the Palestinian Authority, and the Secretary-General's Envoy to the Quartet: ROBERT H. SERRY (Netherlands).

Special Co-ordinator of the Joint Mission of the United Nations and the Organisation for the Prohibition of Chemical Weapons: SIGRID KARG (Netherlands).

Further Special Representatives and other high-level appointees of the UN Secretary-General are listed in entries on UN peacekeeping and peacebuilding missions and under Offices and Departments of the UN Secretariat. The Secretary-General also appoints distinguished figures in the worlds of arts and sports as Messengers of Peace, as a means of focusing global attention on the UN's activities.

General Assembly

The General Assembly was established as a principal organ of the UN under the UN Charter. It first met on 10 January 1946. It is the main deliberative organ of the UN, and the only one composed of representatives of all the member states. Each delegation consists of not more than five representatives and five alternates, with as many advisers as may be required. It has specific responsibility for electing the Secretary-General and members of other UN councils and organs, and for approving the UN budget and the assessments for financial contributions by member states. It is also empowered to make recommendations (but not binding decisions) on questions of international security and co-operation.

The regular session of the General Assembly commences each year in mid-September. After the election of its President and other officers, the Assembly opens its General Debate, a two-week period during which the head of each delegation makes a formal statement of his or her government's views on major world issues. Since 1997 the Secretary-General has presented his report on the work of the UN at the start of the General Debate. The Assembly then begins examination of the principal items on its agenda: it acts directly on some agenda items, but most business is handled by the six Main Committees, which study and debate each item and present draft resolutions to the Assembly. After a review of the report of each Main Committee, the Assembly formally approves or rejects the Committee's recommendations. On designated 'important questions', such as recommendations on international peace and security, the admission of new members to the UN, or budgetary questions, a two-thirds majority is needed for adoption of a resolution. Other questions may be decided by a simple majority. In the Assembly, each member has one vote.

Special sessions of the Assembly may be held to discuss issues which require particular attention (e.g. illicit drugs) and 'emergency special sessions' may also be convened to discuss situations on which the UN Security Council has been unable to reach a decision.

The Assembly's 55th session (from September 2000) was designated as the Millennium Assembly. In early September a Millennium Summit of UN heads of state or government was convened to debate 'The Role of the United Nations in the 21st Century'. The Summit issued the UN Millennium Declaration, identifying the values and principles that should guide the organization in key areas including peace, development, environment, human rights, protection of the vulnerable, and the special needs of the African continent; and specified six fundamental values underlying international relations: freedom; equality; solidarity; tolerance; respect for nature; and a sense of shared responsibility for the global economy and social development. The summit adopted the following so-called Millennium Development Goals (MDGs), each incorporating specific targets to be attained by 2015: the eradication of extreme poverty and hunger; attainment of universal primary education; promotion of gender equality and empowerment of women; reduction of child mortality rates; improvement in maternal health rates; combating HIV/AIDS, malaria and other diseases; ensuring environmental sustainability; and the development of a global partnership for development. A five-year review conference of the Millennium Declaration was convened in September 2005 at the level of heads of state and of government.

In March 2005 the Secretary-General presented to the General Assembly a report entitled *In Larger Freedom: Towards Development, Security and Human Rights for All*. The report focused on three main pillars, defined as: 'Freedom from Want', urging developing countries to improve governance and combat corruption, and industrialized nations to increase funds for development assistance and debt relief and to provide immediate free market access to all exports from least developed countries; 'Freedom from Fear', urging states to agree a new consensus on security matters and adopting a definition of an act of terrorism as one 'intended to cause death or serious bodily harm to civilians or non-combatants with the purpose of intimidating a population or compelling a government or an international organization to do or abstain from doing any act'; and 'Freedom to Live in Dignity', urging the international community to support the principle of 'responsibility to protect'. The report also detailed a number of recommendations for strengthening the UN, which were subsequently considered by the September 2005 World Summit of UN heads of state. In December the General Assembly authorized the establishment of an intergovernmental advisory Peacebuilding Commission, which had been recommended by the World Summit. The Assembly and Security Council also authorized at that time the creation of a Peacebuilding Fund. In March 2006 the Assembly authorized the establishment of a new Human Rights Council to replace the Commission on Human Rights. Both the Peacebuilding Commission and Human Rights Council were inaugurated in June. In September the Assembly adopted the UN Global Counter-Terrorism Strategy and plan of action.

In October 2008, in view of the ongoing international financial crisis, the President of the General Assembly announced that a body would be established to review the global financial system, including the role of the World Bank and the IMF. The first plenary meeting of the resulting Commission of Experts of the President of the UN General Assembly on Reforms of the International Monetary and Financial System was held in January 2009, and, in September, the Commission issued a report addressing the origins of, and outlining recommendations for the future global response to, the ongoing crisis; the latter included proposals to establish a new global reserve system, a new global credit facility to complement the IMF, a new global co-ordination council, and an International Debt Restructuring Court. In June the General Assembly convened a UN Conference on the World Financial and Economic Crisis and its Impact on Development.

In September 2009 the General Assembly adopted, by consensus, its first resolution on the 'Responsibility to Protect', promoting efforts to protect the world's population from genocide, war crimes, ethnic cleansing and other crimes against humanity.

World leaders participating in the 65th session of the General Assembly, commencing in September 2010, adopted a document entitled 'Keeping the Promise: United to Achieve the MDGs'. The UN Secretary-General was requested to report annually on progress until 2015, and was mandated to recommend means of advancing the UN development agenda thereafter. A High-level Panel was appointed by the Secretary-General in July 2012 to advise on the pursuit of the post-2015 global development agenda. In September 2013 a special event on the MDGs, convened by the General Assembly, requested that a summit be convened in September 2015 to adopt a series of follow-on goals to build on and supersede the MDGs.

The UN Conference on Sustainable Development, convened in Rio de Janeiro, Brazil, in June 2012, determined to create a new high-level intergovernmental forum to promote system-wide co-ordination and coherence of sustainable development policies, and to follow up the implementation of sustainable development objectives, replacing the UN Commission on Sustainable Development. The High-level Political Forum was established in July 2013, and met for the first time at the start of the 68th General Assembly, in September. In January 2013 the General Assembly established an Open Working Group to draft a proposal on the Sustainable Development Goals (SDGs).

In September 2012 the General Assembly held its first High Level Meeting on the Rule of Law, which was attended by some 80 heads of state and government. A High-level Dialogue on International Migration and Development was convened in October 2013, during the 68th Assembly session.

In late March 2014 the General Assembly adopted a non-binding resolution that declared invalid the referendum that had been held in mid-March in the hitherto Ukrainian autonomous territory of Crimea, concerning secession from Ukraine.

President of 68th Session (from Sept. 2013): Dr JOHN W. ASHE (Antigua and Barbuda).

MAIN COMMITTEES

There are six Main Committees, on which all members have a right to be represented. Each Committee includes an elected Chairperson and two Vice-Chairs.

First Committee: Disarmament and International Security.

Second Committee: Economic and Financial.

Third Committee: Social, Humanitarian and Cultural.

Fourth Committee: Special Political and Decolonization.

Fifth Committee: Administrative and Budgetary.

Sixth Committee: Legal.

OTHER SESSIONAL COMMITTEES

General Committee: f. 1946; composed of 28 mems, including the Assembly President, the 21 Vice-Presidents of the Assembly and the Chairs of the six Main Committees.

Credentials Committee: f. 1946; composed of nine mems appointed at each Assembly session.

POLITICAL AND SECURITY MATTERS

Special Committee on Peacekeeping Operations: f. 1965; 34 appointed mems.

Disarmament Commission: f. 1978 (replacing body f. 1952); 61 mems.

UN Scientific Committee on the Effects of Atomic Radiation: f. 1955; 21 mems.

Committee on the Peaceful Uses of Outer Space: f. 1959; 61 mems; has a Legal Sub-Committee and a Scientific and Technical Sub-Committee.

Ad Hoc Committee on the Indian Ocean: f. 1972; 44 mems.

Committee on the Exercise of the Inalienable Rights of the Palestinian People: f. 1975; 25 mems.

Special Committee on the Implementation of the Declaration on Decolonization: f. 1961; 24 mems.

Ad Hoc Committee on Terrorism: f. 1996.

DEVELOPMENT

Commission on Science and Technology for Development: f. 1992; 33 mems.

Committee on Energy and Natural Resources Development: f. 1998; 24 mems.

United Nations Environment Programme (UNEP) Governing Council: f. 1972; 58 mems.

LEGAL QUESTIONS

International Law Commission: f. 1947; 34 mems elected for a five-year term; originally established in 1946 as the Committee on the Progressive Development of International Law and its Codification.

Advisory Committee on the UN Programme of Assistance in Teaching, Study, Dissemination and Wider Appreciation of International Law: f. 1965; 25 mems.

UN Commission on International Trade Law: f. 1966; 36 mems.

Special Committee on the Charter of the United Nations and on the Strengthening of the Role of the Organization: f. 1975; composed of all UN mems.

There is also a UN Administrative Tribunal and a Committee on Applications for Review of Administrative Tribunal Judgments.

ADMINISTRATIVE AND FINANCIAL QUESTIONS

Advisory Committee on Administrative and Budgetary Questions: f. 1946; 16 mems appointed for three-year terms.

Committee on Contributions: f. 1946; 18 mems appointed for three-year terms.

International Civil Service Commission: f. 1972; 15 mems appointed for four-year terms.

Committee on Information: f. 1978, formerly the Committee to review UN Policies and Activities; 95 mems.

There is also a Board of Auditors, Investments Committee, UN Joint Staff Pension Board, Joint Inspection Unit, UN Staff Pension Committee, Committee on Conferences, and Committee for Programme and Co-ordination.

SUBSIDIARY BODIES

Human Rights Council: f. 2006, replacing the fmr Commission on Human Rights (f. 1946); mandated to promote universal respect for the protection of all human rights and fundamental freedoms for all; addresses and makes recommendations on situations of violations of human rights; promotes the effective co-ordination and mainstreaming of human rights within the UN system; supports human rights education and learning and provides advisory services, technical assistance and capacity-building support; serves as a forum for dialogue on thematic issues connected with human rights; makes recommendations to the General Assembly for the advancement of international human rights law; promotes the full implementation of human rights obligations undertaken by states; aims to contribute, through dialogue and co-operation, towards the prevention of human rights violations, and to ensure prompt responses to human rights emergencies; the Human Rights Council Advisory Committee functions as a think tank under the direction of the Council; in March 2011 the Council established an Independent International Commission of Inquiry (CoI) on Syria to address the human rights situation in that country; the CoI's first report was published in Nov., and regular updates have been issued subsequently; an emergency meeting convened at the beginning of June 2012 on the deteriorating situation in Syria adopted a resolution condemning the use of force against civilians as 'outrageous', condemning the Syrian authorities for failure to protect, and to promote the rights of, all Syrians, and calling for the CoI on Syria to conduct a special investigation into the recent shelling of a residential neighbourhood (which had resulted in the deaths of some 108 civilians), with a view to holding to account those responsible for 'violations that may amount to crimes against humanity'; in Aug. the CoI on Syria issued a report which concluded that both Syrian government forces and opposition combatants had committed crimes against humanity (murder and torture), war crimes and gross violations of international human rights and humanitarian law, including unlawful killing, indiscriminate attacks against civilian populations and acts of sexual violence; in March 2013 the UN Secretary-General announced the establishment of a UN mission to initiate an investigation into the alleged use of chemical weapons in the Syrian conflict; the mandate of the mission, which arrived in Syria on 18 Aug., was subsequently extended to assess the alleged use on 21 Aug. of chemical weapons against civilians in the rebel-held area of Ghouta, Damascus, that reportedly resulted in up to around 1,400 deaths; the UN General Assembly adopted a resolution in May that urged rapid progress in the attainment of a political transition in Syria, while also condemning the use by the Syrian authorities of heavy weaponry, and the ongoing 'widespread and systematic' violations of human rights; in June the CoI reported that the incidence of war crimes and gross human rights violations was continuing to escalate, with government forces and affiliated militias allegedly carrying out systematic and widespread crimes against humanity against civilians, while anti-government armed militia were also accused of committing war crimes, particularly in the Aleppo area, including hostage-taking, torture, extrajudicial executions, and pillage; the CoI also found that there were reasonable grounds to believe that chemical weapons had been used in the conflict, without specifying the side responsible; the Commission reiterated its consistent position that a political settlement was the only means of curtailing the violent conflict; the sixth report of the CoI on Syria, released in mid-September, urged the pursuit of a political settlement to the conflict, and maintained that any international military action undertaken in response to the gas attack that occurred on 21 Aug., against civilians in Ghouta, Damascus, would intensify the crisis within Syria and would adversely affect the achievement of a political settlement; in Dec. the Council issued a report on enforced disappearances in Syria; in Jan. 2013 a report of the findings of an International Fact-Finding Mission on Israeli Settlements—appointed in July 2012 by the Council—was published; a CoI on the Democratic People's Republic of Korea (North Korea), appointed by the Council in March 2013, with a mandate to review the human rights situation in that country, issued in Feb. 2014 a final report which found that systematic abuses of human rights—including persecution on political, ethnic, religious and gender grounds, arbitrary imprisonment, torture, sexual violence, forced movements of populations, 'knowingly causing prolonged starvation', and executions—were being directed by policies established 'at the highest level of state'; the North Korean Supreme Leader, Kim Jong Un, was warned that he and elements of his regime faced international prosecution; in Jan. 2014 the Council met in special session on, and appointed an independent expert to examine, the human rights situation in the Central African Republic; panel discussions undertaken during the 25th regular session of the Council, held in March 2014, addressed topics including prevention approaches within the UN system; the death penalty; the promotion and protection of civil society space; the rights of the child; the rights of persons with disabilities; and combating sexual violence in the DRC; in that month the Council deployed a human rights monitoring team throughout Ukraine to investigate reported gross violations of human rights, and—through establishing an impartial factual account of ongoing events there—to attempt to prevent partisan manipulations of the truth and thereby calm tensions; the first cycle of the Universal Periodic Review, an assessment of the human rights situation in all mem. states, was undertaken during 2006–11; the second cycle, covering 2012–16, was launched in May 2012; 47 mems; Pres. (2014) BAUDELAIRE NDONG ELLA (Gabon).

Peacebuilding Commission: f. 2006; inaugural meeting held in June 2006; an intergovernmental advisory body, subsidiary simultaneously to both the General Assembly and the Security Council; mandated to focus international attention on reconstruction, institution building and sustainable development in countries emerging from conflict and to advise on and propose integrated strategies for post-conflict recovery; in July 2010 a report was issued, *Review of the United Nations Peacebuilding Architecture*, based upon extensive consultations with UN member states and with other stakeholders; the Commission's agenda in 2014 was addressing the situations in Burundi, Central African Republic, Guinea, Guinea-Bissau, Liberia and Sierra Leone; 31 mem. states; Chair. ANTONIO DE AGUIAR PATRIOTA (Brazil).

Peacebuilding Fund: f. 2006; finances (through the Immediate Response Facility and the Peacebuilding Recovery Facility) projects in countries that are on the agenda of the Peacebuilding Commission, or that have been declared eligible for assistance by the Secretary-General; initiatives in receipt of funding must fulfil at least one of the following criteria: they respond to imminent threats to a peace process, build or strengthen national capacities to promote coexistence and peaceful resolution of conflict, stimulate economic revitalization facilitating peace, or re-establish essential administrative services; the Fund is replenished by voluntary contributions; its guidelines were revised in 2009; in 2014 the Fund was supporting 222 projects in 22 countries.

Security Council

The Security Council was established as a principal organ under the UN Charter, tasked with promoting international peace and security in all parts of the world; its first meeting was held on 17 January 1946.

MEMBERS

Permanent members: People's Republic of China, France, Russia, United Kingdom, USA, known as the P-5. The remaining 10 members are normally elected (five each year) by the General Assembly for two-year periods (five countries from Africa and Asia, two from Latin America, one from Eastern Europe, and two from Western Europe and others).

Non-permanent members in 2014: Argentina, Australia, Luxembourg, Republic of Korea and Rwanda (term expires 31 December 2014); and Chad, Chile, Lithuania, Nigeria, and Jordan (term expires 31 December 2015).

Rotation of the Presidency in 2014: Jordan (January); Lithuania (February); Luxembourg (March); Nigeria (April); Republic of Korea (May); Russia (June); Rwanda (July); United Kingdom (August); USA (September); Argentina (October); Australia (November); Chad (December).

Organization

The Security Council has the right to investigate any dispute or situation which might lead to friction between two or more countries, and such disputes or situations may be brought to the Council's attention either by one of its members, by any member state, by the General Assembly, by the Secretary-General or even, under certain conditions, by a state which is not a member of the UN.

The Council has the right to recommend ways and means of peaceful settlement and, in certain circumstances, the actual terms of settlement. In the event of a threat to or breach of international peace or an act of aggression, the Council has powers to take 'enforcement' measures in order to restore international peace and security. These include severance of communications and of economic and diplomatic relations and, if required, military action.

The Council is organized to be able to function continuously. The Presidency of the Council is held monthly in turn by the member states in English alphabetical order. Each member of the Council has one vote. On procedural matters decisions are made by the affirmative vote of any nine members. For decisions on other matters the required nine votes must include the votes of the five permanent members. This is the rule of 'great power unanimity' popularly known as the 'veto' privilege. In practice, an abstention by one of the permanent members is not regarded as a veto. Any member, whether permanent or non-permanent, must abstain from voting in any decision concerning the pacific settlement of a dispute to which it is a party. Any member of the UN that is party to a dispute under consideration by the Council may participate in the Council's discussions without a vote.

The allocation of the Security Council's permanent seats reflects the post-Second World War international situation. It is envisaged that reforms to the Council would establish a more equitable regional representation and recognize the current global balance of power. Agreement on the size and composition of an expanded Security Council has been hindered by conflicting national and regional demands. Brazil, India, Japan and Germany (the Group of Four—G4) have requested the status of permanent members without veto rights; while Italy, Pakistan and other middle-ranking countries (known as 'Uniting for Consensus') have requested a 25-member Council with 10 new non-permanent seats; and the African Union (AU) has contended that African states should receive two permanent seats with veto power, and that there should be four further new permanent seats and five non-permanent seats. The report of the High-Level Panel on Threats, Challenges and Change issued in December 2004, stated that the role of the developed countries that contribute most to the UN financially (in terms of contributions to assessed budgets), militarily (through participation in peacekeeping operations), and diplomatically should be reflected in the Council's decision-making processes, as well as the interests of the broader membership. In February 2007 the General Assembly appointed five ambassadors to advance the process of Security Council reform by hosting negotiations on the following five key issues: categories of membership; veto power; regional representation; the size of an enlarged Council; and the working methods of the Council and its relationship with the General Assembly. In February 2009 intergovernmental negotiations on Security Council reform were initiated. The 10th round of negotiations commenced in December 2013.

Activities

As the UN organ primarily responsible for maintaining peace and security, the Security Council is empowered to deploy UN forces in the event that a dispute leads to fighting. It may also authorize the use of military force by a coalition of member states or a regional organization. The Council then monitors closely all peacekeeping and political missions and the situations in countries where missions are being undertaken, and authorizes extensions of their mandates accordingly. In June 2006 an intergovernmental advisory UN Peacebuilding Commission was inaugurated as a subsidiary advisory body of both the Security Council and the General Assembly, its establishment having been authorized by the Security Council and General Assembly, acting concurrently, in December 2005. The annual reports of the Commission were to be submitted to the Security Council for debate.

During 2013 major priorities of the Council's formal agenda included consideration of African issues, such as ongoing crises in the Central African Republic (CAR), the Great Lakes region (particularly relating to the activities in the Democratic Republic of the Congo—DRC of the March 23 Movement—M23), Guinea-Bissau, Mali, and Somalia; the ongoing civil war in Syria; monitoring developments in, inter alia, Afghanistan, the Democratic Republic of Korea (North Korea), Timor-Leste, Bosnia and Herzegovina, Cyprus and Kosovo; and monitoring post-conflict situations (including Burundi, Côte d'Ivoire, Liberia and Libya). During 2012–13 the Security Council adopted 51 resolutions; issued 22 presidential statements; and convened some 195 formal meetings (of which 174 were public).

In late February 2014 the Council convened in emergency session to discuss the political unrest in Ukraine and escalation of tensions following the movement of Russian troops into the autonomous region of Crimea. Further 'urgent' meetings of the Council were convened early March. In mid-March the Council failed to adopt a tabled resolution reaffirming the sovereignty, independence, unity and territorial integrity of Ukraine, and declaring as invalid the referendum that was held in Crimea shortly afterwards (on 16 March) on a proposal that the territory should secede from Ukraine and apply to join Russia. While some 13 Council member states voted in favour of the failed resolution, Russia—which was continuing to deploy a military presence in Crimea—vetoed it, maintaining that it did not regard the holding of the referendum as invalid. China abstained from the vote. The proposal presented in the disputed Crimean referendum was approved by more than 95% of those who voted (representing around 75% of the eligible electorate), and on 17 March the Crimean legislature voted to submit an application for the territory to join Russia, on the basis that it would retain a degree of autonomy. Meanwhile, the Russian President, Vladimir Putin, signed a degree that recognized Crimea as a 'sovereign and independent state'. The UN Secretary-General expressed deep concern at the secession referendum, and encouraged all parties to pursue a negotiated solution guided by the principles of the UN Charter, including respecting the unity and sovereignty of Ukraine; shortly afterwards he visited both Russia and Ukraine. In mid-April an emergency session of the Council was held, at Russia's request, to address the escalation in eastern Ukraine of unrest between the national security forces and armed supporters of union with Russia.

Sanctions and International Military Action: The Security Council may—as provided for under Chapter VII of the UN Charter—take enforcement measures as a means of targeting regimes and entities that are deemed to threaten international peace and security, in situations where diplomatic efforts aimed at achieving a resolution to the situation have failed. The offending entities are expected to comply with a set of objectives issued by the Security Council aimed at restoring order. Such enforcement measures encompass mandatory economic and trade and/or other sanctions (such as financial or diplomatic restrictions, arms embargoes and bans on travel), and also, in certain cases, international military action. The sanctions that took effect against the Taliban leadership in Afghanistan and al-Qa'ida in January 2001 were the first to entail mandatory monitoring of the humanitarian impact of sanctions on the local population, in particular the most vulnerable groups. The UN Secretary-General established an informal working group in April 2000 to. In December 2006 an informal working group mandated to evaluate and refine policy on the design and application of sanctions recommended that resolutions enforcing sanctions should clearly specify intended goals and targets, include incentives to reward partial compliance, and focus in particular on the finances and movements of leaders (so-called smart sanctions). Humanitarian exceptions may now be embodied in Security Council resolutions. In December 2006 the Security Council adopted a resolution requesting the UN Secretary-General to establish a procedure to provide for the removal or exemption ('delisting') of an individual or entity from sanctions lists. In December 2009 the Council adopted a further resolution establishing the Office of the Ombudsperson, tasked with reviewing requests from individuals, groups, undertakings or entities seeking to be removed from the al-Qa'ida Sanctions List.

In March 2014 the Security Council adopted Resolution 2146, condemning the illegal exportation of crude oil from Libya, and imposing sanctions against any vessel—to be designated by the Sanctions Committee established pursuant to Resolution 1970 (March 2011) on Libya—that was implicated in transporting such a cargo.

Counter-Terrorism: On 12 September 2001 the Security Council expressed its unequivocal condemnation of the terrorist attacks against targets in the USA, which had occurred on the previous day. It expressed its readiness to combat terrorism and reiterated the right to individual or collective self-defence in accordance with the UN Charter. At the end of September the Council adopted Resolution 1373, establishing a Counter-Terrorism Committee (CTC) to monitor a range of measures to combat international terrorism, including greater international co-operation and information exchange and suppressing the financing of terrorist groups. A special session of the Council at ministerial level was convened on the issue of terrorism in November. In January 2003 the Council met at ministerial level to discuss international terrorism. The meeting adopted a resolution urging intensified efforts to combat terrorism and full co-operation with the CTC. The CTC has made efforts to strengthen contacts with international, regional and sub-regional organizations, and in March 2003 it convened a meeting of 57 such groupings and agreed on a co-ordinated approach to the suppression of terrorism. A follow-up meeting was convened in March 2004. In that month the Council adopted a resolution to strengthen the CTC by classifying it as a special subsidiary body of the Council, headed by a Bureau and assisted by an Executive Directorate (the Counter-Terrorism Committee Executive Directorate—CTED). In April the Council adopted Resolution 1540—which considered the threat posed by the possible acquisition and use by non-state actors, particularly terrorists, of weapons of mass destruction, and urged all states to establish controls to prevent the proliferation of such weapons—and established the '1540 Committee' to monitor its implementation. The December 2004 report of the High-Level Panel on Threats, Challenges and Change stated that, confronted by a terrorism 'nightmare scenario', the Council would need to take earlier, more proactive and more decisive action than hitherto.

Counter-Piracy: A Contact Group on Piracy off the Coast of Somalia (CGPCS), established in January 2009 to facilitate discussion and the co-ordination of actions among states and organizations engaged in suppressing piracy off the coast of Somalia, reports periodically on its progress to the Security Council. In January 2011 an Special Adviser to the UN Secretary-General, in a briefing to the Security Council, proposed 25 comprehensive measures to address the issue, including the establishment of specialized piracy courts in the region, and the promotion of regional economic development programmes, with a view to finding solutions on land, also, to the ongoing criminal activities at sea. In October 2011 and February 2012 the Council adopted, respectively, Resolutions 2018 and 2039 concerning acts of piracy committed in the Gulf of Guinea. Resolution 2039 urged Gulf of Guinea states to convene a summit on the development of a collective maritime security strategy, including a legal framework to facilitate the prosecution of individuals alleged to be engaged in armed piracy.

Somalia: In February 2007 the Security Council endorsed the deployment of the African Union Mission in Somalia (AMISOM), which had been established by the AU in January, with a mandate to contribute to the political stabilization of Somalia; the Security Council proposed that the mission should eventually be superseded by a UN operation focusing on the post-conflict restoration of Somalia. In January 2009 the Council mandated the UN Support Office for AMISOM (UNSOA) to provide a logistics capacity support package for the Mission. In December 2010 the Council, concerned at continuing unrest and terrorist attacks in Somalia, requested the AU to increase the mission's numbers to 12,000. A Strategic Concept for the mission was endorsed by the Council in January 2012. In the following month the Council voted unanimously further to strengthen the mission, to comprise 17,700 troops, and to expand its areas of operation. The resolution also banned trade in charcoal with Somalia, having identified that commodity as a significant source of revenue for militants. The Council decided that the arms embargo on Somalia (first imposed in 1992) would not apply to equipment (excepting heavy weaponry) to be used for the development of the national security forces. In May 2013 the Council authorized the establishment of the UN Assistance Mission in Somalia (UNSOM), to provide strategic policy advice on peacebuilding and state building; to assist the Government with capacity building and with the co-ordination of international support; and to monitor and help to prevent human rights abuses. In November 2013 the Council requested the AU to increase the mission's military strength to a maximum of 22,126 uniformed personnel, with a view to improving its efficacy against al-Shabaab militants.

South Sudan and Sudan: In July 2004 the Security Council imposed an arms embargo against non-governmental entities and individuals—including the Janjaweed militias—in Darfur, Sudan, and demanded that the Sudanese Government disarm the militias. In July 2007 the Security Council authorized the deployment of the AU/UN Hybrid Operation in Darfur, and in 2014 the Council was continuing to consult closely on the Darfur situation with the UN Secretariat, the AU and the Sudanese Government. The Council authorized the establishment of the UN Interim Security Force for Abyei in June 2011, with a mandate including the protection of civilians and humanitarian personnel in the Abyei region (disputed territory located at Sudan's border with South Sudan), and in July it authorized the UN Mission in South Sudan (UNMISS), to support the consolidation of peace in South Sudan, which in that month became independent from Sudan. In April 2012 the Council, concerned at escalating tensions between Sudan and South Sudan, demanded that the two states redeploy their forces from Abyei (Sudan); that they withdraw forces from their joint border and immediately end mounting cross-border violence; that Sudanese rebels should vacate oilfields in Heglig (Sudan); that Sudan should cease aerial bombardments of South Sudan; and that a summit should be convened between the two states to resolve outstanding concerns. In late December 2013, following the onset in mid-December of violent inter-ethnic disturbances in South Sudan, the Security Council condemned reported violations of human rights by all parties to the conflict, as well as attacks upon UNMISS personnel and UN facilities, and demanded an immediate cessation of hostilities and initiation of dialogue.

Other Sub-Saharan Africa: In May 2012 the Security Council imposed a travel ban against five military officers implicated in a coup in April against the legitimately elected Guinea-Bissau authorities. The Council demanded that the Guinea-Bissau military leadership take immediate steps to restore constitutional order and relinquish authority. In December 2013 the Council expressed regret at the postponement from November of planned presidential and legislative elections that were to mark the end of a transitional period and the restoration of legitimate democratic rule in Guinea-Bissau. (These were eventually held in April 2014.) The Council strongly deplored repeated interference by the military in civilian affairs in that country, urging the armed forces to demonstrate respect for constitutional order, including the electoral process.

In June 2012 the Council issued a presidential statement strongly condemning ongoing attacks perpetrated in Central African states by insurgents of the Lord's Resistance Army (LRA). The statement also welcomed collaboration with the AU in combating the LRA, and the development of a UN regional strategy to address the situation.

In November 2013 the Council welcomed the defeat by DRC security forces of the M23 militia that had been active in eastern DRC.

In December 2012, in response to the occupation of northern Mali from January of that year by radical Islamist militants, and the overthrow of the elected Mali Government in a *coup d'état* in March, the Council adopted Resolution 2085, which condemned the continued interference by members of Mali's security forces in the work of the national transitional authorities (appointed in April), and—taking note of the endorsement in late 2012 by the Economic Community of West African States (ECOWAS) and the AU of a Strategic Concept for the Resolution of the Crisis in Mali, and of a Joint Strategic Concept of Operations for the International Military Force and the Malian Defence and Security Forces—authorized, accordingly, the deployment of an AU-led International Support Mission in Mali (AFISMA) for an initial period of one year. AFISMA was mandated to help rebuild the capacity of Mali's security forces; to support the Mali authorities in reclaiming occupied northern areas of the country; and also to support the national authorities in establishing a secure environment for the delivery of humanitarian assistance and the voluntary return of displaced civilians. Owing to rapid territorial gains by rebel forces in early January 2013, the consequent declaration of a state of emergency by the Mali Government and deployment of French troops ('Opération Serval') in support of the Mali security forces, AFISMA (initially to have been established in September) was inaugurated in mid-January. Resolution 2056, adopted in July 2012, had called for the development of a UN integrated strategy for the Sahel region. In April 2013 the Council authorized the establishment of a UN Multidimensional Integrated Stabilization Mission in Mali, comprising up to 12,640 personnel, which assumed operations from AFISMA with effect from 1 July.

In December 2013 the Council adopted Resolution 2127, authorizing the deployment, for an initial 12-month period, of a new International Support Mission in the Central African Republic (MISCA) to counter increased sectarian violence and violations of human rights in that country. MISCA, to be led by the African Union and supported by a strengthened contingent of French troops already stationed in the CAR, was mandated to use all necessary measures to protect civilians, to restore state authority and to support the provision of humanitarian assistance. Resolution 2127 also imposed an embargo on the sale or supply of arms and related materiel to the CAR and established a Security Council Committee to monitor implementation of the measures.

In October 2013 the AU decided to convene a Contact Group to engage with the Council on all concerns of the AU connected to its relationship with the International Criminal Court.

Lebanon: In April 2005 the Council authorized the establishment of an independent commission to assist the Lebanese authorities with their investigation into a terrorist attack perpetrated in February that had killed 23 people, including the former Prime Minister of that country, Rafik Hariri. In October the investigating commission reported that it suspected officials and other individuals from both Lebanon and Syria of involvement in the fatal attack. Consequently, in that month the Security Council adopted a resolution imposing travel and economic sanctions against such suspected individuals, and requiring the Syrian authorities to detain named Syrian suspects and to co-operate fully and unconditionally with the commission. In March 2006 the Council adopted a resolution requesting the UN Secretary-General to negotiate an agreement with the Lebanese Government on the establishment of an international tribunal to try those suspected of involvement in the February 2005 terrorist attack. The resulting agreement on the Special Tribunal for Lebanon was endorsed by the Security Council in May 2007. The Tribunal, based in The Hague, Netherlands, comprises both international and Lebanese judges and applies Lebanese (not international) law. In February 2012 the UN Secretary-General extended the mandate of the Special Tribunal for a further three years, with effect from 1 March.

Syria: In February 2012 the People's Republic of China and Russia vetoed a Security Council resolution to endorse a proposed peace plan that had been agreed in late January by ministers of the League of Arab States (Arab League) to end the ongoing and escalating conflict in Syria. In mid-February Arab League ministers proposed the creation of a joint peacekeeping mission to Syria. Towards the end of that month the Secretaries-General of the UN and of the Arab League appointed Kofi Annan—formerly the UN Secretary-General—as their Joint Special Envoy on the Syrian Crisis. A six-point peace plan proposed in March by Annan was accepted, towards the end of that month, by the Syrian Government. In mid-April the Security Council adopted, unanimously, a resolution authorizing an advance team of up to 30 unarmed military observers to monitor a ceasefire by all parties to the Syrian violence, pending the deployment of a full ceasefire supervision mission. Soon afterwards the UN Secretary-General reported to the Security Council that, as violence had escalated since the attempt to impose a ceasefire, and Syrian forces had not withdrawn from urban areas, a full team of 300 unarmed observers should be promptly deployed. Consequently, on 21 April, the Security Council unanimously authorized the establishment of the UN Supervision Mission in Syria (UNSMIS), initially for a 90-day period. Repeated violations of the terms of the peace plan continued, however, to be reported. In late May the Security Council issued a statement unanimously condemning—as an 'outrageous use of force against the civilian population' constituting a violation of applicable international law—the indiscriminate massacre (confirmed by UNSMIS observers), of an estimated 108 men, women and children, and the wounding of many more, resulting from the shelling of a residential neighbourhood—the rebel-controlled village of El-Houleh, near Homs—allegedly by forces loyal to the Syrian regime. The Council also condemned the killing of civilians in El-Houleh by shooting at close range and by severe physical abuse. Reiterating its full support to the efforts of the Joint Special Envoy for the implementation of his six-point plan, the Council demanded that the Syrian Government immediately cease the use of heavy weapons in population centres, and return its troops to their barracks. In early June at least an estimated further 78 people were reported to have been killed in the western village of Qbeir, by pro-government militants, following the shelling of the area by government forces; UNSMIS observers en route to the site of the atrocity were reported to have been shot at. The Security Council, while united behind the six-point plan, remained divided in its approach to the situation, with China and Russia refusing to countenance any external actions aimed at influencing regime change in Syria. At the end of June the Secretaries-General of the UN and Arab League, as well as the ministers responsible for foreign affairs of China, France, Russia, the United Kingdom, the USA, Turkey, Iraq, Kuwait, Qatar, and the High Representative of the European Union for Foreign Affairs and Security Policy, gathered in Geneva as the 'Action Group for Syria', under the chairmanship of the then UN-Arab League Joint Special Envoy, to address the situation in Syria. In mid-July, by which time the violence in Syria had further intensified, and the situation was deemed to be a 'civil war', China and Russia voted against a draft Council resolution that would have imposed sanctions on the Syrian regime; Pakistan and South Africa abstained from the vote. On 2 August, in view of the failure of the parties to the Syrian conflict to adhere to the six-point peace plan, and of the divisions within the Security Council over Syria, Annan announced that he would step down as Joint Special Envoy at the end of that month. On the following day a resolution was adopted by the UN General Assembly that condemned the use of heavy weaponry by the Syrian authorities, urged the parties to the conflict to cease acts of violence, and demanded the implementation of relevant Security Council resolutions. Meanwhile, the UN Secretary-General expressed regret concerning the divisions that were weakening the collective authority of the Council, emphasizing the paramount importance of the needs of the people of Syria. The Security Council decided in mid-August not to extend the mandate of UNSMIS beyond 19 August, and the mission was terminated accordingly. At the beginning of September Lakhdar Brahimi took office as the new Joint Special Representative of the UN and Arab League. In early October, in view of escalating tensions at the Syrian-Turkish border—including an incident in which five Turkish civilians were killed, and others injured, by Syrian cross-border mortar fire—the Security Council emphasized the serious impact of the crisis on the security of neighbouring states and on regional peace and stability. The Council asked the Syrian Government fully to respect the territorial integrity of adjoining states. The Joint Special Representative, meanwhile, engaged in discussions with the Syrian and Turkish authorities. Shortly afterwards the Council strongly condemned terrorist attacks—claimed by the al-Qa'ida-affiliated militant Islamist grouping Jebhat al-Nusra—that had been targeted at the city centre of Aleppo, causing numerous civilian fatalities and injuries. The Council and the UN Secretary-General strongly condemned a bomb attack in Beirut, Lebanon, on 19 October, that resulted in eight fatalities, including the death of a senior commander in the Lebanese military, potentially destabilizing that country; it was feared that the conflict in Syria might ignite wider regional tensions. On the following day the Joint Special Representative entered into negotiations with the parties to the Syrian conflict aimed at initiating a temporary ceasefire during the upcoming Muslim festival of Id al-Adha; it was announced on 24 October that this had been achieved, although the truce was not adhered to. In December the Joint Special Representative initiated trilateral discussions with the USA and Russia in an attempt to advance possible solutions for an end to the hostilities; however, the Security Council remained deadlocked into 2014 with regard to action on Syria. The second meeting of the Action Group for Syria, 'Geneva II', was convened by the UN in January 2014, meeting first in Montreux, Switzerland and later in Geneva. In early February both sides agreed to a temporary ceasefire in Homs to enable the evacuation of trapped civilians and the distribution of humanitarian assistance. The negotiations ended without any further agreement in mid-February.

In January 2013 more than 50 UN member states, led by Switzerland, signed a letter urging the UN Security Council to refer the situation in Syria to the International Criminal Court. In March the UN Secretary-General announced that a mission comprising UN weapons experts, in co-operation with specialists from the World Health Organization and the Organisation for the Prohibition of Chemical Weapons (OPCW), would initiate an investigation into the alleged use of chemical weapons in the Syrian conflict. (Syria was not a signatory to the 1992 Convention on the Prohibition of the Development, Production, Stockpiling and Use of Chemical Weapons and on their Destruction, and the presence in that country of stockpiles of chemical nerve agents had been alleged.) At the end of that month the Secretary-General appointed a Swedish scientist, Åke Sellström, to head the mission. During March the Security Council condemned a terrorist attack on a mosque in Damascus, which killed more than 40 civilians. A resolution adopted in May by the General Assembly urged swift progress in the attainment of a political transition in Syria, while also repeating its condemnation of the use by the Syrian authorities of heavy weaponry, and condemning the ongoing 'widespread and systematic' violations of human rights. On 18 August the Sellström-led mission arrived in Syria to investigate three previously reported chemical attacks. The alleged use on 21 August of chemical weapons against unarmed civilians in the rebel-held area of Ghouta, Damascus, prompted widespread international condemnation. In the immediate aftermath of the incident several thousand patients were treated for apparently neurotoxic symptoms, and up to around 1,400 fatalities were reported. The UN Secretary-General expressed shock at the atrocity and announced his intention immediately to initiate an impartial and thorough investigation into the situation, urging the Syrian Government promptly to confirm its willingness to co-operate with the existing UN chemical weapons inspection mission. On 24–25 August 2013 the High Representative for Disarmament Affairs engaged in this respect with representatives of the Syrian authorities, and from 26–30 August the UN mission visited the site of the attack, to examine the scene and to take relevant soil and biological samples. Meanwhile, the Security Council P-5 remained deeply divided over the situation in Syria. President Obama of the USA had previously, in August 2012, stated that the use in the conflict of chemical or biological weaponry by the Syrian

Government would represent the transgression of a 'red line' that might provoke US military intervention, while following the August 2013 atrocity the French and United Kingdom governments indicated that the level of severity of the ongoing humanitarian crisis might necessitate the organization of international military action against the Syrian regime even without a UN mandate. The Chinese and Russian authorities, however, urged restraint and warned against prejudging the inspection mission's findings, with Russia maintaining that any attempt to initiate military intervention against Syria without a mandate from the Security Council would represent a grave violation of international law and risk inflicting potentially catastrophic consequences on countries near to Syria. Towards the end of August the British parliament, recalled to consider an appropriate response to the atrocity, voted against initiating military action against Syria. In early September the Russian minister of foreign affairs, US Secretary of State and Joint UN-Arab League Joint Special Representative for Syria gave consideration to a proposal by Russia that Syria should surrender its chemical stockpiles to international control. Soon afterwards the Syrian regime notified the UN Secretary-General that it was taking measures to accede to the 1992 Chemical Weapons Convention and would observe the obligations imposed by the Convention prior to its national entry into force. In mid-September the Sellström weapons inspection team issued its report on the 21 August atrocity, finding 'clear and convincing evidence' of the use of surface-to-surface rockets containing sarin gas in Ghouta, Damascus, and that chemical weapons had been used on a relatively large scale generally during the Syrian conflict, including against children. On 27 September 2013 intensive diplomatic efforts culminated in the Security Council adopting, unanimously, Resolution 2118, which aimed to eliminate Syria's chemical weapons and initiate a Syrian-led peace process to end the conflict. The resolution authorized the immediate implementation of a weapons monitoring and destruction plan, formulated by the OPCW, and the imposition of punitive measures if any party attempts to use, develop, produce, acquire, stockpile, retain, or transfer chemical weapons. In mid-October the Security Council authorized the deployment of a joint UN-OPCW mission tasked with implementing Resolution 2118, including supervising the destruction by the Syrian authorities, by end-June 2014, of Syria's chemical weapons stockpiles and production facilities. The mandate of the mission—led by a civilian Special Co-ordinator, and primarily based in Cyprus—was to be implemented over three phases.

North Korea: In October 2006 the Security Council adopted a resolution demanding that North Korea abandon all programmes related to nuclear weapons, ballistic missiles and other weapons of mass destruction in a complete, verifiable and irreversible manner. An embargo was imposed by the Council on the supply of arms, military technology and luxury goods to that country, and the foreign assets of personnel connected to its weapons programme were frozen. In April 2009 the Council strongly condemned a long-range missile test conducted by North Korea, in violation of the October 2006 resolution. In June 2009 the Council adopted a resolution that deplored a further nuclear test conducted by North Korea, in late May, imposed a total embargo on arms exports from, and strengthened the prohibition on the importation of armaments into, that country. In December 2012 the Council condemned the successful launch of a rocket by North Korea earlier in that month. In March 2013 the Council imposed further sanctions—freezing the assets of and imposing travel restrictions against three North Korean individuals and two firms connected to the North Korean military—in reaction to an underground nuclear detonation had been conducted in the previous month at the Punngye-ri nuclear testing facility.

Iran: In December 2006 the Security Council imposed sanctions against Iran, including an embargo related to that country's nuclear and ballistic missile programmes and punitive measures targeted at individuals and entities connected to the programmes. In March 2007 the Council adopted a further resolution imposing a ban on the export of arms from Iran, and, in March 2008, an additional resolution was adopted authorizing inspections of any cargo to and from Iran suspected of concealing prohibited equipment; strengthening the monitoring of Iranian financial institutions; and adding names to the existing list of individuals and companies subject to asset and travel restrictions. A resolution adopted in June 2010 strengthened the sanctions further.

Iraq: Resolution 1483, adopted by the Council in May 2003, following the overthrow in April of the Saddam Hussain regime by a multinational force, authorized the withdrawal of economic sanctions against Iraq (first imposed in August 1990), with the exception of the embargo on trade in arms, and supported the formation by the Iraqi people, assisted by the occupying powers under unified command and a new Special Representative of the Secretary-General, of an Iraqi-run interim administration. In August of that year the Council authorized the establishment of the UN Assistance Mission for Iraq (UNAMI), which was mandated to support the Secretary-General in fulfilling his responsibilities under Resolution 1483. In October the Council authorized a multinational peacekeeping force, under unified command, to help maintain security in Iraq and to support UNAMI and the institutions of the Iraqi interim administration. In November the Council adopted a resolution that authorized the establishment of a sanctions committee to identify those individuals and entities holding the outstanding financial assets of the former Saddam Hussain regime. Resolution 1546, adopted by the Council in June 2004, endorsed the newly formed Iraq Interim Government and outlined a timetable for Iraq's transition to democratic government. The Council welcomed the elections held in January 2005 to the new Iraq Transitional National Assembly, while reaffirming the role of the Special Representative of the Secretary-General and UNAMI in support of Iraqi efforts to promote national dialogue. The Council has reiterated demands for the repatriation of all Kuwaiti and third country nationals who had been missing since the 1990 Gulf War and for the return of their property. In March 2013 the Head of UNAMI briefed the Council on issues including the spillover into Iraqi territory of the ongoing conflict in neighbouring Syria, progress towards the normalization of Iraq's relations with Kuwait, and continuing acts of terrorism affecting civilians in Iraq. In January 2014 the Council adopted a presidential statement deploring recent fighting between pro-government forces and al-Qaida-affiliated militants in al-Anbar province, which had prompted more than 300,000 to leave their homes. By January 2014 some US $44,500m. had been disbursed to more than 1.5m. claimants by a compensation fund established by the Council in May 1991 to assist victims of Iraqi aggression in that respect.

Israel and Palestine: The Council provides a forum for discussion of the situation in the Middle East and violence in the West Bank and Gaza and in Israel and to support a comprehensive and just settlement to the situation. In March 2002 the Council adopted Resolution 1397, which envisaged two separate states of Israel and Palestine existing within secure and recognized borders. In November 2003 the Council endorsed the adoption, in April, by the so-called Quartet comprising envoys from the UN, the European Union (EU), Russia and USA of a 'performance-based roadmap to a permanent two-state solution to the Israeli-Palestinian conflict'. In July 2005 the Council convened an open debate on the situation in the Middle East, at the request of Arab member states of the UN. In December 2006 the Council endorsed a presidential statement expressing deep concern over the continuing insecurity in the Middle East and restating the key role of the Quartet. The UN Secretary-General attended a conference held in Annapolis, Maryland, USA, in November 2007, at which participants agreed to implement their respective obligations under the 2003 roadmap to achieving a two-state solution to the Israeli-Palestinian conflict, and a statement of 'joint understanding' was made by the Israeli and Palestinian leaders. Direct talks been the two sides, however, stalled. In December 2008 the Security Council adopted a resolution in which it reaffirmed support for the agreements and negotiations resulting from the Annapolis summit, and urged an intensification of efforts to achieve a peaceful two-state outcome. In January 2009, in response to the intensive bombardment of the Gaza Strip by Israeli forces that commenced in late December 2008 with the stated aim of ending rocket attacks launched by Hamas and other militant groups on Israeli targets, the Security Council adopted Resolution 1860, in which it expressed grave concern at the escalation of violence and stressed that Palestinian and Israeli civilian populations must be protected. In May 2009 the Council convened an open debate on the Middle East, at the level of ministers responsible for foreign affairs, and expressed support for an initiative of the Quartet, and other interested parties, to hold a conference in Moscow; this was subsequently held in March 2010. In September 2011 the Council met to consider Palestine's application in that month for full UN membership; although that process stalled, Palestine was, in November 2012, recognized as an observer state (implying full statehood) of the UN General Assembly. An attempt in September 2011 by Quartet diplomats to instigate new Israeli–Palestinian direct negotiations was unsuccessful. An open debate on the Middle East situation, convened by the Council in July 2012, urged the prompt resumption of negotiations on a two-state outcome; some members of the Council condemned the construction of Israeli settlements in Palestinian territory.

Yemen: In October 2011 the Council adopted Resolution 2014, in which it expressed grave concern at the deterioration in the security situation in Yemen, and condemned ongoing violations there of human rights. In Resolution 2051, adopted in June 2012, the Council reiterated concern at the overall situation in Yemen, urging the full and prompt implementation of an ongoing peace initiative sponsored by the Gulf Cooperation Council. the need for the full and timely implementation of the Gulf Cooperation Council. The Council issued a statement in February 2013 welcoming the launch, in March, of a process of National Dialogue on the future of that country. In January of that year the Council undertook a special mission to Yemen. In February 2014 the Council unanimously adopted a resolution authorizing the imposition of sanctions against any individual or organization that was deemed to be a threat to peace, security or stability—and thereby to be undermining the ongoing political transition—in Yemen.

Kosovo: In February 2008 the Council met in emergency session in reaction to Kosovo's unilateral declaration of independence from Serbia. Pending new guidance from the Council, Resolution 1244 governing the UN Interim Administration in Kosovo and Metohija (UNMIK) was to remain in force; following the enactment of a new Kosovan Constitution in June, providing for the transfer of executive powers from the UN to the elected Kosovan authorities and for an EU police and justice mission to assume supervisory responsibilities from the UN, the Council met to discuss a proposal of the UN Secretary-General for the reconfiguration of UNMIK. Discussions on the future status of Kosovo remain a priority for the Security Council.

Afghanistan: In February 2006 the Security Council endorsed the Afghanistan Compact, which had been adopted in the previous month as a framework for the partnership between Afghanistan and the international community. In June 2008 the Council adopted a resolution in which it expressed concern at the smuggling into Afghanistan of chemicals used for refining heroin. The Security Council has addressed the situation in Afghanistan at regular intervals, and in June 2012 held a debate on Afghanistan at which it was briefed by the Special Representative of the Secretary-General and Head of the UN Assistance Mission in Afghanistan (UNAMA, established in March 2002) on the situation in the country. The SSRG urged full international support for the transition ('Inteqal') to Afghan responsibility and ownership of its own governance, security and development efforts. In March 2014 the Security Council extended UNAMA's mandate until March 2015, and committed to continuing to lead and support international civilian efforts in Afghanistan beyond 2014, including the provision of assistance to future electoral processes. In October 2013 the Council extended for the last time, until 31 December 2014, the mandate of the International Security Assistance Force in Afghanistan. (Thereafter a NATO training mission, 'Resolute Support', was to maintain a presence in Afghanistan.)

Other Activities: In recent years the Council has made statements, adopted resolutions and held open debates on a number of other ongoing themes, including the protection of children from the effects of armed conflict; the protection of civilians in armed conflict situations; curbing the proliferation of small arms and light weapons; women; the role of the UN in supporting justice and the rule of law; security sector reform; non-proliferation of weapons of mass destruction; the relationship between the Council and regional organizations; the role of the Council in addressing humanitarian crises; and the role of the UN in post-conflict national reconciliation.

SPECIAL SUBSIDIARY BODIES

Counter-Terrorism Committee (CTC): f. 2001, pursuant to Security Council Resolution 1373 (2001) and, in March 2004, in accordance with Resolution 1535 (2004), elevated to a special subsidiary body; comprises a Plenary (composed of the Council member states) and a Bureau; assisted by an Executive Directorate (the Counter-Terrorism Committee Executive Directorate—CTED, which became operational in Dec. 2005); since Sept. 2005 the CTC has also been mandated to monitor member states' implementation of Resolution 1624 (2005), concerning incitement to commit acts of terrorism; Chair. RAIMONDA MURMOKAITĖ (Lithuania); Exec. Dir, Counter-Terrorism Exec. Directorate JEAN-PAUL LABORDE (France).

The UN Peacebuilding Commission, which was inaugurated in June 2006, its establishment having been authorized by the Security Council and General Assembly in December 2005, is a subsidiary advisory body of both the Council and Assembly.

COMMITTEES

In April 2014 there were three **Standing Committees**, each composed of representatives of all Council member states:

Committee of Experts on Rules of Procedure (studies and advises on rules of procedure and other technical matters);

Committee on the Admission of New Members;

Committee on Council Meetings away from Headquarters.

Ad hoc Committees, which are established as needed, comprise all Council members and meet in closed session:

Governing Council of the UN Compensation Commission established by Security Council Resolution 692 (1991);

1540 Committee established pursuant to Security Council Resolution 1540 (2004).

Within this category are the Sanctions Committees, which may be established to oversee economic or political enforcement measures, imposed by the Security Council to maintain or restore international peace and security. At April 2014 the following committees were operational:

Security Council Committee established pursuant to Resolution 2140 (2014) concerning Yemen;

Security Council Committee established pursuant to Resolution 2127 (2013) concerning the Central African Republic;

Security Council Committee established pursuant to Resolution 2048 (2012) concerning Guinea-Bissau;

Security Council Committee established pursuant to Resolutions 1267 (1999) and 1989 (2011) concerning al-Qa'ida and associated individuals and entities;

Security Council Committee established pursuant to Resolution 1988 (2011) concerning the Taliban in Afghanistan;

Security Council Committee established pursuant to Resolution 1970 (2011) concerning the Libyan Arab Jamahiriya;

Security Council Committee established pursuant to Resolution 1737 (2006) concerning Iran;

Security Council Committee established pursuant to Resolution 1718 (2006) concerning the Democratic People's Republic of Korea;

Security Council Committee established pursuant to Resolution 1636 (2005) concerning Syria;

Security Council Committee established pursuant to Resolution 1591 (2005) concerning Sudan;

Security Council Committee established pursuant to Resolution 1572 (2004) concerning Côte d'Ivoire;

Security Council Committee established pursuant to Resolution 1533 (2004) concerning the Democratic Republic of the Congo;

Security Council Committee established pursuant to Resolution 1521 (2003) concerning Liberia;

Security Council Committee established pursuant to Resolution 1518 (2003) concerning the financial assets of the former Iraqi regime;

Security Council Committee established pursuant to Resolution 751 (1992) concerning Somalia and Resolution 1907 (2009) concerning Eritrea.

Office of the Ombudsperson of the 1267/1989 Committee: Rm TB-08041D, UN Plaza, New York, NY 10017, USA; f. Dec. 2009; reviews requests from individuals, groups, undertakings or entities seeking to be removed from the al-Qa'ida Sanctions List; Ombudsperson KIMBERLY PROST (Canada).

In June 1993 an Informal Working Group on Documentation and other procedural questions was established. An Informal Working Group on General Issues on Sanctions was established in 2000 to consider ways of improving the effectiveness of UN sanctions and a Working Group on Peacekeeping Operations was established in January 2001. In March 2002 an Ad Hoc Working Group on Conflict Prevention and Resolution in Africa was established. A Working Group established (in October 2004) pursuant to Resolution 1566 was mandated to consider practical measures to be imposed upon individuals, groups or entities involved in or associated with terrorist activities, other than those designated by the Committee on al-Qa'ida and the Taliban; and the possibility of establishing an international fund to compensate victims of terrorist acts and their families. A Working Group on Children and Armed Conflict was established in July 2005.

AD HOC INTERNATIONAL TRIBUNALS

INTERNATIONAL RESIDUAL MECHANISM FOR CRIMINAL TRIBUNALS—MICT

The Residual Mechanism was established by Security Council Resolution 1966 (December 2010) to undertake some essential functions of the International Tribunal for the Former Yugoslavia (ICTY) and of the International Criminal Tribunal for Rwanda (ICTR) pending and after their planned closure. The Residual Mechanism comprises a branch that is based in Arusha, Tanzania (MICT Arusha Branch, which commenced operations on 1 July 2012), and a branch based in The Hague, Netherlands (operational from 1 July 2013). The Mechanism is mandated to operate for an initial period of four years from the first commencement date (1 July 2012), and to conduct any appeals against Tribunal judgments filed following its entry into operation.

President of the Residual Mechanism: THEODOR MERON (USA).

Prosecutor of the Residual Mechanism: HASSAN BUBACAR JALLOW (The Gambia).

Registrar of the Residual Mechanism: JOHN HOCKING (Australia).

INTERNATIONAL CRIMINAL TRIBUNAL FOR THE FORMER YUGOSLAVIA—ICTY

Address: Registry: Public Information Unit, POB 13888, 2501 EW The Hague, Netherlands.

Telephone: (70) 512-5343; **fax:** (70) 512-5355; **internet:** www.icty.org.

In May 1993 the Security Council, acting under Article VII of the UN Charter, adopted Resolution 827, which established an ad hoc 'war crimes' tribunal. The so-called International Tribunal for the Prosecution of Persons Responsible for Serious Violations of International Humanitarian Law Committed in the Territory of the Former Yugoslavia (also referred to as the International Criminal Tribunal for the former Yugoslavia—ICTY) was inaugurated in The Hague, Netherlands, in November. The ICTY consists of a Chief Prosecutor's office, and 16 permanent judges, of whom 11 sit in three trial chambers and five sit in a seven-member appeals chamber (with the remaining two appeals chamber members representing the ICTR). In addition, a maximum at any one time of nine *ad litem* judges, drawn from a pool of 27, serve as required. Public hearings were initiated in November 1994. The first trial proceedings commenced in May 1996, and the first sentence was imposed by the Tribunal in November. In July and November 1995 the Tribunal formally charged the Bosnian Serb political and military leaders Radovan Karadžić and Gen. Ratko Mladić, on two separate indictments, with genocide, crimes against humanity, violation of the laws and customs of war and serious breaches of the Geneva Conventions. In July 1996 the Tribunal issued international warrants for their arrest. Amended indictments, confirmed in May 2000, and announced in October and November, respectively, included the withdrawal of the fourth charge against Mladić. Karadžić was eventually detained in July 2008, and Mladić was captured in May 2011. In April 2000 Momčilo Krajišnik, a senior associate of Karadžić, was detained by the ICTY, charged with genocide, war crimes and crimes against humanity. Biljana Plavšić, another former Bosnian Serb political leader, surrendered to the Tribunal in January 2001, also indicted on charges of genocide, war crimes and crimes against humanity. In the following month three Bosnian Serb former soldiers were convicted by the ICTY of utilizing mass rape and the sexual enslavement of women as instruments of terror in wartime. In February 2003 Plavšić was sentenced to 11 years' imprisonment, having pleaded guilty in October 2002 to one of the charges against her (persecutions: a crime against humanity). (Under a plea agreement reached with the Tribunal the remaining charges had been withdrawn.) In mid-1998 the ICTY began investigating reported acts of violence against civilians committed by both sides in the conflict in the southern Serbian province of Kosovo and Metohija. In early 1999 there were reports of large-scale organized killings, rape and expulsion of the local Albanian population by Serbian forces. In April ICTY personnel visited refugee camps in neighbouring countries in order to compile evidence of the atrocities. In May the President of the then Federal Republic of Yugoslavia (FRY, which was renamed Serbia and Montenegro in February 2003, and divided into separate states of Montenegro and Serbia in 2006), Slobodan Milošević, was indicted, along with three senior government ministers and the chief-of-staff of the army, charged with crimes against humanity and violations of the customs of war committed in Kosovo since 1 January 1999. In June, following the establishment of an international force to secure peace in Kosovo, the ICTY established teams of experts to investigate alleged atrocities at 529 identified grave sites. In April 2001 Milošević was arrested by the local authorities in Belgrade. Under increasing international pressure, the Federal Government approved his extradition in June, and he was immediately transferred to the ICTY, where he was formally charged with crimes against humanity committed in Kosovo in 1999. A further indictment of crimes against humanity committed in Croatia during 1991–92 was confirmed in October 2001, and a third indictment, which included charges of genocide committed in Bosnia and Herzegovina in 1991–95, was confirmed in November 2001. In February 2002 the Appeals Chamber ordered that the three indictments be considered in a single trial. The trial commenced later in that month. Milošević, however, continued to protest against the alleged illegality of his arrest and refused to recognize the jurisdiction of the Court. The case was delayed repeatedly owing to the ill health of the defendant, and in March 2006 he died. In August 2001 the ICTY passed its first sentence of genocide, convicting a former Bosnian Serb military commander, Gen. Radislav Kristić, for his role in the deaths of up to 8,000 Bosnian Muslim men and boys in Srebrenica in July 1995. In January 2003 Fatmir Limaj, an ethnic Albanian deputy in the Kosovo parliament and former commander of the Kosovo Liberation Army (KLA), was indicted by the ICTY on several counts of crimes against humanity and war crimes that were allegedly committed in mid-1998 against Serb and Albanian detainees at the KLA's Lapusnik prison camp. Limaj was arrested in Slovenia in February 2003 and transferred to ICTY custody in March. In July 2011 Serbian authorities arrested Goran Hadžic, who had been the last remaining indictee at large. At April 2014 the ICTY had indicted a total of 161 people. Of those who had appeared in proceedings before the Tribunal, 18 had been acquitted, 74 had received a final guilty sentence, and 13 had been referred to national jurisdictions. Some 48 people had completed their sentences. At that time proceedings were ongoing against 20 people accused by the Tribunal, including four who were on trial, and 16 at the appeals stage. Under the ICTY's completion strategy certain outstanding essential functions of the Tribunal were, on 1 July 2013, taken over by the International Residual Mechanism for Criminal Tribunals. The ICTY assisted with the establishment of the War Crimes Chamber within the Bosnia and Herzegovina state court, which became operational in March 2005, and also helped Croatia to strengthen its national judicial capacity to enable war crimes to be prosecuted within that country.

President of the ICTY: THEODOR MERON (USA).

ICTY Prosecutor: SERGE BRAMMERTZ (Belgium).

ICTY Registrar: JOHN HOCKING (Australia).

INTERNATIONAL CRIMINAL TRIBUNAL FOR RWANDA—ICTR

Address: Registry: Arusha International Conference Centre, POB 6016, Arusha, Tanzania.

Telephone: (212) 963-2850; **fax:** (212) 963-2848; **e-mail:** ictr-press@un.org; **internet:** www.ictr.org.

In November 1994 the Security Council adopted Resolution 955, establishing the ICTR to prosecute persons responsible for genocide and other serious violations of humanitarian law that had been committed in Rwanda and by Rwandans in neighbouring states. Its temporal jurisdiction was limited to the period 1 January to 31 December 1994. UN Secretary Council Resolution 977, adopted in February 1995, determined that the seat of the Tribunal would be located in Arusha, Tanzania. The Tribunal consists of 11 permanent judges, of whom nine sit in four trial chambers and two sit in the seven-member appeals chamber that is shared with the ICTY and based at The Hague, Netherlands. A high security UN Detention Facility, the first of its kind, was constructed within the compound of the prison in Arusha and opened in 1996. In August 2002 the UN Security Council endorsed a proposal by the ICTR President to elect a pool of 18 *ad litem* judges to the Tribunal with a view to accelerating its activities. The first plenary session of the Tribunal was held in The Hague in June 1995; formal proceedings at its permanent headquarters in Arusha were initiated in November. The first trial of persons charged by the Tribunal commenced in January 1997, and sentences were imposed in July. In September 1998 the former Rwandan Prime Minister, Jean Kambanda, and a former mayor of Taba, Jean-Paul Akayesu, both Hutu extremists, were found guilty of genocide and crimes against humanity; Kambanda subsequently became the first person to be sentenced under the 1948 Convention on the Prevention and Punishment of the Crime of Genocide. In October 2000 the Tribunal rejected an appeal by Kambanda. In 2001 two ICTR investigators employed on defence teams were arrested and charged with genocide, having been found to be working at the Tribunal under assumed identities. Relations between the Rwandan Government and the ICTR deteriorated in 2002, with the then Chief Prosecutor accusing the Rwandan authorities of failing to facilitate the travel of witnesses to the Tribunal and withholding access to documentary materials, and counter-accusations by the Rwandan Government that the Tribunal's progress was too slow and that Rwandan witnesses attending the Tribunal had not received sufficient protection. Reporting to the UN Security Council in July, the then Chief Prosecutor alleged that the Rwandan refusal to co-operate ensued from her recent decision to indict former members of the Tutsi-dominated Rwanda Patriotic Army for human rights violations committed against Hutus in 1994. In January 2004 a former minister of culture and education, Jean de Dieu Kamuhanda, was found guilty on two counts of genocide and extermination as a crime against humanity. In the following month Samuel Imanishimwe, a former military commander, was convicted on seven counts of genocide, crimes against humanity and serious violations of the Geneva Conventions. In December 2008 Théoneste Bagosora, Aloys Ntabakuze and Anatole Nsengiyumva, former high-ranking military commanders, were found guilty of genocide, crimes against humanity and war crimes, and were each sentenced to life imprisonment. In May 2012 Callixte Nzabonimana, a former Minister of Youth, was convicted of genocide, conspiracy and incitement to commit genocide, and extermination as a crime against humanity, and sentenced to life imprisonment. In December Augustin Ngirabatware, a former Minister of Planning, was sentenced to 35 years imprisonment for crimes concerning genocide, and rape and extermination as crimes against humanity. By April 2014 the Tribunal had delivered 55 judgments concerning 75 accused, of whom 12 were acquitted, and 16 were appealing their convictions. At that time two cases were being tried in France under French national jurisdiction and eight cases had been transferred to the Rwandan national court system. Nine fugitives wanted by the Tribunal remained at large. On 1 July 2012 the International Residual Mechanism for Criminal Tribunals (MICT) Arusha Branch began to take over outstanding essential functions of the Tribunal; all ICTR responsibilities were to be transferred to MICT by 31 December 2014.

Both the ICTY and ICTR have been supported by teams of investigators and human rights experts working in the field to collect forensic and other evidence in order to uphold indictments. Evidence of mass graves resulting from large-scale unlawful killings has been uncovered in both regions.

President of the ICTR: VAGN JOENSEN (Denmark).

ICTR Prosecutor: HASSAN BUBACAR JALLOW (The Gambia).

ICTR Registrar: BONGANI MAJOLA (South Africa).

Trusteeship Council

The Trusteeship Council (comprising the People's Republic of China—a non-active member until May 1989, France, Russia, the United Kingdom and the USA) was established to supervise United Nations Trust Territories through their administering authorities and to promote the political, economic, social and educational advancement of their inhabitants towards self-government or independence. On 1 October 1994 the last territory remaining under UN trusteeship, the Republic of Palau (part of the archipelago of the Caroline Islands), declared its independence under a compact of free association with the USA, its administering authority. The Security Council terminated the Trusteeship Agreement on 10 November, having determined that the objectives of the agreement had been fully attained. On 1 November the Trusteeship Council formally suspended its operations; thereafter it was to be convened on an extraordinary basis as required. The report of the UN Secretary-General entitled 'In Larger Freedom: Towards Development, Security and Human Rights for All', issued in March 2005, proposed that the Trusteeship Council should be terminated.

Economic and Social Council—ECOSOC

ECOSOC promotes world co-operation on economic, social, cultural and humanitarian problems.

MEMBERS

Fifty-four members are elected by the General Assembly for three-year terms: 18 are elected each year. Membership is allotted by regions as follows: Africa 14 members, Western Europe and other developed countries 13, Asia 11, Latin America 10, Eastern Europe 6.

BUREAU

The Bureau, with responsibility for formulating the agenda and programme of work for the Council, is elected by the Council at its first meeting of the year. It comprises a President and four Vice-Presidents, each representing different regions.

President: MARTIN SAJDIK (Austria) (2014).

ACTIVITIES

The Council meets annually for a four-week substantive session in July, alternately in New York, USA, and Geneva, Switzerland. It has a co-ordinating function between the UN and the specialized agencies, and also makes consultative arrangements with approved voluntary or non-governmental organizations which work within the sphere of its activities (around 3,200 organizations had consultative status in 2014). The Council has functional and regional commissions to carry out much of its detailed work. ECOSOC's purview extends to more than 70% of the human and financial resources of the UN system. The Council was given a leading role in following up the implementation of the Monterrey Consensus, adopted by the March 2002 International Conference on Financing for Development.

In July 2007 ECOSOC organized the first of a series of annual ministerial-level progress reviews (AMRs) of agreed development goals, in particular the Millennium Development Goals (MDGs); under the AMR process a series of global and regional preparatory meetings is convened prior to the main review, which is held during the annual session of the Council. The theme of the 2014 AMR was 'Addressing ongoing and emerging challenges for meeting the MDGs in 2015 and for sustaining development gains in the future'. A new UN High-level Political Forum was inaugurated in September 2013, replacing, in accordance with a decision of the June 2012 UN Conference on Sustainable Development, the former UN Commission for Sustainable Development. The new Forum was to meet annually at ministerial level under the auspices of ECOSOC, and from 2016 was to conduct, also under ECOSOC auspices, regular reviews relating to the follow-up and implementation of sustainable development commitments and objectives. Consequently the AMR process was to be terminated in 2015. When required ECOSOC organizes meetings to assess and promote co-ordinated responses to threats to development, such as famines, epidemics and major natural disasters.

Every year ECOSOC holds high-level consultations with the International Monetary Fund, World Bank, World Trade Organization and the UN Conference on Trade and Development. The 2014 meeting was held in April, in New York, on the theme 'Coherence, co-ordination and co-operation in the context of financing for sustainable development and the post-2015 development agenda'.

DEVELOPMENT CO-OPERATION FORUM (DCF)

The Development Co-operation Forum (DCF) is mandated to advance the implementation of all internationally agreed development goals and to promote dialogue to find effective ways of supporting international development. It is convened every two years, in New York, with participation by representatives of UN bodies, development agencies, regional development banks, civil society and the private sector. The first Forum was held in June–July 2008. The second and third DCFs were convened in June 2010 and July 2012, respectively, and the fourth was scheduled for July 2014.

YOUTH FORUM

The first ECOSOC Youth Forum was convened in May 2012, with participation by young delegates including business people, students and representatives of youth organizations. The Forum emphasised the importance of addressing youth unemployment and was conducted through two interactive dialogues, on education and training, and on creating jobs to ensure a sustainable future. The second Forum was held in March 2013, on the theme 'Shaping tomorrow's innovators: Leveraging science, technology, innovation and culture for today's youth'.

FUNCTIONAL COMMISSIONS

Commission on Crime Prevention and Criminal Justice: f. 1992; aims to formulate an international convention on crime prevention and criminal justice; 40 mems.

Commission on Narcotic Drugs: f. 1946; mainly concerned in combating illicit traffic; 53 mems; there is a Sub-Commission on Illicit Drug Traffic and Related Matters in the Near and Middle East.

Commission on Population and Development: f. 1946; advises the Council on population matters and their relation to socio-economic conditions; 47 mems.

Commission on Science and Technology for Development: f. 1992; works on the restructuring of the UN in the economic, social and related fields; administration of the Commission undertaken by UNCTAD; 43 mems.

Commission for Social Development: f. 1946 as the Social Commission; advises ECOSOC on issues of social and community development; 46 mems.

Commission on the Status of Women: f. 1946; aims at equality of political, economic and social rights for women, and supports the right of women to live free of violence; 45 mems.

Statistical Commission: Standardizes terminology and procedure in statistics and promotes the development of national statistics; 24 mems.

United Nations Forum on Forests: f. 2000; composed of all states mems of the UN and its specialized agencies.

REGIONAL COMMISSIONS

(see United Nations Regional Commissions)

Economic Commission for Africa (ECA).

Economic Commission for Europe (ECE).

Economic Commission for Latin America and the Caribbean (ECLAC).

Economic and Social Commission for Asia and the Pacific (ESCAP).

Economic and Social Commission for Western Asia (ESCWA).

STANDING COMMITTEES

Committee on Negotiations with Intergovernmental Agencies: f. 1946.

Committee on Non-Governmental Organizations: f. 1946; 19 mems.

Committee for Programme and Co-ordination: f. 1962; 34 mems.

EXPERT BODIES

Committee for Development Policy: f. 1965 (as Cttee for Devt Planning), renamed in 1988; 24 mems serving in a personal capacity for three-year terms.

Committee of Experts on International Co-operation in Tax Matters: f. 2004; 25 mems serving in a personal capacity.

Committee of Experts on Public Administration: f. 1967 (as Group of Experts in Public Admin. and Finance), renamed 2002; 24 mems serving in a personal capacity.

Committee of Experts on the Transport of Dangerous Goods and on the Globally Harmonized System of Classification and Labelling of Chemicals: 37 mems serving as governmental experts.

Committee on Economic, Social and Cultural Rights: f. 1985; 18 mems serving in a personal capacity.

Permanent Forum on Indigenous Issues: f. 2000; 16 mems serving in a personal capacity.

United Nations Group of Experts on Geographical Names: f. 1972; 23 mems serving as governmental experts.

There are two ad hoc bodies: the open-ended working group on informatics and the open-ended intergovernmental group of experts on energy and sustainable development. Other ad hoc mechanisms in 2014 were advisory groups on African countries emerging from conflict, an ad hoc advisory group on Haiti, and the UN Public-Private Alliance for Rural Development.

RELATED BODIES

International Narcotics Control Board: f. 1964; 13 mems.

Programme Co-ordination Board for the Joint UN Programme on HIV/AIDS (UNAIDS): f. 1994; 22 mems.

UNDP/UNFPA Executive Board: 36 mems, elected by ECOSOC.

UN-Habitat Governing Council: 58 mems, elected by ECOSOC.

UNHCR Executive Committee: 53 mems, elected by ECOSOC.

UNICEF Executive Board: 36 mems, elected by ECOSOC.

WFP Executive Board: one-half of the 36 mems are elected by ECOSOC, one-half by FAO; governing body of the World Food Programme.

International Court of Justice

Address: Peace Palace, Carnegieplein 2, 2517 KJ The Hague, Netherlands.

Telephone: (70) 3022323; **fax:** (70) 3649928; **e-mail:** information@icj-cij.org; **internet:** www.icj-cij.org.

Established in 1945, the Court is the principal judicial organ of the UN. All members of the UN are parties to the Statute of the Court.

THE JUDGES

(April 2014; in order of precedence)

	Term Ends*
President: PETER TOMKA (Slovakia)	2021
Vice-President: BERNARDO SEPÚLVEDA -AMOR (Mexico)	2015
Judges:	
HISASHI OWADA (Japan)	2021
RONNY ABRAHAM (France)	2015
KENNETH KEITH (New Zealand)	2015
MOHAMED BENNOUNA (Morocco)	2015
LEONID SKOTNIKOV (Russia)	2015
ANTÔNIO AUGUSTO CANÇADO TRINDADE (Brazil)	2018
ABDULQAWI AHMED YUSUF (Somalia)	2018
CHRISTOPHER GREENWOOD (United Kingdom)	2018
XUE HANQIN (People's Republic of China)	2021
JOAN E. DONOGHUE (USA)	2015
GIORGIO GAJA (Italy)	2021
JULIA SEBUTINDE (Uganda)	2021
DALVEER BHANDARI (India)	2018

* Each term ends on 5 February of the year indicated.

Registrar: PHILIPPE COUVREUR (Belgium).

The Court is composed of 15 judges, each of a different nationality, elected with an absolute majority by both the General Assembly and the Security Council. Representation of different legal systems of the world are borne in mind in their election. Candidates are nominated by national panels of jurists.

The judges are elected for nine years and may be re-elected; elections for five seats are held every three years. The Court elects its President and Vice-President for each three-year period. Members may not have any political, administrative, or other professional occupation, and may not sit in any case with which they have been otherwise connected than as a judge of the Court. For the purposes of a case, each side—consisting of one or more states—may, unless the Bench already includes a judge with a corresponding nationality, choose a person from outside the Court to sit as a judge on terms of equality with the Members. Judicial decisions are taken by a majority of the judges present, subject to a quorum of nine Members. The President has a casting vote.

FUNCTIONS

The International Court of Justice operates in accordance with a Statute which is an integral part of the UN Charter. Only states may be parties in cases before the Court; those not parties to the Statute may have access under conditions laid down by the Security Council.

The Jurisdiction of the Court comprises:

1. All cases which the parties refer to it jointly by special agreement (indicated in the list below by a stroke between the names of the parties);

2. All matters concerning which a treaty or convention in force provides for reference to the Court through the inclusion of a jurisdictional clause. Some 300 agreements, both bilateral and multilateral, have been notified to the Court's Registry, for example: Treaty of Peace with Japan (1951); European Convention for Peaceful Settlement of Disputes (1957); Single Convention on Narcotic Drugs (1961); International Convention on the Elimination of All Forms of Racial Discrimination (1966); Protocol relating to the Status of Refugees (1967); Convention on the Suppression of the Unlawful Seizure of Aircraft (1970); Convention on the Elimination of All Forms of Discrimination against Women (1979); Convention against Torture and Other Cruel, Inhuman or Degrading Treatment or Punishment (1984); International Convention for the Suppression of the Financing of Terrorism (1999);

3. Legal disputes between states which have recognized the jurisdiction of the Court as compulsory for specified classes of dispute. Declarations by the following 69 states accepting the compulsory jurisdiction of the Court are in force (although many with reservations): Australia, Austria, Barbados, Belgium, Botswana, Bulgaria, Cambodia, Cameroon, Canada, the Democratic Republic of the Congo, Costa Rica, Côte d'Ivoire, Cyprus, Denmark, Djibouti, Dominica, the Dominican Republic, Egypt, Estonia, Finland, The Gambia, Germany, Georgia, Greece, Guinea, Guinea-Bissau, Haiti, Honduras, Hungary, India, Ireland, Japan, Kenya, Lesotho, Liberia, Liechtenstein, Lithuania, Luxembourg, Madagascar, Malawi, Malta, Mauritius, Mexico, the Netherlands, New Zealand,

Nicaragua, Nigeria, Norway, Pakistan, Panama, Paraguay, Peru, the Philippines, Poland, Portugal, Senegal, Slovakia, Somalia, Spain, Sudan, Suriname, Swaziland, Sweden, Switzerland, Timor-Leste, Togo, Uganda, United Kingdom and Uruguay.

CONTENTIOUS CASES

Since 1946 some 156 cases have been referred to the Court relating to legal disputes or legal questions. Some were removed from the list as a result of settlement or discontinuance, or on the grounds of a lack of basis for jurisdiction.

Judgments

Judgments are without appeal, but are binding only for the particular case and between the parties. States appearing before the Court undertake to comply with its Judgment. If a party to a case fails to do so, the other party may apply to the Security Council, which may make recommendations or decide upon measures to give effect to the Judgment.

Pending Cases

In April 2014 the following contentious cases were under consideration, or pending before the Court: a request by Slovakia for an additional judgment in the dispute with Hungary concerning the Gabčíkovo–Nagymaros Hydroelectric Project (initial Judgment having been delivered in Sept. 1997); further deliberation of the case brought by the DRC against Uganda concerning armed activities on its territory (initial Judgment having been delivered in Dec. 2005); a case brought by Croatia against Serbia concerning the application of the 1948 Convention on the Prevention and Punishment of the Crime of Genocide (Judgment on the preliminary objections regarding jurisdiction and admissibility having been delivered in Nov. 2008); a case brought by Costa Rica against Nicaragua for allegedly violating Costa Rica's territorial integrity during the construction of a canal and through interference in the San Juan River; a case brought by Nicaragua against Costa Rica concerning alleged violations of Nicaraguan sovereignty and major environmental damages to its territory through the construction of a road in Costa Rica alongside the San Juan River; proceedings initiated by Nicaragua against Colombia relating to alleged violations of its sovereignty and maritime zones; proceedings brought by Bolivia concerning the obligation of Chile to negotiate the 'sovereign access of Bolivia to the Pacific Ocean'; and a case brought by Timor-Leste against Australia relating to the alleged seizure by Australian state agents of confidential documents and data belonging to the Timor-Leste authorities.

ADVISORY OPINIONS

Advisory opinions on legal questions may be requested by the General Assembly, the Security Council or, if so authorized by the Assembly, other UN organs or specialized agencies. Matters on which the Court has delivered an Advisory Opinion at the request of the UN General Assembly include the following: Condition of Admission of a State to Membership in the UN; Competence of the General Assembly for the Admission of a State to the United Nations; Interpretation of the Peace Treaties with Bulgaria, Hungary and Romania; International Status of South West Africa; Reservations to the Convention on the Prevention and Punishment of the Crime of Genocide; Effect of Awards of Compensation Made by the United Nations Administrative Tribunal (UNAT); Western Sahara; Application for Review of UNAT Judgment No. 333; Applicability of the Obligation to Arbitrate under Section 21 of the United Nations Headquarters Agreement of 26 June 1947 (relating to the closure of the Observer Mission to the United Nations maintained by the Palestine Liberation Organization); Legality of the Use or Threat of Nuclear Weapons; and Legal Consequences of the Construction of a Wall by Israel in the Occupied Palestinian Territory (delivered in July 2004); and the legality of a unilateral declaration of independence by the Provisional Institutions of Self-Government of Kosovo (delivered in July 2010).

An Advisory Opinion has been given at the request of the Security Council: Legal Consequences for States of the continued presence of South Africa in Namibia (South West Africa) notwithstanding Security Council resolution 276 (1970).

In 1989 (at the request of the UN Economic and Social Council—ECOSOC) the Court gave an Advisory Opinion on the Applicability of Article 6, Section 22, of the Convention on the Privileges and Immunities of the United Nations. The Court has also, at the request of the UN Educational, Scientific and Cultural Organization (UNESCO), given an Advisory Opinion on Judgments of the Administrative Tribunal of the International Labour Organization (ILO) upon Complaints made against UNESCO, and on the Constitution of the Maritime Safety Committee of the Inter-Governmental Maritime Consultative Organization (IMCO), at the request of IMCO. In July 1996 the Court delivered an Advisory Opinion on the Legality of the Use by a State of Nuclear Weapons in Armed Conflict, requested by the World Health Organization. In April 1999 the Court delivered an Advisory Opinion, requested by ECOSOC, on the Difference Relating to Immunity from Legal Process of a Special Rapporteur of the Commission on Human Rights. In February 2012 the Court delivered an Advisory Opinion, requested by the International Fund for Agricultural Development, relating to a Judgment rendered by the Administrative Tribunal of the ILO.

Finance

The UN budget appropriation for the Court for the two-year period 2014–15 amounted to US $52.3m.

Publications

Acts and Documents, No. 6 (contains Statute and Rules of the Court and Practice Directions).

Bibliography (annually).

Pleadings (Written Pleadings and Statements, Oral Proceedings, Correspondence).

Reports (Judgments, Opinions and Orders).

Yearbook.

UNITED NATIONS REGIONAL COMMISSIONS

Economic Commission for Europe—ECE

Address: Palais des Nations, 1211 Geneva 10, Switzerland.

Telephone: 229174444; **fax:** 229170505; **e-mail:** info.ece@unece.org; **internet:** www.unece.org.

ECE was established in 1947 as one of the earliest of the five regional economic commissions set up by the UN Economic and Social Council (ECOSOC). The Commission promotes pan-European and transatlantic economic integration. It provides a multilateral forum for dialogue and co-operation on economic and sectoral issues for governments from European countries, as well as Central Asian republics, the USA, Canada and Israel. It provides analysis, policy advice and assistance to governments, gives focus to UN global mandates on economic issues, and establishes norms, standards and conventions to facilitate international co-operation within and outside the region.

MEMBERS

Albania	Lithuania
Andorra	Luxembourg
Armenia	Macedonia, former Yugoslav republic
Austria	Malta
Azerbaijan	Moldova
Belarus	Monaco
Belgium	Montenegro
Bosnia and Herzegovina	Netherlands
Bulgaria	Norway
Canada	Poland
Croatia	Portugal
Cyprus	Romania
Czech Republic	Russia
Denmark	San Marino
Estonia	Serbia
Finland	Slovakia
France	Slovenia
Georgia	Spain
Germany	Sweden
Greece	Switzerland
Hungary	Tajikistan
Iceland	Turkey
Ireland	Turkmenistan
Israel	Ukraine
Italy	United Kingdom
Kazakhstan	USA
Kyrgyzstan	Uzbekistan
Latvia	
Liechtenstein	

Organization

(April 2014)

COMMISSION

The Commission, the highest decision-making body of the organization, holds biennial formal sessions in Geneva, Switzerland, to review the economic situation and decide on activities for the coming two years. The 65th session was held in April 2013. As well as taking strategic decisions the Commission provides a forum for senior-level dialogue on regional economic development policy.

EXECUTIVE COMMITTEE

The Executive Committee prepares the formal sessions of the Commission, implements the decisions of the Commission, and acts on behalf of the Commission between the sessions of that body. The Executive Committee also reviews and approves the programmes of work of the sectoral committees, which report at least once a year to the Executive Committee.

SECRETARIAT

The Secretariat services the meetings of the Commission and its sectoral committees and publishes periodic surveys and reviews, including a number of specialized statistical bulletins. The Executive Secretary carries out secretarial functions for the executive bodies of several regional conventions and their protocols.

Executive Secretary: MICHAEL MØLLER (Denmark) (acting).

SECTORAL COMMITTEES

There are Committees on Economic Co-operation and Integration; Environmental Policy; Housing and Land Management; Inland Transport; Sustainable Energy; Timber; and Trade. There is also a Conference of European Statisticians.

Activities

The guiding principle of ECE activities is the promotion of sustainable economic growth among its member countries. To this end it provides a forum for communication among states; negotiates international legal instruments concerning trade, transport and the environment; and supplies statistics and economic and environmental analysis. The 59th session of ECE, convened in February 2004, commissioned a comprehensive, external evaluation of the state of ECE, in view of implications arising from the enlargement of the European Union (EU) and ongoing developments in member states with economies in transition. The report, which was published in June 2005, included the following recommendations: more effective governance and management of the Commission, including restructuring work divisions and sub-programmes and identifying specialized areas of competence; raising the political profile of the Commission; co-ordinating the regional implementation of the UN Millennium Development Goals; improving co-operation with other organizations, in particular a partnership with the UN Development Programme (UNDP) and with other regional commissions; and strengthening the participation of the private sector and non-governmental organizations in the Commission. Greater priority was to be given to the environment and transport, and to the specific problems affecting countries with economies in transition. The 61st session of ECE, convened in December 2005, adopted the resulting Work Plan on ECE Reform. The 64th session of ECE, held in March 2011, focused on the Commission's role in promoting pan-European economic integration, addressing in particular the regional transport and trade infrastructure, and energy co-operation. The 65th session, convened in April 2013, included a high-level debate on the theme 'Enabling the shift to a sustainable future'. In November ECE participated in Post-2015 Europe and Central Asia Regional Consultations that were held, in Istanbul, Turkey, to contribute to drafting the post-2015 development agenda.

ECONOMIC CO-OPERATION AND INTEGRATION AND GREEN ECONOMY

The programme on Economic Co-operation and Integration, which is implemented by the Committee on Economic Co-operation and Integration, has the following thematic focuses: strengthening the competitiveness of member states' economies by promoting the knowledge-based economy and innovation; facilitating the development of entrepreneurship and the emergence of new enterprises; facilitating effective regulatory policies and corporate governance, including those in the financial sector; promoting public-private partnerships for domestic and foreign investment; maintaining intellectual property rights; and other relevant aspects of international economic co-operation and integration. At its inaugural session in September 2006 the Committee adopted a programme of work and established three teams of specialists, on innovation and competitiveness policies, on intellectual property, and on public-private partnerships (PPPs), which support programme implementation in these thematic areas. The third session of the Committee, held in December 2008, determined to enhance the practical dimension of its work, in particular the capacity-building activities in transition economies. An International Centre of Excellence (ICoE) on PPPs was established in Geneva in 2011, under the aegis of ECE. In September 2012 an international conference agreed to establish a Regional Centre of Excellence to promote PPPs in Montenegro and South-East Europe, under the auspices of the ICoE. In the following month ECE, with other agencies and the Philippines Government, agreed to establish an International Specialist Centre on PPPs in Health, in Manila, Philippines. A meeting of the ICoE and other international PPP centres, held in June 2013, decided that the ICoE should develop standards and recommendations on international best practices in the use of PPPs in the development of infrastructure and in improving the delivery of social services in sectors including transport, water management, renewable energy and broadband/

ICT. Since 2006 ECE has hosted, jointly with the World Bank Institute and the Asian Development Bank, an annual global meeting, 'PPP Days', of PPP practitioners and experts.

ECE periodically convenes Green Economy seminars. The fourth, held in November 2012, addressed trends and challenges confronting European cities relating to transport, energy and ageing populations. In September 2013 ECE launched an internet-based Green Economy Toolbox, outlining guidelines and policy recommendations for use by governments, entrepreneurs, academics and other stakeholders, relating to the transformation to a green economy in areas including environmental protection, energy, housing, innovation, and transport.

The UN Special Programme for the Economies of Central Asia (SPECA)—begun in 1998, and managed from the ESCAP Sub-regional Office for North and Central Asia, based in Almatı, Kazakhstan—is implemented jointly by ECE and ESCAP: SPECA helps the participating countries to strengthen regional co-operation, particularly in the areas of water resources, energy and transport, and creates incentives for economic development and integration into the economies of Asia and Europe. ECE also provides technical assistance to the Southeast European Co-operative Initiative. In May 2013 a tripartite Memorandum of Understanding was concluded between ECE, ESCAP and the Eurasian Economic Community, committing to future co-operation between the three groupings.

ENVIRONMENT

ECE facilitates and promotes co-operation among member governments in developing and implementing policies for environmental protection, the rational use of natural resources, and sustainable development. It supports the integration of environmental policy into sectoral policies, seeks solutions to environmental problems, particularly those of a transboundary nature, and assists in strengthening environmental management capabilities, particularly in countries in transition. A programme of Environmental Performance Reviews helps individual countries to improve the effectiveness of environmental management and policies. The Committee on Environmental Policy brings governments together to formulate policy and provides a forum for the exchange of experience and good practices. It facilitates and prepares the Environment for Europe process, the focus of which is a ministerial-level conference normally held every four years (the 2011 meeting was held in September, in Astana, Kazakhstan, addressing two main themes: 'Sustainable Management of Water and Water-related Ecosystems' and 'Greening the Economy: Mainstreaming the Environment into Economic Development'). ECE also supports, with the European Office of WHO, a Pan-European Programme (PEP) on transport, health and the environment, and sponsors a programme co-ordinating efforts to develop education for sustainable development in the ECE region. ECE has negotiated five environmental conventions, for which it serves as the secretariat: the Convention on Long-range Transboundary Air Pollution (the LRTAP, which entered into force in 1983 and has been extended by eight protocols); the Convention on the Protection and Use of Transboundary Watercourses and International Lakes (also known as the Water Convention, 1996, two protocols); the Convention on Environmental Impact Assessment in a Transboundary Context (Espoo Convention, 1997, one protocol, which entered into force in July 2010); the Convention on the Transboundary Effects of Industrial Accidents (2000, one protocol) and the Convention on Access to Information, Public Participation in Decision-making and Access to Justice in Environmental Matters (Aarhus Convention, 2001). A Protocol (to the Aarhus Convention) on Pollutant Release and Transfer Registers (PRTRs), which was adopted in May 2003, entered into force in October 2009. All UN member states are encouraged to accede to the Protocol. In July 2011 the meeting of the parties to the Aarhus Convention determined to encourage accession to the Convention, also, by states outside the ECE region. In December 2011—within the context of an amendment adopted in 2003 that, upon ratification, would extend the Water Convention to extra-regional members—ECE organized a high-level conference to promote greater co-operation between European and Asian countries in the management and protection of transboundary waters. In May 2012 representatives of Central Asian ECE member states endorsed the a plan on 'Development of the regional cooperation to ensure water quality in Central Asia', based in principle on the Water Convention. In February 2013 the 2003 amendment to the Water Convention entered into force, opening the Convention to ratification by all UN member states. In June 2013 ECE convened a workshop in Buenos Aires, Argentina, with participation by Latin American countries, to raise awareness in that region of transboundary co-operation under the Water Convention. In May 2012 amendments were adopted to the LRTAP's Gothenburg Protocol to Abate Acidification, Eutrophication and Ground-level Ozone that incorporated national emission reduction commitments to be attained by 2020 for main air pollutants, including 'fine particulate matter'. In December 2012 the parties to the LRTAP's 1998 Protocol on Heavy Metals (relating to reductions in emissions of cadmium, lead and mercury) adopted amendments setting tighter particulate matter emissions limits.

FORESTRY AND TIMBER

ECE's Timber Committee works closely with the FAO's European Forestry Commission to promote sustainable forest management. It compiles data and analyses long-term trends and prospects for forestry and timber; keeps under review developments in the forest industries, including environmental and energy-related aspects; and publishes an annual market review of forest products. The Committee meets annually to review the programme, as well as to discuss policy and market trends and outlook. Assistance in the form of workshops and expert advice is provided to help countries that are undergoing economic transition to develop their forestry sectors. In March 2010 ECE and FAO launched a study of the state of forests and forestry management in Europe; the results were collated in the 2011 edition of the *State of Europe's Forests*, which was issued in June of that year. In December 2013 ECE and FAO jointly adopted the Rovaniemi Action Plan for the Forest Sector in a Green Economy, which represents a tool for initiating actions to promote forests a sustainable source of a wide range of renewable products, while maintaining their vitality. In February 2014 the ECE Executive Committee approved an ECE-FAO Integrated Programme of Work on Forests to be undertaken during 2014–17, which was to cover areas including forest policy, statistics, sustainable forest products, wood energy, monitoring of forests, communication on forests, and green jobs.

HOUSING, LAND MANAGEMENT AND POPULATION

The Committee organizes sub-regional workshops and seminars, and provides policy advice in the form of country profiles on the housing sector and land administration reviews, undertaken by experts. The Committee works to improve housing conditions as well as spatial planning and land administration policy. In particular, it promotes the provision of adequate housing, both in the Eastern European countries undergoing socio-economic transition and in deprived neighbourhoods in Western Europe. The Committee and its Working Party on Land Administration prepare guidance on urban renewal, condominium management, housing finance, land administration, social housing and energy efficiency in housing. The Committee organizes sub-regional workshops and seminars, and provides policy advice, through its country profiles on the housing sector and land administration reviews, which are prepared by teams of experts. In 2008 the Real Estate Market Advisory Group was established to support the Working Party on Land Administration's activities and to help to structure a sustainable housing market. In April 2011 ECE published an Action Plan for Energy Efficient Housing in the UNECE Region, aimed at introducing institutional, technological and cultural changes needed to improve energy efficiency in the housing sector.

ECE tracks demographic and societal change through its Population Unit. In November 2007 ECE organized a Conference on Ageing to discuss the implications of regional fertility rates that had fallen below replacement level. A new Working Group on Ageing was established, and convened for its inaugural meeting in December 2008, to undertake a programme of action to counter the challenges of ageing societies. A Ministerial Conference on Ageing was held, in Vienna, Austria, in September 2012. In July 2013 ECE and the UN Population Fund jointly organized a high-level regional review conference of the International Conference on Population Development.

STATISTICS

The Conference of European Statisticians (CES) and ECE's Statistical Division have the task of co-ordinating international statistical activities in the region, by reviewing the most topical statistical areas, identifying gaps and duplication, and looking for issues not hitherto addressed. The CES plenary sessions and seminars offer a forum for senior statisticians, often leading to work in new areas and the preparation of new standards and recommendations. The CES and the Statistical Division work to develop methodology in compiling and disseminating economic, social and demographic statistics, for example in harmonizing methods of compiling gross domestic product, national accounts and other economic indicators; measuring the distorting effect of globalization on national statistical systems; and finding sound methods of measuring sustainable development. The Division helps countries, especially those undergoing economic transition, to improve their statistical systems in accordance with the UN Fundamental Principles of Official Statistics, by advising on legislation and institutions and on how to ensure the independence and impartiality of official statistics. It maintains an online statistical database, allowing comparison of major economic and social indicators, and publishes guidelines on the editing of statistical data. In June 2013 the CES endorsed a series of recommendations aimed at establishing a framework and set of indicators for measuring regional sustainable development.

SUSTAINABLE ENERGY

Through its Committee on Sustainable Energy, subsidiary bodies and projects, ECE works to promote a sustainable energy development strategy for the region, with the following objectives: sustained access to high quality energy services for all individuals in the ECE region; security of energy supplies in the short, medium and long term; facilitating the transition to a more sustainable energy future and reducing health and environmental impacts resulting from the production, transport and use of energy; promoting well-balanced energy network systems across the region, tailored to optimize operating efficiencies and overall regional co-operation; ensuring sustained improvements in energy efficiency, in production and use, particularly in countries with economies in transition; and, in the context of post-EU enlargement, integrating energy restructuring, legal, regulatory and energy pricing reforms, as well as the social dimension, into energy policy-making. Activities include labelling classification systems and related legal and policy frameworks; liberalization of energy markets, pricing policies and supply security; harmonization of energy policies and practices; rational use of energy, efficiency and conservation; energy infrastructure, including interconnection of gas networks; cleaner electricity production from coal and other fossil fuels; the Energy Efficiency 21 Project (GEE21, the first meeting of which was convened in July 2009); the promotion and development—through the UNECE Gas Centre programme—of a market-based gas industry in countries with economies in transition; and providing technical assistance and operational activities in energy to countries with economies in transition. In December 2011 ECE convened a regional preparatory meeting for the United Nations Conference on Sustainable Development (the so-called Rio+20 conference), which was held in June 2012.

TRADE

ECE's Committee on Trade aims to focus on the facilitation of international trade by means of simpler and better-integrated trade procedures, electronic business methods, common agricultural quality standards, and the harmonization of technical regulations. The Committee works closely with other organizations, and provides a forum for dialogue between the public and the private sector. The UN Centre for Trade Facilitation and Electronic Business (UN/CEFACT, established in 2002 as part of ECE) works to reduce delays and costs in international transactions by simplifying procedures. ECE's Working Party on Agricultural Quality Standards develops and updates commercial quality standards for fruit, vegetables and other agricultural products, in co-operation with the Organisation for Economic Co-operation and Development (OECD), and promotes the application of these standards through regional seminars and workshops. The Working Party on Regulatory Co-operation and Standardization Policies aims to harmonize product regulations and standards, the diversity of which can seriously impede trade. It has developed an international model for technical harmonization to assist countries wishing to standardize their rules on specific products or sectors. In December 2011 the ECE Executive Committee established a new group of experts, within the Working Party, to develop a set of recommendations on the application of risk management to regulatory work. ECE's Advisory Group on Market Surveillance aims to combat the proliferation of counterfeit and pirated goods.

In December 2011 ECE hosted a Global Trade Facilitation Conference, organized by the five UN regional commissions, which requested the commissions to prepare a roadmap to develop and enhance 'Single Window' facilities and information exchange in global supply chains.

TRANSPORT

ECE aims to promote a coherent, efficient, safe and sustainable transport system through the development of international agreements, conventions, norms and standards relating to road, rail, inland water and combined transport. These international legal instruments, which are developed by specialized intergovernmental working parties with participation from, among others, transport equipment manufacturers, consumers and road users, include measures for improving vehicle safety and limiting vehicle emissions, simplifying border crossing procedures, improving road traffic safety, setting the conditions for developing coherent infrastructure networks, and providing for the safe transport of dangerous goods. One of the working groups, the World Forum for Harmonization of Vehicle Regulations, has global participation and meets twice a year. ECE addresses transport trends and economics and compiles transport statistics, and provides a forum for the exchange of technical and legal expertise in the field of inland transport. In 2005, a Master Plan was elaborated for investment in the Trans-European Motorway (TEM) and the Trans-European Railway (TER) projects, with the aim of improving the road and rail networks in 21 Central, Eastern and South-Eastern European countries. A revision of the Master Plan was adopted in 2007. In July 2009 ECE signed an agreement with Slovakia to host the central project office of the TER initiative. In April 2010 the national co-ordinators for the TEM and TER projects in 13 countries adopted a new Innsbruck Initiative for safe, secure, prosperous and environmentally friendly transport. Objectives of the Innsbruck Initiative, which were to be incorporated into the TEM and TER work plans for 2011–15, included the development of transport infrastructure to improve safety, environmental performance and security; encouraging measures conducive to secure and safe transport, and promoting the proper design of transport infrastructure; supporting interoperability between transport modes, intermodal connections and combined transport systems; and promoting the introduction of Intelligent Transport Systems, with a particular focus on increasing transport safety and security, and minimizing traffic congestion and air pollution. Another project, undertaken jointly with ESCAP, aims to develop Euro-Asian transport links. In February 2008 ECE established a Group of Experts on Hinterland Connections of Seaports to study the effectiveness of existing container management and inland transport connections with seaports, and to compile a set of recommendations. In October 2012, at the annual session of the Working Party on Inland Water Transport, ECE published an updated survey on the status of inland navigation in the region, the *Inventory of Main Standards and Parameters of the pan-European Inland Waterway Network (E Waterways)*. A Conference on Improving Road Safety in South-Eastern Europe, organized by ECE, was held in Halkida, Greece, in June 2009. ECE and the other UN regional commissions were to play a key role in implementing the UN Decade of Action for Road Safety, covering the period 2011–20, which aimed to reduce the rate of road fatalities.

Finance

The proposed appropriation for ECE's regular budget in 2014–15 was US $71.7m.

Publications

Report of the Conference of European Statisticians (annually).
Trade Promotion Directory (annually).
UNECE Report (annually).
UNECE Weekly.
UNECE Compendium of Legal Instruments, Norms and Standards.
UNECE Countries in Figures.
Statistical bulletins, reports, performance reviews, country profiles, standards, agreements, recommendations, discussion papers, guidelines and manuals.

Economic and Social Commission for Asia and the Pacific—ESCAP

Address: United Nations Bldg, Rajadamnern Nok Ave, Bangkok 10200, Thailand.

Telephone: (2) 288-1234; **fax:** (2) 288-1000; **e-mail:** unisbkk .unescap@un.org; **internet:** www.unescap.org.

The Commission was founded in 1947, at first to assist in post-war reconstruction, and subsequently to encourage the economic and social development of Asia and the Far East; it was originally known as the Economic Commission for Asia and the Far East (ECAFE). The title ESCAP was adopted after a reorganization in 1974. ESCAP's main objectives are to promote inclusive and sustainable economic and social development in Asia and the Pacific, and to help member countries to achieve internationally agreed development goals.

MEMBERS

Afghanistan	Korea, Democratic People's Republic	Philippines
Armenia	Korea, Republic	Russia
Australia	Kyrgyzstan	Samoa
Azerbaijan	Laos	Singapore
Bangladesh	Malaysia	Solomon Islands
Bhutan	Maldives	Sri Lanka
Brunei	Marshall Islands	Tajikistan
Cambodia	Micronesia, Federated States	Thailand
China, People's Republic	Mongolia	Timor-Leste
Fiji	Myanmar	Tonga
France	Nauru	Turkey
Georgia	Nepal	Turkmenistan
India	Netherlands	Tuvalu
Indonesia	New Zealand	United Kingdom
Iran	Pakistan	USA
Japan	Palau	Uzbekistan
Kazakhstan	Papua New Guinea	Vanuatu
Kiribati		Viet Nam

ASSOCIATE MEMBERS

American Samoa	Hong Kong	Northern Mariana Islands
Cook Islands	Macao	
French Polynesia	New Caledonia	
Guam	Niue	

Organization

(April 2014)

COMMISSION

The main legislative organ of ESCAP is the Commission, which meets annually at ministerial level to examine the region's problems, to review progress, to establish priorities and to decide upon the recommendations of the Executive Secretary or the subsidiary bodies of the Commission. It reports to the UN Economic and Social Council (ECOSOC). Ministerial and intergovernmental conferences on specific issues may be held on an ad hoc basis with the approval of the Commission, although no more than one ministerial conference and five intergovernmental conferences may be held during one year.

COMMITTEES AND SPECIAL BODIES

Specialized committees and special bodies have been established to advise the Commission and help to oversee the work of the Secretariat. They meet every two years, while any sub-committees meet in the intervening years. There are Committees on Macroeconomic Policy, Poverty Reduction and Inclusive Development; Trade and Investment; Transport; Environment and Development; Information and Communications Technology; Disaster Risk Reduction; Social Development; and Statistics. Two special bodies cover Least Developed and Landlocked Developing Countries; and Pacific Island Developing Countries.

In addition, an Advisory Committee of permanent representatives and other representatives designated by members of the Commission functions as an advisory body; it generally meets every month.

SECRETARIAT

The Secretariat operates under the guidance of the Commission and its subsidiary bodies. It consists of the Office of the Executive Secretary and two servicing divisions, covering administration and programme management, in addition to the following substantive divisions: Environment and Development; Information and Communications Technology and Disaster Risk Reduction; Macroeconomic Policy and Development; Social Development; Statistics; Trade and Investment; and Transport.

Executive Secretary: Dr SHAMSHAD AKHTAR DETHO (Pakistan).

SUB-REGIONAL OFFICES

ESCAP Pacific Operations Centre (EPOC): Private Mail Bag, Suva, Fiji; tel. 3319669; fax 3319671; e-mail epoc@un.org; internet www.unescap.org/epoc; f. 1984, relocated to Fiji 2005; responsible for ESCAP's sub-programme on Development of Pacific Island Countries and Territories; assists Pacific island governments in forming and implementing national sustainable development strategies, particularly poverty reduction programmes that create access to services by socially vulnerable groups; conducts research, promotes regional co-operation and knowledge-sharing, and provides advisory services, training and pilot projects; Dir IOSEFA MAIAVA (Samoa).

Sub-regional Office for East and North-East Asia: I-Tower, 6th/7th Floors, 24-4 Songdo-dong, Yeonsu-gu Incheon 406-840, Republic of Korea; tel. (32) 458-6600; fax (32) 458-6699; e-mail vanlaere@un.org; internet northeast-sro.unescap.org; f. 2010; covers activities in the People's Republic of China, Japan, the Democratic People's Republic of Korea, the Republic of Korea, Mongolia and Russia; Dir KILAPARTI RAMAKRISHNA.

Sub-regional Office for North and Central Asia (SONCA): 68A Amangeldy St, Almatı, Kazakhstan; tel. (727) 2503930; internet northcentral-sro.unescap.org; f. 2011; SONCA covers Afghanistan, Azerbaijan, Armenia, Georgia, Kazakhstan, Kyrgyzstan, Russia, Tajikistan, Turkmenistan and Uzbekistan, and co-ordinates the UN Special Programme for the Economies of Central Asia (SPECA), supported both by ESCAP and the UN Economic Commission for Europe; Head of Office Dr NIKOLAY POMOSHCHNIKOV.

Sub-regional Office for South and South-West Asia: POB 4575, C-2 Qutab Institutional Area, New Delhi 110 016, India; tel. (11) 30973700; fax (11) 26856274; internet sswa.unescap.org; f. 2011; serves Afghanistan, Bangladesh, Bhutan, India, Iran, Maldives, Nepal, Pakistan, Sri Lanka and Turkey; Dir Dr NAGESH KUMAR (India).

Activities

ESCAP acts as a UN regional centre, providing the only intergovernmental forum that includes the whole of Asia and the Pacific, and executing a wide range of development programmes through technical assistance, advisory services to governments, research, training and information. The Commission's 69th session, convened in April–May 2013, with a focus on building resilience to economic shocks and natural disasters, endorsed a new regional agenda aimed at establishing the foundations of a future of inclusive, equitable, resilient and sustainable prosperity; and concluded with the first ever review by Executive Secretaries of all the UN regional commissions of their role in promoting South-South co-operation in support of sustainable and inclusive global development.

In December 2013 a Ministerial Conference on Regional Economic Co-operation and Integration in Asia and the Pacific, convened in Bangkok under ESCAP auspices, with representation from 36 member countries, adopted the Bangkok Declaration on Regional Economic Co-operation and Integration in Asia and the Pacific, outlining a road map towards the creation of a regional economic community, which was to provide for an integrated regional market, financial co-operation, full energy and transport connectivity, and improved resilience to the risk of natural disasters.

SOCIAL DEVELOPMENT

ESCAP's Social Development Division, comprises three sections: Social Protection and Integration; Social Policy and Population; and Gender Equality. The Division aims to assess and respond to regional trends and challenges in social development, and to help member countries to build more inclusive societies, through social and financial policies and measures promoting social protection, social inclusion, gender equality and development. The Social Protection and Integration Section aims to strengthen the capacity of public and non-government institutions to address the problems of marginalized social groups and to promote initiatives to provide income to the poor. The Gender Equality Section promotes the advancement of women by helping to improve their access to education, economic resources, information and communication technologies and decision-making; it is also committed to combating violence against women, including trafficking. The Social Policy and Population Section focuses on issues concerning ageing, youth, disability, migration and population. Activities include providing technical assistance to national population programmes; promoting the rights of people with disabilities; supporting improvement of access to social services by poor people; and helping governments to form policies that take into account the increasing proportion of older people in the population. In May 2013 ESCAP co-chaired, with the International Organization for Migration (IOM), an Asia-Pacific Regional Preparatory Meeting for the High-level Dialogue on International Migration and Development, which was hosted in early October by the 68th session of the UN General Assembly.

The Division implements global and regional mandates, such as the Programme of Action of the World Summit for Social Development and the Jakarta Plan of Action on Human Resources Development. In February 2014 the inaugural session of a new working group on the Asian and Pacific Decade of Persons with Disabilities (2013–22) adopted a five-year road map for the implementation of the Incheon Strategy to 'Make the Right Real' for Persons with Disabilities in Asia and the Pacific, which was adopted in November 2012, and incorporates a set of regional disability-inclusive development goals. ESCAP undertook regional preparations for the World Summit on Sustainable Development, which was held in Johannesburg, South Africa, in August–September 2002. In following up the summit ESCAP undertook to develop a biodiversity park, which was officially inaugurated in Rawalpindi, Pakistan, in January 2005. The Commission prepares specific publications relating to population and implements the Programme of Action of the 1994 International Conference on Population and Development (ICPD). The Secretariat co-ordinates the Asia-Pacific Population Information Network (POPIN). The sixth Asia and Pacific Population Conference (APPC), convened in September 2013, in Bangkok, under the auspices of ESCAP and the UN Population Fund, adopted an Asian and Pacific Ministerial Declaration on Population and Development, which was to represent the region's contribution to 'ICPD Beyond 2014', a review of the 1994 ICPD to be concluded during 2014 by the UN General Assembly. In September 2004 ESCAP convened a senior-level intergovernmental meeting on the regional review and implementation of the Beijing Platform for Action (Beijing+10), relating to gender equality. A further intergovernmental review meeting, Beijing+15, was hosted by ESCAP in November 2009. In September 2011 ESCAP hosted the inaugural meeting of an Asia-Pacific Regional Advisory Group on Women, Peace and Security, which was established in the previous year to support the effective implementation throughout the region of UN Security Council Resolution 1325 relating to the impact of conflict on women and girls and their role in peacebuilding. The 67th Commission, meeting in Bangkok, in May 2011, pledged commitment to protecting the poor and vulnerable sectors of the region's population from the after-shocks of economic and natural crises. In February 2012 ESCAP hosted a high-level intergovernmental meeting which endorsed an action plan towards greater regional co-operation in achieving global commitments to address and eliminate HIV/AIDS.

ENVIRONMENT AND DEVELOPMENT

ESCAP is concerned with strengthening national capabilities to achieve environmentally sound and sustainable development by integrating economic concerns, such as the sustainable management of natural resources, into economic planning and policies. The Environment and Development Division comprises sections on Energy Security, Environment and Development Policy, and Water Security. Activities include the promotion of integrated water resources development and management, including water quality and conservation and a reduction in water-related natural disasters; strengthening the formulation of policies in the sustainable development of land and mineral resources; and the consideration of energy resource options, such as rural energy supply, energy conservation and the planning of power networks. The Division administers a North-East Asia Sub-regional Programme for Environmental Co-operation (NEASPEC). Through the Division ESCAP prepares a report entitled *Environmental Sustainability in Asia and the Pacific* which is published at five-yearly intervals. ESCAP helps to organize a ministerial conference on environment and development, also convened every five years. The Division collates information on issues related to climate change, conducts regional seminars on adapting to climate change, and provides training in clean technology and guidance on reduction of harmful gas emissions. In March 2008 ESCAP organized an inaugural meeting of the Asia-Pacific Regional Platform on Climate Change and Development. In the following month ESCAP organized the first Asia-Pacific Mayors' Forum on Environmentally Sustainable Urban Infrastructure Development, held in Ulsan, South Korea. In June 2011 ESCAP hosted an Asia-Pacific Urban Forum, in Bangkok, which was convened on the theme 'Cities of opportunity: Partnerships for an inclusive and sustainable future'. In September an expert group meeting on sustainable energy development in Asia and the Pacific, organized by ESCAP, with other UN agenices, focused on the need for developing national policies in the region aimed at ensuring universal access to clean and efficient energy services, as a means of advancing poverty reduction and improving health and well-being.

In May 2010 the 66th Commission, convened in Incheon, adopted a Declaration urging countries to strengthen and adopt 'green growth' strategies, in order to support recovery from the global economic and financial crisis and to achieve sustainable economic and social development. The sixth ministerial conference on environment and development, convened in Astana, Kazakhstan, in September–October, adopted a Ministerial Declaration on Green Growth, committing member countries to promoting environmentally sustainable economic growth and development. The conference also adopted a Regional Implementation Plan for Sustainable Development in Asia and the Pacific, covering the period 2011–15, and a Green Bridge Initiative to promote environmental partnerships and co-operation between Europe and Asia. In February 2012 ESCAP's Committee on Environment and Development endorsed the so-called Seoul Outcome, which was concluded in October 2011 by the Asia-Pacific Regional Preparatory Meeting, held in South Korea, for the UN Conference on Sustainable Development ('Rio+20'—convened in June 2012, in Rio de Janeiro, Brazil).

In May 2013 ESCAP convened, in Vladivostok, Russia, the inaugural meeting of an Asian and Pacific Energy Forum (APEF), at which ministers responsible for energy in 34 member countries adopted the APEF/Vladivostok Plan of Action, with the aim of strengthening co-operation in order to enhance energy security and the sustainable use of energy throughout the region. In September the leaders of 11 Pacific ESCAP member states, meeting on the sidelines of the UN General Assembly, signed a Declaration on Establishing a Pacific Regional Data Repository for Sustainable Energy for All.

INFORMATION AND COMMUNICATIONS TECHNOLOGY AND DISASTER RISK REDUCTION

ESCAP's Information and Communications Technology (ICT) and Disaster Risk Reduction Division aims to strengthen capacity for access to and the application of ICT, in order to enhance socio-economic development and maximize the benefits of globalization. It supports the development of cross-sectoral policies and strategies, and also supports regional co-operation aimed at sharing knowledge between advanced and developing economies and in areas such as cyber-crime and information security. In May 2005 the Commission approved the establishment, in South Korea, of the Asian and Pacific Training Centre for ICT for Development (APCICT); it was inaugurated in June 2006. The Division organized several conferences in preparation for the second phase of the World Summit on the Information Society (WSIS), which took place in November 2005, and co-ordinates regional activities aimed at achieving WSIS targets for the widespread use of ICT by 2015. It helps members to include space technology in their development planning, for example the use of satellites in meteorology, disaster prevention, remote sensing and distance learning. In August 2007 the Division hosted an international meeting on the use of space technology to combat avian influenza and other infectious diseases. A meeting of national policy-makers on disaster management was convened in March 2008 to discuss access to satellite information as a means of predicting and managing natural disasters. In September 2010 a Regional Co-operative Mechanism on Disaster Monitoring and Early Warning, Particularly Drought was established. An expert group meeting to consider priority areas for the mechanism was convened in Beijing, People's Republic of China, in March 2011.

The Division's policy with relation to disaster risk reduction is guided by the Hyogo Framework for Action, covering the period 2005–15, which was adopted by the World Conference on Disaster Reduction, held in Kobe, Hyogo, Japan, in January 2005. The accompanying Declaration, adopted by the Conference, emphasized the need to develop and strengthen regional strategies and operational mechanisms in order to ensure rapid and effective disaster response. A new Committee on Disaster Risk Reduction convened for an inaugural session in March 2009; participants agreed to strengthen information and knowledge-sharing in relation to risk reduction. During 2012 ESCAP worked with the International Strategy for Disaster Reduction to produce an *Asia and Pacific Disaster Report*, which was published in October. In December Asian and Pacific countries, meeting under ESCAP auspices, adopted a five-year Regional Plan of Action for the application of space technology for addressing natural disasters and achieving sustainable development goals in the region.

ESCAP administers the voluntary, multi-donor trust fund that was inaugurated in late 2005 to assist reconstruction, and to support national and regional efforts to develop a tsunami early warning system: the Regional Integrated Multi-Hazard Early Warning System for Africa and Asia (RIMES). In March 2011 ESCAP and the government of Thailand, the founding donor of the Fund, signed an agreement to expand the mandate of the Fund and rename it as the Multi-Donor Trust Fund for Tsunami, Disaster and Climate Preparedness in Indian Ocean and South-East Asian Countries. In June 2012 the first ministerial conference on RIMES, meeting in New Delhi, India, determined to develop a financial mechanism to finance the System. In 2011, in May and December, ESCAP helped to organize expert meetings to consider the experiences of the tsunami and earthquake in Japan, in March of that year, and observe lessons for regional disaster preparedness. In February 2012 ESCAP hosted a forum to reflect on the experiences of the extensive flooding which caused large-scale economic and humanitarian devastation in parts of South-East Asia in 2011. In May 2012 the 68th session of the Commission endorsed the Asia-Pacific Years of Action for Applications of Space Technology and the Geographic Information System (GIS) for Disaster Risk Reduction and Sustainable Development, 2012–17; this was formally launched in October 2012.

MACROECONOMIC POLICY AND DEVELOPMENT

The work of the Division is undertaken by the following sections: Development Policy, and Macroeconomic Policy and Analysis. The Division aims to increase the understanding of the economic and social development situation in the region, with particular attention given to the attainment of the Millennium Development Goals (MDGs), sustainable economic growth, poverty alleviation, the integration of environmental concerns into macroeconomic decisions and policy-making processes, and enhancing the position of the region's disadvantaged economies, including those Central Asian countries undergoing transition from a centrally planned economy to a market economy. The Division is responsible for the provision of technical assistance, and the production of relevant documents and publications. It publishes the *Economic and Social Survey of Asia and the Pacific*, and policy briefs. The 63rd Commission, meeting in Almatı, Kazakhstan, in May 2007, endorsed a regional plan, developed by ESCAP, the UN Development Programme (UNDP) and the Asian Development Bank (ADB), to help poorer member countries to achieve the MDGs. Assistance was to be provided in the following areas: knowledge and capacity building; expertise; resources; advocacy; and regional co-operation in delivering public goods (including infrastructure and energy security). The Commission also approved a resolution urging greater investment in health care in all member countries. In 2009 the Macroeconomic Policy and Development Division co-ordinated the preparation of a joint report of all five UN Regional Commissions, entitled *The Global Economic and Financial Crisis: Regional Impacts, Responses and Solutions*, which was published in May. In February 2010 a regional report on achieving the MDGs acknowledged the impact of the crisis and highlighted the need to strengthen social protection throughout the region. In December 2011 ESCAP hosted a meeting of senior officials to address the implementation of the Istanbul Programme of Action for the Least Developed Countries for the Decade 2011–20 in the Asia-Pacific region.

An annual regional review on progress towards achieving the MDGs is prepared by the Commission. In August 2013 ESCAP and the Government of Thailand convened, in Bangkok, the Asia-Pacific Ministerial Dialogue: From the MDGs to the UN Development Agenda beyond 2015, representing the first gathering of ministers from the region to address the UN's future development framework.

STATISTICS

ESCAP's Statistics Division provides training and advice in priority areas, including national accounts statistics, poverty indicators, gender statistics, population censuses and surveys, and the strengthening and management of statistical systems. It supports co-ordination throughout the region of the development, implementation and revision of selected international statistical standards, and, in particular, co-ordinates the International Comparison Programme (ICP) for Asia and the Pacific (part of a global ICP initiative). The Division disseminates comparable socio-economic statistics, with increased use of the electronic media, promotes the use of modern technology in the public sector and trains senior-level officials in the effective management of ICT. Training is provided by the Statistical Institute for Asia and the Pacific.

TRADE AND INVESTMENT

ESCAP aims to help members to benefit from globalization by increasing global and regional flows of trade and investment. Its Trade and Investment Division provides technical assistance and advisory services. It aims to enhance institutional capacity building; gives special emphasis to the needs of least developed, landlocked and island developing countries, and to Central Asian countries that are in transition to a market economy, in accelerating their industrial and technological advancement, promoting their exports, and furthering their integration into the region's economy; supports the development of electronic commerce and other information technologies in the region; and promotes the intra-regional and inter-subregional exchange of trade, investment and technology through the strengthening of institutional support services such as regional information networks. In March 2013 ESCAP and other partners supported the Government of Laos in convening a meeting, in Vientiane, Laos, of UN representatives and senior government officials from landlocked developing countries in Asia and the Pacific and Europe, which addressed means of promoting full participation in global trade by landlocked developing countries, as well as other socio-economic consequences of not having direct access to maritime ports.

The Division functions as the secretariat of the Asia-Pacific Trade Agreement (APTA), concluded in 1975 to promote regional trade through mutually agreed concessions by the participating states (in 2014 they comprised Bangladesh, China, India, South Korea, Laos, Mongolia and Sri Lanka). Since 2004 the Division has organized an annual Asia-Pacific Business Forum (2013: held in November, in Bangkok, Thailand), involving representatives of governments, the private sector and civil society. It operates the Asia-Pacific Trade and Investment Agreements Database, the Trade and Transport Facilitation Online Database and an online directory of trade organizations, and publishes the *Asia-Pacific Trade and Investment Review* twice a year. The Division acts as the Secretariat of the Asia-Pacific Research and Training Network on Trade (ARTNeT), established in 2004, which aims to enhance the region's research capacity. ESCAP, with the World Trade Organization (WTO), implements a technical assistance programme, helping member states to implement WTO agreements and to participate in ongoing multilateral trade negotiations. In March 2009 ESCAP launched the UN Network of Experts for Paperless Trade in Asia and the Pacific (UN NExT).

TRANSPORT

ESCAP's Transport Division aims to improve the regional movement of goods and people, and to assist member states to manage and to benefit from globalization. The Division has three sections: Transport Infrastructure; Transport Facilitation and Logistics; and Transport Policy and Development (incorporating a sub-programme on Tourism). In April 2008 the ESCAP Commission determined to establish a Forum of Asian Ministers of Transport to provide strategic guidance for the development of efficient, reliable and cost-effective transport services throughout the region. The inaugural meeting of the Forum was held in December 2009, in Bangkok, and the second Forum was convened in November 2013. Principal infrastructure projects undertaken by the Transport Division have been the development of the Trans-Asian Railway and of the Asian Highway road network. Other activities are aimed at improving the planning process in developing infrastructure facilities and services, in accordance with the Regional Action Programme of the New Delhi Action Plan on Infrastructure Development in Asia and the Pacific (which was adopted at a ministerial conference held in October 1996), and at enhancing private sector involvement in national infrastructure development through financing, management, operations and risk-sharing. The Division aims to reduce the adverse environmental impact of the provision of infrastructure facilities and to promote more equitable and easier access to social amenities. An Intergovernmental Agreement on the Asian Highway Network (adopted in 2003, identifying some 143,000 km of roads in 32 countries) came into effect in July 2005. At October 2013 the working group on the highway network estimated that more than nearly 12,000 km of the highway network did not meet the minimum standards set by the Agreement. In November 2005 ESCAP organized an intergovernmental meeting to conclude a draft agreement on the establishment of a Trans-Asian Railway Network. The intergovernmental accord was adopted in April 2006, and entered into force in June 2009, by April 2014 it had received 22 signatures and been ratified by 18 member states. The network was to comprise some 114,000 km of rail routes over 28 countries (80,900 km over 26 countries had been achieved by 2014). The first meeting of a working group on the Trans-Asian Railway Network was held in December, in Bangkok. In 2004 ESCAP and the UN Economic Commission for Europe (ECE) initiated a project for developing Euro-Asian transport linkages, aiming to identify and overcome the principal obstacles (physical and otherwise) along the main transport routes linking Asia and Europe. In November 2006 the Ministerial Conference on Transport, held in Busan, South Korea, adopted the Busan Declaration, which outlined a long-term development strategy for regional transport and identified investment priorities. The meeting also adopted a Ministerial Declaration on Road Safety which pledged to implement safety measures to save some 600,000 lives in the region in the period 2007–15. In May 2012 the 68th session of the Commission endorsed phase II of a Regional Action Programme for Transport Development in Asia and the Pacific, covering 2012–16 (phase I having been implemented during 2007–11), and a Regional Strategic Framework for the Facilitation of International Road Transport. In May 2013 the Commission adopted the Intergovernmental Agreement on Dry Ports, which had been formulated to promote the development of dry ports along the Asian Highway and Trans-Asian Railway networks. A formal signing ceremony for the Agreement took place in November. In June a Policy Dialogue on Strengthening Transport Connectivity among Countries of South and Southwest Asia gave consideration to the development of a masterplan aimed at accelerating sub-regional connectivity.

ESCAP's tourism concerns include the development of human resources, improved policy planning for tourism development, greater investment in the industry, and minimizing the environmental impact of tourism. A Network of Asia-Pacific Education and Training Institutes in Tourism, established in 1997, comprised 261 institutes and organizations in 45 countries and states in 2014.

CO-OPERATION WITH OTHER ORGANIZATIONS

ESCAP works with other UN agencies and non-UN international organizations, non-governmental organizations, academic institutions and the private sector; such co-operation includes joint planning of programmes, preparation of studies and reports, participating in meetings, and sharing information and technical expertise. In 2001 ESCAP, with the ADB and UNDP, established a tripartite regional partnership to promote the MDGs; a report on implementation of the goals was prepared by the partnership and published in June 2005 prior to a global review, conducted at the UN

General Assembly in September. A Memorandum of Understanding (MOU) was signed by ESCAP and the ADB in May 2004 with an emphasis on achieving poverty reduction throughout the region. In May 2007 ESCAP endorsed a regional plan developed by the partnership with the aim of addressing regional challenges (in particular those faced by poorer countries) to the achievement of the MDGs. A High-level Subregional Forum on Accelerating Achievement of the Millennium Development Goals in South Asia was organized by the partnership in February 2012. The UN Special Programme for the Economies of Central Asia (SPECA), begun in 1998, is implemented jointly by ESCAP and ECE, and managed from ESCAP's Subregional Office for North and Central Asia. In May 2013 ESCAP, ECE and the Eurasian Economic Community signed a tripartite MOU on strengthening co-operation in areas including sustainable development and environmental protection, the efficient use of water and energy resources, the development of transport networks, trade facilitation, and business development. In June 2008 ESCAP signed an MOU with the IOM to provide for greater co-operation and co-ordination on international migration issues. In November 2013 ESCAP signed an MOU with the Organisation for Economic Co-operation and Development (OECD) during a joint conference concerned with regional co-operation to advance responsible business practices.

Special Programme for the Economies of Central Asia (SPECA): c/o 68A Amangeldy St, Almatı, Kazakhstan; tel. (727) 2503930; internet northcentral-sro.unescap.org; launched in 1998 by the presidents of Central Asian states, SPECA is supported jointly by ESCAP and ECE. It aims to strengthen sub-regional co-operation by enabling the discussion of regional issues and offering technical assistance. Six project working groups cover: transport and border crossing; water and energy resources; trade; knowledge-based development; statistics; and gender and economy. SPECA is managed from ESCAP's Sub-regional Office for North and Central Asia. The SPECA Economic Forum meets annually in conjunction with the sessions of the SPECA Governing Council, composed of the national co-ordinators of member countries. The 2013 Forum was convened in Almatı, in November.

REGIONAL INSTITUTIONS

Centre for Sustainable Agricultural Machination (CSAM): A-7/F, China International Science and Technology Convention Centre, 12 Yumin Rd, Chaoyang District, Beijing 100029, People's Republic of China; tel. (10) 8225-3581; fax (10) 8225-3584; e-mail info@un-csam.org; internet www.un-csam.org; f. 1977 as the Regional Network for Agricultural Engineering and Machinery, elevated to regional centre (as the Asian and Pacific Centre for Agricultural Engineering and Machinery) in 2002; present name adopted in Oct. 2012; aims to achieve, through sustainable agricultural mechanization, resilient, inclusive production gains, improved rural livelihoods and poverty alleviation. Active mems: Bangladesh, People's Republic of China, Fiji, India, Indonesia, Iran, Democratic People's Republic of Korea, Republic of Korea, Mongolia, Nepal, Pakistan, Philippines, Sri Lanka, Thailand, Viet Nam; Dir BING ZHAO (China); publ. *CSAM Policy Brief* (quarterly).

Asian and Pacific Centre for Transfer of Technology (APCTT): APCTT Bldg, POB 4575, C-2 Qutab Institutional Area, New Delhi 110 016, India; tel. (11) 30973700; fax (11) 26856274; e-mail postmaster.apctt@un.org; internet www.apctt.org; f. 1977 to assist countries of the ESCAP region by strengthening their capacity to develop, transfer and adopt technologies relevant to the region, and to identify and promote regional technology development and transfer; operates Business Asia Network (www.business-asia.net) to promote technology-based co-operation, particularly between small and medium-sized enterprises; Dir MICHAEL WILLIAMSON; publs *Asia Pacific Tech Monitor*, *VATIS Updates on Biotechnology*, *Food Processing*, *Ozone Layer Protection*, *Non-Conventional Energy*, *Waste Management* (each every 2 months).

Asian and Pacific Training Centre for ICT for Development (APCICT): I-Tower, 24-4 Songdo-dong, Yeonsu-gu Incheon 406-840, Republic of Korea; tel. (32) 245-1700; fax (32) 245-7712; e-mail info@unapcict.org; internet www.unapcict.org; f. 2006 to provide training to ICT policy-makers and professionals, advisory services and analytical studies, to promote best practices in the field of ICT, and to contribute to narrowing the digital divide in the region; developed an Academy of ICT Essentials for Government Leaders, a virtual Academy, and an e-Collaborative hub; Dir HYUEN-SUK RHEE.

Centre for Alleviation of Poverty through Sustainable Agriculture (CAPSA): Jalan Merdeka 145, Bogor 16111, Indonesia; tel. (251) 343277; fax (251) 336290; e-mail capsa@uncapsa.org; internet www.uncapsa.org; f. 1981 as CGPRT Centre, current name adopted 2010; initiates and promotes socio-economic and policy research, training, dissemination of information and advisory services to enhance food security in Asia and the Pacific; Dir Dr KATINKA WEINBERGER (Germany).

Statistical Institute for Asia and the Pacific (SIAP): JETRO-IDE Building, 2–2 Wakaba 3-chome, Mihama-ku, Chiba-shi, Chiba 2618787, Japan; tel. (43) 2999782; fax (43) 2999780; e-mail staff@unsiap.or.jp; internet www.unsiap.or.jp; f. 1970 as Asian Statistical Institute, present name adopted 1977; became a subsidiary body of ESCAP in 1995; provides training in official statistics to government statisticians; Dir MARGARITA GUERRERO.

ASSOCIATED BODIES

ESCAP/WMO Typhoon Committee: Av. de 5 de Outubro, Coloane, Macao, SAR, People's Republic of China; tel. 88010531; fax 88010530; e-mail info@typhooncommittee.org; internet www.typhooncommittee.org; f. 1968; an intergovernmental body affiliated to ESCAP and regional body of the Tropical Cyclone Programme of the World Meteorological Organization; promotes disaster preparedness, trains personnel on meteorology, hydrology and disaster risk reduction and co-ordinates research. The committee's programme is supported by national resources and also by other international and bilateral assistance; Mems: Cambodia, People's Republic of China, Democratic People's Republic of Korea, Republic of Korea, Hong Kong SAR, Japan, Laos, Macao SAR, Malaysia, Philippines, Singapore, Thailand, USA, Viet Nam; Sec. OLAVO RASQUINHO.

WMO/ESCAP Panel on Tropical Cyclones: PTC Secretariat, Meteorological Complex, Pitras Buk. Rd, Sector H-8/2, Islamabad 44000, Pakistan; tel. (51) 9250367; fax (51) 9250368; e-mail PTC.Sectt@ptc-wmoescap.org; internet www.ptc-wmoescap.org; f. 1972 to mitigate damage caused by tropical cyclones in the Bay of Bengal and the Arabian Sea; mems: Bangladesh, India, Maldives, Myanmar, Oman, Pakistan, Sri Lanka, Thailand; Sec. ARIF MAHMOOD.

Finance

For the two-year period 2014–15 ESCAP's programme budget, an appropriation from the UN budget, was US $103.8m. The regular budget is supplemented annually by funds from various sources for technical assistance.

Publications

Annual Report.
Asia-Pacific Development Journal (2 a year).
Asia-Pacific in Figures (annually).
Asia-Pacific Population Journal (3 a year).
Asia-Pacific Regional MDGs Report.
Asia-Pacific Trade and Investment Report (annually).
Asia and Pacific Disaster Report.
Bulletin on Asia-Pacific Perspectives (annually).
Directory of Trade and Investment-Related Organizations.
Economic and Social Survey of Asia and the Pacific (annually).
Environment and Sustainable Development News (quarterly).
Environmental Sustainability in Asia and the Pacific (every 5 years).
ESCAP Energy News (2 a year).
ESCAP Human Resources Development Newsletter (2 a year).
ESCAP Population Data Sheet (annually).
ESCAP Tourism Review (annually).
Foreign Trade Statistics of Asia and the Pacific (every 2 years).
Key Economic Developments and Prospects in the Asia-Pacific Region (annually).
Macroeconomic Policy and Development Division Policy Briefs.
Population Headliners (several a year).
Poverty Alleviation Initiatives (quarterly).
Socio-Economic Policy Brief (several a year).
Statistical Indicators for Asia and the Pacific (quarterly).
Statistical Newsletter (quarterly).
Statistical Yearbook for Asia and the Pacific.
Technical Co-operation Yearbook.
Transport and Communications Bulletin for Asia and the Pacific (annually).
Water Resources Journal (annually).
Manuals; country and trade profiles; commodity prices; statistics; Atlas of Mineral Resources of the ESCAP Region (country by country).

Economic Commission for Latin America and the Caribbean—ECLAC

Address: Edif. Naciones Unidas, Avda Dag Hammarskjöld 3477, Vitacura, Casilla 179-D, Santiago, Chile.

Telephone: (2) 2102000; **fax:** (2) 2080252; **e-mail:** dpisantiago@eclac.cl; **internet:** www.eclac.cl.

ECLAC was established (as the UN Economic Commission for Latin America, current name adopted in 1984) in 1948 to co-ordinate policies for the promotion of economic development in the Latin American region.

MEMBERS

Antigua and Barbuda	El Salvador	Paraguay
Argentina	France	Peru
Bahamas	Germany	Portugal
Barbados	Grenada	Saint Christopher and Nevis
Belize	Guatemala	Saint Lucia
Bolivia	Guyana	Saint Vincent and the Grenadines
Brazil	Haiti	Spain
Canada	Honduras	Suriname
Chile	Italy	Trinidad and Tobago
Colombia	Jamaica	United Kingdom
Costa Rica	Japan	USA
Cuba	Korea, Republic	Uruguay
Dominica	Mexico	Venezuela
Dominican Republic	Netherlands	
Ecuador	Nicaragua	
	Panama	

ASSOCIATE MEMBERS

Anguilla	Cayman Islands	Puerto Rico
Aruba	Curaçao	Turks and Caicos
Bermuda	Guadaloupe	United States Virgin Islands
British Virgin Islands	Martinique	
	Montserrat	

Organization

(April 2014)

COMMISSION

The Commission, comprising representatives of every member state, normally meets every two years at ministerial level. It considers matters relating to the economic and social development of the region, reviews activities of the organization, and adopts programmes of work. The 34th session was held in San Salvador, El Salvador, in August 2012; the 35th session was scheduled to be convened in Lima, Peru, in May 2014. Member states may meet between Commission meetings in an ad hoc Committee of the Whole. The Commission has established the following ad hoc and permanent bodies:

Caribbean Development and Co-operation Committee;
Committee of High-level Government Experts;
Committee on Central American Economic Co-operation;
Committee on South-South Co-operation;
Regional Conference on Population and Development;
Regional Conference on Women;
Regional Council for Planning of ILPES;
Statistical Conference of the Americas.

SECRETARIAT

The Secretariat employs more than 500 staff and is headed by the Offices of the Executive Secretary and of the Secretary of the Commission. ECLAC's work programme is carried out by the following divisions: Economic Development (including a Development Studies Unit); Economic and Social Planning (ILPES, see below); Financing for Development; International Trade and Integration; Natural Resources and Infrastructure (including a Transport Unit); Population (CELADE, see below); Production, Productivity and Management (including an Agricultural Development Unit, a joint ECLAC/UNIDO Industrial and Technological Development Unit and a Unit on Investment and Corporate Strategies); Social Development; Statistics; Programme Planning and Operations; Sustainable Development and Human Settlements; and Gender Affairs. There are also a Development Studies Unit and a Public Information and Web Services Section.

Executive Secretary: Alicia Bárcena Ibarra (Mexico).

SUB-REGIONAL OFFICES

Caribbean: 1 Chancery Lane, POB 1113, Port of Spain, Trinidad and Tobago; tel. 224-8000; fax 623-8485; e-mail registry@eclacpos.org; internet www.eclacpos.org; f. 1956; covers non-Spanish-speaking Caribbean countries; functions as the secretariat for the Caribbean Development and Co-operation Committee; Dir Diane Quarless (Jamaica).

Central America and Spanish-speaking Caribbean: Edif. Corporativo MCS, Av. Miguel de Cervantes Saavedra 193, piso 12, Col. Granada. Del. Miguel Hidalgo, CP11520, México, DF; tel. (55) 4170-5600; fax (55) 5531-1151; e-mail registromexico@cepal.org; internet www.cepal.org.mx; f. 1951; covers Central America and Spanish-speaking Caribbean countries; Dir Hugo E. Beteta.

There are also national offices, in Buenos Aires, Argentina; Brasília, Brazil; Bogotá, Colombia; and Montevideo, Uruguay; and a liaison office in Washington, DC, USA.

Activities

ECLAC collaborates with regional governments in the investigation and analysis of regional and national economic problems, and provides guidance in the formulation of development plans. The activities of its different divisions include research, monitoring of trends and policies, and comparative studies; analysis; publication of information; provision of technical assistance; organizing and participating in workshops, seminars and conferences; training courses; and co-operation with national, regional and international organizations, including non-governmental organizations and the private sector. ECLAC's 29th session, held in Brasília, Brazil, in May 2002, adopted the Brasília Resolution, which outlined a strategic agenda to meet the challenges of globalization. Proposed action included the consolidation of democracy, strengthening social protection, the formulation of policies to reduce macroeconomic and financial vulnerability, and the development of sustainable and systemic competitiveness in order to build, gradually, an international social agenda based on rights.

The 34th session of the Commission, convened in August 2012, in San Salvador, El Salvador, proposed the implementation of structural changes to diversify the region's economies and to promote social equality and environmental sustainability, and presented a report entitled *Structural Change for Equality: An Integrated Development View*. In June 2013 a ministerial meeting on Innovation and Structural Change in Latin America, organized by ECLAC in Rio de Janeiro, Brazil, adopted the Rio de Janeiro Declaration on promoting strategies and industrial policies aimed at boosting inclusive regional development. The priority areas addressed by ECLAC's work programme for the two-year period 2014–15 were: improving macroeconomic stability, and enhancing policies aimed at reducing vulnerability and mitigating the effects of economic and financial crises; strengthening access to financing for development, and enhancing the financial architecture at all levels; increasing the region's productive potential, with a particular emphasis on innovation and new technologies; advancing—through trade, regional integration and co-operation—the region's position in the global economy; improving social equality, reducing social risks and strengthening gender mainstreaming in public policies; enhancing policies on sustainable development, improving energy efficiency, addressing the impacts of climate change, facilitating implementation of the outcomes of the June 2012 UN Conference on Sustainable Development, and reducing vulnerability in key sectors; reinforcing public management, particularly through progressive fiscal policies; and improving institution-building related to the management of global and transboundary issues, and to the provision of public goods at the regional level.

ECLAC works closely with other UN agencies and with other regional and multinational organizations. In January 2010 ECLAC offered its total co-operation in the immediate humanitarian tasks resulting from the earthquake that caused extensive damage and loss of life in Haiti and in any future reconstruction process. In March, following a massive earthquake in Chile, ECLAC established a joint working group, with the UN Development Programme

(UNDP), the Office for the Co-ordination of Humanitarian Affairs (OCHA) and the Chilean authorities, to define priority areas for emergency funding.

ECLAC supports member countries in negotiations of bilateral or sub-regional free trade agreements, in particular with the USA. In January 2002 ECLAC hosted an Interregional Conference on Financing for Development, held in Mexico City, Mexico, which it had organized as part of the negotiating process prior to the World Summit on Financing for Development, held in March. In June senior representatives of ECLAC, UNDP, the World Bank and the Inter-American Development Bank (IADB) agreed to co-ordinate activities in pursuit of the Millennium Development Goals. In July 2004 the 30th session of the Commission approved the establishment of an intergovernmental forum to monitor the implementation of decisions emerging from the World Summit on Sustainable Development, held in Johannesburg, South Africa, in September 2002. In January 2006 ECLAC organized the first Regional Implementation Forum on Sustainable Development, as mandated by the UN Commission on Sustainable Development. In June 2012 the ECLAC Executive Secretary and the President of the People's Republic of China discussed the creation of a new China-Latin America Cooperation Forum, with a view to strengthening inter-regional relations. In July ECLAC, the Latin American Integration Association, and the Corporación Andina de Fomento concluded an inter-agency co-operation agreement on establishing a Latin America/Asia-Pacific Observatory, which was to analyse systematically economic relations between the countries of those regions, with a view to strengthening inter-regional co-operation.

A regional ministerial meeting convened, at the request of the Commission, in June 2005, in Rio de Janeiro, approved a Regional Action Plan—eLAC 2007—to support national and regional projects that incorporate information and communications technology for use in economic and social development in the region. A second plan, eLAC2010, was adopted by ministers in February 2008, to assist countries to attain the global targets identified by the World Summit on the Information Society (WSIS, convened held in two instalments, in December 2003, in Geneva, Switzerland, and in November 2005, in Tunis, Tunisia). The first Follow-up Meeting of eLAC2010 was convened in April 2009. A third Ministerial Conference on the Information Society in Latin America and the Caribbean was held in Lima, Peru, in November 2010, at which a new action plan, eLAC2015, was approved. ECLAC serves as the technical secretariat for a regional dialogue on the costs of international connections, broadband services and digital inclusion, which was inaugurated in August 2010. In May 2011 ECLAC launched a new Regional Broadband Observatory (ORBA), which aims to facilitate public policy decision-making with regard to the provision of broadband services, and in October ECLAC organized its first so-called School for broadband policy-makers. In that month, the fourth meeting of the regional dialogue on broadband endorsed ORBA proposals relating to minimum download speeds and connectivity. In April 2013 the fourth Ministerial Conference on the Information Society in Latin America and the Caribbean was convened in Montevideo, Uruguay. Ministers and representatives from 15 countries reaffirmed their commitment to the targets outlined in eLAC2015 and agreed to strengthen regional collaboration to develop further the digital economy.

In November 2003 a Regional Intergovernmental Conference on Ageing was convened, in Santiago, to further the objectives of a World Assembly on Ageing that had been held in Madrid, Spain, in April 2002. A second Regional Intergovernmental Conference on Ageing was held in Brasília, in December 2007, and a third was held in May 2012, in San José, Costa Rica, on the theme 'Ageing, Solidarity and Social Protection: Time to Move Towards Equality'. The 2012 Conference adopted the San José Letter on the rights of the elderly, expressing regional commitment to the eradication of all forms of discrimination, and to establishing networks for the protection of old people. In November 2013 ECLAC organized the seventh Statistical Conference of the Americas (SCA), which is convened every two years to promote the development and improvement of national statistics (in particular their comparability), and to encourage co-operation between national statistical offices and regional and international organizations. ECLAC organizes an annual competition to encourage small-scale innovative social projects in local communities. In July 2009 ECLAC signed an agreement with the UN World Tourism Organization to strengthen co-operation in measuring and analysing tourism statistics and indicators. In January 2010 ECLAC initiated a joint project with the IADB to conduct an economic analysis of the impact of climate change on the region. A database on coastal dynamics in Latin America and the Caribbean, for use in planning on coastal vulnerability and the impact of climate change, was initiated in October 2013 jointly by ECLAC, the Spanish Government and the University of Cantabria (Spain). In January 2012 ECLAC and the Union of Universities of Latin America and the Caribbean signed a five-year co-operation agreement providing a framework for collaboration between officials and consultants in the shared goal of improving research, debate and training of professionals. ECLAC acts as the secretariat for the Observatory on Gender Equality for Latin America and the Caribbean, which was established in 2008 and is supported by partners including UN Women and the UN Population Fund. In October 2013 the 12th session of ECLAC's Regional Conference on Women adopted the Santo Domingo Consensus on progress towards gender equality, which focused on the linkage between economic autonomy and women's rights, and detailed actions aimed at building a technological, scientific and digital culture geared towards the economic advancement of women and girls. The Consensus also addressed the elimination of violence, female political participation, and sexual and reproductive rights.

In August 2013 ECLAC, with support from the UN Population Fund, hosted the inaugural gathering of the Regional Conference on Population and Development in Latin America and the Caribbean; the meeting adopted the Montevideo Consensus on Population and Development, setting out a series of measures related to eight priority areas for action identified in the regional agenda to follow up the Programme of Action of the International Conference on Population and Development beyond 2014.

In July 2006 Japan became the first Asian nation to be granted full membership of ECLAC. The membership of the Republic of Korea was formally approved in July 2007.

Latin American and Caribbean Institute for Economic and Social Planning (Instituto Latinoamericano y del Caribe de Planificacion Economica y Social—ILPES): Edif. Naciones Unidas, Avda Dag Hammarskjöld 3477, Vitacura, Casilla 179-D, Santiago, Chile; tel. (2) 2102507; fax (2) 2066104; e-mail ilpes@cepal.org; internet www.eclac.cl/ilpes; f. 1962; supports regional governments through the provision of training, advisory services and research in the field of public planning policy and co-ordination; Dir JORGE MATTAR MÁRQUEZ (Mexico).

Latin American Demographic Centre (Centro Latinoamericano y Caribeno de Demografia—CELADE): Edif. Naciones Unidas, Avda Dag Hammarskjöld 3477, Casilla 179-D, Santiago, Chile; tel. (2) 2102021; fax (2) 2080196; e-mail celade@eclac.cl; internet www.eclac.cl/celade; f. 1957, became an autonomous entity within ECLAC in 1971 and was fully incorporated into ECLAC as its Population Division in 1997; provides technical assistance to governments, universities and research centres in demographic analysis, population policies, integration of population factors in development planning, and data processing; conducts courses on demographic analysis for development and various national and regional seminars; provides demographic estimates and projections, documentation, data processing, computer packages and training; Dir DIRK JASPERS-FAIJER (Netherlands).

Finance

For the two-year period 2014–15 ECLAC's proposed regular budget, an appropriation from the UN, amounted to US $116.7m. In addition, extra-budgetary activities are financed by governments, other organizations, and UN agencies.

Publications

(in English and Spanish)

CEPAL Review (3 a year).

Challenges / Desafíos (2–3 a year, with UNICEF).

Demographic Observatory (2 a year).

ECLAC Notes (quarterly).

Economic and Social Panorama of the Community of Latin American and Caribbean States.

Economic Survey of Latin America and the Caribbean (annually).

FAL Bulletin (Trade Facilitation and Transport in Latin America) (monthly, electronic).

Foreign Investment in Latin America and the Caribbean (annually).

Latin America and the Caribbean in the World Economy (annually).

Latin American Economic Outlook (annually).

Macroeconomic Report on Latin America and the Caribbean (annually).

Notas de Población (2 a year).

Preliminary Overview of the Economies of Latin America and the Caribbean (annually).

Statistical Yearbook for Latin America and the Caribbean.

Studies, reports, bibliographical bulletins.

Economic Commission for Africa—ECA

Address: Menelik II Ave, POB 3001, Addis Ababa, Ethiopia.

Telephone: (11) 5517200; **fax:** (11) 5514416; **e-mail:** ecainfo@uneca.org; **internet:** www.uneca.org.

ECA was founded in 1958 by a resolution of the UN Economic and Social Council (ECOSOC). The Commission promotes sustainable socio-economic development in Africa and aims to advance economic integration among African countries, and international co-operation in support of Africa's development.

MEMBERS

Algeria	Eritrea	Niger
Angola	Ethiopia	Nigeria
Benin	Gabon	Rwanda
Botswana	The Gambia	São Tomé and Príncipe
Burkina Faso	Ghana	Senegal
Burundi	Guinea	Seychelles
Cameroon	Guinea-Bissau	Sierra Leone
Cape Verde	Kenya	Somalia
Central African Republic	Lesotho	South Africa
Chad	Liberia	South Sudan
Comoros	Libya	Sudan
Congo, Democratic Republic	Madagascar	Swaziland
Congo, Republic	Malawi	Tanzania
Côte d'Ivoire	Mali	Togo
Djibouti	Mauritania	Tunisia
Egypt	Mauritius	Uganda
Equatorial Guinea	Morocco	Zambia
	Mozambique	Zimbabwe
	Namibia	

Organization

(April 2014)

CONFERENCE OF AFRICAN MINISTERS

The Conference, which meets every year, is attended by ministers responsible for finance, planning and economic development, representing the governments of member states, and is the main deliberative body of the Commission. The Commission's responsibility to promote concerted action for the economic and social development of Africa is vested primarily in the Conference, which considers matters of general policy and the priorities to be assigned to the Commission's programmes, considers inter-African and international economic policy, and makes recommendations to member states in connection with such matters.

SECRETARIAT

The Secretariat serves the Conference of Ministers and the meetings of the Commission's subsidiary bodies, and implements the resolutions and programmes adopted there. It comprises the Office of the Executive Secretary and (following a radical restructuring, which took effect in March 2013) the following divisions: Gender; Governance; Innovation and Technology; Macroeconomic Policy; Natural Resource Management; Regional Integration and Trade; Social Development; and Capacity Development and Special Initiatives. An Office of Partnerships includes teams from the African Union (AU) and the New Partnership for Africa's Development (NEPAD).

Executive Secretary: Dr Carlos Lopes (Guinea-Bissau).

AFRICAN POLICY CENTRES

The following are focal points for continental policy making and programming:

African Centre for Statistics;

African Climate Policy Centre;

African Institute for Economic Development and Planning;

African Minerals Development Centre;

African Trade Policy Centre;

Land Policy Initiative.

SUB-REGIONAL OFFICES

The Sub-regional Offices (SROs) aim to enable member states to play an effective role in the process of African integration. They promote the production and use of high-quality statistical data by national statistical offices, and develop and maintain sub-regional repositories of statistical information that support the Commission's analytical and research activities. The SROs also provide advisory services to member states, RECs and sub-regional development stakeholders, and aim to build the capacity of member states to formulate evidence-based plans and policies in support of economic and social transformation.

Central Africa: POB 14935, Yaoundé, Cameroon; tel. 2222-0861; fax 2223-3185; e-mail sroca@uneca.org; internet www.uneca.org/sro-ca.

East Africa: POB 4654, Kigali, Rwanda; tel. 586549; fax 586546; e-mail easrdc@uneca.org; internet www.uneca.org/sro-ea.

North Africa: BP 2062 Rabat Ryad, Morocco; tel. (3) 771-78-29; fax (3) 771-27-02; e-mail srdc-na@uneca.org; internet www.uneca.org/sro-na.

Southern Africa: POB 30647, Lusaka, Zambia; tel. (1) 228502; fax (1) 236949; e-mail srdcsa.uneca@uneca.org; internet www.uneca.org/sro-sa.

West Africa: POB 744, Niamey, Niger; tel. 72-29-61; fax 72-28-94; e-mail srdcwest@eca.ne; internet www.uneca.org/sro-wa.

ECA-AFDB-AU JOINT SECRETARIAT SUPPORT OFFICE

In 2010 the tripartite partnership of ECA, the Commission of the African Union and the African Development Bank (AfDB)established a Joint Secretariat Support Office (JSSO), based at ECA headquarters, to promote stronger institutional and programmatic linkages between the three institutions, and to establish common positions on issues such as climate change and the development of the regional infrastructure.

Activities

The Commission's activities are focused on two pillars: promoting regional integration in support of the visions and priorities of the AU, through research and policy analysis on regional integration issues, capacity building, and the provision of technical assistance to the institutions (including the regional economic communities) underpinning the regional integration agenda; and on meeting emerging global challenges and the special needs of Africa, with particular emphasis on achieving the Millennium Development Goals. The Secretariat is guided in its efforts by major regional strategies, including the Abuja Treaty on the establishment of an African Economic Community, the UN System-wide Support to the AU and the New Partnership for Africa's Development (NEPAD—approved in 2006), and the Framework, Roadmap and Architecture for Fast Tracking the Establishment of a Continental Free Trade Area, and an Action Plan for Boosting Intra-African Trade, adopted in January 2012 by AU leaders. The following regional economic communities are regarded as pillars of continental economic integration: the Common Market for Eastern and Southern Africa (COMESA), the East African Community (EAC) and the Southern African Development Community (SADC) (which together form the EAC-COMESA-SADC Tripartite FTA initiative); the Communauté Économique des États de l'Afrique Centrale (CEEAC), the Economic Community of West African States (ECOWAS), the Intergovernmental Authority on Development (IGAD), and the Union of the Arab Maghreb.

Meeting in January 2013 the ECA Executive Secretary, the Chairperson of the AU Commission, and the President of the AfDB addressed the future challenges and priorities confronting Africa, and issued a communiqué outlining means of co-ordinating organizational activities aimed at supporting continental socio-economic transformation over the coming 50 years. In May AU heads of state and government outlined a vision and eight ideals to represent pillars for the economic and social transformation of the continent. These were to be translated into concrete actions and objectives by a joint ECA-AU-AfDB programme known as Agenda 2063, within the context of which a series of African Development Goals (ADGs) were to be developed; it was envisaged that Agenda 2063, which was being drafted by the three pan-African bodies in early 2014, would be finalized by June. In May 2013 the AfDB endorsed a new Africa50-Fund, which was to finance, in partnership with regional institutions, transformational projects with a focus on enhancing the transcontinental infrastructure.

In March 2013 African ministers of finance, planning and economic development agreed a revised ECA strategic framework to guide the Commission through 2014–15, rooted in a transformative regional agenda that aimed, over the long term, to upgrade African economies from low-income to middle-income status. Shortly afterwards the sixth joint annual meeting of ECA ministers of finance, planning and economic development and AU ministers of economics and finance issued a unanimous statement urging the pursuit of commodity based-industrialization as a stimulus for Africa's structural transformation.

GENDER

ECA aims to improve the socio-economic prospects of women through the promotion of equal access to resources and opportunities, and equal participation in decision-making. An African Centre for Gender and Development was established in 1975 to service all national, sub-regional and regional bodies involved in development issues relating to gender and the advancement of women. The Centre manages the African Women's Development Fund, which was established in June 2000. An African Women's Rights Observatory, launched in 1995, monitors gender equality and the advancement of women. An African Gender and Development Index, measuring how far member states had met their commitments towards international agreements on gender equality and women's advancement, was inaugurated in January 2005; the most recent Index, reflecting the state of progress in 2011, was issued in January 2012. The African Women's Decade, covering 2010–20, was launched in October 2010 on the theme 'Grassroots approach to gender equality and women's empowerment'. In March 2014 ECA initiated a new Continent-Wide Initiative on Gender Equality and Women's Empowerment.

GOVERNANCE

ECA aims to improve member states' capacity for good governance and development management. The Commission provides support for the African Peer Review Mechanism, a NEPAD initiative whereby participating member governments mutually assess compliance with a number of codes, standards and commitments that uphold good governance and sustainable development. ECA assists civil society organizations to participate in governance; supports the development of private sector enterprises; and helps to improve public administration in member states. To achieve these aims the Commission provides technical assistance and advisory services, conducts studies, and organizes training workshops, seminars and conferences at national, sub-regional and regional levels for ministers, public administrators and senior policy-makers, as well as for private and non-governmental organizations (NGOs). The Commission and the AU jointly provide support to the African Governance Forum (AGF) process, which is implemented through the UN Development Programme's Regional Bureau for Africa; such fora have been convened periodically since 1997. AGF VIII, addressing the theme 'Democracy, Elections, and the Management of Diversity in Africa', was held in Gaborone, Botswana, in 2012. In 2005 the first *African Governance Report (AGR-1)* was published by ECA, monitoring progress towards good governance in 27 countries. *AGR-2*, issued in August 2009, found improvements over the past few years in the observance of human rights and the rule of law, as well as in competitive electoral politics and the scope of political representation. Advances were also judged to have been made in economic governance, public sector management, private sector development and corporate governance, while weaknesses were highlighted in the management of the tax system and in service delivery, and corruption was cited as a major challenge to achieving sustainable economic progress and development in Africa. *AGR-3*, addressing elections and diversity management in Africa, was released in August 2013. A *Mutual Review of Development Effectiveness in Africa Report (MRDE)* is jointly compiled by ECA's Governance Division and the Organisation for Economic Co-operation and Development (OECD); the Review considers progress achieved hitherto in delivering commitments made by African countries and their development partners, and outlines future key priorities. The 2013 edition was issued in November.

INNOVATION AND TECHNOLOGY

The Innovation and Technology Division has responsibility for co-ordinating the implementation of the Harnessing Information Technology for Africa project, and for implementing the African Information Society Initiative (AISI), which was founded in 1996 and supports the development of the pan-continental information and communications infrastructure. ECA was given responsibility for the Task Force on e-Government, mandated by the second session of the World Summit on Information Society (WSIS), convened in Tunis, Tunisia, in November 2005. The Commission maintains the Africa Knowledge for Development Networks, an internet-based platform for promoting knowledge sharing on regional economic and social development. In July 2009 the first International Conference on African Digital Libraries and Archives, held under ECA auspices, urged the establishment of an ECA African Digital Library and Archives Programme. In February of that year representatives of UN agencies, NEPAD, the AU, and media executives, convened the first Regional Media Dialogue, in The Vaal, South Africa, at the end of which they adopted a Consensus Declaration and series of recommendations relating to the increasing role of the media in Africa's development. A second Regional Media Dialogue, held in June 2011, in Maseru, Lesotho, adopted the Maseru Declaration, recommending the development of a continent-wide framework for structured engagement with the media. In September 2012 the Division launched a new African Forum for Geospatial Information Systems (GIS), aimed at enhancing the capacity of African media professionals to promote GIS. In October 2011 ECA, with the AU, launched a new Africa Internet Governance Forum (AfIGF), in accordance with the recommendations of the WSIS. ECA hosts the AfIGF's secretariat. The inaugural meeting of the AfIGF, held in October 2012, in Cairo, Egypt, urged regional collaboration to combat cybercrime. The second Forum was convened in September 2013, in Nairobi, Kenya, and the third was to be convened in July 2014, in Abuja, Nigeria. In June 2013 a meeting of experts on cyber legislation from member states in eastern, southern and northern Africa, held under the auspices of ECA, the AU, and relevant regional economic communities, adopted the Addis Ababa Declaration on the harmonization of cyber legislation in Africa. ECA has provided technical support to the AU in developing a new AU Convention on Cybersecurity.

In August 2012 ECA and the UN Institute for Training and Research launched a series of free internet-based e-Learning courses aimed at supporting the objective of establishing a Continental Free Trade Area by 2017. The Commission supports the Electronic Rural School in Local Languages (ERELA) programme, administered by the Government of Finland with the aim of promoting learning and use of communications technologies in local African mother tongues.

In March 2008 ECA organized a conference entitled Science with Africa to link African science-based organizations and businesses with their global counterparts; the second Science with Africa conference, held in June 2010, adopted a set of recommendations on how African countries might leverage science and technology to carry forward their development agenda. In September 2012 ECA launched a new Access to Scientific Knowledge in Africa (ASKIA) online portal, providing scientific and socio-economic information of relevance to scientists, policy-makers, and other researchers in the region.

Since 2007 ECA has organized biennial Technology in Government in Africa (TIGA) awards, with the objective of recognizing the effective use by regional governments and institutions of ICTs for public service delivery. In 2011 ECA, jointly with the Switzerland-based African Innovation Foundation, launched an annual Innovation Prize for Africa (IPA), which aims to reward regional innovation in the areas of science, technology and engineering.

MACROECONOMIC POLICY

ECA advocates for a sound regional macroeconomic policy framework, with the aim of supporting and enabling inclusive growth, private sector development, value addition, employment, sustainable development, and the transformation of the region's economies from low-income to middle-income status. The Commission supports the economic development of member states through the collection and analysis of data; the preparation of annual economic surveys; the compilation of reports on regional economic conditions, governance and development management; the production of regional and national policy studies covering economic reforms, international and illicit financial flows, domestic resource mobilization, external debt, and exchange rate management; and the dissemination of best practices relating to specific aspects of economic management.

In June 2009 ECA and the AU hosted, in Cairo, a joint meeting of African ministers of finance and economic affairs, which considered the impact on the region of the global crisis. During that month a joint report of all five UN Regional Commissions, entitled *The Global Economic and Financial Crisis: Regional Impacts, Responses and Solutions*, was launched. In October 2010 ECA, the AU and the AfDB established a Joint Secretariat (based at ECA headquarters) to enhance coherence and collaboration in support of Africa's development agenda. In May 2011 ECA launched the *ECA LDC Monitor*, an internet-based tool aimed at assessing economic progress in member least developed countries. The theme of the 2014 *Economic Report on Africa*, released by ECA and the AU Commission in April of that year, was 'Dynamic Industrial Policy in Africa—Innovative Institutions, Effective Processes and Flexible Mechanisms'. ECA, the AfDB, OECD and UNDP jointly prepare an annual *African Economic Outlook*: the focus of the 2013 edition was 'Structural Transformation and Natural Resources'. Since 2006 ECA and AfDB have organized an annual African Economic Conference (AEC), aimed at enabling an exchange of ideas among economists and policy-makers on development policy. The eighth AEC was held in Johannesburg, South Africa, in October 2013, on the theme 'Regional Integration in Africa'.

ECA's African Institute for Economic Development and Planning (IDEP), founded in 1962, undertakes pan-African capacity development and training programmes, and also conducts policy research and dialogue initiatives. The African Centre for Statistics was established in 2006 to encourage the use of statistics in national planning, to provide training and technical assistance for the compilation, analysis and dissemination of statistics, and to assist member states with the compilation of population censuses. An Advisory Board on Statistics in Africa, comprising 15 experts from national statistical offices, sub-regional bodies and training institutes, meets annually to advise ECA on statistical developments in Africa and guide its activities. The Statistical Commission for Africa (StatCom-Africa), comprising representatives of national statistical offices, regional and international institutions and development partners, meets every two years as the principal body overseeing statistical development in Africa, with annual working groups monitoring progress and deciding on activities. In January 2012 StatCom-Africa, meeting in Cape Town, South Africa, adopted the Robben Island Declaration on Statistical Development, which aimed to strengthen methods of data collection and analysis, of harmonizing statistics in Africa and upgrading the system of national accounts. ECA assists its member states in population data collection and data processing; analysis of demographic data obtained from censuses or surveys; training demographers; formulation of population policies and integrating population variables in development planning, through advisory missions and through the organization of national seminars on population and development; and in dissemination of demographic information. The first conference of African ministers responsible for civil registration was convened in August 2010, in Addis Ababa, and the second was held in September 2012, in Durban, South Africa. ECA commemorates African Statistics Day annually on 18 November.

SOCIAL DEVELOPMENT

ECA undertakes research and develops tools and guidelines in support of the formulation, implementation and evaluation of regional and national policies aimed at achieving inclusive, equitable and sustainable development. The Commission provides information on global processes on social policy, including on the International Conference on Population and Development and the development of the UN's post-2015 development agenda. A Regional Conference on Population and Development Beyond 2014 was convened in Addis Ababa, under ECA auspices, during late September–early October 2013.

A Commission on HIV/AIDS and Governance in Africa, with its secretariat based at ECA headquarters, was launched in September 2003. The Commission, an initiative of the UN Secretary-General, was mandated to assess the impact of the HIV/AIDS pandemic on national structures and African economic development and to incorporate its findings in a Final Report; this was issued in October 2005.

NATURAL RESOURCE MANAGEMENT

ECA conducts research in support of policy, legal and regulatory frameworks underpinning the management of natural resources in Africa. ECA works to strengthen regional and national human and institutional capacities and to widen stakeholder participation in the protection of Africa's environment and in the management of mineral resources. The Commission promotes the use of science and technology in achieving sustainable development.

In 2006, with the AU and the AfDB, the Commission established a 10-year Climate for Development in Africa Programme (Clim-Dev Africa) to improve the collection of climate-related data and assist in forecasting and risk management. ECA provides the technical secretariat for Clim-Dev Africa. In December 2007 ECA announced the establishment of an African Climate Policy Centre (ACPC), to help member states to incorporate climate-related concerns in their development policies so as to counter the impact of climate change. Since 2011 Clim-Dev Africa has launched annual Climate Change and Development in Africa Conferences (CCDAs): CCDA-3 was held in Addis Ababa, in October 2013, with a focus on the effectiveness of policies on climate resilience in Africa, and the impact of current climate-related frameworks. In September 2012 a series of ACPC workshops on upgrading hydro-meteorological networks and recovering hydro-meteorological data was initiated.

ECA assists member states in the assessment and use of water resources and the development of river and lake basins common to more than one country. ECA encourages co-operation between countries with regard to water issues and collaborates with other UN agencies and regional organizations to promote technical and economic co-operation in this area. In 1992, on the initiative of ECA, the Interagency Group for Water in Africa (now UN-Water/Africa) was established to co-ordinate and harmonize the water-related activities of the UN and other organizations on the continent. ECA has been particularly active in efforts to promote the integrated development of the water resources of the Zambezi river basin and of Lake Victoria.

ECA aims to advance the development of Africa's extensive mineral and energy resources, focusing on promoting co-operation, integration and public–private sector partnerships; facilitating policy decisions and dissemination of best practices; and supporting capacity building. The Commission's Energy Programme provides assistance to member states in the development of indigenous energy resources and the formulation of energy policies to extricate member states from continued energy crises. In May 2004 ECA was appointed as the secretariat of a UN-Energy/Africa initiative which aimed to facilitate the exchange of information, good practices and knowledge-sharing among UN organizations and with private sector companies, NGOs, power utilities and other research and academic institutions. In December 2013 ECA and the AU jointly organized the third conference of African ministers responsible for mineral resources development. An African Minerals Development Centre (AMDC)—established by ECA, the AU, the AfDB and UNDP—was inaugurated during the conference; based in Maputo, Mozambique, the AMDC was mandated to implement the African Mining Vision, endorsed in February 2009 by AU heads of state. The conference also adopted the Business Plan of the AMDC, and emphasized the need for African states to seize the opportunity presented by high commodity prices and competition for Africa's mineral resources in support of the socio-economic transformation of the continent, as envisaged by Agenda 2063.

ECA promotes food security in African countries through raising awareness of the relationship between population, food security, the environment and sustainable development; encouraging the advancement of science and technology in member states; and providing policy analysis support and technical advisory services aimed at strengthening national population policies. In March 2010 ECA issued a report urging member countries to build upon the outcomes of the Abuja Food Security Summit, organized by the AU in December 2006, by establishing a common market of strategic food and agricultural commodities.

In 2006 ECA, the AU and the AfDB established the Land Policy Initiative (LPI), a joint programme that promotes equitable access to, and the efficient and sustainable utilization of land. The LPI's Secretariat is based at ECA headquarters, and is assisted by an African Task Force on Land. An LPI Framework and Guidelines on Land Policy in Africa was finalized in 2009. The LPI aims to advance women's secure access to land, and the recognition of African customary land rights.

In October 2011 ECA organized an Africa Regional Preparatory Conference in advance of the UN Conference on Sustainable Development, which was convened in Rio de Janeiro, Brazil, in June 2012, The Preparatory Conference noted emerging challenges to sustainable development in Africa, including low adaptive capacity to the effects of climate change; increasing severe biodiversity loss, desertification and land degradation, aggravated by the effects of climate change; and rapid urbanization. It urged the international community to meet its commitments to the continent in terms of transfer of financial and technological resources, and committed African states to enhancing efforts to improve national governance and development effectiveness, and to formulating national strategies for sustainable development. ECA, in collaboration with other agencies, compiles periodically a Sustainable Development Report on Africa (SDRA).

REGIONAL INTEGRATION AND TRADE

ECA supports the implementation of the AU's regional integration agenda, through research; policy analysis; strengthening capacity and the provision of technical assistance to the regional economic communities; and working on transboundary initiatives and activities across a variety of sectors. In October 2008 ECA launched an Observatory on Regional Integration in Africa, an internet-based repository of knowledge and information aimed at supporting the activities of policy-makers, member states, regional economic communities, and other stakeholders. ECA conducts research and outreach activities aimed at ensuring best practice in trade policy development and undertakes research and dissemination activities on bilateral and international trade negotiations with a view to helping African countries to benefit from globalization through trade. In July 2012 ECA, the AU and the AfDB issued their fifth joint *Assessing Regional Integration in Africa* report (ARIA V), which addressed the ongoing process towards establishing, by 2017, an operational Continental Free Trade Area. The African Trade Policy Centre (ATPC), established in 2003, aims to strengthen the human, institutional and policy capacities of African governments to formulate and implement sound trade policies and participate more effectively in international trade negotiations. The Centre takes both a national and regional perspective, and provides a rapid response to technical needs arising from ongoing trade negotiations. In November 2011 the ATPC organized the first Africa Trade Forum (ATF). During ATF II, held in September 2012 on the theme 'Boosting Intra-Africa Trade and Establishing the Continental Free Trade Area', the ATPC launched a new Africa Corridor Management Alliance (ACMA), with the aim of making more efficient the cost of moving goods through Africa's trade and transit corridors, and across international borders. Issues to be addressed by the ACMA included unofficial fees, roadblocks, and corruption; as well as variance in national laws relating to vehicle standards and inspection requirements; inefficient administrative procedures; and delays in the clearance of goods at ports.

ECA and the World Bank jointly co-ordinate the sub-Saharan Africa Transport Programme (SSATP), established in 1987, which aims to facilitate policy development and related capacity building in the continent's transport sector. In April 2012 ECA formally invited the AU Commission to join the SSATP Board. A meeting of all participants in the programme is held annually. The regional Road Management Initiative (RMI) under the SSATP seeks to encourage a partnership between the public and private sectors to manage and maintain road infrastructure more efficiently and thus to improve country-wide communications and transportation activities. An Urban Mobility component of the SSATP aims to improve sub-Saharan African urban transport services, while a Trade and Transport component aims to enhance the international competitiveness of regional economies through the establishment of more cost-effective services for shippers. The Railway Restructuring element focuses on the provision of financially sustainable railway enterprises. The first session of a forum on Central African regional integration, organized by the ECA SRO for Central Africa, took place in November 2009, in Douala, Cameroon. The second session was held in May–June 2012, also in Douala, on the theme 'Sub-regional Trade and Transport Infrastructure Development in Central Africa'. The first African Road Safety Conference, held in Accra, Ghana, in February 2007, by African ministers responsible for transport and health, reaffirmed road safety as a key development priority and pledged to set and achieve measurable national targets for road safety and the prevention of traffic injuries in all member states. In November 2011 the second African Road Safety Conference, convened by ECA within the framework of the SSATP, approved an Action Plan, which aimed to halve the number of road crash fatalities by 2020. A meeting of experts convened in September 2011 to review the development of interconnected Trans-African Highways (TAH) reported that by that time the TAH comprised some nine principal axes of roads across the continent, but that about one-quarter of an envisaged final network was yet to be constructed. The meeting recommended the adoption of an intergovernmental agreement on the TAH, and adopted a series of 10 recommendations aimed at accelerating the development of the highways interconnection initiative.

SPECIAL INITIATIVES AND CAPACITY DEVELOPMENT

ECA provides guidance to the policy-making organs of the UN and the AU on the formulation of policies supporting the achievement of Africa's development objectives. It contributes to the work of the General Assembly and of specialized agencies by providing an African perspective in the preparation of development strategies. The former UN System-wide Special Initiative on Africa, covering the decade 1995–2006, aimed to mobilize resources and to implement a series of political and economic development objectives; the Initiative was followed by the UN System-wide Support to the AU and NEPAD, launched in 2006. NEPAD was established by the AU in 2001, and ECA was assigned the task of co-ordinating UN support for NEPAD at the regional level. In February 2010 a new NEPAD Planning and Co-ordination Committee (NPCC) was established as a technical body of the AU, to replace the former NEPAD Secretariat, with the aim of improving the implementation of NEPAD projects at country level. In April 2010 ECA and the NPCC concluded a Memorandum of Understanding strengthening collaboration between the two bodies.

Joint meetings of ECA ministers of economy, planning and economic development and AU ministers of economy and finance are convened annually, in March. In October 1999 the first African Development Forum (ADF)—initiated by ECA as a process to formulate an agenda for effective sustainable development in African countries—was organized in Addis Ababa. Regular ADF meetings are held, each addressing a specific development issue. ADF VIII was convened in October 2012, on the theme 'Governing and Harnessing Natural Resources for Africa's Development'. In March 2011 ECA launched the Africa Platform for Development Effectiveness (APDEv, accessible at www.africa-platform.org), a multi-stakeholder platform and organizing mechanism for policy-makers in the continent.

In March 2009 the Coalition for Dialogue on Africa (CoDA) was launched, by ECA, the AU and the AfDB, as an independent African forum to serve as an umbrella for all existing fora on Africa. ECA hosts its secretariat. CoDA meetings, including a multi-stakeholder dialogue forum, were convened in Tunis, in November, to consider Africa's recovery from the global economic and financial crisis, and regional integration. In February 2010 CoDA met, again in Tunis, to discuss transforming the Coalition into a fully independent, non-governmental African initiative, with a chief executive; and to develop a work programme. A CoDA policy forum was held in Abidjan, Côte d'Ivoire, in May, on 'Financing Regional Integration in Africa'. Meeting in October 2010, on the sidelines of ADF VII, CoDA urged African leaders to continue to pursue participation multinational negotiations on climate change. A CoDA policy forum on foreign direct investments in land in Africa was convened in Lisbon, Portugal, in June 2011.

Finance

ECA's proposed regular budget for the two-year period 2014–15, an appropriation from the UN budget, was US $151.6m.

Publications

Africa Climate Policy Bulletin.

African Economic Outlook (annually, with the AfDP, OECD and UNDP).

African Gender and Development Index.

African Governance Report.

African Review Report on Chemicals.

African Statistical Yearbook.

African Women's Report.

Africa Youth Report.

Assessing Regional Integration in Africa (with the AU and AfDB).

ECA Policy Brief.

Eastern Africa News (issued by the SRO for East Africa).

Echos d'Afrique Centrale (issued by the SRO for Central Africa).

Economic Report on Africa.

Insight ECA-SA (issued by the SRO for Southern Africa).

MDG Report: Assessing Progress in Africa.

Mutual Review of Development Effectiveness in Africa (jointly with OECD).

Sustainable Development Report on Africa (every 2 years).

Country reports, policy and discussion papers, reports of conferences and meetings, training series, working paper series.

Economic and Social Commission for Western Asia—ESCWA

Address: Riad el-Solh Sq., POB 11-8575, Beirut, Lebanon.

Telephone: (1) 981301; **fax:** (1) 981510; **e-mail:** webmaster-escwa@un.org; **internet:** www.escwa.un.org.

The UN Economic Commission for Western Asia was established in 1974 by a resolution of the UN Economic and Social Council (ECOSOC), to provide facilities of a wider scope for those countries previously served by the UN Economic and Social Office in Beirut (UNESOB). The name Economic and Social Commission for Western Asia (ESCWA) was adopted in 1985.

MEMBERS

Bahrain
Egypt
Iraq
Jordan
Kuwait
Lebanon
Libya
Morocco
Oman
Palestine
Qatar
Saudi Arabia
Sudan
Syria
Tunisia
United Arab Emirates
Yemen

Organization

(April 2014)

COMMISSION

The Commission meets every two years in ministerial session to determine policy and establish work directives. Representatives of UN bodies and specialized agencies, regional organizations, other UN member states, and non-governmental organizations having consultative status with ECOSOC may attend as observers. The 27th ministerial session of the Commission was convened in May 2012. The 28th session was to be held in June 2014, in Amman, Jordan.

PREPARATORY COMMITTEE

The Committee reviews programming issues and presents recommendations in that regard to the sessions of the Commission. It is the principal subsidiary body of the Commission and functions as its policy-making structure.

SUBSIDIARY COMMITTEES

Seven specialized inter-governmental committees—on Energy, Liberalization, Social Development, Statistics, Transport, Water Resources, and Women—report on their areas of specialization to the Preparatory Committee and assist the Committee in formulating ESCWA's medium-term work programmes: they meet every two years, except for the Committee on Transport, which meets annually.

ADVISORY COMMITTEE

The Advisory Committee, which comprises heads of member states' diplomatic missions in the country hosting each quarterly meeting, and a senior representative from the host country, fulfils a consultative role, while providing a means of communication between member governments and the ESCWA Secretariat.

Technical Committee

The Technical Committee, made up of senior officials from member countries, convenes every six months, with a mandate to advise and assist the Secretariat in formulating strategy and future priorities and implementing programmes of work. Additionally, a Consultative Committee on Scientific Technological Development and Technological Innovation meets every two years. It comprises experts from public institutions, the private sector, civil society and research centres.

SECRETARIAT

The Secretariat comprises an Executive Secretary, a Deputy Executive Secretary, and the following administrative and programme divisions: Administrative Services; Economic Development and Globalization; Information and Communications Technology; Programme Planning and Technical Co-operation; Social Development; Statistics; and Sustainable Development and Productivity. Each division is headed by a Chief, who is accountable to the Executive Secretary. In addition, there is an ESCWA Centre for Women, and a Unit for Emerging and Conflict Related Issues.

Executive Secretary: RIMA KHALAF (Jordan).

Activities

ESCWA aims to support development and to further economic co-operation and integration in western Asia. ESCWA undertakes or sponsors studies of economic, social and development issues of the region, collects and disseminates information, and provides advisory services to member states in various fields of economic and social development. It also organizes conferences and intergovernmental and expert group meetings and sponsors training workshops and seminars. ESCWA adopts biennial strategic frameworks as the basis for its programme planning.

Much of ESCWA's work is carried out in co-operation with other UN bodies, as well as with other international and regional organizations, for example the League of Arab States (Arab League), the Cooperation Council for the Arab States of the Gulf (GCC) and the Organization of Islamic Cooperation (OIC). In May 2009 ESCWA co-hosted, with the International Labour Organization and the Syrian Government, a Regional High-Level Consultative Forum on the Impacts of the International Financial Crisis on the ESCWA Member Countries. The meeting adopted the Damascus Declaration, comprising a set of proposals for member countries to respond more effectively to the crisis, including support for greater investment in the region by ESCWA's sovereign wealth funds, adopting fiscal stimulus policies, and strengthening the efficiency of their regulatory frameworks. The Forum identified ESCWA as being key to enhancing the participation of Arab and Islamic financial institutions in member countries' efforts to counter the effects of the crisis. In June 2013 ESCWA and the Arab League concluded a Memorandum of Understanding, reflecting new modalities of co-operation with respect to emerging regional challenges. Henceforth ESCWA was to participate in ministerial sessions and meetings of the Economic and Social Council of the League.

In June 2011 ESCWA hosted the 15th meeting of a Regional Co-ordination Mechanism for Arab States, at which regional directors and officials from more than 20 UN agencies and other international and regional organizations considered the recent political and social reforms in several Arab countries. The grouping reaffirmed its commitment to strengthening co-operation in order to support more inclusive and sustainable development in the region. It also resolved to establish a new thematic working group to achieve greater regional integration. In mid-2011 ESCWA undertook an internal review of its work programmes in order to enhance its capacity to address the emerging needs of societies in transition. In January 2012 the UN Secretary-General addressed a High-level Meeting on Reform and Transition to Democracy, organized by ESCWA. The meeting emphasized the need to incorporate human rights and principles of social justice as essential elements of future economic strategies in countries in the region in order to secure democracy, as well as to protect and promote the empowerment of women and to stimulate youth employment opportunities. ESCWA's 27th ministerial session was convened in May, on the theme 'The role of participation and social justice in achieving sustainable and balanced development'. In February 2013 a High-Level Meeting on Beyond Populism: Economic Challenges and Opportunities in Democratic Transitions was convened, under ESCWA auspices, in Rabat, Morocco. In February 2014 ESCWA issued a report entitled *Arab Integration: a 21st Century Development Imperative*, which considered progress achieved by Arab citizens towards the attainment of inalienable human rights in the context of the so-called Arab Spring, and explored means of promoting a dynamic regional economic environment.

ECONOMIC DEVELOPMENT AND GLOBALIZATION

Through its Economic Development and Globalization Division ESCWA aims to assist member states to achieve sustainable economic development in the region and to integrate more fully into the world economy. A Financing for Development Team aims to assist member countries to implement the recommendations of the Monterrey Consensus, adopted at the International Conference on Financing for Development, held in Monterrey, Mexico, in March 2002. Other concerns are to encourage domestic, intra-regional and foreign investment, to facilitate transboundary flows of goods, services, people and capital, by integrating regional markets (for example through the Greater Arab Free Trade Area) and to support member countries with debt management. The Division's Trade Team works to advance regional trading integration, as well as greater participation of the region in the multilateral trading system. It acts as a forum for member countries in preparation for multilateral trade negotiations, such as those within the Doha Round of negotiations under the World Trade Organization. An Economic Analysis Team aims to increase the capacity of member countries to co-ordinate economic policies. It makes continuous assessments of the region's macroeconomic performances; conducts economic research, modelling and forecasting; monitors the region's progress towards the UN Millennium Development Goals (MDGs); and disseminates its findings to support dialogue at various regional meetings. The Division aims to help member countries to increase their exports and to encourage domestic and foreign investment. The work of the Division's Transport Team includes the development of an integrated transport system in the Arab Mashreq region; development of a regional transport information system; formation of national and regional transport and trade committees, representing both the private and public sectors; simplification of cross-border trading procedures; and the use of electronic data exchange for more efficient transport and trade. In May 2008 the 25th ministerial session of the Commission adopted a Convention on International Multi-modal Transport of Goods in the Arab Mashreq.

The first Arab Economics Forum was convened by ESCWA in November 2012, in Beirut, Lebanon, with participation by academics, experts and policy-makers from the ESCWA region, as well as from neighbouring countries in Europe and Asia. The Forum was funded by the European Union. In April 2013 ESCWA launched a new regional Infrastructure Investments and Public-Private Partnerships (PPP) Initiative, in co-operation with the Geneva-based ECE International Centre of Excellence on PPPs. Under the Initiative a regional PPP network and PPP specialist centres (including on Islamic finance, renewable energy and infrastructure) were to be established.

EMERGING AND CONFLICT-RELATED ISSUES

In January 2006 a Unit for Emerging and Conflict-related Issues (ECRI) was established to consolidate and develop ESCWA's activities in conflict and post-conflict countries and areas, including Iraq, the Palestinian territories and, initially, southern Lebanon. Following the Israeli military strikes that targeted the Lebanese bases of the militant Shi'a organization Hezbollah in July–August of that year, the mandate of ECRI was expanded to cover all of Lebanon. ECRI's priority areas include analysis and policy formulation for reducing the causes of conflict; capacity building to improve the effectiveness of public administration and the rule of law; forging partnerships among civic entities at local and regional level; and working with other ESCWA divisions to meet the special needs of countries affected by conflicts. ESCWA administers an E-Caravan mobile computer school programme, to provide information and communications technology (ICT) training to communities in southern Lebanon. Other projects include the provision of regional and local 'networking academies' in Iraq, to give training in information technology; the Smart Communities Project, providing modern technology for villages in Iraq; the improvement of statistics related to gender in Iraq; and the support of the Coalition of Arab-Palestinian Civil Society Organizations. Regional expert group meetings organized by ECRI have included 'Strengthening Good Governance Practices in Conflict Affected Countries: Current Priorities and Future Interventions', and 'Policies for Peacebuilding and Conflict Prevention in Western Asia'. In September 2011 ESCWA hosted an expert group meeting, in part chaired by ECRI, to consider the impact of conflict on progress towards achieving the MDGs in countries in the region. In the following month ECRI contributed to a seminar on participatory governance in crisis-affected Arab countries. In July 2012 ESCWA hosted a round-table discussion on 'Reconciliation, Reform and Resilience' in post-conflict Lebanon.

ESCWA CENTRE FOR WOMEN

The ESCWA Centre for Women was established in October 2003. Its main focus of activities is the empowerment and advancement of women. It also aims to incorporate issues relating to gender in regional projects and programmes. The Centre monitors developments, compiles country profiles on the status of women, provides support for formulating relevant legislation, raises awareness by publishing reports and studies, and organizes conferences. In December 2003 ESCWA issued its first *Status of Arab Women* report; this was to assess the situation of Arab women at two-yearly intervals. The 2011 edition focused on equal participation in decision-making. In September 2008 the ESCWA Secretary-General launched a guide entitled *Gender in the Millennium Development Goals*, which summarized the key regional gender issues in the context of each MDG and provided a statistical framework for evaluating and following up adherence to international agreements relating to gender equality, in the context of reporting progress in achieving (by 2015) the Arab MDGs. In 2012 the Centre's activities included organizing a seminar on 'Women in the Arab Uprisings' (in January), participating in a regional collaborative workshop on 'Women in Computing in the Arab World' (in March), convening a sub-regional workshop on strengthening legislative frameworks to address violence against women (in April), organizing a workshop on 'Women in Arab Parliaments' (in July), and (in December) organizing a training workshop on developing national action plans for the implementation of UN Security Council Resolution 1325 (2000), relating to the role of women in conflict management, conflict resolution, and sustainable peace. During 2013 the Centre compiled reports on combating domestic violence against women and girls, including through the establishment of multisectoral partnerships, and on trafficking in women and children in the Arab region.

INFORMATION AND COMMUNICATIONS TECHNOLOGY

The Information and Communications Technology Division works to increase the capabilities of ESCWA member countries in harnessing ICT in support of sustainable development and regional integration. It aims to narrow the so-called digital gap between Arab countries and other regions, and, consequently, to improve the competitiveness of local industries and the effectiveness of local services. It supports the formation of ICT policies and infrastructure, by providing technical assistance, pilot projects, studies and meetings of experts. ESCWA was responsible for advising member countries on the implementation of recommendations issued by the first phase of the World Summit on the Information Society (WSIS), held in December 2003, and on preparations for the second phase of the Summit, which was convened in Tunis, Tunisia, in November 2005. As a follow-up to the Summit, ESCWA undertook to collate a profile of the region's information society based on national profile reports. A Regional Follow-up to the Outcome of the WSIS was held in Damascus, Syria, in June 2009. In November ESCWA organized a regional workshop on Arabic domain names and internet governance, held in Sharm el-Sheikh, Egypt. In July 2011 ESCWA co-organized, with the Arab League and International Telecommunication Union, a Partnership Building Forum for the Implementation of the Arab Top Level Domains. The inaugural meeting of a new Arab Internet Governance Forum (AIGF)—established under the auspices of ESCWA and the Arab League—was convened in October 2012, in Kuwait. The 26th session of the Commission, held in May 2010, resolved to establish an ESCWA Technology Centre, in order to strengthen member states' ICT capabilities. The Centre was inaugurated, in El Hassan Science City, Jordan, in November 2011. In May 2012 the 27th Commission session launched a set of directives on Cyber Legislation. In 2012 ESCWA undertook a Digital Arabic Content Survey, which analysed the use of Arabic language content by ICT sector companies.

SOCIAL DEVELOPMENT

ESCWA's Social Development Division encourages regional co-operation in promoting comprehensive and integrated social policies, so as to achieve greater social equality and well-being, and to alleviate poverty, social exclusion, gender imbalances and social tension. It advises governments on the importance of integrating social analysis into policy-making, identifies methods for the effective formulation, implementation and monitoring of social policy, and assists national and regional research on social development. ESCWA's objectives with regard to population are to increase awareness and understanding of links between population factors and poverty, human rights and the environment, and to strengthen the capacities of member states to analyse and assess demographic trends and migration. In the area of social participatory development ESCWA aims to further the alleviation of poverty and to generate a sustainable approach to development through greater involvement of community groups, institutions and users of public services in decision-making. The Division's work on social policy in the city analyses urban problems, such as poverty, unemployment, violence, and failure to integrate vulnerable and marginal groups, and aims to assist policy-makers in ensuring that all city-dwellers have equal access to public services. ESCWA provides a forum for preparatory and follow-up meetings to global conferences. In December 2011 ESCWA organized a second regional review meeting of the International Plan of Action on Ageing, which resulted from the World Assembly, held in Madrid, Spain in 2002. In May 2010 ESCWA's 26th ministerial session emphasized the need to secure employment opportunities for young people. Efforts to increase the involvement of young people, and of women, in development programmes were also promoted, in particular at a time when the region was attempting to recover from the effects of the global financial and economic crisis. In 2010 an estimated 60% of the region's population were under 25 years of age. In November 2011 ESCWA organized an inter-regional seminar on 'Participatory Development and Conflict Resolution: Path of Democratic Transition and Social Justice', to address aspects of the political and social changes taking place in several countries in the region.

STATISTICS

ESCWA helps to develop the statistical systems of member states in accordance with the UN Fundamental Principles of Official Statistics, in order to improve the accuracy and comparability of economic and social data, and to make the information more accessible to planners and researchers. It aims to improve human and institutional capacities, in particular in the use of statistical tools for data analysis, to expand the adoption and implementation of international statistical methods, and to promote co-operation to further the regional harmonization of statistics. ESCWA assists members in preparing for population and housing censuses, in accordance with the UN 2010 World Population and Housing Census Programme. In December 2011 ESCWA hosted a workshop on Population Census Preparedness. A Trade and Transport Statistics Team compiles, processes and disseminates statistics on international trade and transport within the region, and assists member countries to develop their statistical capacity in this sector.

SUSTAINABLE DEVELOPMENT AND PRODUCTIVITY

The work of ESCWA's Sustainable Development and Productivity Division is undertaken by four teams, covering: energy for sustainable development; water and environment; technology and enterprise development; and sustainable agriculture and rural development. ESCWA aims to counter the problem of an increasing shortage of freshwater resources and deterioration in water quality resulting from population growth, agricultural land use and socio-economic development, by supporting measures for more rational use and conservation of water resources, and by promoting public awareness of and community participation in water and environmental protection projects. The Division assists governments in the formulation and implementation of capacity-building programmes and the development of surface and groundwater resources. ESCWA promotes greater co-operation among member and non-member countries in the management and use of shared water resources, and supports the Arab Integrated Water Resources Management Network (AWARENET, comprising some 120 research and training institutes). in September 2013 ESCWA and the German Federal Institute for Geosciences and Natural Resources launched an Inventory of Shared Water Resources in Western Asia, which aimed to identify and review the state of transboundary surface and groundwater resources in the Middle East. ESCWA supports co-operation in the establishment of electricity distribution and supply networks throughout the region and promotes the use of alternative sources of energy and the development of new and renewable energy technologies. It places a special emphasis on increasing the access of poor people to cheap energy and water, and on the creation of new jobs. The Division promotes the application of environmentally sound technologies in order to achieve sustainable development, as well as measures to recycle resources, minimize waste and reduce the environmental impact of transport operations and energy use. ESCWA collaborates with national, regional and international organizations in monitoring and reporting on emerging environmental issues and to pursue implementation of Agenda 21, which was adopted at the June 1992 UN Conference on Environment and Development, with particular regard to land and water resource management and conservation. In July 2011 ESCWA hosted a regional meeting concerned with 'Economic Policies Supporting the Transition to a Green Economy in the Arab Region'. In September ESCWA hosted a conference on 'The Role of Green Industries in Promoting Socio-Economic Development in the Arab Countries'. In February 2012 ESCWA organized, jointly with the International Food Policy Research Institute, an international conference on food security in the Arab region. In April 2014 ESCWA organized an Arab High Level Forum on Sustainable Development, in Amman, Jordan, with participation by government officials, UN agencies, the Arab League, financing institutions, and civil society; the Forum addressed the formulation of a post-2015 development agenda, including a proposed Arab Strategic Framework for Sustainable Development.

ESCWA, in co-operation with the Arab League and the UN Environment Programme's Office for West Asia, organized a series of preparatory meetings to formulate a regional strategy for the UN Conference on Sustainable Development (Rio+20), which was held in Rio de Janeiro, Brazil, in June 2012. In May 2013 a Regional Arab Implementation Meeting, in Dubai, United Arab Emirates, issued the Dubai Document addressing the regional implementation of the 2012 Conference outcomes.

Finance

ESCWA's proposed regular budget allocation from the UN budget for the two years 2014–15 was US $70.2m.

Publications

ESCWA Annual Report.

Annual Review of Developments in Globalization and Regional Integration.

Arab Integration: A 21st Century Development Imperative.

the Arab Millennium Development Goals Report 2013.

Arab Society: a Compendium of Social Statistics.

Country and Regional Profiles for Sustainable Development Indicators.

ESCWA Centre for Women Newsletter (monthly).

Estimates and Forecasts for GDP Growth in the ESCWA Region.

External Trade Bulletin of the ESCWA Region (annually).

International Comparison Program Newsletter.

Outlook of the Information Society in the Arab Region.

Review of Industry in ESCWA Member Countries.

Review of Information and Communications Technology and Development.

Status of Arab Women Report (every 2 years).

Survey of Economic and Social Developments in the ESCWA Region.

Transport Bulletin.

Weekly News.

ESCWA publishes reports, case studies, assessments, guides and manuals on the subjects covered by its various Divisions.

OTHER UNITED NATIONS BODIES

Office for the Co-ordination of Humanitarian Affairs—OCHA

Address: United Nations Plaza, New York, NY 10017, USA.

Telephone: (212) 963-1234; **fax:** (212) 963-1312; **e-mail:** ochany@un.org; **internet:** www.unocha.org.

OCHA was established in January 1998 as part of the UN Secretariat, and has a mandate to mobilize and co-ordinate international humanitarian assistance and to provide policy and other advice on humanitarian issues. It replaced the Department of Humanitarian Affairs, established in 1992.

Organization

(April 2014)

OCHA has headquarters in New York, USA, and in Geneva, Switzerland. It maintains regional support offices in Dakar, Senegal (for West Africa), Johannesburg, South Africa (Southern Africa) and Nairobi, Kenya (Central and East Africa); and deploys regional disaster response advisers in Panama (for Latin America and the Caribbean), Kobe, Japan (Asia), and Suva, Fiji (the Pacific). OCHA also maintains field presences in Africa, Europe, Asia and Latin America. In 2014 there were 1,900 staff posts, of which one-third were based at headquarters.

Under-Secretary-General for Humanitarian Affairs and Emergency Relief Co-ordinator: VALERIE AMOS (United Kingdom).

Deputy Emergency Relief Co-ordinator: KYUNG-WHA KANG (Republic of Korea).

Activities

OCHA's mandate is to work with UN agencies, governments, intergovernmental humanitarian organizations and non-governmental organizations (NGOs) to ensure that a prompt, co-ordinated and effective response is provided to complex emergencies and natural disasters. OCHA monitors developments throughout the world and undertakes contingency planning. It liaises with UN Resident Co-ordinators, Humanitarian Co-ordinators and country teams, and reaches agreement with other UN bodies regarding the division of responsibilities, which may include field missions to assess requirements, organizing inter-agency Consolidated Appeals for financial assistance, and mobilizing other resources. The Emergency Relief Co-ordinator is the principal adviser to the UN Secretary-General on humanitarian issues. He chairs the Inter-Agency Standing Committee (IASC), which co-ordinates and administers the international response to humanitarian disasters and the development of relevant policies. The Co-ordinator also acts as Convener of the Executive Committee for Humanitarian Affairs, which provides a forum for humanitarian agencies, as well as the political and peacekeeping departments of the UN Secretariat, to exchange information on emergency situations and humanitarian issues. In view of the serious challenges posed by the increasing frequency and intensity of extreme natural hazard events, combined with other developing 'mega-trends', such as the ongoing global crisis in food price levels, OCHA aims (in co-operation with governments and development agencies) to place a stronger focus on disaster risk reduction (DRR) and preparedness and on increasing national disaster management capacities; and also on enabling the international emergency response system to respond successfully to these greater requirements. Under OCHA's strategic framework covering the period 2014–17 the Office aimed to enhance the predictability and accountability of its humanitarian co-ordination, information management, and financing services to partners in the field.

OCHA participates in the High Level Task Force (HLTF) on the Global Food Crisis, which was established in April 2008 by the UN Secretary-General to promote a unified response to soaring food and fuel prices and other factors adversely affecting the supply and accessibility of food, and to formulate a Comprehensive Framework for Action.

OCHA's Early Warning Unit identifies and monitors potentially emerging humanitarian crises, as well as humanitarian emergencies at risk of deterioration and potentially resurgent humanitarian emergencies. Analysis by the Unit determines the at-risk areas to which inter-agency contingency planning missions should be directed.

OCHA maintains internet-based Integrated Regional Information Networks (IRINs). The first IRIN desk was created in 1995 in Nairobi, Kenya (now the IRIN headquarters), to disseminate information on the humanitarian situation in Central and East Africa. Additional IRINs have since been established in Johannesburg, South Africa; Dakar, Senegal; Dubai, United Arab Emirates; and Bangkok, Thailand. The IRINs provide news coverage (in English, French and Arabic) of a total of 70 countries in sub-Saharan Africa, the Middle East and Asia. A complementary service, ReliefWeb, launched in 1996, monitors crises and publishes information on the internet.

OCHA's Humanitarian Emergency and Response Co-ordination branches (based, respectively, at the New York and Geneva headquarters) co-operate in mobilizing and co-ordinating international emergency assistance. The Response Co-ordination branch facilitates and participates in situation assessment missions; prepares briefings and issues Situation Reports to inform the international community on ongoing humanitarian crises, the type and level of assistance required and action being undertaken; and provides administrative support to OCHA field offices. The Emergency Services branch, based at the Geneva headquarters, undertakes disaster preparedness activities and manages international rapid response missions in the field. UN Disaster Assessment and Co-ordination (UNDAC) teams, established by OCHA with the aid of donor governments, are available for immediate deployment to help to determine requirements and to co-ordinate assistance in those countries affected by disasters, for example by establishing reliable telecommunications and securing other logistical support. OCHA maintains a Central Register of Disaster Management Capacities, which may be available for international assistance. In addition, a stockpile of emergency equipment and supplies is maintained at the UN Humanitarian Response Depot in Brindisi, Italy, ready for immediate dispatch. The Field Co-ordination Support Section of the Emergency Services Branch acts as the secretariat of INSARAG, an intergovernmental network dealing with urban search and rescue (USAR) issues. INSARAG facilitates information exchange, defines standards for international USAR assistance, and develops methodology for international co-ordination in earthquake response. A joint OCHA/UN Environment Programme (UNEP) Environment Unit mobilizes and co-ordinates international assistance in environmental emergency situations. A UN inter-agency Displacement and Protection Support Section, reporting to the Emergency Relief Co-ordinator, was established in 2007 to strengthen and co-ordinate the inter-agency collaborative response to the plight of people displaced from their homes by civil conflict and natural disasters.

The focal point within the UN system for co-ordinating disaster reduction activities in the socio-economic, humanitarian and development fields is the International Strategy for Disaster Reduction (ISDR), which has an Inter-Agency Secretariat (UN/ISDR) based in Geneva. In January 2005 the UN/ISDR organized the second World Conference on Disaster Reduction, held in Kobe, Japan, which launched the International Early Warning Programme (IEWP), comprising UN bodies and agencies including the ISDR, UNEP, the World Food Programme (WFP) and the World Meteorological Organization (WMO). (The first such conference was held in Yokohama, Japan, in May 1994.) The IEWP was to improve global resilience to natural disasters (such as droughts, wildland fires, volcanic eruptions, earthquakes, tsunamis—tidal waves, floods and hurricanes) by improving the exchange of observational data, promoting education on disaster preparedness, and ensuring an effective response mechanism to be activated on the issue of warnings. The Kobe Conference also adopted the Hyogo Declaration and the Hyogo Framework of Action (HFA) covering the period 2005–15, which had the following strategic goals: integrating DRR into sustainable development policies and planning; development and strengthening of institutions, mechanisms and capacities to build resilience to hazards; and the systematic incorporation of risk reduction approaches into the implementation of emergency preparedness, response and recovery programmes. In July 2008 OCHA, in collaboration with UN/ISDR, issued guidelines for governments, local authorities and other stakeholders on the implementation of Priority Five of the HFA: 'Disaster Preparedness for Effective Response at all Levels'. OCHA has joint responsibility, with UNICEF and WFP, for managing emergency telecommunications assistance under the co-ordinated 'Cluster Approach' to providing humanitarian assistance to IDPs developed by the IASC in 2005. In 2011 the ISDR recorded 302 natural disasters, which resulted in the deaths of some 29,782 people. In early 2012 the ISDR initiated consultations on formulating a blueprint on a post-2015 DRR framework in advance of the third World Conference on Disaster Reduction, scheduled to be held in March 2015, once again in Japan (Sendai City). UN/ISDR organizes the Global Platform for Disaster Risk Reduction, which was launched in 2007 as a biennial forum on information exchange and building partnerships with the objective of improving the implementation of DRR and strengthening the resilience of communities against disasters. The fourth session of the Global Platform convened in Geneva, in May 2013.

OCHA facilitates the inter-agency Consolidated Appeals Process (CAP), which aims to organize a co-ordinated response to resource mobilization following humanitarian crises. Participants in the process include UN bodies and agencies and other international governmental and NGOs (including the International Red Cross and Red Crescent Movement). Under guidelines adopted by the IASC in 1994, the CAP was clearly defined as a programming mechanism rather than simply an appeal process. Technical guidelines adopted in 1999 established a framework for developing a Common Humanitarian Action Plan (CHAP) to address a crisis, co-ordinating the relevant inter-agency appeal (on the basis of the CHAP), and preparing strategic monitoring reports. CAP appeals seeking an estimated US $12,900m. (the largest ever total amount requested) were issued in December 2013, under OCHA's Overview of Global Humanitarian Response for 2014; they contained action plans relating to complex humanitarian crises affecting some 52m. people and involving more than 500 globally active humanitarian organizations. By far the largest appeal ($6,500m.) was for alleviating the humanitarian situation in Syria and in neighbouring countries that were hosting Syrian refugees; this represented the greatest ever appeal for a single crisis. The next most substantial appeals were for South Sudan ($1,100m.), Sudan ($995m.), Somalia ($928m.), Democratic Republic of the Congo ($832m.), and the Philippines ($791m.). From 2014 OCHA replaced its previous annual single consolidated CAP document with a series of country documents to be produced in sequence, comprising a national humanitarian needs overview, a strategic response plan (including the country strategy and relevant cluster plans), and periodic monitoring bulletins.

In December 2005 the UN General Assembly adopted a resolution establishing a new Central Emergency Response Fund (CERF), expanding the former Central Emergency Revolving Fund (founded in 1991) to comprise a US $450m. grant facility, in addition to the existing $50m. revolving element, with a view to ensuring a more predictable and timely response to humanitarian crises. Both the grant and revolving facilities are financed by voluntary contributions from member states. Up to two-thirds of the grant facility can be allocated to life-saving rapid response initiatives. The upgraded Fund, administered on behalf of the UN Secretary-General by the Emergency Relief Co-ordinator in consultation with humanitarian agencies and relevant humanitarian co-ordinators, had three principle objectives: promotion of early action and response to save lives in the case of newly emerging crises or deterioration of existing complex crises, through an initial injection of funds before further donor contributions become available; enhanced response to time-crucial requirements based on demonstrable needs; and strengthening core elements of humanitarian response in underfunded crises. UN agencies and their implementing partners were to be able to access the Fund within 72 hours of the onset of a crisis. The new CERF became operational in March 2006, and by 2014 had raised more than $3,300m. from 124 donor states. During 2013 the CERF allocated $482m. in assistance to 15 humanitarian agencies active in 45 countries and territories. In 2013 some 63.8% of CERF resources were allocated to rapid response operations, and the remainder were allocated to underfunded and neglected emergencies. In November the CERF issued $25m. to fund immediate humanitarian relief for the survivors of Typhoon Haiyan in the Philippines.

OCHA organizes Emergency Response Funds (ERFs) to respond to unforeseen humanitarian planning requirements; and Common Humanitarian Funds (CHFs) to provide a predictable pool of funding for critical humanitarian situations. Some 13 ERFs and five CHFs (for the Central African Republic, DRC, Somalia, South Sudan and Sudan) were operational in 2014.

In December 2013 OCHA issued the 2014 Syria Humanitarian Assistance Response Plan-Syria Regional Response Plan (SHARP-RRP), for which the SHARP element—aiming to support the humanitarian requirements of 9.3m. Syrians in critical need—required funding of US $2,276m., and the RRP element—with a projected 6.8m. beneficiaries in neighbouring countries (including 4.1m. Syrian refugees, and also the host communities supporting them)—required funding of $4,200m.

In November 2013 OCHA co-ordinated a UN 'flash appeal' for US $301m. (increased to $348m. later in that month) to provide immediate humanitarian aid for the survivors of the devastating Typhoon Haiyan in the Philippines.

GLOBAL CLUSTER LEADS

IASC co-ordinates agency assistance to IDPs through a 'Cluster Approach' (initiated in 2005); this currently comprises 11 core areas of humanitarian activity, with designated global cluster lead agencies, as follows:

Camp Co-ordination/Management: UNHCR, conflict situations; IOM, natural disasters.

Early Recovery: UNDP.

Education: UNICEF; Save The Children.

Emergency Shelter: UNHCR, conflict situations; International Federation of Red Cross and Red Crescent Societies, natural disasters.

Emergency Telecommunications: OCHA; WFP.

Food Security: FAO; WFP.

Health: WHO.

Logistics: WFP.

Nutrition: UNICEF.

Protection: UNHCR.

Water, Sanitation and Hygiene: UNICEF.

Finance

OCHA's budgetary requirements for 2014 were estimated at US $331.8m. In that year OCHA was allocated an appropriation of $14.5m. from the UN regular budget.

Publications

Annual Report.

Overview of Global Humanitarian Response.

OCHA News (weekly).

Associated Body

Inter-Agency Secretariat of the International Strategy for Disaster Reduction—UN/ISDR: International Environment House II, 7–9 Chemin de Balexert, 1219 Châtelaine, Geneva 10, Switzerland; tel. 229178907; fax 229178964; e-mail isdr@un.org; internet www.unisdr.org; operates as secretariat of the International Strategy for Disaster Reduction (ISDR), adopted by UN member states in 2000 as a strategic framework aimed at guiding and co-ordinating the efforts of humanitarian organizations, states, intergovernmental and non-governmental organizations, financial institutions, technical bodies and civil society representatives towards achieving substantive reduction in disaster losses, and building resilient communities and nations as the foundation for sustainable development activities; UN/ISDR promotes information sharing to reduce disaster risk, and serves as the focal point providing guidance for the implementation of the Hyogo Framework for Action (HFA), adopted in 2005 as a 10-year plan of action for protecting lives and livelihoods against disasters; organizes the biennial sessions of the Global Platform for Disaster Risk Reduction (fourth session: held in May 2013, in Geneva); in early 2012 UN/ISDR launched a consultative process on a post-2015 disaster risk reduction framework, to be adopted by the third World Conference on Disaster Reduction (to be convened in March 2015 in Sendai City, Japan); it is also a co-leader of the global consultations on addressing conflict and fragility in the post-2015 development framework; UN/ISDR implements a 'Making Cities Resilient' campaign in view in increasing urbanization; Head, Special Representative of the UN Secretary-General for Disaster Risk Reduction MARGARETA WAHLSTRÖM.

Office of the United Nations High Commissioner for Human Rights—OHCHR

Address: Palais des Nations, 1211 Geneva 10, Switzerland.

Telephone: 229179000; **fax:** 229179022; **e-mail:** infodesk@ohchr.org; **internet:** www.ohchr.org.

The Office is a body of the UN Secretariat and is the focal point for UN human rights activities. Since 1997 it has incorporated the Centre for Human Rights. OHCHR is guided by relevant resolutions of the General Assembly, the Charter of the United Nations, the Universal Declaration of Human Rights and subsequent human rights instruments, the Vienna Declaration and programme of action adopted by the 1993 World Conference on Human Rights, and the outcome document of the 2005 World Summit of the General Assembly.

Organization

(April 2014)

HIGH COMMISSIONER

In December 1993 the UN General Assembly decided to establish the position of a United Nations High Commissioner for Human Rights (UNHCHR) following a recommendation of the World Conference on Human Rights, held in Vienna, Austria, in June of that year. The High Commissioner, who is the UN official with principal responsibility for UN human rights activities, is appointed by the UN Secretary-General, with the approval of the General Assembly, for a four-year term in office, renewable for one term.

High Commissioner: Navanethem Pillay (South Africa).

Deputy High Commissioner: Flavia Pansieri (Italy).

ADMINISTRATION

OHCHR's Executive Direction and Management comprises the following units: the Executive Office of the High Commissioner; the Policy, Planning, Monitoring, and Evaluation Section; the Communications Section; the Civil Society Unit; the Field Safety and Security Section; and the Donor and External Relations Section. OHCHR's headquarters contains the following four substantive Divisions: Field Operations and Technical Co-operation; Research and Right to Development; Special Procedures; and the Human Rights Council and Treaties Division. There is also a Programme Support and Management Services unit, and a branch office in New York, USA, that aims to ensure that human rights issues are fully integrated into the broader UN development and security agenda.

FIELD PRESENCES

A substantial structure of field presences has developed to promote human rights and support UN peacemaking, peacekeeping and peacebuilding activities. In 2014 there were OHCHR regional offices in Addis Ababa, Ethiopia (covering East Africa); Bangkok, Thailand (South-East Asia); Beirut, Lebanon (the Middle East); Bishkek, Kyrgyzstan (Central Asia); Panama City, Panama (Central America); Santiago, Chile (South America); Pretoria, South Africa (Southern Africa); and Suva, Fiji (the Pacific); as well as an OHCHR Regional Centre for Human Rights and Democracy for Central Africa, based in Yaoundé, Cameroon. OHCHR country offices with human rights promotion and protection mandates were being maintained in Angola, Bolivia, Cambodia, Colombia, Guatemala, Mexico, Nepal, the Palestinian territories, Serbia (including Kosovo), Togo and Uganda.

Activities

OHCHR's mandate incorporates the following functions and responsibilities: the promotion and protection of human rights throughout the world; the reinforcement of international co-operation in the field of human rights; the promotion of universal ratification and implementation of international standards; the establishment of a dialogue with governments to ensure respect for human rights; and co-ordination of efforts by other UN programmes and organs to promote respect for human rights. Upon request OHCHR undertakes assessments of national human rights needs, in consultation with governments. Through the provision of guidance and training it supports the establishment of independent national human rights institutions. The Office may also study and react to cases of serious violations of human rights, and may undertake diplomatic efforts to prevent violations. It produces educational and other information material to enhance understanding of human rights. OHCHR co-operates with academic bodies and non-governmental organizations working in the area of human rights. Its strategic management plan for the four-year period 2014–17 focused on the following six thematic priorities: strengthening international human rights mechanisms; integrating human rights in development and in the economic sphere; early warning and protection of human rights in situations of conflict, violence and insecurity; enhancing equality and countering discrimination, in particular discrimination on the grounds of race, gender or religion, and against those who are marginalized; combating impunity and strengthening accountability and the rule of law; and widening the democratic space.

The Office offers support and expertise to the UN system's human rights monitoring mechanisms, including the Human Rights Council (established in 2006) and the Universal Periodic Review (UPR, also established in 2006, to assess, cyclically, the human rights situation in all UN member states). OHCHR supports the committees that observe implementation of the following core international human rights treaties: the International Covenant on Civil and Political Rights, which entered into force in 1976; the International Covenant on Economic, Social and Cultural Rights (1976); the Convention against Torture and Other Cruel, Inhuman or Degrading Treatment or Punishment (1987); the Optional Protocol of the Convention against Torture (2006); the Convention on the Rights of the Child (1990) and its optional Protocols on Involvement of Children in Armed Conflict, on Sale of Children, Child Prostitution and Child Pornography, and (in effect from April 2014) on a Communications Procedure—allowing individual children to submit complaints about specific violations of their human rights under the Convention; the International Convention on the Protection of the Rights of All Migrant Workers and Members of Their Families (1990); the Convention on the Rights of Persons with Disabilities (2008); and the International Convention for the Protection of All Persons from Enforced Disappearance (2010). An Optional Protocol to the International Covenant on Economic, Social and Cultural Rights entered into force in May 2013, providing for a mechanism enabling individuals and groups to file complaints with the UN relating to violations by states parties of citizens' economic, social and cultural rights. OHCHR provided technical support for the establishment, in January 2014, of a UN Independent Commission of Inquiry into reports of human rights violations committed in the Central African Republic during 2013. In February the High Commissioner urged all parties to the developing conflict in Ukraine to exercise maximum restraint, and called for an urgent investigation to establish facts and accountabilites in that situation; the Human Rights Council dispatched an investigative team to Ukraine in the following month.

OHCHR was the lead agency in undertaking preparations for the World Conference against Racism, Racial Discrimination, Xenophobia and Related Intolerance, convened in Durban, South Africa, in August–September 2001. A Durban Review Conference, convened in Geneva, Switzerland, in April 2009, issued an Outcome Document which identified further measures and initiatives aimed at combating and eliminating, with OHCHR involvement, manifestations of racism, racial discrimination, xenophobia and related intolerance. Major current issues identified at that time included the concept of defamation of religions within the existing framework of international human rights law, as a matter of incitement to religious hatred; improving understanding of different legislative patterns and judicial practices worldwide; slow progress towards eradicating extreme poverty and hunger and the effects of the global financial and food crises and of climate change, all deemed to have disproportionately severe effects on already vulnerable population groups; growing diversification of societies exacerbated by competition for scarce resources, placing migrants at increased risk of racism; and attitudes engendered by increasing implementation of counter-terrorism measures.

OHCHR assisted with the preparation of the International Convention for the Protection of All Persons from Enforced Disappearance, which was opened for signature in February 2007 and entered into force in December 2010. The fourth session of the Committee on Enforced Disappearances, responsible for reviewing implementation of the Convention, was held in April 2013. By April 2014 the Convention had been ratified by 42 states.

The Office promotes adherence to the Second Optional Protocol to the International Covenant on Civil and Political Rights, Aiming at the Abolition of the Death Penalty, which had been ratified by 80 states by April 2014; states where the Protocol is binding are obliged not to conduct executions or extradite individuals to a country where the death penalty is enforced, to take all necessary steps towards definitively abolishing the death penalty, and to report on their efforts in this respect.

OHCHR acts as the secretariat for three grant-making humanitarian funds: the UN Voluntary Fund for Victims of Torture (established in 1981); the Voluntary Fund for Indigenous Populations (established in 1985); and the Voluntary Fund on Contemporary Forms of Slavery (established in 1991).

OHCHR field offices and operations undertake a variety of activities, such as training and other technical assistance, support for Special Rapporteurs (usually appointed by the Commission on Human Rights to investigate human rights emergencies), monitoring and fact-finding. Increasingly they provide support to conflict prevention, peacemaking, peacekeeping and peacebuilding activities. OHCHR co-operates with the UN Department of Peacekeeping Operations and Department of Political Affairs in developing the human rights component of peacekeeping and peacebuilding missions. At April 2014 OHCHR was concerned with 37 thematic mandates, and with the following 14 country mandates (serviced by the Field Operations and Technical Co-operation Division): Belarus (mandate established in 2012; and most recently extended in 2013), Cambodia (mandate established in 1993; 2013), Central African Republic (2013), Côte d'Ivoire (2011; 2013), Eritrea (2012; 2013), Haiti (1995; 2013), Iran (2011; 2013), Democratic Republic of Korea (2004; 2013), Mali (2013), Myanmar (1992; 2013), Palestinian Territories (1993, to be maintained pending 'the end of the Israeli occupation'), Somalia (1993; 2013), Syria (2011), and Sudan (2009; 2013).

The OHCHR Quick Response Desk co-ordinates urgent appeals for assistance in addressing human rights emergencies. The High Commissioner issues reports on human rights emergencies to the Commission on Human Rights.

TECHNICAL CO-OPERATION PROGRAMME

The UN Technical Co-operation Programme in the Field of Human Rights was established in 1955 to assist states, at their request, to strengthen their capacities in the observance of democracy, human rights, and the rule of law. Examples of work undertaken within the framework of the programme include training courses and workshops on good governance and the observance of human rights, expert advisory services on the incorporation of international human rights standards into national legislation and policies and on the formulation of national plans of action for the promotion and protection of human rights, fellowships, the provision of information and documentation, and consideration of promoting a human rights culture. In recent years the Programme, one of the key components of OHCHR's activities, has expanded to undertake UN system-wide human rights support activities, for example in the area of peacekeeping.

Finance

OHCHR's activities are financed from the regular budget of the UN, as well as by voluntary contributions (which are channelled through the Trust Fund for the Support of the Activities of the UNHCHR and the Voluntary Fund for Technical Co-operation in the Field of Human Rights), and the three humanitarian trust funds administered by the Office. For the two years 2014–15 the projected regular budget appropriation for OHCHR amounted to US $174.8m.

Publications

A Handbook for Civil Society.

Annual Report.

Fact sheet series.

Human Rights Quarterly.

Human rights study series.

Professional training series.

Other reference material, reports, proceedings of conferences, workshops, etc.

UN Women—United Nations Entity for Gender Equality and the Empowerment of Women

Address: 304 East 45th St, 15th Floor, New York, NY 10017, USA.

Telephone: (212) 906-6400; **fax:** (212) 906-6705; **internet:** www.unwomen.org.

The UN Entity for Gender Equality and the Empowerment of Women, referred to most commonly as UN Women, was established by the UN General Assembly in July 2010 in order to strengthen the UN's capacity to promote gender equality, the empowerment of women, and the elimination of discrimination against women and girls. It commenced operations on 1 January 2011, with a universal mandate covering all countries.

Organization

(April 2014)

EXECUTIVE BOARD

The Executive Board comprises representatives from 41 countries around the world who serve on a rotating basis. The first Board was elected, by the UN Economic and Social Council, in November 2010 for an initial three-year term. A five-member Bureau was elected by the Board in December.

SECRETARIAT

Executive Director and Under-Secretary-General: PHUMZILE MLAMBO-NGCUKA (South Africa).

Deputy Executive Directors: LAKSHMI PURI (India), JOHN HENDRA (Canada).

REGIONAL OFFICES

There are Regional Offices for East and Southern Africa (based in Nairobi, Kenya); West and Central Africa (in Dakar, Senegal); the Americas and Caribbean (in Panama City, Panama); the Arab States (in Cairo, Egypt); and for Asia and the Pacific (in Bangkok, Thailand). The establishment of a Regional Office for Europe and Central Asia, in Istanbul, Turkey, was under way in 2014. There are also UN Women Liaison Offices in Brussels, Belgium; Copenhagen, Denmark (for the Nordic countries); Addis Ababa, Ethiopia (for the African Union); Osaka, Japan; and Madrid, Spain; 15 Sub-regional Offices; and Country Offices and Programme Presences worldwide.

Activities

UN Women was established in order to consolidate the resources and mandates of existing UN bodies working to promote gender equality. It incorporated the functions of the Office of the Special Adviser on Gender Issues and Advancement of Women, the Division for the Advancement of Women of the Secretariat, the United Nations Development Fund for Women (UNIFEM) and the International Research and Training Institute for the Advancement of Women (INSTRAW).

UN Women supports deliberations on international policy, standards and norms by UN member states in intergovernmental bodies such as the Commission on the Status of Women (CSW). It also co-ordinates UN system-wide efforts to achieve gender equality, and assists countries with putting international standards into practice. In all areas of activity UN Women aims to promote implementation of internationally agreed standards as incorporated, for example, in the Convention on the Elimination of All Forms of Discrimination against Women (1979); the Beijing Declaration and Platform for Action (approved at the Fourth World Conference on Women, held in 1995); the Millennium Declaration (2000); and UN Security Council commitments such as Resolution 1325 (2000) on women, peace and security.

The core areas of activity of UN Women are identified as Violence against Women; Peace and Security; Leadership and Participation; Economic Empowerment; Making National Plans and Budgets Gender-Responsive; Human Rights; and the Millennium Development Goals (MDGs). The organization aims to work with national partners, regional organizations and UN country teams to extend the necessary expert technical, practical and advocacy assistance to further gender equality efforts. Civil society organizations are actively encouraged to collaborate with UN Women. In May 2012 UN Women launched a Global Civil Society Advisory Group, comprising advocates for women's rights and experts on gender issues, which was to facilitate UN Women-civil society dialogue.

The Entity's strategic plan for 2014–17, adopted by the Executive Board in September 2013, had the following programmatic priorities: women lead and participate in decision-making at all levels; women, especially the poorest and most excluded, are economically empowered and benefit from development; women and girls live a life free from violence; peace and security and humanitarian action are shaped by women's leadership and participation; governance and national planning fully reflect accountability for gender equality commitments and priorities; and keeping in place a comprehensive and dynamic set of global norms, policies and standards on gender equality and women's empowerment.

In June 2012 UN Women—maintaining that the most effective strategy in addressing HIV/AIDS is the empowerment of women and the guaranteeing of women's rights—became the 11th co-sponsor of the Joint United Nations Programme on HIV/AIDS (UNAIDS).

The first International Day of the Girl Child was commemorated on 11 October 2012, on the theme 'End Child Marriage'. UN Women participated—with UNICEF, the UN Population Fund (UNFPA) and the Global Partnership to Ending Child Marriage ('Girls Not Brides')—in a high-level panel discussion on that subject at UN headquarters, New York USA. There were estimated at that time to be some 70m. married girls under the age of 18 worldwide; child marriage is seen as disruptive to education, limiting to girls' opportunities, as well as jeopardizing health and placing girls at increased risk of abuse.

Through the UN Women Training Centre training programmes in gender equality and the empowerment of women are offered to UN system personnel, in close co-ordination with the UN Staff College, UNITAR and other UN training institutions. In May 2013 UN Women launched a new UN Women Expert and Trainer Roster online database, representing a global pool of experts on gender issues.

International Women's Day is celebrated annually on 8 March.

VIOLENCE AGAINST WOMEN

UN Women advocates for strengthening legislation and the implementation of legislation aimed at preventing violence against women, including physical, sexual, psychological and economic abuses of power. UN Women works to combat the organized trafficking of females; child marriage; female genital mutilation/cutting; and the use of rape as a weapon of warfare. In March 2013 participants in the 57th session of the CSW adopted a landmark set of 'Agreed Conclusions' that condemned pervasive violence against women and girls, pledged to end impunity and to improve evidence collection and victim response mechanisms; and proposed the establishment of multi-sectoral services for female survivors of violence, including in the areas of provision of health and psychological support services, and protection of the right to sexual and reproductive health.

Under its grant-making cycle covering 2014–17, the UN Women's Trust Fund to End Violence Against Women, established in 1997, allocated US $8m. to 17 initiatives in 18 countries and territories, aimed at 2.7m. beneficiaries. Cumulatively, by the end of 2012, the Fund had delivered more than $86m. to 351 initiatives in 128 countries and territories.

In November 2010 UNIFEM, operating as part of UN Women, inaugurated a new initiative, the Global Safe Cities Free of Violence Against Women and Girls Programme. By the end of 2013 15 cities were participating in the initiative.

UN Women supports a public campaign ('Say NO—UNiTE'), which was launched in 2008 by the UN Secretary-General to end violence against women. The UN Entity maintains the Virtual Knowledge Centre to End Violence against Women and Girls (accessible at www.endvawnow.org), envisaged as a global one-stop resource for formulating and implementing anti-violence programmes.

PEACE AND SECURITY

UN Women estimates that civilians and in particular women and children represent up to 90% of casualties in conflict situations. Women and girls in such situations are adversely affected by the devastation of local infrastructures, and may also be subjected to sexual violence, which is sometimes deployed systematically. The impact of conflict and sexual violence can, in turn, prevent women and girls from accessing education and attaining economic independence or participation in governance and peace-building activities. In 2011 UN Women reported that fewer than 6% of national reconstruction budgets made specific provision for the particular needs of women and girls, and that, since 1992, fewer than 10% of peace negotiators had been female.

UN Women promotes the role of women in peacemaking, peacekeeping and peacebuilding activities, and works to advance the development of gender-sensitive early warning strategies to prevent the outbreak of conflict, to combat conflict-related sexual violence, to strengthen advocacy and gender-sensitive programming in the areas of security and justice, and to increase the inclusion of women and gender perspectives in post-conflict and humanitarian planning. UN Women has played a leading role in the development of an interagency framework for implementing and monitoring UN Security Council Resolution 1325 (adopted in October 2000), which urged the full and equal participation of women in peacebuilding efforts, and consideration of the protection needs of women and girls during conflict, and in post-conflict rehabilitation and recovery initiatives. Resolution 1325 is complemented by Resolution 1820 (adopted in June 2008), urging the cessation of conflict-related sexual violence and of related impunity; by Resolution 1888 (September 2009), with a focus on building the UN's and member states' leadership and other institutional capacities to end conflict-related sexual violence; and Resolution 1960 (December 2010), mandating the UN Secretary-General to establish arrangements for monitoring sexual violence in conflict situations and to list parties suspected of complicity in such violence.

In January 2014 UN Women, with the Government of the Netherlands, organized a Conference on Promoting Syrian Women's Engagement in the Syrian Political Process.

LEADERSHIP AND PARTICIPATION

The 2014 edition of the UN Women/Inter-Parliamentary Union annual *Women in Politics Map*, issued in March and giving data as of 1 January, reported that the global average of female representation in legislatures at that time was 21.8%. Rwanda and Andorra had reached the benchmark of 50% or more female parliamentary representation (Rwanda having become in September 2008 the first state to achieve this). Only 35 countries worldwide had achieved female parliamentary representation of 30% or more. At sub-regional level the Nordic countries had the highest level of female representation in legislatures (at 42%) and also of women holding ministerial posts (48.9%). The Americas had the highest regional percentage of female ministers (22.9%), followed by Africa (20.4%); meanwhile the Pacific and the Arab countries had the lowest percentage, at 8.7% and 8.3%, respectively. At that time there were only 18 female elected heads of state or government worldwide. UN Women supports national efforts to advance women's political leadership, including through constitutional reforms and through special temporary measures to raise the number of women in political positions. It supports women in acquiring the skills needed to be effective politicians, and by ensuring that election management bodies respond to women's concerns. In March 2012 the Executive Director of UN Women urged the broader use of quotas to expand participation by women in parliaments.

Jointly with other partners, including IPU and the UN Development Programme (UNDP), UN Women supports the International Knowledge Network of Women in Politics, an online resource on female political participation, launched in 2007 (accessible at iknowpolitics.org).

UN Women's multi-donor Fund for Gender Equality (established in 2009) aims to support women in attaining political and economic empowerment. The Fund focuses its support on women's organizations, civil society groups, and governments, and distributes two types of grant: catalytic grants, aimed at accelerating progress in advancing gender equality; and implementation grants, aimed at consolidating existing gender equality infrastructures. Under the Fund's second grant-making cycle, covering 2011–12, 53 grants were made, totalling US $17m.

ECONOMIC EMPOWERMENT

UN Women advocates for economic empowerment as a women's right, promoting it as a significant benefit for societies and economies. The Entity supports countries with enacting legislation and implementing policies aimed at increasing women's access to economic resources, and at establishing services that support sustainable livelihoods. UN Women works to strengthen women's rights to inheritance and land, to increase their access to decent work and to credit, and also to support the empowerment of female migrant workers.

In October 2011 a Social Protection Floor Advisory Group, launched in August 2010 by the International Labour Organization and the World Health Organization, and chaired by UN Women's Executive Director, issued a report entitled *Social Protection Floor for a Fair and Inclusive Globalization*.

In September 2011 UN Women and the World Food Programme (WFP) announced a joint initiative to provide income generating opportunities for women in rural areas, and in September 2012 UN Women, FAO, the International Fund for Agricultural Development and WFP launched 'Accelerating Progress Toward the Economic Empowerment of Rural Women', a five-year initiative that was to be implemented initially in Ethiopia, Guatemala, Kyrgyzstan, Liberia, Nepal, Niger and Rwanda.

NATIONAL PLANNING AND BUDGETING

UN Women advocates for provisions on gender equality to be integrated into national and local policies, plans, budgets and statistical data, and for gender equality to be a priority in channelling development assistance. UN Women provides support to national institutions that aim to make advancements for women.

MILLENNIUM DEVELOPMENT GOALS

UN Women supports the 'Global Strategy for Women's and Children's Health', launched by heads of state and government participating in the September 2010 UN Summit on the MDGs; some US $40,000m. has been pledged towards the health of women and children and achieving goals (iv) Reducing Child Mortality and (v) Improving Maternal Health. UN Women is contributing to the formulation of a post-2015 UN system-wide development agenda.

Finance

The Entity's annual budget is financed by mainly by voluntary contributions (forecast at US $690.0m. in 2014–15), and UN Women also receives an appropriation from the regular UN budget (projected at $15.3m. in that biennium). Total available resources for that period were projected at $925.6m. Total programme expenditure of $515.1m. was proposed for 2014–15.

From 2014–17 UN Women, UNDP, UNICEF and UNFPA were to maintain synchronized strategic planning cycles.

Publications

Annual Report.

Progress of the World's Women (every 2 years).

Women in Politics Map (with the IPU, annually).

Words to Action (quarterly).

World Survey on the Role of Women in Development (every 5 years).

United Nations Children's Fund—UNICEF

Address: 3 United Nations Plaza, New York, NY 10017, USA.

Telephone: (212) 326-7000; **fax:** (212) 887-7465; **e-mail:** info@unicef.org; **internet:** www.unicef.org.

UNICEF was established in 1946 as the UN International Children's Emergency Fund, to meet the emergency needs of children in post-war Europe. In 1950 its mandate was expanded to respond to the needs of children in developing countries. In 1953 the General Assembly decided that UNICEF should become a permanent branch of the UN system, with an emphasis on programmes giving long-term benefits to children everywhere, particularly those in developing countries. UNICEF was awarded the Nobel Peace Prize in 1965.

Organization

(April 2014)

EXECUTIVE BOARD

The Executive Board, as the governing body of UNICEF, comprises 36 member governments from all regions, elected in rotation for a three-year term by the Economic and Social Council (ECOSOC). The Board establishes policy, reviews programmes and approves expenditure. It reports to the UN General Assembly through ECOSOC.

SECRETARIAT

The Executive Director of UNICEF is appointed by the UN Secretary-General in consultation with the Executive Board. The administration of UNICEF and the appointment and direction of staff are the responsibility of the Executive Director, under policy directives laid down by the Executive Board, and under a broad authority delegated to the Executive Director by the Secretary-General. Around 85% of UNICEF staff positions are based in field offices.

Executive Director: ANTHONY LAKE (USA).

Deputy Executive Director: JOHANNA (YOKA) BRANDT (Netherlands).

UNICEF OFFICES

UNICEF has a network of eight regional and 127 field offices serving 155 countries and territories. Its offices in Tokyo, Japan, and Brussels, Belgium, support fund-raising activities; UNICEF's supply division is administered from the office in Copenhagen, Denmark. A research centre concerned with advocacy for child rights and development is based in Florence, Italy.

Belgium: Keizerinlaan 66, 1000 Brussels, Belgium; tel. (2) 230-59-70; fax (2) 230-34-62; e-mail brussels@unicef.org; internet unicef.be.

Japan: UNICEF House, 4-6-12 Takanawa, Minato-ku, Tokyo 108-8607, Japan; tel. (3) 5467-4431; fax (3) 5467-4437; e-mail tokyo@unicef.org; internet www.unicef.or.jp.

Regional Office for the Americas and the Caribbean: Apdo 0843-03045, Panamá, Panama; tel. (507) 301-7400; fax (507) 301.7370; e-mail panama@unicef.org; internet www.uniceflac.org.

Regional Office for Central and Eastern Europe and the Commonwealth of Independent States: Palais des Nations, 1211 Geneva 10, Switzerland; tel. 229095433; fax 229095909; e-mail ceecis@unicef.org; internet www.unicef.org/ceecis.

Regional Office for East Asia and the Pacific: POB 2-154, Bangkok 10200, Thailand; tel. (2) 3569499; fax (2) 2803563; e-mail asiapacificinfo@unicef.org; internet www.unicef.org/eapro.

Regional Office for Eastern and Southern Africa: POB 44145, Nairobi, Kenya 00100; tel. (20) 7621234; fax (20) 7622678; e-mail unicefesaro@unicef.org; internet www.unicef.org/esaro.

Regional Office for the Middle East and North Africa: POB 1551, 11821 Amman, Jordan; tel. (6) 5502400; fax (6) 5538880; e-mail menaro@unicef.org; internet www.unicef.org/jordan.

Regional Office for South Asia: POB 5815, Leknath Marg, Kathmandu, Nepal; tel. (1) 4417082; fax (1) 4419479; e-mail rosa@unicef.org; internet www.unicef.org/rosa.

Regional Office for West and Central Africa: POB 29720, Dakar-Yoff, Senegal; tel. 33-869-58-58; fax 33-820-89-64; e-mail mdawes@unicef.org; internet www.unicef.org/wcaro.

UNICEF Innocenti Research Centre: Piazza SS. Annunziata 12, 50122 Florence, Italy; tel. (055) 20330; fax (055) 2033220; e-mail florence@unicef.org; internet www.unicef-irc.org; f. 1988; undertakes research in two thematic areas: Social and economic policies and children; and Child protection and implementation of international standards for children; Dir GORDON ALEXANDER.

UNICEF Supply Division: Oceanvej 10–12, 2100 Copenhagen, Denmark; tel. 45-33-55-00; fax 35-26-94-21; e-mail supply@unicef.org; internet www.unicef.org/supply; responsible for overseeing UNICEF's global procurement and logistics operations.

UNICEF New York Supply Centre: UNICEF House, 3 UN Plaza, New York, NY 10017 USA; tel. (212) 326-7490; fax (212) 326-7477.

Further strategic supply hubs are located in Dubai, United Arab Emirates; Douala, Cameroon; Colón, Panama; and Shanghai, People's Republic of China.

NATIONAL COMMITTEES

UNICEF is supported by 36 National Committees, mostly in industrialized countries, whose volunteer members raise money through various specific campaigns and activities, including the sale of greetings cards and collection of foreign coins. The Committees also undertake advocacy and awareness campaigns on a number of issues and provide an important link with the general public.

Activities

UNICEF is dedicated to the well-being of children, adolescents and women and works for the realization and protection of their rights within the frameworks of the Convention on the Rights of the Child (adopted by the UN General Assembly in 1989, and by 2014 was almost universally ratified), and of the Convention on the Elimination of All Forms of Discrimination Against Women (adopted by the UN General Assembly in 1979). Promoting the full implementation of the Conventions, UNICEF aims to ensure that children worldwide are given the best possible start in life and attain a good level of basic education, and that adolescents are given every opportunity to develop their capabilities and participate successfully in society. The Fund also provides relief and rehabilitation assistance in emergencies. Through its extensive field network UNICEF undertakes, in co-ordination with governments, local communities and other aid organizations, programmes in health, nutrition, education, water and sanitation, the environment, gender issues and development. Emphasis is placed on low-cost, community-based programmes. UNICEF programmes are increasingly focused on supporting children and women during critical periods of their life, when intervention can make a lasting difference. Since the 1950s UNICEF has engaged the services of prominent individuals as Goodwill Ambassadors and Advocates, who can use their status to attract attention to particular causes and support UNICEF's objectives. UNICEF advocates for increased focus on children in national budgets and development plans.

In 2002 a UN General Assembly Special Session on Children adopted a declaration and plan of action based on the concept 'A World Fit for Children'. The plan of action resolved to work towards the attainment by 2015 of 21 new goals and targets supporting the UN Millennium Development Goals (MDGs) in the areas of education, health and the protection of children; these included a reduction in mortality rates for infants and children under five by two-thirds; a reduction in maternal mortality rates by three-quarters; a reduction by one-third in the rate of severe malnutrition among children under the age of five; and enrolment in primary education by 90% of children. UNICEF supports the Global Strategy for Women's and Children's Health, launched by heads of state and government participating in the September 2010 UN Summit on the MDGs. The Fund's medium-term strategic plan for the period 2014–17, endorsed by the Executive Board in September 2013, aimed to realize the rights of children everywhere, including the most disadvantaged, and focused on the following seven pillars: young child survival and development; basic education and gender equality; HIV/AIDS and children; child protection from violence, exploitation and abuse; policy advocacy and partnerships for children's rights; and humanitarian action. The 2014–17 plan was underpinned by seven implementation strategies relating to: capacity development; evidence generation and evidence-based policy dialogue and advocacy; partnerships; South-South triangular co-operation; the identification and promotion of innovation; support to integration and cross-sectoral linkages; and service delivery. UNICEF co-leads the following five of the 11 global thematic consultations on the post-2015 development agenda: addressing inequalities; conflict, disaster and violence; education; health; and water. In September 2012 UNICEF organized the inaugural forum of a new Global Partnership on Children with Disabilities, which aimed to include issues pertaining to disabled children in the post-2015 development agenda.

YOUNG CHILD SURVIVAL AND DEVELOPMENT

In 2012 UNICEF allocated some 53% of total programme assistance to young child survival and development. In 2012 UNICEF estimated that around 6.6m. children under five years of age died (compared with some 20m. child mortalities in 1960 and 13m. in 1990)—mainly in developing countries (four-fifths of such premature deaths occurring in sub-Saharan African and South Asia, and representing a mortality rate 48 deaths per 1,000 live births). The majority of such deaths were from largely preventable causes, such as birth asphyxia, diarrhoea, malaria, pneumonia and prematurity. More than one-third of all deaths of children under five in that year occurred in India (22% of all deaths) and Nigeria (13%). In 2004 UNICEF, the World Health Organization (WHO), the World Bank and the UN Population Division established an Inter-agency Group for Child Mortality Estimation (IGME), to advance work on monitoring progress towards meeting the MDG on reducing child mortality; it produces updated child mortality data each year. In September 2005 UNICEF, WHO and other partners launched the Partnership for Maternal, Newborn and Child Health, which aimed to accelerate progress towards the attainment of the MDGs to reduce child and maternal mortality. In June 2012 UNICEF, and the Ethiopian, Indian and US Governments launched Committing to Child Survival: A Promise Renewed; the initiative, administered from a small secretariat hosted by UNICEF, that aimed to terminate preventable child mortality through the pursuit of the following goals: mobilizing political leadership; achieving consensus on a global roadmap of proven strategies; and driving sustained collective action and mutual accountability.

In 2010 the Partnership supported the UN Secretary-General to launch a new Global Strategy for Women's and Children's Health. Immunization is an outstandingly successful and cost-effective health intervention, and therefore UNICEF has worked with WHO and other partners to increase global immunization coverage against the following six diseases: measles, poliomyelitis, tuberculosis, diphtheria, whooping cough and tetanus. In 2000 UNICEF, WHO, the World Bank and a number of public and private sector partners launched the Global Alliance for Vaccines and Immunization (GAVI), subsequently renamed the GAVI Alliance, which aims to protect children of all nationalities and socio-economic groups against vaccine-preventable diseases. GAVI's strategy includes improving access to sustainable immunization services, expanding the use of existing vaccines, accelerating the development and introduction of new vaccines and technologies and promoting immunization coverage as a focus of international development efforts. From 2006 a Global Immunization Meeting was convened annually by UNICEF, WHO and GAVI Alliance partners. In 2006 UNICEF, WHO and other partners launched the Global Immunization Vision and Strategy (GIVS), a global 10-year framework, covering 2006–15, aimed at reducing deaths due to vaccine-preventable diseases by at least two-thirds compared to 2000 levels, by 2015; and increasing national vaccination coverage levels to at least 90%. (In 2011 the global child vaccination coverage rate was estimated at 83%.) In May 2012 the 65th World Health Assembly endorsed a Global Vaccine Action Plan (GVAP), building on the GIVS, which aimed to facilitate more equitable access to vaccines by 2020.

UNICEF works to improve safe water supply, sanitation and hygiene, and thereby reduce the risk of diarrhoea and other water-borne diseases. UNICEF places great emphasis on increasing the testing and protection of drinking water at its source as well as in the home. UNICEF, the World Bank and other partners participate in the Global Public-Private Partnership for Handwashing with Soap, which was established in 2001 with the aim of empowering communities in developing countries to prevent diarrhoea and respiratory infections through the promotion of the practice of thorough hand-washing with soap. In 2006 UNICEF and partners established the Global Task Force on Water and Sanitation with the aim of providing all children with access to safe water, and accelerating progress towards MDG targets on safe drinking water and basic sanitation.

UNICEF-assisted programmes for the control of diarrhoeal diseases promote the low-cost manufacture and distribution of prepackaged salts or home-made solutions. The use of 'oral rehydration therapy' has risen significantly in recent years, and is believed to prevent more than 1m. child deaths annually. During 1990–2000 diarrhoea-related deaths were reduced by one-half. UNICEF also promotes the need to improve sanitation and access to safe water supplies in developing nations in order to reduce the risk of diarrhoea and other water-borne diseases (see 20/20 initiative). To control acute respiratory infections, another leading cause of death in children under five in developing countries, UNICEF works with WHO in training health workers to diagnose and treat the associated diseases. A report released by UNICEF in July 2012 entitled *Pneumonia and diarrhoea: tackling the deadliest diseases for the world's poorest children*, stated that pneumonia and diarrhoea account for nearly one-third of deaths among children under the age of five globally.

At the UN General Assembly Special Session on Children, in 2002, goals were set to reduce measles deaths by 50%. Expanded efforts by UNICEF, WHO and other partners led to a reduction in worldwide measles deaths by 78% between 2000 and 2008. Around 1m. children die from malaria every year, mainly in sub-Saharan Africa. In October 1998 UNICEF, together with WHO, the UN Development Programme (UNDP) and the World Bank, inaugurated a new global campaign, Roll Back Malaria, to fight the disease. UNICEF is actively engaged in developing effective ways of distributing highly subsidized insecticide-treated mosquito nets at the local level, thereby increasing the proportion of children and pregnant women who use them.

According to UNICEF estimates, around 25% of children under five years of age are underweight, while each year malnutrition contributes to more than one-third of the child deaths in that age group and leaves millions of others with physical and mental disabilities. UNICEF supports national efforts to reduce malnutrition, for example, fortifying staple foods with micronutrients, widening women's access to education, improving the nutritional status of pregnant women, strengthening household food security and basic health services, providing food supplies in emergencies, and promoting sound childcare and feeding practices. Since 1991 more than 19,000 hospitals in about 130 countries have been designated 'baby-friendly', having implemented a set of UNICEF and WHO recommendations entitled '10 steps to successful breastfeeding'. The Executive Director of UNICEF chairs the Lead Group of the Scaling Up Nutrition (SUN) initiative, which convened its first meeting in April 2012, and comprises 27 national leaders and agencies jointly providing strategic guidance with a view to improving child and maternal nutrition. SUN, initiated in 2009, and co-ordinated by the UN Secretary-General's Special Representative for Food Security and Nutrition, aims to increase the coverage of interventions that improve nutrition during the first 1,000 days of a child's life (such as exclusive breastfeeding, optimal complementary feeding practices, and provision of essential vitamins and minerals); and to ensure that national nutrition plans are implemented and that government programmes take nutrition into account. The activities of SUN are guided by the Framework for Scaling up Nutrition, which was published in April 2010 and subsequently endorsed by more than 100 partners, including UN agencies, governments, research institutions, and representatives of civil society and of the private sector; and by the SUN Roadmap, finalized in September 2010.

BASIC EDUCATION AND GENDER EQUALITY

In 2012 UNICEF allocated 20% of total programme assistance to basic education and gender equality. UNICEF considers education to be a fundamental human right, and works to ensure all children receive equal access to quality education. UNICEF participated in and fully supports the objectives and framework for action adopted by the World Education Forum in Dakar, Senegal, in April 2000, including the Education for All initiative. UNICEF was assigned formal responsibility within the initiative for education in emergencies, early childhood care and technical and policy support. UNICEF advocates the implementation of the Child Friendly School model, designed to facilitate the delivery of safe, quality education. UNICEF, in partnership with UNESCO, has developed an Essential Learning Package to support countries to reduce disparities in the provision of basic education. The initiative was implemented for the first time by Burkina Faso in 2003, and has since been adopted by a further 11 countries in West and Central Africa.

On 11 October UNICEF celebrates the International Day of the Girl Child (approved by the UN General Assembly in December 2011); the theme in 2013 was 'innovating for girls' education'.

UNICEF leads and acts as the secretariat of the United Nations Girls' Education Initiative (UNGEI), which aims to increase the enrolment of girls in primary schools in more than 100 countries. It is estimated that more than 100m. school-age children worldwide, of whom more than one-half are girls, remain deprived of basic education. In May 2010 UNGEI convened the first international conference on 'Engendering Empowerment: Education and Equality' ('E4'), in Dakar, Senegal. The E4 conference unanimously adopted the Dakar Declaration on Accelerating Girls' Education and Gender Equality, in which it urged that increased focus should be placed on accelerating access to education for the most socially deprived girls, deemed to be the most disadvantaged group in education.

The first *A Promise Renewed: Progress Report* issued in September 2013 by the Committing to Child Survival: A Promise Renewed initiative noted the linkage between advances in female educational attainment and recent reductions in under-five mortality, stating that maternal education tended to lead to economic benefits; to access to better housing and sanitation; to delayed marriage and childbirth, and better family planning; and to improved access to preventive and curative health services as well as increased confidence in using them, all of which impacted positively on child survival, and also on mothers' own health and survival.

UNICEF estimates that more than 500,000 women die every year during pregnancy or childbirth, largely because of inadequate health care. For every maternal death, approximately 30 further women suffer permanent injuries or chronic disabilities as a result of complications during pregnancy or childbirth. Under the Global Partnership for Maternal, Newborn and Child Health, UNICEF works with WHO, the UN Population Fund (UNFPA) and other partners in countries with high maternal mortality to improve maternal health and prevent maternal and newborn death through the integration of a continuum of home, community, outreach and facility-based care, embracing every stage of maternal, newborn and child health. UNICEF and partners work with governments and policy-makers to ensure that antenatal and obstetric care is a priority in national health plans. UNICEF's activities in this area have included support for obstetric facilities and training in, and advocacy of, women's health issues, such as ending child marriage, eliminating female genital mutilation/cutting (FGM/C), preventing malaria and promoting the uptake of tetanus toxoid vaccinations and iron and folic acid supplements among pregnant women. UNICEF promotes access to family planning services and recommends that births per mother should be spaced at least two years apart, as short birth spacing tends to raise the risk of prematurity and low birth weight. It discourages a culture of early marriage and adolescent motherhood as this typically leads to girls ceasing their education, thereby losing potential economic and health benefits, and being at greater risk of suffering potentially life-threatening complications in pregnancy and childbirth, and of having premature or low birth weight babies. In 2013 UNICEF reported that the risk of maternal death was 2.7 times higher among women with no education than among women having more than 12 years of education.

In July 2013 UNICEF released *Female Genital Mutilation / Cutting: A statistical overview and exploration of the dynamics of change*, based on comprehensive surveys undertaken in 29 countries in Africa and the Middle East. The report estimated that, while support for the practice was declining, some 30m. girls were at risk of undergoing FGM/C over the next decade. FGM/C was reported to be almost universal in Djibouti, Egypt, Guinea and Somalia. As a means of eliminating the tradition the report recommended working with rather than against local cultural traditions; revising attitudes about FGM/C; promoting a critical mass of public opposition to the practice; increasing exposure of groups that still practice FGM/C to groups that do not; promoting the abandonment of FGM/C alongside improved status and opportunities for girls; and continuing to gather data to inform future related policies and programmes.

HIV/AIDS AND CHILDREN

UNICEF is concerned about the danger posed by HIV/AIDS to the realization of children's rights and aims to provide expertise, support, logistical co-ordination and innovation towards ending the epidemic and limiting its impact on children and their mothers. In 2012 it was estimated that 3.4m. children under the age of 15 were living with HIV/AIDS worldwide. During 2011 some 330,000 children under the age of 15 were estimated to have been newly infected with HIV, while 230,000 died as a result of AIDS and AIDS-related illnesses. Around 17m. children worldwide have lost one or both parents to AIDS, and as a result of HIV/AIDS many children have suffered poverty, homelessness, discrimination, and loss of education and other life opportunities. UNICEF's priorities in this area include prevention of infection among young people (through, for example, support for education programmes and media campaigns); reduction in mother-to-child transmission; care and protection of orphans and other vulnerable children; and care and support for children, young people and parents living with HIV/AIDS. UNICEF works closely in this field with governments and co-operates with other UN agencies in the Joint UN Programme on HIV/AIDS (UNAIDS). Young people aged 15–24 are reported to account for around 45% of new HIV infections worldwide. UNICEF advocates Life Skills-Based Education as a means of empowering young people to cope with challenging situations and of encouraging them to adopt healthy patterns of behaviour. In October 2005 UNICEF launched Unite for Children, Unite against AIDS, a campaign that was to provide a platform for child-focused advocacy aimed at reversing the spread of HIV/AIDS amongst children, adolescents and young people; and to provide a child-focused framework for national programmes based on the following four 'pillars' (known as the 'Four Ps'): the prevention of mother-to-child HIV transmission; improved provision of paediatric treatment; prevention of infection among adolescents and young people; and protection and support of children affected by HIV/AIDS. In November 2010 UNICEF issued its fifth *Children and AIDS: A Stocktaking Report*, detailing ongoing progress and challenges. In October 2010 UNICEF issued its first Mother-Baby Pack, containing drugs to prevent mother-to-child transmission of HIV in the poorest households. UNICEF supports the Global Plan towards the Elimination of New HIV Infections among Children by 2015 and Keeping Their Mothers Alive, which was endorsed in June 2011 by a UN High Level Meeting on HIV/AIDS, and aims to reduce by 90% of new HIV infections among children, and halve the number of deaths among their mothers.

At December 2011 it was estimated that of the total cases of children aged 0–14 years living with HIV/AIDS, 3.1m. were in sub-Saharan Africa, 150,000 in South and South-East Asia, 60,000 in Latin America and the Caribbean, 15,000 in the Middle East and North Africa, 17,600 in Europe and Central Asia, 16,000 in East Asia, 4,500 in North America and 3,600 in the Pacific region.

CHILD PROTECTION FROM VIOLENCE, EXPLOITATION AND ABUSE

In 2012 some 11% of total programme resources were allocated to child protection. UNICEF is actively involved in global-level partnerships for child protection, including the Inter-Agency Coordination Panel on Juvenile Justice; the Inter-Agency Working Group on Unaccompanied and Separated Children; the Donors' Working Group on Female FGM/C; the Better Care Network; the Study on Violence Against Children; the Inter-Agency Standing Committee (IASC) Task Force on Protection from Sexual Exploitation and Abuse in Humanitarian Crises; and the IASC Task Force on Mental Health and Psychological Support in Emergency Settings.

UNICEF estimated in 2012 that only around 65% of children aged below five had been officially registered at birth, and that many others had no proof of registration. The regions with the lowest levels of birth registration are Asia (accounting for 59% of unregistered children worldwide) and sub-Saharan Africa (37%). The three countries with the lowest birth registration levels in 2012 were Somalia (3% of births registered), Liberia (4%), and Ethiopia (7%). Nearly one-third of unregistered children worldwide live in India. UNICEF promotes universal registration in order to prevent the abuse of children without proof of age and nationality, for example through trafficking, forced labour, early marriage and military recruitment. The Fund provides advocacy and technical support for the enactment of legislation, policies and standards that advance free and universal birth registration. In 2012 it supported the registration at birth of around 30m. children in some 75 countries. The Fund has promoted the organization of birth registration data in rural areas of developing countries through RapidSMS text messaging.

UNICEF estimates that some 158m. children aged from five–14 years are engaged in child labour, while around 1.2m. children worldwide are trafficked each year. The Fund works with the International Labour Organization and other partners to promote an end to exploitative and hazardous child labour, and supports special projects to provide education, counselling and care in developing countries. UNICEF promotes ratification of the Optional Protocol to the Convention on the Rights of the Child on the sale of children, child prostitution and child pornography. The Fund co-sponsored and actively participated in the Third Congress Against Commercial Sexual Exploitation of Children, held in Rio de Janeiro, Brazil, in November 2008.

More than 250,000 children are involved in armed conflicts as soldiers, porters and forced labourers. UNICEF encourages ratification of the Optional Protocol to the Convention on the Rights of the Child on the involvement of children in armed conflict, which was adopted by the General Assembly in May 2000 and entered into force in February 2002, and bans the compulsory recruitment of combatants below the age of 18. The Fund also urges states to make unequivocal statements endorsing 18 as the minimum age of voluntary recruitment to the armed forces. UNICEF, with Save the Children, co-chairs the Steering Group of the Paris Principles, which aims to support the implementation of a series of 'Commitments and Guidelines'—first endorsed by an international conference convened by UNICEF and the French Government in Paris, France, in February 2007—to end the recruitment of children, support the release of children from the armed forces and facilitate their reintegration into civilian life. In March 2014 the UN Secretary-General launched a campaign entitled 'Children, Not Soldiers', and to be supported by UNICEF, that promoted the goal of zero use by 2016 of children in government armed forces; at that time eight government security forces were alleged to be recruiting children. By the end of 2012 105 countries had voluntarily signed up to the Paris Commitments. It is estimated that landmines kill and maim between 8,000 and 10,000 children every year. UNICEF supports mine awareness campaigns, and promotes the full ratification of the Convention on the Prohibition of the Use, Stockpiling, Production and Transfer of Anti-Personnel Mines and on their Destruction, which was adopted in December 1997 and entered into force in March 1999. By April 2014 the Convention had been ratified by 161 countries.

POLICY AND ADVOCACY AND PARTNERSHIPS FOR CHILDREN'S RIGHTS

In 2012 UNICEF allocated some 9% of total programme assistance to policy and advocacy and partnerships for children's rights.

The Fund promotes the collection and analysis of statistical data relating to the well being of children. UNICEF's annual publication *The State of the World's Children* presents such data annually; the theme of the 2014 report, issued in January, was 'Every child counts', with a focus on the importance of collecting, disseminating and monitoring credible data in realizing children's rights. UNICEF's Multiple Indicator Cluster Survey (MICS) method of data collection, initiated in 1995, analyses data on child protection, education, health (including HIV and AIDS), nutrition, and water and sanitation, and is a main tool used in measuring progress towards the achievement of the UN MDGs. The fifth MICS round was being undertaken during 2012–14. During 2012 UNICEF developed a new Multiple Overlapping Deprivation Analysis (MODA) tool to assess poverty and inequalities within countries. In recent years the Fund has become increasingly concerned about the number of children who are not included in statistical information on development markers, and who have become isolated from vital services owing to factors such as urbanization, political volatility, natural disasters, and environmental challenges.

Since 2005 young people from the Group of Eight (G8) industrialized nations and selected emerging countries (including Brazil, China, Egypt, India, Mexico and South Africa) have participated in a Junior 8 (J8) summit, which is organized with support from UNICEF on the fringes of the annual G8 summit. The J8 summits have addressed issues including education, energy, climate change, HIV/AIDS, the global financial crisis, and tolerance. Since 2010 G(irls)20 summits have been convened alongside summits of G20 leaders; the participants represent the G20 countries, and include, also, young female representatives of the African Union and European Union.

UNICEF aims to break the cycle of poverty by advocating for increased development aid to developing countries, and aims to help poor countries obtain debt relief and to ensure access to basic social services. In May 2012 UNICEF initiated its first Social Protection Strategic Framework, promoting child-sensitive inclusive social protection systems.

Through this focus area, UNICEF seeks to work with partners to strengthen capacities to design and implement cross-sectoral social and economic policies, child-focused legislative measures and budgetary allocations that enable countries to meet their obligations under the Convention on the Rights of the Child and the Convention on the Elimination of All Forms of Discrimination against Women. UNICEF has identified the following priority areas of support to 'upstream' policy work: child poverty and disparities; social budgeting; decentralization; social security and social protection; holistic legislative reform for the two Conventions; and the impact of migration on children.

HUMANITARIAN RESPONSE

UNICEF provides emergency relief assistance to children and young people affected by conflict, natural disasters and food crises. In situations of violence and social disintegration the Fund provides support in the areas of education, health, mine-awareness and psychosocial assistance, and helps to demobilize and rehabilitate child soldiers. In 2012 UNICEF responded to 286 humanitarian challenges in 79 countries. In February 2014 UNICEF launched its largest ever appeal, for nearly US $2,200m. to support the urgent requirements of 59m. children in 50 territories affected by conflict, natural disasters, and other complex emergencies that year.

UNICEF's emergency education assistance includes the provision of 'school-in-a-box' kits in refugee camps and the reconstruction of school buildings. In the area of health the Fund co-operates with WHO to arrange 'days of tranquillity' in order to facilitate the immunization of children in conflict zones. Psychosocial assistance activities include special programmes to support traumatized children and help unaccompanied children to be reunited with parents or extended families.

In January 2014 UNICEF expressed deep concern over the use of children as combatants in the ongoing armed conflict in South Sudan, urging all relevant parties not to permit the use of children in fighting and immediately to release any child soldiers.

In December 2013 UNICEF condemned extreme violence being perpetrated against children caught in violent unrest in Bangui, Central African Republic (CAR), as well as the ongoing recruitment of children into militant groups. At that time UNICEF was providing sanitation facilities and essential medical supplies and safe water to families that had been displaced by the conflict. The Fund was also establishing safe spaces for children. In January 2014 UNICEF supported and monitored an integrated vaccination campaign—covering immunization against polio and measles, as well as the provision of vitamin A supplements, de-worming medication, and malnutrition screening—that aimed to reach more than 210,000 displaced children in Bangui. (Internally displaced persons in the CAR then numbered around 935,000, while in December 2013 alone around two-thirds of residents of Bangui were reportedly displaced from their homes.) In early 2014 UNICEF and partners established temporary learning spaces to enable some 20,000 displaced children in Bangui to continue their educations.

In January 2014 UNICEF, with UNHCR and other partners, initiated a 'No Lost Generation' strategy, which envisaged raising US $1,000m. from voluntary donations to improve the situation of Syrian children affected by long-term civil war. By that time more than 3m. Syrian children had been displaced from their homes within Syria, and a further 1.2m. were sheltering as refugees in neighbouring countries (Lebanon, Jordan, Turkey, Iraq and Egypt). The strategy aimed to offer safe, uninterrupted education; protection from exploitation, abuse and violence; social cohesion opportunities; and psychological and psychosocial support. In February 2014 UNICEF supported a report issued by the UN Secretary-General concerning children and armed conflict in Syria, which cited very grave violations perpetrated against children during the course of the civil war. The Fund supported the UN Secretary-General in demanding an immediate end to the targeting of innocent children and civilians, including the use of weaponry that causes indiscriminate and disproportionate harm. In early 2014 UNICEF and WHO were undertaking an emergency campaign, initiated in November 2013, that aimed to immunize more than 23m. children in the Middle East against polio, following the detection of the poliovirus in Egypt, Israel, the Palestinian Territories, and within Syria.

In November 2013 UNICEF initiated an emergency operation to deliver critical supplies to support more than 1m. children in areas of the Philippines that had been devastated by Typhoon Haiyan. Health kits, water, therapeutic food for children, and hygiene kits were provided from supplies already within the country, and UNICEF airlifted in a further essential items from its Supply Division in Copenhagen, Denmark, including medical kits, water purification tablets, soap, tarpaulins, micronutrient supplements, school-in-a-box kits, tents (to serve as classrooms and safe spaces for children), recreation kits and pharmaceutical products.

Since 1998 UNICEF's humanitarian response has been structured within a framework of identified Core Commitments for Children in Humanitarian Action (CCCs). Revised CCCs were issued in April 2010 to reflect new humanitarian structures and best practices. The revised CCCs incorporated UNICEF's commitment to working in partnership with international organizations, national authorities and civil society in order to strengthen risk reduction, disaster preparedness and response, and early recovery. During 2005 the

UN's Inter-Agency Standing Committee (IASC), concerned with co-ordinating the international response to humanitarian disasters, developed a concept of organizing agency assistance to IDPs through the institutionalization of a 'Cluster Approach', comprising 11 core areas of activity. UNICEF is the lead agency for the clusters on Education (jointly with Save The Children); Nutrition; and Water, Sanitation and Hygiene. In addition, it leads the Gender-based Violence Area of Responsibility sub-cluster (jointly with UNFPA) and the Child Protection Area of Responsibility sub-cluster within the Protection Cluster.

Finance

UNICEF is funded by voluntary contributions from governments and non-governmental and private sector sources. UNICEF's income is divided into contributions for 'regular resources' and for 'other resources' (for special purposes, including expanding the outreach of country programmes of co-operation, and ensuring capacity to deliver critical assistance to women and children, for example during humanitarian crises). In September 2013 the Executive Board adopted an integrated budget in support of the Fund's strategic plan covering 2014–17, under which proposed programme expenditure amounted to US $14,800m. Total resources for 2014–17 were projected at $18,600m., comprising $6,200m. in regular resources and $12,400m. in other resources.

From 2014–17 UNICEF, UNDP, UNFPA and UN Women were to maintain synchronized strategic planning cycles.

Publications

Committing to Child Survival: A Promise Renewed—Progress Report.

Progress for Children.

The State of the World's Children (annually).

UNICEF Annual Report.

UNICEF at a Glance.

UNICEF Humanitarian Action for Children Report (annually).

Reports and studies; series on children and women; nutrition; education; children's rights; children in wars and disasters; working children; water, sanitation and the environment; analyses of the situation of children and women in individual developing countries.

United Nations Conference on Trade and Development—UNCTAD

Address: Palais des Nations, 1211 Geneva 10, Switzerland.

Telephone: 229171234; **fax:** 229170057; **e-mail:** unctadinfo@unctad.org; **internet:** www.unctad.org.

UNCTAD was established in December 1964. It is the principal instrument of the UN General Assembly concerned with trade and development, and is the focal point within the UN system for integrated treatment of trade and development and interrelated issues of finance, technology, investment, and sustainable development. It aims to help developing countries—particularly least developed countries, small island developing states, landlocked developing countries, economies in transition, and the so-called structurally weak, vulnerable and small economies—to maximize their trade and development opportunities, especially in view of the increasing globalization and liberalization of the world economy.

Organization

(April 2014)

CONFERENCE

The Conference is the organization's highest policy-making body and meets every four years at ministerial level to formulate major policy guidelines and to decide on UNCTAD's mandate and work priorities. The 13th session took place in Doha, Qatar, in April 2012; the 14th session was scheduled to be convened in Peru, in 2016. As well as its 194 members, many intergovernmental and non-governmental organizations participate in UNCTAD's work as observers.

TRADE AND DEVELOPMENT BOARD

The Trade and Development Board oversees the activities of UNCTAD in between conferences. The Board comprises elected representatives from 153 member states and is responsible for ensuring the overall consistency of UNCTAD's activities, as well as those of its subsidiary bodies. The Board meets in a regular annual session lasting about 10 days, at which it examines global economic issues. It may also meet a further three times a year to deal with urgent policy issues and to address institutional matters.

COMMISSIONS

The Trade and Development Board has two Commissions: the Trade and Development Commission; and the Investment, Enterprise and Development Commission. The role of the Commissions is to conduct policy dialogues, to consider the reports of expert meetings, to manage and recommend for approval the work programmes of expert meetings within their purview, and to promote and strengthen synergies among UNCTAD's three pillars of work: research and analysis; technical co-operation; and intergovernmental consensus-building. Each Commission holds one session per year. In addition to the Intergovernmental Group of Experts on Competition Law and Policy and the Intergovernmental Working Group of Experts on International Standards of Accounting and Reporting, the Commissions may convene up to eight expert meetings a year on specific issues. Of the eight, six have now been established as multi-year expert meetings and cover issues such as commodities, transport and trade facilitation, investment, enterprises and science, technology and innovation, services, and South-South co-operation.

SECRETARIAT

The UNCTAD secretariat undertakes policy analysis; monitoring, implementation and follow-up of decisions of intergovernmental bodies; technical co-operation in support of UNCTAD's policy objectives; and information exchanges and consultations of various types. It comprises the following divisions: Globalization and Development Strategies; Investment and Enterprise Development; International Trade in Goods and Services, and Commodities; Technology and Logistics; Africa, Least Developed Countries and Special Programmes; and Management.

Secretary-General: Mukhisa Kituyi (Kenya).

Deputy Secretary-General: Petko Draganov (Bulgaria).

Activities

In April 2012 the 13th session of the Conference (UNCTAD XIII), convened in Doha, Qatar, adopted two outcome documents, the Doha Manar and the Doha Mandate. The Doha Manar ('beacon' in Arabic) represented a declaration of support for UNCTAD's planned promotion during 2012–16 of inclusive development through commerce and structural change, and noted the need to strengthen the organization's impact. The Doha Mandate reaffirmed work priorities determined in April 2008, in Accra, Ghana, by UNCTAD XII, and established directions on policy analysis, and the ongoing role of UNCTAD in the context of fostering more inclusive and sustainable economic growth. During 2012–16 UNCTAD was to work to maximize the positive impact of globalization and trade on development; to enhance its programme activities relating to the special needs of the African continent, and of least developed Countries (LDCs), small island developing states, landlocked developing countries, and other structurally weak, vulnerable and small economies; to assist transit developing countries with their special challenges in relation to infrastructure and transport; to make a contribution to the implementation and follow-up to the outcomes of relevant global conferences; and to continue to contribute to the achievement of internationally agreed development goals.

UNCTAD has a clear mandate to assist with the implementation of the Istanbul Programme of Action for LDCs, which resulted from the fourth UN Conference on the LDCs, held in May 2011; the Mauritius Strategy on the Programme of Action for the Sustainable Development of Small Island Developing States, adopted by the UN Conference on Small Islands held in Port Louis, Mauritius, in January 2005; and the Almatı Programme of Action, that was adopted in August 2003 by the International Ministerial Conference of Landlocked and Transit Developing Countries and Donor Countries and International Financial and Development Institutions on Transit Transport Co-operation. UNCTAD emphasizes the importance of providing financial access to developing countries.

UNCTAD, with the World Trade Organization (WTO), leads an initiative on promoting trade—combating protectionism, including through the conclusion of the Doha Round, and by strengthening aid-for-trade financing-for-trade initiatives—the third of nine activities that were launched in April 2009 by the UN System Chief Executives Board for Co-ordination (CEB), with the aim of alleviating the impact on poor and vulnerable populations of the then developing global economic crisis. Since 2009 UNCTAD has also provided advisory services to the G20 nations in relation to macroeconomic and development policies, including on volatility in commodity prices, employment, global economic governance, and investment.

In February 2012 the UNCTAD Secretary-General issued a report entitled *Development-led Globalization: Towards Sustainable and Inclusive Development Paths*, in which he urged a change of direction in the global economic system—a 'global new deal'—to enable more stable and inclusive economic progress. 'Development-centred globalization' was also the theme of UNCTAD XIII (in April). During UNCTAD XIII the Secretary-General recommended the inclusion of two new initiatives in the follow-up to the UN Conference on Sustainable Development (Rio+20), which was convened in June: the establishment of a Global Trade and Green Economy Forum, a new institutional space where evidence-based dialogue and solution sharing could be fostered with a view to addressing 'green protectionism'; and the creation of a scheme to support developing countries with identifying green export opportunities.

An UNCTAD Panel of Eminent Persons was established in 2005 to advise UNCTAD's Secretary-General on means of enhancing the Conference's development role and impact; the first report of the Panel was issued in June 2006. The Panel was reconvened from late 2011 and, in May 2013, released a second report entitled *Addressing Key Economic Issues to Advance Sustainable Development: Ideas for Actions*, which recommended the creation, under UNCTAD auspices, of a Development Observatory of Global Economic and Financial Governance, with the aim of safeguarding the interests of developing countries during reforms to the global economic and financial framework.

In July 2012 and July 2013 ad hoc expert group meetings on consumer protection were convened at UNCTAD headquarters, with the aim of reviewing and updating the non-binding UN Guidelines for Consumer Protection (adopted by the UN General Assembly in April 1985), including providing for increased transparency and disclosure in financial services. The UNCTAD Secretariat was to present a report on the interface between competition and consumer policies to a review conference on consumer protection that was scheduled to be held in 2015.

UN conferences on cocoa, jute, olive oil, restrictive business practices and tropical timber are convened periodically under UNCTAD auspices.

INTERNATIONAL TRADE IN GOODS AND SERVICES, AND COMMODITIES

In working to secure development gains from participation in international trade and globalization, the Division on International Trade in Goods and Services, and Commodities monitors and assesses trends in the international trading system from a development perspective. Among other activities, each year UNCTAD prepares an assessment of key developments in the international trading system for consideration and deliberation by the Trade and Development Board and the UN General Assembly. The Division quantifies the positive interaction between trade and development, and has developed the Trade and Development Index (TDI), covering 125 countries, as a diagnostic tool for policy-makers and researchers. It supports international trade and trade negotiations, and provides assistance to developing countries in clarifying and exploring the development dimension of the international trading system, particularly the WTO Doha Round negotiations, and in strengthening regional economic integration. It promotes South-South trade, including through trade finance, and through servicing the 1989 Global System of Trade Preferences among Developing Countries (GSTP) Agreement. In December 2010 the parties to the GSTP, meeting in Foz do Iguaçu, Brazil, adopted the São Paulo Round Protocol to Agreement, which was deposited with UNCTAD. UNCTAD aims to increase the participation of developing countries in global services trade. Support is given to developing countries to enhance their knowledge of issues of particular concern to them relating to services, to assess the contribution of services to development, and to reform and formulate regulatory and institutional frameworks focused on building supply capacity. UNCTAD works to increase developing countries' participation in new and dynamic sectors of global trade, including creative products and industries, and serves as a global centre of excellence in managing trade data, statistics and related analytical software. A Trade Analysis Branch (TAB) of the Division on International Trade in Goods and Services, and Commodities undertakes policy-oriented analytical work aimed at improving the understanding of relevant and emerging issues in international trade. UNCTAD maintains an Agricultural Trade Policy Simulation Model (ATPSM); and helps countries to set up competition policies and laws, and to develop voluntary norms to combat anti-competitive practices in national and global markets and to promote consumer welfare. UNCTAD is the focal point of work on competition policy and related consumer welfare within the UN system and hosts an annual meeting of an Intergovernmental Group of Experts on Competition Law and Policy. In 2005 UNCTAD established ad hoc voluntary peer reviews on competition law and policy. Developing countries are also helped to design policies and strategies to strengthen their competitive productive capacities and trade-related infrastructures. UNCTAD aims to promote the achievement through trade of the UN Millennium Development Goals, and to promote UN system-wide coherence on trade matters. It services a number of UN task forces and co-ordination mechanisms to facilitate greater synergy and co-operation in the UN's development work. A joint UN Environment Programme/UNCTAD Capacity Building Task Force on Trade, Environment and Development aims to strengthen the capacities of countries to address issues relating to trade, the environment and development. UNCTAD also supports research and technical assistance in a range of subjects linking trade and the environment, including organic agriculture, the use of renewable energy technologies and the protection of traditional knowledge. The 2013 edition of the triennial *Trade and Environment Review*, issued in September, was subtitled 'Wake up before it is too late: Make agriculture truly sustainable now for food security in a changing climate'. With FAO and other agencies the WTO participates in the Agricultural Market Information System (AMIS), founded in 2011 to improve market transparency and help stabilize food price volatility.

UNCTAD and the WTO jointly manage the International Trade Centre (ITC), based in Geneva, Switzerland, which helps developing countries and countries with economies in transition to achieve sustainable human development through the export of goods and services.in In March 2014 UNCTAD and the ITC signed a Memorandum of Understanding on jointly assisting developing countries in the implementation of the WTO Trade Facilitation Agreement concluded in December 2013.

UNCTAD convenes an annual Global Services Forum, at which representatives of governments, business and academia gather to share best practices and to establish partnerships aimed at fostering growth in the services sector and sustainable development. The 2014 Forum was to be held in late May–early June, in Beijing, People's Republic of China.

INVESTMENT AND ENTERPRISE DEVELPMENT

As the focal point of the UN system on matters related to investment UNCTAD promotes the understanding of key issues, particularly matters related to foreign direct investment (FDI) and enterprise development. The Division on Investment and Enterprise (DIAE) also assists developing countries, in particular LDCs and countries with special needs, in formulating and implementing active policies aimed at boosting productive capacities and international competitiveness and in participating more fully in international investment agreements (IIAs). In order to accomplish this objective, the DIAE carries out research and policy analysis on the development impact of FDI in the areas of IIAs, national FDI policies, intellectual property, and enterprise development and business facilitation. An *IIA Monitor* is published four times a year. Technical assistance includes organizing seminars for policy-makers and the training of trade negotiators, some of it through a distance-learning programme. The annual *World Investment Report (WIR)* is a main point of reference for policy-makers and practitioners in this area, providing data on issues pertaining to FDI and transnational corporations (TNCs), as well as analysing trends and developments in FDI, examining the implications of activities by TNCs in relation to these trends, and assessing consequent international and national policy issues of relevance to developing countries. The 2013 edition of *WIR*—issued in June and subtitled *Global value chains: investment and trade for development* —made recommendations to governments of developing economies on efficiently channelling investment to enable the achievement of progress up global value chains. UNCTAD's *Global Investment Trends Monitor* reports three times a year on the state of global FDI inflows; the January 2014 edition reported that these had increased by 11% in 2013, representing a return to pre-global economic crisis levels. The DIAE also assists developing countries in establishing an enabling policy framework for attracting and benefiting from FDI. In this respect, UNCTAD supports these nations in undertaking Investment Policy Reviews (IPRs), objective analyses of how national policy, regulatory and institutional systems attract or inhibit FDI; by 2014 some 35 IPRs had been implemented. UNCTAD also assists developing countries in implementing the recommendations of IPRs. Other capacity-building programmes include assistance to developing countries in collecting, improving, and harmonizing statistics on FDI; in negotiating international investment agreements; in investment promotion and facilitation; and in linking foreign affiliates and domestic enterprises. UNCTAD is also mandated to provide a platform for international dialogue on best practices in investment policies, and supports developing countries in promoting their enterprise development, through upgrading entrepreneurship, harmonizing international accounting and reporting standards, developing competitive insurance markets, and through an e-tourism initiative. UNCTAD's Empretec programme, initiated in 32 developing countries worldwide, trains and encourages entrepreneurs. The DIAE also services the Intergovernmental Group of Experts on International Standards on Accounting and Reporting (ISAR), which aims to assist developing countries and economies in transition with the implementation of best practices in corporate transparency and accounting. Since 2008 UNCTAD has organized a World Investment Forum, held every two years, to promote dialogue among government ministers, corporate executives, investors and heads of investment promotion agencies on investment-related issues and challenges. The fourth Forum was to be convened in Sea Island, Georgia, USA, in May 2014.

GLOBALIZATION AND DEVELOPMENT STRATEGIES

UNCTAD works to promote policies and strategies at national and international levels, and analyses issues related to globalization, international trade and finance, in support of economic management for sustainable development. Every September UNCTAD publishes its flagship *Trade and Development Report (TDR)*. The 2013 *TDR* focused on income inequality. Through its Debt Management and Financial Analysis System (DMFAS), a joint programme with the World Bank, UNCTAD provides assistance to developing countries on debt management, helping debtor countries to analyse data, make projections, and plan strategies for debt repayment and reorganization with the help of modern information technology. By 2014 the programme had supported 69 countries. UNCTAD provides training for operators and senior officials to raise awareness of institutional reforms that might be necessary for effective debt management. UNCTAD also supports developing countries in their negotiations on debt owed to developed countries' governments, in the context of the Paris Club, and every year it provides a report on the external debt of developing countries to the UN General Assembly. Since 1995 UNCTAD has also provided technical assistance to support the Palestinian people and the development of the Palestinian economy; it determined in 2008 to intensify support to Palestine in order to alleviate economic and social hardships and to strengthen its state-building efforts.

TECHNOLOGY AND LOGISTICS

Within the UN system UNCTAD provides intellectual leadership and serves as a source of expertise in the areas of science, technology, innovation and information and communication technologies. Substantive and technical servicing is provided to the Commission on Science and Technology for Development (CSTD), and work is undertaken in the areas of science, technology and innovation policy, as well as technology transfer. In the area of information and communication technologies (ICTs), relevant mandates are implemented through policy research, and providing support to enable the participation of developing countries and transition economies in international discussions and policy debates. Furthermore, technical assistance projects are undertaken with a view to helping build the capacity of developing countries in the areas of science, technology, innovation and ICTs. UNCTAD's annual *Information Economy Report* tracks recent ICT trends and assesses strategies to enhance the development impact of these technologies in developing countries. The 2013 edition focused on the potential benefits for developing countries of cloud computing. UNCTAD's Virtual Institute on Trade and Development, established in 2004, aims to strengthen capacities at universities in developing and transition countries for the teaching and researching of trade issues. In June 2004 UNCTAD launched an e-tourism initiative to help small economies and island developing countries reach their full tourism development potential using ICTs. UNCTAD conducts a regular three-week flagship course on trade and development, 'Key Issues on the International Economic Agenda', that was initiated in 2001. UNCTAD's work on trade logistics focuses on research and analysis, technical assistance and consensus building. Analytical studies and reports are prepared in the field of transport, and advice is provided to advance developing country policy-makers' and traders' understanding of international trade mechanisms and frameworks. The ASYCUDA programme software, adopted by more than 90 countries worldwide, helps to automate customs procedures and further facilitate trade transactions.

AFRICA AND SPECIAL PROGRAMMES

Development of Africa: UNCTAD undertakes analysis of African socio-economic issues and uses its findings to advance global understanding of that continent's development challenges, and to promote action at national, regional and international levels with a view to accelerating both regional development and greater participation by African countries in the global economy; UNCTAD co-operates closely with the New Partnership for Africa's development (NEPAD), with a particular focus on its agriculture, market access and diversification areas of activity; UNCTAD also participates in the annual regional consultations of UN agencies active in Africa. Since 2000 UNCTAD has published an annual *Economic Development in Africa Report*; the 2013 edition, released in July, focused on 'Intra-African trade: unleashing private-sector dynamism'.

Landlocked Developing Countries: in 2014 there were 31 LLDCs, of which 15 were located in Africa, 12 were in Asia, two were in Latin America, and three were in Europe; LLDCs experience strong challenges to growth and development owing to factors including poor physical infrastructure, weak institutional and productive capacities, small domestic markets, remoteness from maritime ports and therefore world markets, and high vulnerability to external shocks; the need to transport goods through neighbouring territory tends to incur high transaction costs resulting in reduced competitiveness; UNCTAD's multidimensional approach to landlocked states includes developing adequate national transport networks and efficient transit systems, promoting regional or subregional economic integration, and encouraging FDI in economic activities that are not distance-sensitive. In 1995 the Global Framework for Transit Transport Co-operation between Landlocked and Transit Developing Countries and the Donor Community was endorsed by the UN General Assembly, with a view to enhancing transit systems and enabling LLDCs to reduce their marginalization from world markets. In 2003 the UN convened an international ministerial conference, in Almatı, Kazakhstan, which aimed to enhance transit transport co-operation between landlocked and transit developing countries. The resulting Declaration and Almatı Programme of Action addressed infrastructure development and maintenance, transit policy issues, and trade facilitation measures. UNCTAD participates in the implementation of the Almatı Programme of Action through analytical work on the transit transport and related development problems confronting LLDCs, and also through the provision of technical assistance to these countries in areas such as trade facilitation and electronic commerce. In 2005 the first meeting of LLDC Ministers responsible for trade, convened in Asunción, Paraguay, adopted the Asunción Platform for the Doha Development Round, which aimed to harmonize the positions of LLDCs in multilateral trade negotiations. A 10-Year Review Conference of the Almatı Programme of Action was to be held in 2014.

LDCs: UNCTAD aims to give particular attention to the needs of the world's 49 LDCs, the large majority of which (35) are in Africa; the UN has since 1971 (using established criteria based on gross national income per capita, weak human assets, and economic vulnerability) classified as LDCs states that are deemed highly disadvantaged in their development processes; in view of the UN's recognition of the particular challenges confronting LDCs, the development partners of these countries have adopted certain special support measures aimed at: reducing LDCs' competitive disadvantages in the global economy; supporting the development of LDCs' physical infrastructure and human resources; and enhancing their institutional capacities; LDC-specific treatment is focused on three main areas of international co-operation: the multilateral trading system (where special concessions, such as non-reciprocal market access preferences, are granted to LDCs); development financing (where donors are expected to give especially favourable consideration to LDCs when making decisions on concessionary financing); and technical assistance (with priority being given to LDCs under all UN development programming); UNCTAD's ninth session, held in April–May 1996, determined that particular attention be given to the problems of the LDCs in all areas of UNCTAD's work. In April 2008 the 12th session emphasized the urgent need to take global action to protect the world's poor from the ongoing global financial and food crises and ensuing global recession. UNCTAD XIII, convened in April 2012, noted with concern that LDCs remained vulnerable to external shocks (for example relating to natural disasters and to food, fuel, and economic and financial crises), and to the adverse impacts of climate change, and so urged a redoubling of efforts to enhance international support to them. UNICEF is a partner—with the IMF, the International Trade Centre, the UN Development Programme, the World Bank and the WTO—in the Enhanced Integrated Framework (EIF) for trade-related assistance to LDCs, a multi-donor programme which aims to support greater participation by LDCs in the global trading system; EIF funding is channelled through a dedicated EIF Trust Fund. The EIF replaced in 2007, and builds upon, a former Integrated Framework, which was established in 1997. Four UN Conferences on the LDCs have been convened under UNCTAD auspices, in 1981, 1990, 2001 and 2011. LDC IV, held in

İstanbul, Turkey, in May 2011, approved the Istanbul Programme of Action, which included a provision that national parliaments should be engaged in debating development strategies as well as in overseeing their implementation, and had the ultimate objective of enabling at least one-half of then current LDCs to graduate from LDC status by 2020. UNCTAD publishes an annual *Least Developed Countries Report*, which in 2013 was issued in November, with a focus on the theme 'Growth with employment for inclusive and sustainable development'.

Small Island Developing States (SIDS): since 1974 the UN has recognized the particular problems of SIDS, which are deemed to be at greater risk of marginalization from the global economy than many other developing countries, owing to adverse consequences arising from their small size; remoteness from large markets (resulting in high transport costs); high economic vulnerability to economic and natural shocks beyond domestic control; fragile ecosystems and high exposure to globally induced phenomena such as rises in sea levels; and frequently unstable agricultural production, owing to increased exposure to natural disasters; there is no formal listing of SIDS, but, for analytical purposes, UNCTAD uses an unofficial list comprising 29 SIDS; the first Global Conference on the Sustainable Development of SIDS (held in Barbados, in April–May 1994) adopted a Programme of Action for the Sustainable Development of SIDS; an International Meeting to Review the Implementation of the Programme of Action (convened in Mauritius, in January 2005) approved the Mauritius Strategy for the Further Implementation of the Programme of Action for the Sustainable Development of SIDS, which addressed the serious disadvantages suffered by many SIDS in the global economy; a High-level Review Meeting on the implementation of the Mauritius Strategy, convened in September 2010, adopted an Outcome Document reaffirming commitment to supporting SIDS' development efforts, acknowledging the significant threat posed to SIDS by climate change and sea level rises, and recognizing the need to advance internationally a preventive approach towards alleviating the effects of natural disasters on SIDS, including reducing risks and properly integrating risk management into development policies. A second Global Conference on Small Island States was to be convened in September 2014, in Apia, Samoa.

SPECIAL UNIT ON COMMODITIES

UNCTAD's Special Unit on Commodities provides analysis and technical co-operation and builds international consensus among member states on deepening understanding of the relationship between commodity production and trade and poverty reduction. Major areas of activity include focusing on making the commodity sector an instrument of poverty reduction by facilitating the access of small and poor commodity producers to markets; supporting diversification towards higher-value products and encouraging the stronger parts of the value chain to support the weaker parts; promoting the use of market-based instruments for generating finance, particularly for the disadvantaged parts of the value chain; focusing on the role of exchanges as facilitators for commodity-based development; publishing statistics; finding ways to enable producers to meet both official and private sector standards; developing ways of promoting broad-based economic development and diversification in mining-dependent areas; enhancing activities dealing with energy, particularly oil and gas, and organizing annual conferences on oil and gas trade and finance in Africa; and convening and servicing UN conferences relating to international commodity bodies. UNCTAD convenes annually a Global Commodities Forum; the fifth Forum was held in April 2014, on the theme 'Global value chains, transparency, and commodity-based development'.

CHIEF EXECUTIVES BOARD (CEB) INTER-AGENCY CLUSTER ON TRADE AND PRODUCTIVE CAPACITY

UNCTAD leads the UN's CEB Inter-agency Cluster on Trade and Productive Capacity, which was established in April 2007 to co-ordinate trade and development operations at national and regional levels within the UN system. Other partner organizations in the Cluster are: UNIDO, UNDP, FAO, the International Trade Centre, WTO, the five UN Regional Commissions, UNEP, UNOPS, and (since December 2010) the UN Commission on International Trade Law. The Cluster has participated in pilot activities under the *Delivering as One* process.

Finance

The operational expenses of UNCTAD are borne by the regular budget of the UN, and amount to approximately US $68m. annually. Technical co-operation activities, financed from extra-budgetary resources, amount to some $40m. annually.

Publications

Development and Globalization: Facts and Figures.
Economic Development in Africa Report.
Global Investment Trends Monitor (3 a year).
Information Economy Report.
Least Developed Countries Report (annually).
Review of Maritime Transport (annually).
Trade and Development Report (annually).
Trade and Environment Review.
UNCTAD Handbook of Statistics (annually, also available online).
World Commodity Survey.
World Investment Report (annually).
Policy briefs, other abstracts, reviews and reports.

United Nations Development Programme—UNDP

Address: One United Nations Plaza, New York, NY 10017, USA.
Telephone: (212) 906-5300; **fax:** (212) 906-5364; **e-mail:** hq@undp.org; **internet:** www.undp.org.

UNDP was established in 1965 by the UN General Assembly. Its central mission is to help countries to eradicate poverty and achieve a sustainable level of human development, an approach to economic growth that encompasses individual well-being and choice, equitable distribution of the benefits of development, and conservation of the environment. UNDP co-ordinates global and national efforts to achieve the UN Millennium Development Goals, and is contributing to the formulation of a post-2015 UN system-wide development framework.

Organization

(April 2014)

UNDP is responsible to the UN General Assembly, to which it reports through the Economic and Social Council (ECOSOC).

EXECUTIVE BOARD

The Executive Board is responsible for providing intergovernmental support to, and supervision of, the activities of UNDP and the UN Population Fund (UNFPA). It comprises 36 members: eight from Africa, seven from Asia and the Pacific, four from Eastern Europe, five from Latin America and the Caribbean and 12 from Western Europe and other countries. Members serve a three-year term.

SECRETARIAT

Offices and divisions at the Secretariat include an Operations Support Group; Offices of the United Nations Development Group, the Human Development Report, Development Studies, Audit and Performance Review, Evaluation, and Communications; and Bureaux for Crisis Prevention and Recovery; Partnerships; Development Policy; and Management. Five regional bureaux, all headed by an assistant administrator, cover Africa; Asia and the Pacific; the Arab states; Latin America and the Caribbean; and Europe and the Commonwealth of Independent States. UNDP's Administrator (the third most senior UN official, after the Secretary-General and the Deputy Secretary-General) is in charge of strategic policy and overall co-ordination of UN development activities (including the chairing of the UN Development Group), while the Associate Administrator supervises the operations and management of UNDP programmes.

Administrator: HELEN CLARK (New Zealand).

Associate Administrator: (vacant).

Assistant Administrator and Director of the Bureau for Crisis Prevention and Recovery: JORDAN RYAN (USA).

Assistant Administrator and Director of the Bureau for Development Policy a.i.: MAGDY MARTÍNEZ-SOLMÁN (Spain).

Assistant Administrator and Director of the Bureau of External Relations and Advocacy: MICHAEL O'NEILL (United Kingdom).

Assistant Administrator and Director of the Bureau of Management: JENS WANDEL (Denmark).

COUNTRY OFFICES

In almost every country receiving UNDP assistance there is an office, headed by the UNDP Resident Representative, who usually also serves as the UN Resident Co-ordinator and Humanitarian Co-ordinator, responsible for the co-ordination of all UN technical assistance, humanitarian operations and development activities in that country, so as to ensure the most effective use of UN and international aid resources.

Activities

UNDP works as the UN's global development network, advocating for change and connecting countries to knowledge, experience and resources to help people to build a better life. In 2014 UNDP was active in 177 countries. It provides advisory and support services to governments and UN teams with the aim of advancing sustainable human development and building national development capabilities. Assistance is mostly non-monetary, comprising the provision of experts' services, consultancies, equipment and training for local workers. Developing countries themselves contribute significantly to the total project costs in terms of personnel, facilities, equipment and supplies. UNDP also supports programme countries in attracting aid and utilizing it efficiently.

In 1997 the UNDP Administrator was appointed to chair the UN Development Group (UNDG), which promotes coherent policy at country level through the system of UN Resident Co-ordinators, the Common Country Assessment mechanism (CCA, a process for evaluating national development needs), and the UN Development Assistance Framework (UNDAF, for planning and co-ordination development operations at country level, based on the CCA). UNDP maintains a series of Thematic Trust Funds to channel support to priority programme activities.

UNDP's 2014–17 Strategic Plan, adopted in September 2013, focused the organization's work around the following desired outcomes: inclusive and sustainable development and growth; stronger systems of democratic governance; strengthened delivery of universal basic services; faster progress in reducing gender inequality; enabling member states to reduce the likelihood of conflict and natural disasters; promoting the rapid return to sustainable development pathways in post-conflict and post-natural disaster scenarios; and the prioritization of poverty, inequality and exclusion in development debates and actions at all levels. UNDP's development activities were to place particular emphasis on: people living in poverty (as defined by UNDP's Multidimensional Poverty Index, the global US $1.25 per day poverty line, and national poverty lines); and groups experiencing the greatest social inequalities and exclusion, especially women, female-headed households and youth. The principal focal areas of work under the Strategic Plan were: how to adopt sustainable development pathways; how to build and/or strengthen inclusive and effective democratic governance; and how to build resilience.

UNDP, jointly with the World Bank, leads an initiative on 'additional financing for the most vulnerable', the first of nine activities that were launched in April 2009 by the UN System Chief Executives Board for Co-ordination (CEB), with the aim of alleviating the impact on poor and vulnerable populations of the developing global economic crisis.

MILLENNIUM DEVELOPMENT GOALS

UNDP, through its leadership of the UNDG and management of the Resident Co-ordinator system, has a co-ordinating function as the focus of UN system-wide efforts to achieve the so-called Millennium Development Goals (MDGs), pledged by UN member governments attending a summit meeting of the UN General Assembly in September 2000. The objectives were to establish a defined agenda to reduce poverty and improve the quality of lives of millions of people and to serve as a framework for measuring development. There are eight MDGs, as follows, for which one or more specific targets have been identified:

i) to eradicate extreme poverty and hunger, with the aim of reducing by 50% (compared with the 1990 figure) the number of people with an income of less than US $1 a day and those suffering from hunger by 2015, and to achieve full and productive employment and decent work for all, including women and young people;

ii) to achieve universal primary education by 2015;

iii) to promote gender equality and empower women, in particular to eliminate gender disparities in primary and secondary education by 2005 and at all levels by 2015;

iv) to reduce child mortality, with a target reduction of two-thirds in the mortality rate among children under five by 2015 (compared with the 1990 level);

v) to improve maternal health, specifically to reduce by 75% the numbers of women dying in childbirth and to achieve universal access to reproductive health by 2015 (compared with the 1990 level);

vi) to combat HIV/AIDS, malaria and other diseases, with targets to have halted and begun to reverse the incidence of HIV/AIDS, malaria and other major diseases by 2015 and to achieve universal access to treatment for HIV/AIDS for all those who need it by 2010;

vii) to ensure environmental sustainability, including targets to integrate the principles of sustainable development into country policies and programmes, to reduce by 50% (compared with the 1990 level) the number of people without access to safe drinking water by 2015, and to achieve significant improvement in the lives of at least 100m. slum dwellers by 2020;

viii) to develop a global partnership for development, including an open, rule-based, non-discriminatory trading and financial system, and efforts to deal with international debt, to address the needs of least developed countries (LDCs) and landlocked and small island developing states, to provide access to affordable, essential drugs in developing countries, and to make available the benefits of new technologies.

UNDP plays a leading role in efforts to integrate the MDGs into all aspects of UN activities at country level and to ensure that the MDGs are incorporated into national development strategies. UNDP supports efforts by countries, as well as regions and sub-regions, to report on progress towards achievement of the goals, and on specific social, economic and environmental indicators, through the formulation of MDG reports. These form the basis of an annual global report, issued by the UN Secretary-General. UNDP also works to raise awareness of the MDGs and to support advocacy efforts at all levels. UNDP provides administrative and technical support to the Millennium Project, an independent advisory body established by the UN Secretary-General in 2002 to develop a practical action plan to achieve the MDGs. Financial support of the Project is channelled through a Millennium Trust Fund, administered by UNDP. In January 2005 the Millennium Project presented its report, based on extensive research conducted by teams of experts, which included recommendations for the international system to support country level development efforts and identified a series of 'Quick Wins' to bring conclusive benefit to millions of people in the short-term. International commitment to achieve the MDGs by 2015 was reiterated at a World Summit, convened in September 2005. In December 2006 UNDP and the Spanish Government concluded an agreement on the establishment of the MDG Achievement Fund (MDG-F), which aims to support the acceleration of progress towards the achievement of the MDGs and to enhance co-operation at country level between UN development partners. UNDP and the UN Department of Economic and Social Affairs (UNDESA) are lead agencies in co-ordinating the work of the MDG Gap Task Force, which was established by the UN Secretary-General in May 2007 to track, systematically and at both international and country level, existing international commitments in the areas of official development assistance, market access, debt relief, access to essential medicines and technology. In November the UN, in partnership with two major US companies, launched an online MDG Monitor to track progress and to support organizations working to achieve the goals. In September 2010 UNDP launched the MDGs Acceleration Framework, which aimed to support countries in identifying and overcoming barriers to eradicating extreme poverty and achieving sustainable development. The 2013 edition of the *Millennium Development Goals Report*, issued in July of that year, reported that progress towards achieving the MDGs remained uneven between regions, countries, and also between population groups within countries, with communities living in poverty or in rural areas facing unfair disadvantage.

POST-2015 DEVELOPMENT FRAMEWORK

In January 2012 the UN Secretary-General established a UN System Task Team—led jointly by the UNDP Administrator-General and the UN Under-Secretary-General for Economic and Social Affairs—which supports system-wide consultations in 11 thematic areas, each led by specified UN agencies, on the advancement of the post-2015 global development agenda. In May and July, respectively, the Co-Chairs and membership were announced of a new High-level Panel to Advise on the Global Development Agenda Beyond 2015, and in September 2012 the Panel's Executive Secretary was appointed and the Panel's inaugural meeting was held, on the sidelines of the UN General Assembly. In May 2013 the Panel presented to the UN Secretary-General a draft document entitled *A New Global Partner-*

ship: Eradicate Poverty and Transform Economies through Sustainable Development, which set out a universal agenda to eradicate extreme poverty globally by 2030, and to pursue and deliver sustainable development. The Panel consulted closely with a working group of experts tasked by the UN Conference on Sustainable Development (convened in June 2012) to formulate a series of Sustainable Development Goals. In September 2013 a special event on the MDGs, convened by the UN General Assembly, requested that a summit meeting be held in September 2015 to adopt a set of follow-on Development Goals that would build on and supersede the MDGs. In March 2014 the UNDG announced that a series of Dialogues on Implementation of the Post-2015 Development Agenda were to be initiated in, at first, some 50 countries, with participation by policy makers, and representatives of civil society, local communities and the private sector; the Dialogues were to be supplemented by internet-based public consultations.

The thematic areas in which consultations were under way in 2013–14 are as follows:

i) Conflict and fragility: led by UNDP, UNICEF, the UN Peacebuilding Support Office and the Inter-Agency Secretariat of the International Strategy for Disaster Reduction;

ii) Education, led by UNESCO and UNICEF;

iii) Energy, led by UN-Energy, the Sustainable Energy for All initiative of the UN Secretary-General, UNDP, UNIDO, UNDESA, and the World Bank;

iv) Environmental sustainability, led by UNDP and UNEP;

v) Food security and Nutrition, led by WFP and FAO;

vi) Governance, led by UNDP and OHCHR;

vii) Growth and employment, led by UNDP, the ILO and UNDESA;

viii) Health, led by WHO and UNICEF;

ix) Inequalities, led by UNDP, the ILO and UNDESA;

x) Population dynamics, led by UNFPA, UN-Habitat, the International Organization for Migration and UNDESA;

xi) Water, facilitated by UN-Water, and co-led by UNICEF and UNDESA.

DEMOCRATIC GOVERNANCE

UNDP supports national efforts to ensure efficient and accountable governance, to improve the quality of democratic processes, and to build effective relations between the state, the private sector and civil society, which are essential to achieving sustainable development. As in other practice areas, UNDP assistance includes policy advice and technical support, the capacity building of institutions and individuals, advocacy and public information and communication, the promotion and brokering of dialogue, and knowledge networking and sharing of good practices.

UNDP works to strengthen parliaments and other legislative bodies as institutions of democratic participation. It assists with constitutional reviews and reform, training of parliamentary staff, and capacity building of political parties and civil organizations as part of this objective. In April 2012, jointly with the Inter-Parliamentary Union, UNDP released the *Global Parliamentary Report*, which addressed means of improving strategies to meet public expectations of parliaments. UNDP undertakes missions to help prepare for and ensure the conduct of free and fair elections. It helps to build the long-term capacity of electoral institutions and practices within a country, for example by assisting with voter registration, the establishment of electoral commissions, providing observers to verify that elections are free and fair, projects to educate voters, and training journalists to provide impartial election coverage.

Within its justice sector programme UNDP supports projects to improve access to justice, in particular for the poor and disadvantaged, and to promote judicial independence, legal reform and understanding of the legal system. UNDP also works to promote access to information, the integration of human rights issues into activities concerned with sustainable human development, and support for the international human rights system.

UNDP is mandated to assist developing countries to fight corruption and improve accountability, transparency and integrity (ATI). It has worked to establish national and international partnerships in support of its anti-corruption efforts and used its role as a broker of knowledge and experience to uphold ATI principles at all levels of public financial management and governance. UNDP publishes case studies of its anti-corruption efforts and assists governments to conduct self-assessments of their public financial management systems. UNDP leads the new secretariat of the International Aid Transparency Initiative, which was inaugurated, in collaboration with other members of the multi-stakeholder steering committee, in September 2013.

In March 2002 a UNDP Governance Centre was inaugurated in Oslo, Norway, to enhance the role of UNDP in support of democratic governance and to assist countries to implement democratic reforms in order to achieve the MDGs. The Centre undertakes analysis of governance projects and emerging issues, and provides training programmes and workshops. The Democratic Governance Network allows discussion and the sharing of information. An iKnow Politics Network, supported by UNDP, aims to help women become involved in politics.

POVERTY REDUCTION

UNDP aims to promote sustainable human development by ensuring that national development policies emphasize the needs of the poor and marginalized, and by supporting developing countries in integrating human rights principles and standards into the design and implementation of development policies (on the basis that equal opportunities and freedoms are conducive to the promotion of economic growth with an inclusive impact). Activities aimed at facilitating poverty eradication include support for capacity-building programmes and initiatives to generate sustainable livelihoods, for example by improving access to credit, land and technologies, and the promotion of strategies to improve education and health provision for the poorest elements of populations (especially women and girls). UNDP aims to help governments to reassess their development priorities and to design initiatives for sustainable human development. Following the introduction, in 1999, by the World Bank and IMF of Poverty Reduction Strategy Papers (PRSPs), UNDP has helped governments to draft these documents, and, since 2001, has linked the papers to efforts to achieve and monitor progress towards the MDGs. In 2004 UNDP inaugurated the International Poverty Centre for Inclusive Growth (IPC-IG), in Brasília, Brazil, which fosters the capacity of countries to formulate and implement poverty reduction strategies and encourages South-South co-operation in all relevant areas of research and decision-making. In particular, the Centre aims to assist countries to meet MDGs through research into and implementation of pro-poor policies that encourage social protection and human development, and through the monitoring of poverty and inequality. UNDP's Secretariat hosts the UN Office for South-South Cooperation, which was established, as the Special Unit for South-South Cooperation, by the United Nations General Assembly in 1978.

UNDP country offices support the formulation of national human development reports (NHDRs), which aim to facilitate activities such as policy-making, the allocation of resources, and monitoring progress towards poverty eradication and sustainable development. In addition, the preparation of Advisory Notes and Country Co-operation Frameworks by UNDP officials helps to highlight country-specific aspects of poverty eradication and national strategic priorities. Since 1990 UNDP has published an annual *Human Development Report*, incorporating a Human Development Index, which ranks countries in terms of human development, using three key indicators: life expectancy, adult literacy and basic income required for a decent standard of living. The Report also includes a Human Poverty Index and a Gender-related Development Index, which assesses gender equality on the basis of life expectancy, education and income. The 2013 edition of the Report, *The Rise of the South: Human Progress in a Diverse World*, was released in April. UNDP proposed to the June 2012 UNCSD a future 'Sustainable Human Development Index', which would recognize the impact on future generations of contemporary development, and place a high value on factors such as dignity and sustainability, alongside economic development. Jointly with the International Labour Organization (ILO), UNDP operates a Programme on Employment for Poverty Reduction, which undertakes analysis and studies, and supports countries in improving their employment strategies. In March 2012 the first Global Human Development Forum was convened, under UNDP auspices, in İstanbul, Turkey; delegates (comprising experts on development, and representatives of the UN, governments, the private sector and civil society) adopted the Istanbul Declaration, urging that the global development agenda should be redrafted, and calling for concerted global action against social inequities and environmental degradation.

In March 2014 UNDP launched its first ever Youth Strategy ('Empowered Youth, Sustainable Future'), which made recommendations for the engagement of young people and a wide range of partners in addressing youth empowerment issues globally.

UNDP is committed to ensuring that the process of economic and financial globalization, including national and global trade, debt and capital flow policies, incorporates human development concerns. It aimed to ensure that the Doha Development Round of World Trade Organization (WTO) negotiations should achieve an expansion of trade opportunities and economic growth to less developed countries. UNDP is a partner—with the IMF, the International Trade Centre, the UN Conference on Trade and Development (UNCTAD), the World Bank and the WTO—in the Enhanced Integrated Framework (EIF) for trade-related assistance to LDCs, a multi-donor programme which aims to support greater participation by LDCs in the global trading system; EIF funds are channelled through a dedicated EIF Trust Fund.

UNDP has a leading role in the World Alliance of Cities Against Poverty, which was inaugurated in 1996 as a network of municipal authorities committed to addressing and co-operating on the challenges of urbanization, including poor housing, transport, the management of waste disposal, water supply and sanitation. The eighth global Forum of the Alliance convened in Dublin, Ireland, in February 2013.

UNDP sponsors the International Day for the Eradication of Poverty, held annually on 17 October.

ENVIRONMENT AND ENERGY

UNDP aims to strengthen national capacities to implement effective and sustainable environmental management policies and practices, including addressing the challenges of climate change. Together with the UN Environment Programme (UNEP) and the World Bank, UNDP is an implementing agency of the Global Environment Facility (GEF), which was established in 1991 to finance international co-operation in projects to benefit the environment.

In November 2013 UNDP, with UNEP and the UNFCC, issued a joint publication, *Guidance for NAMA Design: Building on Country Experiences*, which outlined practical means by which governments and organizations might design and implement Nationally Appropriate Mitigation Actions (NAMAs) aimed at mitigating greenhouse gas emissions.

UNDP recognizes that desertification, land degradation and drought (DLDD) are major causes of rural poverty and promotes sustainable land management, drought preparedness and reform of land tenure as means of addressing the problem. It also aims to reduce poverty caused by land degradation through implementation of environmental conventions at national and international level. In June 2009 UNDP and the Secretariat of the UN Convention to Combat Desertification in Those Countries Experiencing Serious Drought and/or Desertification, Particularly in Africa (UNCCD) agreed a pilot strategic working partnership, based on the UNCCD's strategic priorities in combating DLDD and on UNDP's implementation support capabilities at the national level. A formal UNDP/UNCCD programme of co-operation was concluded in March 2012. UNDP is also concerned with sustainable management of forestries, fisheries and agriculture. Since 1992 UNDP has administered a Small Grants Programme, funded by the GEF, to support community-based initiatives concerned with biodiversity conservation, prevention of land degradation and the elimination of persistent organic pollutants. The Equator Initiative, inaugurated in 2002, as a partnership between UNDP and representatives of governments, civil society and businesses, aims to reduce poverty in communities along the equatorial belt by fostering local partnerships, harnessing local knowledge and promoting conservation and sustainable practices. UNDP is a partner agency of the Climate and Clean Air Coalition to Reduce Short Lived Climate Pollutants (SLCPs), which was launched in February 2012 with the aim of combating SLCPs, including methane, black carbon and certain hydrofluorocarbons. UNDP also implements projects funded by the International Climate Initiative (launched in 2008 by the German Government).

In December 2005 UNDP (in collaboration with Fortis, a private sector provider of financial services) launched the MDG Carbon Facility, whereby developing countries that undertake projects to reduce emissions of carbon dioxide, methane and other gases responsible for global warming may sell their 'carbon credits' to finance further MDG projects. The first projects under the MDG Carbon Facility were inaugurated in February 2008, in Uzbekistan, the former Yugoslav republic of Macedonia, Yemen and Rwanda.

UNDP supports efforts to promote international co-operation in the management of chemicals. It was actively involved in the development of a Strategic Approach to International Chemicals Management which was adopted by representatives of 100 governments at an international conference convened in Dubai, United Arab Emirates, in February 2006. UNDP also assists countries to integrate the 'sound management of chemicals' into national development planning.

UNDP works to ensure the effective governance of freshwater and aquatic resources, and promotes co-operation in transboundary water management, ocean and coastal management, efforts to promote safe sanitation and community water supplies. In 1996 UNDP, with the World Bank and the Swedish International Development Agency, established a Global Water Partnership to promote and implement water resources management. UNDP, with the GEF, supports a range of projects which incorporate development and ecological requirements in the sustainable management of international waters. including the Global Mercury Project, a project for improved municipal waste-water management in coastal cities of the African, Caribbean and Pacific states, a Global Ballast Water Management Programme and an International Waters Learning Exchange and Resources Network.

CRISIS PREVENTION AND RECOVERY

UNDP collaborates with other UN agencies jn to promote relief and development efforts in countries in crisis, in order to secure the foundations for sustainable human development and thereby increase national capabilities to prevent or mitigate future crises. In particular, UNDP is concerned to achieve reconciliation, reintegration and reconstruction in affected countries, as well as to support emergency interventions and management and delivery of programme aid. It aims to facilitate the transition from relief to longer-term recovery and rehabilitation. Special development initiatives in post-conflict countries include the demobilization of former combatants and destruction of illicit small armaments, rehabilitation of communities for the sustainable reintegration of returning populations and the restoration and strengthening of democratic institutions. UNDP established a mine action unit within its Bureau for Crisis Prevention and Recovery in order to strengthen national and local de-mining capabilities including surveying, mapping and clearance of anti-personnel landmines. It also works to increase awareness of the harm done to civilians by cluster munitions, and participated in the negotiations that culminated in the entry into force in August 2010 of the international Convention on Cluster Munitions. UNDP works closely with UNICEF to raise awareness and implement risk reduction education programmes, and manages global partnership projects concerned with training, legislation and the socio-economic impact of anti-personnel devices. UNDP's '8-Point Agenda', adopted in 2005, aims to improve the security of women and girls in conflict situations and promote their participation in post-crisis recovery processes. In late 2006 UNDP began to administer the then newly established UN Peacebuilding Fund of the UN Peacebuilding Support Office. During 2008 UNDP developed a new global programme aimed at strengthening the rule of law in conflict and post-conflict countries; the programme placed particular focus on women's access to justice, institution building and transitional justice.

In 2006 UNDP launched an Immediate Crisis Response programme (known as 'SURGE') aimed at strengthening its capacity to respond quickly and effectively in the recovery phase following a conflict or natural disaster. Under the programme Immediate Crisis Response Advisors—UNDP staff with special expertise in at least one of 12 identified areas, including early recovery, operational support and resource mobilization—are swiftly deployed, in a 'SURGETeam', to UNDP country offices dealing with crises.

UNDP is the focal point within the UN system for strengthening national capacities for natural disaster reduction (prevention, preparedness and mitigation relating to natural, environmental and technological hazards). UNDP's Bureau of Crisis Prevention and Recovery, in conjunction with the Office for the Co-ordination of Humanitarian Affairs and the secretariat of the International Strategy for Disaster Reduction, oversees the system-wide Capacity for Disaster Reduction Initiative (CADRI), which was inaugurated in 2007. UNDP was actively involved in preparations for the second World Conference on Disaster Reduction, which was held in Kobe, Japan, in January 2005. Following the Kobe Conference UNDP initiated a new Global Risk Identification Programme. During 2005 the Inter-Agency Standing Committee, concerned with co-ordinating the international response to humanitarian disasters, developed a concept of providing assistance through a 'Cluster Approach', comprising core areas of activity (see OCHA). UNDP was designated the lead agency for the Early Recovery cluster, linking the immediate needs following a disaster with medium- and long-term recovery efforts. UNDP has participated in a series of consultations on a successor arrangement for the Hyogo Framework for Action that were launched in 2012 by the UN International Strategy for Disaster Reduction (UN/ISDR—the focal point of UN disaster planning); it was envisaged that the post-Hyogo arrangement (expected to be adopted by the third World Conference on Disaster Reduction, to be held in March 2015 in Sendai City, Japan) would specify measurable outcomes of disaster risk reduction planning, in addition to detailing processes, and that, in view of rapidly increasing urbanization globally, it would have a focus on building safer cities. UNDP hosts the Global Risk Identification Programme (GRIP), initiated in 2007 to support activities worldwide aimed at identifying and monitoring disaster risks. Jointly with a German postal and delivery company, UNDP also administers a 'Get Airports Ready for Disaster' programme to train local officials and formulate post-disaster preparedness strategies. In August 2012 the UNDP Administrator, stating that disaster risk management should become central to development planning, announced that UNDP disaster reduction assistance would be doubled over the next five years.

HIV/AIDS

UNDP regards the HIV/AIDS pandemic as a major challenge to development. It advocates making HIV/AIDS a focus of national planning and national poverty reduction strategies; supports decentralized action against HIV/AIDS at the community level; helps to strengthen national capacities at all levels to combat the disease; and aims to link support for prevention activities, education and treatment with broader development planning and responses. UNDP places a particular focus on combating the spread of HIV/AIDS through the promotion of women's rights. UNDP is a co-sponsor, jointly with the World Health Organization (WHO) and other UN bodies, of the Joint UN Programme on HIV/AIDS (UNAIDS), which became operational on 1 January 1996. UNAIDS co-ordinates UNDP's HIV and Development Programme. UNDP works in partnership with the Global Fund to Fight HIV/AIDS, Tuberculosis and Malaria, in particular to support the local principal recipient of grant financing and to help to manage fund projects.

Finance

From 2014–17 UNDP, UNICEF, UNFPA and UN Women were to maintain synchronized strategic planning cycles.

Publications

Annual Report of the Administrator.
Choices (quarterly).
Human Development Report (annually).
Poverty Report (annually).
Results-Oriented Annual Report.

Associated Funds and Programmes

UNDP is the central funding, planning and co-ordinating body for technical co-operation within the UN system. A number of associated funds and programmes, financed separately by means of voluntary contributions, provide specific services through the UNDP network. UNDP manages a trust fund to promote economic and technical co-operation among developing countries.

GLOBAL ENVIRONMENT FACILITY (GEF)

The GEF, which is managed jointly by UNDP, the World Bank (which hosts its secretariat) and UNEP, began operations in 1991 and was restructured in 1994. Its aim is to support projects in the six thematic areas of climate change; the conservation of biological diversity; the protection of international waters; reducing the depletion of the ozone layer in the atmosphere; arresting land degradation; and addressing the issue of persistent organic pollutants. Capacity building to allow countries to meet their obligations under international environmental agreements, and adaptation to climate change, are priority cross-cutting components of these projects. The GEF acts as the financial mechanism for the Convention on Biological Diversity and the UN Framework Convention on Climate Change. UNDP is responsible for capacity building, targeted research, pre-investment activities and technical assistance. UNDP also administers the Small Grants Programme of the GEF, which supports community-based activities by local non-governmental organizations, and the Country Dialogue Workshop Programme, which promotes dialogue on national priorities with regard to the GEF; by April 2014 the Small Grants Programme had co-financed around 3,700 community projects in more than 165 countries. In that month donor countries pledged US $4,430m. for the sixth periodic replenishment of GEF funds (GEF-6), covering the period 2015–18.

Chair. and CEO: Dr Naoko Ishii (Japan).

Executive Co-ordinator of UNDP-GEF Unit: Yannick Glemarec; 304 East 45th St, 9th Floor, New York, NY 10017, USA; fax (212) 906-6998; e-mail gefinfo@undp.org; internet www.undp.org/gef.

MDG ACHIEVEMENT FUND (MDG-F)

The Fund, established in accordance with an agreement concluded in December 2006 between UNDP and the Spanish Government, aims to support the acceleration of progress towards the achievement of the MDGs and to advance country-level co-operation between UN development partners. The Fund operates through the UN development system and focuses mainly on financing collaborative UN activities addressing multi-dimensional development challenges. The Spanish Government provided initial financing to the Fund of nearly €528m., adding some €90m. in September 2008. By 2013 some 130 programmes were under way in 50 countries, in the thematic areas of children and nutrition; climate change; conflict prevention; culture and development; economic governance; gender equality and women's empowerment; and youth employment.

Senior Adviser, MDG-F Secretariat: Paloma Duran; MDG-F Secretariat, c/o UNDP, One United Nations Plaza, New York, NY 10017, USA; tel. (212) 906-6180; fax (212) 906-5364; e-mail pb.mdgf.secretariat@undp.org; internet www.mdgfund.org.

MONTREAL PROTOCOL

Through its Montreal Protocol/Chemicals Unit UNDP collaborates with public and private partners in developing countries to assist them in eliminating the use of ozone-depleting substances (ODS), in accordance with the Montreal Protocol to the Vienna Convention for the Protection of the Ozone Layer, through the design, monitoring and evaluation of ODS phase-out projects and programmes. In particular, UNDP provides technical assistance and training, national capacity building and demonstration projects and technology transfer investment projects.

PROGRAMME OF ASSISTANCE TO THE PALESTINIAN PEOPLE (PAPP)

PAPP, established in 1978, is committed to strengthening institutions in the Israeli-occupied Territories and emerging Palestinian autonomous areas, to creating employment opportunities and to stimulating private and public investment in the area to enhance trade and export potential. Examples of PAPP activities include the following: construction of sewage collection networks and systems in the northern Gaza Strip; provision of water to 500,000 people in rural and urban areas of the West Bank and Gaza; construction of schools, youth and health centres; support to vegetable and fish traders through the construction of cold storage and packing facilities; and provision of loans to strengthen industry and commerce. In January 2009, in response to the intensive bombardment of the Gaza Strip by Israeli forces during December 2008–January 2009, with the stated aim of ending rocket attacks launched by Hamas and other militant groups on Israeli targets ('Operation Cast Lead'), PAPP distributed food packages to more than 30,000 Palestinians in the territory who were not served by UNRWA. In September 2011 PAPP launched a Consolidated Plan of Assistance, covering the period 2012–14, which aimed to support the Palestinian people in the following areas: energy resources; transport and management systems; affordable and adequate housing; education; public health services and systems; and heritage conservation.

UNDP Special Representative in the Occupied Palestinian Territories: Frode Mauring (Norway); POB 51359, Jerusalem; tel. (2) 6268200; fax (2) 6268222; e-mail registry.papp@undp.org; internet www.undp.ps.

UNDP DRYLANDS DEVELOPMENT CENTRE (DDC)

The Centre, based in Nairobi, Kenya, was established in February 2002, superseding the former UN Office to Combat Desertification and Drought (UNSO). (UNSO had been established following the conclusion, in October 1994, of the UN Convention to Combat Desertification in Those Countries Experiencing Serious Drought and/or Desertification, Particularly in Africa; in turn, UNSO had replaced the former UN Sudano-Sahelian Office.) The DDC was to focus on the following areas: ensuring that national development planning takes account of the needs of communities based in drylands (arid, semi-arid and dry sub-humid areas, with vulnerable ecoystems), particularly in poverty reduction strategies; helping countries to cope with the effects of climate variability, especially drought, and to prepare for future climate change; and addressing local issues affecting the utilization of resources. The DDC delivers UNDP's Integrated Drylands Development Programme, currently in its second phase focusing on mainstreaming drylands issues and climate change adaptation and mitigation into national policy and development frameworks; building the capacity of drylands communities to address environmental, economic and socio-cultural challenges; and supporting drylands communities through improved local governance, management and utilization of natural resources.

UN Gigiri Compound, United Nations Ave, POB 30552, 00100 Nairobi, Kenya; tel. (20) 7624640; fax (20) 7624648; e-mail ddc@undp.org; internet www.undp.org/drylands.

UNDP-UNEP POVERTY-ENVIRONMENT INITIATIVE (UNPEI)

UNPEI, inaugurated in February 2007, supports countries in developing their capacity to launch and maintain programmes that mainstream poverty-environment linkages into national development planning processes, such as MDG achievement strategies and PRSPs. In May 2007 UNDP and UNEP launched the Poverty-Environment Facility (UNPEF) to co-ordinate, and raise funds in support of, UNPEI. In 2014 UNPEI was supporting programmes in 19 countries, and also providing technical advice across all regions.

UN Gigiri Compound, United Nations Ave, POB 30552, 00100 Nairobi, Kenya; e-mail facility.unpei@unpei.org; internet www.unpei.org.

UNITED NATIONS CAPITAL DEVELOPMENT FUND (UNCDF)

The Fund was established in 1966 and became fully operational in 1974. It invests in poor communities in LDCs through local governance projects and microfinance operations, with the aim of increasing such communities' access to essential local infrastructure and services and thereby improving their productive capacities and self-reliance. UNCDF encourages participation by local people and local governments in the planning, implementation and monitoring of projects. The Fund aims to promote the interests of women in community projects and to enhance their earning capacities. UNCDF helps to develop financial services for poor communities and supports UNDP's MicroStart initiative, which assists private sector and community-based initiatives aimed at generating employment opportunities. In November 2008 UNCDF launched MicroLead, a fund (initially amounting to US $26m.) that provides loans to leading microfinance institutions and other financial service providers (MFIs/FSPs) in developing countries; MicroLead was also to focus on the provision of early support to countries in post-conflict situations. In September 2011 UNCDF and the MasterCard Foundation agreed a $23m. six-year expansion of MicroLead with a focus on sub-Saharan Africa. In October 2012 MicroLead was extended into Myanmar, with a $7m. grant from LIFT Myanmar (a multi-donor trust fund).

Executive Secretary: MARC BICHLER (Luxembourg); Two United Nations Plaza, 26th Floor, New York, NY 10017, USA; fax (212) 906-6479; e-mail info@uncdf.org; internet www.uncdf.org.

UNITED NATIONS OFFICE FOR SOUTH-SOUTH COOPERATION

The Office was established as the Special Unit for South-South Cooperation in 1978 by the UN General Assembly and is hosted by UNDP. It was renamed, as above, in 2012 in order to strengthen the work of the body within the UN. The Office aims to co-ordinate and support South-South co-operation in the political, economic, social, environmental and technical areas, and to support 'triangular' collaboration on a UN system-wide and global basis. It organizes the annual UN Day for South-South Cooperation (12 September), and manages the UN Trust Fund for South-South Cooperation (UNFSC) and the Perez-Guerrero Trust Fund for Economic and Technical Co-operation among Developing Countries (PGTF), as well as undertaking programmes financed by UNDP.

Director: YIPING ZHOU (People's Republic of China); 304 East 45th St, 12th Floor, New York, NY 11017, USA; tel. (212) 906-6944; fax (212) 906-6352; e-mail ssc.info@undp.org; internet ssc.undp.org.

UNITED NATIONS VOLUNTEERS (UNV)

The United Nations Volunteers is an important source of middle-level skills for the UN development system supplied at modest cost, particularly in the LDCs. Volunteers expand the scope of UNDP project activities by supplementing the work of international and host country experts and by extending the influence of projects to local community levels. UNV also supports technical co-operation within and among the developing countries by encouraging volunteers from the countries themselves and by forming regional exchange teams comprising such volunteers. UNV is involved in areas such as peacebuilding, elections, human rights, humanitarian relief and community-based environmental programmes, in addition to development activities.

The UN International Short-term Advisory Resources (UNISTAR) Programme, which is the private sector development arm of UNV, has increasingly focused its attention on countries in the process of economic transition. Since 1994 UNV has administered UNDP's Transfer of Knowledge Through Expatriate Nationals (TOKTEN) programme, which was initiated in 1977 to enable specialists and professionals from developing countries to contribute to development efforts in their countries of origin through short-term technical assignments. In March 2000 UNV established an Online Volunteering Service to connect development organizations and volunteers using the internet; in 2012 11,037 online volunteers, working on 16,196 assignments, made their skills available through the Online Volunteering Service.

In December 2011 UNV issued the first *State of the World's Volunteerism Report*, on the theme 'Universal Values for Global Well-being'.

By 2014 the total number of people who had served as UNVs amounted to around 40,000, deployed to more than 140 countries. During 2012 some 6,807 national and international UNVs were deployed in 127 countries, on 6,912 assignments.

Executive Co-ordinator: RICHARD DICTUS (Netherlands); POB 260111, 53153 Bonn, Germany; tel. (228) 8152000; fax (228) 8152001; e-mail information@unvolunteers.org; internet www.unv.org.

United Nations Environment Programme—UNEP

Address: POB 30552, Nairobi 00100, Kenya.

Telephone: (20) 621234; **fax:** (20) 623927; **e-mail:** unepinfo@unep.org; **internet:** www.unep.org.

UNEP was established in 1972 by the UN General Assembly, following recommendations of the 1972 UN Conference on the Human Environment, in Stockholm, Sweden, to encourage international co-operation in matters relating to the human environment.

Organization

(April 2014)

GOVERNING COUNCIL

The main functions of the Governing Council (which meets every two years in ordinary sessions, with special sessions taking place in the alternate years) are to promote international co-operation in the field of the environment and to provide general policy guidance for the direction and co-ordination of environmental programmes within the UN system. In December 2012 the UN General Assembly resolved to expand UNEP's Governing Council from 58 members to universal representation of all UN member states. The first meeting of the enlarged Council was held in February 2013 on the theme 'Rio+20: From Outcome to Implementation'. A Global Ministerial Environment Forum (first convened in 2000) meets annually as part of the Governing Council's regular and special sessions. The Governing Council is assisted in its work by a Committee of Permanent Representatives.

SECRETARIAT

Offices and divisions at UNEP headquarters in Nairobi, Kenya, include the Offices of the Executive Director and Deputy Executive Director; the Secretariat for Governing Bodies; Offices for Evaluation and Oversight, Programme Co-ordination and Management, Resource Mobilization, and Global Environment Facility Co-ordination; and Divisions of Communications and Public Information, Early Warning and Assessment, Environmental Policy Implementation, Technology, Industry and Economics, Regional Co-operation, and Environmental Law and Conventions.

Executive Director: ACHIM STEINER (Germany).

Deputy Executive Director: IBRAHIM THIAW (Mauritania).

REGIONAL OFFICES

UNEP maintains six regional offices. These work to initiate and promote UNEP objectives and to ensure that all programme formulation and delivery meets the specific needs of countries and regions. They also provide a focal point for building national, sub-regional and regional partnerships and enhancing local participation in UNEP initiatives. A co-ordination office has been established at headquarters to promote regional policy integration, to co-ordinate programme planning, and to provide necessary services to the regional offices.

Africa: POB 30552, Nairobi, Kenya; tel. (20) 7624292; fax (20) 7624489; e-mail roa.information.officer@unep.org; internet www.unep.org/roa.

Asia and the Pacific: United Nations Bldg, 2nd Floor, Rajadamnern Nok Ave, Bangkok 10200, Thailand; tel. (2) 288-2314; fax (2) 280-3829; e-mail uneproap@un.org; internet www.unep.org/roap.

Europe: 11–13 chemin des Anémones, 1219 Châtelaine, Geneva, Switzerland; tel. 229178279; fax 229178024; e-mail roe@unep.org; internet www.unep.ch/roe.

Latin America and the Caribbean: Ciudad del Saber, Edif. 103, Avda Morse, Corregimiento de Ancón, Ciudad de Panamá, Panama;

tel. 305-3100; fax 305-3105; e-mail enlace@pnuma.org; internet www.pnuma.org.

North America: 900 17th St NW, Suite 506, Washington, DC 20006, USA; tel. (202) 785-0465; fax (202) 785-2096; e-mail uneprona@un.org; internet www.rona.unep.org.

UNEP New York Office: DC-2 Bldg, Room 0803, Two United Nations Plaza, New York, NY 10017, USA; tel. (212) 963-8210; fax (212) 963-7341; e-mail unepnyo@un.org; internet www.unep.org/newyork.

West Asia: POB 10880, Manama, Bahrain; tel. 17812777; fax 17825110; e-mail uneprowa@unep.org.bh; internet www.unep.org/rowa.

OTHER OFFICES

Basel, Rotterdam and Stockholm Conventions, Secretariat: 11–13 chemin des Anémones, 1219 Châtelaine, Geneva, Switzerland; tel. 229178729; fax 229178098; e-mail brs@brsmeas.org; internet www.basel.int; www.pic.int; www.pops.int; Exec. Sec. Kerstin Stendahl (Finland).

Convention on International Trade in Endangered Species of Wild Fauna and Flora (CITES), Secretariat: 15 chemin des Anémones, 1219 Châtelaine, Geneva, Switzerland; tel. 229178139; fax 227973417; e-mail info@cites.org; internet www.cites.org; Sec.-Gen. John Scanlon (Australia).

Global Programme of Action for the Protection of the Marine Environment from Land-based Activities: GPA Co-ordination Unit, UNEP, POB 30552, 00100 Nairobi, Kenya; tel. (20) 7621206; fax (20) 7624249; internet www.gpa.unep.org.

Mediterranean Action Plan on the Implementation of the Barcelona Convention, Secretariat: Leoforos Vassileos Konstantinou 48, POB 18019, 11610 Athens, Greece; tel. (210) 7273100; fax (210) 7253196; e-mail unepmedu@unepmap.gr; internet www.unepmap.org.

Multilateral Fund for the Implementation of the Montreal Protocol, Secretariat: Suite 4100, 1000 De La Gauchetière St, Montréal, QC H3B 4W5, Canada; tel. (514) 282-1122; fax (514) 282-0068; e-mail secretariat@unmfs.org; internet www.multilateralfund.org; Chief Officer Eduardo Ganem (Mexico).

Regional Co-ordinating Unit for East Asian Seas: UN Bldg, 2nd Floor, Rajadamnern Nok Ave, Bangkok 10200, Thailand; tel. (2) 288-1860; fax (2) 281-2428; e-mail kleesuwan.unescap@un.org; internet www.cobsea.org; Co-ordinator Dr Ellik Adler (Israel).

Regional Co-ordinating Unit for the Caribbean Environment Programme: 14–20 Port Royal St, Kingston, Jamaica; tel. 922-9267; fax 922-9292; e-mail rcu@cep.unep.org; internet www.cep.unep.org; Co-ordinator Nelson Andrade Colmenares.

UNEP/CMS (Convention on the Conservation of Migratory Species of Wild Animals), Secretariat: Platz der Vereinten Nationen 1, 53113 Bonn, Germany; tel. (228) 8152402; fax (228) 8152449; e-mail secretariat@cms.int; internet www.cms.int; Exec. Sec. Bradnee Chambers.

UNEP Division of Technology, Industry and Economics: 15 rue de Milan, 75441 Paris, Cedex 09, France; tel. 1-44-37-14-50; fax 1-44-37-14-74; e-mail unep.tie@unep.fr; internet www.unep.org/dtie; Dir Tim Kasten (USA) (acting).

UNEP International Environmental Technology Centre (IETC): 2–110 Ryokuchi koen, Tsurumi-ku, Osaka 538-0036, Japan; tel. (6) 6915-4581; fax (6) 6915-0304; e-mail ietc@unep.org; internet www.unep.org/ietc; Dir Surendra Shrestha.

UNEP Ozone Secretariat: POB 30552, Nairobi, Kenya; tel. (20) 762-3851; fax (20) 762-0335; e-mail ozoneinfo@unep.org; internet ozone.unep.org; services both the 1985 Vienna Convention for the Protection of the Ozone Layer and its 1987 Montreal Protocol; Exec. Sec. Tina Birbili (Greece).

UNEP Post-Conflict and Disaster Management Branch: 11–15 chemin des Anémones, 1219 Châtelaine, Geneva, Switzerland; tel. 229178530; fax 229178064; e-mail postconflict@unep.org; internet www.unep.org/disastersandconflicts; Chief Officer Henrik Alexander Slotte.

UNEP Risoe Centre on Energy, Environment and Sustainable Development: Risoe Campus, Technical University of Denmark, Frederiksborgvej 399, Bldg 142, POB 49, 4000 Roskilde, Denmark; tel. 46-77-51-29; fax 46-32-19-99; e-mail unep@risoe.dtu.dk; internet uneprisoe.org; f. 1990 as the UNEP Collaborating Centre on Energy and Environment; supports UNEP in the planning and implementation of its energy-related policy and activities; provides technical support to governments towards the preparation of national Technology Needs Assessments on climate change adaptation; Head John M. Christensen.

UNEP-SCBD (Convention on Biological Diversity, Secretariat): 413 St Jacques St, Suite 800, Montréal, QC, H2Y 1N9, Canada; tel. (514) 288-2220; fax (514) 288-6588; e-mail secretariat@cbd.int; internet www.cbd.int; Exec. Sec. Braulio Ferreira de Souza Dias (Brazil).

UNEP Secretariat for the UN Scientific Committee on the Effects of Atomic Radiation: Vienna International Centre, Wagramerstr. 5, POB 500, 1400 Vienna, Austria; tel. (1) 26060-4330; fax (1) 26060-5902; e-mail malcolm.crick@unscear.org; internet www.unscear.org; Sec. Dr Malcolm Crick.

Activities

UNEP aims to maintain a constant watch on the changing state of the environment; to analyse trends; to assess problems using a wide range of data and techniques; and to undertake or support projects leading to environmentally sound development. It plays a catalytic and co-ordinating role within and beyond the UN system; many UNEP projects are implemented in co-operation with other UN agencies. About 45 intergovernmental organizations outside the UN system and 60 international non-governmental organizations (NGOs) have official observer status on UNEP's Governing Council, and, through the Environment Liaison Centre in Nairobi, Kenya, UNEP is linked to more than 6,000 non-governmental bodies concerned with the environment. UNEP also sponsors international conferences, programmes, plans and agreements regarding all aspects of the environment.

In February 1997 the Governing Council, at its 19th session, adopted a ministerial declaration (the Nairobi Declaration) on UNEP's future role and mandate, which recognized the organization as the principal UN body working in the field of the environment and as the leading global environmental authority, setting and overseeing the international environmental agenda. In June a special session of the UN General Assembly was convened to review the state of the environment and progress achieved in implementing the objectives of the UN Conference on Environment and Development (UNCED—known as the Earth Summit), that had been held in Rio de Janeiro, Brazil, in June 1992. UNCED had adopted Agenda 21 (a programme of activities to promote sustainable development in the 21st century) and the so-called Rio+5 meeting adopted a Programme for Further Implementation of Agenda 21 in order to intensify efforts in areas such as energy, freshwater resources and technology transfer. The meeting confirmed UNEP's essential role in advancing the Programme and as a global authority promoting a coherent legal and political approach to the environmental challenges of sustainable development. UNEP played a leading role in preparing for the World Summit on Sustainable Development (WSSD), held in August–September 2002 in Johannesburg, South Africa, to assess strategies for strengthening the implementation of Agenda 21. Governments participating in the conference adopted the Johannesburg Declaration and WSSD Plan of Implementation, in which they strongly reaffirmed commitment to the principles underlying Agenda 21 and also pledged support to all internationally agreed development goals, including the UN Millennium Development Goals (MDGs) adopted by governments attending a summit meeting of the UN General Assembly in September 2000. A UN Conference on Sustainable Development (UNCSD—also referred to as Earth Summit 2012 and Rio+20), was convened in June 2012, again in Rio de Janeiro, with participation by more than 100 heads of state and government, and by an estimated 50,000 representatives of international agencies, NGOs, civil society groups, and the private sector. The meeting determined to strengthen the institutional framework and intergovernmental arrangements for sustainable development and to establish a high-level intergovernmental forum to promote system-wide co-ordination and coherence of sustainable development policies and to follow up the implementation of sustainable development objectives. UNCSD determined that UNEP's role should be strengthened as the lead agency in setting the global environmental agenda and co-ordinating UN system-wide implementation of the environmental dimension of sustainable development. It resolved to request the UN General Assembly, during its 67th session (commencing in September 2012), to adopt a resolution that would upgrade UNEP by establishing universal membership of the Governing Council; ensuring increased financial resources to enable the Programme to fulfil its mandate; strengthening UNEP's participation in the main UN co-ordinating bodies; and empowering UNEP to lead efforts to develop UN system-wide strategies on the environment. The resolution was approved by the General Assembly in December. The participants in UNCSD endorsed an outcome document, entitled *The Future We Want*, which reaffirmed commitment to working towards an economically, socially and environmentally sustainable future, and to the eradication of poverty as an indispensable requirement for sustainable development; and deemed the implementation of green economy policy options, in the context of sustainable development and poverty eradication, to be an important tool for achieving sustainable development. UNCSD approved a set of Sustainable Development Goals (SDGs), setting global targets in sustainable development challenges; it was envisaged that the SDGs would complement the post-2015 UN development agenda. A 10-year framework on sustainable consumption and production was also announced, and the Conference decided to develop a new global wealth indicator that was to incorporate more dimensions than gross national product (the traditional indicator). UNCSD invited all UN agencies and entities to mainstream sustainable development in their mandates, programmes, and strategies. The importance of enhancing the participation of developing countries in international economic decision-making was emphasized. UNEP was to provide the Secretariat with a 10-Year Framework of Programmes (YFP) on Sustainable Consumption and Production that was adopted by the UNCSD participating states. A World Congress on Justice, Governance and Law for Environmental Sustainability, which convened during the Conference, with participation by leading judges, prosecutors and auditor generals, adopted a landmark series of principles to guide the Advancement of Justice, Governance and Law for Environmental Sustainability. During 2012 UNEP established a nine-member International Advisory Council, comprising senior judges, auditors and academics, with a mandate to provide strategic guidance to the international community in improving the legal foundations for achieving international environmental goals.

In July 2013 a High-level Political Forum, which had been proposed by UNCSD to build on the work of, and eventually replace, the UN Commission on Sustainable Development, was established. The inaugural meeting of the Forum was held in late September, at the start of the 68th session of the UN General Assembly. It was to be convened annually at ministerial level under the auspices of ECOSOC, and every four years at the level of heads of state and government.

In May 2000 UNEP initiated an annual Global Ministerial Environment Forum (GMEF), with participation by environment ministers and other senior government delegates. The 2013 session, held in February, at UNEP's Nairobi headquarters, determined to discontinue gatherings of the Forum.

CLIMATE CHANGE

UNEP worked in collaboration with the World Meteorological Organization (WMO) to formulate the 1992 UN Framework Convention on Climate Change (UNFCCC), with the aim of reducing the emission of gases that have a warming effect on the atmosphere (known as greenhouse gases). In 1998 UNEP and WMO established the Intergovernmental Panel on Climate Change (IPCC), as an objective source of scientific information about the warming of the earth's atmosphere.

UNEP's climate change-related activities have a particular focus on strengthening the capabilities of countries (in particular developing countries) to integrate climate change responses into their national development processes, including improving preparedness for participating in UN Reduced Emissions from Deforestation and Forest Degradation (UN-REDD) initiatives; Ecosystem Based Adaptation; and Clean Tech Readiness. UN-REDD, launched in September 2008 as a collaboration between UNEP, the UN Development Programme (UNDP) and FAO, aims to enable donors to pool resources (through a trust fund established for that purpose) to promote a transformation of forest resource use patterns. In August 2011 UN-REDD endorsed a Global Programme Framework covering 2011–15. Leaders from countries in the Amazon, Congo and Borneo-Mekong forest basins participated, in June 2011, in the Summit of Heads of State and Government on Tropical Forest Ecosystems, held in Brazzaville, Republic of the Congo; the meeting issued a declaration recognising the need to protect forests in order to combat climate change, and to conduct future mutual dialogue. In that month UNEP issued a report focusing on the economic benefits of expanding funding for forests.

In September 2012 UNEP and INTERPOL jointly reported that 50%–90% of logging in certain countries of the Amazon basin, Central Africa and South-East Asia was being conducted by organized criminal groups, posing a significant threat to efforts aimed at combating climate change, conserving wildlife, and eradicating poverty. Illegal logging was reported to account at that time for at least 15% of the total global trade in tropical timber products. A related increase in violence against indigenous forest dwellers in affected areas was also reported.

UNEP is a founding member of the Climate and Clean Air Coalition to Reduce Short Lived Climate Pollutants (SLCPs), which was launched in February 2012 as an international partnership, with the aim of reducing SLCPs, including methane and black carbon, to counter their negative impact on human health, crop yields and global warming. By April 2014 the partnership comprised 36 governments and 44 institutes and international organizations.

UNEP's Technology Needs Assessment and Technology Action Plan aims to support some 35–45 countries with the implementation of improved national Technology Needs Assessments within the framework of the UNFCCC, involving, inter alia, detailed analysis of mitigation and adaptation technologies, and prioritization of these technologies. The UNEP Risoe Centre of Denmark supports governments in the preparation of these Assessments. It was announced in February 2013 that UNEP would lead a consortium, including the UN Industrial Development Organization (UNIDO) and other agencies, as the hosts of a new Climate Technology Centre and Network (CTCN), which was to accelerate the transfer of climate-related technology and expertise to developing nations.

UNEP encourages the development of alternative and renewable sources of energy, as part of its efforts to mitigate climate change. To achieve this, UNEP has created the Global Network on Energy for Sustainable Development, linking 21 centres of excellence in industrialized and developing countries to conduct research and exchange information on environmentally sound energy technology resources. UNEP's Rural Energy Enterprise Development (REED) initiative (operating within Africa as AREED) helps the private sector to develop affordable 'clean' energy technologies, such as solar crop-drying and water-heating, wind-powered water pumps and efficient cooking stoves. UNEP is a member of the Global Bioenergy Partnership initiated by the G8 group of industrialized countries to support the sustainable use of biofuels. Through its Transport Programme UNEP promotes the use of renewable fuels and the integration of environmental factors into transport planning, leading a worldwide Partnership for Clean Fuels and Vehicles, a Global Fuel Economy Initiative, and a Non Motorised Transport 'Share the Road' scheme. Meanwhile, UNDP's Sustainable Buildings and Construction Initiative promotes energy efficiency in the construction industry. In conjunction with UN-Habitat, UNDP, the World Bank and other organizations and institutions, UNEP promotes environmental concerns in urban planning and management through the Sustainable Cities Programme, and projects concerned with waste management, urban pollution and the impact of transportation systems. In June 2012 UNEP and other partners inaugurated a new Global Initiative for Resource-Efficient Cities, which aimed to lower pollution levels, advance efficiency in the utilization of resources (including through the promotion of energy-efficient buildings), and reduce infrastructure costs in urban areas worldwide with populations in excess of 500,000.

During 2007 UNEP (with WMO and the WTO) convened a second International Conference on Climate Change and Tourism, together with two meetings on sustainable tourism development and a conference on global eco-tourism. In June 2009 UNEP and WTO jointly issued a report entitled *Trade and Climate Change*, reviewing the intersections between trade and climate change from the perspectives of the science of climate change; economics; multilateral efforts to combat climate change; and the effects on trade of national climate change policies.

GREEN ECONOMY

In October 2008, in response to the global economic, fuel and food crises that escalated during that year, UNEP launched the 'Green Economy Initiative' (GEI), which aimed to mobilize and refocus the global economy towards investments in clean technologies and the natural infrastructure (for example the infrastructures of forests and soils), with a view to, simultaneously, combating climate change and promoting employment. The UNEP Executive Director stated that the global crises were in part related to a broad market failure that promoted speculation while precipitating escalating losses of natural capital and nature-based assets, compounded by an over-reliance on finite, often subsidized fossil fuels. The three principal dimensions of the GEI were the compilation of the *Green Economy Report*, to provide an analysis of how public policy might support markets in accelerating the transition towards a low-carbon green economy; the Green Jobs Initiative, a partnership launched by UNEP, the International Labour Organization and the International Trade Union Confederation in 2007 (and joined in 2008 by the International Organisation of Employers); and the Economics of Ecosystems and Biodiversity (TEEB) partnership project, focusing on valuation issues. In April 2009 the UN System Chief Executives Board for Co-ordination (CEB) endorsed the GEI as the fourth of nine UN initiatives aimed at alleviating the impact of the global economic crisis on poor and vulnerable populations. UNEP participates in the SEED Initiative, a global partnership for action on sustainable development and the green economy that was launched collaboratively with UNDP and the International Union for the Conservation of Nature at the 2002 WSSD. SEED supports innovative locally driven small-scale businesses that actively work towards providing social and environmental benefits. A Green Economy Coalition was established in 2008 as a loose grouping of UNEP and other UN agencies, research institutes, business interests, trade unions, and NGOs, with the aim of promoting environmental sustainability and social equity.

In February 2013 UNEP, the ILO, UNIDO and the United Nations Institute for Training and Research launched the Partnership for Action on Green Economy (PAGE), which aimed, during the period 2013–20, to support 30 countries in developing national green economy strategies aimed at generating employment and skills, promoting clean technologies, and reducing environmental risks and poverty.

In June 2009 UNEP welcomed the 'Green Growth' declaration of Organisation for Economic Co-operation and Development (OECD), which urged the adoption of targeted policy instruments to promote green investment, and emphasized commitment to the realization of an ambitious and comprehensive post-2012 global climate agreement. In January 2012 UNEP, OECD, the World Bank, and the Global Green Growth Institute (established in June 2010 in Seoul, Republic of Korea—South Korea) launched the Green Growth Knowledge Platform. The Platform, accessible at www.greengrowthknowledge.org, aims to advance efforts to identify and address major knowledge gaps in green growth theory and practice, and to support countries in formulating and implementing policies aimed at developing a green economy.

In January 2011 UNEP and the World Tourism Organization launched the Global Partnership for Sustainable Tourism, also comprising other UN agencies, OECD, 18 governments, and other partners, with the aim of guiding policy and developing projects in the area of sustainable tourism, providing a global platform for discussion, and facilitating progress towards a green economy.

UNEP Finance Initiatives (FI) is a programme encouraging banks, insurance companies and other financial institutions to invest in an environmentally responsible way: an annual FI Global Roundtable meeting is held, together with regional meetings. In April 2007 UNEP hosted the first annual Business for Environment (B4E) meeting, on corporate environmental responsibility, in Singapore; the 2013 meeting was held in April, in New Delhi, India. During 2007 UNEP's Programme on Sustainable Consumption and Production (SCP) established an International Panel for Sustainable Resource Management (comprising experts whose initial subjects of study were to be the environmental risks of biofuels and of metal recycling), and initiated forums for businesses and NGOs in this field. In May 2011 the International Panel issued a *Decoupling Report* that urged the separation of the global economic growth rate from the rate of natural resource consumption. The report warned that, by 2050, without a change of direction, humanity's consumption of minerals, ores, fossil fuels and biomass were on course to increase three-fold. In 2014 UNEP launched an online Global SCP Clearinghouse, to facilitate access to information and promote new innovations relating to SCP.

In 1994 UNEP inaugurated the International Environmental Technology Centre (IETC), based in Osaka, Japan. The Centre promotes and implements environmentally sound technologies for disaster prevention and post-disaster reconstruction; sustainable production and consumption; and water and sanitation (in particular waste-water management and more efficient use of rainwater).

EARLY WARNING AND ASSESSMENT

The Nairobi Declaration resolved that the strengthening of UNEP's information, monitoring and assessment capabilities was a crucial element of the organization's restructuring, in order to help to establish priorities for international, national and regional action, and to ensure the efficient and accurate dissemination of information on emerging environmental trends and emergencies.

UNEP's Division of Early Warning and Assessment analyses the world environment, provides early warning information and assesses global and regional trends. It provides governments with data and helps them to use environmental information for decision-making and planning. Major assessments undertaken by UNEP include the International Assessment of Agricultural Science and Technology for Development; the Solar and Wind Energy Resource Assessment; the Regionally Based Assessment of Persistent Toxic Substances; the Land Degradation Assessment in Drylands; and the Global Methodology for Mapping Human Impacts on the Biosphere (GLOBIO) project.

UNEP's Global Environment Outlook (GEO) process of environmental analysis and assessment, launched in 1995, is supported by an extensive network of collaborating centres. The fifth 'umbrella' report on the GEO process (*GEO-5*) was issued in June 2012, just in advance of the UN Conference on Sustainable Development. The fifth report assessed progress achieved towards the attainment of some 90 environmental challenges, and identified four objectives—the elimination of the production and use of ozone layer-depleting substances; the removal of lead from fuel; access to improved water supplies; and promoting research into reducing pollution of the marine environment—as the areas in which most progress had been made. Little or no progress, however, was found to have been attained in the pursuit of 24 objectives, including managing climate change, desertification and drought; and deterioration was found to have occurred in the state of the world's coral reefs. In recent years regional and national GEO reports have been issued focusing on Africa, the Andean region, the Atlantic and Indian oceans, Brazil, the Caucasus, Latin America and the Caribbean, North America, and the Pacific; and the following thematic GEO reports have been produced: *The Global Deserts Outlook* (2006) and *The Global Outlook for Ice and Snow* (2007).

UNEP's Global International Waters Assessment (GIWA) considers all aspects of the world's water-related issues, in particular problems of shared transboundary waters, and of future sustainable management of water resources. UNEP is also a sponsoring agency of the Joint Group of Experts on the Scientific Aspects of Marine Environmental Pollution and contributes to the preparation of reports on the state of the marine environment and on the impact of land-based activities on that environment. The UNEP-World Conservation Monitoring Centre (UNEP-WCMC), established in June 2000 in Cambridge, United Kingdom, manages and interprets data concerning biodiversity and ecosystems, and makes the results available to governments and businesses. In October 2008 UNEP-WCMC, in partnership with the IUCN, launched the World Database on Protected Areas (WDPA), which details the world's terrestrial and marine protected areas. In 2007 the Centre undertook the 2010 Biodiversity Indicators Programme, with the aim of supporting decision-making by governments so as to reduce the threat of extinction facing vulnerable species. UNEP is a partner in the International Coral Reef Action Network—ICRAN, which was established in 2000 to monitor, manage and protect coral reefs worldwide.

In June 2010 delegates from 85 countries, meeting in Busan, South Korea, at the third conference addressing the creation of a new Intergovernmental Science-Policy Platform on Biodiversity and Ecosystem Services (IPBES), adopted the Busan Outcome Document finalizing details of the establishment of the IPBES; the Outcome Document was subsequently approved by the UN General Assembly. The Platform, inaugurated in April 2012, was to undertake, periodically, assessments, based on current scientific literature, of biodiversity and ecosystem outputs beneficial to humans, including timber, fresh water, fish and climatic stability.

DISASTERS AND CONFLICTS

UNEP aims to minimize environmental causes and consequences of disasters and conflicts, and supports member states in combating environmental degradation and natural resources mismanagement, deeming these to be underlying risk factors for conflicts and natural hazards. UNEP promotes the integration of environmental concerns into risk reduction policy and practices. UNEP undertakes assessments to establish the risks posed by environmental impacts on human health, security and livelihoods, and provides field-based capacity building and technical support, in countries affected by natural disaster and conflict.

An independent report of the Senior Advisory Group to the UN Secretary-General on Civilian Capacity in the Aftermath of Conflict, issued in February 2011, identified natural resources (such as minerals, oil, gas and timber) as a key area of focus. The report designated UNEP as the lead agency for identifying best practices in managing natural resources in support of peacebuilding. In December 2013 a UN report entitled *The Role of Natural Resources in Disarmament, Demobilization and Reintegration—Addressing Risks and Seizing Opportunities*, indicated that the incorporation of a focus on the fair management and distribution of natural resources into plans for post-conflict reintegration and recovery might help mitigate potential future conflicts, such as disputes over territory or water.

ENVIRONMENTAL GOVERNANCE

UNEP promotes international environmental legislation and the development of policy tools and guidelines in order to achieve the sustainable management of the world environment. It helps governments to implement multilateral environmental agreements, and to report on their results. At national level it assists governments to develop and implement appropriate environmental instruments and aims to co-ordinate policy initiatives. Training in various aspects of environmental law and its applications is provided. UNEP supports the development of new legal, economic and other policy instruments to improve the effectiveness of existing environmental agreements. It updates a register of international environmental treaties, and publishes handbooks on negotiating and enforcing environmental law. It acts as the secretariat for a number of regional and global environmental conventions. In June 2011 UNEP launched the Multilateral Environmental Agreements Information and Knowledge Management Initiative, which aimed to expand the sharing of information on more than 12 international agreements relating to the protection of the environment.

UNEP is the principal UN agency for promoting environmentally sustainable water management. It regards the unsustainable use of water as one of the most urgent environmental issues, and estimates that two-thirds of the world's population will suffer chronic water shortages by 2025, owing to growing populations, decreasing quality of water because of pollution, and increasing requirements of industries and agriculture. In 2000 UNEP adopted a new water policy and strategy, comprising assessment, management and co-ordination components. The Global International Waters Assessment is the primary framework for the assessment component. The management component includes the Global Programme of Action (GPA) for the Protection of the Marine Environment from Land-based Activities (adopted in November 1995), which focuses on the effects of pollution on freshwater resources, marine biodiversity and the coastal ecosystems of small island developing states. UNEP promotes international co-operation in the management of river basins and coastal areas and for the development of tools and guidelines to achieve the sustainable management of freshwater and coastal resources. During 2014 UNEP was undertaking preparations for the first International Environment Forum for Basin Organizations, scheduled to be convened in November, in Bangkok, Thailand. UNEP provides scientific, technical and administrative support to facilitate the implementation and co-ordination of 13 regional seas conventions and associated regional plans of action. UNEP's Regional Seas Programme aims to protect marine and coastal ecosystems, particularly by helping governments to put relevant legislation into practice.

UNEP was instrumental in the drafting of a Convention on Biological Diversity (CBD) to preserve the immense variety of plant and animal species, in particular those threatened with extinction. The Convention entered into force at the end of 1993; by April 2014 192 states and the European Union (EU) were parties to the CBD. The CBD's Cartagena Protocol on Biosafety (so called as it had been addressed at an extraordinary session of parties to the CBD convened in Cartagena, Colombia, in February 1999) was adopted at a meeting of parties to the CBD in January 2000, and entered into force in September 2003; by April 2014 the Protocol had been ratified by 166 states parties. The Protocol regulates the transboundary movement and use of living modified organisms resulting from biotechnology, in order to reduce any potential adverse effects on biodiversity and human health. It established an Advanced Informed Agreement procedure to govern the import of such organisms. Prior to the Protocol's entry into force, UNEP undertook a major project aimed at supporting developing countries to assess the potential health and environmental risks and benefits of genetically modified (GM) crops. The sixth conference of parties (COP) to the CBD, held in April 2002, adopted detailed voluntary guidelines concerning access to genetic resources and sharing the benefits attained from such resources with the countries and local communities where they originate; a global work programme on forests; and a set of guiding principles for combating alien invasive species. In October 2010 the 10th COP, meeting in Nagoya, Japan, approved the Nagoya-Kuala Lumpur Supplementary Protocol to the CBD, with a view to establishing an international regime on access and benefit sharing (ABS) of genetic resources, alongside a strategic 10-year Strategic Plan for Biodiversity, comprising targets and timetables to combat loss of the planet's nature-based resources. The Supplementary Protocol was opened for signature in March 2011, and by April 2014 had been signed by 92 states and ratified by 29. The 12th COP to the CBD, convened in October 2012, in Hyderabad, India, agreed that developed countries should double by 2015 resources dedicated towards biodiversity protection. The conference pledged to focus particular attention towards the sustainable management of marine areas, such as the Sargasso Sea and Tonga archipelago, and determined formally to classify marine areas of ecological or biological significance. The UN Decade on Biodiversity was being celebrated during 2011–20. UNEP supports co-operation for biodiversity assessment and management in selected developing regions and for the development of strategies for the conservation and sustainable exploitation of individual threatened species (e.g. the Global Tiger Action Plan). It also provides assistance for the preparation of individual country studies and strategies to strengthen national biodiversity management and research. UNEP administers the Convention on International Trade in Endangered Species of Wild Flora and Fauna (CITES), which entered into force in 1975 and comprised 180 states parties at April 2014. CITES, whose states parties meet in conference every three years, regulates international trade in nearly 35,000 species of plants and animals, as well as products and derivatives therefrom. The Convention has special programmes on the protection of elephants (including an African Elephant Action Plan, finalized in 2010), falcons, great apes, hawksbill turtles, sturgeons, tropical timber (jointly with the International Tropical Timber Organization), and big leaf mahogany. Meeting in St Petersburg, Russia, in November 2010, at the International Tiger Forum, the heads of the UN Office on Drugs and Crime, CITES, the World Customs Organization, INTERPOL and the World Bank jointly approved the establishment of a new International Consortium on Combating Wildlife Crime (ICCWC), with the aim of combating the poaching of wild animals and illegal trade in wild animals and wild animal products. The 2013 CITES conference, which was held in March, in Bangkok, strengthened the international regime covering trade in precious tropical hardwoods (including rosewoods and ebonies; with special procedures to be implemented for musicians travelling with instruments made therefrom); tortoises and turtles; five species of shark that are harvested for their fins or meat; manta rays (whose gill plates are traded); elephants (including stronger controls on e-commerce, and stricter monitoring of ivory stockpiles); rhinoceros; and big cats (with a focus on trophy leopard hunting). The conference agenda focused on means of combating the over-exploitation of marine and forest reserves, and escalating wildlife crime, determined to consider the use of the GEF as a financial instrument for the Convention, and declared 3 March as annual World Wildlife Day. ICCWC organized the first global meeting of wildlife enforcement networks on the sidelines of the conference.

In December 1996 the Lusaka Agreement on Co-operative Enforcement Operations Directed at Illegal Trade in Wild Flora and Fauna entered into force, having been concluded under UNEP auspices in order to strengthen the implementation of the CBD and CITES in Eastern and Central Africa. UNEP and UNESCO jointly co-sponsor the Great Apes Survival Project (GRASP), which was launched in May 2001. GRASP supports, in 23 'great ape range states' (of which 21 are in Africa and two—Indonesia and Malaysia—in South-East Asia), the conservation of gorillas, chimpanzees, orang-utans and bonobos. GRASP's first intergovernmental meeting, held in Kinshasa, Democratic Republic of the Congo in September 2005, was attended by representatives of governments of great ape habitat states, donor and other interested states, international organizations, NGOs, and private sector and academic interests. The meeting adopted a Global Strategy for the Survival of Great Apes, and the Kinshasa Declaration pledging commitment and action towards achieving this goal. GRASP, CITES and the World Association of Zoos and Aquariums jointly declared 2009 the Year of the Gorilla. A UNEP-GRASP report issued in March 2013, entitled *Stolen Apes: The Illicit Trade in Chimpanzees, Gorillas, Bonobos and Orangutans*, urged the enforcement of protection areas, stating that nearly 3,000 live great apes were being trafficked annually from habitats in Africa and South-East Asia, that more than 22,200 great apes were trafficked and/or killed during 2005–11, and that their habitats were being eroded by up to 5% annually.

The Convention on the Conservation of Migratory Species of Wild Animals (CMS, also referred to as the Bonn Convention), concluded under UNEP auspices in 1979, aims to conserve migratory avian, marine and terrestrial species throughout the range of their migration. The secretariat of the CMS is hosted by UNEP. At April 2014 there were 119 states parties to the Convention. A number of agreements and Memorandums of Understanding (MOUs) concerning conservation have been concluded under the CMS. Agreements cover the conservation of African-Eurasian Migratory Waterbirds (1999), Populations of European Bats (1994), Small Cetaceans of the Baltic, North-East Atlantic, Irish and North Seas (1994), Cetaceans of the Black Seas, Mediterranean and Contiguous Atlantic Area (2001), Seals in the Wadden Sea (1991), Albatrosses and Petrels (2004), and Gorillas and their Habitiats (2008). MOUs cover the conservation of the Siberian Crane (1993), the Slender-billed Curlew (1994), Marine Turtles of the Atlantic Coast of Africa (1999), Marine Turtles of the Indian Ocean and South-east Asia (2001), the Great Bustard (2001), the Bukhara Deer (2002), the Aquatic Warbler (2003), the West African Elephant (2005), the Saiga Antelope (2005), Pacific Island Cetaceans (2006), the Ruddy-headed Goose (2006), Grassland Birds (2007), Atlantic Populations of the Mediterranean Monk Seal (2007), Dugongs (2007), the Manatee and Small Cetaceans of Western Africa and Macaronesia (2008), Migratory Birds of Prey in Africa and Eurasia (2008), High Andean Flamingos and their Habitats (2008), Migratory Sharks (2010), and the Southern Huemul (2010). In August 2012 the conference of parties to the CMS determined to develop a new strategic plan to guide the Convention over the period 2015–23.

In October 1994 87 countries, meeting under UN auspices, signed a Convention to Combat Desertification (see UNDP Drylands Development Centre), which aimed to provide a legal framework to counter the degradation of arid regions. An estimated 75% of all drylands have suffered some land degradation, affecting approximately 1,000m. people in 110 countries. UNEP continues to support the implementation of the Convention, as part of its efforts to protect land resources. UNEP also aims to improve the assessment of dryland degradation and desertification in co-operation with governments and other international bodies, as well as identifying the causes of degradation and measures to overcome these.

ECOSYSTEM MANAGEMENT

The Millennium Ecosystem Assessment, a scientific study of the state of 24 ecosystems, that was commissioned by the UN Secretary-General in 2001, found that 15 of the ecosystems under assessment were being used unsustainably, thereby inhibiting, particularly in developing countries, the achievement of the UN MDGs of reducing poverty and hunger. UNEP's Ecosystem Management Programme aims to develop an adaptive approach that integrates the management of forests, land, freshwater and coastal systems, focusing on sustaining ecosystems to meet future ecological needs, and to enhance human well-being. UNEP places particular emphasis on six ecosystem services deemed to be especially in decline: climate regulation; water regulation; natural hazard regulation; energy; freshwater; nutrient cycling; and recreation and ecotourism. Secondary importance is given to water purification and waste treatment; disease regulation; fisheries; and primary production. UNEP supports national and regional governments to build capacity in order to promote the role of sustainably managed ecosystems in support of social and economic development; to determine which ecosystem services to prioritize; and to incorporate an ecosystem management approach into their national and developmental planning and investment strategies.

In February 2012 UNEP and the Chinese Academy of Sciences (CAS) signed an agreement to establish the International Ecosystem Management Partnership of the United Nations Environment Programme (UNEP-IEMP), a new global centre on ecosystem management to be based in Beijing, with a mandate to promote ecosystem management in developing nations.

HARMFUL SUBSTANCES AND HAZARDOUS WASTE

UNEP administers the Basel Convention on the Control of Transboundary Movements of Hazardous Wastes and their Disposal, which entered into force in 1992 with the aim of preventing the uncontrolled movement and disposal of toxic and other hazardous wastes, particularly the illegal dumping of waste in developing countries by companies from industrialized countries. At April 2014 179 countries and the EU were parties to the Convention.

In February 2004 a new international convention on prior informed consent (PIC) for hazardous chemicals and pesticides in international trade entered into force, having been formulated and promoted by UNEP, in collaboration with FAO. The Convention aimed to reduce risks to human health and the environment by restricting the production, export and use of hazardous substances and enhancing information exchange procedures. UNEP played a leading role in formulating a multilateral agreement to reduce and ultimately eliminate the manufacture and use of Persistent Organic Pollutants (POPs), which are considered to be a major global environmental hazard. The Stockholm Convention on POPs, targeting 12 particularly hazardous pollutants, was adopted by 127 countries in May 2001 and entered into force in May 2004. In May 2009 the fourth conference of parties to the Stockholm Convention agreed on a list of nine further POPs; these were incorporated into the Convention in an amendment that entered into force in August 2010.

In January 2013, meeting in Geneva, Switzerland, more than 140 governments finalized the Minamata Convention on Mercury, which provides for controls relating to the usage, release, mining, import and export, and safe storage of mercury, and for the phasing-out by 2020 of the production of several mercury-containing products. The Convention—which had been under negotiation since February 2009—was adopted and opened for signature at a meeting convened in Minamata, Japan, in October 2013. By April 2014 the Convention had been signed by 97 countries and ratified by one (the USA). Pending the entry into force of the Convention, requiring 50 ratifications, a voluntary Global Mercury Partnership addresses activities related to combating mercury pollution. A Global Alliance to Eliminate Lead Paint was endorsed in May 2009 by the second International Conference on Chemicals Management, with the aim of minimizing occupational exposure to, and preventing children's exposure to paints containing lead. The Global Alliance convened in May 2010 (in Geneva) and in July 2012 (in Bangkok).

UNEP was the principal agency in formulating the 1987 Montreal Protocol to the Vienna Convention for the Protection of the Ozone Layer (1985), which provided for a 50% reduction in the production of chlorofluorocarbons (CFCs) by 2000. An amendment to the Protocol was adopted in 1990, which required complete cessation of the production of CFCs by 2000 in industrialized countries and by 2010 in developing countries. The Copenhagen Amendment, adopted in 1992, stipulated the phasing out of production of hydrochlorofluorocarbons (HCFCs) by 2030 in developed countries and by 2040 in developing nations. Subsequent amendments aimed to introduce a licensing system for all controlled substances, and imposed stricter controls on the import and export of HCFCs, and on the production and consumption of bromochloromethane (Halon-1011, an industrial solvent and fire extinguisher). In September 2007 the states parties to the Vienna Convention agreed to advance the deadline for the elimination of HCFCs to 2020 in developed countries and to 2030 in developing countries. A Multilateral Fund for the Implementation of the Montreal Protocol was established in June 1990 to promote the use of suitable technologies and the transfer of technologies to developing countries, and support compliance by developing countries with relevant control measures. UNEP, UNDP, the World Bank and UNIDO are the sponsors of the Fund, which by February 2012 had approved financing for more than 6,875 projects and activities in 145 developing countries at a cost of more than US $2,800m. The eighth replenishment of the Fund, covering the period 2012–14, raised $400m. in new contributions from donors. In September 2009 the Montreal Protocol, with 196 states parties, became the first agreement on the global environment to attain universal ratification. UNEP's OzonAction branch promotes information exchange, training and technological awareness, helping governments and industry in developing countries to undertake measures towards the cost-effective phasing-out of ozone-depleting substances.

UNEP encourages governments and the private sector to develop and adopt policies and practices that are cleaner and safer, make efficient use of natural resources, incorporate environmental costs, ensure the environmentally sound management of chemicals, and reduce pollution and risks to human health and the environment. In collaboration with other organizations UNEP works to formulate international guidelines and agreements to address these issues. UNEP also promotes the transfer of appropriate technologies and organizes conferences and training workshops to provide sustainable production practices. Relevant information is disseminated through the International Cleaner Production Information Clearing House. By 2014 more than 50 National Cleaner Production Centres (NCPCs), and, in Latin America, a regional network of cleaner production centres, had been established, under a joint UNEP/UNIDO programme that was launched in 1994 to promote the use and development of environmentally sustainable technologies and to build national capacities in cleaner production. In October 2009 UNIDO and UNEP endorsed the creation of the global network for Resource Efficient and Cleaner Production (RECPnet), with the aim of utilizing the capabilities of NCPCs in developing and transition countries. RECPnet was launched in November 2011. In October 1998 UNEP adopted an International Declaration on Cleaner Production, with a commitment to implement cleaner and more sustainable production methods and to monitor results. UNEP was a co-founder (in 1997) of the Global Reporting Initiative, which, with participation by corporations, business associations and other organizations, develops guidelines for voluntary reporting by companies on their economic, environmental and social performance. In 2002 UNEP, with the Society of Environmental Toxicology and Chemistry, launched the Life Cycle Initiative (currently in its third phase covering 2012–16), which evaluates the impact of products over their entire life cycle (from manufacture to disposal) and aims to assist governments, businesses and other consumers with adopting environmentally sound policies and practice, in view of the upward trend in global consumption patterns.

In accordance with a decision made by UNEP's Governing Council in February 2002, a Preparatory Committee for the Development of a Strategic Approach to International Chemicals Management was established; the work of the Committee culminated in the first session, held in February 2006, in Dubai, United Arab Emirates, of the International Conference on Chemicals Management (ICCM-1), comprising governments and intergovernmental and non-governmental organizations. ICCM-1 adopted the Strategic Approach to International Chemicals Management (SAICM), a policy framework to promote the sound management of chemicals in support of the objective (determined by the 2002 WSSD) of ensuring that, by 2020, chemicals are produced and used in ways that minimize significant adverse impacts on the environment and human health. ICCM-2, convened in May 2009, in Geneva, reviewed the implementation of the SAICM and adopted 20 indicators to measure its future progress. ICCM-3, held in September 2012, in Nairobi, evaluated data on the 20 indicators. UNEP provides technical support for implementing the Convention on Persistent Organic Pollutants, encouraging the use of alternative pesticides, and monitoring the emission of pollutants through the burning of waste. In September 2012 UNEP published the *Global Chemical Outlook*, highlighting the effect of chemicals on human health and the environment, and assessing the negative impact on emerging and developing economies.

In March 2013 UNEP and WHO issued a joint report entitled *State of the Science of Endocrine Disrupting Chemicals*, which assessed the potential disrupting effects on the human hormone system and the environment of synthetic chemicals found in many household products.

GLOBAL ENVIRONMENT FACILITY

UNEP, together with UNDP and the World Bank, is an implementing agency of the Global Environment Facility (GEF), established in 1991 to help developing countries and those undergoing economic transition to meet the costs of projects that benefit the environment in six specific areas: biological diversity; climate change; international waters; depletion of the ozone layer; land degradation; and persistent organic pollutants. Important cross-cutting components of these projects include capacity building to allow countries to meet their obligations under international environmental agreements, and adaptation to climate change. UNEP services the Scientific and Technical Advisory Panel, which provides expert advice on GEF programmes and operational strategies.

COMMUNICATIONS AND PUBLIC INFORMATION

UNEP's public education campaigns and outreach programmes promote community involvement in environmental issues. Further communication of environmental concerns is undertaken through coverage in the press, broadcasting and electronic media, publications, an information centre service and special promotional events, including World Environment Day (celebrated on 5 June; slogan in 2013: 'Think.Eat.Save. Reduce Your Footprint'—relating to an anti-food wastage theme), the Focus on Your World photography competition, and the awarding of the annual Sasakawa Prize (to recognize distinguished service to the environment by individuals and groups) and of the Champions of the Earth awards (for outstanding environmental leaders from each of UNEP's six regions). An annual Global Civil Society Forum (preceded by regional consultative meetings) is held in association with UNEP's Governing Council meetings. UNEP's Tunza programme for children and young people includes conferences, online discussions and publications. The Online Access to Research in the Environment, a UNEP-led initiative, provides access to more than 17,000 peer reviewed scientific journals, online books, and other resources, for use by some 6,000 environmental institutions in 109 low- and middle-income countries. UNEP co-operates with the International Olympic Committee, the Commonwealth Games organizing body and international federations for football, athletics and other sports to encourage 'carbon neutral' sporting events and to use sport as a means of outreach.

Finance

Project budgetary resources approved by the Governing Council for UNEP's activities during 2012–13 totalled US $474m. UNEP is allocated a contribution from the regular budget of the United Nations, and derives most of its finances from voluntary contributions to the Environment Fund and to trust funds.

Publications

Annual Report.

CBTF (Capacity Building Task Force on Trade, Environment and Development) Newsletter.

DEWA / GRID Europe Quarterly Bulletin. E+ (Energy, Climate and Sustainable Development).

Emissions Gap Report.

The Environment and Poverty Times.

Global Chemicals Outlook.

Great Apes Survival Project Newsletter.

Green Economy Report.

IETC (International Environmental Technology Centre) Insight.

Life Cycle Initiatives Newsletter.

Our Planet (quarterly).

Planet in Peril: Atlas of Current Threats to People and the Environment.

ROA (Regional Office for Africa) News (2 a year).

Tourism Focus (2 a year).

RRC.AP (Regional Resource Centre for Asia and the Pacific) Newsletter.

Sustainable Consumption Newsletter.

Tunza (quarterly magazine for children and young people).

UNEP Chemicals Newsletter.

UNEP Year Book (annually).

World Atlas of Biodiversity.

World Atlas of Coral Reefs.

World Atlas of Desertification.

Studies, reports (including the *Global Environment Outlook* series), legal texts, technical guidelines, etc.

Associated Bodies

Intergovernmental Panel on Climate Change (IPCC): c/o WMO, 7 bis, ave de la Paix, 1211 Geneva 2, Switzerland; tel. 227308208; fax 227308025; e-mail ipcc-sec@wmo.int; internet www.ipcc.ch; established in 1988 by the World Meteorological Organization (WMO) and UNEP; comprises some 3,000 scientists as well as other experts and representatives of all UN member governments. Approximately every five years the IPCC assesses all available scientific, technical and socio-economic information on anthropogenic climate change. The IPCC provides, on request, scientific, technical and socio-economic advice to the Conference of the Parties to the UN Framework Convention on Climate Change (UNFCCC) and to its subsidiary bodies, and compiles reports on specialized topics, such as *Aviation and the Global Atmosphere*, *Regional Impacts of Climate Change*, and *Managing the Risks of Extreme Events and Disasters to Advance Climate Change Adaptation*. The IPCC informs and guides, but does not prescribe, policy. The IPCC's *Fourth Assessment Report*, the final instalment of which was issued in Nov. 2007, concluded that increases in global average air and ocean temperatures, widespread melting of snow and ice, and the rising global average sea level, demonstrate that the warming of the climate system is unequivocal; that observational evidence from all continents and most oceans indicates that many natural systems are being affected by regional climate changes; that a global assessment of data since 1970 has shown that it is likely that anthropogenic warming has had a discernable influence on many physical and biological systems; and that other effects of regional climate changes are emerging. The *Fourth Assessment Report* was awarded a share of the Nobel Peace Prize for 2007. In Jan. 2010 the IPCC accepted criticism that an assertion in the 2007 *Report*, concerning the rate at which Himalayan glaciers were melting, was exaggerated, and in Feb. 2010 the Panel agreed that the *Report* had overstated the proportion of the Netherlands below sea level. Later in that month it was announced that an independent board of scientists would be appointed to review the work of the IPCC. In May 2011 a meeting of delegates from IPCC member states determined that a 13-member executive committee, under the leadership of the IPCC Chairman, should be established to supervise the day-to-day operations of the Panel and to consider matters requiring urgent action. Publication of the *Fifth Assessment Report* of the IPCC was phased, with three Working Group reports released in Sept. 2013, and in March and April 2014, and a Synthesis Report due in Oct.; the Sept. 2013 report presented new research on the physical science basis of climate change, and concluded that it was virtually certain there will be more extremes of temperatures and a continued rise in sea levels; the March 2014 report stated emphatically that the impacts of global warming were likely to be 'severe, pervasive and irreversible'—including on food security, the availability of fresh water, and in terms of increasing occurrence of extreme natural events—and that human adaptation strategies (such as the construction of defences against flooding) would be essential as means of partially mitigating the economic and societal consequences; and the report released in April stressed that increasing numbers of policies on arresting climate change had failed to prevent the recent rapid acceleration in the growth of greenhouse gas emissions, but found that, were major institutional and technological changes introduced aimed at reducing emissions from energy production and use, buildings, industry, human settlements, land use, and transport, it would be possible to limit the increase in global mean temperature to the goal of 2° Celsius above pre-industrial levels.

Chair.: RAJENDRA K. PACHAURI (India).

United Nations Convention to Combat Desertification in Those Countries Experiencing Serious Drought and/or Desertification, Particularly in Africa, Secretariat (UNCCD): Platz der Vereinten Nationen 1, 53113 Bonn, Germany; tel. (228) 815-2800; fax (228) 815-2898; e-mail secretariat@unccd.int; internet www.unccd.int; the UN Conference on Environment and Development, convened in June 1992, in Rio de Janeiro, Brazil, endorsed an integrated approach to addressing the issue of accelerating desertification, with an emphasis on promoting sustainable development at the community level, and requested the UN General Assembly to establish a negotiating committee to draft the Convention; consequently, UNCCD was adopted in June 1994, and came into force in Dec. 1996. In Oct. 1998 a Global Mechanism was established under UNCCD, to provide strategic advisory services to developing countries on means of attracting and increasing investments in sustainable land management, for example by channelling investments from innovative financial sources such as micro-finance and climate change funds. The eighth session of the UNCCD Conference of the Parties (COP), held in Sept. 2007, in Madrid, Spain, adopted The Strategy, a 10-year strategic plan and framework, which aimed to enhance the implementation of the Convention, with a focus on forging global partnerships towards the reversal and prevention of desertification and land degradation, and on establishing a global framework to support the development and implementation of national and regional poverty reduction policies. COP 10, convened in Oct. 2011, in Changwon, Republic of Korea, adopted the Changwon Initiative, to complement activities being undertaken in accordance with The Strategy, including enhancing UNCCD scientific processes; mobilizing additional resources and facilitating partnership arrangements; and supporting a global framework for the promotion of best practice. COP 11 was held in Windhoek, Namibia, in Sept.–Oct. 2013; the meeting agreed to establish a Science Policy Interface to facilitate the communication of scientific findings to policy-makers. COP 12 was scheduled to be convened in Turkey, in 2015. By April 2014 UNCCD had been ratified by 194 states and the EU.

Executive Secretary: MONIQUE BARBUT (France).

United Nations Framework Convention on Climate Change, Secretariat (UNFCCC): Haus Carstanjen, Martin-Luther-King-Str. 8, 53175 Bonn, Germany; tel. (228) 815-1000; fax (228) 815-1999; e-mail secretariat@unfccc.int; internet unfccc.int; the World Meteorological Organization (WMO) and UNEP worked together to formulate the Convention, in response to the first report of the IPCC, issued in August 1990, which predicted an increase in the concentration of greenhouse gases (i.e. carbon dioxide and other gases that have a warming effect on the atmosphere) owing to human activity. The UNFCCC was signed in May 1992 and formally adopted at the UN Conference on Environment and Development, held in June. It entered into force in March 1994, committing countries to submitting reports on measures being taken to reduce the emission of greenhouse gases and recommended stabilizing these emissions at 1990 levels by 2000; however, this was not legally binding. Following the second session of the Conference of the Parties (COP) of the Convention, held in July 1996, multilateral negotiations ensued to formulate legally binding objectives for emission limitations. At the third COP, held in Kyoto, Japan, in Dec. 1997, 38 industrial nations endorsed mandatory reductions of combined emissions of the six major gases by an average of 5.2% during the five-year period 2008–12, to pre-1990 levels. The so-called Kyoto Protocol was to enter into force on being ratified by at least 55 countries party to the UNFCCC, including industrialized countries with combined emissions of carbon dioxide in 1990 accounting for at least 55% of the total global greenhouse gas emissions by developed nations. The fourth COP, convened in Buenos Aires, Argentina, in Nov. 1998, adopted a plan of action to promote implementation of the UNFCCC and to finalize the operational details of the Kyoto Protocol. These included the Clean Development Mechanism, by which industrialized countries may obtain credits towards achieving their reduction targets by assisting developing countries to implement emission-reducing measures, and a system of trading emission quotas. Agreement on the implementation of the Buenos Aires action plan was not achieved until the second session of the sixth COP, held in Bonn in July 2001. The seventh COP, convened in Marrakesh, Morocco, in Oct.–Nov., formally adopted the decisions reached in July, and elected 15 members to the Executive Board of the Clean Development Mechanism. In March 2002 the USA (the most prolific national producer of harmful gas emissions) announced that it would not ratify the Kyoto Protocol. The Kyoto Protocol eventually entered into force on 16 Feb. 2005, 90 days after its ratification by Russia. Negotiations commenced in May 2007 on establishing a new international arrangement eventually to succeed the Kyoto Protocol. Participants in COP 13, convened in Bali, Indonesia, in Dec. 2007, adopted the Bali Roadmap, detailing a two-year process leading to the planned conclusion of the schedule of negotiations in Dec. 2009. The UN Climate Change Conference (COP 14), convened in Poznań, Poland, in Dec. 2008, finalized the Kyoto Protocol's Adaptation Fund, which was to finance projects and programmes in developing signatory states that were particularly vulnerable to the adverse effects of climate change. Addressing the Conference, the UN Secretary-General urged the advancement of a 'Green New Deal', to address simultaneously the ongoing global climate and economic crises. COP 15 was held, concurrently with the fifth meeting of parties to the Kyoto Protocol, in Copenhagen, Denmark, in Dec. 2009. Heads of state and government and other delegates attending the Conference approved the Copenhagen Accord, which determined that international co-operative action should be taken, in the context of sustainable development, to reduce global greenhouse gas emissions so as to hold the ongoing increase in global temperature below 2°C. It was agreed that enhanced efforts should be undertaken to reduce vulnerability to climate change in developing countries, with special reference to least developed countries, small island states and Africa. Developed countries agreed to pursue the achievement by 2020 of strengthened carbon emissions targets, while developing nations were to implement actions to slow down growth in emissions. A Green Climate Fund was to be established to support climate change mitigation actions in developing countries, and a Technology Mechanism was also to be established, with the aim of accelerating technology development and transfer in support of climate change adaptation and mitigation activities. COP 16, convened, concurrently with the sixth meeting of parties to the Kyoto Protocol, in Cancún, Mexico, in Nov.–Dec. 2010, adopted several decisions, which included mandating the establishment of a Cancún Adaptation Framework and associated Adaptation Committee, and approving a work programme which was to consider approaches to environmental damage linked to unavoidable impacts of climate change in vulnerable countries, as well as addressing forms of adaptation action, such as: strengthening the resilience of ecological systems; undertaking impact, vulnerability and adaptation assessments; engaging the participation of vulnerable communities in ongoing processes; and valuing traditional indigenous knowledge alongside the best available science. UN system-wide activities to address climate change are co-ordinated by an action framework established by the UN Chief Executives Board for Co-ordination under the UN *Delivering as One* commitment. COP 17, held in Durban, South Africa, in Nov.–Dec. 2011 concluded with an agreement on a 'Durban Platform for Enhanced Action'. The Platform incorporated agreements to extend the Kyoto provisions regarding emissions reductions by industrialized nations for a second phase, to follow on from the expiry at end-2012 of the first commitment phase, and to initiate negotiations on a new, inclusive global emissions arrangement, to be concluded in 2015, that would come into effect in 2020 with 'legal force'. During the conference sufficient funds were committed to enable the inauguration of the Green Climate Fund, and a commitment was concluded to establish the Adaptation Committee. In Dec. 2012 COP 18, convened in Doha, Qatar, approved an amendment of the Kyoto Protocol to initiate a second commitment period of eight years and endorsed the timetable for negotiating a new climate agreement by May 2015 (with a meeting of world heads of state to be convened in 2014). States parties committed to reducing greenhouse gas emissions by at least 18% below 1990 levels during 2013–20. COP 18 also secured a commitment by developed nations to mobilize US $100,000m. by 2020 to support climate change adaptation and mitigation initiatives in affected developing countries. It was envisaged that the Green Climate Fund would become fully operational in 2014, based in Sondgo, South Korea. As at April 2014 the Kyoto Protocol had 192 states parties (191 countries and the European Community). The USA has not signed the Protocol. Canada withdrew its participation with effect from Dec. 2012. In Nov. 2013 states participating in COP 19, convened in Warsaw, Poland, agreed to intensify immediate actions to combat climate change and to confirm national commitments to reducing greenhouse gas emissions in advance of the 2015 deadline to conclude a new legally binding treaty.

Executive Secretary: CHRISTIANA FIGUERES (Costa Rica).

United Nations High Commissioner for Refugees—UNHCR

Address: CP 2500, 1211 Geneva 2 dépôt, Switzerland.

Telephone: 227398111; **fax:** 227397312; **e-mail:** unhcr@unhcr.org; **internet:** www.unhcr.org.

The Office of the High Commissioner was established in 1951 to provide international protection for refugees and to seek durable solutions to their problems. In 1981 UNHCR was awarded the Nobel Peace Prize.

Organization

(April 2014)

HIGH COMMISSIONER

The High Commissioner is elected by the United Nations General Assembly on the nomination of the Secretary-General, and is responsible to the General Assembly and to the UN Economic and Social Council (ECOSOC).

High Commissioner: ANTÓNIO MANUEL DE OLIVEIRA GUTERRES (Portugal).

Deputy High Commissioner: THOMAS ALEXANDER ALEINIKOFF (USA).

EXECUTIVE COMMITTEE

The Executive Committee of the High Commissioner's Programme (ExCom), established by ECOSOC, gives the High Commissioner policy directives in respect of material assistance programmes and advice in the field of international protection. In addition, it oversees UNHCR's general policies and use of funds. ExCom, which comprises representatives of 87 states, meets once a year.

ADMINISTRATION

Headquarters, based in Geneva, Switzerland, include the Executive Office, comprising the offices of the High Commissioner, the Deputy High Commissioner and the two Assistant High Commissioners (for Operations and Protection). The Inspector General, the Director of the UNHCR liaison office in New York, and the Director of the Ethics Office report directly to the High Commissioner. The principal administrative Divisions cover International Protection; Programme and Support Management; Emergency Security and Supply; Financial and Administrative Management; Human Resources Management; External Relations; and Information Systems and Telecommunications. A UNHCR Global Service Centre, based in Budapest, Hungary, provides administrative support to the headquarters. There are five regional bureaux covering Africa, Asia and the Pacific, Europe, the Americas, and North Africa and the Middle East. In 2014 UNHCR employed around 7,140 regular staff, of whom about 85% were working in the field. At that time there were around 450 UNHCR offices in 123 countries.

Activities

The competence of the High Commissioner extends to any person who, owing to well-founded fear of being persecuted for reasons of race, religion, nationality, social group or political opinion, is outside the country of his or her nationality and is unable or, owing to such fear or for reasons other than personal convenience, remains unwilling to accept the protection of that country; or who, not having a nationality and being outside the country of his or her former habitual residence, is unable or, owing to such fear or for reasons other than personal convenience, is unwilling to return to it. This competence may be extended, by resolutions of the UN General Assembly and decisions of ExCom, to cover certain other 'persons of concern'. Although its core mandate relates to refugees, UNHCR also supports people who are threatened with displacement, and those who have been displaced from their homes inside their own country (i.e. with similar needs to those of refugees but who have not crossed an international border); these include—additionally to conflict-affected populations—people displaced by natural disasters, environmental degradation and the detrimental effects of climate change.

In July 2006 UNHCR issued a '10 Point Plan of Action on Refugee Protection and Mixed Migration' (*10 Point Plan*), detailing the following areas in which UNHCR might make an impact in supporting member states with the development of comprehensive migration strategies: co-operation among key players; data collection and analysis; protection-sensitive entry systems; reception arrangements; mechanisms for profiling and referral; differentiated processes and procedures; solutions for refugees; addressing secondary movements; return of non-refugees and alternative migration options; and information strategy. A revised version of the document was published in January 2007. UNHCR aims to address the fundamental causes of refugee flows, and has urged recognition and comprehension of the broad patterns of global displacement and migration, and of the mixed nature of many 21st-century population flows, which often comprise economic migrants, refugees, asylum seekers. and victims of trafficking requiring detection and support.

During 2005 the UN's Inter-Agency Standing Committee (IASC), concerned with co-ordinating the international response to humanitarian disasters, developed a concept of organizing agency assistance to internally displaced persons (IDPs) through the institutionalization of a 'Cluster Approach', currently comprising 11 core areas of activity. UNHCR is the lead agency for the clusters on Camp Co-ordination and Management (in conflict situations; the International Organization for Migration leads that cluster in natural disaster situations), Emergency Shelter, and (jointly with OHCHR and UNICEF) Protection. The IASC maintains a series of *Guidelines on Mental Health and Psychosocial Support in Emergency Settings*.

In 2009 UNHCR launched the first annual Global Needs Assessment (GNA), with the aim of mapping comprehensively the situation and needs of populations of concern falling under the mandate of the Office, to provide a blueprint for planning and decision-making for itself, governments and other partners.

UNHCR's global strategic priorities in 2014–15 were: promoting a favourable protection environment; fair processes and documentation; security from violence and exploitation; basic needs and services; community empowerment and self reliance; and durable solutions.

A Policy Development and Evaluation Service (PDES) reviews systematically UNHCR's operational effectiveness. In 2013 the PDES supported the formulation and implementation of the Office's policy on refugee protection and solutions in urban areas, by undertaking a global survey on the implementation of urban refugee policy; establishing internet-based compilation of effective operational practices in urban areas; and by implementing a review of an urban refugee programme then ongoing in New Delhi, India. It has also recently given consideration to areas including emergency response capabilities; protection and solutions; protracted refugee situations; sexual and gender-based violence; and refugee youth.

At December 2012 the total global population of concern to UNHCR, based on provisional figures, amounted to 35.8m. At that time the refugee population worldwide totalled 10.5m., of whom 6.7m. were being assisted by UNHCR. UNHCR was also concerned with some 525,941 recently returned refugees, 17.7m. IDPs, 1.5m. returned IDPs, 3.3m. stateless persons, and 936,740 asylum seekers. UNHCR maintains an online statistical population database.

World Refugee Day, sponsored by UNHCR, is held annually on 20 June. The theme in 2014 was to be 'One family torn apart by war is too many'.

INTERNATIONAL PROTECTION

In the exercise of its mandate UNHCR seeks to ensure that refugees and asylum seekers are protected against *refoulement* (forcible return), that they receive asylum, and that they are treated according to internationally recognized standards. The Office discourages the detention and encampment of refugees and asylum seekers, as this restricts their freedom of movement and opportunities to become self-reliant. UNHCR pursues these objectives by a variety of means that include promoting the conclusion and ratification by states of international instruments for the protection of refugees. The Office supervises the application of, and actively encourages states to accede to, the 1951 United Nations Convention relating to the Status of Refugees (with 145 parties at April 2014) and its 1967 Protocol (which had 146 parties at that time). These define the rights and duties of refugees and contain provisions dealing with a variety of matters that affect their day-to-day lives. Important provisions for the treatment of refugees are also contained in a number of instruments adopted at the regional level, including the 1969 Convention Governing the Specific Aspects of Refugee Problems, the European Agreement on the Abolition of Visas for Refugees, and the 1969 American Convention on Human Rights. In October 2009 African Union (AU) member states adopted the AU Convention for the Protection and Assistance of IDPs in Africa, the first legally binding international treaty providing legal protection and support to internally displaced populations. An increasing number of states have also adopted domestic legislation and/or administrative measures to implement the international instruments, particularly in the field of procedures for the determination of refugee status. UNHCR seeks to ensure swift, fair asylum procedure systems. The Office works in countries of origin and countries of asylum to ensure that policies, laws and practices comply with international standards, and in situations of forced displacement it advocates for the adoption of fair practices ensuring the protection of populations of concern.

UNHCR has sought to address the specific needs of refugee women, children, and elderly refugees, and prioritizes their needs in its programme planning and implementation. The Office actively seeks solutions to support refugees residing in urban areas (who by 2014 represented more than one-half of all refugees). It has attempted to deal with the problem of military attacks on refugee camps, by adopting and encouraging the acceptance of a set of principles to ensure the refugee safety. The post of Senior Adviser to the High Commissioner on Gender Issues was established in 2004, and in June 2011 UNHCR issued an updated strategy on Action against Sexual and Gender-Based Violence. UNHCR gives consideration to the environmental impact of its assistance programmes.

UNHCR has increasingly placed a focus on statelessness (lack of legal nationality), and promotes new accessions to the 1951 Convention Relating to the Status of Stateless Persons and the 1961 Convention on the Reduction of Statelessness, while maintaining that a significant proportion of the global stateless population has not hitherto been systematically identified. The Office promotes improved procedures for identifying stateless people on their territories, enhancing civil registration systems, and raising awareness of the options available to stateless people. Some US $79m. was allocated by the Office in 2013 to 61 projects on addressing statelessness.

ASSISTANCE ACTIVITIES

The first phase of an assistance operation uses UNHCR's capacity of emergency response. This enables UNHCR to address the immediate needs of refugees at short notice, for example, by employing specially trained emergency teams and maintaining stockpiles of basic equipment, medical aid and materials. A significant proportion of UNHCR expenditure is allocated to the next phase of an operation, providing 'care and maintenance' in stable refugee circumstances. This assistance can take various forms, including the provision of clean water, sanitation, medical care, shelter, and relief items (for example household goods, jerry cans, sleeping mats and blankets). UNHCR organizes, or else supports, refugee registration. Also covered in many instances are basic services, including education, counselling, and assistance with asylum applications. UNHCR is one of the 10 co-sponsors of UNAIDS, and promotes access for displaced populations to HIV/AIDS prevention services, treatment, and care.

As far as possible, assistance is geared towards the identification and implementation of durable solutions to refugee problems—this being the second statutory responsibility of UNHCR. Such solutions generally take one of three forms: voluntary repatriation; local integration; or resettlement onwards to a third country. UNHCR supports the implementation of the Guidance Note on Durable Solutions for Displaced Persons, adopted in 2004 by the UN Development Group.

Where voluntary repatriation, generally the preferred solution, is feasible, the Office assists refugees to overcome obstacles preventing their return to their country of origin. This may be done through negotiations with governments involved, and by arranging transport for and providing basic assistance packages to repatriating refugees, and also by implementing or supporting local integration or reintegration programmes in their home countries, including Quick Impact Projects aimed at income generation and at the restoration of local infrastructures. Some 526,000 refugees repatriated voluntarily to their home countries in 2012. Similarly, UNHCR works to enable local communities support returned IDPs.

When voluntary repatriation is not an option, efforts are made to assist refugees to integrate locally and to become self-supporting in their countries of asylum. This may be done either by granting loans to refugees, or by assisting them, through vocational training or in other ways, to learn a skill and to establish themselves in gainful occupations. One major form of assistance to help refugees re-establish themselves outside camps is the provision of housing.

In cases where resettlement through emigration is the only viable solution to a refugee problem, UNHCR negotiates with governments in an endeavour to obtain suitable resettlement opportunities, to encourage liberalization of admission criteria and to draw up special immigration schemes. During 2012 an estimated 71,000 refugees were resettled under UNHCR auspices.

EAST ASIA AND THE PACIFIC

Increasing mixed migratory flows to urban areas of the People's Republic of China have been reported in recent years. Refugees and asylum seekers in that country depend upon UNHCR for registration, refugee status determination, and practical support, as, although China has acceded to the 1951 Convention relating to the Status of Refugees and to its 1967 Protocol, it has not as yet enacted comprehensive national legislation in support of their implementation.

UNHCR has advocated for the accession of the Hong Kong Special Administrative Region—which attracts mixed inflows of refugees, asylum seekers and economic migrants—to the 1951 Refugees Convention. A 'unified screening mechanism' for the assessment of claims to protection from *refoulement* was initiated by the Hong Kong authorities in March 2014.

Inter-communal tensions between Rohingya Muslim and Buddhist residents of the northern Rakhine region of Myanmar (which have persisted over many years) escalated significantly, into violent conflict, in the second half of 2012, causing large-scale internal displacement and flight from the country. Meanwhile, from 2011 until the adoption of a peace accord between militants and the Government in October 2013, violent unrest destabilized Myanmar's northern Kachin region, resulting in further population displacement. In 2014 UNHCR was maintaining 12 offices in Myanmar, where it was supporting some 500,000 IDPs, of whom 140,000 (mainly Rohingya) were encamped in Rakhine, 100,000 in Kachin, 60,000 in Shan, and 230,000 in southeastern Myanmar. UNHCR was advocating for the right to citizenship of more than 800,000 stateless individuals in the country, including a majority of the IDPs. Significant outflows of Rohingya Muslims from Myanmar towards Indonesia, Malaysia and Thailand took place in recent years. At the end of 2013 some 128,000, mainly ethnic Karen and Kayah, Myanma refugees were sheltering in nine camps in Thailand close to the Thailand-Myanmar border. Thailand (which was also accommodating a stateless population totalling of around 500,000 at end-2013) had not by that time ratified the 1951 Refugee Convention and it had not established domestic legislation on refugees or highly functioning asylum procedures. In 2014 UNHCR aimed to prepare for and monitor spontaneous returns of Myanmar refugees from Thailand. During 2005–12 more than 80,000 refugees in Thailand were resettled to third countries. At end-2013 there were more than 95,000 UNHCR-assisted Myanma refugees living in urban situations in Malaysia; as Malaysia has not acceded to the 1951 Refugee Convention and lacks a legal framework for managing asylum cases UNHCR was working in 2014 to improve the protection environment there. In addition, an estimated 31,000 long-term Myanma refugees (Rohingya) were receiving basic care from UNHCR in two camps (Nayapara and Kutupalong) in south-eastern Bangladesh, having fled persecution in Rakhine in the 1990s. In 2014 UNHCR was aiming to improve the conditions of a further estimated 200,000 unregistered Myanma refugees living outside its camps in Bangladesh. In 2012 UNHCR facilitated the resettlement to third countries of 17,400 Myanma refugees, the main beneficiaries by nationality in that year under its global resettlement programme.

UNHCR endeavours to facilitate safe passage to the Republic of Korea for people who have fled from the Democratic People's Republic of Korea to China and other countries in the region.

With a view to deterring increasing mixed inflows of migrants and asylum seekers travelling by sea (so-called irregular maritime arrivals—IMAs) Australia has in recent years adopted strict asylum legislation, policies and processes, including the conclusion in August 2012 of bilateral arrangements with Nauru and Papua New Guinea that provide for the transfer of IMAs to offshore camps there for processing. UNHCR has repeatedly expressed concern over the transfer arrangement and over the absence of adequate protection standards for the detained transferees. In 2014 UNHCR aimed to advocate for broader domestic understanding of asylum and refugee issues in Australia and New Zealand; to monitor the protection environment for asylum seekers arriving in those countries; to advocate for access to effective and fair refugee status determination processes; to advocate for a reduction in the use of detention, which it deems to be harmful to the physical and psycho-social well-being of asylum seekers; and to promote increased intake of people recommended for resettlement. In February of that year UNHCR welcomed a commitment by the Australian authorities to investigate a disturbance that arose at the Manus Island detention centre in Papua New Guinea, resulting in the death of one asylum seeker and injuries to several others.

The Bali Process on People Smuggling, Trafficking in Persons and Related Transnational Crime (Bali Process), launched in February 2002, comprises a series of UNHCR-supported initiatives, including capacity-building workshops, that aim to raise awareness of people smuggling throughout the Asia-Pacific region; to promote the enactment of national legislation aimed at combating this; to address its root causes; to improve intelligence sharing and enhance co-operation among law enforcement agencies, and between border agencies; and to support states in adopting best practices in asylum management. Bali Process ministerial review conferences were held in April 2003, April 2009, March 2011 and April 2013. The March 2011 conference adopted a Regional Co-operation Framework (RCF), which aimed to strengthen regional collaboration in safeguarding the protection of refugees while simultaneously countering irregular population movements. In September 2012 a regional support office was inaugurated in Bangkok, Indonesia, to assist the implementation of the RCF.

SOUTH ASIA

From the late 1970s civil strife in Afghanistan resulted in massive population displacements, reaching a peak in 1990, by which time nearly 6.3m. refugees had fled from that country into neighbouring Pakistan and Iran. The international political crisis that emerged in September 2001, leading to the launch in October of military action directed by a US-led global coalition against targets in the Taliban-administered areas of Afghanistan, prompted further population movements. At that time the Office initiated an emergency relief operation to assist Afghan refugees and IDPs, while substantially reinforcing its presence in Iran and Pakistan. It was estimated that from October 2001–January 2002 some 50,000 Afghan refugees entered Pakistan officially, while about 150,000 crossed into the country at unofficial border points. Much smaller movements into Iran were reported. Spontaneous repatriations also occurred during that period (reportedly partly owing to the poor conditions at many camps in Pakistan), and UNHCR-assisted IDP returns were also undertaken. From November 2001 UNHCR implemented humanitarian operations within Afghanistan, including the implementation of QIPs and the distribution of supplies. In March 2002 tripartite accords on repatriation were concluded by UNHCR with the Afghan authorities and with Iran and Pakistan. During 2002–early 2014 more than 5.7m. refugees returned voluntarily to Afghanistan from Pakistan and Iran; of these, some 4.6m. were assisted by UNHCR. Limited socio-economic opportunities in Afghanistan have, however, adversely impacted the reintegration of returnees. Where possible UNHCR provides them with a cash grant (equivalent to US $150 in 2013), offers counselling on health, legal and social matters, and monitors their situation. Particular focus is placed upon the situation of returnee women and on the prevention of gender-based violence, and on encouraging the return of professional workers, especially doctors and teachers. UNHCR aims to strengthen the capacity of the Afghan Government to manage the return and sustainable reintegration of refugees and IDPs, and—with a focus on areas of high returns—works to promote an environment conducive to sustainable reintegration. In May 2012 a regional stakeholders conference on Afghanistan endorsed a new 'Solutions Strategy for Afghan Refugees' (SSAR), negotiated during 2011 by UNHCR, Afghanistan, Iran and Pakistan, and based on the pillars of voluntary repatriation, sustainable reintegration in Afghanistan, and support for refugee-hosting communities. In June 2013 UNHCR, Afghanistan and Pakistan met to address the situation of 1.6m. Afghan refugees whose right to remain in Pakistan was due to expire at that time; the Pakistan authorities agreed to extend this until 31 December 2015. At 31 December 2013 Iran was hosting around 800,000 UNHCR-assisted Afghan refugees. At that time at least 2.4m. unregistered Afghan migrants were also believed to be residing in Pakistan and Iran. It is estimated that around one-half of the Afghan refugees in neighbouring countries were not born in Afghanistan. In early 2014 there were some 600,000 Afghan IDPs. The relocation of significant numbers of IDPs and returnees from rural to urban areas was reported in 2013, placing considerable strain on housing and local services. UNHCR envisaged that the planned withdrawal of international security forces from Afghanistan by the end of 2014 might further restrict the already challenging humanitarian operational environment, including unreliable access to vulnerable communities, and thus adversely affect the Agency's programme delivery in the country; and that any deterioration in the already fragile security situation might prompt further population displacement.

At the end of 2013 UNHCR was assisting around 520,000 people who had been displaced from their homes by ongoing insecurity in the Federally Administered Tribal Areas and Khyber Pakhtunkhwa area of Pakistan. The Agency, whose movements have been restricted by the fragile security situation, was in 2014 supporting three camps accommodating more than 80,000 of the IDPs. It was also assisting 330,000 recently returned IDPs, and undertaking protection activities in areas including registration and civil documentation support.

In 1991–92 large numbers of people of Nepalese ethnic origin ('Lhotshampasas') living in Bhutan sought refuge from alleged persecution by fleeing to eastern Nepal. In December 2000 Bhutan and Nepal reached agreement on a joint verification mechanism for the repatriation of the refugees, and the first verification of Bhutanese refugees was undertaken in March 2001; progress towards repatriation, however, subsequently stalled. In November 2007—at which time Nepal was still hosting nearly 110,000 Bhutanese refugees—UNHCR initiated a large-scale operation, in co-operation with the International Organization for Migration (IOM) and the governments of Nepal and a core group of resettlement countries (Australia, Canada, Denmark, the Netherlands, New Zealand, Norway, the United Kingdom and the USA), to resettle as many as possible of the Bhutanese refugees, with a view to providing a durable solution to their situation. By the end of December 2013 around 83,000 of the refugees had been resettled (with the USA receiving the largest number); 34,000 Bhutanese remained, meanwhile, at two camps in eastern Nepal. In 2014 UNHCR planned to facilitate the resettlement of up to a further 7,000 Bhutanese refugees from Nepal. The Office was at that time advocating for the Nepalese authorities to simplify the national visa waiver process, in order to facilitate the departures of refugees accepted for resettlement. During 2007 the Nepalese Government extended citizenship to some 2.6m. of the 3.5m. stateless people hitherto resident in Nepal.

During 1983–2001 hostilities between the Sri Lankan Government and Tamil separatists resulted in the displacement of more than 1m. Sri Lankan Tamil refugees (who sought shelter in India) and IDPs. Ongoing efforts by UNHCR to repatriate the refugees were disrupted in late 1995 by an offensive by Sri Lankan government troops against the northern Jaffna peninsula, which caused a massive displacement of the local Tamil population. Increasing insecurity from late 1999 prompted further population movements. However, following the conclusion of a cease-fire agreement between the Sri Lankan Government and Tamil separatists in February 2002, the number of spontaneous returns accelerated. From April 2006 conflict between Tamil separatists and the Sri Lankan Government escalated once again, prompting a new wave of internal displacement and refugee movements to India, and in January 2008 the 2002 cease-fire agreement was abrogated, further intensifying the situation. More than 335,000 Sri Lankans were newly displaced during April 2006–February 2009; UNHCR screened, registered and provided emergency accommodation for affected civilians, advised the Sri Lankan authorities, and monitored the human rights situation. In May 2009 the Sri Lankan Government declared an end to military operations against the Tamil separatists. The largest camp for displaced persons in Sri Lanka, Menik Farm, was closed in September 2012. In 2013 UNHCR shifted its priorities in Sri Lanka towards reintegration support, including the promotion of self-reliance for returnees. The Office continues to monitor the protection needs of Sri Lankans remaining in protracted displacement (unable to return home owing to issues with housing and land—numbering 93,482 at end-2012), and to advocate for the rights of all persons of concern, including by promoting civil documentation and land and property rights. In 2014 the Office was working to facilitate voluntary repatriation for the 67,000 Sri Lankan refugees still accommodated in camps in southern India. At end-December 2012 India's total refugee population of some 185,656 also included 100,003 refugees from China (mainly Tibetans).

CENTRAL ASIA

In the early 2000s UNHCR implemented an initiative to integrate locally up to 10,000 Tajik refugees of Kyrgyz ethnic origin in Kyrgyzstan and 12,500 Tajik refugees of Turkmen origin in Turkmenistan; this process was facilitated by the conclusion in mid-2003 of a Kyrgyz-Tajik agreement on a simplified procedure for citizenship acquisition. From 1 July 2006 UNHCR terminated refugee status for exiled Tajiks, although the Office continued to support their voluntary repatriation. By the end of that year most of the former Tajik refugees in Kyrgyzstan and Turkmenistan had become naturalized citizens of those countries, as planned; in 2008 all remaining Tajik refugees in Kyrgyzstan were granted Kyrgyz citizenship. UNHCR has helped the Kyrgyz authorities to integrate the former Tajiks. UNHCR ascertained that there were 15,473 stateless people residing in Kyrgyzstan at the end of 2012, either without documentation or holding expired USSR passports; the Office and the Kyrgyz authorities have aimed to work together to support applications by the stateless individuals for Kyrgyz citizenship. In August 2012 Turkmenistan acceded to the 1961 Convention on the Reduction of Statelessness.

From late 2001 about 9,000 Afghan refugees repatriated from Tajikistan under the auspices of UNHCR and the IOM. UNHCR expressed concern following the adoption by the Tajikistan authorities in May 2002 of refugee legislation that reportedly contravened the 1951 Convention relating to the Status of Refugees and its 1967 Protocol. During 2006 nearly 1,500 Afghan refugees were resettled from Tajikistan to third countries, leaving a remaining Afghan refugee population in that country of about 1,000; UNHCR subsequently pursued durable solutions for their local integration. Increasing numbers of Afghan asylum seekers fled to Tajikistan in 2010, however, and by 2014 Tajikistan was reported to be accommodating in total around 4,000 refugees and asylum seekers, of whom the majority were of Afghan origin. The refugees and asylum seekers were not permitted at that time to reside in Tajikistan's major urban centres. In 2013 UNHCR supported the Tajik authorities with the establishment of a modern refugee registration framework, and with revising national citizenship legislation. During 2014, in view of the planned withdrawal of international security forces from Afghanistan by the end of that year, UNHCR was to assist Tajikistan—which, it was envisaged, might consequently be particularly at risk of receiving a new influx of asylum seekers—with improving its emergency preparedness capabilities.

UNHCR has reported in recent years that compliance with the 1951 Convention is problematic in the Central Asia region, and that national preoccupations with perceived cross-border threats and domestic security have adversely impacted asylum policy and the protection of refugees. A Regional Ministerial Conference on Refugee Protection and International Migration in Central Asia, organized by UNHCR, with IOM and the Kazakh authorities, in March 2011, adopted the Almatı Declaration, in which participants determined to draft a regional framework for co-operation in the efficient management of mixed migration flows and refugee issues. The first meeting of National Co-ordinators from Central Asia, arranged by UNHCR in Almatı, in September 2012, adopted the consequent regional co-operation framework and a regional action plan on refugee protection, and determined to establish in Almatı the secretariat of the developing so-called Almatı Process on Migration; the core countries of the process were Afghanistan, China, Iran, Kazakhstan, Kyrgyzstan, Pakistan, Tajikistan and Turkmenistan. The meeting also tasked UNHCR, IOM and the Kazakhstan Government with organizing a second Regional Ministerial Conference on Refugee Protection and International Migration in Central Asia; this was convened in June 2013. In February UNHCR and IOM organized a meeting under the Almatı Process relating to operational aspects of managing regional population movements. In May 2012 UNHCR, the Organization of Islamic Cooperation and the Government of Turkmenistan organized the first OIC International Ministerial Conference on Refugees in the Muslim World, in Aşgabat.

The Office's priorities in Central Asia in 2014 included protection of refugees and asylum seekers; ensuring the compliance of refugee status determination procedures with international standards, while also seeking durable solutions and promoting the self-reliance of refugees; preserving asylum space within mixed migratory flows, through ongoing support to the Almatı Process; preventing and reducing statelessness while advocating for accession to the 1951 Convention Relating to the Status of Stateless Persons and the 1961 Convention on the Reduction of Statelessness; and developing an optimal response capacity to deal with emergencies, with a particular focus on the possibility of an influx of Afghans into the region, given the evolving security situation in that country.

NORTH AFRICA AND THE MIDDLE EAST

Given the lack of progress in achieving a settlement agreement for Western Sahara, UNHCR co-ordinates humanitarian assistance for around 90,000 vulnerable Sahrawi refugees accommodated, in a protracted situation ongoing since 1975, in five camps in the Tindouf area of Algeria; the Sahrawi refugees are heavily dependent on external assistance as there are few opportunities for income generation in the remote camps. In 2014 UNHCR was continuing to provide them with protection and basic relief items, and to implement a confidence-building programme that it launched in 2004 with the aim of restoring family and community links, and reducing the risk of psychological isolation; by 2014 around 12,000 people had participated in family visits under the programme.

UNHCR operates eight offices, in Yemen, which has historically received refugees fleeing political instability and intermittent drought in the Horn of Africa. At 31 December 2012 Yemen was hosting an estimated 237,182, mostly Somali refugees (about 95% of the total); the majority of these were residing in urban areas, while some 20,000 were accommodated in the al-Kharaz camp. Some 22,300 new Somali refugees arrived in Yemen in 2012. Ongoing violent conflict in northern Yemen has also generated internal displacement, and at the end of 2012 there were an estimated 385,320 IDPs. A regional conference on asylum and migration from the Horn of Africa to Yemen, convened in November 2013 by the Yemeni authorities, with support from UNHCR and IOM, issued a declaration urging improved support for countries of origin and host countries, and better international management of mixed migration. In 2014, when continuing insecurity and fragile economic and socio-political conditions in the country were creating a challenging humanitarian operational space, UNHCR's priorities in Yemen included strengthening the protection environment for asylum seekers, refugees, IDPs and returnees; pursuing durable solutions (with a focus on the protracted IDP presence in northern areas); providing basic services for camp-based refugees; promoting self-reliance, for example through vocational-skills training and access to income-generating activities; and promoting access to education and health services.

In March 2003 UNHCR and the International Federation of Red Cross and Red Crescent Societies signed an agreement to co-operate in providing humanitarian relief in Iraq and neighbouring countries. From mid-2003, following the overthrow of the Saddam Hussain regime by a US-led force, UNHCR developed plans for the eventual phased repatriation of more than 500,000 of the large population of Iraqis exiled worldwide, and for the return to their homes of some 800,000 IDPs. The Office assumed responsibility for assisting about 50,000 refugees from other countries (including some 34,000 Palestinians—of whom an estimated 11,740 remained in 2013) who had been supported by the previous Iraqi administration but were now suffering harassment; many had abandoned their homes in Iraq owing to insufficient security and inadequate supplies. Negotiations with Iran were initiated in mid-2003 to enable Iranian refugees to repatriate across the Iraq–Iran border. From March–May 2003, and following a devastating bomb attack in August on the UN headquarters in Baghdad, all international UN humanitarian personnel were withdrawn from Iraq, leaving national staff to conduct operations on the ground. During 2003–05 some 315,000 spontaneous returns by Iraqi refugees and asylum seekers and 496,000 returns by IDPs were reported. However, owing to the ongoing unstable security situation, UNHCR and the Iraqi Interim Government (inaugurated in June 2004) discouraged Iraqi refugees from returning home, and UNHCR warned governments hosting Iraqi refugees against repatriation, as well as advising continued protection of Iraqi asylum seekers. During 2006–07, owing to escalating violent sectarian unrest, it was reported that more than 1.5m. Iraqis had become newly displaced and that many people—including skilled and professional workers—had left Iraq, further inhibiting the national recovery process. In April 2007 an International Conference on Addressing the Humanitarian Needs of Refugees and Internally Displaced Persons inside Iraq and in Neighbouring Countries was convened in Geneva by the UN High Commissioner for Refugees. UNHCR remains highly concerned for foreign refugees remaining in Iraq (totalling 98,822 at end-2012). UNHCR has a small international presence (re-established in March 2008) in Baghdad, Basrah, Erbil, Kirkuk and Mosul, as well as 18 Protection and Assistance Centres, six Return Integration and Community Centres, and 40 mobile teams. Through its network of offices UNHCR monitors population movements and the well-being of refugees, IDPs and returnees throughout Iraq. At 31 December 2012, the total Iraqi IDP population amounted to 1.1m., around 219,000 IDPs having returned to their homes during that year. The Office provides returnees, in accordance with a case-by-case approach, with counselling, limited transportation and livelihood grants. UNHCR's priorities in Iraq in 2014 included advocating for a strengthened social safety net for vulnerable populations; providing advocacy, protection interventions and basic assistance to IDPs in newly and protracted displacement situations; capacity building of state and NGO partners; enhanced monitoring and assessment of the protection environment; assessing the international protection needs of former inmates of Camp New Iraq (also known as Camp Ashraf); enhancing its response to sexual and gender-based violence; and providing outreach activities to Syrian refugees in urban areas. UNHCR maintains (in northern Iraq) an emergency stockpile of basic non-food items to support Syrian refugees in Iraq. A Comprehensive Plan to End Displacement, developed in 2012 by the Iraqi authorities with UNHCR support, was being implemented in 2014, providing for shelter programmes in areas of displacement, and improved access to basic services, livelihoods and employment in areas of return.

At the end of 2012 UNHCR reported that there was an Iraqi refugee population of 471,418 in Syria (62,727 UNHCR-assisted) and 63,037 (27,814 UNHCR-protected) in Jordan, as well as smaller groups of Iraqis in other neighbouring countries. In 2010 UNHCR and the Syrian Government concluded a Co-operation Agreement providing the legal basis for the Office's activities in that country, which have included the pursuit of accelerated departures and resettlement opportunities for the most vulnerable Iraqi refugees. The violent unrest that emerged in Syria from 2011, and escalated during 2012–14, disrupted resettlement activities and prompted an acceleration in returns to Iraq; some 56,930 Iraqis were reported to have repatriated voluntarily from Syria in 2012 (only 8,960 of these UNHCR-assisted). A new secondary displacement was developing within Iraq, as many returnees were unable to go back to their places of origin. In 2014 UNHCR was working to ensure the basic protection of Iraqi refugees remaining in Syria; implementing programmes aimed at meeting their basic food and shelter requirements; and providing them with monthly cash assistance. During 2014 UNHCR was closely monitoring the Iraqi refugee population in Jordan, to ensure that their protection needs were still being met, given that recent large inflows of Syrian refugees were placing additional strain on local infrastructures and services.

An appeal for some US $6,500m. was made in December 2013 to fund the 2014 edition of the Syria Humanitarian Assistance Response Plan-Syria Regional Response Plan (SHARP-RRP); UNHCR and other humanitarian agencies were co-ordinating and implementing the RRP, which aims to assist Syrians who have fled to neighbouring countries (which have continued to keep their borders open to the influx), as well as supporting host communities. By April 2014 some 2,585,370 Syrian refugees (of a total 2,633,287 persons of concern) had been registered by UNHCR in neighbouring countries. At that time 953,626 Syrian refugees were registered in Lebanon (where the total Syrian population of concern was estimated to exceed 1m.), 667,636 in Turkey, 588,979 in Jordan, 219,579 in Iraq, and 135,853 in Egypt. In 2014 a UNHCR presence in Jordan was managing the overcrowded Za'atri refugee camp, near Mafraq, which opened in July 2012 with capacity for around 60,000 residents, and was by early 2014 accommodating around 120,000 Syrian refugees. A second, smaller camp, Mrajeeb al-Fhood, was opened near Zarqa in April 2013. The majority of Syrian refugees in Jordan were based outside camps, mainly in northern areas. In 2014 the Office aimed to promote in Jordan timely refugee registration (enabling prompt access to basic services) and a favourable protection environment, to work to mitigate the impact of the influx of Syrian refugees on local communities, and to offer technical assistance to the Jordanian authorities to reinforce the capacity of national institutions. UNHCR was assisting the Lebanese authorities in 2014 with building capacity to support refugees and to prevent statelessness; the Office was also working to ensure the timely registration of Syrian refugees in Lebanon; providing them with shelter and essential non-food items; promoting access to health services and education; providing income-generating and vocational training activities aimed at supporting self-reliance within the refugee community; and supporting the overall protection environment in host communities. Although there were no formal refugee camps in Lebanon, several informal tented encampments were operating in 2014. In 2014 UNHCR was focusing on registration and protection activities for Syrian refugees in Iraq (more than 90% of whom were sheltering in the Kurdistan region); targeting protection and support interventions at refugees living, often in substandard conditions, outside camps (accounting for around three-fifths of all Syrian refugees in Iraq) and their host communities; providing outreach support to Syrian refugees in urban areas; and monitoring the provision of essential assistance and services in refugee camps (the largest of which was Domiz camp, in Dohuk, Kurdistan, accommodating 108,118 Syrian refugees by February 2014). Meanwhile, at that time, UNHCR was also providing essential material and technical assistance to the Turkish authorities to enable them to register and protect Syrian refugees, accommodated in 21 camps and in host communities in that country. Within Syria—where, by April 2014, the IDP population had reached at least 6.5m., and a total of 9.3m. people were reported to be in urgent need of support as a consequence of the ongoing conflict—UNHCR, within the SHARP framework, is responsible for the provision of support to IDPs in the areas of shelter and non-food items, as well as providing protection, financial assistance, health, community services, and registration and counselling services. UNHCR has also assisted Syrian IDPs through cash-for-shelter activities. At 31 December 2012 Syria was also accommodating a significant population of stateless people, totalling 221,000.

In January 2014 UNHCR, UNICEF and other partners, initiated a 'No Lost Generation' strategy, which envisaged raising US $1,000m.

from voluntary donations to improve the situation of more than 3m. children affected by the long-term civil war.

In 2014 UNHCR was developing a new Central Mediterranean Sea Initiative, with a view to enhancing local responsibility-sharing arrangements and sea rescue mechanisms, in response to high numbers of dangerous journeys by sea being undertaken by refugees and economic migrants, especially on routes from North Africa to Italy and Malta. These have resulted in significant numbers of fatalities in recent years, including, in October 2013, the deaths of more than 300 African migrant passengers on a boat that sank in the vicinity of the Italian Mediterranean island of Lampedusa. Many migrants and refugees crossing the Mediterranean have originated in Eritrea and Somalia, and recently increasing numbers of Egyptians, Libyans, Syrians and Syria-based Palestinian refugees have attempted boat journeys across the Mediterranean.

During 2008 the Iranian authorities initiated an online refugee registration process, referred to as Amayesh, under which the details of more than 900,000 people were registered; identity cards were issued to refugees registered under the scheme, and, subsequently, temporary work permits began to be issued to Amayesh card holders with a view to finding temporary solutions in Iran for the Afghan refugees. The data collated under Amayesh also supported UNCHR's planning processes. By the end of December 2013 around 804,000 UNHCR-assisted Afghan refugees remained in Iran (in addition to about 1m. unregistered Afghan migrants), almost entirely based in urban and semi-urban areas. In 2014 UNHCR was focusing on the provision of assistance to Afghan refugees in Iran in areas including education, poverty alleviation and livelihoods, with a view to enabling the refugees to reintegrate successfully into Afghan society following their return to their home country.

SUB-SAHARAN AFRICA

UNHCR has provided assistance to refugees and internally displaced populations in many parts of the continent where civil conflict, violations of human rights, drought, famine or environmental degradation have forced people to flee their home regions. The majority of African refugees and returnees are located in countries that are themselves suffering major economic problems and are thus unable to provide the basic requirements of the uprooted people. At 31 December 2012 there were an estimated 6.4m. people of concern to UNHCR in eastern Africa and the Horn of Africa; 4.4m. in Central Africa and the Great Lakes region; 900,000 in West Africa; and 300,000 in Southern Africa.

The Horn of Africa, afflicted by famine and long-term internal conflict, has suffered large-scale population movements in recent decades. During 1992–mid-2006 more than 1m. Somalis (of whom about 485,000 received UNHCR assistance) returned to their country, having sought sanctuary in neighbouring states following the January 1991 overthrow of the former Somali president Siad Barre. There was, at 31 December 2012, a Somalian IDP population totalling more than 1.1m. UNHCR is responsible for co-ordinating the UN's emergency shelter and protection clusters in Somalia. Severe food insecurity in southern areas of Somalia that escalated in 2011 exacerbated further the ongoing humanitarian crisis in that country. At September 2012 3.8m. Somalis were estimated to be food-insecure, and many Somali rural households were reported to have migrated in search of food and support towards the conflict-affected Somali capital, Mogadishu, and into neighbouring countries. Following a declaration of a state of famine in July 2011 UNHCR distributed more than 27,000 emergency assistance packages to 174,000 IDPs in southern Somalia and Mogadishu, and supported nearly 270,000 IDPs throughout the country through the provision of emergency relief items such as blankets, mattresses, kitchen sets, and plastic sheeting. Despite the inauguration of a new President and federal administration in Somalia in the second half of 2012 the humanitarian situation in parts of the country has subsequently remained fragile. The Office's priorities within Somalia for 2014 were shifting from the provision of assistance towards the pursuit of durable solutions for people of concern, including the assisted return of IDPs and refugees to their communities of origin, or to other selected integration areas; the provision of shelter and livelihood opportunities; and the implementation of community-based projects to benefit both returnees and their host communities. The Office's durable solutions strategy was being pursed within the context of the New Deal Compact for Somalia, adopted in September 2013 by stakeholders in Somalia, and of UNHCR's Global Initiative on Somali Refugees, inaugurated in November by the High Commissioner on Refugees. In 2014 UNHCR was also to continue to supply basic services to populations of concern; to provide technical support to the new federal authorities on the development of an efficient asylum framework; to advocate for the adoption of international protection conventions, and for equal access to justice; to identify and provide protection for people of concern within larger mixed migratory flows; to provide protection from sexual and gender-based violence; and to conduct registration, documentation and community outreach activities for refugee populations in Somaliland and Puntland. UNHCR maintains a presence in those two territories, and envisaged that by the end of 2014 it would be conducting its activities from a fully functional main office in Mogadishu and from eight field offices.

There was at 31 December 2012 an estimated total Somali refugee population of 1.1m., sheltering in nearby countries, principally Kenya and Yemen. During 2007 Kenya enacted a Refugee Act that provided for a more active state role in managing the registration and status determination of refugees. UNHCR assists the Kenyan authorities with strengthening the response capacity of national and local institutions and with finding durable solutions for refugees. By April 2014 some 343,694 Somali refugees were accommodated under UNHCR protection at North-East Kenya's Dadaab complex of camps, comprising the Hagadera, Dagahaley, Ifo, Ifo East, Ifo West and Kambioos camps; Hagadera (with around 104,376 Somali residents) was the largest of the camps. In early 2014 around 30,000 further Somali refugees were living in Nairobi, the Kenyan capital, and some 54,000 Somalis were sheltering at the Kakuma camp, in Turkana, North-Western Kenya. It was hoped that the inauguration in August 2012 of a new Somali federal administration might lead to an environment conducive to the voluntary repatriation of Somali refugees from Kenya. By the end of 2013 the Kakuma camp was accommodating in total 125,000 refugees, and required additional land for expansion, having received a sharply increased inflow of new refugees, predominantly originating in South Sudan, during 2012–13; the outbreak of violent conflict in that country from mid-December 2013–mid-January 2014 prompted an escalation in South Sudanese refugee arrivals, with around 300 reported to have crossed the border into Kenya daily during that period. In 2014 UNHCR was responding to protection needs at Kakuma, and was developing the provision of basic services and infrastructure to enable the newly registered refugee population to be effectively supported. There were an estimated 412,000 Kenyan IDPs at 31 December 2012.

At 31 December 2012 an estimated 527,800 Sudanese were exiled as refugees, mainly in South Sudan, Chad, Ethiopia, Kenya and Uganda, owing to a history of civil unrest in southern Sudan and the emergence in early 2003 of a new conflict zone in the western Sudanese province of Darfur. Discord in 2012 between and Sudan and South Sudan (which had become independent in July 2011) has caused further population displacement. In February 2006 UNHCR and Sudan signed tripartite agreements with Ethiopia, the Democratic Republic of the Congo (DRC) and the Central African Republic (CAR) to provide a legal framework for the repatriation of Sudanese refugees remaining in those countries. In August 2011 the Sudanese Government amended legislation to deprive of Sudanese citizenship all individuals who acquired the nationality of newly independent South Sudan. UNHCR has repeatedly expressed concern over the implications of this for significant numbers of people of mixed Sudanese/South Sudanese origin living in border areas. Mounting tensions during the first half of 2012 in disputed border areas between Sudan and South Sudan caused increasing numbers of Sudanese to flee to South Sudan, and also to Ethiopia. By February 2014 South Sudan was accommodating—mainly in the Upper Nile and Unity regions—233,363 registered refugees, of whom the majority (211,721) were from Sudan. Insecurity within South Sudan (persistent inter-ethnic clashes, and, most particularly, the violent conflict that erupted there in December 2013–early 2014) have caused significant population displacement; by February 2014 some 738,000 people had been displaced within South Sudan since December 2013 (of whom about three-fifths were sheltering in or around UN compounds), and more than 130,000 South Sudanese had fled to neighbouring countries (of whom 79,460 had sought shelter in Uganda, 42,366 in Ethiopia, 27,612 in Sudan, and 18,020 in Kenya). In early 2014 UNHCR was supporting the construction of new camps and the expansion of existing ones in the countries receiving significant inflows of South Sudanese refugees. Despite the conclusion in mid-January of a ceasefire agreement between militants and the South Sudanese authorities, South Sudan remained highly insecure in February, prompting UNHCR in that month to issue a non-return advisory, urging states receiving South Sudanese refugees to continue to extend protection to all, with the exception of people accused of committing serious violations of human rights. Since 2008 violent attacks committed by Ugandan Lord's Resistance Army rebels on communities in the (now) South Sudan-Sudan-CAR-DRC-Sudan border region have caused significant population displacement.

In response to a severe breakdown in law and order in the CAR, caused by a rebel offensive, initiated in December 2012, that culminated in the overturning of the legitimately elected Government in March 2013 and the inauguration as President in August of the coup leader, an estimated 935,000 people had become displaced within that country by early 2014, many sheltering in informal displacement sites. Furthermore, around 65,000 CAR refugees had fled by that time into neighbouring countries, creating a total CAR refugee population in the region of nearly around 240,000 (of whom 86,000 were in Cameroon, 80,000 in Chad, and 60,000 in the DRC). Intense violent conflict that erupted in the CAR capital, Bangui, from early

December 2013 had, by January 2014, displaced up to two-thirds of Bangui's population. In 2014 UNHCR was strengthening its monitoring, protection activities, and advocacy on behalf of the internally displaced population, while supplying non-food items and shelter support to the most vulnerable IDPs, and providing assistance aimed at keeping children in education. Furthermore, the Office was registering the CAR refugees in nearby countries, facilitating their transferral to camps, providing them with documentation, and distributing basic assistance.

From April 2003 more than 200,000 refugees from Sudan's western Darfur region sought shelter across the Sudan-Chad border, having fled an alleged campaign of killing, rape and destruction of property conducted by pro-government militias against the indigenous population. In addition, 2m.–3m. people became displaced within Darfur itself. The Office organized airlifts of basic household items to the camps, aimed to improve and expand refugees' access to sanitation, health care and education, to manage supplementary and therapeutic feeding facilities in order to combat widespread malnutrition, to provide psychosocial support to traumatized refugees, and to promote training and livelihood programmes. The Chad-Darfur operation has been hampered by severe water shortages resulting from the arid environment of the encampment areas, necessitating costly UNHCR deliveries of stored water, and by intense insecurity. A significant deterioration during 2004–09 in the security situation in the eastern areas of Chad bordering Darfur, as well as in Darfur itself, led to further population displacement in the region, including the displacement of significant numbers of Chadians. At December 2012 there were also around 90,000 Chadian IDPs and 35,000 returned IDPs who had fled inwards from the Chad-Sudan border region. UNHCR established a presence within western Darfur in June 2004, and in 2012 the Office provided protection assistance to around 2.7m. displaced and returned Darfurians, as well as Chadian refugees, in the region. Following the establishment of the AU/UN Hybrid Operation in Darfur (UNAMID) in December 2007, UNHCR opened a liaison office near the UNAMID base in northern Darfur. UNHCR teams have undertaken efforts to train Sudanese managers of camps in Darfur in the areas of protection and human rights. The Office has also established in the area a number of women's centres providing support to survivors of sexual violence, and several centres for IDP youths, as well as rehabilitating conflict-damaged schools. In 2012 a gradual shift in UNHCR programming from a primarily protection-oriented, camp-based approach to pursuing durable solutions was initiated; this was ongoing in 2014. Nevertheless, insecurity continued to prevail, and during 2013 400,000 people were newly displaced in the territory.

Since the 1990s the Great Lakes region of central Africa has experienced massive population displacement, causing immense operational challenges and demands on the resources of international humanitarian and relief agencies. From late 1998 substantial numbers of DRC nationals fled escalating civil conflict to neighbouring countries (mainly Tanzania and Zambia) or were displaced within the DRC. Meanwhile, the DRC, in turn, was hosting a significant refugee population. In view of the conclusion, in December 2002, of a peace agreement, UNHCR planned for eventual mass refugee returns. Owing to incessant rebel activity, insecurity continued to prevail, however, during 2003–14, in north-eastern areas of the DRC, resulting in further population displacements; by the end of 2013 it was estimated that the DRC had 2.7m. IDPs, around four-fifths of whom were living with host families or in spontaneous settlements. As lead agency of the protection cluster in the DRC, UNHCR responsibility for directing shelter and camp co-ordination activities. During 2012 militants of the Kivu-based 23 March Movement (known as 'M23') became increasingly active in north-eastern DRC, clashing with government forces and intensifying the ongoing population displacement; M23 forces eventually surrendered to the DRC security forces in early November 2013. By February 2014 there were more than 400,000 IDPs in Katanga, south-eastern DRC, where during 2012–14 so-called Mai Mai Kata Katanga insurgents, seeking Katanga's secession from the DRC, were clashing with security forces; from 2013 the Mai Mai Kata Katanga pursued a scorched earth policy, involving the burning of villages, in Manono, Mitwaba and Pweto districts. At the end of 2012 some 57,857 DRC refugees were sheltering in neighbouring Rwanda (all UNHCR-assisted), while 127,021 had fled to Uganda (also all supported by UNHCR). A further 41,349 were in Burundi and 63,330 were in Tanzania. In September 2005 UNHCR and the DRC and Tanzanian Governments signed a tripartite agreement on facilitating refugee returns of DRC refugees from Tanzania, and, during 2005–early 2012 UNHCR assisted 60,000 such returns. A tripartite agreement on assistance was concluded by the Burundian and Tanzanian Governments and UNHCR in August 2003. In April 2010 the UN High Commissioner for Refugees expressed gratitude to the Tanzanian authorities for offering citizenship to 162,000 long-standing Burundian refugees. In April–November 2012 the residents of Tanzania's Mtabila refugee camp were repatriated to Burundi and in December that camp was closed. UNHCR concluded similar tripartite accords in 2003 with the Rwandan Government and other states hosting Rwandan refugees, paving the way subsequently for significant voluntary refugee returns to Rwanda. From 30 June 2013 refugee status for people who fled Rwanda before 31 December 1998 was terminated. In 2012 UNHCR assisted a total of 11,200 refugee returns to that country. The major populations of concern to UNHCR in the Great Lakes region at 31 December 2012 were, provisionally, as follows: 2.7m. IDPs, 304,600 returned IDPs and 509,396 refugees in the DRC; 78,948 IDPs in Burundi; and 97,470 refugees in Rwanda. Meanwhile there was a refugee population of only 1,130 in Tanzania, very significantly reduced from 602,088 at end-2004. The DRC was the country of origin of the largest number of asylum seekers worldwide in 2012, with 52,100 new applications made by DRC in nationals in that year.

UNHCR's activities in assisting refugees in West Africa have included a focus on the prevention of sexual and gender-based violence in refugee camps and collaboration with other agencies to ensure continuity between initial humanitarian assistance and long-term development support. UNHCR provided assistance to 120,000 people displaced by the extreme insecurity that developed in Côte d'Ivoire from September 2002. About 25,000 Côte d'Ivoire refugees fled to southern Liberia, and others sought shelter in Ghana, Guinea and Mali. In addition, between November and January 2003 an estimated 40,000 Liberian refugees in Côte d'Ivoire repatriated, in both spontaneous and partly UNHCR-assisted movements, having suffered harassment since the onset of the conflict. UNHCR initiated a number of Quick Impact Projectss aimed at rehabilitating the infrastructure of communities that were to receive returned Côte d'Ivoire refugees. As a consequence of unrest that erupted in Côte d'Ivoire following a disputed presidential election held in October–November 2010, an estimated 200,000 people became displaced from their homes in western Côte d'Ivoire, and some 150,000 Ivorian nationals fled to Liberia, during December 2010–April 2011. In response to the influx of Côte d'Ivoire refugees into Liberia, UNHCR facilitated the registration of the new refugees and mobilized the delivery of food aid and non-food relief items, as well as material for constructing a campsite. At 31 December 2012 there were 72,845 returned refugees and 96,010 returned IDPs in Côte d'Ivoire. UNHCR planned to facilitate a further 20,000 Ivorian returns, principally from Ghana and Liberia, in 2014. During that year the Office aimed to support the modernization of Côte d'Ivoire's civil registration processes. In June 2012 UNHCR terminated refugee status for Liberians who had fled their country owing to violent insecurity during 1989–2003, and, in 2014 the Office was addressing related exemption applications, as well as supporting local integration and voluntary repatriation programmes for affected Liberians. During 2014 UNHCR aimed to resolve four small long-standing refugee situations in West Africa, involving Ghanaians in Togo; Togolese in Benin and Ghana, Chadian refugees in Niger; and Mauritanian refugees in Mali and Senegal.

Violent unrest that erupted in northern Mali in mid-January 2012 led, by the end of 2013, to the internal displacement of around 165,000 people (residing in spontaneous settlements or with host communities), and an influx of an estimated 175,000 Malian refugees into neighbouring countries, including Mauritania (which received around 74,000), Niger (50,000) and Burkina Faso (also 50,000). From the onset of the emergency UNHCR deployed assistance teams to the neighbouring countries, conducted rapid needs assessments, and co-ordinated assistance focused on protection and the delivery of non-food items (such as family tents) to refugees. During 2013, particularly in view of an international military intervention in January and the deployment from July of the UN Multi-dimensional Integrated Stabilization Mission in Mali, the security situation ameliorated somewhat, enabling the implementation of humanitarian operations in northern areas of the country (excluding Kidal, which remained highly unstable). In 2014 UNHCR planned to strengthen its presence in Gao and Timbuktu in order to assist IDPs, and to prepare for an envisaged 15,000 refugee returns; repatriation programmes were to be established in neighbouring countries to assist refugees wishing to return—conditions there permitting—to Mali.

THE AMERICAS AND THE CARIBBEAN

UNHCR's activities in Central and South America are guided by the Mexico Plan of Action (MPA), adopted in November 2004. The MPA aims to address ongoing population displacement problems in Latin America, with a particular focus on the humanitarian crisis in Colombia and the border areas of its neighbouring countries (see below), and the increasing numbers of refugees concentrated in urban centres in the region. The Cities of Solidarity pillar of the MPA assists UNHCR with facilitating the local integration and self-sufficiency of people in urban areas who require international protection; the Borders of Solidarity pillar addresses protection at international borders; and the Resettlement in Solidarity pillar promotes co-operation in resettling refugees. In November 2010 regional leaders adopted the Brasília Declaration on the Protection of Refugees and Stateless Persons in the Americas, in which they committed to revitalizing the MPA pillars. During 2014 UNHCR and states in the region were devising a new plan of action, to cover the period 2015–24, which was to supersede the MPA.

UNHCR supports the 'Puebla Process', which was launched in March 1996 to promote regional co-operation on migration, and comprises the governments of Belize, Canada, Costa Rica, the Dominican Republic, El Salvador, Guatemala, Honduras, Mexico, Nicaragua, Panama and the USA. A Regional Conference on Refugee Protection and International Migration in the Americas, held in San José, Costa Rica, in November 2009, addressed key protection challenges in the context of an environment characterized by complex mixed migratory population movements.

In 1999 the Colombian Government approved an operational plan proposed by UNHCR to address a massive population displacement that had arisen in that country (escalating significantly from 1997), as a consequence of ongoing long-term internal conflict and alleged human rights abuses committed by paramilitary groups. Although the military capacity of the Colombian security forces improved in the 2000s, leading to the demobilization of significant numbers of militants, insecurity and population displacement persisted, exacerbated by a rise in organized crime and by the emergence of new illegal armed groups. Some 230,000 Colombians were newly displaced in 2012. Indigenous and Afro-Colombian peoples in remote, rural districts, particularly along the Pacific Coast, in central areas, in Antioquia, and in border areas neighbouring Ecuador and Venezuela, have been particularly vulnerable. Intra-urban displacement among 1.7m. Colombian urban IDPs has also caused concern. Gang conflict, sexual and gender-based violence, forced recruitment, forced disappearances, extortion and murder have been prevalent. In 2014 UNHCR aimed to explore possible viable solutions to the displacement situation in the context of an ongoing peace dialogue between the Government and the Fuerzas Armadas Revolucionarias de Colombia (FARC, the largest Colombian rebel group), and of the Law on Victims and Land Restitution, which was adopted in June 2011 to enable victims of forced displacement to claim reparations for and restitution of their holdings. Despite the dialogue, FARC elements and other armed militants continued to destabilize the country and to prompt continuing displacement; some 61 large population displacements were recorded in 2013. Within Colombia UNHCR's protection activities have included ensuring an adequate, functioning legal framework for the protection of IDPs and enabling domestic institutions to supervise compliance with national legislation regarding the rights of IDPs; strengthening representation for IDPs and other vulnerable people; and working with the authorities to promote sustainable solutions, with a focus on self-reliance and local integration (particularly as more than one-half of registered IDPs have assembled in urban areas and are unlikely to return to their native communities). UNHCR has also advised on public policy formulation in the areas of emergency response, IDP registration, health, education, housing, income generation and protection of policy rights; and provided technical assistance to national and local authorities. The Office has co-operated with UNICEF to improve the provision of education to displaced children. UNHCR, jointly with UNDP, has implemented since 2010 a Transitional Solutions Initiative, under which methodologies for sustainable solutions in 17 communities are being developed, with a focus on local integration, relocation and returnee processes. UNHCR works to provide legal protection and educational and medical support to around 500,000 Colombians who have fled to but not sought asylum in neighbouring countries. The Office's strategy for supporting countries receiving displaced Colombians (of whom the majority were not registered as refugees) has included border-monitoring activities, entailing the early warning of potential refugee movements, and provision of detailed country-of-origin data. UNHCR has offered technical assistance in relation to the Colombia-Ecuador Neighborhood Commission, established in 1989 and reactivated, following a period of inactivity, in November 2010. During 2014 UNHCR was to monitor the implementation of recently reformed, more restrictive asylum procedures in Ecuador, where, since 2000, asylum has been requested by some 160,000 people (nearly all Colombians). In 2014 UNHCR aimed to help refugees in that country secure access to education, health care, banking, government programmes, and employment. In that year the Office aimed to support the Venezuelan authorities with enhancing registration and documentation procedures. At the end of 2012 around 3.9m. IDPs within Colombia remained of concern to UNHCR. (In June 2013 Colombia's Constitutional Court determined to revise statistics on displacement upwards to reflect hitherto unrecognized cases caused by violence perpetrated by militia post-demobilization.) At end-2012 Ecuador was sheltering 54,000 Colombian refugees (of whom 1,500 were newly registered in 2012), while a further 68,300 Colombians were reported to be in a refugee-like situation in that country but had not sought official protection. It was reported that around 1,000 Colombians were crossing the border into Ecuador every month at the end of 2013, and that mainly they were settling in poorer, fragile districts. Some 203,600 Colombian refugees and persons in a refugee-like situation were sheltering in Venezuela at 31 December 2012. In 2014 UNHCR's presence in Colombia included 11 field offices and a branch office in Bogotá.

In the aftermath of the devastating earthquake that struck Haiti in January 2010, UNHCR provided assistance to the international humanitarian response operation in the areas of camp registration and profiling matters; shelter co-ordination; and supporting OHCHR in its efforts to assist the displaced population outside Port-au-Prince and earthquake survivors living outside registered camps. UNHCR also implemented a number of QIPs, and provided material support to Haitian evacuees in the neighbouring Dominican Republic. In June 2010 UNHCR opened an office in Santo Domingo, Dominican Republic. In July 2011 UNHCR and OHCHR urged governments to suspend all involuntary returns to Haiti, owing to the ongoing fragile protection environment in that country and continuing massive displacement; it was reported at the end of 2012, however, that the request by UNHCR and OHCHR had not been widely heeded. By the end of 2013 some 300,000 individuals displaced by the 2010 earthquake remained in camps, reportedly in slum-like conditions, while others were sheltering in nearby spontaneous settlements. In 2014 UNHCR's activities in Haiti were to focus on the provision of documentation and on the development of the civil registry, with a view to reducing risk of statelessness; and on improving protection for victims of sexual and other gender-based violence, with a particular focus on gay, lesbian, bisexual, transgender and intersex individuals. In the Dominican Republic the Office was to assist with the processing of a backlog of asylum claims, and was to continue to support the basic needs of refugees, while pursuing durable solutions for those of undetermined nationality or at risk of statelessness. It is of concern to UNHCR that a significant number of descendants of migrant Haitians born outside Haiti, as well as children unable to acquire nationality from their mothers under existing legislation governing nationality, are stateless or are at risk of becoming so in the Caribbean region.

In May 2013 UNHCR and the IOM organized a Caribbean regional conference, in Nassau, Bahamas, on promoting co-operation and identification of good practices in the protection of vulnerable persons in mixed migration flows. In 2014 UNHCR was to follow up the conference by supporting several Caribbean states with establishing or enhancing national asylum systems and more protection-sensitive migration management strategies.

Canada and the USA are major resettlement destinations for refugees. UNHCR provides counselling and legal services for asylum seekers in these countries. At 31 December 2012 the estimated refugee populations totalled 163,756 in Canada and 262,023 in the USA, while asylum seekers numbered 32,643 and 18,926, respectively. In 2014 UNHCR was seeking to expand resettlement take-up, and to improve the integration prospects of resettled refugees in those two countries.

CENTRAL AND SOUTH-EASTERN EUROPE

In July 2002 the heads of state of Bosnia and Herzegovina, Croatia and the Federal Republic of Yugoslavia (FRY, which was renamed Serbia and Montenegro in 2003, and was divided into separate sovereign states of Montenegro and Serbia in June 2006) met in Sarajevo with a view to resolving a number of outstanding issues from the conflict in the former Yugoslavia, including the return of remaining refugees. In January 2005 the concerned parties adopted the Sarajevo Declaration, committing to resolve remaining population displacement issues through the 'Sarajevo Process' (also referred to as the '3x3 Initiative'). The repossession by their rightful owners and reconstruction of illegally appropriated properties have been key issues for returned refugees to the region. In January 2011 the UN High Commissioner for Refugees appointed a personal envoy to assist the governments of Bosnia and Herzegovina, Croatia, Montenegro and Serbia in developing a binding common commitment to address the region's protracted population displacement; in November those countries' ministers of foreign affairs signed a joint declaration reaffirming this commitment, and paving the way for the development of a Regional Housing Programme (RHP) to pursue housing solutions for 74,000 vulnerable refugees in the region. By December 2012 there was still an estimated total Bosnian refugee population of 51,822, of whom some 4,779 were receiving assistance from UNHCR. The majority of the Bosnian refugees were residing in Germany (23,460) and in Serbia (16,418). At end-2012 there were also 13,449 IDPs of concern to UNHCR in Bosnia and Herzegovina. UNHCR was supporting the implementation of the ongoing RHP in 2014. In June 2013 the European Union (EU) adopted a Common European Asylum System (CEAS), establishing common asylum standards for its member states (including Croatia); during 2014 UNHCR aimed to raise regional awareness of the CEAS, and also to support EU member states with incorporating CEAS standards into domestic legal frameworks.

Throughout the region UNHCR is concerned to reduce and prevent statelessness, and to promote respect for the basic rights of stateless people. The Office has undertaken a civil registration programme for undocumented IDPs in Kosovo and Serbia, particularly members of

Roma, Ashkali and Egyptian communities in Kosovo, deemed to be at risk of statelessness. In early 2014 there were still around 97,000 IDPs in need of durable solutions in Serbia. In addition, Serbia was hosting nearly 60,000 refugees, of whom more than two-thirds were from Croatia, and the majority of the remainder from Bosnia and Herzegovina. UNHCR has expanded its durable solution programmes for IDPs in Serbia, by assisting with the construction of social housing, by providing cash grants to help people to move to the new accommodation, and by organizing self-reliance projects. In early 2014 around 17,400 people remained displaced within Kosovo, of whom the majority were in the Mitrovica area. UNHCR's work plan in Kosovo in 2014 was concerned with strengthening asylum procedures; building the capacity of the authorities to manage mixed migratory flows and to enable the identification of individuals requiring international protection, and to identify and support stateless individuals; providing legal assistance to secure civil status documentation for persons of concern; supporting the authorities in implementing durable solutions for refugees and IDPs; and supporting community-level reconciliation, with a focus on the role and situation of women.

EASTERN EUROPE

In June 2007, following the publication in June 2006 of its *10 Point Plan* for assisting member states with the management of refugee protection and mixed migration, UNHCR issued a '10 Point Plan of Action on Refugee Protection and Mixed Migration for Countries along the Eastern and South-Eastern Borders of European Union Member States', providing a framework for discussion between UNHCR and the governments of Belarus, Moldova and Ukraine, and also clarifying UNHCR's operational relationship in that subregion with the IOM and non-governmental organizations. In 2014 UNHCR was implementing the EU-supported Asylum Quality Initiative in Eastern Europe and the South Caucasus, which was initiated in April 2013 and aimed, over a two-year period, to improve decision making on the determination of refugee status. During 2014 the Office continued to engage closely with regional consultative processes including the Panel on Migration and Asylum of the EU Eastern Partnership, the Budapest Process, and the Prague Process.

The dissolution of the former Soviet Union had led to significant numbers of stateless people in Eastern Europe; at the end of 2012 UNHCR estimated that up to 250,000 people in the region were without a citizenship. During 2003–10 more than 600,000 stateless people in Russia were accepted as citizens; there remained some 178,000 stateless people in Russia at the end of 2012.

In the early 1990s UNHCR co-ordinated international humanitarian efforts to assist some 500,000 people displaced by the conflict between Armenia and Azerbaijan. Of the 12 emergency camps established, the last were closed in December 2007. At 31 December 2012 Azerbaijan was still supporting an IDP population totalling 600,336. During 2014 it was to give priority to strengthening the national asylum system, and aimed to enhance existing refugee legislation to extend protection to any person who, while not qualifying as a refugee, would be at real risk of harm if returned to their home country. UNCHR also aimed to promote access to employment opportunities for refugees in Azerbaijan, particularly in urban areas, to strengthen their self-reliance.

In Georgia, where almost 300,000 people left their homes as a result of civil conflict from 1991, UNHCR has attempted to encourage income-generating activities among the displaced population, to increase the Georgian Government's capacity to support those people and to assist the rehabilitation of people returning to their areas of origin. In July 2008 the Georgian authorities adopted a National IDP Action Plan, drafted with support from UNHCR, which was expected to provide a basis for future durable solutions. During August of that year UNHCR provided humanitarian assistance, including the distribution of blankets, jerrycans and kitchen sets, to people affected by a period of violent insecurity that escalated in July between Georgian and South Ossetian separatist forces, further intensifying in early August when Georgia launched a military offensive on the South Ossetian capital Tskhinvali, a stronghold of the separatists, and Russian forces responded by supporting the South Ossetian counter-attack and by crossing into Georgian territory. The heightened insecurity resulted in the temporary displacement of some 134,000 people within Georgia and of nearly 35,000 from South to North Ossetia (Russian Federation). In the following month, once the conflict had abated, UNHCR teams began regular visits to assess the humanitarian situation in villages in the Georgia–South Ossetia buffer zone area north of the Georgian town of Gori. More than 32,000 of those who had fled from South to North Ossetia returned to their homes swiftly. There were 279,778 Georgian IDPs at 31 December 2012, including about 22,000 people who remained displaced by the August 2008 conflict. In 2014 UNHCR aimed to support Georgia in reducing statelessness and in strengthening and implementing its national legislative framework and action plans relating to populations of concern, while focusing on durable outcomes for refugees through naturalization and local integration, and pursuing local integration for IDPs.

During 2003–10 some 255,000 IDPs were reported to have returned to the Russian separatist republic of Chechnya (the Chechen Republic of Ichkeriya) from elsewhere in the Russian Federation, having fled civil unrest from the mid-1990s. UNHCR conducted regular missions into Chechnya to monitor and support the reintegration of the IDPs. UNHCR has also conducted interviews of returnees to Chechnya from neighbouring Ingushetiya in order to ensure that their returns have been voluntary rather than enforced. It was estimated at January 2013 that a displaced Chechen and North Ossetian population of around 10,000 remained in Chechnya, Dagestan and Ingushetiya. In September of that year the Chechen authorities refuted German media reports that up to 10,000 Chechens had recently requested political asylum in Germany.

CO-OPERATION WITH OTHER ORGANIZATIONS

UNHCR works closely with other UN agencies, intergovernmental organizations and non-governmental organizations (NGOs) to increase the scope and effectiveness of its operations. Within the UN system UNHCR co-operates, principally, with WFP in the distribution of food aid, UNICEF and WHO in the provision of family welfare and child immunization programmes, OCHA in the delivery of emergency humanitarian relief, UNDP in development-related activities and the preparation of guidelines for the continuum of emergency assistance to development programmes, and the Office of the UN High Commissioner for Human Rights. UNHCR also has close working relationships with the International Federation of Red Cross and Red Crescent Societies and the International Organization for Migration. UNHCR planned to engage with 740 NGOs as implementing partners in 2014–15. UNHCR engages private sector businesses in supporting its activities through the provision of (cash and 'in kind') donations, loaned expertise, and marketing related to designated causes. The Office maintains a private sector partnerships unit, in London, United Kingdom.

TRAINING

UNHCR organizes training programmes and workshops to enhance the capabilities of field workers and non-UNHCR staff, in the following areas: the identification and registration of refugees; people-orientated planning; resettlement procedures and policies; emergency response and management; security awareness; stress management; and the dissemination of information through the electronic media.

Finance

The United Nations' regular budget finances a proportion of UNHCR's administrative expenditure. The majority of UNHCR's programme expenditure (about 98%) is funded by voluntary contributions, mainly from governments. The Private Sector and Public Affairs Service aims to increase funding from non-governmental donor sources, for example by developing partnerships with foundations and corporations. Following approval of the Unified Annual Programme Budget any subsequently identified requirements are managed in the form of Supplementary Programmes, financed by separate appeals. UNHCR's projected funding requirements for 2014 totalled US $5,307.8m. The proposed field programme budget for that year was projected at $4,460.7m., of which 42.4% was to be allocated to operations in sub-Saharan Africa, 34.3% to the Middle East and North Africa, 13.0% to Asia and the Pacific, 7.7% to Europe, and 2.5% to the Americas.

Publications

Assessing Mental Health and Psychosocial Needs and Resources: Toolkit for Humanitarian Settings.

Global Trends (annually).

Refugees (quarterly, in English, French, German, Italian, Japanese and Spanish).

Refugee Resettlement: An International Handbook to Guide Reception and Integration.

Refugee Survey Quarterly.

Refworld (annually).

Sexual and Gender-based Violence Against Refugees, Returnees and Displaced Persons: Guidelines for Prevention and Response.

The State of the World's Refugees (every 2 years).

Statistical Yearbook (annually).

UNHCR Handbook for Emergencies.

Press releases, reports.

Statistics

POPULATIONS OF CONCERN TO UNHCR BY REGION
('000 persons, at 31 December 2012, provisional figures)

	Refugees*	Asylum seekers	Returned refugees†	Others of concern‡
Africa	3,068	422	274	8,782
Asia	5,060	93	251	10,045
Europe	1,522	328	1	1,105
Latin America/ Caribbean	381	22	0	3,949
North America	426	52	—	—
Oceania	41	12	—	—
Total	10,500	928	526	23,881

* Includes persons recognized as refugees under international law, and also people receiving temporary protection and assistance outside their country but who have not been formally recognized as refugees.
† Refugees who returned to their place of origin during 2012.
‡ Mainly internally displaced persons (IDPs), former IDPs who returned to their place of origin during 2012, and stateless persons.

POPULATIONS OF CONCERN TO UNHCR BY COUNTRY*
('000 persons, at 31 December 2012, provisional figures)

	Refugees†	Asylum seekers	Returned refugees†	Others of concern†
Africa				
Burundi	41.8	10.1	4.4	80.1
Cameroon	100.0	3.3	—	—
CAR	14.0	2.4	9.0	171.8
Chad	373.7	0.2	0.1	131.0
Congo, Democratic Repub.	65.1	1.8	71.9	3,045.5
Côte d'Ivoire	100.7	11.2	72.8	141.3
Ethiopia	75.0	38.7	0.0	4.8
Kenya	8.9	1.5	—	412.0
Mali	149.9	1.8	0.0	227.9
Rwanda	97.5	10.2	11.2	0.1
Somalia	1,136.1	33.0	0.0	1,143.2
South Sudan	87.0	18.7	2.3	345.7
Sudan	569.2	21.5	19.5	1,964.9
Zimbabwe	22.1	38.4	0.0	57.9
Asia				
Afghanistan	16.2	0.1	98.6	1,384.5
Bangladesh	230.7	0.0	—	—
China, People's Republic‡	301.0	0.0	—	—
Egypt	109.9	17.0	—	0.1
India	185.7	3.6	—	—
Iran	868.2	0.2	0.0	—
Iraq	98.8	4.9	82.3	1,470.0
Israel	48.5	5.7	—	0.0
Jordan	302.7	2.9	—	—
Kyrgyzstan	4.9	0.4	—	187.5
Lebanon	133.9	1.9	—	—
Libya	7.1	6.6	1.1	236.9
Malaysia	90.2	11.7	—	120.0
Myanmar		—	—	1,238.5
Pakistan	1,638.5	3.3	0.0	814.2
Sri Lanka	0.1	0.3	1.5	138.1
Philippines	0.1	0.0		343.5
Syria	576.5	2.2	68.6	221.0
Thailand	84.5	14.6	—	506.2
Turkey	267.1	14.1	—	10.9
Yemen	237.2	6.5	—	492.2
Europe				
Azerbaijan	1.5	0.1	—	603.9
Bosnia and Herzegovina	6.9	0.0	0.3	170.2
Estonia	0.1	0.0	—	94.2
France	217.9	49.9	—	1.2
Georgia	0.5	0.5	—	280.9
Germany	589.7	85.6	—	5.7
Latvia	0.1	0.2	—	280.8
Russian Federation	3.2	0.8	0.0	187.1
Serbia and Kosovo	66.4	0.3	0.2	237.8
Sweden	92.9	18.0	—	9.6
United Kingdom	149.8	18.9	—	0.2
Latin America/ Caribbean				
Colombia	0.2	0.1	0.0	3,943.5
Ecuador	123.8	14.6	—	—
Venezuela	203.6	0.9	—	—
North America				
Canada	163.8	32.6	—	—
USA	262.0	19.0	—	—

* The list includes only those countries having 100,000 or more persons of concern to UNHCR.
† See table above for definitions.
‡ Excluding Hong Kong Special Administrative Region.

ORIGIN OF MAJOR POPULATIONS OF CONCERN TO UNHCR*
('000 persons, 31 December 2012, provisional figures)

Origin	Population of concern to UNHCR
Colombia	4,356.3
Afghanistan	4,122.4
Sudan	2,574.8
DRC	3,613.5
Syria	2,846.7
Iraq	2,203.0
Somalia	2,313.5

* Data exclude (some 4,919,917 at 31 December 2012) Palestinian refugees who come under the mandate of UNRWA, although (at 31 December 2012) 94,918 Palestinians who are outside the UNRWA area of operation, for example those in Iraq and Lebanon, are considered to be of concern to UNHCR.

United Nations Human Settlements Programme—UN-Habitat

Address: POB 30030, 00100 Nairobi, Kenya.
Telephone: (20) 7623120; **fax:** (20) 7623477; **e-mail:** infohabitat@unhabitat.org; **internet:** www.unhabitat.org.

UN-Habitat was established as the United Nations Centre for Human Settlements, UNCHS-Habitat, in October 1978, on the recommendation of the First UN Conference on Human Settlements, Habitat I, convened in Vancouver, Canada, in May–June 1976, in order to service the intergovernmental Commission on Human Settlements. It became a full UN programme in January 2002, serving as a focus for human settlements and sustainable urban development activities in the UN system.

Organization

(April 2014)

GOVERNING COUNCIL

The Governing Council (formerly the Commission on Human Settlements) meets once every two years and has 58 members, serving for four years. Sixteen members are from Africa, 13 from Asia, 10 from Latin America and the Caribbean, six from Eastern European countries, and 13 from Western European and other countries. The Committee of Permanent Representatives to UN-Habitat, which meets at least four times a year, functions as an inter-sessional subsidiary body of the Governing Council. The Governing Council reports to the UN General Assembly through the UN Economic and Social Council.

SECRETARIAT

The Secretariat services the Governing Council, implements its resolutions and ensures the integration and co-ordination of technical co-operation, research and policy advice. It comprises Offices of the Executive Director, of Management, and of External Relations, a Project Office, and Branches of Urban Legislation, Land and Governance, Urban Planning and Design, Urban Economy, Urban Basic Services, Housing and Slum Upgrading, Risk Reduction and Rehabilitation, and Research and Capacity Building.

Executive Director: Dr JOAN CLOS (Spain).

Deputy Executive Director: AISA KIRABO KACYIRA (Rwanda).

REGIONAL OFFICES

Regional Office for Africa and the Arab States: POB 30030, Nairobi, Kenya 00100; tel. (20) 623221; fax (20) 623904; e-mail roaas@unhabitat.org; internet www.unhabitat.org/roaas.

Regional Office for Asia and the Pacific: ACROS Fukuoka Bldg, 8th Floor 1-1-1 Tenjin, Chuo-ku Fukuoka 810, Japan; tel. (92) 724-7121; fax (92) 724-7124; e-mail habitat.fukuoka@unhabitat.org; internet www.fukuoka.unhabitat.org.

Regional Office for Latin America and the Caribbean: Rua Rumânia 20, Cosme Velho 22240-140, Rio de Janeiro, Brazil; tel. (21) 3235-8550; fax (21) 3235-8566; e-mail rolac@onuhabitat.org; internet www.onuhabitat.org.

In addition, there are Liaison and Information Offices in Geneva, Switzerland; Brussels, Belgium; Budapest, Hungary; New York, USA; Beijing, the People's Republic of China; Cairo, Egypt; Moscow, Russia; and Chennai, India.

Activities

Since 2008 at least one-half of the world's population has been resident in towns and cities (compared with about one-third in 1950, and forecast to rise to 70% by 2050). UN-Habitat supports and conducts capacity building and operational research with regard to urban growth, provides technical co-operation and policy advice, and disseminates information with the aim of strengthening the development and management of human settlements. It is mandated to support the UN Millennium Development Goals (MDGs) of halving, by 2015, the proportion of people without sustainable access to safe drinking water and improving significantly the lives of at least 100m. slum dwellers by 2020.

UN-Habitat provides the leadership and serves as a focal point for the implementation of the Habitat Agenda, which was adopted as a Global Plan of Action to achieve 'adequate shelter for all' and 'sustainable human settlements development in an urbanizing world' by the Second UN Conference on Human Settlements, convened in Istanbul, Turkey, in June 1996. A special session of the UN General Assembly, entitled Istanbul + 5, held in June 2001, adopted a Declaration on Cities and Other Human Settlements in the New Millennium that reaffirmed commitment to the objectives of the Habitat Agenda and urged an intensification of efforts towards eradicating widespread poverty and promoting good governance. The special session resolved to increase international co-operation in several other areas, including addressing HIV/AIDS, urban crime and violence, environmental issues, and the problems posed by conflicts and refugees; and recommended the enhancement of the status and role of UNCHS (Habitat). Consequently, in December the General Assembly authorized the elevation of the body to a full UN programme with a strengthened mandate to address and implement the Habitat Agenda and, in January 2002, UN-Habitat was inaugurated. The Third UN Conference on Human Settlements, Habitat III, is scheduled to be held in 2016. An Interagency Co-ordinating Committee for Habitat III was inaugurated in July 2013. UN-Habitat hosts the secretariat of and co-ordinates the World Urban Campaign, a partnership and advocacy platform for cities. In March 2014 the World Urban Campaign released *The City We Need*, representing a blueprint for the principles essential to the development of model sustainable cities in the 21st century; the document emphasized the linkages between urbanization and development challenges such as climate change and extreme poverty. UN-Habitat participates in fora of the World Alliance of Cities Against Poverty (WACAP), a global network of more than 900 cities, with a focus on the development, through public-private partnerships, of sustainable social inclusion and the provision of universal access to basic services in urban environments. The eighth WACAP forum was convened in February 2013.

UN-Habitat participated in the preparatory process for the UN Conference on Sustainable Development (Rio+20), which was convened in June 2012, in Rio de Janeiro, Brazil. In April 2011 the Governing Council adopted a resolution on 'Sustainable urban development through expanding equitable access to land, housing, basic services and infrastructure', underpinning UN-Habitat's contribution to Rio+20. 'Cities' were identified by the Conference Secretariat as one of the most critical sustainable development issues. In May 2013 UN-Habitat and United Cities and Local Government organized a meeting of a Global Taskforce for the Post-2015 Development Agenda and Towards Habitat III, with participation by representatives of local and regional authorities; the gathering stressed commitment to ending extreme poverty in all its forms and to reducing social inequalities, in the context of sustainable development.

A Safer Cities Programme was initiated in 1996 to prevent and address urban violence through capacity building at the local government and city level. In November 2010 UN-Habitat, working with UNIFEM, now part of UN Women, inaugurated a Global Safe Cities for Women and Girls Programme. Pilot projects were initiated in the poorest areas of five cities: Quito (Ecuador); Cairo (Egypt); New Delhi (India); Port Moresby (Papua New Guinea); and Kigali (Rwanda). From 2011 Global Safe Cities activities were extended to Beirut (Lebanon); Dushanbe (Tajikistan); Metro Manila (Philippines); Marrakesh (Morocco); Nairobi (Kenya); Rio de Janeiro (Brazil); San José (Costa Rica); Tegucigalpa (Honduras); and from February 2013 Dublin, Ireland, joined the initiative. In September 2012 UN-Habitat's Executive Director inaugurated a Global Network on Safer Cities, to enhance collaborative efforts to reduce crime and violence in cities.

During 2014 UN-Habitat was undergoing organizational restructuring to realign with the seven focus areas of its new strategic plan covering the period 2014–19. The following cross-cutting issues were to be integrated into the work of all focus areas: gender; youth; climate change; and human rights.

World Habitat Day is celebrated annually on the first Monday in October, to raise awareness of the state of human settlements; the theme for 2014 was to be 'Changing Cities, Building Opportunities'.

URBAN LEGISLATION, LAND AND GOVERNANCE

UN-Habitat provides policy and operational support to governments and city authorities with respect to legislation, land use and governance that fosters equitable and sustainable urban development.

The UN Housing Rights Programme (UNHRP), launched jointly by UN-Habitat and OHCHR in April 2002, supports states and other stakeholders with the implementation of their Habitat Agenda commitments to realizing the universal right to adequate housing. In 2004 UN-Habitat established an Advisory Group on Forced Evictions, with a mandate to monitor forced evictions of people with no or inadequate legal security of tenure, and to identify and promote alternatives including *in situ* upgrading of accommodation and negotiated resettlement. UN-Habitat's programme on Rapid Urban Sector Profiling for Sustainability (RUSPS) involves an accelerated action-oriented assessment of urban conditions in particular cities in seven thematic areas (governance; slums; gender and HIV/AIDS; urban environment; local economic development; basic urban services; and cultural heritage), with a view to developing and implementing tailor-made urban poverty reduction policies. UN-Habitat's Global Campaign for Secure Tenure and Global Campaign on Urban Governance both emphasize urban poverty reduction.

UN-Habitat facilitates the Global Land Tool Network, a global partnership (comprising 63 national and regional organizations, research institutions, finance bodies and professional organizations, as at April 2014) which aims to contribute to poverty alleviation through land reform, improved land management and security of tenure. In August 2013 UN-Habitat launched a new Participatory and Inclusive Land Re-adjustment (PILaR) service for national governments and local authorities to address urban land use and slum upgrading issues.

URBAN PLANNING AND DESIGN

The challenges of rapid urban expansion include ineffective development controls, traffic congestion, an expansion of informal housing, and environmental pollution. UN-Habitat aims to support local authorities and national governments to achieve more sustainable urban development through improved urban planning legislation, implementation and design initiatives. A particular focus is on supporting cities to plan for future challenges relating to climate change.

UN-Habitat implements a programme entitled 'Localizing Agenda 21' (LA21), to assist local authorities in developing countries to achieve more sustainable development and to address local environmental and infrastructure-related problems. The Programme targets secondary cities and supports city-to-city co-operation initiatives. A Sustainable Cities Programme, operated jointly with the UN Environment Programme (UNEP), is concerned with incorporating environmental issues into urban planning and management, in order to ensure sustainable and equitable development. The Programme is active in some 30 cities worldwide, although a prepared series of policy guidelines is used in many others. Some 95% of the Programme's resources are spent at city level to strengthen the capacities of municipal authorities and their public, private and community sector partners in the field of environmental planning and management, with the objective that the concepts and approaches of the Programme are replicated throughout the region.

UN-Habitat supported the development of a Sustainable Urban Development Network (SUD-Net) which aims to mobilize local, regional and global partners to achieve a multilateral and interdisciplinary approach to sustainable urban development. SUD-Net envisaged strengthening capacity building at the local level, involving the local community in decision-making, and promoting knowledge sharing and the exchange of good practices. A Cities in Climate Change Initiative was established in 2008 as a component of SUD-Net. It aimed to work with local governments and other bodies involved in the environmental planning and management process in order to address problems relating to climate change and to reduce greenhouse gas emissions. In September 2010 UN-Habitat, with UNEP and the World Bank, launched an International Standard for Determining Greenhouse Gas Emissions for Cities. In December, prior to the 16th COP of the UNFCCC, held in Cancún, Mexico, UN-Habitat joined with five other UN agencies in declaring their commitment to work to counter climate change. In September 2011 the first annual 'Shelter Academy', a gathering of mayors and senior local government officials from Africa, Asia and Latin America, met in Rotterdam, Netherlands, to discuss the challenges that climate change presents to port cities.

URBAN ECONOMY AND MUNICIPAL FINANCE

With more than half of the world's population living in cities and urban areas, these need to be able to support their expanding populations and to contribute to local economic development. UN-Habitat provides technical assistance for the development of effective urban strategies, in particular policies to promote the creation of employment opportunities for young people and women (who are often disadvantaged by discriminatory practices). UN-Habitat encourages incentive schemes to stimulate local investment in infrastructure and basic services and to generate jobs.

The September 2005 World Summit of UN heads of state approved the development of a Slum Upgrading Facility (SUF) to improve access to credit and other resources for slum dwellers, in order to improve their homes and living conditions. Pilot projects were subsequently established in Ghana, Indonesia, Sri Lanka and Tanzania. Within each project Local Finance Facilities have been established, both at city and national level, to help communities to access credit from local commercial banks.

In April 2007 the Governing Council approved the establishment of a trust fund—the Experimental Reimbursable Seeding Operations and Other Innovative Mechanism (ERSO)—to support the financing of loans and credits for low-income housing, infrastructure and settlements upgrading. In November 2008 a new Opportunities Fund for Urban Youth-Led Development was inaugurated.

URBAN BASIC SERVICES

UN-Habitat is committed to increasing the numbers of people living in urban areas who have access to adequate basic services. The organization works with local authorities and partner countries to strengthen policies and institutional frameworks to achieve this. The main areas of activity focus on water and sanitation; urban waste management; urban mobility; and urban energy. During 2014–19 UN-Habitat aimed to strengthen collaboration with regional finance institutions, in particular the African Development Bank, the Asian Development Bank (ADB) and the Inter-American Development Bank, to stimulate investment into urban basic services.

In October 2002 UN-Habitat launched a Water and Sanitation Trust Fund, with the aim of supporting the goal of halving the proportion of the world's population lacking access to basic sanitation or clean water by 2015, that was set by the World Summit on Sustainable Development (WSSD), held in Johannesburg, South Africa, during August–September 2002 to assess strategies for strengthening the implementation of Agenda 21. In April 2013 UN-Habitat's Governing Council determined that the Trust Fund should expand its remit and be renamed the Urban Basic Services Trust Fund. UN-Habitat water and sanitation activities include promoting policy dialogue, information exchange, water education and raising awareness; monitoring progress towards achieving the MDG targets on improving access to safe water and sanitation; and designing replicable model-setting initiatives, i.e. the Lake Victoria Region Water and Sanitation Initiative and the Mekong Regional Water and Sanitation Initiative. A Managing Water for African Cities Programme, jointly co-ordinated by UN-Habitat and UNEP, promotes efficient water demand management, capacity building to alleviate the environmental impact of urbanization on freshwater resources, information exchange on water management and conservation issues, and the exchange of best practices in urban water management. In March 2003 UN-Habitat and the ADB signed an agreement on the establishment of a parallel Water for Asian Cities Programme.

In accordance with decisions adopted at the fourth World Water Forum, held in Mexico, in March 2006, UN-Habitat hosted from 2007 the secretariat of the Global Water Operators' Partnership Alliance (GWOPA). The first international conference of the GWOPA was convened in Zaragoza, Spain, in December 2009. In June 2012 it was announced that the municipality of Barcelona, Spain, would host the GWOPA secretariat for the next five years. GWOPA supports the establishment and development of regional Water Operators' Partnerships, and supports training and capacity-building activities. The Alliance, in collaboration with Google and an international benchmarking network, has developed a Geo-Referenced Utility Benchmarking System (GRUBS) as a means of presenting utility performance (benchmarking) data in a searchable format online. The benchmarking of service providers was a key component of a separate h2.O Monitoring Services to Inform and Empower Initiative which aimed to improve methodologies for monitoring the urban environment and acquiring data and to enhance the effectiveness of investment planning. The project also envisaged the development and application of Urban Inequity Surveys and Citizen Report Cards.

UN-Habitat administers a Global Energy Network for Urban Settlements (GENUS) which aims to support and encourage partnerships between the public and private sector, governmental and non-governmental organizations, and other international, national and civil society agencies concerned with improving energy access for the urban poor, in order to advance best practices, technologies and capacity building. GENUS workshops are convened regularly, most recently in New Delhi, India, in October 2012, with a focus on improving informal transport to facilitate mobility for the poor.

In October 2013 participants attending the first forum of a multi-stakeholder Global Wastewater Initiative agreed that it should be co-chaired by UN-Habitat and UNEP.

HOUSING AND SLUM UPGRADING

In 2013 UN-Habitat estimated that more than 860m. people were living in slums, compared with 725m. in 2000. UN-Habitat aims to counter this expansion by supporting greater supply and affordibility of new housing, alongside local and national programmes to improve the housing conditions and quality of life in existing slums. It is committed to providing technical assistance to city, regional and national authorities to formulate and implement schemes to build more, affordable housing where it is required to contribute to sustainable urban development, and to prevent the emergence of new slums. It also aims to involve residents and grass-roots organizations in housing development and slum upgrading projects.

An international conference organized in November 2012 by UN-Habitat and the Government of Morocco on the theme 'Making Slums History' adopted the Rabat Declaration on Making Slums History, reaffirming the irreversibility of the process of urbanization and its positive impact in advancing human development and poverty reduction; recognizing the need to promote inclusive strategies aimed at the full integration of slums into the political, economic, social and cultural dimensions of cities; and committing to 10 key related actions, including the development and implementation of inclusive urban policies, legislation, and national housing strategies; the expansion of financial and human resources for slum upgrading and prevention; and strengthening multi-sectoral dialogue prior to the Habitat III conference scheduled to take place in 2016.

RISK REDUCTION AND REHABILITATION

UN-Habitat contributes to relief, rehabilitation and development activities undertaken in areas affected by natural disaster and civil conflict. Within the inter-agency emergency response system UN-Habitat provides shelter, water and sanitation under the Emergency Shelter and Early Recovery 'clusters'. UN-Habitat also provides assessment and technical support both as disaster prevention and preparedness and during post-disaster reconstruction. UN-Habitat's Settlements Recovery Programme operates in the immediate aftermath of a disaster to assist humanitarian efforts and to introduce elements of sustainable recovery. It aims to involve affected local populations in rehabilitation efforts, a so-called People's Process of Recovery. In April 2013 UN-Habitat nominated 10 cities across the world that were to collaborate, with other international partners, under a City Resilience Profiling Programme to develop more effective tools to measure and manage urban resilience to risk.

An international conference on post-emergency shelter reconstruction, organized by UN-Habitat in partnership with government donors, was convened in Colombo, Sri Lanka, in March 2014. The conference aimed to emphasize the role of homeowners and local groups in restoring communities and securing their sustainable future following a disaster.

RESEARCH AND CAPACITY DEVELOPMENT

UN-Habitat maintains a Global Urban Observatory (GUO) to monitor implementation of the Habitat Agenda, to report on and support local and national plans of action and ongoing research and development, and to conduct assessments of the impact of urban development. The GUO operates through a global network of regional, national and local urban observatories, and through partner institutions that provide training and other capacity-building expertise. It also maintains the GUO databases of global urban indicators, statistics and city profiles. The Observatory works closely with the Best Practices and Local Leadership Programme, which was established in 1997 to support the implementation of the Habitat Agenda through the use of information and networking. In April 2011 UN-HABITAT launched www.urbangateway.org, a forum for knowledge sharing among urban policy-makers and managers globally.

Through its Strengthening Training Institutions programme UN-Habitat supports regional and national training institutions by organizing regional workshops to develop capacity-building strategies and training needs assessments; by designing new training manuals and other tools; by developing, jointly with partners, generic training manuals and handbooks; by educating trainers; and by supporting institutions with the design and implementation of national training programmes. In addition, UN-Habitat supports training and other activities designed to strengthen management development (in particular in the provision and maintenance of services and facilities) at the local and community level.

In November 2004 UN-Habitat hosted the first meeting of the Global Research Network on Human Settlements (HS-Net). HS-Net acts as a forum for human settlements researchers, research institutions and networks, and advises the UN-Habitat Secretariat on the preparation of its two flagship reports, the *Global Report on Human Settlements* and *State of the World's Cities*. UN-Habitat has also prepared regional state of cities reports. In 2014–19, as part of the UN's Delivering as One approach, UN-Habitat was to work with UNICEF and WHO to establish a data collection system and to improve analysis of urban issues in developing countries.

UN-Habitat has, since 2008, developed and supported a network of universities to promote greater collaboration with regard to urban research and training and to enhance the effectiveness of research and training undertaken. The second global meeting of the so-called Habitat Partner University Initiative—subsequently renamed the Habitat UNI (University Network Initiative)—was convened in May 2013, and attended by representatives of 40 institutions.

UN-Habitat provides the secretariat of the World Urban Forum (WUF), the first of which was held in April–May 2002, in Nairobi, with participation by national governments and Habitat Agenda partners. The Forum represented a merger of the former Urban Environment Forum and International Forum on Urban Poverty. It aims to promote international co-operation in shelter and urban development issues, and convenes to consider important issues relating to urban settlements every two years. The seventh WUF was held in Medellín, Colombia, in April 2014, on the theme 'Urban Equity in Development—Cities for Life'. Since 2006 a youth forum has been convened prior to the main Forum. In 2010 this was restructured as the World Urban Youth Assembly further to promote youth-led development.

ASSOCIATED BODY

Cities Alliance: 1818 H St, NW, Washington, DC, 20433 USA; tel. (202) 473-9233; fax (202) 522-3224; e-mail info@citiesalliance.org; internet www.citiesalliance.org; f. 1999, jointly by Habitat and the World Bank, as a coalition of local authorities, govts and development orgs; aims to reduce urban poverty and improve the effectiveness of urban development co-operation and urban investment; in Sept. 2000 the UN Millennium Summit endorsed the Alliance's new Cities without Slums action plan as a target within its MDGs, i.e. 'by 2020, to have achieved a significant improvement in the lives of at least 100m. slum dwellers'; facilitates collaboration between govts and authorities to achieve best practices in slum upgrading initiatives; supports the formulation of city development strategies (CDS) in order to promote equitable and sustainable urban growth; in 2009 established a new CDS sub-group to develop a CDS conceptual framework; mems: UNEP, UN-Habitat, the World Bank, the European Union, Shack/Slumdwellers International, United Cities and Local Government, World Association of the Major Metropolises (Metropolis), 16 national govts; assoc. mems: the ILO, UNDP; Man. WILLIAM COBBETT.

Finance

UN-Habitat's work programme is financed from the UN regular budget, and from voluntary contributions to the UN Habitat and Human Settlements Foundation and to the Programme's technical co-operation activities. The approved general purpose budget for the two-year period 2014–15 amounted to US $45.6m.; in addition, a special purposes budget amounted to $123.3m.

Publications

Global Report on Human Settlements (every 2 years).
State of the World's Cities (every 2 years).
State of African Cities.
State of Arab Cities.
State of Asian Cities.
State of China's Cities.
State of Latin American and Caribbean Cities.
UMP e-Newsletter (quarterly).
UN-Habitat Global Activities Report (annually).
UN-Habitat Vision on Urbanization.
Urban World (quarterly).
Technical reports and studies, occasional papers, bibliographies, directories.

United Nations Office on Drugs and Crime—UNODC

Address: Vienna International Centre, POB 500, 1400 Vienna, Austria.

Telephone: (1) 26060-0; **fax:** (1) 263-33-89; **e-mail:** info@unodc.org; **internet:** www.unodc.org.

UNODC was established in November 1997 (as the Office for Drug Control and Crime Prevention—ODCCP) to strengthen the UN's integrated approach to issues relating to drug control, crime prevention and international terrorism; the Office was renamed in October 2002.

Organization

(April 2014)

UNODC comprises the following four divisions: Operations; Treaty Affairs; Policy Analysis and Public Affairs; and Management. There are UNODC liaison offices in Brussels, Belgium, and New York, USA, and there are more than 50 UNODC field offices covering more than 150 countries worldwide, with a particular regional focus on Africa; Central America and the Caribbean; Central Asia; East Asia and the Pacific; the Middle East, and South-East Europe. In October 2012 UNODC and the Government of Mexico established a UNODC liaison and partnership office in that country.

Executive Director: YURI FEDOTOV (Russia).

Activities

UNODC aims to provide in-depth expertise and extensive resources and tools for combating international crime, drugs-trafficking and terrorism. The Office manages the Global Programme on Organized Crime, which analyses emerging transnational criminal organizations and assist countries to formulate strategies to combat that problem. The Office conducts evidence-based research to support policy-making; helps to strengthen criminal justice institutions and the rule of law; offers assistance in the establishment and setting of best practices; and assists governments with building capacity to establish and sustain safe, stable societies. UNODC also develops integrated approaches to eradicate or alleviate conditions that encourage criminal activities, and works in partnership with governments, international agencies and other stakeholders to address the challenges posed by drugs, crime and terrorism and to rehabilitate people affected by these. UNODC leads regional and transnational initiatives aimed at strengthening the rule of law, stability and development, and at disrupting transnational organized crime. Trafficking—most significantly in illicit drugs, but also in natural resources, weaponry, counterfeit goods and human beings—is regarded as the primary pillar of global criminal networks which utilize advances in technology, communications and transportation to operate across international borders, while profits raised through transnational organized criminal activity are, in some cases, also used to support terrorist groupings.

ORGANIZED CRIME AND TRAFFICKING

At a special session of the General Assembly, held in June 1998, heads of state and representatives of some 150 countries adopted a global strategy, formulated on the basis of UN International Drug Control Programme (UNDCP) proposals, to reduce significantly the production of and demand for illicit substances over the next decade. UNDCP subsequently launched the Global Assessment Programme on Drug Abuse (GAP), which aimed to establish one global and nine regional drug abuse data systems to collect and evaluate data on the extent of and patterns of illegal substance abuse. In March 2009 UNODC reviewed progress since the 1998 General Assembly special session and adopted a Draft Political Declaration and Plan of Action on the future of drug control. The Declaration recognized that countries have a shared responsibility for solving the global drugs problem, and recommended a 'balanced and comprehensive approach', an emphasis on human rights, and a focus on health as a basis for international drugs policy. The Action Plan proposed some 30 solutions to problems in the following six areas of concern: reducing drug abuse and dependence; reducing the illicit supply of drugs; control of precursors and of amphetamine-type stimulants; international co-operation to eradicate the illicit cultivation of crops and to provide alternative development; countering money-laundering; and judicial co-operation. UNODC supports national monitoring systems that assess the extent and evolution of illicit crops in the world's principal drugs-growing countries: Bolivia, Colombia and Peru (coca); Afghanistan, Laos and Myanmar (opium); and Morocco (cannabis). Crop surveys are facilitated by a combination of satellite sensing (with the assistance of the European Space Agency), aerial surveillance and ground-level surveys, which provide a reliable collection and analysis mechanism for data on the production of illicit substances.

UNODC promotes implementation of the following major treaties which govern the international drug control system: the Single Convention on Narcotic Drugs (1961) and a Protocol amending the Convention (1972); the Convention on Psychotropic Substances (1971); and the UN Convention against Illicit Traffic in Narcotic Drugs and Psychotropic Substances (1988). Among other important provisions, these treaties aim to restrict severely the production of narcotic drugs, while ensuring an adequate supply for medical and scientific purposes, to prevent profits obtained from the illegal sale of drugs being diverted into legal usage and to secure the extradition of drugs-traffickers and the transfer of proceedings for criminal prosecution. The Office assists countries to adapt their national legislation and drug policies to facilitate their compliance with these conventions and to enhance co-ordinated intergovernmental efforts to control the movement of narcotic drugs. It services meetings of the International Narcotics Control Board (INCB), an independent body responsible for promoting and monitoring government compliance with the provisions of the drug control treaties, and of the Commission on Narcotic Drugs, which is the main policy-making organ within the UN system on issues relating to international drug abuse control. The 52nd session of the Commission on Narcotic Drugs, held at UNODC headquarters in March 2009, adopted a Political Declaration and Plan of Action on International Co-operation towards an Integrated and Balanced Strategy to Counter the World Drug Problem. The INCB is promoting co-ordinated global action to prevent illicit internet sales of internationally controlled prescription drugs by so-called online pharmacies. The increasing occurrence globally of abuse of prescription drugs was reported on by the INCB in February 2010. In February 2013 a high-level conference on illicit trafficking in fraudulent medicines was held in Vienna, Austria, with participation by representatives of UNODC, INTERPOL and the World Customs Organization (WCO).

In March 2013 UNODC issued a technical report on New Psychoactive Substances (NPS). NPS, also known as 'legal highs', are deemed to pose a threat to public health but are not covered by the scope of the 1961 Single Convention on Narcotic Drugs or the 1971 Convention on Psychotropic Substances. In June 2013 UNODC initiated an early warning advisory mechanism with respect to NPS, providing up-to-date information and identification techniques, and detailing adverse effects, as well as outlining legislative measures being pursued worldwide. The Office is compiling manuals to assist with their identification. The 2013 edition of UNODC's *World Drug Report*, issued in June, addressed the increased use of NPS, and also growing abuse of prescription drugs.

In October 2004 UNODC and the WCO launched a joint Container Control Programme aimed at improving port control measures in developing countries and building local capacity to detect illicit container shipments. In 2012 some 11 metric tons of cocaine, 17 tons of cannabis, and 434 tons of precursor chemicals were seized under the Programme which, in 2014, was being implemented in 41 countries. During 2010 UNODC launched the Airport Communication Project (AIRCOP), initially focusing on 10 international airports, located in West Africa, Brazil and Morocco. Under the Project, Joint Airport Interdiction Task Forces (JAITFs) were to be established with connections to international law enforcement databases and communication networks, to enable information sharing, including the instantaneous transmission between international airports of operational information on passengers and cargo, in order to facilitate the interception of illicit cargo.

UNODC promotes research and undertakes studies of new forms of crime prevention, in collaboration with the UN Interregional Crime and Justice Research Institute (UNICRI). It also maintains a UN Crime and Justice Information Network database (UNCJIN), which provides information on national crime statistics, publications and links to other relevant intergovernmental agencies and research and academic institutes.

UNODC manages a Global Programme against Trafficking in Human Beings (trafficking in human beings for sexual exploitation or forced labour is regarded as the fastest-growing area of international organized crime). In March 2007 UNODC and partners initiated the UN Global Initiative to Fight Human Trafficking (UN.GIFT), with the aim of raising awareness worldwide of the phenomenon, promoting effective preventative measures, and improving law enforcement methods. In February 2008 UN.GIFT organized the Vienna Forum to Fight Human Trafficking, with participation by UN member states and agencies, other international organizations, academics, and representatives of the private sector and civil society. In February 2009 UNODC issued the *Global Report on Trafficking in Persons*, which used data drawn from 155 countries to compile an assessment of the worldwide scope of human-trafficking and ongoing means of combating it. The Report included an overview of trafficking patterns, of legal steps taken in response, and also country-specific information on reported trafficking and prosecutions. The Report found sexual exploitation to be the most common purpose of human-trafficking (representing 79% of incidences), followed by forced labour (18%), although it was stated that the prevalence of trafficking for forced labour may be under-represented. About one-fifth of known trafficking victims were reported to be children. Intra-regional and domestic trafficking were found to be more common than long-distance trafficking in persons. In March 2009 UNODC launched the Blue Heart Campaign against Human Trafficking, which aimed to use the media and the social networking arena to raise awareness of global trafficking. UNODC administers a UN Voluntary Trust Fund for Victims of Trafficking in Persons, which was established in November 2010 to support the objectives of a new UN Global Plan of Action to Combat Trafficking in Persons, adopted by the UN General Assembly in July of that year.

In September 2013 UNODC convened a group of experts to review the role played by the use of new information technologies in the abuse and exploitation of children, and to consider measures that had hitherto proven effective in combating this.

CORRUPTION

UNODC assisted with the formulation of the UN Convention against Corruption (UNCAC), which was opened for signature in December 2003 in Mérida, Mexico, and entered into force in December 2005; the implementation of UNCAC in signatory states is monitored systematically under a review mechanism established in November 2009. In April 2012 UNODC launched the Integrity Initial Public Offering (IPO) initiative,enablinb private companies and investors to finance efforts by developing countries to combat corruption, which is regarded as a major obstacle to sustainable development. The fifth meeting of the Conference of the Parties to UNCAC was convened in Panama City, Panama, in November 2013.

In October 2008 UNODC and INTERPOL signed a joint agreement establishing the first International Anti-Corruption Academy; the Academy, based in Laxenburg, Austria, provides training to police personnel, government officials, academics and representatives of non-governmental organizations (NGOs) and private sector entities. In September 2011 UNODC launched TRACK (Tools and Resources for Anti-Corruption Knowledge), an internet-based anti-corruption portal.

The UN Global Programme against Money Laundering (GPML), established in March 1999, assists governments with formulating legislation against money-laundering and establishing and maintaining appropriate frameworks to counter the problem. GPML activities include the provision of technical assistance, training, and the collection, research and analysis of crime data. GPML, in collaboration with other governmental organizations, law enforcement agencies and academic institutions, co-ordinates the International Money Laundering Information Network (IMoLIN), an internet-based information resource. IMoLIN incorporates the Anti-Money Laundering International Database (a comprehensive database on money-laundering legislation throughout the world that constituted a key element in the Office's activities in support of the elaboration of UNTOC). At the first GPML Forum, held in the Cayman Islands in March 2000, the governments of 31 participating 'offshore' financial centres agreed in principle to adopt internationally accepted standards of financial regulation and measures against money-laundering.

In 2007 UNODC and the World Bank jointly launched the Stolen Asset Recovery (StAR) initiative, which aimed to address the theft of public assets from developing countries, and to promote direct government-to-government assistance. In April 2009 the G20 recommended that StAR review and propose mechanisms to strengthen international co-operation relating to asset recovery.

International Anti-Corruption Day is celebrated annually on 9 December.

CRIME PREVENTION AND CRIMINAL JUSTICE

UNODC focuses on strengthening the rule of law—particularly in conflict and post-conflict countries, breaking cycles of organized crime, and combating urban and armed crime, against a background of globalization where, increasingly, international approaches to combating organized crime are required. The Office develops tools to identify and measure trends in transnational criminal activity and resources aimed at assisting policy-makers in addressing challenging trends.

The Office assists countries in establishing the necessary national legal frameworks to underpin the implementation of the UN Convention against Transnational Organized Crime (UNTOC, also known as the Palermo Convention), which was opened for signature in December 2000 at a UN conference on combating organized crime held in Sicily, Italy, and entered into force in September 2003. UNTOC has three additional Protocols: the Protocol to Prevent, Suppress and Punish Trafficking in Persons, especially Women and Children (entered into force in December 2003, sometimes referred to as the 'Trafficking Protocol'); the Protocol against the Smuggling of Migrants by Land, Air and Sea (entered into force in January 2004); and the Protocol against the Illicit Manufacturing and Trafficking in Firearms, Their Parts and Components and Ammunition (entered into force in July 2005).

The Office oversees the application of international standards and norms relating to criminal justice, for example the Minimum Rules for the Treatment of Prisoners, Conventions against Torture, and Other Cruel, Inhuman or Degrading Treatment or Punishment, and Safeguards Guaranteeing the Protection of the Rights of Those Facing the Death Penalty. UNODC provides assistance to states in the area of penal reform, placing particular emphasis on training prison staff and responding to the needs of women and vulnerable prisoners.

UNODC has contributed to organization of regional preparatory meetings for successive UN Congresses on Crime Prevention and Criminal Justice; the 12th Congress was convened in April 2010, in Salvador, Brazil, and the 13th was to be held in 2015, in Qatar.

COUNTER-PIRACY ACTIVITIES

UNODC supports states in the Horn of Africa with the implementation of the UNTOC and other relevant international instruments in order to deter maritime piracy. During 2009 UNODC and the European Commission launched a joint counter-piracy programme (CPP), with a focus on Kenya, the Maldives, Mauritius, Seychelles and Tanzania. The CPP supports efforts to detain and prosecute piracy suspects, and supports financial intelligence units and law enforcement agencies in East Africa and the Horn of Africa. By 2013 prosecutions related to alleged acts of piracy numbered 290 in Puntland and 94 in Somaliland (both in Somalia); 164 in Kenya, 129 in Yemen; 124 in the Seychelles; and 119 in India. In February 2012 UNODC's Executive Director reported that, in 2011, pirates made US $170m. in ransom money from hijacking vessels, that the laundering of the proceeds of piracy was causing consumer prices to rise steeply in the Horn of Africa, and that illicit money flows linked to piracy were also being reinvested into other criminal activities, involving drugs, weaponry, alcohol-smuggling, and human-trafficking. UNODC, the World Bank and INTERPOL are jointly compiling a report on illicit financial flows linked to piracy. During November 2011 the UN Secretary-General sent an assessment mission—jointly led by UNODC and the UN Department of Political Affairs—to several Gulf of Guinea states (Benin, Nigeria, Gabon and Angola) to determine the scope of the threat of piracy in the region.

HEALTH

UNODC co-operates closely with other international, regional and NGOs and maintains dialogue with agencies advocating drug abuse control. It is a co-sponsor of the Joint Programme on HIV/AIDS (UNAIDS), which was established on 1 January 1996. UNODC's participation is in recognition of the importance of international drug control efforts in preventing the spread of HIV/AIDS.

UNODC supports member states in implementing drug use prevention interventions (in particular through the Global Youth Network against Drug Abuse and the Global Initiative on Primary Prevention of Substance Abuse) and in providing drug dependence treatment and care services. In 2005 UNODC launched Treatnet, a network of drug treatment clinics, which in 2014 was active in Latin America, Africa, the Middle East, Central Asia and South-East Asia.

ALTERNATIVE DEVELOPMENT

UNODC's Alternative Development Programme supports projects to create alternative sources of income for farmers economically dependent on the production of illicit narcotic crops. In 2014 such projects were being implemented in Afghanistan (Strengthening provincial capacity for drug control); Bolivia (Sustainable and integrated management of natural resources in the tropics of Cochabamba and the Yungas of La Paz, and Vocational training and promotion of microenterprise in the Yungas of La Paz); Colombia (Strengthening of alternative development productive projects, and Support to monitor and implement the integrated and sustainable illicit crop reduction and alternative development strategy in Colombia); Laos (Increasing food security and promoting licit crop production and small farmer enterprise development in Houaphan province, and Phongsaly alternative development fund); Myanmar (Food security); and Peru (Alternative development with an environmental approach in Apurimac-Ene and south-eastern valleys and in Pichis Palcazu, Aguaytia and Huallaga, and Sustainable agricultural development to reduce poverty through environmentally sustainable approaches and gender empowerment). A South-East Asia regional project—Increasing food security and promoting legal crop production and small-farmer development enterprise development in Laos and Myanmar—was also under way. In March 2012 UNODC and the UN Industrial Development Organization signed a Memorandum of Understanding on establishing a strategic partnership aimed at promoting grass-roots development and alternative livelihoods in poor rural communities hitherto dependent on the cultivation of illegal drugs crops.

TERRORISM PREVENTION

The UNODC's Terrorism Prevention Branch, established in 1999, researches trends in terrorist activity and provides legal and technical assistance to countries to improve their capabilities to investigate and prevent acts of terrorism. The Branch promotes international co-operation in combating the problem, and has researched the connections between terrorist activity and other forms of crime. The Branch supports states in ratifying universal legal instruments against terrorism, and in the development and application of national legislation in support of the implementation of these. A comprehensive global database on global terrorism, including counter-terrorism conventions, national criminal laws and relevant case laws, was launched by UNODC in June 2009. In October 2012 UNODC and the UN Counter-Terrorism Implementation Task Force (established in 2005) jointly published *The Use of the Internet for Terrorist Purposes*, providing practical guidelines on investigating and prosecuting cases of terrorism involving use of the internet for raising finance; distributing propaganda; recruiting, training and inciting followers; and gathering and disseminating information of practical use in terrorist activities.

An online UNODC/INTERPOL training course, aimed at people engaged in international co-operation against terrorism, was launched in October 2009.

WILDLIFE AND FOREST CRIME

Meeting in St Petersburg, Russia, in November 2010, at the International Tiger Forum, the heads of UNODC, the Convention on International Trade in Endangered Species of Wild Fauna and Flora (CITES), the WCO, INTERPOL and the World Bank jointly approved the establishment of an International Consortium on Combating Wildlife Crime (ICCWC), with the aim of combating the poaching of wild animals and illegal trade in wild animals and wild animal products. In September 2013 UNODC's Executive Director urged member states to strengthen efforts to combat poaching and illicit wildlife-trafficking, stating that this represented an area of transnational organized crime that was being undertaken on a massive scale, and was driving certain species close to extinction, as well as disturbing fragile ecosystems and adversely affecting local livelihoods and social and economic development.

REGIONAL ACTIVITIES

Afghanistan is the source of more than 90% of global opium supplies. UNODC and Afghan government sources jointly estimated that in 2013 some 209,000 ha of land in Afghanistan was under opium poppy cultivation (significantly higher than the 2012 total of 154,000 ha), with most of the cultivation focused on southern and western provinces of the country, where insecurity prevailed. Around 80% of opiates produced in Afghanistan are smuggled out of that country by transnational organized criminal groups via Iran and Pakistan, with the remainder being routed through central Asian countries; illegal trafficking threatens regional security and development and enriches criminal networks. In May 2003, at a Ministerial Conference on Drug Routes from Central Asia to Europe, convened in Paris, France, UNODC played a leading role in launching the Paris Pact, a partnership of more than 50 countries and international organizations aimed at combating the traffic in and consumption of Afghan opiates and related problems in affected countries along the Afghan opiates-trafficking routes. In October 2007, within the frame of the Paris Pact, UNODC organized a meeting of senior international counter-narcotics officials, in Kabul, Afghanistan, aimed at strengthening efforts to restrict the supply of illicit drugs from Afghanistan. UNODC supports the Central Asia Regional Information and Co-ordination Centre (CARICC), which was established in Almatı, Kazakhstan, in February 2006, to combat illicit drugs-trafficking in that region. In April UNODC and the Collective Security Treaty Organization (then comprising Armenia, Belarus, Kazakhstan, Kyrgyzstan, Russia and Tajikistan; Uzbekistan joined in June) signed a protocol on developing joint projects and sharing information with the aim of addressing drugs-trafficking, terrorism and transborder crime in Central Asia. In December 2008 UNODC launched the Rainbow Strategy, a regional initiative comprising seven operational plans (covering areas such as precursor chemicals, border management, financial flows, and drug abuse prevention and treatment), aimed at facilitating the implementation of the Paris Pact. The Triangular Initiative, organized by UNODC and launched in June 2007, promotes drugs control co-operation between Afghanistan, Iran and Paksistan. In December 2011 UNODC launched a new regional programme for Afghanistan and neighbouring countries. Meeting in February 2012 partners in the Paris Pact adopted the Vienna Declaration on committing to act in a 'balanced and comprehensive manner' against the illicit Afghan opium trade. In February 2013 a survey on patterns of corruption in Afghanistan, issued jointly by UNODC and the Afghan authorities, reported that, in 2012, at least one-half of Afghan citizens had paid a bribe to state officials.

In 2010 UNODC, INTERPOL and the WCO launched the Airport Communication Project (AIRCORP), to improve airport intelligence and data sharing at airports in Latin America, Africa and Europe, with a view to halting the air transportation of illegal drugs from Latin America through West Africa.

In July 2009 UNODC, other UN agencies, the Economic Community of West African States and INTERPOL launched the West Africa Coast Initiative (WACI), which aimed to build national and regional capacities to combat drugs-trafficking and organized crime in, initially, four pilot post-conflict countries: Côte d'Ivoire, Guinea-Bissau, Liberia and Sierra Leone. In February 2010 the pilot countries signed the 'WACI–Freetown Commitment', endorsing the implementation of the initiative, and agreeing to establish specialized transnational crime units on their territories. WACI activities were subsequently to be expanded to Guinea.

In December 2010 UNODC and the League of Arab States launched a five-year Regional Programme on Drug Control, Crime Prevention and Criminal Justice Reform for the Arab States, covering the period 2011–15, and based, similarly, on the following pillars: countering illicit trafficking, organized crime and terrorism; promoting justice and integrity; and drug use prevention and improving health.

In April 2014 a new UNODC regional programme was launched in support of the Crime and Security Strategy of the Caribbean Community.

In July 2013 UNODC initiated a new Voluntary Reporting System on Migrant Smuggling and Related Conduct (VRS-MSRC) in South-east Asia, representing an internet-based data collection and sharing system for use by state authorities in the region, with a view to informing strategic analysis and policy direction at the national, regional and inter-regional levels. In November 2013 UNODC launched a new Regional Programme for South-East Asia and the Pacific, to guide its activities there during 2014–17, with a focus on transnational organized crime and illicit trafficking; anti-corruption; terrorism prevention; criminal justice; and drugs, health and alternative development.

Finance

UNODC receives an allocation from the regular budget of the UN (US $43.9m. in 2014–15), although voluntary contributions from member states and private organizations represent the majority (about 90%) of its resources.

Publications

Afghanistan Opium Survey (annual).
eNews@UNODC (electronic newsletter).
Global Report on Crime and Justice.
Global Report on Trafficking in Persons.
Multilingual Dictionary of Narcotic Drugs and Psychotropic Substances Under International Control.
Serious Organized Crime Threat Assessment Handbook.
Technical Series.
The United Nations and Juvenile Justice: A Guide to International Standards and Best Practices.
UNODC Counter-Piracy Programme Brochure.
UNODC Update (quarterly).
World Drug Report.

United Nations Peacekeeping

Address: Department of Peacekeeping Operations, Room S-3727B, United Nations, New York, NY 10017, USA.

Telephone: (212) 963-8077; **fax:** (212) 963-9222; **internet:** www.un.org/Depts/dpko/.

United Nations peacekeeping operations have been conceived as instruments of conflict control. The UN has used these operations in various conflicts, with the consent of the parties involved, to maintain international peace and security, without prejudice to the positions or claims of parties, in order to facilitate the search for political settlements through peaceful means. Each operation is established with a specific mandate, which requires periodic review by the UN Security Council. In 1988 the United Nations Peacekeeping Forces were awarded the Nobel Peace Prize.

United Nations peacekeeping operations fall into two categories: peacekeeping forces and observer missions. Both must at all times maintain complete impartiality and avoid any action that might affect the claims or positions of the parties. Peacekeeping forces are composed of contingents of military and civilian personnel, made available by member states. These forces assist in preventing the recurrence of fighting, restoring and maintaining peace, and promoting a return to normal conditions. To this end, peacekeeping forces are authorized as necessary to undertake negotiations, persuasion, observation and fact-finding. They conduct patrols and interpose physically between the opposing parties. Peacekeeping forces are permitted to use their weapons only in self-defence.

Military observer missions are composed of officers who are made available, on the Secretary-General's request, by member states. A mission's function is to observe and report to the Secretary-General (who, in turn, informs the Security Council) on the maintenance of a ceasefire, to investigate violations and to do what it can to improve the situation.

In January 2013 the Security Council adopted Resolution 2086, which endorsed an evolving approach to peacekeeping that aims to facilitate peacebuilding and the advancement of sustainable stability and development in post-conflict countries. Peacekeeping missions have increasingly multidimensional mandates, focusing on, inter alia, strengthening national security sectors and the rule of law, building institutions of government, implementing programmes aimed at reintegrating former combatants into civilian society, and promoting reconciliation and inclusive political processes.

The UN's peacekeeping forces and observer missions are financed in most cases by assessed contributions from member states. (The exceptions are the UN Peacekeeping Force in Cyprus, which is funded partly by voluntary contributions; and the UN Military Observer Group in India and Pakistan and the UN Truce Supervision Organization, financed from the UN regular budget.) At 28 February 2014 outstanding assessed contributions to the peacekeeping budget amounted to some US $2,360m.

By April 2014 the UN had deployed a total of 69 peacekeeping operations, of which 13 were authorized in the period 1948–88 and 56 since 1988. At 28 February 2014 122 countries were contributing some 98,056 uniformed personnel to the 15 operations that were ongoing at that time, of whom 83,154 were peacekeeping troops, 13,056 police and 1,846 military observers.

In 2014 the DPKO was also directly supporting the UN Assistance Mission in Afghanistan, a political and peacebuilding mission that was established in March 2002.

African Union (AU)/UN Hybrid Operation in Darfur—UNAMID

Address: El Fasher, Sudan.

Joint AU-UN Special Representative: Dr Mohamed Ibn Chambas (Ghana).

Force Commander: Lt-Gen. Paul Ignace Mella (Tanzania).

Police Commissioner: Hester Andriana Paneras (South Africa).

Establishment and Mandate: UNAMID was established by a resolution of the UN Security Council in July 2007, with a mandate to take necessary action to support the implementation and verification of the Darfur Peace Agreement signed in May 2006 by the Sudanese Government and a rebel faction in Darfur, southern Sudan. UNAMID was also mandated to protect civilians, to provide security for humanitarian assistance, to support an inclusive political process, to contribute to the promotion of human rights and rule of law, and to monitor and report on the situation along the borders with Chad and the Central African Republic. An AU-UN Joint Mediation Support Team for Darfur (JMST) and a Tripartite Committee on UNAMID (including representatives of the UN, the AU and Government of Sudan) meet periodically.

Activities, 2007–10: UNAMID assumed command of the AU Mission in Sudan, comprising 10 battalions, in December 2007. In February 2008 UNAMID's Joint Special Representative signed a status of forces agreement with the minister responsible for foreign affairs of Sudan, covering logistical aspects of the mission. In March UNAMID police units conducted their first confidence-building patrols in areas under rebel control in northern Darfur. In July the UN designated Darfur a 'security phase four' area (permitting the UN to relocate staff temporarily pending an improvement in the security situation). A new joint AU-UN Chief Mediator was appointed in June, and a Joint Support Co-ordination Mechanism (JSCM) Office in Addis Ababa, Ethiopia, comprising liaison officers and communications equipment, was established in November to ensure effective consultation between the UN and AU headquarters. In February 2009 the UN Secretary-General reported that UNAMID's operational capabilities were limited by lack of critical and key military enabling equipment, logistical constraints, and the reluctance of many troop- and police-contributing countries to deploy to it well-trained personnel and efficient contingent-owned equipment. In addition, there was concern at restrictions on the movement of troops and on the issuing of visa and vehicle licence applications that were being imposed by the Sudanese authorities. In early 2009 an escalation of violence in the Mahajeriya region of southern Darfur resulted in the displacement of some 46,000 people, the majority of whom moved to the Zam Zam refugee camp near El Fasher. UNAMID undertook to deliver daily water supplies, as well as to conduct protection patrols in and around the camp. The mission provided security and other logistical support to help to ensure the continued distribution of humanitarian assistance following the expulsion from the country, in March, of 13 international non-governmental organizations (NGOs) and the dissolution of three national NGOs by the Sudanese authorities (who claimed that they had collaborated with investigations being conducted by the International Criminal Court). From late 2009 UNAMID provided logistical support to the Government's disarmament, demobilization and rehabilitation programme. In January 2010 the UN Secretary-General reported that the capability of UNAMID batallions in Darfur continued to be a cause of concern, with a number of units not having sufficient major equipment. UNAMID assisted the former UN Mission in Sudan and the Sudanese authorities with transporting electoral materials to remote locations and with training more than 10,000 local police officers in preparation for the municipal, legislative and presidential elections that were held in April.

In February and March 2010, respectively, two of the rebel groupings that had been operating in Darfur signed framework agreements with the Sudanese Government aimed at resolving the conflict. During May violent unrest in Darfur caused nearly 600 fatalities, the highest number since the deployment of the mission. UNAMID strengthened security measures and provided additional medical care in some of the larger camps for internally displaced persons (IDPs) where inter-tribal conflict was becoming a major security concern. In August UNAMID and the Sudanese Government agreed to establish a joint committee to resolve problems in Kalma camp, which hosted some 82,000 IDPs. In late August a consultative meeting of representatives of UNAMID, the AU, the USA and the Sudanese President agreed that UNAMID and the Sudanese Government would work closely together to improve the security situation in Darfur and to support stabilization and development of the region.

2011–14: In May 2011 an All-Darfur Stakeholders' Conference was convened, with support from UNAMID, in Doha, Qatar, to consider a draft peace agreement that had been formulated by the JMST. Participants in the Conference endorsed a communiqué providing for the draft document (the Doha Document for Peace in Darfur—DDPD) to form the basis for achieving a permanent ceasefire and comprehensive Darfurian peace settlement. In July the Sudanese Government and the 'Liberation and Justice Movement', an alliance of rebel groupings, signed an accord on the adoption of the DDPD. Shortly afterwards, the two sides also signed a Protocol on the Political Participation of the Liberation and Justice Movement and Integration of its Forces. Meanwhile, UNAMID, a participant in the DDPD Implementation Follow-on Commission, prepared, with civil society representatives, a plan for the dissemination throughout Darfur of information on the Document. In August UNAMID chaired the first meeting of a ceasefire Commission established under the provisions of the DDPD.

In May 2011 UNAMID and humanitarian agencies active in Darfur launched Operation Spring Basket, aimed at enhancing access to remote parts of Darfur and thereby providing humanitarian aid to around 400,000 beneficiaries. UNAMID continued to implement Quick Impact Projects in Darfur, in support of the education sector, infrastructure and local facilities. The mission, where requested, provides logistical and security support to humanitarian agencies assisting returnees to West Darfur. The formation in 2011 of a subcommittee comprising UNAMID and Sudanese government security entities led to a significant decrease in restrictions on the movements of UNAMID security patrols in the latter part of the year. There were continued reports of criminal attacks on UN personnel, including the theft of UNAMID vehicles, during 2008–14.

In March 2012 UNAMID completed an operation to verify positions held by former rebels; information acquired during the verification operation was to be used by the ceasefire Commission in disarmament, demobilization, and reintegration/integration planning. In June UNAMID and the DDPD signatories agreed to revise the Document's schedule of implementation (extending by one year all previously determined deadlines). During April–June UNAMID provided technical and logistical support towards the convening of 55 workshops aimed at widely disseminating the Doha Document. In July the Security Council authorized a reconfiguration of UNAMID, entailing a reduction in the mission's numbers to be implemented over a period of 12–18 months. The largest UNAMID presence was to be confined henceforth to areas of Darfur with the highest risk of insecurity. The mission was to make more frequent and longer patrols, with expanded use of temporary operating bases, and was to be more rapidly deployable. The Security Council demanded that all parties to the conflict in Darfur immediately cease acts of violence, and effect a permanent ceasefire and comprehensive peace settlement based on the DDPD. From mid-2012–early 2014 a trend towards inter-communal resource-based conflict developed, with a particular focus on competition for access to arable land and to gold and petroleum deposits in central and southern Darfur. During 2012 UNAMID assisted with the staging of a series of workshops—aimed at assessing Darfur's economic recovery, development and poverty eradication requirements—that were organized by a Darfur Joint Assessment Mission initiated in May by the Darfur local authorities and international partners. A new Special Prosecutor for crimes committed in Darfur, appointed by the Sudan Government in June, announced in December that investigations had been opened into some 10 cases, included criminal acts committed against UNAMID personnel. In January 2013 UNAMID delivered humanitarian assistance to IDPs in North Darfur, following the mass displacement earlier that month of thousands of civilians, arising from violent unrest in Jabel Amir gold mining area. A further humanitarian operation was undertaken in April to deliver essential supplies to some 20,000 people displaced by renewed fighting in Labado and Muhajeria, East Darfur. In that month UNAMID and the AU's High-Level Panel on Darfur endorsed a strategy, formulated by the mission, which aimed to advance internal dialogue in Darfur, and in accordance with which a committee of stakeholders was to be established to prepare and conduct the continuing consultations; a concept note, communications strategy and roadmap for the initiative were adopted in December. In July the Security Council extended UNAMID's mandate until 31 August 2014. During 2013 UNAMID facilitated conferences addressing the root causes of inter-communal conflict, in El Fasher, El Geneina, Khartoum, Nyala and Zalingei, with participation by community leaders, local authorities, and civil society representatives.

Operational Strength: UNAMID's operational strength at 28 February 2014 comprised 14,354 troops, 330 military observers and 4508 police; the mission was supported by 404 UN Volunteers and (at 30 November 2013) by 1,060 international civilian personnel and 2,957 local civilian staff.

Finance: The budget for UNAMID amounted to US $1,335.2m. for the period 1 July 2013–30 June 2014, funded from a Special Account comprising assessed contributions from UN member states.

United Nations Disengagement Observer Force—UNDOF

Address: Camp Faouar, Syria.

Force Commander: Maj.-Gen. IQBAL SINGH SINGHA (India).

Establishment and Mandate: UNDOF was established for an initial period of six months by a UN Security Council resolution in May 1974, following the signature in Geneva, Switzerland, of an Agreement on Disengagement of Forces between Israel and Syria. The mandate has since been extended by successive resolutions. The initial task of the mission was to take over territory evacuated in stages by the Israeli troops, in accordance with the disengagement agreement, to hand over territory to Syrian troops, and to establish an area of separation on the Golan Heights. Indirect peace talks between Israel and Syria on reaching a comprehensive peace agreement providing for the withdrawal of the Israeli presence from the Golan Heights were initiated in May 2008, but were discontinued in December, owing to the Israeli military offensive initiated against the Gaza strip at that time; by 2014 the ongoing civil war in Syria rendered their prompt resumption unlikely.

Activities: UNDOF continues to monitor the area of separation; it carries out inspections of the areas of limited armaments and forces; uses its best efforts to maintain the ceasefire; carries out de-mining activities; and undertakes activities of a humanitarian nature (for example it has arranged the transfer of prisoners and war dead between Syria and Israel). The Force operates exclusively on Syrian territory.

During 2011 demonstrations by anti-Government protesters in Syria extended to the area of UNDOF's operations. As the uprising within Syria descended into civil war—and, in violation of the 1974 agreement on disengagement of forces, the Syrian armed forces expanded their deployment in the mission's area of operations—UNDOF strengthened its force protection measures, including the fortification of its positions. In mid-May and early June groups of Palestinian protesters gathered at a site known as the 'family shouting place', opposite the village of Majdal Chams in the area of limitation on the Israeli-occupied Golan side. UNDOF monitored the proceedings using armoured patrols, engaged with the Syrian and Israeli militaries, and attempted to diffuse tensions. During 2012–14 UNDOF's area of operations continued to be affected by the ongoing deep instability in Syria. Significant population movements were noted: for example, in July 2012 more than 800 Syrian civilians vacated Jabbata al Khashab, in the area of separation, seeking shelter in villages further south. UNDOF protested against all violations of the 1974 Agreement on Disengagement of Forces and continued to monitor the area of separation through the use of fixed positions and patrols, attempting to ensure the exclusion from it of military forces; the mission also undertook fortnightly inspections of equipment and force levels in the areas of limited armaments and forces. On several occasions UNDOF provided direct emergency medical treatment, including to wounded Syrian opposition and national military personnel; the mission also provided assistance to the Syrian Red Crescent.

In March 2013 armed Syrian opposition combatants stopped and detained 21 UNDOF peacekeepers, in the al-Jimla area. The UN Secretary-General and Security Council strongly condemned the action and demanded the immediate and unconditional release of the mission personnel; the detainees were released soon afterwards. In June the UN Security Council expressed concern that military activities impinging upon the area of separation, in violation of the 1974 Agreement on Disengagement of Forces, had the potential to escalate tensions between Israel and Syria, and requested the UN Secretary-General to ensure that UNDOF was sufficiently equipped to fulfil its mandate in a safe and secure way. Reporting on the mission's activities in September and again in December, the Secretary-General noted the occurrence of heavy clashes between the Syrian military and opposition forces close to UNDOF positions, causing mission personnel to seek shelter, and he also noted several reports of firing across the ceasefire line by the parties to the Syrian conflict and also—with prior notification to UNDOF—by the Israeli military claiming retaliation. UNDOF continued to man static positions and to undertake constant observation to ensure the exclusion of all military forces from the area of separation. From July the Observer Group Golan set up several temporary observation posts along the ceasefire line with a view to enhancing the Force's situational awareness of the area of separation. In December the UN Security Council strongly condemned recent intense fighting in the area of separation and called upon all parties to the Syrian conflict to cease military actions in UNDOF's area of operations, reiterating the destabilizing potential of such violations.

Operational Strength: At 28 February 2014 the mission comprised 1,243 troops, supported by 146 international and local civilian personnel (as at 30 November 2013). Military observers of UNTSO's Observer Group Golan help UNDOF in the performance of its tasks, as required.

Finance: The General Assembly appropriation for the operation over the period 1 July 2013–30 June 2014 amounted to US $48.0m.

United Nations Interim Administration Mission in Kosovo—UNMIK

Address: Priština, Kosovo.

Special Representative of the UN Secretary-General and Head of Office: FARID ZARIF (Afghanistan).

Establishment and Mandate: In June 1999, following the end of 15 months of armed conflict in Kosovo, the UN Security Council adopted Resolution 1244, which outlined the terms of a political settlement for the southern Serbian province, and provided for the deployment of international civilian and security personnel. The security presence, termed the Kosovo Peace Implementation Force (KFOR), was to be led by NATO, while the UN was to oversee all civilian operations. UNMIK was established under the terms of Resolution 1244 as the supreme legal and executive authority in Kosovo, with responsibility for all civil administration and for facilitating the reconstruction and rehabilitation of the province as an autonomous region. For the first time in a UN operation other organizations were mandated to co-ordinate aspects of the mission in Kosovo, under the UN's overall jurisdiction. The four key elements, or Pillars, of UNMIK were (I) humanitarian affairs (led by UNHCR); (II) civil administration; (III) democratization and institution-building (the Organization for Security and Co-operation in Europe—OSCE); and (IV) economic reconstruction (European Union—EU). At the end of the first year of UNMIK's presence the element of humanitarian assistance was phased out. A new Pillar (I), concerned with police and justice, was established in May 2001, under the direct leadership of the UN. The mission's priorities are to promote security, stability and respect for human rights in Kosovo. Regional UNMIK offices are located in Mitrovica, Skopje (former Yugoslav republic of Macedonia), and Belgrade (Serbia).

Activities, 1999–2002: In December 1999 the leaders of the three main political groupings in Kosovo agreed on provisional power-sharing arrangements with UNMIK. The so-called Kosovo-UNMIK Joint Interim Administrative Structure established an eight-member executive Interim Administrative Council and a framework of administrative departments. In January 2000 UNMIK oversaw the inauguration of the Kosovo Protection Corps, a civilian agency comprising mainly former members of the newly demilitarized Kosovo Liberation Army, which was to provide an emergency response service and a humanitarian assistance capacity, to assist in de-mining operations and contribute to rebuilding local infrastructure. During mid-2000 UNMIK organized the voter registration process for municipal elections, which were held in October. In December the Supreme Court of Kosovo was inaugurated, comprising 16 judges appointed by the UN Secretary-General's Special Representative (SRSG). During 2000 UNMIK police and KFOR co-operated in conducting joint security operations; the establishment of a special security task force to combat ethnically motivated political violence, comprising senior UNMIK police and KFOR members, was agreed in June. From January 2001 UNMIK international travel documents were distributed to Kosovars without Yugoslav passports. From June, in response to ongoing concern at violence between ethnic Albanians and security forces in the former Yugoslav republic of Macedonia (FYRM), UNMIK designated 19 authorized crossing points at Kosovo's international borders with Albania and the FYRM, and its boundaries with Montenegro and Serbia. In May the SRSG signed the Constitutional Framework on Interim Self-Government, providing for the establishment of a Constitutional Assembly. UNMIK undertook efforts to register voters and to continue to facilitate the return of displaced persons to their home communities. The last session of the Kosovo Transitional Council was held in October, and a general election was conducted, as scheduled, in the following month. In December the SRSG inaugurated the new 120-member Assembly. In February 2002 the SRSG negotiated an agreement with the leaders of the main political parties that resolved a deadlock in establishing an Interim Government. Accordingly, in March, the new President, Prime Minister and Interim Government were inaugurated, enabling the commencement of the process of developing self-governing institutions. In November the mission established the UNMIK Administration—Mitrovica (UAM), superseding parallel institutions that had operated hitherto in Serb-dominated northern Mitrovica, and thereby extending UNMIK's authority over all Kosovo. During that month a second series of municipal elections took place.

2003–05: In March 2003 a Transfer Council was established with responsibility for transferring competencies from UNMIK to the provisional institutions of self-government (PISG). In June UNMIK, with the UN Development Programme (UNDP), launched a Rapid Response Returns Facility (RRRF) to assist returnees from inside and outside Kosovo through the provision of housing and socio-economic support. In October the SSRG mediated an agreement between Kosovan and Serb leaders, supported by the international Contact Group on the Balkans, to pursue a process of direct dialogue.

In December 2003 the SRSG and the Kosovan Prime Minister jointly launched *Standards for Kosovo*, drafted by the UN and partners and detailing eight fundamental democratic standards to be applied in the territory. Leaders of the Serb community declined to participate in the process. At the end of March 2004 the SRSG and then Prime Minister Rexhapi launched the Kosovo Standards Implementation Plan, outlining 109 standards and goals, as a mechanism for reviewing the standards and assessing the progress of the PISG. In mid-March rioting erupted in Kosovska Mitrovica and violent clashes between Serb and Albanian communities occurred throughout the province. After two days of serious incidents 19 civilians were reported to have been killed and an estimated 4,100 people from the Kosovan Serb, Roma and Ashkali communities had been displaced. In addition, 730 houses and 36 sites of cultural or religious importance had been damaged or destroyed. UNMIK undertook to restore the confidence of the affected communities, to assist with the reconstruction of damaged infrastructure, and to investigate the organizers and main perpetrators of the violence. It also initiated a review of its own operational procedures, as well as the conduct of local politicians. The priority areas for the mission were identified as providing a secure environment, including the protection of minorities, and ensuring the success of the Standards Implementation Plan. In August a newly appointed SRSG also re-emphasized the need to stimulate the local economy. In September UNMIK established a Financial Information Centre to help to deter money-laundering and other related offences. UNMIK assisted in preparations for legislative elections, held in October, and supported efforts to ensure a large and representative voter turnout. In November the SRSG met the newly elected political leaders and agreed on the establishment of new ministries for energy and mining, local government, and returns and communities. In the following month the SRSG and the new Prime Minister, Ramush Haradinaj, concluded an agreement on making the Standards a priority for the Kosovan Government and on action for their implementation. In January 2005 a new UNMIK Senior Adviser on Minority Issues was appointed in order to assist the Government's efforts to integrate fully minorities into Kosovan society. In March Haradinaj resigned following notification of his indictment by the International Criminal Tribunal for the former Yugoslavia. UNMIK supported the establishment of a coalition administration, and announced the establishment of a new body to promote political consensus within the province. The first meeting of the so-called Kosovo Forum, to which all political leaders were invited, was convened in June. In October the UN Secretary-General recommended that political negotiations on the future status of the province commence. A Special Envoy for the Future Status Process, Martii Ahtisaari, was appointed in the following month. In December new UNMIK regulations provided for the establishment of Ministries of Justice and of Internal Affairs.

2006–09: In August 2006 the Interim Government approved the European Partnership Action Plan, which replaced the Kosovo Standards Implementation Plan as the basic reference document concerning standards. Negotiations on the future status of Kosovo were organized by the Special Envoy for the Future Status Process during 2006, and in February 2007 he presented a Settlement Proposal to the relevant parties. The provisional Proposal, which provided for a Kosovan constitution, flag and national anthem and for Kosovo to apply for independent membership of international organizations, while remaining under close international supervision, was rejected by many Kosovan Serbs on the grounds that it appeared to advance the advent of a fully independent Kosovo, and also by extremist Kosovan Albanian elements since it did not guarantee immediate full independence. During violent protests against the proposals organized by radical Kosovo Albanians two protesters were killed by Kosovan and UNMIK police, leading to the resignations of the UNMIK Police Commissioner and the Kosovan Minister of Internal Affairs. The Special Envoy pursued further discussions with all parties; however, in March he abandoned the Proposal. In July a troika of the Contact Group on Kosovo, comprising representatives of the EU, Russia and USA, was established to undertake intensive negotiations to determine a final status for the province. UNMIK monitored the preparation for and conduct of a general election in Kosovo, held in November.

In February 2008 UNMIK appealed for restraint following a declaration of independence from Serbia, announced by the newly inaugurated Kosovan Assembly. In the following month the mission condemned a violent attack, by Serbian protesters, against a Court in northern Mitrovica, and subsequent clashes with UNMIK and KFOR personnel who regained control of the building. In early April the UN Secretary-General confirmed that UNMIK and the provisions of Security Council Resolution 1244 remained in effect and should be adhered to by the Kosovan and Serbian authorities. In June a new Kosovan Constitution entered in force, providing for the transfer of executive powers from the UN to the elected authorities and for an EU police and justice mission to assume supervisory responsibilities from the UN. The UN Secretary-General confirmed that UNMIK was to be reconfigured; however, Serbian opposition to the Constitution and political divisions within the UN Security Council regarding the governance of the territory had prevented a new resolution from being agreed. The EU pillar of the mission was terminated on 30 June. UNMIK worked closely with the EU to establish and deploy the EU Rule of Law Mission in Kosovo (EULEX), under the overall authority of the UN. In June the issuance of UNMIK travel documents was terminated as a result of a decision by the Kosovan authorities to produce national passports. EULEX assumed responsibility for police and judicial functions in December, and reached full operational capacity in April 2009. During 2009–10 UNMIK reoriented its field presence to focus on areas occupied by ethnic non-Albanians.

2010–14: In July 2010 the International Court of Justice ruled that Kosovo had legitimately seceded from Serbia in February 2008. In mid-2010 UNMIK, jointly with the UN Kosovo Team, developed a new UN Strategic Framework for Kosovo, which was endorsed in September. With a view to diffusing local tensions in northern areas, UNMIK facilitated a new security co-ordination forum from 2011, comprising KFOR, EULEX, the OSCE and northern Kosovo Serb leaders. In January 2012 UNMIK and partners re-established regular meetings of a lapsed Human Rights International Contact Group on Kosovo. In May the Kosovo authorities inaugurated a new Mitrovica North Administrative Office (MNAO) and announced the termination, from July, of financing towards the salaries of local staff of the UNMIK Administration—Mitrovica (UAM, established in 2002), having from 2011 significantly reduced funding to the UAM. UNMIK maintained that it had not been appropriately consulted on the downgrading of the UAM, which was, nevertheless, to continue, without local staff, to pursue a role in the areas of conflict prevention, mediation and facilitation. The first high-level meeting between the Prime Ministers of Serbia and Kosovo was convened, under EU auspices, in October 2012, in Brussels, Belgium; the dialogue continued in early 2014, and included, in February 2013, contact at presidential level. In April 2013 both parties signed a 15-point 'First agreement on principles governing the normalization of relations'. (UNMIK was to support its implementation.) In November–December mayoral elections took place, and municipal elections were also held in November, for the first time under a single legislative framework throughout Kosovo. During 2013 UNMIK continued to facilitate dialogue among all Kosovar communities, to monitor the implementation of the Council of Europe Framework Convention for the Protection of National Minorities, and to promote the rule of law. The mission provided document-certification services, and supported the continuing investigatory process into the situation of persons (numbering 1,721 at January 2014) still reported missing from the 1998–99 conflict. In co-operation with UNESCO, UNMIK continued to monitor the protection of cultural and religious heritage sites; in September 2013 a new Cultural Heritage Council was established in Prizren, Kosovo. The mission also co-operated with the International Criminal Police Organization, facilitating the issuance of several 'Red Notices' (wanted persons alerts), as well as assisting with a number of extraditions. An escalation of violent incidents was reported in northern Kosovo in the first half of that year, but the security situation subsequently calmed, and municipal elections took place relatively peacefully in November. During 2010–14 UNMIK continued its efforts to facilitate the participation of Kosovo in international and regional arrangements and conferences. In October 2013 the EU—having determined in June that sufficient progress had been achieved in the territory in the areas of rule of law, public administration, protection of minorities, and trade—initiated negotiations with the Kosovo authorities on the adoption of a Stabilization and Association Agreement.

Operational Strength: At 28 February 2014 UNMIK comprised eight military officers and seven civilian police officers, in addition to 27 UN Volunteers, and (as at 30 November 2013) 114 international and 211 local civilian staff.

Finance: The General Assembly proposed the apportionment of US $45m. to the Special Account for UNMIK to finance the operation during the period 1 July 2013–30 June 2014.

United Nations Interim Force in Lebanon—UNIFIL

Address: Naqoura, Lebanon.

Force Commander and Chief of Mission: Maj.-Gen. PAOLO SERRA (Italy).

Maritime Task Force Commander: Rear Admiral WALTER EDUARDO BOMBARDA (Brazil).

Establishment and Mandate: UNIFIL was established by UN Security Council Resolution 425 in March 1978, following an invasion of Lebanon by Israeli forces. The force was mandated to confirm the withdrawal of Israeli forces, to restore international peace and security, and to assist the Government of Lebanon in ensuring the return of its effective authority in southern Lebanon. UNIFIL also extended humanitarian assistance to the population of the area, particularly following the second Israeli invasion of Lebanon in 1982. UN Security Council Resolution 1701, approved in August 2006—following an eruption of conflict in July between the Israeli armed forces and Hezbollah militia—expanded the mission's mandate to include monitoring the ceasefire between the two sides, supporting the deployment of Lebanese troops in southern Lebanon, and facilitating humanitarian activities and safe returns of internally displaced persons (IDPs). Resolution 1701 also authorized the establishment of a UNIFIL Maritime Task Force. Regular tripartite meetings take place between the UNIFIL Force Commander and senior officials from the Lebanese and Israeli security forces.

Activities, 2000–2005: In April 2000 the Israeli Government formally notified the UN Secretary-General of its intention to comply with Security Council Resolution 425, requiring the unconditional withdrawal of its forces from southern Lebanon. In mid-June the UN Secretary-General confirmed that Israeli forces had fully evacuated from southern Lebanon. UNIFIL patrolled the area vacated by the Israeli forces, monitored the line of withdrawal (the so-called Blue Line), undertook de-mining activities, and continued to provide humanitarian assistance. From August the Lebanese Government deployed a Joint Security Force to the area and began re-establishing local administrative structures and reintegrating basic services into the rest of the country. However, the authorities declined to deploy military personnel along the border zone, on the grounds that a comprehensive peace agreement with Israel would first need to be achieved. In November, following two serious violations of the Blue Line in the previous month by both Israeli troops and Hezbollah militia, the Security Council urged the Lebanese Government to take effective control of the whole area vacated by Israel and to assume international responsibilities. In January 2001 the UN Secretary-General reported that UNIFIL no longer exercised control over the area of operations. The Security Council endorsed his proposals to reconfigure the Force in order to focus on its remaining mandate of maintaining and observing the ceasefire along the line of withdrawal; this was completed by the end of 2002. During 2002 and 2003 UNIFIL helped to clear areas of land of anti-personnel devices and to assist the integration of the formerly occupied zone into the rest of the country. In July 2004 UNIFIL representatives, with other UN officials, worked to defuse tensions following an alleged Hezbollah sniper attack against Israeli forces and subsequent Israeli violations of Lebanese airspace. At the end of that year the UN expressed concern at further repeated violations of the Blue Line from both sides. A serious breach of the ceasefire occurred in May 2005. In June UNIFIL reported attacks on Israeli troop positions by Hezbollah militia and a forceful response by the Israeli Defence Force. In November UNIFIL brokered a ceasefire following further hostilities across the Blue Line, initiated by Hezbollah; however, there were reports of a missile attack on Israeli positions in the following month.

2006–14: In mid-July 2006 a full-scale conflict erupted between the Israeli armed forces and Hezbollah, following the capture by Hezbollah of two Israeli soldiers, and the killing of three others. An estimated 1,000 Lebanese civilians were killed and 900,000 displaced from their homes during the unrest. A ceasefire between Hezbollah and Israel entered into effect in mid-August, following the adoption by the UN Security Council of Resolution 1701. The provisions of the resolution demanded 'the immediate cessation by Hezbollah of all attacks and the immediate cessation by Israel of all offensive military operations' in Lebanon; welcomed a recent decision of the Lebanese Government to deploy 15,000 armed troops in southern Lebanon; increased the Force's authorized troop strength to a maximum of 15,000; and expanded its mandate to include monitoring the ceasefire, supporting the Lebanese troop deployment in southern Lebanon, facilitating humanitarian access to civilian communities, and assisting voluntary and safe returns of people displaced by the conflict. Resolution 1701 also (at the request of the Lebanese authorities) established a UNIFIL Maritime Task Force (MTF)—the first naval task force to participate in a UN peacekeeping mission—which was deployed from October to support the Lebanese Navy in monitoring and securing Lebanon's territorial waters and coastline, and preventing the unauthorized entry of arms by sea into Lebanon. In September 2006 a new Strategic Military Cell, reporting to the Under-Secretary-General for Peacekeeping Operations, was established to provide military guidance to UNIFIL. A UN Mine Action Co-ordination Centre of South Lebanon was also established to co-ordinate efforts to locate and destroy unexploded munitions.

A review of UNIFIL's operational effectiveness was conducted in late 2009; in February 2010 recommendations were issued, on the basis of the review, on means of making the Force in future more task-oriented and flexible. The review also emphasized the need to formalize a mechanism for regular strategic dialogue between UNIFIL and the Lebanese armed forces. In August the Force Commander convened an extraordinary tripartite meeting with senior representatives of the Lebanese Armed Forces and the Israeli Defence Forces, following a violent encounter along the Blue Line.

In February 2011 UNIFIL conducted a large-scale disaster preparedness exercise with the Lebanese Armed Forces in the Tyre area. The UN Security Council strongly condemned a terrorist attack perpetrated against a UNIFIL convoy near Saida in July, injuring six peacekeepers. At the beginning of August Lebanese and Israeli forces briefly exchanged fire across the Blue Line in the Wazzani River area; UNIFIL subsequently investigated the incident, and made a number of recommendations aimed at preventing a recurrence.

UNIFIL has repeatedly reported and protested Israeli violations of Lebanese airspace—mainly by unmanned vehicles, but also by fighter aircraft. In May 2013 Hezbollah combatants openly participated in a battle in western Syria. A breach of the Blue Line by four Israeli soldiers in August, during which they engaged with Hezbollah fighters on Lebanese territory, was deemed by UNIFIL to be a serious violation of the ceasefire and of Security Council Resolution 1701, by both the Israelis and Hezbollah. Shortly afterwards, four rockets were aimed across the Blue Line towards Israel from the Tyre area of Lebanon; on the following day the Israeli forces mounted a retaliatory attack back across the Blue Line. UNIFIL investigated the rocket attack—for which a Lebanese militant group claimed responsibility—and declared it to be a further serious violation of the ceasefire and Resolution 1701. More rockets were launched towards Israel from southern Lebanon in December, provoking retaliatory artillery fire by the Israeli forces. UNIFIL investigated the incident, and, in co-operation with the Lebanese armed forces, intensified its patrols in the area.

In September 2013 UNIFIL's Force Commander participated in the inaugural meeting of the International Support Group for Lebanon, held at the UN's New York headquarters, under the chairmanship of the UN Secretary-General, to consider means of supporting stability in Lebanon, in view of the impact on the country's resources of the ongoing civil war in neighbouring Syria (by April 2014 Lebanon was accommodating 953,626 registered Syrian refugees, and also an influx of Palestinians who had been registered as refugees in Syria). The meeting acknowledged UNIFIL's ongoing support to the Lebanese security forces in maintaining peace along the Blue Line, and also welcomed a strategic dialogue plan concluded by UNIFIL and the Lebanese security forces as a component of the Lebanese security forces' ongoing capabilities development plan.

UNIFIL patrols its area of operations daily on foot and in vehicles, as well as regularly by helicopter. The mission and the Lebanese armed forces also jointly conduct daily co-ordinated activities (including capability exercises, training exercises on land and at sea, and counter-rocket-launching operations) in addition to operating seven checkpoints on the Litani River in southern Lebanon. UNIFIL works to mark visibly the Blue Line, involving the clearance of minefields, measuring co-ordinates, and constructing Blue Line markers (by October 2013 180 markers had been verified). The UNIFIL MTF continues to work closely with the Lebanese Navy in training and capacity-building activities, and to conduct maritime surveillance operations. During October 2006–April 2014 the Task Force hailed some 56,817 vessels and referred 4,738 vessels to the Lebanese authorities for further inspections.

UNIFIL provides regular community services in its area of operations, including dental, medical, veterinary and educational assistance, and the implementation of Quick Impact Projects.

Operational Strength: At 28 February 2014 the Force comprised 10,200 military personnel; it was supported (at 30 November 2013) by 315 international and 634 local civilian staff. UNIFIL is assisted in its tasks by military observers of the United Nations Truce Supervision Organization (q.v.).

Finance: The General Assembly appropriation for the operation for the period 1 July 2013–30 June 2014 amounted to US $492.6m.

United Nations Interim Security Force for Abyei—UNISFA

Address: Abyei Town, Sudan.

Head of Mission and Force Commander: Maj.-Gen. YOHANNES GEBREMESKEL TESFAMARIAM (Ethiopia).

Establishment and Mandate: UNISFA was established by UN Security Resolution 1990 on 27 June 2011, and is mandated to protect civilians and humanitarian personnel in the disputed Abyei region (located at Sudan's border with South Sudan); to facilitate the free movement of humanitarian aid; to monitor and verify the redeployment of government and rebel forces from the Abyei Area; to participate in relevant Abyei Area bodies; to provide de-mining assistance and advice on technical matters; to strengthen the capacity of the Abyei Police Service; and, as necessary, to provide—in co-operation with the Abyei Police Service—security for the regional oil infrastructure. In December the UN Security Council expanded UNISFA's mandate to include assisting all parties in ensuring the observance of the Safe Demilitarized Border Zone, and advising, and supporting the operational activities of, the Joint Border Verification and Monitoring Mechanism (the creation of the Zone and Mechanism having been outlined in Agreements concluded in June 2011); facilitating liaison between the parties; and supporting the parties, when requested, in developing effective bilateral management mechanisms along the border. UNISFA pursues contact with local community leaderships, and works to promote inter-community dialogue. The mandate of the mission has been successively extended.

Activities, 2011–14: Under the auspices of the 'Friends of Abyei', chaired by the Resident Co-ordinator in Sudan, a planning team, comprising representatives of UN agencies, donor and international non-governmental organizations, developed during 2011 a humanitarian joint recovery programming strategy for Abyei; it was envisaged that people displaced by the violence in Abyei would only be returned there following the planned withdrawal of forces and the full deployment of UNISFA. At the end of June 2011 the parties to the conflict in Abyei signed an Agreement on Border Security, in which they reaffirmed commitment to a Joint Political and Security Mechanism, established under an agreement concluded in December 2010; and provided for the establishment of a Safe Demilitarized Border Zone, and Joint Border Verification and Monitoring Mechanism, pending the resolution of the status of disputed areas; UNISFA was mandated from December 2011 to provide force protection for Monitoring Mechanism. Since its inauguration UNISFA has conducted regular air and ground patrols, and has established permanent operating bases in Abyei Town, Agok, and Diffra. In February 2012 South Sudan and Sudan signed a Memorandum of Understanding on non-aggression and co-operation, committing each state to respecting the other's sovereignty and territorial integrity. In the following month the UN Secretary-General reported that the security situation in Abyei remained tense, owing to the continued presence—of unauthorized Sudanese armed forces, South Sudanese police, and rebels in the area; as well as owing to ongoing large-scale nomadic migration, and returns of internally displaced persons. In April 2012, as tensions continued and violent clashes mounted, the UN Security Council demanded that Sudan and South Sudan redeploy their forces from Abyei; that the two sides withdraw forces from their joint border and cease escalating cross-border violence with immediate effect, with the support of UNISFA and through the establishment of a demilitarized border zone; that Sudanese rebels should vacate oilfields in Heglig (Sudan); that Sudan should cease aerial bombardments of South Sudan; and that a summit should be convened between the two states to resolve outstanding concerns. During April the African Union (AU) High-Level Implementation Panel (AUHIP) on Sudan (established in October 2009 and mandated to assist the relevant Sudanese parties with the implementation of the January 2005 Comprehensive Peace Agreement, presented to both parties a draft Joint Decision for Reduction of Tension, providing for the immediate cessation of hostilities between the two states, and the withdrawal of armed forces of each state from the territory of the other. At the end of April 2012 and in early May, respectively, South Sudan and Sudan agreed to abide by a seven-point Roadmap for Action by Sudan and South Sudan, approved in late April by the AU Peace and Security Council. The AU Roadmap provided for (i) the immediate cessation of all hostilities; (ii) the unconditional withdrawal of all armed forces to their respective sides of the border; (iii) the activation, within one week from the adoption of the Roadmap, of all necessary border security mechanisms; (iv) cessation of harbouring of, and support to, rebel groups active against the other state; (v) the activation of an ad hoc Committee to investigate complaints made by one party against the other; (vi) immediate cessation of hostile propaganda and inflammatory statements in the media, and against property, cultural and religious symbols belonging to the nationals of the other state; and (vii) implementation of pending aspects of the June 2011 Temporary Arrangements for the Administration and Security of the Abyei Area, most particularly the redeployment of all Sudanese and South Sudanese forces out of Abyei. In accordance with its commitment to the Roadmap, South Sudan withdrew its forces from Abyei in early May 2012, with logistical support and protection from UNISFA; and, also with mission assistance, Sudan withdrew its military and most police from the area at, respectively, the end of May and beginning of June. However, in early 2014 a presence of up to 150 Sudanese police, equipped with small arms, remained in Abyei, guarding infrastructures at the Diffra oil fields, in contravention of the June 2011 Agreement. On 27 September 2012 the Sudan and South Sudan Governments concluded an agreement that committed each state to renouncing war and to implementing all previously negotiated security arrangements; the two Governments determined to achieve the full operation of the Joint Border Verification and Monitoring Mechanism, and to achieve the full redeployment of all forces from the Safe Demilitarized Border Zone, and the full demilitarization of Abyei. In that month the AUHIP proposed that a referendum should be held in October 2013 on the final determination of the status of Abyei. An implementation matrix for the 27 September 2012 agreement—aimed at activating agreed security mechanisms and finalizing both sides' full withdrawal, by 5 April 2013, from the Safe Demilitarized Border Zone—was concluded between Sudan and South Sudan in March 2013. From late March UNISFA monitored the troop withdrawal; violations of the bilateral agreement by both countries were, however, subsequently reported. In mid-March Sudan and South Sudan reached agreement on restarting South Sudanese petroleum exports through Sudan. In May 2013 the UN Security Council authorized an increase in UNISFA's strength to 5,326 troops; the additional peacekeepers were to be tasked with providing protection for border patrols by the Joint Border Verification and Monitoring Mechanism. In September South Sudan and Sudan determined to establish the centreline of the Safe Demilitarized Border Zone, in accordance with the proposal of an AU technical team; subsequently, however, little further progress was achieved in plotting the centreline. Against a background of continuing hostilities along the border between the Sudanese security forces and Sudan People's Liberation Movement/North militants, the Joint Border Verification and Monitoring Mechanism remained below par in 2013–early 2014, as the full deployment of the additional UNISFA troops authorized in May 2013 had not yet been achieved. A referendum on the future status of Abyei was held at the end of October, but—against the wishes of the AU and outside the context and negotiations framework of the AUHIP's proposal of September 2012—was organized and conducted on a unilateral basis by an Abyei Referendum Task Force comprising only members of the Ngok Dinka community. Following the referendum the Task Force unilaterally declared that 99.99% of eligible voters had elected for Abyei to be a part of South Sudan, and declared that this was to be the case with immediate effect. The unilateral referendum heightened inter-community tensions, and a seasonal migration from Sudan of nomadic Misseriya pastoralists into the area, as well as a disorganized influx of 6,000 people from South Sudan, contributed to the fragility and increasing volatility of the security situation. UNISFA worked to ensure that the Misseriya migration was conducted calmly, and pursued a dialogue with the Ngok Dinka and Misseriya communities on establishing strategies and monitoring procedures aimed at eliminating weaponry from Abyei. Where possible UNISFA has disarmed groups in possession of weapons.

Operational Strength: At 28 February 2014 UNISFA comprised 3,955 troops, 133 military observers, and 23 police officers; it was supported by 19 UN Volunteers, and (as at 30 November 2013) by 127 international and local civilian personnel.

Finance: The approved budget for the operation for the period 1 July 2013–30 June 2014 was US $290.6m.

United Nations Military Observer Group in India and Pakistan—UNMOGIP

Address: Rawalpindi, Pakistan (November–April); Srinagar, India (May–October).

Head of Mission and Chief Military Observer: Maj.-Gen. YOUNG-BUM CHOI (Republic of Korea).

Establishment and Mandate: The Group was established in 1948 by UN Security Council resolutions aiming to restore peace in the region of Jammu and Kashmir, the status of which had become a matter of dispute between the Governments of India and Pakistan. Following a ceasefire that came into effect in January 1949 the military observers of UNMOGIP were deployed to assist in its observance. There is no periodic review of UNMOGIP's mandate.

Activities: In 1971, following the signature of a new ceasefire agreement, India claimed that UNMOGIP's mandate had lapsed, since it was originally intended to monitor the agreement reached in 1949. Pakistan, however, regarded UNMOGIP's mission as unchanged, and the Group's activities have continued, although they have been somewhat restricted on the Indian side of the 'line of control', which was agreed by India and Pakistan in 1972.

Operational Strength: At 28 February 2014 there were 42 military observers deployed on both sides of the 'line of control'; the mission was supported by 68 international and local civilian personnel (as at 30 November 2013).

Finance: The approved budget for the operation for the two-year period 2014–15 was US $19.6m., covered by the regular budget of the United Nations.

United Nations Mission for the Referendum in Western Sahara—MINURSO

Address: el-Aaiún, Western Sahara.

Special Representative of the UN Secretary-General and Chief of Mission: WOLFGANG WEISBROD-WEBER (Germany).

Force Commander: Maj.-Gen. IMAM EDY MULYONO (Indonesia).

Establishment and Mandate: In April 1991 the UN Security Council endorsed the establishment of MINURSO to verify a ceasefire in the disputed territory of Western Sahara, to promote security and stability, and to implement a settlement plan, involving the repatriation of Western Saharan refugees (in co-ordination with UNHCR), the release of all Sahrawi political prisoners, and the organization of a referendum on the future of the territory. Western Sahara is claimed by Morocco, the administering power since 1975, and by the Algerian-supported (and based) Frente Popular para la Liberación de Saguia el Hamra y Río de Oro—Frente Polisario. Although originally envisaged for January 1992, the referendum was postponed indefinitely. Although, by 2014, the referendum remained postponed, the mission has continued to monitor the ceasefire, support confidence-building measures, and reduce the threat of mines and unexploded ordnances.

Activities, 1997–2000: In 1997 the Secretary-General of the UN appointed James Baker, a former US Secretary of State, as his Personal Envoy to the region to revive efforts to negotiate a resolution to the dispute. Direct talks were initiated in June, in Lisbon, Portugal, under the auspices of the UN, and attended by Algeria and Mauritania in an observer capacity. In September the two sides concluded an agreement which aimed to resolve the outstanding issues of contention, including a commitment by both parties to identify, for the purposes of the proposed referendum, eligible Sahrawi voters on an individual basis, in accordance with the results of the last official census in 1974, and a code of conduct to ensure the impartiality of the poll. The process of voter identification resumed in December 1997, and by September 1998 the initial identification process had been completed. However, the controversial issue of the eligibility of 65,000 members of three Saharan tribal groups remained unresolved. In October the Security Council endorsed a series of measures to advance the referendum, including a strengthened Identification Commission to consider requests from any applicant from the three disputed tribal groups on an individual basis. In November, following a visit to the region by the UN Secretary-General, the Frente Polisario accepted the proposals, and in March 1999 the Moroccan Government signed an agreement with the UN to secure the legal basis of the MINURSO operation. In July the UN published the first part of a provisional list of qualified voters. An appeals process then commenced, in accordance with the settlement plan. In November almost 200 Moroccan prisoners of war were released by the Frente Polisario, following a series of UN-led negotiations. The identification of applicants from the three disputed Saharan tribal groups was completed at the end of December. In January 2000 the second, final part of the provisional list of qualified voters was issued, and a six-week appeals process ensued.

2001–06: In June 2001 the Personal Envoy of the UN Secretary-General elaborated a draft Framework Agreement on the Status of Western Sahara as an alternative to the settlement plan. The draft Agreement, which envisaged the disputed area remaining part of Morocco, but with substantial devolution of authority, was rejected by the Frente Polisario and Algeria. In January 2002 the Secretary-General's Personal Envoy visited the region and met with leaders of both sides. He welcomed the release by the Frente Polisario of a further 115 Moroccan prisoners, but urged both sides to release all long-term detainees. In July the Frente Polisario released a further 101 Moroccan prisoners, leaving a total of 1,260 long-term detainees, of whom 816 had been held for more than 20 years. During February–November 2003 the Frente Polisario released 643 more prisoners. Morocco continued to detain 150 Sahrawi prisoners. In January the Secretary-General's Personal Envoy presented to both sides and to the Governments of neighbouring states a new arrangement for a political settlement, providing for self-determination, that had been requested by Resolution 1429 of the Security Council. In July the Frente Polisario accepted the so-called Peace Plan for Self-Determination of the People of Western Sahara. This was, however, rejected by the Moroccan Government in April 2004.

In March 2004 MINURSO co-operated with UNHCR to implement a family visits programme, providing for exchange of contacts of relatives divided by the dispute. MINURSO provided transport and other logistical support for the scheme, which was intended to be part of a series of humanitarian confidence-building measures. James Baker resigned as Personal Envoy of the Secretary-General in June. In September the Special Representative of the UN Secretary-General, who had assumed responsibility for pursuing a political solution, held his first series of formal meetings with all parties to the dispute. In July 2005 the Secretary-General appointed a new Personal Envoy for Western Sahara, Peter van Walsum, who undertook his first visit to heads of state in the region in October in an attempt to review the 2003 Peace Plan. The Frente Polisario released all remaining Moroccan prisoners in August 2005.

2007–14: Direct talks between representatives of the Moroccan Government and the Frente Polisario, attended by representatives of Algeria and Mauritania, were held in June 2007 under the auspices of the Personal Envoy of the UN Secretary-General in Manhasset, NY, USA. Further rounds of negotiations were conducted in August, and in January and March 2008. In February 2009 the newly appointed Personal Envoy, Christopher Ross, visited the region for the first time to meet with representatives of the Moroccan Government, Frente Polisario authorities and the Group of Friends of Western Sahara (France, Russia, Spain, the United Kingdom and USA). In August an informal meeting of the main parties, held in Dürnstein, Austria, secured a commitment by the Moroccan Government and the Frente Polisario to continue negotiations as soon as possible. At a second informal meeting, held in Westchester County, NY, USA, in February 2010, both parties agreed once again to continue with negotiations; however, an impasse remained, concerning the issue of self-determination, with the Frente Polisario requesting a referendum for Western Sahara that would present multiple options, including independence, and the Moroccan Government favouring a negotiated autonomy for the area. Talks held at regular intervals between November–July 2011 failed to achieve any significant progress. Informal negotiations were renewed in March 2012, at the Greentree Estate, in Manhasset, again without progression. In October–November Ross visited Algeria, Morocco, Western Sahara, Mauritania, France and Spain, with a view to evaluating the preceding nine rounds of negotiations. Concluding that convening a further round of informal bilateral negotiations in the near future would not advance a solution, Ross determined to embark upon a period of constructive shuttle diplomacy. In early 2013 he undertook a series of visits to the capitals of the Group of Friends nations, and to Germany and Switzerland, seeking international backing for the negotiations process. In March–April he visited Algeria and Morocco. In April the UN Secretary-General, reporting to the Security Council, agreed that—given the Moroccan Government and Frente Polisario were unwilling at that time to consider compromises to their respective positions—it would be unproductive in the immediate future to hold a further round of informal talks on advancing the negotiations process. In that month the Moroccan Government announced its objection to a proposal by the USA that MINURSO's mandate should be expanded to include the investigation and monitoring of the human rights situation in Western Sahara. During 2013 both sides to the conflict raised concerns that the then ongoing violent unrest in nearby Mali might spill over into the region and might contribute to radicalizing Western Saharan refugee camps. In January 2014 the Special Envoy, during a visit to the region, reaffirmed the postponement of bilateral talks pending improved prospects of progress.

In 2014 MINURSO was continuing to conduct ground and aerial patrols, including air reconnaissance, while maintaining good communications with the Royal Moroccan Army and the Frente Polisario. The mission continued to monitor a temporary deployment line comprising 326 observation posts of the Royal Moroccan Army, positioned some 15 km to the west of the 'Berm' (the 2,700 km-long Moroccan-built wall separating the Moroccan- and Frente Polisario-controlled areas).

MINURSO has headquarters in the north and south of the disputed territory. There are liaison offices in Tindouf, Algeria—which was established in order to maintain contact with the Frente Polisario and the Algerian Government—and in Dakhla, Western Sahara. The mission's military component is deployed at nine team sites.

Operational Strength: At 28 February 2014 MINURSO comprised 201 military observers, 23 troops and four police officers; it was supported by 15 UN Volunteers, and (at 30 November 2013) by 96 international and 168 local civilian personnel.

Finance: The General Assembly appropriation to cover the cost of the mission for the period 1 July 2013–30 June 2014 amounted to US $60.5m.

United Nations Mission in Liberia—UNMIL

Address: Monrovia, Liberia.

Special Representative of the UN Secretary-General and Head of Mission: KARIN LANDGREN (Sweden).

Force Commander: Maj.-Gen. LEONARD MURIUKI NGONDI (Kenya).

Police Commissioner: JOHN NIELSEN (USA).

Establishment and Mandate: UNMIL was authorized by the UN Security Council in September 2003 to support the implementation of the ceasefire accord agreed in June and the Comprehensive Peace Agreement concluded in August by the parties to the conflict in

Liberia. UNMIL, then with an authorized maximum strength of 15,000 military personnel, was mandated to assist with the development of an action plan for the disarmament, demobilization, reintegration and, where appropriate, repatriation of all armed groups and to undertake a programme of voluntary disarmament; to protect civilians and UN personnel, equipment and facilities; to support humanitarian and human rights activities; to support the implementation of national security reforms; and, in co-operation with the Economic Community of West African States (ECOWAS) and other partners, to assist the National Transitional Government (inaugurated in October) with the training of a national police force and the restructuring of the military. Troops were also mandated to assist with the rehabilitation of damaged physical infrastructure, in particular the road network. On 1 October UNMIL assumed authority from an ECOWAS-led multinational force in Liberia. In accordance with Resolution 2066, adopted by the Security Council in September 2012, the mission's mandated priorities include supporting the solidification of peace and stability; supporting the transition to full ownership of policing responsibilities by the national police; assisting with the reform and restructuring of the justice sector; combating impunity for perpetrators of sexual and gender-based violence; promoting the participation of women in conflict prevention, conflict resolution and peacebuilding; and enhancing co-operation with theUN Operation in Côte d'Ivoire.

Activities, 2003–10: The programme for disarmament, demobilization, rehabilitation and reintegration (DDRR), was initiated in December 2003. A training programme for the country's new police service was inaugurated in July 2004, and the first UN-trained police officers were deployed at the end of the year. (By 2014 more than 4,200 officers had graduated from the UN police training programme.)

UNMIL provided technical assistance to the National Elections Commission, which, in April 2005, initiated a process of voter registration in preparation for presidential and legislative elections that were held in October–November 2005. UNMIL also undertook a large-scale civic education campaign in support of the democratic election process. In October UNMIL, with the Transitional Government, established a Joint National Security Operations Centre. In 2006 UNMIL strengthened its focus on the rule of law, economic recovery and good governance. It also pledged to support the new Government in efforts to remove UN sanctions against sales of rough diamonds and to become a member of the Kimberley Process Certification Scheme by providing air support for surveillance and mapping activities in mining areas. Throughout 2006 and 2007 UNMIL personnel undertook projects to rehabilitate and construct roads and bridges, police stations, courtrooms and educational facilities. The mission also initiated, with the support of other UN agencies, a scheme to create employment throughout the country. In April 2007 the UN Security Council removed the embargo against sales of diamonds from Liberia, and in the following month UNMIL transferred control of the regional diamond certification office to the national authorities.

In September 2006 the UN Security Council endorsed a recommendation by the Secretary-General that a consolidation, drawdown and withdrawal plan for UNMIL should be developed and implemented; the consolidation phase was completed in December 2007. In September the Security Council endorsed a plan to reduce UNMIL's military component by 2,450 troops between October and September 2008, and to reduce the number of police officers by 498 in the period April 2008–December 2010. UNMIL continued to monitor and control security incidents, local demonstrations, cross-border activities and drugs-trafficking. In June 2009 the UN Secretary-General issued a special report recommending a further reduction of UNMIL's military component, of some 2,029 troops, in the period October 2009–May 2010, and that UNMIL's mandate be revised to enable it to support the authorities in preparing for presidential and legislative elections, to be held in late 2011. In accordance with a UN Security Council resolution adopted in September 2009, UNMIL, the UN country team in Liberia, the Liberian National Electoral Commission, and other stakeholders subsequently developed a multi-sector electoral assistance project, with a view to supporting the planned elections. In July 2009 an UNMIL training programme for the new Armed Forces of Liberia was initiated. The Liberian Government officially assumed responsibilities for the development of the Armed Forces of Liberia in January 2010. In February UNMIL troops intervened to restore order in Lofa County, in north-western Liberia, following widespread inter-ethnic violence, during which four people died and several churches and mosques were set on fire. In September the SRSG reported that the security situation in the country was stable, but remained fragile. She observed that the country required greater national reconciliation and more progress towards resolving issues concerning access to land, strengthening public confidence in the justice system and developing an independent security sector. The third stage of UNMIL's drawdown was completed, as planned, in May. In September 2010 the UN Security Council authorized UNMIL to assist the Liberian Government with staging the 2011 elections, through the provision of logistical support, co-ordination of international electoral assistance, and support for Liberian institutions and political parties.

2011–14: UNMIL strengthened its monitoring in 2011 of electoral, legal, political, public information, security and human rights matters prior to the elections conducted in October–November. The mission also co-ordinated international assistance to the electoral process through a Donor Co-ordination Group. In early 2012 a technical assessment mission sent by the UN Secretary-General found that, in spite of the successful staging of the elections, the security situation in Liberia remained fragile, and that there remained high levels of violent crime. Causes that were cited included an inadequate justice system and other weak state institutions; large numbers of unemployed, unskilled former combatants; ethnic divisions; and disputes over land ownership. In April the UN Secretary-General recommended a gradual reduction of UNMIL's strength, by around 4,200 troops, to be implemented in three phases during 2012–15. It was envisaged that thereafter a residual presence of about 3,750 troops would remain. Meanwhile, during that period, the mission was gradually to reconfigure, consolidating its presence in the capital, Monrovia, and in the Liberia–Côte d'Ivoire border area. In September 2012 the UN Security Council authorized the first phase of the proposed reduction (by 1,900) in the mission's strength, to be implemented over the period October 2012–September 2013. UNMIL was to continue to support the Liberian Government's efforts towards consolidating peace and stability and protecting civilians; and was also to support the Government in facilitating the transfer of full responsibility for security to the national police force, by strengthening the police's ability to manage personnel, and improving training programmes. Furthermore, the mission was to assist with the reform and restructuring of the justice sector; with combating impunity for perpetrators of sexual and gender-based violence; promoting the participation of women in conflict prevention, conflict resolution and peacebuilding; and was to enhance its ongoing co-operation with UNOCI with regard to the stabilization of Liberia–Côte d'Ivoire border area.

From May 2011 the Liberian military, supported by UNMIL, increased its presence along the Liberia–Côte d'Ivoire border, and UNMIL and UNOCI intensified inter-mission co-ordination, including undertaking joint border patrols under the so-called Operation Mayo. In June UNMIL and UNOCI conducted a joint assessment mission in western Côte d'Ivoire. In June 2012 the heads of UNMIL and UNOCI, and government representatives from Liberia and Côte d'Ivoire, held a quadripartite meeting, in Abidjan, Côte d'Ivoire, on developing a strategy to enhance joint border security, following a fatal attack on UNOCI troops, and other fatal incidents, perpetrated in the border area during that month. Liberia closed the border, excepting for humanitarian purposes, for nine months from July 2012. A second quadripartite meeting was convened in April 2013, in Monrovia.

In early 2014 UNMIL and UNOCI were jointly developing, within UNOCI's authorized military strength, a quick reaction capability, which was to be equipped to respond immediately both to incidents arising within Côte d'Ivoire and from mid-2015 to emerging security crises in Liberia, as well as the wider sub-region.

Operational Strength: At 28 February 2014 UNMIL comprised 5,749 troops, 136 military observers, and 1,561 police officers, supported by 221 UN Volunteers, and (as at 30 November 2013) by 420 international civilian personnel and 860 local civilian staff.

Finance: The General Assembly appropriation to the Special Account for UNMIL amounted to US $476.3m. for the period 1 July 2013–30 June 2014.

United Nations Mission in South Sudan—UNMISS

Address: Juba, Sudan.

Special Representative of the Secretary-General: HILDE JOHNSON (Norway).

Force Commander: Maj.-Gen. DELALI JOHNSON SAKYI (Ghana).

Establishment and Mandate: UNMISS was established in July 2011 upon the independence of South Sudan. The mission succeeded the former UN Mission in the Sudan (UNMIS). UNMISS is mandated to support the consolidation of peace, thereby fostering longer-term state-building and economic development; to support the South Sudan authorities with regard to conflict prevention, mitigation, and the protection of civilians; and to develop the new Government's capacity to provide security, to establish the rule of law, and to strengthen the security and justice sectors.

Activities, 2011–14: From July 2011 UNMISS liaised with the South Sudan Government and provided good offices to facilitate inclusive consultative processes involving all the stakeholders invested in nation-building. The mission responded to a request by the South Sudan authorities to support the development of a national security strategy; cleared and opened (by November) some 121 km of road, through its Mine Action Service; and assisted, with the UN Development Programme (UNDP), the South Sudan Disarmament, Demobilization and Reintegration Commission in preparing a disarmament, demobilization and reintegration (DDR) policy, as well as contributing to the construction of a DDR transitional facility in Wau, South Sudan, to support—through the provision of skills training—the reintegration into society of demobilized former combatants. UNMISS supported the new Government's ratification of principal international human rights treaties, and monitored the harmonization of the national legislative framework with international human rights standards. In early August UNMISS and the Government of South Sudan signed a status-of-forces agreement guaranteeing the mission's freedom of movement throughout the new country; subsequently, however, UNMISS reported several restrictions on its movements. From the inception of UNMISS its forces were deployed mainly in response to violent unrest in the politically volatile Jonglei State. Further UNMISS deployments from 2011 included deterrence operations in Western Equatoria, and a mission to support the integration of rebel forces in Pibor. UNMISS police activities focused on training and advising the new South Sudan Police Service.

From January 2012 relations between South Sudan and Sudan deteriorated significantly, owing to factors including the disputed delineation of the two countries' joint border; mutual accusations of support for anti-government rebel militia groups; control over the territory of Abyei; and the dependence at that time of landlocked South Sudan (which has significant oilfields) on the use of Sudanese infrastructure for the export of petroleum. In February South Sudan and Sudan signed a Memorandum of Understanding on non-aggression and co-operation, committing each state to respecting the other's sovereignty and territorial integrity. In early April an African Union (AU) High-Level Implementation Panel (AUHIP) on Sudan (established in October 2009) presented to both parties a draft Joint Decision for Reduction of Tension, providing for the immediate cessation of hostilities between the two states, and the withdrawal of armed forces of each state from the territory of the other. Shortly afterwards the UN Security Council made several demands of both parties, including that they redeploy their forces from forward positions and end cross-border violence with immediate effect; that Sudan should cease aerial bombardments of South Sudan; that South Sudan and Sudan should redeploy forces from Abyei; and that a summit should be convened between the two states to resolve outstanding concerns. In mid-April an UNMISS support base was among buildings damaged by an aerial bombardment by Sudanese forces of Mayom, in Unity State, South Sudan, which resulted in several fatalities in that settlement. In early and late May, respectively, South Sudan and Sudan withdrew their forces from Abyei, in accordance with a seven-point Roadmap for Action by Sudan and South Sudan that was approved in late April by the AU Peace and Security Council (see under the UN Interim Security Force for Abyei). On 27 September 2012 South Sudan and Sudan reached agreement on reviewing effective mechanisms for metering supplies of petroleum, and determined to establish a committee, under AU auspices, that would review oil sector-related payments and technical matters, as a means of avoiding future disputes and enabling the resumption of South Sudanese petroleum production. In mid-December an UNMISS helicopter was shot down by South Sudanese rebel forces, killing four mission personnel. The attack was strongly condemned by the UN Secretary-General. An implementation matrix for the 27 September 2012 co-operation agreement—aimed at activating agreed security mechanisms and finalizing both sides' full withdrawal from the border area—was concluded between South Sudan and Sudan in March 2013. In mid-March South Sudan and Sudan reached agreement on reinstating South Sudanese petroleum exports through Sudan, and, in early April, oil production was restarted in South Sudan, although full output was not expected to resume until mid-2014.

In mid-December 2013 a power struggle between President Salva Kiir and his former deputy, Riek Machar, and incorporating their respective ethnic political bases, culminated in the eruption of violent unrest in Juba, the South Sudanese capital; fierce fighting almost immediately spread to Jonglei, and the crisis soon escalated into full-scale conflict, fought largely along ethnic lines. An attack against an UNMISS camp in Akobo, eastern Jonglei, in mid-December, caused a number of casualties, including the deaths of two mission peacekeepers. In late December, following the onset of the crisis, the UN Security Council—condemning reported violations of human rights by all parties to the conflict, as well as threats made to and attacks upon UNMISS personnel and UN facilities—demanded an immediate cessation of hostilities and initiation of dialogue; demanded that all parties co-operate with UNMISS, in particular with respect to its mandate to protect civilians; and determined, as an urgent temporary measure to support the protection of civilians and delivery of humanitarian assistance, to increase the mission's overall force strength to up to 12,500 troops and 1,323 police officers. If necessary supplementary troops were to be transferred from other missions. Agreements on Cessation of Hostilities and on the Status of Detainees were concluded on 23 January 2014, and from mid-February the rebels and government pursed a dialogue aimed at resolving the situation; each side accused the other, meanwhile, of violating the ceasefire. UNMISS conducted numerous military and police patrols at that time. At mid-February nearly 723,000 people remained displaced from their homes within South Sudan (of these nearly 80,000 were sheltering at eight UNMISS bases), and a further 145,000 had fled to neighbouring countries (with Ethiopia receiving the majority of refugees).

The UNMISS HRD has continued to monitor the observance of human rights in the emerging nation, to undertake capacity building initiatives in collaboration with the Southern Sudan Human Rights Commission and other partners, and to report on potential threats against the civilian population and violations of international humanitarian law. Following the outbreak of violent conflict in December 2013, and associated reports of widespread human rights abuses, the HRD's investigation capacity was strengthened.

UNMISS, although not mandated to pursue militants of the Lord's Resistance Army (LRA—active in parts of South Sudan, as well as of Uganda, the Central African Republic and the Democratic Republic of the Congo), supports the AU-Regional Task Force (AU-RTF), launched in March 2012 to combat the LRA, and shares relevant information with UNISFA and UNAMID. UNMISS has also co-operated with UNISFA and UNAMID to support the migration of pastoralists in the sensitive South Sudan–Sudan border area. UNMISS provides administrative and logistical support to UNISFA through its logistics hub, based in Wau, a liaison office in Juba, and a presence in Malakal.

Operational Strength: At 28 February 2014 UNMISS comprised 7,327 troops, 152 military observers and 1,015 police officers; it was supported by 406 UN Volunteers and (as at 30 November 2013) by 869 international and 1,333 local civilian personnel.

Finance: The approved budget for the mission amounted to US $924.4m. for the period 1 July 2013–30 June 2014, funded from a Special Account comprising assessed contributions from UN member states.

United Nations Multidimensional Integrated Stabilization Mission in the Central African Republic—MINUSCA

Address: Bangui, Central African Republic.

Establishment and Mandate: MINUSCA was authorized in April 2014 by UN Security Council 2149, for an initial period of one year, in view of the ongoing security, humanitarian, human rights and political crisis in the Central African Republic (CAR), and the regional implications thereof. MINUSCA immediately subsumed the responsibilities of the former UN Integrated Peacebuilding Office in the CAR (BINUCA, established in January 2010), and was—on 15 September 2014—to take over the military and policing functions of the African Union (AU)-led International Support Mission to the CAR (MISCA).

In October 2013 the Security Council adopted Resolution 2121, which expressed deep concern over ongoing total breakdown in law and order in the CAR. In view of the mounting violent unrest caused by a rebel offensive, initiated in December 2012, that culminated in the overturning of the legitimately elected CAR Government of President François Bozizé in March 2013 and the inauguration as President in August of Michel Djotodia, the coup leader, Resolution 2121 updated the mandate of the former BINUCA (hitherto focused on supporting, inter alia, governance reforms, electoral processes and disarmament activities) to assist with the implementation of peace accords (the 'Libreville agreements') that were adopted in January 2013 by the parties to the conflict, and of the so-called N'Djamena roadmap, adopted in April, both of which established the basis for a peaceful political resolution to the crisis, defining a transition process towards national elections. In October 2013 the Security Council also approved the deployment (which took effect in December) of MISCA, under AU leadership and with the support of the French military 'Opération Sangaris'. In January 2014 the Council authorized the European Union to establish a temporary operation in the CAR in support of MISCA.

MINUSCA was mandated, as its first priority, to protect civilians; as well as to support the ongoing transition process in the CAR; facilitate humanitarian assistance; promote and protect human rights; promote justice and the rule of law; and support disarmament, demobilization, reintegration and repatriation processes. The mission was to co-operate with a panel of experts established by the Council in August 2013 to monitor the situation in the CAR. Opération Sangaris was instructed to use all necessary means to support MINUSCA, and the Council authorized MINUSCA—under limited circumstances and exceptionally—to adopt urgent temporary measures to maintain law and order and combat impunity. Military enablers were to be deployed to MINUSCA before the assumption in September of military authority from MISCA.

In April 2014 the appointment of a Special Representative of the UN for the Central African Republic and Head of Mission was pending.

Operational Strength: Security Council Resolution 2149 authorized the deployment to the mission of up to 10,000 military personnel (including 240 military observers) and 1,800 police.

United Nations Multidimensional Integrated Stabilization Mission in Mali—MINUSMA

Address: Bamako, Mali.

Special Representative of the Secretary-General and Head of Mission: ALBERT (BERT) GERARD KOENDERS (Netherlands).

Force Commander: Maj.-Gen. JEAN BOSCO KAZURA (Rwanda).

Establishment and Mandate: On 1 July 2013 MINUSMA—authorized in April by the UN Security Council—assumed the authority of the former African Union (AU)-led International Support Mission in Mali (AFISMA, authorized by the Council in December 2012). MINUSMA was mandated to support the re-establishment of state authority in Mali and to stabilize key population centres, especially in northern areas; to support the Mali transitional authorities in implementing a transitional road map towards the full restoration of constitutional order, democratic processes and national unity, including promoting national political dialogue and the electoral process; to protect civilians and UN personnel; to promote and protect human rights; to help to create a suitable environment for the civilian-led delivery of humanitarian assistance; to support the transitional authorities, in co-operation with UNESCO, in protecting Mali's cultural sites; and—taking into account the referral by the Mali transitional authorities of the situation in that country since January 2012 to the International Criminal Court—to provide support in bringing to justice individuals accused of serious violations of international humanitarian law. MINUSMA was mandated to use all necessary means to address threats to the implementation of its mandate, acting either alone or in co-operation with the Malian security forces. The Security Council also authorized troops from the French Opération Serval to intervene, upon the request of the Secretary-General, in support of elements of MINUSMA if under imminent and serious threat. MINUSMA was mandated to comprise up to 11,200 military and 1,440 police personnel.

Activities: MINUSMA provided assistance to the Malian security forces, and offered security support to vote counting centres, during the conduct of two rounds of presidential elections that were held in late July and early August 2013. Further logistical and security support was provided during two rounds of legislative elections that were held, peacefully, in November and December. MINUSMA also worked to promote female participation in the electoral process. In late 2013 the security situation in northern areas of the country deteriorated. In October, in an attack claimed by the militant grouping al-Qa'ida in the Arab Maghreb, an explosive device was detonated at a MINUSMA checkpoint, killing seven people, including two mission peacekeepers, and in December a further two mission peacekeepers were killed by a vehicle-borne explosive device. On several occasions French troops deployed to Opération Serval intervened to assist MINUSMA personnel. In early 2014 MINUSMA was assisting the Malian authorities with the design of a strategy for the cantonment of armed groups—the preliminary stage of an envisaged programme of disarming, demobilizing and reintegrating former combatants—and the mission was also providing logistical support to the cantonment process. At that time MINUSMA was providing training in human rights and international law for mission personnel, members of non-governmental and civil society organizations, the national police, and the military.

Operational Strength: At 28 February 2014 MINUSMA comprised 6,137 troops and 956 police officers, supported by 58 UN Volunteers, and (at 30 November 2013) by 287 international and 113 local civilian staff.

Finance: The approved budget for the mission amounted to US $366.8m. for the period 1 July 2013–30 June 2014.

United Nations Operation in Côte d'Ivoire—UNOCI

Address: Abidjan, Côte d'Ivoire.

Special Representative of the Secretary-General and Head of Mission: AICHATOU MINDAOUDOU SOULEYMANE (Niger).

Force Commander: Maj.-Gen. MUHAMMAD IQBAL ASI (Pakistan).

Police Commissioner: Maj.-Gen. JEAN MARIE BOURRY (France).

Establishment and Mandate: UNOCI was authorized by the UN Security Council in February 2004 and began operations in April. It was mandated to observe and monitor the implementation of the Linas-Marcoussis Accord, signed by the parties to the conflict in Côte d'Ivoire in January 2003, and hitherto supported by the UN Mission in Côte d'Ivoire (MINUCI), forces of the Economic Community of West African States—ECOWAS and French peacekeeping troops. UNOCI was authorized also to assist with the disarmament, demobilization and reintegration of rebel groups, to protect civilians and UN personnel, institutions and equipment, and to support ongoing humanitarian and human rights activities. With a contingent of the French Licorne peacekeeping force, UNOCI was to monitor a so-called Zone of Confidence then separating the two areas of the country under government and rebel control. The mission's mandate was subsequently adjusted to address evolving challenges, including the political and security crisis that followed the disputed presidential elections that took place in November 2010 in Côte d'Ivoire. Security Council Resolution 2112, adopted in July 2013, mandated UNOCI, inter alia, to focus on the protection of civilians; to address outstanding security challenges, including in border areas; to support the Côte d'Ivoire authorities in the implementation of a national disarmament, demobilization and reintegration programme; to support the reconstitution and reform of security institutions; to monitor ongoing sanctions; to assist with the provision of humanitarian assistance; to promote compliance with international humanitarian and human rights law; and to support the extension of state authority throughout the country.

Activities, 2003–06: In July 2003 all parties, attending a meeting of West African heads of state that had been convened by the UN Secretary-General and the President of Ghana, endorsed the Accra III Agreement identifying means of implementing the Linas-Marcoussis Accord. In August UNOCI launched a radio station, in accordance with its mandate, to assist the process of national reunification, and in the following month it established secure transit routes between the areas under government and rebel control.

In November 2004 government troops violated the ceasefire and the Zone of Confidence by launching attacks against rebel Forces Nouvelles in the north of the country. An emergency session of the UN Security Council, convened following an escalation of the hostilities and a fatal air strike on a French peacekeeping unit, urged both sides to refrain from further violence. Security deteriorated in the south of the country when French troops destroyed the government air force, prompting rioting in the capital, Abidjan, and violence directed towards foreign nationals. UNOCI assisted with the evacuation of foreign residents and provided secure refuge for other personnel. In November the Security Council imposed an immediate embargo on the sale or supply of armaments to Côte d'Ivoire and demanded a cessation of hostilities and of the use of media broadcasts to incite hatred against foreigners. In December UNOCI commenced joint patrols with government forces to uphold security in Abidjan.

In April 2005 UNOCI troops were deployed to the border regions with Liberia and Ghana in order to support implementation of the UN-imposed arms embargo. UNOCI troops also monitored the withdrawal of heavy weaponry by both government forces and the Forces Nouvelles. In June the UN Security Council authorized an increase in UNOCI's military and civilian police components, as well as the redeployment of troops from other missions in the region in order to restore security in the country. In October UNOCI conducted joint border patrols with UN forces in Liberia to monitor movements of combatants and weapons.

2007–11: In January 2007 the Security Council formally enlarged UNOCI's mandate to co-ordinate with UNMIL to monitor the arms embargo and to conduct a voluntary repatriation and resettlement programme for foreign former combatants. The Council's resolution also defined UNOCI's mandate as being to monitor the cessation of hostilities and movements of armed groups; to assist programmes for the disarmament, demobilization and reintegration of all combatants; to disarm and dismantle militias; to support population identification and voter registration programmes; to support reform of the security sector and undertake other activities aimed at upholding law and order; to support humanitarian assistance and the promotion of human rights; and to provide technical support for the conduct of free and fair elections. A new political agreement to work towards national reconciliation was signed by leaders of the opposing parties in Ouagadougou, Burkina Faso, in March. Accordingly, the Zone of Confidence was to be dismantled and replaced by a UN-monitored 'green line'. UNOCI organized a series of meetings to ensure the support of traditional leaders for the peace process. The process of disarmament was officially launched at the end of July. The redeployment of UNOCI troops from the former Zone of Confidence was completed by late July 2008, when the last observation post was officially closed. In the following month UNOCI, in collaboration with the UN Development Programme, initiated a scheme of 'micro projects' to help to reduce poverty and youth unemployment and facilitate the reintegration of former combatants.

During 2010 UNOCI developed, jointly with the Côte d'Ivoire military and French Licorne force, a co-ordinated plan for helping to ensure the security of the long-postponed planned presidential election. At the end of September the UN Security Council approved a temporary increase in UNOCI's authorized military and police personnel from 8,650 to 9,150, to be deployed with immediate effect. The first round of the presidential election was held on 31 October, and, following certification of the results of the first round by the SRSG on 12 November, a second electoral round was contested by the two forerunners on 28 November. (The incumbent President, Laurent Gbagbo, had received the most votes at the first round, but by a margin that did not constitute an outright victory.) At the beginning of December the electoral commission, supported by the UN, confirmed that Gbagbo's opponent, Alassane Ouattara, had won the presidential election; on the following day, however, the national constitutional council rejected the final results, declaring Gbagbo to be the winner. International opinion, including the UN, the AU and ECOWAS, continued to endorse Ouattara as the rightfully elected new Ivorian President, and the UN Secretary-General and French Government rejected demands by Gbagbo, who refused to concede defeat to Ouattara, that UNOCI and Licorne troops should leave Côte d'Ivoire. From mid-December serious violent unrest erupted, and, into early 2011, numerous fatalities were reported, as well as obstructions to the movement and activities of UNOCI peacekeepers, and attacks on UN personnel and on the UNOCI headquarters. In mid-January 2011 the Security Council authorized the deployment of an additional 2,000 military personnel to UNOCI, until end-June 2011, and extended the temporary additional military and police capabilities authorized in September 2010.

On 30 March 2011 the UN Security Council adopted Resolution 1975, urging all Ivorian parties to respect the will of the electorate and to acknowledge the election of Ouattara as Côte d'Ivoire President. Resolution 1975 emphasized that UNOCI might use 'all necessary measures' in executing its mandate to protect civilians under threat of attack. On the following day forces loyal to Ouattara advanced on Abidjan, while UNOCI peacekeepers took control of the capital's airport. In early April UNOCI and Licorne forces directed fire at pro-Gbagbo heavy artillery and armoured vehicles. UNOCI and Licorne air strikes were later undertaken against pro-Gbagbo heavy weaponry, reportedly inflicting significant damage on the presidential palace. On 11 April forces loyal to Ouattara arrested Gbagbo, with assistance from Licorne; Gbagbo and his entourage were then placed under UNOCI guard. Ouattara was eventually inaugurated as President in May.

In May 2011 the UN Secretary-General dispatched a mission to assess the situation in Côte d'Ivoire. The Secretary-General subsequently recommended that UNOCI play a greater role in helping the national authorities to stabilize the security situation, with a particular focus on Abidjan and western (including border) areas. Accordingly, UNOCI was to increase joint patrols with the Côte d'Ivoire military and police; to facilitate the resumption of law enforcement responsibilities by the police and gendarmerie; to deter the activities of militias; and to assist in the protection of civilians. UNOCI was also to continue to collect, secure and dispose of weaponry; and to assist in de-mining activities. It was recommended that UNOCI, in close co-operation with the UN Mission in Liberia (UNMIL), should enhance its support to the Côte d'Ivoire and Liberian authorities to monitor and address cross-border security challenges, and should increase patrols of the Côte d'Ivoire-Liberia border area (under the so-called Operation Mayo). It was also recommended that UNOCI should provide assistance for the development of a UN justice support programme; support the capacity development for the police, gendarmerie and corrections officers; deploy an expert to work with the authorities on security sector reform; assist the Government in developing a new national programme for demobilization, disarmament and reintegration of combatants, and dismantling of militias, that would be tailored to the post-April 2011 context; continue to support the registration and profiling of former combatants; support the organization and conduct of the legislative elections; and strengthen its human rights monitoring activities. UNOCI provided logistical and security support to facilitate the conduct of legislative elections that were held in Côte d'Ivoire in December 2011.

2012–14: In March 2012, having considered the findings of an assessment mission sent to Côte d'Ivoire in February, the UN Secretary-General recommended a reduction in UNOCI's authorized strength, and decided that the mission should adjust the scope of its deployment to cover more remote areas and to intensify its engagement with local communities. In June the heads of UNOCI and UNMIL, and government representatives from Côte d'Ivoire and Liberia, held a quadripartite meeting, in Abidjan, on developing a strategy to enhance joint border security, following a fatal attack on UNOCI troops, and other fatal incidents, recently perpetrated in the border area. Joint UNOCI-UNMIL meetings subsequently were conducted on a fortnightly basis. During the second half of 2012 the national security situation deteriorated, as insurgents, allegedly pledging allegiance to the former Gbagbo regime, attacked the national security forces in the Abidjan area, and also at Côte d'Ivoire's borders with Ghana and Liberia, with the aim of destabilizing the Ouattara Government; the attacks resulted in serious civilian displacement, and also a number of fatalities. A second quadripartite meeting was convened in April 2013, in Monrovia, Liberia. In June the UN Secretary-General reported that UNOCI would receive the capacity to deploy unarmed, unmanned aerial systems, with a view to enhancing the mission's situational awareness. In July UNOCI's mandate was extended until 30 June 2014, by which time troop numbers were to be reduced to 7,137; depending upon the security environment, as well as the development of the Government's capacity to assume the mission's security functions, a further reduction by June 2015 to 5,437 military personal remained under consideration. In mid-2013 President Ouattara announced his intention to contest the next presidential elections, which were scheduled to be held in October 2015. By December 2013 around 5,500 of an identified 74,068 eligible former combatants had been disarmed and demobilized; it was envisaged that the national disarmament, demobilization and reintegration programme would continue until mid-2015. UNOCI was supporting the implementation of the programme in western areas. In early 2014 UNOCI and UNMIL were jointly developing, within the UNOCI authorized military strength, a quick reaction capability, which was to be equipped to respond immediately to incidents arising within Côte d'Ivoire, and—from mid-2015, once an ongoing process to downsize UNMIL's military strength had been completed—to react to emerging security crises in Liberia and the wider sub-region. Planning was also under way for the envisaged process of transferring civil society-related and security responsibilities from UNOCI to the Côte d'Ivoire authorities. It was hoped that donor resources would be forthcoming to strengthen the capacity of the national authorities, to facilitate this process.

Operational Strength: At 28 February 2014 UNOCI had an operational strength of 7,957 troops, 182 military observers and 1,316 police officers; it was supported by 150 UN Volunteers, and (as at 30 November 2013) by 400 international and 762 local civilian personnel.

Finance: The General Assembly appropriated US $584.5m. to finance the mission during the period 1 July 2013–30 June 2014.

United Nations Organization Stabilization Mission in the Democratic Republic of the Congo—MONUSCO

Address: Kinshasa, Democratic Republic of the Congo.

Liaison offices are situated in Kampala (Uganda), Kigali (Rwanda) and Pretoria (South Africa). A logistics base is located in Entebbe, Uganda.

Special Representative of the UN Secretary-General and Chief of Mission: Martin Kobler (Germany).

Force Commander: Lt-Gen. Carlos Alberto dos Santos Cruz (Brazil).

Police Commissioner: Brig.-Gen. Pascal Champion (France).

Establishment and Mandate: MONUSCO's deployment was authorized in May 2010, under Security Council Resolution 1925, to reflect a new phase in the ongoing peace process in the Democratic Republic of the Congo (DRC) MONUSCO was inaugurated on 1 July, succeeding the former UN Mission in the DRC (MONUC), which had been active since August 1999. MONUSCO was to use all necessary means to carry out its mandate, which focused on protecting civilians and humanitarian personnel, as well as protecting UN staff, facilities, installations and equipment; supporting the DRC regime in efforts towards stabilizing the country and consolidating peace, including supporting its International Security and Stabilization Support Strategy (ISSSS), helping with strengthening the capacity of the military and with police reforms, supporting disarmament, demobilization and rehabilitation (DDR) activities, developing and implementing a multi-year joint UN justice support programme, consolidating state authority in areas freed from the control of armed militia, providing technical and logistics support for local and national elections at the request of the Government, and monitoring the arms embargo against rebel militia active in the DRC; providing human rights training to DRC government officials, security service personnel, journalists, and civil society organizations; and advancing child protection, combating sexual violence, and promoting the representation of women in decision-making roles. MONUSCO was to focus its military forces in eastern areas of the DRC, while maintaining a reserve force that could be deployed elsewhere at short notice. MONUSCO screens DRC battalion commanders for human rights violations prior to the provision of logistical and other support. In 2014, with a view to enabling MONUSCO to focus more sharply on its core responsibilities, the transfer of responsibility of certain non-military tasks to the UN's DRC country team was envisaged.

Activities, 2010–14: From mid-2010 MONUSCO implemented several Quick Impact Projects. The mission continued to support the Government's DDR initiative, and, through its regional radio network, aimed to encourage defections from the Lord's Resistance Army (LRA) rebel group. In July MONUSCO established a mobile base in Beni, North Kivu province, in order to enhance security for humanitarian personnel working to provide essential medical and food assistance to an estimated 90,000 people who had been temporarily displaced by an escalation of fighting in that area between the national armed forces and the Ugandan rebel group, the Allied Democratic Forces. In September MONUSCO initiated special patrols in North Kivu to enhance civilian protection following a series of violent attacks, including mass rapes, by illegal armed groups. MONUSCO provided technical advice, logistical support, and police electoral security training, during the preparation for legislative and presidential elections that were held in November–December 2011, as well as providing security patrols before, during and after the electoral process. (The outcome of the presidential election was disputed.) During 2011 MONUSCO documented several hundred reported violations of human rights linked to the electoral process, affecting, in particular, political opposition supporters, journalists and human rights defenders.

MONUSCO and the national armed forces launched the joint military operations 'Amani Kamilifu' and 'Radi Strike' in February and March 2012, respectively, targeting militants in the Kivu provinces. MONUSCO undertook several military operations in 2012 to protect civilians in LRA-affected areas, and supported an initiative of the national armed forces to encourage LRA members to enter a disarmament, demobilization, repatriation, resettlement and reintegration process. The mission was tasked with assisting a newly created African Union (AU)-Regional Task Force, which was mandated to combat the LRA, through the provision of logistical support to the Force's Dungu (Haut-Uele) Joint Intelligence and Operations Centre. Militants of the newly formed Kivu-based 23 March Movement (known as 'M23') became increasingly active from May 2012, clashing with government forces and causing mass population displacement. In response to reports in mid-2012 of systematic targeted massacres of civilians by armed groups at that time in North Kivu, the UN Joint Human Rights Office in the DRC (UNJHRO)—comprising representatives of MONUSCO and UNHCR—conducted several missions to affected areas to interview witnesses and verify the crimes. In June the UN Security Council expressed great concern at the deteriorating humanitarian situation in eastern DRC and at the ongoing human rights abuses against civilians, and urged the UN presence, the DRC authorities and other relevant bodies to provide security, medical, humanitarian, and other support to victims. Meanwhile, MONUSCO and partners were also undertaking efforts to provide training to the DRC security forces in child/youth protection and protection from sexual and gender-based violence, as well as in human rights. In late August 2012 the Special Representative of the Secretary-General expressed deep concern over alleged further systematic massacres of civilians in Masisi, North Kivu. During May–August UNJHRO verified 45 attacks on some 30 communities in the Masisi area. In September three UN integrated offices were launched, under the authority of UN Area Co-ordinators, in Matadi (Bas-Congo), Mbuji-Mayi (Kasai Oriental) and Kananga (Kasai Occidental), in place of previous MONUSCO offices, signifying the first phase of the transition process towards an emphasis on peace-building. In November MONUSCO deployed attack helicopters and ground infantry support vehicles in order to support the Congolese army and to protect civilians against an escalation of fighting by M23 in North Kivu. The UN Security Council, meeting in emergency session, condemned the resumption of violence and consequent displacement of the civilian population. At the end of November MONUSCO mobilized 17 rapid reaction units with the intent of monitoring the withdrawal of M23 troops to an internationally agreed Neutral Zone some 20 km outside of Goma. MONUSCO troops also escorted national police forces to key locations within that city with a view to restoring lawful control. M23, however, did not withdraw to the Neutral Zone, but continued to occupy Munighi Heights, at a distance of some 3 km from Goma's airport. In early December, in accordance with the terms of a 24 November communiqué of the International Conference of the Great Lakes Region (ICGLR), representatives of M23 and the DRC Government initiated a dialogue, mediated by the Ugandan Minister for Defence, Crispus Kiyonga. By early 2013 police numbers in Goma had been restored, with support from MONUSCO, to the pre-M23-occupation level of around 3,500. Meanwhile, in northern Katanga, insurgents seeking Katanga's secession from the DRC clashed during late 2012 with national forces, causing significant population displacement there. In January 2013 the UN Secretary-General sent his Military Adviser to the Great Lakes region to co-ordinate the regional and UN approaches to future security arrangements in eastern DRC. In late February the leaders of 11 African countries, meeting in Addis Ababa, Ethiopia, signed the Peace, Security and Cooperation Framework for the DRC and the Region, which aimed to stabilize the Great Lakes region; the UN, the AU, the ICGLR and Southern African Development Community (SADC) were to act as a guarantors of the Framework. The signatories to the Framework committed to protect the future territorial sovereignty and the peace and stability of the DRC.

In March 2013, at the request of the UN Secretary-General, the Security Council authorized the establishment of a new Force Intervention Brigade (FIB), to be deployed under the umbrella of MONUSCO's operations, and under the direct command of the MONUSCO Force Commander, with a mandate to confront urgent threats to security by conducting targeted offensive operations against any armed militia perpetrating violence in eastern areas of that country, including foreign armed groups active in the region; and to disable and disarm such militia and reduce the threat posed by them to state authority and civilian security. Based in North Kivu, the FIB was to comprise a total of 3,069 peacekeeping troops, and was to comprise three infantry battalions, one artillery unit, and one special force and reconnaissance company. A new Special Envoy for the Great Lakes Region, appointed in March, was to co-ordinate the implementation of these objectives. From May the new Force was deployed, in the form of a brigade from SADCBRIG, the SADC's regional standby force, comprising troops from Malawi, South Africa and Tanzania. (In December 2012 an extraordinary summit of SADC heads of state and government had agreed in principle to the deployment of SADCBRIG, within the framework of any international operation in eastern DRC.) In late July 2013 the FIB was activated for the first time to enforce a security zone around Goma, with rebel forces there ordered to surrender their weaponry and join the DDR and—where appropriate—repatriation process. In the following month civilians in Goma organized a demonstration to demand an expansion northwards of the new security zone. In September the ICGLR granted MONUSCO permanent representation on its Expanded Joint Verification Mechanism (a military monitoring team) and appealed to MONUSCO to provide logistical support to the Mechanism. The full deployment of the FIB was completed in early October. Towards the end of that month the Brigade assisted the DRC security forces in a robust action against M23 rebels, starting in the Kibumba area, to the north of Goma. In early November the DRC armed forces gained control over former M23 strongholds, causing the remaining M23 combatants to flee, with many crossing into Rwanda and Uganda. On 5 November the M23 declared the end of its rebellion in eastern DRC, and indicated that it would pursue its grievances through political mechanisms. The announcement was welcomed by the Security Council. In November–early December a so-called Kampala dialogue took place between the DRC Government and the M23 leadership, culminating in the signing of final declarations by the parties, representing a political resolution to issues including the cantonment and DDR of former combatants. An amnesty was to be granted by the DRC authorities, except to former M23 elements suspected of having perpetrated serious contraventions of international humanitarian law. MONUSCO was to assist efforts to restore state authority in areas that had been destabilized by the rebel grouping, and to support the DDR process. The mission was continuing to provide logistical support to the DRC armed forces throughout the country and to undertake extensive patrols, including jointly with the DRC armed forces, throughout the Kivus, and Orientale, Maniema and Katanga provinces. In 2014 MONUSCO aimed to strengthen its active presence in eastern DRC, while maintaining an antenna presence in areas not affected by armed conflict. With a view to enabling MONUSCO to focus more sharply on its core responsibilities, the transfer of certain tasks from the mission's remit to the scope of the UN's DRC country team was envisaged, in areas including humanitarian de-mining, technical elections support, capacity building, and justice and corrections (where, for example, MONUSCO had hitherto provided advice and support to the military and civilian judicial authorities relating to the deployment of mobile courts).

In June 2012 the Security Council requested MONUSCO to undertake a strategic review—identifying a clear strategy and schedule for its implementation—of the DRC Government's ISSSS (the framework, developed in 2008–09, for establishing sustainable national security forces, and for consolidating state authority in eastern DRC). In January 2013 the UN Secretary-General announced a revised ISSSS, covering the period 2013–17, based on the five pillars of democratic dialogue; security and justice; restoration of state authority; return, reintegration and socio-economic recovery; and combating gender-based violence.

Operational Strength: At 28 February 2014 MONUSCO comprised 19,558 troops, 502 military observers and 1,185 police officers (including formed police units); it was supported by 556 UN Volunteers and (as at 30 November 2013) by 990 international and 2,979 local civilian personnel. The mission's Force Intervention Brigade, authorized in March 2013, numbers 3,069 troops.

Finance: The authorized budget for the mission amounted to US $1,456.4m. for the period 1 July 2013–30 June 2014, funded from a Special Account comprising assessed contributions from UN member states.

United Nations Peacekeeping Force in Cyprus—UNFICYP

Address: Nicosia, Cyprus.

Special Representative of the UN Secretary-General and Chief of Mission: LISA M. BUTTENHEIM (USA).

Force Commander: Maj.-Gen. CHAO LIU (People's Republic of China).

Establishment and Mandate: UNFICYP was established in March 1964 by a UN Security Council resolution to prevent a recurrence of fighting between the Greek and Turkish Cypriot communities, and to contribute to the maintenance of law and order. The Force controls a 180-km buffer zone, established (following the Turkish intervention in 1974) between the ceasefire lines of the Turkish forces and the Cyprus National Guard. It is mandated to investigate and act upon all violations of the ceasefire and buffer zone, as well as to perform humanitarian functions, such as facilitating the supply of electricity and water across the ceasefire lines. The UN Secretary-General's good offices have supported the conduct of negotiations between the Greek and Turkish Cypriot leaders. In reports to the Security Council the UN Secretary-General has consistently recognized UNFICYP as being indispensable to maintaining calm on the island and to creating the best conditions for his good offices.

Activities, 2000–08: In January 2002 a new series of direct talks between the Greek Cypriot and Turkish Cypriot leaders commenced, under the auspices of the UN Secretary-General's Special Adviser. In November the UN Secretary-General submitted for consideration a document providing the basis for a comprehensive settlement agreement. A revised version of the draft settlement plan document was presented to the leaders of the two communities during a visit by the Secretary-General to Cyprus in February 2003. He urged both sides to put this to separate simultaneous referendums at the end of March, in the hope that, were the settlement plan approved, Cyprus would be able to accede to the European Union (EU) in a reunited state on 1 May 2004. Progress stalled, however, at a meeting between the two sides held in early March 2003 in The Hague, Netherlands. In April the Security Council adopted a resolution calling upon both parties to continue to work towards a settlement using the Secretary-General's plan as the unique basis for future negotiations. In February 2004 the Greek Cypriot and Turkish Cypriot leaders committed themselves to the Secretary-General's settlement plan. Negotiations on settling outstanding differences were chaired by the Secretary-General's Special Adviser for Cyprus throughout March and a finalized text was presented at the end of that month. The proposed Foundation Agreement was subsequently approved by two-thirds of Turkish Cypriot voters in a referendum held in April, but rejected by some 75% of Greek Cypriot voters. In June the Secretary-General determined to undertake a comprehensive review of UNFICYP's mandate and force levels, in view of the political developments on the island. In October the Security Council endorsed the recommendations of the Secretary-General's review team, which included a reduction in the mission's authorized strength from 1,230 to 860 military personnel and an increase in the deployment of civilian police officers from 44 to 69.

In July 2006 the Turkish Cypriot leader and the Greek Cypriot President meeting under the auspices of the UN Secretary-General, agreed on a set of principles and decisions aimed at reinstating the negotiating process. UNFICYP hosted a second meeting of the leaders of the two communities in September 2007. They agreed on a need to initiate a settlement process and confirmed that they would continue a bi-communal dialogue under UN auspices. In March 2008 the Special Representative of the UN Secretary-General (SRSG) convened a meeting of the two leaders, who agreed to the establishment of technical committees and working groups in preparation for detailed political negotiations. The leaders also agreed to reopen a crossing between the two communities at Ledra Street, Nicosia. A ceremony to mark the event was held in early April. In July the two leaders agreed in principle on the issue of a single sovereignty and citizenship and initiated a review of the technical committees and working groups. Full negotiations on a political settlement for the island were inaugurated in September, supported by the UN Secretary-General's Special Adviser on Cyprus, Alexander Downer.

2009–14: By August 2009 the two leaders had met 40 times in the preceding 12-month period, discussing issues concerning governance and power sharing, the EU, security and guarantees, territory, property, and economic matters. The second round of full negotiations commenced in September, and by September 2010 a further 44 meetings had been conducted. UNFICYP personnel during that year focused efforts on the maintenance of the military status quo, demining, and the facilitation of civilian activities in the buffer zone. In October the Limnitis/Yesilirmak crossing point was reopened. In November the UN Secretary-General met directly with the two leaders in order to reinvigorate the settlement discussions. A further meeting between the Secretary-General and the leaders of the two communities was convened in January 2011, at which both sides agreed to intensify efforts to reach substantive agreement on outstanding core issues of contention. In July a tripartite meeting of the Secretary-General and the Greek Cypriot and Turkish Cypriot leaders agreed on an intensified schedule of regular negotiations, with enhanced engagement by the UN. In October 2011 and January 2012 further tripartite meetings were held, in Greentree, NY, USA, aimed at assessing progress made in the ongoing negotiations, and at addressing unresolved core issues, especially related to power-sharing, contentious property ownership issues, territory and citizenship. Bilateral meetings continued, in Nicosia, in February–March 2012, but were reported at that time by the UN Secretary-General to be almost deadlocked on outstanding core issues. In April the Special Adviser of the Secretary-General indicated that the UN's participation in negotiations would be reduced to the level of technical-level discussions and confidence-building measures, pending the achievement of significant progress in bilateral discussions between the Greek and Turkish Cypriot leaders. In January 2013 the Security Council urged both communities to continue to pursue negotiations on reunification, to increase the participation of civil society representatives in the negotiations process, and to engage with UNFICYP on the demarcation of a buffer zone. In May the Special Adviser of the UN Secretary-General hosted a meeting between Nicos Anastasiades, the new Greek Cypriot leader, and his Turkish counterpart, Derviş Eroğlu. Thereafter the Special Adviser met both leaders several times with a view to overcoming the impasse reached in the negotiations process; momentum towards restarting talks was stalled at that time by disagreement between the two sides over the content of a proposed common declaration—on positions with respect to sovereignty, citizenship and state personality—that the Greek Cypriot leadership regarded as a precondition for continuing negotiations. In November UNFICYP organized an informal social event that gathered for the first time the Greek Cypriot and Turkish Cypriot mayors of Nicosia, and their councillors. In late January 2014 the UN Security Council urged the two sides to implement military and social confidence-building measures, and to reach agreement on the pursuit of negotiations. In early February the two leaderships finally agreed a roadmap to guide the negotiations, and, consequently, UN-mediated formal talks recommenced soon afterwards, in Nicosia.

During the second half of 2013 UNFICYP issued more than 860 permits for civilian activities, including farming, in the buffer zone; delivered weekly humanitarian assistance to 347 Greek Cypriots and 120 members of the Roman Catholic Maronite community in northern Cyprus; provided support to Greek Cypriot schools in the Karpas peninsula, in the north; undertook home visits to Turkish Cypriots requiring assistance in the south; addressed legal and humanitarian issues relating to the detention of four Turkish Cypriots in the south; and facilitated 42 religious events, and also some 51 civil society activities in support of bi-communal co-operation.

Operational Strength: At 28 February 2014 UNFICYP had an operational strength of 857 troops and 67 police officers, supported by 149 international and local civilian staff (as at 30 November 2013).

Finance: The General Assembly appropriated US $56.6m. to the Special Account for UNFICYP to supplement voluntary donations in financing the period 1 July 2013–30 June 2014.

United Nations Stabilization Mission in Haiti—MINUSTAH

Address: Port-au-Prince, Haiti.

Special Representative of the UN Secretary-General and Head of Mission: SANDRA HONORÉ (Trinidad and Tobago).

Force Commander: Lt-Gen. JOSE LUIZ JABORANDY , Jr (Brazil).

Police Commissioner: LUIS MIGUEL CARRILHO (Portugal).

Establishment and Mandate: In February 2004 the UN Security Council authorized the establishment of a Multinational Interim Force (MIF) to help to secure law and order in Haiti, where political tensions had escalated prior to the resignation of President Jean-Bertrand Aristide. In April the Security Council agreed to establish MINUSTAH, which was to assume authority from the MIF with effect from 1 June. MINUSTAH was mandated to create a stable and secure environment, to support the transitional government in institutional development and organizing and monitoring elections, and to monitor the human rights situation. Among its declared objectives was the improvement of living conditions of the population through security measures, humanitarian actions and economic development.

Activities, 2004–09: During 2004 mission civil support units covering electoral assistance, child protection, gender, civil affairs, human rights, and HIV/AIDS became operational. MINUSTAH forces worked to stabilize the security situation in the country, including by reducing the criminal activities of armed groups in poorer urban areas. In June 2005 the Security Council approved a temporary reinforcement of MINUSTAH to provide increased security in advance of planned local, legislative and presidential elections; the mission also deployed experts to train electoral agents and supervisors. After some delay the presidential and first round of legislative elections were conducted in early February 2006, with MINUSTAH officers providing security during the voting process and maintaining order as the results were being clarified. The mission subsequently pledged to support a post-election process of national dialogue and reconciliation and measures to strengthen the country's police force in order to re-establish law and order in areas of the capital, Port-au-Prince. A second round of voting in the legislative election was conducted in April. In August the UN Security Council determined that the mission should strengthen its role in preventing crime and reducing community violence, in particular kidnappings and other activities by local armed groups. In February 2007 MINUSTAH launched a large-scale operation in the Cité Soleil quarter of Port-au-Prince in order to extend its security presence in the most vulnerable locations and to counter the activities of criminal gangs. At the same time UN personnel helped to rehabilitate education, youth and medical facilities in those areas. In April MINUSTAH provided security and logistical support during the conduct of local municipal and mayoral elections. By November an estimated 9,000 local police officers had graduated from MINUSTAH training institutes. In April 2008 there were violent local demonstrations concerning the rising cost of living, during which several MINUSTAH personnel were attacked and property was damaged. A contingent of the mission subsequently distributed food aid to some 3,000 families in the poorest quarters of the capital. In August–September MINUSTAH personnel undertook emergency relief and rehabilitation activities, including evacuation of local residents and the distribution of humanitarian aid, to assist some of the 800,000 people affected by tropical storms which struck the country consecutively during a period of three weeks. From mid-2008 MINUSTAH strengthened its presence along the country's border with the Dominican Republic to counter illegal drugs-trafficking and improve security in the region. In December the mission undertook its first joint operation with the local police authorities to seize illegal drugs. During 2009 MINUSTAH, as well as implementing projects aimed at reducing violence in the community, provided technical security capacity-building support to the national police.

2010–14: In January 2010 a major earthquake struck Haiti, and destroyed the MINUSTAH headquarters in Port-au-Prince. Subsequently it was confirmed that 102 mission staff had been killed, among them Hédi Annabi, the then Special Representative of the UN Secretary-General, his deputy, and the acting police commissioner for the mission. Later in January the UN Security Council adopted a resolution increasing the strength of the mission, to enable it to support the immediate recovery, reconstruction and stability efforts in Haiti. The temporary deployment of an additional 680 police officers was authorized by the Security Council in June. MINUSTAH extended technical, logistical and administrative assistance to the country's authorities in preparation for presidential and legislative elections, which were conducted in November. MINUSTAH contributed to efforts to restore order and to maintain stability following violent reactions to preliminary election results in December. The mission developed a revised security strategy to ensure a stable environment for the second round of voting in the presidential election, held in March 2011. In January of that year MINUSTAH launched a major initiative, with the national police force, to seize known criminals, as well as to support vulnerable young people in some of the most socially fragile urban areas through the provision of skills training, income-generating activities, and the implementation of psychosocial initiatives. A five-year Haitian National Police Development Plan, finalized in March 2012 jointly by MINUSTAH's police component and the national police service, aimed to strengthen the national police force by 2016 to a minimum of 15,000 serving officers. In October 2012, in response to the onset of Hurricane Sandy, MINUSTAH co-ordinated with other organizations to support local authorities in executing the rapid evacuations of more than 17,000 people from areas at risk of severe flood and wind damage.

From October 2010 MINUSTAH provided logistical support to counter a severe outbreak of cholera, including the construction of temporary treatment centres, public education efforts, transportation of personnel, emergency medicines and supplies, and the distribution of potable water in affected areas. In January 2011 the UN Secretary-General appointed a panel of independent experts to assess the outbreak amid widespread speculation within the country that a contingent of MINUSTAH troops was the source. A claim for compensation was brought against the UN in November on behalf of victims of the cholera outbreak; in February 2013, however, the compensation claim was formally rejected by the UN Secretary-General. In December 2012 the UN Secretary-General appointed a Special Adviser for Community-based Medicine and Lessons from Haiti to support existing national elimination efforts through investment in prevention, treatment, and education, with a focus on the provision of clean drinking water and sanitation systems, and of an oral cholera vaccine.

In October 2011 the UN Security Council authorized a reduction in the mission's authorized strength by 1,600 personnel, to be completed by mid-2012, in order to redress the mission's post-earthquake expansion. A further reduction in the mission's strength, to 6,270 troops and 2,601 police officers, was authorized by the Council in October 2012; and in October 2013 the Council endorsed another reduction in troop numbers, to 5,021, while maintaining the police component of 2,601 personnel. At the time the mission's mandate was extended until October 2014.

During 2012 MINUSTAH and the UN country team in Haiti finalized a new integrated strategic framework covering 2013–16, which was aligned with the Haiti Government's strategic priorities for that period; the framework focused on strengthening Haitian institutions to manage the delivery of basic social services; and the ongoing downsizing of the mission. In April 2013 a MINUSTAH and the Haiti authorities established a joint workshop to monitor the gradual transfer of responsibilities from the mission to the Government. In May, against a background of dissatisfaction from some civil society and politcal stakeholders with the continuing presence of the mission, the Haiti Senate passed a non-binding resolution requesting the progressive withdrawal of the mission.

Meanwhile MINUSTAH continued to monitor the security situation during 2013–early 2014, conducting joint operations with the national police in the most challenging districts of Port-au-Prince, supporting police development efforts, and implementing initiatives aimed at addressing high levels of youth unemployment, criminal gang activities, and weak security institutions. MINISTAH military and police components maintained a presence in camps accommodating nearly 279,000 people who remained homeless in the aftermath of the 2010 earthquake, as well as in fragile urban districts.

Operational Strength: At 28 February 2014 MINUSTAH comprised 5,794 troops and 2,413 police officers; there was also a support team of 169 UN Volunteers and (as at 30 November 2013) 373 international civilian staff and 1,242 local civilian staff.

Finance: The mission is financed by assessments in respect of a Special Account. The approved budget for the period 1 July 2013–30 June 2014 amounted to US $576.6m.

United Nations Truce Supervision Organization—UNTSO

Address: Government House, Jerusalem.

Head of Mission and Chief-of-Staff: Maj.-Gen. MICHEL FINN (Ireland).

Establishment and Mandate: UNTSO was established initially to supervise the truce called by the UN Security Council in Palestine in May 1948 and has assisted in the application of the 1949 Armistice Agreements. Its activities have evolved over the years, in response to developments in the Middle East and in accordance with the relevant resolutions of the Security Council. There is no periodic renewal procedure for UNTSO's mandate. UNTSO maintains liaison offices in Beirut, Lebanon; Ismailia, Egypt; and Damascus, Syria.

Activities: UNTSO observers attach to and assist UN peacekeeping forces in the Middle East. The mission maintains offices in Beirut, Lebanon and Damascus, Syria. In addition, UNTSO operates a number of outposts in the Sinai region of Egypt to maintain a UN presence there. UNTSO observers have been available at short notice to deploy to and form the nucleus of newly authorized peacekeeping operations.

Military Strength: The operational strength of UNTSO at 28 February 2014 was 160 military observers, supported by 95 international and 138 local civilian staff (as at 30 November 2013).

Finance: UNTSO expenditures are covered by the regular budget of the United Nations. The appropriation for the two-year period 2014–15 was US $74.3m.

United Nations Peacebuilding

Address: Department of Political Affairs, United Nations, New York, NY 10017, USA.

Telephone: (212) 963-1234; **fax:** (212) 963-4879; **internet:** www.un.org/Depts/dpa.

The Department of Political Affairs provides support and guidance to UN peacebuilding operations and political missions working in the field to prevent and resolve conflicts or to promote enduring peace in post-conflict societies. The Department also supports envoys and advisers bearing the UN Secretary-General's 'good offices' for the resolution of conflicts or implementation of other UN mandates.

The World Summit of UN heads of state held in September 2005 approved recommendations made by the UN Secretary-General in his March 2005 report entitled *In Larger Freedom: Towards Development, Security and Human Rights for All* for the creation of an intergovernmental advisory Peacebuilding Commission. In December the UN Security Council and General Assembly authorized the establishment of the Commission; it was inaugurated, as a special subsidiary body of both the Council and Assembly, in June 2006. A multi-year standing peacebuilding fund, financed by voluntary contributions from member states and mandated to support post-conflict peacebuilding activities, was established in October 2006. A Peacebuilding Support Office was established within the UN Secretariat to administer the fund, as well as to support the Commission.

In 2014 the Peacebuilding Commission was actively concerned with the situation in six African countries: Burundi; Central African Republic; Guinea; Guinea-Bissau; Liberia; and Sierra Leone.

The UN Assistance Mission in Afghanistan is directed by the Department of Peacekeeping Operations.

Office of the Special Representative of the UN Secretary-General for West Africa—UNOWA

Address: BP 23851 Dakar-Ponty, 5 ave Carde, Immeuble Caisse de sécurité sociale, Dakar, Senegal.

Telephone: (221) 849-07-29; **fax:** (221) 842-50-95.

Special Representative of the UN Secretary-General: SAID DJINNIT (Algeria).

Establishment and Mandate: UNOWA was established in January 2002 to elaborate an integrated approach by the United Nations to the prevention and management of conflict in West Africa; and to promote peace, security and development in the sub-region. UNOWA is also mandated to facilitate the implementation of the 10 October 2002 ruling of the International Court of Justice relating to land and maritime boundaries between Cameroon and Nigeria; the Cameroon-Nigeria Mixed Commission, chaired by the Special Representative of the Secretary-General (SRSG) has met regularly since December 2002 in this respect. UNOWA's mandate has been successively renewed, most recently for three years until 31 December 2016.

Activities: UNOWA supports the development of a regional harmonized approach to disarmament, demobilization and reintegration in West Africa, and its projects have included an initiative to address cross-border challenges, such as mercenaries, child-soldiers and small arms proliferation. UNOWA also aims to support and facilitate a sub-regional approach to issues that impact stability in West Africa, in particular electoral processes and the transfer of power. UNOWA works with the Economic Community of West African States (ECOWAS), whose projects embrace security sector reform (identified as a key priority for the sub-region), small arms, transborder co-operation, etc. A trilateral partnership between UNOWA, the European Union (EU) and ECOWAS has also been established. In July 2009 UNOWA, with the UN Office on Drugs and Crime, the UN Department of Peacekeeping Operations and INTERPOL, inaugurated a West Africa Coast Initiative (WACI) to support efforts by ECOWAS to counter the problem of illicit drugs trafficking, organized crime, and drug abuse in West Africa. WACI provides advice, equipment, technical assistance and specialized training, and supports the establishment of Transnational Crime Units in each country. In March 2013 WACI's Programme Advisory Committee adopted a revised regional strategy for the Initiative. UNOWA, with the UN Office for the Co-ordination of Humanitarian Affairs (OCHA), has worked to address economic, political, security and humanitarian problems that confront the populations of certain border areas in West Africa through the development of integrated, multi-agency strategies in respect of four border clusters: Guinea/Côte d'Ivoire/Liberia/Sierra Leone (Guinea Forestière); Mali/Burkina Faso/Côte d'Ivoire/Ghana; Mauritania/Mali/Niger; and Senegal/The Gambia/Guinea-Bissau. UNOWA works closely with OCHA in strengthening the UN's regional humanitarian response. It is also concerned to promote respect for human rights and to support the full consideration of gender issues in conflict management and peacebuilding activities.

In May 2011 UNOWA organized a Regional Conference on Elections and Stability in West Africa, in Praia, Cape Verde; the Conference adopted the Praia Declaration on Elections and Stability in West Africa, identifying practical recommendations for improving electoral processes in the region. A round-table meeting was convened in September, in New York, USA, by UNOWA and the International Peace Institute, further to discuss issues raised by the Conference. In the following month UNOWA supported the organization by the West African Human Rights Defenders Network of a panel discussion on the role of civil society organizations in elections; as a consequence of the panel discussion, civil society organizations in the subregion adopted a roadmap for the implementation of the Praia Declaration.

In December 2011 UNOWA, jointly with the Office of the UN High Commissioner for Human Rights (OHCHR), ECOWAS, the African Union, the Mano River Union (which comprises Côte d'Ivoire, Guinea, Liberia and Sierra Leone), and the Organisation Internationale de la Francophonie, convened a Regional Conference on Impunity, Justice and Human Rights in West Africa, in Bamako, Mali; the Conference adopted the Bamako Declaration and a strategic framework, outlining recommendations aimed at strengthening good governance and the rule of law, in order to promote stability and development in West Africa. A Regional Forum on Media, Peace and Security in West Africa, organized by UNOWA, together with ECOWAS and the Francophonie, in Abidjan, Côte d'Ivoire, in June 2012, with participation by representatives of government, regional and international organizations, and by media professionals, adopted a set of recommendations on the role of the media in peace and security, with a view to fostering mutual capacity building and collaboration among regional stakeholders.

In June 2013 regional heads of state attending a summit in Yaoundé, Cameroon, on combating maritime piracy in the Gulf of Guinea, that was organized jointly by regional governments, UNOWA, UNOCA, and sub-regional organizations, formally adopted and opened for signature a Code of Conduct concerning the Prevention and Repression of Piracy, Armed Robbery against Ships, and Illegal Maritime Activities in West and Central Africa.

Following the overthrow of the legitimate governments of Mali and Guinea-Bissau in March and April 2012, respectively, the SRSG devoted his good offices to promoting a return to civilian rule and constitutional order in those countries (in the case of Guinea-Bissau he acted in co-operation with the SRSG to that country). UNOWA continued to work at supporting the consolidation of democratic processes and institutions throughout the region, with a particular focus on Guinea, Senegal and Togo; and at managing election-related tensions in the region.

In June 2013 a high-level meeting, held in Dakar, Senegal, and co-chaired by the SRSG, the President of the ECOWAS Commission, and the Secretary-General of the Mano River Union, initiated the process of formulating a security strategy for the Mano River Union, as requested in recent resolutions of the UN Security Council.

Operational Strength: At 31 January 2014 UNOWA comprised two military advisers, and (as at 31 October 2013) 22 international civilian and 16 local civilian personnel.

Office of the United Nations Special Co-ordinator for Lebanon—UNSCOL

Address: UN House, Riad el-Solh Sq., POB 11, 8577 Beirut, Lebanon.

Special Co-ordinator for Lebanon: DEREK PLUMBLY (United Kingdom).

Establishment and Mandate: UNSCOL was established in February 2007, replacing the Office of the Personal Representative of the UN Secretary-General for southern Lebanon (established in August 2000). The Office co-ordinates the UN presence in Lebanon and is the focal point for the core group of donor countries supporting Lebanon. The Office works closely with the expanded UN peacekeeping mission in Lebanon, UNIFIL. The Special Co-ordinator is responsible for supervising implementation of Security Council Resolution 1701, which was adopted in August 2006, and called for a cessation of hostilities in Lebanon.

In September 2013 the inaugural meeting of a new International Support Group for Lebanon—held at the UN New York headquarters, under the chairmanship of the UN Secretary-General, to consider means of supporting stability in Lebanon in view of the impact on the country's resources of the ongoing crisis in neighbouring

Syria—urged UNSCOL and UNIFIL to work with the Lebanese security forces to activate co-ordination mechanisms in support of the security forces' ongoing capabilities development plan, and also in support of a strategic dialogue concluded between UNIFIL and the security forces as a component part of the plan.

Operational Strength: At 30 November 2013 UNSCOL comprised 21 international civilian and 61 local civilian personnel.

Office of the United Nations Special Co-ordinator for the Middle East Peace Process—UNSCO

Address: Gaza; Jerusalem; Ramallah.

Special Co-ordinator for the Middle East Peace Process: ROBERT R. SERRY (Netherlands).

Establishment and Mandate: UNSCO was established in June 1994 after the conclusion of the Declaration of Principles on Interim (Palestinian) Self-Government Arrangements—the Oslo Accord. UNSCO was to seek, during the transition process envisaged by the Declaration, to ensure 'an adequate response to the needs of the Palestinian people and to mobilize financial, technical, economic and other assistance'. In 1995 UNSCO's mandate was reconfigured as the Office of the Special Co-ordinator for the Middle East Peace Process and Personal Representative of the Secretary-General to the Palestine Liberation Organization and the Palestine (National) Authority (PA).

Activities: The Office has been mandated to assist in all issues related to the humanitarian situation confronting the Palestinian people, and supports negotiations and the implementation of political agreements. The Regional Affairs Unit (RAU) of the Office assists in the fulfilment of that part of the Office's mandate that requires it to co-ordinate its work and to co-operate closely with all of the parties to the Middle East peace process, including the Governments of Israel, Lebanon, Syria, Jordan and Egypt, the PA, Palestinian civil society, the League of Arab States, and individual Arab states that have assumed a key role in facilitating the peace process. The Special Co-ordinator also collaborates closely with key international actors, in particular those that, together with the UN, constitute the Middle East Quartet, i.e. the European Union, Russia and the USA, and serves as the Envoy of the UN Secretary-General to the Quartet. The RAU also provides technical support for the organization of free, fair and transparent Palestinian elections. In addition to the RAU, UNSCO maintains a Media Office and a Co-ordination Unit.

Operational Strength: At 30 November 2013 UNSCO comprised 25 international civilian and 30 local civilian personnel.

United Nations Assistance Mission in Afghanistan—UNAMA

Address: POB 5858, Grand Central Station, New York, NY 10163-5858, USA.

Telephone: (813) 246000; **fax:** (831) 246069; **e-mail:** spokesperson-unama@un.org; **internet:** www.unama.unmissions.org.

Special Representative of the UN Secretary-General: JÁN KUBIŠ (Slovakia).

Deputy Special Representative of the UN Secretary-General, Political Affairs: NICHOLAS (FINK) HAYSOM (South Africa).

Deputy Special Representative of the UN Secretary-General, Relief, Recovery and Reconstruction: MARK BOWDEN (United Kingdom).

Establishment and Mandate: UNAMA was established by the UN Security Council in March 2002. During March 2002–September 2005 the Mission was authorized to fulfil tasks assigned to the UN under the December 2001 Bonn Agreement on provisional arrangements for Afghanistan. Subsequently UNAMA assumed responsibility for assisting the Afghan Government with the implementation of an Afghanistan Compact, which was adopted by the London Conference on Afghanistan, convened in early 2006, as a framework for co-operation between the Afghan authorities, the UN and the international community. From July 2010 UNAMA supported the Afghanistan National Development Strategy: Prioritization and Implementation Plan ('Kabul Process'), which was endorsed by an International Conference on Afghanistan, convened in that month under UN auspices in Kabul, the Afghan capital. The Kabul Process aimed to facilitate the transition to full Afghan leadership and ownership in 2014, alongside strengthened international partnership and regional co-operation, improved Afghan governance, economic growth, enhanced capabilities of Afghan security forces, and protection for the rights of all Afghan citizens, including women and girls. UNAMA's support to the Kabul Process was to include the provision of electoral assistance to the independent Afghan electoral commissions; fostering national political dialogue and regional engagement; promoting regional co-operation, though confidence-building measures and a Kabul Silk Road initiative (inaugurated in early 2010 by the SRSG to promote informal dialogue between the Government, the UN and Ambassadors of neighbouring countries); and co-ordinating UN and international aid in support of the Government's national development and governance priorities. Peace-building tasks that fall under UNAMA's political mandate include the prevention and resolution of conflicts; building confidence and the promotion of national reconciliation; monitoring the political and human rights situation; and investigating human rights violations. In 2014 UNAMA maintained 13 field offices in Afghanistan. In November 2010 the UN signed an agreement with the Kuwaiti Government establishing a UNAMA/UNAMI Integrated Support Office in that country.

Activities: UNAMA co-ordinates all of the activities of the UN system, whose programme of work is determined by Afghan needs and priorities. Nineteen UN agencies work together with their Afghan government counterparts and with national and international NGO partners. The Paris International Conference in Support of Afghanistan, convened in June 2008, agreed that UNAMA should expand its efforts to co-ordinate international activities in Afghanistan and endorsed a new Afghanistan National Development Strategy. In early 2009 UNAMA established a new political unit to co-ordinate efforts, in collaboration with local political parties, observers and civil society organizations, to promote a free and fair environment for the presidential and provincial council elections that were held in August. The London International Conference in Support of Afghanistan, convened in January 2010, renewed the commitment of the international community and Afghan authorities to the implementation of a reform-oriented nation-building agenda. UNAMA was mandated to support the Kabul Process, endorsed by an International Conference on Afghanistan that was convened in July, in Kabul (q.v.). In October 2010 the SRSG met members of a new High Peace Council, and concluded an agreement to provide technical and practical assistance to the Council in support of the process of national peace and reconciliation. An international conference on Afghanistan held in Bonn, Germany, in December, confirmed long-term commitment to supporting Afghanistan through a newly designated Transformation Decade, to cover 2015–24. In May 2012 the Afghanistan authorities, the Special Representative and the heads of all UN agencies active in Afghanistan met to consider the direction of their collaboration during the process of transferring ownership of security, development and governance agendas to the Afghan Government. The parties determined to hold regular fora henceforth. In July international and Afghan stakeholders attending the Tokyo Conference on Afghanistan adopted the Tokyo Mutual Accountability Framework, covering commitment to good governance, development, representational democracy and elections, rule of law, human rights, and integrity of public finance, and improving aid effectiveness, during Afghanistan's Transformation Decade. UNAMA participated in defining a new steering committee, which was to convene at ministerial and ambassadorial levels, in order to drive dialogue in the implementation of the Framework. In 2013–14 UNAMA assisted an ongoing Afghan People's Dialogue on Peace, primarily by organizing a series of focus group discussions across the country which were to form the basis of provincial roadmaps for peace. UNAMA supported the organization of presidential and provincial council elections that were held in early April 2014, as well as providing capacity building and technical assistance to the Independent Election Commission and Independent Electoral Complaints Commission, and promoting freedom of the media.

UNAMA's human rights unit monitors the situation of Afghan civilians, and investigates and reports on womens' rights, the situation of detainees, and on the protection of civilians in armed conflict. In October 2011 UNAMA released a report that concluded that allegations by prisoners of mistreatment and torture at several Afghan state detention facilities were credible, while detailing several key recommendations aimed at preventing the recurrence of such ill treatment. An updated report, issued in January 2013, and based on interviews of 635 pre-trial detainees and convicted prisoners—including 105 children—conducted during October 2011–October 2012—found credible and reliable evidence that more than one-half of the interviewees had been tortured or otherwise ill treated. UNAMA's *2013 Annual Report on Protection of Civilians in Armed Conflict*, issued in February 2014, found that civilian fatalities arising from the Afghan conflict numbered 2,959 in 2013, with about one-third of civilian casualties caused by the use of improvised explosive devices, 27% by ground engagements, and 15% by suicide and complex attacks; some 74% of civilian casualties were attributed to actions taken by anti-government forces.

Operational Strength: At 31 January 2014 UNAMA comprised 18 military advisers, four police personnel and 69 UN Volunteers; there were, in addition, 381 international civilian and 1,339 local civilian personnel (as at 31 October 2013).

United Nations Assistance Mission for Iraq—UNAMI

Address: Amman, Jordan.

Telephone: (6) 5504700; **fax:** (6) 5504705; **e-mail:** unami-information@un.org; **internet:** unami.unmissions.org.

Special Representative of the UN Secretary-General for Iraq: NICKOLAY MLADENOV (Bulgaria).

Deputy Special Representative of the UN Secretary-General for Political, Electoral and Constitutional Support: GYÖRGY BUSZTIN (Hungary).

Deputy Special Representative of the UN Secretary-General for Development and Humanitarian Support: Dr JACQUELINE BADCOCK (United Kingdom).

Establishment and Mandate: UNAMI was established by UN Security Council Resolution 1500 (14 August 2003) to co-ordinate and support humanitarian efforts in post-conflict Iraq. Later in August terrorist attacks on the UNAMI headquarters in Baghdad killed the newly appointed Special Representative of the UN Secretary-General (SRSG) for Iraq (and UN High Commissioner for Human Rights), Sergio Vieira de Mello, and 21 other UN personnel. UN international staff were subsequently withdrawn from Iraq, and, until the formation of the Iraqi Interim Government at the end of June 2004, UNAMI operated primarily from outside the country (from Cyprus, Jordan and Kuwait). UNAMI consists of two 'pillars'—political, and reconstruction and development—and a Human Rights Office (HRO). Generally, the work of the political pillar is carried out in support of the good offices and facilitation role of the SRSG. The political office also supports, as necessary, the HRO and the reconstruction and development pillar. In April–May 2004 the UN helped to establish an Independent Electoral Commission of Iraq (IECI). In accordance with the mandate afforded it under UN Security Council Resolution 1546 (June 2004), UNAMI assisted in the convening of an Iraqi national conference in August, including in the selection of a Consultative Council. UNAMI is mandated, under Resolution 1546, 'to promote the protection of human rights, national reconciliation, and judicial and legal reform in order to strengthen the rule of law in Iraq'. Through two units, the HRO monitors and reports on the human rights situation (jointly with the Office of the UN High Commissioner for Human Rights) and addresses the reconstruction of Iraqi national human rights institutions. HRO activities include providing technical support and training to the ministries of justice, defence and human rights; the establishment of a national centre for missing and disappeared persons in Iraq; and the establishment of a national human rights institution. UNAMI is also mandated to promote dialogue and effective procedures to resolve disputed international boundaries.

In August 2007 the UN Security Council approved Resolution 1770, which expanded UNAMI's mandate to incorporate a responsibility to promote, support and facilitate the implementation of the International Compact, as well as the co-ordination and delivery of humanitarian assistance, and to support and advise on national reconciliation efforts.

In November 2010 the UN signed an agreement with the Kuwaiti Government establishing a UNAMI/UNAMA Integrated Support Office in that country.

Activities: In January 2005 elections were held in Iraq to form a Transitional National Assembly that would be charged with drafting a permanent constitution, as well as to help establish a Transitional Government and presidency. UNAMI's electoral unit assisted and advised the IECI in relation to the organization and conduct of the elections. In early 2007 UNAMI facilitated and observed the process of reconfiguring the IECI as the Independent High Electoral Commission (IHEC), and subsequently the mission supported the IHEC in capacity and institution building. UNAMI provided technical support to the IHEC in respect of provincial and national legislative elections that were conducted in 2009–10 and provincial elections held in April and June 2013, and in the preparation of legislative elections scheduled to be held at the end of April 2014. UNAMI participates in meetings of the IHEC Board of Commissioners, and has served in an impartial advisory capacity in the process of selecting commissioners.

With regard to reconstruction and development, UNAMI aims to address the long-term challenge of achieving sustainable food security; to strengthen the overall quality of education and service delivery at all levels; to support policy development, and preserve and conserve the tangible and intangible Iraqi cultural heritage; to improve the human development situation in Iraq and promote good governance by strengthening institutional capacity, contributing to the creation of employment opportunities and providing policy advice; to support the national health strategy of the Iraqi Ministry of Health in meeting basic health needs; to formulate and implement programmes on institutional/policy reform, capacity building, and service provision necessary to rehabilitate and develop the infrastructure of human settlements; and to support the Iraqi authorities in providing adequate assistance and effective protection to uprooted populations in Iraq, and to assist them in preventing new displacement as well as in achieving durable solutions. UNAMI works closely with other UN agencies, funds and programmes to co-ordinate assistance activities through the UN Country Team for Iraq.

UNAMI endorsed the International Compact for Iraq, a five-year framework for co-operation between Iraq and the international community jointly chaired by the Iraqi Government and the UN Secretariat, that was launched in May 2007. In May 2010 the UN and the Iraqi Government adopted a UN Development Assistance Framework covering the period 2011–14. The Framework identified as priority areas for UN support inclusive economic growth; environmental management; promoting good governance and protection of human rights; ensuring access to improved basic services for all; and investment in the capacities of women, youth and children to enable their full participation in all aspects of life in Iraq. During 2011–early 2014 UNAMI, with UNHCR, monitored the situation at the Iraq–Syria border, as increasing numbers of refugees crossed into Iraq in flight from the ongoing civil war in Syria. In 2014 UNAMI and UNHCR were continuing to pursue durable solutions for individuals within Iraq with identified international protection needs.

In July 2013 the UN Secretary-General reported that heightening inter-sectarian tensions, demonstrations and unrest were posing a significant threat to stability and security in Iraq. During that year an increase in direct attacks on civilian populations by terrorist and armed groups was reported. UNAMI, in response, sought to create space for and mediate political dialogue. In early September the mission strongly condemned an outbreak of violent unrest at Camp Ashraf, in eastern Iraq, which resulted in the deaths of 52 inmates, and urged the Iraqi authorities to establish forthwith a board of inquiry into the incident. The majority of the camp's exiled Iranian refugees had already been relocated to Camp Hurriya near Baghdad. In December a rocket attack on that camp killed three civilians. In early January 2014 the UN Secretary-General appointed a Special Adviser to work with UNAMI and UNHCR to relocate the estimated 3,200 residents of Camp Hurriya to locations outside of Iraq. UNAMI reports civilian casualty figures on a monthly basis; in February 2014 the mission stated that, in January—in all areas of Iraq excluding, owing to issues with verification, the western region of al-Anbar, where conflict was ongoing between security forces and militants—618 civilians (including 178 civilian police) had been killed, as well as 115 members of the Iraqi security forces, with 297 of the fatalities occurring in Baghdad. With less certainty the mission estimated that a further 138 civilian fatalities had occurred in al-Anbar in that month.

Operational Strength: At 31 January 2014 UNAMI personnel (based in Iraq, Jordan and Kuwait) comprised 272 troops and three police officers; they were assisted by 333 international civilian staff and 473 local civilian staff (as at 31 October 2013).

United Nations Office in Burundi—BNUB

Address: BP 6899, Gatumba Rd, Bujumbura, Burundi.

Telephone: 22205165; **internet:** binub.unmissions.org.

Special Representative of the UN Secretary-General and Head of Office: PARFAIT ONANGA-ANYANGA (Gabon).

Establishment and Mandate: BNUB (Bureau des Nations Unies au Burundi) was established on 1 January 2011, as a successor to the UN Integrated Office in Burundi (BINUB), which had operated in the country since 2007. BNUB represented a commitment by the UN to maintaining a scaled-down presence in the country, for an initial 12-month period, in order to support the country's progress towards peace consolidation and long-term development. BNUB mandate included support for the efforts of the Burundi Government to strengthen the independence, capacities and legal frameworks of key national institutions, in accordance with international standards and principles; facilitating political dialogue and promoting justice and reconciliation within Burundi's society; and strengthening national capacities to promote and protect human rights and the needs of the most vulnerable population. The Office was to work to ensure effective co-ordination among UN agencies in Burundi.

In February 2013 the UN Security Council urged BNUB to support the Burundi authorities in fostering dialogue and an inclusive environment in preparation for the planned staging of legislative and presidential elections in 2015. In March 2013 BNUB organized a workshop on 'elements for a credible roadmap towards the organization of inclusive, transparent, free and fair elections in 2015', with participation by the main political actors in Burundi; a workshop on the implementation of the roadmap was convened by BNUB in

November 2013. In October the mission supported a workshop aimed at training media correspondents in pre-election coverage. In January 2014 the UN Secretary-General requested the Burundi authorities to reconsider their expressed preference for the mission to terminate by August. He asked the Security Council to consider two alternative options, should the Burundian authorities not reconsider their position: either the replacement of BNUB by an interim mission with a more focused mandate, pending the transfer of responsibilities to the UN country team for Burundi, or the appointment of a special envoy tasked with promoting and facilitating dialogue between the country's main political actors.

Operational Strength: At 31 January 2014 BNUB comprised one military adviser, one police officer, and three UN Volunteers; as at 31 October 2013 the mission was supported by 38 international and 52 local civilian staff.

United Nations Integrated Peacebuilding Office in Guinea-Bissau—UNIOGBIS

Address: UN Bldg, CP 179, Rua Rui Djassi, Bissau, Guinea-Bissau.

Telephone: 20-36-18; **fax:** 20-36-13; **internet:** uniogbis.unmissions.org.

Special Representative of the UN Secretary-General and Head of Office: José Ramos-Horta (Timor-Leste).

Establishment and Mandate: Established to assist the Peacebuilding Commission in its multi-dimensional engagement with Guinea-Bissau, UNIOGBIS first became operational in January 2010, succeeding the former UN Peacebuilding Office in Guinea-Bissau (UNOGBIS). In May 2013, in view of a coup perpetrated in April 2012, the mandate of UNIOGBIS was adjusted to support a process leading to the restoration of constitutional order.

Activities: From 2003 the work of UNOGBIS, which preceded UNIOGBIS, focused on transition to civilian rule in the aftermath of a military coup that took place in that year. UNOGBIS was mandated by the UN Security Council to promote national reconciliation, respect for human rights and the rule of law; to support national capacity for conflict prevention; to encourage reform of the security sector and stable civil-military relations; to encourage government efforts to suppress trafficking in small arms; and to collaborate with a 'comprehensive peacebuilding strategy' to strengthen state institutions and mobilize international resources. In June 2009 the UN Security Council endorsed the establishment of UNIOGBIS, which succeeded UNOGBIS from 1 January 2010. From mid-2010 UNIOGBIS facilitated the preparation of meetings of security and defence forces, as part of a National Reconciliation Conference process. It also worked to enhance the co-ordination and effectiveness of international assistance aimed at advancing defence and security sector reform, co-operated with the UN Mine Action Service to assess the country's weapons and ammunition stockpiles, supported a constitutional review process, and supported the national authorities to combat human-trafficking, drugs-trafficking and other areas of organized crime. In 2011 the Office provided technical and financial assistance to the National Technical Independent Mixed Commission, responsible for the selection of police officers. In September a model police station, established with support from UNIOGBIS, was inaugurated in Bissau. In May 2012 the Special Representative of the UN Secretary-General (SRSG) expressed strong concern over the impact on civilian living standards of a political crisis that had emerged following a military coup in the previous month against the legitimate Guinea-Bissau authorities. The SRSG, in co-operation with the SRSG to West Africa (see UNOWA), devoted his good offices following the April coup to promoting a return to civilian rule and constitutional order in Guinea-Bissau. In November UNIOGBIS and the Guinea-Bissau Supreme Court jointly published a comprehensive compendium of criminal laws that aimed to assist all actors in the justice sector. The mission, with other partners, issued a manual on human rights for the military in December. In May 2013 the UN Security Council adjusted the mandate of UNIOGBIS to support an inclusive political dialogue and national reconciliation process that was to lead to the full restoration of constitutional order. The process was to comprise two phases, the first culminating in presidential and legislative elections, and the second focusing on post-election stability, and on strengthening state and democratic governance architecture. UNIOGBIS was mandated to facilitate the establishment of an environment conducive to holding free, fair and transparent elections, and to assist with the strengthening of state institutions. The envisaged presidential and legislative elections were postponed from November, and were eventually held in mid-April 2014. In early February, at the conclusion of the voter registration process, the SRSG noted that some 91% of potential voters had been registered.

Operational Strength: At 31 January 2014 UNIOGBIS comprised 16 police officers, two military advisers and six UN Volunteers; in addition, there were 47 international civilian and 40 local civilian personnel (as at 31 October 2013).

United Nations Assistance Mission in Somalia—UNSOM

Address: Mogadishu, Somalia.

Internet: www.unsom.org.

Special Representative of the UN Secretary-General and Head of Mission: Nicholas Kay (United Kingdom).

Establishment and Mandate: The UN Assistance Mission in Somalia (UNSOM) was authorized by the UN Security Council in May 2013, under Resolution 2102, to supersede the former Political Office for Somalia (established in 1995). UNSOM was mandated to provide UN 'good offices' functions in support of the peace and reconciliation process of the Federal Government of Somalia (inaugurated in August 2012); to support the Federal Government and the AU Mission in Somalia through the provision of strategic policy advice on peacebuilding and state-building; to assist the Government with capacity building in the areas of human rights and rule of law, and with the co-ordination of international support; and to monitor and help to prevent abuses of human rights and of humanitarian law. UNSOM, which was established in June 2013, is mandated to deploy a presence across Somalia as requested by the Federal Government and, in early 2014, was maintaining offices in Mogadishu, Baidoa, Garoowe (Puntland), and Kismayo. A further office in Hargeisa (Somaliland) was not active, owing to local objections to its mandate.

Activities: From mid-2013 the SRSG undertook a series of mediation and good offices activities aimed at promoting reconciliation and dialogue, engaging with local leaders, the Federal Government, and international partners, including the Intergovernmental Authority on Development. In September an integrated UN constitutional support team was established, comprising UNSOM, the UN Development Programme and other UN bodies involved in assisting the ongoing constitution-making process in Somalia. During that month a Conference on a New Deal for Somalia, organized in Brussels, Belgium, by the European Union and the Somali Federal Government, endorsed a New Deal Compact for Somalia, which listed 'inclusive politics' as its primary peacebuilding and statebuilding objective. UNSOM and the AU Mission in Somalia (AMISOM) convene periodic leadership meetings, aimed at strengthening co-ordination.

Operational Strength: At 31 January 2014 UNSOM comprised six military advisers and three police, supported (as at 31 October 2013) by 32 international civilian and 18 local civilian staff.

United Nations Regional Centre for Preventive Diplomacy for Central Asia—UNRCCA

Address: Aşgabat, Archabil Shaeli 43, Turkmenistan.

Telephone: (12)-48-16-12; **fax:** (12) 48-16-07; **e-mail:** UNRCCA-DPA@un.org; **internet:** unrcca.unmissions.org.

Special Representative of the UN Secretary-General and Head of Office: Miroslav Jenča (Slovakia).

Establishment and Mandate: The Centre was inaugurated in December 2007, with the objective of assisting and supporting the governments of Kazakhstan, Kyrgyzstan, Tajikistan, Turkmenistan and Uzbekistan to enhance their conflict prevention capacities through dialogue, confidence-building measures and partnerships, in order to respond to existing threats and emerging challenges in the Central Asian region. The Centre is administered by the UN Department of Political Affairs.

Activities: The Centre monitors and analyses the situation in Central Asia, including maintaining close contact with the UN Assistance Mission in Afghanistan, to attain early warning of potential conflict, co-ordinates the efforts of international agencies to promote sustainable development and conflict prevention, facilitates the implementation of regional and international agreements and frameworks of action, and organizes training, workshops and seminars. For the period 2012–14 the Centre identified the following as priority areas of activity: liaising with the governments of the region and, with their concurrence, with other parties concerned on issues relevant to preventive diplomacy; monitoring and analysing the situation on the ground and providing the UN Secretary-General with current information related to conflict prevention efforts; maintaining contacts with relevant regional organizations, encouraging their peacemaking efforts and initiatives, and facilitating co-ordination and information exchange with due regard to their specific mandates; providing a political framework and leadership for the preventive activities of the UN country teams in the region, and supporting the efforts of the Resident Co-ordinators; maintaining close contact with the UN Assistance Mission in Afghanistan to ensure a comprehensive and integrated analysis of the situation in the region. In December 2010 UNRCCA, with the UN Counter-Terrorism Implementation Task Force and the European Union, convened the first of a series of expert meetings on measures to combat terrorism in Central Asia. In November 2011 UNRCCA organized a high-level international meeting, in Aşgabat, aimed at strengthening regional counter-terrorism co-operation on the basis of the Global Counter-Terrorism Strategy that had been adopted in September 2006 by the UN General Assembly. The meeting approved a joint action plan for Central Asian countries on the implementation of the Global Strategy. In October 2012 the Centre hosted the fourth annual meeting of deputy ministers of foreign affairs of Central Asian countries, in Bishkek, Kyrgyzstan, at which recent UNRCCA activities were reviewed and measures to enhance regional co-operation were discussed. An international conference on 'Neutrality and Preventive Diplomacy: Bases for Peace and Security' was staged jointly by UNRCCA and the Turkmenistan Government in Aşgabat in December. During 2013 the Centre organized a series of seminars on regional transboundary water systems. In April UNRCCA convened, in Dushanbe, Tajikistan, a seminar on 'Challenges in addressing the illicit drugs problem in Central Asia in the context of withdrawal of international forces from Afghanistan in 2014'.

Operational Strength: At 31 October 2013 the Centre was served by eight international civilian personnel and by two local civilian staff members.

United Nations Regional Office for Central Africa—UNOCA

Address: BP 23773, Cité de la Démocratie, Villas 55–57, Libreville, Gabon.

Telephone: (241) 741-401; **fax:** (241) 741-402.

Special Representative of the UN Secretary-General: ABOU MOUSSA (Chad).

Establishment and Mandate: UNOCA—covering the 10 member states of the Communauté économique des états de l'Afrique centrale (CEEAC): Angola, Burundi, Cameroon, Central African Republic (CAR), Chad, Democratic Republic of the Congo (DRC), Republic of the Congo, Equatorial Guinea, Gabon, and São Tomé and Príncipe—was inaugurated in March 2011, having been established through an exchange of letters, finalized in August 2010, between the UN Secretary-General and the UN Security Council. UNOCA is mandated to extend the UN's good offices and other assistance to regional states and organizations in support of preventive diplomacy and the consolidation of peace. The Office is also mandated to work closely with UN and other entities to address cross-border challenges, such as organized crime, trafficking in arms, and the activities of armed groups (including the Lord's Resistance Army—LRA). In February 2014 the UN Security Council extended UNOCA's mandate until 31 August 2015.

Activities: UNOCA's priority areas of activity include supporting conflict mediation, and, where requested, assisting with the peaceful conduct of elections in the region; facilitating cohesion in the general work of the UN in the region, including in partnership with other agencies, such as UNDP, UNODC, UN Women and OHCHR; promoting activities in partnership with the private sector and civil society networks; co-ordinating UN efforts in the region against armed groups; undertaking studies on regional challenges and threats; providing technical assistance aimed at advancing early warning and mediation capabilities; helping to build the capacity of CEEAC; promoting the formulation of a regional integrated approach to addressing cross-border insecurity; and combating maritime insecurity in the Gulf of Guinea.

In June 2013 regional heads of state attending a summit in Yaoundé, Cameroon, on combating maritime piracy in the Gulf of Guinea, that was organized jointly by regional governments, UNOCA, UNOWA, and sub-regional organizations, formally adopted and opened for signature a Code of Conduct concerning the Prevention and Repression of Piracy, Armed Robbery against Ships, and Illegal Maritime Activities in West and Central Africa.

In June 2012 a Regional Strategy to Address the Threat and Impact of the Activities of the LRA—developed by UNOCA to address the challenges posed by the LRA to civilians residing in the CAR, DRC, South Sudan, and in Uganda—was endorsed by the Security Council. The Strategy has the following priority objectives: (i) supporting the full operationalization and implementation of the ongoing African Union (AU) regional co-operation initiative against the LRA; (ii) enhancing efforts to protect civilians; (iii) expanding ongoing disarmament, demobilization, repatriation, resettlement and reintegration activities across all LRA-affected areas; (iv) supporting a co-ordinated humanitarian and child protection response in these areas; and (v) assisting governments combating the LRA in the areas of peacebuilding, human rights, rule of law and development. The Council requested the UN Secretary-General to report back in a single document on progress being made by UNOCA, by the Regional Strategy, and by other actors in the region, towards combating the LRA. In February 2013 UNOCA organized a meeting of stakeholders to assess priorities in the implementation of the June 2012 Regional Strategy. During a jointly undertaken visit to Bangui, CAR, and Juba, South Sudan, in late-October–early November 2013, the Special Representative of the UN Secretary-General and the AU's Special Envoy on the LRA urged LRA combatants to cease their activities and return to normal life, and also to acknowledge the need to establish favourable conditions for the restoration of peace and security in the CAR. In January 2014 the Office helped to organize a workshop on police and security, which adopted a series of measures—informed by the UN Global Counter-Terrorism Strategy (adopted in September 2006 by the UN General Assembly)—aimed at combating terrorism and arms proliferation in the region.

Operational Strength: At 31 January 2014 the Office comprised one military adviser, supported (as at 31 October 2013) by 17 international civilian and eight local civilian personnel.

United Nations Support Mission in Libya—UNSMIL

Address: Tripoli, Libya.

Special Representative of the UN Secretary-General: TAREK MITRI (Lebanon).

Establishment and Mandate: Following the outbreak of conflict in Libya in February 2011, UNSMIL was established in September, with a mandate to support Libya's transitional authorities in restoring public security and the rule of law; promoting inclusive political dialogue and national reconciliation; and embarking upon the process of drafting a new constitution and preparing for democratic elections. UNSMIL was also mandated to support the Libyan authorities in extending state authority, through the strengthening of emerging accountable institutions; restoring public services; promoting and protecting human rights (particularly for vulnerable groups); supporting transitional justice; taking the immediate steps required to initiate economic recovery; and co-ordinating support that may be requested from other multilateral and bilateral actors. In March 2012 the UN Security Council modified the mission's mandate to include assisting the Libyan authorities to define national needs and priorities; managing the process of democratic transition; promoting the rule of law and monitoring and protecting human rights, particularly those of women and vulnerable groups; restoring public security; countering the illicit proliferation of all arms and related materiel of all types, in particular man-portable surface-to-air missiles; co-ordinating international assistance; and building government capacity across all relevant sectors. In December 2012 UNSMIL, the Libyan authorities and the UN Development Programme organized a conference on 'Truth and Reconciliation in Libya: the Way Forward'. In May 2013 the mission urged the active participation of women in the ongoing constitution-drafting process.

Operational Strength: At 31 January 2014 the Office was served by 11 police officers and three UN Volunteers, as well as (as at 31 October 2013) by 151 international civilian and 81 local civilian staff members.

United Nations Population Fund—UNFPA

Address: 605 Third Ave, New York, NY 10158, USA.

Telephone: (212) 297-5000; **fax:** (212) 370-0201; **e-mail:** hq@unfpa.org; **internet:** www.unfpa.org.

Created in 1967 as the Trust Fund for Population Activities, UNFPA was established as a Fund of the UN General Assembly in 1972 ('the UN Fund for Population Activities') and was made a subsidiary organ of the UN General Assembly in 1979. In 1987 the organization's name was changed to the UN Population Fund (retaining the same acronym). UNFPA works to achieve a world in which every pregnancy is wanted, every child is safe, and every young person's potential is fulfilled.

Organization

(April 2014)

EXECUTIVE DIRECTOR

The Executive Director is responsible for the overall direction of the Fund, working closely with governments, other UN bodies and agencies, and non-governmental and international organizations to ensure the most effective programming and use of resources in population activities.

Executive Director: Dr Babatunde Osotimehin (Nigeria).

Deputy Executive Director (Management): Anne-Birgitte Albrectsen (Denmark).

Deputy Executive Director (Programme): Kate Gilmore (Australia).

EXECUTING AGENCIES

UNFPA provides financial and technical assistance to developing countries and countries with economies in transition, at their request. In many projects assistance is extended through member organizations of the UN system, although projects are executed increasingly by national governments themselves. The Fund may also call on the services of international, regional and national non-governmental and training organizations, as well as research institutions. In addition, UNFPA's multidisciplinary country technical services teams, composed of experts from the UN, its specialized agencies and non-governmental organizations, assist countries at all stages of project/programme development and implementation. The technical services teams include advisers on HIV/AIDS, who work to integrate HIV prevention into activities supported by UNFPA, as well as advisers on advocacy, reproductive and sexual health, and gender.

FIELD ORGANIZATION

UNFPA operates field offices, each headed by an UNFPA Representative, in some 112 countries. In other countries UNFPA uses the UN Development Programme's field structure of Resident Representatives as the main mechanism for performing its work. The field offices assist governments in formulating requests for aid and co-ordinate the work of the executing agencies in any given country or area. UNFPA has five regional offices, located in Bangkok, Thailand; Cairo, Egypt; İstanbul, Turkey; Johannesburg, South Africa; and Panama City, Panama; and five liaison offices, in Brussels, Belgium; Copenhagen, Denmark; Geneva, Switzerland; Tokyo, Japan; and Washington, DC, USA.

Activities

UNFPA aims to promote health, in particular reproductive health, and gender equality as essential elements of long-term sustainable development. It aims to assist countries, at their request, to formulate policies and strategies to reduce poverty and support development and to collect and analyse population data to support better understanding of their needs. UNFPA's activities are broadly defined by the Programme of Action adopted by the International Conference on Population and Development (ICPD), which was held in Cairo, Egypt, in September 1994; UNFPA was designated the lead agency in following up the objectives of Programme of Action, which envisaged universal access to reproductive health care services and family planning services, a reduction in infant, child and maternal mortality, a reduction in the rate of HIV infection, improving life expectancy at birth, and universal access to primary education for all children. The Programme also emphasized the necessity of empowering and educating women, in order to achieve successful sustainable human development. A special session of the UN General Assembly (ICPD+5), held in June–July 1999 to assess progress in achieving the objectives of the Cairo Conference, identified several key actions for further implementation of the Programme of Action. Several new objectives were adopted by the special session, including working towards universal availability of contraceptives and reproductive health care services. The ICPD objectives were incorporated into the Millennium Development Goals (MDGs), agreed in September 2000 by a summit of UN heads of state or government, and have been included in national development frameworks and poverty reduction strategies. The 10th and 15th anniversaries of the ICPD were commemorated by meetings of the General Assembly convened in October 2004 and October 2009, respectively. In February 2012 UNFPA launched a new website, icpdbeyond2014.org, providing formal updates on progress made under the IPCD Programme of Action. In May 2012 UNFPA helped to organize the fifth International Parliamentarians Conference on Population and Development, in İstanbul, Turkey, with participation by lawmakers from 110 countries (the first such gathering having been held in November 2002 in Ottawa, Canada); the Conference adopted the Istanbul Declaration reaffirming commitment to the principles and goals of the 1994 Cairo Conference, and pledging to attempt to allocate at least 10% of national development and development assistance budgets towards population and reproductive health programmes. In December 2012 UNFPA convened an ICPD Beyond 2014 Global Youth Forum, in Bali, Indonesia, with participation by more than 600 on-site youth leaders and representatives of governments and international agencies, as well as by some 2,500 virtual delegates. The Forum released the Bali Global Youth Forum Declaration, relating to youth rights. It was estimated at that time that around 43% of the global population was aged between 0–24 years.

UNFPA's strategic plan for the period 2014–17, adopted by the Executive Board in September 2013, aimed to advance the availability and use of integrated sexual and reproductive health services; to promote a focus on the sexual health services and educational needs of adolescents, in particular young adolescent girls, in national development policies and programmes; to advance gender quality and women's and girls' empowerment and reproductive rights, including for the most vulnerable populations; and to integrate evidence-based analysis on population dynamics into national policies and international development agendas. In 2013 UNFPA co-led global consultations on formulating a post-2015 development framework in the thematic area of population and dynamics; an outcome report on the consultations was to be issued in 2014. In October 2013 UNFPA launched an advocacy platform for the post-2015 development framework, 'Empowering People to Ensure a Sustainable Future for All', with a focus on incorporating the principles of the 1994 ICPD into the future development mandate.

REPRODUCTIVE HEALTH AND RIGHTS

UNFPA recognizes that improving reproductive health is an essential requirement for improving the general welfare of the population and the basis for empowering women and achieving sustainable social and economic development. The ICPD succeeded in raising the political prominence of reproductive health issues and stimulating consideration by governments of measures to strengthen and restructure their health services and policies. In October 2007 the UN General Assembly officially incorporated the aim of achieving, by 2015, universal access to reproductive health into the target for Goal 5 of the MDGs. UNPFA supports the 'Every Woman Every Child' campaign and the Global Strategy for Women's and Children's Health, both launched in September 2010 at the commencement of the 65th session of the UN General Assembly. The campaign aimed to mobilize global action to address major health challenges and thereby save the lives of 16m. women and children by 2015, and the Global Strategy represents a roadmap for identifying principal areas requiring enhanced funding, strengthened policy and improved service delivery. UNFPA encourages the integration of family planning into all maternal, child and other reproductive health care. Its efforts to improve the quality of these services include support for the training of health care personnel and promoting greater accessibility to education and services. Many reproductive health projects focus on the reduction of maternal mortality—i.e. deaths related to pregnancy and childbirth, of which around 500,000 occur annually, leaving children motherless and vulnerable. Maternal mortality was included as a central objective of the ICPD Programme, and recognized as a legitimate element of international human rights instruments concerning the right to life/survival. Projects to reduce maternal deaths have focused on improving accessibility to essential obstetric care and ensuring the provision of skilled attendance to women in labour. The ICPD reported that a major cause of maternal deaths was unsafe abortions, and urged governments to confront the issue as a major public health concern. UNFPA was an active member of a core planning group of international organizations and partnerships that organized the first Women Deliver conference, held in London, United Kingdom, in October 2007. Participants, including government ministers and representatives of organizations, private sector foundations and non-government bodies, endorsed a final commitment to increase investment in women's health and to make improving maternal health a development priority. A second Women Deliver conference was convened in June 2010, in Washington, DC, USA, and the third was held in May 2013 in Kuala Lumpur, Malaysia. UNFPA's Maternal Health Thematic Fund, launched in February 2008, aims to support efforts in 75 developing countries to improve maternal health care. In addition to maternal deaths, an estimated 10m.–15m. women suffer serious or long-lasting illnesses or disabilities as a result of inadequate care in pregnancy and childbirth. In 2003 UNFPA launched a Global Campaign to End Fistula, which aims to improve the prevention and treatment of this obstetric condition in 30 countries in Africa and Asia and to achieve its elimination. UNFPA supports research into contraceptives and training in contraceptive technology. UNFPA organizes studies on national contraceptive requirements and aims to ensure an adequate supply of contraceptives and reproductive health supplies to developing countries. In March 2012 UNFPA and UNICEF launched a Commission on Life-saving Commodities for Women and Children, which was to have participation by public, private and civil society stakeholders worldwide, and aimed to improve access to essential health supplies. UNFPA encourages partnerships between private sector interests and the governments of developing nations, with a view to making affordable commercial contraceptive products more easily available to consumers and thereby enabling governments to direct subsidies at the poorest sectors of society.

UNFPA is a co-sponsor of the Joint UN Programme on HIV/AIDS (UNAIDS), and is the UNAIDS convening agency with responsibility for young people and for condom programming, as well as taking a leading role in the UNAIDS inter-agency task team on gender and HIV/AIDS. UNFPA gives special attention to the specific needs of adolescents, for example through education and counselling initiatives, and to women in emergency situations. The Fund maintains that meeting the reproductive health needs of adolescents is an urgent priority in combating poverty and HIV/AIDS. Through the joint Adolescent Girls Initiative, UNFPA, UNICEF and the World Health Organization promote policy dialogues in 10 countries. In May 2012 UNFPA welcomed a landmark resolution adopted by the UN Commission on Population and Development concerning the sexual and reproductive health, and reproductive rights, of adolescents and youth.

UNFPA takes a lead role in an emergency situation, following natural disaster or conflict, in providing basic supplies and services to protect reproductive health, in particular in the most vulnerable groups, i.e. young girls and pregnant women. It also helps to conduct rapid health assessments and censuses, supports counselling, education and training activities, and the construction of clinics and other health facilities, following humanitarian crises. UNFPA works with local authorities to prevent an escalation of sexual violence and to ensure that rapid and appropriate treatment and care is given to survivors of sexual violence. In November 2013 UNFPA appealed for US $30m. to fund efforts in the Philippines to provide emergency obstetric care and the protection of women and girls in communities devastated by Typhoon Haiyan.

POPULATION AND DEVELOPMENT

UNFPA promotes work on population as a central component of the goals of the international community to eradicate poverty and achieve sustainable development. UNFPA helps countries to formulate and implement comprehensive population policies as a part of any sustainable development strategies. Research, educational and advocacy activities are undertaken to focus on specific aspects of development and population concern, for example migration, ageing and environmental sustainability. UNFPA provides assistance and training for national statistical offices in undertaking basic data collection, for example censuses and demographic surveys. UNFPA also provides assistance for analysis of demographic and socio-economic data, for research on population trends and for the formulation of government policies. A *State of World Population* report is published annually. The 2013 edition, issued in November of that year, was subtitled 'Motherhood in Childhood: Facing the Challenge of Adolescent Pregnancy'. UNFPA supports a programme of fellowships in demographic analysis, data processing and cartography. In October 2012 UNFPA released a report, *Ageing in the Twenty-first Century: A Celebration and a Challenge*, which envisaged that the global numbers of people over 60 years of age would exceed 1,000m. within the next decade.

GENDER EQUALITY

A fundamental aspect of UNFPA's mission is to achieve gender equality, in order to promote the basic human rights of women and, through the empowerment of women, to support the elimination of poverty. Incorporated into all UNFPA activities are efforts to improve the welfare of women, in particular by providing reproductive choice, to eradicate gender discrimination, and to protect women from sexual and domestic violence and coercion. The Fund aims to encourage the participation of women at all levels of decision- and policy-making and supports programmes that improve the access of all girls and women to education and grant women equal access to land, credit and employment opportunities. UNFPA supports the eradication of female genital mutilation and cutting (FGM/C); UNFPA, jointly with UNICEF and the Italian Government, organized international conference on FGM/C in October 2013, in Rome, Italy. UNFPA actively participates in efforts to raise awareness of and implement Resolution 1325 of the UN Security Council, adopted in October 2000, which addresses the impact of armed conflict on women and girls, the role of women in peacebuilding, and gender dimensions in peace processes and conflict resolution. Other activities are directed at particular issues concerning girls and adolescents and projects to involve men in reproductive health care initiatives. Concurrently with the commemoration of the first International Day of the Girl Child, held on 11 October 2012, UNFPA released a report entitled *Marrying Too Young: End Child Marriage*, detailing prevalence and trends relating to child marriage in developing countries.

Finance

UNFPA is supported entirely by voluntary contributions from governments and private donors. The Fund's total resources available for programme implementation in 2014–17 were forecast at US $4,235.3m. Institutional expenditure over that period was projected at $664.1m.

From 2014–17 UNFPA, UNDP, UNICEF and UN Women were to maintain synchronized strategic planning cycles.

Publications

Annual Report.

Global Programme to Enhance Reproductive Health Commodity Security (annually).

Maternal Health Thematic Fund (annually).

State of the World's Midwifery.

State of World Population (annually).

Reports, technical publications, guidelines and manuals.

United Nations Relief and Works Agency for Palestine Refugees in the Near East—UNRWA

Address: Gamal Abd al-Nasser St, Gaza City.

Telephone: (8) 2887701; **fax:** (8) 2887707.

Address: Bayader Wadi Seer, POB 140157, Amman 11814, Jordan.

Telephone: (6) 5808100; **fax:** (6) 5808335; **e-mail:** unrwa-pio@unrwa.org; **internet:** www.unrwa.org.

UNRWA was established by the UN General Assembly to provide relief, health, education and welfare services for Palestine refugees in the Near East, initially on a short-term basis. UNRWA began operations in May 1950 and, in the absence of a solution to the refugee problem, its mandate has subsequently been extended by the General Assembly.

Organization

(April 2014)

UNRWA employs an international staff of about 120 and more than 24,200 local staff, mainly Palestine refugees. The Commissioner-General is the head of all UNRWA operations and reports directly to the UN General Assembly. UNRWA has no governing body, but its activities are reviewed annually by 21-member Advisory Commission (with national membership of the Commission reflecting the funding commitments of the governments concerned). The Palestinian authorities, the European Community and the League of Arab States participate in the Commission as observers.

Commissioner-General: PIERRE KRÄHENBÜHL (Switzerland).

Deputy Commissioner-General: MARGOT B. ELLIS (USA).

FIELD OFFICES

Each field office is headed by a director and has departments responsible for education, health and relief and social services programmes, finance, administration, supply and transport, legal affairs and public information. Operational support officers work in Gaza and the West Bank to monitor and report on the humanitarian situation and facilitate UNRWA field activities.

Gaza: POB 61, Gaza City; Al Azhar Rd, Rimal Quarter, Gaza City; tel. (8) 2887457; fax (8) 2887219; Dir ROBERT TURNER.

Jordan: POB 143464, 11814 Amman; tel. (6) 5809100; fax (6) 5809134; Dir MARTA COLBURN.

Lebanon: POB 11-0947, Beirut 1107 2060; Bir Hassan, Ghobeiri, opp. City Sportive, Beirut; tel. (1) 840490; fax (1) 840466; e-mail lebanon@unrwa.org; Dir ANN DISMORR.

Syria: POB 4313, Damascus; UN Compound, Mezzah Highway/ Beirut Rd, Damascus; tel. (11) 6133035; fax (11) 6133047; Dir MICHAEL KINGSLEY-NYINAH.

West Bank: POB 19149, Jerusalem; Sheik Jarrah Qtr, East Jerusalem; tel. (2) 5890400; fax (2) 5322714; Dir FELIPE SANCHEZ.

There are UNRWA liaison offices in Brussels, Belgium (for the European Union); Cairo, Egypt; Geneva, Switzerland; and New York and Washington, DC, USA.

Activities

ASSISTANCE ACTIVITIES

Since 1950 UNRWA has been the main provider of relief, health, education and social services for Palestine refugees in Lebanon, Syria, Jordan, the West Bank and the Gaza Strip. To be eligible for assistance, a refugee must reside in one of the five areas in which UNRWA operates and be in need. A refugee's descendants who fulfil certain criteria are also eligible for UNRWA assistance. Following the renewal of Arab–Israeli hostilities in the Middle East in June 1967, hundreds of thousands of people fled from the fighting and from Israeli-occupied areas to east Jordan, Syria and Egypt. UNRWA provided emergency relief for displaced refugees and was additionally empowered by a UN General Assembly resolution to provide 'humanitarian assistance, as far as practicable, on an emergency basis and as a temporary measure' for those persons other than Palestine refugees who were newly displaced and in urgent need. In practice, UNRWA lacked the funds to aid the other displaced persons and the main burden of supporting them devolved on the Arab governments concerned. UNRWA's emergency humanitarian support activities for Palestinian refugees include the provision of basic food and medical supplies; the implementation of a programme of emergency workdays, which aims to provide employment and income for labourers with dependants, while improving the local infrastructure; the provision of extra schooling days to make up for those missed because of the conflict, trauma counselling for children, and post-injury rehabilitation; and the reconstruction of shelters. In June 2004 UNRWA and the Swiss Government hosted an international conference, convened in Geneva, aimed at addressing the humanitarian needs of Palestinian refugees; further to a decision of the conference a Department of Infrastructure and Camp Improvement was established at UNRWA headquarters, to address the deteriorating living conditions in many camps. In recent years diminishing funding has necessitated a retrenchment of the Agency's assistance activities, with the average annual spending per refugee falling by about one-half since 1975.

At 1 July 2013 UNRWA was providing essential services to 5.0m. registered refugees, and 373,624 other registered persons. Of the total number of registered refugees, about 29% were living in 58 camps serviced by the Agency (of which 19 were in the West Bank; 12 in Lebanon; 10 in Jordan; nine in Syria; and eight in Gaza), while the remaining refugees had settled in local towns and villages of the host countries. UNRWA's three principal areas of activity are 'Acquired knowledge and skills', 'A long and healthy life', and 'A decent standard of living'. Some 82% of the Agency's 2014–15 regular budget was devoted to these three operational programmes.

In the 2012/13 school year there were 491,641 pupils enrolled in 703 UNRWA schools, and 22,701 educational staff. UNRWA also operated nine vocational and teacher-training centres, which provided a total of 7,024 training places, and two other educational sciences faculties. Technical co-operation for the Agency's education programme is provided by UNESCO. In March 2012 UNRWA convened an international conference in Brussels, Belgium, on the theme 'Engaging Youth: Palestine Refugees in a Changing Middle East', and published a list of 10 'Youth Commitments' through which the Agency was to strengthen its support to young Palestinian refugees. These included: expanding a pilot skills programme; providing enhanced vocational training and micro-finance opportunities; promoting fundraising towards scholarships; and increasing co-operation with global youth initiatives.

At 1 July 2013 there were 138 primary health care units providing outpatient medical care, disease prevention and control, maternal and child health care and family planning services, of which 108 also offered dental care and a further 124 had laboratory services. At that time the number of health staff totalled 3,011. UNRWA also operates a hospital in the West Bank and offers assistance towards emergency and other secondary treatment, mainly through contractual agreements with non-governmental and private hospitals. Technical assistance for the health programme is provided by the World Health Organization (WHO). UNRWA offers mental health care to refugees, in particular children, experiencing psychological stress. The Agency aims to provide essential environmental health services. Nearly all camp shelters are connected to water networks, and nearly 90% are connected to sewerage networks.

'Decent standard of living' services comprise the distribution of food rations, the provision of emergency shelter and the organization of welfare programmes for the poorest refugees (at 1 July 2013 some 294,736 refugees, or nearly 6% of the total registered refugee population, were eligible to receive special social safety net assistance; of these, 107,354 resided in the Gaza Strip). In 2013 UNRWA provided technical and financial support to 59 women's programme centres and 35 community-based rehabilitation centres.

In order to encourage Palestinian self-reliance the Agency issues grants to ailing businesses and loans to families who qualify as special hardship cases. UNRWA's microfinance programme, launched in 1991, promotes income-generating opportunities for Palestinian refugees as well as for low-income communities living near refugee populations. Under the programme (available to refugees in the Occupied Territories, Jordan and Syria) credit and complimentary financial services are extended to small- and micro-business owners, and to households, with the objective of creating sustainable employment, and with a particular focus on empowering women and children. By July 2013 some 311,142 loans, with a total estimated value of US $350m., had been awarded under the programme.

UNRWA Microfinance Department Headquarters: POB 19149, Jerusalem; 21 Zalman Sharagi St, Sheikh Jarrah Qtr, East Jerusalem; tel. (2) 5890221; fax (2) 5890230; the microfinance programme also operates through national field offices and several local branch offices; announced in Feb. 2012 a new 'Mubadarati' initiative that was to provide loans to young entrepreneurs in the West Bank and Gaza.

RECENT EMERGENCIES

From the commencement, in 2000, of the so-called second Palestinian al-Aqsa *intifada*, and Israel's restriction from that time on the issuing of permits to enter or leave Gaza to only medical humanitarian cases, UNRWA became the lead agency with responsibility for the co-ordination and delivery of emergency assistance, as well as for monitoring the immediate needs of the local populations, and launched successive emergency appeals for assistance to Palestinian refugees in Gaza and the West Bank. The UNRWA Commissioner-General repeatedly expressed deep concern at the worsening humanitarian situation in the Palestinian territories, at the demolition of homes in Gaza and the West Bank by Israeli military forces, at the entry restrictions imposed by Israel against the Gaza Strip, which were causing extreme food shortages, and at restrictions on the movements of UN international staff within Gaza, which were severely impeding the Agency's activities. UNRWA repeatedly expressed concern at the construction by Israel, from 2002, of the West Bank security fence, or barrier, which was estimated to affect some 200,000 people through loss of land, water, agricultural resources and education, and hindered UNRWA's ability to provide and distribute humanitarian assistance. UNRWA has continued to monitor closely the construction and impact of the barrier.

From 2008–14 UNRWA was overseeing the rehabilitation of the Nahr el-Bared camp in Lebanon, which had been extensively damaged from May 2007 by fighting between Lebanese government and rebel forces; the reconstruction of the camp was to provide 5,000 houses, 1,500 shops, six school complexes and sufficient public space, with the aim of accommodating 27,000 Palestinian refugees.

In late December 2008, in response to the intensive bombardment of the Gaza Strip by Israeli forces that commenced at that time with the stated aim of ending rocket attacks launched by Hamas and other militant groups on Israeli targets, the UNRWA Commissioner-General expressed horror at the extensive destruction and loss of life caused by the Israeli action and, while recognizing Israel's legitimate security concerns, urged the Israeli military to cease the bombardment and to respect all international conventions regarding the protection of non-combatants in times of conflict to which Israel is a signatory. At the end of December UNRWA reported that Israeli air strikes had inflicted significant damage to Gaza's fragile infrastructure and had destroyed its public service capacity. The Agency, which had suspended its food assistance during the second half of December owing to insufficient supplies, demanded that border crossings be reopened permanently. At the beginning of January 2009 Israeli forces initiated a ground invasion of Gaza.

In early January 2009 the UN Secretary-General urged an immediate ceasefire in Gaza and denounced as unacceptable recent Israeli attacks on three UNRWA-run schools that had resulted in a substantial number of civilian fatalities and injuries. At that time around 25 UNRWA schools were serving as temporary shelters to Palestinians who had been displaced by the ongoing violence. Soon afterwards UNRWA suspended its movements through Gaza (including food distribution) owing to Israeli air strikes on humanitarian convoys that had caused several fatalities. On 8 January the UN Security Council demanded an immediate ceasefire in Gaza, culminating in the full withdrawal of Israeli forces; the unimpeded provision throughout Gaza of food, fuel and medical treatment; improved international arrangements to prevent arms and ammunition smuggling; intra-Palestinian reconciliation; and renewed efforts to achieve a comprehensive long-term peace between Israel and Palestine. In mid-January UNRWA's field headquarters in Gaza was struck and set alight by Israeli shells that reportedly contained incendiary white phosphorus; the UN Secretary-General protested strongly against the attack. On 18 January Israel ceased hostilities and completed a withdrawal from the territory a few days later. By that time the Israeli offensive had reportedly killed 1,340 people in Gaza (including 460 children and 106 women), and had wounded some 5,320 people (including 1,855 children and 795 women). At the height of the crisis UNRWA provided refuge for 50,896 Palestinians in 50 shelters. In early March the UN Secretary-General appealed to international donors participating in the International Conference on the Palestinian Economy and Gaza Reconstruction, convened in Sharm el-Sheikh, Egypt, for contributions to support and rebuild Gaza.

At the end of May 2010 the UNRWA Commissioner-General and the UN Special Co-ordinator for the Middle East Peace Process issued a joint statement strongly condemning an attack perpetrated at that time by Israeli security forces against a flotilla of vessels that was travelling through international waters with the aim of carrying humanitarian aid to Gaza; the Israeli action resulted in the deaths of nine civilians. The joint statement stressed that such fatalities would be avoidable if Israel were to terminate its blockade of Gaza.

Air and naval strikes by the Israeli security forces, as well as incursions into the Gaza Strip and search and arrest operations in refugee camps, continued to be reported during 2011–13, and during 2013 several incidents of settler-on-settler violence were reported in the West Bank. Owing to political instability in Egypt during 2013 the Gaza Strip became further isolated and its resources further strained. Significantly reduced movements were reported at the Rafah border linking the Strip with Egypt, and from mid-2013 the Egyptian authorities initiated a campaign to destroy, on security grounds, a series of underground tunnels that had, since the imposition in June 2007 of the Israeli blockade on Gaza, represented illegal entry points through which some essential fuel, construction materials and consumer goods had been delivered. During the second half of 2013 construction activities in Gaza consequently slowed, and fuel costs escalated. UNRWA's 2014 Emergency Appeal (for US $300m.), issued in December 2013, to fund activities in support of Palestinian refugees in the Gaza Strip (to which $254m. of the total was allocated) and the West Bank ($45m.), recognized the following three strategic objectives: mitigating the increase of food insecurity among already food-insecure refugees and those facing acute shocks; upholding the rights of refugees facing acute crises and violations of international humanitarian law; and ensuring effective implementation of the Agency's humanitarian response, in co-ordination with relevant stakeholders. The Appeal document noted that some 56% Palestinian refugee households in Gaza were food-insecure at that time, with a further 14% vulnerable to food insecurity, and that in 2012 the rate of unemployment among refugees in Gaza had stood at 32.7%, representing one of the highest levels in the world, with some 55.9% of young people in the territory reported to be unemployed. During 2014 UNRWA, jointly with the World Food Programme, was to pilot a new emergency food and voucher assistance system in the West Bank, aimed at meeting the basic food requirements of some 10,000 food-insecure refugee households. Meanwhile, emergency cash-for-work assistance activities, offering both skilled and unskilled positions, were also to be offered there, placing a strong emphasis on the inclusion of female refugees. During 2014 the Agency was to seek to meet the basic food requirements of some 790,000 food-insecure refugees in Gaza, aiming to ensure that the 'abject poor' received 78% and the 'absolute poor' 40% of daily calorific requirements. Small school meals were to be provided for some 240,000 children in Gaza through an ongoing school feeding programme, and the nutritional needs of pregnant women and infants under two years of age were to be prioritized. 'Summer fun weeks', aimed at strengthening the emotional, mental and physical coping capabilities and resilience of some 130,000 refugee schoolchildren, were to be funded in Gaza.

In 2014 UNRWA was working to provide essential services and supplies to conflict-affected Palestinian refugees in Syria. Following the emergence of civil conflict in that country, in early 2011, the Syrian authorities ceased to provide health services to resident Palestinian refugees, leaving UNRWA as the sole health service provider. At December 2013 540,000 Palestinian refugees remained in Syria, of whom 270,000 were displaced (the majority of these in the Damascus area), and 440,000 were deemed by the Agency to require urgent humanitarian assistance. An estimated 80,000 Palestinian refugees were reported to have fled to neighbouring countries, or beyond, by that time. In December 2013 UNRWA appealed, through its Syria Regional Crisis Response Plan, for US $417.4m. to support emergency activities during January–December 2014 relating to Palestinian refugees within Syria (who were to be allocated $310m.), as well as those who had fled Syria to alternative refuge in Lebanon ($90.4m.) and in Jordan ($14.6m.); furthermore $2.4m. was to fund regional management and emergency response activities in respect of Palestinian refugees from Syria who were sheltering elsewhere in the region. During 2014 the Agency aimed to provide cash assistance for food security, non-food items (NFIs) and shelter to 539,000 (nearly all) Palestinian refugees in Syria; to supply NFI kits (covering bedding, clothes and hygiene) to 244,340 of the Palestinian refugees; to give a monthly ration of basic food commodities to up to 440,000 refugees, as well as daily school meals for 45,000 schoolchildren; and to provide shelter support to 109,940 Syria-based Palestinians.

In November 2013 the UNRWA Commissioner-General stated that six of the 12 camps in Syria accommodating Palestinian refugees had become 'battlegrounds' in the ongoing civil war, and were frequently inaccessible to UNRWA personnel. The Agency has repeatedly urged the Syrian authorities to afford protection to all civilians, including refugees, to ensure the safety of humanitarian personnel, and to comply with its obligations under international law. During November UNRWA reiterated an appeal to be allowed access to an estimated 18,000 refugees still residing in Yarmouk, a suburb of Damascus, to whom the delivery of humanitarian assistance had been prevented since July. It was reported in December that since September at least 15 Palestinian refugees had died of hunger at Yarmouk, and a further 89 reportedly starved in the first five weeks of 2014. At the end of January 2014 UNRWA succeeded in distributing milk for infants, bread and food parcels to 1,026 refugee families there.

Statistics

REFUGEES REGISTERED WITH UNRWA*
(1 July 2013)

Country	Number	% of total
Jordan	2,034,527	40
Gaza Strip	1,221,110	24
West Bank	748,899	17
Syria	507,904	10
Lebanon	444,480	9
Total	4,976,920	100

* Additionally, UNRWA was providing assistance at to some 373,624 eligible other registered persons.

Finance

UNRWA is financed almost entirely by voluntary contributions from governments and the European Union, the remainder being provided by UN bodies, non-governmental organizations, business corporations and private sources, which also contribute to extra-budgetary activities. UNRWA's projected regular budget for 2014–15, covering recurrent expenditure on sectoral activities, totalled US $1,362m., of which 52% was allocated to the sector 'Acquired knowledge and skills', 19% to 'A long and healthy life', and 11% to a 'Decent standard of living'. The ongoing crisis in Syria has placed extreme pressure on the Agency's resources.

Publications

Annual Report of the Commissioner-General of UNRWA.

Reports on labour markets, microfinance, youth outreach, etc.

United Nations Training and Research Institutes

United Nations Institute for Disarmament Research—UNIDIR

Address: Palais des Nations, 1211 Geneva 10, Switzerland.

Telephone: 229173186; **fax:** 229170176; **e-mail:** unidir@unog.ch; **internet:** www.unidir.org.

UNIDIR was established by the General Assembly in 1980 to undertake independent research on disarmament and related problems, particularly international security issues. UNIDIR's statute as an autonomous institution within the UN became effective on 1 January 1985. The Director of UNIDIR reports annually to the General Assembly on the activities of the Institute. The UN Secretary-General's Advisory Board on Disarmament Studies functions as UNIDIR's Board of Trustees.

The work of the Institute is based on the following objectives: to provide the international community with more diversified and complete data on problems relating to international security, the armaments race and disarmament in all fields; to promote informed participation by all states in disarmament efforts; to assist ongoing negotiations on disarmament, and continuing efforts to ensure greater international security at a progressively lower level of armaments, in particular nuclear weapons, by means of objective studies and analyses; and to conduct long-term research on disarmament in order to provide a general insight into the problems involved and to stimulate new initiatives for negotiations. UNIDIR's activities are grouped into the following five programmatic areas: weapons of mass destruction; weapons of societal disruption; security and society; emerging threats; and improving processes and practices.

The work programme of UNIDIR is reviewed annually and is subject to approval by its Board of Trustees. UNIDIR organizes conferences, workshops and seminars on a range of issues; in 2014 these included space security and cyber stability. Examples of ongoing research projects in 2014 include: Transparency and Accountability in Nuclear Disarmament; Measuring, Prioritizing and Evaluating Efforts to Implement Small Arms and Light Weapons (SALW) controls; Technological Development and Autonomy: the Implications of Drones and Robots for Security and Arms Control; Humanitarian Impact of Nuclear Weapons (phase II); Facilitating the Process for the Development of an International Code of Conduct for Outer Space Activities; and Understanding Disarmament. Research projects are conducted within the Institute, or commissioned to experts or research organizations. The Institute offers a research fellowship programme focusing on topics relating to regional security. UNIDIR maintains a database on research institutes (DATARIs) in the field of international security.

The Institute organizes (jointly with the Quaker United Nations Office and the Centre on Conflict, Development and Peacebuilding of the Graduate Institute of International and Development Studies) the Geneva Forum, which aims to serve as a focal point for discussion of disarmament and arms control issues, engaging government and non-governmental officials, UN personnel, media representatives and academics.

UNIDIR supported the preparatory meetings that led to the UN Conferences on the Arms Trade Treaty (ATT) that were held in July 2012 and March 2013, both in New York, USA, in pursuit of the development of a legally binding instrument to guide the import, export and transfer of conventional weapons. The March 2013 gathering failed to achieve consensus among all 193 UN member states on the text of the finalized treaty. Nevertheless, in early April the ATT was presented to the UN General Assembly, where it was adopted by a majority of member states. The ATT (which required 50 ratifications to enter into force, and by April 2014 had 118 signatories and 31 states parties) aims to ban weapons trading conducted in violation of arms embargoes; where weapons might be used in perpetrating acts of genocide or terrorism, or other crimes against humanity; or where they might enter the black market. The Treaty's scope covers battle tanks, armoured combat vehicles, attack helicopters, combat aircraft, large-calibre artillery systems, warships, missiles and missile launchers, and small arms and light weapons.

UNIDIR is financed mainly by voluntary contributions from governments and public or private organizations. A contribution to the costs of the Director and staff may be provided from the UN regular budget.

Director: THERESA A. HITCHENS (USA).

Publications: *Annual Report*, *Disarmament Forum* (quarterly), *UNIDIR Highlights*, research reports (6 a year), research papers (irregular).

United Nations Institute for Training and Research—UNITAR

Address: Palais des Nations, 1211 Geneva 10, Switzerland.

Telephone: 229178400; **fax:** 229178047; **e-mail:** info@unitar.org; **internet:** www.unitar.org.

UNITAR was established in 1963, as an autonomous body within the UN, in order to provide training for diplomats and other officials and to enhance the effectiveness of the UN. UNITAR's training activities, including seminars, workshops, distance and online training, and fellowships, are now open to any professional working in the relevant field. UNITAR has offices in New York, USA, in Hiroshima, Japan, and in Brasília, Brazil, to provide specialist or regional training activities.

UNITAR's Training Department is focused on three main areas of activity: peace, security and diplomacy; environment; and governance. The Peace, Security and Diplomacy Unit incorporates programmes on multilateral diplomacy, international law, peacemaking and conflict prevention, and peacekeeping training. The Environment Unit manages programmes concerning environmental governance and law, chemicals and waste management, climate change, and biodiversity. Within the Governance Unit are programmes on public finance and trade, and on e-governance. The Unit also administers the Decentralized Co-operation Programme, which operates partly through a network of International Training Centres for Local Actors (CIFAL) to train local authorities in issues relating to sustainable development, the efficient management of local services, and urbanization.

UNITAR's Research Department is concerned with the application of new technologies to training and knowledge systems innovation. It administers the UNITAR Operational Satellite Applications Programme (UNOSAT) which aims to ensure that information from satellite earth observation is available and used effectively by relief and development organizations, as well as to help to monitor human rights and security and to support territorial planning. UNOSAT's humanitarian rapid mapping service, developed in 2003, provides rapid acquisition and processing of satellite imagery for use by agencies co-ordinating emergency relief, as well as recovery and rehabilitation efforts.

UNITAR organizes the annual retreats of the UN Secretary-General, and of the Departments of Peacekeeping Operations and of Political Affairs. The Institute also organizes an annual seminar of the Special Representatives of the UN Secretary-General. UNITAR's Geneva Lecture Series, inaugurated in April 2008, aims to generate public awareness and engage leading personalities in a consideration of global challenges; Martti Ahtisaari, the former President of Finland, and José Ramos-Horta, the former President of Timor-Leste, jointly presented the 2013 session, convened in November on means of securing peace.

In February 2013 UNITAR, with the UN Environment Programme, the International Labour Organization and the UN Industrial Development Organization, launched the Partnership for Action on Green Economy (PAGE), which aimed, over the period 2013–20, to support 30 countries in developing national green economy strategies aimed at generating employment and skills, promoting clean technologies, and reducing environmental risks and poverty.

UNITAR is financed by voluntary contributions from UN member states, by donations from foundations and other non-governmental sources, and by income generated by its Reserve Fund.

Executive Director a.i.: SALLY FEGAN-WYLES (Ireland).

United Nations Interregional Crime and Justice Research Institute—UNICRI

Address: Viale Maestri del Lavoro 10, 10127 Turin, Italy.

Telephone: (011) 6537111; **fax:** (011) 6313368; **e-mail:** information@unicri.it; **internet:** www.unicri.it.

The Institute was established in 1968 as the United Nations Social Defence Research Institute. Its present name was adopted in 1989. The Institute undertakes research, training and information activities in the fields of crime prevention and criminal justice, at international, regional and national levels. UNICRI maintains a Liaison Office in Rome, Italy, to strengthen collaboration with local institutions and civil bodies and with UN agencies.

In collaboration with national governments, UNICRI aims to establish a reliable base of knowledge and information on organized and emerging crime; to identify strategies for the prevention and control of crime, within the framework of contributing to socio-economic development and protecting human rights; and to design systems to support policy formulation, implementation and evaluation. The Institute has the following thematic areas of activity: countering the threat of organized crime to security and development; increasing the efficiency of criminal justice systems and protection of vulnerable groups; promoting international criminal law and practice; sharing best practices, building capacity to promote human rights and improving access to services; security governance and countering the appeal of terrorism; and training and advanced education: building capacity in crime prevention and criminal justice. Areas of focus in 2014 included chemical, biological, radiological and nuclear risks mitigation; cyber crime; illicit trafficking in precious metals; environmental crime, including countering electronic waste ('waste electrical and electronic equipment'—WEEE); urban security; security during major events; counter-terrorism; addressing gender issues in drug abuse and its treatment; combating trafficking in women and children; combating counterfeit medicines; domestic violence; and juvenile justice.

The Programme maintains a Security Governance/Counter Terrorism Laboratory, which provides support to the International Permanent Observatory (IPO) on Security during Major Events, as well as other regional security efforts (i.e. an IPO Americas network and the European House of Major Events Security—'the House', a project of the European Union (EU) that commenced in 2012); and participates in the UN Counter-Terrorism Implementation Task. The Security Governance/Counter Terrorism Laboratory has three regional offices (inaugurated in 2009): in Lucca, Italy, to specialize in dialogue and innovation; in Lisbon, Portugal, to promote technical projects on public/private partnerships; and in Boston, USA, to focus on security in the urban environment. Jointly with the International Maritime Organization, UNICRI maintains a database on court decisions related to acts of maritime piracy. UNICRI manages a Training and Advanced Education Department, which administers educational courses, a summer school on migration, and a Masters of Law in International Crime and Justice. In June 2009 UNICRI opened an office at the University of Pomezia, Italy, to conduct postgraduate, master's and other specialized training courses. UNICRI, with the International Criminal Tribunal for the former Yugoslavia and the OSCE Office for Democratic Institutions and Human Rights, supports the EU-funded War Crimes Justice Project, aimed at strengthening the capacity of national judiciaries in the Balkans to process war crimes trials.

UNICRI organizes workshops and conferences, and promotes the exchange of information through its international documentation centre on criminology.

UNICRI is funded by the United Nations Crime Prevention and Criminal Justice Fund, which is financed by voluntary contributions from UN member states, non-governmental organizations, academic institutions and other concerned bodies.

Director: Dr Jonathan Lucas (Seychelles).

Publications: *F3–Freedom from Fear* (online journal, in collaboration with the Max Planck Institute for Foreign and International Criminal Law), *World Criminological Directory*, training materials, reports, research studies.

United Nations Research Institute for Social Development—UNRISD

Address: Palais des Nations, 1211 Geneva 10, Switzerland.

Telephone: 229173020; **fax:** 229170650; **e-mail:** info@unrisd.org; **internet:** www.unrisd.org.

UNRISD was established in 1963 as an autonomous body within the UN, to conduct multidisciplinary research into the social dimensions of contemporary problems affecting development.

The Institute aims to provide governments, development agencies, grass-roots organizations and scholars with a better understanding of how development policies and processes of economic, social and environmental change affect different social groups.

UNRISD research is undertaken in collaboration with a network of national research teams drawn from local universities and research institutions. UNRISD aims to promote and strengthen research capacities in developing countries. Its main focus areas are the eradication of poverty; the promotion of democracy and human rights; environmental sustainability; gender equality; and the effects of globalization. During 2010–14 UNRISD's research agenda 'Social Development in an Uncertain World' covered two main themes: 'social policies for inclusive and sustainable development' and 'political and institutional dynamics of social development'. In February 2013 the Institute published three briefing papers relating to the ongoing formulation of the post-2015 global development agenda, focusing on combating poverty; inequalities; and social policy and employment.

The Institute is supported by voluntary grants from governments, and also receives financing from other UN organizations, and from various other national and international agencies.

Director: Dr Sarah Cook (United Kingdom).

Publications: *Conference News*, *e-Bulletin* (quarterly), *UNRISD News* (2 a year), discussion papers and monographs, special reports, programme and occasional papers.

United Nations System Staff College—UNSSC

Address: Viale Maestri del Lavoro 10, 10127 Turin, Italy.

Telephone: (011) 6535906; **fax:** (011) 6535901; **e-mail:** info@unssc.org; **internet:** www.unssc.org.

In July 2001 the UN General Assembly approved a statute for the College, which was mandated to provide knowledge management, training and continuous learning opportunities for all UN personnel, with a view to developing UN system-wide co-operation and operational effectiveness. The College formally began operations on 1 January 2002. It aims to promote the exchange of knowledge and shared learning, to administer learning and training workshops, to provide support and expert advice, and to act as a clearing house for learning activities. It provides an online orientation course for new UN staff members and provides extensive learning support to the Resident Co-ordinators. A UN Leaders Programme, focusing on strategic leadership theory, practice and skills, was inaugurated in May 2009. In 2014 the College's activities were organized under the following programmes: Development, Gender and Human Rights; Peace and Security; UN Coherence (including a focus on the *Delivering as One* agenda); the UN Leadership Exchange (an annual gathering open to all UN Under-Secretaries-General, Assistant Secretaries-General and Assistant Directors-General); and the UN Learning Lab (focusing on the application of innovation and technology to knowledge management)

The UNSSC is financed by a combination of course fees, voluntary grants from governments and contributions in kind from various UN organizations in the form of staff secondments.

Director: Dr Jafar Javan (USA).

United Nations University—UNU

Address: 53–70, Jingumae 5-chome, Shibuya-ku, Tokyo 150-8925, Japan.

Telephone: (3) 5467-1212; **fax:** (3) 3499-2828; **e-mail:** mbox@unu.edu; **internet:** www.unu.edu.

The University is sponsored jointly by the UN and UNESCO. It is an autonomous institution within the UN, guaranteed academic freedom by a charter approved by the General Assembly in 1973. It is governed by a 28-member University Council of scholars and scientists, of whom 24 are appointed by the Secretary-General of the UN and the Director-General of UNESCO (who, together with the Executive Director of UNITAR, are ex officio members of the Council; the Rector is also on the Council). The University works through networks of collaborating institutions and individuals. UNU undertakes multidisciplinary research on problems that are the concern of the UN and its agencies, and works to strengthen research and training capabilities in developing countries. It administers joint graduate and international postgraduate courses and organizes an advanced seminar series and a global seminar series, which aims to generate awareness about contemporary global issues and the role of the UN in addressing them. In January 2009 UNU established an Institute for Sustainability and Peace, which integrated the academic activities of two main programme areas: peace and governance; and environment and sustainable development. The Institute aims to promote a transdisciplinary approach to issues affecting human security and sustainability.

The University oversees a network of research and training centres and programmes worldwide, comprising: the UNU Institute for Environment and Human Security (UNU-EHS), based in Bonn, Germany; the World Institute for Development Economics Research (UNU-WIDER) in Helsinki, Finland; the Economic and Social Research and Training Centre on Innovation and Technology (UNU-MERIT) in Maastricht, Netherlands; the International Institute for Software Technology (UNU-IIST) in Macao; the UNU Institute for Natural Resources in Africa (UNU-INRA) in Accra, Ghana (with a mineral resources unit in Lusaka, Zambia); the UNU Programme for Biotechnology in Latin America and the Caribbean (UNU-BIOLAC), based in Caracas, Venezuela; the International Leadership Institute (UNU-ILI) in Amman, Jordan; the Institute of Advanced Studies (UNU-IAS), based in Yokohama, Japan; the UNU International Network on Water, Environment and Health (UNU-INWEH) in Hamilton, Canada; the UNU Programme on Comparative Regional Integration Studies (UNU-CRIS), in Bruges, Belgium; the UNU Food and Nutrition Programme for Human and Social Development (UNU-FNP), based at Cornell University, USA; the UNU International Institute for Global Health (UNU-IIGH), based in Kuala Lumpur, Malaysia; the UNU Geothermal Training Programme (UNU-GTP), UNU Land Restoration Training Programme

(UNU-LRT), and UNU Fisheries Training Programme (UNU-FTP), all in Reykjavík, Iceland; the UNU Institute in Barcelona, Spain (UNU-Barcelona, focusing on globalization, culture and mobility); the UNU Institute for Integrated Management of Material Fluxes and Resources (UNU-FLORES), based in Dresden, Germany; and the International Institute for Software Technology (UNU-IIST), based in Macau. In 1993 the UNU established a research centre focusing on international conflict (INCORE), as a joint project with the University of Ulster, United Kingdom.

The UNU Centre in Tokyo, Japan, co-ordinates much of the activities of the UNU and ensures close co-operation with the UN system. It is also supported by a Vice-Rectorate in Europe, based in Bonn, Germany, which is also responsible for promoting UNU's presence in Africa. In December 2008 the UNU Council approved an initiative to 'twin' institutes, in order to promote greater collaboration between centres in developed and less developed regions. The first twinning arrangement has linked the Institute for Sustainability and Peace with UNU-INRA, in Ghana, and it is envisaged that the UNU Institute for Integrated Management of Material Fluxes and Resources (UNU-FLORES) will be twinned with a planned institute to be based in Maputo, Mozambique.

UNU is financed by voluntary contributions from UN member states.

Rector: Dr DAVID M. MALONE (Canada).

Publications: *Our World 2.0* (online magazine), *UNU Update* (regular online newsletter), *UNU Press Newsletter* (quarterly), journals, abstracts, research papers.

University for Peace—UPEACE

Address: POB 138-6100, San José, Costa Rica.

Telephone: 2205-9000; **fax:** 2249-1929; **e-mail:** info@upeace.org; **internet:** www.upeace.org.

The University was established in 1980 to conduct research on, inter alia, disarmament, mediation, the resolution of conflicts, the preservation of the environment, international relations, peace education and human rights. The Council of the University (the governing body, comprising 17 members) was reconstituted in March 1999, meeting for the first time since 1994, and initiated a programme of extensive reforms and expansion. A programme of short courses for advanced international training was reintroduced in 2001. In 2000 a Centre and Policy Institute was established in Geneva, Switzerland, and an Institute for Media, Peace and Security was inaugurated, with administrative headquarters in Paris, France. In 2001 the World Centre for Research and Training in Conflict Resolution was established in Bogotá, Colombia. In December 2006 UPEACE inaugurated a Human Rights Centre, which aimed to conduct research, education and training in theory and practice of human rights issues. A UPEACE Centre for Executive Education offers seminars and workshops to business executives and other professionals in fields concerning leadership, conflict resolution and peace education. In 2014 regular master's degrees were available in Environment, Development and Peace (also with specializations in Sustainable Food Systems, Climate Change Policy, Environmental Security and Governance, and Sustainable Natural Resource Management); Gender and Peacebuilding; International Law and Human Rights; International Law and the Settlement of Disputes; International Peace Studies; Media, Peace and Conflict Studies; Peace Education; Responsible Management and Sustainable Economic Development; and Urban Governance and Peace.

UPEACE aims to develop a global network of partner institutions. A Central Asia Programme, concerned with education in peacebuilding and conflict prevention in the former Soviet Central Asia, was initiated in 2000. In January 2002 the University launched an Africa Programme, which aims to build African capacity for education, training and research on matters related to peace and security. A UPEACE Academic Advisory Council, mandated to improve the organization of the University's academic programme and build partnerships and networks with other academic institutions for collaboration in the areas of both teaching and research, was inaugurated in May 2003. From 2013 UPEACE offered a Master of Arts (MA) under the Asian Peacebuilders Scholarship (APS) programme, a dual degree with the Japanese Nippon Foundation and the Ateneo de Manila University, the Philippines. An MA dual degree in Natural Resources and Sustainable Development is conducted with the American University in Washington, DC, USA. UPEACE aims to strengthen education capacities in developing countries. In September 2007 UPEACE, in collaboration with the Government of the Netherlands, initiated a programme to promote the teaching of peace and conflict studies in the Horn of Africa, the Middle East and South Asia. In November 2009 UPEACE signed a partnership agreement with the Peace and Sport international forum, based in Monaco, under which both organizations determined to establish a Joint Master's Degree in Sustainable Peace through Sport.

Rector: Dr FRANCISCO R. ARAVENA (USA).

Publications: *Peace and Conflict Monitor*, *Peace and Conflict Review* (2 a year), *African Peace and Conflict Journal* (quarterly).

World Food Programme—WFP

Address: Via Cesare Giulio Viola 68, Parco dei Medici, 00148 Rome, Italy.

Telephone: (06) 65131; **fax:** (06) 6513-2840; **e-mail:** wfpinfo@wfp.org; **internet:** www.wfp.org.

WFP, the principal food assistance organization of the UN, became operational in 1963. It aims to alleviate acute hunger by providing emergency relief following natural or man-made humanitarian disasters, and supplies food assistance in post-disaster situations, and to vulnerable populations in developing countries to improve nutrition and eradicate chronic undernourishment, and to further social advancement through developing assets and promoting the self-reliance of poor families and communities.

Organization

(April 2014)

EXECUTIVE BOARD

The governing body of WFP is the Executive Board, comprising 36 members, 18 of whom are elected by the UN Economic and Social Council (ECOSOC) and 18 by the Council of the Food and Agriculture Organization (FAO). The Board meets four times each year at WFP headquarters, in Rome, Italy.

SECRETARIAT

WFP's Executive Director is appointed jointly by the UN Secretary-General and the Director-General of FAO and is responsible for the management and administration of the Programme. Around 90% of WFP staff members work in the field. WFP administers some 87 country offices, and maintains six regional bureaux, located in Bangkok, Thailand (for Asia), Cairo, Egypt (for the Middle East, Central Asia and Eastern Europe), Panama City, Panama (for Latin America and the Caribbean), Johannesburg, South Africa (for Southern Africa), Kampala, Uganda (for Central and Eastern Africa), and Dakar, Senegal (for West Africa). A Vulnerability Analysis and Mapping (VAM) unit is maintained within the Secretariat.

Executive Director: ERTHARIN COUSIN (USA).

Activities

WFP, which is the frontline UN agency in combating hunger, focuses its efforts on the world's poorest countries, and aims to provide at least 90% of its total assistance to those designated as 'low-income food-deficit'. During 2012 WFP food assistance, distributed through development projects, emergency operations (EMOPs) and protracted relief and recovery operations (PRROs), benefited some 97.2m. people, including 82.1m. women and children, and 6.5m. internally displaced persons (IDPs), in 80 countries. Total food deliveries in 2012 amounted to 3.5m. metric tons. The four principal objectives of WFP's strategic plan governing its activities during 2014–17 were saving lives and protecting livelihoods in emergencies; supporting food security and nutrition and building livelihoods in fragile settings and in the aftermath of emergencies; reducing risk and enabling people, communities and countries to meet their own food and nutrition needs; and reducing undernutrition and breaking the intergenerational cycle of hunger.

Since 2008 WFP has shifted its primary focus from the supply of food towards the provision of food assistance. The implementation, where possible, of targeted cash and voucher schemes as an efficient alternative to food rations, has reduced the Programme's food transportation and storage costs as well as helping to sustain local economies. Vouchers are considered to be relatively easy to monitor, and also may be flexibly increased or reduced depending upon the severity of an emergency situation. There were some 6m. beneficiaries of cash and voucher programmes in 2012. WFP continues to provide basic rations in emergency situations, and special nutrition support where needed. It is WFP policy to buy food as near to where it is needed as possible. In cases where food donations are received, they must meet internationally agreed standards applicable to trade in food products. Basic WFP rations comprise basic food items (staple foods such as wheat flour or rice; pulses such as lentils and chickpeas; vegetable oil fortified with vitamins A and D; sugar; and iodized salt). Where possible basic rations are complemented with special products designed to improve the nutritional intake of beneficiaries. These include fortified blended foods, principally Corn Soya Blend, containing important micronutrients; Super Cereals; ready-to-use foods, principally peanut-based pastes enriched with vitamins and minerals trade-marked as Plumpy'Doz and Plumpy'Sup, which are better suited to meeting the nutritional needs of young and moderately malnourished children; high energy biscuits, distributed in the first phases of emergencies when cooking facilities may be scarce; micronutrient powder ('sprinkles'), which can be used to fortify home cooking; and compressed food bars, given out during disaster relief operations when the distribution and preparation of local food is not possible. Some 9.8m. children were in receipt of special nutrition support in 2012.

WFP aims to address the causes of chronic malnourishment, which it identifies as poverty and lack of opportunity. It emphasizes the role played by women (who are most likely to sow, reap, harvest and cook household food) in combating hunger, and endeavours to address the specific nutritional needs of women, to increase their access to food and development resources, and to promote girls' education. WFP estimates that females represent four-fifths of people engaged in farming in Africa and three-fifths of people engaged in farming in Asia, and that globally women are the sole breadwinners in one-third of households. Increasingly WFP distributes food assistance through women, believing that vulnerable children are more likely to be reached in this way. WFP also urges the development of new food assistance strategies as a means of redressing global inequalities and thereby combating the threat of conflict and international terrorism.

With other UN agencies, governments, research institutions, and representatives of civil society and of the private sector, WFP supports the Scaling up Nutrition (SUN) initiative, which was initiated in 2009, under the co-ordination of the UN Secretary-General's Special Representative for Food Security and Nutrition, with the aim of increasing the coverage of interventions that improve nutrition during the first 1,000 days of a child's life (such as exclusive breastfeeding, optimal complementary feeding practices, and provision of essential vitamins and minerals); and ensuring that nutrition plans are implemented at national level, and that government programmes take nutrition into account. In 2013–14 WFP, FAO, and the International Fund for Agricultural Development (IFAD) were participating in global consultations on formulating a post-2015 development framework in the thematic area of food and nutrition.

The Programme, which is a co-sponsor of the Joint UN Programme on HIV/AIDS (UNAIDS) also focuses resources on supporting the nutrition and food security of households and communities affected by HIV/AIDS, and on promoting food security as a means of mitigating extreme poverty and vulnerability and thereby combating the spread and impact of HIV/AIDS.

WFP is a participant in the High Level Task Force (HLTF) on the Global Food Security Crisis, which was established by the UN Secretary-General in April 2008 with the aim of addressing the global impact of soaring levels of food and commodity prices, and of formulating a comprehensive framework for action. In January 2009 the HLTF determined to establish a Global Partnership for Agriculture, Food Security and Nutrition. During 2009 the long-standing Committee on World Food Security (CFS), open to member states of WFP, FAO and IFAD, underwent reform, becoming a central component of the new Global Partnership; thereafter the CFS was tasked with influencing hunger elimination programmes at global, regional and national level, taking into account that food security relates not just to agriculture but also to economic access to food, adequate nutrition, social safety nets and human rights. WFP participated in a World Summit on Food Security, organized by FAO, in Rome, in November 2009, which aimed to secure greater coherence in the global governance of food security and set a 'new world food order'. WFP, with FAO, IFAD and other agencies, contributes to the Agriculture Market Information System, established in 2011 to improve transparency in agricultural markets and contribute to stabilizing food price volatility. WFP, with FAO and IFAD, implements a food security initiative to strengthen feeding programmes and expand support to farmers in developing countries, the second of nine activities that were launched in April 2009 by the UN System Chief Executives Board for Co-ordination (CEB), with the aim of alleviating the impact on poor and vulnerable populations of the global economic crisis. WFP also solely leads an initiative on emergency activities to meet humanitarian needs and promote security, the seventh of the CEB activities launched in April 2009.

In November 2014 WFP, FAO and the World Health Organization (WHO), in co-operation with the HLTF, and other partners, were to organize the Second International Conference on Nutrition (ICN2, ICN1 having been convened in December 1992), at FAO headquarters in Rome. ICN2, with participation by senior policymakers in areas including agriculture and health, representatives of UN and other international agencies, and of civil society, was to review progress achieved since 1992 towards improving nutrition, and to consider future policy options in that area, taking into account advances in science and technology and changes to food systems.

WFP has developed a range of mechanisms to enhance its preparedness for emergency situations (such as conflict, drought and other natural disasters) and to improve its capacity for responding effectively to crises as they arise. Through its Vulnerability Analysis and Mapping (VAM) project, WFP aims to identify potentially vulnerable groups by providing information on food security and the capacity of different groups for coping with shortages, and to enhance emergency contingency-planning and long-term assistance objectives. VAM—co-ordinated from a dedicated unit at the WFP Secretariat in Rome, and also comprising, in 2014, more than 150 analysts worldwide—produces food security analysis reports, guidelines, reference documents and maps. VAM's online Food and Commodity Price Data Store, launched in 2001, provides data on the most commonly consumed staples in 1,226 markets in 75 countries. The key elements of WFP's emergency response capacity comprises its strategic stores of food and logistics equipment (drawn from 'stocks afloat': ships loaded with WFP food supplies that can be re-routed to assist in crisis situations; development project stocks redesignated as emergency project contingency reserves; and in-country borrowing from national food reserves enabled by bilateral agreements); standby arrangements to enable the rapid deployment of personnel, communications and other essential equipment; and the Augmented Logistics Intervention Team for Emergencies (ALITE), which undertakes capacity assessments and contingency-planning. When engaging in a crisis WFP dispatches an emergency preparedness team to quantify the amount and type of food assistance required, and to identify the beneficiaries of and the timescale and logistics (e.g. means of transportation; location of humanitarian corridors, if necessary; and designated food distribution sites, such as refugee camps, other emergency shelters and therapeutic feeding centres) underpinning the ensuing EMOP. Once the EMOP has been drafted, WFP launches an appeal to the international donor community for funds and assistance to enable its implementation. WFP special operations are short-term logistics and infrastructure projects that are undertaken to facilitate the movement of food aid, regardless of whether the food is provided by the Agency itself. Special operations typically complement EMOPs or longer rehabilitation projects.

During 2000 WFP led efforts, undertaken with other UN humanitarian agencies, for the design and application of local UN Joint Logistics Centre facilities, aimed at co-ordinating resources in an emergency situation. In 2001 a UN Humanitarian Response Depot was opened in Brindisi, Italy, under the direction of WFP experts, for the storage of essential rapid response equipment. Since 2003 WFP has been mandated to provide aviation transport services to the wider humanitarian community. During 2005 the UN's Inter-Agency Standing Committee (IASC), concerned with co-ordinating the international response to humanitarian disasters, developed a concept of organizing agency assistance to IDPs through the institutionalization of a 'Cluster Approach', currently comprising 11 core areas of activity. WFP was designated the lead agency for the clusters on Emergency Telecommunications (jointly with the Office for the Co-ordination of Humanitarian Affairs—OCHA—and UNICEF) and Logistics. A new cluster on Food Security, established in 2011, is led jointly by WFP and FAO, and aims to combine expertise in food aid and agricultural assistance in order to boost food security and to improve the resilience of food-insecure disaster-affected communities.

WFP aims to link its relief and development activities to provide a continuum between short-term relief and longer-term rehabilitation and development. In order to achieve this objective, WFP aims to promote capacity-building elements within relief operations, e.g. training, income-generating activities and environmental protection measures; and to integrate elements that strengthen disaster mitigation into development projects, including soil conservation, reafforestation, irrigation infrastructure, and transport construction and rehabilitation. In all its projects WFP aims to assist the most vulnerable groups (such as nursing mothers and children) and to ensure that beneficiaries have an adequate and balanced diet. Through its development activities, WFP aims to alleviate poverty in developing countries by promoting self-reliant families and communities. No individual country is permitted to receive more than 10% of the Programme's available development resources. WFP's Food-for-Assets development operations pay workers living in poverty with food in return for participation in self-help schemes and labour-intensive projects, with the aim of enabling vulnerable households and communities to focus time and resources on investing in lasting assets with which to raise themselves out of poverty (rather than on day-to-day survival). Food-for-Assets projects provide training in new techniques for achieving improved food security (such as training in new agricultural skills or in the establishment of home gardening businesses); and include, for example, building new irrigation or terracing infrastructures; soil and water conservation activities; and allocating food rations to villagers to enable them to devote time to building schools and clinics. In areas undermined by conflict WFP offers food assistance as an incentive for former combatants to learn new skills and reintegrate into society. In 2012 some 15.1m. people were in receipt of food from WFP as an incentive to build assets, attend training, strengthen resilience to shocks and preserve livelihoods. WFP focuses on providing good nutrition for the first 1,000 days of life, from the womb to two years of age, in order to lay the foundations for a healthy childhood and adulthood. WFP's '1,000 days plus' approach supports children over the age of two through school feeding activities, which aim to expand educational opportunities for poor children (given that it is difficult for children to concentrate on studies without adequate food and nutrition, and that food-insecure households frequently have to choose between educating their children or making them work to help the family to survive), and to improve the quality of the teaching environment. During 2012 school feeding projects benefited 24.7m. children. As an incentive to promote the education of vulnerable children, including orphans and children with HIV/AIDS, and to encourage families to send their daughters to school, WFP also implements 'take-home ration' projects, under which it provides basic food items to certain households, usually including sacks of rice and cans of cooking oil. WFP's Purchase for Progress (P4P) programme, launched in September 2008, expands the Programme's long-term 'local procurement' policy, enabling smallholder and low-income farmers in developing countries to supply food to WFP's global assistance operations. Under P4P farmers are taught techniques and provided with tools to enable them to compete competitively in the market-place. P4P also aims to identify and test specific successful local practices that could be replicated to benefit small-scale farmers on a wider scale. P4P pilot initiatives were undertaken in 20 countries, in Africa, Latin America and Asia during 2008–13, and in 2014 the programme was entering its post-pilot phase; by that time WFP had established links under P4P with some 1,000 farmers' organizations representing more than 1.1m. farmers worldwide.

Since 1999 WFP has been implementing PRROs, where the emphasis is on fostering stability, rehabilitation and long-term development for victims of natural disasters, displaced persons and refugees. PRROs are introduced no later than 18 months after the initial EMOP and last no more than three years. When undertaken in collaboration with UNHCR and other international agencies, WFP has responsibility for mobilizing basic food commodities and for related transport, handling and storage costs.

In January 2010 WFP appealed for US $475.3m. to fund a complex emergency humanitarian operation in response to the earthquake that caused devastation in Haiti in that month. In February WFP hosted a high-level meeting in Rome to launch a global partnership aimed at developing a future food security plan for Haiti, where, even prior to the 2010 emergency, one-third of the population was estimated by WFP to be vulnerable to food insecurity, owing to persistent political and civil unrest, successive natural disasters (including hurricanes), high food prices, and poor infrastructure. The impact of further adverse natural events in 2012, including, in October, Hurricane Sandy, resulted in some 1.5m. Haitians being declared 'severely food insecure' by the end of that year. Prolonged drought in 2013 aggravated the food security crisis. WFP, in response, distributed take-home rations, via schools and health centres, to 200,000 Haitians. During April 2014–March 2017 a $118.6m. PRRO was under way in Haiti that aimed to respond to the needs of more than 2m. affected and at-risk people in the most food insecure and disaster-prone districts, with a focus on saving lives, rebuilding livelihoods and enhancing resilience to shocks.

In March 2011 WFP and the Brazilian authorities inaugurated a Centre of Excellence Against Hunger, in Brasília, Brazil, which aimed to utilize techniques used in a long-term Brazilian initiative known as Fome Zero (Zero Hunger) to support other countries in ending malnutrition and hunger. The Centre is a global reference point on school meals, nutrition and food security. In 2014 its activities were focused on 18 countries in Africa and Asia.

In 2010 and, again, from early 2012, the Sahel region of West Africa (including parts of Niger, Mali, Mauritania, Burkina Faso, Chad, Gambia, northern Nigeria and Senegal) was affected by severe drought, causing acute food insecurity. In early 2012, in response, WFP targeted emergency food assistance at some 3.3m. beneficiaries in Niger, 750,000 in Mali, and 400,000 Mauritanians. The situation in northern areas of Mali was exacerbated from March by violent conflict. Following the conclusion of a peace accord, in June 2013, between the Malian Government and rebels active in northern areas, IDPS and refugees (who had sought shelter in neighbouring countries, mainly Burkino Faso, Mauritania and Niger) began to return to their communities of origin. An EMOP 'Assistance for Crisis-Affected Populations in Mali: IDPs, Host Families and Fragile Communities' was being undertaken during February 2013–December 2014, and aimed to benefit more than 1.3m. food-insecure people throughout Mali, including 900,000 in the northern regions of Gao, Kidal, Mopti and Timbuktu. Meanwhile, WFP's country programme in Mali, initiated in 2008 and ongoing in 2014, was reoriented predominantly towards resilience building activities in the south of the country. From mid-2012 heavy rainfall in Niger devastated food crops, further disrupting food security in that country; a three-year PRRO being implemented there during January 2014–December 2016, at a total cost of US $1,018m. was providing food transfers, and cash and vouchers for some 7m. beneficiaries, and had the following objectives: reducing the impact of seasonal stresses and preventing a peak in acute malnutrition and mortality; increasing access to assets and food through land regeneration, water harvesting and local purchases; supporting integrated safety nets, with a focus on treating acute malnutrition in children under the age of five and in pregnant and lactating women, and on improving access to and retention in education. A $562m. PRRO was assisting 2.6m. vulnerable people in Chad (including refugees from the Central African Republic—CAR) during January 2013–December 2014).

Drought-affected communities in the Horn of Africa are a particular focus of WFP's sub-Saharan Africa activities. By mid-2011, as a result of crop failure and livestock loss following two consecutive seasons of poor rainfall, a severe drought prevailed in the Horn of Africa, with southern Somalia, in particular, a focus of humanitarian emergency. The situation in Somalia was exacerbated by the inaccessibility of extensive rebel-controlled areas, and high food prices which had further limited access to adequate nutrition. During the period July 2011–early February 2012 the UN declared a state of famine in two southern Somali regions. Sufficient rain during October–December 2012, a small reduction in food prices, and the beneficial impact of humanitarian operations improved the food security situation somewhat in Somalia in the first half of 2013. Over the three-year period 2013–15 WFP was implementing a US $917m. PRRO, which targeted 2.9m. beneficiaries in Somalia, with a focus on strengthening food and nutrition security and enhancing resilience. During January 2013–December 2014 a $71m. special operation focusing on the provision of humanitarian air services in Somalia and Kenya was also under way. A PRRO assisting 556,000 refugees in Kenya was being undertaken over the three-year period October 2011–September 2014. WFP had planned to initiate a full PRRO in January 2014 in South Sudan to shift its focus there from emergency to development assistance. Following the outbreak of violent conflict in that country in mid-December 2014, however, WFP launched a $324.1m. emergency operation, covering January–September 2014, to supply food aid to 400,000 vulnerable people. The core recovery-focused elements of the planned PRRO—such as school feeding and food-for-assets activities—were postponed, pending an amelioration in the security situation, while relief elements incorporated into that operation, including food and nutrition support to Sudanese refugees sheltering in South Sudan and IDPs in the disputed Abyei area, were to be implemented immediately. A PRRO being undertaken in Ethiopia during January 2012–June 2015 aimed to improve the nutritional status of 5.9m. beneficiaries, at a total cost of $1,500m.

During January–December 2014 WFP was implementing a US $106.9m. emergency operation that aimed to assist 1.25m. beneficiaries in the CAR where violent conflict had prompted massive population displacement and had adversely affected crop production, livestock, and livelihoods. The operation was to be implemented in two phases: from January–April the urgent provision of food assistance to those in immediate need was to be prioritized; and subsequently WFP was to establish an integrated food and nutrition safety net for moderately food-insecure communities, as well as providing support for basic health and education services.

In June 2013 the Executive Board approved a US $474m. PRRO, covering the period July 2013–December 2015, which targets food assistance to 4.2m. beneficiaries in the DRC, including people displaced by ongoing armed conflict, hard-pressed communities hosting IDPs, and members of other vulnerable malnourished groups, particularly in the provinces of North Kivu, South Kivu, Kasai Occidental, Kasai Oriental, Katanga and Maniema.

In October 2011 WFP initiated an EMOP (costing, by early 2014, US $1,500m.) to assist people affected by the violent unrest within Syria, through the distribution of supplementary food rations covering (from January 2013) 80% of daily energy requirements. In January 2013 the UN declared the humanitarian crisis in Syria to be a system-wide 'Level Three' emergency. Accordingly, by 2014 WFP had increased the number of target beneficiaries of the EMOP from 2.5m. at the start of 2013 to 4.25m. However, maintaining access to all the beneficiaries identified under the programme was—owing to the intensity of the conflict and consequent logistical difficulties—proving highly challenging, as was achieving sustainable funding of the magnitude required to maintain the operation. In 2014 WFP was providing food rations, including canned food, cooking oil, flour, pulses and sugar within Syria, and was also working with UNICEF to provide nutritionally enriching food products to children with, and at risk of, malnutrition. Jointly with UNHCR, WFP was providing emergency fuel support to displacement sites. During July 2012–December 2014 WFP was implementing a logistics and telecommunications augmentation and co-ordination programme in support of operations being undertaken by humanitarian agencies to assist populations affected by the protracted Syrian crisis. The Agency has co-ordinated with other agencies, including UNHCR and the Red Cross, to facilitate rapid relief transport and delivery capabilities there. During the same period an EMOP, costing $1,745m., was being undertaken—within the framework of the UNHCR-led UN inter-agency Syria Regional Response Plan—to provide food assistance to vulnerable Syrians sheltering in nearby Egypt, Iraq, Jordan, Lebanon and Turkey. Beneficiaries of the EMOP (in January 2014 estimated to number 2.7m., including 2.3m. refugees—registered and awaiting registration—and host communities) were given, on a monthly basis, vouchers to purchase food items from local markets, with a view to supporting local economies; the operation also aimed to provide school-feeding assistance to 10,000 Syrian refugee children during each month of its duration. In 2014 WFP continued to refine its emergency preparedness and response in countries receiving Syrian refugees, and was focusing the EMOP towards achieving better targeted, more efficient assistance throughout the region; working with governments, host communities and refugees to define sustainable means of addressing evolving longer-term requirements; and providing support to vulnerable local communities in the refugee-hosting countries. WFP has distributed food vouchers to Syrian refugees sheltering in the large Za'atri camp in Jordan, enabling them to select food items, including fresh produce, from designated camp shops.

WFP estimates that around one-third of Palestinian households (and more than one-half of Gaza Strip residents) are food insecure. A US $1.3m. special operation was under way during June 2013–May 2015 to strengthen the food security co-ordination platform in the Palestinian territories, within the framework of a new UN Food Security Sector for Palestine, established in December 2012. From 1 January 2012–30 June 2014 WFP was implementing a $115m. EMOP to provide food assistance to the non-refugee population of the Gaza Strip (numbering 542,600 people). A PRRO supporting vulnerable and marginalized groups in the West Bank was being undertaken during 1 January 2011–30 June 2014; the $174m. scheme was to help some 324,500 beneficiaries annually, focusing on meeting immediate food needs, enhancing food consumption, and improving dietary diversity, and aimed to promote long-term resilience by supporting the re-establishment of agricultural livelihoods in conflict-affected areas. WFP was implementing an EMOP in Yemen during January 2013–June 2014 to provide emergency food and nutrition support to some 5.1m. food-insecure and conflict-affected people, at a total cost to WFP of $315m. A survey produced in March 2012 by WFP—in conjunction with UNICEF and the Yemen authorities—on the food situation in that country, reported that levels of hunger had doubled since 2009. A PRRO was being undertaken in that country during 1 January 2013–31 December 2014 aimed at providing food assistance to 131,000 refugees sheltering there.

During August 2010–July 2015 WFP was undertaking a development programme aimed at improving access to education for some 370,000 vulnerable children in Tajikistan, and during the period 1 January 2011–31 December 2013 it implemented a project aimed at assisting tuberculosis patients and their families in that country. A development programme to support sustainable school feeding was being undertaken in Armenia during mid-2010–mid-2016.

WFP is active in Afghanistan, where violent conflict and natural disasters (mainly severe drought) have caused massive and protracted population displacement and food insecurity. Restricted humanitarian access, limited institutional capacities, devastated infrastructure, and the country's landlocked geography have contributed to a crisis in which, by early 2014, about one-third of the population were estimated by WFP to be food-insecure. It was envisaged that the withdrawal of international security forces from Afghanistan by the end of 2014 would render the operating environment even more fragile. WFP was implementing a PRRO in Afghanistan during 1 January 2014–31 December 2016, which aimed to assist 3.7m. beneficiaries, at a total cost to the Programme of US $497m. The PRRO aimed to enhance food security and nutrition among IDPs and returnees; natural disaster-affected communities; persons affected by acute economic stresses; communities, families and individuals affected by successive shocks; and moderately malnourished children under five years of age, and pregnant and nursing women. A PRRO, costing $34.8m., was being implemented during January 2013–December 2014 to support relief and recovery activities—benefiting up to 325,000 people annually—in formerly conflict-afflicted areas of Sri Lanka. A PRRO providing food assistance to 8.3m. beneficiaries in Pakistan was being implemented during the period 1 January 2013–31 December 2015, with a particular focus on flood-affected communities in Balochistan, Khyber Pakhtunkhwa, and the Federally Administered Tribal Areas of Pakistan.

The food situation in the Democratic People's Republic of Korea (North Korea) has required substantial levels of emergency food supplies in recent years, owing to natural disasters and consistently poor harvests. During 1995–99 an estimated 1.5m.–3.5m. people died of starvation in North Korea. In August 2005 by the North Korean regime requested that WFP shift the focus of its activities in the country from emergency relief to development activities. However, in June 2008 a WFP/FAO Rapid Food Security Assessment found that North Koreans' access to food had deteriorated significantly since 2007, particularly for urban households in areas of low industrial activity, who had been severely affected by rising food and fuel prices, reductions in food rationing and decreasing rates of employment. WFP subsequently undertook a $503.6m. EMOP during the period September 2008–June 2010, while stating that comprehensive interventions were required to improve agricultural production in North Korea, and that, conditions permitting, humanitarian assistance would be reduced following the expiry of the emergency operation, and a long-term development approach be resumed. Accordingly, in June 2010, a new PRRO was approved, initially covering the two-year period until June 2012. In view of worsening food insecurity caused by high rainfall in 2010 and a harsh winter over 2010–11, the North Korean Government made a formal appeal to WFP in January 2011 requesting emergency food assistance. WFP, FAO and UNICEF conducted an inter-agency rapid food security assessment of the country during February–March. WFP undertook an EMOP covering 1 April 2011–30 June 2012, which aimed to support some 3.5m. vulnerable people (mainly women and children), incorporating and expanding activities launched under the PRRO initiated in June 2010. The PRRO was suspended during the implementation of the EMOP, and was relaunched in July 2012, for a one-year period terminating on 30 June 2013. On the basis of a nutrition survey recently conducted across North Korea, WFP initiated in July 2013 a two-year, $200m. PRRO which was to provide nutritional support to 2.4m. vulnerable North Korean women and children, with a particular focus on young children and pregnant and breastfeeding women.

A PRRO to reduce food insecurity and undernutrition in Myanmar (targeting 1.6m. individuals), at a cost of US $167.7m., was being implemented during the three-year period 1 January 2013–31 December 2015. During 2012–15 WFP was implementing a $69m. country programme in Laos in support of government efforts to reduce childhood stunting and micronutrient deficiencies; the programme was expected to reach 751,000 beneficiaries. In June 2011 WFP approved a country programme for Cambodia covering the period 2011–16, aimed at improving food security. During the period 1 May 2012–30 April 2014 WFP implemented a $73m. PRRO to assist returnees and other conflict-affected households in conflict-affected central Mindanao, Philippines, and to support national capacity development on disaster preparedness and response. The PRRO was strengthened in December 2012 to take into account devastation caused in that month to the region by Typhoon Bopha. In November 2013 WFP launched an EMOP, covering the six months until 13 May 2014, to provide immediate life-saving food assistance (including rice and high energy biscuits), supplementary feeding, and food-for-work and cash-for-work opportunities to some 2.5m. people in the Philippines affected by the so-called super Typhoon Haiyan.

Finance

The Programme is funded by voluntary contributions from donor countries, intergovernmental bodies such as the European Commission, and the private sector. Contributions are made in the form of commodities, finance and services (particularly shipping). Commitments to the International Emergency Food Reserve, from which WFP provides the majority of its food supplies, and to the Immediate Response Account of the IEFR, are also made on a voluntary basis by donors. WFP's projected operational requirements for 2014 amounted to some US $5,857m.

Publications

Cost of Hunger in Africa series.
Emergency Food Security Assessment Handbook.
Food and Nutrition Handbook.
State of Food Insecurity in the World (annually, with FAO and IFAD).
World Hunger Series.
Year in Review.

SPECIALIZED AGENCIES WITHIN THE UN SYSTEM

Food and Agriculture Organization of the United Nations—FAO

Address: Viale delle Terme di Caracalla, 00100 Rome, Italy.

Telephone: (06) 5705-1; **fax:** (06) 5705-3152; **e-mail:** fao-hq@fao.org; **internet:** www.fao.org.

FAO, the first specialized agency of the UN to be founded after the Second World War, aims to raise levels of nutrition and achieve food security for all; to eliminate poverty and facilitate economic and social progress for all; and to promote the sustainable management and utilization of natural resources (land, water, air, climate and genetic) for the benefit of present and future generations. FAO serves as a co-ordinating agency for development programmes in the whole range of food and agriculture, including forestry and fisheries. It helps developing countries to promote educational and training facilities and to create appropriate institutions.

MEMBERS

FAO has 191 member nations; the European Union is a member organization. The Faroe Islands and Tokelau are associate members.

Organization

(April 2014)

CONFERENCE

The governing body is the FAO Conference of member nations. It meets every two years, formulates policy, determines the organization's programme and budget on a biennial basis, and elects new members. It also elects the Director-General of the Secretariat and the Independent Chairman of the Council. Regional conferences are also held each year.

COUNCIL

The FAO Council is composed of representatives of 49 member nations, elected by the Conference for rotating three-year terms. It is the interim governing body of FAO between sessions of the Conference, and normally holds at least five sessions in each biennium. There are eight main Governing Committees of the Council: the Finance, Programme, and Constitutional and Legal Matters Committees, and the Committees on Commodity Problems, Fisheries, Agriculture, Forestry, and World Food Security.

HEADQUARTERS

The Office of the Director-General includes the Office of Evaluation; Office of the Inspector-General; Legal Office; Ethics Office; Office for Communication, Partnerships and Advocacy; and Office of Strategy, Planning and Resources Management. There are Departments covering: Agriculture and Consumer Protection; Economic and Social Development; Fisheries and Aquaculture; Forestry; Natural Resources Management and Environment; Corporate Services, Human Resources and Finance; and Technical Co-operation.

Director-General: Dr José Graziano da Silva (Brazil).

REGIONAL OFFICES

FAO maintains five regional offices (see below), 10 sub-regional offices, five liaison offices (in Yokohama, Japan; Washington, DC, USA; Geneva, Switzerland, and New York, USA: liaison with the UN; and Brussels, Belgium: liaison with the European Union), and more than 130 country offices.

Africa: POB 1628, Accra, Ghana; tel. (21) 675000; fax (21) 668427; e-mail fao-raf@fao.org; internet www.fao.org/world/regional/raf/index_en.asp; a biennial Regional Conference for Africa (ARC) is convened (2014: Tunis, Tunisia, in March); Regional Rep. Bukar Tijani (Nigeria).

Asia and the Pacific: Maliwan Mansion, 39 Phra Atit Rd, Bangkok 10200, Thailand; tel. (2) 697-4000; fax (2) 697-4445; e-mail fao-rap@fao.org; internet www.fao.org/world/regional/rap; a biennial Regional Conference for Asia and the Pacific (APRC) is convened (2014: Ulan Bator, Mongolia, in March); Regional Rep. Hiroyuki Konuma (Japan).

Europe and Central Asia: 1068 Budapest, Benczur u. 34, Hungary; tel. (1) 461-2000; fax (1) 351-7029; e-mail fao-seur@fao.org; internet www.fao.org/europe; a biennial Regional Conference for Europe (ERC) is convened (2014: Bucharest, Romania, in March–April); Regional Rep. Tony Alonzi.

Latin America and the Caribbean: Avda Dag Hammarskjöld 3241, Casilla 10095, Vitacura, Santiago, Chile; tel. (2) 923-2100; fax (2) 923-2101; e-mail fao-rlc@field.fao.org; internet www.rlc.fao.org; a biennial Regional Conference for Latin America and the Caribbean (LARC) is convened (2014: Santiago, Chile); Regional Rep. Raúl Osvaldo Benítez (Argentina).

Near East: 11 El-Eslah el-Zerai St, Dokki, POB 2223, Cairo, Egypt; tel. (2) 3316000; fax (2) 7495981; e-mail fao-rne@fao.org; internet www.fao.org/world/Regional/RNE/index_en.htm; a biennial Regional Conference for the Near East (NERC) is convened (2014: Rome, Italy, in Feb.); Regional Rep. Abdessalam Ould Ahmed (Mauritania).

Activities

FAO focuses on four priority areas of activity: serving as a knowledge network; sharing policy expertise; providing a neutral forum for nations; and bringing knowledge directly to the field. The Organization pursues the following five strategic objectives: helping to eliminate hunger, food insecurity and malnutrition; making agriculture, forestry and fisheries more productive and sustainable; reducing rural poverty; enabling inclusive and efficient agricultural and food systems; and increasing the resilience of livelihoods to disasters. World Food Day, commemorating the foundation of FAO, is held annually on 16 October.

ECONOMIC AND SOCIAL DEVELOPMENT

The Economic and Social Development Department comprises divisions of Agricultural Development; Economics; Statistics; Trade and Markets; and Gender, Equity and Rural Employment. The Department's priority areas of focus are: the world food situation; investment in agriculture; long-term perspectives in agriculture; gender right to food; and food volatility in agricultural markets.

FAO provides a focal point for economic research and policy analysis relating to food security and sustainable development. FAO's long-term commitment to reducing hunger was in recent years based on the objectives of the Rome Declaration on World Food Security and the World Food Summit Plan of Action adopted by the World Food Summit, convened under FAO auspices in November 1996, and aiming to halve by 2015 the number of people (around 800m.) then afflicted by undernutrition; this objective was subsequently incorporated into a Strategic Framework for the period 2000–15 that was approved by the FAO Conference in November 1999, and also into the UN Millennium Development Goals (MDGs). The commitment was further reaffirmed by World Food Summit: Five Years Later, held in June 2002 to review the 1996 conference. In 2013–14 FAO, the World Food Programme (WFP), and the International Fund for Agricultural Development (IFAD) were participating in global consultations on formulating a post-2015 development framework in the thematic area of food and nutrition. In April 2014 the three agencies identified five future targets, to be achieved through the development of innovative partnerships: promoting access to adequate food all year round for all people; ending malnutrition in all its forms with special attention to stunting; making all food production systems more productive, sustainable, resilient and efficient; securing access for all small food producers, especially women, to adequate inputs, knowledge, productive resources and services; and promoting more efficient post-production food systems that reduce by one-half the global rate of food loss and waste. The 2013 edition of the joint FAO-IFAD-WFP annual *State of Food Insecurity in the World* report, released in October, found that, during 2011–13, some 842m. people globally were suffering from chronic malnutrition, of whom around 826m. resided in developing countries.

With a view to countering an escalation from 2006 in commodity prices, FAO launched, in October 2007, an online Global Forum on

Food Security and Nutrition; and inaugurated, in December of that year, an Initiative on Soaring Food Prices, which sought to boost food production in low-income developing countries by improving smallholders' access to agricultural supplies. In April 2008 the UN Secretary-General appointed FAO's Director-General as Vice-Chairman of a High Level Task Force (HLTF) on the Global Food Security Crisis. A High Level Conference on World Food Security and the Challenges of Climate Change and Bioenergy that was hosted in June by FAO adopted a Declaration on Food Security, urging the international donor community to increase investment in rural development, agriculture and agribusiness in developing countries and countries with economies in transition. During 2009 the long-standing Committee on World Food Security (CFS), open to member states of FAO, the WFP and IFAD, underwent reform, becoming a central component of a new Global Partnership for Agriculture, Food Security and Nutrition; thereafter the CFS was tasked with influencing hunger elimination programmes at global, regional and national level, taking into account that food security relates not just to agriculture but also to economic access to food, adequate nutrition, social safety nets and human rights. The CFS appoints the steering committee of the High Level Panel of Experts on Food Security and Nutrition, established in October 2009. In July of that year the FAO Director-General welcomed the Food Security Initiative—with commitments of US $20,000m.—approved in that month by leaders of the Group of Eight (G8) industrialized nations. In November FAO organized a World Summit on Food Security, in Rome, which adopted the Five Rome Principles for Sustainable Global Food Security: (i) investment in country-owned plans aimed at channelling resources to efficient results-based programmes and partnerships; (ii) fostering strategic co-ordination at the national, regional and global level to improve governance, promote better allocation of resources, avoid duplication of efforts and identify response gaps; (iii) striving for a comprehensive twin-track approach to food security comprising direct action to combat hunger in the most vulnerable, and also medium- and long-term sustainable agricultural, food security, nutrition and rural development programmes to eliminate the root causes of hunger and poverty, including through the progressive realization of the right to adequate food; (iv) ensuring a strong role for the multilateral system by sustained improvements in efficiency, responsiveness, co-ordination and effectiveness of multilateral institutions; and (v) ensuring sustained and substantial commitment by all partners to investment in agriculture and food security and nutrition, with provision of necessary resources in a timely and reliable fashion, aimed at multi-year plans and programmes. In November 2014 FAO, WFP and the World Health Organization (WHO), in co-operation with the HLTF, and other partners, were to organize the Second International Conference on Nutrition (ICN2, ICN1 having been convened in December 1992), at FAO headquarters in Rome, Italy. ICN2, with participation by senior policy-makers in areas including agriculture and health, representatives of UN and other international agencies, and of civil society, was to review progress achieved since 1992 towards improving nutrition, and to consider future policy options in that area, taking into account advances in science and technology and changes to food systems.

FAO, with WFP and IFAD, leads an initiative to strengthen feeding programmes and expand support to farmers in developing countries, the second of nine activities that were launched in April 2009 by the UN System Chief Executives Board for Co-ordination (CEB), with the aim of alleviating the impact on poor and vulnerable populations of the developing global economic crisis. In May 2010 FAO launched an online petition entitled the *1billionhungry project*, with the aim of raising awareness of the plight of people worldwide suffering from chronic hunger. In May 2012 the CFS endorsed a set of landmark Voluntary Guidelines on the Responsible Governance of Tenure of Land, Fisheries and Forests in the Context of National Food Security, with the aim of supporting governments in safeguarding the rights of citizens to own or have access to natural resources. The FAO Director-General welcomed a new 'Zero Hunger Challenge' initiative announced by the UN Secretary-General in the following month, which aimed to eliminate malnutrition through measures such as boosting the productivity of smallholders, creating sustainable food systems, and reducing food wastage. In January 2013 FAO and the International Finance Corporation signed a Memorandum of Understanding (MOU) jointly to promote responsible private investment in agribusiness, and to promote the development of economic opportunities for rural communities.

In February 2011 FAO's Food Price Index recorded the highest levels of global food prices since 1990 (reaching 238 points). In June agriculture ministers from G20 countries adopted an action plan aimed at stabilizing food price volatility and agriculture, with a focus on improving international policy co-ordination and agricultural production; promoting targeted emergency humanitarian food reserves; and developing, under FAO auspices, an Agricultural Market Information System (AMIS) to improve market transparency and help to stabilize food price volatility. FAO maintains, additionally to the Food Price Index—which averaged 212.8 points in March 2014—price indices for cereal, dairy, oils and fats, meat, and sugar.

FAO produces studies and reports on agricultural development, the impact of development programmes and projects, and the world food situation, as well as on commodity prices, trade and medium-term projections. It supports the development of methodologies and guidelines to improve research into food and agriculture and the integration of wider concepts, such as social welfare, environmental factors and nutrition, into research projects. In November 2004 the FAO Council adopted a set of voluntary Right to Food Guidelines, and established a dedicated administrative unit, that aimed to 'support the progressive realization of the right to adequate food in the context of national food security' by providing practical guidance to countries in support of their efforts to achieve the 1996 World Food Summit commitment and MDG relating to hunger reduction. FAO's Statistical Division assembles, analyses and disseminates statistical data on world food and agriculture and aims to ensure the consistency, broad coverage and quality of available data. The Division advises member countries on enhancing their statistical capabilities. It maintains FAOSTAT (accessible at faostat.fao.org) as a core database of statistical information relating to nutrition, fisheries, forestry, food production, land use, population, etc. A new Global Land Cover SHARE (GLC-SHARE) database was initiated in March 2014, which was to monitor trends in global land coverage, categorized into: artificial surfaces (accounting for 0.6% of land coverage at that time), bare soils (15.2%), croplands (12.6%), forests (27.7%), grasslands (13%), herbacious vegetation (1.3%), inland water bodies (2.6%), mangroves (0.1%), shrubs (9.5%), snow and glaciers (9.7%), and sparse vegetation (7.7%). GLC-SHARE was also to be utilized in assessing the impact of climate change on food production, and in land-use planning activities. In 2004 FAO developed a new statistical framework, CountrySTAT, to provide for the organization and integration of statistical data and metadata from sources within a particular country. By 2014 CountrySTAT systems had been established in 25 developing countries. FAO's internet-based interactive World Agricultural Information Centre (WAICENT) offers access to agricultural publications, technical documentation, codes of conduct, data, statistics and multimedia resources. FAO compiles and co-ordinates an extensive range of international databases on agriculture, fisheries, forestry, food and statistics, the most important of these being AGRIS (the International Information System for the Agricultural Sciences and Technology) and CARIS (the Current Agricultural Research Information System).

In 1999 FAO signed an MOU with UNAIDS on strengthening co-operation to combat the threat posed by the HIV/AIDS epidemic to food security, nutrition and rural livelihoods. FAO is committed to incorporating HIV/AIDS into food security and livelihood projects, to strengthening community care and to highlighting the importance of nutrition in the care of those living with HIV/AIDS.

FAO's Special Programme for Food Security (SPFS), initiated in 1994, assists low-income countries with a food deficit to increase food production and productivity as rapidly as possible, primarily through the widespread adoption by farmers of improved production technologies, with emphasis on areas of high potential. Under the Programme, which promotes South-South co-operation, some 40 bilateral co-operation agreements are in effect. In 2014 some 62 countries were categorized formally as 'low-income food-deficit'.

FAO's Global Information and Early Warning System (GIEWS), which become operational in 1975, monitors and maintains a database on the crop and food outlook at the global, regional, national and sub-national level in order to detect emerging food supply difficulties and disasters and to ensure rapid intervention in countries experiencing food supply shortages. It publishes regular reports on the weather conditions and crop prospects in sub-Saharan Africa and in the Sahel region, issues special alerts which describe the situation in countries or sub-regions experiencing food difficulties, and recommends an appropriate international response. The publication *Crop Prospects and Food Situation* reviews the global situation, and provides regional updates and a special focus on countries experiencing food crises and requiring external assistance, on a quarterly basis. *Food Outlook*, issued in June and November, analyses developments in global food and animal feed markets.

AGRICULTURE AND CONSUMER PROTECTION

The Department of Agriculture and Consumer Protection comprises the following divisions: Animal Production and Health; Food Safety and Quality; Plant Production and Protection; Rural Infrastructure and Agro-Industries; and the Joint FAO/IAEA Division of Nuclear Techniques in Food and Agriculture.

FAO is concerned to improve crop and grassland and pasture productivity and to develop sustainable agricultural systems. It provides member countries with technical advice for plant improvement, the application of plant biotechnology, the development of integrated production systems and rational grassland management. There are groups concerned with the main field cereal crops, i.e. rice, maize and wheat, which inter alia identify means of enhancing production, collect and analyse relevant data and promote collaboration between research institutions, government bodies and other farm management organizations. In 1985 and 1990 FAO's International Rice Commission endorsed the use of hybrid rice, and it has subsequently assisted member countries to acquire the necessary technology and training to develop hybrid rice production. FAO actively promotes the concept of Conservation Agriculture, which aims to minimize the need for mechanical soil tillage or additional farming resources and to reduce soil degradation and erosion.

FAO is also concerned with the development and diversification of horticultural and industrial crops, for example oil seeds, fibres and medicinal plants. FAO collects and disseminates data regarding crop trials and new technologies. It has developed an information processing site, Ecocrop, to help farmers to identify appropriate crops and environmental requirements.

FAO's plant protection service incorporates a range of programmes concerned with the control of pests and the use of pesticides. Negotiations initiated in 1996 under the auspices of FAO and the UN Environment Programme (UNEP) culminated in September 1998 in the adoption of the Rotterdam Convention on the Prior Informed Consent Procedure for Certain Hazardous Chemicals and Pesticides in International Trade, which required that hazardous chemicals and pesticides banned or severely restricted in at least two countries should not be exported unless explicitly agreed by the importing country. The treaty entered into force in February 2004. In November 2002 FAO launched a revised International Code of Conduct on the Distribution and Use of Pesticides (first adopted in 1985) to reduce the inappropriate distribution and use of pesticides and other toxic compounds, particularly in developing countries. FAO co-operates with UNEP to provide secretariat services for the Convention. FAO has promoted the use of Integrated Pest Management (IPM) initiatives to encourage the use, at the local level, of safer and more effective methods of pest control, such as biological control methods and natural predators.

FAO hosts the secretariat of the International Plant Protection Convention (first adopted in 1951, revised in 1997) which aims to prevent the spread of plant pests and to promote effective control measures. The secretariat helps to define phytosanitary standards, promote the exchange of information and extend technical assistance to contracting parties (181 at April 2014).

FAO's Animal Production and Health Division is concerned with the control and management of major animal diseases, and, in recent years, with safeguarding humans from livestock diseases. Other programmes are concerned with the contribution of livestock to poverty alleviation, the efficient use of natural resources in livestock production, the management of animal genetic resources, promoting exchange of information, and mapping the global distribution of livestock.

The Emergency Prevention System for Transboundary Animal and Plant Pests and Diseases (EMPRES) was established in 1994 to strengthen FAO's activities in the prevention, early warning, control and, where possible, eradication of pests and highly contagious livestock diseases (which the system categorizes as epidemic diseases of strategic importance, such as rinderpest or foot-and-mouth; diseases requiring tactical attention at international or regional level, e.g. Rift Valley fever; and emerging diseases, e.g. bovine spongiform encephalopathy—BSE). EMPRES has a desert locust component, and has published guidelines on all aspects of desert locust monitoring. A web-based EMPRES Global Animal Disease Information System (EMPRES-i) aims to support veterinary services through the timely release of disease information to enhance early warning and response to transboundary animal diseases, including emergent zoonoses. In November 2004 FAO established a specialized Emergency Centre for Transboundary Animal Disease Operations (ECTAD) to enhance FAO's role in assisting member states to combat animal disease outbreaks and in co-ordinating international efforts to research, monitor and control transboundary disease crises. In May 2004 FAO and the World Organization for Animal Health (OIE) signed an agreement to clarify their respective areas of competence and improve co-operation, in response to an increase in contagious transboundary animal diseases (such as foot-and-mouth disease and avian influenza). The two bodies agreed to establish a global framework on the control of transboundary animal diseases, entailing improved international collaboration and circulation of information. In 2006 FAO, the OIE and WHO launched a Global Early Warning and Response System for Major Animal Diseases, including Zoonoses (GLEWS). In October of that year FAO inaugurated a Crisis Management Centre to co-ordinate (in close co-operation with the OIE) the organization's response to major emergencies related to animal or food health.

In June 2011 the FAO Conference adopted a resolution declaring global freedom from rinderpest, following long-term efforts by the FAO-led Global Rinderpest Eradication Programme in pursuit of that goal. FAO and the OIE adopted two resolutions during 2011 relating to the destruction/safe storage of remaining stocks of rinderpest virus and on banning the use of the live virus in research. In July 2013, however, FAO and the OIE, having established a set of strict criteria and procedures, lifted the ban on the use of live rinderpest virus for approved research purposes. In June 2012 a conference convened in Bangkok, Thailand, under the auspices of FAO, the OIE and the Thai Government, endorsed a new Global Foot and Mouth Disease Control Strategy.

In September 2004 FAO and WHO declared an ongoing epidemic in certain East Asian countries of the H5N1 strain of highly pathogenic avian influenza (HPAI) to be a 'crisis of global importance': the disease was spreading rapidly through bird populations and was also transmitting to human populations through contact with diseased birds (mainly poultry). In April 2005 FAO and the OIE established a joint Network of Expertise on Animal Influenza (OFFLU) to exchange data and provide expert technical advice on avian, equine and swine influenza. In the following month FAO, with WHO and the OIE, launched a global strategy for the progressive control of avian influenza. In October 2008, at the sixth international ministerial conference on avian influenza, convened in Sharm el-Sheikh, Egypt, FAO, with WHO, UNICEF, the OIE, the World Bank and the UN System Influenza Co-ordinator, presented a new strategic framework within the concept of a 'One World, One Health' policy focused on caring for the health of animals, humans, and the ecosystems that support them. The framework aimed to advance co-operation with respect to emerging infectious diseases, to strengthen animal and public health surveillance and to enhance response mechanisms. During 2003–14 outbreaks of H5N1 were recorded in 63 countries and territories, and more than 400m. domestic and wild birds consequently died or were culled. FAO warned in January 2013—at which time the virus remained endemic in parts of Asia and the Middle East—that the implementation of global health measures aimed at monitoring and controlling H5N1 and other diseases of animal origin (with particular reference to Peste des Petits Ruminants, affecting goats and sheep) was being put at risk by national budgetary restrictions arising from the ongoing global economic downturn. In 2014 FAO was monitoring, and providing preparedness and response support in relation to, an outbreak that arose in poultry and wild birds in China in early 2013 of the highly pathogenic H7N9 virus. Meanwhile the OFFLU was analysing the genetic sequence of the new virus to determine its characteristics, including its response to antivirals.

In December 2011 the conference of parties to the Convention on Migratory Species (CMS) established a Scientific Task Force on Wildlife and Ecosystem Health, with FAO participation, reflecting the ongoing 'One World, One Health' policy; a Task Force on Avian Influenza and Wild Birds, established under the CMS in August 2005, was to continue as a core focus area within the larger Scientific Task Force.

In December 2013 FAO issued a report entitled *World Livestock 2013: Changing Disease Landscapes*, which stated that in recent years some 70% of new diseases emerging in humans were of animal origin, and frequently related to the increasingly intensive production of and trade in animal-sourced nutrition. The report outlined how agricultural expansion into formerly wild areas, thereby promoting the transfer of pathogens—in both directions—between livestock and wildlife; population growth combined with persisting poverty; and modern globe-spanning food supply chains have affected the emergence of disease, its transference across species boundaries, and its spread. The report recommended a more holistic approach to managing the animal-human-environment interface.

FAO is committed to promoting food quality and safety in all different stages of food production and processing. It supports the development of integrated food control systems by member states, which incorporate aspects of food control management, inspection, risk analysis and quality assurance. The joint FAO/WHO Codex Alimentarius Commission, established in 1962, aims to protect the health of consumers, ensure fair trade practices and promote the co-ordination of food standards activities at an international level. The Commission maintains databases of standards for food additives, and for maximum residue levels of veterinary drugs and pesticides. In July 2001 the Commission agreed the first global principles for assessing the safety of foods derived from biotechnology (i.e. genetically modified—GM—foods), and approved a series of maximum levels of environmental contaminants in food. In June 2004 FAO published guidelines for assessing possible risks posed to plants by living modified organisms. In March 2014 the FAO warned that, as a result of increasing production of GM crops worldwide, and in the absence of an international agreement clarifying mutually accepted standards with regard to the presence of GM organisms (GMOs), rising incidents of low levels of GMOs were being reported in traded shipments of food and animal feed. In 2007 FAO published a *Toolkit* to help countries to develop and implement national systems on biosecurity (i.e. the prevention, control and management of risks to animal, human and plant life and health) and to enhance biosecurity capacity.

FAO aims to assist member states to enhance the efficiency, competitiveness and profitability of their agricultural and food enterprises. FAO extends assistance in training, capacity building and the formulation of agribusiness development strategies. It promotes the development of effective 'value chains', connecting primary producers with consumers, and supports other linkages within the agribusiness industry. Similarly, FAO aims to strengthen marketing systems, links between producers and retailers and training in agricultural marketing, and works to improve the regulatory framework for agricultural marketing. FAO promotes the use of new technologies to increase agricultural production and extends a range of services to support mechanization, including training, maintenance, testing and the promotion of labour-saving technologies. Other programmes are focused on farm management, post-harvest management, food and non-food processing, rural finance, and rural infrastructure. FAO helps to reduce immediate post-harvest losses, through the introduction of improved processing methods and storage systems.

FAO's Joint Division with the International Atomic Energy Agency (IAEA) is concerned with the use of nuclear techniques in food and agriculture. It co-ordinates research projects, provides scientific and technical support to technical co-operation projects and administers training courses. A joint laboratory in Seibersdorf, Austria, is concerned with testing biotechnologies and in developing non-toxic fertilizers (especially those that are locally available) and improved strains of food crops (especially from indigenous varieties). In the area of animal production and health, the Joint Division has developed progesterone-measuring and disease diagnostic kits. Other sub-programmes of the Joint Division are concerned with soil and water, plant breeding and nutrition, insect pest control and food and environmental protection.

NATURAL RESOURCES MANAGEMENT AND ENVIRONMENT

FAO's Natural Resources Management and Environment Department is mandated to provide leadership, knowledge, and technical and policy advice regarding the sustainable use of the planet's land, water, genetic resources and biodiversity; to improve responses to challenges to the global environment that affect food and agriculture, including climate change and land degradation; to address issues related to bioenergy; and to serve as a neutral forum for dialogue on the sustainable use of natural resources. The Department comprises two divisions: Climate, Energy and Tenure, and Land and Water. FAO hosts the secretariat of the Commission on Genetic Resources for Food and Agriculture, established in 1983, with a mandate to address the impact of biodiversity on food and agriculture.

The Climate, Energy and Tenure Division supports member states to develop adaptive capacities in the agriculture, fisheries and forestry sectors to enhance the resilience of agricultural systems to climate change (which increases the risk of crop and livestock failure in fragile ecosystems, causing changing growing conditions and an increase in extreme weather events); and to promote sustainable agricultural practices aimed at reducing the emission of greenhouse gases. The Division serves as the secretariat for FAO interdepartmental working groups on climate change and on bioenergy. Emissions can also be reduced by sustainable agricultural practices. In 2006 FAO established the International Bioenergy Platform to serve as a focal point for research, data collection, capacity building and strategy formulation by local, regional and international bodies concerned with bioenergy. FAO also serves as the secretariat for the Global Bioenergy Partnership, which was inaugurated in May 2006 to facilitate the collaboration between governments, international agencies and representatives of the private sector and civil society in the sustainable development of bioenergy. In 2012 FAO initiated a new Energy-Smart Food for people and climate (ESF) programme, which aims to support states in promoting energy-smart agrifood systems, through the identification, development and implementation of energy, water, food security and climate-smart strategies that promote agricultural growth and rural development. FAO has also developed a Sustainable Bioenergy Support Package, to promote good practices and monitoring of bioenergy development.

FAO aims to enhance the sustainability of land and water systems, and to secure agricultural productivity, through the improved tenure, management, development and conservation of those natural resources. The organization promotes equitable access to land and water resources and supports integrated land and water management, including river basin management and improved irrigation systems. FAO has developed AQUASTAT as a global information system concerned with water and agricultural issues, comprising databases, country and regional profiles, surveys and maps. AquaCrop, CropWat and ClimWat are further productivity models and databases which have been developed to help to assess crop requirements and potential yields. Since 2003 FAO has participated in UN Water, an inter-agency initiative to co-ordinate existing approaches to water-related issues. In August 2012 FAO launched an initiative entitled 'Coping with water scarcity: An action framework for agriculture and food security', which aimed to support the improved management of water resources in agricultural production, including through the development of irrigation schemes, the recycling and re-using of waste water, and the implementation of measures to reduce water pollution.

FAO is concerned with the conservation and sustainable use of plant and animal genetic resources. It works with regional and international associations to develop seed networks, to encourage the use of improved seed production systems, to elaborate quality control and certification mechanisms and to co-ordinate seed security activities, in particular in areas prone to natural or man-made disasters. FAO has developed a World Information and Early Warning System (WIEWS) to gather and disseminate information concerning plant genetic resources for food and agriculture and to undertake periodic assessments of the state of those resources. FAO is also developing, as part of the WIEWS, a Seed Information Service to extend information to member states on seeds, planting and new technologies. In November 2001 the FAO Conference adopted the International Treaty on Plant Genetic Resources for Food and Agriculture ('the Seed Treaty'), with the aim of providing a framework to ensure access to plant genetic resources and to related knowledge, technologies, and—through the Treaty's Benefit-sharing Fund (BSF)—funding. The Seed Treaty entered into force in June 2004, and had 131 parties (130 contracting states and the European Union) by April 2014. The BSF assists poor farmers in developing countries with conserving, and also adapting to climate change, their most important food crops. By 2014 around 1,750 gene banks had been established worldwide, storing more than 7m. plant samples, covering both food crops and related wild variants. In January of that year FAO published a series of voluntary standards to guide the activities of the gene banks.

FAO's Agro-Ecological Zoning (AEZ) methodology, developed jointly with the International Institute for Applied Systems Analysis, is the main tool used for land resources assessment; agro-ecological zones are defined as homogenous and contiguous areas possessing similar soil, land and climate characteristics. FAO's database of Global Agro-Ecological Zones (GAEZ) is updated periodically.

FAO is the UN lead agency of an initiative, 'Education for Rural People', which aims to improve the quality of and access to basic education for people living in rural areas and to raise awareness of the issue as an essential element of achieving the MDGs. FAO also hosts the secretariat of the Global Forum on Agricultural Research, which was established in 1996 as a collaboration of research centres, non-governmental and private sector organizations and development agencies. The Forum aims to strengthen research and promote knowledge partnerships concerned with the alleviation of poverty, the increase in food security and the sustainable use of natural resources. Furthermore FAO hosts the secretariat of the Science Council of the Consultative Group on International Agricultural Research (CGIAR), which, specifically, aims to enhance and promote the quality, relevance and impact of science within the network of CGIAR research centres and to mobilize global scientific expertise.

A High-level Meeting on National Drought Policy, organized in March 2013, in Geneva, Switzerland, by FAO, WMO, and the UN Convention to Combat Desertification, issued a declaration that urged governments to develop and implement national drought management policies consistent with their development objectives, and provided supporting scientific and policy guidance.

FISHERIES AND AQUACULTURE

FAO's Fisheries and Aquaculture Department comprises divisions of fisheries and aquaculture policy and economics; and fisheries and aquaculture resources use and conservation. Fish was estimated in 2014 to be the primary source of protein for 17% of the global population, and for about one-quarter of the populations of 'low-income food-deficit' countries. Aquaculture contributes almost one-third of annual global fish landings (predicted to rise to three-fifths by 2030), and accounts for nearly one-half of fish consumed by humans (forecast at two-thirds by 2030). FAO reported record global production, of 160m. metric tons, in 2013 from both wild capture fisheries and aquaculture, with exports of fish totalling an estimated US $136,000m. in that year. In February 2014 FAO, the World Bank and the International Food Policy Research Institute issued a report entitled *Fish to 2030: Prospects for Fisheries and Aquaculture*, which emphasized the predominant directional flow in fish exports from developing to developed countries, and predicted that by 2030 China would account for 38% of global consumption of food fish.

FAO undertakes extensive monitoring, publishing every two years *The State of World Fisheries and Aquaculture*, and collates and maintains relevant databases. It formulates country and regional profiles and has developed a specific information network for the fisheries sector, GLOBEFISH, which gathers and disseminates information regarding market trends, tariffs and other industry issues. FAO aims to extend technical support to member states with regard to the management and conservation of aquatic resources, and other measures to improve the utilization and trade of products, including the reduction of post-harvest losses, preservation marketing and quality assurance. FAO works to ensure that small-scale fishing communities (accounting for around 90% of the sector's work force) reap equitable benefits from the dynamic international trade in fish and fish products, and to explore the development of new markets to ensure that maximum economic and nutritional benefits are derived from by-products, such as fish heads, backbones and viscera (which have a particularly high content of essential fatty acids, minerals and vitamins, and therefore can be used in commercial fish oil and mineral supplements, and to combat micronutrient deficiencies in developing countries).

FAO aims to facilitate and secure the long-term sustainable development of fisheries and aquaculture, in both inland and marine waters, and to promote its contribution to world food security. In March 1995 a ministerial meeting of fisheries adopted the Rome Consensus on World Fisheries, which identified a need for immediate action to eliminate overfishing and to rebuild and enhance depleting fish stocks. In November the FAO Conference adopted a Code of Conduct for Responsible Fishing (CCRF), which incorporated many global fisheries and aquaculture issues (including fisheries resource conservation and development, fish catches, seafood and fish processing, commercialization, trade and research) to promote the sustainable development of the sector. In February 1999 the FAO Committee on Fisheries adopted new international measures, within the framework of the Code of Conduct, in order to reduce over-exploitation of the world's fish resources, as well as plans of action for the conservation and management of sharks and the reduction in the incidental catch of seabirds in longline fisheries. The voluntary measures were endorsed at a ministerial meeting, held in March, which issued a declaration to promote the implementation of the Code of Conduct and to achieve sustainable management of fisheries and aquaculture. Several international plans of action (IPOA) have been elaborated within the context of the CCRF: the IPOA for Conservation and Management of Sharks (IPOA-Sharks, 1999); the IPOA for the Management of Fishing Capacity (IPOA-Capacity, 1999); the IPOA for Reducing Incidental Catch of Seabirds in Longline Fisheries (IPOA-Seabirds, 1999); and the IPOA to Prevent, Deter and Eliminate Illegal, Unreported and Unregulated Fishing (IPOA-IUU, 2001). FAO has prepared guidelines to support member countries with implementing IPOAs and has encouraged states to develop national plans of action to complement the international plans. FishCode, an interregional assistance programme, supports developing countries in implementing the CCRF.

In 2001 FAO estimated that about one-half of major marine fish stocks were fully exploited, one-quarter under-exploited, at least 15% over-exploited, and 10% depleted or recovering from depletion. IUU was estimated to account for up to 30% of total catches in certain fisheries. In October FAO and the Icelandic Government jointly organized the Reykjavík Conference on Responsible Fisheries in the Marine Ecosystem, which adopted a declaration on pursuing responsible and sustainable fishing activities in the context of ecosystem-based fisheries management (EBFM). EBFM involves determining the boundaries of individual marine ecosystems, and maintaining or rebuilding the habitats and biodiversity of each of these so that all species will be supported at levels of maximum production. In March 2005 FAO's Committee on Fisheries adopted voluntary guidelines for the so-called eco-labelling and certification of fish and fish products, i.e. based on information regarding capture management and the sustainable use of resources. In November 2009 an Agreement on Port State Measures to Prevent, Deter and Eliminate Illegal, Unreported and Unregulated Fishing, negotiated by the Committee, and denying port access to fishing vessels involved in IUU activities, was endorsed by the FAO Conference. In May 2011 FAO initiated a Technical Consultation on flag state performance, aimed at assessing the performance of flag states, and establishing means of preventing vessels from flying the flags of irresponsible states. Voluntary Guidelines for Flag State Performance were approved by a session of the Technical Consultation that was held in February 2013. FAO was committed to supporting the development of the guidelines and providing assistance to countries to implement them effectively. The guidelines were to be presented to the Committee on Fisheries at its next session in June 2014.

FAO promotes aquaculture as a valuable source of animal protein and income-generating activity for rural communities. It has undertaken to develop an ecosystem approach to aquaculture and works to integrate aquaculture with agricultural and irrigation systems. In February 2000 FAO and the Network of Aquaculture Centres in Asia and the Pacific (NACA) jointly convened a Conference on Aquaculture in the Third Millennium, which adopted the Bangkok Declaration and Strategy for Aquaculture Beyond 2000. In September 2010 FAO and NACA convened the Global Conference on Aquaculture, in Phuket, Thailand, on the theme 'Farming the Waters for People and Food'; the Global Conference adopted a set of recommendations on further advancing aquaculture. In October 2012 development agencies, governments and research institutions launched a new three-year project 'Aquaculture for Food Security, Poverty Alleviation and Nutrition' (AFSPAN)—under FAO management and with funding by the European Union—with the aim of advancing understanding of the role of aquaculture in maintaining food security in poorer countries, and using that knowledge to develop sustainable policies for improving livelihoods. The establishment of a new Global Aquaculture Advancement Partnership (GAAP), comprising governments, UN agencies, non-governmental organizations and private sector interests, and tasked with pursuing sustainable solutions to meeting the growing global demand for fish products, was to be presented to FAO's Committee on Fisheries for approval in June 2014.

In 2014—building on a Blue Economy model that arose from the June 2012 UN Conference on Sustainable Development, and emphasizes sustainable ocean management—FAO was developing a new 'Blue Growth Initiative', through which it was to assist countries with drafting and implementing national Blue Economy and growth agendas.

FORESTRY

FAO's Forestry Department comprises divisions of forest economics, policy and products; and forest assessment, management and conservation.

FAO is committed to the sustainable management of trees, forests and forestry resources. It aims to address the critical balance of ensuring the conservation of forests and forestry resources while maximising their potential to contribute to food security and social and economic development. In March 2009 the Committee on Forestry approved a new 10-year FAO Strategic Plan for Forestry, replacing a previous strategic plan initiated in 1999. The new plan, which was 'dynamic' and was to be updated regularly, covered the social, economic and environmental aspects of forestry. The first World Forest Week, sponsored by FAO, was held in March 2009, and the first World Forest Day, sponsored by FAO and the UN Forum on Forests, was observed on 21 March 2013. In May 2013 FAO hosted an International Conference on Forests for Food Security and Nutrition.

FAO assists member countries to formulate, implement and monitor national forestry programmes, and encourages the participation of all stakeholders in developing plans for the sustainable management of tree and forest resources. FAO also helps to implement national assessments of those programmes and of other forestry activities. At a global level FAO undertakes surveillance of the state of the world's forests and publishes a report every two years. A separate *Forest Resources Assessment* is published every five years; the process to compile the 2015 edition was initiated in June 2011. In 2012 FAO issued a report on *The State of the World's Forest Genetic Resources*. FAO maintains the Forestry Information System (FORIS).

In September 2008 FAO, with UNEP and the UN Development Programme, launched the UN Collaborative Programme on Reducing Emissions from Deforestation and Forest Degradation in Developing Countries (UN-REDD), with the aim of enabling donors to pool resources (through a trust fund established for that purpose) to promote a transformation of forest resource use patterns. In August 2011 UN-REDD endorsed a Global Programme Framework covering 2011–15.

FAO is a member of the Collaborative Partnership on Forests, an informal, voluntary arrangement among 14 agencies with significant forestry programmes, which was established in April 2004 on the recommendation of the UN's Economic and Social Council. FAO organizes a World Forestry Congress, generally held every six years; the 14th Congress was to be held in September 2015, in Durban, South Africa.

TECHNICAL CO-OPERATION

The Technical Co-operation Department has responsibility for FAO's operational activities, including policy and programme development assistance to member countries; the mobilization of resources; investment support; field operations; emergency operations and rehabilitation; and the Technical Co-operation Programme.

FAO provides policy advice to support the formulation, implementation and evaluation of agriculture, rural development and food security strategies in member countries. It administers a project to assist developing countries to strengthen their technical negotiating skills, in respect to agricultural trade issues. FAO also aims to co-ordinate and facilitate the mobilization of extra-budgetary funds from donors and governments for particular projects. It administers a range of trust funds, including a Trust Fund for Food Security and Food Safety, established in 2002 to generate resources for projects to combat hunger, and the Government Co-operative Programme. FAO's Investment Centre, established in 1964, aims to promote greater external investment in agriculture and rural development by assisting member countries to formulate effective and sustainable projects and programmes. The Centre collaborates with international financing institutions and bilateral donors in the preparation of projects, and administers cost-sharing arrangements, with, typically, FAO funding 40% of a project. The Centre is a co-chair (with the German Government) of the Global Donor Platform for Rural Development, which was established in 2004, comprising multilateral, donor and international agencies, development banks and research institutions, to improve the co-ordination and effectiveness of rural development assistance.

FAO's Technical Co-operation Programme, which was inaugurated in 1976, provides technical expertise and funding for small-scale projects to address specific issues within a country's agriculture, fisheries or forestry sectors. An Associate Professional Officers programme co-ordinates the sponsorship and placement of young professionals to gain experience working in an aspect of rural or agricultural development.

FAO was designated the lead agency for directing activities under the International Year of Family Farming (2014), which aimed to reposition small-scale family farming at the centre of national agricultural, environmental and social policies.

The Technical Co-operation Division co-ordinates FAO's emergency operations, concerned with all aspects of disaster and risk prevention, mitigation, reduction and emergency relief and rehabilitation, with a particular emphasis on food security and rural populations. FAO works with governments to develop and implement disaster prevention policies and practices. It aims to strengthen the capacity of local institutions to manage and mitigate risk and provides technical assistance to improve access to land for displaced populations in countries following conflict or a natural disaster. Other disaster prevention and reduction efforts include dissemination of information from the various early warning systems and support for adaptation to climate variability and change, for example by the use of drought-resistant crops or the adoption of conservation agriculture techniques. Following an emergency FAO works with governments and other development and humanitarian partners to assess the immediate and longer-term agriculture and food security needs of the affected population. It has developed an Integrated Food Security and Humanitarian Phase Classification Scheme to determine the appropriate response to a disaster situation. Emergency co-ordination units may be established to manage the local response to an emergency and to facilitate and co-ordinate the delivery of inter-agency assistance. In order to rehabilitate agricultural production following a natural or man-made disaster FAO provides emergency seed, tools, other materials and technical and training assistance. Under the UN's cluster approach to co-ordinating the international response to humanitarian disasters with a focus on core areas of activity, FAO and WFP jointly lead the Food Security cluster, which was established in 2011, and aims to combine expertise in agricultural assistance and food aid to improve the resilience of food-insecure disaster-affected communities. FAO also contributes the agricultural relief and rehabilitation component of the UN's Consolidated Appeals Process (CAP), which aims to co-ordinate and enhance the effectiveness of the international community's response to an emergency. In April 2004 FAO established a Special Fund for Emergency and Rehabilitation Activities to enable it to respond promptly to a humanitarian crisis before making an emergency appeal for additional resources.

FAO Statutory Bodies and Associated Entities

(based at the Rome headquarters, unless otherwise indicated)

Advisory Committee on Fisheries Research: f. 1961 to study, and advise the FAO Director-General on FAO's work in all areas of fisheries research, including conservation and management of inland and marine fishery resources, advancing fish productivity through the advancement of aquaculture and of wild resources, and the utilization of fishery resources for human nutrition; mems: 8 experts selected to represent a broad subject matter and geographical representation.

African Commission on Agricultural Statistics: c/o FAO Regional Office for Africa, POB 1628, Accra, Ghana; e-mail Eloi .OuedraogoATfao.org; f. 1961 to advise member countries on the development and standardization of food and agricultural statistics; 22nd session: Nov.–Dec. 2011, in Addis Ababa, Ethiopia; 37 mem. states.

African Forestry and Wildlife Commission: c/o FAO Regional Office for Africa, POB 1628, Accra, Ghana; e-mail foday.bojang@fao .org; f. 1959 to advise on the formulation of forest policy and to review and co-ordinate its implementation on a regional level; to exchange information and advise on technical problems; 19th session: Feb. 2014, Namibia; 42 mem. states.

Agricultural Market Information System (AMIS): AMIS Secretariat, FAO, Viale delle Terme di Caracalla, 00153 Rome, Italy; tel. (6) 5705-2057; fax (6) 5705-3152; e-mail amis-secretariat@fao.org; internet www.amis-outlook.org; f. 2011 to improve transparency in agricultural markets and contribute to stabilizing food price volatility; a partnership of FAO, the International Food Policy Research Institute, IFAD, OECD, UNCTAD, the World Bank, WFP, WTO, and the UN High Level Task Force on the Global Food Security Crisis (f. 2008).

Agriculture, Land and Water Use Commission for the Near East (ALAWUC): c/o FAO Regional Office for the Near East, POB 2223, Cairo, Egypt; f. 2000 by merger of the Near East Regional Commission on Agriculture and the Regional Commission on Land and Water Use in the Near East; seventh session of ALAWUC held in May 2012, in Cairo, Egypt; 23 mem. states.

Animal Production and Health Commission for Asia and the Pacific: c/o FAO Regional Office, Maliwan Mansion, 39 Phra Atit Rd, Bangkok 10200, Thailand; internet www.aphca.org; f. 1975 to support national and regional livestock production and research; 36th session: Oct. 2012, in Negombo, Sri Lanka; 17 mem. states.

Asia and Pacific Commission on Agricultural Statistics: c/o FAO Regional Office, Maliwan Mansion, 39 Phra Atit Rd, Bangkok 10200, Thailand; e-mail rap-statistics.fao.org; f. 1963; reviews recent developments in agricultural statistical systems, provides a platform for the exchange of ideas relating to the state of food and agricultural statistics in the region; 25th session: Feb. 2014, in Vientiane, Laos; senior officials responsible for the development of agricultural statistics from 25 mem. states.

Asia and Pacific Plant Protection Commission: c/o FAO Regional Office, Maliwan Mansion, Phra Atit Rd, Bangkok 10200, Thailand; f. 1956 (new title 1983) to strengthen international co-operation in plant protection to prevent the introduction and spread of destructive plant diseases and pests; 23 mem. states.

Asia-Pacific Fishery Commission: c/o FAO Regional Office, Maliwan Mansion, 39 Phra Atit Rd, Bangkok 10200, Thailand; f. 1948 to develop fisheries, encourage and co-ordinate research, disseminate information, recommend projects to governments, propose standards in technique and management measures; 20 mem. states.

Asia-Pacific Forestry Commission: internet www.apfcweb.org; f. 1949 to advise on the formulation of forest policy, and review and co-ordinate its implementation throughout the region; to exchange information and advise on technical problems; 29 mem. states.

Codex Alimentarius Commission (Joint FAO/WHO Food Standards Programme): e-mail codex@fao.org; internet www .codexalimentarius.org; f. 1962 to make proposals for the co-ordination of all international food standards work and to publish a code of international food standards; Trust Fund to support participation by least developed countries was inaugurated in 2003; there are numerous specialized Codex committees, e.g. contaminants in foods, food additives, food hygiene, food import and export inspection and certification systems, food labelling, nutrition and foods for special dietary uses, pesticide and veterinary drug residues, spices and culinary herbs, and processed fruits and vegetables; intergovernmental task forces may be appointed; had established by April 2014 212 food standards and 127 guidelines, codes of practice, limits and principles relating to food production and processing; 185 mem. states and the EU; 221 observers.

Commission for Controlling the Desert Locust in Southwest Asia: internet www.fao.org/ag/locusts/SWAC; f. 1964 to carry out all possible measures to control plagues of the desert locust in Afghanistan, India, Iran and Pakistan; 28th session: Dec. 2012, New Delhi, India; 4 mem. states.

Commission for Controlling the Desert Locust in the Central Region: c/o FAO Regional Office for the Near East, POB 2223, Cairo, Egypt; e-mail eclo@fao.org; internet www.fao.org/ag/locusts/en/info/info/index.html; covers north-eastern Africa and the Middle East; reported in Sept. 2012 that limited expansion of the locust population might occur in Red Sea coastal areas of Yemen that had received recent rainfall; 28th session: Nov. 2012, Jeddah, Saudi Arabia; 16 mem. states.

Commission for Controlling the Desert Locust in the Western Region: 30 rue Asselah Hocine, BP 270, Algiers, Algeria; e-mail clcpro@fao.org; internet www.clcpro-empres.org; f. 2002; covers north-western Africa; has implemented a preventive control programme to strengthen locust surveillance and control in member countries (first phase: 2006–11; second phase 2011–14); and has advocated to help member countries to establish autonomous national locust control units; works closely with EMPRES; sixth session: March 2012, Tunis, Tunisia; 10 mem. states.

Commission for Inland Fisheries of Latin America: c/o FAO Regional Office for Latin America and the Caribbean, Avda Dag Hammarskjöld 3241, Casilla 10095, Vitacura, Santiago, Chile; f. 1976 to promote, co-ordinate and assist national and regional fishery and limnological surveys and programmes of research and development leading to the rational utilization of inland fishery resources; 13th session: Dec. 2013, in Buenos Aires, Argentina; 21 mem. states.

Commission on Genetic Resources for Food and Agriculture: internet www.fao.org/ag/cgrfa/en; f. 1983 as the Commission on Plant Genetic Resources, renamed in 1995; provides a forum for negotiation on the conservation and sustainable utilization of genetic resources for food and agriculture, and the equitable sharing of benefits derived from their use; 14th session: April 2013, in Rome; 175 mem. states and the EU.

Commission on Livestock Development for Latin America and the Caribbean: c/o FAO Regional Office for Latin America and the Caribbean, Avda Dag Hammarskjöld 3241, Casilla 10095, Vitacura, Santiago, Chile; f. 1986; 32nd conference: March 2012, in Asunción, Paraguay; 24 mem. states.

Commission on Phytosanitary Measures: f. 1997 as the governing body of the revised International Plant Protection Commission; ninth session of the Commission: March–April 2014, Rome.

Committee for Inland Fisheries and Aquaculture of Africa (CIFAA): c/o FAO Regional Office for Africa, POB 1628, Accra, Ghana; internet www.fao.org/fishery/rfb/cifaa; f. 1971 to promote improvements in inland fisheries and aquaculture in Africa; the 16th session of CIFAA, convened in November 2010, in Maputo, Mozambique, proposed that the role of the Committee should be re-examined; consequently, a working group was established to make recommendations on the future direction of the Committee, and, in March 2012, an FAO-New Partnership for Africa seminar was held in Cape Town, South Africa, to discuss the review of CIFAA; 38 mem. states.

Emergency Prevention System for Transboundary Animal and Plant Pests and Diseases (EMPRES): e-mail vincent.martin@fao.org; internet www.fao.org/ag/againfo/programmes/en/empres.html; f. 1994 to strengthen FAO's activities in prevention, early warning, control and eradication of pests and highly contagious livestock diseases; maintains an internet-based EMPRES Global Animal Disease Information System (EMPRES-i).

European Commission on Agriculture: c/o FAO Regional Office for Europe and Central Asia, 1068 Budapest, Benczur u. 34, Hungary; f. 1949 to encourage and facilitate action and co-operation in technological agricultural problems among member states and between international organizations concerned with agricultural technology in Europe; also monitors the activities of the European System of Cooperative Research Networks in Agriculture (ESCORENA) and the Working Party on Women and the Family in Rural Development (WPW); 38th session: Bucharest, Romania, in April 2014; 54 mem. states and the EU.

European Commission for the Control of Foot-and-Mouth Disease: internet www.fao.org/ag/againfo/commissions/eufmd; f. 1953 to promote national and international action for the control of the disease in Europe and its final eradication; 35 mem. states.

European Forestry Commission: f. 1947 to advise on the formulation of forest policy and to review and co-ordinate its implementation on a regional level; to exchange information and to make recommendations; 27 mem. states.

European Inland Fisheries Advisory Commission: internet www.fao.org/fi/body/eifac/eifac.asp; f. 1957 to promote improvements in inland fisheries and to advise member governments and FAO on inland fishery matters; 27th session: Oct. 2012, in Hämeenlinna, Finland; 34 mem. states and the EU.

Fishery Committee for the Eastern Central Atlantic: f. 1967 to promote improvements in inland fisheries in the Eastern Central Atlantic area between Cape Spartel (Morocco) and the Congo River; 20th session: March 2012, in Rabat, Morocco; 33 mem. states and the EU.

General Fisheries Commission for the Mediterranean: internet www.gfcm.org; f. 1949 (as the General Fisheries Council for the Mediterranean, name changed with adoption of amendments to the GFCM agreement in 1997) to develop aquatic resources, to encourage and co-ordinate research in the fishing and allied industries, to assemble and publish information, and to recommend the standardization of equipment, techniques and nomenclature; covers the Mediterranean, Black Sea and connecting waters; 37th session: May 2013, in Croatia; 23 mem. states and the EU.

Governing Body of the International Treaty on Plant Genetic Resources (Seed Treaty): e-mail pgrfa-treaty@fao.org; internet www.planttreaty.org; f. 2004 to oversee the implementation of the Seed Treaty; fourth session: March 2011, Nusa Dua, Bali; 126 mem. states and the EU.

International Poplar Commission: internet www.fao.org/forestry/ipc/en; f. 1947 to study scientific, technical, social and economic aspects of poplar and willow cultivation; to promote the exchange of ideas and material between research workers, producers and users; to arrange joint research programmes, congresses, study tours; to make recommendations to the FAO Conference and to National Poplar Commissions; 24th session: Oct.–Nov. 2012, in Dehradun, India; 37 mem. states.

International Rice Commission (IRC): internet www.fao.org/ag/irc; f. 1949 to promote national and international action on production, conservation, distribution and consumption of rice, except matters relating to international trade; supports the International Task Force on Hybrid Rice, the Working Group on Advanced Rice Breeding in Latin America and the Caribbean, the Interregional Collaborative Research Network on Rice in the Mediterranean Climate Areas, and the Technical Co-operation Network on Wetland Development and Management/Inland Valley Swamps; in July 2012 27 experts from 22 IRC member countries convened a Global Rice Roundtable, in Le Corum, Montpelier, France, to consider possible future directions of the IRC; 62 mem. states (accounting for around 93% of global rice production).

Latin American and Caribbean Forestry Commission: c/o FAO Regional Office for Latin America and the Caribbean, Avda Dag Hammarskjöld 3241, Casilla 10095, Vitacura, Santiago, Chile; internet www.fao.org/forestry/31106/en/; f. 1948 to advise on formulation of forest policy and review and co-ordinate its implementation throughout the region; to exchange information and advise on technical problems; meets every two years; 28th session: Sept. 2013; 35 mem. states.

Near East Forestry and Range Commission: c/o FAO Regional Office for the Near East, 11 El-Eslah el-Zerai St, Dokki, POB 2223, Cairo, Egypt; f. 1953 to advise on formulation of forest policy and review and co-ordinate its implementation throughout the region; to exchange information and advise on technical problems; 21st session: Jan. 2014, Cairo; 27 mem. states.

North American Forestry Commission: internet www.fs.fed.us/global/nafc/welcome.html; f. 1959 to advise on the formulation and co-ordination of national forest policies in Canada, Mexico and the USA; to exchange information and to advise on technical problems; 27th session: Oct. 2013, USA; 3 mem. states.

South West Indian Ocean Fisheries Commission: c/o FAO Sub-regional Office for Southern Africa, POB 3730, Harare, Zimbabwe; internet www.fao.org/fishery/rfb/swiofc/en; f. 2004 to promote the sustainable development and utilization, through proper management, of living marine resources; 12 mem. states.

Silva Mediterranea: e-mail silva.mediterranea@fao.org; internet www.fao.org/forestry/silvamed; f. 1911, became a statutory body of FAO in 1948; FAO committee on Mediterranean forestry issues convened under the auspices of the FAO Forestry Commissions for Africa, Europe, and Near-East; 26 mem. states and the EU.

Western Central Atlantic Fishery Commission: c/o FAO Regional Office for Latin America and the Caribbean, Avda Dag Hammarskjöld 3241, Casilla 10095, Vitacura, Santiago, Chile; f. 1973 to assist international co-operation for the conservation, development and utilization of the living resources, especially shrimps, of the Western Central Atlantic; 15th session: March 2014, in Port-of-Spain, Trinidad and Tobago.

The Committee on Commodity Problems (see Council) has several subsidiary intergovernmental groups, on: bananas and tropical fruits; citrus fruit; grains; hard fibres; jute, kenaf and allied fibres; meat and dairy products; oilseeds, oils and fats; rice; surplus disposal; and tea.

Finance

FAO's Regular Programme, which is financed by contributions from member governments, covers the cost of FAO's Secretariat, its Technical Co-operation Programme (TCP) and part of the cost of several special action programmes. The regular budget for the two-year period 2014–15 totalled US $1,006m. Much of FAO's technical assistance programme and emergency (including rehabilitation) support activities are funded from extra-budgetary sources, predominantly by trust funds that come mainly from donor countries and international financing institutions; voluntary donor contributions to FAO were projected at around $1,400m. in 2014–15.

Publications

Commodity Review and Outlook (annually).
Crop Prospects and Food Situation (5/6 a year).
Desert Locust Bulletin.
Ethical Issues in Food and Agriculture.
FAO Statistical Yearbook (annually).
FAOSTAT Statistical Database (online).
Food Outlook (2 a year).
Food Safety and Quality Update (monthly; electronic bulletin).
Forest Resources Assessment (every 5 years).
The State of Agricultural Commodity Markets (every 2 years).

The State of Food and Agriculture (annually).
The State of Food Insecurity in the World (annually, with IFAD and WFP).
The State of World Fisheries and Aquaculture (every 2 years).
The State of the World's Forests (every 2 years).
Unasylva (quarterly).
Yearbook of Fishery Statistics.
Yearbook of Forest Products.
Commodity reviews, studies, manuals. A complete catalogue of publications is available at www.fao.org/icatalog/inter-e.htm.

International Atomic Energy Agency—IAEA

Address: POB 100, Wagramerstrasse 5, 1400 Vienna, Austria.
Telephone: (1) 26000; **fax:** (1) 26007; **e-mail:** official.mail@iaea.org; **internet:** www.iaea.org.

The IAEA is an intergovernmental organization, established in 1957 in accordance with a decision of the UN General Assembly. Although it is autonomous, the IAEA is administratively a member of the UN, and reports on its activities once a year to the UN General Assembly. Its main objectives are to enlarge the contribution of atomic energy to peace, health and prosperity throughout the world and to ensure, so far as it is able, that assistance provided by it or at its request or under its supervision or control is not used in such a way as to further any military purpose. The 2005 Nobel Peace Prize was awarded, in two equal parts, to the IAEA and to the Agency's Director-General.

MEMBERS

The IAEA has 162 members. Some 72 intergovernmental and non-governmental organizations have formal agreements with the IAEA.

Organization

(April 2014)

GENERAL CONFERENCE

The Conference, comprising representatives of all member states, convenes each year for general debate on the Agency's policy, budget and programme. It elects members to the Board of Governors, and approves the appointment of the Director-General; it admits new member states.

BOARD OF GOVERNORS

The Board of Governors consists of 35 member states elected by the General Conference. It is the principal policy-making body of the Agency and is responsible to the General Conference. Under its own authority, the Board approves all safeguards agreements, important projects and safety standards.

SECRETARIAT

The Secretariat, comprising some 2,470 staff, is headed by the Director-General, who is assisted by six Deputy Directors-General. The Secretariat is divided into six departments: Technical Co-operation; Nuclear Energy; Nuclear Safety and Security; Nuclear Sciences and Applications; Safeguards; and Management. A Standing Advisory Group on Safeguards Implementation advises the Director-General on technical aspects of safeguards.

Director-General: YUKIYA AMANO (Japan).

Activities

The Agency's activities are supported by three pillars: technology (assisting research on and practical application of atomic energy for peaceful uses), safety, and verification (ensuring that special fissionable and other materials, services, equipment and information made available by the Agency or at its request or under its supervision are not used for any non-peaceful purpose).

TECHNICAL CO-OPERATION AND TRAINING

The IAEA provides assistance in the form of experts, training and equipment to technical co-operation projects and applications worldwide, with an emphasis on radiation protection and safety-related activities. Training is provided to scientists, and experts and lecturers are assigned to provide specialized help on specific nuclear applications. The IAEA supported the foundation in September 2003 of the World Nuclear University, comprising a global network of institutions that aim to strengthen international co-operation in promoting the safe use of nuclear power in energy production, and in the application of nuclear science and technology in areas including sustainable agriculture and nutrition, medicine, fresh water resources management and environmental protection.

FOOD AND AGRICULTURE

In co-operation with FAO, the Agency conducts programmes of applied research on the use of radiation and isotopes in fields including efficiency in the use of water and fertilizers; improvement of food crops by induced mutations; eradication or control of destructive insects by the introduction of sterilized insects (radiation-based Sterile Insect Technique); improvement of livestock nutrition and health; studies on improving efficacy and reducing residues of pesticides, and increasing utilization of agricultural wastes; and food preservation by irradiation. The programmes are implemented by the Joint FAO/IAEA Division of Nuclear Techniques in Food and Agriculture and by the FAO/IAEA Agriculture and Biotechnology Laboratory, based at the IAEA's laboratory complex in Seibersdorf, Austria. A Training and Reference Centre for Food and Pesticide Control, based at Seibersdorf, supports the implementation of national legislation and trade agreements ensuring the quality and safety of food products in international trade. The Agency's Marine Environment Laboratory (IAEA-MEL), in Monaco, studies radionuclides and other ocean pollutants. In June 2012 IAEA announced the establishment of a new Ocean Acidification International Coordination Centre (OA-ICC), under the management of IAEA-MEL, with a mandate to facilitate, promote and communicate global actions on ocean acidification.

LIFE SCIENCES

In co-operation with the World Health Organization (WHO), the IAEA promotes the use of nuclear techniques in medicine, biology and health-related environmental research, provides training, and conducts research on techniques for improving the accuracy of radiation dosimetry.

The IAEA/WHO Network of Secondary Standard Dosimetry Laboratories (SSDLs) comprises 81 laboratories in 62 member states. The Agency's Dosimetry Laboratory in Seibersdorf performs dose inter-comparisons for both SSDLs and radiotherapy centres. The IAEA undertakes maintenance plans for nuclear laboratories; national programmes of quality control for nuclear medicine instruments; quality control of radioimmunoassay techniques; radiation sterilization of medical supplies; and improvement of cancer therapy in low- and middle-income countries through the IAEA Programme of Action for Cancer Therapy (PACT), inaugurated in 2004. By the end of 2012 47 member states had received imPACT (integrated missions of the Programme of Action for Cancer) reviews, which provide comprehensive assessments of national cancer control capabilities and support radiotherapy capacity building. In May 2009 the IAEA and WHO launched a new Joint Programme on Cancer Control, aimed at enhancing efforts to fight cancer in the developing world. In June 2010 the inaugural meeting took place of an IAEA Advisory Group on Increasing Access to Radiotherapy Technology (AGaRT) in low- and middle-income countries.

PHYSICAL AND CHEMICAL SCIENCES

The Agency's programme on physical sciences includes industrial applications of isotopes and radiation technology; application of nuclear techniques to mineral exploration and exploitation; radiopharmaceuticals; and hydrology, involving the use of isotope techniques for assessment of water resources. Nuclear data services are provided, and training is given for nuclear scientists from developing countries. The Physics, Chemistry and Instrumentation Laboratory in Seibersdorf supports the Agency's research in human health, industry, water resources and environment. The Abdus Salam International Centre for Theoretical Physics, based in Trieste, Italy, operates in accordance with a tripartite agreement in force between the IAEA, UNESCO and the Italian Government.

NUCLEAR POWER

In 2014 there were 435 nuclear power plants in operation and 72 reactors under construction worldwide. Nuclear power accounts for about 13% of total electrical energy generated globally. The IAEA helps developing member states to introduce nuclear-powered electricity-generating plants through assistance with planning, feasibility studies, surveys of manpower and infrastructure, and safety measures. The Agency also assesses life extension and decommissioning strategies for ageing nuclear power plants; there were in 2014 some 149 decommissioned reactors in a state of permanent shutdown. IAEA issues publications on numerous aspects of nuclear power, and provides training courses on safety in nuclear power plants and other topics. An energy data bank collects and disseminates information on nuclear technology, and a power reactor information system monitors the technical performance of nuclear power plants. The use of nuclear technology in seawater desalination and of radiation hydrology techniques to provide potable water are addressed. IAEA has since 1992 been actively engaged in the process to develop an International Thermonuclear Experimental Reactor (ITER), to expand the use of fusion energy. In October 2007 the ITER International Organization—comprising the European Union (EU), People's Republic of China, India, Japan, Republic of Korea (South Korea), Russia and the USA—was inaugurated, with responsibility for constructing, operating and decommissioning the reactor. The construction phase commenced in 2010, in Cadarache, France, and it is envisaged that the reactor will enter fully into operation by 2026. In May 2001 the International Project on Innovative Nuclear Reactors and Fuel Cycles (INPRO) was inaugurated. INPRO, which has 40 members (38 IAEA member states and the European Commission), aims to promote nuclear energy as a means of meeting future sustainable energy requirements and to facilitate the exchange of information by member states to advance innovations in nuclear technology. The IAEA is a permanent observer at the Generation IV International Forum (GIF), which was inaugurated in 2000 to undertake research and development activities aimed at developing the feasibility and performance capabilities of next generation nuclear energy systems, which are expected to become commercially available during 2030–40. In 2010 the IAEA established an Integrated Nuclear Infrastructure Group (ING), which aimed to integrate information from disparate databases to enable more effective planning; to offer training in the use of planning tools; to provide legislative assistance; and to provide guidance on ensuring self-assessment capabilities among governmental and operating organizations. Integrated Nuclear Infrastructure Review (INIR) missions are conducted in member states, and in 2012 a new INIR methodology was introduced. An advisory Technical Working Group on Nuclear Power Infrastructure was also initiated during 2010. In that year the Executive Board endorsed the establishment of a Low Enriched Uranium (LEU) Bank, to be funded from extra-budgetary sources, with the aim of supplying LEU for the purpose of nuclear power generation to states affected by a supply disruption of LEU to nuclear power plants. The Bank was to represent a mechanism of last resort, to be used (upon advance payment) by national authorities unable to secure LEU either from the commercial market or state-to-state arrangements.

An IAEA International Ministerial Conference on Nuclear Energy in the 21st Century, with a focus on the role of nuclear energy in climate change mitigation and on meeting increasing global demand for energy, was convened in June 2013 in St Petersburg, Russia, with support from the OECD Nuclear Energy Agency and the Russian Government.

RADIOACTIVE WASTE MANAGEMENT

The Agency provides practical help to member states in the management of radioactive waste. The Waste Management Advisory Programme (WAMAP) was established in 1987, and undertakes advisory missions in member states. A code of practice to prevent the illegal dumping of radioactive waste was drafted in 1989, and another on the international transboundary movement of waste was drafted in 1990. A ban on the dumping of radioactive waste at sea came into effect in 1994, under the Convention on the Prevention of Marine Pollution by Dumping of Wastes and Other Matters; the IAEA was to determine radioactive levels, for purposes of the Convention, and to provide assistance to countries for the safe disposal of radioactive wastes. A new category of radioactive waste—very low level waste (VLLW)—was introduced in the early 2000s. A VLLW repository, at Morvilliers, France, became fully operational in 2004. The Agency has issued modal regulations for the air, sea and land transportation of all radioactive materials.

In September 1997 the IAEA adopted a Joint Convention on the Safety of Spent Fuel Management and on the Safety of Radioactive Waste Management. The first internationally binding legal device to address such issues, the Convention was to ensure the safe storage and disposal of nuclear and radioactive waste, during both the construction and operation of a nuclear power plant, as well as following its closure. The Convention entered into force in June 2001, and had been ratified by 69 parties at April 2014.

NUCLEAR SAFETY

The IAEA's nuclear safety programme encourages international co-operation in the exchange of information, promoting implementation of its safety standards and providing advisory safety services. It includes the IAEA International Nuclear and Radiological Event Scale (INES), which measures the severity of nuclear events, incidents and accidents; the Incident Reporting System; an emergency preparedness programme (which maintains an Emergency Response Centre, located in Vienna, Austria); operational safety review teams; the International Nuclear Safety Group (INSAG); the Radiation Protection Advisory Team; and a safety research co-ordination programme. The safety review teams provide member states with advice on achieving and maintaining a high level of safety in the operation of nuclear power plants, while research programmes establish risk criteria for the nuclear fuel cycle and identify cost-effective means to reduce risks in energy systems. A new version of the INES, issued in July 2008, incorporated revisions aimed at providing more detailed ratings of activities including human exposure to sources of radiation and the transportation of radioactive materials.

The nuclear safety programme promotes a global safety regime, which aims to ensure the protection of people and the environment from the effects of ionizing radiation and the minimization of the likelihood of potential nuclear accidents, etc. Through the Commission on Safety Standards (which has sub-committees on nuclear safety standards, radiation safety standards, transport safety standards and waste safety standards) the programme establishes IAEA safety standards and provides for their application. In September 2006 the IAEA published a new primary safety standard, the Fundamental Safety Principles, representing a unified philosophy of nuclear safety and protection that was to provide the conceptual basis for the Agency's entire safety standards agenda. The IAEA's *Safety Glossary Terminology Used in Nuclear Safety and Radiation Protection* is updated regularly. In 2010 IAEA established a Global Safety Assessment (G-SAN), facilitating collaboration between experts worldwide with the aim of harmonizing nuclear safety.

The Convention on the Physical Protection of Nuclear Material, signed in 1980, commits contracting states to ensuring the protection of nuclear material during transportation within their territory or on board their ships or aircraft; amendments aimed at strengthening the Convention were adopted in July 2005.

Following a serious accident at the Chernobyl nuclear power plant in Ukraine (then part of the USSR) in April 1986, two conventions were formulated by the IAEA and entered into force in October. The first, the Convention on Early Notification of a Nuclear Accident, commits parties to provide information about nuclear accidents with possible transboundary effects at the earliest opportunity (it had 117 parties by April 2014); and the second, the Convention on Assistance in the Case of a Nuclear Accident or Radiological Emergency, commits parties to endeavour to provide assistance in the event of a nuclear accident or radiological emergency (this had 111 parties by April 2014). During 1990 the IAEA organized an assessment of the consequences of the Chernobyl accident, undertaken by an international team of experts, who reported to an international conference on the effects of the accident, convened at the IAEA headquarters in Vienna in May 1991. In February 1993 INSAG published an updated report on the Chernobyl incident, which emphasized the role of design factors in the accident, and the need to implement safety measures in the RBMK-type reactor. In March 1994 an IAEA expert mission visited Chernobyl and reported continuing serious deficiencies in safety at the defunct reactor and the units remaining in operation. An international conference reviewing the radiological consequences of the accident, 10 years after the event, was held in April 1996, co-sponsored by the IAEA, WHO and the EC. The last of the Chernobyl plant's three operating units was officially closed in December 2000. During the 2000s the IAEA offered a wide range of assistance with the decommissioning of Chernobyl. In November 2008 the IAEA and other UN agencies approved a UN Action Plan on Chernobyl to 2016, which had been developed by the UN Development Programme (UNDP), and was envisaged as a framework for the regeneration of affected areas of Ukraine, Belarus and Russia.

An International Convention on Nuclear Safety, which was adopted at an IAEA conference in June 1994, and entered into force in October 1996, applies to land-based civil nuclear power plants: adherents commit themselves to fundamental principles of safety, and maintain legislative frameworks governing nuclear safety.

In October 2003 a protocol entered into force that revised the 1963 Vienna Convention on Civil Liability for Nuclear Damage, fixing the minimum limit of liability for the operator of a nuclear reactor at 300m. Special Drawing Rights (SDRs, the accounting units of the IMF) in the event of an accident. The amended protocol also extended the length of time during which claims may be brought for loss of life or injury. The International Expert Group on Nuclear Liability (INLEX) was also established in 2003. A Convention on Supplementary Compensation for Nuclear Damage established a further compensatory fund to provide for the payment of damages following an accident; contributions to the Fund were to be calculated on the basis of the nuclear capacity of each member state. The Convention had four contracting states by April 2014.

In May 2001 the IAEA convened an international conference to address the protection of nuclear material and radioactive sources from illegal trafficking. In September, in view of the perpetration of major terrorist attacks against targets in the USA during that month, the IAEA General Conference adopted a resolution that emphasized the importance of the physical protection of nuclear material in preventing its illicit use or the sabotage of nuclear facilities and nuclear materials. Three main potential threats were identified: the acquisition by a terrorist group of a nuclear weapon; acquisition of nuclear material to construct a nuclear weapon or cause a radiological hazard; and violent acts against nuclear facilities to cause a radiological hazard. In March 2002 the Board of Governors approved in principle an action plan to improve global protection against acts of terrorism involving nuclear and other radioactive materials. The plan addressed the physical protection of nuclear materials and facilities; the detection of malicious activities involving radioactive materials; strengthening national control systems; the security of radioactive sources; evaluation of security and safety at nuclear facilities; emergency response to malicious acts or threats involving radioactive materials; ensuring adherence to international guidelines and agreements; and improvement of programme co-ordination and information management. In March 2003 the IAEA organized an International Conference on Security of Radioactive Sources, held in Vienna. In April 2005 the UN General Assembly adopted the International Convention for the Suppression of Acts of Nuclear Terrorism. The Convention, which opened for signature in September of that year and entered into force in July 2007, established a definition of acts of nuclear terrorism and urged signatory states to co-operate in the prevention of terrorist attacks by sharing information and providing mutual assistance with criminal investigations and extradition proceedings. Under the provisions of the Convention it was required that any seized nuclear or radiological material should be held in accordance with IAEA safeguards. By the end of 2012 a total of 2,331 incidents had been reported to the Illicit Trafficking Database (ITDB) since its creation in 1995; of the 160 incidents that were reported to have occurred during 2012, 17 involved illegal possession of and attempts to sell nuclear material or radioactive sources; 24 involved reported theft or loss; and 119 concerned discoveries of uncontrolled material, unauthorized disposals, and inadvertent unauthorized shipments and storage. The ITDB had 120 participant states in that year. In July 2012 ITDB participant states convened to discuss means of improving the sharing of information on incidents of unauthorized activities involving radioactive materials.

In June 2004 the IAEA Board of Governors approved an international action plan on the decommissioning of nuclear facilities (revised in 2007). In September 2007 the IAEA launched a Network of Centres of Excellence for Decommissioning. In 2014 the Agency was managing four ongoing international projects related to safe decommissioning. IAEA works to enhance the exchange of information between countries with decommissioning programmes under development and those that have decommissioning experience.

In October 2008 the IAEA inaugurated the International Seismic Safety Centre (ISSC), within the Agency's Department of Safety and Security. The ISSC was to serve as a focal point for avoiding and mitigating the consequences of extreme seismic events on nuclear installations worldwide, and was to be supported by a committee of high-level experts in the following areas: geology and tectonics; seismology; seismic hazard; geotechnical engineering; structural engineering; equipment; and seismic risk. In March 2011, in the aftermath of the severe earthquake and tsunami flooding that had struck and severely damaged the Fukushima Daiichi nuclear power plant, the Japanese authorities requested IAEA support in monitoring the effects of the ensuing release of radiation on the environment and on human health. Accordingly, the IAEA dispatched radiation monitoring teams to Japan to provide assistance to local experts, with a particular focus on: worker radiation protection; food safety; marine and soil science; and Boiling Water Reactor (BWR) technology. In late March the IAEA, FAO and WHO issued a joint statement on food safety issues following the Fukushima nuclear emergency, emphasizing their commitment to mobilizing knowledge and expertise in support of the Japanese authorities. During late May–early June an IAEA team comprising 20 international experts visited Japan to assess the ongoing state of nuclear safety in that country. The emergency phase of the Fukushima accident ended with the attainment of Cold Shutdown Condition, in mid-December 2011. In 2011–14 the IAEA issued regular status reports on the situation at Fukushima Daiichi, covering environmental radiation monitoring; workers' exposure to radiation; and ongoing conditions at the plant. In February 2014 the IAEA presented an independent assessment, compiled at the request of the Japanese authorities, of that country's ongoing Mid-and-Long-Term Roadmap towards decommissioning Fukushima Daiichi. The report offered technical and policy advice on issues including the management of increasing volumes of contaminated water at the site, as well as fuel removal, and waste storage.

In June 2011, in view of the Fukushima Daiichi accident, the IAEA Ministerial Conference on Nuclear Safety adopted a Ministerial Declaration which formed the basis of the first IAEA Action Plan on Nuclear Safety. The Plan, which was unanimously endorsed in September by the 55th General Conference, emphasized greater transparency in nuclear safety matters and the improvement of safety regimes, including the strengthening of peer reviews, emergency and response mechanisms, and national regulatory bodies. Safety standards were to be reviewed and an assessment of the vulnerabilities of nuclear power plants was to be undertaken. In March 2012 the IAEA convened an International Experts' Meeting on Reactor and Spent Fuel Safety, and in June a meeting of experts was held on Enhancing Transparency and Communications Effectiveness in the Event of a Nuclear or Radiological Emergency, resulting in a 12-point Plan of Action. In September the IAEA and the World Association of Nuclear Operators signed a new Memorandum of Understanding, to reflect enhanced co-operation in the aftermath of the Fukushima Daiichi event. A ministerial conference on nuclear safety convened jointly by the IAEA and the Japanese Government in Fukushima in December 2012, with participation by representatives of 117 states and 13 international organizations, aimed to share lessons learnt and knowledge gained from the Fukushima Daiichi accident. In January–February 2013 the IAEA organized an International Experts' Meeting on Decommissioning and Remediation After a Nuclear Accident, within the context of implementation of the 2011 IAEA Action Plan on Nuclear Safety.

In May 2011 the IAEA convened a technical meeting on the theme 'Newly Arising Threats in the Cybersecurity of Nuclear Facilities'; the meeting proposed revisions to current international guidance relating to computer security at nuclear facilities, and recommended that the Agency undertake further reviews of current security guidance and identify best practices relating to cybersecurity in nuclear installations.

The IAEA Director-General attended a series of international Nuclear Security Summits that were convened in April 2010 (in Washington, DC, USA), in March 2012 (Seoul, South Korea), and in March 2014 (The Hague, Netherlands) to address means of securing nuclear material and preventing nuclear terrorism; addressing the 2014 meeting, he urged states to avail themselves fully of the services offered by the IAEA in the field of nuclear security.

DISSEMINATION OF INFORMATION

The International Nuclear Information System (INIS), which was established in 1970, provides a computerized indexing and abstracting service. Information on the peaceful uses of atomic energy is collected by member states and international organizations and sent to the IAEA for processing and dissemination (see list of publications below). The IAEA also co-operates with FAO in an information system for agriculture (AGRIS) and with the World Federation of Nuclear Medicine and Biology, and the non-profit Cochrane Collaboration, in maintaining an electronic database of best practice in nuclear medicine. The IAEA Nuclear Data Section provides cost-free data centre services and co-operates with other national and regional nuclear and atomic data centres in the systematic worldwide collection, compilation, dissemination and exchange of nuclear reaction data, nuclear structure and decay data, and atomic and molecular data for fusion.

SAFEGUARDS

The Treaty on the Non-Proliferation of Nuclear Weapons (known also as the Non-Proliferation Treaty or NPT), which entered into force in 1970, requires each 'non-nuclear-weapon state' (one which had not manufactured and exploded a nuclear weapon or other nuclear explosive device prior to 1 January 1967) which is a party to the Treaty to conclude a safeguards agreement with the IAEA (an IAEA comprehensive safeguards agreement—CSA). Under such an agreement, the state undertakes to accept IAEA safeguards on all nuclear material in all its peaceful nuclear activities for the purpose of verifying that such material is not diverted to nuclear weapons or other nuclear explosive devices. In May 1995 the Review and Extension Conference of parties to the NPT agreed to extend the NPT indefinitely, and reaffirmed support for the IAEA's role in verification and the transfer of peaceful nuclear technologies. At the next review conference, held in April–May 2000, the five 'nuclear-weapon states'—China, France, Russia, the United Kingdom and the USA—issued a joint statement pledging their commitment to the ultimate goal of complete nuclear disarmament under effective international controls. A further review conference was convened in May 2005. The 2010 review conference, held in May of that year, unanimously adopted an outcome document containing a 22-point action plan aimed at advancing nuclear disarmament, non-proliferation and the peaceful uses of nuclear energy over the following five years. The Conference also proposed that a regional conference should be convened to address means of eliminating nuclear and other weapons of mass destruction in the Middle East; resolved that the nuclear-weapon states should commit to further efforts to reduce and ultimately eliminate all types of nuclear weapons, including through unilateral, bilateral, regional and multilateral measures, with specific emphasis on the full implementation of the Treaty on Measures for the Further Reduction and Limitation of Strategic Offensive Arms (known as the New START Treaty), signed by the Presidents of Russia and the USA in April 2010 (and in effect from February 2011); and determined that the Conference on Disarmament should immediately establish a subsidiary body to address nuclear disarmament within the context of an agreed and comprehensive programme of work. At April 2014 185 non-nuclear-weapon states and the five nuclear-weapon states were parties to the NPT. A number of non-nuclear-weapon states, however, had not complied, within the prescribed time limit, with their obligations under the Treaty regarding the conclusion of the relevant safeguards agreement with the Agency.

The five nuclear-weapon states have concluded safeguards agreements with the Agency that permit the application of IAEA safeguards to all their nuclear activities, excluding those with 'direct national significance'. A Comprehensive Nuclear Test Ban Treaty (CTBT) was opened for signature in September 1996, having been adopted by the UN General Assembly. The Treaty was to enter into international law upon ratification by all 44 nations with known nuclear capabilities. A verification body, the Comprehensive Nuclear-Test-Ban Treaty Organization (CTBTO), was to be established upon the Treaty's entry into force; meanwhile, an interim Preparatory Commission for the CTBTO, based in Vienna, became operational in 1997. By April 2014 183 countries had signed the CTBT and 162 had ratified it, including 36 of the 44 states with known nuclear capabilities (known as the 'Annex II states', of which the remaining eight were China, Egypt, Iran, Israel, and the USA, which were at that time signatories to the CTBT; and the Democratic People's Republic of Korea—North Korea, India, and Pakistan, which had not signed the Treaty). In October 1999 ratification of the CTBT was rejected by the US Senate. President Obama of the USA indicated in April 2009 that ratification of the Treaty would be pursued by his regime. The May 2010 NPT review conference determined that all nuclear-weapon states should undertake to ratify the CTBT, and emphasized that, pending the entry into force of the CTBT, all states should refrain from conducting test explosions of nuclear weapons.

To enable the Agency to be able to conclude that all nuclear material in a state is channelled towards peaceful activities both a CSA and an Additional Protocol to the CSA must be in effect. Additional Protocols, which were introduced from 1997, bind member states to provide inspection teams with improved access to information concerning existing and planned nuclear activities, and to allow access to locations other than known nuclear sites within the country's territory. By 31 December 2012 119 states and the European Atomic Energy Community (Euratom) had ratified Additional Protocols to their safeguards agreements. At the end of 2012 some 114 states had both a CSA and an Additional Protocol in force. Integrated Safety Assessments of Research Reactors (INSARR) missions are conducted in member states, on the basis of IAEA safety standards, and, during 2012, a programme of complementary Operation and Maintenance Assessment for Research Reactors (OMARR) missions was initiated.

Several regional nuclear weapons treaties require their member states to conclude CSAs with the IAEA, including the Treaty for the Prohibition of Nuclear Weapons in Latin America (Tlatelolco Treaty, with 33 states parties at April 2014); the South Pacific Nuclear-Free Zone Treaty (Rarotonga Treaty, 13 states parties at April 2014); the Treaty in the South-East Asia Nuclear-Weapon Free Zone (Treaty of Bangkok, adopted in 1995, 10 states parties at April 2014); and the African Nuclear-Weapon Free Zone Treaty (Pelindaba Treaty, adopted in 1996, with 37 states parties at April 2014). In September 2006 experts from Kazakhstan, Kyrgyzstan, Tajikistan, Turkmenistan and Uzbekistan adopted the Treaty of Semipalatinsk on establishing a Central Asian Nuclear Weapon Free Zone (CANWFZ); all five states subsequently ratified this. At the end of 2012 664 IAEA safeguards agreements were in force with 179 states, covering 692 nuclear facilities. During that year the Agency conducted 1,965 inspections. Expenditure on the Safeguards Regular Budget for 2012 was €121.2m., and extra-budgetary programme expenditure amounted to €25.5m. The IAEA maintains an imagery database of nuclear sites, and has installed digital surveillance systems (including unattended and remote monitoring capabilities) at sites to replace obsolete analogue systems: by the end of 2012 some 1,283 cameras were connected to 591 systems, operating at 252 facilities in 33 countries.

Under a long-term strategic plan for safeguards, covering the period 2012–23, the IAEA aims to develop the concept of a safeguards approach that is driven by outcomes and customized to the circumstances of individual states, and thereby to move away from a prescriptive facility-based approach.

The IAEA's Safeguards Analytical Laboratory (at the Seibersdorf complex) analyses nuclear fuel cycle samples collected by IAEA safeguards inspectors. A new Nuclear Material Laboratory was inaugurated at Seibersdorf in September 2013.

In April 1992 North Korea ratified a safeguards agreement with the IAEA. Subequently, however, that country refused to permit full access to all its facilities for IAEA inspectors to ascertain whether material capable of being used for the manufacture of nuclear weapons was being generated and stored. In June 1994 the IAEA Board of Governors halted IAEA technical assistance to North Korea because of continuous violation of the NPT safeguards agreements. In the same month North Korea withdrew from the IAEA (though not from the NPT); however, it allowed IAEA inspectors to conduct safeguards activities at its Yongbyon nuclear site. In October the Governments of North Korea and the USA concluded an agreement whereby the former agreed to halt construction of two new nuclear reactors, on condition that it received international aid for the construction of two 'light water' reactors (which could not produce materials for the manufacture of nuclear weapons). North Korea also agreed to allow IAEA inspections of all its nuclear sites, but only after the installation of one of the light water reactors had been completed (entailing a significant time lapse). From 1995 the IAEA pursued technical discussions with the North Korean authorities as part of the Agency's efforts to achieve the full compliance with the IAEA safeguards agreement; however, little overall progress was achieved, owing to the obstruction of inspectors by the authorities in that country, including their refusal to provide samples for analysis. In accordance with a decision of the General Conference in September 2001, IAEA inspectors subsequently resumed a continuous presence in North Korea. However, in December 2002, following repeated requests by the IAEA that North Korea verify the accuracy of reports that it was implementing an undeclared uranium enrichment programme, the authorities disabled IAEA safeguards surveillance equipment placed at three facilities in Yongbyon and took measures to restart reprocessing capabilities at the site, requesting the immediate withdrawal of the Agency's inspectors. In early January 2003 the IAEA Board of Governors adopted a resolution deploring North Korea's non-co-operation and urging its immediate and full compliance with the Agency. Shortly afterwards, however, North Korea announced its withdrawal from the NPT, while stating that it would limit its nuclear activities to peaceful purposes. In February the IAEA found North Korea to be in further non-compliance with its safeguards agreement, and condemned the reported successful reactivation of the Yongbyon reactor. In August a series of six-party talks on the situation was launched, involving North Korea, China, Japan, the Republic of Korea (South Korea), Russia and the USA, under the auspices of the Chinese Government. In September 2004 the General Conference adopted a resolution that urged North Korea to dismantle promptly and completely any nuclear weapons programme and to recognize the verification role of the Agency, while strongly encouraging the ongoing diplomatic efforts to achieve a peaceful outcome. In February 2005 North Korea suspended its participation in the six-party talks, and asserted that it had developed nuclear weapons as a measure of self-defence. The talks resumed during July–September, when the six parties signed a joint statement, in which North Korea determined to resume its adherence to the NPT and Agency safeguards, and consequently to halt its development of nuclear weapons; the USA and South Korea affirmed that no US nuclear weapons were deployed on the Korean Peninsula; the five other parties recognized North Korea's right to use nuclear energy for peaceful purposes, and agreed to consider at a later date the provision of a light water reactor to that country; and all parties undertook to promote co-operation in security and economic affairs. A timetable for future progress was to be established at the next phase of the six-party talks, the first session of which convened briefly in early November; North Korea, however, subsequently announced that it would only resume the talks pending the release by the USA of recently frozen financial assets. In July 2006 the UN Security Council condemned a recent ballistic missile test by North Korea, noting the potential of such missiles to be used for delivering nuclear, chemical or biological payloads, and urged that country to return immediately to the six-party talks without precondition and work towards the implementation of the September 2005 joint statement. In early 2006 October the IAEA Director-General expressed serious concern in response to an announcement by North Korea that it had conducted a nuclear test. In mid-October the Security Council adopted Resolution 1718, demanding that North Korea suspend all activities related to its ballistic missile programme, abandon all nuclear weapons and existing nuclear programmes, abandon all other existing weapons of mass destruction and ballistic missile programmes in a complete, verifiable and irreversible manner, and return to the six-party talks. The Council also imposed sanctions against North Korea.

The six-party talks were resumed in February 2007, and resulted in an ad hoc agreement by all the participants that North Korea would shut down and seal—for the purpose of eventual abandonment—the Yongbyon facility, and would invite back IAEA personnel to conduct all necessary monitoring and verifications; that North Korea would discuss with the other parties a list of all its nuclear programmes; that it would enter into negotiations with the USA aimed at resolving pending bilateral issues and moving toward full diplomatic relations; that the USA would initiate the process of removing the designation of North Korea as a state sponsor of terrorism; that North Korea and Japan would start negotiations aimed at normalizing their relations; and that the parties would agree to co-operate in security and economic affairs (as detailed under the September 2005 joint statement). In the latter regard, the parties agreed to the provision of emergency energy assistance to North Korea. In July 2007 an IAEA team visited the country and verified the shutdown of the Yongbyon facility. Upon the resumption of the six-party talks in September, the participants adopted an agreement wherein North Korea resolved to disable permanently its nuclear facilities.

In April 2009 a long-range rocket test conducted by North Korea, in violation of UN Security Council Resolution 1718, was unanimously condemned by the Council. North Korea responded by announcing its withdrawal from the six-party talks; withdrawing from the ad hoc agreement concerning the Yongbyon facility reached in February 2007; stating its intention to restart the Yongbyon facility; and ceasing, with immediate effect, all co-operation with the IAEA. Accordingly, IAEA inspectors removed all seals and surveillance equipment from the Yongbyon complex and departed the country. A further nuclear test conducted by North Korea in May 2009 was deplored by the Security Council, which, in June, strengthened the sanctions regime against that country (in Resolution 1874), and demanded that it rejoin the NPT. Reporting to the Board of Governors in June and September the IAEA Director-General urged all concerned parties to continue to work through diplomatic channels for a comprehensive solution that would bring North Korea back to the NPT and address that country's security concerns and humanitarian, economic and political requirements. In September 2011 the 55th IAEA Conference expressed concern at reports of the construction of a new uranium enrichment facility and light water reactor in North Korea. It was announced at the end of February 2012 that North Korea, under new leadership since December 2011, had agreed to suspend uranium enrichment and nuclear testing, and to permit the return of IAEA inspectors, in return for significant provision of food aid from the USA. In March 2012 the North Korean authorities formally invited the IAEA to send a delegation to discuss technical issues relating to verifying activities at Yongbyon. In April the USA suspended the January agreement following a failed long-range missile launch, which North Korea declared to be an attempt to send a satellite into orbit. The UN Security Council condemned the launch as a violation of UN resolutions. The IAEA Director-General announced in June that no delegation would be sent to North Korea in the immediate future. In August the IAEA reported that satellite imagery indicated that, since 2011, North Korea had made significant progress in the construction of a light water atomic reactor with the potential to extend the country's capacity to produce material for the construction of nuclear weapons. It was also reported that North Korea had traded nuclear technology with Libya, Syria, and possibly also with Myanmar and Pakistan. In December 2012 the UN Security Council condemned the successful launch of a rocket by North Korea earlier in that month (reportedly to put a weather satellite into orbit), which was undertaken in violation of the ban on ballistic missile development by that country authorized in Resolutions 1718 and 1874. In February 2013 the IAEA Director-General described as 'deeply regrettable' an announcement by the North Korean state media that an underground nuclear detonation had been conducted in that month at the Punngye-ri nuclear testing facility. In March, in response, the Security Council imposed further sanctions against North Korean entities. Although no IAEA verification activities could be conducted in North Korea during April 2009–early 2014, the Agency repeatedly urged that country to offer full co-operation in implementing its safeguards agreement, as well as to implement fully all relevant UN Security Council resolutions.

In September 2003 the IAEA adopted a resolution demanding that the Iranian Government sign, ratify and fully implement an Additional Protocol to its CSA promptly and unconditionally. The Agency also urged Iran to suspend its uranium enrichment and reprocessing activities, pending satisfactory application of the provisions of the Additional Protocol. Iran issued a declaration of its nuclear activities in October, and, in December, signed an Additional Protocol and agreed to suspend uranium enrichment processing. The Agency dispatched inspectors to Iran from October to conduct an intensive verification process. In April 2004 the IAEA Director-General visited Iran and concluded an agreement on a joint action plan to address the outstanding issues of the verification process. Iran provided an initial declaration under the (as yet unratified) Additional Protocol in May. In June, however, the Director-General expressed his continued concern at the extent of Iranian co-operation with IAEA inspectors. In September the Board of Governors adopted a resolution in which it strongly regretted continuing enrichment-related and reprocessing activities by Iran and requested their immediate suspension. The Director-General announced in late November that the suspension had been verified. In August 2005 the Agency adopted a resolution condemning Iran for resuming uranium conversion. In the following month a further resolution was adopted by the Board of Governors, in support of a motion by the EU, citing Iran's non-compliance with the NPT and demanding that Iran accelerate its co-operation with the Agency regarding the outstanding issues. In February 2006 the Board of Governors adopted a resolution that recalled repeated failures by Iran to comply with its obligations under its NPT safeguards agreement, expressed serious concern at the nature of Iran's nuclear programme, and urged that, with a view to building confidence in the exclusively peaceful nature of the programme, Iran should suspend fully all activities related to uranium enrichment (reportedly resumed in January) and reprocessing; ratify and fully implement the Additional Protocol agreed in 2003; and implement transparency measures extending beyond its formal arrangements with the Agency. The resolution requested the IAEA Director-General to report the steps required of Iran to the UN Security Council and to inform the Security Council of all related IAEA documents and resolutions. In response, the Iranian authorities declared that they would suspend all legally non-binding measures imposed by the IAEA, including containment and surveillance measures provided for under the Additional Protocol, and that consequently all IAEA seals and cameras should be removed from Iranian sites by mid-February 2006. At the end of July the UN Security Council, having reviewed the relevant information provided by the IAEA Director-General, issued Resolution 1696, in which it demanded that Iran suspend all enrichment-related and reprocessing activities, including research and development, within a period of one month, and stipulated that non-compliance might result in the imposition on Iran of economic and diplomatic sanctions. The resolution requested that the IAEA Director-General submit to the Council at the end of August a report on Iran's response. The report, which was made public in mid-September, found that Iran had not suspended its enrichment-related activities and was still not in compliance with the provisions of the Additional Protocol. In December the Security Council imposed sanctions against Iran, and in March 2007 the Council imposed a ban on the export of arms from that country.

In June 2007 the IAEA Director-General and the Iranian authorities agreed to develop within 60 days a plan on the modalities for resolving outstanding safeguards implementation issues; accordingly, in August, a workplan on this area (also detailing procedures and timelines) was finalized. At that time the IAEA declared that previous Agency concerns about plutonium reprocessing activities in Iran were now resolved, as its findings had verified earlier statements made by the Iranian authorities. In February 2008 the IAEA Board of Governors reported that Iran was still pursuing its uranium enrichment activities, and that the Iranian Government needed to continue to build confidence about the scope and purported peaceful nature of its nuclear programme. Consequently, in the following month, the UN Security Council adopted a new resolution on Iran in which it professed concern for the proliferation risk presented by the Iranian nuclear programme and authorized inspections of any cargo to and from Iran suspected of transporting prohibited equipment; and strengthened sanctions against Iran.

In May 2008 the IAEA Director-General, at the request of the UN Security Council, circulated a report to both the Security Council and the IAEA Board of Governors on the *Implementation of the NPT Safeguards Agreement and Relevant Provisions of Security Council Resolutions 1737 (2006), 1747 (2007), and 1803 (2008) in the Islamic Republic of Iran*, which concluded that there remained several areas of serious concern, including an ongoing 'green salt' project; high explosives testing; a missile re-entry vehicle project; some procurement activities of military-related institutions; outstanding substantive explanations regarding information with a possible military dimension; and Iran's continuing enrichment-related activities. In September the UN Security Council adopted a new resolution that reiterated demands that Iran cease enriching uranium. Reporting on the situation in February 2009, the IAEA Director-General stated that Iran continued to enrich uranium. Iran was urged once again to implement its Additional Protocol and other transparency measures.

In September 2009 the IAEA was informed by Iran that a second uranium enrichment facility was under construction in its territory; the Iranian authorities stated that the facility was to be used for peaceful purposes. The IAEA determined to send safeguards inspectors to examine the plant, located at the Fordo underground site near Qom, south-west of Tehran. In November the IAEA Board of Governors adopted a resolution urging Iran to suspend immediately construction at Fordo; to engage with the IAEA on resolving all outstanding issues concerning its nuclear programme; to comply fully and without qualification with its safeguards obligations, specifically to provide requested clarifications regarding the purpose of the Fordo enrichment plant and the chronology of its design and construction; and to confirm that no other undeclared facilities were planned or under construction. A report by the IAEA Secretary-General issued in February 2010 stated that, while the IAEA continued to verify the non-diversion of declared nuclear material in Iran, the Iranian authorities had not provided the necessary degree of co-operation to enable the Agency to confirm that all nuclear material in Iran was not being diverted for military purposes. In June the UN Security Council adopted Resolution 1929 further strengthening the UN sanction regime against Iran. Resolution 1929 also established a panel of experts to assist with monitoring and enforcing the implementation of the Iran sanctions. In November 2011 the IAEA Board of Governors adopted a resolution expressing 'deep and increasing concern' over the unresolved issues regarding the Iranian nuclear programme and calling upon Iran to engage seriously and without preconditions in discussions aimed at restoring international confidence in the exclusively peaceful nature of its nuclear activities. With a view to intensifying dialogue, senior IAEA experts visited Iran in late January–early February 2012, and again in late February. On both occasions the IAEA team requested, but was denied, access to the military complex at Parchin, south-east of Tehran, which was suspected to be the site of an explosives containment vessel; clarification of unresolved issues relating to possible military dimensions of Iran's nuclear programme was not achieved. An IAEA report on the Iran situation, issued in late February, found that uranium enrichment had increased three-fold since late 2011, in particular at the underground site at Fordo near Qom; it was maintained by the Iranian authorities, however, that this material was required for a medical research reactor. The report also claimed that the installation of centrifuges at the Natanz uranium enrichment plant, in central Iran, had accelerated. In late August the IAEA reported that Iran's Fordo nuclear installation had, since May, doubled production capacity. The IAEA Board of Governors adopted a resolution in September that urged Iran fully and promptly to comply with all requirements set by the Board and with all that country's obligations established by relevant resolutions of the UN Security Council. Several rounds of talks between representatives of the IAEA and the Iranian authorities on developing a structured approach to communications were convened from May 2012–September 2013, and, in November, IAEA and Iran agreed a Joint Statement on a Framework for Co-operation. In January 2014 the IAEA Board of Governors endorsed a joint plan of action with Iran, that had been concluded later in November 2013 by the Governments of China, France, Germany, Russia, the United Kingdom and the USA (the '5+1 Group'). In accordance with the plan, which was envisaged as a long-term comprehensive solution aimed at ensuring that Iran's nuclear programme remained exclusively peaceful, the IAEA was to monitor and verify an initial series of voluntary measures that were to be implemented by Iran by 15 May 2014. In February, in the context of the new Framework for Co-operation, the IAEA and Iran reviewed the progress so far achieved in implementing the agreed measures.

The IAEA Conference adopted a resolution in September 2009 that expressed concern about Israel's nuclear capabilities and called upon Israel to accede to the NPT and to place all its nuclear facilities under comprehensive IAEA safeguards. In July 2013 an INSARR mission was sent to Israel to conduct a peer review of the safety of a reactor at the centrally located Soreq Nuclear Research Center.

In June 2011 the IAEA Board of Governors adopted a resolution noting with serious concern the conclusion of the Agency that a building destroyed at Dair Alzour, Syria, in September 2007, was very likely an undeclared nuclear reactor; the resolution requested Syria to remedy urgently non-compliance with its Safeguards Agreement and called upon that country promptly to bring into force and implement an Additional Protocol to its CSA. IAEA officials visited Syria in October 2011 to pursue the matter, but were not granted sufficient access to locations believed to be functionally related to the Dair Alzour site. In November the IAEA Director-General demanded that Syria co-operate fully with the Agency in connection with unresolved issues relating to Dair Alzour and other locations. In August 2012 the Board of Governors reiterated this request.

In November 2011 the IAEA convened, in Vienna, a Forum on the Experience of Possible Relevance to the Creation of a Nuclear-Weapon-Free-Zone in the Middle East.

NUCLEAR FUEL CYCLE

The Agency promotes the exchange of information between member states on technical, safety, environmental, and economic aspects of nuclear fuel cycle technology, including uranium prospecting and the treatment and disposal of radioactive waste; it provides assistance to member states in the planning, implementation and operation of nuclear fuel cycle facilities and assists in the development of advanced nuclear fuel cycle technology. The Agency operates a number of databases and a simulation system related to the nuclear fuel cycle through its Integrated Nuclear Fuel Cycle Information System (iNFCIS). Every two years, in collaboration with OECD, the Agency prepares estimates of world uranium resources, demand and production.

Finance

The Agency is financed by regular and voluntary contributions from member states. Expenditure approved under the regular budget for 2014 amounted to some €349.8m., while the target for voluntary contributions to replenish IAEA's Technical Co-operation Fund (TCF) in that year was €90.3m. In July 2013 the Executive Board agreed to establish a new Working Group on Financing the Agency's Activities, to address means of ensuring sufficient and predictable resources for the TCF. The IAEA Peaceful Uses Initiative (PUI), launched in 2010, raises extra-budgetary contributions for Agency activities in the peaceful uses of nuclear technology.

Publications

Annual Report.
Atoms for Peace.
Fundamental Safety Principles.
Human Health Series.
IAEA Bulletin (quarterly).
IAEA Safety Glossary Terminology Used in Nuclear Safety and Radiation Protection.
INSAG Series.
Legal Series.
Meetings on Atomic Energy (quarterly).
The Nuclear Fuel Cycle Information System: A Directory of Nuclear Fuel Cycle Facilities.
Nuclear Data Newsletter.
Nuclear Energy Series.
Nuclear Fusion (monthly).
Nuclear Safety Review (annually).
Nuclear Security Series.
Nuclear Technology Review (annually).
Panel Proceedings Series.
Proceedings Series.
Publications Catalogue (annually).
Safeguards Implementation Report (annually).
Safety Series.
Technical Cooperation Report (annually).
Technical Reports Series.

International Bank for Reconstruction and Development—IBRD (World Bank)

Address: 1818 H St, NW, Washington, DC 20433, USA.

Telephone: (202) 473-1000; **fax:** (202) 477-6391; **e-mail:** pic@worldbank.org; **internet:** www.worldbank.org.

The IBRD was established in December 1945. Initially, it was concerned with post-war reconstruction in Europe; since then its aim has been to assist the economic development of member nations by making loans where private capital is not available on reasonable terms to finance productive investments. Loans are made either directly to governments, or to private enterprises with the guarantee of their governments. The World Bank, as it is commonly known, comprises the IBRD and the International Development Association (IDA). The affiliated group of institutions, comprising the IBRD, IDA, the International Finance Corporation (IFC), the Multilateral Investment Guarantee Agency (MIGA) and the International Centre for Settlement of Investment Disputes (ICSID), is referred to as the World Bank Group, and aims to eradicate extreme poverty, and pursue shared prosperity, while promoting environmentally sustainable development.

MEMBERS

There are 188 members. Only members of the International Monetary Fund (IMF) may be considered for membership in the World Bank. Subscriptions to the capital stock of the Bank are based on each member's quota in the IMF, which is designed to reflect the country's relative economic strength. Voting rights are related to shareholdings.

Organization

(April 2014)

Officers and staff of the IBRD serve concurrently as officers and staff in IDA. The World Bank has offices in New York, Brussels, Paris (for Europe), Frankfurt, London, Geneva and Tokyo, as well as in more than 100 countries of operation. Country Directors are located in some 30 country offices.

BOARD OF GOVERNORS

The Board of Governors consists of one Governor appointed by each member nation. Typically, a Governor is the country's finance minister, central bank governor, or a minister or an official of comparable rank. The Board normally meets once a year.

EXECUTIVE DIRECTORS

With the exception of certain powers specifically reserved to them by the Articles of Agreement, the Governors of the Bank have delegated their powers for the conduct of the general operations of the World Bank to a Board of Executive Directors which performs its duties on a full-time basis at the Bank's headquarters. There are 25 Executive Directors (see table below); each Director selects an Alternate. Six Directors are appointed by the six members having the largest number of shares of capital stock, and the rest are elected by the Governors representing the other members. The President of the Bank is Chairman of the Board.

The Executive Directors fulfil dual responsibilities. First, they represent the interests of their country or groups of countries. Second, they exercise their authority as delegated by the Governors in overseeing the policies of the Bank and evaluating completed projects. Since the Bank operates on the basis of consensus (formal votes are rare), this dual role involves frequent communication and consultations with governments so as to reflect accurately their views in Board discussions.

The Directors consider and decide on Bank policy and on all loan and credit proposals. They are also responsible for presentation to the Board of Governors at its Annual Meetings of an audit of accounts, an administrative budget, the *Annual Report* on the operations and policies of the World Bank, and any other matter that, in their judgement, requires submission to the Board of Governors. Matters may be submitted to the Governors at the Annual Meetings or at any time between Annual Meetings.

PRINCIPAL OFFICERS

The principal officers of the Bank are the President of the Bank, three Managing Directors, two Senior Vice-Presidents and 25 Vice-Presidents.

President and Chairman of Executive Directors: Dr Jim Yong Kim (USA).

Managing Directors: Sri Mulyani Indrawati (Indonesia), Caroline Anstey (United Kingdom), Bertrand Badré (France).

Special Envoy on MDGs and Financial Development: Mahmoud Mohieldin (Egypt).

Activities

The World Bank's primary objectives are the achievement of sustainable economic growth and the reduction of poverty in developing countries. In the context of stimulating economic growth the Bank promotes both private sector development and human resource development and has attempted to respond to the growing demands by developing countries for assistance in these areas. In September 2001 the Bank announced that it was to become a full partner in implementing the UN Millennium Development Goals (MDGs), and was to make them central to its development agenda. The objectives, which were approved by governments attending a special session of the UN General Assembly in September 2000, represented a new international consensus to achieve determined poverty reduction targets. The Bank was closely involved in preparations for the International Conference on Financing for Development, which was held in Monterrey, Mexico, in March 2002. The meeting adopted the Monterrey Consensus, which outlined measures to support national development efforts and to achieve the MDGs. During 2002/03 the Bank, with the IMF, undertook to develop a monitoring framework to review progress in the MDG agenda. The first *Global Monitoring Report* was issued by the Bank and the IMF in April 2004 and has since been published annually. In 2013 the Bank, with other agencies, co-led global consultations on formulating a post-2015 development framework in the thematic area of energy.

In October 2007 the Bank's President defined the following six strategic themes as priorities for Bank development activities: the poorest countries; fragile and post-conflict states; middle-income countries; global public goods; the Arab world; and knowledge and learning. In May 2008 the Bank established a Global Food Crisis Response Programme (GFRP) to assist developing countries affected by the escalating cost of food production. In December the Bank resolved to establish a new facility to accelerate the provision of funds, through IDA, for developing countries affected by the global decline in economic and financial market conditions. The Bank participated in the meeting of heads of state and government of the Group of 20 (G20) leading economies, that was held in Washington, DC, USA, in November 2008 to address the global economic situation, and pursued close collaboration with other multinational organizations, in particular the IMF and the Organisation for Economic Co-operation and Development (OECD), to analyse the impact of the ongoing economic instability. During early 2009 the Bank elaborated its operational response to the global economic crisis. Three operational platforms were devised to address the areas identified as priority themes, i.e. protecting the most vulnerable against the effects of the crisis; maintaining long-term infrastructure investment programmes; and sustaining the potential for private sector-led economic growth and employment creation. Consequently, a new Vulnerability Financing Facility was established, incorporating the GFRP and a new Rapid Social Response Programme, to extend immediate assistance to the poorest groups in affected low- and middle-income countries. Infrastructure investment was to be supported through a new Infrastructure Recovery and Assets Platform, which was mandated to release funds to secure existing infrastructure projects and to finance new initiatives in support of longer-term economic development. Private sector support for infrastructure projects, bank recapitalization, microfinance, and trade financing was to be led by IFC.

The Bank's efforts to reduce poverty include the compilation of country-specific assessments and the formulation of country assistance strategies (CASs) to review and guide the Bank's country programmes. In 1998/99 the Bank's Executive Directors endorsed a Comprehensive Development Framework (CDF) to effect a new approach to development assistance based on partnerships and country responsibility, with an emphasis on the interdependence of the social, structural, human, governmental, economic and environmental elements of development. The CDF, which aimed to enhance the overall effectiveness of development assistance, was formulated after a series of consultative meetings organized by the Bank and attended by representatives of governments, donor agencies, financial institutions, non-governmental organizations (NGOs), the private sector and academics. In December 1999 the Bank introduced a new approach to implement the principles of the CDF, as part of its strategy to enhance the debt relief scheme for heavily indebted poor countries (HIPCs, q.v.). Applicant countries were requested to formulate, in consultation with external partners and other stakeholders, a results-oriented national strategy to reduce poverty, to be presented in the form of a Poverty Reduction Strategy Paper (PRSP). In cases where there might be some delay in issuing a full PRSP, it was permissible for a country to submit a less detailed 'interim' PRSP (I-PRSP) in order to secure the preliminary qualification for debt relief. The approach also requires the publication of annual progress reports. In 2001 the Bank introduced a new Poverty Reduction Support Credit to help low-income countries to implement the policy and institutional reforms outlined in their PRSP. Increasingly, PRSPs have been considered by the international community to be the appropriate country-level framework to assess progress towards achieving the MDGs.

The Bank's annual publication *World Development Report* addresses specific aspects of development. The 2014 edition, published in October 2013, focused on the theme 'Managing Risk for Development'.

In September 2011 the Bank introduced a Corporate Scorecard, which uses a framework of performance indicators to monitor the IBRD and IDA's ongoing progress and achievement of development results. In April 2012 an interactive internet-based version of the Corporate Scorecard was initiated.

FINANCIAL OPERATIONS

IBRD capital is derived from members' subscriptions to capital shares, the calculation of which is based on their quotas in the IMF. At 30 June 2013 the total subscribed capital of the IBRD was US $223,181m., of which the paid-in portion was $13,434m. (6.0%); the remainder is subject to call if required. Most of the IBRD's lendable funds come from its borrowing, on commercial terms, in world capital markets, and also from its retained earnings and the flow of repayments on its loans. IBRD loans carry a variable interest rate, rather than a rate fixed at the time of borrowing.

IBRD loans usually have a 'grace period' of five years and are repayable over 15 years or fewer. Loans are made to governments, or must be guaranteed by the government concerned, and are normally made for projects likely to offer a commercially viable rate of return. In 1980 the World Bank introduced structural adjustment lending, which (instead of financing specific projects) supports programmes and changes necessary to modify the structure of an economy so that it can restore or maintain its growth and viability in its balance of payments over the medium term.

The IBRD and IDA together made 276 new lending and investment commitments totalling US $31,547m. during the year ending 30 June 2013, compared with 253 (amounting to $35,335m.) in the previous year. During 2012/13 the IBRD alone approved commitments totalling $15,249m. (compared with $20,582m. in the previous year), of which $4,769m. (31%) was allocated to projects in Latin America and the Caribbean, $4,591m. (30%) to Europe and Central Asia, and $3,661m. (24%) to East Asia and the Pacific. Disbursements by the IBRD in the year ending 30 June 2013 amounted to $15,830m. (For details of IDA operations, see the separate chapter on IDA.)

IBRD operations are supported by medium- and long-term borrowings in international capital markets. During the year ending 30 June 2012 the IBRD's net income amounted to –US $676m.

In September 1996 the World Bank/IMF Development Committee endorsed a joint initiative to assist HIPCs to reduce their debt burden to a sustainable level, in order to make more resources available for poverty reduction and economic growth. A new Trust Fund was established by the World Bank in November to finance the initiative. The Fund, consisting of an initial allocation of US $500m. from the IBRD surplus and other contributions from multilateral creditors, was to be administered by IDA. In early 1999 the World Bank and the IMF initiated a comprehensive review of the HIPC initiative. By April meetings of the Group of Seven (G7) industrialized nations and of the governing bodies of the Bank and IMF indicated a consensus that the scheme needed to be amended and strengthened, in order to allow more countries to benefit from the initiative, to accelerate the process by which a country may qualify for assistance, and to enhance the effectiveness of debt relief. In June the G7 and Russia (known as the G8), meeting in Cologne, Germany, agreed to increase contributions to the HIPC Trust Fund and to cancel substantial amounts of outstanding debt, and proposed more flexible terms for eligibility. In September the Bank and the IMF reached an agreement on an enhanced HIPC scheme. During the initial phase of the process to ensure suitability for debt relief, each applicant country should formulate a PRSP, and should demonstrate prudent financial management in the implementation of the strategy for at least one year, with support from the IMF and IDA. At the pivotal 'decision point' of the process, having thus developed and successfully applied the poverty reduction strategy, applicant countries still deemed to have an unsustainable level of debt were to qualify for interim debt relief from the IMF and IDA, as well as relief on highly concessional terms from other official bilateral creditors and multilateral institutions. During the ensuing 'interim period' countries were required successfully to implement further economic and social development reforms, as a final demonstration of suitability for securing full debt relief at the 'completion point' of the scheme. Data produced at the decision point was to form the base for calculating the final debt relief (in contrast to the original initiative, which based its calculations on projections of a country's debt stock at the completion point). In the majority of cases a sustainable level of debt was targeted at 150% of the net present value (NPV) of the debt in relation to total annual exports (compared with 200%–250% under the original initiative). Other countries with a lower debt-to-export ratio were to be eligible for assistance under the scheme, providing that their export earnings were at least 30% of GDP (lowered from 40% under the original initiative) and government revenue at least 15% of GDP (reduced from 20%). In March 2005 the Bank and the IMF implemented a new Debt Sustainability Framework in Low-income Countries to provide guidance on lending to low-income countries and to improve monitoring and prevention of the accumulation of unsustainable debt. In June ministers responsible for finance of the G8 proposed providing additional resources to achieve the full cancellation of debts owed by eligible HIPCs to assist those countries to meet their MDG targets. Countries that had reached their completion point were to qualify for immediate assistance. In July the heads of state and government of G8 countries requested that the Bank ensure the effective delivery of the additional funds and provide a framework for performance measurement. In September the Bank's Development Committee and the International Monetary and Financial Committee of the IMF endorsed the proposal, subsequently referred to as the Multilateral Debt Relief Initiative (MDRI). The Committees agreed to protect the financial capability of IDA, as one of the institutions (with the IMF and the African Development Bank) which was to meet the additional cancellation commitments, and to develop a monitoring programme. At 31 December 2012 assistance committed under the HIPC initiative amounted to an estimated $76,000m. (in end-2011 NPV terms), of which the World Bank Group had committed $14,800. At that time the estimated costs of the MDRI amounted to $39,900m. in nominal value terms, of which the Bank Group's share amounted to an estimated $24,100m. By October 2013 35 countries (Afghanistan, Benin, Bolivia, Burkina Faso, Burundi, Cameroon, Central African Republic, Comoros, Côte d'Ivoire, Democratic Republic of the Congo, Republic of Congo, Ethiopia, The Gambia, Ghana, Guinea, Guinea-Bissau, Guyana, Haiti, Honduras, Liberia, Madagascar, Malawi, Mali, Mauritania, Mozambique, Nicaragua, Niger, Rwanda, São Tomé and Príncipe, Senegal, Sierra Leone, Tanzania, Togo, Uganda and Zambia) had reached completion point under the enhanced HIPC initiative, while a further one country had reached decision point. In addition, four countries were deemed eligible, or potentially eligible, for the initiative.

In January 2012 the Bank launched the Program for Results (PforR), a new lending instrument that links the disbursement of funds to the delivery of pre-defined results. By October 2013 eight PforR projects had been approved and a further 16 were under consideration.

During 2000/01 the World Bank strengthened its efforts to counter the problem of HIV and AIDS in developing countries. In November 2001 the Bank appointed its first Global HIV/AIDS Adviser. In September 2000 a new Multi-Country HIV/AIDS Programme for Africa (MAP) was launched, initially with US $500m., in collaboration with UNAIDS and other major donor agencies and NGOs. In February 2002 the Bank approved an additional $500m. for a second phase of MAP. A MAP initiative for the Caribbean, with a budget of $155m., was launched in 2001. The Bank has undertaken research into the long-term effects of HIV/AIDS, and hosts the Global HIV/AIDS Monitoring and Evaluation Support Team of UNAIDS. In November 2004 the Bank launched an AIDS Media Center to improve access to information regarding HIV/AIDS, in particular to journalists in developing countries. It has also established a resource library to strengthen HIV/AIDS monitoring and evaluation systems. In July 2009 the Bank published a report, with UNAIDS, concerned with the impact of the global economic crisis on HIV prevention and treatment programmes. A new regional report on HIV/AIDS in the Middle East and North Africa, entitled *Time for Strategic Action*, was published in June 2010.

In March 2007 the Board of Executive Directors approved an action plan to develop further its Clean Energy for Development Investment Framework, which had been formulated in response to a request by the G8 heads of state, meeting in Gleneagles, United Kingdom, in July 2005. The action plan focused on efforts to improve access to clean energy, in particular in sub-Saharan Africa; to accelerate the transition to low carbon emission development; and to support adaptation to climate change. In October 2008 the Bank Group endorsed a new Strategic Framework on Development and Climate Change, which aimed to guide the Bank in supporting the efforts of developing countries to achieving growth and reducing poverty, while recognizing the operational challenges of climate change. In June 2010 the Bank appointed a Special Envoy to lead the Bank's representation in international discussions on climate change. In February 2012 the Bank supported the establishment of a Global Partnership for Oceans.

In February 2012 the Bank opened a new Global Centre on Conflict, Security and Development in Nairobi, Kenya, in order to enhance its support for the poorest people living in some 30 countries considered 'fragile' or affected by conflict. The Centre was to help co-ordinate development efforts in those countries, to improve the efficiency of financial support, and to serve as a focus for experts and practitioners to share knowledge and experience.

TECHNICAL ASSISTANCE AND ADVISORY SERVICES

In addition to providing financial services, the Bank also undertakes analytical and advisory services, and supports learning and capacity building, in particular through the World Bank Institute, the Staff Exchange Programme and knowledge-sharing initiatives. The Bank has supported efforts, such as the Global Development Gateway, to disseminate information on development issues and programmes, and, since 1988, has organized the Annual Bank Conference on Development Economics (ABCDE) to provide a forum for the exchange and discussion of development-related ideas and research. The 2013 gathering was held, in June, on the theme 'Risk and Vulnerability'. In September 1995 the Bank initiated the Information for Development Programme (InfoDev) with the aim of fostering partnerships between governments, multilateral institutions and private sector experts in order to promote reform and investment in developing countries through improved access to information technology.

The provision of technical assistance to member countries has become a major component of World Bank activities. The economic and sector work (ESW) undertaken by the Bank is the vehicle for considerable technical assistance and often forms the basis of CASs and other strategic or advisory reports. In addition, project loans and credits may include funds earmarked specifically for feasibility studies, resource surveys, management or planning advice, and training. The World Bank Institute has become one of the most important of the Bank's activities in technical assistance. It provides training in national economic management and project analysis for government officials at the middle and upper levels of responsibility. It also runs overseas courses aiming to build up local training capability, and administers a graduate scholarship programme. Technical assistance (usually reimbursable) is also extended to countries that do not need Bank financial support, e.g. for training and transfer of technology. The Bank encourages the use of local consultants to assist with projects and to strengthen institutional capability.

The Project Preparation Facility (PPF) was established in 1975 to provide cash advances to prepare projects that may be financed by the Bank. In 1992 the Bank established an Institutional Development Fund (IDF), which became operational on 1 July; the purpose of the Fund was to provide rapid, small-scale financial assistance, to a maximum value of US $750,000, for capacity-building proposals. In 2002 the IDF was reoriented to focus on good governance, in particular financial accountability and system reforms.

ECONOMIC RESEARCH AND STUDIES

In the 1990s the World Bank's research, conducted by its own research staff, was increasingly concerned with providing information to reinforce the Bank's expanding advisory role to developing countries and to improve policy in the Bank's borrowing countries. The principal areas of current research focus on issues such as maintaining sustainable growth while protecting the environment and the poorest sectors of society, encouraging the development of the private sector, and reducing and decentralizing government activities.

Consultative Group on International Agricultural Research (CGIAR): founded in 1971 under the sponsorship of the World Bank (which provides its secretariat), FAO and UNDP. The International Fund for Agricultural Development (IFAD) is also a co-sponsor. The Group was established to raise funds for international agricultural research work for improving crops and animal production in developing countries, and works in partnership with governments, international and regional organizations, private businesses and foundations to support 15 research centres; during 2010 CGIAR implemented a major reorganization: a CGIAR Fund, of which the Bank was nominated as trustee, was established as a multi-trust fund to administer donations to the various programmes, while a Consortium, governed by a 10-member board, was established to unite the strategic and funding supervision of the research centres; a new Independent Science Partnership Council was also established to promote the quality, relevance and impact of science in CGIAR and to advise on strategic scientific issues; Chair. CGIAR Fund Council RACHEL KYTE (United Kingdom); Chair. CGIAR Consortium Bd CARLOS PÉREZ DEL CASTILLO (Uruguay).

CO-OPERATION WITH OTHER ORGANIZATIONS

The World Bank co-operates with other international partners with the aim of improving the impact of development efforts. It collaborates with the IMF in implementing the HIPC scheme and the two agencies work closely to achieve a common approach to development initiatives. The Bank has established strong working relationships with many other UN bodies, in particular through a mutual commitment to poverty reduction objectives. In May 2000 the Bank signed a joint statement of co-operation with OECD. The Bank holds regular consultations with other multilateral development banks and with the European Union with respect to development issues. The Bank-NGO Committee provides an annual forum for discussion with NGOs. Strengthening co-operation with external partners was a fundamental element of the Comprehensive Development Framework, which was adopted in 1998/99 (see above). In 2001/02 a Partnership Approval and Tracking System was implemented to provide information on the Bank's regional and global partnerships. In June 2007 the World Bank and the UN Office on Drugs and Crime launched a joint Stolen Asset Recovery (StAR) initiative, as part of the Bank's new Governance and Anti-Corruption (GAC) strategy. In April 2009 the G20 recommended that StAR review and propose mechanisms to strengthen international co-operation relating to asset recovery. The first global forum on stolen asset recovery and development was convened by StAR in June 2010.

The Bank is a partner, with the IMF, the UN Conference on Trade and Development (UNCTAD), UNDP, the World Trade Organization (WTO) and the International Trade Commission, in the Enhanced Integrated Framework (EIF) for trade-related assistance to least developed countries (LDCs), which aims to facilitate greater participation by LDCs in the global trading system; EIF activities are supported by a dedicated EIF Trust Fund. The EIF replaced in 2007, and builds upon, a previous Integrated Framework, established in 1997. In 1997 a Partnerships Group was established to strengthen the Bank's work with development institutions, representatives of civil society and the private sector. The Group established a new Development Grant Facility, which became operational in October, to support partnership initiatives and to co-ordinate all of the Bank's grant-making activities. The Bank establishes and administers trust funds, open to contributions from member countries and multilateral organizations, NGOs, and private sector institutions, in order to support development partnerships. By 30 June 2012 the Bank had a portfolio of 1,064 active trust funds, with assets of some US $29,200m.

In June 1995 the World Bank joined other international donors (including regional development banks, other UN bodies, Canada, France, the Netherlands and the USA) in establishing a Consultative Group to Assist the Poorest (CGAP), with the aim of channelling funds to the most needy through grass-roots agencies. An initial credit of approximately US $200m. was committed by the donors. The Bank manages the CGAP Secretariat, which is responsible for the administration of external funding and for the evaluation and approval of project financing. The CGAP provides technical assistance, training and strategic advice to microfinance institutions and other relevant bodies. As an implementing agency of the Global Environment Facility (GEF) the Bank assists countries to prepare and supervise GEF projects relating to biological diversity, climate change and other environmental protection measures. It is an example of a partnership in action which addresses a global agenda, complementing Bank country assistance activities. Other funds administered by the Bank include the Global Program to Eradicate Poliomyelitis, launched during the financial year 2002/03, the Least Developed Countries Fund for Climate Change, established in September 2002, an Education for All Fast-Track Initiative Catalytic Trust Fund, established in 2003/04, and a Carbon Finance Assistance Trust Fund, established in 2004/05. In 2006/07 the Bank established a Global Facility for Disaster Reduction and Recovery. In September 2007 the Bank's Executive Directors approved a Carbon Partnership Facility and a Forest Carbon Partnership Facility to support its climate change activities. In May 2008 the Bank inaugurated the Global Food Crisis Response Programme (GFRP) to provide financial support, with resources of some $1,200m., to help to meet the immediate needs of countries affected by the escalating cost of food production and by food shortages. Grants and loans were to be allocated on the basis of rapid needs assessments, conducted by the Bank with FAO, the World Food Programme and IFAD. As part of the facility a Multi-Donor Trust Fund was established to facilitate co-ordination among donors and to leverage financial support for the rapid delivery of seeds and fertilizer to small-scale farmers. In April 2009 the Bank increased the resources available under the GFRP to $2,000m. By March 2013 $1,560m. had been approved under the GFRP for initiatives in 49 countries, of which some $1,390m. had been disbursed. In April 2010 a new trust fund was established to support a Global Agriculture and Food Security Programme (GAFSP), with total donations amounting to $900m. from the Governments of Canada, Republic of Korea, Spain and the USA and the Bill and Melinda Gates Foundation. By September 2013 10 donors (additionally the Governments of Australia, Ireland, Japan, the Netherlands, and the United Kingdom) had pledged some $1,300m. in funding to the GAFSP, and resources of $912m. had been allocated to support projects in 25 countries worldwide. The Bank is a partner agency of the Climate and Clean Air Coalition to Reduce Short Lived Climate Pollutants (SLCPs), which was launched in February 2012 with the aim of combating SLCPs, including methane, black carbon and certain hydrofluorocarbons.

The Bank is a lead organization in providing reconstruction assistance following natural disasters or conflicts, usually in collaboration with other UN agencies or international organizations, and through special trust funds. In May 2011 the Bank co-hosted, with the Global Facility for Disaster Reduction and Recovery and the UN International Strategy for Disaster Reduction, the first World Reconstruction Conference, which concluded an agreement to develop a framework for international co-operation in post disaster recovery and reconstruction. In November 2001 the Bank worked with UNDP and the Asian Development Bank (ADB) to assess the needs of Afghanistan following the removal of the Taliban authorities in that country. At an International Conference on Reconstruction Assistance to Afghanistan, held in Tokyo, Japan, in January 2002, the Bank's President proposed extending US $500m. in assistance over a 30-month period, and providing an immediate amount of $50m.–$70m. in grants. In May an Afghanistan Reconstruction Trust Fund was established to provide a co-ordinated financing mechanism to support the interim administration in that country. The Bank is the Administrator of the Trust, which is managed jointly by the Bank, the ADB, the Islamic Development Bank and UNDP. By May 2010 contributions to the Trust Fund amounted to $4,361.2m., pledged by 30 countries, of which $3,715.4m. was paid-in. Disbursements under the Fund amounted to $3,112.0m. at that time. In May 2003 a Bank representative participated in an international advisory and monitoring board to assess reconstruction and development needs following international conflict in Iraq and removal of its governing regime. In October the Bank, with the UN Development Group, published a report identifying 14 priority areas for reconstruction, with funding requirements of $36,000m. over the period 2004–07, which was presented to an international donor conference held later in that month. The conference, held in Madrid, Spain, approved the establishment of an International Reconstruction Fund Facility for Iraq to channel international donations and to co-ordinate reconstruction activities. In January 2004 the Bank's Board of Executive Directors authorized the Bank to administer an integral part of the facility, the Iraq Trust Fund (ITF), to finance a programme of emergency projects and technical assistance. By January 2009 the ITF was financing 18 project grants, amounting to $481.6m. The Bank was a partner, with the Iraqi Government, the UN Secretariat, the IMF and other financial institutions, in the International Compact with Iraq, a five-year framework for co-operation that was launched in May 2007. At the end of 2004 the Bank responded immediately to assist countries affected by a massive earthquake and subsequent tsunami which devastated many coastal areas of some 14 countries in the Indian Ocean. Bank staff undertook assessments and other efforts to accelerate recovery planning, mobilize financial support and help to co-ordinate relief and recovery efforts. Some $672m. was allocated by the Bank, mainly in grants to be directed to Indonesia, Sri Lanka and the Maldives, for the first phase of reconstruction efforts. By June 2005 the Bank had committed more than $835m. to countries affected by the tsunami, in particular to repair damaged services, to assist the reconstruction of housing and to restore livelihoods. The Bank administers a Multi-Donor Trust Fund for Aceh and North Sumatra that was established by the Indonesian Government to manage some $500m. in pledged aid. By 30 September 2009 $685.2m. had been pledged for the Multi-Donor Trust Fund, of which some $399m. had been disbursed. In October 2005 the Bank, with the ADB, undertook a preliminary damage and needs assessment following a massive earthquake in north-west Pakistan. The cost of the disaster was estimated at $5,200m., with initial reconstruction funding requirements of $3,500m. An international donors' conference was convened in November. In February 2007 the Bank approved a new framework policy to accelerate the response to a disaster or emergency situation in order to fund essential recovery and rehabilitation activities. In January 2010 the Bank issued $100m. in immediate emergency funding to support recovery efforts in Haiti following an earthquake which caused extensive damage and loss of life. By June the Bank had extended some $479m. in grants to support Haiti reconstruction and rehabilitation; at the end of May it cancelled the remaining $36m. outstanding debt owed by Haiti. The Bank acts as trustee of a multi-donor Haiti Reconstruction Fund, which was established in March at an international donors' conference.

The Bank has worked with FAO, the World Health Organization (WHO) and the World Organisation of Animal Health (OIE) to develop strategies to monitor, contain and eradicate the spread of highly pathogenic avian influenza. In September 2005 the Bank organized a meeting of leading experts on the issue and in November it co-sponsored, with FAO, WHO and the OIE, an international partners' conference, focusing on control of the disease and preparedness planning for any future related influenza pandemic in humans. In January 2006 the Bank's Board of Directors approved the establishment of a funding programme (the Global Program for Avian Influenza Control and Human Pandemic Preparedness and Response—GPAI), with resources of up to US $500m., to assist countries to combat the disease. Later in that month the Bank co-sponsored, with the European Commission and the People's Republic of China, an International Ministerial Pledging Conference on Avian and Human Pandemic Influenza (AHI), convened in Beijing. Participants pledged some $1,900m. to fund disease control and pandemic preparedness activities at global, regional and country levels. Commitments to the AHI facility amounted to $126m. at January 2009. In June the Bank approved an additional $500m. to expand the GPAI in order to fund emergency operations required to prevent and control outbreaks of the new swine influenza variant pandemic (H1N1).

EVALUATION

The Independent Evaluation Group is an independent unit within the World Bank. It conducts Country Assistance Evaluations to assess the development effectiveness of a Bank country programme, and studies and publishes the results of projects after a loan has been fully disbursed, so as to identify problems and possible improvements in future activities. In addition, the department reviews the Bank's global programmes and produces the *Annual Review of Development Effectiveness*. In 1996 a Quality Assurance Group was established to monitor the effectiveness of the Bank's operations and performance. In March 2009 the Bank published an Action Plan on Aid Effectiveness, based on the Accra Agenda for Action that had been adopted in September 2008 during the Third High Level Forum on Aid Effectiveness, held in Ghana.

In September 1993 the Bank established an independent Inspection Panel, consistent with the Bank's objective of improving project implementation and accountability. The Panel, which began operations in September 1994, was to conduct independent investigations and report on complaints from local people concerning the design, appraisal and implementation of development projects supported by the Bank. By October 2013 the Panel had received 91 formal requests for inspection.

IBRD INSTITUTIONS

World Bank Institute (WBI): founded in March 1999 by merger of the Bank's Learning and Leadership Centre, previously responsible for internal staff training, and the Economic Development Institute (EDI), which had been established in 1955 to train government officials concerned with development programmes and policies. The new Institute aimed to emphasize the Bank's priority areas through the provision of training courses and seminars relating to poverty, crisis response, good governance and anti-corruption strategies. The Institute supports a Global Knowledge Partnership, which was established in 1997 to promote alliances between governments, companies, other agencies and organizations committed to applying information and communication technologies for development purposes. Under the EDI a World Links for Development programme was also initiated to connect schools in developing countries with partner establishments in industrialized nations via the internet. In 1999 the WBI expanded its programmes through distance learning, a Global Development Network, and use of new technologies. A new initiative, Global Development Learning Network (GDLN), aimed to expand access to information and learning opportunities through the internet, video conferences and organized exchanges. The WBI had also established 60 formal partnership arrangements with learning centres and public, private and NGOs to support joint capacity building programmes; many other informal partnerships were also in place. During 2009/10 new South-South and middle-income country (MIC)–OECD Knowledge Exchange facilities were established. In 2014 the WBI was focusing its work on the following areas: climate change; fragile and conflict-affected states; governance; growth and competitiveness; health systems; public-private partnerships in infrastructure; and urban development; Vice-Pres. SANJAY PRADHAN (India); publs *Annual Report*, *Development Outreach* (quarterly), other books, working papers, case studies.

International Centre for Settlement of Investment Disputes (ICSID): founded in 1966 under the Convention of the Settlement of Investment Disputes between States and Nationals of Other States. The Convention was designed to encourage the growth of private foreign investment for economic development, by creating the possibility, always subject to the consent of both parties, for a Contracting State and a foreign investor who is a national of another Contracting State to settle any legal dispute that might arise out of such an investment by conciliation and/or arbitration before an impartial, international forum. The governing body of the Centre is its Administrative Council, composed of one representative of each Contracting State, all of whom have equal voting power. The President of the World Bank is (ex officio) the non-voting Chairman of the Administrative Council. At April 2014 some 470 cases had been registered with the Centre, of which 283 had been concluded and 187 were pending consideration. At that time 150 countries had signed and ratified the Convention to become ICSID Contracting States; Sec.-Gen. MEG KINNEAR (Canada).

Publications

African Development Indicators (annually).
Annual Report on Portfolio Performance.
Atlas of Global Development.
Commodity Markets Outlook (quarterly).
Doing Business (annually).
Environment Matters (annually).
Global Development Finance (annually).
Global Economic Prospects (2 a year).
Global Financial Development Report (annually).
Global Monitoring Report (annually).
ICSID Annual Report.
ICSID Review—Foreign Investment Law Journal (2 a year).
Inequality in Focus (quarterly).
International Debt Statistics (annually).
Joint External Debt Hub.
Poverty Reduction and the World Bank (annually).
Research News (quarterly).
Results and Performance of the World Bank Group (annually).
Staff Working Papers.
The World Bank and the Environment (annually).
World Bank Annual Report.
World Bank Economic Review (3 a year).
World Bank Research Observer.
World Development Indicators (annually).
World Development Report (annually).

Statistics

LENDING OPERATIONS, BY SECTOR
(projects approved, year ending 30 June; US $ million)

	2012	2013
Agriculture, fishing and forestry	3,134	2,112
Education	2,959	2,731
Energy and mining	5,000	3,280
Finance	1,764	2,055
Health and other social services	4,190	4,363
Industry and trade	1,352	1,432
Information and communication	158	228
Public administration, law and justice	8,728	7,991
Transportation	4,445	5,135
Water, sanitation and flood protection.	3,605	2,220
Total	35,355	31,547

IBRD INCOME AND EXPENDITURE
(year ending 30 June; US $ million)

Revenue	2011	2012	2013
Income from loans	2,470	2,585	2,380
Income from investments and securities	367	214	241
Other income	1,540	1,590	1,625
Total income	4,377	4,389	4,246

Expenditure	2011	2012	2013
Borrowing expenses	1,687	1,652	1,483
Administrative expenses	1,711	1,631	1,761
Contributions to special programmes	147	133	147
Provision for loan losses	45	–189	22
Other financial expenses	1	1	1
Total	3,591	3,417	3,392
Operating income	1,023	783	876
Effects of adjustment and accounting charge	–93	–1,459	–658
Net income	930	–676	218

IBRD LOANS AND IDA CREDITS APPROVED, BY SECTOR AND REGION
(1 July 2012–30 June 2013; US $ million)

Sector	Africa	East Asia and Pacific	South Asia	Europe and Central Asia	Latin America and the Caribbean	Middle East and North Africa	Total
Agriculture, fishing and forestry	970	185	231	199	324	203	2,112
Education	626	579	609	74	639	204	2,731
Energy and mining	1,218	736	263	332	140	591	3,280
Finance	36	313	127	1,215	154	210	2,055
Health and other social services	997	542	1,061	630	891	243	4,363
Industry and trade	258	271	168	483	164	88	1,432
Information and communications	106	35	24	5	3	55	228
Public administration, law and justice	1,782	1,428	1,037	1,326	2,084	334	7,991
Transportation	1,843	1,098	553	916	694	31	5,135
Water, sanitation and flood protection	410	1,061	401	140	111	98	2,220
Total	8,245	6,247	4,474	5,320	5,204	2,058	31,547
of which: IBRD	42	3,661	378	4,591	4,769	1,809	15,249
IDA	8,203	2,586	4,096	729	435	249	16,298

IBRD OPERATIONS AND RESOURCES, 2009–13
(years ending 30 June; US $ million)

	2008/09	2009/10	2010/11	2011/12	2012/13
Loans approved	32,911	44,197	26,737	20,582	15,247
Gross disbursements	18,565	28,855	21,879	19,777	16,030
New medium- to long-term borrowings	39,092	31,696	28,790	38,406	22,146
Net income	3,114	–1,077	930	–676	218
Subscribed capital	189,918	189,943	193,732	205,394	223,181
Loans outstanding	105,698	120,103	132,459	136,325	143,776

Source: World Bank, *Annual Report 2013*.

EXECUTIVE DIRECTORS AND THEIR VOTING POWER
(April 2014)

		IBRD		IDA	
Executive Director	Casting votes of	Total votes	% of total	Total votes	% of total
Appointed:					
(Vacant)	USA	306,789	15.13	2,461,716	10.47
Hideaki Suzuki	Japan	166,044	8.19	2,044,447	8.69
Shixin Chen	People's Republic of China	107,194	5.28	495,213	2.11
Ingrid G. Hoven	Germany	93,101	4.59	1,320,461	5.61
Hervé de Villeroche	France	82,892	4.09	908,581	3.86
Gwen Hines	United Kingdom	82,892	4.09	1,409,037	5.99
Elected:					
Gino Alzetta (Belgium)	Austria, Belarus†, Belgium, Czech Republic, Hungary, Kosovo, Luxembourg, Slovakia, Slovenia, Turkey	105,361	5.19	1,096,922	4.66
Juan José Bravo Moises (Mexico)	Costa Rica, El Salvador, Guatemala, Honduras, Mexico, Nicaragua, Spain, Venezuela†	86,608	4.27	550,758	2.34
Frank Heemskerk (Netherlands)	Armenia, Bosnia and Herzegovina, Bulgaria†, Croatia, Cyprus, Georgia, Israel, the former Yugoslav republic of Macedonia, Moldova, Montenegro, Netherlands, Romania†, Ukraine	85,598	4.22	1,102,354	4.69
Alister Smith (Canada)	Antigua and Barbuda†, Bahamas, Barbados Belize, Canada, Dominica, Grenada, Guyana, Ireland, Jamaica†, Saint Christopher and Nevis, Saint Lucia, Saint Vincent and the Grenadines	81,596	4.02	1,036,431	4.41
Michael Willcock (Australia)	Australia, Cambodia, Kiribati, Republic of Korea, Marshall Islands, Federated States of Micronesia, Mongolia, New Zealand, Palau, Papua New Guinea, Samoa, Solomon Islands, Tuvalu, Vanuatu	81,019	3.99	920,978	3.92
Mukesh N. Prasad (India)	Bangladesh, Bhutan, India, Sri Lanka	73,526	3.63	914,385	3.89
Satu-Leena Santala (Finland)	Denmark, Estonia, Finland, Iceland, Latvia, Lithuania, Norway, Sweden	69,049	3.40	1,257,142	5.34
Roberto Tan (Philippines)	Brazil, Colombia, Dominican Republic, Ecuador, Haiti, Panama, Philippines, Suriname†, Trinidad and Tobago	66,957	3.30	819,206	3.48
Piero Cipollone (Italy)	Albania, Greece, Italy, Malta†, Portugal, San Marino†, Timor-Leste	65,312	3.22	779,931	3.32
Omar Bougara (Algeria)	Afghanistan, Algeria, Ghana, Iran, Morocco, Pakistan, Tunisia	62,600	3.09	615,572	2.62
Jorg Frieden (Switzerland)	Azerbaijan, Kazakhstan, Kyrgyzstan, Poland, Serbia, Switzerland, Tajikistan, Turkmenistan†, Uzbekistan	59,673	2.94	1,055,120	4.49
Sundaran Annamalai (Malaysia)	Brunei†, Fiji, Indonesia, Laos, Malaysia, Myanmar, Nepal, Singapore, Thailand, Tonga, Viet Nam	57,090	2.81	708,992	3.01
Merza H. Hasan (Kuwait)	Bahrain†, Egypt, Iraq, Jordan, Kuwait, Lebanon, Libya, Maldives, Oman, Qatar†, Syria, United Arab Emirates, Yemen	53,809	2.65	533,599	2.27
Vadim Grishin	Russia	46,431	2.49	73,197	0.31
(Vacant)	Saudi Arabia	46,431	2.29	772,020	3.28
Cesar Guido Forcieri (Argentina)	Argentina, Bolivia, Chile, Paraguay, Peru, Uruguay†	42,308	2.09	348,598	1.48
Agapito Mendes Dias (São Tomé and Príncipe)	Benin, Burkina Faso, Cameroon, Cape Verde, Central African Republic, Chad, Comoros, Democratic Republic of the Congo, Republic of the Congo, Côte d'Ivoire, Djibouti, Equatorial Guinea, Gabon, Guinea, Mali, Mauritania, Mauritius, Niger, São Tomé and Príncipe, Senegal, Togo	36,340	1.75	1,008,504	4.29
Denny Kalyalya (Zambia)	Botswana, Burundi, Eritrea, Ethiopia, The Gambia, Kenya, Lesotho, Liberia, Malawi, Mozambique, Namibia†, Rwanda, Seychelles†, Sierra Leone, South Sudan, Sudan, Swaziland, Tanzania, Uganda, Zambia, Zimbabwe	36,230	1.79	1,062,147	4.52
Mansur Muhtar (Nigeria)	Angola, Nigeria, South Africa	33,430	1.65	225,692	0.96

Note: Guinea-Bissau (1,140 votes in IBRD and 44,500 in IDA), Madagascar (2,022 votes in IBRD and 54,982 in IDA), and Somalia (1,152 votes in IBRD and 10,506 in IDA) did not participate in the 2012 regular election of Executive Directors.
† Member of the IBRD only (not IDA).

International Development Association—IDA

Address: 1818 H Street, NW, Washington, DC 20433, USA.
Telephone: (202) 473-1000; **fax:** (202) 477-6391; **internet:** www.worldbank.org/ida.

IDA began operations in November 1960. Affiliated to the International Band for Reconstruction and Development (IBRD), IDA advances capital to the poorer developing member countries on more flexible terms than those offered by the IBRD.

MEMBERS

IDA has 172 members.

Organization

(April 2014)

Officers and staff of the IBRD serve concurrently as officers and staff of IDA.

President and Chairman of Executive Directors: Dr JIM YONG KIM (USA).

Activities

IDA assistance is aimed at the poorer developing countries (i.e. those with a 2012 annual gross national income (GNI) per caput of less than US $1,205 qualified for assistance in 2013/14) in order to support their poverty reduction strategies. Under IDA lending conditions, credits can be extended to countries whose balance of payments could not sustain the burden of repayment required for IBRD loans. Terms are more favourable than those provided by the IBRD; since 1 July 2011 the maturity of credits has been 25 or 40 years, with a grace period of five or 10 years. In 2014 82 countries were eligible for IDA assistance, including 13 small island economies with a 2012 GNI per caput greater than $1,205, but which would otherwise have little or no access to Bank funds, and 18 so-called blend borrowers which are entitled to borrow from both IDA and the IBRD.

IDA's total development resources, consisting of members' subscriptions and supplementary resources (additional subscriptions and contributions), are replenished periodically by contributions from the more affluent member countries. In March 2013 negotiations on the 17th replenishment of IDA funds (IDA17) commenced, in Paris, France. Participants determined that the overarching theme of IDA17 should be maximizing development impact, including leveraging the collective resources of the World Bank Group, and the following areas of focus be 'special themes': climate change; fragile and conflict-affected states; gender; inclusive growth; and regional transformative initiatives. Replenishment meetings were subsequently held in Managua, Nicaragua, in July, and in Washington, DC, USA, in October. An agreement was concluded in December, at a meeting convened in Moscow, Russia. The IDA17 replenishment was supported by 46 donor countries, and amounted to US $52,000m., to cover the period 1 July 2014–30 June 2017.

During the year ending 30 June 2013 new IDA commitments amounted to US $16,298 for 184 projects, compared with $14,753m. for 160 projects in the previous year. Of total IDA assistance during 2012/13 $8,203m. (50%) was for Africa and $4,096m. (25%) for South Asia. In that financial year some 37% of lending was for infrastructure projects, 26% for social sector projects, and 22% for projects in the area of public administration and law.

In December 2008 the Bank's Board of Executive Directors approved the Financial Crisis Response Fast Track Facility, to accelerate the provision of up to US $2,000m. of IDA15 resources to help the poorest countries to counter the impact of the global economic and financial crisis. The first operations approved under the Facility, in February 2009, were for Armenia (amounting to $35m.) and the Democratic Republic of the Congo ($100m.) in support of employment creation and infrastructure development initiatives and meeting the costs of essential services. In December the Board of Executive Directors approved a pilot Crisis Response Window to deploy an additional $1,300m. of IDA funds to support the poorest countries affected by the economic crisis until the end of the IDA15 period (30 June 2011), with the aim of assisting those countries to maintain spending on sectors critical to achieving the Millennium Development Goals. Permanent funding for the Crisis Response Window, which additionally was to assist low-income countries to manage the impact of natural disasters, was agreed as part of the IDA16 replenishment accord in December 2010. In mid-2011 $250m. was allocated from the Crisis Response Window to provide relief and longer-term rehabilitation assistance to areas of the Horn of Africa affected by severe drought. In September the World Bank announced that $30m. of those funds were to be disbursed through UNHCR in order to improve basic facilities in settlements occupied by persons displaced as a result of the drought. In December the World Bank's Board of Executive Directors approved the establishment of an Immediate Response Mechanism in order to accelerate the provision of assistance to IDA-eligible countries following a natural disaster or economic crisis.

IDA administers a Trust Fund, which was established in November 1996 as part of a World Bank/IMF initiative to assist heavily indebted poor countries (HIPCs). In September 2005 the World Bank's Development Committee and the International Monetary and Financial Committee of the IMF endorsed a proposal of the Group of Eight (G8) industrialized nations to cancel the remaining multilateral debt owed by HIPCs that had reached their completion point under the scheme (see IBRD). In December IDA convened a meeting of donor countries to discuss funding to uphold its financial capability upon its contribution to the so-called Multilateral Debt Relief Initiative (MDRI). IDA's participation in the scheme was approved by the Board of Executive Directors in March 2006 and entered into effect on 1 July. During IDA16 US $3,512m. was allocated to the provision of debt relief under the MDRI, $1,320m. under the HIPC initiative and a further $383m. to finance arrears clearance operations. At December 2013 the estimated cost of the HIPC initiative, in end-2012 nominal present value terms, was $74,300m., of which IDA commitments totalled $14,400m.; IDA's contribution to the MDRI was estimated at $35,500m. in nominal value terms (or some 68% of the total cost of the MDRI). By April 2014 35 countries had reached completion point to receive assistance under the initiative.

Publication

Annual Report.

Statistics

IDA OPERATIONS AND RESOURCES, 2008–12
(years ending 30 June; US $ million)

	2008/09	2009/10	2010/11	2011/12	2012/13
Commitments	14,041*	14,550	16,269	14,753	16,298
Disbursements	9,219	11,460	10,282	11,061	11,228
Number of projects	176	190	230	160	184

* Includes an HIPC grant of US $45.5m.
Source: World Bank, *Annual Report 2013*.

International Finance Corporation—IFC

Address: 2121 Pennsylvania Ave, NW, Washington, DC 20433, USA.

Telephone: (202) 473-3800; **fax:** (202) 974-4384; **e-mail:** information@ifc.org; **internet:** www.ifc.org.

IFC was founded in 1956 as a member of the World Bank Group to stimulate economic growth in developing countries by financing private sector investments, mobilizing capital in international financial markets, and providing technical assistance and advice to governments and businesses.

MEMBERS

IFC has 184 members.

Organization

(April 2014)

IFC is a separate legal entity in the World Bank Group. Executive Directors of the World Bank also serve as Directors of IFC. The President of the World Bank is ex officio Chairman of the IFC Board of Directors, which has appointed him President of IFC. Subject to his overall supervision, the day-to-day operations of IFC are conducted by its staff under the direction of the Executive Vice-President. The senior management team includes 10 Vice-Presidents responsible for regional and thematic groupings. At the end of June 2013 IFC had 4,015 staff members, of whom 57% were based in field offices in 99 countries.

PRINCIPAL OFFICERS

President: Dr JIM YONG KIM (USA).

Executive Vice-President: JIN-YONG CAI (People's Republic of China).

REGIONAL AND INDUSTRY DEPARTMENTS

IFC's regional departments cover sub-Saharan Africa; East Asia and the Pacific; South Asia; Central and Eastern Europe; Southern Europe and Central Asia; Latin America and the Caribbean; and the Middle East and North Africa. They aim to develop strategies for member countries, promote businesses, and strengthen relations with governments and the private sector. The Industry Departments include Agribusiness; Environment and Social Development; Global Capital Markets Development; Global Financial Markets; Global Information and Communications Technologies (jointly managed with the World Bank); Global Manufacturing and Services; Health and Education; Infrastructure; Oil, Gas, Mining and Chemicals (jointly managed with the World Bank); Private Equity and Investment Funds; and Syndication and Resource Mobilization.

REGIONAL AND RESIDENT MISSIONS

There are Regional and Resident Missions in Australia, Bangladesh, Brazil, Cambodia, People's Republic of China, Dominican Republic, Egypt, Guyana, Haiti, India, Kazakhstan, Laos, Liberia, Mongolia, Russia, Serbia, South Africa, Sri Lanka, Trinidad and Tobago, Turkey, United Arab Emirates and Viet Nam. There are also Special Representatives in France, Germany and the United Kingdom (for Europe), an office in Tokyo, Japan, and other programme co-ordinators, managers and investment officers in more than 50 additional countries.

Activities

IFC aims to promote economic development in developing member countries by assisting the growth of private enterprise and effective capital markets. It finances private sector projects, through loans, the purchase of equity, quasi-equity products, and risk management services, and assists governments to create conditions that stimulate the flow of domestic and foreign private savings and investment. IFC may provide finance for a project that is partly state-owned, provided that there is participation by the private sector and that the project is operated on a commercial basis. IFC also mobilizes additional resources from other financial institutions, in particular through syndicated loans, thus providing access to international capital markets. IFC provides a range of advisory services to help to improve the investment climate in developing countries and offers technical assistance to private enterprises and governments. From late 2008 IFC's overriding concern was to respond effectively to the difficulties facing member countries affected by the global economic and financial crisis and to maintain a sustainable level of development. In particular it aimed to preserve and create employment opportunities, to support supply chains for local businesses, and to provide credit. During 2014–16 IFC's activities were guided by a roadmap, which identified five strategic 'pillars' as priority areas of activity: strengthening the focus on frontier markets (i.e. the lowest income countries or underdeveloped regions of middle-income countries, and fragile and conflict-affected countries); addressing climate change, and securing environmental and social sustainability; promoting private sector growth in infrastructure, including education, health, water, and the food supply chain; developing local financial markets through institution building, the use of innovative financial products and mobilization, and focusing on micro, small and medium enterprises; and establishing and maintaining long-term client relationships with firms in developing countries, using the full range of IFC's products and services, and assisting their cross-border growth. Gender was a cross-cutting theme, and a special emphasis was placed on job creation.

To be eligible for financing projects must be profitable for investors, as well as financially and economically viable; must benefit the economy of the country concerned; and must comply with IFC's environmental and social guidelines. IFC aims to promote best corporate governance and management methods and sustainable business practices, and encourages partnerships between governments, non-governmental organizations and community groups. In 2001/02 IFC developed a Sustainability Framework to help to assess the longer-term economic, environmental and social impact of projects; following an 18-month consulation process an updated Sustainability Framework came into effect on 1 January 2012. In 2002/03 IFC assisted 10 international banks to draft a voluntary set of guidelines (the Equator Principles), based on IFC's environmental, social and safeguard monitoring policies, to be applied to their global project finance activities. In September 2009 IFC initiated a Performance Standards Review Process to define new standards to be applied within the Equator Principles framework. At April 2014 78 financial institutions had signed up to the Equator Principles.

In November 2004 IFC announced the establishment of a Global Trade Finance Programme (GTFP), with initial funding of some US $500m., which aimed to support small-scale importers and exporters in emerging markets, and to facilitate South–South trade in goods and services, by providing guarantees for trade transactions, as well as extending technical assistance and training to local financial institutions. Additional funding of $500m. was approved in January 2007, and in October 2008. In December, as part of a set of measures to support the global economy, the Board of Directors approved an expansion of the GTFP, doubling its funding to $3,000m. By August 2013 more than 250 global and regional confirming banks operating in around 100 countries were participating in the Programme. Other initiatives included the establishment of an Infrastructure Crisis Facility to provide investment for existing projects affected by a lack of private funding, and a new Bank Capitalization Fund (to be financed, up to $3,000m., with the Japan Bank for International Co-operation) to provide investment and advisory services to banks in emerging markets. In May 2009 IFC established an Asset Management Company, as a wholly owned subsidiary, to administer the Capitalization Fund. In February of that year IFC inaugurated a Microfinance Enhancement Facility, with a German development bank, to extend credit to microfinancing institutions and to support lending to low-income borrowers, with funds of up to $500m. IFC committed $1,000m. in funds to a new Global Trade Liquidity Program (GTLP), which was inaugurated by the World Bank Group in April, with the aim of mobilizing support of up to $50,000m. in trade transactions through financing extended by governments, other development banks and the private sector. In October IFC established a Debt and Asset Recovery Program to help to restore stability and growth by facilitating loan restructuring for businesses and by investing in funds targeting distressed assets and companies. IFC pledged to contribute $1,550m. to the Program over a three-year period, and aimed to mobilize resources through partnerships with other international financial institutions and private sector companies. IFC's first Green Bond was issued in April 2010 (maturing in April 2014). Proceeds from IFC Green Bonds—amounting to $3.5m. by April 2014—have been invested in energy efficient, renewable energy, and other climate-friendly projects. Two $1m. green bonds were issued, in February and November 2013. During 2011/12 IFC launched a Critical Commodities Finance Program, which aimed to expand agricultural-commodity trade finance in developing countries, providing up to $18,000m. in trade over a period of three years.

IFC's authorized capital is US $2,580m. (In July 2010 the Board of Directors recommended a special capital increase of $130m., to raise authorized capital from $2,450 to the current $2,580m; the increase took effect on 27 June 2012, having received the approval of the

Board of Governors.) At 30 September 2013 paid-in capital was $2,403m. The World Bank was originally the principal source of borrowed funds, but IFC also borrows from private capital markets. IFC's net income amounted to $1,018m. (after a $340m. grant transfer to IDA) in 2012/13, compared with $1,328m. in 2011/12 (after a $330m. transfer to IDA). In December 2008 the Board of Directors approved a Sovereign Funds Initiative to enable IFC to raise and manage commercial capital from sovereign funds.

In the year ending 30 June 2013 project financing approved by IFC amounted to US $24,853m. for 612 projects in 113 countries (compared with $20,358m. for 576 projects in the previous year). Of the total approved in 2012/13, $18,349m. was for IFC's own account, while $6,540m. was in the form of loan syndications and parallel loans, underwriting of securities issues and investment funds and funds mobilized by the IFC Asset Management Company. Generally, IFC limits its financing to less than 25% of the total cost of a project, but may take up to a 35% stake in a venture (although never as a majority shareholder). Disbursements for IFC's account amounted to $9,971m. in 2012/13.

In 2012/13 the largest proportion of investment commitments, for IFC's account, was allocated to Latin America and the Caribbean, receiving 26%, while sub-Saharan Africa received 19%, Europe and Central Asia 18%, East Asia and the Pacific received 16%, the Middle East and North Africa 12%, and South Asia 9%. In that year 29% of total financing committed (the largest allocation) was for global financial markets. Other commitments included infrastructure (19%) and manufacturing (13%).

IFC's Advisory Services are a major part of the organization's involvement with member countries to support the development of private enterprises and efforts to generate funding, as well as to enhance private sector participation in developing infrastructure. Advisory services cover the following five main areas of expertise: the business enabling environment (i.e. improving the investment climate in a country); access to financing (including developing financing institutions, improving financial infrastructure and strengthening regulatory frameworks); infrastructure (mainly encouraging private sector participation); environment and social sustainability; and corporate advice (in particular in support of small and medium-sized enterprises—SMEs). In December 2008 the Board of Directors determined to provide additional funding to IFC advisory services in order to strengthen the capacity of financial institutions and governments to respond to the crisis in the global financial markets. At 30 June 2013 there were more than 660 active Advisory Service projects in 105 countries; some 65% of projects were being implemented in IDA countries, and 18% in fragile and conflict-affected areas. Total expenditure on Advisory Services during that year amounted to US $232m. IFC manages, jointly financed with the World Bank and MIGA, the Foreign Investment Advisory Service (FIAS), which provides technical assistance and advice on promoting foreign investment and strengthening the country's investment framework at the request of governments. Under the Technical Assistance Trust Funds Program (TATF), established in 1988, IFC manages resources contributed by various governments and agencies to provide finance for feasibility studies, project identification studies and other types of technical assistance relating to project preparation. In 2004 a Grassroots Business Initiative was established, with external donor funding, to support businesses that provide economic opportunities for disadvantaged communities in Africa, Latin America, and South and South-East Asia. Since 2002 IFC has administered an online SME Toolkit to enhance the accessibility of business training and advice. By 2014 the service was available in 18 languages.

Since 2004 IFC has presented an annual Client Leadership Award to a chosen corporate client who most represents IFC values in innovation, operational excellence and corporate governance.

Publications

Annual Report.

Doing Business (annually).

Lessons of Experience (series).

Other handbooks, discussion papers, technical documents, policy toolkits, public policy journals.

Statistics

IFC OPERATIONS AND RESOURCES, 2011–13
(fiscal years ending 30 June; US $ million, unless otherwise stated)

	2011	2012	2013
Approved investments			
Number of new projects	518	576	612
Total investment programme*	18,660	20,358	24,853
Commitments for IFC's own account	12,186	15,462	18,349
Disbursements			
Total financing disbursed	8,744	10,568	12,113
For IFC's own account	6,715	7,981	9,971
Resources and income			
Borrowings	38,211	44,665	44,869
Paid-in capital	2,369	2,372	2,403
Retained earnings	16,367	17,695	18,713
Net income	1,579	1,328	1,018

* Including parallel loans, structured finance, other mobilization and IFC initiatives, and IFC Asset Management Company.

Source: IFC, *Annual Report 2013*.

Multilateral Investment Guarantee Agency—MIGA

Address: 1818 H Street, NW, Washington, DC 20433, USA.

Telephone: (202) 473-6163; **fax:** (202) 522-2630; **internet:** www.miga.org.

MIGA was founded in 1988 as an affiliate of the World Bank. Its mandate is to encourage the flow of foreign direct investment to, and among, developing member countries, through the provision of political risk insurance and investment marketing services to foreign investors and host governments, respectively.

MEMBERS

MIGA has 180 member countries. Membership is open to all countries that are members of the World Bank.

Organization

(April 2014)

MIGA is legally and financially separate from the World Bank. It is supervised by a Council of Governors (comprising one Governor and one Alternate of each member country) and an elected Board of Directors (of no less than 12 members).

President: Dr Jim Yong Kim (USA).

Executive Vice-President: Keiko Honda (Japan).

Activities

The convention establishing MIGA took effect in April 1988. Authorized capital was initially set at 100,000 shares, equivalent to US $1,082m. The convention provided for an automatic increase of capital stock upon the admission of new members. In April 1998 the Board of Governors endorsed an increase in MIGA's capital base, amounting to $700m. callable capital and $150m. paid-in capital. A grant of $150 was transferred from the IBRD as part of the General Capital Increase (GCI) package. A subscription period then ensued, covering April 1999–March 2003. By 30 June 2013 some $749.9m. of the GCI had been subscribed (of which $132.3m. was paid-in and $617.5m. callable). At that time MIGA's capital base comprised 186,359 shares, equivalent to $2,016m. (Comoros and São Tomé and Príncipe were granted membership in 2012/13.) At 30 June 2013 total subscriptions to the capital stock amounted to $1,916.3m., of which $365.6m. was paid-in.

MIGA's activities are guided by four strategic priorities: promoting foreign direct investment into the world's poorest countries; complex projects; South–South investments; and assisting conflict-affected and fragile economies. Eligible investments are guaranteed against losses resulting from non-commercial risks, under the following main categories:

(i) transfer risk resulting from host government restrictions on currency conversion and transfer;

(ii) risk of loss resulting from legislative or administrative actions of the host government;

(iii) repudiation by the host government of contracts with investors in cases in which the investor has no access to a competent forum;

(iv) the risk of armed conflict and civil unrest;

(v) risk of a sovereign not honouring a financial obligation or guarantee.

Before guaranteeing any investment, MIGA must ensure that it is commercially viable, contributes to the development process and is not harmful to the environment. The MIGA/IFC Office of the Compliance Advisor/Ombudsman (established in the fiscal year 1998/99) considers the concerns of local communities directly affected by MIGA- or IFC-sponsored projects. In February 1999 the Board of Directors approved an increase in the amount of political risk insurance available for each project, from US $75m. to $200m. During 2003/04 MIGA established a new fund, the Invest-in-Development Facility, to enhance the role of foreign investment in attaining the Millennium Development Goals. In 2005/06 MIGA supported for the first time a project aimed at selling carbon credits gained by reducing greenhouse gas emissions; it provided $2m. in guarantee coverage to the El Salvador-based initiative. In April 2009 the Board of Directors approved modifications to MIGA's policies and operational regulations in order to enhance operational flexibility and efficiency, in particular in the poorest countries and those affected by conflict. In November 2010 the Council of Governors endorsed amendments to MIGA's convention (the first since 1988) to broaden the eligibility for investment projects and to enhance the effectiveness of MIGA's development impact. In April 2013 the Board of Directors approved a new Conflict-Affected and Fragile Economies Facility, with the aim of providing political risk insurance to enable projects to be implemented in challenging environments that might assist with reconstruction, bring in capital, and generate employment.

During the year ending 30 June 2013 MIGA issued 47 investment insurance contracts for 30 projects with a value of US $2,781m. (compared with 66 contracts amounting to $2,657m. in 2011/12). Around three-quarters of guarantees went to projects in IDA countries. Since 1990 the total investment guarantees issued amounted to some $30,000m., through 1,143 contracts in support of 727 projects.

MIGA works with local insurers, export credit agencies, development finance institutions and other organizations to promote insurance in a country, to ensure a level of consistency among insurers and to support capacity building within the insurance industry. MIGA also offers investment marketing services to help to promote foreign direct investment in developing countries and in transitional economies, and to disseminate information on investment opportunities. MIGA's annual flagship report *World Investment and Political Risk*, is the focal point of the Agency's knowledge dissemination of resources on political risk management and insurance. In early 2007 MIGA's technical assistance services were amalgamated into the Foreign Advisory Investment Service (FIAS, see IFC), of which MIGA became a lead partner, along with IFC and the World Bank. During 2000/01 an office was established in Paris, France, to promote and co-ordinate European investment in developing countries, in particular in Africa and Eastern Europe. In 2002, to facilitate foreign investment in sub-Saharan Africa and Asia, MIGA opened offices in Johannesburg, South Africa and in Singapore. The role of Regional Director for Asia and the Pacific was created in August 2010 to head a new Asian Hub, operating from offices in Singapore, Hong Kong SAR and the People's Republic of China.

An Afghanistan Investment Guarantee Facility, administered by MIGA, has, since July 2004, provided political risk guarantees for foreign investors in that country.

MIGA administers a West Bank and Gaza Investment Guarantee Trust Fund, which was inaugurated in November 2008 to encourage greater private sector investment in those territories, and is co-sponsored by the European Investment Bank, the Japanese Government and the Palestinian (National) Authority. During 2012/13 some US $4.5m. in guarantees was issued through the Fund in support of two projects.

Publications

Annual Report.

MIGA News (online newsletter; every 2 months).

World Investment and Political Risk (annually).

Other guides, brochures and regional briefs.

International Civil Aviation Organization—ICAO

Address: 999 University St, Montréal, QC H3C 5H7, Canada.

Telephone: (514) 954-8219; **fax:** (514) 954-6077; **e-mail:** icaohq@icao.int; **internet:** www.icao.int.

ICAO was founded in 1947, following the adoption, in Chicago, USA, in 1944, of the Convention on International Civil Aviation. As the global forum for civil aviation co-operation, ICAO aims to facilitate sustainable growth of the civil aviation system. ICAO develops, accordingly, Standards and Recommended Practices that are encoded in annexes to the 1944 Convention, and aviation policies; undertakes compliance audits, studies and analysis; provides assistance to member states; and helps to build aviation capacity.

MEMBERS

ICAO has 191 contracting states.

Organization

(April 2014)

ASSEMBLY

Composed of representatives of all member states, the Assembly is the ICAO's legislative body and meets at least once every three years. It reviews the work of the organization, sets out the work programme for the next three years, approves the budget and determines members' contributions. The 38th Assembly took place in September–October 2013.

COUNCIL

Composed of representatives of 36 member states, elected by the Assembly. It is the executive body, and establishes and supervises subsidiary technical committees and makes recommendations to member governments; meets in virtually continuous session; elects the President, appoints the Secretary-General, and administers the finances of the organization. The Council is assisted by the Air Navigation Commission, the Air Transport Committee, the Committee on Joint Support of Air Navigation Services, the Finance Committee, the Committee on Unlawful Interference and the Technical Co-operation Committee. The functions of the Council are:

(i) to adopt Standards and Recommended Practices and incorporate them as annexes to the Chicago Convention on International Civil Aviation;

(ii) to arbitrate between member states on matters concerning aviation and implementation of the Convention;

(iii) to investigate any situation which presents avoidable obstacles to development of international air navigation;

(iv) to take whatever steps are necessary to maintain safety and regularity of operation of international air transport;

(v) to provide technical assistance to the developing countries under the UN Development Programme and other assistance programmes.

President of the Council: Dr Olumuyiwa Benard Aliu (Nigeria).

SECRETARIAT

The Secretariat, headed by a Secretary-General, is divided into five main divisions: the Air Navigation Bureau, the Air Transport Bureau, the Technical Co-operation Bureau, the Legal Bureau, and the Bureau of Administration and Services.

Secretary-General: Raymond Benjamin (France).

REGIONAL OFFICES

Asia and Pacific: 252/1 Vibhavadi-Rangsit Rd, Ladyao, Chatuchak, Bangkok 10900, Thailand; tel. (2) 537-8189; fax (2) 537-8199; e-mail apac@icao.int; internet www.icao.int/apac; Regional Dir Arun Mishra.

Eastern and Southern Africa: Limuru Rd, Gigiri, POB 46294, Nairobi, Kenya; tel. (20) 7622395; fax (20) 7623028; e-mail icaoesaf@

icao.int; internet www.icao.int/esaf; Regional Dir MESHESHA BELAYNEH.

European and North Atlantic: 3 bis Villa Émile-Bergerat, 92522 Neuilly-sur-Seine Cedex, France; tel. 1-46-41-85-85; fax 1-46-41-85-00; e-mail icaoeurnat@paris.icao.int; internet www.paris.icao.int; f. 1944; Regional Dir LUIS FONSECA DE ALMEIDA.

Middle East: POB 85, Cairo Airport Post Office Terminal One, Cairo 11776, Egypt; tel. (2) 267-4840; fax (2) 267-4843; e-mail icaomid@cairo.icao.int; internet www.icao.int/mid; Regional Dir MOHAMED R. M. KHONJI.

North America, Central America and the Caribbean: Apdo Postal 5-377, CP 06500, México, DF, Mexico; tel. (55) 5250-3211; fax (55) 5203-2757; e-mail icaonacc@icao.int; internet www.icao.int/nacc; Regional Dir L. J. MARTIN.

South America: ave Víctor Andrés Belaúnde 147, San Isidro, Lima, Peru; tel. (1) 611-8686; fax (1) 611-8689; e-mail icaosam@icao.int; internet www.icao.int/sam; Regional Dir FRANKLIN HOYER.

Western and Central Africa: Leopold Sedar Senghor International Airport, POB 38050, Dakar, Senegal; tel. 869-2424; fax 820-3259; e-mail icaowacaf@dakar.icao.int; internet www.icao.int/wacaf; Regional Dir MAM SAIT JALLOW.

Activities

During the period 2014–16 ICAO was pursuing the following strategic objectives: to enhance global civil aviation safety (the Organization's most fundamental guiding priority), within the framework of its Global Aviation Safety Plan (GASP); to increase—within the framework of the Global Air Navigation Capacity and Efficiency Plan—the capacity of and improve the efficiency of the global civil aviation system; to enhance global civil aviation security and facilitation; to foster the development of a sound and economically viable civil aviation system; and to minimize the adverse environmental effects of civil aviation activities. In October 2013 member states agreed to develop a market-based measure (MBM) scheme for international aviation, to be implemented by 2020.

ICAO Worldwide Air Transport Conferences have been convened periodically since April 1977, with participation by representatives of member states, international organizations, and aviation industry interests; the sixth Conference, was convened in March 2013, in Montréal.

SAFETY

Through the GASP, initiated in 1998, and periodically revised, most recently in October 2013, the ICAO aims to ensure and enhance all aspects of air safety. The following are priority areas of activity: policy and standardization; monitoring key safety trends and indicators; safety analysis; and implementing targeted safety programmes. ICAO also supports programmes to assist the victims of aircraft accidents. A Universal Safety Oversight Audit Programme (USOAP) became operational on 1 January 1999, providing for mandatory, systematic and harmonized safety audits regularly to be undertaken in member states in fields including the airworthiness of aircraft, flight operations and personnel licensing, with results to be compiled in an Audit Findings and Differences Database. In 2003 an International Financial Facility for Aviation Safety (IFFAS), to provide funds to states to adhere to ICAO safety-related standards, became effective in 2003. In October 2004 the Assembly recognized the USOAP as having significantly contributed to raising the level of safety oversight worldwide and endorsed its expansion, from 1 January 2005, to incorporate, in a new comprehensive systems approach (CSA), all safety-related provisions of the annexes to the Chicago Convention. A first cycle of USOAP audits was undertaken during 2002–07, and a second cycle was implemented during the period January 2008–December 2013. A meeting of Directors-General of Civil Aviation, convened by ICAO in March 2006 to identify ways to achieve improvements in aviation safety standards, endorsed a Global Strategy for Aviation Safety; determined that safety-related information, including the results of audits within the USOAP, should be shared among states, the public and other interested parties; and endorsed Part I of a Global Aviation Safety Roadmap, delivered to ICAO in December of 2005 by the Industry Safety Strategy Group, which identified mid- and long-term goals related to air-safety oversight and regulation matters. In December 2006 Part II of the Roadmap was finalized, outlining strategies for achieving these objectives. In September 2007 the Assembly endorsed a new Comprehensive Regional Implementation Plan for Aviation Safety in Africa, which had been formulated by African governments, with representatives of the local civil aviation authorities and air industry. In March 2012 the ICAO Council adopted Standards related to remotely piloted aircraft (RPA) systems. In May ICAO, with the International Air Transport Association, the African Airlines Association, and other partners, convened an aviation safety summit to develop a Strategic Improvement Action Plan, which was to be implemented in Africa during the period 2012–15, with a view to strengthening regulatory oversight and enhancing safety performance. In September 2010 ICAO, the European Union (EU), the US Department of Transportation, and the International Air Transport Association, formally approved the establishment of a new Global Safety Information Exchange (GSIE), with the aim of improving the overall level of international aviation safety. The 19th annex to the 1944 Chicago Convention, consolidating Standards and Recommended Practices on safety management, entered into force in November 2013. In May 2014 ICAO was to convene a special meeting of state and industry experts to address the global tracking of airline flights, in view of the loss in March of a Malaysia Airlines passenger plane.

In December 2011 ICAO released the first *State of Global Aviation Safety* report, addressing global aviation safety performance. The report envisaged that the volume of scheduled aviation traffic worldwide (which, in 2013, reached a record 33m. departures), would rise to 52m. annually by 2030. Annual air passenger numbers (estimated at 3,100m. in 2013) were expected to exceed 6,000m. by 2030.

ICAO maintains a Flight Safety Information Exchange (FSIX) website at cfapp.icao.int/fsix, to help to disseminate safety-related information, including aviation safety and security audits, such as USOAP findings. The main subject areas cover safety oversight information; resolving safety deficiencies; regional regulations; and safety management.

In April 2010, in view of the eruption of the Eyjafjallajökull volcano, in Iceland, ICAO established the International Volcanic Ash Task Force (IVATF), to establish a co-ordinated region-wide operational approach to volcanic ash emergencies. In the following month the Task Force agreed a common working agenda to improve contingency plans for preventing accidents in the wake of any future eruption, as well as minimizing disruptions of service and severe economic impact on the airline industry. In March 2012 ICAO issued a manual entitled *Flight Safety and Volcanic Ash*, which was based on the work of the Task Force, and aimed to provide air transport operators with a scientific basis for future post-volcanic eruption decision-making. In June the IVATF delivered a series of recommendations and practical tools—including a template for Air Traffic Management (ATM) Volcanic Ash Contingency Plans—aimed at mitigating the impact on international aviation of any future volcanic events.

NAVIGATION

ICAO's Air Navigation Bureau develops technical studies for the Air Navigation Commission, as well as recommendations for Standards and Recommended Practices relating to the safety, regularity and efficiency of international air navigation. Areas of activity include meteorology, automated data interchange systems, accident investigation and prevention, aviation medicine and air traffic management. In March 1998 the ICAO Council adopted the first edition of a Global Air Navigation Plan (GANP), addressing Communications, Navigation, Surveillance (CNS)/ATM Systems. An international conference convened in Rio de Janeiro, Brazil, to consider implementation of the CNS/ATM systems, urged greater financing and co-operation between states to ensure that the CNS/ATM becomes the basis of a global ATM system. An Air Traffic Management Operational Concept Panel, which was to develop Standards and Recommended Practices for the development of an integrated ATM system, was convened for the first time in March–April 1999. In October 1998 the Assembly adopted a Charter on the Rights and Obligations of States relating to Global Navigation Satellite Systems (GNSS) to serve as an interim framework on the GNSS. A long-term legal framework on principles governing the GNSS, including an international convention, remains under consideration. The 11th Air Navigation Conference, convened by ICAO in September–October 2003, in Montréal, endorsed an operational concept for a globally harmonized air navigation system that aimed to enhance safety and reduce airspace and airport congestion. In 2005 ICAO assisted countries and international organizations to develop preparedness strategies with regard to the threat of a pandemic of highly pathogenic avian influenza. A new World Air Services Agreements (WASA) database was launched in 2011, holding more than 2,500 summaries of bilateral 'open skies' air services agreements, and arrangements at regional level. Some 130 new air services agreements were signed at the ICAO's 2012 Air Services Negotiation Conference (ICAN 2012), held in December, in Jeddah, Saudi Arabia. In April 2009 ICAO and major global aviation stakeholders adopted a declaration calling for the rapid implementation of Performance-based Navigation (PBN), a new air navigation concept setting clear performance targets for specific flight operations, and emphasizing the use of accurate satellite-based navigation aids, with the aim of contributing further to improving the safety, efficiency and sustainability of the global air transport system; all of the ICAO Regional Offices have established PBN task forces, which, with a global PBN Task Force, support countries' implementation of PBN. In February 2013 the first World ATM Congress was held, in Madrid, Spain. A revised GANP, the

ICAO Global Air Navigation Capacity and Efficiency Plan—covering the period 2013–28, and giving states the flexibility to adopt performance upgrades suited to their specific operational environments—was endorsed by the ICAO Council in October 2013.

SECURITY

The 1963 Tokyo Convention on Offences and Certain Other Acts Committed On Board Aircraft addresses unruly behaviour committed by airline passengers (other than hijacking, sabotage etc.). In 2000 ICAO developed model legislation relating to unruly passengers. A protocol to the Tokyo Convention, adopted by a Diplomatic Conference convened in April 2014, expanded jurisdiction over on board offences to the state in which the aircraft operator was based, and also to the state of landing. In October 1998 a protocol to the Chicago Convention, prohibiting the use of weapons against civil aircraft in flight, entered into effect. Following the terrorist attacks perpetrated against targets in the USA in September 2001, involving the use of hijacked aircraft as weapons, the 33rd Assembly—held in September–October—adopted a Declaration on the Misuse of Civil Aircraft as Weapons of Destruction and Other Terrorist Acts involving Civil Aviation. The Declaration urged a review of ICAO's aviation security programme and consideration of the initiation of a programme to audit airport security arrangements and member states' civil aviation security programmes. In October the Council established a Special Group on Aviation War Risk Insurance to make recommendations on the development of a co-ordinated and long-term approach in this area. A proposal by the Special Group concerning the establishment of a Global Scheme on Aviation War Risk Insurance (Globaltime), to be provided by a non-profit entity with initial multilateral government support, was approved in principle by the Council in May 2002. A high-level ministerial conference, convened under ICAO auspices in February of that year, endorsed a global Aviation Security Plan of Action and reaffirmed the responsibility of states to ensure aviation security on their territories. The Plan provided for the development of an effective global response to emerging threats; strengthened security-related provisions of the Convention on International Civil Aviation; and enhanced co-ordination of regional and sub-regional audit programmes. In June a Universal Security Audit Programme (USAP) was launched, as part of the Aviation Security Plan of Action, to help to identify and correct deficiencies in the implementation of security-related standards. The first round of security audits of all contracting states was completed by the end of 2007, and a second USAP round was implemented during 2008–13. A new Implementation Support and Development Branch was established in June 2007 to support member states with significant safety oversight or security deficiencies and to help to implement correction action plans. In September 2010 the Diplomatic Conference on Aviation Security, convened under ICAO auspices in Beijing, People's Republic of China, adopted two new international legal instruments: the Convention on the Suppression of Unlawful Acts Relating to International Civil Aviation, and the Protocol Supplementary to the Convention for the Suppression of Unlawful Seizure of Aircraft. In October 2010 the Assembly adopted the ICAO Declaration on Aviation Security, which included a roadmap aimed at further protecting global air transport from terrorist and other security threats, through the development of security screening procedures and increased capacity-building assistance. In the following month the Chicago Convention annex on security was amended to enhance air cargo security standards.

ICAO convened regional aviation security conferences in New Delhi, India in September 2011; Dakar, Senegal, in October 2011; Moscow, Russia, in November 2011; Kuala Lumpur, Malaysia, in January 2012; Caracas, Venezuela, in February 2012; and Manama, Bahrain, in April 2012, under a process that culminated in a high-level global security conference, which was held in Montréal in September. The conference issued a communiqué on aviation security in which it requested ICAO further to address emerging issues, such as the security of air navigation services and facilities; landside security; and cyber threats.

ICAO is developing a globally interoperable system of Machine Readable Travel Documents (MRTDs), incorporating biometric identification data, in order to enhance airport and international security, and has provided technical assistance to support the efforts of contracting states to develop MRTDs. ICAO's objective that all states issue machine readable passports by 1 April 2010 was not universally met. The Organization has specified 24 November 2015 as the obligatory deadline for universal machine readable compliance, by which time non-machine readable documents are to be phased out.

ECONOMIC DEVELOPMENT

ICAO aims to foster the development of a sound and economically viable—while environmentally and socially sustainable—civil aviation system of airlines, airports and air navigation service providers, providing freedom to travel and affordable access to mobility; fair and equal opportunities for states and air transport users; support for sustainable global and regional economic development; a long-term reasonable rate of return for air transport industry; and the efficient use of existing and future resources and technologies.

In March 2013 the sixth ICAO Worldwide Air Transport Conference agreed several economic regulatory objectives intended to guide efforts to deliver a more competitive and sustainable international aviation sector over the next 10 years; these included enhanced liberalization of airline ownership and control, increased air cargo liberalization, further convergence of consumer protection regimes for passengers and airlines, and minimizing state taxes and other charges on air travel and transport.

ENVIRONMENTAL PROTECTION

ICAO activities with respect to the environment are primarily focused on areas that require a co-ordinated international approach, i.e. aircraft noise and engine emissions. International standards and guidelines for noise certification of aircraft and international provisions for the regulation of aircraft engine emissions have been adopted and published in Annex 16 to the Chicago Convention. ICAO provides briefings and written submissions to meetings of the parties to the United Nations Framework Convention on Climate Change (UNFCCC), having been recognized in the 1997 Kyoto Protocol to the UNFCCC as the global body through which industrialized nations were to pursue the limitation or reduction of so-called greenhouse gas emissions from international aviation. In early 1999 the ICAO Council endorsed a reduction by 16%, applicable to new engine designs from 2003, in the permissible levels of nitrogen oxides emitted by aircraft engines; further reduced limits were approved in 2004. During July 2008–June 2009 ICAO convened four meetings of a Group on International Aviation and Climate Change, which developed an action plan to address aircraft emissions, and adopted a global aspirational target of an annual 2% improvement in aircraft fuel efficiency. By the end of 2012 54 ICAO member states, representing 75.45% of international air traffic, had submitted to ICAO national action plans to reduce carbon dioxide emissions from international aviation. In June 2001 the Council adopted a stricter noise standard (applicable from 1 January 2006) for jet and large propeller-driven aircraft, as well as new noise limits for helicopters and new provisions concerning re-certification. In October the Assembly approved a series of measures developed by the Committee concerning a balanced approach to aircraft noise and based on the following elements: quieter aircraft; land-use planning and management in the vicinity of airports; operational procedures for noise abatement; and operating restrictions. In 2008 the CAEP launched a series of Independent Expert (IE) reviews to establish technology and operational mid-term (i.e. 10-year) and long-term (20-year) objectives for progress in the reduction of noise, fuel burn and the emission of nitrogen oxides.

ICAO's first Environmental Report was published in September 2007, covering technical and policy aspects of aviation's impact on the environment. In October 2010 the 37th session of the ICAO Assembly adopted a resolution aimed at reducing the impact of aviation emissions on climate change, and providing a roadmap for action until 2050.

ICAO's online Carbon Emissions Calculator, launched in June 2008, estimates the carbon dioxide emissions from air travel for use in devising carbon footprint offset programmes.

ICAO SPECIFICATIONS

These are contained in annexes to the Chicago Convention, and in three sets of Procedures for Air Navigation Services (PANS Documents). The specifications are periodically revised in keeping with developments in technology and changing requirements. The 19 annexes to the Convention include personnel licensing, rules relating to the conduct of flights, meteorological services, aeronautical charts, air-to-ground communications, safety management, safety specifications, identification, air traffic control, rescue services, environmental protection, security and the transporting of dangerous goods. Technical Manuals and Circulars are issued to facilitate implementation.

TECHNICAL CO-OPERATION

ICAO's Technical Co-operation Bureau promotes the implementation of ICAO Standards and Recommended Practices, including the CNS/ATM (see above) and safety oversight measures, and assists developing countries in the execution of various projects, financed by UNDP and other sources. The TRAINAIR programme helps institutions to develop a standard aviation training package, and promotes international co-operation in training and course development.

ICAO works in close co-operation with other UN bodies, such as the World Meteorological Organization, the UNFCCC, the International Telecommunication Union, the Universal Postal Union, the World Health Organization (WHO) and the International Maritime Organization. Non-governmental organizations which also participate in ICAO's work include the International Air Transport Association, the Airports Council International, the International Federation of

Air Line Pilots' Associations, and the International Council of Aircraft Owner and Pilot Associations. In June 2003 ICAO published measures for preventing the spread by air travel of Severe Acute Respiratory Syndrome (SARS) and other contagious diseases, based on guidelines issued by WHO, and in 2009 ICAO supported member states in developing effective, globally harmonized national aviation contingency plans aimed at controlling the spread of pandemic (H1N1) 2009 (swine flu).

Finance

ICAO is financed mainly by contributions from member states. The authorized budget for the triennium 2014–16 totalled C $286.5m. (allocated as follows: $92.8m. in 2014, $94.7m. in 2015, and $99.0m. in 2016).

Publications

Annual Report of the Council.
Aviation Training Directory.
Directory of National Civil Aviation Administrations (online database).
ICAO Environmental Report.
ICAO Journal (6 a year).
Safety Report.
State of Global Aviation Safety.
World of Civil Aviation.
Conventions, agreements, rules of procedures, regulations, technical publications and manuals.

International Fund for Agricultural Development—IFAD

Address: Via Paolo di Dono 44, 00142 Rome, Italy.
Telephone: (06) 54591; **fax:** (06) 5043463; **e-mail:** ifad@ifad.org; **internet:** www.ifad.org.

IFAD was established in 1977, following a decision by the 1974 UN World Food Conference, with a mandate to combat hunger and eradicate poverty on a sustainable basis in the low-income, food-deficit regions of the world. Funding operations began in January 1978.

MEMBERS

IFAD has 172 members.

Organization

(April 2014)

GOVERNING COUNCIL

Each member state is represented in the Governing Council (the Fund's highest authority) by a Governor and an Alternate. Sessions are held annually with special sessions as required. The Governing Council elects the President of the Fund (who also chairs the Executive Board) by a two-thirds' majority for a four-year term. The President is eligible for re-election.

EXECUTIVE BOARD

Consists of 18 members and 18 alternates, elected by the Governing Council, who serve for three years. The Executive Board is responsible for the conduct and general operation of IFAD and approves loans and grants for projects; it holds three regular sessions each year. An independent Office of Evaluation reports directly to the Board.

The governance structure of the Fund is based on the classification of members. Membership of the Executive Board is distributed as follows: eight List A countries (i.e. industrialized donor countries), four List B (petroleum-exporting developing donor countries), and six List C (recipient developing countries), divided equally among the three Sub-List C categories (i.e. for Africa, Europe, Asia and the Pacific, and Latin America and the Caribbean).

President and Chairman of Executive Board: KANAYO F. NWANZE (Nigeria).

DEPARTMENTS

IFAD has three main administrative departments, each headed by an Assistant President: Finance and Administration; Programme Management (with five regional Divisions and a Technical Advisory Division); and External Affairs (including a Policy Division, a Communication Division and a Resource Mobilization Unit). Offices of the General Counsel and of Internal Audit report to the Office of the President and Vice-President.

Activities

IFAD provides financing primarily for projects designed to improve food production systems in developing member states and to strengthen related policies, services and institutions. In allocating resources IFAD is guided by the need to increase food production in the poorest food-deficit countries; the potential for increasing food production in other developing countries; and the importance of improving the nutrition, health and education of the poorest people in developing countries, i.e. small-scale farmers, artisanal fishermen, nomadic pastoralists, indigenous populations, rural women, and the rural landless. All projects emphasize the participation of beneficiaries in development initiatives, both at the local and national level. Issues relating to gender and household food security are incorporated into all aspects of its activities. IFAD has worked towards achieving the Millennium Development Goals (MDGs), in particular in relation to reducing, by 2015, the proportion of people living in extreme poverty. During 2013–14 IFAD, FAO and WFP were jointly discussing the development of a post-2015 framework in the area of food and nutrition.

In May 2011 the Executive Board adopted IFAD's Strategic Framework for 2011–15, in which it reiterated its commitment to improving rural food security and nutrition, and enabling the rural poor to overcome their poverty. The 2011–15 Strategic Framework was underpinned by five strategic objectives: developing a natural resource and economic asset base for poor rural communities, with improved resilience to climate change, environmental degradation and market transformation; facilitating access for the rural poor to services aimed at reducing poverty, improving nutrition, raising incomes and building resilience in a changing environment; supporting the rural poor in managing profitable, sustainable and resilient farm and non-farm enterprises and benefiting from decent employment opportunities; enabling the rural poor to influence policies and institutions that affect their livelihoods; and enabling institutional and policy environments that support agricultural production and the related non-farm activities.

From 2009 IFAD implemented a new business model, with the direct supervision of projects, and maintaining a stable presence in countries of operations, as its two main pillars. Consequently, by 2011 the Fund directly supervised some 93% of the projects it was funding, compared with 18% in 2007.

IFAD is a participant in the High Level Task Force (HLTF) on the Global Food Security Crisis, which was established by the UN Secretary-General in April 2008 and aims to address the impact of soaring global levels of food and fuel prices and to formulate a comprehensive framework for action. In June IFAD participated in the High-Level Conference on World Food Security and the Challenges of Climate Change and Bioenergy, convened by FAO in Rome, Italy. The meeting adopted a Declaration on Food Security, which noted an urgent need to develop the agricultural sectors and expand food production in developing countries and countries with economies in transition, and for increased investment in rural development, agriculture and agribusiness. In January 2009 the HLTF participated in a follow-up high-level meeting convened in Madrid, Spain, which agreed to initiate a consultation process with regard to the establishment of a Global Partnership for Agriculture, Food Security and Nutrition. During 2009 the long-standing Committee on World Food Security (CFS), open to member states of IFAD, FAO, and the World Food Programme (WFP), underwent reform, becoming a central component of the new Global Partnership; thereafter the CFS was tasked with influencing hunger elimination programmes at the global, regional and national level, taking into account that food security relates not just to agriculture but also to economic access to food, adequate nutrition, social safety nets and human rights. IFAD contributes, with FAO, WFP and other agencies, to a new Agricultural Market Information System (AMIS), which was agreed by a meeting of agriculture ministers from G20 countries, held in June 2011 to increase market transparency and to address the stabilization of food price volatility. IFAD welcomed a commitment made, in May 2012, by G8 heads of state and government and leaders of African countries, to supporting a New Alliance for Food Security and Nutrition; the Alliance was to promote sustainable and inclusive agricultural growth over a 10-year period. The 2013 edition of the joint IFAD-FAO-WFP annual *State of Food Insecurity in the World* report, released in October, addressed the multidimensional nature of the determinants and outcomes of food insecurity, and demonstrated the importance of mainstreaming food security and nutrition in public policies and programmes.

IFAD, with FAO and WFP, leads an initiative on ensuring food security by strengthening feeding programmes and expanding support to farmers in developing countries, the second of nine activities that were launched in April 2009 by the UN System Chief Executives Board for Co-ordination (CEB), with the aim of alleviating the impact on poor and vulnerable populations of the developing global economic crisis.

In September 2012 IFAD, FAO, WFP and UN Women launched 'Accelerating Progress Toward the Economic Empowerment of Rural Women', a five-year initiative that was to be implemented initially in Ethiopia, Guatemala, Kyrgyzstan, Liberia, Nepal, Niger and Rwanda.

In March 2010 the Executive Board endorsed a new IFAD Climate Change Strategy, under which the Fund aimed to create a climate-smart portfolio, and to support smallholder farmers increase their resilience to climate change. In October 2012 a new Adaptation for Smallholder Agriculture Programme (ASAP) became operational; under the ASAP finance for climate adaptation initiatives was to be integrated into IFAD-supported investments.

IFAD is a leading repository of knowledge, resources and expertise in the field of rural hunger and poverty alleviation. In 2001 it renewed its commitment to becoming a global knowledge institution for rural poverty-related issues. Through its technical assistance grants, IFAD aims to promote research and capacity building in the agricultural sector, as well as the development of technologies to increase production and alleviate rural poverty. In 1996 IFAD supported the establishment of the Support Group of the Global Forum on Agricultural Research (GFAR), which facilitates dialogue between research centres and institutions, farmers' organizations, non-governmental bodies, the private sector and donors. In recent years IFAD has been increasingly involved in promoting the use of communication technology to facilitate the exchange of information and experience among rural communities, specialized institutions and organizations, and IFAD-sponsored projects. Within the strategic context of knowledge management, IFAD has supported initiatives to establish regional electronic networks, such as Electronic Networking for Rural Asia/Pacific (ENRAP, conducted over three phases during the period 1998–2010), and FIDAMERICA in Latin America and the Caribbean (conducted over four phases during 1995–2009), as well as to develop other lines of communication between organizations, local agents and the rural poor.

In February 2014 IFAD and the global consumer goods enterprise Unilever concluded a five-year public-private partnership agreement (the first such contract to be signed by IFAD), with the aim of co-operating in improving the livelihoods of smallholder farmers, and consequently food security, globally.

In April 2013 IFAD and the World Bank jointly organized a session of the Global Forum on Remittances (GFR2013), on the theme: 'Sending money home to Asia'. The first GFR was established in 2005.

IFAD is empowered to make both loans and grants. Loans are available on highly concessionary, hardened, intermediate and ordinary terms. Highly concessionary loans carry no interest but have an annual service charge of 0.75% and a repayment period of 40 years; loans approved on hardened terms carry no interest charge, have an annual service charge of 0.75%, and are repaid over 20 years; intermediate loans are subject to a variable interest charge, equivalent to 50% of the interest rate charged on World Bank loans, and are repaid over 20 years; and ordinary loans carry a variable interest charge equal to that levied by the World Bank, and are repaid over 15–18 years. New Debt Sustainability Framework (DSF) grant financing was introduced in 2007 in place of highly concessional loans for heavily indebted poor countries (HIPCs). In 2012 highly concessionary loans represented some 33% of total lending in that year, DSF grants 32%, ordinary loans 30%, and intermediate loans 4%. Research and technical assistance grants are awarded to projects focusing on research and training, and for project preparation and development. In order to increase the impact of its lending resources on food production, the Fund seeks as much as possible to attract other external donors and beneficiary governments as cofinanciers of its projects. In 2012 external co-financing accounted for some 29.1% of all project funding, while domestic contributions, i.e. from recipient governments and other local sources, accounted for 22.4%.

The IFAD Indigenous Peoples Assistance Facility was created in 2007 to fund microprojects that aim to build upon the knowledge and natural resources of indigenous communities and organizations. Under IFAD's Policy on Engagement with Indigenous Peoples, adopted by the Executive Board in September 2009, an Indigenous Peoples' Forum was established in February 2011; this was to be hosted by IFAD and to convene every two years. The inaugural session of the Forum was held in February 2013. In September 2010, the Executive Board approved the establishment of a new Spanish Food Security Cofinancing Facility Trust Fund (the 'Spanish Trust Fund'), which is used to provide loans to IFAD borrower nations. On 31 December 2010 the Spanish Government provided, on a loan basis, €285.5m. to the Spanish Trust Fund.

In November 2006 IFAD was granted access to the core resources of the HIPC Trust Fund, administered by the World Bank, to assist in financing the outstanding debt relief on post-completion point countries participating in the HIPC debt relief initiative (see under IBRD). By April 2014 36 of 39 eligible countries had passed their decision points, thereby qualifying for HIPC debt relief assistance from IFAD; of those countries 35 had reached completion point, thereby qualifying for full and irrevocable debt reduction.

At the end of 2012 total IFAD loans approved since 1978 amounted to US $13,811.7m. for 924 projects. During the same period the Fund approved 2,486 research and technical assistance grants, at a cost of $869.0m. In 2012 IFAD approved 36 loans and 17 DSF grants, amounting in total to $968.0m., for a total of 33 projects. The financing of one project through the ASAP Trust Fund was approved, at a cost of $4.9m. Research and technical assistance grants amounting to $69.1m. were awarded, bringing the total financial assistance approved in 2012 to $1,042.0m., compared with $997.6m. in the previous year.

The regional distribution of project financing in 2012 was as follows: US $130.9m. for four projects in Eastern and Southern Africa (or 13.2% of the total committed in that year); $345.1m. for 10 operations in Asia and the Pacific (34.9%); $268.9m. for seven projects in Western and Central Africa (27.2%); $93.9m. for four projects in the Near East, North Africa and Europe (9.5%); and $149.6m. for eight projects in Latin America and the Caribbean (15.1%).

IFAD's development projects usually include a number of components, such as infrastructure (e.g. improvement of water supplies, small-scale irrigation and road construction); input supply (e.g. improved seeds, fertilizers and pesticides); institutional support (e.g. research, training and extension services); and producer incentives (e.g. pricing and marketing improvements). IFAD also attempts to enable the landless to acquire income-generating assets: by increasing the provision of credit for the rural poor, it seeks to free them from dependence on the capital market and to generate productive activities.

In addition to its regular efforts to identify projects and programmes, IFAD organizes special programming missions to selected countries to undertake a comprehensive review of the constraints affecting the rural poor, and to help countries to design strategies for the removal of these constraints. In general, projects based on the recommendations of these missions tend to focus on institutional improvements at the national and local level to direct inputs and services to small farmers and the landless rural poor. Monitoring and evaluation missions are also sent to check the progress of projects and to assess the impact of poverty reduction efforts.

The Fund supports projects that are concerned with environmental conservation, in an effort to alleviate poverty that results from the deterioration of natural resources. In addition, it extends environmental assessment grants to review the environmental consequences of projects under preparation. IFAD administers the Global Mechanism of the 1996 Convention to Combat Desertification in those Countries Experiencing Drought and Desertification, particularly in Africa. The Mechanism mobilizes and channels resources for the implementation of the Convention, and IFAD is its largest financial contributor. IFAD is an executing agency of the Global Environmental Facility, specializing in the area of combating rural poverty and environmental degradation.

During 1998 the Executive Board endorsed a policy framework for the Fund's provision of assistance in post-conflict situations, with the aim of achieving a continuum from emergency relief to a secure basis from which to pursue sustainable development. In September 2012 a High Level Expert Forum on Food Insecurity in Protracted Crises, convened by IFAD, FAO and WFP within the framework of the CFS, drafted an Agenda for Action. The document recommended utilizing integrated strategies—with a focus on building resilience—to address food insecurity in protracted crises, i.e. integrating food security into peacebuilding and governance initiatives at the national and regional level, and integrating food security into regional and global initiatives aimed at improving governance and addressing vulnerability.

IFAD co-operates with other agencies and partners within the context of the Global Partnership for Effective Development Co-operation, established by the Fourth High Level Forum on Aid Effectiveness, convened in Busan, Republic of Korea, in November–December 2011. Since the late 1990s IFAD has established partnerships within the agribusiness sector, with a view to improving performance at project level, broadening access to capital markets, and encouraging the advancement of new technologies. In

October 2001 IFAD became a co-sponsor of the Consultative Group on International Agricultural Research (CGIAR). In November 2009 IFAD and the Islamic Development Bank concluded a US $1,500m. framework co-financing agreement for jointly financing priority projects during 2010–12 in many of the 52 countries that had membership of both organizations.

Finance

In accordance with the Articles of Agreement establishing IFAD, the Governing Council periodically undertakes a review of the adequacy of resources available to the Fund and may request members to make additional contributions. In February 2012 a target of US $1,500m. was set for the ninth replenishment of IFAD funds (IFAD9), covering the period 2013–15. IFAD9 became effective on 30 November 2012. (A Fund replenishment becomes effective upon receipt of one-half of the funds pledged; by the end of December 2012 member states had pledged 92% of the ninth replenishment target.) The provisional regular budget for administrative expenses for 2013 amounted to $144.1m., while some $3.7m. was budgeted in that year to the Fund's capital budget.

Publications

Annual Report.
Rural Poverty Report.
Staff Working Papers (series).
State of Food Insecurity in the World (annually, with FAO and WFP).

International Labour Organization—ILO

Address: 4 route des Morillons, 1211 Geneva 22, Switzerland.

Telephone: 227996111; **fax:** 227988685; **e-mail:** ilo@ilo.org; **internet:** www.ilo.org.

The ILO was founded in 1919 to work for social justice as a basis for lasting peace. It carries out this mandate by promoting decent living standards, satisfactory conditions of work and pay and adequate employment opportunities. In 1946 the ILO became a specialized agency associated with the UN. It was awarded the Nobel Peace Prize in 1969. The ILO's tripartite structure gives representation to employers' and workers' organizations alongside governments.

MEMBERS

The ILO has 185 members.

Organization

(April 2014)

INTERNATIONAL LABOUR CONFERENCE

The supreme deliberative body of the ILO, the Conference meets annually in Geneva, Switzerland, with a session devoted to maritime questions when necessary. National delegations are composed of two government delegates, one employers' delegate and one workers' delegate. Non-governmental delegates can speak and vote independently of the views of their national government. The Conference elects the Governing Body and adopts International Labour Conventions and Recommendations. Every two years the Conference adopts the ILO Budget. The 102nd session of the Conference was held in June 2013, and the 103rd session was to take place in May–June 2014.

GOVERNING BODY

The ILO's executive council meets three times a year in Geneva to decide policy and programmes. It is composed of 28 government members, 14 employers' members and 14 workers' members. Ten of the titular government seats are held permanently by 'states of chief industrial importance': Brazil, the People's Republic of China, France, Germany, India, Italy, Japan, Russia, the United Kingdom and the USA. The remaining 18 are elected from other countries every three years. Employers' and workers' members are elected as individuals, not as national candidates.

Among the Committees formed by the Governing Body are the Programme, Financial and Administrative Committee; the Building Sub-Committee; the Committee on Freedom of Association; the Committee on Legal Issues and International Labour Standards; the Sub-Committee on Multinational Enterprises; the Committee on Employment and Social Policy; the Committee on Sectoral and Technical Meetings and Related Issues; the Committee on Technical Co-operation; the Working Party on the Social Dimension of Globalization; and the Working Party on the Functioning of the Governing Body and the International Labour Conference.

Chairperson: (2013–14) VICTORIA MARINA VELÁSQUEZ DE AVILÉS (El Salvador).

Employers' Vice-Chairperson: DANIEL FUNES DE RIOJA (Argentina).

Workers' Vice-Chairperson: LUC CORTEBEECK (Belgium).

INTERNATIONAL LABOUR OFFICE

The International Labour Office is the ILO's secretariat, operational headquarters and publishing house. It is staffed in Geneva and in the field by about 2,500 people of some 110 nationalities. Operations are decentralized to regional, area and branch offices in nearly 40 countries.

Director-General: GUY RYDER (United Kingdom).

ADMINISTRATIVE TRIBUNAL

The Tribunal comprises seven judges, of differing nationalities, who are appointed to a renewable three-year term by the International Labour Conference, on the recommendation of the Governing Body. The Tribunal examines employment-related complaints from officials of the International Labour Office and of more than 50 other international organizations that have recognized its jurisdiction. The Tribunal, which is served by a Registry, meets, at ILO headquarters, for two sessions a year.

REGIONAL OFFICES

Africa: Africa Hall, 6th Floor, Menelik II Ave, Addis Ababa, Ethiopia; tel. (11) 544-4480; fax (11) 544-5573; e-mail addisababa@ilo.org.

Arab States: POB 11-4088, Beirut, Lebanon; tel. (1) 752400; fax (1) 752405; e-mail beirut@ilo.org.

Asia and the Pacific: POB 2-349, Bangkok 10200, Thailand; tel. (2) 881234; fax (2) 883062; e-mail bangkok@ilo.org.

Europe and Central Asia: 4 route des Morillons, 1211 Geneva 22, Switzerland; tel. 227996666; fax 227996061; e-mail europe@ilo.org.

Latin America and the Caribbean: Apdo Postal 14–124, Lima, Peru; tel. (1) 6150300; fax (1) 6150400; e-mail oit@oit.org.pe.

Activities

The ILO pursues the goal of 'Decent Work for All' and promotes a Decent Work Agenda (adopted in 1999), which has four basic pillars: employment creation, as the principal route out of poverty; rights at work, which empower men and women to escape from poverty; social protection, which safeguards against poverty; and tripartism and social dialogue, regarding the participation of employers' and workers' organizations as of key importance in shaping government policy for poverty reduction. Gender equality is a cross-cutting objective. Through the Decent Work Agenda the ILO has supported the UN's Millennium Development Goals. In 2013 the ILO co-led global consultations on the advancement of the post-2015 international development framework in the thematic areas of growth and employment; and addressing inequalities.

STANDARDS AND FUNDAMENTAL PRINCIPLES AND RIGHTS AT WORK

One of the ILO's primary functions is the adoption by the International Labour Conference of conventions and recommendations setting minimum labour standards. Through ratification by member states, conventions create binding obligations to put their provisions into effect. Recommendations provide guidance as to policy and practice. By April 2014 a total of 189 conventions, five protocols, and 202 recommendations had been adopted, ranging over a wide field of social and labour matters. Together they form the International Labour Code. The Committee of Experts on the Application of Conventions and Recommendations and the Conference Committee on the Application of Standards monitor the adoption of international labour standards. In June 1998 the Conference adopted a Declaration on Fundamental Principles and Rights at Work, establishing four fundamental (core) labour standards: freedom of association, the abolition of forced labour, the abolition of child labour, and the elimination of discrimination in employment promotion, training and the protection of workers. All member states are obliged to observe these standards, whether or not they have ratified the corresponding international conventions. The following eight ILO core conventions have been identified by the Governing Body as being fundamental to the rights of people at work, irrespective of the levels of development of individual member states: (relating to the core labour standard of freedom of association) Freedom of Association and Protection of the Right to Organise Convention (No. 87), Right to Organise and Collective Bargaining Convention (No. 98); (abolition of forced labour) Forced Labour Convention (No. 29), Abolition of Forced Labour Convention (No. 105); (equality) Equal Remuneration Convention (No. 100), Discrimination (Employment and Occupation) Convention (No. 111); (elimination of child labour) Minimum Age Convention (No. 138), Worst Forms of Child Labour Convention (No. 182). By April 2014 some 138 countries had ratified all of the core conventions; three member states, the Marshall Islands, Palau and Tuvalu, had ratified none of them. Since 2008 the following four conventions have been designated as priority 'governance conventions' (i.e. having particular significance from the perspective of governance): the Labour Inspection Convention (No. 81); Employment Policy Convention (No. 122); Labour Inspection (Agriculture) Convention (No. 129); and the Tripartite Consultation (International Labour Standards) Convention (No. 144).

In May 2003 the ILO issued the first global report on discrimination at work, *Time for Equality at Work*, compiled as a follow-up to the 1998 Declaration on Fundamental Principles and Rights at Work; *Equality for Work: The Continuing Challenge* was published in June 2011. In June 2012 the ILO released a *Global Estimate of Forced Labour*, which found that 20.9m. people globally (of whom 5.5m. were under 18 years of age) were trapped in forced labour, including through debt bondage and trafficking. Of an estimated 18.7m. people reported to be exploited in the private economy, some 14.2m. were believed to be trapped in activities such as domestic work, agriculture, construction and manufacturing (for example barely rewarded sweatshop work), and 4.5m. were believed to be victims of forced sexual exploitation. The ILO estimated that a further 2.2m. people were being exploited in organized forms of forced labour that failed to meet global standards, imposed, for example, by prisons or by the military.

The ILO, working closely with UNICEF, encourages member states to ratify and to implement relevant international standards on child labour. In June 1999 the International Labour Conference adopted the Worst Forms of Child Labour Convention (No. 182); the convention entered into force in November 2000. By April 2014 it had been ratified by 178 states. A Global Conference on Child Labour, held in The Hague, Netherlands, in May 2010, and organized jointly by the ILO and the Government of the Netherlands, adopted a roadmap to strengthen the global effort to eliminate the worst forms of child labour. In November the ILO Governing Body endorsed a new Global Plan of Action for achieving the elimination of the worst forms of child labour by 2016. By 2014 the ILO's International Programme for the Elimination of Child Labour (IPEC, established in 1992) was operational in 88 countries, of which more than 60 had signed a Memorandum of Understanding (MOU) with the ILO. Under IPEC emphasis was placed on the elimination of the most severe forms of labour such as hazardous working conditions and occupations, child prostitution and trafficking of children. In addition, IPEC gives special attention to children who are particularly vulnerable, for example those under 12 years of age. IPEC published a resource guide on child trafficking and sexual exploitation to coincide with the third World Congress against Sexual Exploitation of Children and Adolescents, convened in Rio de Janeiro, Brazil, in November 2008. The ILO-sponsored World Day against Child Labour is held annually on 12 June.

In June 2011 the International Labour Conference adopted a Convention on Decent Work for Domestic Workers, establishing global standards for up to 100m. domestic labourers worldwide; the Convention entered into force in September 2013 (one year after its second ratification). By April 2014 13 states had ratified the Convention.

The ILO's Maritime Labour Convention (MLC), adopted in February 2006, and establishing labour protection and comprehensive rights for seafarers, entered into force in August 2013.

EMPLOYMENT

The ILO aims to monitor, examine and report on the situation and trends in employment throughout the world, and considers the effects on employment and social justice of economic trade, investment and related phenomena. ILO leads an initiative on promoting a 'Global Jobs Pact', the fifth of nine activities that were launched in April 2009 by the UN System Chief Executives Board for Co-ordination (CEB), with the aim of alleviating the impact on poor and vulnerable populations of the global economic crisis that emerged from 2008. The Pact, a co-ordinated labour recovery strategy, based on promoting sustainable enterprises, was endorsed by the International Labour Conference in June 2009. In September, addressing a summit meeting of G20 leaders held in Pittsburgh, Philadelphia, USA, which had welcomed the Pact, the ILO Director-General applauded the G20 leaders' stated commitment to implementing economic recovery plans that emphasized decent work and prioritized employment growth. In October the ILO reported that workers employed by and through temporary labour agencies were particularly badly affected by the continuing financial and economic crisis. The June 2010 session of the International Labour Conference urged governments to place employment and social protection at the centre of economic recovery policies. In June 2011 the ILO published a study entitled *The Global Crisis: Causes, responses and challenges*, focusing on the role that well-designed employment and social policies should play in promoting job creation and equitable economic growth. In December 2011 the ILO and the MasterCard Foundation launched Work4Youth, a partnership aimed at promoting decent work among young people. In January 2012 the ILO Director-General—addressing a panel on 'Averting a Lost Generation' at the annual meeting of the World Economic Forum, convened in Davos-Klosters, Switzerland—strongly urged the development of a new policy paradigm to promote inclusive employment opportunities for unemployed youth. An ILO Action Plan on youth employment was adopted by the ILO in June of that year. Youth unemployment was the central theme of the 2013 session of the International Labour Conference, which was held in June. In April the ILO and World Bank released a joint report entitled *Inventory of Policy Responses to the Financial and Economic Crisis*, and a companion web-based data tool that provided a detailed record of policies that had been implemented by governments during 2008–10 with a view to limiting the economic and social impacts of the global crisis and to boosting employment. It was envisaged that stocktaking and reviewing past crisis response measures would facilitate the design of efficient and effective policies to address future economic downturns.

In January 2014 the ILO estimated that nearly 202m. workers worldwide were unemployed in 2013 (an increase of 29m. over 2007, prior to the impact of the continuing global economic and jobs downturn) and reported that around 48% of workers globally were in vulnerable employment. In addition, it was estimated that around 375m. workers worldwide were living on or less than US $1.25 a day (categorized as 'working poor'). The rate of global youth unemployment was estimated at 13.1% in 2013.

In February 2002 the ILO established a World Commission on the Social Dimension of Globalization to consider means of utilizing economic globalization to stimulate economic growth and reduce poverty. The Commission issued its final report, entitled *A Fair Globalization*, in February 2004; this was endorsed by the 92nd International Labour Conference, held in June. In March 2003 the ILO adopted the Global Employment Agenda, a comprehensive framework for managing changes to employment derived from the developing global economy, through investment in knowledge and skills, maintaining a healthy labour market and ensuring adequate social safety nets. In June 2008, as the outcome of tripartite consultations based on the work of the World Commission on the Social Dimension of Globalization and its final report, the *ILO Declaration on Social Justice for a Fair Globalization*, building on the Philadelphia Declaration (1944) and the Declaration on Fundamental Principles and Rights at Work (1998), was adopted by the International Labour Conference. The Declaration placed the Decent Work Agenda at the core of ILO activities.

The ILO's programme sector on skills, knowledge and employability supports governments in structuring policies for improved investment in learning and training for enhanced employability, productivity and social inclusion. The programme focuses on promoting access to training and decent work for specific groups, such as youths, the disabled, and workers in the informal economy, and on protecting the rights of the elderly. The Job Creation and Enterprise Development Programme aims to assist governments, employers, workers and other related groups with fostering a successful business environment, for example through the identification and implementation of appropriate policies, legal frameworks and management strategies, the promotion of access to business development and training services, and the promotion of local economic development programmes. It also incorporates a specific programme to promote the development of micro- and small enterprises, in co-operation with governments, communities and other social partners. The ILO's Gender Promotion Programme aims to promote effective gender mainstreaming and is responsible for a global programme for the creation of more and better jobs for women and men. The programme assists countries to develop and implement National Action Plans to achieve this objective. A programme on crisis response and reconstruction addresses the effect on employment of armed conflicts, natural disasters, social movements or political transitions, and financial and economic disruptions. The impact of current global financial and economic trends on employment creation, poverty alleviation and social exclusion are addressed by the ILO's Social Finance Programme. The programme works to reduce vulnerability, to create jobs through enterprise development, and to make financial policies more employment-sensitive, for example by providing information on microfinance and promoting microfinance institutions, and by conducting research on the impact of financial sector liberalization on the poor.

The Multinational Enterprise Programme is responsible for the promotion of and follow-up to the Tripartite Declaration of Principles concerning Multinational Enterprises and Social Policy, which was adopted in 1977 and amended in 2000. The Declaration provides international guidelines, agreed by governments and employers' and workers' organizations, on investment policy and practice. The programme is also responsible for co-ordinating work on corporate social responsibility, as well as for the ILO's participation in the Global Compact, an initiative of the UN Secretary-General originating in 2000, comprising leaders in the fields of business, labour and civil society who undertook to promote human rights, the fundamental principles of the ILO, and protection of the environment.

The ILO maintains technical relations with the IMF, the World Bank, Organisation for Economic Co-operation and Development (OECD), the World Trade Organization (WTO) and other international organizations on global economic issues, international and national strategies for employment, structural adjustment, and labour market and training policies. In May 2011 the ILO and OECD signed an MOU on strengthening mutual co-operation. In September of that year the ILO and WTO jointly issued a publication entitled *Making Globalization Socially Sustainable*.

In 2007 the ILO, the UN Environment Programme (UNEP) and the International Trade Union Confederation launched in partnership the Green Jobs Initiative (the International Organisation of Employers joined in 2008). The Initiative aims to promote the creation of decent jobs as a consequence of new environmental policies required to transform ongoing global environmental challenges. In September 2008 it released a report entitled *Green Jobs: Towards Decent Work in a Sustainable, Low-Carbon World*, the first comprehensive study on the impact of the emergent 'green economy' on the labour market. In February 2013 the ILO, with UNEP, the UN Industrial Development Organization (UNIDO) and the UN Institute for Training and Research, launched the Partnership for Action on Green Economy (PAGE), which aimed, over the period 2013–20, to support 30 countries in developing national green economy strategies aimed at generating employment and skills, promoting clean technologies, and reducing environmental risks and poverty.

SOCIAL PROTECTION

Access to an adequate level of social protection is recognized in the ILO's 1944 Declaration of Philadelphia, as well as in a number of international labour standards, as a basic right of all individuals. The ILO aims to enable countries to extend social protection to all groups in society and to improve working conditions and safety at work. The fundamental premise of the ILO's programme sector on socio-economic security is that basic security for all is essential for productive work and human dignity in the future global economy. The achievement of basic security is deemed to entail the attainment of basic humanitarian needs, including universal access to health services and a decent level of education. The programme focuses on the following dimensions of work-based security: the labour market (the provision of adequate employment opportunities); employment (for example, protection against dismissal); occupational security (the opportunity to develop a career); work (protection against accidents, illness and stress at work); skills; income; and representation (the right to collective representation in the labour market, through independent trade unions and employers' associations, etc.). The ILO's Social Security Policy and Development Branch assists member states and constituents in the design, reform and implementation of social security policies based on the principles embodied in international labour standards, with a special focus on developing strategies to extend social security coverage. The Branch provides general research and analysis of social security issues; extends technical assistance to member states for designing, reforming and expanding social security schemes; provides services to enable community-based organizations to develop their own social security systems; promotes and oversees the implementation of ILO standards on social security; develops training programmes and materials; and disseminates information. The Financial, Actuarial and Statistical Services Branch aims to improve the financial planning, management and governance of national social security schemes and social protection systems. In June 2003 the ILO inaugurated a Global Campaign on Social Security and Coverage for All, with a particular focus on the informal economy. The ILO estimates that only one-fifth of the world's population has sufficient social security coverage. The key operational tool of the Campaign is the ILO's STEP (Strategies and Tools against Social Exclusion and Poverty) Programme which undertakes field work, research, training and the dissemination of knowledge to help to extend social protection and combat social exclusion. The International Social Security Association (ISSA), based at ILO headquarters, unites social security agencies and organizations, with the aim of supporting excellence in social security administration as a means of promoting the social dimension in the era of rapid economic globalization. In March 2013 the ILO and ISSA signed an MOU on strengthening co-operation in advancing and promoting social security.

The ILO's Programme on Safety and Health at Work and the Environment aims to protect workers in hazardous occupations; to provide protection to vulnerable groups of workers outside the scope of normal protection measures; to improve the capacity of governments and employers' and workers' organizations to address workers' well-being, extend the scope of occupational health care etc.; and to ensure that policy-makers recognize and document the social and economic impact of implementing measures that enhance workers' protection. The ILO Guidelines on Occupational Safety and Health Management Systems (ILO-OSH 2001) provides a framework of action at an international, national and organizational level. The ILO's Conditions of Work Branch conducts research and provides advocacy, training and technical co-operation to governments and employers' and workers' organizations in areas such as wages, working time, maternity protection and life outside of work. The International Migration Branch focuses on protecting the rights, and promoting the integration, of migrant workers, forging international consensus on the management of migration, and furthering knowledge of international migration. In December 2010 the ILO and the OSCE jointly published a study entitled *Strengthening Migration Governance*.

The ILO's Global Programme on HIV/AIDS and the World of Work, formally established in November 2000, issued a code of practice in May 2001, focusing on prevention, management and mitigation of the impact of HIV/AIDS on the world of work, support for HIV/AIDS-affected workers, and eliminating discrimination on the basis of perceived HIV status. The ILO is a co-sponsor of the Joint UN Programme on HIV/AIDS (UNAIDS), which was established on 1 January 1996 to co-ordinate and strengthen worldwide action against HIV/AIDS. The ILO adopted a Code of Practice on HIV/AIDS and the World of Work in October 2005. In June 2010 the International Labour Conference adopted a new international labour standard on HIV/AIDS, representing the first international human rights instrument related to HIV/AIDS and employment. A new ILO list of occupational diseases was adopted by the Governing Body in March 2010; this aimed to assist member countries with the prevention, recording, notification and, where applicable, compensation of illnesses caused by work.

The ILO, with the World Health Organization, leads the Social Protection Floor initiative, the sixth activity launched in April 2009 by CEB, to alleviate the effects of the global economic crisis. In October 2011 a Social Protection Floor Advisory Group, launched in August 2010 under the initiative, issued a report entitled *Social Protection Floor for a Fair and Inclusive Globalization*, which urged that basic income and services should be guaranteed for all, stating that this would promote both stability and economic growth globally. A landmark Recommendation on a Social Protection Floor for All was adopted by the International Labour Conference in June 2012.

In December 2011 the ILO launched the ILO Global Business and Disability Network, a new global knowledge-sharing platform (accessible at www.businessanddisability.org), which was aimed at promoting the inclusion of people with disabilities in the workplace.

The ILO sponsors the World Day for Safety and Health at Work, held annually on 28 April.

SOCIAL DIALOGUE

This area was identified as one of the four strategic objectives in order to concentrate and reinforce the ILO's support for strengthening the process of tripartism, the role and activities of its tripartite constituents (i.e. governments, employers and workers' organizations), and, in particular, their capacity to engage in and to promote the use of social dialogue. The ILO recognizes that the enactment of labour laws, and ensuring their effective enforcement, collective bargaining and other forms of co-operation are important means of promoting social justice. It aims to assist governments and employers' and workers' organizations to establish sound labour relations, to adapt labour laws to meet changing economic and social needs, and to improve labour administration. In August 2006 the ILO inaugurated a joint programme with the International Finance Corporation, 'Better Work', to improve labour standards within a competitive global market; a second phase of the programme was initiated in 2009.

The Social Dialogue, Labour Law and Labour Administration Department maintains an International Observatory of Labour

Law which provides information concerning national labour legislation and facilitates the dissemination of information regarding development in labour law throughout the world. The Department also supports the training and professional development of labour court judges and publishes the proceedings of meetings of European labour court judges.

A Committee on Freedom of Association examines allegations of abuses committed against trade union organizations and reports to the Governing Body. Reports of failure to implement the Freedom of Association and Protection of the Right to Organize Convention, 1948 (No. 87) are considered by the International Labour Conference.

INSTITUTES

International Institute for Labour Studies (IILS): 4 route des Morillons, 1211 Geneva 22, Switzerland; tel. 227996128; fax 227998542; e-mail inst@ilo.org; internet www.ilo.org/inst/lang–en/index.htm; f. 1960; promotes the study and discussion of policy issues of concern to the ILO and its constituents, i.e. governments, employers and workers. The core theme of the Institute's activities is the interaction between labour institutions, development and civil society in a global economy. It identifies emerging social and labour issues by developing new areas for research and action, and encourages dialogue on social policy between the tripartite constituency of the ILO and the international academic community and other experts. The Institute maintains research networks, conducts courses, seminars and social policy forums, and supports internships and visiting scholar and internship programmes. The ILO Director-General is Chairman of the Board of the Institute; Dir RAYMOND TORRES.

International Training Centre of the ILO (ITC-ILO): Viale Maestri del Lavoro 10, 10127 Turin, Italy; tel. (011) 693-6111; fax (011) 663-8842; e-mail communications@itcilo.org; internet www.itcilo.org; f. 1964 by the ILO to offer advanced training facilities for managers, trainers and social partners, and technical specialists from ILO mem. states; became operational in 1965; the Centre has been increasingly used by its partners to provide training for improving the management of development and for building national capacities to sustain development programmes; through training and learning the ITC-ILO develops human resources and institutional capacity in pursuit of the ILO's goal of decent work for men and women; Exec. Dir PATRICIA O'DONOVAN.

Finance

The proposed regular budget for the two years 2014–15 was US $857.8m.

Publications

(in English, French and Spanish unless otherwise indicated)

Asia-Pacific Labour Market Update (2 a year).

Bulletin of Labour Statistics (quarterly).

Global Employment Trends.

Global Employment Trends for Women.

Global Employment Trends for Youth.

Global Wage Report.

International Labour Review (quarterly).

Key Indicators of the Labour Market (2 a year).

Labour Law Documents (selected labour and social security laws and regulations; 3 a year).

Official Bulletin (3 a year).

Reports (for the annual sessions of the International Labour Conference, etc.; also in Arabic, Chinese and Russian).

World Labour Report (every 2 years).

World of Work (magazine issued in several languages; 5 a year).

Yearbook of Labour Statistics.

International studies, surveys, works of practical guidance or reference (on questions of social policy, manpower, industrial relations, working conditions, social security, training, management development, etc.). Also maintains a database on international labour standards, ILOLEX, a database on national labour law, NATLEX, and a database on labour statistics, ILOSTAT, all in electronic form.

International Maritime Organization—IMO

Address: 4 Albert Embankment, London, SE1 7SR, United Kingdom.

Telephone: (20) 7735-7611; **fax:** (20) 7587-3210; **e-mail:** info@imo.org; **internet:** www.imo.org.

The Inter-Governmental Maritime Consultative Organization (IMCO) began operations in 1959, as a specialized agency of the UN to facilitate co-operation among governments on technical matters affecting international shipping. Its main functions are the achievement of safe, secure and efficient navigation, and the control of pollution caused by ships and craft operating in the marine environment. IMCO became IMO in 1982.

MEMBERS

IMO has 170 members and three associate members.

Organization

(April 2014)

ASSEMBLY

The Assembly consists of delegates from all member countries, who each have one vote. Associate members and observers from other governments and the international agencies are also present. Regular sessions are held every two years. The 28th session was convened in London, United Kingdom, in November–December 2013.

The Assembly is responsible for the election of members to the Council and approves the appointment of the Secretary-General of the Secretariat. It considers reports from all subsidiary bodies and decides the action to be taken on them; it votes the agency's budget and determines the work programme and financial policy. The Assembly also recommends to members measures to promote maritime safety and security, and to prevent and control maritime pollution from ships.

COUNCIL

The Council is the governing body of the Organization between the biennial sessions of the Assembly. Its members, representatives of 40 states, are elected by the Assembly for a term of two years. The Council appoints the Secretary-General; transmits reports by the subsidiary bodies, including the Maritime Safety Committee, to the Assembly, and reports on the work of the Organization generally; submits budget estimates and financial statements with comments and recommendations to the Assembly. The Council normally meets twice a year.

Facilitation Committee: The Facilitation Committee deals with measures to facilitate maritime travel and transport and matters arising from the 1965 Facilitation Convention. Membership is open to all IMO member states.

MARITIME SAFETY COMMITTEE

The Maritime Safety Committee is open to all IMO members. The Committee meets at least once a year and submits proposals to the Assembly on technical matters affecting the safety of shipping. In December 2002 a conference of contracting states to the 1974 International Convention for the Safety of Life at Sea (see below) adopted a series of security measures relating to the international maritime and port industries that had been formulated by the Safety Committee in view of the major terrorist attacks perpetrated against targets in the USA in September 2001. A Department for Member State Audit and Implementation Support was established within the Committee in January 2012. Sub-committees of the Marine Safety Committee cover: bulk liquids and gases (also a sub-committee of the Marine Environment Protection Committee); carriage of dangerous goods, solid cargoes and containers; fire protection; flag state implementation (also a sub-committee of the Marine Environment Protection Committee); radiocommunications and search and rescue; safety of navigation; ship design and equipment; stability and load lines and fishing vessel safety; and standards of training and watchkeeping.

LEGAL COMMITTEE

Established by the Council in June 1967 to deal initially with legal issues connected with the loss of the tanker *Torrey Canyon,* and subsequently with any legal problems laid before IMO. Membership is open to all IMO member states.

MARINE ENVIRONMENT PROTECTION COMMITTEE

Established by the eighth Assembly (1973) to co-ordinate IMO's work on the prevention and control of marine pollution from ships, and to assist IMO in its consultations with other UN bodies, and with international organizations and expert bodies in the field of marine pollution. Membership is open to all IMO members.

TECHNICAL CO-OPERATION COMMITTEE

Evaluates the implementation of projects for which IMO is the executing agency, and generally reviews IMO's technical assistance programmes. Established in 1965 as a subsidiary body of the Council, and formally institutionalized by means of an amendment to the IMO constitution in 1984. Membership is open to all IMO member states.

SECRETARIAT

The Secretariat consists of the Secretary-General (who serves a four-year term of office), and a staff appointed by the Secretary-General and recruited on as wide a geographical basis as possible. The Secretariat comprises the following divisions: Administrative; Conference; Legal Affairs and External Relations; Marine Environment; Maritime Safety; and Technical Co-operation.

Secretary-General: KOJI SEKIMIZU (Japan).

Activities

The 27th regular session of the Assembly, held in London, United Kingdom, in November 2011, approved a new Strategic Plan to guide the Organization during the period 2012–17, with a focus on areas including the environmental impact of global shipping activities; the elimination of substandard shipping; piracy; and the implementation of effective measures to alleviate the humanitarian impact of piracy, and to address seaborne migration and stowaways. The 28th regular Assembly, convened in November–December 2013, also in London, adopted a mandatory audit scheme aimed at assessing and supporting the performance, under relevant IMO treaties, of member states as flag, port and coastal states.

From 2005 IMO brought to the attention of the UN Security Council serious concerns over acts of piracy and armed robbery being perpetrated against ships off the coast of Somalia and in the Gulf of Aden; and serious concerns were also subsequently raised about armed pirate attacks on ships in the Gulf of Guinea. In June, October and December 2008, November 2009, April and November 2010, April and November 2011, and February 2012, the Security Council adopted successive resolutions on combating piracy. The issue was also one of the focal areas of a UN General Assembly resolution on 'Oceans and the law of the sea', adopted in February 2009. A high-level sub-regional meeting of states from the Western Indian Ocean, the Gulf of Aden and Red Sea areas, held under IMO auspices in Djibouti, in January 2009, adopted the Djibouti Code of Conduct concerning the Repression of Piracy and Armed Robbery. The Code, which by April had been signed by 20 of the 21 countries eligible as signatories, promotes the implementation of those aspects of relevant UN Security Council resolutions, and of the February 2009 General Assembly resolution on oceans and the law of the sea, which fall within IMO's area of competence. Signatories to the Code (which is supported by a dedicated trust fund) have agreed to co-operate lawfully in the apprehension, investigation and prosecution of people suspected of committing or facilitating acts of piracy; in the seizure of suspect vessels; in the rescue of ships, persons and property subject to acts of armed robbery; and to collaborate in the conduct of security operations. The Code also provides for sharing related information on matters related to maritime security. Meeting in May–June 2009 the Maritime Safety Committee approved revised guidance to governments, and also to shipowners, ship operators, ship masters and crews, on suppressing piracy. In December 2009 the IMO Assembly adopted a resolution supporting UN Security Council efforts to combat piracy, and also adopted a revised code of practice for investigating crimes of piracy and armed robbery against ships. The November 2011 IMO Assembly adopted a further resolution on 'combating piracy and armed robbery against ships in waters off the coast of Somalia', urging universal compliance with guidance promulgated by the Organization on preventive, evasive and defensive measures; encouraging governments to decide, as a matter of national policy, whether ships entitled to fly their flag should be authorized to carry privately contracted armed security personnel; strongly encouraging port and coastal states to promulgate their national policies on the embarkation, disembarkation and carriage of privately contracted armed security personnel and security-related equipment; and urging governments to ensure that owners and operators of ships entitled to fly their flags take fully into account the welfare of seafarers affected by piracy. In May 2012 the IMO hosted a Conference on Capacity Building to Counter Piracy off the Coast of Somalia, at which the Organization signed five strategic partnerships with UN agencies and the European Union relating to building maritime infrastructure and law enforcement capacity, and to the implementation of the Djibouti Code of Conduct. In January 2013 the IMO Secretary-General proposed the target of halving, by 2015, the number of lives lost at sea (which had exceeded 1,000 in 2012), and eradicating pirate attacks. IMO supported the Economic Community of West Africa States (ECOWAS) and the Communauté économique des états de l'Afrique centrale in drafting a new Code of Conduct concerning the Prevention and Repression of Piracy, Armed Robbery against Ships, and Illegal Maritime Activities in West and Central Africa; the Code was formally adopted and opened for signature at a meeting of regional heads of state convened in June 2013, in Yaoundé, Cameroon. IMO was to support the implementation of the new Code, which in July had 22 signatories, and was to establish a multi-donor trust fund to finance the implementation of maritime security projects in western and central Africa.

In December 2009 the 26th session of the Assembly determined that from 2015 the IMO's Member State Audit Scheme, aimed at comprehensively assessing national implementation of IMO instruments, should become mandatory.

In May 2010 the Maritime Safety Committee adopted a set of 'goal-based standards' (GBS)—structural standards conforming to functional requirements that had been developed by the Committee—with which, thereafter, newly constructed oil tankers and bulk carriers were to comply. The GBS were the first standards set by IMO for ship construction. At that time the Committee also adopted guidelines giving IMO a role in verifying compliance with the provisions of the International Convention for the Safety of Life at Sea (SOLAS). In July 2011 states parties to the MARPOL Convention adopted amendments to Annex VI (relating to prevention of air pollution from ships) to make mandatory the Energy Efficiency Design Index (EEDI), for new ships, of 400 gross tonnage and above, and the Ship Energy Efficiency Management Plan (SEEMP) for all ships. The revised regulations entered into force on 1 January 2013.

In June 2013 IMO convened an IMO Symposium on the Future of Ship Safety, which recommended that the Organization conduct a full review of the existing maritime safety regulatory framework.

In June 2010 five new navigational areas (NAVAREAs) and meteorological areas (METAREAs), delineated by IMO and the World Meteorological Organization (WMO) respectively, were established in Arctic waters, expanding the World Wide Navigational Warning System (WWNWS) into the region and thereby enabling ships operating there to receive necessary information about navigational and meteorological hazards. In 2013 the Sub-Committee on Ship Design and Equipment was developing a new mandatory Polar Code, which was to supplement relevant instruments, including MARPOL and SOLAS, to take into account risks specific to ships operating in remote and environmentally extreme polar waters.

In September 2010 IMO launched a new Seafarers' Rights International Centre, located at the London headquarters of the International Transport Workers' Federation.

In November 2011 IOM, jointly with the Intergovernmental Oceanographic Commission, UN Development Programme, and FAO, released *The Blueprint for Ocean and Coastal Sustainability*, aimed at improving the management of oceans and coastal areas.

IMO sponsors an annual Day of the Seafarer, held on 25 June. World Maritime Day is celebrated annually on 23 September; the theme for 2014 was 'IMO Conventions: Effective Implementation'.

CONVENTIONS

(of which IMO is the depository)

Convention on Facilitation of International Maritime Traffic, 1965: came into force in March 1967.

International Convention on Load Lines, 1966: came into force in July 1968; Protocol, adopted in 1988, came into force in Feb. 2000; numerous other amendments.

International Convention on Tonnage Measurement of Ships, 1969: Convention embodies a universal system for measuring ships' tonnage. Came into force in 1982.

International Convention relating to Intervention on the High Seas in Cases of Oil Pollution Casualties, 1969: came into force in May 1975; a Protocol adopted in 1973 came into force in 1983.

International Convention on Civil Liability for Oil Pollution Damage, 1969: came into force in June 1975; amended by Protocols of 1976, 1984 and 1992 (which was to replace the original Convention); further amendments to the 1992 Protocol, adopted in 2000, came into force in Nov. 2003.

International Convention on the Establishment of an International Fund for Compensation for Oil Pollution Damage, 1971: came into force in Oct. 1978; amended by Protocols of 1976, 1984 and 1992 (which replaced the original Convention); further amendments to the 1992 Protocol, adopted in 2000, came into force in Nov. 2003; a Protocol to establish a Supplementary Fund was adopted in 2003 and came into force in March 2005.

Convention relating to Civil Liability in the Field of Maritime Carriage of Nuclear Material, 1971: came into force in 1975.

Special Trade Passenger Ships Agreement, 1971: came into force in 1974.

Convention on the International Regulations for Preventing Collisions at Sea, 1972: came into force in July 1977; numerous amendments.

Convention on the Prevention of Marine Pollution by Dumping of Wastes and Other Matter ('London Convention'), 1972: came into force in Aug. 1975; numerous amendments, including, in 1993, to incorporate a ban on low-level nuclear waste, which came into force in Feb. 1994; Protocol, which was to replace the original Convention, adopted in 1996.

Hong Kong International Convention for the Safe and Environmentally Sound Recycling of Ships, 2009: adopted in May 2009, and opened for signature during Sept. 2009–Aug. 2010; was to enter into force 24 months after ratification by 15 states representing 40% of global merchant shipping by gross tonnage.

International Convention for Safe Containers, 1972: came into force in Sept. 1977.

International Convention for the Prevention of Pollution from Ships, 1973: (as modified by the Protocol of 1978, known as MARPOL 73/78); came into force in Oct. 1983; extended to include regulations to prevent air pollution in Sept. 1997; came into force in May 2005; a revised MARPOL Annex VI: Prevention of Air Pollution from Ships was adopted in Oct. 2008 and entered into force in July 2010; further amendments to Annex VI entered into effect in May 2005 (establishing a Baltic Sea Emission Control Area—ECA), in Nov. 2007 (creating a North Sea ECA), in Aug. 2012 (providing for a North American ECA), and in Jan. 2014 (establishing a USA/Caribbean Sea ECA); a revised MARPOL Annex III: Prevention of Pollution from Packaged Goods, and a revised MARPOL Annex V: Regulations for the Prevention of Pollution by Garbage from Ships, were approved in Oct. 2010; in July 2011 a revision to Annex I, banning heavy fuel oil from the Antarctic region, was adopted.

International Convention for the Safety of Life at Sea (SOLAS), 1974: came into force in May 1980; a Protocol drawn up in 1978 came into force in May 1981; a second Protocol, of 1988, came into force in Feb. 2000; amendments including special measures to enhance maritime safety came into force in July 2004; further amendments strengthening international passenger ship safety regulations entered into force in July 2010; and the International Code for the Application of Fire Test Procedures became mandatory on 1 July 2012; draft amendments requiring the mandatory staging of safety drills for newly embarked passengers prior to or immediately upon a ship's departure (proposed in response to the sinking of the cruise ship *Costa Concordia* off the Italian coast in Jan. 2012, which had resulted in numerous fatalities) were adopted in June 2013; amendments relating to lifeboat safety entered in to force in Jan. 2013.

Athens Convention relating to the Carriage of Passengers and their Luggage by Sea, 1974: came into force in April 1987.

Cape Town Agreement, 2012: adopted in Oct. 2012, superseding the 1993 Torremolinos Protocol relating to the 1977 International Convention for the Safety of Fishing Vessels (the 1993 Protocol never having entered into force, owing to failure to meet its aggregate fleet requirement); was opened for signature in Feb. 2013, and was to enter into force 12 months after ratification by at least 22 states with an aggregate fleet of at least 3,600 vessels of 24 m in length.

Convention on the International Maritime Satellite Organization, 1976: came into force in July 1979.

Convention on Limitation of Liability for Maritime Claims, 1976: came into force in Dec. 1986; a Protocol came into force in May 2004.

International Convention on Standards of Training, Certification and Watchkeeping (STCW) for Seafarers, 1978: came into force in April 1984; restructured by amendments that entered into force in Feb. 1997, and further amendments adopted in June 2010; countries deemed to be implementing the Convention fully are recorded on a so-called white list.

International Convention on Maritime Search and Rescue, 1979: came into force in June 1985.

Convention for the Suppression of Unlawful Acts against the Safety of Maritime Navigation, 1988: came into force in March 1992. Further Protocol adopted in Oct. 2005.

Protocol for the Suppression of Unlawful Acts against the Safety of Fixed Platforms located on the Continental Shelf, 1988: came into force in March 1992; further Protocol adopted in Oct. 2005.

International Convention on Salvage, 1989: came into force in July 1996.

International Convention on Oil Pollution, Preparedness, Response and Co-operation, 1990: came into force in May 1995.

International Convention on Maritime Liens and Mortgages, 1992: came into force in Sept. 2004.

International Convention on Standards on Training, Certification and Watchkeeping for Fishing Vessel Personnel (STCW-F), 1995: entered into force in Sept. 2012.

International Convention on Liability and Compensation for Damage in Connection with the Carriage of Hazardous and Noxious Substances by Sea, 1996: will come into force 18 months after 12 states of which four have not less than 2m. units of gross tonnage have become parties thereto.

International Convention on Civil Liability for Bunker Oil Pollution Damage, 2001: entered into force Nov. 2008.

International Convention on the Control of Harmful Antifouling Systems on Ships, 2001: entered into force Sept. 2008.

International Convention for the Control and Management of Ships' Ballast Water and Sediments, 2004: will come into force 12 months after 30 states representing not less than 35% of the world's merchant shipping tonnage have become parties thereto.

Maritime Labour Convention, 2006: entered into force in Aug. 2013.

Nairobi International Convention on the Removal of Wrecks, 2007: was to enter into force on 14 April 2015.

Port State Control Agreements: Paris Memorandum of Understanding (MOU) on Port State Control, 1982 (covering Europe and the North Atlantic); Viña del Mar Agreement, 1992 (Latin America); Tokyo MOU, 1993 (Asia and the Pacific); Caribbean MOU, 1996; Mediterranean MOU, 1997; Indian Ocean MOU, 1998; Abuja MOU, 1999 (West and Central Africa); Black Sea, MOU, 2000; and the Riyadh MOU, 2005 (Gulf region). An International Ship and Port Facility Security Code was adopted under IMO auspices in December 2002 and entered into force in July 2004. The sixth workshop for the administrators of Port State Control agreements was convened by IMO in July 2013.

TRAINING INSTITUTES

IMO International Maritime Law Institute (IMLI): POB 31, Msida, MSD 1000, Malta; tel. 21319343; fax 21343092; e-mail info@imli.org; internet www.imli.org; f. 1988; provides degree courses, other training courses, study and research facilities for specialists in maritime law; promotes the development and dissemination of knowledge and expertise in the international legal regime of merchant shipping and related areas; Dir Prof. DAVID J. ATTARD; publs *IMLI News*, *IMLI e-News*, *IMLI Global Directory*.

World Maritime University (WMU): POB 500, Citadellsvägen 29, 201 24 Malmö, Sweden; tel. (40) 356300; fax (40) 128442; e-mail info@wmu.se; internet www.wmu.se; f. 1983; offers postgraduate courses in maritime affairs, a master's and doctoral programme and professional development courses; undertakes various research projects; Pres. Dr BJÖRN KJERFVE (USA/Sweden); publs *WMU News*, *WMU Handbook*, *WMU Journal of Maritime Affairs* (2 a year), several books on maritime issues.

OTHER AFFILIATED BODIES

Partnership in Environmental Management for the Seas of East Asia (PEMSEA): POB 2502, Quezon City, 1165 Philippines; tel. (2) 9292992; fax (2) 9269712; e-mail info@pemsea.org; internet www.pemsea.org; administered by UNOPS in conjunction with UNDP and the Global Environment Facility; aims to build interagency, intersectoral and intergovernmental partnerships for the implementation of the Sustainable Development Strategy for the Seas of East Asia (SDS-SEA).

Regional Marine Pollution Emergency Response Centre for the Mediterranean Sea (REMPEC): Maritime House, Lascaris Wharf, Valletta VLT 1921, Malta; tel. 21337296; fax 21339951; e-mail rempec@rempec.org; internet www.rempec.org; f. 1976 as the Regional Oil Combating Centre for the Mediterranean Sea; administered by IMO in conjunction with the Regional Seas Programme of the UN Environment Programme (UNEP); aims to develop measures to prevent and combat pollution from ships in the Mediterranean; a partner in the Mediterranean Decision Support System for Marine Safety (MEDESS-4MS) project, dedicated to the strengthening of maritime safety by mitigating the risks and impacts associated with oil spills; Dir FRÉDÉRIC HÉBERT (France).

Regional Marine Pollution Emergency, Information and Training Center for the Wider Caribbean Region: Fokkerweg 26, Willemstad Curaçao, Netherlands Antilles; tel. 461-4012; fax 461-1996; e-mail rempeitc@cep.unep.org; internet cep.unep.org/racrempeitc; f. 1995; aims to help prevent and respond to major pollution incidents in the region's marine environment; administered by IMO in conjunction with UNEP's Regional Seas Programme.

Finance

Contributions are received from the member states, with the amount paid calculated according to the tonnage of a member state's merchant fleet. The 10 top contributors in 2010 were: Panama, Liberia, the Bahamas, Marshall Islands, the United Kingdom, Greece, Singapore, Malta, Japan and the People's Republic of China. The budget appropriation for the two years 2014–15, approved by the Assembly in December 2013, amounted to £64.3m., comprising £31.7m. for 2014 and £32.6m. for 2015.

Publications

IMO News (quarterly).

Ships' Routeing.

Numerous specialized publications, including international conventions of which IMO is the depository.

International Monetary Fund—IMF

Address: 700 19th St, NW, Washington, DC 20431, USA.

Telephone: (202) 623-7000; **fax:** (202) 623-4661; **e-mail:** publicaffairs@imf.org; **internet:** www.imf.org.

The IMF was established at the same time as the World Bank in December 1945, to promote international monetary co-operation, to facilitate the expansion and balanced growth of international trade and to promote stability in foreign exchange.

MEMBERS

The IMF has 188 members.

Organization

(April 2014)

Managing Director: CHRISTINE LAGARDE (France).

First Deputy Managing Director: DAVID LIPTON (USA).

Deputy Managing Directors: NAOYUKI SHINOHARA (Japan), MIN ZHU (People's Republic of China).

Special Adviser to the Managing Director: NEMAT SHAFIK (Egypt/United Kingdom/USA) (until 1 Aug. 2014).

BOARD OF GOVERNORS

The highest authority of the Fund is exercised by the Board of Governors, on which each member country is represented by a Governor and an Alternate Governor. The Board normally meets once a year. The Board of Governors has delegated many of its powers to the Executive Directors. However, the conditions governing the admission of new members, adjustment of quotas and the election of Executive Directors, as well as certain other important powers, remain the sole responsibility of the Board of Governors. The voting power of each member on the Board of Governors is related to its quota in the Fund (see tahble below).

In September 1999 the Board of Governors adopted a resolution to transform the Interim Committee of the Board of Governors (established in 1974) into the International Monetary and Financial Committee (IMFC). The IMFC, which held its inaugural meeting in April 2000, comprises 24 members, representing the same countries or groups of countries as those on the Board of Executive Directors (see below). It advises and reports to the Board on matters relating to the management and adaptation of the international monetary and financial system, sudden disturbances that might threaten the system and proposals to amend the Articles of Agreement, but has no decision-making authority.

The Development Committee (the Joint Ministerial Committee of the Boards of Governors of the World Bank and the IMF on the Transfer of Real Resources to Developing Countries, created in 1974, with a structure similar to that of the IMFC) reviews development policy issues and financing requirements.

BOARD OF EXECUTIVE DIRECTORS

The 24-member Board of Executive Directors, responsible for the day-to-day operations of the Fund, is in continuous session in Washington, DC, USA, under the chairmanship of the Fund's Managing Director or Deputy Managing Directors. The USA, United Kingdom, Germany, France and Japan each appoint one Executive Director. There is also one Executive Director each from the People's Republic of China, Russia and Saudi Arabia, while the remainder are elected by groups of all other member countries. As in the Board of Governors, the voting power of each member is related to its quota in the Fund, but in practice the Executive Directors normally operate by consensus. In December 2010 the Board of Governors endorsed a proposal to amend the composition of the Board of Executive Directors in order to increase the representation of emerging dynamic economies and developing countries. The proposal, which required ratification of an Amendment to the Articles of Agreement by members holding 85% of the total voting power, also provided for Board to be fully elected.

The Managing Director of the Fund serves as head of its staff, which is organized into departments by function and area. In 2013 the Fund employed some 2,400 staff members from 144 countries.

REGIONAL REPRESENTATION

There is a network of regional offices and Resident Representatives in more than 90 member countries. In addition, special information and liaison offices are located in Tokyo, Japan (for Asia and the Pacific), in New York, USA (for the United Nations), and in Europe (Paris, France; Geneva, Switzerland; Belgium, Brussels; and Warsaw, Poland, for Central Europe and the Baltic states).

Offices in Europe: c/o 64–66 ave d'Iéna, 75116 Paris, France; tel. 1-40-69-30-70; fax 1-47-23-40-89; Dir CHRISTIAN MUMSSEN.

Regional Office for Asia and the Pacific: 21F Fukoku Seimei Bldg, 2-2-2, Uchisaiwai-cho, Chiyodu-ku, Tokyo 100, Japan; tel. (3) 3597-6700; fax (3) 3597-6705; f. 1997; Dir ODD PER BREKK (Norway).

Regional Office for Central Europe and the Baltics: 00-108 Warsaw, 37C Zielna, Poland; tel. (22) 3386700; fax (22) 3386500; e-mail cee-office@imf.org; f. 2005; Senior Regional Rep. JAMES ROAF.

Activities

The purposes of the IMF, as defined in the Articles of Agreement, are:

(i) To promote international monetary co-operation through a permanent institution which provides the machinery for consultation and collaboration on monetary problems;

(ii) To facilitate the expansion and balanced growth of international trade, and to contribute thereby to the promotion and maintenance of high levels of employment and real income and to the development of members' productive resources;

(iii) To promote exchange stability, to maintain orderly exchange arrangements among members, and to avoid competitive exchange depreciation;

(iv) To assist in the establishment of a multilateral system of payments in respect of current transactions between members and in the elimination of foreign exchange restrictions which hamper the growth of trade;

(v) To give confidence to members by making the general resources of the Fund temporarily available to them, under adequate safeguards, thus providing them with the opportunity to correct maladjustments in their balance of payments, without resorting to measures destructive of national or international prosperity;

(vi) In accordance with the above, to shorten the duration of and lessen the degree of disequilibrium in the international balances of payments of members.

In joining the Fund, each country agrees to co-operate with the above objectives. In accordance with its objective of facilitating the expansion of international trade, the IMF encourages its members to accept the obligations of Article VIII, Sections two, three and four, of the Articles of Agreement. Members that accept Article VIII undertake to refrain from imposing restrictions on the making of payments and transfers for current international transactions and from engaging in discriminatory currency arrangements or multiple currency practices without IMF approval. By April 2014 some 90% of members had accepted Article VIII status.

In 2000/01 the Fund established an International Capital Markets Department to improve its understanding of financial markets and a separate Consultative Group on capital markets to serve as a forum for regular dialogue between the Fund and representatives of the private sector. In mid-2006 the International Capital Markets Department was merged with the Monetary and Financial Systems Department to create the Monetary and Capital Markets Department, with the intention of strengthening surveillance of global financial transactions and monetary arrangements. In June 2008 the Managing Director presented a new Work Programme, comprising the following four immediate priorities for the Fund: to enable member countries to deal with the current crises of reduced economic growth and escalating food and fuel prices, including efforts by the Fund to strengthen surveillance activities; to review the Fund's lending instruments; to implement new organizational tools and working practices; and to advance further the Fund's governance agenda.

The deceleration of economic growth in the world's major economies in 2007 and 2008 and the sharp decline in global financial market conditions, in particular in the second half of 2008, focused international attention on the adequacy of the governance of the international financial system and of regulatory and supervisory frameworks. The IMF aimed to provide appropriate and rapid financial and technical assistance to low-income and emerging economies most affected by the crisis and to support a co-ordinated, multinational recovery effort. The Fund worked closely with the Group of 20 (G20) leading economies to produce an Action Plan, in November 2008, concerned with strengthening regulation, transparency and integrity in financial markets and reform of the international financial system. In March 2009 the IMF released a study on the 'Impact of the Financial Crisis on Low-income Countries', and in that month convened, with the Government of Tanzania, a high-level conference, held in Dar es Salaam, to consider the effects of the global financial situation on African countries, as well as areas for future partnership and growth. Later in that month the Executive Board approved a series of reforms to enhance the effectiveness of the Fund's lending framework, including new conditionality criteria, a new flexible credit facility and increased access limits.

In April 2009 a meeting of G20 heads of state and government, convened in London, United Kingdom, determined to make available substantial additional resources through the IMF and other multinational development institutions in order to strengthen global financial liquidity and support economic recovery. There was a commitment to extend US $250,000m. to the IMF in immediate bilateral financial contributions (which would be incorporated into an expanded New Arrangements to Borrow facility) and to support a general allocation of special drawing rights (SDRs), amounting to a further $250,000m. It was agreed that additional resources from sales of IMF gold were to be used to provide $6,000m. in concessional financing for the poorest countries over the next two to three years. The G20 meeting also resolved to implement several major reforms to strengthen the regulation and supervision of the international financial system, which envisaged the IMF collaborating closely with a new Financial Stability Board. In September G20 heads of state and government endorsed a Mutual Assessment Programme, which aimed to achieve sustainable and balanced growth, with the IMF providing analysis and technical assistance. In January 2010 the IMF initiated a process to review its mandate and role in the 'post-crisis' global economy. Short-term priorities included advising countries on moving beyond the policies they implemented during the crisis; reviewing the Fund's mandate in surveillance and lending, and investigating ways of improving the stability of the international monetary system; strengthening macro-financial and cross-country analyses, including early warning exercises; and studying ways to make policy frameworks more resilient to crises. In November 2011 G20 heads of state and government, meeting in Cannes, France, agreed to initiate an immediate review of the Fund's resources, with a view to securing global financial stability which had been undermined by high levels of debt in several eurozone countries. In December European Union heads of state and government agreed to allocate to the IMF additional resources of up to $270,000m. in the form of bilateral loans.

During 2012–13 the Executive Board approved the modalities to enable bilateral borrowing from member countries as a means of supplementing both quota resources and the institution's standing borrowing arrangements; by 30 April 2013 25 such bilateral agreements had been signed by the Board, and a further 13 states had committed to providing resources in this way. Furthermore, the Board had signed bilateral borrowing agreements with 14 member states aimed specifically at supporting the Fund's concessional financing. The Fund was, meanwhile, reviewing means of ensuring more sustainable long-term funding of its concessional finanancing.

A joint meeting of the IMFC, G20 ministers responsible for finance and governors of central banks, convened in April 2012, in Washington, DC, welcomed a decision in March by eurozone member states to strengthen European firewalls through broader reform efforts and the availability of central bank swap lines, and determined to enhance IMF resources for crisis prevention and resolution, announcing commitments from G20 member states to increasing, by more than US $430,000m., resources to be made available to the IMF as part of a protective firewall to serve the entire IMF membership. Additional resources pledged by emerging economies (notably by the People's Republic of China, Brazil, India, Mexico and Russia) at a meeting of G20 heads of state and government held in June, in Los Cabos, Baja California Sur, Mexico, raised the universal firewall to $456,000m. Meeting in October, in Tokyo, Japan, the IMFC urged national policy-makers to implement policies agreed in recent months aimed at restarting economic growth and promoting job creation. The global economy was reported to have decelerated to a greater extent than had been previously anticipated: a contraction in output in the eurozone was noted, and, additionally, a slowdown in economic activity in many other advanced economies and also in emerging markets and developing economies, reflecting weaker external and domestic demand, and also in some cases the impact of policies aimed at addressing inflationary pressures.

In 2011 the IMF prepared a series of pilot reports assessing the potential 'spillover' impact on economic partners of the domestic economic policies pursued by the so-called Systemic five (S5) major economies—China, the eurozone, Japan, the United Kingdom and the USA. In July 2012 the first annual consolidated *Spillover Report* was published. The 2013 edition, issued in July of that year, found that the S5 economies were operating below potential, and focused on their need to find policies that would close their output gaps (the difference between actual and potential output) without over-stimulating or over-tightening—through spillovers—external economies. In July 2012 the Executive Board gave consideration to a pilot *External Sector Report*, analysing the external positions of 28 systemic economies and the eurozone.

The IMF's annual evaluation of the eurozone, undertaken by a dedicated IMF mission in May–June 2012, in accordance with Article IV of the Articles of Agreement, found the area's financial crisis to have reached a critical stage, with markets remaining under acute stress; the mission recommended the forceful pursuit of stronger European Economic and Monetary Union, accompanied by wide-ranging structural reforms aimed at advancing economic growth. A major IMF assessment of the financial soundness of the eurozone, published in March 2013, and based on visits to regional oversight institutions conducted in November and December 2012, as well as analysis of individual member country reports, urged eurozone policy-makers and banks to intensify their efforts across a wide range of areas, including building strong bank capital buffers; maintaining momentum towards creating an effective banking union; and creating promptly a stronger financial oversight framework.

In September 2011 the IMF joined other international financial institutions active in the Middle East and North Africa region to endorse the so-called Deauville Partnership, established by the Group of Eight (G8) industrialized nations in May to support political and economic reforms being undertaken by several countries, notably Egypt, Jordan, Morocco and Tunisia. The Fund was committed to supporting those countries to maintain economic and financial stability, and to promote inclusive growth.

SPECIAL DRAWING RIGHTS

The SDR was introduced in 1970 as a substitute for gold in international payments, and was intended eventually to become the principal reserve asset in the international monetary system. SDRs are allocated to members in proportion to their quotas. In October 1996 the Executive Board agreed to a new allocation of SDRs in order to achieve their equitable distribution among member states (i.e. all members would have an equal number of SDRs relative to the size of their quotas). In particular, this was deemed necessary since 38 countries that had joined the Fund since the last allocation of SDRs in 1981 had not yet received any of the units of account. In September 1997, at the annual meeting of the Executive Board, a resolution approving a special allocation of SDR 21,400m. was passed, in order to ensure an SDR to quota ratio of 29.32%, for all member countries. The proposed Fourth Amendment to the Articles of Agreement was to come into effect following its acceptance by 60% of member countries, having 85% of the total voting power. The final communiqué of the G20 summit meeting, held in April, endorsed the urgent ratification of the Fourth Amendment. In August the Amendment entered into force, having received approval by the USA. The special allocation, equivalent to some US $33,000m., was implemented on 9 September.

In August 2009 the Board of Governors approved a third general allocation of SDRs, amounting to SDR 161,200m., which become available to all members, in proportion to their existing quotas, effective from 28 August.

From 1974 to 1980 the SDR was valued on the basis of the market exchange rate for a basket of 16 currencies, belonging to the members with the largest exports of goods and services; since 1981 it has been based on the currencies of the five largest exporters (France, Germany, Japan, the United Kingdom and the USA), although the list of currencies and the weight of each in the SDR valuation basket is revised every five years. In January 1999 the IMF incorporated the new currency of the European Economic and Monetary Union, the euro, into the valuation basket; it replaced the French and German currencies, on the basis of their conversion rates with the euro as agreed by the EU. From 1 January 2006 the relative weights assigned to the currencies in the valuation basket were redistributed. The value of the SDR averaged US $1.51973 in 2013, and at 8 April 2014 stood at $1.54571.

The Second Amendment to the Articles of Agreement (1978) altered and expanded the possible uses of the SDR in transactions with other participants. These 'prescribed holders' of the SDRs have the same degree of freedom as Fund members to buy and sell SDRs and to receive or use them in loans, pledges, swaps, donations or settlement of financial obligations.

QUOTAS

Each member is assigned a quota related to its national income, monetary reserves, trade balance and other economic indicators. A member's subscription is equal to its quota and is payable partly in SDRs and partly in its own currency. The quota determines a member's voting power, which is based on one vote for each SDR 100,000 of its quota plus the 250 votes to which each member is entitled. A member's quota also determines its access to the financial resources of the IMF, and its allocation of SDRs.

Quotas are reviewed at intervals of not more than five years, to take into account the state of the world economy and members' different rates of development. Special increases, separate from the general review, may be made in exceptional circumstances. In June 1990 the Board of Governors authorized proposals for a Ninth General Review of quotas. At the same time the Board stipulated that the quota increase, of almost 50%, could occur only after the Third Amendment of the IMF's Articles of Agreement had come into effect. The amendment provides for the suspension of voting and other related rights of members that do not fulfil their obligations under the Articles. By September 1992 the necessary proportion of IMF members had accepted the amendment, and it entered into force in November. The 10th General Review of quotas was concluded in December 1994, with the Board recommending no further increase in quotas. In October 1996 the Fund's Managing Director advocated an increase in quotas under the latest review of at least two-thirds in the light of the IMF's reduced liquidity position. (The IMF had extended unprecedentedly large amounts in stand-by arrangements during the period 1995–96, notably to Mexico and Russia.) In January 1998 the Board of Governors adopted a resolution in support of an increase in quotas of 45%. The required consent of member states constituting 85% of total quotas had been granted by January 1999 to enable the 11th General Review of Quotas to enter into effect. The 12th General Review was initiated in December 2001, and was concluded at the end of January 2003 without an increase in quotas. The 13th General Review was concluded, without an increase in quotas, in January 2008. In September 2006 the Board of Governors adopted a resolution on Quota and Voice Reform in the IMF, representing a two-year reform package aimed at improving the alignment of the quota shares of member states to represent more accurately their relative positions in the global economy and also to enhance the participation and influence of emerging market and low-income countries. An immediate ad hoc quota increase was approved for China, the South Korea, Mexico and Turkey. In March 2008 the Executive Board approved a second round of ad hoc quota increases as part of the proposed extensive reform of the governance and quota structure, which also committed the Fund to regular, five-yearly realignments of quotas. The proposals were to come into effect upon being accepted by member states representing 85% of total votes. In April 2009 G20 heads of state and government further endorsed the quota and voice reform measures and urged the IMF to complete a general review of quotas by January 2011. The 2008 Quota and Voice Reform agreement entered into effect in March 2011, providing for quota increases for 54 member countries with emerging or dynamic economies and an increase in basic votes for low-income countries, in order to strengthen their participation mechanism. In November 2010 the Executive Board responded to a request by the G20 for a further realignment of quotas, and in December the Board of Governors endorsed an agreement concluding the 14th General Review of Quotas to provide for a 100% increase in quotas, to some SDR 476,800m., and adjustment of quota shares to ensure appropriate representation for emerging economies and developing countries. The agreement included a commitment to undertake a comprehensive review of the quota formula by January 2013 (this was achieved) and to conclude a 15th General Review—on the basis of the comprehensive review—by January 2014 (this deadline was subsequently postponed until January 2015). The reforms required acceptance of three-fifths of members representing 85% of voting power in order to enter into effect. By March 2014 144 members accounting for 76.40% of the Fund's voting power had accepted the amendment. At April total quotas in the Fund amounted to SDR 238,120.6m.

RESOURCES

Members' subscriptions form the basic resource of the IMF. They are supplemented by borrowing. Under the General Arrangements to Borrow (GAB), established in 1962, the Group of Ten industrialized nations (G10—Belgium, Canada, France, Germany, Italy, Japan, the Netherlands, Sweden, the United Kingdom and the USA) and Switzerland (which became a member of the IMF in May 1992 but which had been a full participant in the GAB from April 1984) undertake to lend the Fund as much as SDR 17,000m. in their own currencies to assist in fulfilling the balance of payments requirements of any member of the group, or in response to requests to the Fund from countries with balance of payments problems that could threaten the stability of the international monetary system. In 1983 the Fund entered into an agreement with Saudi Arabia, in association with the GAB, making available SDR 1,500m., and other borrowing arrangements were completed in 1984 with the Bank for International Settlements, the Saudi Arabian Monetary Agency, Belgium and Japan, making available a further SDR 6,000m. In 1986 another borrowing arrangement with Japan made available SDR 3,000m. In May 1996 GAB participants concluded an agreement in principle to expand the resources available for borrowing to SDR 34,000m., by securing the support of 25 countries with the financial capacity to support the international monetary system. The so-called New Arrangements to Borrow (NAB) was approved by the Executive Board in January 1997. It was to enter into force, for an initial five-year period, as soon as the five largest potential creditors participating in NAB had approved the initiative and the total credit arrangement of participants endorsing the scheme had reached at least SDR 28,900m. While the GAB credit arrangement was to remain in effect, the NAB was expected to be the first facility to be activated in the event of the Fund's requiring supplementary resources. In July 1998 the GAB was activated for the first time in more than 20 years—and for the last time to date—in order to provide funds of up to US $6,300m. in support of an IMF emergency assistance package for Russia (the first time the GAB had been used for a non-participant). The Fund's long-standing arrangement with Saudi Arabia to make available SDR 1,500m. if required under the GAB was most recently extended to December 2018. The NAB became effective in November 2008, and was called upon for the first time as part of an extensive programme of support for Brazil, which was adopted by the IMF in December. (In March 1999, however, the activation was cancelled.) In November 2008 the Executive Board initiated an assessment of IMF resource requirements and options for supplementing resources in view of an exceptional increase in demand for IMF assistance. In February 2009 the Board approved the terms of a borrowing agreement with the Government of Japan to extend some SDR 67,000m. (some $100,000m.) in supplemental funding, for an initial one-year period. In April G20 heads of state and government resolved to expand the NAB facility, to incorporate all G20 economies, in order to increase its resources by up to SDR 367,500m. ($500,000m.). The G20 summit meeting held in September confirmed that it had contributed the additional resources to the NAB. In April 2010 the IMF's Executive Board approved the expansion and enlargement of NAB borrowing arrangements; these came into effect in March 2011, having completed the ratification process. By April 2014 38 members or state institutions were participating in the NAB, and had committed SDR 369,997m. in supplementary resources.

FINANCIAL ASSISTANCE

The Fund makes resources available to eligible members on an essentially short-term and revolving basis to provide members with temporary assistance to contribute to the solution of their payments problems. Before making a purchase, a member must show that its balance of payments or reserve position makes the purchase necessary. Apart from this requirement, reserve tranche purchases (i.e. purchases that do not bring the Fund's holdings of the member's currency to a level above its quota) are permitted unconditionally. Exchange transactions within the Fund take the form of members' purchases (i.e. drawings) from the Fund of the currencies of other members for the equivalent amounts of their own currencies.

With further purchases, however, the Fund's policy of conditionality means that a recipient country must agree to adjust its economic policies, as stipulated by the IMF. All requests other than for use of the reserve tranche are examined by the Executive Board to determine whether the proposed use would be consistent with the Fund's policies, and a member must discuss its proposed adjustment programme (including fiscal, monetary, exchange and trade policies) with IMF staff. New guidelines on conditionality, which, inter alia, aimed to promote national ownership of policy reforms and to introduce specific criteria for the implementation of conditions given different states' circumstances, were approved by the Executive Board in September 2002. In March 2009 the Executive Board approved reforms to modernize the Fund's conditionality policy, including greater use of pre-set qualification criteria and monitoring structural policy implementation by programme review (rather than by structural performance criteria).

Purchases outside the reserve tranche are made in four credit tranches, each equivalent to 25% of the member's quota; a member must reverse the transaction by repurchasing its own currency (with SDRs or currencies specified by the Fund) within a specified time. A credit tranche purchase is usually made under a Stand-by Arrangement with the Fund, or under the Extended Fund Facility. A Stand-by Arrangement is normally of one or two years' duration, and the amount is made available in instalments, subject to the member's observance of 'performance criteria'; repurchases must be made within three-and-a-quarter to five years. In March 2012 the Executive Board approved an amendment to the Extended Fund Facility permitting extended arrangements to be approved from the start for up to a maximum of four years (the Facility had hitherto been approved for up to three years, with the possibility of a subsequent one-year extension). The member must submit detailed economic programmes and progress reports for each year; repurchases must be made within four-and-a-half to 10 years. In October 1994 the Executive Board approved an increase in members' access to IMF resources, on the basis of a recommendation by the then Interim Committee. The annual access limit under IMF regular tranche drawings, Stand-by Arrangements and Extended Fund Facility credits was increased from 68% to 100% of a member's quota, with the cumulative access limit set at 300%. In March 2009 the Executive Board agreed to double access limits for non-concessional loans to 200% and 600% of a member's quota for annual and cumulative access respectively. In 2012/13 regular funding arrangements approved (and augmented) amounted to SDR 75,111.6m. (compared with SDR 52,601.2m. in the previous financial year, SDR 129,628m. in 2010/11, and SDR 74,175m. in 2009/10).

In October 1995 the Interim Committee of the Board of Governors endorsed recent decisions of the Executive Board to strengthen IMF financial support to members requiring exceptional assistance. An Emergency Financing Mechanism was established to enable the IMF to respond swiftly to potential or actual financial crises, while additional funds were made available for short-term currency stabilization. The Mechanism was activated for the first time in July 1997, in response to a request by the Philippines Government to reinforce the country's international reserves, and was subsequently used during that year to assist Thailand, Indonesia and South Korea. It was used in 2001 to accelerate lending to Turkey. In September 2008 the Mechanism was activated to facilitate approval of a Stand-by Arrangement amounting to SDR 477.1m. for Georgia, which urgently needed to contain its fiscal deficit and undertake rehabilitation measures following a conflict with Russia during the previous month. In November the Board approved a Stand-by Arrangement of SDR 5,169m., under the Emergency Financing Mechanism procedures, to support an economic stabilization programme in Pakistan, one for Ukraine, amounting to SDR 11,000m., and another of SDR 10,538m. for Hungary, which constituted 1,015% of its quota, to counter exceptional pressures on that country's banking sector and the Government's economic programme. An arrangement for Latvia, amounting to SDR 1,522m., was approved in the following month. In May 2010 the Board endorsed a three-year Stand-by Arrangement for Greece amounting to SDR 26,400m., accounting for some 2,400% of that country's new quota (under the 2008 quota reform). The Arrangement was approved under the Emergency Financing Mechanism, as part of a joint financial assistance package with the eurozone countries, which aimed to alleviate Greece's sovereign debt crisis and to support an economic recovery and reform programme. In July 2011 the Fund completed a fourth review of the country's economic performance under the Stand-by Arrangement, enabling a further disbursement of SDR 2,900m. In March 2012, following the cancellation of the Stand-by Arrangement, the Executive Board approved an allocation of SDR 23,800m. to be distributed over four years under the Extended Fund Facility—representing access to IMF resources amounting to 2,159% of Greece's quota—in support of the country's ongoing economic adjustment programme; some SDR 1,400m, was to be disbursed immediately. An IMF-European Central Bank (ECB)-European Commission review mission to Greece, conducted in March 2014, reported positively that the Greek economy was stabilizing and that fiscal targets were being met. An allocation of SDR 19,465.8m., to be distributed over three years, was approved in December 2010 for Ireland under the Emergency Financing Mechanism, in conjunction with a eurozone assistance programme for that country aimed at supporting the restoration of stability in its financial sector. In May 2011 the Fund allocated SDR 23,742m. to Portugal over three years under the Extended Fund Facility, again under the Emergency Financing Mechanism and in tandem with a wider eurozone package of assistance that was supporting the Portuguese Government's ongoing economic adjustment programme. In March 2013 the IMF Managing Director, the President of the ECB, and eurozone ministers responsible for finance agreed, in principle, to develop a joint programme of support to alleviate the sovereign debt crisis in Cyprus. In early April an IMF team and the Cypriot authorities reached a provisional agreement on the terms of a €10,000m. finance package that included a three-year SDR 891m. (equivalent to around €1,000m.) IMF allocation under the Extended Fund Facility; the arrangement was approved by the Board of Executive Directors in May. In March 2014 an IMF mission that had been dispatched to assess the economic situation in Ukraine approved, subject to endorsement by the Executive Board, a Stand-by Arrangement that would—depending on the amount of other bilateral and multilateral funding raised—total from US $14,000m.–18,000m. Prior to consideration of the proposal by the Executive Board, envisaged to occur in April, the Ukraine interim authorities were expected to adopt a comprehensive package of actions aimed at stabilizing the domestic economy and establishing conditions that would promote sustained growth.

In October 2008 the Executive Board approved a new Short-Term Liquidity Facility (SLF) to extend exceptional funds (up to 500% of quotas) to emerging economies affected by the turmoil in international financial markets and economic deceleration in advanced economies. Eligibility for lending under the new Facility was to be based on a country's record of strong macroeconomic policies and having a sustainable level of debt. In March 2009 the Executive Board decided to replace the SLF with a Flexible Credit Line (FCL) facility, which, similarly, was to provide credit to countries with very strong economic foundations, but was also to be primarily considered as precautionary. In addition, it was to have a longer repayment period (of up to five years) and have no access 'cap'. The first arrangement under the FCL was approved in April for Mexico, making available funds of up to SDR 31,528m. for a one-year period. In August 2010 the duration of the FCL, and credit available through it, were increased, and a Precautionary Credit Line (PCL) was established for member states with sound economic policies that had not yet meet the requirements of the FCL. In November 2011 the PCL was replaced by a new, more flexible Precautionary and Liquidity Line (PLL), which was to be made available to countries 'with sound economic fundamentals' and 'sound policies', for use in broader circumstances than the PCL, including as insurance against shocks and as a short-term liquidity window; PLL arrangements may have a duration of either six months or 1–2 years. During 2010/11 (in January 2011) an FCL, amounting to SDR 19,160m., was approved for Poland, and one further FCL arrangement, amounting to SDR 3,870m., was approved in 2011/12, for Colombia. In 2012/13 successor FCLs were approved for Mexico (in November 2012, amounting to SDR 47,292m.), and for Poland (in January 2013, amounting to SDR 22,000m.). One PLL was approved in 2012/13 (in August 2012) for Morocco, amounting to SDR 4,117m.

In January 2010 the Fund introduced new concessional facilities for low-income countries as part of broader reforms to enhance flexibility of lending and to focus support closer to specific national requirements. The three new facilities aimed to support country-owned programmes to achieve macroeconomic positions consistent with sustainable poverty reduction and economic growth. They carried zero interest rate, although this was to be reviewed every two years. An Extended Credit Facility (ECF) succeeded the existing PRGF to provide medium-term balance of payments assistance to low-income members. ECF loans were to be repayable over 10 years, with a five-and-a-half-year grace period. A Standby Credit Facility (SCF) replaced the high-access component of a former Exogenous Shocks Facility (operational from January 2006–December 2009) in order to provide short-term balance of payments financial assistance in response to the adverse economic impact of events beyond government control, including on a precautionary basis. SCF loans were to be repayable over eight years, with a grace period of four years. A new Rapid Credit Facility was to provide rapid financial assistance to PRGF-eligible members requiring urgent balance of payments assistance, under a range of circumstances. Loans were repayable over 10 years, with a five-and-a-half-year grace period. A Post-Catastrophe Debt Relief (PCDR) Trust was established in June 2010 to enable the Fund—in the event of a catastrophic disaster—to provide debt relief to any vulnerable low-income eligible member state in order to free up resources to meet exceptional balance of payments needs. In November 2011 a new Rapid Financing Instrument (RFI) was launched, for which all member states were to be eligible, and which was to support urgent balance of payments requirements, including those arising from exogenous shocks such as commodity price changes, natural disasters, and post-conflict and other fragile situations. Low-income member states may also make use of a non-financial Policy Support Instrument (PSI), providing access to IMF monitoring and other support aimed at consolidating economic performance.

During 2012/13 members' purchases from the general resources account amounted to SDR 10,587m., compared with SDR 32,270m. in the previous year. Outstanding IMF credit at 30 April 2013 totalled SDR 90,182m., compared with SDR 94,182m. in 2011/12. The largest users of IMF credit during the 2012/13 financial year were Greece, Ireland and Portugal.

During the financial year 2012/13 a new Stand-by Arrangement for approved (in August 2012) for Jordan, amounting to SDR 1,364m., to be disbursed over 36 months.

IMF participates in the initiative to provide exceptional assistance to heavily indebted poor countries (HIPCs), in order to help them to achieve a sustainable level of debt management. The initiative was formally approved at the September 1996 meeting of the Interim Committee, having received the support of the 'Paris Club' of official creditors, which agreed to increase the relief on official debt from 67% to 80%. In all 41 HIPCs were identified, of which 33 were in sub-Saharan Africa. Resources for the HIPC initiative were channelled through the PRGF Trust. In early 1999 the IMF and the World Bank initiated a comprehensive review of the HIPC scheme, in order to consider modifications of the initiative and to strengthen the link between debt relief and poverty reduction. A consensus emerged among the financial institutions and leading industrialized nations to enhance the scheme, in order to make it available to more countries, and to accelerate the process of providing debt relief. In September the IMF Board of Governors expressed its commitment to undertaking an off-market transaction of a percentage of the Fund's gold reserves (i.e. a sale, at market prices, to central banks of member countries with repayment obligations to the Fund, which were then to be made in gold), as part of the funding arrangements of the enhanced HIPC scheme; this was undertaken during the period December 1999–April 2000. Under the enhanced initiative it was agreed that countries seeking debt relief should first formulate, and successfully implement for at least one year, a national poverty reduction strategy (see above). In May 2000 Uganda became the first country to qualify for full debt relief under the enhanced scheme. In September 2005 the IMF and the World Bank endorsed a proposal by G8 to achieve the cancellation by the IMF, IDA and the African Development Bank of 100% of debt claims on countries that had reached completion point under the HIPC initiative, in order to help them to achieve their Millennium Development Goals. The debt cancellation was to be undertaken within the framework of a Multilateral Debt Relief Initiative (MDRI). The IMF's Executive Board determined, additionally, to extend MDRI debt relief to all countries with an annual per caput GDP of US $380, to be financed by IMF's own resources. Other financing was to be made from existing bilateral contributions to the PRGF Trust Subsidy Account. In December the Executive Board gave final approval to the first group of countries assessed as eligible for 100% debt relief under the MDRI, including 17 countries that had reached completion point at that time, as well as Cambodia and Tajikistan. The initiative became effective in January 2006 once the final consent of the 43 contributors to the PRGF Trust Subsidy Account had been received. By October 2013 a total of 37 countries had qualified for MDRI relief. As at December 2012 the IMF had committed some $6,500m. in debt relief under the HIPC initiative, of a total of $76,000m. pledged for the initiative (in end-2011 net present value terms); at that time the cost to the IMF of the MDRI amounted to some $4,200m. (in nominal value terms). In June 2010 the Executive Board approved the establishment of a Post-Catastrophe Debt Relief Trust (PCDR Trust) to provide balance of payments assistance to low-income members following an exceptional natural disaster.

The IMF is a partner in the Enhanced Integrated Framework (EIF) for trade-related assistance to Least Developed Countries (LDCs), a multi-donor programme which aims to support greater participation by LDCs in the global trading system.

SURVEILLANCE

Under its Articles of Agreement, the Fund is mandated to oversee the effective functioning of the international monetary system. Accordingly, the Fund aims to exercise firm surveillance over the exchange rate policies of member states and to assess whether a country's economic situation and policies are consistent with the objectives of sustainable development and domestic and external stability. The Fund's main tools of surveillance are regular, bilateral consultations with member countries conducted in accordance with Article IV of the Articles of Agreement, which cover fiscal and monetary policies, balance of payments and external debt developments, as well as policies that affect the economic performance of a country, such as the labour market, social and environmental issues and good governance, and aspects of the country's capital accounts, and finance and banking sectors. In April 1997 the Executive Board agreed to the voluntary issue of Press Information Notices (PINs) following each member's Article IV consultation, to those member countries wishing to make public the Fund's views. Other background papers providing information on and analysis of economic developments in individual countries continued to be made available. The Executive Board monitors global economic developments and discusses policy implications from a multilateral perspective, based partly on World Economic Outlook reports and Global Financial Stability Reports. In addition, the IMF studies the regional implications of global developments and policies pursued under regional fiscal arrangements. The Fund's medium-term strategy, initiated in 2006, determined to strengthen its surveillance policies to reflect new challenges of globalization for international financial and macroeconomic stability. The IMF, with the UN Department for Economic and Social Affairs, leads an initiative to strengthen monitoring and analysis surveillance, and to implement an effective warning system, one of nine initiatives that were endorsed in April 2009 by the UN System Chief Executives Board for Co-ordination (CEB), with the aim of alleviating the impact of the global crisis on poor and vulnerable populations. In September 2010 the Executive Board decided that regular financial stability assessments, within the Financial Sector Assessment Programme framework (see below), were to be a mandatory exercise for 25 jurisdictions considered to have systemically important financial sectors. In July 2012 the Executive Board adopted a Decision on Bilateral and Multilateral Surveillance (the so-called Integrated Surveillance Decision), which aimed to strengthen the legal framework underpinning surveillance activities. In September the Board endorsed a Financial Surveillance Strategy detailing steps towards further strengthening the financial surveillance framework.

In April 1996 the IMF established the Special Data Dissemination Standard (SDDS), which was intended to improve access to reliable economic statistical information for member countries that have, or are seeking, access to international capital markets. In March 1999 the IMF undertook to strengthen the Standard by the introduction of a new reserves data template. By April 2013 71 countries had subscribed to the Standard. The eurozone also voluntarily issues metadata in SDDS format. The financial crisis in Asia, which became apparent in mid-1997, focused attention on the importance of IMF surveillance of the economies and financial policies of member states and prompted the Fund further to enhance the effectiveness of its surveillance through the development of international standards in order to maintain fiscal transparency. In December 1997 the Executive Board approved a new General Data Dissemination System (GDDS), to encourage all member countries to improve the production and dissemination of core economic data. The operational phase of the GDDS commenced in May 2000. By April 2013 107 countries were actively participating in the GDDS. The Fund maintains a Dissemination Standards Bulletin Board, which aims to ensure that information on SDDS subscribing countries is widely available.

In April 1998 the then Interim Committee adopted a voluntary Code of Good Practices on Fiscal Transparency: Declaration of Principles, which aimed to increase the quality and promptness of official reports on economic indicators, and in September 1999 it adopted a Code of Good Practices on Transparency in Monetary and Financial Policies: Declaration of Principles. The IMF and World Bank jointly established a Financial Sector Assessment Programme (FSAP) in May 1999, initially as a pilot project, which aimed to promote greater global financial security through the preparation of confidential detailed evaluations of the financial sectors of individual countries. In September 2009 the IMF and World Bank determined to enhance the FSAP's surveillance effectiveness with new features, for example introducing a risk assessment matrix, targeting it more closely to country needs, and improving its cross-country analysis and perspective. As part of the FSAP Fund staff may conclude a Financial System Stability Assessment (FSSA), addressing issues relating to macroeconomic stability and the strength of a country's financial system. A separate component of the FSAP are Reports on the Observance of Standards and Codes (ROSCs), which are compiled after an assessment of a country's implementation and observance of internationally recognized financial standards.

In March 2000 the IMF Executive Board adopted a strengthened framework to safeguard the use of IMF resources. All member countries making use of Fund resources were to be required to publish annual central bank statements audited in accordance with internationally accepted standards. It was also agreed that any instance of intentional misreporting of information by a member country should be made public. In the following month the Executive Board approved the establishment of an Independent Evaluation Office (IEO) to conduct objective evaluations of IMF policy and operations. The Office commenced activities in July 2001. In January 2010 the Office published a report on IMF Interactions with Member Countries. A paper on the IMF's Role in the Run-up to the Current Financial and Economic Crisis was issued by the Office in 2011.

In April 2001 the Executive Board agreed on measures to enhance international efforts to counter money-laundering, in particular through the Fund's ongoing financial supervision activities and its programme of assessment of offshore financial centres (OFCs). In November the IMFC, in response to the terrorist attacks against targets in the USA, which had occurred in September, resolved, inter alia, to strengthen the Fund's focus on surveillance, and, in particular, to extend measures to counter money-laundering to include the funds of terrorist organizations. It determined to accelerate efforts to assess offshore centres and to provide technical support to enable poorer countries to meet international financial standards. In March 2004 the Board of Directors resolved that an anti-money laundering and countering the financing of terrorism (AML/CFT) component be introduced into regular OFC and FSAP assessments conducted by the Fund and the World Bank. In May 2008 the IMF's Executive Board agreed to integrate the OFC programme into the FSAP.

TECHNICAL ASSISTANCE

Technical assistance is provided by special missions or resident representatives who advise members on every aspect of economic management, while more specialized assistance is provided by the IMF's various departments. In 2000/01 the IMFC determined that technical assistance should be central to the IMF's work in crisis prevention and management, in capacity building for low-income countries, and in restoring macroeconomic stability in countries following a financial crisis. Technical assistance activities subsequently underwent a process of review and reorganization to align them more closely with IMF policy priorities and other initiatives.

The IMF delivers some technical assistance, aimed at strengthening local capacity in economic and financial management, through regional centres. The first, established in 1993, was a Pacific Financial Technical Assistance Center, located in Fiji. A Caribbean Regional Technical Assistance Centre (CARTAC), located in Barbados, began operations in November 2001. In October 2002 an East African Regional Technical Assistance Centre (East AFRITAC), based in Dar es Salaam, Tanzania, was inaugurated and West AFRITAC was launched in May 2003, to serve Francophone West African countries. (In 2012 West AFRITAC relocated from Bamako, Mali to Abidjan, Côte d'Ivoire.) AFRITAC West 2 was inaugurated in March 2014, to cover the non-Francophone West African countries. Central AFRITAC was launched in Libreville, Gabon, in 2007, and AFRITAC South (serving Southern Africa and the Indian Ocean) was inaugurated in October 2011, in Port Louis, Mauritius. In October 2004 a new technical assistance centre for the Middle East (METAC) was inaugurated, based in Beirut, Lebanon. A Regional Technical Assistance Centre for Central America, Panama and the Dominican Republic (CAPTAC-DR), was inaugurated in June 2009, in Guatemala City, Guatemala. In September 2002 the IMF signed a Memorandum of Understanding with the African Capacity Building Foundation to strengthen collaboration, in particular within the context of a new IMF Africa Capacity-Building Initiative.

In May 2009 the IMF launched the first of a series of Topical Trust Funds (TTFs—providing support to member states towards addressing economic policy challenges), on Anti-Money Laundering and Combating the Financing of Terrorism. In May 2011 two further TTFs were created, on Tax Policy and Administration, and on Managing Natural Resource Wealth.

In May 2012, following the merger of the former IMF Institute (established in 1964) and Office of Technical Assistance Management, a new Institute for Capacity Development was inaugurated, to provide technical assistance and training to support member countries with developing the capacity of national economic and financial institutions. The IMF is a co-sponsor, with the Austrian authorities, the European Bank for Reconstruction and Development, Organisation for Economic Co-operation and Development and the World Trade Organization, of the Joint Vienna Institute, which was opened in the Austrian capital in October 1992 and which trains officials from former centrally planned economies in various aspects of economic management and public administration. In May 1998 an IMF-Singapore Regional Training Institute was inaugurated, in collaboration with the Singaporean Government, in order to provide training for officials from the Asia-Pacific region. In 1999 a Joint Regional Training Programme, administered with the Arab Monetary Fund, was established in the United Arab Emirates, and during 2000/01 a joint training programme for Chinese government officials was established in Dalian, Liaoning Province. A Joint Regional Training Centre for Latin America became operational in Brasília, Brazil, in 2001. In July 2006 a Joint India-IMF Training Programme was inaugurated in Pune, India. In May 2011 a new IMF-Middle East Center for Economics and Finance was inaugurated in Kuwait.

Publications

Annual Report.

Balance of Payments Statistics Yearbook.

Civil Society Newsletter (quarterly).

Direction of Trade Statistics (quarterly and annually).

Emerging Markets Financing (quarterly).

F & D—Finance and Development (quarterly).

Financial Statements of the IMF (quarterly).

Global Financial Stability Report (2 a year).

Global Monitoring Report (annually, with the World Bank).

Government Finance Statistics Yearbook.

Handbook on Securities Statistics (published jointly by IMF, BIS and the European Central Bank).

IMF Commodity Prices (monthly).

IMF Financial Activities (weekly, online).

IMF in Focus (annually).

IMF Research Bulletin (quarterly).

IMF Survey (monthly, and online).

International Financial Statistics (monthly and annually).

Joint BIS-IMF-OECD-World Bank Statistics on External Debt (quarterly).

Quarterly Report on the Assessments of Standards and Codes.

Spillover Report (annually).

Staff Papers (quarterly).

World Economic Outlook (2 a year).

Other country reports, regional economic outlooks, economic and financial surveys, occasional papers, pamphlets, books.

Statistics

QUOTAS
(SDR million)

	April 2014
Afghanistan	161.9
Albania	60.0
Algeria	1,254.7
Angola	286.3
Antigua and Barbuda	13.5
Argentina	2,117.1
Armenia	92.0
Australia	3,236.4
Austria	2,113.9
Azerbaijan	160.9
Bahamas	130.3
Bahrain	135.0
Bangladesh	533.3
Barbados	67.5
Belarus	386.4
Belgium	4,605.2
Belize	18.8
Benin	61.9
Bhutan	6.3
Bolivia	171.5
Bosnia and Herzegovina	169.1
Botswana	87.8
Brazil	4,250.5
Brunei	215.2
Bulgaria	640.2
Burkina Faso	60.2
Burundi	77.0
Cambodia	87.5
Cameroon	185.7
Canada	6,369.2
Cape Verde	11.2
Central African Republic	55.7
Chad	66.6
Chile	856.1
China, People's Republic	9,525.9
Colombia	774.0
Comoros	8.9
Congo, Democratic Republic	533.0
Congo, Republic	84.6
Costa Rica	164.1
Côte d'Ivoire	325.2
Croatia	365.1
Cyprus	158.2
Czech Republic	1,002.2
Denmark	1,891.4
Djibouti	15.9
Dominica	8.2
Dominican Republic	218.9
Ecuador	347.8
Egypt	943.7
El Salvador	171.3

—continued	April 2014
Equatorial Guinea	52.3
Eritrea	15.9
Estonia	93.9
Ethiopia	133.7
Fiji	70.3
Finland	1,263.8
France	10,738.5
Gabon	154.3
The Gambia	31.1
Georgia	150.3
Germany	14,565.5
Ghana	369.0
Greece	1,101.8
Grenada	11.7
Guatemala	210.2
Guinea	107.1
Guinea-Bissau	14.2
Guyana	90.9
Haiti	81.9
Honduras	129.5
Hungary	1,038.4
Iceland	117.6
India	5,821.5
Indonesia	2,079.3
Iran	1,497.2
Iraq	1,188.4
Ireland	1,257.6
Israel	1,061.1
Italy	7,882.3
Jamaica	273.5
Japan	15,628.5
Jordan	170.5
Kazakhstan	365.7
Kenya	271.4
Kiribati	5.6
Korea, Republic	3,366.4
Kosovo	59.0
Kuwait	1,381.1
Kyrgyzstan	88.8
Laos	52.9
Latvia	142.1
Lebanon	266.4
Lesotho	34.9
Liberia	129.2
Libya	1,123.7
Lithuania	183.9
Luxembourg	418.7
Macedonia, former Yugoslav republic	68.9
Madagascar	122.2
Malawi	69.4
Malaysia	1,773.9
Maldives	10.0
Mali	93.3
Malta	102.0
Marshall Islands	3.5
Mauritania	64.4
Mauritius	101.6
Mexico	3,625.7
Micronesia, Federated States	5.1
Moldova	123.2
Mongolia	51.1
Montenegro	27.5
Morocco	588.2
Mozambique	113.6
Myanmar	258.4
Namibia	136.5
Nepal	71.3
Netherlands	5,162.4
New Zealand	894.6

—continued	April 2014
Nicaragua	130.0
Niger	65.8
Nigeria	1,753.2
Norway	1,883.7
Oman	237.0
Pakistan	1,033.7
Palau	3.1
Panama	206.6
Papua New Guinea	131.6
Paraguay	99.9
Peru	638.4
Philippines	1,019.3
Poland	1,688.4
Portugal	1,029.7
Qatar	302.6
Romania	1,030.2
Russia	5,945.4
Rwanda	80.1
Saint Christopher and Nevis	8.9
Saint Lucia	15.3
Saint Vincent and the Grenadines	8.3
Samoa	11.6
San Marino	22.4
São Tomé and Príncipe	7.4
Saudi Arabia	6,985.5
Senegal	161.8
Serbia	467.7
Seychelles	10.9
Sierra Leone	103.7
Singapore	1,408.0
Slovakia	427.5
Slovenia	275.0
Solomon Islands	10.4
Somalia	44.2
South Africa	1,868.5
South Sudan	123.0
Spain	4,023.4
Sri Lanka	413.4
Sudan	169.7
Suriname	92.1
Swaziland	50.7
Sweden	2,395.5
Switzerland	3,458.5
Syria	293.6
Tajikistan	87.0
Tanzania	198.9
Thailand	1,440.5
Timor-Leste	10.8
Togo	73.4
Tonga	6.9
Trinidad and Tobago	335.6
Tunisia	286.5
Turkey	1,455.8
Turkmenistan	75.2
Tuvalu	1.8
Uganda	180.5
Ukraine	1,372.0
United Arab Emirates	752.5
United Kingdom	10,738.5
USA	42,122.4
Uruguay	306.5
Uzbekistan	275.6
Vanuatu	17.0
Venezuela	2,659.1
Viet Nam	460.7
Yemen	243.5
Zambia	489.1
Zimbabwe	353.4

FINANCIAL ACTIVITIES
(SDR million, year ending 30 April)

Type of Transaction	2008	2009	2010	2011	2012	2013
Total disbursements	1,952	17,082	22,488	27,529	33,336	11,466
Purchases by facility (General Resources Account)*	1,468	16,363	21,087	26,616	32,270	10,587
Loans under PRGF/ECF/ESF arrangements	484	719	1,402	914	1,066	879
Repurchases and repayments	3,324	2,301	764	3,412	4,002	15,050
Repurchases	2,905	1,833	275	2,268	3,561	14,587
SAF/PRGF/ECF/ESF loan repayments	419	468	489	1,144	441	463
Total outstanding credit provided by Fund (end of year)	9,844	24,625	46,349	70,421	99,689	96,105
Of which:						
General Resources Account	5,896	20,426	41,238	65,539	94,182	90,182
SAF Arrangements	9	9	9	9	9	9
PRGF/ ECF/ESF Arrangements†	3,873	4,124	5,037	4,807	5,432	5,848
Trust Fund	66	66	66	66	66	66

* Including reserve tranche purchases.
† Including Saudi Fund for Development associated loans.
Source: IMF, *Annual Report 2013*.

BOARD OF EXECUTIVE DIRECTORS
(April 2014)

Director	Casting Votes of	Total Votes	%
Appointed:			
MEG LUNDSAGER	USA	421,961	16.75
DAIKICHI MOMMA	Japan	157,022	6.23
HUBERT TEMMEYER	Germany	146,392	5.81
HERVÉ JODON DE VILLEROCHE	France	108,122	4.29
STEVE FIELD	United Kingdom	108,122	4.29
Elected:			
MENNO SNEL (Netherlands)	Armenia, Belgium, Bosnia and Herzegovina, Bulgaria, Croatia, Cyprus, Georgia, Israel, Luxembourg, the former Yugoslav republic of Macedonia, Moldova, Montenegro, Netherlands, Romania, Ukraine	165,496	6.57
JOSE ROJAS (Venezuela)	Colombia, Costa Rica, El Salvador, Guatemala, Honduras, Mexico, Spain, Venezuela	123,469	4.90
ANDREA MONTANINO (Italy)	Albania, Greece, Italy, Malta, Portugal, San Marino	106,404	4.22
WIMBOH SANTOSO (Indonesia)	Brunei, Cambodia, Fiji, Indonesia, Laos, Malaysia, Myanmar, Nepal, Philippines, Singapore, Thailand, Tonga, Viet Nam	99,023	3.93
TAO ZHANG	People's Republic of China	95,996	3.81
JONG-WON LOON (Republic of Korea)	Australia, Kiribati, Republic of Korea, Marshall Islands, Federated States of Micronesia, Mongolia, New Zealand, Palau, Papua New Guinea, Samoa, Seychelles, Solomon Islands, Tuvalu, Uzbekistan, Vanuatu	91,302	3.62
THOMAS HOCKIN (Canada)	Antigua and Barbuda, The Bahamas, Barbados, Belize, Canada, Dominica, Grenada, Ireland, Jamaica, Saint Christopher and Nevis, Saint Lucia, Saint Vincent and the Grenadines	90,672	3.60
AUDUN GROENN (Norway)	Denmark, Estonia, Finland, Iceland, Latvia, Lithuania, Norway, Sweden	85,615	3.40
MOMODOU BAMBA SAHO (The Gambia)	Angola, Botswana, Burundi, Eritrea, Ethiopia, The Gambia, Kenya, Lesotho, Liberia, Malawi, Mozambique, Namibia, Nigeria, Sierra Leone, South Africa, South Sudan, Sudan, Swaziland, Tanzania, Uganda, Zambia, Zimbabwe	82,989	3.29
A. SHAKOUR SHAALAN (Egypt)	Bahrain, Egypt, Iraq, Jordan, Kuwait, Lebanon, Libya, Maldives, Oman, Qatar, Syria, United Arab Emirates, Yemen	80,061	3.18
JOHANN PRADER (Austria)	Austria, Belarus, Czech Republic, Hungary, Kosovo Slovakia, Slovenia, Turkey	73,478	2.92
RAKESH MOHAN (India)	Bangladesh, Bhutan, India, Sri Lanka	70,693	2.81
FAHAD IBRAHIM ALSHATHRI	Saudi Arabia	70,592	2.80
DANIEL HELLER (Switzerland)	Azerbaijan, Kazakhstan, Kyrgyzstan, Poland, Serbia, Switzerland, Tajikistan, Turkmenistan	69,818	2.77
PAULO NOGUEIRA BATISTA, Jr (Brazil)	Brazil, Cape Verde, Dominican Republic, Ecuador, Guyana, Haiti, Nicaragua, Panama, Suriname, Timor-Leste, Trinidad and Tobago	65,844	2.61
ALEKSEI V. MOZHIN	Russia	60,191	2.39
JAFAR MOJARRAD (Iran)	Afghanistan, Algeria, Ghana, Iran, Morocco, Pakistan, Tunisia	57,071	2.26
ALVARO ANDRES ROJAS (Chile)	Argentina, Bolivia, Chile, Paraguay, Peru, Uruguay	46,317	1.84
KOSSI ASSIMAIDOU (Togo)	Benin, Burkina Faso, Cameroon, Central African Republic, Chad, Comoros, Democratic Republic of the Congo, Republic of the Congo, Côte d'Ivoire, Djibouti, Equatorial Guinea, Gabon, Guinea, Mali, Mauritania, Mauritius, Niger Rwanda, São Tomé and Príncipe, Senegal, Togo	39,069	1.55

Note: The total number of votes does not include the votes of Guinea-Bissau, Madagascar and Somalia (amounting to 0.16% of the total of vote in the General Department and the Special Drawing Rights Department), as these countries did not participate in the 2012 election of Executive Directors.

International Telecommunication Union—ITU

Address: Place des Nations, 1211 Geneva 20, Switzerland.
Telephone: 227305111; **fax:** 227337256; **e-mail:** itumail@itu.int; **internet:** www.itu.int.

Founded in 1865, ITU became a specialized agency of the UN in 1947. It aims to encourage world co-operation for the improvement and national use of telecommunications to promote technical development, to harmonize national policies in the field, and to promote the extension of telecommunications throughout the world.

MEMBERS

ITU has 193 member states. More than 700 scientific and technical companies, public and private operators, broadcasters and other organizations are also ITU members.

Organization

(April 2014)

PLENIPOTENTIARY CONFERENCE

The supreme organ of ITU; it normally meets every four years. The main tasks of the Conference are to elect ITU's leadership, establish policies, revise the Constitution and Convention, and approve limits on budgetary spending. The 2010 Conference was held in Guadalajara, Mexico, in October; the 2014 Conference was scheduled to be convened in Busan, Republic of Korea, in October–November.

WORLD CONFERENCES ON INTERNATIONAL TELECOMMUNICATIONS

World Conferences on International Telecommunications (WCITs) are held at the request of members and after approval by the Plenipotentiary Conference. The World Conferences are authorized to review and revise the International Telecommunications Regulations (ITRs—most recently agreed in 1998) applying to the provision and operation of international telecommunications services. A WCIT was convened in December 2012, in Dubai, United Arab Emirates, to review and renegotiate the 1988 ITRs. Separate Conferences are held by the Union's three sectors (see below): Radiocommunication Conferences (every two or three years); Telecommunication Standardization Assemblies (every four years or at the request of one-quarter of ITU members); and Telecommunication Development Conferences (every four years).

ITU COUNCIL

The Council meets annually in Geneva, Switzerland, and is composed of 48 members elected by the Plenipotentiary Conference.

The Council ensures the efficient co-ordination and implementation of the work of the Union in all matters of policy, administration and finance, in the interval between Plenipotentiary Conferences, and approves the annual budget.

GENERAL SECRETARIAT

The Secretary-General is elected by the Plenipotentiary Conference and is assisted by a Co-ordination Committee that also comprises the Deputy Secretary-General and the Directors of the three sector Bureaux. The General Secretariat comprises the Office of the Secretary-General; the ITU Telecom Secretariat (guiding and organizing high-level debate for the global ICT community); and departments of Conferences and Publications; Financial Resources Management; Human Resources Management; Information Services; and Strategic Planning and Members. The Secretariat employs some 800 staff.

Secretary-General: HAMADOUN I. TOURÉ (Mali).

Deputy Secretary-General: HOULIN ZHAO (People's Republic of China).

Executive Manager of the Telecom Secretariat: BLAISE JUDJA-SATO (USA).

Constitution and Convention

Between 1865 and 1992 each Plenipotentiary Conference adopted successive Conventions of ITU. A new Constitution and Convention were signed at the Additional Plenipotentiary Conference held in December 1992, in Geneva, Switzerland, and entered into force on 1 July 1994; these were partially amended by the following three Plenipotentiary Conferences, held in Kyoto, Japan, in 1994, Minneapolis, USA, in 1998, and Marrakesh, Morocco, in 2002. The Constitution contains the fundamental provisions of ITU, whereas the Convention contains other provisions which complement those of the Constitution and which, by their nature, require periodic revision.

The Constitution establishes the purposes and structure of the Union, contains the general provisions relating to telecommunications and special provisions for radio, and deals with relations with the UN and other organizations. The Convention establishes the functioning of the Union and the three sectors, and contains the general provisions regarding conferences and assemblies. Both instruments are further complemented by the Radio Regulations (the most recent revisions of which were adopted in February 2012) and the International Telecommunications Regulations (the most recent revisions of which entered into force on 1 July 1990).

Activities

In December 2012 a World Conference on International Communications, convened in Dubai, United Arab Emirates, and attended by delegates from 151 member states, endorsed new International Telecommunication Regulations (ITRs), updating those previously set down in 1988. The new ITRs included provisions to secure freedom of expression, to assist developing countries to enhance their telecommunications infrastructure, to promote accessibility to persons with disabilities, to limit unsolicited bulk electronic communications, and to improve the energy efficiency of telecommunications networks. The ITRs were signed by 89 states; dissenting states included the USA, Canada and the United Kingdom, citing opposition to governmental regulation of the internet.

In December 1992 an Additional Plenipotentiary Conference, convened in Geneva, Switzerland, determined that ITU should be restructured into three sectors corresponding to its main functions: standardization; radiocommunication; and development. The ordinary Plenipotentiary Conference, held in November 1998, in Minneapolis, USA, approved the active involvement of ITU in governance issues relating to the internet, and recommended that a World Summit on the Information Society (WSIS, see below) be convened, given the rapid developments in that field. The 2006 Conference, held in November, in Antalya, Turkey, endorsed ITU's essential role in 'Bridging the Digital Divide' and in leading the multi-stakeholder process for the follow-up and implementation of relevant WSIS objectives. In October 2010 the Plenipotentiary Conference, held in Guadalajara, Mexico, adopted strategic and financial plans to govern the Union over the period 2012–15, as well as a series of resolutions concerning, inter alia, enhanced collaboration with relevant international organizations and regional registries in the development of Internet Protocol-based networks and internet governance, the implementation of a programme of work on confirmity and interoperability, bridging the standardization gap between developed and developing countries, supporting further Next Generation Network (NGN) development and its deployment in developing countries, promoting collation of information relating to human exposure to electromagnetic fields, and the establishment of a new Council Working Group on internet-related public policy issues.

ITU's Telecom division organizes major global and regional conferences which bring together governments, non-governmental bodies and representatives of the telecommunications industry. An ITU World Telecoms conference is held annually. The 2013 conference was held in Bangkok, Thailand, in November, on the theme 'Embracing Change in a Digital World'. The 2014 conference was scheduled to be convened in Doha, Qatar, in December.

The Global Cybersecurity Agenda (GCA) was inaugurated in May 2007, as part of ITU's commitments to implement the WSIS 'Action Line' on building confidence and security in the use of information and communication technologies. It aimed to provide a framework for international co-operation to enhance confidence in and the security of the information society, structured on the following five work areas: legal measures; technical and procedural measures; organizational structures; capacity building; and international co-operation. In September 2008 ITU signed a Memorandum of Understanding (MOU) with the International Multilateral Partnership against Cyber Threats (IMPACT) to collaborate in efforts to strengthen cybersecurity and to transfer the operations and administration of the GCA to IMPACT. In November ITU inaugurated a Child Online Protection (COP) initiative, to be incorporated into the GCA framework, in order to address the specific cybersecurity issues relating to young people. A COP Global Initiative was launched in November 2010 to promote the implementation, through national action plans, industry codes of conduct, awareness training etc., of previously developed strategies and guidelines. In May 2011 ITU signed an MOU with the UN Office on Drugs and Crime (UNODC) to promote co-operation at a global level to counter cyber crime. At the same time a separate MOU was signed with Symantec, a private provider of security intelligence and systems management. An agreement to establish an ITU Regional Cybersecurity Centre in Nigeria was signed in July 2013. In that month the ITU Secretary-General expressed concern over the risk to smartphone usage posed by cyber criminals through malicious apps, malware and SIM cloning. A new Global Cybersecurity Index, initiated in April 2014 by ITU and a USA-based market intelligence company, ranks the relative strengths of national cybersecurity strategies.

ITU, with the UN Industrial Development Organization (UNIDO) and the World Intellectual Property Organization (WIPO), leads an initiative on promoting technology and innovation, the eighth of nine activities that were launched in April 2009 by the UN System Chief Executives Board for Co-ordination (CEB), with the aim of alleviating the impact on poor and vulnerable populations of the developing global economic crisis.

In May 2010 ITU, with UNESCO, established a UN Broadband Commission for Digital Development, to comprise high-level representatives of governments, industry and international agencies concerned with the effective deployment of broadband networks as an essential element of economic and social development objectives. The Commission released its first annual report, with a series of recommendations for the rapid development of broadband worldwide, in September, prior to the UN Millennium Development Goal Review Summit. A second report, focusing on bringing high-speed connectivity to the poorest communities, was issued in June 2011. In September 2012 the Commission published a report focusing on the achievement of digital inclusion for all. At that time the Commission also established a new working group on broadband and gender. In March 2013 the new group established a target mandating 'gender equality in broadband access by the year 2020', noting that women tended to have less access to technology than men, particularly in low-income environments. The working group's first report, published in September 2013, reviewed the large and expanding gender gap in access to and use of ICT. The Broadband Commission's 2013 annual report, released also in September, addressed the development of mobile broadband technologies, stating that mobile broadband subscriptions relating to wifi-connected laptops, smartphones and tablets had grown to be three times as common as conventional fixed broadband subscriptions, while also noting that these were most prevalent in developed countries, with more than 90% of people in the least developed countries continuing to be unconnected to broadband internet. The report stressed the need to prioritize the role of broadband internet as a tool for bridging urgent development gaps in areas including education, environmental management, gender empowerment and health. In February 2013 the Commission issued a report on *Technology, Broadband and Education: Advancing the Education for All Agenda*, which addressed the potential of broadband networks for extending the reach of education in the developing world. A task force was launched by the Commission in March to address the technology dimension of the UN's proposed post-2015 development agenda and series of Sustainable Development Goals.

ITU has developed training materials that aim to advance ICT literacy among women and girls and aim to encourage the use of ICTs in support of women's economic activities. In November 2012 ITU launched 'Tech Needs Girls', a campaign that promotes technology as a means of empowering women and girls. In March 2013 ITU announced that it would become an official supporting agency and partner of a mobile technology-based educational initiative known as 'Smart Woman', which offers learning in areas including communications, and financial and health matters, to working women in developing economies. In that month the Broadband Commission agreed the target 'gender equality in broadband access by 2020', aimed at redressing a measureable disparity between female and male broadband access in developing countries and also (to a lesser extent) in the developed world.

ITU publishes an annual report entitled *Measuring the Information Society*, which includes an ICT Development Index (IDI), measuring the state of ICT development worldwide (covering 155 countries in the 2013 edition, released in September of that year). The IDI also measures levels of 'digital nativism', representing the national proportion of people aged 15–24 years who have spent at least five years actively using the internet; the 2013 IDI reported the level of digital nativism in high-income countries to have exceeded 90% globally, while the average in low-income countries was around 6%. The report also features an ICT Price Basket, reflecting the combined cost of mobile-cellular, fixed-telephone and fixed-broadband tariffs.

WORLD SUMMIT ON THE INFORMATION SOCIETY

ITU took a lead role in organizing the WSIS, which was held, under the auspices of the UN Secretary-General, in two phases: the first took place in Geneva in December 2003, and the second in Tunis, Tunisia in November 2005. The Geneva meeting, attended by representatives of 175 countries, recognized the central role of ITU in building an information society and approved a Declaration of Principles and Plan of Action, which urged co-operation by public and private sector stakeholders, civil society interests and UN agencies in encouraging new projects and partnerships aimed at bridging the so-called international digital divide. It entrusted ITU with addressing issues relating to cybersecurity. The second meeting adopted the Tunis Agenda for the Information Society, which called upon the UN Secretary-General to establish an Internet Governance Forum (IGF), with a view to establishing a more inclusive dialogue on global internet policy. In March 2006 the UN Secretary-General announced that a small secretariat would be formed to assist with convening the planned Forum, the first session of which was held in Athens, Greece, in October–November. IGFs have subsequently been organized annually. (The 2013 IGF was convened in Bali, Indonesia, in October.) ITU hosts an annual WSIS Forum, in May, to address issues relating to follow-up and implementation by all stakeholders in the process. A UN Group on the Information Society was established in April 2006 to address UN implementation of the WSIS Plan of Action. A WSIS+10 Review meeting was convened in February 2013, hosted by UNESCO at its headquarters in Paris, France.

RADIOCOMMUNICATION SECTOR

The role of the sector (ITU-R) is globally to manage, and to ensure the equitable and efficient use of, the radio frequency spectrum by all radiocommunication services, including those that use satellite orbits (the latter being in increasing demand from fixed, mobile, amateur, broadcasting, emergency telecommunications, environmental monitoring and communications services, global positioning systems, meteorology and space research services). The sector also conducts studies, and adopts recommendations on sector issues. The *Radio Regulations*, which first appeared in 1906, include general rules for the assignment and use of frequencies and the associated orbital positions for space stations. They include a Table of Frequency Allocations (governing the use of radio frequency bands between 9 kHz and 400 GHz) for the various radio services (*inter alia*, radio broadcasting, television, radio astronomy, navigation aids, point-to-point service, maritime mobile, amateur). They are reviewed and revised by periodic World Radiocommunication Conferences. The technical work on issues to be considered by the conferences is conducted by Radiocommunication Assemblies, on the basis of recommendations made by Study Groups. These groups of experts study technical questions relating to radiocommunications, according to a study programme formulated by the Assemblies. The Assemblies may approve, modify or reject any recommendations of the Study Groups, and are authorized to establish new groups and to abolish others. The procedural rules used in the application of the Radio Regulations may be considered by a Radio Regulations Board, which may also perform duties relating to the allocation and use of frequencies and consider cases of interference. ITU-R is responsible for defining and recommending standards and frequency arrangements for international mobile telecommunications (IMT), in collaboration with governments, industry and the private sector. In October 2007 the Radiocommunication Assembly agreed to define as 'IMT-Advanced' new systems and capabilities that extend beyond the existing 'IMT 2000' systems. In January 2012 the Radiocommunication Assembly specified standards for IMT-Advanced technologies and agreed that 'LTE-Advanced' and WirelessMAN-Advanced' met the criteria for classification as IMT-Advanced.

The January 2012 Radiocommunication Assembly determined to conduct further studies on the development of a continuous time standard, aimed at replacing the current system of 'Coordinated Universal Time' (UTC), and repressing the use of 'leap seconds' that is standardized within UTC. In December 2013 ITU-R announced a draft Recommendation for next-generation personalized 'immersive' audio systems, enabling audiences to be enveloped by audio effects that track both laterally and vertically across screens.

The administrative work of the sector is the responsibility of the Radiocommunication Bureau, which is headed by an elected Director, who is assisted by an Advisory Group. The Bureau co-ordinates the work of Study Groups, provides administrative support for the Radio Regulations Board, and works alongside the General Secretariat to prepare conferences and to provide relevant assistance to developing countries. The Bureau maintains the Maritime Mobile Access and Retrieval System (MARS), which provides access to operational information registered in the ITU maritime database.

Director: FRANÇOIS RANCY (France).

TELECOMMUNICATION STANDARDIZATION SECTOR

The Telecommunication Standardization sector (ITU-T) studies technical, operational and tariff issues in order to standardize telecommunications throughout the world. The sector's conferences adopt ITU-T Recommendations, aimed at guaranteeing the effective provision of telecommunication services. Recommendations may be approved outside of the four-year interval between conferences if a sectoral Study Group (comprising private and public sector experts) concludes such action to be urgent. Study Groups are engaged in the following areas of interest: operational aspects of service provision, networks and performance; tariff and accounting principles; telecommunication management; protection against electromagnetic environmental effects; outside plant and related indoor installations; integrated broadband cable networks and television and sound transmission; signalling requirements and protocols; performance and quality of service; NGN; optical and other transport network infrastructures; multimedia terminals, systems and applications; security, languages and telecommunications softwares; and mobile telecommunications networks. The Telecommunication Standardization Advisory Group (TSAG) reviews sectoral priorities, programmes, operations and administrative matters, and establishes, organizes and provides guidelines to the Study Groups.

The 2004 World Telecommunication Standardization Assembly (WTSA), convened in October, in Florianópolis, Brazil, adopted an action plan for addressing the global standardization gap. Consequently a Group on Bridging the Standardization Gap (BSG) was established within the TSAG. The 2008 WTSA was held in Johannesburg, South Africa, in October; it was preceded for the first time by a Global Standards Symposium that addressed means of enabling increased participation by developing countries in the standards making process, as well as considering challenges to the standards agenda, such as accessibility and climate change. ITU Global Standards Initiatives cover: Identity Management; Internet Protocol; Television; and NGN. The 2008 WTSA, inter alia, resolved to reduce greenhouse gas emissions arising from the use of ICTs, established a BSG Fund and approved a new academia category of membership of the sector. The 2012 WTSA was convened in November, in Dubai. The meeting adopted a resolution concerned with upholding non-discriminatory access and use of internet resources in all member states. Other resolutions adopted covered e-health, software-defined networks, and e-waste. ITU-T's Recommendation L.1000, adopted in June 2011, provided for the introduction of a universal power adapter and charger solution for mobile phones and other ICT devices, with the aim of significantly reducing e-waste, device duplication and energy consumption. In December 2013 Recommendation L.1002 was approved, providing for a universal charger for laptop computers, and a standard on green batteries for smartphones was also agreed at that time, with a view to reducing further the global volume of e-waste. In February 2014 ITU organized a workshop on the 'Internet of Things—Trends and Challenges in Standardization', to prepare the way for drafting future technical ITU-T Recommendations aimed at assisting the operation of networks supporting fast-developing machine-to-machine communication (M2M).

Preparations for conferences and other meetings of the sector are made by the Telecommunication Standardization Bureau. It administers the application of conference decisions, as well as relevant provisions of the International Telecommunications Regulations. The Bureau is headed by an elected Director, who is assisted by an Advisory Group. The Director reports to conferences and to the ITU Council on the activities of the sector.

Director: MALCOLM JOHNSON (United Kingdom).

TELECOMMUNICATION DEVELOPMENT SECTOR

The sector's objectives are to facilitate and enhance telecommunications development by offering, organizing and co-ordinating technical co-operation and assistance activities, to promote the development of telecommunication infrastructure, networks and services in developing countries, to facilitate the transfer of appropriate technologies and the use of resources, and to provide advice on issues specific to telecommunications. The sector implements projects under the UN development system or other funding arrangements. In January 2005 ITU launched an initiative to establish a network of some 100 Multipurpose Community Telecentres in 20 African countries, with the aim of providing broader access to ICTs. A global development initiative entitled 'Connect the World' was introduced by ITU in June, with the aim of providing access to ICTs to 1,000m. people without connectivity, within the context of the WSIS agenda to encourage new projects and partnerships to bridge the digital divide. The first in a series of regional summits was held in October 2007 in Kigali, Rwanda, with the aim of mobilizing the human, financial and technical resources required to close ICT gaps throughout Africa; 'Connect CIS', was convened in Minsk, Belarus, in November 2009, 'Connect Americas' in Panama City, Panama, in July 2012, and 'Connect Asia-Pacific' in Bangkok, Thailand, in November 2013. Since 2001 ITU has supported the establishment of Internet Training Centres, by working in partnership with multinational and local private companies and training institutes. By 2014 around 80 Centres had been established under the initiative.

The sector regularly holds conferences to encourage international co-operation in the development of telecommunications, and to determine strategies for development. Conferences consider the result of work undertaken by Study Groups on issues of benefit to developing countries, including development policy, finance, network planning and operation of services. The fourth World Telecommunication Development Conference (WTDC), convened in March 2006, in Doha, addressed development priorities in the context of the Digital Divide, and the promotion of international co-operation to strengthen telecommunication infrastructure and institutions in developing countries. The fifth WTDC, held in Hyderabad, India, in May–June 2010, adopted the Hyderabad Action Plan, detailing strategies for fostering future global ICT and telecommunications development. Availability of NGN and extensive access to broadband services, wireless technologies and the internet were deemed to be catalysts for advancing a global information society and worldwide economic, social and cultural development. The sixth WTDC was held in March–April 2014, in Sharm el-Sheikh, Egypt, on the theme 'Broadband for sustainable development'.

ITU aims to support international humanitarian efforts in the event of an emergency by deploying temporary telecommunications and assessing the damage to the information infrastructure and its rehabilitation needs. ITU played a key role in drafting and promoting the Tampere Convention on the Provision of Telecommunication Resources for Disaster Mitigation and Relief Operations that was signed in 1998 and entered into force in January 2005. The Convention facilitates the deployment and use of telecommunications equipment in an emergency situation, in particular by removing regulatory barriers.

The administrative work of the sector is conducted by the Telecommunication Development Bureau, which may also study specific problems presented by a member state. The Director of the Bureau reports to conferences and the ITU Council, and is assisted by an Advisory Board.

Director: BRAHIMA SANOU (Burkina Faso).

Finance

The budget for the two-year period 2014–15 amounted to 327.1m. Swiss francs.

Publications

ICT-Eye.

ITU Global Directory.

ITU News (10 a year).

ITU Yearbook of Statistics (annually).

Measuring the Information Society.

Operational Bulletin.

The World in 2013: ICT Facts and Figures.

Trends in Telecommunication Reform (annually).

WSIS Stocktaking Report (annually).

Conventions, databases, statistics, regulations, technical documents and manuals, conference documents.

United Nations Educational, Scientific and Cultural Organization—UNESCO

Address: 7 place de Fontenoy, 75352 Paris 07 SP, France.

Telephone: 1-45-68-10-00; **fax:** 1-45-67-16-90; **e-mail:** bpi@unesco.org; **internet:** www.unesco.org.

UNESCO was established in 1946 and aims to contribute, through education, the sciences, culture, communication and information, to the building of peace and the eradication of poverty, and to advancing sustainable development and intercultural dialogue.

MEMBERS

UNESCO has 195 members and nine associate members.

Organization

(April 2014)

GENERAL CONFERENCE

The supreme governing body of the Organization, the Conference meets in ordinary session once in two years and is composed of representatives of the member states. It determines policies, approves work programmes and budgets and elects members of the Executive Board.

EXECUTIVE BOARD

The Board, comprising 58 members, prepares the programme to be submitted to the Conference and supervises its execution; it meets twice a year.

SECRETARIAT

UNESCO is headed by a Director-General, appointed for a four-year term. Assistant Directors-General are responsible for education; natural sciences; social and human sciences; culture; communication and information; external relations and co-operation; and administration.

Director-General: IRINA BOKOVA (Bulgaria).

CO-OPERATING BODIES

In accordance with UNESCO's constitution, national Commissions have been set up in most member states, which help to integrate work within the member states and the work of UNESCO. Most members also have their own permanent delegations to UNESCO. UNESCO aims to develop partnerships with cities and local authorities.

FIELD CO-ORDINATION

UNESCO maintains a network of offices to support a more decentralized approach to its activities and enhance their implementation at field level. Cluster offices provide the main structure of the field co-ordination network. These cover a group of countries and help to co-ordinate between member states and with other UN and partner agencies operating in the area. In 2014 there were 17 cluster offices covering 113 states. In addition 27 national offices serve a single country, including those in post-conflict situations or economic transition and the nine most highly populated countries. The regional bureaux provide specialized support at the national level.

REGIONAL BUREAUX

Regional Bureau for Education in Africa (BREDA): 12 ave L. S. Senghor, BP 3311, Dakar, Senegal; tel. 849-23-23; fax 823-86-23; e-mail dakar@unesco.org; internet www.dakar.unesco.org; Dir ANN THERESE NDONG-JATTA.

Regional Bureau for Sciences in Africa: POB 30592, Nairobi, Kenya; tel. (20) 7621-234; fax (20) 7622-750; e-mail nairobi@unesco.org; internet www.unesco-nairobi.org; f. 1965 to execute UNESCO's regional science programme, and to assist in the planning and execution of national programmes; Dir MOHAMMED DJELID.

Regional Bureau for Education in the Arab States: POB 5244, Cité Sportive, Beirut, Lebanon; tel. (1) 850013; fax (1) 834854; e-mail beirut@unesco.org; internet www.unesco.org/en/beirut; Dir HAMED AL-HAMMAMI.

Regional Bureau for Sciences in the Arab States: 8 Abdel Rahman Fahmy St, Garden City, Cairo 11511, Egypt; tel. (2) 7945599; fax (2) 7945296; e-mail cairo@unesco.org; internet www.unesco.org/new/en/cairo/natural-sciences; also covers informatics; Dir Dr TAREK GALAL SHAWKI.

Regional Bureau for Science and Culture in Europe and North America: Palazzo Zorzi, 4930 Castello, 30122 Venice, Italy; tel. (041) 260-1511; fax (041) 528-9995; e-mail veniceoffice@unesco.org; internet www.unesco.org/venice; Dir YOLANDE VALLE-NEFF (France).

Regional Bureau for Culture in Latin America and the Caribbean (ORCALC): Calzada 551, esq. D, Vedado, Havana 4, Cuba; tel. (7) 833-3438; fax (7) 833-3144; e-mail habana@unesco.org; internet www.unesco.org/new/es/havana; f. 1950; activities include research and programmes of cultural development and cultural tourism; maintains a documentation centre and a library of 14,500 vols; Dir HERMAN VAN HOOFF; publs *Oralidad* (annually), *Boletín Electrónico* (quarterly).

Regional Bureau for Education in Latin America and the Caribbean (OREALC): Calle Enrique Delpiano 2058, Providencia, Santiago, Chile; Casilla 127, Correo 29, Providencia, Santiago, Chile; tel. (2) 472-4600; fax (2) 655-1046; e-mail santiago@unesco.org; internet www.unesco.org/santiago; f. 1963; Dir JORGE SEQUEIRA.

Regional Bureau for Science for Latin America and the Caribbean: Calle Dr Luis Piera 1992, 2°, Casilla 859, 11000 Montevideo, Uruguay; tel. 2413 2075; fax 2413 2094; e-mail orcyt@unesco.org.uy; internet www.unesco.org.uy; also cluster office for Argentina, Brazil, Chile, Paraguay, Uruguay; Dir JORGE GRANDI.

Regional Bureau for Education in Asia and the Pacific: POB 967, Bangkok 10110, Thailand; tel. (2) 391-0577; fax (2) 391-0866; e-mail bangkok@unescobkk.org; internet www.unescobkk.org; Dir GWANG-JO KIM.

Regional Science Bureau for Asia and the Pacific: UNESCO Office, Jalan Galuh II 5, Kebayoran Baru, Jakarta 12110, Indonesia; tel. (21) 7399818; fax (21) 72796489; e-mail jakarta@unesco.org; internet www.unesco.or.id; Dir HUBERT J. GIJZEN.

Activities

In the implementation of all its activities UNESCO aims to contribute to achieving the UN Millennium Development Goal (MDG) of halving levels of extreme poverty by 2015, as well as other MDGs concerned with education and sustainable development. During October 2012–March 2013 UNESCO, with UNICEF, co-led a series of global consultations on formulating a post-2015 development framework in the thematic area of education.

In November 2013 the General Conference approved a new medium-term strategy for the period 2014–21. The strategy had two overarching objectives: contributing to lasting peace; and contributing to sustainable development and the eradication of poverty, and designated UNESCO's five primary functions, to be implemented at global, regional and national levels, as: serving as a laboratory of ideas and generating innovative proposals and policy advice in its fields of competence; developing and reinforcing the global agenda in its fields of competence through policy analysis, monitoring and bench-marking; setting norms and standards in its fields of competence and supporting and monitoring their implementation; strengthening international and regional co-operation in its fields of competence, and fostering alliances, intellectual co-operation, knowledge sharing and operational partnerships; and providing advice for policy development and implementation, and developing institutional and human capacities. UNESCO's strategic objectives during 2017–21 were defined as:

- developing education systems to foster quality lifelong learning opportunities for all;
- empowering learners to be creative and responsible global citizens;
- shaping the future education agenda;
- promoting the interface between science, policy and society and ethical and inclusive policies for sustainable development;
- strengthening international science co-operation for peace, sustainability and social inclusion;
- supporting inclusive social development and promoting intercultural dialogue and the rapprochement of cultures;
- protecting, promoting and transmitting heritage;
- fostering creativity and the diversity of cultural expressions;
- promoting freedom of expression, media development and universal access to information and knowledge.

The 2014–21 strategy reaffirmed UNESCO's commitment to its global priority areas of activity 'Priority Africa' and 'Priority Gender Equality'; aimed to mainstream specific interventions in relation to youth, most marginalized social groups, least developed countries (LDCs), small island developing states (SIDS); and focused on contributing to building knowledge societies, including through the use of the internet and other information and communication technologies (ICTs). The Organization continued to be committed to responding to post-conflict and post-natural disaster situations.

Under the focal area 'Priority Africa' UNESCO's activities are aimed at addressing emerging continental challenges such as the need for education, training and social and occupational integration; to build knowledge societies to effect the transition to a knowledge economy; to build inclusive, peaceful and resilient societies given that the core traditional foundation on which social cohesion has traditionally rested is eroding; and establishing conditions for the preservation and promotion of durable collective peace and security.

During 2014–21 UNESCO was implementing a Priority Gender Equality Action Plan, representing a roadmap for the implementation of gender mainstreaming and gender-specific programming across the Organization's activities and programmes.

EDUCATION

UNESCO recognizes education as an essential human right, and is committed under its medium-term strategy for 2014–21 to developing education systems to foster quality lifelong learning opportunities for all; to empowering learners to be creative and responsible global citizens; and shaping the future education agenda.

UNESCO leads and co-ordinates global efforts in support of 'Education for All' (EFA), which was adopted as a guiding principle of UNESCO's contribution to development following a world conference, convened in March 1990. In April 2000 several UN agencies, including UNESCO and UNICEF, and other partners sponsored the World Education Forum, held in Dakar, Senegal, to assess international progress in achieving the goal of Education for All and to adopt a strategy for further action (the 'Dakar Framework'), with the aim of ensuring universal basic education by 2015. An EFA Global Action Plan was formulated in 2006 to reinvigorate efforts to achieve EFA objectives and, in particular, to provide a framework for international co-operation and better definition of the roles of international partners and of UNESCO in leading the initiative. In September 2012 the UN Secretary-General launched 'Education First', a new initiative aimed at increasing access to education, and the quality thereof, worldwide. An EFA Global Monitoring Report is prepared periodically; the 2013/14 edition (released in January 2014), focused on the importance of investing in teachers and educational reforms to promote equitable learning, and stated that some 250m. children worldwide were receiving a poor quality education and therefore failing to acquire basic skills. The focus of many of UNESCO's initiatives are the nine most highly populated developing countries (Bangladesh, Brazil, the People's Republic of China, Egypt, India, Indonesia, Mexico, Nigeria and Pakistan), known collectively as the E-9 (Education-9) countries.

UNESCO advocates 'Literacy for All' as a key component of Education for All, regarding literacy as essential to basic education and to social and human development. A Literacy Initiative for Empowerment (LIFE) was developed as an element of a UN Literacy Decade (2003–12) to accelerate efforts in some 35 countries where illiteracy is a critical challenge to development. UNESCO is the co-ordinating agency for the UN Decade of Education for Sustainable Development (2005–14), through which it aims to establish a global framework for action and strengthen the capacity of education systems to incorporate the concepts of sustainable development into education programmes. In November 2014 UNESCO was to organize, with the Government of Japan, a UNESCO World Conference on Education for Sustainable Development, in Okayama, Japan, to assess the implementation of the UN Decade.

The April 2000 World Education Forum recognized the global HIV/AIDS pandemic to be a significant challenge to the attainment of Education for All. UNESCO, as a co-sponsor of UNAIDS, takes an active role in promoting formal and non-formal preventive health education. Through a Global Initiative on HIV/AIDS and Education (EDUCAIDS) UNESCO aims to develop comprehensive responses to HIV/AIDS rooted in the education sector, with a particular focus on vulnerable children and young people. An initiative covering the 10-year period 2006–15, the Teacher Training Initiative in sub-Saharan Africa, has aimed to address teacher shortages in that region (owing to HIV/AIDS, armed conflict and other causes) and to improve the quality of teaching.

Under the medium-term strategy for 2014–21 UNESCO aimed to promote expanded access to learning opportunities throughout the life cycle and through multiple pathways (formal education, non-formal and informal learning), and was to promote inclusive and rights-based learning systems reflecting the diversity of all learners. During 2014–18 priority was to be given to areas in which UNESCO has a strong comparative advantage: literacy; technical and vocational education and training; and higher education.

A key priority area of UNESCO's education programme is to foster quality education for all, through formal and non-formal educational opportunities. It assists members to improve the quality of education provision through curricula content, school management and teacher training. UNESCO aims to expand access to education at all levels and to work to achieve gender equality. In particular, UNESCO aims to strengthen capacity building and education in natural, social and human sciences and promote the use of new technologies in teaching and learning processes. In May 2010 UNESCO, jointly with the International Telecommunication Union (ITU), established a Broadband Commission for Digital Development, to comprise high level representatives of governments, industry and international agencies concerned with the effective deployment of broadband networks as an essential element of economic and social development objectives. The 2013 edition of the Commission's flagship report, *State of Broadband*, released in September, addressed the expansion of wireless broadband.

The Associated Schools Project (ASPnet—comprising nearly 9,600 institutions in 180 countries in 2014) has, since 1953, promoted the principles of peace, human rights, democracy and international co-operation through education. It provides a forum for dialogue and for promoting best practices. At tertiary level UNESCO chairs a University Twinning and Networking (UNITWIN) initiative, which was established in 1992 to establish links between higher education institutions and to foster research, training and programme development. A complementary initiative, Academics Across Borders, was inaugurated in November 2005 to strengthen communication and the sharing of knowledge and expertise among higher education professionals. In October 2002 UNESCO organized the first Global Forum on International Quality Assurance, Accreditation and the Recognition of Qualifications to establish international standards and promote capacity building for the sustainable development of higher education systems.

Within the UN system UNESCO is responsible for providing technical assistance and educational services in the context of emergency situations. This includes establishing temporary schools, providing education for refugees and displaced persons, as well as assistance for the rehabilitation of national education systems. In Palestine, UNESCO collaborates with the UN Relief and Works Agency for Palestine Refugees in the Near East (UNRWA) to assist with the training of teachers, educational planning and rehabilitation of schools.

NATURAL SCIENCES

UNESCO recognizes the essential role of science (including mathematics, engineering and technology) as a foundation for achieving the eradication of extreme poverty and ensuring environmental sustainability. In June 2012, in advance of the UN Conference on Sustainable Development (Rio+20), which was convened later in that month, UNESCO, with the International Council of Scientific Unions and other partners, participated in a Forum on Science, Technology and Innovation (STI) for Sustainable Development, addressing the role to be played by science and innovation in promoting sustainable development, poverty eradication, and the transition to a green economy. UNESCO hosts a Scientific Advisory Board, comprising 26 eminent scientists, that was inaugurated in January 2014, on the recommendation of the UN Secretary-General, to provide advice to the UN leadership on the use of STI in the advancement of sustainable development.

Under UNESCO's medium-term strategy for 2014–21 the Organization was to continue to provide through its science programmes policy advice on STI, as well as to strengthen member states' STI capacities, and to enhance international scientific co-operation for the advancement of inclusive sustainable development. Furthermore, UNESCO was to exercise leadership in ocean and fresh water issues, and was to develop holistic solutions to climate change adaptation and disaster risk reduction.

In November 1999 the General Conference endorsed a Declaration on Science and the Use of Scientific Knowledge and an agenda for action, which had been adopted at the World Conference on Science, held in June–July 1999, in Budapest, Hungary. By leveraging scientific knowledge, and global, regional and country level science networks, UNESCO aims to support sustainable development and the sound management of natural resources. It also advises governments on approaches to natural resource management, in particular the collection of scientific data, documenting and disseminating good practices and integrating social and cultural aspects into management structures and policies. UNESCO's Man and the Biosphere Programme supports a worldwide network of biosphere reserves (comprising 621 biosphere reserves in 117 countries, including 12 transboundary sites, in April 2014), which aim to promote environmental conservation and research, education and training in biodiversity and problems of land use (including the fertility of tropical soils and the cultivation of sacred sites). The third World Congress of

Biosphere Reserves, held in Madrid, Spain, in February 2008, adopted the Madrid Action Plan, which aimed to promote biosphere reserves as the main internationally designated areas dedicated to sustainable development. UNESCO also supports a Global Network of National Geoparks (100 in 30 countries in 2014) which was inaugurated in 2004 to promote collaboration among managed areas of geological significance to exchange knowledge and expertise and raise awareness of the benefits of protecting those environments. Member geoparks must have effective management structures that facilitate sustainable development, with a particular emphasis on sustainable tourism. UNESCO organizes regular International Geoparks Conferences; the sixth was to be held in Stonehammer, Canada, in September 2014.

UNESCO promotes and supports international scientific partnerships to monitor, assess and report on the state of Earth systems. With the World Meteorological Organization and the International Council of Science, UNESCO sponsors the World Climate Research Programme, which was established in 1980 to determine the predictability of climate and the effect of human activity on climate. UNESCO hosts the secretariat of the World Water Assessment Programme, which prepares the periodic *World Water Development Report*. UNESCO is actively involved in the 10-year project, agreed by more than 60 governments in February 2005, to develop a Global Earth Observation System of Systems (GEOSS). The project aims to link existing and planned observation systems in order to provide for greater understanding of the earth's processes and dissemination of detailed data, for example predicting health epidemics or weather phenomena or concerning the management of ecosystems and natural resources. UNESCO's Intergovernmental Oceanographic Commission (UNESCO-IOC) serves as the Secretariat of the Global Ocean Observing System. The International Geoscience Programme, undertaken jointly with the International Union of Geological Sciences (IUGS), facilitates the exchange of knowledge and methodology among scientists concerned with geological processes and aims to raise awareness of the links between geoscience and sustainable socio-economic development.

From 2005 UNESCO-IOC developed a Tsunami Early Warning and Mitigation System in the North-eastern Atlantic, the Mediterranean and Connected Seas (NEAMTWS), which conducted its first tsunami training exercise (NEAMWave12) in November 2012.

In March 2013 a Caribbean Tsunami Warning Exercise was conducted under the auspices of UNESCO-IOC, with the aim of testing the tsunami reaction capacity of some 32 countries in the Caribbean and adjacent regions. A similar warning and preparedness exercise was conducted with 39 Pacific Rimcountries in May.

UNESCO is committed to contributing to international efforts to enhance disaster preparedness and mitigation. Through education UNESCO aims to reduce the vulnerability of poorer communities to disasters and improve disaster management at local and national levels. It also co-ordinates efforts at an international level to establish monitoring networks and early warning systems to mitigate natural disasters, in particular in developing tsunami early warning systems in Africa, the Caribbean, the South Pacific, the Mediterranean Sea and the North-East Atlantic similar to those already established for the Indian and Pacific oceans. Other regional partnerships and knowledge networks were to be developed to strengthen capacity building and the dissemination of information and good practices relating to risk awareness and mitigation and disaster management. Disaster education and awareness were to be incorporated as key elements in the UN Decade of Education for Sustainable Development. UNESCO is also the lead agency for the International Flood Initiative, which was inaugurated in January 2005 at the World Conference on Disaster Reduction, held in Kobe, Japan. The Initiative aims to promote an integrated approach to flood management in order to minimize the damage and loss of life caused by floods, mainly with a focus on research, training, promoting good governance and providing technical assistance. The sixth International Conference on Flood Management was to be convened in São Paulo, Brazil, in September 2014.

With the International Council of Scientific Unions and the Third World Academy of Sciences, UNESCO operates a short-term fellowship programme in the basic sciences and an exchange programme of visiting lecturers.

SOCIAL AND HUMAN SCIENCES

UNESCO is mandated to contribute to the worldwide development of the social and human sciences and philosophy, which it regards as of great importance in policy-making and maintaining ethical vigilance. The structure of UNESCO's Social and Human Sciences programme takes into account both an ethical and standard-setting dimension, and research, policy-making, action in the field and future-oriented activities.

A priority area of UNESCO's work programme on Social and Human Sciences has been to promote principles, practices and ethical norms relevant for scientific and technological development. The programme fosters international co-operation and dialogue on emerging issues, as well as raising awareness and promoting the sharing of knowledge at regional and national levels. UNESCO supports the activities of the International Bioethics Committee (IBC—a group of 36 specialists who meet under UNESCO auspices) and the Intergovernmental Bioethics Committee, and hosts the secretariat of the 18-member World Commission on the Ethics of Scientific Knowledge and Technology (COMEST), established in 1999, which aims to serve as a forum for the exchange of information and ideas and to promote dialogue between scientific communities, decision-makers and the public.

The priority Ethics of science and technology element aims to promote intergovernmental discussion and co-operation; to conduct explorative studies on possible UNESCO action on environmental ethics and developing a code of conduct for scientists; to enhance public awareness; to make available teaching expertise and create regional networks of experts; to promote the development of international and national databases on ethical issues; to identify ethical issues related to emerging technologies; to follow up relevant declarations, including the Universal Declaration on the Human Genome and Human Rights; and to support the Global Ethics Observatory, an online worldwide database of information on applied bioethics and other applied science- and technology-related areas (including environmental ethics) that was launched in December 2005 by the IBC.

UNESCO itself provides an interdisciplinary, multicultural and pluralistic forum for reflection on issues relating to the ethical dimension of scientific advances, and promotes the application of international guidelines. In May 1997 the IBC approved a draft version of a Universal Declaration on the Human Genome and Human Rights, in an attempt to provide ethical guidelines for developments in human genetics. The Declaration, which identified some 100,000 hereditary genes as 'common heritage', was adopted by the UNESCO General Conference in November and committed states to promoting the dissemination of relevant scientific knowledge and co-operating in genome research. In October 2003 the General Conference adopted an International Declaration on Human Genetic Data, establishing standards for scientists working in that field, and in October 2005 the General Conference adopted the Universal Declaration on Bioethics and Human Rights. At all levels UNESCO aims to raise awareness and foster debate about the ethical implications of scientific and technological developments and to promote exchange of experiences and knowledge between governments and research bodies.

UNESCO recognizes that globalization has a broad and significant impact on societies. It is committed to strengthening the links between research and policy formulation by national and local authorities, in particular concerning poverty eradication. In that respect, UNESCO promotes the concept that freedom from poverty is a fundamental human right. In 1994 UNESCO initiated an international social science research programme, the Management of Social Transformations (MOST), to promote capacity building in social planning at all levels of decision-making. In 2003 the Executive Board approved a continuation of the programme but with a revised strategic objective of strengthening links between research, policy and practice. UNESCO's medium-term strategy for 2014–21 emphasized the role played by the social sciences in deepening understanding of barriers to equitable participation and inclusion at all career levels.

UNESCO aims to monitor emerging social or ethical issues and, through its associated offices and institutes, formulate preventative action to ensure they have minimal impact on the attainment of UNESCO's objectives. As a specific challenge UNESCO is committed to promoting the International Convention against Doping in Sport, which entered into force in 2007. UNESCO also focuses on the educational and cultural dimensions of physical education and sport and their capacity to preserve and improve health.

Fundamental to UNESCO's mission is the rejection of all forms of discrimination. It disseminates information aimed at combating racial prejudice, works to improve the status of women and their access to education, promotes equality between men and women, and raises awareness of discrimination against people affected by HIV/AIDS, in particular among young people. In 2004 UNESCO inaugurated an initiative to enable city authorities to share experiences and collaborate in efforts to counter racism, discrimination, xenophobia and exclusion. As well as the International Coalition of Cities against Racism, regional coalitions were to be formed with more defined programmes of action. An International Youth Clearing House and Information Service (INFOYOUTH) aims to increase and consolidate the information available on the situation of young people in society, and to heighten awareness of their needs, aspirations and potential among public and private decision-makers. Supporting efforts to facilitate dialogue among different cultures and societies and promoting opportunities for reflection and consideration of philosophy and human rights, for example the celebration of World Philosophy Day, are also among UNESCO's fundamental aims.

CULTURE

In undertaking efforts to preserve the world's cultural and natural heritage UNESCO has attempted to emphasize the link between culture and development. In December 1992 UNESCO established the World Commission on Culture and Development; the first World Conference on Culture and Development was held in June 1999, in Havana, Cuba. In November 2001 the General Conference adopted the UNESCO Universal Declaration on Cultural Diversity, which affirmed the importance of intercultural dialogue in establishing a climate of peace. UNESCO's medium-term strategy for 2014–21 placed a particular focus on addressing challenges in achieving gender equality in cultural life, including difficulties faced by women in attaining senior management positions and decision-making roles; unequal value attributed to the roles of women and men in heritage protection and transmission; unequal opportunities for women to share their creativity with audiences; limitations on freedom of expression based on gender; and unequal access to technical and entrepreneurial training, as well as to financial resources, based on gender.

UNESCO aims to promote cultural diversity through the safeguarding of heritage and enhancement of cultural expressions. In January 2002 UNESCO inaugurated the Global Alliance on Cultural Diversity, to promote partnerships between governments, non-governmental bodies and the private sector with a view to supporting cultural diversity through the strengthening of cultural industries and the prevention of cultural piracy. An International Convention on the Protection of the Diversity of Cultural Expressions, approved by the General Conference in 2005, entered into force in March 2007.

UNESCO's World Heritage Programme, inaugurated in 1978, aims to protect historic sites and natural landmarks of outstanding universal significance, in accordance with the 1972 UNESCO Convention Concerning the Protection of the World Cultural and Natural Heritage, by providing financial aid for restoration, technical assistance, training and management planning. The medium-term strategy for 2008–13 acknowledged that new global threats may affect natural and cultural heritage. It also reinforced the concept that conservation of sites contributes to social cohesion. States parties compile 'Tentative Lists', detailing sites under consideration for nomination to the formal 'World Heritage List'; at April 2014 some 172 countries had compiled Tentative Lists, comprising some 1,598 prospective sites. During mid-2013–mid-2014 the World Heritage List comprised 981 sites globally, of which 759 had cultural significance, 193 were natural landmarks, and 29 were of 'mixed' importance. Examples include the Great Barrier Reef (in Australia); the Galapagos Islands (Ecuador); Chartres Cathedral (France); the Taj Mahal at Agra (India); Auschwitz concentration camp (Poland); the historic sanctuary of Machu Picchu (Peru); Robben Island (South Africa); the Serengeti National Park (Tanzania), and the archaeological site of Troy (Turkey). UNESCO also maintains a 'List of World Heritage in Danger', comprising 44 sites in April 2014, in order to attract international attention to sites particularly at risk from the environment or human activities. In February 2013, following reports in the previous month that numerous historic manuscripts had been set on fire in Timbuktu, Mali, and that at least three mausoleums there had recently been destroyed, UNESCO adopted a US $11m. action plan to guide future reconstruction activities in that country, and to provide training in the conservation of cultural heritage (including ancient manuscripts and intangible heritage). Six sites in Syria: the ancient city of Damascus; the site of Palmyra; the ancient city of Bosra; the ancient city of Aleppo; Crac des Chevaliers and Qal'at Salah El-Din; and ancient villages of northern Syria were added in June of that year to the List of World Heritage in Danger.

UNESCO supports the safeguarding of humanity's non-material 'intangible' heritage, including oral traditions, music, dance and medicine. An Endangered Languages Programme was initiated in 1993. By 2014 the Programme estimated that, of the more than 6,000 languages spoken worldwide, about one-half were endangered. It works to raise awareness of the issue, for example through publication of the *Atlas of the World's Languages in Danger of Disappearing*, to strengthen local and national capacities to safeguard and document languages, and administers a Register of Good Practices in Language Preservation. In October 2003 the UNESCO General Conference adopted a Convention for the Safeguarding of Intangible Cultural Heritage, which provided for the establishment of an intergovernmental committee and for participating states to formulate national inventories of intangible heritage. The Convention entered into force in April 2006 and the intergovernmental committee convened its inaugural session in November. A Representative List of the Intangible Cultural Heritage of Humanity, inaugurated in November 2008, comprised, at April 2014, 282 elements ('masterpieces of the oral and intangible heritage of humanity') deemed to be of outstanding value; these included Chinese calligraphy; falconry; several dances, such as the tango, which originated in Argentina and Uruguay, and the dances of the Ainu in Japan; Turkish coffee culture and tradition; craftsmanship of Horezu ceramics in Romania; and the Ifa divination system in Nigeria. The related List of Intangible Cultural Heritage in Need of Urgent Safeguarding comprised 31 elements at April 2014, including the Naqqāli form of story-telling in Iran, the Saman dance in Sumatra, Indonesia; earthenware pottery-making skills in Kgatleng District, Botswana; and the Qiang New Year Festival in Sichuan Province, China. UNESCO's culture programme also aims to safeguard movable cultural heritage and to support and develop museums as a means of preserving heritage and making it accessible to society as a whole.

In November 2001 the General Conference authorized the formulation of a Declaration against the Intentional Destruction of Cultural Heritage. In addition, the Conference adopted the Convention on the Protection of the Underwater Cultural Heritage, covering the protection from commercial exploitation of shipwrecks, submerged historical sites, etc., situated in the territorial waters of signatory states. UNESCO also administers the 1954 Hague Convention on the Protection of Cultural Property in the Event of Armed Conflict and the 1970 Convention on the Means of Prohibiting and Preventing the Illicit Import, Export and Transfer of Ownership of Cultural Property. In 1992 a World Heritage Centre was established to enable rapid mobilization of international technical assistance for the preservation of cultural sites. Through the World Heritage Information Network, a worldwide network of more than 800 information providers, UNESCO promotes global awareness and information exchange.

From 2001 the UNESCO World Heritage Centre, International Council on Monuments and Sites, and the Working Party for the Documentation and Conservation of Buildings, Sites and Neighbourhoods of the Modern Movement launched the Programme on Modern Heritage, aimed at identifying and documenting 19th- and 20th-century built heritage (including architecture, town planning and landscape design). The World Heritage Centre convened a series of Regional Meetings on Modern Heritage subsequently, and was, in 2014, collating and publishing the outcomes of these.

UNESCO aims to support the development of creative industries and or creative expression. Through a variety of projects UNESCO promotes art education, supports the rights of artists, and encourages crafts, design, digital art and performance arts. In October 2004 UNESCO launched a Creative Cities Network to facilitate public and private sector partnerships, international links, and recognition of a city's unique expertise. In 2014 the following cities were participating in the Network: Aswan (Egypt), Fabriano (Italy), Hangzhou (China), Icheon (Republic of Korea—South Korea), Kanazawa (Japan), Santa Fe (Mexico) as UNESCO Cities of Craft and Folk Art; Beijing (China), Berlin (Germany), Buenos Aires (Argentina), Graz (Austria), Montreal (Canada), Nagoya (Japan), Kobe (Japan), Seoul (Republic of Korea), Shanghai (China), Shenzhen (China), Saint-Etienne (France) as UNESCO Cities of Design; Chengdu (China), Jeonju (South Korea), Östersund (Sweden), Popayan (Colombia), Zahlé (Lebanon) as UNESCO Cities of Gastronomy; Dublin (Republic of Ireland), Edinburgh (United Kingdom), Iowa City (USA), Kraków (Poland), Melbourne (Australia), Norwich (United Kingdom), Reykjavik (Iceland) as UNESCO Cities of Literature; Bogotá (Colombia), Bologna (Italy), Brazzaville (Republic of Congo), Ghent (Belgium), Glasgow (United Kingdom), Seville (Spain) as UNESCO Cities of Music; Bradford (United Kingdom) and Sydney (Australia) as UNESCO Cities of Film; and Lyon (France) as a UNESCO City of Media Arts. A Creative Cities Summit was convened in Beijing, in October 2013. UNESCO is active in preparing and encouraging the enforcement of international legislation on copyright, raising awareness on the need for copyright protection to uphold cultural diversity, and is contributing to the international debate on digital copyright issues and piracy.

Within its ambition of ensuring cultural diversity, UNESCO recognizes the role of culture as a means of promoting peace and dialogue. Several projects have been formulated within a broader concept of Roads of Dialogue. In Central Asia a project on intercultural dialogue follows on from an earlier multidisciplinary study of the ancient Silk Roads trading routes linking Asia and Europe, which illustrated many examples of common heritage. Other projects include a study of the movement of peoples and cultures during the slave trade, a Mediterranean Programme, the Caucasus Project and the Arabia Plan, which aims to promote worldwide knowledge and understanding of Arab culture. UNESCO has overseen an extensive programme of work to formulate histories of humanity and regions, focused on ideas, civilizations and the evolution of societies and cultures. These have included the *General History of Africa, History of Civilizations of Central Asia,* and *History of Humanity*. UNESCO endeavoured to consider and implement the findings of the Alliance of Civilizations, a high-level group convened by the UN Secretary-General that published a report in November 2006. UNESCO signed a Memorandum of Understanding with the Alliance during its first forum, convened in Madrid, Spain, in January 2008.

COMMUNICATION AND INFORMATION

UNESCO regards information, communication and knowledge as being at the core of human progress and well-being. It advocates the concept of inclusive, equitable, open and participatory knowledge societies, based on the principles of freedom of expression (through traditional, contemporary and new forms of media—including the internet), universal access to information and knowledge, respect for cultural and linguistic diversity, and equal access to quality education. UNESCO determined to consolidate and implement this concept, in accordance with the Declaration of Principles and Plan of Action adopted by the second phase of the World Summit on the Information Society (WSIS) in November 2005. UNESCO hosted the WSIS+10 Review meeting, in February 2013 (the first WSIS phase having taken place in December 2003), in Paris, on the theme 'Towards Knowledge Societies for Peace and Sustainable Development'. Under UNESCO's 2014–21 medium-term strategy member states were to be supported in exploiting the use of ICTs, information and data flows, and the Organization was to continue to stimulate debate on the ethical, political and societal challenges to building sustainable knowledge societies.

A key strategic objective of building inclusive knowledge societies is enhancing universal access to communication and information. At the national and global level UNESCO promotes the rights of freedom of expression and of access to information. It promotes the free flow and broad diffusion of information, knowledge, data and best practices, through the development of communications infrastructures, the elimination of impediments to freedom of expression, and the development of independent and pluralistic media, including through the provision of advisory services on media legislation, particularly in post-conflict countries and in countries in transition. UNESCO recognizes that the so-called global digital divide, in addition to other developmental differences between countries, generates exclusion and marginalization, and that increased participation in the democratic process can be attained through strengthening national communication and information capacities. UNESCO promotes policies and mechanisms that enhance provision for marginalized and disadvantaged groups to benefit from information and community opportunities. Activities at local and national level include developing effective 'infostructures', such as libraries and archives and strengthening low-cost community media and information access points, for example through the establishment of Community Multimedia Centres (CMCs). Many of UNESCO's principles and objectives in this area are pursued through the Information for All Programme, which entered into force in 2001. It is administered by an intergovernmental council, the secretariat of which is provided by UNESCO. UNESCO also established, in 1982, the International Programme for the Development of Communication (IPDC), which aims to promote and develop independent and pluralistic media in developing countries, for example by the establishment or modernization of news agencies and newspapers and training media professionals, the promotion of the right to information, and through efforts to harness informatics for development purposes and strengthen member states' capacities in this field. In March 2013 the IPDC approved funding for 63 new media development projects in developing and emerging countries worldwide. In 2011, on the basis of discussions held at the 2010 session of the Internet Governance Forum (established by the second phase of the WSIS to support the implementation of the Summit's mandate) UNESCO published a report entitled *Freedom of Connection-Freedom of Expression: the Changing Legal and Regulatory Ecology Shaping the Internet*. UNESCO has engaged with the Freedom Online Coalition, launched in December 2011 by the first Freedom Online Conference, held in The Hague, Netherlands, with the objective of facilitating global dialogue regarding the role of governments in furthering freedom on the internet. The second Freedom Online Conference was convened in Nairobi, Kenya, in September 2012, and the third Conference was held in Tunis, Tunisia, in June 2013, by which time the Freedom Online Coalition had 21 member states.

UNESCO supports cultural and linguistic diversity in information sources to reinforce the principle of universal access. It aims to raise awareness of the issue of equitable access and diversity, encourage good practices and develop policies to strengthen cultural diversity in all media. In 2002 UNESCO established Initiative B@bel as a multidisciplinary programme to promote linguistic diversity, with the aim of enhancing access of under-represented groups to information sources as well as protecting underused minority languages. In December 2009 UNESCO and the Internet Corporation for Assigned Names and Numbers (ICANN) signed a joint agreement which aimed to promote the use of multilingual domain names using non-Latin script, with a view to promoting linguistic diversity. UNESCO's Programme for Creative Content supports the development of and access to diverse content in both the electronic and audio-visual media. The Memory of the World project, established in 1992, aims to preserve in digital form, and thereby to promote wide access to, the world's documentary heritage. Documentary material includes stone tablets, celluloid, parchment and audio recordings. By April 2014 299 inscriptions had been included on the project's register; five inscriptions originated from international organizations, including the Archives of the ICRC's former International Prisoners of War Agency, 1914–23, submitted by the ICRC, and inscribed in 2007; the League of Nations Archives, 1919–46, submitted by the UN Geneva Office, and inscribed in 2009; and documentary heritage of the International Commission for the International Tracing Service (ITS), submitted by the ITS, and inscribed in 2013. In September 2012 UNESCO organized an international conference on the 'Memory of the World in the Digital Age: Digitization and Preservation', in Vancouver, Canada. The conference adopted the Vancouver Declaration, emphasizing that every individual should be guaranteed access to information, including in digital format, and that digital information should be available in the long term. UNESCO also supports other efforts to preserve and disseminate digital archives and, in 2003, adopted a Charter for the Preservation of Digital Heritage. In April 2009 UNESCO launched the internet based World Digital Library, accessible at www.wdl.org, which aims to display primary documents (including texts, charts and illustrations), and authoritative explanations, relating to the accumulated knowledge of a broad spectrum of human cultures.

UNESCO promotes freedom of expression, of the press and independence of the media as fundamental human rights and the basis of democracy. It aims to assist member states to formulate policies and legal frameworks to uphold independent and pluralistic media and infostructures and to enhance the capacities of public service broadcasting institutions. In regions affected by conflict UNESCO supports efforts to establish and maintain an independent media service and to use it as a means of consolidating peace. UNESCO also aims to develop media and information systems to respond to and mitigate the impact of disaster situations, and to integrate these objectives into wider UN peacebuilding or reconstruction initiatives. UNESCO is the co-ordinating agency for 'World Press Freedom Day', which is held annually on 3 May; it also awards an annual World Press Freedom Prize. A conference convened in Tunis, in celebration of the May 2012 World Press Freedom Day—held on the theme 'New Voices: Media Freedom Helping to Transform Societies', with a focus on the transition towards democracy in several countries of North Africa and the Middle East—adopted the Carthage Declaration, urging the creation of free and safe environments for media workers and the promotion of journalistic ethics. The Declaration also requested UNESCO to pursue implementation of the UN Plan of Action on the Safety of Journalists and the Issue of Impunity, which had been drafted with guidance from UNESCO, and endorsed in April by the UN System Chief Executives Board for Co-ordination. UNESCO maintains an Observatory on the Information Society, which provides up-to-date information on the development of new ICTs, analyses major trends, and aims to raise awareness of related ethical, legal and societal issues. UNESCO promotes the upholding of human rights in the use of cyberspace.

UNESCO promotes the application of ICT for sustainable development. In particular it supports efforts to improve teaching and learning processes through electronic media and to develop innovative literacy and education initiatives, such as the ICT-Enhanced Learning (ICTEL) project. UNESCO also aims to enhance understanding and use of new technologies and support training and ongoing learning opportunities for librarians, archivists and other information providers.

Finance

UNESCO's activities are funded through a regular budget provided by contributions from member states and extra-budgetary funds from other sources, particularly the UN Development Programme, the World Bank, regional banks and other bilateral Funds-in-Trust arrangements. UNESCO co-operates with many other UN agencies and international non-governmental organizations.

In response to a decision, in late October 2011, by a majority of member states participating in the UNESCO General Conference to admit Palestine as a new member state, the USA decided to withhold from UNESCO significant annual funding. In the following month UNESCO launched an Emergency Multi-Donor Fund, as a channel for donations made by international donors with the aim of addressing the funding shortfall.

UNESCO's Regular Programme budget for the two-year period 2014–15 was US $507m.

Publications

(mostly in English, French and Spanish editions; Arabic, Chinese and Russian versions are also available in many cases)

Atlas of the World's Languages in Danger (online).

Best Practices of Island and Coastal Biospheres.

CI Newsletter.

Encyclopedia of Life Support Systems (online).

Education for All Global Monitoring Report.

International Review of Education (quarterly).

International Social Science Journal (quarterly).

Memory of the World, The Treasures that Record our History from 1700 BC to the Present Day.

Museum International (quarterly).

Nature and Resources (quarterly).

Prospects (quarterly review on education).

UNESCO Courier (quarterly).

UNESCO Science Report.

UNESCO World Atlas of Gender Equality in Education.

World Heritage Review (quarterly).

World Science Report (every 2 years).

Books, databases, video and radio documentaries, statistics, scientific maps and atlases.

Specialized Institutes and Centres

Abdus Salam International Centre for Theoretical Physics: Strada Costiera 11, 34151 Trieste, Italy; tel. (040) 2240111; fax (040) 224163; e-mail sci_info@ictp.it; internet www.ictp.it; f. 1964; promotes and enables advanced study and research in physics and mathematical sciences; organizes and sponsors training opportunities, in particular for scientists from developing countries; aims to provide an international forum for the exchange of information and ideas; operates under a tripartite agreement between UNESCO, IAEA and the Italian Government; Dir FERNANDO QUEVEDO (Guatemala).

International Bureau of Education (IBE): POB 199, 1211 Geneva 20, Switzerland; tel. 229177800; fax 229177801; e-mail doc .centre@ibe.unesco.org; internet www.ibe.unesco.org; f. 1925, became an intergovernmental organization in 1929 and was incorporated into UNESCO in 1969; the Council of the IBE is composed of representatives of 28 member states of UNESCO, designated by the General Conference; the Bureau's fundamental mission is to deal with matters concerning educational content, methods, and teaching/learning strategies; an International Conference on Education is held periodically; Dir CLEMENTINA ACEDO (Venezuela); publs *Prospects* (quarterly review), *Educational Innovation* (newsletter), educational practices series, monographs, other reference works.

UNESCO Institute for Information Technologies in Education: 117292 Moscow, ul. Kedrova 8, Russia; tel. (499) 129-29-90; fax (499) 129-12-25; e-mail liste.info.iite@unesco.org; internet iite .unesco.org; f. 1988; the Institute aims to formulate policies regarding the development of, and to support and monitor the use of, information and communication technologies in education; it conducts research and organizes training programmes; Dir a.i. DENDEV BADARCH.

UNESCO Institute for Lifelong Learning: Feldbrunnenstr. 58, 20148 Hamburg, Germany; tel. (40) 448-0410; fax (40) 410-7723; e-mail uil@unesco.org; internet www.unesco.org/uil/index.htm; f. 1951, as the Institute for Education; a research, training, information, documentation and publishing centre, with a particular focus on adult basic and further education and adult literacy; Dir ARNE CARLSEN (Denmark).

UNESCO Institute for Statistics: CP 6128, Succursale Centre-Ville, Montréal, QC, H3C 3J7, Canada; tel. (514) 343-6880; fax (514) 343-5740; e-mail uis.information@unesco.org; internet www.uis .unesco.org; f. 2001; collects and analyses national statistics on education, science, technology, culture and communications; Dir HENDRIK VAN DER POL (Netherlands).

UNESCO Institute for Water Education: Westvest 7, 2611 AX Delft, Netherlands; tel. (15) 2151715; fax (15) 2122921; e-mail info@ unesco-ihe.org; internet www.unesco-ihe.org; f. 2003; activities include education, training and research; and co-ordination of a global network of water sector organizations; advisory and policy-making functions; setting international standards for postgraduate education programmes; and professional training in the water sector; Rector Prof. ANDRÁS SZÖLLÖSI-NAGY (Hungary).

UNESCO-UNEVOC International Centre for Technical and Vocational Education and Training: UN Campus, Platz der Vereinten Nationen 1, 53113 Bonn, Germany; tel. (228) 8150-100; fax (228) 8150-199; e-mail unevoc@unesco.org; internet www.unevoc .unesco.org; f. 2002; the centre assists member states to strengthen and upgrade their technical vocational education and training (TVET) systems; promotes high-quality lifelong technical and vocational education, with a particular focus on young people, girls and women, and the disadvantaged; Head SHYAMAL MAJUMDAR (India).

UNESCO International Institute for Capacity Building in Africa (UNESCO–IICBA): ECA Compound, Africa Ave, POB 2305, Addis Ababa, Ethiopia; tel. (11) 5445284; fax (11) 514936; e-mail info@unesco-iicba.org; internet www.unesco-iicba.org; f. 1999 to promote capacity building in the following areas: teacher education; curriculum development; educational policy, planning and management; and distance education; Dir ARNALDO NHAVOTO.

UNESCO International Institute for Educational Planning (IIEP): 7–9 rue Eugène Delacroix, 75116 Paris, France; tel. 1-45-03-77-00; fax 1-40-72-83-66; e-mail info@iiep.unesco.org; internet www .iiep.unesco.org; f. 1963; serves as a world centre for advanced training and research in educational planning; aims to help all member states of UNESCO in their social and economic development efforts, by enlarging the fund of knowledge about educational planning and the supply of competent experts in this field; legally and administratively a part of UNESCO, the Institute is autonomous, and its policies and programme are controlled by its own Governing Board, under special statutes voted by the General Conference of UNESCO; a satellite office of the IIEP is based in Buenos Aires, Argentina; Dir (vacant).

UNESCO International Institute for Higher Education in Latin America and the Caribbean: Avda Los Chorros con Calle Acueducto, Edif. Asovincar, Altos de Sebucán, Apdo 68394, Caracas 1062-A, Venezuela; tel. (212) 286-0555; fax (212) 286-0527; e-mail iesalc@unesco.org.ve; internet www.iesalc.unesco.org.ve; CEO PEDRO HERNÁN HENRÍQUEZ GUAJARDO (Chile).

United Nations Industrial Development Organization—UNIDO

Address: Vienna International Centre, Wagramerstr. 5, POB 300, 1400 Vienna, Austria.

Telephone: (1) 260260; **fax:** (1) 2692669; **e-mail:** unido@unido.org; **internet:** www.unido.org.

UNIDO began operations in 1967, as an autonomous organization within the UN Secretariat, and became a specialized agency of the UN in 1985. UNIDO's objective is to promote sustainable industrial development in developing nations and states with economies in transition. It aims to assist such countries to integrate fully into the global economic system by mobilizing knowledge, skills, information and technology to promote productive employment, competitive economies and sound environment.

MEMBERS

UNIDO has 171 member states.

Organization

(April 2014)

GENERAL CONFERENCE

The General Conference, which consists of representatives of all member states, meets once every two years. It is the chief policy-making organ, and reviews UNIDO's policy concepts, strategies on industrial development and budget. The 15th regular session of the General Conference was held in December 2013, in Lima, Peru.

INDUSTRIAL DEVELOPMENT BOARD

The Board consists of 53 members elected by the General Conference for a four-year period. It reviews the implementation of the approved work programme, the regular and operational budgets and other General Conference decisions, and, every four years, recommends a candidate for the post of Director-General to the General Conference for appointment.

PROGRAMME AND BUDGET COMMITTEE

The Committee, consisting of 27 members elected by the General Conference for a two-year term, assists the Industrial Development Board in preparing work programmes and budgets.

SECRETARIAT

The Secretariat comprises the office of the Director-General and three divisions, each headed by a Managing Director: Programme Development and Technical Co-operation; Programme Co-ordination and Field Operations; and Administration. In 2014 UNIDO employed nearly 700 regular staff members at its headquarters and other established offices.

Director-General: LI YONG (People's Republic of China).

FIELD REPRESENTATION

UNIDO has 12 regional offices, 17 country offices (some covering more than one country), and 17 country desks. UNIDO's field activities throughout the world are assisted annually by around 2,800 experts.

Activities

UNIDO bases its assistance on two core functions: serving as a global forum for generating and disseminating industry-related knowledge; and designing and implementing technical co-operation programmes in support of its clients' industrial development efforts. The two core functions are complementary and mutually supportive: policy-makers benefit from experience gained in technical co-operation projects, while, by helping to define priorities, UNIDO's analytical work identifies where technical co-operation will have greatest impact. Its assistance is also underpinned by the following three thematic priorities: poverty reduction through productive activities; trade capacity building; and environment and energy. The comprehensive services provided by UNIDO cover:

(i) Industrial governance and statistics;

(ii) Promotion of investment and technology;

(iii) Industrial competitiveness and trade;

(iv) Private sector development;

(v) Agro-industries;

(vi) Sustainable energy and climate change;

(vii) the Montreal Protocol;

(viii) Environment management.

UNIDO promotes the achievement by 2015 of all the Millennium Development Goals (MDGs) adopted by the September 2000 UN Millennium Summit, with a particular focus on using industrial development in support of: eradicating extreme poverty and hunger; promoting gender equality and empowering women; ensuring environmental protection; and developing a global partnership for development. In December 2005 the 11th session of the General Conference adopted a *Strategic Long-term Vision Statement* covering the period 2005–15, focused on promoting the UNIDO's three thematic priorities. In 2013 UNIDO, with other agencies including the World Bank, the UN Development Programme (UNDP)and UN-Energy, co-led global consultations on advancing a post-2015 development framework in the thematic area of energy. In December 2013 UNIDO's General Conference, convened in Lima, Peru, adopted a Declaration which emphasized the Organization's renewed commitment towards achieving inclusive and sustainable industrial development.

UNIDO participates in the UN System Chief Executives' Board for Co-ordination—CEB's Inter-Agency Cluster on Trade and Productive Capacity, chaired by the UN Conference on Trade and Development (UNCTAD) and also comprising UNDP, FAO, the International Trade Centre (ITC), the World Trade Organization (WTO) and the UN regional commissions; the Cluster, in line with the UN's *Delivering as One* agenda, aims to co-ordinate trade and development operations at the national and regional levels within the UN system.

UNIDO, with the International Telecommunication Union (ITU) and the World Intellectual Property Organization (WIPO), leads an initiative on promoting technology and innovation, the eighth of nine activities that were launched in April 2009 by the CEB, with the aim of alleviating the impact on poor and vulnerable populations of the developing global economic crisis.

UNIDO also supports collaborative efforts between countries with complementary experience or resources in specific sectors. The investment and technology promotion network publicizes investment opportunities, provides information to investors and promotes business contacts between industrialized and developing countries and economies in transition. UNIDO is increasingly working to achieve investment promotion and transfer of technology and knowledge among developing countries. The organization has developed several databases, including the Biosafety Information Network Advisory Service (BINAS), the Business Environment Strategic Toolkit (BEST), Industrial Development Abstracts (IDA, providing information on technical co-operation), and the International Referral System on Sources of Information (IRS).

UNIDO publishes an annual *Connectedness Index*, measuring and ranking national 'knowledge networks' to assist private sector policy makers; the 2012 report was subtitled 'Networks for Prosperity: Connecting development knowledge beyond 2015'.

UNIDO has helped to establish and operate the following International Technology Centres: the International Centre for Science and High Technology (based in Trieste, Italy); the International Centre for Advancement of Manufacturing Technology (Bangalore, India); the UNIDO Regional Centre for Small Hydro Power (Trivandum, India); the Centre for the Application of Solar Energy (Perth, Australia); the International Centre of Medicine Biotechnology (Obolensk, Russia); the International Materials Assessment and Application Centre (Rio de Janeiro, Brazil); the International Centre for Materials Technology Promotion (Beijing, People's Republic of China); and the Shenzhen International Technology Promotion Centre (also in China).

UNIDO promotes South-South industrial co-operation. UNIDO Centres for South-South Industrial Co-operation (UCSSICs) are maintained in New Delhi, India (established in February 2007), and in Beijing (established July 2008).

POVERTY REDUCTION THROUGH PRODUCTIVE ACTIVITIES

UNIDO provides support to policy-making bodies in developing countries to promote competitive industries and private sector development, with a particular focus on: the creation of competitiveness intelligence units in major public and private sector institutions; and the establishment of industrial observatories, with the role of monitoring global trade and industry trends, and benchmarking national and company performance. During 2007 UNIDO introduced an online private sector development toolkit, to provide support to policy-makers.

Encouraging foreign direct investment, and promoting technology transfer and technology diffusion projects aimed at strengthening developing countries' national innovation systems, are key elements of UNIDO's poverty reduction strategy.

UNIDO implements a programme for small and medium-sized enterprise (SME) cluster development, which aims to enhance linkages between small businesses and support institutions, in order to assist them with realizing their full growth potential. A Rural and Women's Entrepreneurship Development Programme promotes businesses in developing countries with a particular focus on women and youth. UNIDO recognizes that agro-based industries play a major role in the transition from traditional rural to competitive manufacturing-based economies, and therefore supports the development of the skills and technologies required to advance those industries in developing countries. In the area of food-processing programmes have been initiated to upgrade agro-based value chains, and to open market channels for agro-products. Through its efforts to strengthen developing countries' food supplies and facilitate access to markets, technology and investment, UNIDO also contributes to UN system-wide efforts to address the ongoing global food security crisis. In April 2008 UNIDO, jointly with FAO, the International Fund for Agricultural Development and the Indian Government, organized the Global Agro-Industries Forum: Improving Competitiveness and Development Impact, convened in New Delhi, India; and in November UNIDO helped to organize an International Conference on Sharing Innovative Agribusiness Solutions, held in Cairo, Egypt. The organization also implements projects aimed at restoring agro-industries that have been adversely affected by violent conflict and natural disasters, and has undertaken studies and projects aimed at strengthening the textile and garment industries.

In March 2012 UNIDO and the UN Office on Drugs and Crime (UNODC) signed a Memorandum of Understanding on establishing a strategic partnership aimed at promoting grass-roots development and alternative livelihoods in poor rural communities hitherto dependent on the cultivation of illegal drugs crops.

UNIDO provides advice to governmental agencies and industrial institutions to improve the management of human resources. It also undertakes training projects to develop human resources in specific industries, and aims to encourage the full participation of women in economic progress through gender awareness programmes and practical training to improve women's access to employment and business opportunities.

UNIDO participated in the Third United Nations Conference on the Least Developed Countries (LDC-III), held in Brussels, Belgium, in May 2001. The Organization launched a package of 'deliverables' (special initiatives) in support of the Programme of Action adopted by the Conference, which emphasized the importance of productive capacity in the international development agenda. These related to energy, market access (the enablement of LDCs to participate in international trade), and SME networking and cluster development (with a particular focus on agro-processing and metal-working). LDC-IV was convened in May–June 2011 in Istanbul, Turkey.

UNIDO places a major focus on industrialization in Africa, the advancement of which is regarded as essential to that continent's full integration into the global economy; challenges include the prevalence there of LDCs, limited industrial skills and technological capabilities, weak support from institutions, inadequate financing and underdeveloped domestic and regional markets. UNIDO welcomed the African Union Action Plan for the Accelerated Industrial Development of Africa, which was launched in January 2008, and promotes African regional integration as beneficial for the industrialization of the continent. UNIDO plays a leading role in coordinating Africa Industrialization Day, held annually on 20 November. UNIDO has developed national programmes for 24 African countries; these have emphasized capacity building for the enhancement of industrial competitiveness and private sector development, which is regarded as a major priority for the transformation of African economies. The basic philosophy has been to identify, jointly with key stakeholders in major industrial sub-sectors, the basic tools required to determine their national industrial development needs and priorities. This process has facilitated the definition and establishment of comprehensive national medium- and long-term industrial development agendas. In March 2010 UNIDO convened a high-level conference, in Abuja, Nigeria, on means of developing agribusiness and agro-industries in Africa; the conference endorsed a new African Agribusiness and Agro-industries Development Initiative (known as '3ADI'), a programme framework and funding mechanism enabling public and private sector interests to mobilize resources for investment in development of the African agri-food sector.

TRADE CAPACITY BUILDING

UNIDO implements programmes that build industrial capacities, in both public and private institutions, to formulate policies and strategies for developing trade competitiveness. The organization has developed a comprehensive programme to improve deficiencies in standards, metrology, accreditation and conformity infrastructure, to help developing countries overcome technical barriers while improving product quality, to meet the standards required in the global trading arena. UNIDO also helps countries to comply with global sanitary and phyto-sanitary standards. Efforts in the area of post-conflict rebuilding of quality infrastructures have been undertaken. UNIDO's industrial business development services—such as business incubators, rural entrepreneurship development and SME cluster development—for SME support institutions are aimed at enabling SMEs to play a key role in economic growth. Aid-for-trade activities are undertaken, including programmes that link debt swaps to trade-related technical co-operation. UNIDO assists with the establishment of export consortia, through which SMEs can pool knowledge, financial resources and contacts to improve their export potential while also reducing costs. Promotion of business partnership has been strengthened through a worldwide network of investment and technology promotion offices, investment promotion units, and subcontracting and partnership exchanges. UNIDO contributes to the UN Global Compact aimed at promoting corporate social responsibility.

UNIDO has pursued efforts to overcome the so-called digital divide between and within countries. It has helped to develop electronic and mobile business for SMEs in developing countries and economies in transition. It has also launched an internet-based electronic platform, UNIDO Exchange, for sharing intelligence and fostering business partnerships. UNIDO's Technology Foresight initiative, launched in 1999, involves the systematic visualization of long-term developments in the areas of science, technology, industry, economy and society, with the aim of identifying technologies capable of providing future economic and social benefits. The initiative is being implemented in Asia, Latin America and the Caribbean, and in Central and Eastern Europe and the CIS.

In March 2002, while participating in the International Conference on Financing and Development, held in Monterrey, Mexico, UNIDO launched an initiative designed to facilitate access to international markets for developing countries and countries with transitional economies by assisting them in overcoming barriers to trade.

ENVIRONMENT AND ENERGY

UNIDO's Energy and Climate Change Branch supports patterns of energy use by industry that are environmentally sustainable and likely to mitigate climate change. UNIDO encourages energy efficiency and implements a programme to promote access to renewable sources of energy, essential for conducting modern productive activities. UNIDO has organized a number of conferences relating to renewable energy. In April 2009 a report was issued entitled *UNIDO and Renewable Energy: Greening the Industrial Agenda*, outlining the organization's renewable energy promotion efforts. In June 2012 UNIDO participated in the UN Conference on Sustainable Development (Rio+20). UNIDO's Lighting up Rural Africa programme develops small hydropower projects for rural electrification and industrial usage. The Global Mercury Project focuses on reducing mercury pollution caused by artisanal gold mining, and a Participatory Control of Desertification and Poverty Reduction in the Arid and Semi-Arid High Plateau Ecosystems of Eastern Morocco scheme, jointly developed with IFAD, promotes natural regeneration and efficient land use. UNIDO is engaged in capacity building activities for developing biotechnology projects. In October 2010 UNIDO participated in the fourth global ministerial conference on renewable energy, which took place in New Delhi, on the theme 'Upscaling and Mainstreaming Renewables for Energy Security, Climate Change and Economic Development'; the first, second and third conferences had been held in Bonn, Germany, in June 2004; in Beijing, in November 2005; and Washington, DC, USA, in March 2008. In June 2012 UNIDO, with the UN Environment Programme (UNEP) and the UN Global Compact, launched a new Green Industry Platform, which aimed to mainstream climate, environmental and social dimensions into business operations; the membership of the Advisory Board of the Platform was announced in November. In February 2013 UNIDO, with UNEP, the International Labour Organization (ILO) and the UN Institute for Training and Research launched the Partnership for Action on Green Economy (PAGE), which aimed, over the period 2013–20, to support 30 countries in developing national green economy strategies aimed at generating employment and skills, promoting clean technologies, and reducing environmental risks and poverty.

In September 2009 UNIDO, with UNEP, the ILO, ESCAP and the Philippines Government organized the International Conference on Green Industry in Asia, in Manila; the conference adopted the Manila Declaration and Framework for Action, detailing measures aimed at reducing the resource-intensity and carbon emissions of Asian industries. UNIDO subsequently focused on developing a series of activities aimed at assisting the implementation of the Framework in those Asian countries wishing to implement it, including the preparation of green industry policy guidelines and of country status reports on eco-efficiency. Green industry pilot programmes were to be undertaken in Asia and elsewhere.

As one of the implementing agencies of the Multilateral Fund for the Implementation of the Montreal Protocol, UNIDO implements projects that help developing countries to reduce the use of ozone-depleting substances. From 2007 UNIDO contributed to the formulation of national plans in support of the phasing out (by 2030) of the production of hydrochlorofluorocarbons (HCFCs). It is also involved in implementing the Kyoto Protocol of the Framework Convention on Climate Change (relating to greenhouse gas emissions) in old factories worldwide. UNIDO has helped to develop 10 national ozone units responsible for designing, monitoring and implementing programmes to phase out ozone-depleting substances. By 2014 more than 50 National Cleaner Production Centres (NCPCs), and, in Latin America, a regional network of cleaner production centres, had been established, under a joint UNIDO/UNEP programme that was launched in 1994 to promote the use and development of environmentally sustainable technologies and to build national capacities in cleaner production. In October 2009 UNIDO and UNEP endorsed the creation of the global network for Resource Efficient and Cleaner Production (RECPnet), with the aim of utilizing the capabilities of NCPCs in developing and transition countries. RECPnet was launched in November 2011. In February 2010 UNIDO, in partnership with the Norwegian Government and the Global Carbon Capture and Storage Institute, launched a project aimed at developing a global technology roadmap for carbon capture and storage for industrial processes. UNIDO is a partner agency of the Climate and Clean Air Coalition to Reduce Short Lived Climate Pollutants (SLCPs), which was launched in February 2012 with the aim of combating SLCPs, including methane, black carbon and certain hydrofluorocarbons.

The Director-General of UNIDO serves as the chairperson of UN-Energy, the inter-agency mechanism that aims to promote system-wide co-operation in the UN's response to energy-related issues. UNIDO, on behalf on UN-Energy, identifies areas for collaboration between the UN and private sector in addressing challenges posed by climate change and the achievement of sustainable development.

UNIDO, jointly with the Government of Austria and the Austria-based International Institute of Applied Systems Analysis, has since 2009 organized the biennial Vienna Energy Forum (VEF). The 2013 VEF, held in May, addressed the energy dimension of the outcome document of the June 2012 Rio+20 conference.

In December 2007 the General Conference endorsed a Strategic Approach to International Chemicals Management. A programme promoting chemical leasing encourages improved co-operation between chemicals producers and users, and helps companies to comply with environmental regulations. UNIDO has supported countries with the preparation of national implementation plans for the effective removal of persistent organic pollutants. The organization has undertaken a number of technical assistance projects and schemes aimed at helping countries to adopt energy management standards, and has also co-operated with the International Organization for Standardization on the development of an international energy management standard.

UNIDO and UN-Energy supported the UN Global Compact in organizing the annual Private Sector Forum, held in September 2011, in New York, USA, at which the UN Secretary-General launched a new initiative, Sustainable Energy for All by 2030, and a high-level group responsible for its implementation. In September 2012 the UN Secretary-General appointed the then Secretary-General of UNIDO as his Special Representative for Sustainable Energy for All.

The 2013 edition of UNIDO's annual *Industrial Development Report*, issued in December of that year, highlighted the importance of the role played by manufacturing globally, both in employment generation and in achieving inclusive and sustainable industrial development.

Finance

The provisional regular budget for the two years 2014–15 amounted to €176.5m., financed mainly by assessed contributions payable by member states. There was an operational budget of some €32.7m. for the same period, financed mainly by voluntary contributions. The Industrial Development Fund is used by UNIDO to finance development projects that fall outside the usual systems of multilateral funding.

Publications

Annual Report.
Connectedness Index.
Development of Clusters and Networks of SMEs.
Industrial Development Report.
International Yearbook of Industrial Statistics (annually).
Making It: Industry for Development (quarterly).
Manual for the Evaluation of Industrial Projects.
Reforming the UN System—UNIDO's Need-Driven Model.
UNIDO Times (electronic newsletter).
Several other manuals, guidelines, numerous working papers and reports.

Universal Postal Union—UPU

Address: Case Postale 13, 3000 Bern 15, Switzerland.
Telephone: 313503111; **fax:** 313503110; **e-mail:** info@upu.int; **internet:** www.upu.int.

The General Postal Union was founded by the Treaty of Berne (1874), beginning operations in July 1875. Three years later its name was changed to the Universal Postal Union. In 1948 the UPU became a specialized agency of the UN. The UPU promotes the sustainable development of high-quality, universal, efficient and accessible postal services.

MEMBERS

The UPU has 192 members.

Organization

(April 2014)

CONGRESS

The supreme body of the Union is the Universal Postal Congress, which meets, in principle, every four years. Congress focuses on general principles and broad policy issues. It is responsible for the Constitution (the basic act of the Union), the General Regulations (which contain provisions relating to the application of the Constitution and the operation of the Union), changes in the provision of the Universal Postal Convention, approval of the strategic plan and budget parameters, formulation of overall policy on technical co-operation, and for elections and appointments. Amendments to the Constitution are recorded in Additional Protocols, of which there are currently seven. The 25th Universal Postal Congress was held in Doha, Qatar, during September–October 2012.

COUNCIL OF ADMINISTRATION

The Council meets annually in Bern, Switzerland. It is composed of a Chairman and representatives of 41 member countries of the Union elected by the Universal Postal Congress on the basis of an equitable geographical distribution. It is responsible for supervising the affairs of the Union between Congresses. The Council also considers policies that may affect other sectors, such as standardization and quality of service, provides a forum for considering the implications of governmental policies with respect to competition, deregulation and trade-in-service issues for international postal services, and considers intergovernmental aspects of technical co-operation. The Council approves the Union's budget, supervises the activities of the International Bureau and takes decisions regarding UPU contacts with other international agencies and bodies. It is also responsible for promoting and co-ordinating all aspects of technical assistance among member countries. The Council has subsidiary project groups covering Trade Facilitation, Financial Inclusion, Acts of the Union, the Universal Postal Service, and Interconnectivity.

POSTAL OPERATIONS COUNCIL (POC)

As the technical organ of the UPU, the POC, which holds annual sessions and comprises 40 elected member countries, is responsible for the operational, economic and commercial aspects of international postal services. The POC has the authority to amend and enact the Detailed Regulations of the Universal Postal Convention, on the basis of decisions made at Congress. It promotes the studies undertaken by some postal services and the introduction of new postal products. It also prepares and issues recommendations for member countries concerning uniform standards of practice. On the recommendation of the 1999 Beijing Congress the POC established a Standards Board with responsibility for approving standards relating to telematics, postal technology and Electronic Data Interchange (EDI). The POC aims to assist national postal services to modernize postal products, including letter and parcel post, financial services and expedited mail services. A Products Strategy and Integration sub-group of the POC, established on the recommendation of the 2012 Doha Congress, is developing an integrated approach to the physical post services sector. Revised regulations on letter-post and parcel international regulations entered into force on 1 January 2014.

CONSULTATIVE COMMITTEE

The Consultative Committee, established in September 2004 by the 23rd (Bucharest) Congress, provides a platform for dialogue between postal industry stakeholders and represents the interests of the wider international postal sector. It has 27 members, comprising non-governmental organizations (NGOs) representing customers, delivery service providers, workers' organizations, suppliers of goods and services to the postal sector and other organizations. Membership of the Committee is open to NGOs with an interest in international postal services, representing customers, delivery service providers, suppliers of goods and services to the postal sector, and workers' organizations; and also to private companies with an interest in international postal services, such as private operators, direct marketers, international mailers, and printers. All members are extended full observer status in all organs of the Union. The Committee convenes twice a year, in Bern, to coincide with meetings of the Council of Administration and the Postal Operations Council.

DIRECT MARKETING ADVISORY BOARD

The Direct Marketing Advisory Board (formerly the Direct Mail Advisory Board, renamed by the 2012 Doha Congress) has 47 members, including posts and private companies and associations.

INTERNATIONAL BUREAU

The day-to-day administrative work of the UPU is executed through the International Bureau, which provides secretariat and support facilities for the UPU's bodies. It serves as an instrument of liaison, information and consultation for the postal administration of the member countries and promotes technical co-operation among Union members. It also acts as a clearing house for the settlement of accounts between national postal administrations for inter-administration charges related to the exchange of postal items and international reply coupons. The Bureau supports the technical assistance programmes of the UPU, organizes regular conferences and workshops, and serves as an intermediary between the UPU, the UN, its agencies and other international organizations, customer organizations and private delivery services. Increasingly, the Bureau has assumed a greater role in postal administration, through two co-operatives: the Telematics Co-operative and the Express Mail Service (EMS) Co-operative. The Telematics Co-operative, with voluntary participation by public, semi-public, and private postal operators, supports the use of new technologies in the improvement and expansion of postal services. Its operational arm is the Postal Technology Centre (PTC, supported by five Regional Support Centres worldwide), which manages three core activities: Post*Net, a global postal communication network, using EDI to provide monitoring services, a track-and-trace system, and postal remuneration and billing; the International Postal System (IPS), an integrated international mail management system, providing automated processing of dispatches and end-to-end tracking of items; and the International Financial System (IFS), a software application facilitating international money order services. The EMS Co-operative, comprising (at April 2014) 175 EMS designated operators covering 85% of global EMS traffic, regulates the provision of a high-quality, competitive global EMS service, and operates through an EMS Unit. Seven UPU Regional Project Co-ordinators support the implementation of postal development projects worldwide.

Director-General of the International Bureau: Bishar Abdirahman Hussein (Kenya).

Deputy Director-General: Pascal-Thierry Clivaz (Switzerland).

Activities

The essential principles of the Union are the following:

(i) to develop social, cultural and commercial communication between people through the efficient operation of the postal services;

(ii) to guarantee freedom of transit and free circulation of postal items;

(iii) to ensure the organization, development and modernization of the postal services;

(iv) to promote and participate in postal technical assistance between member countries;

(v) to ensure the interoperability of postal networks by implementing a suitable policy of standardization;

(vi) to meet the changing needs of customers;

(vii) to improve the quality of service.

In addition to the Constitution and the General Regulations, the Universal Postal Convention is also a compulsory Act of the UPU (binding on all member countries), in view of its importance in the postal field and historical value. The Convention and its Detailed Regulations contain the common rules applicable to the international postal service and provisions concerning letter- and parcel-post. The Detailed Regulations are agreements concluded by the national postal administrations elected by Congress to the POC. The POC is empowered to revise and enact these, taking into account decisions made by Congress.

The 24th Congress, convened in Geneva, Switzerland, in July–August 2008, adopted a new Postal Payment Services Agreement and its Regulations (the original version of which was adopted by the 1999 Beijing Congress to replace the former Money Orders, Giro and Cash-on-Delivery Agreements). The Agreement (adherence to which is optional for UPU member states) aims to enable postal operators to operate faster, more secure and more accessible electronic money transfer services to communities without access to banks or other formal money transfer networks.

In recent years the UPU has reviewed its activities and has focused on the following factors underlying the modern postal environment: the growing role played by technology; the expanding reach of the effects of globalization; and the need to make the customer the focus of new competitive strategies. In October 2002 the UPU organized a Strategy Conference entitled 'Future Post', at which delegates representing governments and postal services addressed challenges confronting the postal industry. The 23rd Congress, held in September–October 2004, adopted the Bucharest World Postal Strategy, detailing a number of objectives to be pursued in the postal sector over the next four years; a new package of proposals for so-called terminal dues; a new quality of standards and targets for international mail services; a resolution relating to security, the combating of terrorism and prevention of money-laundering through use of the mail network; and a proposal to amend the UPU Convention to recognize legally the Electronic Postmark as an optional postal service. In July–August 2008 the 24th Congress adopted the Nairobi Postal Strategy to guide the Union's activities during 2009–12. The Strategy focused on modernizing global postal services at all levels, in terms of institutional reform, improvement in the quality of service, security of postal services, and promoting a universal postal service (UPS); and also in terms of raising awareness of the impact of postal services on the environment and climate change. The UPU Secretary-General stated during the 24th Congress that UPU's future agenda would focus on e-commerce, technological development, intelligent mail, facilitation of international trade and exchanges, electronic money transfers, sustainable development, international co-operation, postal infrastructure at the service of development policies, and improvements to the UPS. The 24th Congress determined to establish minimum security standards and processes for postal operators, and to invite postal administrations to co-operate more closely with customs authorities to identify counterfeit or pirated articles dispatched through the mail. In December 2009 UPU released the results of its first worldwide survey of greenhouse gas emissions generated by postal operations. At the UN Climate Change Conference, held in Copenhagen, Denmark, later in that month, UPU pledged to promote more environmentally friendly methods of processing and delivering mail. In January 2012 UPU released a study monitoring the development of postal e-services, which were divided into e-post services (such as internet-access points in post offices, postal electronic mailboxes and online direct mail); e-finance services (electronic invoicing, electronic remittances, electronic bill payments); e-commerce services (online subscriptions to periodicals, secure web certificates); and e-government services (including electronic payment of retirement pensions, online passport applications, electronic customs documents).

In October 2012 the 25th Congress adopted the Doha Postal Strategy for the period 2013–16, which was to navigate the UPU, and to provide guidance to member states' governments and postal authorities in developing national postal strategies and policies, within a changing environment of rapidly evolving technologies and consumer habits—including increasing electronic substitution for postal mail, diversification by communications media, and development of e-commerce. The Strategy had four main objectives: to improve the efficient interoperability of international postal networks; to provide postal sector-related technical expertise; to promote diversification of innovative products and services in the postal network's physical, financial and digital/electronic dimensions; and to foster sustainable development of the postal sector. The Strategy recognized that the concept of a universal postal service should be more broadly understood than hitherto, and the UPU was to be developed as a principal forum for exchanging ideas, best practices, and the development of analytical tools (such as statistics).

In April 2011 a new UPU inter-committee security group, with participation by postal operators and international organizations, met for the first time to pursue the development and application of global postal security standards.

In November 2011 a new UPU Emergency and Solidarity Fund (ESF) became operational; the ESF was to facilitate the recovery of basic postal services in countries affected by natural disaster and armed conflict, and was to be financed by voluntary contributions from governments and postal sector partners. The ESF was activated in December 2013 in view of devastating damaged caused to the Philippines postal infrastructure by Typhoon Haiyan.

POSTAL ENVIRONMENT

The 2004 Bucharest Congress approved a UPU policy on extraterritorial offices of exchange (ETOEs), defined as offices of facilities operated by or in connection with a postal operator on the territory of another country for the commercial purpose of drawing business in markets outside its national territory. The Council of Administration's WTO Issues Project Group monitors developments on trade in services, keeps member states informed on trade developments, and promotes awareness of WTO issues of interest to the UPU. In recent years the UPU has been concerned with developing the role of the postal sector in the modern information society and in reducing the digital divide between industrialized and developing nations. The

UPU pursues the following objectives in line with the Geneva Plan of Action adopted during the first phase of the World Summit on the Information Society convened in December 2003: facilitating, through the global postal infrastructure, unprecedented access to knowledge and ICTs; advancing the physical, electronic and financial dimensions of the global postal network; transferring postal administrations' expertise in physical communications management to the internet (particularly in the areas of identity management and spam control); and helping to build confidence and security in the use of ICTs. At the World Telecommunication Development Conference, convened in Hyderabad, India, in May–June 2010, the UPU, jointly with the International Telecommunication Union, launched a publication on innovation in the postal sector, entitled *ICTs, New Services and Transformation of the Post*. The UPU conducts market analysis to assist postal administrations in adapting to globalization and technological advances in world markets. A Postal Economics Programme implemented by the UPU conducts economic research aimed at analysing the uneven postal sector development of developing countries and providing growth models for the postal sectors of developing countries. In recent years the UPU has focused on the role of postal administrations in supporting the use of e-commerce activities by micro- and small enterprises in least developed and developing countries.

In October 2003 a new UPU clearing system (UPU*Clearing) became operational to enable postal operators to exchange bills electronically. During 2004 the UPU sponsored an application to the Internet Corporation for Assigned Names and Numbers (ICANN) to obtain a top-level internet domain, .post, for use, inter alia, by national and other postal operators, postal-related organizations, regional associations, UPU-regulated services, and trademarks and brand names. Negotiations between ICANN and the UPU on contract terms for the .post domain were concluded in October 2009 and an agreement was signed in December. The 2012 Doha Congress established a .post user group, which was to support the management of the domain name.

In March 2007 the UPU and the International Air Transport Association signed a Memorandum of Understanding on developing and harmonizing standards and increasing the use of technologies (such as bar coding, radio frequency identification, and the processing of electronic data) to improve air mail flows.

UPU helps to organize a regular World Postal Business Forum, which addresses postal sector challenges and trends; the 2014 Forum was to be convened in September, in Stockholm, Sweden, concurrently with the 18th annual POST-EXPO, an exhibition displaying recent post-related technological innovations and systems.

POSTAL DEVELOPMENT

The UPU's International Bureau undertakes quality tests on postal products and services worldwide, monitoring some 900 international links through the use of test letters and parcels; the Bureau also publishes end-to-end delivery standards. The UPU sends consultants to selected countries to promote the implementation of improvements in quality of service. The first phase of testing a new performance-measuring facility, the Global Monitoring System (GMS), was initiated in August 2009 by postal operators in 21 countries. The GMS commenced operations in January 2010.

The UPU has conducted research into the effects of postal sector regulatory reforms. The UPU's Integrated Postal Reform and Development Plan (IPDP) aims to enhance co-operation in promoting postal sector reform; under IPDP guidelines the principal aim of the postal sector reform process is to ensure that the state obligation to provide the UPS is met, and that the conditions required to modernize the postal sector are established, with a view to benefiting both individual citizens and business. Through its programme on development co-operation the UPU provides postal technical assistance to developing member countries. The 2008 Congress and the Nairobi Postal Strategy promoted the regional implementation of global development strategies; UPU implements a Regional Development Plan (RDP) aimed at providing a coherent framework for regional development activities.

The UPU has undertaken projects to develop human resources in the postal sector. It has developed guides, training materials and training models through its Trainpost programme, and organizes capacity-building training workshops in developing countries and on a regional basis. The UPU promotes environmental sustainability in the postal sector, encouraging recycling programmes and the use of environment-friendly products and resources. The UPU has produced guidelines on cost accounting to be used as a management tool by postal administrations.

The 1999 Congress approved the establishment of a Quality of Service Fund, which was to be financed by industrialized member countries (by a 7.5% increase in dues) in order to support service improvement projects in developing member states. The Fund became operative in 2001 and had by the end of 2012 approved 600 projects, benefiting some 150 national postal services. The 2008 Congress determined to extend the Fund's period of operation (originally to have expired in that year) to 2016. In October 2013 UPU, with other partners, organized a global forum on financial inclusion for development, which emphasized the role of post offices in providing financial services for around 2,700m. impoverished and rural 'unbanked' people globally, who are excluded from more mainstream financial institutions.

Finance

All of the UPU's regular budget expenses are financed by member countries, based on a contribution class system. The UPU's annual budget amounts to some 37m. Swiss francs.

Publications

Postal Statistics.

*POST*Info* (online newsletter of postal technology centre).

Union Postale (quarterly).

UPU EDI Messaging Standards.

UPU Technical Standards.

Other guides and industry reports.

World Health Organization—WHO

Address: 20 ave Appia, 1211 Geneva 27, Switzerland.

Telephone: 227912111; **fax:** 227913111; **e-mail:** info@who.int; **internet:** www.who.int.

WHO, established in 1948, is the lead agency within the UN system concerned with the protection and improvement of public health.

MEMBERS

WHO has 194 members.

Organization

(April 2014)

WORLD HEALTH ASSEMBLY

The Assembly meets in Geneva, Switzerland, once a year. It is responsible for policy-making and the biennial budget; appoints the Director-General; admits new members; and reviews budget contributions. The 67th Assembly was to be convened in May 2014.

EXECUTIVE BOARD

The Board is composed of 34 health experts designated by a member state that has been elected by the World Health Assembly to serve on the Board; each expert serves for three years. The Board meets at least twice a year to review the Director-General's programme, which it forwards to the Assembly with any recommendations that seem necessary. It advises on questions referred to it by the Assembly and is responsible for putting into effect the decisions and policies of the Assembly. It is also empowered to take emergency measures in case of epidemics or disasters. Meeting in November 2011 the Board agreed several proposed organizational reforms aimed at improving health outcomes, achieving greater coherence in global health matters, and promoting efficiency and transparency throughout WHO.

Chairman: Prof. JANE HALTON (Australia).

SECRETARIAT

Director-General: Dr MARGARET CHAN (People's Republic of China).

Deputy Director-General: Dr ANARFI ASAMOA-BAAH (Ghana).

Assistant Directors-General: Dr BRUCE AYLWARD (Canada) (Polio, Emergencies and Country Collaboration), FLAVIA BUSTREO (Italy) (Family, Women's and Children's Health), OLEG CHESTNOV (Russia) (Non-communicable Diseases and Mental Health), KEIJI FUKUDA (USA) (Health Security), MOHAMED ABDI JAMA (Somalia) (General Management), MARIE-PAULE KIENY (France) (Health Systems and Innovation), HIROKI NAKATANI (Japan) (HIV/AIDS, TB, Malaria and Neglected Tropical Diseases).

PRINCIPAL OFFICES

Each of WHO's six geographical regions has its own organization, consisting of a regional committee representing relevant member states and associate members, and a regional office staffed by experts in various fields of health.

Africa Office: Cité du Djoue BP 06, Brazzaville, Republic of the Congo; tel. 83-91-00; fax 83-95-03; e-mail regafro@whoafro.org; internet www.afro.who.int; Dir Dr LUÍS GOMES SAMBO (Angola).

Americas Office: Pan-American Health Organization, 525 23rd St, NW, Washington, DC 20037, USA; tel. (202) 974-3000; fax (202) 974-3663; e-mail postmaster@paho.org; internet www.paho.org; also administers The Caribbean Epidemiology Centre (CAREC); concluded in Oct. 2012 a Practical Arrangement with the IAEA, covering collaboration in areas including quality and safety in radiation medicine, radiological safety, radiological security and emergencies, and environmental medicine; Dir Dr CARISSA ETIENNE (Dominica).

Eastern Mediterranean Office: POB 7608, Abdul Razzak al Sanhouri St, Cairo (Nasr City) 11371, Egypt; tel. (2) 2765000; fax (2) 6702492; e-mail postmaster@emro.who.int; internet www.emro.who.int; Dir Dr ALA ALWAN (Iraq).

Europe Office: 51 Marmorvej, 2100 Copenhagen Ø, Denmark; tel. 45-33-70-00; fax 45-33-70-01; e-mail postmaster@euro.who.int; internet www.euro.who.int; Dir ZSUZSANNA JAKAB (Hungary).

International Health Regulations Coordination—WHO Lyon Office: 58 ave Debourg, 69007 Lyon, France; tel. 4-72-71-64-70; fax 4-72-71-64-71; e-mail ihrinfo@who.int; internet www.who.int/ihr/lyon/en/index.html; supports (with regional offices) countries in strengthening their national surveillance and response systems, with the aim of improving the detection, assessment and notification of events, and responding to public health risks and emergencies of international concern under the International Health Regulations.

South-East Asia Office: World Health House, Indraprastha Estate, Mahatma Gandhi Rd, New Delhi 110002, India; tel. (11) 23370804; fax (11) 23379507; e-mail registry@searo.who.int; internet www.searo.who.int; Dir Dr POONAM KHETRAPAL SINGH.

Western Pacific Office: POB 2932, Manila 1000, Philippines; tel. (2) 5288001; fax (2) 5211036; e-mail pio@wpro.who.int; internet www.wpro.who.int; Dir Dr SHIN YOUNG SOO (Republic of Korea).

WHO Centre for Health Development: I. H. D. Centre Bldg, 9th Floor, 5–1, 1-chome, Wakinohama-Kaigandori, Chuo-ku, Kobe, Japan; tel. (78) 230-3100; fax (78) 230-3178; e-mail wkc@who.int; internet www.who.int/kobe_centre/en/; f. 1995 to address health development issues; Dir ALEX ROSS (USA).

WHO European Office for Investment for Health and Development: Castello 3252, 30122 Venice, Italy; tel. (041) 279-3865; fax (041) 279-3869; e-mail info@ihd.euro.who.int; f. 2003; aims to develop a systematic approach to the integration of social and economic factors into European countries' development strategies.

Activities

WHO is the UN system's co-ordinating authority for health (defined as 'a state of complete physical, mental and social well-being and not merely the absence of disease and infirmity'). WHO's objective is stated in its constitution as 'the attainment by all peoples of the highest possible level of health'. In May 2013 the 66th World Health Assembly adopted the Organization's 12th General Programme of Work, to guide its activities during 2014–19; this was underpinned by six leadership priorities: advancing universal health coverage; addressing unfinished and future challenges (beyond 2015) in respect of the health-related Millennium Development Goals (MDGs); addressing the challenge of non-communicable diseases and mental health, violence and injuries and disabilities; implementing the provisions of the International Health Regulations; increasing access to essential, high-quality and affordable medical products; and addressing the social, economic and environmental determinants of health as a means of reducing health inequities within and between countries. WHO's core functions, emphasized in the 2014–19 programme of work, are to provide leadership on global public health matters, in partnership, where necessary, with other agencies; to help to shape the global health research agenda; to set, and monitor the implementation of, norms and standards; to articulate ethical and evidence-based policy options; to provide technical and policy support to member countries; and to monitor and assess health trends. Aid is provided in emergencies and natural disasters. The 12th General Programme of Work takes into account global challenges to health, including the negative impact on public spending on health of the continuing economic downturn in a number of developed countries; rapid unplanned urbanization, particularly in low? and middle?income countries (simultaneously providing new opportunities for the Organization of health provision and increased risks of social exclusion and inequity); health risks associated with economic migration; the potential health and social impact of a worldwide high level of youth unemployment; and pressure on the global environment, including significant loss of biodiversity, and climate change (potentially affecting fundamental requirements for health, including clean urban air, safe drinking water, a secure and nutritious food supply, and protection from extreme weather events).

WHO has developed a structured system of formulating and disseminating international standards of health issues. Its so-called Family of International Classifications (WHO-FIC) includes the *International Classification of Diseases (ICD)*, providing an etiological framework of health conditions, and currently in its 10th edition (11th revision due in 2017); and the complementary *International Classification of Functioning, Disability and Health (ICF)*, which describes how people live with their conditions. The WHO-FIC Network, comprising WHO collaborating centres that have been designated to work on international classifications, the WHO regional offices, and relevant departments of the Organization's headquarters, meets on an annual basis (in 2014 in Barcelona, Spain, in October), and develops, disseminates and maintains the WHO-FIC. Globally there are more than 800 WHO collaborating centres in more than 80 countries; networks of centres covering specific areas of expertise have been established, including (as well as those designated for developing international classifications) communicable diseases, food safety, nursing and midwifery, nutrition, occupational health, prevention of injuries and violence, radiation, tobacco control, and traditional medicine.

WHO keeps diseases and other health problems under constant surveillance, promotes the exchange of prompt and accurate information and of notification of outbreaks of diseases, and administers the International Health Regulations (the most recently revised version of which entered into force in June 2007). WHO undertakes to collect and disseminate health data and undertake statistical analyses and comparative studies in such diseases as cancer, heart disease and mental illness; set standards for the quality control of drugs, vaccines and other substances affecting health, and communicate reports or any known adverse reactions to drugs to all member states; formulate health regulations for international travel; and promote improved environmental conditions, including housing, sanitation and working conditions.

In October 2013 the WHO Director-General convened an informal consultation of WHO stakeholders to discuss the development of a robust framework to guide WHO's extensive engagement with non-state actors, i.e. entities that participate or act in international and national relations, possessing the power to influence and cause change, while not belonging to any state, such as private commercial interests, non-governmental organizations (NGOs), philanthropic foundations, and academic institutions, and including, for example, the influential GAVI Alliance and Global Fund to Fight AIDS, TB and Malaria. In January 2014 the Executive Board gave consideration to the draft framework under development, which outlined five key overarching principles to guide any such engagement, as follows: interaction between WHO and non-state actors must demonstrate a clear benefit to public health; must respect the intergovernmental nature of WHO, with no non-state actor expecting to have the same decision-making privileges as WHO's member states; must support WHO's ethos of basing the development of norms, standards, policies and strategies on the systematic use of scientific evidence, free from the influence of any form of—commercial or otherwise—bias or vested interest; must be actively managed, so as to reduce any form of risk to WHO (including conflicts of interest); and must be underpinned by transparency and inclusiveness. It was envisaged that further consultations on the draft framework would be conducted during 2014.

A global programme of collaborative research and exchange of scientific information is carried out in co-operation with about 1,200 national institutions. Particular emphasis is given to the widespread communicable diseases of the tropics, and the countries directly concerned are assisted in developing their research capabilities. WHO negotiates and sustains national and global partnerships. It may propose international conventions and agreements, or promote the development and testing of new technologies, tools and guidelines. WHO assists in developing an informed public opinion on matters of health.

WHO has contributed to the pursuit, by 2015, of the UN MDGs, with particular responsibility for the MDGs of reducing child mortality (with a target reduction of two-thirds in the mortality rate among children under the age of five); improving maternal health (with a specific goal of reducing by 75% the numbers of women dying in childbirth); and combating HIV/AIDS, malaria and other diseases. In addition, it has directly supported the following millennium 'targets': halving the proportion of people suffering from malnutrition; halving the proportion of people without sustainable access to safe drinking water and basic sanitation; and providing access, in co-operation with pharmaceutical companies, to affordable, essential drugs in developing countries. In 2013 WHO, with UNICEF, co-led consultations on formulating a post-2015 development framework in the thematic area of health.

During 2005 the UN's Inter-Agency Standing Committee (IASC), concerned with co-ordinating the international response to humanitarian disasters, developed a concept of organizing agency assistance to internally displaced persons through the institutionalization of a 'Cluster Approach', comprising 11 core areas of activity. WHO was designated the lead agency for the Health Cluster. The 65th World Health Assembly, convened in May 2012, adopted a resolution endorsing WHO's role as Health Cluster lead and urging international donors to allocate sufficient resources towards health sector activities during humanitarian emergencies.

WHO, with the International Labour Organization (ILO), leads the Social Protection Floor initiative, the sixth of nine activities that were launched in April 2009 by the UN System Chief Executives Board for Co-ordination (CEB), with the aim of alleviating the impact on poor and vulnerable populations of the global economic downturn. In October 2011 a Social Protection Floor Advisory Group, launched in August 2010 under the initiative, issued a report entitled *Social Protection Floor for a Fair and Inclusive Globalization*, which urged that basic incomes and services should be guaranteed for all, stating that this would promote both stability and economic growth globally. WHO is the sponsoring agency for the Health Workforce Decade (2006–15).

COMMUNICABLE DISEASES

WHO aims to reduce the burden of infectious and parasitic communicable diseases, HIV/AIDS, tuberculosis (TB), malaria, neglected tropical diseases and vaccine-preventable diseases, identifying these as a major obstacle to social and economic progress, particularly in developing countries, where, in addition to disabilities and loss of productivity and household earnings, they cause nearly one-half of all deaths. Emerging and re-emerging diseases, those likely to cause epidemics, increasing incidence of zoonoses (diseases or infections passed from vertebrate animals to humans by means of parasites, viruses, bacteria or unconventional agents), attributable to factors such as environmental changes and changes in farming practices, outbreaks of unknown etiology, and the undermining of some drug therapies by the spread of antimicrobial resistance, are main areas of concern. In recent years WHO has noted the global spread of communicable diseases through international travel, voluntary human migration and involuntary population displacement.

WHO's Global Alert and Response (GAR) framework aims to provide an effective international system for co-ordinated response to epidemics and other public health emergencies, underpinned by strong national public health systems. In 2000 WHO and several partner institutions in epidemic surveillance established the Global Outbreak Alert and Response Network (GOARN), which maintains constant vigilance regarding outbreaks of disease, and links worldwide expertise—for example through co-ordinated regional and global Emerging and Dangerous Pathogens Laboratory Networks, that cover both the human and animal sectors—to provide an immediate response capability. WHO aims to strengthen biorisk reduction capacity, biosecurity, and readiness for outbreaks of dangerous and emerging pathogens. The Organization assists member states in the development and implementation of domestic capacities for epidemic preparedness and response through strengthening national laboratory capacities and early warning alert and response mechanisms; promoting relevant national and international training programmes; promoting standardized approaches in relation to epidemic-prone infections, such as cholera; influenza; meningitis; plague (in its bubonic, pneumonic and septicemic presentations), which can be carried to humans by infected rodents and domestic cats; Severe Acute Respiratory Syndrome (SARS), viral haemorrhagic fevers (including the Crimean-Congo, Ebola, Lassa and Marburg types), which are spread by direct contact with infected blood, body fluids and tissues, including of wild animals; and yellow fever. In July 2011 WHO launched the Global Infection Prevention and Control (GIPC) Network, which provides technical support to member states through the dissemination of epidemic-prone infection prevention and control policies and guidance; the compilation of relevant indicators; and generic training curricula.

Combating the human immunodeficiency virus/acquired immunodeficiency syndrome (HIV/AIDS), TB and malaria are organization-wide priorities and, as such, are supported not only by their own areas of work but also by activities undertaken in other areas. TB is the principal cause of death for people infected with the HIV virus and an estimated one-third of people living with HIV/AIDS globally are co-infected with TB. In July 2000 a meeting of the Group of Seven industrialized nations and Russia, convened in Genoa, Italy, announced the formation of the Global Fund to Fight AIDS, TB and Malaria (as previously proposed by the UN Secretary-General and recommended by the World Health Assembly).

Some 95% of those known to be infected with HIV/AIDS live in developing countries, and AIDS-related illnesses are the leading cause of death in sub-Saharan Africa. It is estimated that around 30m. people worldwide died of AIDS during 1981–2011. WHO supports governments to develop effective health sector responses to the HIV/AIDS epidemic through enhancing their planning and managerial capabilities, implementation capacity, and health systems resources. The Joint UN Programme on HIV/AIDS (UNAIDS) became operational on 1 January 1996, sponsored by WHO and other UN agencies; the UNAIDS secretariat is based at WHO headquarters. In May 2000 the World Health Assembly adopted a resolution urging WHO member states to improve access to the prevention and treatment of HIV-related illnesses and to increase the availability and affordability of drugs. A WHO-UNAIDS HIV Vaccine Initiative was launched in that year. In July 2012 WHO published the first report detailing levels of HIV drug resistance in low- and middle-income countries; the overall rate was estimated at that time to be 6.8%. WHO guidelines on the use of antiretroviral therapy (ART) were first released in 2002, and have subsequently been revised, with the most recent update released in June 2013. In the following month UNAIDS initiated the Treatment 2015 framework, aimed at facilitating the provision by 2015 of ART to some 15m. people infected with HIV. At mid-2013 it was reported that around 10m. people requiring ART globally had access to the treatment.

In May 2011 the 64th World Health Assembly adopted a new Global Health Sector Strategy on HIV/AIDS, covering 2011–15, which aimed to promote greater innovation in HIV prevention, diagnosis, treatment, and the improvement of care services to facilitate universal access to care for HIV patients. In December 2011 the UN General Assembly adopted a Political Declaration on HIV/AIDS, outlining 10 targets to be attained by 2015: reducing by 50% sexual transmission of HIV; reducing by 50% HIV transmission among people who inject drugs; eliminating new HIV infections among children, and reducing AIDS-related maternal deaths; ensuring that at least 15m. people living with HIV are receiving ART; reducing by 50% TB deaths in people living with HIV; reaching annual global investment of at least US $22,000m. in combating AIDS in low- and medium-resource countries; eliminating gender inequalities and increasing the capacity of women and girls to self-protect from HIV; promoting the adoption of legislation and policies aimed at eliminating stigma and discrimination against people living with HIV; eliminating HIV-related restrictions on travel; strengthening the integration of the AIDS response in global health and development efforts.

The total number of people worldwide living with HIV/AIDS at December 2011 was estimated at 34m., including some 2.7m. children under 15 years of age. It was reported that 2.5m. people were newly infected during that year. At December 2011 an estimated 23.5m. people in sub-Saharan Africa were estimated to have HIV/AIDS, of whom around 1.7m. were newly infected during that year. Swaziland had the highest national HIV prevalence rate in the world in 2011 (with around one-quarter of the population infected), and more people were living with HIV/AIDS in South Africa than in any other country globally (an estimated 5.6m.). Meanwhile, 3m. people were living with AIDS in Nigeria, 1.6m. both in Kenya and Tanzania, and 1.4m. in Mozambique and in Uganda. In December 2012 UNAIDS reported that, although prevalence rates remained high, the number of new HIV infections fell during 2001–11—by 73% in Botswana, by 71% in Malawi, by 68% in Namibia, by 58% in Zambia, and by 50% in Zimbabwe—indicating the successful impact of prevention and treatment programmes.

Joint UN Programme on HIV/AIDS (UNAIDS): 20 ave Appia, 1211 Geneva 27, Switzerland; tel. 227913666; fax 227914187; e-mail communications@unaids.org; internet www.unaids.org; f. 1996 to lead, strengthen and support an expanded response to the global HIV/AIDS pandemic; activities focus on prevention, care and support, reducing vulnerability to infection, and alleviating the socio-economic and human effects of HIV/AIDS; launched the Global Coalition on Women and AIDS in Feb. 2004; guided by UN Security Council Resolution 1308, focusing on the possible impact of AIDS on social instability and emergency situations, and the potential impact of HIV on the health of international peacekeeping personnel; by the MDGs adopted in Sept. 2000; by the Declaration of Commitment on HIV/AIDS agreed in June 2001 by the first Special Session of the UN General Assembly on HIV/AIDS, which acknowledged the AIDS epidemic as a 'global emergency'; and the Political Declaration on HIV/AIDS, adopted by the June 2006 UN General Assembly High Level Meeting on AIDS; in Nov. 2012 UNAIDS appointed Aung San Suu Kyi as Global Advocate for Zero Discrimination; in Dec. 2013 a fourth international replenishment meeting secured funding of US $12,000m. for the three-year period 2014–16; co-sponsors: WHO,

UN Women, UNICEF, UNDP, UNFPA, UNODC, the ILO, UNESCO, the World Bank, WFP, UNHCR; Exec. Dir MICHEL SIDIBÉ (Mali).

According to WHO estimates, one-third of the world's population carries the TB bacillus. In 2011 this generated 8.7m. new active cases (13% in people co-infected with HIV), and killed 1.4m. people (430,000 of whom were also HIV-positive). Some 22 countries account for four-fifths of global TB cases. The largest concentration of TB cases is in South-East Asia. WHO provides technical support to all member countries, with special attention given to those with high TB prevalence, to establish effective national tuberculosis control programmes. WHO's strategy for TB control includes the use of the expanded DOTS (direct observation treatment, short-course) regime, involving the following five tenets: sustained political commitment to increase human and financial resources and to make TB control in endemic countries a nationwide activity and an integral part of the national health system; access to quality-assured TB sputum microscopy; standardized short-course chemotherapy for all cases of TB under proper case-management conditions; uninterrupted supply of quality-assured drugs; and maintaining a recording and reporting system to enable outcome assessment. Simultaneously, WHO is encouraging research with the aim of further advancing DOTS, developing new tools for prevention, diagnosis and treatment, and containing new threats (such as the HIV/TB co-epidemic). Inadequate control of DOTS in some areas, leading to partial and inconsistent treatments, has resulted in the development of drug-resistant and, often, incurable strains of TB. The incidence of so-called Multidrug Resistant TB (MDR-TB) strains has risen in recent years; an estimated 3.7% of new TB cases were reported to be MDR in 2011. MDR-TB cases occur most frequently in the People's Republic of China, India, Russia and South Africa; it was reported in 2011 that in Russia around 20% of new cases and 46% of cases presenting for retreatment were MDR. WHO has developed DOTS-Plus, a specialized strategy for controlling the spread of MDR-TB in areas of high prevalence. By the end of 2011 some 84 countries had reported at least one case of Extensive Drug Resistant TB (XDR-TB), defined as MDR-TB plus resistance to any fluoroquinolone, and to any of the three second-line anti-TB drugs. XDR-TB is believed to be most prevalent in Eastern Europe and Asia. TB cases resistant to all drugs have been reported in Europe and in Iran. In 2007 WHO launched the Global MDR/XDR Response Plan, which aimed to expand diagnosis and treatment to cover, by 2015, some 85% of TB patients with MDR-TB.

The 'Stop TB' partnership, launched by WHO in 1999, in partnership with the World Bank, the US Government and a coalition of NGOs, co-ordinates the Global Plan to Stop TB, which represents a roadmap for TB control covering the period 2006–15. The Global Plan aims to facilitate the achievement of the MDG of halting and beginning to reverse by 2015 the incidence of TB by means of access to quality diagnosis and treatment for all; to supply ART to 3m. TB patients co-infected with HIV; to treat nearly 1m. people for MDR-TB (this target was subsequently altered by the 2007 Global MDR/XDR Response Plan); to develop a new anti-TB drug and a new vaccine; and to develop rapid and inexpensive diagnostic tests at the point of care. A second phase of the Global Plan, launched in late 2010 and covering 2011–15, updated the Plan to take account of actual progress achieved since its instigation in 2006. The Global TB Drug Facility, launched by 'Stop TB' in 2001, aims to increase access to high-quality anti-TB drugs for sufferers in developing countries. In 2007 'Stop TB' endorsed the establishment of a Global Laboratory Initiative with the aim of expanding laboratory capacity.

In October 2013 WHO and partners launched the 'Roadmap for childhood TB: towards zero deaths', recommending 10 actions aimed at eradicating childhood deaths from TB, including incorporating the needs of children and adolescents into TB research, policy development and clinical practices; making use of critical intervention strategies, such as contact tracing and preventive therapy; implementing policies to enable early diagnosis and ensuring an uninterrupted supply of high-quality anti-TB medicines for children; addressing research gaps, and closing all funding gaps relating to childhood TB; and establishing partnerships to study and evaluate the best strategies for preventing, managing and treating childhood TB. Some US $120m. was pledged at that time in new donor funding towards addressing childhood TB (including $40m. allocated to the provision of ARTs for children co-infected with TB and HIV).

In October 1998 WHO, jointly with UNICEF, the World Bank and UNDP, formally launched the Roll Back Malaria (RBM) programme. The disease acutely affects at least 350m.–500m. people, and kills an estimated 1m. people, every year. Some 85% of all malaria cases occur in sub-Saharan Africa. It is estimated that the disease directly causes nearly one-fifth of all child deaths in that region. The Democratic Republic of the Congo and Nigeria have the highest levels of infection in sub-Saharan Africa. The global RBM Partnership, linking governments, development agencies, and other parties, aims to mobilize resources and support for controlling malaria. The RBM Partnership Global Strategic Plan for the period 2005–15, adopted in November 2005, listed steps required to intensify malaria control interventions with a view to by 2015 75% reduction in malaria morbidity and mortality over levels at 2005. WHO recommends a number of guidelines for malaria control, focusing on the need for prompt, effective antimalarial treatment, and the issue of drug resistance; vector control, including the use of insecticide-treated bed nets; malaria in pregnancy; malaria epidemics; and monitoring and evaluation activities. WHO, with several private and public sector partners, supports the development of more effective anti-malaria drugs and vaccines through the 'Medicines for Malaria' venture. A draft Global Technical Strategy for Malaria Control and Elimination, to cover the period 2016–25, was under development in 2014.

During 2012–20 WHO was implementing a global strategy for the prevention and control of the mosquito-borne dengue virus, the incidence of which has increased significantly in humans in recent years, with at least 50m. new cases arising annually, resulting in some 20,000 deaths, in more than 100 endemic countries, particularly in the Asia-Pacific region and Latin America. The strategy focuses on improving—through co-ordinated epidemiological and entomological surveillance—outbreak prediction and detection, and on the deployment of locally-adapted vector control measures. The Special Programme for Research and Training in Tropical Diseases, established in 1975 and sponsored jointly by WHO, UNDP and the World Bank, as well as by contributions from donor countries, involves a worldwide network of some 5,000 scientists working on the development and application of vaccines, new drugs, diagnostic kits and preventive measures, and applied field research on practical community issues affecting the target diseases. In May 2013 the 66th World Health Assembly adopted a resolution on Neglected Tropical Diseases that urged member states to ensure country ownership of prevention, control, elimination and eradication programmes, urged international partners to supply adequate funding in support of these, and encouraged the development of new technologies aimed at supporting vector control and infection prevention.

From March 2003 WHO began to co-ordinate an international investigation into the global spread of SARS, a previously unknown atypical pneumonia. In 2014 WHO was monitoring the spread of Middle East respiratory syndrome coronavirus (MERS-CoV), a related acute respiratory condition; by 27 January 2014 180 laboratory-confirmed cases of MERS-CoV had been reported to WHO since September 2012, and 77 of those affected had died. The reported cases had arisen in Jordan, Qatar, Saudi Arabia and the United Arab Emirates (UAE). Laboratory-confirmed cases had also been reported in France, Italy, Tunisia and the United Kingdom, relating to patients who had recently been in the source region, or had been transferred to a third country for care. From the end of 2003 WHO was monitoring the spread through several Asian countries of the virus H5N1 (a rapidly mutating strain of zoonotic highly pathogenic avian influenza—HPAI) that was transmitting to human populations through contact with diseased birds, mainly poultry. It was then greatly feared that H5N1, which has since become endemic among poultry in parts of Asia and Africa, might mutate into a form transmissable from human to human, although WHO reported in 2014 that, by then, H5N1 still did not appear to transmit easily among people. In March 2005 WHO issued a *Global Influenza Preparedness Plan*, and urged all countries to develop national influenza pandemic preparedness plans and to stockpile antiviral drugs. In May, in co-operation with FAO and the World Organisation for Animal Health (OIE), WHO launched a Global Strategy for the Progressive Control of Highly Pathogenic Avian Influenza. A conference on Avian Influenza and Human Pandemic Influenza that was jointly organized by WHO, FAO, the OIE and the World Bank in November 2005 issued a plan of action identifying a number of responses for disease control, preparedness, response and vaccine research. WHO has continued to report on cases of H5N1 on a monthly basis, and by 24 January 2014 a total of 650 human cases of H5N1 had been laboratory confirmed, in Azerbaijan, Bangladesh, Cambodia, China, Djibouti, Egypt, Indonesia, Iraq, Laos, Myanmar, Nigeria, Pakistan, Thailand, Turkey and Viet Nam, resulting in 386 deaths. Two further general subtypes of avian influenza—H7 and H9—have also been reported in humans. In April 2013 WHO and the Chinese authorities deployed a joint mission to investigate and make recommendations concerning the control of an outbreak of H7N9 in humans that had emerged in February in China. By 21 January 2014 209 cases of H7N9 in humans had been reported to WHO. These were mainly concentrated in two waves, occurring during February–May 2013, and from October of that year onwards, and had resulted in 46 fatalities.

In April 2009 GOARN sent experts to Mexico to work with health authorities there in response to an outbreak of confirmed human cases of a new variant of swine influenza A(H1N1) that had not previously been detected in animals or humans. In late April, by which time cases of the virus had been reported in the USA and Canada, the Director-General of WHO declared a 'public health emergency of international concern'. All countries were instructed to activate their national influenza pandemic preparedness plans. On

11 June WHO declared a global pandemic (phase six on the Organization's warning scale, characterized by human-to-human transmission in two or more WHO regions). In August 2010 the WHO Director-General declared that transmission of the new H1N1 virus had entered a post-pandemic phase. In May 2011 the 64th World Health Assembly adopted a Pandemic Influenza Preparedness (PIP) Framework, which aimed to broaden access to anti-influenza vaccines.

WHO works with animal health sector partners at the human–animal interface at national level to identify and reduce animal health and public health risks, with a strong focus on pigs, as they can become infected with influenza viruses from a variety of different hosts (including birds and humans), and can act as a 'mixing vessel', generating new reassortant viruses that, it is feared, may spread easily among humans. In the context of avian influenza, WHO in August 2013 initiated a so-called 'Four-Way Linking Project' in H5N1-endemic countries to assess health risks arising at the human–animal interface, as a means of supporting effective national disease control measures; it was envisaged that the project might subsequently be adapted to address other priority zoonotic diseases.

In 1988 the World Health Assembly launched the Global Polio Eradication Initiative (GPEI), which aimed, initially, to eradicate poliomyelitis by the end of 2000; this target was subsequently extended to the end of 2018. Co-ordinated periods of Supplementary Immunization Activity (SIA, facilitated in conflict zones by the negotiation of so-called days of tranquility), including National Immunization Days (NIDs), Sub-National Immunization Days (SNIDs), mop-up campaigns, VitA campaigns (Vitamin A is administered in order to reduce nutritional deficiencies in children and thereby boost their immunity), and Follow up/Catch up campaigns, have been employed in combating the disease, alongside the strengthening of routine immunization services. Since the inauguration of the GPEI WHO has declared the following regions 'polio-free': the Americas (1994); Western Pacific (2000); and Europe (2002). Furthermore, type 2 wild poliovirus has been eradicated globally (since 1999), although a type 2 circulating vaccine-derived poliovirus (cVDPV) was reported to be active in northern Nigeria during 2006–early 2010. In January 2004 ministers responsible for health of affected countries, and global partners, meeting under the auspices of WHO and UNICEF, adopted the Geneva Declaration on the Eradication of Poliomyelitis, in which they made a commitment to accelerate the drive towards eradication of the disease, by improving the scope of vaccination programmes. In February 2007 the GPEI launched an intensified eradication effort aimed at identifying and addressing the outstanding operational, technical and financial barriers to eradication. The May 2008 World Health Assembly adopted a resolution urging all remaining polio-affected member states to achieve the vaccination of every child. Some 223 polio cases were confirmed worldwide in 2012, of which 217 were in the then three polio-endemic countries (Nigeria, 122 cases, Pakistan, 58 cases, and Afghanistan, 35 cases), and six cases were recorded in non-endemic countries (Chad and Niger). (In 1988, by comparison, 35,000 cases had been confirmed in 125 countries, with the actual number of cases estimated at around 350,000.) In April 2013, acting upon a request made in May 2012 by the 65th World Health Assembly, the GPEI issued a new Polio Eradication and Endgame Strategic Plan covering the period 2013–18. Under the Plan countries were urged to ensure the administration of at least one dose of inactivated poliovirus vaccine (IPV), and—with a view to eliminating the risk of vaccine-associated polio outbreaks—to begin the phased removal of oral polio vaccines. In November 2013 the GAVI Alliance determined to add IPV to its routine immunisation programme, in support of the Plan. In March 2014 the WHO South-East Asia region was certified by an independent commission to be polio-free.

In 1996 an African Programme for Onchocerciasis Control (APOC), covering 19 African countries, became operational, with funding co-ordinated by the World Bank and with WHO as the executing agency. In January 2014 the APOC entered a two-year transition period which was to culminate, in 2016, in the establishment of a new entity that was to support African countries in the elimination of onchocerciasis, lymphatic filariasis, and other neglected tropical diseases.

The Onchocerciasis Elimination Programme in the Americas (OEPA), launched in 1992, co-ordinates work to control the disease in six Latin American countries where it is endemic. South American trypanosomiasis ('Chagas disease') is endemic in Central and South America, causing the deaths of some 45,000 people each year and infecting a further 16m.–18m. A regional intergovernmental commission is implementing a programme to eliminate Chagas from the Southern Cone region of Latin America. In July 2007, to combat the expansion of Chagas disease into some European countries, the Western Pacific, and the USA, as well as the re-emergence of the disease in areas such as the Chaco, in Argentina and Bolivia, where it was thought to have been eradicated, WHO established a Global Network for Chagas Disease Elimination.

WHO is committed to the elimination of leprosy. The use of a highly effective combination of three drugs (known as multi drug therapy—MDT) resulted in a reduction in the number of leprosy cases worldwide from 10m.–12m. in 1988 to 181,941 registered cases in January 2012. In 2013 leprosy remained endemic in parts of Brazil, Indonesia, Philippines, Democratic Republic of the Congo, India, Madagascar, Mozambique, Nepal and Tanzania. The Global Alliance for the Elimination of Leprosy was launched in November 1999 by WHO, in collaboration with governments of affected countries and several private partners, to support the eradication of the disease through the provision of free MDT treatment; WHO's Enhanced Global Strategy for Further Reducing the Disease Burden Due to Leprosy was being implemented during 2011–15 through national programmes in the remaining endemic countries, with the aim of reducing the global rate of new leprosy cases with Grade 2 (visible) disabilities per 100,000 of the population by at least 35% by end-2015, compared with the situation in 2010. In 1998 WHO launched the Global Buruli Ulcer Initiative, which aimed to co-ordinate control of and research into Buruli ulcer, another mycobacterial disease. In July of that year the Director-General of WHO and representatives of more than 20 countries, meeting in Yamoussoukro, Côte d'Ivoire, signed a declaration on the control of Buruli ulcer; a further declaration was signed in March 2009 by WHO's Regional Director for Africa, representatives of affected countries, and other stakeholders.

The objective of providing immunization for all children by 1990 was adopted by the World Health Assembly in 1977. Six diseases (measles, whooping cough, tetanus, poliomyelitis, tuberculosis and diphtheria) became the target of the Expanded Programme on Immunization (EPI), in which WHO, UNICEF and many other organizations collaborated. As a result of massive international and national efforts, the global immunization coverage increased from 20% in the early 1980s to the targeted rate of 80% by the end of 1990, and stood at 83% at the end of 2011. WHO's Strategic Advisory Group of Experts (SAGE) on Immunization was established in 1999 to guide the Organization on vaccines and immunization for all age groups, including on formulating global policies and strategies relating to technology; research and development; the delivery of immunization; and its linkages with other health interventions. In 2006 WHO, UNICEF and other partners launched the Global Immunization Vision and Strategy (GIVS), a global 10-year framework, covering 2006–15, aimed at increasing national vaccination coverage levels, for all ages, to at least 90% by 2015. In May 2012 the 65th World Health Assembly endorsed a Global Vaccine Action Plan (GVAP), building on the GIVS, which aimed to facilitate more equitable access to vaccines by 2020.

In recent years WHO has been concerned with the problem of Antimicrobial Resistance (AMR): the spread of infections caused by micro-organisms (including bacteria, viruses and certain parasites)—'super-pathogens'—that are resistant to conventional treatments (antibiotics, antivirals and antimalarials), such as multidrug-resistant TB, multidrug- and cephalosporin-resistant gonorrhea, and hospital-acquired infections such as methicillin-resistant Staphylococcus Aureus (MRSA). First-line medicines are increasingly failing, with second-line agents proving generally more costly, more toxic, and less effective, causing WHO to warn of the imminent advent of a post-antibiotic era. In 2011 WHO issued a six-point policy package on AMR, and in September 2013 a Strategic and Technical Advisory Group was established, to advise WHO on its co-ordination role in combating AMR, and to help develop a Global Action Plan on AMR; it was envisaged that the Plan would be presented in May 2014 to the World Health Assembly for approval. The Plan was to address contributory factors to the spread of AMR, such as over-prescribing (caused by the vested commercial interests of some private providers), the use of antimicrobials in livestock reared for human consumption, weak national drug policies and regulatory agencies in many developing countries, and the commonplace open-market purchase of non-prescribed antimicrobial medicines in some countries.

NON-COMMUNICABLE DISEASES AND MENTAL HEALTH

WHO's activities in the area of non-communicable diseases (NCDs) and mental health aim—through health promotion and risk reduction, prevention, treatment and monitoring of NCDs and their risk factors—to reduce the burden of heart disease, cancer, lung disease, diabetes, mental disorders, disability, and injuries. The surveillance, prevention and management of NCDs, tobacco, and mental health are organization-wide priorities. Tobacco use, unhealthy diet and physical inactivity are regarded as common, preventable risk factors for the four most prominent NCDs, i.e. cardiovascular diseases, cancer, chronic respiratory disease and diabetes. It is estimated that these NCDs are collectively responsible for an estimated 35m. deaths—60% of all deaths—globally each year, and that up to 80% of cases of heart disease, stroke and type 2 diabetes, and more than one-third of cancers, could be prevented by eliminating shared risk factors, the main ones being tobacco use, unhealthy diet, physical inactivity and harmful use of alcohol. WHO aims to monitor the global epidemiological situation of NCDs, to co-ordinate multinational research activities concerned with prevention and care, and to analyse determining factors such as gender and poverty. In May 2013 the 66th World Health Assembly endorsed a Global Action Plan for 2013–20 for the Prevention and Control of NCDs, incorporating nine targets for reducing the impact of NCDs, as well as a monitoring framework. In July 2013 the UN Economic and Social Council adopted a resolution requesting the UN Secretary-General to establish an inter-agency UN Task Force on the Prevention and Control of NCDs. The Task Force, convened and led by WHO, held its inaugural meeting in October, and was to support the implementation of the 1999 WHO Framework Convention on Tobacco Control (q.v.) and also to co-ordinate the activities of all UN organizations in implementing the Global Action Plan for 2013–20 for the Prevention and Control of NCDs.

In May 2004 the World Health Assembly endorsed a Global Strategy on Diet, Physical Activity and Health; it is estimated that more than 1,000m. adults worldwide are overweight, and of these some 300m. are clinically obese, carrying a raised risk of contracting chronic diseases. WHO has studied obesity-related issues in co-operation with the International Association for the Study of Obesity (IASO). The International Task Force on Obesity, affiliated to the IASO, aims to encourage the development of new policies for managing obesity.

In March 2014, with a view to reducing levels of obesity and dental decay, WHO launched a public consultation on a draft update to its most recent (2002) guideline on the intake of sugars. Under the new proposed guideline—which stressed the often hidden presence of sugars in processed foods—monosaccharides (including glucose and fructose), disaccharides (such as sucrose or table sugar), and naturally present sugars (for example in honey and fruit juices) should provide less than 10% of total energy intake per day, while the benefits were emphasized of a reduction to below 5% of daily energy intake.

WHO's programmes for diabetes mellitus, chronic rheumatic diseases and asthma assist with the development of national initiatives, based upon goals and targets for the improvement of early detection, care and reduction of long-term complications. WHO's cardiovascular diseases programme aims to prevent and control the major cardiovascular diseases, which are responsible for more than 14m. deaths each year. It is estimated that one-third of these deaths could have been prevented with existing scientific knowledge.

The Cancer Control is Programme is concerned with the prevention of cancer, improving its early detection and treatment, and ensuring care of all cancer patients in need. In May 2009 WHO and the International Atomic Energy Agency launched a Joint Programme on Cancer Control, aimed at enhancing efforts to fight cancer in the developing world. Inter-agency collaboration on combating cancer was intensified following the Political Declaration on the Prevention and Control of NCDs made in September 2011 by a High-level Meeting of the UN General Assembly. WHO is a co-sponsor of the Global Day Against Pain, which is held annually on 11 October to highlight the need for improved pain management and palliative care for sufferers of diseases such as cancer and AIDS, with a particular focus on patients living in low-income countries with minimal access to opioid analgesics, and to promote recognition of access to pain relief as a basic human right.

In April 2014 WHO issued its first guidelines on the treatment of chronic Hepatitis C infections, with a view to reducing the number of deaths globally (estimated at up to 500,000 annually) from Hepatitis C-related cirrhosis and cancer of the liver.

The WHO Human Genetics Programme manages genetic approaches for the prevention and control of common hereditary diseases and of those with a genetic predisposition representing a major health factor. The Programme also concentrates on the further development of genetic approaches suitable for incorporation into health care systems, as well as developing a network of international collaborating programmes.

WHO's health promotion division promotes decentralized and community-based health programmes and is concerned with developing new approaches to population ageing and encouraging healthy lifestyles and self-care. It also seeks to relieve the negative impact of social changes such as urbanization, migration and changes in family structure upon health. Several health promotion projects have been undertaken, in collaboration between WHO regional and country offices and other relevant organizations, including the Global School Health Initiative, to bridge the sectors of health and education and to promote the health of school-age children; the Global Strategy for Occupational Health, to promote the health of the working population and the control of occupational health risks; Community-based Rehabilitation, aimed at providing a more enabling environment for people with disabilities; and a communication strategy to provide training and support for health communications personnel and initiatives. In 2000 WHO, UNESCO, the World Bank and UNICEF adopted the joint Focusing Resources for Effective School Health (FRESH Start) approach to promoting life skills among adolescents.

WHO supports the UN Convention, and its Optional Protocol, on the Rights of Persons with Disabilities, which came into force in May 2008, and seeks to address challenges that prevent the full participation of people with disabilities in the social, economic and cultural lives of their communities and societies; at that time the WHO Director-General appointed a Taskforce on Disability to ensure that WHO was reflecting the provisions of the Convention in its programme of work. In December 2011 WHO and the World Bank jointly released the first *World Report on Disability*, focusing on the areas of health care, rehabilitation, education, employment and support services, and detailing a number of recommendations for governments aimed at creating environments that would enable people with disabilities to flourish. The WHO Disability Assessment Schedule, introduced in November 2012, measures health and disability across six areas: cognition (understanding and communicating); mobility; self-care (hygiene, dressing, eating and coping alone); interaction with other people; life activities (including domestic responsibilities, leisure, education and work); and participation in community life. In May 2013 the 66th World Health Assembly adopted a resolution urging member states to develop national action plans for the implementation of the Convention on the Rights of Persons with Disabilities.

In February 1999 WHO initiated the programme, 'Vision 2020: the Right to Sight', which aimed to eliminate avoidable blindness (estimated to be as much as 80% of all cases) by 2020. Blindness was otherwise predicted to increase by as much as two-fold, owing to the increased longevity of the global population. In May 2013 the 66th World Health Assembly endorsed a Global Action Plan, covering 2014–19, that focused on improving eye health, reducing avoidable visual impairment, and securing access to rehabilitation services.

In 2012 WHO estimated that tobacco would lead to more than 8m. deaths annually by 2030 (through lung cancer, heart disease, chronic bronchitis and other effects). The Tobacco or Health Programme aims to reduce the use of tobacco, by educating tobacco-users and preventing young people from adopting the habit. In May 1999 the World Health Assembly endorsed the formulation of a Framework Convention on Tobacco Control (FCTC) to help to combat the increase in tobacco use (although a number of tobacco growers expressed concerns about the effect of the convention on their livelihoods). The FCTC entered into force in February 2005. In 2008 WHO published a comprehensive analysis of global tobacco use and control, the *WHO Report on the Global Tobacco Epidemic*, which designated abuse of tobacco as one of the principal global threats to health, and predicted that during the latter part of the 21st century the vast majority of tobacco-related deaths would occur in developing countries. The report identified and condemned a tobacco industry strategy to target young people and adults in the developing world, and detailed six key proven strategies, collectively known as the 'MPOWER package', aimed at combating global tobacco use: monitoring tobacco use and implementing prevention policies; protecting people from tobacco smoke; offering support to people to enable them to give up tobacco use; warning about the dangers of tobacco; enforcing bans on tobacco advertising, promotion and sponsorship; and raising taxes on tobacco. The MPOWER package supports countries in building on their obligations under the FCTC. The FCTC obligates its states parties to require 'health warnings describing the harmful effects of tobacco use' to appear on packs of tobacco and their outside packaging, and recommends the use of warnings that contain pictures. WHO provides technical and other assistance to countries to support them in meeting this obligation through the Tobacco Free Initiative. WHO encourages governments to adopt tobacco health warnings meeting the agreed criteria for maximum effectiveness in convincing consumers not to smoke. In November 2012 the fifth Conference of the Parties to the FCTC adopted a Protocol to Eliminate Illicit Trade in Tobacco Products. This was opened for signature in January 2013 and required ratification by 40 member states to enter into force.

WHO defines mental health as a 'state of well-being in which every individual realizes his or her own potential, can cope with the normal stresses of life, can work productively and fruitfully, and is able to make a contribution to her or his community'. WHO's Mental Health Programme is concerned with mental health problems that include unipolar and bipolar affective disorders, psychosis, epilepsy, dementia, Parkinson's disease, multiple sclerosis, drug and alcohol dependency, and neuropsychiatric disorders such as post-traumatic stress disorder, obsessive compulsive disorder and panic disorder. WHO aims to increase awareness of mental health issues and promote improved mental health services and primary care. In October 2008 WHO launched the so-called mental health Gap Action Programme (mhGAP), which aimed to improve services addressing mental, neurological and substance use disorders, with a special focus on low and middle income countries. A main focus of mhGAP concerns forging strategic partnerships to enhance countries' capacity to combat stigma commonly associated with mental illness, reduce the burden of mental disorders, and promote mental health. In August 2013 WHO extended mhGAP to incorporate new clinical protocols and guidelines aimed at supporting health care workers in treating post-traumatic stress disorder. In May of that year the 66th World Health Assembly adopted a Mental Health Action Plan covering the period 2013–20, with the objectives of strengthening effective mental health leadership and governance; providing comprehensive, integrated and responsive mental health and social care services in community-based settings; implementing strategies for mental health prevention and promotion; and strengthening information systems, evidence and research. In December 2013 WHO launched MiNDbank, an online platform consolidating international resources and national legislation, policies, and service standards relating to mental health, substance abuse, disability, human rights, general health and development. WHO is a joint partner in the Global Campaign against Epilepsy: Out of the Shadows, which aims to advance understanding, treatment, services and prevention of epilepsy worldwide.

The Substance Abuse Programme addresses the misuse of all psychoactive substances, irrespective of legal status. WHO provides technical support to assist countries in formulating policies with regard to the prevention and reduction of the health and social effects of psychoactive substance abuse, and undertakes epidemiological surveillance and risk assessment, advocacy and the dissemination of information, strengthening national and regional prevention and health promotion techniques and strategies, the development of cost-effective treatment and rehabilitation approaches, and also encompasses regulatory activities as required under the international drugs-control treaties in force. In May 2010 WHO endorsed a new global strategy to reduce the harmful use of alcohol; this promoted measures including taxation on alcohol, minimizing outlets selling alcohol, raising age limits for those buying alcohol, and the employment of effective measures to deter people from driving while under the influence of alcohol.

PROMOTING HEALTH THROUGH THE LIFE COURSE

WHO's aims to reduce morbidity and mortality and improve health during pregnancy, childbirth, the neonatal period, childhood and adolescence; to improve sexual and reproductive health; and to promote active and healthy ageing. Activities take into consideration the need to address the social and environmental determinants of health (a main priority of WHO), and internationally agreed development goals, in particular the health?related MDGs. In October 2011 WHO convened a global conference on the social determinants of health, in Rio de Janeiro, Brazil; the conference adopted the Rio Political Declaration on Social Determinants of Health, expressing commitment to reducing inequities in health and health care provision. The eighth Global Conference on Health Promotion, convened by WHO and the Finnish Government in June 2013, in Helsinki, Finland, issued the Helsinki Statement on Health in All Policies, aimed at promoting health in all levels of national policy-making.

WHO aims to improve access to sustainable health care for all by strengthening health systems and fostering individual, family and community development. Activities include newborn care; child health, including promoting and protecting the health and development of the child through such approaches as promotion of breast-feeding and use of the mother-baby package, as well as care of the sick child, including diarrhoeal and acute respiratory disease control, and support to women and children in difficult circumstances; the promotion of safe motherhood and maternal health; adolescent health, including the promotion and development of young people and the prevention of specific health problems; women, health and development, including addressing issues of gender, sexual violence, and harmful traditional practices; and human reproduction, including research related to contraceptive technologies and effective methods. In addition, WHO aims to provide technical leadership and co-ordination on reproductive health and to support countries in their efforts to ensure that people: experience healthy sexual development and maturation; have the capacity for healthy, equitable and responsible relationships; can achieve their reproductive intentions safely and healthily; avoid illnesses, diseases and injury related to sexuality and reproduction; and receive appropriate counselling, care and rehabilitation for diseases and conditions related to sexuality and reproduction.

WHO supports the Global Strategy for Women's and Children's Health, launched by heads of state and government participating in the September 2010 UN Summit on the MDGs; some US $40,000m. has been pledged towards women's and child's health and achieving goals (iv) Reducing Child Mortality and (v) Improving Maternal Health. In May 2012 the World Health Assembly adopted a resolution on raising awareness of early marriage (entered into by more than 30% of women in developing countries) and adolescent pregnancy, and the consequences thereof for young women and infants.

In September 1997 WHO, in collaboration with UNICEF, formally launched a programme advocating the Integrated Management of Childhood Illness (IMCI). IMCI recognizes that pneumonia, diarrhoea, measles, malaria and malnutrition cause some 70% of the approximately 11m. childhood deaths each year. WHO encourages national programmes aimed at reducing childhood deaths as a result of diarrhoea, particularly through the use of oral rehydration therapy and preventive measures. In November 2009 WHO and UNICEF launched a Global Action Plan for the Prevention and Control of Pneumonia. In April 2013 WHO and UNICEF launched a new Integrated Global Action Plan for the Prevention and Control of Pneumonia and Diarrhoea, focusing on interventions such as improved nutrition and maintaining a clean environment to protect children from contracting both diseases. Accelerated efforts by WHO to promote vaccination against measles through its Measles Initiative (subsequently renamed the Measles and Rubella Initiative), established in 2001, contributed to a three-quarters' reduction in global mortality from that disease during the period 2000–10. In April 2012 WHO and other partners launched a global strategy that aimed to eliminate measles deaths and congenital rubella syndrome.

WHO seeks to monitor the advantages and disadvantages for health, nutrition, environment and development arising from the process of globalization; to integrate the issue of health into poverty reduction programmes; and to promote human rights and equality. WHO collaborates with FAO, WFP, UNICEF and other UN agencies in pursuing its objectives relating to nutrition and food safety. It has been estimated that 780m. people worldwide cannot meet basic needs for energy and protein, more than 2,000m. people lack essential vitamins and minerals, and that 170m. children are malnourished. In December 1992 WHO and FAO hosted an international conference on nutrition, at which a World Declaration and Plan of Action on Nutrition was adopted to make the fight against malnutrition a development priority. WHO aims to support the enhancement of member states' capabilities in dealing with their nutrition situations, and addressing scientific issues related to preventing, managing and monitoring protein-energy malnutrition; micronutrient malnutrition, including iodine deficiency disorders, vitamin A deficiency, and nutritional anaemia; and diet-related conditions and NCDs such as obesity (increasingly affecting children, adolescents and adults, mainly in industrialized countries), cancer and heart disease. In 1990 the World Health Assembly resolved to eliminate iodine deficiency (believed to cause mental retardation); a strategy of universal salt iodization was launched in 1993. In collaboration with other international agencies, WHO is implementing a comprehensive strategy for promoting appropriate infant, young child and maternal nutrition, and for dealing effectively with nutritional emergencies in large populations. Areas of emphasis include promoting health care practices that enhance successful breastfeeding; appropriate complementary feeding; refining the use and interpretation of body measurements for assessing nutritional status; relevant information, education and training; and action to give effect to the International Code of Marketing of Breast-milk Substitutes. (WHO reported in July 2013 that only 37 countries worldwide had adopted legislation reflecting all the recommendations of the International Code.) The food safety programme aims to protect human health against risks associated with biological and chemical contaminants and additives in food. With FAO, WHO establishes food standards (through the work of the Codex Alimentarius Commission and its subsidiary committees) and evaluates food additives, pesticide residues and other contaminants and their implications for health. The programme provides expert advice on such issues as food-borne diseases and pathogens (e.g. bovine spongiform encephalopathy, campylobacter, escherichia coli, listeria, and salmonella), production methods (e.g. aquaculture) and food biotechnology (e.g. genetic modification). WHO also addresses the methods of producing, processing and preparing foods that contribute to the incidence (especially in parts of East and South-East Asia and Latin America) of foodborne trematode infections (parasitic infections caused by flatworms). WHO's Global Foodborne Infections Network (GNP), established in 2001, and currently guided by a strategic plan covering 2011–15, promotes integrated laboratory-based surveillance and intersectoral collaboration among human health, veterinary and food-related entitities. In July 2001 the Codex Alimentarius Commission adopted the first global principles for assessing the safety of genetically modified (GM) foods. In March 2002 an intergovernmental task force established by the Commission finalized 'principles for the risk analysis of foods derived from biotechnology', which were to provide a framework for assessing the safety of GM foods and plants. A Codex Trust Fund, initiated in 2003, assists the efficient participation of developing countries in the work of the Commission. WHO supports, with other UN agencies, governments, research institutions, and representatives of civil society and of the private sector, the initiative on Scaling up Nutrition (SUN), which was initiated in 2009, under the co-ordination of the UN Secretary-General's Special Representative for Food Security and Nutrition, with the aim of increasing the coverage of interventions that improve nutrition during the first 1,000 days of a child's life (such as exclusive breast-feeding, optimal complementary feeding practices, and provision of essential vitamins and minerals); and ensuring that nutrition plans are implemented at national level, and that government programmes take nutrition into account. The activities of SUN are guided by the Framework for Scaling up Nutrition, which was published in April 2010, and by the SUN Roadmap, finalized in September 2010.

In November 2014 WHO, FAO, WFP, and other partners, were to organize the Second International Conference on Nutrition (ICN2, ICN1 having been convened in December 1992), at FAO headquarters in Rome, Italy. ICN2, with participation by senior policy-makers in areas including agriculture and health, representatives of UN and other international agencies, and of civil society, was to review progress achieved since 1992 towards improving nutrition, and to consider future policy options in that area, taking into account advances in science and technology and changes to food systems.

WHO's programme area on environmental health undertakes a wide range of initiatives to tackle the increasing threats to health and well-being from a changing environment, especially in relation to air pollution, water quality, sanitation, protection against radiation, management of hazardous waste, chemical safety and housing hygiene. In October 2013 WHO's subsidiary International Agency for Research on Cancer formally classified outdoor air pollution as carcinogenic to humans, having concluded that there is sufficient evidence to link exposure to outdoor pollution with lung and also bladder cancer. Particulate matter within outdoor air pollution was evaluated separately and also classified as carcinogenic to humans. In March 2014 WHO reported that in 2012 exposure to air pollution (both outside and indoors) was the cause of some 7m. deaths worldwide, establishing air pollution as the largest single global environmental health risk. In addition to increased risk of cancer, raised susceptibility to cardiovascular diseases was attributed to air pollution. WHO supports the Global Alliance against Chronic Respiratory Diseases, established in March 2006. In 2012 it was estimated that some 783m. people worldwide had no access to clean drinking water, while a further 2,500m. people are denied suitable sanitation systems. WHO helped to launch the Water Supply and Sanitation Council in 1990 and regularly updates its *Guidelines for Drinking Water Quality*. In rural areas the emphasis continues to be on the provision and maintenance of safe and sufficient water supplies and adequate sanitation, the health aspects of rural housing, vector control in water resource management, and the safe use of agrochemicals. In urban areas assistance is provided to identify local environmental health priorities and to improve municipal governments' ability to deal with environmental conditions and health problems in an integrated manner; promotion of the 'Healthy City' approach is a major component of the programme. Other programme activities include environmental health information development and management, human resources development, environmental health planning methods, research and work on problems relating to global environment change, such as UV-radiation. The WHO Global Strategy for Health and Environment provides the framework for programme activities.

WHO forecasts that by 2050 nearly 2,000m. people globally will be aged over 60 years. In June 2010 WHO launched the Global Network of Age-Friendly Cities, as part of a broader response to the ageing of populations worldwide. The Network aims to support cities in creating urban environments that would enable older people to remain active and healthy. The first International Conference on Age-Friendly Cities was convened in September 2011, in Dublin, Ireland; the second was held in Québec, Canada, in September 2013 on the theme 'Living and Aging Together in our Community'.

In March 1996 WHO's Centre for Health Development opened at Kobe, Japan. The Centre researches health developments and other determinants to strengthen policy decision-making within the health sector.

HEALTH SYSTEMS

WHO supports the strengthening of health systems, with a focus on the development of integrated quality service delivery; robust financing mechanisms; universal health coverage; strengthening well trained human resources for health; reliable health information systems; promoting access to and facilitating transfer of affordable, quality, safe, and efficacious health technologies; ensuring well maintained facilities and logistics to deliver quality medicines and technologies; and promoting health systems research. Through the generation and dissemination of evidence WHO aims to assist policy-makers to assess health needs, choose intervention strategies, design policy and monitor performance, and thereby improve the performance of national health systems. International and national dialogue on health policy are also promoted. WHO appoints and administers the secretariat of the Alliance for Health Policy and Systems Research, initiated in 1999 with the aim of improving health and health systems in developing countries. In 2010 the Alliance broadened its core focus from the areas of human resources for health, health financing, and the role of non-state health actors (of particular concern in low-income and fragile states), to launch a project supporting new research and analysis on access to medicines.

WHO works to develop national drugs policies and global guidelines, and, through collaboration with member countries, promotes access to essential drugs of good quality at low cost, the rational use of medicines, and compliance with international drug control requirements. Other activities include global and national operational research in the pharmaceutical sector, and the development of technical tools for problem solving, management and evaluation. WHO promotes worldwide co-operation on blood safety and clinical technology, supporting states in ensuring access (based on Voluntary Non-Remunerated Donation) to safe blood, blood products and transfusions, as well as injections, and health care technologies. The WHO Blood Regulators Network, established in 2006, provides a forum for the exchange of information among leading international authorities with responsibility for the regulation of blood, blood products and related in vitro diagnostic devices. Activities are undertaken related to quality assurance and safety of biologicals; vaccine development; vaccine assessment and monitoring; access to technologies; and the development of policies and strategies aimed at maximizing the use of vaccines.

In January 1999 the Executive Board adopted a resolution on WHO's Revised Drug Strategy which placed emphasis on the inequalities of access to pharmaceuticals, and also covered specific aspects of drugs policy, quality assurance, drug promotion, drug donation, independent drug information and rational drug use. Plans of action involving co-operation with member states and other international organizations were to be developed to monitor and analyse the pharmaceutical and public health implications of international agreements, including trade agreements. In May 2001 the World Health Assembly adopted a resolution urging member states to promote equitable access to essential drugs, noting that this was denied to about one-third of the world's population, particularly in less developed countries. WHO participates in the 'Accelerating Access' initiative, which aims to expand access to care, support and advanced antiretroviral therapy (ART) for people with HIV/AIDS. WHO hosts the secretariat of the International HIV Treatment Access Coalition, founded in December 2002 by governments, (NGOs, donors and others to facilitate access to ART for people in low- and middle-income countries. In September 2006, Brazil, Chile, France, Norway and the United Kingdom launched UNITAID, an international drug purchase facility aiming to provide sustained, strategic market intervention, with a view to reducing the cost of medicines for priority diseases and increasing the supply of drugs and diagnostics. WHO supports national drug-regulatory authorities and drug-procurement agencies and facilitates international pharmaceutical trade through the exchange of technical information and the harmonization of internationally respected norms and standards. In particular, it publishes the *International Pharmacopoeia (Ph. Int.)*, the *Consultative List of International Nonproprietary Names for Pharmaceutical Substances*, and annual and biennial reports of Expert Committees responsible for determining relevant international standards for the manufacture and specification of pharmaceutical and biological products in international commerce. It provides information on the safety and efficacy of drugs, with particular regard to counterfeit and substandard projects, to health agencies and providers of health care, and it maintains the pharmaceuticals section of the UN *Consolidated List of Products whose Consumption and/or Sale have been Banned, Withdrawn, Severely Restricted or Not Approved by Governments*. The *WHO Model List of Essential Medicines* is updated about every two years and is complemented by corresponding model prescribing information; the 17th *Model List* was published in March 2011, alongside the third *Model List of Medicines for Children*. The *WHO Model Formulary* (current edition: 2008) provides detailed information on the safe and effective use of all essential drugs. The first *WHO Model Formulary for Children*, listing more than 240 essential medicines, as well as recommended usage, dosage, adverse effects and contra-indications, for treating children between the age of 0–12, was issued in June 2010. *WHO Drug Information*, published quarterly, provides current news on drug development and regulation.

In May 2013 the World Health Assembly determined to establish an open-ended working group to address means of eliminating so-called Substandard/Spurious/Falsely-labelled/Falsified/Counterfeit (SSFFC) medical products.

WHO supports member states in the integration of traditional medicine (TM, also referred to as complementary or alternative medicine—CAM) into national health care systems and in the appropriate use of traditional medicine, through the provision of technical guidelines, standards and methodologies. In May 2002 WHO adopted a strategy on the regulation of TM/CAM. A WHO Congress on TM was held in November 2008, in Beijing, China.

The WHO International Clinical Trials Registry Platform, established in August 2005, links clinical trials worldwide (i.e. all research studies that assign human participants to health-related interventions, with a view to evaluating the health outcomes of these), and aims to ensure complete transparency of clinical research and its accessibility to all those involved in health care decision-making.

WHO reports that 2m. children die each year of diseases for which common vaccines exist. A comprehensive survey, *State of the World's Vaccines and Immunization*, was published by WHO, jointly with UNICEF, in 1996; revised editions of the survey were issued in 2003 and 2010. In 1999 WHO, UNICEF, the World Bank and a number of public and private sector partners formed the Global Alliance for Vaccines and Immunization (GAVI), which aimed to expand the provision of existing vaccines and to accelerate the development and introduction of new vaccines and technologies, with the ultimate goal of protecting children of all nations and from all socio-economic backgrounds against vaccine-preventable diseases.

WHO co-ordinates the Health InterNetwork Access to Research Initiative (HINARI), which was launched in July 2001 to enable relevant authorities in developing countries to access biomedical journals through the internet at no or greatly reduced cost, in order to improve the worldwide circulation of scientific information; by 2014 around 13,000 journals and 28,800 e-books were being made available to health institutions in more than 100 countries. A virtual Healthy Academy provides eLearning courses, on topics such as HIV/AIDS; malaria; oral health; and safer food. The WHO e-Library of Evidence for Nutrition Actions (eLENA) provides evidence-informed guidelines and recommendations for nutrition interventions. WHO Patient Safety (launched in 2004 as the World Alliance on Patient Safety, and subsequently renamed) facilitates the development of patient safety policy and practice across all WHO member states. In May 2011 WHO launched a new internet-based Global Health Observatory, a repository of data on health topics, which also provides online access to WHO's annual *World Health Statistics*. In May 2013 the 66th World Health Assembly adopted a resolution on e-Health standardization and interoperability, noting the importance of health data in underpinning the efficient functioning of health systems and services, as well as the need to protect the security of such information and the privacy of personal clinical data.

PREPAREDNESS, SURVEILLANCE AND RESPONSE

WHO contributes to human security by working to support the preparedness, surveillance and effective response to disease outbreaks, acute public health emergencies, and the effective management of health-related aspects of humanitarian disasters. Within the UN system, WHO co-ordinates the international response to emergencies and natural disasters in the health field, in close co-operation with other agencies and within the framework set out by the Office for the Co-ordination of Humanitarian Affairs. In this context, WHO provides expert advice on epidemiological surveillance, control of communicable diseases, public health information and health emergency training. Its emergency preparedness activities include co-ordination, policy-making and planning, awareness-building, technical advice, training, publication of standards and guidelines, and research. Its emergency relief activities include organizational support, the provision of emergency drugs and supplies and conducting technical emergency assessment missions. WHO aims to strengthen the national capacity of member states to reduce the adverse health consequences of disasters, including conflict, natural disasters, food insecurity. In responding to emergency situations, WHO always tries to develop projects and activities that will assist the national authorities concerned in rebuilding or strengthening their own capacity to handle the impact of such situations. WHO appeals through the UN's inter-agency Consolidated Appeals Process (CAP) for funding for its emergency humanitarian operations.

Since the major terrorist attacks perpetrated against targets in the USA in September 2001, WHO has focused renewed attention on the potential malevolent use of bacteria (such as bacillus anthracis, which causes anthrax), viruses (for example, the variola virus, causing smallpox) or toxins, or of chemical agents, in acts of biological or chemical terrorism. In September 2001 WHO issued draft guidelines entitled 'Health Aspects of Biological and Chemical Weapons'. In March 2013 the UN Secretary-General announced that a mission comprising UN weapons experts, in co-operation with specialists from WHO and the Organisation for the Prohibition of Chemical Weapons, would initiate an investigation into the alleged misuse of chemical weapons by combatants in the ongoing conflict in Syria. In mid-September the mission issued a report on the alleged use on 21 August of chemical weapons against unarmed civilians in the rebel-held area of Ghouta, Damascus, causing significant injuries and fatalities, in which it found 'clear and convincing evidence' of the use of surface-to-surface rockets containing sarin gas, and that chemical weapons had been used on a relatively large scale generally during the Syrian conflict, including against children.

WHO's work in the promotion of chemical safety is undertaken in collaboration with the ILO and UNEP through the International Programme on Chemical Safety (IPCS), the Central Unit for which is located in WHO. The Programme provides internationally evaluated scientific information on chemicals, promotes the use of such information in national programmes, assists member states in establishment of their own chemical safety measures and programmes, and helps them strengthen their capabilities in chemical emergency preparedness and response and in chemical risk reduction. WHO administers the Inter-organization Programme for the Social Management of Chemicals, established in 1995 jointly with UNEP, the ILO, FAO, WHO, the World Bank, the UN Industrial Development Organization (UNIDO) and OECD, in order to strengthen international co-operation in the field of chemical safety.

Through its International EMF Project WHO is compiling a comprehensive assessment of the potential adverse effects on human health deriving from exposure to electromagnetic fields (EMF). In May 2011 the International Agency for Research on Cancer, an agency of WHO, classified radiofrequency EMF as possibly carcinogenic to humans, on the basis of an increased risk of glioma (malignant brain cancer) associated with the use of wireless phones.

In March 2013 WHO and UNEP issued a joint report entitled *State of the Science of Endocrine Disrupting Chemicals*, which assessed the potential disrupting effects on the human hormone system and the environment of synthetic chemicals found in many household products.

HEALTH DAYS

World Health Day is observed on 7 April every year, and is used to promote awareness of a particular health topic ('Vector-borne diseases', in 2014). World Leprosy Day is held every year on 30 January, World TB Day on 24 March, World No Tobacco Day on 31 May, World Heart Day on 24 September, World Mental Health Day on 10 October, World Diabetes Day, in association with the International Diabetes Federation, on 14 November, World AIDS Day on 1 December, and World Asthma Day on 11 December.

ASSOCIATED AGENCY

International Agency for Research on Cancer: 150 Cours Albert Thomas, 69372 Lyon Cedex 08, France; tel. 4-72-73-84-85; fax 4-72-73-85-75; e-mail com@iarc.fr; internet www.iarc.fr; established in 1965 as a self-governing body within the framework of WHO, the Agency organizes international research on cancer. It has its own laboratories, maintains the IARC Biobank, and runs a programme of research on the environmental factors causing cancer. Mems: Australia, Belgium, Canada, Denmark, Finland, France, Germany, India, Ireland, Italy, Japan, South Korea, Netherlands, Norway, Russia, Spain, Sweden, Switzerland, United Kingdom, USA; Dir Dr CHRISTOPHER WILD (United Kingdom).

Finance

WHO's regular budget is provided by assessment of member states and associate members. An additional fund for specific projects is provided by voluntary contributions from members and other sources, including UNDP and UNFPA.

A total programme budget of US $3,977m. was approved for the two years 2014–15; of the total some $841m. (21%) was allocated to communicable diseases; $700m. (18%) to polio eradication; $684m. (17%) to corporate services and enabling functions; $531m.(13%) to health systems; $388m. (10%) to promoting health through the life course; $318m. (8%) to non-communicable diseases; and $228m. (6%) to outbreak and response.

Publications

Bulletin of WHO (monthly).

Eastern Mediterranean Health Journal (annually).

Global Tuberculosis Report.

International Classification of Diseases.

International Classification of Functioning, Disability and Health—ICF.

International Classification of Health Interventions.

International Pharmacopoeia.

International Travel and Health.

Model List of Essential Medicines (every 2 years).

Pan-American Journal of Public Health (annually).

Weekly Epidemiological Record.

Western Pacific Surveillance and Response.

WHO Drug Information (quarterly).

WHO South-East Asia Journal of Public Health.

World Health Statistics.

WHO Model Formulary.

WHO Report on the Global Tobacco Epidemic.

World Health Report (annually).

World Cancer Report (every 5–6 years).

World Malaria Report (annually, with UNICEF).

Technical report series; guidelines; catalogues of specific scientific, technical and medical fields available.

World Intellectual Property Organization—WIPO

Address: 34 chemin des Colombettes, BP 18, 1211 Geneva 20, Switzerland.

Telephone: 223389111; **fax:** 227335428; **e-mail:** wipo.mail@wipo.int; **internet:** www.wipo.int.

WIPO was established by a Convention signed in Stockholm, Sweden, in 1967, which came into force in 1970. It became a specialized agency of the UN in December 1974.

MEMBERS

WIPO has 187 members.

Organization

(April 2014)

GENERAL ASSEMBLY

The General Assembly is one of the three WIPO governing bodies, and is composed of all states that are party to the WIPO Convention and that are also members of any of the WIPO-administered Unions (see below). The Assembly meets in ordinary session once a year to agree on programmes and budgets. It elects the Director-General, who is the executive head of WIPO. Prior to the adoption of a new Treaty, the General Assembly may convene a Diplomatic Conference (a high-level meeting of member states) to finalize negotiations.

CONFERENCE

All member states are represented in the Conference, which meets in ordinary session once every two years.

CO-ORDINATION COMMITTEE

Countries belonging to the Committee are elected from among the member states of WIPO, the Executive Committee of the International Union for the Protection of Industrial Property (Paris Union, relating to the Paris Convention), the Executive Committee of the International Union for the Protection of Literary and Artistic Works (Berne Union, relating to the Berne Convention, also see below), and, ex officio, Switzerland. It meets in ordinary session once a year.

ASSEMBLIES OF THE UNIONS

The Assemblies of member states of the Paris Union, the Berne Union, the other Unions of WIPO-administered international agreements (the Budapest Union, Hague Union, Lisbon Union, Locarno Union, Madrid Union—Marks, Nice Union, PCT (Patent Co-operation Treaty) Union, Strasbourg Agreement Concerning the International Patent Classification—IPC—Union, and Vienna Union), and the Assemblies of member states of the Rome Convention Intergovernmental Committee, the Patent Law Treaty, WIPO Copyright Treaty, and of the WIPO Performances and Phonograms Treaty) also contribute to the WIPO decision-making process. Meetings of the WIPO Assemblies are preceded by a two-day high-level ministerial gathering ('ministerial segment').

INTERNATIONAL BUREAU

The International Bureau, as WIPO's secretariat, prepares the meetings of the various bodies of WIPO and the Unions, mainly through the provision of reports and working documents. It organizes the meetings, and sees that the decisions are communicated to all concerned, and, as far as possible, that they are carried out.

The International Bureau implements projects and initiates new ones to promote international co-operation in the field of intellectual property. It acts as an information service and publishes reviews. It is also the depository of most of the treaties administered by WIPO.

Separate Geneva-based regional bureaux, under the co-ordination of the International Bureau, channel technical assistance to member states in the Middle East, Africa, the Far East and Australasia, and Latin America and the Caribbean. WIPO also maintains external offices in Rio de Janeiro, Brazil; Tokyo, Japan; and Singapore, with further offices under consideration for Moscow, Russia; Beijing, People's Republic of China; New York, USA; and in Africa.

Director-General: FRANCIS GURRY (Australia).

There are four ad hoc Standing Committees, comprising experts, on Law of Patents; Law of Trademarks, Industrial Designs and Geographical Indications; Copyright and Related Rights; and Information Technologies. A Standing Committee may establish a working group to examine specific issues in detail. There is also a Committee on Development and Intellectual Property, and an Advisory Committee on Enforcement. Some 250 non-governmental organizations have observer status at WIPO. WIPO has co-ordination offices in Brussels, Belgium; Toyko, Japan; Singapore; and New York, USA.

Activities

WIPO works to ensure that the rights of creators and owners of intellectual property (IP), 'creations of the mind', are protected throughout the world, with a view to facilitating the advancement of science, technology and the arts and promoting international trade. IP comprises two principal branches: industrial property (patents and other rights in technological inventions, rights in trademarks, industrial designs—constituting the ornamental or aesthetic aspect of an article, geographical indications—including appellations of origin, etc.) and copyright and related rights (covering literary, musical, artistic and photographic works; and also the rights of performing artists in their performances, of producers of phonograms in their recordings, and of broadcasters and performers in their audiovisual media broadcasts). IP rights enable the owner of a copyright, patent or trademark (the 'creator') to benefit from their work. In December 2008 member states adopted a revised strategic framework for WIPO comprising the following nine strategic goals: promoting the balanced evolution of the international normative framework for IP; providing premier global IP services; facilitating the use of IP for development; co-ordinating and developing a global IP infrastructure; developing as a world reference source for IP information and analysis; promoting international co-operation on building respect for IP; addressing IP in relation to global policy issues; developing a responsive communications interface between WIPO, its member states and all stakeholders; and developing an efficient administrative and financial support structure to enable the organization better to deliver its programmes.

In October 2008 a WIPO strategic realignment programme (SRP) was launched, which was to introduce a corporate culture and to review WIPO's strategic objectives, structures, programmes and resources, to enable it to fulfill its mandate more effectively. In September 2010 member states endorsed proposed reforms and adopted a new medium-term strategic plan for 2011–15, based on the organization's nine strategic goals.

WIPO administers and encourages member states to sign and enforce international treaties relating to the protection of IP, of which the most fundamental are the Paris Convention for the Protection of Industrial Property (1883), the Berne Convention for the Protection of Literary and Artistic Works (1886), and the Patent Co-operation Treaty (PCT).

WIPO's Advisory Committee on Enforcement (ACE, established in October 2002) co-ordinates with other organizations and the private sector to enforce IP rights by combating piracy and counterfeiting; promoting public education; implementing national and regional training programmes for relevant stakeholders; and facilitating, through its IPEIS Electronic Forum, the exchange of information on enforcement issues. WIPO helps to organize the periodic Global Congress on Combating Counterfeiting and Piracy, which was established in 2004 as an international forum of senior public sector representatives and business leaders who gather to develop strategies against counterfeiting and piracy.

WIPO organizes an annual World Intellectual Property Day, held on 26 April, to promote discussion of and demonstrate the role of intellectual property in encouraging innovation and creativity. The theme for the Day in 2014 was 'Movies—A Global Passion'.

GLOBAL IP INFRASTRUCTURE

The co-ordination and development of a global IP infrastructure, to enhance the worldwide promotion of science, new technologies and innovation, was one of the new strategic goals approved by WIPO member states in December 2008. In September 2009 a WIPO global symposium of IP authorities met to discuss means of establishing a more accessible, digital and borderless global IP infrastructure. The infrastructure comprises the following 'pillars': IP institutions and authorities; capacity building and networking; electronic data interchange among IP offices; international classifications in the fields of trademarks and industrial design; standards and technical agreements; the organization's PatentScope, and Global Brand databases (the latter comprising 12.7m. data records at April 2014); services; and an information-sharing forum (the Global Symposium of IP Authorities, of which the third was convened in September 2011).

DEVELOPING LAWS AND STANDARDS

One of WIPO's major activities is the progressive development and harmonization of IP laws, standards, and practices among its member states, in the areas of industrial property law and copyright law.

The organization prepares new treaties and undertakes the revision of the existing treaties that it administers. WIPO administers international classifications established by treaties and relating to inventions, marks and industrial designs: periodically it reviews these to ensure their improvement in terms of coverage and precision. WIPO also carries out studies on issues in the field of IP that could be the subject of model laws or guidelines for implementation at national or international levels. The organization seeks to simplify and harmonize national IP legislation and procedures (for example through implementation of the Trademark Law Treaty, 1994, and development of the Patent Law Treaty, 2000) in order to make the registration of IP more easily accessible.

WIPO implements two programmes that provide legal and technical assistance on the formulation of strong IP laws and systems specifically to, respectively, developing countries and countries with economies in transition.

WIPO DIGITAL AGENDA

WIPO promotes the development of the use of Information and Communication Technology (ICT) for storing, accessing and using valuable IP data, and to provide a forum for informed debate and for the exchange of expertise on IP. The rapid advancement of digital communications networks has posed challenges regarding the protection and enforcement of IP rights. WIPO has undertaken a range of initiatives to address the implications for copyright and industrial property law, and for electronic commerce transcending national jurisdictions. WIPO's Electronic Commerce Section co-ordinates programmes and activities relating to the IP aspects of electronic commerce. In September 1999 WIPO organized the first International Conference on Electronic Commerce and IP; the 'WIPO Digital Agenda', which establishes a series of guidelines and objectives, was launched by the Organization at the Conference. The second International Conference on Electronic Commerce and IP was held in September 2001. In January 2001, under its Digital Agenda, WIPO launched WIPOnet, a global digital network of IP information sources capable of transmitting confidential data. The Organization also manages WIPO Gold, launched in June 2010 as an online repository of searchable IP data, and maintains WIPO Lex, an online search facility for IP national laws and treaties.

IP FOR DEVELOPMENT

WIPO aims to support governments and organizations in establishing policies and structures to harness the potential of IP for development. In 2005 WIPO founded an Office for Strategic Use of IP for Development (OSUIPD), which comprises the following four divisions: the Creative Industries Division; the IP and Economic Development Division; the IP and New Technologies Division; and the Small and Medium-Sized Enterprises (SMEs) Division. The OSUIPD supports member states—with a particular focus on developing countries and those with economies in transition—in successfully utilizing the IP system for cultural, economic and social development; assists SMEs; and aims to enhance capacity in the area of managing IP assets.

WIPO has organized a number of international and national seminars on the strategic use of intellectual property (IP) for economic and social development. In April 2012 WIPO and the UN Industrial Development Organization (UNIDO) agreed to strengthen co-operation relating to IP in the areas of science and technology, promoting innovation, private sector development, and building trade capacity.

In September 2007 WIPO member states adopted the WIPO Development Agenda. The Agenda comprises a series of recommendations that incorporate 45 agreed proposals covering the following six clusters of activities: Technical Assistance and Capacity Building; Norm-setting, Flexibilities, Public Policy and Public Knowledge; Technology Transfer, ICT and Access to Knowledge; Assessments, Evaluation and Impact Studies; Institutional Matters including Mandate and Governance; and Other Issues (for example, ensuring that IP enforcement is viewed within the context of broader societal interests). A Committee on Development and IP was established in October 2007 to formulate a work programme for the implementation of these recommendations, and to monitor their implementation. The OSUIPD co-operates closely with all departments of WIPO involved in the implementation of the Development Agenda.

WIPO aims to modernize national IP systems. It offers technical assistance to increase the capabilities of developing countries to benefit from the international IP framework, with a view to promoting the optimal use of human and other resources and thereby contributing to national prosperity. WIPO supports governments with IP-related institution building, human resources development, and preparation and implementation of legislation. The OSUIPD helps countries to formulate national IP strategies. The WIPO Worldwide Academy, established in March 1998, undertakes training, teaching and research on IP matters, focusing particularly on developing countries. The Academy maintains a Distance Learning Centre using online facilities, digital multimedia technology and video conferencing. WIPO's Information and Documentation Centre holds extensive reference materials. Under its Digital Agenda WIPO aims to assist the integration of developing countries into the internet environment, particularly through the use of WIPOnet (see above). In March 2007 WIPO helped to organize the first annual symposium for IP academies, in Rio de Janeiro, Brazil, which established the Global Network of IP Academies (GNIPA) as a framework for co-operation. The sixth GNIPA symposium was convened in May 2013, in Tokyo, Japan.

WIPO advises countries on obligations under the World Trade Organization's agreement on Trade-Related Aspects of IP Rights (TRIPS). The two organizations have jointly implemented a technical co-operation initiative to assist least developed countries with harmonizing their national legislative and administrative structures in compliance with the TRIPS accord.

WIPO presented a programme of action to the Third UN Conference on the Least Developed Countries (LDCs-III, held in Brussels, Belgium in May 2001), which was aimed at strengthening LDCs' IP systems. In May 2009 WIPO launched a Japan-funded programme aimed at promoting the use of IP in Africa and LDCs as a catalyst for economic and commercial development. Representatives of LDCs attending a WIPO high-level forum on the strategic use of intellectual property for prosperity and development, held in July 2009, reaffirmed commitment to integrating IP and innovation strategies into their national development planning. WIPO participated in the preparation of LDC-IV, which was held in May 2011, in Istanbul, Turkey. The inaugural annual conference on South-South Cooperation on IP and Development was held, under WIPO auspices, in September 2012. In March 2013 WIPO organized an African Conference on the Strategic Importance of Intellectual Property Policies to Foster Innovation, Value Creation and Competitiveness, in Dar es Salaam, Tanzania, with participation by regional ministers responsible for science and technology, research and development institutions, business interests, and the Japanese national patent office.

WIPO, with the International Telecommunication Union (ITU) and UNIDO, leads an initiative on promoting technology and innovation, the eighth of nine activities that were launched in April 2009 by the UN System Chief Executives Board for Co-ordination (CEB), with the aim of alleviating the impact on poor and vulnerable populations of the developing global economic crisis. WIPO and the graduate business school INSEAD jointly release an annual *Global Innovation Index (GII)*, which ranks economies according to their innovation capabilities and results; this is complemented by a *Global Innovation Efficiency Index*, which ranks countries according to their relative strengths in turning innovation into economic output. Switzerland, followed by Sweden and the United Kingdom, headed the 2013 GII, which was released in July.

In June 2011 WIPO launched a project to establish a common digital platform across 11 countries in West Africa, with the aim of simplifying the identification of protected musical works in that region.

In October 2011 a new WIPO Re:Search initiative was launched—with participation by pharmaceutical companies, research institutions and the non-profit organization BIO Ventures for Global Health, and the World Health Organization as technical adviser—with the aim of advancing the development of treatments for hitherto neglected tropical diseases through the establishment of partnerships between interested parties. In June 2013 WIPO, jointly with WHO and the WTO, convened a symposium to consider the use of new incentives and collaborative innovation models aimed at advancing the research and development of new medical and pharmaceutical products, to meet constantly evolving market requirements globally.

COPYRIGHT AND RELATED RIGHTS

Through its Copyright and Related Rights sector WIPO works on the development of international norms and standards in the area of copyright and related rights (these being legal concepts and instruments that both protect the rights of creators of works and aim to contribute to national development); and also actively promotes, through the organization of meetings and seminars, the so-called WIPO Internet Treaties (the WIPO Copyright Treaty—WCT and WIPO Performances and Phonograms Treaty—WPPT), which were enacted as part of the WIPO Digital Agenda with the aim of updating copyright law in the light of new digital technologies.

In May 2011 WIPO and the International Council of Museums (ICOM) signed a Memorandum of Understanding on collaboration in the management of IP options, and in the mediation of disputes, in the area of cultural heritage and museums, with a particular focus on copyright issues, traditional knowledge and traditional cultural expressions, and the digitization of cultural artifacts.

In June 2013 WIPO convened, in Marrakesh, Morocco, a diplomatic conference which adopted the Marrakesh Treaty to Facilitate Access to Published Works for Persons Who Are Blind, Visually Impaired, or Otherwise Print Disabled.

SMALL AND MEDIUM-SIZED ENTERPRISES

A programme focusing on the IP concerns of SMEs was approved by the WIPO General Assembly in September 2000. An International Forum on IP and SMEs, organized jointly by WIPO and the Italian Government in Milan, Italy in February 2001, adopted the Milan Plan of Action for helping SMEs to benefit fully from the IP system. WIPO publishes a number of guides and manuals aimed specifically at SMEs.

TRADITIONAL KNOWLEDGE, EXPRESSIONS OF FOLKLORE, GENETIC RESOURCES

In view of the advances in technology and economic globalization in recent years WIPO has focused increasingly on the relationship between IP and issues such as traditional knowledge (TK), biological diversity, environmental protection and human rights. In April 2000 the organization convened its first Meeting on IP and Genetic Resources (GR). A WIPO Intergovernmental Committee on IP and GR, TK and Folklore (IGC) was established in September of that year. In January 2002 an international forum organized by WIPO adopted the Muscat Declaration on IP and TK, recognizing the contribution of TK to international co-operation. In October 2005 the WIPO Voluntary Fund for Accredited Indigenous and Local Communities was inaugurated with a view to supporting the participation of accredited indigenous and local communities in the work of the IGC. In December 2006 the 10th session of the IGC identified 10 key questions relating to the protection of traditional cultural expressions (TCE) and expressions of folklore (EoF), and to the protection of TK. In December 2007 WIPO convened a round table on building the capacity of indigenous communities in the area of IP, TK, GR and TCE. The 12th session of the IGC, convened in February 2008, determined to prepare a working document that was to identify any gaps in, the existing provisions at international level providing protection for TCE/EoF; and that was to consider means of addressing any gaps identified. The resulting 'gap analyses' were reviewed by the 13th IGC session, convened in October of that year. In July 2009 the 14th session of the IGC agreed on the future negotiation and adoption of an internationally legally binding instrument aimed at ensuring the effective protection of biodiversity, TK, GR and TCEs. Text-based negotiations on the proposed international legal framework were initiated in May 2010, and, in February 2012, the 20th session of the IGC consolidated proposals arising from the negotiations into a single text. In October 2013 the WIPO General Assembly requested the IGC to submit to the 2014 General Assembly the final text of the proposed international legal instrument.

WIPO's Creative Heritage Project supports indigenous communities and cultural institutions with the employment of new digital technologies to record and archive expressions of their heritage, and provides support in protecting local rights regarding the authorization of third party use of this material. The Project manages the WIPO Creative Heritage Digital Gateway, an internet portal to collections of indigenous cultural heritage. WIPO has commissioned surveys of existing IP-related codes, policies and practices relating to the safeguarding of, access to, and control over cultural heritage, with a view to using these as a basis for the development of guidelines and best practices.

ENFORCEMENT OF IP RIGHTS

WIPO's Advisory Committee on Enforcement (ACE) provides technical assistance and co-ordinates with other organizations and with the private sector to combat counterfeiting and piracy activities; provides public education; supports the implementation of national and regional training programmes; and promotes the exchange of information on enforcement issues.

ARBITRATION AND MEDIATION CENTRE

A WIPO Arbitration and Mediation Centre became operational in October 1994 to facilitate the settlement of IP disputes between private parties. Since its inception the Centre has deliberated on more than 210 requests for arbitration (relating to, inter alia, patent infringements, patent licenses, software licenses, distribution agreements for pharmaceutical products, research and development agreements, trademark co-existence agreements, consultancy agreements, and joint venture agreements); and more than 70 requests for mediation (relating to, inter alia, patent disputes, software/ICT, copyright, trademark co-existence, employment issues in an IP context, and engineering disputes). The Centre organizes workshops and assists in the development of WIPO model contract clauses and industry-specific resolution schemes. The Centre offers parties to disputes the option of using the WIPO Electronic Case Facility which provides for secure web-based filing, storing and retrieval of case-related submissions.

The Centre also offers a Domain Name Dispute Resolution service, which plays a leading role in reviewing cases of conflict between trademarks and internet domain names (such as com, .net, .org, and .info), and some 70 country code top-level domains (ccTLDs) that have engaged the Centre as their dispute resolution service provider. The service is provided in accordance with the Uniform Domain Name Dispute Resolution Policy (UDRP) that was, on WIPO's recommendation, adopted by the Internet Corporation for Assigned Names and Numbers—ICANN in October 1999. WIPO's first Internet Domain Name Process, a series of international consultations, undertaken in 1999, issued several recommendations for controlling the abuse of trademarks on the internet. A second Internet Domain Name Process, completed in 2001, addressed the improper registration of other identifiers ('cybersquatting'), including standard non-proprietary names for pharmaceutical substances, names and acronyms of intergovernmental organizations, geographical indications and terms, and trade names. In addition to UDRP cases, the Centre deals with cases relating to registrations in the start-up phase of new domains, in accordance with so-called Sunrise policies. Cumulatively during 2000–12 more than 25,500 UDRP cases, relating to some 47,000 separate domain names, and involving parties from more than 150 countries, were administered by WIPO under UDRP procedures. WIPO publishes an online Legal Index of WIPO UDRP Panel Decisions and also maintains an online database of cybersquatting cases: a record 2,884 complaints regarding alleged cybersquatting, covering 5,084 internet domain names, were filed with the Centre in 2012, with retail, fashion, and banking and finance representing the top three areas of complaint. Evidence of cybersquatting was found in more than 90% of adjudicated cases in that year.

INTERNATIONAL REGISTRATION SERVICES

WIPO maintains the following international registration services:

International registration of trademarks: operating since 1893; during 2013 there were 46,829 registrations of trademarks; publ. *WIPO Gazette of International Marks* (every two weeks).

International deposit of industrial designs: operating since 1928; during 2013 2,990 applications were made for deposits, renewals and prolongations of industrial designs; publ. *International Designs Bulletin* (weekly).

International applications for patents: operating since 1978; provisionally, 205,300 record copies of international applications for patents under the PCT were received in 2013, with the fastest area of growth in the area of electronic machinery; publ. *World Intellectual Property Indicators* (annually), *PCT Year Review*, *Weekly Published PCT Data*.

WIPO-ADMINISTERED TREATIES

Intellectual Property Treaties

(status at April 2014)

The IP Treaties administered by WIPO define internationally agreed basic standards of IP protection in each member state.

Paris Convention for the Protection of Industrial Property: signed 20 March 1883, last revised in 1967; 175 states parties.

Berne Convention for the Protection of Literary and Artistic Works: signed 9 Sept. 1886, last revised in 1971; 167 states parties.

Madrid Agreement for the Repression of False or Deceptive Indications of Source on Goods: signed 14 April 1891; 36 states parties.

Marrakesh Treaty to Facilitate Access to Published Works for Persons Who Are Blind, Visually Impaired, or Otherwise Print Disabled: signed 28 June 2013; 51 signatories.

Rome Convention for the Protection of Performers, Producers of Phonograms and Broadcasting Organizations: signed 26 October 1961; 92 states parties.

Phonograms Convention for the Protection of Producers of Phonograms against Unauthorized Duplication of their Phonograms: signed 29 October 1971; 78 states parties.

Brussels Convention Relating to the Distribution of Programme-carrying Signals Transmitted by Satellite: signed 21 May 1974; 37 states parties.

Nairobi Treaty on the Protection of the Olympic Symbol: signed 26 September 1981; 50 states parties.

Trademark Law Treaty: signed 27 October 1994; 53 states parties.

WIPO Copyright Treaty (WCT): signed 20 December 1996; 91 states parties.

WIPO Performances and Phonograms Treaty (WPPT): signed 20 December 1996; 92 states parties.

Patent Law Treaty, 2000: entered into force 28 April 2005; 36 states parties.

Singapore Treaty on the Law of Trademarks: entered into force 16 March 2009; 36 states parties.

Washington Treaty on Intellectual Property in Respect of Integrated Circuits: signed 26 May 1989; three ratifications.

Beijing Treaty on Audiovisual Performances: signed 26 June 2012; 59 signatories, two ratifications.

Global Protection System Treaties
(status at April 2014)

WIPO administers a small number of treaties, listed below, that cover inventions (patents), trademarks and industrial designs, under which one international registration or filing has effect in any of the relevant signatory states. The services provided by WIPO under its so-called Global Protection System treaties simplify the registration process and reduce the cost of making individual applications or filings in each country in which protection for a given IP right is sought. The most widely used of these treaties is the PCT, under which a single international patent application is valid in all signatory countries selected by the applicant. The PCT system has expanded rapidly in recent years. The PCT-SAFE (Secure Applications Filed Electronically) system became operational in February 2004, safeguarding the electronic filing of patent applications. Patent applications can be accessed through WIPO's PatentScope search facility. The corresponding treaties concerning the international registration of trademarks and industrial designs are, respectively, the Madrid Agreement (and its Protocol), and the Hague Agreement. From 1 January 2010 the earliest of the three Acts of the Hague Agreement (the 1934 London Act, deemed to be obsolete) was suspended to streamline the administration of the Agreement. In October 2012 the WIPO Assembly determined to expedite the development of a new treaty aimed at simplifying standards for the registration of industrial designs.

Madrid Agreement Concerning the International Registration of Marks: signed 14 April 1891; 56 states parties.

The Hague Agreement Concerning the International Registration of Industrial Designs: signed 16 November 1925; 62 states parties.

Lisbon Agreement for the Protection of Appellations of Origin and their International Registration: signed 31 October 1958; 28 states parties.

Patent Co-operation Treaty (PCT): signed 19 June 1970; 148 states parties.

Budapest Treaty on the International Recognition of the Deposit of Micro-organisms for the Purposes of Patent Procedure: signed 28 April 1977; 79 states parties.

Protocol Relating to the Madrid Agreement Concerning the International Registration of Marks: signed 28 June 1989; 91 contracting states.

International Classification Treaties
(status at April 2014)

The International Classification Treaties administered by WIPO create classification systems that organize information concerning inventions, trademarks and industrial designs. The International Classification treaties have established permanent committees of experts mandated periodically to revise and update the classification systems.

Locarno Agreement Establishing an International Classification for Industrial Designs: signed 8 October 1968; 53 states parties.

Nice Agreement Concerning the International Classification of Goods and Services for the Purposes of the Registration of Marks: signed 15 June 1957; 84 states parties.

Strasbourg Agreement Concerning the International Patent Classification (IPC): signed 24 March 1971; 62 states parties.

Vienna Agreement Establishing an International Classification of the Figurative Elements of Marks: signed 12 June 1973; 32 states parties.

Finance

The approved budget for the two years 2014–15 amounted to 673.2m. Swiss francs. More than 90% of WIPO's revenue derives from the international registration systems maintained by the organization; the remainder derives mainly from contributions by member states.

Publications

Les appellations d'origine (annually, in French).
Global Innovation Index (annually, co-published with INSEAD).
Hague Yearly Review.
Intellectual Property Statistics.
International Designs Bulletin (weekly).
PCT Newsletter (monthly).
PCT Yearly Review.
WIPO Gazette of International Marks (weekly, in English and French).
WIPO Handbook.
WIPO IP Facts and Figures.
WIPO Magazine (every 2 months).
WIPO Overview.
World Intellectual Property Indicators (annually).
World Intellectual Property Report.
A collection of industrial property and copyright laws and treaties; a selection of publications related to intellectual property.

World Meteorological Organization—WMO

Address: 7 bis, ave de la Paix, CP 2300, 1211 Geneva 2, Switzerland.
Telephone: 227308111; **fax:** 227308181; **e-mail:** wmo@wmo.int; **internet:** www.wmo.int.

WMO was established in 1950 and was recognized as a Specialized Agency of the UN in 1951, operating in the fields of meteorology, climatology, operational hydrology and related fields, as well as their applications.

MEMBERS

WMO has 191 members.

Organization
(April 2014)

WORLD METEOROLOGICAL CONGRESS

The supreme body of the organization, the Congress, is convened every four years and represents all members; it adopts regulations, and determines policy, programme and budget. The 16th Congress was held in May–June 2011. An extraordinary session of the Congress was convened at the end of October 2012.

EXECUTIVE COUNCIL

The Council has 37 members and meets at least once a year to prepare studies and recommendations for the Congress; it supervises the implementation of Congress resolutions and regulations, informs members on technical matters and offers advice.

SECRETARIAT

The Secretariat acts as an administrative, documentary and information centre; undertakes special technical studies; produces publications; organizes meetings of WMO constituent bodies; acts as a link between the meteorological and hydrometeorological services of the world, and provides information for the general public. The WMO Secretariat hosts the secretariat of the intergovernmental Group on Earth Observations (GEO), which was founded by participants at the Earth Observation Summit convened in Washington, DC, USA, in July 2003.

Secretary-General: MICHEL JARRAUD (France).
Deputy Secretary-General: JEREMIAH LENGOASA (South Africa).

REGIONAL ASSOCIATIONS

Members are grouped in six Regional Associations (Africa, Asia, Europe, North America, Central America and the Caribbean, South America and the South-West Pacific), whose task is to co-ordinate meteorological activity within their regions and to examine questions referred to them by the Executive Council. Sessions are held at least once every four years.

TECHNICAL COMMISSIONS

The Technical Commissions are composed of experts nominated by the members of WMO Sessions are held at least once every four years.

The Commissions cover the following areas: Atmospheric Sciences; Aeronautical Meteorology; Agricultural Meteorology; Basic Systems; Climatology; Instruments and Methods of Observation; Hydrology; Oceanography and Marine Meteorology.

Activities

In June 2011 the 16th World Meteorological Congress determined that WMO's five priority areas of activity during 2011–15 would be developing the newly endorsed Global Framework for Climate Services; enhancing the agency's contribution to disaster risk reduction; improving observation and information systems; strengthening developing countries' capacity to share in scientific advances and their applications; and advancing the efficiency of meteorological services in the aviation sector. The 16th Congress also recommended that WMO should prepare a cross-cutting Capacity Development Strategy to co-ordinate and enhance existing capacity building activities.

WORLD WEATHER WATCH (WWW) PROGRAMME

Combining facilities and services provided by the members, the Programme's primary purpose is to make available meteorological and related geophysical and environmental information enabling them to maintain efficient meteorological services. Facilities in regions outside any national territory (outer space, ocean areas and Antarctica) are maintained by members on a voluntary basis. In May 2007 the 15th WMO Congress made a number of decisions aimed at improving the WWW Programme, including instruments and observation methods and assisting developing countries to strengthen their operational capacities. WMO's World Weather Information Services website (worldweather.wmo.int) provides weather observations in nine languages. WMO's Severe Weather Forecasting Demonstration Project (SWFDP), established in 2006, aims to strengthen the capacity of National Meteorological and Hydrological Services (NMHSs) in developing and least developed countries to deliver improved warnings of severe weather.

Antarctic Activities: co-ordinates WMO activities related to the Antarctic, in particular the surface and upper-air observing programme, plans the regular exchange of observational data and products needed for operational and research purposes, studies problems related to instruments and methods of observation peculiar to the Antarctic, and develops appropriate regional coding practices. Contacts are maintained with scientific bodies dealing with Antarctic research and with other international organizations on aspects of Antarctic meteorology.

Data Management: monitors the integration of the different components of the WWW Programme, with the intention of increasing the efficiency of, in particular, the Global Observing System, the Global Data Processing System and the Global Telecommunication System. The Data Management component of the WWW Programme develops data handling procedures and standards for enhanced forms of data representation, in order to aid member countries to process large volumes of meteorological data.

Emergency Response Activities: assists national meteorological services to respond effectively to man-made environmental emergencies, particularly nuclear accidents, through the development, co-ordination and implementation of WMO/International Atomic Energy Agency (IAEA) established procedures and response mechanisms for the provision and exchange of observational data and specialized transport model products.

WMO and other agencies support UNESCO's International Oceanographic Commission with implementing tsunami warning systems for the Caribbean region, Indian Ocean, north-eastern Atlantic, Mediterranean and connected seas, and the Pacific. In the immediate aftermath of the devastating earthquake and tsunami flooding that struck Japan in March 2011, disabling the Fukushima Daiichi nuclear power plant, WMO, in partnership with the IAEA, undertook weather forecast monitoring.

Global Data Processing and Forecasting System: consists of World Meteorological Centres (WMCs) in Melbourne (Australia), Moscow (Russia) and Washington, DC (USA); 40 Regional/Specialized Meteorological Centres (RSMCs); and 191 National Meteorological Centres. The WMCs and RSMCs provide analyses, forecasts and warnings for exchange on the Global Telecommunications System. Some centres concentrate on the monitoring and forecasting of environmental quality and special weather phenomena, such as tropical cyclones, monsoons, droughts, etc., which have a major impact on human safety and national economies. These analyses and forecasts are designed to assist the members in making local and specialized forecasts.

WMO Integrated Global Observing System (WIGOS): makes simultaneous observations at around 10,000 land stations and 1,300 upper-air stations. Meteorological information is also received from 3,000 aircraft, 4,000 ships, 1,200 drifting ocean buoys, and 17 meteorological satellites (both polar orbiting and geostationary).

Global Telecommunication System: provides telecommunication services for the rapid collection and exchange of meteorological information and related data; comprises a network of dedicated satellites, and the Main Telecommunication Network (MTN) of the three WMCs, 15 Regional Meteorological Telecommunication networks and WMO's 191 NMHSs.

Instruments and Methods of Observation Programme: promotes the worldwide standardization of meteorological and geophysical instruments and methods of observation and measurement to meet agreed accuracy requirements. It provides related guidance material and training assistance in the use and maintenance of the instruments.

System Support Activity: provides guidance and support to members in the planning, establishment and operation of the WWW Programme. It includes training, technical co-operation support, system and methodology support, operational WWW evaluations, advanced technology support, an operations information service, and the WWW Programme referral catalogue.

GLOBAL ATMOSPHERE WATCH (GAW)

GAW is a worldwide system—comprising a network of 29 global stations in remote areas of the world, more than 400 regional stations, and around 100 other contributing stations—that integrates monitoring and research activities involving the long-term measurement of atmospheric composition, and is intended to serve as an early warning system to detect further changes in atmospheric concentrations of greenhouse gases, changes in the ozone layer and associated ultraviolet radiation, and in long-range transport of pollutants, including acidity and toxicity of rain, as well as the atmospheric burden of aerosols. In recent years the GAW network's measurements of atmospheric compounds and related parameters have been complemented by those of satellite programmes with almost global coverage. GAW is the main contributor of data on chemical composition and surface ultraviolet radiation to the GCOS. Through GAW, WMO has collaborated with the UN Economic Commission for Europe (ECE) and has been responsible for the meteorological part of the Monitoring and Evaluation of the Long-range Transmission of Air Pollutants in Europe. In this respect, WMO has arranged for the establishment of two Meteorological Synthesizing Centres (Oslo, Norway, and Moscow, Russia) which provide daily analysis of the transport of pollution over Europe. GAW also focuses on atmospheric chemistry studies, prepares scientific assessments and encourages integrated environmental monitoring. Quality Assurance/Science Activity Centres have been established to ensure an overall level of quality in GAW. Atmospheric composition information is maintained by a series of six GAW World Data Centres: the World Data Center for Remote Sensing of the Atmosphere (in Wessling, Germany), and further centres covering ozone and UV (in Toronto, Canada); solar radiation (St Petersburg, Russia); greenhouse gases (Tokyo, Japan); aerosols (Kjeller, Norway); and precipitation chemistry (Silver Spring, USA). GAW's Urban Environment Meteorological Research Programme (GURME) assists NMHSs in dealing with regional and urban pollution monitoring and forecasting, through the provision of guidelines and information on the requisite measuring and modelling infrastructures, and by bringing together NMHSs, regional and city administrations and health authorities. GURME is being developed in co-operation with the World Health Organization (WHO).

WORLD WEATHER RESEARCH PROGRAMME (WWRP)

The WWRP promotes the development and application of improved weather forecasting techniques. The Programme is primarily concerned with forecasting weather events that have the potential to cause considerable socio-economic dislocation. Advances in forecasting capability are pursued through a combination of improved scientific understanding (gained through field experiments and research), forecast technique development, the demonstration of new forecasting capabilities, and the transfer of these advances to all NMHSs in conjunctionwith related training through various Research Development Projects (RDPs) and Forecast Demonstration Projects (FDPs). In particular, THORPEX: a Global Atmospheric Research Programme, is being developed and implemented as part of the WWRP to accelerate improvements in the accuracy of 1–14-day weather forecasts in order to achieve social and economic benefits. The Programme builds upon ongoing advances within the basic research and operational forecasting communities. It aims to make progress by enhancing international collaboration between these communities and with users of forecast products.

HYDROLOGY AND WATER RESOURCES PROGRAMME

The overall objective of this major Programme is to apply hydrology to meet the needs of sustainable development and use of water and related resources; for the mitigation of water-related disasters; and to ensure effective environment management at national and international levels. The 16th World Meteorological Congress determined that the Programme should be strengthened to meet a growing need for sustainable water resources management. The Programme consists of the following mutually supporting component programmes:

Programme on Basic Systems in Hydrology (BSH): provides the basis and framework for the majority of the scientific and technical aspects of WMO activities in hydrology and water resources. The BSH covers the collection, transmission and storage of data, the transfer of operationally proven technology through the Hydrological Operational Multipurpose System (HOMS), and the development of the World Hydrological Cycle Observing System (WHYCOS), with the aim of improving countries' capacity to supply reliable water-related data, and manage and exchange accurate and timely water resources information.

Programme on Forecasting and Applications in Hydrology (FAH): covers aspects of the Hydrology and Water Resources Programme relating to hydrological modelling and forecasting, and to the application of hydrology in studies of global change. The FAH organizes activities in support of water resources development and management, and hazard mitigation, and promotes interdisciplinary co-operation to enhance flood forecasting at the national, regional and global level. The Programme is linked to the World Climate and Tropical Cyclone programmes.

Programme on Capacity Building in Hydrology and Water Resources (CBH): provides a framework under which National Hydrological Services (NHSs) are supported in their institutional development, through education and training activities, development of guidance material, assistance in the preparation of water legislation, reorganization of services and changes in administrative and legal frameworks.

WORLD CLIMATE PROGRAMME

The 16th World Meteorological Congress (2011) adopted a restructured and strengthened World Climate Programme (WCP, initiated in 1979), and decided that it would be a key programme in the delivery of the newly endorsed Global Framework for Climate Services. The WCP is supported by the Global Climate Observing System (GCOS), which provides comprehensive observation of the global climate system, involving a multidisciplinary range of atmospheric, oceanic, hydrologic, cryospheric and biotic properties and processes. The objectives of the WCP are to use existing climate information to improve economic and social planning; to improve the understanding of climate processes through research, so as to determine the predictability of climate and the extent of humankind's influence on it; and to detect and warn governments of impending climate variations or changes, either natural or man-made, which may significantly affect critical human activities.

Co-ordination of the overall Programme is the responsibility of WMO, together with direct management of the WCDMP and WCASP. The UN Environment Programme (UNEP) has accepted responsibility for the WCIRP, while the WCRP is jointly administered by WMO, the International Council for Science (ICSU) and UNESCO's Intergovernmental Oceanographic Commission. Other organizations involved in the Programme include FAO, WHO, and the Consultative Group on International Agricultural Research (CGIAR). In addition, the WCP supports the WMO/UNEP Intergovernmental Panel on Climate Change and the implementation of international agreements, such as the UN Framework Convention on Climate Change, and co-ordinates climate activities within WMO.

Global Framework for Climate Services (GFCS): the third World Climate Conference, convened in August–September 2009, resolved to establish the GFCS, to act as a platform for dialogue on climate change between providers of climate services (for example national meteorological and hydrometeorological services) and service users, such as policy-makers and farmers. The new Framework, developed by a High-level Task Force, was endorsed by the 16th World Meteorological Congress in June 2011. An extraordinary session of the World Meteorological Congress that was convened in October 2012 adopted a draft implementation plan for the new Global Framework.

World Climate Research Programme (WCRP): organized jointly with the Intergovernmental Oceanographic Commission of UNESCO and the ICSU, to determine to what extent climate can be predicted, and the extent of man's influence on climate. Its three specific objectives are establishing the physical basis for weather predictions over time ranges of one to two months; understanding and predicting the variability of the global climate over periods of several years; and studying the long-term variations and the response of climate to natural or man-made influence over periods of several decades. Studies include: changes in the atmosphere caused by emissions of carbon dioxide, aerosols and other gases; the effect of cloudiness on the radiation balance; the effect of ground water storage and vegetation on evaporation; the Arctic and Antarctic climate process; and the effects of oceanic circulation changes on the global atmosphere. Incorporates core projects on: Climate and Cryosphere (CliC); Climate Variability and Predictability (CLIVAR); the Global Energy and Water Exchanges Experiment (GEWEX); and Stratospheric Processes And their Role in Climate (SPARC).

Global Climate Observing System (GCOS): aims to ensure that data on climate are obtained and made available for climate system monitoring and climate change detection and attribution; assessing impacts of, and vulnerability to, climate variability and change, e.g. extreme events, terrestrial ecosystems, etc., and analysing options for adaptation; research to improve understanding, modelling and prediction of the climate system; and application to sustainable economic development. The strategy of the GCOS has been to work with its international and regional partners and to engage countries both directly and through international fora such as WMO, other GCOS sponsors and the UN Framework Convention on Climate Change (UNFCCC).

World Climate Services Programme (WCSP): aims to enhance the availability of and access to reliable data; and focuses on climate monitoring, watch and prediction; climate system operation and infrastructure; and climate adaptation and risk management. The WCSP acts as the climate services information system component of the GFCS.

OTHER PROGRAMMES

Agricultural Meteorology Programme: the study of weather and climate as they affect agriculture and forestry, the selection of crops and their protection from disease and deterioration in storage, soil conservation, phenology and physiology of crops and productivity and health of farm animals; the Commission for Agricultural Meteorology supervises the applications projects and also advises the Secretary-General in his efforts to co-ordinate activities in support of food production. There are also special activities in agrometeorology to monitor and combat drought and desertification, to apply climate and real-time weather information in agricultural planning and operations, and to help improve the efficiency of the use of human labour, land, water and energy in agriculture; close co-operation is maintained with FAO, centres of CGIAR and UNEP. The 16th World Meteorological Congress (2011) approved the use of a standardized meteorological drought index to enhance drought monitoring and early warning systems.

Aeronautical Meteorology Programme: provides operational meteorological information required for safe, regular and efficient air navigation, as well as meteorological assistance to non-real-time activities of the aviation industry. The Programme is implemented at the global, regional and national level, the Commission for Aeronautical Meteorology (CAeM) playing a major role, taking into account relevant meteorological developments in science and technology, studying aeronautical requirements for meteorological services, promoting international standardization of methods, procedures and techniques, and considering requirements for basic and climatological data as well as aeronautical requirements for meteorological observations and specialized instruments and enhanced understanding and awareness of the impact of aviation on the environment. Activities under this Programme are carried out, where relevant, with the International Civil Aviation Organization (ICAO) and in collaboration with users of services provided to aviation.

Disaster Risk Reduction (DDR) Programme: through its scientific and technical programmes and network of meteorological and climate centres, WMO provides observational, monitoring, prediction and early warning services in respect of a wide range of weather-, climate- and water-related hazards (of which 8,835 occurrences were reported globally during 1970–2012, causing some 1.9m. fatalities and also significant economic damage). In accordance with the global Hyogo Framework for Action, covering 2005–15, which aims to build the resilience of nations and communities to disasters, and promotes a shift of focus from emergency response to a more proactive and systematic approach to risk reduction, WMO's DDR programme aims to ensure the integration of relevant DDR activities across WMO's programming.

Education and Training Programme: WMO assists members to develop adequately trained staff to meet their responsibilities for providing meteorological and hydrological information services. Activities include surveys of the training requirements of member states, the development of appropriate training programmes, the monitoring and improvement of the network of 23 Regional Meteorological Training Centres, the organization of training courses, seminars and conferences and the preparation of training materials. The Programme also arranges individual training programmes and the provision of fellowships. The Panel of Experts on Education and Training was established by the Executive Council to serve as an advisory body on all aspects of technical and scientific education and of training in meteorology and operational hydrology.

Marine Meteorology and Oceanography Programme: undertakes operational monitoring of the oceans and the maritime atmosphere; collection, exchange, archival recording and management of marine data; processing of marine data, and the provision of marine meteorological and oceanographic services in support of the safety of life and property at sea and of the efficient and economic operation of all sea-based activities. The joint WMO/Intergovernmental Oceanographic Commission (IOC) Technical Commission for Oceanography and Marine Meteorology (JCOMM) has broad responsibilities in the overall management of the Programme. Many programme elements are undertaken jointly with the IOC, within the context of JCOMM, and also of the Global Ocean Observing System (GOOS). Close co-operation also occurs with the International Maritime Organization (IMO), as well as with other bodies both within and outside the UN system.

Programme for the Least Developed Countries (LDCs): has as its long-term objective enhancement of the capacities of the NMHSs of LDCs so that they can contribute efficiently and in a timely manner to socio-economic development efforts. Priority areas are poverty alleviation and natural disaster preparedness and mitigation. Specific projects will be developed for individual countries and at a subregional level for countries in Africa, Asia and the Pacific.

Public Weather Services Programme: the Programme assists members in providing reliable and effective weather and related services for the benefit of the public. The main objectives of the Programme are to strengthen members' capabilities to meet the needs of the community through the provision of comprehensive weather and related services, with particular emphasis on public safety and welfare; and to foster a better understanding by the public of the capabilities of national meteorological services and how best to use their services.

Regional Programme: WMO's Regional Programme cuts across the other major WMO programmes of relevance to the regions and addresses meteorological, hydrological and other geophysical issues which are unique to and of common concern to a region or group of regions. It provides a framework for the formulation of most of the global WMO Programmes and serves as a mechanism for their implementation at the national, subregional and regional levels. The Programme provides support to the WMO regional associations and contributes to the development of NMHSs through capacity building and other priority activities identified by members or relevant economic groups and organizations within the respective regions.

Space Programme: the 14th WMO Congress, held in 2003, initiated this cross-cutting programme to increase the effectiveness of, and contributions from, satellite systems for WMO activities. Congress recognized the critical importance of data, products and services provided by the expanded space-based component of the GCOS. The 53rd session of the Executive Council adopted a landmark decision to expand the space-based component of the GCOS to include appropriate research and development (R&D) and environmental satellite missions. The Congress agreed that the Commission for Basic Systems should continue to play a leading role, in full consultation with the other technical commissions for the Space Programme. Anticipated benefits from the Programme include an increasing contribution to the development of the GCOS, as well as to that of other WMO-supported programmes and associated observing systems, through the provision of continuously improved data, products and services, from both operational and R&D satellites. The Programme also aims to facilitate and promote the wider availability and meaningful utilization worldwide of such improved data. The 16th Congress agreed to pursue the development of an architecture for climate monitoring from space.

Tropical Cyclone Programme: established in response to UN General Assembly Resolution 2733 (XXV), aims to develop national and regionally co-ordinated systems to ensure that the loss of life and damage caused by tropical cyclones and associated floods, landslides and storm surges are reduced to a minimum. The Programme supports the transfer of technology, and includes five regional tropical cyclone bodies covering more than 60 countries, to improve warning systems and collaboration with other international organizations in activities related to disaster mitigation. The 16th World Meteorological Congress determined that the Programme should be strengthened to provide capacity-building support to LDCs and small island developing states.

Voluntary Co-operation Programme (VCP): WMO assists members in implementing the WWW Programme to develop an integrated observing and forecasting system. Member governments contribute equipment, services and fellowships for training, in addition to cash donations.

WMO also carries out assistance projects under Trust Fund arrangements, financed by national authorities, either for activities in their own country or in a beneficiary country and managed by the UN Development Programme (UNDP), the World Bank, regional development banks, the European Union and others. WMO provides assistance to UNDP in the development of national meteorological and hydrological services, in the application of meteorological and hydrological data to national economic development, and in the training of personnel.

WMO INFORMATION SYSTEM (WIS)

The WIS became operational in January 2012 as a single co-ordinated global infrastructure responsible for telecommunications and data management, aimed at expanding the global exchange of weather, climate and water data. It was conceived as a pillar of WMO's activities for managing and moving weather, climate and water information in the 21st century. The core infrastructure of the WIS comprises Global Information System Centres (GISCs), numbering 15 at April 2014.

INTERNATIONAL POLAR DECADE AND GLOBAL CRYOSPHERE WATCH

WMO considers the polar regions (including the 'Third Pole'—the Himalayan and Tibetan Plateau) as extremely important in terms of their impact on global weather, water and climate. The 16th World Meteorological Congress (2011) agreed to work with other international organizations to organize a future International Polar Decade. The 16th Congress also supported the need to establish an observational framework for polar regions, including an Antarctic Observing Network; determined to support a Global Integrated Polar Prediction System; and decided to develop, with international partners, the Global Cryosphere Watch. The Congress emphasized the significance, in terms of climate change prediction, of the cryosphere—i.e. water in its frozen state, including snow cover, sea, lake and river ice, glaciers, ice caps, ice sheets and permafrost, spanning all latitudes, in approximately 100 countries.

CO-OPERATION WITH OTHER BODIES

Within the UN *Delivering as One* process WMO and UNESCO were assigned the lead role in developing a Climate Knowledge Base. WMO, in addition, has concluded a number of formal agreements and working arrangements with international organizations both within and outside the UN system, at the intergovernmental and non-governmental level. As a result, WMO participates in major international conferences convened under the auspices of the UN or other organizations. In 1988 WMO, jointly with UNEP, established the Intergovernmental Panel on Climate Change as an advisory scientific body concerned with assessing and reporting the scientific, technical and socio-economic information relating to climate change. In response to the first report of the Panel, published in 1990, WMO and UNEP worked together to formulate the UNFCCC, which was signed in May 1992 and entered into force in March 1994. Other co-sponsored programmes are the World Climate Research Programme, the Global Climate Observing System, and the Global Ocean Observing System.

INTERNATIONAL DAY

World Meteorological Day is observed every year, normally on 23 March. The theme for 2014 was 'Weather and climate: engaging youth'.

Finance

WMO is financed by contributions from members on a proportional scale of assessment. For the 16th financial period, the four years 2012–15, a regular budget of 276m. Swiss francs was approved, and voluntary resources were projected at 175m. Swiss francs. Outside this budget, WMO implements a number of projects as executing agency for UNDP or else under trust fund.

Publications

Greenhouse Gas Bulletin (annually).

MeteoWorld.

WMO Bulletin (quarterly in English, French, Russian and Spanish).

World Climate News.

Reports, technical regulations, manuals and notes and training publications.

World Tourism Organization—UNWTO

Address: Capitán Haya 42, 28020 Madrid, Spain.

Telephone: (91) 5678100; **fax:** (91) 5713733; **e-mail:** omt@unwto.org; **internet:** www.world-tourism.org.

UNWTO was formally established in 1975 following transformation of the International Union of Official Travel Organisations into an intergovernmental body, in accordance with a resolution of the UN General Assembly approved in 1969. UNWTO became a specialized agency of the UN in December 2003. It aims to promote and develop sustainable tourism, in particular in support of socio-economic growth in developing countries.

MEMBERS

156 member states, six territories as associate members, 418 affiliate members.

Organization

(April 2014)

GENERAL ASSEMBLY

The General Assembly meets every two years to approve the budget and programme of work of the organization and to consider issues of concern for the tourism sector. It consists of representatives of all full and associate members; affiliate members and representatives of other international organizations participate as observers. The 20th General Assembly was convened in Livingstone (Zambia) and Victoria Falls (Zimbabwe), in August 2013.

EXECUTIVE COUNCIL

The Council, comprising 29 members elected by the General Assembly, is the governing body responsible for supervising the activities of the organization. It meets twice a year. The following specialized committees are subsidiary organs of the Council and advise on management and programme content: Programme; Budget and Finance; Statistics and Macroeconomic Analysis of Tourism; Market Intelligence and Promotion; Sustainable Development of Tourism; and Quality Support and Trade. In addition, there is a World Committee on Tourism Ethics and a Sub-committee for the Review of Applications for Affiliate Membership.

REGIONAL COMMISSIONS

There are six regional commissions, comprising all members and associate members from that region, which meet at least once a year to determine UNWTO's priorities and future activities in the region. The commissions cover Africa, the Americas, East Asia and the Pacific, Europe, the Middle East, and South Asia.

SECRETARIAT

The Secretariat is responsible for implementing UNWTO's work programme. The Secretary-General is supported by three Executive Directors, all based at headquarters, in Madrid, Spain. A regional support office for Asia and the Pacific is based in Osaka, Japan. Six regional representatives, based at the Secretariat, support national tourism authorities, act as a liaison between those authorities and international sources of finance, and represent the body at national and regional events.

Secretary-General: Taleb Rifai (Jordan).

AFFILIATE MEMBERS

UNWTO is unique as an intergovernmental body in extending membership to operational representatives of the industry and other related sectors, for example transport companies, educational institutions, insurance companies, publishing groups. A UNWTO Education Council aims to support UNWTO's education and human resource development activities. It undertakes research projects, grants awards for innovation and the application of knowledge in tourism, and co-ordinates a tourism labour market observatory project. The UNWTO Business Council groups together the affiliate members from the private sector and aims to promote and facilitate partnerships between the industry and governments. A third group of the affiliate membership is the UNWTO Destinations Council, which acts as an operational body supporting the UNWTO Destination Management programme with particular concern for issues relevant to tourist destinations, for example local tourism marketing, economic measurements and management of congestion.

Chair. of Board of UNWTO Affiliate Members (2014–15): Miguel Mirones Díez (Spain).

Activities

UNWTO promotes the development of responsible, sustainable and universally accessible tourism within the broad context of contributing to economic development, international prosperity and peace and respect for human rights. As a UN specialized agency UNWTO aims to emphasize the role of tourism as a means of supporting socio-economic development and achieving the UN Millennium Development Goals (MDGs). Through its network of affiliated members UNWTO extends its activities and objectives to the private sector, tourism authorities and educational institutions. In October 2008 the Executive Council approved the establishment of a Tourism Resilience Committee, which was to consider the response of the tourism industry to the deterioration of the global economy and the role of tourism in economic stimulus programmes. The Committee convened for the first time in January 2009. In September UNWTO published a *Roadmap for Recovery* which highlighted the role of tourism and travel in job creation and economic recovery, including its contribution to creating a 'green economy'. Ministers responsible for tourism of several industrialized and developing economies determined to form a grouping to promote the Roadmap at high-level international discussions. Meetings of the so-called T.20 were subsequently convened, with the full support of UNWTO, in Johannesburg, South Africa, in February 2010; in Buyeo, Republic of Korea (South Korea), in October of that year; in Paris, France, in October 2011; Mérida, Mexico, in May 2012; and London, United Kingdom, in November 2013. The 5th T.20 meeting focused, in particular, on advances in visa facilitation, and in reducing remaining barriers to tourist movements, in view of recognition given by G20 leaders, at their June 2012 gathering in Los Cabos, Mexico, to the role played by travel and tourism in stimulating job creation, and economic growth and development. March 2011 UNWTO, with the Government of Andorra, organized an inaugural Global Tourism Forum, which brought together representatives of international agencies, private sector companies, and other partners, to promote the role of tourism in a sustainable global economic recovery and to harness collective support for the competitive and responsible development of the tourism sector.

DEVELOPMENT ASSISTANCE

UNWTO aims to support member states to develop and promote their tourism industry in order to contribute to socio-economic growth and poverty alleviation. Activities to transfer technical skills and knowledge to developing countries are fundamental tasks for the organization. It aims to assist member countries to develop tourism plans and strategies and helps to secure and manage specific development projects, hotel classification in Bolivia and statistics development in Botswana. Other aspects of developing tourism concern the involvement of local communities, fostering public-private partnerships and the preservation of cultural and natural heritage.

In September 2002 at the World Summit on Sustainable Development, held in Johannesburg, South Africa, UNWTO, in collaboration with the UN Conference on Trade and Development (UNCTAD), launched the Sustainable Tourism-Eliminating Poverty (ST-EP) initiative. It aimed to encourage social, economic and ecologically sustainable tourism with the aim of alleviating poverty in the world's poorest countries. In September 2004 UNWTO signed an agreement with South Korea providing for the establishment of a ST-EP Foundation in the capital, Seoul. UNWTO has conducted a series of capacity-building seminars and other training activities concerning tourism and poverty alleviation, within the framework of the ST-EP initiative. It convenes an annual ST-EP forum, in Berlin, Germany, to involve a range of tourism agencies and companies in the scheme. Project identification missions have been conducted in some 30 developing countries with a focus on local-level tourism development and small-scale entrepreneurial schemes. In October 2012 ministers responsible for tourism, conservation officials and representatives of the private sector participating in the first Pan-African Conference on Sustainable Tourism Management in African National Parks and Protected Areas, convened by UNWTO in Arusha, Tanzania, adopted the Arusha Declaration on Sustainable Tourism in African National Parks. The Declaration emphasized the importance of good governance in the management of park tourism, of knowledge sharing between national authorities, and of encouraging involvement by local communities.

MARKET, COMPETITIVENESS AND STATISTICS

UNWTO aims to ensure that quality standards and safety and security aspects are incorporated into all tourism products and services. It is also concerned with the social impact of tourism and the regulatory trading framework. UNWTO has formulated international standards for tourism measurement and reporting. It compiles comprehensive tourism statistics and forecasts. A Tourism Satellite Account (TSA) was developed to analyse the economic impact of tourism. It was endorsed by the UN Statistical Commission in 2000 and is recognized as a framework for providing internationally comparable data. (An updated Recommended Methodological Framework was introduced in 2008.) The TSA is also considered by UNWTO to be a strategic project within the broader objective of developing a system of tourism statistics. In October 2005 a world conference on TSAs, held in the Iguazu region of Argentina, Brazil and Paraguay, agreed on 10 defined objectives to extend and develop the use of TSAs. Further international conferences on tourism statistics have been held in Málaga, Spain, in October 2008, and in Bali, Indonesia, in March–April 2009.

UNWTO assists governments and tourist professionals to identify, analyse and forecast tourism trends and to assess the relative performance of each country's tourism industry. The organization also assists member states with tourism promotion through marketing tools and the formulation of tourism development strategies. A Market Intelligence and Promotion Committee was formally established in October 2002. Following the terrorism attacks against targets in the USA in September 2001 a Tourism Recovery Committee was established to monitor events affecting tourism, to help to restore confidence in the industry and to strengthen UNWTO activities concerned with safety and security.

In 1991 UNWTO's General Assembly approved a series of Recommended Measures for Tourism Safety which member states were encouraged to apply. UNWTO has established a Safety and Security in Tourism Network to consider aspects of the recommended measures and to facilitate collaboration between institutions and experts concerned with safety and security issues. The Network publishes national factsheets on safety and security in countries and tourist destinations, compiled by a designated national tourism administration focal point, for use by tourism professionals and the general public. Other essential quality standards promoted by the organization are hygiene and food safety, accessibility, product and pricing transparency and authenticity. UNWTO is also concerned with ensuring that tourist activities are in keeping with the surrounding environment.

In January 2005 the Executive Council convened its first emergency session following the December 2004 tsunami which devastated many coastal areas in the Indian Ocean. The Council, meeting in Phuket, Thailand, along with other regional organizations, private sector representatives and tourism experts, adopted an action plan to support the recovery of the tourism sector in many of the affected areas, to help to restore tourist confidence in the region and to rehabilitate tourism infrastructure, in particular in Thailand, the Maldives, Indonesia and Sri Lanka. A co-ordinating unit to oversee the longer-term projects was established in February 2005 and its functions were integrated into UNWTO's broader emergency response framework in mid-2006. In 2005 UNWTO pledged its commitment to working with governments and the private sector to incorporate tourism concerns into preparedness programmes relating to the threat of highly pathogenic avian influenza. A Tourism Emergency Response Network (TERN) was established in April 2006 as a grouping of travel organizations committed to supporting UN efforts to respond to avian influenza and the threat of a potential human pandemic. UNWTO maintains a tourism emergency tracking system, which identifies recent outbreaks of the disease. In 2008 UNWTO developed a new online service, SOS.travel, to support crisis preparedness and management within the tourist industry and to enable individual travellers to enhance their own personal safety and security.

UNWTO participates as an observer at the World Trade Organization (WTO) on issues relating to trade in tourism services, with particular concern to negotiations under the General Agreement on Trade in Services for a separate annex on tourism. UNWTO hosts a voluntary working group on liberalization.

In March 2013 UNWTO and the International Civil Aviation Organization (ICAO) signed a Joint Statement on Aviation and Tourism, in which they made a commitment towards closer co-operation in areas of shared priority.

In order to generate awareness of tourism among the international community UNWTO sponsors a World Tourism Day, held each year on 27 September. The theme of the 2014 events—to be hosted by Mexico—was to be 'Tourism and Development in the Community'.

SUSTAINABLE TOURISM DEVELOPMENT

UNWTO aims to encourage and facilitate the application of sustainable practices within the tourism industry. It publishes guides on sustainable development and compilations for good practices for use by local authorities. UNWTO has also published manuals for tourism planning at regional, national and local level and has organized seminars on planning issues in developing countries. UNWTO actively promotes voluntary initiatives for sustainability including labelling schemes, certification systems and awards.

UNWTO publishes a series of compilations of good practices for small and medium-sized businesses involved with ecotourism. In May 2002 a World Ecotourism Summit was convened in Québec, Canada, within the framework of the International Year of Ecotourism (led by UNWTO and the UN Environment Programme—UNEP). The organization welcomed the adoption in December 2012 by the UN General Assembly of a resolution that urged member states to pursue policies aimed at the 'promotion of ecotourism for poverty eradication and environmental protection'. UNWTO sponsored the first International Conference on Climate Change and Tourism, which was held in Djerba, Tunisia, in April 2003. A final declaration of the conference urged that UNWTO take the lead in focusing international attention on the issue and called upon all parties to continue research efforts, to encourage sustainability in tourism, to generate awareness and to implement defined actions. The second International Conference on Climate Change and Tourism, organized by UNWTO, UNEP and the World Meteorological Organization (WMO), was convened in Davos, Switzerland, in October 2007. The meeting concluded the Davos Declaration, which urged greater action by the tourism sector to respond to the challenges of climate change, for example by employing new energy efficiency technologies, in order to support the objectives of the MDGs. An UNWTO Consulting Unit on Tourism and Biodiversity was established in 2006 to provide consulting services to member states relating to biodiversity-based tourism. UNWTO supported the development of a new initiative to promote responsible and sustainable tourism, which was inaugurated as the 'Live the Deal' global campaign during the 15th Conference of the Parties to the UN Framework Convention on Climate Change, held in Copenhagen, Denmark, in December 2009. UNWTO was a co-organizer of official events on Tourism for a Sustainable Future and Green Innovation in Tourism, held on the sidelines of the UN Conference on Sustainable Development, which was convened in Rio de Janeiro, Brazil, in June 2012.

In 2004 UNWTO initiated the Global Observatory on Sustainable Tourism (GOST) programme, with the aim of better monitoring and implementing sustainable tourism practices, and establishing a network of local observatories. By April 2014 five observatories were operational in the People's Republic of China (at Chengdu, Huangshan, Kanas, Yangshuo, and Zhangjiajie); and an Observatory of the Aegean Islands was operational in Greece (launched in April 2013). In January 2011 UNWTO and UNEP launched the Global Partnership for Sustainable Tourism, also comprising other UN agencies, the Organisation for Economic Co-operation and Development, 18 governments, and other partners, with the aim of guiding policy and developing projects in the area of sustainable tourism, providing a global platform for discussion, and facilitating progress towards a green economy.

In May 2011 UNWTO participated in a special event on Tourism for Sustainable Development and Poverty Reduction, which was organized at the fourth UN Conference on Least Developed Countries (LDC-IV), held in İstanbul, Turkey. Tourism is a major source of export earnings in more than one-half of LDCs.

In 1997 a Task Force for the Protection of Children from Sexual Exploitation in Tourism was established by UNWTO as a forum for governments, industry associations and other organizations to work together with the aim of identifying, preventing and eradicating the sexual exploitation of children. In March 2007 the mandate of the Task Force was expanded to include protection of children and young people against all forms of exploitation in tourism, including child labour and trafficking. In November 2008 the Task Force, meeting during the World Travel Market in London, United Kingdom, inaugurated a new 'Protect Children Campaign' to generate awareness of the abuse of children and to harness global support for its protection efforts. In 1999 the General Assembly adopted a Global Code of Ethics for Tourism. The Code, which was endorsed by a special resolution of the UN General Assembly in 2001, aims to protect resources upon which tourism depends and to ensure that the economic benefits of tourism are distributed equitably. In 2011 UNWTO initiated a campaign to promote adherence by private tourism enterprises and associations to Code. A World Committee on Tourism Ethics, established in 2003 to support the implementation of the Code, meets on an annual basis. A permanent secretariat for the Committee was inaugurated in November 2008. In February 2014 the Committee approved a four-year action plan focusing on the exploitation of children in all its forms; trafficking; poaching and illegal trading in wildlife; accessible tourism for all; the promotion of fair models of all-inclusive holidays; and addressing unfounded, unjust ratings on travel review portals that potentially negatively impact the reputation of companies and destinations. In March 2000 UNWTO, with UNESCO and UNEP, established a Tour Operators Initiative to encourage socially responsible tourism development within the industry.

UNWTO and the Turkish Government organized a Global Summit on City Tourism in November 2012, in İstanbul, Turkey, on the theme 'Catalysing Economic Development and Social Progress'.

In November 2007 the General Assembly resolved to appoint the organization's first Special Adviser on Women and Tourism. In

March 2008 UNWTO launched an Action Plan to Empower Women through Tourism.

In 1994 UNWTO, in co-operation with UNESCO, initiated a project to promote tourism, in support of economic development, along the traditional Silk Road trading routes linking Asia and Europe. In October 2004 a Silk Road Tourism Office was opened in Samarkand, Uzbekistan. In December 2008 UNWTO, in collaboration with UNDP, initiated a UN Silk Road City award scheme further to promote tourism and development along the trading route. In October 2009 the General Assembly adopted the Astana Declaration in support of a Silk Road Initiative, which aimed to promote the tourism potential of the countries along the Silk Road. At the fifth international meeting of participants in the Silk Road project, convened in Samarkand, in October 2010, representatives of 26 countries endorsed UNWTO's development of a Silk Road Action Plan. An updated Silk Road Action Plan was approved at a ministerial meeting held in March 2012, in Berlin, Germany. An UNWTO Silk Road ministerial meeting convened in March 2013, also in Berlin, announced a new joint UNWTO-UNHCR 'Silk Road Heritage Corridors' tourism strategy project, aimed at safeguarding and raising the profile of the region's heritage sites and intangible cultural heritage. The sixth international meeting on Silk Road Toruism, organized by UNWTO and the Chinese authorities in August 2013, in Dunhuang, China, was held alongside a Silk Road International Tourism Festival. In 1995 UNWTO and UNESCO launched the Slave Route project to stimulate tourism and raise cultural awareness in several West African countries. In October 2007 UNWTO hosted an International Conference on Tourism, Religion and the Dialogue of Cultures, in Córdoba, Spain, to contribute to the discussion and promotion of the UN initiative for an Alliance of Civilizations.

EDUCATION AND KNOWLEDGE MANAGEMENT

UNWTO is committed to supporting education and training within the tourism industry and to developing a network of specialized research and training institutes. Most activities are undertaken by the UNWTO Education Council and the Themis Foundation. A specialized office concerned with human resource development was opened in September 2003, in Andorra. In September 2010 UNWTO inaugurated a Knowledge Network (UNWTO.Know) of institutes, universities, and public and private organizations, with the aim of facilitating a broad approach to the development of tourism policy, governance and practices. The inaugural meeting of UNWTO.Know took place in Madrid, Spain, in January 2011. In June of that year the Network organized the UNWTO Algarve Forum, held in Vilamoura, Portugal, with participation by more than 300 representatives from the tourism sector, as well as academics. The Forum, conceived as a means of bridging theory and practice in tourism, adopted the Algarve Consensus, detailing guidelines and policy programmes aimed at directing the future development and good governance of the sector. By 2014 UNWTO.Know comprised more than 130 institutions from 40 countries. In October 2012 UNWTO and partners launched a Global Partnership for the Hotel Industry, with the aim of sharing best practices and finding common positions on challenges such as hotel quality.

UNWTO Themis Foundation: Avinguda Dr Vilanova 9, Edif. Thaïs 4c, Andorra la Vella, Andorra; tel. 802600; fax 829955; e-mail wto.themis@andorra.ad; internet themis.unwto.org; aims to promote quality and efficiency in tourism education and training. Works closely with the human resource development programme of UNWTO and promotes UNWTO's specialized training products and services, in particular the TedQual certification and the Practicum programme for tourism officials; Exec. Dir OMAR VALDEZ.

INFORMATION AND COMMUNICATIONS

In January 2004 UNWTO hosted the first World Conference on Tourism Communications. Regular regional conferences have since been organized, within the framework of a Special Programme for Capacity Sharing in International Tourism Communications (TOURCOM), to enhance the capacity of regional and national tourism authorities to apply international standards and best practices to the promotion and communication of tourism.

UNWTO aims to act as a clearing house of information for the tourist industry. A UNWTO Documentation Centre collates extensive information on tourism activities and promotes access to and exchange of information among member states and affiliated partners. The Centre offers access to tourism legislation and other regulatory procedures through its LEXTOUR database on the internet. The Centre also administers a tourism information database (INFODOCTOUR).

Finance

The budget for the two-year period 2014–15 amounted to €26.6m.

Publications

Annual Report (annually).
Compendium of Tourism Statistics.
Global Report on the Meetings Industry.
Tourism Highlights (annually).
Yearbook of Tourism Statistics.
UNWTO News (monthly).
UNWTO World Tourism Barometer (3 a year).
Other research or statistical reports, studies, guidelines and fact-sheets.

AFRICAN DEVELOPMENT BANK—AfDB

Address: Statutory Headquarters: rue Joseph Anoma, 01 BP 1387, Abidjan 01, Côte d'Ivoire.

Telephone: 20-20-48-22; **fax:** 20-21-31-00; **e-mail:** afdb@afdb.org; **internet:** www.afdb.org.

Address: Temporary Relocation Agency: 15 ave du Ghana, angle des rues Pierre de Coubertin et Hedi Nouira, BP 323, 1002 Tunis Belvédère, Tunisia.

Telephone: (71) 103-900; **fax:** (71) 351-933.

Established in 1964, the Bank began operations in July 1966, with the aim of financing economic and social development in African countries. The Bank's headquarters are officially based in Abidjan, Côte d'Ivoire. Since February 2003, however, in view of ongoing insecurity in Côte d'Ivoire, the Bank's operations have been conducted, on a long-term temporary basis, from Tunis, Tunisia. In May 2013 the Bank's Board of Governors approved a roadmap for a structured return to Côte d'Ivoire by the end of 2014.

REGIONAL MEMBERS

Algeria	Equatorial Guinea	Namibia
Angola	Eritrea	Niger
Benin	Ethiopia	Rwanda
Botswana	Gabon	São Tomé and Príncipe
Burkina Faso	The Gambia	Senegal
Burundi	Ghana	Seychelles
Cameroon	Guinea	Sierra Leone
Cape Verde	Guinea-Bissau	Somalia
Central African Republic	Kenya	South Africa
Chad	Lesotho	South Sudan
Comoros	Liberia	Sudan
Congo, Democratic Republic	Libya	Swaziland
Congo, Republic	Madagascar	Tanzania
Côte d'Ivoire	Malawi	Togo
Djibouti	Mali	Tunisia
Egypt	Mauritania	Uganda
	Mauritius	Zambia
	Morocco	Zimbabwe
	Mozambique	

There are also 26 non-African members.

Organization

(April 2014)

BOARD OF GOVERNORS

The highest policy-making body of the Bank, which also elects the Board of Directors and the President. Each member country nominates one Governor, usually its Minister of Finance and Economic Affairs, and an alternate Governor or the Governor of its central bank. The Board meets once a year. The 2013 meeting was held in Marrakesh, Morocco, in May; the 2014 was scheduled to be convened in Kigali, Rwanda, in May.

BOARD OF DIRECTORS

The Board, elected by the Board of Governors for a term of three years, is responsible for the general operations of the Bank and meets on a weekly basis. The Board has 20 members.

OFFICERS

The President is responsible for the organization and the day-to-day operations of the Bank under guidance of the Board of Directors. The President is elected for a five-year term and serves as the Chairperson of the Board of Directors. The President oversees the following senior management: Chief Economist; Vice-Presidents of Finance, Corporate Services, Country and Regional Programmes and Policy, Sector Operations, and Infrastructure, Private Sector and Regional Integration; Auditor General; General Counsel; Secretary-General; and Ombudsman. Bank field offices are located in around 35 member countries. In January 2011 a Permanent Committee on the Review and Implementation of the Decentralization was established. In accordance with a Roadmap on Decentralization, adopted by the Board of Directors in April 2011, and covering the period 2011–16, greater responsibility for portfolio management was to be transferred to the Bank's field offices; the Bank's presence in fragile states was to be enhanced; and five regional resource centres were to be established with the aim of consolidating regional capacity. The Bank's first external representation office (for Asia) was inaugurated in Tokyo, Japan, in October 2012, and two further external representation offices were also to be opened: for the Americas, to be based in Washington, DC, USA; and for Europe, to be based in Brussels, Belgium.

Executive President and Chairperson of Board of Directors: DONALD KABERUKA (Rwanda).

FINANCIAL STRUCTURE

The African Development Bank (AfDB) Group of development financing institutions comprises the African Development Fund (ADF) and the Nigeria Trust Fund (NTF), which provide concessionary loans, and the AfDB itself. The Group uses a unit of account (UA), which, at December 2012, was valued at US $1.53692.

The capital stock of the Bank was at first exclusively open for subscription by African countries, with each member's subscription consisting of an equal number of paid-up and callable shares. In 1978, however, the Governors agreed to open the capital stock of the Bank to subscription by non-regional states on the basis of nine principles aimed at maintaining the African character of the institution. The decision was finally ratified in May 1982, and the participation of non-regional countries became effective on 30 December. It was agreed that African members should still hold two-thirds of the share capital, that all loan operations should be restricted to African members, and that the Bank's President should always be a national of an African state. In May 1998 the Board of Governors approved an increase in capital of 35%, and resolved that the non-African members' share of the capital be increased from 33.3% to 40%. In May 2010 the Board of Governors approved a general capital increase of 200%. At 31 December 2012 the Bank's authorized capital was UA 66,980.0m. (compared with UA 66,054.5m. at the end of 2011); subscribed capital at the end of 2012 was UA 65,220.0m. (of which the paid-up portion was UA 4,960.0m.).

Activities

At the end of 2012 the Bank Group had approved total lending of UA 72,202.8m. since the beginning of its operations in 1967. In 2012 the Group approved 199 lending operations amounting to UA 4,253.8m. compared with UA 5,720.3m. in the previous year. Of the total amount approved in 2012 UA 3,602.8m. was for loans and grants, UA 248.0m. for heavily indebted poor countries (HIPC) debt relief, UA 133.9m. for equity participation and UA 269.0m. for special funds. Of the total loans and grants approved in 2012, UA 1,763.5m. (49%) was for infrastructure projects (of which UA 889.7m. was for energy supply initiatives); UA 604.2m. (17%) was for transport projects; UA 505.4m. (14%) for multisector projects; and UA 402.8m. (11%) for projects in the finance sector. Some 31% of Bank Group loan and grant approvals in 2012 were allocated to countries in North Africa, 12.8% to Southern Africa, 12.4% to East Africa, 12.2% to West Africa, and 8.8% to Central Africa.

In 2006 the Bank established a High Level Panel of eminent personalities to advise on the Bank's future strategic vision. The Panel issued its report, *Investing in Africa's Future—The AfDB in the 21st Century*, in February 2008. A Roadmap on Development Effectiveness was approved by the Board in March 2011, focusing on areas deemed most likely to bring about transformational change, including strengthening transparency and accountability, and accelerating decentralization. The Bank's Strategy for 2013–22, adopted in April 2013, focused on achieving inclusive growth and promoting the transition to green growth, with infrastructure development, regional integration, private sector development, governance and accountability, and skills and technology designated as core areas of priority. Further areas of special emphasis included fragile states, gender, agriculture, and food security. In mid-2008 the Bank established an African Food Crisis Response initiative to extend accelerated support to members affected by the sharp increase in the cost of food and food production. The initiative aimed to reduce short-term food poverty and malnutrition, with funds of some UA 472.0m., and to support long-term sustainable food security, with funding of UA 1,400m.

In November 2008 the Bank hosted a special conference of African ministers responsible for finance and central bank governors to consider the impact on the region of the contraction of the world's major economies and the recent volatility of global financial markets. The meeting determined to establish a Committee of African Finance Ministers and Central Bank Governors, comprising 10 representatives from each Bank region, with a mandate to examine further the impact of the global financial crisis on Africa, to review the responses by member governments, and to develop policy options. The so-called Committee of Ten (C10) convened for its inaugural meeting in Cape Town, South Africa, in January 2009. In March the Bank's Board of Directors endorsed four new initiatives to help to counter the effects of the global economic crisis: the establishment of an Emergency Liquidity Facility, with funds of some US $1,500m., to assist members with short-term financing difficulties; a Trade Finance Initiative, with funds of up to $1,000m., to provide credit for trade financing operations; a Framework for the Accelerated Resource Transfer of ADF Resources; and enhanced policy advisory support. The Bank also agreed to contribute $500m. to a multinational Global Trade Liquidity Program, which commenced operations in mid-2009. In September the Bank initiated a consultative process for a sixth general capital increase. An increase of 200% was endorsed by a committee of the governing body representing the Bank's shareholders, meeting in April 2010, to enable the Bank to sustain its increased level of lending. The capital increase was formally approved by the Board of Governors in May. The C10 adopted a paper in March 2009 that outlined the major concerns of African countries in preparation for the meeting of heads of state of the Group of 20 (G20) major economies, held in London, United Kingdom, in early April. The third meeting of the Committee, held in Abuja, Nigeria, in July, reviewed economic indicators and developments since the G20 meeting and appealed for all commitments to low-income countries pledged at the summit to be met. The Committee also issued a series of messages for the next G20 summit meeting, held in Pittsburgh, PA, USA, in September, including a request for greater African participation in the G20 process and in international economic governance. The fourth meeting of the C10, convened in February 2010, determined that it should meet formally two times a year, with other informal meetings and meetings of deputies to be held in between; the Secretariat of the Committee was to be provided by the AfDB.

In May 2011 the Group of Eight (G8) industrialized nations, in collaboration with regional and international financial institutions and the governments of Egypt and Tunisia, established a Deauville Partnership to support political and economic reforms being undertaken by several countries in North Africa and the Middle East, notably Egypt, Jordan, Morocco and Tunisia. The AfDB supported the establishment of the Partnership and was to chair a Co-ordination Platform. In September Kuwait, Qatar, Saudi Arabia, Turkey and the United Arab Emirates joined the Partnership.

Since 1996 the Bank has collaborated closely with international partners, in particular the World Bank, in efforts to address the problems of HIPCs (see IBRD). Of the 41 countries identified as potentially eligible for assistance under the scheme, 33 were in sub-Saharan Africa. Following the introduction of an enhanced framework for the initiative, the Bank has been actively involved in the preparation of Poverty Reduction Strategy Papers, that provide national frameworks for poverty reduction programmes. In April 2006 the Board of Directors endorsed a Multilateral Debt Relief Initiative (MDRI), which provided for 100% cancellation of eligible debts from the ADF, the IMF and the International Development Association to secure additional resources for countries to help them attain their Millennium Development Goals (MDGs). ADF's participation in the MDRI, which became effective in September, was anticipated to provide some UA 5,570m. (US $8,540m.) in debt relief.

The Bank contributed funds for the establishment, in 1986, of the Africa Project Development Facility, which assists the private sector in Africa by providing advisory services and finance for entrepreneurs: it was managed by the International Finance Corporation (IFC), until replaced by the Private Enterprise Partnership for Africa in April 2005. In 1989 the Bank, in co-ordination with IFC and the UN Development Programme (UNDP), created the African Management Services Company (AMSCo), which provides management support and training to private companies in Africa. The Bank is one of three multilateral donors, with the World Bank and UNDP, supporting the African Capacity Building Foundation, which was established in 1991 to strengthen and develop institutional and human capacity in support of sustainable development activities. The Bank hosts the secretariat of an Africa Investment Consortium, which was inaugurated in October 2005 by several major African institutions and donor countries to accelerate efforts to develop the region's infrastructure. An Enhanced Private Sector Assistance Initiative was established, with support from the Japanese Government, in 2005 to support the Bank's strategy for the development of the private sector. The Initiative incorporated an Accelerated Co-financing Facility for Africa and a Fund for African Private Sector Assistance. In October 2010 the Board of Directors agreed to convert the Fund into a multi-donor trust fund.

In November 2006 the Bank Group, with the UN Economic Commission for Africa (ECA), organized an African Economic Conference (AEC), which has since become an annual event. The eighth AEC was held in Johannesburg, South Africa, in October 2013, with a focus on enhancing regional integration to generate economic benefits throughout Africa.

In March 2000 African ministers responsible for water resources endorsed an African Water Vision and a Framework for Action to pursue the equitable and sustainable use and management of water resources in Africa in order to facilitate socio-economic development, poverty alleviation and environmental protection. An African Ministers' Council on Water (AMCOW) was established in April 2002 to provide the political leadership and focus for implementation of the Vision and the Framework for Action. AMCOW requested the Bank to establish and administer an African Water Facility Special Fund, in order to provide the financial requirements for achieving their objectives; this became operational in December. In March the Bank approved a Rural Water Supply and Sanitation Initiative to accelerate access in member countries to sustainable safe water and basic sanitation, in order to meet the requirements of several MDGs. In March 2008 the Bank hosted the first African Water Week, organized jointly with AMCOW. The Bank co-ordinated and led Africa's regional participation in the Sixth World Water Forum, which was held in Marseilles, France, in March 2012. The Bank was actively involved in preparing for the fifth Africa Carbon Forum, which was convened in Abidjan, Côte d'Ivoire, in July 2013 (previous fora having been held in September 2008, March 2010, July 2011 and April 2012).

The Bank hosts the secretariat of the Congo Basin Forest Fund, which was established in June 2008, as a multi-donor facility, with initial funding from Norway and the United Kingdom, to protect and manage the forests in that region. The Bank also hosts the secretariat of an African Fertilizer Financing Mechanism (AFFM), established in 2007 to boost agricultural productivity, food security, and the sustainable management of natural resources in Africa. The inaugural meeting of the AFFM Governing Council was convened in November 2009; the second Governing Council meeting was hosted by the Bank in March 2013.

In April 2014 the Board of Directors endorsed the establishment of an Africa Climate Change Fund, which was to be hosted by the Bank, and was to assist the transition of African countries towards climate-resilient and low-carbon development.

Through the Migration and Development Trust Fund, launched in 2009, the Bank supports the development of financial services for migrant workers, and facilitates channelling remittances towards productive uses in workers' countries of origin.

The Bank provides technical assistance to regional member countries in the form of experts' services, pre-investment feasibility studies, and staff training. Much of this assistance is financed through bilateral trust funds contributed by non-African member states. The Bank's African Development Institute provides training for officials of regional member countries in order to enhance the management of Bank-financed projects and, more broadly, to strengthen national capacities for promoting sustainable development. The Institute also manages an AfDB/Japan Fellowship programme that provides scholarships to African students to pursue further education. In 1990 the Bank established the African Business Round Table (ABR), which is composed of the chief executives of Africa's leading corporations. The ABR aims to strengthen Africa's private sector, promote intra-African trade and investment, and attract foreign investment to Africa. The ABR is chaired by the Bank's Executive President. The AfDB, jointly with the French media concern Groupe Jeune Afrique, organizes the Africa CEO Forum; the first forum was convened in November 2012, in Geneva, Switzerland, and the second, with participation by 680 CEOs, financiers and journalists, was staged in March 2014, also in Geneva.

A joint secretariat supports co-operation activities between the African Union (AU), ECA and the AfDB. In March 2009 a new Coalition for Dialogue on Africa was inaugurated by the Bank, ECA and the AU. In 1999 a Co-operation Agreement was formally concluded between the Bank and the Common Market for Eastern and Southern Africa. In March 2000 the Bank signed a Memorandum of Understanding (MOU) on its strategic partnership with the World Bank. Other MOUs were signed during that year with the United Nations Industrial Development Organization, the World Food Programme, and the Union of the Arab Maghreb. In September 2008 the Bank supported the establishment of an African Financing Partnership, which aimed to mobilize private sector resources through partnerships with regional development finance institutions. The Bank hosts the secretariat of the Partnership. It also hosts the secretariat of the Making Finance Work for Africa Partnership, which was established, by the G8, in October 2007, in order to support the development of the financial sector in the sub-Saharan region. In December 2010 the Bank signed an MOU with the Islamic Development Bank to promote economic development in common member countries through co-financing and co-ordinating projects in priority areas. It signed an MOU with the European Bank for Reconstruction and Development in September 2011. The Bank is actively involved in the New Partnership for Africa's Development (NEPAD), established in 2001 to promote sustainable development and eradicate poverty throughout the region. Since 2004 it has been a strategic partner in NEPAD's African Peer Review Mechanism. In 2007 the Bank approved an investment of US $50m. in the first edition of the Pan-African Development Fund (PAIDF 1), which supported the development of a joint AU-NEPAD Program for Infrastructure Development in Africa (PAID), investing in the continental energy, health care, ICT, sanitation, transport and water infrastructures.. In December 2013 the Board of Directors approved an equity participation of up to $25m. in PAIDF 2. In early 2014 the AfDB, the AU and ECA were jointly developing Agenda 2063, a vision to guide the economic and social transformation of Africa during the next 50 years, within the context of which a series of African Development Goals (ADGs) were being formulated. Agenda 2063 was to be finalized by June 2014. In May 2013 the Board of Governors endorsed a new Africa50Fund, which was to finance, in partnership with regional institutions, transformational projects with a focus on enhancing the trans-continental infrastructure.

AFRICAN DEVELOPMENT BANK

The Bank makes loans at a variable rate of interest, which is adjusted twice a year, plus a commitment fee of 0.75%. Lending approved amounted to UA 2,080.5m. for 48 operations in 2012, including resources allocated under the HIPC debt relief initiative, the Post-conflict Country Facility, and equity participations, compared with UA 3,689.4m., for 59 operations, in the previous year. Lending for private sector projects amounted to UA 753m. in 2012. Since October 1997 fixed and floating rate loans have been made available.

AFRICAN DEVELOPMENT FUND

The Fund commenced operations in 1974. It grants interest-free loans to low-income African countries for projects with repayment over 50 years (including a 10-year grace period) and with a service charge of 0.75% per annum. Grants for project feasibility studies are made to the poorest countries.

In October 2010 donor countries agreed to increase contributions to the Fund by 10.6%, to some US $9,350m., covering the period 2011–13 (ADF-12). ADF-12 was to support ongoing institutional reform and capacity building, as well as efforts to stimulate economic growth in Africa's lowest income countries. Operational priorities included climate change adaptation and mitigation measures, regional economic integration, and private sector development. The first replenishment meeting for ADF-13 was held in Tunis, Tunisia, in February 2013 and a second meeting was held in June. In late September 27 donor countries concluded an agreement on ADF-13, replenishing the Fund by $7,300m. for the period 2014-15.

In 2012 lending under the ADF amounted to UA 1,890.2m. for 98 projects, compared with UA 1,831.9m. for 87 projects in the previous year.

NIGERIA TRUST FUND

The Agreement establishing the NTF was signed in February 1976 by the Bank and the Government of Nigeria. The Fund is administered by the Bank and its loans are granted for up to 25 years, including grace periods of up to five years, and carry 0.75% commission charges and 4% interest charges. The loans are intended to provide financing for projects in co-operation with other lending institutions. The Fund also aims to promote the private sector and trade between African countries by providing information on African and international financial institutions able to finance African trade.

Operations under the NTF were suspended in 2006, pending a detailed assessment and consideration of the Fund's activities which commenced in November. The evaluation exercise was concluded in July 2007 and an agreement was reached in November to authorize the Fund to continue activities for a further 10-year period. Three operations, amounting to UA 14.1m., were approved in 2012.

Publications

Annual Development Effectiveness Review.
AfDB Business Bulletin (10 a year).
AfDB Statistics Pocketbook.
African Competitiveness Report.
African Development Report (annually).
African Development Review (3 a year).
African Economic Outlook (annually, with OECD).
Annual Report.
African Statistical Journal (2 a year).
Annual Procurement Report.
Compendium of Statistics on Bank Group Operations (annually).
Economic Research Papers.
Gender, Poverty and Environmental Indicators on African Countries (annually).
OPEV Sharing (quarterly newsletter).
Quarterly Operational Summary.
Selected Statistics on African Countries (annually).
Summaries of operations and projects, background documents, Board documents.

Statistics

SUMMARY OF BANK GROUP OPERATIONS
(millions of UA)

	2011	2012	Cumulative total*
AfDB approvals†			
Number	59	48	1,366
Amount	3,689.43	2,080.46	41,777.96
Disbursements	1,868.79	2,208.17	24,618.55
ADF approvals†			
Number	87	98	2,572
Amount	1,831.86	1,890.17	29,430.22
Disbursements	1,296.65	1,169.60	17,268.11
NTF approvals			
Number	3	3	85
Amount	10.88	14.10	396.31
Disbursements	8.67	1.76	237.50
Special Funds‡			
Number	35	50	158
Amount approved	188.12	269.00	598.30
Group total†			
Number	184	199	4,184
Amount approved	5,720.29	4,253.75	72,202.76
Disbursements	3,174.11	3,379.53	42,124.15

* Since the initial operations of the three institutions (1967 for the AfDB, 1974 for the ADF and 1976 for the NTF).
† Approvals include loans and grant operations, private and public equity investments, emergency operations, HIPC debt relief, loan reallocations and guarantees, the Post-Conflict Country Facility and the Fragile States Facility.
‡ Includes the African Water Fund, the Rural Water Supply and Sanitation Initiative, the Global Environment Facility, the Congo Basin Forest Fund, the Fund for African Private Sector Assistance, and the Migration and Development Trust Fund.

BANK GROUP APPROVALS BY SECTOR, 2012

Sector	Number of projects	Amount (millions of UA)
Agriculture and rural development	20	308.1
Social	21	535.3
Education	8	191.6
Health	6	3.7
Other	7	330.1
Infrastructure	46	1,763.5
Water supply and sanitation	13	269.7
Energy supply	14	889.7
Communication	—	—
Transportation	19	604.2
Finance	4	402.8
Multisector	43	505.4
Industry, mining and quarrying	1	97.7
Environment	—	—
Total (loans and grants)	135	3,602.8
HIPC debt relief	5	248.0
Equity participations	9	133.9
Special funds	50	269.0
Other approvals	64	650.9
Total approvals	199	4,253.8

Source: African Development Bank, *Annual Report 2012*.

AFRICAN UNION—AU

Address: Roosevelt St, Old Airport Area, POB 3243, Addis Ababa, Ethiopia.

Telephone: (11) 5517700; **fax:** (11) 5517844; **e-mail:** webmaster@africa-union.org; **internet:** au.int.

In May 2001 the Constitutive Act of the African Union entered into force. In July 2002 the AU became fully operational, replacing the Organization of African Unity (OAU), which had been founded in 1963. The AU aims to support unity, solidarity and peace among African states; to promote and defend African common positions on issues of shared interest; to encourage human rights, democratic principles and good governance; to advance the development of member states by encouraging research and by working to eradicate preventable diseases; and to promote sustainable development and political and socio-economic integration, including co-ordinating and harmonizing policy between the continent's various 'regional economic communities'.

MEMBERS*

Algeria	Eritrea	Nigeria
Angola	Ethiopia	Rwanda
Benin	Gabon	São Tomé and Príncipe
Botswana	The Gambia	Senegal
Burkina Faso	Ghana	Seychelles
Burundi	Guinea	Sierra Leone
Cameroon	Guinea-Bissau	Somalia
Cape Verde	Kenya	South Africa
Central African Republic†	Lesotho	South Sudan
Chad	Liberia	Sudan
Comoros	Libya	Swaziland
Congo, Democratic Republic	Madagascar	Tanazania
Congo, Republic	Malawi	Togo
Côte d'Ivoire	Mali	Tunisia
Dijbouti	Mauritania	Uganda
Egypt†	Mauritius	Zambia
Equatorial Guinea	Mozambique	Zimbabwe
	Namibia	
	Niger	

* The Sahrawi Arab Democratic Republic (SADR–Western Sahara) was admitted to the OAU in February 1982, following recognition by more than one-half of the member states, but its membership was disputed by Morocco and other states which claimed that a two-thirds' majority was needed to admit a state whose existence was in question. Morocco withdrew from the OAU with effect from November 1985, and has not applied to join the AU. The SADR ratified the Constitutive Act in December 2000 and is a full member of the AU.

† In April 2012 Guinea-Bissau was suspended from participation in meetings of the Union following a military coup, pending the restoration of constitutional order. In March 2013 the Central African Republic's participation was suspended, also after a military coup. Following the overthrow of the elected Egyptian regime in July of that year, that country was also suspended from participation in meetings of the Union.

Note: The Constitutive Act stipulates that member states in which Governments accede to power by unconstitutional means are liable to suspension from participating in the Union's activities and to the imposition of sanctions by the Union.

Organization

(April 2014)

ASSEMBLY

The Assembly, comprising heads of state and government, is the supreme organ of the Union and meets at least once a year (with alternate sessions held in Addis Ababa, Ethiopia) to determine and monitor the Union's priorities and common policies and to adopt its annual work programme. Resolutions are passed by a two-thirds' majority, procedural matters by a simple majority. Extraordinary sessions may be convened at the request of a member state and on approval by a two-thirds' majority. A chairperson is elected at each meeting from among the members, to hold office for one year. The Assembly ensures compliance by member states with decisions of the Union, adopts the biennial budget, appoints judges of the African Court of Human and Peoples' Rights, and hears and settles disputes between member states. The first regular Assembly meeting was held in Durban, South Africa, in July 2002, and a first extraordinary summit meeting of the Assembly was convened in Addis Ababa in February 2003. An extraordinary session of the Assembly took place in October 2013, in Addis Ababa, with a focus on 'Africa's relationship with the International Criminal Court'. The 22nd ordinary session of the Assembly was held in January 2014, also in Addis Ababa, on the theme 'Agriculture and Food Security'.

Chairperson: (2014/15) MOHAMED OULD ABDEL AZIZ (Pres. of Mauritania).

EXECUTIVE COUNCIL

Consists of ministers responsible for foreign affairs and others and meets at least twice a year (in February and July), with provision for extraordinary sessions. The Council's Chairperson is the minister of foreign affairs (or another competent authority) of the country that has provided the Chairperson of the Assembly. Prepares meetings of, and is responsible to, the Assembly. Determines the issues to be submitted to the Assembly for decision, co-ordinates and harmonizes the policies, activities and initiatives of the Union in areas of common interest to member states, and monitors the implementation of policies and decisions of the Assembly.

PERMANENT REPRESENTATIVES COMMITTEE

The Committee, which comprises ambassadors accredited to the AU, meets at least once a month. It is responsible to the Executive Council, which it advises, and whose meetings, including matters for the agenda and draft decisions, it prepares.

COMMISSION

The Commission is the permanent secretariat of the organization. It comprises a Chairperson (elected for a four-year term of office by the Assembly), Deputy Chairperson and eight Commissioners (responsible for peace and security; political affairs; infrastructure and energy; social affairs; human resources, science and technology; trade and industry; rural economy and agriculture; and economic affairs) who are elected on the basis of equal geographical distribution. Members of the Commission serve a term of four years and may stand for re-election for one further term of office. The Commission represents the Union under the guidance of, and as mandated by, the Assembly and the Executive Council, and reports to the Executive Council. It deals with administrative issues, implements the decisions of the Union, and acts as the custodian of the Constitutive Act and Protocols, and other agreements. Its work covers the following domains: control of pandemics; disaster management; international crime and terrorism; environmental management; negotiations relating to external trade; negotiations relating to external debt; population, migration, refugees and displaced persons; food security; socio-economic integration; and all other areas where a common position has been established by Union member states. It has responsibility for the co-ordination of AU activities and meetings.

Chairperson: Dr NKOSAZANA DLAMINI-ZUMA (South Africa).

SPECIALIZED TECHNICAL COMMITTEES

There are specialized committees for monetary and financial affairs; rural economy and agricultural matters; trade, customs and immigration matters; industry, science and technology, energy, natural resources and environment; infrastructure; transport, communications and tourism; health, labour and social affairs; and education, culture and human resources. These have responsibility for implementing the Union's programmes and projects.

PAN-AFRICAN PARLIAMENT

The Pan-African Parliament comprises five deputies (including at least one woman) from each AU member state, presided over by an elected President assisted by four Vice-Presidents. The President and Vice-Presidents must equitably represent the central, northern, eastern, southern and western African states. The Parliament convenes at least twice a year; an extraordinary session may be called by a two-thirds' majority of the members. The Parliament currently has only advisory and consultative powers. Its eventual evolution into an institution with full legislative authority is planned. The Parliament is located in Midrand, South Africa.

President: BETHEL NNAEMEKA AMADI (Nigeria).

AFRICAN COURT OF JUSTICE AND HUMAN RIGHTS

An African Court of Human and Peoples' Rights (ACHPR) was created following the entry into force in January 2004 of the Protocol to the African Charter on Human and Peoples' Rights Establishing the ACHPR (adopted in June 1998). In February 2009 a protocol (adopted in July 2003) establishing an African Court of Justice entered into force. The Protocol on the Statute of the African Court of Justice and Human Rights, aimed at merging the ACHPR and the

African Court of Justice, was opened for signature in July 2008, and had, by April 2014, been ratified by five states.

PEACE AND SECURITY COUNCIL

The Protocol to the Constitutive Act of the African Union Relating to the Peace and Security Council of the African Union entered into force on 26 December 2003; the 15-member elected Council was formally inaugurated in May 2004. It acts as a decision-making body for the prevention, management and resolution of conflicts.

ECONOMIC, SOCIAL AND CULTURAL COUNCIL

The Economic, Social and Cultural Council (ECOSOCC), inaugurated in March 2005, was to have an advisory function and to comprise representatives of civic, professional and cultural bodies at national, regional and diaspora levels. Its main organs were to be an elected General Assembly; Standing Committee; Credential Committee; and Sectoral Cluster Communities, to formulate opinions and influence AU decision-making in the following 10 areas: peace and security; political affairs; infrastructure and energy; social affairs and health; human resources, science and technology; trade and industry; rural economy and agriculture; economic affairs; women and gender; and cross-cutting programmes. It is envisaged that the Council will strengthen the partnership between member governments and African civil society. The General Assembly was inaugurated in September 2008.

NEW PARTNERSHIP FOR AFRICA'S DEVELOPMENT (NEPAD)

NEPAD Planning and Co-ordination Agency (NPCA): POB 1234, Halfway House, Midrand, 1685 South Africa; tel. (11) 256-3600; fax (11) 206-3762; e-mail media@nepad.org; internet www.nepad.org; f. Feb. 2010, as a technical body of the AU, to replace the former NEPAD Secretariat, with the aim of improving the country-level implementation of projects; NEPAD was launched in 2001 as a long-term strategy to promote socio-economic development in Africa; adopted Declaration on Democracy, Political, Economic and Corporate Governance and the African Peer Review Mechanism in June 2002; the July 2003 AU Maputo summit decided that NEPAD should be integrated into AU structures and processes; a special 'Brainstorming on NEPAD' summit, held in Algiers, Algeria in March 2007, issued a 13-point communiqué on the means of reforming the Partnership; a further Review Summit on NEPAD, convened in Dakar, Senegal, in April 2008, reaffirmed the centrality of NEPAD as the overarching developmental programme for Africa; principal thematic areas of activity in 2014 were Agriculture and food security; Climate change and natural resource management; Regional integration and infrastructure; Human development; and Economic and corporate governance; major cross-cutting issues were: Gender, Capacity development, and ICT; the UN allocated US $17m. in support of NEPAD under its 2014–15 budget; CEO Dr IBRAHIM ASSANE MAYAKI.

PROPOSED INSTITUTIONS

In 2014 three financial institutions, for managing the financing of programmes and projects, remained to be established: an African Central Bank; an African Monetary Fund; and an African Investment Bank. In January 2014 the Executive Council determined that the headquarters of a proposed African Institute for Remittances should be located in Kenya. The establishment of the Institute, agreed in 2010, was being supported by the European Commission, World Bank, International Organization for Migration and the African Development Bank.

Activities

In May 1963 30 African heads of state adopted the Charter of the Organization of African Unity (OAU). In May 1994 the Abuja Treaty Establishing the African Economic Community (AEC, signed in June 1991) entered into force.

An extraordinary summit meeting, convened in September 1999, in Sirte, Libya, at the request of the then Libyan leader Col Muammar al-Qaddafi, determined to establish an African Union, based on the principles and objectives of the OAU and AEC, but furthering African co-operation, development and integration. Heads of state declared their commitment to accelerating the establishment of regional institutions, including a pan-African parliament, a court of human and peoples' rights and a central bank, as well as the implementation of economic and monetary union, as provided for by the Abuja Treaty Establishing the AEC. In July 2000 at the annual OAU summit meeting, held at Lomé, Togo, 27 heads of state and government signed the draft Constitutive Act of the African Union, which was to enter into force one month after ratification by two-thirds of member states' legislatures; this was achieved on 26 May 2001. The Union was inaugurated, replacing the OAU, on 9 July 2002, at a summit meeting of heads of state and government held in Durban, South Africa, after a transitional period of one year had elapsed since the endorsement of the Act in July 2001. During the transitional year, pending the transfer of all assets and liabilities to the Union, the OAU Charter remained in effect. A review of all OAU treaties was implemented, and those deemed relevant were retained by the AU. The four key organs of the AU were launched in July 2002. Morocco is the only African country that is not a member of the AU. The AU aims to strengthen and advance the process of African political and socio-economic integration initiated by the OAU. The Union operates on the basis of both the Constitutive Act and the Abuja Treaty.

The AU has the following areas of interest: peace and security; political affairs; infrastructure and energy; social affairs; human resources, science and technology; trade and industry; rural economy and agriculture; and economic affairs. In July 2001 the OAU adopted a New African Initiative, which was subsequently renamed the New Partnership for Africa's Development (NEPAD). NEPAD, which was officially launched in October, represents a long-term strategy for socio-economic recovery in Africa and aims to promote the strengthening of democracy and economic management in the region. The heads of state of Algeria, Egypt, Nigeria, Senegal and South Africa played leading roles in its preparation and management. In June 2002 NEPAD heads of state and government adopted a Declaration on Democracy, Political, Economic and Corporate Governance and announced the development of an African Peer Review Mechanism (APRM). Meeting during that month the Group of Seven industrialized nations and Russia (known as the G8) welcomed the formation of NEPAD and adopted an Africa Action Plan in support of the initiative. The inaugural summit of the AU Assembly, held in Durban, in July 2002, issued a Declaration on the Implementation of NEPAD, which urged all member states to adopt the Declaration on Democracy, Political, Economic and Corporate Governance and to participate in the peer review process. By 2014 some 16 nations had joined the APRM process, which was assessing states' conduct in the areas of democracy and political governance; economic governance and management; corporate governance; and socio-economic development. The summit meeting of the AU Assembly convened in Maputo, Mozambique, in July 2003 determined that NEPAD should be integrated into AU structures and processes. In March 2007 a special NEPAD summit held in Algiers, Algeria, issued a 13-point communiqué on the best means of achieving this objective without delay. The centrality of NEPAD as the overarching developmental programme for Africa was reaffirmed by a further summit meeting, convened in Dakar, Senegal, in April 2008, which also published a number of further key decisions aimed at guiding the future orientation of the Partnership. In February 2010 African leaders approved the establishment of the NEPAD Planning and Co-ordination Agency (NPCA), a technical body of the AU, to replace the former NEPAD Secretariat, with the aim of improving the implementation of projects at country level. The Chairperson of the African Union Commission (AUC) exercises supervisory authority over the NPCA. NEPAD's Programme for Infrastructure Development in Africa (PIDA), of which the African Development Bank (AfDB) is the executing agency, aims to develop the continental energy, information and communications technology (ICT), transport and transboundary water resources infrastructures. Some 80 programmes and projects aimed at regional integration, with a particular focus on developing the continental infrastructure, were being undertaken in the context of an AU/NEPAD African Action Plan (AAP) covering the period 2010–15.

The eighth AU Assembly, held in January 2007 in Cairo, Egypt, adopted a decision on the need for a 'Grand Debate on the Union Government', concerned with the possibility of establishing an AU Government as a precursor to the eventual creation of a United States of Africa. The ninth Assembly, convened in July in Accra, Ghana, adopted the Accra Declaration, in which AU heads of state and government expressed commitment to the formation of a Union Government of Africa and ultimate aim of creating a United States of Africa, and pledged, as a means to this end, to accelerate the economic and political integration of the African continent; to rationalize, strengthen and harmonize the activities of the regional economic communities; to conduct an immediate audit of the organs of the AU ('Audit of the Union'); and to establish a ministerial committee to examine the concept of the Union Government. A panel of eminent persons was subsequently established to conduct the proposed institutional Audit of the Union; the panel became operational at the beginning of September, and presented its review to the 10th Assembly, which was held in January–February 2008 in Addis Ababa, Ethiopia. A committee comprising 10 heads of state was appointed to consider the findings detailed in the review.

In March 2005 the UN Secretary-General issued a report on the functioning of the UN which included a clause urging donor nations to focus particularly on the need for a 10-year plan for capacity building within the AU. The UN System-wide Support to the AU and

NEPAD was launched in 2006, following on from the UN System-wide Special Initiative on Africa, which had been undertaken over the decade 1996–2005.

In May 2012, with a view to increasing the involvement in the African development agenda of people of African origin living beyond the continent, the AU hosted the first Global African Diaspora Summit, in Midrand, South Africa.

In May 2013 the 21st ordinary session of the Assembly, which commemorated 50 years since the 1963 foundation of the former OAU, adopted a Strategic Plan to guide the activities of the Union during 2014–17. The Plan focused on the following priority areas: human capacity development in health, education, research, science, technology and innovation; agriculture and agro processing; inclusive economic development through industrialization, infrastructure development, agriculture and trade and investment; peace, stability and good governance; mainstreaming women and youth into all activities; resource mobilization; building a people-centred AU through active communication and branding; and strengthening the institutional capacity of the Union and its organs. In January 2014 AU heads of state and government adopted the Common African Position Document on the Post-2015 Development Agenda.

AGENDA 2063

The May 2013 session of the Assembly issued a 50th Anniversary Solemn Declaration, in which African heads of state and government outlined a vision and eight ideals to represent pillars for the economic and social transformation of the continent over the coming 50 years. These were to be translated into concrete actions and objectives by a joint AU-AfDB-Economic Commission for Africa (ECA) programme known as Agenda 2063, which in early 2014 was being drafted by the three pan-African bodies. Within the context of Agenda 2063, which was to be finalized by June 2014, a series of African Development Goals (ADGs) were being formulated. In May 2013 the AfDB endorsed a new Africa50Fund, which was to finance, in partnership with regional institutions, transformational projects with a focus on enhancing the trans-continental infrastructure.

PEACE AND SECURITY

The Protocol to the Constitutive Act of the African Union Relating to the Establishment of the Peace and Security Council, adopted by the inaugural AU summit of heads of state and government in July 2002, entered into force in December 2003, superseding the 1993 Cairo Declaration on the OAU Mechanism for Conflict Prevention, Management and Resolution. The Protocol provides for the development of a collective peace and security framework (known as the African Peace and Security Architecture). This includes a 15-country Peace and Security Council, operational at the levels of heads of state and government, ministers responsible for foreign affairs, and permanent representatives, to be supported by a five-member advisory Panel of the Wise, a Continental Early Warning System, an African Standby Force (ASF) and a Peace Fund (superseding the OAU Peace Fund, which was established in June 1993). In March 2004 the Executive Council elected 15 member states to serve on the inaugural Peace and Security Council. The activities of the Peace and Security Council include the promotion of peace, security and stability; early warning and preventive diplomacy; peacemaking mediation; peace support operations and intervention; peacebuilding activities and post-conflict reconstruction; and humanitarian action and disaster management. The Council was to implement the common defence policy of the Union, and to ensure the implementation of the 1999 OAU Convention on the Prevention and Combating of Terrorism (which provided for the exchange of information to help to counter terrorism and for signatory states to refrain from granting asylum to terrorists). Member states were to set aside standby troop contingents for the planned ASF, which was to be mandated to undertake observation, monitoring and other peace support missions; to deploy in member states as required to prevent the resurgence or escalation of violence; to intervene in member states as required to restore stability; to conduct post-conflict disarmament and demobilization and other peacebuilding activities; and to provide emergency humanitarian assistance. The Council was to harmonize and co-ordinate the activities of other regional security mechanisms. An extraordinary AU summit meeting, convened in Sirte, in February 2004, adopted a declaration approving the establishment of the multinational ASF, comprising five regional brigades—the Central African Multinational Force, the Eastern Africa Standby Force, the Economic Community of West Africa (ECOWAS) Standby Force, the North African Regional Capability, and the Southern African Development Community (SADC) Standby Brigade—to be deployed in African-led peace support operations. A Policy Framework Document on the establishment of the ASF and the Military Staff Committee was approved by the third regular summit of AU heads of state, held in July 2004. It was envisaged that the ASF, which is composed of rapidly deployable multidimensional military, police and civilian capabilities, would become fully operational by 2015. In October 2010 the ASF conducted an exercise known as 'AMANI AFRICA', with pan-continental participation, in Addis Ababa. A roadmap on achieving the full operationalization of the ASF (ASF Roadmap III) was finalized in April 2011.

The extraordinary OAU summit meeting convened in Sirte, in September 1999 determined to hold a regular ministerial Conference on Security, Stability, Development and Co-operation in Africa (CSSDCA): the first CSSDCA took place in Abuja, Nigeria, in May 2000. The CSSDCA process provides a forum for the development of policies aimed at advancing the common values of the AU and AEC in the areas of peace, security and co-operation. In December 2000 OAU heads of state and government adopted the Bamako Declaration, concerned with arresting the circulation of small arms and light weapons (SALW) on the continent. It was envisaged that the Central African Convention for the Control of SALW, their Ammunition, Parts and Components that can be used for their Manufacture, Repair or Assembly (Kinshasa Convention), adopted by Central African states in April 2010, would contribute to the AU's SALW control capacity. In September 2011 AU member states, met in Lomé, to debate a draft strategy on SALW control and to elaborate an African Common Position on global negotiations towards a comprehensive Arms Trade Treaty (ATT, to guide trade in conventional weapons). In May 2012 an African Regional Consultation on the ATT was organized at AU headquarters by the Regional Centre for Peace and Disarmament in Africa (UNREC, a subsidiary of the UN Office for Disarmament Affairs). The ATT was eventually adopted by the UN General Assembly in April 2013.

In January 2005 the AU Non-Aggression and Common Defence Pact was adopted to promote co-operation in developing a common defence policy and to encourage member states to foster an attitude of non-aggression. The Pact, which entered into force in December 2009, establishes measures aimed at preventing inter- and intra-state conflicts and arriving at peaceful resolutions to conflicts. It also sets out a framework defining, inter alia, the terms 'aggression' and 'intervention' and determining those situations in which intervention may be considered an acceptable course of action. As such, the Pact stipulates that an act, or threat, of aggression against an individual member state is to be considered an act, or threat, of aggression against all members states.

In recent years the AU has been involved in peacemaking and peacebuilding activities in several African countries and regions. An AU Special Representative on Protection of Civilians in Armed Conflict Situations in Africa was appointed in September 2004. Since July 2006 an AU Policy on Post-Conflict Reconstruction and Development (PRCD) has been pursued since July 2006. In July 2012 a new African Solidarity Initiative was launched, with the aim of mobilizing support among member states for countries emerging from conflict, in line with the PCRD.

In April 2006, following talks in Abuja, AU mediators submitted a proposed peace agreement to representatives of the Sudanese Government and rebel groups; the so-called Darfur Peace Agreement (DPA) was signed on 5 May. In August the UN Security Council expanded the mandate of the then UN Mission in Sudan (UNMIS) to provide for its deployment to Darfur, in order to enforce a cease-fire and support the implementation of DPA. The Council also requested the UN Secretary-General to devise jointly with the AU, in consultation with the parties to the DPA, a plan and schedule for a transition from AMIS to a sole UN operation in Darfur. The Sudanese Government, however, initially rejected the concept of an expanded UN peacekeeping mission, on the grounds that it would compromise national sovereignty. Eventually, in late December, the UN, the AU and the Sudanese Government established a tripartite mechanism which was to facilitate the implementation of a UN-formulated three-phase approach, endorsed by the AU Peace and Security Council in November, that would culminate in a hybrid AU/UN mission in Darfur. In January 2007 UNMIS provided AMIS with supplies and extra personnel under the first ('light') phase of the approach; the second ('heavy') phase, finalized in that month, was to involve the delivery of force enablers, police units, civilian personnel and mission support items. UNMIS continued to make efforts to engage the non-signatories of the DPA in the political process in Darfur. In June the AU and UN special representatives for Darfur defined a political roadmap to lead eventually to full negotiations in support of a peaceful settlement to the sub-regional conflict. In August the first AU/UN-chaired 'pre-negotiation' discussions with those rebel groups in Darfur that were not party to the DPA approved an agreement on co-operation in attempting to secure a settlement.

In June 2007 the Sudanese Government agreed to support unconditionally the deployment of the AU/UN Hybrid Operation in Darfur (UNAMID); UNAMID was authorized by the UN Security Council in the following month, with a mandate to take necessary action to support the implementation and verification of the May 2006 Darfur Peace Agreement, to protect civilians, to provide security for humanitarian assistance, to support an inclusive political process, to contribute to the promotion of human rights and rule of law, and to monitor and report on the situation along the borders with Chad and the Central African Republic (CAR). UNAMID assumed command of AMIS in December 2007. An AU-UN Joint Mediation Support Team for Darfur (JMST) and a Tripartite Committee on UNAMID (including representatives of the AU, the UN and the Government of Sudan), meet periodically. A joint AU-UN Chief Mediator, based at UNAMID headquarters in El Fasher, was appointed in June 2008. A Joint Support Co-ordination Mechanism (JSCM) Office in Addis Ababa, comprising liaison officers and communications equipment, was established in November to ensure effective consultation between AU headquarters and the UN. In March 2009 an AU High-Level Panel on Darfur was established to address means of securing peace, justice, and reconciliation in Darfur. The panel issued a report of its findings and recommendations in October; a key recommendation was the creation of a hybrid court, comprising both AU and Sudanese judges, to prosecute crimes against humanity committed in Darfur. During October a new AU High-Level Implementation Panel (AUHIP) on Sudan was established, with a mandate to support the implementation of all AUPD recommendations, and to assist the relevant Sudanese parties with the implementation of the January 2005 CPA. (See under UN Peacekeeping for further information on UNAMID and joint AU-UN progress towards achieving peace in Sudan.)

From January 2011, when a referendum was held on future self-determination for South Sudan, violent tensions escalated significantly in Abyei, and had, by July, when South Sudan's independence was achieved, displaced some 113,000 people. In July UNMIS was succeeded by the UN Mission in South Sudan (UNMISS). A further UN mission, the UN Interim Security Force for Abyei (UNISFA), was established in June. The 'Temporary Arrangements for the Administration and Security of the Abyei Area'—an accord adopted in mid-June by the Sudanese Government and rebels, governing the withdrawal of their respective forces from Abyei—vested responsibility for supervising security and stability in the region in an Abyei Joint Oversight Committee, comprising members from each party to the conflict, and also an AU Facilitator. From January 2012 relations between South Sudan and Sudan deteriorated significantly. In early April the AUHIP, facilitating discussions between the two sides, presented to both parties a draft Joint Decision for Reduction of Tension, providing for the immediate cessation of hostilities and the withdrawal of armed forces of each state from the territory of the other. In accordance with a seven-point Roadmap for Action by Sudan and South Sudan, approved in late April by the AU Peace and Security Council, and aimed at normalizing relations between the two states, both militaries were withdrawn from Abyei by the end of May. (See UNISFA for further details.)

In January 2007 the Peace and Security Council authorized the deployment of an AU Mission in Somalia (AMISOM), with a mandate to contribute to the political stabilization of Somalia. In the following month the UN Security Council endorsed AMISOM, and proposed that it should eventually be superseded by a UN operation focusing on the post-conflict restoration of that country. AMISOM became operational in May 2007. In mid-September 2009 the AU strongly condemned terrorist attacks that were perpetrated against the AMISOM headquarters in Mogadishu, Somalia, killing more than 20 people, including the Deputy Force Commander of the Mission, and injuring a further 40. In October 2010 Flt Lt Jerry Rawlings, the former President of Ghana, was appointed as the AU High Representative on Somalia. AMISOM reached its then mandated strength of 8,000 troops in November 2010. In the following month the UN Security Council, concerned at continuing unrest and terrorist attacks, requested the AU to increase the mission's numbers to 12,000. In January 2012 the Peace and Security Council adopted a Strategic Concept for future AMISOM Operations, and in late February the Security Council voted unanimously to enhance the mission further, to comprise 17,731 troops, and to expand its areas of operation. At that time the Council also banned trade in charcoal with Somalia, having identified that commodity as a significant source of revenue for militants. In November 2013 the UN Security Council extended AMISOM's mandate until October 2014 and requested that the AU increase its troop strength to 22,136 for a period of 18–24 months, with a view to improving its efficacy against the militant group al-Shabaab—'The Youth'.

In November 2008 the AU and International Conference on the Great Lakes Region (ICGLR) jointly convened, in Nairobi, Kenya, with participation by the UN Secretary-General, a regional summit on ongoing heightened insecurity in eastern regions of the DRC. Meeting on the sidelines of the July 2012 Assembly summit, the Presidents of the Democratic Republic of the Congo (DRC) and Rwanda agreed in principle to the deployment in eastern DRC of an international force with a mandate to suppress armed rebels active in that area. Meanwhile the AU Commission Chairperson stated the willingness of the AU to contribute to such a force. Following the launching by opposition 'M23' forces of an offensive in North Kivu on 19 November 2012 the AU Peace and Security Council issued a communiqué requesting an immediate, unconditional end to the hostilities. In late February 2013 the AU hosted a summit meeting at which heads of state of 11 African countries signed a Peace, Security and Cooperation Framework for the DRC and the Region, which aimed to stabilize the Great Lakes area. With the UN, SADC and the ICGLR, the AU was to act as a guarantor of the Framework, in an 11+4 format. The signatories to the Framework committed to protect the future territorial sovereignty and the peace and stability of the DRC. In late March the UN Security Council authorized the establishment of a new Force Intervention Brigade (FIB), to be deployed under the umbrella of the existing UN Organization Stabilization Mission in the DRC, with a mandate to confront urgent threats to security in eastern areas of the country. The AU welcomed the defeat, in early November, of the M23, achieved by DRC armed forces with FIB assistance, while continuing to monitor the security situation in eastern DRC.

In November 2011 the Peace and Security Council authorized an AU Regional Cooperation Initiative for the Elimination of the Lord's Resistance Army (AU RCI-LRA), with three components: (i) a Joint Coordination Mechanism, based in Bangui, CAR, and chaired by the AU Commissioner for Peace and Security, with participation by the ministers responsible for defence of LRA-affected countries, and responsibility for strategic co-ordination with all affected states and actors; (ii) a 5,000-strong Regional Task Force (RTF), comprising national contingents from LRA-affected countries, headquartered in Yambio, South Sudan, with four liaison officers based at a Joint Intelligence and Operations Centre, in Dungu, DRC; and (iii) a Joint Operations Centre, reporting to the RTF Commander, and comprising 30 officers engaged in integrated planning and monitoring activities. The AU RCI-LRA was officially launched in March 2012. (The LRA is active in parts of Uganda, the CAR, the DRC and South Sudan.) An AU Special Envoy on the LRA, Francisco Caetano José Madeira (Director of the Algiers-based African Centre for Study and Research on Terrorism), was appointed in November 2011. In late October–early November 2013 the AU Special Envoy on the LRA and the Special Representative of the UN Secretary-General for Central Africa jointly visited Bangui, CAR, and Juba, South Sudan; they urged LRA combatants to cease their activities and return to normal life, and also to acknowledge the need to establish favourable conditions for the restoration of peace and security in the deeply destabilized CAR. During 2012–13 actions by the AU RCI-LRA reportedly achieved the removal of two of five main LRA commanders, as well as a downward turn in the numbers of LRA abductions and killings, and a significant increase in the number of defections from the rebel grouping.

Following the overthrow of the legitimate Government of Mali by the military in March 2012 that country was suspended (until November) from participation in AU activities. The AU Commission, recalling the 'fundamental principle of the intangibility of borders inherited by the African countries at their accession to independence' expressed its 'total rejection' of a unilateral declaration, made in early April by separatist militants of the National Movement for the Liberation of Azawad, who, supported by Islamist forces, had just seized land in the Kidal, Gao and Tombouctou regions of northern Mali, that this was, henceforth, to be known as the independent entity of Azawad. The Commission affirmed the AU's full support for efforts being undertaken by ECOWAS to protect Mali's unity and territorial integrity, both through mediation and through the then envisaged deployment there of an ESF presence in that country. In early September the Peace and Security Council expressed deep concern at the occupation of northern Mali by terrorist and militant groups, and condemned violations of human rights being committed there, while welcoming an initiative of the African Commission on Human and People's Rights to investigate the situation. The Council strongly condemned the activities of the Movement for Oneness and Jihad in West Africa, and condemned its reported presence in northern Mali. In October–November AU and ECOWAS leaders endorsed both a Strategic Concept for the Resolution of the Crisis in Mali, and a Joint Strategic Concept of Operations for the International Military Force and the Malian Defence and Security Forces. In December the UN Security Council approved a resolution authorizing the deployment, by September 2013, of an AU-led International Support Mission in Mali (AFISMA) for an initial period of one year. AFISMA was mandated to help to rebuild the capacity of Mali's security forces; to support the Malian authorities in reclaiming occupied northern areas of the country; and also to support the national authorities in establishing a secure environment for the delivery of humanitarian assistance and the voluntary return of displaced civilians. Owing to rapid territorial gains by the rebel forces in early January 2013, and the consequent declaration of a state of emergency by the Malian transitional authorities and deployment of French troops (Opération Serval) in support of the Malian security forces, AFISMA's deployment was advanced to mid-January. In April the UN Security Council authorized the deployment, from 1 July, of the UN Multidimensional Integrated Stabilization Mission in Mali (MINUSMA), superseding AFISMA. In June a long-term observer/expert mission was sent to Mali in advance of the two rounds of presidential elections that were held there in late July and early August.

In early July 2013, in response to the overthrow in a coup d'etat of the elected Egyptian president, Mohamed Morsi, the AU Peace and Security Council suspended Egypt from participation in meetings of the AU and authorized the establishment of an International Consultative Forum on Egypt (ICF-Egypt), also with Arab League and UN participation, to address and facilitate a co-ordinated response to the crisis. Furthermore, the Chairperson of the AU Commission immediately appointed an AU High-Level Panel for Egypt—under the leadership of Alpha Oumar Konaré, the former President of Mali and former Chairperson of the AU Commission—with a mandate to engage with Egyptian stakeholders, with a view to stimulating constructive political dialogue towards national reconciliation and a prompt return to constitutional order. The Panel aimed to consolidate advancements to the democratic process that had been attained since the popular uprising that had occurred in Egypt in January–February 2011 resulting in the overthrow of the authoritarian regime of former President Hosni Mubarak. The July 2013 suspension of Egypt represented the first suspension of one of the Union's principal financially contributing nations.

In response to mounting sectarian violence and human rights violations caused by a rebel offensive, initiated in December 2012, that culminated in the overturning of the legitimately elected CAR Government of President François Bozizé in March 2013 and the inauguration as President in August of the coup leader Michel Djotodia, the UN Security Council approved, in October, the deployment of a new peacekeeping force to the CAR. During October the AU Peace and Security Council adopted a concept of operations for the consequent AU-led International Support Mission to the CAR (MISCA). The UN Security Council authorized the deployment of MISCA in December. The mission—with support from a strengthened contingent of French troops that had already been stationed in the CAR—was mandated to use all necessary measures to protect civilians, to restore state authority and to support the provision of humanitarian assistance. An existing Mission for the Consolidation of Peace in the CAR (MICOPAX), which had operated under the auspices of the Communauté économique des états de l'Afrique centrale since July 2008, transferred authority to MISCA on 19 December. It was envisaged that authority over MISCA might eventually be transferred to the UN. In late January 2014 the UN Security Council authorized the deployment of a 1000-strong EU force in the CAR, tasked with securing part of Bangui, the capital, for the conduct of humanitarian operations; by late March, however, the EU operation had not yet commenced. In April, in view of the continuing crisis in the CAR, the UN Security Council authorized the creation of the UN Multidimensional Integrated Stabilization Mission in the Central African Republic (MINUSCA), which was mandated to protect civilians; as well as to support the ongoing transition process in the CAR; facilitate humanitarian assistance; promote and protect human rights; promote justice and the rule of law; and support disarmament, demobilization, reintegration and repatriation processes. From 15 September 2014 MINUSCA was to take over the military and policing functions of MISCA.

The EU assists the AU financially in the areas of peace and security, institutional development, governance, and regional economic integration and trade. In June 2004 the European Commission activated for the first time its newly established Africa Peace Facility (APF), which represents the main source of funding to the African peace and security agenda, and has, since 2007, provided short-term crisis response funding, as well as contributing to longer-term peace and security institutional capacity building in connection with the AU and other African regional economic communities, in the areas of conflict prevention, post-conflict stabilization, and accelerating decision making and co-ordination processes. During 2007–13 APF funds were channelled as follows: €600m. to peace support operations (the Fund's core area of activity); €100m. towards the operationalization of the African Peace and Security Architecture and Africa-EU dialogue; €40m. for unforeseen contingencies; and €15m. towards early response. It was announced in March 2012 that €11.4m. would be allocated through the APF over the period 1 February 2012–31 January 2014 towards the training of the ASF, and towards the establishment of an African e-library comprising documentation of relevance to the Force.

When activated the APF's Early Response Mechanism (ERM) provides, in crisis situations, financing within a deadline of two weeks in support of mediation and fact-finding missions. In May 2013 AU heads of state and government endorsed the African Immediate Crisis response Capacity (AICRC), which aims to to provide Africa with a highly reactive military capacity to be deployed promptly in crisis situations.

INFRASTRUCTURE, ENERGY AND THE ENVIRONMENT

Meeting in Lomé, in July 2001, OAU heads of state and government authorized the establishment of an African Energy Commission (AFREC), with the aim of increasing co-operation in energy matters between Africa and other regions. AFREC was launched in February 2008. It was envisaged at that time that an African Electrotechnical Standardization Commission would also become operational, as a subsidiary body of AFREC.

In 1964 the OAU adopted a Declaration on the Denuclearization of Africa, and in April 1996 it adopted the African Nuclear Weapons Free Zone Treaty (also known as the Pelindaba Treaty), which identifies Africa as a nuclear weapons-free zone and promotes co-operation in the peaceful uses of nuclear energy; the Pelindaba Treaty entered into force in July 2009.

In 1968 OAU member states adopted the African Convention on the Conservation of Nature and Natural Resources. The Bamako Convention on the Ban of the Import into Africa and the Control of Transboundary Movement and Management of Hazardous Wastes within Africa was adopted by OAU member states in 1991 and entered into force in April 1998.

In June 2010 a consultative meeting was convened between the AU, the Common Market for Eastern and Southern Africa (COMESA), the Intergovernmental Authority on Development (IGAD), and other regional partners, aimed at advancing co-ordination and harmonization of their activities governing the environment. It was envisaged that the AU would facilitate the development of a comprehensive African Environmental Framework, to guide pan-continental and regional economic community environmental activities. At that time the AU was in the process of integrating two regional fora—the African Ministerial Conference on Water (AMCOW) and the African Ministerial Conference on the Environment (AMCEN)—into its structures, as specialized institutes.

In February 2007 the first Conference of African Ministers responsible for Maritime Transport was convened to discuss maritime transport policy in the region. A draft declaration was submitted at the Conference, held in Abuja, outlining the AU's vision for a common maritime transport policy aimed at 'linking Africa' and detailing programmes for co-operation on maritime safety and security and the development of an integrated transport infrastructure. The subsequently adopted Abuja Maritime Transport Declaration formally provided for an annual meeting of ministers responsible for maritime transport, to be hosted by each region in turn. In July 2009 the AU Assembly decided to establish an African Agency for the Protection of Territorial and Economic Waters of African Countries. In June 2011 a task force was inaugurated to lead the development and implementation of a new '2050 Africa's Integrated Maritime Strategy' (2050 Aim-Strategy); the Strategy was to address maritime challenges affecting the continent, including the development of aquaculture and offshore renewable energy resources; unlawful activities, such as illegal fishing, acts of maritime piracy (particularly in the Gulfs of Aden and Guinea), and trafficking in arms and drugs; and environmental pressures, such as loss of biodiversity, degradation of the marine environment, and climate change. The first Conference of African Ministers responsible for Maritime-related Affairs was held in April 2012, alongside a workshop on developing the 2050 AIM-Strategy. In January 2014 AU heads of state and government adopted a 2050 AIM Strategic Plan of Action.

In January 2012 the Executive Council endorsed a new African Civil Aviation Policy; and also endorsed the African Action Plan for the UN 2011–20 Decade of Action on Road Safety.

In February 2009 AU heads of state adopted the Africa Mining Vision (AMV), which promotes the contribution of mining to sustainable local development, aiming to ensure that employees and communities benefit from industrial mining enterprises, and that priority is given to the protection of local environments. An African Minerals Development Centre, based in Maputo, with a mandate to implement the AMV, was inaugurated in December 2013.

POLITICAL AND SOCIAL AFFAIRS

The African Charter on Human and People's Rights, which was adopted by the OAU in 1981 and entered into force in October 1986, provided for the establishment of an 11-member African Commission on Human and People's Rights, based in Banjul, The Gambia. A Protocol to the Charter, establishing an African Court of People's and Human Rights, was adopted by the OAU Assembly of Heads of State in June 1998 and entered into force in January 2004. In February 2009 a protocol (adopted in July 2003) establishing an African Court of Justice entered into force. The Protocol on the Statute of the African Court of Justice and Human Rights, aimed at merging the African Court of Human and Peoples' Rights and the African Court of Justice, was opened for signature in July 2008. A further Protocol, relating to the Rights of Women, was adopted by the July 2003 Maputo Assembly. The African Charter on the Rights and Welfare of the Child was opened for signature in July 1990 and entered into force in November 1999. A Protocol to the Abuja Treaty Establishing the AEC relating to the Pan-African Parliament, adopted by the OAU in March 2001, entered into force in December 2003. The Parliament was inaugurated in March 2004 and was, initially, to exercise advisory and consultative powers only, although its eventual evolution into an institution with full legislative powers is envisaged. In March 2005 the advisory Economic, Social and Cultural Council was inaugurated.

In April 2003 AU ministers responsible for labour and social affairs requested the AU Commission to develop, in consultation with other stakeholders, a pan-African Social Policy Framework (SPF). The SPF, finalized in November 2008, identified the following thematic social issues: population and development; social protection; labour and employment; education; health; HIV/AIDS, tuberculosis (TB), malaria and other infectious diseases; the family; children, adolescents and youth; migration; agriculture, food and nutrition; ageing; disability; gender equality and women's empowerment; culture; urban development; environmental sustainability; the impact of globalization and trade liberalization; and good governance, anti-corruption and rule of law. The following areas of focus: drug abuse and crime prevention; civil conflict; foreign debt; and sport were given special consideration under the Framework. Recommendations were outlined in the SPF that were aimed at supporting AU member states in formulating and implementing national social policies.

The July 2002 inaugural summit meeting of AU heads of state and government adopted a Declaration Governing Democratic Elections in Africa, providing guidelines for the conduct of national elections in member states and outlining the AU's electoral observation and monitoring role. In April 2003 the AU Commission and the South African Independent Electoral Commission jointly convened an African Conference on Elections, Democracy and Governance. In February 2012 a new African Charter on Democracy, Elections and Governance entered into force, having been ratified at that time by 15 AU member states.

In recent years several large population displacements have occurred in Africa, mainly as a result of violent conflict. In 1969 OAU member states adopted the Convention Governing the Specific Aspects of Refugee Problems in Africa, which entered into force in June 1974 and had been ratified by 45 states at April 2014. The Convention promotes close co-operation with UNHCR. The AU maintains a Special Refugee Contingency Fund to provide relief assistance and to support repatriation activities, education projects, etc., for displaced people in Africa. In October 2009 AU member states participating in a regional Special Summit on Refugees, Returnees and internally displaced persons (IDPs) in Africa, convened in Kampala, Uganda, adopted the AU Convention for the Protection and Assistance of IDPs in Africa, the first legally binding international treaty providing legal protection and support to people displaced within their own countries by violent conflict and natural disasters; the Convention entered into force in December 2012, and by April 2014 had been ratified by 22 countries.

The AU aims to address pressing health issues affecting member states, including the eradication of endemic parasitic and infectious diseases and improving access to medicines. In May 2006, an AU Special Summit on HIV/AIDS, TB and Malaria was convened, in Abuja (following a previous summit, convened in March 2001). The Special Summit adopted the Abuja Call for Accelerated Action on HIV/AIDS, TB and Malaria, and, in September of that year AU ministers responsible for health adopted the Maputo Plan of Action for the Operationalisation of the Continental Policy Framework for Sexual and Reproductive Health, covering 2007–10, aimed at advancing the goal of achieving universal access to comprehensive sexual and reproductive health services in Africa; in July 2010 the Plan was extended over the period 2010–15. In January 2012 the 18th AU Assembly meeting decided to revitalize AIDS Watch Africa (AWA), an advocacy platform established in April 2001, and hitherto comprising several regional heads of states, to be henceforth an AU Heads of State and Government Advocacy and Accountability Platform with continent-wide representation. AWA's mandate was to be extended to cover, also, TB and malaria. In March 2012 NEPAD and UNAIDS signed an agreement on advancing sustainable responses to HIV/AIDS, health and development across Africa. In July 2013 AU heads of state and government, participating in a Special Summit on HIV/AIDS, TB and Malaria, convened in Abuja, issued the Abuja Declaration on Actions Towards the Elimination of HIV/AIDS, TB and Malaria in Africa by 2030, and determined to establish an African Centre for Disease Control and Prevention, to be based in Addis Ababa. An AU Scientific, Technical and Research Commission is based in Abuja.

In July 2004 the Assembly adopted the Solemn Declaration on Gender Equality in Africa (SDGEA), incorporating a commitment to reporting annually on progress made towards attaining gender equality. The first conference of ministers responsible for women's affairs and gender, convened in Dakar, in October 2005, adopted the Implementation Framework for the SDGEA, and Guidelines for Monitoring and Reporting on the SDGEA, in support of member states' reporting responsibilities. An African Girls and Young Women Dialogue with African Leaders, convened at the January 2014 AU Assembly, issued a set of recommendations detailing gender-based priorities and requirements in the context of the formulation of a post-2015 global development agenda.

The seventh AU summit, convened in Banjul, in July 2006, adopted the African Youth Charter, providing for the implementation of youth policies and strategies across Africa, with the aim of encouraging young African people to participate in the development of the region and to take advantage of increasing opportunities in education and employment. The Charter outlined the basic rights and responsibilities of youths, which were divided into four main categories: youth participation; education and skills development; sustainable livelihoods; and health and well-being. The Charter, which entered into force in August 2010, also details the obligations of member states towards young people. In September 2013 representatives of the AU, the AfDB, ECA and International Labour Organization (ILO), gathered at the AU headquarters, signed a declaration of intent on 'creating employment for accelerating youth development and empowerment' through a new Joint Youth Employment Initiative for Africa. A Youth Forum on Accelerating Youth Employment in Africa was convened on the sidelines of the January 2014 meeting of the AU Authority.

AU efforts to combat human trafficking are guided by the 2006 Ouagadougou Action Plan to Combat Trafficking in Human Beings. In June 2009 the AU launched AU COMMIT, a campaign aimed at raising the profile of human trafficking on the regional development agenda. It was estimated at that time that nearly 130,000 people in sub-Saharan Africa and 230,000 in North Africa and the Middle East had been recruited into forced labour, including sexual exploitation, as a result of trafficking; many had also been transported to Western Europe and other parts of the world.

In December 2012 the AU adopted a Plan of Action on Drug Control and Crime Prevention covering the period 2003–17.

In October 2013 an extraordinary summit of the AU Assembly, convened on the theme 'Africa's relationship with the International Criminal Court', determined that—in order to safeguard the constitutional order, stability and integrity of member states—no trial proceedings ought to be commenced or continued before any international court or tribunal against any serving AU head of state or government, or against anybody acting in such capacity, during her or his term of office. The summit specifically requested the Court to defer until after the expiry of their terms of office the indictments that were issued in 2011 against the serving President of Kenya, Uhuru Muigai Kenyatta, and his Vice-President, William Samoei Ruto, in relation to violent unrest that followed the December 2007 presidential elections there. The summit decided to convene an Executive Council Contact Group to engage with the UN Security Council on all concerns of the AU regarding its relationship with the Court, including the deferral of the Kenyan cases, and the arrest warrant issued by the Court in 2009 against President Omar al-Bashir of Sudan, concerning his alleged responsibility for the perpetration of war crimes in Darfur. Furthermore, the Assembly adopted, inter alia, a declaration of solidarity with Kenya in view of a terrorist attack perpetrated in September 2013 by al-Shabaab militants at a Nairobi shopping mall; and a declaration on the recent accidental sinking of a boat carrying African migrants to Europe in the vicinity of the Italian Mediterranean island of Lampedusa, causing more than 300 fatalities.

TRADE, INDUSTRY AND ECONOMIC CO-OPERATION

In April 2000 the first EU-Africa summit of heads of state and government was held in Cairo, with participation also by Morocco. The summit adopted the Cairo Plan of Action, which addressed areas including economic integration, trade and investment, private sector development in Africa, human rights and good governance, peace and security, and development issues such as education, health and food security. The second EU-Africa summit meeting was initially to have been held in April 2003 but was postponed, owing to disagreements concerning the participation of President Mugabe of Zimbabwe, against whom the EU had imposed sanctions. Held eventually (with participation by Mugabe) in December 2007, in Lisbon, Portugal, the second EU-Africa Summit adopted a Joint Africa-EU Strategy (JAES), outlining a long-term vision of the future partnership between the two regions. The third EU-Africa Summit, held in November 2010, in Tripoli, confirmed commitment to the JAES and adopted an action plan on co-operation, covering 2011–13. Enhancing the JAES and the implementation of agreed action programmes, and expanding engagement with civil society stakeholders, were on the agenda of the fourth Africa-EU Summit, convened in April 2014, in Brussels, Belgium. A fifth EU-Africa Business Forum was organized in September 2012, also in Brussels. A Joint Africa-EU Task Force meets regularly, most recently in October 2013, to consider areas of co-operation.

Co-operation between African states and the People's Republic of China is undertaken within the framework of the Forum on China-Africa Co-operation (FOCAC). The first FOCAC ministerial conference was held in October 2000; the second in December 2003; the third (organized alongside a China-Africa leaders' summit) in November 2006; the fourth in November 2009; and the fifth in July 2012. During the fifth FOCAC the Chinese President announced strengthened China-Africa co-operation in the following priority areas: support for sustainable development in Africa, including investment in the development of transnational and transregional infrastructure, agricultural technology, manufacturing, and small and medium-sized enterprises; implementation of an 'African Talents Program', which was to provide skills training; capacity building in meteorological infrastructure, in the protection and management of forests, and in water supply projects; and the implementation of a new 'Initiative on China-Africa Cooperative Partnership for Peace and Security'. Africa–USA trade is underpinned by the US African Growth and Opportunity Act, adopted in May 2000 to promote the development of free market economies in Africa. Regular Africa-EU and Africa-South America ('ASA') summits are convened. The second ASA summit, convened by the AU and Union of South American Nations—UNASUR in Porlamar, Margarita Island, Venezuela, in September 2009, adopted the Margarita Declaration and Action Plan, covering issues of common concern, including combating climate change, and developing an alternative financial mechanism to address the global economic crisis. The third ASA summit took place in May 2012, in Malabo, Equatorial Guinea.

The AU aims to reduce obstacles to intra-African trade and to reverse the continuing disproportionate level of trade conducted by many African countries with their former colonial powers. In June 2005 an AU conference of Ministers of Trade was convened, in Cairo, to discuss issues relating to the development of trade in Africa, particularly in the context of the World Trade Organization's (WTO) Doha Work Programme. The outcome of the meeting was the adoption of the Cairo Road Map on the Doha Work Programme, which addressed several important issues including the import, export and market access of agricultural and non-agricultural commodities, development issues and trade facilitation.

The 1991 Abuja Treaty Establishing the AEC initially envisaged that the Economic Community would be established by 2028, following a gradual six-phase process involving the co-ordination, harmonization and progressive integration of the activities of all existing and future sub-regional economic unions. (The AU recognizes the following eight so-called regional economic communities, or RECs, in Africa: the COMESA, the East African Community—EAC and SADC, which together comprise the EAC-COMESA-SADC Tripartite FTA initiative; the Communauté Economique des Etats de l'Afrique Centrale—CEEAC, ECOWAS, the IGAD, and the Union of the Arab Maghreb. The subsidiary RECs are the Communauté Economique et Monétaire de l'Afrique Centrale—CEMAC, the Community of Sahel-Saharan States—CEN-SAD, the Economic Community of the Great Lakes Countries, the Indian Ocean Commission—IOC, the Mano River Union, the Southern African Customs Union, and the Union Economique et Monétaire Ouest-Africaine—UEMOA.) The inaugural meeting of the AEC took place in June 1997. In July 2007 the ninth AU Assembly adopted a Protocol on Relations between the AU and the RECs, aimed at facilitating the harmonization of policies and ensuring compliance with the schedule of the Abuja Treaty.

In January 2012 the 18th summit of AU leaders endorsed a new Framework, Roadmap and Architecture for Fast Tracking the Establishment of a Continental Free Trade Area (CFTA), and an Action Plan for Boosting Intra-African Trade. The summit determined that the implementation of the CFTA process should follow these milestones: the finalization by 2014 of the EAC-COMESA-SADC Tripartite FTA initiative; the completion during 2012–14 of other REC FTAs; the consolidation of the Tripartite and other regional FTAs into the CFTA initiative during 2015–16; and the establishment of an operational CFTA by 2017. The January 2012 summit invited ECOWAS, CEEAC, CEN-SAD and the Union of the Arab Maghreb to draw inspiration from the EAC-COMESA-SADC Tripartite initiative and to establish promptly a second pole of regional integration, thereby accelerating continental economic integration. The summit also recognized the need to strengthen the AU's institutional framework for sustainable development, deeming that promoting the transition to 'green' and 'blue' economies would accelerate continental progress towards sustainable development.

In February 2008 the AU Assembly endorsed the AU Action Plan for the Accelerated Industrial Development of Africa, which had been adopted in September 2007 by the first extraordinary session of the Conference of African Ministers of Industry. The Action Plan details a set of programme and activities aimed at stimulating a competitive and sustainable industrial development process.

A roadmap and plan of action for promoting microfinance in Africa was finalized in 2009.

In January 2012 AU leaders endorsed a new action plan on Boosting Intra-African Trade (BIAT), which aimed to reduce transit times between member states.

In October 2010 the AU, ECA and the AfDB established a Joint Secretariat to enhance coherence and collaboration in support of Africa's development agenda.

RURAL ECONOMY AND AGRICULTURE

In July 2003 the second Assembly of heads of state and government adopted the Maputo Declaration on Agriculture and Food Security in Africa, focusing on the need to revitalize the agricultural sector and to combat hunger on the continent by developing food reserves based on African production. The leaders determined to deploy policies and budgetary resources to remove current constraints on agricultural production, trade and rural development; and to implement the Comprehensive Africa Agriculture Programme (CAADP). The CAADP, which is implemented through NEPAD, focuses on the four pillars of sustainable land and water management; market access; food supply and hunger; and agricultural research. CAADP heads of state have agreed the objective of allocating at least 10% of national budgets to investment in agricultural productivity. The CAADP aims by 2015 to achieve dynamic agricultural markets between African countries and regions; good participation in and access to markets by farmers; a more equitable distribution of wealth for rural populations; more equitable access to land, practical and financial resources, knowledge, information, and technology for sustainable development; development of Africa's role as a strategic player in the area of agricultural science and technology; and environmentally sound agricultural production and a culture of sustainable management of natural resources.

In December 2006 the AU adopted the Great Green Wall of the Sahara and Sahel Initiative, comprising a set of cross-sectoral actions and interventions (including tree planting) that were aimed at conserving and protecting natural resources, halting soil degradation, reducing poverty, and increasing land productivity in some 20 countries in the Sahara and Sahel areas.

The AU's Programme for the Control of Epizootics (PACE) has co-operated with FAO to combat the further spread of the Highly Pathogenic Avian Influenza (H5N1) virus, outbreaks of which were reported in poultry in several West African countries in the 2000s; joint activities have included establishing a regional network of laboratories and surveillance teams and organizing regional workshops on H5N1 control.

In July 2009 the 13th regular session of the Assembly issued a Declaration on Land Issues and Challenges in Africa, and the Sirte Declaration on Investing in Agriculture for Economic Growth and Food Security. The Sirte Declaration urged member states to review their land sector policies, and determined to undertake studies on the establishment of an appropriate institutional framework, and to launch an African Fund for Land Policy, in support of these efforts.

In January 2011 the Executive Council endorsed the Accelerated African Agribusiness and Agro-Industries Development Initiative (3ADI), which had been launched at a high-level conference on the development of agribusiness and agro-industries in Africa, convened in Abuja, Nigeria, in March 2010. The framework for the implementation of the 3ADI is the Strategy for the Implementation of the AU Plan of Action for the Accelerated Industrial Development of Africa (AIDA), adopted by African ministers responsible for industry, in October 2008; the Ministerial Action Plan for the Least Developed Countries (LDCs), adopted in December 2009 by LDC ministers responsible for industry and trade; and the Abuja Declaration on Development of Agribusiness and Agro-industries in Africa, adopted by the March 2010 Abuja high-level conference. The initiative aims to mobilize private sector investment, from domestic, regional and international sources, in African agribusiness and agro-industrial development, with the long-term objective of achieving, by 2020, highly productive and profitable agricultural value chains.

The First Conference of African Ministers of Fisheries and Aquaculture (CAMFA) was convened in September 2010, in Banjul. In January 2011 the Executive Council urged member states to adopt and integrate ecosystem approaches in their national and regional fisheries management plans; to strengthen measures to address Illegal, Unreported and Unregulated (IUU) fishing; and to eliminate barriers to intra-regional trade in fish and fishery products.

HUMANITARIAN RESPONSE

In December 2005 a ministerial conference on disaster reduction in Africa, organized by the AU Commission, adopted a programme of action for the implementation of the Africa Regional Strategy for Disaster Risk Reduction (2006–15), formulated in the context of the Hyogo Framework of Action that had been agreed at the World Conference on Disaster Reduction held in Kobe, Japan, in January 2005. A second ministerial conference on disaster reduction, convened in April 2010, urged all member states, and the RECs, to take necessary measures to implement the programme of action. In August 2010 the AU and the UN Office for the Co-ordination of Humanitarian Affairs signed an agreement detailing key areas of future co-operation on humanitarian issues, with the aim of strengthening the AU's capacity in the areas of disaster preparedness and response, early warning, co-ordination, and protection of civilians affected by conflict or natural disaster.

Finance

The 2014 budget, adopted by the Executive Council in July 2012, totalled US $308m., comprising an operational budget of $138m. and a programme budget $170m. Some 75% of the operational budget is financed by contributions—of 15% of the total each—from Algeria, Egypt, Libya, Nigeria and South Africa. Around 90% of programme budgetary funding derives from the AU's international development partners. The inaugural meeting of a new AU Foundation was convened in February 2014; the Foundation aimed to mobilize voluntary contributions for financing continent-wide priorities.

Specialized Agencies

African Academy of Languages (ACALAN): BP 10, Koulouba-Bamako, Mali; tel. 2023-84-47; fax 2023-84-47; e-mail acalan@acalan.org; internet www.acalan.org; f. 2006 to foster continental integration and development through the promotion of the use—in all domains—of African languages; aims to restore the role and vitality of indigenous languages (estimated to number more than 2,000), and to reverse the negative impact of colonialism on their perceived value; implements a Training of African Languages Teachers and Media Practitioners Project; a core programme is the promotion of the Pan-African Masters and PhD Program in African Languages and Applied Linguistics (PANMAPAL), inaugurated in 2006 at the University of Yaoundé 1 (Cameroon), Addis Ababa University (Ethiopia), and at the University of Cape Town (South Africa); has identified some 41 'Vehicular Cross-Border Languages'; Vehicular Cross-Border Language Commissions were to be established for 12 of these: Beti-fang and Lingala (Central Africa); Kiswahili, Somali and Malagasy (East Africa); Standard modern Arab and Berber (North Africa); Chichewa/Chinyanja and Setswana (Southern Africa); and Hausa, Mandenkan and Fulfulde (West Africa); in Dec. 2011 organized a workshop on African languages in cyberspace; ACALAN is developing a linguistic atlas for Africa; Exec. Dir Prof. SOZINHO FRANCISCO MATSINHE.

African Civil Aviation Commission (AFCAC): 1 route de l'Aéroport International LSS, BP 2356, Dakar, Senegal; tel. 859-88-00; fax 820-70-18; e-mail secretariat@afcac.org; internet www.afcac.org; f. 1969 to co-ordinate civil aviation matters in Africa and to co-operate with ICAO and other relevant civil aviation bodies; promotes the devt of the civil aviation industry in Africa in accordance with provisions of the 1991 Abuja Treaty; fosters the application of ICAO Standards and Recommended Practices; examines specific problems that might hinder the devt and operation of the African civil aviation industry; 53 mem. states; promotes co-ordination and better utilization and devt of African air transport systems and the standardization of aircraft, flight equipment and training programmes for pilots and mechanics; organizes working groups and seminars, and compiles statistics; Sec.-Gen. IYABO O. SOSINA.

African Risk Capacity Agency: Merafe House, 11 Naivasha Rd, Sunninghill, 2157 Johannesburg, South Africa; tel. (11) 517-1642; internet www.africanriskcapacity.org; f. 2012 under the African Risk Capacity Establishment Agreement (which had 22 signatories at Sept. 2013); aims to finance risk resistance and contingency measures; uses satellite weather surveillance and WFP-developed software to assess, and disburse immediate funding to, member states affected by a natural disaster; Dir Dr RICHARD WILCOX (USA) (acting).

African Telecommunications Union (ATU): ATU Secretariat, POB 35282 Nairobi, 00200 Kenya; tel. (20) 4453308; fax (20) 4453359; e-mail sg@atu-uat.org; internet www.atu-uat.org; f. 1999 as successor to Pan-African Telecommunications Union (f. 1977); promotes the rapid devt of information communications in Africa, with the aim of making Africa an equal participant in the global information society; works towards universal service and access and full inter-country connectivity; promotes devt and adoption of appropriate policies and regulatory frameworks; promotes financing of devt; encourages co-operation between members and the exchange of information; advocates the harmonization of telecommunications policies; 46 national mems, 18 associate mems comprising fixed and mobile telecoms operators; Sec.-Gen. ABDOULKARIM SOUMAILA.

Pan-African Institute of Education for Development (IPED): POB 35527, Yaoundé Bastos, Cameroon; tel. (237) 22-20-82-35; e-mail gs@paidafrica.org; internet www.paidafrica.org/en; f. 1973, became specialized agency in 1986, present name adopted 2001; undertakes educational research and training, focuses on co-operation and problem-solving, acts as an observatory for education; responsible for Education Management Information Systems under the Second Decade for Education for Africa (2006–15); publs *Bulletin d'Information* (quarterly), *Revue africaine des sciences de l'éducation* (2 a year), *Répertoire africain des institutions de recherche* (annually).

Pan-African News Agency (PANAPRESS): BP 4056, ave Bourguiba, Dakar, Senegal; tel. 869-12-34; fax 824-13-90; e-mail panapress@panapress.com; internet www.panapress.com; f. 1979 as PanAfrican News Agency, restructured under current name in 1997; regional headquarters in Khartoum, Sudan; Lusaka, Zambia; Kinshasa, Democratic Republic of the Congo; Lagos, Nigeria; Tripoli, Libya; began operations in May 1983; receives information from national news agencies and circulates news in Arabic, English, French and Portuguese; publs *Press Review*, *In-Focus*.

Pan-African Postal Union (PAPU): POB 6026, Arusha, Tanzania; tel. (27) 2543263; fax (27) 2543265; e-mail sg@papu.co.tz; internet www.upap-papu.org; f. 1980 to extend members' co-operation in the improvement of postal services; 43 mem. countries; Sec.-Gen. YOUNOUSS DJIBRINE (Cameroon); publ. *PAPU News*.

ANDEAN COMMUNITY OF NATIONS

(COMUNIDAD ANDINA DE NACIONES—CAN)

Address: Paseo de la República 3895, San Isidro, Lima 27; Apdo 18-1177, Lima 18, Peru.

Telephone: (1) 7106400; **fax:** (1) 2213329; **e-mail:** contacto@comunidadandina.org; **internet:** www.comunidadandina.org.

The Acuerdo de Cartagena (the Cartagena Agreement), also referred to as the Grupo Andino (Andean Group) or the Pacto Andino (Andean Pact), was established in 1969. In March 1996 member countries signed a Reform Protocol of the Cartagena Agreement, in accordance with which the Andean Group was superseded in August 1997 by the Andean Community of Nations (CAN). The Community was to promote greater economic, commercial and political integration within a new Andean Integration System (Sistema Andino de Integración), comprising the organization's bodies and institutions.

MEMBERS

Bolivia	Colombia	Ecuador	Peru

Note: Argentina, Brazil, Chile, Paraguay and Uruguay are associate members. Mexico, Panama and Spain have observer status. Venezuela withdrew from the Community in April 2006.

Organization

(April 2014)

ANDEAN PRESIDENTIAL COUNCIL

The presidential summits, which had been held annually since 1989, were formalized under the 1996 Reform Protocol of the Cartagena Agreement as the Andean Presidential Council. The Council is the highest-level body of the Andean Integration System, and provides the political leadership of the Community.

COMMISSION

The Commission consists of a plenipotentiary representative from each member country, with each country holding the presidency in turn. The Commission is the main policy-making organ of the Andean Community, and is responsible for co-ordinating Andean trade policy.

COUNCIL OF FOREIGN MINISTERS

The Council of Foreign Ministers meets annually or whenever it is considered necessary, to formulate common external policy and to co-ordinate the process of integration.

GENERAL SECRETARIAT

In August 1997 the General Secretariat assumed the functions of the Board of the Cartagena Agreement. The General Secretariat is the body charged with implementation of all guidelines and decisions issued by the bodies listed above. It submits proposals to the Commission for facilitating the fulfilment of the Community's objectives. The Secretary-General is elected by the Council of Foreign Ministers for a five-year term, and has enhanced powers to adjudicate in disputes arising between member states, as well as to manage the sub-regional integration process. There are three Directors-General.

Secretary-General: PABLO GUZMÁN LAUGIER (Bolivia).

PARLIAMENT

Parlamento Andino: Avda Caracas, No. 70A-61, Bogotá, Colombia; tel. (1) 217-3357; fax (1) 348-2805; e-mail carias@parlamentoandino.org; internet www.parlamentoandino.org; f. 1979; comprises five members from each country, elected by direct voting, and meets in each capital city in turn; makes recommendations on regional policy; Pres. (2013–14) PEDRO DE LA CRUZ (Ecuador); Sec.-Gen. Dr RUBÉN VÉLEZ.

COURT OF JUSTICE

Tribunal de Justicia de la Comunidad Andina: Juan de Dios Martínez Mera 34-380 y Portugal, Sector Iglesia de Fátima, Quito, Ecuador; tel. (2) 3331417; e-mail tjca@tribunalandino.org.ec; internet www.tribunalandino.org.ec; f. 1979, began operating in 1984; a protocol approved in May 1996 (which came into force in August 1999) modified the Court's functions; its main responsibilities are to resolve disputes among member countries and interpret community legislation; comprises one judge from each member country, appointed for a six-year renewable period; the Presidency is assumed annually by each judge in turn; Pres. Dr LEONOR PERDOMO PERDOMO (Colombia); Sec.-Gen. Dr GUSTAVO GARCÍA BRITO.

Activities

In March 1996 heads of state, meeting in Trujillo, Peru, signed the Reform Protocol of the Cartagena Agreement, providing for the establishment of the Andean Community of Nations, which was to have greater ambitious economic and political objectives than the previous framework for Andean integration, the Grupo Andino (Andean Group). Consequently, in August 1997 the Andean Community was inaugurated, and the Group's Junta was replaced by a new General Secretariat, headed by a Secretary-General with enhanced executive and decision-making powers. In January 2003 the Community heads of state, convened in Quirama, Colombia, endorsed a strategic direction for the Andean integration process based on developing the Andean common market, common foreign policy and social agenda, physical integration, and sustainable development.

In February 2010 the Council of Foreign Ministers approved a new Andean Strategic Agenda, which was supported by a New Andean Strategic Agenda Implementation Plan, and focused on 12 priority strategic areas: citizen participation; common foreign policy; trade integration and economic complementation, and promotion of production, trade and sustainable consumption; physical integration and border development; social development; environment; tourism; security; culture; co-operation; energy integration and natural resources; and development of the Community's institutions.

In June 2012 Colombia and Peru, together with Chile and Mexico, inaugurated the Pacific Alliance, aimed at furthering economic integration.

ANTI-CORRUPTION AND DEMOCRACY

A sub-regional workshop to formulate an Andean Plan to Fight Corruption was held in April 2005, organized by the General Secretariat and the European Commission. Heads of state expressed their commitment to the Plan in mid-2007, and in September 2008 Offices of the Controller General and other supervisory bodies in Andean countries agreed its implementation. The Plan aims to promote a region-wide culture of legality, the adoption of common positions in relation to the implementation of international conventions, transparency in public administration, and the strengthening of regional control bodies. The Andean Community Secretariat monitors elections in member states; in 2014 a mission was sent to observe local elections held in Ecuador during February.

CULTURE

An Andean Council of Education Ministers and Persons Responsible for Cultural Policy was established in July 2004. Common policies and mechanisms for the registration, conservation, surveillance and return of member states' cultural heritage were also adopted in that month. In March 2010 representatives of Andean cultural authorities determined to initiate an Andean Development Plan for Cultural Industries. In March 2012 the inaugural meeting of a new Andean Council of Ministers of Culture launched the Plan, covering 2012–15, with a focus on the areas of cultural information, cultural and artistic training, and the promotion and dissemination of culture. The Community's online cultural portal, CULTURANDE, was to be enhanced. A Permanent Working Network on Andean Cinema was established in February 2010.

DRUGS CONTROL

At the 13th presidential summit, held in Valencia, Venezuela, in June 2001, heads of state adopted an Andean Co-operation Plan for the Control of Illegal Drugs and Related Offences. In July 2005 the Council of Foreign Ministers approved an Andean Alternative Development Strategy, which aimed to support sustainable local development initiatives, including alternatives to the production of illicitcrops. In August 2009 the Council approved a financing agreement with the European Union (EU) to implement an anti-illegal drugs programme in the Andean Community. In June 2012 a joint CAN-EU-Pan American Health Organization programme known as 'Familias Fuertes' ('Strong Families') was initiated, with the aim of preventing drugs use and associated risk behaviours among adolescents in the region. In November a High-Level International Conference on Alternative Development, convened at the Community's headquarters, considered a draft Andean Strategy for Jointly Addressing the Global Drug Problem during 2012–19, which was to promote sustainable alternative development in illicit crop cultivation areas.

ENVIRONMENT

In March–April 2005 the first meeting of an Andean Community Council of Ministers of the Environment and Sustainable Development was convened, in Paracas, Peru. Successive Andean Environmental Agendas have aimed to strengthen the capacities of member countries with regard to environmental and sustainable development issues, in particular biodiversity, climate change and water resources. The 2012–16 Agenda—adopted by CAN ministers responsible for the environment and sustainable development in April 2012, alongside an action plan for the implementation of the Andean Strategy for Integrated Management of Water Resources—provides, inter alia, for the strengthening of biodiversity management, with a focus on protected areas; the promotion of joint initiatives on biosafety; the strengthening of national processes aimed at protecting traditional knowledge; improving the exchange of information on conservation and biodiversity; the development of joint actions in relation to the implementation of the Nagoya Protocol on Access to Genetic Resources and the Fair and Equitable Sharing of Benefits Arising from their Utilization; the development of an Andean Plan of Action on Climate Change; and promoting responsible and efficient water use, advancing the prevention of water pollution, evaluating the impact of climate variability on Andean water resources, and developing appropriate adaptation measures. In September 2012 CAN launched a new 'One Amazon' campaign, aimed at raising awareness of the environmentally strategic importance of the Amazon ecosystem.

In June 2007 the Secretariat signed an agreement with Finland to develop a regional biodiversity programme in the Amazon region of Andean member countries (BioCAN); the implementation of BioCAN was approved in February 2013 by a meeting of the Council of Foreign Ministers. Pilot projects implemented during 2012–13 included developing an Amazon Regional Information Platform (PIRAA), and formulating norms for wildlife management, and guidelines for land zoning and for the sustainable use of Amazonian biodiversity. Also in 2012 BioCAN supported workshops of Andean Community wildlife officials and experts that aimed to address, respectively, proposals for an appropriate sub-regional co-ordination mechanism to combat illegal trafficking in wild Amazonian flora and fauna; and the management of Amazonian areas, with a special focus on priority species. In October 2007 the Secretariat organized Clima Latino, hosted by two city authorities in Ecuador, comprising conferences, workshops and cultural events at which climate change was addressed. The Community represented member countries at the conference of parties to the UN Framework Convention on Climate Change (UNFCCC), held in Bali, Indonesia, in December, and demanded greater international political commitment and funding to combat the effects of climate change, in particular to monitor and protect the Amazon rainforest. In November 2011, at a special meeting of the Andean Council of Presidents in Bogotá, Colombia, heads of state asserted their intention to work together to reach a common position for the UN Conference on Sustainable Development (Rio+20), which was held in June 2012.

In July 2002 an Andean Committee for Disaster Prevention and Relief (CAPRADE) was established to help to mitigate the risk and impact of natural disasters in the sub-region, and to implement the

Andean Strategy for Disaster Prevention and Relief, which was approved by the Council of Foreign Ministers in July 2004. A new Strategy for Natural Disaster Prevention and Relief was approved in August 2009, which aimed to link activities for disaster prevention and relief to those related to the environmental agenda, climate change and integrated water management. An Andean University Network in Risk Management and Climate Change promotes information exchange between some 32 institutions.

INDUSTRY AND ENERGY

During 2003 efforts were undertaken to establish an Andean Energy Alliance, with the aim of fostering the development of integrated electricity and gas markets, as well as developing renewable energy sources, promoting 'energy clusters' and ensuring regional energy security. The first meeting of ministers responsible for energy, electricity, hydrocarbons and mines, convened in Quito, Ecuador, in January 2004, endorsed the Alliance. In August 2011 representatives of Andean electricity regulatory bodies, including that of Chile, agreed upon transitional arrangements to provide for trade in surplus electricity and greater interconnectivity. Andean Community heads of state, meeting in Bogotá, in November, pledged to boost the integration of regional energy. In February 2012 the Community held the first meeting of representatives of mining and environment authorities to discuss issues relating to illegal mining activities, in order to promote co-ordinated efforts against those activities, and to initiate the development of a legal directive to counter illegal mining.

RURAL DEVELOPMENT AND FOOD SECURITY

The 12th Andean presidential summit, held in June 2000, authorized the adoption of an Andean Common Agricultural Policy, which included measures to harmonize trade policy instruments and legislation on animal and plant health. The meeting also concluded a plan of action for its implementation. In January 2002, at a special Andean presidential summit, it was agreed that all countries in the bloc would adopt price stabilization mechanisms for agricultural products. In July 2004 Andean ministers responsible for agriculture approved a series of objectives and priority actions to form the framework of a Regional Food Security Policy. Also in July Andean heads of state endorsed the Andean Rural Development and Agricultural Competitiveness Programme to promote sub-regional efforts in areas such as rural development, food security, production competitiveness, animal health and technological innovation. In October 2005 ministers responsible for trade and for agriculture approved the establishment of the Fund for Rural Development and Agricultural Productivity to finance the Programme. In June 2013 Community agriculture ministers approved a set of common strategic guidelines and objectives that were to guide joint efforts to advance sub-regional rural and agricultural development. The ministers also established an Andean Rural Territorial Development Committee to advise on the implementation of an Integral Subregional Rural Territorial Development Program.

REGIONAL SECURITY

In June 2002 Community ministers responsible for defence and for foreign affairs approved an Andean Charter for Peace and Security, establishing principles and commitments for the formulation of a policy on sub-regional security, the establishment of a zone of peace, joint action in efforts to counter terrorism, and the limitation of external defence spending. Other provisions included commitments to eradicate illegal trafficking in firearms, ammunition and explosives, to expand and reinforce confidence-building measures, and to establish verification mechanisms to strengthen dialogue and efforts in those areas. In January 2003 the Community concluded a co-operation agreement with INTERPOL providing for collaboration in combating national and transnational crime, and in June the presidential summit adopted an Andean Plan for the Prevention, Combating and Eradication of Small, Light Weapons. In July 2004 the Council of Foreign Ministers adopted Policy Guidelines on Andean Common External Security.

SOCIAL INTEGRATION

The first Andean Social Summit, organized in April 1994 by the Andean Parliament, adopted a non-binding Andean Social Charter. The second Andean Social Summit was convened in February 1999. Participants in the third Andean Social Summit, organized by the Andean Parliament in May 2012, endorsed an updated Andean Social Charter, incorporating additional provisions covering human mobility and the rights of migrants; Andean ethical and moral values (including protection for modern as well as traditional family configurations); disability; female empowerment; access to decent housing for senior citizens; urban renewal; guaranteed rights to all gender identities and sexual orientations; environmental issues; food security; and corporate social responsibility.

Several formal agreements and institutions have been established within the framework of the Andean Integration System to enhance social development and welfare. In June 2000 the 12th presidential summit instructed the Andean institutions to prepare individual programmes aimed at consolidating implementation of the Community's integration programme and advancing the development of the social agenda, in order to promote greater involvement of representatives of civil society. In June 2003 ministers responsible for foreign affairs and for foreign trade adopted 16 legal provisions aimed at giving maximum priority to the social dimension of integration within the Community, including a measure providing for mobility of workers between member countries. In July 2004 Community heads of state declared support for a new Andean Council of Social Development Ministers. Other bodies established in 2003/04 included Councils of Ministers of Education and of Ministers responsible for Cultural Policies, and a Consultative Council of Municipal Authorities. A new Andean passport system, which had been approved in 2001, entered into effect in December 2005. An Integral Plan for Social Development, first approved by the Council of Foreign Ministers in September 2004, has remained under development. In August 2009 the Council of Foreign Ministers endorsed the establishment of an Andean Council of Authorities of Women's Affairs as a forum for regional consideration of equal opportunities and gender issues. In September 2012 the Council approved priority actions aimed, inter alia, at combating violence against women, promoting women's political participation and economic autonomy, and preventing adolescent pregnancy, within the framework of a new Andean Programme for Gender Equality and Equal Opportunities. In April 2013 six indicators were adopted by the Council with the aim of harmonizing measurements of political participation by women. In July 2011 Andean ministers responsible for social development approved 11 Andean Social Development Objectives, which they pledged to achieve by 2019, and a new Andean Economic and Social Cohesion Strategy to support the accomplishment of those targets. In November 2012 CAN ministers responsible for labour—with a view to facilitating workers' employability in any of the four member states—endorsed the establishment of a new Andean Employment Network (Red ANDE), which was to match labour supply and demand within member states; approved new regulations aimed at ensuring equal labour conditions in the member states; and also determined to promote the regional mutual labour skills certification mechanism (CERTIANDINA). Social and labour policies in the Community are analysed through an Andean Labour Observatory Pilot Plan implemented under the auspices of the Convenio Simón Rodríguez. In that month the Commission determined to expand science and technology programmes in member states, with a view to developing human capital regionally.

An Andean Charter for the Promotion and Protection of Human Rights was adopted by the Presidential Council in July 2002. In June 2007 Community heads of state approved the establishment of a Working Committee on Indigenous People's Rights. A Consultative Council of Indigenous Peoples of the Andean Community was founded in September to promote the participation of representatives of indigenous communities in the Andean integration process. In November 2010 the first Andean Meeting of Racial Equality Bodies was held, and during 2011 national meetings were convened in member countries aimed at enhancing the participation of people of African descent in the activities of the Community. A Working Committee on Peoples of African Descent in the Andean Community was launched in August 2011.

TOURISM

Tourist arrivals in the CAN region rose from around 2.7m. in 2002 to some 6.2m. in 2011. In December 2010 the Andean Committee of Tourism Authorities (comprising representatives of national tourism authorities) approved an Agenda for Tourism Development in the Andean Community, covering the period 2011–15, which aimed to develop the region as a major global tourism destination, by facilitating tourist flows between member states and promoting innovative tourism products. The development of an information system on the Community tourism sector is under way, with the objective of establishing a tourism observatory.

TRADE AND MACROECONOMY

The Caracas Declaration of May 1991 provided for the establishment of an Andean free trade area (AFTA), which entered into effect (excluding Peru) in February 1993. Heads of state also agreed in May 1991 to create a common external tariff (CET), to standardize member countries' trade barriers in their dealings with the rest of the world, and envisaged the eventual creation of an Andean common market. In November 1994 ministers responsible for trade and integration, meeting in Quito, concluded a final agreement on a four-tier structure of external tariffs (although Bolivia was to retain a two-level system). The CET agreement came into effect on 1 February 1995, covering 90% of the region's imports. In June 1997 an agreement was concluded to provide for Peru's integration into AFTA. The Peruvian Government determined to eliminate customs duties on some 2,500 products with immediate effect. The process of incorporating Peru into AFTA was completed by January 2006.

In May 1999 the 11th presidential summit agreed to establish the Andean Common Market by 2005; the Community adopted a policy on border integration and development to prepare the border regions of member countries for the envisaged free circulation of people, goods, capital and services, while consolidating sub-regional security. In June 2001 the Community agreed to recognize national identification documents issued by member states as sufficient for tourist travel in the sub-region. Community heads of state, meeting in January 2002 at a special Andean presidential summit, agreed to consolidate and improve the free trade zone by mid-2002 and apply a new CET. To facilitate this process a common agricultural policy was to be adopted and macro-economic policies were to be harmonized. In October member governments determined the new tariff levels applicable to 62% of products and agreed the criteria for negotiating levels for the remainder. Although the new CET was to become effective on 1 January 2004, this date was subsequently postponed. In January 2006 ministers responsible trade approved a working programme to define the Community's common tariff policy, which was to incorporate a flexible CET. The value of intra-Community trade totalled some US $9,261m. in 2011, and increased to $10,349m. in 2012.

In November 2012 the Commission adopted a new work plan which detailed several priority areas of trade-related activity, including the promotion of industrial complementarity and production chains between the Andean states; certification of organic products; and macroeconomic co-ordination of the regional response to the global economic downturn.

In May 2011 the Commission approved the establishment of an Andean Committee on Micro, Small and Medium-sized Enterprises (MSMEs), mandated to advise and support the Commission and General Secretariat in efforts to support MSMEs. At the same time the Commission endorsed the establishment of an Andean Observatory on MSMEs as a mechanism for monitoring the development and needs of MSMEs in the sub-region, as well as the impact of corporate policy instruments on their competitiveness.

An Andean Business Meeting is convened periodically to promote inter-regional trade.

TRANSPORT AND COMMUNICATIONS

The Andean Community has pursued efforts to improve infrastructure throughout the region. An 'open skies' agreement, giving airlines of member states equal rights to airspace and airport facilities within the grouping, was signed in May 1991. In June 1998 the Commission approved the establishment of an Andean Commission of Land Transportation Authorities, to oversee the operation and development of land transportation services. Similarly, an Andean Committee of Water Transportation Authorities was established to ensure compliance with Community regulations regarding ocean transportation activities. The Community aims to facilitate the movement of goods throughout the region by the use of different modes of transport ('multimodal transport') and to guarantee operational standards. It also intends to harmonize Community transport regulations and standards with those of Mercosur countries.

In August 1996 a regulatory framework was approved for the development of a commercial Andean satellite system. In December 1997 the General Secretariat approved regulations for granting authorization for the use of the system; the Commission subsequently granted the first Community authorization to an Andean multinational enterprise (Andesat), comprising 48 companies from all five member states. In 1994 the Community initiated efforts to establish digital technology infrastructure throughout the Community: the resulting Andean Digital Corridor comprises ground, underwater and satellite routes providing a series of cross-border interconnections between the member countries. In May 1999 the Andean Committee of Telecommunications Authorities agreed to remove all restrictions to free trade in telecommunications services (excluding sound broadcasting and television) by 1 January 2002. The Committee also determined to formulate provisions on interconnection and the safeguarding of free competition and principles of transparency within the sector. In November 2006 the Andean Community approved a new regulatory framework for the commercial exploitation of the Andean satellite system belonging to member states. In February 2014 the Community concluded an agreement with the Netherlands-based company SES World Skies on the construction of a satellite, which, once launched and operational, was to provide high power satellite capacity to Andean telecommunications operators, broadcasters and service providers, over a 15-year period.

Asociación de Empresas de Telecomunicaciones de la Comunidad Andina (ASETA): Calle La Pradera E7–41 y San Salvador, Casilla 17-1106042, Quito, Ecuador; tel. (2) 256-3812; fax (2) 256-2499; e-mail aseta@aseta.org; internet www.aseta.org; f. 1974; coordinates improvements in national telecommunications services, in order to contribute to the further integration of the countries of the Andean Community; Sec.-Gen. MARCELO LÓPEZ ARJONA.

EXTERNAL RELATIONS

In 1999 the Council of Foreign Ministers approved guidelines establishing the principles, objectives and mechanisms of a common foreign policy. In July 2004 Andean ministers responsible for foreign affairs approved new guidelines for an Andean common policy on external security. The ministers, meeting in Quito, also adopted a Declaration on the Establishment of an Andean Peace Zone, free from nuclear, chemical or biological weapons. In April 2005 the Community Secretariat signed a Memorandum of Understanding with the Organization for the Prohibition of Chemical Weapons, which aimed to consolidate the Andean Peace Zone, assist countries to implement the Chemical Arms Convention and promote further collaboration between the two groupings.

A co-operation agreement with the EU was signed in April 1993, establishing a Mixed Commission to further deliberation and co-operation between the two organizations. A Euro-Andean Forum is held periodically to promote mutual co-operation, trade and investment. In February 1998 the Community signed a co-operation and technical assistance agreement with the EU in order to combat drugs-trafficking. At the first summit meeting of Latin American and Caribbean (LAC) and EU leaders held in Rio de Janeiro, Brazil, in June 1999, Community-EU discussions were held on strengthening economic, trade and political co-operation and on the possibility of concluding an Association Agreement. Following the second LAC and EU summit meeting, held in May 2002 in Madrid, Spain, a Political Dialogue and Co-operation Agreement was signed in December 2003. In May 2004 a meeting of the two sides held during the third LAC-EU summit, in Guadalajara, Mexico, confirmed that an EU-CAN Association Agreement was a common strategic objective. In January 2005 an ad hoc working group was established in order to undertake a joint appraisal exercise on regional economic integration. The fourth LAC and EU summit meeting, held in Vienna, Austria, in May 2006, approved the establishment of an EU-LAC Parliamentary Assembly; this was inaugurated in November. Negotiations on an Association Agreement were formally inaugurated at the meeting of Andean heads of state held in Tarifa, Bolivia, in June 2007, and the first round of negotiations was held in September. In May 2008 heads of state of the Andean Community confirmed that they would continue to negotiate the agreement as a single group; however, in December the EU announced that it was to commence separate free trade agreement negotiations with Colombia and Peru. Bolivia criticized the decision as undermining the Andean integration process. In March 2010 the EU-CAN Mixed Commission agreed on a programme of co-operation in 2011–13, with funding commitments of €17.5m. for projects concerned with economic integration, countering illicit drugs production and trafficking, and environmental protection. An EU-CAN summit meeting was held in Madrid in May 2010. In June 2012 Colombia and Peru concluded a Multi-Party Commercial Agreement with the EU; reservations were expressed at that time by the EU concerning progress on human rights and environmental protection in those countries.

In August 2002 a new US Andean Trade Preference and Drug Eradication Act provided duty free access for more than 6,000 products from the Andean Community with the objective of supporting legal trade transactions in order to help to counter the production and trafficking of illegal narcotic drugs. The Act was initially scheduled to expire in December 2006, but has been periodically extended by the US Congress. In December 2008 the US President suspended Bolivia's eligibility under the Act owing to its failure to meet its counternarcotics requirements.

In March 2000 the Andean Community concluded an agreement to establish a political consultation and co-operation mechanism with the People's Republic of China. At the first ministerial meeting within this framework, which took place in October 2002, it was agreed that consultations would be held thereafter on a biennial basis. The first meeting of the Council of Foreign Ministers with the Chinese Vice-President took place in January 2005.

In April 1998, at the 10th Andean presidential summit, an agreement was signed with Panama establishing a framework for negotiations providing for the conclusion of a free trade accord by the end of 1998 and for Panama's eventual associate membership of the Community. A political dialogue and co-operation agreement, a requirement for Panama's associate membership status, was signed by both sides in September 2007. Mexico was invited to assume observer status in September 2004. In November 2006 Mexico and the Andean Community signed an agreement to establish a mechanism for political dialogue and co-operation in areas of mutual interest. The first meeting of the mechanism was held in New York, USA, in September 2007. In November 2004 the Community signed a framework agreement with the Central American Integration System

(SICA) to strengthen dialogue and co-operation between the two blocs of countries. In January 2011 the Secretaries-General of the two organizations, meeting in San Salvador, El Salvador, determined to reactivate the agreement and pursue greater collaboration.

The Community signed a framework agreement with Mercosur on the establishment of a free trade accord in April 1998. Although negotiations between the Community and Mercosur were subsequently delayed, bilateral agreements between the countries of the two groupings were extended. In September 2000 leaders of the Community and Mercosur, meeting at a summit of Latin American heads of state, determined to relaunch negotiations, with a view to establishing a free trade area. In July 2001 ministers responsible for foreign affairs of the two groupings approved the establishment of a formal mechanism for political dialogue and co-ordination in order to facilitate negotiations and to enhance economic and social integration. In December 2003 Mercosur and the Andean Community signed an Economic Complementary Agreement providing for free trade provisions, according to which tariffs on 80% of trade between the two groupings were to be phased out by 2014 and tariffs to be removed from the remaining 20% of, initially protected, products by 2019. The accord did not enter into force in July 2004, as planned, owing to delays in drafting the tariff reduction schedule. Members of the Latin American Integration Association (Aladi) remaining outside Mercosur and the Andean Community—Cuba, Chile and Mexico—were to be permitted to apply to join the envisaged larger free trade zone. In July 2005 the Community granted Argentina, Brazil, Paraguay and Uruguay associate membership of the grouping, as part of efforts to achieve a reciprocal association agreement. Chile was granted observer status in December 2004, and in September 2006 was formally invited to join the Community as an associate member. In December the first meeting of the CAN-Chile Joint Commission was convened in Cochabamba, Bolivia. An agreement on Chile's full participation in all Community bodies and mechanisms was approved in July 2007. In February 2010 ministers responsible for foreign affairs of the Community and Mercosur agreed to establish a CAN–Mercosur Mixed Commission to facilitate enhanced co-operation between the countries of the two organizations.

In April 2007, at the first South American Energy Summit, held in Margarita Island, Venezuela, heads of state endorsed the establishment of a Union of South American Nations (UNASUR) to be the lead organization for regional integration; UNASUR was to have political decision-making functions, supported by a small Quito-based permanent secretariat, and was to co-ordinate on economic and trade matters with the Andean Community, Mercosur and Aladi. At a summit meeting convened in May 2008, in Brasília, a constitutional document formally establishing UNASUR was signed. In December Brazil hosted a Latin American and Caribbean Summit on Integration and Development, which aimed to strengthen the commitment by all countries in the region to work together in support of sustainable development. The meeting issued the Salvador Declaration, which pledged support to strengthen co-operation among the regional and sub-regional groupings, to pursue further consultation and joint efforts to counter regional effects of the global financial crisis, and to promote closer collaboration on issues including energy, food security, social development, physical infrastructure and natural disaster management. The first informal meeting of the General Secretariat of the Andean Community and UNASUR was held in January 2010, in Lima, Peru.

At a special meeting of the Andean Council of Presidents, held in Bogotá, in November 2011, heads of state agreed to strengthen the CAN, and requested that the then acting Secretary-General of the Community identify jointly, with the General Secretariats of both Mercosur and UNASUR, common and complementary elements and differences prior to the future convergence of the three processes. In January 2012 the process of listing complementary elements commenced. Meeting in June 2013 Andean Community ministers responsible foreign affairs and of foreign trade established a high-level working group which was mandated to submit a proposal to the Council of Foreign Ministers that was to cover the Community's new vision, strategic guidelines and priority areas of action.

The Community participated in the first and second editions of a new Meeting of Regional and Subregional Integration Mechanisms and Bodies, held, respectively, in August 2012, in Montevideo, Uruguay, and in November, in Santiago, Chile, with the aim of defining and deepening integration in Latin America and the Caribbean. In November it was reported that the UN Economic Commission for Latin America and the Caribbean (ECLAC) was to undertake a study relating to institution building by the Community in the context of ongoing developments in the continental integration process.

Spain was awarded observer status at the Community in August 2011.

INSTITUTIONS

Consejo Consultivo de Pueblos Indígenos de la Comunidad Andina (Consultative Council of Indigenous Peoples of the Andean Community): Paseo de la República 3895, Lima, Peru; tel. (1) 4111400; fax (1) 2213329; f. 2007; comprising an indigenous representative from each mem. country; first meeting held in Sept. 2008; normally meets twice a year; aims to strengthen the participation of indigenous peoples in the sub-regional integration process.

Consejo Consultivo Empresarial Andino (Andean Business Advisory Council): Asociación Nacional de Industriales, Calle 73, No. 8–13, Bogotá, Colombia; tel. (1) 3268500; fax (1) 3473198; e-mail jnarino@andi.com.co; first meeting held in Nov. 1998; an advisory institution within the framework of the Sistema Andino de Integración; comprises elected representatives of business orgs; advises Community ministers and officials on integration activities affecting the business sector; Chair. LUÍS CARLOS VILLEGAS ECHEVERRI (Colombia).

Consejo Consultivo Laboral Andino (Andean Labour Advisory Council): Paseo de la República 3832, Of. 502, San Isidro, Lima 27, Peru; tel. (1) 6181701; fax (1) 6100139; e-mail cutperujcb@gmail.com; f. 1998; an advisory institution within the framework of the Sistema Andino de Integración; comprises elected representatives of labour orgs; advises Community ministers and officers on related labour issues; Pres. CÉRVULO BAUTISTA MATOMA (Colombia).

Convenio Andrés Bello (Andrés Bello Agreement): Calle 93B 17-49, Bogotá, Colombia; tel. and fax (1) 644-9292; fax (1) 644-9292; internet www.convenioandresbello.org; f. 1970, modified in 1990; aims to promote integration in the educational, technical and cultural sectors; a new Inter-institutional Co-operation Agreement was signed with the Secretariat of the CAN in Aug. 2003; mems: Bolivia, Chile, Colombia, Cuba, Dominican Republic, Ecuador, Mexico, Panama, Paraguay, Peru, Spain, Venezuela; Exec. Sec. MÓNICA LÓPEZ CASTRO (Colombia).

Convenio Hipólito Unanue (Hipólito Unanue Agreement): Edif. Cartagena, Paseo de la República 3832, 3°, San Isidro, Lima, Peru; tel. (1) 2210074; fax (1) 2222663; e-mail contacto@conhu.org.pe; internet www.orasconhu.org; f. 1971 on the occasion of the first meeting of Andean ministers responsible for health; became part of the institutional structure of the Community in 1998; aims to enhance the devt of health services, and to promote regional co-ordination in areas such as environmental health, disaster preparedness and the prevention and control of drug abuse; Exec. Sec. Dr CAROLINE CHANG CAMPOS (Ecuador).

Convenio Simón Rodríguez (Simón Rodríguez Agreement): Paseo de la República 3895, esq. Aramburú, San Isidro, Lima 27, Peru; tel. (1) 4111400; fax (1) 2213329; promotes a convergence of social and labour conditions throughout the Community, for example, working hours and conditions, employment and social security policies, and promotes the participation of workers and employers in the sub-regional integration process; Protocol of Modification signed in June 2001, and had by 2014 been ratified by all member states apart from Colombia; analyses Community social and labour policies through the ongoing Andean Labour Observatory Pilot Plan.

Corporación Andina de Fomento (CAF) (Andean Development Corporation): Torre CAF, Avda Luis Roche, Altamira, Apdo 5086, Caracas, Venezuela; tel. (212) 2092111; fax (212) 2092444; e-mail infocaf@caf.com; internet www.caf.com; f. 1968, began operations in 1970; aims to encourage the integration of the Andean countries by specialization and an equitable distribution of investments; conducts research to identify investment opportunities, and prepares the resulting investment projects; gives technical and financial assistance; and attracts internal and external credit; in July 2012 the CAF signed an inter-agency co-operation agreement, with ECLAC and the Latin American Integration Association, on establishing a new Latin America/Asia-Pacific Observatory, which was to analyse relevant economic data with a view to strengthening co-operation between the two regions; auth. cap. US $10,000m.; subscribed or underwritten by the governments of mem. countries, or by public, semi-public and private sector institutions authorized by those govts; the Board of Directors comprises representatives of each country at ministerial level; mems: the Andean Community, Argentina, Brazil, Chile, Costa Rica, Jamaica, Mexico, Panama, Paraguay, Spain, Trinidad and Tobago, Uruguay, Venezuela, and 14 private banks in the Andean region; has subsidiary offices in Buenos Aires, Argentina; La Paz, Bolivia; Brasília, Brasil; Bogotá, Colombia; Quito, Ecuador; Lima, Peru; Madrid, Spain; and Montevideo, Uruguay; Exec. Pres. ENRIQUE GARCÍA RODRÍGUEZ (Bolivia).

Fondo Latinoamericano de Reservas (FLAR) (Latin American Reserve Fund): Avda 82 12–18, 7°, POB 241523, Bogotá, Colombia; tel. (1) 634-4360; fax (1) 634-4384; e-mail info@flar.net; internet www.flar.net; f. 1978 as the Fondo Andino de Reservas to support the balance of payments of member countries, provide credit, guarantee loans, and contribute to the harmonization of monetary and financial policies; adopted present name in 1991, in order to allow the admission of other Latin American countries; in 1992 the Fund began extending credit lines to commercial cos for export financing; it is administered by an Assembly of the ministers responsible for finance and economic affairs of the mem. countries, and a Board of Directors comprising the Presidents of the central banks of the mem. states; mems: Bolivia, Colombia, Costa Rica, Ecuador, Peru, Uruguay, Venezuela; subscribed cap. US $2,343.8m. cap. p.u. $2,034.1m. (31 Dec. 2011); Exec. Pres. ANA MARÍA CARRASQUILLA.

Universidad Andina Simón Bolívar (Simón Bolívar Andean University): Real Audiencia 73, Casilla 545, Sucre, Bolivia; tel. (4) 6460265; fax (4) 6460833; e-mail uasb@uasb.edu.bo; internet www.uasb.edu.bo; f. 1985; institution for postgraduate study and research; promotes co-operation between other universities in the Andean region; branches in Quito (Ecuador), La Paz (Bolivia), Caracas (Venezuela) and Cali (Colombia); Pres. (Sucre Office) JOSÉ LUIS GUITIÉRREZ SARDÁN; Pres. (Quito Office) ENRIQUE AYALA MORA.

Publications

Reports, working papers, sector documents, council proceedings.

ARAB FUND FOR ECONOMIC AND SOCIAL DEVELOPMENT—AFESD

Address: POB 21923, Safat, 13080 Kuwait.

Telephone: 24959000; **fax:** 24815760; **e-mail:** hq@arabfund.org; **internet:** www.arabfund.org.

Established in 1968 by the Economic Council of the Arab League, the Fund began its operations in 1974. It participates in the financing of economic and social development projects in the Arab states.

MEMBERS

All member countries of the League of Arab States.

Organization

(April 2014)

BOARD OF GOVERNORS

The Board of Governors consists of a Governor and an Alternate Governor appointed by each member of the Fund. The Board of Governors is considered as the General Assembly of the Fund, and has all powers.

BOARD OF DIRECTORS

The Board of Directors is composed of eight Directors elected by the Board of Governors from among Arab citizens of recognized experience and competence. They are elected for a renewable term of two years.

The Board of Directors is charged with all the activities of the Fund and exercises the powers delegated to it by the Board of Governors.

Director-General and Chairman of the Board of Directors: ABDLATIF YOUSUF AL-HAMAD (Kuwait).

FINANCIAL STRUCTURE

The Fund's authorized capital is 800m. Kuwaiti dinars (KD) divided into 80,000 shares having a value of KD 10,000 each. In April 2008 the Board of Governors approved a transfer of KD 1,337m. from the Fund's additional capital reserves to paid-up capital, increasing subscribed capital from KD 663m. to KD 2,000m. At 31 December 2012 shareholders' equity amounted to KD 2,808.6m. (including KD 808.6m. in reserves).

Activities

Pursuant to the Agreement Establishing the Fund (as amended in 1997 by the Board of Governors), the purpose of the Fund is to contribute to the financing of economic and social development projects in the Arab states and countries by:

1. Financing economic development projects of an investment character by means of loans granted on concessionary terms to governments and public enterprises and corporations, giving preference to projects which are vital to the Arab entity, as well as to joint Arab projects;

2. Financing private sector projects in member states by providing all forms of loans and guarantees to corporations and enterprises (possessing juridical personality), participating in their equity capital, and providing other forms of financing and the requisite financial, technical and advisory services, in accordance with such regulations and subject to such conditions as may be prescribed by the Board of Directors;

3. Forming or participating in the equity capital of corporations possessing juridical personality, for the implementation and financing of private sector projects in member states, including the provision and financing of technical, advisory and financial services;

4. Establishing and administering special funds with aims compatible with those of the Fund and with resources provided by the Fund or other sources;

5. Encouraging, directly or indirectly, the investment of public and private capital in a manner conducive to the development and growth of the Arab economy;

6. Providing expertise and technical assistance in the various fields of economic development.

The Fund co-operates with other Arab organizations in preparing regional studies and conferences, for example in the areas of human resource development, demographic research and private sector financing of infrastructure projects. It also acts as the secretariat of the Co-ordination Group of Arab National and Regional Development Financing Institutions. These organizations work together to produce a *Joint Arab Economic Report*, which considers economic and social developments in the Arab states. The 2012 edition of the Report was themed 'Opportunities and Challenges of Access to Financial and Banking Services and Financing in the Arab World'. The Fund has, since 2011, organized jointly with the World Bank annual Arab Development Symposiums. The inaugural Symposium was held in March 2011, in Kuwait; the second, convened in June 2012, also in Kuwait, focused on the developmental role of micro, small and medium-sized enterprises in inclusive economic growth, job creation and poverty reduction. In September 2011 the Fund endorsed the so-called Deauville Partnership, which had been established by the Group of Eight (G8) industrialized countries in May in order to assist countries in the Middle East and North Africa undergoing social and economic transformations. The Fund joined some nine other international financial institutions active in the region to establish a Co-ordination Platform to facilitate and promote collaboration among the institutions extending assistance under the Partnership.

During 2012 the Fund approved 13 loans, totalling KD 379m., to help 12 new and one previously financed public sector projects in nine member countries. One private sector project was appraised in 2012: a storage services initiative in Egypt. At the end of that year total lending since 1974 amounted to KD 7,958.1m., which had helped to finance 499 projects in 17 Arab countries. In 2012 33% of financing was for transport and telecommunications projects, while 27% was for projects in the energy and electricity sector. During the period 1974–2012 70% of project financing was for infrastructure sector projects and 20% for projects in the productive sectors.

In 2012 the Fund extended 14 inter-Arab and national grants, totalling KD 2.8m., providing for technical assistance, training, research activities and other emergency assistance programmes. The cumulative total number of grants provided by the end of 2012 was 1,009, with a value of KD 183.4m.

In December 1997 AFESD initiated an Arab Fund Fellowships Programme, which aimed to provide grants to Arab academics to conduct university teaching or advanced research. During 2010 the Fund contributed US $100m. to a new Special Account to finance small and medium-sized private sector projects in Arab countries, which had first been proposed in January 2009. The Fund administers the Account, and hosted its inaugural meeting in October 2010.

Publications

Annual Report.

Joint Arab Economic Report (annually).

Statistics

LOANS BY SECTOR

	2012		1974–2012
Sector	Amount (US $ million)	%	%
Infrastructure sectors	292.0	77.0	69.7
Transport and telecommunications	124.0	32.7	26.3
Energy and electricity	103.0	27.2	33.1
Water and sewerage	65.0	17.1	10.3
Productive sectors	0.0	0.0	20.0
Industry and mining	0.0	0.0	5.8
Agriculture and rural development	0.0	0.0	14.2
Social services	42.0	11.1	7.6
Other	45.0	11.9	2.7
Total	379.0	100.0	100.0

Source: AFESD, *Annual Report 2012*.

ARAB MONETARY FUND

Address: Arab Monetary Fund Bldg, Corniche Rd, POB 2818, Abu Dhabi, United Arab Emirates.

Telephone: (2) 6171400; **fax:** (2) 6326454; **e-mail:** centralmail@amfad.org.ae; **internet:** www.amf.org.ae.

The Agreement establishing the Arab Monetary Fund was approved by the Economic Council of Arab States in Rabat, Morocco, in April 1976 and entered into force on 2 February 1977.

MEMBERS

Algeria	Morocco
Bahrain	Oman
Comoros	Palestine
Djibouti	Qatar
Egypt	Saudi Arabia
Iraq*	Somalia*
Jordan	Sudan*
Kuwait	Syria
Lebanon	Tunisia
Libya	United Arab Emirates
Mauritania	Yemen

* From July 1993 loans to Iraq, Somalia and Sudan were suspended as a result of non-repayment of debts to the Fund. Sudan was readmitted in April 2000, following a settlement of its arrears; a Memorandum of Understanding, to incorporate new loan repayments was concluded in September 2001. An agreement to reschedule Iraq's outstanding arrears was concluded in 2008. In 2011 an agreement was signed with Comoros concerning the settlement of that country's debt to the Fund. Somalia and Syria were in arrears at end-2012.

Organization

(April 2014)

BOARD OF GOVERNORS

The Board of Governors is the highest authority of the Arab Monetary Fund. It formulates policies on Arab economic integration and the liberalization of trade among member states. The Board of Governors is composed of a governor and a deputy governor appointed by each member state for a term of five years. It meets at least once a year; meetings may also be convened at the request of half the members, or of members holding half of the total voting power.

BOARD OF EXECUTIVE DIRECTORS

The Board of Executive Directors exercises all powers vested in it by the Board of Governors and may delegate to the Director-General such powers as it deems fit. It is composed of the Director-General and eight non-resident directors elected by the Board of Governors. Each director holds office for three years and may be re-elected.

DIRECTOR-GENERAL

The Director-General of the Fund is appointed by the Board of Governors for a renewable five-year term, and serves as Chairman of the Board of Executive Directors.

The Director-General supervises Committees on Loans, Investments, and Administration. Other offices include the Economic and Technical Department, the Economic Policy Institute, the Investment Department, the Legal Department, an Internal Audit Office, and the Finance and Computer Department.

Director-General and Chairman of the Board of Executive Directors: Dr ABDULRAHMAN BIN ABDULLAH AL-HAMIDY.

FINANCE

The Arab Accounting Dinar (AAD) is a unit of account equivalent to three IMF Special Drawing Rights (SDRs). (The average value of the SDR in 2012 was US $1.53169, and in 2013 it was US $1.51973.)

In April 1983 the authorized capital of the Fund was increased from AAD 288m. to AAD 600m. The new capital stock comprised 12,000 shares, each having the value of AAD 50,000. At the end of 2012 total paid-up capital was AAD 596.04m.

CAPITAL SUBSCRIPTIONS
(million Arab Accounting Dinars, 31 December 2012)

Member	Paid-up capital
Algeria	77.90
Bahrain	9.20
Comoros	0.45
Djibouti	0.45
Egypt	58.80
Iraq	77.90
Jordan	9.90
Kuwait	58.80
Lebanon	9.20
Libya	24.69
Mauritania	9.20
Morocco	27.55
Oman	9.20
Palestine	3.96
Qatar	18.40
Saudi Arabia	88.95
Somalia	7.35
Sudan	18.40
Syria	13.25
Tunisia	12.85
United Arab Emirates	35.30
Yemen	28.30
Total*	596.04

* Excluding Palestine's share (AAD 3.96m.), which was deferred by a Board of Governors' resolution in 1978.

Activities

The creation of the Arab Monetary Fund was seen as a step towards the goal of Arab economic integration. It assists member states in balance of payments difficulties, and also has a broad range of aims.

The Articles of Agreement define the Fund's aims as follows:

(*a*) to correct disequilibria in the balance of payments of member states;

(*b*) to promote the stability of exchange rates among Arab currencies, to render them mutually convertible, and to eliminate restrictions on current payments between member states;

(*c*) to establish policies and modes of monetary co-operation to accelerate Arab economic integration and economic development in the member states;

(*d*) to tender advice on the investment of member states' financial resources in foreign markets, whenever called upon to do so;

(*e*) to promote the development of Arab financial markets;

(*f*) to promote the use of the Arab dinar as a unit of account and to pave the way for the creation of a unified Arab currency;

(*g*) to co-ordinate the positions of member states in dealing with international monetary and economic problems; and

(*h*) to provide a mechanism for the settlement of current payments between member states in order to promote trade among them.

The Arab Monetary Fund functions both as a fund and a bank. It is empowered:

(*a*) to provide short- and medium-term loans to finance balance of payments deficits of member states;

(*b*) to issue guarantees to member states to strengthen their borrowing capabilities;

(*c*) to act as intermediary in the issuance of loans in Arab and international markets for the account of member states and under their guarantees;

(*d*) to co-ordinate the monetary policies of member states;

(*e*) to manage any funds placed under its charge by member states;

(*f*) to hold periodic consultations with member states on their economic conditions; and

(*g*) to provide technical assistance to banking and monetary institutions in member states.

Loans are intended to finance an overall balance of payments deficit and a member may draw up to 75% of its paid-up subscription, in convertible currencies, for this purpose unconditionally (automatic loans). A member may, however, obtain loans in excess of this limit, subject to agreement with the Fund on a programme aimed at reducing its balance of payments deficit (ordinary and extended loans, equivalent to 175% and 250% of its quota, respectively). From 1981 a country receiving no extended loans was entitled to a loan under the Inter-Arab Trade Facility (discontinued in 1989) of up to 100% of its quota. In addition, a member has the right to borrow under a compensatory loan in order to finance an unexpected deficit in its balance of payments resulting from a decrease in its exports of goods and services or a large increase in its imports of agricultural products following a poor harvest. In 2009 the access limit was doubled to 100% of paid-up capital.

Automatic and compensatory loans are repayable within three years, while ordinary and extended loans are repayable within five and seven years, respectively. Loans are granted at concessionary and uniform rates of interest that increase with the length of the period of the loan. In 1996 the Fund established the Structural Adjustment Facility, initially providing up to 75% of a member's paid-up subscription and later increased to 175%. This may include a technical assistance component comprising a grant of up to 2% of the total loan. In 2009, in order to enhance the flexibility and effectiveness of its lending to meet the needs of member countries affected by the global financial crisis, the Fund determined to extend an access limit of 175% for lending for both the public finance sector and for the financial and banking sector under the Structural Adjustment Facility. In 2007 the Fund established an Oil Facility to assist petroleum-importing member countries to counter the effects of the escalation in global fuel prices. Eligible countries were entitled to borrow up to 200% of their paid-up subscription under the new Facility. A new Short Term Liquidity Facility was approved in 2009 to provide resources to countries with previously strong track records undergoing financial shortages owing to the sharp contraction in international trade and credit.

During the period 1978–2012 the Fund extended 160 loans, amounting to AAD 1,600m., to 14 countries. In 2012 the Fund approved lending of AAD 118m. (compared with AAD 116m. in 2011), including an automatic loan, amounting to AAD 7.4m., for Jordan; a compensatory loan (AAD 24m.) and an ordinary loan (AAD 21m.), extended to Yemen; an automatic loan (AAD 9.6m.), a compensatory loan (AAD 12.8m.) and a loan under the Structural Adjustment Facility (AAD 16.0m.) in the public finance sector, for Tunisia; and an AAD 27.4m. compensatory loan for Morocco, which aimed to support the financing of the purchase of agricultural imports.

The Fund's technical assistance activities are extended through either the provision of experts to the country concerned or in the form of specialized training of officials of member countries. In view of the increased importance of this type of assistance, the Fund established, in 1988, the Economic Policy Institute (EPI), which offers regular training courses and specialized seminars for middle-level and senior staff, respectively, of financial and monetary institutions of the Arab countries. During 2012 the EPI organized 13 training events, attended by 369 people. In April 1999 the Fund signed a Memorandum of Understanding with the International Monetary Fund (IMF) to establish a joint regional training programme. The Fund also co-operates with the IMF in conducting workshops and technical advice missions under the Arab Credit Reporting Initiative and the Arab Debt Markets Development Initiative.

AMF collaborates with Arab Fund for Economic and Social Development (AFESD), the League of Arab States and the Organization of Arab Petroleum Exporting Countries (OAPEC) in writing and publishing a *Joint Arab Economic Report*. The Fund also co-operates with AFESD, with the technical assistance of the IMF and the World Bank, in organizing an annual seminar. The Fund provides the secretariat for the Council of Arab Central Banks, comprising the governors of central banks and the heads of the monetary agencies in Arab countries, and also serves as the technical secretariat of the Board of Arab ministers repsonsible for finance. In 1991 the Council established the Arab Committee on Banking Supervision. In 2005 the Council inaugurated a second technical grouping, the Arab Committee on Payments and Settlements Systems. In September 2011 the Fund endorsed the so-called Deauville Partnership, which had been established by the Group of Eight (G8) industrialized countries in May in order to assist countries in the Middle East and North Africa undergoing social and economic transformations. The Fund joined some nine other international financial institutions active in the region to establish a Co-ordination Platform to facilitate and promote collaboration among the institutions extending assistance under the Partnership.

TRADE PROMOTION

Arab Trade Financing Program (ATFP): POB 26799, Arab Monetary Fund Bldg, 7th Floor, Corniche Rd, Abu Dhabi, United Arab Emirates; tel. (2) 6316999; fax (2) 6316793; e-mail finadmin@atfp.ae; internet www.atfp.org.ae; f. 1989 to develop and promote trade between Arab countries and to enhance the competitive ability of Arab exporters; operates by extending lines of credit to Arab exporters and importers through national agencies (some 198 agencies designated by the monetary authorities of 19 Arab and five other countries); the Arab Monetary Fund provided 56% of ATFP's authorized capital of US $500m; participation was also invited from private and official Arab financial institutions and joint Arab/foreign institutions; administers the Inter-Arab Trade Information Network (IATIN), and organizes Buyers-Sellers meetings to promote Arab goods; by the end of 2012 the Program had extended lines of credit with a total value of $9,200m; Chair. and Chief Exec. Dr Jassim Abdullah al-Mannai; publ. *Annual Report* (Arabic and English).

Publications

Annual Report.

Arab Capital Markets (quarterly).

Arab Countries: Economic Indicators (annually).

Foreign Trade of the Arab Countries (annually).

Joint Arab Economic Report (annually).

Money and Credit in the Arab Countries.

National Accounts of the Arab Countries (annually).

Statistical Bulletin of Arab Countries.

Reports on commodity structure (by value and quantity) of member countries' imports from and exports to other Arab countries; other studies on economic, social, management and fiscal issues.

Statistics

LOANS APPROVED, 1978–2012

Type of loan	Number of loans	Amount (AAD '000)
Automatic	60	362,126
Ordinary	12	125,751
Compensatory	16	130,785
Extended	24	340,344
Structural Adjustment Facility	27	430,162
Oil Facility	3	32,489
Inter-Arab Trade Facility (cancelled in 1989)	11	64,730
Total	153	1,550,487

LOANS APPROVED, 2012

Borrower	Type of loan	Amount (AAD '000)
Jordan	Automatic loan	7,365
Morocco	Compensatory loan	27,350
Tunisia	Automatic loan	9,562
	Compensatory loan	12,750
	Structural Adjustment Facility	15,935
Yemen	Compensatory loan	24,000
	Ordinary loan	21,000

Source: *Annual Report 2012*.

ASIA-PACIFIC ECONOMIC COOPERATION—APEC

Address: 35 Heng Mui Keng Terrace, Singapore 119616.

Telephone: 68919600; **fax:** 68919690; **e-mail:** info@apec.org; **internet:** www.apec.org.

APEC was initiated in November 1989, in Canberra, Australia, as an informal consultative forum. Its aim is to promote multilateral economic co-operation on issues of trade and investment.

MEMBERS

Australia	Japan	Philippines
Brunei	Korea, Republic	Russia
Canada	Malaysia	Singapore
Chile	Mexico	Taiwan*
China, People's Republic	New Zealand	Thailand
Hong Kong	Papua New Guinea	USA
Indonesia	Peru	Viet Nam

* Admitted as Chinese Taipei.

Note: APEC has three official observers: the Association of Southeast Asian Nations (ASEAN) Secretariat; the Pacific Economic Cooperation Council; and the Pacific Islands Forum Secretariat. Observers may participate in APEC meetings and have full access to all related documents and information.

Organization

(April 2014)

ECONOMIC LEADERS' MEETINGS

The first meeting of APEC heads of government was convened in November 1993, in Seattle, Washington, USA. Subsequently, each annual meeting of APEC ministers responsible for foreign affairs and for economic affairs has been followed by an informal gathering of the leaders of the APEC economies, at which the policy objectives of the grouping are discussed and defined. The 21st Economic Leaders' Meeting was convened in October 2013, in Nusa Dua, Bali, Indonesia. Subsequent Meetings were to take place in Beijing, People's Republic of China, in 2014, the Philippines (2015) and Peru (2016).

MINISTERIAL MEETINGS

APEC ministers responsible for foreign affairs and for economic affairs meet annually. These meetings are hosted by the APEC Chair, which rotates each year, although it was agreed, in 1989, that alternate Ministerial Meetings were to be convened in an ASEAN member country. A Senior Officials' Meeting (SOM) convenes regularly between Ministerial Meetings to co-ordinate and administer the budgets and work programmes of APEC's committees and working groups. Other meetings of ministers are held on a regular basis to enhance co-operation in specific areas.

SECRETARIAT

In 1992 the Ministerial Meeting, held in Bangkok, Thailand, agreed to establish a permanent secretariat to support APEC activities. The Secretariat became operational in February 1993. The office of Chief of Staff, based at the Secretariat and tasked with co-ordinating and assisting programmatic work, was established in November 2013.

Executive Director: Dr ALAN BOLLARD (New Zealand).

Chief of Staff: IRENE SIM (Australia).

COMMITTEES

Budget and Management Committee (BMC): f. 1993 as Budget and Administrative Committee, present name adopted 1998; advises APEC senior officials on budgetary, administrative and managerial issues. The Committee reviews the operational budgets of APEC committees and groups, evaluates their effectiveness and conducts assessments of group projects. APEC projects may be self-funded, or else financed through: the Operational Account, the Trade and Investment Liberalisation and Facilitation Account, or (in the case of capacity-building programmes in developing economies) the APEC Support Fund.

Committee on Trade and Investment (CTI): f. 1993 on the basis of a Declaration signed by ministers meeting in Seattle, Washington, USA, in order to facilitate the expansion of trade and the development of a liberalized environment for investment among member countries; undertakes initiatives to improve the flow of goods, services and technology in the region. Supports Industry Dialogues to promote collaboration between public and private sector representatives in the following areas of activity: Automotive; Chemical; Non-ferrous Metal; and Life Sciences Innovation (a Life Sciences Innovation Forum was established in 2002). An Investment Experts' Group was established in 1994, initially to develop non-binding investment principles. In May 1997 an APEC Tariff Database was inaugurated, with sponsorship from the private sector. A Market Access Group was established in 1998 to administer CTI activities concerned with non-tariff measures. In 2001 the CTI finalized a set of nine non-binding Principles on Trade Facilitation, which aimed to help eliminate procedural and administrative impediments to trade and to increase trading opportunities. A Trade Facilitation Action Plan (TFAP) was approved in 2002. By 2005 a strategy was adopted to systematize transparency standards. The successor TFAP II was endorsed by APEC Leaders in September 2007. In 2007 the Electronic Commerce Steering Group, established in 1999, became aligned to the CTI. An Investment Facilitation Action Plan (IFAP) was initiated in 2008, with the aim of assisting investment flows into the region. The seventh edition of the official *Guide to the Investment Regimes of the APEC Member Economies* was published in January 2011.

Economic Committee (EC): f. 1994; aims to enhance APEC's capacity to analyse economic trends and to research and report on issues affecting economic and technical co-operation in the region. In addition, the Committee is considering the environmental and development implications of expanding population and economic growth. From 2011 the EC held a series of symposia and workshops aimed at capacity building for the APEC New Strategy for Structural Reform (ANSSR, approved in November 2010 by the 18th Leaders' Meeting).

SOM Steering Committee on ECOTECH (SCE): f. 1998 to assist the SOM with the co-ordination of APEC's economic and technical co-operation programme (ECOTECH); reconstituted in 2006, with an enhanced mandate to undertake greater co-ordination and oversee project proposals of the working groups; monitors and evaluates project implementation and also identifies initiatives designed to strengthen economic and technical co-operation in infrastructure.

ADVISORY COUNCIL

APEC Business Advisory Council (ABAC): Philamlife Tower, 43rd Floor, 8767 Paseo de Roxas, Makati City, 1226 Metro Manila, Philippines; tel. (2) 8454564; fax (2) 8454832; e-mail abacsec@pfgc.ph; internet www.abaconline.org; an agreement to establish ABAC, comprising up to three senior representatives of the private sector from each APEC member economy, was concluded at the Ministerial Meeting held in Nov. 1995. ABAC is mandated to advise member states on the implementation of APEC's Action Agenda and on other business matters, and to provide business-related information to APEC fora. ABAC meets three or four times each year and holds an annual CEO Summit alongside the annual APEC Economic Leaders' Meeting; Exec. Dir NING GAONING (People's Republic of China) (2014); Dir of ABAC Secretariat ANTONIO I. BASILIO.

Activities

APEC is focused on furthering objectives in three key areas, or 'pillars': trade and investment liberalization; business facilitation; and economic and technical co-operation. It was initiated in 1989 as a forum for informal discussion between the then six Association of Southeast Asian Nations (ASEAN) members and their six dialogue partners in the Pacific, and, in particular, to promote trade liberalization in the Uruguay Round of negotiations, which were being conducted under the General Agreement on Tariffs and Trade (GATT). The Seoul Declaration, adopted by ministers meeting in the Republic of Korea (South Korea) in November 1991, defined the objectives of APEC.

ASEAN countries were initially reluctant to support any more formal structure of the forum, or to admit new members, owing to concerns that it would undermine ASEAN's standing as a regional grouping and be dominated by powerful non-ASEAN economies. In August 1991 it was agreed to extend membership to the People's Republic of China, Hong Kong and Taiwan (subject to conditions imposed by China, including that a Taiwanese official of no higher than vice-ministerial level should attend the annual meeting of ministers responsible for foreign affairs). Mexico and Papua New Guinea acceded to the organization in November 1993, and Chile joined in November 1994. The summit meeting held in November 1997 agreed that Peru, Russia and Viet Nam should be admitted to APEC at the 1998 meeting, but imposed a 10-year moratorium on further expansion of the grouping.

Meeting in Osaka, Japan, in November 1995, APEC heads of government adopted the Osaka Action Agenda as a framework to achieve the commitments of the Bogor Declaration. Part One of the Agenda identified action areas for the liberalization of trade and investment and the facilitation of business, for example, customs procedures, rules of origin and non-tariff barriers. Each member economy was to ensure the transparency of its laws, regulations and procedures affecting the flow of goods, services and capital among APEC economies and to refrain from implementing any trade protection measures. A second part of the Agenda was to provide a framework for further economic and technical co-operation between APEC members in areas such as energy, transport, infrastructure, small and medium-sized enterprises (SMEs) and agricultural technology. In order to resolve a disagreement concerning the inclusion of agricultural products in the trade liberalization process, a provision for flexibility was incorporated into the Agenda, taking into account diverse circumstances and different levels of development in APEC member economies. Liberalization measures were to be implemented from January 1997 (three years earlier than previously agreed). Each member economy was to prepare an Individual Action Plan (IAP) on efforts to achieve the trade liberalization measures, that were to be reviewed annually.

In November 1996 the Economic Leaders' Meeting, held in Subic Bay, Philippines, approved the Manila Action Plan for APEC, which incorporated the IAPs and other collective measures aimed at achieving the trade liberalization and co-operation objectives of the Bogor Declaration, as well as the joint activities specified in the second part of the Osaka Agenda. Heads of government also endorsed a US proposal to eliminate tariffs and other barriers to trade in information technology (IT) products by 2000 and determined to support efforts to conclude an agreement to this effect at the forthcoming World Trade Organization (WTO) conference; however, they insisted on the provision of an element of flexibility in achieving trade liberalization in this sector.

The 1997 Economic Leaders' Meeting, held in Vancouver, Canada, in November, was dominated by concern at the financial instability that had affected several Asian economies during that year. The final declaration of the summit meeting endorsed a framework of measures that had been agreed by APEC deputy ministers of finance and central bank governors at an emergency meeting convened in the previous week in Manila, Philippines (the so-called Manila Framework for Enhanced Asian Regional Cooperation to Promote Financial Stability). The meeting, attended by representatives of the IMF, the World Bank and the Asian Development Bank (ADB), committed all member economies receiving IMF assistance to undertake specified economic and financial reforms, and supported the establishment of a separate Asian funding facility to supplement international financial assistance (although this was later rejected by the IMF). APEC ministers of finance and governors of central banks were urged to accelerate efforts for the development of the region's financial and capital markets and to liberalize capital flows in the region. Measures were to include strengthening financial market supervision and clearing and settlement infrastructure, the reform of pension systems, and promoting co-operation among export credit agencies and financing institutions. The principal item on the Vancouver summit agenda was an initiative to enhance trade liberalization, which, the grouping insisted, should not be undermined by the financial instability in Asia; 15 economic sectors were identified for 'early voluntary sectoral liberalization' ('EVSL').

The region's economic difficulties remained the principal topic of discussion at the Economic Leaders' Meeting held in Kuala Lumpur, Malaysia, in November 1988. A final declaration reiterated their commitment to co-operation in pursuit of sustainable economic recovery and growth, in particular through the restructuring of financial and corporate sectors, promoting and facilitating private sector capital flows, and efforts to strengthen the global financial system. Other initiatives approved included an Agenda of APEC Science and Technology Industry Cooperation into the 21st Century, and an Action Programme on Skills and Development in APEC. Japan's persisting opposition to a reduction of tariffs in the fish and forestry sectors prevented the conclusion of tariff negotiations under the EVSL scheme, and it was therefore agreed that responsibility for managing the tariff reduction element of the initiative should be transferred to the WTO.

The September 1999 Economic Leaders' Meeting considered measures to sustain the economic recovery in Asia and endorsed the APEC Principles to Enhance Competition and Regulatory Reform (for example, transparency, accountability, non-discrimination) as a framework to strengthen APEC markets and to enable further integration and implementation of the IAPs. An APEC Business Travel Card scheme, facilitating business travel within the region, was inaugurated in 1999, having been launched on a trial basis in 1997; card holders receive fast-track passage through designated APEC immigration processing lanes at major airports, and multiple short term-entry entitlements to participating economies. By 2014 more than 120,000 individuals were registered under the scheme, in which all 21 APEC economies were participating fully. (Russia joined the scheme in May 2013.) The November 2011 Leaders' Meeting determined to launch an APEC Travel Facilitation Initiative, which was to address means of facilitating faster, easier and more secure travel through the region.

The Economic Leaders' Meeting for 2000, held in Brunei in November, endorsed a plan of action to promote the utilization of advances in information and communications technologies (ICTs) in member economies, for the benefit of all citizens. A proposal that the Democratic People's Republic of Korea (North Korea) be permitted to participate in APEC working groups was approved at the meeting.

The 2001 Economic Leaders' Meeting, held in October, in Shanghai, China, condemned the terrorist attacks against targets in the USA of the previous month and resolved to take action to combat the threat of international terrorism. The meeting declared terrorism to be a direct challenge to APEC's vision of free, open and prosperous economies, and concluded that the threat made the continuing move to free trade, with its aim of bolstering economies, increasing prosperity and encouraging integration, even more of a priority. Leaders emphasized the importance of sharing the benefits of globalization, and adopted the Shanghai Accord, which identified development goals for APEC and clarified measures for achieving the Bogor goals within the agreed timetable. A process of IAP Peer Reviews was initiated. (By late 2005 the process had been concluded for each member economy.) The meeting also outlined the e-APEC Strategy developed by the e-APEC Task Force established after the Brunei Economic Leaders' meeting. Considering issues of entrepreneurship, structural and regulatory reform, competition, intellectual property rights and information security, the strategy aimed to facilitate technological development in the region. Finally, the meeting adopted a strategy document relating to infectious diseases in the Asia-Pacific region, which aimed to promote a co-ordinated response to combating HIV/AIDS and other contagious diseases.

In September 2002 a meeting of APEC ministers responsible for finance was held in Los Cabos, Mexico. Ministers discussed the importance of efforts to combat money-laundering and the financing of terrorism. The 2002 Economic Leaders' Meeting, held in the following month, also in Los Cabos, issued a statement on the implementation of APEC standards of transparency in trade and investment liberalization and facilitation. Leaders also issued a statement on fighting terrorism and promoting growth. In February the first conference to promote the Secure Trade in the APEC Region (STAR) initiative was convened in Bangkok, Thailand, and attended by representatives of all APEC member economies as well as senior officers of private sector companies and relevant international organizations. STAR conferences have since been held at regular one to two year intervals.

The 2003 Economic Leaders' Meeting, convened in October, in Bangkok, considered means of advancing the WTO's stalled Doha Round of trade negotiations and noted progress made hitherto in facilitating intra-APEC trade. The meeting also addressed regional security issues, reiterating the Community's commitment to ensuring the resilience of APEC economies against the threat of terrorism. The Leaders adopted the Bangkok Declaration on Partnership for the Future, which identified the following areas as priority concerns for the group: the promotion of trade and investment liberalization; enhancing human security; and helping people and societies to benefit from globalization. The Bangkok meeting also issued a statement on health security, which expressed APEC's determination to strengthen infrastructure for the detection and prevention of infectious diseases, as well as the surveillance of other threats to public health, and to ensure a co-ordinated response to public health emergencies, with particular concern to the outbreak, earlier in the year, of Severe Acute Respiratory Syndrome (SARS).

In September 2005 APEC ministers responsible for finance, meeting in Jeju, South Korea, discussed two main issues: the increased importance of capital flows among member economies, particularly those from worker remittances; and the challenge presented by the region's ageing population. The meeting resolved to promote capital account liberalization and to develop resilient and efficient capital markets. It also adopted the Jeju Declaration on Enhancing Regional Cooperation against the Challenges of Population Ageing, in which it acknowledged the urgency of such domestic reforms such as creating sustainable pension systems, providing an increased range of savings products and improving financial literacy. In November the 13th Economic Leaders' Meeting endorsed a Busan Roadmap to the Bogor Goals, which outlined key priorities and frameworks. Particular focus was drawn to support for the multilateral trading system, efforts to promote high quality regional trade agreements and free trade agreements, and strengthened collective and individual action plans. It also incorporated a Busan Business Agenda and commitments to a strategic approach to capacity building and to a pathfinder approach to promoting trade and investment in the region, through work on areas such as intellectual property rights, anti-corruption, secure trade and trade facilitation.

The 14th Economic Leaders' Meeting, held in Hanoi, Viet Nam, in November 2006, reaffirmed support for the stalled negotiations on the WTO's Doha Development Agenda; adopted the Hanoi Action Plan on the implementation of the 2005 Busan Roadmap; endorsed the APEC Action Plan on Prevention and Response to Avian and Influenza Pandemics; and expressed strong concern at the nuclear test conducted by North Korea in October.

The participants at the 15th Economic Leaders' Meeting, convened in Sydney, Australia, in September 2007, adopted a Declaration on Climate Change, Energy Security and Clean Development, wherein they acknowledged the need to ensure energy supplies to support regional economic growth while also preserving the quality of the environment. The Declaration incorporated an Action Agenda and agreements to establish an Asia-Pacific Network for Energy Technology and an Asia-Pacific Network for Sustainable Forest Management and Rehabilitation, while committing to increase regional forest coverage to 20m. ha by 2020. The Economic Leaders also issued a statement once again affirming the need successfully to resolve the stalled WTO Doha Development Round; endorsed a report on means of further promoting Asia-Pacific economic integration; agreed to examine the options and prospects for the development of a Free Trade Area of the Asia-Pacific (FTAAP); welcomed efforts by the Economic Committee to enhance the implementation of the LAISR; endorsed the second Trade Facilitation Action Plan (under which a 5% reduction in business and trade transaction costs was achieved by the end of 2010); determined to strengthen the protection and enforcement of intellectual property rights in the region; and approved a set of Anti-corruption Principles for the Public and Private Sectors, and related codes of conduct.

The 16th Economic Leaders' Meeting, held in November 2008, in Lima, Peru, addressed the implications for the region of the then deteriorating global economic situation. The APEC Leaders urged the promotion of good Corporate Social Responsibility (CSR) practices in the region; commended the progress made hitherto in examining the prospects for establishing the proposed FTAAP; and urged ministers of finance to examine more fully means of optimizing linkages between private infrastructure finance and economic growth and development. Expressing deep concern at the impact on the region of volatile global food prices, and at food shortages in some developing economies, the meeting determined to support the regional implementation of the Comprehensive Framework for Action of the UN Task Force on the Global Food Security Crisis, and to increase technical co-operation and capacity-building measures aimed at fostering the growth of the agricultural sector.

Convened in November 2009, in Singapore, the 17th Economic Leaders' Meeting expressed support for the goals of the Group of Twenty (G20) Framework for Strong, Sustainable and Balanced Growth (adopted in September), and adopted a Declaration on a New Growth Paradigm for a Connected Asia-Pacific in the 21st Century, aimed at navigating a future post-global economic crisis landscape. The Meeting also reaffirmed commitment to addressing issues related to the threat of climate change; and welcomed the implementation of a peer review of energy efficiency in APEC economies.

The first APEC Ministerial Meeting on Food Security, held in October 2010, in Niigata, Japan, endorsed a new APEC Action Plan on Food Security. In May 2011 APEC and the World Bank concluded a Memorandum of Understanding on strengthening collaboration on food safety in the Asia-Pacific region. In November 2010 the 18th Economic Leaders' Meeting, held in Yokohama, Japan, endorsed the APEC New Strategy for Structural Reform (ANSSR), representing a comprehensive long-term framework for promoting high-quality growth in the region. Under the ANSSR progress was to be achieved in the areas of structural reform; human resource and entrepreneurship development; human security; green growth; and the development of a knowledge-based economy. The Meeting also endorsed a report and issued an assessment on the state of progress towards achieving the Bogor Goals. Leaders reaffirmed strong commitment to pursuing the proposed FTAAP and towards achieving a successful conclusion to the Doha Development Agenda, while determining to refrain from adopting protectionist measures until 2014.

In September 2011 a session of APEC ministers, senior government officials and private sector leaders, meeting in San Francisco, USA, adopted the San Francisco Declaration on Women and the Economy, outlining means of realizing the as yet untapped full potential of women to contribute to the regional economy, and welcoming the establishment of an APEC Policy Partnership on Women and the Economy (PPWE), which had been endorsed by senior officials in May.

The 19th Leaders' Meeting, convened in Honolulu, Hawaii, in November 2011, adopted the Honolulu Declaration 'Toward a Seamless Regional Economy', which, inter alia, pledged to monitor implementation of the San Francisco Declaration; instructed regional officials to consider new approaches to the still stalled negotiations on concluding the Doha Development Round; reaffirmed commitment to anti-protectionism; determined to advance a set of policies to promote market-driven innovation policy; committed to implementing plans towards the establishment of an APEC New Strategy for Structural Reform and a voluntary APEC Cross Border Privacy Rules System; committed, further, to promoting green growth, including through encouraging member economies to develop an APEC List of Environmental Goods contributing directly to the Community's sustainable development objectives; aspired to reduce regional energy intensity by 45% by 2035, to take specific steps to promote energy-smart low-carbon communities, and to incorporate low-emissions development strategies into national economic growth plans; and determined to enhance the role of the private sector in APEC, through greater contribution to its working groups and the establishment of new public-private policy partnerships.

The second APEC Ministerial Meeting on Food Security, convened in May 2012, in Kazan, Russia, adopted the Kazan Declaration on APEC Food Security, representing a comprehensive assessment of member states' food security issues, and an updated framework for addressing them. In June APEC ministers responsible for trade, also meeting in Kazan, issued a statement outlining specific measures being taken to promote regional economic recovery and sustainable growth; and also issued a Statement on Supporting the Multilateral Trading System and Resisting Protectionism. In July APEC ministers responsible for the environment, meeting in Khabarovsk, Russia, issued the Khabarovsk Statement on Environment, outlining an updated framework for co-operation in addressing the following key environmental issues: conservation of biological diversity; sustainable use of natural resources; sustainable management of water resources and transboundary watercourses; transboundary air pollution and climate change; and support for green growth. At the end of July the USA became the first participant in the new APEC Cross Border Privacy Rules System, which aims to promote APEC-wide compatibility in privacy policies, lower regulatory compliance costs, and consumer protection. The 20th Economic Leaders' Meeting, convened in September, in Vladivostok, Russia, reaffirmed a commitment to achieving, by 2015, a 10% improvement in the performance of the regional food supply chain; endorsed the APEC List of Environmental Goods that had been proposed by the November 2011 meeting (comprising some 54 items on which tariffs were to be reduced to 5% by the end of 2015); and welcomed the recent establishment of a new APEC Policy Partnership on Science, Technology and Innovation. The Meeting encouraged member economies to consider using new Organisation for Economic Co-operation and Development (OECD) Guidelines for Financial Education in Schools, and also to consider participating in 2015 in OECD's evaluatory Programme for International Student Assessments (PISA), to measure youth financial literacy. Leaders welcomed progress achieved so far in the implementation of the ANSSR.

The 21st Economic Leaders' Meeting, held in October 2013, in Bali, Indonesia, reiterated a shared commitment towards a seamless regional economy; tasked member states' senior officials with recommending means of deepening APEC's engagement with international and regional co-operation fora and processes; reaffirmed commitment to attaining, by 2020, the Bogor Goals, and towards achieving the proposed FTAAP; and extended from 2014 to 2016 the regional moratorium on the adoption of protectionist measures. The Meeting also endorsed a Proposal on Capacity-Building Activities to Assist Implementation of APEC's Environmental Goods Commitments, and established an APEC Public-Private Partnership on Environmental Goods and Services (PPEGS), representing a platform for enhanced dialogue in that area. (The inaugural meeting of the PPEGS was to take place in 2014.) The Leaders (with the US President being represented by his Secretary of State) endorsed an APEC Multi-Year Plan on Infrastructure Development and Investment, covering 2013–16. The Plan aimed to support member economies in enhancing the investment environment, promoting public-private partnerships, and improving government capacity and co-ordination in delivering infrastructure projects. The Meeting also approved a new Food Security Road Map towards 2020.

WORKING GROUPS

APEC's structure of working groups aims to promote practical and technical co-operation in specific areas, and to help implement individual and collective action plans in response to the directives of the Economic Leaders and meetings of relevant ministers.

Agricultural Technical Co-operation (ATCWG): formally established as an APEC expert's group in 1996, and incorporated into the system of working groups in 2000. The ATCWG aims to enhance the role of agriculture in the economic growth of the region and to promote co-operation in the following areas: conservation and utilization of plant and animal genetic resources; research, development and extension of agricultural biotechnology; processing, marketing, distribution and consumption of agricultural products; plant and animal quarantine and pest management; development of an agricultural finance system; sustainable agriculture; and agricultural technology transfer and training. The ATCWG has primary responsibility for undertaking recommendations connected with the implementation of the APEC Food System, which aims to improve the efficiency of food production, supply and trade within member economies. The ATCWG has conducted projects on human resource development in post-harvest technology and on capacity building, safety assessment and communication in biotechnology. A high-level policy dialogue on agricultural biotechnology was initiated in 2002. Following the outbreak of so-called avian flu and its impact on the region's poultry industry, in 2004 it was agreed that the ATCWG would develop the enhanced biosecurity planning and surveillance capacity considered by APEC's member economies as being essential to protect the region's agricultural sector from the effects of future outbreaks of disease. A quarantine regulators' seminar on Implementing Harmonised Arrangements for Ensuring Effective Quarantine Treatments, and an APEC Workshop on Avian Influenza Risks in the Live Bird Market System, were organized in 2008; and in August 2009 a symposium on the Approach of Organic Agriculture: New Markets, Food Security and a Clean Environment was held. In April 2010 a *Report on Developing and Applying a Traceability System in Agriculture Production and Trade* was issued. The ATCWG contributed to the development of the APEC Action Plan on Food Security, which was endorsed by the October 2010 APEC Ministerial Meeting on Food Security. The 15th ATCWG meeting, held in Washington, DC, USA, in February 2011, agreed to promote agricultural technical transfer and co-operation within the APEC region; consequently, in November, an APEC Agricultural Technology Transfer Forum was held, in Beijing, China, on the theme 'Strengthening Agricultural Technology Transfer for Food Security in the APEC Region'. In March 2012 a web-based Asia-Pacific Food Security Information Platform (APIP) was launched. Workshops on food security, the application of remote sensing and geographic information system technology on crops productivity, and sustainable land management to enhance food production, were convened, respectively, in September, October and November 2012.

Anti-corruption and Transparency (ACT): the ACT was upgraded to a working group in March 2011, having been established as a task force in 2004. The Ministerial Meeting, held in Santiago, Chile, in November 2004, endorsed the establishment of the ACT to implement an APEC Course of Action on Fighting Corruption and Ensuring Transparency. Following its establishment the ACT worked to promote ratification and implementation of the UN Convention against Corruption, to strengthen measures to prevent and combat corruption and to sanction public officials found guilty of corruption, to promote public-private partnerships, and to enhance co-operation within the region to combat problems of corruption. An APEC Anti-Counterfeiting and Piracy Initiative was launched in mid-2005. In June 2007 the ACT approved a Code of Conduct for Business, in collaboration with ABAC, a set of Conduct Principles for Public Officials, and Anti-corruption Principles for the Public and Private Sectors. In February 2010 the ACT endorsed the final result of a project entitled 'Stocktaking of Bilateral and Regional Arrangements on Anti-corruption Matters Between/Among APEC Member Economies'. The 17th meeting of the ACT group was convened in June 2013, in Medan, Indonesia. A joint ACT-Experts Group on Illegal Logging and Associated Trade conference was also held in June, in Medan. The ACT is undertaking an APEC-ASEAN Pathfinder Project on Combating Corruption and Illicit Trade. In January 2014 an APEC Round Table Discussion on Anti-Corruption and Public Sector Governance was convened in Taiwan, and in February a Workshop on International Recovery of the Proceeds of Corruption was held, in Ningbo, China.

Counter Terrorism Working Group (CTWG): the CTWG seceded in 2013 the former Counter Terrorism Task Force; the first meeting of the CTWG was held in February 2014, in Ningbo, China, and the second was to be convened in Qingdao, also in China, in May; focal areas in 2014 included secure travel (covering bus security training; and developing regional trusted traveller and advance passenger information systems); secure finance (protecting designated non-financial businesses and professions from terrorist financing); secure supply trains; secure infrastructure; and participation by the CTWG in the ninth Secure Trade in the APEC Region conference, to be held in September.

Emergency Preparedness (EPWG): established in March 2005, as a special task force, in response to the devastating natural disaster that had occurred in the Indian Ocean in late December 2004; upgraded to a working group in 2010. The EPWG is mandated to co-ordinate efforts throughout APEC to enhance disaster management capacity building, to strengthen public awareness regarding natural disaster preparedness, prevention and survival, and to compile best practices. An APEC Senior Disaster Management Co-ordinator Seminar, convened in Cairns, Australia, in August 2007, and comprising representatives of APEC member economies and of international humanitarian organizations, determined to support the development of a three- to five-year emergency preparedness strategic plan. In October 2011 the EPWG organized a workshop on 'school earthquake and tsunami safety in APEC economies'. The sixth APEC Senior Disaster Management Officials Forum (known until 2011 as the Emergency Management CEOs' Forum), convened in October 2012, in Vladivostok, Russia, addressed lessons learned from the earthquakes in New Zealand and Japan, in February and March 2011, respectively. In particular, the Forum highlighted the importance of private sector participation in the response to the New Zealand disaster and, in the case of Japan, efforts to promote public awareness. The seventh APEC Senior Disaster Management Officials Forum, held in August 2013, in Bali, Indonesia, endorsed a document on 'Improving Disaster Risk Reduction and Resiliency in the APEC Region'. The eighth Forum was to take place in October 2014, in Beijing, China.

Energy (EWG): APEC ministers responsible for energy convened for the first time in August 1996 to discuss major energy challenges confronting the region. The main objectives of the EWG, established in 1990, are: the enhancement of regional energy security and improvement of the fuel supply market for the power sector; the development and implementation of programmes of work promoting the adoption of environmentally sound energy technologies and promoting private sector investment in regional power infrastructure; the development of energy efficiency guidelines; and the standardization of testing facilities and results. The EWG is supported by four expert groups, on clean fossil energy, efficiency and conservation, energy data and analysis, and new and renewable energy technologies; and by two task forces, on energy trade and investment, and biofuels. The inaugural meeting of a business network established by the EWG to improve relations and communications with the private sector took place in April 1999. In May 2000 APEC energy ministers meeting in San Diego, California, USA, launched the APEC 21st Century Renewable Energy Initiative, which aimed to encourage co-operation in and advance the utilization of renewable energy technologies, envisaging the establishment of a Private Sector Renewable Energy Forum. In June 2003 APEC ministers responsible for energy agreed on a framework to implement APEC's Energy Security Initiative, a strategy aimed at responding to temporary supply disruptions and at addressing the broader challenges facing the region's energy supply by means of longer-term policy. In 2004, amid challenges to energy security and unusually high oil prices, the EWG was instructed by APEC Economic Leaders to accelerate the implementation of the Energy Security Initiative. Meeting in May 2007 in Darwin, Australia, on the theme 'Achieving Energy Security and Sustainable Development through Efficiency, Conservation and Diversity', ministers responsible for energy directed the EWG to formulate a voluntary Energy Peer Review Mechanism. The ministers welcomed the work of the Asia-Pacific Partnership on Clean Development and Climate, launched in January 2006 by Australia, China, India, Japan, South Korea and the USA. In June 2010 energy ministers gathered, in Fukui, Japan, on the theme 'Low Carbon Path to Energy Security'. Pursuant to the Osaka Action Agenda adopted by APEC Economic Leaders in 1995, the Asia Pacific Energy Research Centre (APERC) was established in July 1996 in Tokyo, Japan; APERC's mandate and programmes focus on energy sector development in APEC member states. APERC maintains a comprehensive regional Energy Database. Meeting in Kaohsiung, Taiwan, in October 2011, the EWG set a target to reduce APEC regional energy intensity by 45% by 2035; this was endorsed by the November 2011 Leaders' Meeting. In March 2012 the EWG, convened in Kuala Lumpur, Malaysia, discussed an 'Action Agenda to move APEC toward an Energy Efficient, Sustainable, Low-Carbon Transport Future', which had been adopted by the first APEC Joint Transportation and Energy Ministerial Conference, convened in September 2011, in San Francisco, USA. In June 2012 APEC ministers, meeting in St Petersburg, Russia, issued the St Petersburg Declaration on Energy Security, representing a framework for addressing regional and global energy challenges. In November the EWG, meeting in Washington, DC, nominated Danang City, Viet Nam, as the forthcoming case study for APEC's ongoing Low Carbon Model Town Project (LCMT, launched in 2010, with Tianjin Yujiapu, China, as the first model town); San Borja (Peru) was to be considered subsequently by the LCMT. The 45th EWG meeting, held in March 2013, in Koh Samui, Thailand, addressed policy responses to energy supply disruptions, within the context of the APEC Energy Security Initiative. An APEC Conference on Clean, Renewable and Sustainable Use of Energy was convened in September–October 2013, in Bali, Indonesia.

Health: in October 2003 a Health Task Force (HTF) was established, on an ad hoc basis, to implement health-related activities, including a Health Safety Initiative, and to address health issues perceived as potential threats to the region's economy, trade and security, in particular emerging infectious diseases. The HTF convened for the first time in Taiwan, in April 2004. It was responsible for enhancing APEC's work on preventing, preparing for and mitigating the effects of highly pathogenic avian influenza (avian flu) and any future related human influenza pandemic. In May 2006 a Ministerial Meeting on Avian and Influenza Pandemics, held in Da Nang, Viet Nam, endorsed an APEC Action Plan on the Prevention of and Response to Avian and Influenza Pandemics. In June 2007 APEC ministers of health, meeting in Sydney, Australia, determined to reconstitute the HTF as the Health Working Group. The Group convened for its first official meeting in February 2008. Meeting in June 2010, the HWG identified the following priority areas: enhancing preparedness for combating vector-borne diseases, including avian and human pandemic influenza, and HIV/AIDS; capacity building in the areas of health promotion and prevention of lifestyle-related diseases; improving health outcomes through advances in health information technologies; and strengthening health systems in each member economy. An APEC High-Level Meeting on Health and the Economy, convened in June 2012, in St Petersburg, Russia, urged APEC ministers responsible for to factor good health as a source of economic growth and development into budgetary processes. In July 2013 the HWG adopted a strategic plan to cover the period 2013–15. Joint meetings of the HWG and APEC's Life Sciences Innovation Forum (LSIF) have been held in March 2011, June 2012, and September 2013. In July 2013 an inaugural HWG/LSIF Roundtable Dialogue on Traditional Medicines, the first HWG/LSIF Dialogue on Mental Health, and the first HWG/LSIF Joint Dialogue on Health Associated Infections were convened. A meeting of APEC ministers responsible for health held in September 2013 issued a statement on Health and the Economy, agreeing that health is a critical component of economic and trade development and cooperation.

Human Resources Development (HRD): established in 1990; comprises three networks: the Capacity Building Network, with a focus on human capacity building, including management and technical skills development and corporate governance; the Education Network, promoting effective learning systems and supporting the role of education in advancing individual, social and economic development; and the Labour and Social Protection Network, concerned with promoting social integration through the strengthening of labour markets, the development of labour market information and policy, and improvements in working conditions and social safety net frameworks. The HRD undertakes activities through these networks to implement ministerial and leaders' directives. A voluntary network of APEC study centres links higher education and research institutions in member economies. Private sector participation in the HRD has been strengthened by the establishment of a network of APEC senior executives responsible for human resources management. Recent initiatives have included a cyber-education cooperation project, a workshop on advanced risk management, training on the prevention and resolution of employment and labour disputes, and an educators' exchange programme on the use of information technology in education. Meeting in February 2012, in Moscow, Russia, the HRD adopted the Moscow Initiative on fostering public-private partnership in the working group's activities. A seminar on strengthening the social protection system was convened in July, in the Philippines.

Oceans and Fisheries (OFWG): formed in 2011 by the merger of the former Fisheries Working Group (FWG) and Marine Resource Conservation Working Group (MRCWG); promotes initiatives within APEC to protect the marine environment and its resources, and to maximize the economic benefits and sustainability of fisheries resources for all APEC members; previously the FWG and MRCWG had held a number of joint sessions focusing on areas of common interest, such as management strategies for regional marine protected areas, fishery resources and aquaculture; exotic marine species introduction; capacity building in the fields of marine and fishery resources and coral reef conservation; combating destructive fishing practices; aquaculture; and information sharing. The OFWG was to implement the October 2010 Paracas Declaration on Healthy Oceans and Fisheries Management Towards Food Security, focusing on sustainable development and protection of the marine environment, which built upon the previous Seoul Oceans Declaration (2002) and Bali Plan of Action (2005). The September 2012 Vladivostok APEC Leaders' Meeting reaffirmed commitment to enhancing co-operation to combat illegal, unreported and unregulated fishing and associated trade; to working towards sustainable management of marine ecosystems; to improving capture fisheries management and sustainable aquaculture practices; and to facilitating sustainable, open and fair trade in products of fisheries and aquaculture.

Small and Medium Enterprises (SMEWG): established in 1995, as the Ad Hoc Policy Level Group on SMEs, with a temporary mandate to oversee all APEC activities relating to the SME sector (which, by 2013, represented around 90% of all businesses in the APEC region). It supported the establishment of an APEC Centre for Technical Exchange and Training for Small and Medium Enterprises, which was inaugurated at Los Baños, near Manila, Philippines, in September 1996. The group was redesignated as a working group, with permanent status, in 2000. In August 2002 the SMEWG's action plan was revised to include an evaluation framework to assist APEC and member economies in identifying and analysing policy issues. In the same month a sub-group specializing in micro-enterprises was established. The first APEC Incubator Forum was held in July–August 2003, in Taiwan, to promote new businesses and support their early development. In 2004 the APEC SME Coordination Framework was finalized. The 12th APEC SME ministerial meeting, held in Daegu, South Korea, in September 2005, adopted the Daegu Initiative on SME Innovation Action Plan, which provided a framework for member economies to create economic and policy environments more suitable to SME innovation. In 2006 the APEC Private Sector Development Agenda was launched. The sixth APEC SME Technology Conference and Fair was convened in June–July 2010, in Fuzhou, China. In August 2012 APEC ministers responsible for SMEs endorsed a new four-year SME Strategic Plan for the period 2013–16, covering the following priority areas: building management capability, entrepreneurship and innovation; financing the business environment; and market access and internationalization. Meeting in September 2013, APEC ministers responsible for SMEs released a statement on SMEs and Women, and a further statement on enhancing SME global competitiveness.

Telecommunications and Information (TEL): incorporates three steering groups concerned with different aspects of the development and liberalization of the sector—liberalization; ICT development; and security and prosperity. Activities are guided by directives of ministers responsible for telecommunications, who first met in 1995, in South Korea, and adopted a Seoul Declaration on Asia Pacific Information Infrastructure (APII). The second ministerial meeting, held in Gold Coast, Australia, in September 1996, adopted more detailed proposals for liberalization of the sector in member economies. In June 1998 ministers, meeting in Singapore, agreed to remove technical barriers to trade in telecommunications equipment (although Chile and New Zealand declined to sign up to the arrangement). At their fourth meeting, convened in May 2000 in Cancún, Mexico, ministers approved a programme of action that included measures to bridge the 'digital divide' between developed and developing member economies, and adopted the APEC Principles on International Charging Arrangements for Internet Services and the APEC Principles of Interconnection. The fifth ministerial meeting, held in May 2002, issued a Statement on the Security of Information and Communications Infrastructures; a compendium of IT security standards has been disseminated in support of the Statement. A Mutual Recognition Arrangement Task Force (MRATF) (under the Liberalization steering group) implements a mutual recognition arrangement for conformity assessment of telecommunications equipment. The November 2008 Leaders' Meeting endorsed an APEC Digital Prosperity Checklist, with the aim of promoting ICT as a means of fuelling economic growth. An Asia-Pacific Information Infrastructure (APII) Testbed Network Project, which aimed to facilitate researchers' and engineers' work and to promote the use of new generation internet, and a Stock-Take on Regulatory Convergence are also ongoing. The ninth meeting of APEC ministers responsible for telecommunications, convened in St Petersburg, Russia, in August 2012, issued the St Petersburg Declaration, which outlined means of increasing co-operation to promote widespread access to and secure use of ICT in the Asia-Pacific region. In July 2013 senior officials representing APEC, G20 and ASEAN member states, alongside private sector representatives, held a roundtable meeting to consider possible future co-operation in undertaking projects related to connectivity and infrastructure development. During the period 2010–15 TEL was implementing a Strategic Action Plan, with a focus on universal broadband access.

Tourism (TWG): established in 1991, with the aim of promoting the long-term sustainability of the tourism industry, in both environmental and social terms. The TWG administers a Tourism Information Network and an APEC International Centre for Sustainable Tourism. The first meeting of APEC ministers responsible for tourism, held in South Korea in July 2000, adopted the Seoul Declaration on the APEC Tourism Charter. The TWG's work plan is based on four policy goals inherent in the Seoul Declaration, namely the removal of impediments to tourism business and investment; increased mobility of visitors and increased demand for tourism goods and services; sustainable management of tourism; and enhanced recognition of tourism as a vehicle for economic and social development. At a meeting of the TWG in April 2001, APEC and the Pacific Asia Travel Association (PATA) adopted a Code for Sustainable Tourism, designed for adoption and implementation by a variety of tourism companies and government agencies. It urges members to conserve the natural environment, ecosystems and biodiversity; respect local traditions and cultures; conserve energy; reduce pollution and waste; and ensure that regular environmental audits are carried out. In 2004 the TWG published a report on Best Practices in Safety and Security to Safeguard Tourism against Terrorism. The fourth meeting of ministers responsible for tourism, held in Hoi An, Viet Nam, in October 2006, adopted the Hoi An Declaration on Tourism, which aimed to promote co-operation in developing sustainable tourism and investment in the region, with a focus on the following areas: encouragement of private sector participation in a new APEC Tourism and Investment Forum, and the promotion of the APEC Tourism Fair, both of which were to be held on the sidelines of tourism sector ministerial meetings; and liberalization of the air routes between the cultural heritage sites of APEC member states. In April 2008 ministers, meeting in Lima, Peru, adopted the Pachacamac Declaration on Responsible Tourism. Meeting in May 2011 the TWG agreed to increase private sector involvement in future meetings. The seventh meeting of ministers responsible for tourism, held in July 2012, in Khabarovsk, Russia, issued the Khabarovsk Declaration on Tourism Facilitation, representing a roadmap for advancing policies to facilitate cross-border tourist flows and strengthen the overall development of the tourism sector. APEC Guidelines on Ensuring Tourist Safety were endorsed in September by the 20th Economic Leaders' Meeting. The eighth meeting of APEC tourism ministers was to be held in August 2014, in Macau.

Transportation (TPTWG): undertakes initiatives to enhance the efficiency and safety of the regional transportation system, in order to facilitate the development of trade. The TPTWG focuses on three main areas: improving the competitiveness of the transportation industry; promoting a safe and environmentally sound regional transportation system; and human resources development, including training, research and education. The TPTWG has published surveys, directories and manuals on all types of transportation systems, and has compiled an inventory on regional co-operation on oil spills preparedness and response arrangements. A Road Transportation Harmonization Project aims to provide the basis for common standards in the automotive industry in the Asia-Pacific region. The TPTWG has established an internet database on ports and the internet-based Virtual Centre for Transportation Research, Development and Education. It plans to develop a regional action plan on the implementation of Global Navigation Satellite Systems, in consultation with the relevant international bodies. A Special Task Force was established by the TPTWG in 2003 to assist member economies to implement a new International Ship and Port Facility Security Code, sponsored by the International Maritime Organization, which entered into force on 1 July 2004. In April 2004 an Aviation Safety Experts' Group met for the first time since 2000. In July 2004 the fourth meeting of APEC ministers of transport directed the TPTWG to prepare a strategy document to strengthen its activities in transport liberalization and facilitation. A Seminar on Post Tsunami Reconstruction and Functions of Ports Safety was held in 2005. The sixth APEC Transportation ministerial meeting, convened in Manila, Philippines, in April 2009, issued a joint ministerial statement detailing the following future focus areas for the TPTWG: liberalization and facilitation of transport services; seamless transportation services; aviation safety and security; land transport and mass transit safety and security; maritime safety and security; sustainable transport; industry involvement; and information sharing. The seventh meeting of APEC ministers responsible for transport, convened in September 2011, in San Francisco, USA, pledged to advance greener, more energy-efficient co-operation. The first APEC Joint Transportation and Energy Ministerial Conference, also convened in September, in San Francisco, adopted an Action Agenda to move APEC toward an Energy Efficient, Sustainable, Low-Carbon Transport Future. A special APEC Transportation Ministerial Meeting, convened in August 2012, in St Petersburg, Russia, adopted a Declaration on the Development of Integrated Supply Chains for Innovative Growth in the Asia-Pacific Region. The eighth meeting of APEC ministers of transport, convened in September 2013, focused on the promotion of infrastructure investment.

OTHER GROUPS

Experts Group on Illegal Logging and Associated Trade: inaugural meeting was held in February 2012, in Moscow, Russia. The Group aims to promote trade in legally harvested forest products from the APEC region; to act as a policy platform on combating illegal logging and associated trade; and to promote activities aimed at building capacity in the regional forestry sector (which accounts for some 80% of global trade in forest products, according to FAO). The terms of reference of the Experts Group were adopted by the first meeting of APEC ministers responsible for forestry, convened in September 2011, in Beijing, China; that meeting—recognizing that forestry has the potential to be a leading sector in achieving green growth—also reaffirmed a commitment made by the September 2007 APEC Leaders' Meeting to increase forest cover in the region by 20m. ha by 2020. An Asia-Pacific Network for Sustainable Forest Management and Rehabilitation (APFNet) was endorsed by the September 2007 Leaders' Meeting, and inaugurated in that month. Meeting in January 2013, in Jakarta, Indonesia, the Group endorsed a multi-year strategic plan aimed at strengthening policy dialogue; advancing knowledge on technical matters related to combating illegal logging and associated trade; enhancing member economies' capacity to address illegal logging and associated trade; improving relevant law enforcement co-operation; collaborating with international and regional organizations involved in promoting sustainable forest management and forest rehabilitation; and promoting trade in legally harvested forest products. Meeting in Cusco, Peru, in August 2013, APEC ministers responsible for forestry issued the Cusco Statement, which recognized the vital role played by forests in member economies, and listed 17 aspirations aimed at addressing ongoing challenges related to green growth and to sustainable development.

Mining Task Force (MTF): the first meeting of the MTF was convened in May 2008, in Arequipa, Peru. The Task Force was to provide a unified, cohesive mining, minerals and metals forum for APEC member economies. Its ongoing work programme includes undertaking a study on means of attracting investment to the regional mining sector, with a particular focus on investment; the regulatory framework; and the availability of skilled workforces. A Conference on Sustainable Development of the Mining Sector in the APEC Region was held in July 2009, in Singapore. Meeting in June 2012 APEC ministers responsible for mining issued a joint statement that recognized the significance of sustainable development in mining, covering areas including industry and social responsibility; investment in mining; innovations and environmental issues in mining and metallurgy; and the activities of the MTF. An APEC ministerial meeting on mining was scheduled to be held in June 2014, in Beijing, China.

Policy Partnership on Science, Technology and Innovation (PPSTI): established in 2012, replacing the former Working Group on Industrial Science and Technology (ISTWG). The PPSTI aims to strengthen collaboration between member states in the areas of science, research, technology and innovation; to enhance member economies' innovative capacities; to help to build human capacity and develop infrastructure to support the commercialization of ideas; and to develop policy frameworks and foster an enabling environment for innovation. In September 2012 the 20th Economic Leaders' meeting urged ABAC to nominate private sector representatives to the PPSTI, and to participate actively in the activities of the Partnership; the Leaders instructed the PPSTI to draft—with the support of ABAC—an action plan identifying short- and long-term objectives. Innovation Policy Dialogues were to be conducted through the PPSTI. The former ISTWG helped to establish an APEC Virtual Centre for Environmental Technology Exchange in Japan; a Science and Technology Industrial Parks Network; an International Molecular Biology Network for the APEC Region; an APEC Centre for Technology Foresight, based in Thailand; the APEC Science and Technology Web, an online database; and an Emerging Infections Network (EINet), based at the University of Washington, Seattle, USA. In April 2012 an APEC Conference on Innovation and Trade was convened in Singapore, with the aim of promoting cross-border innovation. An Innovation Technology Dialogue on Nanotechnologies for Energy Efficiency was held in the following month, in Kazan,

Russia. The inaugural meeting of APEC Chief Science Advisors and Equivalents was held in June 2013, in Medan, Indonesia.

Policy Partnership on Women and the Economy (PPWE): established in May 2011 as a public-private mechanism to integrate gender considerations into APEC activities, replacing the former Gender Focal Point Network (GFPN, established in 2002); provides policy advice on gender issues and promotes gender equality; aims to provide linkages between the APEC secretariat, working groups, and economies, to advance the economic integration of women in the APEC region for the benefit of all members; at the inaugural meeting of the PPWE, convened in San Francisco, USA, in September 2011, member states address four policies areas regarded as key in increasing economic participation by women: access to capital; access to markets; capacity and skills building; and women's leadership; the meeting also adopted terms of reference and endorsed the San Francisco Declaration on Women and the Economy, urging APEC member states to take concrete actions to realize the full potential of women and integrate them more fully into APEC economies; an APEC Women's Entrepreneurship Summit was held in September–October 2010, in Gifu, Japan; in 2005 the GFPN recommended that women's participation in the APEC Business Advisory Council (ABAC) should be increased, following which several member economies have nominated at least one female delegate to ABAC; a *Gender Experts List* and a *Register of Best Practices on Gender Integration* are maintained. APEC ministers participating in an APEC Women and the Economy Forum, convened in St Petersburg, Russia, in June 2012, issued a statement on supporting female empowerment and decreasing gender barriers in the APEC region's innovation economy: analysis of women's participation in business, innovation, and social aspects of the economy was to be undertaken, in particular through the collection of gender-disaggregated data.

Publications

ABAC Report to APEC Leaders (annually).
APEC at a Glance (annually).
APEC Business Travel Handbook.
APEC Economic Policy Report.
APEC Energy Demand and Supply Outlook (every three to four years).
APEC Energy Handbook (annually).
APEC Energy Overview (annually).
APEC Energy Statistics (annually).
APEC Outcomes and Outlook.
Guide to the Investment Regimes of the APEC Member Economies (every three years).
Key APEC Documents (annually).
Towards Knowledge-based Economies in APEC.
Trade and Investment Liberalization in APEC.
Working group reports, regional directories, other irregular surveys.

ASIAN DEVELOPMENT BANK—ADB

Address: 6 ADB Ave, Mandaluyong City, 0401 Metro Manila, Philippines; POB 789, 0980 Manila, Philippines.

Telephone: (2) 6324444; **fax:** (2) 6362444; **e-mail:** information@adb.org; **internet:** www.adb.org.

The ADB commenced operations in December 1966. The Bank's principal functions are to provide loans and equity investments for the economic and social advancement of its developing member countries, to give technical assistance for the preparation and implementation of development projects and programmes and advisory services, to promote investment of public and private capital for development purposes, and to respond to requests from developing member countries for assistance in the co-ordination of their development policies and plans.

MEMBERS

There are 48 member countries and territories within the ESCAP region and 19 others (see list of subscriptions below).

Organization

(April 2014)

BOARD OF GOVERNORS

All powers of the Bank are vested in the Board, which may delegate its powers to the Board of Directors except in such matters as admission of new members, changes in the Bank's authorized capital stock, election of Directors and President, and amendment of the Charter. One Governor and one Alternate Governor are appointed by each member country. The Board meets at least once a year. The 47th meeting was scheduled to be convened in Astana, Kazakhstan, in May 2014.

BOARD OF DIRECTORS

The Board of Directors is responsible for general direction of operations and exercises all powers delegated by the Board of Governors, which elects it. Of the 12 Directors, eight represent constituency groups of member countries within the ESCAP region (with about 65% of the voting power) and four represent the rest of the member countries. Each Director serves for two years and may be re-elected.

Three specialized committees (the Audit Committee, the Budget Review Committee and the Inspection Committee), each comprising six members, assist the Board of Directors in exercising its authority with regard to supervising the Bank's financial statements, approving the administrative budget, and reviewing and approving policy documents and assistance operations.

The President of the Bank, though not a Director, is Chairman of the Board.

Chairman of Board of Directors and President: TAKEHIKO NAKAO (Japan).

Vice-Presidents: WENCAI ZHANG (People's Republic of China), STEPHEN P. GROFF (USA), BINDU LOHANI (Nepal), LAKSHMI VENKATACHALAM (India), THIERRY DE LONGUEMAR (France), BRUCE DAVIS (Australia).

ADMINISTRATION

The Bank had 3,045 staff at 31 December 2012.

Five regional departments cover Central and West Asia, East Asia, the Pacific, South Asia, and South-East Asia. Other departments and offices include Anti-corruption and Integrity, Central Operations Services, Co-financing Operations, Economics and Research, Private Sector Operations, Regional and Sustainable Development, Risk Management, Strategy and Policy.

There are Bank Resident Missions in Afghanistan, Armenia, Azerbaijan, Bangladesh, Bhutan, Cambodia, the People's Republic of China, Georgia, India, Indonesia, Japan, Kazakhstan, Kyrgyzstan, Laos, Mongolia, Myanmar, Nepal, Pakistan, Papua New Guinea, Sri Lanka, Tajikistan, Thailand, Timor-Leste, Turkmenistan, Uzbekistan and Viet Nam, all of which report to the head of the regional department. In addition, the Bank maintains a Country Office in the Philippines, an Extended Mission in Myanmar, a Special Liaison Office in Timor-Leste, a Pacific Liaison and Co-ordination Office in Sydney, Australia, and a South Pacific Sub-Regional Mission, based in Fiji. Representative Offices are located in Tokyo, Japan, Frankfurt am Main, Germany (for Europe), and Washington, DC, USA (for North America).

INSTITUTE

ADB Institute (ADBI): Kasumigaseki Bldg, 8th Floor, 2–5 Kasumigaseki 3-chome, Chiyoda-ku, Tokyo 100-6008, Japan; tel. (3) 3593-5500; fax (3) 3593-5571; e-mail info@adbi.org; internet www.adbi.org; f. 1997 as a subsidiary body of the ADB to research and analyse long-term development issues and to disseminate development practices through training and other capacity-building activities; Dean NAOYUKI YOSHINO (Japan).

FINANCIAL STRUCTURE

The Bank's ordinary capital resources (which are used for loans to the more advanced developing member countries) are held and used entirely separately from its Special Funds resources. In May 2009 the Board of Governors approved a fifth General Capital Increase (GCI V), increasing the Bank's resources by some 200% to US $165,000m. GCI V was concluded in January 2012, at which time the Bank had received subscriptions equivalent to 99.6% of the shares authorized under the Increase.

At 31 December 2012 the position of subscriptions to the capital stock was as follows: authorized US $163,512m.; subscribed $162,129m.

The Bank also borrows funds from the world capital markets. Total borrowings during 2012 amounted to US $15,067m. (compared with $14,446m. in 2011). At 31 December 2012 total outstanding debt amounted to $64,279m.

In July 1986 the Bank abolished the system of fixed lending rates, under which ordinary operations loans had carried interest rates fixed at the time of loan commitment for the entire life of the loan. Under the present system the lending rate is adjusted every six months, to take into account changing conditions in international financial markets.

Activities

Loans by the ADB are usually aimed at specific projects. In responding to requests from member governments for loans, the Bank's staff assesses the financial and economic viability of projects and the way in which they fit into the economic framework and priorities of development of the country concerned. In 1985 the Bank decided to expand its assistance to the private sector, hitherto comprising loans to development finance institutions, under government guarantee, for lending to small and medium-sized enterprises (SMEs); a programme was formulated for direct financial assistance, in the form of equity and loans without government guarantee, to private enterprises. During the early 1990s the Bank expanded its role as project financier by providing assistance for policy formulation and review and promoting regional co-operation, while placing greater emphasis on individual country requirements. During that period the Bank also introduced a commitment to assess development projects for their impact on the local population and to avoid all involuntary resettlement where possible and established a formal procedure for grievances, under which the Board may authorize an inspection of a project by an independent panel of experts, at the request of the affected community or group. The currency instability and ensuing financial crises affecting many Asian economies in 1997/98 prompted the Bank to reflect on its role in the region. The Bank resolved to strengthen its activities as a broad-based development institution, rather than solely as a project financier, through lending policies, dialogue, co-financing and technical assistance.

In November 1999 the Board of Directors approved a new overall strategy objective of poverty reduction, which was to be the principal consideration for all future Bank activities. The strategy incorporated key aims of supporting sustainable, grass-roots based economic growth, social development and good governance. From 2000 the Bank refocused its country strategies, projects and lending targets to complement the poverty reduction strategy. In addition, it initiated a process of consultation to formulate a long-term strategic framework, based on the target of reducing by 50% the incidence of extreme poverty by 2015, one of the so-called Millennium Development Goals (MDGs) identified by the UN General Assembly. A review of the strategy, initiated at the end of 2003, concluded that more comprehensive, results-oriented monitoring and evaluation be put in place. It also recommended a closer alignment of Bank operations with national poverty reduction strategies and determined to include capacity development as a new overall thematic priority for the Bank, in addition to environmental sustainability, gender and development, private sector development and regional co-operation. In mid-2004 the Bank initiated a separate reform agenda to incorporate the strategy approach 'Managing for development results' throughout the organization. In July 2006 the Bank adopted a strategy to promote regional co-operation and integration in order to combat poverty through collective regional and cross-border activities.

In May 2008 the Board of Governors, convened in Madrid, Spain, endorsed a new long-term strategic framework to cover the period 2008–20 ('Strategy 2020'), replacing the previous 2001–15 strategic framework, in recognition of the unprecedented economic growth of recent years and its associated challenges, including the effect on natural resources, inadequate infrastructure to support economic advances, and widening disparities both within and between developing member countries. Under the strategy the Bank determined to refocus its activities onto three critical agendas: inclusive economic growth; environmentally sustainable growth; and regional integration. It determined also to initiate a process of restructuring its operations into five core areas of specialization, to which some 80% of lending was to be allocated by 2012: infrastructure; environment, including climate change; regional co-operation and integration; financial sector development; and education. The Bank resolved to act as an agent of change, stimulating economic growth and widening development assistance, for example by supporting the private sector with more risk guarantees, investment and other financial instruments, placing greater emphasis on good governance, promoting gender equality and improving accessibility to and distribution of its knowledge services. It also committed to expanding its partnerships with other organizations, including with the private sector and other private institutions.

In September 2008 the Bank organized a high-level conference, attended by representatives of multilateral institutions, credit rating agencies, regulatory and supervisory bodies and banks to discuss and exchange ideas on measures to strengthen the region's financial markets and contain the global financial instability evident at that time. In March 2009 the Bank hosted a South Asia Forum on the Impact of the Global Economic and Financial Crisis. At the end of that month the Bank expanded its Trade Finance Facilitation Program (TFFP, inaugurated in 2004) to support the private sector by increasing its exposure limit to guarantee trade transactions from US $150m. to $1,000m. In May 2009 the Board of Governors approved a general capital increase of some 200% to enable the Bank to extend the lending required to assist countries affected by the global economic downturn, as well as to support the longer-term development objectives of Strategy 2020. In June 2009 the Board of Directors approved a new Countercyclical Support Facility, with resources of $3,000m., to extend short-term, fast-disbursing loans to help developing member countries to counter the effects of the global financial crisis. Countries eligible for the funds were required to formulate a countercyclical development programme, to include plans for investment in public infrastructure or social safety net initiatives. The Board approved an additional $400m., to be made available through the Asian Development Fund (ADF), for countries with no access to the Bank's ordinary capital resources. In April 2000 the Bank announced that some new loans would be denominated in local currencies, in order to ease the repayment burden on recipient economies.

In 2012 the Bank's financing operations amounted to US $21,571m., compared with $21,716m. in the previous year. Of the total amount approved in 2012, $11,718m. was for 134 loans, of which loans from ordinary capital resources totalled $9,402m., while loans from the ADF amounted to $2,316m. In 2012 the Bank approved 27 grants amounting to $697m. financed mainly by the ADF, as well as by other Special Funds and bilateral and multilateral sources. It also approved funding of $151m. for 237 technical assistance projects, $131m. for three equity investments, and $403m. in guarantees for two projects. During 2012 $8,272m. of the total financing approved came from co-financing partners, for 203 investment and technical assistance projects, compared with $7,695m. in 2011.

The Bank co-operates with other international organizations active in the region, particularly the World Bank, the IMF, the UN Development Programme (UNDP) and Asia-Pacific Economic Cooperation (APEC), and participates in meetings of aid donors for developing member countries. In May 2001 the Bank and UNDP signed a Memorandum of Understanding (MOU) on strategic partnership, in order to strengthen co-operation in the reduction of poverty, for example the preparation of common country assessments and a common database on poverty and other social indicators. Also in 2001 the Bank signed an MOU with the World Bank on administrative arrangements for co-operation, providing a framework for closer co-operation and more efficient use of resources. In May 2004 the Bank signed a revised MOU with ESCAP to enhance co-operation activities to achieve the MDGs. In November 2011 the Bank signed an MOU with the European Bank for Reconstruction and Development (EBRD) to strengthen co-operation in their mutual countries of operation. In early 2002 the Bank worked with the World Bank and UNDP to assess the preliminary needs of the interim administration in Afghanistan, in preparation for an International Conference on Reconstruction Assistance to Afghanistan, held in January, in Tokyo, Japan. The Bank pledged to work with its member governments to provide highly concessional grants and loans of some US $500m. over two-and-a-half years, with a particular focus on road reconstruction, basic education, and agricultural irrigation rehabilitation. In June 2008, at an international donors' conference held in Paris, France, the Bank pledged up to $1,300m. to finance infrastructure projects in Afghanistan in the coming five years. A new policy concerning co-operation with non-governmental organizations (NGOs) was approved by the Bank in 1998. The Bank administers an NGO Centre to provide advice and support to NGOs on involvement in country strategies and development programmes.

In June 2004 the Bank approved a new policy to provide rehabilitation and reconstruction assistance following disasters or other emergencies. The policy also aimed to assist developing member countries with prevention, preparation and mitigation of the impact of future disasters. At the end of December the Bank announced assistance amounting to US $325m. to finance immediate reconstruction and rehabilitation efforts in Indonesia, the Maldives and Sri Lanka, which had been severely damaged by the tsunami that had spread throughout the Indian Ocean as a result of a massive earthquake that had occurred close to the west coast of Sumatra, Indonesia. Of the total amount $150m. was to be drawn as new lending commitments from the ADF. Teams of Bank experts undertook to identify priority operations and initiated efforts, in co-operation with governments and other partner organizations, to prepare for more comprehensive reconstruction activities. In accordance with the 2004 policy initiative, an interdepartmental task force was established to co-ordinate the Bank's response to the disaster. In January 2005, at a Special ASEAN Leaders' Meeting, held in Jakarta, Indonesia, the Bank pledged assistance amounting to $500m.; later in that month the Bank announced its intention to establish a $600m. Multi-donor Asian Tsunami Fund to accelerate the provision of reconstruction and technical assistance to countries most affected by the disaster. In March 2006 the Bank hosted a high-level co-ordination meeting on rehabilitation and reconstruction assistance to tsunami-affected countries. In October the Bank, with representatives of the World Bank, undertook an immediate preliminary damage and needs assessment following a massive earthquake in north-western Pakistan, which also affected remote parts of Afghanistan and India. The report identified relief and reconstruction requirements totalling some $5,200m. The Bank made an initial contribution of $80m. to a Special Fund and also pledged concessional support of up to $1,000m. for rehabilitation and reconstruction efforts in the affected areas. In August 2010 the Bank announced that it was to extend up to $2,000m. in emergency rehabilitation and reconstruction assistance to Pakistan, large areas of which had been severely damaged by flooding. The Bank agreed to undertake, jointly with the World Bank, a damage and needs assessment to determine priority areas of action.

The Bank has actively supported regional, sub-regional and national initiatives to enhance economic development and promote economic co-operation within the region. The Bank is the main co-ordinator and financier of a Greater Mekong Sub-region (GMS) programme, initiated in 1992 to strengthen co-operation between Cambodia, China, Laos, Myanmar, Thailand and Viet Nam. Projects undertaken have included transport and other infrastructure links, energy projects and communicable disease control. The first meeting of GMS heads of state was convened in Phnom Penh, Cambodia, in November 2002. A second summit was held in Kunming, China, in July 2005, and a third summit in Vientiane, Laos, in March 2008. The fourth meeting of GMS heads of state, convened in December 2011, adopted a GMS Strategic Framework, covering the period 2012–22. In June 2008 a GMS Economic Corridors Forum (ECF-1) was held, in Kunming, to accelerate development of economic corridors in the sub-region. A second Forum was convened in Phnom Penh, in September 2009, a third in Vientiane, in June 2011, and ECF-4 was held in June 2012, in Mandalay, Myanmar, on the theme 'Towards Implementing the New GMS Strategic Framework (2012–22): Expanding, Widening, and Deepening Economic Corridors in the GMS'. ECF-5 was convened in Bangkok, Thailand, in August 2013. Other sub-regional initiatives supported by the Bank include the Central Asian Regional Economic Co-operation (CAREC) initiative, the South Asia Sub-regional Economic Cooperation (SASEC) initiative, the Indonesia, Malaysia, Thailand Growth Triangle (IMT-GT), and the Brunei, Indonesia, Malaysia, Philippines East ASEAN Growth Area (BIMP-EAGA).

SPECIAL FUNDS

The Bank is authorized to establish and administer Special Funds. The Asian Development Fund (ADF) was established in 1974 in order to provide a systematic mechanism for mobilizing and administering resources for the Bank to lend on concessionary terms to the least-developed member countries. Since 1 January 1999 all new project loans are repayable within 32 years, including an eight-year grace period, while quick-disbursing programme loans have a 24-year maturity, also including an eight-year grace period. The previous annual service charge was redesignated as an interest charge, totalling 1%–1.5% per annum on all loans, and including a portion to cover administrative expenses. In July 2012 the Board of Governors adopted a resolution providing for the 10th replenishment of ADF resources (ADF XI), towards which donors had, in March, committed resources totalling US $12,400m. to cover the four-year period 2013–16. The total amount included replenishment of the Technical Assistance Special Fund (TASF).

The Bank provides technical assistance grants from its TASF. The fifth replenishment of its resources was approved in July 2012 for the period 2013–16. By the end of 2012 the Fund's total resources amounted to US $1,892m. During 2012 $128m. was approved under the TASF project preparation, advisory and capacity development activities. The Japan Special Fund (JSF) was established in 1988 to provide finance for technical assistance by means of grants, in both the public and private sectors. The JSF aims to help developing member countries to restructure their economies, enhance the opportunities for attracting new investment, and recycle funds. The Japanese Government had committed a total of 112,900m. yen (equivalent to some $973.7m.) to the JSF by the end of 2012. The Bank administers the ADB Institute Special Fund, which was established to finance the ADB Institute's operations. By 31 December 2012 cumulative commitments to the Special Fund amounted to 20,600m. yen and A$1.6m. (or $194.4m.).

In February 2007 the Bank established, with an initial $40.0m., the Regional Co-operation and Integration Fund to fund co-operation and integration activities. By the end of 2012 the Fund's total resources amounted to $53.1m., of which $1.7m. was uncommitted. In April 2008 the Bank established a Climate Change Fund, with an initial contribution of $40.0m. By 31 December 2012 total resources amounted to $51.2m., of which $7.9m. was uncommitted. In April 2009 the Bank's Board of Directors approved the establishment of an Asia Pacific Disaster Response Fund (APDRF) to extend rapid assistance to developing countries following a natural disaster. Some $40.0m. from the Asian Tsunami Fund was transferred to inaugurate the APDRF, which was mandated to provide grants of up to $3.0m. to fund immediate humanitarian relief operations. The APDRF was used in September to provide assistance for more than 300,000 families in the Philippines affected by extensive flooding and damage to infrastructure caused by a tropical storm. In the following month the Bank approved $1.0m. from the Fund to support emergency efforts in Samoa, following an earthquake and tsunami. In August 2010 $3.0m. was approved under the APDRF to extend immediate emergency assistance following devastating flooding in Pakistan. At that time the Bank established a special flood reconstruction fund to administer donor contributions for relief and rehabilitation efforts in Pakistan. At 31 December 2012 the APDRF's total resources amounted to $40.2m., of which $10.3m. remained uncommitted. In November 2012 the Executive Board approved a new pilot Disaster Response Facility, within the ADF.

TRUST FUNDS

The Bank also manages and administers several trust funds and other bilateral donor arrangements. The Japanese Government funds the Japan Scholarship Program, under which 2,968 scholarships had been awarded to recipients from 35 member countries between 1988 and 2012. In May 2000 the Japan Fund for Poverty Reduction was established, with an initial contribution of 10,000m. yen (approximately US $92.6m.) by the Japanese Government, to support ADB-financed poverty reduction and social development activities. During 2011 the Fund expanded its scope of activity to provide technical assistance grants. By the end of 2012 cumulative resources available to the Fund totalled $561.6m. In March 2004 a Japan Fund for Public Policy Training was established, with an initial contribution by the Japanese Government, to enhance capacity building for public policy management in developing member countries.

The majority of grant funds in support of the Bank's technical assistance activities are provided by bilateral donors under channel financing arrangements (CFAs), the first of which was negotiated in 1980. CFAs may also be processed as a thematic financing tool, for example concerned with renewable energy, water or poverty reduction, enabling more than one donor to contribute. A Co-operation Fund for Regional Trade and Financial Security Initiative was established in July 2004, with contributions by Australia, Japan and the USA, to support efforts to combat money-laundering and the financing of terrorism. Other financing partnerships facilities may also be established to mobilize additional financing and investment by development partners. In November 2006 the Bank approved the establishment of an Asia Pacific Carbon Fund (within the framework of a Carbon Market Initiative) to finance clean energy projects in developing member countries. To complement this Fund a new Future Carbon Fund was established, in July 2008, to provide resources for projects beyond 2012 (when the Kyoto Protocol regulating trade in carbon credits was to expire). In December 2006 the Bank established a Water Financing Partnership Facility to help to achieve the objectives of its Water Financing Program. In April 2007 a Clean Energy Financing Partnership Facility (CEFPF) was established, further to provide investment in clean energy projects for developing member countries. An Asian Clean Energy Fund and an Investment Climate Facilitation Fund were established in 2008 within the framework of the CEFPF. A separate Carbon Capture and Storage Fund was established, under the CEFPF, with funding from the Australian Government, in July 2009. In November the Bank, with funding from the United Kingdom, initiated a five-year strategic partnership to combat poverty in India. In the following month the Bank established a multi-donor Urban Financing Partnership Facility. In November 2010 the Board of Directors approved the establishment of an Afghanistan Infrastructure Trust Fund, to be administered by the Bank, to finance and co-ordinate donor funding for infrastructure projects in that country.

In April 2010 the Board of Directors agreed to allocate US $130m. to a new Credit Guarantee and Investment Facility, established by ASEAN + 3 governments, with a further capital contribution of some $570m., in order to secure longer-term financing for local businesses and to support the development of Asian bond markets.

Finance

Internal administrative expenses were budgeted at US $610.3m. for 2014.

Publications

ADB Institute Newsletter.
Annual Report.
Asia Bond Monitor (quarterly).
Asia Capital Markets Monitor (annually).
Asia Economic Monitor (2 a year).
Asian Development Outlook (annually; an *Update* is published annually).
Asian Development Review (2 a year).
Basic Statistics (annually).
Development Asia (2 a year).
Key Indicators for Asia and the Pacific (annually).
Pension Systems in East and Southeast Asia: Promoting Fairness and Sustainability.
Sustainability Report.
Studies and technical assistance reports, information brochures, guidelines, sample bidding documents, staff papers.

Statistics

SUBSCRIPTIONS AND VOTING POWER
(31 December 2012)

Country	Voting power (% of total)	Subscribed capital (% of total)
Regional:		
Afghanistan	0.33	0.03
Armenia	0.54	0.30
Australia	4.93	5.79
Azerbaijan	0.65	0.45
Bangladesh	1.12	1.02
Bhutan	0.30	0.01
Brunei	0.58	0.35
Cambodia	0.34	0.05
China, People's Republic	5.45	6.44
Cook Islands	0.30	0.00
Fiji	0.35	0.07
Georgia	0.57	0.34
Hong Kong	0.73	0.55
India	5.36	6.33
Indonesia	4.65	5.44
Japan	12.78	15.61
Kazakhstan	0.94	0.81
Kiribati	0.30	0.00
Korea, Republic	4.33	5.05
Kyrgyzstan	0.54	0.30
Laos	0.31	0.01
Malaysia	2.48	2.72
Maldives	0.30	0.00
Marshall Islands	0.30	0.00
Micronesia, Federated States	0.30	0.00
Mongolia	0.31	0.02
Myanmar	0.73	0.55
Nauru	0.30	0.00
Nepal	0.42	0.15
New Zealand	1.53	1.54
Pakistan	2.04	2.18
Palau	0.30	0.00
Papua New Guinea	0.37	0.09
Philippines	2.21	2.38
Samoa	0.30	0.00
Singapore	0.57	0.34
Solomon Islands	0.30	0.01
Sri Lanka	0.76	0.58
Taiwan	1.17	1.09
Tajikistan	0.53	0.29
Thailand	1.39	1.36
Timor-Leste	0.31	0.01
Tonga	0.30	0.00
Turkmenistan	0.50	0.25
Tuvalu	0.30	0.00
Uzbekistan	0.84	0.67
Vanuatu	0.30	0.01
Viet Nam	0.57	0.34
Sub-total	65.16	63.54
Non-regional:		
Austria	0.57	0.34
Belgium	0.57	0.34
Canada	4.48	5.23
Denmark	0.57	0.34
Finland	0.57	0.34
France	2.16	2.33
Germany	3.76	4.33
Ireland	0.57	0.34
Italy	1.75	1.81
Luxembourg	0.57	0.34
Netherlands	1.12	1.03
Norway	0.57	0.34
Portugal	0.39	0.11
Spain	0.57	0.34
Sweden	0.57	0.34
Switzerland	0.77	0.58
Turkey	0.57	0.34
United Kingdom	1.93	2.04
USA	12.78	15.60
Sub-total	34.84	36.46
Total	100.00	100.00

LOAN APPROVALS BY SECTOR

Sector	2012 Amount (US $ million)	2012 %	1968–2012 Amount
Agriculture and natural resources	1,040.1	8.9	21,482.5
Education	277.6	2.3	6,946.4
Energy	2,600.9	22.2	39,500.0
Finance	775.0	6.6	21,292.7
Health and social protection	70.0	0.6	3,922.9
Industry and trade	184.9	1.6	4,772.9
Public sector management	1,435.6	12.3	15,945.7
Transport and information and communication technology (ICT)	3,666.2	31.3	48,391.5
Water supply and other municipal infrastructure and services	1,206.3	10.3	16,433.1
Multi-sector	461.0	3.9	12,647.5
Total	11,717.6	100.0	191,427.3

APPROVALS BY COUNTRY, 2012
(US $ million)

Country	Ordinary Capital loans	ADF loans	Total approvals*
Bangladesh	435.1	657.5	1,634.6
China, People's Republic	1,809.0	—	2,102.0
India	2,290.0	—	3,112.0
Indonesia	1,232.8	—	1,287.6
Kazakhstan	496.3	—	694.6
Pakistan	343.1	74.0	1,074.9
Philippines	750.0	—	1,063.2
Thailand	214.7	657.5	1,634.6
Uzbekistan	363.0	232.0	3,305.5
Viet Nam	822.2	462.9	3,112.0
Regional	40.0	2.6	478.6
Other developing member states	605.6	866.9	2,747.5
Total	9,401.7	2,315.9	21,571.3

* Includes guarantees, equity investments, grants, technical assistance financing and co-financing.

Source: Asian Development Bank, *Annual Report 2012*.

ASSOCIATION OF SOUTHEAST ASIAN NATIONS—ASEAN

Address: 70A Jalan Sisingamangaraja, POB 2072, Jakarta 12110, Indonesia.

Telephone: (21) 7262991; **fax:** (21) 7398234; **e-mail:** www.asean.org/information/contact-us (contact form); **internet:** www.asean.org.

ASEAN was established in August 1967 in Bangkok, Thailand, to accelerate economic progress and to increase the stability of the South-East Asian region. The first ASEAN summit meeting was convened in February 1976 at which a Treaty of Amity and Co-operation in South-East Asia and a Declaration of ASEAN Concord were adopted. In November 2007 its 10 members signed an ASEAN Charter, which, upon its entry into force on 15 December 2008 (following ratification by all member states), formally accorded the grouping the legal status of an intergovernmental organization.

MEMBERS

Brunei	Malaysia	Singapore
Cambodia	Myanmar	Thailand
Indonesia	Philippines	Viet Nam
Laos		

Organization

(April 2014)

SUMMIT MEETING

The summit meeting is the highest authority of ASEAN, bringing together the heads of state or government of member countries. The first meeting was held in Bali, Indonesia, in February 1976. The new ASEAN Charter specified that summit meetings were to be convened at least twice a year, hosted by the member state holding the Chairmanship of the organization (a position that rotates on an annual basis; 2014: Myanmar). The 23rd summit meeting was held in October 2013, in Bandar Seri Begawan, Brunei.

ASEAN CO-ORDINATING COUNCIL

The inaugural meeting of the Council was convened in December 2008, upon the entering into force of the new ASEAN Charter. Comprising the ministers responsible for foreign affairs of member states, the Council meets at least twice a year to assist in the preparation of summit meetings, to monitor the implementation of agreements and summit meeting decisions and to co-ordinate ASEAN policies and activities.

ASEAN COMMUNITY COUNCILS

Three new Community Councils were established within the framework of the ASEAN Charter in order to pursue the objectives of the different pillars of the grouping and to enhance regional integration and co-operation. The ASEAN Political-Security Community Council, the ASEAN Economic Community Council and the ASEAN Socio-Cultural Community Council each meet at least twice a year, chaired by the appropriate government minister of the country holding the ASEAN Chairmanship. Each Council oversees a structure of Sectoral Ministerial Bodies, many of which had established mandates as ministerial meetings, councils or specialized bodies.

COMMITTEE OF PERMANENT REPRESENTATIVES

The Committee, according to the new Charter, comprises a Permanent Representative appointed, at ambassadorial level, by each member state. Its functions include supporting the work of ASEAN bodies, liaising with the Secretary-General, and facilitating ASEAN co-operation with external partners.

SECRETARIATS

A permanent secretariat was established in Jakarta, Indonesia, in 1976 to form a central co-ordinating body. The Secretariat comprises the Office of the Secretary-General and Bureaux relating to Economic Integration and Finance, External Relations and Co-ordination, and Resources Development. The Secretary-General holds office for a five-year term and is assisted by four Deputy Secretaries-General, increased from two in accordance with the new ASEAN Charter. Two were to remain as nominated positions, rotating among member countries for a non-renewable term of three years; the two new positions of Deputy Secretary-General were to be openly recruited on a renewable three-year term. Each member country is required to maintain an ASEAN National Secretariat to co-ordinate implementation of ASEAN decisions at the national level and to raise awareness of the organization and its activities within that country. Since July 2009 a regular ASEAN Secretariat Policy Forum has been convened, with the aim of promoting public debate on the activities of the Secretariat. An administrative unit supporting the ASEAN Regional Forum is based at the secretariat.

ASEAN Committees in Third Countries (composed of heads of diplomatic missions) may be established to promote ASEAN's interests and to support the conduct of relations with other countries and international organizations.

Secretary-General: LE LUONG MINH (Viet Nam).

Deputy Secretary-General, for the ASEAN Political Security Community: NYAN LYNN (Myanmar).

Deputy Secretary-General, for the ASEAN Economic Community: Dr LIM HONG HIN (Brunei).

Deputy Secretary-General, for the ASEAN Socio-Cultural Community: ALICIA DELA ROSA BALA (Philippines).

Deputy Secretary-General, for Community and Corporate Affairs: Dr A. K. P. MOCHTAN (Indonesia).

Activities

In October 2003 ASEAN leaders adopted a declaration known as Bali Concord II, which committed signatory states to the creation of an ASEAN Economic Community, an ASEAN Security Community and an ASEAN Socio-Cultural Community. In December 2005 heads of state determined to establish a High Level Task Force to formulate a new ASEAN Charter. The finalized document, codifying the principles and purposes of the grouping and according it the legal status of an intergovernmental organization, was signed in November 2007 by ASEAN heads of government attending the 13th summit meeting, convened in Singapore. The Charter entered into force on 15 December, having been ratified by each member state. The occasion was commemorated at a Special ASEAN Foreign Ministers' Meeting, convened at the Secretariat, which consequently became the inaugural meeting of the new ASEAN Co-ordinating Council.

In March 2009, at the end of the 14th summit meeting, held in Cha-am and Hua Hin, Thailand, ASEAN heads of state and government signed the Cha-am Hua Hin Declaration on the Roadmap for an ASEAN Community (2009–15), comprising Blueprints on the ASEAN Political Security, Economic, and Socio-cultural Communities as well as a second Initiative for ASEAN Integration Work Plan. The meeting also issued a Statement on the Global Economic and Financial Crisis, which emphasized the need for co-ordinated policies and joint actions to restore financial stability and to safeguard economic growth in the region.

In October 2010 ASEAN heads of state, meeting in Hanoi, Viet Nam, adopted a Master Plan on ASEAN Connectivity, which identified priority projects to enhance communications and community-building in three dimensions: physical; institutional; and people-to-people. The November 2011 meeting of ASEAN heads of state, held in Bali, Indonesia, agreed to consider the possibility of developing a Connectivity Master Plan Plus in future, with the aim of expanding the Connectivity initiative beyond the immediate ASEAN region. The meeting also adopted a declaration on Bali Concord III, promoting a common ASEAN platform on global issues of common interest and concern, based on a shared ASEAN global view. The 20th ASEAN summit meeting, held in April 2012, in Phnom Penh, Cambodia, adopted the Phnom Penh Declaration on ASEAN: One Community, One Destiny and the Phnom Penh Agenda on ASEAN Community Building. A Bali Concord III Plan of Action for the period 2013–17 was approved by the 21st summit meeting, convened in November 2012, in Phnom Penh. The 23rd summit meeting, held in October 2013, in Bandar Seri Begawan, Brunei, determined to strengthen the ASEAN Secretariat and to review the various organs, processes and institutions of ASEAN co-operation, to ensure the organization's continuing centrality in the evolving regional architecture. The summit adopted the Bandar Seri Begawan Statement on the ASEAN Community's Post-2015 Vision, tasking the Co-ordinating Council with formulating by the 27th summit, to be convened in 2015, a vision of ASEAN's onwards development.

TRADE AND ECONOMIC CO-OPERATION

In January 1992 heads of government, meeting in Singapore, signed an agreement to create an ASEAN Free Trade Area (AFTA) by 2008.

In accordance with the agreement, a common effective preferential tariff (CEPT) scheme came into effect in January 1993, covering all manufactured products, including capital goods, and processed agricultural products (which together accounted for two-thirds of intra-ASEAN trade). In September 1994 ASEAN ministers of economic affairs agreed to accelerate the implementation of AFTA, advancing the deadline for its entry into operation from 2008 to 1 January 2003. Tariffs were to be reduced to 0%–5% within seven to 10 years, or within five to eight years for products designated for accelerated tariff cuts. In July 1995, Viet Nam was admitted as a member of ASEAN and was granted until 2006 to implement the AFTA trade agreements. In December 1995 heads of government, meeting in Bangkok, Thailand, agreed to extend liberalization to certain service industries, including banking, telecommunications and tourism. In July 1997 Laos and Myanmar became members of ASEAN and were granted a 10-year period, from 1 January 1998, to comply with the AFTA schedule.

In December 1998, meeting in Hanoi, Viet Nam, heads of government approved a Statement on Bold Measures, detailing ASEAN's strategies to deal with the economic crisis that had prevailed in the region since late 1997. These included incentives to attract investors, for example a three-year exemption on corporate taxation, accelerated implementation of the ASEAN Investment Area (AIA), and advancing the AFTA deadline, for the original six members, to 2002, with some 85% of products to be covered by the arrangements by 2000, and 90% by 2001. In April 1999 Cambodia, on being admitted as a full member of ASEAN, signed an agreement to implement the tariff reduction programme over a 10-year period, commencing 1 January 2000. Cambodia also signed a declaration endorsing the commitments of the 1998 Statement on Bold Measures. In May 2000 Malaysia was granted a special exemption to postpone implementing tariff reductions on motor vehicles for two years from 1 January 2003. In November 2000 a protocol was approved permitting further temporary exclusion of products from the CEPT scheme for countries experiencing economic difficulties.

On 1 January 2002 AFTA was formally realized among the original six signatories (Brunei, Indonesia, Malaysia, the Philippines, Singapore and Thailand), which had achieved the objective of reducing to less than 5% trade restrictions on 96.24% of products on the inclusion list. By 1 January 2005 tariffs on just under 99% of products on the 2005 CEPT 'inclusion list' had been reduced to the required 0%–5% range among the original signatory countries, with the average tariff standing at 1.93%. With regard to Cambodia, Laos, Myanmar and Viet Nam, some 81% of products fell within the 0%–5% range. On 1 August 2008 comprehensive revised CEPT rules of origin came into effect.

To complement AFTA in facilitating intra-ASEAN trade, member countries committed to the removal of non-tariff barriers (such as quotas), the harmonization of standards and conformance measures, and the simplification and harmonization of customs procedures. In June 1996 the Working Group on Customs Procedures completed a draft legal framework for regional co-operation, designed to simplify and harmonize customs procedures, legislation and product classification. The agreement was signed in March 1997 at the inaugural meeting of ASEAN ministers responsible for finance. (Laos and Myanmar signed the customs agreement in July and Cambodia assented to it in April 1999.) In 2001 ASEAN finalized its system of harmonized tariff nomenclature, implementation of which commenced in the following year. In November the summit meeting determined to extend ASEAN tariff preferences to ASEAN's newer members from January 2002, under the ASEAN Integration System of Preferences (AISP), thus allowing Cambodia, Laos, Myanmar and Viet Nam tariff-free access to the more developed ASEAN markets earlier than the previously agreed target date of 2010. In April 2002 ASEAN ministers responsible for economic affairs signed an agreement to facilitate intra-regional trade in electrical and electronic equipment by providing for the mutual recognition of standards (for example, testing and certification). The agreement was also intended to lower the costs of trade in those goods, thereby helping to maintain competitiveness.

In November 2000 heads of government endorsed an Initiative for ASEAN Integration (IAI), which aimed to reduce economic disparities within the region through effective co-operation, with a particular focus on assisting the newer signatory states, i.e. Cambodia, Laos, Myanmar and Viet Nam. In July 2002 the ASEAN Ministerial Meeting (AMM) endorsed a first IAI Work Plan, with the following priority areas: human resources development; infrastructure; information and communications technology (ICT); and regional economic integration. Much of the funding for the Initiative came from ASEAN's external partners, including Australia, India, Japan, Norway and South Korea. A second IAI Work Plan, covering the period 2009–15, was adopted by ASEAN heads of state and government in March 2009.

In December 1995 ASEAN ministers responsible for trade adopted the ASEAN Framework Agreement on Services (AFAS), providing for enhanced co-operation in services among member states. By 2014 eight packages of services liberalization commitments had been approved under the AFAS; additionally, since 2005, several 'mutual recognition arrangements' had been adopted, enabling the mutual recognition between the qualifications of member states' professional services suppliers. Full liberalization of services was scheduled to be achieved in 2015.

The Bali Concord II, adopted in October 2003, affirmed commitment to existing ASEAN economic co-operation frameworks, including the Hanoi Plan of Action (and any subsequently agreed regional plans of action) and the IAI, and outlined plans for the creation, by 2020, of an integrated ASEAN Economic Community (AEC), entailing the harmonization of customs procedures and technical regulations by the end of 2004; the removal of non-tariff trade barriers and the establishment of a network of free trade zones by 2005; and the progressive withdrawal of capital controls and strengthening of intellectual property rights. An ASEAN legal unit was to be established to strengthen and enhance existing dispute settlement systems. (A Protocol on Enhanced Dispute Settlement Mechanism was signed in November 2004.) The free movement of professional and skilled workers would be facilitated by standardizing professional requirements and simplifying visa procedures, with the adoption of a single ASEAN visa requirement envisaged by 2005. In November 2004 the 10th meeting of ASEAN heads of state, held in Vientiane, Laos, endorsed—as the successor to the Hanoi Plan of Action—a new Vientiane Action Programme (VAP), with commitments to deepening regional integration and narrowing the development gap within the grouping. An ASEAN Development Fund was to be established to support the implementation of the VAP and other action programmes. The leaders adopted two plans of action (concerning security and sociocultural affairs) to further the implementation of the Bali Concord II regarding the establishment of a three-pillared ASEAN Community, which included the AEC. An ASEAN Framework Agreement for Integration of the Priority Sectors and its Protocols was also signed. Import duties (on 85% of products) were to be eliminated by 2007 for the original members (including Brunei) and by 2012 for newer member states in 11 sectors, accounting for more than 50% of intra-ASEAN trade in 2003. A Blueprint and Strategic Schedule for realizing the AEC by 2015 was approved by ASEAN ministers of economic affairs in August 2007 and was signed by ASEAN heads of state, meeting in November. During 2008 ASEAN developed a 'scorecard' mechanism to track the implementation of the Blueprint by member countries. In March 2009 heads of state agreed that the new Roadmap for an ASEAN Community should replace the VAP. In May 2010 an ASEAN Trade in Goods Agreement entered into force, which aimed to consolidate all trade commitments and tariff liberalization schedules. In October 2013 the 23rd ASEAN summit confirmed that 79.7% of the measures set by the AEC Blueprint had been implemented.

In November 1999 an informal meeting of leaders of ASEAN countries, the People's Republic of China, Japan and the Republic of Korea (South Korea) (the so-called ASEAN + 3) issued a Joint Statement on East Asian Co-operation, in which they agreed to strengthen regional unity, and addressed the long-term possibility of establishing an East Asian common market and currency. In July 2000 ASEAN + 3 ministers responsible for foreign affairs convened an inaugural formal summit in Bangkok, and in October ASEAN + 3 ministers responsible for economic affairs agreed to hold their hitherto twice-yearly informal meetings on an institutionalized basis. In November an informal meeting of ASEAN + 3 leaders approved further co-operation in various sectors and initiated a feasibility study into a proposal to establish a regional free trade area. In May 2001 ASEAN + 3 ministers responsible for economic affairs endorsed a series of projects for co-operation in ICT, environment, small and medium-sized enterprises (SMEs), Mekong Basin development, and harmonization of standards. ASEAN + 3 ministers of foreign affairs declared their support in July 2003 for other regional initiatives, namely an Asia Co-operation Dialogue, which was initiated by the Thai Government in June, and an Initiative for Development in East Asia (IDEA), which had been announced by the Japanese Government in January. An IDEA ministerial meeting was convened in Tokyo, Japan, in August. ASEAN + 3 ministers of labour have convened periodically since 2000, to address employment generation, labour market monitoring, labour mobility, social protection, tripartite co-operation, and (since 2006) occupational safety and health. In September the sixth consultation between ASEAN + 3 ministers responsible for economic affairs was held, at which several new projects were endorsed, including two on e-commerce. During 2004 an ASEAN + 3 Unit was established in the ASEAN Secretariat. In November the ASEAN summit meeting agreed to convene a meeting of an East Asia Summit (q.v.), to be developed in parallel with the ASEAN + 3, or APT, framework. In November 2012 a commemorative summit was held, in Phnom Penh, to mark 15 years since the first meeting of APT heads of state.

In October 2008 ASEAN heads of state held a special meeting, in Beijing, China, to consider the impact on the region of the deceleration of growth in the world's most developed economies and the ongoing instability of global financial markets. The meeting was followed by a specially convened ASEAN + 3 summit to discuss further regional co-operation to counter the impact of the crisis. In April 2010 ASEAN heads of state, convened in Hanoi, adopted an ASEAN Strategy for Economic Recovery and Development to ensure sustainable recovery from the global financial and economic crisis. Leaders determined to strengthen efforts to enhance financial monitoring and surveillance, to foster infrastructure and sustainable development, to pursue regional communications connectivity, and to achieve regional economic integration.

In August 2010 an inaugural meeting of ministers responsible for economic affairs of Cambodia, Laos, Myanmar and Viet Nam (the so-called CLMV countries) was convened, in Da Nang, Viet Nam, further to strengthen intra-economic and trade relations. In particular, the meeting considered measures to enhance trade promotion and to narrow the development gap between the CLMV countries and other countries in the region. Meeting for the fourth time in August 2012, in Siem Riep, Cambodia, the CLMV ministers endorsed a CLMV Action Plan 2013, covering some 15 priority activities in the areas of economy and trade, human resource development, and co-ordination.

FINANCE AND INVESTMENT

In October 1998 ministers of economic affairs, meeting in Manila, Philippines, signed a Framework Agreement on an ASEAN Investment Area (AIA), which was to provide for equal treatment of domestic and other ASEAN direct investment proposals within the grouping by 2010, and of all foreign investors by 2020. The meeting also confirmed that an ASEAN Surveillance Process (ASP) would be implemented with immediate effect, to monitor the economic stability and financial systems of member states; the ASP required the voluntary submission of economic information by all members to a Jakarta, Indonesia-based monitoring committee. The ASP and the Framework Agreement on the AIA were incorporated into the Hanoi Plan of Action, adopted by heads of state in December 1998. The summit meeting also resolved to accelerate reforms, particularly in the banking and financial sectors, in order to strengthen the region's economies, and to promote the liberalization of the financial services sector. In March 1999 ASEAN ministers of trade and industry, meeting in Phuket, Thailand, as the AIA Council, agreed to open their manufacturing, agriculture, fisheries, forestry and mining industries to foreign investment. Investment restrictions affecting those industries were to be eliminated by 2003 in most cases, although Laos and Viet Nam were granted until 2010. In addition, ministers adopted a number of measures to encourage investment in the region, including access to three-year corporate income tax exemptions, and tax allowances of 30% for investors. The AIA agreement formally entered into force in June 1999, having been ratified by all member countries. In September 2001 ministers agreed to accelerate the full realization of the AIA for non-ASEAN investors in manufacturing, agriculture, forestry, fishing and mining sectors. The date for full implementation was advanced to 2010 for the original six ASEAN members and to 2015 for the newer members. In August 2007 the AIA Council determined to revise the Framework Agreement on the AIA in order to implement a more comprehensive investment arrangement in support of the establishment of the AEC; consequently a new ASEAN Comprehensive Investment Agreement (ACIA) entered into force in March 2012. An ASEAN investment website, and an *ACIA Guidebook for Businesses* and *ACIA Handbook for Investment Promotion Agencies* were launched at an introductory forum on the ACIA, which took place in March 2013, in Kuala Lumpur, Malaysia.

In May 2000, ASEAN + 3 ministers responsible for economic affairs, meeting in Chiang Mai, Thailand, proposed the establishment of an enhanced currency swap mechanism, enabling countries to draw on liquidity support to defend their economies during balance of payments difficulties or speculative currency attacks and to prevent future financial crises. The so-called Chiang Mai Initiative Multilateralization (CMIM) on currency swap arrangements was formally approved by ASEAN + 3 ministers responsible for finance in May 2001. In August 2003 ASEAN + 3 finance ministers agreed to establish a Finance Co-operation Fund, to support ongoing economic reviews relating to projects such as the CMIM. An Asian Bond Markets Initiative (ABMI) was launched by ASEAN + 3 countries in 2003 to develop local currency denominated bond markets. In February 2009 ministers of finance of ASEAN + 3 countries convened a special meeting, in Phuket, to consider the impact on the region of the global economic and financial crisis, and issued an Action Plan to Restore Economic and Financial Stability of the Asian Region. Ministers agreed to expand the CMIM (from US $80,000m. to $120,000m.) and to establish an independent regional surveillance unit to strengthen economic monitoring. The CMIM entered into force in March 2010. In May ASEAN + 3 finance ministers, convened in Tashkent, Uzbekistan, announced the launch, within the ABMI framework, of a Credit Guarantee and Investment Facility, with an initial capital of $700m., as a trust fund of the Asian Development Bank. Ministers also acknowledged that agreement had been reached on the establishment, in Singapore, of an ASEAN + 3 Macroeconomic Research Office, to monitor and analyse regional economies and to support the effectiveness of the CMIM. The Office was inaugurated in April 2011. In May 2012 ASEAN + 3 ministers of finance and governors of central banks, meeting in Manila, agreed further to expand the CMIM (from $120,000m. to $240,000m.), and to initiate a crisis prevention mechanism: the CMIM Precautionary Line (CMIM-PL); they also adopted an ABMI New Roadmap+, aimed at enhancing the Bond Markets Initiative.

POLITICS AND SECURITY

In 1971 ASEAN members endorsed a declaration envisaging the establishment of a Zone of Peace, Freedom and Neutrality (ZOPFAN) in the South-East Asian region. This objective was incorporated in the Declaration of ASEAN Concord, which was adopted at the first summit meeting of the organization, held in Bali, in February 1976. Heads of state also signed a Treaty of Amity and Co-operation, establishing principles of mutual respect for the independence and sovereignty of all nations, non-interference in the internal affairs of one another and settlement of disputes by peaceful means. The Treaty was amended in December 1987 by a protocol providing for the accession of Papua New Guinea and other non-member countries in the region. In January 1992 ASEAN leaders agreed that there should be greater co-operation on security matters within the grouping, and that ASEAN's post-ministerial conferences (PMCs) should be used as a forum for discussion of questions relating to security with dialogue partners and other countries. In July 1992 Viet Nam and Laos signed ASEAN's Treaty of Amity and Co-operation. Cambodia acceded to the Treaty in January 1995 and Myanmar signed it in July.

The ASEAN member states are parties to the treaty establishing a South-East Asia Nuclear-Weapon Free Zone (SEANWFZ), which was adopted by heads of government in December 1995 and entered into force in March 1997. The SEANWFZ, covering the territories, continental shelves and offshore economic exclusion zones of each state party, entered into force in March 1997, and in July 1999 China and India agreed to observe its terms. The treaty prohibits the manufacture or storage of nuclear weapons within the region; individual signatories have the power to decide whether to allow port visits or transportation of nuclear weapons by foreign powers through territorial waters. In May 2001 ASEAN and the five nuclear-weapon states (China, France, Russia, the United Kingdom and the USA, known as the P5) initiated negotiations on a protocol providing for their accession to the SEANWFZ. The envisaged adoption of the protocol in July 2012 was postponed, reportedly owing to reservations on the part of France, Russia, the United Kingdom and the USA relating to the precise definition of the Zone, sovereignty matters, and the rights of foreign ships and aircraft passing through the Zone.

In February 2013 ASEAN member countries issued a statement expressing deep concern about the impact on regional security in view of reports that the Democratic People's Republic of Korea (North Korea) had in that month conducted an underground nuclear test at its Punngye-ri testing facility. North Korea was urged to comply fully with its obligations under relevant UN Security Council resolutions.

In 1999 ASEAN established a special committee to formulate a code of conduct for the South China Sea to be observed by all claimants to the disputed Spratly Islands (namely China, Viet Nam, Taiwan, Brunei, Malaysia and the Philippines). In November 2002 ASEAN and China's ministers responsible for foreign affairs adopted a Declaration on the Conduct (DOC) of Parties in the South China Sea, agreeing to promote a peaceful environment and durable solutions for the area, to resolve territorial disputes by peaceful means, to refrain from undertaking activities that would aggravate existing tensions (such as settling unpopulated islands and reefs), and to initiate a regular dialogue of defence officials. The South China Sea has significant resources of oil, natural gas, and minerals, and, as well as the Spratly Islands, other disputed territories there include the Paracel Islands (claimed by China, Taiwan and Viet Nam), and the Scarborough Shoal (a reef area claimed by China, the Philippines, and Taiwan). In December 2004 in Kuala Lumpur, at the first senior officials' meeting between ASEAN and China on the implementation of the DOC, it was agreed to adopt the Terms of Reference of the newly established joint working group as a step towards enhancing security and stability in the South China Sea. In July 2011 Guidelines on the Implementation of the DOC were agreed by senior officials from ASEAN and China. During April–May 2012 tensions escalated significantly between the Philippines and China concerning territorial rights in the Scarborough Shoal area. In early July ASEAN ministers responsible for foreign affairs reiterated the need to implement the DOC and agreed a draft legally binding Code of Conduct (COC) in the South China Sea; however, at the 19th ASEAN Regional Forum, held in that month, China—declaring that conditions were not at that time conducive for finalizing the draft Code—refrained from signing it, and ASEAN ministers failed to agree a common position on addressing the situation. Later in that month the foreign ministers issued a Statement on the Six-Point

Principles in the South China Sea, reaffirming member states' commitment to: the full implementation of the DOC; the 2011 Guidelines for the Implementation of the DOC; the early conclusion of the COC; full respect for universally recognized principles of international law, with particular reference to the 1982 UN Convention on the Law of the Sea; the continued exercise by all parties of self-restraint; and the peaceful resolution of disputes, in accordance with universally recognized principles of international law. In November 2012 the 15th ASEAN-China Summit issued a joint statement reaffirming commitment to implementing the DOC. Formal high-level consultations between ASEAN and China aimed at finalizing the COC were initiated in September 2013.

In 1997 the efforts of ASEAN ministers responsible for foreign affairs to negotiate a political settlement to ongoing internal conflict in Cambodia marked a significant shift in diplomatic policy from one of non-interference in the internal affairs of other countries towards one of 'constructive intervention'. Most participants in the July 1998 AMM agreed to pursue a policy of 'enhanced interaction', and to maintain open dialogue within the grouping. In September 1999 the unrest prompted by the popular referendum on the future of East Timor (now Timor-Leste) and the resulting humanitarian crisis highlighted the unwillingness of some ASEAN member states to intervene in other member countries and undermined the political unity of the grouping. A compromise agreement, enabling countries to act on an individual basis rather than as representatives of ASEAN, was formulated prior to an emergency meeting of ministers of foreign affairs, held in October. Malaysia, the Philippines, Singapore and Thailand declared their support for the establishment of a multinational force to restore peace in East Timor and committed troops to participate in the Australian-led operation. At their informal summit in November heads of state approved the establishment of an ASEAN Troika, which was to be constituted as an ad hoc body comprising the ministers responsible for foreign affairs of the Association's current, previous and future chairmanship with a view to providing a rapid response mechanism in the event of a regional crisis.

On 12 September 2001 ASEAN issued a ministerial statement on international terrorism, condemning the attacks of the previous day in the USA and urging greater international co-operation to counter terrorism. The seventh summit meeting in November issued a Declaration on a Joint Action to Combat Terrorism. The summit encouraged member countries to sign (or ratify) the International Convention for the Suppression of the Financing of Terrorism, to strengthen national mechanisms against terrorism, and to work to deepen co-operation, particularly in the area of intelligence exchange. The summit noted the need to strengthen security co-operation to restore investor confidence. In its Declaration and other notes, the summit explicitly rejected any attempt to link terrorism with religion or race, and expressed concern for the suffering of innocent Afghanis during the US military action against the Taliban authorities in Afghanistan. The summit's final Declaration was worded so as to avoid any mention of the US action, to which Muslim ASEAN states such as Malaysia and Indonesia were strongly opposed. In November 2002 the eighth summit meeting adopted a Declaration on Terrorism, reiterating and strengthening the measures announced in the previous year. (See, also, Transnational Crime.)

The ASEAN Charter that entered into force in December 2008 envisaged the establishment of a new ASEAN human rights body, to extend, for the first time within the grouping, a formal structure for the promotion and protection of human rights and fundamental freedoms. The ensuing ASEAN Intergovernmental Commission on Human Rights (AICHR), composed of a national expert representative from each member state, held its inaugural meeting at the ASEAN Secretariat in March–April 2010. An ASEAN Human Rights Declaration (AHRD), which had been drafted by the AICHR, was adopted by the 21st summit of ASEAN heads of state, in November 2012. An ASEAN Institute for Peace and Reconciliation was also inaugurated at the meeting, held in Phnom Penh.

In July 2009 the AMM urged the authorities in Myanmar to release all political detainees, including the main opposition leader Aung San Suu Kyi, in order to enable them to participate freely in elections scheduled to be conducted in 2010. In August 2009 Thailand, acting in its capacity as the ASEAN Chair, expressed deep disappointment at the sentencing of Aung San Suu Kyi for allegedly breaching the terms of her house arrest. (Aung San Suu Kyi eventually was released in November 2010.)

ASEAN Regional Forum (ARF): In July 1993 the meeting of ASEAN ministers responsible for foreign affairs sanctioned the establishment of a forum to discuss and promote co-operation on security issues within the region, and, in particular, to ensure the involvement of China in regional dialogue. The ARF was informally initiated during that year's PMC, comprising the ASEAN countries, its dialogue partners (at that time Australia, Canada, the European Community, Japan, South Korea, New Zealand and the USA), and China, Laos, Papua New Guinea, Russia and Viet Nam. The first formal meeting of the ARF was conducted in July 1994, following the AMM held in Bangkok, and it was agreed that the ARF would be convened on an annual basis. The 1995 meeting, held in Brunei, in August, attempted to define a framework for the future of the Forum. It was perceived as evolving through three stages: the promotion of confidence-building (including disaster relief and peacekeeping activities); the development of preventive diplomacy; and the elaboration of approaches to conflict. The third ARF, convened in July 1996, which was attended for the first time by India and Myanmar, agreed a set of criteria and guiding principles for the future expansion of the grouping. In particular, it was decided that the ARF would only admit as participants countries that had a direct influence on the peace and security of the East Asia and Pacific region. The ARF held in July 1997 reviewed progress made in developing the first two 'tracks' of the ARF process, through the structure of inter-sessional working groups and meetings. Mongolia was admitted into the ARF at its meeting in July 1998. India rejected a proposal that Pakistan attend the meeting to discuss issues relating to both countries' testing of nuclear weapons. The meeting ultimately condemned the testing of nuclear weapons in the region, but declined to criticize specifically India and Pakistan. At the seventh meeting of the ARF, convened in Bangkok, in July 2000, North Korea was admitted to the Forum. The meeting considered the impact of globalization, including the possibilities for greater economic interdependence and also for a growth in transnational crime. The eighth ARF meeting in July 2001, in Hanoi, pursued these themes, and also discussed the widening development gap between nations. The meeting agreed to enhance the role of the ARF Chairman, enabling him to issue statements on behalf of ARF participants and to organize events during the year. The ninth ARF meeting, held in Bandar Seri Begawan, in July 2002, assessed regional and international security developments, and issued a statement of individual and collective intent to prevent any financing of terrorism. The statement included commitments by participants to freeze the assets of suspected individuals or groups, to implement international financial standards and to enhance co-operation and the exchange of information. In October the Chairman, on behalf of all ARF participants, condemned the terrorist bomb attacks committed against tourist targets in Bali. An administrative unit supporting the ARF was established within the ASEAN Secretariat in June 2004. Pakistan joined the ARF in the following month. In November the first ARF Security Policy Conference was held in Beijing. The Conference recommended developing various aspects of bilateral and multilateral co-operation, including with regard to non-traditional security threats. Timor-Leste and Bangladesh became participants in the ARF in July 2005. In July 2006 the ARF issued statements on 'co-operation in fighting cyber attacks and terrorist misuse of cyber space'; and on disaster management and emergency responses, determining to formulate guidelines for enhanced co-operation in humanitarian operations. In January 2007 an ARF maritime security shore exercise was conducted, in Singapore. In March the first ARF Defense Ministers Retreat was convened, in Bali. The 14th ARF, held in Manila, in July, approved the establishment of a 'Friends of the Chair' mechanism, comprising three ministers, to promote preventive diplomacy and respond rapidly to political crises. In July 2008 the 15th ARF determined further to strengthen co-operation in natural disaster preparedness and relief operations and resolved to organize training in those areas and a disaster relief exercise. At that time North Korea acceded to ASEAN's Treaty of Amity and Co-operation. The USA acceded to the Treaty in July 2009, and Canada and Turkey acceded in July 2010. In July 2009, the ARF marked its 15th anniversary by adopting a Vision Statement for the period up to 2020. It reaffirmed its commitment to 'building a region of peace, friendship and prosperity' and proposed measures to strengthen the ARF and to develop security-based partnerships. The 17th meeting of the ARF, convened in Hanoi, in July 2010, adopted a Plan of Action to implement the Vision Statement 2020. In July 2012 the 19th Forum, meeting in Phnom Penh, failed to agree a concluding statement, following failure among participating ministers responsible for foreign affairs to establish a common position concerning the pursuit of a draft Code of Conduct in the South China Sea. The 20th Forum, convened in July 2013, noted the Statement on the Six-Point Principles in the South China Sea that was concluded by ASEAN ministers in July 2012 following the 19th Forum, and agreed to strengthen preventive diplomacy training in the region.

Since 2000 the ARF has published the *Annual Security Outlook*, to which participating countries submit assessments of the security prospects in the region.

In October 2010 the first so-called ASEAN Defence Ministers' Meeting (ADMM)-Plus was held, in Hanoi, incorporating ASEAN ministers and their counterparts from eight dialogue partner ('Plus') countries, i.e. Australia, China, India, Japan, South Korea, New Zealand, Russia and the USA. The new body aimed to complement the work of the ARF. ADMM-Plus experts' working groups have been established on disaster management; maritime security; counter-terrorism; peacekeeping; and military medicine. The first ADMM-Plus Humanitarian Assistance and Disaster Relief/Military Medicine Exercise was conducted in June 2013, in Brunei. The second ADMM-Plus meeting took place in Bandar Seri Begawan, in August of that year, and the third was to be organized in 2015. An ASEAN Defence Senior Officials' Meeting (ADSOM)-Plus is convened annually.

TRANSNATIONAL CRIME

The first ASEAN Ministerial Meeting on Transnational Crime (AMMTC) was convened in June 1999. Regular meetings of senior officials and ministers were subsequently held. The third AMMTC, in October 2001, considered initiatives to combat transnational crime, which was defined as including terrorism, trafficking in drugs, arms and people, money-laundering, cyber crime, piracy and economic crime. In May 2002 ministers responsible for transnational crime issues convened a Special Ministerial Meeting on Terrorism, in Kuala Lumpur. The meeting approved a work programme to implement a plan of action to combat transnational crime, including information exchange, the development of legal arrangements for extradition, prosecution and seizure, the enhancement of co-operation in law enforcement, and the development of regional security training programmes. In a separate initiative Indonesia, Malaysia and the Philippines signed an agreement on information exchange and the establishment of communication procedures. Cambodia acceded to the agreement in July. In November 2004 ASEAN leaders adopted an ASEAN Declaration against Trafficking in Persons, Particularly Women and Children, which aimed to strengthen co-operation to prevent and combat trafficking, through, inter alia, the establishment of a new regional focal network, information-sharing procedures and standardized immigration controls. In May 2011 ASEAN leaders issued a joint statement on enhancing co-operation against trafficking in persons in South-East Asia. An ASEAN Convention on Trafficking in Persons (ACTIP) was being finalized in 2014. The Plan of Action of the ASEAN Security Community (envisaged by the Bali Concord II) had as its five key areas: political development; shaping and sharing of norms; conflict prevention; conflict resolution; and post-conflict peacebuilding. In November 2004 eight member countries, namely Brunei, Cambodia, Indonesia, Malaysia, Laos, the Philippines, Singapore and Viet Nam, signed a Treaty on Mutual Legal Assistance in Criminal Matters in Kuala Lumpur.

In January 2007 ASEAN leaders, meeting in Cebu, Philippines, signed an ASEAN Convention on Counter Terrorism. The Convention entered into force in May 2011, having received the required ratification by six member states: Brunei, Cambodia, the Philippines, Singapore, Thailand and Viet Nam.

INDUSTRY

The ASEAN-Chambers of Commerce and Industry (CCI) aims to enhance ASEAN economic and industrial co-operation and the participation in these activities of the private sector. In March 1996 a permanent ASEAN-CCI secretariat became operational at the ASEAN Secretariat. An ASEAN Business Advisory Council held its inaugural meeting in April 2003. An ASEAN Business-Investment Summit (ASEAN-BIS) has been held annually since 2003; the 2013 Summit was convened in Brunei, in August.

An ASEAN Industrial Co-operation (AICO) scheme was initiated in 1996 to encourage companies in the ASEAN region to undertake joint manufacturing activities prior to the full implementation of the CEPT scheme: products derived from the first phase of AICO arrangements (the majority of which were in the automotive sector) benefited immediately from a preferential tariff rate of 0%–5%. In April 2004 ASEAN ministers responsible for the economy signed a Protocol to Amend the Basic Agreement on the AICO Scheme, which aimed to maintain its relevance. As from 1 January 2005 the tariff rate for Brunei, Cambodia, Indonesia, Laos, Malaysia and Singapore was 0%; for the Philippines 0%–1%, for Thailand 0%–3% and for Myanmar and Viet Nam 0%–5%. ASEAN has initiated studies of new methods of industrial co-operation within the grouping, with the aim of achieving further integration.

The ASEAN Consultative Committee on Standards and Quality (ACCSQ) aims to promote the understanding and implementation of quality concepts. ACCSQ comprises three working groups: standards and information; conformance and assessment; and testing and calibration. An ASEAN Intellectual Property Rights (IPR) Action Plan covering the period 2011–15 aims, inter alia, to promote a balanced IP system taking into account the varying levels of development of member states, to develop national or regional legal and policy infrastructures to address the evolving demands of the IP landscape, and to ensure that IP is utilized as a tool for innovation and development.

The Hanoi Plan of Action, which was adopted by ASEAN heads of state in December 1998, incorporated a series of initiatives to enhance the development of SMEs, including training and technical assistance, co-operation activities and greater access to information. In September 2004 ASEAN ministers responsible for economic affairs approved an ASEAN Policy Blueprint for SME Development 2004–14, first proposed by a working group in 2001, which comprised strategic work programmes and policy measures for the development of SMEs in the region. The Strategic Action Plan for ASEAN SME Development 2010–15, endorsed by ministers in August 2010, provided for the establishment of ASEAN SME Regional Development Fund. The first meeting of a new ASEAN SME Advisory Board was held in Singapore, in June 2011. A *Directory of ASEAN Innovative SMEs* was published in November 2012.

In January 2007 senior officials concluded a five-year ASEAN plan of action to support the development and implementation of national occupational safety and health frameworks. In May 2010 ASEAN ministers responsible for labour adopted a Work Programme for the period 2010–15, which aimed to support the realization of the ASEAN Community and to further the objectives of achieving adequate social protection for all workers in the region and fostering productive employment.

FOOD, AGRICULTURE AND FORESTRY

In February–March 2009 ASEAN heads of state, meeting in Cha-am and Hua Hin, adopted an Integrated Food Security Framework and a Strategic Plan of Action on Food Security in the ASEAN Region. An ASEAN-FAO Regional Conference on Food Security was held in Bangkok, in May. In October 2010 ministers endorsed the transformation of the ASEAN + 3 Emergency Rice Reserve—launched in 2003, in place of a previous emergency rice reserve scheme established in 1979—into a permanent mechanism; the ensuing Three Emergency Rice Reserve (APTERR) was inaugurated in October 2011.

In June 2011 the ministerial session of the ASEAN-Southeast Asian Fisheries Development Center Conference on Sustainable Fisheries for Sustainable Development adopted a resolution on Sustainable Fisheries for Food Security for the ASEAN Region Towards 2020, to be implemented through individual and collective efforts among member states.

Co-operation in forestry is focused on joint projects, funded by ASEAN's dialogue partners, which include a Forest Tree Seed Centre, an Institute of Forest Management and the ASEAN Timber Technology Centre. In 2005 an Ad Hoc Experts Working Group on International Forest Policy Processes was created, to support the development of ASEAN joint positions and approaches on regional and international forest issues. An ASEAN Social Forestry Network was also established in that year. In November 2007 ASEAN ministers responsible for forestry issued a statement on strengthening forest law enforcement and governance.

There is an established ASEAN programme of training and study exchanges for farm workers, agricultural experts and members of agricultural co-operatives. In December 1998 heads of state determined to establish an ASEAN Food Security Information Service to enhance the capacity of member states to forecast and manage food supplies. In 1999 ministers responsible for agriculture endorsed guidelines on assessing risk from genetically modified organisms in agriculture, to ensure a common approach. In October 2004 ministers of agriculture and forestry endorsed the establishment of an ASEAN Highly Pathogenic Avian Influenza (HPAI) Taskforce, to co-ordinate regional co-operation for the control and eradication of HPAI. In October 2010 ASEAN ministers of agriculture and forestry endorsed a Roadmap Towards an HPAI-Free ASEAN Community by 2020, as a strategic framework to address avian influenza and other transboundary and zoonotic diseases of significant priority to the region. The human health dimension of HPAI is monitored by the ASEAN Experts Group on Communicable Diseases, through the ASEAN + 3 programme on emerging infectious diseases. In November 2006 an agreement establishing a new ASEAN Animal Health Trust Fund was signed by ASEAN ministers of agriculture and forestry. In November 2007 ministers responsible for agriculture and forestry agreed to establish an ASEAN Network on Aquatic Animal Health Centres, to strengthen diagnostic and certification measures of live aquatic animals within the region.

ASEAN + 3 ministers responsible for agriculture and forestry met for the first time in October 2001, and discussed issues of poverty alleviation, food security, agricultural research and human resource development. An ASEAN + 3 Cooperation Strategy (APTCS) on food, agriculture and forestry covering the period 2011–15 focuses on the following strategic areas: strengthening food security; biomass energy development; sustainable forest management; climate change mitigation and adaptation; animal health and disease control; and cross-cutting issues.

MINERALS AND ENERGY

The ASEAN Centre for Energy, based in Jakarta, Indonesia, provides an energy information network, promotes the establishment of interconnecting energy structures among ASEAN member countries, supports the development of renewable energy resources and encourages co-operation in energy efficiency and conservation. An ASEAN Energy Business Forum is held annually, attended by representatives of the energy industry in the private and public sectors. In November 1999 a Trans-ASEAN Gas Pipeline Task Force was established. In July 2002 ASEAN ministers responsible for energy signed a Memorandum of Understanding (MOU) to implement the Trans-ASEAN Gas Pipeline Project, involving seven interconnections. The Trans-Thai-Malaysia Gas Pipeline became operational in early 2005. In July 2003 ASEAN ministers agreed that the final report, published in March, of an ASEAN Interconnection Masterplan Study (AIMS) working group should be used henceforth as the reference document for the implementation of electricity interconnection projects within the region; an updated Study, AIMS II, was completed in 2010. An MOU on the regional power grid initiative, providing for the establishment of an ASEAN Power Grid Consultative Committee, was signed by ministers of energy, meeting in August 2007. Nine electricity interconnection projects were scheduled for completion by 2015, with six further projects to be completed thereafter. In June 2004 the first meeting of ASEAN + 3 ministers responsible for energy was convened. Later in that year a permanent Secretariat of the Heads of ASEAN Power Utilities/Authorities (HAPUA) was established, on a three-year rotation basis. In July 2009 ministers of energy adopted an ASEAN Plan of Action for Energy Cooperation (APAEC), covering the period 2010–15.

A Framework of Co-operation in Minerals was adopted by an ASEAN working group of experts in August 1993. The group has also developed a programme of action for ASEAN co-operation in the development and utilization of industrial minerals, to promote the exploration and development of mineral resources, the transfer of mining technology and expertise, and the participation of the private sector in industrial mineral production. The programme of action is implemented by an ASEAN Regional Development Centre for Mineral Resources, based in Bandung, Indonesia, which also conducts workshops and training programmes relating to the sector. In August 2005 ASEAN ministers responsible for minerals held an inaugural meeting, in Kuching, Malaysia. A second meeting was convened, in October 2008, in Manila; and a third in December 2011, in Hanoi. An ASEAN Minerals Co-operation Action Plan for 2011–15 aimed to promote information sharing on minerals; to facilitate and enhance trade and investment in the sector; and to promote environmentally and socially sustainable practices.

TRANSPORT

ASEAN objectives for the transport sector include developing multi-modal transport, harmonizing road transport laws and regulations, improving air space management and developing ASEAN legislation for the carriage of dangerous goods and waste by land and sea. In September 1999 ASEAN ministers responsible for transport adopted a Ministerial Understanding on the Development of the ASEAN Highway Network Project, which aimed to upgrade the signage and standards on all designated national routes, with all routes to be 'class I' or 'primary' standard by 2020. A Framework Agreement on Facilitation of Goods in Transit entered into force in October 2000. In September 2002 ASEAN ministers responsible for transport signed Protocol 9 on Dangerous Goods, one of the implementing protocols under the Framework Agreement, which provided for the simplification of procedures for the transportation of dangerous goods within the region using internationally accepted rules and guidelines. A roadmap to support the development of an integrated and competitive maritime transport sector in the ASEAN region was signed by ministers of transport in November 2007. At the same time an agreement to strengthen co-operation in maritime cargo and passenger transport was signed with China. The November 2008 meeting of ministers responsible for transport concluded an ASEAN Framework Agreement on the Facilitation of Inter-State Transport. In November 2010 ASEAN ministers adopted the ASEAN Transport Action Plan, 2011–15, which incorporated measures to support the realization of the AEC by 2015 and the regional transport priorities of the Master Plan on ASEAN Connectivity.

In September 2002 ASEAN senior transport officials signed an MOU on air freight services, which represented the first stage in full liberalization of air freight services in the region. The Action Plan for ASEAN Air Transport Integration and Liberalization 2005–15 was adopted in November 2004. In February 2009 and October 2010, respectively, ministers approved the seventh and eighth packages of commitments for the air and transport sectors under the 1995 ASEAN Framework Agreement on Services. The ASEAN Multilateral Agreement on Air Services (MAAS), and six protocols, were signed in May 2009. The Master Plan for ASEAN Connectivity, adopted by heads of state in October 2010, incorporated objectives for the development and implementation of an ASEAN Single Aviation Market, as well as an ASEAN Single Shipping Market, by 2015. In November 2010 the ASEAN Multilateral Agreement on the Full Liberalisation of Passenger Air Services (MAFLPAS), with two Protocols, were signed. Meeting in January 2012 ministers responsible for transport issued a Declaration on the Adoption of the Implementation Framework of the ASEAN Single Aviation Market (ASAM), which was to guide ASEAN's aviation sector activities to 2015 and beyond, covering areas including the liberalization of air services, alignment of aviation safety and security processes, and harmonization of air traffic management.

TELECOMMUNICATIONS

ASEAN aims to achieve interoperability and interconnectivity in the telecommunications sector. In November 2000 ASEAN heads of government approved an e-ASEAN Framework Agreement to promote and co-ordinate e-commerce and internet utilization. The Agreement incorporated commitments to develop and strengthen ASEAN's information infrastructure, in order to provide for universal and affordable access to communications services. Tariff reduction on ICT products was to be accelerated, with the aim of eliminating all tariffs in the sector by 2010. In July 2001 the first meeting of ASEAN ministers responsible for telecommunications (TELMIN) was held, in Kuala Lumpur, during which a Ministerial Understanding on ASEAN co-operation in telecommunications and ICT was signed. In September ASEAN ministers responsible for economic affairs approved a list of ICT products eligible for the gradual elimination of duties under the e-ASEAN Framework Agreement. During 2001 ASEAN continued to develop a reference framework for e-commerce legislation. In September 2003 the third ASEAN telecommunications ministerial meeting adopted a declaration incorporating commitments to harness ASEAN technological advances, create digital opportunities and enhance ASEAN's competitiveness in the field of ICT. The ministers also endorsed initiatives to enhance cybersecurity, including the establishment of computer emergency response teams in each member state. In August 2004 an ASEAN ICT Fund was established to accelerate implementation of the grouping's ICT objectives. At the fifth meeting of ministers responsible for telecommunications, held in Hanoi, in September 2005, the Hanoi Agenda on Promoting Online Services and Applications was adopted. 'ASEANconnect', a web portal collating all essential information and data regarding ICT activities and initiatives within ASEAN, was also launched. In August 2007 ASEAN ministers responsible for telecommunications, convened in Siem Reap, Cambodia, endorsed a commitment to enhance universal access of ICT services within ASEAN, in particular to extend the benefits of ICT to rural communities and remote areas. At the same time ministers met their counterparts from China, Japan and South Korea to strengthen co-operation in ICT issues. An ASEAN Connectivity Initiative, approved by ASEAN heads of state in October 2009, envisaged greater investment and targets for co-operation in ICT, as well as transport, energy and cross-border movement of goods and people. In September 2011 ASEAN and the Asian Development Bank signed an agreement to establish the Malaysia-based ASEAN Infrastructure Fund (AIF), which was to channel funding to support regional infrastructure development and MPAC. The AIF was launched in April 2012 and by December 2013 had received contributions totalling US $485m.; it was envisaged that the Fund would finance six projects per year. The AIF's inaugural loan, of $25m., was granted in that month towards developing power links and expanding transmission networks between Bali and Java, Indonesia. In January 2011 ASEAN ministers responsible for telecommunications adopted an ASEAN ICT Masterplan 2015 ('AIM2015'). In November 2012 the 12th TELMIN meeting reaffirmed commitment to developing an ASEAN Broadband Corridor, provided for under AIM2015.

SCIENCE AND TECHNOLOGY

ASEAN's Committee on Science and Technology (COST) supports co-operation in food science and technology, meteorology and geophysics, microelectronics and ICT, biotechnology, non-conventional energy research, materials science and technology, space technology applications, science and technology infrastructure and resources development, and marine science. There is an ASEAN Science Fund, used to finance policy studies in science and technology and to support information exchange and dissemination.

The Hanoi Plan of Action, adopted in December 1998, envisaged a series of measures aimed at promoting development in the fields of science and technology, including the establishment of networks of science and technology centres of excellence and academic institutions, the creation of a technology scan mechanism, the promotion of public and private sector co-operation in scientific and technological (particularly ICT) activities, and an increase in research on strategic technologies. In September 2001 the ASEAN Ministerial Meeting on Science and Technology, convened for its first meeting since 1998, approved a new framework for the implementation of ASEAN's Plan of Action on Science and Technology, which aimed to help less developed member countries to become competitive in the sector and integrate into regional co-operation activities. In September 2003 ASEAN and China inaugurated a Network of East Asian Think-tanks to promote scientific and technological exchange. In November 2004 a Ministerial Meeting on Science and Technology decided to establish an ASEAN Virtual Institute of Science and Technology with the aim of developing science and technology human resources in the region. An ASEAN Plan of Action on Science and Technology for 2012–17 covers food security; an early warning system for natural disasters; biofuels; development and application of open source software; and climate change.

ENVIRONMENT

In June 2002 ASEAN ministers responsible for the environment signed an Agreement on Transboundary Haze Pollution, which was intended to provide a legal basis for the Regional Haze Action Plan that had been endorsed in 1997 to address the environmental problems resulting from forest fires. The Agreement, which entered into force in November 2003, required member countries to co-operate in the prevention and mitigation of haze pollution, for example, by responding to requests for information by other states and facilitating the transit of personnel and equipment in case of disaster. The Agreement also provided for the establishment of an ASEAN Co-ordination Centre for Transboundary Haze Pollution Control. The first conference of parties to the Agreement was held in November 2004. An ASEAN Specialized Meteorological Centre, based in Singapore, plays a primary role in long-range climatological forecasting, early detection and monitoring of fires and haze. In August 2005, guided by the ASEAN Agreement on Transboundary Haze Pollution, member countries activated bilateral and regional mechanisms to exchange information and mobilize resources to deal with severe fires in Sumatra (Indonesia), peninsular Malaysia and southern Thailand. In September 2007 ASEAN ministers agreed to establish a sub-regional Technical Working Group to focus on addressing land and forest fires in the northern part of the region.

In May 2001 ministers responsible for the environment launched the ASEAN Environment Education Action Plan (AEEAP), with the aim of promoting public awareness of environmental and sustainable development issues. The current phase of AEEAP covers 2008–15. In November 2003 ASEAN + 3 ministers responsible for the environment agreed to prioritize environmental activities in the following areas: environmentally sustainable cities; global environmental issues; land and forest fires and transboundary haze pollution; coastal and marine environment; sustainable forest management; freshwater resources; public awareness and environmental education; promotion of green technologies and cleaner production; and sustainable development monitoring and reporting. The Vientiane Action Plan incorporated objectives for environmental and natural resource management for the period 2004–10. In September 2005 the ASEAN Centre for Biodiversity, funded jointly by ASEAN and the European Union (EU), was inaugurated in La Union, near Manila, following on from an ASEAN Regional Centre for Biodiversity Conservation, was established in February 1999. The ACB is supported by an ASEAN Biodiversity Fund, which is funded by ASEAN member states on a voluntary basis, and by other approved governments and agencies. In September 2005 ministers of the environment approved an ASEAN Strategic Plan of Action on Water Resources Management. The ASEAN summit meeting convened in November 2007 issued a final Declaration on Environmental Sustainability, which incorporated specific commitments to strengthen environmental protection management, to respond to climate change and to work towards the conservation and sustainable management of natural resources. A Special Ministerial Meeting on the environment was held in Hua Hin, in September 2009. The meeting reviewed ongoing programmes and approved the establishment of an ASEAN Working Group on Climate Change. In the following month ASEAN ministers responsible for the environment endorsed the terms of reference of an ASEAN Climate Change Initiative and adopted a Singapore Resolution on Environmental Sustainability and Climate Change, recognizing the need for closer co-operation in responding to climate change. In April 2010 ASEAN heads of state, meeting in Hanoi, adopted a Leaders' Statement on Joint Response to Climate Change, which reaffirmed ASEAN's commitment to securing a new legally binding agreement on carbon emissions and to strengthening ASEAN efforts to counter and respond to climate change. In November 2010 ASEAN ministers responsible for agriculture and forestry endorsed an ASEAN Multi-Sectoral Framework on Climate Change: Agriculture and Forestry Towards Food Security.

In October 2009 an ASEAN-China Environmental Protection Cooperation Strategy, covering 2009–15, was adopted. A China-ASEAN Environmental Cooperation Centre (CAEC), inaugurated in May 2011, in Beijing, was to support the implementation of the Strategy.

In December 2003 ASEAN members adopted a Declaration on ASEAN Heritage Parks (AHPs), which aimed to strengthen co-operation on the development and implementation of regional conservation and management action plans. The first AHP Conference was convened in September 2004, in Khao Yai National Park, Thailand; the second in April 2007, in Sabah, Malaysia; the third in June 2010, in Brunei; and the fourth in October 2013, in Tagaytay City, Philippines. There were 33 AHPs in 2014.

SOCIAL WELFARE AND DEVELOPMENT

The Plan of Action for the ASEAN Socio-Cultural Community (envisaged in the Bali Concord II) was adopted by ASEAN leaders in November 2004. The first ASEAN + 3 Ministerial Meeting for social welfare and development was convened in Bangkok, in December, at which it was agreed that the three key areas of co-operation were to be the promotion of a community of caring societies in the region; developing policies and programmes to address the issue of ageing; and addressing human resource development in the social sector. In July 2005 it was agreed to establish an ASEAN Development Fund, to which each member country would make an initial contribution of US $1m. An ASEAN Commission on the Promotion and Protection of the Rights of Women and Children was inaugurated in April 2010. A Strategic Framework and Plan of Action for Social Welfare, Family and Children for the period 2011–15 had the following objectives: promoting the welfare of children by safeguarding their rights, ensuring their survival and their full development; protecting children from abuse, discrimination and exploitation; protecting the elderly by supporting community-based support systems to supplement the role of the family as primary caregiver; strengthening regional co-operation to promote self-reliance of older persons and persons with disabilities; strengthening national social welfare and social protection national capacities; and developing family support and family life education programmes. The 23rd ASEAN summit, held in October 2013, in Bandar Seri Begawan, adopted declarations on the elimination of violence against women and children.

ASEAN supports efforts to combat drug abuse and illegal drugs-trafficking. It aims to promote education and drug-awareness campaigns throughout the region, and administers a project to strengthen the training of personnel involved in combating drug abuse. In July 1998 ASEAN ministers of foreign affairs signed a Joint Declaration for a Drug-Free ASEAN, which envisaged greater co-operation among member states, in particular in information exchange, educational resources and legal procedures, in order to eliminate the illicit production, processing and trafficking of narcotic substances by 2020. (This deadline was subsequently advanced to 2015.) In April 2012 ASEAN leaders adopted a Declaration on Drug Free ASEAN 2015.

An ASEAN task force on AIDS has been operational since March 1993. The seventh ASEAN summit meeting, held in November 2001, declared work on combating HIV and AIDS to be a priority. Heads of government expressed their readiness to commit the necessary resources for prevention and care, and to attempt to obtain access to cheaper drugs. An ASEAN Co-operation Forum on HIV/AIDS was held in February 2003, in Bangkok. An East Asia and Pacific Consultation on Children and AIDS was convened in March 2006 and identified nine urgent actions to respond to children affected by HIV/AIDS. In April 2003 a Special ASEAN Leaders' Meeting on Severe Acute Respiratory Syndrome (SARS) endorsed the establishment of an ad hoc ministerial-level Joint Task Force to follow-up and monitor the implementation of a series of co-operation measures approved by ministers of health, including public information and education campaigns, health and immigration control procedures, and the establishment of an early warning system on emerging infectious diseases. In June 2006 ASEAN ministers responsible for health adopted a declaration entitled 'ASEAN Unity in Health Emergencies'. In June 2008 ASEAN inaugurated an internet-based information centre on emerging infectious diseases in the ASEAN + 3 countries to exchange data relating to infection outbreaks and surveillance. In May 2009 ASEAN + 3 health ministers convened a Special Meeting on Influenza A(H1N1), an emerging strain of swine flu that posed a serious threat to humans. The meeting agreed to strengthen surveillance and effective responses; to implement national pandemic preparedness plans; and to ensure effective public communication. It urged regional co-operation to promote surveillance and the transfer of technology, in relation to the production of vaccines.

In November 2011 ASEAN ministers approved a new framework action plan on rural development and poverty eradication, covering the period 2011–15, to address the following priorities: sustainable rural development and rural economic growth; food security and food sovereignty amid climate change; social protection and safety nets; development of infrastructure and human resources in rural areas; constituency building for rural development and poverty eradication; and monitoring and evaluation of the poverty reduction in the region.

In January 1992 the ASEAN summit meeting resolved to establish an ASEAN University Network (AUN); a draft AUN Charter and Agreement were adopted in 1995. The Network aims to strengthen co-operation within the grouping, develop academic and professional human resources and transmit information and knowledge. At the seventh ASEAN summit in November 2001 heads of government agreed to establish the first ASEAN University, in Malaysia. In August 2005 it was agreed to convene a regular ASEAN Ministerial Meeting on education; the first meeting was held in March 2006. In

March 2007 ministers responsible for education determined to restart an ASEAN Student Exchange Programme. An ASEAN + 3 Plan of Action on Education: 2010–17 is being implemented. The seventh Ministerial Meeting on education was convened in July 2012, alongside the first formal ASEAN + 3 and East Asia Summit ministerial meetings.

In January 2007 ASEAN heads of government signed a Declaration on the Protection and Promotion of the Rights of Migrant Workers, which mandated countries to promote fair and appropriate employment protection, payment of wages, and adequate access to decent working and living conditions for migrant workers. A Committee on the Implementation of the ASEAN Declaration held its inaugural meeting in September 2008.

DISASTER MANAGEMENT AND HUMANITARIAN ASSISTANCE

An ASEAN Committee on Disaster Management was established in 2003 and worked to formulate a framework for co-operation in disaster management and emergency response. In January 2005 a Special ASEAN Leaders' Meeting was convened in Jakarta, to consider the needs of countries affected by an earthquake and devastating tsunami that had occurred in the Indian Ocean in late December 2004. The meeting, which was also attended by the UN Secretary-General, the President of the World Bank and other senior envoys of donor countries and international organizations, adopted a Declaration on Action to Strengthen Emergency Relief, Rehabilitation, Reconstruction and Prevention on the Aftermath of Earthquake and Tsunami Disaster. In July 2005 an ASEAN Agreement on Disaster Management and Emergency Response (AADMER) was signed in Vientiane. The Agreement stated as its objective the provision of mechanisms that would effectively reduce the loss of life and damage to the social, economic and environmental assets of the region and the response to disaster emergencies through concerted national efforts and increased regional and international co-operation. The AADMER entered into force in December 2009, having been ratified by each member state. The first meeting of the conference of parties to the AADMER, held in March 2012, determined to establish financial procedures for the operationalization of an ASEAN Disaster Management and Emergency Relief Fund, provided for under the Agreement. In March 2009 ASEAN heads of state resolved that, in the event of a major disaster in a member state, the Secretary-General would act as the ASEAN Humanitarian Assistance Co-ordinator. Meeting in Bali, in November 2011, ASEAN ministers responsible for foreign affairs signed an agreement on the establishment of an ASEAN Coordinating Centre for Humanitarian Assistance on disaster management (AHA Centre); this was inaugurated in Jakarta, in March 2012.

In November 2013 ASEAN mobilized an emergency rapid assessment and dispatched personnel from the AHA Centre, to review the immediate humanitarian needs of survivors of Typhoon Haiyan in the Philippines.

TOURISM

National tourist organizations from ASEAN countries meet regularly to assist in co-ordinating the region's tourist industry, and a Tourism Forum is held annually to promote the sector. (Malaysia hosted the January 2014 Forum, in Kuching.) The first formal meeting of ASEAN ministers responsible for tourism was held in January 1998, in Cebu, Philippines. The meeting adopted a Plan of Action on ASEAN Co-operation in Tourism, which aimed to promote intra-ASEAN travel, greater investment in the sector, joint marketing of the region as a single tourist destination and environmentally sustainable tourism. In January 1999 the second tourism ministerial meeting agreed to appoint country co-ordinators to implement various initiatives, including research to promote the region as a tourist destination in the 21st century, and to develop a cruise ship industry; and the establishment of a network of ASEAN Tourism Training Centres to develop new skills and technologies in the tourist industry. The third meeting of ministers responsible for tourism, held in Bangkok, in January 2000, agreed to reformulate the Visit ASEAN Millennium Year initiative as a long-term Visit ASEAN programme. Ministers responsible for tourism from the ASEAN + 3 countries attended the ministerial meeting for the first time in January 2002. In November the eighth summit of heads of state adopted a framework agreement on ASEAN co-operation in tourism, aimed at facilitating domestic and intra-regional travel. ASEAN national tourism organizations signed an implementation plan for the agreement in May 2003, when they also announced a Declaration on Tourism Safety and Security. In January 2011 ASEAN ministers of tourism approved a new ASEAN Tourism Strategic Plan for the period 2011–15. The Plan envisaged promoting the region as a single tourist destination, developing a set of ASEAN tourism standards with a certification process, and enabling visitors to travel throughout the region with a single visa.

CULTURE AND INFORMATION

Regular workshops and festivals are held in visual and performing arts, youth music, radio, television and films, and print and interpersonal media. In addition, ASEAN administers a News Exchange and provides support for the training of editors, journalists and information officers. In 2000 ASEAN adopted new cultural strategies, with the aim of raising awareness of the grouping's objectives and achievements, both regionally and internationally. The strategies included producing ASEAN cultural and historical educational materials; promoting cultural exchanges; and achieving greater exposure of ASEAN cultural activities and issues in the mass media. An ASEAN Youth Camp was held for the first time in that year, and subsequently has been organized on an annual basis. An ASEAN Youth Forum is convened on the sidelines of the ASEAN summit meeting. ASEAN ministers responsible for culture and arts (AMCA) met for the first time in October 2003. The fourth ministerial meeting was convened, with their ministerial counterparts from the ASEAN + 3 countries, in Clark, Angelus City (Pampanga province), Philippines, in March 2010. The fourth ASEAN Festival of Arts was held concurrently, on the theme 'The Best of ASEAN', while Clark was named as the first ASEAN City of Culture (Cebu and Singapore were subsequently declared Cities of Culture). In April 2014 an ASEAN-China Cultural Exchange Year was inaugurated.

In July 1997 ASEAN ministers responsible for foreign affairs endorsed the establishment of an ASEAN Foundation to promote awareness of the organization and greater participation in its activities; this was inaugurated in July 1998 and is based at the ASEAN secretariat building (www.aseanfoundation.org). The ASEAN Secretariat and Metro TV (Indonesia) jointly produce *ASEAN Today*, a monthly half-hour television broadcast.

EXTERNAL RELATIONS

ASEAN's external relations have been pursued through a dialogue system, initially with the objective of promoting co-operation in economic areas with key trading partners. The system has been expanded in recent years to encompass regional security concerns and co-operation in other areas, such as the environment. The ARF emerged from the dialogue system, and more recently the formalized discussions of ASEAN with China, Japan and South Korea (ASEAN + 3) has evolved as a separate process with its own strategic agenda. In February 2000 a meeting of ASEAN heads of state and the Secretary-General of the United Nations (UN) took place in Bangkok. (A second ASEAN-UN summit was held in September 2005, in New York, USA, and a third was convened in October 2010, in Hanoi.) In December 2006 the UN General Assembly granted ASEAN permanent observer status at its meetings.

In December 2005 the first East Asia Summit (EAS) meeting was convened, following the ASEAN leaders' meeting in Kuala Lumpur. It was attended by ASEAN member countries, China, Japan, South Korea (the '+ 3' countries), India, Australia and New Zealand; Russia participated as an observer. The meeting agreed to pursue co-operation in areas of common interest and determined to meet annually. It concluded a Declaration on Avian Influenza Prevention, Control and Response. At the second EAS meeting, held in Cebu, in January 2007, a Declaration on East Asian Energy Security was adopted. An inaugural meeting of East Asian ministers responsible for energy was convened in August. The third summit meeting was convened in Singapore, in November; it issued the Singapore Declaration on Climate Change, Energy and the Environment and held discussions on issues of mutual concern. A statement by EAS heads of state, issued in June 2009 declared their support for efforts to counter the global economic and financial crisis, including measures agreed by the Group of 20 (G20) industrialized and emerging economies, completion of the Doha Round of the World Trade Organization (WTO), and a Comprehensive Economic Partnership in East Asia Initiative. The fourth EAS was convened in October, in Cha-am and Hua Hin, and the fifth in October 2010, in Hanoi. Russia and the USA participated fully in the EAS for the first time at the sixth summit meeting, held in Bali, in November 2011. The seventh EAS was held in November 2012, in Phnom Penh. Climate change, disaster management, energy and food security, and sustainable development were addressed by the eighth EAS, held in October 2013, in Brunei. The first meeting of EAS ministers responsible for education was convened in July 2012, in Yogyakarta, Indonesia.

In November 2012 ASEAN heads of state initiated negotiations with its free trade area partner countries (i.e. Australia, China, India, Japan, South Korea and New Zealand) to establish a Regional Comprehensive Economic Partnership.

European Union: A Joint Co-operation Committee meets annually (most recently in January 2014), under the terms of a co-operation agreement, signed in 1980 to strengthen trade links and increase co-operation in the scientific and agricultural spheres. A joint Business Council was launched in December 1983 to promote private sector co-operation. In 2001 an ASEAN-EU Business Network was established to develop political and commercial contacts between the two sides. An ASEAN-EU Business Summit meeting was convened for the first time in May 2011, in Jakarta; the second was held in April 2012, in Phnom Penh; the third in March 2013, in Hanoi; and the fourth in February 2014, in Phuket, Thailand. The first meeting of ministers responsible for economic affairs from both groupings took place in October 1985.

In May 1995 ASEAN and EU senior officials endorsed an initiative to strengthen relations between the two economic regions within the framework of an Asia-Europe Meeting of heads of government (ASEM). The first ASEM was convened in Bangkok, in March 1996, at which leaders approved a new Asia-Europe Partnership for Greater Growth. The second ASEM summit meeting, held in April 1998, focused heavily on economic concerns. In February 1997 ministers of foreign affairs of countries participating in ASEM met in Singapore. Despite ongoing differences regarding human rights issues, in particular concerning ASEAN's granting of full membership status to Myanmar and the situation in East Timor (which precluded the conclusion of a new co-operation agreement), the Ministerial Meeting issued a final joint declaration, committing both sides to strengthening co-operation and dialogue on economic, international and bilateral trade, security and social issues. The third ASEM summit meeting was convened in Seoul, South Korea in October 2000. At the 14th ASEAN-EU Ministerial Meeting, held in Brussels, in January 2003, delegates adopted an ASEAN-EU Joint Declaration on Co-operation to Combat Terrorism. An ASEM seminar on combating terrorism was held in Beijing, in October. In February 2003 the EU awarded €4.5m. under the ASEAN-EU Programme on Regional Integration Support (APRIS) to enhance progress towards establishing AFTA. (The first phase of the APRIS programme was concluded in September 2006, and a second three-year phase, APRIS II, was initiated in November with a commitment by the EU of €7.2m.) In April 2003 the EU proposed the creation of a regional framework, the Trans-Regional EU-ASEAN Trade Initiative (TREATI), to address mutual trade facilitation, investment and regulatory issues. In January 2004 a joint statement was issued announcing a roadmap for implementing the TREATI and an EU-ASEAN work plan for that year. The fifth ASEM meeting of heads of state and government was held in Hanoi, in October, attended for the first time by the 10 new members of the EU and by Cambodia, Laos and Myanmar. At the session of the Joint Co-operation Committee held in February 2005, in Jakarta, it was announced that the European Commission's communication entitled 'A New Partnership with Southeast Asia', issued in July 2003, would form the basis for the development of the EU's relations with ASEAN, along with Bali Concord II and the VAP. Under the new partnership, the TREATI would represent the framework for dialogue on trade and economic issues, whereas the READI (Regional EC ASEAN Dialogue Instrument) would be the focus for non-trade issues. The sixth ASEM, convened in Helsinki, Finland, in September 2006, on the theme '10 Years of ASEM: Global Challenges and Joint Responses', was attended for the first time by the ASEAN Secretariat, Bulgaria, India, Mongolia, Pakistan and Romania. The participants adopted a Declaration on Climate Change, aimed at promoting efforts to reach consensus in international climate negotiations, and the Helsinki Declaration on the Future of ASEM, detailing guidelines and practical recommendations for developing future ASEM co-operation. A Declaration on an Enhanced Partnership was endorsed in March 2007 and a plan of action to pursue strengthened co-operation was adopted at an ASEAN-EU summit meeting held in November. The seventh ASEM summit, convened in Beijing, in October 2008, issued a Declaration on Sustainable Development, focusing on the MDGs, climate change and energy security, and social cohesion. In May 2009 ASEAN and EU ministers responsible for foreign affairs signed a declaration committing both sides to completing EU accession to the Treaty of Amity and Co-operation as a priority. (This was achieved in July 2012.) Australia, New Zealand and Russia acceded to the grouping during the eighth ASEM, held in October 2010, in Brussels. The 19th ASEAN-EU Ministerial Meeting, held in April 2012, in Bandar Seri Begawan, adopted the Bandar Seri Begawan Plan of Action to Strengthen the ASEAN-EU Enhanced Partnership (2013–17), which aimed to give co-operation and dialogue a more strategic focus. The ninth ASEM summit was convened in Vientiane, in November 2012 on the theme 'Friends for Peace, Partners for Prosperity'. Bangladesh, Norway and Switzerland were admitted into the grouping, bringing the number of member partners to 51 (including the ASEAN Secretariat and the European Commission). ASEM-10 was to be held in October 2014, in Milan, Italy.

People's Republic of China: Efforts to develop consultative relations between ASEAN and China were initiated in 1993. Joint Committees on economic and trade co-operation and on scientific and technological co-operation were subsequently established. The first formal consultations between senior officials of the two sides were held in April 1995. In July 1996, in spite of ASEAN's continued concern at China's territorial claims to the Spratly Islands in the South China Sea, China was admitted to the PMC as a full dialogue partner. In February 1997 a Joint Co-operation Committee was established to co-ordinate the China-ASEAN dialogue and all aspects of relations between the two sides. Relations were further strengthened by the decision to form a joint business council to promote bilateral trade and investment. China participated in the informal summit meeting held in December, at the end of which both sides issued a joint statement affirming their commitment to resolving regional disputes through peaceful means. Subsequently, China has been a key founding member of the ASEAN + 3 process. An ASEAN-China Experts Group was established in November 2000, to consider future economic co-operation and free trade opportunities. The Group held its first meeting in April 2001 and proposed a framework agreement on economic co-operation and the establishment of an ASEAN-China free trade area within 10 years (with differential treatment and flexibility for newer ASEAN members). Both proposals were endorsed at the seventh ASEAN summit meeting in November 2001. In November 2002 an agreement on economic co-operation was concluded by the ASEAN member states and China. The Framework Agreement on Comprehensive Economic Co-operation between ASEAN and China entered into force in July 2003, and envisaged the establishment of an ASEAN-China Free Trade Area (ACFTA) by 2010 (with the target for the newer member countries being 2015). The Agreement provided for strengthened co-operation in key areas including agriculture, information and telecommunications, and human resources development. It was also agreed to implement the consensus of the Special ASEAN-China Leaders' Meeting on SARS, held in April 2003, and to set up an ASEAN + 1 special fund for health co-operation. In October China acceded to the Treaty on Amity and Co-operation and signed a joint declaration with ASEAN on Strategic Partnership for Peace and Prosperity on strengthening co-operation in politics, economy, social affairs, security and regional and international issues. It was also agreed to continue consultations on China's accession to the SEANWFZ and to expedite the implementation of the Joint Statement on Co-operation in the Field of Non-Traditional Security Issues and the Declaration on the Conduct of Parties in the South China Sea. In 2013 ASEAN declared that it aimed to intensify negotiations to conclude a Code of Conduct in the South China Sea, in order to enhance peace, stability and prosperity in the region; a programme of formal consultation commenced in September. In November 2004 ASEAN and China signed the Agreement on Trade in Goods and the Agreement on Dispute Settlement Mechanism of the Framework Agreement on Comprehensive Economic Co-operation, to be implemented from 1 July 2005. A Plan of Action to Implement ASEAN-China Joint Declaration on Strengthening Strategic Partnership for Peace and Prosperity was also adopted by both parties at that time. In August 2005 ASEAN signed an MOU with China on cultural co-operation. An ASEAN-China Agreement on Trade in Services was signed in January 2007, within the Framework Agreement on Comprehensive Economic Co-operation, and entered into force on 1 July. The final component of the Framework Agreement, an ASEAN-China Investment Agreement, was signed in August 2009. Accordingly, ACFTA entered fully into effect on 1 January 2010. In November 2007 the ASEAN-China summit resolved that the environment should be included as a priority area for future co-operation and endorsed agreements concluded earlier in that month to strengthen co-operation in aviation and maritime transport. An ASEAN-China Environmental Co-operation Centre was formally inaugurated in Beijing, in May 2011. In October 2012 China opened a mission to ASEAN, based in Jakarta.

Japan: The first meeting between the two sides at ministerial level was held in October 1992. At this meeting, and subsequently, ASEAN requested Japan to increase its investment in member countries and to make Japanese markets more accessible to ASEAN products, in order to reduce the trade deficit with Japan. Since 1993 ASEAN-Japanese development and cultural co-operation has expanded under schemes including the Inter-ASEAN Technical Exchange Programme, the Japan-ASEAN Co-operation Promotion Programme and the ASEAN-Japan Friendship Programme. In December 1997 Japan, attending the informal summit meeting in Malaysia, agreed to improve market access for ASEAN products and to provide training opportunities for more than 20,000 young people in order to help develop local economies. In December 1998 ASEAN heads of government welcomed a Japanese initiative to allocate US $30,000m. to promote economic recovery in the region. In mid-2000 a new Japan-ASEAN General Exchange Fund was established to promote and facilitate the transfer of technology, investment and personnel. In November 1999 Japan, with China and South Korea, attending an informal summit meeting of ASEAN, agreed to strengthen economic and political co-operation with the ASEAN countries, to enhance political and security dialogue, and to implement joint infrastructure and social projects. Japan participated in the first official ASEAN + 3 meeting of ministers responsible for foreign affairs, which was convened in July 2000. In October 2003 ASEAN and Japan signed a Framework for Comprehensive Partnership. In December Japan concluded a joint action plan with ASEAN with provisions on reinforcing economic integration within ASEAN and enhancing competitiveness, and on addressing terrorism, piracy and other transnational issues. Negotiations on an ASEAN-Japan Comprehensive Economic Partnership Agreement were initiated in April 2005 and concluded in November 2007. The accord was signed in April 2008 and entered into force on 1 December. In July 2004 Japan acceded to the Treaty on Amity and Co-operation. In November the ASEAN-Japan summit meeting adopted the ASEAN-Japan Joint Declaration for Co-operation in the Fight Against International Terrorism. In July 2008 ASEAN concluded a formal partnership agreement with the new Japan International Co-operation Agency, with the aim of working together to strengthen ASEAN integration and development. In April 2011 a Special ASEAN-Japan Ministerial Meeting was convened, in Jakarta, to reaffirm mutual support, in particular in respect to Japan's recovery from a massive earthquake in the previous month. In November the ASEAN-Japan summit meeting adopted a Joint Declaration for Enhancing ASEAN-Japan Strategic Partnership for Prospering Together, and also adopted the ASEAN-Japan Plan of Action for its implementation during the period 2011–15.

Australia and New Zealand: In 1999 ASEAN and Australia undertook to establish the ASEAN-Australia Development Co-operation Programme (AADCP), to replace an economic co-operation programme that had begun in 1974. In August 2002 the two sides signed a formal MOU on the AADCP. It was to comprise three core elements, with assistance amounting to $A45m.: a Program Stream, to address medium-term issues of economic integration and competitiveness; a Regional Partnerships Scheme for smaller collaborative activities; and the establishment of a Regional Economic Policy Support Facility within the ASEAN Secretariat. In July 2009 ASEAN and Australia signed an MOU on the implementation of a seven-year second phase of the AADCP.

In September 2001 ASEAN ministers responsible for economic affairs signed a Framework for Closer Economic Partnership (CEP) with their counterparts from Australia and New Zealand (the Closer Economic Relations—CER—countries), and agreed to establish a Business Council to involve the business communities of all countries in the CEP. In November 2004 a Commemorative Summit, marking 30 years of dialogue between the nations, took place between ASEAN leaders and those of Australia and New Zealand at which it was agreed to launch negotiations on a free trade agreement. In July 2005 New Zealand signed ASEAN's Treaty of Amity and Co-operation; Australia acceded to the Treaty in December. In August 2007 the Australian and ASEAN ministers responsible for foreign affairs signed a Joint Declaration on a Comprehensive Partnership, and in November they agreed upon a plan of action to implement the accord. An agreement establishing an ASEAN–Australia–New Zealand free trade area (AANZFTA) was negotiated during 2008 and signed in Cha-am/Hua Hin, in February 2009; the AANZFTA entered into force on 1 January 2010. An ASEAN-New Zealand Joint Declaration on Comprehensive Partnership for the period 2010–15 was signed by ministers of foreign affairs of both sides in July 2010. The inaugural meeting of an ASEAN-CER Integration Partnership Forum held in June 2011, in Kuala Lumpur. The second Forum took place in May 2012, in Manila, and the third was convened in June 2013, in Cairns, Australia.

South Asia: In July 1993 both India and Pakistan were accepted as sectoral partners, providing for their participation in ASEAN meetings in trade, transport and communications and tourism. An ASEAN-India Business Council was established, and met for the first time, in New Delhi, India, in February 1995. In 1995 the ASEAN summit meeting agreed to enhance India's status to that of a full dialogue partner; India was formally admitted to the PMC in July 1996. At a meeting of the ASEAN-India Working Group in March 2001 the two sides agreed to pursue co-operation in new areas, such as health and pharmaceuticals, social security and rural development. The first ASEAN-India consultation between ministers responsible for economic affairs, which took place in September 2002, resulted in the adoption as a long-term objective, of the ASEAN-India Regional Trade and Investment Area. The first ASEAN-India summit at the level of heads of state was held in Phnom Penh, in November. In October 2003 India acceded to the Treaty of Amity and Co-operation and signed a joint Framework Agreement on Comprehensive Economic Co-operation. The objectives of the Agreement included strengthening and enhancing economic, trade and investment co-operation; liberalizing and promoting trade in goods and services; and facilitating economic integration within ASEAN. It was also agreed that negotiations would begin on establishing an ASEAN-India Regional Trade and Investment Area (RTIA), including a free trade area, for Brunei, Indonesia, Malaysia, Singapore and Thailand. A Partnership for Peace, Progress and Shared Prosperity was signed at the third ASEAN-India summit, held in November 2004. At the sixth summit meeting, held in November 2007, it was noted that annual bilateral ASEAN-India trade had reached US $20,000m. ASEAN-India agreements on trade in goods and on a dispute settlement mechanism were concluded in August 2008. The agreement on trade in goods was signed by both sides in August 2009, enabling the RTIA to enter into force on 1 January 2010. The inaugural annual Delhi Dialogue, aimed at advancing engagement between India and the ASEAN region, was held in January 2009. In December 2012 an ASEAN-India Commemorative Summit was held, in New Delhi, to mark 20 years of co-operation, at that time ASEAN-India relations were elevated to a Strategic Partnership. A meeting of the Delhi Dialogue was convened in March 2014 to address translating the Vision Statement into concrete activities in areas including culture, education, science and technology, sports, and youth co-operation.

An ASEAN-Pakistan Joint Business Council met for the first time in February 2000. In early 2001 both sides agreed to co-operate in projects relating to new and renewable energy resources, ICT, agricultural research and transport and communications. Pakistan acceded to the Treaty on Amity and Co-operation in July 2004. In January 2007 Timor-Leste acceded to the Treaty; Sri Lanka and Bangladesh acceded in August.

In February 2013 ASEAN and the South Asian Association for Regional Cooperation held discussions on future co-operative activities between the two organizations in areas including agriculture, disaster management, energy, poverty alleviation, combating illegal trafficking in narcotics and in persons, and trade and investment.

Republic of Korea: In July 1991 the Republic of Korea (South Korea) was accepted as a 'dialogue partner' in ASEAN, and in December a joint ASEAN-Korea Chamber of Commerce was established. South Korea participated in ASEAN's informal summit meetings in December 1997 and November 1999, and took part in the first official ASEAN + 3 meeting of ministers responsible for foreign affairs, convened in July 2000. South Korea's assistance in the field of ICT has become particularly valuable in recent years. In March 2001, in a sign of developing co-operation, ASEAN and South Korea exchanged views on political and security issues in the region for the first time. South Korea acceded to the Treaty on Amity and Co-operation in November 2004. A Framework Agreement on Comprehensive Economic Co-operation, providing for the establishment of an ASEAN-Korea Free Trade Area, was signed in December 2005, eliminating tariffs on some 80% of products, with effect from 1 January 2010. In May 2006 governments of both sides (excluding Thailand, owing to a dispute concerning trade in rice) signed an Agreement on Trade in Goods. An ASEAN–Korea agreement on trade in services entered into force in May 2009. An ASEAN-Korea Investment Agreement was signed in June. An ASEAN-Korea joint plan of action was being implemented during 2011–15.

Russia: In March 2000 the first ASEAN-Russia business forum opened in Kuala Lumpur. In July 2004 ASEAN and Russia signed a Joint Declaration to Combat International Terrorism, while in November Russia acceded to the Treaty of Amity and Co-operation. The first ASEAN-Russia summit meeting was held in December 2005. The leaders agreed on a comprehensive programme of action to promote co-operation between both sides during the period 2005–15. This included commitments to co-operate in areas including counter-terrorism, human resources development, finance and economic activities and science and technology. In July 2008 both sides adopted a roadmap to further implementation of the comprehensive programme of action.

USA and Canada: In 1990 ASEAN and the USA established an ASEAN-US Joint Working Group, the purpose of which was to review ASEAN's economic relations with the USA and to identify measures by which economic links could be strengthened. In recent years, dialogue has increasingly focused on political and security issues. In August 2002 ASEAN ministers responsible for foreign affairs met with their US counterpart, and signed a Joint Declaration for Co-operation to Combat International Terrorism. At the same time, the USA announced the ASEAN Co-operation Plan, which was to include activities in the fields of ICT, agricultural biotechnology, health, disaster response and training for the ASEAN Secretariat. In July 2009 the USA signed ASEAN's Treaty of Amity and Co-operation. The first official ASEAN meeting with the US President took place in November, in Singapore. Both sides resolved to enhance collaboration and to establish an ASEAN-US Eminent Persons Group. A second ASEAN-US Leaders' Meeting was held in September 2010, and a third in November 2011. In November 2012, the fourth ASEAN-US Leaders' Meeting agreed to institutionalize the gatherings as an annual summit, the first of which took place in October 2013. The heads of state initiated a US-ASEAN Expanded Economic Engagement (E3) project to expand trade and investment opportunities and endorsed the US-ASEAN Innovation in Science through Partners in Regional Engagement (INSPIRE).

In July 2009 a PMC + 1 session adopted a Joint Declaration on an ASEAN-Canada Enhanced Partnership 2010–15. A Plan of Action to implement the initiative was concluded in July 2010; at that time Canada also acceded to the Treaty of Amity and Co-operation. The first meeting of an ASEAN-Canada Joint Co-ordination Committee (AC-JCC) to oversee progress in implementing the Plan of Action was held in April 2013, in Bangkok; a second meeting was convened in April 2014.

Latin America: The first ASEAN-Mercosur Ministerial Meeting, held in November 2008, in Brasília, Brazil, agreed that a region-to-region Roadmap and Action Plan should be drafted, covering areas of mutual interest. In December 2010 the first annual ASEAN-Latin America Business Forum was convened; the second took place in June 2012, in Jakarta. In November 2012 Brazil became the first Latin American country to accede to the Treaty of Amity and Co-operation. In January 2013 the Argentine Minister of Foreign Affairs stated his country's willingness to host a second ASEAN-Mercosur Ministerial Meeting, with a view to bringing to fruition the proposed bi-regional Roadmap and Plan of Action.

Indo-China: In June 1996 ministers of ASEAN countries, and of Cambodia, China, Laos and Myanmar adopted a framework for ASEAN-Mekong Basin Development Cooperation (AMBDC). The initiative aimed to strengthen the region's cohesiveness, with greater co-operation on issues such as drugs-trafficking, labour migration and terrorism, and to facilitate the process of future expansion of ASEAN. Groups of experts and senior officials were to be convened to consider funding issues and proposals to link the two regions, including a gas pipeline network, rail links and the establishment of a common time zone. In December 1996 the working group on rail links appointed a team of consultants to conduct a feasibility study of the proposals. The completed study was presented at the second AMBDC ministerial conference, convened in Hanoi, in July 2000. At the November 2001 summit China pledged US $5m. to assist with navigation along the upper stretches of the Mekong River, while other means by which China could increase its investment in the Mekong Basin area were considered. At the meeting South Korea was invited to become a core member of the grouping. The AMBDC meets annually, most recently in August 2013. Other growth regions sponsored by ASEAN include the Brunei, Indonesia, Malaysia, Philippines, East ASEAN Growth Area (BIMP-EAGA), the Indonesia, Malaysia, Singapore Growth Triangle (IMS-GT), and the West-East Corridor within the Mekong Basin Development initiative.

Gulf States: In June 2009 ASEAN ministers responsible for foreign affairs held an inaugural meeting with their counterpart from the Cooperation Council for the Arab States of the Gulf (GCC). The meeting, convened in Manama, Bahrain, adopted a GCC-ASEAN Joint Vision as a framework for future co-operation between the two groupings. A second meeting, held in Singapore, in May–June 2010, approved an ASEAN–GCC Action Plan to guide co-operation during the two-year period 2010–12. Meeting in October 2012 ASEAN and GCC ministers responsible for foreign affairs extended the Plan into 2013, and established several joint working groups aimed at strengthening joint activities. ASEAN-GCC co-operation was reaffirmed by the third joint meeting of foreign affairs, held in November 2013, in Manama; and a fourth ministerial meeting was to be held during 2014, in Myanmar.

Publications

Annual Report.
Annual Security Report.
ASEAN Investment Report (annually).
ASEAN State of the Environment Report.
ASEAN Updates.
Directory of ASEAN Innovative SMEs.

Public Information Series, briefing papers, documents series, educational materials.

BANK FOR INTERNATIONAL SETTLEMENTS—BIS

Address: Centralbahnplatz 2, 4002 Basel, Switzerland.
Telephone: 612808080; **fax:** 612809100; **e-mail:** email@bis.org; **internet:** www.bis.org.

The BIS was founded pursuant to the Hague Agreements of 1930 to promote co-operation among national central banks, assistance with the management and investment of their foreign exchange and gold reserves, and trustee and agency functions; in addition, the Bank provides facilities for international financial operations.

Organization

(April 2014)

GENERAL MEETING

A General Meeting is held annually in June and is attended by representatives of the central banks of countries in which shares have been subscribed. The central banks of the following 60 authorities are entitled to attend and vote at BIS General Meetings: Algeria, Argentina, Australia, Austria, Belgium, Bosnia and Herzegovina, Brazil, Bulgaria, Canada, Chile, the People's Republic of China, Colombia, Croatia, Czech Republic, Denmark, Estonia, Finland, France, Germany, Greece, Hong Kong SAR, Hungary, Iceland, India, Indonesia, Ireland, Israel, Italy, Japan, Republic of Korea (South Korea), Latvia, Lithuania, Luxembourg, the former Yugoslav republic of Macedonia, Malaysia, Mexico, the Netherlands, New Zealand, Norway, Peru, the Philippines, Poland, Portugal, Romania, Russia, Saudi Arabia, Serbia, Singapore, Slovakia, Slovenia, South Africa, Spain, Sweden, Switzerland, Thailand, Turkey, United Arab Emirates, the United Kingdom and the USA. The European Central Bank became a BIS shareholder in December 1999.

BOARD OF DIRECTORS

The Board of Directors is responsible for the conduct of the Bank's operations at the highest level. It comprises the Governors in office of the central banks of Belgium, France, Germany, Italy, and the United Kingdom, as well as the Chairman of the Board of Governors of the US Federal Reserve System. Each of those six ex officio members may appoint another director of the same nationality. The Bank's statutes provide for the election to the Board of not more than nine Governors of other member central banks. As at April 2014 those of Brazil, Canada, the People's Republic of China, India, Japan, Mexico, the Netherlands, Sweden and Switzerland and the President of the European Central Bank were elected members of the Board. In June 2005 an extraordinary general meeting amended the statutes to abolish the position of President of the Bank, which had been jointly vested with chairmanship of the Board since 1948.

Chairman of the Board: CHRISTIAN NOYER (France).

MANAGEMENT

At July 2013 the Bank employed some 647 staff members, from 54 countries. The main departments are the General Secretariat, the Monetary and Economic Department and the Banking Department. In July 1998 the BIS inaugurated its first overseas administrative unit, the Representative Office for Asia and the Pacific, which is based in Hong Kong. A Regional Treasury dealing room became operational at the Hong Kong office in October 2000, with the aim of improving access for Asian central banks to BIS financial services during their trading hours. In November 2002 a Representative Office for the Americas was inaugurated in Mexico City, Mexico.

General Manager: JAIME CARUANA (Spain).

Representative Office for Asia and the Pacific: Two International Finance Centre, 78th Floor, 8 Finance St, Central, Hong Kong, Special Administrative Region, People's Republic of China; tel. 28787100; fax 28787123.

Representative Office for the Americas: Torre Chapultepec, Rubén Darío 281, 17th Floor, Col. Bosque de Chapultepec, Del. Miguel Hidalgo, 11580 Mexico, D.F., Mexico; tel. (55) 91380290; fax (55) 91380299; e-mail americas@bis.org.

Activities

The BIS is an international financial institution whose role is to promote international monetary and financial co-operation, and to fulfil the function of a 'central banks' bank'. Although it has the legal form of a company limited by shares, it is an international organization governed by international law, and enjoys special privileges and immunities in keeping with its role (a Headquarters Agreement was concluded with Switzerland in 1987). The participating central banks were originally given the option of subscribing the shares themselves or arranging for their subscription in their own countries. In January 2001, however, an extraordinary general meeting amended the Bank's statutes to restrict ownership to central banks. Accordingly, all shares then held by private shareholders (representing 14% of the total share capital) were repurchased; an additional compensation payment was awarded by a decision in September 2003 of the Hague Arbitral Tribunal (provided for in the 1930 Hague Agreements).

FINANCE

Until the end of the 2002/03 financial year the Bank's unit of account was the gold franc. An extraordinary general meeting in March 2003 amended the Bank's statutes to redenominate the Bank's share capital in Special Drawing Rights (SDRs), the unit of account of the IMF, in order to enhance the efficiency and transparency of the Bank's operations. The meeting decided that the nominal value of shares would be rounded down from SDR 5,696 at 31 March 2003 to SDR 5,000, entailing a reduction of 12.2% in the total share capital. The excess of SDR 92.1m. was transferred to the Bank's reserve funds. The authorized capital of the Bank at 31 March 2013 was SDR 3,000m., divided into 600,000 shares of equal value.

BANKING OPERATIONS

In 2014 some 140 international financial institutions and central banks from all over the world had deposits with the BIS, representing around 3% of world foreign exchange reserves.

The BIS uses the funds deposited with it partly for lending to central banks. Its credit transactions may take the form of swaps against gold; covered credits secured by means of a pledge of gold or marketable short-term securities; credits against gold or currency deposits of the same amount and for the same duration held with the BIS; unsecured credits in the form of advances or deposits; or standby credits, which in individual instances are backed by guarantees given by member central banks.

The BIS also engages in traditional types of investment: funds not required for lending to central banks are placed in the market as deposits with commercial banks and purchases of short-term negotiable paper, including Treasury bills. Increasingly, the Bank has developed its own investment services for central banks, including short-term products and longer-term financial instruments.

Central banks' monetary reserves often need to be available at short notice, and need to be placed with the BIS at short term, for fixed periods and with clearly defined repayment terms. The BIS has to match its assets to the maturity structure and nature of its commitments, and must therefore conduct its business with special regard to maintaining a high degree of liquidity.

The Bank's operations must be in conformity with the monetary policy of the central banks of the countries concerned. It is not permitted to make advances to governments or to open current accounts in their name. Real estate transactions are also excluded.

INTERNATIONAL MONETARY CO-OPERATION

Governors of central banks meet every two months for discussions at the BIS to co-ordinate international monetary policy and to promote stability in the international financial markets. There is close co-operation with the IMF and the World Bank. The BIS participates as an observer in meetings of the so-called Group of 10 (G10) industrialized nations (see IMF). It hosts the secretariat of the Committee on the Global Financial System, which has 22 member central banks, and is mandated to undertake systematic short-term monitoring of global financial system conditions, longer-term analysis of the functioning of financial markets, and the articulation of policy recommendations aimed at improving market functioning and promoting stability. A Markets Committee (formerly known as the Committee on Gold and Foreign Exchange) comprises senior officials responsible for market operations in 21 central banks. It meets regularly to consider developments in foreign exchange and related financial markets, possible future trends and short-run implications of events on market functioning. In 1990 a Committee on Payment and Settlement Systems was established to monitor and analyse developments in domestic payment, settlement and clearing systems, and cross-border and multi-currency systems. It has 25 member central banks, and meets three times a year. The Irving Fisher Committee on Central Bank Statistics, a forum of central bank users and compilers of statistics, has operated under the auspices of the BIS since January 2006.

In 1974 the Governors of central banks of the G10 set up the Basel Committee on Banking Supervision (whose secretariat is provided by the BIS) to co-ordinate banking supervision at international level. The Committee pools information on banking supervisory regulations and surveillance systems, including the supervision of banks' foreign currency business, identifies possible danger areas and proposes measures to safeguard the banks' solvency and liquidity. An International Conference of Banking Supervisors is held every two years. In 1997 the Committee published new guidelines, entitled Core Principles for Effective Banking Supervision, that were intended to provide a comprehensive set of standards to ensure sound banking. A Financial Stability Institute was established in 1999, jointly by the BIS and Basel Committee, to enhance the capacity of central banks and supervisory bodies to implement aspects of the Core Principles, through the provision of training programmes and other policy workshops. In June 2004 the Committee approved a revised framework of the International Convergence of Capital Measurement and Capital Standards (also known as Basel II), which aimed to promote improvements in risk management and strengthen the stability of the financial system. An updated version of the revised framework, and also a new version of the 1996 Amendment to the Capital Accord to incorporate market risks, were issued in November 2005. The updated versions also incorporated a paper concerned with trading activities and the treatment of double default effects prepared by a joint working group of the Committee and the International Organization of Securities Commissions. In October 2006 the International Conference of Banking Supervisors endorsed an enhanced version of the Core Principles (and its associated assessment methodology), incorporating stricter guidelines to counter money-laundering and to strengthen transparency. The Basel II capital framework began to be implemented by countries and banks from 1 January 2007. The Committee's Accord Implementation Group undertook to promote full implementation of the accord, to provide supervisory guidance and review procedures. In January 2009 the Committee proposed a package of enhanced measures to strengthen the Basel II capital framework. In June the Committee agreed to broaden its membership to include representatives from the Group of 20 (G20) countries not currently in the Committee, i.e. Argentina, Indonesia, Saudi Arabia, South Africa and Turkey. In addition, Hong Kong SAR, and Singapore were invited to become members. The first meeting of the expanded Committee, convened in July, approved the enhancements to the Basel II capital framework. In July 2010 a reformed capital framework programme, Basel III, was agreed by Committee's Group of Central Bank Governors and Heads of Supervision. In September 2010 the Group announced further agreements substantially to strengthen global capital requirements, including raising common equity levels in relation to risk-weighted assets, and introducing capital conservation buffers from 2016. The regulatory framework was endorsed by a meeting of the G20 heads of state and government held in Seoul, South Korea, in November 2010. Basel III's transitional period became effective from 1 January 2013, initially in 11 member jurisdictions; the regulations were to be phased in gradually, with some elements, for example those concerning full capital requirements, not becoming mandatory until 1 January 2019.

BIS working groups have studied aspects of highly leveraged, or unregulated, institutions, offshore financial centres, short-term capital flows, deposit insurance schemes, and measures to promote implementation of international standards. The BIS hosts the secretariat of the Financial Stability Board, established in April 2009 by a meeting of G20 heads of state and government to supersede the former Financial Stability Forum (which, in turn, was created in February 1999 by ministers of finance and governors of the central banks of the Group of Seven—G7—industrialized nations to strengthen co-operation among the world's largest economies and economic bodies, in order to improve the monitoring of international finance). The new Board—with participation by all G20 economies, as well as Spain and the European Commission—had an expanded mandate to develop and implement strengthened financial regulation and supervision. Its inaugural meeting was convened in June. Since January 1998 the BIS has hosted the secretariat of the International Association of Insurance Supervisors, which aims to promote co-operation within the insurance industry with regard to effective supervision and the development of domestic insurance markets. It also hosts the secretariat of the International Association of Deposit Insurers, founded in May 2002.

RESEARCH

The Bank's Monetary and Economic Department conducts research, particularly into monetary and financial questions; collects and publishes data on securities markets and international banking developments; and administers a Data Bank for central banks. In 2004 the BIS established a Central Bank Research Hub to promote and facilitate the dissemination of economic research published by central banks. Statistics on aspects of the global financial system are published regularly, including details on international banking activities, international and domestic securities markets, derivatives, global foreign exchange markets, external debt, and payment and settlement systems. The Bank is a co-sponsor, with the UN, Euro Banking Association, Eurostat, the Organisation for Economic Co-operation and Development (OECD), the IMF and the World Bank, of the Statistical Data and Metadata Exchange initiative, established in June 2002.

AGENCY AND TRUSTEE FUNCTIONS

Throughout its history the BIS has undertaken various duties as Trustee Fiscal Agent or Depository with regard to international loan agreements. In October 2005 the BIS served in an escrow agent role in a loan with the Central Bank of Nigeria; the arrangement was terminated upon the final release of funds in February 2007.

In April 1994 the BIS assumed new functions in connection with the rescheduling of Brazil's external debt, which had been agreed by the Brazilian Government in November 1993. In accordance with two collateral pledge agreements, the BIS acts in the capacity of Collateral Agent to hold and invest collateral for the benefit of the holders of certain US dollar-denominated bonds, maturing in 15 or 30 years, which have been issued by Brazil under the rescheduling arrangements. The Bank acts in a similar capacity for Peru, in accordance with external debt agreements concluded in November 1996 and a collateral agreement signed with the BIS in March 1997, and for Côte d'Ivoire, under a restructuring agreement signed in May 1997 and collateral agreement signed in March 1998.

Publications

Annual Report.

BIS Consolidated Banking Statistics (every 6 months).

BIS Papers (series).

Central Bank Survey of Foreign Exchange and Derivatives Market Activity (every 3 years).

Handbook on Securities Statistics (with the European Central Bank and IMF).

International Journal of Central Banking (quarterly).

Joint BIS-IMF-OECD-World Bank Statistics on External Debt (quarterly).

Progress Report on Basel III Implementation.

Quarterly Review.

Regular OTC Derivatives Market Statistics (every 6 months).

Statistics

STATEMENT OF ACCOUNT
(In SDR millions; 31 March 2013)

Assets		%
Gold and gold deposits	35,367.1	16.7
Cash and on sight a/c with banks	6,884.1	3.2
Treasury bills	46,694.1	22.0
Loans and advances	19,676.8	9.3
Securities	91,112.8	43.0
Miscellaneous	12,217.5	5.8
Total	211,952.4	100.0

Liabilities		%
Deposits (gold)	17,580.9	8.3
Deposits (currencies)	166,160.3	78.4
Accounts payable	5,335.3	2.5
Other liabilities	3,890.1	1.8
Shareholders' equity	18,985.8	9.0
Total	211,952.4	100.0

Source: BIS, *Annual Report*.

CARIBBEAN COMMUNITY AND COMMON MARKET—CARICOM

Address: POB 10827, Turkeyen, Greater Georgetown, Guyana.
Telephone: (2) 222-0001; **fax:** (2) 222-0171; **e-mail:** registry@caricom.org; **internet:** www.caricom.org.

CARICOM was formed in 1973 by the Treaty of Chaguaramas, signed in Trinidad, as a movement towards unity in the Caribbean; it replaced the Caribbean Free Trade Association (CARIFTA), founded in 1965. A revision of the Treaty of Chaguaramas (by means of nine separate Protocols), in order to institute greater regional integration and to establish a CARICOM Single Market and Economy (CSME), was instigated in the 1990s and completed in July 2001. The single market component of the CSME was formally inaugurated on 1 January 2006.

MEMBERS

Antigua and Barbuda	Jamaica
Bahamas*	Montserrat
Barbados	Saint Christopher and Nevis
Belize	Saint Lucia
Dominica	Saint Vincent and the Grenadines
Grenada	Suriname
Guyana	Trinidad and Tobago
Haiti	

* The Bahamas is a member of the Community but not the Common Market.

ASSOCIATE MEMBERS

Anguilla	Cayman Islands
Bermuda	Turks and Caicos Islands
British Virgin Islands	

Note: In April 2014 applications for associate membership by French Guiana, Guadeloupe, Martinique, and Curaçao and St. Maarten were under consideration. Colombia, Dominican Republic, Mexico, Puerto Rico, and Venezuela have observer status with the Community.

Organization

(April 2014)

HEADS OF GOVERNMENT CONFERENCE AND BUREAU

The Conference is the final authority of the Community and determines policy. It is responsible for the conclusion of treaties on behalf of the Community and for entering into relationships between the Community and international organizations and states. Decisions of the Conference are generally taken unanimously. Heads of government meet annually, although inter-sessional meetings may be convened.

At a special meeting of the Conference, held in Trinidad and Tobago in October 1992, participants decided to establish a Heads of Government Bureau, with the capacity to initiate proposals, to update consensus and to secure the implementation of CARICOM decisions. The Bureau became operational in December, comprising the Chairman of the Conference, as Chairman, as well as the incoming and outgoing Chairmen of the Conference, and the Secretary-General of the Conference, in the capacity of Chief Executive Officer.

COMMUNITY COUNCIL OF MINISTERS

In October 1992 CARICOM heads of government agreed that a Caribbean Community Council of Ministers should be established to replace the existing Common Market Council of Ministers as the second highest organ of the Community. Protocol I amending the Treaty of Chaguaramas, to restructure the organs and institutions of the Community, was formally adopted at a meeting of CARICOM heads of government in February 1997 and was signed by all member states in July. The inaugural meeting of the Community Council of Ministers was held in Nassau, Bahamas, in February 1998. The Council consists of ministers responsible for community affairs, as well as other government ministers designated by member states, and is responsible for the development of the Community's strategic planning and co-ordination in the areas of economic integration, functional co-operation and external relations.

COURT OF JUSTICE

Caribbean Court of Justice (CCJ): 134 Henry St, POB 1768, Port of Spain, Trinidad and Tobago; tel. 623-2225; fax 627-1193; e-mail info@caribbeancourtofjustice.org; internet www.caribbeancourtofjustice.org; inaugurated in April 2005; an agreement establishing the Court was formally signed by 10 member countries in February 2001, and by two further states in February 2003; in January 2004 a revised agreement on the establishment of the CCJ, which incorporated provision for a Trust Fund, entered into force; serves as a tribunal to enforce rights and to consider disputes relating to the CARICOM Single Market and Economy; intended to replace the Judicial Committee of the Privy Council as the Court of Final Appeal (effective for Barbados, Belize and Guyana at April 2014); Pres. Sir DENNIS BYRON (Saint Christopher and Nevis).

MINISTERIAL COUNCILS

The principal organs of the Community are assisted in their functions by the following bodies, established under Protocol I amending the Treaty of Chaguaramas: the Council for Trade and Economic Development (COTED); the Council for Foreign and Community Relations (COFCOR); the Council for Human and Social Development (COHSOD); and the Council for Finance and Planning (COFAP). The Councils are responsible for formulating policies, promoting their implementation and supervising co-operation in the relevant areas.

SECRETARIAT

The Secretariat is the main administrative body of the Caribbean Community. The functions of the Secretariat are to service meetings of the Community and of its Committees; to take appropriate follow-up action on decisions made at such meetings; to carry out studies on questions of economic and functional co-operation relating to the region as a whole; to provide services to member states at their request in respect of matters relating to the achievement of the objectives of the Community. The Secretariat incorporates Directorates, each headed by an Assistant Secretary-General, for Trade and Economic Integration; Foreign and Community Relations; Human and Social Development; and CARIFORUM.

Secretary-General: IRWIN LAROCQUE (Dominica).

Activities

The Heads of Government meeting, convened in Montego Bay, Jamaica, in July 2010, agreed to establish a seven-member high-level committee to draft proposals on a new governance structure for CARICOM, in order to address concerns regarding the implementation of community decisions. The report, entitled *Turning around CARICOM: Proposals to restructure the Secretariat*, was presented to heads of government, convened for an inter-sessional meeting in Paramaribo, Suriname, in March 2012.

ECONOMIC CO-OPERATION

The Caribbean Community's main field of activity is economic integration, by means of a Caribbean Common Market. The Secretariat and the Caribbean Development Bank undertake research on the best means of tackling economic difficulties, and meetings of the chief executives of commercial banks and of central bank officials are also held with the aim of strengthening regional co-operation. In March 2009 heads of government, meeting in Belize City, Belize, resolved to pursue a regional strategy to counter the effects on the region of the severe global economic and financial downturn. A new Heads of Government Task Force on the Regional Financial and Economic Crisis held its inaugural meeting in August, in Jamaica.

In 1989 the Conference of Heads of Government agreed to implement, by July 1993, a series of measures to encourage the creation of a single Caribbean market. These included the establishment of a CARICOM Industrial Programming Scheme; the inauguration of the CARICOM Enterprise Regime; facilitation of travel for CARICOM nationals within the region; full implementation of the rules of origin and the revised scheme for the harmonization of fiscal incentives; free movement of skilled workers; removal of all remaining regional barriers to trade; establishment of a regional system of air and sea transport; and the introduction of a scheme for regional capital movement. In August 1990 CARICOM heads of government mandated the governors of CARICOM members' central banks to begin a study of the means to achieve monetary union within CARICOM; they also institutionalized biannual meetings of CARICOM ministers responsible for finance and senior finance officials.

The initial deadline of 1991 for the establishment of a common external tariff (CET—first agreed in 1984) was not achieved. At a special meeting, held in October 1992, CARICOM heads of government agreed to reduce the maximum level of tariffs from 45% to between 30% and 35%, to be in effect by 30 June 1993 (the level was to be further lowered, to 25%–30% by 1995). The Bahamas, however, was not party to these trading arrangements (since it is a member of the Community but not of the Common Market), and Belize was granted an extension for the implementation of the new tariff levels. At the Heads of Government Conference, held in July 1995 in Guyana, Suriname was admitted as a full member of CARICOM and acceded to the treaty establishing the Common Market. It was granted until 1 January 1996 for implementation of the tariff reductions. The 1995 Conference approved additional measures to promote the single market. The free movement of skilled workers was to be permitted from 1 January 1996. At the same time an agreement on the mutual protection and provision of social security benefits was to enter into force. In July 1996 heads of government agreed to extend the provisions of free movement to sportsmen and women, musicians and others working in the arts and media.

In July 1997 the Conference, meeting in Montego Bay, Jamaica, determined to accelerate economic integration, with the aim of completing a single market by 1999. At the meeting 11 member states signed Protocol II amending the Treaty of Chaguaramas, which constituted a central element of a CARICOM Single Market and Economy (CSME), providing for the right to establish enterprises, the provision of services and the free movement of capital and labour throughout participating countries. In July 1998, at the meeting of heads of government, held in Saint Lucia, an agreement was signed with the Insurance Company of the West Indies to accelerate the establishment of a Caribbean Investment Fund, which was to mobilize foreign currency from extra-regional capital markets for investment in new or existing enterprises in the region. Some 60% of all funds generated were to be used by CARICOM countries and the remainder by non-CARICOM members of the Association of Caribbean States. In November 2000 a special consultation on the single market and economy was held in Barbados, involving CARICOM and government officials, academics, and representatives of the private sector, labour organizations, the media, and other regional groupings. In February 2001 heads of government agreed to establish a new high-level sub-committee to accelerate the establishment of the CSME and to promote its objectives. The sub-committee was to be supported by a Technical Advisory Council, comprising representatives of the public and private sectors. By June all member states had signed and declared the provisional application of Protocol II.

In October 2001 CARICOM heads of government, convened for a special emergency meeting, considered the impact on the region's economy of the terrorist attacks perpetrated against targets in the USA in the previous month. The meeting resolved to enhance aviation security, implement promotion and marketing campaigns in support of the tourist industry, and approach international institutions to assist with emergency financing. The economic situation, which had been further adversely affected by the reduced access to the European Union (EU) banana market, the economic downturn in the USA, and the effects on the investment climate of the OECD Harmful Taxation Initiative, was considered at the Heads of Government Conference, held in Guyana, in July 2002.

On 1 January 2006 the single market component of the CSME was formally inaugurated, with Barbados, Belize, Guyana, Jamaica, Suriname and Trinidad and Tobago as active participants. Six more countries (Antigua and Barbuda, Dominica, Grenada, Saint Christopher and Nevis, Saint Lucia, Saint Vincent and the Grenadines) formally joined the single market in July. At the same time CARICOM heads of government approved a contribution formula allowing for the establishment of a regional development fund. The Caribbean Development Fund (CDF), launched in mid-2008, with initial finances of US $60m. commenced full operations in August 2009. In February 2011 heads of government signed an agreement to enable the CDF to grant funds on preferential terms to low-income member countries. In March 2013 a $3.5m. CSME Standby Facility was launched, to be administered by the Caribbean Development Bank.

In February 2007 an inter-sessional meeting of the Conference of Heads of Government, held in Saint Vincent and the Grenadines, approved a timetable for the full implementation of the CSME: phase I (mid-2005–08) for the consolidation of the single market and the initiation of a single economy; phase II (2009–15) for the consolidation and completion of the single economy process, including the harmonization and co-ordination of economic policies in the region and the establishment of new institutions to implement those policies. In July 2007 CARICOM heads of government endorsed the report, *Towards a Single Development Vision and the Role of the Single Economy*, on which the elaboration of the CSME was based. In January 2008 a Caribbean Competition Commission was inaugurated, in Paramaribo, Suriname, to enforce the rules of competition within the CSME. In February Haiti signed the revised Treaty of Chaguaramas.

In December 2007 a special meeting of the Conference of Heads of Government, convened in Georgetown, Guyana, considered issues relating to regional poverty and the rising cost of living in member states. The meeting resolved to establish a technical team to review the CET on essential commodities to determine whether it should be removed or reduced to deter inflationary pressures. The meeting also agreed to review the supply and distribution of food throughout the region, including transportation issues affecting the price of goods and services, and determined to expand agricultural production and agro-processing. Efforts to harness renewable energy sources were to be strengthened to counter rising fuel prices.

REGIONAL INTEGRATION

In July 1992 a West Indian Commission, established to study regional political and economic integration, recommended that CARICOM should remain a community of sovereign states (rather than a federation), but should strengthen the integration process and expand to include the wider Caribbean region. It recommended the formation of an Association of Caribbean States (ACS), to include all the countries within and surrounding the Caribbean Basin. In November 1997 the Secretaries-General of CARICOM and the ACS signed a Co-operation Agreement to formalize the reciprocal procedures through which the organizations work to enhance and facilitate regional integration. Suriname was admitted to CARICOM in July 1995. In July 1997 the Heads of Government Conference agreed to admit Haiti as a member, although the terms and conditions of its accession to the organization were not finalized until July 1999. In July 2001 the CARICOM Secretary-General formally inaugurated a CARICOM Office in Haiti, which aimed to provide technical assistance in preparation for Haiti's accession to the Community. In January 2002 a CARICOM special mission visited Haiti, following an escalation of the political violence that had started in the previous month. Ministers responsible for foreign affairs emphasized the need for international aid for Haiti when they met their US counterpart in February. Haiti was admitted as the 15th member of CARICOM at the Heads of Government Conference, held in July. It hosted a meeting of CARICOM heads of government for the first time in February 2013.

In July 1998 heads of government expressed concern at the hostility between the Government and opposition groupings in Guyana. The two sides signed an agreement, under CARICOM auspices, and in September a CARICOM mediation mission visited Guyana to promote further dialogue. CARICOM has declared its support for Guyana in its territorial disputes with Venezuela and Suriname. A CARICOM electoral observer mission monitored the conduct of a general election in Guyana in November 2011.

In February 1997 Community heads of government signed a new Charter of Civil Society for the Community, which set out principles in the areas of democracy, government, parliament, freedom of the press and human rights. In July 2002 a conference was held, in Liliendaal, Guyana, attended by representatives of civil society and CARICOM heads of government. The meeting issued a statement of principles on 'Forward Together', recognizing the role of civil society in meeting the challenges to the region. It was agreed to hold regular meetings and to establish a task force to develop a regional strategic framework for pursuing the main recommendations of the conference. In February 2007 an inter-sessional meeting of CARICOM heads of government determined to add security (including crime) as a fourth pillar of regional integration, in addition to those identified: economic integration; co-ordination of foreign policy; and functional co-operation.

CO-ORDINATION OF FOREIGN POLICY

The co-ordination of foreign policies of member states is listed as one of the main objectives of the Community in its founding treaty. Activities include strengthening member states' position in international organizations; joint diplomatic action on issues of particular interest to the Caribbean; joint co-operation arrangements with third countries and organizations; and the negotiation of free trade agreements with third countries and other regional groupings. In April 1997 CARICOM inaugurated a Caribbean Regional Negotiating Machinery (CRNM) body, based in Kingston, Jamaica, to co-ordinate and strengthen the region's presence at external economic negotiations. The main areas of activity were negotiations to establish a Free Trade Area of the Americas (FTAA—now stalled), ACP relations with the EU, and multilateral trade negotiations under the World Trade Organization (WTO). In July 2009 the CRNM was renamed the Office of Trade Negotiations, reporting directly to the Council for Trade and Economic Development; its mandate was expanded to include responsibility for all external trade negotiations on behalf of the Community, with immediate priority to be placed on negotiations with Canada. Since 2001 CARICOM has conducted regular meetings with representatives of the UN. The sixth meeting, convened in July 2011, agreed to revise the existing Regional Strategic Framework for co-operation and to initiate negotiations towards a more effective mechanism for UN activities in the region.

In July 1991 Venezuela applied for membership of CARICOM, and offered a non-reciprocal free trade agreement for CARICOM exports to Venezuela, during an initial five-year period. In October 1993 the newly established Group of Three (G-3—Colombia, Mexico and Venezuela) signed joint agreements with CARICOM and Suriname on combating drugs-trafficking and on environmental protection. In June 1994 CARICOM and Colombia concluded an agreement on trade, economic and technical co-operation, which, inter alia, gives special treatment to the least developed CARICOM countries.

In 1992 Cuba applied for observer status within CARICOM, and in July 1993 a joint commission was inaugurated to establish closer ties between CARICOM and Cuba and provide a mechanism for regular dialogue. In July 1997 the heads of government agreed to pursue consideration of a free trade accord between the Community and Cuba. A Trade and Economic Agreement was signed by the two sides in July 2000, and in February 2001 a CARICOM office was established in Cuba. At the first meeting of heads of state and government in December 2002, convened in Havana, Cuba, it was agreed to commemorate the start of diplomatic relations between the two sides, some 30 years previously, on 8 December each year as Cuba/CARICOM Day. The second summit meeting, held in December 2005 in Bridgetown, Barbados, agreed to strengthen co-operation in education, culture and the environment, access to health care and efforts to counter international terrorism. A second meeting of CARICOM-Cuba ministers responsible for foreign affairs was convened in May 2007 (the first having taken place in July 2004). The third meeting at the level of heads of state and government was held in December 2008 in Santiago de Cuba, Cuba. CARICOM leaders urged the new US administration to reconsider its restrictions on trade with Cuba. A similar appeal was made at the fourth summit meeting, convened in December 2011, in Port of Spain, Trinidad and Tobago. The meeting also focused on collaboration with regard to the illegal trafficking of drugs and small arms.

In August 1998 CARICOM and the Dominican Republic signed a free trade accord, covering trade in goods and services, technical barriers to trade, government procurement, and sanitary and phytosanitary measures and standards. A protocol to the agreement was signed in April 2000, following the resolution of differences concerning exempted items. The accord was ratified by the Dominican Republic in February 2001 and entered partially into force on 1 December. A Task Force to strengthen bilateral relations was established in 2007 and held its first meeting in November 2008. In November 2001 the CARICOM Secretary-General formally inaugurated a Caribbean Regional Technical Assistance Centre (CARTAC), in Barbados, to provide technical advice and training to officials from member countries and the Dominican Republic in support of the region's development. The Centre's operations are managed by the IMF.

In March 2000 heads of government issued a statement supporting the territorial integrity and security of Belize in that country's ongoing border dispute with Guatemala. CARICOM subsequently urged both countries to implement the provisions of an agreement signed in November and has continued to monitor the situation regularly.

In February 2002 the first meeting of heads of state and of government of CARICOM and the Central American Integration System (SICA) was convened in Belize City. The meeting aimed to strengthen co-operation between the groupings, in particular in international negotiations, efforts to counter transnational organized crime, and support for the regions' economies. In 2002 a joint CARICOM-Spain commission was inaugurated to foster greater co-operation between the two parties. In August 2012 a new CARICOM-Spain Joint Fund was launched, and, within its framework, a number of regional projects were approved. In March 2004 CARICOM signed a free trade agreement with Costa Rica.

In March 2006 a CARICOM-Mexico Joint Commission signed an agreement to promote future co-operation, in particular in seven priority areas. The first summit-level meeting between heads of state and government of Mexico and CARICOM was held in February 2010, in Riviera Maya, Mexico. In February 2007 the Secretaries-General of CARICOM and SICA signed a plan of action on future co-operation between the two groupings. A second CARICOM-SICA meeting of heads of state and of government was convened in May, in Belize. The meeting endorsed the plan of action and, in addition, instructed their ministers responsible for foreign affairs and for trade to pursue efforts to negotiate a free trade agreement, to be based on that signed by CARICOM with Costa Rica. Trade negotiations were formally inaugurated in August. The third CARICOM-SICA summit meeting was convened in El Salvador, in August 2011. A joint declaration recognized the need to develop transport and cultural links, and detailed measures to strengthen co-operation in international environmental negotiations, combating transnational crime, disaster management, the prevention of non-communicable diseases, and the management of migratory fish stocks in the Caribbean Sea.

In March 2006 CARICOM ministers responsible for foreign affairs met with the US Secretary of State and agreed to strengthen co-operation and enhance bilateral relations. In June 2007 a major meeting, the 'Conference on the Caribbean: a 20/20 Vision', was held in Washington, DC, USA. A series of meetings was held to consider issues and challenges relating to CARICOM's development and integration efforts and to the strengthening of relations with other countries in the region and with the USA. An Experts' Forum was hosted by the World Bank, a Private Sector Dialogue was held at the headquarters of the Inter-American Development Bank, and a Diaspora Forum was convened at the OAS. A summit meeting of CARICOM heads of government and then US President George W. Bush was held in the context of the Conference, at which issues concerning trade, economic growth and development, security and social investment were discussed. A second Conference on the Caribbean was held in New York, USA, in June 2008. A meeting of CARICOM foreign ministers with the US Secretary of State was held in June 2010, in Barbados, at which a series of commitments was concluded to enhance co-operation on a range of issues including energy security, climate change, health and trade relations.

In November 2013 CARICOM signed a Memorandum of Understanding with UNESCO, providing a framework for future co-operation in areas including assessment of natural hazards, heritage preservation and the development of national cultural policies, promotion of inclusive education, and implementation of the Plan of Action for the Sustainable Development of Small Island Developing States.

In July 2013 CARICOM heads of government determined that, with respect to the pursuit of reparations for historic acts of slavery and native genocide, national reparations committees should be established in every member state, and that the chairperson of each of these should participate in a new CARICOM Reparations Commission. The first CARICOM Regional Reparations Conference was held in September, in St Vincent and the Grenadines. In March 2014 CARICOM heads of state or government endorsed a new Caribbean Reparatory Justice Programme (CRJP) as the basis for future regional discussions on reparations. Priority areas of the CRJP included seeking a full apology from the governments of European countries that were implicated in the transatlantic slave trade; the initiation of an educational programme to address illiteracy; the establishment of Caribbean cultural institutions; and a debt cancellation initiative.

CRIME AND SECURITY

In December 1996 CARICOM heads of government determined to strengthen comprehensive co-operation and technical assistance to combat illegal drugs-trafficking. The Conference decided to establish a Caribbean Security Task Force to help to formulate a single regional agreement on maritime interdiction, incorporating agreements already concluded by individual members. A Regional Drugs Control Programme at the CARICOM Secretariat aims to co-ordinate regional initiatives with the overall objective of reducing the demand and supply of illegal substances.

In July 2000 the Heads of Government meeting issued a statement strongly opposing the OECD Harmful Tax Initiative, under which punitive measures had been threatened against 35 countries, including CARICOM member states, if they failed to tighten taxation legislation. The meeting also condemned a separate list, issued by OECD's Financial Action Task Force on Money Laundering (FATF), which identified 15 countries, including five Caribbean states, of failing to counter effectively international money-laundering. The statement reaffirmed CARICOM's commitment to fighting financial crimes and support for any necessary reform of supervisory practices or legislation, but insisted that national taxation jurisdictions, and specifically competitive regimes designed to attract offshore business, was not a matter for OECD concern. CARICOM remained actively involved in efforts to counter the scheme, and in April 2001 presented its case to the US President. In September the FATF issued a revised list of 19 'unco-operative jurisdictions', including Dominica, Grenada, Saint Christopher and Nevis, and Saint Vincent and the Grenadines. In early 2002 most Caribbean states concluded a provisional agreement with OECD to work to improve the transparency and supervision of 'offshore' sectors.

In July 2001 heads of government resolved to establish a task force to be responsible for producing recommendations for a forthcoming meeting of national security advisers. In October heads of government convened an emergency meeting in Nassau, Bahamas, to consider the impact of the terrorist attacks against the USA that had occurred in September. The meeting determined to convene immediately the so-called Task Force on Crime and Security in order to implement new policy directives. It was agreed to enhance co-ordination and collaboration of security services throughout the region, in particular in intelligence gathering, analysis and sharing in relation to crime, illicit drugs and terrorism, and to strengthen security at airports, seaports and borders. In July 2002 heads of government agreed on a series of initiatives recommended by the Task Force to counter the escalation in crime and violence. These included strengthening border controls, preparing national anti-crime master plans, establishing broad-based National Commissions on law and order and furthering the exchange of information and intelligence.

In July 2005 CARICOM heads of government endorsed a new Management Framework for Crime and Security, which provided for regular meetings of a Council of Ministers responsible for national security and law enforcement, a Security Policy Advisory Committee, and the establishment of an Implementation Agency for Crime and Security (IMPACS). In July 2007 CARICOM heads of government agreed in principle to extend these security efforts, including the introduction of a voluntary CARICOM Travel Card, CARIPASS, to facilitate the establishment of a single domestic space. An agreement to implement CARIPASS was signed by heads of state and government meeting in Dominica, in March 2010.

In April 2010 US President Barack Obama announced a Caribbean Basin Security Initiative (CBSI), which was to structure its regional security policy around a bilateral partnership with CARICOM, in particular to advance public safety and security, substantially to reduce the trafficking of illicit substances and to promote social justice. In the following month an inaugural Caribbean-US Security Co-operation Dialogue was held, in Washington, DC, to pursue discussion of the CBSI. The first meeting of a CBSI Commission was convened in Kingston, in November. Also in November, at the second meeting of the CARICOM-US Security Co-operation Dialogue, held in the Bahamas, officials agreed to facilitate region-wide information sharing, and to develop a regional juvenile justice policy.

In September 2011 a delegation from the UN Office on Drugs and Crime met with officials from IMPACS in Trinidad and Tobago. Discussions centred on strengthening regional forensics capacity, the proliferation of illegal guns, human trafficking, smuggling of migrants, and money-laundering. The establishment of an INTERPOL Liaison Office within IMPACS is under consideration.

INDUSTRY, ENERGY AND THE ENVIRONMENT

A protocol relating to the CARICOM Industrial Programming Scheme (CIPS), approved in 1988, is the Community's instrument for promoting the co-operative development of industry in the region. Protocol III amending the Treaty of Chaguaramas, with respect to industrial policy, was opened for signature in July 1998. The Secretariat has established a national standards bureau in each member country to harmonize technical standards. In 1999 members agreed to establish a new CARICOM Regional Organisation for Standards and Quality (CROSQ), as a successor to the Caribbean Common Market Standards Council. The agreement to establish CROSQ, to be located in Barbados, was signed in February 2002.

The CARICOM Alternative Energy Systems Project provides training, assesses energy needs and conducts energy audits. Implementation of a Caribbean Renewable Energy Development Programme, a project initiated in 1998, commenced in 2004. The Programme aimed to remove barriers to renewable energy development, establish a foundation for a sustainable renewable energy industry, and to create a framework for co-operation among regional and national renewable energy projects. A Caribbean Renewable Energy Fund was established to provide equity and development financing for renewable energy projects. In March 2013 the Council for Trade and Economic Development (COTED) endorsed a new Regional Energy Policy to strengthen energy efficiency and support the adoption of renewable sources of energy throughout the Community.

In January 2001 (COTED) approved the development of a specialized CARICOM agency to co-ordinate the gathering of information and other activities relating to climate change. The Caribbean Community Climate Change Centre became operational in early 2004 and was formally inaugurated, in Belmopan, Belize, in August 2005. It serves as an official clearing house and repository of data relating to climate change in the Caribbean region, provides advice to governments and other expertise for the development of projects to manage and adapt to climate change, and undertakes training. The results of the Centre's Mainstreaming Adaptation to Climate Change (MACC) Project were presented to governments at a Caribbean Climate Change Conference, held in Saint Lucia, in March 2009. In June 2012, during the UN Conference on Sustainable Development, held in Rio de Janeiro, Brazil, the Centre, the Indian Ocean Commission and the Secretariat of the Pacific Regional Environment Programme signed two agreements on co-operation in addressing climate change and promoting sustainable development.

In July 2008 CARICOM heads of government established a Task Force on Climate Change and Development to consider future action in relation to developments in energy and climate change, and in particular food insecurity caused by global rising food and fuel prices. The inaugural meeting of the Task Force was held in November, in Saint Lucia. In March 2012 CARICOM heads of government endorsed an Implementation Plan for the Regional Framework for Achieving Development Resilient to Climate Change, to cover the period 2011–21.

TRANSPORT, COMMUNICATIONS AND TOURISM

A Multilateral Agreement Concerning the Operations of Air Services within the Caribbean Community entered into force in November 1998, providing a formal framework for the regulation of the air transport industry and enabling CARICOM-owned and -controlled airlines to operate freely within the region. In July 1999 heads of government signed Protocol VI amending the Treaty of Chaguaramas providing for a common transportation policy, with harmonized standards and practices, which was to be an integral component of the development of a single market and economy. In November 2001 representatives of national civil aviation authorities signed a MOU, providing for the establishment of a regional body, the Regional Aviation Safety Oversight System. This was succeeded, in July 2008, by a Caribbean Aviation Safety and Security Oversight System upon the signing of an agreement by Barbados, Guyana, Saint Lucia and Trinidad and Tobago.

In 1989 a Caribbean Telecommunications Union was established to oversee developments in regional telecommunications. In July

2006 the Conference of Heads of Government, convened in Saint Christopher and Nevis, mandated the development of C@ribNET, a project to extend the availability of high-speed internet access throughout the region. In May 2007 the inaugural meeting of a Regional Information Communications and Technology Steering Committee was held, in Georgetown, Guyana, to determine areas of activity for future co-operation in support of the establishment of a Caribbean Information Society. In July 2012 government representatives, potential investors and organizations from nine CARICOM member states participated in a multi-stakeholder meeting on the sidelines of a 'Connect to the Americas Summit', which was convened, under the auspices of the International Telecommunication Union, in Panama City, Panama, to address the promotion of digital inclusion and means of accelerating secure and affordable access to broadband connectivity across the continent. In March 2014 it was announced that a CARICOM Single Information Communication Technology (ICT) Space, and Digital Agenda 2025, would be developed.

In 1997 CARICOM heads of government requested ministers responsible for tourism to meet regularly to develop tourism policies. A regional summit on tourism was held in the Bahamas in December 2001. A new Caribbean passport, introduced in January 2005, is issued by all 12 member countries participating in the CSME. In February 2013 representatives of regional and international tourism agencies met in Managua, Nicaragua, to develop a Regional Agenda for Sustainable Tourism in the Greater Caribbean.

AGRICULTURE AND FISHERIES

In July 1996 the CARICOM summit meeting agreed to undertake wide-ranging measures in order to modernize the agricultural sector and to increase the international competitiveness of Caribbean agricultural produce. The CARICOM Secretariat was to support national programmes with assistance in policy formulation, human resource development and the promotion of research and technology development in the areas of productivity, marketing, agri-business and water resources management. Protocol V amending the Treaty of Chaguaramas, which was concerned with agricultural policy, was opened for signature by heads of government in July 1998. In July 2002 heads of government approved an initiative to develop a CARIFORUM Special Programme for Food Security. CARICOM Governments have continually aimed to generate awareness of the economic and social importance of the banana industry to the region, in particular within the framework of the WTO multilateral trade negotiations.

In July 2005 CARICOM heads of government issued a statement protesting against proposals by the European Commission, issued in the previous month, to reform the EU sugar regime. Particular concern was expressed at a proposed price reduction in the cost of refined sugar of 39% over a four-year period. The heads of government insisted that, in accordance with the ACP-EU Cotonou Agreement, any review of the Sugar Protocol was required to be undertaken with the agreement of both parties and with regard to safeguarding benefits. In December CARICOM heads of government held a special meeting to discuss the EU sugar and banana regimes, in advance of a ministerial meeting of the WTO, held in Hong Kong that month. The Conference reiterated the potentially devastating effects on regional economies of the sugar price reduction and proposed new banana tariffs, and expressed the need for greater compensation and for the WTO multilateral negotiations to address fairly issues of preferential access. Negotiations between the ACP Caribbean signatory countries (the so-called CARIFORUM) and the EU on an Economic Partnership Agreement (EPA) to succeed the Cotonou Agreement, which had commenced in April 2004, were concluded in December 2007. In January 2008 CARICOM's Council for Trade and Economic Development resolved to conduct an independent review of the new agreement. The EPA was signed (initially, with the exception of Guyana and Haiti) in October. The first meeting of a new CARIFORUM-EU Trade and Development Committee was convened in July 2011 within the framework of the EPA. The text of a new Joint Caribbean-EU Partnership Strategy was concluded by CARIFORUM and the EU in November 2012, representing a framework for future co-operation in areas such as regional integration, climate change, natural disasters, crime, security, the reconstruction of Haiti, and joint action in multilateral fora. In March 2013 a US $3.5m. EPA Standby Facility was launched, to be administered by the Caribbean Development Bank.

A Caribbean Regional Fisheries Mechanism was established in 2002 to promote the sustainable use of fisheries and aquaculture resources in the region. It incorporates a Caribbean Fisheries Forum, which serves as the main technical and scientific decision-making body of the Mechanism. In March 2010 a Caribbean Agricultural Health and Food Safety Agency (CAHFSA) was inaugurated in Paramaribo.

HEALTH AND SOCIAL POLICY

In 1984 CARICOM and the Pan American Health Organization launched 'Caribbean Co-operation in Health' with projects to be undertaken in six main areas: environmental protection, including the control of disease-bearing pests; development of human resources; chronic non-communicable diseases and accidents; strengthening health systems; food and nutrition; maternal and child health care; and population activities. A second phase of the initiative commenced in 1992. In 2001 CARICOM established the Pan-Caribbean Partnership against HIV/AIDS (PANCAP), with the aim of reducing the spread and impact of HIV and AIDS in member countries. In February 2002 PANCAP initiated regional negotiations with pharmaceutical companies to secure reductions in the cost of anti-retroviral drugs.

In July 2001 heads of government, meeting in the Bahamas, issued the Nassau Declaration on Health, advocating greater regional strategic co-ordination and planning in the health sector and institutional reform, as well as increased resources. In February 2006 PANCAP and UNAIDS organized a regional consultation on the outcomes of country-based assessments of the HIV/AIDS crisis that had been undertaken in the region, and formulated a Regional Roadmap for Universal Access to HIV and AIDS Prevention, Care, Treatment and Support over the period 2006–10. A special meeting of COHSOD, convened in June 2006, in Trinidad and Tobago, issued the Port of Spain Declaration on the Education Sector Response to HIV and AIDS, which committed member states to supporting the Roadmap through education policy. In September 2007 a special regional summit meeting on chronic non-communicable diseases was held in Port of Spain, Trinidad and Tobago. In July 2008 CARICOM heads of government endorsed a new Caribbean Regional Strategy Framework on HIV and AIDS for the period 2008–12. In March 2010 Caribbean heads of government approved the establishment of a Caribbean Public Health Agency (CARPHA), which was intended to promote a co-ordinated approach to public health issues, in accordance with the Nassau Declaration. CARPHA was legally established in July 2011, began operations in January 2013, and was officially launched in July of that year. The Agency represents a merger of five former regional bodies: the Caribbean Environmental Health Institute, Caribbean Epidemiology Centre, Caribbean Food and Nutrition Institute, Caribbean Health Research Council, and Caribbean Regional Drug Testing Laboratory.

CARICOM education programmes have included the improvement of reading in schools through assistance for teacher training and ensuring the availability of low-cost educational material throughout the region. In March 2004 CARICOM ministers responsible for education endorsed the establishment of a Caribbean Knowledge and Learning Network (CKLN) to strengthen tertiary education institutions throughout the region and to enhance knowledge sharing. The CKLN was formally inaugurated in July, in co-operation with the OECS, in Grenada. A Caribbean Vocational Qualification was introduced in 2007. In March 2010, during an intersessional meeting of the Heads of Government Conference, convened in Dominica, an Agreement Establishing a Caribbean Knowledge and Learning Network Agency (CKLNA) was opened for signature, providing for the establishment of the Network as a full CARICOM institution. In July 2012, at the 23rd ordinary meeting of the Conference, held in Gros Islet, St Lucia, an Amendment to the Agreement Establishing the CKLNA was adopted, with the aim of establishing a more efficient organizational structure for the planned Agency.

From the late 1990s youth activities have been increasingly emphasized by the Community. These have included new programmes for disadvantaged youths, a mechanism for youth exchange and the convening of a Caribbean Youth Parliament. CARICOM organizes a biennial Caribbean Festival of Arts (CARIFESTA). CARIFESTA XI took place in Suriname, in August 2013. A CARICOM Regional Sports Academy was inaugurated, in Paramaribo, in March 2012. In October of that year the CARICOM Secretariat, in partnership with the UN Development Programme, convened a sub-regional meeting on youth gangs and violence, in Guyana; the meeting addressed the first phase of a new CARICOM Social Development and Crime Prevention Plan, which aimed to enhance the capacity of youth and community members to implement programmes aimed at addressing youth gang formation and violence, and to improve livelihood opportunities for marginalized young people.

In March 2014 CARICOM heads of state or government determined to establish a commission that was to be tasked with shaping the CARICOM strategy on human resource development.

EMERGENCY ASSISTANCE

A Caribbean Disaster Emergency Response Agency (CDERA) was established in 1991 to co-ordinate immediate disaster relief, primarily in the event of hurricanes. In January 2005, meeting on the sidelines of the fifth Summit of the Alliance of Small Island States, in Port Louis, Mauritius, the Secretaries-General of CARICOM, the

Commonwealth, the Pacific Islands Forum and the Indian Ocean Commission determined to take collective action to strengthen the disaster preparedness and response capabilities of their member countries in the Caribbean, Pacific and Indian Ocean areas. In September 2006 CARICOM, the EU and the Caribbean ACP states signed a Financing Agreement for Institutional Support and Capacity Building for Disaster Management in the Caribbean, which aimed to support CDERA by providing €3.4m. to facilitate the implementation of revised legislation, improved co-ordination between countries in the region and the increased use of information and communications technology in emergency planning. A new Caribbean Catastrophe Risk Insurance Facility (CCRIF), a multi-country initiative enabling participating states to draw funds for responding immediately to adverse natural events, such as earthquakes and hurricanes, became operational in June 2007, with support from international donors, including the Caribbean Development Bank and the World Bank. In September 2009 a new Caribbean Disaster Emergency Management Agency (CDEMA) formally replaced the CDERA, which had 18 participating states.

In January 2010 CARICOM provided immediate assistance to Haiti, after a massive earthquake caused extensive damage and loss of life in the country. A Tactical Mission was deployed to assess relief requirements and logistics, in particular in providing health services. A Special Co-ordinator, to be based in Haiti, was appointed to ensure the effectiveness of the Community's assistance, working closely with CDEMA and other international relief efforts. At the International Donors' Conference Towards a New Future for Haiti, held in New York, in March, UN member countries and other international partners pledged US $5,300m. in support of an Action Plan for the National Recovery and Development of the country. CARICOM pledged to support the Haitian Government in working with the international community and to provide all necessary institutional and technical assistance during the rehabilitation process. CARICOM was represented on the Board of the Interim Commission for the Reconstruction of Haiti, inaugurated in June, following a World Summit on the Future of Haiti, held to discuss the effective implementation of the Action Plan.

INSTITUTIONS

The following are among the institutions formally established within the framework of CARICOM:

Assembly of Caribbean Community Parliamentarians: c/o CARICOM Secretariat; an intergovernmental agreement on the establishment of a regional parliament entered into force in August 1994; inaugural meeting held in Barbados in May 1996. Comprises up to four representatives of the parliaments of each member country, and up to two of each associate member. It aims to provide a forum for wider community involvement in the process of integration and for enhanced deliberation on CARICOM affairs; authorized to issue recommendations for the Conference of Heads of Government and to adopt resolutions on any matter arising under the Treaty of Chaguaramas.

Caribbean Agricultural Research and Development Institute (CARDI): UWI Campus, St Augustine, Trinidad and Tobago; tel. 645-1205; fax 645-1208; e-mail infocentre@cardi.org; internet www.cardi.org; f. 1975; aims to contribute to the competitiveness and sustainability of Caribbean agriculture by generating and transferring new and appropriate technologies and by developing effective partnerships with regional and international entities; Exec. Dir Dr ARLINGTON CHESNEY; publs *CARDI Weekly*, *CARDI Review*, technical bulletin series.

Caribbean Association of Professional Statisticians: f. 2013 as a forum addressing statistical issues and developments, and promoting research on statistical methodology and its applications.

Caribbean Centre for Development Administration (CARICAD): Weymouth Corporate Centre, 1st Floor, Roebuck St, St Michael, Barbados; tel. 427-8535; fax 436-1709; e-mail info@caricad.net; internet www.caricad.net; f. 1980; aims to assist governments in the reform of the public sector and to strengthen their managerial capacities for public administration; promotes the involvement of the private sector, NGOs and other bodies in all decision-making processes; Exec. Dir JENNIFER ASTAPHAN.

Caribbean Community Climate Change Centre (5Cs): Lawrence Nicholas Bldg, 2nd Floor, Ring Rd, POB 563, Belmopan, Belize; tel. 822-1094; fax 822-1365; e-mail evalladares@caribbeanclimate.bz; internet www.caribbeanclimate.bz; f. 2005 to co-ordinate the region's response to climate change; Exec. Dir Dr KENRICK LESLIE.

Caribbean Competition Commission: Hendrikstraat 69, Paramaribo, Suriname; tel. 491439; fax 530639; e-mail senioradmin@ccc.sr; internet www.caricomcompetitioncommission.com; f. 2008; mandated to enforce the rules of competition of the CARICOM Single Market and Economy; Chair. Dr KUSHA HARAKSINGH (Trinidad and Tobago).

Caribbean Disaster Emergency Management Agency (CDEMA): Bldg 1, Manor Lodge, Lodge Hill, St Michael, Barbados; tel. 425-0386; fax 425-8854; e-mail cdema@cdema.org; internet www.cdema.org; f. 1991; aims to respond with immediate assistance following a request by a participating state in the event of a natural or man-made disaster; co-ordinates other relief efforts; assists states to establish disaster preparedness and response capabilities; incorporates national disaster organizations, headed by a co-ordinator, in each participating state; Exec. Dir RONALD JACKSON.

Caribbean Examinations Council: The Garrison, St Michael, BB14038, Barbados; tel. 227-1700; fax 429-5421; e-mail cxcezo@cxc.org; internet www.cxc.org; f. 1972; develops syllabuses and conducts examinations for the Caribbean Advanced Proficiency Examination (CAPE), the Caribbean Secondary Education Certificate (CSEC), the Caribbean Certificate of Secondary Level Competence (CCSLC) and the Caribbean Primary Exit Assessment (CPEA); mems: govts of 16 English-speaking countries and territories; Registrar and CEO Dr DIDACUS JULES.

Caribbean Meteorological Organization (CMO): 27 O'Connor St, Woodbrook, Port of Spain, Trinidad and Tobago; tel. 622-4711; fax 622-0277; e-mail cmohq@cmo.org.tt; internet www.cmo.org.tt; f. 1973 as successor to the British Caribbean Meteorological Service (founded 1951) to co-ordinate regional activities in meteorology, operational hydrology and allied sciences; became a specialized institution of CARICOM in 1973; comprises a Council of Government Ministers, a Headquarters Unit, the Caribbean Meteorological Foundation and the Caribbean Institute for Meteorology and Hydrology, located in Barbados; mems: govts of 16 countries and territories represented by the National Meteorological and Hydrometeorological Services; Co-ordinating Dir TYRONE W. SUTHERLAND.

Caribbean Public Health Agency (CARPHA): 16–18 Jamaica Blvd, Federation Park, Port of Spain, Trinidad and Tobago; tel. 622-4261; e-mail postmaster@carpha.org; internet carpha.org; f. 2011 (began operations in 2013) as a new single public health agency for the region, representing a merger of the fmr Caribbean Environmental Health Institute, Caribbean Epidemiology Centre, Caribbean Food and Nutrition Institute, Caribbean Health Research Council, and Caribbean Regional Drug Testing Laboratory; aims to facilitate emergency responses to natural disasters, such as hurricanes, earthquakes and flooding; to provide surveillance and management of non-communicable conditions prevalent in the region, such as cancer, diabetes, heart disease and obesity; to provide surveillance and management of communicable diseases, including HIV/AIDS and TB; to address surveillance and prevention of injuries, violence and employment-related conditions; and to contribute to global health agreements and compliance with international health regulations; pursues a people-centred and evidence-based approach to address regional public health challenges; provides specialized laboratory services; issues guidelines, handbooks, reports and alerts on regional public health issues; Exec. Dir Dr C. JAMES HOSPEDALES (Trinidad and Tobago).

Caribbean Telecommunications Union (CTU): Victoria Park Suites, 3rd Floor, 14–17 Victoria Sq., Port of Spain, Trinidad and Tobago; tel. 627-0281; fax 623-1523; internet www.ctu.int; f. 1989; aims to co-ordinate the planning and development of telecommunications in the region; encourages the development of regional telecommunications standards, the transfer of technology and the exchange of information among national telecommunications administrations; membership includes mems of CARICOM and other countries in the region, private sector orgs and NGOs; Sec.-Gen. BERNADETTE LEWIS (Trinidad and Tobago).

CARICOM Implementation Agency for Crime and Security (IMPACS): Sagicor Bldg, Ground Floor, 16 Queen's Park West, Port of Spain, Trinidad and Tobago; tel. 622-0245; fax 628-9795; e-mail enquiries@caricomimpacs.org; internet www.caricomimpacs.org; f. 2006 as a permanent institution to co-ordinate activities in the region relating to crime and security; incorporates two sub-agencies: a Joint Regional Communications Centre and a Regional Intelligence Fusion Centre; a Regional Integrated Ballistic Information Network was initiated in 2013; Exec. Dir FRANCIS FORBES (Jamaica).

CARICOM Regional Organisation for Standards and Quality: Baobab Towers, Warrens, St Michael, Barbados; tel. 622-7670; fax 622-7678; e-mail crosq.caricom@crosq.org; internet www.crosq.org; f. 2002; aims to enhance and promote the implementation of standards, infrastructure and quality verification throughout the region and liaise with international standards orgs; CEO WINSTON BENNETT.

Council of Legal Education: c/o Gordon St, St Augustine, Trinidad and Tobago; tel. 662-5860; fax 662-0927; internet www.clecaribbean.com; f. 1971; responsible for the training of members of the legal profession; administers law schools in Jamaica, Trinidad and Tobago, and the Bahamas; mems: govts of 12 countries and territories; Chair. JACQUELINE SAMUELS BROWN.

ASSOCIATE INSTITUTIONS

Caribbean Development Bank: POB 408, Wildey, St Michael, Barbados; tel. 431-1600; fax 426-7269; e-mail info@caribank.org; internet www.caribank.org; f. 1969 to stimulate regional economic growth through support for agriculture, industry, transport and other infrastructure, tourism, housing and education; in May 2010 the Board of Governors approved an ordinary capital increase of US $1,000m., including a paid-up component of $216m.; in 2012 new loans approved totalled $104m. bringing the cumulative total to $4,082.2m.; total assets $1,640.8m. (31 Dec. 2012); mems: 27 mems, incl. 19 regional mem. states, Colombia, Mexico, Venezuela (non-borrowing regional mems), and Canada, the People's Republic of China, Germany, Italy, United Kingdom (non-regional mems); Pres. Dr. WILLIAM WARREN SMITH (Jamaica).

Caribbean Law Institute Centre: Caricom Research Bldg, Faculty of Law, University of the West Indies, Cave Hill Campus, Cave Hill, Barbados; tel. (246) 417-4652; e-mail clic@cavehill.uwi.edu; internet www.cavehill.uwi.edu/clic/clic.asp; f. 1988 to harmonize and modernize commercial laws in the region; Dir Prof. VELMA NEWTON.

Other Associate Institutions of CARICOM, in accordance with its constitution, are the University of Guyana, the University of the West Indies and the Secretariat of the Organisation of Eastern Caribbean States.

Publications

CARICOM Perspective (annually).

CARICOM View (6 a year).

CENTRAL AMERICAN INTEGRATION SYSTEM

(SISTEMA DE LA INTEGRACIÓN CENTROAMERICANA—SICA)

Address: Final Blv. Cancillería, Ciudad Merliot, Distrito El Espino, Antiguo Cuscatlán La Libertad, San Salvador, El Salvador.

Telephone: 2248-8800; **fax:** 2248-8899; **e-mail:** info@sica.int; **internet:** www.sica.int.

Founded in December 1991, when the heads of state of six Central American countries signed the Protocol of Tegucigalpa to the agreement establishing the Organization of Central American States (f. 1951), creating a new framework for regional integration. A General Secretariat of the Sistema de la Integración Centroamericana was inaugurated in February 1993 to co-ordinate the process of political, economic, social cultural and environmental integration and to promote democracy and respect for human rights throughout the region. In September 1997 Central American Common Market (CACM) heads of state, meeting in the Nicaraguan capital, signed the Managua Declaration in support of further regional integration and the establishment of a political union.

MEMBERS

Belize	El Salvador	Nicaragua
Costa Rica	Guatemala	Panama
Dominican Republic	Honduras	

Note: Argentina, Australia, Brazil, Chile, the People's Republic of China, Colombia, Ecuador, the European Union, France, Germany, the Holy See, Italy, Japan, the Republic of Korea, Mexico, Peru, Spain, Taiwan, United Kingdom, Uruguay and the USA have observer status with SICA.

Organization

(April 2014)

SUMMIT MEETINGS

The meetings of heads of state of member countries serve as the supreme decision-making organ of SICA.

COUNCIL OF MINISTERS

Ministers responsible for foreign affairs of member states meet regularly to provide policy direction for the process of integration.

Executive Committee

Comprises a government representative of each member state tasked with ensuring the implementation of decisions adopted by heads of state or the Council of Ministers, and with overseeing the activities of the General Secretariat.

CONSULTATIVE COMMITTEE

The Committee comprises representatives of business organizations, trade unions, academic institutions and other federations concerned with the process of integration in the region. It is a fundamental element of the integration system and assists the Secretary-General in determining the organization's policies.

GENERAL SECRETARIAT

The General Secretariat of SICA was established in February 1993 to co-ordinate the process of enhanced regional integration. It comprises Directorates-General of Social Integration, Economic Integration, and of Environmental Affairs.

In February 1998 heads of state resolved to establish a Unified General Secretariat to integrate the institutional aspects of the grouping in a single office, to be located in San Salvador, El Salvador. A new headquarters for the organization was inaugurated in July 2011.

Secretary-General: HUGO MARTÍNEZ BONILLA (El Salvador).

CORE INSTITUTIONS

Central American Parliament (PARLACEN)

12 Avda 33-04, Zona 5, 01005 Guatemala City, Guatemala; tel. 2424-4600; fax 2424-4610; e-mail guatemala@parlacen.int; internet www.parlacen.org.gt.; officially inaugurated in 1991; comprises 20 elected representatives of the Domincan Republic, El Salvador, Guatemala, Honduras, Nicaragua and Panama, as well as former Presidents and Vice-Presidents of mem. countries; Haiti, Mexico, Puerto Rico, Venezuela and Taiwan have observer status; Pres. PAULA RODRÍGUEZ (Guatemala); publ. *Foro Parlamentario*.

Central American Court of Justice

Apdo Postal 907, Managua, Nicaragua; tel. 266-6273; fax 266-4604; e-mail cortecen@ccj.org.ni; internet portal.ccj.org.ni.; officially inaugurated in 1994; tribunal authorized to consider disputes relating to treaties agreed within the regional integration system; in February 1998 Central American heads of state agreed to limit the number of magistrates in the Court to one per country; Sec.-Gen. Dr ORLANDO GUERRERO MAYORGA

SPECIALIZED SECRETARIATS

In addition to those listed below, various technical or executive secretariat units support meetings of ministerial Councils, concerned, inter alia, with women, housing, health and finance.

Secretaría General de la Coordinación Educativa y Cultural Centroamericana (SG-CECC): 400m este y 25m norte de la Iglesia Santa Teresita en Barrio Escalante, 262-1007 San José, Costa Rica; tel. 2283-7629; fax 2283-7719; e-mail sgcecc@racsa.co.cr; internet www.sica.int/cecc; f. 1982; promotes development of regional programmes in the fields of education and culture; Sec.-Gen. MARÍA EUGENIA PANIAGUA PADILLA.

Secretaría de Integración Económica Centroamericana (SIECA): 4A Avda 10–25, Zona 14, Apdo 1237, 01901 Guatemala City, Guatemala; tel. 2368-2151; fax 2368-1071; e-mail info@sieca.int; internet www.sieca.int; f. 1960 to assist the process of economic integration and the creation of a Central American Common Market (CACM—established by the organization of Central American States under the General Treaty of Central American Economic Integration, signed in December 1960 and ratified by Costa Rica, Guatemala, El Salvador, Honduras and Nicaragua in September 1963); supervises the correct implementation of the legal instruments of economic integration, conducts relevant studies at the request of the CACM, and arranges meetings; comprises departments covering the working of the CACM: negotiations and external trade policy; external co-operation; systems and statistics; finance and administration; also includes a unit for co-operation with the private sector and finance institutions, and a legal consultative committee; Sec.-Gen. CARMEN GISELA VERGERA (Panama); publs *Anuario Estadístico Centroamericano de Comercio Exterior*, *Carta Informativa* (monthly), *Cuadernos de la SIECA* (2 a year), *Estadísticas Macroeconómicas de Centroamérica* (annually), *Series Estadísticas Seleccionadas de Centroamérica* (annually), *Boletín Informativo* (fortnightly).

Secretaría de Integración Turística Centroamericana (SITCA): Final Blv. Cancillería, Distrito El Espino, Ciudad Merliot, Antiguo Cuscatlán La Libertad, El Salvador; tel. 2248-8837; fax 2248-8897; e-mail info.stcct@sica.int; internet www.sica.int/cct; f. 1965 to develop regional tourism activities; provides administrative support to the Central American Tourism Council, comprising national ministers and directors responsible for tourism; Dir SHANTANNY ANASHA CAMPBELL LEWIS (Nicaragua).

Secretaría de la Integración Social Centroamericana (SISCA): Final Blv. Cancillería, Distrito El Espino Ciudad Merliot, Antiguo Cuscatlán La Libertad, El Salvador; tel. 2248-8857; fax 2248-6943; e-mail info.sisca@sica.int; internet www.sica.int/sisca; f. 1995; co-ordinates various intergovernmental secretariats, including regional councils concerned with social security, sport and recreation, and housing and human settlements; Sec. ANA HAZEL ESCRICH CAÑAS (Costa Rica).

Secretaría del Consejo Agropecuario Centroamericano (SCAC): 600m noreste del Cruce de Ipis-Coronado, San Isidro de Coronado, Apdo Postal 55-2200, San José, Costa Rica; tel. 2216-0303; fax 2216-0285; e-mail info.cac@sica.int; internet www.sica.int/cac; f. 1991 to determine and co-ordinate regional policies and programmes relating to agriculture and agroindustry; Exec. Sec. JULIO CALDERÓN ARTIEDA.

Secretaría Ejecutiva de la Comisión Centroamericana de Ambiente y Desarrollo (SE-CCAD): Final Blv. Cancillería, Distrito El Espino Ciudad Merliot, Antiguo Cuscatlán La Libertad, El Salvador; tel. 2248-8843; fax 2248-8899; e-mail info.ccad@sica.int; internet www.sica.int/ccad; f. 1989 to enhance collaboration in the promotion of sustainable development and environmental protection; Exec. Sec. NELSON ORLANDO TREJO AGUILAR (Honduras).

Secretaría Ejecutiva del Consejo Monetario Centroamericano (SECMCA) (Central American Monetary Council): 400m suroeste de la Rotonda La Bandera, Barrio Dent, Contiguo al BANHVI, San José, Costa Rica; tel. 2280-9522; fax 2524-1062; e-mail secma@secmca.org; internet www.secmca.org; f. 1964 by the presidents of Central American central banks, to co-ordinate monetary policies; Exec. Sec. WILLIAM CALVO VILLEGAS; publs *Boletín Estadístico* (annually), *Informe Económico* (annually).

OTHER SPECIALIZED INSTITUTIONS

Agriculture and Fisheries

Organismo Internacional Regional de Sanidad Agropecuaria (OIRSA) (International Regional Organization of Plant Protection and Animal Health): Calle Ramón Belloso, Final Pasaje Isolde, Colonia Escalón, Apdo (01) 61, San Salvador, El Salvador; tel. 2209-9200; fax 2263-1128; e-mail oirsa@oirsa.org; internet www.oirsa.org; f. 1953 for the prevention of the introduction of animal and plant pests and diseases unknown in the region; research, control and eradication programmes of the principal pests present in agriculture; technical assistance and advice to the ministries of agriculture and livestock of member countries; education and qualification of personnel; mems: Belize, Costa Rica, Dominican Republic, El Salvador, Guatemala, Honduras, Mexico, Nicaragua, Panama; Exec. Dir EDWIN MAURICIO ARAGÓN ROJAS.

Unidad Coordinadora de la Organización del Sector Pesquero y Acuícola del Istmo Centroamericano (OSPESCA) (Organization of Fishing and Aquaculture in Central America): Final Blv. Cancillería, Distrito El Espino, Ciudad Merliot, Antiguo Cuscatlán La Libertad, El Salvador; tel. 2248-8841; fax 2248-8899; e-mail info.ospesca@sica.int; internet www.sica.int/ospesca; f. 1995, incorporated into SICA in 1999; Regional Co-ordinator MARIO GONZÁLEZ RECINOS.

Education, Health and Sport

Consejo Superior Universitario Centroamericano (CSUCA) (Central American University Council): Avda Las Américas 1–03, Zona 14, International Club Los Arcos, 01014 Guatemala City, Guatemala; tel. 2502-7500; fax 2502-7501; e-mail sg@csuca.org; internet www.csuca.org; f. 1948 to guarantee academic, administrative and economic autonomy for universities and to encourage regional integration of higher education; maintains libraries and documentation centres; Council of 32 mems; mems: 18 universities, in Belize, Costa Rica (four), Dominican Republic, El Salvador, Guatemala, Honduras (two), Nicaragua (four) and Panama (four); Sec.-Gen. Dr JUAN ALFONSO FUENTES SORIA; publs *Estudios Sociales Centroamericanos* (quarterly), *Cuadernos de Investigación* (monthly), *Carta Informativa de la Secretaría General* (monthly).

Consejo del Istmo Centroamericano de Deportes y Recreación (CODICADER) (Committee of the Central American Isthmus for Sport and Recreation): Juan Díaz, Vía José Agustín Arango, Instituto Panameño de Deportes, Apartado Postal 00066, Panama; tel. 500-5480; fax 500-5484; e-mail dgeneral@pandeportes.gob.pa; internet www.sica.int/sisca/codicader; f. 1992; Pres. RAMÓN CARDOZE.

Instituto de Nutrición de Centro América y Panamá (INCAP) (Institute of Nutrition of Central America and Panama): Calzada Roosevelt 6–25, Zona 11, Apdo Postal 1188-01901, Guatemala City, Guatemala; tel. 2472-3762; fax 2473-6529; e-mail info.incap@sica.int; internet www.sica.int/incap; f. 1949 to promote the development of nutritional sciences and their application and to strengthen the technical capacity of member countries to reach food and nutrition security; provides training and technical assistance for nutrition education and planning; conducts applied research; disseminates information; maintains library (including about 600 periodicals); administered by the Pan American Health Organization and the World Health Organization; mems: CACM mems, Belize and Panama; Dir CAROLINA SIÚ; publ. *Annual Report*.

Energy and the Environment

Secretaría Ejecutiva de la Comisión Regional de Recursos Hidráulicos (SE-CRRH): 500 mts norte, 200 oeste y 25 norte de Super Blvd Pavas, San José, Costa Rica; tel. 2231-5791; fax 2296-0047; e-mail secretaria@recursoshidricos.org; internet www.recursoshidricos.org; f. 1966; mems: Belize, Costa Rica, El Salvador, Guatemala, Honduras, Nicaragua, Panama.

Secretaría Ejecutiva del Consejo de Electrificación de América Central (CEAC) (Central American Electrification Council): Apdo 0816, 01552 Panamá, Panama; tel. 2211-6175; fax 501-3990; e-mail jfisher@etesa.com.pa; internet www.ceaconline.org; f. 1985; Exec. Sec. JORGE FISHER MILLER.

Finance

Banco Centroamericano de Integración Económica (BCIE) (Central American Bank for Economic Integration): Blv. Suyapa, Contigua a Banco de Honduras, Apdo 772, Tegucigalpa, Honduras; tel. 2240-2243; fax 2240-2231; e-mail MNunez@bcie.org; internet www.bcie.org; f. 1961 to promote the economic integration and balanced economic development of member countries; finances public and private development projects, particularly those related to industrialization and infrastructure; auth. cap. US $2,000m; regional mems: Costa Rica, El Salvador, Guatemala, Honduras, Nicaragua; non-regional mems: Argentina, Colombia, Dominican Republic, Mexico, Panama, Spain, Taiwan; Exec. Pres. NICK RISCHBIETH GLÖE; publs *Annual Report*, *Revista de la Integración y el Desarrollo de Centroamérica*.

Organización Centroamericana y del Caribe de Entidades Fiscalizadores Superiores (OCCEFS) (Organization of Central American and Caribbean Supreme Audit Institutions): Tribunal Superior de Cuentas de la República de Honduras, Centro Cívico Gubernamental, Col. Las Brisas Comayagüela, Honduras; tel. and fax 234-5210; e-mail info.occefs@sica.int; internet www.sica.int/occefs; f. 1995 as the Organización Centroamericana de Entidades Fiscalizadores Superiores, within the framework of the Organización Latinoamericana y del Caribe de Entidades Fiscalizadoras Superiores; assumed present name in 1998; aims to promote co-operation among members, facilitate exchange of information, and provide technical assistance; Exec. Sec. JORGE BOGRÁN RIVERA (Honduras).

Public Administration

Centro de Coordinación para la Prevención de Desastres Naturales en América Central (CEPREDENAC): Avda Hincapié 21–72, Zona 13 Guatemala City, Guatemala; tel. and fax 2390-0200; fax 2390-0202; e-mail info.cepredenac@sica.int; internet www.sica.int/cepredenac; f. 1988, integrated into SICA in 1995; aims to strengthen the capacity of the region to reduce its vulnerability to natural disasters; Exec. Sec. NOEL BARILLAS.

Instituto Centroamericano de Administración Pública (ICAP) (Central American Institute of Public Administration): Apdo Postal 10025-1000, San José, Costa Rica; tel. 2234-1011; fax 2225-2049; e-mail info@icap.ac.cr; internet www.icap.ac.cr; f. 1954 by the five Central American Republics and the UN, with later participation by Panama; the Institute aims to train the region's public servants, provide technical assistance and carry out research leading to reforms in public administration.

Science and Technology

Comisión para el Desarrollo Científico y Tecnológico de Centroamérica y Panamá (CTCAP) (Committee for the Scientific and Technological Development of Central America and Panama): 3A Avda 13–28, Zona 1, Guatemala City, Guatemala; tel. and fax 2228-6019; fax 2360-2664; e-mail info.ctcap@sica.int; internet www.sica.int/ctcap; f. 1976; Pres. ROSA MARÍA AMAYA FABIÁN DE LÓPEZ.

Security

Comisión Centroamericana Permanente para la Erradicación de la Producción, Tráfico, Consumo y Uso Ilícitos de Estupefacientes y Sustancias Psicotrópicas y Delitos Conexos (CCP): Blv. Suyapa, Colonia Florencia Norte, Edificio Florencia, Oficina 412, Tegucigalpa, Honduras; tel. 235-6349; e-mail ccp@ccpcentroamerica.org; f. 1993; supports regional efforts to combat the production, trafficking and use of illicit substances, and related crimes; Exec. Sec. OSCAR ROBERTO HERNÁNDEZ HIDALGO.

Transport and Communications

Comisión Centroamericana de Transporte Marítimo (COCATRAM): Frente al costado oeste del Hotel Mansión Teodolinda, Barrio Bolonia, Apdo Postal 2423, Managua, Nicaragua; tel. 222-3667; fax 222-2759; e-mail info@cocatram.org.ni; internet www.cocatram.org.ni; f. 1981; Exec. Dir OTTO NOACK SIERRA; publ. *Boletín Informativo*.

Comisión de Telecomunicaciones de Centroamérica (COMTELCA) (Commission for Telecommunications in Central America): Col. Palmira, Edif. Alpha 608, Avda Brasil, Apdo 1793, Tegucigalpa, Honduras; tel. 2220-1011; fax 2220-1197; e-mail sec@comtelca.org; internet www.comtelca.org; f. 1966 to co-ordinate and improve the regional telecommunications network; Dir-Gen. RAFAEL A. MARADIAGA.

Corporación Centroamericana de Servicios de Navegación Aérea (COCESNA) (Central American Air Navigation Services Corporation): Apdo 660, 150 sur de Aeropuerto de Toncontín, Tegucigalpa, Honduras; tel. 2234-3360; fax 2234-2488; e-mail notam@cocesna.org; internet www.cocesna.org; f. 1960; offers radar air traffic control services, aeronautical telecommunications services, flight inspections and radio assistance services for air navigation; provides support in the areas of safety, aeronautical training and aeronautical software; Exec. Pres. BAYARDO PAGOADA FIGUEROA.

Activities

In June 1990 the presidents of Costa Rica, El Salvador, Guatemala, Honduras and Nicaragua signed a declaration appealing for a revitalization of CACM, as a means of promoting lasting peace in the region. In December the presidents committed themselves to the creation of an effective common market. They requested the support of multilateral lending institutions through investment in regional development, and the cancellation or rescheduling of member countries' debts. In December 1991 the heads of state of the five Central American Common Market (CACM) countries and Panama signed the Protocol of Tegucigalpa; in February 1993 the General Secretariat of SICA was inaugurated to co-ordinate the integration process in the region.

In May 2008 Brazil was invited to become an observer of SICA. In June 2009 the Council of Ministers agreed to admit Japan as an extra-regional observer of the grouping. The agreement was formalized with the Japanese Government in January 2010. The Republic of Korea was approved as an observer at the meeting of heads of state held in July 2011. In June, meanwhile, at the International Conference in Support of the Regional Strategy for Central America and Mexico, the US Secretary of State announced that the USA was to apply for regional observer status with SICA. This was approved at the SICA summit meeting held in December, and granted by the signing of a Memorandum of Understanding in May 2012. At the December 2011 meeting Australia and France became extra-regional observers; Peru was admitted with regional observer status in February 2012. An agreement formally admitting the Holy See as an observer was concluded in January 2013. Applications for observer status by Colombia, Ecuador, Haiti, the United Kingdom and Uruguay were approved by SICA heads of state and government in December 2012. Ecuador and Uruguay were admitted, accordingly, March 2013, and Colombia in September, as regional observers, and in June the United Kingdom became an extra-regional observer. Also in June, the Dominican Republic became the eighth full member of SICA.

In December 2011 SICA heads of state and government mandated regional ministers responsible for women's affairs to formulate a Regional Policy on Gender Equality and Equity; this remained under development in 2014.

TRADE AGREEMENTS AND EXTERNAL RELATIONS

In November 1997, at a special summit meeting of CACM heads of state, an agreement was reached with the president of the Dominican Republic to initiate a gradual process of incorporating that country into the process of Central American integration, with the aim of promoting sustainable development throughout the region. A free trade accord with the Dominican Republic was concluded in April 1998, and formally signed in November. At a meeting of heads of state in June 2013, the Dominican Republic became the eighth full member of the grouping.

In April 2001 Costa Rica concluded a free trade accord with Canada; the other four CACM countries commenced negotiations with Canada in November with the aim of reaching a similar agreement. In February 2002 Central American heads of state convened an extraordinary summit meeting in Managua, Nicaragua, at which they resolved to implement measures to further the political and economic integration of the region. The leaders determined to pursue initial proposals for a free trade accord with the USA, a Central American Free Trade Area (CAFTA), during the visit to the region of the then US President, George W. Bush, in the following month, and, more generally, to strengthen trading relations with the European Union (EU). They also pledged to resolve all regional conflicts by peaceful means. Earlier in February the first meeting of heads of state or government of Central American and Caribbean Community and Common Market (CARICOM) countries took place in Belize, with the aim of strengthening political and economic relations between the two groupings. The meeting agreed to work towards concluding common negotiating positions, for example in respect of the World Trade Organization.

Negotiations on CAFTA between the CACM countries and the USA were initiated in January 2003. An agreement was concluded between the USA and El Salvador, Guatemala, Honduras and Nicaragua in December, and with Costa Rica in January 2004. Under the resulting US-Central America Free Trade Agreement some 80% of US exports of consumer and industrial goods and more than 50% of US agricultural exports to CAFTA countries were to become duty-free immediately upon its entry into force, with remaining tariffs to be eliminated over a 10-year period for consumer and industrial goods and over a 15-year period for agricultural exports. Almost all CAFTA exports of consumer and industrial products to the USA were to be duty-free on the Agreement's entry into force. The Agreement was signed by the US Trade Representative and CACM ministers responsible for trade and economy, convened in Washington, DC, USA, in May 2004. It required ratification by all national legislatures before entering into effect. Negotiations on a US-Dominican Republic free trade agreement, to integrate the Dominican Republic into CAFTA, were concluded in March and the agreement was signed in August. The so-called CAFTA-DR accord was formally ratified by the USA in August 2005. Subsequently, the agreement entered into force with El Salvador on 1 March 2006, Honduras and Nicaragua on 1 April, Guatemala on 1 July, the Dominican Republic on 1 March 2007, and Costa Rica on 1 January 2009.

In May 2006 a meeting of EU and Central American heads of state resolved to initiate negotiations to conclude an Association Agreement. The first round of negotiations was concluded in San José, Costa Rica, in October 2007. In April 2009 the seventh round of negotiations, being held in Tegucigalpa, Honduras, was suspended when the delegation from Nicaragua withdrew from the talks. Negotiations to conclude the accord resumed in February 2010; Panama participated in the negotiations as a full member for the first time in March and an agreement was finalized in May. It provided for immediate duty-free access into the EU for some 92% of Central American products into the EU (48% for EU goods entering Central America), with the remainder of tariffs (on all but 4% of products) being phased out over a 15-year period. The accord also incorporated new import quotas for meat, dairy products and rice, and market access agreements for car manufacturers and the service industry. The Association Agreement, which included 'pillars' concerned with political dialogue and co-operation, as well as trade, was initialled in March 2011 and formally signed by both sides in June 2012. On 1 August 2013 trade liberalization measures became operational between the EU and Honduras, Nicaragua and Panama. Guatemala acceded to the trade accord in December. In that month the EU was granted observer status.

In February 2007 the Secretaries-General of SICA and CARICOM signed a plan of action to foster greater co-operation in areas including foreign policy, international trade relations, security and combating crime, and the environment. Meetings of ministers responsible for foreign affairs and for the economy and foreign trade were convened in the same month at which preparations were initiated for trade negotiations between the two groupings. In May the second Central American-CARICOM summit meeting was convened, in Belize City, Belize. Heads of state and of government endorsed the efforts to enhance co-operation between the organizations and approved the elaboration of a free trade agreement, based on the existing bilateral accord signed between CARICOM and Costa Rica. Formal negotiations were inaugurated at a meeting of ministers responsible for trade in August. In December 2010 SICA heads of state, meeting in Belize, resolved to strengthen co-operation with CARICOM and the Association of Caribbean States (ACS). The third meeting of SICA and CARICOM heads of state or government was held in August 2011, in San Salvador, El Salvador. Also in August, the OAS convened a high-level meeting of CEOs and business executives from the two blocs to discuss measures to expand trade and investment in the region following the global economic downturn. In July 2013 SICA's Secretary-General stated that the grouping was to seek agreements with CARICOM and the Union of South American Nations (UNASUR).

A framework agreement with the Andean Community was signed with SICA in November 2004 to strengthen dialogue and co-operation between the two blocs of countries. In January 2011 the Secretaries-General of the two organizations, meeting in San Salvador, determined to reactivate the agreement and pursue greater collaboration.

In May 2008 SICA heads of state and government met their Brazilian counterparts in San Salvador. The summit meeting reaffirmed the willingness of both sides to enhance political and economic co-operation with the grouping of Southern Common Market (Mercosur) countries and determined to establish mechanisms, in particular, to promote trade and political dialogue.

ECONOMIC INTEGRATION AND FINANCIAL CO-OPERATION

In March 2002 Central American leaders adopted the San Salvador Plan of Action for Central American Economic Integration, establishing several objectives as the basis for the future creation of a regional customs union, with a single tariff. CACM heads of state, meeting in December in Costa Rica, adopted the Declaration of San José, supporting the planned establishment of the Central American customs union. Negotiations on technical aspects of the proposed union—the development of which was a regional commitment made by SICA under the Association Agreement concluded in 2012 with the EU—were ongoing in 2013–14.

In January 2007 the Treaty on Payment Systems and the Liquidation of Assets in Central America and the Dominican Republic was presented to the Secretary-General of SICA. The treaty aimed to increase greater financial co-operation and further develop the financial markets in the region.

In December 2008 a summit meeting, convened in San Pedro Sula, Honduras, adopted a plan of urgent measures to address the effects of the global economic and financial downturn, including a commitment of greater investment in infrastructure projects and the establishment of a common credit fund. Heads of state ratified an agreement to establish a Central American Statistical Commission (Centroestad) to develop a regional statistics service, provide technical statistical assistance to member countries and harmonize national and regional statistics.

INTEGRATED DISASTER RISK MANAGEMENT, ENERGY AND CLIMATE CHANGE

In December 1994 SICA and the USA signed a joint declaration (CONCAUSA), covering co-operation in the following areas: conservation of biodiversity; sound management of energy; environmental legislation; and sustainable economic development. In June 2001 both sides signed a renewed and expanded CONCAUSA, now also covering co-operation in addressing climate change, and in disaster preparedness.

In June 2001 the heads of state and representatives of Belize, Costa, Rica, El Salvador, Guatemala, Honduras, Mexico, Nicaragua and Panama, meeting within the framework of the 'Tuxtla dialogue mechanism' (so-called after an agreement signed in 1991 between Mexico and Central American countries to strengthen co-ordination between the parties) agreed to activate a Puebla-Panamá Plan (PPP) to promote sustainable social and economic development in the region and to reinforce integration efforts among Central America and the southern states of Mexico (referred to as Mesoamerica). In June 2008 the 10th Tuxtla summit meeting, convened in Villahermosa, Mexico, agreed to establish the Mesoamerican Integration and Development Project to supersede the PPP. The new Project was to incorporate ongoing initiatives on highways and infrastructure and implement energy, electricity and information networks.

In 1997 a Mesoamerican Biological Corridor was inaugurated, with the aim of preserving sub-regional biodiversity, enhancing ecosystems and landscape connectivity, and promoting productive sustainable processes to improve local communities' quality of life.

Representatives of SICA and of Colombia, the Dominican Republic and Mexico adopted the Declaration of Romana in June 2006, wherein they agreed to implement the Mesoamerican Energy Integration Program, aimed at developing regional oil, electricity and natural gas markets, promoting the use of renewable energy, and increasing electricity generation and interconnection capacity across the region. In the following month, SICA member states approved the legal framework for the Central American Electrical Connection System (known as SIEPAC), which was to be co-funded by the Central American Bank for Economic Integration and the Inter-American Development Bank.

In November 2007 SICA heads of state endorsed a Sustainable Energy Strategy for Central America 2020. Its main areas of concern were access to energy by the least advantaged populations; the rational and efficient use of energy; renewable sources of energy; biofuels for the transport sector; and climate change. The SICA Secretary-General participates in the Supervisory Board of the Energy and Environment Partnership with Central America, which was established in 2002, and convenes regional sustainable energy fora (most recently in October 2013, in Panama), with the aim of promoting the use of renewable energy, and contributing to sustainable development and to the mitigation of the impacts of climate change.

SICA heads of state adopted, in December 2010, the Regional Strategy for Climate Change (ERCC), to accelerate efforts to reduce the region's vulnerability to natural disasters and the effects of climate change. At the third SICA-CARICOM meeting, held in San Salvador, El Salvador, in August 2011, heads of state welcomed an initiative by Panama to establish a Regional Humanitarian Logistic Assistance Centre to respond to emergency situations in the region within 24 to 48 hours. The meeting recognized the need to strengthen transport and cultural links and detailed measures to bolster co-operation in international environmental negotiations and disaster management. In December, at the summit meeting of SICA heads of state, environmental preservation and tackling natural disasters were central to the agenda, and members agreed to adopt the constitution of a Central American Fund for the Promotion of Integrated Risk Management to provide technical assistance and resources as needed. In June 2012 SICA heads of state and government approved a plan of action under which regional joint regional initiatives implemented within the framework of the ERCC were to be strengthened and multiplied.

HEALTH AND TOURISM

At the meeting of CACM heads of state in December 2002, the establishment of a new Central American Tourism Agency was announced. In July 2011 SICA heads of state declared 2012 to be the Central American Year of Sustainable Tourism.

In June 2008 the SICA summit meeting, convened in San Salvador, reiterated concerns regarding escalating petroleum and food prices, and welcomed several initiatives concerned with strengthening the region's food security. During the SICA-CARICOM heads of state meeting in El Salvador, in August 2011, it was agreed that the two organizations would collaborate on the early detection (and prevention) of non-communicable diseases. In February 2013 a meeting of the secretaries of SICA national focal points on food security and nutrition was convened, with the aim of developing a regional food security framework.

REGIONAL SECURITY

In March 2005 SICA ministers responsible for security, defence and the interior resolved to establish a special regional force to combat crime, drugs and arms trafficking and terrorism. In June 2008 SICA heads of state and government, convened in San Salvador, agreed to establish a peacekeeping operations unit within the secretariat in order to co-ordinate participation in international missions.

In June 2008 the US Congress approved US $65m. to fund a Central American initiative to counter drugs-trafficking and organized crime, as part of a larger agreement arranged with the Mexican Government (the so-called Mérida Initiative). The scheme was subsequently relaunched as the Central American Regional Security Initiative, with additional approved funds of some $100m. to provide equipment, training, and technical assistance to build the capacity of Central American institutions to counter crime. In February 2010, at a meeting of the Inter-American Development Bank (IDB), several countries and other multilateral organizations determined to establish a Group of Friends for Central American Security, in order to support the region to counter organized crime. In March 2011 the US President, Barack Obama, announced the establishment of a Central American Citizen Security Partnership to strengthen law enforcement and to provide young people with alternatives to organized crime.

In 2011 an Ad Hoc Regional Expert Task Force was established to help to elaborate a regional security strategy, in advance of an international conference, convened in Guatemala City, Guatemala, in June. At the International Conference in Support of the Regional Security Strategy for Central America and Mexico, the US Secretary of State committed US $300m. in support of security initiatives, including more specialized police units and a new SICA Regional Crime Observatory. Negotiations to formulate a Central American Security Strategy (Estrategia de Seguridad de Centroamérica—ESCA), based on 22 priority projects identified at the International

Conference, recommenced in September. ESCA's main activities were to incorporate combating crime and preventing violence, rehabilitation of offenders, prison management, and institutional strengthening. In February 2012 the IDB hosted a meeting of the SICA Security Commission and the so-called Group of Friends of the Central America Security Strategy to inaugurate an initial eight ESCA projects. A high-level debate on promoting and implementing the Security Strategy was conducted at the UN in New York, USA, in May. In February 2013 the Mexican President attended a meeting of SICA heads of state, convened in San Jose, to discuss joint efforts to counter organized crime in the region. The summit meeting determined to establish a specialized secretariat to focus on regional security issues. In April 2014 SICA signed a strategic agreement with the UN High Commissioner for Refugees to strengthen co-ordination in issues concerning the protection of forcibly displaced persons, enhancing national legal frameworks and disseminating international refugee legislation.

COMMON MARKET FOR EASTERN AND SOUTHERN AFRICA—COMESA

Address: COMESA Centre, Ben Bella Rd, POB 30051, 101101 Lusaka, Zambia.

Telephone: (1) 229725; **fax:** (1) 225107; **e-mail:** info@comesa.int; **internet:** www.comesa.int.

The COMESA treaty was signed by member states of the Preferential Trade Area for Eastern and Southern Africa (PTA) in November 1993. COMESA formally succeeded the PTA in December 1994. COMESA aims to strengthen regional economic and social development, with the ultimate aim of merging with the other regional economic communities of the African Union.

MEMBERS

Burundi	Malawi
Comoros	Mauritius
Congo, Democratic Republic	Rwanda
Djibouti	Seychelles
Egypt	South Sudan
Eritrea	Sudan
Ethiopia	Swaziland
Kenya	Uganda
Libya	Zambia
Madagascar	Zimbabwe

Organization

(April 2014)

AUTHORITY

The Authority of the Common Market is the supreme policy organ of COMESA, comprising heads of state or government of member countries. The inaugural meeting of the Authority took place in Lilongwe, Malawi, in December 1994. The 17th summit meeting was convened in February 2014, in Kinshasa, Democratic Republic of the Congo, on the theme 'Consolidating Intra-COMESA Trade through Micro, Small and Medium Enterprise Development'.

COUNCIL OF MINISTERS

Each member government appoints a minister to participate in the Council. The Council monitors COMESA activities, including supervision of the Secretariat, recommends policy direction and development, and reports to the Authority.

A Committee of Governors of Central Banks advises the Authority and the Council of Ministers on monetary and financial matters.

COURT OF JUSTICE

The sub-regional Court is vested with the authority to settle disputes between member states and to adjudicate on matters concerning the interpretation of the COMESA treaty. The Court is composed of seven judges, who serve terms of five years' duration. The Court was restructured in 2005 to comprise a First Instance division and an Appellate division.

President: NZAMBA KITONGA (Kenya).

SECRETARIAT

COMESA's Secretariat comprises the following divisions: Administration; Budget and finance; Gender and social affairs; Infrastructure development; Investment promotion; Private sector development; and Trade customs and monetary affairs. There are also units at the Secretariat dealing with legal and institutional affairs, and climate change.

Secretary-General: SINDISO NDEMA NWENGYA (Zimbabwe).

Activities

COMESA aims to promote economic and social progress, co-operation and integration, and eradicate poverty, in member states. A strategic plan, endorsed by the COMESA Authority at its 14th summit meeting convened in August 2010, governs COMESA's medium-term goals and activities during the period 2011–15, prioritizing integration; enhancing productive capacity for global competitiveness; infrastructure development; cross-cutting issues such as gender and social development, climate change, statistics, peace and security, knowledge-based capacity and human capital; co-operation and partnership; and institutional development. COMESA supports capacity building activities and the establishment of other specialized institutions.

From COMESA's establishment there were concerns on the part of member states, as well as other regional non-member countries, in particular South Africa, of adverse rivalry between COMESA and the Southern African Development Community (SADC) and of a duplication of roles. In 1997 Lesotho and Mozambique terminated their membership of COMESA owing to concerns that their continued participation in the organization was incompatible with their SADC membership. Tanzania withdrew from COMESA in September 2000, reportedly also in view of its dual commitment to that organization and to SADC. In June 2003 Namibia announced its withdrawal from COMESA. The summit meeting of COMESA heads of state or government held in May 2000 expressed support for an ongoing programme of co-operation by the Secretariats of COMESA and SADC aimed at reducing the duplication of roles between the two organizations, and urged further mutual collaboration. A co-ordinating task force was established in 2001, and was joined by the East African Community (EAC) in 2005, as the EAC became involved in the REC co-operation programme. The Regional Trade Facilitation Programme covering Southern and Eastern Africa, and based in Pretoria, South Africa, provides secretariat services to the Task Force.

TRADE, CUSTOMS AND MONETARY AFFAIRS

In May 1999 COMESA established a Free Trade Area (FTA) Committee to facilitate and co-ordinate preparations for the creation of the common market envisaged under the COMESA treaty. An extraordinary summit of COMESA heads of state or government, held in October 2000, inaugurated the FTA, with nine initial members: Djibouti, Egypt, Kenya, Madagascar, Malawi, Mauritius, Sudan, Zambia and Zimbabwe. Burundi and Rwanda became members of the FTA in January 2004, and Swaziland undertook in April to seek the concurrence of the Southern African Customs Union, of which it is also a member, to allow it to participate in the FTA. Trading practices within the FTA have been fully liberalized, including the elimination of non-tariff barriers, thereby enabling the free internal movement of goods, services and capital. In early 2014 it was reported that some 40% of intra-COMESA trade was generated through micro, small and medium-sized enterprises (MSMEs). Ethiopia and Uganda were expected to ratify instruments of accession to the FTA by end-2014. In May 2007 the Authority endorsed the establishment of an 'Aid for Trade' unit in the COMESA Secretariat, which was to assist countries with the identification and implementation of projects aimed at removing trade-related supply constraints. A COMESA Competition Commission, based in Blantyre, Malawi, was inaugurated in December 2008. The COMESA Customs Union (CU), with a common external tariff set at 0% for capital goods and raw materials, 10% for intermediate goods and 25% for finished products, was launched at the 13th annual summit meeting of the Authority, in June 2009. It was envisaged at that time that the CU would become fully operational after a transition period of three years; however, the 16th meeting of the Authority, in November 2012, determined to extend the transition period by a further two years. In February 2014 COMESA heads of state and government took note of a significant increase in intra-community trade to US $19,300m. in 2012. A Protocol establishing the COMESA Fund, which assists member states in addressing structural imbalances in their economies, came into effect in November 2006. COMESA plans to form an economic community (entailing monetary union and the free movement of people between member states) by 2018. In March 2011 a COMESA Monetary Institute was inaugurated, in Nairobi, Kenya, to enhance the implementation of a monetary co-operation programme, in support of an eventual monetary union. In January 2013 the African Development Bank published a study, *Facilitating Multilateral Fiscal Surveillance in the Monetary Union Context with Focus on the COMESA Region*, which outlined concrete proposals for the establishment of the planned monetary union. A regional payments and settlement system (REPSS), headquartered in Lusaka, Zambia, became operational in October 2012, and facilitates the swift, cost-efficient transfer of funds between traders in COMESA member states, through the pre-funding of commercial bank accounts held within, and guaranteed by, participating central banks.

In October 2008 the first tripartite COMESA-EAC-SADC summit was convened, in Kampala, Uganda, to discuss the harmonization of policy and programme work by the three regional communities. Leaders of the 26 countries attending the Kampala summit approved a roadmap towards the formation of a common FTA and the eventual establishment of a single African Economic Community (a long-term objective of African Union—AU—co-operation). A COMESA-EAC-SADC Joint Competition Authority was established at the tripartite summit. At the second tripartite summit, held in June 2011, in Johannesburg, South Africa, negotiations were initiated on the establishment of the proposed COMESA-EAC-SADC Tripartite FTA. In January 2012 AU leaders endorsed a new Framework, Roadmap and Architecture for Fast Tracking the Establishment of a Continental FTA (referred to as CFTA), and an Action Plan for Boosting Intra-African Trade, which planned for the consolidation of the COMESA-EAC-SADC Tripartite FTA with other regional FTAs into the CFTA initiative during 2015–16; and the establishment of an operational CFTA by 2017. COMESA has co-operated with other sub-regional organizations to finalize a common position on co-operation between African ACP countries and the European Union (EU) under the Cotonou Agreement (concluded in June 2000, see the chapter on the EU). The COMESA Customs Bond Guarantee Scheme facilitate the movement of goods through the region, and provides the necessary customs security and guarantee to transit countries.

In June 2013 a pilot version of a new COMESA Virtual Trade Facilitation System (CVTFS) was launched to cover routes from Mombasa, Kenya to the Democratic Republic of the Congo (DRC), Rwanda and Uganda, and in August the CVTFS pilot was extended to cover the Djibouti–Addis Ababa, Ethiopia–Khartoum,Sudan–Juba, South Sudan trade corridor; preparations are under way to extend the CVTFS further, across the Malawi–Zambia–Zimbabwe trade corridor.

In August 2013 the Court ruled that Mauritius had breached the terms of the COMESA treaty by imposing a customs duty, relating to imports of car paint from Egypt, during the period November 2001–November 2010; the Mauritius Government was ordered to refund the duties that it had levied.

In February 2014 COMESA heads of state and government held a round table discussion on using natural resources as an anchor for economic transformation.

AGRICULTURE

A regional food security programme aims to ensure continuous adequate food supplies. COMESA works with private sector interests through the AU Comprehensive African Agricultural Development Programme (CAADP) to improve agricultural performance. The CAADP undertook efforts in 2008 to strengthen regional capacity to address food insecurity, promoting robust markets and long-term competitiveness. COMESA maintains a Food and Agricultural Marketing Information System (FAMIS), providing up-to-date data on the sub-regional food security situation. The organization supports the establishment of common agricultural standards and phytosanitary regulations throughout the region in order to stimulate trade in food crops. In March 2005 more than 100 standards on quality assurance, covering mainly agricultural products, were adopted. Meeting for the first time in November 2002, COMESA ministers responsible for agriculture determined to formulate a regional policy on genetically modified organisms. At their second meeting, held in October 2004, ministers agreed to prioritize agriculture in their development efforts, and—in accordance with a Declaration of the AU—the objective of allocating at least 10% of national budgets to agriculture and rural development. In September 2008 COMESA ministers responsible for agriculture launched the Alliance for Commodity Trade in Eastern and Southern Africa (ACTESA), with the aim of integrating small farmers into national, regional and international markets. ACTESA became a specialized agency of COMESA in June 2009. In March 2010 COMESA and ACTESA signed an agreement aimed at accelerating the implementation of regional initiatives in agriculture, trade and investment. In 2014 COMESA member states were harmonizing policies aimed at combating aflatoxin contamination of grain crops in the region.

CLIMATE CHANGE ADAPTATION AND ENVIRONMENT

Following a recommendation by the AU, in January 2007, that climate change adaptation strategies should be integrated into African national and sub-regional development planning and activities, COMESA launched a Climate Change Initiative, which aims to improve economic and social resilience to the impacts of climate change. In July 2010 COMESA, the EAC and SADC adopted a five-year Tripartite Programme on Climate Change Adaptation and Mitigation in the COMESA-EAC-SADC region. A tripartite agreement for the implementation of the Programme was signed by the three parties in July 2012. In June 2013 COMESA initiated baseline data collection activities under the Programme in 10 regional pilot countries.

In June 2010 a consultative meeting was convened between COMESA, the AU, the Intergovernmental Authority on Development (IGAD), and other regional partners, aimed at advancing co-ordination and harmonization of their activities related to the environment.

INVESTMENT PROMOTION AND PRIVATE SECTOR DEVELOPMENT

The COMESA Regional Investment Agency, based in Cairo, Egypt, was inaugurated in June 2006, its founding charter having been adopted in June 2005 by the 10th summit meeting of the Authority. An Agreement on the establishment of a COMESA Common Investment Area (CCIA) was adopted by the Authority at its May 2007 summit meeting.

In February 2000 a COMESA economic forum was convened in Cairo. A COMESA Business Council was inaugurated in 2003, with a mandate to provide a policy and advocacy platform for regional private sector interests. The ninth COMESA Business Partnerships Forum and Linkages Fair was organized in February 2014, in Kinshasa, DRC, on the sidelines of the 17th summit of the Authority. The COMESA RIA sponsors an annual investment forum, and in May 2013 organized the first Africa Global Business Forum in Dubai, United Arab Emirates, jointly with the Dubai Chamber of Commerce and Industry. In August 2012 the COMESA Business Council, together with the Kenyan authorities, organized the first COMESA Sustainable Tourism Development Forum, on the theme 'Shaping the Future of Tourism in COMESA'. In February 2014 COMESA heads of state and government adopted a new COMESA MSME Strategy, and urged member states to support the participation of female entrepreneurs in policy making roles. A new COMESA Women Economic Empowerment Fund was under development in 2014.

In June 2012 COMESA the first meeting of COMESA ministers responsible for science, technology and innovation decided to establish an Innovation Council, which was to adopt knowledge practices from around the world to assist member states in the research and development of information technology. Members of the Innovation Council were appointed at the 16th meeting of heads of state and government, in November, which also endorsed the establishment of an Innovation Fund and an annual Innovation Award. The Innovation Council was formally inaugurated in April 2013.

In February 2014 COMESA heads of state and government tasked the Secretariat with drafting, by June, a regional common industrialization policy.

INFRASTRUCTURE DEVELOPMENT

In March 2012 COMESA announced that it aimed to raise US $1,000m. in funding for a new COMESA Infrastructure Fund, which was to support trade-related infrastructure projects in the region. In March 2014 the management of the Fund was transferred to the Eastern and Southern Africa Trade and Development Bank.

An Eastern Africa Power Pool (EAPP) has been established by COMESA, comprising Burundi, the DRC, Djibouti, Ethiopia, Kenya, Sudan, Tanzania and Uganda. COMESA and SADC have the joint objective of eventually linking the EAPP and the Southern Africa Power Pool. COMESA maintains a priority list of regional infrastructure projects, and, in 2008, launched an interactive database recording the status of the projects. In March 2009 a new Regional Association of Energy Regulators for Eastern and Southern Africa was launched.

A COMESA Telecommunications Company (COMTEL) was registered in May 2000. In January 2003 the Association of Regulators of Information and Communication for Eastern and Southern Africa was launched, under the auspices of COMESA. COMESA is developing a regional e-Government programme to provide for the greater dissemination of government information through, for example, the internet, mobile telephones and radios. It was envisaged that e-Government activities would promote civic engagement and make government operations more transparent and accountable.

Organization-wide initiatives to facilitate travel in the region include a scheme for third-party motor vehicle insurance, a road customs declaration document, and a system of regional traveller's cheques.

GENDER AND SOCIAL AFFAIRS

A new Gender and Social Affairs division of the COMESA Secretariat was established in 2008, with the aim of facilitating increased involvement by COMESA in areas related to social development, including health, education, youth affairs, and migration and labour. A COMESA Social Charter is being drafted, with the aiming of incorporating social dimensions into the regional integration agenda, through the identification of economic- and social rights-related benchmarks. The planned Charter was to provide a regional platform for the promotion of the AU Commission's 2008 pan-African Social Development Framework (q.v.); and was to help guide the formulation of member states' national development strategies.

REGIONAL SECURITY

In May 1999 the COMESA Authority resolved to establish a Committee on Peace and Security comprising ministers responsible for foreign affairs from member states. It was envisaged that the Committee would convene at least once a year to address matters concerning regional stability. (Instability in certain member states was regarded as a potential threat to the successful implementation of the FTA.) The Committee met for the first time in 2000. It was announced in September 2002 that the COMESA Treaty was to be amended to provide for the establishment of a formal conflict prevention and resolution structure to be governed by member countries' heads of state. COMESA participates, with other regional economic communities in the AU's Continental Early Warning System, and has, since 2008, taken part in joint technical meetings and training sessions in this respect. In June 2009 COMESA inaugurated the regional COMWARN early warning system, which was to monitor indicators of vulnerability to conflict in member states. The seventh meeting of the Committee, held in November 2006, recommended the establishment of a COMESA Committee of Elders, which was to undertake preventive peacebuilding assignments; the Committee of Elders held its inaugural meeting in December 2011. In November 2013 COMESA ministers responsible for justice adopted rules of procedure for the Committee of Elders, aimed at guiding its peacebuilding activities.

COMESA deploys teams of observers to monitor elections held in member states. In July 2013 representatives of Election Management Bodies (EMBs) in COMESA member states met to consider the establishment of a COMESA EMBs Forum. A joint COMESA-EAC-IGAD observer mission was dispatched to monitor a general election that took place in Kenya in March of that year. In July a COMESA observer mission was sent to monitor a harmonized general election in Zimbabwe, and, in September, observer teams were also dispatched to observe legislative elections held in Rwanda and in Swaziland.

Finance

COMESA is financed by member states.

Publications

Annual Report of the Council of Ministers.

Asycuda Newsletter.

COMESA Journal.

COMESA Trade Directory (annually).

COMESA Trade Information Newsletter (monthly).

e-COMESA (monthly newsletter).

Demand/supply surveys, catalogues and reports.

COMESA Institutions

African Trade Insurance Agency (ATI): POB 10620, 00100-GPO, Nairobi, Kenya; tel. (20) 27269999; fax (20) 2719701; e-mail info@ati-aca.org; internet www.ati-aca.org; f. 2001 to promote trade and investment activities throughout the region; mems: 13 African countries; CEO GEORGE ODUORI OTIENO.

Alliance for Commodity Trade in Eastern and Southern Africa (ACTESA): Corporate Park, Alick Nkhata Rd, Lusaka, 10101 Zambia; tel. 211-253572; e-mail info@actesacomesa.org; internet www.actesacomesa.org; f. 2008, became a specialized agency of COMESA in June 2009; aims to integrate small farmers into national, regional and international markets; CEO Dr ARGENT CHUULA (Zambia).

COMESA Business Council: COMESA Centre, Ben Bella Rd, POB 30051, 101101 Lusaka, Zambia; e-mail info@comesabusinesscouncil.org; internet www.comesabusinesscouncil.org; f. 2003 as a private sector policy and advocacy platform; aims to influence policy at the highest level of decision-making within the COMESA region; Chair. Dr AMANY ASFOUR (Egypt).

COMESA Leather and Leather Products Institute (LLPI): POB 2358, 1110 Addis Ababa, Ethiopia; tel. (11) 4390928; fax (11) 4390900; e-mail comesa.llpi@ethionet.et; internet www.comesa-llpi.org/index.php; f. 1990 as the PTA Leather Institute; mems: 17 COMESA mem. states; Chair. Dr M. CHARLES MOTURI; Dir Dr MWINYIKIONE MWINYIHIJA.

COMESA Regional Investment Authority (COMESA-RIA): 3 Salah Salem Rd, Nasr City, Cairo, Egypt; tel. (2) 405-5428; fax (2) 405-5421; e-mail info@comesaria.org; internet www.comesaria.org; Chair. CHALIMBA PHIRI; Man. HEBA SALAMA.

Compagnie de réassurance de la Zone d'échanges préférentiels (ZEP-RE) (PTA Reinsurance Co): ZEP-RE Place, Longonot Rd, Upper Hill, POB 42769, 00100 Nairobi, Kenya; tel. (20) 2738221; fax (20) 2738444; e-mail mail@zep-re.com; internet www.zep-re.com; f. 1992 (began operations on 1 Jan. 1993); provides local reinsurance services and training to personnel in the insurance industry; total assets US $154.1m. (2012); Chair. WILLIAM ERIO; Man. Dir RAJNI VARIA.

East African Power Pool (EAPP): Bole Sub City, Gulz Aziz Bldg, Addis Ababa Ethiopia; tel. (11) 6183694; fax (11) 6183694; e-mail eapp@eappool.org; internet www.eappool.org/eng/about.html; in Feb. 2005 energy ministers from Burundi, DRC, Egypt, Ethiopia, Kenya, Rwanda and Sudan signed the Inter-Governmental Memorandum of Understanding on the establishment of the Eastern Africa Power Pool (EAPP); EAPP was adopted by COMESA as a specialized institution in 2006; Tanzania and Libya joined in 2010 and 2011, respectively; Exec. Sec. JASPER ODUOR.

Eastern and Southern African Trade and Development Bank: NSSF Bldg, 22nd/23rd Floor, Bishop's Rd, POB 48596, 00100 Nairobi, Kenya; tel. (20) 2712250; fax (20) 2711510; e-mail official@ptabank.org; internet www.ptabank.org; f. 1983 as PTA Development Bank; aims to mobilize resources and finance COMESA activities to foster regional integration; promotes investment and co-financing within the region; in March 2014 assumed responsibility for managing the COMESA Infrastructure Fund; in Jan. 2003 the US dollar replaced the UAPTA (PTA unit of account) as the Bank's reporting currency; shareholders: 15 COMESA mem. states, the People's Republic of China, Somalia, Tanzania and the African Development Bank; auth. cap. US $3,000m. (April 2014); Pres. and CEO TADESSE ADMASSU (Ethiopia).

Federation of National Associations of Women in Business in Eastern and Southern Africa (FEMCOM): Off Queens Drive, Area 6, Plot No. 170, POB 1499, Lilongwe, Malawi; tel. (1) 205-908; e-mail info@femcomcomesa.org; internet www.femcomcomesa.org; f. 1993; autonomous secretariat launched in 2009; aims to promote programmes that integrate women into regional trade and development activities, with a particular focus on the areas of agriculture, fishing, energy, communications, industry, mining, natural resources, trade, services, and transport; has chapters in all COMESA mem. states; Exec. Dir KATHERINE NYANGUI ICHOYA.

THE COMMONWEALTH

Address: Commonwealth Secretariat, Marlborough House, Pall Mall, London, SW1Y 5HX, United Kingdom.

Telephone: (20) 7747-6500; **fax:** (20) 7930-0827; **e-mail:** info@commonwealth.int; **internet:** www.thecommonwealth.org.

The Commonwealth is a voluntary association of independent sovereign states, comprising about one-quarter of the world's population, linked by a common history and values, and by concern for the vulnerable.

The Commonwealth Secretariat, established by Commonwealth Heads of Government in 1965, operates as an intergovernmental organization at the service of all Commonwealth countries.

MEMBERS*

Antigua and Barbuda	Kiribati	Samoa
Australia	Lesotho	Seychelles
Bahamas	Malawi	Sierra Leone
Bangladesh	Malaysia	Singapore
Barbados	Maldives	Solomon Islands
Belize	Malta	South Africa
Botswana	Mauritius	Sri Lanka
Brunei	Mozambique	Swaziland
Cameroon	Namibia	Tanzania
Canada	Nauru	Tonga
Cyprus	New Zealand	Trinidad and Tobago
Dominica	Nigeria	Tuvalu
Ghana	Pakistan	Uganda
Grenada	Papua New Guinea	United Kingdom
Guyana	Rwanda	Vanuatu
India	Saint Christopher and Nevis	Zambia
Jamaica	Saint Vincent and the Grenadines	
Kenya		

* Ireland, South Africa and Pakistan withdrew from the Commonwealth in 1949, 1961 and 1972, respectively. In October 1987 Fiji's membership was declared to have lapsed (following the proclamation of a republic there). It was readmitted in October 1997, but was suspended from participation in meetings of the Commonwealth in June 2000. Fiji was formally readmitted to Commonwealth meetings in December 2001 following legislative elections in August–September. However, following a further military coup in December 2006, Fiji was once again suspended from participation in meetings, and, in September 2009, was fully suspended. In March 2014 Fiji's suspension reverted to a ban on participation in meetings. Pakistan rejoined the Commonwealth in October 1989. However, it was suspended from participation in meetings during the periods October 1999–May 2004 and November 2007–May 2008. South Africa rejoined in June 1994. Nigeria's membership was suspended in November 1995; it formally resumed membership in May 1999, when a new civilian government was inaugurated. In 1995 Mozambique became a member, the first to have no historical or administrative connection with another Commonwealth country. Tuvalu, previously a special member of the Commonwealth with the right to participate in all activities except full Meetings of Heads of Government, became a full member in September 2000. In March 2002 Zimbabwe was suspended from participation in meetings of the Commonwealth. Zimbabwe announced its withdrawal from the Commonwealth in December 2003. Rwanda was admitted to membership of the Commonwealth in November 2009. In June 2011 Nauru was reinstated as a full member of the Commonwealth, having been classed as a 'member in arrears' from 2003. The Gambia withdrew from the Commonwealth in October 2013. Possible future membership for South Sudan, which attained independence in July 2011, is under consideration.

Australian External Territories

Ashmore and Cartier Islands	Coral Sea Islands Territory
Australian Antarctic Territory	Heard Island and the McDonald Islands
Christmas Island	Norfolk Island
Cocos (Keeling) Islands	

New Zealand Dependent and Associated Territories

Cook Islands	Ross Dependency
Niue	Tokelau

United Kingdom Overseas Territories

Anguilla	Gibraltar
Bermuda	Isle of Man
British Antarctic Territory	Montserrat
British Indian Ocean Territory	Pitcairn Islands
British Virgin Islands	Saint Helena, Ascension, Tristan da Cunha
Cayman Islands	South Sandwich Islands
Channel Islands	Turks and Caicos Islands
Falkland Islands	

HEADS OF STATE AND HEADS OF GOVERNMENT

All Commonwealth countries accept Queen Elizabeth II as the symbol of the free association of the independent member nations and as such the Head of the Commonwealth. Some 33 member states are republics. In 21 of those the offices of Head of State and Head of Government are combined: Botswana, Cameroon, Cyprus, Ghana, Guyana, Kenya, Kiribati, Malawi, the Maldives, Mozambique, Namibia, Nauru, Nigeria, Rwanda, Seychelles, Sierra Leone, South Africa, Sri Lanka, Tanzania, Uganda and Zambia. The two offices are separated in the remaining 11: Bangladesh, Dominica, Fiji, India, Malta, Mauritius, Pakistan, Samoa, Singapore, Trinidad and Tobago and Vanuatu.

Of the monarchies, the Queen is Head of State of the United Kingdom and of 15 others, in each of which she is represented by a Governor-General: Antigua and Barbuda, Australia, the Bahamas, Barbados, Belize, Canada, Grenada, Jamaica, New Zealand, Papua New Guinea, Saint Christopher and Nevis, Saint Lucia, Saint Vincent and the Grenadines, Solomon Islands and Tuvalu. Brunei, Lesotho, Malaysia, Swaziland and Tonga are also monarchies, where the traditional monarch is Head of State.

HIGH COMMISSIONERS

Governments of member countries are represented in other Commonwealth countries by High Commissioners, who have a status equivalent to that of Ambassadors.

Organization

(April 2014)

The Commonwealth is not a federation: there is no central government nor are there any rigid contractual obligations such as bind members of the UN. In December 2012 Commonwealth heads of government adopted a non-binding Charter of the Commonwealth, and, in March 2013, it was signed by Queen Elizabeth II and launched throughout the Commonwealth.

MEETINGS OF HEADS OF GOVERNMENT

Commonwealth Heads of Government Meetings (CHOGMs) are private and informal and operate by consensus. The emphasis is on consultation and exchange of views for co-operation. A communiqué is issued at the end of every meeting. Meetings are normally held every two years in different capitals in the Commonwealth. The 2013 meeting was held in November, in Colombo, Sri Lanka; Malta was to host the 2015 meeting.

OTHER CONSULTATIONS

The Commonwealth Ministerial Action Group on the Harare Declaration was formed in 1995 to support democracy in member countries. It comprises a group of nine ministers responsible for foreign affairs, with rotating membership.

Commonwealth ministers responsible for finance meet in the week prior to the annual meetings of the IMF and the World Bank. Ministers responsible for civil society, education, the environment, foreign affairs, gender issues, health, law, tourism and youth also hold regular meetings.

Biennial conferences of representatives of Commonwealth small states are convened.

Senior officials—cabinet secretaries, permanent secretaries to Heads of Government and others—meet regularly in the year between meetings of Heads of Government to provide continuity and to exchange views on various developments.

COMMONWEALTH SECRETARIAT

The Secretariat organizes consultations between governments and runs programmes of co-operation. Meetings of Heads of Government, ministers and senior officials decide these programmes and provide overall direction. A Board of Governors, on which all eligible member governments are represented, meets annually to review the Secretariat's work and approve its budget. The Board is supported by an Executive Committee which convenes four times a year to monitor implementation of the Secretariat's work programme. The Secretariat is led by a Secretary-General, elected by Heads of Government. The Secretariat has observer status at the UN.

The Secretariat's divisional structure is as follows: Legal and constitutional affairs; Political affairs; Corporate services; Communications and public affairs; Strategic planning and evaluation; Economic affairs; Governance and institutional development; Social transformation programmes; Gender affairs; Youth affairs; and Special advisory services. In addition there are units responsible for human rights; and for technical co-operation and strategic response; and an Office of the Secretary-General.

Secretary-General: KAMALESH SHARMA (India).

Deputy Secretaries-General: MMASEKGOA MASIRE-MWAMBA (Botswana) (Political, Legal and Constitutional and Youth Affairs, and Human Rights)), DEODAT MAHARAJ (Trinidad and Tobago) (Economic Affairs, Trade and Debt, Social Development, and Public Sector Governance), GARY DUNN (Australia) (Corporate Affairs) (from mid-May 2014).

Activities

In July 2010, in view of a decision of the 2009 summit meeting of Commonwealth Heads of Government meeting, a Commonwealth Eminent Persons Group was inaugurated, with a mandate to make recommendations on means of strengthening the organization. The summit of Heads of Government held in Perth, Australia, in October 2011, agreed that a Charter of the Commonwealth, proposed by the Eminent Persons Group, embodying the principles contained in previous summit declarations, should be drafted, in consultation with member governments and civil society organizations; the new Commonwealth Charter was adopted by Heads of Government in December 2012, and signed by the Head of the Commonwealth, Queen Elizabeth II, in March 2013.

The November 2013 summit of Commonwealth Heads of Government was noted for the representation by only 27 Heads of State or Government of the 50 member countries that attended, owing to concerns regarding the human rights record of the Sri Lankan authorities hosting the meeting.

STRATEGIC PLAN

A Strategic Plan to guide the Secretariat during 2013/14–2016/17, and aimed at creating a more dynamic contemporary organization, in line with the newly adopted Commonwealth Charter, was endorsed by Commonwealth Heads of Government in November 2013. The Plan takes into consideration the following three longer term objectives: strong democracy, rule of law, promotion and protection of human rights, and respect for diversity; inclusive growth and sustainable development; and maintaining a well-connected and networked Commonwealth; and focuses on six strategic outcomes:

i. Democracy: greater adherence to Commonwealth political values and principles;

ii. Public institutions: more effective, efficient and equitable public governance;

iii. Social development: enhanced positive impact of social development;

iv. Youth: enhanced integration of, and appreciation of the value of, youth in political and developmental processes;

v. Development (pan-Commonwealth): more effective frameworks for inclusive economic growth and social and sustainable development;

vi. Development (small states and vulnerable states): strengthened resilience.

The Plan—which is underpinned by a Strategic Results Framework comprising intermediate outcomes and indicators—provides for a reduction in the scope of activities undertaken by the Secretariat; increased use of information and communication technologies; the promotion of strategic partnerships; enhanced collaboration between member states; and, where appropriate, the promotion of external assistance.

PROMOTING PEACE, DEMOCRACY AND CONSENSUS BUILDING

The Commonwealth Secretariat's Political Affairs Division, together with the Office of the Secretary-General, and assisted by the divisions on Legal and Constitutional Affairs, Governance and Institutional Development, and Communications and Public Affairs, as well as the Human Rights Unit, delivers the organization's work in promoting peace, democracy and consensus building. The Commonwealth promotes best practice, issues publications and organizes workshops and conferences aimed at strengthening democratic values, and provides, upon request, technical assistance in member states.

Through his good offices the Commonwealth Secretary-General works at promoting political dialogue in member states, fostering greater democratic space for political and civil actors, and strengthening institutions. The Secretary-General's good offices may involve discreet 'behind the scenes' diplomacy, sometimes conducted by Special Envoys, to prevent or resolve conflict and assist other international efforts to promote political stability. Advisers may be appointed in support of the organization's long-term promotion of democracy.

The Commonwealth, often working alongside observation teams from regional organizations, monitors the preparations for and conduct of parliamentary, presidential or other elections in member countries at the request of national election management bodies or governments. Furthermore, it offers peer support to enhance the functioning of the electoral process, and assists with the strengthening of institutions between elections. In May 2010 a Commonwealth Network of National Election Management Bodies was inaugurated; the Network aims to enhance collaboration among institutions and to promote good practice in election management. Meetings convened under the auspices of the Network during 2011–13 addressed issues including voter education and registration, electoral participation, independence of election management bodies, and campaign financing. A Junior Election Professionals Initiative was launched in June 2013, under the direction of the Network, with a view to strengthening democratic culture in member states and building national electoral administration capacity.

In 2013 Commonwealth Observer Groups were dispatched to monitor a general election in Kenya (in March); legislative elections in Pakistan (in May); and a presidential election held in the Maldives, legislative elections in Rwanda, a general election in Swaziland, and provincial elections in northern Sri Lanka (all in September). A Group was sent to observe parliamentary elections that were held in the Maldives, in March 2014.

In November 1995 Commonwealth Heads of Government, convened in New Zealand, formulated and adopted the Millbrook Commonwealth Action Programme on the Harare Declaration, to promote adherence by member countries to the fundamental principles of democracy and human rights (as proclaimed in the Harare Declaration, adopted in October 1991). The Programme incorporated a framework of measures to be pursued in support of democratic processes and institutions, and actions to be taken in response to violations of the Harare Declaration principles, in particular the unlawful removal of a democratically elected government. A Commonwealth Ministerial Action Group on the Harare Declaration (CMAG) was established in December 1995 to implement this process. In March 2002 Commonwealth leaders expanded CMAG's mandate to enable it to consider action against serious violations of the Commonwealth's core values perpetrated by elected administrations as well as by military regimes. In October 2011 the Perth CHOGM agreed a series of reforms aimed at strengthening further the role of CMAG in addressing serious violations of Commonwealth political values; these included clearer guidelines and time frames for engagement when the situation in a country causes concern, with a view to shifting from a reactive to a more proactive role. The unjustified postponement of elections, systematic violation of human rights, abrogation of constitutions, undermining of the rule of law and independence of the judiciary, suppression of media freedoms, and closing of the national political space were specified as events that might cause investigation by CMAG.

In November 2013 Heads of Government reconstituted CMAG's membership to comprise over the next biennium the ministers responsible for foreign affairs of Cyprus, Guyana, India, New Zealand, Pakistan, Sierra Leone, Solomon Islands, Sri Lanka (ex officio as Chair in Office) and Tanzania.

In February 2012 CMAG placed the Maldives on its formal agenda, having considered a report from a Commonwealth ministerial mission that reviewed an allegedly forced transfer of presidential power, in early February, between former President Mohamed Nasheed and the incumbent President Mohamed Waheed Hassan Manik. CMAG urged the initiation of immediate dialogue between the two sides, with a view to setting a date for early elections, and welcomed the appointment of a Special Envoy of the Commonwealth Secretary-General to address the situation in the Maldives. (Sir Donald McKinnon, who had been Secretary-General of the Commonwealth during 2000–08, assumed the role of Special Envoy on 1 March 2012.) CMAG also placed in abeyance the Maldives' ongoing Group membership, owing to its inclusion on the Group's formal agenda. In June the Group welcomed a commitment made in May by the Maldives authorities towards strengthening, and making more representative, a Commission of National Inquiry mandated to investigate the February events; the reformed Commission was relaunched in mid-June, with the support of the good offices of the Commonwealth

Special Envoy. In late August the Commission released a report which concluded that Nasheed had resigned voluntarily from the presidency, and which therefore found the transfer of power to President Waheed to have occurred legitimately, while also stating that certain acts of police brutality had occurred during the transfer period, and that these required further investigation. The Commonwealth Secretary-General welcomed the report, finding the inquiry to have been conducted in an objective and credible manner. The Commonwealth was to continue supporting the strengthening of democratic institutions, processes and dialogue in the Maldives. Meeting in late September CMAG determined to reinstate the Maldives as a member of the Group and to remove that country from its formal agenda, placing it henceforth in the 'Matters of Interest to CMAG' section. In November 2013 CMAG, noting the successful conduct of a first round presidential election followed by a delay in the second round poll in breach of a constitutional deadline, placed the Maldives back on its formal agenda pending the credible conclusion of the electoral process and inauguration of a new president. This was achieved a few days later, when, accordingly, CMAG removed the Maldives from its agenda.

In December 2006, following the overthrow of the Fijian Government by the military, an extraordinary meeting of CMAG determined that Fiji should be suspended from meetings of the Commonwealth, pending the reinstatement of democratic governance. In April 2009 the Commonwealth Secretary-General condemned the unconstitutional conduct of the Fijian authorities in abrogating the Constitution, dismissing the judiciary and announcing that democratic elections were to be postponed to 2014, following a judgment by Fiji's Court of Appeal declaring the appointment of the current interim government to be unlawful and urging the prompt restoration of democracy. Meeting at the end of July 2009, CMAG demanded that the Fijian regime reactivate by 1 September the Commonwealth- and UN-mediated political dialogue process, leading to the staging of elections no later than October 2010. At the beginning of September 2009 the Commonwealth Secretary-General announced that the Fijian regime had not acted to meet CMAG's demands and that Fiji's Commonwealth membership was consequently fully suspended with immediate effect. In April 2012 CMAG welcomed an announcement by the Fiji Government that a constitutional consultation process would be undertaken leading to the staging, by September 2014, of national elections; CMAG reaffirmed the willingness of the Commonwealth to provide technical assistance in support of constitutional consultations and election preparations. Meeting in September 2012 CMAG welcomed the completion of the first phase of voter registration for the 2014 elections, and also the commencement of the constitutional consultation process, while urging the Fiji authorities to address continuing restrictions on human rights and the rule of law. In April 2013, however, CMAG expressed regret over deviation by the Fiji Government from the agreed constitutional process, and encouraged the authorities to ensure that steps be taken towards restoring constitutional democracy. Meeting in March 2014 CMAG welcomed the progress made in Fiji towards holding the elections scheduled for September, including the promulgation of a new constitution; the establishment of an independent Electoral Commission; the enrolment of more than 540,000 voters; and the commencement of a dialogue between the Commission and political stakeholders. The Group determined that Fiji's hitherto full suspension from the Commonwealth should—pending the restoration of full democracy—be reduced to a suspension from the meetings of the councils of the organization, thereby enabling Fiji to participate in activities such as the Commonwealth Games.

RULE OF LAW

The Commonwealth Secretariat works to strengthen the rule of law underpinning strong and accountable democratic governance in member states. The Legal and Constitutional Affairs Division offers assistance with legislative drafting; with the placement and training of judges and other legal experts; with the training of prosecutors and police; and in the provision of judicial education. The Division also promotes and facilitates co-operation and the exchange of information among member governments on legal matters, and assists in combating corruption and financial and organized crime, in particular transborder criminal activities. The Division organizes the triennial meeting of ministers, Attorneys-General and senior ministry officials concerned with the legal systems in Commonwealth countries. It has also implemented schemes for co-operation on extradition, the protection of material cultural heritage, mutual assistance in criminal matters and the transfer of convicted offenders within the Commonwealth. It liaises with the Commonwealth Magistrates' and Judges' Association, the Commonwealth Legal Education Association, the Commonwealth Lawyers' Association (with which it helps to prepare the triennial Commonwealth Law Conference for the practising profession), the Commonwealth Association of Legislative Counsel, and with other international non-governmental organizations (NGOs). The Division provides in-house legal advice for the Secretariat.

HUMAN RIGHTS

The Commonwealth's human rights programme is managed by the Secretariat's Human Rights Unit. The Unit provides technical assistance towards the establishment and capacity building of national human rights institutions in member states; facilitates the exchange of best practice on human rights matters; and raises awareness and promotes human rights education. It also strengthens the capacities of member states to participate in the UN's Universal Periodic Review (which assesses, cyclically, the human rights situation in all UN member states).

In May 2013 the Human Rights Unit convened a Commonwealth Roundtable on Reconciliation, aimed at enhancing awareness and promoting exchanges of best practice with regard to transitional justice and reconciliation. and with participation by representatives of Government, civil society organizations and national human rights institutions from Kenya, Rwanda, Sierra Leone, South Africa, Sri Lanka, Uganda and the United Kingdom. The Unit organizes an annual Commonwealth Forum of National Human Rights Institutions (the 2014 meeting was held in March, in Geneva, Switzerland).

GOVERNANCE AND PUBLIC SECTOR DEVELOPMENT

The Commonwealth Secretariat's Governance and Institutional Development Division provides support to member states in strengthening the so-called political administrative interface between elected politicians and senior public officials. The Secretariat offers advice, training and other expertise in order to build capacity in the national public institutions of member states, and promotes the effective use of information and communication technologies in governance and public sector development. The Secretariat convenes post-election victory retreats, with participation by ministers and senior government officials, aimed at promoting good governance through the promotion of confidential discussions and experience sharing. The Commonwealth promotes the development of local government and fiscal decentralization in member states. A Commonwealth Cybercrime Initiative, launched by Commonwealth Heads of Government in October 2011, aims to ensure that member countries have appropriate legal frameworks in place to combat cybercrime. A Commonwealth Conference on Public Administration in Very Small States was convened in April 2013.

An Association of Anti-Corruption Agencies in Commonwealth Africa was established in 2011; in February 2013, under the auspices of the Association, an Africa Anti-Corruption Centre was established in Gaborone, Botswana.

ECONOMIC DEVELOPMENT

The Commonwealth's Economic Development Programme is managed by the Economic Affairs Division and Special Advisory Services Division, with—as a priority focus is the empowerment of women and young people—support from the Gender Affairs Section and the Youth Affairs Division. The Economic Affairs Division organizes and services the annual meetings of Commonwealth ministers responsible for finance and the ministerial group on small states (accounting for 32 of the Commonwealth member states) and assists in servicing the biennial meetings of Heads of Government. It engages in research and analysis on economic issues of interest to member governments and organizes seminars and conferences of government officials and experts.

The Commonwealth has consistently urged improved responsiveness by some international organizations mandated to promote economic stability, and has promoted greater representation for developing countries in international economic decision-making, with particular reference to the IMF and the World Bank. In June 2008 Commonwealth Heads of Government expressed concern that many Commonwealth countries were failing to meet the Millennium Development Goal (MDG) targets, and resolved to strengthen existing networks of co-operation: in particular, they undertook to take measures to improve the quality of data used in policy-making, and to strengthen the links between research and policy-making. A Commonwealth Partnership Platform Portal was established to provide practical support for sharing ideas and best practices.

The Secretariat advises member states on the development of sound debt management policies and strategies. Through its Debt Recording and Management System (DRMS)—an integrated debt recording, monitoring and analysing tool, which was first used in 1985, and updated in 2002—it aims to assist both member and non-member countries in managing sovereign debt; by 2014 the DRMS had been used by 61 states. The DRMS is complemented by 'Horizon', a software tool that assists member states in undertaking prudent sovereign debt management; and by the Securities Auctioning System (CS-SAS), which was initiated in 2008 to support institutions involved in securities auctions to manage all phases of that process.

The Economic Affairs Division actively supports developing Commonwealth countries to participate in the multilateral trading system, including in World Trade Organization (WTO) negotiations, and promotes policy discourse on issues related to the WTO's Aid for Trade initiative. In July 2013 it issued a comprehensive review entitled 'Aid For Trade: Effectiveness, Current Issues and Future Directions'. Active engagement within the G20 Development Working Group is also pursued, to promote the concerns of small and vulnerable states. The Division is assisting the ACP group of countries to negotiate economic partnership agreements with the European Union (EU). It supports developing countries in strengthening their links with international capital markets and foreign investors, and services groups of experts on economic affairs that have been commissioned by governments to report on, among other things, protectionism; obstacles to the North-South negotiating process; reform of the international financial and trading system; the debt crisis; management of technological change; the impact of change on the development process; environmental issues; women and structural adjustment; and youth unemployment.

The Economic Affairs Division addresses the specific needs of, and provides technical assistance to, small states, with a focus on trade, vulnerability, environment, politics and economics. In June 2010 the first Commonwealth Biennial Small States Conference was convened, in London, comprising representatives of small states from the Africa, Asia-Pacific and Caribbean regions. In January 2011 a new Commonwealth Small States Office was inaugurated in Geneva; the Office provides subsidized office space for the Geneva-based diplomatic missions of Commonwealth small states, and business facilities for both diplomatic personnel and visiting delegations from small member states, and has a resident Trade Adviser. The second Commonwealth Biennial Global Small States Conference was held in September 2012, again in London; participating representatives of small states discussed the development of sustainable economies, job creation and improving livelihoods, agreeing that 'green growth' might act as a vehicle for progress. In June 2013 a technical workshop was convened with a focus on strengthening resilience in small states, including developing an index to measure countries' capacities to absorb external shocks caused by adverse global economic conditions, extreme weather events, and natural disasters. The third Biennial Global Small States Conference, convened in March 2014, in St Lucia, focused on building the resilience of small states in the areas of debt, economic development, governance, environmental management, and social cohesion. The Secretariat's Political Affairs Division manages a joint office in New York, USA, to enable small states to maintain a presence at the UN.

In November 2005 Commonwealth Heads of Government endorsed a new Commonwealth Action Programme for the Digital Divide and approved the establishment of a special fund to enable implementation of the programme's objectives to make available to all the benefits of new information technologies. Accordingly, a Commonwealth Connects programme was established in August 2006 to develop partnerships and to help to strengthen the use of and access to information technology in all Commonwealth countries; a Commonwealth Connects web portal was launched at the October 2011 Heads of Government summit.

The Commonwealth Secretariat provides assistance to member states on negotiations relating to the delimitation of maritime boundaries, and on issues related to the law of the sea. It also assists member states in the area of natural resources management, including in the preparation of policy, and legislative and contractual arrangements for the governance of extractive industries development, and the negotiation of investment terms.

The summit of Heads of Government held in Perth, Australia, in October 2011, issued the Perth Declaration on Food Security Principles, reaffirming the universal right to safe, sufficient and nutritious food.

ENVIRONMENTALLY SUSTAINABLE DEVELOPMENT

The Commonwealth's Environmentally Sustainable Development Programme is managed by the Economic Affairs Division, working with the Office of the Secretary-General, the Special Advisory Services Division, and the Technical Cooperation and Strategic Response Unit. The Economic Affairs Division undertakes analytical research, partnership building and skill-building activities to assist member states in managing their risk and identifying opportunities for environmentally sustainable growth.

The Commonwealth Climate Change Action Plan, adopted by Heads of Government in November 2007, acknowledged that climate change posed a serious threat to the very existence of some small island states within the Commonwealth, and to the low-lying coastal areas of others. It offered support for the UN Framework Convention on Climate Change, and recognized the need to overcome technical, economic and policy-making barriers to reducing carbon emissions, to using renewable energy, and to increasing energy efficiency. The Plan undertook to assist developing member states in international negotiations on climate change; to support improved land use management, including the use of forest resources; to investigate the carbon footprint of agricultural exports from member countries; to increase support for the management of natural disasters in member countries; and to provide technical assistance to help least developed members and small states to assess the implications of climate change and adapt accordingly. A Commonwealth expert group on climate finance was established in June 2013, to assess and propose remedies for the challenges faced by small and vulnerable states in accessing and disbursing climate finance. The Secretariat pursues strategic partnerships with regional institutions representing small states—such as the Caribbean Community Climate Change Centre, Indian Ocean Commission and Secretariat of the Pacific Regional Environment Programme—aimed at building institutional capacities in climate financing and sustainable development.

In October 2012 the Commonwealth launched *Integrating Sustainable Development into International Investment Agreements: A Guide for Developing Country Negotiators*, intended as a handbook for developing member states to use in navigating the international investment agreements that support their development needs.

In November 2013 Heads of Government adopted the Colombo Declaration on Sustainable, Inclusive and Equitable Development, in which they expressed commitment to developing supportive global policies aimed at addressing climate change mitigation and adaptation, food security, poverty, inequalities in trade, predictable and sufficient finances, investments, knowledge and technology transfers, and processes promoting growth with equity.

In early 2014 a technical working group convened by the Commonwealth Secretariat was reviewing issues relating to resilience building in small island states, including the effectiveness of national policy frameworks and of the international financing and capacity agenda, in advance of the third Global Conference on the Sustainable Development of Small Island States, scheduled to be convened in September, in Apia, Samoa.

The Iwokrama International Centre for Rainforest Conservation and Development, managed by the Commonwealth Secretariat and the Guyanese authorities, promotes environmentally balanced, sustainable tropical rainforest management.

HUMAN AND SOCIAL DEVELOPMENT

The Commonwealth Secretariat's Social Transformation Programmes Division is primarily responsible for managing activities in the area of human and social development, covering health, education and gender equality. Gender equality is a cross-cutting theme that is integrated across the Secretariat's activities.

Ministerial, technical and expert group meetings and workshops, are convened regularly to foster co-operation on health matters, and to promote the exchange of health information and expertise. Studies are commissioned, and professional and technical advice is provided to member states. The Secretariat supports the work of regional health organizations. The priority areas of focus with regard to health are: e-health; health worker migration; HIV/AIDS; maternal and child health; non-communicable diseases; and mental health. A Commonwealth Advisory Committee on Health advises the Secretariat on public health matters.

The Commonwealth Secretariat works to improve the quality of and access to basic education in member states; to strengthen science, technology and mathematics education; to improve the quality of management in institutions of higher learning and basic education; to enhance—in accordance with the Pan-Commonwealth Framework on Professional Standards for Teachers and School Leaders—the performance of educational staff; to strengthen examination assessment systems; and to promote the movement of students between Commonwealth countries. Advancing inclusive education—focusing on reaching excluded and underperforming groups—is a priority area of activity. Support for education is also offered in difficult circumstances, such as areas affected by conflict or natural disasters, and mitigating the impact of HIV and AIDS on education. Collaboration between governments, the private sector and other NGOs is promoted. A meeting of Commonwealth ministers responsible for education, held at the end of August 2012, in Port Louis, Mauritius, discussed means of achieving education-related MDGs by 2015 and considered priorities for the Commonwealth's contribution to a post-2015 development framework. The meeting was synchronized with parallel fora for Commonwealth teachers, post-secondary and tertiary education leaders, young people, and stakeholders.

The Commonwealth Plan of Action for Gender Equality, covering the period 2005–15, supports efforts towards achieving the 1995 MDGs, and the objectives of gender equality adopted by the 1995 Beijing Declaration and Platform for Action and the follow-up Beijing+5 review conference, held in 2000, and Beijing+10 in 2005. Gender equality, poverty eradication, promotion of human rights, and strengthening democracy are recognized as intrinsically interrelated, and the Plan has a particular focus on the advancement of gender mainstreaming in the following areas: democracy, peace and conflict; human rights and law; poverty eradication and economic empowerment; and HIV/AIDS. Commonwealth Women's Affairs Ministers Meetings (WAMMs) have been held every three years since 1985; the 10th WAMM was convened in Dhaka, Bangladesh, in June 2013, on the theme 'Women's Leadership for Enterprise'.

YOUTH

The Secretariat's Youth Affairs Division administers the Commonwealth Youth Programme (CYP), which was initiated in 1973 to promote the involvement of young people in the economic and social development of their countries. (Young people under the age of 30 represent around 60% of the citizens of the Commonwealth.) The CYP is funded by dedicated voluntary contributions from governments. The Programme's activities are in three areas: Youth Enterprise and Sustainable Livelihoods; Governance, Development and Youth Networks; and Youth Work Education and Training. Regional centres are located in Zambia (for Africa), India (for Asia), Guyana (for the Caribbean), and Solomon Islands (for the Pacific). The Programme administers a Youth Study Fellowship scheme, a Youth Project Fund, a Youth Exchange Programme (in the Caribbean), and a Youth Development Awards Scheme. It also holds conferences and seminars, carries out research and disseminates information. The CYP Diploma in Youth Development Work is offered by partner institutions in 45 countries, primarily through distance education. The Commonwealth Youth Credit Initiative, initiated in 1995, provides funds and advice for young entrepreneurs setting up small businesses. A Plan of Action for Youth Empowerment, covering the period 2007–15, was approved by the sixth meeting of Commonwealth ministers responsible for youth affairs, held in Nassau, Bahamas, in May 2006. The Commonwealth Youth Games are normally held at four-yearly intervals (2015: Samoa). In September 2012 a Commonwealth Pacific Youth Leadership and Integrity Conference was convened in Honiara, Solomon Islands. A new pan-Commonwealth Student Association was launched in August of that year. The first Commonwealth Conference on the Education and Training of Youth Workers was held in Pretoria, South Africa, in March 2013. In September the first Commonwealth Youth Development Index was launched, comprising indicators measuring development and empowerment with respect to young people globally. In November Heads of Government, meeting in Sri Lanka, adopted the Magampura Declaration of Commitment to Young People. The enhanced integration of, and appreciation of the value of, youth in political and developmental processes was the fourth strategic objective stipulated under the Commonwealth's Strategic Plan for 2013/14–2016/17, adopted in November 2013; accordingly, national and pan-Commonwealth frameworks aimed at advancing the social, political and economic empowerment of young people, and the further development of youth-led initiatives, were to be promoted during the term of the Plan.

TECHNICAL ASSISTANCE

Commonwealth Fund for Technical Co-operation (CFTC): f. 1971 to facilitate the exchange of skills between member countries and to promote economic and social devt; it is administered by the Commonwealth Secretariat and financed by voluntary subscriptions from member governments. The CFTC responds to requests from member governments for technical assistance, such as the provision of experts for short- or medium-term projects, advice on economic or legal matters, and training programmes. Public sector devt, allowing member states to build on their capacities, is the principal element in CFTC activities. This includes assistance for improvement of supervision and combating corruption; improving economic management, for example by advising on exports and investment promotion; strengthening democratic institutions, such as electoral commissions; and improvement of education and health policies. The CFTC also administers the Langkawi awards for the study of environmental issues, which is funded by the Canadian Government; the CFTC's annual budget amounts to £29m., supplemented by external resources through partnerships.

Finance

Member governments meet the costs of the Secretariat through subscriptions on a scale related to income and population.

Publications

Commonwealth News (weekly e-mail newsletter).

Commonwealth Human Rights Law Digest.

Commonwealth Law Bulletin (quarterly).

Global (electronic magazine).

Report of the Commonwealth Secretary-General (every 2 years).

Small States Digest (periodic newsletter).

Numerous reports, studies and papers (catalogue available).

Commonwealth Organizations

(in the United Kingdom, unless otherwise stated)

The two principal intergovernmental organizations established by Commonwealth member states, apart from the Commonwealth Secretariat itself, are the Commonwealth Foundation and the Commonwealth of Learning. In 2013 there were nearly 90 other professional or advocacy organizations bearing the Commonwealth's name and associated with or accredited to the Commonwealth, a selection of which are listed below.

PRINCIPAL INTERGOVERNMENTAL ORGANIZATIONS

Commonwealth Foundation: Marlborough House, Pall Mall, London, SW1Y 5HY; tel. (20) 7930-3783; fax (20) 7839-8157; e-mail foundation@commonwealth.int; internet www.commonwealthfoundation.com; f. 1966; intergovernmental body promoting people-to-people interaction, and collaboration within the non-governmental sector of the Commonwealth; supports non-governmental orgs, professional asscns and Commonwealth arts and culture; funds are provided by Commonwealth govts; Chair. Sir ANAND SATYANAND (New Zealand); Dir VIJAY KRISHNARAYAN (Trinidad and Tobago); publ. *Commonwealth People* (quarterly).

Commonwealth of Learning (COL): 1055 West Hastings St, Suite 1200, Vancouver, BC V6E 2E9, Canada; tel. (604) 775-8200; fax (604) 775-8210; e-mail info@col.org; internet www.col.org; f. 1987 by Commonwealth Heads of Government to promote the devt and sharing of distance education and open learning resources, including materials, expertise and technologies, throughout the Commonwealth and in other countries; implements and assists with national and regional educational programmes; acts as consultant to international agencies and national govts; conducts seminars and studies on specific educational needs; convened the seventh Pan-Commonwealth Forum on Open Learning in Dec. 2013, in Abuja, Nigeria; core financing for COL is provided by Commonwealth govts on a voluntary basis; COL has an annual budget of approx. C $12m; Pres. and CEO Prof. ASHA KANWAR (India); publ. *Connections*.

The following represents a selection of other Commonwealth organizations:

ADMINISTRATION AND PLANNING

Commonwealth Association for Public Administration and Management (CAPAM): 291 Dalhousie St, Suite 202, Ottawa, ON K1N 7E5, Canada; tel. (819) 956-7952; fax (613) 701-4236; e-mail capam@capam.org; internet www.capam.org; f. 1994; aims to promote sound management of the public sector in Commonwealth countries and to assist those countries undergoing political or financial reforms; an international awards programme to reward innovation within the public sector was introduced in 1997, and is awarded every two years; more than 1,200 individual mems and 80 institutional memberships in some 80 countries; Pres. PAUL ZAHRA (Malta); Exec. Dir and CEO GAY HAMILTON (Canada).

Commonwealth Association of Planners: c/o Royal Town Planning Institute in Scotland, 18 Atholl Crescent, Edinburgh, EH3 8HQ; tel. (131) 229-9628; fax (131) 229-9332; e-mail annette.odonnell@rtpi.org.uk; internet www.commonwealth-planners.org; aims to develop urban and regional planning in Commonwealth countries, to meet the challenges of urbanization and the sustainable devt of human settlements; Pres. CHRISTINE PLATT (South Africa); Sec.-Gen. CLIVE HARRIDGE (United Kingdom).

Commonwealth Local Government Forum: 16A Northumberland Ave, London, WC2N 5AP; tel. (20) 7389-1490; fax (20) 7389-1499; e-mail info@clgf.org.uk; internet www.clgf.org.uk; works to promote democratic local govt in Commonwealth countries, and to encourage good practice through confs, programmes, research and the provision of information; regional offices in Fiji, India and South Africa; Sec.-Gen. CARL WRIGHT.

AGRICULTURE AND FORESTRY

Commonwealth Forestry Association: The Crib, Dinchope, Craven Arms, Shropshire, SY7 9JJ; tel. (1588) 672868; e-mail cfa@cfa-international.org; internet www.cfa-international.org; f. 1921; produces, collects and circulates information relating to world forestry and promotes good management, use and conservation of forests and forest lands throughout the world; mems: 1,200; Chair. JOHN INNES (Canada); Pres. JIM BALL (United Kingdom); publs *International Forestry Review* (quarterly), *Commonwealth Forestry News* (quarterly), *Commonwealth Forestry Handbook* (irregular).

Royal Agricultural Society of the Commonwealth: Royal Highland Centre, Ingleston, Edinburgh, EH28 8NF; tel. (131) 335-6200; fax (131) 335-6229; e-mail info@therasc.com; internet www.therasc.com; f. 1957 to promote devt of agricultural shows and good farming practice, in order to improve incomes and food production in Commonwealth countries; Chair. Lord VESTEY.

Standing Committee on Commonwealth Forestry: Forestry Commission, 231 Corstorphine Rd, Edinburgh, EH12 7AT; tel. (131) 314-6405; fax (131) 316-4344; e-mail commonwealth.standing-committee@forestry.gsi.gov.uk; internet www.cfc2010.org; f. 1923 to provide continuity between Commonwealth Forestry Conferences (usually held every four years), and to provide a forum for discussion on any forestry matters of common interest to mem. govts which may be brought to the Committee's notice by any mem. country or org.; 54 mems; 2010 Conference: Edinburgh, United Kingdom, in June; Sec. JONATHAN TAYLOR.

BUSINESS

Commonwealth Business Council: 18 Pall Mall, London, SW1Y 5LU; tel. (20) 7024-8200; fax (20) 7024-8201; e-mail info@cbcglobal.org; internet www.cbcglobal.org; f. 1997 by the Commonwealth Heads of Government Meeting to promote co-operation between govts and the private sector in support of trade, investment and devt; the Council aims to identify and promote investment opportunities, in particular in Commonwealth developing countries, to support countries and local businesses to work within the context of globalization, to promote capacity building and the exchange of skills and knowledge (in particular through its Information Communication Technologies for Development programme), and to encourage co-operation among Commonwealth members; promotes good governance; supports the process of multilateral trade negotiations and other liberalization of trade and services; represents the private sector at govt level; CEO PETER CALLAGHAN.

EDUCATION AND CULTURE

Association of Commonwealth Universities (ACU): Woburn House, 20-24 Tavistock Sq., London, WC1H 9HF; tel. (20) 7380-6700; fax (20) 7387-2655; e-mail info@acu.ac.uk; internet www.acu.ac.uk; f. 1913; promotes international co-operation and understanding; provides assistance with staff and student mobility and devt programmes; researches and disseminates information about universities and relevant policy issues; organizes major meetings of Commonwealth universities and their representatives; acts as a liaison office and information centre; administers scholarship and fellowship schemes; operates a policy research unit; mems: c. 500 universities in 36 Commonwealth countries or regions; Sec.-Gen. Prof. JOHN WOOD; publs include *Yearly Review*, *Commonwealth Universities Yearbook*, *ACU Bulletin* (quarterly), *Who's Who of Executive Heads: Vice-Chancellors, Presidents, Principals and Rectors*, *International Awards*, student information papers (study abroad series).

Commonwealth Association of Museums: 10023 93 St, Edmonton, Alberta T5H 1W6, Canada; tel. and fax (780) 424-2229; e-mail catherinec.cole@telus.net; internet www.maltwood.uvic.ca/cam; f. 1974; professional asscn working for the improvement of museums throughout the Commonwealth; encourages links between museums and assists professional devt and training through distance learning, workshops and seminars; general assembly held every three years; mems in 38 Commonwealth countries; Pres. ROOKSANA OMAR.

Commonwealth Association of Science, Technology and Mathematics Educators (CASTME): 7 Lion Yard, Tremadoc Rd, London, SW4 7NQ; tel. (20) 7819-3936; e-mail admin@castme.org.uk; internet www.castme.org.uk; f. 1974; special emphasis is given to the social significance of education in these subjects; organizes an Awards Scheme to promote effective teaching and learning in these subjects, and biennial regional seminars; Chair. COLIN MATHESON; publ. *CASTME Journal* (3 a year).

Commonwealth Council for Educational Administration and Management: 86 Ellison Rd, Springwood, NSW 2777, Australia; tel. and fax (2) 4751-7974; e-mail admin@cceam.org; internet www.cceam.org; f. 1970; aims to foster quality in professional devt and links among educational administrators; holds national and regional confs, as well as visits and seminars; mems: 28 affiliated groups representing 3,000 persons; Pres. Prof. FRANK CROWTHER; Exec. Dir JENNY LEWIS; publ. *International Studies in Educational Administration* (2 a year).

Commonwealth Education Trust: New Zealand House, 6th Floor, 80 Haymarket, London, SW1Y 4TE; tel. (20) 7024-9822; fax (20) 7024-9833; e-mail info@commonwealth-institute.org; internet www.commonwealtheducationtrust.org; f. 2007 as the successor trust to the Commonwealth Institute; funds the Centre of Commonwealth Education, established in 2004 as part of Cambridge University; supports the Lifestyle of Our Kids (LOOK) project initiated in 2005 by the Commonwealth Institute (Australia); Chief Exec. JUDY CURRY.

Institute of Commonwealth Studies: South Block, 2nd Floor, Senate House, Malet Street, London, WC1E 7HU; tel. (20) 7862-8844; fax (20) 7862-8813; e-mail ics@sas.ac.uk; internet commonwealth.sas.ac.uk; f. 1949 to promote advanced study of the Commonwealth; provides a library and meeting place for postgraduate students and academic staff engaged in research in this field; offers postgraduate teaching; Dir PHILIP MURPHY; publs *Annual Report*, *Collected Seminar Papers*, *Newsletter*, *Theses in Progress in Commonwealth Studies*.

HEALTH AND WELFARE

Commonwealth Medical Trust (COMMAT): BMA House, Tavistock Sq., London, WC1H 9JP; tel. (20) 7272-8492; e-mail office@commat.org; internet www.commat.org; f. 1962 (as the Commonwealth Medical Association) for the exchange of information; provision of techical co-operation and advice; formulation and maintenance of a code of ethics; promotes the Right to Health; liaison with WHO and other UN agencies on health issues; meetings of its Council are held every three years; mems: medical asscns in Commonwealth countries; Dir MARIANNE HASLEGRAVE.

Commonwealth Nurses' Federation: c/o Royal College of Nursing, 20 Cavendish Sq., London, W1G 0RN; tel. (20) 7647-3593; fax (20) 7647-3413; e-mail jill@commonwealthnurses.org; internet www.commonwealthnurses.org; f. 1973 to link national nursing and midwifery asscns in Commonwealth countries; aims to influence health policy, develop nursing networks, improve nursing education and standards, and strengthen leadership; inaugural Conference held in March 2012 (in London); Exec. Sec. JILL ILIFFE.

Commonwealth Organization for Social Work: Halifax, Canada; tel. (902) 455-5515; e-mail moniqueauffrey@eastlink.ca; promotes communication and collaboration between social workers in Commonwealth countries; provides network for information and sharing of expertise; Sec.-Gen. MONIQUE AUFFREY (Canada).

Commonwealth Pharmacists Association: 1 Lambeth High St, London, SE1 7JN; tel. (20) 7572-2216; fax (20) 7572-2504; e-mail admin@commonwealthpharmacy.org; internet www.commonwealthpharmacy.org; f. 1970 (as the Commonwealth Pharmaceutical Association) to promote the interests of pharmaceutical sciences and the profession of pharmacy in the Commonwealth; to maintain high professional standards, encourage links between members and the creation of nat. asscns; and to facilitate the dissemination of information; holds confs (every four years) and regional meetings; mems: pharmaceutical asscns from over 40 Commonwealth countries; Pres. RAYMOND ANDERSON (United Kingdom); publ. *Quarterly Newsletter*.

Commonwealth Society for the Deaf (Sound Seekers): UCL Ear Institute, 332–336 Gray's Inn Rd, London, WC1X 8EE; tel. (20) 7833-0035; fax (20) 7233-5800; e-mail admin@sound-seekers.org.uk; internet www.sound-seekers.org.uk; f. 1959; undertakes initiatives to establish audiology services in developing Commonwealth countries, including mobile clinics to provide outreach services; aims to educate local communities in aural hygiene and the prevention of ear infection and deafness; provides audiological equipment and organizes the training of audiological maintenance technicians; conducts research into the causes and prevention of deafness; Chief Exec. LUCY CARTER; publ. *Annual Report*.

Royal Commonwealth Ex-Services League: Haig House, 199 Borough High St, London, SE1 1AA; tel. (20) 3207-2413; fax (20) 3207-2115; e-mail mgordon-roe@commonwealthveterans.org.uk; internet www.commonwealthveterans.org.uk; links the former service orgs in the Commonwealth, assists former servicemen of the Crown who are resident abroad; holds confs every four years; 56 mem. orgs in 48 countries; Grand Pres. HRH The Duke of EDINBURGH; publ. *Annual Report*.

Sightsavers (Royal Commonwealth Society for the Blind): Grosvenor Hall, Bolnore Rd, Haywards Heath, West Sussex, RH16 4BX; tel. (1444) 446600; fax (1444) 446688; e-mail info@sightsavers.org; internet www.sightsavers.org; f. 1950 to prevent blindness and restore sight in developing countries, and to provide education and community-based training for incurably blind people; operates in collaboration with local partners in some 30 developing countries, with high priority given to training local staff; Chair. Lord NIGEL CRISP; Chief Exec. Dr CAROLINE HARPER; publ. *Sightsavers News*.

INFORMATION AND THE MEDIA

Commonwealth Broadcasting Association: 17 Fleet St, London, EC4Y 1AA; tel. (20) 7583-5550; fax (20) 7583-5549; e-mail cba@cba.org.uk; internet www.cba.org.uk; f. 1945; general confs are held every two years (2014: Glasgow, United Kingdom, in May); mems: c. 100 in more than 50 countries; Pres. MONEEZA HASHMI; Sec.-Gen.

SALLY-ANN WILSON; publs *Commonwealth Broadcaster* (quarterly), *Commonwealth Broadcaster Directory* (annually).

Commonwealth Journalists Association: c/o Canadian Newspaper Association, 890 Yonge St, Suite 200, Toronto, ON M4W 3P4, Canada; tel. (416) 575-5377; fax (416) 923-7206; e-mail pat.perkel@commonwealthjournalists.com; internet www.commonwealthjournalists.com; f. 1978 to promote co-operation between journalists in Commonwealth countries, organize training facilities and confs, and foster understanding among Commonwealth peoples; Exec. Dir PATRICIA PERKEL; publ. *Newsletter* (3 a year).

CPU Media Trust (Association of Commonwealth Newspapers, News Agencies and Periodicals): e-mail webform@cpu.org.uk; internet www.cpu.org.uk; f. 2008 as a 'virtual' org. charged with carrying on the aims of the Commonwealth Press Union (CPU, f. 1950, terminated 2008); promotes the welfare of the Commonwealth press; Chair. GUY BLACK.

LAW

Commonwealth Lawyers Association: c/o Institute of Advanced Legal Studies, 17 Russell Sq., London, WC1B 5DR; tel. (20) 7862-8824; fax (20) 7862-8816; e-mail cla@sas.ac.uk; internet www.commonwealthlawyers.com; f. 1983 (fmrly the Commonwealth Legal Bureau); seeks to maintain and promote the rule of law throughout the Commonwealth, by ensuring that the people of the Commonwealth are served by an independent and efficient legal profession; upholds professional standards and promotes the availability of legal services; organizes events including a Commonwealth Law Conference every two years (2015: Glasgow, United Kingdom); Pres. MARK STEPHENS; publ. *The Commonwealth Lawyer*.

Commonwealth Legal Advisory Service: c/o British Institute of International and Comparative Law, Charles Clore House, 17 Russell Sq., London, WC1B 5DR; tel. (20) 7862-5151; fax (20) 7862-5152; e-mail contact@biicl.org; internet www.biicl.org; f. 1962; financed by the British Institute and by contributions from Commonwealth govts; provides research facilities for Commonwealth govts and law reform commissions; publ. *New Memoranda* series.

Commonwealth Legal Education Association: c/o Legal and Constitutional Affairs Division, Commonwealth Secretariat, Marlborough House, Pall Mall, London, SW1Y 5HX; tel. (20) 7747-6415; fax (20) 7004-3649; e-mail clea@commonwealth.int; internet www.clea-web.com; f. 1971 to promote contacts and exchanges and to provide information regarding legal education; Gen. Secs PATRICIA MCKELLAR, MICHAEL BROMBY; publ. *Commonwealth Legal Education Association Newsletter* (2 a year).

Commonwealth Magistrates' and Judges' Association: Uganda House, 58–59 Trafalgar Sq., London, WC2N 5DX; tel. (20) 7976-1007; fax (20) 7976-2394; e-mail info@cmja.org; internet www.cmja.org; f. 1970 to advance the administration of the law by promoting the independence of the judiciary, to further education in law and crime prevention and to disseminate information; confs and study tours; corporate membership for asscns of the judiciary or courts of limited jurisdiction; assoc. membership for individuals; Sec.-Gen. Dr KAREN BREWER; publs *Commonwealth Judicial Journal* (2 a year), *CMJA News*.

PARLIAMENTARY AFFAIRS

Commonwealth Parliamentary Association: Westminster House, Suite 700, 7 Millbank, London, SW1P 3JA; tel. (20) 7799-1460; fax (20) 7222-6073; e-mail hq.sec@cpahq.org; internet www.cpahq.org; f. 1911 to promote understanding and co-operation between Commonwealth parliamentarians; an Executive Committee of 35 MPs is responsible to annual Gen. Assembly; 176 brs in national, state, provincial and territorial parliaments and legislatures throughout the Commonwealth; holds annual Commonwealth Parliamentary Conferences and seminars; also regional conferencs and seminars; Chair. Sir ALAN HASELHURST; Sec.-Gen. Dr WILLIAM F. SHIJA; publ. *The Parliamentarian* (quarterly).

SCIENCE AND TECHNOLOGY

Commonwealth Association of Architects: POB 1166, Stamford, PE2 2HL; tel. and fax (1780) 238091; e-mail info@comarchitect.org; internet www.comarchitect.org; f. 1964; aims to facilitate the reciprocal recognition of professional qualifications; to provide a clearing house for information on architectural practice; and to encourage collaboration. Plenary confs every three years; regional confs are also held; 38 societies of architects in various Commonwealth countries; Pres. RUKSHAN WIDYALANKARA; Exec. Dir TONY GODWIN; publs *Handbook, Objectives and Procedures: CAA Schools Visiting Boards, Architectural Education in the Commonwealth* (annotated bibliography of research), *CAA Newsnet* (2 a year), a survey and list of schools of architecture.

Commonwealth Engineers' Council: c/o Institution of Civil Engineers, One Great George St, London, SW1P 3AA; tel. (20) 7222-7722; e-mail secretariat@ice.org.uk; internet www.cec.ice.org.uk; f. 1946; links and represents engineering institutions across the Commonwealth, providing them with an opportunity to exchange views on collaboration and mutual support; holds international and regional confs and workshops; mems: 45 institutions in 44 countries; Sec.-Gen. NEIL BAILEY.

Commonwealth Telecommunications Organization: 64-66 Glenthorne Rd, London, W6 0LR; tel. (20) 8600-3800; fax (20) 8600-3819; e-mail info@cto.int; internet www.cto.int; f. 1967 as an international devt partnership between Commonwealth and non-Commonwealth govts, business and civil society orgs; aims to help to bridge the digital divide and to achieve social and economic devt by delivering to developing countries knowledge-sharing programmes in the use of information and communication technologies in the specific areas of telecommunications, broadcasting and the internet; convened in March 2014, in London, jointly with the Commonwealth Secretariat, the first forum of Commonwealth ICT ministers, to discuss recommendations on pan-Commonwealth cyber-governance; Sec.-Gen. Prof. TIM UNWIN; publs *CTO Update* (quarterly), *Annual Report*, *Research Reports*.

Conference of Commonwealth Meteorologists: c/o International Branch, Meteorological Office, FitzRoy Rd, Exeter, EX1 3PB; tel. (1392) 885680; fax (1392) 885681; e-mail commonwealth@metoffice.gov.uk; internet www.commonwealthmet.org; links national meteorological and hydrological services in Commonwealth countries.

SPORT AND YOUTH

Commonwealth Games Federation: 138 Piccadilly, 2nd Floor, London, W1J 7NR; tel. (20) 7491-8801; fax (20) 7409-7803; e-mail info@thecgf.com; internet www.thecgf.com; the Games were first held in 1930 and are now held every four years; participation is limited to competitors representing the mem. countries of the Commonwealth; 2014 games: Glasgow, United Kingdom (in July); mems: 72 affiliated bodies; Pres. HRH Prince IMRAN (Malaysia); CEO MICHAEL HOOPER.

Commonwealth Student Association: c/o Youth Affairs Division, Commonwealth Secretariat, Marlborough House, Pall Mall, London, SW1Y 5HX; tel. (20) 7747-6462; e-mail o.said@commonwealth.int; internet cmmnwlthstdnt.tumblr.com/CSA; f. 2012; aims to serve as a forum for student orgs throughout the Commonwealth; a strategic plan was launched in Feb. 2013, which prioritized building the capacity of national student orgs and their leaders to influence education policy; a nine-member steering committee is elected from student leaders across the Commonwealth; Chair. STANLEY NJOROGE.

Commonwealth Youth Exchange Council (CYEC): 7 Lion Yard, Tremadoc Rd, London, SW4 7NQ; tel. (20) 7498-6151; fax (20) 7622-4365; e-mail mail@cyec.org.uk; internet www.cyec.org.uk; f. 1970; promotes contact between groups of young people of the United Kingdom and other Commonwealth countries by means of educational exchange visits, provides information for organizers and allocates grants; provides host govts with technical assistance for delivery of the Commonwealth Youth Forum, held every two years; since July 2011 administers the Commonwealth Teacher Exchange Programme (CTEP); mems: 222 orgs, 134 local authorities, 88 voluntary bodies; Dir of Programmes HELEN JONES MBE; publs *Contact* (handbook), *Exchange* (newsletter), *Final Communiqués* (of the Commonwealth Youth Forums), *Safety and Welfare* (guidelines for Commonwealth Youth Exchange groups).

RELATIONS WITHIN THE COMMONWEALTH

Commonwealth Countries League: 37 Priory Ave, Sudbury, HA0 2SB; tel. (19) 2382-1364; e-mail info@ccl-int.org; internet www.ccl-int.org; f. 1925; aims to secure equality of liberties, status and opportunities between women and men and to promote friendship and mutual understanding throughout the Commonwealth; promotes women's political and social education and links together women's orgs in most countries of the Commonwealth; an education sponsorship scheme was established in 1967 to finance the secondary education of bright girls from lower-income backgrounds in their own Commonwealth countries; the CCL Education Fund sponsors 300–400 girls throughout the Commonwealth; in March 2011 the Fund launched the 'A Thousand Schools for a Thousand Girls' initiative, aiming to increase to 1,000 the number of girls sponsored annually; Exec. Chair. MAJORIE RENNIE; publs *News Update* (3 a year), *Annual Report*.

Commonwealth War Graves Commission: 2 Marlow Rd, Maidenhead, SL6 7DX; tel. (1628) 634221; fax (1628) 771208; internet www.cwgc.org; casualty and cemetery enquiries; e-mail casualty.enq@cwgc.org; f. 1917 (as Imperial War Graves Commission); responsible for the commemoration in perpetuity of the 1.7m. members of the Commonwealth Forces who died during the wars of

1914–18 and 1939–45; provides for the marking and maintenance of war graves and memorials at some 23,000 locations in 150 countries; mems: Australia, Canada, India, New Zealand, South Africa, United Kingdom; Pres. HRH The Duke of KENT; Dir-Gen. ALAN PATEMAN-JONES.

Council of Commonwealth Societies: c/o Royal Commonwealth Society, 7 Lion Yard, Tremadoc Rd, London, SW4 7NQ; tel. (20) 7766-9206; fax (20) 7622-4365; e-mail ccs@rcsint.org; internet www.rcsint.org/day; f. 1947; provides a forum for the exchange of information regarding activities of member orgs which promote understanding among countries of the Commonwealth; organizes the observance of and promotes Commonwealth Day (held annually on the second Monday in March; 2014 theme: 'Team Commonwealth'), produces educational materials relating to the occasion, and co-ordinates the distribution of the Commonwealth Day message by Queen Elizabeth II; seeks to raise the profile of the Commonwealth; mems: 30 official and unofficial Commonwealth orgs; Chair. Lord ALAN WATSON.

Royal Commonwealth Society: Award House, 7–11 St Matthew St, London SW1P 2JT, United Kingdom; tel. (20) 3727-4300; fax (20) 7930-9705; e-mail info@thercs.org; internet www.thercs.org; f. 1868; aims to improve the lives and prospects of Commonwealth citizens across the world; the society is constituted by Royal Charter (most recently amended in 2013) and as a charity; organizes meetings and seminars on topical issues, projects for young people, a youth leadership programme, and cultural and social events; Chair. CLAIRE WHITAKER; Dir MICHAEL LAKE; publs *RCS Exchange* (3 a year), conference reports.

Royal Over-Seas League: Over-Seas House, Park Place, St James's St, London, SW1A 1LR; tel. (20) 7408-0214; fax (20) 7499-6738; e-mail info@rosl.org.uk; internet www.rosl.org.uk; f. 1910 to promote friendship and understanding in the Commonwealth; club houses in London and Edinburgh; membership is open to all British subjects and Commonwealth citizens; Dir-Gen. Maj.-Gen. RODDY PORTER; publ. *Overseas* (quarterly).

Victoria League for Commonwealth Friendship: 55 Leinster Sq., London, W2 4PW; tel. (20) 7243-2633; fax (20) 7229-2994; e-mail enquiries@victorialeague.co.uk; internet www.victorialeague.co.uk; f. 1901; aims to further personal friendship among Commonwealth peoples and to provide hospitality for visitors; maintains Student House, providing accommodation for students from Commonwealth countries; has branches elsewhere in the UK and abroad; Chair. LYN D. HOPKINS; Gen. Man. DOREEN HENRY; publ. *Annual Report*.

COMMONWEALTH OF INDEPENDENT STATES—CIS

Address: 220030 Minsk, Kirava 17, Belarus.

Telephone: (17) 222-35-17; **fax:** (17) 227-23-39; **e-mail:** cr@cis.minsk.by; **internet:** www.cis.minsk.by.

The Commonwealth of Independent States (CIS) is a voluntary association of 11 states, established at the time of the collapse of the USSR in December 1991.

MEMBERS

Armenia	Moldova
Azerbaijan	Russia
Belarus	Tajikistan
Kazakhstan	Ukraine
Kyrgyzstan	Uzbekistan

Note: Azerbaijan formally became a member of the CIS in September 1993. Georgia was admitted to the CIS in December 1993. In August 2009 Georgia's membership was terminated. Ukraine ratified the foundation documents that established the CIS in 1991 but has not yet ratified the CIS Charter. Turkmenistan has associate membership, reduced from full membership in August 2005.

Organization

(April 2014)

COUNCIL OF HEADS OF STATE

This is the supreme body of the CIS, on which all the member states of the Commonwealth are represented at the level of head of state, for discussion of issues relating to the co-ordination of Commonwealth activities and the development of the Minsk Agreement. Decisions of the Council are taken by common consent, with each state having equal voting rights. The Council meets at least once a year. An extraordinary meeting may be convened on the initiative of the majority of Commonwealth heads of state. An ordinary meeting of the Council was held in November 2013, in St Petersburg, Russia. The chairmanship of the Council is normally rotated among member states. Ukraine, which had been granted the 2014 chairmanship, declined in March to continue in that role, in protest against Russia's decision to recognize independent statehood for the autonomous region of Crimea (hitherto a part of Ukraine). In early April Belarus assumed the 2014 chairmanship.

COUNCIL OF HEADS OF GOVERNMENT

This Council convenes for meetings at least once every three months; an extraordinary sitting may be convened on the initiative of a majority of Commonwealth heads of government. The two Councils may discuss and take necessary decisions on important domestic and external issues, and may hold joint sittings.

Working and auxiliary bodies, composed of authorized representatives of the participating states, may be set up on a permanent or interim basis on the decision of the Council of Heads of State and the Council of Heads of Government.

EXECUTIVE COMMITTEE

The Executive Committee was established by the Council of Heads of State in April 1999 to supersede the previous Secretariat, the Interstate Economic Committee and other working bodies and committees, in order to improve the efficient functioning of the organization. The Executive Committee co-operates closely with other CIS bodies including the councils of ministers responsible for foreign affairs and defence; the Economic Council; Council of Border Troops Commanders; the Collective Security Council; the Secretariat of the Council of the Inter-parliamentary Assembly; and the Inter-state Committee for Statistics.

Executive Secretary and Chairman of the Executive Committee: SERGEI N. LEBEDEV (Russia).

Activities

On 8 December 1991 the heads of state of Belarus, Russia and Ukraine signed the Minsk Agreement, providing for the establishment of a Commonwealth of Independent States. Formal recognition of the dissolution of the USSR was incorporated in a second treaty (the Alma-Ata Declaration), signed by 11 heads of state in the then Kazakh capital, Alma-Ata (Almatı), later in that month.

In March 1992 a meeting of the CIS Council of Heads of Government decided to establish a commission to examine the resolution that 'all CIS member states are the legal successors of the rights and obligations of the former Soviet Union'. Documents relating to the legal succession of the Soviet Union were signed at a meeting of heads of state in July. In April an agreement establishing an Inter-parliamentary Assembly of the Member States of the CIS (IPA-CIS), signed by Armenia, Belarus, Kazakhstan, Kyrgyzstan, Russia, Tajikistan and Uzbekistan, was published. The first Assembly was held in Bishkek, Kyrgyzstan, in September, attended by delegates from all these countries, with the exception of Uzbekistan. Normally the Assembly meets twice annually at the Tavricheskiy Palace (the seat of the pre-1917 Revolution Russian legislature), in St Petersburg, Russia.

A CIS Charter was adopted at the meeting of the heads of state in Minsk, Belarus, in January 1993. The Charter, providing for a defence alliance, an inter-state court and an economic co-ordination committee, was to serve as a framework for closer co-operation and was signed by all of the members except for Turkmenistan and Ukraine; by 2014 Ukraine had still not signed the Charter.

In May 1994 the CIS and the UN Conference on Trade and Development signed a co-operation accord. A similar agreement was concluded with the UN Economic Commission for Europe in June 1996. Working contacts have also been established with the International Labour Organization, UN High Commissioner for Refugees, the World Health Organization and the European Union (EU). In June 1998 the IPA-CIS approved a decision to sign the European Social Charter (see Council of Europe); a declaration of co-operation between the Assembly and the OSCE Parliamentary Assembly was also signed.

In April 1996 the Council of Heads of Government approved a long-term plan for the integrated development of the CIS, incorporating measures for further socio-economic, military and political co-operation. Meeting in April 1999 the Council of Heads of Government adopted guidelines for restructuring the CIS and for the future development of the organization. Economic co-operation was to be a priority area of activity, and in particular, the establishment of a free trade zone. An informal CIS 10-year 'jubilee' summit, convened in November 2001, adopted a statement identifying the collective pursuit of stable socio-economic development and integration on a global level as the organization's principal objectives. A summit of heads of state convened in January 2003 agreed that the position of Chairman of the Council of Heads of State (hitherto held by consecutive Russian presidents) should be rotated henceforth among member states.

At the 2007 CIS summit meeting, held in Dushanbe, Tajikistan, in October, CIS heads of state (excluding those of Georgia and Turkmenistan) adopted the 'Concept for Further Development of the CIS' and an action plan for its implementation. Azerbaijan endorsed the document, but reserved the right to abstain from implementing certain clauses. The Concept cited the 'long-term formation of an integrated economic and political association' as a major objective of the Commonwealth, and determined that the multi-sector nature of the organization should be retained and that the harmonized development of its interacting spheres should continue to be promoted. Further goals detailed in the Concept included supporting regional socio-economic stability and international security; improving the economic competitiveness of member states; supporting the accession of member states to the World Trade Organization (WTO); improving regional living standards and conditions; promoting inter-parliamentary co-operation; increasing co-operation between national migration agencies; harmonizing national legislation; and standardizing CIS structures and bodies. The state chairing the Council of Heads of State was to have responsibility for co-ordinating the implementation of the Concept.

In mid-August 2008, following a period of conflict between Georgian and Russian forces earlier in that month, Georgia announced its intention to withdraw from the CIS; this came into effect in August 2009.

The 2011 summit meeting, held in September, in Dushanbe (with participation by Azerbaijan, Belarus and Uzbekistan only at prime ministerial level) gave consideration to a report analysing progress during the first 20 years of the CIS.

CIS heads of state, gathered in May 2013 at a summit meeting in Minsk, signed a series of documents aimed at further developing and deepening inter-regional co-operation across all main spheres of activity. The heads of state also reviewed an interstate programme of innovation co-operation, ongoing during 2012–20, which supported 11 projects in areas including, aerospace and transportation systems, energy efficiency, environmental management, health care, information and communication technologies, manufacturing technology nano-industry, and security.

In May 2009 the heads of state or government of Armenia, Azerbaijan, Belarus, Georgia, Moldova and Ukraine, and representatives of the EU and the heads of state or government, and other representatives, of its member states, convened in Prague, Czech Republic, issued a Joint Declaration on establishing an Eastern Partnership. The main goal of the Eastern Partnership (to be facilitated through a specific Eastern dimension of the EU's European Neighbourhood Policy) was, through EU support for political and socio-economic reforms in interested partner countries, to create the necessary conditions to accelerate political association and further economic integration with the EU.

Member states of the CIS have formed alliances of various kinds among themselves, thereby potentially undermining the unity of the Commonwealth. Belarus, Kazakhstan, Kyrgyzstan, Russia and Tajikistan are members of the Eurasian Economic Community (EurAsEC), inaugurated in October 2001. Azerbaijan, Georgia, Moldova and Ukraine co-operated increasingly from the late 1990s as the GUAM group. Uzbekistan was a member of the group during the period April 1999–May 2005, during which time it was known as 'GUUAM'. Meeting in Kyiv, Ukraine, in May 2006 the heads of state of Azerbaijan, Georgia, Moldova and Ukraine adopted a charter formally inaugurating GUAM as a full international organization and renaming it Organization for Democracy and Economic Development—GUAM. The heads of state suggested at that time that the GUAM countries might withdraw from the CIS. In April 2003 Armenia, Belarus, Kazakhstan, Kyrgyzstan, Tajikistan and Russia established the Collective Security Treaty Organization. In 1994 Kazakhstan, Kyrgyzstan, Tajikistan and Uzbekistan formed the Central Asian Economic Community. In February 2002 those countries relaunched the grouping as the Central Asian Co-operation Organization (CACO). Russia joined the organization in 2004. In October 2005, at a summit of CACO leaders in St Petersburg, it was announced that the organization would be merged with EurAsEC. This was achieved in January 2006 with the accession to EurAsEC of Uzbekistan, which had hitherto been the only member of CACO that did not also belong to the Community. In November 2008 Uzbekistan announced the suspension of its membership of EurAsEC.

Tensions emerged within the CIS in early 2014, following the deployment by Russia in February of troops to the hitherto Ukrainian autonomous region of Crimea. In March Ukraine renounced its 2014 chairmanship of the CIS Council of Heads of State, in view of Russia's recognition of the emphatically pro-independence outcome of a controversial referendum held in Crimea (illegally under Ukraine and international law) on the question of the territory's secession from Ukraine, and the adoption immediately following the referendum by the Russian President, Vladimir Putin, of a degree that recognized Crimea as a 'sovereign and independent state'. Decisions taken by the Crimean legislature following the disputed referendum included submitting an application for the territory to join Russia, replacing the Ukrainian currency (hryvnya) with the Russian rubl, adopting Moscow time (GMT+4) in place of Kyiv time, and permitting Crimean soldiers to join the Russian military. It was reported at that time that Ukraine was considering withdrawing from the CIS. Meeting in early April CIS ministers of foreign affairs urged Ukraine to remain within the organization, and emphasized the need for the continuation of multi-stakeholder dialogue, with a view to stabilizing the situation in that country.

ECONOMIC AFFAIRS AND TRADE

The CIS Charter, adopted in January 1993, provided for the establishment of an economic co-ordination committee. In May all member states, with the exception of Turkmenistan, adopted a declaration of support for increased economic union and, in September, agreement was reached by all states except Ukraine and Turkmenistan on a framework for economic union, including the gradual removal of tariffs and creation of a currency union. Turkmenistan was subsequently admitted as a full member of the economic union in December 1993 and Ukraine as an associate member in April 1994.

At the Council of Heads of Government meeting in September 1994 all member states, except Turkmenistan, agreed to establish an Inter-state Economic Committee to implement economic treaties adopted within the context of an economic union. The establishment of a payments union to improve the settlement of accounts was also agreed. In April 1998 CIS heads of state resolved to incorporate the functions of the Inter-state Economic Committee, along with those of other working bodies and sectional committees, into a new CIS Executive Committee.

Guidelines adopted by the Council of Heads of State in April 1999 concerning the future development of the CIS identified economic co-operation and the establishment of a free trade zone as priority areas for action. An annual St Petersburg International Economic Forum was inaugurated by the IPA-CIS in 1997, and was in 2006 recognized as the major economic summit of the CIS. In 2013 the Forum was held in June, on the theme 'Future of the Global Economy'. Improving the economic competitiveness of member states was a primary focus of the 'Concept for the Integrated Economic Development of the CIS' that was adopted by the organization's October 2007 summit meeting. In October 2009 a CIS Economic Development Strategy until 2020 was endorsed by CIS heads of state gathered in Chişinău, Moldova; the summit also discussed strengthening member states' co-operation in combating the impact of the global financial crisis, and adopted a joint action plan of related measures.

In March 1998 Russia, Belarus, Kazakhstan and Kyrgyzstan signed an agreement establishing a customs union, which was to be implemented in two stages. In February 1999 Tajikistan signed the 1998 agreement to become the fifth member of the customs union. In October 1999 the heads of state of the five member states of the customs union approved a programme to harmonize national legislation to create a single economic space, and in May 2000 they determined to raise the status of the customs union to that of an interstate economic organization; in October the leaders consequently signed the founding treaty of EurAsEC. Under the new structure member states aimed to formulate a unified foreign economic policy, and, taking into account existing customs agreements, collectively to pursue the creation of the planned single economic space. In the following month the five member governments signed an agreement enabling visa-free travel within the new Community, which was formally inaugurated in October 2001. (Earlier in 2000 Russia had withdrawn from a CIS-wide visa-free travel arrangement agreed in 1992. Kazakhstan, Turkmenistan and Uzbekistan subsequently withdrew from that agreement, and Belarus announced its intention to do so in 2005.)

In June 2000 the Council of Heads of State adopted a plan and schedule for the implementation of priority measures related to the creation of the long-proposed free trade zone. In September 2003 the leaders of Belarus, Kazakhstan, Russia and Ukraine (Union of Four) reached an agreement on establishing the framework for a Common Economic Space (CES), envisaging the creation of a free trade zone and the gradual harmonization of tariffs, customs and transport legislation. While participation at each stage would remain optional, decisions would be obligatory and certain areas of sovereignty would eventually be ceded to a council of heads of state and a commission. The Union of Four accord entered into force in April 2004. Meeting on the sidelines of the CIS summit held in October 2007, EurAsEC leaders determined to establish a fully operational customs union over the next three years, with Belarus, Kazakhstan and Russia as the founding members, and Kyrgyzstan, Tajikistan and Uzbekistan to join at a later date, once they had achieved the requisite accession conditions. Ukraine, which was also committed to participation in the GUAM Free Trade Zone, was not an active participant in the negotiating process on the CES. Despite significant growth in the gross domestic product of the poorer states of the CIS at that time (Armenia, Azerbaijan, Georgia, Kyrgyzstan, Moldova, Tajikistan and Uzbekistan, then known as the CIS-7), in April 2005 the IMF called for greater harmonization of trade rules within the CIS, as well as liberalization of transit policies and the removal of non-tariff barriers. The customs union between Russia, Belarus and Kazakhstan finally entered into formal existence on 1 January 2010, when a common external tariff was adopted; on 1 July 2010 a harmonized customs code came into force. In September 2013 Armenia announced its intention (supported by Russia) to join the so far tripartite customs union. In December 2010 the heads of state of Russia, Belarus and Kazakhstan signed several agreements aimed at finalizing the establishment of the planned CES, and in November 2011 they signed a declaration on Eurasian economic integration and adopted a roadmap outlining integration processes aimed at creating a Eurasian Economic Union, to be established, provisionally, by 1 January 2015, and to be based on the customs union and proposed CES. In October 2011, in St Petersburg, the leaders of Russia, Armenia, Belarus, Kazakhstan, Kyrgyzstan, Moldova, Tajikistan and Ukraine (therefore all CIS states except for Azerbaijan, Uzbekistan and Turkmenistan) signed an Agreement establishing the CIS Free Trade Area—CISFTA; this aimed to simplify trade and economic relations, and to regulate a free trade regime, replacing several previous multilateral agreements and around 100 bilateral agreements. The CISFTA Agreement entered into force in September 2012. A protocol providing for Uzbekistan's accession to the CISFTA was signed in May 2013. By April 2014 the CISFTA Agreement had been ratified by Armenia, Belarus, Kazakhstan, Moldova, Russia, Ukraine and Uzbekistan. Under the CISFTA accord all import tariffs, with the exception of those on sugar, were to be eliminated by 1 January 2015; meanwhile, negotiations were to be initiated on phasing out existing export tariffs. In October 2011 CIS leaders also adopted an accord on basic principles of currency regulation and currency controls within the CIS. The development of a supplementary accord on free trade in services is under consideration.

In January 1993, at the signing of the CIS Charter, the member countries endorsed the establishment of a new Inter-state Bank to facilitate payments between the republics and to co-ordinate monetary credit policy.

In December 2000, in accordance with the CSR and Treaty of Union, the Presidents of Belarus and Russia signed an agreement providing for the adoption by Belarus of the Russian currency from 1 January 2005, and for the introduction of a new joint Union currency by 1 January 2008; the adoption by Belarus of the Russian currency was, however, subsequently postponed. Following the entry into formal existence on 1 January 2010 of the customs union between Belarus, Russia and Kazakhstan, the introduction of a new common currency unit for the members of the union was under consideration.

REGIONAL SECURITY

At a meeting of heads of government in March 1992 agreements on settling interstate conflicts were signed by all participating states (except Turkmenistan). At the same meeting an agreement on the status of border troops was signed by five states. In May a five-year Collective Security Treaty was signed. In July further documents were signed on collective security and it was agreed to establish joint forces to intervene peacefully in CIS disputes. (CIS peacekeeping forces were sent into Tajikistan, and Abkhazia, Georgia during 1993–2000, and 1994–2009, respectively.) In December 1993 the Council of Defence Ministers agreed to establish a secretariat to co-ordinate military co-operation. In November 1995 the Council of Defence Ministers authorized the establishment of a Joint Air Defence System, to be co-ordinated largely by Russia. In April 1999 Armenia, Belarus, Kazakhstan, Kyrgyzstan, Russia and Tajikistan signed a protocol to extend the Collective Security Treaty (while Azerbaijan, Georgia and Uzbekistan then withdrew from the agreement). In April 1998 the Council proposed drawing up a draft programme for military and technical co-operation between member countries and also discussed procedures advising on the use and maintenance of armaments and military hardware. The programme was approved by CIS heads of state in October 2002.

In June 2000 the Councils of Heads of State and Government issued a declaration concerning the maintenance of strategic stability and adopted a short-term programme for combating international terrorism (perceived to be a significant threat in Central Asia). In June 2001 a CIS Anti-terrorism Centre was established in Moscow. A Central Asian subdivision of the CIS Anti-Terrorism Centre was established in Bishkek, in October 2002. In October 2001, in response to the major terrorist attacks perpetrated in September against targets in the USA, the parties to the Collective Security Treaty adopted a new anti-terrorism plan. In December 2002 the committee of the Collective Security Treaty member countries adopted a protocol on the exchange of expertise and information on terrorist organizations and their activities. In April 2003 the signatory states determined to establish the Collective Security Treaty Organization (CSTO); ratification of its founding documents was completed by September, when it applied for UN observer status (granted in December 2004). The CIS summit in September 2003 approved draft decisions to control the sale of portable anti-aircraft missiles and to set up a joint co-ordination structure to address illegal immigration. During September 2004 the CIS Council of Heads of State determined to establish a Security Council, comprising the ministers responsible for foreign affairs and for defence, and heads of security and border control.

The signatory countries to the Collective Security Treaty have participated in regular joint military exercises. A summit meeting of CSTO leaders held in October 2007 endorsed documents enabling the future establishment of CSTO joint peacekeeping forces and the creation of a co-ordination council for the heads of member states' emergency response agencies. In February 2009 the participating states in the CSTO determined to develop a rapid reaction military force, which would be deployed to combat terrorists and in response to regional emergencies. In February 2009 Belarus and Russia signed an agreement on establishing a joint integrated air defence system, and in January 2013 a similar accord was concluded between Russia and Kazakhstan. A meeting of the Council of Defence Ministers held in June 2009, in Moscow, addressed conceptual approaches to the development of military co-operation among CIS countries until 2015. Leaders participating in the 2010 summit meeting, convened in December, in Moscow, signed an agreement on advancing military co-operation until 2015, as well as concluding agreements addressing CIS common border policy; trafficking in humans and drugs; terrorism; and combating extremist terrorist activity. In March 2010 the Secretaries-General of the CSTO and the UN signed a declaration on co-operation, giving the CSTO full recognition as a regional security organization, similar to that accorded to NATO; future possible areas of co-operation were identified as conflict prevention and resolution, countering terrorism and transnational crime, and combating illegal arms-trafficking. In December CSTO ministers of defence and foreign affairs resolved to commit forces to collective peacekeeping activities in cases of emergency: the first CSTO peacekeeping training exercise ('Undefeatable Brotherhood') was launched in October 2012, in Kazakhstan. In September 2012 the CSTO and UN Department of Peacekeeping Operations signed a memorandum of co-operation providing for the future expansion of collaboration on peacekeeping activities, including increased participation by CSTO member states in UN-mandated peacekeeping missions. Uzbekistan (which joined the CSTO in June 2006) suspended its membership of the Organization in June 2012. Meeting in Kaliningrad, Russia, in July of that year, the CIS Council of Defence Ministers focused once again on the development of an integrated air defence architecture; Uzbekistan sent a delegation to the gathering, and subsequently confirmed that—despite distancing itself from the CSTO—it would continue to participate in the CIS Joint Air Defence System. The participants approved proposals for the Chistoye Nebo (Clear Sky) joint command staff training exercise that was subsequently conducted in October, in airspace over Kazakhstan, Kyrgyzstan and Tajikistan, and agreed on joint training exercises to be implemented by CIS states during 2013; these included 'Combat Community 2013', a joint live-fire tactical exercise that was conducted in Ashuluk, Russia, with the objective of strengthening the command and control systems of CIS militaries. In December 2012 CIS heads of state, meeting in Aşgabat, Turkmenistan, gave consideration to issues including enhancing co-operation in countering drugs-trafficking, other organized crime, and terrorism.

The CIS participates in the Paris Pact—a partnership of more than 50 countries and international organizations aiming to combat the traffic in and consumption of Afghan opiates and related problems in affected countries along the Afghan opiates-trafficking routes—that was launched in May 2003 at a Ministerial Conference on Drug Routes from Central Asia to Europe, convened in Paris, France. An Agreement on the Co-operation of the CIS Member States in Combating Trafficking in Persons, Human Organs and Tissues was adopted in November 2005 and has been ratified by Azerbaijan, Armenia, Belarus, Kyrgyzstan and Russia. In August 2005 CIS member states adopted a blueprint on joint co-operation in combating terrorism and extremism; the blueprint provided for the exchange of relevant information between member states and for the extradition of individuals suspected of financing or committing terrorist acts. In October 2009 CIS heads of states approved a number of additional measures for strengthening border control.

OTHER ACTIVITIES

An agreement on legislative co-operation was signed at an inter-parliamentary conference in January 1992; joint commissions were established to co-ordinate action on economy, law, pensions, housing, energy and ecology. The CIS Charter, formulated in January 1993, provided for the establishment of an interstate court. In October 1994 a Convention on the rights of minorities was adopted at the meeting of the heads of state; this has been ratified by Azerbaijan, Armenia, Belarus, Kyrgyzstan and Tajikistan. In May 1995, at the sixth plenary session of the IPA-CIS, several acts to improve co-ordination of legislation were approved, relating to migration of labour, consumer rights, and the rights of prisoners of war; revised legislation on labour migration and the social protection of migrant workers was adopted in November 2005. A CIS Convention on Human Rights and Fundamental Freedoms, adopted at that time, and incorporating the Statute of a proposed CIS Commission on Human Rights, has been ratified by Belarus, Kyrgyzstan, Russia and Tajikistan. In November 2006 an agreement on the protection of participants in the criminal justice system was signed by eight member states. In October 2007 CIS heads of state (excluding those of Georgia and Turkmenistan) adopted determined to establish a special body to oversee migration in the region. In November 2008 the CIS Convention on the Legal Status of Working Migrants and their Families was signed by the heads of member states. In September 2011 CIS heads of states addressed a programme on co-operation in combating illegal migration during 2012–14. CIS leaders meeting in Moscow in May 2005 agreed to sign a declaration aimed at enhancing co-operation between CIS members in the humanitarian, cultural and scientific spheres. The October 2009 Chişinău summit meeting addressed advancing co-operation in the humanitarian sphere.

The creation of a Council of Ministers of Internal Affairs was approved at the heads of state meeting in January 1996; the Council was to promote co-operation between the law enforcement bodies of member states. The IPA-CIS has approved a number of model laws, relating to areas including banking and financial services; charity; defence; ecology, the economy; education; the regulation of refugee problems; combating terrorism; and social issues, including obligatory social insurance against production accidents and occupational diseases. The harmonization of legislation related to information security in the CIS is under consideration.

In December 2010 CIS heads of state endorsed the CIS Strategy for International Youth Co-operation until 2020; In November 2013 CIS heads of state approved an action plan guiding the implementation of the Strategy during 2014–15.

The CIS has held a number of discussions relating to the environment. In July 1992 agreements were concluded to establish an Inter-state Ecological Council. 2013 was recognized as the Year of Ecological Culture and Environment in the CIS. In May 2013 CIS heads of government signed an agreement relating to the co-ordination of inter-state co-operation on the use of nuclear energy for peaceful purposes, and endorsed the creation of a regional data bank of patents and innovations. In November 2013 CIS heads of state, convened in St Petersburg, adopted a concept of co-operation between member states in the area of renewable energy, and a priority action plan for its implementation.

In July 1992 CIS member states agreed to establish Mir, an inter-state television and radio company. In February 1995 the IPA-CIS established a Council of Heads of News Agencies, in order to promote the concept of a single information area. In October 2002 a decision was made by CIS heads of government to enhance mutual understanding and co-operation between members countries through Mir radio and television broadcasts. A Connect CIS Summit was convened by the International Telecommunications Union and partners in Minsk, in November 2009, with participation by CIS leaders and representatives from businesses and financial institutions, with the aim of mobilizing the financial and technical resources required to facilitate a swift regional transition towards a digital infrastructure and services. The Summit urged greater investment in regional ICT broadband access. In October 2013 a meeting of CIS media representatives was convened, in Chişinău, Moldova, to address the onwards development of cyber space.

The CIS Election Monitoring Organization (CIS-EMO) was established—and registered as a non-governmental organization—in September 2003, to observe primarily elections conducted in the post-Soviet space. From March 2005 Ukraine temporarily suspended its participation in CIS-EMO, owing to discrepancies in the findings of the observers of that body with those of the OSCE during the Ukrainian presidential election that was held in October and December 2004. In 2013 CIS-EMO teams monitored presidential elections held in Armenia in February, in Azerbaijan in October, and in Tajikistan, in November; and legislative elections held in Turkmenistan in December. The CIS Convention on Democratic Elections Standards, Electoral Rights and Freedoms in Member States, adopted in October 2002, has been ratified by Armenia, Kyrgyzstan, Moldova, Russia and Tajikistan.

In November 2013 CIS heads of state approved a strategy for co-operation in the field of tourism until 2020, including the creation of a common CIS tourist space.

ASSOCIATED BODIES

Interparliamentary Assembly of Member Nations of the Commonwealth of Independent States (IPA-CIS): Shpalernaya 47, Tavricheskiy Palace, St Petersburg, 191015 Russia; tel. (812) 326-69-45; fax (812) 272-22-48; e-mail kanz@iacis.ru; internet www.iacis.ru; f. 1992; the first Assembly was held in Bishkek, Kyrgyzstan, in Sept. 1992; the activities of the IPA-CIS are organized by the IPA-CIS Council; in Feb. 2006 the IPA-CIS Council determined to establish the International Institute of Monitoring Democracy Development, Parliamentarianism and Suffrage Protection for the Citizens of the IPA-CIS Member Nations; the Institute trains election officials and researches best practices in election observation. In 2013 IPA-CIS observation missions monitored presidential elections held in Armenia (in Feb.), in Azerbaijan (in Oct.), and in Tajikistan (in Nov.); and legislative elections held in Turkmenistan in Dec., and a mission was sent to observe the parliamentary elections held in Serbia in March 2014; the Assembly organizes the annual St Petersburg International Economic Forum; the inaugural meeting of the Youth IPA-CIS Assembly was convened, at IPA-CIS headquarters, in March of that year; mem. parliaments: Armenia, Azerbaijan, Belarus, Kazakhstan, Kyrgyzstan, Moldova, Russia, Tajikistan and Ukraine; the Afghanistan parliament has observer status; Sec.-Gen. ALEXEY SERGEEV.

Interstate Bank: 15 Shukhov St, Moscow, 115162, Russia; tel. (495) 954-92-58; fax (495) 954-70-12; e-mail info@isbnk.org; internet www.isbnk.org; f. 1993 by 10 CIS member states to facilitate payments between the republics and to co-ordinate monetary credit policy, and in general to promote the development of member economies; managed by a Council comprising the governors of central banks, and governmental representatives, of the founding members; has direct access to the national payment systems of six countries: Armenia, Belarus, Kazakhstan, Kyrgyzstan, Russia and Tajikistan; implements arrangements for combating laundering of proceeds from crime; mems: Armenia, Belarus, Kazakhstan, Kyrgyzstan, Moldova, Russia, Tajikistan, Turkmenistan, Uzbekistan, Ukraine; Pres. IGOR G. SOUVOROV.

COOPERATION COUNCIL FOR THE ARAB STATES OF THE GULF

Address: POB 7153, Riyadh 11462, Saudi Arabia.

Telephone: (1) 482-7777; **fax:** (1) 482-9089; **internet:** www.gcc-sg.org.

More generally known as the Gulf Cooperation Council (GCC), the organization was established on 25 May 1981 by six Arab states. Its charter describes the GCC as providing the means for realizing co-ordination, integration and co-operation in all economic, social and cultural affairs.

MEMBERS*

Bahrain	Oman	Saudi Arabia
Kuwait	Qatar	United Arab Emirates

* In December 2001 the Supreme Council admitted Yemen (which applied to join the organization as a full member in 1996) as a member of the GCC's Arab Bureau of Education for the Gulf States, as a participant in meetings of GCC ministers responsible for health and for labour and social affairs, and, alongside the GCC member

states, as a participant in the biennial Gulf Cup football tournament. In September 2008 Yemen's inclusion in future GCC development planning was approved and Yemen was admitted to GCC control and auditing apparatuses. Negotiations were ongoing on the full accession of Yemen to the GCC by 2016. In May 2011 the GCC invited Jordan and Morocco to submit membership applications.

Organization

(April 2014)

SUPREME COUNCIL

The Supreme Council is the highest authority of the GCC. It comprises the heads of member states and holds one regular session annually, and in emergency session if demanded by two or more members. The Council also convenes an annual consultative meeting. The Presidency of the Council is undertaken by each state in turn, in alphabetical order. The Supreme Council draws up the overall policy of the organization; it discusses recommendations and laws presented to it by the Ministerial Council and the Secretariat General in preparation for endorsement. The GCC's charter provided for the creation of a commission for the settlement of disputes between member states, to be attached to and appointed by the Supreme Council. The Supreme Council convenes the commission for the settlement of disputes on an ad hoc basis to address altercations between member states as they arise. The 34th annual meeting of the Supreme Council was convened in December 2013 in Kuwait City, Kuwait.

CONSULTATIVE COMMISSION

The Consultative Commission, comprising 30 members (five from each member state) nominated for a three-year period, acts as an advisory body, considering matters referred to it by the Supreme Council. In 2013 the creation of a regulatory authority to oversee food and drugs in the GCC states; the establishment of a joint GCC specialized centre for public and preventative health; the development of a GCC media strategy; the creation of mechanisms aimed at combating corruption and removing obstacles to development; and children's cultural programmes were given consideration by the Commission.

COMMISSION FOR THE SETTLEMENT OF DISPUTES

The Commission for the Settlement of Disputes is formed by the Supreme Council for each case, on an ad hoc basis in accordance with the nature of each specific dispute.

MINISTERIAL COUNCIL

The Ministerial Council consists of the ministers responsible for foreign affairs of member states (or other ministers acting on their behalf), meeting every three months, and in emergency session if demanded by two or more members. It prepares for the meetings of the Supreme Council, and draws up policies, recommendations, studies and projects aimed at developing co-operation and co-ordination among member states in various spheres. GCC ministerial committees have been established in a number of areas of co-operation; sectoral ministerial meetings are held periodically.

SECRETARIAT GENERAL

The Secretary-General is appointed by the Supreme Council for a three-year term renewable once. The position is rotated among member states in order to ensure equal representation. The Secretariat, which assists member states to implement recommendations by the Supreme and Ministerial Councils, and prepares reports and studies, budgets and accounts, comprises the following divisions and departments: Political Affairs; Economic Affairs; Human and Environmental Affairs; Military Affairs; Security; Legal Affairs; the Office of the Secretary-General; Finance and Administrative Affairs; a Patent Bureau; an Administrative Development Unit; an Internal Auditing Unit; an Information Centre; and a Telecommunications Bureau (based in Bahrain). Five Assistant Secretaries-General are appointed by the Ministerial Council upon the recommendation of the Secretary-General. There is a GCC delegation office in Brussels, Belgium.

Secretary-General: ABDUL LATIF BIN RASHID AL-ZAYANI (Bahrain).

Activities

ARAB GULF UNION COUNCIL

In December 2011 the 32nd summit of the Supreme Council welcomed a proposal by King Abdullah of Saudi Arabia specifying that the basis of GCC collaboration should progress from the stage of co-operation to full political, economic and military union (as an 'Arab Gulf Union Council'). The summit directed the Ministerial Council to form a specialized commission, to comprise three members from each member state, to study the proposal. The initiative was regarded as a means of consolidating the organization in view of the Arab uprisings of 2011 and consequent changed regional political landscape. At the inaugural meeting of the commission, held in February 2012, the GCC Secretary-General noted that the full economic integration of member states would precede political union. An extraordinary summit of GCC heads of state was held in May to discuss the initiative, which, at that time, was most strongly supported by the Governments of Saudi Arabia and Bahrain. In December 2013 Oman publicly expressed its opposition to the proposal.

COMPREHENSIVE DEVELOPMENT STRATEGY FOR 2010–25

In December 1998 the Supreme Council approved a long-term strategy for regional development, covering the period 2000–25, aimed at achieving integrated, sustainable development in all member states and the co-ordination of national development plans. Meeting in December 2010 the 31st summit of GCC heads of state adopted a revised comprehensive development strategy for member states, covering 2010–25. The updated strategy identified several ongoing challenges including: promoting integration over competition, and collective over national development efforts, within the grouping; scarcity of water resources in the region, the high salinity content in local water, and the high cost of alternative water resources; limitations on cultivating farming lands; the disproportionate engagement of national citizens in state employment and dependence on foreign workers in the non-governmental labour market; incompatibility between educational and training goals and the needs of the labour market (the region has a large non-resident population); investment decline in certain sectors, and migration of national capital abroad owing to limited local investment opportunities; the existence of budgetary deficits; the potential impacts of climate change on the environment; and global development, security and economic challenges. The following strategic goals were outlined: pursuing a framework enabling sustainable development; ensuring adequate water for development needs; achieving self-sufficiency in meeting the security and defence needs of the GCC development process; achieving integrated economic partnership; eliminating sources of vulnerability from the GCC economic environment; deriving maximum benefit from infrastructure facilities; technical and scientific capacity building; enhancing social development in the areas of education and training, health, and intellectual and cultural development; and enhancing the productivity of the GCC labour force.

ECONOMIC CO-OPERATION

In December 2001 the Supreme Council, meeting in Muscat, Oman, adopted a new agreement on regional economic union ('Economic Agreement Between the Arab GCC States'), superseding the original 1981 Unified Economic Agreement. The new accord brought forward the deadline for the establishment of the proposed customs union to 1 January 2003 and provided for a standard tariff level of 5% for foreign imports (with the exception of 53 essential commodities previously exempted by the Supreme Council). The agreement also provided for the introduction, by January 2010, of a GCC single currency, linked to the US dollar (this deadline, however, was not met).

The GCC customs union was launched, as planned, on 1 January 2003. In July the GCC entered into negotiations with Yemen on harmonizing economic legislation. In December 2005 the Supreme Council approved standards for the introduction of the planned single currency. The GCC Common Market was inaugurated on 1 January 2008. Oman and the United Arab Emirates (UAE) withdrew from the process to introduce a single currency in 2007 and 2009, respectively. An accord on Gulf Monetary Union was signed in June 2009 by Bahrain, Kuwait, Qatar and Saudi Arabia, and was approved by the 30th meeting of the Supreme Council, held in Kuwait in December. In May 2010 the GCC Secretary-General stated that the introduction of the single currency was unlikely to occur for at least five years.

In April 1993 GCC central bank governors agreed to establish a joint banking supervisory committee, in order to devise rules for GCC banks to operate in other member states. In December 1997 GCC heads of state authorized guidelines to this effect. These were to apply only to banks established at least 10 years previously with a share capital of more than US $100m.

The 29th summit meeting, held in Muscat, in December 2008, discussed the ongoing global financial crisis, and directed relevant ministerial committees to intensify co-ordination among member states to mitigate the negative impact of the global situation on the region's economies.

In April 2014 the GCC inaugurated GCC-Stat, a Muscat-based centre that was to provide national statistical and other data for member states.

TRADE AND INDUSTRY

In December 1992 the Supreme Council endorsed Patent Regulations for GCC member states to facilitate regional scientific and technological research. A GCC Patent Office for the protection of intellectual property in the region was established in 1998. In December 2006 the Supreme Council endorsed a system to unify trademarks in GCC states.

In December 2001 the Supreme council adopted unified procedures and measures for facilitating the intra-regional movement of people and commercial traffic, as well as unified standards in the areas of education and health care. In August 2003 the GCC adopted new measures permitting nationals of its member states to work in, and to seek loans from financial institutions in, any other member state. In December 2005 the Supreme Council approved a plan to unify member states' trade policies. The Council adopted further measures aimed at facilitating the movement of people, goods and services between member countries, with consideration given to environmental issues and consumer protection, and agreed to permit GCC citizens to undertake commercial activities in all member states.

AGRICULTURE

The GCC states aim to achieve food security through the best utilization of regional natural resources. A unified agricultural policy for GCC countries, initially endorsed in 1985, was revised in December 1996. Unified agricultural quarantine laws were adopted by the Supreme Council in December 2001. In 2006 an agreement was entered into with FAO on the regional implementation of a technical programme on agricultural quarantine development, aimed at protecting the agricultural sector from plant disease epidemics. A permanent committee on fisheries aims to co-ordinate national fisheries policies, to establish designated fishing periods and to undertake surveys of the fishing potential in the Arabian (Persian) Gulf. In December 2010 the summit meeting of GCC leaders called for a comprehensive review of agricultural sector development, with a focus on policies aimed at preserving water resources; the regional scarcity of water, and its high saline content, have been an area of concern.

COMMUNICATIONS, INFORMATION AND TRANSPORT

GCC ministers responsible for telecommunications, posts and information technology, and for information, convene regularly. The 2001 Economic Agreement provided for member states to take all necessary means to ensure the integration of their telecommunication policies, including telephone, post and data network services. A simplified passport system was approved in 1997 to facilitate travel between member countries. In December 2006 the Supreme Council requested that all GCC members conclude studies on the implementation of a GCC rail network, which was to interconnect all member states, with a view to enhancing economic development. It was announced in 2010 that the GCC states would invest nearly US $119,600m. in infrastructure projects during 2010–20, of which 90% was to be allocated to developing the regional rail infrastructure. A report, issued in April 2011, on the status of GCC infrastructure development schemes, stated that some $452m. of infrastructure projects were under way in the region. It was envisaged that increased expenditure on infrastructure projects, representing a diversification from petroleum-based growth, might strengthen the regional economy during the ongoing global economic slowdown.

In December 2012 the 33rd GCC summit meeting, held in Manama, Bahrain, approved the creation of a GCC commission for civil aviation.

ENERGY AND ENVIRONMENT

GCC ministers responsible for petroleum hold occasional co-ordination meetings to discuss the agenda and policies of the Organization of the Petroleum Exporting Countries (OPEC), to which all six member states belong. In November 2003 ministers responsible for petroleum determined to develop a GCC Common Mining Law.

The Unified Economic Agreement provided for the establishment and co-ordination of an infrastructure of power-generating stations and desalination plans. The 2001 Economic Agreement also stressed that member states should adopt integrated economic policies with regard to developing the basic utilities infrastructure. In December 1997 GCC heads of state declared that work should commence on the first stage of the plan to integrate the electricity networks of the six member countries, under the management of an independent authority. The estimated cost of the project was more than US $6,000m. The Gulf Council Interconnection Authority was established in 1999, with its headquarters in Dammam, Saudi Arabia. In 2001 a GCC Electric Interconnection Commission was established, which was to support the project. The first phase of the project was completed, and in trial operation, by 2009.

In February 2001 GCC ministers responsible for water and electricity determined to formulate a common water policy for the region. Ministers responsible for electricity and water approved an Electric Interconnection Agreement in November 2009, setting out the relations between the contracting parties. A GCC conference on Power and Water Desalination was convened in Qatar in October 2011. A Common Water Emergency Plan is under development.

In December 2006 the Supreme Council declared its intention to pursue the use of nuclear energy technology in the GCC region. The Council commissioned a study to develop a joint nuclear energy programme, but emphasized that any development of this technology would be for peaceful purposes only and fully disclosed to the international community.

In December 2001 GCC member states adopted the Convention on the Conservation of Wildlife and their Natural Habitats in the Countries of the GCC; the Convention entered into force in April 2003. In December 2007 the Supreme Council adopted a green environment initiative, aimed at improving the efficiency and performance of environmental institutions in member states.

REGIONAL SECURITY

Although no mention of defence or security was made in the original charter, the summit meeting which ratified the charter also issued a statement rejecting any foreign military presence in the region. The Supreme Council meeting in November 1981 agreed to include defence co-operation in the activities of the organization: as a result, ministers responsible for defence met in January 1982 to discuss a common security policy, including a joint air defence system and standardization of weapons. In November 1984 member states agreed to form the Peninsula ('Al Jazeera') Shield Force for rapid deployment against external aggression, comprising units from the armed forces of each country under a central command to be based in north-eastern Saudi Arabia.

In December 2000 GCC leaders adopted a joint defence pact aimed at enhancing the grouping's defence capability. The pact formally committed member states to defending any other member states from external attack, envisaging the expansion of the Peninsula Shield Force from 5,000 to 22,000 troops and the creation of a new rapid deployment function within the Force. In addition, the pact established a Joint Military Committee to promote co-operation in joint military exercises and co-ordination in the field of military industries. In March 2001 the GCC member states inaugurated the first phase of the long-envisaged joint air defence system. In December GCC heads of state authorized the establishment of a supreme defence council, comprising member states' ministers responsible for defence, to address security-related matters and supervise the implementation of the joint defence pact. The council was to convene on an annual basis. Meeting in emergency session in early February 2003 GCC ministers for defence and foreign affairs agreed to deploy the Peninsula Field Force in Kuwait, in view of the then impending US military action against neighbouring Iraq. The full deployment of 3,000 Peninsula Shield troops to Kuwait was completed in early March; the force was withdrawn two months later. In December 2005 the Supreme Council, meeting in Abu Dhabi, UAE, agreed that the Peninsula Shield Force should be reconstituted. Proposals to develop the Force were endorsed by the 2006 heads of state summit, held in December, in Riyadh, Saudi Arabia. In December 2009 the 30th Supreme Council meeting ratified a new defence strategy that included upgrading the capabilities of the Peninsula Shield, undertaking joint military projects, and pursuing co-operation in combating the illegal trade of armaments to GCC member states.

In 1992 Iran extended its authority over the island of Abu Musa, which it had administered under a joint arrangement with the UAE since 1971. In September 1992 the GCC Ministerial Council condemned Iran's continued occupation of the island and efforts to consolidate its presence, and reiterated support of UAE sovereignty over Abu Musa, as well as the largely uninhabited Greater and Lesser Tunb islands (also claimed by Iran). All three islands are situated in the approach to the Strait of Hormuz, through which petroleum exports are transported. The GCC has condemned repeated military exercises conducted by Iran in the waters around the disputed islands as a threat to regional security and a violation of the UAE's sovereignty. Successive GCC summit meetings have restated support for the UAE's right to regain sovereignty over the three islands (and over their territorial waters, airspace, continental shelf and economic zone). In December 2010 the 31st summit meeting stated disappointment at the failure of repeated contacts with Iran over the matter. The meeting welcomed international efforts to engage with Iran over its controversial nuclear programme, particularly by the 5+1 Group (comprising the People's Republic of China, France, Germany, Russia and the United Kingdom). In December 2012 the 33rd summit meeting urged Iran to co-operate with the International Atomic Energy Agencyy (IAEA), deeming that its nuclear programme threatened international as well as regional security. In December 2013 the 34th summit meeting welcomed the adoption in November by Iran and the 5+1 Group of a joint plan of action (to be monitored by the IAEA) that aimed to ensure that Iran's nuclear programme remained exclusively peaceful. The meeting also welcomed a recent rapprochement between the Iranian authorities and the GCC, and emphasized the importance of closer co-operation on the basis of the principles of good neighbourliness, non-interference in internal affairs, respect for the sovereignty of countries in the region, and the absence of threats of the use of force. The Supreme Council renewed emphasis on the continued Iranian occupation of the Abu Musa and the Greater and Lesser Tunbs.

In March 2011, in response to a request from the Bahrain Government following a series of violent clashes between opposition protesters and security forces in that country, the GCC dispatched a contingent of Peninsula Shield Force troops (numbering some 1,000 from Saudi Arabia and 500 from the UAE, with more than 100 armoured vehicles), to Bahrain to protect strategic facilities and to help maintain order.

The December 2005 summit of GCC heads of state issued a statement declaring that the Gulf region should be free of weapons of mass destruction.

In December 2009 the 30th Supreme Council meeting emphasized the GCC's support for Iraq's sovereignty, independence and territorial integrity, on non-interference in Iraq's internal affairs, and on the preservation of its Arab and Islamic identity; and urged inclusive national reconciliation. The meeting also stated concern over acts of marine piracy in the Gulf of Aden, the Red Sea and other regional waterways, and emphasized the need to intensify co-operation in challenging the perpetrators. The December 2010 summit meeting expressed appreciation at efforts made by the GCC naval forces in combating maritime piracy and protecting shipping corridors.

In July 2007 the Ministerial Council determined to establish a GCC Disaster Control Center; a team of experts in disaster management was to be established there. In December 2010 the GCC summit approved a regional plan of action to prepare for and respond to radiation risks.

In December 2013 the 34th GCC summit mandated the Joint Military Committee to establish a unified military command, in order to strengthen the grouping's regional security structures. A joint police force was also endorsed. The summit meeting announced the establishment of a Gulf Academy for Strategic and Security Studies, in the UAE, to enhance understanding of issues including missile defence, border security and counter terrorism.

In early March 2014 Bahrain, Saudi Arabia and the UAE announced that they had recalled their ambassadors from Qatar, and requested Qatar to desist from supporting any party that aimed to 'threaten the security or stability of any GCC member'. It was reported that they deemed their security to be endangered by alleged support by Qatar for antagonistic media campaigns conducted by Islamist elements.

EXTERNAL RELATIONS

In June 1988 an agreement was signed by the GCC and European Community (EC) ministers responsible for economic co-operation; this took effect from January 1990. Under the accord a joint ministerial council (meeting on an annual basis) was established, and working groups were subsequently created to promote co-operation in several specific areas. Negotiations on formulating a free trade agreement commenced in October 1990. GCC heads of state, meeting in December 1997, condemned statements issued by the European Parliament, as well as by other organizations, regarding human rights issues in member states and insisted they amounted to interference in GCC judicial systems. In January 2003 the GCC established a customs union, which was a precondition of the proposed GCC-European Union (EU, as the restructured EC was now known) free trade agreement. Negotiations on the agreement, initiated in 2003, were suspended by the GCC in May 2010, owing to a dispute over export duties; by 2014 the negotiations had not been formally restarted, although informal contacts were ongoing. In June 2013 the GCC and EU concluded a joint work programme for the period 2013–16 that aimed to deepen bilateral co-operation in areas including disaster management, education, energy, the environment, health and tourism. In July 2009 the GCC and the European Free Trade Association (EFTA) adopted a bilateral free trade agreement.

In September 1994 GCC ministers responsible for foreign affairs decided to end the secondary and tertiary embargo on trade with Israel. In December 1996 the foreign ministers of the Damascus Declaration states, convened in Cairo, Egypt, requested the USA to exert financial pressure on Israel to halt the construction of settlements on occupied Arab territory. In December 2001 GCC heads of state issued a statement holding Israeli government policy responsible for the escalating crisis in the Palestinian territories. The consultative meeting of heads of state held in May 2002 declared its support for a Saudi-proposed initiative aimed at achieving a peaceful resolution of the crisis. GCC heads of state summits have repeatedly urged the international community to encourage Israel to sign the Nuclear Non-Proliferation Treaty. In December 2012 the 33rd GCC summit welcomed the granting of observer status to Palestine by the UN General Assembly in the previous month.

In June 1997 ministers responsible for foreign affairs of the Damascus Declaration states agreed to pursue efforts to establish a free trade zone throughout the region, which they envisaged as the nucleus of a future Arab common market. Meanwhile, the Greater Arab Free Trade Area, an initiative of the League of Arab States, entered into effect on 1 January 2005.

The GCC-USA Economic Dialogue, which commenced in 1985, convenes periodically as a government forum to promote co-operation between the GCC economies and the USA. Since the late 1990s private sector interests have been increasingly represented at sessions of the Dialogue. It was announced in March 2001 that a business forum was to be established under the auspices of the Dialogue, to act as a permanent means of facilitating trade and investment between the GCC countries and the USA.

In December 2008 an agreement establishing a GCC-Singapore Free Trade Area (GSFTA) was signed, in Doha, Qatar. An inaugural meeting of ministers responsible for foreign affairs of the GCC and the Association of Southeast Asian Nations (ASEAN) was held in June 2009, in Manama. The meeting adopted a GCC-ASEAN Joint Vision as a framework for future co-operation between the two groupings. A second meeting, held in Singapore, in May–June 2010, approved an ASEAN-GCC Action Plan, to guide co-operation during the two-year period 2010–12. Meeting in October 2012 GCC and ASEAN foreign affairs ministers extended the Plan into 2013, and established several joint working groups aimed at strengthening joint activities. GCC-ASEAN co-operation was reaffirmed by the third joint meeting of foreign affairs, held in November 2013, in Manama. A fourth ministerial meeting was to be held during 2014, in Myanmar.

The GCC Secretary-General denounced the major terrorist attacks that were perpetrated in September 2001 against targets in the USA. Meeting in an emergency session in mid-September, in Riyadh, GCC ministers responsible for foreign affairs agreed to support the aims of the developing international coalition against terrorism. Meanwhile, however, member states urged parallel international resolve to halt action by the Israeli security forces against Palestinians. In December the Supreme Council declared the organization's full co-operation with the anti-terrorism coalition. In December 2006 the Supreme Council determined to establish a specialized security committee to counter terrorism.

In March 2011 GCC leaders issued a statement urging the League of Arab States to take measures to protect citizens in Libya from the effects of violent measures against opposition elements being taken at that time by the regime of the then Libyan leader Col Muammar al-Qaddafi. In October the Council met in emergency session to discuss ongoing violent unrest in Syria, where suppression by the regime of anti-government protests during that year had resulted in more than 3,000 civilian fatalities. In early 2012 all GCC member states withdrew their diplomatic presence from Syria in protest at the Syrian regime's violent suppression of mass anti-government protests. In December the 33rd summit formally recognized the National Coalition for Syrian Revolutionary and Opposition Forces, formed in November, as the 'sole lawful representative' of the Syrian people. The 34th summit, convened in December 2013, condemned the Syrian President, Bashar al-Assad, for his government's ongoing attacks against the civilian population; the meeting also urged the withdrawal of all foreign forces from Syria.

In April 2011, in response to mounting political unrest in Yemen, the GCC proposed a mediation plan whereby President Saleh of Yemen would resign and receive immunity from prosecution, anti-Government activists would desist from protesting, and a new government of national unity would be appointed, pending the staging of a presidential election within two months of Saleh's proposed withdrawal. Saleh, however, refused to sign the plan at that time, and, in late May, the GCC mediation attempt was suspended. In September Saleh indicated that he might be willing to approve the plan although opposition elements expressed scepticism that Saleh would fully adhere to the peace initiative. In October the UN Security Council unanimously approved a resolution that expressed serious concern over the worsening security situation in Yemen; demanded that all sides immediately reject the use of violence to achieve their political goals; and called on all parties to sign the GCC peace initiative. In late November President Saleh finally signed the GCC-mediated agreement. Accordingly, Saleh relinquished his constitutional powers and, in February 2012, presidential elections were held.

In November 2012 GCC ministers responsible for foreign affairs and their counterparts from Jordan and Morocco, meeting in Manama, Bahrain, endorsed a joint co-operation initiative; a meeting of GCC foreign ministers was convened in July 2013 in order to develop plans for implementing the initiative.

CULTURAL CO-OPERATION

The GCC Folklore Centre, based in Doha, was established in 1983 to collect, document and classify the regional cultural heritage, publish research, sponsor and protect regional folklore, provide a database on Gulf folklore, and to promote traditional culture through education. The December 2005 summit of heads of state adopted the Abu Dhabi Declaration, which stressed that member states should place a strong focus on education and on the development of human resources in order better to confront global challenges. Periodically cultural fora are held, including ones on folklore (most recently in 2001); poetry (2004); drama (2009); and intellectual matters (2006). An occasional Exhibition of Creative Arts and Arabic Calligraphy is convened, most recently in 2006. A Strategy for GCC Youth was approved by the 33rd GCC summit in December 2012.

FINANCE

All member states contribute equal amounts to the functioning of the GCC.

ASSOCIATED BODIES

Gulf Investment Corporation (GIC): POB 3402, Safat 13035, Kuwait; tel. 2225000; fax 2225010; e-mail gic@gic.com.kw; internet www.gic.com.kw; f. 1983 by the six mem. states of the GCC, each contributing 16.6% of the total capital; total assets US $6,292m. (Dec. 2012); investment chiefly in the Gulf region, financing industrial projects (including pharmaceuticals, chemicals, steel wire, aircraft engineering, aluminium, dairy produce and chicken-breeding); provides merchant banking and financial advisory services, and in 1992 was appointed to advise the Kuwaiti Government on a programme of privatization; CEO and Chief Investment Officer IBRAHIM A. AL-QADHI; publ. *The GIC Gazetteer* (annually).

Gulf International Bank: POB 1017, ad-Dowali Bldg, 3 Palace Ave, Manama 317, Bahrain; tel. 17534000; fax 17522633; e-mail info@gibbah.com; internet www.gibonline.com; f. 1976 by the six GCC states and Iraq; became a wholly owned subsidiary of the GIC (without Iraqi shareholdings) in 1991; in April 1999 a merger with Saudi Investment Bank was concluded; total assets US $21,156.9m. (31 December 2013); CEO Dr YAHYA ALYAHYA.

Publications

Consumer Price Index in GCC States (annually).
GCC News (monthly, available online in Arabic).
GCC: A Statistical Glance.
Statistical Bulletin (annually).

COUNCIL OF THE BALTIC SEA STATES—CBSS

Address: Slussplan 9, POB 2010, 103 11 Stockholm, Sweden.
Telephone: (8) 440-19-20; **fax:** (8) 440-19-44; **e-mail:** cbss@cbss.org; **internet:** www.cbss.org.

The CBSS was established in 1992 to develop co-operation between member states.

MEMBERS

Denmark	Iceland	Poland
Estonia	Latvia	Russia
Finland	Lithuania	Sweden
Germany	Norway	

The European Commission also has full membership status.
Observers: Belarus, France, Italy, the Netherlands, Romania, Slovakia, Spain, Ukraine, United Kingdom, USA.

Organization

(April 2014)

PRESIDENCY

The presidency is occupied by member states for one year, on a rotating basis (1 July 2013–30 June 2014: Finland). Summit meetings of heads of government are held every two years. The ninth summit meeting was convened in Stralsund, Germany, in May 2012, and the 10th was to take place in Turku, Finland, in May 2014.

MINISTERIAL COUNCIL

The Council comprises the ministers responsible for foreign affairs of each member state and a representative of the European Commission. The Council meets every two years and aims to serve as a forum for guidance, direction of work and overall co-ordination among participating states. The 18th session of the Council was convened in Pionersky, Kaliningrad, Russia, in June 2013. Chairmanship of the Council rotates annually among member states and is responsible for co-ordinating the Council's activities between ministerial sessions, with assistance from the Committee of Senior Officials. (Other ministers also convene periodically, on an ad hoc basis by their own decision.)

COMMITTEE OF SENIOR OFFICIALS—CSO

The Committee consists of senior officials of the ministries of foreign affairs of the member states and of the European Commission. It serves as the main discussion forum and decision-making body for matters relating to the work of the Council, and monitors, facilitates and aims to co-ordinate the activities of all structures for CBSS co-operation. The Chairman of the Committee, from the same country serving as President of the CBSS, meets regularly with the previous and future Chairmen. The so-called Troika aims to maintain information co-operation, promote better exchange of information, and ensure more effective decision-making. The CSO monitors the work of the Expert Group on Nuclear and Radiation Safety; the Task Force against Trafficking in Human Beings; the Expert Group on Co-operation on Children at Risk; the Expert Group on Youth Affairs; the Lead Country Function of the EuroFaculty Project in Pskov (in Russia); the Expert Group on Maritime Policy; and the Expert Group on Sustainable Development—Baltic 21.

SECRETARIAT

The Secretariat provides technical and organizational support to the chairmanship, structures and working bodies of the Ministerial Council; co-ordinating CBSS activities; manages the CBSS archives and information databases; and maintains contacts with governments and other organizations operational in the region. The Secretariat includes a Children's Unit, and it hosts the Secretariat of Northern Dimension Partnership in Public Health and Social Well-being.

Director-General: JAN LUNDIN (Sweden).

Activities

The CBSS was established in March 1992 as a forum to enhance and strengthen co-operation between countries in the Baltic Sea region. At a meeting of the Council in Kalmar, Sweden, in July 1996, ministers adopted an Action Programme as a guideline for CBSS activities. The main programme areas covered stable and participatory political development; economic integration and prosperity; and protection of the environment. The third summit meeting of CBSS heads of government, held at Kolding, Denmark, in April 2000, recommended a restructuring of the organization to consolidate regional intergovernmental, multilateral co-operation in all sectors. In June the ninth meeting of the CBSS Council approved the summit's recommendations. Heads of government attending the seventh summit of Baltic Sea States, held in Riga, Latvia, in June 2008, endorsed a Declaration on the Reform of the CBSS, listing the following five future priority areas of co-operation for member states: environment (which may include climate change); economic development; energy; education and culture; and civil security and the human dimension. The 15th ministerial session, held in Helsingør, Denmark, in June 2009, endorsed new terms of reference of the CBSS and of its Secretariat, updated in view of the 2008 Declaration on the

Reform of the CBSS. Meeting in Vilnius, Lithuania, in June 2010, the eighth summit of heads of government adopted the Vilnius Declaration on 'A Vision for the Baltic Region by 2020'. In May 2012 the ninth summit meeting endorsed a decision of the Committee of Senior Officials to establish a Project Support Facility, to be administered by the Secretariat.

At the first Baltic Sea States summit, held in Visby, Sweden, in May 1996, heads of government agreed to establish a Task Force on Organized Crime to counter drugs-trafficking, strengthen judicial co-operation, increase the dissemination of information, impose regional crime prevention measures, improve border controls and provide training. The Task Force's mandate has been successively renewed, most recently, by the 10th Baltic Sea States summit, until 31 December 2016. In January 1998 the second summit meeting, convened in Riga, Latvia, agreed to enhance co-operation in the areas of civic security and border control. The third Baltic Sea summit, held in April 2000, authorized the establishment of a Task Force on Communicable Disease Control, which was mandated to formulate a joint plan aimed at improving disease control throughout the region, and also to strengthen regional co-operation in combating the threat to public health posed by a significant increase in communicable diseases, in particular HIV/AIDS. The Task Force presented its final report to the CBSS summit meeting held in June 2004. It was recognized that some of the structures of the Task Force could be pursued through the Northern Dimension Partnership in Public Health and Social Well-Being (NDPHS, see below). A Task Force against Trafficking in Human Beings was established in November 2006.

The Council has founded a number of groups, comprising experts in specific fields, which aim to report on and recommend action on issues of concern to the Council (see under the Committee of Senior Officials). In January 2009 the Council inaugurated the CBSS EuroFaculty Pskov programme, aimed at upgrading business/economics education at two higher education institutions in the western Russian Pskov region (bordering Estonia and Latvia); a second phase of the programme commenced in October 2012. A CBSS EuroFaculty programme was implemented during 2000–07 at the Immanuel Kant State University in Kaliningrad, Russia.

A Baltic Business Advisory Council was established in 1996 with the aim of facilitating the privatization process in the member states in transition and promoting small and medium-sized enterprises. A Roadmap on Investment Promotion, drafted by the Working Group on Economic Co-operation, was approved by the sixth summit meeting of CBSS heads of government, held in Reykjavik, Iceland, in June 2006. A Ministerial Conference on Trade and Economy was held in Stockholm, Sweden, in May 2007. In May 2012 the CBSS signed a Memorandum of Understanding with three regional banking groups to establish a Pilot Financial Initiative to support sustainable economic development, initially in north-west Russia. In November the CBSS Secretariat co-hosted an international conference, held in Kaliningrad, on the theme 'Fostering Small and Medium Enterprises in the Baltic Sea Region: Financing, Public Private Partnership, Innovations'.

The environmental state of the Baltic Sea, which is one of the world's busiest shipping routes, and associated issues such as eutrophication, overfishing, unsustainable production, and marine littering, are priority areas of concern. In January 2001 the Council agreed to establish a unit in the CBSS secretariat to implement Baltic 21, the regional variant (adopted by the CBSS in 1998) of Agenda 21, the programme of action agreed by the UN Conference on Environment and Development, held in Rio de Janeiro, Brazil, in June 1992. From January 2010 Baltic 21 was integrated into the structure of the CBSS as the Expert Group on Sustainable Development—Baltic 21. The Expert Group and BASREC co-hosted an event on the sidelines of the June 2012 UN Conference on Sustainable Development (Rio+20). The 16th session of the Ministerial Council, held in June 2011, in Oslo, Norway, endorsed a new CBSS Strategy on Sustainable Development for 2010–15, with a focus on the following four strategic areas of co-operation: climate change; sustainable urban and rural development; sustainable consumption and production; and innovation and education for sustainable development. In June 2010 funding was approved by the Baltic Sea Region Programme of the European Union (EU) for a new Baltic Sea Region Climate Change Adaptation Strategy (BALTADAPT), to be implemented, with participation by 11 partners from seven countries, under the auspices of Baltic 21. The CBSS convened a high-level Policy Forum on Climate Change Adaptation in Berlin, Germany, in April 2012. The Baltic Sea Region Energy Co-operation (BASREC) has its own secretariat function and council of senior energy officials, administered by the CBSS Secretariat. BASREC also has ad hoc groups on electricity markets, gas markets, energy efficiency and climate change. The 17th, extraordinary, ministerial session, held in February 2012, adopted a Declaration on Energy Security, highlighting future areas of policy focus. These included: diversification; reciprocity; security of supplies; environmental aspects and sustainability; and nuclear safety standards. The promotion of the sustainable and balanced spatial development of the region is addressed within the framework of the Visions and Strategies around the Baltic Sea (VASAB) co-operation.

The CBSS organizes annual co-ordination meetings to provide a forum and framework of co-operation for its strategic partners in the Baltic Sea area, including the B7 Baltic Island Network (comprising the seven largest Baltic Sea islands), the Baltic Development Forum, the Baltic Sea Forum, the Helsinki Commission and the Union of the Baltic Cities. The CBSS seeks synergies with the Arctic Council, the Barents Euro-Arctic Council, the Nordic Council of Ministers, and the EU's Northern Dimension co-operation framework. The Council contributed to the implementation of Northern Dimension Action Plans (NDAPs) for 2000–03 and 2004–06. In 2006 the CBSS prepared and presented to the European Commission a survey on the future of Northern Dimension co-operation. This contributed to the development of a long-term Northern Dimension Policy Framework Document that was adopted, alongside a Political Declaration on the Northern Dimension, in November 2006, in place of the previous NDAPs, with a view to renewing the co-operation. The first ministerial meeting of the renewed Northern Dimension co-operation was convened in St Petersburg, Russia, in October 2008. Ongoing Northern Dimension initiatives that are supported by CBSS member states include the Northern Dimension Environment Partnership (NDEP), established in 2001; the NDPHS, which was established in 2003; and the development of a Northern Dimension Partnership on Transport and Logistics, approved in October 2008. An EU Strategy for the Baltic Sea Region (EUSBSR) was adopted by the European Council in October 2009. In January 2012 the CBSS Secretariat became lead partner of a EUSBSR flagship project on macro-regional risk scenarios and gaps identification.

Finance

The Secretariat is financed by contributions of the governments of the Council's 11 member states. Ongoing activities and co-operation projects are funded through voluntary contributions from member states on the basis of special contribution schemes. Some €2.7m. was budgeted in 2013 for core Secretariat expenditure, the Expert Group on Sustainable Development—Baltic 21, the Task Force against Trafficking in Human Beings, and a new Project Support Facility (receiving an allocation of €1m.).

Publications

Annual Report.
Balticness Light (quarterly).

COUNCIL OF EUROPE

Address: Ave de l'Europe, 67075 Strasbourg Cedex, France.

Telephone: 3-88-41-20-33; **fax:** 3-88-41-27-45; **e-mail:** private .office@coe.int; **internet:** hub.coe.int.

The Council, founded in May 1949, aims to achieve greater unity within Europe; to protect human rights, pluralist democracy and the rule of law; to consolidate democratic stability in Europe by supporting political, legislative and constitutional reform; to promote awareness and the development of Europe's cultural identity and also of its diversity; and to develop common solutions to ongoing challenges facing European society. Membership has risen from the original 10 to 47.

MEMBERS*

Albania	Lithuania
Andorra	Luxembourg
Armenia	Macedonia, former Yugoslav republic
Austria	Malta
Azerbaijan	Moldova
Belgium	Montenegro
Bosnia and Herzegovina	Monaco
Bulgaria	Netherlands
Croatia	Norway
Cyprus	Poland
Czech Republic	Portugal
Denmark	Romania
Estonia	Russia
Finland	San Marino
France	Serbia
Georgia	Slovakia
Germany	Slovenia
Greece	Spain
Hungary	Sweden
Iceland	Switzerland
Ireland	Turkey
Italy	Ukraine
Latvia	United Kingdom
Liechtenstein	

* Belarus is a state candidate for membership of the Council of Europe. Canada, the Holy See, Japan, Mexico and the USA have observer status with the Committee of Ministers. The parliaments of Canada, Israel and Mexico have observer status with the Parliamentary Assembly.

Organization

(April 2014)

COMMITTEE OF MINISTERS

The Committee consists of the ministers responsible for foreign affairs of all member states (or their deputies, who are usually ministers' permanent diplomatic representatives in Strasbourg, France); it decides all matters of internal organization, makes recommendations to governments and draws up conventions and agreements with binding effect; it also discusses matters of political concern, such as European co-operation, compliance with member states' commitments, in particular concerning the protection of human rights, and considers possible co-ordination with other institutions, such as the European Union (EU) and the Organization for Security and Co-operation in Europe (OSCE). The Committee meets weekly at deputy ministerial level and once a year (in May or November) at ministerial level. Six two-day meetings are convened each year to supervise the execution of judgments of the European Court of Human Rights.

CONFERENCES OF SPECIALIZED MINISTERS

There are 20 Conferences of specialized ministers, meeting regularly for intergovernmental co-operation in various fields.

PARLIAMENTARY ASSEMBLY

President: ANNE BRASSEUR (Luxembourg).

Secretary-General of the Parliamentary Assembly: WOJCIECH SAWICKI (Poland).

Chairman of the Socialist Group: ANDREAS GROSS (Switzerland).

Chairman of the Group of the European People's Party: PEDRO AGRAMUNT (Spain).

Chairman of the Alliance of Liberals and Democrats for Europe: JORDI XUCLÁ I COSTA (Spain).

Chairman of the European Democrat Group: ALEXEY PUSHKOV (Russia).

Chairman of the Unified European Left Group: TINY KOX (Netherlands).

Members are elected or appointed by their national parliaments from among the members thereof; political parties in each delegation follow the proportion of their strength in the national parliament. Members speak on their own behalf rather than representing their governments. At April 2014 the Assembly had 318 members (and 318 substitutes): 18 each for France, Germany, Italy, Russia (suspended, q.v.) and the United Kingdom; 12 each for Poland, Spain, Turkey and Ukraine; 10 for Romania; seven each for Belgium, the Czech Republic, Greece, Hungary, the Netherlands, Portugal and Serbia; six each for Austria, Azerbaijan, Bulgaria, Sweden and Switzerland; five each for Bosnia and Herzegovina, Croatia, Denmark, Finland, Georgia, Moldova, Norway and Slovakia; four each for Albania, Armenia, Ireland and Lithuania; three each for Cyprus, Estonia, Iceland, Latvia, Luxembourg, the former Yugoslav republic of Macedonia, Malta, Montenegro and Slovenia; and two each for Andorra, Liechtenstein, Monaco and San Marino. The parliaments of Canada, Israel and Mexico have permanent observer status. (Belarus's special 'guest status' was suspended in January 1997.)

The Assembly meets in ordinary session once a year. The session is divided into four parts, generally held in the last full week of January, April, June and September. The Assembly submits Recommendations to the Committee of Ministers, passes Resolutions, and discusses reports on any matters of common European interest. It is also a consultative body to the Committee of Ministers, issuing Opinions (for example on membership applications and draft treaties), and it elects the Secretary-General, the Deputy Secretary-General, the Secretary-General of the Assembly, the Council's Commissioner for Human Rights, and the members of the European Court of Human Rights.

The parliament of Morocco (since June 2011) and the Palestine National Council (since October 2011) hold 'Partner for Democracy' status at the Parliamentary Assembly, which aims to provide democracy-building support to national legislatures in regions neighbouring the Council of Europe area.

In mid-March 2014 the President of the Parliamentary Assembly condemned 'in the strongest possible terms' Russia's decision to recognize the independence of the hitherto Ukrainian autonomous territory of Crimea, and to incorporate the territory into the Russian Federation. Later in that month the Assembly President led a delegation to Kyiv, Ukraine, to assess the situation in that country. An urgent debate on threats to the functioning of democratic institutions in Ukraine was held in April. Subsequently, the Assembly resolved to suspend the voting rights of the Russian delegation, given that the annexation of Crimea was contradictory to the commitments that country had made when joining the organization, as well as its right to be represented in the Assembly's leading bodies, and its right to participate in election observation missions, effective until the end of the 2014 session.

Standing Committee: represents the Assembly when it is not in session, and may adopt Recommendations to the Committee of Ministers and Resolutions on behalf of the Assembly. Consists of the President, Vice-Presidents, Chairmen of the Political Groups, Chairmen of the Ordinary Committees and Chairmen of national delegations. Meetings are usually held at least twice a year.

Ordinary Committees: political affairs; legal and human rights; economic affairs and development; social, health and family affairs; culture, science and education; environment, agriculture, and local and regional affairs; migration, refugees and population; rules of procedure and immunities; equal opportunities for women and men; honouring of obligations and commitments by member states of the Council of Europe.

SECRETARIAT

The Secretariat incorporates the Secretariats and Registry of the institutions of the Council. There are Directorates of Communication, Internal Oversight, External Relations, Policy Planning, Political Advice, and Legal Advice and Public International Law; the following Directorates-General: Human Rights and Rule of Law, General Democracy, Administration, and Programmes; and a Treaty Office.

Secretary-General: THORBJØRN JAGLAND (Norway).

Deputy Secretary-General: GABRIELLA BATTAINI-DRAGONI (Italy).

EUROPEAN COURT OF HUMAN RIGHTS

The Court was established in 1959 under the European Convention on Human Rights. It has compulsory jurisdiction and is competent to consider complaints lodged by states parties to the European Convention and by individuals, groups of individuals or non-governmental organizations (NGOs) claiming to be victims of breaches of the Convention's guarantees. The Court comprises one judge for each contracting state. The Court sits in three-member Committees, empowered to declare applications inadmissible in the event of unanimity and where no further examination is necessary, seven-member Chambers, and a 17-member Grand Chamber. Chamber judgments become final three months after delivery, during which period parties may request a rehearing before the Grand Chamber, subject to acceptance by a panel of five judges. Grand Chamber judgments are final. The Court's final judgments are binding on respondent states and their execution is supervised by the Committee of Ministers. Execution of judgments includes payment of any pecuniary just satisfaction awarded by the Court, adoption of specific individual measures to erase the consequences of the violations found (such as striking out of impugned convictions from criminal records, reopening of judicial proceedings, etc.), and general measures to prevent new similar violations (e.g. constitutional and legislative reforms, changes of domestic case-law and administrative practice, etc.). When the Committee of Ministers considers that the measures taken comply with the respondent state's obligation to give effect to the judgment, a final resolution is adopted that terminates the supervision of the case. In June 2009 the Court adopted a new policy establishing seven categories of case, and aiming to focus resources on the cases ('priority applications') deemed to be most important. The EU Treaty of Lisbon, which entered into force in December 2009, committed the EU to pursuing accession to the Court. During 2013 the Court delivered 916 judgments concerning 3,659 applications; in 87% of those judgments at least one violation of the European Convention of Human Rights was found to have been perpetrated by the respondent. Of the total number of judgments delivered in 2013, Russia was the focus of 129, Turkey of 124, Romania (of 88), Ukraine (69), and Hungary (41).

In mid-March 2014—in view of Russia's formal recognition of the hitherto Ukrainian autonomous independent territory of Crimea as an 'independent and sovereign state'—the interim authorities in Ukraine lodged with the Court an inter-state application against Russia, and formally requested from the Court an interim measure indicating to the Russian authorities that, inter alia, they should refrain from implementing measures that might threaten the well-being of the civilian population of Ukraine. On the grounds that the ongoing situation in Ukraine presented a serious risk of violations of the European Convention of Human Rights, the Court President at that time urged both Russia and Ukraine to refrain from taking any measures, in particular military actions, that might entail breaches of the rights of Ukraine's civilian population under the Convention.

President: DEAN SPIELMANN (Luxembourg).

CONGRESS OF LOCAL AND REGIONAL AUTHORITIES OF THE COUNCIL OF EUROPE (CLRAE)

The Congress was established in 1994, incorporating the former Standing Conference of Local and Regional Authorities, in order to protect and promote the political, administrative and financial autonomy of local and regional European authorities by encouraging central governments to develop effective local democracy. The Congress comprises two chambers—a Chamber of Local Authorities and a Chamber of Regions—with a total membership of 318 elected representatives (and 318 elected substitutes). Annual sessions are mainly concerned with local government matters, regional planning, protection of the environment, town and country planning, and social and cultural affairs. A Standing Committee, drawn from all national delegations, meets between plenary sessions of the Congress. Four Statutory Committees (Institutional; Sustainable Development; Social Cohesion; Culture and Education) meet twice a year in order to prepare texts for adoption by the Congress.

The Congress advises the Council's Committee of Ministers and the Parliamentary Assembly on all aspects of local and regional policy and co-operates with other national and international organizations representing local government. The Congress monitors implementation of the European Charter of Local Self-Government, which was opened for signature in October 1985 and entered into effect in December 1987, and provides common standards for effective local democracy. An Additional Protocol to the European Charter of Local Self-Government, on the right to participate in the affairs of a local authority, was adopted in November 2009 and entered into force in June 2012.

In May 2005 the Congress concluded an agreement with the EU Committee of the Regions on co-operation in ensuring local and regional democracy and self-government. In October 2011 the Congress, after giving consideration to two reports on means of strengthening the impact of the European Charter of Local Self-Government, determined to establish a 'unified European space of common standards' for local democracy.

The Congress produces 'monitoring reports' on the state of local democracy in member countries, and is responsible for the monitoring of local and regional elections and for setting standards in electoral matters. In October 2012 the Congress adopted the following three priority objectives for the four-year period 2013–16: raising the quality of local and regional democracy and human rights; rising to the new challenges resulting from the economic and financial crisis; and developing co-operation and partnerships.

In March 2011 the President of the Congress expressed concern about a recent declaration by 48 mayors from the Czech Republic that designated the Roma community as 'socially inadaptable', deeming this to be counter-productive to progress towards social integration. In September the Congress convened a Summit of Mayors on Roma, in Strasbourg, with participation by representatives of European municipalities, regions, institutions and networks, and Roma and traveller organizations. The Summit issued a final Declaration which supported the establishment of a new European Alliance of Cities and Regions for Roma Inclusion, with a view to enhancing future co-operation.

In October 2012 the Congress adopted a resolution and recommendation urging the Protection of Children against Sexual Exploitation and Sexual Abuse in the organization of regional social, health and welfare services.

The 26th plenary session of the Congress, held in late March 2014, adopted a declaration rejecting the validity of the recent referendum held in Ukraine's autonomous territory of Crimea. The Congress offered to send a delegation to Ukraine and to pursue a dialogue with Russia.

Secretary-General: ANDREAS KIEFER (Austria).

Activities

In an effort to harmonize national laws, to put the citizens of member countries on an equal footing and to pool certain resources and facilities, the Council of Europe has concluded a number of conventions and agreements covering particular aspects of European co-operation. From 1989 the Council undertook to increase co-operation with all countries of the former Eastern bloc and to facilitate their accession to the organization. Heads of state or government of member countries convened for the first time in October 1993, in Vienna, Austria. In October 1997 they met for the second time, in Strasbourg, France, with the aim of formulating a new social model to consolidate democracy throughout Europe. The third (and most recent) meeting of heads of state or government, held in Warsaw, Poland, in May 2005, issued a Final Declaration and an Action Plan defining the principal tasks of the Council over the coming years as: promoting human rights and the rule of law, strengthening the security of European citizens and fostering co-operation with other international and European organizations. The Council's activities have the following cross-cutting themes: children's rights; democracy; intercultural dialongue; and combating violence. Combating the social marginalization of Roma minority communities has pre-occupied the Council increasingly in recent years. In January 2011 the Parliamentary Assembly adopted a resolution recommending that a Council of Europe summit should be convened with the aim of redefining the role of the Council and giving it a new political impetus.

The Committee of Ministers condemned the referendum conducted in mid-March 2014 by the Crimean authorities, in violation of Ukrainian legislation, and deplored Russia's decision to grant admittance to the territory. At the beginning of April the Committee of Ministers adopted a report issued by the Advisory Committee on the Framework Convention for National Minorities that stated deep concern over the safety and access to rights of minority populations in Crimea, with particular reference to individuals belonging to the Crimean Tatar and Ukrainian communities.

HUMAN RIGHTS

The protection of human rights is one of the Council of Europe's basic goals, to be achieved in four main areas: the effective supervision and protection of fundamental rights and freedoms; identification of new threats to human rights and human dignity; development of public awareness of the importance of human rights; and promotion of human rights education and professional training. The most significant treaties in this area include the European Convention for the Protection of Human Rights and Fundamental Freedoms (European Convention on Human Rights) (which was adopted in 1950 and entered into force in 1953); the European Social Charter; the European Convention for the Prevention of Torture and Inhuman or Degrading Treatment or Punishment; the Framework Convention for the Protection of National Minorities; the European Charter for Regional or Minority Languages; and the Convention on Action against Trafficking in Human Beings.

The Steering Committee for Human Rights is responsible for intergovernmental co-operation in the field of human rights and fundamental freedoms; it works to strengthen the effectiveness of systems for protecting human rights and to identify potential threats and challenges to human rights. The Committee has been responsible for the elaboration of several conventions and other legal instruments including the following protocols to the European Convention on Human Rights: Protocol No. 11, which entered into force in November 1998, resulting in the replacement of the then existing institutions—the European Commission of Human Rights and the European Court of Human Rights—by a single Court, working on a full-time basis; Protocol No. 12, which entered into force in April 2005, enforcing a general prohibition of discrimination; No. 13, which entered into force in July 2003, guaranteeing the abolition of the death penalty in all circumstances, including in time of war (Europe is the only continent where capital punishment is not applied, all European states having either outlawed or instituted a moratorium on executions); No. 14, which entered into force on 1 June 2010, aiming to enhance the effectiveness of the Court by improving implementation of the European Convention on Human Rights at national level and the processing of applications, and accelerating the execution of the Court's decisions; No. 15—opened for signature in June 2013—which emphasized states' margin of appreciation in applying the Convention, and the subsidiarity of the Convention to the safeguarding of human rights at national level; and No. 16, adopted in October of that year, which allowed the highest courts and tribunals of a contracting party to request advisory opinions from the European Court of Human Rights on questions of principle relating to the interpretation or application of the rights and freedoms defined in the Convention and its protocols.

The EU Treaty of Lisbon, which entered into force in December 2009, provided for accession by the EU to the European Convention on Human Rights. Formal negotiations on EU accession commenced in July 2010. Since 2011 a Joint Informal Body, comprising members of the Parliamentary Assembly and members of the European Parliament, has met periodically to discuss the accession process.

The Council of Europe Commissioner for Human Rights (whose office was established by a resolution of the Council's Committee of Ministers in May 1999) promotes respect for human rights in member states.

In May 2012 the Commissioner emphasized the importance of effective national human rights structures—including independent commissions, equality bodies, ombudsmen, and police complaints mechanisms—in protecting vulnerable sectors of society during the period of economic and social austerity that was ongoing in many European countries. In the following month the Commissioner stressed the need for human rights-based assessments of the impact on children of state-authorized austerity measures and poverty alleviation policies. In November the Commissioner urged an end to evictions of Roma from settlements in member states, noting that these tended to be undertaken without the safeguard of social protection and integration planning, and that they were therefore perpetuating cycles of social exclusion. In February 2013 the Commissioner drew attention to increasing numbers of alleged racist crimes and incidents of so-called hate speech being reported in Greece, stating that the relevant Greek authorities must put into effect relevant anti-racism legislation and end impunity in this respect, and that they should act to promote social integration. In January 2014 the Commissioner made a statement condemning as deeply discriminatory selective abortions of female foetuses, determining that the practice—reported to be responsible for distorted birth rates by gender in countries including Albania, Armenia, Azerbaijan, Georgia, Kosovo and Montenegro—arises from the disadvantaged status of women in society, and should be banned by law. In the following month the Commissioner stated that excessive force had been used by Ukraine law enforcement officers against anti-government protesters during armed interventions, and subsequent confrontations, during the period end-November 2013–end-January 2014.

In 2014 the particular focus areas of the Commissioner's human rights focus were children's rights; the economic crisis; lesbian, gay and transgender rights; media freedom; migration; persons with disabilities; post-war justice; and Roma and travellers.

Commissioner for Human Rights: NILS MUIŽNIEKS (Latvia).

EUROPEAN COMMITTEE FOR THE PREVENTION OF TORTURE AND INHUMAN OR DEGRADING TREATMENT OR PUNISHMENT (CPT)

The Committee was established under the 1987 Convention for the Prevention of Torture as an integral part of the Council of Europe's system for the protection of human rights. The Committee, comprising independent experts, aims to examine the treatment of persons deprived of their liberty with a view to strengthening, if necessary, the protection of such persons from torture and from inhuman or degrading treatment or punishment. It conducts periodic visits to police stations, prisons, detention centres, and all other sites where persons are deprived of their liberty by a public authority, in all states parties to the Convention, and may also undertake ad hoc visits when the Committee considers them necessary. After each visit the Committee drafts a report of its findings and any further advice or recommendations, based on dialogue and co-operation. By April 2014 the Committee had published 306 reports and had undertaken 357 visits (214 periodic and 143 ad hoc).

President: LATIF HÜSEYNOV (Azerbaijan).

EUROPEAN SOCIAL CHARTER

The European Social Charter, in force since 1965, is the counterpart of the European Convention on Human Rights, in the field of protection of economic and social rights. A revised Charter, which amended existing guarantees and incorporated new rights, was opened for signature in May 1996, and entered into force on 1 July 1999. By April 2014 27 member states had ratified the Charter and 33 had ratified the revised Charter. Rights guaranteed by the Charter concern all individuals in their daily lives in matters of housing, health, education, employment, social protection, movement of persons and non-discrimination. The European Committee of Social Rights considers reports submitted to it annually by member states. It also considers collective complaints submitted in the framework of an Additional Protocol (1995), providing for a system which entered into force in July 1998, permitting trade unions, employers' organizations and non-governmental organizations (NGOs) to lodge complaints about alleged violations of the Charter. The Committee, composed of 15 members, decides on the conformity of national situations with the Charter. When a country does not bring a situation into conformity, the Committee of Ministers may, on the basis of decisions prepared by a Governmental Committee (composed of representatives of each Contracting Party), issue recommendations to the state concerned, inviting it to change its legislation or practice in accordance with the Charter's requirements.

President of the European Committee of Social Rights: Prof. LUIS JIMENA QUESADA (Spain).

FRAMEWORK CONVENTION FOR THE PROTECTION OF NATIONAL MINORITIES

In 1993 the first summit meeting of Council of Europe heads of state and government, held in Vienna, mandated the Committee of Ministers to draft 'a framework convention specifying the principle that States commit themselves to respect in order to assure the protection of national minorities'. A special committee was established to draft the so-called Framework Convention for the Protection of National Minorities, which was then adopted by the Committee in November 1994. The Convention was opened for signature in February 1995, entering into force in February 1998. Contracting parties (39 states at April 2014) are required to submit reports on the implementation of the treaty at regular intervals to an Advisory Committee composed of 18 independent experts. The Advisory Committee adopts an opinion on the implementation of the Framework Convention by the contracting party, on the basis of which the Committee of Ministers adopts a resolution. A Conference entitled 10 Years of Protecting National Minorities and Regional or Minority Languages was convened in March 2008 to review the impacts of, and the role of regional institutions in implementing, both the Framework Convention and the Convention on Minority Languages. In October 2010 a high-level meeting of the Council of Europe adopted the Strasbourg Declaration on Roma, detailing guiding principles and priorities to encourage the empowerment and inclusion of Roma/Gypsy people in Europe (who are estimated to number 10m.–12m.).

Head, Secretariat: MICHÈLE AKIP.

RACISM AND INTOLERANCE

In October 1993 heads of state and of government, meeting in Vienna, resolved to reinforce a policy to combat all forms of intolerance, in response to the increasing incidence of racial hostility and intolerance towards minorities in European societies. A European Commission against Racism and Intolerance (ECRI) was established by the summit meeting to analyse and assess the effectiveness of legal, policy and other measures taken by member states to combat these problems. It became operational in March 1994. The European conference against racism, held in October 2000, requested that ECRI should be reinforced and, in June 2002, the Committee of Ministers of the Council of Europe adopted a new Statute for ECRI that consolidated its role as an independent human rights monitoring body focusing on issues related to racism and racial discrimination. Members of ECRI are appointed on the basis of their recognized expertise in the field; they are independent and impartial in fulfilling their mandate. ECRI undertakes activities in three programme areas: country-by-country approach; work on general themes; and relations with civil society. In the first area of activity, ECRI analyses the situation regarding racism and intolerance in each of the member states, in order to advise governments on measures to combat these problems. In December 1998 ECRI completed a first round of reports for all Council members. A second series of country reports was completed in December 2002, a third monitoring cycle, focusing on implementation and 'specific issues', was undertaken during 2003–07, a fourth series of country reports was compiled during 2008–12, and the fifth round was under way during 2013–18. ECRI's work on general themes includes the preparation of policy recommendations and guidelines on issues of importance to combating racism and intolerance. ECRI also collects and disseminates examples of good practices relating to these issues. Under the third programme area ECRI aims to disseminate information and raise awareness of the problems of racism and intolerance among the general public.

EQUALITY BETWEEN WOMEN AND MEN

The Steering Committee for Equality between Women and Men (CDEG—an intergovernmental committee of experts) is responsible for encouraging action at both national and Council of Europe level to promote equality of rights and opportunities between the two sexes. Assisted by various specialist groups and committees, the CDEG is mandated to establish analyses, studies and evaluations, to examine national policies and experiences, to devise concerted policy strategies and measures for implementing equality and, as necessary, to prepare appropriate legal and other instruments. It is also responsible for preparing the European Ministerial Conferences on Equality between Women and Men. The main areas of CDEG activities are the comprehensive inclusion of the rights of women (for example, combating violence against women and trafficking in human beings) within the context of human rights; the issue of equality and democracy, including the promotion of the participation of women in political and public life; projects aimed at studying the specific equality problems related to cultural diversity, migration and minorities; positive action in the field of equality between men and women and the mainstreaming of equality into all policies and programmes at all levels of society. Following a decision of the meeting of heads of state or government convened in Warsaw in May 2005, a Council of Europe Task Force to Combat Violence against Women, including Domestic Violence was established. In June 2006 the Committee of Ministers adopted the Blueprint of the Council of Europe Campaign to Combat Violence against Women, including Domestic Violence, which had been drafted by the Task Force. A Convention on Preventing and Combating Violence against Women and Domestic Violence was adopted in May 2011, and was to enter into force following its 10th ratification (it had 24 signatories and nine ratifications at April 2014). In May 2009 the Council of Europe published a *Handbook on the Implementation of Gender Budgeting*. A new Council of Europe Gender Equality Commission was inaugurated in June 2012.

MEDIA AND COMMUNICATIONS

Implementation of the Council of Europe's work programme concerning the media is undertaken by the Steering Committee on the Media and New Communication Services (CDMC), which comprises senior government officials and representatives of professional organizations, meeting in plenary session twice a year. The CDMC is mandated to devise concerted European policy measures and appropriate legal instruments. Its underlying aims are to further freedom of expression and information in a pluralistic democracy, and to promote the free flow of information and ideas. The CDMC is assisted by various specialist groups and committees. Policy and legal instruments have been developed on subjects including exclusivity rights; media concentrations and transparency of media ownership; protection of journalists in situations of conflict and tension; independence of public service broadcasting, protection of rights holders; legal protection of encrypted television services; media and elections; protection of journalists' sources of information; the independence and functions of broadcasting regulatory authorities; and coverage of legal proceedings by the media. These policy and legal instruments (mainly in the form of non-binding recommendations addressed to member governments) are complemented by the publication of studies, analyses and seminar proceedings on topics of media law and policy. The CDMC has also prepared a number of international binding legal instruments, including the European Convention on Transfrontier Television (adopted in 1989 and ratified by 34 countries by April 2014), the European Convention on the Legal Protection of Services Based on or Consisting of Conditional Access (ratified by 10 countries at April 2014), and the European Convention Relating to Questions on Copyright Law and Neighbouring Rights in the Context of Transfrontier Broadcasting by Satellite (ratified by three countries at April 2014).

In March 2005 the Council's Committee of Ministers adopted a declaration on freedom of expression and information in the media in the context of the fight against terrorism. A declaration on the independence and functions of regulatory authorities for the broadcasting sector was adopted by the Committee of Ministers in March 2008. In that month the Committee also adopted a Recommendation on the Use of Internet Filters aimed at promoting a balance between freedom of expression and the protection of children against harmful material published on the internet.

SOCIAL COHESION

The European Committee for Social Cohesion (CDCS), established by the Committee of Ministers in 1998, has the following responsibilities: to co-ordinate, guide and stimulate co-operation between member states with a view to promoting social cohesion in Europe; to develop and promote integrated, multidisciplinary responses to social issues; and to promote the social standards embodied in the European Social Charter and other Council of Europe instruments, including the European Code of Social Security. In 2002 the CDCS published the *Report on Access to Social Rights in Europe*, concerning access to employment, housing and social protection. The Committee supervises an extensive programme of work on children, families and the elderly. In March 2004 the Committee of Ministers approved a revised version of the Council's Strategy for Social Cohesion (adopted in July 2000).

The European Code of Social Security and its Protocol entered into force in 1968; by April 2014 the Code had been ratified by 21 states and the Protocol by seven states. These instruments set minimum standards for medical care and the following benefits: sickness; old age; unemployment; employment injury; family; maternity; invalidity; and survivor's benefit. A revision of these instruments, aiming to provide higher standards and greater flexibility, was opened for signature in 1990 but by April 2014 had only been ratified by one member state (the Netherlands).

The European Convention on Social Security, in force since 1977, currently applies in Austria, Belgium, Italy, Luxembourg, the Netherlands, Portugal, Spain and Turkey; most of the provisions apply automatically, while others are subject to the conclusion of additional multilateral or bilateral agreements. The Convention is concerned with establishing the following four fundamental principles of international law on social security: equality of treatment; unity of applicable legislation; conservation of rights accrued or in course of acquisition; and payment of benefits abroad. In 1994 a Protocol to the Convention, providing for the enlargement of the personal scope of the Convention, was opened for signature; by April 2014 it had been ratified only by Portugal.

In May 2011 a Group of Eminent Persons, appointed by the Secretary-General, released a report entitled *Living Together: Combining Freedom and Diversity in 21st-Century Europe*, which identified threats to the values of the Council of Europe deriving from rising intolerance and increasing diversity in European populations, and outlined proposed responses.

HEALTH

Through a series of expert committees, the Council aims to ensure constant co-operation in Europe in a variety of health-related fields, with particular emphasis on health services and patients' rights. These efforts are supplemented by the training of health personnel. Recommendations adopted by the Committee of Ministers in the area of health cover blood, cancer control, disabilities, health policy development and promotion, health services, the protection of human rights and dignity of persons with mental disorders, the organization of palliative care, the role of patients, transplantation, access to health care by vulnerable groups, and the impact of new information technologies on health care.

A Partial Agreement in the Social and Public Health Field aims to protect the consumer from potential health risks connected with commonplace or domestic products, including asbestos, cosmetics, flavouring substances, pesticides, pharmaceuticals and products that have a direct or indirect impact on the human food chain, and also has provisions on the integration of people with disabilities. Two European treaties have been concluded within the framework of this Partial Agreement: the European Agreement on the Restriction of the use of Certain Detergents in Washing and Cleaning Products, and the Convention on the Elaboration of a European Pharmacopoeia (establishing legally binding standards for medicinal substances, auxiliary substances, pharmaceutical preparations, vaccines for human and veterinary use and other articles). The latter Convention entered into force in eight signatory states in May 1974 and by April 2014 had been ratified by 37 states and the EU. The World Health Organization (WHO), the Taiwan Food and Drug Administration, and seven European and 17 non-European states, participate (as at April 2014) as observers in the sessions of the European Pharmacopoeia Commission. In 1994 a procedure on certification of suitability to the *European Pharmacopoeia* monographs for manufacturers of substances for pharmaceutical use was established. A network of official control laboratories for human and veterinary medicines was established in 1995, open to all signatory countries to the Convention and observers at the Pharmacopoeia Commission. The seventh edition of the *European Pharmacopoeia*, in force since 1 January 2011, is updated regularly in its electronic version, and includes more than 2,000 harmonized European standards, or 'monographs', 268 general methods of analysis and 2,210 reagents.

The 1992 Recommendation on a Coherent Policy for People with Disabilities contains the policy principles for the rehabilitation and integration of people with disabilities. This model programme recommends that governments of all member states develop comprehensive and co-ordinated national disability policies taking account of prevention, diagnosis, treatment education, vocational guidance and training, employment, social integration, social protection, information and research. It has set benchmarks, both nationally and internationally. The 2001 Resolution on New Technologies recommends formulating national strategies to ensure that people with disabilities benefit from new technologies. In April 2006 the Council of Europe Committee of Ministers adopted a Recommendation endorsing a recently drafted Council of Europe action plan for 2006–15, with the aim of promoting the rights and full participation of people with disabilities in society and of improving the quality of life of people with disabilities in Europe.

In the co-operation group to combat drug abuse and illicit drugs trafficking (Pompidou Group), 37 states work together, through meetings of ministers, officials and experts, to counteract drug abuse and to improve drug detection in European airports. The Group follows a multidisciplinary approach embracing, in particular, legislation, law enforcement, prevention, treatment, rehabilitation and data collection. In January 2007 the Group initiated an online register of ongoing drug research projects; revised versions of the register have subsequently been released.

A new Council of Europe Convention on the Counterfeiting of Medical Products and Similar Crimes Involving Threats to Public Health ('Medicrime Convention') was opened for signature in October 2011 and had 21 signatories and three ratifications at April 2014.

Improvement of blood transfusion safety and availability of blood and blood derivatives has been ensured through European Agreements and guidelines. Advances in this field and in organ transplantation are continuously assessed by expert committees.

In April 1997 the first international convention on biomedicine was opened for signature at a meeting of ministers responsible for health of member states, in Oviedo, Spain. The so-called Convention for the Protection of Human Rights and the Dignity of Human Beings with Respect to the Applications of Biology and Medicine incorporated provisions on scientific research, the principle of informed patient consent, organ and tissue transplants and the prohibition of financial gain and disposal of a part of the human body. It entered into force on 1 November 1999.

POPULATION AND MIGRATION

The European Convention on the Legal Status of Migrant Workers, in force since 1983, has been ratified by Albania, France, Italy, Moldova, the Netherlands, Norway, Portugal, Spain, Sweden, Turkey and the Ukraine. The Convention is based on the principle of equality of treatment for migrant workers and the nationals of the host country as to housing, working conditions, and social security. An international consultative committee monitors the application of the Convention.

The European Committee on Migration is responsible for activities concerning Roma/Gypsies in Europe, in co-ordination with other relevant Council of Europe bodies. In December 2004 a European Roma and Travellers Forum, established in partnership with the Council of Europe, was inaugurated. The eighth Council of Europe conference of ministers responsible for migration affairs, convened in Kyiv, Ukraine, in September 2008, adopted a final declaration on pursuing an integrated approach to addressing economic migration, social cohesion and development. In May 2011 a consultation meeting on Council of Europe activities in the area of migration, addressing the human rights dimension of migration, procedures for asylum and return, and questions relating to the social integration of migrants, was convened in Athens, Greece, with participation by experts and representatives of the UN High Commissioner for Refugees and the EU Fundamental Rights Agency.

In May 2006 the Council of Europe adopted a Convention on the avoidance of statelessness in relation to state succession. It was reported in August 2011 by the Council's Commissioner for Human Rights that there were at that time up to 589,000 stateless people in Europe. In January 2013 the Commissioner urged member governments to act in the best interests of children without citizenship, deeming citizenship as the right to have political—and often also economic and social—rights, and stating that statelessness was being transmitted inter-generationally, particularly among minorities, the displaced, refugees, orphans, the illiterate, and within the poorest sectors of society.

The European Population Committee, an intergovernmental committee of scientists and government officials responsible for population matters, monitors and analyses population trends throughout Europe and informs governments, research centres and the public of demographic developments and their impact on policy decisions. It compiles an annual statistical review of regional demographic developments and publishes the results of studies on population issues.

LEGAL AFFAIRS

The European Committee on Legal Co-operation develops co-operation between member states in the field of law, with the objective of harmonizing and modernizing public and private law, including administrative law and the law relating to the judiciary. The Committee is responsible for expert groups which consider issues relating to administrative law, efficiency of justice, family law, nationality, information technology and data protection.

Numerous conventions and Recommendations have been adopted, and followed up by appropriate committees or groups of experts, on matters which include efficiency of justice; nationality; legal aid; rights of children; data protection; information technology; children born out of wedlock; animal protection; adoption; information on foreign law; and the legal status of NGOs.

In December 1999 the Convention for the Protection of Human Rights and the Dignity of Human Beings with Respect to the Applications of Biology and Medicine: Convention on Human Rights and Biomedicine entered into force, as the first internationally binding legal text to protect people against the misuse of biological and medical advances. It aims, through a series of principles and rules, to preserve human dignity and identity, rights and freedoms. Additional protocols develop the Convention's general provisions by means of specialized texts. A Protocol prohibiting the medical cloning of human beings was approved by Council heads of state and government in 1998 and entered into force in March 2001. A Protocol on the transplantation of human organs and tissue was opened for signature in January 2002 and entered into force in May 2006, and a Protocol concerning biomedical research opened for signature in January 2005 and entered into force in September 2007. Work on draft protocols relating to protection of the human embryo and foetus, and genetics was ongoing in 2014. A Recommendation on xenotransplantation was adopted by the Committee of Ministers in 2003.

The Council of Europe is concerned with balancing the free flow of information, and increasingly efficient centralization of personal data through the computerization of personal records, with citizens' fundamental right to privacy and data protection. In October 1985 the Convention for the Protection of Individuals with regard to Automatic Processing of Personal Data (referred to as 'Convention 108') entered into force; in 2014 this Convention—regarded as a cornerstone of privacy legislation in Europe, and also as a global standard—was being modernized. In November 2001 an Additional Protocol to Convention 108 was opened for signature, concerning supervisory authorities and transborder data flows; this entered into force in July 2004. The monitoring committee of the Convention has been increasingly focused on the development of technologies such as biometric identification, smart cards and video surveillance, and has, accordingly, produced guidelines on the application of data protection principles in respect to these techniques. Furthermore, the potential for linking state databases with those of other agencies, such as insurance companies and banks; and risks associated with the transborder transfer of information through the internet have become priority areas of focus.

In 2001 the European Committee for Social Cohesion (CDCS) approved three new conventions on contact concerning children, legal aid, and 'Information Society Services'. In 2002 the CDCS approved a Recommendation on mediation on civil matters and a resolution establishing the European Commission for the Efficiency of Justice (CEPEJ). The aims of the CEPEJ are: to improve the efficiency and functioning of the justice system of member states, with a view to ensuring that everyone within their jurisdiction can enforce their legal rights effectively, increasing citizen confidence in the system; and to enable better implementation of the international legal instruments of the Council of Europe concerning efficiency and fairness of justice.

A Convention on Contact concerning Children was adopted in May 2003. It entered into force in September 2005 and by April 2014 had been ratified by eight states. A Convention on the Protection of Children against Sexual Exploitation and Sexual Abuse was adopted in July 2007 and entered into force in July 2010; by April 2014 it had received 30 ratifications.

The Consultative Council of European Judges has prepared a framework global action plan for judges in Europe. In addition, it has contributed to the implementation of this programme by the adoption of opinions on standards concerning the independence of the judiciary and the irremovability of judges, and on the funding and management of courts.

A Committee of Legal Advisers on Public and International Law (CAHDI), comprising the legal advisers of ministers responsible for foreign affairs of member states and of several observer states, is authorized by the Committee of Ministers to examine questions of public international law, and to exchange and, if appropriate, to co-ordinate the views of member states. The CAHDI functions as a European observatory of reservations to international treaties. Recent activities of the CAHDI include the preparation of a Recommendation on reactions to inadmissible reservations to international treaties, the publication of a report on state practice with regard to state succession and recognition, and another on expression of consent of states to be bound by a treaty.

With regard to crime, expert committees and groups operating under the authority of the European Committee on Crime Problems have prepared conventions on such matters as extradition, mutual assistance, recognition and enforcement of foreign judgments, transfer of proceedings, suppression of terrorism, transfer of prisoners, compensation payable to victims of violent crime, money-laundering, confiscation of proceeds from crime and corruption.

A Convention on Cybercrime, adopted in 2001, entered into force in July 2004 and by April 2014 had received 42 ratifications. In 2003 member states concluded an additional Protocol to the Convention relating to the criminalization of acts of a racist and xenophobic nature committed through computer systems; this entered into force in March 2006 and had been ratified by 20 countries at April 2014. The Council of Europe organizes an annual conference on cybercrime (in 2013 this was held in December, in Strasbourg). In March 2014 the Council of Europe and the EU initiated a joint project on Global Action on Cybercrime (GLACY).

A Multidisciplinary Group on International Action against Terrorism, established in 2001, elaborated a protocol that updated the 1977 European Convention on the Suppression of Terrorism. In 2002 the Council's Committee of Ministers adopted a set of 'guidelines on Human Rights and the Fight against Terrorism'. In 2003 a Committee of Experts on Terrorism (CODEXTER) was inaugurated, with a mandate to oversee and co-ordinate the Council's counter-terrorism activities in the legal field. CODEXTER formulated the Council of Europe Convention for the Prevention of Terrorism, which was opened for signature in May 2005 and entered into force in June 2007. By April 2014 the Convention for the Prevention of Terrorism had been ratified by 31 member states. In 2006 the Council of Europe launched a campaign to combat trafficking, which seeks to raise awareness of the extent of trafficking in Europe and to emphasize the measures that can be taken to prevent it. The campaign also promotes participation in the Convention on Action against Trafficking in Human Beings; the Convention entered into force in February 2008 and, by April 2014, had been ratified by 42 countries. Parties to the Convention are monitored by the Group of Experts on Action against Trafficking in Human Beings (GRETA). In October 2013 GRETA urged recognition of the following principles: more countries should sign the Convention; anti-trafficking efforts should focus on every type of trafficking, for example trafficking for labour exploitation (including forced begging) and for organ removal; the private sector and media should play a greater role in helping to prevent trafficking; and the effectiveness of anti-trafficking measures should be subject to thorough independent assessment.

The Group of States Against Corruption (GRECO) became operational in 1999 and became a permanent body of the Council in 2002. At April 2014 it had 49 members (including the USA). A monitoring mechanism, based on mutual evaluation and peer pressure, GRECO assesses members' compliance with Council instruments for combating corruption, including the Criminal Law Convention on Corruption, which entered into force in July 2002 (and by April 2014 had been ratified by 45 states), and its Additional Protocol (which entered into force in February 2005). The evaluation procedure of GRECO is confidential but it has become practice to make reports public after their adoption. GRECO's First Evaluation Round was completed during 2001–02, and the Second Evaluation Round was conducted during 2003–06. The Third Evaluation Round, which was undertaken during 2007–11, covered member states' compliance with, inter alia, requirements of the Criminal Law Convention on Corruption and its Additional Protocol, and the area of transparency of political party funding. GRECO's Fourth Evaluation Round was under way in 2014, having commenced in January 2012. In May GRECO urged member states to establish transparent systems for regulating the funding of political parties and election campaigns. In 2012 GRECO, for the first time, considered the prevention of corruption among members of parliament and of judiciaries in member states; Estonia, Finland, Latvia, Poland, Slovenia and the United Kingdom were the first countries to be evaluated in this respect. In January 2013 the Council of Europe Secretary-General warned that widespread corruption was damaging European citizens' trust in the rule of law, and recommended that the Council place a special focus on combating corruption and supporting governments with the implementation of judicial reforms; on protecting freedom of expression and of the media; on combating intolerance and hate speech; and on promoting diversity and protecting minorities. A report published in March 2014 on Ukraine's follow-up to recommendations made during GRECO's third round of evaluations found that only three of 16 recommendations had been sufficiently addressed, and that of six recommendations that had not been implemented at all most concerned the theme of transparency of party funding.

The Select Committee of Experts on the Evaluation of Anti-Money Laundering Measures (MONEYVAL) became operational in 1998. It is responsible for mutual evaluation of the anti-money-laundering measures in place in 30 Council of Europe states that are not members of the Financial Action Task Force (FATF), or else have joined FATF but wish to continue to be evaluated by MONEYVAL. The MONEYVAL mechanism is based on FATF practices and procedures. States are evaluated against the relevant international standards in the legal, financial and law enforcement sectors. In the legal sector this includes evaluation of states' obligations under the Council of Europe Convention on Laundering, Search, Seizure and Confiscation of the Proceeds from Crime and on the Financing of Terrorism, which entered into force in May 2008. With effect from 1 January 2011 MONEYVAL was elevated to the status of an independent monitoring mechanism, reporting directly to the Committee of Ministers. After the terrorist attacks against targets in the USA on 11 September 2001, the Committee of Ministers adopted revised terms of reference, which specifically include the evaluation of measures to combat the financing of terrorism. MONEYVAL's ongoing fourth round of evaluations, initiated in October 2009, is focused more rigidly on core FATF Recommendations. The full evaluations of MONEYVAL are confidential, but summaries of adopted reports are made public.

A Criminological Scientific Council, composed of specialists in law, psychology, sociology and related sciences, advises the Committee and organizes criminological research conferences and colloquia. A Council for Penological Co-operation organizes regular high-level conferences of directors of prison administrations and is responsible for collating statistical information on detention and community sanctions in Europe. The Council prepared the European Prison Rules in 1987 and the European Rules on Community Sanctions (alternatives to imprisonment) in 1992. A Council for Police Matters was established in 2002.

In May 1990 the Committee of Ministers adopted a Partial Agreement to establish the European Commission for Democracy through Law, to be based in Venice, Italy. The so-called Venice Commission was enlarged in February 2002 and in April 2014 comprised all Council of Europe member states in addition to Kyrgyzstan (which joined in 2004), Chile (2005), the Republic of Korea (2006), Algeria and Morocco (2007), Israel and Tunisia (2008), Peru and Brazil (2009), Mexico (2010), Kazakhstan (2012), and the USA (2013). The Commission is composed of independent legal and political experts, mainly senior academics, supreme or constitutional court judges, members of national parliaments, and senior public officers. Its main activity is constitutional assistance and it may supply opinions upon request, made through the Committee of Ministers, by the Parliamentary Assembly, the Secretary-General or any member states of the Commission. Other states and international organizations may request opinions with the consent of the Committee of Ministers. The Commission is active throughout the constitutional domain, and has worked on issues including legislation on constitutional courts and national minorities, electoral law and other legislation with implications for national democratic institutions. In March 2014 the Council of Europe Secretary-General requested two urgent opinions from the Venice Commission, concerning: the compatibility with constitutional principles of the decision of the Supreme Council of the Autonomous Republic of Crimea in Ukraine to hold a referendum on becoming a constituent territory of the Russian Federation or restoring Crimea's constitution of 1992, and on the compatibility with international law of the draft Federal Constitutional Law of the Russian Federation on 'Amending the Federal Constitutional Law on the procedure of admission to the Russian Federation and creation of a new subject of the Russian Federation in its composition'. The creation of the Council for Democratic Elections institutionalized co-operation in the area of elections between the Venice Commission, the Parliamentary Assembly of the Council of Europe, and the CLRAE. The Commission disseminates its work through the Uni-Dem (University for Democracy) programme of seminars, the CODICES database, and the *Bulletin of Constitutional Case-Law*. In May 2005 Council heads of state decided to establish a new Forum for the Future of Democracy, with the aim of strengthening democracy and citizens' participation.

The promotion of local and regional democracy and of transfrontier co-operation constitutes a major aim of the Council's intergovernmental programme of activities. The Steering Committee on Local and Regional Democracy (CDLR) serves as a forum for representatives of member states to exchange information and pursue co-operation in order to promote the decentralization of powers, in accordance with the European Charter on Local Self-Government. The CDLR's principal objectives are to improve the legal, institutional and financial framework of local democracy and to encourage citizen participation in local and regional communities. The CDLR publishes comparative studies and national reports, and aims to identify guidelines for the effective implementation of the principles of subsidiarity and solidarity. Its work also constitutes a basis for the provision of aid to Central and Eastern European countries in the field of local democracy. The CDLR undertakes the preparation and follow-up of Conferences of Ministers responsible for local and regional government.

Intergovernmental co-operation with the CDLR is supplemented by specific activities aimed at providing legislative advice, supporting reform and enhancing management capabilities and democratic participation in European member and non-member countries. These activities are specifically focused on the democratic stability of Central and Eastern European countries. The programmes for democratic stability in the field of local democracy draw inspiration from the European Charter of Local Self-Government, operating at three levels of government: at intergovernmental level, providing assistance in implementing reforms to reinforce local or regional government, in compliance with the Charter; at local or regional level, co-operating with local and regional authorities to build local government capacity; and at community level, co-operating directly with individual authorities to promote pilot initiatives. Working methods include awareness-raising conferences; legislative opinion involving written opinions, expert round tables and working groups; and seminars, workshops and training at home and abroad. Since May 2013 (when it was signed by San Marino) the Treaty covers all 47 Council of Europe member states.

In October 2007 the 15th session of the conference of European ministers responsible for local and regional government adopted the Valencia Declaration, recommitting to efforts to support local and regional democracy and endorsing a new Council of Europe Strategy on Innovation and Good Governance at Local Level. The 15th session also determined to draft an additional protocol to the European Charter on Local Self-Government consolidating at European level the right to democratic participation, citizens' right to information, and the duties of authorities relating to these rights; this was opened for signature in November 2009. The 16th session, held in Utrecht, Netherlands, in October 2009, adopted the Utrecht Declaration on Good Local and Regional Governance in Turbulent Times: The Challenge of Change. In October 2012 the Council of Europe convened the first World Forum for Democracy, in Strasbourg, on the theme 'Bridging the gap: democracy between old models and new realities'. The second Forum, held in November 2013, also in Strasbourg, addressed 'Re-wiring democracy: connecting institutions and citizens in the digital age'.

The policy of the Council of Europe on transfrontier co-operation between territorial communities or authorities is implemented through two committees. The Committee of Experts on Transfrontier Co-operation, working under the supervision of the CDLR, aims to monitor the implementation of the European Outline Convention on Transfrontier Co-operation between Territorial Communities or Authorities; to make proposals for the elimination of obstacles, in particular of a legal nature, to transfrontier and interterritorial co-operation; and to compile 'best practice' examples of transfrontier co-operation in various fields of activity. In 2002 the Committee of Ministers adopted a Recommendation on the mutual aid and assistance between central and local authorities in the event of disasters affecting frontier areas. A Committee of Advisers for the development of transfrontier co-operation in Central and Eastern Europe is composed of six members appointed or elected by the Secretary-General, the Committee of Ministers and the CLRAE. Its task is to guide the promotion of transfrontier co-operation in Central and Eastern European countries, with a view to fostering good neighbourly relations between the frontier populations, especially in particularly sensitive regions. Its programme comprises: conferences and colloquies designed to raise awareness on the Outline Convention; meetings in border regions between representatives of local communities with a view to strengthening mutual trust; and legal assistance to, and restricted meetings with, national and local representatives responsible for preparing the legal texts for ratification and/or implementation of the Outline Convention. The priority areas outlined by the Committee of Advisers include South-East Europe, northern Europe around the Baltic Sea, the external frontiers of an enlarged EU, and the Caucasus.

EDUCATION, CULTURE AND HERITAGE

The European Cultural Convention covers education, culture, heritage, sport and youth. Programmes on education, higher education, culture and cultural heritage are managed by four steering committees. A new Council of Europe cultural governance observatory, CultureWatchEurope is under development, with a mandate to monitor the follow-up to all relevant Council of Europe Conventions; to act as a forum for the exchange of information on culture, and on cultural and natural heritage; to observe ongoing relevant policies, practices, trends and emerging issues; to highlight good practice; and to analyse and advise on policy.

The education programme comprises projects on education for democratic citizenship and human rights, history teaching, intercultural dialogue, instruments and policies for plurilingualism, the education of European Roma/Gypsy children, teaching remembrance—education for the prevention of crimes against humanity, and the 'Pestalozzi' training programme for education professionals. The Council of Europe's main focus in the field of higher education is, in co-operation with the EU, on the Bologna Process, which was launched in 1999 with the aim of establishing a European Higher Education Area, including education networks and student exchanges at all levels. In May 2007 the Council of Europe and the EU signed a Memorandum of Understanding confirming mutual co-operation in the promotion of democratic citizenship and human rights education and reaffirming commitment to the Bologna Process. In April 2009 ministers responsible for higher education in the member countries of the Bologna Process adopted the priorities for the European Higher Education Area until 2020, with an emphasis on the importance of lifelong learning, expanding access to higher education, and mobility. In March 2010 the Bologna Process ministers for higher education adopted the Budapest-Vienna Declaration officially launching the European Higher Education Area. Other Council of Europe activities in the area of education include the partial agreement for the European Centre for Modern Languages located in Graz, Austria, the Network for School Links and Exchanges, and the European Schools Day competition, organized in co-operation with the EU.

In December 2000 the Committee of Ministers adopted a Declaration on Cultural Diversity, formulated in consultation with other organizations (including the EU and UNESCO), which created a framework for developing a European approach to valuing cultural diversity. A European Charter for Regional or Minority Languages entered into force in 1998, with the aim of protecting regional or minority languages, which are considered to be a threatened aspect of Europe's cultural heritage. The Charter provides for a monitoring system enabling states, the Council of Europe and individuals to observe and follow up its implementation. The meeting of heads of state or government convened in Warsaw, in May 2005 identified intercultural dialogue as a means of promoting tolerance and social cohesion; this was supported by the Faro Declaration on the Council of Europe's Strategy for Developing Intercultural Dialogue adopted by ministers responsible for culture convened in Faro, Portugal, in October of that year. In May 2008 the Council of Europe organized, in Liverpool, United Kingdom, a conference on intercultural cities, which addressed replacing a multicultural approach to cultural diversity with an intercultural outlook, encouraging interaction between and hybridization of cultures, with a view to generating a richer common cultural environment. A new Council of Europe Intercultural Cities Programme was launched at the conference. In that month the Committee of Ministers adopted a *White Paper on Intercultural Dialogue* which stated that clear reference to the universal values of democracy, human rights, and the rule of law must underpin the use of intercultural dialogue as a means of addressing the complex issues raised by increasingly culturally diverse societies. In April 2010 the Council of Europe, European Commission, OSCE, UNESCO, UNICEF and Hungary-based Roma Education Fund established an International Task Force for the Education of Roma, aimed at improving the educational situation an social inclusion of Roma, Sinti and 'Travellers'. In November 2012 the Council of Europe reported that Roma children were receiving segregated and substandard education, and were subjected to lower teacher expectations, in the school systems of a majority of member states, perpetuating cycles of social marginalization and poverty.

The Framework Convention on the Value of Cultural Heritage for Society (known as the Faro Framework Convention), which entered into force in June 2011, establishes principles underpinning the use and development of heritage in Europe in the globalization era.

The European Audiovisual Observatory, established in 1992, collates and circulates information on legal, production, marketing and statistical issues relating to the audiovisual industry in Europe, in the four sectors of film, television, video and DVD, and new media. The European Convention for the Protection of Audiovisual Heritage and its Protocol were opened for signature in November 2001; the first document entered into force in January 2008, and the second in April 2014. The Eurimages support fund, in which 36 member states participate, helps to finance the co-production of films. The Convention for the Protection of the Architectural Heritage and the Protection of the Archaeological Heritage provide a legal framework for European co-operation in these areas. The European Heritage Network is being developed to facilitate the work of professionals and state institutions and the dissemination of good practices in 43 countries of the states parties to the European Cultural Convention.

YOUTH

In 1972 the Council of Europe established the European Youth Centre (EYC) in Strasbourg. A second residential centre was created in Budapest, Hungary, in 1995. The centres, run with and by international non-governmental youth organizations representing a wide range of interests, provide about 50 residential courses a year (study sessions, training courses, symposia). A notable feature of the EYC is its decision-making structure, by which decisions on its programme and general policy matters are taken by a Programming Committee composed of an equal number of youth organizations and government representatives. The ninth Council of Europe Conference of Ministers responsible for Youth was held in St Petersburg, Russia, in September 2012.

The European Youth Foundation (EYF) aims to provide financial assistance to European activities of non-governmental youth organizations and began operations in 1973. Since that time more than 300,000 young people have benefited directly from EYF-supported activities. The Steering Committee for Youth conducts research in youth-related matters and prepares for ministerial conferences.

In 1997 the Council of Europe and the European Youth Information and Counselling Agency (EYRICA) concluded a partnership agreement on developing the training of youth information workers. EYRICA maintains SHEYRICA, an online platform supporting youth information workers. In November 2004 the EYRICA General Assembly adopted the European Youth Information Charter; in 2014 some 13,000 EYRICA youth workers were providing young people with general information in accordance with the principles of the Charter. EYRICA comprised 25 member organizations in that year, as well as seven affiliated and two co-operating organizations, which were active in more than 7,500 youth information centres in 28 countries.

SPORT

The Committee for the Development of Sport, founded in 1977, oversees sports co-operation and development on a pan-European basis, bringing together all the 50 (as at April 2014) states parties to the European Cultural Convention. Its activities focus on the implementation of the European Sport Charter and Code of Sports Ethics (adopted in 1992 and revised in 2001), the role of sport in society, the provision of assistance in sports reform to new member states in Central and Eastern Europe, and the practice of both recreational and high-level sport. A Charter on Sport for Disabled Persons was adopted in 1986. The Committee also prepares the Conferences of European Ministers responsible for Sport (usually held every four years) and has been responsible for drafting two important conventions to combat negative influences on sport. The European Convention on Spectator Violence and Misbehaviour at Sport Events (1985) provides governments with practical measures to ensure crowd security and safety, particularly at football matches. The Anti-Doping Convention (1989) has been ratified by 52 countries (as at April 2014); it is also open to non-European states. In May 2007 the Committee of Ministers adopted the Enlarged Partial Agreement on Sport (EPAS), which aimed to develop a framework for a pan-European platform of intergovernmental sports co-operation and to set international standards. By April 2014 EPAS had 36 member states, and 24 sports organizations as non-governmental partners.

ENVIRONMENT AND SUSTAINABLE DEVELOPMENT

In 1995 the Pan-European Biological and Landscape Diversity Strategy (PEBLDS), formulated by the Committee of Ministers, was endorsed at a ministerial conference of the UN Economic Commission for Europe, which was held in Sofia, Bulgaria. The Strategy is implemented jointly by the Council of Europe and UNEP, in close co-operation with the EU. In particular, it provides for implementation of the Convention on Biological Diversity. It promotes the development of the Pan-European Ecological Network (PEEN), supporting the conservation of a full range of European ecosystems, habitats, species and landscapes, and physically linking core areas through the preservation (or restoration) of ecological corridors.

The Convention on the Conservation of European Wildlife and Natural Habitats (Bern Convention), which was signed in 1979 and entered into force in June 1982, gives total protection to 693 species of plants, 89 mammals, 294 birds, 43 reptiles, 21 amphibians, 115 freshwater fishes, 113 invertebrates and their habitats. The Convention established a network of protected areas known as the 'Emerald Network'; the Network is being developed in partnership with the EU, and has also been extended to Africa (Burkino Faso, Morocco, Senegal and Tunisia). The Council awards the European Diploma for protection of sites of European significance, supervises a network of biogenetic reserves, and co-ordinates conservation action for threatened animals and plants. A European Convention on Landscape, to provide for the management and protection of the natural and cultural landscape in Europe, was adopted by the Committee of Ministers in 2000 and entered into force in July 2004.

Regional disparities constitute a major obstacle to the process of European integration. Conferences of ministers responsible for regional/spatial planning (CEMAT) are held to discuss these issues. In 2000 they adopted guiding principles for sustainable development of the European continent and, in 2001, a resolution detailing a 10-point programme for greater cohesion among the regions of Europe. In September 2003 the 13th CEMAT, convened in Ljubljana, Slovenia, agreed on strategies to promote the sustainable spatial development of the continent, including greater public participation in decision-making, an initiative to revitalize the countryside and efforts to prevent flooding. The 14th meeting was held in Portugal, in October 2006, and the 15th was convened in July 2010, in Moscow, Russia, on the theme 'Challenge of the Future: Sustainable Spatial Development of the European Continent in a Changing World'.

EXTERNAL RELATIONS

Agreements providing for co-operation and exchange of documents and observers have been concluded with the UN and its agencies, and with most of the European intergovernmental organizations and the Organization of American States (OAS). Relations with non-member states, other organizations and NGOs are co-ordinated by the Directorate-General of Political Affairs. In 2001 the Council and European Commission signed a joint declaration on co-operation and partnership, which provided for the organization and funding of joint programmes.

Israel, Canada and Mexico are represented in the Parliamentary Assembly by observer delegations, and certain European and other non-member countries participate in or send observers to certain meetings of technical committees and specialized conferences at intergovernmental level. Full observer status with the Council was granted to the USA in 1995, to Canada and Japan in 1996 and to Mexico in 1999. The Holy See has had a similar status since 1970.

The European Centre for Global Interdependence and Solidarity (the 'North-South Centre') was established in Lisbon, Portugal, in 1990, in order to provide a framework for European co-operation in this area and to promote pluralist democracy and respect for human rights. The Centre is co-managed by parliamentarians, governments, NGOs and local and regional authorities. Its activities are divided into three programmes: public information and media relations; education and training for global interdependence; and dialogue for global partnership. The Centre organizes workshops, seminars and training courses on global interdependence and convenes international colloquies on human rights.

The partial agreement on the Co-operation Group for the Prevention of, Protection Against, and Organisation of Relief in Major Natural and Technological Disasters (EUR-OPA), adopted in 1987, facilitates co-operation between European and non-European southern Mediterranean countries, covering knowledge of hazards, risk prevention, risk management, post-crisis analysis and rehabilitation. At April 2014 there were 26 parties to the Agreement.

Since 1993 the Council of Europe and EU have jointly established a co-operative structure of programmes to assist the process of democratic reform in Central and Eastern European countries that were formerly under communist rule. Several joint programmes are country-specific. Sub-regional multilateral thematic programmes are also implemented, for example on developing the Emerald Network for Nature Protection sites (2012–16) and promoting minority rights in South-East Europe (2011–14).

Finance

The budget is financed by contributions from members on a proportional scale of assessment (using population and gross domestic product as common indicators). The budget for 2013 totalled €240m.

Publications

Activities Report (in English and French).

The Bulletin (newsletter of the CLRAE, quarterly).

Bulletin On Constitutional Case-Law (3–4 times a year, in English and French).

The Council of Europe: 800 million Europeans (introductory booklet).

Education Newsletter (3 a year).

The Europeans (electronic bulletin of the Parliamentary Assembly).

The Fight Against Terrorism, Council of Europe Standards (in English and French).

Human Rights and the Environment (in English, French and Italian).

Human Rights Information Bulletin (3 a year, in English and French).

Iris (legal observations of the European audiovisual observatory, monthly).

Naturopa (2 a year, in 15 languages).

Recent Demographic Developments in Europe (annually, in English and French).

Social Cohesion Developments (3 a year).

Yearbook of Film, Television and Multimedia in Europe (in English and French).

Associated Bodies

Council of Europe Development Bank (CEB): 55 ave Kléber, 75116 Paris, France; tel. 1-47-55-55-00; fax 1-47-55-37-82; e-mail info@coebank.org; internet www.coebank.org; f. April 1956 as the Council of Europe Resettlement Fund, subsequently renamed as the Council of Europe Social Development Fund, with the present name adopted in Nov. 1999; a multilateral development bank with a social development mandate; grants loans for investment projects with a social purpose: priority projects seek to solve social problems related to the presence of refugees, displaced persons or forced migrants; additionally, the Bank finances projects in other fields contributing directly to strengthening social cohesion in Europe, including job creation and preservation in small and medium-sized enterprises; social housing; improving urban living conditions; health and education infrastructure; managing the environment; and supporting public infrastructure; established in 2008 a Human Rights Trust Account to finance technical projects in the field of human rights protection; at 31 Dec. 2013 this had received total contributions of €10.9m; total assets: €24.5m. (2013); in 2013 the Bank approved new projects with a value of €3,100m; Governor ROLF WENZEL (Germany).

European Centre for Global Interdependence and Solidarity (North-South Centre): Avda da República 15, 4º Andar, 1050-185 Lisbon, Portugal; tel. (21) 358-40-30; fax (21) 358-40-37; e-mail nscinfo@coe.int; internet www.coe.int/t/dg4/nscentre; f. 1990; launched the Council of Europe North-South prize in 1995; co-sponsors, with the European Youth Forum, the Spanish Government, and other partners the University on Youth and Development, a youth event convened annually, since 2000, in Mollina, Spain; launched the first Africa-Europe Youth Summit in Dec. 2007; supported the establishment, in 2009, of the annual African University on Youth and Development; an Africa-Europe Youth Cooperation Action Plan was being implemented by the Centre during 2012–15; mems: 23 states, including (beyond the European membership) Cape Verde and Morocco; Exec. Dir FRANCISCO SEIXAS DA COSTA (Portugal).

Group of States against Corruption (GRECO): GRECO Secretariat, Council of Europe Directorate-General of Human Rights and the Rule of Law, 67075 Strasbourg Cedex, France; fax 3-88-41-29-55; e-mail webmaster.greco@coe.int; internet www.coe.int/greco; f. 1999 to support and monitor (through a process of mutual evaluation and peer pressure) states' compliance with Council of Europe anti-corruption standards; participation is open to states outside of the Council of Europe membership; mems: 49 states (48 European countries and the USA); Exec. Sec. WOLFGANG RAU (Germany).

ECONOMIC COMMUNITY OF WEST AFRICAN STATES—ECOWAS

Address: ECOWAS Executive Secretariat, 101 Yakubu Gowon Crescent, PMB 401, Asokoro, Abuja, Nigeria.

Telephone: (9) 3147647; **fax:** (9) 3147646; **e-mail:** info@ecowas.int; **internet:** www.ecowas.int.

The Treaty of Lagos, establishing ECOWAS, was signed in May 1975 by 15 states, with the object of promoting trade, co-operation and self-reliance in West Africa. Outstanding protocols bringing certain key features of the Treaty into effect were ratified in November 1976. Cape Verde joined in 1977. A revised ECOWAS treaty, to accelerate economic integration and to increase political co-operation, was signed in July 1993.

MEMBERS

Benin	Ghana	Niger
Burkina Faso	Guinea	Nigeria
Cape Verde	Guinea-Bissau	Senegal
Côte d'Ivoire	Liberia	Sierra Leone
The Gambia	Mali	Togo

Organization

(April 2014)

AUTHORITY OF HEADS OF STATE AND GOVERNMENT

The Authority is the supreme decision-making organ of the Community, with responsibility for its general development and realization of its objectives. The Chairman is elected annually by the Authority from among the member states. The Authority meets at least once a year in ordinary session. The 44th ordinary session was convened in March 2014, in Yamoussoukro, Côte d'Ivoire.

COUNCIL OF MINISTERS

The Council consists of two representatives from each member country; the chairmanship is held by a minister from the same member state as the Chairman of the Authority. The Council meets at least twice a year, and is responsible for the running of the Community.

ECOWAS COMMISSION

The ECOWAS Commission, formerly the Executive Secretariat, was inaugurated in January 2007, following a decision to implement a process of structural reform taken at the January 2006 summit meeting of the Authority. In July 2013 the Commission—elected for a four-year term, which may be renewed once only—was enlarged from nine to 15 members. It comprises a President, a Vice-President and 13 other Commissioners, responsible for finance; macroeconomic policy; trade, customs, and free movement; agriculture, environment and water resources; infrastructure; political affairs, peace and security; social affairs and gender; general administration and conferences; human resources management; education, science and culture; energy and mines; telecommunications and information technology; and industry and private sector promotion.

President: KADRÉ DÉSIRÉ OUÉDRAOGO (Burkina Faso).

ECOWAS PARLIAMENT

The inaugural session of the 120-member ECOWAS Parliament, based in Abuja, Nigeria, was held in November 2000. The January 2006 summit meeting of the Authority determined to restructure the Parliament, in line with a process of wider institutional reform. The number of seats was reduced from 120 to 115 and each member of the Parliament was to be elected for a four-year term (reduced from five years). The second legislature was inaugurated in November 2006. There is a co-ordinating administrative bureau, comprising a speaker and four deputy speakers, and there are also eight standing committees (reduced in number from 13) covering each of the Parliament's areas of activity.

Speaker: IKE EKWEREMADU (Nigeria).

ECOWAS COURT OF JUSTICE

The Court of Justice, established in January 2001, is based in Abuja, and comprises seven judges who serve a five-year renewable term of office. At the January 2006 summit meeting the Authority approved the creation of a Judicial Council, comprising qualified and experienced persons, to contribute to the establishment of community laws. The Authority also approved the inauguration of an appellate division within the Court. The judges hold (non-renewable) tenure for four years. In March 2013 the President of the ECOWAS Court of Justice formally recommended the establishment of an ECOWAS appellate body.

President: NANA AWA DABOYA (Togo).

Registrar: TONY ANENE-MAIDOH (Ghana).

Activities

ECOWAS aims to promote co-operation and development in economic, social and cultural activities, to raise the standard of living of the people of the member countries, to increase and maintain economic stability, to improve relations among member countries and to contribute to the progress and development of Africa. ECOWAS is committed to abolishing all obstacles to the free movement of people, services and capital, and to promoting: harmonization of agricultural policies; common projects in marketing, research and the agriculturally based industries; joint development of economic and industrial policies and elimination of disparities in levels of development; and common monetary policies.

Initial slow progress in achieving many of the aims of ECOWAS aims was attributed, inter alia, to the reluctance of some governments to implement policies at the national level and their failure to provide the agreed financial resources; to the high cost of compensating loss of customs revenue; and to the existence of numerous other intergovernmental organizations in the region (in particular the Union Economique et Monétaire Ouest-Africaine—UEMOA, which replaced the Francophone Communauté Economique de l'Afrique de l'Ouest in 1994). In respect of the latter obstacle to progress, however, ECOWAS and UEMOA resolved in February 2000 to create a single monetary zone (see below). In October ECOWAS and the European Union (EU) held their first joint high-level meeting, at which the EU pledged financial support for ECOWAS's economic integration programme, and in April 2001 it was announced that the IMF had agreed to provide technical assistance for the programme.

A revised treaty for the Community was drawn up by an ECOWAS Committee of Eminent Persons in 1991–92, and was signed at the ECOWAS summit conference that took place in Cotonou, Benin, in July 1993. The treaty designated the achievement of a common market and a single currency as economic objectives, while in the political sphere it envisaged the establishment of an ECOWAS parliament, an economic and social council, and an ECOWAS court of justice to enforce Community decisions (see above). The treaty also formally assigned the Community with the responsibility of preventing and settling regional conflicts. At a summit meeting held in Abuja, Nigeria, in August 1994, ECOWAS heads of state and government signed a protocol agreement for the establishment of a regional parliament. The meeting also adopted a Convention on Extradition of non-political offenders. The new ECOWAS treaty entered into effect in August 1995, having received the required number of ratifications. A draft protocol providing for the creation of a mechanism for the prevention, management and settlement of conflicts, and for the maintenance of peace in the region, was approved by ECOWAS heads of state and government in December 1999. In December 2000 Mauritania, a founding member, withdrew from the Community.

In May 2002 the ECOWAS Authority met in Yamoussoukro, Côte d'Ivoire, to develop a regional plan of action for the implementation of the New Partnership for Africa's Development (NEPAD). In January 2006 the Authority, meeting in Niamey, Niger, commended the recent establishment of an ECOWAS Project Development and Implementation Unit, aimed at accelerating the implementation of regional infrastructural projects in sectors such as energy, telecommunications and transport. Also at that meeting the Authority approved further amendments to the revised ECOWAS treaty to provide for institutional reform.

In June 2007 the Authority adopted a long-term ECOWAS Strategic Vision, detailing the proposed establishment by 2020 of a region-wide West African borderless, stateless space and single economic community. In January 2008 the Authority adopted a comprehensive strategy document proposing several initiatives and programmes aimed at reducing poverty in West Africa. The Authority also approved the establishment of a statistics development support fund, and the ECOWAS Common Approach on Migration.

TRADE AND MONETARY UNION

In 1990 ECOWAS heads of state and government agreed to adopt measures that would create a single monetary zone and remove barriers to trade in goods that originated in the Community. ECOWAS regards monetary union as necessary to encourage investment in the region, since it would greatly facilitate capital transactions with foreign countries. In September 1992 it was announced that, as part of efforts to enhance monetary co-operation and financial harmonization in the region, the West African Clearing House was to be restructured as the West African Monetary Agency (WAMA). As a specialized agency of ECOWAS, WAMA was to be responsible for administering an ECOWAS exchange rate system (EERS) and for establishing the single monetary zone. In July 1996 the Authority agreed to impose a common value-added tax (VAT) on consumer goods, in order to rationalize indirect taxation and to stimulate greater intra-Community trade. In August 1997 ECOWAS heads of state and government authorized the introduction of a regional travellers' cheque scheme. (The scheme was formally inaugurated in October 1998, and the cheques, issued by WAMA in denominations of a West African Unit of Account and convertible into each local currency at the rate of one Special Drawing Right—SDR—see IMF—entered into circulation on 1 July 1999.) In December 1999 the ECOWAS Authority determined to pursue a 'Fast Track Approach' to economic integration, involving a two-track implementation of related measures. In April 2000 seven, predominantly anglophone, ECOWAS member states—Cape Verde, The Gambia, Ghana, Guinea, Liberia, Nigeria and Sierra Leone—issued the Accra Declaration, in which they agreed to establish a second West African monetary union (the West African Monetary Zone—WAMZ) to co-exist initially alongside UEMOA, which unites eight, mainly francophone, ECOWAS member states. As preconditions for adopting a single currency and common monetary and exchange rate policy, the member states of the second West African monetary union were (under the supervision of a newly established ECOWAS Convergence Council, comprising member states' ministers responsible for finance and central bank governors) to attain a number of convergence criteria, including a satisfactory level of price stability; sustainable budget deficits; a reduction in inflation; and the maintenance of an adequate level of foreign exchange reserves. The two complementary monetary unions were expected to harmonize their economic programmes, with a view to effecting an eventual merger, as outlined in an action plan adopted by ECOWAS and UEMOA in February 2000. The ECOWAS Authority summit held in December 2000, in Bamako, Mali, adopted an Agreement Establishing the WAMZ, approved the establishment of a West African Monetary Institute to prepare for the formation of a West African Central Bank (WACB), and determined that the harmonization of member countries' tariff structures should be accelerated to facilitate the implementation of the planned customs union. In December 2001 the Authority determined that the currency of the WAMZ (and eventually the ECOWAS-wide currency) would be known as the 'eco' and authorized the establishment during 2002 of an exchange rate mechanism. This was achieved in April. Meeting in November 2002 the heads of state and government determined that a forum of WAMZ ministers responsible for finance should be convened on a regular basis to ensure the effective implementation of fiscal policies. In May 2004 ECOWAS and UEMOA signed an agreement that provided for the establishment of a Joint Technical Secretariat to enhance the co-ordination of their programmes.

Owing to slower than anticipated progress in achieving the convergence criteria required for monetary union, past deadlines for the inauguration of the WAMZ and launch of the 'eco' were not met. In May 2009 the Convergence Council adopted a roadmap towards realizing the single currency for West Africa by 2020. The roadmap (of which an updated version was released in March 2010) envisaged that during 2014 the WACB, WAMZ Secretariat and West African Financial Supervisory Agency would be established, and that the WAMZ monetary union would finally to enter into effect before or at the start of 2015, with the 'eco' scheduled to enter into circulation in January 2015. In October 2011 the Convergence Council adopted supplementary acts to facilitate the process of establishing the single currency. The documents included the Guideline on the Formation of a Multi-year Programme on Convergence with ECOWAS; and the Draft Supplementary Act on Convergence and Macroeconomic Stability Pact among Member States, the latter constituting a formal commitment by signatories to ensure economic policy co-ordination, to strengthen economic convergence and to increase macroeconomic stability. In October 2013 ECOWAS heads of state and government appointed the Presidents of Ghana and Niger to advance the implementation of the roadmap, and in January 2014 an extraordinary session of the Council noted that poor performance achieved hitherto on macroeconomic convergence, and the delayed implementation of roadmap activities, were undermining the likely achievement of the 2015 deadline for WAMZ monetary union. An updated version of the roadmap was to be submitted to the Council of Ministers for approval.

In December 2011 a meeting of the Joint ECOWAS-UEMOA Management Committee of the ECOWAS common external tariff (CET), established in July 2006, agreed on a timetable for concluding a draft CET. Accordingly, in March 2013 ECOWAS ministers responsible for finance endorsed a new five-band regional tariff regime, covering some 5,899 tariff lines, under which a rate of 5% duty was to be applied to 2,146 lines designated as basic raw materials and capital goods; 10% to 1,373 lines designated as intermediate products; and a 20% tariff would be levied on 2,165 lines categorized as final consumer products. A new 1.5% community integration levy (whose scope was to be subject to further discussions) was to replace the existing ECOWAS community levy and UEMOA community solidarity levy, to help ensure uniformity in port charges. In January of that year a new West African Capital Markets Integration Council (WACMIC) was inaugurated; the WACMIC was to govern the integration of regional capital markets, and was envisaged as a pillar of a proposed West African Common Investment Market. An extraordinary summit of the ECOWAS Authority was convened in October 2013, in Dakar, Senegal, to address in detail matters of critical importance to the consolidation of the regional market, and to the Community levy. The summit meeting endorsed the final structure of the CET, which was to enter into effect on 1 January 2015, and authorized the establishment of a task force on trade liberation.

In December 1992 ECOWAS ministers agreed on the institutionalization of an ECOWAS trade fair, in order to promote trade liberalization and intra-Community trade. The first trade fair was held in Dakar, Senegal, in 1995; the seventh was held in Accra, in October–November 2013. In September 2011 an ECOWAS Investment Forum was held in Lagos, Nigeria (following an inaugural event held in Brussels, Belgium, in the previous year), during which member states were called upon to implement measures to reduce risk and improve investor confidence and the business climate. A further Investment Forum was staged in Accra, Ghana, in August 2012. ECOWAS business fora are organized periodically (the fourth, with a focus on information and communication technology—ICT, was held in 2013, in The Gambia). During 2013–14 ECOWAS was implementing a Business Incubators for African Women Entrepreneurs project, with a particular focus on agri-business, agro-processing and handicrafts. In December 2013 the ECOWAS Council of Ministers approved the establishment of an ECOWAS Investment Guarantee/Reinsurance Agency, which was to be endowed with authorized capital of US $1,000m., and to be tasked with mitigating political risks associated with investing in the region.

An extraordinary meeting of ministers responsible for trade and industry was convened in May 2008 to discuss the impact on the region of the rapidly rising cost at that time of basic food items. In December the ECOWAS Authority warned that the ongoing global financial crisis might undermine the region's economic development, and called for a regional strategy to minimize the risk. In June 2012 the Authority endorsed measures aimed at finding a durable resolution to the ongoing food security crisis in the Sahel region, that had been agreed by an ECOWAS-UEMOA Permanent Inter-State Committee on Drought Control in the Sahel high-level meeting convened earlier in that month; these included the development of a regional food reserve. The Authority also urged the international community to mobilize resources required to support affect communities in the Sahel, and welcomed a new Partnership for Resilience in the Sahel initiative, launched earlier in that month by the EU. In November the Commission initiated a programme aimed at promoting regional food self-sufficiency and reducing food imports into the region.

TRANSPORT AND TELECOMMUNICATIONS

In July 1992 the ECOWAS Authority formulated a Minimum Agenda for Action for the implementation of Community agreements regarding the free movement of goods and people, for example the removal of non-tariff barriers, the simplification of customs and transit procedures and a reduction in the number of control posts on international roads. However, implementation of the Minimum Agenda was slow. In April 1997 Gambian and Senegalese finance and trade officials concluded an agreement on measures to facilitate the export of goods via Senegal to neighbouring countries, in accordance with ECOWAS protocols relating to inter-state road transit arrangements. A Brown Card scheme provides recognized third-party liability insurance throughout the region. In January 2003 Community heads of state and government approved the ECOWAS passport; by 2014 the passport was being issued by 10 member states.

In February 1996 ECOWAS and several private sector partners established ECOAir Ltd, based in Abuja, which was to develop a regional airline. In December 2007, following a recommendation by the Authority, a new Togo-based regional airline, ASKY (Africa Sky) was established, which initiated operations in January 2010. In October 2011 West African ministers responsible for transport concluded a series of measures to establish a common regulatory regime for the airline industry in order to improve the viability of regional airlines and to support regional integration. A regional shipping company, ECOMARINE, commenced operations in February 2003; this was, however, inactive in 2014.

A long-standing ECOWAS vision for the development of an integrated regional road network comprises: the Trans-West African Coastal Highway, connecting Lagos, Nigeria, with Nouackchott, Mauritania (4,767 km), and envisaged as the western part of an eventual Pan-African Highway; and the Trans-Sahelian Highway, linking Dakar, Senegal, with N'Djamena, Chad (4,633 km). In November 2012 ECOWAS and the People's Republic of China concluded an agreement on regional infrastructure development and economic co-operation, which incorporated Chinese support in advancing the Trans-West African Coastal Highway project. In July 2013 the inaugural meeting was convened of an ECOWAS steering committee to guide the implementation of the 1,028-km Abidjan–Lagos corridor road project, linking Lagos (Nigeria), Cotonou (Benin), Lomé (Togo), Accra (Ghana) and Abidjan (Côte d'Ivoire) as well as several other sea ports; it was envisaged that the construction phase of the project would commence in 2016. In September 2013 the steering committee agreed to mobilize funding for the initiative.

A West African Telecommunications Regulators' Association was established, under the auspices of ECOWAS, in September 2000. The January 2006 summit meeting of the Authority approved a new Special Fund for Telecommunications to facilitate improvements to cross-border telecommunications connectivity. In May ECOWAS ministers responsible for information and telecommunications agreed guidelines for harmonizing the telecommunications sector. In January 2007 ECOWAS leaders adopted a regional telecommunications policy and a regulatory framework that covered areas including interconnection to ICT and services networks, licence regimes, and radio frequency spectrum management. A common, liberalized ECOWAS telecommunications market is envisaged. In October 2008 ECOWAS ministers responsible for telecommunications and ICT adopted regional legislation on combating cybercrime. In October 2011 ECOWAS ministers, meeting in Yamoussoukro, adopted a series of priority projects to be undertaken during the next five years, including the elaboration of a regulation on access to submarine cable landing stations and national rights of way. The meeting recommended the establishment of a Directorate of Telecoms-ICT and Post sectors, in order to improve ECOWAS's operational capacity and to enhance the planning and monitoring of these sectors at Community level.

ECONOMIC AND INDUSTRIAL DEVELOPMENT

In June 2010 the Council of Ministers adopted the West African Common Industrial Policy (WACIP), and a related action plan and supplementary acts. WACIP aimed to diversify and expand the regional industrial production base by supporting the creation of new industrial production capacities as well as developing existing capacities. WACIP envisaged the expansion of intra-ECOWAS trade from 13% to 40% by 2030, through enhancing skills, industrial competitiveness and quality infrastructure, with a particular focus on the areas of information, communications and transport.

In September 2008 the inaugural meeting was convened of an ECOWAS-China economic and trade forum, which aimed to strengthen bilateral relations and discuss investment possibilities; a second forum was convened in March 2012, in Accra. In November ECOWAS and China signed a framework agreement aimed at fostering economic co-operation on trade, services, investment and infrastructure development, and at enhancing technical and industrial co-operation.

In November 1984 ECOWAS heads of state and government approved the establishment of a private regional investment bank, Ecobank Transnational Inc. ECOWAS has a 10% share in the bank, which is headquartered in Lomé.

In late 2007 the 600-km West African Gas Pipeline—extending from Lagos, Nigeria, to Takoradi, Ghana—became operational, an agreement on financing its construction having been concluded in August 1999 by Nigeria, Ghana, Togo and Benin, and also two petroleum companies operating in Nigeria. The implementation of a planned energy exchange scheme, known as the West African Power Pool Project (WAPP), is envisaged as a means of efficiently utilizing the region's hydro-electricity and thermal power capabilities by transferring power from surplus producers to countries unable to meet their energy requirements. An ECOWAS Energy Protocol, establishing a legal framework for the promotion of long-term co-operation in the energy sector, was adopted in 2003. In May of that year the Community decided to initiate the first phase of WAPP, to be implemented in Benin, Côte d'Ivoire, Ghana, Niger, Nigeria and Togo, at an estimated cost of US $335m. In January 2005 the Authority endorsed a revised masterplan for the implementation of WAPP, which was scheduled to be completed by 2020. In July 2005 the World Bank approved a $350m. facility to support the implementation of WAPP; this became fully operational in January 2006.

In November 2008 the Authority approved the establishment of a Regional Centre for Renewable Energy and Energy Efficiency (ECREEE, and also endorsed the establishment of an ECOWAS Regional Electricity Regulatory Authority (based in Accra). The Authority also adopted a joint ECOWAS/UEMOA action plan on priority regional infrastructure projects. ECREEE was inaugurated in 2009, and a Secretariat was established in July 2010, in Praia, Cape Verde. In September 2011 the ECOWAS Commission signed a €2.3m. grant contract with the EU for an ECREEE project on energy efficiency in West Africa.

In April 2009 ministers responsible for the development of mineral resources endorsed an ECOWAS Directive on the Harmonization of Guiding Principles and Policies in the Mining Sector. An ad hoc committee convenes periodically to monitor the implementation of the Directive.

REGIONAL SECURITY

The revised ECOWAS treaty, signed in July 1993, incorporates a separate provision for regional security, requiring member states to work towards the maintenance of peace, stability and security. In December 1997 an extraordinary meeting of ECOWAS heads of state and government was convened in Lomé, to consider the future stability and security of the region. It was agreed that a permanent mechanism should be established for conflict prevention and the maintenance of peace. ECOWAS leaders also reaffirmed their commitment to pursuing dialogue to prevent conflicts, co-operating in the early deployment of peacekeeping forces and implementing measures to counter trans-border crime and the illegal trafficking of armaments and drugs.

In December 1999 ECOWAS heads of state and government, meeting in Lomé, approved a draft protocol to the organization's treaty, providing for the establishment of a Permanent Mechanism for the Prevention, Management and Settlement of Conflicts and the Maintenance of Peace in the Region, and for the creation of a

Mediation and Security Council, to comprise representatives of 10 member states, elected for two-year terms. The Council was to be supported by an advisory Council of Elders (also known as the Council of the Wise), comprising 32 eminent statesmen from the region; this was inaugurated in July 2001. In January 2003 the Council of Elders was recomposed as a 15-member body with a representative from each member state. In December 2006 a Technical Committee of Experts on Political Affairs, Peace and Security was established as a subsidiary body of the Mediation and Security Council.

An ECOWAS Warning and Response Network (ECOWARN) assesses threats to regional security. In June 2004 the Community approved the establishment of the ECOWAS Standby Force (ESF), comprising 6,500 troops, including a core rapid reaction component, the ECOWAS Task Force, numbering around 2,770 soldiers (deployable within 30 days). The ECOWAS Defence and Security Commission approved the operational framework for the ESF in April 2005. A training exercise for the logistics component of the ESF was conducted, in Ouagadougou, Burkina Faso, in June 2009.

In January 2005 the Authority authorized the establishment of a humanitarian depot, to be based in Bamako, and a logistics depot, to be based in Freetown, Sierra Leone, with a view to expanding regional humanitarian response capacity. In December 2009 the Sierra Leone Government allocated land for the construction of the planned Freetown depot, and, in February 2011, ECOWAS signed Memorandums of Understanding with the World Food Programme (WFP) and with the Government of Mali relating to the planned creation of the Bamako ECOWAS Humanitarian Depot, which, once established, was to provide storage for food and non-food items, and for emergency equipment. An ECOWAS Emergency Response Team was established in 2007.

In June 2006 the Authority adopted the ECOWAS Convention on Small Arms and Light Weapons, their Ammunitions and other Materials, with the aim of regulating the importation and manufacture of such weapons. The ECOWAS Small Arms Control Programme (ECOSAP) was inaugurated in that month. Based in Bamako, ECOSAP aims to improve the capacity of national and regional institutions to reduce the proliferation of small weapons across the region. During 1999 ECOWAS member states established the Intergovernmental Action Group Against Money Laundering in Africa (GIABA), which was mandated to combat drugs-trafficking and money-laundering throughout the region; a revised regulation for GIABA adopted by the Authority in January 2006 expanded the Group's mandate to cover regional responsibility for combating terrorism. Representatives from ECOWAS member states met in Ouagadougou, in September 2007 to draft a new West African strategy for enhanced drug control. In October 2008—during a High-level Conference on Drugs Trafficking as a Security Threat to West Africa, convened by ECOWAS jointly with the UN Office on Drugs and Crime (UNODC) and the Cape Verde Government, in Praia, Cape Verde—the Executive Director of UNODC warned that West Africa was at risk of becoming an epicentre for drugs-trafficking, representing a serious threat to public health and security in the region. He proposed the establishment of a West African intelligence-sharing centre, and urged the promotion of development and the strengthening of the rule of law as a means of reducing regional vulnerability to drugs and crime. At the Conference ECOWAS adopted the Praia Political Declaration on Drugs Trafficking and Organized Crime in West Africa, and approved an ECOWAS Regional Response Plan. In April 2009 ECOWAS ministers with responsibility for issues relating to trafficking in persons adopted a policy aimed at establishing a legal mechanism for protecting and assisting victims of trafficking. In July 2009 ECOWAS, UNODC, other UN agencies, and INTERPOL launched the West Africa Coast Initiative (WACI), which aimed to build national and regional capacities to combat drugs-trafficking and organized crime in, initially, four pilot post-conflict countries: Côte d'Ivoire, Guinea-Bissau, Liberia and Sierra Leone. In February 2010 the pilot countries signed the 'WACI-Freetown Commitment', endorsing the implementation of the initiative, and agreeing to establish specialized transnational crime units on their territories. It was envisaged that WACI activities would be expanded to Guinea. In March 2010 ECOWAS, the African Union (AU), the International Organization for Migration (IOM) and UNODC launched an initiative to develop a roadmap for implementing in West Africa the Ouagadougou Action Plan to Combat Trafficking in Human Beings (adopted by the AU in 2006). In February 2013 the Authority reaffirmed commitment to the 2008 Praia Political Declaration on Drugs Trafficking and Organized Crime in West Africa, and extended by two years the Regional Response Plan. At that time the Authority also endorsed a new ECOWAS Counter-Terrorism Strategy and Implementation Plan, and Political Declaration on a Common Position against Terrorism.

In October 2006 it was reported that ECOWAS planned to introduce a series of initiatives in each of the member states under a Peace and Development Project (PADEP). The Project intended to foster a 'culture of peace' among the member states of ECOWAS, strengthening social cohesion and promoting economic integration, democracy and good governance.

In March 2008 an ECOWAS Network of Electoral Commissions (ECONEC), comprising heads of member states' institutions responsible for managing elections, was established, to provide electoral support to member states and also to serve as a regional platform for the exchange of best practices in the management of elections. In October 2012 ECONEC adopted an action plan aimed at improving electoral processes to facilitate the conduct of free, fair and transparent elections and advancing democracy in the region.

In July 2013 a team of 80 ECOWAS observers was dispatched to monitor parliamentary elections that took place in Togo, in September a team observed legislative elections held in Guinea, and in November ECOWAS observers monitored legislative elections in Mali.

Meeting in June 2012 the Authority expressed concern at the rise in terrorist activities in the Sahel region, and also in Nigeria. ECOWAS has developed a Sahel Strategy, which aims to counter weak governance, poverty, terrorism, organized crime and trafficking in the region.

In June 2013 the President of the ECOWAS Commission, the UN Special Representative for West Africa, and the Secretary-General of the Mano River Union (which comprises Côte d'Ivoire, Guinea, Liberia and Sierra Leone), co-chaired a high-level meeting, in Dakar, Senegal, which initiated the process of formulating a security strategy for the Mano River Union, as requested in recent resolutions of the UN Security Council.

Piracy in the Gulf of Guinea: In April 2011 ECOWAS initiated a series of regional measures to combat the increased incidence of piracy, in co-operation with the Communauté économique des états de l'Afrique centrale (CEEAC—Economic Community of Central African States). In October the UN Security Council adopted Resolution 2018 which urged ECOWAS, CEEAC and the Gulf of Guinea Commission to develop a comprehensive regional action plan against piracy and armed robbery at sea. Accordingly, in June 2013 regional heads of state attending a summit held in Yaoundé, Cameroon, on combating maritime piracy in the Gulf of Guinea, formally adopted and opened for signature a Code of Conduct concerning the Prevention and Repression of Piracy, Armed Robbery against Ships, and Illegal Maritime Activities in West and Central Africa, that had been drafted by ECOWAS and CEEAC and the Gulf of Guinea Commission. The Authority expressed concern in June 2012 at increased acts of piracy, illegal trafficking activities (relating to drugs, weapons and human beings), and environmental degradation in the Gulf of Guinea. In July 2013 the Authority directed the ECOWAS Commission to facilitate the urgent adoption of a new ECOWAS Integrated Maritime Strategy.

Guinea-Bissau: In March 2009 ECOWAS Chiefs of Defence agreed to deploy a multidisciplinary group to monitor and co-ordinate security sector reforms in Guinea-Bissau, following the assassinations of the military Chief of Staff and President of that country at the beginning of the month. The ECOWAS Chiefs of Defence also demanded a review of ECOWAS legislation on conflict prevention and peacekeeping. In November 2010 ECOWAS and the Comunidade dos Países de Língua Portuguesa (CPLP) adopted an ECOWAS-CPLP roadmap on reform of the defence and security sector in Guinea-Bissau. In March 2012 an 80-member ECOWAS observation mission monitored the first round of a presidential election held in Guinea-Bissau. In mid-April, before the planned second round of the election, scheduled for later in that month, a military junta usurped power by force and established a Transitional National Council (TNC), comprising military officers and representatives of political parties that had been in opposition to the legitimate government. The ECOWAS Commission strongly condemned the military coup and denounced the establishment of the TNC. An ECOWAS high-level delegation visited Guinea-Bissau in mid-April to hold discussions with the military leadership. An extraordinary summit meeting of ECOWAS heads of state and government convened in late April decided to deploy troops from the ESF to Guinea-Bissau in support of a swift restoration of constitutional order. Sanctions, including economic measures and targeted individual penalties, were to be imposed if the military continued to obstruct the democratic process. The summit meeting urged the military leadership to release civilians who had been detained during the coup and to ensure the safety of officials from the former legitimate administration. The meeting stipulated that democratic elections should be held in Guinea-Bissau within 12 months. A seven-nation Contact Group on Guinea-Bissau (comprising Benin, Cape Verde, The Gambia, Guinea, Senegal and Togo, and chaired by Nigeria) was established by the extraordinary summit, with a mandate to follow up its decisions. At the end of April diplomatic, economic and financial sanctions were imposed on military leaders and their associates in Guinea-Bissau, in view of the failure at that time of talks between the Contact Group and Guinea-Bissau stakeholders to secure an arrangement for restoring constitutional rule within a 12-month period. A 620-strong ESF contingent (the ECOWAS Mission in Guinea-Bissau—ECOMIB) was deployed in May. At the end of June the ECOWAS Authority endorsed new transitional organs established in Guinea-Bissau and withdrew the sanctions that had been imposed in April. In February 2013 the ECOWAS Authority urged the AU Commission to produce as soon as possible a consolidated report of a Joint Assessment Mission undertaken in Guinea-Bissau in December 2012 by ECOWAS, the AU, the CPLP, the UN and the EU. (The report was published in March 2013.) In June the ECOWAS Council of Ministers took note of gradual ongoing progress towards stability in Guinea-Bissau, including an agreement adopted in April by national stakeholders, and the formation in early June of an inclusive transitional government. The Council of Ministers also welcomed a decision taken in May by ECOWAS, the AU, the CPLP, the UN and the EU to organize a follow-up joint mission to Guinea-Bissau; this was undertaken in July. In July the ECOWAS Authority extended the mandate of ECOMIB until 16 May 2014. Legislative and presidential elections were held in Guinea-Bissau in April.

Mali: In mid-March 2012 the President of the ECOWAS Commission led a fact-finding mission to Mali, in view of escalating unrest in northern areas of that country arising from attacks by separatist militants of the National Movement for the Liberation of Azawad (MNLA). The Commission condemned all acts of violence committed by the MNLA. In late March ECOWAS heads of state and government convened an extraordinary summit to discuss the recent illegal overthrow, by the Comité National de Redressement pour la Démocratie et la Restauration de l'Etat (CNRDRE), of the legitimate government of Mali's elected President Amadou Touré, and also to address the separatist violence ongoing in the north of the country. The regional leaders suspended Mali from participating in all decision-making bodies of ECOWAS pending the restoration of constitutional order, and imposed sanctions (including a ban on travel and an assets freeze) on members of the CNRDRE and their associates. The summit appointed President Blaise Compaoré of Burkina Faso as ECOWAS mediator, with a mandate to facilitate dialogue between the legitimate Mali Government and the CNRDRE regime on achieving a return to civilian rule, and also on means of terminating the northern rebellion. Meanwhile, in early April, MNLA rebels, assisted by Islamist forces, seized land in the Kidal, Gao and Tombouctou regions of northern Mali, unilaterally declaring this to be the independent entity of Azawad. At that time the Commission denounced a Declaration of Independence by the MNLA for the North of Mali, reminding all militants that Mali is an 'indivisible entity', and stating that ECOWAS would be prepared to use all necessary measures, including force, to ensure Mali's territorial integrity. On 6 April representatives of the CNRDRE and the ECOWAS mediation team, under the chairmanship of Compaoré, signed an accord that was intended to lead to a return to full constitutional rule; the accord entailed the appointment of a new interim president, who was to lead a transitional administration pending the staging of democratic elections. Accordingly, an interim president, Dioncounda Traoré, was sworn in on 12 April, and ECOWAS sanctions against Mali were withdrawn. The CNRDRE, however, subsequently appeared to influence the political process: in late April Traoré announced a new government, which included three posts held by military officers and no ministers from the former Touré government.

An extraordinary summit meeting of ECOWAS heads of state and government convened in late April 2012 decided to deploy troops from the ESF to Mali to support a swift restoration of constitutional order. Sanctions, including economic measures and targeted individual penalties, were to be imposed if the military continued to obstruct the democratic process. The summit meeting urged military leaders in both countries to release civilians who had been detained during the coup and to ensure the safety of officials from the former legitimate administration. The meeting stipulated that democratic elections should be held in Mali within 12 months. Meeting in early May an extraordinary summit of the Authority condemned violent clashes that had erupted in Bamako, the Malian capital, from the end of April, and welcomed the availability of the President of Nigeria, Goodluck Jonathan, to assist, as 'Associate Mediator', Compaoré in pursuing a negotiated resolution to the conflict in northern Mali. Later in May the President of the Commission condemned a violent assault on Traoré, the interim Malian President, by opponents protesting against the length of his term of office. At the end of that month the President of the Commission reaffirmed support to the transitional authorities and warned that sanctions would be imposed on those deemed to be disrupting the transitional process. ECOWAS heads of state and government attending a consultative meeting on the situation in Mali that was organized in early June, in Lomé, on the sidelines of the 16th UEMOA summit, strongly condemned acts of rape, robbery, and killing, and the desecration of cultural sites, allegedly being perpetrated by armed groups in northern Mali. The meeting urged the Community and the AU to seek UN Security Council approval for the deployment of an international military presence in Mali.

Meeting in late June 2012 the Authority reaffirmed all previous decisions on Mali, and noted with deep concern that terrorist groups—such as Boko Haram, al-Shabaab ('The Youth'), al-Qa'ida au Maghreb islamique, and the Unity Movement for Jihad in West Africa—were aiming to establish a safe haven in the north of the country. In early July a committee of ECOWAS culture experts urged the Mali separatists to respect and ensure the preservation of the cultural heritage under occupation in Timbuktu, Gao and Kidal. In September 2012 the Mediation and Security Council recommended the imposition of targeted sanctions against individuals or groups found to be obstructing the political transition in Mali, or to be perpetuating insecurity in northern areas of the country. In October–November ECOWAS and AU leaders endorsed both a Strategic Concept for the Resolution of the Crisis in Mali, and a Joint Strategic Concept of Operations for the International Military Force and the Malian Defence and Security Forces. In December, consequently, the UN Security Council approved Resolution 2085 authorizing the deployment, by September 2013, of the AU-led International Support Mission in Mali (AFISMA). AFISMA was mandated to help rebuild the capacity of Mali's security forces; to support the Mali authorities in reclaiming occupied northern areas of the country; and also to support the national authorities in establishing a secure environment for the delivery of humanitarian assistance and the voluntary return of displaced civilians. In January 2013 an ECOWAS working group was established to co-ordinate the activities of the Commission in implementing Resolution 2085. Owing to rapid territorial gains by the rebel forces early in that month, and the consequent declaration of a state of emergency by the Mali transitional authorities and deployment of French troops (Opération Serval) in support of the Mali security forces, AFISMA's deployment was advanced to mid-January. In order to review the modalities for AFISMA's accelerated deployment, an extraordinary session of the Authority was convened soon afterwards, with observer participation by representatives of the AU Commission, the EU, the UN Secretary-General's Special Representative to West Africa, and of several non-member African countries, European states, and the USA and Canada. The Authority applauded France for acting to halt the advance of extremist groupings in Mali, and directed the President of the Commission to undertake high-level consultations with the Government of Mali, the AU and the UN with respect to establishing a Joint Co-ordination Mechanism on Resolution 2085. At the end of February the Mediation and Security Council, in response to a request by the Malian authorities, endorsed the proposed transformation of AFISMA into a UN peacekeeping operation, and recommended that ECOWAS should collaborate with the AU in the pursuit of this objective. Accordingly, in April, the UN Security Council authorized the deployment, from 1 July, of the UN Multidimensional Integrated Stabilization Mission in Mali (MINUSMA), to supersede AFISMA. Meeting at the end of February the Authority welcomed the adopted in January by the Malian authorities of a transitional roadmap towards the restoration of democracy. In June the President of the ECOWAS Commission welcomed the conclusion by representatives of the Transitional Government and rebels active in northern Mali of a preliminary agreement on holding presidential elections without delay, and on initiating an inclusive peace dialogue. A team of 250 ECOWAS monitors was dispatched in July to observe the two rounds of presidential polls, which were held at the end of that month and in early August.

AGRICULTURE AND THE ENVIRONMENT

The Community enforces a certification scheme for facilitating the monitoring of animal movement and animal health surveillance and protection in the sub-region. In February 2001 ECOWAS ministers responsible for agriculture adopted an action plan for the formulation of a common agricultural policy, as envisaged under the ECOWAS treaty. An ECOWAS Regional Agricultural Policy (ECOWAP) was endorsed by the January 2005 Authority summit. In January 2006 the Authority approved an action plan for the implementation of ECOWAP. The Policy was aimed at enhancing regional agricultural productivity with a view to guaranteeing food sufficiency and standards. In October 2011 a high-level consultative meeting of ECOWAS and FAO officials determined that ECOWAP was the most effective means of countering the effects of food price increases and volatility. In September 2013 a Togo-based ECOWAS Regional Agency for Agriculture and Food (RAAF) was established, tasked with implementing the technical aspects of regional investment programmes on agriculture, forestry and livestock.

ECOWAS promotes implementation of the UN Convention on Desertification Control and supports programmes initiated at national and sub-regional level within the framework of the treaty. Together with the Permanent Inter-State Committee on Drought Control in the Sahel, ECOWAS has been designated as a project leader for implementing the Convention in West Africa. Other environmental initiatives include a regional meteorological project to enhance meteorological activities and applications, and in particular to contribute to food security and natural resource management in the sub-region. ECOWAS pilot schemes have formed the basis of integrated control projects for the control of floating (or invasive aquatic) weeds in five water basins in West Africa, which had hindered the development of the local fishery sectors. A rural water supply programme aims to ensure adequate water for rural dwellers in order to improve their living standards. The first phase of the project focused on schemes to develop village and pastoral water points in Burkina Faso, Guinea, Mali, Niger and Senegal, with funds from various multilateral donors.

In September 2009 a regional conference, convened in Lomé, to address the potential effects of rapid climate change on regional stability, issued the Lomé Declaration on Climate Change and Protection of Civilians in West Africa, and recommended the establishment of a fund to support communities suffering the negative impact of climate change. In March 2010 ECOWAS ministers responsible for agriculture, environment and water resources adopted a Framework of Strategic Guidelines on the Reduction of Vulnerability and Adaptability to Climate Change in West Africa, outlining the development of regional capacities to build up resilience and adaptation to climate change and severe climatic conditions. ECOWAS supports the development and implementation by member states of Nationally Appropriate Mitigation Actions.

In September 2013 ECOWAS ministers responsible for forestry and wildlife, gathered in Abidjan, adopted a Convergence Plan for the Sustainable Management and Utilization of Forest Ecosystems in West Africa, aimed at protecting regional forests and woodlands, which cover a total surface area of about 72.1m. ha (representing some 14% of the total land area). The ministers also adopted the Sub-regional Action Programme for Combating Desertification in West Africa.

SOCIAL PROGRAMME

The following organizations have been established within ECOWAS: the Organization of Trade Unions of West Africa, which held its first meeting in 1984; the West African Universities' Association, the ECOWAS Youth and Sports Development Centre (EYSDC), the ECOWAS Gender Development Centre (EGDC), and the West African Health Organization (WAHO), which was established in 2000 by merger of the West African Health Community and the Organization for Co-ordination and Co-operation in the Struggle against Endemic Diseases. ECOWAS and the European Commission jointly implement the West African Regional Health Programme, which aims to improve the co-ordination and harmonization of regional health policies, with a view to strengthening West African integration. In December 2001 the ECOWAS summit of heads of state and government adopted a plan of action aimed at combating trafficking in human beings and authorized the establishment of an ECOWAS Criminal Intelligence Bureau. In March 2009 ECOWAS ministers responsible for education, meeting in Abuja, identified priority activities for advancing the regional implementation of regional activities relating to the AU-sponsored Second Decade of Education in Africa (2006–15). In the following month ECOWAS ministers responsible for labour and employment adopted a regional labour policy. In February 2012 the ECOWAS Commission and the International Labour Organization determined to collaborate in order to address the challenges of child labour in West Africa. The Commission resolved to harmonize national action plans relating to child labour and to formulate a regional strategy. Since 2010 the EYSDC has organized the biennial 'ECOWAS Games' (August 2014: Yamoussoukro, Côte d'Ivoire).

Specialized Agencies

ECOWAS Bank for Investment and Development (EBID): BP 2704, 128 blvd du 13 janvier, Lomé, Togo; tel. 22-21-68-64; fax 22-21-86-84; e-mail bidc@bidc-ebid.org; internet www.bidc-ebid.org; f. 2001, replacing the former ECOWAS Fund for Co-operation, Compensation and Development; comprises two divisions, a Regional Investment Bank and a Regional Development Fund; Pres. Bashir M. Ifo.

West African Monetary Agency (WAMA): 11–13 ECOWAS St, PMB 218, Freetown, Sierra Leone; tel. 224485; fax 223943; e-mail wamao@amao-wama.org; internet www.amao-wama.org; f. 1975 as West African Clearing House; agreement founding WAMA signed by governors of ECOWAS central banks in March 1996; administers transactions between its eight mem. central banks in order to promote sub-regional trade and monetary co-operation; administers ECOWAS travellers' cheques scheme. Mems: Banque Centrale des Etats de l'Afrique de l'Ouest (serving Benin, Burkina Faso, Côte d'Ivoire, Guinea-Bissau, Mali, Niger, Senegal, Togo) and the central banks of Cape Verde, The Gambia, Ghana, Guinea, Liberia, Nigeria and Sierra Leone; Dir-Gen. Prof. Mohamed Ben Omar Ndiaye; publ. *Annual Report*.

West African Monetary Institute (WAMI): Gulf House, Tetteh Quarshie Interchange, Cantonments 75, Accra, Ghana; tel. (30) 2743801; fax (30) 2743807; e-mail info@wami-imao.org; f. by the ECOWAS Authority summit in December 2000 to prepare for the establishment of a West African Central Bank, scheduled for 2014; Dir-Gen. Abwaku Englama (Nigeria).

West African Health Organization (WAHO): 01 BP 153 Bobo-Dioulasso 01, Burkina Faso; tel. and fax (226) 20-97-01-00; e-mail wahooas@fasonet.bf; internet www.wahooas.org; f. 2000 by merger of the West African Health Community (f. 1978) and the Organization for Co-ordination and Co-operation in the Struggle against Endemic Diseases (f. 1960); aims to harmonize mem. states' health policies and to promote research, training, the sharing of resources and diffusion of information; Dir-Gen. Dr Crespin Xavier (Niger); publ. *Bulletin Bibliographique* (quarterly).

West African Power Pool (WAPP): 06 BP 2907, Zone des Ambassades, PK 6 Cotonou, Benin; tel. 21-37-41-95; fax 21-37-41-96; e-mail info@ecowapp.org; internet www.ecowapp.org; f. 1999; new organization approved as a Specialized Agency in Jan. 2006; inaugural meeting held in July 2006; aims to facilitate the integration, by 2020, of the power systems of member nations into a unified regional electricity market; Gen. Sec. Amadou Diallo; publ. *WAPP Newsletter*.

Finance

Under the revised treaty, signed in July 1993, ECOWAS was to receive revenue from a community tax, based on the total value of imports from member countries. In March 2013 ECOWAS ministers responsible for finance agreed that a new 1.5% community integration levy should be agreed as a replacement for the existing ECOWAS community levy and UEMOA community solidarity levy. In practice Nigeria provides around two-thirds of the annual budget.

Publications

Annual Report.
Contact.
ECOWAS National Accounts.
ECOWAS News.
ECOWAS Newsletter.
West African Bulletin.

ECONOMIC COOPERATION ORGANIZATION—ECO

Address: 1 Golbou Alley, Kamranieh St, POB 14155-6176, Tehran, Iran.

Telephone: (21) 22831733; **fax:** (21) 22831732; **e-mail:** registry@ecosecretariat.org; **internet:** www.ecosecretariat.org.

ECO was established in 1985 as the successor to the Regional Cooperation for Development, founded in 1964.

MEMBERS

Afghanistan	Kyrgyzstan	Turkey
Azerbaijan	Pakistan	Turkmenistan
Iran	Tajikistan	Uzbekistan
Kazakhstan		

The 'Turkish Republic of Northern Cyprus' has been granted special guest status.

Organization

(April 2014)

SUMMIT MEETING

The first summit meeting of heads of state and of government of member countries was held in Tehran, Iran, in February 1992. Summit meetings are generally held at least once every two years. The 12th summit was held in October 2012, in Baku, Azerbaijan, and the 13th was to be convened in Islamabad, Pakistan, in 2014.

COUNCIL OF MINISTERS

The Council of Ministers, comprising ministers responsible for foreign affairs of member states, is the principal policy- and decision-making body of ECO. It meets at least once a year.

REGIONAL PLANNING COUNCIL

The Council, comprising senior planning officials or other representatives of member states, meets at least once a year. It is responsible for reviewing programmes of activity and evaluating results achieved, and for proposing future plans of action to the Council of Ministers.

COUNCIL OF PERMANENT REPRESENTATIVES

Permanent representatives or Ambassadors of member countries accredited to Iran meet regularly to formulate policy for consideration by the Council of Ministers and to promote implementation of decisions reached at ministerial or summit level.

SECRETARIAT

The Secretariat is headed by a Secretary-General, who is supported by two Deputy Secretaries-General. The following Directorates administer and co-ordinate the main areas of ECO activities: Trade and investment; Transport and communications; Energy, minerals and environment; Agriculture, industry and tourism; Project and economic research and statistics; Human resources and sustainable development; and International relations. The Secretariat services sectoral ministerial meetings held by regional ministers responsible for agriculture; energy and minerals; environment; finance and economy; health; industry; trade and investment; and transport and communications.

Secretary-General: SHAMIL ALESKEROV (Azerbaijan).

Activities

The Regional Cooperation for Development (RCD) was established in 1964 as a tripartite arrangement for economic co-operation between Iran, Pakistan and Turkey. ECO replaced the RCD in 1985, and seven additional members were admitted to the organization in November 1992. The main objectives of co-operation are advancing the sustainable economic development of member states; the development of the regional transport and communications infrastructure; economic liberalization and privatization; the progressive removal of trade barriers and the promotion of intra-regional trade; advancing the region's role in global trade, and the gradual integration of member states' economies with the global economy; the mobilization and utilization of the region's material resources; the interconnection of power grids in the region; the effective utilization of the region's agricultural and industrial potential; regional co-operation on narcotics control; ecological and environmental co-operation; strengthening regional cultural ties; and pursuing mutually beneficial co-ooperation with regional and international organizations. The third ECO summit meeting, held in Islamabad, Pakistan, in March 1995, endorsed the creation of an ECO eminent persons group. In September 1996, at an extraordinary meeting of the ECO Council of Ministers, held in İzmir, Turkey, member countries signed a revised Treaty of İzmir, the organization's founding charter. The seventh ECO summit, held in İstanbul, in October 2002, adopted the Istanbul Declaration, which outlined a strengthened and more proactive economic orientation for the organization. Meeting in October 2005, in Astana, Kazakhstan, the ECO Council of Ministers adopted a document entitled *ECO Vision 2015*, detailing basic policy guidelines for the organization's activities during 2006–15, and setting a number of targets to be achieved in the various areas of regional co-operation. At the 11th summit meeting, held in İstanbul, in December 2010, it was reported that Iraq had applied to join ECO. The Organization's 20th anniversary summit meeting, held in October 2012, in Baku, Azerbaijan, granted observer status at its summit meetings to the 'Turkish Republic of Northern Cyprus'.

A regional Chamber of Commerce and Industry was established in 1993. In March 1995, in order to enhance and facilitate trade throughout the region, heads of state and of government signed the Transit Trade Agreement (which entered into force in December 1997); and an Agreement on the Simplification of Visa Procedures for Businessmen of ECO Countries (which came into effect in March 1998). Convening in conference for the first time in March 2000, ECO ministers responsible for trade signed a Framework Agreement on ECO Trade Cooperation (ECOFAT), which established a basis for the expansion of intra-regional trade. The Framework Agreement envisaged the eventual adoption of an accord providing for the gradual elimination of regional tariff and non-tariff barriers between member states. The so-called ECO Trade Agreement (ECOTA) was endorsed at the eighth ECO summit meeting, held in Dushanbe, Tajikistan, in September 2004; ECOTA entered into force in April 2008, having been ratified by Afghanistan, Iran, Pakistan, Tajikistan and Turkey. An ECO Trade and Development Bank, headquartered in İstanbul (with main branches in Tehran, Iran, and Islamabad) commenced operations in 2008. The organization maintains ECO TradeNet, an internet-based repository of regional trade information.

A meeting of ministers of industry, convened in November 2005, approved an ECO plan of action on privatization, envisaging enhanced technical co-operation between member states, and a number of measures for increasing cross-country investments; and adopted a declaration on industrial co-operation. The first meeting of the heads of ECO member states' national statistics offices, convened in January 2008 in Tehran, adopted the ECO Framework of Cooperation in Statistics and a related plan of action. In May 2011 the Permanent Steering Committee on Economic Research, meeting for the first time, adopted the ECO Plan of Action for Economic Research. An ECO College of Insurance was inaugurated in 1990, and, in February 2010, the statutes of an ECO Reinsurance Company, to be based in Karachi, Pakistan, were approved. The first meeting of ECO Heads of Tax Administrations was convened in January 2013, in Tehran.

Co-operation in the area of transport and communications—including the building of road and rail links—is of particular regional importance, given that seven ECO member states are landlocked. Relevant activities are guided by the 1993 Quetta Plan of Action and Istanbul Declaration, and by the Almatı Outline Plan for the Development of Transport Sector in the ECO Region, which was adopted in October 1993 by the first meeting of ECO ministers responsible for transport. In March 1995 ECO heads of state or government concluded formal agreements on the establishment of a regional joint shipping company (now operational) and airline; the latter project was terminated in May 2001 by the Council of Ministers, owing to its unsustainable cost, and replaced by a framework agreement on co-operation in the field of air transport. An extraordinary ECO summit meeting, held in Aşgabat, Turkmenistan, in May 1997, adopted the Aşgabat Declaration, emphasizing the importance of the development of the transport and communications infrastructure and the network of transnational petroleum and gas pipelines through bilateral and regional arrangements in the ECO area. In May 1998, at the fifth summit meeting, held in Almatı, Kazakhstan, ECO heads of state and of government signed a Transit Transport Framework Agreement (TTFA); this entered into force in May 2006.

In October 2012 the Council of Ministers endorsed the Charter of the Parliamentary Assembly of the Economic Cooperation Organization Countries (PAECO). PAECO's inaugural conference was convened in Islamabad, in February 2013; a Women Parliamentarians' Meeting was held within the framework of the conference. The second PAECO conference was to take place in Afghanistan in 2014. The Assembly was to have a permanent secretariat, which was to be based in Islamabad and was to be financed by the Pakistan Government.

ECO ministers responsible for agriculture, convened in July 2002, in Islamabad, adopted a declaration on co-operation in the agricultural sector, which specified that member states would contribute to agricultural rehabilitation in Afghanistan, and considered instigating a mechanism for the regional exchange of agricultural and cattle products. In December 2004, meeting in Antalya, Turkey, ministers approved the Antalya Declaration on ECO Cooperation in Agriculture and adopted an ECO plan of action on drought management and mitigation. In March 2007, meeting in Tehran, ECO ministers approved the concept of an ECO Permanent Commission for Prevention and Control of Animal Diseases and Control of Animal Origin Food-Borne Diseases (ECO-PCPCAD). An ECO Veterinary Commission (ECO-VECO) was established, in Tehran, in October 2012. ECO implements a Regional Programme for Food Security (RPFS), supported by FAO, which comprises nine regional components, as well as a country programme for community-based food production in Afghanistan.

In April 2007 an ECO experts' group convened to develop a work plan on biodiversity in the ECO region with the aim of promoting co-operation towards achieving a set of agreed biodiversity targets over the period 2007–15. The ECO member states agreed, in July 2008, to establish the ECO Seed Association (ECOSA); ECOSA hosted its first international seed trade conference in December 2009, and thereafter regular conferences have been held (the fifth was convened in

October 2013, in Bishkek, Kyrgyzstan). In December 2008 the first ECO expert meeting on tourism adopted a plan of action on ECO co-operation in the field of ecotourism, which covered the period 2009–13. In June 2011 ECO ministers responsible for the environment adopted a Framework Plan of Action on Environmental Cooperation and Global Warming, covering the period 2011–15. The ECO Institute of Environmental Science and Technology (ECO-IEST), hosted by the Karaj, Iran-based University of the Environment, was established in February 2011. In September 2007 the ECO Regional Center for Risk Management of Natural Disasters was inaugurated in Mashhad, Iran, tasked with promoting inter-regional co-operation in drought early warning and monitoring activities. The sixth ECO International Conference on Disaster Risk Management was convened in February 2012, in Kabul, Afghanistan, and the seventh was to be held in Qabala, Afghanistan, in June 2014.

In February 2006 a high-level group of experts on health was formed; its first meeting, held in the following month, focused on the spread of avian influenza in the region. The first ECO ministerial meeting on health, convened in February 2010, considered means of enhancing co-operation on health issues with regard to attaining the relevant UN Millennium Development Goals, and addressed strengthening co-operation in the areas of blood transfusion and pharmaceuticals. The meeting adopted the Baku Declaration, identifying key priority areas for future ECO area health co-operation.

A Tehran-based ECO Cultural Institute was inaugurated in 2000. In December 2011 the ECO Science Foundation was established in Islamabad. An ECO Educational Institute commenced operations in April 2012, in Ankara, Turkey.

ECO has co-operation agreements with several UN agencies and other international organizations in development-related activities. In December 2007 the ECO Secretary-General welcomed, as a means of promoting regional peace and security, the inauguration of the UN Regional Centre for Preventive Diplomacy in Central Asia (UNRCCA), based in Aşgabat. In that month ECO and the Shanghai Cooperation Organization signed a Memorandum of Understanding (MOU) on mutual co-operation in areas including trade and transportation, energy and environment, and tourism. An ECO-International Organization on Migration MOU on co-operation was concluded in January 2009. In March 2011 ECO, the UN Economic Commission for Europe and the Islamic Development Bank signed a trilateral MOU on co-operation. ECO has been granted observer status at the UN, the Organization of Islamic Cooperation and the World Trade Organization.

ECO prioritizes activities aimed at combating the cultivation of and trade in illicit drugs in the region (which is the source of more than one-half of global seizures of opium, with more than 90% of global opium production occurring in Afghanistan, and many ECO member states are used in transit for its distribution). An ECO-UNODC Drug Control and Co-ordination Unit (ECO-DOCCU) was inaugurated, in Tehran, in July 1999. In May 1998 ECO heads of state and of government adopted an MOU to help combat the cross-border trafficking of illegal goods. The inaugural meeting of heads of INTERPOL of ECO member states was held in June 2010, in Tehran, and, in August, the first conference of ECO police chiefs with responsibility for anti-narcotics was convened, also in Tehran. In February 2013 representatives of ECO-DOCCU and ECO member states participated in an experts' group meeting on the scientific detection of crime, convened by INTERPOL in Tehran. In November 2012 a meeting of heads of anti-corruption organizations and ombudsmen of the ECO member states, held in Dushanbe, approved the Statute of the ECO Regional Center for Cooperation of Anti-Corruption Agencies and Ombudsmen (RCCACO).

In November 2001 the UN Secretary-General requested ECO to take an active role in efforts to restore stability in Afghanistan and to co-operate closely with his special representative in that country. ECO operates a Special Fund for the Reconstruction of Afghanistan, which was established in April 2004; by 2013 more than US $11m. had been pledged to the Fund, under which four ECO projects—targeted towards the education and health sectors—had been approved. ECO envisages connecting Afghanistan to the regional railroad system.

Finance

Member states contribute to a centralized administrative budget.

Publications

ECO Annual Economic Report.
ECO Bulletin (quarterly).
ECO Economic Journal.
ECO Environment Bulletin.
ECO Statistical Report.

EUROPEAN BANK FOR RECONSTRUCTION AND DEVELOPMENT—EBRD

Address: One Exchange Square, London, EC2A 2JN, United Kingdom.

Telephone: (20) 7338-6000; **fax:** (20) 7338-6100; **e-mail:** generalenquiries@ebrd.com; **internet:** www.ebrd.com.

The EBRD was founded in May 1990 and inaugurated in April 1991. Its object is to contribute to the progress and the economic reconstruction of the countries of Central and Eastern Europe, and, from 2011–12, transitional economies in the Southern and Eastern Mediterranean, that undertake to respect and put into practice the principles of multi-party democracy, pluralism, the rule of law, respect for human rights and a market economy.

MEMBERS

Countries of Operations:

Albania	Moldova
Armenia	Mongolia
Azerbaijan	Montenegro
Belarus	Morocco*
Bosnia and Herzegovina	Poland
Bulgaria	Romania
Estonia	Russia
Georgia	Serbia
Hungary	Slovakia
Jordan*	Slovenia
Kazakhstan	Tajikistan
Kosovo	Tunisia*
Kyrgyzstan	Turkey
Latvia	Turkmenistan
Lithuania	Ukraine
Macedonia, former Yugoslav republic	Uzbekistan

Other EU members†:

Austria	Ireland
Belgium	Italy
Croatia	Luxembourg
Cyprus	Malta
Czech Republic	Netherlands
Denmark	Portugal
Finland	Spain
France	Sweden
Germany	United Kingdom
Greece	

EFTA‡ members:

Iceland	Norway
Liechtenstein	Switzerland

Other countries:

Australia	Republic of Korea
Canada	Mexico
Egypt*	New Zealand
Israel	USA
Japan	

* Jordan and Tunisia were admitted as members of the EBRD in December 2011; on 1 November 2013 those two countries, as well as Morocco (a founding member of the Bank) became countries of operation. The granting of country of operations status to Egypt (also a founding member) is under consideration.

† The European Union (EU) and the European Investment Bank (EIB) are also shareholder members in their own right.

‡ European Free Trade Association.

Organization

(April 2014)

BOARD OF GOVERNORS

The Board of Governors, to which each member appoints a Governor (normally the minister of finance of that country) and an alternate, is the highest authority of the EBRD. It elects the President of the Bank. The Board meets each year. The 2013 meeting was held in Istanbul, Turkey, in May, concurrently with an EBRD Business Forum. The 2014 meeting was to be convened in Warsaw, Poland, in May.

BOARD OF DIRECTORS

The Board, comprising 23 directors elected by the Board of Governors for a three-year term, is responsible for the organization and operations of the EBRD.

ADMINISTRATION

The EBRD's operations are conducted by its Banking Department, headed by the First Vice-President. Four other Vice-Presidents oversee departments of Finance; Risk Management; Human Resources and Corporate Services; and Policy. Other offices include Internal Audit; Communications; the Evaluation Department; and Offices of the President, the Secretary-General, the General Counsel, the Chief Economist and the Chief Compliance Officer. A structure of country teams, industry teams and operations support units oversee the implementation of projects. The EBRD has 34 local offices in 27 countries. At December 2012 there were 1,257 staff at the Bank's headquarters (76%) and 392 staff in the Resident Offices.

President: Sir SUMA CHAKRABARTI (United Kingdom).

First Vice-President: PHILIP BENNETT (United Kingdom/USA).

FINANCIAL STRUCTURE

In May 2010 EBRD shareholders agreed to increase the Bank's capital from €20,000m. to €30,000m., through use of a temporary increase in callable capital of €9,000m. and a €1,000m. transfer from reserves to paid-in capital. At 31 December 2012 paid-in capital amounted to €6,202m.

Activities

The Bank was founded to assist the transition of the economies of Central Europe, Southern and Eastern Europe and the Caucasus, and Central Asia and Russia towards a market economy system, and to encourage private enterprise. The Agreement establishing the EBRD specifies that 60% of its lending should be for the private sector, and that its operations do not displace commercial sources of finance. The Bank helps the beneficiaries to undertake structural and sectoral reforms, including the dismantling of monopolies, decentralization, and privatization of state enterprises, to enable these countries to become fully integrated in the international economy. To this end, the Bank promotes the establishment and improvement of activities of a productive, competitive and private nature, particularly small and medium-sized enterprises (SMEs), and works to strengthen financial institutions. It mobilizes national and foreign capital, together with experienced management teams, and helps to develop an appropriate legal framework to support a market-orientated economy. The Bank provides extensive financial services, including loans, equity and guarantees, and aims to develop new forms of financing and investment in accordance with the requirements of the transition process. In 2006 the Bank formally began to implement a strategy to withdraw, by 2010, from countries where the transition to a market economy was nearing completion, i.e. those now members of the European Union (EU), and strengthen its focus on and resources to Russia, the Caucasus and Central Asia. New operations in the Czech Republic were terminated at the end of 2007. Mongolia and Montenegro became new countries of operations in 2006. In November 2008 Turkey, which had been a founding member of the Bank, became the 30th country of operations. In November 2012 the Board of Governors approved Kosovo's membership of the Bank, which came into effect in December. In May 2011 the Group of Eight (G8) major industrialized nations declared their support for an expansion of the Bank's geographical mandate to support transitional economies in the Southern and Eastern Mediterranean (SEMED) region. In March the Bank signed a new Memorandum of Understanding (MOU) with the European Investment Bank (EIB) and European Commission to enhance co-operation in activities outside of the EU region. MOUs with the African Development Bank and the Islamic Development Bank were signed in September. At that time the EBRD joined other international financial institutions active in the Middle East and North Africa region to endorse the so-called Deauville Partnership, established by the G8 in May to support political and economic reforms being undertaken by several countries, notably Egypt, Jordan, Morocco and Tunisia. Jordan and Tunisia were admitted as members of the EBRD in January 2012; during that year a process was under way to enable those two countries, as well as Egypt and Morocco (both founding members of the Bank), to become countries of operations. It was envisaged that the EBRD would be able to invest up to €2,500m. annually across the four countries, with a focus on the development of SMEs, in order to stimulate job creation, entrepreneurship and growth. Initial flows of grant-funded technical assistance to the planned four new countries of operations commenced in late 2011; a dedicated SEMED Investment Special Fund (ISF), facilitating investments in the four countries, was established in February 2012. In September the Bank's Board of Directors approved the first three projects to be implemented in the SEMED region, in Jordan, Morocco and Tunisia. In accordance with an agreement concluded in December between the Bank and the Tunisian authorities on the establishment of a permanent local EBRD presence in that country. Permanent EBRD offices were opened in Tunisia, in June 2013, and in Jordan, in October. In that month the EBRD Chief Economist and World Bank Chief Economist for the Middle East and North Africa, jointly addressing the aftermath of the 2011 'Arab Awakening', reported that the poor macroeconomic fundamentals of transition countries in the region, an underestimation of those countries' emerging needs, slow progress on reform, and continuing political instability had constrained the use of resources committed under the Deauville Partnership. They recommended that new financial assistance should be linked to long-term reforms; to the provision of technical support to ensure the channelling of funding towards productive investment in short-term, employment-generating public-works programmes and also in longer-term infrastructure projects; to the development of broad frameworks for trade, investment and regulatory reform; and to policy and institutional support aimed at improving governance. The EBRD was hosting the rotating secretariat of the Partnership during 2014. On 1 November 2013 the Board of Governors granted countries of operation status to Jordan, Morocco and Tunisia; with immediate effect those countries' assets and capital resources hitherto held in the SEMED ISF were transferred to the balance sheet of the EBRD. Egypt, meanwhile, retained its status as a potential country of operations, and projects there continued to be funded through the SEMED ISF.

In the year ending 31 December 2012 the EBRD approved 393 operations, involving funds of €8,920m. compared with €9,051m. for 380 operations in the previous year. During 2012 some 41% of project financing committed was allocated the energy and infrastructure sectors, 32% to the financial sector, including loans to SMEs through financial intermediaries, while 28% was for the corporate sector, including agribusiness, manufacturing, property, tourism, telecommunications and new media. Some 29% of the Bank's commitments in 2012 was for projects in Russia, 17% for Eastern Europe and the Caucasus, 17% for countries in South-Eastern Europe, 14% for Central Europe and the Baltic states, 12% for Turkey, 10% for Central Asia, and 2% for the southern and eastern Mediterranean. By the end of 2012 the Bank had approved 3,644 projects, with financial commitments of €78,916m., since it commenced operations. In addition, the Bank had mobilized external resources amounting to an estimated €155,644m., bringing the total project value to €235,387m.

In 1999 the Bank established a Trade Facilitation Programme to extend bank guarantees in order to promote trading capabilities, in particular for SMEs. An increasing number of transactions are intra-regional arrangements. In December 2008 the Bank's Board of Directors agreed to expand the Programme's budget for 2009, from €800m. to €1,500m., in order to provide exceptional assistance to countries affected by the global deceleration of economic growth and contraction in credit markets. During 2009, however, the Programme was less widely used than anticipated, owing to a sharp decline in foreign trade transactions and a reluctance on the part of local banks to expose themselves to more risk. In 2012 the Bank financed 1,870 trade transactions under the Programme, amounting to €1,100m. (compared with 1,616 transactions amounting to around €1,000m. in the previous year). In February 2009 the Bank established a Corporate Support Facility, with funds of €250m., to assist medium-sized businesses to counter the economic downturn. In the same month the EBRD, with the World Bank and the EIB, inaugurated a Joint International Financial Institutions (IFI) Action Plan to support the banking systems in Central and Eastern Europe and to finance lending to businesses in the region affected by the global economic crisis. Under the Plan the Banks initially committed €24,500m. over a two-year period. The IFI Action Plan was concluded in March 2011, at which time €33,200m. had been provided under the joint initiative, including €8,100m. released by the EBRD. A parallel plan, the European Banking Co-ordination Initiative (the 'Vienna Initiative'), was initiated in 2008–09 to promote dialogue between authorities in emerging European economies, official multilateral donors and private banks. In early 2010 the Bank initiated a Local Currency and Capital Market Initiative ('Vienna Plus') aimed at addressing the regional impact of new global regulatory standards on bank capital adequacy and liquidity, as well as the challenges confronting emerging economies in managing non-performing loans. The EBRD chaired a committee, established under the Initiative framework, concerning local currency finance development, and in 2011 co-chaired, with the World Bank, a new committee on the challenges of implementing the Basel III capital framework programme. During the second half of 2011, at which time financial crisis in several eurozone countries raised the risk of contagion in the financial sectors of many of the EBRD's countries of operations, the Bank took a lead role in developing the second phase of the Vienna Initiative, 'Vienna 2.0'; this was launched in January 2012, with a focus on fostering home-host co-ordination on cross-border banking activities, and on limiting systemic risks from parent bank deleveraging, in Central and Eastern Europe. In November the Bank, with the World Bank and the EIB, endorsed a new Joint IFI Action Plan to support economic recovery, growth and restructuring in 17 Central and Eastern European countries. The Plan, which was developed within the context of the Vienna Initiative, included funding commitments of €30,000m. for the period 2013–14, of which the EBRD pledged €4,000m. in loans, equity and trade financing.

In April 2004 an initiative was launched by the EBRD to increase its activities in several low-income countries in Eastern Europe and Central Asia (Armenia, Azerbaijan, Belarus, Georgia, Kyrgyz Republic, Moldova, Mongolia, Tajikistan, Turkmenistan and Uzbekistan), known 'Early Transition Countries' (ETCs). The initiative was focused in particular on stimulating private sector business development, market activity and on the financing of small-scale projects. In November the Bank established a multi-donor ETC Fund to administer donor pledges and grant financing in support of EBRD projects in those countries. In 2006 Mongolia was incorporated into the ETC grouping. In 2007 the Bank's resident office in Tbilisi, Georgia, was transformed into a regional focal point for specialized activities in the Caucasus and Moldova. Belarus and Turkmenistan joined the ETC programme in 2009 and 2010 respectively. During 2012 Bank commitments for the ETCs increased substantially to more than €1,000m. for 100 projects. Financing from the ETC Fund amounted to €79.6m. during 2004–12. In May 2011 an ETC Local Currency Lending Programme was initiated, with donor support from the ETC Fund, Switzerland, the USA, and the EBRD Shareholders Special Fund. By late 2013 local currency loans equivalent to US $300m. had been approved under the Programme, which has been introduced in Armenia, Georgia, Kyrgyzstan, Moldova, Mongolia, and Tajikistan.

In late March 2014 the EBRD Board of Directors determined to increase and broaden the scope of its investments in Ukraine. In April two projects for that country were approved: a €150m.framework facility, and (subject to the Ukraine Government's agreement on a macro-economic stabilization programme with the International Monetary Fund) €200m. funding for the rehabilitation of road approaches to Kyiv, the Ukrainian capital.

High priority is given to attracting external finance for Bank-sponsored projects, in particular in countries at advanced stages of transition, from government agencies, international financial institutions, commercial banks and export credit agencies. The EBRD's Technical Co-operation Funds Programme (TCFP) aims to facilitate access to the Bank's capital resources for countries of operations by providing support for project preparation, project implementation and institutional development. Resources for technical co-operation originate from regular TCFP contributions, specific agreements and contributions to Special Funds. The Baltic Investment Programme, which is administered by Nordic countries, consists of two special funds to co-finance investment and technical assistance projects in the private sectors of Baltic states. The Funds are open to contributions from all EBRD member states. The Russia Small Business Fund (RSBF) was established in 1994 to support local SMEs through similar investment and technical co-operation activities. In November 2006 a new Western Balkans Fund was established as a multi-donor facility to support economic growth and the business environment in Albania, Bosnia and Herzegovina, the former Yugoslav republic of Macedonia, Montenegro and Serbia (including Kosovo). A Western Balkans Local Enterprise Facility was also established in 2006. In November 2009 a Western Balkans Investment Framework was inaugurated by the EBRD, the European Commission, the European Investment Bank and the Council of Europe Development Bank, to co-ordinate the leverage and use of donor funds in support of priority projects in the region. In mid-2008 the Bank established a Neighbourhood Investment Facility to provide technical assistance and grants mainly for infrastructure projects. An Investment Facility for Central Asia was launched in June 2010 to provide additional grant funding for energy and environmental sustainability projects in Kazakhstan, Kyrgyzstan, Tajikistan, Turkmenistan and Uzbekistan. An EBRD Moldovan Residential Energy Efficiency Financing Facility was established in October 2012. Other financing mechanisms that the EBRD uses to address the needs of the region include Regional Venture Funds, which invest equity in privatized companies, in particular in Russia, and provide relevant management assistance, and the Central European Agency Lines, which disburse lines of credit to small-scale projects through local intermediaries. It was announced in August 2012 that the EBRD was to be a cornerstone investor in Elbrus Capital Fund II, a new private equity mechanism that was to invest mainly in SMEs in Russia and neighbouring countries; the Bank was to provide up to one-quarter of aggregate commitments to the Fund. In December 2012 the EBRD adopted a strategy for Russia, covering the period 2013–15, which prioritized reforms and investment aimed at promoting diversification and modernization of the economy; innovation; private sector development; the development of less advanced regions; improving finance for SMEs; supporting urban renewal; and enhancing the quality of services.

An Enterprise Growth Programme—EGP (formerly the Turn-Around Management initiative, and renamed in 2011) provides practical assistance to senior managers of industrial enterprises to facilitate the expansion of businesses in a market economy. A Small Business Support Team—SBS (known until 2011 as the Business Advisory Services scheme) complements the Enterprise Growth Programme by undertaking projects to improve competitiveness, strategic planning, marketing and financial management in SMEs. In 2011 the SBS raised €23.9m. from donors for several new initiatives and ongoing programmes in all regions. During the second half of that year the EGP and SBS conducted feasibility studies in Egypt, Morocco and Tunisia, which were in the process of becoming countries of operation, and in late 2011 two EGP projects were initiated in Egypt. In May 2008 the Bank agreed to establish a Shareholders Special Fund (SSF), with resources of €115m., in order to support technical co-operation and grant operations. Further allocations of resources, including of €150m. in May 2010, brought the total committed by the Bank to €295m. by the end of that year.

In 2001 the EBRD collaborated with other donor institutions and partners to initiate a Northern Dimension Environmental Partnership (NDEP) to strengthen and co-ordinate environmental projects in northern Europe. The Partnership, which became operational in November 2002, includes a 'nuclear window' to address the nuclear legacy of the Russian Northern Fleet. The Bank administers the NDEP Support Fund, as well as a number of other funds specifically to support the promotion of nuclear safety: the Nuclear Safety Account (NSA), a multilateral programme of action established in 1993; the Chornobyl (Chernobyl) Shelter Fund (CSF), established in 1997; and International Decommissioning Support Funds (IDSFs), which have enabled the closure of nuclear plants for safety reasons where this would otherwise have been prohibitively costly, in Bulgaria, Lithuania and Slovakia. In 1997 a CSF-financed Chornobyl Unit 4 Shelter Implementation Plan (SIP) was initiated to assist Ukraine in stabilizing the protective sarcophagus covering the damaged Chornobyl reactor. The first-stage Unit 4 shelter was completed in December 2006. A contract for construction of a New Safe Confinement (NSC) of the destroyed Unit 4 was signed in 2007; the NSC was scheduled to be completed by October 2015.

The EBRD's founding Agreement specifies that all operations are to be undertaken in the context of promoting environmentally sound and sustainable development. It undertakes environmental audits and impact assessments in areas of particular concern, which enable the Bank to incorporate environmental action plans into any project approved for funding. An Environment Advisory Council assists with the development of policy and strategy in this area. In May 2006 the Bank launched the first, three-year, phase of a Sustainable Energy Initiative (SEI), committing to invest in energy efficiency and renewable energy projects in the region. A second phase of the SEI (SEI-2) was initiated in 2009, with enhanced activities in areas including transport energy efficiency, climate change adaptation and the stationary use of biomass. SEI-3, with a financing target of €4,500m.–€6,500m., was launched in May 2012, focusing on projects in areas including large industry energy efficiency; cleaner energy supply; municipal infrastructure energy efficiency; support to carbon market development in the region; energy efficiency of buildings; biomass energy; gas flaring reduction; transport energy efficiency, and climate change adaptation. Over the period 2006–end-2012 the Bank invested more than €10,000m. in SEI projects. A separate Multilateral Carbon Credit Fund was established, in December 2006, in co-operation with the EIB, providing a means by which countries may obtain carbon credits from emission-related projects. By 2013 the Fund was fully subscribed with resources totalling €208.5m. In December 2009 the Bank contributed €25m. to a new joint Southeast Europe Energy Efficiency Fund (SE4F), which aimed to expand the availability of and access to sustainable energy finance in the western Balkans and Turkey. A new multi-donor EBRD Water Fund, with a particular focus on water projects in Central Asia, was established in July 2010.

Publications

Annual Report.
Donor Report (annually).
Economics of Transition (quarterly).
Financial Report (annually).
Law in Transition (2 a year).
People and Projects (annually).
Sustainability Report (annually).
Transition Report (annually).
Working papers, fact sheets.

Statistics

BANK COMMITMENTS BY SUB-REGION AND COUNTRY
(in € million)

	2012	Cumulative to 31 Dec. 2012
Central Europe and the Baltic States		
Croatia	210	2,749
Czech Republic	0	1,137
Estonia	4	543
Hungary	75	2,663
Latvia	4	575
Lithuania	37	640
Poland	672	6,063
Slovakia	185	1,787
Slovenia	28	765
Sub-total	1,215	16,952
South-Eastern Europe		
Albania	69	732
Bosnia and Herzegovina	125	1,474
Bulgaria	246	2,661
Macedonia, former Yugoslav republic	157	1,085
Montenegro	5	66
Kosovo	39	323
Romania	612	6,110
Serbia	612	3,106
Sub-total	1,522	15,557
Eastern Europe and the Caucasus		
Armenia	94	613
Azerbaijan	83	1,554
Belarus	185	1,049
Georgia	103	1,719
Moldova	102	733
Ukraine	934	8,148
Sub-total	1,500	13,817
Central Asia		
Kazakhstan	374	4,588
Kyrgyzstan	16	414
Mongolia	419	690
Tajikistan	46	285
Turkmenistan	14	172
Uzbekistan	2	741
Sub-total	871	6,891
Southern and Eastern Mediterranean		
Egypt	10	10
Jordan	123	123
Morocco	23	23
Tunisia	25	25
Sub-total	181	181
Russia	2,582	22,943
Turkey	1,049	2,576
Total	8,920	78,916

Note: Financing for regional projects is allocated to the relevant countries.

Source: EBRD, *Annual Report 2012*.

EUROPEAN SPACE AGENCY—ESA

Address: 8–10 rue Mario Nikis, 75738 Paris Cedex 15, France.
Telephone: 1-53-69-76-54; **fax:** 1-53-69-75-60; **e-mail:** contactesa@esa.int; **internet:** www.esa.int.

ESA was established in 1975 to provide for, and to promote, European co-operation in space research and technology, and their applications, for exclusively peaceful purposes. It replaced the European Space Research Organisation (ESRO) and the European Launcher Development Organisation (both founded in 1962).

MEMBERS*

Austria	Luxembourg
Belgium	Netherlands
Czech Republic	Norway
Denmark	Poland
Finland	Portugal
France	Romania
Germany	Spain
Greece	Sweden
Ireland	Switzerland
Italy	United Kingdom

* Estonia, Hungary, Latvia, and Slovenia have 'European Cooperating State' status. Canada has signed an agreement for close co-operation with ESA, including representation on the ESA Council. Cyprus, Israel, Latvia and Slovakia have also signed Cooperation Agreements.

Organization

(April 2014)

COUNCIL

The Council is composed of representatives of all member states. It is responsible for formulating the policy (the 'European Span Plan'), and meets at ministerial or delegate level.

ADMINISTRATION

ESA's activities are divided into the following 10 Directorates, each headed by a Director who reports directly to the Director-General: Earth Observation Programmes; Technical and Quality Management; Launchers; Human Spaceflight; Resources Management; Legal Affairs and External Relations; Science and Robotic Exploration; Telecommunications and Integrated Applications; Galileo Programme and Navigation-related Activities; Operations; and Infrastructure.

Director-General: JEAN-JACQUES DORDAIN (France).

ESA CENTRES

European Astronaut Centre (EAC): Köln, Germany. As a subsidiary of the Directorate of Human Spaceflight, manages all European astronaut activities and trains European and international partner astronauts on the European elements of the International Space Station. The Centre employs 16 European astronauts.

European Centre for Space Applications and Telecommunications (ESCAT): Harwell, United Kingdom. Manages activities related to integrated applications, telecommunications, climate change, technology and science.

European Space Astronomy Centre (ESAC): Villanueva de la Canada, Spain. A centre of excellence for space science and a base for ESA astrophysics and solar system missions. Hosts a virtual observatory.

European Space Operations Centre (ESOC): Darmstadt, Germany. Responsible for all satellite operations and the corresponding ground facilities and communications networks.

European Space Research and Technology Centre (ESTEC): Noordwijk, Netherlands. ESA's principal technical establishment, at which the majority of project teams are based, together with the space science department and the technological research and support engineers; provides the appropriate testing and laboratory facilities.

European Space Research Institute (ESRIN): Frascati, Italy. Responsible for the corporate exploitation of Earth observation data from space.

ESA has liaison offices in Brussels, Belgium; Moscow, Russia; and Washington, DC, USA, as well as offices in Houston, Texas, USA, to support International Space Station activities, and at the Guyana Space Centre, located in Kourou, French Guyana. ESA owns the launch and launcher production facilities at Kourou. ESA's Redu Centre in Belgium tests satellites, and incorporates the Space Weather Data Centre. The Agency also operates ground/tracking stations around the world.

Activities

ESA's tasks are to define and put into effect a long-term European space policy of scientific research and technological development and to encourage all members to co-ordinate their national programmes with those of ESA to ensure that Europe maintains a competitive position in the field of space technology. ESA's basic activities cover studies on future projects; technological research; and shared technical investments, information systems and training programmes. These, and the science programme, are mandatory activities to which all members must contribute; other programmes are optional and members may determine their own level of participation. In November 2000 the ESA Council and the Council of the European Union (EU) endorsed a European strategy for space, which aimed to strengthen the foundation for European space activities; advance scientific knowledge; and to use the technical capabilities developed in connection with space activities to secure wider economic and social benefits. In May 2004 a framework agreement entered into force providing the legal basis for structured co-operation between ESA and the European Commission. This provided for a co-ordinating ESA-European Commission secretariat, and for joint consultations between the ESA Council and the EU Council (known as the Space Council). The European Space Policy was adopted in May 2007, providing a common political framework for space activities in Europe. In June 2011 ESA and the European Defence Agency concluded an administrative arrangement on co-operation.

In addition to its relations with the EU, ESA is committed to pursuing international co-operation to achieve its objective of developing the peaceful applications of space technology. The Agency has observer status with the UN Committee on the Peaceful Uses of Outer Space, and co-operates closely with the UN's Office of Outer Space Affairs (in particular through the organization of a training and fellowship programme), EUMETSAT, and with the US National Aeronautics and Space Administration (NASA) and the Russian Federal Space Agency ('Roscosmos'). In 2003 ESA and the Russian Government signed an Agreement on Co-operation and Partnership in the Exploration and Use of Outer Space for Peaceful Purposes, succeeding a similar agreement concluded with the USSR in 1990. ESA is a partner in the International Space Station (ISS), which was initiated by the US Government in 1984, and subsequently developed as a wider project by Canada, Europe, Japan, Russia and the USA. In September 2012 ESA and the European Investment Bank concluded an agreement establishing a new Space for Mediterranean Countries Initiative, tasked with delivering satellite-based services aimed at bridging the digital divide and stimulating economic growth in the Mediterranean region.

In March–April 2009 ESA convened the fifth European Conference on Space Debris. In October 2012 the first ESA orbital debris test radar was inaugurated in Santorcaz, Spain; the radar was to detect space debris that might be hazardous to space navigation, and was to be used to develop future debris warning services.

SCIENCE AND ROBOTIC EXPLORATION

The Science Programme is a mandatory activity of the Agency and forms the basis of co-operation between member states. Among successful scientific satellites and probes subsequently launched by ESA are the Giotto probe, launched in 1985 to study the composition of Halley's comet and reactivated in 1990 to observe the Grigg-Skjellerup comet in July 1992; and Hipparcos, which, between 1989 and 1993, determined the precise astronomic positions and distances of more than 1m. stars. In November 1995 ESA launched the Infrared Space Observatory (the operational phase of which lasted until April 1998, and was followed by a post-operational period ending in 2006), which successfully conducted pre-planned scientific studies providing data on galaxy and star formation and on interstellar matter. ESA collaborated with NASA in the Ulysses space project (a solar polar mission that was launched in October 1990 and terminated in June 2009, as the spacecraft's orbital path became too far removed from the Earth to allow sufficient transmission of data); the Solar and Helispheric Observatory (SOHO, launched in December 1995 to study the internal structure of the sun); and the Hubble Space Telescope. The Agency is committed to co-operation with NASA on the JWST (James Webb Space Telescope), the successor of the Hubble Space telescope, scheduled to be launched in 2018. In May 2012 ESA took delivery of the Mid InfraRed Instrument (MIRI), the first instrument that it had commissioned for the JWST. In October 1997 the Huygens space probe was launched under the framework of a joint NASA–ESA project (the Cassini/Huygens mission) to study the planet Saturn and its largest moon, Titan, where it landed in January 2005. In August 2009 ESA and NASA agreed in principle to establish a Mars Exploration Joint Initiative (MEJI), which was to launch (in 2016, 2018 and 2020) landers and orbiters to conduct astrobiological, geological, geophysical and other investigations; samples were to be returned to Earth from Mars during the 2020s. In March 2013 ESA and Roscosmos agreed to work in partnership on the ExoMars programme, under which two missions were to be launched, in 2016 and 2018, with the aim of investigating whether life has ever existed on Mars. The LISA Pathfinder mission was to be conducted with NASA.

In December 1999 the X-Ray Multimirror Mission (XMM–Newton) was launched from Kourou, French Guyana. It was envisaged that XMM–Newton, the most powerful X-ray telescope ever placed in orbit, would investigate the origin of galaxies, the formation of black holes, etc. Four cluster satellites, launched from Baikonur, Russia, in July–August 2000, were, in association with SOHO, to explore the interaction between the Earth's magnetic field and electrically charged particles transported on the solar wind. In October 2002 INTEGRAL (International Gamma-Ray Astrophysical Laboratory) was successfully launched by a Russian Proton vehicle, to study the most violent events perceptible in the Universe.

ESA's space missions are an integral part of its long-term science programme, Horizon 2000, which was initiated in 1984. In 1994 a new set of missions was defined, to enable the inclusion of projects using new technologies and participation in future international space activities, which formed the Horizon 2000 Plus extension covering the period 2005–16. Together they were called Horizons 2000.

In November 2003 the Science Programme Committee initiated a new long-term space science programme, Cosmic Vision, initially to cover the period 2004–14. Under the programme three main projects—Astrophysics, Solar System Science, and Fundamental Physics—were to be developed in production groups, missions within each to be built synergistically, where possible using common technologies and engineering teams. Projects included Herschel, exploring the infrared and microwave Universe (the Herschel Space Observatory, designed to investigate the formation of stars and galaxies, was operational during May 2009–April 2013); Planck, studying the cosmic microwave background (launched in May 2009); Gaia, the ultimate galaxy mapper (launched in December 2013); Rosetta (launched in March 2004, to rendezvous with and land on a comet; reactivated in January 2014 after a 31-month 'hibernation' to continue its mission, which was scheduled to conclude in December 2015); Mars Express, a Mars orbiter carrying the Beagle 2 lander (launched in 2003; contact with Beagle 2 was, however, lost in January 2004); Venus Express, a Venus orbiter (launched 2005, entered into orbit around Venus in April 2006); SMART-1, which was to demonstrate solar propulsion technology while on course to the Moon (launched 2003); BepiColombo, a mission to Mercury (to be launched in 2014); and SMART-2, a technology demonstration mission.

In accordance with a new phase of Cosmic Vision, focusing on 2015–25, further missions were to be undertaken, including LISA Pathfinder, a joint mission with NASA, searching for gravitational waves (to be launched in 2015); and Solar Orbiter, which aimed to take a closer look at the Sun (to be launched in 2017). Other missions under consideration included Cross-Scale (Investigating Multi-scale Coupling in Space Plasmas); Euclid (mapping the geometry of the dark universe; to be launched in 2019); Plato (next generation planet finder); Spica (an infrared space telescope for cosmology and astrophysics); JUICE (detailed observation of Jupiter and three of its moons: Callisto, Europa and Ganymede; to be launched in 2022, with arrival at the Jupiter system scheduled for 2030); and Xeus/Ixo (X-ray observatory for the extreme and evolving universe).

EARTH OBSERVATION

ESA has contributed to the understanding and monitoring of the Earth's environment through its satellite projects. From 1977–2002 ESA launched seven Meteosat spacecraft (financed and owned by EUMETSAT, but ESA-operated until December 1995) into geosynchronous orbit, to provide continuous meteorological data, mainly for the purposes of weather forecasting. The first, second and third Meteosat Second Generation (MSG) satellites—MSG-1, MSG-2, and MSG-3—were launched in August 2002, December 2005, and July 2012, respectively. In 2014 ESA and EUMETSAT were developing a more advanced Meteosat Third Generation (MTG) operational geostationary meteorological satellite system, which was to be inaugurated in 2018. ESA and EUMETSAT have also collaborated on the METOP/EPS (EUMETSAT Polar System) programme, to provide observations from polar orbit. The first METOP satellite was launched in October 2006, and the second in September 2012.

ENVISAT, the largest and most advanced European-built observation satellite, was launched in February 2002 from Kourou, French Guyana, with the aim of monitoring exceptional natural events, such as volcanic eruptions, and of providing detailed assessments of the impact of human activities on the Earth's atmosphere, as well as of land and coastal processes. In April 2012 contact with ENVISAT was lost and in the following month that mission was terminated.

In June 1998 the ESA Council approved the initiation of activities related to the Living Planet Programme, designed to increase understanding of environmental issues. In May 1999 the Council committed funds for a research mission, CryoSat, to be undertaken, in order to study the impact of global warming on polar ice caps. However, the launch of CryoSat was aborted in October 2005. A recovery plan, completed in February 2006, provided for the development of a CryoSat-2 mission, with the same objectives; CryoSat-2 was eventually launched in April 2010. The Gravity Field and Steady-State Ocean Circulation Explorer (GOCE) mission, launched in March 2009 and concluded in November 2013, used a unique measurement technique to recover geodetic precision data on the Earth's gravity field. ESA is responsible for the space component of the European Commission's Copernicus initiative (previously known as the Global Monitoring for Environment and Security programme), and in April 2014 launched the first ('Sentinel-1a') of a series of Sentinel earth observation satellites. In November 2008 the Council approved a Space Situational Awareness (SSA) preparatory programme, to develop a capability to monitor potentially hazardous objects and natural phenomena; the SSA became fully operational in 2012. In April 2013 a new ESA Space Weather Coordination Centre (SSCC) was inaugurated in Brussels, Belgium, within the framework of the SSA; an SSCC helpdesk was to provide expert support for satellite operators, the telecommunications and navigation sectors, and government agencies and research institutes on solar weather, ionospheric weather, and on the state of the geomagnetic and the orbital radiation environments.

ESA Earth Explorer missions aim to enhance understanding of the Earth's system with a view to supporting efforts to address the challenges posed by ongoing global change, i.e. climate change and also the large-scale impact on the Earth of the growing human population and continued economic expansion. The Agency has selected six such missions, of which three are 'Core' (responding to specific areas of public concern) and three are 'Opportunity' (quick implementation missions aimed at addressing areas of immediate environmental concern). The Core missions are as follows: GOCE; the Atmospheric Dynamics Mission (ADM)-Aeolus, scheduled to be launched in 2015 to demonstrate measurements of vertical wind profiles from space; and the Earth Clouds Aerosols and Radiation Explorer (EarthCARE), which, once launched in 2015, will aim to improve the representation and understanding of the Earth's radiative balance in climate and numerical forecast models. The Opportunity missions are the Soil Moisture and Ocean Salinity (SMOS) mission, launched in November 2009, which aims to further understanding of the Earth's water cycle; CryoSat-2; and Swarm, launched in November 2013, which was to produce the best survey to date of the geomagnetic field and its temporal evolution.

As part of the Treaty Enforcement Services using Earth Observation (TESEO) initiative, agreed in 2001, ESA satellites provide data for a wide range of environmental activities including monitoring wetlands, ensuring compliance with Kyoto Protocol emission targets and combating desertification. Similarly, ESA has agreements with UNESCO to protect wildlife and sites of historic interest, in support of the Convention Concerning the Protection of the World Cultural and Natural Heritage.

TELECOMMUNICATIONS AND INTEGRATED APPLICATIONS

ESA commenced the development of communications satellites in 1968. These have since become the largest markets for space use and have transformed global communications, with more than 100 satellites circling the Earth for the purposes of telecommunications. The main series of operational satellites developed by ESA are the European Communications Satellites (ECS), based on the original orbital test satellite and used by EUTELSAT, and the Maritime Communications Satellites (MARECS), which have been leased for operations to the mobile satellite company, Inmarsat.

An Advanced Relay and Technology Mission Satellite (ARTEMIS) was developed by ESA to test and operate new telecommunications techniques, and to enable the relay of information directly between satellites. ARTEMIS was launched in July 2001. In May 1999 the Council approved funding for a satellite multimedia programme, Advanced Research in Telecommunications Systems (Artes), which aimed to support the development of satellite systems and services for delivering information through high-speed internet access. Ongoing in 2014 were Artes-1 (focused on strategic analysis); Artes-3–4 (seeking to improve the near-term competitiveness of the satcom industry through the development of equipment including terminals, processors and antennas for ground or space); Artes-5 (seeking to develop a more sustained long-term technological basis for European industrial effectiveness, and divided into Artes-5.1, involving projects initiated by and also fully funded by the Agency, and Artes-5.2, comprising projects initiated by industry and 75% ESA-funded); Artes-7, dedicated to the implementation of an European Data Relay Satellite (EDRS) system; Artes-8, focused on the development of the Alphasatis satellite that, with Inmarsat, was to incorporate the first stage of the Alphabus multi-purpose geostationary communications platform; Artes-10, a satellite-based communication system that was to complement a new EU air traffic management system; Artes-11, aimed at developing the Small GEO System, a satellite incorporating advanced payload technology; Artes-20, dedicated to the development, implementation and pilot operations of Integrated Applications (combined satellite operations); Artes-21, developing the Automatic Identification System, a short-range coastal tracking system.

GALILEO PROGRAMME AND NAVIGATION-RELATED ACTIVITIES

ESA and the European Commission have collaborated to design and develop a European global satellite and navigation system, Galileo. The project aimed to provide a highly accurate global positioning service by means of 30 satellites (of which 27 were to be operational and three active spares), a global network of 20 Galileo Sensor Stations (GSSs), and two Galileo Control Centres (GCCs), based in Europe. ESA, in co-operation with the European Commission and EUROCONTROL, implements the EGNOS System, the European contribution to the Global Navigation Satellite System phase 1 (GNSS-1) that was to provide an improved navigation and positioning service for all users of the (American) GPS and (Russian) GLONASS systems. The GNSS aimed to use the Galileo, GPS and GLONASS systems to provide an integrated satellite navigation service of unprecedented accuracy and global coverage under civilian control. The first four operational Galileo satellites were launched in 2011–12.

LAUNCHERS

The European requirement for independent access to space first manifested itself in the early 1970s against the background of strategic and commercial interests in telecommunications and Earth observation. As a consequence, and based on knowledge gained through national programmes, ESA began development of a space launcher. The resulting Ariane rocket was first launched in December 1979. The project, which incorporated four different launchers; Ariane-1 to Ariane-4, subsequently became an essential element of ESA's programme activities and, furthermore, developed a successful commercial role in placing satellites into orbit. From 1985 ESA worked to develop the more powerful Ariane-5 launcher, which has been in commercial operation since 1999, launched from the ESA facility at the Guyana Space Centre. Ariane-5 undertook seven missions during 2012. In December 2000 the ESA Council approved the Vega Small Launcher Development and the P80 Advanced Solid Propulsion Stage programmes. The first Vega launch took place in February 2012. A Future Launcher Preparatory Programme (FLPP) was being defined.

HUMAN SPACEFLIGHT

ESA supports space research in the life and physical sciences through its microgravity programmes. A considerable scientific output has been achieved in key areas such as crystal growth, solidification physics, fluid sciences, thermophysical properties, molecular and cell biology, developmental biology, exobiology and human physiology. The Agency's main contributions to the ISS have been the Columbus Laboratory (launched in February 2008); and the 'Jules Verne', 'Johannes Kepler', 'Edoardo Amaldi' and 'Albert Einstein' unmanned Automated Transfer Vehicles (ATVs), launched in March 2008, February 2011, March 2012 and June 2013, respectively; these provide logistical support to the ISS. The fifth ATV,

'Georges Lemaître', was to be launched in June 2014. The Columbus laboratory accommodates European multi-user research facilities: Biolab; Fluid Science Laboratory, European Physiology Modules, Material Science Laboratory (all developed within the Microgravity Facilities for the Columbus Programme); and European Drawer Rack and European Stowage Rack (both within the ISS Utilization Programme). In the framework of the ISS agreements with the USA, ESA is allocated 51% usage of Columbus, the remainder being allocated to NASA. In addition to the experiment accommodation capabilities on Columbus, the European Zero-G Airbus, operated under ESA contract by Novespace, provides European researchers short-duration access to microgravity conditions for a wide variety of experiments, ranging from precursor experiments for the ISS to student experiments. Droptowers and sounding rockets provide additional short-duration opportunities. The ESA Directorate of Human Spaceflight also provides European researchers with flight opportunities on unmanned Russian Foton and Bion capsules.

Finance

All member states contribute to ESA's mandatory programme activities on a scale based on their national income, and are free to decide on their level of commitment in optional programmes. The total budget for 2014 amounted to €4,102.1m., with €915.9m. (22.3%) allocated to earth observation, €630.2m. (15.4%) to navigation, €617.4m. (15.1%) to launchers, €506.5m. (12.3%) to the scientific programme, and €370.9m. (9.0%) to human spaceflight.

Publications

ECSL News.
ESA Annual Report.
ESA Bulletin (quarterly).
Monographs and conference proceedings.

EUROPEAN UNION—EU

The European Coal and Steel Community (ECSC) was created by a treaty signed in Paris, France, on 18 April 1951 (effective from 25 July 1952) to pool the coal and steel production of the six original members. It was regarded as a first step towards a united Europe. The European Economic Community (EEC) and European Atomic Energy Community (Euratom) were established by separate treaties signed in Rome, Italy, on 25 March 1957 (effective from 1 January 1958), the former to create a common market and to approximate economic policies, the latter to promote growth in nuclear industries. The common institutions of the three Communities were established by a treaty signed in Brussels, Belgium, on 8 April 1965 (effective from 1 July 1967).

The EEC was formally changed to the European Community (EC) under the Treaty on European Union (effective from 1 November 1993, and renamed from December 2009, see below), although in practice the term EC had been used for several years to describe the three Communities together. The new Treaty established a European Union (EU), which introduced citizenship thereof and aimed to increase intergovernmental co-operation in economic and monetary affairs; to establish a common foreign and security policy; and to introduce co-operation in justice and home affairs. The EU was placed under the supervision of the European Council (comprising heads of state or of government of member countries), while the EC continued to exist, having competence in matters relating to the Treaty of Rome and its amendments.

The Treaty of Paris establishing the ECSC expired on 23 July 2002, resulting in the termination of the ECSC legal regime and procedures and the dissolution of the ECSC Consultative Committee. The ECSC's assets and liabilities were transferred to the overall EU budget, while rights and obligations arising from international agreements drawn up between the ECSC and third countries were devolved to the EC.

With the entry into force, on 1 December 2009, of the Treaty of Lisbon amending the Treaty on European Union and the Treaty establishing the European Community, the Treaty on European Union was renamed the Treaty on the Functioning of the European Union, with all references to the European 'Community' changed to the 'Union'. Euratom continued to exist, alongside the EU.

Meetings of the principal organs take place in Brussels, Luxembourg and Strasbourg, France. The Treaty of Lisbon provided for the posts of President of the European Council and High Representative of the Union for Foreign Affairs and Security Policy; and for an 18-month troika comprising groups of three successive governments holding the rotating six-month presidency of the Council of the European Union.

Presidency of the Council of the European Union: Greece (January–June 2014); Italy (July–December 2014); Latvia (January–June 2015).

President of the European Council: HERMAN VAN ROMPUY (Belgium).

High Representative of the Union for Foreign Affairs and Security Policy: CATHERINE ASHTON (United Kingdom).

Secretary-General of the Council of the European Union: UWE CORSEPIUS (Germany).

President of the European Commission: JOSÉ MANUEL DURÃO BARROSO (Portugal).

President of the European Parliament: MARTIN SCHULZ (Germany).

MEMBERS

Austria	Germany*	Netherlands*
Belgium*	Greece	Poland
Bulgaria	Hungary	Portugal
Croatia	Ireland	Romania
Cyprus	Italy*	Slovakia
Czech Republic	Latvia	Slovenia
Denmark	Lithuania	Spain
Estonia	Luxembourg*	Sweden
Finland	Malta	United Kingdom
France*		

* Original members.

ENLARGEMENT

The six original members (Belgium, France, Germany, Italy, Luxembourg and the Netherlands) were joined in the European Communities (later the European Union—EU) on 1 January 1973 by Denmark, Ireland and the United Kingdom, and on 1 January 1981 by Greece. In a referendum held in February 1982, the inhabitants of Greenland voted to end their membership of the Community, entered into when under full Danish rule. Greenland's withdrawal took effect from 1 February 1985. Portugal and Spain became members on 1 January 1986. Following the reunification of Germany in October 1990, the former German Democratic Republic immediately became part of the Community, although a transitional period was allowed before certain Community legislation took effect there. Austria, Finland and Sweden became members on 1 January 1995.

At the Copenhagen summit on 13 December 2002, an historic agreement was reached when the European Council agreed that 10 candidate countries, comprising eight in Central and Eastern Europe (the Czech Republic, Estonia, Hungary, Latvia, Lithuania, Poland, Slovakia and Slovenia), and Malta and Cyprus, should join the EU on 1 May 2004. The leaders of the 10 new member states signed the accession treaty in Athens, Greece, on 16 April 2003. The Treaty of Athens had to be ratified by all 25 states prior to accession on 1 May 2004. The 15 existing member states opted to ratify the Treaty in parliament whereas the future member states, except Cyprus (the Cypriot Parliament unanimously approved accession to the EU on 14 July 2003), adopted the Treaty by referendum. Under the terms of the Treaty, only the Greek Cypriot sector of Cyprus was to be admitted to the EU in the absence of a settlement on the divided status of the island, although the EU made clear its preference for the accession of a united Cyprus. In April 2004, however, in a referendum on a UN-proposed reunification settlement held only a few days before Cyprus was scheduled to join the EU, some 76% of Greek Cypriot voters rejected the proposal. At the same time, some 65% of Turkish Cypriot voters endorsed the settlement. Both communities would have had to approve the proposed reunification in order for Cyprus to commence its membership of the EU undivided. Consequently, only the Greek sector of the island assumed EU membership from 1 May.

Romania submitted its formal application for EU membership on 22 June 1995, while Bulgaria applied for membership on 14 December. Following the Helsinki European Council's decision in December 1999, accession negotiations started with Romania and Bulgaria in February 2000. The Commission concluded in November 2003 that Bulgaria had a functioning market economy and would be able to perform within the EU in the near future provided it continued to implement its reform programme. In October 2004 a report by the

European Commission described Romania as a functioning market economy, although it confirmed that endemic corruption, ethnic minority rights and human trafficking remained, inter alia, areas of concern in both countries. In the same strategy document, the Commission proposed a new clause in accession treaties under which membership negotiations could be suspended if candidate countries failed to fulfil the economic and political criteria established in Copenhagen, Denmark, in December 2002, according to which a prospective member must be a stable democracy, respecting human rights, the rule of law, and the protection of minorities; have a functioning market economy; and adopt the common rules, standards and policies that make up the body of EU law. Bulgaria and Romania provisionally completed formal negotiations in June and December 2004, respectively, and this was confirmed at the Brussels European Council meeting of 17 December. The Commission formally approved the accession applications of Romania and Bulgaria on 22 February 2005. Bulgaria and Romania signed a joint accession treaty on 25 April. In September 2006 the Commission recommended that Romania and Bulgaria should accede to the EU as planned; both countries formally became members of the Union on 1 January 2007, with the entry into force of their joint accession treaty.

Croatia submitted its application for membership of the EU in February 2003, and membership negotiations commenced in October 2005. Negotiations were completed in June 2011, and Croatia signed an accession treaty on 9 December. Croatia acceded to full membership of the EU on 1 July 2013, following approval of EU membership by a referendum held in that country in January 2012.

Turkey, which had signed an association agreement with the EC in 1963 (although this was suspended between 1980 and 1986, following a military coup), applied for membership of the EU on 14 April 1987. As a populous, predominantly Muslim nation, with a poor record on human rights and low average income levels, Turkey encountered objections to its prospective membership, which opponents claimed would disturb the balance of power within the EU and place an intolerable strain on the organization's finances. The Helsinki (Finland) European Council of 1999, however, granted Turkey applicant status and encouraged it to undertake the requisite political and economic reforms for eventual membership. By accelerating the pace of reforms, Turkey had made significant progress towards achieving compliance with the so-called Copenhagen criteria by 2004, including far-reaching reforms of the Constitution and the penal code. Turkish ambitions for EU membership were adversely affected in April 2004 by the failure of the UN plan for the reunification of Cyprus, which was rejected in a referendum by the Greek Cypriots in the south of the island (see above). Cyprus has been divided since 1974 when Turkey invaded the northern third of the country in response to a Greek-sponsored coup aiming to unite the island with Greece. Turkey refuses to recognize the Greek Cypriot Government and is the only country to recognize the Government of the northern section of the country, known as the 'Turkish Republic of Northern Cyprus', where it has 30,000 troops deployed. The requirement for the successful resolution of all territorial disputes with members of the EU meant that failure to reach a settlement in Cyprus remained a significant impediment to Turkey's accession to the EU, although the Turkish authorities had expressed strong support for the peace plan. In December 2004, however, the EU agreed to begin accession talks with Turkey in early October 2005, although it specified a number of conditions, including the right to impose 'permanent safeguard' clauses in any accession accord. The safeguard clauses related to the freedom of movement of Turkish citizens within the EU (seeking to allay fears about large numbers of low-paid Turkish workers entering other EU member states) and restrictions on the level of subsidy available to Turkey for its infrastructure development or agriculture. The EU warned that negotiations could last between 10 and 15 years and that eventual membership was not guaranteed. Turkey was also obliged to sign a protocol to update its association agreement with the EU prior to accession negotiations in October, to cover the 10 new members that had joined the organization in May 2004, including Cyprus. The Turkish Government had previously refused to grant effective recognition to the Greek Cypriot Government and, although it signed the protocol at the end of July 2005, it still insisted that the extension of the association agreement did not constitute formal recognition. In a report issued in November 2006, the Commission demanded that Turkey open its ports to Cypriot ships by mid-December, in compliance with its agreement to extend its customs union to the 10 new member states in 2005. Turkey announced that there could be no progress on this issue until the EU implemented a regulation drafted in 2004 to end the economic isolation of the 'Turkish Republic of Northern Cyprus', the adoption of which had been blocked by Cyprus. In December 2006, therefore, the EU Council stipulated that talks would not commence in eight policy areas affected by the restrictions placed on Cypriot traffic by Turkey. In its 2011 annual report on enlargement strategy and progress, the Commission expressed regret that negotiations had not opened in any new policy areas for over a year. Negotiations have opened in 14 of the total of 33 policy areas, with talks provisionally closed in one area; eight areas remain blocked

At a summit of EU leaders in Brussels in December 2005, the former Yugoslav Republic of Macedonia (FYRM) was granted candidate status, joining Croatia and Turkey. However, no date was established for the initiation of accession negotiations. A summit of the Council convened in June 2008 determined that, as a precondition of the FYRM's accession, an ongoing dispute with Greece concerning its name (Macedonia also being the name of a region of Greece) must be satisfactorily resolved. Montenegro applied for EU membership in December 2008, and the European Council confirmed Montenegro's status as a candidate country in December 2010. In October 2011 the European Commission declared that Montenegro had fulfilled the political and economic criteria needed to begin EU membership negotiations. Upon the Commission's recommendation, the European Council agreed in December to initiate the accession process, and negotiations commenced on 29 June 2012. In July 2009 Iceland's legislature voted to apply for EU membership, and membership negotiations commenced in July 2010. Popular support for EU membership in Iceland subsequently declined, however, and by the beginning of 2013 talks on just 11 of the 35 negotiating areas had been closed. In mid-2013 Iceland's new Government decided to suspend EU membership negotiations.

Serbia applied for EU membership in December 2009, and in October 2011 the European Commission recommended to the Council that Serbia should be granted candidate status. On 1 March 2012 the European Council agreed officially to give Serbia the status of a candidate country for EU membership; accession negotiations commenced in late January 2014. Albania submitted a membership application in April 2009. In October 2013 the European Commission recommended that Albania be offered candidate status, which was approved by the European Parliament in December; however, the General Affairs Council deferred making a decision on Albania's status until June 2014.

INSTITUTIONAL REFORM

In February 2002 a Convention on the Future of Europe was opened in Brussels, Belgium, chaired by former French President Valéry Giscard d'Estaing. The Convention, which had been agreed upon at the Laeken summit in December 2001, when the European Council adopted the Declaration on the Future of the European Union, included in its remit 60 or more topics aimed at reforming EU institutions to ensure the smooth functioning of the Union after enlargement. The full text of the draft constitutional treaty was submitted to the Council of the European Union in July 2003. The draft was discussed at the Intergovernmental Conference (IGC), which was composed of the representatives of the member states and the accession countries, from October to December.

Heads of state and of government attending an EU summit held in Brussels, in December 2003, failed to agree the final text of the proposed constitution, owing to conflicting views over the issue of voting rights. At a summit meeting held in Brussels, in June 2004, the heads of state and of government of the then 25 EU member states approved a draft constitutional treaty, having reached a compromise over voting rights. The draft constitutional treaty was formally signed in Rome, Italy, in October by the heads of state or of government of the 25 member states and the three candidate countries of Bulgaria, Romania and Turkey, although it remained subject to ratification by each member nation (either by a vote in the national legislature or by a popular referendum). The future of the constitutional treaty became uncertain following its rejection in national referendums held in France and the Netherlands, in May and June 2005, respectively, and seven countries (the Czech Republic, Denmark, Finland, Ireland, Portugal, Sweden and the United Kingdom) announced plans to postpone a national referendum.

In June 2007, at a summit in Brussels, the European Council agreed to convene an IGC to draft a new treaty. At an informal summit of the European Council held in Lisbon, Portugal, in mid-October, agreement was reached on the final text of a new reform treaty. The resulting Treaty of Lisbon amending the Treaty on European Union and the Treaty establishing the European Community was signed in Lisbon, on 13 December, by the heads of state or of government of the 27 member states. The Treaty of Lisbon revised existing treaties, and retained much of the content of the abandoned constitutional treaty, including its scheme for Council of the European Union voting rights (whereby measures would require the support of at least 55% of EU states, representing at least 65% of the total population, see below; this aimed to ensure that smaller member states—particularly the newer, Eastern European members—could not be overruled by a small but powerful group of senior members). During 2008 the parliaments of most member states voted to ratify the Treaty. However, in June voters in Ireland, which was constitutionally bound to conduct a popular referendum on the issue, rejected ratification. In December the European Council agreed to a number of concessions, including the removal of a provision in the Treaty for a reduction in the number of European Commissioners (see below), and relating to taxation, the family, and state neutrality, with the aim of securing its ratification by all EU member states by the end of 2009. A new referendum, held in Ireland in early October 2009, approved the Treaty. In early November, following a ruling by the Constitutional Court of the Czech Republic that its provisions were compatible with the country's Constitution, the Czech Republic became the final EU country to ratify the Treaty of Lisbon. The Treaty entered into force on 1 December 2009.

Principal Elements of the Treaty of Lisbon

The Treaty of Lisbon (formally known as the Treaty of Lisbon amending the Treaty on European Union and the Treaty establishing the European Community) sought to redefine the functions and procedures of the institutions of the EU. It created a High Representative of the Union for Foreign Affairs and Security Policy (appointed by the European Council by qualified majority with the agreement of the President of the Commission) to represent the EU internationally, combining the former roles of EU Commissioner responsible for external relations and EU High Representative for the Common Foreign and Security Policy (although foreign policy remains subject to a national veto). The High Representative of the Union for Foreign Affairs and Security Policy is mandated by the Council, but is also one of the Vice-Presidents of the Commission and chairs the External Relations Council. The Lisbon Treaty also provided for the creation of a new permanent president of the European Council, elected by the European Council for a period of two years and six months, renewable once; the creation of this role aimed to promote coherence and continuity in policy-making. The system of a six-month rotating presidency was retained for the different Council formations (except for the External Relations Council, chaired by the High Representative of the Union for Foreign Affairs and Security Policy). A new system of fixed 18-month troikas (groups of three presidencies) was introduced, sharing the presidencies of most configurations of the Council, to facilitate overall co-ordination and continuity of work. The Lisbon Treaty provided for a revised system of qualified majority voting in the Council (see Council of the European Union). The European Parliament's legislative powers wee consolidated under the Treaty, which granted the Parliament the right of co-decision with the Council of the European Union in an increased number of policy areas, giving it a more prominent role in framing legislation. The maximum number of seats in the European Parliament was raised to 751 (to be fully effective from 2014, see European Parliament). The European Commission retained its composition of one commissioner for each member state. The Treaty establishing the European Community (also known as the Treaty of Rome) was renamed as the Treaty on the Functioning of the European Union, with references to the 'Community' replaced by 'Union'. The Lisbon Treaty sought to improve democracy and transparency within the Union, introducing the right for EU citizens to petition the Commission to introduce new legislation and enshrining the principles of subsidiarity (that the EU should only act when an objective can be better achieved at supranational level, implying that national powers are the norm) and proportionality (that the action should be proportional to the desired objective). National parliaments are given the opportunity to examine EU legislation to ensure that it rests within the EU's remit, and legislation may be returned to the Commission for reconsideration if one-third of member states find that a proposed law breaches these principles. The Treaty of Lisbon enabled enhanced co-operation for groups numbering at least one-third (i.e. currently nine) of the member states. The Treaty provided a legal basis for the EU defence force, with a mutual defence clause, and included the stipulation that the EU has the power to sign treaties and sit on international bodies as a legal entity in its own right. The new framework also provided for the establishment of a European public prosecutor's office to combat EU fraud and cross-border crime and the right to dual citizenship (i.e. of the EU as well as of a member state), and included arrangements for the formal withdrawal of a member state from the EU.

Union Institutions

The EU provides an information service, Europe Direct, online at europa.eu/europedirect/index_en.htm.

EUROPEAN COMMISSION

Address: 200 rue de la Loi, 1049 Brussels, Belgium.

Telephone: (2) 299-11-11; **fax:** (2) 295-01-38; **e-mail:** forename.surname@ec.europa.eu; **internet:** ec.europa.eu.

Please note: in an e-mail address, when the forename and/or the surname are composed of more than one word, the different words are linked by a hyphen. If help is needed, you may send a message to address-information@ec.europa.eu requesting the correct e-mail address of the correspondent.

MEMBERS OF THE COMMISSION
(2010–14)

President: JOSÉ MANUEL DURÃO BARROSO (Portugal).

Vice-President and High Representative of the Union for Foreign Affairs and Security Policy: CATHERINE ASHTON (United Kingdom).

Vice-President, responsible for Justice, Fundamental Rights and Citizenship: VIVIANE REDING (Luxembourg).

Vice-President, responsible for Competition: JOAQUÍN ALMUNIA (Spain).

Vice-President, responsible for Transport: SIIM KALLAS (Estonia).

Vice-President, responsible for the Digital Agenda: NEELIE KROES (Netherlands).

Vice-President, responsible for Industry and Entrepreneurship: ANTONIO TAJANI (Italy).

Vice-President, responsible for Inter-Institutional Relations and Administration: MAROŠ ŠEFČOVIČ (Slovakia).

Commissioner, responsible for the Environment: JANEZ POTOČNIK (Slovenia).

Commissioner, responsible for Economic and Monetary Affairs and the Euro: OLLI REHN (Finland).

Commissioner, responsible for Development: ANDRIS PIEBALGS (Latvia).

Commissioner, responsible for Internal Market and Services: MICHEL BARNIER (France).

Commissioner, responsible for Education, Culture, Multilingualism and Youth: ANDROULLA VASSILIOU (Cyprus).

Commissioner, responsible for Taxation and Customs Union, Audit and Anti-Fraud: ALGIRDAS ŠEMETA (Lithuania).

Commissioner, responsible for Trade: KAREL DE GUCHT (Belgium).

Commissioner, responsible for Health: ANTONIO BORG (Malta).

Commissioner, responsible for Consumer Policy: NEVEN MIMICA (Croatia).

Commissioner, responsible for Research, Innovation and Science: MÁIRE GEOGHEGAN-QUINN (Ireland).

Commissioner, responsible for Financial Programming and Budget: JANUSZ LEWANDOWSKI (Poland).

Commissioner, responsible for Maritime Affairs and Fisheries: MARIA DAMANAKI (Greece).

Commissioner, responsible for International Co-operation, Humanitarian Aid and Crisis Response: KRISTALINA GEORGIEVA (Bulgaria).

Commissioner, responsible for Energy: GÜNTHER H. OETTINGER (Austria).

Commissioner, responsible for Regional Policy: JOHANNES HAHN (Austria).

Commissioner, responsible for Climate Action: CONNIE HEDEGAARD (Denmark).

Commissioner, responsible for Enlargement and European Neighbourhood Policy: ŠTEFAN FÜLE (Czech Republic).

Commissioner, responsible for Employment, Social Affairs and Inclusion: LÁSZLÓ ANDOR (Hungary).

Commissioner, responsible for Home Affairs: CECILIA MALMSTRÖM (Sweden).

Commissioner, responsible for Agriculture and Rural Development: DACIAN CIOLOŞ (Romania).

The European Commission, like the European Parliament and Council of the European Union, was established in the 1950s under the EU's founding Treaties. The functions of the Commission are four-fold: to propose legislation to the European Parliament and the Council of the European Union; to implement EU policies and programmes adopted by the European Parliament and to manage and implement the budget; to enforce European law, in conjunction with the Court of Justice, in all the member states; and to represent the EU in international affairs and to negotiate agreements between the EU and other organizations or countries.

A new Commission is appointed for a five-year term, normally within six months of the elections to the European Parliament. The Governments of the member states agree on an individual to designate as the new Commission President. The President-designate then selects the other members of the Commission, following discussions with the member state Governments. In the performance of their duties, the members of the Commission are forbidden to seek or accept instructions from any government or other body, or to engage in any other paid or unpaid professional activity. The nominated President and other members of the Commission must be approved as a body by the European Parliament before they can take office.

…pproved, the Commission may nominate a number of its …rs as Vice-President. Any member of the Commission, if he … no longer fulfils the conditions required for the performance of …r her duties, or commits a serious offence, may be declared removed from office by the Court of Justice. The Court may, furthermore, on the petition of the Council of the European Union or of the Commission itself, provisionally suspend any member of the Commission from his or her duties. The European Parliament has the authority to dismiss the entire Commission by adopting a motion of censure. The number of members of the Commission may be amended by a unanimous vote of the Council of the European Union.

The members of the Commission, also known as the College, meet once a week and a collective decision is made on policy following a presentation by the relevant Commissioner. The Commission's staff is organized into Directorates-General and Services. The Directorates-General are each responsible for a particular policy area and they devise and draft the Commission's legislative proposals, which become official when adopted by the Commission.

In January 1999 Commissioners accused of mismanagement and corruption retained their positions following a vote of censure by Parliament. However, Parliament appointed a five-member Committee of Independent Experts to investigate allegations of fraud, mismanagement and nepotism within the Commission. In March two new codes of conduct for Commissioners were announced, and the Committee published a report that criticized the Commission's failure to control the administration of the budget and other measures implemented by each department. As a consequence of the report the Commission agreed, collectively, to resign, although Commissioners retained their positions, and exercised limited duties, until their successors were appointed. In late March EU heads of state and of government nominated Romano Prodi, the former Italian Prime Minister, as the next President of the Commission. His appointment, and that of his interim team of Commissioners, were duly ratified by Parliament in September, subject to conditions that formed the foundation of a future inter-institutional agreement between Parliament and the Commission. The Commission retained its powers, but undertook to be more open in its dealings with the Parliament.

In November 2005, in response to diminishing public confidence in EU institutions, the Commission launched the European Transparency Initiative, with the aim of strengthening ethical rules for EU policy-makers, increasing the transparency of lobbying and ensuring the openness of the institutions.

Meanwhile, on 1 May 2004, following the accession of 10 new member states, the 20 existing members of the Commission were joined by 10 new members (one from each new member state). For the first six months of their term of office, although considered full members, they worked alongside existing Commissioners and were not allocated their own departments. From 1 November, when a new Commission was to begin its mandate, there were to be 25 members of the Commission, one from each member state as stipulated by the Treaty of Nice (prior to 1 May, large countries had been permitted two Commissioners, while smaller countries had one). In late October, however, the incoming President of the European Commission, José Manuel Durão Barroso, withdrew his proposed team of commissioners, in order to avoid defeat in the investiture vote in the European Parliament. The reconstituted Commission (two members were replaced and one was allocated a new portfolio) was approved by the European Parliament and took office on 22 November. In January 2007, following the accession of Bulgaria and Romania, the number of Commissioners increased to 27. As it was feared that too large an increase in the number of Commissioners would be prejudicial to collective responsibility, it was initially determined that from 2014 the number would be reduced to a level determined by the Council. However, in December 2008, in response to Ireland's rejection of the Lisbon Treaty in a national referendum in June, the European Council agreed a number of legal guarantees intended to address voters' objections, including a commitment that every member state would have one Commissioner. (The Irish electorate approved the Treaty in October 2009, and it entered into force in December of that year.)

The second Barroso Commission, for 2010–14, was approved by the European Parliament in January 2010 and inaugurated in the following month. The mandate of the previous commission (that should have expired in October 2009) had been lengthened temporarily to accommodate delays in the appointment of the new Commission that were caused by the later than anticipated entry into force of the Lisbon Treaty. John Dalli, the Maltese European Commissioner, responsible for Health and Consumer Policy, resigned in October 2012, following fraud allegations; he was replaced by Antonio Borg in the following month. Following Croatia's accession to the EU in July 2013, the number of Commissioners increased to 28. Responsibility for Health and Consumer Policy was divided between two roles, with the new Croatian Commissioner taking responsibility for Consumer Policy; Borg retained responsibility for Health.

DIRECTORATES-GENERAL AND SERVICES

Policies

Directorate-General for Agriculture and Rural Development: 130 rue de la Loi, 1049 Brussels; tel. (2) 299-11-11; fax (2) 299-17-61; e-mail agri-library@ec.europa.eu; internet ec.europa.eu/dgs/agriculture; Dir-Gen. JERZY B. PŁEWA.

Directorate-General for Budget: 45 ave d'Auderghem, 1049 Brussels; tel. (2) 299-11-11; fax (2) 295-95-85; e-mail budget@ec.europa.eu; internet ec.europa.eu/dgs/budget; Dir-Gen. HERVÉ JOUANJEAN.

Directorate-General for Climate Action: 200 rue de la Loi, 1049 Brussels; e-mail ec.europa.eu/dgs/clima/contact_en.htm (contact form); internet ec.europa.eu/clima/news; f. Feb. 2010; Dir-Gen. JOS DELBEKE.

Directorate-General for Communications Networks, Content and Technology (DG Connect): 200 rue de la Loi, 1049 Brussels; tel. (2) 299-93-99; fax (2) 298-55-90; e-mail cnect-desk@ec.europa.eu; internet ec.europa.eu/dgs/connect/index_en.htm; Dir-Gen. PAUL ROBERT MADELIN.

Directorate-General for Competition: Place Madou 1, 1049 Brussels; tel. (2) 299-11-11; fax (2) 295-01-28; e-mail infocomp@ec.europa.eu; internet ec.europa.eu/dgs/competition; f. 1958; Dir-Gen. ALEXANDER ITALIANER.

Directorate-General for Economic and Financial Affairs: Ave de Beaulieu 1, 1160 Brussels; tel. (2) 299-11-11; fax (2) 298-08-23; e-mail staffdir@ec.europa.eu; internet ec.europa.eu/economy_finance; Dir-Gen. MARCO BUTI.

Directorate-General for Education and Culture: 70 rue Joseph II, 1049 Brussels; tel. (2) 299-11-11; fax (2) 295-60-85; e-mail eac-info@ec.europa.eu; internet ec.europa.eu/dgs/education_culture; Dir-Gen. JAN TRUSZCZYŃSKI.

Directorate-General for Employment, Social Affairs and Inclusion: 200 rue de la Loi, 1049 Brussels; tel. (2) 299-11-11; e-mail ec.europa.eu/social/contact (contact form); internet ec.europa.eu/social; Dir-Gen. MICHEL SERVOZ.

Directorate-General for Energy: 200 rue de la Loi, 1049 Brussels; tel. (2) 299-11-11; fax (2) 295-01-50; e-mail ec.europa.eu/energy/contact/index_en.htm (contact form); internet ec.europa.eu/energy; Dir-Gen. DOMINIQUE RISTORI.

Directorate-General for Health and Consumers: 4 rue Breydel, 1049 Brussels; tel. (2) 299-11-11; fax (2) 296-62-98; e-mail sanco-mailbox@ec.europa.eu; internet ec.europa.eu/dgs/health_consumer; Dir-Gen. PAULA TESTORI COGGI.

Directorate-General for Home Affairs: 46 rue du Luxembourg, 1050 Brussels; tel. (2) 299-11-11; fax (2) 296-74-81; e-mail forename.surname@ec.europa.eu; internet ec.europa.eu/dgs/home-affairs; Dir-Gen. STEFANO MANSERVISI.

Directorate-General for Internal Market and Services: 2 rue de Spa, 1000 Brussels; tel. (2) 299-11-11; e-mail markt-info@ec.europa.eu; internet ec.europa.eu/dgs/internal_market; Dir-Gen. JONATHAN FAULL.

Directorate-General for Justice: 200 rue de la Loi, 1049 Brussels; tel. (2) 299-11-11; fax (2) 296-74-81; e-mail forename.surname@ec.europa.eu; internet ec.europa.eu/justice; Dir-Gen. FRANÇOISE LE BAIL.

Directorate-General for Maritime Affairs and Fisheries: 99 rue de Joseph II, 1000 Brussels; tel. (2) 299-11-11; fax (2) 299-30-40; e-mail fisheries-info@ec.europa.eu; internet ec.europa.eu/dgs/maritimeaffairs_fisheries; Dir-Gen. LOWRI EVANS.

Directorate-General for Mobility and Transport (DG Move): 24–28 rue Demot, 1040 Brussels; tel. (2) 299-11-11; fax (2) 295-01-50; e-mail move-infos@ec.europa.eu; internet ec.europa.eu/transport; Dir-Gen. ALFRED MATTHIAS RUETE.

Directorate-General for Regional and Urban Policy: 1 ave de Beaulieu, 1160 Brussels; tel. (2) 299-11-11; fax (2) 296-60-03; e-mail regio-info@ec.europa.eu; internet ec.europa.eu/dgs/regional_policy; Dir-Gen. WALTER DEFFAA.

Directorate-General for Research and Innovation: 21 rue du Champ de Mars, 1050 Brussels; tel. (2) 299-11-11; fax (2) 295-82-20; e-mail research@cec.eu.int; internet ec.europa.eu/research; Dir-Gen. ROBERT-JAN SMITS.

Enterprise and Industry Directorate-General: 45 ave d'Auderghem, 1049 Brussels; tel. (2) 299-11-11; fax (2) 296-99-30; e-mail entr-general-information@ec.europa.eu; internet ec.europa.eu/enterprise; Dir-Gen. DANIEL CALLEJA CRESPO.

Environment Directorate-General: 5 ave de Beaulieu, 1160 Brussels; tel. (2) 299-11-11; fax (2) 299-11-05; e-mail envinfo@ec.europa.eu; internet ec.europa.eu/environment; Dir-Gen. KARL-FRIEDRICH FALKENBERG.

Taxation and the Customs Union Directorate-General: 79 rue Joseph II, 1000 Brussels; tel. (2) 299-11-11; fax (2) 295-07-56; e-mail librarian-information@ec.europa.eu; internet ec.europa.eu/taxation_customs; Dir-Gen. HEINZ ZOUREK.

External Relations

Directorate-General for Enlargement: 15 rue de la Loi, 1049 Brussels; tel. (2) 299-11-11; fax (2) 296-84-90; e-mail elarg-info@ec.europa.eu; internet ec.europa.eu/enlargement; Dir-Gen. CHRISTIAN DANIELSSON.

Directorate-General for Trade (DG Trade): 170 rue de la Loi, 1049 Brussels; tel. (2) 299-11-11; fax (2) 299-10-29; e-mail trade-unit3@ec.europa.eu; internet ec.europa.eu/trade; Dir-Gen. JEAN-LUC DEMARTY.

Directorate-General for Development and Co-operation (EuropeAid): 41 rue de la Loi, 1040 Brussels; tel. (2) 299-35-20; fax (2) 296-49-26; e-mail development@ec.europa.eu; internet ec.europa.eu/europeaid; Dir-Gen. FERNANDO FRUTUOSO DE MELO.

Humanitarian Aid and Civil Protection Office (ECHO): 88 rue d'Arlon, 1040 Brussels; tel. (2) 299-11-11; fax (2) 295-45-44; e-mail echo-info@ec.europa.eu; internet ec.europa.eu/echo; Dir-Gen. CLAUS SØRENSEN.

Service for Foreign Policy Instruments: 200 rue de la Loi, 1049 Brussels; tel. (2) 584-11-11; e-mail fpi-intranet-updates@ec.europa.eu; internet ec.europa.eu/dgs/fpi; Dir TUNG-LAI MARGUE.

General Services

Directorate-General for Communication: 200 rue de la Loi, 1049 Brussels; tel. (2) 299-11-11; fax (2) 295-01-43; e-mail comm-web@ec.europa.eu; internet ec.europa.eu/dgs/communication; Dir-Gen. GREGORY PAULGER.

European Anti-Fraud Office: 30 rue Joseph II, 1000 Brussels; tel. (2) 299-11-11; fax (2) 296-08-53; e-mail olaf-courrier@ec.europa.eu; internet ec.europa.eu/anti_fraud; Dir-Gen. GIOVANNI KESSLER.

Eurostat (Statistical Office of the European Communities): Bâtiment Joseph Bech, 11 rue Alphonse Weicker, 2721 Luxembourg; tel. 43-01-33-444; fax 43-01-35-349; e-mail eurostat-pressoffice@ec.europa.eu; internet epp.eurostat.ec.europa.eu; Dir-Gen. WALTER RADERMACHER.

Joint Research Centre (JRC): 200 rue de la Loi, 1049 Brussels; tel. (2) 299-11-11; fax (2) 295-01-46; e-mail jrc-info@ec.europa.eu; internet ec.europa.eu/dgs/jrc/index.cfm; Dir-Gen. VLADIMIR ŠUCHA.

Office for Official Publications of the European Communities (Publications Office): 2 rue Mercier, 2985 Luxembourg; tel. (2) 29-29-43-210; fax (2) 29-29-44-604; e-mail info@publications.europa.eu; internet www.publications.europa.eu; Dir-Gen. MARTINE REICHERTS.

Secretariat-General: 200 rue de la Loi, 1049 Brussels; tel. (2) 299-11-11; fax (2) 296-05-54; e-mail sg-info@ec.europa.eu; internet ec.europa.eu/dgs/secretariat_general; Sec.-Gen. CATHERINE DAY.

Internal Services

Bureau of European Policy Advisers (BEPA): 200 rue de la Loi, 1049 Brussels; tel. (2) 299-11-11; fax (2) 295-23-05; e-mail bepa-info@ec.europa.eu; internet ec.europa.eu/dgs/policy_advisers; Head JEAN-CLAUDE THÉBAULT.

Data Protection Officer of the European Commission: 1049 Brussels; tel. (2) 226-87-50; fax (2) 296-38-91; e-mail data-protection-officer@ec.europa.eu; internet ec.europa.eu/dataprotectionofficer; Data Protection Officer PHILIPPE RENAUDIÈRE.

Directorate-General for Human Resources and Security: 200 rue de la Loi, 1049 Brussels; tel. (2) 299-11-11; fax (2) 299-62-76; e-mail forename.surname@ec.europa.eu; internet ec.europa.eu/dgs/human-resources/index_en.htm; Dir-Gen. IRÈNE SOUKA.

Directorate-General for Informatics (DIGIT): rue Alcide de Gasperi, 2920 Luxembourg; tel. (2) 299-11-11; e-mail digit-europa@ec.europa.eu; internet ec.europa.eu/dgs/informatics; Dir-Gen. STEPHEN QUEST.

Directorate-General for Interpretation: 100 rue Belliard, 1040 Brussels; tel. (2) 299-11-11; e-mail scic-euroscic@ec.europa.eu; internet ec.europa.eu/dgs/scic; Head of Service MARCO BENEDETTI.

Directorate-General for Translation (DGT): 1 rue de Genève, 1140 Brussels; tel. (2) 299-11-11; fax (2) 296-97-69; e-mail dgt-webmaster@ec.europa.eu; internet ec.europa.eu/dgs/translation; Dir-Gen. RYTIS MARTIKONIS.

European Personnel Selection Office (EPSO): Ave de Cortenbergh 80, 1049 Brussels; tel. (2) 299-31-31; fax (2) 295-74-88; internet europa.eu/epso; Dir NICHOLAS D. BEARFIELD.

Internal Audit Service (IAS): 200 rue de la Loi, 1049 Brussels; tel. (2) 299-11-11; fax (2) 295-41-40; e-mail ias-europa@ec.europa.eu; internet ec.europa.eu/dgs/internal_audit/index_en.htm; Internal Auditor of the European Commission PHILIPPE TAVERNE.

Legal Service: 200 rue de la Loi, 1049 Brussels; tel. (2) 299-11-11; fax (2) 296-30-86; e-mail oib-info@ec.europa.eu; internet ec.europa.eu/dgs/legal_service; Dir-Gen. LUIS ROMERO REQUENA.

Office for the Administration and Payment of Individual Entitlements (PMO): 27 rue de la Science, 1049 Brussels; fax (2) 299-11-11; internet ec.europa.eu/pmo; Dir MARC LEMAÎTRE.

Office for Infrastructure and Logistics in Brussels (OIB): 23 rue Père de Deken, 1049 Brussels; tel. (2) 296-44-52; fax (2) 296-43-10; e-mail oib-info@ec.europa.eu; internet ec.europa.eu/oib/index_en.htm; Dir MARC MOULIGNEAU (acting).

Office for Infrastructure and Logistics in Luxembourg (OIL): Jean Monnet bldg, rue Alcide de Gasperi, 2920 Luxembourg; e-mail oil-cad@ec.europa.eu; internet ec.europa.eu/oil/index_en.htm; Dir MARIAN O'LEARY.

EUROPEAN COUNCIL

Address: Justus Lipsius Bldg, 175 rue de la Loi, 1048 Brussels, Belgium.

Telephone: (2) 281-61-11; **fax:** (2) 281-69-34; **internet:** www.european-council.europa.eu.

The European Council was the name used to describe summit meetings of the heads of state or of government of the EU member states, their ministers responsible for foreign affairs, and senior officials of the European Commission. The Council met at least twice a year, in the member state that exercised the Presidency of the Council of the European Union, or in Brussels. Until 1975 summit meetings were held less frequently, on an ad hoc basis, usually to adopt major policy decisions regarding the future development of the Community. In answer to the evident need for more frequent consultation at the highest level, it was decided at the summit meeting held in Paris, France, in December 1974 to convene the meetings on a regular basis, under the rubric of the European Council. There was no provision made for the existence of the European Council in the Treaty of Rome, but its position was acknowledged and regularized in the Single European Act (1987). Its role was further strengthened in the Treaty on European Union, which entered into force on 1 November 1993. As a result of the Treaty, the European Council became directly responsible for common policies within the fields of common foreign and security policy and justice and home affairs.

Under the Treaty of Lisbon, which came into force at the beginning of December 2009, the European Council became an institution shaping the EU's development and defining its political priorities. In November, prior to the entry into force of the Treaty, an informal meeting of EU heads of state and of government had elected Herman Van Rompuy of Belgium to the new position of President of the European Council, for a period of two years and six months, renewable once. He took office upon the entry into force of the Treaty; in March 2012 Van Rompuy was appointed for a second term of office, which commenced on 1 June. The European Council comprises the heads of state or of government of the member states, together with its President and the President of the Commission; the High Representative of the Union for Foreign Affairs and Security Policy is also involved in the activities of the European Council, which performs no legislative function, and meets twice every six months, as convened by its President. If required, the President may convene special meetings of the European Council.

COUNCIL OF THE EUROPEAN UNION

Address: Justus Lipsius Bldg, 175 rue de la Loi, 1048 Brussels, Belgium.

Telephone: (2) 281-61-11; **fax:** (2) 281-73-97; **e-mail:** press.office@consilium.europa.eu; **internet:** www.consilium.europa.eu.

The Council of the European Union (until November 1993 known formally as the Council of Ministers of the European Communities and still sometimes referred to as the Council of Ministers) is the only institution that directly represents the member states. It is the EU's principal decision-making body, acting, as a rule, only on proposals made by the Commission, and has six main responsibilities: to approve EU legislation (in many fields it legislates jointly with the European Parliament); to co-ordinate the broad economic policies of the member states; to conclude international agreements between the EU and one or more states or international organizations; to approve the EU budget (in conjunction with the European Parliament); to develop the EU's Common Foreign and Security Policy, on the basis of guidelines drawn up by the European Council; and to co-ordinate co-operation between the national courts and police forces in criminal matters. The Council is composed of representatives of the member states, each Government delegating to it one of its members, according to the subject to be discussed (the Council has 10 different configurations). These meetings are generally referred to as the Agriculture and Fisheries Council, the Transport, Telecommunications and Energy Council, etc. The General Affairs and External

Relations Council, the Economic and Financial Affairs Council and the Agriculture and Fisheries Council each normally meet once a month. The Presidency is exercised for a term of six months by each member of the Council in rotation. A new, fixed 18-month troika system (groups of three presidencies) was introduced under the Treaty of Lisbon, which entered into force on 1 December 2009. The upcoming group of presidencies is as follows: Italy, July–December 2014; Latvia, January–July 2015; Luxembourg, July–December 2015. The troika shares the presidencies of most configurations of the Council, with the aim of facilitating overall co-ordination and continuity of work.

The Treaty of Rome prescribed three types of voting (depending on the issue under discussion): simple majority; qualified majority; and unanimity. Amendments to the Treaty of Rome (the Single European Act), effective from July 1987, restricted the right of veto, and were expected to accelerate the development of a genuine common market: they allowed proposals relating to the dismantling of barriers to the free movement of goods, persons, services and capital to be approved by a majority vote in the Council, rather than by a unanimous vote. Unanimity was still required, however, for certain areas, including harmonization of indirect taxes, legislation on health and safety, veterinary controls, and environmental protection; individual states retained control over immigration rules and the prevention of terrorism and of drugs-trafficking. The Treaty of Amsterdam, which came into force on 1 May 1999, extended the use of qualified majority voting (QMV) to a number of areas previously subject to unanimous decision. Under the terms of the Treaty of Nice, which came into force on 1 February 2003, a further range of areas (mostly minor in nature and relating to appointments to various EU institutions) that had previously been subject to national vetoes became subject to QMV. With the expansion of the EU to 25 members in 2004, and subsequently to 27 members in 2007 and to 28 members in 2013, and the consequent reduced likelihood of unanimity in Council decisions, the use of QMV in an even broader range of decisions was intended to minimize so-called policy drag. The 2009 Lisbon Treaty provided for the further extension of QMV, which was newly defined, to areas that had previously been subject to national vetoes (from 2014, see below).

The Single European Act introduced a 'co-operation procedure' whereby a proposal adopted by a qualified majority in the Council must be submitted to the European Parliament for approval: if the Parliament rejects the Council's common position, unanimity shall be required for the Council to act on a second reading, and, if the Parliament suggests amendments, the Commission must re-examine the proposal and forward it to the Council again. A 'co-decision procedure' was introduced in 1993 by the Treaty on European Union. The procedure allowed a proposal to be submitted for a third reading by a so-called Conciliation Committee, composed equally of Council representatives and members of the European Parliament. The Treaty of Amsterdam simplified the co-decision procedure, and extended it to matters previously resolved under the co-operation procedure, although the latter remained in place for matters concerning economic and monetary union.

Under the Treaty of Amsterdam, the Secretary-General of the Council also took the role of High Representative, responsible for the co-ordination of the common foreign and security policy. The Council Secretary-General is supported by a policy planning and early warning unit.

The Treaty of Nice addressed institutional issues that remained outstanding under the Treaty of Amsterdam and that had to be settled before the enlargement of the EU in 2004, and various other issues not directly connected with enlargement. The main focus of the Treaty was the establishment of principles governing the new distribution of seats in the European Parliament, the new composition of the Commission and a new definition of QMV within the Council of the European Union. From 1 May 2004 (when the 10 accession states joined the EU) until 31 October, there were transitional arrangements for changing the weighting of votes in the Council. In accordance with the provisions incorporated in the Treaty of Nice, from 1 November the new weighting system was as follows: France, Germany, Italy and the United Kingdom 29 votes each; Poland and Spain 27 votes each; the Netherlands 13 votes; Belgium, the Czech Republic, Greece, Hungary and Portugal 12 votes each; Austria and Sweden 10 votes each; Denmark, Finland, Ireland, Lithuania and Slovakia seven votes each; Cyprus, Estonia, Latvia, Luxembourg and Slovenia four votes each; and Malta three votes. A qualified majority was reached if a majority of member states (in some cases a two-thirds' majority) approved and if a minimum of 232 votes out of a total of 321 was cast in favour (which was 72.3% of the total—approximately the same share as under the previous system). In addition, a member state could request confirmation that the votes in favour represented at least 62% of the total population of the EU. Should this not be the case, the decision would not be adopted by the Council. The number of weighted votes required for the adoption of a decision (referred to as the 'qualified majority threshold') was to be reassessed on the accession of any additional new member state. Accordingly, in January 2007, with the accession of Romania and Bulgaria, which were allocated, respectively, 14 and 10 votes, the 'qualified majority threshold' was increased to 255 votes, which represented 73.9% of the new total of 345 votes. It was widely purported that the voting system according to the Treaty of Nice was overly complicated and that it gave undue power to certain less populous countries, notably Spain and Poland (which both held 27 votes each, compared with Germany, which, with a population of at least twice the size of those in Spain and Poland, controlled 29 votes). In July 2013, with the accession of Croatia (which was allocated seven votes), the qualified majority threshold was raised to 260 votes, which continued to represent 73.9% of the increased total of 352, to be cast by at least 15 member states. A member state may, additionally, demand evidence that the qualified majority represents at least 62% of the EU's population.

Reforms approved under the 2009 Treaty of Lisbon provided for the extension and redefinition of QMV in the Council of the European Union and the ending of the system of national vetoes in a number of further policy areas (including combating climate change, energy, emergency aid, and security). From November 2014 a qualified majority was to be defined as representing at least 55% of the members of the Council, composed of at least 16 of them and representing member states comprising at least 65% of the EU's population (although a blocking minority would have to include at least four member states). However, in cases where the Council is not acting on the basis of a Commission proposal, the qualified majority threshold is to be 72% of the members of the Council (that is, 21 member states), representing at least 65% of the EU population. The Lisbon Treaty includes a provision allowing the European Council to agree, by unanimity and subject to prior unanimous approval by national legislatures, to introduce QMV in an area currently requiring unanimity (except in a small number of areas including defence, foreign policy and taxation), thus obviating the need for treaty change.

GENERAL SECRETARIAT

Secretary-General of the Council of the European Union: Uwe Corsepius (Germany).

Secretary-General's Private Office: Head of Cabinet Marek Mora.

Legal Service: Dir-Gen./Legal Adviser Hubert Legal.

Directorates-General:

A (Administration): Dir-Gen. William Shapcott.

B (Agriculture, Fisheries, Social Affairs and Health): Dir-Gen. Ángel Boixareu Carrera.

C (Foreign Affairs, Enlargement and Civil Protection): Dir-Gen. Leonardo Schiavo.

D (Justice and Home Affairs): Dir-Gen. Rafael Fernández-Pita y González.

E (Environment, Education, Transport and Energy): Dir-Gen. Jarosław Pietras.

F (Communication and Transparency): Dir-Gen. Reijo Kempinnen.

G (Economic Affairs and Competitiveness): Dir-Gen. Carsten Pillath.

PERMANENT REPRESENTATIVES OF MEMBER STATES

Austria: Walter Grahammer; 30 ave de Cortenberg, 1040 Brussels; tel. (2) 234-51-00; fax (2) 235-63-00; e-mail bruessel-ov@bmeia.gv.at.

Belgium: Dirk Wouters; 61–63 rue de la Loi, 1040 Brussels; tel. (2) 233-21-11; fax (2) 231-10-75; e-mail dispatch.belgoeurop@diplobel.fed.be.

Bulgaria: Dimiter Tzantchev; 49 sq. Marie-Louise, 1000 Brussels; tel. (2) 235-83-01; fax (2) 374-91-88; e-mail info@bg-permrep.eu; internet www.bg-permrep.eu.

Croatia: Mato Škrabalo; 50 ave des Arts, 1000 Brussels; tel. (2) 507-54-11; fax (2) 646-56-64; e-mail hr.perm.rep@mvep.hr; internet eu.mfa.hr.

Cyprus: Kornelios S. Korneliou; 61 ave de Cortenberg, 1000 Brussels; tel. (2) 739-51-11; fax (2) 735-45-52; e-mail cy.perm.rep@mfa.gov.cy.

Czech Republic: Martin Povejsil; 15 rue Caroly, 1050 Brussels; tel. (2) 213-91-11; fax (2) 213-91-86; e-mail eu.brussels@embassy.mzv.cz; internet www.czechrep.be.

Denmark: Jeppe Tranholm-Mikkelsen; 73 rue d'Arlon, 1040 Brussels; tel. (2) 233-08-11; fax (2) 230-93-84; e-mail brurep@um.dk.

Estonia: Matti Maasikas; 11–13 rue Guimard, 1040 Brussels; tel. (2) 227-39-10; fax (2) 227-39-25; e-mail firstname.surname@mfa.ee; internet www.eu.estemb.be.

Finland: Pilvi-Sisko Vierros-Villeneuve; 100 rue de Trèves, 1040 Brussels; tel. (2) 287-84-11; fax (2) 287-84-05; e-mail sanomat.eue@formin.fi; internet www.finland.eu.

France: PHILIPPE ETIENNE; 14 place de Louvain, 1000 Brussels; tel. (2) 229-82-11; fax (2) 230-99-50; e-mail courrier.bruxelles-dfra@diplomatie.gouv.fr; internet www.rpfrance.org.

Germany: PETER TEMPEL; 8–14 rue Jacques de Lalaing, 1040 Brussels; tel. (2) 787-10-00; fax (2) 787-20-00; e-mail info@eu-vertretung.de; internet www.eu-vertretung.de.

Greece: THEODOROS N. SOTIROPOULOS; 19–21 rue Jacques de Lalaing, 1040 Brussels; tel. (2) 551-56-11; fax (2) 551-56-51; e-mail mea.bruxelles@rp-grece.be; internet www.greekembassy-press.be.

Hungary: PÉTER GYÖRKÖS; 92–98 rue de Trèves, 1040 Brussels; tel. (2) 234-12-00; fax (2) 230-43-51; e-mail sec.beu@mfa.gov.hu; internet www.hunrep.be.

Ireland: DECLAN KELLEHER; 50 rue Froissart, 1040 Brussels; tel. (2) 230-85-80; fax (2) 230-32-03; e-mail irlprb@dfa.ie; internet www.irelandrepbrussels.be.

Italy: STEFANO SANNINO; 5–11 rue du Marteau, 1000 Brussels; tel. (2) 220-04-11; fax (2) 219-34-49; e-mail rpue@rpue.esteri.it; internet www.italiaue.esteri.it.

Latvia: ILZE JUHANSONE; 23 ave des Arts, 1000 Brussels; tel. (2) 238-31-00; fax (2) 238-32-50; e-mail permrep.eu@mfa.gov.lv; internet www.mfa.gov.lv/brussels.

Lithuania: RAIMUNDAS KAROBLIS; 41–43 rue Belliard, 1040 Brussels; tel. (2) 771-01-40; fax (2) 401-98-77; e-mail office@eurep.mfa.lt; internet www.eurep.mfa.lt.

Luxembourg: CHRISTIAN BRAUN; 75 ave de Cortenberg, 1000 Brussels; tel. (2) 737-56-00; fax (2) 737-56-10; e-mail forename.surname@mae.etat.lu.

Malta: MARLENE BONNICI; 25 rue d'Archimède, 1000 Brussels; tel. (2) 343-01-95; fax (2) 343-01-06; e-mail maltarep@gov.mt.

Netherlands: PIETER DE GOOIJER; 4–10 ave de Cortenberg, 1040 Brussels; tel. (2) 679-15-11; fax (2) 679-17-75; e-mail bre@minbuza.nl; internet www.eu-nederland.be.

Poland: MAREK PRAWDA; 139 rue Stevin, 1000 Brussels; tel. (2) 780-42-00; fax (2) 780-42-97; e-mail bebrustpe@msz.gov.pl; internet www.brukselaeu.polemb.net.

Portugal: DOMINGOS FEZAS VITAL; 12 ave de Cortenberg, 1040 Brussels; tel. (2) 286-42-11; fax (2) 231-00-26; e-mail reper@reper-portugal.be; internet www.reper-portugal.be.

Romania: MIHNEA IOAN MOTOC; 12 rue Montoyer, 1000 Brussels; tel. (2) 700-06-40; fax (2) 700-06-41; e-mail bru@rpro.eu; internet www.ue.mae.ro.

Slovakia: IVAN KORČOK; 79 ave de Cortenberg, 1000 Brussels; tel. (2) 743-68-11; fax (2) 743-68-88; e-mail eu.brussels@mzv.sk; internet www.mzv.sk/szbrusel.

Slovenia: RADO GENORIO; 44 rue du Commerce, 1000 Brussels; tel. (2) 213-63-00; fax (2) 213-63-01; e-mail spbr@gov.si; internet www.mzz.gov.si.

Spain: ALFONSO DASTIS QUECEDO; 52 blvd du Régent, 1000 Brussels; tel. (2) 509-86-11; fax (2) 511-19-40; e-mail reper.bruselasue@reper.maec.es; internet www.es-ue.org.

Sweden: ANDERS AHNLID; 30 place de Meeûs, 1000 Brussels; tel. (2) 289-56-45; fax (2) 289-56-00; e-mail anders.ahnlid@gov.se; internet www.sweden.gov.se/sb/d/2250.

United Kingdom: IVAN ROGERS; 10 ave d'Auderghem, 1040 Brussels; tel. (2) 287-82-11; fax (2) 282-89-00; e-mail ukrep@fco.gov.uk; internet ukeu.fco.gov.uk/en.

Preparation and co-ordination of the Council's work (with the exception of agricultural issues, which are handled by the Special Committee on Agriculture) is entrusted to a Committee of Permanent Representatives, which meets in Brussels on a weekly basis and which comprises the permanent representatives of the member countries to the Union (who have senior ambassadorial status). A staff of national civil servants assists each ambassador.

EUROPEAN EXTERNAL ACTION SERVICE—EEAS

Address: Capital Bldg, Rond-point Schuman, 1000 Brussels, Belgium.

Telephone: (2) 584-11-11; **internet:** www.eeas.europa.eu.

The Treaty of Lisbon, which entered into force at the beginning of December 2009, created the new position of High Representative of the Union for Foreign Affairs and Security, to which Catherine Ashton was appointed for a five-year term. In July 2010 the European Parliament approved the creation of the European External Action Service (EEAS), which was formally established at the beginning of December, as the EU's foreign policy and diplomatic service. The High Representative of the Union for Foreign Affairs and Security Policy, who is also a Vice-President of the Commission, is responsible for the co-ordination of the EEAS, and chairs monthly meetings of the Foreign Affairs Council, which comprises EU ministers responsible for foreign affairs, for defence and for development. The EEAS, an independent body, incorporated functions of the Commission and the Council that had hitherto been responsible for foreign affairs, and has its own budget. The EEAS comprises seven departments, each headed by a managing director: (i) Asia and the Pacific; (ii) Africa; (iii) Europe and Central Asia; (iv) North Africa, Middle East, Arabian Peninsula, Iran and Iraq; (v) Americas; (vi) global and multilateral issues; and (vii) crisis response and operational co-ordination.

High Representative of the Union for Foreign Affairs and Security Policy: CATHERINE ASHTON (United Kingdom).

Executive Secretary-General: PIERRE VIMONT (France).

Chief Operating Officer: DAVID O'SULLIVAN (Ireland).

EUROPEAN PARLIAMENT

Address: Centre Européen, Plateau du Kirchberg, BP 1601, 2929 Luxembourg.

Telephone: 4300-1; **fax:** 4300-22457; **internet:** www.europarl.europa.eu.

PRESIDENT AND MEMBERS

President: MARTIN SCHULZ (Germany).

Members: Members of the Parliament are elected for a five-year term by direct universal suffrage and proportional representation by the citizens of the member states. Members sit in the Chamber in transnational political, not national, groups. The Parliament elected in June 2009 was initially composed of 736 members; the Treaty of Lisbon, which entered into force on 1 December 2009, however, makes provision for a total of 751 seats.

The European Parliament has three main roles: sharing with the Council of the European Union the power to legislate; holding authority over the annual Union budget (again, jointly with the Council), including the power to adopt or reject it in its entirety; and exercising a measure of democratic control over the executive organs of the EU, the Commission and the Council. Notably, it has the power to dismiss the European Commission as a whole by a vote of censure (requiring a two-thirds' majority of the votes cast, which must also be a majority of the total parliamentary membership). The Parliament does not exercise the authority, however, to dismiss individual Commissioners. Increases in parliamentary powers were brought about through amendments to the Treaty of Rome. The Single European Act, which entered into force on 1 July 1987, introduced, in certain circumstances where the Council normally adopts legislation through majority voting, a co-operation procedure involving a second parliamentary reading, enabling the Parliament to amend legislation. EU agreements with third countries require parliamentary approval. The Treaty on European Union, which came into force in November 1993, introduced the co-decision procedure, permitting a third parliamentary reading (see the Council of the European Union). The Treaty also gives the Parliament the right potentially to veto legislation, and allows it to approve or reject the nomination of Commissioners (including the President of the Commission). The Parliament appoints the European Ombudsman from among its members, who investigates reports of maladministration in EU institutions. The Treaty of Amsterdam, which entered into force in May 1999, expanded and simplified the Parliament's legislative role. The co-decision procedure between the Parliament and the Council was extended into a wider range of policy areas. The Treaty also stipulated that the President of the Commission must be formally approved by the Parliament. In addition, international agreements, treaty decisions and the accession of new member states all require the assent of the Parliament. The Treaty of Nice, which came into force in February 2003, further extended the use of co-decision and introduced a new distribution of seats in the Parliament. The Treaty of Lisbon again extended the Parliament's right of co-decision with the Council, and made provision for a maximum number of seats of 751 (750 voting members and the President), with each member state being entitled to a minimum of six and a maximum of 96 seats, on a proportional basis (see below). Under the Treaty 18 additional seats were allocated to 12 member states, while Germany was to lose three of its former seats.

The Parliament elected in June 2009, prior to the entry into force of the Lisbon Treaty in December, initially comprised the 736 members provided for by the Nice Treaty. However, in December 2008 EU heads of state and of government had agreed a compromise composition for the 2009–14 Parliament, which was to comprise the 736 members elected in June 2009 (including the three extra German representatives elected legitimately under the terms of the Nice Treaty), plus the 18 additional members provided for by the Lisbon Treaty, thereby temporarily raising the total number of members to 754. In order to enable the 18 additional members (who would technically hold observer status, to enable their participation in the 2009–14 Parliament) to assume their responsibilities, a transitional change to the Lisbon Treaty was required. On 17 June 2010 the European Council agreed to launch an Intergovernmental Conference to negotiate the required amendment. The amendment was adopted six days later, subject to ratification by the national legislatures of member states. Ratification was completed in November 2011, and the amendment entered into force on 1 December.

The distribution of seats among the 27 members provided for by the Lisbon Treaty is as follows: Germany 96 members (with, exceptionally, 99, in accordance with the provisions of the Nice Treaty, to hold seats during 2009–14); France 74 (compared with 72 provided for under the Nice Treaty); the United Kingdom 73 (including one additional member); Italy 73 (one additional member); Spain 54 (four); Poland 51 (one); Romania 33; the Netherlands 26 (one); Portugal (one), Belgium, the Czech Republic, Greece and Hungary 22 each; Sweden 20 (two additional members); Austria 19 (two); Bulgaria 18 (one additional member); Denmark, Finland and Slovakia 13 each; Ireland and Lithuania 12 each; Latvia nine (one); Slovenia eight (one); and Malta (with one additional member), Cyprus, Estonia and Luxembourg six each. In April 2013 Croatia held its first elections to the Parliament, to select 12 members to serve until new parliamentary elections in May 2014.

Political Groups

	Distribution of seats (July 2013)
Group of the European People's Party (Christian Democrats) (EPP)	275
Group of the Progressive Alliance of Socialists and Democrats (S/D)	195
Group of the Alliance of Liberals and Democrats for Europe (ALDE)	84
Group of the Greens/European Free Alliance (Verts/EFA)	58
European Conservatives and Reformists Group (ECR)	56
Confederal Group of the European United Left/ Nordic Green Left (GUE/NGL)	36
Europe of Freedom and Democracy Group (EFD)	33
Non-affiliated (NA)	29
Total	766

With effect from June 2009 the minimum number of members required to form a political group under the Parliament's rules of procedure has been fixed at 25, from a minimum of seven member states (previously 20 members were required from a minimum of six member states).

The Parliament has an annual session, divided into around 12 one-week meetings, attended by all members and normally held in Strasbourg, France. The session opens with the March meeting. Committee meetings, political group meetings and additional plenary sittings of the Parliament are held in Brussels, Belgium, while the parliamentary administrative offices are based in Luxembourg.

The budgetary powers of the Parliament (which, together with the Council of the European Union, forms the Budgetary Authority of the EU) were increased to their present status by a treaty of 22 July 1975. Under this treaty the Parliament can amend non-agricultural spending and reject the draft budget, acting by a majority of its members and two-thirds of the votes cast. The Parliament debates the draft budget in two successive readings, and it does not come into force until it has been signed by the President of the Parliament. The Parliament's Committee on Budgetary Control monitors how the budget is spent, and each year the Parliament decides whether to approve the Commission's handling of the budget for the previous financial year (a process technically known as 'granting a discharge').

The Parliament is run by a Bureau comprising the President, 14 Vice-Presidents elected from its members by secret ballot to serve for two-and-a-half years, and the five members of the College of Quaestors. The Conference of Presidents is the political governing body of the Parliament, with responsibility for formulating the agenda for plenary sessions and the timetable for the work of parliamentary bodies, and for establishing the terms of reference and the size of committees and delegations. It comprises the President of the Parliament and the Chairmen of the political groups.

The majority of the Parliament's work is conducted by 20 Standing Parliamentary Committees, which correspond to different policy areas and various European Commission agencies: Foreign Affairs (including Human Rights and Security and Defence); Development; International Trade; Budgets; Budgetary Control; Economic and Monetary Affairs; Employment and Social Affairs; Environment, Public Health and Food Safety; Industry, Research and Energy; Internal Market and Consumer Protection; Transport and Tourism; Regional Development; Agriculture and Rural Development; Fisheries; Culture and Education; Legal Affairs; Civil Liberties, Justice and Home Affairs; Constitutional Affairs; Women's Rights and Gender Equality; Petitions.

The first direct elections to the European Parliament took place in June 1979, and Parliament met for the first time in July. The second elections were held in June 1984 (with separate elections held in Portugal and Spain in 1987, following the accession of these two countries), the third in June 1989, and the fourth in June 1994. Direct elections to the European Parliament were held in Sweden in September 1995, and in Austria and Finland in October 1996. The fifth European Parliament was elected in June 1999, and the sixth in June 2004, following the mass accession of 10 new member states in May of that year. Elections to the seventh European Parliament were held on 4–7 June 2009; the rate of participation by the electorate was 43.1%.

EUROPEAN OMBUDSMAN

Address: 1 ave du Président Robert Schuman, BP 30403, 67001 Strasbourg Cedex, France.

Telephone: 3-88-17-23-13; **fax:** 3-88-17-90-62; **e-mail:** euro-ombudsman@europarl.eu.int; **internet:** www.ombudsman.europa.eu.

The position was created by the Treaty on European Union (the Maastricht Treaty), and the first Ombudsman took office in July 1995. The Ombudsman is appointed by the European Parliament (from among its own members) for a renewable five-year term (to run concurrently with that of the European Parliament). The Ombudsman is authorized to receive complaints (from EU citizens, businesses and institutions, and from anyone residing or having their legal domicile in an EU member state) regarding maladministration in Community institutions and bodies (except in the Court of Justice and Court of First Instance), to make recommendations, and to refer any matters to the Parliament. The Ombudsman submits an annual report on their activities to the European Parliament.

European Ombudsman: EMILY O'REILLY (Ireland).

COURT OF JUSTICE OF THE EUROPEAN UNION

Address: Cour de justice de l'Union européenne, Blvd Konrad Adenauer, Kirchberg, 2925 Luxembourg.

Telephone: 4303-1; **fax:** 4303-2600; **e-mail:** info@curia.europa.eu; **internet:** curia.europa.eu.

As the EU's judicial institution, the Court of Justice acts as a safeguard of EU legislation and has jurisdiction over cases concerning member states, EU institutions, undertakings or individuals. EU legislation has been technically known as European Union law since the entry into force in December 2009 of the Treaty of Lisbon, which invested the EU with legal personality; prior to that it was known as Community law. The Court ensures uniform interpretation and application of European Union law throughout the EU. The 28 Judges and the eight Advocates-General are each appointed for a renewable term of six years. The role of the Advocates-General is—publicly and impartially—to deliver reasoned opinions on the cases brought before the Court. There is normally one Judge per member state, whose name is put forward by the Government of that member state. These proposed appointments are then subject to a vote in the Council of the European Union. For the sake of efficiency, when the Court holds a plenary session only 15 Judges—sitting as a 'Grand Chamber'—have to attend. The President of the Court, who has overall charge of the Court's work and presides at hearings and deliberations, is elected by the Judges from among their number for a renewable term of three years. The majority of cases are dealt with by one of the 10 chambers, each of which consists of a President of Chamber and three or four Judges. The Court may sit in plenary session in cases of particular importance or when a member state or Union institution that is a party to the proceedings so requests. Judgments are reached by a majority vote and are signed by all Judges involved in the case, irrespective of how they voted. The Court has jurisdiction to award damages. It may review the legality of acts (other than recommendations or opinions) of the Council, the Commission or the European Central Bank, of acts adopted jointly by the European Parliament and the Council, and of Acts adopted by the Parliament and intended to produce legal effects vis-à-vis third parties. It is also competent to give judgment on actions by a member state, the Council or the Commission on grounds of lack of competence, of infringement of an essential procedural requirement, of infringement of a Treaty or of any legal rule relating to its application, or of misuse of power. The Court of Justice may hear appeals, on a point of law only, from the Court of First Instance.

The Court is empowered to hear certain other cases concerning contractual and non-contractual liability and disputes between member states in connection with the objects of the Treaties. It also gives preliminary rulings at the request of national courts on the interpretation of the Treaties, of Union legislation, and of the Brussels Convention on Jurisdiction and the Enforcement of Judgments in Civil and Commercial Matters.

President of the Court of Justice: VASSILIOS SKOURIS (Greece).

Vice-President of the Court of Justcie: KOEN LENAERTS (Belgium).

Registrar: ALFREDO CALOT ESCOBAR (Spain).

GENERAL COURT

Address: Cour de justice de l'Union européenne, Blvd Konrad Adenauer, 2925 Luxembourg.

Telephone: 4303-1; **fax:** 4303-2600; **e-mail:** info@curia.europa.eu; **internet:** curia.europa.eu.

The General Court was established, as the Court of First Instance of the European Communities, by the European Council by a decision of October 1988, and began operations in 1989. Its current name was adopted following the entry into force of the Treaty of Lisbon on 1 December 2009. In order to help the Court of Justice to deal with the thousands of cases brought before it and to offer citizens better legal protection, the General Court (which, although independent, is attached to the Court of Justice) deals with cases brought by individuals, legal entities and member states against the actions of EU institutions. The decisions of the General Court may be subject to appeal to the Court of Justice, on issues of law, within two months. As with the Court of Justice, the composition of the General Court is based on 28 Judges (one from each member state, appointed for a renewable term of six years) and one President (elected from among the 28 Judges for a renewable period of three years); the General Court has eight chambers. The General Court has no permanent Advocates-General.

Within the framework of the Treaty of Nice, which provided for the creation of additional judicial panels in specific areas, in November 2004 the Council decided to establish the Civil Service Tribunal in order to reduce the number of cases brought before the Tribunal of First Instance. The specialized Tribunal, which had been fully constituted by December 2005, exercises jurisdiction in the first instance in disputes between the EU and its staff. Its decisions are subject to appeal on questions of law only to the General Court and, in exceptional cases, to review by the European Court of Justice. The Council appoints the Tribunal's seven Judges for a period of six years, and the President is elected by the Judges from among their number for a period of three years. The Council is charged with ensuring that as many member states as possible are represented in the Tribunal.

President of the General Court: MARC JAEGER (Luxembourg).

Registrar: EMMANUEL COULON (France).

President of the Civil Service Tribunal: SEAN VAN RAEPENBUSCH (Belgium).

EUROPEAN COURT OF AUDITORS—ECA

Address: 12 rue Alcide de Gasperi, 1615 Luxembourg.

Telephone: 4398-1; **fax:** 4393-42; **e-mail:** eca-info@eca.europa.eu; **internet:** www.eca.europa.eu.

The European Court of Auditors was created by the Treaty of Brussels, which was signed on 22 July 1975, and commenced its duties in late 1977. It was given the status of an institution on a par with the Commission, the Council, the Court of Justice and the Parliament by the Treaty on European Union. It is the institution responsible for the external audit of the resources managed by the EU. The entry into effect of the Treaty of Lisbon in 2009 confirmed the Court's mandate and status as an institution of the EU; in addition, the Treaty introduced changes to the way funds are managed. It consists of 28 members (one from each member state), who are appointed for renewable six-year terms (under a qualified majority voting system) by the Council of the European Union, after consultation with the European Parliament (in practice, however, the Council simply endorses the candidates put forward by the member states). The members elect the President of the Court from among their number for a renewable term of three years.

The Court is organized and acts as a collegiate body. It adopts its decisions by a majority of its members. Each member, however, has a direct responsibility for the audit of certain sectors of Union activities.

The Court examines the accounts of all expenditure and revenue of the EU and of any body created by them in so far as the relevant constituent instrument does not preclude such examination. It examines whether all revenue has been received and all expenditure incurred in a lawful and regular manner and whether the financial management has been sound. The audit is based on records, and if necessary is performed directly in the institutions of the Union, in the member states and in other countries. In the member states the audit is carried out in co-operation with the national audit bodies. The Court of Auditors draws up an annual report after the close of each financial year. The Court provides the European Parliament and the Council with a statement of assurance as to the reliability of the accounts, and the legality and regularity of the underlying transactions. It may also, at any time, submit observations on specific questions (usually in the form of special reports) and deliver opinions at the request of one of the institutions of the Union. It assists the Parliament and the Council in exercising their powers of control over the implementation of the budget, in particular within the framework of the annual discharge procedure, and gives its prior opinion on financial regulations, on the methods and procedure whereby budgetary revenue is made available to the Commission, and on the formulation of rules concerning the responsibility of authorizing officers and accounting officers and concerning appropriate arrangements for inspection.

President: VÍTOR MANUEL SILVA CALDEIRA (Portugal).

Secretary-General: EDUARDO RUIZ GARCÍA (Spanish).

EUROPEAN CENTRAL BANK—ECB

Address: Kaiserstr. 29, 60311 Frankfurt am Main, Germany; Postfach 160319, 60066 Frankfurt am Main, Germany.

Telephone: (69) 13440; **fax:** (69) 13446000; **e-mail:** info@ecb.europa.eu; **internet:** www.ecb.int/home/html/index.en.html.

The European Central Bank (ECB) was formally established on 1 June 1998, replacing the European Monetary Institute, which had been operational since January 1994. The Bank has the authority to issue the single currency, the euro, which replaced the European Currency Unit (ECU) on 1 January 1999, at the beginning of Stage III of Economic and Monetary Union (EMU), in accordance with the provisions of the Treaty on European Union (the Maastricht Treaty). One of the ECB's main tasks is to maintain price stability in the euro area or eurozone (i.e. in those member states that have adopted the euro as their national currency). This is achieved primarily by controlling the money supply and by monitoring price trends.

In mid-September 2012 the European Commission proposed that, in response to the crisis in the eurozone, and as part of plans for the introduction of a banking union, the powers of the ECB should be considerably expanded, to enable it to act as a so-called Single Supervisory Mechanism (SSM). In mid-December the Council endorsed plans for the SSM to hold responsibility for the supervision of some 200 majors banks (those with assets of more than €30,000m., or 20% of national gross domestic product) in operation throughout the eurozone. The SSM was to co-operate closely with national regulatory authorities, with the aim of safeguarding financial stability. In March 2013 the European Parliament and the Council reached political agreement on the SSM package, and in October the EU Council formally adopted a regulation on the creation of an ECB-led SSM, which was to commence operations in November 2014. An interinstitutional agreement with the European Parliament on the ECB's role within the framework of the SSM entered into force in November 2013. In mid-December Danièle Nouy was appointed as Chair of the Supervisory Board of the SSM, for a five-year term, from 1 January 2014. Meanwhile, in July 2013 the Commission had proposed a complementary Single Resolution Mechanism (SRM) to centralize the fundamental responsibilities and resources for managing failing banks in the eurozone, and throughout the banking union's member states. In March 2014 the European Parliament and the Council came to a provisional agreement on the proposed SSR

The Bank's leadership is provided by an Executive Board, appointed by common agreement of the presidents or prime ministers of the 18 eurozone countries for a non-renewable term of eight years (it should be noted that the Statute of the European System of Central Banks—ESCB—provides for a system of staggered appointments to the first Executive Board for members other than the President in order to ensure continuity). The Executive Board is responsible for the preparation of meetings of the Governing Council, the implementation of monetary policy in accordance with the guidelines and decisions laid down by the Governing Council and for the current business of the ECB. The ECB and the national central banks of all EU member states together comprise the ESCB. The Governing Council, which is the ECB's highest decision-making body and which consists of the six members of the Executive Board and the governors of the central banks of eurozone member countries, usually meets twice a month. The prime mission of the Governing Council is to define the monetary policy of the eurozone, and, in particular, to fix the interest rates at which the commercial banks can obtain money from the ECB. The General Council is the ECB's third decision-making body; it comprises the ECB's President, the Vice-President and the governors of the central banks of all EU member states.

President: MARIO DRAGHI (Italy).

Vice-President: VITOR MANUEL RIBEIRO CONSTÂNCIO (Portugal).

EUROPEAN INVESTMENT BANK—EIB

Address: 100 blvd Konrad Adenauer, 2950 Luxembourg.

Telephone: 4379-1; **fax:** 4377-04; **e-mail:** info@eib.org; **internet:** www.eib.org.

The European Investment Bank (EIB) is the EU's long-term financing institution, and was created in 1958 by the six founder member states of the European Economic Community. The shareholders are the member states of the EU, which have all subscribed to the bank's capital. The bulk of the EIB's resources comes from borrowings, principally public bond issues or private placements on capital markets inside and outside the Union. The EIB works on the basis of a three-year operational plan, which is approved by its Board of Directors and revised annually. The plan for 2012–14 aimed to respond to the consequences of the economic crisis, while pursuing an efficient transition to a more environmentally friendly, sustainable economy.

The EIB's principal task, defined by the Treaty of Rome (now known as the Treaty on the Functioning of the European Union), is to work on a non-profit basis, making or guaranteeing loans for investment projects that contribute to the balanced and steady development of EU member states. Throughout the Bank's history, priority has been given to financing investment projects that further regional development within the Union. The EIB also finances projects that improve communications, protect and improve the environment, promote urban development, strengthen the competitive position of industry and encourage industrial integration within the Union, support the activities of small and medium-sized enterprises (SMEs), and help to ensure the security of energy supplies. Following a recommendation of the Lisbon European Council in March 2000 for greater support for SMEs, the Board of Governors set up the EIB Group, consisting of the EIB and the European Investment Fund. Some 90% of EIB financing is allocated to projects within the EU, but the EIB also provides finance for developing countries in Africa, the Caribbean and the Pacific, under the terms of the Cotonou Agreement (see p. 324), the successor agreement to the Lomé Convention; for countries in the Mediterranean region, under a Euro-Mediterranean investment facility established in 2002; and for candidate and potential candidate countries. Lending outside the EU is usually based on Union agreements, but exceptions have been made for specific projects in certain countries, such as Russia.

The Board of Governors of the EIB, which usually meets once a year, lays down general directives on credit policy, approves the annual report and accounts and decides on capital increases. The Board of Directors meets once a month, and has sole power to take decisions in respect of loans, guarantees and borrowings. The Bank's President presides over meetings of the Board of Directors. The day-to-day management of operations is the responsibility of the Management Committee, which is the EIB's collegiate executive body and recommends decisions to the Board of Directors. The Audit Committee is an independent body, which reports to the Board of Governors regarding the management of operations and the maintenance of the Bank's accounts.

Board of Governors: The Board of Governors comprises one minister (usually the minister with responsibility for finance or economic affairs) from each member state.

Chair.: Edward Scicluna (Malta).

Board of Directors: The Board of Directors consists of 28 directors, appointed for a renewable five-year term, with one director appointed by each member state and one by the European Commission. There are 18 alternates, also appointed for a renewable five-year term, meaning that some of these positions will be shared by groupings of countries. Since 1 May 2004 decisions have been taken by a majority consisting of at least one-third of members entitled to vote and representing at least 50% of the subscribed capital.

Management Committee: Comprises the President and seven Vice-Presidents, nominated for a renewable six-year term by the Board of Directors and approved by the Board of Governors. The President presides over the meetings of the Management Committee but does not vote.

President: Werner Hoyer (Germany).

Audit Committee: The Audit Committee is composed of six members, appointed by the Governors for a non-renewable six-year term of office.

Chair.: (vacant).

EUROPEAN INVESTMENT FUND—EIF

Address: 15 Ave J. F. Kennedy 2968 Luxembourg.

Telephone: 2485-1; **fax:** 2485-81200; **e-mail:** info@eif.org; **internet:** www.eif.org.

The European Investment Fund (EIF) was founded in 1994 as a specialized financial institution to support the growth of small and medium-sized enterprises (SMEs). Its operations are focused on helping SMEs to gain access to equity, through investment in funds that support SMEs, and on guarantee activities. The Fund makes use of risk-sharing principles. The Joint European Resources for Micro to Medium Enterprises (JEREMIE) initiative, which was launched in 2006, enables EU member countries and regions to use structural funds to obtain financing that is specifically targeted to support SMEs. Technical assistance is also offered under the Joint Action to Support Microfinance Institutions in Europe (JASMINE) initiative, launched in 2008; another initiative is the European Progress Microfinance Facility. The European Investment Fund is operational in the member states of the EU, and candidate and potential candidate countries, and in the member countries of the European Free Trade Association.

Chief Executive: Pier Luigi Gilibert (Italy).

EUROPEAN STABILITY MECHANISM—ESM

Address: 6A Circuit de la Foire, 1347 Luxembourg.

Telephone: (352) 2609620; **e-mail:** info@esm.europa.eu; **internet:** www.esm.europa.eu.

The European Stability Mechanism (ESM) was established by a treaty signed on 2 February 2012 by representatives of the then 17 eurozone member countries, meeting in Brussels, Belgium, and replacing a treaty signed in July 2011. The ESM was conceived as an international financial institution, the purpose of which is to make available financial assistance to member countries, where necessary, in order to ensure financial stability. The ESM was inaugurated on 8 October 2012, when the Board of Governors, comprising eurozone ministers responsible for finance, held its first meeting. The ESM superseded two temporary funding programmes: the European Financial Stability Facility (EFSF) and the European Financial Stabilization Mechanism (EFSM), which remained responsible only for lending approved prior to the establishment of the ESM.

Managing Director of the ESM: Klaus Regling (Germany).

Chairman of Board of Governors and President of Eurogroup: Jeroen Dijsselbloem (Netherlands).

EUROPEAN ECONOMIC AND SOCIAL COMMITTEE—EESC

Address: 99 rue Belliard, 1040 Brussels.

Telephone: (2) 546-90-11; **fax:** (2) 513-48-93; **e-mail:** info@eesc.europa.eu; **internet:** www.eesc.europa.eu.

The Committee was set up by the 1957 Rome Treaties. It is advisory and is consulted by the Council of the European Union or by the European Commission, particularly with regard to agriculture, free movement of workers, harmonization of laws and transport, as well as legislation adopted under the Euratom Treaty. In certain cases consultation of the Committee by the Commission or the Council is mandatory. In addition, the Committee has the power to deliver opinions on its own initiative.

The Committee has a tripartite structure with members belonging to one of three groupings: the Employers' Group; the Workers' Group; and the Various Interests' Group, which includes representatives of social, occupational, economic and cultural organizations. The Committee is appointed for a renewable term of four years by the unanimous vote of the Council of the European Union. The 353 members are nominated by national governments, but are appointed in their personal capacity and are not bound by any mandatory instructions. The existing mandate began in October 2010, and will run until September 2015. Germany, France, Italy and the United Kingdom have 24 members each; Spain and Poland have 21; Romania, 15; Belgium, Bulgaria, Greece, the Netherlands, Portugal, Austria, Sweden, the Czech Republic and Hungary 12; Croatia, Denmark, Ireland, Finland, Lithuania and Slovakia nine; Estonia, Latvia and Slovenia seven; Luxembourg and Cyprus six; and Malta five. The Committee is served by a permanent and independent General Secretariat, headed by the Secretary-General.

President: Henri Malosse (France).

Secretary-General: Luís Planas Puchades (Spain).

COMMITTEE OF THE REGIONS—COR

Address: 99–101 rue Belliard, 1040 Brussels.

Telephone: (2) 282-22-11; **fax:** (2) 282-23-25; **e-mail:** info@cor.europa.eu; **internet:** www.cor.europa.eu.

The Treaty on European Union provided for a committee to be established, with advisory status, comprising representatives of regional and local bodies throughout the EU. The first meeting of the CoR was held in March 1994. It may be consulted on EU proposals concerning economic and social cohesion, trans-European networks, public health, education and culture, and may issue an opinion on any issue with regional implications. The CoR meets in plenary session five times a year.

The entry into force of the Lisbon Treaty, in December 2009, empowered the CoR, on the basis of a simple majority vote, to challenge at the European Court of Justice any new EU legislation—relating to the policy areas where the Committee may be consulted—that is deemed to infringe the principle of 'subsidiarity', i.e. that decisions should be taken as closely as possible to the citizens.

The number of members of the CoR is equal to that of the European Economic and Social Committee, currently 353. Members are appointed for a term of five years by the Council, acting unanimously on the proposals from the respective member states. The Committee elects its principal officers from among its members for a two-year term.

President: RAMÓN LUIS VALCÁRCEL SISO (Spain).

Secretary-General: DANIEL JANSSENS (acting) (Belgium).

AGENCIES

In March 2008 the European Commission published a document entitled 'European Agencies: The Way Forward', and an inter-institutional working group, comprising representatives of the European Parliament, the Council and the Commission, and chaired by the Commission, was consequently established to discuss proposals to improve the coherence, effectiveness and accountability of the EU's decentralized agencies. Hitherto, the decentralized agencies had been established on a case-by-case basis, and differed widely with respect to governance, functioning and oversight. A non-binding, so-called common approach was agreed by the three institutions in June 2012, which provided, inter alia, for the creation of new agencies to be preceded by an impact assessment; gave criteria for the selection of agency headquarters; provided for five-yearly evaluations; and endorsed balanced governance. In 2011 the 31 decentralized agencies received €737m. from the EU budget.

Decentralized Agencies

Agency for the Co-operation of Energy Regulators—ACER

1000 Ljubljana, Trg republike 3, Slovenia; tel. (8) 2053400; fax (8) 2053413; e-mail info@acer.europa.eu; internet www.acer.europa.eu; f. 2011; ACER aims to facilitate cross-border energy trade, to co-ordinate the activities of national energy regulators and to help to prevent conflict between them, in order to encourage competition and to ensure fair prices for both consumers and businesses. The agency's opening coincided with the entry into force of the EU's third energy package on the internal market.

President: ALBERTO POTOTSCHNIG (Italy).

Body of European Regulators for Electronic Communications—BEREC

2nd Floor, Z. A. Meierovica Bulv. 14, Rīga 1050, Latvia; tel. 6611-7590; e-mail berec@berec.europa.eu; internet berec.europa.eu.

Established by a regulation of the European Parliament in Nov. 2009, replacing the European Regulators Group (ERG).

Administrative Manager: ANDO REHEMAA (Estonia).

Community Plant Variety Office—CPVO

3 blvd Maréchal Foch, POB 10121, 49000 Angers, France; tel. 2-41-25-64-00; fax 2-41-25-64-10; e-mail cpvo@cpvo.europa.eu; internet www.cpvo.europa.eu/main/en.

Began operations in April 1995, with responsibility for granting intellectual property rights for plant varieties. Supervised by an Administrative Council, and managed by a President, appointed by the Council of the European Union. A Board of Appeal has been established to consider appeals against certain technical decisions taken by the Office. Publishes an annual report listing valid Community plant variety rights, their owners and their expiry dates.

President: MARTIN EKVAD (Sweden).

European Agency for the Management of Operational Co-operation at the External Borders—FRONTEX

Rondo ONZ 1, 00-124 Warsaw, Poland; tel. (22) 2059500; fax (22) 2059501; e-mail frontex@frontex.europa.eu; internet www.frontex.europa.eu.

Established by a regulation of the European Parliament in October 2004, the Agency's primary responsibility is the creation of an integrated border management system, in order to ensure a high and uniform level of control and surveillance. The Agency began operations on 1 May 2005.

Executive Director: Col ILKKA PERTTI JUHANI LAITINEN (Finland).

European Agency for the Operational Management of Large-Scale IT Systems in the Area of Freedom, Security and Justice—IT AGENCY

EU House, Rävala pst 4, 10143 Tallinn, Estonia

The agency, which began operations on 1 December 2012, was established to provide operational management of large-scale IT systems in the area of home affairs. It was to have operational management responsibility for the Schengen Information System (SIS II), which entered into operation on 9 April 2013.

Executive Director: KRUM GARKOV (Bulgaria).

European Agency for Safety and Health at Work—EU-OSHA

Gran Vía 33, 48009 Bilbao, Spain; tel. (94) 4794360; fax (94) 4794383; e-mail information@osha.europa.eu; internet osha.europa.eu/en/front-page/view.

Began operations in 1996. Aims to encourage improvements in the working environment, and to make available all necessary technical, scientific and economic information for use in the field of health and safety at work. The Agency supports a network of Focal Points in the member states of the EU, in the member states of the European Free Trade Association and in the candidate states of the EU.

Director: Dr CHRISTA SEDLATSCHEK (Austria).

European Aviation Safety Agency—EASA

Postfach 101253, 50452 Köln, Germany; Ottoplatz 1, 50679 Köln, Germany; tel. (221) 8999000; fax (221) 8999099; e-mail info@easa.europa.eu; internet www.easa.europa.eu/home.php.

Established by a regulation of the European Parliament in July 2002; the mission of the agency is to establish and maintain a high, uniform level of civil aviation safety and environmental protection in Europe. The Agency commenced full operations in September 2003, and moved to its permanent seat, in Köln, Germany, in November 2004.

Executive Director: PATRICK KY (France).

European Centre for the Development of Vocational Training—Cedefop

POB 22427, 551 02 Thessaloníki, Greece; Evropis 123, 570 01 Thessaloníki, Greece; tel. (30) 2310490111; fax (30) 2310490049; e-mail info@cedefop.europa.eu; internet www.cedefop.europa.eu.

Established in 1975, Cedefop assists policy-makers and other officials in member states and partner organizations in issues relating to vocational training policies, and assists the European Commission in the development of these policies. Manages a European Training Village internet site (www.trainingvillage.gr/etv/default.asp).

Director: JAMES CALLEJA (Malta).

European Centre for Disease Prevention and Control—ECDC

17183 Stockholm, Sweden; Tomtebodavägen 11A, Solna, Sweden; tel. (8) 586-01000; fax (8) 586-01001; e-mail info@ecdc.europa.eu; internet www.ecdc.europa.eu.

Founded in 2005 to strengthen European defences against infectious diseases. It works with national health protection bodies to develop disease surveillance and early warning systems across Europe.

Director: Dr MARC SPRENGER (Netherlands).

European Chemicals Agency—ECHA

Annankatu 18, Helsinki, Finland; POB 400, 00121 Helsinki, Finland; tel. (9) 686180; e-mail press@echa.europa.eu; internet echa.europa.eu.

The European Chemicals Agency (ECHA) was established by regulations of the European Parliament and the European Council in 2006, and became fully operational in June 2008. The objective of the ECHA is to supervise and undertake the technical, scientific and administrative aspects of the Registration, Evaluation, Authorization and Restriction of Chemicals throughout the EU and in Iceland, Liechtenstein and Norway. It also supports and runs a national helpdesk, and disseminates information on chemicals to the public.

Executive Director: GEERT DANCET (Finland).

European Defence Agency—EDA

17–23 rue des Drapiers, 1050 Brussels, Belgium; tel. (2) 504-28-00; fax (2) 504-28-15; e-mail info@eda.europa.eu; internet www.eda.europa.eu.

Founded in July 2004 and became operational in 2005; aims to help member states to improve their defence capabilities for crisis management under the European Security and Defence Policy. The Steering Board is composed of the ministers responsible for defence of 26 member states (all states, except Denmark).

Head of the Agency and Chairman of the Steering Board: CATHERINE ASHTON (United Kingdom).

Chief Executive: CLAUDE-FRANCE ARNOULD (France).

European Environment Agency—EEA

6 Kongens Nytorv, 1050 Copenhagen K, Denmark; tel. 33-36-71-00; fax 33-36-71-99; e-mail eea@eea.europa.eu; internet www.eea.europa.eu.

Became operational in 1994, having been approved in 1990, to gather and supply information to assist the drafting and implementation of EU policy on environmental protection and improvement. Iceland, Liechtenstein, Norway, Switzerland and Turkey are also members of the Agency. The Agency publishes frequent reports on the state of the environment and on environmental trends.

Executive Director: Prof. HANS BRUYNINCKX (Belgium).

European Fisheries Control Agency—EFCA

Edificio Odriozola, Avda García Barbón, 36201 Vigo, Spain; tel. (98) 6120610; fax (98) 6125234; e-mail efca@efca.europa.eu; internet cfca.europa.eu/pages/home/home.htm.

Established in April 2005 to improve compliance with regulations under the 2002 reform of the Common Fisheries Policy. The EFCA aims to ensure the effectiveness of enforcement by sharing EU and national methods of fisheries' control, monitoring resources and co-ordinating activities.

Executive Director: PASCAL SAVOURET (France).

European Food Safety Authority—EFSA

Via Carlo Magno 1A, 43126 Parma, Italy; tel. (39-0521) 036111; fax (39-0521) 036110; e-mail info@efsa.europa.eu; internet www.efsa.europa.eu.

Established by a regulation of the European Parliament in February 2002 and began operations in May 2003; the primary responsibility of the Authority is to provide independent scientific advice on all matters with a direct or indirect impact on food safety. The Authority will carry out assessments of risks to the food chain and scientific assessment on any matter that may have a direct or indirect effect on the safety of the food supply, including matters relating to animal health, animal welfare and plant health. The Authority also gives scientific advice on genetically modified organisms, and on nutrition in relation to EU law.

Executive Director: Dr BERNHARD URL (Austria) (acting).

European Foundation for the Improvement of Living and Working Conditions—EUROFOUND

Wyattville Rd, Loughlinstown, Dublin 18, Ireland; tel. (1) 2043100; fax (1) 2826456; e-mail postmaster@eurofound.europa.eu; internet www.eurofound.europa.eu.

Established in 1975, the Foundation aims to provide information and advice on European living and working conditions, industrial relations, and the management of change to employers, policy-makers, governments and trade unions, by means of comparative data, research and analysis. In 2001 the Foundation established the European Monitoring Centre on Change to help to disseminate information and ideas on the management and anticipation of change in industry and enterprise.

Director: JUAN MENÉNDEZ-VALDÉS (Spain).

European GNSS Supervisory Authority—GSA

Janovského 438/2, 17000 Prague 7, Czech Republic; tel. 234766000; e-mail info@gsa.europa.eu; internet www.gsa.europa.eu.

The European GNSS Supervisory Authority (GSA) was established in July 2004, to oversee all public interests relating to European Global Navigation Satellite System (GNSS) programmes. On 1 January 2007 the GSA officially took over the tasks previously assigned to the Galileo Joint Undertaking, which had been established in May 2002 by the EU and the European Space Agency to manage the development phase of the Galileo programme. The strategic objectives of the GSA include the achievement of a fully operational Galileo system, capable of becoming the world's leading civilian satellite navigation system, and Europe's only GNSS.

Executive Director: CARLO DES DORIDES (Italy).

European Institute for Gender Equality—EIGE

Švitrigailos g. 11M, 03228 Vilnius, Lithuania; tel. (5) 239-4140; e-mail eige.sec@eige.europa.eu; internet eige.europa.eu.

The European Institute for Gender Equality was established in May 2007, initially in Brussels, Belgium, to help EU member states and institutions to promote gender equality, combat gender discrimination and disseminate information on gender issues. The institute collects and interprets relevant data, to develop methodologies and tools to help to integrate gender across all policy areas, to facilitate discussion and the adoption of best practices, and to raise awareness of gender issues. The institute comprises a management board, which is the decision-making body, together with a consultative experts' forum. The budget for 2007–13 was €52.5m.

Director: VIRGINIJA LANGBAKK (Estonia).

European Judicial Co-operation Unit—EUROJUST

Maanweg 174, 2516 The Hague, Netherlands; tel. (70) 4125000; fax (70) 4125005; e-mail info@eurojust.europa.eu; internet eurojust.europa.eu.

Established in 2002 to improve co-operation and co-ordination between member states in the investigation and prosecution of serious cross-border and organized crime. The EUROJUST College is composed of one member (a senior prosecutor or judge) nominated by each member state.

President of the College: MICHÈLE CONINSX (Belgium).

Administrative Director: KLAUS RACKWITZ (Germany).

European Maritime Safety Agency—EMSA

Cais do Sodré, 1249-206 Lisbon, Portugal; tel. (21) 1209200; fax (21) 1209210; e-mail information@emsa.europa.eu; internet www.emsa.europa.eu.

Established by a regulation of the European Parliament in June 2002; the primary responsibility of the Agency is to provide technical and scientific advice to the Commission in the field of maritime safety and prevention of pollution by ships, and, from April 2012, oil and gas rigs. The Agency held its inaugural meeting in December 2002, and in December 2003 it was decided that the permanent seat of the Agency would be Lisbon, Portugal. Norway and Iceland are also members of EMSA.

Executive Director: MARKKU MYLLY (Finland).

European Medicines Agency—EMA

7 Westferry Circus, Canary Wharf, London, E14 4HB, United Kingdom; tel. (20) 7418-8400; fax (20) 7418-8416; e-mail info@ema.europa.eu; internet www.ema.europa.eu.

Established in 1995 for the evaluation, authorization and supervision of medicinal products for human and veterinary use; was being restructured in 2013.

Executive Director: GUIDO RASI (Sweden).

European Monitoring Centre for Drugs and Drug Addiction—EMCDDA

Cais do Sodré, 1249-289 Lisbon, Portugal; tel. (21) 1210200; fax (21) 1210380; e-mail info@emcdda.europa.eu; internet www.emcdda.europa.eu.

Founded in 1993 and became fully operational at the end of 1995, with the aim of providing member states with objective, reliable and comparable information on drugs and drug addiction in order to assist in combating the problem. The Centre co-operates with other European and international organizations and non-EU countries. The Centre publishes an *Annual Report on the State of the Drugs Problem in Europe*. A newsletter, *Drugnet Europe*, is published quarterly.

Executive Director: WOLFGANG GÖTZ (Germany).

European Police College—CEPOL

CEPOL House, Bramshill, Hook, Hampshire, RG27 0JW, United Kingdom; tel. (1256) 60-26-68; fax (1256) 60-29-96; e-mail secretariat@cepol.europa.eu; internet www.cepol.europa.eu.

Founded in 2005 to help to create a network of senior police officers throughout Europe, to encourage cross-border co-operation in combating crime, and to improve public security and law and order through the organization of training activities and research. There were plans to relocate CEPOL to Budapest, Hungary, during 2014.

Director: Dr FERENC BÁNFI (Hungary).

European Police Office—EUROPOL

POB 90850, 2509 The Hague, Netherlands; Eisenhowerlaan 73, 2517 The Hague, Netherlands; tel. (70) 3025000; fax (70) 3025896; e-mail info@europol.europa.eu; internet www.europol.europa.eu.

Established in 1992, EUROPOL is a law enforcement organization that aims to aid EU member states to combat organized crime, by handling criminal intelligence throughout Europe and promoting co-operation between the law enforcement bodies of member countries; became a full EU agency, with an enhanced mandate for combating international crime, in Jan. 2010.

Director: ROB WAINWRIGHT (United Kingdom).

European Railway Agency—ERA

120 rue Marc Lefrancq, 59300 Valenciennes, France; tel. 3-27-09-65-00; fax 3-27-33-40-65; e-mail press-info@era.europa.eu; internet www.era.europa.eu.

Established by a regulation of the European Parliament in April 2004; the primary responsibility of the Agency is to reinforce the safety and interoperability of railways in the EU.

Executive Director: MARCEL VERSLYPE (Belgium).

European Training Foundation—ETF

Villa Gualino, Viale Settimio Severo 65, 10133 Turin, Italy; tel. (011) 630-22-22; fax (011) 630-22-00; e-mail info@etf.europa.eu; internet www.etf.europa.eu

The Foundation, which was established in 1990 and became operational in 1994, provides policy advice to the European Commission and to the EU's partner countries, to support vocational education and training reform. The ETF works in the countries surrounding the EU, which are involved either in the European Neighbourhood Partnership Instrument, or in the enlargement process under the Instrument for Pre-accession Assistance. The ETF also works in a number of other countries from Central Asia. The ETF also gives technical assistance to the European Commission for the implementation of the Trans-European Mobility Programme for University Studies (TEMPUS), which focuses on the reform of higher education systems in partner countries.

Director: MADLEN SERBAN (Romania).

European Union Agency for Fundamental Rights—FRA

Schwarzenbergplatz 11, 1040 Vienna, Austria; tel. (1) 580300; fax (1) 58030699; e-mail information@fra.europa.eu; internet fra.europa.eu

Founded in March 2007, replacing the European Monitoring Centre on Racism and Xenophobia (EUMC). The Agency aims to provide assistance to EU member states on fundamental rights matters during the application of EU law. The FRA continues the work of the EUMC on racism, xenophobia, anti-Semitism and related intolerance, and utilizes its experience of data collection methods and co-operation with governments and international organizations. In addition, the FRA places significant emphasis on increasing public awareness of rights issues and on co-operation with civil society.

Director: MORTEN KJAERUM (Denmark).

European Union Agency for Network and Information Security—ENISA

POB 1309, 710 01 Heraklion, Crete, Greece; Science and Technology Park of Crete, Vassilika Vouton, 700 13 Heraklion, Crete, Greece; tel. (2810) 391280; fax (2810) 391410; e-mail info@enisa.europa.eu; internet www.enisa.europa.eu.

Established by a regulation of the European Parliament in March 2004; commenced operations in 2005. The primary responsibilities of the Agency are to promote closer European co-ordination on the security of communications networks and information systems and to provide assistance in the application of EU measures in this field. The agency publishes a quarterly magazine.

Executive Director: Dr UDO HELMBRECHT (Germany).

European Union Institute for Security Studies—EUISS

100 ave de Suffren, 75015 Paris, France; tel. 1-56-89-19-30; fax 1-56-89-19-31; e-mail institute@iss.europa.eu; internet www.iss.europa.eu.

Established by a Council Joint Action in July 2001, and inaugurated in January 2002. The Institute aims to help to implement and develop the EU's Common Foreign and Security Policy (CFSP), and carries out political analysis and forecasting. The Institute produces several publications: the Chaillot Papers, occasional papers and a quarterly newsletter, as well as books containing in-depth studies of specialized topics.

Director: ANTONIO MISSIROLI (Italy).

European Union Satellite Centre—EUSC

Avda de Cadiz 457, Torréjon de Ardoz, 28850 Madrid, Spain; tel. (91) 6786000; fax (91) 6786006; e-mail info@eusc.europa.eu; internet www.eusc.europa.eu.

Established by a Council Joint Action in July 2001 and operational from 1 January 2002. The Centre is dedicated to providing material derived from the analysis of satellite imagery in support of the Common Foreign and Security Policy.

Director: TOMAŽ LOVRENČIČ (Slovenia).

Office for Harmonization in the Internal Market (Trade Marks and Designs)—OHIM

Avda de Europa 4, 03008 Alicante, Spain; tel. (96) 5139100; fax (96) 5131344; e-mail information@oami.europa.eu; internet oami.europa.eu.

Established in 1993 to promote and control trade marks and designs throughout the EU.

President: ANTÓNIO CAMPINOS (Portugal).

Translation Centre for the Bodies of the European Union—CdT

12E rue Guillaume Kroll, 1882 Luxembourg; tel. 4217-11-1; fax 4217-11-220; e-mail cdt@cdt.europa.eu; internet www.cdt.europa.eu.

Established in 1994 to meet the translation needs of other decentralized Union agencies.

Director: MARIE-ANNE FERNÁNDEZ (acting) (Spain).

EURATOM Agencies and Bodies

Euratom Supply Agency

EUFO 2161, rue Alcide de Gasperi, 2920 Luxembourg; Complexe Euroforum, 10 rue Robert Stumper, 2557 Luxembourg; tel. 4301-37147; fax 4301-38139; e-mail esa-aae@ec.europa.eu; internet ec.europa.eu/euratom/index.html.

The Euratom Supply Agency commenced operations in 1960, having been established by the Euratom Treaty to ensure the regular and equitable supply of nuclear energy throughout EU member states.

Director-General: STAMATIOS TSALAS (Belgium).

European Joint Undertaking for ITER and the Development of Fusion Energy—Fusion for Energy

2 Josep Pla, Torres Diagonal Litoral, Edificio B3, 08019 Barcelona, Spain; tel. (93) 320-18-00; fax (93) 489-75-37; e-mail info@f4e.europa.eu; internet fusionforenergy.europa.eu.

The Agency was established in 2007, as a Joint Undertaking under the European Atomic Energy Community (Euratom) Treaty, by a decision of the Council of the European Union (see Energy). Its members comprise the EU member states, Euratom and Switzerland.

Director: HENRIK BINDSLEV (Denmark).

Executive Agencies are established for a pre-determined length of time. There are currently six such agencies in operation: the Education, Audiovisual and Culture Executive Agency (EACEA); the European Research Council Executive Agency (ERCEA); the Executive Agency for Small and Medium-Sized Businesses (EASME); the Consumers, Health and Food Executive Agency (Chafea); the Research Executive Agency (REA); and the Innovation and Networks Executive Agency (INEA).

Activities of the Union

STRATEGIC FRAMEWORK

Meeting in March 2000, the European Council launched the Lisbon Strategy, which was elaborated at subsequent meetings of the Council and rested on three 'pillars': an economic pillar preparing for a transition to a competitive, knowledge-based economy, with a focus on research and development; a social pillar that covered investment in human resources and combating social exclusion, with a focus on education, training and employment policy; and an environmental pillar, focused on disconnecting economic growth from the depletion of natural resources.

On 17 June 2010 the Council adopted the Europe 2020 strategic policy framework, the successor to the Lisbon Strategy, which seeks to consolidate the Lisbon Strategy's achievements with respect to economic growth and the creation of jobs. EU-wide targets were agreed in five policy areas. By 2020 at least 75% of those aged between 20 and 64 years are to be in employment; 3% of the EU's total gross domestic product is to be invested in research and innovation; greenhouse gas emissions are to be reduced by at least 20%, compared with levels in 1990, with 20% of energy produced to be renewable, and with energy efficiency to be increased by 20%; at least 40% of those aged between 30 and 34 years are to have completed higher education, and 10% more children are to complete their schooling; and there are to be at least 20m. fewer people living in, or threatened by, poverty and social exclusion.

AGRICULTURE

Agriculture (including rural development) is by far the largest single item on the EU budget, accounting for 41% of annual expenditure in 2012, although this represented a significant reduction compared with 1985, when agriculture accounted for 73% of expenditure.

Co-operation in the EU has traditionally been at its most highly organized in the area of agriculture. The Common Agricultural Policy (CAP), which took effect from 1962, was originally devised to ensure food self-sufficiency for Europe following the food shortages of the post-war period and to ensure a fair standard of living for the agricultural community. Its objectives are described in the Treaty of Rome, now the Treaty on the Functioning of the EU. The markets for agricultural products have been progressively organized following three basic principles: unity of the market (products must be able to circulate freely within the Union and markets must be organized according to common rules); EU preference (products must be protected from low-cost imports and from fluctuations on the world market); and common financial responsibility: the European Agricultural Guarantee Fund (which replaced the European Agricultural Guidance and Guarantee Fund in 2007) finances the export of agricultural products to third countries, intervention measures to regulate agricultural markets, and direct payments to farmers.

Agricultural prices in the EU are, in theory, fixed each year at a common level, taking into account the rate of inflation and the need to discourage surplus production of certain commodities. Export subsidies are paid to enable farmers to sell produce at the lower world market prices without loss. When market prices of certain cereals, sugar, some fruits and vegetables, dairy produce and meat fall below a designated level, the EU intervenes, and buys a quantity, which is then stored until prices recover.

Serious reform of the CAP began in 1992, following strong criticism of the EC's agricultural and export subsidies during the Uruguay Round of negotiations on the General Agreement on Tariffs and Trade (GATT, see World Trade Organization—WTO) in 1990. In May ministers adopted a number of reforms, which aimed to transfer the Community's agricultural support from upholding prices to maintaining farmers' incomes, thereby removing the incentive to overproduce. Intervention prices were reduced, and farmers were compensated by receiving additional grants, which, in the case of crops, took the form of a subsidy per hectare of land planted. To qualify for these subsidies, arable farmers (except for those with the smallest farms) were obliged to remove 15% of their land from cultivation (the 'set-aside' scheme). Incentives were given for alternative uses of the withdrawn land (e.g. forestry).

In March 1999, at the Berlin European Council, the EU Heads of Government concluded an agreement on a programme, Agenda 2000, which aimed to reinforce Community policies and to restructure the financial framework of the EU with a view to enlargement. In terms of agriculture, it was decided to continue the process of agricultural reform with particular emphasis on environmental concerns, safeguarding a fair income for farmers, streamlining legislation and decentralizing its application. A further element of reform was the increased emphasis on rural development, which was described as the 'second pillar' of the CAP in Agenda 2000. The objective was to restore and increase the competitiveness of rural areas, through supporting employment, diversification and population growth. In addition, producers were to be rewarded for the preservation of rural heritage. Forestry was recognized as an integral part of rural development (hitherto, EU treaties had made no provision for a comprehensive common forestry policy).

The accession of 10 new states to the EU in May 2004 had major implications for the CAP, as the enlargement doubled the EU's arable land area and its farming population. In October 2002 it was agreed that the enlargement process would be part-funded by a deal to maintain farm subsidies at 2006 levels until 2013, with a 1% annual correction for inflation, and that the new members would be offered direct farm payments at 25% of the level paid to existing member states, rising in stages to 100% over 10 years. Meanwhile, in July 2002 the Commissioner responsible for Agriculture, Rural Development and Fisheries had proposed severing the link between direct payments to farmers and production ('decoupling'). The proposal was, however, vigorously opposed by the main beneficiaries of the existing system, in particular France. A revised plan was submitted, which restored the link between subsidies and production for certain products while still adhering to the principle of decoupling.

The compromise deal for CAP reform was agreed in June 2003, and the agreement was ratified by the Council of the European Union and the accession states in September. Production-linked subsidies were to be replaced by a Single Farm Payment, subsidies previously received, rather than tied to current production levels, and were also to be linked to environmental, food safety and animal welfare standards. Obligatory decoupling was only partial for beef, cereal and mutton, with production still accounting for as much as 25% of payments for cereals and as much as 40% for beef. Overall, however, 90% of payments would no longer be linked to production. The agreement contained a commitment to reduce all payments above €5,000 a year by 3% in 2005, by 4% in 2006 and by 5% in 2007. Increased resources were to be directed towards rural development projects, protecting the environment and improvements to food quality; organic farmers and those offering high-quality produce with special guarantees were to receive grants of up to €3,000 a year for five years. Under the principle of 'modulation', an increasing percentage of direct farm subsidies was to be retained by individual member states to finance rural development measures. The equivalent of at least 80% of the funds gathered in each member state (90% in Germany) was to be spent in that country. Implementation of the CAP reforms agreed in June 2003 commenced on 1 January 2005.

Meanwhile, in April 2004 the EU Council of Ministers of Agriculture reached agreement for CAP reform of the olive oil, cotton, hops and tobacco sectors, extending the principle of decoupling aid from production to these commodities. The agreement also provided for a significant share of the existing production-linked payments to be transferred to the Single Farm Payment (which was provided independently of production), although production-linked subsidies were permitted of up to 60% for tobacco, 40% for olive oil, 35% for cotton and 25% for hops. Moreover, full decoupling in the tobacco sector was to be introduced progressively over the four years to 2010 and rural development aid was to finance conversion to other crops in tobacco-producing areas. The remaining production aid for olive oil was to be directed at maintaining olive groves with environmental or social value. In September 2006 the European Court of Justice annulled the CAP provisions on cotton, proposing a slightly revised reform of the support scheme in November 2007. The new proposal maintained the support arrangements agreed in 2004 (i.e. production-linked subsidies of up to 35%), but provided for additional funding for support measures in cotton-producing regions and the creation of a 'label of origin' to enhance the promotion of EU cotton.

The EU agreed reforms to the sugar industry in November 2005, following a WTO ruling earlier in the year (after an action brought by Brazil, Australia and Thailand) that the existing level of subsidy breached legal limits. In 2005 the EU sugar sector continued to be characterized by large subsidies, high internal prices, and imports by African, Caribbean and Pacific (ACP) countries on favourable terms under quotas. The EU produced large surpluses of sugar, which were disposed of on the world market to the detriment of more competitive producers, notably developing countries. The reforms, which were implemented from July 2006, included the gradual reduction of the internal EU market price (which was three times the international price for the commodity in 2005) by 36% by 2009, and direct aid payments of €6,300m. over the four years of the phased introduction of the reforms to EU sugar producers as compensation. A fundamental element in the reform of the EU sugar sector was the establishment of a restructuring fund, financed by sugar producers, to ease the transition to greater competitiveness. The objective was to remove a total of some 6m. metric tons of sugar quota during the four-year reform period. Amendments to the sugar-restructuring scheme were adopted in October 2007 in an attempt to encourage greater participation and, by the conclusion of the reform period in early 2009, some 5.8m. tons of sugar quota had been renounced.

At the Doha Round of the WTO in Hong Kong in December 2005, agreement was reached on the elimination of export subsidies on farm goods by the end of 2013. This represented a concession by the EU but was three years later than the date sought by the USA and developing countries.

A new regulation laying down specific rules concerning the fruit and vegetable sector was adopted in September 2007 and entered into force in January 2008. Notable reforms included the integration of the sector into the Single Farm Payment scheme; the requirement that producer organizations allocate at least 10% of their annual expenditure to environmental concerns; an increase in EU funding for the promotion of fruit and vegetable consumption and for organic production; and the abolition of export subsidies for fruit and vegetables. In April ministers responsible for agriculture adopted a new regulation on the reform of the wine sector. The regulation provided, inter alia, for the inclusion of the sector in the Single Farm Payment scheme, while distillation subsidies were to be gradually withdrawn by 2012, releasing funds for measures such as wine promotion in third countries and the modernization of vineyards and cellars. In addition, the regulation provided for the introduction of a voluntary, three-year scheme, under which wine producers were to receive subsidies, with the aim of removing surplus and uncompetitive wine from the market.

In May 2008 the European Commission proposed a number of regulations to reform and simplify the CAP further in 2009–13, including additional reductions in production-linked payments and increased funding for rural development. In November 2008 the European Council, as part of a CAP 'Health Check', reached agreement on the proposed reforms, which raised the rate of decoupling in those countries that maintained the link between subsidy and production; provided for reform of the dairy sector; abolished the set-aside scheme from 2009; and provided for payments to farms qualifying for subsidies of at least €5,000 a year to be reduced gradually, so that by 2012 10% of funds (compared with the existing 5%) would be transferred to the rural development budget (large-scale farms would be required to transfer a greater proportion of funds). Milk quotas were to be increased by 1% per year in 2009–13, before their eventual expiry in 2015.

As a result of severe decline in dairy prices from 2008, in June 2009 the Commissioner for Agriculture and Rural Development established a High Level Experts' Group on Milk (HLG), which sought to identify medium- and long-term measures for stabilizing the dairy market and incomes, given the expiry of milk quotas from 1 April 2015. The HLG identified significant problems in the supply chain. In September 2010 its proposals for addressing the problems were endorsed by the Council. The so-called Milk Package entered into force fully in October 2012, and was to remain in force until 2020. The agreement increased transparency, and allowed member states, inter alia, to introduce obligatory, freely negotiated, written contracts between farmers and processors, with the possibility of contracts for a limited volume of milk being negotiated collectively by groups of farmers, in producer organizations.

In mid-November 2010 the European Commission launched the consultation process on further reform of the CAP with the adoption of a communication entitled *The CAP towards 2020: Meeting the food, natural resources and territorial challenges of the future*, based on the results of public debate on the issue of CAP reform, which had been summarized at a conference held in Brussels, Belgium, in July 2010. In mid-October 2011 the Commission announced a set of legislative proposals aimed at simplifying the CAP from 2014, while ensuring greater transparency, and the long-term sustainability, competitiveness and diversity of the agricultural sector. Political agreement on the reform of the CAP was reached between the European Commission, the Council and the European Parliament in late June 2013, and agreement on outstanding funding issues for 2014–20 was reached between the three institutions in late September. In mid-December, following approval by the Parliament in the previous month, the Council formally adopted four basic regulations for the reformed CAP, and the transition arrangements for its implementation from 2014 (some elements were not to come into operation until 2015). The regulations provided for the administration of the CAP to be simplified, and transparency increased. The budget for agricultural research and innovation was to be increased two-fold, supported by the creation of a new European Innovation Partnership. Direct payments were to be distributed more equitably: by 2019 no single member state was to receive less than 75% of the EU average; only practising farmers would be eligible for income support, and incentives were to be introduced for younger farmers to enter the sector (some 65% of farmers were at least 55 years of age). Sugar quotas were to be removed by the end of 2017. Improved tools for managing economic crises were to be introduced: the Commission would be able to intervene temporarily to manage the volume of agricultural products in the market; a 'crisis reserve' was to be established; and farmers were to be encouraged to take part in risk-prevention schemes. A 'greening' component was to be introduced, to reward environmental competitiveness by directing up to 30% of the value of direct payments towards encouraging better use of natural resources, through crop diversification; the preservation of grassland; and the conservation of 5% (potentially rising to 7%) of areas of ecological interest from 2018 (or the introduction of measures deemed to be of equivalent environmental worth).

Food safety is a significant issue in the EU, especially since the first case of bovine spongiform encephalopathy (BSE), a transmissible disease that causes the brain tissue to degenerate, was diagnosed in cattle in the United Kingdom in 1986. The use of meat and bone meal (MBM) in animal feed was identified as possibly responsible for the emergence of the disease, and was banned for use in cattle feed in the United Kingdom in 1988. MBM was banned throughout the EU from 1994 for ruminants and in December 2000 for all animals. The possible link between BSE and new variant Creutzfeldt-Jakob disease (vCJD), a degenerative brain disease that affects humans, led to a collapse in consumer confidence in the European beef market in 1996. By the end of 2011 176 people had contracted vCJD in the United Kingdom, the location of the vast majority of cases.

In July 1997 ministers responsible for agriculture voted to introduce a complete ban on the use for any purpose of 'specified risk materials' (i.e. those parts and organs most likely to carry the BSE prion disease agent) from cattle, sheep and goats. The ban was implemented in January 1999. The scope of legislation on undesirable substances in animal feed was extended in May 2002, to cover additives. In May 2001 new legislation was adopted by the European Parliament and the Agriculture Council that consolidated much of the existing legislation on BSE and other transmissible spongiform encephalopathies (TSEs) in bovine, ovine and caprine animals. The new TSE Regulation, which replaced previous emergency legislation and clarified the rules for the prevention, control and eradication of TSEs, came into force on 1 July. Every year the Commission approves programmes aimed at monitoring, controlling and eradicating animal diseases, with a special focus on zoonoses, which are transmissible from animal carriers to humans.

The EU's Food and Veterinary Office was established in April 1997 to ensure that the laws on food safety, animal health and welfare, and plant health are applied in all member states. The office carries out audits and checks on food safety in member states and in third countries exporting agricultural produce to the EU. Legislation establishing the European Food Safety Authority (EFSA) was signed in January 2002; the body provides independent scientific advice and support on matters with a direct or indirect impact on food safety. It has no regulatory or judicial power, but co-operates closely with similar bodies in the member states. In September 2007 the European Commission adopted a communication setting out the EU's animal health strategy for 2007–13. The aims of the new strategy were: to ensure a high level of public health and food safety by reducing the risks posed to humans by problems with animal health; to promote animal health by preventing or reducing the incidence of animal diseases, thus also protecting farming and the rural economy; to improve economic growth, cohesion and competitiveness in animal-related sectors; and to promote farming and animal welfare practices that prevent threats to animal health and minimize the environmental impact of raising animals. In January 2012 the European Commission adopted a new animal health strategy for 2012–15, the objective of which was to improve animal welfare throughout the EU, by adopting new, comprehensive legislation on animal welfare, while strengthening existing actions.

In June 1995 the Agriculture Council agreed to new rules on the welfare of livestock during transport. The agreement, which came into effect in 1996, limited transport of livestock to a maximum of eight hours in any 24-hour period, and stipulated higher standards for their accommodation and care while in transit. A ban on veal crates came into effect in January 1998. In April 2001 the Commission adopted new rules for long-distance animal transport, setting out the required standards of ventilation, temperature and humidity control. A new regulation further improving the welfare of animals during transportation was adopted in December 2004. In June 1999 EU ministers responsible for agriculture agreed to end egg production from hens kept in barren battery cages within the EU from 1 January 2012. A new directive laying out minimum standards for the protection of pigs, including provisions banning the use of individual stalls for pregnant sows and gilts, increasing their living space, and allowing them to have permanent access to materials for rooting, was applicable from January 2003 to holdings newly built or rebuilt, and from January 2013 to all holdings. A similar directive was adopted in June 2007 for the protection of chickens kept for meat production, laying out minimum standards in areas such as stocking density, lighting, litter and ventilation; it required implementation by member states within three years. Following 13 years of negotiations, in November 2002 agreement was finally reached between the European Parliament and the member states to ban the sale, import and export of virtually all cosmetic products tested after 11 March 2009 on animals in the EU, and to halt from 11 March 2013 all animal testing for cosmetics. In October 2009 the European Commission adopted a report that outlined options for labelling products with the objective of enabling consumers to identify good animal welfare practices and to provide an economic incentive to producers to make advances in the area of animal welfare. The report considered the possible future establishment of an animal welfare-orientated European Network of Reference Centres to provide technical support for the development and implementation of animal welfare policies, including in the areas of certification and labelling.

The EU has adopted a number of protective measures to prevent the introduction of organisms harmful to plants and plant products. Regulations governing the deliberate release of genetically modified organisms (GMOs) into the environment have been in force since October 1991, with an approval process based on a case-by-case analysis of the risks to human health and the environment. A total of 18 GMOs were authorized for use in the EU under this directive. An updated directive took effect in October 2002, which introduced principles for risk assessment, long-term monitoring requirements and full labelling and traceability obligations for food and feed containing more than 0.9% GM ingredients. A further regulation adopted by the Commission in January 2004 specified a system to identify and trace each GMO product used in the production of all food and animal feeds, completing the EU's regulatory framework on the authorization, labelling and traceability of GMOs. All of the accession states had adopted EU regulations on GM products by 2004, despite fears raised by environmental groups that inadequate testing facilities would prevent the implementation of effective labelling procedures. By June 2009 15 EU member states had adopted specific legislation on the co-existence of GMOs with conventional and organic crops. In March 2010 the European Commission announced that Amflora, a genetically modified potato, had been authorized for cultivation in the EU for industrial use.

In 2004 the Commission, with support from the Council, presented a European action plan for organic food and farming, comprising 21 measures, aimed at promoting the development of organic farming in the EU. The Council also adopted a regulation improving legal protection for organic farming methods and established a programme on the conservation, collection and utilization of genetic resources in agriculture. In 2005 the Commission adopted a proposal for new regulations defining objectives and principles for organic production, clarifying labelling rules and regulating imports. The new regulation on production and labelling was adopted in June 2007 and came into force on 1 January 2009. The new rules concerning imports of organic foods were approved in December 2006. From July 2010 all pre-packaged EU organic products were required to carry an EU organic food logo.

In January 2013 it emerged that horsemeat had been covertly used as an ingredient in processed meat products in Ireland, and it subsequently became evident that wrongly labelled food had been supplied throughout Europe. In mid-February extensive tests were ordered on meat products throughout the EU, and in March a new, five-point plan identified actions to be implemented over the short, medium and longer term in order to rectify shortcomings in the EU's food supply chain (see Consumer Protection and Health).

FISHERIES

The Common Fisheries Policy (CFP) came into effect in January 1983 after seven years of negotiations, particularly concerning the problem of access to fishing grounds. The CFP confirmed a 200-mile (370-km) zone around the regional coastline (excluding the Mediterranean) within which all members had access to fishing, and allowed exclusive national zones of six miles with access between six and 12 miles from the shore for other countries according to specified historic rights. Rules furthering conservation (e.g. standards for fishing tackle) were imposed under the policy, with checks by a Community fisheries inspectorate. A body of inspectors answerable to the Commission monitored compliance with the quotas and with technical measures in Community and some international waters.

In December 1992 EC ministers agreed to extend the CFP for a further 10-year period. Two years later ministers concluded a final agreement on the revised CFP, allowing Spain and Portugal to be integrated into the policy by 1 January 1996. A compromise accord was reached regarding access to waters around Ireland and off south-west Great Britain (referred to as the 'Irish box'), by means of which up to 40 Spanish vessels were granted access to 80,000 sq miles of the 90,000 sq mile area. However, the accord was strongly opposed by Irish and British fishermen. In October 1995 ministers responsible for fisheries agreed a regime to control fishing in the 'Irish box', introducing stricter controls and instituting new surveillance measures.

The organization of fish marketing involves common rules on size, weight, quality and packing and a system of guide prices established annually by the Council of the European Union. Fish are withdrawn from the market if prices fall too far below the guide price, and compensation may then be paid to the fishermen. Export subsidies are paid to enable the export of fish onto the lower-priced world market, and import levies are imposed to prevent competition from low-priced imports. A new import regime took effect from May 1993. This enabled regional fishermen's associations to increase prices to a maximum of 10% over the Community's reference price, although this applied to both EU and imported fish.

In June 1998 the Council of the European Union overcame long-standing objections from a number of member states and adopted a ban on the use of drift nets in the Atlantic Ocean and the Mediterranean Sea, in an attempt to prevent the unnecessary deaths of marine life such as dolphins and sharks. The ban, which was introduced in January 2002, partially implemented a 1992 UN resolution demanding a complete cessation of driftnet fishing. A series of compensatory measures aimed to rectify any short-term detrimental impact on EU fishing fleets. In March 2004 the Council approved a ban on the use of drift nets in the Baltic Sea, and, in April, it adopted a regulation stipulating the use of active acoustic deterrent devices on fishing nets throughout most EU waters to prevent dolphins and porpoises from becoming fatally entangled in the nets.

With concern over stocks continuing to mount (it was calculated in the early 2000s that cod stocks in the North Sea had fallen to one-10th of their level at 1970), in June 2002 the Commission proposed to establish a procedure for setting annual total allowable catches (TACs) so as to achieve a significant increase in mature fish stocks, with limits on the fishing effort fixed in accordance with the TACs. The Commission also proposed the temporary closure of areas where endangered species had congregated, and more generous EU aid for the decommissioning of vessels (aid for the modernization of vessels, which tends to increase the fishing catch, was to be reduced). By 2002 the Commission had also been alerted to the critical depletion of deep-sea species, the commercialization of which had become increasingly attractive in the 1990s as other species became less abundant. For the first time, in December 2002, the Commission introduced catch limits for deep-water fish species, complemented by a system of deep-sea fishing permits (TACs for deep-sea fishing are revised every two years). In 2004 the Commission extended the scope of the use of TACs to more fish stocks and introduced a number of closed areas for heavily depleted species.

Initially structural assistance actions for fisheries were financed by the European Agricultural Guidance and Guarantee Fund (which was replaced by the European Agricultural Guarantee Fund in 2007). Following the reform of funding programmes in 1993, a separate fund, the Financial Instrument for Fisheries Guidance (FIFG), was set up. The instrument's principal responsibilities included the decommissioning of vessels and the creation, with foreign investors, of joint ventures designed to reduce the fishing effort in EU waters. The fund also supported the building and modernization of vessels, developments in the aquaculture sector, and the creation of protected coastal areas. From January 2007 the FIFG was replaced by the simplified European Fisheries Fund, covering the period 2007–13, which provided financial support to facilitate the implementation of the CFP (see below).

Radical reform of the CFP, aimed at ensuring the sustainable development of the industry, was announced during 2002. The Commission proposed a new multi-annual framework—which was to replace the existing Multi-Annual Guidance Programme—for the efficient conservation of resources and the management of fisheries, incorporating environmental concerns. The new measures were introduced on 1 January 2003, replacing the basic rules that had governed the CFP since 1993, and substantially amending structural assistance in the fisheries sector under the FIFG. The new framework provided for a long-term approach to attaining and maintaining fish stocks, designed to encourage member states to achieve a better balance between the fishing capacity of their fleets and available resources. Under the terms of the new framework quotas for catches of cod, whiting and haddock were substantially reduced, fishermen were guaranteed only nine days a month at sea (with provision to extend this to 15 days in some circumstances), and public funding for the renewal or modernization of fishing boats was abolished after 2004 (with the exception of funding for the provision of aid to improve security and working conditions on board). In addition, measures were announced to develop co-operation among the various fisheries authorities and to strengthen the uniformity of control and sanctions throughout the EU. The Commission inspectors had their powers extended to ensure the equity and efficacy of the enforcement of EU regulations. In an attempt to compensate for the ongoing decline of the EU fishing fleet, a number of socio-economic measures were introduced, including the provision of aid from member states to fishermen and vessel owners who had temporarily to halt their fishing activities and the granting of aid to fishermen to help them retrain to convert to professional activities outside the fisheries sector, while permitting them to continue fishing on a part-time basis. A new regulation setting up an emergency fund to encourage the decommissioning of vessels (known as the 'Scrapping Fund') was also adopted.

In July 2004 the Council adopted a common framework on the establishment of regional advisory councils (RACs), as part of the 2002 reform, to enable scientists, fishermen and other interested parties to work together to identify ways of maintaining sustainable fisheries. In November 2004 the first RAC, for the North Sea, was instituted in Edinburgh, Scotland. The Pelagic RAC and the North Western Waters RAC, based, respectively, in Amsterdam, Netherlands, and Dublin, Ireland, were created in August and September 2005. A Baltic Sea RAC, based in Copenhagen, Denmark, was set up in March 2006. The RAC for Long Distance Waters and the RAC for the South Western Waters were established in March and April 2007, while the last RAC (for the Mediterranean Waters) was established in September 2008. During 2006, for the first time, TACs and quotas for the Baltic Sea were discussed separately from those covering other Community waters. Meanwhile, in March 2005 the European Commission announced its decision to initiate a consultation process on a new integrated EU maritime policy aimed at developing the potential of the maritime economy in an environmentally sustainable manner. In October 2007 the Commission presented a communication on integrated maritime policy, which was endorsed by the Council in December. An accompanying action plan included fisheries-related initiatives such as a scheme to strengthen international co-operation against destructive deep-sea fishing practices and measures to halt imports of illegal fisheries products.

In April 2005, to improve further compliance with the CFP as reformed in 2002, the Council of Ministers agreed to establish a Community Fisheries Control Agency (CFCA). The Agency, through the implementation of joint deployment plans, aims to strengthen the uniformity and effectiveness of enforcement of fisheries regulations by pooling EU and individual countries' means of control and monitoring and by co-ordinating enforcement activities. The CFCA (now the European Fisheries Control Agency—EFCA) adopted five joint deployment plans for 2009, three of which covered the regulated fisheries in the North Atlantic, and cod fisheries in the Baltic, North Sea and adjacent areas; and two of which covered the cod fisheries in Western Waters, and the regulated fisheries in waters beyond the national fisheries jurisdiction in the North Eastern Atlantic.

In July 2006, in order to facilitate, within the framework of the CFP, a sustainable European fishing and aquaculture industry, the Agriculture and Fisheries Council adopted a regulation on the establishment of a European Fisheries Fund (EFF), which replaced the FIFG on 1 January 2007. The Fund was to support the industry as it adapted its fleet in order to make it more competitive, and to promote measures to protect the environment. It was also to assist the communities that were most affected by the resulting changes to diversify their economic base. The EFF was to remain in place for seven years, with a total budget of some €3,800m. The regulation also set forth detailed rules and arrangements regarding structural assistance, including an obligation on all member states to draw up a national strategic plan for their fisheries sectors. Assistance was henceforth to be channelled through a single national EFF programme.

In January 2009 the European Commission adopted the first EU Plan of Action for the Conservation and Management of Sharks, which also aimed to protect related species, such as skates and rays, and was to apply wherever the EU fleet operates, both within and outside European waters. At the beginning of January 2010 a framework of new rules to strengthen the CFP control system entered into force, in accordance with which no country was to be given preferential treatment over another, thereby promoting, it was envisaged, a culture of compliance throughout the sector. The framework comprised three separate, yet inter-related, regulations on: combating illegal, unreported and unregulated (IUU) fishing; authorizations for the EU fleet operating outside EU waters; and

establishing a control system for ensuring compliance with CFP rules. Under the new IUU regulation, all marine fishery products traded with the EU were to be certified and their origin traceable under a comprehensive catch certification scheme.

Legally bound to review some areas of the CFP by 2012, and concerned to address depleted stock levels and fleet overcapacity, the European Commission launched a consultation process on CFP reform in April 2009; following the termination of the consultations in December, the Commission published a report in April 2010. Five structural failings of the CFP were identified: the issue of fleet overcapacity; the need to refocus the CFP on the ecological sustainability of fish stocks and the minimization of 'discards' (dead fish or other marine organisms caught in excess of quotas that are dumped overboard, having been caught unintentionally); the desire to adapt fisheries governance away from centralized control, towards regionalized implementation of principles; involving the sector in resource management and implementation of the CFP; and developing a culture of compliance with rule. The Commission published its draft proposals for reform in July 2011. The proposals provided for returning fish stocks to sustainable levels by 2015, using a multi-annual, ecosystem approach. The proposals provided for the establishment of clear targets and timetables to prevent overfishing, and to benefit small-scale fisheries, while providing transferrable fishing concessions. In December 2011 the European Commission proposed the establishment of a new European Maritime and Fisheries Fund (EMFF) to co-ordinate the EU's maritime and fisheries policies in 2014–20, replacing the EFF. The EMFF, which was expected to have a budget of some €6,500m., was to be responsible for implementing the objectives of the revised CFP, assisting fishermen to adapt to more sustainable methods of fishing and helping coastal areas to diversify their economies. In February 2013 EU ministers responsible for fisheries agreed gradually to introduce a ban on discards between 2014 and 2017. Discards of fish living near the surface (pelagic fish) were to be banned by 2015, while discards of deep-sea (demersal) fish were to be banned by 2016; Mediterranean stocks were to be exempt from the ban until 2017 and, controversially, southern member states were to be permitted to continue to discard up to 7% of catches beyond 2017. Political agreement on the revised CFP was reached in May 2013; it was approved by the Council in October, and in December the European Parliament voted officially to adopt the reformed CFP, which came into effect on 1 January 2014. In late January political agreement on the EMFF was reached between the European Parliament and the Council.

Bilateral fisheries agreements have been signed with other countries (Norway, Iceland and the Faroe Islands) allowing limited reciprocal fishing rights and other advantages ('reciprocity agreements'), and with some African and Indian Ocean countries and Pacific Islands that receive technical and financial assistance in strengthening their fishing industries in return for allowing EU boats to fish in their waters ('fisheries partnership agreements'). Following the withdrawal of Greenland from the Community in February 1985, Community vessels retained fishing rights in Greenland waters, in exchange for financial compensation. In recent years, however, owing to growing competition for scarce fish resources, it has become increasingly difficult for the EU to conclude bilateral fisheries agreements giving its fleets access to surplus fish stocks in the waters of third countries.

RESEARCH AND INNOVATION

In the amendments to the Treaty of Rome, effective from July 1987 (now the Treaty on the Functioning of the European Union), a section on research and technology (subsequently restyled 'research and innovation') was included for the first time, defining the extent of Community co-operation in this area. Most of the funds allocated to research and innovation are granted to companies or institutions that apply to participate in EU research programmes.

In December 2006 the Council adopted a decision establishing the Seventh Framework Programme for research and technological development (FP7), and also established the Seventh Framework Programme of Euratom, for nuclear research and training activities in 2007–11, with a budget of €2,702m. A budget of €48,770m. was approved for the four specific programmes into which FP7 had been structured: co-operation (€32,413m.); ideas (to be implemented by the European Research Council—ERC—€7,510m.); people (€4,750m.); and capacities (€4,097m.). Joint technology initiatives (JTIs), in which industry, research organizations and public authorities would form public-private partnerships to pursue common research objectives, were a major new element of FP7. In December 2007 the Council adopted resolutions establishing ARTEMIS, a JTI involving research into embedded computer systems (specialized computer components dedicated to a specific task that are part of a larger system); the Clean Sky JTI, which aimed to develop environmentally sound and reasonably priced aircraft; the Innovative Medicines Initiative (IMI), which aimed to attract pharmaceutical research and development to Europe, in order to improve access to the newest and most effective medicines; and Nanoelectronics Technologies 2020 (ENIAC), a JTI which aimed to develop European nanoelectronic capabilities. In May 2008 the Council approved the establishment of the Fuel Cells and Hydrogen JTI, which aims to develop new hydrogen energy and fuel cell technologies for use in transport, and stationary and portable applications.

In February 2006 the Commission recommended the establishment of a European Institute of Technology (EIT), to promote excellence in higher education, research and innovation, and based on a Europe-wide network of 'knowledge and innovation communities' (partnerships comprising higher education institutions, research organizations, companies and other interested parties). The EU's contribution to the EIT was forecast at €308.7m. during 2008–13. A directive on the establishment of the EIT (known by this time as the European Institute of Innovation and Technology) came into force in April 2008, and the inaugural meeting of the EIT's 18-member governing board took place in September. In April 2010 the EIT's headquarters moved to Budapest, Hungary.

In October 2010 the Commission adopted a communication on the new Innovation Union, part of the 10-year Europe 2020 Strategy, designed to help the EU economy to recover from the economic crisis, by encouraging global competitiveness and innovation. From 2014 FP7 was superseded by Horizon 2020, a financial instrument to aid implementation of the Innovation Union. Horizon 2020, which was to have a budget of €80,000m. for 2014–20, combined the funding previously provided through the FP7 and the innovation part of the Competitiveness and Innovation Framework Programme.

In January 2000 the Commission launched an initiative to establish a European Research Area (ERA). The aim was to promote the more effective use of scientific resources within a single area, in order to enhance the EU's competitiveness and create jobs. Detailed plans for the creation of the ERC, as an independent funding body for science, were incorporated in the FP7 agenda. The ERC commenced operations in February 2007, with a budget of €7,500m. The ERC's Dedicated Implementation Structure, the Council's executive agency responsible for applying the strategies and methodologies defined by the Scientific Council, became operational in July 2009. The mandate of the European Research Area Committee (now European Research Area and Innovation Committee) was approved by the Council in May 2010; the Committee replaced the Scientific and Technical Research Committee (CREST) established in 1995, and provides strategic policy advice to the Council, the Commission and the EU member states on research and innovation issues of relevance to the ERA.

The EU is making efforts to integrate space science into its research activities, and has increasingly been collaborating with the European Space Agency (ESA). In September 2000 the EU and ESA adopted a joint European strategy for space, and in the following year the two bodies established a joint task force. In November 2003 negotiations on a framework agreement for structured co-operation between the EU and ESA were concluded. The European Space Policy, providing a common political framework for space activities in Europe, was adopted in May 2007. The European Commission, ESA and Eurocontrol developed the European Geostationary Navigation Overlay Service (EGNOS), the first pan-European satellite navigation system, which extends the US Global Positioning System (GPS) system, and is suitable for use in challenging navigational situations in which safety is critical (for example, guiding boats through narrow channels). In April 2009 ownership of EGNOS was transferred to the European Commission. In October the European Commission announced the launch of the free EGNOS Open Service. The European Commission and ESA are also collaborating to design and develop a European satellite and navigation system, Galileo, to consist of about 30 satellites, a global network of tracking stations, and central control facilities in Europe. The European Global Navigation Satellite System Supervisory Authority (GSA) aims to use the Galileo, GPS and Global Navigation Satellite systems to provide a global, integrated satellite navigation service under civilian control.

The Joint Research Centre (JRC) was established under the European Atomic Energy Community. Directed by the European Commission, but relying for much of its funding on individual contracts, the JRC is a collection of seven institutes, based at five different sites around Europe—Ispra, Italy; Geel, Belgium; Karlsruhe, Germany; Seville, Spain; and Petten, Netherlands. While nuclear research and development remain major concerns of the institutes, their research efforts have diversified substantially over the years. The JRC identified seven priority areas to be addressed under FP7: food safety; biotechnology, chemicals and health; the environment (including climate change and natural disasters); energy and transport; nuclear energy, safety and security; the Lisbon Strategy, information society and rural development; and internal and external security, anti-fraud measures and development aid. Nuclear work accounts for about one-quarter of all JRC activities, with the share accounted for by non-nuclear work increasing. The JRC also provides technical assistance to applicant countries. The JRC's budget for the FP7 period was €1,751m. for non-nuclear activities and €517m. for nuclear activities.

In 2005 the Enterprise and Industry Directorate-General launched the PRO INNO ('Promoting innovation in Europe') initiative, which aimed to foster trans-European co-operation between national and sub-national innovation programmes and activities. The INNO-Policy TrendChart provides detailed information about innovation trends in 39 countries in Europe, the Mediterranean region, North America and Asia. In order to analyse the EU's performance, the Commission used a set of performance indicators to draw up a so-called European Innovation Scoreboard (EIS). After the adoption by the Commission of the Innovation Union in October 2010, the EIS was re-established as the Innovation Union Scoreboard (IUS), in order to monitor implementation of the Innovation Union. The IUS for 2013, published in March, uses 24 research and innovation-related indicators, and covers all EU member states, as well as Iceland, the former Yugoslav republic of Macedonia, Norway, Serbia, Switzerland and Turkey. Sweden, Germany, Denmark and Finland were designated 'European innovation leaders', outperforming the rest of Europe. However, when compared with major global competitor nations, a significant gap remained between the EU and the superior performance in innovation of Japan, the Republic of Korea (South Korea) and the USA.

The EU also co-operates with non-member countries in bilateral research projects. The Commission and 38 (mainly European) countries—including EU members as individuals—participate, as full members, in the EUREKA programme of research and development in market-orientated industrial technology, which was launched in 1985; in addition to the full members, South Korea is designated a EUREKA associated country, and Albania and Bosnia and Herzegovina participate in EUREKA projects through a network of National Information Points. EUREKA (the acronym of the European Research Co-ordination Agency), sponsors projects focusing on robotics, engineering, information technology and environmental science, allows resources to be pooled and promotes collaboration. Most of EUREKA's funding is provided by private sources. The Community research and development information service (CORDIS) disseminates findings in the field of advanced technology.

ENERGY

The treaty establishing the European Atomic Energy Community (Euratom) came into force on 1 January 1958. This was designed to encourage the growth of the nuclear energy industry in the Community by conducting research, providing access to information, supplying nuclear fuels, building reactors and establishing common laws and procedures. A common market for nuclear materials was introduced in 1959 and there is a common insurance scheme against nuclear risks. In 1977 the Commission began granting loans on behalf of Euratom to finance investment in nuclear power stations and the enrichment of fissile materials. An agreement with the International Atomic Energy Agency (IAEA) entered into force in the same year, to facilitate co-operation in research on nuclear safeguards and controls. The EU's Joint Research Centre (JRC, see Research and Innovation) conducts research on nuclear safety and the management of radioactive waste.

The Joint European Torus (JET) is an experimental thermonuclear machine designed to pioneer new processes of nuclear fusion, using the 'Tokamak' system of magnetic confinement to heat gases to very high temperatures and bring about the fusion of tritium and deuterium nuclei. Fusion is the source of power for stars and is viewed as a 'cleaner' approach to energy production than nuclear fission and fossil fuels. Switzerland is also a member of the JET project (formally inaugurated in 1984), which is based in Culham, United Kingdom, and which is funded by the European Commission. In 1991 JET became the first fusion facility in the world to achieve significant production of controlled fusion power. The European Fusion Development Agreement (EFDA), which entered into force in March 1999, and a new JET implementing agreement, which came into force in January 2000, provide the framework for the collective use of the JET facilities. In 1988 work began with representatives of Japan, the former USSR and the USA on the joint design of an International Thermonuclear Experimental Reactor (ITER), based on JET but with twice its capacity. In mid-2005 the six participant teams in the ITER project (the People's Republic of China, the EU—represented by Euratom, Japan, the Republic of Korea, Russia and the USA), organized under the auspices of the IAEA, agreed that the vast trial reactor would be located in Cadarache, in southern France. In 2005 India also became a full partner in the project. The main aim of ITER is to demonstrate the potential for fusion to generate electrical power (ITER would be the first fusion experiment with a net output of power) as well as to collect the data required to design and operate the first electricity-producing plant. In March 2007 the Council established the European Joint Undertaking for ITER and the Development of Fusion Energy (Fusion for Energy) to manage the EU's contribution to ITER. Overall responsibility for ITER was formally assumed by the newly established ITER International Fusion Energy Organization in November, following the ratification of a joint implementation agreement by all seven participants in the project. The construction of the project was expected to be accomplished during 2011–16, after which the reactor would remain operational for 20 years, at a total estimated cost of €10,000m., of which the EU was to contribute about 50%.

Legislation on the completion of the 'internal energy market', adopted in 1990, aimed to encourage the sale of electricity and gas across national borders by opening national networks to foreign supplies, obliging suppliers to publish their prices and co-ordinating investment in energy. Ministers responsible for energy reached agreement in June 1996 on rules for the progressive liberalization of the electricity market. In December 1997 the Council agreed rules to allow the gas market to be opened up in three stages, over a 10-year period. In 2000 European electricity and gas energy regulators established the Council of European Energy Regulators (CEER), a not-for-profit association that promotes voluntary co-operation. In 2001 the Commission amended the timetable for liberalizing the electricity and gas markets: by 2003 all non-domestic consumers were to have the freedom to choose their electricity supplier; by 2004 non-domestic consumers were to have the freedom to choose their gas supplier; and by 2005 all consumers, domestic and non-domestic, would be able to choose both suppliers. In June 2002 the European Council confirmed amended target dates for the complete two-stage liberalization of the markets: opening up by July 2004 for non-domestic users and by July 2007 for domestic users. The European Regulators Group for electricity and gas (ERGEG) was established in November 2003 to act as an advisory group of independent national regulatory authorities to assist the European Commission in consolidating the internal market for electricity and gas. In early 2006 the ERGEG launched a regional initiative which created three gas and seven electricity zones within the EU. The initiative focused on removing barriers to market integration at a regional level, in order to facilitate the creation of a single competitive market. In 2011 ERGEG was superseded by the Agency for the Co-operation of Energy Regulators (ACER), based in Ljubljana, Slovenia.

In October 2005 the EU signed a treaty establishing an Energy Community, which entered into force in July 2006, and extended the EU's internal energy market to South-Eastern Europe and further afield (contracting parties to the treaty comprise Albania, Bosnia and Herzegovina, Croatia, Kosovo, the former Yugoslav Republic of Macedonia, Montenegro and Serbia). Armenia, Georgia, Norway and Turkey have been admitted as observers. The treaty, which aimed to facilitate the creation of an integrated pan-European market for electricity and gas, required the signatories to adopt EU energy regulations. The treaty provided for the liberalization of electricity and gas markets within participating countries by 2008 for non-domestic users, and by 2015 for domestic users. The World Bank estimated that this planned extension of the single European market for electricity and gas would lead to investment of €21,000m. in energy infrastructure in South-Eastern Europe over 15 years.

The Commission has consistently urged the formation of an effective overall energy policy. The five-year programmes, SAVE and SAVE II, introduced in 1991 and 1995, respectively, aimed to establish energy efficiency (e.g. reduction in the energy consumption of vehicles and the use of renewable energy) as a criterion for all EU projects. SAVE was integrated into Energy, Environment and Sustainable Development (EESD), initiated under the Fifth Framework Programme (FP5) for 1998–2002 and subsequently incorporated into a new, overarching plan, Intelligent Energy for Europe (IEE), which was adopted by the Commission for 2003–06 as part of the Sixth Framework Programme (FP6). IEE aimed to strengthen the security of supply and to promote energy efficiency and renewable energy sources (RES) such as wind, solar, biomass and small-scale hydropower. IEE was expanded under a new Competitiveness and Innovation Framework Programme (CIP), in conjunction with the Seventh Framework Programme (FP7) for research during 2007–13. Under CIP, IEE II incorporated three separate elements: energy efficiency (SAVE); RES for the production of electricity and heat (ALTENER); and the energy aspects of transport (STEER); IEE 2 was allocated a budget of €730m. The EU Sustainable Energy Europe Campaign, covering 2005–11, sought to accelerate private investment in sustainable energy technologies, to spread best practices, and to encourage alliances among sustainable energy stakeholders. From 2014 the activities supported by IEE were incorporated into the EU's research and innovation programme, Horizon 2020.

In order to help the EU to meet its joint commitment under the Kyoto Protocol to reduce greenhouse gas emissions by 8% from 1990 levels by 2012, and to encourage the use of more efficient energy technologies, in July 2003 the Council established the Emissions Trading Scheme, now Emissions Trading System (ETS). Under the scheme, which came into force in January 2005, individual companies were allocated a free greenhouse gas emission allowance by national governments. If they reduced emissions beyond their allocated quota, they would be allowed to sell their credits on the open market. During the first phase, covering 2005–07, ETS was only applied to large industrial and energy undertakings in certain sectors and only covered carbon dioxide emissions. Several member states opted to extend the scope of ETS for the second trading period

(2008–12), and it incorporated revised rules for monitoring and reporting, more stringent restrictions on emissions, and an increased number of combustion sources. The third trading period (2013–20) introduced significant changes. Notably, an EU-wide cap on emissions replaced the national targets hitherto in place. Auctioning (as opposed to free allocation), became the default method for the allocation of allowances; in 2013 over 40% of allowances were to be auctioned, and this proportion was to increase gradually on an annual basis.

In January 2007 the Commission attempted to initiate a more coherent integration of the EU energy and climate policies by incorporating in its proposals a comprehensive series of measures addressing the issue of climate change, while emphasizing the interdependency between security of supply and the promotion of sustainable energy sources. The measures included the establishment of a biennial Strategic Energy Review to monitor progress in all aspects of energy policy, which was to constitute the basis for future action plans to be adopted by the Council and the Parliament. The Council endorsed the proposals in March; it also stated that its strategic objective was to limit the increase in the average global temperature to no more than 2°C above pre-industrial levels. The EU was to commit itself to reducing its greenhouse gas emissions by 20% (compared with their 1990 levels) by 2020. At the same time, the renewable energy sector was to supply 20% of EU energy by 2020, compared with 6.6% in 1990, and the share of biofuels in overall consumption of energy by the transport sector was to increase by 10%, also by 2020. New legislation was to facilitate the market penetration of renewable energy sources, while individual member states were to decide whether to develop their nuclear electricity sectors. The development of a European strategic energy technology plan was agreed, with the aim of increasing research into sustainable technologies (including low-carbon technology) by 50% by 2014. In November 2007 the Commission launched the European Strategic Energy Technology Plan (SET-Plan), in which it outlined plans to introduce six new industrial initiatives, focusing on wind power; solar power; biofuels; carbon dioxide capture, transport and storage; the electricity grid (including the creation of a centre to implement a research programme on the European transmission network); and sustainable nuclear fission. In December 2011 the Commission adopted a communication entitled *Energy Roadmap 2050*, with the aim of facilitating implementation of reductions in greenhouse gases to between 80% and 95% below 1990 levels by 2050, while simultaneously ensuring the security of energy supplies and competitiveness. In March 2013 the Commission published a progress report on renewable energy, following the adoption of legislation on renewable energy in 2009. The majority of member states had experienced significant growth in the usage of renewable energy sources; by 2010 renewable energy accounted for 12.7% of EU energy supplies.

Ministers responsible for energy from the EU member states and 12 Mediterranean countries agreed at a meeting held in June 1996 in Trieste, Italy, to develop a Euro-Mediterranean gas and electricity network. The first Euro-Med Energy Forum was held in May 1997, and an action plan for 1998–2002 was adopted in May 1998. In May 2003 the ministers responsible for energy of the Euro-Med partnership (including the ministers from the 10 accession states) adopted a declaration launching the Second Regional Energy Plan (2003–06). An Energy Forum took place in September 2006, to agree on priorities for 2007–10. The fifth Euro-Med ministerial conference on energy, held in Cyprus in December 2007, endorsed an action plan for further energy co-operation, covering 2008–13. Priorities included the harmonization of regional energy markets and legislation; the promotion of sustainable development in the energy sector; and the development of initiatives of common interest in areas such as infrastructure, investment financing and research and development. In December 2013 a meeting of Euro-Med ministers for energy took place in Brussels, Belgium. The need to strengthen regional energy co-operation to enhance energy efficiency in the Mediterranean basin was discussed, with the aim of increasing socio-economic development and aiding the transition to low-carbon, energy efficient economies of the region.

The EU promotes trans-European networks (TENs, see also Transport), with the aim of developing European energy, telecommunications and transport through the interconnection and opening up of national networks. In 2003 a revision of the guidelines for the TEN-Energy (TEN-E) programme was undertaken to take into account the priorities of the enlarged EU. The revised guidelines, adopted by the Council in July 2006, sought to enhance the security of energy supplies in Europe; to strengthen the internal energy market of the enlarged EU; to support the modernization of energy systems in partner countries; to increase the share of renewable energies, in particular in electricity generation; and to facilitate the realization of major new energy infrastructure projects. The TEN-E networks policy, in particular, aimed to secure and diversify additional gas import capacity from sources in Russia, the Caspian Basin, northern Africa and the Middle East. The budget agreed for the TEN-E programme for 2007–13 totalled €155m. In October 2011 the European Commission published a proposal for a regulation on guidelines for trans-European energy infrastructure, which aimed to ensure the completion of energy networks (12 priority corridors were identified) and storage facilities by 2020. In November 2013 the European Parliament approved the EU's new infrastructure policy. A new Connecting Europe Facility (CEF) for the fields of transport, energy and telecommunications was introduced, with funding of €5,850m. to be made available for improvements to trans-European energy infrastructure in 2014–20. In January 2014 an Innovation and Networks Executive Agency commenced operations in Brussels, to manage the principal funding programmes relating to transport, energy and digital policy.

EU member states are required to maintain minimum stocks of crude oil and/or petroleum products. In accordance with a European Council Directive issued in September 2009 member states had to ensure, by 31 December 2012, that these corresponded to at least 90 days of average daily net imports or to 61 days of average daily internal consumption. A Green Paper of March 2006, entitled 'Towards a European strategy for the security of energy supply', re-emphasized the links between security of supply, the creation of a liberalized, integrated EU energy market and the development of sustainable energy. To protect energy supplies against the risk of natural catastrophes, terrorist threats, political risks and rising oil and gas prices, it recommended the following measures: the development of smart electricity networks; the establishment of a European Energy Supply observatory to monitor supply and demand patterns in EU energy markets; improved network security through increased collaboration and exchange of information between transmission system operators under an overarching European centre of energy networks; a solidarity mechanism to ensure rapid assistance to any member state confronted by damage to its essential infrastructure; and common standards to protect infrastructure and the development of a common European voice to promote partnerships with third countries. In May 2007 an EU Network of Energy Security Correspondents was launched to provide early warnings, and thus enhance the EU's ability to react to pressure on external energy security.

In mid-June 2009 the Council formally adopted a new liberalization agreement for the EU's gas and electricity markets, the Third Energy Package (the Second Energy Package had been agreed in 2003), which was to enter into effect in 2011–13, and which established common rules for the internal markets in gas and electricity; included regulations on conditions for access to natural gas transmission networks and the network for cross-border exchanges in electricity; and provided for the establishment of ACER. The Third Energy Package aimed to separate energy supply and production from network operations; ensure fair competition both within the EU, and with respect to third countries; strengthen the national energy regulators; and create European Networks of Transmission Operators for electricity (ENTSO-E) and for gas (ENTSO-G). In July the new ENTSO-E took over all the operational tasks of the six existing European Transmission System Operators associations. The new ENTSO-G was established at the beginning of December, and comprises 33 Transmission System Operators from 22 European countries in an effort to facilitate progress towards the creation of a single energy market.

In November 2010 the Commission adopted a communication entitled *Energy 2020: A strategy for competitive, sustainable and secure energy*, which defined the Commission's energy priorities for the next 10 years, focusing on the need to save energy; to ensure a competitive market with secure energy supplies; to promote technological advances; and to encourage effective international negotiation. In early February 2011 the first EU energy summit was held, in Brussels, Belgium, at which an agreement was adopted on a number of strategic energy-related areas. In particular, the summit concluded that work should be undertaken to develop a transparent, rule-governed relationship with Russia. The summit also made clear its intention to promote investment in renewable energy, and sustainable low-carbon technologies; to accelerate the liberalization of energy markets, in order to bring them into accordance with EU law (about one-half of the EU member states had liberalized their energy markets, but only Denmark had fully implemented the latest legislation; some 60 infringement proceedings had been brought against member states for failing to open up their markets); to improve adherence to the 2020 20% energy-efficiency target (which aimed to reduce the use of greenhouse gases by 20%, to increase the proportion of renewable energy used to 20%, and to improve overall energy efficiency by 20% by 2020); and to investigate the potential extraction and use of unconventional fossil fuel sources, such as shale gas and oil shale, favoured, in particular, by Poland.

ENTERPRISE AND INDUSTRY

Industrial co-operation was the earliest activity of the Community. The treaty establishing the European Coal and Steel Community (ECSC) came into force in July 1952, and by the end of 1954 nearly all barriers to trade in coal, coke, steel, pig iron and scrap iron had been removed. The ECSC treaty expired in July 2002, and the provisions of the ECSC treaty were incorporated in the EEC treaty, on the grounds that it was no longer appropriate to treat the coal and steel sectors separately.

In the late 1970s and 1980s measures were adopted radically to restructure the steel industry in response to a dramatic reduction in world demand for steel. During the 1990s, however, new technologies and modern production processes were introduced, and the European steel sector showed signs of substantial recovery. Privatization and cross-border mergers also improved the industry's competitive performance, and by the 2000s Europe was a competitive global exporter. In March 2004 the European Commission and major stakeholders in the European steel industry launched the European Steel Technology Platform, the long-term aim of which was to help the sector to meet the challenges of the global marketplace, changing supply and demand patterns, environmental objectives, and the simplification of EU and national legislation and regulation in this field. In addition, the May 2004 enlargement of the EU increased the need for extensive restructuring of the steel industries. The steel industry played a relatively larger role in the 10 new member states, compared with the existing 15 members. In 2008 the European steel industry produced 198m. metric tons of steel, compared with some 160m. tons in the early 2000s. The industry directly employed around 420,000 EU citizens (with several times this number employed in the steel-processing, -usage and -recycling industries) in 2008. However, from 2009 the global economic downturn resulted in a decline in production. In December 2012 the European Parliament recommended the establishment of a tripartite body comprising representatives of trade unions, the steel industry and the Commission, to aid the development of the industry, and to avert the threat of its possible relocation outside the EU. In June 2013 the European Commission published an Action Plan for the steel industry. The demand for steel had declined by 27% since the beginning of the economic crisis, and sectoral employment had decreased by 10% between 2007 and 2011; none the less, the EU remained the second largest producer of steel worldwide.

The European textiles and clothing industry has been seriously affected by overseas competition. From 1974 the Community participated in the Multi-Fibre Arrangement (MFA, see World Trade Organization—WTO), to limit imports from low-cost suppliers overseas. However, as a result of the Uruguay Round of GATT (General Agreement on Tariffs and Trade) trade negotiations, the quotas that existed under the MFA were progressively eliminated during 1994–2004 in accordance with an Agreement on Textiles and Clothing. A report published by the Commission in 2000 established future priorities for the sector. Particular importance was attached to ensuring a smooth transition to the quota-free world environment (from 1 January 2005), to enable third countries currently exporting to the EU to maintain their competitive position, and to secure for EU textiles and clothing industries in third countries market access conditions similar to those offered by the EU. A high-level group on textiles and clothing, established by the Commission, published a report in September 2006, which sought, inter alia, to chart the likely development of the sector up to 2020. The report noted that a Commission statement released in mid-2006 had indicated that the anticipated disruptive impact of the liberalization of Chinese textiles exports to the EU had been confined to a fairly restricted range of product categories. The People's Republic of China's share of exports to the EU of products in the liberalized categories had risen markedly, but the statement noted, too, that China was becoming an important growth market for exports of textiles and clothing from the EU. In October 2007 the European Commission agreed not to renew quotas on textiles from China, but instead to introduce a system of monitoring imports. Trade in textiles and clothing was fully liberalized from January 2009, and China continued to increase its market share in Europe.

Production in EU member states' shipyards fell drastically from the 1970s, mainly as a result of competition from shipbuilders in the Far East. In the first half of the 1980s a Council directive allowed for subsidies to help tp reorganize the shipbuilding industry and to increase efficiency, but subsequently rigorous curbs on state aid to the industry were introduced. State aid was eventually withdrawn in early 2001. From 2000 construction activity increased somewhat. However, the number of new orders declined sharply from the latter half of 2008 as a result of the global economic downturn.

Harmonization of national company law to form a common legal structure within the Union has led to the adoption of directives on disclosure of information, company capital, internal mergers, the accounts of companies and of financial institutions, the division of companies, the qualification of auditors, single-member private limited companies, mergers, takeover bids, and the formation of joint ventures.

The European Patent Convention (EPC) was signed in 1973 and entered into force in 1977. Revisions to the Convention were agreed in November 2000, and a revised EPC entered into force on 13 December 2007. In June 1997 the Commission published proposals to simplify the European patent system through the introduction of a unitary Community patent, to remove the need to file patent applications with individual member states. Upon the entry into force in December 2009 of the Lisbon Treaty, which provided a new legal basis for the establishment of unitary intellectual property titles within the EU, the proposed Community patent was renamed the EU patent. During that month the European Council agreed a draft regulation on the EU patent, in accordance with which it was envisaged that the EU would accede to the EPC (which would require further revision to the Convention), and the European Patent Office (EPO, based in Munich, Germany) would grant EU patents with unitary effect throughout the territory of the EU. Infringement and validity issues relating to the planned EU patent were to be addressed by a proposed European and EU Patents Court. On 11 December 2012 the European Parliament approved the so-called patent package, comprising two draft regulations, on increased co-operation to facilitate unitary patent protection and associated translation arrangements, and an agreement on the establishment of a Unified Patent Court, which prepared the way for the introduction of a European patent with unitary effect. The agreement establishing the Unitary Patent Convention (UPC) was signed in mid-February 2013, and was to enter into force following its ratification by a minimum of 13 EU member states, including France, Germany and the United Kingdom. The UPC was intended to apply throughout the participating EU member states (Italy and Spain did not intend to take part in the Convention), and was to be gradually introduced from 2015.

An Office for Harmonization in the Internal Market (OHIM), based in Alicante, Spain, was established in December 1993, and is responsible for the registration of Union trademarks and for ensuring that these receive uniform protection throughout the EU.

The liberalization of public procurement has played an important role in the establishment of the internal market. From January 1993 the liberalization of procurement was extended to include public utilities in the previously excluded sectors of energy, transport, drinking water and telecommunications. In 1996 the Commission launched the Système d'information pour les marchés publics (SIMAP) programme, to provide information on rules, procedures and opportunities in the public procurement market, and to encourage the optimum use of information technology in public procurement. In 2002 the European Parliament adopted a regulation aimed at simplifying the rules on procurement of contract notices, by introducing a single system for classifying public procurement, to be used by all public authorities; a regulation updating the classification system was adopted in November 2007. The European Public Procurement Network was established in January 2003. The objective of this network, which comprises all EU member states, EU candidate countries, European Economic Area (EEA) members, Switzerland and other European countries, was to strengthen the application of public procurement rules through a mutual exchange of experience. Reforms to the EU's public procurement directives were adopted in 2004 in an attempt to make the often complex rules more transparent, efficient and comprehensible. In November 2007 a directive was adopted with the aim of improving the effectiveness of review procedures concerning the award of public contracts. In April 2012 the Commission adopted a communication outlining a strategy for a full transition to e-procurement (procurement by electronic means of communication) throughout the EU by mid-2016.

In 1990 the European Council adopted two directives with the aim of removing the tax obstacles encountered by companies operating across borders: the Merger Directive was designed to reduce tax measures that could hamper business reorganization and the Parent-Subsidiary Directive abolished double taxation of profit distributed between parent companies in one member state and their subsidiaries in others. In October 2001 the European Council adopted two legislative instruments enabling companies to form a European Company (known as a Societas Europaea—SE). A vital element of the internal market, the legislation gave companies operating in more than one member state the option of establishing themselves as single companies, thereby able to function throughout the EU under one set of rules and through a unified management system; companies might be merged to establish an SE. The legislation was aimed at making cross-border enterprise management more flexible and less bureaucratic, and at helping to improve competitiveness. In July 2003 the Council adopted similar legislation enabling co-operatives to form a European Co-operative Society (Societas Cooperativa Europaea—SCE). In September 2004 the Commission established a working group to advance the development of a common consolidated corporate tax base. In February 2005 the Council approved an amendment to the Merger Directive of 1990, extending its provisions to cover a wider range of companies, including SEs and SCEs. A directive aimed at facilitating cross-border mergers of limited liability companies was adopted by the European Parliament and the Council in October 2005. The establishment of SPEs from mid-2008 (see below) aimed to facilitate the operation of small and medium-sized enterprises (SMEs) across borders.

In March 1996 the Commission agreed new guidelines for state aid to SMEs. A Charter for Small Enterprises, approved in June 2000,

aimed to support SMEs in areas such as education and training, the development of regulations, and taxation and financial matters, and to increase representation of the interests of small businesses at national and EU level. In November 2005 the Commission launched a new policy framework for SMEs, proposing specific actions in five areas: promoting entrepreneurship and skills; improving SMEs' access to markets; simplifying regulations; improving SMEs' growth potential; and strengthening dialogue and consultation with SME stakeholders. A new Competitiveness and Innovation Framework Programme (CIP), targeted primarily at SMEs, was formally approved by the Council of the European Union in October 2006. The CIP for 2007–13 had an overall budget of €3,621m., and was divided into three operational programmes: the Entrepreneurship and Innovation Programme (EIP); the Information Communication Technologies Policy Support Programme (ICT-PSP); and the Intelligent Energy Europe Programme (IEE). In January 2007 the Commission launched an action programme aimed at reducing unnecessary administrative burdens on companies, primarily SMEs, by one-quarter by 2012. In addition, 10 'fast-track' measures were identified, which, it was estimated, would reduce the burden on businesses by €1,300m. per year. In June 2008 the Commission adopted the Small Business Act for Europe (SBA), which was endorsed by the EU Council of Ministers in December. The SBA aimed further to streamline bureaucratic procedures for SMEs, and to enable businesses to establish a European Private Company (Societas Privata Europaea—SPE), which would operate according to uniform principles in all member states, thereby simplifying procedures for SMEs operating across borders. By 2010 there were more than 20m. SMEs in the EU, accounting for 99% of all EU enterprises. In February 2011 the results of a review of the SBA's work in 2008–10 was published. The review concluded that some 100,000 SMEs had benefited from the CIP; a new late payment directive required public authorities to pay suppliers within 30 days, improving cash flow; the resources (both financial and in terms of time taken) required to establish a new SME had been reduced; simplified online procedures and opportunities for joint bidding had facilitated the participation of SMEs in public procurement; and the establishment of a new EU SME Centre in China had helped SMEs to access Chinese markets. The review also identified a number of priority areas for further action: the need to assist SMEs in accessing finance, for investment and growth, as well as targeted measures aimed at making investors more aware of the benefits of SMEs; improving regulation; enhancing the ability of SMEs fully to utilize the common market, with proposals for a Common Consolidated Corporate Tax Base, measures to facilitate cross-border debt recovery, and a revision of the European standardization system to make it more accessible to SMEs; and assisting SMEs in dealing with the issues of globalization and climate change. A new programme, COSME, for the Competitiveness of Enterprises and Small and Medium-sized Enterprises, was to be implemented in 2014–20, with an anticipated budget of some €2,300m. COSME was to support SMEs by facilitating access to finance and to markets; providing support to entrepreneurs; and helping to ensure favourable condition for the conception and growth of businesses. The European Business Angels Network provides a means of introduction between SMEs and investors and encourages the exchange of expertise.

The European Investment Bank provides finance for small businesses by means of 'global loans' to financial intermediaries. A mechanism providing small businesses with subsidized loans was approved by ministers in April 1992.

The Enterprise Europe Network, launched in February 2008, comprises contact points providing information and advice to businesses, in particular SMEs, on EU matters, in more than 50 countries, including the EU member states, EU candidate countries, members of the EEA, and other participating third countries. The EU's other information services for business include the Community Research and Development Information Service (CORDIS, see Research and Innovation) and the internet-based Your Europe: Business, which brings together advice and data from various sources. In addition, more than 150 accredited Business and Innovation Centres (BICs) operate in the EU countries, with a mission to promote entrepreneurship and the creation of innovative businesses, and to assist existing companies to enhance their prospects through innovation.

The Commission adopted a Multiannual Programme for Enterprise and Entrepreneurship (MAP) covering 2001–05, aimed particularly at SMEs. Stronger measures were proposed for the protection of intellectual property rights (IPRs), and the harmonization of legislation on IPRs was advocated (differences between national laws in this respect could constitute protectionist barriers to the EU's principle of free movement of goods and services). In April 2004 a directive was adopted on the enforcement of IPRs, to make it easier to enforce copyrights, patents and trademarks in the EU and to punish those who tampered with technical mechanisms designed to prevent copying or counterfeiting. In January 2007 the MAP, which had been extended until the end of 2006, was succeeded by an Entrepreneurship and Innovation Programme under the CIP for 2007–13. In October 2012 the Commission adopted an initiative for industrial policy, entitled 'A stronger European industry for growth and economic recovery'.

COMPETITION

The Treaty of Rome establishing the European Economic Community (now the Treaty on the Functioning of the European Union—TFEU) provided for the creation of a common market based on the free movement of goods, persons, services and capital. The EU's competition policy aims to guarantee the unity of the internal market, by providing access to a range of high-quality goods and services, at competitive prices. The Commission has wide investigative powers in the area of competition policy. It may act on its own initiative, or after a complaint from a member state, firm or individual, or after being notified of agreements or planned state aid. Before taking a decision, the Commission organizes hearings; its decisions can be challenged before the Court of First Instance and the Court of Justice, or in national courts.

The TFEU prohibits any state aid that distorts or threatens to distort competition in the common market (e.g. by discriminating in favour of certain firms or the production of certain goods); however, some exceptions are permitted where the proposed aid may have a beneficial impact in overall Union terms. As an integral part of competition policy, control of state aid, including balancing the negative effects of aid on competition with its positive effects on the common interest, helps to maintain competitive markets. The procedural rules on state aid were consolidated and clarified in a regulation in 1999, and provided for several exemptions, notably regarding the provision of aid to small and medium-sized enterprises and for training. The EU has drawn up 'regional aid maps' designed to concentrate aid in those regions with the most severe development problems. A State Aid Action Plan (SAAP), covering the five-year period 2005–09, was adopted by the Commission in June 2005. The SAAP streamlined procedures (which had become increasingly complex) to provide member states with a clear state aid framework. It promoted targeting state aid towards improving the competitiveness of European industry and towards the creation of sustainable jobs, and provided for aid to be utilized as a means of achieving objectives of common interest. Amid widespread recession, in December 2008 the European Commission adopted a Temporary Framework for State Aid, which aimed to assist member states in co-ordinating the provision of credit facilities to businesses until 2010 (later extended until the end of 2011), in order to protect and restore their viability in the long term. In December 2011 the Commission revised and extended rules governing state aid to financial institutions during the ongoing economic crisis. The rules sought to ensure that the State would be properly remunerated should member states agree to recapitalize banks using methods where remuneration was not fixed in advance (for example, ordinary shares). A revised methodology was also agreed concerning the remuneration of guarantees for banks' funding needs, to ensure that the fees paid by banks reflected their intrinsic risk, rather than the risk related to the member state concerned or the market as a whole. The rules were to apply for as long as required by market conditions, and were amended in August 2013. Meanwhile, in February 2012 the Commission published a guidance paper on state aid-compliant financing, and restructuring and privatization of state-owned enterprises. Since 2001 the Commission has analysed state aid granted by member states in its State Aid Scoreboard. According to the Scoreboard published in December 2013, and excluding targeted crisis measures and aid to the railways sector, the total amount of state aid granted by EU member states in 2012 was some €67,158m., equivalent to 0.5% of EU gross domestic product, compared with €65,793m. in 2011. The Commission acts to recover any illegal or incompatible state aid.

The TFEU prohibits agreements and concerted practices between firms resulting in the prevention, restriction or distortion of competition within the common market. This ban applies both to horizontal agreements (between firms at the same stage of the production process) and vertical agreements (between firms at different stages). The type of agreements and practices that are prohibited include price-fixing; imposing conditions on sale; seeking to isolate market segments; imposing production or delivery quotas; agreements on investments; establishing joint sales offices; market-sharing agreements; creating exclusive collective markets; agreements leading to discrimination against other trading parties; collective boycotting; and voluntary restraints on competitive behaviour. Certain types of co-operation considered to be positive, such as agreements promoting technical and economic progress, may be exempt.

In addition, mergers that would significantly impede competition in the common market are banned. The Commission examines prospective mergers in order to decide whether they are compatible with competition principles. In July 2001 the EU blocked a merger between two US companies for the first time, on the grounds that EU companies would be adversely affected. In December the Commission launched a review of its handling of mergers and acquisitions, focusing on the speed of decisions and on bringing European competition standards in line with those in the USA and elsewhere. A new merger regulation was adopted in January 2004 and came into force in May, introducing some flexibility into the time frame for investigations into proposed mergers. In December 2013 the Commission adopted measures to simplify procedures for reviewing mergers, with effect from 1 January 2014.

The Commission seeks to abolish monopolies in the networks supplying basic services to member states. In June 2002 the Council adopted a directive on the opening up of postal services. Liberalization has also been pursued in the gas and electricity, telecommunications and transport sectors. In July the Commission approved a plan to open the car industry to greater competition, by applying new EU-wide rules for car sales, giving car dealers the freedom to operate anywhere in the EU. The reforms came into effect in October 2005. In January 2007 the Commission adopted the final report of an inquiry into competition in the gas and electricity markets, concluding that consumers and businesses were disadvantaged by inefficiency and expense. Particular problems identified were high levels of market concentration; vertical integration of supply, generation and infrastructure, leading unequal access to and insufficient investment in infrastructure; and possible collusion between operators to share markets. The Commission sought to take action in individual cases, within the framework of anti-trust, merger control and state aid regulations, and to improve the regulatory framework for energy liberalization. The adoption of the final report was accompanied by the adoption of a comprehensive package of measures to establish a New Energy Policy for Europe, with the aim of combating climate change and prompting energy security and competitiveness within the EU. The final report of an inquiry into the retail banking sector, published in January 2007, indicated a number of concerns in the markets for payment cards, payments systems and retail banking products. In particular, the report noted that there were large variations in merchant and interchange fees for payment cards, barriers to entry into the markets for payment systems and credit registers, impediments to customer mobility and product tying. The final report of an inquiry into the business insurance sector, published in September, raised concerns about the widespread practice of premium alignment in the reinsurance and coinsurance markets when more than one insurer is involved in covering a single risk and about lack of transparency in the remuneration of insurance brokers, as well as the risk of conflicts of interest jeopardizing the objectivity of brokers' advice to clients.

In February 2006 the European Parliament adopted a draft directive aimed at opening up the services sector to cross-border competition. The Parliament notably amended the directive so that a company offering services in another country would be governed by the rules and regulations of the country in which the service was being provided (rather than those of the company's home country, as the Commission had favoured). The Parliament agreed a list of legitimate reasons that a country could cite for restricting the activities of foreign service providers, such as national security, public health and environmental protection. Following its adoption by the Council of the European Union, the directive entered into force in December.

In 2003 the Commission worked to establish detailed provisions for a modernized framework for anti-trust and merger control in advance of the enlargement of the EU in May 2004. In that month major changes to EU competition law and policy (including substantive and procedural reform of the European Community Merger Regulation) entered into force. As part of the reforms, national competition authorities, acting as a network, and national courts were to become much more involved in the enforcement of competition rules, and companies were to be required to conduct more self-assessment of their commercial activities. In March the US Department of Justice had criticized the EU's anti-trust action against the US computer software company Microsoft. The European Commission imposed a fine of €497m. and instructed the company to disclose elements of its programming to facilitate the development of competitive products. In July 2006 the Commission imposed a fine of €280.5m. on Microsoft, and threatened to impose heavier penalties, for the company's failure to comply with the EU's demand that it should provide complete information to permit interoperability between its Windows operating system and rival products. In October 2007 Microsoft indicated that it would accept the Court's ruling and comply with the Commission's demands. In December 2009 the Commission made legally binding, for five years from March 2010, a commitment by Microsoft to offer its consumers a choice of web browser beyond Microsoft's own Internet Explorer, and, thereby, to remove a long-term obstacle to competition and innovation. Meanwhile, in May 2009 the Commission imposed a fine of €1,060m. on the Intel Corporation, after concluding that it had abused its strong position in the central processing unit (CPU) market by making reimbursements to computer manufacturers that bought CPUs from Intel, and by making direct payments to Europe's largest computer retailer, Media Saturn Holding, on condition that its stock solely comprised computers containing Intel CPUs. In addition, Intel made direct payments to computer manufacturers to postpone or halt the launch of specific products containing competitors' CPUs and to restrict the sales avenues available to such products.

In mid-January 2008 the Commission initiated an inquiry into the pharmaceuticals sector, in response to indications that fewer new medicines were entering the market, and that the launch of generic medicines appeared to be subject to unnecessary delays. In July 2009 the Commission adopted the final report of the sector inquiry into pharmaceuticals, which confirmed that originator companies use a variety of methods to extend the commercial life of their products prior to generic entry, and which confirmed a decline in the number of new medicines reaching the market. The Commission planned to increase monitoring of pharmaceuticals companies in order to identify breaches of anti-trust legislation in the sector, to identify defensive patenting strategies and to monitor settlements that limit or delay the market entry of generic drugs.

In February 2013 the Commission announced its intention to launch a case against France and Luxembourg at the Court of Justice, claiming that their imposition of reduced rates of value-added tax (VAT) on sales of e-books distorted competition within the internal market and served to benefit major internet retailers. The Commission sought to formulate a draft proposal on VAT regulations for those providing e-services by the end of 2013, with the objective of introducing parity in the rules applying to e-books and traditional printed books by 2015. In January 2014 the Commission launched anti-trust proceedings to examine licensing agreements between a number of large US film studios and principal European subscription television broadcasters, in order to ascertain whether such agreements prevent broadcasters from providing cross-border services.

The international affairs unit of the Directorate-General for Competition co-operates with foreign competition authorities and promotes competition instruments in applicant countries, where it also provides technical assistance. The unit works within the framework of international organizations such as the World Trade Organization (WTO), the Organisation for Economic Co-operation and Development (OECD) and the UN Conference on Trade and Development (UNCTAD). Dedicated co-operation agreements on competition policy have been signed with the USA, Canada and Japan, while other forms of bilateral co-operation on competition issues exist with a number of other countries and regions. In addition, in 2001 the European Commission was a founding member of the International Competition Network, an informal forum for competition authorities from around the world.

TELECOMMUNICATIONS, INFORMATION TECHNOLOGY AND BROADCASTING

In 1991 the Council adopted a directive requiring member states to liberalize their rules on the supply of telecommunications terminal equipment, thus ending the monopolies of national telecommunications authorities. In the same year, the Council adopted a plan for the gradual introduction of a competitive market in satellite communications; a directive relating to the liberalization of satellite telecommunications equipment and services came into force in late 1994, but allowed for deferment until 1 January 1996. In October 1995 the European Commission adopted a directive liberalizing the use of cable telecommunications, requiring member states to permit a wide range of services, in addition to television broadcasts, on such networks. The EU market for mobile telephone networks was opened to full competition as a result of a directive adopted by the Commission in January 1996, which obliged member states to abolish all exclusive and special rights in this area, and establish open and fair licensing procedures for digital services. All the major EU telecommunications markets were, in principle, open to competition from 1998.

In February 2000 the Commission requested that national competition authorities, telecommunications regulators, mobile network operators and service providers give information on conditions and price structures for national and international mobile services. In response to concerns regarding the increased cost for EU citizens of using a mobile telephone when travelling in another EU country, a new regulation fixing a maximum rate for so-called roaming charges entered into force in June 2007. In order to enhance the transparency of retail prices, mobile telephony providers were also required to inform their customers of the charges applicable to them when making and receiving calls in another member state. In July 2012 a new roaming regulation came into effect, which amended the application of roaming charges for EU mobile telephone users by imposing new maximum rates and, from July 2014, enables travellers to temporarily change telephone operators, and use less expensive roaming services abroad, or transfer to a rival domestic roaming services provider while travelling. In September 2013 the Commission adopted a legislative proposal for a Connected Continent, which sought approval from the European Parliament and the Council for the creation a single market for mobile telephone usage, by introducing new regulations and market incentives to encourage mobile telephone operators to extend their domestic usage plans (for both telephone and mobile internet services) to consumers throughout the EU by 2016.

In July 2000 a comprehensive reform of the regulatory framework for telecommunications—the 'telecoms package'—was launched. The reform aimed to update EU regulations to take account of changes in the telecommunications, media and information technology (IT) sectors. The Commission aimed to develop a single regulatory framework for all transmission networks and associated services, in order to exploit the full potential for growth, competition and job creation. The Commission recommended, as a priority, the introduction of a regulation on unbundled access to the local loop (the final connection of telephone wires into the home). The regulation obliged incumbent operators to permit shared and full access to the local loop by the end of 2000. In December 2001 the European Parliament voted to adopt a compromise telecoms package. This gave the Commission powers to oversee national regulatory regimes and, in some cases, to overrule national regulatory authorities. The package included a framework directive and three specific directives (covering issues of authorization, access and interconnection, universal service and users' rights) and measures to ensure harmonized conditions in radio spectrum policy. By the end of 2003 the EU regulatory framework for electronic communications had been completely implemented; during subsequent years, however, the Commission initiated legal proceedings against a number of member states for either their failure fully to transpose the new rules of competition in their national laws or for incorrect implementation of the framework. In November 2009 the European Parliament and the Council of Ministers agreed a reform of the EU's telecommunications rules. New rules, to be fully incorporated into national legislation by June 2011, provided consumers with more choice by reinforcing competition between operators; promoting investment in new communication infrastructures, notably by freeing radio spectrum for wireless broadband services; and making communication networks more reliable and more secure, for example by introducing new measures to combat unsolicited e-mail, viruses, etc. To improve regulation and competition, and reinforce co-operation between national telecommunications regulators in an attempt to facilitate the creation of pan-European services, a new Body of European Regulators for Electronic Communications was inaugurated in January 2010.

The '.eu' top-level domain name, aimed at giving individuals, organizations and companies the option of having a pan-European identity for their internet presence, was launched in December 2005, when registration commenced for applicants with prior rights, such as trademark holders and public bodies; registration was open to all from April 2006. According to data from the European Registry of Internet Domain Names (EURid), at the end of February 2013 the number of registered '.eu' domain names was 3.7m.

Information and communication technologies (ICT) was one of the main themes of the co-operation programme of the Seventh Framework Programme for research, technological development and demonstration activities (FP7, covering 2007–13)—see Research and Innovation. The development of ICT was allocated €9,050m. in the budget for 2007–13. Aims included strengthening Europe's scientific and technology base in ICTs; stimulating innovation through ICT use; and ensuring that progress in ICTs was transformed into benefits for citizens, businesses, industry and governments. The Interchange of Data between Administrations (IDA) initiative supported the rapid electronic exchange of information between EU administrations—in January 2005 the IDA was renamed the Interoperable Delivery of pan-European eGovernment Services to Public Administrations, Businesses and Citizens (IDAbc) programme. From 2014 the framework programme was absorbed into Horizon 2020, a financial instrument for the implementation of the Innovation Union, part of the Europe 2020 initiative, which aims to safeguard and develop the EU's competitiveness worldwide.

An action plan promoting safer use of the internet, extended in March 2002 until December 2004, aimed to combat illegal and harmful content on global networks. In December 2004 the EU approved a new programme, called Safer Internet Plus (2005–08), to promote safer use of the internet and new online technologies and to combat illegal and harmful content (particularly child pornography and violent and racist material). The renewed Safer Internet programme for 2009–13 was awarded a budget of €55m., and aimed to combat both illegal content and harmful conduct such as the 'grooming' of children by paedophiles (whereby an adult establishes contact with a child via the internet, under false pretences, with the intention of arranging a meeting with that child for the purposes of committing a sexual offence) and bullying.

In October 2003 new digital privacy legislation aimed at combating unwanted commercial e-mails (known collectively as 'spam') came into force across the EU. The new rules required companies to gain consent before sending e-mails and introduced a ban on the use of spam throughout the EU. It was widely recognized, however, that concerted international action was required, since most of the spam entering Europe originated from abroad (particularly from the USA). In February 2005 13 European countries agreed to share information and pursue complaints across borders in an effort to combat unsolicited e-mails. A European Network and Information Security Agency (now European Union Agency for Network and Information Security, ENISA) became fully operational in October 2004. The main aims of the Agency, which is based in Heraklion, Greece, are to promote closer European co-ordination on information security and to provide assistance in the application of EU measures in this field. ENISA periodically monitors anti-spam activities.

In 1991 a directive ('Television without Frontiers') came into force, establishing minimum standards for television programmes to be broadcast freely throughout the Community: limits were placed on the amount of time devoted to advertisements, a majority of programmes broadcast were to be from the Community, where practicable, and governments were allowed to forbid the transmission of programmes considered morally harmful. In November 2002 the Commission adopted a communication on the promotion and distribution of television programmes. In July 2003 the Commission reiterated proposals (originally presented at the Lisbon summit in March 2000) to help film and audiovisual production companies to have access to external funding from banks and other financial institutions by covering some of the costs of the guarantees demanded by these institutions and/or part of the cost of a loan ('discount contract loan') for financing the production of their works. In May 2005 the Commission urged EU member states to accelerate the changeover from analogue to digital broadcasting, and set a target of 2012 for shutting down analogue services. In December 2005 the Commission proposed a modernization of the Television without Frontiers directive in view of rapid technological and market developments in the audiovisual sector. A reduction in the regulatory burden on providers of television and similar services was envisaged, as well as the introduction of more flexible rules on advertising. National rules on the protection of minors, against incitement to hatred and against surreptitious advertising would be replaced with an EU-wide minimum standard of protection. The proposals distinguished between so-called linear services (e.g. scheduled broadcasting via traditional television, the internet or mobile cellular telephones) and non-linear services, such as on-demand films or news, which would be subject only to a basic set of minimum principles. The modernized Television without Frontiers directive, renamed the Audiovisual Media Services without Frontiers directive, was adopted by the European Parliament in November 2007. The deadline for implementation of the legislation by member states was December 2009, although this was not universally met. In July 2007 the Commission adopted a strategy urging member states and industry to facilitate and accelerate the introduction of mobile television (the transmission of traditional and on-demand audiovisual content to a mobile device), encouraging the use of DVB-H (Digital Video Broadcasting for Handhelds) technology as the single European standard. In March 2010 the European Parliament and the Council adopted a directive on Audiovisual Media Services, with the aim of implementing a cross-border framework for audiovisual media services, thereby strengthening the EU's market for both production and distribution, and ensuring fair competition.

The MEDIA programme was introduced in 1991 to provide financial support to the television and film industry. MEDIA 2007, covering the period 2007–13, was formally adopted by the European Parliament and the Council in November 2007, with a budget of €755m. MEDIA 2007's principal objectives were to preserve and enhance European cultural diversity and its cinematographic and audiovisual heritage, and to guarantee Europeans' access to it and foster intercultural dialogue; to increase the circulation of European audiovisual works both within and outside the EU; and to reinforce the competitiveness of the European audiovisual sector within the framework of an open and competitive market. In January 2011 the Commission launched a loan guarantee mechanism, the MEDIA Production Guarantee Fund, within the framework of MEDIA 2007; the Fund was to facilitate access to bank credits for European audiovisual companies during 2011–13. In November 2011 the European Commission proposed a programme called Creative Europe, to supersede the Culture and MEDIA programmes, with a proposed budget of €1,400m. for 2014–20; the new programme entered into force on 1 January 2014.

In October 2009 the European Commission published a report on cross-border consumer e-commerce that detailed concerns with ongoing barriers to completing online purchases across EU borders and so to achieving progress towards the creation of a digital single market. Difficulties were, in particular, caused by traders not shipping their products to certain countries or not offering suitable means for cross-border payment; the countries where consumers were least able to buy cross-border products online were Belgium, Bulgaria, Latvia and Romania. By 2007 the majority of EU households had internet access (55%), and this had increased to 73% by 2011; at 2011 43% of people aged between 16 and 74 years had used the internet to purchase goods and services. In October 2013 the Commission published guidelines for businesses concerning new rules on value-added tax (VAT) for telecommunications and e-services, which are to come into force in 2015. Under the new legislation, VAT is be charged based on the location of customer, rather than the service provider, as part of efforts to reduce complications relating to cross-border taxation and administration for businesses operating in the single market.

In March 2010 the European Commission launched the Europe 2020 strategy, which established the Digital Agenda for Europe as one of seven principal initiatives. The Digital Agenda for Europe, which replaced the i2010 initiative, aimed to exploit the full economic and social potential of ICT resources, in particular the internet, in order to promote innovation and economic growth, through the creation of a digital single market. The Commission identified seven principal objectives: the creation of a new single, online market; improved standards and interoperability for ICT; enhanced trust and security for those using the internet; improved access to very fast internet speeds; improved research and innovation; improved digital literacy; and using ICT to address issues of importance to society throughout Europe, such as mitigating rising health costs and digitizing the EU's cultural heritage. The Connecting Europe Facility (CEF) provides funding of €1,000m. for 2014–20, primarily for investment in cross-border, public IT services, for example, eProcurement and eHealth, and for a limited number of broadband projects.

TRANSPORT

The establishment of a common transport policy was stipulated in the Treaty of Rome (renamed the Treaty on the Functioning of the European Union in 2009), with the aim of gradually standardizing national regulations hindering the free movement of traffic, such as the varying safety and licensing rules, diverse restrictions on the size of lorries, and frontier-crossing formalities. A White Paper in 1992 set out a common transport policy for the EU. The paper proposed the establishment of trans-European networks (TENs) to improve transport, telecommunications and energy infrastructure throughout the Community, as well as the integration of transport systems and measures to protect the environment and improve safety.

In March 2011 the Commission published a new White Paper on Transport Policy for a Single European Transport Area, which aimed to create a competitive and environmentally efficient transport system by 2050. The Commission detailed 40 separate initiatives for the next decade with the objective of building a competitive transport system to increase mobility; removing barriers; and aiding economic growth and employment. The proposals sought to reduce substantially Europe's dependence on imported petroleum and to reduce carbon emissions in the transport sector by 60% by 2050. Principal goals for fulfilment by 2050 included: removing conventionally fuelled cars from cities; ensuring that 40% of aviation fuels used were sustainable, low-carbon fuels; and reducing shipping emissions by at least 40%.

In November 2013 the European Parliament approved the EU's new infrastructure policy, and voted to increase funding for its transport programme three-fold for 2014–20, under the new Connecting Europe Facility (CEF) for the fields of transport, energy and telecommunications, to €26,300m. The new policy aimed to create a core transport network by 2030, which was to comprise nine principal corridors: two running North–South; three running East–West; and four running diagonally. The transport network aimed to reduce congestion, improve safety and result in faster journey times. Related projects included the SESAR programme (see below), and the European Rail Traffic Management System (ERTMS—see below).

The overall aim of the EU's trans-European transport network (TEN-T) policy, which included so-called intelligent transport systems and services, was to unite the various national networks into a single European network, by eliminating bottlenecks and adding missing links. As a result of the accession of 10 new member states in 2004, a further 16 TEN-T projects, in addition to 14 ongoing projects, were identified as being priorities for the enlarged Union. The Commission estimated that all 30 TEN-T projects would require investment of €225,000m. for completion by 2020. The total cost of completing the TEN-T was estimated at €600,000m. A Trans-European Transport Network Executive Agency (TEN-T EA) was established in November 2006 to manage priority projects. The first annual ministerial conference on the future of TEN-T, held in October 2009, with participation by delegates from the EU member states, the Balkans, the Western Mediterranean and Africa, and from Norway, Switzerland, Russia and Turkey, determined to strengthen co-operation to facilitate the creation of a sustainable infrastructure network, and outlined common priorities until 2020. In October 2010 the Commission published the first mid-term review of the TEN-T programme. Of the 92 large-scale infrastructure projects under way, 48 were deemed to be making sufficient progress to reach completion in December 2013, as planned; a further 39 projects were given a revised deadline of 2015, while the remaining five were to be cancelled. It has been estimated that the completion of TEN-T could reduce transport-generated carbon dioxide emissions by 6.3m. metric tons per year by 2020. In January 2014 a new Innovation and Networks Executive Agency commenced operations in Brussels, Belgium, managing major funding programmes relating to transport, energy and digital policy, and replacing the TEN-T EA.

In 1991 directives were adopted by the Council on the compulsory use of safety belts in vehicles weighing less than 3.5 metric tons. Further regulations applying to minibuses and coaches were introduced in 1996. In November 2002 the European Parliament adopted a directive on speed limitation devices for certain categories of motor vehicles, including haulage vehicles and passenger vehicles carrying more than eight passengers. In March 2006 the European Parliament and the Council adopted a regulation reducing maximum driving times and increasing obligatory rest periods for professional drivers and a directive increasing the number of checks on lorries; the new legislation entered into force in April 2007.

In 1992 ministers responsible for transport approved an 'open skies' arrangement that would allow any EC airline to operate domestic flights within another member state (with effect from 1 April 1997). In November 2002 the European Court of Justice ruled that bilateral open skies treaties, or Air Services Agreements (ASAs), between countries were illegal if they discriminated against airlines from other member states; the ruling was in response to a case brought by the Commission against eight member states that had concluded such agreements with the USA. In response to the ruling, in June 2003 the Commission and member states identified two ways of resolving the issues: either bilateral negotiations between each member state concerned and its partners, amending each bilateral ASA separately, or single 'horizontal' agreements negotiated by the Commission on behalf of the member states. Each horizontal agreement aims to amend the relevant provisions of all existing bilateral ASAs in the context of a single negotiation with one third country. By May 2006 separate bilateral negotiations had led to changes with 39 partner states, representing the correction of 69 bilateral agreements, while by December 2007 horizontal negotiations had led to changes with 32 partner states. In 2004–05 the Commission initiated infringement proceedings against a number of member states that were persisting in maintaining discriminatory bilateral air agreements with the USA. At the same time the Commission was conducting negotiations with the USA in an attempt to conclude an overall open skies agreement, under which a common aviation area would be created. In November 2005 a preliminary agreement was concluded with the USA, and in early March 2007 EU and US negotiators concluded a draft accord. The EU-US aviation agreement, encompassing some 60% of global air traffic, was approved by EU ministers responsible for transport later in March and formally signed in April.

In June 2006 the European Council signed a political agreement with the eight new EU member states from Central and South-Eastern Europe, Bulgaria, Romania, Norway, Iceland and the countries of the Western Balkans on the creation of a European Common Aviation Area (ECAA). The establishment of the ECAA involved the harmonization of standards and regulations on safety, security, competition policy, social policy and consumer rights, as well as the establishment of a single market for aviation.

In July 1994, despite EU recommendations for tighter controls on subsidies awarded to airlines, as part of efforts to increase competitiveness within the industry, the Commission approved substantial subsidies that had been granted by the French and Greek governments to their respective national airlines. Subsequently, the Commission specified that state assistance could be granted to airlines 'in exceptional, unforeseen circumstances, outside the control of the company'. In October 2001 the Commission proposed to establish common rules in the field of civil aviation security, to strengthen public confidence in air transport following the terrorist attacks on the USA in the previous month. Issues addressed included securing cockpits, improving air–ground communications and using video cameras in aircraft. Member states also agreed to incorporate into Community law co-operation arrangements on security measures. These measures covered control of access to sensitive areas of airports and aircraft, control of passengers and hand luggage, control and monitoring of hold luggage, and training of ground staff. In October 2006 the Commission adopted a regulation restricting the liquids that air passengers were allowed to carry beyond certain screening points at airports and onto aircraft. The new regulation, introduced in response to the threat posed to civil aviation security by home-made liquid explosives, was applied to all flights departing from member states' airports.

In July 2002 the European Parliament adopted a regulation creating a European Aviation Safety Agency (EASA). The EASA (which officially opened its permanent seat in Köln, Germany, in December 2004) covered all aircraft registered in member states, unless agreed otherwise. The Commission has also formulated ground rules for inquiries into civil air incidents and has issued proposals for assessing the safety of aircraft registered outside the EU. In April 2008 a regulation entered into force that extended the responsibilities of the EASA, particularly regarding control over pilots' licences and the regulation of airlines based in third countries operating in the EU. In December 2005 EU ministers responsible for transport approved a regulation introducing a Europe-wide 'blacklist' of unsafe airlines and granting passengers the right to advance information about the identity of the air carrier operating their flight.

In December 1999 the Commission presented a communication on streamlining air traffic management (ATM) to create a Single European Sky (SES), of which the overall aim was to restructure the EU's airspace on the basis of traffic, rather than national frontiers. In December 2002 EU ministers responsible for transport agreed on a package of measures under which the separate European ATM providers would be regulated as a single entity, and EU airspace over 28,500 ft (approximately 8,690 m) would be under unified control. A first package of SES legislation (SES I), bringing ATM under the common transport policy, was adopted by the European Parliament and Council in April 2004. In November 2005 the European Commission launched SESAR, a Single European Sky industrial and technological programme to develop a new ATM system. The project consisted of three phases: the definition phase (2005–07), costing €60m. (co-funded by the Commission and the European Organisation for the Safety of Air Navigation—EUROCONTROL); the development phase (2008–13), estimated to cost around €300m. per year (co-funded by the Commission, EUROCONTROL and the industry); and the deployment phase (2014–20), to be financed by the industry. A regulation creating the SESAR Joint Undertaking, a public-private entity managing the development stage of the project, was formally approved by the Council and Parliament in February 2007. Meanwhile, in April 2006 a directive was adopted on the introduction of a Community air traffic controller licence, with the aim of raising safety standards and improving the operation of the ATM system. In March 2009 the Council adopted a decision endorsing a new SESAR ATM Master Plan as the initial version of a planned European ATM Master Plan. Also during that month the European Parliament approved a second package of SES legislation (SES II), incorporating improvements aimed at addressing environmental challenges and fuel cost efficiency.

In 1986 progress was made towards the establishment of a common maritime transport policy, with the adoption of regulations on unfair pricing practices, safeguard of access to cargoes, application of competition rules and the eventual elimination of unilateral cargo reservation and discriminatory cargo-sharing arrangements. In December 1990 the Council approved, in principle, the freedom for shipping companies to provide maritime transport anywhere within the Community. Cabotage by sea began to be introduced from January 1993 and was virtually complete by January 1999. Cabotage was also introduced in the inland waterways transport sector in 1993. By January 2000 the inland waterways market had been liberalized, although obstacles to the functioning of the single market subsequently persisted, including differing technical regulations among member states. The 2001 White Paper on European Transport Policy proposed the development of Motorways of the Sea, which aimed to shift a proportion of freight traffic from the road system to short sea shipping, or to a combination of short sea shipping and other modes of transport in which road journeys were minimized. In March 2005 the European Commission launched a consultation process on a new integrated EU maritime policy aimed at developing the potential of the maritime economy in an environmentally sustainable manner. The commissioners responsible for sea-related policies were charged with preparing a consultation paper addressing all economic and recreational maritime activities, such as shipping, fishing, oil and gas extraction, use of wind and tidal power, shipbuilding, tourism and marine research. The resultant Green Paper was adopted by the Commission in June 2006. Following the conclusion of a consultation process based on the document, in October 2007 the Commission presented a communication on its vision for the integrated maritime policy, which was endorsed by the Council in December. An accompanying action plan included initiatives such as a European strategy for marine research; national integrated maritime policies; an integrated network for maritime surveillance; a European marine observation and data network; and a strategy to mitigate the effects of climate change on coastal regions. In January 2009 the Commission published its objectives for EU maritime policy until 2018, which focused primarily on the provision of cost-efficient maritime transport services compatible with efforts to sustain economic growth throughout the EU and global economies; and ensuring the long-term competitiveness of the EU's shipping sector, by developing its ability to create both value and employment throughout the EU.

In March 2000 the Commission adopted a communication on the safety of the sea-borne oil trade. It proposed the introduction of a first package of short-term measures to strengthen controls, including the right to refuse access to substandard ships, more stringent inspections and a generalization of the ban on single-hull oil tankers. In May the Commission adopted a proposal to harmonize procedures between bulk carriers and terminals, in order to reduce the risk of accidents caused by incorrect loading and unloading. In the same month the Commission signed a Memorandum of Understanding (MOU) with several countries on the establishment of the Equasis database, intended to provide information on the safety and quality of ships. In December the Commission set out a second package of safety measures, broad agreement was reached on the first package, and the EU agreed to accelerate the gradual introduction of double-hull tankers (single-hull tankers were being phased out from the end of 2010). In June 2002 the European Parliament established by regulation the European Maritime Safety Agency (the permanent seat of which was to be located in Lisbon, Portugal); its tasks were to include preparing legislation in the field of maritime safety, co-ordination of investigations following accidents at sea, assisting member states in implementing maritime safety measures, and providing assistance to candidate countries. In March 2004 the Agency was given additional responsibility for combating pollution caused by ships. In November 2005 the Commission proposed a third package of maritime safety measures, including a requirement that member states ensure that ships flying their flags comply with international standards; an improvement in the quality and effectiveness of ship inspections, with increased targeting of vessels deemed to pose the greatest risk and less frequent inspections of high-quality ships; and an obligation that member states designate an independent authority responsible for the prior identification of places of refuge for ships in distress. The Commission noted that the EU had become a major maritime power, accounting for some 25% of the world's fleet.

In April 1998 the Commission published a report on railway policy, with the aim of achieving greater harmonization, the regulation of state subsidies and the progressive liberalization of the rail-freight market. In October 1999 EU ministers responsible for transport concluded an agreement that was regarded as a precursor to the full liberalization and revitalization of the rail freight market. Rail transport's share of the total freight market had declined substantially since the 1970s, but in terms of environmental protection and safety transport of freight by rail was greatly preferable to road haulage. The agreement provided for the extension of access to a planned core Trans-European Rail Freight Network (covering some 50,000 km), with a charging system designed to ensure optimum competitiveness. During 2000–04 the EU adopted three 'railway packages', which dealt with the progressive deregulation of the rail market. Other measures included developing a common approach to rail safety; upholding principles of interoperability; and setting up a European Railway Agency (ERA). The ERA opened in Lille/Valenciennes, France, in June 2005, with aim of reinforcing the safety and interoperability of railways in the EU. In March 2005 the Commission and representatives of the rail industry signed an MOU on the deployment of the ERTMS single European rail signalling system) on a major part of the European network to enhance safety and reduce infrastructure costs in the longer term; existing national systems were to be gradually withdrawn within 10–12 years. In December 2006 the Commission presented a communication proposing measures to remove technical and operational barriers to international rail activities, with the aim of making the rail industry more competitive, particularly in relation to road and air transport; the simplification of procedures for the approval of locomotives for operational service across the EU; and the extension of the powers of the ERA. In January 2013 the Commission adopted proposals on a fourth railway package, which focused on four principal areas. First, the package proposed transferring substantial administrative responsibility from individual member states to the ERA, in order to help new operators to enter the market and to reduce costs (it was anticipated that railway companies could save some €500m. by 2025 if the ERA were to become a so-called one-stop shop for authorizing trains and issuing safety certificates). Second, it was proposed that the provision of domestic rail passenger services be opened up to private companies across the EU from December 2019, with the aim of improving quality and choice, and increasing passenger rail traffic. At early 2013 only Sweden and the United Kingdom had fully liberalized their rail markets, while Austria, the Czech Republic, Germany, Italy and the Netherlands had undertaken partial liberalization. Third, the role of independent track managers was to be strengthened, with such managers to be given responsibility for all core functions (for example, infrastructure planning, daily operations, maintenance and timetables) in order to enable networks to be run in an efficient and non-discriminatory manner at EU level. Finally, the proposals emphasized the need to invest in maintaining a skilled workforce.

A directive adopted in April 2004 aimed to establish an electronic toll collection system across the EU that would apply to roads, tunnels, bridges, ferries and urban congestion-charging schemes. Notably, all new electronic toll systems brought into service from 1 January 2007 were required to use at least one of three prescribed existing technologies.

JUSTICE AND HOME AFFAIRS

Under the Treaty on European Union, EU member states undertook to co-operate in the areas of justice and home affairs, particularly in relation to the free movement of people between member states. Issues of common interest were defined as asylum policy; border controls; immigration; drug addiction; fraud; judicial co-operation in civil and criminal matters; customs co-operation; and police co-operation for the purposes of combating terrorism, drugs-trafficking and other serious forms of international crime. In view of the sensitivity of many of the issues involved in this sphere, the EU affords great weight to the positions and opinions of individual states. There tends to be a greater degree of flexibility than in other areas, and requirements are frequently less stringent.

The EU's draft Charter of Fundamental Rights, which was signed in December 2000, outlines the rights and freedoms recognized by the EU. It includes civil, political, economic and social rights, with each based on a previous charter, convention, treaty or jurisprudence. The charter may be used to challenge decisions taken by the Community institutions and by member states when implementing EU law. A reference to the charter, making it legally binding, was included in the Treaty of Lisbon amending the Treaty on European Union and the Treaty establishing the European Community (previously known as the Reform Treaty), which was signed in December 2007 and entered into force in December 2009. A protocol to the Treaty of Lisbon limited the application of the charter in the United Kingdom and Poland to rights recognized by national legislation in those countries. In June 2005 the European Commission adopted a proposal for a regulation establishing an EU Agency for Fundamental Rights. The regulation was adopted in its final form in February 2007, allowing the establishment of the Agency, as the successor to the European Monitoring Centre on Racism and Xenophobia, on 1 March. In April the specific programme Fundamental Rights and Citizenship was established under the framework programme Fundamental Rights and Justice. With a budget of €94m. for 2007–13, the Programme aimed to promote the development of a European society based on respect for fundamental rights; to strengthen civil society organizations and to encourage a dialogue with them regarding fundamental rights; to combat racism, xenophobia and anti-Semitism; and to improve contacts between legal, judicial and administrative authorities and the legal professions.

In March 2000 an action programme to develop a European strategy for the prevention and control of organized crime was adopted. A European crime prevention network was formally established in May 2001. There are also agreements within the EU on co-operation between financial intelligence units and between police forces for the purposes of combating child pornography. The EU ran the FALCONE programme—a series of incentives, training opportunities and exchanges for those responsible for the fight against organized crime in individual member states. The STOP (sexual treatment of persons) programme operated a similar system for those responsible for combating trade in humans and the sexual exploitation of children. In September 2001 member states harmonized their definitions of human trafficking and set common minimum prison sentences. Several programmes, including Grotius II, STOP and FALCONE, were merged into a single framework programme, called AGIS, in January 2003. In 2006 AGIS, which covered police and judicial co-operation in criminal matters, was terminated and succeeded by new programmes, adopted by the Council in February 2007 and covering the period 2007–13, with a focus on internal security (with an overall budget of €745m.) and criminal justice (with an overall budget of some €196m.).

The European Monitoring Centre for Drugs and Drug Addiction (EMCDDA) is based in Lisbon, Portugal. In 2000 Norway became the first non-EU state to be admitted to EMCDDA. The EU is working with other third countries to tackle issues of drugs demand and supply. In December 2004 the European Council endorsed an EU strategy on drugs (2005–12). In December 2012 the Council approved a new strategy on drugs (2013–20), which set out the framework, objectives and priorities for two new, consecutive four-year action plans. A drug prevention and information programme was adopted in September 2007.

In December 2009 the European Council adopted the Stockholm Programme, which aimed to provide a framework in 2010–14 for the creation of an 'open and secure Europe serving and protecting its citizens'. The Programme's objectives were to promote European citizenship and fundamental rights; to achieve a Europe of law and justice; to develop an internal EU security strategy; to promote, through integrated border management and visa policies, access to Europe; to develop a forward-looking and comprehensive European migration and asylum policy; and to develop the external dimension of EU freedom, security and justice policy. Cyber-security (developing a single system for the protection of personal data), combating terrorism and organized crime, and border control were all to be addressed by the new agenda. Ensuring equal rights for migrants, finer monitoring of migration patterns and labour trends, and closer co-operation with non-EU countries on managing migration flows were areas of focus.

In November 2011 the European Commission adopted a proposal for the establishment for 2014–20 of a new Rights, Equality and Citizenship programme to supersede the Fundamental Rights and Justice programme, Daphne III (which combated violence) and the parts of the PROGRESS programme dedicated to non-discrimination and diversity and gender equality. The Rights, Equality and Citizenship programme was adopted by the European Parliament and the Council in mid-December 2013. With a proposed budget of €439m. for 2014–20, the new programme was to protect rights and freedoms within the context of EU law; promote gender equality; and combat discrimination, including funding to increase Roma inclusion. Also in mid-December 2013 a new Justice programme was adopted by the European Parliament and the Council. The programme sought to create a European area of justice, promoting judicial co-operation, providing training for legal professionals, supporting efforts to combat drugs, and supporting the application of Union legislation in the areas of civil law and criminal law, and access to justice throughout Europe. The Justice Programme was the successor to three existing funding programmes (on civil justice, criminal justice and drug prevention and information), and had a budget of €378m. for 2014–20.

A European Police Office (EUROPOL), facilitating the exchange of information between police forces, operates from The Hague, Netherlands. A special EUROPOL unit dealing with the trafficking of illicit drugs and nuclear and radioactive materials began work in 1994. EUROPOL's mandate has been extended to cover illegal immigrants, stolen vehicles, paedophilia and terrorist activities, money-laundering and counterfeiting of the euro and other means of payment. From 1 January 2010 EUROPOL became a full EU agency, with a stronger mandate and enhanced capability for combating serious international crime and terrorism.

The EU convention on extradition, signed by ministers of justice in September 1996 prior to ratification by national governments, simplified and accelerated procedures in this area, reduced the number of cases where extradition could be refused, and made it easier to extradite members of criminal organizations. In November 1997 the Commission proposed an extension to European law to allow civil and commercial judgments made in the courts of member states to be enforced throughout the whole of the EU. A regulation on the mutual recognition and enforcement of such judgments came into force in March 2001 across the EU, with the exception of Denmark. In 2000 a convention on mutual assistance in criminal matters (such as criminal hearings by video and telephone conference and cross-border investigations) was adopted.

The Grotius-Civil programme of incentives and exchanges for legal practitioners was established in 1996. It was designed to aid judicial co-operation between member states by improving reciprocal knowledge of legal and judicial systems. The successor programme, Grotius II, focused on general and criminal law. In February 2002 the EU established a 'Eurojust' unit, composed of prosecutors, magistrates and police officers from member states, to help to co-ordinate prosecutions and support investigations into incidences of serious organized crime. A European Police College (CEPOL) has also been created, initially consisting of a network of existing national training institutes; in December 2003, however, the European Council decided that a permanent CEPOL institution would be established at Bramshill in the United Kingdom. CEPOL was formally established as an EU agency in 2005.

Measures related to the abolition of customs formalities at intra-community frontiers were completed by mid-1991, and entered into force in January 1993. In June 1990 Belgium, France, Germany, Luxembourg and the Netherlands, meeting in Schengen, Luxembourg, signed a convention to implement an earlier agreement (concluded in 1985 at the same location), abolishing frontier controls on the free movement of persons from 1993. Delay in the establishment of the Schengen Information System (SIS), providing a computer network on suspect persons or cargo for use by the police forces of signatory states, resulted in the postponement of the implementation of the new agreement. Seven countries (Belgium, France, Germany, Luxembourg, the Netherlands, Portugal and Spain) agreed to implement the agreement with effect from March 1995. Frontier controls at airports on those travelling between the seven countries were dismantled during a three-month transition period, which ended on 1 July (although France retained all of its land-border controls until March 1996, when border controls with Spain and Germany were lifted, although controls on borders with the Benelux countries were retained owing to fear over the transportation of illicit drugs). Italy joined the 'Schengen Group' in October 1997, and Austria in December. Border controls for both countries were removed in 1998. Denmark, Finland and Sweden (and non-EU members Norway and Iceland) were admitted as observers of the accord from 1 May 1996, and all five countries joined the Schengen Group in March 2001. Meanwhile, in March 1999 signatories of the Schengen accords on visa-free border crossings began to waive visa requirements with Estonia, Latvia and Lithuania. The Treaty of Amsterdam, which came into effect on 1 May, incorporated the so-called Schengen *acquis* (comprising the 1985 agreement, 1990 convention and additional accession protocols and executive decisions), in order to integrate it into the framework of the EU. The Treaty permitted the United Kingdom and Ireland to maintain permanent jurisdiction over their borders and rules of asylum and immigration. Countries acceding to the EU after 2000 were automatically to adhere to the Schengen arrangements. In February 2002 the Council approved Ireland's participation in some of the provisions of the Schengen *acquis*.

Following the enlargement of the EU in May 2004, border controls between the 15 existing members and the 10 new members remained in force until 2007. Although the 10 new states technically belonged to the Schengen Agreement, the Commission decided that the SIS computer network was not large enough to incorporate data from 10 more countries. Work on a new computerized information system, SIS II, began in 2002 but suffered delays. Pending deployment of SIS II, a modified version of SIS, named SISone4ALL, was introduced to allow the extension of the Schengen area to proceed. SIS II became operational in April 2013. In December 2007 the provisions of the Schengen Agreement were applied to the land and sea borders of nine of the 10 countries that joined the EU in 2004, with controls at airports removed, accordingly, in March 2008. The inclusion of Cyprus in the Schengen area was postponed. The admission of Bulgaria and Romania (which were both subject to ongoing concerns regarding their progress in combating corruption and organized crime) to the Schengen area was vetoed in both December 2010 and September 2011. Switzerland, a non-EU member, joined the Schengen area in December 2008, and Liechtenstein was expected to join in the future. At the end of February 2013 the Commission proposed a so-called smart border package to streamline and strengthen border-control procedures for those entering the EU. A proposed Registered Traveller Programme (RTP) sought to permit certain categories of frequent travellers to enter the EU with simplified border checks, and an Entry/Exit System (EES) was to be installed to record exactly where and when third country nationals entered the EU. The proposed package required approval by the Council and the European Parliament, with implementation envisaged for 2018.

In November 2000 the Commission adopted a communication outlining a common asylum procedure and providing for a uniform status, valid throughout the EU, for persons granted asylum. In March 2001 a common list of countries whose citizens required visas to enter the EU was adopted. The EU has also developed the so-called Eurodac database for co-ordinating information on the movements of asylum seekers; Eurodac allows for the comparison of fingerprints of refugees. In April 2004 the Council adopted a directive establishing a common European definition of a refugee, aimed at curtailing movement from state to state until one is reached that is prepared to give protection. In February 2002 the European Council adopted a comprehensive plan to combat illegal immigration. Priority areas included visa policy, readmission and repatriation policies, the monitoring of borders, the role of Europol and penalties. A European Agency for the Management of Operational Co-operation at the External Borders of the European Union (FRONTEX) was established by a regulation of the European Parliament in October 2004, the primary responsibility of which was the creation of an integrated border management system. The Agency commenced operations on 1 May 2005, with its seat at Warsaw, Poland. In June 2004 the Council adopted a decision concerning the development of a system for the exchange of visa data between member states, the Visa Information System (VIS). The VIS was intended to enhance the internal security of member states and contribute to the fight against illegal immigration. In September 2005 the Commission presented a package of measures on asylum and immigration. The proposals included the application of common standards to the return of illegal immigrants, the adoption of a more coherent approach to the integration of migrants, the encouragement of migrants to contribute to the development of their home countries, and the introduction of Regional Protection Programmes to assist refugees remaining in their regions of origin and their host countries. In December, in a move towards the creation of a common European asylum system, the Justice and Home Affairs Council adopted a directive on asylum procedures, setting minimum standards for granting and withdrawing refugee status, as well as an action plan on preventing human trafficking. A new framework programme entitled Solidarity and Management of Migration Flows was adopted in December 2006 with the aim of improving management of migratory flows at EU level. The programme was divided into four specific policy areas, each with its own financial instrument: the control and surveillance of external borders (External Borders Fund, €1,820m.); the return of third country nationals residing illegally in the EU (European Return Fund, €676m.); the integration of legally resident third country nationals (European Integration Fund, €825m.); and asylum (European Refugee Fund—first established in 2000—€699m.). In June 2008 the Commission adopted a communication on principles, actions and tools relating to a common immigration policy for Europe, and a policy plan on asylum. The latter provided the framework for the second phase of the creation of the common European asylum system. In December the European Parliament and Council of the EU adopted a directive on determining common standards and procedures for returning illegally staying third country nationals from member states, and, in May 2009, the Council adopted a directive on the enforcement of sanctions and measures against employers engaging illegal immigrants. It was estimated at that time that up to 8m. illegal immigrants were residing in the EU. A new European Migration Network, fully established following a directive of the Council adopted in May 2008, having been launched in 2003 as a pilot project, aims to provide current and comparable information on migration and asylum. In November 2011 the EU Immigration Portal was launched, to provide practical information for foreign nationals interested in moving to the EU, or seeking to move between EU countries. In December the Single Permit Directive was adopted, establishing rights for non-EU workers residing lawfully in an EU member state.

EDUCATION, TRAINING AND CULTURE

The Treaty of Rome (renamed the Treaty on the Functioning of the European Union with the entry into force of the Treaty of Lisbon in 2009), although not covering education directly, gave the Community the role of establishing general principles for implementing a common vocational training policy. The Treaty on European Union urged greater co-operation on education policy, including encouraging exchanges and mobility for students and teachers, distance learning and the development of European studies. The Bologna Process was launched in 1999 with the aim of establishing a European Higher Education Area, including education networks and student exchanges. In May 2007 the EU and the Council of Europe signed a memorandum of understanding confirming mutual co-operation in the promotion of democratic citizenship and human rights education and their joint commitment to the Bologna Process. In April 2009 ministers responsible for higher education in the member countries of the Bologna Process adopted the priorities for the European Higher Education Area until 2020, with an emphasis on the importance of lifelong learning, expanding access to higher education, and mobility. In March 2010 the Bologna Process ministers responsible for higher education adopted the Budapest-Vienna Declaration, officially launching the European Higher Education Area. Meanwhile, in May 2009 the Council had adopted Education and Training 2020 (ET 2020), a strategic framework for European co-operation in education and training, which identified four principal objectives: to facilitate lifelong learning and mobility; to improve the quality of education and training; to promote equality, social cohesion and citizenship; and to help develop creativity and innovation in education and training. ET 2020 also provided for support for the Bologna intergovernmental process, which focuses on higher education.

The postgraduate European University Institute (EUI) was founded in Florence, Italy, in 1972, with departments of history and civilization, economics, law, and political and social sciences. The EUI is also the depository for the historical archives of the EC institutions. An Academy of European Law was founded within the EUI in 1990, and in 1992 the Robert Schuman Centre for Advanced Studies was established to develop inter-disciplinary and comparative postdoctoral research. The Jean Monnet programme, which supports institutions and activities in the field of European integration, finances the establishment of Jean Monnet chairs at universities throughout the world; the programme targets disciplines in which EU developments are an increasingly important part of the subject studied—e.g. European law, European economic and political integration, and the history of the European construction process. The establishment of a network of Jean Monnet Centres of Excellence was approved in 1998; the network was extended beyond Europe in 2001, and by the end of 2013 it was active in 72 countries worldwide.

The EU's Lifelong Learning Programme, an integrated action programme covering 2007–13, and with an overall budget of €6,970m., incorporated as sub-programmes four existing educational and training initiatives—Comenius (for schools), Erasmus (for higher education), Grundtvig (for adult education) and the Leonardo da Vinci programme—as well as the Jean Monnet programme, and introduced the Transversal programme to facilitate activities involving more than one area of education, such as language learning and innovation in information and communication technologies. An educational information network, Eurydice began operations in 1980, providing data on and analyses of European national education systems and policies, co-ordinated by an Education, Audiovisual and Culture Executive Agency in Brussels, Belgium. The Leonardo da Vinci programme was introduced in 1994 to help European citizens to enhance their skills and to improve the quality and accessibility of vocational training; the programme ran until 2013.

The Erasmus educational exchange programme, launched in 1987, enables students throughout Europe to travel to other EU countries to study and work as part of their degree programme. The first Erasmus Mundus programme ran from 2004–08 as a global mobility programme, promoting inter-cultural co-operation, and the EU as a centre of academic excellence, by enabling students and academics living outside the EU to pursue Masters or doctorate programmes at EU universities. In October 2008 the European Parliament approved a second Erasmus Mundus programme for 2009–13, with an estimated budget of €950m.

The EU's Youth in Action programme, with a total budget of €885m., covered the period 2007–13, replacing the previous Youth programme for 2000–06. Objectives of Youth in Action included fostering a sense of citizenship, solidarity and mutual understanding in young people; enhancing the quality of support systems for youth activities; and promoting European co-operation in youth policy.

Covering 2007–13, the fourth phase of the Trans-European Mobility Scheme for University Studies (Tempus, the first phase of which was launched in 1990) aimed to support the modernization of higher education, and to create an area of co-operation between institutions in EU member countries and partner countries surrounding the EU. Tempus IV covered 27 partner countries in the Western Balkans, Eastern Europe and Central Asia, North Africa and the Middle East. The European Training Foundation (ETF), which was established in Turin, Italy, in 1995, and the mandate of which was revised in December 2008, sought to support developing and transition countries in the promotion of human capital development, i.e. advancing skills and competences through the improvement of vocational education and training systems.

In November 2013 the European Parliament approved Erasmus+, a new, seven-year programme, which was to have a budget of €14,700m. Erasmus+ was to include all the existing programmes for education, training, youth and sport, including the Lifelong Learning Programme (and its associated sub-programmes), Youth in Action and five international co-operation initiatives (Erasmus Mundus, Tempus, Alfa, Edulink and a programme for co-operation with industrialized countries).

The European Centre for the Development of Vocational Training (Centre Européen pour le Développement de la Formation Professionnelle—CEDEFOP) was established in Berlin, Germany, in 1975. The centre relocated to Thessaloníki, Greece, in 1995. The EUROPASS programme, which was officially launched in February 2005 and which brought into a single framework several existing tools for the transparency of diplomas, certificates and competences, was aimed at promoting both occupational mobility, between countries as well as across sectors, and mobility for learning purposes. In September 2006 the Commission proposed the establishment of a European qualifications framework (EQF), based on eight reference levels of qualifications, with the aim of further promoting mobility and lifelong learning. Member states were required to relate their own qualifications systems to the EQF by 2010, and by 2012 every new qualification issued in the EU was to have a reference to the appropriate EQF level. The EQF was formally adopted in April 2008.

The EU's Culture 2007 programme, covering the period 2007–13, and with a total budget of some €400m., replaced a previous Culture 2000 agenda, and focused on three priorities: the mobility of those working in the cultural sector; the transnational circulation of works of art; and intercultural dialogue. In November 2007 the Council endorsed the first European strategy for culture policy, which had three main objectives: the promotion of cultural diversity and intercultural dialogue; the promotion of culture as a catalyst for creativity; and the promotion of culture as a vital element in the EU's international relations. The EU's Culture programme supported several prizes, awarded in recognition of excellence in architecture, cultural heritage, literature and music. In November 2008 the Europeana project was launched, funded by the European Commission, with the aim of creating an online digital library to make Europe's cultural heritage accessible to the public (www.europeana.net).

In November 2011 the European Commission proposed a programme called Creative Europe, to supersede the Culture and MEDIA (see Telecommunications, Information Technology and Broadcasting) programmes, with a proposed budget of €1,400m. for 2014–20; the new programme was approved by the European Parliament in November 2013, and entered into force on 1 January 2014.

The European City of Culture initiative was launched in 1985 (and renamed the European Capital of Culture initiative in 1999). Member states nominate one or more cities in turn, according to an agreed chronological order. The capitals of culture are then formally selected by the Council on the recommendation of the Commission, taking into account the view of a selection panel. Since 2009 there have been two annual capitals of culture from member states, including one from the new, post-May 2004, membership, plus a maximum of one city from European non-member countries. Umeå (Sweden) and Rīga (Latvia) were selected as capitals for culture for 2014; Mons (Belgium) and Plzeň (the Czech Republic) for 2015; and San Sebastián (Spain) and Wrocław (Poland) for 2016.

EMPLOYMENT, SOCIAL AFFAIRS AND INCLUSION

The Single European Act, which entered into force in 1987, added to the original Treaty of Rome articles that emphasized the need for 'economic and social cohesion' in the Community, i.e. the reduction of disparities between the various regions. This was to be achieved principally through the existing 'structural funds'—the European Regional Development Fund, the European Social Fund, and the Guidance Section of the European Agricultural Guidance and Guarantee Fund, which was replaced by the European Fund for Agricultural Development in 2007. In 1988 the Council declared that Community operations through the structural funds, the European Investment Bank (EIB) and other financial instruments should have five priority objectives: promoting the development and structural adjustment of the less-developed regions (where gross domestic product per head was less than 75% of the Community average); converting the regions, frontier regions or parts of regions seriously affected by industrial decline; combating long-term unemployment among people above the age of 25 years; providing employment for young people (under the age of 25); and with a view to the reform of the Common Agricultural Policy (CAP), speeding up the adjustment of agricultural structures and promoting the development of rural areas.

In 1989 the Commission proposed a Charter of Fundamental Social Rights of Workers (later known as the Social Charter), covering freedom of movement, fair remuneration, improvement of working conditions, the right to social security, freedom of association and collective wage agreements, the development of participation by workers in management, and sexual equality. The Charter was approved (with some modifications) by the heads of government of all Community member states, except the United Kingdom, in December. On the insistence of the United Kingdom, the chapter on social affairs of the Treaty on European Union, negotiated in December 1991, was omitted from the Treaty to form a separate protocol (the Community Charter of Fundamental Social Rights for Workers, or so-called Social Charter, complete with an opt-out arrangement for the United Kingdom). In September 1994 ministers adopted the first directive to be approved under the Social Charter, concerning the establishment of mandatory works councils in multinational companies; this came into force in September 1996. In April 1996 the Commission proposed that part-time, fixed-term and temporary employees should receive comparable treatment to permanent, full-time employees. A directive ensuring equal treatment for part-time employees was adopted by the Council in December 1997. A directive on parental leave, the second directive to be adopted under the Social Charter, provided for a statutory minimum of three months' unpaid leave to allow parents to care for young children, and was adopted in June 1996. In May 1997 the new Government of the United Kingdom approved the Social Charter, which was to be incorporated into the Treaty of Amsterdam. The Treaty, which entered into force in May 1999, consequently removed the opt-out clause and incorporated the Social Chapter in the revised Treaty of Rome (renamed the Treaty on the Functioning of the European Union in December 2009). In December 1999 the Council adopted amendments extending the two directives adopted under the Charter to include the United Kingdom.

The EU's Europe 2020 initiative was adopted by the Council in mid-June 2010, with a focus on economic growth and the creation of jobs; Europe 2020 sought to ensure that by 2020 at least 75% of those aged between 20 and 64 years were to be in employment. In mid-September 2010 an initiative called Youth on the Move was launched, as part of efforts to improve access to education and employment for young people. In late November the Commission published its Agenda for new skills and jobs, with the aim of increasing the pace of reform to add flexibility and security to the labour market ('flexicurity'); to equip people with the skills required in employment, both currently and in the future; to improve the quality of employment; to guarantee improved working conditions; and to improve conditions for job creation. In April 2012, in response to high rates of unemployment throughout Europe, the European Commission launched a new Employment Package; in December a Youth Employment Package for 2014–20 was announced. In April 2013 the Council adopted the so-called Youth Guarantee, a programme of reform to be partly financed by the European Social Fund. The Youth Guarantee seeks to ensure that all people under the age of 25 years have access to employment, further education or a training scheme within four months of becoming unemployed or leaving education. By January 2014 17 countries had submitted Implementation Plans for the Youth Guarantee. The overall, seasonally adjusted EU unemployment rate was 10.7% in December 2013, compared with 10.8% in December 2012. The rate of unemployment in the eurozone was 12.0% in December 2013, compared with 11.9% in December 2012.

The Treaty of Amsterdam authorized the European Council to take action against all types of discrimination. Several directives and programmes on gender equality and equal opportunities have been approved and the Commission has initiated legal proceedings against a number of member states before the European Court of Justice for infringements. In June 2000 the Council adopted a directive implementing the principle of equal treatment regardless of racial or ethnic origin in employment, education, social security, health care and access to goods and services. This was followed in November by a directive establishing a framework for equal treatment regardless of religion or belief, disability, age or sexual orientation. A joint seminar was held in February 2004, in Brussels,

Belgium, by the Commission and the European Jewish Congress, to discuss Jewish community concerns that anti-Semitism was increasing in Europe. In June 2005 the Commission presented a framework strategy on non-discrimination and equal opportunities, aimed at ensuring the full implementation and enforcement by member states of anti-discrimination legislation. In March 2007 the EU Agency for Fundamental Rights (FRA), based in Vienna, Austria, replaced the former European Monitoring Centre on Racism and Xenophobia (EUMC). The FRA, which immediately assumed the mandate of the EUMC regarding racism and xenophobia, was gradually to develop knowledge, expertise and work programmes in respect of other fundamental rights. The Agency maintains an information network (the European Information Network on Racism and Xenophobia) and a database. In December 2006 the Council and the Parliament approved the establishment of a European Institute for Gender Equality, which was founded in 2007; initially temporarily located in Brussels, it is now based in Vilnius, Lithuania.

In April 2010 the Commission issued a communication in support of the social and economic integration of the Roma community of Europe (which numbers between 10m. and 12m. people, and has encountered widespread discrimination). In April 2011 the Commission adopted an EU Framework for National Roma Integration Strategies by 2020, in order to promote the formulation of targeted and coherent national, regional and local integration policy, and to compel each EU member state to develop a national strategy focused on the welfare of the Roma population. In May 2012 the Commission published an initial assessment of the strategies that had been put into place, which focused on four principal areas: ensuring that all Roma children complete primary education; ensuring equal access to employment; ensuring equal access to health care; and to ensure equal access to housing and public utilities. The Commission concluded that although member states were making efforts to put into practice equitable policies targeting the Roma population, further work was necessary by national governments.

Numerous directives on health and safety in the workplace have been adopted by the Community. The Major Accident Hazards Bureau (MAHB), which was established in 1996 and is based at the Joint Research Centre in Ispra, Italy, helps to prevent and to mitigate industrial accidents in the EU. To this end, MAHB maintains a Major Accident Reporting System database and a Community Documentation Centre on Industrial Risk. There is also a European Agency for Health and Safety at Work, which was established in 1995 in Bilbao, Spain. The Agency has a health and safety information network composed of 'focal points' in each member state, in the candidate countries and in the four European Free Trade Association (EFTA) states.

In June 1993 the Working Time Directive (WTD) was approved, restricting the working week to a maximum duration of 48 hours, except where overtime arrangements are agreed with trade unions. The WTD also prescribed minimum rest periods and a minimum of four weeks' paid holiday a year. However, certain categories of employee were exempt from the maximum 48-hour week rule, including those in the transport sector, those employed in offshore oil extraction, fishermen and junior hospital doctors. In April 2000 agreement was reached on gradually extending some or all of the rights of the WTD to cover most excluded workers. A Road Transport Directive, which applies to mobile workers who participate in road transport activities covered by EU drivers' hours rules, was adopted in March 2002 and took effect in March 2005. In January 2004 the Commission launched a review of the WTD following an increase in the use of its opt-out clause by a number of member states. In May 2005, however, in a first reading, the European Parliament voted in favour of proposals to phase out the opt-out clause (except for the police, army and emergency services, and chief executive officers and senior managers) and to count all on-call time as working time, although members agreed with the Commission regarding the use of a one-year reference period for calculating the average working week. In December 2008 the European Parliament voted to phase out the WTD opt-out clause within three years of the entry into force of a revised directive; however, negotiations on WTD reform subsequently broke down. A European Commission report published in December 2010 indicated that five member states (Bulgaria, Cyprus, Estonia, Malta and the United Kingdom) permitted the opt-out to be used, without restriction on sector, while 11 further member states allowed, or were introducing, limited use of the opt-out clause. In contrast, four member states made use of the opt-out clause in 2003.

The European Foundation for the Improvement of Living and Working Conditions (Eurofound), which was established in Dublin, Ireland, in 1975, undertakes four-year research and development programmes in the fields of employment, sustainable development, equal opportunities, social cohesion, health and well-being, and participation. Prior to the EU's enlargement in May 2004, Eurofound made available wide-ranging new data and analysis on living and working conditions in the existing member states and in the accession and candidate states. The Foundation utilizes monitoring tools including the European Industrial Relations Observatory, the European Working Conditions Observatory, and the European Monitoring Centre on Change. Every four years Eurofound conducts surveys on Quality of Life in Europe; and surveys are also carried out on European Working Conditions; and on European companies.

All 15 of the longer-standing members of the EU (EU-15), except the United Kingdom, Ireland and Sweden, planned to impose at least a two-year period of restriction on immigrants from the eight formerly communist new member states (EU-8—the Czech Republic, Estonia, Hungary, Latvia, Lithuania, Poland, Slovenia and Slovakia) after their accession to the EU in May 2004, to prevent their labour markets being saturated with inexpensive labour. Workers from the new member states Malta and Cyprus were allowed into existing EU countries without any restrictions. All EU-15 states were required to apply EU legislation on free movement and open their labour markets to the EU-8 in 2011, and EU labour markets were opened to workers from Bulgaria and Romania on 1 January 2014. In the United Kingdom, in particular, concerns were expressed over the potential adverse social impact of an influx of Bulgarian and Romanian migrant workers, and in late 2013 the British Prime Minister, David Cameron, announced plans to restrict access to unemployment benefits for migrant workers. A European Commission report published in 2009 estimated that the number of EU-8 nationals residing in EU-15 countries had risen from around 900,000 before enlargement to some 1.9m. in 2007, with Ireland and the United Kingdom as the main destination for new workers; meanwhile, over the same period, the number of Bulgarian and Romanian workers resident in EU-15 states was estimated to have increased from about 700,000 to nearly 1.9m., with Italy and Spain as the principal destination countries.

An employment body, European Employment Services (EURES), launched in 1994, maintains a web portal and operates as a network of more than 750 specialist advisers across Europe, who (with the co-operation of national public employment services, trade unions, employers' organizations, local authorities, etc., and with access to a detailed database) provide the three basic EURES services of information, guidance and placement to both job seekers and employers interested in the European job market. EURES has a particularly effective role to play in cross-border regions where there are significant degrees of cross-border commuting by employees. EURES, which covers the countries of the European Economic Area (EEA) and Switzerland, also provides a public database of employment vacancies and a database through which job seekers can make their curricula vitae available to a wide range of employers.

A European Social Protection Committee was established in June 2000. In addition, the EU administers the Mutual Information System on Social Protection in the EU member states, as well as Iceland, Liechtenstein, Norway and Switzerland. In February 2005 the European Commission launched a Social Agenda for modernizing the EU's social model. The Agenda focused on providing jobs and equal opportunities for all and ensuring that the benefits of the EU's growth and employment creation schemes reached all levels of society. A renewed Agenda was adopted by the European Commission in July 2008. Meanwhile, a new programme for employment and social solidarity (PROGRESS) had been established to provide financial support for the implementation of the objectives set out in the Social Agenda. With an overall budget of €743m. for 2007–13, PROGRESS replaced four previous programmes that had expired in 2006 and covered the policy areas of social protection and inclusion; employment; non-discrimination; gender equality; and working conditions.

In late June 2013 the European Parliament and the Council reached political agreement on a new programme for Employment and Social Innovation (EaSI), with a proposed budget of €815m. for 2014–20. The EaSI programme sought to support measures by member states to develop and implement social reforms, and incorporated the PROGRESS and EURES programmes, and the European Progress Microfinance Facility (launched in 2010 to facilitate the provision of small loans for the establishment of businesses).

The Charter of Fundamental Rights (CFR) was proclaimed at the Nice Summit of the European Council in December 2000. The text of the CFR consists of seven chapters, covering dignity, freedoms, equality, solidarity, citizens' rights, justice and general provisions. No new rights were created as part of the CFR; rather, it presents in a single document the existing rights and freedoms enjoyed by EU citizens through the European Convention on Human Rights, the Charter of Fundamental Social Rights of Workers and various other EU treaties. The CFR became legally binding following the entry into force in December 2009 of the Treaty of Lisbon. (A protocol limited the application of the CFR in the Czech Republic, Poland and the United Kingdom.) In February 2010 the EU, a single legal entity under the terms of the Lisbon Treaty, acceded to the European Convention on Human Rights (ECHR), thereby enabling the European Court of Human Rights to verify future EU compliance with the provisions of the ECHR.

The EU disability strategy has three main areas of focus: co-operation between the Commission and the member states; the full participation of people with disabilities; and ensuring disability issues are fully recognized in policy formulation (particularly with regard to employment). Ongoing EU activities relating to disability include dialogue with the European Disability Forum and a European Day of Disabled People, which takes place in December each year. A disability action plan for 2004–10 aimed to enhance the economic and social integration of people with disabilities. In November 2010 the Commission launched the EU Disability Strategy 2010–20, which established plans for the forthcoming decade. In the Strategy's first five years the Commission aimed to improve accessibility to goods and services for people with disabilities, and to consider proposing a European Accessibility Act; help disabled people to exercise their right to vote; use the European Platform Against Poverty to reduce the risk of poverty; ensure that the European Social Fund offered ongoing support to disability-related projects; carry out data collection with the aim of improving opportunities for the employment of disabled people; develop policies to ensure inclusive education; facilitate the mutual recognition of disability cards and related entitlements throughout Europe; and promote the rights of people with disabilities through the EU's external action.

CONSUMER PROTECTION AND HEALTH

Consumer protection is one of the stated priorities of EU policy, and has been implemented via a series of action programmes covering areas such as safety of products and services (e.g. food additives, safety of toys and childcare articles, packaging and labelling of goods), protecting consumers' economic and legal interests, and promoting consumer representation. A number of measures have been taken to strengthen consumer power, by promoting consumer associations and drawing up a requirement for fair commercial practices. The EU consumer policy strategy for 2007–13 was adopted in March 2007, subtitled 'Empowering consumers, enhancing their welfare, effectively protecting them'. Proposals for a new consumer policy programme for 2014–20, with a budget of some €197m., were adopted by the Commission in November 2011. The programme sought to increase the safety of products through market surveillance; improve the information provided to consumers, including awareness of their rights; consolidate consumer rights and strengthen redress, in particular, by means of alternative dispute resolution; and strengthen enforcement of cross-border rights.

In December 2009 the European Commission adopted a new set of Rapid Alert System for Non-Food Consumer Products (known as RAPEX) guidelines. The RAPEX system (inaugurated in 2004, and its scope extended in 2010 and 2013) aids the effective and timely exchange of information between member states of measures taken to restrict or prevent the marketing or use of products deemed to pose a risk to the health and safety of consumers, professionals and public interests. The Commission publishes a weekly report of recent RAPEX notifications. In July 2009 a new Toy Safety Directive entered into force, which aimed to ensure that toys produced in and/or sold to consumers in the EU meet the highest safety requirements, and limits the amounts of certain chemicals that may be contained in materials used in the production of toys.

The European Food Safety Authority was established to assume responsibility for providing the Commission with scientific advice on food safety. With a wide brief to cover all stages of food production and supply right through to consumers, the Authority has been based in Parma, Italy, since June 2005. In March 2004 the Commission adopted a decision to establish three new scientific steering committees in the fields of consumer products, health and environmental risks, and emerging and newly identified health risks. In July 1998 an Institute for Health and Consumer Protection, attached to the Commission's Joint Research Centre, was established (see ihcp.jrc .ec.europa.eu).

In July 2001 the Commission developed its rules on the labelling and tracing of genetically modified organisms (GMOs, see Agriculture). During 2004 a framework was developed for the creation of international guidelines on the measurement of chemical and biological elements in food and other products. The system aimed to facilitate the detection of GMOs and the measurement of sulphur content in motor fuels. New legislation on the safety of food and animal feed came into force in January 2005. Business operators were required to ensure the safety of their products and apply appropriate systems and procedures to establish the traceability of food, feed, food-producing animals and all substances incorporated into foodstuffs at all stages of production, processing and distribution. An Advisory Group on the Food Chain and Animal and Plant Health was established by the Commission in March and held its inaugural meeting in July. It emerged in January–February 2013 that unregulated horsemeat had been used covertly in processed meat products widely supplied throughout Europe. In March the European Commissioner, responsible for Health Policy, Antonio Borg, announced a five-point plan which identified actions to be implemented over the short, medium and longer term in order to rectify shortcomings in the EU's food supply chain. The actions related to following areas: food fraud; food testing; rules pertaining to the monitoring and issuing of horse passports (with which all horses are issued); official controls, implementation and penalties; and source of origin labelling. In May the Commission proposed new legislation to update and strengthen the agri-food chain, in an effort to improve food safety. In July the EU Food Fraud Network (FFN) was launched, comprising food fraud contact points in each of the 28 EU member states, as well as Iceland, Norway and Switzerland. The FFN, which held two meetings in 2013, provides cross-border administrative support and co-operation, on issues pertaining to financially motivated violations of legislation on food, and by early 2014 had begun to examine potential food fraud cases and to act as a forum for discussion regarding the prioritization of action at the supranational level on food fraud.

A Community Register of Feed Additives (now European Union Register of Feed Additives) was published in November 2005, in accordance with a regulation on additives for use in animal nutrition. A regulation requiring that all health claims on food, drinks or food supplements be substantiated by independent experts was adopted in December 2006. In January of that year new regulations on food and animal feed hygiene, applying to every stage of the food chain, entered into force. At the same time, an EU-wide ban on the use of antibiotics in animal feed to stimulate growth took effect, as part of efforts to reduce the non-essential use of antibiotics in order to address the problem of micro-organisms becoming resistant to traditional medical treatments. In November 2011 the European Commission issued a communication addressed to the European Parliament and the Council on a proposed action plan to address the problems posed by increased anti-microbial resistance, which was understood to be causing annually around 25,000 human fatalities in the EU region.

In January 2005 a European Consumer Centres Network (ECC-Net) was established to provide a single point of contact in each member state for consumers to obtain information about their rights and assistance in pursuing complaints, particularly in cases concerning cross-border purchases. The ECC-NET dealt with 32,000 complaints in 2012, the majority of which (some 60%) related to the purchase of online products.

Legislation increasing the compensation rights of air travellers took effect in February 2005. New rights to compensation and assistance in the event of cancellations or long delays were introduced, compensation was increased for passengers unable to board a flight owing to overbooking by the airline and cover was extended to passengers travelling on charter or domestic flights. In November 2009 the European Commission launched a public consultation on revising EU legislation relating to package travel, to take account of advances made in recent years in internet and low-cost airline usage. Also in that month the Commission published a report on airline charges which found that frequently it had been airline practice to incorporate some basic operational costs (including handling charges, fuel charges and booking fees) into the 'taxes and charges' category, rendering it difficult for consumers to make comparisons between offers or to identify the value of national taxes and airport charges that might be refunded against unused tickets. In July 2013 the Commission issued proposals for an updated directive on Package Holidays and Assisted Travel Arrangements, which was under consideration by the European Parliament and the Council in early 2014.

The Consumer Protection Co-operation Network, comprising public authorities responsible for enforcing legislation to protect the interests of consumers in the event of cross-border disputes, was officially launched in February 2007. The first of a series of EU 'sweeps'—joint investigations and enforcement actions aimed at evaluating compliance with consumer laws in particular markets—was conducted in September, into misleading advertising and unfair practices on airline ticket-selling websites, and in November it was revealed that irregularities had been discovered on more than 50% of the sites checked. Following such investigations, national enforcement authorities act to ensure that companies found to have been compromising consumer rights improve their practices. In September 2010 the results of the second phase of a sweep investigating online distributors of electronic goods (such as mobile cellular telephones, digital cameras and personal music players) were published; 84% of the websites checked for breach of EU consumer legislation in 26 member states, plus Iceland and Norway, were found to comply with EU laws, compared with 44% in 2009. The breaches identified involved misleading information on consumer rights, incorrect tariffs, and failures to provide traders' contact details; such sites were compelled to make adjustments and, if necessary, penalties were imposed. In July 2009 the European Commission published a blueprint for a proposed standardized EU-wide method for classifying and reporting consumer complaints. In November 2011 the Commission adopted a directive on Alternative Dispute Resolution, which sought to ensure that all contractual disputes between consumers and providers could be resolved without recourse to the courts. A new Regulation on Online Dispute Resolution was to create an online presence ('ODR platform') throughout the EU by 2016, to be consulted by both consumers and businesses in order to enable them to settle disputes concerning the online purchase of goods from other EU member countries.

In February 2005 the European Parliament approved a new directive to harmonize the framework across the EU for banning unfair commercial practices. The new legislation, which clarified consumers' rights, banned pressure selling and misleading marketing and facilitated cross-border trade, took effect in December 2007, although only 14 member states had implemented the directive by that time. In February 2003 the Commission adopted an action plan for a more coherent and standardized European contract law. In July 2010 the Commission published a green paper on possible options for the formulation of European contract law, for public consultation. In October 2011 the Commission adopted a proposal for an optional Common European Sales Law, which aimed to simplify cross-border trade for both consumers and businesses by means of a standardized set of rules on contract law.

A programme of action in the field of health, for the period 2008–13, entitled 'Together for Health', was adopted in October 2007, with a budget of €321.5m. Meanwhile, the Commission adopted a new health strategy for the same period with the aims of fostering good health in an ageing Europe, protecting citizens from health threats, and supporting dynamic health systems and new technologies. Proposals for a new health programme for 2014–20, 'Health for Growth', were adopted by the Commission in November 2011, and were expected to be adopted by the Council in mid-2014. The new programme was to have a total budget of €449.4m., and was to focus on the development of innovative and sustainable health systems; facilitating access to improved, safer health care; the promotion of health and the prevention of disease; and protection from cross-border health risks.

In December 2008—in view of estimates that annually 8%–12% of patients admitted to EU hospitals suffered largely preventable harm from the health care they received, including contracting health care-associated infections, such as those caused by the bacterium MRSA (methicillin-resistant staphylococcus aureus)—the Commission adopted a communication and proposal for a Council Recommendation on specific actions that member states could take, either individually, collectively or with the Commission, to improve the safety of patients.

Various epidemiological surveillance systems are in operation, covering major communicable diseases. An early warning and response system to help member states to deal with outbreaks of diseases was in place by the end of 2000. In April 2004 the European Parliament and the Council adopted a regulation establishing a European Centre for Disease Prevention and Control (ECDC), to enable the EU to share its disease control expertise more effectively and to allow multinational investigation teams to be drawn up quickly and efficiently. The Centre, based in Sweden, became operational in May 2005. The ECDC's European Programme for Intervention Epidemiology Training provides training and practical experience in intervention epidemiology at national centres for surveillance and communicable diseases control within the EU.

In September 2009 the European Commission launched a new European Partnership for Action against Cancer, which was to bring together relevant organizations to pool expertise with the aim of reducing the number of new cancer cases arising in the EU by some 15%, by 2020. During 2006–08 the EU member states, and Iceland and Norway, implemented the Vaccine European New Integrated Collaboration Effort (VENICE) project, which aimed to broaden knowledge and best practice on vaccination; a follow-up project, VENICE II, was launched in December 2008 to cover 2009–11. The first European conference on vaccination and immunization, Eurovaccine 2009, was organized and funded by the ECDC, and convened in Stockholm, Sweden, in December 2009.

Under the Treaty on European Union, the EU assumed responsibility for the problem of drug addiction; a European Monitoring Centre for Drugs and Drug Addiction (EMCDDA—see Justice and Home Affairs) was established in Lisbon, Portugal, in 1995. In March 2005 an EU Platform for Action on Diet, Physical Activity and Health was launched, as part of an overall strategy on nutrition and physical activity being developed by the Commission to address rising levels of obesity. The Commission initiated a public consultation in December on how to reduce obesity levels and the prevalence of associated chronic diseases in the EU. In May 2007 the Commission adopted a White Paper on nutrition- and obesity-related health issues, in which it urged food manufacturers to reduce levels of salt, fat and sugar in their products and emphasized the need to encourage Europeans to undertake more physical activity. A European Alcohol and Health Forum, comprising more than 40 businesses and non-governmental organizations, was formed in June to focus on initiatives to protect European citizens from the harmful use of alcohol. In October 2006 the Commission had adopted a communication setting out an EU strategy to support member states in reducing alcohol-related harm.

The European Commission states that tobacco use is the largest single cause of premature death and disease in the EU. In July 2005 an EU directive came into effect that prohibited tobacco advertising in the print media, on radio and over the internet, as well as the sponsorship by tobacco companies of cross-border cultural and sporting events. The directive applied only to advertising and sponsorship with a cross-border dimension. Tobacco advertising on television had already been banned in the EU in the early 1990s. In June 2009, after extensive consultation, the Commission adopted a proposal for a Council recommendation on the introduction of national legislation to protect citizens from exposure to tobacco smoke. In February 2013 the Commission published a report on progress following the Council recommendation of 2009, which noted that all EU countries had made progress towards protecting against exposure to tobacco smoke, although national measures varied widely; the strongest measures had been introduced in Bulgaria, Greece, Hungary, Ireland, Malta, Spain and the United Kingdom. Meanwhile, in December 2012 the European Commission had proposed that the 2001 Tobacco Products Directive be revised. The Commission sought to prohibit the use of cigarettes and tobacco with a so-called characterizing flavour (such as menthol cigarettes), and to ensure that pictorial health warnings appeared on 75% of tobacco packaging (rather than the existing 30%). It also aimed to introduce measures to prevent cross-border online sales to minors, to track illegal trade in tobacco products and to extend the scope of the directive to include currently unregulated products, such as some e-cigarettes and herbal smoking products. In December 2013 the European Parliament and representatives of EU member states reached agreement on the revision of the Tobacco Products Directive, tightening rules pertaining to tobacco and related products, in an effort to reduce their appeal to young people. The Directive was approved by Parliament and the Council in early 2014, and was to come into force in May.

The Food Supplements Directive, which was approved in 2002 and was designed to strengthen controls on the sale of natural remedies, vitamin supplements and mineral plant extracts, came into effect in August 2005. Under the legislation, only vitamins and minerals on an approved list could be used in supplements and restrictions were to be placed on the upper limits of vitamin doses. A Falsified Medicines Directive came into force in January 2013, which improved the safety of medicines through measures to ensure their authenticity and the quality of their ingredients.

In June 2008 an EU high-level conference entitled Together for Mental Health and Well-being launched the European Pact for Mental Health and Well-being, to be implemented during 2009–10 and focusing on five priority areas: prevention of suicide and depression; mental health in youth and education; mental health in workplace settings; mental health in older people; and combating stigma and social exclusion.

In October 2009 the European Commission adopted a strategy and action plan for combating HIV/AIDS in the EU and neighbouring countries in 2009–13, with a focus on the following principal areas: HIV prevention and testing; targeting priority groups most at risk of HIV; and targeting regions with a higher proportion of people at risk. The strategy had the following overall objectives: to reduce new HIV infections across all European countries; to improve patients' access to prevention, treatment and support; and to ameliorate the quality of life of those living with, affected by or most vulnerable to HIV/AIDS in Europe and neighbouring countries.

It was envisaged that the enlargement of the EU in 2004 and 2007 would cause a number of problems for the Union with regard to public health policy given that, in general, the health status indicators of the majority of the accession states compared poorly with the EU average. Some of the new member states, which (with only one or two exceptions) had few resources to spend on health, had serious problems with communicable diseases (particularly HIV/AIDS), and the health systems of most were in need of improvement. In October 2009 the European Commission announced a series of actions aimed at helping member states and other actors to address inequalities in health provision and life expectancy within and between individual EU member states. Member states and stakeholders were to be helped to identify best practices; and the Commission was to publish regular relevant statistics, and also to issue reports on inequalities and their impact and on successful strategies for addressing them. It was to support countries by using EU funds towards improving primary care facilities, water provision, sanitation and housing renewal.

Since 1 January 2006 EU member states have issued European Health Insurance Cards (EHICs), which entitle residents to receive state-provided medical treatment in the event of suffering either an accident or illness while visiting temporarily states within the European Economic Area (EEA) and Switzerland.

ENVIRONMENT

Environmental action by the EU was initiated in 1972. The Maastricht Treaty on European Union, which entered into force in November 1993, gave environmental action policy status, and the Treaty of Amsterdam identified sustainable development as one of the Community's overall aims. In June 1998 European heads of state and government launched the Cardiff Process, requiring the integration of environmental considerations into all EU policies.

In 1990 the EC established the European Environment Agency (EEA, see p. 284) to monitor environmental issues and provide advice. The agency, which is located in Copenhagen, Denmark, and which became operational in November 1994, also provides targeted information to policy-makers and the public and disseminates comparable environmental data. The agency is open to non-EU countries and it was the first EU body to have members from the accession states.

From November 2009 the online European Pollutant Release and Transfer Register (E-PRTR) replaced the former European Pollutant Emission Register (EPER). The E-PRTR provides data (updated annually, with records commencing in 2007) for EU member states on 91 substances released to air, water and land and 65 sectors of industrial activity, including data on transfers of waste and wastewater from industrial facilities to other locations, and data on emissions caused by accidents at industrial facilities. The European Parliament approved legislation in April 2004 aimed at making firms causing pollution liable for the costs of repairing the damage caused to natural habitats, water resources and wildlife. In December 2007 the Commission adopted a new directive on reducing industrial emissions, which was to replace seven existing directives. The directive was intended, inter alia, to tighten emission limits in certain industrial sectors, to introduce minimum standards for environmental inspections of industrial installations and to extend the scope of legislation to cover other polluting activities, such as medium-sized combustion plants.

The EU has approved numerous international instruments relating to the environment, including the Vienna Convention for the Protection of the Ozone Layer, and its protocol, controlling the production of chlorofluorocarbons (CFCs); the Stockholm Convention on Persistent Organic Pollutants; and the Kyoto Protocol. In June 2000 the Commission launched the European Climate Change Programme (ECCP), which aimed to identify and develop a strategy needed to meet commitments under the Kyoto Protocol, and to incorporate climate change concerns into various EU policies. A second phase of the ECCP (under which more than 30 measures had been implemented since its establishment in 2000), ECCP II, was launched in October 2005, with the aim of reviewing the progress of individual member states towards achieving their individual targets on reducing emissions, and developing a framework for EU climate change policy beyond the expiry of the Kyoto Protocol in 2012 (the Protocol was renewed in that year). In January 2007, in a communication ('Limiting Global Climate Change to 2° Celsius: The Way Ahead for 2020 and Beyond'), the Commission set out proposals for climate change management, which were aimed at limiting the increase in the average global temperature to no more than 2°C above pre-industrial levels. In March 2007, at a summit meeting, EU leaders set a number of joint targets as part of the continued effort to combat the effects of global warming, which, together, it was claimed, constituted the Union's first ever comprehensive agreement on climate and energy policy. Consequently, in April 2009, the Council adopted new climate change legislation, committing EU member states to reducing carbon dioxide emissions by 20% in 2013–20, compared with emissions levels in 1990. The Council also agreed to increase the use of renewable energy sources to 20% (10% for transport energy consumption) by 2020, and to increase energy efficiency by 20% by the same date. Meeting in January 2010, the European Council and the European Commission published a joint letter in which they formally stated the willingness of the EU to adhere to emission reduction targets detailed in the non-binding Copenhagen Accord, which had been agreed in December 2009 by heads of state and government and other delegates attending the UN Climate Change Conference that had been convened in Copenhagen, originally with the objective of finalizing negotiations on a successor instrument to the Kyoto Protocol. The Copenhagen Accord determined that international co-operative action should be taken, in the context of sustainable development, to reduce global greenhouse gas emissions so as to hold the ongoing increase in global temperature below 2°C; in accordance with its April 2009 commitments, the EU had pledged a unilateral commitment to reduce the overall emissions by 20% of 1990 levels by 2020, and made a conditional offer to increase this reduction in emissions to 30%, provided that other major emitters agreed to assume their fair share of global emissions reduction efforts.

In February 2010 a Directorate-General for Climate Action was established, to help to mitigate the consequences of climate change, to ensure targets on climate change are met, and to oversee the EU Emissions Trading System (ETS). The ETS, which was launched in January 2005, obliges companies that exceed their allocation of carbon dioxide emissions to buy extra allowances from more efficient companies or incur considerable fines. In November 2006 the Commission initiated a review of the EU ETS, proposing an expansion of its coverage to new sectors and emissions and the further harmonization of its application between member states. Legislation on a revised ETS was adopted by the Commission in April 2009. The revised ETS was to be effective from 2013–20, capping the overall level of permissible emissions, while allowing allowances to be traded as required. The total annual allowance was to decline each year, in order to reduce gradually the overall emissions level; 12% of ETS revenues were to be invested in a fund designed to encourage poorer member states to modernize their industry. Exemptions were to apply to industrial sectors considered to be at risk of 'carbon leakage', through the relocation of factories to countries located outside the EU, or the acquisition of EU industries by non-EU competitors. A directive incorporating the aviation sector into the EU ETS, capping aviation sector emissions from January 2012, entered into force in February 2009. At 2014 non-EU airlines remained temporarily exempt from obligations under the ETS.

In October 2007 the European Commission announced that it had reached an agreement with the three countries of the EEA on linking their respective emissions trading systems. In the same month the Commission became a founding member of the International Carbon Action Partnership, which convenes a Global Carbon Market Forum for countries and regions with mandatory emissions capping and trading systems.

In June 1996 the European Commission agreed a strategy, drawn up in collaboration with the European petroleum and car industries and known as the Auto-Oil Programme, for reducing harmful emissions from road vehicles by between 60% and 70% by 2010 in an effort to reduce air pollution. The programme committed member states to the progressive elimination of leaded petrol by 2000 (with limited exemptions until 2005). From 2000 petrol-powered road vehicles were to be fitted with 'on-board diagnostic' (OBD) systems to monitor emissions. Diesel vehicles were to be installed with OBD systems by 2005. Under Auto-Oil II, the directive was revised in 2003, establishing specifications to come into force on 1 January 2005, with new limits on sulphur content of both petrol and diesel. Moreover, lower limits would come into force for all fuel marketed from December 2009, although there would be limited availability from 2005. In July 1998 the Commission announced plans to reduce pollution from nuclear power stations by reducing emissions of sulphur dioxides, nitrogen oxides and dust by one-half. A new directive limiting the sulphur content of marine fuel came into force in August 2005. In April 2009 the Council and the European Parliament adopted a regulation on setting carbon dioxide emissions performance standards for new passenger cars, as part of an integrated approach to reducing carbon dioxide emissions from light-duty vehicles to no more than 120 g per km by 2012. In January 2013 the Commission announced a new Clean Power for Transport Package, which aimed to facilitate the construction of recharging and refuelling stations across the EU, to facilitate the use of clean fuels (such as electricity, hydrogen and natural gas) for road vehicles. The proposals envisaged, inter alia, the introduction of a minimum number of recharging points for electric cars in each country, with use of a common standard plug; the introduction of a network of hydrogen filling stations, with uniform standards of operation, throughout the 14 existing applicable countries; and an increase in the use of biofuels, while ensuring sustainability.

In September 2005 the Commission presented a thematic strategy on air pollution, prepared under the auspices of Clean Air for Europe (CAFE), a programme of technical analysis and policy development launched in March 2001. While covering all major pollutants, the new air quality policy focused on particulates and ground-level ozone pollution, which were known to pose the greatest risk to human health. The strategy aimed to cut the annual number of premature deaths from pollution-related diseases by almost 40% by 2020, compared with the 2000 level, and also to reduce the area of forests and other ecosystems suffering damage from airborne pollutants. In April 2008 a new air quality directive was approved by the Council, which merged five existing pieces of legislation into a single directive, and imposed limits on fine particle emissions (PM2.5) from vehicles, agriculture and small-scale industry for the first time. Emissions of PM2.5 in urban areas were to be reduced by 20% by 2020, compared with 2010 levels. The Commission estimated that some 370,000 EU citizens died each year from conditions linked to air pollution. A review of legislation on air pollution commenced in 2011, which concluded in December 2013 with the adoption by the Commission of a new CAFE, specifying objectives for air quality until 2030. An amended National Emissions Ceilings Directive was also adopted, which introduced more restrictive maximum levels for national emissions of the six principal pollutants. The Commission also proposed a new directive to minimize pollution from medium-sized combustion installations.

In October 2005 the Commission proposed a strategy to protect the marine environment, which aimed to ensure that all EU marine waters were environmentally healthy by 2021. This was the second of seven thematic strategies to be adopted under the sixth environmental action programme (2002–12). The Commission proposed strategies on the prevention and recycling of waste and the sustainable use of natural resources in December 2005, and on the urban environment in January 2006. In July the Commission proposed a directive aimed at establishing a framework for achieving a more sustainable use of pesticides by reducing the risks posed by pesticides to human health and the environment (its sixth thematic strategy).

In September the Commission adopted a comprehensive strategy dedicated to soil protection, including a proposal for a directive setting forth common principles for soil protection across the EU. A directive on the assessment and management of flood risks entered into force in November 2007, requiring member states to conduct preliminary assessments by 2011 to identify river basins and associated coastal areas at risk of flooding, to develop flood risk maps by 2013 for areas deemed to be at risk, and to establish flood risk management plans for these areas by 2015. In March 2009 the European Commission finalized an EU-wide review of the safety—to consumers, farmers, local residents, passers-by and animals—of existing pesticides used in plant protection products that were on the market before 1993; the review had resulted in the removal from sale of more than two-thirds of the substances assessed.

In September 2000 the EU adopted a directive on end-of-life vehicles (ELVs), containing measures for the collection, treatment, recovery and disposal of such waste. The ruling forced manufacturers to pay for the disposal of new cars from July 2002 and of old cars from January 2007. The directive set recycling and recovery targets, restricted the use of heavy metals in new cars from 2003, and specified that ELVs might only be dismantled by authorized agencies. EU directives on waste electronic and electrical equipment and the restriction of the use of certain hazardous substances in electronic and electrical equipment came into force in February 2003. The directives were based on the premise of producer responsibility and aimed to persuade producers to improve product design in order to facilitate recycling and disposal. Increased recycling of electrical and electronic equipment would limit the total quantity of waste going to final disposal. Under the legislation consumers would be able to return equipment free of charge from August 2005. In order to prevent the generation of hazardous waste, the second directive required the substitution of various heavy metals (lead, mercury, cadmium, and hexavalent chromium) and brominated flame retardants in new electrical and electronic equipment marketed from July 2006. In January 2005 the Commission adopted a new strategy on reducing mercury pollution, which was endorsed by EU ministers responsible for the environment in June. A regulation banning mercury exports from the EU by 2011 was proposed by the Commission in October 2006. In September 2007 a directive was adopted on phasing out, by April 2009, the use of toxic mercury in measuring devices in cases where it could be substituted by safer alternatives.

A regulation revising EU laws on trade in wild animals and plants was adopted by ministers responsible for the environment in December 1996. A series of directives adopted in 2002 formulated new EU policy on the conservation of wild birds, fishing and protection for certain species of whales. Every three years the Commission publishes an official report on the conservation of wild birds. In January 2010 the Commission issued a communication detailing possible future options for biodiversity policy after 2010, to succeed a previous agenda of halting biodiversity loss in the Union by 2010. The communication envisaged a long-term vision, towards 2050, for preserving and, as far as possible, restoring biodiversity, to be preceded by medium-term objectives to be achieved by 2020.

As part of the EU's efforts to promote awareness of environmental issues and to encourage companies to do likewise, the voluntary Eco-Management and Audit Scheme was launched in April 1995. Under the scheme, participating industrial companies undergo an independent audit of their environmental performance. In addition, the EU awards 'eco-labels' for products that limit harmful effects on the environment (including foodstuffs, beverages and pharmaceutical products, among others). The criteria to be met are set by the EU Eco-Labelling Board.

In October 2003 the Commission presented a new environmental policy—the Registration, Evaluation and Authorisation of Chemicals system (REACH)—which was originally intended to collate crucial safety information on tens of thousands of potentially dangerous chemicals used in consumer goods industries. However, following intensive lobbying by the chemical industry sector, the scope of REACH was reduced (for example, the number of chemicals to be tested was cut and the number of chemicals that would require licences was also substantially curtailed). The European Parliament approved the proposed legislation in a first reading in November 2005, and in December the Council reached a political agreement on REACH. Environmentalists criticized ministers for weakening the legislation by relaxing the conditions set by the Parliament for authorization of the most dangerous chemicals. The REACH regulation was formally adopted in December 2006. The European Chemicals Agency, which is responsible for managing REACH, commenced operations in Helsinki, Finland, in June 2007. In December 2008 the Commission adopted a regulation aligning the EU system of classification, labelling and packaging of chemical substances and mixtures to the UN Globally Harmonized System of Classification and Labelling of Chemicals.

The EU's sixth environmental action programme (2002–12), Environment 2010: Our Future, Our Choice, emphasized the continuing importance of the integration of environmental considerations into other EU policies, focusing on four priority areas: climate change, nature and biodiversity; environment; health and quality of life; and the management of natural resources and waste. The programme also identified explicitly the measures required to implement successfully the EU's sustainable development strategy. In addition, it sought to encourage greater public participation in environmental debates.

In May 2007 the Council and Parliament adopted a new funding programme, LIFE+, following on from a LIFE programme established in 1992; LIFE+ was to be the EU's single financial instrument targeting only the environment. With a budget of €2,143m. for the period 2007–13, LIFE+ consists of three thematic components: nature and biodiversity; environment policy and governance; and information and communication. LIFE+ supports projects throughout the EU, as well as in some candidate, acceding and neighbouring countries. Between 1992 and 2009 some 3,316 projects were co-financed by LIFE/LIFE+. In December 2011 the European Commission published proposals for a new LIFE programme, for the period until 2020. The revised LIFE programme, which entered into effect in January 2014, had a budget of some €3,400m.

The environment was one of the 10 themes of the 'co-operation' specific programme of the Seventh Framework Programme (FP7) for research, technological development and demonstration activities covering 2007–13. With a budget of €1,900m., a wide range of environmental research activities were allocated funding under FP7, grouped into four areas: climate change, pollution and risks; sustainable management of resources; environmental technologies; and earth observation and assessment tools for sustainable development. The Institute for Environment and Sustainability, located in Ispra, Italy, was created in 2001 as part of the Joint Research Centre to provide research-based support to the development and implementation of European environmental policies.

Europe 2020 is the EU's strategy for growth until 2020, as part of which the Commission's flagship initiative for a resource-efficient Europe focuses on sustainable growth and a move towards a resource-efficient, low-carbon economy. In March 2011 the Commission adopted detailed proposals concerned with bringing about the transition to a competitive, low-carbon EU economy, by reducing domestic carbon emissions by between 80% and 95% by 2050. A so-called roadmap for a resource-efficient Europe was adopted by the Commission in September.

In December 2012 the Commission announced proposals for a new Environment Action Programme (EAP), entitled 'Living Well, Within the Limits of our Planet', which sought to influence environmental policy until 2020. The new EAP entered into force in January 2014, and focuses on three principal thematic goals: the protection of nature and improvements in ecological resilience; increased sustainable, resource-efficient, low-carbon growth; and addressing environmental health risks. Four principal measures were to facilitate implementation of these objectives: increasing implementation of legislation; improving information, by developing the knowledge base; better-targeted investment for environment and climate policy; and the integration of environmental issues into other policy areas. The programme also sought to make improve the sustainability of EU cities, and to help the EU to address more effectively international environmental and climate challenges.

SECURITY AND DEFENCE

Under the Single European Act, which came into force on 1 July 1987 (amending the Treaty of Rome, now the Treaty on the Functioning of the European Union), it was formally stipulated for the first time that member states should inform and consult each other on foreign policy matters (as was already, in practice, often the case). In June 1992 the Petersberg Declaration of Western European Union (WEU) defined the role of WEU as the defence component of the EU and outlined the 'Petersberg tasks' relating to crisis management, including humanitarian, peacekeeping and peacemaking operations, which could be carried out under WEU authority (now EU authority). In 1992 France and Germany established a joint force called Eurocorps, based in Strasbourg, France, which was later joined by Belgium, Spain and Luxembourg. An agreement was signed in January 1993 that specified that Eurocorps troops could serve under the command of the North Atlantic Treaty Organization (NATO), thus relieving concern, particularly from the United Kingdom and the USA, that the Eurocorps would undermine NATO's role in Europe. In May member states of the Eurocorps agreed to make the Eurocorps available to WEU. The Maastricht Treaty on European Union, which came into force on 1 November, provided for joint action by member governments in matters of common foreign and security policy (CFSP), and envisaged the formation of a European security and defence policy (ESDP), with the possibility of a common defence force, although existing commitments to NATO were to be honoured. The Treaty raised WEU to the rank of an 'integral part of the development of the Union', while preserving its institutional autonomy, and gave it the task of elaborating and implementing decisions and actions with defence implications. In May 1995 WEU ratified the decision by Spain, France, Italy and Portugal to establish land and sea forces, the

European Operational Rapid Force (EUROFOR) and the European Maritime Force (EUROMARFOR) respectively, which were also to undertake the Petersberg tasks under the auspices of WEU. Several other multinational forces also belonged to Forces Answerable to the WEU (FAWEU). At the EU summit in Köln, Germany, in June 1999, EU member states accepted a proposal for the Eurocorps to be placed at the disposal of the EU for crisis response operations. At the end of that year Eurocorps member states agreed to transform the Eurocorps into a rapid reaction corps headquarters available both to the EU and NATO. In 2002 NATO certified the Eurocorps as a NATO high readiness force, which required the headquarters (Eurocorps HQ) to be open to all NATO members as well as those from the EU; thus representatives from Austria, Canada, Finland, Greece, Italy, the Netherlands, Poland, Turkey and the United Kingdom are integrated into Eurocorps HQ.

The Treaty of Amsterdam, which entered into force in May 1999, aimed to strengthen the concept of a CFSP within the Union and incorporated a process of common strategies to co-ordinate external relations with a third party. Under the Amsterdam Treaty, WEU was to provide the EU with access to operational capability for undertaking the so-called Petersberg tasks. In March 1999 representatives of the Commission and NATO held a joint meeting, for the first time, to discuss the conflict in the southern Serbian province of Kosovo. The Treaty introduced the role of High Representative for the CFSP. In April a meeting of NATO Heads of State and of Government determined that NATO's equipment, personnel and infrastructure would be available to any future EU military operation. In June the European Council, meeting in Köln, determined to strengthen the ESDP, stating that the EU needed a capacity for autonomous action, without prejudice to actions by NATO and acknowledging the supreme prerogatives of the UN Security Council. The European Council initiated a process of assuming direct responsibility for the Petersberg tasks, which were placed at the core of the ESDP process. In December, following consultation with NATO, the European Council, meeting in Helsinki, Finland, adopted the European Defence Initiative, comprising the following goal: by 2003 the EU should be able to deploy within 60 days and for a period of up to one year a rapid reaction force, comprising up to 60,000 national troops from member states, capable of implementing the full range of Petersberg tasks. At the Helsinki meeting, the establishment of three permanent military institutions was proposed: a Political and Security Committee (PSC); a Military Committee; and a Military Staff. The PSC, which was fully established by 2001, monitors the international situation, helps to define policies and assess their implementation, encourages dialogue and, under the auspices of the Council, takes responsibility for the political direction of capability development. In the event of a crisis situation, it oversees the strategic direction of any military response, proposes political objectives and supervises their enactment. The Military Committee gives military advice to the PSC, and comprises the chiefs of defence of member states, represented by military delegates. It serves as a forum for military consultation and co-operation and deals with risk assessment, the development of crisis management and military relations with non-EU European NATO members, accession countries, and NATO itself. Meanwhile, the Military Staff, comprising experts seconded by the member states, provides the EU with an early warning capability, takes responsibility for strategic planning for the Petersberg tasks and implements the Military Committee's policies. Permanent arrangements have been agreed for EU-NATO consultation and co-operation in this area. The process of transferring the crisis management responsibilities of WEU to the EU was finalized by July 2001. From January 2007 a new EU Operations Centre (OpsCentre), located in Brussels, Belgium, was available as a third option for commanding EU crisis management missions. Hitherto autonomous EU operations were commanded either with recourse to NATO's command structure or from the national operational headquarters of one of five member states (France, Germany, Greece, Italy and the United Kingdom). Although the EU OpsCentre had a permanent staff of just four core officers, it was envisaged that a total of 103 officers and civilians would be able to begin planning an operation within five days of the Council deciding to activate the centre, achieving full capability to command the operation within 20 days. The EU OpsCentre was activated for the first time in March 2012, to strengthen civilian-military co-operation in the Horn of Africa.

In December 2001 the EU announced that the rapid reaction force was ready to undertake small-scale crisis management tasks. A deal was agreed at the Copenhagen summit in December 2002 on sharing planning resources with NATO. In January 2003 EU forces were deployed for the first time in an international peacekeeping role (when 500 police officers were dispatched to Bosnia and Herzegovina to take over policing duties from the existing UN force). In June 2004 the European Council approved the creation of a European Defence Agency (EDA), which commenced operations later that year. The EDA took responsibility for improving the EU's defence capabilities in relation to crisis management and for promoting co-operation on research and procurement, strengthening the European defence industrial and technological base and developing a competitive European defence equipment market. In November 2007 EU ministers responsible for defence adopted a framework for a joint strategy on defence research and technology.

In June 2000 the EU established a civilian crisis management committee. In the same month the European Council defined four priority areas for civilian crisis management: developing the role of the police; strengthening the rule of law; strengthening civilian administrations; and improving civil protection. In February 2001 the Council adopted a regulation creating a rapid reaction mechanism (RRM) to improve the EU's civilian capacity to respond to crises. The mechanism bypassed cumbersome decision-making processes, to enable civilian experts in fields such as mine clearance, customs, police training, election monitoring, institution building, media support, rehabilitation and mediation to be mobilized speedily. In November 2006 the Council and Parliament adopted a regulation establishing an Instrument for Stability, replacing the RRM.

The common security and defence policy (CSDP), as the ESDP was renamed, remained an integral part of the CFSP under the Treaty of Lisbon, which entered into force, becoming the new legal basis for the CFSP, in December 2009. According to the Lisbon Treaty, the progressive framing of a common defence policy was intended to lead to a common defence, following a unanimous decision of the European Council. A mutual defence clause and a solidarity clause (in the event of a member state becoming the victim of a terrorist attack or natural or man-made disaster) were included, and joint disarmament operations, military advice and assistance, conflict prevention and post-conflict stabilization were added to the Petersberg tasks. The Lisbon Treaty introduced the office of High Representative of the Union for Foreign Affairs and Security Policy (uniting the previous roles of High Representative for the CFSP and External Affairs Commissioner), and provided for the establishment of the European External Action Service (with a diplomatic function, and supporting the work of and reporting to the High Representative). The High Representative leads the External Relations Council, is also a Vice-President of the European Commission, and heads political dialogue with international partners. Most decisions on the CFSP continued to be adopted at intergovernmental level and by consensus of all member states.

In November 2004 EU ministers responsible for defence agreed to create several Battlegroups (BGs) for eventual deployment to crisis areas. BGs were to comprise up to 1,500 troops and were to be capable of being deployed within 10 days of a unanimous decision from EU member states and the creation of a battle plan and would be equipped to stay in an area for up to four months. Each group was to be commanded by a 'lead nation' and associated with a force headquarters. The BGs reached initial operational capacity in January 2005, meaning that at least one was on standby every six months. France, Italy, Spain and the United Kingdom set up their own BGs. The creation of the BGs was partly to compensate for the inadequacies of the rapid reaction force of 60,000 troops, which, while theoretically declared ready for action in May 2003, in practice was adversely affected by shortfalls in equipment, owing to a lack of investment in procurement and research and a failure to co-ordinate purchases among member states. In November 2005 it was announced that 15 BGs would be created, and additional groups were subsequently proposed. In January 2007 the BGs reached full operational capacity, meaning that two BG operations could be undertaken concurrently; no BG deployments had, however, taken place.

The Justice and Home Affairs Council held an emergency meeting in September 2001 following the terrorist attacks on the USA. It determined a number of measures to be taken to improve security in the Community. First, the Council sought to reach a common definition of acts of terrorism, and to establish higher penalties for such acts. The new definition included cyber and environmental attacks. The Council decided that, for the perpetrators of terrorist attacks, as well as those involved in other serious crimes (including trafficking in arms, people and drugs and money-laundering), the process of extradition would be replaced by a procedure for handover based on a European arrest warrant. The member states reached agreement on the arrest warrant in December; under the agreement, covering 32 serious offences, EU countries may no longer refuse to extradite their own nationals. The European arrest warrant had been implemented in all member states by mid-2005. The Council also determined to accelerate the implementation of the convention on mutual assistance in criminal matters and to establish a joint investigation team. Member states were encouraged to ratify the convention on combating the financing of terrorism and to exercise greater rigour in the issuing of travel documents. The heads of the security and intelligence services of member states met in October 2001, in the first EU-wide meeting of this kind, to discuss the co-ordinated action to be taken to curb terrorism. Rapid links were forged with US counterparts—in December Europol signed a co-operation agreement on the exchange of strategic information (excluding personal data) with the USA; in December 2002 the agreement was extended to include the exchange of personal data.

The heads of the EU's anti-terrorist units also held a meeting following the September 2001 attacks, to discuss issues such as joint training exercises, equipment sharing, the joint procurement of equipment and possible joint operations. Prior to these emergency meetings, intelligence and security information had been shared bilaterally and on a small scale. Terrorist bombings in Madrid, Spain, in March 2004 gave added impetus to EU initiatives aimed at improving travel document security and impeding the cross-border movements of terrorists. Following the attacks, the EU created the new position of Counter-terrorist Co-ordinator, the principal responsibilities of whom included enhancing intelligence sharing among EU members and promoting the implementation of agreed EU anti-terrorism measures, some of which had been impeded by the legislative processes of individual member states. The Justice and Home Affairs Council held an extraordinary meeting following the terrorist attacks in London, United Kingdom, in July 2005, at which ministers pledged to accelerate the adoption and implementation of enhanced counter-terrorism measures, focusing on issues such as the financing of terrorism, information sharing by law enforcement authorities, police co-operation and the retention of telecommunications data by service providers. In December the Council adopted a new EU counter-terrorism strategy focused on preventing people embracing terrorism, protecting citizens and infrastructure, pursuing and investigating suspects, and responding to the consequences of an attack. A specific strategy for combating radicalization and the recruitment of terrorists was approved at the same time. The Council also reached agreement on a draft directive on the retention of telecommunications data for a period of between six months and two years for use in anti-terrorism investigations. Police would have access to information about telephone calls, text messages and internet data, but not to the exact content. The directive was approved by the European Parliament later that month. In November 2007 the Commission adopted a series of proposals on the criminalization of terrorist training, recruitment and public provocation to commit terrorist offences, on the prevention of the use of explosives by terrorists and on the use of airline passenger information in law enforcement investigations.

Under the European code of conduct on arms exports, the EU publishes an annual report on defence exports based on confidential information provided by each member state. EU member states must withhold export licences to countries where it is deemed that arms sales might lead to political repression or external aggression. The EU funds projects aimed at the collection and destruction of weapons in countries emerging from conflict. The EU is strongly committed to nuclear non-proliferation. Under its programme of co-operation with Russia, the Union works to dismantle or destroy nuclear, chemical and biological weapons and weapons of mass destruction.

In September 2004 five European ministers responsible for defence signed an agreement in Noordwijk, Netherlands, to establish a police force, which could be deployed internationally for post-conflict peacekeeping duties and maintaining public order. The European Gendarmerie Force (EUROGENDFOR), which was officially inaugurated at its headquarters in Vicenza, Italy, in January 2006, was capable of deploying a mission of up to 800 gendarmes within 30 days, which could be reinforced. A comprehensive operational system for crisis management has been developed, for the use of the EU and other international organizations, including the UN, NATO and the Organization for Security and Co-operation in Europe (OSCE). In 2007 the EGF became involved with EUFOR-Althea (in Bosnia and Herzegovina), and in 2009 the EGF commenced an operational commitment within the NATO Training Mission in Afghanistan, to contribute to the development of the Afghan National Police. In 2010 EUROGENDFOR offered assistance to the UN Mission in Haiti (MINUSTAH), following an earthquake in that country. From December 2008 the EGF comprised members from France, Italy, the Netherlands, Portugal, Romania and Spain; Poland's military gendarmerie is also a partner.

In December 2012 the Presidents of the European Council, the European Commission and the European Parliament travelled to Oslo, Norway, to accept the Nobel Peace Prize, which had been awarded to the EU in October in acknowledgement of its contribution to 'the advancement of peace and reconciliation, democracy and human rights in Europe' after the two world wars of the 20th century.

For details of military operations that the EU has undertaken in third countries, see the specific regional information.

FINANCIAL SERVICES AND CAPITAL MOVEMENTS

Freedom of capital movement and the creation of a uniform financial area were regarded as vital for the completion of the EU's internal market by 1992. In 1987, as part of the liberalization of the flow of capital, a Council directive came into force whereby member states were obliged to remove restrictions on three categories of transactions: long-term credits related to commercial transactions; acquisition of securities; and the admission of securities to capital markets. In June 1988 the Council of Ministers approved a directive whereby all restrictions on capital movements (financial loans and credits, current and deposit account operations, transactions in securities and other instruments normally dealt in on the money market) were to be removed by 1 July 1990. A number of countries were permitted to exercise certain restrictions until the end of 1992, and further extensions were then granted to Portugal and Greece. With the entry into force of the Maastricht Treaty in November 1993, the principle of full freedom of capital movements was incorporated into the structure of the EU.

The EU worked to develop a single market in financial services throughout the 1990s. In October 1998 the Commission drew up a framework for action in the financial services sector. This communication was followed by a Financial Services Action Plan (FSAP) in May 1999, with three strategic objectives: to establish a single market in wholesale financial services; to make retail markets open and secure; and to strengthen the rules on prudential supervision in order to keep pace with new sources of financial risk. The prudential supervision of financial conglomerates (entities offering a range of financial services in areas such as banking, insurance and securities), which were developing rapidly, was identified as an area of particular importance. During 2002 a directive was drawn up on the supplementary supervision of such businesses, in recognition of the increasing consolidation in the financial sector and the emergence of cross-sector financial groups. Individual targets specified in the 1999 FSAP included removing the outstanding barriers to raising capital within the EU; creating a coherent legal framework for supplementary pension funds; and providing greater legal certainty in cross-border securities trading.

In November 2003 the Commission adopted a package of seven measures aiming to establish a new organizational architecture in all financial services sectors. The Commission stressed that this initiative was required urgently if the FSAP was to be implemented and enforced effectively. The deadline of 2005 for the adoption of the FSAP measures was largely met, with 98% of the measures having been completed, and their implementation by member states was closely monitored. In December 2005 the Commission presented its financial services policy for 2005–10, identifying five priorities: to consolidate progress and ensure effective implementation and enforcement of existing rules; to extend the 'better regulation principles' (i.e. transparency, wide consultation and thorough evaluation) to all policy-making; to enhance supervisory co-operation and convergence; to create greater competition between service providers, especially those active in retail markets; and to expand the EU's external influence in globalizing capital markets.

A proposed directive that had been under negotiation for 14 years, which aimed to ensure that shareholders were treated in the same way throughout the EU after takeover bids, and which sought to create a single Community framework governing takeovers, was approved by the European Parliament in December 2003. Following approval by the Council, it came into force in May 2004. A directive enhancing the rights of shareholders of listed companies was adopted in June 2007, with implementation to be undertaken by member states within two years.

A directive on Community banking, adopted in 1977, laid down common prudential criteria for the establishment and operation of banks in member states. A second banking directive, adopted in 1989, aimed to create a single community licence for banking, thereby permitting a bank established in one member country to open branches in any other. The directive entered into force on 1 January 1993. Related measures were subsequently adopted, with the aim of ensuring the capital adequacy of credit institutions and the prevention of money-laundering by criminals. In September ministers approved a directive on a bank deposit scheme to protect account holders. These directives were consolidated into one overall banking directive in March 2000. Non-bank institutions would be eligible for a 'European passport' on compliance with the principles of the EU's first banking directive on the mutual recognition of licences, prudential supervision and supervision by the home member state. Non-bank institutions must also comply with the directive on money-laundering. In May 2001 a directive on the reorganization and closure of failed credit institutions with branches in more than one member state was agreed; it entered into force in May 2004. The capital requirements directive, which was adopted in June 2006, provided for the introduction of a supervisory framework on capital measurement and capital standards in accordance with the Basel II rules agreed by the Basel Committee on Banking Supervision (see Bank for International Settlements—BIS). In October 2008, in response to the crisis in global financial markets, the European Commission proposed amendments to the existing capital requirement directive, revising the rules on bank capital requirements with the aim of reinforcing the stability of the financial system. In September 2009 the directive was adopted by the Council and the European Parliament. The amendments aimed to foster improved risk management among financial institutions, and strengthened the regulatory framework in areas relevant to the causes of the financial and economic crisis in the eurozone, and had to be transposed into national law by the end of October 2010. Meanwhile, in June 2009 the European Council had recommended the establishment of a single rulebook to apply to all financial institutions in the single market. In December 2010 the Basel Committee put forward new regulatory standards on the adequacy and liquidity of bank capital, which were collectively known as Basel III. The existing Capital Requirements Directive was divided into two legislative instruments: a directive governing access to deposit-taking activities, and a regulation establishing the requirements to be adhered to by institutions (together known as CRD IV). Basel III entered into force in mid-July 2013.

In September 2000 a directive was issued governing the actions of non-bank institutions with regard to the issuance of 'electronic money' (money stored on an electronic device, for example a chip card or in a computer memory). The directive authorized non-bank institutions to issue electronic money on a non-professional basis, with the aim of promoting a 'level playing field' with other credit institutions. Other regulations oblige the institutions to redeem electronic money at par value in coins and bank notes, or by transfer without charge. A review of this directive, prompted by various market developments since its introduction, such as the use of pre-paid telephone cards, which some member states considered as electronic money and others did not, was proposed by the Commission in July 2006 and was to follow the approval of the directive on payment services. The directive on payment services, which was adopted in November 2007, provided the legal framework for the creation of the Single Euro Payments Area, an initiative designed to make all electronic payments across the eurozone, for example by credit card, debit card, bank transfer or direct debit, as straightforward, efficient and secure as domestic payments within a single member state. From November 2009 non-bank institutions were also permitted to provide payment services under the new directive, thus opening the market to competition.

In July 1994 the third insurance co-ordination directives, relating to life assurance and non-life insurance, came into effect, creating a framework for an integrated Community insurance market. The directive on the reorganization and winding-up of insurance undertakings was adopted by the EU in February 2001 and came into force in April 2003. The main aim of the directive was to provide greater consumer protection and it formed part of a wider drive to achieve a consistent approach to insolvency proceedings across the EU. A new directive on life assurance was adopted in November 2002, superseding all previous directives in this field. In May 2005 the EU adopted a fifth motor insurance directive, which considerably increased the minimum amounts payable for personal injuries and damage to property and designated pedestrians and cyclists as specific categories of victims who are entitled to compensation. A directive on reinsurance was adopted in November; companies specializing in this area had not previously been specifically regulated by EU legislation. In July 2007 the Commission proposed a thorough reform of EU insurance legislation, which was designed to improve consumer protection, modernize supervision, deepen market integration and increase the international competitiveness of European insurers. The new system, known as Solvency II, would introduce more extensive solvency requirements for insurers, in order to guarantee that they have sufficient capital to withstand adverse events, covering not only traditional insurance risks, but also economic risks, including market risk (such as a fall in the value of an insurer's investments), credit risk (for example when debt obligations are not met) and operational risk (such as malpractice or system failure). In addition, insurers would be compelled to devote significant resources to the identification, measurement and proactive management of risks. The directive on Solvency II (replacing 14 existing directives), was adopted in May 2009 and the new system had been expected to become operational by 1 January 2013, although it was subsequently delayed, and was not expected to be in operation before 2016. The European Insurance and Occupational Pensions Committee works to improve co-operation with national supervisory authorities.

In September 2007 the Council and Parliament adopted a directive designed to harmonize procedural rules and assessment criteria throughout the Community with regard to acquisitions and increases of shareholdings in the banking, insurance and securities sectors. A directive aimed at modernizing and simplifying rules on value-added tax (VAT) for financial and insurance services was proposed by the Commission in November. It was noted that although these services were generally exempt from VAT, the exemption was not being applied uniformly by member states and that a clear definition of exempt services was therefore required.

In May 1993 ministers adopted a directive on investment services, which (with effect from 1 January 1996) allowed credit institutions to offer investment services in any member state, on the basis of a licence held in one state. The 1999 FSAP aimed to achieve the further convergence of national approaches to investment, in order to increase the effectiveness of the 1993 directive. The directive on the market in financial services, which was adopted in April 2004 to replace the 1993 directive, aimed to allow investment firms to operate throughout the EU on the basis of authorization in their home member state and to ensure that investors enjoyed a high level of protection when employing investment firms, regardless of their location in the EU. The directive entered into force in November 2007.

In late 1999 the Commission put forward proposals to remove tax barriers and investment restrictions affecting cross-border pension schemes, as variations among member states in the tax liability of contributions to supplementary pension schemes were obstructing the transfer of pension rights from one state to another, contradicting the Treaty of Rome's principles of free movement. In October 2000 a specific legal framework for institutions for occupational retirement provision (IORPs) was proposed. This seeks to abolish barriers to investment by pension funds and would permit the cross-border management of IORP pension schemes, with mutual recognition of the supervisory methods in force. In September 2003 the occupational pensions directive (IORP directive), which was designed to allow workers of multinational companies to have access to cross-border employer pension schemes, became EU law. Implementation, which had been due within two years, was subject to delays.

In November 1997 the Commission adopted proposals to co-ordinate tax policy among member states. The measures aimed to simplify the transfer of royalty and interest payments between member states and to prevent the withholding of taxes. In February 1999 the European Parliament endorsed a proposal by the Commission to harmonize taxation further, through the co-ordination of savings taxes. In November 2000 ministers responsible for finance agreed on a proposed savings tax directive, the details of which were endorsed in July 2001. This directive set out rules on the exchange of information on savings accounts of individuals resident in one EU country and receiving interest in another. However, in December Austria, Luxembourg and Belgium abandoned the agreement, insisting that they would only comply if other tax havens in Europe, such as Monaco, Liechtenstein and Switzerland, were compelled to amend their banking secrecy laws.

Two proposed directives were issued in November 2000, the first relating to interest and royalties and the second concerning the code of conduct for business taxation. Together with the savings tax directive, these were known as the EU tax package. The EU ministers responsible for finance finally reached agreement on the terms of the package in June 2003. The package consisted of a political code of conduct to eliminate harmful business tax regimes; a legislative measure to ensure an effective minimum level of taxation of savings income; and a legislative measure to eliminate source taxes on cross-border payments of interest and royalties between associated companies. The Council of the EU reached agreement on the controversial savings tax directive (after 15 years of negotiation) in June 2004; the directive entered into force on 1 July 2005. The aim of the directive was to prevent EU citizens from avoiding taxes on savings by keeping their money in foreign bank accounts. Under the directive, each member state would ultimately be expected to provide information to other member states on interest paid from that member state to individual savers resident in those other member states. For a transitional period, Belgium, Luxembourg and Austria were to be allowed to apply a withholding tax instead, at a rate of 15% for the first three years (2005–07), 20% for the subsequent three years (2008–10) and 35% from 1 July 2011. Negotiations had been concluded with Switzerland, Liechtenstein, Monaco, Andorra and San Marino to ensure the adoption of equivalent measures in those countries to allow effective taxation of savings income paid to EU residents.

The May 2000 convention on mutual assistance in criminal matters (see Justice and Home Affairs) committed member states to co-operation in combating economic and financial crime. In May 2001 the Council adopted a framework decision on preventing fraud and counterfeiting in non-cash means of payment, recognizing this as a criminal offence. An EU conference in Paris, France, in February 2002 (which was also attended by representatives of seven candidate countries and Russia) agreed to tackle money-laundering by setting minimum secrecy levels and compelling internet service providers to identify operators of suspect financial deals. Following the terrorist attacks on the USA in September 2001, the EU attempted to accelerate the adoption of the convention combating the financing of terrorism, and began work on a new directive on 'freezing' assets or evidence related to terrorist crimes. In October 2005 a regulation on the compulsory declaration at EU borders of large amounts (i.e. more than €10,000) of cash (including banknotes and cheques) entered into force. The aim of this measure, which applied only to the external borders of the Union, was to prevent the entry into the EU of untraceable money, which could then be used to fund criminal or terrorist activities. A third money-laundering directive (which was extended to cover terrorist financing as well as money-laundering) was also adopted in that month. In November 2006 the Council and Parliament adopted a regulation aimed at ensuring that law enforcement authorities have access to basic information on the payer of transfers of funds in the context of investigating terrorists and tracing their assets.

In February 2001 the Commission launched a complaints network for out-of-court settlements in the financial sector, to help consumers to find amicable solutions in cases where the supplier is in another member state. A directive establishing harmonized rules on the cross-border distance-selling of financial services was adopted in June 2002. The first meeting took place in June 2006 of the Financial Services Consumer Group, a permanent committee, comprising representatives of consumer organizations from each of the member states as well as those active at EU level, established by the Commission to discuss financial services policies and proposals of particular relevance to consumers. In December 2007 the Commission published a White Paper proposing measures to improve the competitiveness and efficiency of European residential mortgage markets by facilitating the cross-border supply and funding of mortgage credit and by increasing the diversity of products available.

The European Commission convened regularly from late 2008 to address the crisis in the eurozone. In October 2008 the President of the European Commission established a high-level group on financial supervision in the EU to decide means of building more effective European and global supervision for financial institutions. Shortly afterwards the heads of state or government of the eurozone countries issued a Declaration on a Concerted European Action Plan of the Euro Area Countries, outlining measures to ensure liquidity for financial institutions and co-operation among European states. In mid-October the European Commission proposed a revision to the deposit guarantee schemes directive, which would increase the minimum protection for bank deposits to €100,000. A summit of the Council held in mid-October urged further concerted and global action to protect the financial market system and the best interests of tax-payers. It emphasized the need for further action to strengthen European and international financial market rules and supervision. In mid-December the European Council approved a European Economic Recovery Plan, outlining a co-ordinated European response to the crisis, involving a three-part approach, based on a new European financial market architecture; a framework plan for the recovery of the real economy, to stimulate jobs and economic growth; and a global response to the financial crisis (see Economic Co-operation). In January 2009 the European Commission adopted decisions aimed at strengthening the supervisory framework for the EU financial markets. The high-level group on financial supervision in the EU, established in October 2008, published a report in February 2009 that analysed the complexity and principal causes of the financial crisis; identified priority areas requiring regulatory change; detailed proposals for far-reaching reforms within the EU aimed at stabilizing the financial markets; and proposals for changes at international level to prevent the recurrence of such a crisis. In mid-March the European Council adopted a common European position, based on constructing a rules- and values-based form of globalization, for a summit of the Group of Twenty (G20), which was held in early April. The Commission participated in the Financial Stability Forum which the April G20 meeting determined to establish, with a mandate to strengthen worldwide financial regulation and supervision; the Forum's inaugural meeting was held in June.

In September 2009, with a view to strengthening EU financial supervision, the Commission adopted proposals for the creation of a European Systemic Risk Board (ESRB), which was to monitor and assess risks to the stability of the financial system as a whole; and a European System of Financial Supervisors (ESFS), which would have the capacity to address recommendations and warnings issued to member states and to the European supervisory authorities. The ESFS was to comprise three European Supervisory Authorities (ESAs): a European Banking Authority; a European Securities and Markets Authority; and a European Insurance and Occupational Pensions Authority. These authorities were to be responsible for helping to rebuild confidence, develop a single set of financial rules, seek solutions to problems involving cross-border firms, and prevent the accumulation of risks that could undermine the stability of the financial system. In September 2010 the European Parliament endorsed the new supervisory framework, which was confirmed by ministers of the economy and of finance (the ECOFIN Council) in mid-November. The three ESAs and the ESRB were established in January 2011 to replace the supervisory committees hitherto in place.

In September 2011 the President of the European Commission announced proposals to introduce a new, EU-wide, financial transaction tax (FTT). The FTT would apply to transactions between financial institutions, at a rate of 0.1% on equity and debt transactions, and 0.01% on derivatives transactions. In October 2012, however, negotiations failed to result in unanimous support for the FTT, and the Commission proposed that to enable implementation of the tax in the 11 supporting states the principle of 'enhanced co-operation' should be utilized (a procedure permitting a minimum of nine member states to introduce ameliorated co-operation in certain areas). The proposal was approved by the European Parliament in December, and by the Council in January 2013. Accordingly, in mid-February the Commission announced modified proposals for the enactment of the proposed FTT under enhanced co-operation rules; the proposal required approval by all the participating member states, with the agreement of the European Parliament, before its entry into force.

In March 2013 the Council and the European Parliament approved legislation restricting bonus payments payable to those working in the banking sector to no more than the sum of an employee's total annual salary from 2014; the one-to-one ratio could be increased twofold, dependent on the approval of a majority of shareholders. The Parliament also voted in favour of the imposition of an upper limit on bonus payments to fund managers.

ECONOMIC CO-OPERATION

A review of the economic situation is presented annually by the Commission, analysing recent developments and short- and medium-term prospects. Economic policy guidelines for the following year are adopted annually by the Council.

The following objectives for the end of 1973 were agreed by the Council in 1971, as the first of three stages towards European economic and monetary union: the narrowing of exchange rate margins to 2.25%; creation of a medium-term pool of reserves; co-ordination of short- and medium-term economic and budgetary policies; a joint position on international monetary issues; harmonization of taxes; creation of the European Monetary Co-operation Fund (EMCF); and creation of the European Regional Development Fund.

The narrowing of exchange margins (the 'snake') came into effect in 1972; however, Denmark, France, Ireland, Italy and the United Kingdom later floated their currencies, with only Denmark permanently returning to the arrangement. Sweden and Norway also linked their currencies to the 'snake', but Sweden withdrew from the arrangement in August 1977, and Norway withdrew in December 1978.

The European Monetary System (EMS) came into force in March 1979, with the aim of creating closer monetary co-operation, leading to a zone of monetary stability in Europe, principally through an Exchange Rate Mechanism (ERM), supervised by the ministries of finance and the central banks of member states. Not all Community members participated in the ERM: Greece did not join, Spain joined only in June 1989, the United Kingdom in October 1990 and Portugal in April 1992. To prevent wide fluctuations in the value of members' currencies against each other, the ERM fixed for each currency a central rate in European Currency Units (ECUs, see below), based on a 'basket' of national currencies; a reference rate in relation to other currencies was fixed for each currency, with established fluctuation margins. Central banks of the participating states intervened by buying or selling currencies when the agreed margin was likely to be exceeded. Each member placed 20% of its gold reserves and dollar reserves, respectively, into the EMCF, and received a supply of ECUs to regulate central bank interventions. Short- and medium-term credit facilities were given to support the balance of payments of member countries. The EMS was initially put under strain by the wide fluctuations in the exchange rates of non-Community currencies and by the differences in economic development among members, which led to nine realignments of currencies in 1979–83. Subsequently, greater stability was achieved, with only two realignments of currencies between 1984 and 1988. In 1992–93, however, there was great pressure on currency markets, necessitating further realignments; in September 1992 Italian and British membership of the ERM was suspended. In July 1993, as a result of intensive currency speculation on European financial markets (forcing the weaker currencies to the very edge of their permitted margins), the ERM almost collapsed. In response to the crisis, EC ministers responsible for finance decided to widen the fluctuation margins allowed for each currency, except in the cases of Germany and the Netherlands, which agreed to maintain their currencies within the original limits. The new margins were regarded as allowing for so much fluctuation in exchange rates as to represent a virtual suspension of the ERM, although some countries, notably France and Belgium, expressed their determination to adhere as far as possible to the original 'bands' in order to fulfil the conditions for eventual monetary union. In practice, most currencies remained within the former narrower bands during 1994. Austria became a member of the EMS in January 1995, and its currency was subject to ERM conditions. While Sweden decided to remain outside the EMS, Finland joined in October 1996. In November of that year the Italian lira was readmitted to the ERM.

The Intergovernmental Conference on Economic and Monetary Union, initiated in December 1990, was responsible for the drafting of the economic and monetary provisions of the Treaty on European Union, which came into force on 1 November 1993. The principal feature of the Treaty's provisions on Economic and Monetary Union (EMU), which was to be implemented in three stages, was the gradual introduction of a single currency, to be administered by a single central bank.

In December 1995 the European Council confirmed that Stage III of EMU was to begin on 1 January 1999 and confirmed the economic conditions for member states wishing to participate in it. The meeting decided that the proposed single currency would be officially known as the euro. Member countries remaining outside the monetary system, whether or not by choice, would still be part of the single market. Technical preparations for the euro were confirmed during a meeting of the European Council in Dublin, Ireland, in December 1996. The heads of government endorsed the new ERM and the legal framework for the euro, and approved the Stability and Growth Pact (SGP), intended to ensure that member countries maintained strict budgetary discipline. In March 1998 Greece was admitted to the ERM, causing a 14% devaluation of its national currency. In May of that year it was confirmed by a meeting of heads of state and of government that Greece failed to fulfil the conditions required for the adoption of a single currency from 1999. The meeting agreed that existing ERM central rates were to be used to determine the final rates of exchange between national currencies and the euro. A European Central Bank (ECB) was established in June 1998, which was to be accountable to a European Forum, comprising members of the European Parliament and chairmen of the finance committees of the national parliaments of EU member countries.

Although all of the then 15 members of the EU endorsed the principle of monetary union, with France and Germany the most ardent supporters, some countries had political doubts about joining. In October 1997 both the United Kingdom and Sweden confirmed that they would not participate in EMU from 1999. Denmark was also to remain outside the single currency. In May 1998 heads of state and government confirmed that 11 countries would take part in Stage III of EMU. It was agreed that existing ERM central rates were to be used to determine the final rates of exchange between national currencies and the euro.

On 31 December 1998 ministers for economic and financial affairs adopted the conversion rates for the national currencies of the countries participating in the single currency. The euro was formally launched on 1 January 1999. ERM-II, the successor to the ERM, was launched on the same day. Both Greece and Denmark joined ERM-II, but in September 2000 some 53% of Danish voters participating in a national referendum rejected the adoption of the euro. On 1 January 2001 Greece became the 12th EU member state to adopt the euro. In September 2003 the majority of Swedish voters—some 56%—participating in a national referendum chose to reject Sweden's adoption of the euro.

The SGP, endorsed by the European Council in 1996, was instituted with the intention of ensuring that member countries maintain strict budgetary discipline during Stage III of monetary union, of which it was regarded as the cornerstone. Under its original terms, member states were obliged to keep budget deficits within 3% of gross domestic product (GDP), or face fines, and to bring their budgets close to balance by 2004. However, during 2002 the Pact was strongly criticized for being inflexible, when a number of countries could not meet its requirements. In September 2002 the 2004 deadline for reaching a balanced budget was extended by two years, although the 3% limit for budgetary deficit remained, while some concessionary provision was introduced to allow countries with low levels of long-term debt to increase investment spending by running larger short-term budget deficits.

In November 2003 France and Germany, which were both likely to breach the budget deficit of 3% for a third consecutive year, persuaded the EU ministers responsible for finance to suspend the disciplinary procedure (triggered by their failure to meet the 3% limit in 2002) under which they could have faced punitive fines. The refusal of France and Germany to restrict their expenditure provoked anger among some smaller EU countries that had implemented strict austerity programmes in order to comply with the Pact. In January 2004 the European Commission launched a legal action against the Council of Finance Ministers in the European Court of Justice, seeking clarification of whether the Council had acted illegally in temporarily suspending the budget rules. The SGP faced additional pressure with the pending enlargement of the EU, as its framework would have to apply to the 10 candidate countries, even though their economies were very diverse.

All 10 countries that joined the EU on 1 May 2004 (Cyprus, the Czech Republic, Estonia, Hungary, Latvia, Lithuania, Malta, Poland, Slovakia and Slovenia) were obliged to participate in EMU; however, adoption of the euro was dependent on the fulfilment of the same Maastricht convergence criteria as the initial entrants, which comprised conditions regarding inflation, debt, budget deficit, long-term interest rates and exchange rate stability. The exchange rate criteria included the requirement to spend at least two years in ERM-II. Although the currency was permitted to fluctuate 15% either side of a central rate or, by common agreement, within a narrower band, the ECB specified that the limit of 2.25% would be applied when judging whether countries had achieved sufficient stability to join the eurozone. The entry into the eurozone of the new member states was not expected to affect the ECB's monetary policy, as the new member states only accounted for about 5% of the GDP of the enlarged EU. Although many of the new member countries were keen to adopt the euro as soon as possible, the ECB warned of the risks associated with early membership of ERM-II, sharing widespread concerns that the required fiscal austerity and loss of flexibility over exchange rate policy would stifle economic growth in the accession countries. Moreover, currencies would also become vulnerable to speculative attacks once they entered ERM-II. Owing to differences in the economies of the new member states, progress towards adoption of the euro varied significantly. In June 2004 Estonia, Lithuania and Slovenia joined ERM-II. In May 2006, in a specific convergence report drawn up at the request of Slovenia and Lithuania to assess their readiness to adopt the euro, the Commission concluded that Slovenia met all of the conditions for admission to the eurozone, while Lithuania should retain its current status as a member state with a derogation. Slovenia duly adopted the euro on 1 January 2007. Cyprus, Latvia and Malta joined ERM-II on 2 May 2005, followed by Slovakia on 28 November. Cyprus and Malta were admitted to the eurozone on 1 January 2008, Slovakia adopted the euro on 1 January 2009 and Estonia introduced it on 1 January 2011. Latvia adopted the euro on 1 January 2014, increasing the number of countries in the eurozone to 18.

In September 2004 revised figures released by Greece revealed previous gross under-reporting of the country's national budgetary deficit and debt figures. It was subsequently established that Greece had not complied with membership rules for the single currency in 2000, the year in which it qualified to join. Greece received a formal warning from the Commission in December 2004 for publishing inaccurate data concerning its public finances for 1997–2003.

In 2008 a sharp contraction in global credit markets prompted EU Governments to offer widespread financial assistance to support failing banks amid the onset of recession throughout the EU. In mid-November a Group of Twenty (G20) summit meeting was held in Washington, DC, USA, at the EU's instigation, in order to discuss measures to help stimulate economic recovery worldwide, improve the regulation of financial markets, aid international governance, and reject protectionism. In December the European Council adopted a European Economic Recovery Plan (EERP), worth around €200,000m., equivalent to some 1.5% of the EU's total GDP, and representing a co-ordinated response to the situation. The plan aimed to restore consumer and business confidence, to restart lending, and to stimulate investment in EU economies and create jobs, by increasing investments in infrastructure and important sectors of the economy—including the automotive industry, construction and green technologies—while making full use of the flexibility offered in the SGP. The EERP proposed that member states should co-ordinate national budgetary stimulus packages in order to optimize their impact and avoid secondary consequences, as negative effects spread from one country to another. A Commission report on the EU economy issued in September 2009 found the ongoing recession to be the deepest since the 1930s, and stated that a comprehensive, co-ordinated recession 'exit strategy' (emphasizing investment in renewable energy sources and green infrastructure) should be developed, for implementation as soon as economic recovery was apparent.

In April 2009 the Council placed Greece under excessive deficit procedures, setting a deadline of 2010 for correction of the deficit to below 3%, on the basis of a Commission proposal which, in turn, had been based on an estimated Greek budgetary deficit equivalent to 3.7% of GDP in 2008. In December 2009—by which time Greece's 2008 budgetary deficit had been revised up to 7.7% and the 2009 deficit was being estimated at 12.7%, attributable to factors such as the effects of the ongoing economic crisis, absence of corrective measures and fiscal slippage—the Council determined that the Greek authorities had not taken sufficient effective action to correct the deficit. The estimated 12.7% Greek budgetary deficit for 2009 was deemed potentially destabilizing to markets and to the entire eurozone, and the unreliable reporting of public finance statistics was a significant cause of concern. In January 2010 the ECOFIN Council advised the Greek Government to embrace a far-reaching economic reform plan aimed at gradually reducing Greece's budget deficit (by 4% by the end of 2010, initially); the plan was endorsed by the Commission in early February 2010. In early February the European Commission also, using new powers given under the Treaty of Lisbon, imposed a new 'quasi-permanent' surveillance system on the management of Greece's public finances. Furthermore, the Commission issued a formal warning to the Greek authorities regarding the need to pursue policies consistent with the broad economic guidelines adopted by the Council, and launched infringement proceedings against Greece relating to the submission of erroneous statistical data. Soon afterwards EU heads of state and government issued a statement emphasizing that all eurozone members were required to conduct sound national policies in line with agreed rules, while committing the eurozone member states to taking determined and co-ordinated action, if need be, to safeguard financial stability in the eurozone as a whole. In mid-February the Council gave notice to Greece to correct its excessive deficit (to below 3% of GDP) by 2012, setting out a timetable for corrective measures, and issued a formal recommendation to Greece to bring its economic policies into line with broad EU economic policy guidelines and thereby remove the risk of jeopardizing the overall proper functioning of economic and monetary union. In May 2010 the European Commission, the ECB and the IMF reached agreement with Greece on a programme intended to stabilize the Greek economy, in accordance with which funding of €110,000m. would be provided over a period of three years, of which €80,000m. was to originate from the countries of the eurozone. In accordance with the terms of the programme, Greece was required to implement further budget cuts, increase taxation, and carry out substantial reforms of the pensions and social security systems.

In early July 2011 EU ministers of finance approved the disbursement of further lending to Greece, temporarily alleviating the threat of default. In late October EU leaders agreed further emergency measures designed to help resolve the eurozone debt crisis. The agreement provided for the recapitalization of private banks; provided for losses of one-half of the banks' holdings of Greek debt; and increased the financial strength of the European Financial Stability Facility (EFSF—see below). In March 2012 EU ministers of finance approved further lending to Greece by the EU, the ECB and the IMF, worth some €130,000m., in addition to the funds already committed, but not yet disbursed. In November new stringent measures were approved by Greece, and were followed by the adoption of a revised austerity budget. In December the EU-ECB-IMF troika approved the second disbursement under the economic adjustment programme; under revised targets, debt was to be reduced to 124% of GDP (rather than 120%) by 2020, and the troika agreed to provide €26,000m. in additional financing for the period 2012–16, and to cover further gaps provided that the programme was implemented. An EU tranche of €34,300m. was subsequently disbursed; smaller tranches were disbursed in early 2013, and in July 2013 disbursement of the next tranche in aid to Greece was approved, after the Government agreed to implement further large-scale public sector dismissals. In mid-March 2014 it was announced that agreement had been reached on the release of a further €10,000m. in bail-out funds.

Meanwhile, in June 2012 eurozone ministers of finance had agreed to providing lending of up to €100,000m. to recapitalize the Spanish banking sector; in December the Spanish Government requested and received lending amounting to some €39,500m. After Greece, Ireland, Portugal and Spain, in late June Cyprus had became the fifth member of the eurozone to seek emergency EU funding. In mid-March 2013 eurozone ministers of finance approved lending of €10,000m. to Cyprus, contingent on that country's imposition of a levy on bank deposits; however, on 19 March the Cypriot legislature failed to approve a proposed tax on deposits, which had been intended to apply to both large- and small-scale savers. Revised proposals to safeguard the Cypriot banking system and Cyprus's position within the eurozone, through, inter alia, the nationalization of the national pension fund, were rejected by the EU on 22 March. Three days later an agreement was reached between Cyprus and the EU, when EU ministers of finance approved the terms required for the disbursement of lending: deposits under €100,000 were to be exempt from any losses, but larger deposits in the country's two biggest banks, the Bank of Cyprus and the Cyprus Popular Bank (Laiki Bank), were to be frozen and subject to deductions of up to 40%; some of Laiki Bank's assets were to be merged into the Bank of Cyprus, and the institution closed.

In early May 2010 eurozone member states agreed to the establishment of a new, temporary institution, the EFSF, with a lending capacity of €4,400m., which aimed to maintain financial stability in the eurozone through the provision of rapid financial assistance to member countries. In late June heads of state and of government agreed to expand the EFSF's remit and increase its guarantee commitments from €4,400m. to €7,800m., equivalent to a lending capacity of €4,400m. The EFSF's scope was further expanded in late July, and all amendments to the EFSF Framework entered into force in mid-October 2011. The EFSF, based in Luxembourg, was backed by guarantees from 14 of the eurozone's 17 members (Greece, Ireland and Portugal were exempted). Meanwhile, in October 2010 the European Council had agreed to establish a permanent crisis mechanism, the ESM, to safeguard the financial stability of the eurozone. Combined with strengthened economic governance and monitoring, the ESM, which was to have an overall lending capacity of €500,000m., aimed to prevent the development of future crises. In late July 2011 EU heads of state and of government taking part in an emergency Euro Area Summit in Brussels, Belgium, agreed to reduce EFSF interest rates and extend the maturities of future loans issued to Greece, Ireland and Portugal, in an effort to strengthen their financial programmes. On 2 February 2012 representatives of the eurozone countries, meeting in Brussels, signed a treaty providing for the establishment of the ESM, which was inaugurated on 8 October. The EFSF and the associated European Financial Stabilization Mechanism (EFSM) remained responsible only for lending approved prior to the establishment of the ESM.

Meanwhile, on 9 December 2011 the majority of EU member states had reached agreement in principle on new fiscal arrangements, designed to increase fiscal discipline and convergence in the eurozone. The so-called fiscal compact, inter alia, required member states to maintain a balanced budget (or a deficit of no more than 0.5% of nominal GDP). Agreement was reached on increased co-operation on economic policy, and an acceleration of arrangements for the introduction of the ESM. In March 2012 25 heads of state and of government signed the new fiscal compact, which required ratification by 12 eurozone member states; the United Kingdom and the Czech Republic refused to sign the agreement. In Ireland, the fiscal compact was approved by a referendum, which took place at the end of May.

In mid-December 2011 new rules, comprising five regulations and one directive (the 'six-pack'), came into effect, applying to both the procedures within the SGP that are designed to prevent excessive deficits, and the excessive deficit procedure (EDP), which is the corrective branch of the pact. New measures, specifically financial disincentives and fines, were to be applied to non-compliant eurozone members in an effort to strengthen the efficacy of the SGP. At February 2013 25 of the 27 EU member states were, or had been, subject to an EDP (with the exception of Estonia and Sweden). At the end of May supplementary governance reform measures, known as the 'two-pack', entered into force throughout the eurozone. The new measures sought to ensure increased transparency for budgetary decisions, strengthen co-ordination in the euro area from 2014 and recognize the particular needs of the eurozone. They also prepared the way for the possible introduction of additional measures to reinforce EMU at supra-national level.

In mid-December 2012 EU ministers of finance approved plans to deepen and safeguard economic stability through the creation of a banking union, comprising: (i) a single European framework for the supervision of banks, and an associated set of harmonized banking regulations; (ii) a Single Resolution Mechanism to govern and co-ordinate the provision (or withdrawal) of support for failing banks, by means of levies on the sector, rather than through public financing; and (iii) a common system for the protection of bank deposits throughout the EU. Accordingly, the Council endorsed plans for the ECB's powers to be considerably expanded, to enable it to act as a Single Supervisory Mechanism (SSM), with responsibility for the supervision of major banks (those with assets of either more than €30,000m., or equivalent to 20% of national GDP) in operation throughout the eurozone. The SSM was to co-operate closely with national regulatory authorities, with the aim of safeguarding financial stability. With the appointment of a banking supervisor for the eurozone, the ESM would be able to disburse funds directly to banks, rather than through individual central banks. In March 2013 the European Parliament and the Council reached political agreement on the SSM package, and in October the EU formally adopted the creation of an ECB-led SSM, which was expected to come into operation in November 2014. Meanwhile, in July 2013 the European Commission had proposed a new Single Resolution Mechanism (SRM), to complement the SSM. The aim of the SRM would be to centralize the principal responsibilities and resources directed at managing any failing banks in the eurozone, as well as in other member states taking part in the banking union.

The Euro

With the creation of the European Monetary System (EMS) in 1979, a new monetary unit, the European Currency Unit (ECU), was adopted. Its value and composition were identical to those of the European Unit of Account (EUA) already used in the administrative fields of the Community. The ECU was a composite monetary unit, in which the relative value of each currency was determined by the gross national product and the volume of trade of each country. Assigned the function of the unit of account used by the European Monetary Co-operation Fund, the ECU was also used as the denominator for the Exchange Rate Mechanism (ERM); as the denominator for operations in both the intervention and the credit mechanisms; and as a means of settlement between monetary authorities of the European Community. From April 1979 the ECU was also used as the unit of account for the purposes of the Common Agricultural Policy (CAP). From 1981 it replaced the EUA in the general budget of the Community; the activities of the European Development Fund (EDF) under the Lomé Convention; the balance sheets and loan operations of the European Investment Bank (EIB); and the activities of the European Coal and Steel Community (ECSC). In June 1985 measures were adopted by the governors of the Community's central banks, aiming to strengthen the EMS by expanding the use of the ECU, for example, by allowing international monetary institutions and the central banks of non-member countries to become 'other holders' of ECUs. From September 1989 the Portuguese and Spanish currencies were included in the composition of the ECU. The composition of the ECU 'basket' of national currencies was 'frozen' with the entry into force of the Treaty on European Union on 1 November 1993, and remained unchanged until the termination of the ECU on 31 December 1998. (Consequently, the currencies of Austria, Finland and Sweden, on those countries' accession to the EU, were not represented in the ECU basket.)

As part of Stage III of the process of Economic and Monetary Union (EMU), the ECU was replaced by a single currency, the euro (€), on 1 January 1999, at a conversion rate of 1:1. Initially, the euro was used for cashless payments and accounting purposes, while the traditional national currencies, then considered as 'sub-units' of the euro, continued to be used for cash payments. On 1 January 2002 euro coins and banknotes entered into circulation in the then 12 participating countries, and, by the end of February, the former national currencies of all of the participating countries had been withdrawn. The euro's value in national currencies is calculated and published daily, and stood at €1 = US $1.3840 on 16 April 2014, at which time there were 18 participating countries.

A payments settlement system, known as TARGET (Trans-European Automated Real-time Gross Settlement Express Transfer), was introduced for countries participating in EMU on 4 January 1999. An upgraded version of the system, TARGET2, was launched in November 2007. The Single Euro Payments Area, which was introduced gradually from 2008, was designed to enable all electronic payments across the eurozone to be made as efficiently and securely as domestic payments within a single member state.

Three interest rates are set for the eurozone: the rate on the main refinancing operations, providing most of the banking system's liquidity; the rate on the deposit facility, which may be used by banks making overnight deposits with the euro system; and the rate on the marginal lending facility, which offers overnight credit to banks from the euro system. From October 2008 refinancing operations were conducted through a fixed-rate tender procedure, having been conducted as variable rate tenders since June 2000. During the second half of 2008 and early 2009 the ECB considerably reduced interest rates with the aim of stimulating non-inflationary growth and contributing to financial stability. The ECB reduced the fixed refinancing rate progressively from 3.75% in October 2008 to 1.0% at 13 May 2009 (that rate remaining in force until 13 April 2011). The rates set in 2009 represented the lowest eurozone rates (whether variable or fixed) set in the decade since January 1999. On 13 April 2011 the fixed refinancing rate was increased to 1.25%. The fixed refinancing rate was amended to 1.0% on 14 December 2011, to 0.75% on 11 July 2012, to 0.5% on 8 May 2013, and to 0.25% (its lowest recorded rate) from 7 November.

External Relations

CENTRAL AND SOUTH-EASTERN EUROPE

During the late 1980s the extensive political changes and reforms in Eastern European countries led to a strengthening of links with the EC. Agreements on trade and economic co-operation were concluded with several countries. Community heads of government agreed in December 1989 to establish a European Bank for Reconstruction and Development—EBRD, with participation by member states of the Organisation for Economic Co-operation and Development—OECD and the Council for Mutual Economic Assistance, to promote investment in Eastern Europe; the EBRD began operations in April 1991. In the 1990s 'Europe Agreements' were signed with Czechoslovakia, Hungary and Poland (1991), Bulgaria and Romania (1993), Estonia, Latvia and Lithuania (1995), and Slovenia (1996), which led to formal applications for membership of the EU. On 1 May 2004 the Czech Republic, Estonia, Hungary, Latvia, Lithuania, Poland, Slovakia and Slovenia acceded to the EU. Bulgaria and Romania formally joined the EU on 1 January 2007. Croatia joined the EU on 1 July 2013.

In July 2006 an Instrument for Pre-Accession Assistance (IPA) was adopted by the Council, which replaced the former PHARE (Poland/Hungary Aid for Restructuring of Economies) and other such programmes (Instrument for Structural Policies for Pre-Accession—ISPA; Special Accession Programme for Agriculture and Rural Development—SAPARD; Community Assistance for Reconstruction, Development and Stabilisation, with reference to the Western Balkans—CARDS; and the Turkey instrument) from January 2007. The IPA aimed to provide targeted assistance to candidate countries for membership of the EU (at early 2014 the former Yugoslav republic of Macedonia—FYRM, Montenegro, Serbia and Turkey) or potential candidate countries (e.g. Albania and Bosnia and Herzegovina). In March 2008 the Commission launched the Civil Society Facility, a new financing arrangement under the IPA, which aims to support the development of civil society in South-Eastern Europe, by strengthening the political role of civil society organizations; developing cross-border projects; and familiarizing representatives of civil society with EU affairs.

In June 1999 the EU, in conjunction with the Group of Seven industrialized nations and Russia (the Group of Eight—G8), regional governments and other organizations concerned with the stability of the region, launched the Stability Pact for South Eastern Europe, a comprehensive conflict-prevention strategy, which was placed under the auspices of the Organization for Security and Co-operation in Europe (OSCE). In April 2008 the Stability Pact was replaced by a Regional Co-operation Council, based in Sarajevo, Bosnia and Herzegovina.

In September 2002 the European Parliament voted in support of opening negotiations for a Stabilization and Association Agreement (SAA) with Albania, following satisfactory progress in that country, with regard to presidential voting and electoral reform. Negotiations on the signature of an SAA with Albania, which officially commenced at the end of January 2003, were completed in February 2006. The SAA was formally signed in June and entered into force in April 2009; later that month Albania applied for the status of a candidate country for EU membership. In November 2010 the European Commission agreed to introduce visa liberalization for Albania, with effect from mid-December. In October 2012 the European Commission recommended that Albania be offered candidate status, provided that further progress was made in meeting the EU's political criteria. In October 2013 the Commission reported that progress had been made by Albania in fulfilling the political criteria, including in the conduct of legislative elections, and again recommended that it be given candidate status; this decision was approved by the European Parliament in December. Meanwhile, in early December Albania signed a co-operation accord with the European Police Office (Europol), as part of efforts to fight organized crime. Following the opposition of several states, notably the Netherlands, in mid-December the EU General Affairs Council deferred a decision on Albania's candidacy to June 2014, citing the need for additional judicial and public administration reforms.

A co-operation agreement was signed with Yugoslavia in 1980 (but was not ratified until April 1983), allowing tariff-free imports and Community loans. New financial protocols were signed in 1987 and 1991. However, EC aid was suspended in July 1991, following the declarations of independence by the Yugoslav republics of Croatia and Slovenia, and the subsequent outbreak of civil conflict. Efforts were made in the ensuing months by EC ministers responsible for foreign affairs to negotiate a peaceful settlement, and a team of EC observers was maintained in Yugoslavia from July, to monitor successive ceasefire agreements. In October the EC proposed a plan for an association of independent states, to replace the Yugoslav federation: this was accepted by all of the Yugoslav republics except Serbia, which demanded a redefinition of boundaries to accommodate within Serbia all predominantly Serbian areas. In November the application of the Community's co-operation agreements with Yugoslavia was suspended (with exemptions for the republics which co-operated in the peace negotiations). In January 1992 the Community granted diplomatic recognition to the former Yugoslav republics of Croatia and Slovenia, and in April it recognized Bosnia and Herzegovina, while withholding recognition from Macedonia (owing to pressure from the Greek Government, which feared that the existence of an independent Macedonia would imply a claim on the Greek province of the same name). In May EC ambassadors were withdrawn from the Yugoslav capital, Belgrade, in protest against Serbia's support for aggression by Bosnian Serbs against other ethnic groups in Bosnia and Herzegovina, and the Community imposed a trade embargo on Serbia and Montenegro.

In April 1994, following a request from EU ministers responsible for foreign affairs, a Contact Group, consisting of France, Germany, the United Kingdom, the USA and Russia, was initiated to undertake peace negotiations. In the following month ministers responsible for foreign affairs of the USA, Russia and the EU (represented by five member states) jointly endorsed a proposal to divide Bosnia and Herzegovina in proportions of 49% to the Bosnian Serbs and 51% to the newly established Federation of Muslims and Croats. The proposal was rejected by the Bosnian Serb assembly in July and the Muslim-Croat Federation also withdrew its support. In July the EU formally assumed political control of Mostar, in southern Bosnia and Herzegovina, in order to restore the city's administrative infrastructure. In September 1995 the EU supported US-led negotiations in Geneva, Switzerland, to devise a plan to end the conflict in Bosnia and Herzegovina. The plan closely resembled the previous proposals of the Contact Group: two self-governing entities were to be created within Bosnia and Herzegovina, with 51% of territory being allocated to the Muslim-Croat Federation and 49% to Bosnian Serbs. The proposals were finally agreed after negotiations in Dayton, Ohio, USA, in November 1995, and an accord was signed in Paris, France, in December. In January 1996 the EU announced its intention to recognize Yugoslavia (Serbia and Montenegro). During 1996–99 the EU allocated ECU 1,000m. for the repatriation of refugees, restructuring the economy and technical assistance, in addition to ECU 1,000m. in humanitarian aid provided since the beginning of the conflict in the former Yugoslavia.

In 2000 the EU published a roadmap for Bosnia and Herzegovina, outlining measures that must be undertaken by the Government prior to the initiation of a feasibility study on the formulation of an SAA. In September 2002 the Commission reported that Bosnia and Herzegovina had essentially adhered to the terms of the roadmap. In January 2003 a new EU Police Mission (EUPM) took over from the UN peacekeeping force in Bosnia and Herzegovina. This was the first operation under the common European Security and Defence Policy. The EUPM was re-established in 2006 to support the police reform process and to help to combat organized crime; the Mission completed its mandate at the end of June 2012. Meanwhile, on 28 January 2004 the Bosnian Government issued a decree providing for the reunification of Mostar (divided between Croat- and Bosnian-controlled municipalities since 1993) into a single administration, thereby fulfilling one of the major preconditions for the signature of an SAA with the EU. In December 2004 7,000 troops (EUFOR) were deployed under EU command in Bosnia and Herzegovina, taking over from the North Atlantic Treaty Organization (NATO), with a mission (Operation Althea) to ensure stability in the country. From the end of March 2007 EUFOR-Althea was reduced in size, to comprise the Multinational Maneuver Battalion, of around 2,000 troops. Negotiations on an SAA officially commenced in November 2005, and an SAA with the EU was initialled in December 2007, and signed in mid-June 2008. In November 2010 the European Commission agreed to introduce visa liberalization for Bosnia and Herzegovina, with effect from mid-December. Following state and entity elections in October, the failure to establish a state-level government was cited by the European Commission in October 2011 as a major obstacle to progress in reforms. A new state Council of Ministers was finally formed in February 2012. In June negotiations commenced in Brussels, Belgium, which resulted in agreement on a roadmap for the country's membership application; however, the main political parties failed to adopt reforms by the stipulated deadlines. Progress reports on Bosnia and Herzegovina, published in 2012 and 2013, concluded that the authorities had demonstrated little progress in meeting obligations for EU integration. The European Commission expressed concern at the continuing failure of the ruling parties to agree constitutional amendments required by a 2009 ruling of the European Court of Human Rights.

An SAA was signed with Croatia in October 2001. In February 2003 Croatia submitted a formal application for membership of the EU. In December 2004 the European Council announced that negotiations on membership would commence in mid-March 2005, provided that Croatia co-operated fully with the International Criminal Tribunal for the former Yugoslavia (ICTY). The SAA entered into force in February 2005. In early 2005 an outstanding issue between Croatia and the ICTY was the need for the arrest and transfer to The Hague of the retired Gen. Ante Gotovina, who had been in hiding since 2001, when the ICTY charged him with war crimes against ethnic Serbs during a military operation in 1995. The planned accession talks with Croatia were postponed in March 2005, following an official report by the Chief Prosecutor at the ICTY, Carla Del Ponte, which stated that the Croatian authorities had failed to demonstrate full co-operation with the ICTY. However, in early October Del Ponte issued an assessment stating that Croatia's co-operation with the ICTY had improved, and negotiations were initiated. In December Gotovina was apprehended in the Canary Islands, Spain, thereby removing the main perceived obstacle to EU membership. A border dispute with Slovenia threatened progress towards membership from late 2008; however, a referendum held in Slovenia in early June 2010 secured support for the resolution of the dispute by international arbitration. In November the Commission praised Croatia's progress towards meeting the criteria for EU membership, but urged that further efforts be made to combat corruption and organized crime, to undertake administrative reform, protect ethnic minorities and to aid the repatriation of refugees. Croatia completed membership negotiations on 30 June 2011, and signed the Treaty of Accession on 9 December. Accession took place on 1 July 2013, following popular approval of Croatian membership of the EU in a referendum held in late January 2012.

In December 1993 six member states of the EU formally recognized the FYRM as an independent state, but in February 1994 Greece imposed a commercial embargo against the FYRM, on the grounds that the use of the name and symbols (e.g. on the state flag) of 'Macedonia' was a threat to Greek national security. In March, however, ministers responsible for foreign affairs of the EU decided that the embargo was in contravention of EU law, and in April the Commission commenced legal proceedings in the European Court of Justice against Greece. In September 1995 Greece and the FYRM began a process of normalizing relations, after the FYRM agreed to change the design of its state flag. In October Greece ended its economic blockade of the FYRM. A trade and co-operation agreement with the FYRM entered into force in January 1998. In April 2001 an SAA was signed with the FYRM. At the same time, an interim agreement was adopted, allowing for trade-related matters of the SAA to enter into effect in June, without the need for formal ratification by the national parliaments of the EU member states. (The SAA provided for the EU to open its markets to 95% of exports from the FYRM.) However, the FYRM Government was informed that it would be required to deliver concessions to the ethnic Albanian minority population prior to entering into the agreement. On 31 March 2003 a NATO contingent in the FYRM was replaced by an EU-led mission, Operation Concordia, comprising 350 military personnel. It was replaced in December by a 200-member EU police mission, Operation Proxima, which, in addition to maintaining security and combating organized crime, advised the FYRM police forces. Operation Proxima's mandate expired at the end of 2005. The SAA entered into force in April 2004. A formal application for membership of the EU was submitted in March of that year, and the FYRM was granted candidate status in December 2005. In October 2009 the European Commission recommended that accession negotiations with the FYRM commence; however, Greece objected to the initiation of membership negotiations while the dispute over the country's name remained unresolved. In mid-December visa liberalization entered into force for travel within the Schengen area. Despite the FYRM's unresolved dispute with Greece, in March 2012 the FYRM began a preliminary dialogue with the EU, which was designed to reduce the length of any future official membership negotiations.

In 1998 the escalation of violence in the Serbian province of Kosovo (Federal Republic of Yugoslavia—FRY), between Serbs and the ethnic Albanian majority, prompted the imposition of sanctions by EU ministers responsible for foreign affairs. During October the Yugoslav Government allowed a team of international experts to investigate atrocities in the region, under an EU mandate. Several EU countries participated in the NATO military offensive against Yugoslavia, which was initiated in March 1999 owing to the continued repression of ethnic Albanians in Kosovo by Serbian forces. Ministers approved a new series of punitive measures in April. Humanitarian assistance was extended to provide relief for the substantial numbers of refugees who fled Kosovo, in particular to assist the Governments of Albania and the FYRM. In September EU ministers responsible for foreign affairs agreed to ease sanctions against Kosovo and Montenegro. In February 2000 the EU suspended a ban on the Yugoslav national airline. However, restrictions on visas for Serbian officials were reinforced. Kosovo received a total of €474.7m. under EU programmes in 2000, and the EU was the largest financial contributor to the province in 2001.

On 17 February 2008 the Assembly of Kosovo endorsed a declaration establishing the province as a sovereign state, independent from Serbia. Serbia immediately protested that the declaration of independence contravened international law and demanded that it be annulled. The USA extended recognition to Kosovo on the following day, and a large number of EU member nations announced their intention to do so. A supervisory EU mission in Kosovo (the EU Rule of Law Mission in Kosovo—EULEX), to comprise some 1,900 foreign personnel, became operational in 2008 (although full deployment was delayed until April 2009). Following the deployment of EULEX, the UN Mission in Kosovo (UNMIK) had been scheduled to transfer authority to government institutions. However, after both Serbia and Russia challenged the legality of EULEX, it was agreed that the two missions would co-exist under joint command. On 15 June 2008 a new Constitution came into force in Kosovo (Serbia refused to accept its introduction in Serb-dominated northern Kosovo). EULEX assumed responsibility from UNMIK for police and judicial functions in December. In July 2010 the European Parliament adopted a resolution that reiterated its desire for all EU member states to recognize Kosovo's independence, the legality of which was upheld by the advisory opinion of the ICJ later that month. At April 2014 108 UN member nations, including 23 EU member states, had formally recognized Kosovo, and many diplomatic missions in Prishtina had become embassies. However, several EU member states (Cyprus, Greece, Romania, Slovakia and Spain) continued to withhold recognition of Kosovo as an independent state. Meanwhile, in February 2012 the European Commission had proposed the undertaking of a feasibility study for an SAA with Kosovo. In June the mandate of EULEX was extended until mid-2014. In October 2012, following the official attainment of full independence by Kosovo in the previous month, the Commission reported that there was no legal obstacle to the signature of an SAA between Kosovo and the EU, and in June 2013 the Council authorized the initiation of talks on an SAA. Negotiations formally commenced in late October. Notably, relations between Kosovo and Serbia improved in 2013, with the conclusion in April of the 15-point First Agreement of Principles Governing the Normalization of Relations, which was followed, in May, by an implementation plan. In particular, both sides agreed that neither would pose an obstacle to the other's progress in their respective relationships with the EU. Normalization talks, under the aegis of the EU, continued in 2014.

In May 2000 the EU agreed an emergency aid package to support Montenegro against destabilization by Serbia. Following the election of a new administration in the FRY in late 2000, the EU withdrew all remaining sanctions, with the exception of those directed against Milošević and his associates, and pledged financial support of €200m. The FRY was welcomed as a full participant in the stabilization and association process (see below). The EU insisted that the FRY must co-operate fully with the ICTY. Following the arrest of Milošević by the FRY authorities in April 2001, the first part of the EU's aid package for that year (amounting to €240m.) was released. During 2002 EU humanitarian aid to Serbia totalled €37.5m., to assist the large numbers of refugees and displaced persons. Negotiations on an SAA between the State Union of Serbia and Montenegro (as the FRY became known in February 2003) and the EU commenced in November 2005, but were terminated in May 2006, owing to the country's failure fully to co-operate with the ICTY. Following Montenegro's declaration of independence on 3 June 2006, the National Assembly of the Republic of Serbia confirmed that Serbia was the official successor state of the State Union of Serbia and Montenegro. On 12 June the EU recognized Montenegrin independence, and the Serbian Government officially recognized Montenegro as an independent state three days later. At the end of September the National Assembly adopted a new Constitution, which was confirmed by referendum in late October. In early June 2007 the President of the European Commission invited Serbia to resume negotiations on an SAA, following the arrest, within Serbia, of Zdravko Tolimir, a former Bosnian Serb army officer. A visa facilitation and readmission agreement between Serbia and the EU came into force at the beginning of 2008. In late February the EU suspended negotiations with Serbia on an SAA, after violence broke out in Belgrade following the declaration of independence by Kosovo. However, on 29 April EU ministers of foreign affairs signed the SAA, in what was widely perceived as an effort to strengthen popular support for reformist parties contesting the forthcoming elections. The SAA with Serbia was accompanied by a provisional document granting Serbia access to benefits based on the SAA before all EU members had ratified the Agreement; however, its implementation was to be suspended until EU member states agreed unanimously on Serbia's full co-operation with the ICTY. In late July Radovan Karadžić, a former President of Republika Srpska, Bosnia and Herzegovina, whose arrest on charges of war crimes, including genocide, had long been sought by the ICTY, was apprehended in Belgrade. In mid-December 2009 visa liberalization was implemented for Serbian citizens travelling within the Schengen area. In late December Serbia formally applied for membership of the EU. At the end of March 2010 the Narodna skupština (National Assembly) passed a resolution condemning the massacre of up to 8,000 Muslim male civilians by Serb forces in July 1995, in Srebrenica, Bosnia and Herzegovina. In June 2010 the EU agreed to begin the ratification process for the SAA with Serbia, following a positive assessment of Serbia's co-operation with the ICTY. In late July the International Court of Justice (ICJ) issued a non-binding, advisory opinion that Kosovo's declaration of independence on 17 February 2008 had not breached international law, UN Security Council Resolution 1244 or the constitutional framework. Serbia reaffirmed its intention to continue to withhold recognition of independence for Kosovo. In early September 2010, however, the UN General Assembly adopted a joint, non-binding, EU-Serbia resolution, according to which Serbia agreed to participate in direct talks with Kosovo, under the aegis of the EU. Subsequently, in late October EU ministers of foreign affairs agreed to request that the Commission assess Serbia's application for candidacy. In late May 2011 the Serbian authorities arrested the Bosnian Serb former military leader Ratko Mladić in northern Serbia. The arrest of the final major war crimes suspect to be indicted by the ICTY, the Croatian Serb Goran Hadžić, was announced in late July. In October the European Commission issued a report stating that Serbia had made sufficient progress towards meeting EU criteria for a formal recommendation to be made that it become a candidate country. In December, nevertheless, Serbia failed to secure membership status at an EU summit meeting in Brussels owing to the insistence of a number of EU leaders that the issue of Serbia's refusal to recognize Kosovo first be resolved. At the end of February 2012, the Romanian Government unexpectedly presented objections to Serbia's candidacy relating to the treatment of the Vlach ethnic minority in Serbia, which were withdrawn following an agreement between Serbian and Romanian officials. EU heads of state and government officially approved Serbia's candidate status on 1 March (following significant progress in dialogue between Serbian and Kosovo representatives in Brussels), although no date for the beginning of accession negotiations was announced. On 19 April 2013 EU-mediated talks in Brussels resulted in the signature of a provisional accord on the normalization of relations by the premiers of Serbia and Kosovo (the First Agreement of Principles Governing the Normalization of Relations). The agreement confirmed that ethnic Serb-dominated northern Kosovo was to be administered by Kosovo, while retaining autonomy in a number of areas; the deal also provided for both Serbia and Kosovo to seek EU accession without obstruction. Three days later the Commission recommended that Serbia be given a date for the initiation of membership negotiations. In late June the European Council officially endorsed the opening of talks on EU accession with Serbia. The SAA entered into force at the beginning of September 2013, and accession negotiations officially commenced in late January 2014.

Following the declaration of independence by Montenegro in June 2006, the EU Council pledged to develop the relationship of the EU with Montenegro as a sovereign state. The first Enhanced Permanent Dialogue meeting between Montenegro and the EU was held in the Montenegrin capital, Podgorica, in late July. On the same day the Council adopted a mandate for the negotiation of an SAA with Montenegro (based on the previous mandate for negotiations with the State Union of Serbia and Montenegro). Negotiations were initiated in September, and in October 2007 Montenegro signed an SAA with the EU, which entered into force on 1 May 2010. Meanwhile, Montenegro had applied for membership of the EU in December 2008. A visa facilitation and readmission agreement between Montenegro and the EU came into force at the beginning of 2008, and from 19 December 2009 Montenegrin citizens were no longer required to hold a visa to travel within the Schengen area. Following a recommendation by the European Commission in the previous month, in mid-December 2010, at a meeting of the Council, held in Brussels, Montenegro was formally granted the status of a candidate country for EU membership. In March 2011 the European Parliament adopted a resolution commending Montenegro's progress towards EU integration. In October the Commission recommended that accession negotiations be opened with Montenegro, and negotiations duly commenced in late June 2012, following the approval of the European Council.

EASTERN EUROPE, RUSSIA AND THE CIS

In the late 1980s the extensive political changes and reforms in Eastern Europe led to a strengthening of links with the EC. In December 1989 EC heads of government agreed to establish the European Bank for Reconstruction and Development (EBRD) to promote investment in Eastern Europe, with participation by member states of the Organisation for Economic Co-operation and Development (OECD) and the Council for Mutual Economic Assistance (CMEA), which provided economic co-operation and co-ordination in the communist bloc between 1949 and 1991. The EBRD began operations in April 1991. In the same year the EC established the Technical Assistance to the Commonwealth of Independent States (TACIS) programme, to promote the development of successful market economies and to foster democracy in the countries of the former USSR through the provision of expertise and training. (TACIS initially extended assistance to the Baltic states; in 1992, however, these became eligible for assistance under PHARE (Poland/Hungary Aid for Restructuring of Economies) and withdrew from TACIS. Mongolia was eligible for TACIS assistance in 1991–2003, but was subsequently covered by the Asia Latin America—ALA programme.)

In March 2003 the European Commission launched a European Neighbourhood Policy (ENP) with the aim of enhancing co-operation with countries adjacent to the enlarged Union. A new European Neighbourhood and Partnership Instrument (ENPI) replaced TACIS and MEDA (which was concerned with EU co-operation with Mediterranean countries) from 2007. All countries covered by the ENP (Armenia, Azerbaijan, Belarus, Georgia, Moldova, Ukraine and several Mediterranean countries) were to be eligible for support under the ENPI. Russia was not covered by the ENP, and the relationship between Russia and the EU was described as a Strategic Partnership, which was also to be funded by the ENPI. In accordance with the ENP, in December 2004 the EU agreed Action Plans with Moldova and Ukraine, establishing targets for political and economic co-operation. These Plans were adopted by EU ministers responsible for foreign affairs and the two countries concerned in February 2005. ENP Action Plans for Armenia, Azerbaijan and Georgia were developed in 2005 and published in late 2006. A visa facilitation and readmission agreement with Georgia was concluded in January 2011. The EU did not enter into discussions on a Plan with Belarus, stating that it first required the country to hold free and fair elections in order to establish a democratic form of government (see below). The eventual conclusion of more ambitious relationships with partner countries achieving sufficient progress in meeting the priorities set out in the Action Plans (through the negotiation of European Neighbourhood Agreements) was envisaged. On the expiry of the initial Action Plans, new documents were being adopted. From 2014 the ENPI was replaced by the European Neighbourhood Instrument (ENI), for which the European Parliament approved funding of more than €15,000m. during 2014–20.

In June 2007 the European Council adopted The EU and Central Asia: Strategy for a New Partnership, which aimed to develop bilateral and regional co-operation in a wide number of areas. In May 2009 the heads of state or government of Armenia, Azerbaijan, Belarus, Georgia, Moldova and Ukraine, and representatives of the EU and the heads of state or government, and other representatives, of its member states, convened in Prague, Czech Republic, issued a joint declaration on establishing an Eastern Partnership. The Eastern Partnership (facilitated through a specific Eastern dimension of the ENP) aimed, through support for political and socio-economic reforms in interested partner countries, to create the necessary conditions to accelerate political association and further economic integration with the EU. The work programme of the Eastern Partnership was to focus on four principal areas in 2014–17: democracy, good governance and stability; economic integration and convergence with EU policies; energy policy; and contacts between people.

In 1992 EU heads of government decided to replace the agreement on trade and economic co-operation that had been concluded with the USSR in 1989 with new Partnership and Co-operation Agreements (PCAs), providing a framework for closer political, cultural and economic relations between the EU and the former republics of the USSR. An Interim Agreement with Russia on trade concessions came into effect in February 1996, giving EU exporters improved access to the Russian market for specific products, and at the same time abolishing quantitative restrictions on some Russian exports to the EU; a PCA with Russia came into effect in December 1997. In January 1998 the first meeting of the Co-operation Council for the EU-Russia PCA was held, and in July an EU-Russia Space Dialogue was established. In June 1999 the EU adopted a Common Strategy on Russia. This aimed to promote the consolidation of democracy and rule of law in the country; the integration of Russia into the common European economic and social space; and regional stability and security. At the sixth EU-Russia summit, held in October 2000, both parties agreed to initiate a regular energy dialogue, with the aim of establishing an EU-Russia Energy Partnership. However, the status of Kaliningrad, a Russian enclave situated between Poland and Lithuania, became a source of contention as the EU prepared to admit those two countries. Despite opposition from Russia, the EU insisted that residents of Kaliningrad would need a visa to cross EU territory. In November 2002, at an EU-Russia summit meeting held in Brussels, Belgium, a compromise agreement was reached, according to which residents of the enclave were to be issued with multiple-transit travel documentation; the new regulations took effect in July 2003. Also in November 2002, the EU granted Russian exporters market economy status, in recognition of the progress made by Russia to liberalize its economy. At a summit held in St Petersburg, Russia, in May 2003, the EU and Russia agreed to improve their co-operation by creating four 'common spaces' within the framework of the PCA. The two sides agreed to establish a common economic space; a common space for freedom, security and justice; a space for co-operation on external security; and for research, education and culture. However, relations between the EU and Russia remained strained by Russia's opposition to EU enlargement, partly owing to fears of a detrimental effect on the Russian economy, as some of its neighbouring countries (significant markets for Russian goods) were obliged to introduce EU quotas and tariffs. In May 2004, at a bilateral summit held in the Russian capital, Moscow, the EU agreed to support Russia's membership of the World Trade Organization (WTO), following Russia's extension in April of its PCA with the EU to 10 accession states. The Russian President, Vladimir Putin, signed legislation ratifying the Kyoto Protocol of the UN Convention on Climate Change in November, following EU criticism of the country's failure to do so. The Kyoto Protocol entered into force in February 2005. Consultations on human rights took place between the EU and Russia for the first time in March of that year, in Luxembourg. At a summit held in Moscow in May the two sides adopted a single package of roadmaps, to facilitate the creation of the four common spaces in the medium term. As part of the common space on freedom, security and justice, agreements on visa facilitation (simplifying the procedures for issuing short-stay visas) and on readmission (setting out procedures for the return of people found to be illegally resident in the territory of the other party) were reached in October, and were signed at the EU-Russia summit held in Sochi, Russia, in May 2006. In July the Commission approved draft negotiating directives for a new EU-Russia Agreement to replace the PCA, which was to come to the end of its initial 10-year period in December 2007. The PCA remained in force, and was renewed on an annual basis, pending the conclusion of a new agreement. In March 2007 the Commission published a Country Strategy Paper for EU-Russia relations in 2007–13. Associated with the paper was a National Indicative Programme for Russia for 2007–10, which envisaged that financial allocations from the EU to Russia during that period would amount to €30m. annually. At an EU-Russia summit meeting held in Mafra, Portugal, in October 2007, it was agreed to establish a system to provide early warning of threats to the supply of natural gas and petroleum to the EU, following the serious disruption of supplies to EU countries from Russia, via Belarus, in previous years. In November 2008 the European Commission, the USA and 15 other countries attending an energy summit in Baku, Azerbaijan, signed a declaration urging increased co-operation in projects aimed at improving co-operation in energy projects in the Caspian Sea region, in order to diversify supply routes. In January 2009 the European Commission proposed to contribute €250m. towards funding the planned Nabucco gas pipeline, which was to channel about 5%–10% of Europe's gas requirements (originating in the Caspian region and the Middle East, including Azerbaijan, Egypt, Iraq and Turkmenistan) from Erzurum, Turkey, to Baumgarten an der March, Austria. A new Partnership for Modernisation (P4M) was launched following a summit meeting in Rostov, Russia, in May–June 2010; the P4M focused on economic and technical matters, the rule of law and the functioning of the judiciary.

An Interim Agreement with Belarus was signed in March 1996. However, in February 1997 the EU suspended negotiations for the conclusion of the Interim Agreement and for a PCA in view of serious reverses to the development of democracy in that country. EU technical assistance programmes were suspended, with the exception of aid programmes and those considered directly beneficial to the democratic process. In 1999 the EU announced that the punitive measures would be withdrawn gradually upon the attainment of certain benchmarks. In September 2004 the European Parliament condemned President Alyaksandr Lukashenka's attempt to secure a third term of office by scheduling a referendum to change the country's Constitution, which permitted a maximum of two terms. The EU subsequently imposed a travel ban on officials responsible for the allegedly fraudulent legislative elections and the referendum held in Belarus in October, which abolished limits on the number of terms that the President was permitted to serve. As part of efforts to support civil society and democratization, in September the European Commission initiated a €2m. project to increase access in Belarus to independent sources of news and information. In April 2006, following Lukashenka's re-election in the previous month, the EU extended the travel ban imposed in 2004 to include Lukashenka and 30 government ministers and other officials. In November 2006, in a communication to the Belarusian authorities, the EU detailed the benefits that Belarus could expect to gain, within the framework of the European Neighbourhood Policy, were the country to embark on a process of democratization and to show due respect for human rights and the rule of law. In October 2008 EU ministers of foreign affairs agreed to soften sanctions against Belarus, which released three high-profile political prisoners from detention in August, by suspending the travel ban on Lukashenka and other officials. In November 2009 the Council noted positive developments in EU-Belarus relations, with the development of an EU-Belarus Human Rights Dialogue, increased technical co-operation and the country's active participation in the Eastern Partnership. However, owing to a lack of progress with regard to human rights and democracy, the Council agreed to retain restrictive measures in place against a number of Belarusian officials. In January 2012 the EU noted a worsening in the human rights situation in Belarus, and announced that it was to expand its list of banned officials (then numbering 210) to some 336; in response, in February Belarus expelled the head of the EU delegation to that country and the Polish ambassador, and recalled its own ambassadors. The restrictive measures pertaining to Belarus were renewed for a further 12-month period in both October 2012 and October 2013.

In February 1994 the EU Council of Ministers agreed to pursue closer economic and political relations with Ukraine, following an agreement by that country to renounce control of nuclear weapons on its territory. A PCA was signed by the two sides in June. An Interim Trade Agreement with Ukraine came into force in February 1996; this was replaced by a PCA in March 1998. In December 1999 the EU adopted a Common Strategy on Ukraine, aimed at developing a strategic partnership on the basis of the PCA. The Chernobyl (Chornobyl) nuclear power plant closed in December 2000. The EU provided funding to cover the interim period prior to the completion of two new reactors (supported by the EBRD and the European Atomic Energy Community—Euratom) to replace the plant's generating capacity. The EU Action Plan for Ukraine adopted in February 2005 envisaged enhanced co-operation in many areas. At a summit held in the Ukrainian capital, Kyiv, in December, the EU and Ukraine signed agreements on aviation and on Ukraine's participation in the EU's Galileo civil satellite navigation and positioning system and a Memorandum of Understanding (MOU) on increased co-operation in the energy sector. In November 2005 an EU Border Assistance Mission to monitor Ukraine's border with Moldova was launched at the request of both countries' Governments (deployed for an initial period of two years, subsequently extended, and ongoing at 2013). In February 2008 EU ministers responsible for foreign affairs attended a conference on the EU's Black Sea Synergy programme, held in Kyiv. Following the accession to the EU of the littoral states Bulgaria and Romania, the programme aims to improve co-operation between countries bordering the Black Sea, as well as between members of the Black Sea region and the EU. In September, at an EU-Ukraine summit, held in Paris, France, the EU announced plans to commence negotiations towards an Association Agreement with Ukraine, to supersede the PCA. In March 2009 the EU, Ukraine, international financial institutions, gas industry representatives and other partners participated in a Joint EU-Ukraine International Investment Conference on the Rehabilitation of Ukraine's Gas Transit System, to discuss the future modernization of the system, with a view to improving the sustainability, reliability and efficiency of the infrastructure and helping to secure long-term supplies of gas to the rest of Europe. In November an EU-Ukraine Association Agenda was adopted, replacing the EU Action Plan. In March 2011 an MOU on the National Indicative Programme for Ukraine for 2011–13 was signed, allocating some €470m. to Ukraine, focusing on three principal areas: good governance and the rule of law; progress pertaining to the EU-Ukraine Association Agreement (including plans for the creation of a deep and comprehensive free trade area—DCFTA); and sustainable development. An EU-Ukraine free trade agreement was finalized in late October 2011. Meanwhile, in mid-October Yuliya Tymoshenko, a former Prime Minister and the principal political opponent of the President of Ukraine, Viktor Yanukovych, had been sentenced to seven years' imprisonment for abuse of office, after a trial that she claimed was politically motivated, prompting EU concerns over the treatment of opposition politicians. (In January 2013 Tymoshenko was further accused of the murder of a parliamentarian.) The free trade agreement was initialled in March 2012, and a separate agreement on the DCFTA was signed in July. At an EU-Ukraine summit meeting held in Brussels in February 2013 the EU emphasized that urgent reform of the judicial and electoral systems in Ukraine was required if the Association Agreement was to be signed that year. In November Yanukovych decided to sign neither the Association Agreement nor the accompanying agreement on free trade, prompting violent protests in Kyiv, which continued into early 2014. On 20 February 2014 EU ministers responsible for foreign affairs voted in favour of the imposition of sanctions against senior Ukrainian officials, after more than 75 people were reportedly shot and killed by security forces during action to remove demonstrators from central Kyiv on 19–20 February. On 22 February a power-sharing agreement collapsed, and the Ukrainian legislature voted to remove Yanukovych from office, and to release Tymoshenko. On 3 March EU ministers responsible for foreign affairs condemned the violation of Ukraine's sovereignty by Russian armed forces, and two days later the Council adopted sanctions, which sought to facilitate the recovery of Ukrainian state funds. In early March the Commission reached agreement on economic and financial support measures for Ukraine, and import tariffs on Ukrainian goods were subsequently removed. In mid-March the EU imposed asset freezes and visa restrictions against senior Russian officials, and the number of those targeted was increased later that month. The EU condemned the referendum held in the Ukrainian territory of Crimea on 16 March, the results of which supported annexation by Russia, in contravention of the Ukrainian Constitution. On 21 March the political provisions of the Association Agreement were signed by the EU and Ukraine. On 17 April the EU, Russia, Ukraine and the USA concluded an agreement in Geneva, Switzerland, which sought to defuse the increasing tensions in eastern Ukraine.

On 8 August 2008 Georgia launched a military offensive in the separatist republic of South Ossetia, prompting retaliatory intervention by Russia. A ceasefire agreement was brokered four days later, with the assistance of French President Nicolas Sarkozy, whose country held the rotating Presidency of the Council of the EU. However, Russia's failure to withdraw its troops from Georgian territory by the end of August, and its decision to recognize the independence of the republics of South Ossetia and Abkhazia, led EU leaders to postpone talks with Russia on the new EU-Russia agreement, which had been scheduled to commence in September. Russia finally agreed to withdraw its troops from Georgia by 10 October. Meanwhile, in early September EU ministers responsible for foreign affairs reached agreement on the deployment of an EU Monitoring Mission (EUMM) to Georgia from 1 October. EUMM comprised some 350 personnel from 22 countries, and was mandated to monitor adherence to peace agreements, and to contribute to stability throughout Georgia and the surrounding region. In November EU ministers responsible for foreign affairs agreed to resume talks with Russia on the new EU-Russia agreement.

In May 1997 an Interim Agreement with Moldova entered into force; this was replaced by a PCA in July 1998. The first EU-Moldova Co-operation Council meeting was held in the same month in Brussels. Interim Agreements entered into force during 1997 with Kazakhstan (April), Georgia (September) and Armenia (December). In late September 2012 the Council removed sanctions previously imposed on the authorities in the disputed Transnistria region of Moldova, owing to progress made by the new political leadership in fresh negotiations, which commenced in December 2011. An Interim Agreement with Azerbaijan entered into force in March 1999. A PCA with Turkmenistan was signed in May 1998 and an Interim Agreement with Uzbekistan entered into force in June. By the end of that year PCAs had been signed with all the countries of the CIS, except Tajikistan, owing to political instability in that country. All remaining Agreements had entered into force by 1 July 1999, with the exception of those negotiated with Belarus and Turkmenistan. A PCA with Tajikistan was eventually signed in October 2004, and entered into force in January 2010. In June–July 2013 the EU completed negotiations on DCFTAs with Armenia, Georgia and Moldova, as part of negotiations on new Association Agreements with those countries, which were intended to supersede the relevant PCAs. In September the Armenian Government announced its intention to join a customs union, at that time comprising Russia, Belarus and Kazakhstan, and consequently the Association Agreement negotiated with that country was not initialled. The Association Agreements with Georgia and Moldova were signed at the Eastern Partnership summit meeting held in Vilnius, Lithuania, in November. Meanwhile, in 2013 three agreements were reached with Azerbaijan on visa facilitation, readmission and mobility in order to facilitate travel between that country and the EU; they also aimed to assist with managing both legal and illicit migration. In November the European Commission announced plans to provide funds worth some €1,000m. to Kyrgyzstan, Tajikistan, Turkmenistan and Uzbekistan under its Development Co-operation Instrument for 2014–20.

OTHER EUROPEAN COUNTRIES

The members of the European Free Trade Association (EFTA) concluded bilateral free trade agreements with the European Economic Community and the European Coal and Steel Community during the 1970s. On 1 January 1984 the last tariff barriers were eliminated, thus establishing full free trade for industrial products between the Community and EFTA members. Some EFTA members subsequently applied for membership of the EC: Austria in 1989, Sweden in 1991, and Finland, Switzerland and Norway in 1992. Formal negotiations on the creation of a European Economic Area (EEA), a single market for goods, services, capital and labour among EC and EFTA members, began in June 1990, and were concluded in October 1991. The agreement was signed in May 1992 (after a delay caused by a ruling of the Court of Justice of the EC that a proposed joint EC-EFTA court, for adjudication in disputes, was incompatible with the Treaty of Rome; EFTA members then agreed to concede jurisdiction to the Court of Justice on cases of competition involving both EC and EFTA members, and to establish a special joint committee for other disputes). In a referendum in December, Swiss voters rejected ratification of the agreement, and the remaining 18 countries signed an adjustment protocol in March 1993, allowing the EEA to be established without Switzerland (which was to have observer status). The EEA entered into force on 1 January 1994. Despite the rejection of the EEA by the Swiss electorate, the Swiss Government declared its intention to continue to pursue its application for membership of the EU. Formal negotiations on the accession to the EU of Austria, Finland and Sweden began on 1 February, and those on Norway's membership started on 1 April. Negotiations were concluded in March 1994. Heads of government of the four countries signed treaties of accession to the EU in June, which were to come into effect from 1995, subject to approval by a national referendum in each country. Accession to the EU was endorsed by the electorates of Austria, Finland and Sweden in June, October and November 1994, respectively. Norway's accession, however, was rejected in a national referendum (by 52.4% of voters) conducted at the end of November. From 1994 Norway's relations with the EU were based on full participation in the EEA as well as involvement (at non-signatory level) in the EU's Schengen Agreement. Austria, Finland and Sweden became members of the EU on 1 January 1995. Liechtenstein, which became a full member of EFTA in September 1991, joined the EEA on 1 May 1995.

In 1999 Switzerland signed seven bilateral free trade agreements with the EU, mainly relating to trade liberalization (known together as Bilateral I). A referendum was held in March 2001 on whether to begin 'fast-track' accession negotiations with the EU; the motion was rejected by 77% of voters. The first EU-Switzerland summit meeting took place in Brussels, Belgium, in May 2004, after which nine sectoral agreements (together known as Bilateral II, and covering areas such as savings tax, fraud, the Schengen Agreement on border controls and the environment) were signed by the two parties. The participation of Switzerland in the Schengen area and the extension of the agreement on the free movement of persons to the 10 states that joined the EU in May 2004 were approved by Swiss voters in public referendums in June and September 2005. A protocol on these measures and on Bilateral II was signed in October 2004 and entered into force in April 2006. In February 2014 50.3% of voters approved proposals that the country should renegotiate its freedom of movement agreement with the EU, and introduce quotas for immigrants.

Despite the fact that Iceland joined EFTA in 1970 and ratified the EEA in 1993 (although the extension of the single market legislation excluded agriculture and fisheries management, as in Norway and Liechtenstein), it did not thereafter apply for EU membership. Although opposition to Iceland's joining the EU persisted at government level in the first half of the 2000s, relations between the EU and Iceland had generally developed smoothly since 1993—notably, Iceland negotiated participation in the Schengen Agreement (although, as a signatory, it was not involved in decision-making within the agreement). Following a serious economic crisis in Iceland in 2008, in July 2009 the Icelandic Parliament voted in favour of making an application for membership of the EU. Accession negotiations with Iceland opened in July 2010. Public enthusiasm for membership subsequently lessened, however, and by early 2013 negotiations had been closed on only 11 of the 35 negotiating areas. In June 2013 Iceland suspended its negotiations on membership.

In November 2008 the European Commission adopted a communication on the EU and the Arctic Region, which emphasized the adverse effects of climate change and technological activities in that region. The Commission identified three principal goals: to preserve the region, in co-operation with its indigenous population; to encourage the sustainable use of natural resources; and to aid improved multilateral governance. In June 2012 the European Commission adopted a new communication on its Arctic policy, assessing the progress made since 2008, and identifying next steps in three areas: knowledge; responsibility; and engagement.

The EU's Northern Dimension programme covers the Baltic Sea, Arctic Sea and north-west Russia regions. It aims to address the specific challenges of these areas and to encourage co-operation with external states. The Northern Dimension programme operates within the framework of the EU-Russia PCA and the TACIS programme, as well as other agreements and financial instruments. An Action Plan for the Northern Dimension in the External and Cross-border Policies of the EU, covering 2000–03, was adopted in June 2000. The Plan detailed objectives in the following areas of co-operation: environmental protection; nuclear safety and nuclear waste management; energy; transport and border-crossing infrastructure; justice and internal affairs; business and investment; public health and social administration; telecommunications; and human resources development. The first conference of Northern Dimension ministers responsible for foreign affairs was held in Helsinki, Finland, in November 1999. At a ministerial conference on the Northern Dimension held in October 2002, guidelines were adopted for a second Action Plan for the Northern Dimension in the External and Cross-border Policies of the EU, covering 2004–06. The second Action Plan, which was formally adopted in October 2003, set out strategic priorities and objectives in five priority areas: economy and infrastructure; social issues (including education, training and public health); environment, nuclear safety and natural resources; justice and home affairs; and cross-border co-operation. Under the Northern Dimension programme, priority was given to efforts to integrate Russia into a common European economic and social area through projects dealing with environmental pollution, nuclear risks and cross-border organized crime. At a Northern Dimension summit meeting held in Helsinki in November 2006, the leaders of the EU, Iceland, Norway and Russia endorsed a new Policy Framework Document and Northern Dimension Political Declaration, replacing the three-year action plans hitherto in place with a new common regional policy. In October 2009 a Memorandum of Understanding was signed in Naples, Italy, by the European Commission and 11 northern European countries, establishing the Northern Dimension Partnership on Transport and Logistics, which sought to develop important transport links in northern Europe.

The EU Baltic Sea region comprises eight countries (Denmark, Estonia, Finland, Germany, Latvia, Lithuania, Poland and Sweden). The EU's first macro-regional strategy, the EU Strategy for the Baltic Sea Region (EUSBSR), was approved by the European Council in 2009. In March 2012 the Commission proposed three overall objectives for the EUSBSR: (i) save the sea; (ii) connect the region; and (iii) increase prosperity. These were incorporated in the EUSBSR Action Plan. Accordingly, the EUSBSR aims to provide a framework for improving environmental conditions in the region, helping transportation flows, and improving networks for energy and research and innovation, as well as aiding the development of cross-border competition.

A trade agreement with Andorra entered into force on 1 January 1991, establishing a customs union for industrial products, and allowing duty-free access to the EC for certain Andorran agricultural products. A wide-ranging co-operation agreement with Andorra and an agreement on the taxation of savings income were signed in November 2004 and entered into force in July 2005. Similar agreements on the taxation of savings income also took effect in Liechtenstein, Monaco and San Marino in July 2005. Negotiations on a co-operation and customs union agreement between the EC and San Marino were concluded in December 1991; the agreement entered into force in May 2002. The euro became the sole currency in circulation in Andorra, Monaco, San Marino and the Vatican City at the beginning of 2002.

THE MIDDLE EAST AND THE MEDITERRANEAN

A scheme to negotiate a series of parallel trade and co-operation agreements encompassing almost all of the non-member states on the coast of the Mediterranean was formulated by the European Community (EC) in 1972. Association Agreements, intended to lead to customs union or the eventual full accession of the country concerned, had been signed with Greece (which eventually became a member of the Community in 1981) in 1962, Turkey in 1964 and Malta in 1971; a fourth agreement was signed with Cyprus in 1972. (In May 2004 Malta and Cyprus became members of the EU, as the EC became known in May 2003.) These established free access to the Community market for most industrial products and tariff reductions for most agricultural products. Annexed were financial protocols under which the Community was to provide concessional finance. During the 1970s a series of agreements covering trade and economic co-operation were concluded with the Arab Mediterranean countries and Israel, all establishing free access to EC markets for most industrial products. Access for agricultural products was facilitated, although some tariffs remained. In 1982 the Commission formulated an integrated plan for the development of its own Mediterranean regions and recommended the adoption of a new policy towards the non-Community countries of the Mediterranean. This was to include greater efforts towards diversifying agriculture, in order to avoid surpluses of items such as citrus fruits, olive oil and wine (which the Mediterranean countries all wished to export to the Community) and to reduce these countries' dependence on imported food. From 1 January 1993 the majority of agricultural exports from Mediterranean non-Community countries were granted exemption from customs duties.

In June 1995 the European Council endorsed a proposal by the Commission to reform and strengthen the Mediterranean policy of the EU. In November a conference of ministers responsible for foreign affairs of the EU member states, 11 Mediterranean non-member countries (excluding Libya) and the Palestinian authorities was convened in Barcelona, Spain. The conference issued the Barcelona Declaration, outlining the main objective of the partnership, which was to create a region of peace, security and prosperity. The Declaration set the objective of establishing a Euro-Mediterranean free trade area. The process of co-operation and dialogue under this agreement became known as the Euro-Mediterranean Partnership or Barcelona Process until 2008.

In March 2008 the European Council approved a proposal formally to transform the Barcelona Process into a Union for the Mediterranean. In mid-July heads of state and of government from the then 27 EU member states and from the member states and observers of the Barcelona Process attended the Paris Summit for the Mediterranean, at which the new Union for the Mediterranean was officially launched. (Bosnia and Herzegovina, Croatia, Monaco and Montenegro were also admitted to the Union for the Mediterranean.) Six co-operation projects were approved at the summit, which were to focus on improving pollution levels in the Mediterranean; constructing maritime and land highways; civil protection; the creation of a Mediterranean Solar Plan; the establishment of a Euro-Mediterranean University (which was established in Slovenia in June 2008); and the launch of a Mediterranean Business Development Initiative. A meeting of Euro-Mediterranean ministers responsible for foreign affairs, convened in Marseille, in November, endorsed the new Union. A Euro-Mediterranean Regional and Local Assembly (ARLEM) held its inaugural meeting in Barcelona in January 2010, and a Secretariat was established in Barcelona in March.

The European Neighbourhood Policy (ENP) was established by the European Commission in 2004, to enhance co-operation with 16 countries that neighboured the EU following its enlargement. Algeria, Egypt, Israel, Jordan, Lebanon, Libya, Morocco, the Palestinian Autonomous Areas, Syria and Tunisia were covered by the ENP (which became known as the Southern Neighbourhood), which was intended to complement the Barcelona Process, in addition to several countries to the east of the Union (the Eastern Neighbourhood). Under the ENP, the EU negotiated bilateral Action Plans with 12 neighbouring countries, establishing targets for further political and economic co-operation over a three- to five-year period. The Action Plans aimed to build on existing contractual relationships between the partner country and the EU (e.g. an Association Agreement or a Partnership and Co-operation Agreement—PCA). The eventual conclusion of more ambitious relationships with partner countries achieving significant progress in meeting the priorities set out in the Action Plans was envisaged. On the expiry of the initial Action Plans, new documents were being adopted. In October 2008 Morocco was granted advanced status under the ENP, and in November 2012 negotiations for a new ENP Action Plan for 2013–17 were concluded.

The EU's primary financial instrument for the implementation of the Euro-Mediterranean Partnership was the MEDA programme, providing support for the reform of economic and social structures within partnership countries. It was followed by MEDA II, which was granted a budget of €5,350m. for 2000–06. In 2007 a new European Neighbourhood and Partnership Instrument (ENPI) replaced MEDA and the Technical Assistance to the Commonwealth of Independent States (TACIS) programme (which was concerned with EU co-operation with the countries of the former USSR). The ENPI was conceived as a flexible, policy-orientated instrument to target sustainable development and conformity with EU policies and standards. In 2007–13 some €12,000m. was available, within its framework, to support ENP Action Plans and the Strategic Partnership with Russia. An ENPI cross-border co-operation programme covered activities across the external borders of the EU in the south and the east, supported by funds totalling €1,180m. in 2007–13. From 2014 the ENPI was replaced by the European Neighbourhood Instrument (ENI), for which the European Parliament approved funding of more than €15,000m. during 2014–20.

Turkey, which had signed an Association Agreement with the EC in 1963 (although this was suspended between 1980 and 1986 following a military coup), applied for membership of the EU in April 1987 (see Enlargement). Accession talks began in October 2005, and effectively stalled in 2010. In May 2012 the EU and Turkey launched a new 'positive agenda', which sought to identify areas for future bilateral co-operation, and focus resources on them. Such areas included conformity with EU law; political reform; visas, mobility and migration; trade; energy; counter-terrorism; and foreign policy issues.

Co-operation agreements concluded in the 1970s with the Maghreb countries (Algeria, Morocco and Tunisia), the Mashreq countries (Egypt, Jordan, Lebanon and Syria) and Israel covered free access to the Community market for industrial products, customs preferences for certain agricultural products, and financial aid in the form of grants and loans from the EIB. A co-operation agreement negotiated with the Republic of Yemen was non-preferential. In June 1992 the EC approved a proposal to conclude new bilateral agreements with the Maghreb countries, incorporating the following components: political dialogue; financial, economic, technical and cultural co-operation; and the eventual establishment of a free trade area. A Euro-Mediterranean Association Agreement with Tunisia was signed in July 1995 and entered into force in March 1998. A similar agreement with Morocco (concluded in 1996) entered into force in March 2000. (In July 1987 Morocco applied to join the Community, but its application was rejected on the grounds that it is not a European country.) In March 1997 negotiations were initiated between the European Commission and representatives of the Algerian Government on a Euro-Mediterranean Association Agreement that would incorporate political commitments relating to democracy and human rights; this was signed in December 2001 and entered into force in September 2005. An Association Agreement with Jordan was signed in November 1997 and entered into force in May 2002. A Euro-Mediterranean Association Agreement with Egypt (which has been a major beneficiary of EU financial co-operation since the 1970s) was signed in June 2001 and was fully ratified in June 2004. In May 2001 Egypt, together with Jordan, Tunisia and Morocco, issued the Agadir Declaration, in which they determined to establish an Arab Mediterranean Free Trade Zone. The so-called Agadir Agreement on the establishment of a Free Trade Zone between the Arabic Mediterranean Nations was signed in February 2004 and came into force in March 2007. An interim EU Association Agreement with Lebanon was signed in June 2002, and entered into force in April 2006. Protracted negotiations on an Association Agreement with Syria were concluded in October 2004, and a revised version of the Agreement was initialled in December 2008. In May 2011 the EU announced that co-operation with Syria was to be suspended, owing to the violent suppression of anti-Government protests there from March (and subsequent civil conflict—see below). In December 2011 the Council agreed that negotiations could commence towards Deep and Comprehensive Free Trade Agreements with Egypt, Jordan, Morocco and Tunisia. The EU established an election observation mission (EOM) to monitor the legislative elections held in Jordan in January 2013. An EOM observed legislative elections in Algeria in May 2012, and subsequently emphasized the need for increased transparency and for political parties to be given systematic access to the national electoral list. In July 2013 a €10m. programme to support governance in Algeria was adopted by the European Commission.

In January 1989 the EC and Israel eliminated the last tariff barriers to full free trade for industrial products. A Euro-Mediterranean Association Agreement with Israel was signed in 1995, providing further trade concessions and establishing an institutional political dialogue between the two parties. The agreement entered into force in June 2000. In late 2004 an ENP Action Plan on further co-operation was agreed by the EU and Israel; it was adopted by the EU in February 2005 and by the Israeli authorities in April of that year.

Following the signing of the September 1993 Israeli-Palestine Liberation Organization (PLO) peace agreement, the EC committed substantial funds in humanitarian assistance for the Palestinians. A Euro-Mediterranean Interim Association Agreement on Trade and Co-operation was signed with the PLO in February 1997 and entered into force in July. In April 1998 the EU and the Palestinian (National) Authority (PA) signed a security co-operation agreement. The escalation of violence between Israel and the Palestinians from September 2000 resulted in a deterioration in EU-Israel relations. The EU formed part of the Quartet (alongside the UN, the USA and Russia), which was established in July 2002 to monitor and aid the implementation of Palestinian civil reforms, and to guide the international donor community in its support of the Palestinian reform agenda. In late 2004 the EU agreed an Action Plan with the PA; it was adopted by the EU in February 2005 and by the PA in May. In November, on the basis of an agreement reached by Israel and the PA following Israel's withdrawal from Gaza and the northern West Bank, the EU established an EU Border Assistance Mission (EU BAM Rafah), which monitored operations at the Rafah border crossing between Egypt and the Gaza Strip until June 2007. An EU Police Mission for the Palestinian Territories (EUPOL COPPS) commenced operations in January 2006, with an initial three-year mandate, subsequently repeatedly extended, to support the PA in establishing sustainable and effective policing arrangements. At July 2012 the mission comprised 41 international staff and 70 local personnel. In June 2006 EU member states and the European Commission established the Temporary International Mechanism (TIM), an emergency assistance mechanism to provide support directly to the Palestinian people. On 1 February 2008 the European Commission launched a new mechanism, known as PEGASE, with a wider remit than the TIM. PEGASE aimed to support activities in four principal areas: governance (including fiscal reform, security and the rule of law); social development (including social protection, health and education); economic and private sector development; and development of public infrastructure (in areas such as water, the environment and energy). In May 2012 the EU urged progress in the implementation of the 'unity' agreement signed by representatives of 13 Palestinian groups in May 2011, which aimed to result in the formation of a joint administration for the West Bank and Gaza, predominantly comprising figures independent of the two main factions. In September 2012 the European Commission announced funding of €100m. for the Palestinian Autonomous Areas, to be primarily allocated to water and sanitation and support for refugees; total EU funding to Palestine consequently totalled €200m. in 2012. In November the EU Foreign Affairs Council condemned rocket attacks against Israel launched from the Gaza Strip, and urged Israel to seek to ensure the safety of civilians while protecting its population from such attacks. At the end of July 2013 the Quartet welcomed the resumption of direct negotiations between the Israeli and Palestinian sides, with preliminary talks taking place in Washington, DC, USA.

Talks were held with Iran in April 1992 on the establishment of a co-operation accord. In December the Council of Ministers recommended that a 'critical dialogue' be undertaken with Iran, owing to the country's significance to regional security. In April 1997 the 'critical dialogue' was suspended and ambassadors were recalled from Iran, after a German court found the Iranian authorities responsible for having ordered the murder of four Kurdish dissidents in Berlin in 1992. Later that month ministers responsible for foreign affairs resolved to restore diplomatic relations with Iran, in order to protect the strong trading partnership. In November 2000 an EU-Iran Working Group on Trade and Investment met for the first time to discuss the possibility of increasing and diversifying trade and investment. During 2002 attempts were made to improve relations with Iran, as negotiations began in preparation for a Trade and Co-operation Agreement. An eventual trade deal was to be linked to progress in political issues, including human rights, weapons proliferation and counter-terrorism. In mid-2003 the EU (in conformity with US policy) warned Iran to accept stringent new nuclear inspections, and threatened the country with economic repercussions (including the abandonment of the proposed trade agreement) unless it restored international trust in its nuclear programme. A 'comprehensive dialogue' between the EU and Iran (which replaced the 'critical dialogue' in 1998) was suspended by Iran in December 2003. In January 2005 the EU resumed trade talks with Iran after the Iranian authorities agreed to suspend uranium enrichment. However, these talks were halted by the Commission in August, following Iran's resumption of uranium conversion to gas (the stage before enrichment). Following Iran's removal of international seals from a nuclear research facility in January 2006, the EU supported moves to refer Iran to the UN Security Council. In December 2006, in a declaration on Iran, the Council criticized the country's failure to implement measures required by both the International Atomic Energy Agency (IAEA) and the UN Security Council in respect of its nuclear programme, and warned that this failure would be to the detriment of EU-Iran relations. EU trade sanctions against Iran were strengthened in August 2008, after Iran failed to halt its uranium-enrichment programme. In July 2010 EU ministers responsible for foreign affairs adopted a new set of sanctions, prohibiting investment, technical assistance and technology transfers to Iran's energy sector, and also targeting the country's financial services, insurance and transport sectors. Sanctions were strengthened in May 2011. In late 2011 a report published by the IAEA indicated that Iran's ongoing nuclear programme may involve a military component. EU sanctions were further strengthened in January 2012, when a ban on imports of Iranian crude oil was imposed and the assets of the Iranian central bank within the EU were frozen. The EU also has strong concerns over the human rights situation in Iran. As a consequence, the EU imposed sanctions on 61 people believed to be responsible for significant human rights abuses; in March EU ministers responsible for foreign affairs expanded these sanctions to cover a further 17 individuals. In October ongoing concern about Iran's nuclear programme, together with Iran's unwillingness to co-operate with the so-called E3+3 grouping (comprising the People's Republic of China, France, Germany, Russia, the United Kingdom and the USA, and led by the EU's High Representative for Foreign Affairs and Security Policy, Catherine Ashton), prompted the EU further to extend its sanctions regime.

A co-operation agreement between the EC and the countries of the Gulf Cooperation Council (GCC), which entered into force in January 1990, provided for co-operation in industry, energy, technology and other fields. Negotiations on a full free trade pact began in October, but it was expected that any agreement would involve transition periods of some 12 years for the reduction of European tariffs on 'sensitive products' (i.e. petrochemicals). In November 1999 the GCC Supreme Council agreed to establish a customs union (a precondition of the proposed EU-GCC free trade agreement); the union was established in January 2003. At the 20th EU-GCC Joint Council and Ministerial Meeting, held in Luxembourg in June 2010, an EU-GCC Joint Action Programme for 2010–13 was adopted, with the aim of strengthening co-operation in a number of areas, principally economic and financial co-operation; trade and industry; energy and the environment; transport, telecommunications and information technology; education and research; and culture.

The increased tension in the Middle East prior to the US-led military action in Iraq in March 2003 placed considerable strain on relations between member states of the EU, and exposed the lack of a common EU policy on Iraq. In February 2003 the European Council held an extraordinary meeting to discuss the crisis in Iraq, and issued a statement reiterating its commitment to the UN. In April, however, the EU leaders reluctantly accepted a dominant role for the USA and the United Kingdom in post-war Iraq, and Denmark, Spain and the Netherlands announced plans to send peace keeping troops to Iraq. At the Madrid Donors' Conference in October the EU and its accession states pledged more than €1,250m. (mainly in grants) for Iraq's reconstruction. The EU welcomed the handover of power by the Coalition Provisional Authority to the Iraqi Interim Government in June 2004 and supported the holding of elections to the Transitional National Assembly in Iraq in January 2005. An EU integrated rule-of-law mission for Iraq, to provide training in management and criminal investigation to staff and senior officials from the judiciary, the police and the penitentiary, commenced operations in July, with an initial mandate of 12 months. In December 2006 an agreement was signed on the establishment of a European Commission delegation office in the Iraqi capital, Baghdad. In June of that year, in response to the formation of a new Iraqi Government, the Commission set forth its proposals for an EU-wide strategy to govern EU relations with Iraq. The strategy comprised five objectives: overcoming divisions within Iraq and building democracy; promoting the rule of law and human rights; supporting the Iraqi authorities in the delivery of basic services; supporting the reform of public administration; and promoting economic reform. In November negotiations commenced on a trade and co-operation agreement with Iraq; at a round of negotiations on the agreement held in February 2009, participants agreed to upgrade the draft accord to a more comprehensive draft partnership agreement, which would provide for annual ministerial meetings and the establishment of a joint co-operation council. In November the EU and Iraq completed negotiations on the PCA, which was signed in May 2012. Between 2003 and the end of 2008 the EU provided €933m. in reconstruction and humanitarian assistance to Iraq. In November 2010 the EU adopted a Joint Strategy Paper for Iraq for 2011–13, which aimed to assist Iraq in making optimum use of its resources through capacity-building activities relating to good governance; promoting education in order to aid socio-economic recovery; building institutional capacity; water management and agriculture.

A series of large-scale demonstrations in Tunisia, prompted by the self-immolation of a young Tunisian man in protest against state restrictions in mid-December 2010, led President Zine al-Abidine Ben Ali to flee the country in mid-January 2011. An EU-Tunisia Task Force was established to ensure the improved co-ordination of support for Tunisia's political and economic transition, the first meeting of which took place in late September in the capital, Tunis. An Electoral Observation Mission was dispatched to monitor elections to the Constituent Assembly in October 2011. Overall EU financial support for Tunisia was increased to €390m. for 2011–12, focused on facilitating the Government's political and socioeconomic reforms. In February 2014 the Council welcomed the adoption, in the previous month, of a new Constitution in Tunisia.

Mass protests also took place in Egypt in early 2011, which resulted in the resignation of the Egyptian President Lt-Gen. Muhammad Hosni Mubarak on 11 February. The EU dispatched electoral experts to monitor the conduct of the presidential election held in May–June 2012, which concluded that the election took place peacefully and fairly. The EU allocated some €449m. to Egypt in 2011–13, in support of the transition. Further funds, totalling some €5,000m., were made available jointly with the European Investment Bank (EIB) and the European Bank for Reconstruction and Development (EBRD). In late August 2013, following the escalation of violence in Egypt in that month, EU ministers responsible for foreign affairs agreed to suspend the sale of armaments to the country. In February 2014 the Council welcomed the adoption of a new Constitution for Egypt in the previous month.

In mid-February 2011 a series of violent clashes broke out between anti-Government protesters in Libya and armed forces loyal to the Libyan leader, Col Muammar al-Qaddafi. By 22 February it was reported that protesters had taken control of Benghazi and large parts of eastern Libya. At the end of February the Council of the EU adopted a UN Security Council Resolution on Libya, prohibiting the sale to that country of arms and ammunition, and agreed to impose additional sanctions against those responsible for the violent repression of the civilian protests, halting trade in any equipment that could be utilized for such purposes. The Council also imposed a visa ban on several people, including al-Qaddafi and other members of his family, and froze the assets of al-Qaddafi and 25 other people. On 1 April 2011 the Council agreed, in principle, to establish an EU mission in response to the crisis situation in Libya, should its deployment be requested by the UN Office for the Coordination of Humanitarian Affairs (OCHA). After al-Qaddafi went into hiding in late August, and forces in support of the opposition National Transitional Council (NTC) took control of the capital, Tripoli, the European Council agreed measures to support the Libyan economy and to assist the UN mission in Libya. A number of hitherto frozen assets were released in support of humanitarian and civilian needs, and a ban on the use of European air space by Libyan aircraft was removed. At the end of August the EU opened an office in Tripoli. At an international conference held in Paris, France, in early September, the EU agreed to initiate assessments of the needs of the NTC in the fields of security, communication, civil society, border management and procurement, and a further €50m. was to be made available for longer-term support programmes. On 20 October it was confirmed that Qaddafi had been captured and killed during fighting in his home city of Sirte; three days later the NTC declared 'national liberation'. In mid-November the EU's Tripoli office was formally upgraded, becoming the headquarters of the new EU delegation to Libya. EU support to Libya included humanitarian assistance, mobilization of EU civil protection teams, and wide-ranging support for the transitional authorities in, for example, democratic transition and security sector reform. In March 2012 the EU also deployed an expert mission to Libya to advise on border management issues. In January 2013 Libya announced its intention to seek observer status with the Union for the Mediterranean.

Unrest also developed in Yemen in early 2011, with escalating conflict between forces loyal to Saleh and tribal groups, and ongoing protests against Field Marshal Ali Abdullah Saleh's rule in several cities. In late November the EU expressed satisfaction at the signature in Riyadh, Saudi Arabia, of the agreement for political transition signed by President Saleh and senior Yemeni officials, under the auspices of the GCC. The EU provided some €20m. in additional humanitarian aid to Yemen in 2011, and welcomed the presidential election that took place in late February 2012, and the subsequent inauguration of President Field Marshal Abd al-Rabbuh Mansur al-Hadi, prior to legislative elections in 2014. In September 2012 an EU donor conference resulted in pledges worth €170m. in support of Yemen.

After demonstrations commenced in the capital of Bahrain, Manama, in early 2011, the EU urged restraint, and exhorted all parties to take part in negotiations. None the less, protests were violently repressed, and the EU's High Representative dispatched a senior EU envoy to Bahrain for talks. The EU welcomed the establishment, in June, of the Bahrain Independent Commission of Inquiry (BICI)—an independent, international commission of judicial and human rights experts—to investigate both the causes of the unrest and allegations of human rights violations.

Meanwhile, from mid-March 2011 anti-Government protests in Syria were forcibly quashed by the authorities. In response, the EU imposed a number of restrictive measures, including an arms embargo and targeted sanctions, comprising a travel ban and the freezing of assets, against those deemed to be responsible for, or involved with, the repression. The Syrian authorities continued to implement harsh measures in an attempt to quell demonstrations against the rule of President Bashar al-Assad; by mid-October the Office of the UN High Commissioner for Human Rights (OHCHR) estimated that more than 3,000 people had been killed in Syria since protests began. By August 2012 the EU had imposed 17 sets of sanctions on the Syrian authorities. In mid-November the Council expressed its continued support for ongoing efforts to reach a political solution to the situation in Syria. The EU delegation to Syria closed in December, owing to security concerns. In that month the EU Foreign Affairs Council recognized the National Coalition for Syrian Revolutionary and Opposition Forces as the legitimate representatives of the Syrian people. The EU allocated over €400m. in humanitarian aid, while the Commission provided some €100m. to address the long-term consequences of the conflict for the civilian population. In late August 2013 Ashton expressed deep concern at reports of the use of chemical weapons in Syria, and urged intensified diplomatic efforts to bring about a rapid resolution to the civil conflict there. In mid-February 2014 the EU pledged €12m. to help to dismantle and destroy stockpiles of chemical weaponry in Syria.

In late February 2011, at a Senior Officials' meeting to discuss the instability in the Middle East (the 'Arab Spring'), Ashton identified the need to respond in three ways by helping to develop 'deep democracy', through a process of political reform, democratic elections, institution building, measures to combat corruption, and support for the independent judiciary and civil society; through economic development; and by facilitating the movement of people and of communications, while avoiding mass migration. In June a new Task Force for the Southern Mediterranean was established, which aimed to combine expertise from the European External Action Service, the Commission, the European Investment Bank (EIB), the European Bank for Reconstruction and Development (EBRD) and other international financial institutions to act as a focal point for assistance to countries in North Africa experiencing political transformation. The Council appointed an EU Special Representative for the Southern Mediterranean in July, who sought to strengthen the EU's political role in North Africa and the Middle East, to ensure the coherence of EU actions in relation to the region and to support the transition to democracy in the EU's southern neighbourhood. In late September the European Commission agreed to new economic support for the Middle East. The Support for Partnership Reform and Inclusive Growth (SPRING) programme was allocated a budget of €350m. in additional funds for 2011–12, to provide support on a so-called more-for-more basis to those countries that demonstrated progress in implementing democratic reforms. A Civil Society Facility was established, with a budget of €26.4m., to strengthen the capacity of civil society to promote reform and increase public accountability. In November 2013 the Commission announced that the SPRING programme was allocated €150m. for 2013.

SUB-SAHARAN AFRICA

The first Africa-EU summit, representing the institutionalization of Africa-EU dialogue, was convened in April 2000, in Cairo, Egypt. The second summit was held in December 2007, in Lisbon, Portugal (having been postponed from 2003 owing to concerns over the participation of President Robert Mugabe of Zimbabwe, see below). The 2007 Lisbon summit adopted a Joint Africa-EU Strategy as a vision and roadmap, providing an over-arching long-term framework for future political co-operation, to be implemented through successive short-term action plans. The First Action Plan of the Joint Strategy identified eight areas for strategic partnership during 2008–10: peace and security; democratic governance and human rights; trade, regional integration and infrastructure; achievement of the UN Millennium Development Goals (MDGs); energy; climate change; migration, mobility and employment; and science, information society and space. The third Africa-EU summit, with the theme of 'investment, economic growth and job creation' was held in Tripoli, Libya, in November 2010. An action plan for 2011–13 was adopted, focusing on the following principal areas of co-operation: peace and security; democratic governance and human rights; regional integration, trade and infrastructure; the UN's eight MDGs; energy; climate change and the environment; migration, mobility and employment; and science, the information society and space. The fourth Africa-EU summit was held in April 2014, with the theme 'Investing in People, Prosperity and Peace'.

In June 2004 the European Commission activated for the first time its newly established Africa Peace Facility (APF), which provided €12m. in support of African Union (AU) humanitarian and peace-monitoring activities in Darfur (Sudan). In 2007 the EU and the AU agreed to expand the APF to cover the prevention of conflict and post-conflict stabilization, and to facilitate decision-making and co-ordination. APF funds were allocated accordingly: €600m. for Peace Support Operations, the principal focus of the APF; €100m. to aid capacity-building efforts, specifically in the context of the African Peace and Security Architecture and Africa-EU dialogue; €15m. to support the Early Response Mechanism; and €40m. for contingencies.

During 2002 the European Council condemned the worsening human rights situation in Zimbabwe, and imposed a range of targeted sanctions, including a travel ban on and freezing of the assets of certain members of the leadership, an arms embargo, and the suspension of development aid. Sanctions relating to Zimbabwe have been extended repeatedly on an annual basis. In September 2009 an EU delegation visited Zimbabwe for the first time since the imposition of sanctions, and indicated that further progress was needed to end human rights violations there. The majority of the sanctions were extended in February 2010 and February 2011. In February 2012 the EU welcomed developments towards the formation of a Government of National Unity, and agreed to remove sanctions from 51 people and 20 entities with immediate effect. In February 2013 the EU expressed its approval at evidence of progress in the process of reform in Zimbabwe, with an inter-party agreement on a draft constitution, and plans for a referendum, and sanctions were duly further eased. However, in August, following a presidential election that was widely believed to be flawed, EU ministers responsible for foreign affairs agreed to retain remaining sanctions against Zimbabwe until at least February 2014, when most of the remaining sanctions were lifted, with the notable exceptions of the arms embargo and the sanctions in place against President Robert Mugabe and his wife.

The EU, together with, inter alia, the UN Secretary-General, US President Barack Obama, the IMF and the Economic Community of West African States (ECOWAS), recognized Alassane Ouattara as the legitimate victor of a run-off election to decide the presidency of Côte d'Ivoire in November 2010; however, in early December the country's constitutional council released results indicating that incumbent President Laurent Gbagbo had won the election. Widespread disruption and violence followed the disputed elections. In mid-January 2011 the EU imposed sanctions against Côte d'Ivoire, which were subsequently strengthened at the end of that month. Ouattara was officially sworn in as President in May, and EU sanctions on businesses in Côte d'Ivoire were lifted. In July the EU adopted five programmes, which allocated some €125m. to Côte d'Ivoire to support vocational training, road maintenance, health and the management of public finances, and to strengthen civil society organizations.

The political situation in Mali deteriorated in 2012, when a rebellion in the north of the country in January was followed by a *coup d'état* in March. Co-operation with Mali was suspended, but the EU supported regional efforts to reach a peaceful solution to the crisis, and expressed concern at the worsening humanitarian situation there. In 2012 the EU allocated some €337m. to the Sahel region of Africa south of the Sahara (comprising Burkina Faso, northern Cameroon, Chad, Gambia, Mali, Mauritania, Niger, Nigeria and Senegal), which was affected by severe food shortages. Humanitarian aid was expected to reach some 7m. people, in three stages: crisis mitigation and preparedness; emergency response; and recovery/resilience building. The EU dispatched observers to monitor the presidential and legislative elections there in 2013.

The EU maintains several missions in Africa. During June–September 2003 an EU military operation, codenamed Artemis, was conducted in the Democratic Republic of the Congo (DRC). In June 2005 1,400 EUSEC RD Congo peacekeepers were dispatched to attempt to curb ongoing ethnic violence in the DRC; in December 2012 the mandate of EUSEC RD Congo was extended until September 2013. Meanwhile, EUPOL RD Congo was established in 2007 to help with the reform of the country's police force, and to aid its co-operation with the justice system. In October 2007 the Council approved a EUFOR operation (EUFOR Chad/CAR), comprising 3,300 troops, to support a UN mission in eastern Chad and north-eastern Central African Republic (MINURCAT) in efforts to improve security in those regions, where more than 200,000 people from the Darfur region of western Sudan had sought refuge from violence in their own country. The force began deployment in early 2008. In March 2009 EUFOR Chad/CAR's mandate expired and MINURCAT assumed the EU force's military and security responsibilities. In December 2008 Operation EU NAVFOR Somalia—Operation Atalanta, the EU's first maritime military operation, reached its initial operational capacity; Operation EU NAVFOR Somalia was established in support of UN Security Council resolutions aimed at deterring and repressing acts of piracy and armed robbery in waters off the coast of Somalia, and protecting vulnerable vessels in that area (including vessels delivering humanitarian aid to displaced persons in Somalia). The mandate of EU NAVFOR Somalia, due to expire in December 2012, was subsequently extended to December 2014. In February 2010 the Council of the European Union established the EU Training Mission for Somalia (EUTM Somalia), to help to strengthen the Somali transitional federal Government, in particular through providing military training to 2,000 security force recruits; EUTM Somalia became operational in April, and its mandate is due to expire in 2015. EUTM Mali was launched in February 2013 in order to increase the military efficacy of that country's armed forces, through training and reorganization, in an effort to facilitate the restoration of Mali's territorial integrity, under civilian leadership. In mid-April 2014 a civilian mission was established to help to support the security situation in Mali. Meanwhile, in January EU ministers responsible for foreign affairs had approved plans for the preparation of a mission to support internal security in the Central African Republic, as part of its crisis management efforts; humanitarian aid to the country was also to be increased. EUFOR RCA was duly established in February, and formally launched on 1 April.

In mid-June 2012 the Council of the EU approved the establishment of EUAVSEC South Sudan, to strengthen airport security in South Sudan; its mandate expired in January 2014. The establishment of EUCAP SAHEL Niger, with an initial two-year mandate, was approved by the Council in July 2012, as a training, advisory and assistance mission aimed at augmenting the capacity of Niger's security forces to combat terrorism and organized crime. The third, EUCAP NESTOR, was established in mid-July, with a two-year mandate, to develop the maritime capacity of five countries in the Horn of Africa and the Western Indian Ocean. The mission aims to support the rule of law in Somalia and the maritime capacity of Djibouti, Kenya and Seychelles, and eventually Tanzania, and thus complements EU NAVFOR Somalia and EUTM Somalia.

There are EU Special Representatives to the African Union and for the Great Lakes Region.

LATIN AMERICA

A non-preferential trade agreement was signed with Uruguay in 1974, and economic and commercial co-operation agreements with

Mexico in 1975 and with Brazil in 1980. A five-year co-operation agreement with the members of the Central American Common Market and with Panama entered into force in 1987, as did a similar agreement with the member countries (see below) of the Andean Group (now the Andean Community). Co-operation agreements were signed with Argentina and Chile in 1990, and in that year tariff preferences were approved for Bolivia, Colombia, Ecuador and Peru, in support of those countries' efforts to combat drugs-trafficking. In May 1992 an inter-institutional co-operation agreement was signed with the Southern Common Market (Mercado Común del Sur—Mercosur); in the following month the European Community (EC) and the member states of the Andean Group (Bolivia, Colombia, Ecuador, Peru and Venezuela) initialled a new co-operation agreement, which was to broaden the scope of economic and development co-operation and enhance trade relations, and a new co-operation agreement was signed with Brazil. In July 1993 the EC introduced a tariff regime to limit the import of bananas from Latin America, in order to protect the banana-producing countries of the African, Caribbean and Pacific (ACP) group, then linked to the EC by the Lomé Convention. In December 2009, in resolution to a long dispute over the tariff regime, the EU and Latin American states initialled the EU-Latin America Bananas Agreement, which provided for a gradual reduction in the tariff rate—see African, Caribbean and Pacific Countries.

From 1996 the EU, as the EC became in 1993, forged closer links with Latin America, by means of strengthened political ties, an increase in economic integration and free trade, and co-operation in other areas. In April 1997 the EU extended further trade benefits to the countries of the Andean Community. In September 2009 the Commission adopted 'The European Union and Latin America: Global Players in Partnership', updating an earlier communication, published in 2005, on 'A Stronger Partnership between the European Union and Latin America'.

In July 1997 the EU and Mexico concluded an Economic Partnership, Political Co-ordination and Co-operation Agreement (the Global Agreement) and an interim agreement on trade. The accords were signed in December, and entered into effect in 2000. In November 1999 the EU and Mexico concluded a free trade agreement, which provided for the removal of all tariffs on bilateral trade in industrial products by 2007. The first meeting of the Joint Council established by the Economic Partnership, Political Co-ordination and Co-operation Agreement between the EU and Mexico was held in February 2001; further meetings have since been held on a regular basis. In July 2008, in acknowledgement of the gradual strengthening of EU-Mexico relations, the European Commission proposed the establishment of a Strategic Partnership with Mexico. An EU-Mexico summit meeting was held in Comillas, Spain, in May 2010. In May 2007 the European Commission proposed to launch a Strategic Partnership with Brazil, in recognition of its increasing international prominence and strong bilateral ties with Europe. The first EU-Brazil summit was duly held in Lisbon, Portugal, in July.

In November 2002 the EU and Chile signed an association and free trade agreement, which entered into force in March 2005; it provided for the liberalization of trade within seven years for industrial products and 10 years for agricultural products. The first meeting of the Association Council set up by the agreement took place in Athens, Greece, in March 2003.

In late December 1994 the EU and Mercosur signed a joint declaration that aimed to promote trade liberalization and greater political co-operation. In September 1995, at a meeting in Montevideo, Uruguay, a framework agreement on the establishment of a free trade regime between the two organizations was initialled. The agreement was formally signed in December. In July 1998 the European Commission voted to commence negotiations towards an interregional Association Agreement with Mercosur, which would strengthen existing co-operation agreements. Negotiations were initiated in April 2000 (focusing on the three pillars of political dialogue, co-operation, and establishing a free trade area), but were suspended in 2004–10; none the less, political relations were maintained, and notably were extended in May 2008 to include the additional areas of science and technology, infrastructure, and renewable energy.

The first ministerial conference between the EC and the Rio Group of Latin American and Caribbean states took place in April 1991; high-level joint ministerial meetings were held every two years until 2009. The first summit meeting of all EU and Latin American and Caribbean heads of state or government was held in Rio de Janeiro, Brazil, in June 1999, when a strategic partnership was launched. A second EU-Latin America/Caribbean (EU-LAC) summit took place in Madrid, Spain, in May 2002, and covered co-operation in political, economic, social and cultural fields. A political dialogue and co-operation agreement with the Andean Community and its member states was signed in December 2003. At the fourth EU-LAC summit, held in Vienna, Austria, in May 2006, it was decided that negotiations for Association Agreements with Central America and with the Andean Community should be initiated. The summit also endorsed a proposal to establish an EU-Latin America parliamentary assembly. The assembly met for the first time in November. In 2007 the EU concluded negotiations for an Economic Partnership Agreement with the Caribbean Forum (CARIFORUM) grouping of 16 states. In mid-2007 the EU and the Andean Community initiated negotiations on the planned Association Agreement in Tarija, Bolivia. However, negotiations were suspended in June 2008, reportedly owing to divergent views of the aims and scope of the trade provisions. In January 2009 negotiations recommenced between three of the Andean Community countries, Colombia, Ecuador and Peru, with the goal of concluding a multi-party trade agreement; Ecuador provisionally suspended its participation in the negotiations in July. Negotiations were concluded on 1 March 2010, with an agreement on trade between the EU and Colombia and Peru, providing for the liberalization of trade in 65% of industrial products with Colombia, and 80% with Peru. The trade agreement was signed in June 2012. Talks on an Association Agreement between the EU and the countries of Central America (Costa Rica, El Salvador, Guatemala, Honduras, Nicaragua and Panama) commenced in Costa Rica in October 2007, but negotiations were suspended temporarily during 2009 owing to the unstable political situation in Honduras. In May 2010 the EU concluded negotiations on an Association Agreement with Central America, covering three areas: trade; political dialogue; and co-operation. The Association Agreement was signed in Tegucigalpa, Honduras, in June 2012, and approved by the European Parliament in December. In November the Council had endorsed a Joint Caribbean-EU Partnership Strategy, which was conceived at an EU-CARIFORUM summit held in Madrid in May 2010.

In 2010 the Rio Group merged with Cumbres América Latina y Caribe (CALC—internal LAC Summits), under the framework of the Community of Latin American and Caribbean States (CELAC), which began to represent the region in negotiations with third countries and regional grouping. The first EU-CELAC summit meeting took place in Santiago, Chile, in January 2013. An EU-CELAC action plan for 2013–15 was agreed, focusing on the following principal areas: (i) the development of an EU-LAC Knowledge Area, with co-operation and investment in science, research, innovation and technology; (ii) sustainable development, the environment, climate change, biodiversity and energy; (iii) regional integration; (iv) migration; (v) education and employment; (vi) combating drugs; (vii) tackling gender inequalities; and (viii) investment and entrepreneurship. In June 2013 the EU and the Organisation of Eastern Caribbean States established diplomatic relations, in order to promote co-operation between the two organizations.

Cuba remained the only Latin American country that did not have a formal economic co-operation agreement with the EU. In June 1995 a Commission communication advocated greater economic co-operation with Cuba; this policy was criticized by the US Government, which maintained an economic embargo against Cuba. Later that year the EU agreed to make the extent of economic co-operation with Cuba (a one-party state) contingent on progress towards democracy. An EU legation office opened in the Cuban capital, Havana, in March 2003, and the EU supported a renewed application by Cuba to join the successor to the Lomé Convention, the Cotonou Agreement. However, human rights abuses perpetrated by the Cuban regime in April (the imprisonment of a large number of dissidents) led to the downgrading of diplomatic relations with Cuba by the EU, the instigation of an EU policy of inviting dissidents to embassy receptions in Havana (the so-called cocktail wars) and the indefinite postponement of Cuba's application to join the Cotonou Agreement. In May Cuba withdrew its application for membership, and in July the Cuban President, Fidel Castro, announced that the Government would not accept aid from the EU and would terminate all political contact with the organization. In December 2004 the EU proposed a compromise—namely not to invite any Cubans, whether government ministers or dissidents, to future embassy receptions—but reiterated its demand that Cuba unconditionally release all political prisoners who remained in detention (several dissidents had already been released). Cuba announced in January 2005 that it was restoring diplomatic ties with all EU states. At the end of that month the EU temporarily suspended the diplomatic sanctions imposed on Cuba in mid-2003 and announced its intention to resume a 'constructive dialogue' with the Cuban authorities. The EU extended the temporary suspension of diplomatic sanctions against Cuba for one year in June 2005, and annually thereafter. Sanctions were lifted in June 2008, subject to an annual review. In May 2010 the European Commission adopted a country strategy paper on Cuba, which identified three priority areas for intervention: food security; the environment, and adaptation to climate change; and exchanges of expertise, training and studies. In February 2014 EU ministers responsible for foreign affairs endorsed a mandate to initiate efforts to negotiate a political and co-operation agreement with Cuba.

The EU's natural disaster prevention and preparedness programme (Dipecho) has targeted earthquake, flood, hurricane, and volcanic eruption preparedness throughout Latin America and the Caribbean. An earthquake devastated Haiti's infrastructure in January 2010. By March EU humanitarian assistance (including planned pledges), totalled more than €320m. (from member states and the European Commission's Humanitarian Aid Office—ECHO). Emergency relief from ECHO was worth €120m., including €3m. in emergency funding allocated within 24 hours of the earthquake taking place. Following an outbreak of cholera in October, an alert system was put in place, and the Commission approved new funding of some €10m. at the end of December to help to fund the efforts of ECHO to provide support for health staff; to implement preventive strategies, such as the promotion of chlorination and a hygiene-awareness campaign; and to improve the collection and analysis of health-related data. In 2010–13 ECHO contributed a total of €213m. to Haiti.

FAR EAST AND AUSTRALASIA

Relations between the EU and the Association of Southeast Asian Nations (ASEAN) were based on a Co-operation Agreement of 1980. In May 1995 ASEAN and EU senior officials endorsed an initiative to convene an Asia-Europe Meeting of heads of government (ASEM), which takes places every two years. The first ASEM summit was held in March 1996 in Bangkok, Thailand. ASEM VI, convened in Helsinki, Finland, in September 2006, addressed the theme '10 Years of ASEM: Global Challenges and Joint Responses'. The participants adopted a Declaration on Climate Change, aimed at promoting efforts to reach consensus in international climate negotiations, and the Helsinki Declaration on the Future of ASEM, detailing practical recommendations for developing future ASEM co-operation. In March 2007, at an EU-ASEAN ministerial meeting held in Nuremberg, Germany, ASEAN and the EU made the Nuremberg Declaration on an EU-ASEAN Enhanced Partnership, and a Plan of Action was approved to strengthen co-operation during 2007–12. In April 2012 the Bandar Seri Begawan Plan of Action was adopted by both sides, with the objective of strengthening the Enhanced Partnership in 2013–17. In July 2012 the EU acceded to the ASEAN Treaty of Amity and Co-operation.

A trade agreement was signed with the People's Republic of China in 1978 and renewed in May 1985. In June 1989, following the violent repression of the Chinese pro-democracy movement by the Chinese Government, the EC imposed economic sanctions and an embargo on arms sales to that country. In October 1990 it was decided that relations with China should be 'progressively normalized'. The EU has supported China's increased involvement in the international community and, in particular, supported its application for membership of the World Trade Organization (WTO). The first EU-China meeting of heads of government was convened in April 1998. A bilateral trade agreement between the EU and China was concluded in May 2000, removing a major barrier to China's accession to the WTO; this was approved in November 2001. In 2003 an EU-China Comprehensive Strategic Partnership was established. The eighth summit meeting, held in the Chinese capital, Beijing, in September 2005, marked the 30th anniversary of the establishment of EU-China diplomatic relations. During the meeting, the establishment of an EU-China partnership on climate change was confirmed. In October 2006, in a strategy communication, the Commission set forth details of a new agenda for EU-China relations, the priorities of which included support for China's transition towards greater openness and political pluralism. In a separate policy paper, the Commission detailed a new strategy for expanding EU-China relations in the areas of trade and investment. Negotiations for a comprehensive Partnership and Co-operation Agreement (PCA) were launched in January 2007. In January 2009 China and the EU adopted nine agreements aimed at strengthening joint co-operation. At the 12th EU-China summit, held in Nanjing, China, in November, the two sides agreed to make efforts to facilitate the further implementation of the EU-China Joint Declaration on Climate Change, and agreed to strengthen the existing Partnership on Climate Change. At a summit meeting with China, held in Beijing in November 2013, the EU-China 2020 Strategic Agenda of Co-operation was agreed, establishing joint objectives to encourage co-operation in the areas of peace and security, sustainable development, prosperity, and person-to-person exchanges, as part of the EU-China Strategic Partnership.

A framework agreement on trade and co-operation between the EU and the Republic of Korea (South Korea) was signed in 1996 and entered into force in April 2001. In September 1997 the EU joined the Korean Peninsula Energy Development Organization, an initiative founded in 1995 to increase nuclear safety and reduce the risk of nuclear proliferation from the energy programme of the Democratic People's Republic of Korea (North Korea). Meanwhile, in May 2007 the EU and South Korea had commenced negotiations towards the adoption of a free trade agreement, and an agreement was initialled in October 2009. The deal, which provided for the elimination of almost all duties in the agricultural and industrial sectors, was signed formally at an EU-South Korea summit meeting, held in Brussels, Belgium, in October 2010. The agreement was approved by the European Parliament in February 2011, with the addition of a clause ensuring that new Korean legislation on carbon dioxide limits from cars would not damage the interests of European car-makers. The free trade agreement entered into force in July. Meanwhile, in June 2008 negotiations had commenced, aimed at updating the mutual framework agreement. In May 2010 the EU and South Korea signed a new framework agreement on bilateral relations. At the EU-South Korea summit meeting in October the EU and South Korea also agreed further to strengthen their relationship, by forming a Strategic Partnership, which provided for increased commitment to co-operation by both parties. a free trade agreement between the EU and South Korea came into force in July 2011, the first EU trade deal to be concluded with an Asian country.

In September 1999, for the first time, ministerial-level discussions took place between the EU and North Korea at the UN General Assembly. In May 2001 the EU announced that it was to establish diplomatic relations with North Korea to facilitate the Union's efforts in support of reconciliation in the Korean Peninsula and, in particular, in support of economic reform and the easing of the acute food and health problems in North Korea. However, the implementation of a Country Strategy Paper, adopted in March 2002, was suspended, and there no plan for its renewal. In October the EU expressed its deep concern after North Korea admitted that it had conducted a clandestine nuclear weapons programme, in serious breach of the country's international non-proliferation commitments. In the following month the EU stated that failure to resolve the nuclear issue would jeopardize the future development of bilateral relations. In response to North Korea's announcement in October 2006 that it had conducted a nuclear test, the EU strongly condemned the 'provocative' action and urged North Korea to abandon its nuclear programme. In April 2009 the EU strongly condemned North Korea for launching a rocket in contravention of relevant UN Security Council resolutions. In December 2010 the Council reinforced sanctions in place against a number of individuals and entities in North Korea. Sanctions were again strengthened in February 2013, in response to nuclear and ballistic missile tests in North Korea in December 2012 and February 2013, which had been carried out in violation of UN Security Council resolutions.

In June 1992 the EC signed trade and co-operation agreements with Mongolia and Macao, with respect for democracy and human rights forming the basis of envisaged co-operation. In April 2013 a PCA was signed with Mongolia. In November José Barroso visited Mongolia, the first time a President of the European Commission had visited the country. A co-operation accord with Viet Nam entered into force in June 1996, under which the EU agreed to increase quotas for Vietnamese textiles products, to support the country's efforts to join the WTO and to provide aid for environmental and public management projects. In October 2004 the EU and Viet Nam concluded a bilateral agreement on market access in preparation for Viet Nam's accession to the WTO, which took place in January 2007. In addition, an agreement signed in December 2004 lifted all EU quantitative restrictions for Vietnamese textiles. In June 2012 a PCA was signed; in the same month the EU and Viet Nam initiated negotiations on a bilateral free trade agreement. The conclusion of a PCA between the EU and Singapore was announced in June 2013. A bilateral free trade agreement between the EU and Singapore was initialled in September.

Non-preferential co-operation agreements were signed with Laos and Cambodia in April 1997. The agreement with Laos (which emphasized development assistance and economic co-operation) entered into force on 1 December; the agreement with Cambodia was postponed owing to adverse political developments in that country. The EU concluded a textiles agreement with Laos, which provisionally entered into force in December 1998; as a result of the agreement, exports of textiles to the EU from Laos increased significantly. The EU co-operation agreement with Cambodia entered into force in November 1999. EU-Cambodia relations were further enhanced with the opening of an EU delegation in Phnom Penh in early 2002 and a Cambodian embassy in Brussels in late 2004. In September 1999 the EU briefly imposed an arms embargo against Indonesia, which was at that time refusing to permit the deployment of an international peacekeeping force in East Timor (now Timor-Leste). In April 2005 the EU extended preferential trade conditions to Indonesia, which meant that the country would benefit from lower customs duties in certain sectors. From September of that year the EU, together with contributing countries from ASEAN, as well as Norway and Switzerland, deployed a monitoring mission in the Indonesian province of Aceh to supervise the implementation of a peace agreement between the Government of Indonesia and the separatist Gerakan Aceh Merdeka (Free Aceh Movement). Having achieved its aims, the mission was concluded in December 2006. In November 2009 an EU-Indonesia PCA was signed. The EU's long-term assistance strategy for Timor-Leste has focused on stabilization and dialogue, combating poverty, and humanitarian support. The EU country strategy for Timor-Leste during 2008–13 focused on strengthening rural development, with a view to achieving sustained poverty reduction and food security, and supporting the health sector and capacity building.

In October 1996 the EU imposed strict limits on entry visas for Myanma officials, because of Myanmar's refusal to allow the Commission to send a mission to the country to investigate allegations of forced labour. In March 1997 EU ministers responsible for foreign affairs agreed to revoke Myanmar's special trade privileges under the Generalized System of Preferences (GSP). The EU successively extended its ban on arms exports to Myanmar and its prohibition on the issuing of visas. In April 2003 a new 'Common Position' was adopted by the EU, which consolidated and extended the scope of existing sanctions against Myanmar and strengthened the arms embargo; EU sanctions were further extended in April 2004 in view of the military regime's failure to make any significant progress in normalizing the administration of the country and addressing the EU's concerns with regard to human rights. EU ministers responsible for foreign affairs agreed to Myanmar's participation in ASEM V in October at a level below head of government. Following the summit, however, the EU revised the Common Position, further broadening sanctions against Myanmar, as the military regime had failed to comply with certain demands, including the release from house arrest of the opposition leader Aung San Suu Kyi. The Common Position was renewed in April 2006, November 2007 and April 2009. In August an amended Common Position was adopted, extending sanctions to the Myanmar judiciary, following proceedings against Suu Kyi related to alleged violation of the terms of her house arrest. Restrictive measures against Myanmar were renewed in April 2010. Legislative elections in Myanmar in November of that year (which were followed by the release of Suu Kyi) were criticized by the EU and other international observers. However, a civilian Government took power, and a degree of reform was being undertaken. In April 2012 the EU agreed to suspend most of the sanctions in place against Myanmar, in recognition of the significant political changes in that country; an arms embargo remained in place. In September the European Commission adopted a proposal that Myanmar's special trade privileges under the GSP should be restored, owing to the positive political developments in that country; this took effect in July 2013. Meanwhile, in April 2013 EU ministers responsible for foreign affairs had agreed formally to remove all sanctions (with the exception of those relating to military issues) against Myanmar. A joint EU-Myanmar Task Force met in November, with the objective of providing political and economic support for the transition in Myanmar, by means of development aid and investment, parliamentary co-operation and support for the peace process.

In July 1991 the heads of government of Japan and of the EC signed a joint declaration on closer co-operation in both economic and political matters. The European office of the EU-Japan Industrial Co-operation Centre was opened in Brussels in June 1996; the Centre, which was established in 1987 as a joint venture between the Japanese Government and the European Commission, sought to increase industrial co-operation between the EU and Japan. In October 1996 the WTO upheld a long-standing complaint brought by the EU that Japanese taxes on alcoholic spirits discriminated against certain European products. In January 1998 an EU-Japan summit meeting was held, followed by a meeting at ministerial level in October. Subsequent summits have aimed to strengthen dialogue. In March 2013 the EU and Japan initiated negotiations on a free trade agreement.

Regular consultations are held with Australia at ministerial and senior official level. In January 1996 the Commission proposed a framework agreement to formalize the EU's trade and political relationship with that country. In September, however, after the Australian Government had objected to the human rights clause contained in all EU international agreements, negotiations were suspended. In June 1997 a joint declaration was signed, committing both sides to greater political, cultural and economic co-operation. The EU-Australia ministerial consultations convened in Melbourne, Australia, in April 2003, adopted a five-year Agenda for Co-operation. In October 2008 ministers responsible for foreign affairs from the EU and Australia, meeting in Paris, France, adopted a Partnership Framework, outlining future co-operation in the areas of foreign policy and security issues; trade; relations with Asia and the Pacific; environment; and science, technology and education. The Partnership Framework was updated at a meeting of ministers of foreign affairs held in Stockholm, Sweden, in October 2009. In March 1997 New Zealand took a case relating to import duties to the WTO, which later ruled against the EU. A joint declaration detailing areas of co-operation and establishing a consultative framework to facilitate the development of these was signed in May 1999. Mutual recognition agreements were also signed with Australia and New Zealand in 1999, with the aim of facilitating bilateral trade in industrial products. In March 2004 a European Commission Delegation was inaugurated in Wellington, New Zealand. In September 2007 a new joint declaration on relations and co-operation was adopted by the EU and New Zealand, replacing the 1999 joint declaration and 2004 action plan.

SOUTH ASIA

Bilateral non-preferential co-operation agreements were signed with Bangladesh, India, Pakistan and Sri Lanka between 1973 and 1976. A further agreement with India, extended to include co-operation in trade, industry, energy, science and finance, came into force in December 1981. A third agreement, which entered into effect in August 1994, included commitments to develop co-operation between the two sides and improve market access, as well as on the observance of human rights and democratic principles. The first EU-India summit meeting was held in Lisbon, Portugal, in June 2000. In November 2004 the EU and India signed a 'strategic partnership' agreement, which was expected significantly to improve their relationship; the agreement—described as a reflection of 'India's growing stature and influence'—meant that India became a special EU partner alongside the USA, Canada, the People's Republic of China and Russia. An EU-India summit meeting, held in New Delhi, India, in September 2005, adopted a joint action plan to implement the strategic partnership. It was agreed to establish a dialogue on security issues, disarmament and non-proliferation, to increase co-operation in efforts to combat terrorism, and to create a high-level trade group to examine ways of strengthening economic relations. An agreement on India's participation in the EU's Galileo civil satellite navigation and positioning system was also signed. The country strategy paper for 2007–13 allocated funds totalling some €470m. to India, focusing on the implementation of the joint action plan and the country's pursuit of the Millennium Development Goals agreed by UN member Governments in 2000, concentrating on health and education. An EU-India summit was held in Brussels, Belgium, in December 2010, and a joint declaration on international terrorism was adopted. The first India-EU Joint Working Group on Counter-Terrorism met in New Delhi in January 2012. An EU-India summit was held in New Delhi in February, at which participants welcomed the progress that had been made in ongoing negotiations towards the conclusion of an India-EU Broad-based Trade and Investment Agreement, under discussion since mid-2007.

A new accord with Sri Lanka, designed to promote co-operation in areas such as trade, investment and protection of the environment, entered into force in April 1995. In mid-August 2010 the EU temporarily withheld certain trade preferences for Sri Lanka, after an investigation confirmed that three UN conventions relating to human rights had failed to be implemented fully.

The EU has provided support for democracy and peace in Nepal, which formally abolished the monarchy in May 2008, following multi-party legislative elections. In January 2011 a bilateral Memorandum of Understanding on the Multi-Annual Indicative Programme for 2011–13 was signed. Co-operation focuses on three principal areas: education; stability and peacebuilding; and trade and strengthening of economic capacity building.

A new agreement with Pakistan on commercial and economic co-operation entered into force in May 1986; in May 1992 an agreement was signed on measures to stimulate private investment in Pakistan. A draft co-operation agreement was initialled with Pakistan in April 1998. However, following a military coup in Pakistan in October 1999, the agreement was suspended. Political dialogue with Pakistan recommenced on an ad hoc basis in November 2000, and the co-operation agreement was signed in November 2001; a joint statement was issued on the occasion, in which Pakistan reiterated its firm commitment to return to democratic government. The co-operation agreement with Pakistan entered into force in April 2004. The EU pledged assistance for Pakistan amounting to €398m. in 2007–13, compared with €125m. in development co-operation funding granted in 2002–06. In February 2008 the EU deployed an Election Observation Mission to Pakistan, to monitor the conduct of the general election. The first EU-Pakistan summit was held in June 2009, and a second EU-Pakistan summit was held in Brussels in June 2010. In March 2012 the EU and Pakistan endorsed a new, five-year EU-Pakistan engagement plan, which aimed to promote peace and stability in the region through increased engagement in a number of areas, principally political co-operation; security; governance and human rights; trade; and energy. The Council of the EU welcomed the legislative elections of May 2013, which represented the first transition of power between civilian Governments, after the completion of a full term of office, in Pakistan's history.

A new co-operation accord with Bangladesh (which replaced the 1976 commercial co-operation agreement) was signed in May 2000 and came into force in March 2001. In 2007–13, within the framework of a country strategy paper, assistance pledged to Bangladesh totalled €403m.

The EU pledged assistance for the reconstruction of Afghanistan following the removal of the Taliban regime in late 2001, and in 2002 announced development aid of €1,000m. for 2002–06, in addition to humanitarian aid. (By the end of 2006 the total of €1,000m. had been exceeded.) In March 2003 the European Commission hosted, along with the World Bank, the Afghanistan High Level Strategic Forum. The Government of Afghanistan convened the meeting to discuss with its principal partners, donors and multilateral organizations the progress and future vision for state-building in Afghanistan, as well as the long-term funding requirements for reconstruction. In 2004–05 the EU provided substantial support for the election process in Afghanistan, dispatching a Democracy and Election Support

Mission to assess the presidential election, which was held in October 2004, and a full Election Observation Mission to monitor legislative and provincial elections, which took place in September 2005. In November the EU and Afghanistan adopted a joint declaration on a new partnership aimed at promoting Afghanistan's political and economic development and strengthening EU-Afghan relations. Increased co-operation was envisaged in areas such as political and economic governance, judicial reform, counter-narcotics measures, and human rights, while the declaration also provided for a regular political dialogue, in the form of annual meetings at ministerial level. The EU welcomed the launch by the UN-sponsored London Conference on Afghanistan, held on 31 January–1 February 2006, of the Afghanistan Compact, representing a framework for co-operation between the Government of Afghanistan, the UN and the international community for a five-year period. The EU pledged €1,030m. in development assistance to Afghanistan during 2007–13. In May 2007 the Council adopted a Joint Action on an EU police mission to Afghanistan; EUPOL, comprising some 160 police officers, was officially launched on 15 June, and aimed to help develop a police force in Afghanistan that would work to respect human rights and operate within the framework of the rule of law, and to address the issue of police reform at central, regional and provincial levels. In May 2010 the Council extended EUPOL's mandate for a three-year period, terminating at the end of May 2013, and subsequently extended to the end of 2014. Assistance provided by the EU focused on the principal areas of concern identified in the National Development Strategy for Afghanistan, which was adopted by the Paris Declaration at a donors' conference held in France on 12 June 2008, and which included strengthening the judicial system; rural development, to combat narcotics production by promoting alternatives to poppy cultivation; and supporting the health sector. An EU Election Observation Mission was dispatched to monitor the presidential and provincial elections held in Afghanistan in August 2009. In October a Plan for Enhanced EU Engagement in Afghanistan and Pakistan was approved by EU ministers of foreign affairs. The Plan emphasized the need to strengthen sub-national governance, the police and the judiciary in Afghanistan; the importance of co-ordinated EU support for national programmes and the process of reintegration; and support for the electoral structure and the development of democratic institutions. In January 2014 the Council confirmed that the EU would continue its efforts to support civilian policing and justice in Afghanistan; a new strategy for engagement until 2016 was to be formulated.

THE USA AND CANADA

A framework agreement for commercial and economic co-operation between the European Community (EC) and Canada was signed in Ottawa in 1976. It was superseded in 1990 by a Declaration on EC-Canada Relations. In February 1996 the Commission proposed closer ties with Canada and an action plan including early warning to avoid trade disputes, elimination of trade barriers, and promotion of business contacts. An action plan and joint political declaration were signed in December.

Canadian and EU leaders meet regularly at bilateral summits. At the Ottawa summit meeting held in December 1996, a political declaration on EU-Canada relations was adopted, specifying areas for co-operation. At a summit held in Ottawa in March 2004, Canada and the EU adopted a Partnership Agenda to promote political and economic co-operation. In November 2005 Canada and the EU signed an agreement creating a framework for Canada's participation in the EU's crisis management operations. In October 2013 the EU and Canada reached political agreement on a Comprehensive Economic and Trade Agreement.

A number of specific agreements were concluded between the EC and the USA: a co-operation agreement on the peaceful use of atomic energy entered into force in 1959, and agreements on environmental matters and on fisheries came into force in 1974 and 1984, respectively. Additional agreements provide for co-operation in other fields of scientific research and development, while bilateral contacts take place in many areas not covered by a formal agreement. A Transatlantic Declaration on EC-US relations was concluded in November 1990: the two parties agreed to consult each other on important matters of common interest, and to increase formal contacts. A new Transatlantic Agenda for EU-US relations was signed by the US President and the Presidents of the European Commission and the European Council at a meeting in Madrid, Spain, in December 1995. In June 1997 the EU and the USA agreed to introduce a mutual recognition agreement, to enable goods (including medicines, pharmaceutical products, telecommunications equipment and electrical apparatus) undergoing tests in Europe to be marketed in the USA or Canada without the need for further testing. In May 1998, at an EU-US summit held in London, United Kingdom, a new Transatlantic Economic Partnership (TEP) was launched, to remove technical trade barriers, eliminate industrial tariffs, establish a free trade area in services, and further liberalize measures relating to government procurement, intellectual property and investment. (The agricultural and audiovisual sectors were excluded from the TEP.) In June 2005 an EU-US economic summit reached agreement on an initiative to enhance transatlantic economic integration and growth; the first informal EU-US economic ministerial meeting took place in Brussels, Belgium, in November. At an EU-US summit held in April 2007, in Washington, DC, USA, a new Framework for Advancing Transatlantic Economic Integration between the USA and the EU was adopted. A new Transatlantic Economic Council, a political body established to monitor and facilitate bilateral co-operation in order to promote economic integration, met for the first time in November. In November 2009, at an EU-US summit held in Washington, DC, the EU and the USA agreed to relaunch their High Level Consultative Group on Development and to hold annual ministerial meetings to increase co-operation on development policy, initially focused on three areas: food security and agricultural development; climate change; and the Millennium Development Goals. On the margins of the summit, the first meeting of a ministerial-level EU-US Energy Council, which had been launched in September, and aimed to strengthen transatlantic dialogue on energy matters, took place. At a summit meeting held in Washington, DC, in November 2011 the EU and the USA agreed to expand the work of the Transatlantic Economic Council, and to maintain and increase work on energy security and research in the EU-US Energy Council. In February 2012 the EU and the USA announced plans to launch negotiations, with the aim of concluding a new, bilateral trade agreement by 2015. In June 2013 the Council of the EU adopted directives for the negotiation of a Transatlantic Trade and Investment Partnership (TTIP) with the USA. Negotiations commenced in the following month.

Some member states criticized the USA's objections to the establishment of the International Criminal Court (which came into effect in The Hague, Netherlands, in 2003), while there was also criticism of the USA's strategy towards Iraq in early 2003 (see the Middle East and the Mediterranean), as the EU emphasized that only the UN Security Council could determine whether military action in Iraq was justified. The EU-US annual summit held in June, however, emphasized the need for transatlantic co-operation following the overthrow by a US-led coalition force of Saddam Hussain's regime in Iraq, stressing the need to unite against global terrorism and the proliferation of weapons of mass destruction. A visit to several European countries by the US Secretary of State, Condoleezza Rice, in December 2005 was overshadowed by allegations that the USA's Central Intelligence Agency (CIA) had used European airports to transport suspected Islamist militants to secret detention centres in Eastern Europe for interrogation in an illegal programme of so-called extraordinary rendition. Rice acknowledged the practice of rendition, but denied that prisoners were tortured and refused to comment on the alleged existence of CIA prisons in Eastern Europe. The final report of an inquiry by the European Parliament, published in February 2007, rejected extraordinary rendition as an illegal instrument and noted that secret detention facilities may have been located at US military bases in Europe; the Parliament deplored the acquiescence of some member states in illegal CIA operations and the failure of the EU Council of Ministers to co-operate with the inquiry.

Large US technology companies, notably the US internet search engine Google and the social media site Facebook, reportedly risked being adversely affected by a draft General Data Protection Regulation (which aimed to supersede the existing Data Protection Directive in protecting the use of individuals' personal information), proposed by the European Commission in January 2012. The Directive sought to extend EU data protection law to encompass any company located abroad that was involved in processing data pertaining to residents of EU member states; the fundamental principles of the Directive were approved by the Parliament in March 2014. Following revelations, in mid-2013, of large-scale intelligence-gathering programmes by the USA, in November the Commission presented a six-point action plan detailing measures required in order to restore trust in data flows between the EU and the USA, including the rapid adoption of revised data protection legislation; proposals to strengthen the bilateral, voluntary, EU-US 'safe harbor' agreement, reached in 2000, under which US companies pledge to protect the data privacy of EU customers; strengthening data protection safeguards; a commitment to the use of the existing EU-US Mutual Legal Assistance agreement (which entered into effect in 2010) and existing sectoral agreements to secure access to data from the EU; addressing European concerns as part of the ongoing review of surveillance procedures taking place within the USA; and the international promotion of standards pertaining to privacy.

AFRICAN, CARIBBEAN AND PACIFIC (ACP) COUNTRIES

In June 2000, meeting in Cotonou, Benin, heads of state and of government of the EU and African, Caribbean and Pacific (ACP) countries concluded a new 20-year partnership accord between the EU and ACP states. The EU-ACP Partnership Agreement, known as the Cotonou Agreement, entered into force on 1 April 2003 (although many of its provisions had been applicable for a transitional period since August 2000), following ratification by the then 15 EU member states and more than the requisite two-thirds of the ACP countries. Previously, the principal means of co-operation between the European Community (EC) and developing countries were the Lomé Conventions. The First Lomé Convention (Lomé I), which was concluded at Lomé, Togo, in February 1975 and came into force on 1 April 1976, replaced the Yaoundé Conventions and the Arusha Agreement. Lomé I was designed to provide a new framework of co-operation, taking into account the varying needs of developing ACP countries. The Second Lomé Convention entered into force on 1 January 1981 and the Third Lomé Convention on 1 March 1985 (trade provisions) and 1 May 1986 (aid). The Fourth Lomé Convention, which had a 10-year commitment period, was signed in December 1989: its trade provisions entered into force on 1 March 1990, and the remainder entered into force in September 1991.

The Cotonou Agreement was to cover a 20-year period from 2000 and was subject to revision every five years. A financial protocol was attached to the Agreement, which indicated the funds available to the ACP through the European Development Fund (EDF), the main instrument for Community aid for development co-operation in ACP countries. The ninth EDF, covering the initial five-year period from March 2000, provided a total budget of €13,500m., of which €1,300m. was allocated to regional co-operation and €2,200m. was for the new investment facility for the development of the private sector. In addition, uncommitted balances from previous EDFs amounted to a further €2,500m. The new Agreement envisaged a more participatory approach with more effective political co-operation to encourage good governance and democracy, increased flexibility in the provision of aid to reward performance, and a new framework for economic and trade co-operation. Its objectives were to alleviate poverty, contribute to sustainable development and integrate the ACP economies into the global economy. Negotiations to revise the Cotonou Agreement were concluded in February 2005. The political dimension of the Agreement was broadly strengthened and a reference to co-operation in counter-terrorism and the prevention of the proliferation of weapons of mass destruction was included. The revised Cotonou Agreement was signed on 24 June.

Under the provisions of the new accord, the EU was to finalize free trade arrangements (replacing the previous non-reciprocal trade preferences) with the most developed ACP countries during 2000–08, structured around six regional free trade zones, and be designed to ensure full compatibility with World Trade Organization (WTO) provisions. The agreements would be subject to revision every five years. The first general stage of negotiations for the Economic Partnership Agreements (EPAs), involving discussions with all ACP countries regarding common procedures, began in September 2002. The regional phase of EPA negotiations to establish a new framework for trade and investment commenced in October 2003. Negotiations had been scheduled for completion in mid-2007. However, the negotiation period was subsequently extended, and in 2014 negotiations were ongoing.

In March 2010 negotiations were concluded on the second revision of the Cotonou Agreement, which sought to take into account factors including the increasing importance of enhanced regional co-operation and a more inclusive partnership in ACP countries; the need for security; efforts to meet the Millennium Development Goals; the new trade relationship developed following the expiry of trade preferences at the end of 2007; and the need to ensure the effectiveness and coherence of international aid efforts. The second revised Cotonou Agreement was formally signed in Ouagadougou, Burkina Faso, in June 2010, and entered into effect, on a provisional basis, at the beginning of November.

Meanwhile, the EU had launched an initiative to allow free access to the products of the least developed ACP nations by 2005. Stabex and Sysmin, instruments under the Lomé Conventions designed to stabilize export prices for agricultural and mining commodities, respectively, were replaced by a system called FLEX, introduced in 2000, to compensate ACP countries for short-term fluctuations in export earnings. In February 2001 the EU agreed to phase out trade barriers on imports of everything but military weapons from the world's 48 least developed countries, 39 of which were in the ACP group. Duties on sugar, rice, bananas and some other products were maintained until 2009, and withdrawn from October of that year. In May 2001 the EU announced that it was to cancel all outstanding debts arising from its trade accords with former colonies of member states.

A major new programme set up on behalf of the ACP countries and financed by the EDF was Pro€Invest, which was launched in 2002, with funding of €110m. over a seven-year period. In October 2003 the Commission proposed the incorporation of the EDF into the EU budget (it had previously been a fund outside the EU budget, to which the EU member states made direct voluntary contributions). The cost-sharing formula for the member states would automatically apply, obviating the need for negotiations about contributions for the 10th EDF. The Commission proposal was endorsed by the European Parliament in April 2004. The 10th EDF was agreed in December 2005 by the European Council and provided funds of €22,682m. for 2008–13. The Multi-Annual Financial Framework adopted by the Council in December 2013 provided for overall funding of €26,984m. for the 11th EDF in 2014–20.

On 1 July 1993 the EC introduced a regime to allow the preferential import into the Community of bananas from former French and British colonies in the Caribbean. This was designed to protect the banana industries of ACP countries from the availability of cheaper bananas, produced by countries in Latin America. Latin American and later US producers brought a series of complaints before the WTO, claiming that the EU banana import regime was in contravention of free trade principles. The WTO upheld their complaints on each occasion leading to adjustments of the complex quota and tariffs systems in place. Following the WTO authorization of punitive US trade sanctions, in April 2001 the EU reached agreement with the USA and Ecuador on a new banana regime. Under the new accord, the EU was granted the so-called Cotonou waiver, which allowed it to maintain preferential access for ACP banana exports, in return for the adoption of a new tariff-only system for bananas from Latin American countries from 1 January 2006. The Latin American producers were guaranteed total market access under the agreement and were permitted to seek arbitration if dissatisfied with the EU's proposed tariff levels. Following the WTO rejection of EU proposals for tariff levels of €230 and €187 per metric ton (in comparison with existing rates of €75 for a quota of 2.2m. tons and €680 thereafter), in November 2005 the EU announced that a tariff of €176, with a duty-free quota of 775,000 tons for ACP producers, would be implemented on 1 January 2006. In late 2006 Ecuador initiated a challenge to the EU's proposals at the WTO. Twelve other countries subsequently initiated third-party challenges to the proposals at the WTO, in support of the challenge by Ecuador. In April 2008 the WTO upheld the challenge by Ecuador, and ordered the EU to align its tariffs with WTO regulations. In December 2009 representatives from the EU and Latin American countries initialled the Geneva Agreement on Trade in Bananas (GATB), which aimed to end the dispute. Under the Agreement, which made no provision for import quotas, the EU was gradually to reduce its import tariff on bananas from Latin American countries, from €176 per ton to €114 per ton by 2017. In March 2010 the EU also approved the implementation of Banana Accompanying Measures, which aimed to mobilize €190m. to support the 10 main ACP banana-exporting countries in adjusting to the anticipated increase in market competition from Latin America during 2010–13. (ACP countries would continue to benefit from duty- and quota-free access to EU markets.) For their part, Latin American banana-producing countries undertook not to demand further tariff reductions; and to withdraw several related cases against the EU that were pending at the WTO. In response to the Agreement, the US authorities determined to settle ongoing parallel complaints lodged with the WTO against the EU relating to bananas. On 8 November 2012, following the certification by the WTO of the reduced banana tariffs agreed under the GATB, the EU and the 10 main banana-producing countries (Brazil, Colombia, Costa Rica, Ecuador, Guatemala, Honduras, Mexico, Nicaragua, Panama, Peru and Venezuela) signed a Mutually Agreed Solution, ending eight pending banana dispute settlement proceedings at the WTO.

Following a WTO ruling at the request of Brazil, Australia and Thailand in 2005 that the EU's subsidized exports of sugar breached legal limits, reform of the EU's sugar regime was required by May 2006. Previously, the EU purchased fixed quotas of sugar from ACP producers at two or three times the world price, the same price that it paid to sugar growers in the EU. In November 2005 the EU agreed to reform the sugar industry through a phased reduction of its prices for white sugar of 36% by 2009 (which was still twice the market price in 2005).

In June 1995 negotiations opened with South Africa on a Trade, Development and Co-operation Agreement with the EU. The agreement was approved by heads of state and of government in March 1999, and provided for the removal of duties from about 99% of South Africa's industrial exports and some 75% of its agricultural products, and for the liberalization of the South African market for some 86% of EU industrial goods (with protection for the motor vehicle and textiles industries). The accord also introduced increased development assistance for South Africa. The agreement was signed in January 2002, and the liberalization measures had been fully implemented by 2012. Under the terms of the agreement, South Africa was allowed to export 42m. litres of wine per year duty-free to the EU, in exchange for abandoning the use of names such as 'sherry', 'port', 'ouzo' or 'grappa'. In March 1997 the Commission approved a Special Protocol for South Africa's accession to the Lomé Convention, and in April South Africa attained partial membership. Full membership was withheld, as South Africa was not regarded as, in all respects, a developing country. The EU and South Africa launched a strategic partnership in November 2006. In May 2007 the two sides agreed an Action Plan, which aimed to develop political dialogue and increase co-operation on a range of economic, social and other issues. The first EU-South Africa summit meeting was held in Bordeaux, France, in July 2008. Summits were held annually thereafter.

In May 2003 Timor-Leste joined the ACP and the ACP-EC Council of Ministers approved its accession to the ACP-EC Partnership Agreement. Cuba, which had been admitted to the ACP in December 2000, was granted observer status. Cuba withdrew its application to join the Cotonou Agreement in July 2003.

Article 96 of the Cotonou Agreement, which provides for suspension of the Agreement in specific countries in the event of violation of one of its essential elements (respect for human rights, democratic principles and the rule of law), was invoked against Haiti in 2001, and this was extended annually to December 2004. However, relations with Haiti began to be normalized from September of that year.

ACP-EU Institutions

The three institutions of the Cotonou Agreement are the Council of Ministers, the Committee of Ambassadors and the Joint Parliamentary Assembly.

Council of Ministers: comprises the members of the Council of the European Union and members of the EU Commission and a member of the Government of each ACP signatory to the Cotonou Agreement; meets annually.

Committee of Ambassadors: comprises the Permanent Representative of each member state to the EU and a representative of the EU Commission and the Head of Mission (ambassador) of each ACP state accredited to the EU; assists the Council of Ministers and meets regularly, in particular to prepare the session of the Council of Ministers.

Joint Parliamentary Assembly: internet www.europarl.europa.eu/intcoop/acp/10_01/default_en.htm; EU and ACP countries are equally represented; attended by parliamentary delegates from each of the ACP countries and an equal number of members of the European Parliament; two co-presidents are elected by the Assembly from each of the two groups; meets twice a year; 24 vice-presidents (12 EU and 12 ACP) are also elected by the Assembly and with the co-presidents constitute the Bureau of the Joint Parliamentary Assembly, which meets several times a year; Co-Pres LOUIS MICHEL, JOYCE LABOSO.

General Secretariat of the ACP-EU Council of Ministers: 175 rue de la Loi, 1048 Brussels, Belgium; tel. (2) 743-06-00; fax (2) 735-55-73; e-mail info@acp.int; internet www.acp.int; Sec.-Gen. Alhaji MUHAMMAD MUMUNI.

Centre for the Development of Enterprise (CDE): 2 ave Edmond Van Nieuwenhuyse, 1160 Brussels, Belgium; tel. (2) 679-18-11; fax (2) 675-26-03; e-mail info@cde.int; internet www.cde.int/index.aspx; f. 1977 to encourage and support the creation, expansion and restructuring of industrial companies (mainly in the fields of manufacturing and agro-industry) in the ACP states by promoting co-operation between ACP and European companies, in the form of financial, technical or commercial partnership, management contracts, licensing or franchise agreements, sub-contracts, etc.; manages the Pro€Invest programme; Dir PAUL FRIX (acting).

Technical Centre for Agricultural and Rural Co-operation (CTA): Agro Business Park 2, Postbus 380, 6700 AJ Wageningen, Netherlands; tel. (317) 467100; fax (317) 460067; e-mail cta@cta.int; internet www.cta.int; f. 1984 to improve the flow of information among agricultural and rural development stakeholders in ACP countries; Dir MICHAEL HAILU.

ACP Institutions

ACP Council of Ministers: composed of a member of Government for each ACP state or a government-designated representative; the principal decision-making body for the ACP group; meets twice annually; ministerial sectoral meetings are held regularly.

ACP Committee of Ambassadors: the second decision-making body of the ACP Group; it acts on behalf of the Council of Ministers between ministerial sessions and is composed of the ambassadors or one representative from every ACP State.

ACP Secretariat: ACP House, 451 ave Georges Henri, Brussels, Belgium; tel. (2) 743-06-00; fax (2) 735-55-73; e-mail info@acp.int; internet www.acp.int; Sec.-Gen. Alhaji MUHAMMAD MUMUNI (Ghana).

On 15 April 2005 27 ACP countries signed a charter creating the ACP Consultative Assembly, which formalized the existing inter-parliamentary co-operation between the ACP member states.

The ACP States

Angola
Antigua and Barbuda
Bahamas
Barbados
Belize
Benin
Botswana
Burkina Faso
Burundi
Cameroon
Cape Verde
Central African Republic
Chad
Comoros
Congo, Democratic Republic
Congo, Republic
Cook Islands
Côte d'Ivoire
Cuba
Djibouti
Dominica
Dominican Republic
Equatorial Guinea
Eritrea
Ethiopia
Fiji
Gabon
The Gambia
Ghana
Grenada
Guinea
Guinea-Bissau
Guyana
Haiti
Jamaica
Kenya
Kiribati
Lesotho
Liberia
Madagascar
Malawi
Mali
Marshall Islands
Mauritania
Mauritius
Federated States of Micronesia
Mozambique
Namibia
Nauru
Niger
Nigeria
Niue
Palau
Papua New Guinea
Rwanda
Saint Christopher and Nevis
Saint Lucia
Saint Vincent and the Grenadines
Samoa
São Tomé and Príncipe
Senegal
Seychelles
Sierra Leone
Solomon Islands
Somalia
South Africa
Sudan
Suriname
Swaziland
Tanzania
Timor-Leste
Togo
Tonga
Trinidad and Tobago
Tuvalu
Uganda
Vanuatu
Zambia
Zimbabwe

GENERALIZED PREFERENCES

In July 1971 the European Community (EC) introduced a generalized system of preferences (GSP) for tariffs in favour of developing countries, ensuring duty free entry to the EC of all manufactured and semi-manufactured industrial products, including textiles, but subject in certain circumstances to preferential limits. Preferences, usually in the form of a tariff reduction, are also offered on some agricultural products. In 1980 the Council agreed to the extension of the scheme for a second decade (1981–90); at the same time it adopted an operational framework for industrial products, giving individual preferential limits based on the degree of competitiveness of the developing country concerned. From the end of 1990 an interim scheme was in operation, pending the introduction of a revised scheme based on the outcome of the Uruguay Round of General Agreement on Tariffs and Trade (GATT) negotiations on international trade (which were finally concluded in December 1993). From 1977 the EC progressively liberalized GSP access for the least developed countries (LDCs) by according them duty free entry on all products and by exempting them from virtually all preferential limits. In 1992–93 the GSP was extended to Albania, the Baltic states, the Commonwealth of Independent States (CIS) and Georgia; in September 1994 it was extended to South Africa.

In December 1994 the European Council adopted a revised GSP to operate during 1995–98. It provided additional trade benefits to encourage the introduction by governments of environmentally sound policies and of internationally recognized labour standards. Conversely, a country's preferential entitlement could be withdrawn, for example, if it permitted forced labour. Under the new scheme, preferential tariffs amounted to 85% of the common customs duty for very sensitive products (for example, most textiles products), and 70% or 35% for products classified as sensitive (for example, chemicals and electrical goods). The common customs duty was suspended for non-sensitive products (for example, paper, books and cosmetics). In accordance with the EU's foreign policy objective of focusing on the development of the world's poorest countries, duties were eliminated in their entirety (with the exception of arms and ammunition) for 49 LDCs. Duties were also suspended for a further five Latin American countries, conditional on the implementation of campaigns against the production and trade of illegal drugs. The GSP for 1999–2001 largely extended the existing scheme unchanged. The next GSP regulation, for 2002–04 (subsequently extended until the end of 2005), was revised to expand product coverage and improve preferential margins. In May 2003 new regulations were adopted enabling certain countries to be exempted from the abolition of tariff preferences on export of their products to the EU if that sector was judged to be in crisis.

Under the GSP for 2006–08, the coverage of the general arrangement was extended to a further 300 products, mostly in the agriculture and fishery sectors, bringing the total number of products covered to some 7,200. The focus of the new regime was on developing countries most in need. Additional preferences were granted under a new GSP+ incentive scheme to particularly vulnerable countries pursuing good governance and sustainable development policies (judged by their ratification and implementation of relevant international conventions). Bolivia, Colombia, Costa Rica, Ecuador, El Salvador, Georgia, Guatemala, Honduras, Moldova, Mongolia, Nicaragua, Panama, Peru, Sri Lanka and Venezuela were declared eligible for GSP+, which took effect, exceptionally, on 1 July 2005, replacing the special arrangements to combat drugs production and trafficking in force under the previous GSP. Under the GSP for 2009–11, the GSP+ scheme was also retained, as was an initiative in support of the LDCs, Everything but Arms (EBA—introduced in 2001), which granted those countries duty- and quota-free access to EU markets.

In May 2011 the Commission agreed that the existing GSP should remain in place until the end of 2013, while a new GSP was agreed. At the end of October 2012 the EU adopted a revised GSP, which entered into effect on 1 January 2014. The new system targeted fewer countries (89, rather than the previous 111), focusing on the most needy; aimed to strengthen GSP+ and to increase the effectiveness of trade concessions for the LDCs through the EBA scheme; increased the system's transparency and stability; and was to be renewable every 10 years (with the exception of EBA, which did not require renewal). In December 2012 a number of products were identified as being no longer eligible for GSP support from 2014, as they had increased in competitiveness; the list of products was to be reviewed at the end of 2016 (Costa Rica and Ecuador, which qualified for GSP+ arrangements during that period, were to be exempt from the changes). In February 2013 the EU published procedural rules pertaining to applications for GSP+ under the revised GSP. In the same month, it was announced that GSP preferences for Azerbaijan and Iran were to be suspended from 23 February 2014, owing to their level of economic development; additional countries were to cease to benefit from the GSP from 1 January 2015.

AID TO DEVELOPING AND NON-EU COUNTRIES

The main channels for EU aid to developing countries are the Cotonou Agreement and the Mediterranean Financial Protocols, but technical and financial aid and assistance for refugees, training, trade promotion and co-operation in industry, energy, science and technology are also provided to about 30 countries in Asia and Latin America. The European Commission's Humanitarian Aid and Civil Protection Office (ECHO) was established in 1991, with a mandate to co-ordinate the provision of emergency humanitarian assistance and food aid. ECHO, which became fully operational in 1993 and is based in Brussels, Belgium, finances operations conducted by non-governmental organizations (NGOs) and international agencies, with which it works in partnership. Relations between ECHO and its partners are governed by Framework Partnership Agreements (FPAs), which define roles and responsibilities in the implementation of humanitarian operations financed by the EU. In December 2003 ECHO signed an FPA with the International Committee of the Red Cross, the International Federation of Red Cross and Red Crescent Societies, and the national Red Cross societies of the EU member states and Norway. A new FPA with NGOs entered into force on 1 January 2004; this agreement expired on 30 December 2007, and a revised FPA came into force on 1 January 2008. ECHO's relations with UN agencies are covered by a Financial and Administrative Framework Agreement signed in April 2003. ECHO aims to meet the immediate needs of victims of natural and man-made disasters worldwide, in such areas as assisting displaced persons, health, and mine-clearing programmes. In 2012 ECHO committed funds totalling €1,306m. to humanitarian assistance.

In December 2008 the European Council and European Parliament endorsed a new €1,000m. EU Food Facility, aimed at alleviating the global crisis in food security in 2009–11, by supporting agricultural sector programmes and projects in 23 developing countries. In March 2009 the European Commission made its first EU Food Facility financing decision, adopting a €314m. package of projects.

Allocations by ECHO towards sub-Saharan Africa in 2012 totalled €681m., and included €207m. to help populations in Chad, South Sudan and Sudan; €162m. for the Horn of Africa (Djibouti, Ethiopia, Kenya and Somalia); €188m. for the Sahel area of West Africa (Mali, Mauritania and Niger), Côte d'Ivoire, Liberia and Nigeria; and €124m. to help the population of Central and Southern Africa (Angola, the Central African Republic, the Republic of the Congo, the Democratic Republic of the Congo, Lesotho, Malawi, Madagascar and Zimbabwe).

In 2012 ECHO provided €265m. in humanitarian and food aid to support populations in the Middle East and the Mediterranean. This total comprised €156m. to those affected by the crisis in Syria; €42m. to the occupied Palestinian territories; €40m. to Yemen; €10m. to the Iraq crisis; €10m. to Western Sahara; and €7m. to Palestinian refugees in Jordan, Lebanon and Syria.

In 2012 funds totalling €132m. were allocated by ECHO to South Asia: €70m. to Pakistan; €30m. to Afghanistan; €19.3m. to Bangladesh; €7m. to India; €4.5m. to Sri Lanka; and €1m. to Nepal and Bhutan.

In 2012 funds totalling €56m. were allocated by ECHO to South-East and East Asia, of which €30.5m. was allocated to Burma, Myanmar and Thailand.

In 2012 €10m. was allocated to Central Asia, €30m. was allocated to Latin America, and €38m. was allocated to the Caribbean and the Pacific region, including €34m. to Haiti.

Finance

BUDGET

The EU budget, which funds EU policies and finances all the EU institutions, is limited by agreement of all the member states. The Commission puts forward spending proposals, which have to be approved by the European Parliament and the Council of the European Union. The Parliament signs the agreed budget into law. Revenue for the budget comes from customs duties, sugar levies, payments based on value-added tax (VAT) and contributions from the member states based on their gross national income (GNI). The Commission is accountable each year to the European Parliament for its use of EU funds. External audits are carried out by the European Court of Auditors. To combat fraud, the European Anti-Fraud Office (OLAF) was established in June 1999.

The general budget contains the expenditure of the main EU institutions, of which Commission expenditure (covering administrative costs and expenditure on operations) forms the largest proportion. Expenditure is divided into two categories: that necessarily resulting from the Treaties (compulsory expenditure) and other (non-compulsory) expenditure. The budgetary process is aided by the establishment of Financial Perspectives, which are spending plans covering a number of years, thus guaranteeing the security of long-term EU projects and activities. Although the Financial Perspective limits expenditure in each policy area for each of the years covered, a more detailed annual budget still has to be agreed each year. The Commission presents the preliminary draft annual budget in late April or early May of the preceding year and the adopted budget is published in February of the relevant year. If the budget has not been adopted by the beginning of the financial year, monthly expenditure may amount to one-12th of the appropriations adopted for the previous year's budget. The Commission may (even late in the year during which the budget is being executed) revise estimates of revenue and expenditure, by presenting supplementary and/or amending budgets. Expenditure under the general budget is financed by 'own resources', comprising agricultural duties (on imports of agricultural produce from non-member states), customs duties, application of VAT on goods and services, and (since 1988) a levy based on the GNI of member states. Member states are obliged to collect 'own resources' on the Community's behalf.

In May 2006 a new financial framework for the enlarged EU was formally adopted, when the European Parliament, the Council and the Commission signed an inter-institutional agreement on budgetary discipline and sound financial management, which entered into force at the beginning of January 2007. According to the agreement, which was amended in December, the average annual upper limit on payment appropriations for 2007–13 amounted to 1.03% of the GNI of the 27 member states. Meanwhile, in mid-December 2006 the Council adopted new financial regulations, which aimed to improve the management of EU expenditure; the regulations demanded the publication of a list of all those receiving EU funds. All provisions of the Financial Regulation and its Implementing Rules had entered into force by 1 May 2007.

In June 2011 the European Commission proposed increasing the transparency and fairness of the system for financing the EU budget by introducing a new financial transaction tax (FTT). In September the Commission presented a directive on the proposed FTT, which was to be levied on all transactions between financial institutions, provided that at least one of those institutions was located in the EU; it was proposed that the exchange of shares and bonds be taxed at a rate of 0.1%, and derivatives at a rate of 0.01%. Two-thirds of revenue from the FTT was to be directed to the EU budget, thereby reducing the GNI-based contributions of member states, while the remaining one-third would be retained by individual member states. In January 2013 11 member states (including France and Germany) agreed to adopt the new FTT; however, other member states, including the United Kingdom, were strongly opposed to the proposals.

The budget for 2013 was adopted in December 2012. In March 2013 the Commission proposed its first amendment to the 2013 budget, to take into account Croatia's anticipated accession on 1 July; Croatia's proposed national contribution to the EU budget was €211.9m., and an additional €22.4m. in customs duties collected by Croatia were expected to reach the EU budget in 2013.

After talks on the proposed Multi-Annual Financial Framework (MFF) for 2014–20 collapsed in November 2012, the Council reached agreement on the new, long-term EU budget in February 2013. In March, however, the European Parliament rejected the budget, demanding contributions from member states to cover arrears in payments, which had accumulated over the course of preceding budgets. Further negotiations subsequently took place, and new proposals for the MFF for 2014–20 were submitted for endorsement by the European Parliament and the Council in June 2013. The budget provided for a cut in EU expenditure for the first time, representing a reduction of 3.5% in spending commitments and 3.7% in payments, in comparison with the MFF for 2007–13. The Parliament approved the MFF in November, and it was adopted by the Council on 2 December. In mid-November the Council had also approved the agreement reached with the European Parliament for the EU's budget for 2014, which provided for the settlement of payments' arrears accumulated during the previous fiscal year.

FUNDING PROGRAMMES

In July 2006 the Council and the European Parliament adopted five new regulations that were to constitute the legal basis for the pursuit of cohesion objectives in 2007–13. A general regulation indicated common principles and standards for the implementation of three structural funds (principal instruments for financing EU-wide economic and social restructuring, addressing regional disparities and supporting regional development): the European Regional Development Fund (ERDF), the European Social Fund (ESF) and the Cohesion Fund. The regulation on the ERDF defined the scope of its interventions, among them the promotion of private and public investments assisting in the reduction of regional disparities across the EU. Funding priorities were identified as research, innovation, environmental protection and risk prevention. The regulation concerning the ESF determined that it should be implemented in accordance with European employment strategy in 2007–13, and that it should focus on increasing the flexibility of workers and enterprises, enhancing access to and participation in the labour market, reinforcing social inclusion and promoting partnership for reform in the areas of employment and inclusion. In view of its application to member states with a GNI of less than 90% of the Community average, the new regulation concerning the Cohesion Fund extended eligibility for its support to the new member states, in addition to Greece and Portugal. Spain was also to qualify for the Cohesion Fund, but on a transitional basis. A fifth regulation established a European Grouping of Territorial Co-operation, the aim of which was to facilitate cross-border and transnational/inter-regional co-operation between regional and local authorities.

In 2007–13 the ERDF, the ESF and the Cohesion Fund sought to contribute to three objectives: convergence (ERDF, ESF and the Cohesion Fund); regional competitiveness and employment (ERDF and ESF); and European territorial co-operation (ERDF). The convergence objective concerned 84 regions in 17 of the then 27 member states and, on a 'phasing-out' basis, a further 16 regions where per head gross domestic product was only slightly more than the threshold of 75% of the EU average. Indicative allocations for the convergence objective in 2007–13 (expressed in 2004 prices) were €251,100m. The regional competitiveness and employment objective was applicable to 168 regions in the member states, 13 of which were so-called 'phasing-in' regions, eligible for special financial allocations. Indicative allocations for the regional competitiveness and employment objective totalled €49,100m., including €10,400m. for the phasing-in regions. A total of €7,750m. was allocated to the European territorial co-operation objective in 2007–13. Four additional financial instruments were created in 2007: JASPER and JASMINE were developed to provide technical assistance, JEREMIE to improve access to finance for small and medium-sized businesses, and JESSICA to provide support for urban development.

In March 2012 the European Commission published proposals for the introduction of a Common Strategic Framework for the EU's funding programmes in 2014–20. The Common Strategic Framework, covering the ERDF, the ESF, the Cohesion Fund, as well as the European Agricultural Fund for Rural Development (EAFRD) and the European Maritime and Fisheries Fund (EMRF, hitherto the European Fisheries Fund—EFF), provides for the increased co-operation of the various funding programmes in contributing to the Europe 2020 strategy for growth and employment, as well as climate change, energy and social exclusion. The EU's budget for reformed Cohesion Policy in 2014–20 provided for total investment of some €351,800m. A common set of principles governing the European structural and investment funds sought to simplify accounting and administrative procedures, with increased use of 'e-cohesion'. In December 2013 the European Parliament and the Council adopted a directive on common provisions for the EU's funding programmes in 2014–20.

Cohesion Fund

The Treaty on European Union and its protocol on economic and social cohesion provided for the establishment of a Cohesion Fund, which began operating on 1 April 1993, with a mandate to subsidize projects in the fields of the environment and trans-European energy and communications networks in member states with a per head GNI of less than 90% of the Community average. The Fund's total budget for 2007–13 was €61,590m. In 2014–20 the Cohesion Fund was to provide funding of some €66,000m. The Cohesion Fund was to invest in all countries of the region in 2014–20, with the level of support and the national contribution adjusted according to the level of development: less developed regions were defined as those with levels of gross domestic product (GDP) amounting to less than 75% of the EU average; transition regions were those with GDP of between 75% and 90% of the EU average; and more developed regions had GDP of more than 90% of the EU average.

European Agricultural Fund for Rural Development—EAFRD

The EAFRD was created in September 2005 and came into operation at the beginning of 2007. It replaced the Guidance Section of the European Agricultural Guidance and Guarantee Fund (which previously financed the Common Agricultural Policy—CAP) and the rural development measures previously financed under the Guarantee section. It was made responsible for the single financial contribution under the CAP to rural development programmes. In 2014–20 the EAFRD was to contribute to the overall Europe 2020 strategy through the promotion of sustainable rural development, in line with other CAP instruments, cohesion policy and the Common Fisheries Policy.

European Agricultural Guarantee Fund—EAGF

The EAGF was created in September 2005 to replace the Guarantee Section of the European Agricultural Guidance and Guarantee Fund. It came into operation at the beginning of 2007 and was given responsibility for, inter alia, the provision of direct payments to farmers under the CAP, finance for the export of agricultural products to third countries, and intervention measures to regulate agricultural markets.

European Maritime and Fisheries Fund—EMFF

The EMFF, covering the period 2014–20, replaced the European Fisheries Fund, which was established in 1993 (having replaced the Financial Instrument for Fisheries Guidance, established in 1993). The EMFF aims to grant financial support to facilitate the implementation of the Common Fisheries Policy.

European Regional Development Fund—ERDF

Payments began in 1975. The Fund is intended to compensate for the unequal rate of development in different EU regions. It finances investment leading to the creation or maintenance of jobs, improvements in infrastructure, local development initiatives and the business activities of small and medium-sized enterprises (SMEs) in 'least favoured regions'. In 2014–20 investment totalling some €100,000m. was to focus on four principal areas: innovation and research; the digital agenda; support for SMEs; and the introduction of a low-carbon economy.

European Social Fund—ESF

The Fund (established in 1960) provides resources with the aim of combating long-term unemployment and facilitating the integration into the labour market of young people and the socially disadvantaged. It also supports schemes to help workers to adapt to industrial changes. In 2014–20 the ESF was to help support employment, for example through the provision of funds for training, education and social inclusion (a minimum of €70,000m. of ESF funding was to be used in support of these objectives). A new, linked Youth Employment Initiative was to be worth at least €6,000m. during the same period.

European Union Solidarity Fund—EUSF

The EUSF was established in 2002 to support disaster response activities in member states. In July 2013 the European Commission published proposals to simplify and accelerate access to funds under the EUSF.

BUDGET EXPENDITURE: COMMITMENT APPROPRIATIONS
(€ million)

	2013	2014
Smart and inclusive growth	69,246.6	62,788.7
Sustainable growth: natural resources	57,848.8	56,532.5
Security and citizenship	1,894.2	1,668.0
Global Europe	6,811.0	6,251.3
Administration	8,417.8	8,596.7
Compensation	75.0	28.6
Outside the Multi-annual Financial Framework	157.6	200.0
Total	144,450.8	136,065.8

Source: European Union, eur-lex.europa.eu.

REVENUE
(€ million)

Source of revenue	2013	2014
Customs duties and sugar levies	18,777.6	18,211.5
VAT-based resource	15,063.9	17,882.2
Gross National Income-based resource	107,713.1	98,418.7
Other revenue	2,896.2	1,553.4
Total	144,450.8	136,065.8

Source: European Union, eur-lex.europa.eu.

NATIONAL CONTRIBUTION TO THE EU BUDGET

Country	Contribution for 2014 (€ million)	% of total
Austria	2,887.7	2.5
Belgium	3,679.3	3.2
Bulgaria	391.5	0.3
Croatia	414.7	0.4
Cyprus	146.2	0.1
Czech Republic	1,329.1	1.1
Denmark	2,406.5	2.1
Estonia	172.7	0.2
Finland	1,935.0	1.7
France	20,080.5	17.3
Germany	24,776.2	21.3
Greece	1,637.3	1.4
Hungary	899.9	0.8
Ireland	1,297.2	1.1
Italy	14,708.0	12.7
Latvia	223.0	0.2
Lithuania	323.2	0.3
Luxembourg	322.2	0.3
Malta	64.4	0.1
Netherlands	5,444.8	4.7
Poland	3,709.2	3.2
Portugal	1,517.4	1.3
Romania	1,362.3	1.2
Slovakia	682.0	0.6
Slovenia	330.4	0.3
Spain	9,729.2	8.4
Sweden	3,965.9	3.4
United Kingdom	11,865.0	10.2
Total	116,300.9	100.0

Source: European Union, eur-lex.europa.eu.

FRANC ZONE

Address: c/o Direction de la Communication (Service de Presse), Banque de France, 48 rue Croix-des-Petits-Champs, 75049, Paris Cedex 01, France.

Telephone: 1-42-92-39-08; **fax:** 1-42-92-39-40; **e-mail:** infos@banque-france.fr; **internet:** www.banque-france.fr/en/eurosystem-international/franc-zone-and-development-financing.html.

MEMBERS

Benin	Equatorial Guinea
Burkina Faso	France
Cameroon	Gabon
Central African Republic	Guinea-Bissau
Chad	Mali
Comoros	Niger
Republic of the Congo	Senegal
Côte d'Ivoire	Togo

Prior to 1 January 2002, when the transition to a single European currency (euro) was finalized (see below), the Franc Zone also included Metropolitan France, the French Overseas Departments (French Guiana, Guadeloupe, Martinique and Réunion), the French Overseas Collectivité Départementale (Mayotte) and the French Overseas Collectivité Territoriale (St Pierre and Miquelon). The French Overseas Territory (French Polynesia) and the French Overseas Countries (New Caledonia and the Wallis and Futuna Islands) are not members of the Franc Zone, but have continued to use the franc CFP (franc des Comptoirs français du Pacifique, 'French Pacific franc': 1 franc CFP = €0.00839), which is issued by the Institut d'émission d'outre-mer, based in Paris, France.

Apart from Guinea and Mauritania (see below), all of the countries that formerly comprised French West and Equatorial Africa are members of the Franc Zone. The former West and Equatorial African territories are still grouped within the two currency areas that existed before independence, each group having its own variant on the CFA, issued by a central bank: the franc de la Communauté Financière d'Afrique ('franc CFA de l'Ouest'), issued by the Banque Centrale des Etats de l'Afrique de l'ouest—BCEAO, and the franc Coopération financière en Afrique centrale ('franc CFA central'), issued by the Banque des Etats de l'Afrique Centrale—BEAC.

The following states withdrew from the Franc Zone during the period 1958–73: Guinea, Tunisia, Morocco, Algeria, Mauritania and Madagascar. Equatorial Guinea, formerly a Spanish territory, joined the Franc Zone in January 1985, and Guinea-Bissau, a former Portuguese territory, joined in May 1997.

The Comoros, formerly a French Overseas Territory, did not join the Franc Zone following its unilateral declaration of independence in 1975. However, the franc CFA was used as the currency of the new state and the Institut d'émission des Comores continued to function as a Franc Zone organization. In 1976 the Comoros formally assumed membership. In July 1981 the Banque Centrale des Comores replaced the Institut d'Emission des Comores, establishing its own currency, the Comoros franc.

The Franc Zone operates on the basis of agreements concluded between France and each group of member countries, and the Comoros. The currencies in the Franc Zone were formerly linked with the French franc at a fixed rate of exchange. However, following the introduction of the euro (European single currency) in January 1999, the Franc Zone currencies were effectively linked at fixed parity to the euro (i.e. parity was based on the fixed conversion rate for the French franc and the euro). From 1 January 2002, when European economic and monetary union was finalized and the French franc withdrawn from circulation, the franc CFA, Comoros franc, and also the franc CFP, became officially pegged to the euro, at a fixed rate of exchange. All the convertability arrangements previously concluded between France and the Franc Zone remained in force. Therefore, Franc Zone currencies are freely convertible into euros, at the fixed exchange rate, guaranteed by the French Treasury. Each group of member countries, and the Comoros, has its own central issuing bank, with overdraft facilities provided by the French Treasury. Monetary reserves are held mainly in the form of euros. The BCEAO and the BEAC are authorized to hold up to 35% of their foreign exchange holdings in currencies other than the euro. Franc Zone ministers of finance normally meet twice a year to review economic and monetary co-operation.

In September 2000 Franc Zone ministers responsible for finance and central bank governors established the Liaison Committee on Money Laundering in the Franc Zone. The Committee provides a forum for dialogue and exchange of information related to combating money laundering and terrorist financing in the Zone; offers technical support to ensure that local regulations are updated to meet standards set by the Financial Action Task Force on Money Laundering; and raises awareness and conducts training activities for officials in the financial sector, judiciary and police forces in member countries. The Franc Zone was admitted in June 2012 as an observer to the Financial Action Task Force on Money Laundering. Until January of that year the presidency of the Liaison Committee was held by Banque de France; since then it has rotated on an annual basis between the BCEAO, the Banque Centrale des Comores, and BEAC. The Committee meets at least twice a year, and reports on an annual basis to the Franc Zone ministers of finance and central bank governors.

In February 2000 the Union Economique et Monétaire Ouest-Africaine (UEMOA) and the Economic Community of West African States (ECOWAS) adopted an action plan for the creation of a single West African Monetary Zone and consequent replacement of the franc Communauté financière africaine by a single West African currency.

The Banque de France's Franc Zone and Development Financing Studies Division acts as the secretariat for six-monthly meetings of Franc Zone ministers of finance; conducts studies on Franc Zone economies; and produces, in conjunction with the BCEAO, the BEAC and the Banque Centrale des Comores, the *Rapport Annuel de la Zone Franc*. The 2012 report recorded sound overall economic growth of 5.8% was across the Zone during that year, and found that the member countries had benefited from continued high commodity prices, particularly for oil, from buoyant internal demand, and from strong inwards investment. Much improved economic growth—of 6.4% in 2012, compared with 0.9% in the previous year—was recorded in the UEMOA area, with the strong progress attributed to ongoing rapid economic recovery in Côte d'Ivoire, the expansion of investment in several member states, and the strong performance of the agricultural sector. Meanwhile, growth of 5.2% was recorded in the Communauté Economique et Monétaire de l'Afrique Centrale (CEMAC) region in that year, consolidating growth of 5.1% achieved in 2011. Owing to increased taxation revenue, the fiscal deficit contracted in the UEMOA area in 2012; a significant increase in investment expenditure, meanwhile, caused the emergence of a deficit in CEMAC in that year; it was reported that the Zone central banks had, in response, pursued accommodative monetary policies. In October 2013 Franc Zone ministers of finance, central bank governors and presidents of regional institutions, gathered in Paris, launched a joint initiative, developed jointly with the World Bank, which aimed to support member countries of the Zone in strengthening the capabilities of public–private partnerships (PPPs) to develop the regional infrastructure. The next Franc Zone ministerial meeting was held in April 2014, in Malabo, Equatorial Guinea.

Currencies of the Franc Zone

1 franc CFA = €0.00152. CFA stands for Communauté financière africaine in the West African area and for Coopération financière en Afrique centrale in the Central African area. Used in the monetary areas of West and Central Africa, respectively.

1 Comoros franc = €0.00201. Used in the Comoros, where it replaced the franc CFA in 1981.

Central Issuing Banks

Banque Centrale des Comores: place de France, BP 405, Moroni, Comoros; tel. (773) 1814; fax (773) 0349; e-mail secretariat@banque-comores.org; internet www.banque-comores.km; f. 1981; Gov. Mzé Aboudou Mohamed Chanfiou.

Banque des Etats de l'Afrique Centrale (BEAC): 736 ave Mgr François Xavier Vogt, BP 1917, Yaoundé, Cameroon; tel. 223-40-30; fax 223-33-29; e-mail beac@beac.int; internet www.beac.int; f. 1973 as the central bank of issue of Cameroon, the Central African Republic, Chad, Republic of the Congo, Equatorial Guinea and Gabon; a monetary market, incorporating all national financial institutions of the BEAC countries, came into effect on 1 July 1994; Gov. Lucas Abaga Nchama (Equatorial Guinea); Sec.-Gen. Daniel Ngassiki; publs *Rapport Annuel*, *Etudes et statistiques* (monthly).

Banque Centrale des Etats de l'Afrique de l'Ouest (BCEAO): ave Abdoulaye Fadiga, BP 3108, Dakar, Senegal; tel. 839-05-00; fax 823-93-35; e-mail webmaster@bceao.int; internet www.bceao.int; f. 1962; central bank of issue for the mems of UEMOA; mems: Benin, Burkina Faso, Côte d'Ivoire, Guinea-Bissau, Mali, Niger, Senegal and Togo; Gov. Tiémoko Meyliet Kone (Côte d'Ivoire); Sec.-Gen. Fatimatou Zahra Diop; publs *Annual Report*, *Notes d'Information et Statistiques* (monthly), *Annuaire des banques*, *Bilan des banques et établissements financiers* (annually).

Other Franc Zone Institutions

Banque Ouest-Africaine de Développement (BOAD): 68 ave de la Libération, BP 1172, Lomé, Togo; tel. 221-42-44; fax 221-52-67; e-mail boadsiege@boad.org; internet www.boad.org; f. 1973 to promote the balanced development of mem. states and the economic integration of West Africa; a Guarantee Fund for Private Investment in West Africa, established jtly by BOAD and the European Investment Bank in Dec. 1994, aims to guarantee medium- and long-term credits to private sector businesses in the region; in April 2012, jointly with CDC Climat and Proparco (see Agence Française de Développement), BOAD launched the Fonds Carbone pour l'Afrique (FCA), aimed at financing a green economy in West Africa; auth. cap. 1,050,000m. francs CFA; mems: Benin, Burkina Faso, Côte d'Ivoire, Guinea-Bissau, Mali, Niger, Senegal, Togo; Pres. Christian Adovelande (Benin); publs *Rapport Annuel*, *BOAD en Bref* (quarterly).

Bourse Régionale des Valeurs Mobilières (BRVM): 18 rue Joseph Anoma, BP 3802, Abidjan 01, Côte d'Ivoire; tel. 20-32-66-85; fax 20-32-66-84; e-mail brvm@brvm.org; internet www.brvm.org; f. 1998; regional electronic stock exchange; Chair. Gabriel Fal; Gen. Man. Edoh Kossi Amenounve.

Banque de Développement des Etats de l'Afrique Centrale (BDEAC): place du Gouvernement, BP 1177, Brazzaville, Republic of the Congo; tel. 281-18-85; fax 281-18-80; e-mail bdeac@bdeac.org; internet www.bdeac.org; f. 1975; auth. cap. 250,000m. francs CFA (BDEAC's auth. cap. was increased by 100% in 2010); shareholders: Cameroon, Central African Republic, Chad, Republic of the Congo, Gabon, Equatorial Guinea, the AfDB, BEAC, France, Germany and Kuwait; Pres. Michaël Adandé.

Communauté Economique et Monétaire de l'Afrique Centrale (CEMAC): BP 969, Bangui, Central African Republic; tel. and fax 21-61-47-81; fax 21-61-21-35; e-mail secemac@cemac.int; internet www.cemac.int; f. 1998; formally inaugurated as the successor to the Union Douanière et Economique de l'Afrique Centrale (UDEAC, f. 1966) at a meeting of heads of state held in Malabo, Equatorial Guinea, in June 1999; aims to promote the process of sub-regional integration within the framework of an economic union and a monetary union; CEMAC was also to comprise a parliament and sub-regional tribunal; UDEAC established a common external tariff for imports from other countries and administered a common code for investment policy and a Solidarity Fund to counteract regional disparities of wealth and economic development; mems: Cameroon, Central African Republic, Chad, Republic of the Congo, Equatorial Guinea, Gabon; Pres. Pierre Moussa.

Union Economique et Monétaire Ouest-Africaine (UEMOA): BP 543, Ouagadougou 01, Burkina Faso; tel. 31-88-73; fax 31-88-72; e-mail commission@uemoa.int; internet www.uemoa.int; f. 1994; promotes regional monetary and economic convergence, and envisages the eventual creation of a sub-regional common market. A preferential tariff scheme, eliminating duties on most local products and reducing by 30% import duties on many Union-produced industrial goods, became operational on 1 July 1996; in addition, from 1 July, a community solidarity levy of 0.5% (increased to 1% in December 1999) was imposed on all goods from third countries sold within the Union, in order to strengthen UEMOA's capacity to promote economic integration. In June 1997 UEMOA heads of state and government agreed to reduce import duties on industrial products originating in the Union by a further 30%. An inter-parliamentary committee, recognized as the predecessor of a UEMOA legislature, was inaugurated in Mali in March 1998. In September Côte d'Ivoire's stock exchange was transformed into the Bourse regionale des valeurs mobilières, a regional stock exchange serving the Union, in order to further economic integration. On 1 January 2000 internal tariffs were eliminated on all local products (including industrial goods) and a joint external tariff system, in five bands of between 0% and 20%, was imposed on goods deriving from outside the new customs union. Guinea-Bissau was excluded from the arrangement owing to its unstable political situation. The UEMOA member countries also belong to ECOWAS and, in accordance with a decision taken in April 2000, aim to harmonize UEMOA's economic programme with that of a planned second West African monetary union (the West African Monetary Zone—WAMZ), to be established by the remaining—mainly anglophone—ECOWAS member states by January 2015 (as currently scheduled). A merger of the two complementary monetary unions, and the replacement of the franc Communauté financière africaine by a new single West African currency (the 'eco', initially to be adopted by the WAMZ), is eventually envisaged. In January 2003 member states adopted a treaty on the establishment of a UEMOA parliament. In March 2013 ECOWAS ministers of finance endorsed a new region-wide 1.5% community integration levy; it was envisaged that this would eventually replace both the existing UEMOA community solidarity levy and ECOWAS community levy. In January of that year a new West African Capital Markets Integration Council (WACMIC) was inaugurated, to govern the integration of regional capital markets. During 2012–16 UEMOA was implementing a 5,763m.-franc CFA regional economic programme aimed at developing regional infrastructures. UEMOA adopted in March 2009 a Regional Initiative for Sustainable Energy, aiming to meet all regional electricity needs by 2030. A subsidiary mortgage refinancing institution (Caisse Régionale de Refinancement Hypothécaire de l'UEMOA—CRRH-UEMOA) was established in July 2010. A UEMOA Court of Justice, based in Ouagadougou, arbitrates disputes between member states, and between the Union and other bodies. The 17th summit of UEMOA heads of state and government was held in Dakar, Senegal, in Oct. 2013. Mems: Benin, Burkina Faso, Côte d'Ivoire, Guinea-Bissau, Mali, Niger, Senegal and Togo; Pres. CHEIKHE HADJIBOU SOUMARÉ (Senegal).

At a summit meeting in December 1981 leaders of the former UDEAC agreed in principle to establish an economic community of Central African member states: the Communauté Economique des Etats de l'Afrique Centrale—CEEAC began operations in 1985, and includes the members of CEMAC, and also Burundi, Rwanda, São Tomé and Príncipe and the Democratic Republic of the Congo.

French Economic Aid

France's connection with the African Franc Zone countries involves not only monetary arrangements, but also includes comprehensive French assistance in the forms of budget support, foreign aid, technical assistance and subsidies on commodity exports.

Official French financial aid and technical assistance to developing countries is administered by the following agencies:

Agence Française de Développement (AFD): 5 rue Roland Barthes, 75598 Paris Cedex 12, France; tel. 1-53-44-31-31; fax 1-44-87-99-39; e-mail com@afd.fr; internet www.afd.fr; f. 1941; fmrly the Caisse Française de Développement—CFD; French development bank that lends money to member states and former member states of the Franc Zone and several other states, and executes the financial operations of the FSP (see below). Following the devaluation of the franc CFA in January 1994, the French Government cancelled some FFr 25,000m. in debt arrears owed by member states to the CFD. The CFD established a Special Fund for Development and the Exceptional Facility for Short-term Financing to help to alleviate the immediate difficulties resulting from the devaluation. Serves as the secretariat for the Fonds français pour l'environnement mondial (f. 1994). Has, together with private shareholders, an interest in the development investment company PROPARCO (f. 1977). Since 2000 the AFD has been implementing France's support of the World Bank's HIPC initiative; Dir-Gen. ANNE PAUGAM.

Fonds de Solidarité Prioritaire (FSP): c/o Ministry of Foreign and European Affairs, 37 quai d'Orsay, 75351 Paris, France; tel. 1-43-17-53-53; fax 1-43-17-52-03; internet www.diplomatie.gouv.fr; f. 2000, taking over from the Fonds d'aide et de coopération (f. 1959) the administration of subsidies from the French Government to 54 countries of the Zone de solidarité prioritaire; FSP is administered by the French Ministry of Foreign and European Affairs, which allocates budgetary funds to it.

Publications

La Lettre de la Zone Franc (newsletter—issued periodically).

Rapport Annuel de la Zone Franc.

INTER-AMERICAN DEVELOPMENT BANK—IDB

Address: 1300 New York Ave, NW, Washington, DC 20577, USA.

Telephone: (202) 623-1000; **fax:** (202) 623-3096; **e-mail:** pic@iadb.org; **internet:** www.iadb.org.

The Bank was founded in 1959 to promote the individual and collective development of Latin American and Caribbean countries through the financing of economic and social development projects and the provision of technical assistance. From 1976 membership was extended to include countries outside the region.

MEMBERS

Argentina	Ecuador	Nicaragua
Austria	El Salvador	Norway
Bahamas	Finland	Panama
Barbados	France	Paraguay
Belgium	Germany	Peru
Belize	Guatemala	Portugal
Bolivia	Guyana	Slovenia
Brazil	Haiti	Spain
Canada	Honduras	Suriname
Chile	Israel	Sweden
China, People's Rep.	Italy	Switzerland
Colombia	Jamaica	Trinidad and Tobago
Costa Rica	Japan	United Kingdom
Croatia	Republic of Korea	USA
Denmark	Mexico	Uruguay
Dominican Republic	Netherlands	Venezuela

Organization

(April 2014)

BOARD OF GOVERNORS

All the powers of the Bank are vested in a Board of Governors, consisting of one Governor and one alternate appointed by each member country (usually ministers responsible for finance or presidents of central banks). The Board meets annually, with special meetings when necessary. The 55th annual meeting was convened in Costa do Sauípe, Bahía, Brazil, in March 2014.

BOARD OF EXECUTIVE DIRECTORS

The Board of Executive Directors is responsible for the operations of the Bank. It establishes the Bank's policies, approves loan and technical co-operation proposals that are submitted by the President of the Bank, and authorizes the Bank's borrowings on capital markets.

There are 14 Executive Directors and 14 alternates. Each Director is elected by a group of two or more countries, except the Directors representing Canada and the USA. The USA holds 30% of votes on the Board, in respect of its contribution to the Bank's capital. The Board has five permanent committees, relating to Policy and evaluation; Organization, human resources and board matters; Budget, financial policies and audit; Programming; and a Steering Committee.

ADMINISTRATION

In December 2006 the Board of Executive Directors approved a new structure which aimed to strengthen the Bank's country focus and improve its operational efficiency. Three new positions of Vice-Presidents were created. Accordingly the executive structure comprises the President, Executive Vice-President and Vice-Presidents for Countries (with responsibility for four regional departments); Sectors and Knowledge; Private Sector and Non-sovereign Guaranteed Operations; and Finance and Administration. The principal Offices are of the Auditor-General, Outreach and Partnerships, External Relations, Risk Management, and Strategic Planning and Development Effectiveness. An Independent Consultation and Investigation Mechanism, to monitor compliance with the Bank's environmental and social policies, was established in February 2010. The Bank has country offices in each of its borrowing member states, and special offices in Tokyo, Japan (covering Japan, the People's Republic of China and Republic of Korea), and in Madrid, Spain (covering Europe). There are some 1,800 Bank staff (excluding the Board of Executive Directors and the Evaluation Office), of whom almost 30% are based in country offices. The total Bank group administrative expenses for 2013 amounted to US $837m.

President: LUIS ALBERTO MORENO (Colombia).

Executive Vice-President: JULIE T. KATZMAN (USA).

Activities

Loans are made to governments and to public and private entities for specific economic and social development projects and for sectoral reforms. These loans are repayable in the currencies lent and their terms range from 12 to 40 years. Total lending authorized by the Bank amounted to US $230,414m. by the end of 2013. During 2013 the Bank approved loans and guarantees amounting to $13,811m., of which Ordinary Capital loans totalled $13,290m. (compared with a total of $10,799m. in 2012). Disbursements on Ordinary Capital loans amounted to $10,558m. in 2013, compared with $6,882m. in the previous year. Some 168 projects were approved in 2013, of which 148 were investment projects. In October 2008 the Bank announced measures to help to counter the effects on the region of the downturn in the world's major economies and the restrictions on the availability of credit. It resolved to accelerate lending and establish an emergency liquidity facility, with funds of up to $6,000m., in order to sustain regional economic growth and to support social welfare programmes.

In March 2009 the Board of Governors agreed to initiate a capital review, in recognition of unprecedented demand for Bank resources owing to the sharp contraction of international capital markets. An agreement to increase the Bank's authorized capital by US $70,000m. was concluded in March 2010 and endorsed, as the Ninth General Capital Increase (IDB-9), by the Board of Governors in July. Of the total increase, $1,700m. was expected to be paid in by member countries over a five-year period. Under IDB-9, the Bank is mandated to focus by 2015 some 35% of total lending on small and vulnerable countries, and to target lending at the following sectors: Social Policy for Productivity; Global and Regional Integration; Institutions for Growth and Productivity; and Climate Change and Sustainable Energy. In January 2012 member states approved the resolution authorizing IDB-9, and it entered into effect in the following month. At the end of 2013 the subscribed Ordinary Capital stock, including inter-regional capital, which was merged into it in 1987, totalled $128,781m., of which $4,941m. was paid-in and $123,840m. was callable. The callable capital constitutes, in effect, a guarantee of the securities that the Bank issues in the capital markets in order to increase its resources available for lending.

In 2013 operating income amounted to US $881m. At the end of 2013 total borrowings outstanding amounted to $67,460m., compared with $59,754m. at the end of the previous year.

The Fund for Special Operations (FSO) enables the Bank to make concessional loans for economic and social projects where circumstances call for special treatment, such as lower interest rates and longer repayment terms than those applied to loans from the ordinary resources. Assistance may be provided to countries adversely affected by economic crises or natural disasters through a new Development Sustainability Contingent Credit Line (DSL), which was approved by the Board of Directors in September 2012 to replace the previous emergency lending facility. The DSL is capped at a maximum of US $300m. per country, or 2% of a country's gross domestic product (if less), and was developed to provide an efficient response to the types of crisis that may impact the region. In 2013 22 policy-based loans, totalling $4,000m., and one project, were approved under the DSL. In March 2007 the Board of Governors approved a reform of the Bank's concessional lending (at the same time as endorsing arrangements for participation in the Multilateral Debt Relief Initiative, see below), and resolved that FSO lending may be 'blended' with Ordinary Capital loans by means of a parallel lending mechanism. At 31 December 2013 cumulative FSO lending amounted to $19,622m., and in 2013 FSO lending totalled $251m. The terms and conditions of IDB-9, approved by the Board of Governors in July 2010, incorporated a commitment to replenish FSO resources by $479m.

On 1 January 2012 a new Flexible Financing Facility (FFF) entered into effect, which was, thereafter, to be the only financial product platform for approval of all new Ordinary Capital sovereign guaranteed loans.

In June 2007 a new IDB Grant Facility (GRF) was established, funded by transfers from the FSO, to make available resources for specific projects or countries in specific circumstances. By the end of 2013 resources had only been granted to support reconstruction and development in Haiti. In accordance with IDB-9 the Board of Governors may approve transfers of US $200m. from Ordinary Capital to the GRF annually during 2011–20. Consequently, such transfers were approved by the Board of Governors in March 2011, March 2012, and March 2013. During 2013 the Bank approved grants to Haiti from the GRF totalling $188m. In May 2011 the Board of Governors approved a new Small and Medium-sized Enterprises (SME) Financing Facility, with funds of up to $100m. in order to improve access to finance for SMEs, to promote job creation and stimulate economic growth.

In 1998 the Bank agreed to participate in an initiative of the IMF and the World Bank to assist heavily indebted poor countries (HIPCs) to maintain a sustainable level of debt. Also in 1998, following projections of reduced resources for the FSO, borrowing member countries agreed to convert about US $2,400m. in local currencies held by the Bank, in order to maintain a convertible concessional Fund for poorer countries, and to help to reduce the debt-servicing payments under the HIPC initiative. In mid-2000 a committee of the Board of Governors endorsed a financial framework for the Bank's participation in an enhanced HIPC initiative, which aimed to broaden the eligibility criteria and accelerate the process of debt reduction. The Bank was to provide $896m. (in net present value), in addition to $204m. committed under the original scheme, of which $307m. was for Bolivia, $65m. for Guyana, $391m. for Nicaragua and $133m. for Honduras. The Bank assisted the preparation of national Poverty Reduction Strategy Papers, a condition of reaching the 'completion point' of the process. In January 2007 the Bank concluded an agreement to participate in the Multilateral Debt Relief Initiative (MDRI), which had been approved by the World Bank and IMF in 2005 as a means of achieving 100% cancellation of debts for eligible HIPCs. The agreement to support the MDRI was endorsed by the Bank's Board of Governors in March 2007. Under the initiative the eligible completion point countries, along with Haiti (which had reached 'decision point' in November 2006), were to receive additional debt relief amounting to some $3,370m. in principal payments and $1,000m. in future interest payments, cancelling loan balances with the FSO (outstanding as of 31 December 2004). Haiti reached 'completion point' under the HIPC initiative in June 2009. Accordingly, FSO delivered debt relief under the enhanced HIPC initiative and the MDRI amounting to some $419m. The general capital increase, approved in 2010, intended to provide for cancellation of all Haiti's outstanding debts to the Bank. In September 2010 the US Government made available an advance contribution of $204m. to the FSO, enabling the Bank to announce the cancellation of Haiti's outstanding debts, amounting to $484m.

In June 2006 the Bank inaugurated a new initiative, Opportunities for the Majority, to improve conditions for low-income communities throughout the region. Under the scheme the Bank was to support the development of partnerships between communities, private sector bodies and non-governmental organizations to generate employment, deliver services and integrate poorer members of society into the productive economy. During 2013 a total of 10 projects were approved under the initiative with a value of US $100m.

In March 2007 the Bank's Board of Governors endorsed the Sustainable Energy and Climate Change Initiative (SECCI), which aimed to expand the development and use of biofuels and other sources of renewable energy, to enhance energy efficiency and to facilitate adaptation to climate change. A Bank fund, with an initial US $20m. in resources, was established to finance feasibility studies and technical co-operation projects. In November 2009 the Bank signed a Memorandum of Understanding with the Asian Development Bank to support projects and programmes that promote sustainable, low-carbon transport in both regions. In accordance with the priorities of the lending agreement approved along with IDB-9 in July 2010, support for climate change adaptation initiatives and other projects concerned with renewable energy and environmental sustainability was expected to reach 25% of total lending by the end of 2015. In March 2013 the Bank launched a Biodiversity and Ecosystems Services Programme, which was to support projects aimed at leveraging the region's natural capital in pursuit of sustainable development.

The Bank supports a range of consultative groups in order to strengthen donor co-operation with countries in the Latin America and Caribbean region, in particular to co-ordinate emergency relief and reconstruction following a natural disaster or to support peace efforts within a country. In November 2001 the Bank hosted the first meeting of a Network for the Prevention and Mitigation of Natural Disasters in Latin America and the Caribbean, which was part of a regional policy dialogue, sponsored by the Bank to promote broad debate on strategic issues. In April 2006 the Bank established the Disaster Prevention Fund, financed through Ordinary Capital funds, to help countries to improve their disaster preparedness and reduce their vulnerability to natural hazards. A separate Multi-donor Disaster Prevention Trust Fund was established at the end of 2006 to finance technical assistance and investment in preparedness projects.

In July 2004 the Bank co-hosted an international donor conference, together with the World Bank, the European Union (EU) and the UN, to consider the immediate and medium-term needs for Haiti following a period of political unrest. Some US $1,080m. was pledged at the conference, of which the Bank's contribution was $260m. In April 2009 international donors, meeting under the Bank's auspices, pledged further contributions of $324m. to Haiti's economic and social development. In January 2010 the Bank determined to redirect undisbursed funds of up to $90m. to finance priority emergency assistance and reconstruction efforts in Haiti following a devastating earthquake. In March the Board of Governors agreed to cancel Haiti's outstanding debt and to convert undisbursed loans in order to provide grant assistance amounting to $2,000m. over the coming 10 years. In mid-March the Bank organized a conference of representatives of the private sector in Haiti, in preparation for the International Donors' Conference, which was then held at the end of that month in New York, USA. The Bank also supported the Haitian Government in preparing, jointly with the UN, the World Bank and the European Commission, a Preliminary Damage and Needs Assessment report for presentation at the Conference. During 2013 some $186m. of the $188m. committed by the Bank in grants to Haiti was disbursed, in particular to fund activities in the areas of education, private sector development, energy, agriculture, transportation, and water and sanitation.

An increasing number of donor countries have placed funds under the Bank's administration for assistance to Latin America, outside the framework of the Ordinary Resources and the Bank's Special Operations. These include the Social Progress Trust Fund (set up by the USA in 1961); the Venezuelan Trust Fund (set up in 1975); the Japan Special Fund (1988); and other funds administered on behalf of Austria, Belgium, Canada, Chile, Denmark, Finland, France,

Israel, Italy, Japan, the Netherlands, Norway, Portugal, Spain, Sweden, Switzerland, the United Kingdom and the EU. A Program for the Development of Technical Co-operation was established in 1991, which is financed by European countries and the EU.

The Bank provides technical co-operation to help member countries to identify and prepare new projects, to improve loan execution, to strengthen the institutional capacity of public and private agencies, to address extreme conditions of poverty and to promote small- and micro-enterprise development. The Bank has established a special co-operation programme to facilitate the transfer of experience and technology among regional programmes. Technical co-operation operations are mainly financed by income from the FSO and donor trust funds. The Bank supports the efforts of the countries of the region to achieve economic integration and has provided extensive technical support for the formulation of integration strategies in the Andean, Central American and Southern Cone regions. In June 2010 the Bank agreed to collaborate with the Spanish Government, the Bill and Melinda Gates Foundation and the Carlos Slim Health Institute in administering a new 'Salud Mesoamérica 2015' initiative, which aimed to support efforts to achieve the millennium development health objectives in the region over a five-year period. The Bank is a member of the technical co-ordinating committee of the Integration of Regional Infrastructure in South America initiative, which aimed to promote multinational development projects, capacity building and integration in that region. In September 2006 the Bank established a new fund to support the preparation of infrastructure projects, InfraFund, with an initial US $20m. in resources. In 2005 the Bank inaugurated a Trade Finance Facilitation Program (TFFP) to support economic growth in the region by expanding the financing available for international trade activities. The programme was given permanent status in November 2006. In May 2008 the Bank launched a training initiative within the framework of the TFFP. In January 2009 the Bank determined to expand the TFFP to include loans, as well as guarantees, and to increase the programme limit from $400m. to $1,000m. By December 2013 there were more than 90 issuing banks from 21 Latin American and Caribbean countries participating in the programme, and nearly 300 confirming banks worldwide. In September 2009 the Bank supported the establishment, jointly with the Multilateral Investment Fund (MIF), Inter-American Investment Corporation (IIC), the Andean Development Corporation, the US private investment corporation and a Swiss investment management company, of a Microenterprise Growth Facility (MIGROF), which aimed to provide up to $250m. to microfinance institutions in Latin America and the Caribbean.

An Emerging and Sustainable Cities Initiative, initiated by the Bank in 2011, worked in 2013 to support sustainable growth in 26 Latin American cities. The Bank's Biodiversity and Ecosystem Services programme focused in 2013 on the economics of biodiversity systems and means of integrating natural capital in private and public investments. In April 2012 the Bank launched a Citizen Security Initiative, which provides grants for technical co-operation projects aimed at strengthening the effectiveness of public policies in promoting citizen security and justice. A Special Broadband Program, inaugurated in 2013, and supported by US $3.5m. Broadband Fund, promotes increased region-wide adoption of, access to and usage of broadband.

AFFILIATES

Inter-American Investment Corporation (IIC): 1350 New York Ave, NW, Washington, DC 20577, USA; tel. (202) 623-3900; fax (202) 623-2360; e-mail iicmail@iadb.org; internet www.iic.int; f. 1986 as a legally autonomous affiliate of the Inter-American Development Bank, to promote the economic development of the region; commenced operations in 1989; initial capital stock was US $200m., of which 55% was contributed by developing member nations, 25.3% by the USA, and the remainder by non-regional members; in 2001 the Board of Governors of the Bank agreed to increase the IIC's capital to $500m; places emphasis on investment in SMEs without access to other suitable sources of equity or long-term loans; developed FINPYME as an online service to support SMEs and to improve their access to potential sources of financing; in March 2013 launched an $80m. initiative to provide technical assistance aimed at improving the corporate governance of regional SMEs; in 2013 the IIC approved 71 operations with commitments amounting to $415m., with an additional $197m. mobilized from other sources; mems: 45 countries as shareholders; Gen. Man. CARL MUÑANA; publ. *Annual Report* (in English, French, Portuguese and Spanish).

Multilateral Investment Fund (MIF) (Fondo Multilateral de Inversiones (FOMIN)): 1300 New York Ave, NW, Washington, DC 20577, USA; tel. (202) 942-8211; fax (202) 942-8100; e-mail mifcontact@iadb.org; internet www.iadb.org/mif; f. 1993 as an autonomous fund administered by the Bank, to promote private sector development in the region; the 21 Bank members who signed the initial draft agreement in 1992 to establish the Fund pledged to contribute US $1,200m.; the Fund's activities are undertaken through three separate facilities concerned with technical co-operation, human resources development and small enterprise development; resources are targeted at the following core areas of activity: small business development; market functioning; and financial and capital markets; the Bank's Social Entrepreneurship Program makes available credit to individuals or groups without access to commercial or development loans; some $10.6m. was awarded under the programme to fund 12 projects in 2013; in July 2013 launched WEVentureScope, an initiative aimed at evaluating business opportunities for women in the countries of Latin America and the Caribbean; in 2012, jointly with the Nordic Development Fund, the Fund launched EcoMiro, a regional programme providing microfinance institutions in Latin American and the Caribbean with technical assistance to develop green financial products; a Microenterprise Forum, 'Foromic', is held annually (Sept.–Oct. 2013: Guadalajara, Mexico); in April 2005 38 donor countries agreed to establish MIF II, and replenish the Fund's resources with commitments totalling $502m.; MIF II entered into force in March 2007 and was to expire in 2015; in mid-2010 MIF supported the establishment of an Emergency Liquidity Program for Haiti; during 2013 MIF approved $108m. to finance 68 operations; Gen. Man. NANCY LEE; publ. *MicAméricas*.

INSTITUTIONS

Instituto para la Integración de América Latina y el Caribe (INTAL) (Institute for the Integration of Latin America and the Caribbean): Esmeralda 130, 17°, 1035 Buenos Aires, Argentina; tel. (11) 4323-2350; fax (11) 4320-1865; e-mail intal@iadb.org; internet www.iadb.org/intal; f. 1965 under the auspices of the Inter-American Development Bank; undertakes research on all aspects of regional integration and co-operation and issues related to international trade, hemispheric integration and relations with other regions and countries of the world; activities come under four main headings: regional and national technical co-operation projects on integration; policy fora; integration fora; and journals and information; hosts the secretariat of the Integration of Regional Infrastructure in South America (IIRSA) initiative; maintains an extensive Documentation Center and various statistical databases; Dir GRACIELA SCHAMIS; publs *Integración y Comercio/Integration and Trade* (2 a year), *INTAL Monthly Newsletter, Informe Andino/Andean Report, CARICOM Report, Informe Centroamericano/Central American Report, Informe Mercosur/Mercosur Report* (2 a year).

Inter-American Institute for Social Development (INDES): 1350 New York Ave, NW, Washington, DC 20057, USA; fax (202) 623-2008; e-mail bid-indes@iadb.org; internet indes.iadb.org; commenced operations in 1995; aims to support the training of senior officials from public sector institutions and organizations involved with social policies and social services; organizes specialized sub-regional courses and seminars and national training programmes; produces teaching materials and also serves as a forum for the exchange of ideas on social reform; Head JUAN CRISTOBAL BONNEFOY (Chile).

Publications

Annual Report (in English, French, Portuguese and Spanish).

Development in the Americas (series).

Development Effectiveness Overview (annually).

IDB Edu (quarterly).

Latin American and Caribbean Macroeconomic Report.

Puentes (periodic civil society newsletter).

Revelation of Expectations in Latin America (monthly analysis of market expectations of inflation and growth).

Sustainability Report (annually).

Brochure series, occasional papers, working papers, reports.

Statistics

APPROVALS BY SECTOR, 2013*

Sector	Amount (US $ million)	% of total	Number of projects
Infrastructure and environment	4,702	34	53
Agriculture and rural development	227	2	7
Energy	534	4	9
Environment and natural disasters	178	1	6
Sustainable tourism	185	1	5
Transport	2,804	20	20
Water and sanitation	775	6	6
Institutions for development	4,970	36	73
Financial markets	1,614	12	20
Industry	4	0	1
Private firms and SME development	463	3	15
Reform/modernization of the state	2,319	17	26
Science and technology	24	0	1
Urban development and housing	545	4	10
Integration and trade	1,223	9	22
Social sector	3,004	21	19
Education	726	5	6
Health	751	5	5
Social investment	1,527	11	8
Total	10,558	100	167

* Includes loans, guarantees, and operations financed by the IDB Grant Facility, but excludes lending and projects (one in 2013) approved under the DSL.

YEARLY AND CUMULATIVE LOANS AND GUARANTEES, 1961–2013
(US $ million; after cancellations and exchange adjustments)

Country	Total Amount* 2013	Total Amount* 1961–2013	Ordinary Capital 1961–2013	Fund for Special Operations 1961–2013	Funds in Administration 1961–2013
Argentina	1,260.0	33,897.7	33,203.6	644.9	49.2
Bahamas	—	711.4	709.5	—	2.0
Barbados	—	787.6	726.5	40.9	19.0
Belize	—	182.4	182.4	—	—
Bolivia	396.5	5,322.8	2,515.9	2,278.5	78.4
Brazil	3,386.5	47,004.7	45,315.0	1,555.8	133.9
Chile	441.4	6,876.1	6,606.3	204.9	64.9
Colombia	1,054.0	19,652.1	18,750.3	766.0	135.8
Costa Rica	615.5	4,920.5	4,344.3	363.5	212.7
Dominican Republic	661.0	5,544.5	4,708.0	747.8	88.7
Ecuador	502.0	7,630.6	6,555.1	981.4	94.1
El Salvador	360.0	5,129.7	4,183.9	797.9	147.9
Guatemala	196.0	4,846.9	4,026.9	749.7	70.3
Guyana	17.0	1,313.1	251.1	1,055.1	6.9
Haiti	192.0	2,449.3	7.0	1,146.0	1,296.3
Honduras	275.1	4,154.1	1,545.7	2,542.4	66.0
Jamaica	25.0	3,291.3	2,909.8	171.6	209.9
Mexico	2,095.7	33,679.2	32,900.1	559.0	220.1
Nicaragua	236.6	3,635.3	915.4	2,645.8	74.1
Panama	281.5	4,713.9	4,378.0	294.0	41.9
Paraguay	286.3	3,414.7	2,687.6	709.7	17.4
Peru	195.0	10,653.0	9,994.9	434.5	222.6
Suriname	175.0	555.4	499.0	6.4	50.0
Trinidad and Tobago	159.5	2,062.2	2,006.4	30.6	25.2
Uruguay	781.9	6,929.0	6,738.6	104.4	86.0
Venezuela	—	7,617.8	7,443.5	101.4	72.9
Regional	400.0	4,729.6	4,476.7	239.0	13.9
Total	13,997.5	231,703.8	208,581.5	19,622.1	3,500.1

* Includes non-sovereign guaranteed loans, net of participations, and guarantees, as applicable. Excludes the IDB Grant Facility or lines of credit approved and guarantees issued under the Trade Finance Facilitation Program.

Source: Inter-American Development Bank, *Annual Report 2013*.

INTERGOVERNMENTAL AUTHORITY ON DEVELOPMENT—IGAD

Address: Ave Georges Clemenceau, BP 2653, Djibouti.

Telephone: 354050; **fax:** 356994; **e-mail:** igad@igad.org; **internet:** www.igad.org.

IGAD, established in 1996 to supersede the Intergovernmental Authority on Drought and Development (IGADD, founded in 1986), aims to co-ordinate the sustainable socio-economic development of member countries, to combat the effects of drought and desertification, and to promote regional food security. In October 2011 IGAD was granted observer status at the UN General Assembly.

MEMBERS*

Djibouti	Kenya	South Sudan	Uganda
Ethiopia	Somalia	Sudan	

* In April 2007 Eritrea, which joined in 1993 following its proclamation as an independent state, suspended its IGAD membership; the IGAD Council of Ministers has subsequently engaged with Eritrea to promote its return to the organization.

Organization

(April 2014)

ASSEMBLY

The Assembly, consisting of heads of state and of government of member states, is the supreme policy-making organ of the Authority. It holds a regular summit meeting at least once a year. The chairmanship of the Assembly rotates among the member countries on an annual basis.

COUNCIL OF MINISTERS

The Council of Ministers is composed of the minister responsible for foreign affairs and one other minister from each member state. It meets at least twice a year and approves the work programme and the annual budget of the Secretariat.

COMMITTEE OF AMBASSADORS

The Committee of Ambassadors comprises the ambassadors or plenipotentiaries of member states to Djibouti. It convenes as regularly as required to advise and assist the Executive Secretary concerning the interpretation of policies and guidelines and the realization of the annual work programme.

SECRETARIAT

The Secretariat, the executive body of IGAD, is headed by the Executive Secretary, who is appointed by the Assembly for a term of four years, renewable once. In addition to the Office of the Executive Secretary, the Secretariat comprises the following three divisions: Agriculture and Environment; Economic Co-operation; and Political and Humanitarian Affairs, each headed by a director. A workshop was convened in September 2011 to discuss the future organizational restructuring of IGAD.

Executive Secretary: Mahboub Maalim (Kenya).

Activities

IGADD was established in 1986 to combat the effects of aridity and desertification arising from the severe drought and famine that has periodically affected the Horn of Africa. In April 1995, at an extraordinary summit meeting held in Addis Ababa, Ethiopia, heads of state and of government resolved to reorganize and expand the Authority. In March 1996 IGAD was endorsed to supersede IGADD, at a second extraordinary summit meeting of heads of state and of government, held in Nairobi, Kenya. The meeting approved an extended mandate to co-ordinate and harmonize policy in the areas of economic co-operation and political and humanitarian affairs, in addition to its existing responsibilities for food security and environmental protection.

IGAD aims to achieve regional co-operation and economic integration. To facilitate this, IGAD assists the governments of member states to maximize resources and co-ordinates efforts to initiate and implement regional development programmes and projects. IGAD promotes the harmonization of policies relating to agriculture and natural resources, communications, customs, trade and transport; the implementation of programmes in the fields of social sciences, research, science and technology; and effective participation in the global economy. Meetings between IGAD ministers responsible for foreign affairs and the IGAD Partners' Forum (IPF), comprising the grouping's donors, are convened periodically to discuss issues such as food security and humanitarian affairs. In October 2001 delegates from IGAD and representatives of government and civil society in member states initiated a process to establish an IGAD-Civil Society Forum; the founding assembly of the Forum was convened in Nairobi, in July 2003.

In October 2003 the 10th IGAD summit meeting ratified a decision of the eighth summit, held in November 2000, to absorb the Harare, Zimbabwe- and Nairobi-based Drought Monitoring Centre (an initiative of 24 Eastern and Southern African states inaugurated in 1989 under the auspices of the UN Development Programme and the World Meteorological Organization) as a specialized institution of IGAD; the Centre was renamed the IGAD Climate Prediction and Applications Centre (ICPAC). In April 2007 ICPAC was fully integrated into IGAD.

A Protocol establishing the Inter-parliamentary Union of IGAD (IPU-IGAD), signed in February 2004 by the participants in the first meeting of regional speakers of parliament, entered into force in November 2007; IPU-IGAD was to be based in Addis Ababa.

In January 2008 the IGAD Regional AIDS Partnership Program (IRAPP) was launched, with a particular focus on protecting mobile communities (for example pastoralists, internally displaced persons—IDPs, and refugees) at risk of HIV/AIDS. IRAPP was implementing a common regional strategic plan for combating HIV/AIDS, targeting cross-border and mobile populations, over the period 2011–16. Jointly with the World Bank the IGAD Secretariat is developing a mechanism for monitoring the occurrence of HIV/AIDS in member states.

In June 2006 IGAD launched the IGAD Capacity Building Program Against Terrorism (ICPAT), a four-year programme based in Addis Ababa, which aimed to combat the reach of international terrorism through the enhancement of judicial measures and interdepartmental co-operation, improving border control activities, supporting training and information-sharing, and promoting strategic co-operation. In April 2009 a meeting of IGAD ministers responsible for justice, organized by ICPAT, approved a draft IGAD Convention on Extradition, and also a draft Convention on Mutual Legal Assistance. In October 2011 a new IGAD Security Sector Program (ISSP) was launched, focusing on initiatives in the areas of counter-terrorism; organized crime; maritime security; and capacity building of security institutions. In June 2013 an agreement on maritime security was concluded between IGAD and the European Union (EU).

The introduction of an IGAD Gender Peer Review Mechanism was under consideration in 2014; it was envisaged that the Mechanism would be a means of addressing the issue of violence against women in the region as well as other matters relating to women's progress. In December 2009 the first IGAD Women's Parliamentary Conference, convened in Addis Ababa, adopted a declaration on the Enhancement of Women's Participation and Representation in Decision-Making Positions. In April 2011 IGAD convened a conference on women and peace, considering the engagement of women in peacebuilding and security initiatives in the region. In October 2013 an IGAD Regional Strategy on Higher Representation of Women in Decision Making Positions was initiated, and a new regional Women and Peace Forum was established.

FOOD SECURITY AND ENVIRONMENTAL PROTECTION

About 80% of the IGAD sub-region is classified as arid or semi-arid, and some 40% of the region is unproductive, owing to severe environmental degradation. The region suffers from recurrent droughts, which severely impede crop and livestock production. Natural and man-made disasters increase the strain on resources, resulting in annual food deficits. Activities to improve food security and preserve natural resources have included the introduction of remote-sensing services; the development of a Livestock Marketing Information System (LMIS) and of a Regional Integrated Information System (RIIS); the establishment of training and credit schemes for fishermen; research into the sustainable production of drought-resistant, high-yielding crop varieties; transboundary livestock disease control and vaccine production; the control of environmental pollution; the promotion of alternative sources of energy in the home; the management of integrated water resources; the promotion of community-based land husbandry; training programmes in grain marketing;

and the implementation of the International Convention to Combat Desertification.

In June 2008 the IGAD Assembly, meeting at a time of escalating global food prices and shortfalls in regional imports of foodstuffs, issued a Declaration on the Current High Food Price Crisis, in which it resolved to pursue policies aimed at improving sustainable food production; urged IGAD's partners to support regional agricultural development programmes; determined to enhance the regional drought, climate change monitoring, and early warning mechanisms; and announced that a regional emergency reserve fund would be established. In addition the Authority decided to establish a ministerial task force to assess regional emergency food aid requirements with a view to launching an international appeal for assistance. In December 2009 IGAD and the World Food Programme concluded a Memorandum of Understanding (MOU) aimed at enhancing mutual co-operation with a view to improving food and nutrition security in the IGAD region. An executive body, technical committee and co-ordination office were to be established to facilitate the implementation of the MOU.

In November 2011 IGAD and partner countries held a consultative meeting entitled 'Ending Drought Emergencies in the Horn of Africa', in response to ongoing severe drought and an ensuing food security crisis, that had resulted in some 13m. people in the region requiring food assistance. The meeting determined the institutional arrangements for implementing a Horn of Africa IGAD Drought Disaster Resilience and Sustainability Initiative (IDDRSI): Ending Drought Emergencies, which had been launched by regional heads of state in September. The meeting also agreed to establish an IDDRSI Platform, intended as an enhanced partnership with donors facilitating long-term investment—particularly in regional arid and semi-arid lands—to end the recurrence of drought emergencies. A Platform Steering Committee was constituted in February 2013. Meetings of the General Assembly of the IDDRSI were convened in February 2013 and March 2014.

In October 2013 an IGAD Horn of Africa Sustainable Fisheries Task Force was established, tasked with developing a Sustainable Fisheries Management Strategy for the Horn of Africa, aimed at combating the impact on fish stocks of illegal, unregulated and unreported (IUU) fishing in regional waters.

IGAD adopted an Environment and Natural Resources Strategy in April 2007, identifying a number key strategic objectives that were to guide future sub-regional environmental programmes. In June 2010 a consultative meeting was convened between IGAD, the African Union (AU), the Common Market for Eastern and Southern African (COMESA), and other regional partners, aimed at advancing the co-ordination and harmonization of their activities governing the environment.

ECONOMIC CO-OPERATION

The Economic Co-operation division concentrates on the development of a co-ordinated infrastructure for the region, in particular in the areas of transport and communications, to promote foreign, cross-border and domestic trade and investment opportunities. IGAD seeks to harmonize national transport and trade policy and thereby to facilitate the free movement of people, goods and services. The improvements to infrastructure also aim to facilitate more timely interventions in conflicts, disasters and emergencies in the sub-region. Projects under way include the construction of missing segments of the Trans-African Highway and the Pan African Telecommunications Network; the removal of barriers to trade and communications; improvements to ports and inland container terminals; and the modernization of railway and telecommunications services. In November 2000 the IGAD Assembly determined to establish an integrated rail network connecting all member countries. The development of economic co-operation has been impeded by persisting conflicts in the sub-region. In August 2010 an IGAD Business Forum (IBF) was held, in Kampala, Uganda. In May 2013 delegates of IGAD national chambers of commerce and industry met to address strengthening the IBF, the mission of which was defined as representing private sector interests in the regional integration agenda, including facilitating the involvement of the private sector in policy matters, and enhancing public-private partnerships, under the guidance of IGAD Secretariat. A gathering of customs officials and experts on trade from IGAD member states, convened in May 2013, in Kampala, Uganda, endorsed a report on establishing a legal framework and modalities towards the development of 'one-stop' border posts in the IGAD region, with the aim of simplifying border procedures and thereby facilitating intra-regional trade.

POLITICAL AND HUMANITARIAN AFFAIRS

The field of political and humanitarian affairs focuses on conflict prevention, management and resolution through dialogue. The division's primary aim is to restore peace and stability to member countries affected by conflict, in order that resources may be diverted for development purposes. Efforts have been pursued to strengthen capacity for conflict prevention and to relieve humanitarian crises. The ninth IGAD summit meeting, held in Khartoum, Sudan, in January 2002, adopted a protocol to IGAD's founding agreement establishing a conflict early warning and response mechanism (CEWARN). CEWARN, which is based in Addis Ababa, collects and analyses information for the preparation of periodic early warning reports concerning the potential outbreak of violent conflicts in the region. In February 2006 IGAD convened a ministerial conference on refugees, returnees and IDPs, to consider means of addressing the burden posed by population displacement in member states; at that time it was estimated that 11m. people had been forcibly displaced from their homes in the region. In May 2008 IGAD, the AU and the International Organization for Migration jointly organized a workshop, held in Addis Ababa, on inter-state and intra-regional co-operation on migration; an IGAD Regional Consultative Process (IGAD-RCP) on migration was launched, with the aim of building member countries' management capacities. During 2010 IGAD formulated a Regional Migration Policy Framework, detailing strategies for managing migration. The *IGAD Migration Knowledge Series*, reporting on regional patterns of migration and population displacement, was initiated in August 2013. IGAD contributes to efforts to raise awareness of the AU's 2006 Ouagadougou Action Plan to Combat Trafficking in Human Beings, and supports the AU COMMIT campaign, launched in June 2009 to combat human trafficking.

The Executive Secretary of IGAD participated in the first summit meeting of all East African heads of state and government, convened in April 2005 in Addis Ababa; the meeting agreed to establish an Eastern African Standby Brigade (EASBRIG). EASBRIG, the development of which is co-ordinated by IGAD, was to form the regional component of the AU African Standby Force. In November 2009 EASBRIG undertook a field training exercise ('Exercise Amani Carana') in Djibouti.

In 2008 a new IGAD Peace and Security Strategy was devised. In August IGAD chaired the first meeting of the steering committee on Conflict Prevention Management and Resolution (CPMR), comprising IGAD, COMESA and the East African Community (EAC), which aimed to promote a co-ordinated approach to peace and security in the region. In September 2012 IGAD launched a new regional strategy for conflict early warning and response, facilitating information-sharing among member states and joint action against emerging conflict.

Kenya: In February 2008 IGAD heads of state and government convened in Addis Ababa, on the sidelines of the 10th Assembly of the AU, to discuss the violent unrest that had erupted in Kenya in the aftermath of that country's December 2007 disputed general election; following the meeting an IGAD ministerial delegation was dispatched to Kenya as a gesture of regional solidarity with the Kenyan people and with a peace initiative led by the former UN Secretary-General, Kofi Annan. IGAD sent an observer mission to monitor the national referendum on a new draft constitution held in Kenya in August 2010. In March 2013 IGAD observers formed a joint mission with those from the EAC and COMESA to monitor a general election in Kenya. In late September the Executive Secretariat of IGAD issued a message of condolence to the Kenyan Government and people with regard to the terrorist assault that was perpetrated against civilians in a shopping centre in Nairobi, causing an estimated 67 civilian fatalities.

Somalia: In May–August 2000 a conference aimed at securing peace in Somalia was convened in Arta, Djibouti, under the auspices of IGAD. The conference appointed a transitional Somali legislature, which then elected a transitional national president. The eighth summit of IGAD heads of state and government, held in Khartoum, in November, welcomed the conclusion in September of an agreement on reconciliation between the new Somali transitional administration and a prominent opposition alliance, and determined that those member countries that neighboured Somalia (the 'front-line states' of Djibouti, Ethiopia and Kenya) should co-operate in assisting the process of reconstruction and reconciliation in that country. The summit appointed a special envoy to implement IGAD's directives concerning the Somali situation. In January 2002 the ninth IGAD summit meeting determined that a new conference for promoting reconciliation in Somalia (where insecurity continued to prevail) should be convened, under IGAD auspices. The leaders also issued a statement condemning international terrorism and urged Somalia, in particular, to make a firm commitment to eradicating terrorism. The second Somalia reconciliation conference, initiated in October, in Eldoret, Kenya, issued a Declaration on Cessation of Hostilities, Structures and Principles of the Somalia National Reconciliation Process, as a basis for the pursuit of a peace settlement. In February 2003 the conference was relocated to Nairobi, Kenya. In January 2004 the Nairobi conference determined to establish a new parliament; this was inaugurated in August. In January 2005 IGAD heads of state and government authorized the deployment of a Peace Support Mission to Somalia (IGASOM) to assist the transitional federal authorities there, pending the subsequent deployment of an

AU peace force; this arrangement was endorsed in the same month by the AU. In mid-March 2006 the IGAD Assembly reiterated its support for the planned deployment of IGASOM, and urged the UN Security Council to grant an exemption to the UN arms embargo applied to Somalia in order to facilitate the regional peace support initiative. At a consultative meeting on the removal of the arms embargo, convened in mid-April, in Nairobi, representatives of the Somali transitional federal authorities presented for consideration by IGAD and the AU a draft national security and stabilization plan. It was agreed that a detailed mission plan should be formulated to underpin the proposed IGAD/AU peace missions. In January 2007 the AU Peace and Security Council authorized the deployment of the AU Mission in Somalia (AMISOM) in place of the proposed IGASOM.

In December 2008 an IGAD Facilitator for Somalia Peace and Reconciliation was appointed. Meeting in May 2009 an extraordinary session of the IGAD Council of Ministers urged the UN Security Council to impose (except for humanitarian personnel) a no-fly zone over Somalia and blockades on identified Somali seaports, and also to impose targeted sanctions against all those providing assistance to extremists—including foreign forces—who were continuing to attack AMISOM and otherwise to destabilize that country. A further extraordinary meeting of IGAD leaders, convened in June, on the sidelines of the AU summit, in Sirte, Libya, noted with deep concern the continuing poor security situation in Somalia; urged the UN Security Council to consider enabling front-line states to deploy troops to Somalia if necessary; committed IGAD member states individually and collectively to establishing an internal mechanism to effect the sanctions called for in May and to enact legislation aimed at combating piracy; and directed the IGAD Secretariat to accord full support to the grouping's Facilitator for Somalia Peace and Reconciliation. In September IGAD, the UN, the EU, the League of Arab States and the respective Governments of Norway and the USA issued a joint statement strongly condemning suicide car bomb attacks that were perpetrated by Islamic extremists against the AMISOM headquarters in Mogadishu, Somalia, killing more than 20 people, including the Deputy Force Commander of the Mission. The January 2010 IGAD extraordinary summit determined to send a ministerial delegation to selected partner countries and organizations to solicit their support for the Somali transitional federal authorities, and welcomed the imposition by the UN Security Council in December 2009 of punitive sanctions against the Eritrean political and military leadership, who were found to have provided political, financial and logistical support to armed groups engaged in undermining the reconciliation process in Somalia, and to have acted aggressively towards Djibouti. The Kampala Accord, signed in June 2011 by the President of the Somali transitional federal authorities and the Speaker of the transitional legislature, and related roadmap on its implementation, outlined a schedule for national elections, and determined that the IGAD and EAC heads of state, with UN and AU co-operation, should establish a political bureau to oversee and advance the Somali peace process. The January 2012 extraordinary session of the Authority endorsed a new IGAD Somalia Inland Strategy and Action Plan to Prevent and Counter Piracy. In September IGAD congratulated Hassan Sheikh Mohamud and the people of Somalia on his peaceful election as president of a new federal government. In December IGAD adopted a Grand Stabilization Plan for South Central Somalia, under the auspices of the IGAD Facilitator for Somalia Peace and Reconciliation. An extraordinary IGAD summit held in May 2013 welcomed the Somali Federal Government's National Stabilization Plan.

In September 2013 an extraordinary IGAD summit was held on the sidelines of the 'New Deal for Somalia Conference' that was organized in Brussels, Belgium, jointly by the EU and Somali Government. The IGAD summit addressed the New Deal for Somalia under consideration by the Conference, and—emphasizing Somalia's dependence on remittances from the Somali diaspora for sustaining national economic activities—expressed grave concern over a decision by a major United Kingdom-based bank to close, by 30 September, the bank accounts of United Kingdom-based Somali money service businesses (MSBs). IGAD leaders urged the international development community to provide financing for new initiatives aimed at enabling MSBs to continue to serve poor communities.

Sudan and South Sudan: In September 1995 negotiations between the Sudanese Government and opposition leaders were initiated, under the auspices of IGAD, with the aim of resolving the conflict in southern Sudan; these were subsequently reconvened periodically. In March 2001 IGAD's mediation committee on southern Sudan publicized a seven-point plan for a peaceful settlement of the conflict. In June, at a regional summit on the situation in Sudan convened by IGAD, it was agreed that a permanent negotiating forum comprising representatives of the parties to the conflict would be established at the Authority's secretariat. In July 2002 the Sudanese Government and the main rebel grouping in that country signed, under IGAD auspices, in Machakos, Kenya, a protocol providing for a six-year period of autonomy for southern Sudan to be followed by a referendum on self-determination, and establishing that northern Sudan would be governed in accordance with *Shari'a* law and southern Sudan by a secular judicial system. Peace negotiations subsequently continued under IGAD auspices. A ceasefire agreement was concluded by the parties to the conflict in October, to which an addendum was adopted in February 2003, recommending the deployment of an IGAD verification and monitoring team to oversee compliance with the agreement. In September of that year the parties to the conflict signed an accord on interim security arrangements. During 2003–04 IGAD mediated several further accords that paved the way for the conclusion, in January 2005, of a final Comprehensive Peace Agreement (CPA). An extraordinary session of the IGAD Council of Ministers, convened in January 2010, in Addis Ababa, expressed concern regarding the ongoing status of the implementation of the CPA and directed the IGAD Secretariat to develop programmes and seminars aimed at promoting a culture of peace in Sudan. An extraordinary summit meeting of the IGAD Assembly, held in March, directed the IGAD Secretariat to accept an invitation to observe the presidential and legislative elections to be held in Sudan, in April. The meeting also directed the IGAD Secretariat to convene, in collaboration with the IPF and the parties to the CPA, an international Donors' Conference for Sudan.

Following the referendum on self-determination for South Sudan, held in January 2011, and South Sudan's consequent attainment of independence in July, the new nation was admitted to IGAD in November. The 20th extraordinary session of the Authority, held in January 2012, noted with concern deteriorating relations between Sudan and South Sudan, and strongly urged both states to refrain from actions that might undermine the resolution of outstanding issues under the CPA. In February the IGAD Executive Secretary reiterated the position of the AU that a warrant issued in November 2011 by the Kenyan High Court for the arrest of Sudanese President Omar Al-Bashir—indicted by the International Criminal Court on charges of including crimes against humanity and genocide—contravened the interests of peace, stability and economic development in the region, and risked undermining the peace process being undertaken by IGAD in Sudan. In April 2012 the IGAD Executive Secretariat issued a statement expressing deep concern at escalating conflict between Sudan and South Sudan, urging the two sides to adhere to an MOU signed in February on non-aggression and co-operation, and fully supporting the ongoing mediation efforts of an AU High Level and Implementation Panel. In January 2013 an extraordinary session of the Council of Ministers pledged IGAD's continued support for the peace process between the two countries. In late December IGAD convened an extraordinary summit meeting, in Nairobi, Kenya, to consider the outbreak of sectarian conflict in South Sudan and subsequent humanitarian crisis. The heads of state appointed a mediation team to broker a ceasefire between government and opposition forces and to pursue a dialogue for peace. A further extraordinary summit meeting on South Sudan, held at the end of January 2014, welcomed the signing in that month by the South Sudan authorities and armed militants of an Agreement on the Cessation of Hostilities and of a further accord relating to the status of detainees. The meeting urged the expeditious implementation of the agreements, and, in that respect, directed IGAD envoys to establish an IGAD Monitoring and Verification Mechanism (IGAD MVM) in South Sudan. IGAD heads of state and government met once again in an extraordinary summit in mid-March to assess progress made by the IGAD mediation team in South Sudan. The leaders welcomed the adoption in February by the parties to the conflict in South Sudan of a follow-up 'Implementation Modalities' document, and authorized the prompt deployment of a regional Protection and Deterrent Force as part of the IGAD MVM; the AU and UN Security Council were urged to provide necessary support for the mobilization of the Force. IGAD MVM teams commenced operations in South Sudan on 1 April.

Publications

Annual Report.

IGAD Migration Knowledge Series.

IGAD News (2 a year).

Proceedings of the Summit of Heads of State and Government; Reports of the Council of Ministers' Meetings.

Specialized Institutions

Conflict Early Warning and Response Mechanism (CEWARN): off Bole Medhanialem Rd (behind the Millennium Hall), Bole Sub City, Addis Ababa, Ethiopia; tel. (11) 6530977; fax (11) 6614489; internet www.cewarn.org; f. 2002; aims to prevent and mitigate violent conflict in the IGAD member states; has hitherto directed particular attention to cross-border pastoralist and related conflicts; works through a network of Conflict Early Warning and Response Units (CEWERUs), national research institutes (NRIs), and field monitors; focuses its activities in the following geographical clusters: Karamoja Cluster (covering cross-border areas of Ethiopia, Kenya, Sudan and Uganda), Somali Cluster (cross-border areas of Ethiopia, Kenya and Somalia), and Dikhil Cluster (cross-border areas of Djibouti and Ethiopia); in accordance with the new regional strategy for conflict early warning and response launched by IGAD in September 2012, CEWARN was to be strengthened to address a broader range of national and trans-boundary security factors, such as: competition for natural resources and land; migration; displaced populations; internal and international boundaries; climate; environment; ethnicity and religion; and economic variations.

IGAD Climate Prediction and Applications Centre (ICPAC): POB 10304, Nairobi, Kenya; tel. (20) 3514426; fax (20) 2878343; e-mail director@icpac.net; internet www.icpac.net; f. 1989 as the Drought Monitoring Centre and subsequently renamed; became an IGAD specialized institution in 2007; aims to enhance sub-regional and national capacities to utilize climate knowledge for the provision of climate information and prediction, and early warning, and for advancing sustainable development; mems: Burundi, Djibouti, Eritrea, Ethiopia, Kenya, Rwanda, Sudan, Somalia, Tanzania, Uganda.

Other IGAD specialist institutions are the IGAD Capacity Building Program against Terrorism (ICPAT); the IGAD Regional HIV and AIDS Partnership Program (IRAPP); and the IGAD Center for Pastoral Areas and Livestock Development.

INTERNATIONAL CHAMBER OF COMMERCE—ICC

Address: 33–43 ave du President Wilson, 75116 Paris, France.

Telephone: 1-49-53-28-28; **fax:** 1-49-53-28-59; **e-mail:** webmaster@iccwbo.org; **internet:** www.iccwbo.org.

The ICC, founded in 1919, is the primary world business organization, representing enterprises worldwide from all business sectors. The ICC aims to promote cross-border trade and investment and to support enterprises in meeting the challenges and opportunities presented by globalization.

MEMBERS

ICC membership comprises corporations, national professional and sectoral associations, business and employer federations, chambers of commerce, and individuals involved in international business from 130 countries. National Committees or Groups have been formed in some 85 countries and territories to co-ordinate ICC objectives and functions at national level.

Organization

(April 2014)

ICC WORLD COUNCIL

The ICC World Council is the governing body of the organization. It meets twice a year and is composed of members nominated by the National Committees. Ten 'direct' members, from countries where no National Committee exists, may also be invited to participate. The Council elects the Chairman and Vice-Chairman for terms of two years.

Chairman: HAROLD (TERRY) MCGRAW III (USA).

EXECUTIVE BOARD

The Executive Board consists of up to 30 business leaders and ex officio members appointed by the ICC World Council upon recommendation of the Chairman. Members serve for a three-year term, one-third of the members retiring at the end of each year. It ensures the strategic direction of ICC activities and the implementation of its policies, and meets at least three times each year.

INTERNATIONAL SECRETARIAT

The International Secretariat, based at the ICC's Global Headquarters, in Paris, France, is the operational arm of the ICC. It implements the work programme approved by the ICC World Council, providing intergovernmental organizations with commercial views on issues that directly affect business operations. The International Secretariat is led by the Secretary-General, who is appointed by the World Council on the recommendation of the Executive Board, and comprises the following divisions: External communications; Finance, administration and personnel; General services; Information technology; National Committees; Policy and business practices; Publications; and Training and conferences. Regional offices for Asia (based in Singapore), and the Middle East and North Africa (in Doha, Qatar) were inaugurated, respectively, in January 2010 and October 2013.

Secretary-General: JEAN-GUY CARRIER (Canada).

NATIONAL COMMITTEES AND GROUPS

Each affiliate is composed of leading business organizations and individual companies. It has its own secretariat, monitors issues of concern to its national constituents, and draws public and government attention to ICC policies.

WORLD CHAMBERS FEDERATION

The World Chambers Federation (WCF) was established in 1950 (initially as the International Information Bureau of Chambers of Commerce) to bring together national chambers of commerce and business communities. The, which is based at the ICC Global Headquarters, organizes the Chamber's supreme World Chambers Congress every two years; the eighth was convened in Doha, Qatar, in April 2013.

POLICY COMMISSIONS

ICC's Commissions serve as specialized working groups, composed of business experts in those fields, which help to prepare policy and international codes of practice. These cover: Arbitration; Banking; Commercial Law and Practice; Competition; Corporate Responsibility and Anti-corruption; Competition; Customs and Trade Regulation; Digital Economy; Economic Policy; Environment and Energy; Intellectual Property; Marketing and Advertising; Taxation; and Trade and Investment Policy.

ADVISORY GROUPS

Banking Commission Advisory Board;
Corporate Economist Advisory Group;
G20 Advisory Group.

OTHER BODIES

ICC Commercial Crime Services;
ICC Dispute Resolution Services;
ICC Institute of World Business Law;
ICC Research Foundation.

ICC Commercial Crime Services Divisions:

FraudNet: comprises a worldwide network of lawyers specializing in asset tracing and recovery; maintains an international rapid deployment force.

International Maritime Bureau (IMB): a Piracy Reporting Centre provides the most accurate and up-to-date information to shippers regarding pirate activity on the world's oceans.

Financial Investigation Bureau (FIB): works to detect financial fraud before it occurs by allowing banks and other financial institutions access to a database of shared information.

Counterfeiting Intelligence Bureau (CIB): runs a number of initiatives to protect against counterfeiting including Counterforce, Countertech and Countersearch international networks, the Counterfeit Pharmaceutical Initiative, the IHMA's Hologram Image Register and the Universal Hologram Scanner; has developed counterfeiting seizure maps, and a live seizure report.

Activities

The ICC's main activities are setting voluntary rules guiding the conduct of international trade, arbitrating trade disputes, and establishing policy.

The various Policy Commissions of the ICC are composed of more than 500 practising business executives and experts from all sectors of economic life, nominated by National Committees. ICC recommendations must be adopted by a Commission following consultation with National Committees, and then approved by the ICC World

Council or Executive Board, before they can be regarded as official ICC policies. Meetings of Commissions are generally held twice a year. Task Forces are frequently constituted by Commissions to undertake specific projects and report back to their parent body. The Commissions produce a wide array of specific codes and guidelines of direct use to the world business community; formulate statements and initiatives for presentation to governments and international bodies; and comment constructively and in detail on proposed actions by intergovernmental organizations and governments that are likely to affect business.

The ICC works closely with other international organizations. It has undertaken a broad range of activities with the UN, the World Trade Organization (WTO), the European Union (EU) and many other intergovernmental bodies. The ICC presidency meets annually with the leader of the country hosting the Group of Eight (G8) summit to discuss business aspects of the meeting. A Group of 20 (G20) Advisory Group, comprising chief executives from major global corporations and other business leaders, aims to support the effective targeting of G20 policy development. In June 2012 the ICC initiated a G20 Business Scorecard, with the aim of evaluating the G20's performance in response to business recommendations in the areas of financing for growth and development; green growth; trade and investment; and transparency and anti-corruption.

The ICC contributes to combating international crime connected with commerce through its Commercial Crime Services (CCS). Based in London, United Kingdom, the CCS operates according to two basic principles: to prevent and investigate commercial crime and to facilitate the prosecution of criminals involved in such crimes. In July 2008 the ICC issued guidelines on establishing and implementing internal whistleblowing programmes within businesses, aimed at exposing fraud. In March 2009 the ICC, in partnership with Transparency International, the UN Global Compact and the World Economic Forum, launched RESIST (Resisting Extortions and Solicitations in International Transactions), to provide recommendations to assist businesses with responding to attempted solicitation and extortion from clients.

Following the launch of the ICC's Business Action to Stop Counterfeiting and Piracy (BASCAP) initiative in November 2004, more than 150 companies and trade associations have become actively engaged in a set of projects designed to combat counterfeiting and piracy and increase awareness of the economic and social harm such activities cause. (In February 2011 the ICC warned that the global economic and social impacts of counterfeiting and piracy would reach US $1.7m. by 2015, putting at risk 2.5m. legitimate jobs annually.) In March 2008 chief executive officers and senior corporate executives participating in BASCAP convened in New York, USA, with representatives of the World Customs Organization, World Intellectual Property Organization and US Government to discuss means of co-operation in addressing counterfeiting and piracy. In October BASCAP published a set of intellectual property (IP) guidelines aimed at supporting businesses in managing copyright and branded materials, and deterring trade in counterfeit goods. In March 2010 BASCAP noted that jobs in creative industries were under threat from piracy, increasingly caused by illicit use of the internet (so-called digital piracy). An Anti-Counterfeiting Trade Agreement (ACTA) was opened for signature in October 2011. The ICC issues an annual *Intellectual Property Roadmap*.

The International Maritime Bureau (IMB) of the ICC operates the IMB Piracy Reporting Centre (IMB PRC), the world's only manned centre dedicated to the continuous monitoring of armed robberies at sea. The IMB PRC maintains an online Live Piracy Map, which plots recent piracy attacks, attempted attacks, and the positions of suspicious vessels, and compiles a *Live Piracy Report*, detailing incidents of maritime piracy. In January 2014 the IMB PRC reported that in 2013 a total of 264 ships had been attacked by pirates globally (compared with 297 in 2012 and 437 in 2011); of the reported attacks only 15 took place off the coast of Somalia, down from 75 in 2012 and 237 in 2011. Attacks described by the IMB PRC as 'low-level and opportunistic' that were perpetrated in Indonesian anchorages and waters accounted for more than one-half of all reported incidents in 2013.

The ICC provides a framework for settling international commercial disputes. The Commission on Arbitration acts as a forum for experts and also reviews the ICC's dispute settlement services, for example regarding the deployment of new technologies. In 2012 the ICC International Court of Arbitration, which was established in 1923, received 759 requests for arbitration, concerning 2,036 parties from 137 countries. In September 2013 an office of the Court was inaugurated in New York, USA, to administer ICC arbitrations throughout North America. Through professional advice and training support, ICC supported the establishment, in November 2013, of the Jerusalem Arbitration Centre, which was to adjudicate the resolution of commercial disputes between businesses in Israel and the Palestinian Territories. Other ICC services for dispute resolution include its Rules of Arbitration (updated Rules entered into force from 1 January 2012, the Rules having previously been revised in 1998), its Alternative Dispute Resolution, and the International Centre for Expertise. The latter administers ICC Rules of Expertise and Rules for Documentary Credit and Dispute Resolution Expertise (DOCDEX). The International Centre for Expertise administers a dispute resolution procedure in relation to applications received by the Internet Corporation for Assigned Names and Numbers (ICANN)'s ongoing expanded generic TLDs (gTLDs) programme. The ICC's internet-based Dispute Resolution Library (launched in 2008 and upgraded in February 2014) provides online access to ICC documentation on international dispute resolution. Updated ICC Rules of Mediation entered into effect on 1 January 2014.

The ICC's World Chambers Federation (WCF), a global network of chambers of commerce, acts as a platform for interaction and exchange of best practice. It is responsible for the ATA Carnet temporary export document system. The WCF also organizes the biennial World Chambers Congresses. At the sixth Congress, convened in Kuala Lumpur, Malaysia, in June 2009, the WCF signed a co-operation agreement with the UN. The eighth WCF Congress was held in Doha, Qatar, in April 2013, on the theme 'Opportunities for All'. The inaugural ICC World Trade Agenda Summit was held within the framework of the Congress, representing a discussion forum for participants in the ICC Business World Trade Agenda initiative, launched in 2011 to define a policy agenda aimed at advancing progress in the long-standing WTO Doha multilateral trade negotiations. In December 2013 the ICC welcomed the adoption by the ninth WTO Ministerial Conference, convened in Bali, Indonesia, of the Bali Package of measures designed to give renewed impetus to the Doha negotiations.

The ICC has developed rules and guidelines relating to electronic transactions, including guidelines for ethical advertising on the internet and for data protection. It has devised a system of standard trade definitions most commonly used in international sales contracts ('Incoterms'); an updated set of Incoterms—'Incoterms 2010'—entered into force in January 2011. ICC's Model International Sale Contract (most recent version: March 2013) enables businesses and lawyers to establish import-export agreements that are compatible with Incoterms 2010. The Uniform Customs and Practice (UCP) for Documentary Credits, developed by the ICC, and updated most recently in 2007 (the 'UCP 600' edition), is used by banks to finance international trade. New Uniform Rules for Forfaiting (URF) were adopted by the Banking Commission meeting in Mexico City, Mexico, in November 2012 and entered into force on 1 January 2013. ICC's new Uniform Rules for Bank Payment Obligations (URBPOs), a 21st century standard in supply chain finance that governs Bank Payment Obligations transactions worldwide were introduced in March 2013. There are also ICC voluntary codes for eliminating extortion and bribery, and for promoting sound environmental management practices. The first ICC Trade Finance Summit was held in Beijing, People's Republic of China, in October 2011. A new Consolidated ICC Code of Advertising and Marketing Communications was launched in September 2011, detailing standards for marketers selling over the internet, and aimed also at strengthening protection for online consumers. In April 2014 the ICC organized a conference, in Geneva, Switzerland, on Facilitating Trade in the Digital Economy.

The Commission on Banking—the ICC's largest policy commission—supports the global banking industry by providing assistance to policy-makers, drafting universal rules and guidelines (such as the UCP and URF, see above), and compiling relevant publications and market intelligence. In December 2012 a new Banking Commission Advisory Board and Executive Committee were inaugurated to provide strategic direction for the Commission in meeting increasing demands for policy and regulatory support, and for greater transparency and standardization in relation to trade finance products.

In mid-2006 the ICC launched the Business Action to Support the Information Society (BASIS) initiative, which aims to project, at international fora, the global business outlook on issues relating to the information society, such as internet governance, and the use of information and communications technologies in promoting development. BASIS contributes to the annual policy-setting Internet Governance Forum.

In January 2010 the ICC launched a new global framework for responsible environmental marketing communications. The ICC led the engagement of the global business sector in preparations for the UN Conference on Sustainable Development (Rio+20), convened in Rio de Janeiro, Brazil, in June 2012.

In co-operation with the Munich, Germany-based Ifo Institute for Economic Research, the ICC has since 1981 compiled a quarterly *World Economic Survey*, based on the input of more than 1,000 economic experts in 120 countries.

Finance

The ICC is a private, non-profit-making organization financed partly by contributions from National Committees and other members, according to the economic importance of the country that each represents, and partly by revenue from fees for various services and from sales of publications.

Publications

Annual Report.
Annual Review of International Banking Law & Practice.
Documentary Credits Insight (quarterly).
ICC Banking Commission Opinions.
ICC Global Survey on Trade Finance (annually).
ICC-IMF Market Snapshot.
ICC International Court of Arbitration Bulletin.
ICC Trade Register.
Intellectual Property Roadmap (annually).
Live Piracy Report.
World Economic Survey (jointly with the Ifo Institute for Economic Research, quarterly).

Publications on general and technical business and trade-related subjects are also available online.

INTERNATIONAL CRIMINAL COURT—ICC

Address: Maanweg 174, 2516 AB The Hague, Netherlands.
Telephone: (70) 5158515; **fax:** (70) 5158555; **e-mail:** otp.informationdesk@icc-cpi.int; **internet:** www.icc-cpi.int.

The ICC was established by the Rome Statute of the International Criminal Court, adopted by 120 states participating in a UN Diplomatic Conference in July 1998. The Rome Statute (and therefore the temporal jurisdiction of the ICC) entered into force on 1 July 2002, 60 days after ratification by the requisite 60th signatory state in April. The ICC is a permanent, independent body, in relationship with the UN, that aims to promote the rule of law and punish the most serious international crimes. The Rome Statute reaffirmed the principles of the UN Charter and stated that the relationship between the Court and the UN system should be determined by a framework relationship agreement between the states parties to the Rome Statute and the UN General Assembly: under the so-called negotiated relationship agreement, which entered into force in October 2004, upon signature by the Court's President and the Secretary-General of the UN, there was to be mutual exchange of information and documentation to the fullest extent and co-operation and consultation on practical matters, and it was stipulated that the Court might, if deemed appropriate, submit reports on its activities to the UN Secretary-General and propose to the Secretary-General items for consideration by the UN.

The Court comprises the Presidency (consisting of a President and first and second Vice-Presidents), Chambers (including a Pre-Trial Chamber, Trial Chamber and Appeals Chamber) with 18 permanent judges, Office of the Prosecutor (comprising the Chief Prosecutor and up to two Deputy Prosecutors), and Registry. The judges must each have a different nationality and equitably represent the major legal systems of the world, a fair geographical distribution, and a fair proportion of men and women. They are elected by the Assembly of States Parties to the Rome Statute from two lists, the first comprising candidates with established competence in criminal law and procedures and the second comprising candidates with established competence in relevant areas of international law, to terms of office of three, six or nine years. The President and Vice-Presidents are elected by an absolute majority of the judges for renewable three-year terms of office. The Chief Prosecutor is elected by an absolute majority of states parties to the Rome Statute to an unrenewable nine-year term of office.

The Court has established a Trust Fund for Victims (TFV) to finance compensation, restitution, or rehabilitation for victims (individuals or groups of individuals) of crimes under the jurisdiction of the Court. The Fund is administered by the Registry and supervised by an independent board of directors. During 2013 the TFV provided material support, and psychological and physical rehabilitation, to some 110,000 victims. In March of that year the Fund suspended its activities in the Central African Republic (CAR), owing to the deteriorating security situation there. In August 2012 the ICC issued its first decision on reparations for victims, in relation to the conviction in March of that year of Thomas Lubanga (see Situation in the Democratic Republic of the Congo). In March 2013 the TFV's reserve for reparations was raised to €1.8m. (from €1.2m.). More than 8,000 applications for reparations have been received by the Court.

By April 2014 21 cases in eight situations had been brought before the Court. Four situations were being addressed by the Court that had been referred to it by states party to the Rome Statute relating to occurrences on their territories; two situations (in Darfur and Libya) were being pursued that had been referred by the UN Security Council; and investigations *proprio motu* were being conducted into situations in Kenya and Côte d'Ivoire. In June 2013, following a referral from the Comoros Government, the Prosecutor agreed to initiate a preliminary investigation into a raid undertaken on 31 May 2010 by Israeli forces on a flotilla delivering humanitarian aid to Gaza. In February 2014 the Prosecutor opened a preliminary examination into the situation in the CAR since September 2012.

In October 2013 an extraordinary summit of the African Union (AU), convened on the theme 'Africa's relationship with the International Criminal Court', determined that—in order to safeguard the constitutional order, stability and integrity of member states—no trial proceedings ought to be commenced or continued before any international court or tribunal against any serving AU head of state or government, or against anybody acting in such capacity, during her or his term of office. The AU summit specifically requested the Court to defer until after the expiry of their terms of office the ongoing indictments against the serving President of Kenya, Uhuru Muigai Kenyatta, and his Vice-President, William Samoei Ruto. The AU also decided to convene a Contact Group to engage with the UN Security Council on all AU concerns concerning its relationship with the Court, including the proposed deferral of the Kenyan cases, and the arrest warrant issued in 2009 against President Omar al-Bashir of Sudan.

In January 2013 more than 50 UN member states, led by Switzerland, signed a letter urging the UN Security Council to refer the situation in Syria to the ICC.

Situation in Uganda: referred to the Court in January 2004 by the Ugandan Government; the Chief Prosecutor agreed to open an investigation into the situation in July; relates to the long-term unrest in the north of the country; in October 2005 the Court unsealed warrants of arrest (issued in July) against five commanders of the Ugandan Lord's Resistance Army (LRA), including the LRA leader, Joseph Kony; in July 2007 the Court's proceedings against one of the named commanders were terminated on the grounds that he had been killed during LRA rebel activities in August 2006; the other four suspects remained at large at April 2014.

Situation in the Democratic Republic of the Congo (DRC): referred in April 2004 by the DRC Government; the Chief Prosecutor agreed to open an investigation into the situation in June 2004; relates to alleged war crimes; in March 2006 Thomas Lubanga Dyilo, a DRC militia leader, was arrested by the Congolese authorities and transferred to the Court, thereby becoming the first ICC indictee to be captured; Lubanga was charged with conscripting child soldiers, a sealed warrant for his arrest having been issued in February; in July 2007 warrants of arrest were issued for the DRC rebel commanders Germain Katanga and Mathieu Ngudjolo Chui; Katanga was transferred into the custody of the Court in October 2007 and Ngudjolo Chui in February 2008; in April 2008 the Court unsealed a warrant of arrest for the rebel leader Bosco Ntaganda, relating to the exploitation of children under the age of 15 as soldiers during 2002–03; a second warrant for Ntaganda, expanding upon the original charges, was issued in July 2012; in July 2012 a warrant was issued for the arrest of Sylvestre Mudacumura, the commander of the Democratic Forces for the Liberation of Rwanda, relating to war crimes (specifically: cruel treatment; attacking civilians; mutilation; outrages against personal dignity; rape; torture; murder; destruction of property; and pillaging) allegedly committed during the period 20 January 2009–end-September 2010; Lubanga's trial—the first conducted by the Court—commenced in January 2009; the Prosecution concluded its presentation of its case in the trial of Lubanga in July 2009; Lubanga was found guilty in March 2012, in the first verdict given by the Court, and in July of that year he was sentenced to 14 years' imprisonment; the trial in the case of Katanga and Ngudjolo Chui commenced in November 2009; Ngudjolo Chui was acquitted of all charges of war crimes and crimes against humanity in December 2012; in March 2014 Katanga was found guilty of four counts of war crimes and one of crimes against humanity; in December 2011 charges relating to crimes against humanity and other war crimes were withdrawn against Callixte Mbarushimana, an alleged rebel leader who had been arrested by the French authorities in October

2010 and transferred to the custody of the Court in January 2011; in March 2013 Gen. Ntaganda surrendered to the US embassy in Kigali, Rwanda and was transferred to the custody of the Court; Mudacumura remained at large at April 2014.

Situation in the Central African Republic (CAR): referred in January 2005 by the CAR Government; the Chief Prosecutor agreed to open an investigation into the situation in May; relates to war crimes and crimes against humanity allegedly committed during the period October 2002–March 2003; in May 2008 the Court issued a warrant of arrest for Jean-Pierre Bemba Gombo, the leader of the Mouvement du Libération du Congo (the 'Banyamulenge'); Bemba was transferred into the custody of the Court in July 2008, and his trial commenced in November 2010; in November 2013 four men were arrested on charges of corruptly influencing witnesses in the Bemba trial.

Situation in Darfur, Sudan: referred to the Court in March 2005 by the UN Security Council following publication of the report of an International Commission of Inquiry on Darfur; the Chief Prosecutor agreed to open an investigation into the situation in June; relates to the situation prevailing in Darfur since 1 July 2002; the UN Secretary-General handed the Chief Prosecutor a sealed list of 51 names of people identified in the report as having committed crimes under international law; in April 2007 the Court issued warrants for the arrests of Ahmad Harun, a former Sudanese government minister, and Ali Kushayb, a leader of the Sudanese Janjaweed militia, who were both accused of perpetrating war crimes and crimes against humanity; both remained at large at April 2014; in July 2008 the Chief Prosecutor presented evidence that Sudan's President Omar al-Bashir had been responsible for committing alleged war crimes, including crimes against humanity and genocide, in Darfur; an arrest warrant for President al-Bashir was issued by the Court in March 2009; a second arrest warrant for President al-Bashir was issued in July 2010, charging him with genocide against three ethnic groups in Darfur; al-Bashir had not surrendered to the Court at April 2014; in May 2009 a summons was issued against the militia leader Bahr Idriss Abu Garda, who appeared voluntarily before the Court later in that month; the Pre-Trial Chamber examining the Garda case declined, in February 2010, to confirm the charges against him; in June 2010 Abdallah Banda Abakaer Nourain and Saleh Mohammed Jerbo Jamus surrendered voluntarily to the Court, having been accused, with Abu Garda, of attacking the Haskanita AU camp in September–October 2007 and causing the deaths of 12 peacekeeping troops deployed to the former AU Mission in Sudan; on 1 March 2012 the Court issued an arrest warrant for the Sudanese Minister of Defence, Abdelrahim Mohamed Hussein, for crimes against humanity and war crimes committed during August 2003–March 2004, when he was the country's Minister for the Interior, as detailed in the case of Harun and Kushayb; in October 2013 the Court terminated proceedings against Jerbo on the basis of strong evidence that he had died in the previous April; the trial of Banda was scheduled to commence in May 2014.

Situation in Kenya: in November 2009 the Presidency of the Court decided to assign the situation in Kenya (relating to violent unrest that followed the December 2007 presidential elections) to a Pre-Trial Chamber; in July 2009 the International Commission of Inquiry on Post-Election Violence (known also as the Waki Commission), which had been established by the Kenyan Government in February 2008, presented the Court Prosecutor with documentation, supporting materials, and a list of people suspected of being implicated in the unrest, which had resulted in some 1,200 fatalities; on 31 March 2010 Pre-Trial Chamber II granted the Prosecution authorization to open an investigation *proprio motu* into the situation of Kenya; in March 2011 the ICC issued summonses for six Kenyans alleged to be criminally responsible for crimes against humanity, and in April the six accused presented voluntarily to the Court; charges against four of the six: William Samoei Ruto, Joshua arap Sang, Francis Kirimi Muthaura, and Uhuru Muigai Kenyatta were confirmed in January 2012; in March, however, the Court Prosecutor filed to withdraw the charges against Muthaura; Kenyatta was elected as President of Kenya in March 2013; he assumed office, with Ruto as his Vice-President, in early April; trial proceedings against Ruto and arap Sang commenced in September 2013, although the process was adjourned for one week later in that month to enable Ruto to return to Kenya following a terrorist attack on a Nairobi shopping mall; the Kenyatta trial was scheduled to commence in mid-November; in early October the Court issued a warrant for the arrest of Walter Barasar, a Kenyan journalist who was accused of attempting to bribe a prosecution witness in the case against Ruto; shortly afterwards the AU resolved to request the Court to defer proceedings against Kenyatta and Ruto until the expiry of their terms of office in the Kenyan Government, in the interests of Kenya's sovereignty and national stability; at the end of October the Court determined to postpone the commencement of Kenyatta's trial to early February 2014; an indefinite postponement was announced in January further to a request by the prosecution, citing insufficient evidence; in late March the Trial Chamber announced that the Kenyatta trial was to commence on 7 October.

Situation in Libya: referred to the Court in February 2011 by the UN Security Council; in the following month the Prosecutor agreed to open an investigation into the situation in Libya since February 2011; in June 2011 the Court issued arrest warrants against the Libyan leader Col Muammar al-Qaddafi, Saif al-Islam (his son), and Abdullah al-Senussi (his former Head of Military Intelligence), regarding crimes against humanity (murder and persecution) committed in Libya—through the state apparatus and security forces—from 15 February until at least 28 February; in September 2011 the ICC Prosecutor requested INTERPOL to issue a Red Notice for the arrest of the three Libyan indictees; Col Qaddafi was killed during fighting with opposition forces on 20 October; in late November Saif al-Islam was detained in southern Libya; al-Senussi was detained by Mauritanian security forces in mid-March 2012 and was extradited to Libya in September; despite the ICC indictments the Libyan authorities have expressed their intention of bringing al-Islam and al-Senussi to trial within Libya on charges relating to their conduct under the al-Qaddafi regime, and in May 2012 the Libyan National Transitional Council presented a formal challenge to the ICC concerning the admissibility of the Court's case against the two men, on the grounds that the Libyan national judicial system was itself actively investigating their alleged crimes; in May 2013 an ICC Pre-Trial Chamber rejected Libya's challenge to the admissibility of the case against Saif al-Islam, stressing Libya's obligation to transfer him to the Court; in October a Pre-Trial Chamber concluded that the al-Senussi case was inadmissible before the Court and should proceed within Libya.

Situation in Côte d'Ivoire: in early October 2011 an ICC Pre-Trial Chamber agreed, at the request of the Prosecutor, to commence an investigation into alleged crimes committed in Côte d'Ivoire between 28 November 2010 and 12 April 2011, during a period of civil unrest resulting from disputed presidential election results, and to consider also any crimes that may be committed in the future in the context of this situation; in November 2011 the former president, Laurent Gbagbo, who had been in Ivorian custody since April, was transferred to the Court to face charges of crimes against humanity; a warrant for the arrest of his wife, Simone Gbagbo, was issued in February 2012 but only made public in November; Mme Gbagbo was not in the custody of the Court at September 2013; in February 2012 the Court expanded the scope of the Côte d'Ivoire investigation also to include crimes within the jurisdiction of the Court allegedly committed during the period 19 September 2002–28 November 2010; in September 2013 the Court unsealed an arrest warrant, initially issued in December 2011, against Charles Blé Goudé for four counts of crimes against humanity.

Situation in Mali: in January 2013, following a request made in July 2012 by the Government of Mali, the Prosecutor launched a formal investigation into atrocities allegedly perpetrated since January 2012 by armed militants in northern areas of Mali.

The Court conducts an Outreach Programme, which pursues activities (through community, legal, academic, and media divisions) aimed at raising awareness and understanding of the Court's mandate in the communities most affected by the situations and cases being addressed (i.e. currently in the CAR, Darfur—Sudan, the DRC, and Uganda).

By April 2014 122 states had ratified the Rome Statute.

THE JUDGES
(April 2014)

	Term ends*
President: Sang-Hyun Song (Republic of Korea)	2015
First Vice-President: Sanji Mmasenono Monageng (Botswana)	2018
Second Vice President: Cuno Jakob Tarfusser (Italy)	2018
Hans-Peter Kaul (Germany)	2015
Akua Kuenyehia (Ghana)	2015
Erkki Kourula (Finland)	2015
Anita Ušacka (Latvia)	2015
Ekaterina Trendafilova (Bulgaria)	2015
Joyce Aluoch (Kenya)	2018
Christine van den Wyngaert (Belgium)	2018
Silvia Alejandra Fernández de Gurmendi (Argentina)	2018
Kuniko Ozaki (Japan)	2018
Miriam-Defensor Santiago (Philippines)	2021

—continued	Term ends*
HOWARD MORRISON (United Kingdom)	2021
OLGA HERRERA CARBUCCIA (Dominican Republic)	2021
ROBERT FREMR (Czech Republic)	2021
CHILE EBOE-OSUJI (Nigeria)	2021
GEOFFREY ANDREW HENDERSON (Trinidad and Tobago)	2021

* Each term ends on 10 March of the year indicated.

Chief Prosecutor: FATOU B. BENSOUDA (The Gambia).

Registrar: HERMAN VON HEBEL (Netherlands).

Finance

The proposed budget for the International Criminal Court for 2013 amounted to €115.6m.

Publications

ICC Weekly Update (electronic publication).

Booklets, factsheet, official records.

Other International Criminal Tribunals

EXTRAORDINARY CHAMBERS IN THE COURTS OF CAMBODIA—ECCC

Address: National Rd 4, Chaom Chau Commune, Dangkao District, POB 71, Phnom Penh, Cambodia.

Telephone: (23) 861500; **fax:** (23) 861555; **e-mail:** info@eccc.gov.kh; **internet:** www.eccc.gov.kh.

Formally established as the Extraordinary Chambers in the Courts of Cambodia for the Prosecution of Crimes Committed during the Period of Democratic Kampuchea (17 April 1975–6 January 1979), the ECCC was inaugurated in July 2006 on the basis of an agreement concluded in June 2003 between the Cambodian Government and the UN. The ECCC is mandated to prosecute senior leaders of the former Khmer Rouge regime for serious contraventions of Cambodian and international law—including crimes against humanity, genocide and war crimes—committed during the period 17 April 1975–6 January 1979. The ECCC is a hybrid Cambodian tribunal with international participation, combining Cambodian and international judges and personnel. It applies international standards and acts independently of the Cambodian Government and the UN. The ECCC comprises a Pre-Trial Chamber, Trial Chamber and Supreme Court Chamber; an Office of the Co-Prosecutors; an Office of the Co-Investigating Judges; a Defence Support section; a Victims' Unit; and an Office of Administration. The UN Assistance to the Khmer Rouge Trials (UNAKRT) provides technical assistance to the ECCC. Victims may file complaints before the ECCC, and may apply to become Civil Parties to the proceedings. In October 2011 the Court's then International Co-Investigating Judge resigned, citing attempted interference by government officials in the investigation into Cases 003 and 004. His successor submitted his resignation on similar grounds in March 2012. A new International Co-Investigating Judge was appointed in July of that year. In February 2013 the Court determined to annul a previous ruling that had hitherto prevented the prosecution of alleged crimes of conflict-related sexual violence committed under the Khmer Rouge regime, such as rape, sexual slavery, and also forced marriage—which had allegedly been employed systematically with a view to severing traditional family bonds and manipulating citizens' loyalties. The ECCC's budget for 2013 totalled US $35.4m.

Case 001: in February 2009 the ECCC initiated proceedings ('Case 001') against its first defendant, Kaing Guek Eav (also known as 'Duch'), who had been charged under international law with crimes against humanity and grave breaches of the Geneva Conventions, and under Cambodian national law with homicide and torture offences, in relation to his former role under the Khmer Rouge regime as director of Tuol Sleng ('S-21') security centre, where at least 15,000 prisoners had been tortured and executed. The presentation of evidence in the Kaing Guek Eav case was concluded in September 2009, and closing statements were made in November. In July 2010 Kaing Guek Eav was found guilty and sentenced to 35 years of imprisonment; in February 2012, following an appeal in that case, lodged in March 2011, Kaing Guek Eav's sentence was increased to life imprisonment.

Case 002: in September 2010 four other senior figures in the Khmer Rouge regime (Nuon Chea, formerly the Deputy Secretary of the Party of Democratic Kampuchea; Ieng Sary, formerly Minister of Foreign Affairs; Khieu Samphan, formerly President of the State Presidium; and Ieng Thirith, formerly Minister of Social Affairs and Action) were indicted on charges of crimes against humanity, grave breaches of the Geneva Conventions, genocide, and offences under the Cambodian criminal code ('Case 002'). In January 2011 the Pre-Trial Chamber ordered the case to be sent for trial, and an initial hearing was held in June. In September the Trial Chamber issued a Severance Order mandating the division of Case 002 into a series of smaller trials, which were to be tried and adjudicated separately. The first trial ('Case 002/01') was to focus on the forced movement of population and related charges of crimes against humanity. In November the Trial Chamber ordered the unconditional release from detention of Ieng Thirith on the grounds that she was medically unfit to stand trial, having been diagnosed with clinical dementia; trial proceedings against the remaining three defendants commenced on 21 November. In December the Appeals Chamber overturned the decision on Ieng Thirith and ordered that she be re-examined; in September 2012 the original decision permitting Ieng Thirith's release was reinstated, but amended to include several provisos regarding her future movements, contacts and health status. In March 2013 Ieng Sary died of natural causes in detention. At the end of that month Nuon Chea, who was suffering ill health, was deemed by Court-appointed medical specialists to be fit to stand trial. In February, following an appeal by the Prosecutor, the Supreme Court Chamber annulled the September 2011 Severance Order issued by the Trial Chamber, on the grounds that the scope of Case 002/01 as defined by the Trial Chamber was not representative of the charges contained in the overall indictment. In April 2013 the Trial Chamber issued a second Severance Order that limited the scope of Case 002/01 to the forced evacuation of Phnom Penh in April 1975, the execution of former Lon Nol soldiers at the Toul Po Chreu execution site in Pursat immediately after the Khmer Rouge rose to power in 1975, and the second phase of the forced movement of population that was initiated in September 1975; remaining charges under Case 002 were deferred to subsequent trials. In May 2013 Nuon Chea and both Co-Prosecutors filed an appeal against the Trial Chamber's Second Severance Order relating to Case 002; in July, however, this was dismissed by the Supreme Court Chamber. At that time the Supreme Court Chamber also ordered that the evidentiary hearings in the second discrete trial to be conducted under Case 002 ('002/02') should be initiated as soon as possible following the closing submissions in Case 002/01, as well as decreeing that Case 002/02 should include, at a minimum, charges relating to the S-21 security centre, and also to a Khmer Rouge worksite, a co-operative, and to genocide. Furthermore, the Chamber requested that the establishment of a second panel of national and international judges within the Trial Chamber, to consider and adjudicate Case 002/02, should be addressed. The closing statements in Case 002/01 were concluded in October, and it was envisaged that the judgment would be made in the first half of 2014. A memorandum and workplan were issued by the Chamber in December 2013 outlining outstanding issues to be resolved prior to the commencement of hearings in Case 002/02.

Cases 003/004: in September 2009 the International Prosecutor, submitting to the Co-Investigating Judges a confidential list of the names of five additional suspects, requested a formal judicial investigation into two further cases ('Case 003' and 'Case 004'), also relating to alleged atrocities committed during the Period of Democratic Kampuchea; in April 2011 the Co-Investigating Judges notified the Co-Prosecutors of the conclusion of the investigation into Case 003; the investigation was, however, subsequently re-opened; by October 2013 no charges had been brought against the suspects in Cases 003 and 004.

National Co-Prosecutor: CHEA LEANG (Cambodia).

International Co-Prosecutor: NICHOLAS KOUMJIAN (USA).

National Co-Investigating Judge: YOU BUNLENG (Cambodia).

International Co-Investigating Judge: MARK BRIAN HARMON (USA).

SPECIAL TRIBUNAL FOR LEBANON

Address: POB 115, 2260 AC Leidschendam, Netherlands.

Telephone: (70) 800-3400; **e-mail:** stl-pressoffice@un.org; **internet:** www.stl-tsl.org.

In March 2006 the UN Security Council adopted a resolution requesting the UN Secretary-General to negotiate an agreement with the Lebanese Government on the establishment of an international tribunal to try those suspected of involvement in a terrorist attack that, in February 2005, had killed 23 people, including the former Prime Minister of Lebanon, Rafik Hariri. The resulting agreement on the Special Tribunal for Lebanon was endorsed by the Security Council in May 2007. The Tribunal, which became operational on 1 March 2009, comprises both international and Lebanese judges and applies Lebanese (not international) law. On its establishment the Tribunal took over the mandate of a terminated UN International Independent Investigation Commission (UNIIIC), which had been created by a resolution of the Security Council in April 2005 in order to gather evidence and assist the Lebanese authorities in their investigation into the February 2005 attacks, and whose mandate had later been expanded to investigate other assassinations that had occurred before and after the February 2005 attack. A Defence Office has been established within the Tribunal to protect the rights of the suspects, accused and their counsel, providing legal assistance and support where necessary. In January 2011 the Prosecutor submitted to the Pre-Trial Judge an indictment of four suspects—Salim Jamil Ayyash, Mustafa Amine Badreddine, Hussein Hassan Oneissi and Assad Hassan Sabra ('Ayyash et al.')—on charges of conspiracy to commit a terrorist act, in relation to the February 2005 atrocities. The indictment was confirmed in June 2011. In that month the Tribunal passed to the Lebanese authorities arrest warrants for the four suspects. In August the Tribunal also established jurisdiction in the cases concerning terrorist attacks perpetrated on 1 October 2004 against Marwan Hamadeh; on 21 June 2005 against George Hawi; and on 12 July 2005 against Elias el-Murr; accordingly the Lebanese authorities were ordered to transfer to the Tribunal all material relevant to these cases. The Tribunal determined in February 2012 to try the four accused in the case 'Ayyash et al.' *in absentia*, on the grounds that they had apparently absconded. Also in February 2012 the UN Secretary-General extended the mandate of the Special Tribunal for a further three years, with effect from 1 March. In July 2013 it was confirmed that a sealed indictment had been submitted by the Prosecutor against Hassan Habib Merhi, who was also accused of involvement in the February 2005 attack. In December 2013 the Trial Chamber ruled that Merhi should also be tried *in absentia*. Trial proceedings in the case 'Ayyash et al.' opened in January 2014, without the presence of the defendants, who had continued to evade arrest. In February the Chamber ruled that the Merhi case should be amalgamated into that of Ayyash et al. The Tribunal maintains an office in Beirut, Lebanon.

President of the Court: Sir DAVID BARAGWANATH (New Zealand).

Chief Prosecutor: NORMAN FARELL (Canada).

Registrar: DARYL A. MUNDIS (USA).

Head of Defence Office: FRANÇOIS ROUX (France).

RESIDUAL SPECIAL COURT FOR SIERRA LEONE

Address: POB 19536, 2500 CM The Hague, Netherlands.

E-mail: info@rscsl.org; **internet:** www.sc-sl.org.

In December 2013 the Residual Special Court assumed responsibility for the ongoing commitments of the Special Court for Sierra Leone, which had concluded its mandate to prosecute those 'bearing the greatest responsibility for committing violations against humanitarian law' committed in the territory of Sierra Leone since 20 November 1996. The final judgment in the case of Charles Taylor, who became the first former head of state to be found guilty of charges relating to war crimes by an international court, was issued in September 2013. The Residual Special Court, based in The Hague, Netherlands, was authorized to oversee witness protection and sentencing appeals. Sixteen judges were sworn-in to serve the Residual Special Court in early December. The Residual Special Court maintains an office in Freetown, Sierra Leone, that provides witness and victim support.

President of the Court: PHILIP NYAMU WAKI (Kenya).

INTERNATIONAL OLYMPIC COMMITTEE—IOC

Address: Château de Vidy, 1001 Lausanne, Switzerland.

Telephone: 216216111; **fax:** 216216216; **internet:** www.olympic.org.

The IOC was founded in 1894 to ensure the regular celebration of the Olympic Games. The Committee is a non-governmental international organization with the final authority on all questions concerning the Olympic Games and the Olympic Movement.

Organization

(April 2014)

INTERNATIONAL OLYMPIC COMMITTEE

The Committee comprises 115 members—who are representatives of the IOC in their countries and not their countries' delegates to the IOC, and include 15 active Olympic athletes, 15 National Olympic Committee presidents, 15 International Sports Federation presidents, and 70 other individuals—as well as 31 Honorary members and one Honour member. The members meet in session at least once a year: the 125th session was held in September 2013, in Buenos Aires, Argentina. A Nomination Commission examines and reports to the Executive Board on each candidate for membership of the IOC.

There are 204 recognized National Olympic Committees, which are the sole authorities responsible for the representation of their respective countries at the Olympic Games. The IOC may give recognition to International Sports Federations which undertake to adhere to the Olympic Charter, and which govern sports that comply with the IOC's criteria.

An International Council of Arbitration for Sport (ICAS) has been established. ICAS administers the Court of Arbitration for Sport which hears cases brought by competitors.

EXECUTIVE BOARD

The session of the IOC delegates to the Executive Board the authority to manage the IOC's affairs. The President of the Board is elected for an eight-year term, and is eligible for re-election once for an additional term of four years. The Vice-Presidents are elected for four-year terms, and may be re-elected after a minimum interval of four years. Members of the Board are elected to hold office for four years. The Executive Board generally meets four to five times per year.

President: THOMAS BACH (Germany).

Vice-Presidents: NAWAL EL MOUTAWAKEL (Morocco), Sir CRAIG REEDIE (United Kingdom), JOHN D. COATES (Australia).

Members of the Board: GUNILLA LINDBERG (Sweden), CHING-KUO WU (Taiwan), RENÉ FASEL (Switzerland), PATRICK JOSEPH HICKEY (Ireland), CLAUDIA BOKEL (Germany), JUAN ANTONIO SAMARANCH, Jr (Spain), SERGEY BUBKA (Ukraine), WILLI KALTSCHMITT LUJÁN (Guatemala), ANITA L. DEFRANTZ (USA), UGUR ERDENER (Turkey).

IOC COMMISSIONS

Athletes' Commission: f. 1981; comprising active and retired athletes, represents their interests; convenes an Athletes' Forum every two years; may issue recommendations to the Executive Board.

Commission for Culture and Olympic Education: f. 2000 by merger of the Culture Commission (f. 1968) and the IOC Commission for the International Olympic Academy and Olympic Education (f. 1961).

Entourage Commission: f. 2010 to address issues relating to members of Olympic athletes' entourages, such as sports coaches and trainers.

Ethics Commission: f. 1999 to develop and monitor rules and principles to guide the selection of hosts for the Olympic Games, and the organization and execution of the Games; the activities of the Ethics Commission are funded by the Foundation for Universal Olympic Ethics, inaugurated in 2001.

Evaluation Commission: prepares a technical assessment of candidate cities' bids to host the Olympic Games, analysing their suitability.

Finance Commission: aims to ensure the efficient management of the IOC's financial resources.

International Relations Commission: f. 2002 to promote a positive relationship between the Olympic Movement and national governments and public authorities.

Juridical Commission: f. 1974 to provide legal opinions and perform other tasks of a legal nature.

Marketing Commission: helps to perpetuate the work of the Olympic Movement through the provision of financial resources and programmes aimed at protecting and enhancing the Olympic image and Olympic values.

Medical Commission: f. 1967; concerned with the protection of the health of athletes, respect for medical and sport ethics, and equality for all competing athletes; a new Olympic Movement Medical Code entered into force in October 2009.

Nominations Commission: f. 1999 to institute a procedure for electing and re-electing IOC members.

Olympic Philately, Numismatic and Memorabilia Commission: f. 1993; aims to increase awareness of the Olympic ideal through the promotion of Olympic commemorative paraphenalia.

Olympic Programme Commission: reviews, and analyses the Olympic programme of sports, disciplines and events; after each Games develops recommendations on the principles and structure of the programme.

Olympic Solidarity Commission: f. 1971; assists National Olympic Committees (NOCs); responsible for managing and administering the share of television rights allocated to NOCs.

Press Commission: advises Olympic Games organizing committees on the provision of optimum working conditions for the written and photographic media.

Radio and Television Commission: advises Olympic Games organizing committees and national broadcasting organizations on the provision of the optimum working conditions for the broadcast media.

Sport and Environment Commission: f. 1995 to promote environmental protection and sustainable development.

Sport and Law Commission: f. 1996 to act as a forum for discussion of legal issues concerning the Olympic Movement.

Sport for All Commission: f. 1983 to encourage and support the principles of Sport for All; organizes the periodic IOC World Conference Sport for All (2015: Durban, South Africa).

TV Rights and New Media Commission: prepares and implements overall IOC strategy for future broadcast rights negotiations.

Women and Sport Commission: f. 2004 (by transformation of a working group, f. 1995 to advise the Executive Board on policies to promote women in sport).

In addition, co-ordination commissions for specific Olympic Games are founded after the election of a host city to oversee and assist the organizing committee in the planning and management of the Games: in April 2014 co-ordination commissions were in force for Nanjing Youth Olympic Games 2014; Rio de Janeiro Summer Olympic Games 2016; Lillehammer Youth Winter Olympic Games 2016, Pyeongchang Winter Olympic Games 2018, and Tokyo Summer Olympic Games 2020.

OLYMPIC CONGRESS

Olympic Congresses are held periodically, on particular themes, to gather together the different components of the Olympic Movement with the aim of analysing the Movement's strengths and weaknesses and evaluating ongoing opportunities and challenges. The first Congress (Paris, France, 1894) addressed the theme 'Re-establishment of the Olympic Games'; the most recent, the 13th Congress (Copenhagen, Denmark, October 2009) was convened on the theme 'The Role of the Olympic Movement in Society and in all Regions of the World'.

ADMINISTRATION

The administration of the IOC is under the authority of the Director-General, who is appointed by the Executive Board, on the proposal of the President, and is assisted by Directors responsible for the following administrative sectors: international co-operation; Olympic Games co-ordination; finance, marketing and legal affairs; technology; control and co-ordination of operations; communications; and medical.

Director-General: CHRISTOPHE DE KEPPER (Belgium).

Activities

The fundamental principles of the Olympic Movement are:

Olympism is a philosophy of life, exalting and combining, in a balanced whole, the qualities of body, will and mind. Blending sport with culture, education and respect for the environment, Olympism seeks to create a way of life based on the joy found in effort, the educational value of good example and respect for universal fundamental ethical principles.

Under the supreme authority of the IOC, the Olympic Movement encompasses organizations, athletes and other persons who agree to be guided by the Olympic Charter. The criterion for belonging to the Olympic movement is recognition by the IOC.

The goal of the Olympic Movement is to contribute to building a peaceful and better world by educating youth through sport practised without discrimination of any kind and in the Olympic spirit, which requires mutual understanding with a spirit of friendship, solidarity and fair play.

The activity of the Olympic Movement is permanent and universal. It reaches its peak with the bringing together of the athletes of the world at the great sport festival, the Olympic Games.

The Olympic Charter is the codification of the fundamental principles, rules and by-laws adopted by the IOC. It governs the organization and operation of the Olympic movement and stipulates the conditions for the celebration of the Olympic Games. In March 1999, following the publication in January of the results of an investigation into allegations of corruption and bribery, an extraordinary session of the IOC was convened, at which the six Committee members were expelled for violating rules relating to Salt Lake City's bid to host the Olympic Winter Games in 2002; four other members had already resigned. The President of the IOC retained his position after receiving a vote of confidence. The session approved a number of reform measures, including the establishment of a new independent Ethics Commission to oversee bids to host the Olympic Games. In December 1999, having considered the recommendations of the Commission, the IOC adopted 50 reforms aimed at creating a more open, responsive and accountable organization. These included a new permanent procedure for the elimination of member visits to bid cities, the application of terms of office, limiting the expansion of the Summer Games, and the election of 15 active athletes to the IOC membership.

In response to ongoing concern about drugs abuse in sport an independent World Anti-Doping Agency was established by the IOC in November 1999 and, on 1 January 2004, a World Anti-Doping Code entered into effect. Participants attending the World Conference on Doping in Sport, held in Copenhagen, Denmark, in March 2003, adopted the Copenhagen Declaration on Doping in Sport and promoted the Code as the basis for combating such abuses. The Code has subsequently been revised; an updated edition was endorsed in November 2013 by the fourth World Conference on Doping in Sport (convened in Johannesburg, South Africa); the updated Code was to enter into effect on 1 January 2015. In July 2000 the IOC established a subsidiary International Olympic Truce Foundation, and an International Olympic Truce Centre, based in Athens, Greece, with the aim of promoting a culture of peace through the pursuit of sport and the Olympic ideals.

In October 2009 the IOC was granted observer status at the UN. The 13th Olympic Congress, convened in that month, in Copenhagen, approved a set of 66 recommendations with a particular emphasis on youth and athletes, including proposals to promote greater engagement by young people in sport; to improve the protection of athletes medically, psychologically, and in retirement; to make full use of new digital technology, and to establish a digital task force in this respect; and to utilize the Youth Olympic Games as a model for youth competition.

ASSOCIATED BODIES

International Committee for Fair Play: Csörsz út 49-51, Budapest, Hungary; tel. (1) 225-0521; fax (1) 225-0522; e-mail cifp@fairplayinternational.org; internet www.fairplayinternational.org; f. 1963 to defend and promote good sportsmanship; organizes annual World Fair Play Awards; Pres. Dr JENÖ KAMUTI; Sec.-Gen. JEAN DURRY (France).

World Anti-Doping Agency (WADA): Stock Exchange Tower, Suite 1700, 800 Place Victoria, POB 120 Montréal, QC H4Z 1B7, Canada; tel. (514) 904-9232; fax (514) 904-8650; e-mail info@wada-ama.org; internet www.wada-ama.org; f. 1999; aims to promote and co-ordinate efforts to achieve drug-free sport; the World Anti-Doping Program focuses on three pillars: the World Anti-Doping Code (which entered into force on 1 Jan. 2004, and has been subsequently revised—a new edition of the Code was scheduled to enter into effect from Jan. 2015), International Standards, and Models of Best Practice and Guidelines; principal areas of activity are: monitoring compliance with the Code; co-operation with law enforcement; science and medicine (including maintaining and updating annually a List of Prohibited Substances and Methods—detailing those that are prohibited at all times, in competition only, and only for certain sports); anti-doping co-ordination; anti-doping development; education and awareness activities; and athlete outreach; initiated, in 2000, an Independent Observer (IO) programme for the random testing of athletes, and observing and reporting on doping control and results management processes, at major events; and, in 2005, launched the internet-based Anti-Doping Administration and Management System (ADAMS), a clearing house for anti-doping data, such as laboratory results, 'therapeutic use exemptions', and information relating to Anti-Doping Rule Violations (ADRVs); periodically convenes a World Conference on Doping in Sport (the fourth was held in Johannesburg, South Africa, in Nov. 2013); Pres. Sir CRAIG REEDIE (United Kingdom); Dir-Gen. DAVID HOWMAN (New Zealand).

The World Olympics Association, uniting competitors from past Olympic Games, and the International Paralympic Committee are affiliates of the IOC.

THE GAMES OF THE OLYMPIAD

The Olympic Summer Games take place during the first year of the Olympiad (period of four years) that they are to celebrate. They are the exclusive property of the IOC, which entrusts their organization to a host city seven years in advance.

1896 Athens	1968 Mexico City
1900 Paris	1972 Munich
1904 St Louis	1976 Montreal
1908 London	1980 Moscow
1912 Stockholm	1984 Los Angeles
1920 Antwerp	1988 Seoul
1924 Paris	1992 Barcelona
1928 Amsterdam	1996 Atlanta
1932 Los Angeles	2000 Sydney
1936 Berlin	2004 Athens
1948 London	2008 Beijing
1952 Helsinki	2012 London
1956 Melbourne	2016 Rio de Janeiro
1960 Rome	2020 Tokyo
1964 Tokyo	

Olympic sports are governed by recognized International Federations that have adopted and are implementing the WADA Anti-Doping Code, and are admitted to the Olympic programme by decision of the IOC at least seven years before the Games. In September 2013 the 125th IOC session adopted the following core list of Olympic summer sports for inclusion in the 2020 Games: aquatics (including swimming, diving, synchronized swimming and water polo), archery, athletics, badminton, basketball, boxing (including women's boxing, which first entered the programme at the 2012 London Games), canoeing, cycling, equestrian, fencing, field hockey, football, gymnastics, handball, judo, modern pentathlon, rowing, sailing, shooting, taekwondo, table tennis, tennis, triathlon, volleyball and weightlifting. Further sports may be included from an additional list (in 2009 golf and rugby sevens were added to the programme for the 2012 and 2016 Games, and in September 2013 wrestling was added to the summer programme for 2020 and 2024).

OLYMPIC WINTER GAMES

The Olympic Winter Games comprise competitions in sports practised on snow and ice. Since 1994 they have been held in the second calendar year following that in which the Games of the Olympiad take place.

1924 Chamonix	1980 Lake Placid
1928 St Moritz	1984 Sarajevo
1932 Lake Placid	1988 Calgary
1936 Garmisch-Partenkirchen	1992 Albertville
1948 St Moritz	1994 Lillehammer
1952 Oslo	1998 Nagano
1956 Cortina d'Ampezzo	2002 Salt Lake City
1960 Squaw Valley	2006 Turin
1964 Innsbrück	2010 Vancouver
1968 Grenoble	2014 Sochi
1972 Sapporo	2018 Pyeongchang
1976 Innsbrück	

The Winter Games may include biathlon, bobsleigh, curling, ice hockey, luge, skating, and skiing (including Alpine skiing, cross-country skiing, freestyle skiing, Nordic combined skiing, ski jumping and snowboarding).

YOUTH OLYMPIC GAMES

In July 2007 the IOC determined to establish Summer and Winter Youth Olympic Games, in which athletes aged between 14 and 18 years may compete.

2010 Singapore (summer)	2014 Nanjing (summer)
2012 Innsbrück (winter)	2016 Lillehammer (winter)

Finance

The IOC derives marketing revenue from the sale of broadcast rights, the Olympic Partners sponsorship Programme, local sponsorship, ticketing, and licensing. Some 8% of this is retained for the Committee's operational budget, with the remainder allocated to Olympic organizing committees, National Olympic Committees and teams, and international sports federations.

Publications

IOC Newsletter (weekly).

Olympic Review (quarterly).

INTERNATIONAL ORGANIZATION FOR MIGRATION—IOM

Address: 17 route des Morillons, CP 71, 1211 Geneva 19, Switzerland.

Telephone: 227179111; **fax:** 227986150; **e-mail:** info@iom.int; **internet:** www.iom.int.

The Intergovernmental Committee for Migration (ICM) was founded in 1951 as a non-political, humanitarian organization with a predominantly operational mandate, including the handling of humane, orderly and planned migration to meet specific needs of emigration and immigration countries; and the processing and movement of refugees, displaced persons and other individuals in need of international migration services to countries offering them resettlement opportunities, as well as facilitating the voluntary return and reintegration of migrants, refugees and internally displaced persons. In 1989 ICM's name was changed to the IOM. IOM was admitted as an observer to the UN General Assembly in 1992.

MEMBERS

There are 155 member states and 11 observer member states. In addition, 85 international, governmental and non-governmental organizations hold observer status with IOM.

Organization

(April 2014)

COUNCIL

IOM is governed by a Council that is composed of representatives of all member governments, and has the responsibility for making final decisions on policy, programmes and financing.

EXECUTIVE COMMITTEE

An Executive Committee of nine member governments elected by the Council examines and reviews the organization's work; considers and reports on any matter specifically referred to it by the Council; advises the Director-General on any matters that he may refer to it; makes, between sessions of the Council, any urgent decisions on matters falling within the competence of the Council, which are then submitted for approval by the Council; and presents advice or proposals to the Council or the Director-General on its own initiative.

ADMINISTRATION

The Director-General is responsible to the Council and the Executive Committee. There are Departments of International Co-operation and Partnerships, Migration Management, Operations and Emergencies, and Resources Management. In addition, there are special units for Gender Co-ordination and Occupational Health. In recent years IOM has transferred some administrative functions from its headquarters in Geneva, Switzerland, to two administrative centres, located in Manila, Philippines, and Ciudad del Saber, Panama. Nine Regional Offices have been established to formulate regional strategies and plans of action and to provide programmatic and administrative support to the countries within its region. These are located in Dakar, Senegal; Nairobi, Kenya; Pretoria, South Africa; Cairo, Egypt; San José, Costa Rica; Buenos Aires, Argentina; Bangkok, Thailand; Brussels, Belgium; Vienna, Austria. There are Special Liaison Offices in Addis Ababa, Ethiopia and in New York, USA. IOM has more than 250 country and sub-country offices and a field presence in some 480 locations. Four country offices—in Helsinki, Finland; Berlin, Germany; Tokyo, Japan; and Washington, DC, USA—have additional responsibilities for resource mobilization; and five have regional co-ordinating functions (in Canberra, Australia, for the Pacific; Georgetown, Guyana, for the Caribbean; Rome, Italy, for the Mediterranean; Astana, Kazakhstan, for Central Asia; and Bangkok, Thailand, for South Asia).

Director-General: WILLIAM LACY SWING (USA).

Deputy Director-General: LAURA THOMPSON CHACÓN (Costa Rica).

Activities

IOM estimates that migrants comprise some 3.1% of the global population, and that some 15%–20% of migrant movements are unregulated. IOM aims to provide assistance to member governments in meeting the operational challenges of migration, to advance understanding of migration issues, to encourage social and economic development through migration and to work towards effective respect of the human dignity and well-being of migrants. It provides a full range of assistance to, and sometimes de facto protection of, migrants, refugees, internally displaced persons (IDPs) and other individuals in need of international migration services. This includes recruitment, selection, processing, medical examinations, and language and cultural orientation courses, placement, activities to facilitate reception and integration and other advisory services. Since it commenced operations in February 1952 IOM is estimated to have provided assistance to more than 12m. migrants.

IOM supports the efforts of governments and other stakeholders to formulate effective national, regional and global migration management policies and strategies; and conducts research, aimed at guiding migration policy and practice, in areas including migration trends and data, international migration law, migration and development, health and migration, counter-trafficking, labour migration, trade, remittances, irregular migration, integration and return migration. IOM co-ordinates its refugee activities with the UN High Commissioner for Refugees (UNHCR) and with governmental and non-governmental partners. Since 2001 IOM has invited its members, international and non-governmental organizations, representatives of civil society and the private sector, and academics to participate in an annual International Dialogue on Migration (IDM). In 2013 the forum was dedicated to a high-level Diaspora Ministerial Conference, which was held, for the first time, in June to gather information regarding diaspora policies, practices and community needs. The Conference contributed to IOM's preparations for a second High-level Dialogue on International Migration and Development (the first having been held in 2006), convened by the UN General Assembly in October 2013 on the theme 'Making Migration Work'. The focus of the IDM in 2014 was 'Human Mobility and Development: Emerging Trends and New Opportunities for Partnerships'; within its framework a workshop was held in March on 'South-South Migration: Partnering Strategically for Development'.

IOM was a founder member with other international organizations of the inter-agency Global Migration Group (GMG, established as the Geneva Migration Group in April 2003 and renamed in 2006). The GMG provides a framework for discussion among the heads of member organizations on the application of decisions and norms relating to migration, and for stronger leadership in addressing related issues. Since 2007 the GMG has organized a regular Global Forum for Migration and Development (GFMD). The seventh GFMD meeting was scheduled to be held in May 2014 in Stockholm, Sweden. In 2013 the GMG prepared a series of recommendations to be considered by the High-level Dialogue on International Migration and Development, held in October, regarding the incorporation of migration into the post-2015 UN Development Agenda.

Periodic regional consultative processes (RCPs) on migration, with participation by representatives of governments, international organizations and other stakeholders, provide a platform for dialogue and exchange of information on migration-related themes. The following RCPs were active in 2014: the Inter-Governmental Consultations on Migration, Asylum and Refugees (launched in 1985, with 17 member states); the Budapest Process (1991, covering Europe and the Commonwealth of Independent States, with working groups on the Black Sea, Silk Routes and South-Eastern European regions); Puebla Process (1996, Americas and the Caribbean); Inter-Governmental Asia-Pacific Consultations on Refugees, Displaced Persons and Migrants (1996, 34 states and territories); South American Conference on Migration (1999, South America); Migration Dialogue for West Africa (2000, 15 partner countries); Migration Dialogue for Southern Africa (2000, 15 member and nine observer countries); Bali Process on People Smuggling, Trafficking in Persons and Related Transnational Crime (2002, 46 countries and territories); 5+5 Dialogue (2002, Western Mediterranean: Algeria, France, Italy, Libya, Malta, Mauritania, Morocco, Portugal, Spain and Tunisia); Colombo Process (2003, 11 Asian states); Mediterranean Transit Dialogue (2003, with 45 partner states, including the European Union (EU) membership, and Algeria, Cape Verde, Egypt, Ethiopia, Ghana, Kenya, Lebanon, Libya, Mali, Morocco, Niger, Nigeria, Norway, Senegal, Switzerland, Syria, Tunisia and Turkey); IGAD-RCP (2008, the six Intergovernmental Authority on Development—IGAD—member states); the Abu Dhabi dialogue (2008, comprising the 11 Colombo Process countries as well as nine migrant destination countries in Asia and the Middle East); the Prague Process (2009, with 50 members, from the EU, Schengen Area, Eastern Partnership, and from the Western Balkans, Central Asia, Russia and Turkey); and the Almatı Process (formalized in 2012 and comprising the following core participating states: Afghanistan, the People's Republic of China, Iran, Kazakhstan, Kyrgyzstan, Pakistan, Tajikistan and Turkmenistan). Global meetings of the chairmanships of the RCPs have also been convened, under IOM auspices periodically since 2007: the fourth global meeting of RCPs was held in May 2013, in Lima, Peru.

In October 2005 IOM's Director-General inaugurated a new Business Advisory Board, comprising 13 business leaders representing a cross-section of global concerns. It was envisaged that the initiative would promote an effective partnership between IOM and the private sector aimed at supporting the planning, development and implementation of improved mobility policies and practices.

IOM acknowledges a direct link between migration and both climate change and environmental degradation; so-called environmental migration (both cross-border and internal) is particularly prevalent in the world's poorest countries. In March 2011 IOM organized a workshop aimed at assisting the international community in preparing for environmental migration.

IOM supports governments to implement reparation programmes to persons who had been displaced or harmed under previous regimes. IOM implements a Technical Assistance to the Administrative Reparation Programme in Colombia initiative, launched in January 2008, with the aim of supporting the Colombian authorities in compensating—as an act of solidarity—the victims of violence inflicted by illegal armed militia in that country.

Across all its areas of activities IOM aims to support the protection of rights, migration health, the promotion of international migration law, and gender equality. IOM's Migration Health Division aims to ensure that migrants are fit to travel, do not pose a danger to those travelling with them, and that they receive medical attention and care when necessary. IOM also undertakes research and other technical support and policy development activities in the field of health care. Medical screening of prospective migrants is routinely conducted, along with immunizations and specific counselling, e.g. for HIV/AIDS. IOM administers programmes for disabled refugees and undertakes medical evacuation of people affected by conflict. IOM collaborates with government health authorities and relevant intergovernmental and non-governmental organizations. In September 1999 IOM and UNAIDS signed a co-operation framework to promote awareness on HIV/AIDS issues relating to displaced populations, and to ensure that the needs of migrants are incorporated into national and regional AIDS strategies. In October IOM and the World Health Organization signed an agreement to strengthen collaborative efforts to improve the health care of migrants. IOM undertakes diverse initiatives aimed at ensuring the protection of migrant women and girls, who are deemed to be especially vulnerable to exploitation (in unregulated professions, or as victims of trafficking), abuse, violence, and displacement. IOM provides assistance to victims of human trafficking, supports the social reintegration of trafficked young girls and adolescents, offers psychosocial support and family therapy to migrant women who have suffered abuse, and focuses on strengthening community-based prevention mechanisms aimed at ensuring the safety of the migration process. In March 2013 IOM and the International Commission on Missing Persons concluded a co-operation agreement, under which they were jointly to address the migration process, displacement, and human trafficking as causes of people being reported as missing, and to conduct research studies on matters of mutual interest.

MIGRATION AND DEVELOPMENT

IOM places a strategic focus on fostering a deeper understanding of the linkages between migration and development; and on enhancing the benefits that well-managed migration can have for the development, growth and prosperity of migrants' countries of origin and of destination, as well as for the migrants personally. IOM's activities in this area include strengthening the capacity of governments and other stakeholders to engage expatriate migrant communities in development processes in their countries of origin; promoting economic and community development in places from which there is a high level of emigration; enhancing the development impact of remittances; and facilitating the return and reintegration of qualified nationals.

IOM's Migration and Economic/Community Development programme area covers three principal fields of activity. First, IOM seeks to maximize the positive potential from migration for the development of countries of origin and destination, promoting an increase in more development-oriented migration policies, and implementing initiatives aimed at building the capacity of governments and other stakeholders in countries of origin to involve their migrant populations in home country development projects. Second, IOM aims to address the root causes of economically motivated migration by assisting governments and other actors with the strategic focusing of development activities to expand economic opportunities and improve social services and infrastructures in regions experiencing outward or returning migration. Third, IOM promotes data collection, policy dialogue and dissemination of good practices, and pilot project implementation, in the area of remittances (funds sent home by migrant workers, mainly in the form of private money transfers), with the aim of improving the development impact of remittances. IOM helped to organize the Global Consultation on Migration, Remittances and Development: Responding to the Global Economic Crisis from a Gender Perspective, which was convened in June–July 2009, in Switzerland; the meeting adopted a communiqué detailing policy recommendations.

IOM's Capacity Building Through Qualified Human Resources and Experts programme area focuses on the return from abroad and socio-economic reintegration of skilled and qualified nationals. Return and Reintegration of Qualified Nationals (RQN) and similar projects include recruitment, job placement, transport and limited employment support services, and aim to influence the economic and social environment in countries of origin in a manner conducive to further returns. IOM also focuses on the recruitment and selection of highly trained workers and professionals to fill positions in priority sectors of the economy in developing countries for which qualified persons are not available locally, taking into account national development priorities as well as the needs and concerns of receiving communities.

IOM operates the Migration for Development in Africa (MIDA) institutional capacity-building programme, which provides a framework for transferring skills and resources from African migrants to their countries of origin. IOM and the UN Development Programme (UNDP) jointly implement the Qualified Expatriate Somali Technical Support (QUESTS)-MIDA scheme, which aims to engage technical expertise in the areas of policy and legislation, human resources management, and public financial management, among the Somali diaspora, to support the rebuilding of key governance foundations in parts of Somalia. IOM and the EU jointly fund a scheme to support Rwandan students abroad and encourage their return to Rwanda.

In 2011 migrants were estimated to have remitted some US $372,000m. to developing countries of origin. In March 2009 IOM and FAO agreed to collaborate on supporting agricultural projects in home countries funded by remittances from migrants in OECD member states. IOM has initiated a project entitled 'Improving Knowledge of Remittance Corridors and Enhancing Development through Inter-Regional Dialogue and Pilot Projects in South-East Asia and Europe' recognizing the significant impact on development of funds returned to their home countries by migrant workers. The project was to focus particularly on the Philippines and Indonesia.

In April 2006 IOM and the Netherlands Government initiated the Temporary Return of Qualified Nationals (TRQN) project, with the aim of supporting reconstruction and development efforts in Afghanistan, Bosnia and Herzegovina, Kosovo, Montenegro, Serbia, Sierra Leone and Sudan. Under the TRQN, IOM provided logistical and financial assistance to experts originating in any of the target countries who were also nationals of or had residence in the Netherlands, to help them to participate in projects aimed at enriching the target countries. TRQN II was undertaken during July 2009–September 2012. TRQN III commenced in November 2012, with a three-year objective of supporting development efforts in Afghanistan, Armenia, Cape Verde, Georgia, Ghana, Iraq, Morocco, Somalia and South Sudan.

IOM offers Assisted Voluntary Return (AVR) services to migrants and governments, with the aim of facilitating the efficient and humane return and reintegration of migrants who wish to repatriate voluntarily to their countries of origin. Pre-departure, transportation and post-arrival assistance is provided to unsuccessful asylum seekers, migrants in irregular situations, migrants stranded in transit, stranded students, etc. AVR services can be tailored to the particular needs of specific groups, such as vulnerable migrants. IOM established a Stranded Migrant Facility in 2005.

During October 2006–October 2007 IOM implemented the pilot Information on Return and Reintegration in Countries of Origin (IRRiCO) project, which aimed to establish an internet-based database of relevant information in support of voluntary returns and reintegration, for use both by service providers and by migrants considering returning home. IRRiCO II, with the participation of 20 countries of origin and nine European countries, was launched in September 2008.

The IOM Development Fund (founded in 2001 as the '1035 Facility', and renamed in January 2012) supports developing member states and member states with economies in transition with the implementation of migration management capacity-building projects. By early 2014 some 390 projects in 112 member states had been supported by the Fund, at a cost of US $42m.

FACILITATING MIGRATION

Integrated world markets, transnational business networks and the rapid growth of communications technology have contributed to large-scale movements of workers, students, family members, and other migrants. IOM implements programmes that assist governments and migrants with recruitment, language training, pre-departure cultural orientation, pre-consular support services, arrival reception, and integration, and has introduced initiatives in areas including document verification, migrant information, interviews, applicant testing and logistical support. There are three main branches of Facilitating Migration programming: Labour Migration; Migrant Processing and Assistance; and Migrant Integration.

Through its Labour Migration activities, IOM aims to promote regulated orderly labour migration while combating illegal migration and to foster the economic and social development of countries of origin, transit and destination. Jointly with governments and other agencies, IOM has developed specific labour migration programmes that include elements such as capacity building; pre-departure training; return and reintegration support; and regional dialogue and planning.

Through its Migrant Processing and Assistance activities IOM provides assistance to facilitate migration under organized and regular migration schemes that are tailored to meet specific programme needs and cover the different stages of the migration process: information and application, interview and approval, and post-approval (including pre-departure counselling and cultural orientation).

IOM's Migration Integration activities promote strategies aimed at enabling migrants to adjust easily to new environments abroad and focus on the dissemination of information on the rights and obligations of migrants and refugees in home and in host countries, the provision of advisory and counselling services, and the reinforcement of their skills. In addition IOM promotes awareness-raising activities in host societies that highlight the positive contributions that migrants can make, with a view to reducing the risks of discrimination and xenophobia.

REGULATING MIGRATION

IOM aims to counter the growing problem of smuggling and trafficking in migrants, which has resulted in several million people being exploited by criminal agents and employers. IOM aims to provide shelter and assistance for victims of trafficking; to provide legal and medical assistance to migrants uncovered in transit or in the receiving country; and to offer voluntary return and reintegration assistance. The organization maintains the IOM Global Human Trafficking Information Management System (also known as the IOM Global Database), which aims to facilitate the management of assistance for victims of trafficking. IOM organizes mass information campaigns in countries of origin, in order to highlight the risks of smuggling and trafficking, and aims to raise general awareness of the problem. The most common countries of origin covered in the database are Belarus, Bulgaria, the Dominican Republic, Moldova, Romania and Ukraine. IOM also provides training to increase the capacity of governments and other organizations to counter irregular migration.

Through its Technical Co-operation on Migration Division, IOM offers advisory services to governments on the optimum administrative structures, policy, legislation, operational systems and human resource systems required to regulate migration. IOM technical co-operation also focuses on capacity-building projects such as training courses for government migration officials, and analysis of and suggestions for solving emerging migration problems. Throughout these activities, IOM aims to maintain an emphasis on the rights and well-being of migrants, and in particular to ensure that the specific needs of migrant women are incorporated into programmes and policies.

In October 2009 IOM launched a campaign entitled 'What Lies Behind the Things We Buy?', which aimed to draw attention to the use of trafficked and exploited labour in the manufacture of cheap goods.

FORCED MIGRATION

IOM provides services to assist with the resettlement of individuals accepted under regular national immigration programmes. These include supporting the processing of relevant documentation; medical screening; arranging safe transportation; and, in some cases, the provision of language training and cultural orientation. IOM also assists with the voluntary repatriation of refugees, mainly in support of UNHCR's voluntary repatriation activities.

In emergency situations IOM provides transportation and humanitarian assistance to individuals requiring evacuation, as well as providing support to countries of temporary protection. IOM supports internally displaced populations through the provision of emergency shelter and relief materials. Post-emergency movement assistance for returning displaced populations is also provided (mainly IDPs, demobilized soldiers and persons affected by natural disasters). In post-crisis situations IOM actively supports governments in the reconstruction and rehabilitation of affected communities and offers short-term community and micro-enterprise development programmes. In such situations IOM's activities may include health sector assistance and counter-trafficking awareness activities, psychosocial support, capacity building for disaster transportation and logistics; and registration and information management of affected populations.

During 2005 the UN developed a concept of organizing humanitarian agency assistance to IDPs through the institutionalization of a 'Cluster Approach', currently comprising 11 core areas of activity. IOM was designated the lead humanitarian agency for the cluster on Camp Co-ordination and Management in natural disaster situations (UNHCR was to lead that cluster in conflict situations).

In April 2009 IOM was appointed the partner with responsibility for transportation of non-food items (NFIs) in the UN-managed 'common pipeline' operation for Darfur and northern Sudan; during 2012 IOM delivered more than 102,000 NFIs to 10 different humanitarian agencies in Darfur, in support of more than 20,000 households. IOM was responsible for organizing the out-of-country registration and voting process for the referendum on independence for southern Sudan that took place in January 2011; following its attainment of independence in July 2011, South Sudan became a member of IOM. In March 2013 IOM and the Economic Community of the Great Lakes Countries (representing Burundi, the Democratic Republic of the Congo and Rwanda) signed a Memorandum of Understanding on strengthening regional migration policies. Since the start of civil conflict in Syria in 2011 IOM has provided emergency relief to migrants and uprooted IDPs within the country and to displaced persons in neighbouring countries. In early 2014 IOM was organizing about 100 monthly convoys to deliver NFIs within Syria, and was assessing and rehabilitating shelters. IOM was appealing for US $150m. under the broad Syrian Humanitarian Assistance Response Plan (SHARP) and the Regional Response Plan to cover its requirements for 2014; by March, however, only 5% of that sum had been pledged.

Finance

IOM's proposed operational budget for 2014 totalled US $740.6m. In December 2011 the IOM Council approved the establishment of a Migration Emergency Funding Mechanism to facilitate the immediate provision of assistance following a natural disaster or emergency conflict situation, and in particular to cover the cost of international transport for those affected.

Publications

Global Eye on Human Trafficking (quarterly).
International Migration Journal (every 2 months).
IOM Harare Newsletter.
IOM News (quarterly).
Migration and Climate Change.
Migration Health Annual Report.
Migration Initiatives (annually).
Migration Policy Practice (every 2 months).
Report by the Director-General.
World Migration Report (annually).
Research reports, *IOM Info Sheets*, surveys and studies.

INTERNATIONAL RED CROSS AND RED CRESCENT MOVEMENT

The Movement (known as 'Red Cross Red Crescent') is an international independent humanitarian organization, comprising three main components: the International Committee of the Red Cross (ICRC), founded in 1863; the International Federation of Red Cross and Red Crescent Societies (the Federation), founded in 1919; and National Red Cross and Red Crescent Societies in 186 countries; as well as Magen David Adom, an Israeli society equivalent to the Red Cross and Red Crescent Societies. In 1997 all constituent parts of the Movement adopted the Seville Agreement on co-operation in the undertaking of international relief activities. The Agreement excludes activities that are entrusted to individual components by the statutes of the Movement or the Geneva Conventions.

Organization

INTERNATIONAL CONFERENCE

The supreme deliberative body of the Movement, the Conference comprises delegations from the ICRC, the Federation and the National Societies, and of representatives of States Parties to the Geneva Conventions (see below). The Conference's function is to determine the general policy of the Movement and to ensure unity in the work of the various bodies. It usually meets every four to five years, and is hosted by the National Society of the country in which it is held. The 31st International Conference was held in Geneva, Switzerland, in November–December 2011. The 32 International Conference was to take place during 2015.

STANDING COMMISSION

The Commission meets at least twice a year in ordinary session. It promotes harmony in the work of the Movement, and examines matters which concern the Movement as a whole. It is formed of two representatives of the ICRC, two of the Federation, and five members of National Societies elected by the Conference.

COUNCIL OF DELEGATES

The Council comprises delegations from the National Societies, from the ICRC and from the Federation. The Council is the body where the representatives of all the components of the Movement meet to discuss matters that concern the Movement as a whole.

In November 1997 the Council adopted an Agreement on the organization of the activities of the Movement's components. The Agreement aimed to promote increased co-operation and partnership between the Movement's bodies, clearly defining the distribution of tasks between agencies. In particular, the Agreement aimed to ensure continuity between international operations carried out in a crisis situation and those developed in its aftermath.

Fundamental Principles of the Movement

Humanity: The International Red Cross and Red Crescent Movement, born of a desire to bring assistance without discrimination to the wounded on the battlefield, endeavours, in its international and national capacity, to prevent and alleviate human suffering wherever it may be found. Its purpose is to protect life and health and to ensure respect for the human being. It promotes mutual understanding, friendship, co-operation and lasting peace among all peoples.

Impartiality: It makes no discrimination as to nationality, race, religious beliefs, class or political opinions. It endeavours to relieve the suffering of individuals, being guided solely by their needs, and to give priority to the most urgent cases of distress.

Neutrality: In order to continue to enjoy the confidence of all, the Movement may not take sides in hostilities or engage in controversies of a political, racial, religious or ideological nature.

Independence: The Movement is independent. The National Societies, while auxiliaries in the humanitarian services of their governments and subject to national laws, must retain their autonomy so that they may always be able to act in accordance with the principles of the Movement.

Voluntary Service: It is a voluntary relief movement not prompted by desire for gain.

Unity: There can be only one Red Cross or Red Crescent Society in any one country. It must be open to all. It must carry on its humanitarian work throughout the territory.

Universality: The International Red Cross and Red Crescent Movement, in which all National Societies have equal status and share equal responsibilities and duties in helping each other, is worldwide.

International Committee of the Red Cross—ICRC

Address: 19 ave de la Paix, 1202 Geneva, Switzerland.

Telephone: 227346001; **fax:** 227332057; **e-mail:** press.gva@icrc.org; **internet:** www.icrc.org.

Founded in 1863, the ICRC is at the origin of the Red Cross and Red Crescent Movement, and co-ordinates all international humanitarian activities conducted by the Movement in situations of conflict. New statutes of the ICRC, incorporating a revised institutional structure, entered into force in July 1998.

The ICRC is an independent institution of a private character composed exclusively of Swiss nationals. Members are co-opted, and their total number may not exceed 25. The international character of the ICRC is based on its mission and not on its composition.

Organization

(April 2014)

ASSEMBLY

The Assembly is the supreme governing body of the ICRC. It formulates policy, defines the Committee's general objectives and strategies, oversees its activities, and approves its budget and accounts. The Assembly is composed of the members of the ICRC, and is collegial in character. The President and Vice-Presidents of the ICRC hold the same offices in the Assembly.

President: PETER MAURER.

Vice-President: CHRISTINE BEERLI.

ASSEMBLY COUNCIL

The Council (formerly the Executive Board) is a subsidiary body of the Assembly, to which the latter delegates certain of its responsibilities. It prepares the Assembly's activities and takes decisions on matters within its competence. The Council is composed of five members elected by the Assembly and is chaired by the President of the ICRC.

Members: PETER MAURER, CHRISTINE BEERLI, ROLF SOIRON, BRUNO STAFFELBACH, HEIDI TAGLIAVINI.

DIRECTORATE

The Directorate, headed by the Director-General, is the executive body of the ICRC, overseeing the efficient running of the organization and responsible for the application of the general objectives and institutional strategies decided by the Assembly. Members are appointed by the Assembly to serve a four-year term.

Director-General: YVES DACCORD.

Activities

The International Committee of the Red Cross was founded in 1863 in Geneva, Switzerland, by Henry Dunant and four of his friends. The original purpose of the Committee was to promote the foundation, in every country, of a voluntary relief society to assist wounded soldiers on the battlefield (the origin of the National Societies of the Red Cross or Red Crescent), as well as the adoption of a treaty protecting wounded soldiers and all those who come to their rescue. The mission of the ICRC was progressively extended through the Geneva Conventions (see below). The present activities of the ICRC consist in providing legal protection and material assistance to military and civilian victims of wars (international wars, internal strife and disturbances), and in promoting and monitoring the application of international humanitarian law (IHL). The ICRC aims to influence the conduct of all actual and potential perpetrators of violence by seeking direct dialogue with combatants. In 1990 the ICRC was granted observer status at the UN General Assembly. In 2014 the ICRC overall programme of activities covered the following areas:

The protection under IHL of civilians (i.e. individuals who are not participating in hostilities and violent confrontations, including former combatants);

Visiting and ensuring respect for detainees (prisoners of war and interned civilians);

Restoring family links (prevention of disappearances, tracing relatives separated in conflict situations, exchanging family messages and reuniting families), and clarifying the fate of missing persons);

Promoting economic security (working to ensure that conflict-affected households and communities can meet basic needs and maintain or restore sustainable livelihoods); includes the emergency distribution of food and household items, and also programmes aimed at supporting sustainable food production and micro-economic initiatives;

Water and habitat improvement activities (ensuring the sufficient supply, storage and distribution of water; adequate sanitation; restoration and management of electric power; construction, repair and safety of structures; and temporary community facilities);

Health (with a focus on health in prisons, first aid and hospital care, physical rehabilitation, and provision of primary health care);

Safeguarding health care, including protecting patients and health care workers from violence;

Co-operation with National Red Cross and Red Crescent Societies to ensure a rapid and efficient humanitarian response in situations of violence;

Building respect for IHL (through the provision of support to governments in fulfilling their legal obligations, interaction with weapon bearers, and education and outreach activities);

Mine action;

Humanitarian diplomacy and communication;

Building private sector relations;

Development of IHL;

Social research on war.

An ICRC Advisory Service, established in 1996, offers legal and technical assistance to national authorities with incorporating IHL into their national legislation, assists in their implementation of IHL, maintains a database on IHL, and publishes specialist documents. A Documentation Centre has also been established for exchanging information on national measures and activities aimed at promoting humanitarian law in countries. The Centre is open to all states and National Societies, as well as to interested institutions and the general public. With the aim of ensuring that they are knowledgable about and comply with IHL, ICRC delegates meet with weapon bearers present in conflict zones, including the state military and police, armed groups, and the staff of private military companies: in the ICRC maintained relations with the armed forces of 162 countries and with more than 82 armed groups, in some 45 contexts. A Senior Workshop on International Rules Governing Military Operations is organized annually by the ICRC to provide guidance to combatants. The 31st International Conference, convened in November–December 2011 adopted a resolution on 'Strengthening legal protection for victims of armed conflicts', following on from a two-year study of the issue and subsequent consultation process with member states.

The ICRC's Institutional Strategy covering the period 2011–14 focused on the following four priority areas: reinforcing the ICRC's scope of action; strengthening the Committee's contextualized, multidisciplinary response; shaping the debate on legal and policy issues related to the Committee's mission; and optimizing the Committee's performance. The ICRC has noted in recent years that, while some conflicts remain underpinned by territorial or ideological disputes, increasing numbers of conflicts and so-called situations of violence are being fuelled by pressure to secure control over natural resources, and that there is evidence of increasing activity by economically predatory armed elements. Fragile humanitarian situations are complicated by other factors, including weapons proliferation; environmental degradation; mass migration to cities and increased urban violence; and acts of terrorism and anti-terrorism operations. The ICRC has identified two principal challenges to the neutral and independent implementation of its humanitarian activities: developing a refined understanding of the diversity and specificity of armed conflicts and other situations of violence; and addressing meaningfully the many needs of affected civilian populations. During 2011–15 the ICRC was undertaking a Health Care in Danger project, which aimed to enhance protection of the sick and wounded, and address other negative impacts, in cases where illegal and violent acts obstruct the delivery of health provision or endanger health care staff, during armed conflict and other situations of violence.

The ICRC consistently reviews the 1980 UN Convention on prohibitions or restrictions on the use of certain conventional weapons which may be deemed to be excessively injurious or to have indiscriminate effects and its protocols. In September 1997 the ICRC participated in an international conference, held in Oslo, Norway, which adopted the Convention on the Prohibition of the Use, Stockpiling, Production and Transfer of Anti-personnel Mines and on their Destruction. The Convention entered into force on 1 March 1999. In April 1998 the Swiss Government established a Geneva International Centre for Humanitarian Demining, in co-operation with the UN and the ICRC, to co-ordinate the destruction of landmines worldwide. The ICRC was a principal advocate for the formulation of the Convention on Cluster Munitions, which was opened for signature in December 2008, and entered into force on 1 August 2010.

The ICRC participated in drafting the Optional Protocol to the Convention on the Rights of the Child, which was adopted by the UN General Assembly in May 2000 and entered into force in February 2002, raising from 15 to 18 years the minimum age for recruitment in armed conflict. In 2009 the ICRC produced updated field guidelines for its staff working with unaccompanied children, children separated from their relatives, and children associated with armed groups. ICRC supports the Paris Commitments and Guidelines, endorsed by an international conference convened in February 2007, with the aim of ending the recruitment of children, supporting the release of children from the armed forces, and facilitating their reintegration into civilian life.

The ICRC's presence in the field is organized under the following categories: responsive action, aimed at addressing the immediate effects of crises; remedial action, with an emphasis on rehabilitation; and environment building activities, aimed at creating political, institutional, humanitarian and economic situations that are suitable for generating respect for human rights. ICRC operational delegations focus on responsive action and remedial action, while environment-building is undertaken by ICRC regional delegations. The regional delegations undertake humanitarian diplomacy efforts (e.g. networking, promoting IHL and distributing information), logistical support to operational delegations, and their own operations; they also have an early warning function, alerting the ICRC to developing conflict situations. The ICRC targets its activities at the following groups: 'affected populations/persons', comprising civilians affected by confirmed or emerging violent situations of armed conflict, or who are no longer directly involved in such a conflict, people deprived of their freedom, and the wounded and sick (whether civilians or weapon bearers); and institutions and individuals with influence, i.e. official and unofficial authorities, armed forces and other weapon bearers, representatives of civil society, and ICRC National Societies. Groups at risk of exploitation—children (at risk of recruitment), women and girls (at risk of sexual violence), the elderly, the disabled and internally displaced persons (IDPs)—are of particular concern to the ICRC.

The ICRC's 'Family Links' internet pages aim to reunite family members separated by conflict or disaster situations. In February 2003 the ICRC launched 'The Missing', a major initiative that aimed to raise awareness of the issue of persons unaccounted for owing to armed conflict or internal violence. The ICRC assisted with the preparation of the International Convention for the Protection of all Persons from Enforced Disappearance, adopted by the UN General Assembly in December 2006, and representing the first international treaty to prohibit practices facilitating enforced disappearance. Meeting in November 2007 prior to the 30th International Conference, the Council of Delegates adopted the Restoring Family Links Strategy for the International Red Cross and Red Crescent Movement, covering the period 2008–18.

During 2012 ICRC representatives visited some 540,669 prisoners (26,609 individually, of whom 978 were minors, and 829 were female) held in 1,744 places of detention in 97 contexts worldwide, including detainees under the jurisdiction of international courts and tribunals. Some 144,863 messages were collected from and 134,696 distributed to family members separated by conflict; and 209,977 phone calls were facilitated between family members. Some 6,558 individuals who were the subject of other tracing requests were located. A total of 1,811 unaccompanied minors and separated children were reunited with their families, and some 583 demobilized child soldiers were registered in that year. Support was provided to 292 hospitals, 391 other health care facilities, and 111 first aid posts located near combat zones worldwide, benefiting an estimated 7.2m. recipients. Food was distributed by the ICRC in that year to more than 6.3m. beneficiaries and essential household and hygiene items to more than 2.8m. ICRC activities in the areas of water, sanitation and construction benefited more than 22m. people and ICRC sustainable food production programmes and micro-economic initiatives supported more than 2.7m. people. Around 2.5m. people benefited through cash-for-work and other employment programmes, service and training opportunities.

In 2014 the ICRC was actively concerned with around 80 conflicts and was undertaking major operations in (in order of budgetary priority, as envisaged at the start of the year): Syria (provisionally allocated 105.3m. Swiss francs), Afghanistan (82.4m.), the Democratic Republic of the Congo (69.9m.), Somalia (68.1m.), South Sudan (64.1m.), Iraq (60.4m.), Mali (45.3m.), Israel and the Palestinian territories (45.9m.), Israel and the Occupied Territories (43.7m.), Sudan (39.5m.), and Colombia (33.3m.).

During 2011–14 the ICRC, Syrian Arab Red Crescent (SARC) and the International Federation of Red Cross and Red Crescent Societies worked in close co-operation to maximize the efficiency of their response to the humanitarian crisis unfolding in Syria. In 2013 the ICRC, with the SARC, delivered water by truck to more than 108,000 IDPs in Deir Ez-Zor, Homs and rural areas near Damascus; repaired homes, water systems and sanitation facilitation facilities for more than 80,000 IDPs; provided more than 620,000 IDPs with drinking water; implemented a waste and pesticides programme in Aleppo; delivered food assistance to 3.5m. beneficiaries; and supplied household items, such as mattresses, blankets, hygiene kits and kitchen sets. The ICRC also supported mobile health units within Syria, serving mainly IDPs. In March of that year the ICRC stated that all sides in the Syrian conflict were violating the Geneva Conventions, and urged the international community to exert pressure on Syrian combatants to desist from attacking civilians and medical and humanitarian aid workers, and to observe IHL. Meanwhile, the Red Cross and Red Crescent network in neighbouring countries supported the expanding population of refugees who had fled from Syria. The Iraqi Red Crescent provided psychosocial support, first aid, food parcels, water, shelter equipment and hygiene kits to refugees; the Jordanian Red Crescent supported the most vulnerable refugees, including through the provision of relief and health care support, and helped to maintain a 120-bed field hospital; the Lebanese Red Cross made deliveries of emergency medical care, as well as transporting the sick and the wounded to accredited hospitals; and the Turkish Red Crescent worked to provide food, hygiene promotion, sanitation, and shelter to refugees, and in facilitating the transfer of relief supplies into Syria. In Afghanistan, in 2013, the ICRC and Afghan Red Crescent collected more than 16,400 messages, and delivered more than 15,500, mainly between detainees and their families, and installed telephone booths at detention centres and at ICRC field presences to enable contact between separated family members. The ICRC also visited 49,490 detainees at 80 places of detention; distributed clothing, blankets and other essential supplies to around 29,000 detainees; facilitated the return home of 30 former detainees; provided one-month food rations and household items for more than 11,460 IDP families; implemented cash-for-work projects; registered more than 8,900 new patients at its seven physical rehabilitation centres in that country; continued to support two hospitals, in Mirwais and Kandawar; installed and rehabilitated water supply systems; and briefed more than 12,500 weapon bearers, political representatives, religious leaders and community members on its mandate and activities. In conflict-affected North Eastern districts of the DRC, in late-2013–early 2014, the ICRC provided emergency food rations and medicines to prisons; visited former child combatants who had been reunited with their families; worked to improve community access to water; constructed a counselling centre for victims of violence in Nyamilima (in the Rutshuru area); and supported—through the supply of medicines, staff training, and rehabilitation activites—six health centres and two general referral hospitals.

In April 2009 the ICRC and IFRC launched a joint website, www.ourworld-yourmove.org, which aimed to highlight ongoing humanitarian crises.

THE GENEVA CONVENTIONS

Since its inception the ICRC has been a leader in the process of improving and complementing IHL. In 1864, one year after its foundation, the ICRC submitted to the states called to a Diplomatic Conference in Geneva a draft international treaty for 'the Amelioration of the Condition of the Wounded in Armies in the Field'. This treaty was adopted and signed by 12 states, which thereby bound themselves to respect as neutral wounded soldiers and those assisting them. This was the first Geneva Convention.

With the development of technology and weapons, the introduction of new means of waging war, and the manifestation of certain phenomena (the great number of prisoners of war during the First World War; the enormous number of displaced persons and refugees during the Second World War; the internationalization of internal conflicts in recent years), it was considered necessary to develop other international treaties to protect new categories of war victims.

There are now four Geneva Conventions, adopted on 12 August 1949: I—to protect wounded and sick in armed forces on land, as well as medical personnel; II—to protect the same categories of people at sea, as well as the shipwrecked; III—concerning the treatment of prisoners of war; IV—for the protection of civilians in time of war. Two Additional Protocols were adopted on 8 June 1977, for the protection of victims in international armed conflicts (Protocol I) and in non-international armed conflicts (Protocol II). A Third Additional Protocol (Protocol III), endorsing the red crystal—deemed to be a neutral symbol devoid of political or religious connotations—as an additional emblem of the Movement, was adopted on 8 December 2005 and entered into force on 14 January 2007.

By April 2014 195 states were parties to the Geneva Conventions; 173 were parties to Protocol I, 167 to Protocol II and 66 to Protocol III.

Finance

The ICRC's work is financed by a voluntary annual grant from governments parties to the Geneva Conventions, the European Commission, voluntary contributions from National Red Cross and Red Crescent Societies, and by gifts and legacies from private donors. The provisional budget for 2014 allocated 191.7m. Swiss francs to headquarters, and 1,104.4m. Swiss francs to field operations.

Publications

Annual Report.

FORUM series.

The Geneva Conventions (texts and commentaries).

ICRC News (weekly).

International Review of the Red Cross (quarterly in English and French; annually in Arabic, Russian and Spanish).

Red Cross Red Crescent Magazine (quarterly).

The Additional Protocols (texts and commentaries).

The Missing.

Various publications on subjects of Red Cross Red Crescent interest (medical studies, IHL, etc.).

International Federation of Red Cross and Red Crescent Societies

Address: 17 chemin des Crêts, Petit-Saconnex, CP 372, 1211 Geneva 19, Switzerland.

Telephone: 227304222; **fax:** 227330395; **e-mail:** secretariat@ifrc.org; **internet:** www.ifrc.org.

The Federation was founded in 1919 (as the League of Red Cross Societies). It works on the basis of the Principles of the Red Cross and Red Crescent Movement to inspire, facilitate and promote all forms of humanitarian activities by the National Societies, with a view to the prevention and alleviation of human suffering, and thereby contribute to the maintenance and promotion of peace in the world. The Federation acts as the official representative of its member societies in the field. The Federation maintains close relations with many inter-governmental organizations, the UN and its Specialized Agencies, and with non-governmental organizations. It has permanent observer status with the UN.

MEMBERS

National Red Cross and Red Crescent Societies in 188 countries, and Magen David Adom, Israel's equivalent of the Red Cross Society (at April 2014).

Organization

(April 2014)

GENERAL ASSEMBLY

The General Assembly is the highest authority of the Federation and meets every two years in commission sessions (for development, disaster relief, health and community services, and youth) and plenary sessions. It is composed of representatives from all National Societies that are members of the Federation.

GOVERNING BOARD

The Board (formerly the Executive Council) meets every six months and is composed of the President of the Federation, nine Vice-Presidents, representatives of 16 National Societies elected by the Assembly, and the Chairman of the Finance Commission. Its functions include the implementation of decisions of the General Assembly; it also has powers to act between meetings of the Assembly.

President: TADATERU KONOÉ (Japan).

ZONES

International Federation Africa Zone Office: 44 Wierda Rd, West Wierda Valley, 2196 Sandton, Johannesburg, South Africa; tel. (11) 303-9700; fax (11) 884-0230; Dir ALASAN SENGHORE (Gambia).

International Federation Americas Zone Office: Gaillard Ave, Bldg 806, Ciudad del Saber, Clayton, Panama City, Panama; Dir XAVIER CASTELLANOS (Ecuador).

International Federation Asia-Pacific Zone Office: The Amp-Walk Suite, 9.06 (North Block), 218 Jalan Ampang, 50450 Kuala Lumpur, Malaysia; tel. (39) 207-5700; fax (32) 161-0670; Dir JAGAN CHAPAGAIN (Nepal).

International Federation Middle East and North Africa Zone Office: c/o Al Shmeisani, Maroof Al Rasafi St, Bldg 19, Amman, Jordan; tel. (6) 5681060; fax (6) 5694556; Dir ELIAS GHANEM (Lebanon).

International Federation Europe Zone Office: Berkenye u. 13–15, 1025 Budapest, Hungary; tel. (1) 888-4500; fax (1) 336-1516; Dir ANITTA UNDERLIN (Denmark).

GLOBAL SENIOR MANAGEMENT TEAM

Under the Federation's guiding Strategy 2020 responsibility for operational and routine decision-making was transferred in 2010 to the Directors of the Zone offices. The Zone Directors were appointed to the newly established Global Senior Management Team, which also comprises the Secretary-General and Under-Secretaries-General for Governance and Management Services; Humanitarian Values and Diplomacy; and Programme Services.

COMMISSIONS

Development Commission;

Disaster Relief Commission;

Finance Commission;

Health and Community Services Commission;

Youth Commission.

The Commissions meet, in principle, twice a year, before the Governing Board meeting. Members are elected by the Assembly under a system that assures each Society a seat on one Commission.

SECRETARIAT

The Secretariat assumes the statutory responsibilities of the Federation in the field of relief to victims of natural disasters, refugees and civilian populations who may be displaced or exposed to abnormal hardship. In addition, the Secretariat promotes and co-ordinates assistance to National Societies in developing their basic structure and their services to the community. Under the Federation's Strategy 2020 a new business model was adopted for the Secretariat, with the following five business lines: raising humanitarian standards; improving services for vulnerable people; advancing sustainable development; enhancing the Federation's influence and support for its activities; and deepening the tradition of 'togetherness'. Four Business Groups were established, on Programme Services, National Society and Knowledge Development, Governance and Management; Humanitarian Values and Diplomacy; Programme Services; and National Society and Knowledge Development. The Secretary-General nominates honorary and special envoys for specific situations.

Secretary-General: BEKELE GELETA (Canada and Ethiopia).

Activities

In November 2005 the Assembly adopted a Global Agenda, comprising the following objectives which aimed to contribute to the attainment of the UN Millennium Development Goals: to reduce the deaths, injuries and impact of disasters on peoples' lives; to improve methods of dealing with public health crises; to combat intolerance and discrimination; and to build Red Cross and Red Crescent capacity at the community level to prepare for and cope with threats to lives and livelihoods.

In November 2009, following extensive consultation within the Movement, the Assembly adopted Strategy 2020, outlining the Federation's objectives and strategies for the next 10 years. Strategy 2020 focused on a common vision (inspiring, encouraging, facilitating and promoting at all times all forms of humanitarian activities by national societies, with a view to preventing and alleviating suffering and thereby promoting dignity and world peace), and detailed three strategic aims for the Federation and its member national societies: saving lives, protecting livelihoods, and strengthening recovery from disasters and crises; enabling healthy and safe living; and promoting social inclusion and a culture of non-violence and peace. These were to be delivered through three enabling actions: building strong national Red Cross and Red Crescent societies; pursuing humanitarian diplomacy to prevent and reduce vulnerability in a globalized world; and functioning effectively as the International Federation (entailing the decentralization of authority to offices representing five geographical 'Zones').

DISASTER RESPONSE

The Federation supports the establishment of emergency response units, which aim to act effectively and independently to meet the needs of victims of natural or man-made disasters. The units cover basic health care provision, referral hospitals, water sanitation, logistics, telecommunications and information units. The Federation advises National Societies in relief health. A Disaster Relief Emergency Fund (DREF) was established in 1985 to ensure the availability of immediate financial support for emergency response actions. In 2013 DREF's income totalled 21.7m. Swiss francs, and the total funding available to it was 30.3m. Swiss francs; the Fund had an operating budget of 724,924 Swiss francs in that year. During 2005 the UN's Inter-Agency Standing Committee, concerned with co-ordinating the international response to humanitarian disasters, developed a concept of organizing agency assistance to internally displaced persons (IDPs) through the institutionalization of a 'Cluster Approach', comprising nine core areas of activity. The Federation was designated the lead agency for the Emergency Protection (in natural disasters) cluster. In the event of a disaster areas including the following are covered: communicable disease alleviation and vaccination; psychological support and stress management; health education; the provision of medicines; and the organization of mobile clinics and nursing care. The Societies also distribute food and clothing to those in need and assist in the provision of shelter and adequate sanitation facilities and in the management of refugee camps.

In response to the devastation caused to central areas of the Philippines in November 2013 by Typhoon Haiyan, the IFRC, with the ICRC, undertook a three-month emergency relief operation that distributed food, shelter items, water and financial aid to more than 1m. affected people. From February 2014 the focus of activities in the Philippines shifted to rehabilitation, with the objective of supporting 350,000 people in rebuilding their livelihoods. In February the IFRC launched an emergency appeal for 1.1m. Swiss francs to fund the provision of urgent assistance to people affected by the ongoing violent unrest in the Central African Republic, including hygiene promotion; an advocacy campaign to foster inter-community peace; and the construction of 500 latrines in IDP camps and schools. The Central African Red Cross was providing psychosocial support to young people in that country who had witnessed extreme brutality. In the following month the IFRC launched an emergency appeal for 4.7m. Swiss francs, to support the provision of relief assistance to 105,080 people displaced in temporary settlements in Juba and Awerial, South Sudan, in the aftermath of violent conflict that erupted there in December 2013. Ongoing emergency initiatives being implemented by the South Sudan Red Cross addressed hygiene and health promotion, and the management of water distribution points. Further appeals were made at that time to fund assistance to South Sudanese refugees sheltering in neighbouring countries (1.7m. Swiss francs was requested for the Uganda Red Cross Society, and smaller appeals for the Ethiopian and Sudanese national societies). In early 2014 the Ukraine Red Cross Society, owing to the ongoing political turbulence in that country, was receiving funding from the DREF and was on constant alert, providing, when required, first aid both to wounded members of the security forces and protesters.

DEVELOPMENT

The Federation undertakes capacity building activities with the National Societies to train and develop staff and volunteers and to improve management structures and processes, in particular in the area of disaster management. Activities undertaken in the health sector aim to strengthen existing health services and to promote community-based health care and first aid; the prevention of HIV/AIDS and substance abuse; and health education and family planning initiatives. Blood donor programmes are often undertaken by National Societies, sometimes in conjunction with the World Health Organization. The Federation also promotes the establishment and development of education and service programmes for children and for other more vulnerable members of society, including the elderly and disabled. Education projects support the promotion of humanitarian values. In 2014 the largest amount of development funding (55.7m. Swiss francs) was allocated to Africa, followed by Asia and the Pacific (50.7m.).

Finance

The permanent Secretariat of the Federation is financed by the contributions of member Societies on a pro rata basis. Each relief action is financed by separate, voluntary contributions, and development programme projects are also financed on a voluntary basis.

Publications

Annual Report.

Handbook of the International Red Cross and Red Crescent Movement (with the ICRC).

Red Cross Red Crescent Magazine (quarterly).

Weekly News.

World Disasters Report (annually).

Newsletters on several topics; various guides and manuals for Red Cross and Red Crescent activities.

INTERNATIONAL SEABED AUTHORITY—ISA

Address: 14–20 Port Royal St, Kingston, Jamaica.

Telephone: 922-9105; **fax:** 922-0195; **e-mail:** webmaster@isa.org.jm; **internet:** www.isa.org.jm.

The ISA is an autonomous international organization established in accordance with the UN Convention on the Law of the Sea—UNCLOS (which was adopted in April 1982 and entered into force in November 1994) and the Agreement Relating to the Implementation of Part XI of the Convention (which was adopted in 1994 and entered into force in July 1996). The Authority was founded in November 1994 and became fully operational in June 1996.

MEMBERS

There are 166 member states and 32 observer member states and territories.

Organization

(April 2014)

ASSEMBLY

The Assembly is the supreme organ of the Authority, consisting of representatives of all member states who gather for an annual session. In conjunction with the Council, it formulates the Authority's general policies. It elects Council members and members of the Finance Committee. It also approves the budget, submitted by the Council on the recommendation of the Finance Committee. The Assembly's 20th session was to be convened in July 2014.

COUNCIL

The Council, elected by the Assembly for four-year terms, acts as the executive organ of the Authority. It consists of 36 members, comprising the four states that are the largest importers or consumers of seabed minerals, the four largest investors in seabed minerals, the four major exporters of seabed minerals, six developing countries representing special interests, and 18 members covering all the geographical regions.

LEGAL AND TECHNICAL COMMISSION

The Legal and Technical Commission, comprising 25 experts elected for five-year terms, assists the Council by making recommendations concerning seabed activities, assessing the environmental implications of activities in the area, proposing measures to protect the marine environment, and reviewing the execution of exploration contracts.

FINANCE COMMITTEE

The Committee, comprising 15 experts, was established to make recommendations to the Assembly and the Council on all financial and budgetary issues.

SECRETARIAT

The Secretariat provides administrative services to all the bodies of the Authority and implements the relevant work programmes. It comprises the Office of the Secretary-General, Offices of Resources and Environmental Monitoring, Legal Affairs, and Administration and Management. Under the terms of the 1994 Agreement Relating to the Implementation of Part XI of the Convention, the Secretariat is performing the functions of the Enterprise, the organ through which the Authority carries out deep-seabed mining operations (directly or through joint ventures). It is envisaged that the Enterprise will eventually operate independently of the Secretariat.

Secretary-General: NII ALLOTEY ODUNTON (Ghana).

Activities

The Authority, functioning as an autonomous international organization in relationship with the UN, implements the UN Convention on the Law of the Sea. All states parties to the Convention (165 and the European Union as at April 2014) are members. The Convention covers the uses of ocean space: navigation and overflight, resource exploration and exploitation, conservation and pollution, and fishing and shipping; as well as governing conduct on the oceans; defining maritime zones; establishing rules for delineating sea boundaries; assigning legal rights, duties and responsibilities to states; and providing machinery for the settlement of disputes. Its main provisions are as follows:

Coastal states are allowed sovereignty over their territorial waters of up to 12 nautical miles in breadth; foreign vessels are to be allowed 'innocent passage' through these waters;

Ships and aircraft of all states, including landlocked states, are allowed 'transit passage' through straits used for international navigation; states bordering these straits can regulate navigational and other aspects of passage;

Archipelagic states (composed of islands and interconnecting waters) have sovereignty over a sea area enclosed by straight lines drawn between the outermost points of the islands;

Coastal states and inhabited islands are entitled to proclaim a 200-mile exclusive economic zone (EEZ) with respect to natural resources and jurisdiction over certain activities (such as protection and preservation of the environment), and rights over the adjacent continental shelf, up to 350 miles from the shore under specified circumstances;

All states have freedom of navigation, overflight, scientific research and fishing within the EEZ, in addition to the right to lay submarine cables and pipelines, but must co-operate in measures to conserve living resources;

A 'parallel system' is to be established for exploiting the international seabed, where all activities are to be supervised by the International Seabed Authority (ISA); landlocked and geographically disadvantaged states have the right to participate, on an equitable basis, in the exploitation of an appropriate part of the surplus of living resources of the EEZs of coastal states of the same region or sub-region;

Coastal states have sovereign rights over the continental shelf (the national area of the seabed, which can extend up to 200 nautical miles from the shore) for exploring and exploiting its natural resources; the UN Commission on the Limits of the Continental Shelf shall make recommendations to states on the shelf's outer boundaries when it extends beyond 200 miles;

All states parties to the Convention share, through the Authority, the revenue generated from exploiting non-living resources from any part of the continental shelf extending beyond 200 miles; the distribution of revenue is determined according to equitable sharing criteria, taking into account the interests and needs of developing and landlocked states;

States are bound to control pollution and co-operate in forming preventive rules, and incur penalties for failing to combat pollution; states bordering enclosed, or semi-enclosed, waters are bound to co-operate in managing living resources, environmental policies and research activities;

Marine scientific research in the zones under national jurisdiction is subject to the prior consent of the coastal state, but consent may be denied only under specific circumstances;

States are bound to co-operate in the development and transfer of marine technology 'on fair and reasonable terms and conditions' and with proper regard for all legitimate interests;

States are obliged to settle by peaceful means disputes on the application and interpretation of the Convention; disputes must be submitted to a compulsory procedure entailing decisions binding on all parties.

The Convention provides for the establishment of an International Tribunal for the Law of the Sea, which has exclusive jurisdiction over disputes relating to the international seabed area. In July 1994 the UN General Assembly adopted the Agreement Relating to the Implementation of Part XI of the Convention. At April 2014 there were 145 states parties to the Agreement. The original Part XI, concerning the exploitation of the international ocean bed, and particularly the minerals to be found there (chiefly manganese, cobalt, copper and nickel), envisaged as the 'common heritage of mankind', had not been supported by the USA and other industrialized nations on the grounds that countries possessing adequate technology for deep sea mining would be insufficiently represented in the ISA; that the operations of private mining consortia would be unacceptably limited by the stipulations that their technology should be shared with the Authority's 'Enterprise'; and that production should be limited in order to protect land-based mineral producers. Under the 1994 Agreement there was to be no mandatory transfer of technology, the Enterprise was to operate according to commercial principles; and there were to be no production limits, although a compensation fund was to assist land-based producers adversely affected by seabed mining. By April 2014 the USA had not yet ratified either the Convention or the Agreement. An agreement on the implementation of the provisions of the Convention relating to the conservation and management of straddling and highly migratory fish stocks was opened for signature in December 1995 and entered into force in December 2001; by April 2014 it had been ratified by 81 states.

The comprehensive set of rules, regulations and procedures being developed by the ISA to govern prospecting, exploration and exploitation of marine minerals in the international seabed 'Area' (defined as the seabed and subsoil beyond the limits of national jurisdictions) are known as the 'Mining Code'. So far the Mining Code comprises the Regulations for Prospecting and Exploration for Polymetallic Nodules in the Area, adopted by the Authority in July 2000 (and updated by an Annex adopted in July 2013); the Regulations for Prospecting and Exploration for Polymetallic Sulphides, adopted in May 2010; and the Regulations on Prospecting and Exploration for Cobalt-rich Ferromanganese Crusts in the Area, adopted in July 2012 by the 18th session of the Assembly. The Authority maintains a database on polymetallic nodules (POLYDAT) and a central data repository (CDR) for all marine minerals in the seabed. In November 2011 the ISA organized a workshop on 'environmental management needs for exploration and exploitation of deep seabed minerals'. In 2013–14 the Authority was holding a series of workshops aimed at standardizing the taxonomy of macrofauna, megafauna and meiofauna, which tend to be present near polymetallic nodules, polymetallic sulphides and cobalt-rich ferromanganese crusts.

In 2005 the ISA launched a project to make a geological model (comprising a set of digital and hard copy maps and tables describing predicted metal content and abundance of deposits, as well as related error estimates) of the Clarion-Clipperton Fracture Zone (CCZ) exploration area, which is located south-east of Hawaii in the Equatorial North Pacific Ocean and has the largest known deposits worldwide of seabed polymetallic nodules. In December 2009 the Authority organized a workshop aimed at finalizing the CCZ geological model as well as a Prospector's Guide for the Zone. An international workshop was held in November 2010 to advise on the formulation of a CCZ environmental management plan and strategic environmental assessment. A geological model project is under development for the ISA's second designated exploration area, the Central Indian Basin of the Indian Ocean.

Pursuant to the Regulations for Prospecting and Exploration for Polymetallic Nodules in the Area, 17 deep sea exploration contracts have been signed by the ISA and registered pioneer investors. In July 2011, and January and July 2012, companies from, respectively, Nauru, Tonga and Kiribati became the first investors to sign exploration contracts with the ISA relating to polymetallic nodules in areas of the CCZ that have been reserved—in accordance with a provision of UNCLOS—for entities from developing countries. In July 2013 the Council approved two plans of work (submitted by corporations sponsored by the People's Republic of China and Japan) for the exploration of cobalt-rich ferromanganese crusts.

In February 2008 the ISA launched a new Endowment Fund aimed at promoting and supporting collaborative marine scientific research in the international seabed area. The Fund awards fellowships to scientists and technical personnel from developing countries through its Technical Assistance Programme-Marine Scientific Research (TAP-MAR). The ISA also administers short-term training opportunities, provided by ISA contractors, for candidates from developing states. Following the conclusion in June 2009 of a Memorandum of Understanding between the Authority and China, in November China agreed to fund postgraduate studies in marine science at a Chinese university for up to five candidates from ISA developing member states.

Finance

The Authority's budget is adopted by the Assembly on the recommendations of both the Council and the Finance Committee. The budget for the Authority for the biennium 2013–14 was US $14.3m. The administrative expenses of the Authority are met by assessed contributions from its members.

Publications

Basic Texts of the ISA.

Handbook (annually).

The Law of the Sea: Compendium of Basic Documents.

Selected decisions of sessions of the Authority, consultations, documents, rules of procedure, technical reports and studies, etc.

Associated Institutions

The following were also established under the terms of the Convention:

Commission on the Limits of the Continental Shelf: Division for Ocean Affairs and the Law of the Sea, Rm DC2-0450, United Nations, New York, NY 10017, USA; tel. (212) 963-3966; fax (212) 963-5847; e-mail doalos@un.org; internet www.un.org/Depts/los/clcs_new/clcs_home.htm; 21 members, serving a five-year term (currently June 2012–June 2017); responsible for making recommendations regarding the establishment of the outer limits of the continental shelf of a coastal state, where the limit extends beyond 200 nautical miles (370 km); Chair. LAWRENCE FOLAJIMI AWOSIKA (Nigeria).

International Tribunal for the Law of the Sea: Am Internationalen Seegerichtshof 1, 22609 Hamburg, Germany; tel. (40) 35607-0; fax (40) 35607-245; e-mail itlos@itlos.org; internet www.itlos.org; f. 1996; 21 judges; responsible for interpreting the Convention and ruling on disputes brought by states parties to the Convention on matters within its jurisdiction; Registrar PHILIPPE GAUTIER (Belgium).

International Trade Union Confederation—ITUC

Address: 5 blvd du Roi Albert II, bte 1, 1210 Brussels, Belgium.

Telephone: (2) 224-02-10; **fax:** (2) 201-58-15; **e-mail:** info@ituc-csi.org; **internet:** www.ituc-csi.org.

ITUC was established in November 2006 by the merger of the International Confederation of Free Trade Unions (ICFTU, founded in 1949 by trade union federations that had withdrawn from the World Federation of Trade Unions), the World Confederation of Labour (WCL, founded in 1920 as the International Federation of Christian Trade Unions and reconstituted in 1968), and eight national trade union organizations. The principles of trade union democracy and independence are enshrined in ITUC's Constitution.

MEMBERS

There were 325 member organizations in 161 countries and territories with 176m. members (at April 2014).

Organization

(April 2014)

WORLD CONGRESS

The Congress, the highest authority of ITUC, meets in ordinary session at least once every four years. The first Congress was held in Vienna, Austria, in November 2006; the second in Vancouver, Canada, in June 2010, and the third was to convene in Berlin, Germany, in May 2014.

Delegations from national federations vary in size on the basis of their paying membership. The Congress examines past activities and financial reports of the Confederation; reports on the activities of ITUC's regional organizations and on the Council of Global Unions (the structured partnership with the global union federations and TUAC); addresses general policy questions; maps out future plans; considers proposals for amendments to the Constitution and any other proposals submitted by member organizations; and elects the General Council, the General Secretary and the Confederation's three auditors. The General Secretary leads the Secretariat and is an ex officio member of the General Council and of the Executive Bureau.

GENERAL COUNCIL

Elected by the Congress, the General Council comprises 78 members, of whom 70 represent regions (Europe: 24; the Americas: 18; Asia-Pacific: 15; Africa: 11; 'open' regional membership: two); six members are nominated by the Women's Committee; and two members are nominated by the Youth Committee. The Council meets at least once a year and acts as the supreme authority of the Confederation between World Congresses, with responsibility for directing the activities of the Confederation and effecting decisions and recommendations of the Congress. The Council's agenda is prepared by the General Secretary.

The Council has appointed the following Committees: Human and Trade Union Rights; Women's; and Youth.

EXECUTIVE BUREAU

At its first meeting after the regular World Congress the General Council elects an Executive Bureau, comprising the President, the General Secretary and up to 25 members of the General Council. The Executive Bureau is authorized to address questions of urgency that arise between meetings of the General Council, or which are entrusted to it by the General Council. The Bureau meets at least twice a year.

President: MICHAEL SOMMER (Germany).

SECRETARIAT

General Secretary: SHARAN BURROW (Australia).

The General Secretary is supported by two Deputy General Secretaries.

BRANCH OFFICES

ITUC Amman Office: POB 925875, Amman 11190, Jordan; tel. (6) 5824828; fax (6) 5824829; e-mail itucjor@orange.jo; Co-ordinator NEZAM QAHOUSH.

ITUC Geneva Office: 46 ave Blanc, 1202 Geneva, Switzerland; tel. 227384202; fax 227381082; e-mail genevaoffice@ituc-csi.org; Dir RAQUEL GONZALEZ.

ITUC/Global Unions Washington Office: 888 16th St, Washington, DC 20006, USA; tel. (202) 974-8120; fax (202) 974-8122; e-mail washingtonoffice@ituc-csi.org; Rep. PETER BAKVIS.

ITUC/GUF Hong Kong Liaison Office: 1801 18/F Tai Shing Bldg, 498-500 Nathan Rd, Kowloon, Hong Kong SAR, China; tel. 23111077; fax 35421144; e-mail monina@ihlo.org; internet www.ihlo.org; Exec. Dir MONINA WONG.

ITUC Office for the New Independent States: Leninsky Prospect 42, 119119 Moscow, Russia; tel. (495) 938-7356; fax (495) 930-7671; e-mail ituc.mos@gmail.com.

ITUC South-East European Office: 71000 Sarajevo, Topal Osman paše 26/iv, Bosnia and Herzegovina; tel. (33) 715305; fax (33) 664676; e-mail seeoffice@ituc-csi.ba; Co-ordinator ENISA SALIMOVIC.

There are also Permanent Representatives accredited to FAO (Rome), IMO (London), UNIDO and the IAEA (Vienna), and to UNEP and UN-Habitat (Nairobi).

REGIONAL ORGANIZATIONS

African Regional Organisation of ITUC (ITUC-Africa): route Internationale d'Atakpamé, POB 4101, Lomé, Togo; tel. and fax 225-07-10; e-mail info@ituc-africa.org; internet www.ituc-africa.org; f. 2007; Gen. Sec. KWASI ADU-AMANKWAH.

ITUC Regional Organisation for Asia-Pacific (ITUC-AP): 9th Floor, NTUC Centre, One Marina Blvd, Singapore 018989; tel. 63273590; fax 63273576; e-mail gs@ituc-ap.org; internet www.ituc-ap.org; f. 2007; Gen. Sec. NORIYUKI SUZUKI.

Pan-European Regional Council (PERC): 5 blvd du Roi Albert II, bte 1, 1210, Brussels, Belgium; tel. (2) 224-03-19; fax (2) 201-58-15; e-mail perc@ituc-csi.org; internet perc.ituc-csi.org; Gen. Sec. BERNADETTE SEGOL.

Trade Union Confederation of the Americas (TUCA): Rua Formosa 367, Centro CEP 01049-000, São Paulo, Brazil; tel. (11) 21040750; fax (11) 21040751; e-mail sede@csa-csi.org; internet www.csa-csi.org; f. 2008; Gen. Sec. VICTOR BÁEZ MOSQUEIRA.

Activities

ITUC aims to defend and promote the rights of working people by encouraging co-operation between trade unions, and through global campaigning and advocacy. The principal areas of activity are: trade union and human rights; the economy, society and the workplace; equality and non-discrimination; and international solidarity. In November 2006, following its establishment, ITUC ratified an agreement with the so-called Global Unions (global trade union federations) and the Trade Union Advisory Committee to OECD (TUAC) to form a Council of Global Unions, with the aims of promoting trade union membership and advancing common trade union interests worldwide. In 2007 ITUC, the UN Environment Programme and the International Labour Organization launched the Green Jobs Initiative (the International Organisation of Employers joined the partnership in 2008). The Initiative aims to promote the creation of decent jobs as a consequence of progressive policies aimed at meeting ongoing global environmental challenges.

Finance

Affiliated organizations pay an affiliation fee per 1,000 members per annum, which finances ITUC's activities. The Confederation's budget amounts to some €11m. annually.

A Solidarity Fund, financed by contributions from affiliated organizations, supports the development and practice of democratic trade unionism worldwide and assists workers and trade unionists victimized by repressive political measures.

Publications

ITUC Frontlines Report.

ITUC Survey (annually).

Trade Union Focus on Development (monthly newsletter).

Global Union Federations

Building and Wood Workers International (BWI): 54 route des Acacias, 1227 Carouge, Switzerland; tel. 228273777; fax 228273770; e-mail info@bwint.org; internet www.bwint.org; f. 2005 by merger of International Federation of Building and Woodworkers (f. 1934) and World Federation of Building and Wood Workers (f. 1936); mems: 328 national unions with a membership of around 12m. workers in 130 countries; a Congress is held every four years (Dec. 2013: Bangkok, Thailand), which elects the World Council; Pres. PEO SJÖÖ (Sweden); Gen. Sec. ALBERT EMILIO (AMBET) YUSON (Philippines); publ. *BWI Online on the web* (daily).

Education International (EI): 5 blvd du Roi Albert II, 1210 Brussels, Belgium; tel. (2) 224-06-11; fax (2) 224-06-06; e-mail info@ei-ie.org; internet www.ei-ie.org; f. 1993; the fmr World Confederation of Teachers (f. 1962) merged with EI in 2006; aims to represent the causes of teachers and education employees and to promote the development of education; advocates for free quality public education for all, deeming education to be a 'human right and a public good'; regards literacy as the cornerstone of all sustainable societies, and the key to breaking the poverty cycle and halting the spread of HIV/AIDS; mems: 401 orgs representing 30m. teachers and education workers in 172 countries; Pres. SUSAN HOPGOOD (Australia); Gen. Sec. FRED VAN LEEUWEN (Netherlands).

IndustriALL: 54 bis route des Acacias, CP 1516, 1227 Geneva, Switzerland; tel. 223085050; fax 223085055; e-mail info@industriall-union.org; internet www.industriall-union.org; f. 2012 by merger of the International Metalworkers Federation (f. 1893), the International Textile, Garment and Leather Workers' Federation (f. 1970) and the International Federation of Chemical, Energy, Mine and General Workers' Unions (f. 1995); aims to strengthen trade union representation and rights, to counter the power of multinational corporations, to promote social and economic justice worldwide, and to uphold workers' rights and labour standards; mems: 50m. workers in 140 countries; Pres. BERTHOLD HUBER (Germany); Gen. Sec. JYRKI RAINA (Finland).

International Federation of Journalists (IFJ): International Press Centre, 155 rue de la Loi, 1040 Brussels, Belgium; tel. (2) 235-22-00; fax (2) 235-22-19; e-mail ifj@ifj.org; internet www.ifj.org; f. 1952 to link national unions of professional journalists dedicated to the freedom of the press, to defend the rights of journalists, and to raise professional standards; it conducts surveys, assists in trade union training programmes, organizes seminars and provides information; it arranges fact-finding missions in countries where press freedom is under pressure, and issues protests against the persecution and detention of journalists and the censorship of the mass media; holds Congress every three years (June 2013: Dublin, Ireland); mems: 156 unions in more than 100 countries, comprising 600,000 individuals; Pres. JIM BOUMELHA (United Kingdom); Gen. Sec. ELIZABETH (BETH) COSTA (Brazil); publ. *IFJ Direct Line* (every 2 months).

International Transport Workers' Federation (ITF): 49–60 Borough Rd, London, SE1 1DR, United Kingdom; tel. (20) 7403-2733; fax (20) 7357-7871; e-mail mail@itf.org.uk; internet www.itfglobal.org; f. 1896; hosts the Seafarers' Rights International Centre (f. 2010); convened in Sept. 2012, in Casablanca, Morocco, the first of a series of Maritime Roundtables, focusing on building links between dockers' and seafarers unions; organizes and negotiates on behalf of crews working on ships flying Flags of Convenience (FOCs); mems: national trade unions covering 4.5m. workers in around 700 unions in 150 countries; holds Congress every four years; has eight Industrial Sections; Pres. PADDY CRUMLIN (Australia); Gen. Sec. STEPHEN COTTON (United Kingdom) (acting); publ. *Transport International* (quarterly).

International Union of Food, Agricultural, Hotel, Restaurant, Catering, Tobacco and Allied Workers' Associations (IUF): 8 rampe du Pont-Rouge, 1213 Petit-Lancy, Switzerland; tel. 227932233; fax 227932238; e-mail iuf@iuf.org; internet www.iuf.org; f. 1920; mems: 394 affiliated orgs covering about 2.6m. workers in 126 countries; holds Congress every five years (May 2012: Geneva, Switzerland); Gen. Sec. RON OSWALD; publ. bimonthly bulletins.

Public Services International (PSI): 45 ave Voltaire, BP9, 01211 Ferney-Voltaire Cédex, France; tel. 4-50-40-64-64; fax 4-50-40-50-94; e-mail psi@world-psi.org; internet www.world-psi.org; f. 1907; represents public sector employees around the world; PSI is an officially recognized non-governmental organization for the public sector within the ILO; four regional executive committees cover Africa and Arab Countries, Asia and Pacific, Europe, and Inter-America; holds a Congress every five years; the 29th Congress, held in Nov. 2012, in Durban, South Africa, adopted a new PSI Constitution; mems: 650 unions and professional assocns covering 20m. workers in 148 countries; Pres. DAVE PRENTIS (United Kingdom); Gen. Sec. ROSA PAVANELLI (Italy); publ. *Focus* (2 a year).

Union Network International (UNI): 8–10 ave Reverdil, 1260 Nyon, Switzerland; tel. 223652100; fax 223652121; e-mail contact@uniglobalunion.org; internet www.uniglobalunion.org; f. 2000 by merger of Communications International (CI), the International Federation of Commercial, Clerical, Professional and Technical Employees (FIET), the International Graphical Federation (IGF), and Media and Entertainment International (MEI); mems: 900 unions in more than 150 countries, representing 20m. people; activities cover the following sectors: cleaning and security, commerce, finance, gaming, graphical and packaging, hair and beauty, IT and services, media, entertainment and arts, post and logistics, social insurance, telecommunications, tourism, temporary and agency work; fourth World Congress scheduled to be held in Cape Town, South Africa, in Dec. 2014; Gen. Sec. PHILIP J. JENNINGS (United Kingdom); publs *UNIinfo* (quarterly), *UNInet News* (monthly).

INTER-PARLIAMENTARY UNION—IPU

Address: 5 chemin du Pommier, CP 330, 1218 Le Grand Saconnex/Geneva, Switzerland.

Telephone: 229194150; **fax:** 229194160; **e-mail:** postbox@mail.ipu.org; **internet:** www.ipu.org.

Founded in 1889, the IPU aims to promote peace, co-operation and representative democracy by acting as a spokesperson for national parliaments at international level, and by providing a global forum for political dialogue between representatives of national parliaments. It is a repository of knowledge on the role, structure and working methods of national legislatures.

MEMBERS

National parliaments of 164 sovereign states; 10 international parliamentary associations (associate members): the Andean Parliament; Central American Parliament; CEEAC Parliament; East African Legislative Assembly; ECOWAS Parliament; European Parliament; Latin American Parliament; Parliamentary Assembly of the Council of Europe; Transitional Arab Parliament; and UEMOA Inter-Parliamentary Committee. Most member states are affiliated to one of six geopolitical groupings, known as the African, Arab, Asia-Pacific, Eurasia, Latin American and '12-Plus' (European) groups.

Organization

(April 2014)

ASSEMBLY

The Assembly (formerly known as the Inter-Parliamentary Conference and renamed in April 2003) is the main statutory body of the IPU, comprising eight to 10 representatives from each member parliament. It meets twice a year to discuss current issues in world affairs and to make political recommendations. Other specialized meetings of parliamentarians may also be held, on a global or regional basis. The Assembly is assisted by the three plenary Standing Committees: on Peace and International Security; Sustainable Development, Finance and Trade; and Democracy and Human Rights. The 130th Assembly was convened in Geneva, Switzerland, in March 2014.

GOVERNING COUNCIL

The Governing Council (formerly the Inter-Parliamentary Council, renamed in April 2003) comprises two representatives of each member parliament, usually from different political groups. It is responsible for approving membership and the annual programme and budget of the IPU, and for electing the Secretary-General. The Council may consider substantive issues and adopt resolutions and policy statements, in particular on the basis of recommendations from its subsidiary bodies.

President: ABDELWAHAD RADI (Morocco).

MEETING OF WOMEN PARLIAMENTARIANS

The Meeting is a mechanism for co-ordination between women parliamentarians. Convened twice a year, on the occasion of IPU statutory meetings, the Meeting aims to address subjects of common interest, to formulate strategies to develop the IPU's women's programme, to strengthen their influence within the organization and to ensure that women are elected to key positions. The Meeting is assisted by a Co-ordinating Committee.

SUBSIDIARY BODIES

In addition to the thematic Standing Committees of the IPU Assembly, various other committees and groups undertake and co-ordinate IPU activities in specific areas. The following bodies are subsidiary to the IPU Council:

- Standing Committee on Peace and International Security;
- Standing Committee on Sustainable Development, Finance and Trade;
- Standing Committee on Democracy and Human Rights;
- Committee on the Human Rights of Parliamentarians;
- Committee on Middle East Questions;
- Committee on UN Affairs;
- Group of Facilitators for Cyprus;
- Committee to Promote Respect for International Humanitarian Law;
- Advisory Group on HIV/AIDS and Maternal, Newborn and Child Health;
- Co-ordinating Committee of the Meeting of Women Parliamentarians;
- Gender Partnership Group.

The Association of Secretaries-General of Parliaments (ASGP), an autonomous, self-managing body that meets during the IPU Assembly, has consultative status at the IPU.

EXECUTIVE COMMITTEE

The Committee, comprising 17 members and presided over by the President of the Council, oversees the administration of the IPU and advises the Council on membership, policy and programme, and any other matters referred to it.

SECRETARIAT

Secretary-General: ANDERS B. JOHNSSON (Sweden) (until 30 June 2014), MARTIN CHUNGONG (Cameroon) (from 1 July 2014).

Activities

PROMOTION OF REPRESENTATIVE DEMOCRACY

This is one of the IPU's core areas of activity, and covers a wide range of concerns, such as democracy, gender issues, human rights and ethnic diversity, parliamentary action to combat corruption, and links between democracy and economic growth. The IPU sets standards and guidelines, provides technical assistance for strengthening national representative institutions, promotes human rights and the protection of members of parliament, supports partnership between men and women in politics, and promotes knowledge of the functioning of national parliaments.

The IPU aims to improve knowledge of the functioning of national parliaments by gathering and disseminating information on their constitutional powers and responsibilities, structure, and membership, and on the electoral systems used. The IPU also organizes international seminars and gatherings for parliamentarians, officials, academics and other experts to study the functioning of parliamentary institutions. A Technical Co-operation Programme aims to mobilize international support in order to improve the capabilities, infrastructure and technical facilities of national parliaments and enhance their effectiveness. Under the Programme, the IPU may provide expert advice on the structure of legislative bodies, staff training, and parliamentary working procedures, and provide technical equipment and other resources. There is a Parliamentary Resource Centre at IPU headquarters.

In 1993 the Council resolved that the IPU be present at all national elections organized, supervised or verified by the UN. The IPU has reported on the rights and responsibilities of election observers and issued guidelines on the holding of free and fair elections. These include the 1994 *Declaration on Criteria for Free and Fair Elections*, a study entitled *Free and Fair Elections* (initially published in 1994, and re-issued in a new, expanded version in 2006), *Codes of Conduct for Elections*, and *Tools for Parliamentary Oversight* (issued in 2008).

The IPU maintains a special database (PARLINE) on parliaments of the world, giving access to information on the structure and functioning of all existing parliaments, and on national elections. It also maintains a separate database (PARLIT) comprising literature from around the world on constitutional, electoral and parliamentary matters. In April 2012 the IPU, jointly with the UN Development Programme (UNDP), issued the *Global Parliamentary Report*, which addressed means of improving strategies to meet public expectations of parliaments.

In August–September 2000 the IPU organized the first international conference of presiding officers of national parliaments. The second speakers' conference took place in September 2005, and the third in July 2010. The ninth annual meeting of women speakers of parliament, to be organized by the IPU jointly with the Ecuador Parliament, was scheduled to take place in Quito, Ecuador, in September 2014.

In October 2011 the Governing Council adopted the IPU Strategy 2012–17, outlining the three strategic directions of better parliaments and stronger democracies; greater international involvement of parliaments; and repositioning of the IPU as a more effective instrument of parliamentary co-operation.

INTERNATIONAL PEACE AND SECURITY

The IPU aims to promote conflict resolution and international security through political discussion. Certain areas of conflict are monitored on an ongoing basis (for example, Cyprus and the Middle East), while others are considered as they arise. The 127th IPU Assembly, convened in October 2012, in Québec, Canada, issued the Quebec City Declaration, which urged national parliaments to ratify and implement conventions and laws that protect human rights and diversity, and covered issues including combating the marginalization of indigenous peoples; seeking solutions for stateless people; strengthening national frameworks to protect people suffering discrimination; and the adoption of special measures to advance women's full participation in democracy. In December the IPU Secretary-General and the Libyan authorities concluded an agreement under which, from January 2013, the IPU was to support the establishment of parliamentary democracy in post-conflict Libya, including reviewing rules and procedures, advising on the drafting of a new constitution, and conducting training activities, with a special focus on promoting female parliamentary participation. In June the IPU Committee to Promote Respect for International Humanitarian Law (IHL) sent a mission to assess the IHL situation in refugee-hosting countries neighbouring Syria; the mission recommended that IPU member parliaments should ensure that any initiative related to the Syrian refugee crisis covered measures to mitigate the impact of the crisis on host populations. In October the 129th IPU Assembly, in view of the devastating chemical attack perpetrated in Damascus, Syria, in August, adopted by consensus a resolution on the Role of Parliaments in Supervising the Destruction of Chemical Weapons and the Ban on their Use. The IPU dispatched an urgent mission to the Maldives in November, to address means of building trust between state institutions there.

The IPU has worked constantly to promote international and regional efforts towards disarmament, as part of the process of enhancing peace and security. Issues that have been discussed by the Assembly include nuclear non-proliferation, a ban on testing of nuclear weapons, and a global register of arms transfers.

SUSTAINABLE DEVELOPMENT

The Standing Committee for Sustainable Development, Finance and Trade guides the IPU's work in this area, with a broad approach of linking economic growth with social, democratic, human welfare and environmental considerations. Issues of world economic and social development on which the IPU has approved recommendations include employment in a globalizing world, the globalization of economy and liberalization of trade, Third World debt and its impact on the integration of those countries affected into the process of globalization, international mass migration and other demographic problems, and the right to food. The IPU co-operates with programmes and agencies of the UN, in particular in the preparation and follow-up of major socio-economic conferences. Since 2000 the IPU has aimed to bring the UN Millennium Development Goals (MDGs) to the attention of national parliaments. The IPU and UNDP concluded a comprehensive Memorandum of Understanding in November 2007 aimed at expanding mutual co-operation in support of worldwide democratic governance; future areas of co-operation were to cover national budgetary processes; and parliamentary activities aimed at advancing the achievement of the MDGs and at implementing UN treaties and conventions, and strategies aimed at poverty reduction and the empowerment of women. In May 2012 the UN General Assembly adopted a resolution calling for enhanced engagement between the UN, IPU and national parliaments, on major issues such as democracy, peace, development and human rights, and urging the IPU to continue mobilizing efforts aimed at attaining the MDGs, and to encourage parliaments to contribute to formulating post-2015 development objectives. At the end of May 2012 the IPU sponsored an Africa Parliamentary Conference on the MDGs, with a focus on the role of African parliamentarians in accelerating efforts to meet the MDGs and on their participation in discussions on the post-2015 development agenda.

The IPU and the European Parliament jointly organize an annual parliamentary conference on the World Trade Organization (WTO), which addresses issues including access to markets, the development dimension of the multilateral trading system, agriculture and subsidies. The conference aims to add a parliamentary dimension to multilateral co-operation on trade matters and thereby to enhance the transparency of the WTO's activities and to strengthen democracy at international level.

Activities to protect the environment are undertaken within the framework of sustainable development. The IPU monitors the actual measures taken by national parliaments to pursue the objective of sustainable development, as well as emerging environmental problems. In April 2005 the Assembly held an emergency debate on the role of parliaments in the prevention of natural disasters and the protection of vulnerable groups. The IPU participated in the preparations for the June 2012 UN Conference on Sustainable Development (Rio+20), seeking input from member parliaments, and lobbying for the clear presentation in the draft Rio+20 outcome document of the role of parliaments in advancing sustainable development policies.

In November 2007 the IPU, in co-operation with UNDP, UNAIDS and the Philippines legislature, convened the first Global Parliamentary Meeting on HIV/AIDS, at which participating parliamentary representatives addressed the role of national legislatures in responding to the HIV/AIDS pandemic.

In May 2009, in Geneva, Switzerland, the IPU convened a parliamentary conference on the global financial and economic crisis. The role of parliaments in developing South-South and 'triangular' (where two countries form a partnership to assist a third country) co-operation, with a view to accelerating achievement of the MDGs, and parliamentary action to ensure global food security, were addressed by the IPU Assembly in October.

IPU co-ordinated a two-year consultation process aimed at incorporating the concerns of national parliaments into the outcome of the Fourth UN Conference for the Least Developed Countries (LDC IV), convened in İstanbul, Turkey, in May 2011. LDC IV approved the Istanbul Programme of Action, which included a provision that national parliaments should be engaged in debating development strategies as well as in overseeing their implementation.

HUMAN RIGHTS AND HUMANITARIAN LAW

The IPU aims to incorporate human rights concerns, including employment, the rights of minorities, and gender issues, in all areas of activity. The Assembly and specialized meetings of parliamentarians frequently consider and make relevant recommendations on human rights issues. A five-member Committee on the Human Rights of Parliamentarians is responsible for the consideration of complaints relating to alleged violations of the human rights of members of parliament, for example state harassment, intimidation, arbitrary arrest and detention, unfair trial and violation of parliamentary immunity. The Committee conducts hearings and site missions to investigate a complaint and communicates with the authorities of the country concerned. If no settlement is reached at that stage, the Committee may then publish a report for the Governing Council and submit recommendations on specific measures to be adopted. By 2014 the Committee had addressed more than 1,600 cases in around 100 countries. In October 2013 the Governing Council adopted 21 resolutions concerning human rights cases.

The IPU works closely with the International Committee of the Red Cross to uphold respect for IHL. It supports the implementation of the Geneva Conventions and their Additional Protocols, and the adoption of appropriate national legislation. In 1995 the Council adopted a special resolution to establish a reporting mechanism at the parliamentary level to ensure respect for IHL. Consequently, the IPU initiated a world survey on legislative action regarding the application of IHL, as well as efforts to ban anti-personnel landmines. In April and September 1998 the Council adopted special resolutions on parliamentary action to secure the entry into force (achieved in March 1999) and implementation of the Convention on the Prohibition of the Use, Stockpiling, Production and Transfer of

Anti-personnel Mines and on their Destruction, which had been signed by representatives of some 120 countries meeting in Ottawa, Canada, in December 1997.

In February 2008 the IPU and the UN Office on Drugs and Crime (UNODC) jointly organized a Parliamentary Forum on Human Trafficking, convened in Vienna, Austria, in the context of the global Vienna Forum to Fight Human Trafficking; in April 2009 the IPU and UNODC jointly issued *Combating Trafficking in Persons: a Handbook for Parliamentarians*. In April 2010 the Assembly issued a declaration on 'Co-operation and shared responsibility in the global fight against organized crime, in particular drug trafficking, illegal arms trafficking, trafficking in persons, and cross-border terrorism'.

WOMEN IN POLITICS

The IPU, jointly with UN Women, maintains statistical data on female representation in national parliaments, demonstrating progress made towards increasing female representation in parliament since the 1995 Fourth World Conference on Women. The 2014 edition of the IPU/UN Women annual *Women in Politics Map*, issued in March and giving data as of 1 January, reported that the global average of female representation in legislatures at that time was 21.8%. The Americas had the highest regional percentage of female ministers (22.9%), followed by Africa (20.4%), while at sub-regional level the Nordic countries had the highest level of female representation in legislatures (at 42%) and also holding ministerial posts (48.9%).

The IPU aims to promote the participation of women in the political and parliamentary decision-making processes, and, more generally, in all aspects of society. It organizes debates and events on these issues and maintains an online statistical database on women in politics, compiled by regular world surveys, as well as a women in politics bibliographic database. The IPU also actively addresses wider issues of concern to women, such as literacy and education, women in armed conflicts, women's contribution to development, and women in the electoral process. The eradication of violence against women was the subject of a special resolution adopted by the Conference in 1991. The Meeting of Women MPs has monitored efforts by national authorities to implement the recommendations outlined in the resolution. In 1996 the IPU promoted the Framework for Model Legislation on Domestic Violence, formulated by the UN Special Rapporteur on the issue, which aimed to assist national parliaments in preparing legislation to safeguard women. In February 1997 the IPU organized a Specialized Inter-Parliamentary Conference, in New Delhi, entitled 'Towards partnership between men and women in politics'. Following the Conference the IPU established a Gender Partnership Group, comprising two men and two women, within the Executive Committee, to ensure that IPU activities and decisions serve the interests and needs of all members of the population. The Group was authorized to report to the IPU Council. In October 2012 the 127th IPU Assembly adopted an action plan aimed at addressing women's access to, and parity within, national parliaments. In October 2013 the Governing Council adopted a guidance document on gender mainstreaming within the IPU.

The IPU aims to promote the importance of women's role in economic and social development and their participation in politics as a democratic necessity, and recognizes the crucial role of the media in presenting the image of women. Within the context of the 1997 New Delhi Conference, the IPU organized a second Round Table on the Image of Women Politicians in the Media (the first having been convened in November 1989). The debate urged fair and equal representation of women politicians by the media and for governments to revise their communications policies in this respect.

IPU, jointly with UNDP, UN Women and other partners, maintains the International Knowledge Network of Women in Politics (iKNOW Politics, accessible at iknowpolitics.org), an online workspace that has, since March 2007, supported government officials, researchers, etc., in pursuing the objective of advancing female participation in politics.

In 2008 the IPU launched a campaign and work programme to support parliaments to make ending violence against women a priority at national level.

In April 2009 the IPU Assembly discussed means of accelerating progress towards securing the rights of adolescent girls to survival, education, health care, and protection, while emphasizing that the empowerment of adolescent girls belongs at the core of the development agenda and efforts towards achieving the MDGs. In April 2012 the Assembly adopted a resolution on Access to Health as a Basic Right: the Role of Parliaments in Addressing Challenges to Securing the Health of Women and Children.

EDUCATION, SCIENCE AND CULTURE

Activities in these sectors are often subject to consideration by statutory meetings of the Assembly. In October 2003 the IPU and UNESCO launched a network of national focal points linking the IPU's member parliaments and UNESCO, with the aim of circulating information and improving co-operation in the area of education, science, culture and communications.

In November 2006, the IPU and the UN Department of Economic and Social Affairs (UN-DESA) inaugurated the Rome, Italy-based Global Centre for Information and Communication Technologies in Parliament. The Centre, whose establishment had been endorsed at the World Summit of the Information Society held in November 2005 in Tunis, Tunisia, is mandated to act as a clearing house for information, research, innovation, technology and technical assistance, and to promote a structured dialogue among parliaments, centres of excellence, international organizations, civil society, private sector interests, and international donors.

In October 2007 the IPU, in conjunction with the UN-DESA and the Association of Secretaries-General of Parliament, with support from the Global Centre for ICT in Parliament, convened the first World e-Parliament Conference, with participation by parliamentarians, officials, academics and representatives of international organizations and of civil society. The e-Conference aimed to identify best practices in the use of new technologies to modernize parliamentary processes and communications. The IPU has, since 2008, issued a biennial *World e-Parliament Report*. The 2012 edition of the report, released in November, found that parliaments worldwide were increasingly using social media and mobile technologies to increase citizens' engagement and also to facilitate MPs' work.

Finance

The IPU is financed by its members, mainly from assessed contributions from member states. In addition, external financial support, primarily from voluntary donor contributions and UNDP, is received for some special activities. The 2014 annual budget, approved by the Governing Council in October 2013, amounted to 13.7m. Swiss francs.

Publications

Activities of the Inter-Parliamentary Union (annually).
Global Parliamentary Report.
IPU Information Brochure (annually).
IPU Strategy (every 5 years).
Women in Politics Map (annually, with UN Women).
World e-Parliament Report (every 2 years).
Other handbooks, reports and surveys, documents, proceedings of the Assembly.

ISLAMIC DEVELOPMENT BANK

Address: POB 5925, Jeddah 21432, Saudi Arabia.
Telephone: (2) 6361400; **fax:** (2) 6366871; **e-mail:** idbarchives@isdb.org; **internet:** www.isdb.org.

The Bank was established following a conference of Ministers of Finance of member countries of the then Organization of the Islamic Conference (now Organization of Islamic Cooperation—OIC), held in Jeddah in December 1973. Its aim is to encourage the economic development and social progress of member countries and of Muslim communities in non-member countries, in accordance with the principles of the Islamic *Shari'a* (sacred law). The Bank formally opened in October 1975. The Bank and its associated entities—the Islamic Research and Training Institute, the Islamic Corporation for the Development of the Private Sector, the Islamic Corporation for the Insurance of Investment and Export Credit, and the International Islamic Trade Finance Corporation—constitute the Islamic Development Bank Group.

MEMBERS

There are 56 members.

Organization

(April 2014)

BOARD OF GOVERNORS

Each member country is represented by a governor, usually its Minister of Finance, and an alternate. The Board of Governors is the supreme authority of the Bank, and meets annually. The 38th meeting was convened in Dushanbe, Tajikistan, in May 2013, and the 39th meeting was scheduled to be held in Jeddah, Saudi Arabia, in June 2014.

BOARD OF EXECUTIVE DIRECTORS

The Board consists of 18 members, one-half of whom are appointed by the eight largest subscribers to the capital stock of the Bank; the remaining eight are elected by Governors representing the other subscribers. Members of the Board of Executive Directors are elected for three-year terms. The Board is responsible for the direction of the general operations of the Bank.

ADMINISTRATION

President of the Bank and Chairman of the Board of Executive Directors: Dr AHMAD MOHAMED ALI AL-MADANI (Saudi Arabia).

Vice-President Corporate Services and Acting Vice-President Co-operation and Capacity Development: Dr AHMET TIKTIK (Turkey).

Vice-President Finance: Dr ABDULAZIZ BIN MOHAMED BIN ZAHIR AL HINAI (Oman).

Vice-President Operations: BIRAMA BOUBACAR SIDIBE (Mali).

REGIONAL OFFICES

Kazakhstan: 050000 Almatı, Aiteki bi 67; tel. (727) 272-70-00; fax (727) 250-13-03; e-mail idbroa@isdb.org; Dir HISHAM TALEB MAAROUF.

Malaysia: Menara Bank, Pembangunan Bandar Wawasan, Level 13, Jalan Sultan Ismail, 50250 Kuala Lumpur; tel. (3) 26946627; fax (3) 26946626; e-mail ROKL@isdb.org; Dir KUNRAT WIRASUBRATA (acting).

Morocco: Km 6.4, Ave Imam Malik Route des Zaers, POB 5003, Rabat; tel. (3) 7757191; fax (3) 7757260; Dir ABDERRAHAM EL-GLAOUI.

Senegal: 18 blvd de la République, Dakar; tel. (33) 889-1144; fax (33) 823-3621; e-mail RODK@isdb.org; Dir SIDI MOHAMED OULD TALEB.

FINANCIAL STRUCTURE

The Bank's unit of account is the Islamic Dinar (ID), which is equivalent to the value of one Special Drawing Right (SDR) of the IMF (average value of the SDR in 2011 was US $1.57868). In May 2006 the Bank's Board of Governors approved an increase in the authorized capital from ID 15,000m. to ID 30,000m. An increase in the authorized capital, to ID 100,000m., was approved by the Board in May 2013. An increase in subscribed capital, from ID 15,000m. to ID 16,000m. was approved by the Board of Governors in June 2008. In June 2010 the Board of Governors approved a further increase in subscribed capital to ID 18,000m., and an increase to ID 50,000 was approved in May 2013. At 14 November 2012 total committed subscriptions amounted to ID 17,782.6m.

SUBSCRIPTIONS
(million Islamic Dinars, as at 14 November 2012)

Afghanistan	9.93	Maldives	9.23
Albania	9.23	Mali	18.19
Algeria	459.22	Mauritania	9.77
Azerbaijan	18.19	Morocco	91.69
Bahrain	25.88	Mozambique	9.23
Bangladesh	182.16	Niger	24.63
Benin	20.80	Nigeria	1,384.00
Brunei	45.85	Oman	50.92
Burkina Faso	24.63	Pakistan	459.22
Cameroon	45.85	Palestine	19.55
Chad	9.77	Qatar	1,297.50
Comoros	4.65	Saudi Arabia	4,249.60
Côte d'Ivoire	4.65	Senegal	52.80
Djibouti	4.96	Sierra Leone	4.96
Egypt	1,278.67	Somalia	4.96
Gabon	54.58	Sudan	83.21
The Gambia	9.23	Suriname	9.23
Guinea	45.85	Syria	18.49
Guinea-Bissau	4.96	Tajikistan	4.96
Indonesia	406.48	Togo	4.96
Iran	1,491.20	Tunisia	19.55
Iraq	48.24	Turkey	1,165.86
Jordan	78.50	Turkmenistan	4.96
Kazakhstan	19.29	Uganda	24.63
Kuwait	985.88	United Arab Emirates	1,357.20
Kyrgyzstan	9.23	Uzbekistan	4.80
Lebanon	9.77	Yemen	92.38
Libya	1,704.46		
Malaysia	294.01		

Activities

The Bank adheres to the Islamic principle forbidding usury, and does not grant loans or credits for interest. Instead, its methods of project financing are provision of interest-free loans, mainly for infrastructural projects which are expected to have a marked impact on long-term socio-economic development; provision of technical assistance (e.g. for feasibility studies); equity participation in industrial and agricultural projects; leasing operations, involving the leasing of equipment such as ships, and instalment sale financing; and profit-sharing operations. Funds not immediately needed for projects are used for foreign trade financing. Under the Bank's trade financing operations funds are used for importing commodities for development purposes (i.e. raw materials and intermediate industrial goods, rather than consumer goods), with priority given to the import of goods from other member countries. In 2005 the Bank initiated a consultation process, led by a commission of eminent persons, to develop a new long-term strategy for the Bank. A document on the AH 1440 (2020) Vision was published in March 2006. It recommended that the Bank redefine its mandate and incorporate a broad focus on comprehensive human development, with priority concerns to be the alleviation of poverty and improvements to health, education and governance. The new strategy also envisaged greater community involvement in Bank operations and more support given to local initiatives. In October 2008 the Bank organized a forum to consider the impact of the international economic and financial crisis on the Islamic financial system. The meeting resolved to establish a Task Force for Islamic Finance and Global Financial Stability, which met for the first time in January 2009, in Kuala Lumpur, Malaysia. In May the Board of Executive Directors agreed to double ordinary capital resources operations over a three-year period in order to support economic recovery in member countries. In the following month the Board of Governors approved the measure, along with others in support of mitigating the effects of the global financial crisis. During that year the Bank resolved to accelerate implementation of a major reform programme to enhance its relevance and impact in member countries, in accordance with the AH 1440 (2020) Vision. The Bank also adopted a Thematic Strategy for Poverty Reduction and Comprehensive Human Development to focus efforts to achieve the Vision's objectives.

By 14 November 2012 the Bank had approved a total of ID 28,566.3m. (equivalent to some US $42,020.9m.) for project financing since operations began in 1976, including ID 287.1m. ($405.7m.) for technical assistance, in addition to ID 31,172.7m. ($44,073.4m.) for foreign trade financing, and ID 556.4m. ($725.8m.) for special assistance operations, excluding amounts for cancelled operations. Total net approved operations amounted to ID 60,582.6m. ($87,225.6m.) at that time.

During the Islamic year 1433 (27 November 2011–14 November 2012) the Bank approved a net total of ID 6,415.0m., for 386 operations, compared with ID 6,973.0m. for 403 operations in the previous year. Of the total approved in AH 1433 ID 255.3m. was approved for 62 loans, supporting projects concerned with the education and health sectors, infrastructural improvements, and agricultural developments. The Bank approved 77 technical assistance operations during that year in the form of grants and loans, amounting to ID 13.4m. Trade financing approved amounted to ID 2,902.9m. for 57 operations. During AH 1433 the Bank's total disbursements totalled ID 3,672.8m., bringing the total cumulative disbursements since the Bank began operations to ID 40,299.0m.

During AH 1427 the Bank's export financing scheme was formally dissolved, although it continued to fund projects pending the commencement of operations of the International Islamic Trade Finance Corporation (ITFC). The Bank also finances other trade financing operations, including the Islamic Corporation for the Development of the Private Sector (ICD, see below), the Awqaf Properties Investment Fund and the Treasury Department. In addition, a Trade Co-operation and Promotion Programme supports efforts to enhance trade among member countries of the Organization of Islamic Cooperation (OIC). In June 2005 the Board of Governors approved the establishment of the ITFC as an autonomous trade promotion and financing institution within the Bank Group. The inaugural meeting of the ITFC was held in February 2007. In May 2006 the Board of Governors approved a new fund to reduce poverty and support efforts to achieve the UN Millennium Development Goals, in accordance with a proposal of the OIC. It was inaugurated, as the Islamic Solidarity Fund for Development, in May 2007, and became operational in early 2008. By the end of the Islamic year 1433 capital contributions to the Fund amounted to US $1,661m., of a total of $2,661m. that had been pledged by 42 countries.

In AH 1407 (1986/87) the Bank established an Islamic Bank's Portfolio for Investment and Development (IBP) in order to promote the development and diversification of Islamic financial markets and to mobilize the liquidity available to banks and financial institutions. During AH 1428 resources and activities of the IBP were transferred to the newly established ITFC. The Bank's Unit Investment Fund (UIF) became operational in 1990, with the aim of mobilizing additional resources and providing a profitable channel for investments conforming to *Shari'a*. The initial issue of the UIF was US $100m., which was subsequently increased to $325m. The Fund finances mainly private sector industrial projects in middle-income countries and also finances short-term trade operations. The Bank also mobilizes resources from the international financial markets through the issuance of the International Islamic Sukuk bond. In October 1998 the Bank announced the establishment of a new fund to invest in infrastructure projects in member states. The Bank committed $250m. to the fund, which was to comprise $1,000m. equity capital and a $500m. Islamic financing facility. In January 2009 the Bank launched a second phase of the infrastructure fund. In April 2002 the Bank, jointly with governors of central banks and the Accounting and Auditing Organization for Islamic Financial Institutions, concluded an agreement, under the auspices of the IMF, for the establishment of an Islamic Financial Services Board. The Board, to be located in Kuala Lumpur, was intended to elaborate and harmonize standards for best practices in the regulation and supervision of the Islamic financial services industry.

The Bank's Special Assistance Programme was initiated in AH 1400 to support the economic and social development of Muslim communities in non-member countries, in particular in the education and health sectors. It also aimed to provide emergency aid in times of natural disasters, and to assist Muslim refugees throughout the world. Operations undertaken by the Bank are financed by the Waqf Fund (formerly the Special Assistance Account). By the end of the Islamic year 1433 some ID 556.4m. (US $725.8m.) had been approved under the Waqf Fund Special Assistance Programme for 1,440 operations. Other assistance activities include scholarship programmes, technical co-operation projects and the sacrificial meat utilization project (see below). In addition the Bank supports recovery, rehabilitation and reconstruction efforts in member countries affected by natural disasters or conflict.

In October 2002 the Bank's Board of Governors, meeting in Burkina Faso, adopted the Ouagadougou Declaration on the co-operation between the Bank group and Africa, which identified priority areas for Bank activities, for example education and the private sector. The Bank pledged US $2,000m. to finance implementation of the Declaration during the five year period 2004–08. A successor initiative, the IDB Special Programme for the Development of Africa, was endorsed at a summit meeting of the OIC held in March 2008. The Bank committed $4,000m. to the Programme for the next five-year period, 2008–12. By the end of the Islamic year 1433 $5,000m. had been approved under the Programme. During the Islamic year 1431 the Bank initiated a Membership Country Partnership (MCP) Strategy to strengthen dialogue with individual member countries and to contribute more effectively to their medium- and long-term development plans. By the end of AH 1433 eight MCPs were being implemented, in Indonesia, Kazakhstan, Malaysia, Mali, Mauritania, Pakistan, Turkey, and Uganda.

In June 2008 the Board of Governors inaugurated the Jeddah Declaration Initiative, with an allocation of US $1,500m. in funds during a five-year period, to assist member countries to meet the escalating costs of food and to attain greater food security. In November 2009 the Bank concluded a co-financing agreement with the International Fund for Agricultural Development (IFAD), with funds of up to $1,500m., to support priority projects concerned with food security and rural development in the poorest member countries in Africa and Asia. The agreement was signed by the presidents of the two organizations in February 2010. During 2011 the Bank contributed to the preparation of an Action Plan on Food Price Volatility and Agriculture, which was adopted by heads of state and government of the Group of 20 (G20) industrialized and emerging economies in November. The Bank also contributed, through participation in a working group and high-level panel, to the elaboration of a G20 Multilateral Development Bank Infrastructure Action Plan. In April the Bank collaborated with the World Bank Group to inaugurate an Arab Financing Facility for Infrastructure in order to support national and cross-border infrastructure development, in particular through use of public-private partnerships. In September the Bank participated in a meeting of ministers of finance of the Group of Eight (G8) industrialized nations and high-level representatives of international financial institutions active in the Middle East and North Africa region further to support the so-called Deauville Partnership, which had been established in May in order to assist countries in the region undergoing social and economic transformations. The Bank was a founding member of the new Co-ordination Platform to facilitate and promote collaboration among the institutions extending assistance under the Partnership.

In AH 1404 (1983/84) the Bank established a scholarship programme for Muslim communities in non-member countries to provide opportunities for students to pursue further education or other professional training. The programme also assists 12 member countries on an exceptional basis. By the end of the Islamic year 1433 7,652 people had graduated and 3,794 were undertaking studies under the scheme. The Merit Scholarship Programme, initiated in AH 1412 (1991/92), aims to develop scientific, technological and research capacities in member countries through advanced studies and/or research. A total of 860 scholarships had been awarded by the end of AH 1433. In AH 1419 (1998/99) a Scholarship Programme in Science and Technology for IDB Least Developed Member Countries became operational for students in 20 eligible countries. The Bank awards annual prizes for science and technology to promote excellence in research and development and in scientific education.

The Bank's Programme for Technical Co-operation aims to mobilize technical capabilities among member countries and to promote the exchange of expertise, experience and skills through expert missions, training, seminars and workshops. In December 1999 the Board of Executive Directors approved two technical assistance grants to support a programme for the eradication of illiteracy in the Islamic world, and one for self-sufficiency in human vaccine production. The Bank also undertakes the distribution of meat sacrificed by Muslim pilgrims. The Bank was the principal source of funding of the International Centre for Biosaline Agriculture, which was established in Dubai, United Arab Emirates, in September 1999.

BANK GROUP ENTITIES

International Islamic Trade Finance Corporation: POB 55335, Jeddah 21534, Saudia Arabia; tel. (2) 6361400; fax (2) 6371064; e-mail info@isdb.org; internet www.itfc-idb.org; f. 2007; commenced operations Jan. 2008; aims to promote trade and trade financing in Bank member countries, to facilitate access to public and private capital, and to promote investment opportunities; during the Islamic year 1432 the ITFC approved US $3,033m. for 66 trade financing operations; auth. cap. $3,000m.; subs. cap. $750m. (Oct. 2013); CEO Dr WALID AL-WOHAIB.

Islamic Corporation for the Development of the Private Sector (ICD): POB 54069, Jeddah 21514, Saudi Arabia; tel. (2) 6441644; fax (2) 6444427; e-mail icd@isdb.org; internet www.icd-idb.org; f. 1999; to identify opportunities in the private sector, provide financial products and services compatible with Islamic law, mobilize additional resources for the private sector in member countries, and encourage the development of Islamic financing and capital markets; approved 18 projects and eight capital increases, amounting to US $419m., in the Islamic year 1433; the Bank's share of the capital is 50%, member countries 30% and public financial institutions of member countries 20%; auth. cap. $2,000m., subs. cap. $1,000m. (Oct. 2013); mems: 51 countries, the Bank, and five public financial institutions; CEO and Gen. Man. KHALID M. AL-ABOODI.

Islamic Corporation for the Insurance of Investment and Export Credit (ICIEC): POB 15722, Jeddah 21454, Saudi Arabia; tel. (2) 6445666; fax (2) 6379504; e-mail idb.iciec@isdb.org.sa; internet www.iciec.com; f. 1994; aims to promote trade and the flow of investments among member countries of the OIC through the provision of export credit and investment insurance services; a representative office was opened in Dubai, UAE, in May 2010; auth. cap. increased from ID 150m. to ID 400m. in July 2011; mems: 40 mem. states and the Islamic Development Bank (which contributes two-thirds of its capital); CEO Dr ABDEL RAHMAN A. TAHA.

Islamic Research and Training Institute: POB 9201, Jeddah 21413, Saudi Arabia; tel. (2) 6361400; fax (2) 6378927; e-mail irti@isdb.org; internet www.irti.org; f. 1982 to undertake research enabling economic, financial and banking activities to conform to Islamic law, and to provide training for staff involved in development activities in the Bank's member countries; the Institute also organizes seminars and workshops, and holds training courses aimed at furthering the expertise of government and financial officials in Islamic developing countries; Dir-Gen. Dr MOH'D AZMI OMAR (Malaysia); publs *Annual Report*, *Islamic Economic Studies* (2 a year), various research studies, monographs, reports.

Publication

Annual Report.

Statistics

OPERATIONS APPROVED, ISLAMIC YEAR 1433
(27 November 2011–14 November 2012)

Type of operation	Number of operations	Amount (million Islamic Dinars)
Total project financing	281	3,480.6
Project financing	204	3,467.1
Technical assistance	77	13.4
Trade financing operations*	57	2,902.9
Special assistance operations	39	5.3
Total†	386	6,415.0

* Including operations by the ITFC, the ICD, the UIF, Treasury operations, and the Awqaf Properties Investment Fund.
† Excluding cancelled operations.

DISTRIBUTION OF PROJECT FINANCING AND TECHNICAL ASSISTANCE BY SECTOR, ISLAMIC YEAR 1433
(27 November 2011–14 November 2012)

Sector	Number of operations	Amount (million Islamic Dinars)	%
Agriculture	67	476.6	16.9
Education	25	182.6	6.5
Energy	15	802.4	28.5
Finance	56	164.6	5.8
Health	26	306.2	10.9
Industry and mining	3	83.4	3.0
Information and communications	1	0.2	0.0
Public administration	1	0.2	0.0
Trade	1	0.1	0.0
Transportation	8	281.9	10.0
Water, sanitation and urban services	12	521.6	18.5
Total*	215	2,819.8	100.0

* Excluding cancelled operations.

Source: Islamic Development Bank, *Annual Report 1433 H*.

LATIN AMERICAN INTEGRATION ASSOCIATION—LAIA

(ASOCIACIÓN LATINOAMERICANA DE INTEGRACIÓN—ALADI)

Address: Cebollatí 1461, Casilla 20.005, 11200 Montevideo, Uruguay.

Telephone: 2410 1121; **fax:** 2419 0649; **e-mail:** sgaladi@aladi.org; **internet:** www.aladi.org.

The Latin American Integration Association was established in August 1980 to replace the Latin American Free Trade Association, founded in February 1960.

MEMBERS

Argentina	Cuba	Paraguay
Bolivia	Ecuador	Peru
Brazil	Mexico	Uruguay
Chile	Panama	Venezuela
Colombia		

In August 2011 the Council of Ministers approved the admission of Nicaragua as a full member of the Association; the process of concluding the legal requirements for membership was ongoing in 2014.

Observers: People's Republic of China, Costa Rica, Dominican Republic, El Salvador, Guatemala, Honduras, Italy, Japan, Republic of Korea, Pakistan, Portugal, Romania, Russia, San Marino, Spain, Switzerland and Ukraine; also the UN Economic Commission for Latin America and the Caribbean, the UN Development Programme, the Andean Development Corporation, the European Union, the Ibero-American General Secretariat, the Inter-American Development Bank, the Inter-American Institute for Co-operation on Agriculture, the Latin American Economic System, the Organization of American States, and the Pan American Health Organization/World Health Organization.

Organization

(April 2014)

COUNCIL OF MINISTERS

The Council of Ministers of Foreign Affairs is responsible for the adoption of the Association's policies. It meets when convened by the Committee of Representatives.

CONFERENCE OF EVALUATION AND CONVERGENCE

The Conference, comprising plenipotentiaries of the member governments, assesses the integration process and encourages negotiations between members. It also promotes the convergence of agreements and other actions on economic integration. The Conference meets when convened by the Committee of Representatives.

COMMITTEE OF REPRESENTATIVES

The Committee, the permanent political body of the Association, comprises a permanent and a deputy representative from each member country. The Committee is the main forum for the negotiation of ALADI's initiatives and is responsible for the correct implementation of the Treaty and its supplementary regulations. It is supported by several specialized auxiliary bodies and working groups.

GENERAL SECRETARIAT

The General Secretariat is the technical body of the Association; it submits proposals for action, carries out research and evaluates activities. The Secretary-General is elected for a three-year term, which is renewable. There are two Assistant Secretaries-General.

Secretary-General: CARLOS ALBERTO ('CHACHO') ÁLVAREZ (Argentina).

Activities

The Latin American Free Trade Association (LAFTA) was an intergovernmental organization, created by the Treaty of Montevideo in February 1960 with the object of increasing trade between the Contracting Parties and of promoting regional integration, thus contributing to the economic and social development of the member countries. The Treaty provided for the gradual establishment of a free trade area, which would form the basis for a Latin American Common Market. Reduction of tariff and other trade barriers was to be carried out gradually until 1980. In June 1980, however, it was decided that LAFTA should be replaced by a less ambitious and more flexible organization, the Latin American Integration Association (Asociación Latinoamericana de Integración—ALADI), established by the 1980 Montevideo Treaty, which came into force in March 1981, and was fully ratified in March 1982. The Treaty envisaged an area of economic preferences, comprising a regional tariff preference for goods originating in member states (in effect from 1 July 1984) and regional and partial scope agreements (on economic complementation, trade promotion, trade in agricultural goods, scientific and technical co-operation, the environment, tourism, and other matters), taking into account the different stages of development of the members, and with no definite timetable for the establishment of a full common market. By 2011 the estimated total of intra-ALADI trade amounted to US $160,000m.

Certain LAFTA institutions were retained and adapted by ALADI, e.g. the Reciprocal Payments and Credits Agreement (1965, modified in 1982) and the Multilateral Credit Agreement to Alleviate Temporary Shortages of Liquidity, known as the Santo Domingo Agreement (1969, extended in 1981 to include mechanisms for counter-acting global balance of payments difficulties and for assisting in times of natural disaster).

Agreements concluded under ALADI auspices include a regional tariff preference agreement, whereby members allow imports from other member states to enter with tariffs 20% lower than those imposed on imports from other countries, and a Market Opening Lists agreement in favour of the three least developed member states, which provides for the total elimination of duties and other restrictions on imports of certain products. Other 'partial scope agreements' (in which two or more member states participate), include renegotiation agreements (pertaining to tariff cuts under LAFTA); trade agreements covering particular industrial sectors; the agreements establishing the Southern Common Market (Mercado Común del Sur— Mercosur) and the Group of Three (G-3); and agreements covering agriculture, gas supply, tourism, environmental protection, books, transport, sanitation and trade facilitation. A new system of tariff nomenclature, based on the 'harmonized system', was adopted from 1 January 1990 as a basis for common trade negotiations and statistics. General regimes on safeguards and rules of origin entered into force in 1987. The Secretariat convenes meetings of entrepreneurs in various private industrial sectors, to encourage regional trade and co-operation.

ALADI has worked to establish multilateral links or agreements with Latin American non-member countries or integration organizations, and with other developing countries or economic groups outside the continent. In February 1994 the Council of Ministers of Foreign Affairs urged that ALADI should become the co-ordinating body for the various bilateral, multilateral and regional accords (with the Andean Community, Mercosur and G-3, etc.), with the aim of eventually forming a region-wide common market. The General Secretariat initiated studies in preparation for a programme to undertake this co-ordination work. At the same meeting in February there was a serious disagreement regarding the proposed adoption of a protocol to the Montevideo Treaty to enable Mexico to participate in the North American Free Trade Agreement, while remaining a member of ALADI. However, in June the first Interpretative Protocol to the Montevideo Treaty was signed by the Ministers of Foreign Affairs: the Protocol allows member states to establish preferential trade agreements with developed nations, with a temporary waiver of the most favoured nation clause, subject to the negotiation of unilateral compensation. In December 2011 the Secretary-General of ALADI welcomed the establishment of the Community of Latin American and Caribbean States as a further means of strengthening regional integration and of formulating a unified regional position in global fora. In March 2012 ALADI hosted a ministerial meeting, attended by high-level representatives of other regional organizations, which discussed current approaches to development in Latin America.

Mercosur (comprising Argentina, Brazil, Paraguay and Uruguay) aims to conclude free trade agreements with the other members of ALADI. In March 2001 ALADI signed a co-operation agreement with the Andean Community to facilitate the exchange of information and consolidate regional and sub-regional integration. In December 2003 Mercosur and the Andean Community signed an Economic Complementary Agreement, and in April 2004 they concluded a free trade agreement, to come into effect on 1 July 2004 (although later postponed). Those ALADI member states remaining outside Mercosur and the Andean Community would be permitted to apply to join the envisaged larger free trade zone.

In May 2012 ALADI member states met to exchange information and views on sustainability and the Green Economy in advance of the UN Conference on Sustainable Development (Rio+20), which was convened in the following month.

In July 2012 ALADI, the UN Economic Commission for Latin America and the Caribbean, and the Corporación Andina de Fomento concluded an inter-agency co-operation agreement on establishing a Latin America/Asia-Pacific Observatory, which was to analyse systematically economic relations between the countries of both regions, with a view to deepening inter-regional co-operation.

In May 2013 ALADI and the Uruguay Government jointly announced that they were to organize the first ALADI trade and investment meeting—ExpoAladi—in September 2014.

Publications

Estadísticas y Comercio (quarterly, in Spanish).
Noticias ALADI (monthly, in Spanish).
Reports, studies, brochures, texts of agreements.

LEAGUE OF ARAB STATES

Address: POB 11642, Arab League Bldg, Tahrir Sq., Cairo, Egypt.
Telephone: (2) 575-0511; **fax:** (2) 574-0331; **internet:** www.lasportal.org.

The League of Arab States (more generally known as the Arab League) is a voluntary association of sovereign Arab states, designed to strengthen the close ties linking them and to co-ordinate their policies and activities and direct them towards the common good of all the Arab countries. It was founded in March 1945 with the signing of the Pact of the League of Arab States.

MEMBERS

Algeria	Lebanon	Somalia
Bahrain	Libya*	Sudan
Comoros	Mauritania	Syria*
Djibouti	Morocco	Tunisia
Egypt	Oman	United Arab Emirates
Iraq	Palestine†	
Jordan	Qatar	Yemen
Kuwait	Saudi Arabia	

* Libya was suspended from participation in meetings of the League in February 2011. It was readmitted in August following an agreement that the new Libyan Transitional Council would represent the country at the League. In November Syria was suspended from meetings of the League; in November 2012 the League formally recognized the National Coalition for Syrian Revolutionary and Opposition Forces as Syria's 'legitimate representative and main interlocutor with the Arab League'.

† Palestine is considered to be an independent state, and therefore a full member of the League.

Brazil, Eritrea, India and Venezuela have observer status at the League.

Organization

(April 2014)

COUNCIL

The supreme organ of the Arab League, the Council consists of representatives of the member states, each of which has one vote, and a representative for Palestine. The Council meets ordinarily every March, normally at the League headquarters in Cairo, Egypt, at the level of heads of state ('kings, heads of state and emirs'), and in March and September at the level of ministers responsible for foreign affairs. Arab consultative summits may be convoked when deemed necessary to address specific issues. The summit level meeting reviews all issues related to Arab national security strategies, co-ordinates supreme policies of the Arab states towards regional and international issues, reviews recommendations and reports submitted to it by the ministerial meetings, appoints the Secretary-General of the League, and is mandated to amend the League's Pact. Decisions of the Council at the level of heads of state are passed on a consensus basis. Meetings of ministers responsible for foreign affairs assess the implementation of summit resolutions, prepare relevant reports, and make arrangements for subsequent summits. Committees comprising a smaller group of foreign ministers may be appointed to follow up closely summit resolutions. Extraordinary summit meetings may be held at the request of one member state or the Secretary-General, if approved by a two-thirds' majority of member states. Extraordinary sessions of ministers responsible for foreign affairs may be held at the request of two member states or of the Secretary-General. The presidency of ordinary meetings is rotated in accordance with the alphabetical order of the League's member states. Unanimous decisions of the Council are binding upon all member states of the League; majority decisions are binding only on those states that have accepted them.

The Council is supported by technical and specialized committees advising on financial and administrative affairs, information affairs and legal affairs. In addition, specialized ministerial councils have been established to formulate common policies for the regulation and the advancement of co-operation in the following sectors: communications; electricity; environment; health; housing and construction; information; interior; justice; social affairs; tourism; transportation; and youth and sports.

GENERAL SECRETARIAT

The administrative and financial offices of the League. The Secretariat carries out the decisions of the Council, and provides financial and administrative services for the personnel of the League. General departments comprise the Bureau of the Secretary-General; Arab Affairs; Economic Affairs; Information Affairs; Legal Affairs; Palestine Affairs; Political International Affairs; Military Affairs; Social Affairs; Administrative and Financial Affairs; and Internal Audit. In addition, there is a Documentation and Information Centre; an Arab League Centre in Tunis, Tunisia; an Arab Fund for Technical Assistance in African States; a Higher Arab Institute for Translation in Algiers, Algeria; a Music Academy in Baghdad, Iraq; and a Central Boycott Office, based in Damascus, Syria. The following bodies have also been established: an administrative court; an investment arbitration board; and a higher auditing board.

The Secretary-General is appointed at summit meetings of the Council by a two-thirds' majority of the member states, for a five-year, renewable term. He appoints the Assistant Secretaries-General and principal officials, with the approval of the Council. He has the rank of ambassador, and the Assistant Secretaries-General have the rank of ministers plenipotentiary.

Secretary-General: NABIL AL-ARABI (Egypt).

Deputy Secretary-General: AHMED BEN HELLI (Algeria).

DEFENCE AND ECONOMIC CO-OPERATION

Groups established under the Treaty of Joint Defence and Economic Co-operation, concluded in 1950 to complement the Pact of the League.

Economic and Social Council: compares and co-ordinates the economic policies of the member states; supervises the activities of the Arab League's specialized agencies. The Council is composed of ministers of economic affairs or their deputies; decisions are taken by majority vote. The first meeting was held in 1953. In February 1997 the Economic and Social Council adopted the Executive Programme of the League's (1981) Agreement to Facilitate and Develop Trade Among Arab Countries, with a view to establishing a Greater Arab Free Trade Area (see below). The Council's 93nd session: Feb. 2014, Cairo, Egypt.

Joint Defence Council: supervises implementation of those aspects of the treaty concerned with common defence. Composed of ministers responsible for foreign affairs and for defence; decisions by a two-thirds' majority vote of members are binding on all.

Permanent Military Commission: f. 1950; composed of representatives of army general staffs; main purpose: to draw up plans of joint defence for submission to the Joint Defence Council.

An Arab Unified Military Command, established in 1964 to co-ordinate military policies for the liberation of Palestine, is inactive.

ARAB TRANSITIONAL PARLIAMENT

Inaugurated in December 2005, the Arab Transitional Parliament, based in Damascus, comprises 88 members (four delegates from each Arab state, including some representing non-elected bodies). The Transitional Parliament is eventually to be replaced by a Permanent Arab Parliament, a Statute for which remains under discussion. The interim body (which has no legislative function) aims to encourage dialogue between member states and to provide a focal point for joint Arab action.

OTHER INSTITUTIONS OF THE LEAGUE

Other bodies established by resolutions adopted by the Council of the League:

Administrative Tribunal of the Arab League: f. 1964; commenced operations in 1966.

Anti-Human Trafficking Co-ordination Unit: f. 2009.

Arab Fund for Technical Assistance to African Countries: f. 1975 to provide technical assistance for development projects by providing African and Arab experts, grants for scholarships and training, and finance for technical studies.

Central Boycott Office: POB 437, Damascus, Syria; f. 1951 to prevent trade between Arab countries and Israel, and to enforce a boycott by Arab countries of companies outside the region that conduct trade with Israel.

Higher Auditing Board: comprises representatives of seven member states, elected every three years; undertakes financial and administrative auditing duties.

Investment Arbitration Board: examines disputes between member states relating to capital investments.

SPECIALIZED AGENCIES

All member states of the Arab League are also members of the Specialized Agencies, which constitute an integral part of the Arab League. (See also the Arab Fund for Economic and Social Development, the Arab Monetary Fund and the Organization of Arab Petroleum Exporting Countries.)

Arab Academy for Science, Technology and Maritime Transport (AASTMT): POB 1029, Alexandria, Egypt; tel. (3) 5622388; fax (3) 5622525; internet www.aast.edu; f. 1975 as Arab Maritime Transport Academy; provides specialized training in marine transport, engineering, technology and management; Pres. Prof. Dr ISMAIL ABDEL GHAFAR ISMAIL; publs *Maritime Research Bulletin* (monthly), *Journal of the Arab Academy for Science, Technology and Maritime Transport* (2 a year).

Arab Administrative Development Organization (ARADO): 2A El-Hegaz St, POB 2692 al-Horreia, Heliopolis, Cairo, Egypt; tel. (2) 22582444; fax (2) 22580077; e-mail rfaouri@arado.org.eg; internet www.arado.org.eg; f. 1961 (as Arab Organization of Administrative Sciences), became operational in 1969; administration development, training, consultancy, research and studies, information, documentation; promotes Arab and international co-operation in administrative sciences; includes Arab Network of Administrative Information; maintains an extensive digital library; Dir-Gen. Prof. REFAT ABDELHALIM ALFAOURI; publs *Arab Journal of Administration* (biannual), *Management Newsletter* (quarterly), research series, training manuals.

Arab Atomic Energy Agency (AAEA): 7 rue de l'assistance, Cité, El Khadhra, 1003 Tunis, Tunisia; tel. (71) 808400; fax (71) 808450; e-mail aaea@aaea.org.tn; internet www.aaea.org.tn; f. 1988; Dir-Gen. Prof. Dr ABDELMAJID MAHJOUB (Tunisia); publs *The Atom and Development* (quarterly), other publs in the field of nuclear sciences and their applications in industry, biology, medicine, agriculture, food irradiation and seawater desalination.

Arab Bank for Economic Development in Africa (Banque Arabe pour le Développement Economique en Afrique—BADEA): Sayed Abd ar-Rahman el-Mahdi St, POB 2640, Khartoum 11111, Sudan; tel. (1) 83773646; fax (1) 83770600; e-mail badea@badea.org; internet www.badea.org; f. 1973 by Arab League; provides loans and grants to African countries to finance development projects; in 2012 the Bank approved loans and grants totalling US $192m. for 23 development projects, and $8m. for 32 technical assistance operations; by March 2014, total net loan and grant commitments approved since funding activities began in 1975 amounted to $4,630.4m; during 2012 the Bank contributed $2.1m. to the heavily indebted poor countries initiative, bringing the cumulative total to $230.8m. since the scheme commenced in 1997; subscribing countries: all countries of the Arab League, except the Comoros, Djibouti, Somalia and Yemen; recipient countries: all countries of the African Union, except those belonging to the Arab League; Chair. YOUSEF IBRAHEM AL-BASSAM (Saudi Arabia); Dir-Gen. ABDELAZIZ KHELEF (Algeria); publs *Annual Report Co-operation for Development* (quarterly), studies on Afro-Arab co-operation, periodic brochures.

Arab Center for the Studies of Arid Zones and Dry Lands (ACSAD): POB 2440, Damascus, Syria; tel. (11) 5743039; fax (11) 5743063; e-mail email@acsad.org; internet www.acsad.org; f. 1968 to conduct regional research and development programmes related to land and water uses, plant and animal resources, agro-meteorology, and socio-economic studies of arid zones; maintains six research stations; holds confs and training courses and encourages the exchange of information by Arab scientists; Dir-Gen. Dr RAFIK ALI SALEH.

Arab Industrial Development and Mining Organization: rue France, Zanagat al-Khatawat, POB 8019, Rabat, Morocco; tel. (37) 274500; fax (37) 772188; e-mail aidmo@aidmo.org; internet www.aidmo.org; f. 1990 by merger of Arab Industrial Development Organization, Arab Organization for Mineral Resources and Arab Organization for Standardization and Metrology; comprises a 13-member Executive Council, a High Consultative Committee of Standardization, a High Committee of Mineral Resources and a Co-ordination Committee for Arab Industrial Research Centres; a Council of ministers of member states responsible for industry meets every two years; in Sept. 2011 organized, jointly with ESCWA, a conference on 'The Role of Green Industries in Promoting Socio-Economic Development in the Arab Countries'; Dir-Gen. MOHAMED BIN YOUSEF; publs *Arab Industrial Development* (monthly and quarterly newsletters).

Arab Investment & Export Credit Guarantee Corporation: POB 23568, Safat 13096, Kuwait; tel. 4959000; fax 4841240; e-mail info@dhaman.org; internet www.dhaman.org; f. 1974; insures Arab investors for non-commercial risks, and export credits for commercial and non-commercial risks; undertakes research and other activities to promote inter-Arab trade and investment; total assets US $350.1m. (Dec. 2012); mems: 21 Arab countries and four multilateral Arab financial institutions; Chair. NASIR BEN MOHAMAD AL-QUHTANI; Dir-Gen. FAHAD RASHID AL-IBRAHIM; publs *News Bulletin* (quarterly), *Arab Investment Climate Report* (annually).

Arab Labour Organization: POB 814, Cairo, Egypt; tel. (2) 3362721; fax (2) 3484902; internet www.alolabor.org; f. 1965 for co-operation between member states in labour problems; unification of labour legislation and general conditions of work wherever possible; research; technical assistance; social insurance; training, etc; the organization has a tripartite structure: governments, employers and workers; Dir-Gen. AHMAD MUHAMMAD LUQMAN; publs *ALO Bulletin* (monthly), *Arab Labour Review* (quarterly), *Legislative Bulletin* (annually), series of research reports and studies concerned with economic and social development issues in the Arab world.

Arab League Educational, Cultural and Scientific Organization (ALECSO): ave Mohamed V, POB 1120, Tunis, Tunisia; tel. (71) 784-466; fax (71) 784-496; e-mail alecso@alecso.org.tn; internet www.alecso.org.tn; f. 1970 to promote and co-ordinate educational, cultural and scientific activities in the Arab region; implementing a plan for education covering the period 2008–18; regional units: Arab Centre for Arabization, Translation, Authorship, and Publication—Damascus, Syria; Institute of Arab Manuscripts—Cairo, Egypt; Institute of Arab Research and Studies—Cairo, Egypt; Khartoum International Institute for Arabic Language—Khartoum, Sudan; and the Arabization Co-ordination Bureau—Rabat, Morocco; Dir-Gen. MOHAMED-EL AZIZ BEN ACHOUR; publs *Arab Journal of Culture* (2 a year), *Arab Journal of Education* (2 a year), *Arab Journal of Science and Information* (2 a year), *Arab Bulletin of Publications* (annually), *ALECSO Newsletter* (monthly).

Arab Organization for Agricultural Development (AOAD): 7 al-Amarat St, POB 474, Khartoum 11111, Sudan; tel. (1) 83472176; fax (1) 83471402; e-mail info@aoad.org; internet www.aoad.org; f. 1970; began operations in 1972 to contribute to co-operation in agricultural activities, and in the development of natural and human resources for agriculture; compiles data, conducts studies, training and food security programmes; includes Information and Documentation Centre, Arab Centre for Studies and Projects, and Arab Institute of Forestry and Biodiversity; Dir-Gen. Dr TARIQ MOOSA AL-ZADJALI; publs *Agricultural Statistics Yearbook*, *Annual Report on Agricultural Development*, *the State of Arab Food Security* (annually), *Agriculture and Development in the Arab World* (quarterly), *Accession Bulletin* (every 2 months), *AOAD Newsletter* (monthly), *Arab Agricultural Research Journal*, *Arab Journal for Irrigation Water Management* (2 a year).

Arab Satellite Communications Organization (ARABSAT): POB 1038, Diplomatic Quarter, Riyadh 11431, Saudi Arabia; tel. (1) 4820000; fax (1) 4887999; e-mail info@arabsat.com; internet www.arabsat.com; f. 1976; regional satellite telecommunications org. providing broadcast, telecommunications and broadband services to mems and private users; operates six satellites, which cover Arab, European, Central Asian and northern African countries; suspended satellite broadcasts to Syria in June 2012, at the request of the League Council; Pres. and CEO KHALID AHMED BALKHEYOUR.

Arab States Broadcasting Union (ASBU): POB 250, 1080 Tunis Cedex; rue 8840, Centre Urbain Nord, Tunisia; tel. (71) 843445; fax (71) 843054; e-mail asbu-fx@asbu.net; internet www.asbu.net; f. 1969 to promote and study broadcasting, and to exchange expertise and technical co-operation in broadcasting; conducts training and audience research; Multimedia Exchange Network over Satellite (MENOS) network launched in 2009; organizes the biennial Arab Festival for Radio and Television, and an Arab Song Festival every one or two years; 28 active member radio and television orgs, seven participating mems, 19 assoc. mems; Pres. of Exec. Council ISMAIL AL-SHISHTAWI (Egypt); publ. *Arab Broadcasters* (quarterly).

ASSOCIATED BODY

Council of Arab Economic Unity: 1113 Corniche el-Nil, 4th Floor, POB 1 Mohammed Fareed, 11518 Cairo, Egypt; tel. (2) 5755321; fax (2) 5754090; f. 1957 by the Economic and Social Council of the Arab League to co-ordinate measures leading to a customs union subject to a unified administration; conduct market and commodity studies; assist with the unification of statistical terminology and methods of data collection; conduct studies for the formation of new joint Arab companies and federations; and to formulate specific programmes for agricultural and industrial co-ordination and for improving road and railway networks; was to administer the 1962 Arab Economic Unity Agreement; inaugural meeting held in 1964; representatives of member states—usually ministers of economy, finance and trade—meet twice a year; meetings are chaired by the representative of each country for one year on a rotational basis; the Council Secretariat is entrusted with the implementation of the Council's decisions and with proposing work plans, including efforts to encourage participation by member states in the Arab Economic Unity Agreement; the Secretariat also compiles statistics, conducts research and publishes studies on Arab economic problems and on the effects of major world economic trends; has permanent committees on Customs issues; Monetary and finance; Economic; Permanent representatives; and Follow-up; mems: Egypt, Iraq, Jordan, Libya, Mauritania, Palestine, Somalia, Sudan, Syria and Yemen; Sec.-Gen. MOHAMMED AL-RABEE (Yemen).

Activities

In May 2004 the meeting of Arab League heads of state approved a *Pledge of Accord and Solidarity* that committed members to implementing in full decisions of the League. The 22nd Arab League summit meeting, held in Sirte, Libya, in March 2010, approved the formation of a committee comprising the Egyptian, Iraqi, Libyan, Qatari and Yemeni heads of state, and the League Secretary-General, with a mandate to oversee the development of a new structure for joint Arab action. The committee prepared documentation on proposed reforms for consideration by an extraordinary summit of the League that was held in early October, also in Sirte. In early 2012 the League's Secretary-General tasked Lakhdar Brahimi, the former Algerian Minister of Foreign Affairs and UN official (and from August of that year the Joint Special Representative of the League of Arab States and the UN on Syria), to give consideration to reforming the organic structure of the League, and to make a series of recommendations on enhancing the interaction between the League and non-governmental organizations (NGOs); Brahimi submitted his findings to the Secretary-General in January 2013.

From February–August 2011 the League suspended Libya from participation in its meetings owing to the use of military force against opposition movements in that country. In mid-November Syria was suspended from meetings of the League, on similar grounds. The emerging civil unrest in countries in the region, notably, in addition, in Egypt, Tunisia and Yemen, led to the 23rd summit meeting, initially scheduled to be held in March 2011, being postponed until March 2012.

The 23rd summit meeting of Arab League heads of state, convened in Baghdad, Iraq, in March 2012, endorsed, and called for the immediate implementation of, a six-point plan on resolving the Syrian crisis that had been recently proposed by the Arab League-UN Joint Special Envoy on the Syrian Crisis. The UN Secretary-General attended the summit, owing to the inclusion of the Syrian crisis on its agenda. Saudi Arabia, seeking the imposition of stronger measures against the Syrian regime, and having reportedly failed to secure the agreement of the Iraqi Government to invite Syrian opposition representatives to the summit meeting, was represented at the gathering at the level of ambassador. Egypt and Qatar also sent delegates lower than the level of head of state. The Amir of Kuwait participated in the meeting, representing the first visit by a Kuwaiti leader to Baghdad since prior to the 1990 invasion Kuwait by Iraq. Regional water shortages and means of coping with natural disasters were also discussed by the summit.

In November 2012 the League recognized the National Coalition for Syrian Revolutionary and Opposition Forces as Syria's 'legitimate representative and main interlocutor with the Arab League'. Heads of state attending the 24th Arab League summit, convened in Doha, Qatar, in March 2013, addressed an agenda including the continuing conflict in Syria; Palestine; restructuring of the League; and a proposal to establish an Arab fund to finance agricultural development and the implementation of food security plans. Syria was formally represented at the summit by representatives of the National Coalition. The 25th Arab summit, held in late March 2014, in Kuwait, adopted the Kuwait Declaration, which reconfirmed commitment to improving relations through constructive, transparent dialogue; and also undertook to provide technical and financial support to countries undergoing political transition. Syria's seat at the summit was not occupied, and it was announced that it would subsequently remain formally vacant pending the meeting by the Syrian National Coalition of certain 'legal and technical requirements'. Representatives of the Coalition were, however, to be invited 'on an exceptional basis' to a meeting of League ministers of foreign affairs that was scheduled to be held in September.

HUMAN RIGHTS

A Permanent Arab Commission on Human Rights was established in September 1968 as the League's principal political organ for the protection of human rights. The primary focus of the Commission was the pursuit of a settlement to the Arab-Israeli conflict, with less emphasis on addressing human rights issues within League member states. It spent more than 10 years drafting an Arab Charter on Human Rights, which was finally adopted by League heads of state in May 2004. The Charter entered into force in January 2008 and provided for the election of an Arab Human Rights Committee, which was inaugurated in March 2009, with a membership comprising seven men. In March 2011 the League Council adopted a resolution that urged the General Secretariat to prepare a review of the role of the Permanent Commission. In November of that year the League Secretary-General appointed a committee of experts to consider the establishment of an Arab Court on Human Rights. In February 2013 representatives of the League, of human rights-focused NGOs active in the region, and human rights experts from the UN, African Union (AU), Organization of American States (OAS), and Council of Europe, convened in Cairo, Egypt, a conference entitled 'The League of Arab States, human rights and civil society: challenges ahead'. The Conference approved a set of recommendations, focusing on the promotion of an effective human rights protection legislative framework for the Arab region, to be consistent with international human rights standards, including through reforms to the Arab Charter on Human Rights to clarify the League's protection mandate and to ensure engagement with NGOs; strengthening the Arab Human Rights Committee; amending the League's Pact explicitly to mention respect for universal human rights standards; and promoting effective dialogue with independent national, regional and international civil society organizations. The delegates agreed that, were the proposed Arab Court on Human Rights to be created, it should function in accordance with international standards. The establishment of the Arab Court was approved in principle by the March 2013 League summit.

The Arab Human Rights Committee conducted its first reviews of national human rights situations in 2012, addressing Jordan in March, and Algeria in October. The situation in Bahrain was reviewed in February 2013.

The League established an Anti-Human Trafficking Co-ordination Unit in 2009. In March 2010 a regional conference convened in Doha launched an initiative for building national capacities to combat human trafficking in the Arab countries; the League and the UN Office on Drugs and Crime have subsequently supported the implementation of the initiative. The development of an Arab treaty on combating human trafficking and of a database on trafficking are under consideration.

PROMOTING ARAB IDENTITY

In February 2008 Arab ministers of information adopted the Arab League Satellite Broadcasting Charter, establishing principles for the regulation of satellite broadcasting and providing for the withdrawal of permits from channels that broadcast in a manner that might 'damage social harmony, national unity, public order or traditional values', including broadcasting content deemed to be offensive towards Arab leaders or national or religious symbols; erotic content; or content that promotes alcohol or smoking tobacco. Qatar (base of the international satellite broadcaster al-Jazeera) did not sign the Charter at that time.

In early 2012 the League submitted the prospective domain name .arab for registration under the Internet Corporation for Assigned Names and Numbers (ICANN)'s expanded generic top-level domains (gTLD) programme. In October 2013 ICANN announced the introduction of an Arabic script domain suffix.

SECURITY

In April 1998 Arab League ministers responsible for the interior and for justice adopted the Arab Convention for the Suppression of Terrorism, which incorporated security and judicial measures, such as extradition arrangements and the exchange of evidence. The agreement entered into effect in May 2000. An emergency meeting of the League's Council, convened in mid-September 2001 in response to major terrorist attacks on the USA, perpetrated by militant Islamist fundamentalists, condemned the atrocities, while urging respect for the rights of Arab and Muslim US citizens. The Secretary-General subsequently emphasized the need for co-ordinated global anti-terrorist action to have clearly defined goals and to be based on sufficient consultations and secure evidence. He also deplored anti-Islamic prejudice, and stated that US-led action against any Arab state would not be supported and that Israeli participation in an international anti-terrorism alliance would be unacceptable. A meeting of League ministers responsible for foreign affairs in Doha, in October condemned international terrorism but did not express support for retaliatory military action by the USA and its allies. In December a further emergency meeting of League foreign affairs ministers was held to discuss the deepening Middle East crisis. In January 2002 the League appointed a commissioner responsible for promoting dialogue between civilizations. The commissioner was mandated to encourage understanding in Western countries of Arab and Muslim civilization and viewpoints, with the aim of redressing perceived negative stereotypes (especially in view of the Islamist fundamentalist connection to the September 2001 terrorist atrocities). In April 2003 the Secretary-General expressed his regret that the Arab states had failed to prevent the ongoing war in Iraq, and urged the development of a new regional security order. In November the UN Secretary-General appointed the Secretary-General of the League to serve as the Arab region's representative on the UN High-Level Panel on Threats, Challenges and Change. In March 2007 the League's summit meeting resolved to establish an expert-level task force to consider national security issues.

In December 2010 the Arab League and the UN Office on Drugs and Crime jointly launched a five-year Regional Programme on Drug Control, Crime Prevention and Criminal Justice Reform for the Arab States, covering the period 2011–15, and based on the following pillars: countering illicit trafficking, organized crime and terrorism; promoting justice and integrity; and drug prevention and improving health.

In March 2013 the Arab League, the UN Office for Disaster Risk Reduction, the UN Development Programme and other partners organized the First Arab Conference on Disaster Risk Reduction, with participation by 22 Arab states; the Conference launched a new Arab Regional Platform on Disaster Risk Reduction.

TRADE AND ECONOMIC CO-OPERATION

A number of multilateral organizations in industry and agriculture have been formed on the principle that faster development and economies of scale may be achieved by combining the efforts of member states. In industries that are new to member countries Arab Joint Companies are formed, while existing industries are co-ordinated through the establishment of Arab Specialized Unions. The unions are for closer co-operation on problems of production and marketing, and to help companies deal as a group in international markets. The companies are intended to be self-supporting on a purely commercial basis; they may issue shares to citizens of the participating countries. Council of Arab Economic Unity agreements aimed at encouraging Arab investment include an accord on Non-Double Taxation and Income Tax Evasion (adopted in December 1998); an accord on Investment Promotion and Protection (June 2000); and an accord on Investment Dispute Settlement in Arab Countries (December 2000).

In February 1997 the Economic and Social Council adopted the Executive Programme of the (1981) Agreement to Facilitate and Develop Trade Among Arab Countries, with a view to creating a Greater Arab Free Trade Area (GAFTA) which aimed to facilitate and develop trade among participating countries through the reduction (by 10% per year) and eventual elimination of customs duties over a 10-year period, alongside a parallel elimination of trade barriers. In February 2002 the Economic and Social Council agreed to bring forward the inauguration of GAFTA to 1 January 2005. Consequently, customs duties between most member states, which, according to schedule, had been reduced by 50% from January 1998–January 2002, were further reduced by 10% by January 2003, 20% by January 2004, and a final 20% by January 2005; Sudan and Yemen, as less developed economies, were to be subject to a parallel longer schedule of customs reductions. GAFTA (also known as the Pan-Arab Free Trade Area) entered into force, as planned, then with 17 participating countries (accounting for about 94% of the total volume of intra-Arab trade). (In 2009 Algeria became the 18th member of GAFTA.) The Council agreed to supervise the implementation of the free trade agenda and formally to review its progress twice a year. Nevertheless, the level of inter-Arab trade and inter-Arab investments subsequently remained lower than anticipated, reportedly owing to restrictive degrees of bureaucracy and regulation.

In May 2001 Egypt, Jordan, Morocco and Tunisia (all then participants in the Euro-Mediterranean Partnership, relaunched in 2008 as the Union for the Mediterranean—see European Union), while convened in Agadir, Morocco, issued the Agadir Declaration in which they determined to establish an Arab Mediterranean Free Trade Zone. The so-called Agadir Agreement on the establishment of a Free Trade Zone between the Arabic Mediterranean Nations was signed in February 2004, came into force in July 2006, and entered its implementation phase in March 2007. The signatories to the Agadir Agreement are also members of GAFTA.

The inaugural Economic, Development and Social summit meeting of Arab leaders, held in January 2009, in Kuwait, under the auspices of the Arab League, considered means of accelerating progress towards the achievement of Arab economic integration; agreed to create by 2015 a fully functioning Arab Customs Union, and by 2020 a fully functioning Arab Common Market; decided to launch a regional power grid and rail network; and agreed to launch a fund to finance Arab small and medium-sized enterprises (SMEs). Under the Arab Customs Union goods exempt from taxes were to comprise at least 40% of components originating in GAFTA member states. The second Economic, Development and Social summit meeting was convened in January 2011, in Sharm el-Sheikh, Egypt. Participants at the third summit, held in Riyadh, Saudi Arabia, in January 2013, adopted the Riyadh Declaration, in which they determined to activate the fund for SMEs; to strengthen the capacity of joint Arab institutions, including increasing by at least one-half the capital of joint financial institutions; to promote inter-Arab investment; to implement the ongoing Pan-Arab Strategy for Promoting Renewable Energy; to promote the efforts of Arab agencies in pursuing the attainment by 2015 of the UN Millennium Development Goals; and to finalize expeditiously the prerequisites for the full functioning of the Arab Customs Union by 2015, and consequent full implementation of GAFTA. An Arab Private Sector Forum was convened in January 2013, also in Riyadh.

Meeting in October 2012 League ministers responsible for tourism determined to implement a new Arab Tourism Strategy. The proposed establishment of an Arab Youth Centres Observatory and an Arab Youth Training Centre—aimed at monitoring the challenges encountered by young people and facilitating skills development—was on the agenda of the 90th meeting of the Economic and Social Council, held in September 2012.

WATER RESOURCES AND RENEWABLE ENERGY

In January 2009 the Economic, Development and Social Arab summit meeting determined to launch a regional power grid. The inaugural session of an Arab Ministerial Water Council was convened in June of that year. The new Council gave consideration to the development of an Arab Water Strategy; this was launched in March 2011. In October 2010 Arab ministers responsible for electricity adopted a Pan-Arab Strategy for Promoting Renewable Energy, covering the period 2010–30.

ARAB–ISRAELI AFFAIRS

In June 1996 an extraordinary summit conference of Arab League heads of state was convened, the first since 1990, in order to formulate a united Arab response to the election of a new government in Israel. The conference urged Israel to honour its undertaking to withdraw from the Occupied Territories, including Jerusalem, and to respect the establishment of an independent Palestinian state, in order to ensure the success of the peace process. In December 1996 the League convened in emergency session to consider measures to halt any expansion of the Jewish population in the West Bank and Gaza. In March 1997 the Council met in emergency session in response to the Israeli Government's decision to proceed with construction of a new settlement at Har Homa (Jabal Abu-Ghunaim) in East Jerusalem. At the end of March ministers responsible for foreign affairs of Arab League states agreed to cease all efforts to secure normal diplomatic relations with Israel and to close diplomatic offices and missions while construction work continued in East Jerusalem. Mauritania, although a League member state, established full diplomatic relations with Israel in October 1999, prompting protests in a number of Arab countries.

In February 2000 the League strongly condemned an Israeli aerial attack on southern Lebanon. The League welcomed the withdrawal of Israeli forces from southern Lebanon in May, although it subsequently condemned continuing territorial violations by the Israeli military. At an emergency summit meeting convened in October in response to mounting insecurity in Jerusalem and the Occupied Territories, 15 Arab heads of state, senior officials from six countries and Yasser Arafat, the then Palestinian (National) Authority (PA) leader, strongly rebuked Israel, which was accused of inciting the ongoing violent disturbances by stalling the progress of the peace process. The summit determined to 'freeze' co-operation with Israel and requested the formation of an international committee to conduct an impartial assessment of the situation. The summit also endorsed the establishment of an 'al-Aqsa Fund', with a value of US $800m., which was to finance initiatives aimed at promoting the Arab and Islamic identity of Jerusalem, and a smaller 'Jerusalem Intifada Fund' to support the families of Palestinians killed in the unrest.

In March 2001 the League's first ordinary annual summit-level Council was convened, in Amman, Jordan. The summit issued the Amman Declaration, which emphasized the promotion of Arab unity, and demanded the reversal of Israel's 1967 occupation of Arab territories. Heads of state attending the summit requested that the League consider means of reactivating the now relaxed Arab economic boycott of Israel. In May 2001 League ministers responsible for foreign affairs determined that all political contacts with Israel should be suspended in protest at aerial attacks by Israel on Palestinian targets in the West Bank. In July representatives of 13 member countries met in Damascus, under the auspices of the Central Boycott Office. The meeting declared unanimous support for reactivating trade measures against Israeli companies and foreign businesses dealing with Israel. In August an emergency meeting of ministers responsible for foreign affairs of the member states was convened at the request of the Palestinian authorities to consider a unified Arab response to the recent escalation of hostilities and Israel's seizure of institutions in East Jerusalem.

In March 2002 a meeting of League ministers responsible for foreign affairs agreed to support an initiative proposed by Crown Prince Abdullah of Saudi Arabia aimed at brokering a peaceful settlement to the Palestinian–Israeli crisis. The plan—entailing the restoration of 'normal' Arab relations with Israel and acceptance of its right to exist in peace and security, in exchange for a full Israeli withdrawal from the Occupied Territories, the establishment of an independent Palestinian state with East Jerusalem at its capital, and the return of refugees—was unanimously endorsed, as the first pan-Arab Palestinian-Israeli peace initiative, by the summit-level Council held in Beirut in March. The plan urged compliance with UN Security Council Resolution 194 concerning the return of Palestinian refugees to Israel, or appropriate compensation for their property; however, precise details of eligibility criteria for the proposed return, a contentious issue owing to the potentially huge numbers of refugees and descendants of refugees involved, were not elaborated. Conditions imposed by Israel on Yasser Arafat's freedom of movement deterred him from attending the summit. At the end of March the League's Secretary-General condemned the Israeli military's siege of Arafat's presidential compound in Ramallah (initiated in retaliation against a succession of Palestinian bomb attacks on Israeli civilians). In April an extraordinary Council meeting, held at the request of Palestine to consider the 'unprecedented deterioration' of the situation in the Palestinian territories, accused certain states (notably the USA) of implementing a pro-Israeli bias that enabled Israel to act outside the scope of international law and to ignore relevant UN resolutions, and accused Israel of undermining international co-operation in combating terrorism by attempting to equate its actions towards the Palestinian people with recent anti-terrorism activities conducted by the USA. A meeting organized by the Central Boycott Office at the end of April agreed to expand boycott measures. Israel's termination of its siege of Arafat's Ramallah compound in early May was welcomed by the Secretary-General. A Council meeting held in September authorized the establishment of a committee to address the welfare of imprisoned Palestinians and urged the USA and the United Kingdom to reconsider their policies on exporting weaponry to Israel (particularly F-16 military aircraft), while issuing a resolution concerning the danger posed by Israel's possession of weapons of mass destruction.

In November 2003 the League welcomed a UN Security Council resolution endorsing the adoption in April by the so-called Quartet, comprising envoys from the UN, the European Union (EU), Russia and the USA, of a 'performance-based roadmap to a permanent two-state solution to the Israeli–Palestinian conflict'. The 2004 summit meeting of Arab League heads of state, held in Tunis, Tunisia, in May, condemned contraventions of international law by the Israeli Government, in particular continuing settlement activities and the use of unjudicial killings and other violence, and focused on the humanitarian situation of Palestinians recently displaced by large-scale house demolitions in Rafah, Gaza. In January 2005 the League welcomed the election of Mahmud Abbas as the new Executive President of the PA, following the death in November 2004 of Yasser Arafat.

In March 2007 the annual summit meeting of the League reaffirmed the League's support for the 2002 peace initiative proposed by Crown Prince Abdullah of Saudi Arabia, and urged the Israeli authorities to resume direct negotiations based on the principles of the initiative. In July 2007 the ministers responsible for foreign affairs of Egypt and Jordan, representing the League, visited Israel to promote the 2002 initiative. The March 2009 League summit meeting condemned the intensive military assault on Gaza perpetrated by Israeli forces (with the stated aim of ending rocket attacks launched by Hamas and other militant groups on Israeli targets) during late December 2008–mid-January 2009. The summit urged Israel to establish a time frame for committing to the peace process. In October an emergency meeting of the League condemned attacks by the Israeli armed forces on the al-Aqsa Mosque in Jerusalem.

The March 2010 summit meeting, held in Sirte, agreed all Israeli measures seeking to alter the features and demographic, humanitarian and historic situation of occupied Jerusalem to be invalid and unacceptable, while appealing to the international community (particularly the UN Security Council, the EU and UNESCO) to act to save East Jerusalem and maintain the al-Aqsa Mosque. The meeting's final declaration urged that a special session of the UN General Assembly should be held with a view to halting Israeli measures that contravened international law, and mandated the formation of a League legal committee to follow up the issue of the 'judaization' of East Jerusalem and the confiscation of Arab property, and to take these issues before national and international courts with appropriate jurisdiction. In March 2013 the meeting of League heads of state, convened in Doha, approved the establishment of an Arab East Jerusalem Fund, to finance projects and programmes that would maintain the Arab and Islamic character of the city.

In June 2010, in response to an Israeli raid at the end of May on a flotilla of vessels carrying humanitarian aid through international waters towards the Gaza Strip, resulting in nine civilian fatalities, the League Secretary-General demanded the termination of the blockade imposed since 2006 by Israel against Gaza. The League was critical of a UN-commissioned report on the flotilla incident, released in September 2011, which, while concluding that the Israeli army had used 'excessive and unreasonable' force, also found the Israeli naval blockade of Gaza to have been imposed as a 'legitimate security measure' to prevent weapons from reaching Gaza by sea, and found that the flotilla had acted recklessly in attempting to breach the naval blockade.

In July 2011 the recently appointed League Secretary-General, Nabil al-Arabi, announced that the League would encourage the UN to grant full membership to Palestine. In September the Executive President of the PA submitted a formal application to the UN Secretary-General for Palestine's admission to the UN; this, however, was rejected by the UN Security Council. In July 2012 the League mandated an internal committee to prepare a petition to be presented to the UN in support of Palestine's proposed membership. The UN General Assembly granted observer status (and consequently recognition of de facto statehood) to Palestine in November of that year. Later in that month, having met with the Palestinian leadership, al-Arabi announced that the League would continue to pursue the objective of full accession by Palestine to the UN.

In April 2013 a delegation of the League met with the US Secretary of State, in Washington, DC, USA, to discuss the 2002 Saudi Arabia-proposed peace initiative; subsequently, the League delegation indicated that—rather than conforming to the precise land borders in place prior to the 1967 Israeli occupation of Arab territories—the Palestinians might be prepared to consider mutually agreed minor trades in territory in order to resolve the situation with Israel. In mid-May 2013 representatives of the League, Jordan and Palestine requested the UN Security Council, without success, to declare itself as actively engaged in efforts to restart the peace process. In July delegates of the League met again with the US Secretary of State to consider a US initiative to restart the Palestinian-Israeli peace talks; subsequently, the League delegation issued a statement endorsing the initiative, and asserting that any future agreement must be based on a two-state solution, through the establishment of an independent Palestinian state in accordance with boundaries as at 4 June 1967, but reiterating the possibility of limited exchanges of territory of equal value and size. In March 2014 Arab League heads of state reiterated that resolving the Palestinian situation remained the core regional challenge for member states, and announced their 'total rejection' of the expectation of the Israeli Prime Minister, Binyamin Netanyahu, that Israel should be considered as a 'Jewish state' and 'Jewish homeland', deeming this potentially to undermine the perceived right of return of Palestinian refugees.

LIBYA

In mid-February 2011, in protest against violent measures taken by the regime of the Libyan leader Col Muammar al-Qaddafi against opposition groupings, the Libyan delegate to the League resigned his representative position. An emergency session of the League convened soon afterwards suspended Libya from participation in meetings of the League. The League supported the adoption by the UN Security Council, in March, of Resolution 1973, which imposed a no-fly zone in Libya's airspace, strengthened sanctions against the Qaddafi regime, demanded an immediate ceasefire, and authorized member states to take 'all necessary measures to protect civilians and civilian populated areas under threat of attack' by forces loyal to Qaddafi, 'while excluding a foreign occupation force of any form on any part of Libyan territory'. Following the instigation of the UN-mandated military action in Libya, the League Secretary-General reportedly emphasized that the focus of the military intervention ought to be on the protection of civilians and ought not to exceed the mandate to impose a no-fly zone. In August, as opposition forces captured the Libyan capital, Tripoli, the League Secretary-General offered full solidarity to the new Libyan National Transitional Council, as the legitimate representative of the Libyan people. Libya was readmitted to full League membership at the end of that month. The League at that time urged the international community to release all assets and property of the Libyan state, previously blocked by economic sanctions. Following the death of al-Qaddafi in October the Secretary-General urged unity and extended the League's full support for the country's transition.

In September 2012 the Secretary-General of the League condemned an armed attack on the US Consulate in Benghazi, Libya, in which the US Ambassador to Libya and three Consulate personnel were killed. The Secretary-General urged the US Government to denounce a US-produced film deemed to be deeply offensive to Islam, which initially was thought to have been the provocation for the attack.

SYRIA

By August 2011 an estimated 2,200 anti-government street protesters had been killed by security forces—deploying tanks and snipers—during several months of unrest in Syria. A meeting of Arab League ministers responsible for foreign affairs convened in that month issued a statement urging the Syrian regime to act reasonably, stop the ongoing bloodshed, and respect the 'legitimate demands' of the Syrian people. The meeting also determined that the League Secretary-General would visit the Syrian authorities with a peace initiative aimed at resolving the situation through dialogue. Accordingly, talks were held between the Secretary-General and President Bashar al-Assad in the Syrian capital, Damascus, in early September. It was reported that they discussed measures aimed at accelerating political reforms in Syria, and that the League Secretary-General stated his rejection of foreign intervention in the Syrian situation. The League's peace initiative was, however, reportedly rejected by both the Syrian authorities and protesters. In October the Secretary-General led a further delegation to the country, amid an escalation of attacks by the security forces. In mid-November the League, meeting in emergency session, voted to suspend Syria from participation in meetings of the League, and to impose economic and diplomatic sanctions in protest at the violent repression of political opponents and civilian demonstrators by the government, and its failure to implement a peace initiative. The resolution was endorsed by 18 members; Syria, Lebanon and Yemen voted against the suspension (Iraq abstained). The measures came into effect four days later, when no concessions had been made by the Syrian authorities. On 19 December the Syrian authorities reportedly agreed to the League's peace plan to withdraw security forces and heavy weapons from civilian areas, to initiate negotiations with the opposition movement and to release political prisoners. The Arab League was to send an observer mission to the country, with an initial mandate of one month, in order to monitor compliance with the measures. However, within days of the arrival of the first 50 observers, on 26 December, the mission was strongly criticized for its ineffectiveness in preventing further government attacks and its inability to act independently of the authorities to assess accurately the level of violence. In early January 2012 Arab League ministers responsible for foreign affairs met to consider the mission's initial findings and to discuss demands for its withdrawal. The meeting agreed to maintain and to reinforce the mission and demanded that the Syrian authorities co-operate fully. On 22 January League ministers agreed on a plan of action to end the conflict, requiring President Assad to transfer his authority to an interim government within two months, and democratic parliamentary and presidential elections to be conducted within six months. The proposals were rejected, the following day, by the Syrian authorities. The ministerial meeting agreed to extend the monitoring mission. Saudi Arabia, however, decided to withdraw from the operation. On 24 January members of the Gulf Cooperation Council also resolved to withdraw their monitors. A few days later the League announced that it was suspending the mission owing to a sharp deterioration in the security situation in Syria. In early February Russia and the People's Republic of China vetoed a draft resolution at the UN Security Council to endorse the League's peace plan for Syria. In mid-February League ministers adopted a resolution providing for the termination of the suspended monitoring mission; ending diplomatic co-operation with the Syrian regime; and proposing the creation of a joint Arab-UN peacekeeping mission to Syria. Later in that month the Secretaries-General of the League and of the UN appointed Kofi Annan—formerly the UN Secretary-General—as their Joint Special Envoy on the Syrian Crisis; in March Nasser al-Kidwa, a former minister responsible for foreign affairs in the PA, and Jean-Marie Guéhenno, a former UN Under-Secretary-General for Peacekeeping Operations, were appointed as Deputy Joint Special Envoys. Towards the end of February an international conference on the situation in Syria, which had escalated significantly, was convened in Tunis, by the 'Friends of Syria', a coalition initiated by France and the USA, with League support (specifically, with endorsement from Qatar and Saudi Arabia), following China and Russia's veto of the Security Council's draft resolution on Syria. The conference urged the UN to consider establishing a peacekeeping mission for Syria.

In late March 2012 the Syrian Government announced its acceptance of a six-point peace plan proposed earlier in that month by Annan. The plan envisaged: (i) a commitment to working with the Joint Envoy in an inclusive Syrian-led political process aimed at addressing the legitimate aspirations and concerns of the Syrian people; (ii) a UN-monitored ceasefire by all parties, including a commitment by the Syrian regime to withdraw troops and heavy weaponry from population centres; (iii) a commitment to enabling the timely provision of humanitarian assistance to all areas affected by the fighting, and the immediate implementation of a daily two-hour humanitarian pause; (iv) the expedited release of arbitrarily arrested detainees; (v) free access and movement for journalists; and (vi) freedom of association and the right to demonstrate peacefully for all. The plan did not demand explicitly the resignation of Syrian President Assad. Shortly afterwards Arab League heads of state, gathered at a summit meeting in Baghdad, endorsed the plan, and called for its immediate and full implementation. In mid-April the UN Security Council—taking note of an assessment by the Joint Special Envoy that the parties to the Syrian violence appeared to be observing a cessation of fire, and that the Syrian Government had begun to implement its commitments under the plan—authorized an advance team of up to 30 unarmed military observers to monitor the ceasefire, pending the deployment of a full ceasefire supervision mission. Soon afterwards, as violence had escalated since the attempt to impose a ceasefire, and Syrian forces had not withdrawn from urban areas, the UN Secretary-General requested that a full team of 300 unarmed observers should be promptly deployed. Consequently, on 21 April the UN Security Council unanimously authorized the establishment of the UN Supervision Mission in Syria (UNSMIS), initially for a period of 90 days, with a mandate to monitor the cessation of violence and to observe and support the full implementation of the six-point peace plan. Repeated violations of the terms of the peace plan continued, however, to be reported. In late May the UN Security Council issued a statement unanimously condemning—as an 'outrageous use of force against the civilian population' constituting a violation of applicable international law—the indiscriminate massacre (confirmed by UNSMIS observers), of an estimated 108 men, women and children, and the wounding of many more, resulting from the shelling of a residential neighbourhood—the rebel-controlled village of El-Houleh, near Homs—allegedly by Syrian government forces. The Council also condemned the killing of civilians in El-Houleh by shooting at close range and by severe physical abuse. Reiterating its full support to the efforts of the Arab League-UN Joint Special Envoy for the implementation of his six-point plan, the Council demanded that the Syrian Government immediately cease the use of heavy weapons in population centres, and immediately return its troops to their barracks. In early June the 'Free Syrian Army' group of anti-government militants announced that it was no longer committed to the six-point peace plan. Shortly afterwards an estimated further 78 people, again including women and children, were reported to have been killed in the western village of Qbeir, by pro-government militants, following the shelling of the area by government forces. A meeting of the Security Council held soon afterwards, with participation by the Arab League and UN Secretaries-General and the Joint Special Envoy, requested the UN Secretary-General to put forward a range of options for resolving the Syrian crisis. On 16 June, in view of the escalating insecurity, UNSMIS suspended its patrols in Syria, while remaining committed to ending the violence. In June an extraordinary ministerial-level meeting of the League Council requested the Arab Satellite Communications Organization and the Egyptian company Nilesat to suspend broadcasts via Arab Satellites of official and private Syrian television channels. At the end of June the Secretaries-General of the League and UN, as well as the ministers responsible for foreign affairs of China, France, Russia, the United Kingdom, the USA, Turkey, Iraq, Kuwait, Qatar, and the High Representative of the European Union for Foreign Affairs and Security Policy, gathered in Geneva, Switzerland, as the 'Action Group for Syria', under the chairmanship of the then League-UN Joint Special Envoy, to address the situation in Syria. The so-called Geneva I conference agreed that a transitional government of national unity should be established in Syria, including members of both the opposition and the present government, and that this should be tasked with overseeing the drafting of a new constitution and subsequent staging of national elections. In mid-July, by which time the violence in Syria had further intensified, and the situation was deemed to be a civil war, China and Russia vetoed a draft UN Security Council resolution that would have imposed sanctions on the Syrian regime. On 22 July an emergency meeting of Arab ministers responsible for foreign affairs agreed that President Assad should resign and leave the country, and that opposition parties should form a government of national unity. At the beginning of August, in view of the failure of the parties to the Syrian conflict to adhere to the six-point peace plan, and of the divisions within the UN Security Council over Syria, Annan announced that he would step down as Joint Special Envoy at the end of that month; in mid-August the League and UN appointed a Joint Special Representative on Syria, Lakhdar Brahimi, to take office at the beginning of September, and appointed Nasser al-Kidwa (Deputy to Annan) as Deputy Joint Special Representative. The Security Council determined in mid-August not to extend the mandate of UNSMIS beyond 19 August, and the mission was terminated accordingly. In mid-September the new Joint Special Representative visited Damascus to discuss the ongoing, and worsening, crisis with the Syrian President and opposition representatives. In October, in view of mounting tensions between Syria and Turkey (including an incident at the two countries' border at the beginning of the month in which five Turkish civilians were killed, and others injured, by cross-border mortar fire from the Syrian military), the Joint Special Representative engaged in discussions with the Syrian and Turkish authorities. Following a bomb attack in Beirut, on 19 October, that resulted in eight fatalities, including the death of a senior commander in the Lebanese military, potentially destabilizing that country, it was feared that the conflict in Syria might ignite wider regional tensions. On the following day Brahimi entered into negotiations with parties to the Syrian conflict aimed at initiating a temporary ceasefire during the upcoming Muslim festival of Id al-Adha; it was announced on 24 October that this had been agreed. However, the truce, declared on 26 October, was almost immediately broken by a car bomb explosion in Damascus, and within 48 hours at least 100 further violent deaths had been reported.

In November 2012 the League formally recognized the National Coalition for Syrian Revolutionary and Opposition Forces, then under the leadership of Ahmed Moaz al-Khatib, as Syria's 'legitimate representative and main interlocutor with the Arab League'. In February 2013 the participants—including delegates from Arab NGOs—in a conference on human rights challenges to the League urged League member states to sign a letter issued in January by more than 50 UN member states, led by Switzerland, that urged the UN Security Council to refer the situation in Syria to the International Criminal Court (ICC). In early March the League Secretary-General, stated that, as the likelihood of achieving a political solution to Syria's internal conflict had receded, the onwards objective of the League/UN Joint Special Representative should be to support the formation of a Syrian transitional government. At that time League foreign ministers, meeting in Cairo, adopted a resolution urging the National Coalition to nominate an executive body to represent Syria at the impending 24th summit meeting of League heads of state, and thereafter to retain Syria's seat, pending the staging of elections leading to the establishment in that country of a government with a democratic mandate. Lebanon reportedly refused to support the resolution, while reservations were also expressed by Algeria and Iraq. Syria's seat at the 24th League summit of heads of state, convened in March, in Doha, was, consequently, taken by a delegation from the National Coalition, headed by al-Khatib (who shortly before the summit had resigned as the Coalition's leader).

In March 2013 the UN Secretary-General announced that a mission comprising UN weapons experts, in co-operation with specialists from the World Health Organization and the Organisation for the Prohibition of Chemical Weapons (OPCW), would initiate an investigation into the alleged use of chemical weapons in the Syrian conflict; at the end of that month a Swedish scientist, Åke Sellström, was appointed by the UN Secretary-General to head the mission. Addressing the UN Security Council in mid-April the UN-Arab League Joint Special Representative emphasized his continuing pursuit of a political solution to the conflict. On 18 August the Sellström-led mission arrived in Syria to investigate three previously reported chemical attacks. The alleged use on 21 August of chemical weapons against unarmed civilians in the rebel-held area of Ghouta, Damascus, prompted widespread international condemnation. In the immediate aftermath of the incident several thousand patients were treated for apparently neurotoxic symptoms, and up to around 1,400 fatalities were reported. The UN Secretary-General initiated an impartial and thorough investigation into the situation, and from 26–30 August the UN mission visited the site of the attack, to examine the scene and to take relevant soil and biological samples. A meeting of League foreign ministers convened in early September, in Cairo, urged the UN Security Council and the international community to take 'deterrent' measures against the Syrian regime, which it accused of responsibility for the alleged Damascus chemical attack. A meeting held shortly afterwards, in Paris, France, between the US Secretary of State and the leaders of Bahrain, Egypt, Jordan, Kuwait, Morocco, the PA, Qatar and Saudi Arabia, also accused the al-Assad regime of using chemical weapons, and stated that the regime had thereby transgressed an international 'red line'; however, the League member states participating in the meeting did not commit to endorsing a US proposal that punitive military action should be launched against the Syrian regime. It was reported at that time that the participating League states had declared their readiness to sign a statement recently released by 11 G20 member states urging a strong international response in view of the atrocity of 21 August. In early September 2013 the Russian Minister of Foreign Affairs, US Secretary of State and Joint Arab League-UN Special Representative on Syria gave consideration to a proposal by Russia that Syria should surrender its chemical stockpiles to international control. Soon afterwards the Syrian regime notified the UN Secretary-General that it was taking measures to accede to the 1992 Convention on the Prohibition of the Development, Production, Stockpiling and Use of Chemical Weapons and on their Destruction, and would observe the obligations imposed by the Convention prior to its national entry into force. In late September 2013 the UN Security Council adopted a resolution which aimed to initiate a Syrian-led peace process to end the conflict; and, with a view to eliminating Syria's chemical weapons, authorized the immediate implementation of a weapons monitoring and destruction plan, formulated by the OPCW, and the imposition of punitive measures if any party attempts to use, develop, produce, acquire, stockpile, retain, or transfer chemical weapons. In mid-October the UN Security Council authorized the deployment of a joint UN-OPCW mission tasked with supervising the destruction by the Syrian authorities, by end-June 2014, of Syria's chemical weapons stockpiles and production facilities. At that time the Secretaries-General of the League and the OIC urged all parties to the conflict to observe a full ceasefire over the festival of Eid al-Adha. The second gathering of the Action Group for Syria, 'Geneva II', was convened in late January–February 2014, in Montreux, Switzerland, and, later, in Geneva. In early February both sides agreed to a temporary ceasefire in Homs to enable the evacuation of trapped civilians and the distribution of humanitarian assistance; the negotiations failed, however, to achieve further progress. In late March League heads of state urged the pursuit of the peaceful transition of power that had been proposed as a solution to the conflict by the July 2012 Geneva 1 conference, and demanded that the Syrian government cease acts of violence. By April 2014 the number of civilians killed in the conflict since March 2011 was estimated to have exceeded 145,000, and more than 9m. Syrians had become displaced from their homes.

Joint Special Representative of the League of Arab States and the UN on Syria: LAKHDAR BRAHIMI (Algeria).

LATIN AMERICA

The first summit of heads of state and government of the South American-Arab Countries (ASPA) was convened in May 2005, in Brasília, Brazil, and a second ASPA summit was organized in March 2009, in Doha. The third ASPA summit was convened in Lima, Peru, in October 2012, and ASPA IV was to take place in Riyadh during 2015. ASPA also meets at the level of ministers responsible for foreign affairs (every two years, on the sidelines of the UN General Assembly), senior officials (every six months), and in the format of a number of sectoral committees, covering co-operation in the following areas: cultural, economic, environmental, scientific and technological, and social. An Arab-South American Library is being developed in Algiers, Algeria, under the ASPA co-operation initiative. In January 2013 the first ASPA ministerial meeting on energy, held in Abu Dhabi, United Arab Emirates, adopted the Abu Dhabi Declaration on enhanced co-operation.

SUB-SAHARAN AFRICA

In June 2002 the League appointed a special representative to Somalia to assist with the ongoing reconciliation efforts in that country.

In September 2002 the Council established a committee to encourage peace efforts in Sudan. In May 2004 representatives of the League participated in an AU fact-finding mission to assess the ongoing humanitarian crisis in Darfur, Sudan. In August an emergency meeting of League ministers responsible for foreign affairs, convened to address the situation in Darfur, declared support for the Sudanese Government's measures to disarm Arab militias and punish human rights violations there. In November the League was asked to join a panel appointed to monitor the ceasefire agreement that had been adopted in April by the parties to the Darfur conflict. In March 2006 the meeting of heads of state agreed to offer financial support to the AU Mission in Sudan, then deployed to the Darfur region of that country. The summit meeting in March 2007 expressed continued support for all peace accords signed between conflicting parties in Sudan. In March 2009 the summit of heads of state expressed full support and solidarity with Sudan in rejecting the legitimacy of the arrest warrant that had been issued earlier in that month by the ICC against President Omar Al-Bashir of Sudan.

In October 2010 the League and the AU jointly organized an Africa-Arab summit, held in Sirte, the second such meeting since one convened in 1977. Leaders attending the summit endorsed a new Strategic Plan for co-operation, covering the period 2011–15 and agreed to establish a joint Africa-Arab Fund for Disaster Response. The third Africa-Arab summit was held in Kuwait, in November 2013, on the theme 'Partners in Development and Investment', and the fourth was to be hosted by Equatorial Guinea, during 2016.

Finance

The League budgets around US $60m. annually to fund the Secretariat, including a small allocation to the Arab Fund for Technical Assistance in African States. Member states' contributions are determined by a scale of assessments, under which Kuwait and Saudi Arabia each contribute 14% to the total budget (the largest national contributions).

Publications

Arab Perspectives—Sh'oun Arabiyya (monthly).

Journal of Arab Affairs (monthly).

Bulletins of treaties and agreements concluded among the member states, essays, regular publications circulated by regional offices.

NORTH AMERICAN FREE TRADE AGREEMENT—NAFTA

Address: *(Canadian section)* 111 Sussex Drive, 5th Floor, Ottawa, ON K1N 1J1.

Telephone: (613) 992-9388; **fax:** (613) 992-9392; **e-mail:** canada@nafta-sec-alena.org; **internet:** www.nafta-sec-alena.org/canada.

Address: *(Mexican section)* Blvd Adolfo López Mateos 3025, 2°, Col Héroes de Padierna, 10700 México, DF.

Telephone: (55) 5629-9630; **fax:** (55) 5629-9637; **e-mail:** mexico@nafta-sec-alena.org.

Address: *(US section)* 14th St and Constitution Ave, NW, Room 2061, Washington, DC 20230.

Telephone: (202) 482-5438; **fax:** (202) 482-0148; **e-mail:** usa@nafta-sec-alena.org; **internet:** www.nafta-sec-alena.org.

NAFTA developed from the free trade agreement between the USA and Canada that was signed in January 1988 and came into effect on 1 January 1989. Negotiations on the terms of NAFTA, which incorporated Mexico into the free trade area, were concluded in October 1992 and the Agreement was signed in December. It was ratified in November 1993 and entered into force on 1 January 1994. The NAFTA Secretariat is composed of national sections in each member country.

MEMBERS

Canada Mexico USA

MAIN PROVISIONS OF THE AGREEMENT

Under NAFTA almost all restrictions on trade and investment between Canada, Mexico and the USA were removed during the period 1 January 1994–1 January 2008. Tariffs on trade between the USA and Mexico in 94% of agricultural products were eliminated immediately, with trade restrictions on further agricultural products eliminated more gradually.

NAFTA also provided for the phasing out by 2004 of tariffs on automobiles and textiles between all three countries, and for Mexico to open its financial sector to US and Canadian investment, with all restrictions removed by 2008. Mexico was to liberalize government procurement, removing preferential treatment for domestic companies over a 10-year period. Barriers to investment were removed in most sectors, with exemptions for petroleum in Mexico, culture in Canada and airlines and radio communications in the USA. In April 1998 the fifth meeting of the three-member ministerial Free Trade Commission, held in Paris, France, agreed to remove, from 1 August, tariffs on some 600 goods, including certain chemicals, pharmaceuticals, steel and wire products, textiles, toys, and watches. As a result of that agreement, a number of tariffs were eliminated as much as 10 years earlier than had been originally planned.

In transport, it was initially planned that heavy goods vehicles would have complete freedom of movement between the three countries by 2000. However, owing to concerns on the part of the US Government relating to the implementation of adequate safety standards by Mexican truck drivers, the deadline for the free circulation of heavy goods vehicles was not met. In February 2001 a five-member NAFTA panel of experts appointed to adjudicate on the dispute ruled that the USA was violating the Agreement. In December the US Senate approved legislation entitling Mexican long-haul trucks to operate anywhere in the USA following compliance with rigorous safety checks to be enforced by US inspectors.

In the case of a sudden influx of goods from one country to another that adversely affects a domestic industry, the Agreement makes provision for the imposition of short-term 'snap-back' tariffs.

Disputes are to be settled in the first instance by intergovernmental consultation. If a dispute is not resolved within 30 to 40 days, a government may call a meeting of the Free Trade Commission. The Commission's Advisory Committee on Private Commercial Disputes and its Advisory Committee on Private Commercial Disputes Regarding Agricultural Goods recommend procedures for the resolution of such complex disputes. If the Commission is unable to settle an issue a panel of experts in the relevant field is appointed to adjudicate.

ADDITIONAL AGREEMENTS

During 1993, as a result of domestic pressure, the new US Government negotiated two 'side agreements' with its NAFTA partners, which were to provide safeguards for workers' rights and the environment. A Commission for Labor Cooperation was established under the North American Agreement on Labor Cooperation (NAALC) to monitor implementation of labour accords and to foster co-operation in that area. Panels of experts, with representatives from each country, were established to adjudicate in cases of alleged infringement of workers' rights or environmental damage. The panels were given the power to impose fines and trade sanctions, but only with regard to the USA and Mexico; Canada, which was opposed to such measures, was to enforce compliance with NAFTA by means of its own legal system. The Commission for Environmental Cooperation (CEC), initiated in 1994 under the provisions of the 1993 North American Agreement on Environmental Cooperation (which complements the relevant environmental provisions of NAFTA), addresses regional environmental concerns, assists in the prevention of potential trade and environmental conflicts, advises on the environmental impact of trade issues, encourages private sector investment in environmental trade issues, and promotes the effective enforcement of environmental law. During 1994–early 2014 the CEC adopted numerous resolutions, including on the sound management of chemicals, the environmentally sound management and tracking of hazardous wastes and hazardous recyclable materials, the conservation of butterflies and birds, the availability of pollutant release and transfer data, and on co-operation in the conservation of biodiversity. The CEC-financed North American Fund for Environmental Cooperation (NAFEC), established in 1995, supports community environmental projects.

With regard to the NAALC, National Administration Offices have been established in each of the NAFTA countries in order to monitor labour issues and to address complaints about non-compliance with domestic labour legislation. However, punitive measures in the form of trade sanctions or fines (up to US $20m.) may only be imposed in the specific instances of contravention of national legislation regarding child labour, a minimum wage or health and safety standards.

Border Environmental Cooperation Commission (BECC): POB 221648, El Paso, TX 79913, USA; tel. (877) 277-1703; e-mail becc@cocef.org; internet www.cocef.org; f. 1993; supports the co-ordination of projects for the improvement of infrastructure and monitors the environmental impact of NAFTA on the US–Mexican border area; by 31 Dec. 2013 the BECC had certified at total of 227 projects (120 in Mexico and 107 in the USA), at a cost of US $6,985m., and at that time it was actively implementing 76 certified projects; Gen. Man. MARIA ELENA GINER (USA).

Commission for Environmental Cooperation (CEC): 393 rue St Jacques Ouest, Bureau 200, Montréal, QC H2Y IN9, Canada; tel. (514) 350-4300; fax (514) 350-4314; e-mail info@cec.org; internet www.cec.org; f. 1994; Exec. Dir Dr IRASEMA CORONADO (USA); publs *Annual Report*, *North American Environmental Atlas*, *Taking Stock* (annually), industry reports, policy studies.

North American Development Bank (NADB/NADBank): 203 South St Mary's, Suite 300, San Antonio, TX 78205, USA; tel. (210) 231-8000; fax (210) 231-6232; internet www.nadbank.org; f. 1993; mandated to finance environmental and infrastructure projects along the US–Mexican border; at April 2014 the NADB had authorized capital of US $3,000m., subscribed equally by Mexico and the USA, of which $450m. was paid-up; Man. Dir GERÓNIMO GUTIÉRREZ FERNÁNDEZ (Mexico); publs *Annual Report*, *NADBank News*.

NORTH ATLANTIC TREATY ORGANIZATION—NATO

Address: blvd Léopold III, 1110 Brussels, Belgium.

Telephone: (2) 707-41-11; **fax:** (2) 707-45-79; **e-mail:** natodoc@hq.nato.int; **internet:** www.nato.int.

The Atlantic Alliance was established on the basis of the 1949 North Atlantic Treaty as a defensive political and military alliance of a group of European states (then numbering 10) and the USA and Canada. The Alliance aims to provide common security for its members through co-operation and consultation in political, military and economic fields, as well as scientific, environmental, and other non-military aspects. The objectives of the Alliance are implemented by NATO. Since the collapse of the communist governments in Central and Eastern Europe and the dissolution, in 1991, of the Warsaw Treaty of Friendship, Co-operation and Mutual Assistance (the Warsaw Pact), which had hitherto been regarded as the Alliance's principal adversary, NATO has undertaken a fundamental transformation of its structures and policies to meet the new security challenges in Europe and its extended borders.

MEMBERS*

Albania	Greece	Poland
Belgium	Hungary	Portugal
Bulgaria	Iceland	Romania
Canada	Italy	Slovakia
Croatia	Latvia	Slovenia
Czech Republic	Lithuania	Spain
Denmark	Luxembourg	Turkey
Estonia	Netherlands	United Kingdom
France	Norway	USA
Germany		

* Greece and Turkey acceded to the North Atlantic Treaty in 1952, and the Federal Republic of Germany in 1955. France withdrew from the integrated military structure of NATO in 1966, although remained a member of the Atlantic Alliance; in 1996 France resumed participation in some, but not all, of the military organs of NATO. Spain acceded to the Treaty in 1982, but remained outside the Alliance's integrated military structure until 1999. The Czech Republic, Hungary and Poland were formally admitted as members of NATO in March 1999. Bulgaria, Estonia, Latvia, Lithuania, Romania, Slovakia and Slovenia acceded to the Treaty in March 2004. Albania and Croatia were admitted as members in April 2009.

Organization

(April 2014)

NORTH ATLANTIC COUNCIL

The Council, the highest authority of the Alliance, is composed of representatives of the 28 member states. It meets at the level of Permanent Representatives, ministers responsible for foreign affairs, or heads of state and government, and, at all levels, has effective political and decision-making authority. Ministerial meetings are held at least twice a year. Occasional meetings of ministers responsible for defence are also held. At the level of Permanent Representatives the Council meets at least once a week. A meeting of heads of state and government is convened periodically (May 2012: Chicago, USA; September 2014: Newport, Wales, United Kingdom).

The Secretary-General of NATO is Chairman of the Council, and each year a minister of foreign affairs of a member state is nominated honorary President, following the English alphabetical order of countries.

Decisions are taken by common consent and not by majority vote. The Council is a forum for wide consultation between member governments on major issues, including political, military, economic and other subjects, and is supported by the Senior or regular Political Committee, the Military Committee and other subordinate bodies.

PERMANENT REPRESENTATIVES

Albania: LEONARD DEMI.

Belgium: RUDOLF HUYGELEN.

Bulgaria: IVAN NAYDENOV.

Canada: YVES BRODEUR.

Croatia: BORIS GRIGIĆ.

Czech Republic: JIŘÍ ŠEDIVÝ.

Denmark: CARSTEN SØNDERGAARD.

Estonia: LAURI LEPIK.

France: JEAN-BAPTISTE MATTÉI.

Germany: MARTIN ERDMANN.

Greece: MICHAEL-CHRISTOS DIAMESSIS.

Hungary: PÉTER SZTÁRAY.

Iceland: ANNA JÓHANNSDÓTTIR.

Italy: GABRIELE CHECCHIA.

Latvia: MĀRIS RIEKSTIŅŠ.

Lithuania: KĘSTUTIS JANKAUSKAS.

Luxembourg: JEAN-JACQUES WELFRING.

Netherlands: MARJANNE DE KWAASTENIET.

Norway: VEGARD ELLEFSEN.

Poland: JACEK NAJDER.

Portugal: JOÃO MIRA GOMES.

Romania: STELIAN STOIAN.

Slovakia: TOMÁŠ VALÁŠEK.

Slovenia: ANDREJ BENEDEJČIČ.

Spain: MIGUEL AGUIRRE DE CARCER.

Turkey: MEHMET FATIH CEYLAN.

United Kingdom: MARIOT LESLIE (outgoing), ADAM THOMSON (designate).

USA: DOUGLAS E. LUTE.

Note: NATO partner countries are represented by heads of diplomatic missions or liaison officers located at NATO headquarters in Brussels, Belgium.

DEFENCE PLANNING COMMITTEE

Most defence matters are dealt with in the Defence Planning Committee, composed of representatives of all member countries except France. The Committee provides guidance to NATO's military authorities and, within the field of its responsibilities, has the same functions and authority as the Council. It meets regularly at ambassadorial level and assembles twice a year in ministerial sessions, when member countries are represented by their ministers responsible for defence.

NUCLEAR PLANNING GROUP

Ministers responsible for defence of countries participating in the Defence Planning Committee meet regularly in the Nuclear Planning Group (NPG) to discuss specific policy issues relating to nuclear forces, such as safety, deployment issues, nuclear arms control and proliferation. The NPG is supported by a Staff Group, composed of representatives of all members participating in the NPG, which meets at least once a week. The NPG High Level Group, chaired by the USA and comprising national policy-makers and experts, exists as a senior advisory body to the NPG in respect of nuclear policy and planning issues.

OTHER COMMITTEES

There are also committees for political affairs, economics, military medical services, armaments, defence review, science, infrastructure, logistics, communications, civil emergency planning, information and cultural relations, and civil and military budgets. In addition, other committees consider specialized subjects such as NATO pipelines, air traffic management, etc.

INTERNATIONAL SECRETARIAT

The Secretary-General is Chairman of the North Atlantic Council, the Defence Planning Committee and the Nuclear Planning Group, and is the head of the International Secretariat, with staff drawn from the member countries. The Secretary-General proposes items for NATO consultation and is generally responsible for promoting consultation and co-operation in accordance with the provisions of the North Atlantic Treaty.

Secretary-General: ANDERS FOGH RASMUSSEN (Denmark) (until 30 September 2014), JENS STOLTENBERG (Norway) (from 1 October 2014).

Deputy Secretary-General: ALEXANDER VERSHBOW (USA).

Senior Civilian Representative in Afghanistan: MAURITS JOCHEMS (Netherlands).

Special Representative of the Secretary-General for the Caucasus and Central Asia: JAMES APPATHURAI (Canada).

Special Representative for Women: MARI SKÅRE (Norway).

PRINCIPAL DIVISIONS

Division of Defence Investment: responsible for enhancing NATO's defence capacity (including armaments planning, air defence and security investment) by developing and investing in the Alliance's assets and capabilities; Asst Sec.-Gen. Lt-Gen. PATRICK AUROY (France).

Division of Defence Policy and Planning: responsible for defence planning, nuclear policy and defence against weapons of mass destruction; Asst Sec.-Gen. HEINRICH BRAUSS (Germany).

Division of Emerging Security Challenges: co-ordinates the Alliance approach to security issues, including terrorism, the proliferation of weapons of mass destruction, cyber threats, and energy security challenges; Asst Sec.-Gen. SORIN DUCARU (Romania).

Division of Political Affairs and Security Policy: is concerned with regional, economic and security affairs and relations with other international organizations and partner countries; Asst Sec.-Gen. THRASYVOULOS TERRY STAMATOPOULOS (Greece).

Division of Public Diplomacy: responsible for dissemination of information on NATO's activities and policies through the media, the official website and print publications as well as seminars and conferences; manages the Science for Peace and Security programme and the information offices in Russia and Ukraine; Asst Sec.-Gen. KOLINDA GRABAR KITAROVIĆ (Croatia).

Executive Management Division: ensures the efficient running of the International Secretariat and provides support to elements such as conference services, information management and human and financial resources; Asst Sec.-Gen. WAYNE J. BUSH (USA).

Operations Division: responsible for the Alliance's crisis management and crisis management exercising, peacekeeping, deterrence and defence activities, and civil emergency planning and exercises; NATO conducts the following three types of exercise: political/military 'grand strategic exercises' (including crisis management exercises—CMX); military (live exercises with troops/equipment—LIVEX, command post exercises—CPX, and computer-assisted exercises—CAX); and civil emergency planning—CEP and disaster response exercises; incorporates the Euro-Atlantic Disaster Response Coordination Centre (EADRCC) and the NATO Situation Centre; Asst Sec.-Gen. STEPHEN EVANS (United Kingdom).

Military Organization

MILITARY COMMITTEE

Composed of the allied Chiefs-of-Staff, or their representatives, of all member countries, the Military Committee is the highest military body in NATO under the authority of the Council. It meets at least twice a year at Chiefs-of-Staff level and remains in permanent session with Permanent Military Representatives. It is responsible for making recommendations to the Council and Defence Planning Committee and Nuclear Planning Group on military matters and for supplying guidance on military questions to Supreme Allied Commanders and subordinate military authorities. The Committee is supported by an International Military Staff.

Chairman: Gen. KNUD BARTELS (Denmark).

COMMANDS

In June 2011 NATO ministers responsible for defence approved a reform of the existing command structure, in order to enhance its effectiveness and affordability, with the number of command headquarters and personnel to be significantly reduced. In addition to the two strategic commands, of Operations and Transformation, there were to be two main Joint Force Headquarters, each able to deploy a major joint operation into theatre, comprising a Combined Air Operations Centre and static air, land and maritime commands. The Command Structure was to be supported by a Communication and Information Systems Group. Implementation of the reforms was to be completed by 2015.

Allied Command Operations: Casteau, Belgium—Supreme Headquarters Allied Powers Europe—SHAPE; hosts the NATO Special Operations Headquarters, which is assigned to SHAPE under operational command of, and reports directly to, the SACEUR; Supreme Allied Commander Europe—SACEUR Gen. PHILIP M. BREEDLOVE (USA).

Allied Command Transformation: Norfolk, VA, USA; Supreme Allied Commander Transformation—SACT Gen. JEAN-PAUL PALOMÉROS (France).

Activities

The common security policy of the members of the North Atlantic Alliance is to safeguard peace through the maintenance of political solidarity and adequate defence at the lowest level of military forces needed to deter all possible forms of aggression. Each year, member countries take part in a Defence Review, designed to assess their contribution to the common defence in relation to their respective capabilities and constraints. Allied defence policy is reviewed periodically by ministers responsible for defence.

Political consultations within the Alliance take place on a permanent basis, under the auspices of the North Atlantic Council (NAC), on all matters affecting the common security interests of the member countries, as well as events outside the North Atlantic Treaty area.

Co-operation in environmental, scientific and technological fields takes place in the NATO Science Committee and in its Committee on the Challenges of Modern Society. Both these bodies operate an expanding international programme of science fellowships, advance study institutes and research grants. NATO has also pursued co-operation in relation to civil emergency planning. These activities represent NATO's 'Third Dimension'.

Since the 1980s the Alliance has been actively involved in co-ordinating policies with regard to arms control and disarmament issues designed to bring about negotiated reductions in conventional forces, intermediate and short-range nuclear forces and strategic nuclear forces. A Verification Co-ordinating Committee was established in 1990. In April 1999 the summit meeting determined to improve co-ordination on issues relating to weapons of mass destruction through the establishment of a separate centre at NATO headquarters. At a summit meeting of the Conference on Security and Co-operation in Europe (CSCE), later renamed the Organization for Security and Co-operation in Europe (OSCE), in November 1990 the member countries of NATO and the Warsaw Pact signed an agreement limiting Conventional Armed Forces in Europe (CFE), whereby conventional arms would be reduced to within a common upper limit in each zone. The two groups also issued a Joint Declaration, stating that they were no longer adversaries and that none of their weapons would ever be used 'except in self-defence'. In March 1992, under the auspices of the CSCE, the ministers responsible for foreign affairs of the NATO and of the former Warsaw Pact countries (with Russia, Belarus, Ukraine and Georgia taking the place of the USSR) signed the 'Open Skies' treaty. Under this treaty, aerial reconnaissance missions by one country over another were to be permitted, subject to regulation. The eight former Soviet republics with territory in the area of application of the CFE Treaty committed themselves to honouring its obligations in June. In July 1997 the CFE signatories concluded an agreement on Certain Basic Elements for Treaty Adaptation, which provided for substantial reductions in the maximum levels of conventional military equipment at national and territorial level, replacing the previous bloc-to-bloc structure of the Treaty. The Adapted CFE Treaty was concluded and signed in November 1999, at an OSCE meeting held in İstanbul, Turkey. At the same time, a series of agreements or Commitments, was approved which required Russia to withdraw forces from and reduce levels of military equipment in Georgia and Moldova, a process to be monitored by NATO. In April 2007 NATO ministers responsible for foreign affairs held immediate discussions following an announcement by Russia's President that it intended to suspend unilaterally its implementation of CFE obligations. An extraordinary conference of parties to the CFE was convened in June to consider Russia's security concerns; in the following month, however, the Russian Government confirmed that it was to suspend obligations under the Treaty, with effect from mid-December. The Lisbon Summit Declaration, issued by NATO heads of state and government in November 2010, reaffirmed political commitment to the CFE process, but insisted that the existing impasse could not continue indefinitely. In November 2011 NATO CFE allies determined to cease implementing certain CFE obligations with regard to Russia, in view of Russia's continuing unilateral suspension of its obligations under the Treaty.

In June 2001 the first formal meeting of the Military Committees of the European Union (EU) and NATO took place to exchange information relating to the development of EU-NATO security co-operation. In November 2003 NATO and the EU conducted a joint crisis management exercise for the first time. In order to support an integrated security structure in Europe, NATO also co-operates with the OSCE and has provided assistance for the development of the latter's conflict prevention and crisis management activities. In September 2008 a Joint Declaration on UN/NATO Secretariat Co-operation was signed by the Secretaries-General of the two organizations to strengthen practical co-operation, in particular in crisis management. In November 2010 NATO heads of state and government endorsed an Action Plan to incorporate into all aspects of Alliance planning, training and operations the provisions of the UN Security Council Resolution 1325 on Women, Peace and Security.

On 12 September 2001 the NAC agreed to invoke, for the first time, Article 5 of the North Atlantic Treaty, providing for collective self-defence, in response to terrorist attacks against targets in the USA that had taken place on the previous day. The measure was formally implemented in early October after the US authorities presented evidence substantiating claims that the attacks had been directed from abroad. The NAC endorsed eight specific US requests for logistical and military support in its efforts to counter terrorism, including enhanced sharing of intelligence and full access to airfields and ports in member states. It also agreed to dispatch five surveillance aircraft to help to patrol US airspace and directed the standing naval force to the Eastern Mediterranean. In December NATO ministers responsible for defence initiated a review of military capabilities and defences with a view to strengthening its ability to counter international terrorism.

In November 2002 NATO heads of state and government, convened in Prague, Czech Republic, approved a comprehensive reform of the Alliance's capabilities in order to reflect a new operational outlook and enable the transition to smaller, more flexible forces. The command structure was to be reduced and redefined, under operational and functional strategic commands, while a NATO Response Force (NRF), comprising a flexible and interoperable force of readily deployable land, sea and air elements, was to be established. The meeting agreed on further measures to strengthen NATO's capabilities to defend against terrorism and approved a broader commitment to improve and develop modern warfare capabilities. The Prague Summit initiatives were endorsed by a meeting of NATO defence ministers in June 2003. In March 2005 the NAC approved a charter formally to establish an organization to manage an Active Layered Theatre Ballistic Missile Defence programme, which aimed to establish a new collective defence capability. The NRF was inaugurated in October 2003, with a force strength of 9,500 troops. It was intended to enable NATO to react swiftly and efficiently in new areas of operation, such as evacuations, disaster management and counter-terrorism. By October 2004 the NRF had reached its initial operating capacity, comprising some 17,000 troops. It reached its full capacity, of 25,000 troops, in November 2006.

In April 2003 an agreement was signed by six member states—the Czech Republic, Denmark, Germany, the Netherlands, Norway and Poland—formally establishing the Civil-Military Co-operation Group North. The group is based at Budel, Netherlands, and aims to provide NATO commanders with a co-ordinated approach to civil-military co-operation during crises and in post-conflict areas.

In November 2006 NATO heads of state and government, meeting in Riga, Latvia, endorsed and made public a Comprehensive Political Guidance document which aimed to provide a framework and direction for the Alliance in the next 10–15 years. In particular, it identified the likely capability requirements of future operations, the need to respond to new threats and challenges, such as terrorism and the spread of weapons of mass destruction, and the development of relations with non-NATO countries. In June 2007 NATO ministers responsible for defence, meeting to review the transformation of the Alliance's operational capabilities, agreed to assess the political and military implications of a possible redeployment of US missile defences in Europe. In April 2008 a NATO summit meeting, convened in Bucharest, Romania, reviewed progress in transforming the Alliance. It endorsed an Action Plan of proposals to develop and implement a NATO strategy for a comprehensive approach to existing and future security challenges. The meeting recognized the importance of working in partnership with the UN and EU and of strengthening co-operation with other countries and regional alliances. The meeting highlighted issues of arms control, nuclear non-proliferation and disarmament as being of particular concern. NATO's 60th anniversary summit meeting, convened in early April 2009, in Strasbourg, France and Kehl, Germany, adopted a Declaration on Alliance Security, reaffirming the basic values, principles and purposes of the Alliance, and determined to develop a new Strategic Concept that was to define NATO's longer-term role in the 21st century. The process of defining a new Strategic Concept was launched in July at a security conference attended by representatives of allied and partner governments, international organizations, the private sector, and civil society, including non-governmental organizations, academia and the media. In May 2010 a Group of Experts, appointed by the Secretary-General, presented a report to the NAC incorporating an analysis and recommendations for the new Strategic Concept. Further detailed deliberations were pursued over the next few months. The Strategic Concept, entitled *Active Engagement, Modern Defence*, was adopted by NATO heads of state and government, meeting in Lisbon, Portugal, in November. The document identified the challenges posed by the contemporary security environment and sought to enhance NATO's defence and deterrence capacities accordingly, while reaffirming its core tasks of collective defence, crisis management and co-operative security. NATO leaders approved the development of a new European missile defence capability, as well as measures to enhance cyber defence capabilities. They also endorsed an extensive reform of NATO's civil and military command structures, in order to enhance the organization's efficiency and flexibility.

A summit meeting of NATO heads of state and government, convened in May 2012, in Chicago, Illinois, USA, announced readiness to work towards establishing, at the request of the Afghanistan Government, a mission to provide training and assistance to the Afghan Security Forces, including the Afghan Special Operations Forces, following on from the planned departure of the International Security Assistance Force (ISAF, q.v.) at the end of 2014. The summit tasked the Council to commence, immediately, work on the military planning process for the proposed new mission. (A detailed concept to guide the new mission—to be based in five locations in Afghanistan—was endorsed by NATO ministers responsible for defence in June 2013.) The May 2012 summit also endorsed new NATO Policy Guidelines on Counter-Terrorism, mandated the Council to prepare an action plan aimed at improving NATO's terrorist threat awareness capabilities, and endorsed the Chicago Defence Declaration and Defence Package, outlining a vision of, and guidelines towards achieving, a new capabilities objective: 'NATO Forces 2020'—modern, closely connected forces equipped, trained, exercised and commanded in a manner that would enable them to operate jointly, and with partners, in any environment. A new Joint Intelligence, Surveillance and Reconnaissance (JISR) data-gathering initiative was endorsed by the summit. (A revised concept for the JISR was approved in 2013.) A new Connected Forces Initiative was also approved to help to maintain NATO's combat readiness and effectiveness through expanded education and training, increased exercises and improved use of technology. NATO Forces 2020 was to represent a shift in the Alliance's focus from operational engagement to operational preparedness. The summit declared an interim NATO Ballistic Missile Defence (BMD) capacity, and tasked the Council to review on a regular basis the implementation of BMD capabilities.

Meeting in February 2013 NATO ministers responsible for defence agreed that, within the context of the Connected Forces Initiative, launched by in May 2012 by the Alliance's Chicago summit, the role of the NRF should be enhanced following the termination in 2014 of ISAF in Afghanistan. Three partner countries—Finland, Sweden and Ukraine—participated in a series of air, land and maritime exercises, known as 'Steadfast Jazz', undertaken in November 2013 to test the capacity of the NRF. Meanwhile, Georgia was to make forces available to the NRF in 2015.

In late June 2012 a meeting of the Council was held, at the request of Turkey, in accordance with Article 4 of the North Atlantic Treaty—invoked when the territorial integrity, political independence or security of any of the parties is threatened—following the shooting down by Syrian forces of a Turkish military jet; allegedly the attack was not forewarned and the jet was unarmed and in international airspace. The Alliance determined closely to follow the situation in Syria, reiterating the indivisibility of the security of the Alliance. A further Council meeting was held within the Article 4 framework at the beginning of October to address persistent Syrian shelling of Turkish areas close to the two countries' common border, the most recent incident of which had caused five Turkish civilian fatalities and many injuries. The Alliance demanded the immediate cessation of acts of aggression against Turkey and urged Syria to end 'flagrant violations of international law'. In early December NATO ministers responsible for foreign affairs agreed to strengthen Turkey's air defence capabilities along its border with Syria, and, from February 2013 six *Patriot* missile batteries (comprising two Dutch batteries in Adana, two German batteries in Kahramanmaras, and two US batteries in Gaziantep) were deployed defensively under NATO command in southern Turkey. In early February the Secretary-General strongly condemned a bomb attack perpetrated against the US Embassy in Ankara, Turkey, which resulted in a number of fatalities and injuries, and shortly afterwards he condemned a terrorist attack committed at the Turkey–Syria border. A further terrorist attack perpetrated in mid-May that killed at least 46 people in Hatay, Turkey, was also strongly condemned by the Secretary-General. In November NATO ambassadors agreed to maintain the defensive deployment of *Patriot* missiles in southern Turkey throughout 2014. In April 2013, following consideration of the situation in Syria by NATO ministers responsible for foreign affairs, the Secretary-General stated the Alliance's extreme concern over the use of ballistic missiles in the ongoing conflict and at allegations that chemical weapons had been deployed, and noted the potential risk posed by these to the security of the Alliance. Meeting in late August the NAC strongly condemned the use on 21 August of chemical weapons against civilians in Ghouta, Damascus, Syria, and expressed full support for the then ongoing investigation into the atrocity by a mission comprising UN chemical weapons experts, while deploring the Syrian regime's delay in securing access for the UN mission to the site of the attacks. The Council determined to continue closely to review the situation in Syria and to continue to support Turkey in protecting the Alliance's south-eastern border.

In December 2012 the Secretary-General strongly condemned the launch—in direct violation of two resolutions of the UN Security Council—of a ballistic missile by the Democratic Republic of Korea (North Korea); the Secretary-General deemed this to be a provocative act that exacerbated regional tensions, and urged the North Korean authorities to meet their obligations under international law. In February 2013 the NAC condemned an underground nuclear weapons test conducted in that month by North Korea. In April NATO ministers responsible for foreign affairs strongly condemned North Korea's continued development of ballistic missile and nuclear weapons programmes, and urged that country to comply with its international obligations and engage in credible denuclearization discussions.

In early March 2014 a meeting of the NAC was convened, at Poland's request, within the framework of Article 4 of the North Atlantic Treaty, to address the implications for regional stability of ongoing violations by Russia of the territorial integrity and sovereignty of Ukraine. The Council determined to intensify its assessment of the implications of this crisis for Alliance security, and to support all constructive efforts for the conclusion of a peaceful resolution in accordance with the principles of international law. Later in that month the NATO Secretary-General described the Ukraine crisis as a geopolitical 'game-changer', that would require the Alliance to strengthen its economic and military ties, and would in the immediate future necessitate a strengthened commitment to collective defence, a demonstration of strong support towards Ukraine and the wider region, and a clear understanding that, under the changed circumstances, the Alliance would not be able to co-operate as previously with Russia. At the beginning of April NATO formally suspended practical civilian and military co-operation with Russia (see under Partnerships), and tasked Alliance military planners with developing, urgently, a series of additional measures to reinforce the collective defences of member states. In mid-April the NATO Secretary-General announced that the number of sorties by the Alliance's air policing aircraft over the Baltic region would increase with immediate effect, and that warships would be deployed to the Baltic Sea and to the East Mediterranean.

PARTNERSHIPS

In May 1997 a Euro-Atlantic Partnership Council (EAPC) was inaugurated as a successor to the North Atlantic Co-operation Council (NACC), that had been established in December 1991 to provide a forum for consultation on political and security matters with the countries of Central and Eastern Europe, including the former Soviet republics. An EAPC Council was to meet monthly at ambassadorial level and twice a year at ministerial level. The EAPC was to pursue the NACC Work Plan for Dialogue, Partnership and Co-operation and incorporate it into a new Work Plan, which was to include an expanded political dimension of consultation and co-operation among participating states. The Partnership for Peace (PfP) programme, which was established in January 1994 within the framework of the NACC, was to remain an integral element of the new co-operative mechanism. The PfP incorporated practical military and defence-related co-operation activities that had originally been part of the NACC Work Plan. Participation in the PfP requires an initial signature of a framework agreement, establishing the common principles and objectives of the partnership, the submission of a presentation document, indicating the political and military aspects of the partnership and the nature of future co-operation activities and the development of individual partnership programmes establishing country-specific objectives. In June 1994 Russia, which had previously opposed the strategy as being the basis for future enlargement of NATO, signed the PfP framework document, which included a declaration envisaging an 'enhanced dialogue' between the two sides. Despite its continuing opposition to any enlargement of NATO, in May 1995 Russia agreed to sign a PfP Individual Partnership Programme, as well as a framework document for NATO-Russian dialogue and co-operation beyond the PfP. During 1994 a Partnership Co-ordination Cell (PCC), incorporating representatives of all partnership countries, became operational in Mons, Belgium to co-ordinate joint military activities and planning in order to implement PfP programmes. The first joint military exercises with countries of the former Warsaw Pact were conducted in September. NATO began formulating a PfP Status of Forces Agreement (SOFA) to define the legal status of Allies' and partners' forces when they are present on each other's territory; the PfP SOFA was opened for signature in June 1995. The new EAPC was to provide a framework for the development of an enhanced PfP programme, which NATO envisaged would become an essential element of the overall European security structure. Accordingly, the military activities of the PfP were to be expanded to include all Alliance missions and incorporate all NATO committees into the PfP process, thus providing for greater co-operation in crisis management, civil emergency planning and training activities. In addition, all PfP member countries were to participate in the CJTF concept through a structure of Partners Staff Elements, working at all levels of the Alliance military structure. Ministers responsible for defence of NATO and the 27 partner countries were to meet regularly to provide the political guidance for the enhanced Planning and Review Process of the PfP. In December 1997 NATO ministers responsible for foreign affairs approved the establishment of a Euro-Atlantic Disaster Response Co-ordination Centre (EADRCC), and a non-permanent Euro-Atlantic Disaster Response Unit. The EADRCC was inaugurated in June 1998 and immediately commenced operations to provide relief to ethnic Albanian refugees fleeing the conflict in the Serbian province of Kosovo. In November the NAC approved the establishment of a network of PfP training centres, the first of which was inaugurated in Ankara. The centres were a key element of a Training and Education Programme, which was endorsed at the summit meeting in April 1999. A policy of establishing individual PfP Trust Funds was approved in September 2000. These aimed to provide support for military reform and demilitarization activities in partners countries, in particular the destruction of anti-personnel landmines. In November 2002 heads of state and government, meeting in Prague, Czech Republic, endorsed a new initiative to formulate Individual Partnership Action Plans (IPAPs) designed to strengthen bilateral relations with a partner country, improve the effectiveness of NATO assistance in that country, and provide for intensified political dialogue. The İstanbul summit meeting in June 2004 agreed to strengthen co-operation with partner countries in the Caucasus and Central Asia. A Special Representative of the Secretary-General to the two regions was appointed in September. In October the first IPAP was signed with Georgia, with the aim of defining national security and defence objectives, reforms and country-specific NATO assistance. IPAPs were concluded with Azerbaijan in May 2005, Armenia in December, Kazakhstan in January 2006 and with Moldova in May. Bosnia and Herzegovina and Montenegro joined the PfP process in December 2006. (Serbia also joined at that time.) In April 2008 both countries were invited to begin an Intensified Dialogue with NATO. Montenegro concluded an IPAP in June and held its first consultation under the Intensified Dialogue in that month. The IPAP with Bosnia and Herzegovina was concluded in September. In December 2009 NATO ministers responsible for foreign affairs agreed to invite Montenegro to join the Membership Action Plan (MAP), and determined that Bosnia and Herzegovina join the MAP once further institutional reforms had been implemented.

The enlargement of NATO, through the admission of new members from the former USSR and Central and Eastern European countries, was considered to be a progressive means of contributing to the enhanced stability and security of the Euro-Atlantic area. In December 1996 NATO ministers responsible for foreign affairs announced that invitations to join the Alliance would be issued to some former Eastern bloc countries during 1997. The NATO Secretary-General and member governments subsequently began intensive diplomatic efforts to secure Russia's tolerance of these developments. It was agreed that no nuclear weapons or large numbers of troops would be deployed on the territory of any new member country in the former Eastern bloc. In May 1997 NATO and Russia signed the Founding Act on Mutual Relations, Co-operation and Security, which provided for enhanced Russian participation in all NATO decision-making activities, equal status in peacekeeping operations and representation at the Alliance headquarters at ambassadorial level, as part of a recognized shared political commitment to maintaining stability and security throughout the Euro-Atlantic region. A NATO-Russian Permanent Joint Council (PJC) was established under the Founding Act, and met for the first time in July; the Council provided each side with the opportunity for consultation and participation in the other's security decisions, but without a right of veto. In March 1999 Russia condemned NATO's military action against the Federal Republic of Yugoslavia and announced the suspension of all relations within the framework of the Founding Act, as well as negotiations on the establishment of a NATO mission in Moscow. The PJC convened once more in May 2000, and subsequent meetings were held in June and December. In February 2001 the NATO Secretary-General agreed with the then acting Russian President a joint statement of commitment to pursuing dialogue and co-operation. A NATO information office was opened in Moscow in that month. In December an agreement was concluded by NATO ministers responsible for foreign affairs and their Russian counterpart to establish an eventual successor body to the PJC. The new NATO-Russia Council (NRC), in which NATO member states and Russia were to have equal status in decision-making, was inaugurated in May 2002. The Council aimed to strengthen co-operation in issues including counter-terrorism, crisis management, nuclear non-proliferation, and arms control. In April 2005, at an informal meeting of the ministers responsible for foreign affairs of the NRC, Russia signed the PfP Status of Forces Agreement that provides a legal framework for the movement to and from Allied countries, partner countries and Russia of military personnel and support staff. In June a meeting of the Council endorsed Political-Military Guidance towards Enhanced Interoperability between Russian and NATO forces, thereby facilitating the preparation of those forces for possible joint operations. In April 2006 an informal meeting of the Council's ministers responsible for foreign affairs reviewed NATO-Russia co-operation to date and adopted recommendations identifying interoperability, a pilot Afghanistan counter-narcotics project, a co-operative airspace initiative (CAI) and intensified political dialogue as the priority areas for future co-operation. In April 2008 the NRC, meeting at the level of heads of state, determined to extend on a permanent basis the joint project on counter-narcotics training of Afghan and Central Asian personnel and to accelerate the CAI project to ensure it reaches full operational capability by the end of 2009. In June 2008 NATO's Secretary-General urged Russia to withdraw some 400 troops from the Abkhazian region of Georgia and to respect that country's territorial integrity. In August meetings of the NRC were suspended owing to Russia's military action in Georgia, which the Alliance deemed to be 'disproportionate'. In December NATO foreign ministers agreed to initiate a gradual resumption of contacts with Russia. In April 2009 the meeting of NATO heads of state and government determined to resume normal relations with Russia. A meeting of the NRC at ministerial level was convened in June, in Corfu, Greece, at which all sides agreed to resume full political and military co-operation within the framework of the NRC. In December the NRC, meeting at ministerial level, initiated a Joint Review of 21st Century Common Security Challenges. In November 2010 the NRC, meeting at the level of heads of state, agreed on the need for a new strategic partnership, based on the presumption that each side no longer posed a threat to the other. The declaration issued by NATO heads of state and government, meeting at that time in Lisbon, incorporated an invitation to Russia to co-operate with the development of a new European missile defence capability. In April 2011 NRC ministers responsible for foreign affairs initiated a Helicopter Maintenance Trust Fund, under German leadership, aimed at developing the fleet maintenance capacity of the Afghan Air Force. In June the first joint exercise was conducted under the CAI. In July the NRC met in Sochi, Russia. The meeting reaffirmed the commitment of both sides to pursuing co-operation in missile defence, as well as other areas of mutual concern. A second phase of activities supported by the Helicopter Maintenance Trust Fund was initiated by the NRC in April 2013. In September an extraordinary session of the NRC, convened to address the chemical weapons attack perpetrated in August against civilians in Ghouta, Damascus, Syria, condemned the use of chemical weapons, stressing the need for full compliance with the expectations of the international community. The meeting welcomed the recent conclusion of an agreement between the Russian Minister of Foreign Affairs and the US Secretary of State on a framework for the elimination of Syria's chemical weapons stockpiles, and called on the UN Security Council to ensure effective implementation of the framework. In early 2014 projects being implemented within the NRC framework addressed the safe disposal of obsolete and dangerous ammunition in the Kaliningrad area; long-term projects on counter-narcotics training, the stand-off detection of explosives, and developing an improved telemedicine system capability swiftly to support casualties in disaster situations. In early March 2014, meeting to address military activities by Russia on Ukrainian territory and interference in Ukrainian domestic affairs, the NAC urged Russia to de-escalate tensions. In mid-March the NATO Secretary-General condemned as illegal under international law the adoption by President Putin of Russia of legislation aimed at enabling the incorporation of Crimea into the Russian Federation. (See Ukraine.) In late March NATO's Secretary-General stated that, given Russia's recent actions, NATO-Russia co-operation could not continue as previously, and, on 1 April, NATO foreign ministers formally suspended practical civilian and military co-operation with that country. Nevertheless, political dialogue, at ambassadorial level and above, was to continue within the NRC framework, and it was envisaged that co-operation projects related to Afghanistan would proceed unaltered. Russia was urged to reduce to pre-crisis levels its troop numbers in Crimea. The Alliance was to review its relations with Russia in June.

In May 1997 NATO ministers responsible for foreign affairs, meeting in Sintra, Portugal, concluded an agreement with Ukraine providing for enhanced co-operation between the two sides; the so-called Charter on a Distinctive Relationship was signed at the NATO summit meeting held in Madrid, Spain, in July. In May 1998 NATO agreed to appoint a permanent liaison officer in Ukraine to enhance co-operation between the two sides and assist Ukraine to formulate a programme of joint military exercises. The first NATO-Ukraine meeting at the level of heads of state took place in April 1999. A NATO-Ukraine Commission (NUC) met for the first time in March 2000. In February 2005, at a NATO-Ukraine summit meeting, NATO leaders expressed support for Ukraine's reform agenda and agreed to strengthen co-operation with the country. In view of its commitment to strengthened co-operation, NATO announced that it would launch a project, the largest of its kind ever undertaken, to assist Ukraine in the decommissioning of old ammunitions, small arms and light weapons stockpiles. In April NATO invited Ukraine to begin an 'Intensified Dialogue' on its aspirations to NATO membership and on the necessary relevant reforms that it would be required to undertake. In the same month NATO and Ukraine effected an exchange of letters preparing the way for Ukraine to support Operation Active Endeavour (see below). In June talks held between NATO ministers responsible for defence and their Ukrainian counterpart focused on NATO's assistance to Ukraine in the reform of its defence and security sectors. In October the NATO-Ukraine Commission held its first meeting within the framework of the Intensified Dialogue initiated in April. A meeting of the ministers responsible for defence of the NATO-Ukraine Commission held in June 2006 discussed Ukraine's defence policy and the ongoing transformation of the Ukrainian armed forces. In this context, ministers confirmed that the NATO-Ukraine Joint Working Group on Defence Reform should remain a key mechanism. In April 2008 NATO heads of state and government approved, in principle, Ukraine's future membership of the Alliance. The NAC, headed by the Secretary-General, visited Ukraine for a series of meetings in June. In August 2009 a Declaration to Complement the Charter on a Distinctive Partnership between NATO and Ukraine was signed, which emphasized the NUC's role in strengthening political dialogue and co-operation between the two sides and in securing reforms necessary for Ukraine to join the Alliance. In early March 2014, meeting at the request of the interim authorities in Ukraine, the NAC condemned Russia's escalation of military activities in Crimea (hitherto a Ukrainian autonomous territory), and stated grave concern over the recent authorization by the Russian legislature of the use the armed forces on the sovereign territory of Ukraine. The Council emphasized that Russian military action in Ukraine represented a breach of international law and contravened the principles of the PfP and of the NRC, and urged Russia to de-escalate tensions. The NAC determined to pursue continued close consultations with Ukraine within the NUC framework. The NAC declared the referendum on secession from Ukraine, held in Crimea on 17 March, to be an illegal violation of the Ukrainian Constitution and of international law. On the following day the NATO Secretary-General also condemned as illegal under international law the approval by the Russian President of new legislation aimed at enabling the incorporation of Crimea into Russia. NATO co-operation with Russia was formally suspended on 1 April. Meanwhile, NATO determined to intensify its support for strengthening Ukraine's long-term security—including assisting with the modernization of Ukraine's armed forces, and promoting increased participation by Ukraine in Alliance military exercises—and, in general, to deepen co-operation with its partners in Eastern Europe.

In August 2008 an extraordinary meeting of the NAC was convened to discuss an escalation of conflict in Georgia. The meeting expressed solidarity with Georgia's actions to counter attacks by separatist forces in Abkhazia and South Ossetia and deplored as disproportionate the use of force by Russia. Several days later the NAC held a special ministerial meeting to demand a peaceful, lasting solution to the conflict based on respect for Georgia's independence, sovereignty and territorial integrity. The meeting agreed that NATO would support Georgia in assessing damage to civil infrastructure, as well as in re-establishing an air traffic system and advising on cyber defence issues. Ministers also determined to establish a NATO-Georgia Commission, to strengthen co-operation and political dialogue between the two sides and to oversee Georgia's future application for NATO membership. A Framework Document to establish the Commission was signed by NATO's Secretary-General and Georgia's Prime Minister in the Georgian capital, Tbilisi, in September; the inaugural session of the Commission was convened immediately. The first meeting of the Commission at ministerial level was convened in December. In that month NATO ministers responsible for foreign affairs agreed to establish a NATO Liaison Office in Tbilisi. The Office was inaugurated in October 2010 during a visit by the Secretary-General to Georgia. In December 2008 NATO ministers also determined that Georgia should develop an Annual National Programme, replacing its existing IPAP, as a framework for co-operation with the Alliance and the implementation of reforms needed to fulfil membership criteria.

The Madrid summit meeting in July 1997 endorsed the establishment of a Mediterranean Co-operation Group to enhance NATO relations with Egypt, Israel, Jordan, Mauritania, Morocco and Tunisia. The Group was to provide a forum for regular political dialogue between the two groupings and to promote co-operation in training, scientific research and information exchange. In April 1999 NATO heads of state endorsed measures to strengthen the so-called Mediterranean Dialogue. Algeria joined the Mediterranean Dialogue in February 2000. The June 2004 summit meeting determined to enhance the Mediterranean Dialogue and launched a new Istanbul Co-operation Initiative (ICI) aimed at promoting broader co-operation with the Middle East. By April 2007 Bahrain, Kuwait, Qatar and the United Arab Emirates had joined the ICI. In February 2012 an ICI seminar was convened to consider means of deepening the partnership, and to discuss ongoing security challenges in the Middle East and North Africa. In February 2006 NATO and Mediterranean Dialogue partner countries convened their first meeting at the level of ministers responsible for defence. In April, under the chairmanship of NATO's Deputy Secretary-General, the NAC and representatives of the seven Mediterranean Dialogue countries met in Rabat, Morocco, in order to review their co-operation to date and to discuss its future prospects. All countries were encouraged to formulate Individual Co-operation Programmes (ICPs) as a framework for future co-operation. In November NATO heads of state and government, meeting in Riga, inaugurated a NATO Training Co-operation Initiative to extend defence and specialist training and expertise with Mediterranean Dialogue and ICI partner countries. The Initiative aimed to help those countries to strengthen their defence structures and enhance the interoperability of their armed forces with those of the Alliance. Egypt signed an ICP with NATO in October 2007, and Jordan concluded its ICP in April 2009. In April 2011, convened in Berlin, Germany, NATO ministers responsible for foreign affairs approved a More Efficient and Flexible Partnership Policy, providing for '28+' meetings between NATO and partner countries in more flexible formats, beyond and within existing partnership frameworks. Consequently a meeting on Indian Ocean counter-piracy activities was held in September, with participation by representatives of 47 interested states and organizations. In May 2012 Mongolia and NATO agreed an ICP. The NATO summit convened in that month recognized that new standards of consultation and practical co-operation with partner countries had been achieved during the implementation, in 2011, of Operation Unified Protector in Libya, and, agreed to pursue more regular consultations on security issues through the Mediterranean Dialogue and ICI frameworks, as well as through bilateral consultations and the new flexible formats. The summit agreed to consider providing support to partners, where requested, in areas including security institution building, defence modernization, and civil-military relations. An offer by Kuwait to host an ICI Regional Centre was welcomed.

In July 1997 heads of state and government formally invited the Czech Republic, Hungary and Poland to begin accession negotiations. Accession Protocols for the admission of those countries were signed in December and required ratification by all member states. The three countries formally became members of NATO in March 1999. In April the NATO summit meeting, held in Washington, DC, USA, initiated the MAP to extend practical support to aspirant member countries and to formalize a process of reviewing applications. In March 2003 protocols of accession, amending the North Atlantic Treaty, were adopted by the then 19 NATO member states with a view to admitting Bulgaria, Estonia, Latvia, Lithuania, Romania, Slovakia and Slovenia to the Alliance. In March 2004, the protocols of accession having been ratified by all of the member states, those seven countries were formally invited to join NATO and, on 29 March, they acceded to the Treaty. In April 2008 NATO heads of state and government, meeting in Bucharest, invited Albania and Croatia to commence accession negotiations and declared support for Georgia and Ukraine to apply for MAP status. It was also agreed that accession negotiations with the former Yugoslav republic of Macedonia, which joined the MAP programme in 1999, would be initiated as soon as a mutually acceptable solution to the issue over the country's name has been reached with Greece. The Accession Protocols for Albania and Croatia were signed by NATO ministers responsible for foreign affairs in July, and those countries formally acceded to the Treaty on 1 April 2009. Montenegro was invited to join the MAP in December; at that time NATO ministers confirmed that Bosnia and Herzegovina would participate in the MAP as soon as further institutional reforms had been implemented. In April 2010 NATO ministers responsible for foreign affairs invited Bosnia and Herzegovina to join MAP, conditional on the full registration of its defence properties.

In November 2010 the Lisbon summit meeting determined to reform NATO's structure of partnership mechanisms, in order to enhance the flexibility and efficiency of co-operation arrangements.

OPERATIONS

During the 1990s NATO increasingly developed its role as a mechanism for peacekeeping and crisis management. In June 1992 NATO ministers responsible for foreign affairs, meeting in Oslo, Norway, announced the Alliance's readiness to support peacekeeping operations under the aegis of the CSCE on a case-by-case basis: NATO would make both military resources and expertise available to such operations. In July NATO undertook a maritime operation in the Adriatic Sea to monitor compliance with the UN Security Council's resolutions imposing sanctions against the Yugoslav republics of Serbia and Montenegro. In December NATO ministers responsible for foreign affairs expressed the Alliance's readiness to support peacekeeping operations under the authority of the UN Security Council. From April 1993 NATO fighter and reconnaissance aircraft began patrolling airspace over Bosnia and Herzegovina in order to enforce the UN prohibition of military aerial activity over the country. In addition, from July NATO aircraft provided protective cover for troops from the UN Protection Force in Yugoslavia (UNPROFOR) operating in the 'safe areas' established by the UN Security Council. In February 1994 NATO conducted the first of several aerial strikes against artillery positions that were violating heavy weapons exclusion zones imposed around 'safe areas' and threatening the civilian populations. Throughout the conflict the Alliance also provided transport, communications and logistics to support UN humanitarian assistance in the region.

The peace accord for the former Yugoslavia, which was initialled in Dayton, Ohio, USA, in November 1995, and signed in Paris, France, in December, provided for the establishment of a NATO-led Implementation Force (IFOR) to ensure compliance with the treaty, in accordance with a strictly defined timetable and under the authority of a UN Security Council mandate. In December a joint meeting of allied foreign and defence ministers endorsed the military structure for the mission, entitled Operation Joint Endeavour, which was to involve approximately 60,000 troops from 31 NATO and non-NATO countries. IFOR, which constituted NATO's largest military operation, formally assumed responsibility for peacekeeping in Bosnia and Herzegovina from the UN on 20 December.

By mid-1996 the military aspects of the Dayton peace agreement had largely been implemented under IFOR supervision. Substantial progress was achieved in the demobilization of soldiers and militia and in the cantonment of heavy weaponry. During 1996 IFOR personnel undertook many activities relating to the civilian reconstruction of Bosnia and Herzegovina. IFOR assisted the OSCE in preparing for and overseeing the all-Bosnia legislative elections that were held in September, and provided security for displaced Bosnians who crossed the inter-entity boundary in order to vote in their towns of origin. In December NATO ministers responsible for foreign affairs approved a follow-on operation, with an 18-month mandate, to be known as the Stabilization Force (SFOR). SFOR was to be about one-half the size of IFOR, but was to retain 'the same unity of command and robust rules of engagement' as the previous force. Its principal objective was to maintain a safe environment at a military level to ensure that the civil aspects of the Dayton peace accord could be fully implemented, including the completion of the de-mining process, the repatriation of refugees, rehabilitation of local infrastructure and preparations for municipal elections. In February 1998 NATO resolved to establish within SFOR a specialized unit to respond to civil unrest and uphold public security. At the same time the NAC initiated a series of security co-operation activities to promote the development of democratic practices and defence mechanisms in Bosnia and Herzegovina. In October 1999 the NAC agreed to implement a reduction in SFOR's strength to some 20,000 troops, as well as a revision of its command structure, in response to the improved security situation in Bosnia and Herzegovina. In May 2002 NATO determined to reduce SFOR to 12,000 troops by the end of that year, and in December 2003 NATO ministers responsible for defence undertook to reduce NATO's presence to some 7,000 troops by mid-2004. The June 2004 summit meeting determined to terminate SFOR's mandate at the end of 2004, and endorsed a new EU mission, EUFOR, in Bosnia and Herzegovina. NATO maintains a military headquarters in Sarajevo, in order to continue to assist the authorities in Bosnia and Herzegovina in matters of defence reform.

In March 1998 an emergency session of the NAC was convened at the request of the Albanian Government, which was concerned at the deteriorating security of its border region with the Serbian province of Kosovo and Metohija. In June NATO ministers authorized the formulation of plans for air strikes against Serbian targets, which were finalized in early October. However, the Russian Government remained strongly opposed to the use of force and there was concern among some member states over whether there was sufficient legal basis for NATO action without further UN authorization. Nevertheless, in mid-October, following Security Council condemnation of the humanitarian situation in Kosovo, the NAC agreed on limited air strikes against Serbian targets, with a 96-hour delay on the 'activation order'. At the same time the US envoy to the region, Richard Holbrooke, concluded an agreement with President Milošević to implement the conditions of a UN resolution (No. 1199). A 2,000-member international observer force, under the auspices of the OSCE, was to be established to monitor compliance with the agreement, supported by a NATO Co-ordination Unit, based in the former Yugoslav republic of Macedonia (FYRM), to assist with aerial surveillance. In mid-November NATO ambassadors approved the establishment of a 1,200–1,800-strong multinational force, under French command, to assist in any necessary evacuation of OSCE monitors. A NATO Kosovo Verification Command Centre was established in Kumanovo, north-east FYRM, later in that month.

On 24 March 1999 an aerial offensive against the Federal Republic of Yugoslavia (which was renamed 'Serbia and Montenegro' in 2003 and divided into separate states of Montenegro and Serbia in 2006) was initiated by NATO, with the declared aim of reducing that country's capacity to commit attacks on the Albanian population. The first phase of the allied operation was directed against defence facilities, followed, a few days later, by the second phase which permitted direct attacks on artillery positions, command centres and other military targets in a declared exclusion zone south of the 44th parallel. The escalation of the conflict prompted thousands of Albanians to flee Kosovo, while others were reportedly forced from their homes by Serbian security personnel, creating massive refugee populations in neighbouring countries. In early April 1999 NATO ambassadors agreed to dispatch 8,000 troops, as an ACE Mobile Force Land operation (entitled Operation Allied Harbour), to provide humanitarian assistance to the estimated 300,000 refugees in Albania at that time and to provide transportation to relieve overcrowded camps, in particular in border areas. Refugees in the FYRM were to be assisted by the existing NATO contingent (numbering some 12,000 troops by early April), which was permitted by the authorities in that country to construct new camps for some 100,000 displaced Kosovans. An additional 1,000 troops were transferred from the FYRM to Albania in mid-May in order to construct a camp to provide for a further 65,000 refugees. NATO's 50th anniversary summit meeting, held in Washington, DC, in April, was dominated by consideration of the conflict and of the future stability of the region. A joint statement declared the determination of all Alliance members to increase economic and military pressure on President Milošević to withdraw forces from Kosovo. In particular, the meeting agreed to prevent shipments of petroleum reaching Serbia through Montenegro, to complement the embargo imposed by the EU and a new focus of the bombing campaign which aimed to destroy the fuel supply within Serbia. However, there was concern on the part of several NATO governments with regard to the legal and political aspects of implementing the embargo. The meeting failed to adopt a unified position on the use of ground forces. Following further intensive diplomatic efforts to secure a ceasefire in Kosovo, on 9 June a Military Technical Agreement was signed between NATO and the Federal Republic of Yugoslavia, incorporating a timetable for the withdrawal of all Serbian security personnel. On the following day the UN Security Council adopted Resolution 1244, which authorized an international security presence in Kosovo, the Kosovo Peace Implementation Force (KFOR), under NATO command, and an international civilian presence, the UN Interim Administration Mission in Kosovo (UNMIK). The NAC subsequently suspended the air strike campaign, which, by that time, had involved some 38,000 sorties. An initial 20,000 KFOR troops entered Kosovo on 12 June. A few days later an agreement was concluded with Russia, providing for the joint responsibility of Pristina airport with a NATO contingent and for the participation of some 3,600 Russian troops in KFOR, reporting to the country command in each sector. On 20 June the withdrawal of Yugoslav troops from Kosovo was completed, providing for the formal ending of NATO's air campaign. KFOR's immediate responsibility was to create a secure environment to facilitate the safe return of refugees, and, pending the full deployment of UNMIK, to assist the reconstruction of infrastructure and civil and political institutions. In addition, NATO troops were to assist personnel of the international tribunal to investigate sites of alleged violations of human rights and mass graves. In January 2000 NATO agreed that the Eurocorps defence force would assume command of KFOR headquarters in April. In February an emergency meeting of the NAC was convened to review the situation in the divided town of Mitrovicë (Kosovska Mitrovica), northern Kosovo, where violent clashes had occurred between the ethnic populations and five people had died during attempts by KFOR to impose order. The NAC expressed its determination to reinforce KFOR's troop levels. In October KFOR worked with OSCE and UN personnel to maintain a secure environment and provide logistical assistance for the holding of municipal elections in Kosovo. During the year KFOR attempted to prevent the movement and stockpiling of illegal armaments in the region. A Weapons Destruction Programme was successfully conducted by KFOR between April 2000–December 2001; a second programme was initiated in March 2002, while an Ammunition Destruction Programme commenced in January. In July 2003, in view of progress made in the security situation, the withdrawal of the Russian contingent (some 4,800 troops) from KFOR was effected. In March 2004, in response to renewed inter-ethnic violence in Kosovo, NATO deployed additional troops from previously designated operational and strategic reserve forces in order to support operations undertaken by KFOR to protect Kosovar Serbs and other ethnic minorities in addition to ethnic Albanians. In February 2006 direct UN-led talks between Serbian and Kosovo Albanian officials on the future status of Kosovo commenced in Vienna, Austria. In February 2008 Kosovo's newly elected government issued a unilateral declaration of independence from Serbia, supported by many EU countries. NATO's Secretary-General and NAC at that time reaffirmed the commitment to maintain a force in Kosovo and to support any future arrangements. Since 2008 NATO has supported the development of the Kosovo Security Force (KSF), a voluntary, multi-ethnic, lightly-armed crisis response force, with responsibility for conducting civil protection operations that are outside the remit of the Kosovo police—such as explosive ordnance disposal, clearance of hazardous materials, search and rescue operations, and fire-fighting—and supporting the civil authorities in responding to natural disasters. In June 2009 NATO ministers responsible for defence announced a gradual reduction in KFOR troop numbers, given improvements in the security environment, and envisaged the force becoming a minimal 'deterrent presence', with fewer static tasks. On 9 July 2013 the NAC declared that the KSF, then numbering around 2,200 personnel, had reached full operational capability and was fully trained, to NATO standards, to perform the tasks assigned by its mandate. At that time the NATO Secretary-General urged participation in the KSF by members of all communities in Kosovo. NATO was to continue to provide advice and support to the Force through an Alliance Liaison and Advisory Team. By April 2014 there were some 4,704 troops under NATO command in Kosovo (compared with some 15,500 in January 2009), from 24 NATO and eight KFOR partner countries. The schedule of KFOR troop reductions has been assessed continuously by the NAC in accordance with the security situation on the ground, rather than being deadline-driven. In April 2014 NATO reopened Kosovo's upper airspace (closed since the 1999 conflict) to civilian air traffic flights; the Kosovo airspace was to remain under the authority of NATO/KFOR.

In September 2001, following the terrorist attacks against targets in the USA and the decision to invoke Article 5 of the North Atlantic Treaty, NATO redirected the standing naval force to provide an immediate Alliance presence in the Eastern Mediterranean. In the following month Operation Active Endeavour was formally launched, to undertake surveillance and monitoring of maritime trade in the region and to detect and deter terrorist activity, including illegal trafficking. In March 2004 the NAC determined to expand the operation to the whole of the Mediterranean and to seek the support of this extension, through their active participation in the operation, by participants in the EAPC and the PfP programme. An Exchange of Letters between NATO and Russia, concluded in December 2004, facilitated the implementation from February 2006 of joint training activities. In September 2006 NATO authorized the participation of a Russian naval ship in the operation. The NAC approved the active involvement of a Ukrainian ship in the operation in May 2007. By April 2014 more than 115,000 vessels had been monitored under the operation, and some 162 compliant boardings had taken place.

In August 2003 NATO undertook its first mission outside of the Euro-Atlantic area when it assumed command of the UN-mandated ISAF in Afghanistan. In October the office of a Senior Civilian Representative was established to liaise with the national government and representatives of the international community and advance NATO's politico-military objectives in the country. In December NATO ministers responsible for defence agreed progressively to extend ISAF's mission in Afghanistan beyond the capital, Kabul. The transfer of command of the Kunduz Provincial Reconstruction Team (PRT) to NATO in January 2004 represented the first step of that expansion. In June the summit meeting, held in İstanbul, determined to expand ISAF in order to assist the Afghan authorities to extend and exercise authority across the country. A first phase of the mission's expansion, involving the establishment of PRTs in Baghlan, Feyzabad, Mazar-e-Sharif and Meymana, had been completed by October of that year. In December the NAC authorized a second expansionary phase, which envisaged the establishment of four PRTs in western provinces of Afghanistan. This was undertaken in 2005. In September an additional 2,000 NATO troops were temporarily deployed to Afghanistan to provide security during provincial and parliamentary elections, held in that month. In December NATO ministers responsible for foreign affairs endorsed a revised operational plan to incorporate a Stage 3 and Stage 4 Expansion of ISAF. The Stage 3 and Stage 4 Expansions, achieved, respectively, in July and October 2006, entailed extending operations to cover the entire country and establishing 15 additional PRTs, five regional commands and two forward support bases (in Kandahar and Khost). Additional ISAF officers were dispatched to mentor and liaise with national army units, support government programmes to disarm rebel groups and support government and international programmes to counter illicit narcotic production. NATO continued to emphasize immediate reconstruction and development activities, through its civil military co-operation units, working closely with government and local and community leaders, and co-operated with the Pakistani military and Afghan National Army through a Tripartite Commission and a Joint Intelligence and Operations Centre. In September 2006 NATO's Secretary-General signed a declaration with the Afghan President establishing a Framework for Enduring Co-operation in Partnership, committing NATO to long-term support for the country's efforts to secure democratic government and territorial integrity. In June 2008 the Secretary-General participated in an International Conference in Support of Afghanistan, hosted by the French Government in Paris. In April 2009 heads of state and government, and leaders of partner countries contributing to ISAF, attending the NATO summit, issued a Declaration on Afghanistan, in which they stated their long-term commitment to that country, pledged the deployment there of additional military forces for electoral support and for training and mentoring the Afghan National Army, and announced the establishment of a NATO Training Mission in Afghanistan (NTM-A). Further initiatives to enhance the training for Afghan National Security Forces, to improve the command and control structure of ISAF and to deploy NATO airborne warning and control aircraft to Afghanistan, were approved by NATO defence ministers meeting in June. NTM-A was formally established in October. In February 2010 ISAF initiated a joint military offensive with Afghan national security forces, entitled Operation Moshtarak, in order to reassert government authority and to protect the civilian population in southern Helmand province. In April an informal meeting of NATO and ISAF ministers responsible for foreign affairs agreed on a roadmap to structure a transition process ('Inteqal') of handing over full sovereignty to the Afghan authorities. At the same time ministers adopted an Afghan First Policy to strengthen the local Afghan economy. A joint framework for transition to full Afghan ownership of its national security by the end of 2014 was approved at an international conference on Afghanistan, convened in Kabul, in July 2010; a Joint Afghan-NATO Inteqal Board was to recommend districts and provinces that were ready for transition. The transition process was endorsed at the NATO summit meeting in November 2010. Responsibility for security of Bamiyan province, central Lashkar Gah, and Mehter Lam in eastern Afghanistan was transferred to Afghan forces in July 2011. The transition process started in a second tranche of Afghan areas in December 2011. At an International Conference on Afghanistan, held in that month in Bonn, Germany, NATO committed to supporting Afghanistan through its 'Transformation Decade' beyond 2014. In February 2012 a meeting of NATO and ISAF ministers responsible for defence determined that the process of transition to Afghan security ownership was on course, and reaffirmed the objective that the Afghan security forces should have full responsibility for security across the country by the end of 2014. Later in February 2012 ISAF personnel were temporarily withdrawn from government ministries in and around Kabul following the killing of two ISAF officers inside the Afghan Ministry of Interior; violent protests had erupted at that time over reports that US troops based in Afghanistan had unintentionally burned copies of the Koran. The 2012 NATO summit, held in May (shortly after the commencement of the third tranche of the transition process), determined to initiate the planning process for a new mission (to be known as 'Resolute Support') that was to continue training, advising and assisting the Afghan security forces, within the context of the Framework for Enduring Co-operation in Partnership and at the behest of the Afghan Government, following the 2014 transfer of power. At the beginning of September 2012 NATO suspended the training of around 1,000 new recruits to the Afghan Local Police (ALP) and initiated a repeat screening process for existing police, in view of a series of attacks on Alliance personnel that had been perpetrated by ALP members. The fourth tranche of the transition process was announced at the end of December. Ministers responsible for foreign affairs of NATO and ISAF partner states, meeting in April 2013, agreed on means of developing efficient and accountable funding mechanisms to sustain the post-2014 Afghan security forces. In June 2013 a ceremony in Kabul marked the final transfer of command for security operations from ISAF to Afghan national security and military forces, representing the fifth tranche of the transition process. In December negotiations were initiated between NATO and the Afghan authorities on the conclusion of a NATO Status of Forces Agreement, which was to provide a legal context for the eventual deployment, from January 2015, of the Resolute Support mission. At April 2014 ISAF's total troop strength totalled 51,176 from 48 troop contributing nations.

In June 2004 NATO heads of state and government, meeting in İstanbul, agreed to offer assistance to the newly inaugurated Iraqi Interim Government with the training of its security forces. The meeting also endorsed a new NATO Policy on Combating Trafficking in Human Beings, with the aim of supporting the efforts of countries and international organizations to counter the problem. In July a NATO Training Implementation Mission was initiated to undertake the training commitments in Iraq. In December the NAC authorized an expansion of the Mission, of up to 300 personnel, and the establishment of an Iraq Training, Education and Doctrine Centre. The expanded operation was to be called the NATO Training Mission–Iraq (NTM-I). In September 2005 an Iraqi Joint Staff College was inaugurated. In July 2009 NATO and the Iraqi Government signed a long-term agreement regarding the training of Iraqi Security Forces. NTM-I expanded its remit in 2010 to include training of border personnel. NTM-1 was terminated in December 2011. In April 2011 Iraq was granted NATO partner status. It was announced in May 2012 that a NATO Transition Cell had been established in Iraq to support the development of the partnership.

In April 2005 the African Union (AU) requested NATO assistance to support its peacekeeping mission in Darfur, western Sudan, where civil conflict had caused a severe humanitarian crisis. In May the NAC provisionally agreed to provide logistical support for the mission. Further consultations were held with the AU, the UN and the EU. In June the NAC confirmed that it would assist in the expansion of the AU mission (AMIS) by airlifting supplementary AU peacekeepers into the region. No NATO combat troops were to be deployed to Darfur. The first airlifts were undertaken in July and in August NATO agreed to transport civilian police officers. NATO established a Senior Military Liaison Officer team, in Addis Ababa, Ethiopia, to liaise with the AU. In June 2006 the AU requested enhanced NATO assistance for its peacekeeping mission in Darfur, including the certification of troops allocated to the peacekeeping force, assistance with lessons learned and support in the establishment of a joint operations centre. NATO undertook staff training to further the mission's capacity-building activities. In November NATO ministers extended its support for proposals by the AU and UN to undertake a hybrid peacekeeping mission in Darfur. NATO support to AMIS was concluded on 31 December 2007 when the mission was transferred to the UN/AU operation. In June 2007 NATO agreed to support an AU mission in Somalia by providing strategic airlifts for deployment of personnel and equipment. The 2012 NATO summit agreed to extend strategic airlift support, and also maritime life support, to AMISOM, and to support the development of the AU's long-term peacekeeping capabilities, including the African Standby Force. A small NATO military liaison team was based at AU headquarters, in Addis Ababa, Ethiopia, in 2014. In October 2008 NATO ministers responsible for defence, meeting in Budapest, Hungary, agreed to initiate a temporary assignment, Operation Allied Provider, in support of a request by the UN Secretary-General, to protect ships chartered by the World Food Programme to deliver humanitarian aid to Somalia. The mission was also mandated to conduct patrols to deter piracy and other criminal acts against merchant shipping in the high risk areas in the Gulf of Aden. The Operation was concluded in mid-December. NATO resumed its counter-piracy operations in that region in March 2009, under Operation Allied Protector. A successor mission, Operation Ocean Shield, was approved in August and incorporated a new training element to enable countries in the region to strengthen their counter-piracy capabilities. In March 2012 the mandate of Operation Ocean Shield was extended to the end of 2014. A strategic assessment of Operation Ocean Shield undertaken in March 2012 concluded that more robust measures—such as disabling or destroying pirate vessels—should be introduced, with the aim of eroding the pirates' logistics and support base. In September 2013 NATO and Djibouti determined to pursue closer co-operation, including through the establishment of a liaison office in support of Operation Ocean Shield.

In March 2011 NATO initiated Operation Unified Protector, using ships and aircraft operating in the Central Mediterranean, in order to monitor and enforce an arms embargo against the Libyan authorities, which had been imposed by the UN Security Council (Resolution 1973, adopted on 17 March) in response to the violent oppression of an opposition movement in that country. Later in that month NATO members determined to enforce the UN-sanctioned no-fly zone over Libya, alongside a military operation to prevent further attacks on civilians and civilian-populated areas, undertaken by a multinational coalition under British, France and US command. A few days later, on 27 March, NATO member states agreed to assume full command of the operation to protect civilians in Libya (formal transfer of command took place on 31 March). On 28 March NATO's Secretary-General attended an international conference on Libya, held in London, United Kingdom, at which it was agreed to establish a Contact Group to give political guidance to the international community's response to the situation. The first meeting of the Contact Group was held in Doha, Qatar, in April. (The Contact Group was replaced in September by a Group of Friends of the New Libya.) In early June NATO ministers extended Operation Unified Protector for a further 90 days (from 27 June); in September the Operation was extended once again for 90 days. In late October, following the capture by opposition forces of the last remaining government-controlled city, Sirte, and the arrest (and subsequent death) of the Libyan leader, Col Muammar al-Qaddafi, the North Atlantic Council resolved to conclude the Operation with effect from the end of that month. By the time of its conclusion NATO and its partners had conducted more than 26,500 air sorties over Libya, including 9,700 strike missions. Nineteen vessels were deployed during the Operation to monitor and enforce the arms embargo, supported by patrol aircraft. Over 3,100 ships were hailed, 300 boarded and 11 denied transit to port under the Operation. In June 2013 NATO determined to send a team of experts to Libya to identify areas where the Organization might provide assistance in security matters, for example in building security institutions.

NATO Agencies

In July 2012, in accordance with a Reform Plan (approved in June 2011 by NATO ministers responsible for defence) which aimed to realign the Agency structure and consolidate the functions and programmes of the then 14 entities along three major programmatic themes: Support; Communications and information systems; and Procurement, three core bodies—the NATO Support Agency, NATO Communications and Information Agency, and NATO Procurement Organisation—were inaugurated. A new Science and Technology Organization was also established in July 2012. The new agencies were to be developed over three phases: phase I (consolidation, involving the establishment of a streamlined executive management structure, to be undertaken during the second half of 2012); phase II (rationalization; 2013); and phase III (optimization, to be completed by the end of 2014). The future of the pre-existing NATO Standardization Agency was to be reviewed in 2014, and a number of procurement agencies were to continue to exist pending the fulfilment of their mission, or else until participating states agreed to integrate into the new NATO Procurement Organisation; otherwise, all the functions hitherto performed by the outgoing entities were to be transferred immediately to the new Agencies, in some cases as programme offices of the new Agencies. A study was to be undertaken to assess the desirability of, in future, merging the new NATO Support Agency and NATO Procurement Organisation.

Core Agencies:

NATO Communications and Information Agency (NCIA): Bâtiment Z, Ave du Bourget 140, 1110 Brussels, Belgium; tel. (2) 70-78-440; e-mail info@ncia.nato.int; internet www.ncia.nato.int; f. 2012, following the merger of the former NATO Consultation, Command and Control Agency, NATO ACCS Management Agency, NATO Communications and Information System Services Agency, ALTBMD Programme, and certain elements that were previously the responsibility; aims to 'connect forces, NATO and nations', and to provide cyber and missile defence; Gen. Man. Maj.-Gen. (retd) Koen Gijsbers (Netherlands).

NATO Procurement Organisation (NPO): Brussels, Belgium; f. 2012; undergoing 'design phase' during 2012–14, aimed at establishing a holding body in which multinational procurement programmes may be integrated.

NATO Support Agency (NSPA): 11 Rue de la Gare, 8325 Capellen, Luxembourg; tel. 352-30631; fax 352-308721; e-mail pr@nspa.nato.int; internet www.nspa.nato.int; f. 2012, following the merger of the former NATO Maintenance and Supply Agency, Central Europe Pipeline Management Agency, and NATO Airlift Management Agency; NATO's integrated logistics and services provider, NPSA is the executive body of the NATO Support Organisation; has operational centres in France, Hungary, Italy and Luxembourg; Gen. Man. Mike Lyden (USA).

Other Agencies:

NATO Airborne Early Warning Programme Management Agency (NAPMA): POB 8002, 6440 HA Brunssum; Rimburgerweg 30, Bldg 107, 6445 PA Brunssum, Netherlands; tel. (45) 5254373; e-mail info@napma.nato.int; internet www.napma.nato.int; f. 1978; responsible for the management and implementation of the NATO Airborne Early Warning and Control Programme; NAPMA continued to function independently following the July 2012 reform.

NATO Alliance Ground Surveillance Management Agency (NAGSMA): Blvd Leopold III, 1110 Brussels, Belgium; tel. (2) 707-1801; fax (2) 707-1862; e-mail nagsma@nagsma.nato.int; internet www.nagsma.nato.int; f. 2009; the NATO Alliance Ground Surveillance (AGS) system is expected to be fully operational by 2017; NAGSMA continued to function independently following the July 2012 reform.

NATO Eurofighter and Tornado Management Agency (NETMA): c/o Eurofighter Jagdflugzeug GmbH, Am Söldnermoos 17, 85399 Hallbergmoos, Germany; tel. (89) 811-80-0; fax (89) 811-80-1557; e-mail communications@eurofighter.com; internet www.eurofighter.com; replaced the NATO Multirole Combat Aircraft (MRCA) Development and Production Management Agency (f. 1969) and the NATO European Fighter (EF) Aircraft Development, Production and Logistics Management Agency (f. 1987); responsible for the joint development and production of the Eurofighter Typhoon Aircraft and the MRCA (Tornado); NETMA continued to function independently following the July 2012 reform.

NATO Helicopter Management Agency (NAHEMA): Le Quatuor, Bâtiment A, 42 route de Galice, 13082 Aix-en-Provence Cedex 2, France; tel. 4-42-95-92-00; fax 4-42-64-30-50; NAHEMA continued to function independently following the July 2012 reform.

NATO Medium Extended Air Defence System Design and Development, Production and Logistics Management Agency (NAMEADSMA): 620 Discovery Dr., Bldg 1, Suite 300, Hunstsville, AL 35806, USA; tel. (205) 922-3972; fax (205) 922-3900; f. 1996; manages the phases of development of the Medium Extended Air Defence System (MEADS), designed to replace the HAWK and PATRIOT-PAC 3 air defence systems; Tech. Dir Gerhard Brauer.

NATO Science and Technology Organization: BP 25, 7 rue Ancelle, 92201 Neuilly-sur-Seine Cedex, France; tel. 1-55-61-22-00; fax 1-55-61-22-99; internet www.sto.nato.int; f. 2012; Chief Scientist Albert Husniaux (Belgium); Dir Dr René Larose.

NATO Standardization Agency (NSA): 1110 Brussels, Belgium; tel. (2) 707-55-56; fax (2) 707-57-18; e-mail nsa@nsa.nato.int; internet nsa.nato.int; lead agent for the development, co-ordination and assessment of operational standardization, in order to enhance interoperability; initiates, co-ordinates, supports and administers standardization activities conducted under the authority of the NATO Committee for Standardization; NSA was retained after the July 2012 reform, but was to be reviewed in 2014; Dir Dr Cihangir Aksit (Turkey).

Finance

As NATO is an international, not a supra-national, organization, its member countries themselves decide the amount to be devoted to their defence effort and the form which the latter will assume. Thus, the aim of NATO's defence planning is to develop realistic military plans for the defence of the Alliance at reasonable cost. Under the annual defence planning process, political, military and economic factors are considered in relation to strategy, force requirements and available resources. The procedure for the co-ordination of military plans and defence expenditures rests on the detailed and comparative analysis of the capabilities of member countries. All installations for the use of international forces are financed under a common-funded infrastructure programme. In accordance with the terms of the Partnership for Peace strategy, partner countries undertake to make available the necessary personnel, assets, facilities and capabilities to participate in the programme. The countries also share the financial cost of military exercises in which they participate.

Publications

NATO publications (in English and French, with some editions in other languages) include:

NATO Basic Texts.
NATO Handbook.
NATO Ministerial Communiqués.
NATO Review (quarterly, in 24 languages).
NATO Update (monthly, electronic version only).
Secretary-General's Annual Report.
Economic and scientific publications.

ORGANISATION FOR ECONOMIC CO-OPERATION AND DEVELOPMENT—OECD

Address: 2 rue André-Pascal, 75775 Paris Cedex 16, France.

Telephone: 1-45-24-82-00; **fax:** 1-45-24-85-00; **e-mail:** webmaster@oecd.org; **internet:** www.oecd.org.

OECD was founded in 1961, replacing the Organisation for European Economic Co-operation which had been established in 1948 in connection with the Marshall Plan. It constitutes a forum for governments to discuss, develop and attempt to co-ordinate their economic and social policies. The organization aims to promote policies designed to achieve the highest level of sustainable economic growth, employment and increase in the standard of living, while maintaining financial stability and democratic government, and to contribute to economic expansion in member and non-member states and to the expansion of world trade.

MEMBERS

Australia	Hungary	Norway
Austria	Iceland	Poland
Belgium	Ireland	Portugal
Canada	Israel	Slovakia
Chile	Italy	Slovenia
Czech Republic	Japan	Spain
Denmark	Republic of Korea	Sweden
Estonia	Luxembourg	Switzerland
Finland	Mexico	Turkey
France	Netherlands	United Kingdom
Germany	New Zealand	USA
Greece		

Note: Accession talks were ongoing with Colombia and Latvia in April 2014. In mid-March accession talks with Russia were suspended, owing to that country's interference in the domestic affairs of neighbouring Ukraine. The proposed initiation in 2015 of accession discussions with Costa Rica and Lithuania was under consideration in 2014.

The European Commission also takes part in OECD's work. Brazil, the People's Republic of China, India, Indonesia and South Africa are regarded as 'key partner' countries.

Organization

(April 2014)

COUNCIL

The governing body of OECD is the Council, at which each member country is represented. The Council meets from time to time (usually once a year) at ministerial level, with the chairmanship rotated among member states. It also meets regularly at official level, when it comprises the Secretary-General and the Permanent Representatives of member states to OECD. It is responsible for all questions of general policy and may establish subsidiary bodies as required, to achieve the aims of the organization. Decisions and recommendations of the Council are adopted by mutual agreement of all its members.

Heads of Permanent Delegations
(with ambassadorial rank)

Australia: Christopher Barrett.
Austria: Marlies Stubits-Weidinger.
Belgium: Yves Haesendonck.
Canada: Judith Larlocque.
Chile: Ignacio Briones.
Czech Republic: Pavel Rozsypal.
Denmark: Klavs Arnoldi Holm.
Estonia: Marten Kokk.
Finland: Okko-Pekka Salmimies.
France: Pascale Andréani.
Germany: Hans-Juergen Heimsoeth.
Greece: George Prevelakis.
Hungary: Istvan Mikola.
Iceland: Berglind Asgeirstdottir.
Ireland: Michael Forbes.
Israel: Nimrod Barkan.
Italy: Carlo Maria Oliva.
Japan: Kazuo Kodama.
Republic of Korea: Sihyung Lee.
Luxembourg: Paul Dühr.
Mexico: Dionisio Pérez Jácome Friscione.
Netherlands: Noë Van Hulst.
New Zealand: Rosemary Bank.
Norway: Tore Eriksen.
Poland: Pawel Wojciechowski.
Portugal: Paulo Vizeu Pinheiro.
Slovakia: Ingrid Brocková.
Slovenia: Iztok Jarc.
Spain: Ricardo Díez-Hochleitner.
Sweden: Annika Markovic.
Switzerland: Stefan Flückiger.
Turkey: Mithat Rende.
United Kingdom: Nicholas (Nick) Bridge.
USA: (vacant).
European Union: Maria-Francesca Spatolisano.

COMMITTEES

Representatives of all member countries meet in specialized committees to advance policy and consider implementation of activities in specific policy areas. Senior government officials from member countries also attend workshops and expert group meetings to collaborate and support work undertaken by the OECD Secretariat.

SECRETARIAT

The Council, the committees and other bodies in OECD are assisted by an international secretariat of some 2,500 staff, headed by the Secretary-General. There are Directorates for Development Co-operation; Education and Skills; Employment, Labour and Social Affairs; Environment; Financial and Enterprise Affairs; Human Resources; Legal Affairs; Public Affairs and Communications; Public Governance and Territorial Development; Science, Technology and Industry; Statistics; and Trade and Agriculture; as well as an Economics Department; a Centre for Entrepreneurship, SMEs and Local Development; and a Centre for Tax Policy and Administration. There are OECD Centres in Berlin, Germany; Mexico City, Mexico; Tokyo, Japan; and Washington, DC, USA.

Secretary-General: José Ángel Gurría Treviño (Mexico).

Deputy Secretaries-General: Rintaro Tamaki (Japan), Yves Leterme (Belgium), William Danvers (USA).

Chief of Staff and 'Sherpa to the G20': Gabriela Ramos (Mexico).

Executive Director: Anthony Rottier (Australia).

SPECIAL BODIES

Africa Partnership Forum.
Centre for Educational Research and Innovation (CERI).
Development Centre.
Financial Action Task Force.
International Energy Agency.
International Transport Forum.
Nuclear Energy Agency.
Sahel and West Africa Club.

Activities

In May 2011 OECD issued a 50th Anniversary Vision Statement, in which it resolved to adopt a 'New Paradigm for Development', with greater collaboration among members and strengthened partnerships with non-member countries, and to work 'Towards a Global Policy Network'. The Vision Statement acknowledged a transformation of the global economic landscape, and of global economic governance, since the founding of the organization, with developing economies increasingly becoming drivers of economic growth.

In May 2012 the Ministerial Council initiated a New Approaches to Economic Challenges (NAEC) policy agenda, with the aim of advancing the continuous improvement and coherence of OECD analytical frameworks and policy advice. An NAEC work programme was initiated in 2013. Meeting in May the Council adopted the Secretary-General's *Strategic Orientations for 2013 and Beyond*, focusing on the multidimensional impact, inclusiveness and implementation of OECD's future work in the pursuit by member states of 'better policies for better lives'.

ECONOMIC POLICY

OECD aims to promote stable macroeconomic environments in member and non-member countries. The Economics Department works to identify priority concerns for governments and to assess the economic implications of a broad range of structural issues, such as ageing, labour market policies, migration, public expenditure and financial market developments. *Economic Outlook*, analysing the major trends in short-term economic prospects and key policy issues, is published twice a year. The main organ for the consideration and direction of economic policy is the Economic Policy Committee, which meets regularly comprising governments' chief economic advisers and central bankers.

The Economic and Development Review Committee, comprising all member countries, is responsible for surveys of the economic situation and macroeconomic and structural policies of each member country. A report, including specific policy recommendations, is issued every 12 to 18 months on each country, after an examination carried out by the Committee.

In December 2008 OECD published a *Strategic Response to the Global Financial and Economic Crisis* (developed collectively by the OECD Council, Committees and Secretariat), which aimed to address regulatory and policy failures in a comprehensive manner, and focused on strengthening and implementing principles and guidelines, and on identifying regulatory gaps, in the areas of finance, competition and governance; and monitoring developments and identifying policy options to promote the restoration of sustainable long-term growth. From early 2009 OECD co-ordinated an initiative, also involving the International Labour Organization (ILO), the International Monetary Fund (IMF), the World Bank and the World Trade Organization (WTO), to compile *A 'Global Charter'/'Legal Standard', Inventory of Possible Policy Instruments*; this audit of the existing range of economic and social policy instruments, a preliminary version of which was issued in March, was to be a single, coherent repository of policy recommendations, guidelines and principles of best practice, and was regarded as a work in progress aimed at strengthening the regulatory framework. The five organizations contributing to the *Inventory* had been invited by the Group of Eight (G8) summit held in Hokkaido, Japan, in June 2008, to enhance their co-operation. The meeting of the Group of 20 (G20) heads of state and government held, for the first time with OECD participation, in April 2009, determined to relaunch the Financial Stability Board, and issued as its final communiqué a global plan for recovery and reform, outlining commitments that included strengthening financial supervision and regulation and reforming global financial institutions, and supporting consideration of a new charter for promoting sustainable economic development. In June G8 ministers responsible for finance, meeting in Lecce, Italy, endorsed a 'Global Standard for the 21st Century' through the adoption of the Lecce Framework of Common Principles and Standards for Propriety, Integrity and Transparency; the Lecce Framework, as the Global Standard was known thereafter, was supported by OECD and was approved by G8 heads of state and government held in L'Aquila, Italy, in July. It was envisaged that OECD would continue to play a leading role in its development. In April 2011 OECD reported that global economic recovery was advancing and was reaching self-sustaining levels throughout the OECD area. In November, in the context of a serious debt crisis within several eurozone countries, OECD's *Economic Outlook* urged member countries to implement decisive policies, including a substantial increase in the capacity of the European Financial Stability Fund, in order to prevent sovereign defaults, credit contraction and bank failures. OECD economic surveys of the eurozone and EU issued in March 2012 urged far-reaching reforms to taxation systems, education systems, and to product and labour markets, in order to rebalance eurozone economies and restore economic growth and competitiveness. In May OECD launched a new Skills Strategy, which aimed to support governments in boosting employment and building economic resilience through the promotion of skills education and training. In February 2014 OECD produced *OECD forecasts during and after the financial crisis: a post-mortem*, focusing on the need for improved modelling methods and projection making, to minimize future economic forecasting errors; the report found that the interconnecting process of globalization had increased the exposure of domestic economies to external shocks.

STATISTICS

Statistical data and related methodological information are collected from member governments and, where possible, consolidated, or converted into an internationally comparable form. The Statistics Directorate maintains and makes available data required for macroeconomic forecasting, i.e. national accounts, the labour force, foreign trade, prices, output, and monetary, financial, industrial and other short-term statistics. Work is also undertaken to develop new statistics and new statistical standards and systems in areas of emerging policy interest (such as sustainable development). In addition, the Directorate shares with non-member countries member states' experience in compiling statistics. The first World Forum on Statistics, Knowledge and Policy was held in November 2004, in Palermo, Italy. At the second Forum, held in June 2007, in İstanbul, Turkey, the European Commission, the Organization of Islamic Cooperation (OIC), the UN, the UN Development Programme (UNDP) and the World Bank issued the Istanbul Declaration, in which they made a commitment to measuring and fostering the progress of societies with a view to improving policy-making and advancing democracy and the well-being of citizens. The Declaration was subsequently opened to wider signature. A Global Project on Measuring the Progress of Societies, with OECD participation, was launched in 2008. The third World Forum on Statistics, Knowledge and Policy was convened in October 2009, in Busan, Republic of Korea (South Korea), and the fourth Forum was held in October 2012, in New Delhi, India, on the theme 'Measuring well-being for development and policy-making'.

In September 2010 OECD launched the iLibrary, a platform providing comprehensive access to statistical data, working papers, books and journals.

DEVELOPMENT CO-OPERATION

The Development Assistance Committee (DAC) is the principal body through which OECD deals with issues relating to co-operation with developing countries and is one of the key forums in which the major bilateral donors work together to increase their effectiveness in support of sustainable development. The DAC is supported by the Development Co-operation Directorate, which monitors aid programmes and resource flows, compiles statistics and seeks to establish codes of practice in aid. There are also working parties on statistics, aid evaluation, gender equality and development co-operation and environment; and networks on poverty reduction, good governance and capacity development, and conflict, peace and development co-operation. The DAC holds an annual high-level meeting of ministers responsible for international aid, and heads of aid agencies from member governments, with senior officials from the World Bank, the IMF and UNDP.

The DAC's mission is to foster co-ordinated, integrated, effective and adequately financed international efforts in support of sustainable economic and social development. Recognizing that developing countries themselves are ultimately responsible for their own development, the DAC concentrates on how international co-operation can contribute to the population's ability to overcome poverty and participate fully in society. Principal activities include adopting authoritative policy guidelines; conducting periodic critical reviews of members' programmes of development co-operation; providing a forum for dialogue, exchange of experience and the building of international consensus on policy and management issues; and publishing statistics and reports on aid and other resource flows to developing countries and countries in transition. A working set of indicators of development progress has been established by the DAC, in collaboration with experts from UN agencies (including the World Bank) and from developing countries.

In February 2003 OECD/DAC co-sponsored a High-Level Forum on Aid Effectiveness, held in Rome, Italy. The second High-Level Forum, convened in February–March 2005, in Paris, France, endorsed the Paris Declaration on Aid Effectiveness, and agreed a number of country-based action plans, for donor and recipient countries, aimed at improving aid effectiveness. In addition, the meeting reviewed OECD's contribution to achieving the UN Millennium Development Goals, issues relating to development, peace and security, and a report on development effectiveness in the context of the New Partnership for Africa's Development (NEPAD). The Accra Agenda for Action, adopted in September 2008 by the third High-Level Forum convened in Accra, Ghana, included further country-based action plans tailored to advance progress in aid effectiveness. In November–December 2011 the fourth High-Level Forum, convened in Busan, South Korea, reviewed progress in implementing the principles of the Paris Declaration. A Busan Partnership for Effective Development Co-operation was signed to foster a framework for co-operation by developed and developing countries, emerging economies, civil society and private funders. The ensuing Global Partnership for Effective Development Co-operation, was launched in June 2012. In April 2014 the first high-level meeting of the Global Partnership, held in Mexico City, Mexico, addressed means of advancing the initiative in the context of the planned post-2015 development framework.

Since 2006 annual sessions of an OECD Forum on Development have been convened, arranged in thematic cycles: options for more effective development finance (2006–08); domestic resource mobilization for development (2009–10); identifying priorities and best practices in making public expenditure more effective and efficient for development (2011–12); and preparing for the post-2015 world (2013–15).

Development Centre: f. 1962; acts as a forum for dialogue and undertakes research and policy analysis in order to assist the development of policy to stimulate economic and social growth in developing and emerging economies; membership open to both OECD and non-OECD countries.

Sahel and West Africa Club: f. 1976, initially to support countries affected by drought in the Sahel region of Africa; expanded to include other countries in West Africa in 2001; acts as an informal discussion grouping between some 17 African countries and OECD members.

Africa Partnership Forum: f. 2003, following a meeting of heads of state of the G8, in Evian, France; comprises representatives of G8 countries, NEPAD and major bilateral and multilateral development partners; meets twice a year; aims to strengthen efforts in support of Africa's development.

PUBLIC GOVERNANCE AND TERRITORIAL DEVELOPMENT

The Public Governance and Territorial Development Directorate is concerned with identifying changing needs in society and in markets, and with helping countries to adapt their governmental systems and territorial policies. One of the Directorate's primary functions is to provide a forum for exchanging ideas in the area of governance. It is concerned with improving public sector governance through comparative data and analysis, the setting and promotion of standards, and the facilitation of transparency and peer review, as well as to encourage the participation of civil society in public governance. The Public Management Committee serves as a forum for senior officials responsible for the central management systems of government, providing information, analysis and recommendations on public management and governing capacity. A Working Party of Senior Budget Officials is the principal international forum for issues concerning international budgeting. OECD undertakes Reviews of Public Sector Integrity in member and non-member states to assist policy-makers to improve policies, adopt good practices and implement established principles and standards. In March 2012 OECD hosted, in Mexico City a high-level meeting on e-government, which reviewed new digital public sector management tools.

The Territorial Development Policy Committee assists central governments with the design and implementation of more effective, area-based strategies, encourages the emergence of locally driven initiatives for economic development, and promotes better integration of local and national approaches. Generally, the Committee's work programme emphasizes the need for innovative policy initiatives and exchange of knowledge in a wide range of policies, such as entrepreneurship and technology diffusion and issues of social exclusion and urban deprivation. National and regional territorial reviews are undertaken to analyse economic and social trends and highlight governance issues.

TRADE AND AGRICULTURE

Through the Trade and Agriculture Directorate OECD works to support a rules-based multilateral trading system with the objective of promoting further trade liberalization. In addition, it aims to assess government support to the agricultural sector in OECD and principal emerging economies, while assessing the medium-term outlook for agricultural markets and advising on policies for the sustainable use of farm and fisheries resources. OECD undertakes analysis of relevant issues and advises governments, in particular in relation to policy reform, trade liberalization and sustainable agriculture and fisheries. OECD is also a focal point for global efforts in the certification and standardization of products, packaging and testing procedures, though its agricultural codes and schemes.

The OECD Trade Committee supports the continued liberalization and efficient operation of the multilateral trading system, with the aim of contributing to the expansion of world trade on a non-discriminatory basis, and thereby advancing standards of living and sustainable development. Its activities include examination of issues concerning trade relations among member countries as well as relations with non-member countries, and consideration and discussion of trade measures taken by a member country which adversely affect another's interests. The Committee holds regular consultations with civil society organizations.

A Working Party on Export Credits and Credit Guarantees serves as a forum for the discussion and co-ordination of export credit policies. OECD maintains an Export Credit Arrangement, which provides a framework for the use of officially supported export credits, stipulating the most generous financial terms and conditions available. Governments participating in the Arrangement meet regularly. In 2000 the Working Party agreed an Action Statement on Bribery and Officially Supported Export Credits; this was strengthened and converted into an OECD Recommendation in December 2006. In June 2007 the OECD Council adopted a Revised Recommendation on Common Approaches to the Environment and Officially Supported Export Credits (updated from 2003).

The Trade Committee considers the challenges that are presented to the existing international trading system by financial or economic instability, the process of globalization of production and markets and the ensuing deeper integration of national economies. OECD and the WTO have established a joint database that provides information about trade-related technical assistance and capacity building in respect of trade policy and regulation; trade development; and infrastructure. In accordance with the Doha Development Agenda, being pursued by the WTO, OECD is undertaking analysis of the implications on business of the growing number of regional trade agreements and the relationship between those agreements and the multilateral system. OECD hosts an annual Global Forum on Trade. The 2014 Forum was to be convened in May, in Paris, with a focus on resilient economies for inclusive societies.

A Committee for Agriculture reviews major developments in agricultural policies, deals with the adaptation of agriculture to changing economic conditions, elaborates forecasts of production and market prospects for the major commodities, identifies best practices for limiting the impact of agricultural production on the environment, promotes the use of sustainable practices in the sector and considers questions of agricultural development in emerging and transition economies. A separate Fisheries Committee carries out similar tasks in its sector, and, in particular, analyses the consequences of policy measures with a view to promoting responsible and sustainable fisheries. The Directorate administers a Biological Resources in Agriculture programme, which sponsors research fellowships as well as workshops and conferences, to enhance international co-operation in priority areas of agro-food research.

In February 2010 ministers responsible for agriculture from OECD states met, for the first time since 1998, to discuss global food security in relation to issues such as population growth, food demand in affluent industrialized societies, pressure on land and water, and climate change; agriculture ministers from non-member countries with significant agricultural sectors or food markets also participated in the meeting. In January 2011 the OECD Secretary-General stated that volatility in food and commodity prices was undermining efforts to address global poverty and hunger, and was threatening economic growth, and urged governments to co-operate in mitigating extreme swings in market prices. An *OECD-FAO Agricultural Outlook 2011–20* was published in June 2011. OECD, with FAO and other agencies, participates in the Agricultural Market Information System (AMIS), founded in 2011 to improve market transparency and to help to stabilize food price volatility.

ENTREPRENEURSHIP AND LOCAL DEVELOPMENT

In June 2000 OECD convened a Ministerial Conference on Small and Medium-sized Enterprises (SMEs), in Bologna, Italy, and initiated a process to promote SMEs and entrepreneurship policies. Within the context of the so-called Bologna Process, an OECD Global Conference on SME and Entrepreneurship Funding was held in March 2006, in Brasília, Brazil. In July 2004 OECD established a Centre for Entrepreneurship, SMEs and Local Development, responsible for promoting OECD work on entrepreneurship and for bringing together experts in the field. In addition, it disseminates best practices on the design, implementation and evaluation of initiatives to promote entrepreneurship, SMEs and local economic and employment development. The Centre administers OECD's Local Economic and Employment Development programme, which aims to promote the creation of employment through innovative strategies and recommendations to local governments and communities. In June 2012 OECD reported that small business start-up rates—which declined sharply from the onset of the global economic crisis in 2008—were rising slowly towards pre-crisis levels, particularly in the services sector.

A Tourism Committee promotes sustainable growth in the tourism sector and encourages the integration of tourism issues into other policy areas. A Global Forum on Tourism Statistics is convened every two years. In July 2012 OECD reported that the tourism sector was demonstrating resilience to the impact of the global economic and financial crisis, with the strongest regional tourism sector growth occurring in Asia and the Pacific.

FINANCIAL AND ENTERPRISE AFFAIRS

Promoting the efficient functioning of markets and enterprises and strengthening the multilateral framework for trade and investment is the responsibility of the main OECD committees and working groups supported by the Directorate for Financial and Enterprise Affairs. The Directorate analyses emerging trends, provides policy guidelines and recommendations, gives examples of best practice and maintains benchmarks to measure progress.

The Committee on Capital Movements and Invisible Transactions monitors the implementation of the Codes of Liberalization of Invisible Transactions and of Current Invisible Operations as legally binding norms for all member countries. The Committee on International Investment and Multinational Enterprises monitors the OECD Guidelines for Multinational Enterprises, a corporate Code of Conduct recommended by OECD member governments, business and labour units. A Declaration on International Investment and Multinational Enterprises, while non-binding, contains commitments on the conduct and treatment of foreign-owned enterprises established in member countries. It is subject to periodic reviews. Negotiations on a Multilateral Agreement on Investment (MAI), initiated by OECD ministers in 1995 to provide a legal framework for international investment, broke down in October 1998, although 'informal consultation' on the issue was subsequently pursued. In June 2008 the OECD Council, meeting at ministerial level, adopted a Declaration on Sovereign Wealth Funds and Policies for Recipient Countries, to ensure a fair and transparent investment environment. The Declaration was also endorsed by the governments of Chile, Estonia and Slovenia. The development of a non-binding 'Model Investment Treaty', to facilitate negotiations and foster greater consistency in investment procedures, is under consideration by OECD. From March 2013 OECD developed a set of High-level Principles on Long-Term Investment Financing by Institutional Investors, which aimed to promote institutional investment in long-term assets, such as infrastructure and renewable energy projects; these were endorsed in September by G20 ministers responsible for finance and central bank governors.

The Committee on Competition Law and Policy promotes the harmonization of national competition policies, co-operation in competition law enforcement, common merger reporting rules and pro-competitive regulatory reform, the development of competition laws and institutions, and efforts to change policies that restrain competition. The Committee on Financial Markets exercises surveillance over recent developments, reform measures and structural and regulatory conditions in financial markets. It aims to promote international trade in financial services, to encourage the integration of non-member countries into the global financial system, and to improve financial statistics. The Insurance Committee monitors structural changes and reform measures in insurance markets, for example the liberalization of insurance markets, financial insolvency, co-operation on insurance and reinsurance policy, the monitoring and analysis of regulatory and structural developments, and private pensions and health insurance. A working party on private pensions meets twice a year. In 2002 OECD member governments approved guidelines for the administration of private pension funds. Specialized work on public debt is undertaken by the Working Party on Government Debt Management. An OECD Global Forum on Public Debt Management and Emerging Government Securities Markets is convened each year.

An OECD Convention on Bribery of Foreign Public Officials in International Business Transactions entered into force in February 1999; by April 2014 the Convention had been ratified by all OECD member states and seven non-member countries (Argentina, Brazil, Bulgaria, Colombia, Latvia, Russia and South Africa). All signatory states were required to undergo a 'phase I' review of legislation conformity with anti-bribery standards and help to compile a 'phase II' country report assessing the structures in place to enforce these laws and their effectiveness. In May 2009 the OECD Council adopted a Recommendation on the Non-Tax Deductibility of Bribes and in December adopted a Recommendation for Further Combating Bribery of Foreign Public Officials in order to strengthen the existing legal framework for combating bribery and corruption. All signatory states were required to implement the new measures. In 2010 OECD member states, and key partner countries, adopted a Declaration on Propriety, Integrity and Transparency in the Conduct of International Business and Finance.

In March 2011 it was announced that OECD was developing a new initiative, entitled 'clean.gov.biz', to improve the co-ordination of anti-corruption and transparency initiatives, firstly within member countries, and then, in an expanded version, to incorporate all other relevant players, including governments, international organizations, and the private sector.

In May 1999 ministers endorsed a set of OECD Principles for Corporate Governance, covering ownership and control of corporate entities, the rights of shareholders, the role of stakeholders, transparency, disclosure and the responsibilities of boards. In 2000 these became one of the 12 core standards of global financial stability, and they are used as a benchmark by other international financial institutions. A revised set of Principles was published in 2004. OECD collaborates with the World Bank and other organizations to promote good governance worldwide, for example through regional round tables and the Global Corporate Governance Forum. OECD provides the secretariat for the Financial Action Task Force on Money Laundering, which develops and promotes policies to combat money-laundering. In February 2011 the G20 ministers of finance and central bank governors tasked OECD and the Financial Stability Board with developing a new set of principles on consumer protection in financial services. The resulting draft guidelines were agreed at a meeting of G20 ministers in October, and were to be incorporated into a broader regulatory framework.

TAXATION

OECD promotes internationally accepted standards and practices of taxation, and provides a forum for the exchange of information and experience of tax policy and administration. The Committee on Fiscal Affairs is concerned with promoting the removal of tax barriers, monitoring the implementation and impact of major tax reforms, developing a neutral tax framework for electronic commerce, and studying the tax implications of the globalization of national economies. The Centre for Tax Policy and Administration supports the work of the Committee. Other activities include the publication of comparable statistics on taxation and guidelines on transfer pricing, and the study of tax evasion and tax and electronic commerce. OECD is a sponsor, with the IMF and the World Bank, of an International Tax Dialogue. OECD administers a network of Multilateral Tax Centres that provide workshops and a venue for exchanges between national officials and OECD experts.

OECD promotes co-ordinated action for the elimination of so-called harmful tax practices, designed to reduce the incidence of international money-laundering, and the level of potential tax revenue lost by OECD members. In mid-2000 OECD launched an initiative to abolish 'harmful tax systems', identifying a number of offshore jurisdictions as tax havens lacking financial transparency, and inviting these to co-operate by amending national financial legislation. Several of the countries and territories named agreed to follow a timetable for reform, with the aim of eliminating such practices by the end of 2005. Others, however, were reluctant to participate. (The USA also strongly opposed the initiative.) In April 2002 OECD announced that co-ordinated defensive measures would be implemented against non-complying jurisdictions ('unco-operative tax havens') from early 2003. OECD has also highlighted examples of preferential tax regimes in member countries. In May 2009 the Committee removed the remaining three jurisdictions, Andorra, Liechtenstein and Monaco, from the list of unco-operative tax havens, following commitments made by those authorities to implement recommended standards of transparency and effective exchange of information.

OECD convenes a Global Forum on Transparency and Exchange of Information for Tax Purposes to promote co-operation and dialogue with non-member countries. In January 2010 the Global Forum established an Informal Task Force on Tax and Development, comprising business and civil society interests, and non-governmental organizations, from OECD and developing countries. In May 2012 the Informal Task Force launched a 'Tax Inspectors Without Borders' initiative, which aimed to support developing countries in strengthening their tax systems. In March 2010 the Global Forum initiated a peer review process for its member jurisdictions (which numbered 121 by April 2014). In October 2011 the Forum agreed guidelines on the co-ordination of technical assistance, in particular to support smaller jurisdictions to implement standards, and adopted a progress report on international compliance with standards of exchange of tax information. In November G20 countries signed a Protocol amending the Convention on Mutual Administrative Assistance in Tax Matters (first developed by OECD and the Council of Europe in 1988), which aimed to promote exchange of information on tax examinations, evasion and collection between member and non-member states. By April 2014 the Convention had been ratified by

40 states, and the Protocol had 36 ratifications. In February 2013 OECD published a report entitled *Addressing Base Erosion and Profit Shifting*, which identified the extent of taxation avoidance by multinational enterprises. OECD subsequently formulated a Base Erosion and Profit Shifting (BEPS) Action Plan, comprising 15 areas of action, and aimed at strengthening corporate taxation systems and combating corporate tax avoidance globally; the BEPS Plan, presented in July to a gathering of G20 ministers responsible for foreign affairs, was to be passed for endorsement by G20 heads of state and government in September. In June OECD presented to G8 leaders a report entitled *Step Change in Tax Transparency*, detailing four steps required for the establishment of a global automatic exchange of taxation information.

ENVIRONMENT

The OECD Environment Directorate works in support of the Environment Policy Committee (EPOC) on environmental issues. EPOC assesses performance; encourages co-operation on environmental policy; promotes the integration of environmental and economic policies; works to develop principles, guidelines and strategies for effective environmental management; provides a forum for member states to address common problems and share data and experience; and promotes the sharing of information with non-member states. The Directorate conducts peer reviews of environmental conditions and progress. The Directorate aims to improve understanding of past and future trends through the collection and dissemination of environmental data.

OECD programmes and working parties on the environment consider a range of issues, including the harmonization of biotechnology regulation, the environmental impact of production and consumption, natural resource management, trade and investment and the environment, and chemical safety. In some cases working parties collaborate with other Directorates (for example, the working parties on Trade and Environment and on Agriculture and Environment). An Experts Group on Climate Change, based in the Environment Directorate, undertakes studies related to international agreements on climate change.

In May 2001 OECD ministers responsible for the environment, convened in Paris, adopted the OECD Environmental Strategy for the 21st Century, containing recommendations for future work, with a focus on fostering sustainable development, and strengthening co-operation with non-member countries and partnerships with the private sector and civil society. The strategy identified several issues requiring urgent action, such as the generation of municipal waste, increased car and air travel, greenhouse gas emissions, groundwater pollution, and the exploitation of marine fisheries. The meeting endorsed guidelines for the provision of environmentally sustainable transport, as well as the use of a set of key environmental indicators. A review of the key indicators was presented to a meeting of ministers of the environment, convened in April 2004. The *Global Environment Outlook to 2030*, issued in March 2008, indicated that wide-ranging climate change might be achieved without negatively impacting economic growth, if efficient policy instruments were employed. In June 2009 OECD member countries, candidate countries, and key partner countries issued a declaration on 'Green Growth', urging the adoption of targeted policy instruments to promote green investment. OECD launched a Green Growth Strategy in May 2011, providing a flexible policy framework that could be adjusted to suit different national circumstances and stages of development. In March 2012 OECD published *Global Environment Outlook to 2050: Consequences of Inaction*. OECD ministers responsible for the environment meeting in that month considered the following main concerns identified by the report: energy demands; air pollution; natural resources and biodiversity; and global water demand. In January 2012 OECD, jointly with the UN Environment Programme, the World Bank and the Global Green Growth Institute, established a Green Growth Knowledge Platform to compile and disseminate research and policy experience concerning green growth.

SCIENCE, TECHNOLOGY AND INDUSTRY

The Directorate for Science, Technology and Industry aims to assist member countries in formulating, adapting and implementing policies that optimize the contribution of science, technology, industrial development and structural change to economic growth, employment and social development. It provides indicators and analysis on emerging trends in these fields, identifies and promotes best practices, and offers a forum for dialogue.

A Global Science Forum (established in 1992 as the Megascience Forum), convenes a general meeting twice a year for senior science policy officials to identify and pursue opportunities for international co-operation in scientific research. In February 2008 OECD, as part of its International Futures Programme, inaugurated a Global Forum on Space Economics to provide a focus for international debate and co-operation on economic issues affecting the development of space infrastructure and other space-related activities.

Areas considered by the Committee for Scientific and Technological Policy include the management of public research, technology and innovation, and intellectual property rights. A Working Party on Biotechnology was established in 1993 to pursue study of biotechnology and its applications, including issues such as scientific and technological infrastructure, and the relation of biotechnology to sustainable industrial development. Statistical work on biotechnology is undertaken by a Working Party of National Experts on Science and Technology Indicators. A Global Biodiversity Information Facility began operations in 2001 to connect global biodiversity databases in order to make available a wide range of data online. In September 2011 OECD hosted a Global Forum on the Knowledge Economy, which focused on improving national science and innovation policies, and science and innovation for inclusive development.

The Committee for Information, Computer and Communications Policy monitors developments in telecommunications and information technology and their impact on competitiveness and productivity, with an emphasis on technological and regulatory convergence. It also promotes the development of new guidelines and analyses trade and liberalization issues. The Committee maintains a database of communications indicators and telecommunications tariffs. A Working Party on Information Security and Privacy promotes a co-ordinated approach to efforts to enhance trust in the use of electronic commerce. In August 2004 an OECD Task Force was established to co-ordinate efforts to counter unsolicited e-mail ('spam'). OECD supports the Digital Opportunities Task Force (Dot.force) which was established in June 2000 by the G8 to counter the so-called digital divide between developed and less developed countries and between different population sectors within nations. A ministerial meeting on the Future of the Internet Economy was held in Seoul, South Korea, in June 2008. A follow-up High-Level Meeting on the Internet Economy: Generating Innovation and Growth, was convened in June 2011, in Paris.

The Committee on Industry and the Business Environment focuses on industrial production, business performance, innovation and competitiveness in industrial and services sectors, and policies for private sector development in member and selected non-member economies. In recent years the Committee has addressed issues connected with globalization, regulatory reform, SMEs, and the role of industry in sustainable development. Business and industry policy fora explore a variety of issues with the private sector, for example new technologies or environmental strategies for industry, and develop recommendations. The Working Party on SMEs and Entrepreneurship conducts an ongoing review of the contribution of SMEs to growth and employment and carries out a comparative assessment of best practice policies. (See also the Bologna Process.)

The Transport Division of the Directorate for Science, Technology and Industry considers aviation, maritime, shipbuilding, road and intermodal transport issues. Maritime Transport and Steel Committees aim to promote multilateral solutions to sectoral friction and instability based on the definition and monitoring of rules. The Working Party on Shipbuilding seeks to establish normal competitive conditions in that sector, especially through dialogue with non-OECD countries. In January 2004 a new Transport Research Centre was established by merger of OECD's road transport and intermodal linkages research programme and the economic research activities of the European Conference of Ministers of Transport. A new report, entitled *Strategic Transport Infrastructure Needs to 2030* was published in March 2012.

International Transport Forum (ITF): in May 2006 the European Conference of Ministers of Transport agreed to establish and become integrated into a new International Transport Forum; the inaugural meeting of the Forum was held in May 2008, in Leipzig, Germany.

EMPLOYMENT, LABOUR AND SOCIAL AFFAIRS

The Employment, Labour and Social Affairs Committee is concerned with the development of the labour market and selective employment policies to ensure the utilization of human capital at the highest possible level and to improve the quality and flexibility of working life, as well as the effectiveness of social policies. The Committee's work covers such issues as the role of women in the economy, industrial relations, measurements of unemployment, and the development of an extensive social database. The Committee also carries out single-country and thematic reviews of labour market policies and social assistance systems. It has assigned a high priority to work on the policy implications of an ageing population and on indicators of human capital investment. In May 2011 OECD and the ILO signed a Memorandum of Understanding on strengthening mutual co-operation. Both organizations provided analysis and support to the G20 meeting of ministers responsible for labour and employment, held in September 2011, in Cannes, France. The heads of both organizations expressed concern that world unemployment totalled almost 200m. and urged G20 members to prioritize employment and social protection in the policy debate. The 2013 edition of OECD's annual *Employment Outlook*, released in July, envisaged that, owing to faltering economic recovery, the level of unemployment rates in OECD member states would remain high at least until the end of 2014; young and low-skilled people were at particular risk of unemployment. In May 2013 OECD endorsed an Action Plan for Youth, which aimed to address ongoing high levels of youth unemployment, with a focus on improving the skills of disadvantaged young people, and on strengthening education systems.

OECD undertakes analysis of health care and health expenditure issues, and reviews the organization and performance of health systems. A Group on Health was established in January 2005 to direct a programme of work, to be supported by a new Health Division within the Directorate of Employment, Labour and Social Affairs. Social policy areas of concern include benefits and wages, family-friendly policies, and the social effects of population ageing. In 2011 OECD launched a Better Life Index to enhance understanding of the impact of policy options on quality of life; an updated version, Better Life Index 3.0, was released in May 2013.

A Non-Member Economies and International Migration Division works on social policy issues in emerging economies and economies in transition, especially relating to education and labour market reforms and to the economic and social aspects of migration. The Directorate undertakes regular analysis of trends in international migration, including consideration of its economic and social impact, the integration of immigrants, and international co-operation in the control of migrant flows.

In January 2011 OECD issued a study entitled *Housing and the Economy: Policies for Renovation*, which offered governments a roadmap for developing sounder housing policy through the promotion of reforms in areas such as financial sector regulation, taxation, the regulation of rental markets, and the provision of social housing.

EDUCATION

OECD views education as a lifelong activity. The Directorate for Education and Skills focuses on the thematic areas of early childhood and schools; skills beyond schools; innovation in education; and research and knowledge management. Programmes undertaken by the Directorate include a Programme for Co-operation with non-member Economies, the Programme of International Student Assessments, the Programme on Institutional Management in Higher Education and the Programme on Education Building, as well as regular (Programme for International Student Assessment—PISA) peer reviews of education systems. In February 2012 OECD published a report which encouraged governments to increase investment in disadvantaged schools in order to reduce school failure, increase economic growth and help to contribute to a fairer society. A Programme for the International Assessment of Adult Competencies was launched in 2011. In October 2013, in this context, OECD released its first *Survey of Adult Skills*, which measured the skills of adults aged between 16–65 years across 24 countries, and found clear evidence of the beneficial impact on individual employment prospects and quality of life, as well as on national economies and societies, of the development of skills through high-quality initial education and flexible lifelong learning opportunities, while emphasizing that the low-skilled are more likely than others to be unemployed, have lower earnings and suffer poor health. The report offered assistance to policy-makers with setting meaningful national skills targets and developing relevant responses.

Centre for Educational Research and Innovation (CERI): f. 1968; an independently funded programme within the Directorate for Education and Skills; promotes the development of research activities in education, together with experiments of an advanced nature, designed to test innovations in educational systems and to stimulate research and development.

CO-OPERATION WITH NON-MEMBER ECONOMIES

The Centre for Co-operation with Non-Members (CCNM) serves as the focal point for the development of policy dialogue with non-member economies, managing multi-country, thematic, regional and country programmes. These include a Baltic Regional Programme, Programmes for Russia and for Brazil, an Emerging Asian Economies Programme and the OECD Programme of Dialogue and Co-operation with China. The Centre also manages OECD's various Global Forums, which discuss a wide range of specific issues that defy resolution in a single country or region, for example international investment, sustainable development, biotechnology, and trade. The Centre co-ordinates and maintains OECD's relations with other international organizations. An integral part of the CCNM is the joint venture with the European Union, the Support for Improvement in Governance and Management (SIGMA) programme, which aimed to assist the reform of public institutions in transition economies of Central and Eastern Europe.

Non-member economies are invited by the CCNM, on a selective basis, to participate in or observe the work of certain OECD committees and working parties. The Centre also provides a limited range of training activities in support of policy implementation and institution building. In 1994 the OECD Centre for Private Sector Development, based in İstanbul, commenced operations as a joint project between OECD and the Turkish Government to provide policy advice and training to administrators from transitional economies in Eastern Europe, Central Asia and Transcaucasus. Subsequently, the Centre has evolved into a regional forum for policy dialogue and co-operation with regard to issues of interest to transitional economies. The CCNM is also a sponsor of the Joint Vienna Institute, which offers a variety of administrative, economic and financial management courses to participants from transition economies. In May 2007 OECD invited Chile, Estonia, Israel, Russia and Slovenia to initiate discussions with a view to future membership of the organization. So-called 'roadmaps for negotiations' were agreed with those five accession countries in December. Chile, Slovenia, Israel and Estonia formally acceded to OECD in May, July, September and December 2010, respectively.

In 2007 OECD launched an Enhanced Engagement Initiative. Participating ('key partner') countries—Brazil, China, India, Indonesia and South Africa—are encouraged to participate directly in the work of the organization and are important partners in dialogue. The 50th Anniversary Vision Statement adopted in May 2011 by the Ministerial Council placed priority on developing new forms of partnership with each of the key partner countries.

In November 2006 OECD's Trade Union Advisory Committee ratified an agreement with the International Trade Union Confederation and the so-called Global Unions (global trade union federations) to form a Council of Global Unions, in order to promote trade union membership and advance common trade union interests worldwide.

Finance

OECD is funded by its members, with contributions proportional to the national economy. OECD's total budget for 2013 amounted to €354m.

Publications

OECD Annual Report.
African Economic Outlook (annually).
Agricultural Policies in OECD Countries.
Development Co-operation Report (annually).
Economic Policy Reforms (annually).
Energy Balances of Non-OECD Countries (annually).
Energy Balances of OECD Countries (annually).
Geographical Distribution of Financial Flows to Developing countries (annually).
Going for Growth (annually).
International Migration Outlook (annually).
Labour Force Statistics.
Measuring Globalisation.
Measuring Innovation.
OECD Economic Outlook (2 a year).
OECD Economic Surveys (every 12 to 18 months for each country).
OECD Employment Outlook (annually).
OECD Environmental Outlook to 2030.
OECD Factbook (annually).
OECD Information Technology and Communication Outlooks (annually).
OECD Insurance Statistics Yearbook.
OECD International Direct Investment Statistics Yearbook.
OECD Journal (8 a year).
OECD Observer (5 a year).
OECD Science, Technology and Industry Scoreboard.
OECD Tourism Trends and Policies.
OECD Yearbook.
Perspectives on Global Development (annually).

OECD's 'at a glance' series of annual publications cover: aid for trade (jointly with the WTO); entrepreneurship; environment; government; health; national accounts; pensions; regions; society; and space economy, Numerous other specialized reports, working papers, books and statistics on economic and social subjects are also published.

International Energy Agency—IEA

Address: 9 rue de la Fédération, 75739 Paris Cedex 15, France.

Telephone: 1-40-57-65-00; **fax:** 1-40-57-65-09; **e-mail:** info@iea.org; **internet:** www.iea.org.

The Agency was established in 1974 as an autonomous organization within the framework of the OECD to develop co-operation on energy policy among participating countries.

MEMBERS

Australia	Hungary	Portugal
Austria	Ireland	Slovakia
Belgium	Italy	Spain
Canada	Japan	Sweden
Czech Republic	Republic of Korea	Switzerland
Denmark	Luxembourg	Turkey
Finland	Netherlands	United Kingdom
France	New Zealand	USA
Germany	Norway*	
Greece	Poland	

* Norway participates in the IEA under a special agreement.

In October 2010 the Governing Board determined that negotiations should commence on the future admission of Chile to the IEA. The European Commission also takes part in the IEA's work as an observer.

Organization

(April 2014)

GOVERNING BOARD

Composed of ministers or senior officials of the member governments. Meetings are held every two years at ministerial level and five times a year at senior official level. Decisions may be taken by a special weighted majority on a number of specified subjects, particularly concerning emergency measures and emergency reserve commitments; a simple weighted majority is required for procedural decisions and decisions implementing specific obligations in the agreement. Unanimity is required only if new obligations, not already specified in the agreement, are to be undertaken.

STANDING COMMITTEES

The IEA maintains Standing Committees on: Emergency Questions (responsible for IEA oil emergency preparedness, and collective response to supply disruptions); the Oil Market; Long-term Co-operation; Energy Efficiency; and Global Energy Dialogue. The Committee on Energy Research and Technology, which supports international collaboration, is serviced by four expert bodies: Working Parties on Fossil Fuels, Renewable Energy Technologies and Energy End-Use Technologies and a Fusion Power Co-ordinating Committee. The Committee oversees the IEA Energy Technology Network, comprising (in 2014) more than 6,000 experts working in support of global technology collaboration. The Committee on Budget and Expenditure (CBE) advises the Governing Board on resource management and administration of the IEA.

EXECUTIVE OFFICE

The Executive Director is supported by a Deputy Executive Director. The Executive Office comprises the following Directorates: Energy Markets and Security; Sustainable Energy Policies and Technologies; Enhancing Global Dialogue on Energy; and Longer-term Economic and Energy Policy Scenarios and Outlooks.

Executive Director: MARIA VAN DER HOEVEN (Netherlands).

Activities

The Agreement on an International Energy Programme was signed in November 1974 and formally entered into force in January 1976. The Agreement commits the participating countries of the IEA to share petroleum in certain emergencies, to strengthen co-operation in order to reduce dependence on petroleum imports, to increase the availability of information on the petroleum market, to co-operate in the development and co-ordination of energy policies, and to develop relations with the petroleum-producing and other petroleum-consuming countries. At 31 December 2013 IEA countries possessed total reserves of petroleum totalling 2,559m. barrels, from which reserves being held in public stocks—kept exclusively for emergency purposes—were sufficient to cover 28.8 days of forward demand.

The IEA collects, processes and disseminates statistical data and information on all aspects of the energy sector, including production, trade, consumption, prices and greenhouse gas emissions. The IEA promotes co-operation among policy-makers and energy experts to discuss common energy issues, and to enhance research and development and energy technology, with a particular focus on bioenergy; biofuels; carbon capture and storage; clean energy; climate change; coal; electricity; energy poverty; energy security; geothermal energy; heat; hydropower; natural gas; nuclear fission and fusion ocean energy; renewable forms of energy; transport; smart grids; solar energy; and wind power.

The IEA has developed a system of emergency measures to be used in the event of a reduction in petroleum supplies. Under the International Energy Programme, member states are required to stock crude oil equivalent to 90 days of the previous year's net imports. These measures, which also include demand restraint, were to take effect in disruptions exceeding 7% of the IEA or individual country average daily rate of consumption. A more flexible system of response to oil supply disruption has also been developed under the Co-ordinated Energy Response Measures in 1984. IEA member states have collectively made available to the market additional supplies of petroleum in the run-up to the 1991 Gulf War; in September 2005, in response to concerns at interruptions to the supply of petroleum from the Gulf of Mexico, following extensive hurricane damage to oil rigs, pipeline and refineries (that action was terminated in December); and in June 2011, in response to ongoing disruption of oil supplies from Libya. Meeting in Camp David, Maryland, USA, in May 2012, the leaders of the Group of Eight (G8) industrialized nations indicated their readiness to request the IEA to stand by to release emergency oil stocks should international sanctions on Iran (imposed in reaction to international concern at that country's nuclear programme) result in disruption to the global supply.

The IEA undertakes emergency response reviews and workshops, and publishes an Emergency Management Manual to facilitate a co-ordinated response to a severe disruption in petroleum supplies. The Oil Markets and Emergency Preparedness Office monitors and reports on short-term developments in the petroleum market. It also considers other related issues, including international crude petroleum pricing, petroleum trade and stock developments and investments by major petroleum-producing countries.

The IEA promotes international collaboration in the development of energy technology and the participation of energy industries to facilitate the application of new technologies, through effective transfer of knowledge, technology innovation and training. Member states have initiated over 40 Multilateral Technology Initiatives (also referred to as Implementing Agreements), which provide a framework for international collaboration and information exchange in specific areas, including renewable energy, fossil fuels, end-use technologies and fusion power. OECD member states, non-member states, the energy producers and suppliers are encouraged to participate in these Agreements. In May 2011 the IEA issued two roadmaps on solar electricity: the Solar Photovoltaic Roadmap and the Concentrating Solar Power Roadmap; the Agency predicted at that time that by 2050 solar energy could represent up to 25% of global electricity production. In April 2011 the IEA produced its first *Clean Energy Progress Report*, providing an overview of key policy developments in the field of clean energy technologies. Later in April the IEA issued a roadmap on *Biofuels for Transport*, assessing that by 2050 biofuels could provide up to 27% of world transportation fuel. In October 2011 OECD and the IEA released a joint statement in support of reform of fossil fuel subsidies, in order to promote investment in renewable energy and encourage greater energy efficiency. In March 2013 the IEA organized its inaugural Unconventional Gas Forum, with participation by representatives of governments, industry, international agencies and non-governmental organizations. The Forum considered operational best practices for the sustainable development of global unconventional natural gas resources (i.e. gas deposits trapped underground by impermeable rocks, such as shale gas, coal bed methane and tight gas); these have commonly been extracted through the hydraulic fracturing ('fracking') of rock formations, which is alleged by some environmentalists to produce adverse environmental effects.

The IEA Long-Term Co-operation Programme is designed to strengthen the security of energy supplies and promote stability in world energy markets. It provides for co-operative efforts to conserve energy, to accelerate the development of alternative energy sources by means of both specific and general measures, to strengthen research and development of new energy technologies and to remove legislative and administrative obstacles to increased energy supplies. Regular reviews of member countries' efforts in the fields of energy conservation and accelerated development of alternative energy sources assess the effectiveness of national programmes in relation to the objectives of the Agency.

The IEA actively promotes co-operation and dialogue with non-members and international organizations in order to promote global energy security, environmental protection and economic development. The IEA holds bilateral and regional technical meetings and conducts surveys and reviews of the energy situation in non-member countries. Co-operation agreements with key energy-consuming countries, including India and China, are a priority. The Agency also has co-operation agreements with Russia and the Ukraine and works closely with the petroleum-producing countries of the Middle East. In the latter states the IEA has provided technical assistance for the development of national energy legislation, regulatory reform and energy efficiency projects. The IEA is represented on the Executive Committee of the International Energy Forum (formerly the Oil Producer-Consumer Dialogue) to promote greater co-operation and understanding between petroleum producing and consuming countries. It is also active in the Joint Oil Data Initiative, a collaborative initiative of seven international organizations to improve oil data transparency.

Recognizing that ongoing energy trends are not sustainable and that an improved balance should be sought between energy security, economic development, and protection of the environment, the IEA supports analysis of actions to mitigate climate change, studies of the implications of the Kyoto Protocol to the UN Framework Convention on Climate Change (UNFCCC), the development of new international commitments on climate change alleviation, and analysis of policies designed to reduce greenhouse gas emissions, including emissions trading. It is a partner in the Global Bioenergy Partnership and is active in the Renewable Energy and Efficiency Partnership (REEEP). Since 2001 the IEA has organized, with the International Emissions Trading Association and the Electric Power Research Institute, an annual workshop of greenhouse gas emissions trading. The Agency also analyses the regulation and reform of energy markets, especially for electricity and gas. In July 2005 G8 heads of state approved a plan of action mandating a clean, competitive and sustainable energy future. The IEA was requested to make recommendations towards achieving the plan of action and has submitted reports to each subsequent annual summit meeting. In July 2008 the G8 heads of state, convened in Hokkaido, Japan, endorsed an IEA initiative to develop roadmaps for new energy technologies, in particular carbon capture and storage projects. In December 2009 the IEA presented to the UN Climate Change Conference (the 15th conference of parties of the UNFCCC), held in Copenhagen, Denmark, a blueprint for delivering in future on ambitious climate change goals; the Agency also urged participating governments to promote new investment in clean energy. At the 2010 Climate Change Conference, held in December, in Cancún, Mexico, the IEA urged the increased adoption worldwide of clean energy solutions.

In March 2009 the IEA inaugurated a new Energy Business Council, which was mandated to meet twice a year to assess the impact of the global financial crisis on energy markets, and to address climate change and other energy issues.

Publications

CO^2 Emissions from Fuel Combustion (annually).
Coal Information (annually).
Electricity Information (annually).
Energy Balances and Energy Statistics of OECD and non-OECD Countries (annually).
Energy Policies of IEA Countries (annually).
Key World Energy Statistics.
Natural Gas Information (annually).
Natural Gas Market Review (annually).
Oil Information (annually).
Oil Market Report (monthly).
Redrawing the Energy-Climate Map.
Renewables Information (annually).
World Energy Outlook (annually).
Other reports, studies, statistics, country reviews.

OECD Nuclear Energy Agency—NEA

Address: Le Seine Saint-Germain, 12 blvd des Îles, 92130 Issy-les-Moulineaux, France.

Telephone: 1-45-24-82-00; **fax:** 1-45-24-11-10; **e-mail:** nea@oecd-nea.org; **internet:** www.oecd-nea.org.

The NEA was established in 1958 to further the peaceful uses of nuclear energy. Originally a European agency, it has since admitted OECD members outside Europe.

MEMBERS

The NEA has 31 member states.

Organization

(April 2014)

STEERING COMMITTEE FOR NUCLEAR ENERGY

Meets twice a year. Comprises senior representatives of member governments, presided over by a chairman. Reports directly to the OECD Council.

SECRETARIAT

Director-General: LUIS ENRIQUE ECHÁVARRI (Spain) (until 30 April 2014), WILLIAM D. MAGWOOD (USA) (from 1 September 2014).

MAIN COMMITTEES

Committee on Nuclear Regulatory Activities.
Committee on Radiation Protection.
Committee on the Safety of Nuclear Installations.
Committee for Technical and Economic Studies on Nuclear Development and the Fuel Cycle (Nuclear Development Committee).
Nuclear Law Committee.
Nuclear Science Committee.
Radioactive Waste Management Committee.

NEA DATA BANK

The Data Bank was established in 1978, as a successor to the Computer Programme Library and the Neutron Data Compilation Centre. The Data Bank develops and supplies data and computer programmes for nuclear technology applications to users in laboratories, industry, universities and other areas of interest. Under the supervision of the Nuclear Science Committee, the Data Bank collates integral experimental data, and functions as part of a network of data centres to provide direct data services. It was responsible for co-ordinating the development of the Joint Evaluation Fission and Fusion (JEFF) data reference library, and works with the Radioactive Waste Management Division of the NEA on the Thermonuclear Database project (see below).

Activities

The NEA's mission is to assist its member countries in maintaining and further developing, through international co-operation, the scientific, technological and legal bases required for the safe, environmentally friendly and economical use of nuclear energy for peaceful purposes. It maintains a continual survey with the co-operation of other organizations, notably the International Atomic Energy Agency (IAEA), of world uranium resources, production and demand, and of economic and technical aspects of the nuclear fuel cycle.

A major part of the Agency's work is devoted to the safety and regulation of nuclear power, including co-operative studies and projects related to the prevention of nuclear accidents and the long-term safety of radioactive waste disposal systems. The Committee on Nuclear Regulatory Activities contributes to developing a consistent and effective regulatory response to current and future challenges. These challenges include operational experience feedback, increased public expectations concerning safety in the use of nuclear energy, industry initiatives to improve economics and inspection practices, the necessity to ensure safety over a plant's entire life cycle, and new reactors and technology. The Committee on the Safety of Nuclear Installations contributes to maintaining a high level of safety performance and safety competence by identifying emerging safety issues through the analysis of operating experience and research results, contributing to their resolution and, when needed, establishing international research projects. The Radioactive Waste Management Committee assists member countries in the management of radioactive waste and materials, focusing on the development of strategies for the safe, sustainable and broadly acceptable management of all types of radioactive waste, in particular long-lived waste and spent fuel. The Committee on Radiation Protection and Public Health, comprising regulators and protection experts, aims to identify new and emerging issues, analyse their impact and recommend action to address issues and to enhance protection regulation and implementation. It is served by various expert groups and a working party on nuclear emergency matters. The Nuclear Development Committee supports member countries in formulating nuclear energy policy, addressing issues of relevance for governments and the industry at a time of nuclear technology renaissance and sustained government interest in ensuring long-term security of energy supply, reducing the risk of global climate change and pursuing sustainable development. The aim of the nuclear science programme is to help member countries to identify, share, develop and disseminate basic scientific and technical knowledge used to ensure safe and reliable operation of current nuclear systems, as well as to develop next-generation technologies. The main areas covered are reactor physics, fuel behaviour, fuel cycle physics and chemistry, critical safety and radiation shielding. The Nuclear Law Committee (NLC) promotes the harmonization of legislation governing the peaceful uses of nuclear energy in member countries and in selected non-member countries. It supports the modernization and strengthening of national and international nuclear liability regimes. Under the supervision of the NLC, the NEA also compiles, analyses and disseminates information on nuclear law through a regular publications programme and organizes the International School of Nuclear Law educational programme. The NEA co-operates with non-member countries of Central and Eastern Europe and the CIS in areas such as nuclear safety, radiation protection and nuclear law.

During 2011–16 the NEA's activities were guided by a strategic plan that focused on nuclear energy and regulation; radioactive waste management; radiological protection and public health; nuclear science; development and use of nuclear energy; legal affairs; Data Bank services; and information and communication.

In January 2005 a policy group of the Generation IV International Forum (GIF) confirmed arrangements under which the NEA would provide technical secretariat support to the GIF, including the funding of this activity by GIF members through voluntary contributions. The GIF is a major international initiative aimed at developing the next generation of nuclear energy systems. In September 2006 the NEA was selected to perform the technical secretariat functions for the Multinational Design Evaluation Programme (MDEP), which had been established to share the resources and knowledge accumulated by national nuclear regulatory authorities during their assessment of new reactor designs, with the aim of improving both the efficiency and the effectiveness of the process.

The NEA offered its support to the Government of Japan in mid-March 2011, following the destabilization of the Fukushima nuclear power plant by an earthquake and tsunami in that month. In response to the Fukushima incident the Agency activated its Flash-news system, facilitating the swift exchange of information among nuclear regulators, and established a Senior-level Task Group to exchange information, co-ordinate activities and examine the implications for future nuclear plant management. In June the NEA and the French G8 presidency jointly organized a Forum on the Fukushima Daiichi Accident: Insights and Approaches. In January 2012 an NEA panel of experts met with members of the Japanese Advisory Committee for the Prevention of Nuclear Accidents and the special Japanese Task Force for the Reform of Nuclear Safety Regulations and Organizations to discuss improving approaches to the regulation and oversight of nuclear facilities. An Integrated NEA Fukushima Actions for Safety Enhancements programme, headed by the Senior-level Task Group, was expected to publish a report in 2013 on its activities focused on specific areas of nuclear safety, including onsite and offsite accident management, crisis communication, regulatory infrastructure, and radiological protection and public health.

In June 2013 the NEA supported the IAEA, and Russian Government, in hosting an International Ministerial Conference on Nuclear Power in the 21st Century, in St Petersburg, Russia; the Conference had a particular focus on the role of nuclear energy in climate change mitigation and on meeting increasing global demand for energy. In November the NEA and China Atomic Energy Authority concluded a Joint Declaration on Co-operation in the Field of Peaceful Uses of Nuclear Energy; a joint workshop on advancing co-operation was convened in February 2014.

JOINT PROJECTS

The NEA supports joint projects and information exchange programmes that enable interested countries to share the costs of pursuing research or the sharing of data, primarily in the areas of nuclear safety, radioactive waste management and radiation protection.

Finance

The Agency's 2013 budget amounted to some €11.1m., while funding of €3.1m. was made available for the Data Bank. These sums may be supplemented by members' voluntary contributions.

Publications

Annual Report.

NEA News (2 a year).

Nuclear Energy Data (annually).

Nuclear Law Bulletin (2 a year).

Publications on a range of issues relating to nuclear energy, reports and proceedings.

ORGANIZATION FOR SECURITY AND CO-OPERATION IN EUROPE—OSCE

Address: Wallnerstrasse 6, 1010 Vienna, Austria.

Telephone: (1) 514-36-0; **fax:** (1) 514-36-96; **e-mail:** info@osce.org; **internet:** www.osce.org.

The OSCE was established in 1972 as the Conference on Security and Co-operation in Europe (CSCE), providing a multilateral forum for dialogue and negotiation. It produced the Helsinki Final Act of 1975 on East–West relations. The areas of competence of the CSCE were expanded by the Charter of Paris for a New Europe (1990), which transformed the CSCE from an ad hoc forum into an organization with permanent institutions, and the Helsinki Document 1992. In December 1994 the summit conference adopted the new name of OSCE, in order to reflect the organization's changing political role and strengthened secretariat.

PARTICIPATING STATES

Albania
Andorra
Armenia
Austria
Azerbaijan
Belarus
Belgium
Bosnia and Herzegovina
Bulgaria
Canada
Croatia
Cyprus
Czech Republic
Denmark
Estonia
Finland
France
Georgia
Germany
Greece
Hungary
Iceland
Ireland
Italy
Kazakhstan
Kyrgyzstan
Latvia
Liechtenstein
Lithuania
Luxembourg
Macedonia, former Yugoslav republic
Malta
Moldova
Monaco
Mongolia
Montenegro
Netherlands
Norway
Poland
Portugal
Romania
Russia
San Marino
Serbia
Slovakia
Slovenia
Spain
Sweden
Switzerland
Tajikistan
Turkey
Turkmenistan
Ukraine
United Kingdom
USA
Uzbekistan
Vatican City (Holy See)

Organization

(April 2014)

SUMMIT CONFERENCES

Heads of state or government of OSCE participating states convene periodically to set priorities and the political orientation of the organization. The sixth conference was held in İstanbul, Turkey, in November 1999. A seventh summit conference was convened, in Astana, Kazakhstan, in December 2010.

MINISTERIAL COUNCIL

The Ministerial Council (formerly the Council of Foreign Ministers) comprises ministers responsible for foreign affairs of member states. It is the central decision-making and governing body of the OSCE and meets every year in which no summit conference is held. The 20th Ministerial Council was held in Kyiv, Ukraine, in December 2013.

PERMANENT COUNCIL

The Council, which is based in Vienna, Austria, is responsible for day-to-day operational tasks. Members of the Council, comprising the permanent representatives of member states to the OSCE, convene weekly. The Council is the regular body for political consultation and decision-making, and may be convened for emergency purposes.

FORUM FOR SECURITY CO-OPERATION

The Forum for Security Co-operation (FSC), comprising representatives of delegations of member states, meets weekly in Vienna to negotiate and consult on measures aimed at strengthening security and stability throughout Europe. Its main objectives are negotiations on arms control, disarmament, and confidence- and security-building measures (CSBMs); regular consultations and intensive co-operation on matters related to security; and the further reduction of the risks of conflict. The FSC is also responsible for the implementation of CSBMs; the preparation of seminars on military doctrine; the holding of annual implementation assessment meetings; and the provision of a forum for the discussion and clarification of information exchanged under agreed CSBMs.

CHAIRPERSON-IN-OFFICE

The OSCE Chairmanship is held by alternate member states, as designated by the Ministerial Council, for a one-year term. The function of the Chairmanship is executed by the Chairperson-in-Office (CiO)—the minister responsible for foreign affairs of the state holding the Chairmanship—who is vested with overall responsibility for executive action. The CiO is supported by a troika comprising also the preceding and incoming Chairpersons, and also by ad hoc steering groups, and by special or personal representatives mandated to address specific issues, crises or conflicts.

Chairperson-in-Office: DIDIER BURKHALTER (Switzerland) (2014).

SECRETARIAT

The Secretariat comprises the following principal elements: the Conflict Prevention Centre; the Transnational Threats Department (comprising an Action against Terrorism Unit, Strategic Police Matters Unit, and Borders Team); the Office of the Special Representative and Co-ordinator for Combating Trafficking in Human Beings; the Office of the Co-ordinator of OSCE Economic and Environmental Activities; the Gender Section; the Training Section; the External Co-operation Section; a Department of Human Resources; and the Department of Management and Finance, responsible for technical and administrative support activities. The OSCE maintains an office in Prague, Czech Republic, which assists with documentation and information activities.

The Secretary-General is appointed by the Ministerial Council for a three-year term of office. The Secretary-General is the representative of the CiO and is responsible for the management of OSCE structures and operations.

Secretary-General: LAMBERTO ZANNIER (Italy).

Co-ordinator of OSCE Economic and Environmental Activities: Dr HALIL YURDAKUL YIGITGÜDEN (Turkey).

Director of Conflict Prevention Centre: ADAM KOBIERACKI (Poland).

Special Representative of the OSCE Chairperson-in-Office for Conflicts: ANDRII DESHCHYTSIA (Ukraine).

Special Representative and Co-ordinator for Combating Trafficking in Human Beings: MARIA GRAZIA GIAMMARINARO (Italy).

OSCE Specialized Bodies

High Commissioner on National Minorities

POB 20062, 2500 EB The Hague, Netherlands; tel. (70) 3125500; fax (70) 3635910; e-mail hcnm@hcnm.org; internet www.osce.org/hcnm.

The office of High Commissioner on National Minorities was established in December 1992. The High Commissioner is an instrument for conflict prevention, tasked with identifying ethnic tensions that have the potential to develop into conflict, thereby endangering peace, stability or relations between OSCE participating states, and to promote their early resolution. The High Commissioner works in confidence and provides strictly confidential reports to the OSCE CiO. The High Commissioner is appointed by the Ministerial Council, on the recommendation of the Senior Council, for a three-year term.

High Commissioner: ASTRID THORS (Finland).

Office for Democratic Institutions and Human Rights (ODIHR)

Aleje Ujazdowskie 19, 00-557 Warsaw, Poland; tel. (22) 520-06-00; fax (22) 520-06-05; e-mail office@odihr.pl; internet www.osce.org/odihr.

Established in July 1999, the ODIHR has responsibility for promoting human rights, democracy and the rule of law. The Office provides a framework for the exchange of information on and the promotion of democracy building, respect for human rights and elections within OSCE states. In addition, it co-ordinates the monitoring of elections and provides expertise and training on constitutional and legal matters. During 2012 the ODIHR deployed election observers to 14 member states.

Director: JANEZ LENARČIČ (Slovenia).

Office of the Representative on Freedom of the Media

Wallnerstrasse 6, 1010 Vienna, Austria; tel. (1) 512-21-450; fax (1) 512-21-459; e-mail pm-fom@osce.org; internet www.osce.org/fom.

The office was established by a decision of the Permanent Council in November 1997 to strengthen the implementation of OSCE commitments regarding free, independent and pluralistic media.

Representative: DUNJA MIJATOVIĆ (Bosnia and Herzegovina).

Parliamentary Assembly

Radhusstraede 1, 1466 Copenhagen K, Denmark; tel. 33-37-80-40; fax 33-37-80-30; e-mail osce@oscepa.dk; internet www.oscepa.org.

In April 1991 parliamentarians from the CSCE countries agreed on the creation of a pan-European parliamentary assembly. Its inaugural session was held in Budapest, Hungary, in July 1992. The Parliamentary Assembly, which is composed of 320 members from 56 parliaments, meets annually. It comprises a Standing Committee, a Bureau and three General Committees and is supported by a Secretariat in Copenhagen, Denmark.

President: RANKO KRIVOCAPIĆ (Montenegro).

Secretary-General: R. SPENCER OLIVER (USA).

OSCE Related Bodies

Court of Conciliation and Arbitration

Villa Rive-Belle, 266 route de Lausanne, 1292 Chambésy, Geneva, Switzerland; tel. 227580025; fax 227582510; e-mail cca.osce@bluewin.ch; internet www.osce.org/cca.

An OSCE Convention on Conciliation and Arbitration, providing for the establishment of the Court, was concluded in 1992 and entered into effect in December 1994. The first meeting of the Court was convened in May 1995. OSCE states that have ratified the Convention may submit a dispute to the Court for settlement by the Arbitral Tribunal or the Conciliation Commission.

President: Prof. CHRISTIAN TOMUSCHAT (Germany).

Joint Consultative Group (JCG)

The states that are party to the Treaty on Conventional Armed Forces in Europe (CFE), which was concluded within the CSCE framework in 1990, established the Joint Consultative Group (JCG). The JCG, which meets in Vienna, Austria, addresses questions relating to compliance with the Treaty; enhancement of the effectiveness of the Treaty; technical aspects of the Treaty's implementation; and disputes arising out of its implementation. There are currently 30 states participating in the JCG.

Open Skies Consultative Commission

The Commission promotes implementation of the Treaty on Open Skies, which was signed by members of NATO and the former members of the Warsaw Pact (with Russia, Belarus, Ukraine and Georgia taking the place of the USSR) in March 1992. Under the accord, aerial reconnaissance missions by one country over another are permitted, subject to regulation. (The 1,000th observation flight authorized under the Treaty took place at the end of August 2013.) Regular meetings of the Commission are serviced by the OSCE Secretariat.

Activities

Since the adoption in 1975 of the Helsinki Final Act the organization has developed commitments in the following three security 'dimensions': politico-military (covering arms control, combating cybercrime, combating terrorism, conflict prevention and resolution, and military and police reform); economic and environmental (covering combating money-laundering, economies, energy, entrepreneurship, environment and good governance); and human (covering elections, freedom of the media and freedom of expression, human rights, Roma and Sinti affairs, rule of law and tolerance). Cross-cutting commitments include national minorities, gender equality and human trafficking.

In July 1990 heads of government of the member countries of the North Atlantic Treaty Organization (NATO) proposed to increase the role of the CSCE 'to provide a forum for wider political dialogue in a more united Europe'. The Charter of Paris for a New Europe, which undertook to strengthen pluralist democracy and observance of human rights, and to settle disputes between participating states by peaceful means, was signed in November.

In December 1993 a Permanent Committee (later renamed the Permanent Council) was established in Vienna, Austria, providing for greater political consultation and dialogue through its weekly meetings. In December 1994 the summit conference redesignated the CSCE as the Organization for Security and Co-operation in Europe and endorsed the role of the organization as the primary instrument for early warning, conflict prevention and crisis management in the region.

In December 2004 the Ministerial Council, meeting in Sofia, Bulgaria, resolved to establish a Panel of Eminent Persons on Strengthening the Effectiveness of the OSCE; the Panel presented its report, comprising some 70 recommendations, to the Permanent Council in June 2005. In December 2008 the Ministerial Council, convened in Helsinki, determined to pursue a high-level dialogue on strengthening the legal framework of the OSCE.

In December 2010 OSCE heads of state and government, meeting in Astana, Kazakhstan, adopted the Astana Commemorative Declaration: Towards a Security Community, which reaffirmed the core principles and commitments of the organization. The Declaration asserted that commitments in the three security dimensions—i.e. politico-military, economic and environmental, and human—are matters of direct and legitimate concern to all participating states. It urged greater efforts to resolve conflicts and to undertake conflict prevention, to update the Vienna Document 1999, and to enhance energy security dialogue.

Meeting in December 2012, in Dublin, Ireland, the Ministerial Council adopted the Helsinki+40 process, a strategic roadmap aimed at strengthening co-operation among member states prior to the commemoration in 2015 of the 40th anniversary of the adoption of the Helsinki Final Act.

POLITICO-MILITARY DIMENSION

In June 1991 the first meeting of the Council of Foreign Ministers (renamed in 1994 as the Ministerial Council), held in Berlin, Germany, adopted a mechanism for consultation and co-operation in the case of emergency situations, to be implemented by the Council of Senior Officials (CSO; subsequently renamed the Senior Council, which was dissolved in 2006, with all functions transferred to the Permanent Council). A separate mechanism regarding the prevention of the outbreak of conflict was also adopted, whereby a country can demand an explanation of 'unusual military activity' in a neighbouring country. These mechanisms were utilized in July 1991 in relation to the armed conflict in Yugoslavia between the Republic of Croatia and the Yugoslav Government. In August a meeting of the CSO resolved to reinforce the CSCE's mission in Yugoslavia and in September the CSO agreed to impose an embargo on the export of armaments to Yugoslavia. In October the CSO determined to establish an observer mission to monitor the observance of human rights in Yugoslavia.

In January 1992 the Council of Foreign Ministers agreed to alter the Conference's rule of decision-making by consensus in order to allow the CSO to take appropriate action against a participating state 'in cases of clear and gross violation of CSCE commitments'. This development was precipitated by the conflict in Yugoslavia, where the Yugoslav Government was held responsible by the majority of CSCE states for the continuation of hostilities, and, consequently, suspended from the grouping. The meeting also agreed that the CSCE should undertake fact-finding and conciliation missions to areas of tension, with the first such mission to be sent to Nagornyi Karabakh, the largely Armenian-populated enclave in Azerbaijan.

The meeting of heads of state and government, held in Helsinki, Finland, in July 1992, adopted the Helsinki Document, in which participating states defined the terms of future CSCE peacekeeping activities. Conforming broadly to UN practice, operations would be undertaken only with the full consent of the parties involved in any conflict and only if an effective ceasefire were in place. The CSCE may request the use of the military resources of NATO, the Commonwealth of Independent States (CIS), the European Union (EU) or other international bodies. The Helsinki Document declared the CSCE a 'regional arrangement' in the sense of Chapter VIII of the UN's Charter, which states that such a regional grouping should attempt to resolve a conflict in the region before referring it to the Security Council.

The December 1994 summit conference, convened in Budapest, Hungary, adopted a Code of Conduct on Politico-Military Aspects of Security, which set out principles to guide the role of the armed forces in democratic societies. In December 1996 the summit conference convened in Lisbon, Portugal, adopted the Lisbon Declaration on a Common and Comprehensive Security Model for Europe for the 21st Century, committing all parties to pursuing measures to ensure regional security.

The Treaty on Conventional Armed Forces in Europe (CFE), which had been negotiated within the framework of the CSCE, was signed in November 1990 by the member states of NATO and of the Warsaw Pact. The Treaty limits non-nuclear air and ground armaments in the signatory countries. The summit conference that was held in Lisbon, in December 1996 agreed to adapt the CFE Treaty, in order to further arms reduction negotiations on a national and territorial basis. In November 1999 a revised CFE Treaty was signed, providing for a stricter system of limitations and increased transparency, which was to be open to other OSCE states not currently signatories. In December 2007 the Russian Government suspended its obligations under the Treaty.

In September 2001 the Secretary-General condemned terrorist attacks perpetrated against targets in the USA, by militant Islamist fundamentalists. In October OSCE member states unanimously adopted a statement in support of the developing US-led global coalition against international terrorism. In December the Ministerial Council, meeting in Romania, approved the Bucharest Plan of Action outlining the organization's contribution to countering terrorism. An Action against Terrorism Unit was established within the Secretariat to co-ordinate and help to implement the counter-terrorism initiatives. A Personal Representative for Terrorism was appointed by the CiO in January 2002. Also in December 2001 the OSCE sponsored, with the then UN Office for Drug Control and Crime Prevention (ODCCP), an International Conference on Security and Stability in Central Asia, held in Bishkek, Kyrgyzstan. The meeting, which was attended by representatives of more than 60 countries and organizations, was concerned with strengthening efforts to counter terrorism and providing effective support to the Central Asian states. At a Ministerial Council meeting held in Porto, Portugal, in December 2002, the OSCE issued a Charter on Preventing Terrorism, which condemned terrorism 'in all its forms and manifestations' and called upon member states to work together to counter, investigate and prosecute terrorist acts. The Charter also acknowledged the links between terrorism, organized crime and trafficking in human beings. At the same time, a political declaration entitled 'Responding to Change' was adopted, in which member states pledged their commitment to mutual co-operation in combating threats to security. The OSCE's first Annual Security Review Conference was held in Vienna, in July 2003. Security issues were also the subject of the Rotterdam Declaration, adopted by some 300 members of the Parliamentary Assembly in July, which stated that it was imperative for the OSCE to maintain a strong field presence and for field missions to be provided with sufficient funding and highly trained staff. It also recommended that the OSCE assume a role in unarmed peacekeeping operations.

In November 1999 OSCE heads of state and of government, convened in İstanbul, Turkey, signed a new Charter for European Security, which aimed to strengthen co-operation with other organizations and institutions concerned with international security and to formalize existing norms regarding the observance of human rights. The Charter focused on measures to improve the operational capabilities of the OSCE in early warning, conflict prevention, crisis management and post-conflict rehabilitation. Accordingly, Rapid Expert Assistance and Co-operation (REACT) teams were to be established to enable the organization to respond rapidly to requests from participating states for assistance in crisis situations. The REACT programme became operational in April 2001. The 1999 summit meeting also adopted a revised Vienna Document on confidence- and security-building measures and a Platform for Co-operative Security as a framework for co-operation with other organizations and institutions concerned with maintaining security in the OSCE area.

In November 2000 an OSCE Document on Small Arms and Light Weapons was adopted, aimed at curtailing the spread of armaments in member states. At a meeting of the Ministerial Council, convened in Maastricht, in December 2003, member states endorsed a document that aimed to address risks to regional security and stability arising from stockpiles of conventional ammunition through, inter alia, detailing practical steps for their destruction.

In June 2009 OSCE ministers responsible for foreign affairs, meeting in an informal session in Greece, inaugurated the Corfu Process to structure further dialogue on future European security. A Ministerial Declaration on the Corfu Process was adopted by the Ministerial Council in December, which determined to use it to strengthen a free, democratic and integrated Europe. The Declaration was to serve as a roadmap for dialogue focusing on OSCE norms, principles and commitments; conflict resolution; arms control and confidence- and security-building regimes; transnational and multidimensional threats and challenges; common economic and environmental challenges; human rights and fundamental freedoms, as well as democracy and the rule of law; and enhancing the OSCE's effectiveness and interaction with other organizations and institutions. In July 2010 a second informal ministerial meeting, convened in Almatı, Kazakhstan, reviewed progress in implementing the Corfu Process, as well as the OSCE's response to insecurity in Kyrgyzstan. Later in that month the Permanent Council endorsed a decision to deploy a 52-member Police Advisory Group to Kyrgyzstan in order to facilitate law enforcement efforts in areas of ethnic unrest.

In December 2011 the Ministerial Council, convened in Vilnius, Lithuania, adopted a decision on 'enhancing OSCE capabilities in early warning, early action, dialogue facilitation, mediation support and post-conflict rehabilitation on an operational level', tasking the Secretary-General with ensuring that the Secretariat's Conflict Prevention Centre assumes the role of focal point for the systematic collection, collation, analysis and assessment of relevant early warning signals, and calling for increased exchange of information and co-ordination between the OSCE executive structures. Other decisions made by the Council included: enhancing engagement with Afghanistan and Partners for Co-operation; addressing transnational threats; strengthening dialogue on transport; and addressing small arms, light weapons and stockpiles of conventional ammunition. During 2011 the Vienna Document 2011 (VDOC11) was formulated, with a focus on increasing openness and transparency relating to military activities conducted inside the OSCE's 'zone of application' (ZOA—comprising all Europe and parts of Central Asia, including territory, air space, and surrounding sea areas); under a process introduced in 2010, known as Vienna Document PLUS (VD PLUS), the Vienna Document was to be updated henceforth at five-yearly intervals.

A new Transnational Threats Department was inaugurated in the Secretariat in 2012, to co-ordinate OSCE's resources in the areas of policing, counter-terrorism, cybersecurity and border security, and to advance co-operation with NATO, the Collective Security Treaty Organization, the Council of Europe and the EU. An informal working group was established to develop confidence-building measures aimed at reducing the risk of conflict arising from the use of information and communications technologies was established in April 2012; an open-ended working group tasked with addressing the conflict cycle was also formed in that year.

ECONOMIC AND ENVIRONMENTAL DIMENSION

In 1993 the first annual OSCE Economic Forum was convened to focus on the transition to and development of free market economies as an essential aspect of democracy building. In November 1997 the position of Co-ordinator of OSCE Economic and Environmental Activities was created. The annual Forum was renamed as the Economic and Environment Forum in May 2007 to incorporate consideration of environmental security matters. The theme of the 22nd Forum, to be concluded in September 2014, in Prague, Czech Republic, was 'Responding to environmental challenges with a view to promoting cooperation and security in the OSCE area'. The first Preparatory Meeting of the 22nd Forum was convened in January (in Vienna, Austria), and the second was to be held in May (in Montreux, Switzerland).

During July 2003 the first OSCE conference on the effects of globalization was convened in Vienna, attended by some 200 representatives from international organizations. Participants called for the advancement of good governance in the public and private sectors, the development of democratic institutions and the creation of conditions that would enable populations to benefit from the global economy.

In July 2012 the 21st annual session of the Parliamentary Assembly, convened in Monaco, adopted the Monaco Declaration, which set out clear plans of action for OSCE, and member governments and parliaments, in the areas of challenges presented by the global economic crisis, human rights and military transparency. The Declaration, inter alia, called on governments to increase green economic investment; warned against the negative long-term potential impact of continued economic austerity measures; urged the full implementation of VDOC11 and urged the further development of the Vienna Document under the VD PLUS process; urged OSCE member countries to set the highest standard in relation to human rights (in this respect, significant focus was placed on the political situation in Ukraine); and demanded the release of all people imprisoned for their political beliefs.

OSCE, with the UN Environment Programme (UNEP) and other agencies, is a partner in the Environment and Security Initiative (ENVSEC), which was established in 2003 to assess and address environmental challenges that might pose security risks in South-Eastern Europe, Eastern Europe, the Southern Caucasus, and Central Asia.

Since 2002 the OSCE, in co-operation with the Secretariat of the Aarhus Convention, at the UN Economic Commission for Europe (ECE), has supported the establishment of Aarhus Centres and Public Environmental Information Centres in member states, through its field offices and through the Office of the Co-ordinator of OSCE Economic and Environmental Activities. An Aarhus Clearinghouse collates information on legislation and practices relevant to the public's right to access environmental data and participate in decision-making on environmental matters.

HUMAN DIMENSION

In 1993 the First Implementation Meeting on Human Dimension Issues took place. The Meeting, for which the ODIHR serves as a secretariat, provides a now annual forum for the exchange of news regarding OSCE commitments in the fields of human rights and democracy. In November 1997 the Office of the Representative on Freedom of the Media was established in Vienna, to support the OSCE's activities in this field.

The ODIHR is mandated to advise and support member states in integrating Roma and Sinti ethnic minorities, and to address emerging challenges confronting those communities, and to support capacity building activities (for example in the areas of education and civil engagement) aimed at empowering them. An OSCE Action Plan on Improving the Situation of Roma and Sinti within the OSCE Area was endorsed by the Ministerial Council in December 2003, and its implementation is reviewed by the ODIHR. During 2012 the OSCE developed a mentoring network aimed at empowering women from migrant, minority, Roma and Sinti communities.

In February 2001 the ODIHR established an Anti-Trafficking Project Fund to help to finance its efforts to combat trafficking in human beings. In December 2003 the Ministerial Council adopted a new Action Plan to Combat Trafficking in Human Beings. The Council approved the appointment of a Special Representative on Combating Trafficking in Human Beings, mandated to raise awareness of the issues and to ensure member governments comply with international procedures and conventions, and the establishment of a special unit within the Secretariat. In July 2004 the Special Representative organized an international conference to consider issues relating to human trafficking, including human rights, labour, migration, organized crime, and minors. Participants agreed to establish an Alliance against Trafficking in Persons, with the aim of consolidating co-operation among international and non-governmental organizations. In December 2011 the Ministerial Council adopted a declaration on combating all forms of human trafficking. In 2012 the OSCE supported nearly 4,000 people vulnerable to the risk of trafficking.

In June 2012 the OSCE organized a high-level conference on internet governance and freedom, in Dublin, Ireland. A further conference on internet freedom was convened in February 2013, in Vienna. In 2012 the Representative on Freedom of the Media intervened more than 150 times, in 38 member states, to address issues including violence against journalists, and harassment of the media.

In late March 2014 the OSCE Representative on Freedom of the Media expressed concern over the freedom of expression implications of the blocking, upon the order of the Prime Minister of Turkey, of access to the social media website Twitter in that country, as well as restrictions imposed by the Turkish authorities on other internet sites, and urged the immediate lifting of the ban. During that month the OSCE Representative also condemned ongoing extreme censorship, and the continuous closure of Ukrainian television channels, within Crimea. Furthermore, she urged the Ukrainian authorities to withdraw demands that national cable television operators should cease transmitting selected channels broadcast from Russia, expressed outrage over the forced resignation of the acting President of the National Television Company of Ukraine, and urged the interim authorities in that country to strengthen the safety of journalists.

During 2012 the OSCE organized training courses for government officials and parliamentarians in several member countries; advised 13 governments on revising legislation and/or making reforms to their judiciaries; supported the participation of women in the democratic process in eight countries; and supported communities in five countries in the area of water management and conflict resolution.

An OSCE Youth Summit was convened in July 2013 (hosted by Ukraine) with participation by more than 500 representatives from member and partner states.

CO-OPERATION

The OSCE maintains regular formal dialogue and co-operation with certain nominated countries. Afghanistan, Australia, Japan, the

Republic of Korea (South Korea), Mongolia and Thailand have the status of 'Asian Partners for Co-operation' with the OSCE, while Algeria, Egypt, Israel, Jordan, Morocco and Tunisia are 'Mediterranean Partners for Co-operation'. In June 2013 Libya applied for Mediterranean Partner for Co-operation status. Regular consultations are held with these countries in order to discuss security issues of common concern. In October 2004 the OSCE deployed a team of observers to monitor the presidential election in Afghanistan, representing the organization's first election mission in a partner country. In October 2008 OSCE participating states and Mediterranean partner countries convened, in Amman, Jordan, at conference level, to discuss regional security. In the following month a conference was held in the Afghan capital, Kabul, to strengthen co-operation between the OSCE and its Asian partner countries. An OSCE-Japan conference, convened in Tokyo, Japan, in June 2009, considered how the OSCE and Asian partner states should best address global security challenges. In December 2010 OSCE heads of state and government resolved to enhance interaction with its Partners for Co-operation. The annual conference of all OSCE Asian Partners for Co-operation was convened in 2011 in Ulan Bator, Mongolia, in May. The December 2011 Ministerial Conference adopted a decision on Partners for Co-operation, which commended the voluntary reform processes ongoing in some Mediterranean partner countries; reaffirmed the OSCE's readiness, through its executive structures, when requested, to assist the Partners for Co-operation in their voluntary implementation of OSCE norms, principles and commitments; decided to enhance the Partnership for Co-operation by broadening dialogue, intensifying political consultations, strengthening practical co-operation and further sharing best practices, according to the needs and priorities identified by the Partners; and determined to strengthen regular high-level dialogue with the Partners.

The OSCE provides technical assistance to the Southeast European Co-operative Initiative.

FIELD OPERATIONS IN CENTRAL AND SOUTH-EASTERN EUROPE

OSCE Mission in Kosovo: 38000 Priština, Beogradska 32; tel. (38) 500162; fax (38) 240711; e-mail press.omik@osce.org; internet www.osce.org/kosovo; f. July 1999 as an integral component of an international operation, led by the UN, with specific responsibility for democracy- and institution-building; succeeded a 2,000-member OSCE Kosovo Verification Mission (KVM), established to monitor compliance with the terms of a ceasefire between Serbian authorities and ethnic Albanian separatists in the formerly autonomous province of Kosovo and Metohija; in 2013 the Mission was operating five regional centres: in Mitrovica/Mitrovice, Pejë/Peć, Prizren, Gjilan/Gnjilane, and Prishtinë/Priština, as well as more than 30 municipal teams throughout Kosovo; helped to establish and/or administer a police training school and inspectorate, an Institute for Civil Administration, the Department for Democratic Governance and Civil Society, the Office of the Ombudsperson, a Kosovo Centre for Public Safety Education and Development and a Press Council; in early 2002 the Mission initiated training sessions for members of the new Kosovo Assembly; in mid-2004 the Mission initiated an Out-of-Kosovo voting scheme to update the voter registration for forthcoming Assembly elections and, following the election in Oct., the Mission, with other partner organizations co-ordinated under an Assembly Support Initiative, implemented an induction programme for newly elected members; the Mission provided technical assistance for the preparation of national and municipal assembly elections, held in Nov. 2007, and, following the new government's unilateral declaration of independence, issued in Feb. 2008, determined to support the country's new institutions, and monitor their work for compliance with human rights standards; following the reconfiguration of the UN operation in Kosovo, and reduction of its field presence, the OSCE Mission has assumed greater responsibility for monitoring and reporting on the security situation and compliance with human rights standards; a Mission report on the functioning of the Kosovo justice system, released in Jan. 2012, found that improvements were still required to establish a fully independent judiciary; in May the Mission undertook a ballot facilitation operation to enable eligible voters to participate in the Serbian presidential and parliamentary elections; in July the Mission reported that, notwithstanding an advanced legislative framework for the protection and promotion of community rights in effect in Kosovo, limited progress had been achieved in implementing this in support of resident Roma, Ashkali and Egyptian communities; and also in supporting returns and reintegration; enhancing the use of multiple official languages and promoting inter-community dialogue; the provision of education; and in the advancement of socio-economic rights; established seven new local public safety committees in multi-ethnic villages in 2012; during 2012–early 2013 the Mission convened a series of workshops to train lawyers in identifying and addressing hate crimes; Head of Mission JEAN-CLAUDE SCHLUMBERGER (France).

OSCE Mission to Bosnia and Herzegovina: 71000 Sarajevo, Fra Andjela Zvizdovica 1; tel. (33) 752100; fax (33) 442479; e-mail info.ba@osce.org; internet www.oscebih.org; f. Dec. 1995 to achieve the objectives of the peace accords for the former Yugoslavia, in particular to oversee the process of democratization; in 2013 had 14 field offices; helped to organize and monitor national elections, held in Sept. 1996, municipal elections, held in Sept. 1997, elections to the National Assembly of the Serb Republic and to the Bosnian Serb presidency in Nov., a general election, conducted in Sept. 1998, and legislative elections held in Nov. 2000; the Mission's responsibility for elections in the country ended in Nov. 2001 when a new permanent Election Commission was inaugurated, to which the Mission was to provide support; other key areas of Mission activity are the promotion of democratic values, monitoring and promoting respect for human rights, strengthening the legal system, assisting with the creation of a modernized, non-discriminatory education system and establishing democratic control over the armed forces; in Sept. 2004 the agreement on confidence- and security-building measures, mandated under the Dayton peace accords, was suspended in acknowledgement of the country's extensive political reforms and in Dec. the Mission transferred its co-chairmanship of the country's Defence Reform Commission (DRC) to the new NATO headquarters in Sarajevo, although representatives of the Mission continued to be involved in work of the DRC; in June 2008 the Mission concluded a long-term legislative strengthening programme; responsibility for a project to promote greater legislative transparency and accessibility, Open Parliament, was transferred to the national Parliament in July 2009; the Mission supports implementation of the sub-regional arms control agreement, although responsibility for inspection missions was assumed by the national armed forces from Jan. 2010; in 2012 the Mission opened an Aarhus Centre in Sarajevo, to further the environmental agenda; the Mission initiated in Oct. an online mapping tool that collects data on hate crimes, responses to these, and related preventative measures; launched in Feb. 2014 an interactive internet-based War Crimes Case Map; the Mission implements a 'Local First' initiative, aimed at strengthening citizens' participation in local democracy; Head of Mission FLETCHER M. BURTON (USA).

OSCE Mission to Montenegro: 81000 Podgorica, Bul. Svetog Petra Cetinjskog bb; tel. (81) 401401; fax (81) 406431; internet www.osce.org/montenegro; f. June 2006 following the country's declaration of independence from Serbia; in March 2011 the Mission organized a regional conference of ministers responsible for justice and interior affairs in order to strengthen co-operation in judicial and policing matters; in Dec. the Head of Mission and the Montenegro Ministry of Justice concluded a Memorandum of Understanding on judicial reform; in 2012 assisted the Montenegro authorities with the full implementation of legislation governing free access to information; supported in 2012 the implementation of a new criminal procedure code, and assisted the government with the preparation of a new border management strategy; the Mission concluded, in April 2013, an agreement with the Montenegro Government on strengthening OSCE mechanisms of support relating to the promotion of human and minority rights; Head of Mission JANINA HREBICKOVA (Czech Republic).

OSCE Mission to Serbia: 11000 Belgrade, Čakorska 1; tel. (11) 3606100; fax (11) 3606119; e-mail ppiu-serbia@osce.org; internet www.osce.org/serbia; f. Jan. 2001 as the OSCE Mission to the Federal Republic of Yugoslavia (FRY, renamed the OSCE Mission to Serbia and Montenegro in 2003 and divided into two separate Missions in June 2006); the initial mandate of the Mission was to assist in the areas of democracy and protection of human rights and in the restructuring and training of law enforcement agencies and the judiciary, to provide advice to government authorities with regard to reform of the media, and, in close co-operation with the United Nations High Commissioner for Refugees, to facilitate the return of refugees to and from neighbouring countries as well as within the FRY; until Dec. 2011 the Mission provided on-site field support to the Basic Police Training Centre in Sremska Kamenica; in March 2002 the Mission facilitated the census process in southern Serbia; the Mission has supported the formulation and implementation of new procedures to counter organized crime; supports the activities of the Citizen's Protector/Ombudsman, the Commissioner for the Protection of Equality and the Judicial Training Academy; in 2013 the Mission had an office in Bujanovac, southern Serbia, a training facility in Novi Pazar, and an advanced police training centre in Zemun; Head of Mission PETER BURKHARD (Switzerland).

OSCE Presence in Albania: Sheraton Tirana Hotel & Towers, 1st Floor, Sheshi 'Italia', Tirana; tel. (4) 2235993; fax (4) 2235994; e-mail pm-al@osce.org; internet www.osce.org/albania; f. in March 1997 to help to restore political and civil stability, which had been undermined by the collapse of national pyramid saving schemes at the start of the year; from March 1998 to the conclusion of a political settlement for Kosovo and Metohija in mid-1999 the Presence was mandated to monitor the country's borders with the Kosovan region of southern Serbia and to prevent any spillover effects from the escalating crisis; from Sept. 1998 the Presence became the Co-Chair., with the EU, of the international Friends of Albania group; in accordance with an updated mandate, approved in Dec. 2003, the Presence provides advice and support to the Albanian Government regarding democratization, the rule of law, the media, human rights, anti-trafficking, weapons collection, election preparation and monitoring, and the development of civil society; it supports an Economics and Environment Unit and an Elections Unit, which is facilitating the process of electoral reform, including the modernization of the civil registration system; in 2010 the Presence assisted the Albanian Government with drafting legislation concerning parliamentary oversight of the intelligence and security services, and in 2011 it extended technical assistance to the Central Elections Commission in preparing for local government elections, that were conducted in May; the Presence co-organized, in July 2012, jointly with the Albanian authorities, a conference on the development of parliamentary ethical standards and codes, and welcomed, shortly afterwards, the adoption by the Albanian legislature of an amended electoral code—founded on recommendations made by OSCE/ODIHR—while urging its full implementation with respect to parliamentary elections that were held in June 2013; in Feb. 2013 the Presence and OSCE/ODIHR organized an event aimed at encouraging women to compete for leadership roles in the democratic process; in Oct. the Presence organized a regional conference aimed at strengthening co-operation in combating anti-money laundering, corrupton and the financing of terrorism; Head of Presence FLORIAN RAUNIG (Austria).

OSCE Spillover Monitor Mission to Skopje: MK-1000 Skopje, 11 Oktomvri str. 25, QBE Bldg; tel. (2) 3234000; fax (2) 3234234; e-mail info-MK@osce.org; internet www.osce.org/skopje; f. Sept. 1992 to help to prevent the conflict in the former Yugoslavia from destabilizing the former Yugoslav republic of Macedonia, with an initial mandate of overseeing the border region, monitoring human rights and promoting the development of democratic institutions, including an independent media; supports implementation of the Ohrid Framework Agreement, signed in Aug. 2001, initially through the deployment of international confidence-building monitors and police advisers, the recruitment and training of police cadets, and measures to strengthen local self-government; since 2002 the Mission has supported the Office of the Ombudsman, and in June 2007 it initiated a second phase of the support project, including a new public awareness campaign; in early 2009 the Mission worked to strengthen the integrity of the electoral process for presidential and municipal elections that were conducted in March; in April 2010 Skopje missions of the OSCE, the EU, NATO and the USA reiterated the need for full commitment to the Ohrid Framework Agreement and for reinforced political dialogue; a short-term OSCE observer mission monitored parliamentary elections held in June 2011; in July the Mission organized a regional conference on the introduction of legal aid and the improvement of practices to promote access to justice throughout South-Eastern Europe; in March 2012 the Head of Mission condemned recent violent incidents in Skopje; during 2012 the Mission undertook activities aimed at strengthening the capacity of the Ministry of the Interior of the former Yugoslav Republic of Macedonia to address transnational threats, including organizing specialized courses on the role of intelligence-gathering in combating terrorism, and training police officers active in counter-intelligence; the Mission organized roundtable discussions in 18 municipalities during Feb. 2013, with a view to promoting the peaceful and free conduct of local elections that were held in March; Head of Mission RALF BRETH (Germany).

FIELD OPERATIONS IN EASTERN EUROPE AND CENTRAL ASIA

An OSCE Mission to Georgia was established in 1992 to work towards a political settlement between disputing factions within the country. The Mission's mandate was expanded to include monitoring Georgia's borders with Chechnya (in December 1999), Ingushetia (in December 2001), and Dagestan (January 2003). In June 2006 OSCE participating states pledged more than €10m. in support of projects for social and economic rehabilitation in the zone of the Georgian–Ossetian conflict. In August 2008 intensive fighting broke out when Georgian forces entered South Ossetia and attempted to seize control of its capital, Tskhinvali. The resulting counter-attack by Ossetian troops, supported by additional Russian land and air forces, contributed to extensive civilian casualties, population displacement and damage to the region's infrastructure. The OSCE participated in diplomatic efforts to secure a ceasefire and expanded the Mission to Georgia by 100 unarmed military monitoring officers. In October the OSCE met with senior representatives of the UN and EU, in Geneva, Switzerland, to consider the stability and security of the region and the situation of displaced persons. The Mission to Georgia was terminated upon the expiry of its mandate on 31 December 2008, owing to Russia's insistence that the Mission could only be continued with a new mandate excluding any arrangement sustaining Georgia's territorial claims on South Ossetia and Abkhazia, and Georgia's opposition to this. In February 2009, however, the OSCE Permanent Council agreed to extend, until 30 June, the mandate of the OSCE unarmed monitors in Georgia. During 2011–13 the OSCE and UNDP undertook a joint ammunition demilitarization and community security programme in Georgia. An OSCE/ODIHR election observation team observed legislative elections held in Georgia in October 2012; the elections were found to have significantly consolidated democracy, although the team considered the campaigning environment to have been tense and not to have focused sufficiently on concrete political programmes. OSCE/ODIHR deployed an election observation mission to monitor a presidential election held in Georgia in October 2013. The OSCE co-chairs, with the EU and UN, the Geneva International Discussions on Georgia, which have been held regularly since late 2008 to address the consequences of the conflict; the 27th session of the Discussions was convened in March 2014.

In February 2014 the OSCE CiO appointed a Personal Envoy on Ukraine to co-ordinate on the ground, on behalf of the Chairmanship, all ongoing and planned OSCE activities there. In early March 2014 the interim authorities in Ukraine requested the OSCE to send unarmed military observers to visit the autonomous Crimea peninsula, where Russian forces and pro-Russian local militia had seized control of military bases and other strategic locations. The 40-member observer mission was, however, prevented from entering and deploying in the region. The CiO declared as illegal (in relation to both the Ukraine Constitution and relevant international law) the referendum that was held within Crimea on 16 March on secession from Ukraine. On 21 March the OSCE Permanent Council determined immediately to deploy a full OSCE Special Monitoring Mission, initially comprising 100 civilian monitors, throughout Ukraine, for a period of at least six months. The Mission was tasked with gathering information on human rights, assessing the security situation, and fostering dialogue. At that time the OSCE ODIHR established an election mission to observe the conduct of the presidential election scheduled to take place in Ukraine in May. In early April the OSCE Secretary-General expressed concern over mounting violent political unrest in eastern Ukraine, while urging the pursuit of peaceful dialogue. In mid-April the OSCE CiO welcomed the Geneva Statement issued jointly by the ministers of foreign affairs of Russia, Ukraine and the USA, and the High Representative of the EU for Foreign Affairs and Security Policy, which agreed various measures aimed at de-escalating the crisis in Ukraine. The CiO emphasized that the OSCE Special Monitoring Mission was ready to take on responsibility assigned to it under the Statement for assisting the Ukrainian authorities and local communities with the implementation of the agreed measures.

OSCE Centre in Aşgabat: 744005 Aşgabat, Türkmenbasi Shayoly 15, Turkmenistan; tel. (12) 35-30-92; fax (12) 35-30-41; e-mail info_tm@osce.org; internet www.osce.org/ashgabat; f. Jan. 1999 (following a decision of the Permanent Council, in July 1998, to establish a permanent presence in the country); works to support greater collaboration between the authorities and the OSCE and the implementation of OSCE principles, to facilitate contacts with other local and international institutions and organizations working in the region and to assist in arranging regional seminars, events and visits by OSCE personnel; in April 2012 the Centre supported the establishment of a centre in Aşgabat for victims of domestic violence; seminars organized by the Centre in early 2014 addressed gender equality and journalism education; Head of Centre IGO PETROV (Bulgaria).

OSCE Centre in Astana: 010000 Astana, Beibitshilik 10, Kazakhstan; tel. (7172) 32-68-04; fax (7172) 32-83-04; internet www.osce.org/astana; f. June 2007, as successor to an OSCE Centre in Almatı (f. Jan. 1999); mandated to support greater co-operation between the authorities and the OSCE, as well as the implementation of OSCE principles, to facilitate contacts with other local and international institutions and organizations working in the region, to assist in arranging regional seminars, events and visits by OSCE personnel, and to support the Government of Kazakhstan, for example by training officials and raising awareness of OSCE activities; in Jan. 2012 an OSCE/ODIHR observation team monitored legislative elections held in Kazakhstan; the team recommended, in a report released in Sept., the promotion of greater respect for rights of expression, assembly and association, and greater transparency; in June a multi-ethnic policing project was launched, to be implemented jointly by the Centre and the Kazakhstan Government; matters addressed by seminars and courses organized by the Centre in early 2014 included training for judges in combating trafficking in human beings; countering illegal drugs; penal legislation reform; and countering terrorist use of the internet; Head of Centre NATALIA ZARUDNA (Ukraine).

OSCE Centre in Bishkek: 720001 Bishkek, Toktogula 139, Kyrgyzstan; tel. (312) 66-50-15; fax (312) 66-31-69; e-mail pm-kg@osce.org; internet www.osce.org/bishkek; f. Jan. 1999 (following a decision of the Permanent Council, in July 1998, to establish a permanent presence in the country); works to support greater collaboration between the authorities and the OSCE and the implementation of OSCE principles, to facilitate contacts with other local and international institutions and organizations working in the region and to assist in arranging regional seminars, events and visits by OSCE personnel; established a field office in Osh, in 2000, to oversee operations in Kyrgyzstan's southern provinces; supports the OSCE Academy in Bishkek, which was inaugurated in Dec. 2002 as a regional centre for training, research and dialogue, in particular in security-related issues (the Academy has, since 2008, and most recently in Sept. 2013, hosted an annual regional security seminar; following an escalation of civil and political tensions after legislative elections in Feb.–March 2005, the Centre offered to provide a forum for dialogue between the authorities and opposition groups; following political upheaval and civil and ethnic violence in April and June 2010 the Centre worked closely with the interim authorities to alleviate political tension and to promote dialogue and reconciliation; in Sept. the Centre facilitated contacts between political and non-governmental groups and the Head of an OSCE Police Advisory Group, which was deployed from Jan. 2011 in a primarily consultative role; prior to parliamentary elections, held in Oct. 2010, the Centre worked to ensure compliance with an electoral Code of Conduct; the Centre's activities are focused on the following six strategic priority areas: border security and management, including customs training; rule of law; good governance; legislation; environmental protection; and regional co-operation; in March 2012 the Centre co-hosted, jointly with the World Bank, UN Office on Drugs and Crime and the Kyrgyz Government, a workshop on assessing the risk of money-laundering; organized in July an expert meeting for representatives of regional anti-terrorism agencies; convened in April 2013, jointly with OSCE/ODIHR, a roundtable discussion on means of enhancing female participation in political parties, and in Sept. supported a roundtable discussion on the legal and practical aspects of safeguarding freedom of religion or belief; in Aug. the Centre launched a programme aimed at strengthening Kyrgyzstan's capabilities to manage and control small arms and light weapons, as well as stockpiles of conventional ammunition; in Sept. 2013 the Centre signed a Memorandum of Understanding with the Kyrgyzstan State Customs Service on establishing a training centre for customs officials from Kyrgyzstan and Afghanistan; Head of Centre SERGEY KAPINOS (Russia).

OSCE Mission to Moldova: 2012 Chişinău, str. Mitropolit Dosoftei 108; tel. (22) 22-34-95; fax (22) 22-34-96; e-mail moldova@osce.org; internet www.osce.org/moldova; f. Feb. 1993, in order to assist conflicting parties in that country to pursue negotiations on a political settlement for the Transniestrian region, as well as to observe the military situation in the region and to provide advice on issues of human and minority rights, democratization and the repatriation of refugees; the Mission's mandate was expanded in Dec. 1999 to ensure the full removal and destruction of Russian ammunition and armaments and to co-ordinate financial and technical assistance for the withdrawal of foreign troops and the destruction of weapons; in June 2001 the Mission established a tripartite working group, with representatives of the Russian Ministry of Defence and the local authorities in Transnistria, to assist and support the process of disposal of munitions; destruction of heavy weapons began in mid-2002, under the supervision of the Mission; in March 2006 the OSCE CiO expressed concern at the situation along the Transnistrian section of the Moldovan–Ukrainian state border and instructed the Mission to pursue a solution by consulting with all relevant parties; in Jan. 2007 representatives of the OSCE, Russia and Ukraine met, with observers from the EU and USA (i.e. the so-called 5+2 negotiation format), to consider the future of the settlement process and invited chief negotiators from the Moldovan and Transnistrian authorities to initiate mediated discussions in the following month; in Oct. the Mission organized a high-level seminar on confidence- and security-building measures, in support of peace negotiations between Moldova and Transnistria, and in April 2008 the Mission organized a seminar on economic and environmental confidence-building measures, held in Odesa, Ukraine; in Feb. 2009 a Special Representative of the CiO for Protracted Conflicts visited Moldova to promote a resumption of the Transnistrian peace negotiations; an agreement to revive the process was signed by leaders of both sides, meeting in Moscow, Russia, in March; in April the Head of Mission condemned violent demonstrations that occurred following legislative elections; the Mission and the OSCE CiO convened a seminar in June on confidence- and security-building measures in Moldova, with participation by experts and 5+2 process participants; a Trial Monitoring Programme was conducted by the Mission with ODIHR, between March 2006 and Dec. 2009, to observe and enhance Moldova's compliance with OSCE commitments and international legal standards; in June 2010 the Mission signed a Memorandum of Understanding with the Moldovan Government to implement a four-year social integration project for former military personnel from the Transniestrian region; the initiative commenced in Sept; in Feb. 2011 an informal meeting of participants in the 5+2 settlement process agreed a work plan for that year, which included greater bilateral contact, pursuing other confidence-building measures, and resolving outstanding problems of freedom of movement; a further informal round of consultations was held in June, in Moscow; a limited OSCE/ODIHR election observation team was dispatched in May to monitor local elections conducted in the following month; in Sept. an agreement was concluded to restart official talks between the political leaders within the 5+2 framework, which were then initiated, at a meeting in Vilnius, Lithuania, in Nov.; formal meetings subsequently convened in Dublin, in Feb. 2012 and in Vienna, in April, were concerned with the principles and procedures for the negotiating process, and concluded that the dialogue should focus on socio-economic issues, legal issues, humanitarian issues and human rights, and institutional, political and security matters; thereafter meetings were held regularly during 2012–early 2014; in Feb. 2014, in Vienna, a protocol was concluded permitting freedom of movement for permanent residents of Transniestria possessing (non-Moldovan) foreign passports; in July a three-year OSCE-UN Economic Commission for Europe project was initiated which aimed to develop a climate-change adaptation strategy for the Dniester/Nistru basin; Mission offices opened in Tiraspol, in Feb. 1995, and in Bender, in May 2003; Head of Mission JENNIFER LEIGH BRUSH (USA).

OSCE Office in Tajikistan: 734017 Dushanbe, Zikrullo Khojaev 12, Tajikistan; tel. (372) 24-33-38; fax (372) 24-91-59; e-mail cid-tj@osce.org; internet www.osce.org/tajikistan; f. June 2008, as successor to the OSCE Centre in Dushanbe, with an expanded mandate to support the country in efforts to promote the implementation of OSCE principles and commitments, to maintain peace and security, to counter crime, to undertake economic and environmental activities and to develop democratic political and legal institutions, incorporating respect for human rights; a Task Force Meeting, comprising OSCE officials, and representatives of the Tajik Government and civil society, convenes annually to consider the strategic partnership between the OSCE and Tajikistan; the Office implements a Mine Action Programme, initiated in 2004, and in April 2010 inaugurated a new integrated landmine clearance project along the border with Afghanistan; the Office supported the establishment of a human rights ombudsman, and hosts monthly inter-agency human rights sector meetings and an annual Human Dimension Implementation Meeting, attended by representatives of Government and civil society; a counter-terrorism and police unit assists the local law enforcement agencies to combat organized crime, including drugs-trafficking, and terrorism; in May 2009 an OSCE Border Management Staff College (BMSC) was established in Dushanbe to train border security managers and to promote co-operation between OSCE member states and partner countries; in April 2012 the BMSC organized a training course on the implementation of UN Security Council Resolution 1540 concerning the non-proliferation of weapons of mass destruction; in March 2010 the Office signed a Memorandum of Understanding with Tajikistan's Ministry of Economic Development and Trade establishing a Co-ordination Council on Free Economic Zones; the Office facilitates a Dialogue on Human Trafficking, which during 2010, developed a National Action Plan to Combat Human Trafficking; in June 2012 the Office conducted a training course on electoral management for members of Tajikistan's Central Commission for Elections and Referenda; a five-week course to train Tajik and Afghan border officers in detecting and interdicting illegal cross-border movements was organized in Aug.–Sept. 2013; the Office convened in Oct. a roundtable on the use of explosives by terrorists; Head of Office MARKUS MÜLLER (Switzerland).

OSCE Office in Yerevan: 0009 Yerevan, ul. Terian 89, Armenia; tel. (10) 54-58-45; fax (10) 54-10-61; e-mail yerevan-am@osce.org; internet www.osce.org/yerevan; f. July 1999 (began operations in Feb. 2000); the Office works independently of the Minsk Group to promote OSCE principles within the country in order to support political and economic stability, the development of democratic institutions and the strengthening of civil society; a police assistance programme was initiated in 2004, which oversaw the renovation of a police training centre; promotes awareness of human rights, assists the Human Rights Defender's Office and supports Public Monitoring Groups concerned with detention centres; other areas of activity concern legislative reform and good governance, freedom of the media, gender issues and counter-terrorism and money-laundering; in May 2009 the Office, with other partners, organized a high-level forum concerned with discussing Armenian economic policy and addressing the local impact of the global financial crisis; during 2012 the Office provided support to enhance the capacity of the Armenian Human Rights Defender's Office prior to legislative elections held in May of that year (subsequently found by OSCE/ODIHR to have been conducted in a competitive and overall peaceful manner), and a presidential election that was staged in Feb. 2013; the Office assisted the Armenian police in developing a new website, which was launched in Sept. 2012, with the aim of providing greater transparency and enhancing police-citizen interaction; in March 2012 the Head of Office signed a Memorandum of Understanding with Yerevan State University on establishing a Sustainable Development Centre within the University, to support Armenia in implementing UN declarations on sustainable development; in 2013 the Office organized training and workshops in areas including the use of biometric passports to curb the movement of terrorists, public order management, online reporting ethics, civic activism and female political participation, and the use of explosives by terrorists; Head of Office ANDREY SOROKIN (Russia).

OSCE Project Co-ordinator in Baku: 1005 Baku, Nizami küç 96, The Landmark III, Azerbaijan; tel. (12) 497-23-73; fax (12) 497-23-77; e-mail office-az@osce.org; internet www.osce.org/baku; f. Nov. 1999 (as OSCE Office in Baku, began operations in July 2000) to undertake activities concerned with democratization, human rights, economy and the environment, and media; supports a police assistance programme, including a police training school; supports the training of legal professionals and monitors court proceedings and conditions in prisons; workshops and seminars organized by the Office in 2013 were concerned with, inter alia, promoting respect for the rights of detainees, countering human-trafficking, journalists' safety, biodiversity, and, in Aug., in advance of a presidential election held in Oct., non-interference in electoral processes; from 1 Jan. 2014 the Office was redesignated as the OSCE Project Co-ordinator in Baku; Project Co-ordinator ALEXIS CHAHTAHTINSKY (France).

OSCE Project Co-ordinator in Ukraine: 01054 Kyiv, vul. Striletska 16; tel. (44) 492-03-82; fax (44) 492-03-83; internet www.osce.org/ukraine; f. June 1999, as a successor to the OSCE Mission to Ukraine (which had been established in Nov. 1994); responsible for pursuing co-operation between Ukraine and the OSCE and providing technical assistance in areas including legal and electoral reform, freedom of the media, trafficking in human beings, and the work of the human rights Ombudsman; the Project Co-ordinator has developed a Cross-Dimensional Economic-Environmental/Politico-Military Programme, in co-operation with the Ukrainian authorities, in support of the country's objectives of closer integration into European structures; the Programme incorporates activities such as strengthening border security, enhancing national capacity to combat illegal transboundary transportation of hazardous waste, promoting the sustainable management of the Dniestr River basin, and supporting the retraining and integration into civil society of military personnel; a new draft unified Election Code, developed with the support of the Project Co-ordinator, was presented to the Ukrainian parliament in April 2010; convenes an annual roundtable meeting aimed at promoting joint efforts in combating human trafficking between the Ukrainian authorities and diplomatic missions based in Kyiv; in advance of legislative elections that were held at the end of Oct. 2012 the Project Co-ordinator conducted seminars to train administrative court judges in election legislation, supporting the launch (in Oct.) of an internet-based resource aimed at supporting the training of election officials, and implementing an election awareness campaign; in April 2013 the Project Co-ordinator and Ukraine Central Election Commission (CEC) organized a conference in Kyiv to address the proposed development of a training framework for Commission members; in July the Project Co-ordinator, jointly with the CEC, launched a new online training system for election commissioners; from mid-March 2014, at the request of the Ukraine interim authorities, a 15-member team of experts was deployed, under the supervision of the Project Co-ordinator, to identify productive areas for OSCE activities aimed at supporting confidence-building and reconciliation between different elements of Ukrainian society; Project Co-ordinator MADINA JARBUSSYNOVA (Kazakhstan).

OSCE Project Co-ordinator in Uzbekistan: 100000 Tashkent, Afrosiab ko'ch 12B, 4th Floor; tel. (71) 140-04-70; fax (71) 140-04-66; e-mail osce-cit@osce.org; internet www.osce.org/uzbekistan; f. July 2006; works to assist the Government to uphold security and stability, to strengthen socio-economic development and protection of the environment, and to implement other OSCE principles; in Feb. 2011 the Project Co-ordinator formally provided the Uzbek authorities with equipment to implement improvements to the national passport system; training courses and seminars organized by the Project Co-ordinator in 2013 focused, inter alia, on international human rights standards, anti-money-laundering standards, and combating trafficking in illicit drugs and promoting renewable energy; Project Co-ordinator GYÖRGY SZABÓ (Hungary).

Personal Representative of the OSCE Chairperson-in-Office on the Conflict Dealt with by the OSCE Minsk Conference (Nagornyi Karabakh): Tbilisi, Zovreti 15, Georgia; tel. (32) 37-61-61; fax (32) 98-85-66; e-mail persrep@access.sanet.ge; internet www.osce.org/prcio; appointed in Aug. 1995 to represent the CiO in the 11-nation Minsk Group process concerned with the conflict between Armenia and Azerbaijan in relation to the Nagornyi Karabakh region; in 2005–06 the Minsk Group undertook intensive negotiations to formulate a set of basic principles for a peaceful settlement of the conflict, including proposals for the redeployment of Armenian troops, demilitarization of formally occupied territories and a popular referendum to determine the final legal status of the region; in Nov. 2007 the Co-chairs of the Minsk Group presented a Document of Basic Principles for the Peaceful Settlement of the Nagornyi Karabakh Conflict, which has been the basis of subsequent discussions with both sides; in Sept. 2011 the Minsk Group Co-chairs announced a work plan focused on delineating ongoing differences concerning the basic principles; and drafting additional measures aimed at strengthening implementation of the ceasefire implemented since May 1994 in Nagornyi Karabakh; the Minsk Group Co-chairs liaised frequently in 2012–early 2014; the Personal Representative is mandated to assist a High Level Planning Group, which was established in Vienna, to develop a plan for a multinational OSCE peacekeeping operation in the disputed region; Field Assistants of the Personal Representative have been deployed to Baku, Yerevan and Stepanakert/Khankendi; Personal Rep. ANDRZEJ KASPRZYK (Poland); Head of the High Level Planning Group Col MARKUS WIDMER (Switzerland).

OSCE Special Monitoring Mission in Ukraine: established in late March 2014, for a period of at least six months, and tasked with assessing the security situation in Ukraine, gathering information on human rights, and fostering dialogue; initially comprised 100 civilian monitors, with further expansion, to up to 500 monitors, envisaged; by April 10 advance teams had been deployed, to Chernivtsi, Dnepropetrovsk, Donetsk, Ivano-Frankivsk, Kharkiv, Kherson, Kyiv, Luhansk, Lviv and Odessa; from mid-April the Mission was to support the Ukrainian authorities and local communities with the implementation of measures provided for under the Geneva Statement, agreed at that time by the foreign ministers of Russia, Ukraine and the USA, and the High Representative of the EU for Foreign Affairs and Security Policy; Chief Monitor ERTOGRÜL APAKAN (Turkey).

Finance

All activities of the institutions, negotiations, ad hoc meetings and missions are financed by contributions from member states. The unified budget for 2013, adopted in February 2013 by the Permanent Council, amounted to €144.8m.

Publications

Annual Report of the Secretary-General.

The Caucasus: In Defence of the Future.

Decision Manual (annually).

OSCE Handbook.

OSCE Highlights (regular electronic newsletter).

OSCE Newsletter (quarterly, in English and Russian).

Factsheets on OSCE missions, institutions and other structures are published regularly.

ORGANIZATION OF AMERICAN STATES—OAS

(ORGANIZACIÓN DE LOS ESTADOS AMERICANOS—OEA)

Address: 17th St and Constitution Ave, NW, Washington, DC 20006, USA.

Telephone: (202) 370-5000; **fax:** (202) 458-6319; **e-mail:** websection@oas.org; **internet:** www.oas.org.

The ninth International Conference of American States (held in Bogotá, Colombia, in 1948) adopted the Charter of the Organization of American States, creating a successor to the Commercial Bureau of American Republics, founded in 1890, and the Pan-American Union. The purpose of the OAS is to strengthen the peace and security of the continent; to promote human rights and to promote and consolidate representative democracy, with due respect for the principle of non-intervention; to prevent possible causes of difficulties and to ensure the peaceful settlement of disputes that may arise among the member states; to provide for common action in the event of aggression; to seek the solution of political, juridical and economic problems that may arise among the member states; to promote, by co-operative action, their economic, social and cultural development; to achieve an effective limitation of conventional weapons; to devote the largest amount of resources to the economic and social development of the member states; and to confront shared problems such as poverty, terrorism, the trade in illegal drugs, and corruption. The OAS plays a leading role in implementing mandates established by the hemisphere's leaders through the Summits of the Americas.

MEMBERS

Antigua and Barbuda	Guyana
Argentina	Haiti
Bahamas	Honduras
Barbados	Jamaica
Belize	Mexico
Bolivia	Nicaragua
Brazil	Panama
Canada	Paraguay
Chile	Peru
Colombia	Saint Christopher and Nevis
Costa Rica	Saint Lucia
Cuba*	Saint Vincent and the Grenadines
Dominica	Suriname
Dominican Republic	Trinidad and Tobago
Ecuador	USA
El Salvador	Uruguay
Grenada	Venezuela
Guatemala	

* The Cuban Government was suspended from OAS activities in 1962; the suspension was revoked by the OAS General Assembly in June 2009, although Cuba's participation in the organization was to be subject to further review.

Permanent Observers: Albania, Algeria, Angola, Armenia, Austria, Azerbaijan, Belgium, Benin, Bosnia and Herzegovina, Bulgaria, People's Republic of China, Croatia, Cyprus, Czech Republic, Denmark, Egypt, Equatorial Guinea, Estonia, Finland, France, Georgia, Germany, Ghana, Greece, Holy See, Hungary, Iceland, India, Ireland, Israel, Italy, Japan, Kazakhstan, Republic of Korea, Latvia, Lebanon, Lithuania, Luxembourg, Monaco, Morocco, Netherlands, Nigeria, Norway, Pakistan, Philippines, Poland, Portugal, Qatar, Romania, Russia, Saudi Arabia, Serbia, Slovakia, Slovenia, Spain, Sri Lanka, Sweden, Switzerland, Thailand, Tunisia, Turkey, Ukraine, United Kingdom, Vanuatu, Yemen and the European Union.

Organization

(April 2014)

GENERAL ASSEMBLY

The Assembly meets annually and may also hold special sessions when convoked by the Permanent Council. As the highest decision-making body of the OAS, it decides general action and policy. In March 2013 an Extraordinary General Assembly was convened at the OAS headquarters in Washington, DC, USA, to consider means of strengthening the Inter-American human rights system. The 43rd regular session of Assembly was hosted by Guatemala, in Antigua, in June 2013, and the 44th Assembly was to be convened in Asunción, Paraguay, in June 2014.

MEETINGS OF CONSULTATION OF MINISTERS OF FOREIGN AFFAIRS

Meetings are convened, at the request of any member state, to consider problems of an urgent nature and of common interest to member states, or to serve as an organ of consultation in cases of armed attack or other threats to international peace and security. The Permanent Council determines whether a meeting should be convened and acts as a provisional organ of consultation until ministers are able to assemble.

PERMANENT COUNCIL

The Council meets regularly throughout the year at the OAS headquarters comprising representatives of each member state with the rank of ambassador. The office of Chairman is held in turn by each of the representatives, following alphabetical order according to the names of the countries in Spanish. The Vice-Chairman is determined in the same way, following reverse alphabetical order. Their terms of office are three months.

The Council guides ongoing policies and actions and oversees the maintenance of friendly relations between members. It supervises the work of the OAS and promotes co-operation with a variety of other international bodies including the UN. It comprises a General Committee and Committees on Juridical and Political Affairs, Hemispheric Security, Inter-American Summits Management and Civil Society Participation in OAS Activities, and Administrative and Budgetary Affairs. There are also ad hoc working groups.

In January 2012 the Secretary-General presented to the Permanent Council 'A Strategic Vision of the OAS', proposing a refocusing of its core tasks, prioritizing mandates in accordance with the principal strategic objectives, and a rationalization of the use of its financial resources.

GENERAL SECRETARIAT

The Secretariat, the central and permanent organ of the organization, performs the duties entrusted to it by the General Assembly, Meetings of Consultation of Ministers of Foreign Affairs and the Councils. The work of the General Secretariat is undertaken by a Secretariat for Political Affairs; the Executive Secretariat of Integral Development; the Secretariat for Multidimensional Security; the Secretariat for Administration and Finance; the Secretariat for Legal Affairs; and the Secretariat for External Relations. There is an Administrative Tribunal, comprising six elected members, to settle staffing disputes.

Secretary-General: JOSÉ MIGUEL INSULZA (Chile).

Assistant Secretary-General: ALBERT R. RAMDIN (Suriname).

INTER-AMERICAN COUNCIL FOR INTEGRAL DEVELOPMENT (CIDI)

The Council was established in 1996, replacing the Inter-American Economic and Social Council and the Inter-American Council for Education, Science and Culture. Its aim is to promote co-operation among the countries of the region, in order to accelerate economic and social development. An Executive Secretariat for Integral Development provides CIDI with technical and secretarial services and co-ordinates a Special Multilateral Fund of CICI (FEMCIDI), the New Programming Approaches programme, a Hemispheric Integral Development Program, a Universal Civil Identity Program in the Americas, and Migration and Development Innovative Programs. Technical co-operation and training programmes are managed by a subsidiary body of the Council, the Inter-American Agency for Co-operation and Development, which was established in 1999.

Executive Secretary: SHERRY TROSS (USA).

INTER-AMERICAN JURIDICAL COMMITTEE (IAJC)

The Committee's purposes are to serve as an advisory body to the OAS on juridical matters; to promote the progressive development and codification of international law; and to study juridical problems relating to the integration of the developing countries in the hemisphere, and, in so far as may appear desirable, the possibility of attaining uniformity in legislation. It comprises 11 jurists, nationals of different member states, elected for a period of four years, with the possibility of re-election.

Chairman: JOAO CLEMENTE BAENA SOARES (Brazil); Av. Marechal Floriano 196, 3° andar, Palácio Itamaraty, Centro, 20080-002, Rio de Janeiro, Brazil; tel. (21) 2206-9903; fax (21) 2203-2090; e-mail cjioea.trp@terra.com.br.

INTER-AMERICAN COMMISSION ON HUMAN RIGHTS

The Commission was established in 1960 to promote the observance and protection of human rights in the member states of the OAS. It examines and reports on the human rights situation in member countries and considers individual petitions relating to alleged human rights violations by member states. A Special Rapporteurship on the Rights of People of Afro-Descendants, and against Racial Discrimination was established in 2005. Other rapporteurs analyse and report on the rights of children, women, indigenous peoples, migrant workers, prisoners and displaced persons, and on freedom of expression. An OAS Extraordinary General Assembly, held in March 2013, adopted a resolution that provided for refinements to the operations of the Commission with a view to strengthening the Inter-American human rights system.

Executive Secretary: EMILIO ÁLVAREZ ICAZA LONGORIA (Mexico); 1889F St, NW, Washington, DC 20006, USA; tel. (202) 370-9000; fax (202) 458-3992; e-mail cidhdenuncias@oas.org; internet www.cidh.oas.org.

SUBSIDIARY ORGANS AND AGENCIES

Inter-American Committee Against Terrorism (Comité Interamericano Contra el Terrorismo—CICTE): 1889 F St, NW, Washington, DC 20006, USA; tel. (202) 370-4973; fax (202) 458-3857; e-mail cicte@oas.org; internet www.cicte.oas.org; f. 1999 to enhance the exchange of information via national authorities, formulate proposals to assist mem. states in drafting counter-terrorism legislation in all states, compile bilateral, sub-regional, regional and multilateral treaties and agreements signed by member states and promote universal adherence to international counter-terrorism conventions, strengthen border co-operation and travel documentation security measures, and develop activities for training and crisis management; Exec. Sec. NEIL KLOPFENSTEIN (USA).

Inter-American Committee on Ports (Comisión Interamericana de Puertos—CIP): 1889 F St, NW, Washington, DC 20006, USA; tel. (202) 370-9703; fax (202) 458-3517; e-mail cip@oas.org; internet www.oas.org/cip; f. 1998; serves as the permanent inter-American forum to strengthen co-operation on port-related issues among the member states, with the active participation of the private sector; the Committee, comprising 34 mem. states, meets every two years; its Executive Board, which executes policy decisions, meets annually; four technical advisory groups have been established to advise on logistics and competition (formerly port operations), port security, navigation control, and environmental protection; Sec. (vacant).

Inter-American Court of Human Rights (IACHR) (Corte Interamericana de Derechos Humanos): Avda 10, St 45-47 Los Yoses, San Pedro, San José; Postal 6906-1000, San José, Costa Rica; tel. (506) 2527-1600; fax (506) 2234-0584; e-mail corteidh@corteidh.or.cr; internet www.corteidh.or.cr; f. 1979 as an autonomous judicial institution whose purpose is to apply and interpret the American Convention on Human Rights (which entered into force in 1978, and is also known as the Pact of San José); comprises seven jurists from OAS member states; in Sept. 2013 Venezuela withdrew from the American Convention on Human Rights; Pres. HUMBERTO SIERRA PORTO (Colombia); publ. *Annual Report*.

Inter-American Defense Board (Junta Interamericana de Defensa—JID): 2600 16th St, NW, Washington, DC 20441, USA; tel. (202) 939-6041; fax (202) 319-2791; e-mail jid@jid.org; internet www.jid.org; promotes co-operative security interests in the Western Hemisphere; new statutes adopted in 2006 formally designated the Board as an OAS agency; works on issues such as disaster assistance and confidence-building measures directly supporting the hemispheric security goals of the OAS and of regional ministers responsible for defence; also provides a senior-level academic programme in security studies for military, national police and civilian leaders at the Inter-American Defense College; Dir-Gen. Vice Adm. BENTO COSTA LIMA LEITE DE ALBUQUERQUE, Jr (Brazil).

Inter-American Drug Abuse Control Commission (Comisión Interamericana para el Control del Abuso de Drogas—CICAD): 1889 F St, NW, Washington, DC 20006, USA; tel. (202) 458-3178; fax (202) 458-3658; e-mail oidcicad@oas.org; internet www.cicad.oas.org; f. 1986 by the OAS to promote and facilitate multilateral co-operation in the control and prevention of the trafficking, production and use of illegal drugs, and related crimes; reports regularly, through the Multilateral Evaluation Mechanism, on progress against illegal drugs in each mem. state and region-wide; mems: 34 countries; Exec. Sec. PAUL E. SIMONS; publs *Statistical Survey* (annually), *Directory of Governmental Institutions Charged with the Fight Against the Illicit Production, Trafficking, Use and Abuse of Narcotic Drugs and Psychotropic Substances*, *Evaluation of Progress in Drug Control*, *Progress Report on Drug Control—Implementation and Recommendations* (2 a year).

Inter-American Telecommunication Commission (Comisión Interamericana de Telecomunicaciones—CITEL): 1889 F St, NW, Washington, DC 20006, USA; tel. (202) 370-4713; e-mail citel@oas.org; internet www.citel.oas.org; f. 1993 to promote the development and harmonization of telecommunications in the region, in co-operation with governments and the private sector; CITEL has more than 200 associate mems representing private associations or companies, permanent observers, and international organizations; under its Permanent Executive Committee specialized consultative committees focus on telecommunication standardization and radiocommunication, including broadcasting; mems: 34 countries; Exec. Sec. CLOVIS JOSÉ BAPTISTA NETO.

Justice Studies Center of the Americas (Centro de Estudios de Justicia de las Américas): Rodó 1950, Providencia, Santiago, Chile; tel. (2) 2742933; fax (2) 3415769; e-mail info@cejamericas.org; internet www.cejamericas.org; f. 1999; aims to support the modernization of justice systems in the region; Exec. Dir JAIME ARELLANO QUINTANA (Chile).

Pan American Development Foundation (PADF) (Fundación Panamericana para el Desarrollo): 1889 F St, NW, Washington, DC 20006, USA; tel. (202) 458-3969; fax (202) 458-6316; e-mail padf-dc@padf.org; internet www.padf.org; f. 1962 to promote and facilitate economic and social development in Latin America and the Caribbean by means of innovative partnerships and integrated involvement of the public and private sectors; provides low-interest credit for small-scale entrepreneurs, vocational training, improved health care, agricultural development and reafforestation, and strengthening local non-governmental organizations; provides emergency disaster relief and reconstruction assistance; Exec. Dir JOHN A. SANBRAILO.

Activities

STRENGTHENING DEMOCRACY

The OAS promotes and supports good governance in its member states through various activities, including electoral observations, crisis-prevention missions, and programmes to strengthen government institutions and to support a regional culture of democracy. In September 2001 the member states adopted the Inter-American Democratic Charter, which details the essential elements of representative democracy, including free and fair elections; respect for human rights and fundamental freedoms; the exercise of power in accordance with the rule of law; a pluralistic political party system; and the separation and independence of the branches of government. Transparency and responsible administration by governments, respect for social rights, freedom of expression and citizen participation are among other elements deemed by the Charter to define democracy. The 41st General Assembly, held in June 2011, in San Salvador, El Salvador, approved a final Declaration on Citizen Security in the Americas, which incorporated a request to ministers to draft a hemispheric plan of action for consideration the following year. Since 2010 the OAS, jointly with the International Institute for Democracy and Electoral Assistance and Mexican partners, has convened an annual Latin American Democracy Forum; the fourth forum was held in November 2013, in Santiago, Chile, on the theme 'Youth engagement in politics'.

The observation of elections is given high priority by the OAS. Depending on the specific situation and the particular needs of each country, missions vary from a few technical experts sent for a limited time to a large country-wide team of monitors dispatched to observe the full electoral process for an extended period commencing with the political parties' campaigns. The missions present their observations to the OAS Permanent Council, along with recommendations for how each country's electoral process might be strengthened. In October 2012 the Permanent Council approved a resolution to designate 4 February as OAS Electoral Observation Day, to commemorate 50 years since the first mission was dispatched. OAS teams were dispatched to monitor two rounds of a presidential election held in El Salvador in February and March 2014, legislative elections held in Colombia in early March, and legislative elections held in Costa Rica in February, as well a presidential election organized in that country in two rounds, in February and April. Missions were to be sent to observe a presidential election to be held in Colombia, in May, and a parliamentary election to be held in Panama, also in that month.

In February 2004 the Permanent Council authorized the establishment of the OAS Mission to Support the Peace Process in Colombia (MAPP), with a mandate to provide assistance in support of the ongoing process and to advise on, monitor and verify the peacebuilding activities being undertaken by the Colombian authorities; the OAS has undertaken specific projects and measures in support of local initiatives aimed at promoting reconciliation and strengthening democracy.

In June 2012 the Permanent Council determined to send a fact-finding team to investigate the political situation in Paraguay where the president, Fernando Lugo, had been impeached by that country's congress. The team, led by the OAS Secretary-General, visited Paraguay in July, and concluded that any decisions taken by the OAS on the situation there should have as objectives: promoting the completion of the related ongoing domestic judicial process; strengthening the national democratic system during the transition to elections (held in April 2013), through the promotion of public dialogue and support for legal reforms that might be put in place to avoid further crises; and ensuring that the electoral process should be participatory and transparent, and that no reprisals or exclusions should occur in relation to the July 2012 political crisis, in particular reprisals aimed at Lugo or his supporters. In view of the findings of the mission, the OAS Secretary-General determined in early July to deploy an OAS mission to Paraguay to observe the process leading to the April 2013 elections and to facilitate political dialogue.

In early March 2014 the Permanent Council, meeting in special session, at the request of Panama, to consider ongoing anti-government unrest in Venezuela, issued a Declaration of Solidarity and Support for Democratic institutions, Dialogue, and Peace in Venezuela.

In special situations, when both or all member states involved in a dispute ask for its assistance, the OAS plays a longer-term role in supporting countries to resolve bilateral or multilateral issues. In September 2005 Belize and Guatemala signed an agreement at the OAS establishing a framework for negotiations and confidence-building measures to help to maintain good bilateral relations while they sought a permanent solution to a long-standing territorial dispute. Following a series of negotiations under OAS auspices, both sides signed a Special Agreement to resolve the dispute in December 2008. In April 2006 another OAS-supported effort was concluded successfully when El Salvador and Honduras signed an accord settling differences over the demarcation of their common border. In March 2008 a Meeting of Consultation of OAS ministers responsible for foreign affairs was convened following an escalation of diplomatic tension between Colombia and Ecuador resulting from a violation of Ecuador's borders by Colombian soldiers in pursuit of opposition insurgents. The meeting approved a resolution to establish a Good Offices Mission to restore confidence between the two countries and to negotiate an appropriate settlement to the dispute. A Verification Commission of the Good Offices Mission presented a report in July 2009, which included proposals to strengthen bilateral relations. In November 2010 a special meeting of the Permanent Council was convened, at the request of the Costa Rican government, to consider a border dispute with Nicaragua in the San Juan river area. The Council adopted a resolution in support of recommendations of the OAS Secretary-General, who had recently visited the area, to implement various confidence-building measures, including the resumption of bilateral talks on boundary demarcation, the convening of a Binational Committee and strengthening collaborative mechanisms to counter organized crime and arms- and drugs-trafficking.

The OAS aims to combat corruption in recognition of the undermining effect this has on democratic institutions. In 1996 the OAS member states adopted the Inter-American Convention against Corruption, which by 2014 had been ratified or acceded to by 33 member states. In 2002 the treaty's signatory states initiated a peer review process to examine their compliance with the treaty's key provisions. The Follow-Up Mechanism for the Implementation of the Inter-American Convention against Corruption assesses progress and recommends concrete measures that the states parties can implement to improve compliance. Representatives of civil society organizations are also given the opportunity to meet with experts and present information for their consideration. All participating countries have been assessed at least once and the completed progress reports are available to the public. The OAS has also held seminars and training sessions in the region on such matters as improving transparency in government and drafting model anti-corruption legislation. In May 2010 the Follow-up Mechanism organized a Conference on the Progress and Challenges in Hemispheric Co-operation against Corruption, held in Lima, Peru. A second conference was convened in Cali, Colombia, in June 2011. In 2014 the Follow-Up Mechanism was conducting a fourth round of member country evaluations.

In recent years, the OAS has expanded its outreach to civil society. More than 200 non-governmental organizations (NGOs) are registered to take part in OAS activities. Civil society groups are encouraged to participate in workshops and round tables in advance of the OAS General Assembly to prepare proposals and recommendations to present to the member states. This is also the case with Summits of the Americas and the periodic ministerial meetings, such as those on education, labour, culture, and science and technology. NGOs contributed ideas to the development of the Inter-American Democratic Charter and have participated in follow-up work on hemispheric treaties against corruption and terrorism.

The OAS has also focused on strengthening ties with the private sector. In 2006 it concluded a co-operation agreement with the business forum Private Sector of the Americas which aimed to promote dialogue and to support public-private alliances with a view to creating jobs, combating poverty and strengthening development. Business leaders from the region develop proposals and recommendations to present to the OAS General Assembly and to the Summits of the Americas.

DEFENDING HUMAN RIGHTS

Under the Democratic Charter a 'respect for human rights and fundamental freedoms' is deemed to be an essential element of a democracy. The Inter-American Commission on Human Rights and the Inter-American Court of Human Rights are the pillars of a system designed to protect individuals in the Americas who have suffered violations of their rights. A key function of the Commission is to consider petitions from individuals who claim that a state has violated a protected right and that they have been unable to find justice. The Commission brings together the petitioner and the state to explore a 'friendly settlement'. If such an outcome is not possible, the Commission may recommend specific measures to be carried out by the state to remedy the violation. If a state does not follow the recommendations the Commission has the option to publish its report or take the case to the Inter-American Court of Human Rights, as long as the state involved has accepted the Court's compulsory jurisdiction. The Commission convenes for six weeks each year. In July 2011 a special working group was established to review the work of the Commission. An OAS Extraordinary General Assembly convened in March 2013 considered the findings of the working group, and adopted a resolution on refining the operations of the Commission with a view to strengthening the functioning of the Inter-American human rights framework.

In addition to hearing cases the Court may exercise its advisory jurisdiction to interpret the human rights treaties in effect in the region. The Commission, for its part, may conduct an on-site visit to a country, at the invitation of its Government, to analyse and report on the human rights situation. The Commission has also created rapporteurships focusing on particular human rights issues. In 2005 it created a rapporteurship on the rights of persons of African descent and against racial discrimination. Other rapporteurs analyse and report on the rights of children, women, indigenous peoples migrant workers, prisoners and displaced persons, and on freedom of expression. The Commission also has a special unit on human rights defenders. The OAS also works beyond the inter-American human rights system to promote the rights of vulnerable groups. The member states are in the process of negotiating the draft American Declaration on the Rights of Indigenous Peoples, which is intended to promote and protect a range of rights covering such areas as family, spirituality, work, culture, health, the environment, and systems of knowledge, language and communication. A special fund was established for voluntary contributions by member states and permanent observers in order to help cover the costs involved in broadening indigenous participation. The OAS also works to promote and protect women's rights. The Inter-American Commission of Women (CIM), established in 1928, has had an impact on shaping laws and policies in many countries. One of its key initiatives led to the adoption of the Inter-American Convention on the Prevention, Punishment and Eradication of Violence against Women, also known as the Convention of Belém do Pará, which was adopted in 1994 by the OAS General Assembly. Since 2005 parties to the Belém do Pará Convention have participated in a follow-up mechanism designed to determine how the countries are complying with the treaty and progress achieved in preventing and punishing violence against women. In 2006 the CIM also initiated an examination of strategies for reversing the spread of HIV/AIDS among women in the region. The Commission has urged greater efforts to integrate a gender perspective into every aspect of the OAS agenda. In April 2011 and July 2012 the Commission hosted hemispheric fora aiming to promote equal participation of women in the democracies of the Americas. An Inter-American Year of Women was inaugurated in February 2010.

SOCIAL AND ECONOMIC DEVELOPMENT

Combating poverty and promoting social equity and economic development are priority concerns of the OAS, and the OAS pursues these aims in partnership with regional and global agencies, the private sector and the international community. A Strategic Plan for Partnership for Integral Development guided OAS actions in area during 2006–13. In June 2012 the 42nd OAS General Assembly adopted a new Social Charter of the Americas. The 43rd General Assembly, held in June 2013, issued the Declaration of Antigua, which urged governments of the region to promote 'public health, education, and social inclusion', and also adopted the Inter-American Convention against All Forms of Discrimination and Intolerance. OAS development policies and priorities are determined by the organization's political bodies, including the General Assembly, the Permanent Council and the Inter-American Council for Integral Development (CIDI), with direction from the Summits of the Americas. The OAS Executive Secretariat for Integral Development (SEDI) implements the policies through projects and programmes. Specialized departments within SEDI focus on education, culture, science and technology; sustainable development; trade, tourism and competitiveness; and social development and employment. SEDI also supports the regional ministerial meetings on topics such as culture, education, labour and sustainable development that are held periodically as part of the Summit of the Americas process. These regional meetings foster dialogue and strengthen co-operation in specific sectors and ensure that Summit policies are implemented at the national level. The OAS convenes the ministerial meetings, prepares documents for discussion and tracks the implementation of Summit mandates. In June 2009 the General Assembly adopted a resolution committing members to strengthening co-operation to control the spread of communicable diseases, in particular the outbreak of the swine influenza variant pandemic (H1N1), through greater surveillance and other disease control methods.

In June 2008 a technical secretariat was established in Panama City, Panama, to co-ordinate the implementation of an action plan in support of the Decade of the Americas for the Rights and Dignity of Persons with Disabilities (2006–16). The theme of the Decade, which had been inaugurated in Santo Domingo, Dominican Republic, was 'Equality, Dignity, and Participation'. In July 2008 the first Meeting of Ministers and High Authorities of Social Development, within the framework of CIDI, was convened in Valparaiso, Chile.

The OAS Department of Sustainable Development assists member states with formulating policies and executing projects that are aimed at integrating environmental protection with rural development and poverty alleviation, and that ensure high levels of transparency, public participation and gender equity. In December 2006 regional ministers responsible for the environment met in Santa Cruz de la Sierra, Bolivia, to define strategies and goals related to sustainable development, environmental protection, the management of resources and the mitigation of natural disasters. Water resource management projects include initiatives that support member states in managing transboundary water resources in the major river basins of South and Central America, in partnership with the UN Environment Programme (UNEP), the World Bank and the Global Environment Facility (GEF). The OAS is also active in various international fora that address water-related issues.

Projects focusing on natural disasters and climate adaptation include a new programme, launched in April 2006, which is aimed at assisting member countries to reduce the risk of natural disasters, particularly those related to climatic variations that have been linked to rises in sea levels. The OAS also works with CARICOM on the Mainstreaming Adaptation to Climate Change project. Activities include: incorporating risk reduction into development and economic planning; supporting good governance in such areas as the use of appropriate building codes and standards for public and residential buildings; supporting innovative financial instruments related to risk transfer; and supporting regional collaboration with different agencies and organizations.

The OAS serves as the technical secretariat for the Renewable Energy in the Americas initiative, which offers governments access to information on renewable energy and energy-efficient technologies, and facilitates contacts between the private sector and state energy entities in the Americas. The OAS also provides technical assistance for developing renewable energy projects and facilitating their funding.

The Inter-American Biodiversity Information Network (IABIN), which has been supported since 2004 by the GEF, the World Bank and other sources, is a principal focus of OAS biodiversity efforts. The Department of Sustainable Development also supports the work of national conservation authorities in areas such as migratory species and biodiversity corridors. It co-operates with the private sector to support innovative financing through payment for ecological services, and maintains a unique online portal regarding land tenure and land title, which is used throughout the Americas.

In the areas of environmental law, policy and economics the OAS conducts environmental and sustainability assessments to help member states to identify key environmental issues that impact trade. The OAS works with countries to develop priorities for capacity building in such areas as domestic laws, regulations and standards affecting market access of goods and services. Other initiatives include supporting countries in water and renewable energy legislation; supporting efforts towards the more effective enforcement of domestic laws; and facilitating natural disaster risk reduction and relief.

The OAS supports member states at national, bilateral and multilateral level to cope with trade expansion and economic integration. Through its Department of Trade, Tourism and Competitiveness the OAS General Secretariat provides support in strengthening human and institutional capacities, and in enhancing trade opportunities and competitiveness, particularly for micro, small and medium-sized enterprises. One of the Department's key responsibilities is to help member states (especially smaller economies) to develop the capacity they need to negotiate, implement and administer trade agreements and to take advantage of the benefits offered by free trade and expanded markets. Many member states seek assistance from the OAS to meet successfully the challenges posed by increasing globalization and the need to pursue multiple trade agendas. The OAS also administers an Inter-American Foreign Trade Information System, which acts as a repository for information about trade and trade-related issues in the region, including the texts of trade agreements, information on trade disciplines, data, and national legislation. In October 2008 a meeting of Ministers and High Authorities on Science and Technology, convened in Mexico City, Mexico, declared their commitment to co-ordinating activities to promote and enhance policies relating to science, technology, engineering and innovation as tools of development, increasing productivity, and sustainable natural resource management.

A specialized unit for tourism was established in 1996 in order to strengthen and co-ordinate activities for the sustainable development of the tourism industry in the Americas. The unit supports regional and sub-regional conferences and workshops, as well as the Inter-American Travel Congress, which serves as a forum to consider and formulate region-wide tourism policies. The unit also undertakes research and analysis of the industry. In September 2011 the 19th Inter-American Travel Congress, convened in San Salvador, El Salvador, adopted, by consensus, the Declaration of San Salvador for Sustainable Tourism Development in the Americas, recognizing the contribution of the tourism sector towards national efforts to reduce poverty and inequality, to advance standards of living in host communities, and to promote sustainable economic development. The Congress approved the establishment of a Hemispheric Tourism Fund, which was to support poor communities in developing their tourism potential. The inaugural meeting of an Inter-American Tourism Commission was held in August 2012.

In 1998 the OAS approved an Inter-American Programme of Culture to support efforts being undertaken by member states and to promote co-operation in areas such as cultural diversity; protection of cultural heritage; training and dissemination of information; and the promotion of cultural tourism. The OAS also assists with the preparation of national and multilateral cultural projects, and co-operates with the private sector to protect and promote cultural assets and events in the region. In July 2002 the first Inter-American meeting of ministers responsible for culture approved the establishment of an Inter-American Committee on Culture, within the framework of CIDI, to co-ordinate high-level dialogue and co-operation on cultural issues. In November 2006 regional ministers responsible for culture met in Montréal, Canada, to address the contribution of the cultural sector towards promoting development and combating poverty. In 2009 the General Assembly declared 2011 as the Inter-American Year of Culture.

The 42nd General Assembly meeting, held in Cochabamba, Bolivia, in June 2012, adopted the Declaration of Cochabamba on Food Security with Sovereignty in the Americas, committing, inter alia, to promote agricultural development, eradicate hunger and malnutrition, and support inter-American and regional efforts to advance a common agenda on food and nutrition security.

In November 2013 a meeting of OAS ministers responsible for labour and representatives of regional workers and employers, held in in Medellín, Colombia, adopted the Medellin Declaration and Plan of Action on 'Fifty Years of Inter-American Dialogue for the Promotion of Social Justice and Decent Work: Progress and Challenges towards Sustainable Development', which reaffirm regional commitment to the articulation of improved economic and labour policies, with a special emphasis on youth access to the employment market, respect for labour rights, and the provision of vocational training initiatives and employment services.

MULTIDIMENSIONAL SECURITY

The promotion of hemispheric security is a fundamental purpose of the OAS. In October 2003, at a Special Conference on Security convened in Mexico City, Mexico, the member states established a 'multidimensional' approach that recognized both traditional security concerns and threats such as international terrorism, drugs-trafficking, money-laundering, illegal arms dealing, trafficking in persons, institutional corruption and organized crime. In some countries problems such as poverty, disease, environmental degradation and natural disasters increase vulnerability and undermine human security. In March 2006 member states determined to enhance co-operation on defence issues by formally designating the Inter-American Defense Board (IADB) as an OAS agency. Under its new mandate the operations and structure of the IADB were to be in keeping with the OAS Charter and the Inter-American Democratic Charter, including 'the principles of civilian oversight and the subordination of military institutions to civilian authority'. The IADB provides technical and educational advice and consultancy services to the OAS and its member states on military and defence matters. The OAS Secretary-General chairs the Inter-American Committee on Natural Disaster Reduction, which was established in 1999 comprising the principal officers of regional and international organizations concerned with the prevention and mitigation of natural disasters. The Committee met in November 2012 to consider the impact of Hurricane Sandy, in particular in the Bahamas, Haiti, Jamaica and the east coast of the USA.

Following the 11 September 2001 terrorist attacks perpetrated against targets in the USA, the OAS member states strengthened their co-operation against the threat of terrorism. The Inter-American Convention against Terrorism, which seeks to prevent the financing of terrorist activities, strengthen border controls and increase co-operation among law enforcement authorities in different countries, was opened for signature in June 2002 and entered into force in July 2003. At April 2014 it had been signed by all 34 active member states and ratified or acceded to by 24. The Inter-American Committee against Terrorism (CICTE) offers technical assistance and specialized training in key counter-terrorism areas including port security, airport security, customs and border security, and legislation and legal assistance. Through CICTE member countries have also improved co-operation in improving the quality of identification and travel documents, strengthening cybersecurity and adopting financial controls to prevent money-laundering and the funding of terrorist activities. In October 2008 the first meeting of ministers responsible for public security in the Americas was convened, in Mexico City. In June 2009 the General Assembly, meeting in Honduras, adopted the Declaration of San Pedro Sula, promoting the theme 'Towards a Culture of Non-violence'.

The Inter-American Drug Abuse Control Commission (CICAD) seeks to reduce the supply of and demand for illegal drugs, building on the 1996 Anti-Drug Strategy in the Hemisphere. The CICAD Executive Secretariat implements programmes aimed at preventing and treating substance abuse; reducing the supply and availability of illicit drugs; strengthening national drug control institutions; improving practices to control firearms and money-laundering; developing alternate sources of income for growers of coca, poppy and marijuana; and helping member governments to improve the gathering and analysis of data. The Multilateral Evaluation Mechanism (MEM) measures drug control progress in the member states and the hemisphere as a whole, based on a series of objective indicators. Following each evaluation round the MEM process examines how countries are carrying out the recommendations. In June 2009 the OAS General Assembly agreed to initiate a review of the organization's anti-drugs strategy and its instruments to counter drugs-trafficking and abuse. In June 2013 the Assembly issued the Declaration of Antigua Guatemala for a Comprehensive Policy against the World Drug Problem in the Americas.

In 1997 the member states adopted the Inter-American Convention against the Illicit Manufacturing of and Trafficking in Firearms, Ammunition, Explosives, and other Related Materials (known as CIFTA), which, by April 2014, had been ratified by 30 member states. These countries have strengthened co-operation and information sharing on CIFTA-related issues. In 2005 the OAS convened the first meeting of national authorities that make operational decisions on granting export, import and transit licenses for firearms, with a view to creating an information exchange network to prevent illegal manufacturing and trafficking. In June 1999 20 member states signed an Inter-American Convention on Transparency in Conventional Weapons Acquisition; it had been ratified by 15 members by April 2014.

The OAS co-ordinates a comprehensive international programme to remove many thousands of anti-personnel landmines posing a threat to civilians in countries that have been affected by conflict. The OAS oversees the process of identifying, obtaining and delivering the necessary resources, including funds, equipment and personnel; the IADB co-ordinates technical demining operations, working with field supervisors from various countries; and the actual demining is executed by teams of trained soldiers, security forces or other personnel from the affected country. In addition to supporting landmine clearance the OAS Program for Comprehensive Action against Anti-personnel Mines helps with mine risk education; victim assistance and the socio-economic reintegration of formerly mined zones; the establishment of a mine action database; and support for the global ban on the production, use, sale, transfer and stockpiling of anti-personnel landmines. It has also helped to destroy more than 1m. stockpiled mines in Argentina, Colombia, Chile, Ecuador, Honduras, Nicaragua and Peru. By mid-2009 Costa Rica, El Salvador, Guatemala, Honduras and Suriname had declared their territory to be clear of anti-personnel landmines. Nicaragua was officially declared to be free of landmines in June 2010.

The OAS Trafficking in Persons Section organizes seminars and training workshops for law enforcement officials and others to raise awareness on human trafficking, which includes human exploitation, smuggling and other human rights violations. In March 2006 the Venezuelan Government hosted the first Meeting of National Authorities on Trafficking in Persons in order to study ways to strengthen co-operation and to develop regional policies and strategies to prevent human trafficking. Gang violence is another growing public security concern in the region. A second Meeting was convened in Buenos Aires, Argentina, in March 2009.

The OAS, Inter-American Development Bank and OECD jointly implement the Continuous Reporting System on International Migration in the America (SICREMI), which aims rigorously to monitor international migration movements and key policies and programmes being implemented in the region; the first and second SICREMI reports were released in August 2011 and January 2013, respectively.

In June 2010 the 40th meeting of the OAS General Assembly, meeting in Lima, determined to strengthen a collective commitment to peace, security and co-operation, as the principal means of confronting threats to the region.

In June 2012 the 42nd OAS General Assembly issued a Declaration on the Question of the Status of the Islas Malvinas (Falkland Islands), and determined to examine that issue at subsequent sessions. The 43rd General Assembly, held in June 2013, approved a further Declaration on the Malvinas, proposed by Argentina, which reaffirmed that both Argentina and the United Kingdom should resume as soon as possible negotiations over the disputed sovereignty of the islands.

A Meeting of Consultation of OAS ministers responsible for foreign affairs held in late August 2012 adopted a resolution urging Ecuador and the United Kingdom to resolve, through peaceful dialogue, a diplomatic impasse that had ensued from the granting by Ecuador in that month of political asylum to Julian Assange, the Australian founder of WikiLeaks. Assange had sought sanctuary in Ecuador's London embassy to avoid extradition to Sweden, where he was wanted for questioning over alleged sexual misconduct, for fear that he might eventually be extradited to the USA, whose authorities had been investigating the activities of WikiLeaks.

SUMMITS OF THE AMERICAS

Since December 1994, when the First Summit of the Americas was convened in Miami, USA, the leaders of the region's 34 democracies have met periodically to examine political, economic and social development priorities and to determine common goals and forge a common agenda. This process has increasingly shaped OAS policies and priorities and many OAS achievements, for example the adoption of the Inter-American Democratic Charter and the creation of mechanisms to measure progress against illicit drugs and corruption, have been attained as a result of Summit mandates. The Summits of the Americas have provided direction for the OAS in the areas of human rights, hemispheric security, trade, poverty reduction, gender equity and greater civil society participation. The OAS serves as the institutional memory and technical secretariat to the Summit process. It supports the countries in follow-up and planning, and provides technical, logistical and administrative support. The OAS Summits Secretariat co-ordinates the implementation of mandates assigned to the OAS and chairs the Joint Summit Working Group, which includes the institutions of the inter-American system. The OAS also has responsibility for strengthening outreach to civil society to ensure that NGOs, academic institutions, the private sector and other interests can contribute ideas and help to monitor and implement Summit initiatives.

In December 1994 the First Summit of the Americas was convened in Miami. The meeting endorsed the concept of a Free Trade Area of the Americas, and also approved a Plan of Action to strengthen democracy, eradicate poverty and promote sustainable development throughout the region. The OAS subsequently realigned its priorities in order to respond to the mandates emerging from the Summit and developed a new institutional framework for technical assistance and co-operation, although many activities continued to be undertaken by the specialized or associated organizations of the OAS. In 1998, following the Second Summit, held in Santiago, the OAS established an Office of Summit Follow-Up, in order to strengthen its servicing of the meetings, and to co-ordinate tasks assigned to it. The Third Summit, convened in Québec, Canada, in April 2001, reaffirmed the central role of the OAS in implementing decisions of the summit meetings and instructed the organization to pursue the process of reform in order to enhance its operational capabilities, in particular in the areas of human rights, combating trade in illegal drugs, and enforcement of democratic values. The Summit declaration stated that commitment to democracy was a requirement for a country's participation in the summit process. The Third Summit urged the development of an Inter-American Democratic Charter to reinforce OAS instruments for defending and promoting democracy; the Democratic Charter was adopted in September of that year. The Third Summit also determined that the OAS was to be the technical secretariat for the summit process, assuming many of the responsibilities previously incumbent on the host country. Further to its mandate, the OAS established a Summits of the Americas Secretariat, which assists countries in planning and follow-up and provides technical, logistical and administrative support for the Summit Implementation Review Group and the summit process. An interim Special Summit of the Americas was held in January 2004, in Monterrey, Mexico, to reaffirm commitment to the process. The Fourth Summit of the Americas, convened in Mar del Plata, Argentina, in November 2005, approved a plan of action to achieve employment growth and security. The Fifth Summit was held in Port of Spain, Trinidad and Tobago, in April 2009, focusing on the theme 'Securing our citizens' future by promoting human prosperity, energy security and environmental sustainability'. All governments determined to enhance co-operation to restore global economic growth and to reduce social inequalities. The meeting mandated the OAS to pursue various objectives, including the establishment of an Inter-American Social Protection Network, to facilitate the exchange of information with regard to policies, programmes and best practices; the convening of a Conference on Development; organizing regional consultations on climate change; and strengthening the leadership of the Joint Summit Working Group. A Summit of the Americas follow-up and implementation system was inaugurated in January 2010. The Sixth Summit was held in Cartagena, Colombia, in April 2012, on the theme 'Connecting the Americas: Partners for Prosperity'. The meeting mandated the OAS to review its strategies to counter the trafficking of illegal drugs. However, no unanimity was reached on the admission of Cuba to the next summit, scheduled to be convened in Panama, in 2015.

Finance

The OAS regular budget for 2014, approved by the General Assembly in November 2013, amounted to US $82.98m.

Publications

(in English and Spanish)

Américas (6 a year).

Annual Report.

Numerous cultural, legal and scientific reports and studies.

Specialized Organizations and Associated Agencies

Inter-American Children's Institute (Instituto Americano del Niño, la Niña y Adolescentes—IIN): Avda 8 de Octubre 2904, POB 16212, Montevideo 11600, Uruguay; tel. (2) 487-2150; fax (2) 487-3242; e-mail iin@iinoea.org; internet www.iin.oea.org; f. 1927; promotes the regional implementation of the Convention on the Rights of the Child, assists in the development of child-oriented public policies; promotes co-operation between states; and aims to develop awareness of problems affecting children and young people in the region. The Institute organizes workshops, seminars, courses, training programmes and conferences on issues relating to children, including, for example, the rights of children, children with disabilities, and the child welfare system. It also provides advisory services, statistical data and other relevant information to authorities and experts throughout the region. The 20th Pan American Child Congress was convened in Lima, Peru, in September 2009; Dir-Gen. MARÍA DE LOS DOLORES AGUILAR MARMOLEJO; publ. *iinfancia* (annually).

Inter-American Commission of Women (Comisión Interamericana de Mujeres—CIM): 1889 F St, NW, Suite 350 Washington, DC 20006, USA; tel. (202) 458-6084; fax (202) 458-6094; e-mail cim@oas.org; internet www.oas.org/cim; f. 1928 as the first official intergovernmental agency created expressly to ensure recognition of the civil and political rights of women; the CIM is the principal forum for generating hemispheric policy to advance women's rights and gender equality; comprises 34 principal delegates; the Assembly of Delegates, convened every two years, is the highest authority of the Commission, establishing policies and a plan of action for each biennium and electing the seven-mem. Executive Committee; Pres. MARÍA ISABEL CHAMORRO (Costa Rica); Exec. Sec. CARMEN MORENO TOSCANO (Mexico).

Inter-American Institute for Co-operation on Agriculture (IICA) (Instituto Interamericano de Cooperación para la Agricultura): Apdo Postal 55–2200, San Isidro de Coronado, San José, Costa Rica; tel. (506) 216-0222; fax (506) 216-0233; e-mail iicahq@iica.ac.cr; internet www.iica.int; f. 1942 (as the Inter-American Institute of Agricultural Sciences, present name adopted 1980); supports the efforts of mem. states to improve agricultural development and rural well-being; encourages co-operation between regional orgs, and provides a forum for the exchange of experience; Dir-Gen. VÍCTOR M. VILLALOBOS (Mexico).

Pan American Health Organization (PAHO) (Organización Panamericana de la Salud): 525 23rd St, NW, Washington, DC 20037, USA; tel. (202) 974-3000; fax (202) 974-3663; e-mail webmaster@paho.org; internet www.paho.org; f. 1902; co-ordinates regional efforts to improve health; maintains close relations with national health orgs and serves as the Regional Office for the Americas of the World Health Organization; Dir Dr CARISSA ETIENNE (Dominica).

Pan American Institute of Geography and History (PAIGH) (Instituto Panamericano de Geografía e Historia—IPGH): Ex-Arzobispado 29, 11860 México, DF, Mexico; tel. (55) 5277-5888; fax (55) 5271-6172; e-mail secretariageneral@ipgh.org; internet www.ipgh.org; f. 1928; co-ordinates and promotes the study of cartography, geophysics, geography and history; provides technical assistance, conducts training at research centres, distributes publications, and organizes technical meetings; Pres. RIGOBERTO OVIDIO MAGAÑA CHAVARRÍA (El Salvador); Sec.-Gen. RODRIGO BARRIGA VARGAS (Chile); Publs *Revista Cartográfica* (2 a year), *Revista Geográfica* (2 a year), *Revista de Historia de América* (2 a year), *Revista Geofísica* (2 a year), *Revista de Arqueología Americana* (annually), *Folklore Americano* (annually), *Boletín de Antropología Americana* (annually).

ORGANIZATION OF ARAB PETROLEUM EXPORTING COUNTRIES—OAPEC

Address: POB 20501, Safat 13066, Kuwait.

Telephone: 24959000; **fax:** 24959755; **e-mail:** oapec@oapecorg.org; **internet:** www.oapecorg.org.

OAPEC was established in 1968 to safeguard the interests of members and to determine ways and means for their co-operation in various forms of economic activity in the petroleum industry. In 2013 OAPEC member states contributed around 32% of total world petroleum production and an estimated 21% of total global marketed natural gas. In that year OAPEC member states accounted for 55% of total global oil reserves and almost 27% of total global reserves of natural gas.

MEMBERS

Algeria	Kuwait	Saudi Arabia
Bahrain	Libya	Syria
Egypt	Qatar	United Arab Emirates
Iraq		

Organization

(April 2014)

MINISTERIAL COUNCIL

The Council consists normally of the ministers of petroleum of the member states, and forms the supreme authority of OAPEC, responsible for drawing up its general policy, directing its activities and laying down its governing rules. It meets twice yearly, and may hold extraordinary sessions. Chairmanship is on an annual rotating basis.

EXECUTIVE BUREAU

The Bureau assists the Council to direct the management of OAPEC, approves staff regulations, reviews the budget, considers matters relating to the Organization's agreements and activities and draws up the agenda for the Council. The Bureau comprises one senior official from each member state. Chairmanship is by rotation on an annual basis, following the same order as the Ministerial Council chairmanship. The Bureau convenes at least three times a year.

GENERAL SECRETARIAT

The General Secretariat is composed of the Secretary-General's Office; the Arab Centre for Energy Studies (established in 1983), which comprises units of Technical Affairs, and Economics; the Information and Library Department; and the Finance and Administrative Affairs Department.

Secretary-General: ABBAS ALI NAQI (Kuwait).

JUDICIAL TRIBUNAL

The Tribunal comprises seven judges from Arab countries. Its task is to settle differences in interpretation and application of the OAPEC Agreement, arising between members and also between OAPEC and its affiliates; disputes among member countries on petroleum activities falling within OAPEC's jurisdiction and not under the sovereignty of member countries; and disputes that the Ministerial Council decides to submit to the Tribunal.

Activities

OAPEC co-ordinates different aspects of the Arab petroleum industry through joint undertakings. It co-operates with the League of Arab States (Arab League) and other organizations, and attempts to link petroleum research institutes in the Arab states. It organizes or participates in conferences and seminars, many of which are held jointly with non-Arab organizations in order to enhance Arab and international co-operation. OAPEC collaborates with the Arab Fund for Economic and Social Development (AFESD), the Arab Monetary

Fund and the Arab League in compiling the annual *Joint Arab Economic Report*. OAPEC provides training in technical matters and in documentation and information. The General Secretariat also conducts technical and feasibility studies and carries out market reviews.

In association with AFESD, OAPEC organizes the Arab Energy Conference every four years. The conference is attended by OAPEC ministers responsible for petroleum and energy, senior officials from other Arab states, and representatives of invited institutions and organizations concerned with energy issues. The ninth Arab Energy Conference, focusing on the theme 'Energy and Arab Co-operation', was held in Doha, Qatar, in May 2010. The 10th was scheduled to take place in mid-2014, in Tripoli, Libya. OAPEC, with other Arab organizations, participates in the Higher Co-ordination Committee for Higher Arab Action. In June 2012 OAPEC organized a conference, in Abu Dhabi, United Arab Emirates, on 'The development of production capacities of oil in the Arab countries and the current and future role in meeting the global energy demand'.

Finance

The combined General Secretariat and Judicial Tribunal proposed budget for 2013, approved by the Ministerial Council in December 2012, was 2.1m. Kuwaiti dinars.

Publications

Annual Statistical Report.
Energy Resources Monitor (quarterly, Arabic).
OAPEC Monthly Bulletin (Arabic and English editions).
Oil and Arab Cooperation (quarterly, Arabic).
Secretary-General's Annual Report (Arabic and English editions).
Papers, studies, conference proceedings.

OAPEC-Sponsored Ventures

Arab Maritime Petroleum Transport Company (AMPTC): POB 22525, Safat 13086, Kuwait; tel. 24959400; fax 24842996; e-mail amptc.kuwait@amptc.net; internet www.amptc.net; f. 1973 to undertake transport of crude petroleum, gas, refined products and petro-chemicals, and thus to increase Arab participation in the tanker transport industry; owns and operates a fleet of oil tankers and other carriers; also maintains an operations office in Giza, Egypt; auth. cap. US $200m.; Gen. Man. SULAYMAN AL-BASSAM.

Arab Petroleum Investments Corporation (APICORP): POB 9599, Dammam 31423, Saudi Arabia; tel. (3) 847-0444; fax (3) 847-0022; e-mail apicorp@apicorp-arabia.com; internet www.apicorp-arabia.com; f. 1975 to finance investments in petroleum and petrochemicals projects and related industries in the Arab world and in developing countries, with priority being given to Arab joint ventures; projects financed include gas liquefaction plants, petrochemicals, tankers, oil refineries, pipelines, exploration, detergents, fertilizers and process control instrumentation; in Feb. 2013 launched the *Shari'a*-compliant US $150m. APICORP Petroleum Shipping Fund; auth. cap. $2,400m.; paid-up cap. $750m.; shareholders: Kuwait, Saudi Arabia and United Arab Emirates (17% each), Libya (15%), Iraq and Qatar (10% each), Algeria (5%), Bahrain, Egypt and Syria (3% each); CEO and Gen. Man. AHMAD BIN HAMAD AL-NUAIMI.

Arab Company for Detergent Chemicals (ARADET): POB 27064, el-Mansour, Baghdad, Iraq; tel. (1) 541-9341; fax (1) 543-0265; e-mail info@aradetco.com; internet www.aradetco.com; f. 1981; produces and markets linear alkyl benzene; construction of a sodium multiphosphate plant is under way; APICORP holds 32% of shares in the co; auth. cap. 72m. Iraqi dinars; subs. cap. 60m. Iraqi dinars.

Arab Petroleum Services Company (APSCO): POB 12925, Tripoli, Libya; tel. (21) 3409921; fax (21) 3409923; e-mail info@apsco.com.ly; internet apsco.com.ly; f. 1977 to provide petroleum services through the establishment of cos specializing in various activities, and to train specialized personnel; auth. cap. 100m. Libyan dinars; subs. cap. 44m. Libyan dinars.**Arab Drilling and Workover Company:** POB 680, Ring Rd, Wadi Rabee, Beir Ettota, Gasir bin Ghisher, Tripoli, Libya; tel. (21) 5635927; fax (21) 5635926; e-mail info@adwoc.com; internet www.adwoc.com; f. 1980; 40% owned by APSCO; auth. cap. 12m. Libyan dinars; Gen. Man. OMRAN ABUKRAA.

Arab Geophysical Exploration Services Company (AGESCO): POB 84224, Tripoli, Libya; tel. (21) 7155770; fax (21) 7155780; e-mail agesco@agesco-ly.com; internet agesco-ly.com; f. 1985; 40% owned by APSCO; auth. cap. 12m. Libyan dinars; subs. cap. 4m. Libyan dinars; Gen. Man. AHMED ESSED.

Arab Well Logging Company (AWLCO): POB 18528/14 JULY, Baghdad, Iraq; tel. and fax (1) 541-8259; e-mail info@awlco.net; internet www.awlco.net; f. 1983 to provide well-logging services and data interpretation; wholly owned subsidiary of APSCO; auth. cap. 7m. Iraqi dinars.

Arab Shipbuilding and Repair Yard Company (ASRY): POB 50110, Hidd, Bahrain; tel. 17671111; fax 17670236; e-mail asryco@batelco.com.bh; internet www.asry.net; f. 1974 to undertake repairs and servicing of vessels; operates a 500,000-dwt dry dock in Bahrain; two floating docks operational since 1992, and two slipways became operational in 2008; has recently diversified its activities, e.g. into building specialized service boats and upgrading oil rigs; cap. (auth. and subsidized) US $170m.; CEO NILS KRISTIAN BERGE (Norway).

ORGANIZATION OF THE BLACK SEA ECONOMIC COOPERATION—BSEC

Address: Sakıp Sabancı Cad., Müşir Fuad Paşa Yalısı, Eski Tersane 34460 İstinye-Istanbul, Turkey.

Telephone: (212) 229-63-30; **fax:** (212) 229-63-36; **e-mail:** info@bsec-organization.org; **internet:** www.bsec-organization.org.

The Black Sea Economic Cooperation (BSEC) was established in 1992 to strengthen regional co-operation, particularly in the field of economic development. In June 1998, at a summit meeting held in Yalta, Ukraine, participating countries signed the BSEC Charter, thereby officially elevating BSEC to regional organization status. The Charter entered into force on 1 May 1999, at which time BSEC formally became the Organization of the Black Sea Economic Cooperation, retaining the same acronym.

MEMBERS

Albania	Georgia	Russia
Armenia	Greece	Serbia
Azerbaijan	Moldova	Turkey
Bulgaria	Romania	Ukraine

Note: Observer status has been granted to Austria, Belarus, Croatia, the Czech Republic, Egypt, France, Israel, Italy, Poland, Slovakia, Tunisia and the USA. The Black Sea Commission, the BSEC Business Council, the Energy Charter Conference, the European Union, and the International Black Sea Club also have observer status. Sectoral Dialogue Partnership status has been granted to Hungary, Iran, Japan, Jordan, Republic of Korea, Montenegro, Slovenia, the United Kingdom, and six intergovernmental organizations.

Organization

(April 2014)

PRESIDENTIAL SUMMIT

The Presidential Summit, comprising heads of state or government of member states, represents the highest authority of the body. A 20th anniversary summit was convened in İstanbul, Turkey, in June 2012.

COUNCIL

The Council of Ministers of Foreign Affairs is BSEC's principal decision-making organ. Ministers meet twice a year to review progress and to define new objectives. Chairmanship of the Council rotates among members every six months (1 January–31 July 2014:

Bulgaria); the Chairman-in-Office co-ordinates the activities undertaken by BSEC. The Council is supported by a Committee of Senior Officials. Upon the request of the Chairman-in-Office a troika, comprising the current, most recent and next Chairman-in-Office, or their representatives, is convened to consider BSEC's ongoing and planned activities.

PERMANENT INTERNATIONAL SECRETARIAT

The Secretariat's tasks are, primarily, of an administrative and technical nature, and include the maintenance of archives, and the preparation and distribution of documentation. Much of the organization's activities are undertaken by working groups, each headed by an Executive Manager, concerned with organizational matters; budgetary and financial issues; agriculture; banking and finance; combating crime; culture; customs affairs; education; emergency assistance; energy; environmental protection; health; information and communication technologies; institutional renewal and good governance; science and technology; small and medium-sized enterprises; statistics; tourism; trade and economic development; and transport. There are also various ad hoc groups and meetings of experts.

Secretary-General: Dr VICTOR TVIRCUN (Moldova).

Activities

In June 1992, at a summit meeting held in İstanbul, Turkey, heads of state and of government signed the summit declaration on BSEC, and adopted the Bosphorus statement, which established a regional structure for economic co-operation. The grouping attained regional organization status in May 1999. BSEC's main areas of co-operation include transport; communications; trade and economic development; banking and finance; energy; tourism; agriculture and agro-industry; health care and pharmaceuticals; environmental protection; science and technology; the exchange of statistical data and economic information; collaboration between customs authorities; and combating organized crime, drugs-trafficking, trade in illegal weapons and radioactive materials, and terrorism. In order to promote regional co-operation, BSEC also aims to strengthen the business environment by providing support for small and medium-sized enterprises; facilitating closer contacts between businesses in member countries; progressively eliminating obstacles to the expansion of trade; creating appropriate conditions for investment and industrial co-operation, in particular through the avoidance of double taxation and the promotion and protection of investments; encouraging the dissemination of information concerning international tenders organized by member states; and promoting economic co-operation in free trade zones. A Working Group on Culture was established in November 2006 to promote and protect the cultural identity of the region. The Group's activities have focused on safeguarding the region's maritime heritage; promoting the sustainable use of cultural heritage; promoting an interdisciplinary approach to the exploitation of cultural heritage, combining dimensions including tourism and transportation; stimulating creativity and innovation and, as a consequence thereof, economic development. A web portal dedicated to BSEC member states' tangible and intangible cultural heritage, and national protection frameworks, was to be developed.

A BSEC Business Council was established in İstanbul in December 1992 by the business communities of member states. It has observer status at the BSEC, and aims to identify private and public investment projects, maintain business contacts and develop programmes in various sectors. A Black Sea Trade and Development Bank became operational in July 1999, based in Thessaloníki, Greece, to finance and implement joint regional projects. A BSEC Coordination Center for the Exchange of Statistical Data and Economic Information is located in Ankara, Turkey. An International Centre for Black Sea Studies (ICBSS) was established in Athens, Greece, in March 1998, in order to undertake research concerning BSEC, in the fields of economics, industry and technology.

In April 2008 the BSEC Council inaugurated a new €2m. BSEC Hellenic Development Fund to support regional co-operation; guidelines for the operation of the Fund were adopted at a meeting of the Council in October. The Council also adopted the modalities for BSEC fast-track co-operation, aimed at enabling sub-groups of member states to proceed with policies that other member states were unwilling or unable to pursue. The October 2008 meeting of the Council adopted new guidelines on improving the efficiency of the grouping. In November 2012 the first BSEC Tax Forum was held, in Antalya, Turkey, with participation by ministers responsible for finance, senior tax policy officials, tax specialists and academics.

In June 2012 the Council adopted a new BSEC Economic Agenda Towards an Enhanced BSEC Partnership, replacing a previous BSEC Economic Agenda adopted in April 2001; the new Agenda reflected new challenges and opportunities in the global and regional economic environment and outlined 17 priority areas of action.

BSEC aims to foster relations with other international and regional organizations, and has been granted observer status at the UN General Assembly. BSEC supports the Stability Pact for South-Eastern Europe, initiated in June 1999 as a collaborative plan of action by the European Union (EU), the Group of Seven industrialized nations and Russia (the G8), regional governments and other organizations concerned with the stability of the region. In 1999 BSEC agreed upon a platform of co-operation for future structured relations with the EU. The main areas in which BSEC determined to develop co-operation with the EU were transport, energy and telecommunications infrastructure; trade and the promotion of foreign direct investment; sustainable development and environmental protection, including nuclear safety; science and technology; and combating terrorism and organized crime. The Declaration issued by BSEC's decennial anniversary summit, held in İstanbul in June 2002, urged that collaboration with the EU should be enhanced. In April 2005 representatives of BSEC and the EU met in Brussels, Belgium, to address possibilities for such co-operation, focusing in particular on the EU's policy in the Black Sea region and on the development of regional transport and energy networks (see the Alexandroupolis Declaration, below). In June 2007 BSEC heads of state confirmed their commitment to an enhanced relationship with the EU, based on a communication of the European Commission, published in April, entitled *Black Sea Synergy—a New Regional Cooperation Initiative*. In February 2008 a special meeting of the BSEC Council adopted a Declaration on a BSEC-EU Enhanced Relationship. A BSEC-EU Black Sea Regional Strategy was formulated in 2009, promoting BSEC-EU interaction during 2010–13. In March 2010 a Black Sea Environmental Partnership was launched by the EU, to support its efforts, and those of regional partners, including BSEC, to find co-operative approaches towards addressing environmental challenges in areas such as biodiversity conservation, integrated coastal zone and river basin management, and sources of pollution, and towards promoting environmental integration, monitoring and research. BSEC's Secretary-General addressed a stakeholders' conference on Sustainable Development of the Blue Economy of the Black Sea: Enhancing Marine and Maritime Co-operation, which was held in January 2014, in Bucharest, Romania. In 2007 BSEC and the UN Development Programme launched the Black Sea Trade and Investment Promotion Programme (BSTIP), which aims to develop trade and investment linkages among the BSEC member states. In October 2013 the BSEC Secretary-General attended the fourth International Black Sea Economic Forum, hosted by Ukraine.

BSEC has supported implementation of the Bucharest Convention on the Protection of the Black Sea Against Pollution, adopted by Bulgaria, Georgia, Romania, Russia, Turkey and Ukraine in April 1992. In October 1996 those countries adopted the Strategic Action Plan for the Rehabilitation and Protection of the Black Sea (BSSAP), to be implemented by the Commission of the Bucharest Convention. In March 2001 the ministers responsible for transport of BSEC member states adopted a Transport Action Plan, which envisaged reducing the disparities in regional transport systems and integrating the BSEC regional transport infrastructure with wider international networks and projects. In November 2006 BSEC signed a Memorandum of Understanding (MOU) with the International Road Federation. In April 2007 BSEC governments signed an agreement for the co-ordinated development of a 7,100-km-long Black Sea Ring Highway (BSRH). An MOU relating to the development of 'Motorways of the Sea' was also signed. Both accords entered into effect in late 2008. In March 2005 ministers responsible for energy of BSEC member states adopted the Alexandroupolis Declaration, approving a common framework for future collaboration on the creation of a regional energy market, and urging the liberalization of electricity and natural gas markets in accordance with EU directives as a basis for this. An International Scientific Conference of Energy and Climate Change has been convened under BSEC auspices annually since 2008 (most recently in October 2013). The inaugural meeting of a BSEC Green Energy Development Task Force was held in April 2012. In November the Task Force decided to draw up a BSEC Green Strategy Paper and resolved to stage in future a BSEC Conference on Investment Promotion in Green Energy. During November, within the framework of the BSTIP (see above), fora on green markets and agro-logistics were held in İstanbul. BSEC supports the annual Black Sea Oil and Gas Forum; the 2014 session was convened in April, in Bucharest, Romania.

Finance

BSEC is financed by annual contributions from member states on the following scale: Greece, Russia, Turkey and Ukraine each contribute 15% of the budget; Bulgaria, Romania and Serbia contribute 7.5%; the remaining members each contribute 3.5%.

Publication

Black Sea News (quarterly).

Related Bodies

Parliamentary Assembly of the Black Sea (PABSEC): 1 Hareket Kösku, Dolmabahçe Sarayi, Besiktas, 80680 İstanbul, Turkey; tel. (212) 227-6070; fax (212) 227-6080; e-mail pabsec@pabsec.org; internet www.pabsec.org; f. 1993; the Assembly, consisting of the representatives of the national parliaments of mem. states, aims to provide a legal basis for the implementation of decisions within the BSEC framework; comprises three cttees concerning economic, commercial, technological and environmental affairs; legal and political affairs; and cultural, educational and social affairs; the presidency rotates every six months (Dec. 2013–May 2014: Greece); 42nd General Assembly convened in Dec. 2013, in Tbilisi, Georgia; Sec.-Gen. KYRYLO TRETIAK (Ukraine).

Black Sea Trade and Development Bank (BSTDB): 1 Komninon str., 54624 Thessaloníki, Greece; tel. (2310) 290400; fax (2310) 221796; e-mail info@bstdb.org; internet www.bstdb.org; f. 1999; the Bank supports economic devt and regional co-operation by providing trade and project financing, guarantees, and equity for devt projects supporting both public and private enterprises in its mem. countries, in sectors including energy, infrastructure, finance, manufacturing, transport, and telecommunications; by 31 Dec. 2013 the Bank had approved 277 operations with funding of around €3,000m; auth. cap. SDR 3,000m. (April 2014); Pres. ANDREY KONDAKOV (Russia); Sec.-Gen. ORSALIA KALANTZOPOULOS (Greece).

BSEC Business Council: Müsir Fuad Pasa Yalisi, Eski Tersane, 80860 Istinye, İstanbul, Turkey; tel. (212) 229-1144; fax (212) 229-0332; e-mail info@bsec-business.org; internet www.bsecbc.org; f. 1992; aims to secure greater economic integration and to promote investment in the region; in 2000 established the web-based BSEC Business Information Exchange System; Sec.-Gen. MAMMAD ZULFUGAROV (Azerbaijan).

International Centre for Black Sea Studies (ICBSS): 4 Xenophontos Str., 10557 Athens, Greece; tel. (210) 3242321; fax (210) 3242244; e-mail icbss@icbss.org; internet www.icbss.org; f. 1998; aims to foster co-operation among BSEC mem. states and with international partners through applied research and advocacy; hosts the International Black Sea Symposium, an Annual Lecture and other events; the ICBSS is developing the WEB-GIS Observatory Network for the Environmental and Sustainable Development of the Black Sea; Dir-Gen. Dr ZEFI DIMADAMA (Greece); publs *Black Sea Monitor* (quarterly), *Xenophon Paper* series, Policy Briefs.

ORGANIZATION OF ISLAMIC COOPERATION—OIC

Address: Medina Rd, Sary St, POB 178, Jeddah 21411, Saudi Arabia.

Telephone: (2) 690-0001; **fax:** (2) 275-1953; **e-mail:** info@oic-oci.org; **internet:** www.oic-oci.org.

The OIC was formally established, as the Organization of the Islamic Conference, at the first conference of Muslim heads of state convened in Rabat, Morocco, in September 1969; the first conference of Muslim ministers responsible for foreign affairs, held in Jeddah in March 1970, established the General Secretariat; the latter became operational in May 1971. In June 2011 the 38th ministerial conference agreed to change the name of the organization, with immediate effect, to the Organization of Islamic Cooperation (abbreviated, as hitherto, to OIC).

MEMBERS

Afghanistan	Indonesia	Qatar
Albania	Iran	Saudi Arabia
Algeria	Iraq	Senegal
Azerbaijan	Jordan	Sierra Leone
Bahrain	Kazakhstan	Somalia
Bangladesh	Kuwait	Sudan
Benin	Kyrgyzstan	Suriname
Brunei	Lebanon	Syria*
Burkina Faso	Libya	Tajikistan
Cameroon	Malaysia	Togo
Chad	Maldives	Tunisia
Comoros	Mali	Turkey
Côte d'Ivoire	Mauritania	Turkmenistan
Djibouti	Morocco	Uganda
Egypt	Mozambique	United Arab Emirates
Gabon	Niger	Uzbekistan
The Gambia	Nigeria	Yemen
Guinea	Oman	
Guinea-Bissau	Pakistan	
Guyana	Palestine	

* In August 2012 Syria was suspended from participation in the activities of the OIC and also from all its subsidiary organs and specialized and affiliated institutions, in view of the Syrian Government's violent suppression of opposition elements and related acts of violence against civilian communities.

Note: Observer status has been granted to Bosnia and Herzegovina, the Central African Republic, Russia, Thailand, the Muslim community of the 'Turkish Republic of Northern Cyprus', the Moro National Liberation Front (MNLF) of the southern Philippines, the UN, the African Union, the Non-Aligned Movement, the League of Arab States, the Economic Cooperation Organization and the Cooperation Council for the Arab States of the Gulf. The revised OIC Charter, endorsed in March 2008, made future applications for OIC membership and observer status conditional upon Muslim demographic majority and membership of the UN.

Organization

(April 2014)

SUMMIT CONFERENCES

The supreme body of the organization is the Conference of Heads of State ('Islamic summit'), which met in 1969 in Rabat, Morocco, in 1974 in Lahore, Pakistan, and in January 1981 in Makkah (Mecca), Saudi Arabia, when it was decided that ordinary summit conferences would normally be held every three years in future. An extraordinary summit conference was convened in Doha, Qatar, in March 2003, to consider the situation in Iraq. A further extraordinary conference, held in December 2005, in Makkah, Saudi Arabia, determined to restructure the OIC, and, in August 2012, an extraordinary summit was convened, again in Makkah, with a focus on the ongoing civil war in Syria. The 12th ordinary Islamic summit was convened in Cairo, Egypt, in February 2013, and the 13th was to take place in Turkey, during 2016.

CONFERENCE OF MINISTERS OF FOREIGN AFFAIRS

Conferences take place annually, to consider the means of implementing the general policy of the OIC, although they may also be convened for extraordinary sessions.

SECRETARIAT

The executive organ of the organization, headed by a Secretary-General (who is elected by the Conference of Ministers of Foreign Affairs for a five-year term, renewable only once) and four Assistant Secretaries-General (similarly appointed).

In March 2013 a specialized Peace, Security and Mediation Unit was inaugurated at the Secretariat.

Secretary-General: IYAD BIN AMIN MADANI (Saudi Arabia).

At the summit conference in January 1981 it was decided that an International Islamic Court of Justice should be established to adjudicate in disputes between Muslim countries. Experts met in January 1983 to draw up a constitution for the court; however, by 2014 it was not yet in operation.

EXECUTIVE COMMITTEE

The third extraordinary conference of the OIC, convened in Makkah, Saudi Arabia, in December 2005, mandated the establishment of the Executive Committee as a mechanism for following up resolutions of the Conference. It comprises representatives of the OIC host country, the OIC Secretariat, and the summit conference and ministerial conference 'troikas' made up of member countries equally representing the OIC's African, Arab and Asian membership.

STANDING COMMITTEES

Al-Quds Committee: f. 1975 to implement the resolutions of the Islamic Conference on the status of Jerusalem (Al-Quds); it meets at the level of ministers responsible for foreign affairs; maintains the Al-Quds Fund; Chair. King MUHAMMAD VI OF MOROCCO.

Standing Committee for Economic and Commercial Co-operation (COMCEC): f. 1981; Chair. ABDULLAH GÜL (Pres. of Turkey).

Standing Committee for Information and Cultural Affairs (COMIAC): f. 1981; Chair. MACKY SALL (Pres. of Senegal).

Standing Committee for Scientific and Technological Co-operation (COMSTECH): f. 1981; Chair. MAMNOON HUSSAIN (Pres. of Pakistan).

Other committees include the Islamic Peace Committee, the Permanent Finance Committee, the Committee of Islamic Solidarity with the Peoples of the Sahel, the Eight-Member Committee on the Situation of Muslims in the Philippines, the Six-Member Committee on Palestine, the Committee on UN reform, and the ad hoc Committee on Afghanistan. In addition, there is an Islamic Commission for Economic, Cultural and Social Affairs, and there are OIC Contact Groups on Bosnia and Herzegovina, Iraq, Kosovo, Jammu and Kashmir, Mali (established in 2013), Myanmar (formed in 2012), Sierra Leone, and Somalia. A Commission of Eminent Persons was inaugurated in 2005.

OIC Independent Human Rights Commission (IPHRC): f. 2012 to promote the civil, political, social and economic rights enshrined in the covenants and declarations of the OIC, and in universally agreed human rights instruments, in conformity with Islamic values; inaugural session convened in Jakarta, Indonesia (Feb. 2012); second session convened (in Aug.) in Ankara, Turkey, with a focus on the human rights situations in Mali, Myanmar (with regard to the Rohingya Muslim minority), Palestine, and Syria; in Oct. issued a statement strongly condemning an assassination attempt made earlier in that month against the Pakistani schoolgirl Malala Yousufzai, who had campaigned for the recognition of the right to education for girls; the Commission emphasized that access to education remained a fundamental human right and identified the right to education and the rights of women and children as priority areas of activity; OIC human rights instruments include: the *Shari'a* -based Cairo Declaration on Human Rights in Islam (1990) and Covenant on the Rights of the Child in Islam (2005); IPHRC comprises 18 commissioners, equally representing Africa, Asia and the Middle East.

Activities

The OIC's aims, as proclaimed in the Charter (adopted in 1972, with revisions endorsed in 1990 and 2008), are:

(i) To promote Islamic solidarity among member states;

(ii) To consolidate co-operation among member states in the economic, social, cultural, scientific and other vital fields, and to arrange consultations among member states belonging to international organizations;

(iii) To endeavour to eliminate racial segregation and discrimination and to eradicate colonialism in all its forms;

(iv) To take necessary measures to support international peace and security founded on justice;

(v) To co-ordinate all efforts for the safeguard of the Holy Places and support of the struggle of the people of Palestine, and help them to regain their rights and liberate their land;

(vi) To strengthen the struggle of all Muslim people with a view to safeguarding their dignity, independence and national rights;

(vii) To create a suitable atmosphere for the promotion of co-operation and understanding among member states and other countries.

ECONOMIC CO-OPERATION

In 1991 22 OIC member states signed a Framework Agreement on a Trade Preferential System among the OIC Member States (TPS-OIC); this entered into force in 2003, following the requisite ratification by more than 10 member states, and was envisaged as representing the first step towards the eventual establishment of an Islamic common market. A Trade Negotiating Committee was established following the entry into force of the Framework Agreement. The first round of trade negotiations on the establishment of the TPS-OIC, concerning finalizing tariff reduction modalities and an implementation schedule for the Agreement, was held during April 2004–April 2005, and resulted in the conclusion of a Protocol on the Preferential Tariff Scheme for TPS-OIC (PRETAS). In November 2006, at the launch of the second round of negotiations, ministers adopted a roadmap towards establishing the TPS-OIC; the second round of negotiations ended in September 2007 with the adoption of rules of origin for the TPS-OIC. PRETAS entered into force in February 2010. By January 2014 the Framework Agreement had been ratified by 30 OIC member states, and PRETAS had 16 ratifications. In 2014 efforts were under way to enhance the role of the private sector through the promotion of intra-OIC small and medium-sized enterprise clusters, in sectors including agro-food processing, and transportation and logistics.

The first OIC Anti-Corruption and Enhancing Integrity Forum was convened in August 2006 in Kuala Lumpur, Malaysia. In November 2009 a COMCEC Business Forum was held, in Istanbul, Turkey. An International Islamic Business and Finance Summit has been organized annually since 2009, in Kazan, Russia, by the OIC and the Russian Government; 'KAZANSUMMIT 2013' was convened in October 2013. The 14th Trade Fair of the OIC member states took place in Tehran, Iran, in October–November of that year. The ninth World Islamic Economic Forum was convened in London, United Kingdom, in December.

In March 2012 OIC ministers responsible for water approved the OIC Water Vision 2025, providing a framework for co-operation in maximizing the productive use of, and minimizing the destructive impact of, members' water resources. In May 2012 the fifth Islamic Conference of Environment Ministers, convened in Astana, adopted an Islamic Declaration on Sustainable Development.

CULTURAL AND TECHNICAL CO-OPERATION

OIC supports education in Muslim communities throughout the world, and was instrumental in the establishment of Islamic universities in Niger and Uganda. It organizes seminars on various aspects of Islam, and encourages dialogue with the other monotheistic religions. Support is given to publications on Islam both in Muslim and Western countries. In June 1999 an OIC Parliamentary Union was inaugurated; its founding conference was convened in Tehran.

The OIC organizes meetings at ministerial level to consider aspects of information policy and new technologies. An OIC Digital Solidarity Fund was inaugurated in May 2005. Participation by OIC member states in the Fund was promoted at the 11th summit meeting in March 2008, and the meeting also requested each member state to establish a board to monitor national implementation of the Tunis Declaration on the Information Society, adopted by the November 2005 second phase of the World Summit on the Information Society. In August 2011 the OIC organized a Decorative Arts and Calligraphy Exhibition, at its headquarters in Jeddah, Saudi Arabia.

In March 2008 the 11th Islamic summit initiated an Atlas of Islamic World Science and Innovation project, with the aim of mapping trends in, and promoting. science- and technology-based innovation in member states. The most recent country report under the project was compiled for Jordan, and was published in August 2013.

HUMANITARIAN ASSISTANCE

Assistance is given to Muslim communities affected by violent conflict and natural disasters. It was announced in August 2010 that an OIC Emergency Fund for Natural Disasters would be established, to assist survivors of any natural disaster occurring in a Muslim country; the modalities of the establishment of the Fund remain under consideration. The first conference of Islamic humanitarian organizations was convened by the OIC in March 2008, and a second conference, bringing together 32 organizations, took place in April 2009. The third conference, held in March 2010, established a working group to draft a plan aimed at strengthening co-operation between the OIC and other humanitarian organizations active in Afghanistan, Gaza, Darfur, Iraq, Niger, Somalia and Sudan; and also approved the formation of a joint commission which was to study the structure and mechanism of co-operation and co-ordination between humanitarian organizations. The fourth conference was convened in June 2011, on the theme 'Civil Society Organizations in the Muslim World: Responsibilities and Roles'. In May 2012 the first Conference on Refugees in the Muslim World was convened by the OIC, UNHCR and the Turkmen Government, in Aşgabat, Turkmenistan. In November OIC ministers responsible for foreign affairs agreed to grant non-governmental humanitarian relief agencies headquartered in member states consultative status in the Organization. In 2013 OIC worked to enhance co-operation and co-ordination of activities with the UN Office for Humanitarian Affairs (OCHA), with a view to achieving more efficient delivery of humanitarian assistance.

The OIC has established trust funds to assist vulnerable people in Afghanistan, Bosnia and Herzegovina, and Sierra Leone. Humanitarian assistance provided by OIC member states in recent years has included aid to victims of conflict in Darfur, southern Sudan; to Pakistan following severe flooding in August 2010; and to Somalia, in response to severe famine that affected some 3.7m. people in 2011.

The drought-prone countries of the Sahel region (Burkina Faso, Cape Verde, Chad, The Gambia, Guinea, Guinea-Bissau, Mali, Mauritania, Niger and Senegal) receive particular attention. In September 2012 the OIC Secretary-General launched an urgent appeal for Niger and Senegal, as a response to the damage and loss of life caused by sudden heavy rainfall and flooding in August. In October the OIC and OCHA jointly undertook a mission to Burkina Faso, Mali and Niger, to assess the gravity of the ongoing Sahel humanitarian crisis, and to address means of strengthening mutual co-operation. In August 2013 the OIC Secretary-General requested member states to provide urgent assistance to Sudan, in view of severe flooding at that time in the environs of that country's capital, Khartoum. In February 2014 the Islamic Solidarity Fund and the OIC provided humanitarian assistance, including medical drugs, food, non-food items, 250 tents, the sinking of six boreholes, and a power generator, to assist returning refugees in Chad.

In mid-March 2012 a joint OIC-UN team of technical experts was dispatched to Syria to assess the humanitarian impact of the ongoing unrest there and to prepare an evaluation of the level of humanitarian aid required; in April, having considered the findings of the assessment team, the OIC Secretary-General stated that US $70m. in funding was required to assist at least 1m. Syrians at that time.

POLITICAL CO-OPERATION

The OIC gives support to member countries in regaining or maintaining political stability. In January 2009 the OIC and the League of Arab States signed an agreement providing for the strengthening of co-operation and co-ordination in the areas of politics, media, the economy, and in the social and scientific spheres. In June 2011 OIC ministers responsible for foreign affairs adopted the Astana Declaration on Peace, Co-operation and Development, in which they recognized emerging challenges presented by unfolding significant political developments in the Middle East and North Africa (the so-called Arab Spring) and appealed for engagement in constructive dialogue towards peaceful solutions. The Declaration expressed grave concern at the then ongoing conflict in Libya, and at the humanitarian consequences thereof.

The first OIC Conference on Women was held in November 2006, on the theme 'The role of women in the development of OIC member states'. An inaugural Conference of Muslim Women Parliamentarians was convened in January 2012, in Palembang, Indonesia. In December the statute of an OIC Women Development Organization (WDO) was opened for signature; upon entry into force the WDO was to become an OIC specialized agency, to be headquartered in Cairo, and focused on advancing the empowerment of women in member states.

In November 2013 an Islamic conference of ministers responsible for children was convened in Baku, Azerbaijan, on the theme, 'Children and the Challenges of Urbanization in the Islamic World'. An Islamic Conference of Ministers of Youth was convened in March 2014, in Jeddah, Saudi Arabia.

In October 2013 Islamic ministers responsible for health, meeting in Jakarta, Indonesia, adopted the OIC Strategic Health Programme of Action, covering the period 2014–23, and also a plan providing a framework for focused national actions to enable the implementation of the Programme. In February 2014 the OIC inaugurated a new Islamic International Advisory Group on Polio Eradication.

In January 2014 the OIC Secretary-General condemned ongoing violent unrest in the Central African Republic (CAR), which had caused massive population displacement; in March a special envoy of the Secretary-General was appointed to mediate between opposing factions in the CAR. In March the OIC expressed concern for the well being of the Muslim Tatar community in Crimea, in view of that territory's decision—deemed under international law to be illegal—to secede from Ukraine and join Russia.

Afghanistan: In October 2001 OIC ministers responsible for foreign affairs established a fund to assist Afghan civilians, following US-led military attacks on targets in Afghanistan. In mid-2010 the OIC determined to appoint a permanent representative for Afghanistan, to be based in an OIC office in Kabul, the Afghan capital. The OIC Kabul office was inaugurated in January 2011. In March the OIC Secretary-General, addressing the International Contact Group on Afghanistan, stressed OIC support for the High Peace Council, established in Afghanistan in 2010 as a platform for dialogue between the Afghan administration and the Taliban, and stated the willingness of the Organization to contribute to peace in that country. In December 2011, attending the International Conference on Afghanistan, convened in Bonn, Germany, the OIC Secretary-General emphasized that the Organization would continue to support Afghanistan beyond 2014, when NATO forces were scheduled to leave the country.

Iraq: In March 2003 an extraordinary summit conference of Islamic leaders convened in Doha, Qatar, to consider the ongoing Iraq crisis, welcomed the Saddam Hussain regime's acceptance of UN Security Council Resolution 1441 and consequent co-operation with UN weapons inspectors, and emphatically rejected military action against Iraq or threats to the security of any other Islamic state. The conference also urged progress towards the elimination of all weapons of mass destruction in the Middle East, including those held by Israel. In mid-May 2004 the OIC Secretary-General urged combat forces in Iraq to respect the inviolability of that country's holy places. In December 2005 he appealed to the people of Iraq to participate peacefully in the legislative elections that took place later in that month. In October 2006, under OIC auspices, Iraqi representatives, meeting in Jeddah, Saudi Arabia, signed the Mecca Agreement, a 10-point plan aimed at ending ongoing sectarian violence and at safeguarding Iraq's holy places territorial integrity. In April 2012 the OIC Secretary-General announced that a comprehensive plan was being developed to revive the 2006 Mecca Agreement. The OIC Secretary-General has repeatedly appealed for an end to sectarian strife in Iraq. In October 2008 he condemned the persecution of Christians in northern Iraq.

Israel/Palestine: Since its inception the OIC has called for the vacation of Arab territories by Israel, recognition of the rights of Palestinians, and the restoration of Jerusalem to Arab rule. In June 2002 OIC ministers responsible for foreign affairs endorsed the peace plan for the region that had been adopted by the summit meeting of the League of Arab States in March. In May 2004 the Secretary-General of the OIC condemned the ongoing destruction of Palestinian homes by Israeli forces, and consequent population displacement, particularly in Rafah, Gaza. In January 2009 an expanded extraordinary meeting of the Executive Committee, at ministerial level, convened to address the ongoing intensive bombardment of the Gaza Strip that was initiated by Israeli forces in late December 2008 with the stated aim of ending rocket attacks launched by Hamas and other militant groups on Israeli targets. The meeting strongly condemned the Israeli attacks and ensuing destruction and loss of civilian life, and requested the OIC Secretariat to co-ordinate with member states' civil society organizations to provide urgent humanitarian relief to the Palestinian people. In March 2009, while visiting the affected area, the OIC Secretary-General urged the reconciliation of the different Palestinian political factions. In June 2010 an expanded extraordinary ministerial meeting of the Executive Committee condemned the attack by Israeli security forces, at the end of May, against a flotilla of vessels carrying humanitarian aid to Gaza, which had resulted in nine civilian deaths and caused injuries to at least 40 people. The OIC rejected a UN-commissioned report on the flotilla incident, released in September 2011, which—while concluding that the Israeli army had used 'excessive and unreasonable' force—also found the Israeli naval blockade of Gaza to have been imposed as a 'legitimate security measure' to prevent weapons from reaching Gaza by sea, and found that the flotilla had acted recklessly in attempting to breach the naval blockade. The OIC Secretary-General supported efforts to bring the issue of the blockade of Gaza before competent international legal authorities. In late September the OIC Secretary-General condemned a decision by Israel to build 1,100 new housing units in occupied East Jerusalem. During that month the OIC expressed support for the formal request by the Executive President of the Palestinian Authority for Palestine's admission to the UN, and recognition of its independent statehood.

In February 2013 the 12th OIC summit issued a declaration on Palestine which, inter alia, welcomed the decision, in November 2012, of the UN General Assembly to grant Palestine observer status at the UN.

In July 2013 the OIC Secretary-General commended a decision by the European Union to exclude Israeli settlements situated in Palestinian and Arab territories occupied since 1967 from any future agreements made with its member states. In February 2014 the Secretary-General condemned a decision of the Israeli authorities to endorse the construction of 558 new settlement units in Jerusalem, allegedly with a view to altering the demographic reality of the city, and isolating it from its Palestinian surroundings.

Mali: In April 2012 the OIC Secretary-General expressed 'total rejection' of the proclamation by militants in northern Mali of an independent homeland of Azawad. In February 2013 the 12th OIC summit issued a declaration on Mali, in which it strongly condemned the activities of terrorist groups and movements there, including attacks on communities and the destruction of cultural sites, and also condemned the threat to security and stability posed by transnational organized crime and drugs-trafficking networks. The declaration reaffirmed full solidarity with the people of Mali and that country's National Unity Government; urged member states to provide economic assistance to Mali; requested the OIC Secretary-General to elaborate—in consultation with the Mali authorities, the African Union, Economic Community of West African States and other partners—a strategy for post-conflict reconstruction and assistance for that country; and determined to establish an OIC Contact Group on Mali, to monitor future developments. The inaugural meeting of the Contact Group was held in May. The OIC Secretary-General commended the peaceful conduct of the presidential election held in Mali in late July and early August.

Myanmar: In May 2011 the OIC Secretariat hosted a convention of senior leaders of the minority Rohingya Muslim community in the western Rakhine (Arakan) region of Myanmar. The convention established the Arakan Rohingya Union (ARU), which was to seek a political solution to challenges confronting the Rohingya minority, based on the principles of an indivisible Rakhine state, peaceful co-existence with the Buddhist majority population, democracy and human rights, and federalism. In August 2012 OIC heads of state and government, convened in Makkah, Saudi Arabia, determined to form a Contact Group on Myanmar, at ministerial level, and to send an OIC fact-finding mission to Myanmar in September to investigate reports of recent violence and human rights violations against displaced Rohingya Muslims in Rakhine. The OIC heads of state and government also decided to bring before the UN General Assembly concerns about the treatment by the Myanmar authorities of the Rohingya minority. The fact-finding mission visited Myanmar in early September, making extensive contact with the national and Rakhine authorities on means of advancing OIC-Myanmar engagement in the promotion of inter-communal reconciliation. An agreement was signed with the Myanmar authorities to establish a co-ordination and monitoring presence in the Myanmar capital, Yangon, and in Sittwe (in Rakhine), to facilitate the implementation of humanitarian activities in support of the Rohingya minority. The inaugural meeting of the Contact Group, held in September, reviewed a report submitted by the fact-finding mission; representatives of the ARU reported to the Group on the current humanitarian and security situation in Rakhine. The Contact Group concluded that the Rohingya Muslims would benefit from the provision of development projects, as well as humanitarian aid; urged the Myanmar authorities to launch a rehabilitation and reconciliation process in Rakhine and to resettle displaced people in the region; and called for a special session of the UN Human Rights Council, and adoption of a resolution by the UN General Assembly, on the situation in Myanmar. In March 2013 the OIC Secretary-General launched a Global Rohingya Centre, based at OIC headquarters. At the end of that month the Secretary-General urged the Myanmar authorities to act to facilitate an end to ongoing acts of violence being perpetrated against Muslims reportedly by Buddhist nationalist elements. A meeting of the Contact Group, convened in mid-April, condemned the spread of violent conflict in Myanmar, emphasizing the need to respect universally accepted human rights. In July, addressing a congress of the ARU, the OIC Secretary-General urged the Myanmar Government to eradicate all forms of discrimination against Muslims, including legislation adopted in 2005 that imposed a two-child limit on Rohingya Muslim families living in two municipalities in Arakan. In September 2013 the Contact Group determined to table an OIC-sponsored resolution relating to Myanmar during the 68th session of the UN General Assembly. The Group also urged OIC member states and financial institutions to donate funds in support of the Myanmar Rohingya minority, and requested the Myanmar authorities to find a satisfactory solution to the situation of the Rohingya, including relating to their birthrights and legal status (they were at that time regarded by the Myanmar authorities as stateless residents). Meeting in late September OIC foreign ministers condemned continuing violence and violations of human rights in Rakhine, and emphasized the need to restore the right to citizenship of the Rohingya Muslims. In April 2014 the OIC Secretary General expressed concern at the refusal of the Myanmar authorities to permit respondents to self-identify as Rohingya during a recently conducted national population census.

Syria: In December 2011 the OIC Executive Committee convened a ministerial open-ended meeting to address the violent unrest that had prevailed since March in Syria. The OIC Secretary-General strongly condemned mass killings of civilians perpetrated by Syrian security forces in May, June and July 2012. In July the Secretary-General urged the Syrian authorities to place the interests of Syria and the Syrian people above all other considerations. An emergency summit of OIC heads of state and government, convened in Makkah, in August, determined to suspend Syria from participation in the activities of the Organization and from all its subsidiary organs and specialized and affiliated institutions. The summit demanded the immediate implementation of a UN-Arab League peace plan that had been agreed in March by the Syrian authorities and opposition, but was not being observed, and urged the development of a mechanism to facilitate the creation of a Syrian state based on pluralism and democratic values. The summit also urged the UN Security Council to take measures to end the ongoing violence and to pursue a peaceful and lasting solution to the Syrian crisis. Syria's suspension from the OIC was opposed by Iran. In November the OIC welcomed an agreement by the Syrian opposition to establish the Syrian National Coalition of Revolutionary and Opposition Forces. In February 2013 the 12th OIC summit urged a Syrian-led negotiated solution to the ongoing conflict, and reaffirmed support to the UN-Arab League Joint Special Representative on Syria. In mid-September the OIC Secretary-General welcomed the release of the report by a UN weapons inspection team into the deployment, on 21 August, of chemical weapons against civilians in Damascus, Syria, that had caused up to around 1,400 fatalities. Condemning the Damascus atrocity as a war crime and crime against humanity, he emphasized the need to hold to account any party involved in the production, transfer, development, and use of chemical weapons in Syria. In mid-October the Secretaries-General of the League and the OIC urged all parties to the conflict to observe a full ceasefire over the festival of Eid al-Adha. In December an OIC-sponsored Centre for the Treatment of Psychological and Social Shocks was inaugurated in Kayleis, Turkey, to support Syrian refugees in that country. In January 2014 the OIC Secretary-General addressed the Geneva II Syrian peace talks, urging an immediate ceasefire and the creation of a national transitional government.

Combating Terrorism: In December 1994 OIC heads of state adopted a Code of Conduct for Combating International Terrorism, in an attempt to control Muslim extremist groups. The code commits states to ensuring that militant groups do not use their territory for planning or executing terrorist activity against other states, in addition to states refraining from direct support or participation in acts of terrorism. An OIC Convention on Combating International Terrorism was adopted in 1998. In September 2001 the OIC Secretary-General strongly condemned major terrorist attacks perpetrated against targets in the USA. An extraordinary meeting of OIC ministers responsible for foreign affairs, convened in October, in Doha, to consider the implications of the terrorist atrocities, condemned the attacks and declared its support for combating all manifestations of terrorism within the framework of a proposed collective initiative co-ordinated under the auspices of the UN. The meeting, which did not pronounce directly on the recently initiated US-led military retaliation against targets in Afghanistan, urged that no Arab or Muslim state should be targeted under the pretext of eliminating terrorism. In February 2002 the Secretary-General expressed concern at statements of the US Administration describing Iran and Iraq (as well as the Democratic People's Republic of Korea) as belonging to an 'axis of evil' involved in international terrorism and the development of weapons of mass destruction. In April OIC ministers responsible for foreign affairs convened an extraordinary session on terrorism, in Kuala Lumpur, Malaysia. The meeting issued the Kuala Lumpur Declaration, which reiterated member states' collective resolve to combat terrorism; condemned attempts to associate terrorist activities with Islam or any other particular creed, civilization or nationality, and rejected attempts to associate Islamic states or the Palestinian struggle with terrorism; rejected the implementation of international action against any Muslim state on the pretext of combating terrorism; urged the organization of a global conference on international terrorism; and urged an examination of the root causes of international terrorism. The meeting adopted a plan of action on addressing the issues raised in the declaration. Its implementation was to be co-ordinated by a 13-member committee on international terrorism. Member states were encouraged to sign and ratify the Convention on Combating International Terrorism in order to accelerate its implementation. In May 2003 the 30th session of the Conference of Ministers of Foreign Affairs issued the Tehran Declaration, in which it resolved to combat terrorism and to contribute to preserving peace and security in Islamic countries. The Declaration also pledged its full support for the Palestinian cause and rejected the labelling as 'terrorist' of those Muslim states deemed to be resisting foreign aggression and occupation. In April 2009 the heads of law enforcement agencies in OIC member states, gathered in Baku, adopted the Baku Declaration on co-operation in combating transnational organized crime, including international terrorism, extremism, aggressive separatism, and human trafficking. The OIC has repeatedly urged the worldwide adoption of a clear definition of terrorism; in September 2013 the OIC Secretary-General stated that an unambiguous definition should be incorporated into UN counter-terrorism planning.

Supporting Muslim Minorities and Combating Anti-Islamic Feeling: In December 2007 the OIC organized the first International Conference on Islamophobia, aimed at addressing concerns that alleged instances of defamation of Islam appeared to be increasing worldwide (particularly in Europe). Responding to a reported rise in anti-Islamic attacks on Western nations, OIC leaders denounced stereotyping and discrimination, and urged the promotion of Islam by Islamic states as a 'moderate, peaceful and tolerant religion'. The Secretary-General stated in June 2012 that Islamophobia was being exploited in electoral campaigns in Europe, citing the campaigns for the French presidential election held in April–May. An Islamic Observatory on Islamophobia, established in September 2006, has released periodic reports on intolerance against Muslims; the sixth, released in December 2013, and covering the period October 2012–September 2013, claimed that during the period under review symbols and personalities held sacred by Islam continued to be violated, generating a xenophobic environment, particularly in some Western countries. In November 2013 the OIC expressed dismay over reports that the authorities in Angola had banned the practice of Islam.

In March 2011 the UN Human Rights Council adopted by consensus a resolution, that had been presented on behalf of the OIC, on 'Combating intolerance, negative stereotyping, and stigmatization of, and discrimination, incitement to violence and violence against, persons based on religion or belief'. Resolution 16/18 called on UN member states to ensure, inter alia, that public officials avoid discriminating against individuals on the basis of religion or belief; that citizens might manifest their religion; that religious profiling be avoided; and that places of worship be protected. Previous related draft resolutions proposed by the OIC had focused on combating 'defamation of religions', and had been rejected by human rights organizations and by some UN member states on grounds related to the right to freedom of expression. In July 2011 the OIC and the USA jointly launched the Istanbul Process for Combating Intolerance and Discrimination Based on Religion or Belief, and, in December, a joint OIC-USA Conference on Addressing the Istanbul Process was convened in Washington, DC, USA. In June 2013 the inaugural meeting of an OIC Media Forum—tasked with advancing the co-ordination of media oulets in Islamic countries—was held in Ankara, Turkey. An International Conference on Islamophobia: Law and Media, held in Istanbul in September, endorsed the establishment of an Advisory Media Committee to meet under the auspices of the Media Forum.

Reform of the OIC: The 10th OIC summit meeting, held in October 2003, in Putrajaya, Malaysia, issued the Putrajaya Declaration, in which Islamic leaders resolved to enhance Islamic states' role and influence in international affairs. The leaders adopted a plan of action that entailed reviewing and strengthening OIC positions on international issues; enhancing dialogue among Muslim thinkers and policy-makers through relevant OIC institutions; promoting constructive dialogue with other cultures and civilizations; completing an ongoing review of the structure and efficacy of the OIC Secretariat; establishing a working group to address means of enhancing the role of Islamic education; promoting among member states the development of science and technology, discussion of ecological issues, and the role of information communication technology in development; improving mechanisms to assist member states in post-conflict situations; and advancing trade and investment through data-sharing and encouraging access to markets for products from poorer member states. In January 2005 the inaugural meeting of an OIC Commission of Eminent Persons was convened in Putrajaya. The Commission was mandated to make recommendations in the following areas: the preparation of a strategy and plan of action enabling the Islamic community to meet the challenges of the 21st century; the preparation of a comprehensive plan for promoting enlightened moderation, both within Islamic societies and universally; and the preparation of proposals for the future reform and restructuring of the OIC system. In December the third extraordinary OIC summit, convened in Makkah, adopted a 10-Year Programme of Action to Meet the Challenges Facing the Ummah (the Islamic world) in the 21st Century, a related Declaration and a report by the Commission of Eminent Persons. The summit determined to restructure the OIC, and mandated the establishment of an Executive Committee to implement Conference resolutions.

The 11th OIC heads of state summit meeting, held in Dakar, Senegal, in March 2008, endorsed a revised OIC Charter.

Finance

The OIC's activities are financed by mandatory contributions from member states.

Subsidiary Organs

Islamic Centre for the Development of Trade: Complexe Commercial des Habous, ave des FAR, BP 13545, Casablanca, Morocco; tel. (522) 314974; fax (522) 310110; e-mail icdt@icdt-oic.org; internet www.icdt-oic.org; f. 1983 to encourage regular commercial contacts, harmonize policies and promote investments among OIC mems; Dir-Gen. Dr EL HASSANE HZAINE; publs *Tijaris: International and Inter-Islamic Trade Magazine* (every two months), *Inter-Islamic Trade Report* (annually).

Islamic Jurisprudence (Fiqh) Academy: POB 13917, Jeddah, Saudi Arabia; tel. (2) 667-1664; fax (2) 667-0873; internet www.fiqhacademy.org.sa; f. 1982; Gen. Sec. Dr AHMAD KHALED BABACAR.

Islamic Solidarity Fund: c/o OIC Secretariat, POB 1997, Jeddah 21411, Saudi Arabia; tel. (2) 698-1296; fax (2) 256-8185; e-mail info@isf-fsi.org; internet www.isf-fsi.org; f. 1974 to meet the needs of Islamic communities by providing emergency aid and the finance to build mosques, Islamic centres, hospitals, schools and universities; during 2005–13 the Fund supported 389 projects, at a cost of US $29m; Exec. Dir IBRAHIM BIN ABDALLAH AL-KHUZAYEM.

Islamic University in Uganda: POB 2555, Mbale, Uganda; tel. (35) 2512100; fax (45) 433502; e-mail info@iuiu.ac.ug; internet www.iuiu.ac.ug; f. 1988 to meet the educational needs of Muslim populations in English-speaking African countries; second campus in Kampala; mainly financed by the OIC; Rector Dr AHMAD KAWEESA SSENGENDO.

Islamic University of Niger: BP 11507, Niamey, Niger; tel. 20-72-39-03; fax 20-73-37-96; e-mail unislam@intnet.ne; internet www.universite_say.ne; f. 1984; provides courses of study in *Shari'a* (Islamic law) and Arabic language and literature; also offers courses in pedagogy and teacher training; receives grants from Islamic Solidarity Fund and contributions from OIC mem. states; Rector Prof. ABDELJAOUAD SEKKAT.

Islamic University of Technology (IUT): Board Bazar, Gazipur 1704, Dhaka, Bangladesh; tel. (2) 9291254; fax (2) 9291260; e-mail vc@iut-dhaka.edu; internet www.iutoic-dhaka.edu; f. 1981 as the Islamic Centre for Technical and Vocational Training and Resources, named changed to Islamic Institute of Technology in 1994, current name adopted in 2001; aims to develop human resources in OIC mem. states, with special reference to engineering, technology, and technical education; 145 staff and 800 students; library of 30,450 vols; Vice-Chancellor Prof. Dr M. IMTIAZ HOSSAIN; publs *Journal of Engineering and Technology* (2 a year), *News Bulletin* (annually), *News Letter* (6 a year), annual calendar and announcement for admission, reports, human resources development series.

Research Centre for Islamic History, Art and Culture (IRCICA): POB 24, Beşiktaş 34354, İstanbul, Turkey; tel. (212) 2591742; fax (212) 2584365; e-mail ircica@ircica.org; internet www.ircica.org; f. 1980; library of 60,000 vols; Dir-Gen. Prof. Dr HALIT EREN; publs *Newsletter* (3 a year), monographical studies.

Statistical, Economic and Social Research and Training Centre for Islamic Countries (SESRIC): Kudüs Cad. No. 9, Diplomatik Site, 06450, Ankara, Turkey; tel. (312) 4686172; fax (312) 4673458; e-mail oicankara@sesric.org; internet www.sesric.org; became operational in 1978; has a three-fold mandate: to collate, process and disseminate socio-economic statistics and information on, and for the utilization of, its member countries; to study and assess economic and social developments in member countries with the aim of helping to generate proposals for advancing co-operation; and to organize training programmes in selected areas; the Centre also acts as a focal point for technical co-operation activities between the OIC system and related UN agencies; and prepares economic and social reports and background documentation for OIC meetings; Dir-Gen. Dr SAVAŞ ALPAY (Turkey); publs *Annual Economic Report on the OIC Countries*, *Journal of Economic Cooperation and Development* (quarterly), *Economic Cooperation and Development Review* (2 a year), *InfoReport* (quarterly), *Statistical Yearbook* (annually), *Basic Facts and Figures on OIC Member Countries* (annually).

Specialized Institutions

International Islamic News Agency (IINA): King Khalid Palace, Madinah Rd, POB 5054, Jeddah 21422, Saudi Arabia; tel. (2) 665-8561; fax (2) 665-9358; e-mail iina@islamicnews.org; internet www.iinanews.com; f. 1972; distributes news and reports daily on events in the Islamic world, in Arabic, English and French; Dir-Gen. ALI BIN AHMED AL-GHAMDI (acting).

Islamic Educational, Scientific and Cultural Organization (ISESCO): BP 2275 Rabat 10104, Morocco; tel. (37) 566052; fax (37) 566012; e-mail cid@isesco.org.ma; internet www.isesco.org.ma; f. 1982; mems: 52 states; Dir-Gen. Dr ABDULAZIZ BIN OTHMAN ALTWAIJRI; publs *ISESCO Newsletter* (quarterly), *Islam Today* (2 a year), *ISESCO Triennial*.

Islamic Broadcasting Union (IBU): POB 6351, Jeddah 21442, Saudi Arabia; tel. (2) 672-1121; fax (2) 672-2600; e-mail ibu@ibuj.org; internet www.ibuj.org; f. 1975; Dir-Gen. MOHAMED SALEM WALAD BOAKE.

Islamic Organization for Food Security: Astana, Kazakhstan; f. 2013 to co-ordinate, provide technical advice on, and implement OIC policies on agriculture, rural development and food security; also tasked with mobilizing financial resources for developing agriculture and enhancing food security in OIC mem. states.

Organization for the Development of Women in the OIC Member States (WMO): Cairo, Egypt; f. 2012 to address capacity development, and skills and competence building, with respect to the role of women in OIC member states, through mechanisms including education, training and rehabilitation, in accordance with Islamic values; was to become operational following the entry into force of its founding Statute.

Affiliated Institutions

International Association of Islamic Banks (IAIB): King Abdulaziz St, Queen's Bldg, 23rd Floor, Al-Balad Dist, POB 9707, Jeddah 21423, Saudi Arabia; tel. (2) 651-6900; fax (2) 651-6552; f. 1977 to link financial institutions operating on Islamic banking principles; activities include training and research; mems: 192 banks and other financial institutions in 34 countries.

Islamic Chamber of Commerce and Industry: POB 3831, Clifton, Karachi 75600, Pakistan; tel. (21) 5874910; fax (21) 5870765; e-mail icci@icci-oic.org; internet iccionline.net; f. 1979 to promote trade and industry among mem. states; comprises nat. chambers or feds of chambers of commerce and industry; Pres. SALEH ABDULLAH KAMEL; Sec.-Gen. Dr BASSEM AWADALLAH.

Islamic Committee for the International Crescent: POB 17434, Benghazi, Libya; tel. (61) 9095824; fax (61) 9095823; e-mail info@icic-oic.org; internet www.icic-oic.org; f. 1979 to attempt to alleviate the suffering caused by natural disasters and war; Pres. ALI MAHMOUD BUHEDMA.

Islamic Solidarity Sports Federation: POB 5844, Riyadh 11442, Saudi Arabia; tel. (1) 480-9253; fax (1) 482-2145; e-mail issf@awalnet.net.sa; f. 1981; organizes the Islamic Solidarity Games (2013: Jakarta, Indonesia, in Sept.–Oct.); Sec.-Gen. Dr MOHAMMAD SALEH QAZDAR.

OIC Computer Emergency Response Team (OIC-CERT): c/o CyberSecurity Malaysia, 7, Jalan Tasik, The Mines Resort City, 43300 Seri Kembangan, Selangor DArul Ehsan, Malaysia; internet www.ansi.tn/oic-cert/index.html; f. 2009 to enhance co-operation between mem. states' computer emergency response teams; aims to promote the exchange of information, to prevent cyber terrorism and computer crimes, and to advance education and technological research and development.

Organization of Islamic Capitals and Cities (OICC): POB 13621, Jeddah 21414, Saudi Arabia; tel. (2) 698-1953; fax (2) 698-1053; e-mail oiccmak@oicc.org; internet www.oicc.org; f. 1980; aims to preserve the identity and the heritage of Islamic capitals and cities; to achieve and enhance sustainable development in mem. capitals and cities; to establish and develop comprehensive urban norms, systems and plans to serve the growth and prosperity of Islamic capitals and cities and to enhance their cultural, environmental, urban, economic and social conditions; to advance municipal services and facilities in the member capitals and cities; to support mem. cities' capacity-building programmes; and to consolidate fellowship and co-ordinate the scope of co-operation between members; comprises 157 capitals and cities as active mems, eight observer mems and 18 assoc. mems, in Asia, Africa, Europe and South America; Sec.-Gen. OMAR ABDULLAH KADI.

Organization of the Islamic Shipowners' Association: POB 14900, Jeddah 21434, Saudi Arabia; tel. (2) 663-7882; fax (2) 660-4920; e-mail mail@oisaonline.com; internet www.oisaonline.com; f. 1981 to promote co-operation among maritime cos in Islamic countries; in 1998 mems approved the establishment of the Bakkah Shipping Company, to enhance sea transport in the region; Sec.-Gen. Dr ABDULLATIF A. SULTAN.

World Federation of Arab-Islamic Schools: Flat 2, Area 1, Block 28, 10th District, Nasr City, Cairo, Egypt; fax (2) 24728217; f. 1976; supports Arab-Islamic schools worldwide and encourages co-operation between the institutions; promotes the dissemination of the Arabic language and Islamic culture; supports the training of personnel.

ORGANIZATION OF THE PETROLEUM EXPORTING COUNTRIES—OPEC

Address: Helferstorferstrasse 17, 1010 Vienna, Austria.

Telephone: (1) 211-12-3303; **fax:** (1) 216-43-20; **e-mail:** prid@opec.org; **internet:** www.opec.org.

OPEC was established in 1960 to link countries whose main source of export earnings is petroleum. It aims to unify and co-ordinate members' petroleum policies and to safeguard their interests.

OPEC's share of world petroleum production was 43% in 2011 (compared with 54.7% in 1974). OPEC members were estimated to possess 81% of the world's known reserves of crude petroleum in 2011. OPEC members also possessed 48% of known reserves of natural gas, and accounted for 19% of total production of marketed natural gas.

MEMBERS

Algeria	Iraq	Qatar
Angola	Kuwait	Saudi Arabia
Ecuador	Libya	United Arab Emirates
Iran	Nigeria	Venezuela

Organization

(April 2014)

CONFERENCE

The Conference is the supreme authority of the organization, responsible for the formulation of its general policy. It consists of representatives of member countries, who examine reports and recommendations submitted by the Board of Governors. It approves the appointment of Governors from each country and elects the Chairman of the Board of Governors. It works on the unanimity principle, and meets at least twice a year. In September 2000 the Conference agreed that meetings of heads of state or government should be convened every five years.

BOARD OF GOVERNORS

The Board directs the management of OPEC; it implements resolutions of the Conference and draws up an annual budget. It consists of one governor for each member country, and meets at least twice a year.

MINISTERIAL MONITORING COMMITTEE

The Committee is responsible for monitoring price evolution and ensuring the stability of the world petroleum market. As such, it is charged with the preparation of long-term strategies, including the allocation of quotas to be presented to the Conference. The Committee consists of all national representatives, and is normally convened four times a year. A Ministerial Monitoring Sub-committee, reporting to the Committee on production and supply figures, was established in 1993.

ECONOMIC COMMISSION

A specialized body operating within the framework of the Secretariat, with a view to promoting stability in international prices for petroleum at equitable levels; consists of a Board, national representatives and a commission staff; meets at least twice a year.

SECRETARIAT

Secretary-General: ABDALLA SALEM EL-BADRI (Libya).

Office of the Secretary-General: provides the Secretary-General with executive assistance in maintaining contacts with governments, organizations and delegations, in matters of protocol and in the preparation for and co-ordination of meetings.

Legal Office: Provides legal advice, supervises the Secretariat's legal commitments, evaluates legal issues of concern to the organization and member countries, and recommends appropriate action; General Legal Counsel ASMA MUTTAWA.

Research Division: comprises the Data Services Department; the Energy Studies Department; and the Petroleum Market Analysis Department; Dir Dr OMAR S. ABDUL-HAMID.

Support Services Division: responsible for providing the required infrastructure and services to the whole Secretariat, in support of its programmes; has three departments: Administration and IT Services; Finance and Human Resources; and Public Relations and Information; Dir. (vacant).

Activities

OPEC's principal objectives, according to its Statute, are to co-ordinate and unify the petroleum policies of member countries and to determine the best means for safeguarding their individual and collective interests; to seek ways and means of ensuring the stabilization of prices in international oil markets, with a view to eliminating harmful and unnecessary fluctuations, and to provide a steady income to the producing countries, an efficient, economic and regular supply of petroleum to consuming nations, and a fair return on capital to those investing in the petroleum industry.

PRICES AND PRODUCTION

OPEC's five original members (Iran, Iraq, Kuwait, Saudi Arabia and Venezuela) first met following the imposition of price reductions by petroleum companies in the previous month (August 1960). During the 1960s members sought to assert their rights in an international petroleum market that was dominated by multinational companies. Between 1965 and 1967 a two-year joint production programme limited annual growth in output so as to secure adequate prices. During the 1970s member states increased their control over their domestic petroleum industries, and over the pricing of crude petroleum on world markets. In 1971 the five-year Tehran Agreement on pricing was concluded between the six producing countries from the Arabian Gulf region and 23 petroleum companies. In January 1972 petroleum companies agreed to adjust the petroleum revenues of the largest producers after changes in currency exchange rates (Geneva Agreement), and in 1973 OPEC and the petroleum companies agreed to raise posted prices of crude petroleum by 11.9% and installed a mechanism to make monthly adjustments to prices in future (Second Geneva Agreement). In October of that year a pricing crisis occurred when Arab member states refused to supply petroleum to nations that had supported Israel in its conflict with Egypt and Syria earlier in that month. Negotiations on the revision of the Tehran Agreement failed in the same month, and the Gulf states unilaterally declared increases of 70% in posted prices, from US $3.01 to $5.11 per barrel. In December the OPEC Conference decided to increase the price to $11.65 per barrel (despite Saudi Arabian opposition). OPEC's first summit meeting of heads of state or government was held in March 1975, and in September a ministerial meeting agreed to increase prices by 10% for the period to June 1976. Prices remained stable until the end of 1978, when it was agreed that during 1979 prices should increase by an average of 10% in four instalments during the year, to compensate for the effects of the depreciation of the US dollar. The overthrow of the Iranian Government in early 1979, however, led to a new steep increase in petroleum prices.

In March 1982 an emergency meeting of ministers responsible for petroleum agreed (for the first time in OPEC's history) to defend the organization's price structure by imposing an overall production 'ceiling' of 18m. barrels per day (b/d), reducing this to 17.5m. b/d at the beginning of 1983. Quotas were allocated for each member country except Saudi Arabia, which was to act as a 'swing producer' to supply the balancing quantities to meet market requirements. In October 1984 the production ceiling was lowered to 16m. b/d, and in December price differentials for light (more expensive) and heavy (cheaper) crudes were altered in an attempt to counteract price-cutting by non-OPEC producers, particularly Norway and the United Kingdom. During 1985, however, most members effectively abandoned the marker price system, and production in excess of quotas, unofficial discounts and barter deals by members, and price cuts by non-members contributed to a weakening of the market. In August 1986 all members except Iraq agreed upon a return to production quotas (Iraq declined to co-operate after its request to be allocated the same quota as Iran had been refused): total production was to be limited to 14.8m. b/d (16.8m. b/d including Iraq). This measure resulted in an increase in prices to about US $15 per barrel. In December members (except Iraq) agreed to return to a fixed pricing system, at a level of $18 per barrel as the OPEC Reference Basket (ORB) price (based on a 'basket' of, then, seven crudes, not, as hitherto, on a 'marker' crude, Arabian Light) with effect from 1 February 1987, setting a total production limit of 15.8m. b/d. OPEC's role of setting crude oil prices had come to an end, however, and from the late 1980s prices were determined by movements in the international markets, with OPEC's role being to increase or restrain production in order to prevent harmful fluctuations in prices. In June 1987, with prices having stabilized, the Conference decided to limit production to 16.6m. b/d (including Iraq's output) for the rest of the year. The production limit was increased to 18.5m. b/d for the first half of 1989 and, after prices had recovered to about $18 per barrel, to 19.5m. b/d for the second half of 1989, and to 22m. b/d for the first half of 1990.

In May 1990 members resolved to adhere more strictly to the agreed production quotas, in response to a decline in prices. In August Iraq invaded Kuwait (which it had accused, among other grievances, of violating production quotas). Petroleum exports by the two countries were halted by an international embargo, and petroleum prices immediately increased to exceed US $25 per barrel. OPEC ministers promptly allowed a temporary increase in production by other members, of between 3m. and 3.5m. b/d (mostly by Saudi Arabia, the United Arab Emirates—UAE—and Venezuela), to stabilize prices, and notwithstanding some fluctuations later in the year, this was achieved. During 1991 and 1992 ministers attempted to reach a minimum ORB price of $21 per barrel by imposing production limits that varied between 22.3m. b/d and 24.2m. b/d. Kuwait, which resumed production in 1992 after extensive damage had been inflicted on its oil wells during the conflict with Iraq, was granted a special dispensation to produce without a fixed quota until the following year. Ecuador withdrew from OPEC in November 1992, citing the high cost of membership and the organization's refusal to increase Ecuador's production quota. In 1993 a Ministerial Monitoring Sub-committee was established to supervise compliance with quotas, owing to members' persistent over-production. In July of that year discussions between Iraq and the UN on the possible supervised resumption of Iraqi petroleum exports depressed petroleum prices to below $16 per barrel, and at the end of the year prices fell below $14, after the Conference rejected any further reduction in the current limit of 24.5m. b/d, which remained in force during 1994 and 1995, although actual output continued to be well in excess of quotas. In May 1996 the UN and Iraq concluded an agreement allowing Iraq to resume exports of petroleum in order to fund humanitarian relief efforts within Iraq, and OPEC's overall production ceiling was accordingly raised to 25.0m. b/d from June. Gabon withdrew from OPEC in June, citing difficulties in meeting its budgetary contribution. Prices declined during the first half of 1997, falling to a low point of $16.7 per barrel in April, owing to the resumption of Iraqi exports, depressed world demand and continuing over-production: an escalation in political tension in the Gulf region, however, and in particular Iraq's reluctance to co-operate with UN weapons inspectors, prompted a price increase to about $21.2 per barrel in October. The overall production ceiling was raised by about 10%, to 27.5m. b/d, with effect from the beginning of 1998, but during that year prices declined, decreasing to below $12 per barrel from August (demand having been affected by the economic difficulties in South-East Asia), and OPEC imposed a succession of reductions in output, down to 24.4m. b/d from 1 July. Non-member countries concluded agreements with OPEC to limit their production in that year, and in March 1999 Mexico, Norway, Oman and Russia agreed to decrease production by a total of 388,000 b/d, while OPEC's own production limit was reduced to 22.97m. b/d. Evidence of almost 90% compliance with the new production quotas contributed to market confidence that stockpiles of petroleum would be reduced, and resulted in sustained price increases during the second half of the year.

By March 2000 petroleum prices had reached their highest level since 1990, briefly exceeding US $34 per barrel. In that month OPEC ministers agreed to raise output by 1.45m. b/d, in order to ease supply shortages, and introduced an informal price band mechanism that was to signal the need for adjustments in production should prices deviate for more than 20 days from an average bracket of $22–$28 per barrel. Further increases in production took effect in the second half of the year (with five non-OPEC members, Angola, Mexico, Norway, Oman and Russia, also agreeing to raise their output), but prices remained high and there was intense international pressure on OPEC to resolve the situation: in September both the Group of Seven industrialized countries (G7) and the IMF issued warnings about the potential economic and social consequences of sustained high petroleum prices. In that month OPEC heads of state and government, convened in their first summit meeting since 1975, responded by issuing the Caracas Declaration, in which they resolved to promote market stability through their policies on pricing and production, to increase co-operation with other petroleum exporters, and to improve communication with consumer countries. During the first half of 2001, with a view to stabilizing prices that by January had fallen back to around $25 per barrel, the Conference agreed to implement reductions in output totalling 2.5m. b/d, thereby limiting overall production to 24.2m. b/d, with a further reduction of 1m. b/d from 1 September. Terrorist attacks on targets in the USA in September gave rise to market uncertainty, and prices declined further, averaging $17–$18 per barrel in November and December. In September the Conference announced the establishment of a working group of experts from OPEC and non-OPEC petroleum-producing countries, to evaluate future market developments and advance dialogue and co-operation. In December the Conference announced a further reduction in output by 1.5m. b/d (to 21.7m. b/d) from 1 January 2002, provided that non-OPEC producers also reduced their output, which they agreed to do by 462,500 b/d. This output limit was maintained throughout 2002, and the ORB price averaged $24.4 per barrel during the year. From 1 January 2003 the production ceiling was raised to 23m. b/d, but stricter compliance with individual quotas meant a reduction in actual output, and prices rose above the target range, with the ORB price reaching $32 per barrel in February, as a result of the continued interruption of the Venezuelan supply, together with the market's reaction to the likelihood of US-led military action against Iraq. In January the Conference agreed to raise the production ceiling to 24.5m. b/d from 1 February, and in March (when Venezuelan production resumed after industrial action) members agreed to make up from their available excess capacities any shortfall that might result following military action against Iraq. In the event, the war on Iraq that commenced later in that month led to such a rapid overthrow of Saddam Hussain's regime that there were fears that a petroleum surplus, driving down prices, would result, and a production ceiling of 25.4m. b/d was set with effect from the beginning of June: although higher than the previous limit, it represented a 2m. b/d reduction in actual output at that time. The production ceiling of 24.5m. b/d was reinstated from 1 November, in view of the gradual revival of Iraqi exports. The ORB price averaged $28.1 per barrel in 2003. In 2004, however, petroleum prices increased considerably, with the ORB price averaging $36 per barrel over the year, despite OPEC's raising its production ceiling (excluding Iraq's output), in several stages, from the 23.5m. b/d limit imposed from 1 April to 27m. b/d with effect from 1 November. In January 2005 the Conference suspended the $22–$28 price band mechanism, acknowledging this to be unrealistic at that time. The production ceiling was increased to 27.5m. b/d in March and to 28m. b/d in June; nevertheless the ORB price averaged $50.6 per barrel over the year. The March Conference attributed the continuing rise in prices to expectations of strong demand, speculation on the futures markets, and geopolitical tensions; it expressed particular concern that a shortage of effective global refining capacity was also contributing to higher prices by causing 'bottlenecks' in the downstream sector, and announced that members had accelerated the implementation of existing capacity expansion plans. In June an updated ORB was adopted, comprising the following 12 crudes: Saharan Blend (produced by Algeria), Girassol (Angola), Oriente (Ecuador), Iran Heavy (Iran), Basra Light (Iraq), Kuwait Export (Kuwait), Es Sider (Libya), Bonny Light (Nigeria), Qatar Marine (Qatar), Arab Light (Saudi Arabia), Murban (UAE) and Merey (Venezuela). In September the Conference adopted its first Long-Term Strategy for OPEC, setting objectives concerning members' long-term petroleum revenues, fair and stable prices, the role of petroleum in meeting future energy demand, the stability of the world oil market, and the security of regular supplies to consumers. During 2006 petroleum prices continued to rise, with the ORB price averaging $61.1 per barrel for the year. The rise was partly attributable to uncertainty about Iran's future output (since there was speculation that international sanctions might be imposed on that country as a penalty for continuing its nuclear development programme), and to a reduction in Nigeria's production as a result of internal unrest. Existing production targets were maintained until November, when the production ceiling was lowered to 26.3m. b/d, and a further reduction of 500,000 b/d was announced in December. In March 2007 the Conference agreed to maintain the current level of production. Concern over fuel supplies and distribution contributed to steadily rising prices, in spite of OPEC's statements estimating that there were sufficient stock levels to meet demand. In October OPEC's Secretary-General reiterated that the market was well supplied, and attributed the rising prices chiefly to market speculators, with persistent refinery bottlenecks, seasonal maintenance work, ongoing geopolitical problems in the Middle East and fluctuations in the US dollar also continuing to play a role in driving oil prices higher. In November the third OPEC summit meeting of heads of state and government agreed on principles concerning the stability of global energy markets, the role of energy in sustainable development, and the relationship between energy and environmental concerns.

Meeting in March 2008, the Conference again determined to maintain the current production ceiling and in September, once again, the Conference resolved to maintain the production allocations agreed in September 2007 (with an adjustment to include the admission to the organization in late 2007 of both Angola and Ecuador while excluding Indonesia, whose membership was being terminated, resulting in an overall production ceiling of 28.8m. b/d). At 11 July 2008 the ORB price reached a record high of US $147.27 per barrel, although by late October it had decreased to below $60 per barrel. An extraordinary meeting of the Conference, convened at that time, observed that the ongoing global financial crisis was suppressing demand for petroleum. The Conference determined to decrease the production ceiling by 1.5m. b/d, with effect from 1 November. A subsequent extraordinary Conference meeting, held in mid-December, agreed to reduce production further, by 4.7m. b/d from the actual total production in September (29.0m. b/d), with effect from 1 January 2009. By 24 December 2008 the ORB price had fallen to $33.36 per barrel.

The ORB price stabilized in early 2009, fluctuating at around US $40 per barrel during January–mid-March (when a meeting of the Conference determined to maintain current production levels, but urged member states' full compliance with them: this had stood at 79% in February), and rising to around $50 per barrel during mid-March–early May. By mid-June the ORB price had risen to $70.9 per barrel. Meeting in late May the Conference noted that the impact of the ongoing global economic crisis had resulted in a reduction in the global demand for petroleum, this having declined during the second half of 2008 for the first time since the early 1980s. The Conference welcomed the positive effect of recent production decisions in redressing the balance of supply and demand, and decided to maintain current production levels. Reviewing the situation at the next meeting, convened in early September 2009, the Conference observed that the global economic situation continued to be very fragile and that the petroleum market remained over-supplied, and determined once more to maintain existing production levels. When convened again, in December, the Conference expressed concern at the gravity of the global economic contraction, noting that the worldwide demand for petroleum had now declined for two successive years. The March 2010 Conference observed some improvement in the global economy, and projected marginal improvements in global demand for petroleum, but observed, also, that serious threats remained to the economic situation, and that, owing to a forecast increase in petroleum supplies from non-OPEC sources, a third successive year of declining demand for the organization's crude oil was envisaged. The next ordinary meeting of the Conference, held in October, adopted a second Long-Term Strategy for the organization, setting objectives relating to member countries' long-term petroleum revenues; fair and stable prices; future energy demand and OPEC's share in world oil supply; stability of the global oil market; security of regular supply to consumers, and of global demand; and enhancing the collective interests of member states in global negotiations and future multilateral agreements. An extraordinary meeting of the Conference, convened in December, observed that the global economic outlook remained fragile, and, on that basis, agreed to maintain current oil production levels. The next ordinary meeting of the Conference, held in June 2011—following, in the first half of that year, the unforeseen eruption of unrest and uncertainty in several Middle Eastern and North African countries, including Libya (where a significant decline in production was recorded), and a sharp increase in petroleum prices—failed to reach consensus on a proposed agreement to raise output. In December OPEC ministers agreed to maintain the production ceiling at current output levels (some 30m. b/d). Ministers attending the ordinary Conference in mid-June 2012 agreed to maintain the production ceiling, despite marked over-production by some member states and a decline in prices from $122.97 per barrel in mid-March, to $96.02 (on 15 June). Meeting in December the Conference took note of continuing price volatility—reflecting increased speculation in the commodities markets and continuing pessimism concerning the global economy—while deciding further to maintain the 30m. b/d production ceiling. At the end of May 2013 the Conference resolved to maintain the existing production ceiling; in December the Conference again maintained the production ceiling at 30m. b/d. At 16 April 2014 the ORB price stood at $106.06.

ENERGY DIALOGUES

Annual joint 'workshops' are convened jointly by OPEC, the International Energy Agency (IEA) and the International Energy Forum (IEF), bringing together experts, analysts and government officials to discuss aspects of energy supply and demand; the 2014 joint workshop took place in March, in Vienna, Austria, on the theme 'Interactions between Physical and Financial Energy Markets'. In October 2012 OPEC, the IEA and the IEF organized the First Joint Symposium on Gas and Coal Market Outlooks.

Annual formal ministerial meetings of the European Union-OPEC Energy Dialogue have taken place since June 2005, with the aim of exchanging views on energy issues of common interest, including petroleum market developments, and thus contributing to stability, transparency and predictability in the market. The Dialogue is supplemented by roundtable meetings, workshops, joint experts' meetings, and joint study activities. In November 2013 the 10th ministerial Dialogue considered a joint study and roundtable undertaken earlier in the year on 'Potential manpower bottlenecks in the oil and gas industry'; and agreed to organize a joint study and roundtable on challenges facing the petrochemical industry, and also to prepare a joint study on energy efficiency and its potential impact on demand.

Russia (a major producer of petroleum) was given OPEC observer status in 1992, and was subsequently represented at a number of ministerial and other meetings. A formal Energy Dialogue was established in December 2005, providing for annual ministerial meetings, together with technical exchanges, seminars and joint research, on such subjects as petroleum market developments and prospects, data flow, investments across the supply chain, and energy policies. The OPEC-Russia ministerial meeting held in October 2013 addressed market activity, and recent developments concerning the extraction of shale gas and so-called 'tight oil' (also found in rock formations with low permeability, such as shale).

In December 2005 an official dialogue was inaugurated between OPEC and the People's Republic of China (a major customer of OPEC members), with the aim of exchanging views on energy issues, particularly security of supply and demand, through annual ministerial meetings, technical exchanges and energy roundtables.

ENVIRONMENTAL CONCERNS

OPEC has frequently expressed its concern that any measures adopted to avert climate change by reducing the emission of carbon dioxide caused by the consumption of fossil fuels would seriously affect its members' income. In 1998, for example, OPEC representatives attending a conference of the parties to the UN Framework Convention on Climate Change warned that OPEC would claim compensation for any lost revenue resulting from initiatives to limit petroleum consumption, and at subsequent sessions, while expressing support for the fundamental principles of the Convention, OPEC urged that developing countries whose economies were dependent on the export of fossil fuels should not be unfairly treated. In June 2007 OPEC's Secretary-General criticized the industrialized nations' efforts to increase production of biofuel (derived from agricultural commodities) in order to reduce consumption of fossil fuels: he warned that OPEC might reduce its future investment in petroleum production accordingly. In November the third summit meeting of OPEC heads of state and government acknowledged the long-term challenge of climate change, but emphasized the continuing need for stable petroleum supplies to support global economic growth and development, and urged that policies aimed at combating climate change should be balanced, taking into account their impact on developing countries, including countries heavily dependent on the production and export of fossil fuels. The meeting stressed the importance of cleaner and more efficient petroleum technologies, and the development of technologies such as carbon capture and storage.

Finance

OPEC has an annual budget of about €25m.

Publications

Annual Report.
Annual Statistical Bulletin.
Monthly Oil Market Report.
OPEC Bulletin (10 a year).
OPEC Energy Review (quarterly).
World Oil Outlook (annually).
Reports, information papers, press releases.

OPEC FUND FOR INTERNATIONAL DEVELOPMENT

Address: POB 995, 1011 Vienna, Austria.
Telephone: (1) 515-64-0; **fax:** (1) 513-92-38; **e-mail:** info@ofid.org; **internet:** www.ofid.org.

The OPEC Fund for International Development (initially referred to as 'the Fund', more recently as 'OFID') was established 1976 by OPEC member countries, in order to assist developing countries and to promote South-South co-operation. A revised agreement to establish the Fund as a permanent international agency was signed in May 1980.

MEMBERS

Algeria	Iraq	Qatar
Gabon	Kuwait	Saudi Arabia
Indonesia	Libya	United Arab Emirates
Iran	Nigeria	Venezuela

Organization

(April 2014)

ADMINISTRATION

OFID is administered by a Ministerial Council and a Governing Board. Each member country is represented on the Council by its minister of finance. The Board consists of one representative and one alternate for each member country.

Chairman, Ministerial Council: YOUSEF HUSSAIN KAMAL (Qatar).

Chairman, Governing Board: JAMAL NASSER LOOTAH (United Arab Emirates).

Director-General of the Fund: SULEIMAN JASIR AL-HERBISH (Saudi Arabia).

FINANCIAL STRUCTURE

The resources of OFID, whose unit of account is the US dollar, consist of contributions by OPEC member countries, and income received from operations or otherwise accruing to the Fund.

The initial endowment of OFID amounted to US $800m. Its resources have been replenished four times—the Fourth Replenishment, totalling $1,000m., was approved by the Ministerial Council in June 2011. OFID's resources have also been increased by the profits accruing to seven OPEC member countries through the sales of gold held by the International Monetary Fund (IMF). At the end of 2013 the total pledged contributions by member countries amounted to $4,431m., and paid-in contributions totalled some $3,459m.

Activities

The OPEC Fund for International Development (OFID) is a multilateral agency for financial co-operation and assistance. Its objective is to reinforce financial co-operation between OPEC member countries and other developing countries through the provision of financial support to the latter on appropriate terms, to assist them in their economic and social development. OFID was conceived as a collective financial facility which would consolidate the assistance extended by its member countries; its resources are additional to those already made available through other bilateral and multilateral aid agencies of OPEC members. It is empowered to:

(i) Provide concessional loans for balance of payments support;

(ii) Provide concessional loans for the implementation of development projects and programmes;

(iii) Contribute to the resources of other international development agencies;

(iv) Finance technical assistance, research, food aid and humanitarian emergency relief through grants; and

(v) Participate in the financing of private sector activities in developing countries.

The eligible beneficiaries of OFID's assistance are the governments of developing countries other than OPEC member countries, and international development agencies whose beneficiaries are developing countries. OFID gives priority to the countries with the lowest income.

OFID may undertake technical, economic and financial appraisal of a project submitted to it, or entrust such an appraisal to an appropriate international development agency, the executing national agency of a member country, or any other qualified agency. Most projects financed by the organization have been co-financed by other development finance agencies. In each such case, one of the co-financing agencies may be appointed to administer the loan in association with its own. This practice has enabled OFID to extend its lending activities to more than 100 countries and in a simple way, with the aim of avoiding duplication and complications. As its experience grew, OFID increasingly resorted to parallel, rather than joint financing, taking up separate project components to be financed according to its rules and policies. In addition, it started to finance some projects on its own. The loans are not tied to procurement from OFID member countries or from any other countries. The margin of preference for goods and services obtainable in developing countries is allowed on the request of the borrower and within defined limits. OFID assistance in the form of programme loans has a broader coverage than project lending. Programme loans are used to stimulate an economic sector or sub-sector, and assist recipient countries in obtaining inputs, equipment and spare parts. In 2004 a supplementary lending mechanism, a Blend Facility, was established to make available additional resources at higher rates than the standard concessional lending terms. Besides extending loans for project and programme financing and balance of payments support, OFID also undertakes other operations, including grants in support of technical assistance and other activities (mainly research), emergency relief and humanitarian aid, and financial contributions to other international institutions. In 1998 the Fund began to extend lines of credit to support private sector activities in beneficiary countries. The so-called Private Sector Facility aims to encourage the growth of private enterprises, in particular small and medium-sized enterprises (SMEs), and to support the development of local capital markets. A new Trade Finance Facility, to provide loans, lines of credit and guarantees in support of international trade operations in developing countries, was launched in December 2006.

OFID has contributed to the development of an 'Energy for the Poor' initiative launched in June 2008 by a meeting of energy consumers and producers held in Jeddah, Saudi Arabia. In March 2009 OFID participated in a meeting of international finance institutions and development banks to discuss closer co-operation in order to respond more effectively to the global financial and economic crisis. OFID agreed to provide US $30m. to an African sub-fund of the International Finance Corporation's Recapitalization Fund, which aimed to support banks in developing countries. It also participated in a Microfinance Enhancement Facility and, though its Trade Finance Facility, in the World Bank's Global Trade Liquidity Programme. In October 2010 OFID signed a Memorandum of Understanding (MOU) with the World Bank Group in order to strengthen their joint efforts to meet new development challenges, with a particular focus on the need to counter energy poverty (since 2007 a strategic priority of OFID), to improve the management of natural resources, to facilitate trade and to strengthen financial institutions. In May 2011 OFID signed an MOU with the Asian Development Bank, in order to enhance co-operation between the two organizations, and in July it signed an MOU with the Arab Bank for Economic Development in Africa. In December of that year OFID's Director-General, addressing the 20th World Petroleum Congress, convened in Doha, Qatar, recommended that the Fund might act as a hub for efforts by the petroleum sector to promote the global 'Sustainable Energy for All by 2030' initiative that had been launched by the UN Secretary-General in September 2011. In June 2012 the Ministerial Council issued a landmark Ministerial Declaration on Energy Poverty, reaffirming member states' commitment to eradicating global energy poverty, and determining to commit a minimum of $1,000m. to finance the ongoing 'Energy for the Poor Initiative'.

By the end of 2012 OFID had approved a total of US $15,116.3m. since operations began in 1976, of which $10,264.0m. was for public sector loans. Included in the public sector lending is the Fund's contribution to the Heavily Indebted Poor Countries (HIPC) initiative (see World Bank), which by the end of 2012 amounted to $269.8m. Private sector financing totalled $1,759.9m. committed in the same period, while loans committed under the Trade Finance Facility, amounted to $1,522.4m. At that time cumulative disbursements of all loans and operations amounted to $9,582.4m.

Direct loans are supplemented by grants to support technical assistance, food aid and research. By the end of December 2012 grants amounting to US $548.2m., had been committed since operations commenced, including $20m. as a special contribution to the International Fund for Agricultural Development (IFAD) and a further $20m. approved under a Food Aid Special Grant Account, which was established in 2003 to combat famine in Africa. In addition, OFID had committed $1,021.8m. to the resources of IFAD, an IMF Trust Fund and the IMF's Poverty Reduction and Growth Facility (PRGF) Trust.

During the year ending 31 December 2012 the Fund's total commitments amounted to US $1,301.9m. (compared with $758.5m. in the previous year). These commitments included public sector loans, amounting to $676.7m., supporting 39 projects in 32 countries. The largest proportion of loans (41% of the total) was for transportation projects, including the construction or rehabilitation of roads in Bangladesh, Bolivia, Chad, Democratic Republic of the Congo (DRC), Granada, Madagascar, Sierra Leone, Sri Lanka, Suriname, Tajikistan, Uganda and Viet Nam. The energy sector accounted for 32% of the total, for projects including the improvement of electricity generation, transmission and distributions in Cambodia, The Gambia, Kenya, Mauritania, Morocco, Pakistan, Rwanda, Tunisia and Yemen. Projects in the agriculture sector received 12% of the total, including irrigation development projects in the DRC and Egypt, and a project to strengthen farmers' linkages to value chains through the establishment of more efficient production, transport, storage, processing and marketing systems. Public sector loans for the education sector, amounting to 7% of the total, financed projects in the People's Republic of China, Madagascar, Sierra Leone and Zambia. Projects aimed at improving water supply and sanitation were approved for Cuba, Lesotho and Tanzania. A multi-sectoral project was approved for Djibouti, to assist the start-up and expansion of SMEs.

Private sector operations approved during 2012 amounted to US $165.0m., which funded projects in the energy and transportation sectors, and in support of micro, small and medium-sized enterprises. Approvals under the Trade Financing Facility amounted to $441.6m. in 2012 (compared with $117.0m. in 2011). A global risk-sharing guarantee programme amounting to $50.0m. was also concluded during 2012 in co-operation with the United Arab Emirates-based Banque du Commerce et du Placement.

During 2012 OFID approved US $18.5m. in grants. Of the total, $4.5m. was committed from the Special Grant Account for Palestine to support the provision of safe drinking water, to support civil society organizations, and to foster youth employment. Some $4.0m. was approved under OFID's Grant Account for Energy Poverty Operations (approved in 2011 by the Ministerial Council) for projects including several hydro and solar power schemes. A further $2.5m. was approved from the HIV/AIDS Special Account to assist participation by representatives of least developed countries at the 19th International AIDS Conference, held in June 2012 in Washington, DC, USA, and to advance HIV prevention, treatment and patient care activities. Some $4.5m. was approved for technical assistance projects in the agriculture, education, health and sanitation and water supply sectors.

Publications

Annual Report (in Arabic, English, French and Spanish).

OFID Quarterly.

Pamphlet series, author papers, books and other documents.

Statistics

TOTAL APPROVALS IN 2012, BY SECTOR AND REGION
(US $ million)

	Financing approved	%
Sector:		
Agriculture	91.2	7.0
Education and knowledge transfer	46.1	3.5
Emergency activities	1.5	0.1
Energy	382.6	29.4
Finance	181.6	13.9
Health	26.1	2.0
Industry	25.0	1.9
Multi-sector	207.3	15.9
Transportation	275.0	21.1
Water supply and sanitation	35.5	2.7
Telecommunications	30.1	2.3
Total	1,301.9	100.0
Region:		
Africa	558.0	42.9
Asia	438.6	33.7
Latin America and the Caribbean	101.3	7.8
Europe and multi-regional	204.1	15.7

Source: OFID, *Annual Report 2012*.

PACIFIC COMMUNITY

Address: BP D5, 98848 Nouméa, New Caledonia.

Telephone: 26-20-00; **fax:** 26-38-18; **e-mail:** spc@spc.int; **internet:** www.spc.int.

In February 1947 the Governments of Australia, France, the Netherlands, New Zealand, the United Kingdom, and the USA signed the Canberra Agreement establishing the South Pacific Commission, which came into effect in July 1948. (The Netherlands withdrew from the Commission in 1962, when it ceased to administer the former colony of Dutch New Guinea, now Papua, part of Indonesia.) In October 1997 the 37th South Pacific Conference, convened in Canberra, Australia, agreed to rename the organization the Pacific Community, with effect from February 1998. The Secretariat of the Pacific Community (SPC) services the Community, and provides research, technical advice, training and assistance in economic, social and cultural development to the Pacific region. It serves a population of about 6.8m., scattered over some 30m. sq km, more than 98% of which is ocean.

MEMBERS

American Samoa	Niue
Australia	Northern Mariana Islands
Cook Islands	Palau
Fiji	Papua New Guinea
France	Pitcairn Islands
French Polynesia	Samoa
Guam	Solomon Islands
Kiribati	Tokelau
Marshall Islands	Tonga
Federated States of Micronesia	Tuvalu
Nauru	USA
New Caledonia	Vanuatu
New Zealand	Wallis and Futuna Islands

Organization

(April 2014)

CONFERENCE OF THE PACIFIC COMMUNITY

The Conference is the governing body of the Community and is composed of representatives of all member countries and territories. The main responsibilities of the Conference, which meets every two years, are to appoint the Director-General, to determine major national or regional policy issues in the areas of competence of the organization and to note changes to the Financial and Staff Regulations approved by the Committee of Representatives of Governments and Administrations (CRGA). The eighth Conference of the Pacific Community was convened in Suva, Fiji, in November 2013, on the theme 'Enhancing sustainable development in Pacific communities—helping shape the post-2015 agenda'.

COMMITTEE OF REPRESENTATIVES OF GOVERNMENTS AND ADMINISTRATIONS (CRGA)

The CRGA comprises representatives of all member states and territories, having equal voting rights. It meets annually to consider the work programme evaluation conducted by the Secretariat and to discuss any changes proposed by the Secretariat in the context of regional priorities; to consider and approve any policy issues for the organization presented by the Secretariat or by member countries and territories; to make recommendations for the post of Director-General; to approve the administrative and work programme budgets; to approve amendments to the Financial and Staff Regulations; and to conduct annual performance evaluations of the Director-General.

SECRETARIAT

The Secretariat of the Pacific Community (SPC) is headed by a Director-General, supported by three Deputy Directors-General (of whom two are based at the SPC headquarters in Nouméa, New Caledonia, and one is based at the regional office in Suva, Fiji). In October 2009 the CRGA approved a reorganization which was completed by January 2011 and included the transfer to SPC of activities from the Pacific Islands Applied Geoscience Commission (SOPAC), with a view to making SPC the lead co-ordinating agency for the Pacific regional energy sector. The reorganization provided for Secretariat divisions of Applied Geoscience and Technology; Economic Development; Education, Training and Human Development; Fisheries, Aquaculture and Marine Ecosystems; Land Resources; Public Health; and Statistics for Development. A Strategic Engagement Policy and Planning Facility (SEPPF), established in 1998 and expanded in 2007, provides country and programme support; and covers areas including regional co-operation and strategic positioning initiatives; policy analysis, research and mainstreaming of cross-cutting issues; and monitoring and evaluation. The Secretariat provides information services, including library facilities, publications, translation and computer services.

Director-General: Dr Colin Tukuitonga (Niue).

Deputy Directors-General: Cameron Diver (France/New Zealand) (based in Nouméa, New Caledonia), Fabian McKinnon (Canada) (based in Nouméa), Fekitamoeloa Katoa 'Utoikamanu (Tonga) (based in Suva, Fiji).

North Pacific Regional Office: POB 2299, Botanical Garden 2, Kolonia, Pohnpei, Federated States of Micronesia; tel. 320-7523; fax 320-5854; e-mail amenay@spc.int.

Suva Regional Office: Private Mail Bag, Suva, Fiji; tel. 3370733; fax 3370021; e-mail spcsuva@spc.org.fj.

Activities

SPC provides, on request of its member countries, technical assistance, advisory services, information and clearing house services aimed at developing the technical, professional, scientific, research, planning and management capabilities of the regional population. SPC also conducts regional conferences and technical meetings, as well as training courses, workshops and seminars at the regional or country level. It provides small grants-in-aid and awards to meet specific requests and needs of members. In November 1996 the Conference agreed to establish a specific Small Islands States (SIS) fund to provide technical services, training and other relevant activities. The Pacific Community oversees the maritime programme and telecommunications policy activities of the Pacific Islands Forum Secretariat.

The 1999 Conference, held in Tahiti in December, adopted the Déclaration de Tahiti Nui, a mandate that detailed the operational policies and mechanisms of the Pacific Community, taking into account operational changes not covered by the founding Canberra Agreement. The Declaration was regarded as a 'living document' that would be periodically revised to record subsequent modifications of operational policy.

SPC has signed Memorandums of Understanding with the World Health Organization (WHO), the Forum Fisheries Agency, the Melanesian Spearhead Group (in July 2012), the Pacific Islands Private Sector Organization (in March 2013), the South Pacific Regional Environment Programme (SPREP), and several other partners. The organization participates in meetings of the Council of Regional Organizations in the Pacific (CROP). Representatives of SPC and SPREP have in recent years convened periodic meetings to develop regional technical co-operation and harmonization of work programmes.

SPC aims to develop joint country strategies with each of the Pacific Community's member countries and territories, detailing the full scope of its assistance during a defined period.

The eighth Pacific Community Conference, convened in November 2013, in Suva, Fiji, considered expanding the territorial scope of the Community to meet an expression of interest by Timor-Leste for membership, as well as proposals to create 'associate member' and 'observer' membership categories.

APPLIED GEOSCIENCE AND TECHNOLOGY

The reorganization of SPC implemented during 2010 provided for the core work programme of the Pacific Islands Applied Geoscience Commission (SOPAC) to be absorbed into SPC as a new Applied Geoscience and Technology Division. The Division has responsibility for ensuring the productive regional utilization of earth sciences (geology, geophysics, oceanography and hydrology), and comprises the following three technical work programmes: ocean and islands; water and sanitation; and disaster reduction.

In June 2012 SPC and SPREP signed a letter of agreement detailing arrangements for the joint development, by 2015, of an Integrated Regional Strategy for Disaster Risk Management and Climate Change, which was to replace both the then ongoing Pacific Disaster Risk Reduction and Disaster Management Framework for Action 2005–15 and Pacific Islands Framework for Action on Climate Change 2006–15. SPC and the Secretariat of the UN International Strategy for Disaster Reduction (UNISDR) co-convene the Pacific Platform for Disaster Risk Management ('Pacific Platform'), which was established in 2008 to harmonize regional disaster risk management mechanisms. In July 2013 the first joint meeting of the Pacific Platform and the Pacific Climate Change Roundtable (convened biennially, under SPREP auspices) was organized, in Nada, Fiji, jointly by the Fiji Government, SPC, UNISDR, and SPREP. The meeting aimed to contribute to the development of the Integrated Regional Strategy.

ECONOMIC DEVELOPMENT

The Economic Development Division has the following four 'pillars': programmes in the areas of Transport; Energy; Infrastructure and Information; and Communications Technology (ICT). An inaugural Regional Meeting of Ministers for Energy, ICT and Transport was held in April 2011, on the theme of 'Strategic engagement for economic development'.

The Transport Programme comprises the work of the former Regional Maritime Programme (RMP—amalgamated into the main Transport Programme in mid-2011), as well as research and advisory services relating to specific capacity in aviation, and research into transport research. In 2002 the RMP launched the model Pacific Islands Maritime Legislation and Regulations as a framework for the development of national maritime legislation. Since 2006 the Transport Programme has provided the secretariat of the Pacific Maritime Transport Alliance. The inaugural regional meeting of ministers responsible for maritime transport was convened in April 2007. In April 2011 SPC ministers adopted a Framework for Action on Transport Services (FATS) to support all Pacific Islands and Territories (PICTs) to provide regular, safe and affordable air and sea transport services.

The Energy Programme comprises related activities transferred from SOPAC, including its advisory functions and activities relating to petroleum data and information. The Programme co-ordinates and leads work on energy policy, planning, legislation and regulation; petroleum, including procurement, transport, storage and pricing mechanisms; renewable energy production; energy efficiency and conservation; and support for the Pacific Power Association and other relevant bodies regarding to power generation and electric utilities. In April 2011 ministers responsible for energy adopted a Framework for Action on Energy Security in the Pacific and an implementation plan. A new Pacific Centre for Renewable Energy and Energy Efficiency was expected to become operational in the second half of 2014.

The Pacific ICT Outreach (PICTO) Programme, established in January 2010, implements the 'Framework for Action on ICT for Development in the Pacific', endorsed in June 2010 by ministers responsible for ICT; and takes into account initiatives such as the Pacific Regional Infrastructure facility; to implement the Pacific Plan Digital Strategy; to take over work on ICT policy and regulations hitherto undertaken by the Pacific Islands Forum Secretariat; to continue ongoing SPC work relating to submarine cable and satellite communication technology; and to support the ongoing Oceania 'one laptop per child' (OLPC) initiative. In October SPC launched the e-Pacific Island Countries (e-PIC), an online portal providing access to information including country profiles; downloadable documents relating to policy, legal and regulatory matters, publications, news and research materials; a regional forum; and a register of ICT professionals and policy-makers. In April 2011 SPC hosted a Pacific ICT Ministerial Forum, and signed an agreement with the International Telecommunications Union to enhance co-operation between the two organizations and facilitate the implementation of ICT and cyber protection programmes throughout the region. A Pacific Regional Workshop on Cybercrime, was held in Nukúalofa, Tonga, in May.

With other regional partners, including the Pacific Islands Forum and Asian Development Bank, SPC supported the Pacific Conference on the Human Face of the Global Economic Crisis, hosted by the Vanuatu Government in February 2010, in Port Vila, Vanuatu.

In March 2014 SPC and the Australian Government signed the Partnership for Pacific Regionalism and Enhanced Development, covering 2014–23, which initially aimed to support SPC's delivery of regional services in areas including managing coastal fisheries for economic growth; trade in agriculture and forestry among small and medium-sized enterprises; and developing policies and legislation to combat non-communicable diseases in the region.

EDUCATION, TRAINING AND HUMAN DEVELOPMENT

The Division comprises the South Pacific Board for Educational Assessment (SPBEA), the Community Education Training Centre (CETC), the Human Development Programme (HDP), the Regional Media Centre, and the Regional Rights Resource Team.

In January 2010, under the reorganization of SPC implemented in that year, the SPBEA (established in 1980 to develop procedures for assessing national and regional secondary education certificates) was merged into the Community. The SPC regional office in Fiji administers the CETC, which conducts a seven-month training course for up to 40 female community workers annually, with the objective of training women in methods of community development so that they can help others to achieve better living conditions for island families and communities.

The HDP focuses on the areas of gender, youth, and culture. The HDP's Pacific Women's Bureau (PWB) aims to promote the social, economic and cultural advancement of women in the region by assisting governments and regional organizations to include women in the development planning process. The PWB also provides technical and advisory services, advocacy and management support training to groups concerned with women in development and gender and development, and administers the Pacific Women's Information Network (PACWIN). In July 2013 a regional workshop on strengthening women's leadership was convened in Wallis and Futuna, with participation by women from French-speaking Pacific islands and with support from SPC. In the following month SPC helped to organize a workshop, held in Suva, on the formulation of action plans aimed at addressing high rates of violence against women in the region. SPC supported preparations for the 12th Triennial Conference of Pacific Women, which was convened in October, in Rarotonga, Cook Islands, on the theme 'Celebrating our Progress, Shaping our World'. The Pacific Youth Bureau (PYB) co-ordinates the implementation of the Pacific Youth Strategy (PYS), which is updated at five-yearly intervals, most recently to cover the period 2011–15, and aims to develop opportunities for young people to play an active role in society. The PYB provides non-formal education and support for youth, community workers and young adults in community development subjects and provides grants to help young people to find employment. It also advises and assists the Pacific Youth Council in promoting a regional youth identity. At the first Pacific Youth Festival, held in Tahiti in July 2006, a Pacific Youth Charter was formulated, to be incorporated into the PYS. The second Pacific Youth Festival, held in Suva, in July 2009, included discussions on the following issues: promoting healthy living; Pacific identity; adaptation to climate change; and governance, peace and security. In September 2011 the Community published a *State of Pacific Youth Report*, which had been prepared with the Pacific Office of the UN Children's Fund (UNICEF).

The HDP works to preserve and promote the cultural heritage of the Pacific Islands. The Programme assists with the training of librarians, archivists and researchers and promotes instruction in local languages, history and art at schools in the PICTs. SPC acts as the secretariat of the Council of Pacific Arts, which organizes the Festival of Pacific Arts on a four-yearly basis. The 11th Festival was held in June–July 2012 in Solomon Islands, on the theme 'Culture in Harmony with Nature'. In November 2006 the HDP published *Guidelines for developing national legislation for the protection of traditional knowledge and expressions of culture*, with the aim of protecting indigenous Pacific knowledge and cultures. In March 2010 representatives of cultural interests from PICTs met to consider means of strengthening the profile of Pacific culture, including developing a regional cultural strategy, incorporating culture into educational programmes, establishing partnerships at national, regional and international level, and accessing funding for cultural projects. Regional ministers responsible for culture, meeting in July 2012, endorsed the ensuing Pacific Regional Cultural Strategy, representing a regional framework for the formulation and development of policy on culture.

The Regional Media Centre provides training, technical assistance and production materials in all areas of the media for member countries and territories, community work programmes, donor projects and regional non-governmental organizations. The Centre comprises a radio broadcast unit, a graphic design and publication unit and a TV and video unit. The Regional Rights Resource Team provides training, technical support, and policy and advocacy services specifically tailored towards the Pacific region.

FISHERIES, AQUACULTURE AND MARINE ECOSYSTEMS

The Fisheries, Aquaculture and Marine Ecosystems (FAME) Division aims to support and co-ordinate the sustainable development and management of inshore fisheries resources in the region, to undertake scientific research in order to provide member governments with relevant information for the sustainable development and management of tuna and billfish resources in and adjacent to the South Pacific region, and to provide data and analytical services to national fisheries departments. The principal programmes under FAME are the Coastal Fisheries Programme (CFP) and the Oceanic Fisheries Programme (OFP). The development and advisory activities of the CFP are focused within the near territorial and archipelagic waters of the PICTs. The CFP is divided into the following sections: the Reef Fisheries Observatory; sustainable fisheries development; fisheries management; fisheries training; and aquaculture. SPC administers the Pacific Island Aquaculture Network, a forum for promoting regional aquaculture development. During 2007 a Pacific Regional Aquatic Biosecurity Initiative was initiated. In contrast to the CFP, the OFP focuses it activities within 200-mile exclusive economic zones and surrounding waters, and is mandated to equip PICTs with the necessary scientific information and advice for rationally managing and exploiting the regional resources of tuna, billfish and related species. The OFP consists of the following three sections: statistics and monitoring; tuna ecology and biology; and stock assessment and modelling. The statistics and monitoring section maintains a database of industrial tuna fisheries in the region. The OFP contributed research and statistical information for the formulation of the Convention for the Conservation and Management of Highly Migratory Fish Stocks in the Western and Central Pacific, which entered into force in June 2004 and aims to establish a regime for the sustainable management of tuna reserves. Since 2006 the OFP has organized annual tuna Stock Assessment Workshops with participation by senior regional fishery officers. The theme of the fifth Pacific Community Conference, convened in November 2007, was 'The future of Pacific fisheries'; a set of recommendations on managing the regional fisheries was endorsed by that Conference.

SPC hosts the Pacific Office of the WorldFish Center (the International Centre for Living Aquatic Resources Management—ICLARM); SPC and the WorldFish Center have jointly implemented a number of projects. SPC also hosts the Co-ordination Unit of the Coral Reef Initiative for the South Pacific (CRISP), which was launched in January 2005 to address the protection and management of the region's coral reefs.

LAND RESOURCES

The Land Resources Division (LRD) comprises three major programmes: the sustainable management of integrated forest and agriculture systems programme; the biosecurity and trade support programme; and the food security and health programme. The LRD has increasingly decentralized the delivery of its services, which are co-ordinated at country level by personnel within national agricultural systems. The LRD aims to develop the capacity of PICTs in initiatives such as policy analysis and advice, and support for agricultural science and technology. In December 2011 a regional meeting on biosecurity urged increased surveillance concerning alien pest and disease invasion, which at once can derive from international trade, and also risks undermining trade. In February 2012 the LRD organized a workshop aimed at supporting PICTs in strengthening crop production through improved pest management methods, and, at that time, a new regional project on building capacity to develop integrated crop management strategies was launched. SPC hosts the Centre for Pacific Crops and Trees (CePaCT, known prior to 2007 as the Regional Germplasm Centre), which assists PICTs in efforts to conserve and access regional genetic resources. In 2001 the Pacific Community endorsed the Pacific Agricultural Plant Genetic Resources Network, which is implemented by the LRD and other partners. The Pacific Animal Health Information System (PAHIS) provides data on regional livestock numbers and the regional status of animal diseases, and the Pacific Islands Pest List Database provides a register of regional agriculture, forestry and environmental pests. In March 2013 SPC helped to organize a regional conference on the implementation of the FAO/World Organisation for Animal Health Global Framework for the Progressive Control of Transboundary Animal Diseases, held in Nadi, Fiji. The LRD co-ordinates the development of organic agriculture in the Pacific region. In 2008 it adopted the Pacific Organic Standard, and it supports the Pacific Organic and Ethical Trade Community (POETCom), which was launched in 2009 to manage Pacific organic certification. In December 2009 a POETCom technical experts' group met to finalize a farmers' version of the Pacific Organic Standard. POETCom met in May 2012 to formalize its governance framework and to establish an inclusive membership structure. A POETCom information sharing forum was held in July 2013, at the Pacific Community headquarters. The International Fund for Agricultural Development (IFAD) and the International Federation of Organic Agricultural Movement contributed to the development of the Pacific Regional Organic Strategic Plan for 2009–13. In April 2008 Pacific ministers responsible for agriculture and forestry endorsed an action plan for conserving, managing and using the region's forest and tree genetic resources. A new Pacific Island Tree Seed Centre was established in September 2013, in Suva. In September 2009 SPC organized a meeting of heads of forestry agencies in the Pacific, on the theme 'Forests, Climate Change and Markets'; the meeting recommended that SPC support the formulation of a policy framework aimed at facilitating the access of PICTs to funding support offered in the context of REDD+ activities undertaken through the UN Collaborative Programme on Reducing Emissions from Deforestation and Forest Degradation in Developing Countries (UN-REDD), with a view to promoting better conservation and sustainable management of regional forestry resources. Consequently, representatives of PICTs and regional organizations met in April 2012 to consider a new draft Pacific Regional Policy Framework that had been prepared in this respect; the finalized Framework was endorsed in September by regional ministers responsible for agriculture and forestry. During 2012 SPC, through the LRD, supported the contribution of member countries to an FAO report *The State of the World's Forest Genetic Resources*. In October 2010 a multi-agency Food Secure Pacific working group, established in 2008 by SPC, Pacific Islands Forum Secretariat, FAO, UNICEF and WHO, began implementing a new Framework for Action on Food Security in the Pacific, which had been endorsed by a Pacific Food Summit, convened in April 2010, in Port Vila. The seventh Conference of the Pacific Community was held, in November 2011, on the theme 'Climate change and food security: Managing risks for sustainable development'. In July 2013 SPC and FAO organized a workshop aimed at raising regional awareness of the Voluntary Guidelines on the Responsible Governance of Tenure of Land, Fisheries and Forests in the Context of National Food Security, which were endorsed in May 2012 by the FAO-WFP-IFAD Committee on World Food Security.

PUBLIC HEALTH

The Public Health Division aims to implement health promotion programmes; to assist regional authorities to strengthen health information systems and to promote the use of new technology for health information development and disease control; to promote efficient health services management; and to help all Pacific Islanders to attain a level of health and quality of life that will enable them to contribute to the development of their communities. The three main areas of focus of the Public Health Division are non-communicable diseases (NCDs, such as heart disease, cerebrovascular disease and diabetes, which are prevalent in parts of the region); communicable diseases (such as HIV/AIDS, other sexually transmitted infections—STIs, tuberculosis—TB, and vector-borne diseases such as malaria and dengue fever); and public health policy. A Healthy Pacific Lifestyle section aims to assist member countries to improve and sustain health, in particular through advice on nutrition, physical activity and the damaging effects of alcohol and tobacco. The Public Health Surveillance and Communicable Disease Control section is the focal point of the Pacific Public Health Surveillance Network, a regional framework established in 1996 jointly by SPC and WHO, with the aim of sustainably advancing regional public health surveillance and response. SPC operates a project to prevent AIDS and STIs among young people through peer education and awareness. SPC is the lead regional agency for co-ordinating and monitoring the implementation of the Pacific Sexual Health and Wellbeing Shared Agenda, covering 2014–18, which has a particular focus on the rights of groups at risk of poor sexual health. In March 2007 the Pacific Community launched the Oceania Society for Sexual Health and HIV Medicine, a new Pacific network aimed at ensuring access to best practice prevention, treatment, care and support services in the area of sexual health and HIV/AIDS. SPC and WHO jointly organize regular meetings aimed at strengthening TB control in the region. In February 2006 SPC established a Pacific Regional Infection Control Network, based in Fiji, to improve communication and access to expert technical advice on all aspects of infectious diseases and control. During 2006 SPC, in partnership with FAO, WHO and the World Organisation for Animal Health, established the Pacific Regional Influenza Pandemic Preparedness Project (PRIPPP), with the aim of supporting the PICTs in elaborating plans to prepare for outbreaks of avian influenza or other rapidly contagious diseases. A Pacific Community Pandemic Task Force, established under the PRIPPP and comprising human and animal health experts from Pacific governments and international and regional organizations, met for the first time in March 2007 at the Pacific Community headquarters. In July 2009 Pacific ministers of health met to discuss issues including the development of strategies to control and prevent escalating diseases in the region, and the impact on regional nutrition and health of reduced household incomes in view of the global economic crisis. A Pacific Non-communicable Disease Forum, held in Nadi, Fiji, in August, agreed recommendations on action to address the increasing regional prevalence of NCDs (also referred to as 'lifestyle diseases'). In June 2011 SPC, with WHO, organized the ninth meeting of Pacific Island ministers responsible for health, at which it was acknowledged that the escalation in incidence of NCDs remained a priority for all regional governments.

STATISTICS FOR DEVELOPMENT PROGRAMME

The Statistics Programme assists governments and administrations in the region to provide effective and efficient national statistical services through the provision of training activities, a statistical information service and other advisory services. The Programme has three working groups, on Data Collection; Statistical Analysis; and Data Dissemination. A Regional Meeting of Heads of Statistics facilitates the integration and co-ordination of statistical services throughout the region, while the Pacific Regional Information System, initiated by the National Statistics Office of the Pacific Islands and developed with British funding, provides statistical information about member countries and territories. Pacific demographic and health surveys (covering areas including fertility, family planning, maternal and child health, nutrition, and diseases, including HIV/AIDS and malaria), and household income and expenditure surveys are undertaken. In July 2013 Pacific statisticians gathered to consider the formulation of the post-2015 development agenda, and means of measuring progress thereunder.

Finance

SPC has an annual budget of around US $65m., to be funded jointly by Community member states and international donors.

Publications

Annual Report.

Climate Change and Disaster Risk Newsletter (quarterly).

e-Talanoa.

Fisheries Newsletter (quarterly).

Inform'Action (bulletin of Pacific Public Health Surveillance Network).

Pacific Aids Alert Bulletin (quarterly).

Pacific Energiser.

Pacific Maritime Watch.

Report of the Conference of the Pacific Community.

Women in Fisheries Information Bulletin.

Technical publications, statistical bulletins, advisory leaflets and reports.

PACIFIC ISLANDS FORUM

Address: Private Mail Bag, Suva, Fiji.
Telephone: 3312600; **fax:** 3301102; **e-mail:** info@forumsec.org.fj; **internet:** www.forumsec.org.

The Pacific Islands Forum was founded as the gathering of Heads of Government of the independent and self-governing states of the South Pacific; the first annual Forum meeting was held in August 1971, in Wellington, New Zealand. The Pacific Islands Forum Secretariat was established (as the South Pacific Bureau for Economic Co-operation—SPEC) by an agreement signed in April 1973, at the third Forum meeting, in Apia, Western Samoa (now Samoa). SPEC was redesignated as the South Pacific Forum Secretariat in 1988, and the present name was adopted in October 2000, in order to reflect the expansion of its membership since its establishment. The Secretariat aims to enhance the economic and social well-being of the Pacific Islands peoples, in support of the efforts of national governments. In October 2005 the 36th Forum adopted an Agreement Establishing the Pacific Islands Forum, which aimed to formalize the grouping's status as a full intergovernmental organization.

Members

Australia	Niue
Cook Islands	Palau
Fiji*	Papua New Guinea
Kiribati	Samoa
Marshall Islands	Solomon Islands
Federated States of Micronesia	Tonga
Nauru	Tuvalu
New Zealand	Vanuatu

* Fiji was suspended from participation in the Forum in May 2009.

Note: French Polynesia and New Caledonia were admitted to the Forum as associate members in 2006. The ACP Group, American Samoa, the Asian Development Bank, the Commonwealth Secretariat, Guam, the Northern Mariana Islands, Timor-Leste, Tokelau, Wallis and Futuna, the Western and Central Pacific Fisheries Commission, the UN and the World Bank are observers.

Organization

(April 2014)

FORUM OFFICIALS COMMITTEE

The Forum Officials Committee is the Secretariat's executive board, overseeing its activities. It comprises representatives and senior officials from all member countries. It meets twice a year, immediately before the meetings of the Pacific Islands Forum and at the end of the year, to discuss in detail the Secretariat's work programme and annual budget.

FORUM MEETING

Each annual leaders' Forum is chaired by the Head of Government of the country hosting the meeting, who remains as Forum Chairperson until the next Forum. The Forum has no written constitution or international agreement governing its activities nor any formal rules relating to its purpose, membership or conduct of meeting. Decisions are always reached by consensus, it never having been found necessary or desirable to vote formally on issues. In October 1994 the Forum was granted observer status by the UN General Assembly. The 44th Forum was convened in September 2013, in Majuru, Marshall Islands, and the 45th Forum was to be held in July–August 2014, in Palau.

DIALOGUE PLENARY MEETING

From 1989–2006 each annual Pacific Islands Forum meeting was followed by individual dialogues with representatives of selected countries considered to have a long-term interest in the region. A review of the post-Forum dialogues, undertaken in August 2006, recommended that the individual dialogues should be replaced by a new single Post-Forum Dialogue Plenary Meeting, to enable structured communication at ministerial level between Forum and Dialogue countries, and that 'core' dialogue partners, with a special engagement in and commitment to the region, should be identified. The findings of the review were approved in October 2006 by the 37th Forum meeting, and the new post-Forum dialogue structure was initiated following the 38th Forum. In 2014 Canada, the People's Republic of China, Cuba, France, India, Indonesia, Italy, Japan, the Republic of Korea, Malaysia, Philippines, Thailand, the United Kingdom, the USA, and the European Union (EU) had dialogue partner status; an application by Spain for dialogue partner status was under consideration. A separate post-Forum session is convened between the Republic of China (Taiwan) and six of the Forum member states.

SECRETARIAT

The Secretariat acts as the administrative arm of the Forum. It is headed by a Secretary-General, assisted by two Deputy Secretaries-General, and has a staff of some 70 people drawn from the member countries. The Secretariat's Pacific Plan Office services the Pacific Plan Action Committee and supports the overall implementation of the Pacific Plan. A Pacific ACP/EU Co-operation unit assists member states and regional organizations with submitting projects to the EU. A Smaller Island States (SIS) unit was established within the Secretariat in 2006. The Secretariat chairs the Council of Regional Organizations in the Pacific (CROP), an ad hoc committee comprising the heads of 10 regional organizations, which aims to discuss and co-ordinate the policies and work programmes of the various agencies in order to avoid duplication of or omissions in their services to member countries.

Secretary-General: TUILOMA NERONI SLADE (Samoa).

Deputy Secretary-General (Strategic Partnership and Co-ordination): CRISTELLE PRATT (Fiji).

Deputy Secretary-General (Economic Governance and Security): ANDIE FONG TOY (New Zealand).

Activities

The Pacific Islands Forum provides an opportunity for informal discussions to be held on a wide range of common issues and problems and meets annually or when issues require urgent attention.

In February 2007 a Regional Institutional Framework (RIF) Taskforce, comprising representatives of the member states of the Council of Regional Organizations in the Pacific agencies, convened for the first time, under Secretariat auspices. The RIF Taskforce was mandated by the October 2006 Forum to develop an appropriate institutional framework for supporting the implementation of the Pacific Plan.

PACIFIC PLAN

In August 2003 regional leaders attending the 34th Forum, held in Auckland, New Zealand, authorized the establishment of an Eminent Persons Group to consider the future activities and development of the Forum. In April 2004 a Special Leaders' Retreat, also convened in Auckland, in order to review a report prepared by the Group, mandated the development of a new Pacific Plan on Strengthening Regional Co-operation and Integration as a means of addressing the challenges confronting the Pacific Island states. The finalized Pacific Plan, which was endorsed by the October 2005 Forum, incorporates development initiatives that are focused around the four 'pillars' of economic growth, sustainable development, good governance, and regional security and partnerships. It also recognizes the specific needs of Smaller Island States (SIS). The Pacific Plan is regarded as a 'living document', which can be amended and updated continuously to accommodate emerging priorities. The Pacific Plan Action Committee, comprising representatives of the Forum member states and chaired by the Forum Chairperson, has met regularly since January 2006. Regional organizations, working in partnership with national governments and other partners, are responsible for co-ordinating the implementation of—and compiling reports on—many of the specific Pacific Plan initiatives. The 37th Forum leaders' meeting in October 2006 adopted the Nadi Decisions on the Pacific Plan, prioritizing several key commitments in the four pillar areas; these were consequently incorporated into the ('living') Plan during 2007. In October 2007 the 38th Forum adopted a further set of key commitments, the Vava'U Decisions on the Pacific Plan. More key commitments and priority areas, aimed at advancing the Pacific Plan, were adopted by the 40th Forum, in August 2009. In August 2012 leaders attending the 43rd Forum noted an ongoing focus on the relationship between the Plan, the nascent post-2015 global development agenda and new Sustainable Development Goals. The leaders gave consideration to the terms of reference for a planned review of the Plan. The final review report—including a renewed draft of the Plan—was presented to the Forum Secretariat in October 2013. The report presented 36 recommendations to be reviewed by the Leaders, including renaming and reformulating the Plan as the Framework for Pacific Regionalism. The proposed

Framework was to establish manageable regional priority actions, and to be led by a new, efficient Board for Pacific Regionalism (which would replace the Pacific Plan Action Committee).

POLITICAL GOVERNANCE AND SECURITY

The Forum Secretariat organizes and services the gatherings of the Forum, disseminates its views, administers the Forum's observer office at the UN, and aims to strengthen relations with other regional and international organizations. It promotes regional co-operation in law enforcement and legal affairs, and provides technical support for the drafting of legal documents and for law enforcement capacity building.

The Secretariat assists member countries to ratify and implement the 1988 UN Convention against Illicit Trafficking in Narcotic Drugs and Psychotropic Substances. The Honiara Declaration on Law Enforcement Co-operation, adopted by Forum leaders in 1992, stated that security was a prerequisite for attaining the goal of balanced regional economic and social development. At the end of 2001 a conference of Forum ministers responsible for immigration expressed concern at rising levels of human trafficking and illegal immigration in the region, and recommended that member states become parties to the 2000 UN Convention Against Transnational Organized Crime. A Pacific Transnational Crime Co-ordination Centre was established in Suva, Fiji, in 2004, to enhance and gather law enforcement intelligence. In September 2006 the Forum, in co-operation with the USA and the UN Global Programme Against Money Laundering (administered by the UN Office on Drugs and Crime), initiated a programme to provide technical assistance to member states for the development of their national anti-money-laundering and counter-terrorism financing regimes, in accordance with the Pacific Plan's development priority of regional security. Under the Pacific Plan, the Forum Secretariat requested the establishment of a Pacific Islands Regional Security Technical Co-operation Unit to support legislative efforts regarding, inter alia, transnational organized crime, counter-terrorism and financial intelligence.

In July 1995, following a decision of the French Government to resume testing of nuclear weapons in French Polynesia, members of the Forum resolved to increase diplomatic pressure on the Governments of France, the United Kingdom, and the USA to accede to the 1986 South Pacific Nuclear-Free Zone Treaty (Treaty of Rarotonga), prohibiting the acquisition, stationing or testing of nuclear weapons in the region. Following France's decision, announced in January 1996, to end the testing programme four months earlier than scheduled, representatives of the Governments of the three countries signed the Treaty in March.

In September 2008 the first Pacific Islands-European Union (EU) troika ministerial meeting was convened, in Brussels, Belgium, under a new Forum-EU enhanced political dialogue framework, covering areas including regional security and governance, development co-operation, economic stability and growth, the environment, and trade. The second troika ministerial meeting was held in June 2012, in Auckland, New Zealand.

In October 2000 leaders attending the 31st Forum, convened in Tarawa, Kiribati, adopted the Biketawa Declaration, which outlined a mechanism for responding to any security crises that might occur in the region, while also urging members to undertake efforts to address the fundamental causes of potential instability. In August 2003 regional leaders convened at the 34th Forum commended the swift response by member countries and territories in deploying a Regional Assistance Mission to Solomon Islands (RAMSI), which had been approved by Forum ministers of foreign affairs at a meeting held in Sydney, Australia, in June, in accordance with the Biketawa Declaration. In December 2011 the Solomon Islands Government agreed to lead a process under which the military component of RAMSI would be phased out. Accordingly, on 1 July 2013 RAMSI was transformed into a regional policing-only mission, and, from mid-2013 until at least 2017, the newly constituted mission was to focus mainly on building the capacity of the Royal Solomon Islands Police Force. In March 2008 a Pacific Islands Forum Ministerial Contact Group (MCG) on Fiji, comprising the ministers responsible for foreign affairs of Australia, New Zealand, Papua New Guinea, Samoa, Tonga and Tuvalu, was established to facilitate the restoration of democracy and rule of law in that country, where the legitimate Government had been overthrown by the military in December 2006. In January 2009 Forum heads of state and government convened a Special Leaders' Retreat, in Port Moresby, Papua New Guinea, to consider the political situation in Fiji. The meeting resolved to suspend Fiji from the Forum if no date for democratic elections had been set by the interim authorities in that country by 1 May. Fiji's suspension was confirmed in May. Visiting Fiji in early May 2012 the MCG concluded that the ongoing process leading to planned elections in 2014 was encouraging; however, the 43rd Forum, convened in August 2012, determined to maintain Fiji's suspension from participation in Forum meetings. Visiting Fiji once again in April 2013, the MCG noted the work undertaken during 2012 by Fiji's independent Constitution Commission and recalled government assurances that elections would take place no later than September 2014. In September 2013 leaders attending the 44th Forum welcomed the publication of Fiji's new constitution.

The 33rd Forum, held in Suva, in August 2002, adopted the Nasonini Declaration on Regional Security, which recognized the need for immediate and sustained regional action to combat international terrorism and transnational crime, in view of the perceived increased threat to global and regional security following the major terrorist attacks perpetrated against targets in the USA in September 2001. In October 2007 the 37th Forum determined to develop a Regional Co-operation for Counter-Terrorism Assistance and Response model.

In August 2003 regional leaders attending the 34th Forum adopted a set of Forum Principles of Good Leadership, establishing key requirements for good governance, including respect for law and the system of government, and respect for cultural values, customs and traditions, and for freedom of religion.

ECONOMIC GOVERNANCE

The Forum Secretariat extends advice and technical assistance to member countries in policy, development, export marketing, and information dissemination. Trade policy activities are mainly concerned with improving private sector policies, for example investment promotion, assisting integration into the world economy (including the provision of information and technical assistance to member states on World Trade Organization (WTO)-related matters and supporting Pacific Island ACP states with preparations for negotiations on trade partnership with the EU under the Cotonou Agreement), and the development of businesses. The Secretariat aims to assist both island governments and private sector companies to enhance their capacity in the development and exploitation of export markets, product identification and product development. A regional trade and investment database is being developed. The Secretariat co-ordinates the activities of the regional trade offices located in Australia, New Zealand and Japan. A representative trade office in Beijing, People's Republic of China, opened in January 2002. A Forum office was opened in Geneva, Switzerland, in 2004 to represent member countries at the WTO. In April 2005 the Pacific Islands Private Sector Organisation (PIPSO), representing regional private sector interests, was established. The PIPSO Secretariat, hosted by the Forum Secretariat, was inaugurated in April 2007. In August of that year PIPSO organized the first Pacific Islands Business Forum, convened in Nadi, Fiji.

A South Pacific Regional Trade and Economic Co-operation Agreement (SPARTECA) entered into effect in 1981, in order to redress the trade deficit of the Pacific Island countries with Australia and New Zealand. It is a non-reciprocal trade agreement under which Australia and New Zealand offer duty-free and unrestricted access or concessional access for specified products originating from the developing island member countries of the Forum. In 1985 Australia agreed to further liberalization of trade by abolishing (from the beginning of 1987) duties and quotas on all Pacific products except steel, cars, sugar, footwear and garments. In August 1994 New Zealand expanded its import criteria under the agreement by reducing the rule of origin requirement for garment products from 50% to 45% of local content. In response to requests from Fiji, Australia agreed to widen its interpretation of the agreement by accepting as being of local content manufactured products that consist of goods and components of 50% Australian content. In December 2011 Australia and New Zealand agreed to extend to 31 December 2014 the SPARTECA Textile, Clothing and Footwear Provisions Scheme, under which certain goods manufactured in Forum countries may—without meeting all the provisions of SPARTECA—enter Australia and New Zealand tariff-free.

Two major regional trade accords signed by Forum heads of state in August 2001 entered into force in April 2003 and October 2002, respectively: the Pacific Island Countries Trade Agreement (PICTA), providing for the establishment of a Pacific Island free trade area (FTA); and the related Pacific Agreement on Closer Economic Relations (PACER), incorporating trade and economic co-operation measures and envisaging the phased establishment of a regional single market comprising the PICTA FTA and Australia and New Zealand. The FTA was to be implemented over a period of eight years for developing member countries and 10 years for SIS and least developed countries. It was envisaged that negotiations on free trade agreements between Pacific Island states and Australia and New Zealand, with a view to establishing the larger regional single market envisaged by PACER, would commence within eight years of PICTA's entry into force. SPARTECA would remain operative pending the establishment of the larger single market, into which it would be subsumed. Under the provisions of PACER, Australia and New Zealand were to provide technical and financial assistance to PICTA signatory states in pursuing the objectives of PACER. In August 2003 regional leaders attending the 34th Forum agreed, in principle, that the USA and France should become parties to both

PICTA and PACER. In September 2004 Forum trade officials adopted a Regional Trade Facilitation Programme (RTFP), within the framework of PACER, which included measures concerned with customs procedures, quarantine, standards and other activities to harmonize and facilitate trade between Pacific Island states and Australia and New Zealand, as well as with other international trading partners. It was announced in August 2007 that a review of the RTFP was to be undertaken. In March 2008 negotiations commenced on expanding PICTA to include provisions for trade in services as well as trade in goods; a Protocol on trade in services was opened for signature in August 2012. In August 2008 leaders attending the 40th Forum, convened in Cairns, Australia, endorsed the Cairns Compact on Strengthening Development Co-ordination in the Pacific, aimed at improving regional economic and development progress despite the ongoing global economic crisis, and agreed that negotiations on a new regional trade and economic integration agreement (PACER-Plus) should commence forthwith. The participants in the PACER-Plus negotiations (which were ongoing in 2014) were Australia, the Cook Islands, Kiribati, the Marshall Islands, the Federated States of Micronesia, Nauru, New Zealand, Niue, Palau, Papua New Guinea, Samoa, the Solomon Islands, Tonga, Tuvalu and Vanuatu. A meeting of Forum ministers responsible for trade, convened in April 2010, proposed that a shared 10-year strategy for trade and investment promotion should be developed. The April 2010 meeting established a new umbrella body, Pacific Islands Trade and Invest, to cover and develop a co-ordinated corporate strategy for the former Pacific Islands Trade and Investment Commissions, based in Auckland, New Zealand and Sydney, Australia, and trade offices in Beijing, China and Tokyo, Japan. In May 2013 a Memorandum of Understanding to establish a new Pacific Regional Trade and Development Facility was opened for signature.

In January 1997 Japan and the PIF established a series of Pacific Alliance Leaders' Meetings (PALM), hosted by Japan, which are aimed at strengthening mutual economic and political co-operation. PALM-6 was convened in May 2012 in Okinawa, Japan.

In April 2001 the Secretariat convened a meeting of seven member island states—the Cook Islands, the Marshall Islands, Nauru, Niue, Samoa, Tonga and Vanuatu—as well as representatives from Australia and New Zealand, to address the regional implications of Organisation for Economic Co-operation and Development's Harmful Tax Competition Initiative. (OECD had identified the Cook Islands, the Marshall Islands, Nauru and Niue as so-called tax havens lacking financial transparency and had demanded that they impose stricter legislation to address the incidence of international money-laundering in their territories.) The meeting requested OECD to engage in conciliatory negotiations with the listed Pacific Island states. The August 2001 Forum reiterated this stance, proclaiming the sovereign right of nations to establish individual tax regimes, and supporting the development of a co-operative framework to address financial transparency concerns. The Forum is an observer at meetings of the Sydney, Australia-based Asia/Pacific Group on Money Laundering (established in 1997).

The Forum Secretariat aims to co-ordinate and promote co-operation in development activities and programmes throughout the region. It administers a Short Term Advisory Service, which provides consultancy services to help member countries meet economic development priorities, and a Fellowship Scheme to provide practical training in a range of technical and income-generating activities. A Small Island Development Fund aims to assist the economic development of the SIS sub-group of member countries through project financing. A separate fellowship has also been established to provide training to the Kanak population of New Caledonia, to assist in their social, economic and political development. The Secretariat aims to assist regional organizations to identify development priorities and to provide advice to national governments on economic analysis, planning and structural reforms.

The Forum established the Pacific Forum Line and the Association of South Pacific Airlines, as part of its efforts to promote co-operation in regional transport. In May 1998 ministers responsible for aviation in member states approved a new regional civil aviation policy, which envisaged liberalization of air services, common safety and security standards and provisions for shared revenue. The Pacific Islands Air Services Agreement entered into effect in October 2007. In June 2005 the Pacific Islands Civil Aviation and Security Treaty (PICASST) entered into force, establishing a Port Vila, Vanutau-based Pacific Aviation Security Office. In accordance with the Principles on Regional Transport Services, which were adopted by Forum Leaders in August 2004, the Secretariat was to support efforts to enhance air and shipping services, as well as to develop a regional digital strategy.

In August 2004 the 35th Forum adopted a set of Principles on Regional Transport Services, based on the results of a study requested by the 34th Forum, 'to improve the efficiency, effectiveness and sustainability of air and shipping services'.

In August 2008 the 39th Forum welcomed a new Pacific Region Infrastructure Facility initiated by the World Bank, Asian Development Bank and Governments of Australia and New Zealand.

In December 2009 the Forum Secretariat and the World Intellectual Property Organization launched a Traditional Knowledge Action Plan for Forum Island Countries, which sought to protect Pacific traditional knowledge from misuse without compensation to its owners.

In August 2010 the 41st Forum welcomed the outcome of the Pacific Conference on the Human Face of the Global Economic Crisis, which had been convened in February of that year, with participation by policy-makers and civil society and private sector delegates from 16 Pacific Island countries, as well as development partners and representatives of UN agencies and regional organizations, including the Forum Secretariat.

In October 2010 a multi-agency Food Secure Pacific working group, established in 2008 by the Forum Secretariat, the Secretariat of the Pacific Community, FAO, UNICEF and WHO, began implementing a new Framework for Action on Food Security in the Pacific, which had been endorsed by a Pacific Food Summit, convened in April 2010, in Port Vila.

In August 2010 the 41st Forum endorsed a Framework for Action on Energy Security in the Pacific. In September 2011 the 42nd Forum endorsed the Waiheke Declaration on Sustainable Economic Development, which made a commitment to improving energy security in the Pacific, and recognized the importance of focusing efforts on sectors such as tourism, fisheries and agriculture, in which there is comparative advantage. Leaders emphasized maximizing the economic benefit from fisheries, expressed concern at the effect of illegal, unreported and unregulated fishing, and stressed the importance of transport links and secure access to energy. In March 2013 a Pacific Leaders' Energy Summit was convened in Tonga, with a view to advancing the commitments made under the 2011 Waiheke Declaration; a general Pacific Energy Summit was also held in that month, in Auckland.

STRATEGIC PARTNERSHIPS AND CO-ORDINATION

The Forum actively promotes the development of effective international legislation to reduce emissions by industrialized countries of so-called greenhouse gases. Such gases contribute to the warming of the earth's atmosphere (the 'greenhouse effect') and to related increases in global sea levels, and have therefore been regarded as a major threat to low-lying islands in the region. The Secretariat has played an active role in supporting regional participation at meetings of the Conference of the Parties to the UN Framework Convention on Climate Change (UNFCCC), and helps to co-ordinate Forum policy on the environment. With support from the Australian Government, it administers a network of stations to monitor sea levels and climate change throughout the Pacific region. The 29th Forum, held in Pohnpei, Federated States of Micronesia, in August 1998, adopted a Statement on Climate Change, which urged all countries to ratify and implement the gas emission reductions agreed upon by UN member states in December 1997 (the so-called Kyoto Protocol of the UNFCCC), and emphasized the Forum's commitment to further measures for verifying and enforcing emission limitation. In October 2005 the 36th Forum approved the Pacific Islands Framework for Action on Climate Change 2006–15, and noted the need to implement national action plans to address climate change issues. In August 2008 the 39th Forum, held in Alofi, Niue, endorsed the Niue Declaration on Climate Change, which urged international partners to undertake immediate and effective measures to reduce emissions, to use cleaner fuels, and to increase use of renewable energy sources, and directed the Forum Secretariat to work with relevant agencies and member countries and territories in support of a number of commitments, including examining the potential for regional climate change insurance arrangements, and advancing regional expertise in the development and deployment of adaptation technologies. In November 2008 the EU and the Forum Secretariat adopted a joint declaration on co-operating in combating the challenges posed by climate change. The 40th Forum, in August 2009, adopted the Pacific Leaders Call for Action on Climate Change. Following a review of the Framework for Action on Climate Change, undertaken during 2010, a second edition of the Framework was launched in September 2011. In September 2013 the 44th Forum, convened in Majuro, Marshall Islands, endorsed the Majuro Declaration for Climate Leadership, in which—recognizing the unique vulnerability of the Pacific Island states to climate change—they committed to demonstrating climate leadership through a series of targets and actions contributing to the promotion of renewable energy resources and to the urgent reduction and phasing down of greenhouse gas pollution.

In May 2009 Forum Leaders and Government of Japan jointly launched a Pacific Environment Fund (PEC), which is managed by the Forum Secretariat, and supports projects with a focus on sea water desalination and solar power generation.

In August 2002 regional leaders attending the 33rd Forum approved a Pacific Island Regional Ocean Policy, which aimed to ensure the future sustainable use of the ocean and its resources by Pacific Island communities and external partners. A Declaration on Deep Sea Bottom Trawling to Protect Biodiversity on the High Seas was adopted in October 2005 by the 36th Forum. In October 2007 leaders attending the 38th Forum urged increased efforts among Forum members to foster a long-term strategic approach to ensuring the effective management of fish stocks, with a particular focus on tuna, and adopted a related Declaration on Pacific Fisheries Resources. In August 2010 the 41st Forum endorsed both a new Regional Monitoring Control and Surveillance Strategy, adopted by Forum ministers responsible for fisheries in July, as the overarching framework to support regional fisheries management, and also endorsed a new Framework for a Pacific Oceanscape, aimed at ensuring the long-term, co-operative sustainable development, management and conservation of the Pacific. The Framework provides for the creation of a network of national marine reserves; in August 2012, during the 43rd Forum, the Cook Islands inaugurated a new national marine protected zone which, measuring 1.1m. sq km, represented at that time the largest such marine reserve in the world, and, during 2012 Australia announced that it was to expand its national marine protected zone to encompass 3.1m. sq km. Also during the 2012 Forum the leaders of the Cook Islands, Niue, Kiribati, Tokelau, Tuvalu, Nauru and the Marshall Islands signed eight maritime boundary agreements, while Kiribati, the Marshall Islands and Nauru adopted a trilateral treaty relating to the intersection of the exclusive economic zones of the three countries (known as the 'tri-junction point').

In September 1995 the 26th Forum adopted the Waigani Convention, banning the import into the region of all radioactive and other hazardous wastes, and providing controls for the transboundary movement and management of these wastes. Forum leaders have frequently reiterated protests against the shipment of radioactive materials through the region.

In January 2005, meeting on the fringes of the fifth Summit of the Alliance of Small Island States, in Port Louis, Mauritius, the Secretaries-General of the Pacific Islands Forum Secretariat, the Commonwealth, Caribbean Community and Common Market (CARICOM), and the Indian Ocean Commission determined to take collective action to strengthen the disaster preparedness and response capacities of their member countries in the Pacific, Caribbean and Indian Ocean areas. In October 2005 the 36th Forum endorsed the Pacific Disaster Risk Reduction and Disaster Management Framework for Action 2005–15.

In October 2005 the 36th Forum urged the adoption of national and regional avian influenza preparedness measures and considered a proposal to establish a Pacific Health Fund to address issues such as avian influenza, HIV/AIDS, malaria, and non-communicable diseases (NCDs). In June 2011 regional ministers of health issued the Honiara Communiqué on the Pacific Non-Communicable Diseases Crisis, highlighting the impact of a rapid increase in NCDs in the region (the estimated cause of three-quarters of all adult deaths). In September 2011 the 42nd Forum issued a Leaders' Statement on NCDs.

In October 2009 Forum ministers responsible for health approved a new Pacific Regional Strategy on Disability, to cover the period 2010–15.

In August 2012 leaders attending the 43rd Forum adopted a Gender Equality Declaration. In October the first Pacific Regional Action Plan on Women, Peace and Security was initiated. This aimed to promote the active participation of women in conflict prevention and peacebuilding activities, and to develop the necessary frameworks to ensure the protection of women and girls during humanitarian crises and in transitional or post-conflict situations.

Since 2001 the Forum has sent observer groups to monitor elections taking place in member states, and, since 2004, joint election observer missions have been undertaken with the Commonwealth.

SMALLER ISLAND STATES

In 1990 the Cook Islands, Kiribati, Nauru, Niue and Tuvalu, among the Forum's smallest island member states, formed the Forum SIS economic sub-group, which convenes an annual summit meeting to address their specific smaller island concerns. These include, in particular, economic disadvantages resulting from a poor resource base, absence of a skilled workforce and lack of involvement in world markets. Small island member states have also been particularly concerned about the phenomenon of global warming and its potentially damaging effects on the region. In September 1997 the Marshall Islands was admitted as the sixth member of SIS, and Palau was subsequently admitted as the seventh member. In February 1998 senior Forum officials, for the first time, met with representatives of the Caribbean Community and the Indian Ocean Commission, as well as other major international organizations, to discuss means to enhance consideration and promotion of the interests of small island states. An SIS unit, established within the Forum Secretariat in 2006, aims to enable high-profile representation of the SIS perspective, particularly in the development of the Pacific Plan, and to enable the small island member states to benefit fully from the implementation of the Plan. In August 2010 the 41st Forum welcomed the outcome of a Pacific High Level Dialogue (convened in February of that year) on the five-year review conference of the 2005 Mauritius Strategy for the further Implementation of the 1994 Barbados Programme of Action for the Sustainable Development of SIS, which was convened in September 2010. The UN Conference on Sustainable Development, convened in June 2012, in Rio de Janeiro, Brazil, called for a third international conference on SIS to be convened. The third SIS conference was to take place in Samoa, in September 2014. Fiji was designated to host the preparatory meetings for the conference.

Recent Meetings of the Pacific Islands Forum

The 43rd Forum, held in Rarotonga, Cook Islands, in August 2012, noted the progress achieved thus far—through initiatives undertaken in both the productive and enabling sectors—in implementing the 2011 Waiheke Declaration on Sustainable Economic Development, the Pacific Islands Framework for Action on Climate Change, and the Pacific Oceanscape Framework. Leaders also welcomed the recent launch of a new Regional Legislative and Regulatory Framework for Deep Sea Minerals Exploration. The Forum agreed that a review of the Pacific Plan—including an updated draft of the Plan—should be prepared. A Leaders' Gender Equality Declaration was adopted by the Forum.

Heads of Government attending the 44th Forum, held in Majuru, Marshall Islands, in September 2013, emphasized the importance of elaborating a post-2015 global development agenda, and of establishing a series of Sustainable Development Goals, and welcomed an initiative by the Tonga Government to establish a Pacific Regional Data Repository for Sustainable Energy for All (SE4All). The leaders endorsed the Majuro Declaration for Climate Leadership, in which they established a series of targets and actions contributing to the promotion of renewable energy resources and to the phasing down of greenhouse gas pollution. The Forum also welcomed recommendations made to the UN Human Rights Council following visits made by the UN Special Rapporteur in early 2012 to the Marshall Islands and the USA; and supported bilateral and multilateral action to assist the Marshall Islands in its efforts to achieve a just resolution to the US nuclear testing programme.

Finance

The Governments of Australia and New Zealand each contribute some 30% of the annual budget and the remaining amount is shared by the other member Governments. Extrabudgetary funding is contributed mainly by the European Union, Australia, New Zealand, China and Japan. The Forum's 2013 budget amounted to US $111.5m. Following a decision of the 36th Forum a Pacific Fund was established to support the implementation of the Pacific Plan, under the management of the Pacific Plan Action Committee.

Publications

Annual Report.
Forum News (quarterly).
Pacific Plan Progress Report.
Pacific Regional Millennium Development Goals Tracking Report.
Pacific Plan Annual Progress Report.
SPARTECA (guide for Pacific island exporters).
Tracking the Effectiveness of Development Efforts in the Pacific.
Trends and Developments.
Reports of meetings; profiles of Forum member countries.

Overseas Agencies and Affiliated Organizations

Association of South Pacific Airlines (ASPA): POB 9817, Nadi Airport, Nadi, Fiji; tel. 6723526; fax 6720196; e-mail georgefaktaufon@aspa.aero; internet aspa.aero; f. 1979 at a meeting of airlines in the South Pacific, convened to promote co-operation among the mem. airlines for the devt of regular, safe and economical commercial aviation within, to and from the South Pacific; mems: 16

regional airlines, two associates; Chair. DIDIER TAPPERO (New Caledonia).

Forum Fisheries Agency (FFA): POB 629, Honiara, Solomon Islands; tel. (677) 21124; fax (677) 23995; e-mail info@ffa.int; internet www.ffa.int; f. 1979 to promote co-operation in fisheries among coastal states in the region; collects and disseminates information and advice on the living marine resources of the region, including the management, exploitation and development of these resources; provides assistance in the areas of law (treaty negotiations, drafting legislation, and co-ordinating surveillance and enforcement), fisheries development, research, economics, computers, and information management; implements a Vessel Monitoring System, to provide automated data collection and analysis of fishing vessel activities throughout the region; on behalf of its 17 mem. countries, the FFA administers a multilateral fisheries treaty, under which vessels from the USA operate in the region, in exchange for an annual payment; the FFA is implementing the FFA Strategic Plan 2005–20, detailing the medium-term direction of the Agency; Dir JAMES MOVICK (Federated States of Micronesia); publs *FFA News Digest* (every two months), *FFA Reports*, *MCS Newsletter* (quarterly), *Tuna Market Newsletter* (monthly).

Pacific Forum Line: POB 105-612, Auckland 1143, New Zealand; tel. (9) 356-2333; fax (9) 356-2330; internet www.pacificforumline.com; f. 1977 as a joint venture by South Pacific countries, to provide shipping services to meet the special requirements of the region; operates three container vessels; conducts shipping agency services in Australia, Fiji, New Zealand and Samoa, and stevedoring in Samoa; CEO HENNING HANSEN.

Pacific Islands Centre (PIC): Meiji University, 1-1 Kanda-Surugadai, Chiyoda-ku, Tokyo 101-8301, Japan; tel. (3) 3296-4545; e-mail info@pic.or.jp; internet www.pacifictradeinvest.com; f. 1996 to promote and to facilitate trade, investment and tourism among Forum mems and Japan; Dir KANICHIRO SOHMA.

Pacific Islands Private Sector Organization (PIPSO): Lot 3, Goodenough St, Lynica House, Middle Floor, Suva, Fiji Islands; tel. 7736301; fax 3305105; e-mail info@pipso.org.fj; internet www.pipso.org; f. 2005 to represent regional private sector interests; organizes Pacific Islands Business Forum; in March 2013 PIPSO and the Secretariat of the Pacific Community concluded a Memorandum of Understanding aimed at advancing regional economic devt; Chair. PAULA TAUMOEPEAU (Tonga).

Pacific Islands Trade and Invest (Australia): Level 11, 171 Clarence St, Sydney, NSW 20010, Australia; tel. (2) 9290-2133; fax (2) 9299-2151; internet www.pacifictradeinvest.com; f. 1979 as Pacific Islands Trade and Investment Commission (Sydney), current name adopted 2010; assists Pacific Island Governments and business communities to identify market opportunities in Australia and promotes investment in the Pacific Island countries.

Pacific Islands Trade and Invest (China): 5-1-3-1 Tayuan Diplomatic Compound, 1 Xin Dong Lu, Chaoyang District, Beijing 100600, People's Republic of China; tel. (10) 6532-6622; fax (10) 6532-6360; internet www.pacifictradeinvest.com; f. 2001, current name adopted in 2013.

Pacific Islands Trade and Invest (New Zealand): POB 109-395, 5 Short St, Level 3, Newmarket, Auckland, New Zealand; tel. (9) 5295165; fax (9) 5231284; internet www.pacifictradeinvest.com; f. 1988 as Pacific Islands Trade and Investment Commission (New Zealand), current name adopted 2010.

SOUTH ASIAN ASSOCIATION FOR REGIONAL COOPERATION—SAARC

Address: POB 4222, Tridevi Marg, Kathmandu, Nepal.

Telephone: (1) 4221785; **fax:** (1) 4227033; **e-mail:** saarc@saarc-sec.org; **internet:** www.saarc-sec.org.

SAARC was established in 1985 in order to strengthen and accelerate regional co-operation, particularly in economic development.

MEMBERS

Afghanistan	Maldives
Bangladesh	Nepal
Bhutan	Pakistan
India	Sri Lanka

Observers: Australia, People's Republic of China, Iran, Japan, the Republic of Korea, Mauritius, Myanmar, the European Union.

Organization

(April 2014)

SUMMIT MEETING

Heads of state and of government of member states represent the body's highest authority. The 17th summit was held in Addu City, Maldives, in November 2011. The 18th summit was scheduled to convene in Nepal, in November 2014.

COUNCIL OF MINISTERS

The Council of Ministers comprises the ministers responsible for foreign affairs of member countries, who meet twice a year. The Council may also meet in extraordinary session at the request of member states. The responsibilities of the Council include formulation of policies, assessing progress and confirming new areas of co-operation.

STANDING COMMITTEE

The Committee consists of the ministers responsible for foreign affairs of member states. It has overall responsibility for the monitoring and co-ordination of programmes and financing, and determines priorities, mobilizes resources and identifies areas of co-operation. It usually meets twice a year, and submits its reports to the Council of Ministers. The Committee is supported by an ad hoc Programming Committee composed of senior officials, who assist the Standing Committee in matters relating to the selection and financing of regional projects, choosing inter-sectoral priorities, and to confirm the Calendar of Activities. The Programming Committee is also mandated to convene independently of the Standing Committee to co-ordinate the implementation of approved SAARC programmes and activities, and co-ordinates the Governing Boards of the SAARC Regional Centres.

TECHNICAL COMMITTEES

SAARC's six Technical Committees cover Agriculture and Rural Development; Environment; Health and Population Activities; Science and Technology; Transport; and Women, Youth and Children. They are responsible for forming, co-ordinating, implementing and monitoring programmes in their respective areas of focus. Each committee comprises representatives of member states and meets annually.

SECRETARIAT

The Secretariat comprises the Secretary-General and eight Directors, from each member country, responsible for the following working divisions: Media and Integration of Afghanistan; Agriculture and Rural Development; Environment and Science and Technology; Economic, Trade and Finance; Social Affairs; Information and Publications; Administration, Energy and Tourism; and Human Resource Development, Transport and the SAARC Charter. The Secretary-General is appointed by the Council of Ministers, after being nominated by a member state, and serves a three-year term of office.

Secretary-General: ARJUN BAHADUR THAPA (Nepal).

REGIONAL CENTRES

The SAARC Secretariat is supported by 11 Regional Centres, established in member states to promote regional co-operation. Each Centre is managed by a Governing Board comprising representatives from all the member states, the SAARC Secretary-General, and the ministry responsible for foreign affairs of its host government. Each Centre has a Director, who acts as Member Secretary to the Centre's Governing Board, and each Governing Board reports to the SAARC Programming Committee. In July 2012 a meeting of Directors of SAARC Regional Centres, convened in Kathmandu, Nepal, agreed a set of recommendations which were to contribute to an ongoing process (decided in November 2011 by the 17th SAARC summit) of strengthening SAARC mechanisms.

SAARC Agriculture Centre: BARC Complex, New Airport Rd, Farmgate, Dhaka 1215, Bangladesh; tel. (2) 8115353; fax (2) 9124596; internet www.saarcagri.org; f. 1989 as the SAARC Agriculture Information Centre (SAIC), mandate expanded and status upgraded to manage all sub-sections and allied disciplines of agriculture in 2006; aims to network relevant agricultural research and information networks in SAARC member states and to exchange regional technical information to strengthen agricultural research, development and innovation; Dir Dr ABUL KALAM AZAD; publs *SAC Newsletter*, *SAARC Journal of Agriculture*, statistical information, reports on agricultural productivity in member states.

SAARC Coastal Zone Management Centre: Ground Floor, Green Bldg, Handhuvaree Hingun, Malé 20094, Maldives; tel. 3315976; fax 3316088; e-mail admin@sczmc.org; internet www.sczmc.org; f. 2005 to promote the management of the coastal areas of the region; works to promote regional co-operation in the management of coastal ecosystems with a view to their sustainable economic integration in the development planning of the countries in the region; interacts with coastal authorities and international organizations for research, training and awareness activities; Dir IBRAHIM NAEEM.

SAARC Cultural Centre: 224 Baudhaloka Mawatha, Colombo 7, Sri Lanka; tel. (11) 2584451; fax (11) 2584452; e-mail saarc-scc@sltnet.lk; internet www.saarcculture.org; f. 2009 to provide a forum for artistic communities in SAARC member states; aims to establish regional co-operation in the arts by expressing the collective cultural identity of South Asia; Dir G. L. W. SAMARASINGHE; publ. *SAARC Culture* (6 a year).

SAARC Disaster Management Centre: IIPA Campus, I.P. Estate, Mahatma Gandhi Rd, New Delhi 110 002, India; tel. (11) 23765516; fax (11) 23765517; e-mail dir.sdmc@gmail.com; internet www.saarc-sdmc.nic.in; f. 2006; provides policy advice and facilitates strategic learning, research, training, systems development and the exchange of information for effective disaster risk reduction and management in South Asia; Dir Prof. SANTOSH KUMAR; publs *Newsletter* (quarterly), *Journal of South Asia Disaster Studies* (2 a year), *South Asia Disaster Report* (annually).

SAARC Documentation Centre: NISCAIR Bldg, 14 Satsang Vihar Marg, New Delhi 110 067, India; tel. and fax (11) 26863609; e-mail sdc@niscair.res.in; internet www.sdc.gov.in; f. 1994; maintains regional and national databases on various disciplines and development matters; also conducts training courses in information technology to improve information management services; Dir DHAN BAHADUR OLI.

SAARC Energy Centre: House 697, St 43, E-11/4, Islamabad, Pakistan; tel. (51) 2228802; fax (51) 2221937; e-mail info@saarcenergy.org; internet www.saarcenergy.org; f. 2006 to promote the development of energy resources, to expand energy trade in the region, to develop renewable and alternative energy resources, and to promote energy efficiency and conservation; aims to increase cooperation with influential regional bodies such as the Asian Development Bank and the ASEAN Centre for Energy (ACE); Dir HILAL A. RAZA.

SAARC Forestry Centre: POB 1284, Taba, Thimphu, Bhutan; tel. (2) 365148; fax (2) 365190; e-mail iqbal60@gmail.com; internet www.sfc.org.bt; f. 2008 to facilitate regional co-operation in the areas of forestry and environment; aims to address the degradation of forest land and its impact on natural disasters; Dir SANGAY WANGCHUCK; publ. *SAARC Forestry Journal* (annually).

SAARC Human Resource Development Centre: Park Rd, Chak Shehzad, POB 1856, Islamabad, Pakistan; tel. (51) 9255160; e-mail dranis@shrdc.org; internet www.shrdc.org; f. 2007 to undertake research, impart training and share information on issues related to human resource development; assists mem. states with related policies and strategies in an advisory capacity; Dir Dr RIFFAT AYESHA ANIS; publs *Annual Report*, *SAARC Journal of Human Resource Development* (annually), *Newsletter* (2 a year), research studies and training reports.

SAARC Information Centre: POB 26339, Media Village, Kathmandu, Nepal; tel. (1) 4112559; fax (1) 4112569; e-mail director@saarc-sic.org; internet www.saarc-sic.org; e-mail info@saarc-sic.org; f. 2007 to represent SAARC mem. countries in media and information management; aims to promote the development of information sources and facilitate regional co-operation; Dir LAXMI BILAS KOIRALA.

SAARC Meteorological Research Centre: Abhawa Bhaban, Agargaon, Dhaka 1207, Bangladesh; tel. (02) 8181728; fax (02) 8181727; e-mail info@saarc-smrc.org; internet www.saarc-smrc.org; f. 1995 to establish a regional information network on meteorology, hydrology, oceangraphy and the atmospheric sciences; aims to undertake collective research in the SAARC region, to establish modern observation systems to aid weather forecasting, and to monitor the impact of climate change; Dir SHAH ALAM.

SAARC Tuberculosis and HIV/AIDS Centre: Thimi, Bhaktapur, POB 9517, Kathmandu, Nepal; tel. (1) 6631048; fax (1) 6634379; e-mail saarctb@mos.com.np; internet www.saarctb.org; f. 1992 for regional co-operation in health matters; works for the prevention and control of tuberculosis and HIV-related illness in the region by co-ordinating with health authorities and medical bodies in member countries; signed a MOU with the World Health Organization in 2000, works as a Collaborating Centre; Dir Dr KASHI KANT JHA; publ. *SAARC Journal of Tuberculosis, Lung Diseases and HIV/AIDS*.

Activities

In April 2010 the 16th SAARC summit meeting noted the need to develop a SAARC Vision Statement, and determined to organize a South Asia Forum in which to exchange ideas on future regional development. The summit also directed SAARC to establish a working group to organize the creation of a Conclave of SAARC Parliamentarians, and determined to focus more strongly on people-centric development, preservation of environment and better governance. A Steering Committee, comprising representatives of governments, the private sector, academics and civil society, was constituted to elaborate the objectives and guidelines of the South Asia Forum. The inaugural meeting of the Forum took place in New Delhi, India, in September 2011 on the theme 'Integration in South Asia: Moving Towards a South Asian Economic Union'. The 17th SAARC summit, convened in November 2011, in Addu City, Maldives, adopted the Addu Declaration on 'Building Bridges', urging the future strengthening of SAARC mechanisms, including the Secretariat and Regional Centres.

AGRICULTURE, RURAL CO-OPERATION AND FOOD SECURITY

An Agricultural Information Centre (established in 1998) serves as a central institution for the dissemination of knowledge and information in the agricultural sector. It maintains a network of centres in each member state, which provide for the efficient exchange of technical information and for strengthening agricultural research. An extraordinary meeting of SAARC ministers responsible for agriculture, convened in November 2008, adopted a guiding 'SAARC Agriculture Vision 2020', and a roadmap for its achievement. The document identified long-term regional challenges, and priority measures required, including in the areas of natural resource management, augmentation of production, bio-safety and bio-security, food safety, technology development, climate change adaptation, risk mitigation, supporting the livelihoods of small and marginal farmers in farming and non-farm activities, and addressing the threat posed by avian influenza.

Since 2008 SAARC Chief Veterinary Officers (CVOs) have met regularly to address the increasing regional incidence of Transboundary Animal Diseases (TADs—of which some are zoonotic: transferable to humans). The establishment of a Regional Vaccine Bank is under consideration by the SAARC CVOs, and a Roadmap for the Control of TADs has been finalized.

In 2004 the 12th summit meeting determined to establish a Food Bank, incorporating a reserve of wheat and/or rice for use during times of normal food shortages as well as during emergencies. The Intergovernmental Agreement establishing the SAARC Food Bank (SFB) was signed by leaders attending the 14th summit meeting in April 2007. A meeting of the SFB executive board, convened in October 2010, determined to raise the SFB's then authorized total reserve of 241,580 metric tons of food grains to 400,000 tons, in view of ongoing acute regional food insecurity. SAARC's 15th summit meeting, held in Colombo, Sri Lanka, in August 2008, issued the Colombo Statement on Food Security, urging the region—in response to the ongoing global crisis of reduced food availability and rising food prices—to forge greater co-operation with the international community to ensure regional food availability and nutrition security. In November 2011 the 17th SAARC summit adopted an agreement on the establishment of a SAARC Seed Bank, aimed at enhancing regional agricultural productivity.

In June 2009 a working group on biotechnology finalized a programme of co-operation in areas including agricultural, environmental, animal, marine, and industrial biotechnology, bioinformatics, genetically modified organisms and bio-safety, biofertilizers, vaccine production, genomics and proteomics, nanobiotechnology, and stem cell research.

ECONOMIC CO-OPERATION AND TRADE

A Committee on Economic Cooperation, comprising senior trade officials of member states, was established in July 1991 to monitor progress concerning trade and economic co-operation issues. A SAARC Chamber of Commerce (SCCI) became operational in 1992. In April 1993 ministers signed a SAARC Preferential Trading Arrangement (SAPTA), which came into effect in December 1995. At that time the Council resolved that the ultimate objective for member states should be the establishment of a South Asian Free Trade Area (SAFTA), superseding SAPTA. An Agreement on SAFTA was signed in January 2004, at the 12th summit, and on 1 January 2006 it entered into force, with its Trade Liberalization Programme entering into effect on 1 July. The Agreement provided for the phased elimination of tariffs: to 30% in least developed member countries and to 20% in the others over an initial two-year period, and subsequently to 0%–5% over a period of five years. The Agreement established a mechanism for administering SAFTA and for settling disputes at ministerial level. In November 2011 the 17th SAARC summit urged the intensification of efforts to implement SAFTA effectively, and also directed SAARC ministers responsible for finance to draft a proposal on means of facilitating greater regional flow of financial capital and intra-regional long-term investment.

An Agreement on the Establishment of the South Asian Regional Standards Organisation (SARSO), adopted in August 2008, by the 15th summit, entered into force in August 2011; SARSO was to finalize a series of SAARC Regional Standards.

In September 2005 a meeting of SAARC financial experts submitted for further consideration by the Association proposals that an existing South Asian Development Fund should be replaced by a new SAARC Development Fund (SDF), comprising a Social Window (to finance poverty alleviation projects), an Infrastructure Window (for infrastructure development) and an Economic Window (for non-infrastructure commercial programmes). The meeting also considered the possibility of establishing a South Asian Development Bank. A roadmap for the establishment of the SDF was endorsed by the SAARC Council of Ministers in August 2006. The Fund was launched in April 2010 with a secretariat based in Thimphu, Bhutan. In October 2010 the Japanese Government suspended new financing to a SAARC-Japan Special Fund, established in September 1993, through which funds (cumulatively totalling US $4.73m. by 2010) had been channelled to support SAARC symposia and expert meetings on socio-economic matters, especially relating to energy and disaster reduction; the Fund was to terminate operations following the allocation of some $100,000 that remained deposited at that time.

In January 1996 the first SAARC Trade Fair was held, in New Delhi, to promote intra-SAARC commerce. At the same time SAARC ministers responsible for commerce convened for their first meeting to discuss regional economic co-operation. SAARC operates a scheme for the promotion of organized tourism The 11th SAARC Trade Fair and Tourism Mart was held, in Dhaka, Bangladesh, in March–April 2012. In November 2011 the 17th SAARC summit urged the promotion of the region in terms of trade and tourism as 'Destination South Asia'.

A Visa Exemption Scheme, exempting (in 2014) 24 specified categories of person from visa requirements, with the aim of promoting closer regional contact, became operational in March 1992. In February 2011 a meeting of SAARC ministers of foreign affairs agreed to introduce long-term multi-entry visas for certain business people, sports people and journalists. A SAARC citizens' forum promotes interaction among the people of South Asia.

EDUCATION AND CULTURE

Under the SAARC Agenda for Culture, approved in April 2007, the online promotion of regional culture, a SAARC website on culture, and a SAARC exchange programme on culture were to be developed. SAARC film festivals have been convened. A SAARC Cultural Centre was inaugurated in Colombo, in 2009, and organized, in 2013, inter alia, a SAARC Film Festival (in June) and Literary Festival on South Asian Novels (in December).

A SAARC Consortium of Open and Distance Learning was established in 2000. In addition, SAARC operates a fellowships, scholarships and chairs scheme. In August 2010 a SAARC University was inaugurated, based at a campus in New Delhi. The first students graduated in May 2012.

ENERGY

In October 2005 SAARC ministers responsible for energy, convened for the first time, agreed to form an expert group to address the development of energy conservation and energy efficiency measures, and to formulate a regional roadmap thereon. The SAARC Energy Centre, based in Islamabad, Pakistan, was established in March 2006; the Centre promotes the regional development of energy resources, including hydropower, and energy trade; aims to develop renewable and alternative energy resources; and to promote energy efficiency. In March 2007 India hosted a South Asia Energy Dialogue, with participation by experts, academics and other stakeholders. In April 2009 expert groups were announced on oil and gas; electricity; renewable energy; and technology and knowledge sharing. A dedicated task force has finalized a common template on the technical and commercial aspects of regional electricity grid interconnection. In November 2011 the 17th SAARC summit urged the conclusion of an intergovernmental framework agreement on energy co-operation. Furthermore, the summit directed that member states, subject to the approval of national arrangements, should make available an appropriate percentage of national income towards renewable energy investments. A study on SAARC regional power exchange was undertaken during 2012.

ENVIRONMENT

In June 2005 SAARC ministers responsible for the environment met in special session to consider the impact of the devastating earthquake and subsequent massive ocean movements, or tsunamis, that struck in the Indian Ocean at the end of 2004. The meeting reviewed an assessment of the extent of loss and damage in each country, and of the relief and rehabilitation measures being undertaken. Ministers adopted the Malé Declaration on a collective response to large-scale natural disasters, resolving to strengthen early warning and disaster management capabilities in the region, and determined to support the rehabilitation of members' economies, in particular through the promotion of the tourism sector. In February 2006 a SAARC Comprehensive Framework on Disaster Management, covering 2006–15, was finalized. A SAARC Disaster Management Centre, established in October 2006, and headquartered in New Delhi, provides advice on policy, and facilitates capacity building services in areas including strategic learning, research, training, systems development and exchange of information; the Centre has developed roadmaps relating to various aspects of disaster management. In August 2008 the Centre's mandate was expanded to encompass the development of a Natural Disaster Rapid Response Mechanism; in this respect, a SAARC Agreement on Rapid Response to Natural Disasters was adopted in November 2011 by member states' ministers responsible for foreign affairs, in the presence of regional heads of state, at the 17th SAARC summit. India became the first member to ratify the Agreement in August 2012. In July 2008 SAARC ministers of the environment, meeting to discuss climate change, adopted a SAARC Action Plan and Dhaka Declaration on Climate Change, urging close co-operation in developing projects and raising mass awareness of climate change. In April 2010 leaders attending the 16th SAARC summit meeting issued the Thimphu Statement on Climate Change, in which they determined to review the implementation of the 2008 SAARC Action Plan and Dhaka Declaration, and agreed, inter alia, to establish an Intergovernmental Expert Group on Climate Change, with the aim of developing clear policy direction and guidelines for regional co-operation; to direct the Secretary-General to commission a study on 'Climate risks in the region: ways comprehensively to address the related social, economic and environmental challenges'; to implement advocacy and awareness programmes on climate change; to arrange for 10m. trees to be planted in the region during 2010–15; to formulate national plans, and, when appropriate, regional projects, aimed at protecting and safeguarding the SAARC region's archaeological and historical infrastructure from the adverse effects of climate change; to commission SAARC intergovernmental initiatives on the marine and mountain ecosystems, and on evolving monsoon patterns; and to organize a SAARC Intergovernmental Climate-related Disasters Initiative, aimed at integrating climate change adaptation and disaster risk reduction planning mechanisms. The inaugural meeting of the Intergovernmental Expert Group on Climate Change was held in June 2011, in Colombo; and the Group's second meeting took place in April 2012, in Kathmandu. In October 2009 SAARC environment ministers issued the Delhi Statement on Cooperation in Environment, identifying future critical environmental challenges. In April 2010 the 16th SAARC summit adopted the SAARC Convention on Cooperation on Environment. A SAARC Meteorological Research Centre was established in Dhaka, in November 1992. A SAARC Coastal Zone Management Centre, established in 2005, in the Maldives, promotes co-operation relating to the sustainable development of coastal zones. The SAARC Forestry Centre, established in 2008, is headquartered in Bhutan, and focuses on the protection, conservation and prudent utilization of forest resources, through the implementation of sustainable forest management practices.

SOCIAL AFFAIRS

A SAARC Human Resources Development Centre was established in Islamabad, in 1999. In January 2008 a new SAARC database on gender data (the SAARC 'Genderbase') was launched. In November 2011 the 17th SAARC summit urged the establishment of a regional mechanism to ensure the empowerment of women and gender equality in the region. Since 2007 a SAARC Youth Camp has been periodically convened. A Youth Awards Scheme to reward, annually, outstanding achievements by young people has been operational since 1996. A SAARC Young Entrepreneurs Summit was convened in Lahore, Pakistan, in February 2014.

In April 2003 SAARC ministers responsible for health convened an emergency meeting to consider the regional implications of the spread of Severe Acute Respiratory Syndrome (SARS), a previously unknown atypical pneumonia. In November of that year SAARC ministers responsible for health determined to establish a regional surveillance and rapid reaction system for managing health crises and natural disasters. A SAARC Regional Strategy on HIV/AIDS aims to combat the spread of the infection. A SAARC Tuberculosis and HIV/AIDS Centre was inaugurated in November 2007, in Kathmandu.

INFORMATION, COMMUNICATION AND MEDIA

In May 1998 the first conference of SAARC ministers responsible for communications adopted a plan of action on telecommunications. The second conference, held in June 2004, adopted the Revised SAARC Plan of Action on Telecommunications, aiming to promote the enhancement of telecommunication links and utilization of ICTs within the SAARC region; to minimize the digital divide within and between member states; to harness telecommunication technology for social and economic development; and to evolve a co-ordinated approach in international telecommunications fora, including a SAARC common position at the World Summit for Information Society, convened in Tunis, Tunisia, in November 2005. A SAARC Information Centre was inaugurated in Nepal, in 2005. In November 2011 the 17th SAARC summit urged the commemoration of a new SAARC Media Day and staging of a Regional Conference on Media.

POVERTY ALLEVIATION

The 12th summit meeting of heads of state, held in Islamabad, in January 2004, declared poverty alleviation to be the overarching goal of all SAARC activities. The meeting requested the newly reconstituted Independent South Asian Commission on Poverty Alleviation (ISACPA) to continue its work in an advocacy role and to prepare a set of SAARC Development Goals (SDGs). At the meeting heads of state also endorsed a Plan of Action on Poverty Alleviation, and adopted a SAARC Social Charter that had been drafted with assistance from representatives of civil society, academia, non-governmental organizations and government, under the auspices of an intergovernmental expert group, and incorporated objectives in areas including poverty alleviation, promotion of health and nutrition, food security, water supply and sanitation, children's development and rights, participation by women, and human resources development. The 13th SAARC summit meeting, held in Dhaka, in November 2005, declared the SAARC Decade of Poverty Alleviation covering the period 2006–15 and determined to replace SAARC's Three-tier Mechanism on Poverty Alleviation (established in 1995) with a Two-tier Mechanism on Poverty Alleviation, comprising ministers and secretaries responsible for poverty alleviation at national level. The 14th summit meeting, held in New Delhi, in April 2007, acknowledged ISACPA's efforts in elaborating the SDGs and entrusted the Two-tier Mechanism with monitoring progress towards the achievement of these. The 16th summit, held in Thimphu, in April 2010, urged the mainstreaming of the SDGs into member states' national processes.

SECURITY

At the third SAARC summit, held in Kathmandu, in November 1987, member states signed a SAARC Regional Convention on Suppression of Terrorism. The Convention, which entered into force in August 1988, commits signatory countries to the extradition or prosecution of alleged terrorists and to the implementation of preventative measures to combat terrorism. A SAARC Convention on Narcotic Drugs and Psychotropic Substances was signed during the fifth SAARC summit meeting, held in Malé, Maldives, in 1990, and entered into force in November 1993. It is implemented by a co-ordination group of drug law enforcement agencies. In 1992 a SAARC Drug Offences Monitoring Desk (SDOMD) was established, in Colombo, and in 1995 a SAARC Terrorist Offences Monitoring Desk (STOMD) was inaugurated, also in Colombo. In January 2002 the 11th SAARC summit member states adopted a Convention on Preventing and Combating Trafficking in Women and Children for Prostitution; this was being further elaborated in 2012. The 12th summit, in January 2004, adopted an Additional Protocol on Suppression of Terrorism with a view to preventing the financing of terrorist activities. In February 2009 the Council of Ministers issued a Declaration on Cooperation in Combating Terrorism. In August 2008 a new SAARC Convention on Mutual Assistance in Criminal Matters was adopted. Meeting in July 2011 SAARC ministers of the interior addressed for the first time the issue of maritime piracy and security in the region, considering recommendations on measures to considered by future meetings. In February 2012 a high-level group of experts met, in New Delhi, to address means of strengthening anti-terror mechanisms in SAARC countries, including improving the functioning of the STOMD and the SDOMD, and reviewing enabling legislation enacted by member states relating to the SAARC Regional Convention on Suppression of Terrorism and its Additional Protocol, and the SAARC Convention on Narcotic Drugs and Psychotropic Substances. Consideration was also given to the SAARC Convention on Mutual Assistance in Criminal Matters.

TRANSPORT

From October 2004 SAARC implemented, under supervision from the Asian Development Bank (ADB), a Regional Multimodal Transport Study; this was extended in 2007 to cover Afghanistan. In July 2009 SAARC ministers responsible for transport declared 2010–20 as the SAARC Decade of Intra-regional Connectivity. The November 2011 SAARC summit urged the conclusion of a new Regional Railways Agreement.

CO-OPERATION WITH OTHER ORGANIZATIONS

SAARC has signed Memorandums of Understanding with UNICEF and UNCTAD (in 1993); ESCAP (1994); the Asia Pacific Telecommunity (1994); UNDP (1995); the UN Drug Programme (1995); the European Commission (1996); the International Telecommunication Union (1997); the Canadian International Development Agency (1997); WHO (2000); the ADB, FAO, the Joint UN Programme on HIV/AIDS and the UN Population Fund (2004); UNEP and UNESCO (2007); and the UN International Strategy for Disaster Reduction (2008). An informal dialogue at ministerial level has been conducted with ASEAN and the European Union since 1998. SAARC and the WTO hold regular consultations. SAARC's Secretary-General participates in regular consultative meetings of executive heads of sub-regional organizations (including ESCAP, ASEAN, the Economic Cooperation Organization and the Pacific Islands Forum).

Finance

The national budgets of member countries provide the resources to finance SAARC activities. The Secretariat's annual budget is shared among member states according to a specified formula.

Publications

SAARC News (quarterly).

Other official documents, regional studies, reports.

Regional Apex Bodies

Association of Persons of the Legal Communities of the SAARC Countries (SAARCLAW): 495 HSIDC, Udyog Vihar Phase V, N. H. 8, Gurgaon 122016, National Capital Region, India; tel. (124) 4040193; fax (124) 4040194; e-mail info@saarclaw.org; internet www.saarclaw.org; f. 1991; recognized as a SAARC regional apex body in July 1994; aims to enhance exchanges and co-operation among the legal communities of the sub-region and to promote the development of law; Pres. SONAM TOBGYE; Sec.-Gen. HERMANT K. BATRA.

Foundation of SAARC Writers and Literature (FOSWAL): c/o Academy of Fine Arts and Literature, Siri Fort Institutional Area, New Delhi 110 049, India; tel. 26498070; fax 26496542; e-mail afalin@vsnl.net; internet www.foundationsaarcwriters.com; f. 1987; became a SAARC recognized body in 2002; endorsed as a SAARC regional apex body in 2007; has organized major SAARC literary and cultural events, festivals of folklore, and conferences on Buddhism and Sufism; in 2014 it was undertaking a research and documentation project on intangible cultural heritage; Chair. KHUSHWANT SINGH; Exec. Chair. Dr ABID HUSSAIN.

SAARC Chamber of Commerce and Industry (SCCI): House 397, St 64, I-8/3, Islamabad, Pakistan; tel. (51) 4860611; fax (51) 8316024; e-mail info@saarcchamber.org; internet www.saarcchamber.org; f. 1992; promotes economic and trade co-operation throughout the sub-region and greater interaction between the business communities of mem. countries; organizes SAARC Economic Cooperation Conferences and Trade Fairs; Pres. SHRI VIKRAMJIT S. SAHNEY; Sec.-Gen. MUHAMMAD IQBAL TABISH.

South Asia Foundation (SAF): internet www.southasiafoundation.org; f. 2000; granted SAARC regional apex body status in 2006 (renewed 2011); promotes regional co-operation through education and sustainable development; a secular, non-profit and non-political organization, comprising eight autonomous branches in the SAARC mem. countries; a subsidiary South Asia Foundation Documentation and Information Centre, established in 2001, is based at SAF-India, in New Delhi.

South Asia Initiative to End Violence against Children (SAIEVAC): GPO 5850, House No. 122, Sujan Marg, Lazimpat-2, Kathmandu, Nepal; tel. (1) 4420278; fax (1) 4001602; e-mail saievac-sec@saievac.org; internet www.saievac.org; f. 2005 as a regional forum; formally established in 2011 as a SAARC regional apex body, having been endorsed as such by a meeting of SAARC ministers responsible for children, held in June 2010; has the objective of promoting children's welfare and rights and eliminating all forms of violence against children in the South Asia region; organizes a campaign aimed at ending corporal punishment regionally; Dir-Gen. Dr RINCHEN CHOPHEL.

South Asian Federation of Accountants (SAFA): c/o Institute of Chartered Accountants of India, ICAI Bhavan, POB 7100, Indraprastha Marg, New Delhi 110002, India; tel. (11) 23370195; fax (11) 23379334; e-mail safa@icai.org; internet www.esafa.org; f. 1984; recognized as a SAARC regional apex body in Jan. 2002; aims to develop regional co-ordination for the accountancy profession; Pres. ABDUL MANNAN; Sec. T. KARTHIKEYAN.

Associated Body:

Secretariat of the SAARC Development Fund (SDF): POB No. 928, Norzin Lam, Thimphu, Bhutan; tel. (2) 321152; fax (2) 321150; internet www.sdfsec.org; f. 2010; inaugurated by the 16th SAARC summit of heads of state and government; financing in 2012 the following initiatives: Strengthening the livelihood initiative for home-based workers in SAARC Region—phases I and II; Strengthening maternal and child health, including immunization; Scaling up of zero energy cold storage (ZECS) technology for the horticultural commodities in the high hills of SAARC countries; 'Reaching the Unreached': empowering rural communities; study on teacher development as the key to enhancing quality of basic education in selected SAARC countries; the South Asia Initiative to End Violence Against Children (SAIEVAC); and Post-harvest management and value addition of fruits in production catchments in SAARC countries.

Other recognized regional bodies include the South Asian Association for Regional Cooperation of Architects, the Association of Management Development Institutions, the SAARC Federation of University Women, the SAARC Association of Town Planners, the SAARC Cardiac Society, the Association of SAARC Speakers and Parliamentarians, the Federation of Associations of Pediatric Surgeons of SAARC Countries, the Federation of State Insurance Organizations of SAARC Countries, Hindukush Himalayan Grassroots Women's Natural Resources Management, the Radiological Society of SAARC Countries, the SAARC Diploma Engineers Forum, the SAARC Federation of Oncologists, the SAARC Teachers' Federation, the SAARC Surgical Care Society, the South Asia Association of National Scout Organizations, the South Asian Federation of Exchanges, the South Asian Free Media Association, the South Asian Network of Economic Research Institutes, and the South Asian Regional Association of Dermatologists, Venereologists and Leprologists.

SOUTHERN AFRICAN DEVELOPMENT COMMUNITY—SADC

Address: SADC HQ, Plot No. 54385, Private Bag 0095, Gaborone, Botswana.

Telephone: 3951863; **fax:** 3972848; **e-mail:** registry@sadc.int; **internet:** www.sadc.int.

The first Southern African Development Co-ordination Conference (SADCC) was held at Arusha, Tanzania, in July 1979, to harmonize development plans and to reduce the region's economic dependence on South Africa. In August 1992 the 10 member countries of the SADCC signed a Treaty establishing the Southern African Development Community (SADC), which replaced SADCC upon its entry into force in October 1993. The Treaty places binding obligations on member countries, with the aim of promoting economic integration towards a fully developed common market. A Protocol on Politics, Defence and Security Co-operation, regulating the structure, operations and functions of the Organ on Politics, Defence and Security, entered into force in March 2004. A system of SADC national committees, comprising representatives of government, civil society and the private sector, oversees the implementation of regional programmes at country level and helps to formulate new regional strategies.

MEMBERS

Angola	Malawi	South Africa
Botswana	Mauritius	Swaziland
Congo, Democratic Republic	Mozambique	Tanzania
Lesotho	Namibia	Zambia
Madagascar*	Seychelles	Zimbabwe

* Madagascar was suspended from meetings of SADC during March 2009–January 2014.

Organization

(April 2014)

SUMMIT MEETING

The meeting is held at least once a year and is attended by heads of state and government or their representatives. It is the supreme policy-making organ of SADC and is responsible for the appointment of the Executive Secretary. It is managed by a troika system, comprising the current, incoming and previous chairpersons. The 2013 regular SADC summit meeting was convened in Lilongwe, Malawi, in August. An extraordinary summit meeting was held in January 2014, in Addis Ababa, Ethiopia.

Chairperson (2013–14): Dr JOYCE BANDA (Malawi).

COUNCIL OF MINISTERS

Representatives of SADC member countries at ministerial level meet twice a year to oversee the functioning and development of the organization.

SECTORAL AND CLUSTER MINISTERIAL COMMITTEES

These Committees, comprising ministers from each member state, provide policy guidance to the Secretariat, and oversee the activities of the Community Directorates and core areas of integration. The Committees, each in their area of competence, monitor the implementation of the Regional Indicative Strategic Development Plan (RISDP—see below).

STANDING COMMITTEE OF SENIOR OFFICIALS

The Committee, comprising senior officials, usually from the ministry responsible for economic planning or finance, acts as the technical advisory body to the Council. It meets twice a year.

SECRETARIAT

The Secretariat comprises specialized Units and Directorates covering the following priority areas of regional integration: Trade, Industry, Finance and Investment; Infrastructure and Services; Food, Agriculture and Natural Resources; Social and Human Development and Special Programmes; and Policy, Planning and Resource Mobilization. It is headed by an Executive Secretary and two Deputy Executive Secretaries.

Executive Secretary: Dr STERGOMENA LAWRENCE TAX (Tanzania).

SADC TRIBUNAL

The establishment of the SADC Tribunal was provided for under the Treaty establishing SADC and facilitated by a protocol adopted in 2000. The Windhoek, Namibia-based 10-member Tribunal was inaugurated in November 2005. In 2010 the summit meeting suspended the functioning of the Tribunal pending a review of its operations and terms of reference. In August 2012 SADC heads of state and government determined to limit jurisdiction of a new Tribunal to disputes between member states arising from the Treaty, excluding individuals or private companies from seeking its arbitration.

Activities

In July 1979 the first Southern African Development Co-ordination Conference (SADCC) was attended by delegations from Angola, Botswana, Mozambique, Tanzania and Zambia, with participation by representatives from donor governments and international agencies. In April 1980 a regional economic summit was held in Lusaka, Zambia. The meeting approved the Lusaka Declaration, a statement of strategy with the aim of reducing regional economic dependence on South Africa, then in its apartheid period. The 1986 SADCC summit meeting recommended the adoption of economic sanctions against South Africa but failed to establish a timetable for doing so.

In January 1992 a meeting of the SADCC Council of Ministers approved proposals to transform the organization (by then expanded to include Lesotho, Malawi, Namibia and Swaziland) into a fully integrated economic community, and in August the Treaty establishing SADC was signed. Post-apartheid South Africa became a member of SADC in August 1994, thus strengthening the objective of regional co-operation and economic integration. Mauritius became a member in August 1995. In September 1997 SADC heads of state agreed to admit the Democratic Republic of the Congo (DRC) and Seychelles as members of the Community; Seychelles withdrew, however, in July 2004. Madagascar was admitted in August 2005.

The August 2004 summit meeting of heads of state and government, held in Grand Baie, Mauritius, adopted a new Protocol on Principles and Guidelines Governing Democratic Elections, which advocated: full participation by citizens in the political process; freedom of association; political tolerance; elections at regular intervals; equal access to the state media for all political parties; equal opportunity to exercise the right to vote and be voted for; independence of the judiciary; impartiality of the electoral institutions; the right to voter education; the respect of election results proclaimed to be free and fair by a competent national electoral authority; and the right to challenge election results as provided for in the law. Regional elections are monitored by SADC Election Observation Missions (SEOMs); in 2013 SEOMs were dispatched to monitor the constitutional referendum held in Zimbabwe in March 2013; the general election held in that country at the end of July; a legislative election in Swaziland that was organized in September; and the legislative election held in Madagascar in December, and presidential election held in that country, in two rounds, in October and December.

The March 2001 summit meeting endorsed a Common Agenda for the organization, which covered the promotion of poverty reduction measures and of sustainable and equitable socio-economic development, promotion of democratic political values and systems, and the consolidation of peace and security. Furthermore, the establishment of an integrated committee of ministers was authorized; this was mandated to formulate and oversee a Regional Indicative Strategic Development Plan (RISDP), intended as the key policy framework for managing, over a period of 15 years, the SADC Common Agenda; the finalized RISDP was approved by the summit meeting convened in Dar es Salaam, Tanzania, in August 2003. In April 2006 SADC adopted the Windhoek Declaration on a new relationship between the Community and its international co-operating partners. The declaration provides a framework for co-operation and dialogue between SADC and international partners, facilitating the implementation of the SADC Common Agenda. A Consultative Conference on Poverty and Development, organized by SADC and attended by its international co-operating partners, was convened in April 2008, in Port Louis, Mauritius.

A high-level meeting concerned with integrating the objectives of the New Partnership for Africa's Development (NEPAD) into SADC's regional programme activities was convened in August 2004. In December 2008 SADC and NEPAD launched a joint business hub, aimed at consolidating regional private sector investment.

An SADC Vision 2050 was under development in 2014.

REGIONAL SECURITY

In November 1994 SADC ministers of defence, meeting in Arusha, Tanzania, approved the establishment of a regional rapid deployment peacekeeping force, which could be used to contain regional conflicts or civil unrest in member states. The summit meeting of heads of state and government held in August 2007 authorized the establishment of the SADC Standby Brigade (SADCBRIG), with the aim of ensuring collective regional security and stability. SADCBRIG is a pillar of the African Union (AU)'s African Standby Force. SADC's Regional Peacekeeping Training Centre (SADC-RPTC) was established in June 1999 and since August 2005 has been directed by the SADC Secretariat. An SADC Mine Action Committee is maintained to monitor and co-ordinate the process of removing anti-personnel land devices from countries in the region.

In June 1996 SADC heads of state and government, meeting in Gaborone, Botswana, inaugurated an Organ on Politics, Defence and Security (OPDS), with the aim of enhancing co-ordination of national policies and activities in these areas. The stated objectives of the body were, inter alia, to safeguard the people and development of the region against instability arising from civil disorder, inter-state conflict and external aggression; to undertake conflict prevention, management and resolution activities, by mediating in inter-state and intra-state disputes and conflicts, pre-empting conflicts through an early warning system and using diplomacy and peacekeeping to achieve sustainable peace; to promote the development of a common foreign policy, in areas of mutual interest, and the evolution of common political institutions; to develop close co-operation between the police and security services of the region; and to encourage the observance of universal human rights, as provided for in the charters of the UN and the Organization of African Unity (OAU—now AU). The extraordinary summit held in March 2001 determined to develop the OPDS as a substructure of SADC, with sub-divisions for defence and international diplomacy, to be chaired by a member country's head of state, working within a troika system. A Protocol on Politics, Defence and Security Co-operation—to be implemented by an Inter-state Politics and Diplomacy Committee—regulating the structure, operations and functions of the Organ, was adopted and opened for signature in August 2001 and entered into force in March 2004. A Strategic Indicative Plan for the Organ (SIPO) was implemented during 2004–09. A second Plan, SIPO II, covers 2010–15, and has a focus on activities in the areas of defence, the police, politics, public security, and state security; SIPO II was updated during 2012.

The March 2001 extraordinary SADC summit adopted a Declaration on Small Arms, promoting the curtailment of the proliferation of and illicit trafficking in light weapons in the region. A Protocol on the Control of Firearms, Ammunition and Other Related Materials was adopted in August of that year. In July SADC ministers responsible for defence approved a draft regional defence pact, providing for a mechanism to prevent conflict involving member countries and for member countries to unite against outside aggression. In January 2002 an extraordinary summit of SADC heads of state, held in Blantyre, Malawi, adopted a Declaration against Terrorism.

An extraordinary SADC summit meeting convened in March 2007, in Dar es Salaam, Tanzania, mandated the OPDS to assess the political and security situations in the Democratic Republic of the Congo (DRC) and Lesotho. The ministerial committee of the OPDS troika emphasized the need for SADC support to the ongoing post-conflict reconstruction process in the DRC. An extraordinary meeting of the ministerial committee of the OPDS troika, convened in October of that year, resolved to mobilize humanitarian assistance for eastern areas of the DRC in view of an escalation in the violent unrest there, with a particular focus on assisting internally displaced civilians. In November 2008 SADC convoked an extraordinary summit of heads of state or government in response to mounting insecurity in eastern DRC. The summit determined to assist the government of the DRC, if necessary by sending a regional peacekeeping force to the province of North Kivu. In February 2009 it was reported that SADCBRIG was ready to intervene if required in the DRC situation. A large team of SADC observers, comprising more than 200 representatives of Community member states, was sent to monitor the presidential and legislative elections that were held in the DRC in November 2011. In August 2012 SADC heads of state or government urged Rwanda to denounce militants of the Kivu-based 23 March Movement (known as 'M23'), which during 2012 had became highly active in north-eastern DRC, clashing with government forces and causing mass population displacement. SADC determined that a Community mission of security experts should be dispatched to Rwanda to assess the situation; the mission was sent, accordingly, in that month, and reported back to SADC ministers of defence. A meeting of the OPDS ministerial troika, convened in September, urged the parties to the conflict in eastern DRC to seek a negotiated resolution. The OPDS troika also urged co-operation between SADC and the International Conference of the Great Lakes Region (ICGLR) in facilitating dialogue over the eastern DRC crisis. In December an extraordinary summit of SADC heads of state and government agreed in principle to deploy SADCBRIG in eastern DRC, within the framework of a Neutral International Force that had been proposed by the ICGLR. In February 2013 the leaders of 11 African countries (including Angola and South Africa), meeting in Addis Ababa, Ethiopia, signed the Peace, Security and Cooperation Framework for the DRC and the Region, which aimed to stabilize the Great Lakes region; with the UN, the AU and the ICGLR, SADC was to act as a guarantor of the Framework. The signatories to the Framework committed to protect the future territorial sovereignty and the peace and stability of the DRC. In late March, at the request of the UN Secretary-General, the UN Security Council authorized the establishment of a new Force Intervention Brigade (FIB), to be operational in eastern DRC under the auspices of the UN Organization Stabilization Mission in the DRC (MONUSCO); from May the new Brigade was deployed, in the form of a 3,069-strong SADCBRIG force (as endorsed by the December 2012 extraordinary SADC summit), comprising troops from Malawi, South Africa and Tanzania. In early November 2013 the DRC armed forces, with FIB assistance, gained control over former M23 strongholds, causing the remaining M23 combatants to flee, with many crossing into Rwanda and Uganda. On 5 November the M23 declared the end of its rebellion in eastern DRC. In November–early December a so-called Kampala dialogue took place between the DRC Government and the M23 leadership, culminating in the signing, under the auspices of SADC and the ICGLR, of final declarations by the parties. The chairpersons of SADC and the ICGLR signed at that time a joint communiqué in which they commended the conclusion of the declarations and urged the fulfilment of the commitments contained therein. Subsequently MONUSCO supported the restoration of state authority in areas that had been destabilized by the rebel grouping.

In August 2001 SADC established a task force, comprising representatives of five member countries, to address the ongoing political crisis in Zimbabwe. The Community sent two separate observer teams to monitor the controversial presidential election held in Zimbabwe in March 2002; the SADC Council of Ministers team found the election to have been conducted freely and fairly, while the Parliamentary Forum group was reluctant to endorse the poll. Having evaluated both reports, the Community approved the election. An SADC Council of Ministers group was convened to observe the parliamentary elections held in Zimbabwe in March 2005; however, the Zimbabwean Government refused to invite a delegation from the SADC Parliamentary Forum. The Zimbabwean Government claimed to have enacted electoral legislation in accordance with the provisions of the August 2004 SADC Protocol on Principles and Guidelines Governing Democratic Elections (see above). The extraordinary summit meeting of SADC heads of state and government, convened in Dar es Salaam, in March 2007, to address the political, economic, and security situation in the region, declared 'solidarity with the government and people of Zimbabwe' and mandated then President Thabo Mbeki of South Africa to facilitate dialogue between the Zimbabwean government and opposition. Mbeki reported to the ordinary SADC summit held in August of that year that restoring Zimbabwe's capacity to generate foreign exchange through balance of payments support would be of pivotal importance in promoting economic recovery and that SADC should assist Zimbabwe with addressing the issue of international sanctions.

In early March 2008 an SADC election observer team monitored preparations for and the conduct of presidential and national and local legislative elections that were staged in Zimbabwe at the end of that month. In mid-April, at which time the Zimbabwe Electoral Commission had failed to declare the results of the presidental election, prompting widespread international criticism, SADC convened an extraordinary summit to address the electoral outcome. The OPDS presented to the summit a report by the observer team which claimed that the electoral process had been acceptable to all parties. The summit urged the Zimbabwe Electoral Commission to verify and release the results of the elections without further delay and requested President Mbeki of South Africa to continue in his role as Facilitator of the Zimbabwe Political Dialogue. In June an emergency meeting of the OPDS troika, at the level of heads of state, was convened following an announcement by the main opposition candidate, Morgan Tsvangirai, that he was withdrawing from a forthcoming second round of voting in the presidential election owing to an escalation of violence against opposition supporters in that country. In July Mugabe and the leaders of the two main opposition parties signed a Memorandum of Understanding, brokered by President Mbeki, confirming their commitment to pursuing dialogue and forming an inclusive government. An agreement (the Global Political Agreement—GPA) to share executive responsibilities in a government of national unity was concluded and signed in September. In December SADC launched a new Zimbabwe Humanitarian and Development Assistance Framework (ZHDAF), and in January 2009 it established an All Stakeholders Working Committee to implement the ZHDAF. The extraordinary SADC summit convened in March commended political progress recently achieved in Zimbabwe, and established a committee to co-ordinate SADC support, and to mobilize international support for, Zimbabwe's recovery process. The SADC summit held in September urged the termination of all forms of international sanctions against Zimbabwe. Responsibility for managing the ZHDAF was transferred to the Zimbabwe Government in December 2009. The June 2012 emergency SADC summit meeting urged President Zuma of South Africa, the current SADC Facilitator of the Zimbabwe Political Dialogue, and the parties to the GPA, to develop an implementation mechanism and establish a schedule for the implementation of a 'Roadmap to Zimbabwe Elections' which had been agreed by Zimbabwean stakeholders in April 2011. An extraordinary SADC summit meeting held in June 2013 urged a mid-August deadline for the staging of a general election in Zimbabwe. The Community dispatched an observer mission to Zimbabwe in July to oversee the conduct of the election, which was held at the end of that month.

The March 2009 extraordinary summit strongly condemned the unconstitutional actions that led to the forced resignation during that month of the elected President of Madagascar, Mark Ravalomanana, and ensuing transfer of power to the military in that country; the summit suspended Madagascar from participation in the activities of the Community and urged the immediate restoration of constitutional order. In June SADC appointed a Community mediator in the Madagascar constitutional crisis. Negotiations subsequently facilitated by the mediator, under SADC auspices, in Maputo, Mozambique, led, in August, to the conclusion of an agreement on the establishment of a power-sharing administration in Madagascar; the power-sharing accord was not, however, subsequently implemented. In March 2011 SADC mediators proposed a new 'Roadmap Out of the Crisis' for Madagascar, again envisaging a power-sharing interim government; this was approved by SADC heads of state and government at a summit convened in June 2011, and was signed by 10 of 11 Malagasy stakeholders in September. An SADC Liaison Office in Madagascar was established in November to support the implementation of the roadmap. The extraordinary SADC summit convened in June 2012 mandated the Community's mediator and the OPDS ministerial troika to facilitate dialogue between the main Malagasy stakeholders as a matter of urgency in order to ensure the full implementation of the roadmap. In August an SADC delegation visited Madagascar to hold consultations with stakeholders, including the signatories of the roadmap, the prime minister of the transitional administration, the military leadership, church leaders, and representatives of the international community. The SADC extraordinary summit held in June 2013 authorized SADC mediators to continue to engage with stakeholders in Madagascar, in an attempt to advance the political process. Following two rounds of presidential elections, held in October and December 2013, Hery Rajaonarinampianina was confirmed in January 2014 as the legitimately elected President of Madagascar. At the end of that month an extraordinary summit of SADC heads of state and government lifted Madagascar's suspension from participation in meetings of the Community.

TRADE, INDUSTRY AND INVESTMENT

Under the Treaty establishing SADC, efforts were to be undertaken to achieve regional economic integration. The Directorate of Trade, Industry, Finance and Investment aims to facilitate such integration, and poverty eradication, through the creation of an enabling investment and trade environment in SADC countries. Objectives include the establishment of a single regional market; the progressive removal of barriers to the movement of goods, services and people; and the promotion of cross-border investment. SADC supports programmes for industrial research and development and standardization and quality assurance, and aims to mobilize industrial investment resources and to co-ordinate economic policies and the development of the financial sector. In August 1996 SADC member states signed the Protocol on Trade, providing for the establishment of a regional free trade area (FTA), through the gradual elimination of tariff barriers. (Angola and the DRC are not yet signatories to the Protocol.) In October 1999 representatives of the private sector in SADC member states established the Association of SADC Chambers of Commerce, based in Mauritius. The Protocol on Trade entered into force in January 2000, and an Amendment Protocol on Trade came into force in August, incorporating renegotiated technical details on the gradual elimination of tariffs, rules of origin, customs co-operation, special industry arrangements and dispute settlement procedures. In accordance with a revised schedule, some 85% of intra-SADC trade tariffs were withdrawn by 1 January 2008. The SADC Free Trade Area was formally inaugurated at the meeting of heads of state and government, held in Sandton, South Africa, in August 2008; Angola, the DRC, Malawi and Seychelles, however, had not implemented all requirements of the Protocol on Trade and were not yet participating in the FTA. According to the schedule, reaffirmed at the EU–SADC ministerial meeting in 2006, an SADC customs union was to be implemented by 2010 (however, this deadline was not achieved), a common market by 2015, monetary union by 2016, and a single currency was to be introduced by 2018. Annual meetings are convened to review the work of expert teams in the areas of standards, quality, assurance, accreditation and metrology. At an SADC extraordinary summit convened in October 2006 it was determined that a draft roadmap was to be developed to facilitate the process of establishing a customs union. In November 2007 the Ministerial Task Force on Regional Economic Integration approved the establishment of technical working groups to facilitate the development of policy frameworks in legal and institutional arrangements; revenue collection, sharing and distribution; policy harmonization; and a common external tariff. A strategic forum of the Ministerial Task Force, to review the regional economic integration agenda, was convened in February 2010, in Johannesburg, South Africa, immediately prior the Task Force's ninth meeting.

The mining sector contributes about 10% of the SADC region's annual gross domestic product. The principal objective of SADC's programme of action on mining is to stimulate increased local and foreign investment in the sector, through the assimilation and dissemination of data, prospecting activities, and participation in promotional fora. In April 2006 SADC and the EU launched an initiative, in the framework of the EU-SADC Investment Promotion Programme, to facilitate European investment in some 100 mining projects in southern Africa. Other objectives of the mining sector are the improvement of industry training, increasing the contribution of small-scale mining, reducing the illicit trade in gemstones and gold, increasing co-operation in mineral exploration and processing, and minimizing the adverse impact of mining operations on the environment. In February 2000 a Protocol on Mining entered into force, providing for the harmonization of policies and programmes relating to the development and exploitation of mineral resources in the region. SADC supports the Kimberley Process Certification Scheme to prevent trade in illegally mined rough diamonds. (The illicit trade in so-called conflict diamonds and other minerals is believed to have motivated and financed many incidences of rebel activity in the continent, for example in Angola and the DRC.)

In July 1998 a Banking Association was officially constituted by representatives of SADC member states to establish international banking standards and regional payments systems, to organize training and to harmonize banking legislation in the region. In April 1999 governors of SADC central banks determined to strengthen and harmonize banking procedures and technology in order to facilitate the financial integration of the region. Efforts to harmonize stock exchanges in the region were also initiated in 1999.

The summit meeting of heads of state and government held in Maseru, Lesotho, in August 2006 adopted a new Protocol on Finance and Investment. The document, regarded as constituting the main framework for economic integration in Southern Africa, outlined, inter alia, how the region intended to proceed towards monetary union, and was intended to complement the ongoing implementation of the SADC Protocol on Trade and targets contained in the RISDP.

In August 2008 an SADC Protocol on Science, Technology and Innovation was adopted, with the aim of promoting the development and harmonization of regional science and technology activities.

INFRASTRUCTURE AND SERVICES

An SADC Regional Infrastructure Development Master Plan: Vision 2027, intended to be the basis for infrastructure-related co-operation and planning until 2027, was adopted in August 2012 by SADC heads of state and government; the Master Plan—which was to be implemented in three phases, covering 2012–17, 2017–22, and 2022–27—was envisaged as an element of a broader COMESA-EAC-SADC Tripartite Inter-regional Infrastructure Master Plan. In June 2013 a high-level investment conference was held in Maputo, to mobilize resources for the implementation of the Plan.

The Directorate of Infrastructure and Services focuses on transport, communications and meteorology, energy, tourism and water. The SADC Protocol on Transport, Communications and Meteorology, adopted in August 1996, provided, inter alia, for an integrated regional transport policy, an SADC Regional Trunk Road Network, and harmonized regional policies relating to maritime and inland waterway transport; civil aviation; regional telecommunications; postal services; and meterology. An Integrated Transport Committee, and other sub-committees representing the sectors covered by the Protocol, have been established. A Southern African Telecommunications Regional Authority was established in January 1997. In March 2001 the Association of Southern African National Road Agencies was created to foster the development of an integrated regional road transportation system.

SADC development projects have aimed to address missing links and overstretched sections of the regional network, as well as to improve efficiency, operational co-ordination and human resource development, such as management training projects. Other objectives have been to ensure the compatibility of technical systems within the region and to promote the harmonization of regulations relating to intra-regional traffic and trade. SADC's road network constitutes the regions's principal mode of transport for both freight and passengers and is thus vital to the economy. Unsurfaced, low-volume roads account for a substantial proportion of the network and many of these are being upgraded to a sealed standard as part of a wider strategy that focuses on the alleviation of poverty and the pursuit of economic growth and development. In July 1999 a 317-km rail link between Bulawayo, Zimbabwe, and the border town of Beitbridge was opened, administered by SADC as its first build-operate-transfer project.

SADC policy guidelines on 'making information and communications technology (ICT) a priority in turning SADC into an information-based economy' were adopted in November 2001. Policy guidelines and model regulations on tariffs for telecommunications services have also been adopted. An SADC Regional Information Infrastructure was adopted in December 1999, with the aim of linking member states by means of high-capacity digital land and submarine routes. In May 2010 SADC ministers responsible for telecommunications, postal services and ICT adopted a regional e-SADC Strategy Framework, which aimed to utilize ICT for regional socio-economic development and integration. A SADC Digital Broadcasting Migration Forum, convened in Luanda, Angola, in October 2011, to review an SADC Roadmap for Digital Broadcasting Migration, confirmed 31 December 2013 as the SADC Analogue Switch Off (ASO) date, marking the transition from analogue to digital broadcasting. Further fora were subsequently held, to monitor progress of ASO. (The 2013 deadline was not achieved across the region.) In September 2011 SADC endorsed the inaugural Southern Africa Internet Governance Forum (SAIGF), hosted by the South African Government, in Pretoria, and jointly convened by NEPAD and other agencies. SAIGF II was held in Luanda, Angola, in August 2013.

The SADC Drought Monitoring Centre organizes an annual Southern African Regional Climate Outlook Forum (SARCOF), which assesses regional weather prospects. SARCOF-17 was convened in Harare, Zimbabwe, in August 2013.

Areas of activity in the energy sector include joint petroleum exploration, training programmes for the petroleum sector and studies for strategic fuel storage facilities; promotion of the use of coal; development of hydroelectric power and the co-ordination of SADC generation and transmission capacities; new and renewable sources of energy, including pilot projects in solar energy; assessment of the environmental and socio-economic impact of wood-fuel scarcity and relevant education programmes; and energy conservation. In July 1995 SADC ministers responsible for energy approved the establishment of the Southern African Power Pool (SAPP), whereby all member states were to be linked into a single electricity grid. Utilities participating in SAPP aim to provide to consumers in the region an economical and reliable electricity supply. SADC and the Common Market for Eastern and Southern African (COMESA) have the joint objective of eventually linking SAPP and COMESA's Eastern Africa Power Pool. In July 1995 ministers also endorsed a protocol to promote greater co-operation in energy development within SADC, providing for the establishment of an Energy Commission, responsible for 'demand-side' management, pricing, ensuring private sector involvement and competition, training and research, collecting information, etc.; the protocol entered into force in September 1998. In September 1997 heads of state endorsed an Energy Action Plan to proceed with the implementation of co-operative policies and strategies in four key areas of energy: trade; information exchange; training and organizational capacity building; and investment and financing. There are two major energy supply projects in the region: utilities from Angola, Botswana, the DRC, Namibia and South Africa participate in the Western Power Corridor project, approved in October 2002, while a Zambia–Tanzania Inter-connector project is under development. In July 2007 it was announced that a Regional Petroleum and Gas Association would be established, with the aim of promoting a common investment destination with harmonized environmental standards.

The tourism sector operates within the context of national and regional socio-economic development objectives. It comprises four components: tourism product development; tourism marketing and research; tourism services; and human resources development and training. SADC has promoted tourism for the region through trade fairs and investment fora. In September 1997 the legal charter for the establishment of the Regional Tourism Organization for Southern Africa (RETOSA), administered jointly by SADC regional national tourism authorities and private sector operators, was signed by ministers responsible for tourism. RETOSA assists member states to formulate tourism promotion policies and strategies. The development is under way of a region-wide common visa (UNI-VISA) system, aimed at facilitating tourism.

In June 2005 the SADC Council of Ministers endorsed the Transfrontier Conservation Area (TFCA) Development Strategy, aimed at establishing and promoting TFCAs, conservation parks straddling international borders, as premier regional tourist and investment destinations; the Strategy has been implemented in two phases, covering 2005–10, and 'Beyond 2010'.

SADC aims to promote equitable distribution and effective management of the region's water resources, around 70% of which are shared across international borders. A Revised Protocol on Shared Watercourses came into force in September 2003 (updating an earlier Protocol from April 1998). An SADC Regional Water Policy was adopted in August 2005 as a framework for providing the sustainable and integrated development, protection and utilization of national and transboundary water resources. An SADC Multi-Stakeholder Water Dialogue was convened in October 2013, in Lusaka.

A first Regional Strategic Action Plan (RASP I) on Integrated Water Resources Development and Management was implemented during 1999–2004; RASP II was undertaken in 2005–10. RASP III was ongoing during 2011–15, covering three strategic areas: water governance; infrastructure development; and water management.

FOOD, AGRICULTURE AND NATURAL RESOURCES

The Directorate of Food, Agriculture and Natural Resources aims to develop, co-ordinate and harmonize policies and programmes on agriculture and natural resources with a focus on sustainability. The Directorate covers the following sectors: agricultural research and training; inland fisheries; forestry; wildlife; marine fisheries and resources; food security; livestock production and animal disease control; and environment and land management. According to SADC figures, agriculture contributes one-third of the region's gross national product, accounts for about one-quarter of total earnings of foreign exchange and employs some 80% of the labour force. The principal objectives in this field are regional food security, agricultural development and natural resource development.

The Southern African Centre for Co-operation in Agricultural Research (SACCAR), was established in Gaborone, in 1985. It aims to strengthen national agricultural research systems, in order to improve management, increase productivity, promote the development and transfer of technology to assist local farmers, and improve training. Examples of activity include a sorghum and millet improvement programme; a land and water management research programme; a root crop research network; agroforestry research, implemented in Malawi, Tanzania, Zambia and Zimbabwe; and a grain legume improvement programme, comprising separate research units for groundnuts, beans and cowpeas. SADC's Plant Genetic Resources Centre, based near Lusaka, aims to collect, conserve and utilize indigenous and exotic plant genetic resources and to develop appropriate management practices. In November 2009 scientists from SADC member states urged the Community to strengthen and support regional capacity to screen for and detect genetically modified organisms (GMOs), with a view to preventing the uncontrolled influx into the region of GMO products; the results of a survey conducted across the region, released in February 2011, concluded that most Southern African countries lacked sufficient technological capacity to screen for and detect GMOs.

SADC aims to promote inland and marine fisheries as an important, sustainable source of animal protein. Marine fisheries are also considered to be a potential source of income of foreign exchange. SADC ministers of marine fisheries have convened annual meetings since 1993. In May 2002 ministers of marine fisheries expressed concern about alleged ongoing illegal, unregulated and unreported (IUU) fisheries activities in regional waters. The development of fresh water fisheries is focused on aquaculture projects, and their integration into rural community activities. The SADC Fisheries Protocol entered into force in September 2003. Environment and land management activities have an emphasis on sustainability as an essential quality of development. SADC aims to protect and improve the health, environment and livelihoods of people living in the southern African region; to preserve the natural heritage and biodiversity of the region; and to support regional economic development on a sustainable basis. There is also a focus on capacity building, training, regional co-operation and the exchange of information in all areas related to the environment and land management. SADC operates an Environmental Exchange Network and implements a Land Degradation and Desertification Control Programme. Projects on the conservation and sustainable development of forestry and wildlife are under implementation. An SADC Protocol on Forestry was signed in October 2002, and in November 2003 the Protocol on Wildlife Conservation and Law Enforcement entered into force.

Under the food security programme, the Regional Early Warning System aims to anticipate and prevent food shortages through the provision of information relating to the food security situation in member states. As a result of frequent drought crises, SADC member states have agreed to inform the food security sector of their food and non-food requirements on a regular basis, in order to assess the needs of the region as a whole. A programme on irrigation development and water management aims to reduce regional dependency on rain-fed agricultural production, while a programme on the promotion of agricultural trade and food safety aims to increase intra-regional and inter-regional trade with a view to improving agriculture growth and rural incomes. An SADC extraordinary summit on agriculture and food security, held in May 2004 in Dar es Salaam, Tanzania, considered strategies for accelerating development in the agricultural sector and thereby securing food security and reducing poverty in the region. In July 2008 the inaugural meeting was convened of a Task Force of ministers responsible for trade, finance and agriculture, which was established by SADC heads of government earlier in that year in response to rising food prices and production costs. The Task Force agreed upon several measures to improve the food security situation of the SADC region, including increased investment in agriculture and the establishment of a Regional Food Reserve Facility. It also directed the SADC secretariat to develop a regional policy on the production of biofuels. The first Food, Agriculture and Natural Resources cluster ministerial meeting was held in November 2008, in Gaborone, to assess the regional food security situation in view of the ongoing global food security crisis.

The Livestock Sector Unit of the Directorate of Food, Agriculture and Natural Resource co-ordinates activities related to regional livestock development, and implements the Promotion of Regional Integration (PRINT) livestock sector capacity-strengthening programme; the SADC foot-and-mouth disease (FMD) Programme; and the SADC Transboundary Animal Diseases (TADs) project, which aims to strengthen capacity (with a special focus on Angola, Malawi, Mozambique, Tanzania, and Zambia) to control TADs such as FMD, rinderpest, contagious bovine pleuropneumonia, African swine fever, Newcastle disease, avian influenza, Rift Valley Fever, and lumpy skin disease.

In June 2012 SADC member states, meeting in Gaborone, Botswana, adopted common regional priorities and policy in the areas of environment and development in advance of the UN Conference on Sustainable Development (Rio+20), which was convened in Rio de Janeiro, Brazil, later in that month.

SOCIAL AND HUMAN DEVELOPMENT AND SPECIAL PROGRAMMES

Human resources development activities focus on determining active labour market information systems and institutions in the region, improving education policy analysis and formulation, and addressing issues of teaching and learning materials in the region. SADC administers an Intra-regional Skills Development Programme, and the Community has initiated a programme of distance education to enable greater access to education, as well as operating a scholarship and training awards programme. In July 2000 a Protocol on Education and Training, which was to provide a legal framework for co-operation in this sector, entered into force. An extraordinary meeting of ministers responsible for higher education and training, held in June 2012, in Johannesburg, considered means of redressing the comparatively poor level of enrolment in higher education in the SADC region, noting that higher education tends to be the cornerstone of national innovation, socio-economic and human development; the meeting established an SADC Technical Committee on Higher Education and Training and Research and Development and mandated the Committee to formulate a regional strategic plan on higher education and training. In September 1997 SADC heads of state, meeting in Blantyre, endorsed the establishment of a Gender Unit within the Secretariat to promote the advancement and education of women. A Declaration on Gender and Development was adopted. In August 2008 SADC leaders adopted an SADC Protocol on Gender and Development, setting 28 targets on gender equality to be achieved by 2015; the Protocol entered into force in February 2013, having been ratified by two-thirds of member states. A SADC Youth Forum was convened in April 2014, in Lilongwe, Malawi.

An SADC Protocol on Combating Illicit Drugs entered into force in March 1999. In October 2000 an SADC Epidemiological Network on Drug Use was established to enable the systematic collection of narcotics-related data. In November 2011 a joint SADC-UN Office on Drugs and Crime regional progamme entitled 'Making the Region Safer from Drugs and Crime' was initiated.

An SADC Protocol on Health was adopted in August 1999 and entered into force in August 2004. In December 1999 a multi-sectoral sub-committee on HIV/AIDS (which is endemic in the region) was established. In August 2000 the Community adopted a set of guidelines to underpin any future negotiations with major pharmaceutical companies on improving access to and reducing the cost of drugs to combat HIV/AIDS. In July 2003 an SADC special summit on HIV/AIDS, convened in Maseru, Lesotho, and attended by representatives of the World Bank, UNAIDS and the World Health Organization (WHO), issued the Maseru Declaration on HIV/AIDS, identifying priority areas for action, including prevention, access to testing and treatment, and social mobilization. The implementation of the priority areas outlined in the Maseru Declaration is co-ordinated through an SADC Business Plan on HIV/AIDS (currently in a phase covering the period 2010–15), with a focus on harmonizing regional guidelines on mother-to-child transmission and anti-retroviral therapy; and on issues relating to access to affordable essential drugs, including bulk procurement and regional production. The SADC summit held in September 2009 urged member states to intensify their efforts to implement the Maseru Declaration. An SADC Model Law on HIV/AIDS was adopted by the SADC Parliamentary Forum in 2008; the Forum is implementing a Strategic Framework for HIV/AIDS during 2010–15. SADC aims to achieve, by 2015, an 'HIV-Free Generation' and no new infections. In June 2013 the SADC Secretariat, in co-operation with UNDP, formulated a set of indicators aimed at mainstreaming HIV awareness in the following five sectors: economic development; finance; infrastructure; local government; and works and planning. Since 2008 SADC has celebrated an annual Healthy Lifestyles Day, during the last week in February. SADC is implementing a Strategic Plan for the Control of Tuberculosis (TB) In the SADC Region, 2007–15, which aims to address challenges posed by the emergence of Multi-drug Resistant TB (MDR-TB) and Extensive Drug Resistant TB (XDR-TB) strains. SADC supports the Southern Africa Roll Back Malaria Network, which was established in November 2007. SADC member states met in October 2011 to address the elimination of malaria from the region by 2015.

SADC seeks to promote employment and harmonize legislation concerning labour and social protection. Activities include the implementation of International Labour Standards; the improvement of health and safety standards in the workplace; combating child labour; and the establishment of a statistical database for employment and labour issues. In early 2013 SADC ministers responsible for labour and regional employers agreed a set of priorities aimed at promoting the International Labour Organization's Decent Work Agenda across the region.

Following the ratification of the Treaty establishing the Community, regional socio-cultural development was emphasized as part of the process of greater integration. Public education initiatives have been undertaken to encourage the involvement of people in the process of regional integration and development, as well as to promote democratic and human rights' values. Two SADC Artists AIDS Festivals have been organized: the first in Bulawayo, Zimbabwe, in August 2007; and the second in Lilongwe, in December 2009. The first SADC Poetry Festival was convened in November 2009, in

Windhoek, Namibia, with the second held in August 2010, in Gaborone. The creation of an SADC Culture Trust Fund is planned.

EXTERNAL RELATIONS

In July 2004 SADC and the EU approved a roadmap to guide future co-operation, and in October of that year an EU-SADC ministerial 'double troika' meeting took place in The Hague, Netherlands, to mark 10 years of dialogue between the two organizations. At the meeting both SADC and the EU reaffirmed their commitment to reinforcing co-operation with regard to peace and security in Africa. In November 2006, at an EU-SADC double troika meeting held in Maseru, SADC representatives agreed to the development of institutional support to the member states through the establishment of a Human Rights Commission and a new SADC Electoral Advisory Council (SEAC). SEAC became operational in April 2011. The 14th SADC-EU double troika ministerial conference, convened in Brussels, Belgium, in November 2008, discussed the ongoing global financial crisis, and means of addressing volatility in commodity prices and food insecurity in Southern Africa. An EU-SADC Investment Promotion Programme aims to mobilize foreign capital and technical investment in Southern Africa. SADC has co-operated with other sub-regional organizations to finalize a common position on co-operation between African ACP countries and the EU under the Cotonou Agreement (concluded in June 2000).

In 2001 a task force was established to co-ordinate a programme of co-operation between SADC and the COMESA, and in 2005 the East African Community (EAC) became incorporated into the process, which was led thereafter by the COMESA-EAC-SADC Task Force. In October 2008 the first tripartite COMESA-EAC-SADC summit was convened, in Kampala, Uganda, to discuss the harmonization of policy and programme work by the three regional economic communities (RECs). The Kampala summit approved a roadmap towards the formation of a single free trade area and the eventual establishment of a single African Economic Community (a long-term objective of AU co-operation). At the second tripartite summit, held in June 2011, in Johannesburg, negotiations were initiated on the establishment of the proposed COMESA-EAC-SADC Tripartite Free Trade Area. In January 2012 AU leaders endorsed a new Framework, Roadmap and Architecture for Fast Tracking the Establishment of a Continental FTA (referred to as CFTA), and an Action Plan for Boosting Intra-African Trade, which planned for the consolidation of the COMESA-EAC-SADC Tripartite FTA with other regional FTAs into the CFTA initiative during 2015–16; and the establishment of an operational CFTA by 2017. In July 2010 SADC, COMESA and the EAC adopted a tripartite five-year Programme on Climate Change Adaptation and Mitigation in the COMESA-EAC-SADC region. A tripartite agreement for the implementation of the Programme was signed by the three parties in July 2012.

Finance

SADC's administrative budget for 2013–14, approved in October 2012 by the Council of Ministers, amounted to US $65m., to be financed by contributions from member states (45%) and by international co-operating partners (55%).

Publications

Animal Health Bulletin.
Climate Outlook.
Food Security Bulletin.
SADC Annual Report.
SADC Energy Bulletin.
SADC Food Security Update (monthly).
SADC Today (6 a year).

Associated Bodies

Regional Tourism Organisation of Southern Africa (RETOSA): POB 7381, Halfway House, 1685 Midrand, South Africa; tel. (11) 3152420; fax (11) 3159752; e-mail retosa@iafrica.com; internet www.retosa.co.za; f. 1997 to assist SADC member states with formulating tourism promotion policies and strategies; the establishment of a regional tourist visa (UNI-VISA) system aimed at facilitating the the movement of international visitors through the region; RETOSA is administered by a Board comprising representatives of national tourism authorities in SADC mem. states and private sector umbrella bodies in the region.

SADC Parliamentary Forum: 578 Love St, off Robert Mugabe Ave, Windhoek, Namibia; tel. (61) 2870000; fax (61) 254642; e-mail info@sadcpf.org; internet www.sadcpf.org; f. 1996 to promote democracy, human rights and good governance throughout the SADC region, ensuring fair representation for women; endorsed in Sept. 1997 by SADC heads of state as an autonomous institution; a training arm of the Forum, the SADC Parliamentary Leadership Centre, was established in 2005; the Forum frequently deploys missions to monitor parliamentary and presidential elections in the region; adopted, in March 2001, Electoral Norms and Standards for the SADC Region; from the 2000s expanded the scope of its electoral activities beyond observation to guiding the pre- and post-election phases; under the Forum's third Strategic Plan, covering 2011–15, a review of election observation activities and of the 2001 Norms and Standards was to be implemented; programmes are also undertaken in the areas of democracy and governance; HIV/AIDS and public health; regional development and integration; gender equality and empowerment; ICTs; and parliamentary capacity development; the Forum is funded by mem. parliaments, governments and charitable and international organizations; mems: national parliaments of SADC countries, representing more than 3,500 parliamentarians; Sec.-Gen. Dr Esau Chiviya.

SOUTHERN COMMON MARKET—MERCOSUR/ MERCOSUL

(MERCADO COMÚN DEL SUR/MERCADO COMUM DO SUL)

Address: Edif. Mercosur, Luis Piera 1992, 1°, 11200 Montevideo, Uruguay.

Telephone: 2412 9024; **fax:** 2418 0557; **e-mail:** secretaria@mercosur.org.uy; **internet:** www.mercosur.int.

Mercosur (known as Mercosul in Portuguese) was established in March 1991 by the heads of state of Argentina, Brazil, Paraguay and Uruguay with the signature of the Treaty of Asunción. The primary objective of the Treaty is to achieve the economic integration of member states by means of a free flow of goods and services, the establishment of a common external tariff, the adoption of common commercial policy, and the co-ordination of macroeconomic and sectoral policies. The Ouro Preto Protocol, which was signed in December 1994, conferred on Mercosur the status of an international legal entity with the authority to sign agreements with third countries, groups of countries and international organizations.

MEMBERS

Argentina	Brazil	Paraguay	Uruguay	Venezuela

Note: Bolivia, Chile, Colombia, Ecuador, Guyana, Peru and Suriname are associate members. In December 2012 Bolivia signed the adhesion protocol to become a full member of Mercosur. Its admission to the grouping required ratification by each member's legislature.

Organization

(April 2014)

COMMON MARKET COUNCIL

The Common Market Council (Consejo del Mercado Común) is the highest organ of Mercosur and is responsible for leading the integration process and for taking decisions in order to achieve the objectives of the Treaty of Asunción. In December 2010 the Council decided to establish the position of High Representative, with a three-year term-in-office, in order to support the integration process, to promote trade and investment and to represent the grouping internationally.

High Representative: IVÁN RAMALHO (Brazil).

COMMON MARKET GROUP

The Common Market Group (Grupo Mercado Común) is the executive body of Mercosur and is responsible for implementing concrete measures to further the integration process.

TRADE COMMISSION

The Trade Commission (Comisión de Comercio del Mercosur) has competence for the area of joint commercial policy and, in particular, is responsible for monitoring the operation of the common external tariff. The Brasília Protocol may be referred to for the resolution of trade disputes between member states.

CONSULTATIVE ECONOMIC AND SOCIAL FORUM

The Consultative Economic and Social Forum (Foro Consultivo Económico-Social) comprises representatives from the business community and trade unions in the member countries and has a consultative role in relation to Mercosur.

WORKING GROUPS

Technical discussions are held by 12 working groups, directed by Mercosur's incumbent six-monthly rotational chairmanship.

PARLIAMENT

Parlamento del Mercosur: Pablo de María 827, 11200 Montevideo, Uruguay; tel. 2410 9797; e-mail secadministrativa@parlamentodelmercosur.org; internet www.parlamentodelmercosur.org; f. 2005, as successor to the Joint Parliamentary Commission (Comisión Parlamentaria Conjunta); inaugural session held in May 2007; aims to facilitate implementation of Mercosur decisions and regional co-operation; each mem. holds 18 seats; an agreement concluded October 2010 determined that, with effect from 31 December 2014, seats were to be allocated proportional to each country's population.

SECRETARIAT

Director: JEFERSON MIOLA (Brazil).

Activities

In June 1996 Mercosur heads of state, meeting in San Luis de Mendoza, Argentina, endorsed a 'Democratic Guarantee Clause', whereby a country would be prevented from participation in Mercosur unless democratic, accountable institutions were in place. In June 2012 Paraguay was suspended from participation in a regular meeting of heads of state, following the impeachment of that country's president, Fernando Lugo, in a process which the remaining members of Mercosur condemned as a breach of the democratic order. At the meeting, convened in Mendoza, Argentina, the heads of state of Argentina, Brazil and Uruguay determined to suspend Paraguay's membership of the grouping until democratic presidential elections were conducted. It was agreed not to impose economic measures against the country in the mean time. With the suspension from the grouping of Paraguay, whose congress had vetoed the membership of Venezuela, the heads of state announced that Venezuela would be admitted as a full member of Mercosur with effect from 31 July. Following the April 2013 presidential election in Paraguay, Mercosur heads of states agreed at a summit convened in early July, in Montevideo, Uruguay, that Paraguay should be permitted to reintegrate into the grouping following the inauguration on 15 August of its then President-elect, Horacio Cartes. In December, following diplomatic negotiations, both houses of the Paraguay legislature approved Venezuela's adhesion protocol, enabling Paraguay to resume active membership of the grouping.

A regular summit meeting of Mercosur heads of state that had been scheduled to be held in December 2013 was postponed several times, and by mid-April 2014 had still not taken place; initially this was attributed to the then poor health of the Argentinian President, while later postponements were reportedly due to difficulties drafting the agenda. In February 2014, in response to ongoing political unrest in Venezuela, Mercosur issued a statement condemning acts of violence and acts aimed at destabilizing the elected Venezuelan government.

In December 2010 Mercosur heads of state, meeting in Foz do Iguaçú, Brazil, concluded further agreements to accelerate regional integration. These included the appointment of a new High Representative, a Customs Union Consolidation Program, a Strategic Social Action Plan, which aimed to support the eradication of poverty and greater social equality, and a roadmap for the formation of a Mercosur citizenship statute in order to facilitate the free movement of persons throughout the region. A common Mercosur vehicle license plate was endorsed by the summit meeting.

ECONOMIC INTEGRATION

Mercosur's free trade zone entered into effect on 1 January 1995, with tariffs removed from 85% of intra-regional trade. A regime of gradual removal of duties on a list of special products was agreed, while regimes governing trade in the automobile and sugar sectors remained to be negotiated. Mercosur's customs union also came into force at the start of 1995, comprising a common external tariff (CET) of 0%–20%. A list of exceptions from the CET was agreed; these products were to lose their special status and were to be subject to the general tariff system concerning foreign goods by 2006. In December 2012 heads of state agreed that Venezuela could implement the CET in four stages from April 2013, to be concluded by 2016.

In June 1995 Mercosur ministers responsible for the environment agreed to harmonize environmental legislation and to form a permanent sub-group of Mercosur. In December of that year Mercosur presidents affirmed the consolidation of free trade as Mercosur's 'permanent and most urgent goal'. To this end they agreed to prepare norms of application for Mercosur's customs code, accelerate paper procedures and increase the connections between national computerized systems. It was also agreed to increase co-operation in the areas of agriculture, industry, mining, energy, communications, transport and tourism, and finance. At this meeting Argentina and Brazil reached an accord aimed at overcoming their dispute regarding the trade in automobiles between the two countries.

In December 1996 Mercosur heads of state, meeting in Fortaleza, Brazil, approved agreements on harmonizing competition practices (by 2001), integrating educational opportunities for postgraduates and human resources training, standardizing trading safeguards applied against third country products (by 2001) and providing for intra-regional cultural exchanges. An Accord on Sub-regional Air Services was signed at the meeting (including by the heads of state of Bolivia and Chile) to liberalize civil transport throughout the region. In addition, the heads of state endorsed texts on consumer rights. In December 1997 a separate Protocol was signed providing for the liberalization of trade in services and government purchases over a 10-year period. In December 1998 Mercosur heads of state agreed on the establishment of an arbitration mechanism for disputes between members, and on measures to standardize human, animal and plant health and safety regulations throughout the grouping.

The summit meeting held in December 2000 approved criteria, formulated by Mercosur ministers responsible for finance and central bank governors, determining monetary and fiscal targets which aimed to achieve economic convergence, to promote economic stability throughout the region, and to reduce competitive disparities affecting the unity of the grouping. However, unilateral economic action by member governments, in particular to counter economic instability, and bilateral trade disputes have persistently undermined Mercosur's integration objectives. In early 2001 Argentina imposed several emergency measures to strengthen its domestic economy, in contradiction of Mercosur's external tariffs. In February 2002, at a third extraordinary meeting of the Common Market Council, held in Buenos Aires, Mercosur heads of state expressed their support for Argentina's application to receive international financial assistance, in the wake of that country's economic crisis. Although there were fears that the crisis might curb trade and stall economic growth across the region, Argentina's adoption of a floating currency made the prospect of currency harmonization between Mercosur member countries appear more viable. At a summit convened in June 2003, in Asunción, Paraguay, heads of state of the four member countries agreed to strengthen integration of the bloc and to harmonize all import tariffs by 2006, thus creating the basis for a single market. In August 2010 Mercosur heads of state, meeting in San Juan, Argentina, endorsed a new common customs code, incorporating agreements on the redistribution of external customs revenue and elimination of the double taxation on goods imported from outside the group.

In June 2005 Mercosur heads of state announced a US $100m. structural convergence fund to support education, job creation and infrastructure projects in the poorest regions, in particular in Paraguay and Uruguay, in order to remove some economic disparities within the grouping. The meeting also endorsed a multilateral energy project to link gasfields in Camisea, Peru, to existing supply pipelines in Argentina, Brazil and Uruguay, via Tocopilla, Chile. In July 2008 Mercosur heads of state considered the impact of escalating food costs and the production of biofuels. In December a summit meeting, convened in Bahia, Brazil, agreed to establish a $100m. guarantee fund to facilitate access to credit for small and medium-sized businesses operating in the common market in order to alleviate the impact of the global financial crisis.

EXTERNAL RELATIONS

In June 1996 Mercosur heads of state approved the entry into Mercosur of Bolivia and Chile as associate members. An Economic Complementation Accord with Bolivia, which includes Bolivia in Mercosur's free trade zone, but not in the customs union, was signed in December 1995 and was to come into force on 1 January 1997, later extended until 30 April 1997. Measures of the free trade agreement, which was signed in October 1996, were to be implemented during a transitional period commencing on 28 February 1997 (revised from 1 January). Chile's Economic Complementation Accord with Mercosur entered into effect on 1 October 1996, with duties on most products to be removed over a 10-year period (Chile's most sensitive products were given 18 years for complete tariff elimination). Chile was also to remain outside the customs union, but was to be involved in other integration projects, in particular infrastructure projects designed to give Mercosur countries access to both the Atlantic and Pacific Oceans (Chile's Pacific coast was regarded as Mercosur's potential link to the economies of the Far East). In March 1998 the ministers of the interior of Mercosur countries, together with representatives of the Governments of Chile and Bolivia, agreed to implement a joint security arrangement for the border region linking Argentina, Paraguay and Brazil. In particular, the initiative aimed to counter drugs-trafficking, money-laundering and other illegal activities in the area. Procedures to incorporate Chile as a full member of Mercosur were suspended in 2000 following an announcement by the Chilean Government that it had initiated bilateral free trade discussions with the USA, which was considered, in particular by the Brazilian authorities, to undermine Mercosur's unified position at multilateral free trade negotiations. In July 2008 Mercosur and Chile concluded a protocol on trade in services.

In April 1998 Mercosur and the Andean Community signed an accord that committed them to the establishment of a free trade area by January 2000. Negotiations in early 1999 failed to conclude an agreement on preferential tariffs between the two blocs, and the existing arrangements were extended on a bilateral basis. In March the Andean Community agreed to initiate free trade negotiations with Brazil; a preferential tariff agreement was concluded in July. In August 2000 a similar agreement between the Community and Argentina entered into force. In September leaders of the two groupings, meeting at a summit of Latin American heads of state, determined to relaunch negotiations. The establishment of a mechanism to support political dialogue and co-ordination between the two groupings, was approved at the first joint meeting of ministers responsible for foreign affairs in July 2001. In April 2004 Mercosur and the Andean Community signed a free trade accord, providing for tariffs on 80% of trade between the two groupings to be phased out by 2014, and for tariffs to be removed from the remaining 20% of, initially protected, products by 2019. The entry into force of the accord, scheduled for 1 July 2004, was postponed owing to delays in drafting the tariff reduction schedule. Peru became an associate member of Mercosur in December 2003, and Colombia and Ecuador were granted associate membership in December 2004. In July 2004 Mexico was invited to attend all meetings of the organization with a view to future accession to associate membership. In 2005 Mercosur and the Andean Community formulated a reciprocal association agreement, to extend associate membership to all member states of both groupings. In February 2010 ministers responsible for foreign affairs agreed to establish an Andean Community-Mercosur Mixed Commission to facilitate and strengthen co-operation between member countries of both organizations. In December 2005 Bolivia was invited to join as a full member, while Mercosur heads of state agreed to a request by Venezuela (which had been granted associate membership in December 2004) to become a member with full voting rights. The leaders signed a protocol, in July 2006, formally to admit Venezuela to the group. The accord, however, required ratification by each country's legislature, and by mid-2012 the Paraguayan parliament had not endorsed the protocol, as it was blocked by the country's senate. In late June, following the decision to suspend Paraguay's membership of Mercosur, heads of state, meeting in Mendoza, Argentina, agreed to admit Venezuela into the grouping at the end of July. Venezuela was welcomed as the fifth full member of Mercosur by the heads of state of Argentina, Brazil and Uruguay at an Inclusion Ceremony, held in Brazil on 31 July. In December, at a meeting of heads of state in Brasília, Bolivia signed an adhesion protocol formally admitting it into the grouping as a full member. The protocol required ratification by each country's legislature. Paraguay, at that time still suspended from Mercosur, criticized the decision to admit Bolivia without its consent. Guyana and Suriname joined the grouping as associate members in July 2013.

In December 1995 Mercosur and the European Union (EU) signed a framework agreement for commercial and economic co-operation, which provided for co-operation in the economic, trade, industrial, scientific, institutional and cultural fields and the promotion of wider political dialogue on issues of mutual interest. Negotiations between Mercosur and the EU on the conclusion of an Interregional Association Agreement commenced in 1999. Specific discussion of tariff reductions and market access commenced at the fifth round of negotiations, held in July 2001, at which the EU proposed a gradual elimination of tariffs on industrial imports over a 10-year period and an extension of access quotas for agricultural products; however, negotiations stalled in 2005 owing to differences regarding farm subsidies. In July 2008 Mercosur heads of state condemned a new EU immigration policy that would permit the detention and forcible return of illegal immigrants. Leaders attending a Mercosur-EU summit meeting, convened in Madrid, Spain, in May 2010, determined to restart promptly the Association Agreement negotiations. The first discussions took place in Buenos Aires, in July, and subsequently at regular intervals. An announcement made in April 2012 by the Argentine Government that is was to renationalize the petroleum company YPF, of which the Spanish company Repsol had hitherto been the majority shareholder, was expected to impact negatively on the Mercosur–EU negotiations process. In May the EU filed a complaint with the World Trade Organization (WTO) contesting restrictions on imports imposed (since 2005) by Argentina. The ninth round of negotiations on an Association Agreement, were held in October 2012, in Brazil. Further discussions were held in January 2013 on the sidelines of the first EU–Community of Latin American and Caribbean States (CELAC) summit meeting, convened in Santiago, Chile. A technical meeting of Mercosur and EU representatives, held in March 2014, did not make progress on defining a schedule for the exchange of proposals on tariff reductions, which was required to advance the negotiations. In late April it was reported that an agreement had been concluded between Argentina, Brazil, Paraguay and Uruguay for a trade proposal covering 87% of imports to be presented to the next meeting with EU negotiators.

At a summit of Mercosur heads of state convened in July 2013, in Montevideo, Argentina, Brazil, Uruguay and Venezuela announced the recall of their ambassadors from France, Italy, Portugal and Spain, in protest against the diversion from those countries' airspace of a flight carrying the Bolivian President, Evo Morales, following speculation that Edward Snowden, an information specialist wanted for questioning by the US security services, and who had requested political asylum in several Latin American countries, might be on board the aircraft.

Regional integration and co-operation were the principal focus of the sixth summit of the Americas, held in Cartagena, Colombia, in April 2012, on the theme 'Connecting the Americas: Partners for Prosperity'.

In December 2007 Mercosur signed a free trade accord with Israel, which entered into effect in January 2010. At the meeting of heads of state, held in San Miguel de Tucumán, Argentina, in July 2008, a preferential trade agreement was signed with the Southern African Customs Union. Framework agreements on the preparation of free trade accords were also signed with Turkey and Jordan. In June 2009 a preferential trade agreement with India entered into force. A framework agreement on trade with Morocco entered into effect in April 2010. In August Mercosur signed a free trade agreement with Egypt, and in December Mercosur signed a trade and economic co-operation agreement with the Palestinian National Authority and a framework agreement to establish a free trade agreement with Syria. Agreements to establish mechanisms for political dialogue and co-operation were signed with Cuba and Turkey at that time.

Finance

The annual budget for the Secretariat is contributed by the full member states.

Publication

Boletín Oficial del Mercosur (quarterly).

WORLD COUNCIL OF CHURCHES—WCC

Address: 150 route de Ferney, POB 2100, 1211 Geneva 2, Switzerland.

Telephone: 227916111; **fax:** 227910361; **e-mail:** infowcc@wcc-coe.org; **internet:** www.oikoumene.org.

The Council was founded in 1948 to promote co-operation between Christian Churches and to prepare for a clearer manifestation of the unity of the Church.

MEMBERS

There are 35 member Churches in more than 110 countries. Chief denominations: Anglican; Baptist; Congregational; Lutheran; Methodist; Moravian; Old Catholic; Orthodox; Presbyterian; Reformed; and Society of Friends. The Roman Catholic Church is not a member but sends official observers to meetings.

Organization

(April 2014)

ASSEMBLY

The governing body of the World Council, consisting of delegates of the member Churches, it meets every seven years to frame policy and consider some main themes. It elects the Presidents of the Council, who serve as members of the Central Committee. The 10th Assembly was held in Busan, Republic of Korea, in October–November 2013, on the theme 'God of life, lead us to justice and peace'.

CENTRAL COMMITTEE

Appointed by the Assembly to carry out its policies and decisions, the Committee consists of 150 members chosen from Assembly delegates. It meets every 12 to 18 months.

The Central Committee comprises the Programme Committee and the Finance Committee. Within the Programme Committee there are advisory groups on issues relating to communication, women, justice, peace and creation, youth, ecumenical relations, and inter-religious relations. There are also five commissions and boards.

EXECUTIVE COMMITTEE

Consists of the Presidents, the Officers and 20 members chosen by the Central Committee from its membership to prepare its agenda, expedite its decisions and supervise the work of the Council between meetings of the Central Committee. Meets every six months.

Moderator: Dr AGNES ABUOM (Anglican Church of Kenya).

Vice-Moderators: Prof. Dr GENNADIOS OF SASSIMA (Ecumenical Patriarchate of Constantinople), Bishop MARY ANN SWENSON (United Methodist Church, USA).

CONSULTATIVE BODIES

Various bodies, including advisory groups, commissions and reference groups, comprising members from WCC governing bodies and member churches, advise the secretariat on policy direction, implementation and evaluation. The main bodies are the Commissions on Faith and Order (plenary and standing bodies), on World Mission and Evangelism, on Education and Ecumenical Formation, of the Churches on International Affairs, and the Echos Commission on Youth in the Ecumenical Movement.

GENERAL SECRETARIAT

The General Secretariat implements the policies laid down by the WCC and co-ordinates the Council's work. The General Secretariat is also responsible for an Ecumenical Institute, at Bossey, Switzerland, which provides training in ecumenical leadership.

General Secretary: Rev. Dr OLAV FYKSE TVEIT (Norway).

The WCC maintains a liaison office at UN headquarters in New York, USA.

Activities

The ninth WCC Assembly, held in February 2006, approved a reorganization of the WCC's work programme, based on six key areas of activity; these were maintained by the 10th Assembly, convened in October–November 2013. The 10th Assembly adopted a number of joint statements, including on the Politicization of religion and rights of religious minorities; the Human rights of stateless people; Peace and reunification of the Korean peninsula; and Affirming the Christian presence and witness in the Middle East. The Assembly also adopted a resolution urging improved USA-Cuba relations.

THE WCC AND THE ECUMENICAL MOVEMENT IN THE 21ST CENTURY

The WCC aims to support co-operation among member churches and their involvement in the activities of the organization. It also works to enhance partnerships with other regional and international ecumenical organizations to support the ecumenical movement as a whole, and aims to facilitate communication and consultation among relevant bodies with regard to the future of the ecumenical movement. The WCC supported the development of a Global Christian Forum, which convened its first global meeting in November 2007. (The most recent Forum gathering was convened in Manado, Indonesia, in October 2011.) This work programme commits to promote the active participation of young adults in the life of churches and the ecumenical movement, for example through an internship programme at the WCC Secretariat, and to ensure that women, and specific issues concerning them, are fully considered and represented.

UNITY, MISSION, EVANGELISM AND SPIRITUALITY

This work programme is directed and supported by the Commissions on Faith and Order and on World Mission and Evangelism. It aims to promote a 'visible unity' among member churches and to encourage them to address potentially divisive issues and develop mutually acceptable positions. The WCC produces materials to share among churches, such as information on worship and spiritual life practices, and to co-ordinate and promote the annual Week of Prayer for Christian Unity. Other activities aim to confront and overcome any discrimination against ethnic minorities, people with disabilities or other excluded groups within the church and society as a whole. A project entitled 'Towards just and inclusive communities' is being undertaken within the work programme, with a focus on combating discrimination and social exclusion, of, for example, indigenous communities and people with disabilities.

PUBLIC WITNESS: ADDRESSING POWER, AFFIRMING PEACE

The Public Witness programme aims to ensure that the Council's concerns relating to violence, war, human rights, economic injustice, poverty and exclusion are raised and addressed at an international level, including at meetings of UN or other intergovernmental bodies. At regional and local level the Council aims to accompany churches in critical situations in their efforts to defend human rights and dignity, overcome impunity, achieve accountability and build just and peaceful societies. An Ecumenical Accompaniment Programme in Palestine and Israel was inaugurated in August 2002 to provide for individuals to support and protect vulnerable groups in the Occupied Territories and to accompany the Israeli Peace movement. The WCC has established an Israeli/Palestine Ecumenical Forum to bring together churches in the region to develop unified policy positions in support of peace and justice. In February 2014 WCC member churches in South Sudan—where conflict had erupted in December 2013—issued a statement urging the pursuit of comprehensive peace. The WCC convened a meeting with Syrian opposition representatives in mid-February 2014. In the following month the WCC General Secretary expressed deep concern at the ongoing social unrest in Ukraine. The WCC supported a range of activities within the framework of its Decade to Overcome Violence (2001–10); the Decade culminated in an International Ecumenical Peace Convocation, held in May 2011, in Kingston, Jamaica. An International Day of Prayer for Peace is held each year on 21 September.

JUSTICE, *DIAKONIA* AND RESPONSIBILITY FOR CREATION

The Council supports its members' efforts to combat injustice and meet human needs. It aims to strengthen churches' organizational capacities and to strengthen and monitor accountability (and greater understanding) between donors and recipients of resources. It is also committed to strengthening the role of churches in the fields of health and healing, in particular in HIV/AIDS and mental health-related issues. The Council undertakes networking and advocacy activities at an international level and promotes dialogue among church health networks and those of civil society. In 2002 the Council inaugurated the Ecumenical HIV and AIDS Initiative in Africa to inform and assist churches in Africa in their efforts to support communities affected by HIV/AIDS. The WCC participated in the first Summit of High Level Religious Leaders on HIV and AIDS, which was convened in Den Dolder, Netherlands, in March 2010. A WCC Ecumenical

Solidarity Fund provides grants in support of capacity-building efforts, activities to combat racism and other strategic initiatives. The Council aims to strengthen activities relating to migration and racism and to develop new advocacy strategies. The Council provides a forum for discussion and exchange of information on the use of science and new technologies, for example genetically modified seeds and stem cell research. The WCC hosts the secretariat of the Ecumenical Water Network, which aims to highlight issues relating to the scarcity of water resources in many parts of the work and to advocate community-based initiatives to manage resources more effectively. Further programme areas address Eco-justice (exploring linkages between ecological crises and socio-economic injustice); Care for creation and climate justice; and Poverty, wealth and ecology.

EDUCATION AND ECUMENICAL FORMATION

The WCC is committed to supporting ecumenical and faith formation, as well as providing educational opportunities itself. The Ecumenical Institute, in Bossey, Switzerland, offers academic courses, research opportunities and residential programmes, including one for the promotion of inter-faith dialogue. The WCC organizes seminars and workshops to promote good practices in ecumenical formation and leadership training. The Council aims to strengthen theological education through accreditation standards, exchange programmes and modifying curricula. It administers a sponsorship programme to provide opportunities for ecumenical learning in different cultures. In September 2011 the WCC, with Globethics.net, launched the Global Digital Library on Theology and Ecumenism (GlobeTheoLib, accessible at www.globethics.net/gtl), a multilingual theological resource providing access to research materials in theology and related disciplines.

INTER-RELIGIOUS DIALOGUE AND CO-OPERATION

This work programme aims to promote the peaceful co-existence of different faiths and communities within society. It supports inter-faith dialogue and opportunities to develop mutual trust and respect, in particular among women and young people of different faiths. It promotes best practices in inter-religious dialogue and co-operation. The Council encourages reflection on Christianity in an inter-faith society. In 2006 it inaugurated, with the Roman Catholic Church, a process of consultations on religious freedom, to result in the definition of a code of conduct on religious conversion. The Council supports churches in conflict situations to counter religious intolerance or discrimination. It undertakes research, field visits, advocacy work and capacity building in support of churches or communities affected by conflict. During 2011–14 WCC was supporting church leaders in Syria in the pursuit of justice and peace, including through convening dialogues between Christians and Muslims.

Finance

The main contributors to the WCC's budget are the churches and their agencies, with funds for certain projects contributed by other organizations. The WCC's total income (which has decreased significantly in recent years) was estimated at 30.9m. Swiss francs in 2013, and was forecast at 20m. in 2014.

Publications

Annual Review.

Current Dialogue (2 a year).

Ecumenical Review (quarterly).

International Review of Mission (quarterly).

Report of the General Secretary.

WCC e-news (electronic publication).

Catalogue of periodicals, books and audio-visuals.

WORLD FEDERATION OF TRADE UNIONS—WFTU

Address: 40 Zan Moreas St, 11745 Athens, Greece.

Telephone: (21) 09236700; **fax:** (21) 09214517; **e-mail:** info@wftucentral.org; **internet:** www.wftucentral.org.

The Federation was founded in 1945, on a worldwide basis. A number of members withdrew from the Federation in 1949 to establish the International Confederation of Free Trade Unions (now the International Trade Union Confederation).

MEMBERS

Affiliated or associated national federations (including the Trade Unions Internationals) in 126 countries representing some 135m. individuals.

Organization

(April 2014)

WORLD TRADE UNION CONGRESS

The Congress meets every five years. It reviews WFTU's work, endorses reports from the executives, and elects the General Council. The size of the delegations is based on the total membership of national federations. The Congress is also open to participation by non-affiliated organizations. The 16th Congress was held in Athens, Greece, in April 2011.

GENERAL COUNCIL

The General Council meets three times between Congresses, and comprises members and deputies elected by Congress from nominees of national federations. Every affiliated or associated organization and Trade Unions International has one member and one deputy member.

The Council receives reports from the Presidential Council, approves the plan and budget and elects officers.

PRESIDENTIAL COUNCIL

The Council meets twice a year and conducts most of the executive work of WFTU. It comprises a President, elected each year from among its members, the General Secretary and 18 Vice-Presidents.

SECRETARIAT

The Secretariat consists of the General Secretary, and six Deputy General Secretaries. It is appointed by the General Council and is responsible for general co-ordination, regional activities, national trade union liaison, press and information, administration and finance.

WFTU has regional offices in New Delhi, India (for the Asia-Pacific region); Havana, Cuba (the Americas); Johannesburg, South Africa (anglophone Africa); Libreville, Gabon (francophone Africa); Damascus, Syria (the Middle East); Nicosia, Cyprus (Europe); and in Moscow, Russia (the CIS countries).

General Secretary: GEORGE MAVRIKOS (Greece).

Activities

The April 2011 World Trade Union Congress adopted the Athens Pact, concerning the impact on the 'international working class' of the global economic crisis from 2008, regarded by the Congress as a 'deep and multifaceted crisis of the capitalist system', burdening the global labouring class most.

WFTU organizes a militant International Action Day annually on 3 October, with a focus on issues such as the need for affordable food, clean water, housing, free health care and education, and exploitation by multinationals of wealth-producing resources.

In February 2013 WFTU convened a meeting of Pan-African Affiliates and Friends, with participation by 60 trade union leaders from 37 countries; the meeting adopted an Action Plan for Africa, covering 2013–14, which aimed to protect the rights of workers throughout Africa. In October 2013 WFTU organized an international conference on asbestos, in relation to the health and safety of employees.

Finance

Income is derived from affiliation dues, which are based on the number of members in each trade union federation.

Publications

Comments.
Flashes from WFTU.
From the World (electronic news).
Reflects.

Trade Unions Internationals

The following autonomous Trade Unions Internationals (TUIs) are associated with WFTU:

Trade Unions International of Banks, Insurance and Fiscal Unions' Employees (BIFU): c/o All India Bank Employees Asscn, Singapore Plaza, 164 Linghi Chetty St, Chennai 600001, India; tel. (44) 2535-1522; fax (44) 4500-2191; e-mail chv.aibea@gmail.com; Pres. LIKHTAROVITCH ALEXANDRE (Belarus); Gen. Sec. C. H. VENKATACHALAM (India).

Trade Unions International of Pensioners and Retirees (TUI-P&R): Barcelona, Spain; e-mail quimboix@quimboix.es; internet www.pensionistas.info; f. 2014; Pres. DIMOS KOUMPOURIS (Greece); Sec.-Gen. QUIM BOIX (Spain).

Trade Unions International of Public and Allied Employees: off 10A Shankharitola St, Kolkata 700014, India; tel. (33) 2217-7721; fax (33) 2265-9450; e-mail aisgef@dataone.in; internet www.tradeunionindia.org; f. 1949; mems: 34m. in 50 unions in 54 countries; Branch Commissions: State, Municipal, Postal and Telecommunications, Health, Banks and Insurance; Pres. LULAMILE SOTAKA (South Africa); Gen. Sec. SUKOMAL SEN (India); publ. *Information Bulletin*.

Trade Unions International of Teachers' Unions (FISE): 403 Nanak Sai Residency, Hyderabad 500 001, India; tel. (40) 2475-6914; e-mail fise@wftucentral.org; f. 1946; mems: 132 national unions of teachers and educational and scientific workers in 78 countries representing over 24m. individuals; Pres. ORLANDO PEREZ (Venezuela); Gen. Sec. HASSAN ISMAIL (Lebanon); publ. *Teachers of the World* (quarterly, in English).

Trade Unions International of Transport Workers (TUI-Transport): Rua Serra do Japi 31, 03309–000 São Paulo, Brazil; tel. (11) 209-536-05; fax (11) 229-633-03; e-mail info@tui-transport.org; f. 1949; holds International Trade Conference (every four years; 2011: Cyprus) and General Council (annually); mems: 95 unions from 37 countries; Pres. JOSÉ MANUEL OLIVEIRA (Portugal); Gen. Sec. WAGNER FAJARDO (Brazil); publ. *TUI Reporter* (every 2 months, in English and Spanish).

Trade Unions International of Workers in Agriculture, Food, Commerce, Textiles and Allied Industries (UISTAACT): 263 rue de Paris, Case 428, 93514 Montreuil Cedex, France; tel. 1-48-18-83-27; fax 1-48-51-57-49; e-mail uis@fnaf.cgt.fr; Pres. ALIOU NDIAYE (Senegal); Gen. Sec. JULIEN HUCK (France).

Trade Unions International of Workers in the Building, Wood and Building Materials Industries (Union Internationale des Syndicats des Travailleurs du Bâtiment, du Bois et des Matériaux de Construction—UITBB): POB 281, 00101 Helsinki, Finland; tel. (9) 693-1130; fax (9) 693-1020; e-mail rguitbb@kaapeli.fi; internet www.uitbb.org; f. 1949; mems: unions in 60 countries, grouping 2.5m. workers; Pres. ANTONIO LOPÉS DE CARBALHO (Brazil); Gen. Sec. DEBANJAN CHAKRABARTI (India); publ. *Bulletin*.

Trade Unions International of Workers in the Energy, Chemical, Oil and Related Industries (TUI-Energy): c/o 3A Calle Maestro Antonio Caso 45, Col. Tabacalera, 06470 Mexico City, Mexico; tel. (11) 712-0300; e-mail tuienergy@ceppwawu.org.za; f. 1998; Pres. MARTIN ESPARZA FLORES (Mexico); Gen. Sec. SIMON MOFOKENG (South Africa); publ. *Bulletin*.

Trade Unions International Union of Workers in the Mining, the Metallurgy and the Metal industries (TUI-Metal): Pokopandegi Bidea 9, 2º, 20018 San Sebastián, Spain; f. 2008; Pres. P. K. DAS (India); publ. *Bulletin*.

Trade Unions International Union of Workers in Tourism and Hotels (TUI-HOTOUR): Odos Gladstonos 3, 106 77 Athens, Greece; tel. (210) 3830380; fax (210) 3818251; e-mail tui-tourism@hotmail.com; internet www.hotourtui.com; f. 2009; Pres. NGUYEN MANH CUONG (Viet Nam); Sec.-Gen. XRISTOS KATSOTIS (Greece).

WORLD TRADE ORGANIZATION—WTO

Address: Centre William Rappard, 154 rue de Lausanne, 1211 Geneva, Switzerland.

Telephone: 227395111; **fax:** 227314206; **e-mail:** enquiries@wto.org; **internet:** www.wto.org.

The WTO is the legal and institutional foundation of the multilateral trading system. It was established on 1 January 1995, as the successor to the General Agreement on Tariffs and Trade (GATT). The WTO oversees negotiations on trade agreements, monitors the implementation of trade agreements, undertakes dispute procedures, and works to build the trade capacity of developing states.

MEMBERS

At April 2014 there were 159 member governments; of those 34 were officially classified as least developed countries. At that time Yemen's terms of membership had been approved (in December 2013) and its accession to the organization required ratification by the country's legislature. A further 23 applications to join the WTO were either under consideration or awaiting consideration by accession working parties.

Organization

(April 2014)

MINISTERIAL CONFERENCE

The Ministerial Conference is the highest authority of the WTO. It is composed of representatives of all WTO members at ministerial level, and may take decisions on all matters under any of the multilateral trade agreements. The Conference is normally required to meet at least every two years. The ninth Conference was convened in Bali, Indonesia, in December 2013.

GENERAL COUNCIL

The General Council, composed of representatives of all WTO members, is required to report to the Ministerial Conference and conducts much of the day-to-day work of the WTO. The Council convenes as the Dispute Settlement Body, to oversee the trade dispute settlement procedures, and as the Trade Policy Review Body, to conduct regular reviews of the trade policies of WTO members. The Council delegates responsibility to three other major Councils: the Intellectual Property Council (for trade-related aspects of intellectual property rights), the Goods Council (for trade in goods) and the Services Council (trade in services).

TRADE NEGOTIATIONS COMMITTEE

The Committee was established in November 2001 to supervise the agreed agenda of trade negotiations. It operates under the authority of the General Council. A structure of negotiating groups and a declaration of principles and practices for the negotiations were formulated by the Committee in February 2002.

SECRETARIAT

The WTO Secretariat comprised some 640 staff in 2014. Its responsibilities include the servicing of WTO delegate bodies, with respect to negotiations and the implementation of agreements, undertaking accession negotiations for new members and providing technical support and expertise to developing countries.

The WTO Institute for Training and Technical Co-operation, based at the Secretariat, offers courses on trade policy; introduction to the WTO for least developed countries; WTO dispute settlement rules and procedures; and other specialized topics. Other programmes include training-of-trainers schemes and distance-learning services.

Director-General: ROBERTO CARVALHO DE AZEVÊDO (Brazil).

Deputy Directors-General: YI XIAOZHUN (People's Republic of China), KARL-ERNST BRAUNER (Germany), YONOV FREDERICK AGAH (Nigeria), DAVID SHARK (USA).

Activities

The Final Act of the Uruguay Round of General Agreement on Tariffs and Trade (GATT) multilateral trade negotiations, which were concluded in December 1993, provided for extensive trade liberalization measures and for the establishment of a permanent structure to oversee international trading procedures. The Final Act was signed in April 1994, in Marrakesh, Morocco. At the same time a separate accord, the Marrakesh Declaration, was signed by the majority of GATT contracting states, endorsing the establishment of the WTO. The essential functions of the WTO are to administer and facilitate the implementation of the results of the Uruguay Round; to provide a forum for multilateral trade negotiations; to administer the trade dispute settlement procedures; to review national trade policies; and to co-operate with other international institutions, in particular the IMF and the World Bank, in order to achieve greater coherence in global economic policy-making.

The WTO Agreement contains some 29 individual legal texts and more than 25 additional ministerial declarations, decisions and understandings, which cover obligations and commitments for member states, and are based on a number of core principles. An integral part of the Agreement is 'GATT 1994', an amended and updated version of the original GATT Agreement of 1947, which was formally concluded at the end of 1995. Under the 'most favoured nation' (MFN) clause, members are bound to grant to each other's products treatment no less favourable than that accorded to the products of any third parties. A number of exceptions apply, principally for customs unions and free trade areas and for measures in favour of and among developing countries. The principle of 'national treatment' requires goods, having entered a market, to be treated no less favourably than the equivalent domestically produced goods. Secure and predictable market access, to encourage trade, investment and job creation, may be determined by 'binding' tariffs, or customs duties. This process means that a tariff level for a particular product becomes a commitment by a member state, and cannot be increased without compensation negotiations with its main trading partners. Other WTO agreements also contribute to predictable trading conditions by demanding commitments from member countries and greater transparency of domestic laws and national trade policies. By permitting tariffs, while adhering to the guidelines of being non-discriminatory, the WTO aims to promote open, fair and undistorted competition.

The WTO aims to encourage development and economic reform among the increasing number of developing countries and countries with economies in transition participating in the international trading system. These states, particularly the least developed countries (LDCs), have been granted transition periods and greater flexibility to implement certain WTO provisions. Industrial member countries are encouraged to assist developing nations through their trading conditions and by not expecting reciprocity in trade concession negotiations. Since the accession, in August 2012, of Russia to the WTO, all participants in the so-called BRICS informal grouping of large emerging economies, comprising Brazil, Russia, India, the People's Republic of China, and South Africa (which together accounted for some 20% of global gross domestic product—GDP—in 2011), are members of the organization. The WTO reported that 2012 was the first year in which the GDP of developing economies surpassed that of developed economies. It envisages that by 2020—aided by the evolution of supply chains and the possibility of adding value to products at localized stages of production—trade between developing countries will account for one-third of global trade. In January 2012 the WTO and Organisation for Economic Co-operation and Development (OECD) jointly launched a data series measuring trade in value-added rather than gross terms.

Finally, the WTO Agreement recognizes the need to protect the environment and to promote sustainable development. A Committee on Trade and Environment examines the relationship between trade policies, environmental measures and sustainable development and to recommend any appropriate modifications of the multilateral trading provisions. The first WTO Advanced Course on Trade and Environment was held in April 2012, at WTO headquarters in Geneva, Switzerland.

At the 1996 Conference representatives of some 29 countries signed an Information Technology Agreement (ITA), which provides for the elimination of tariffs on the global trade in IT products, including computers, telecommunications products, semiconductors or manufacturing equipment, software, and scientific instruments. By April 2014 there were 78 participants in the ITA, representing some 97% of world trade in IT products; Russia adopted the Agreement in September 2013. Informal negotiations on expanding the product coverage of the ITA were initiated in May 2012. In February 1999 the WTO announced plans to investigate methods of removing non-tariff barriers to trade in IT products, such as those resulting from non-standardization of technical regulations. A work programme on non-tariff measures was approved by the Committee of Participants on the Expansion of Trade in IT Products in November 2000.

At the end of the Uruguay Round a 'built-in' programme of work for the WTO was developed. The final declaration issued from the Ministerial Conference in December 1996 incorporated a text on the contentious issue of core labour standards, although it was emphasized that the relationship between trade and labour standards was not part of the WTO agenda. The text recognized the International Labour Organization (ILO) as having competence in establishing and dealing with core labour standards and endorsed future WTO/ILO co-operation. The declaration also included a plan of action on measures in favour of LDCs, to assist these states in enhancing their trading opportunities. The second Conference, convened in May 1998, agreed to establish a comprehensive work programme to address the issues of electronic commerce. The Conference also supported the creation of a framework of international rules to protect intellectual property rights and provide security and privacy in transactions. Developing countries were assured that their needs in this area would be taken into account.

Formal negotiations on the agenda of a new multilateral trade 'round' commenced in September 1998. While it was confirmed that further liberalization of agriculture and services was to be considered, no consensus was reached (in particular between the Cairns Group of countries and the USA, and the European Union—EU, supported by Japan) on the terms of reference or procedures for these negotiations. In addition, developing countries criticized renewed efforts, mainly by the USA, to link trade and labour standards and to incorporate environmental considerations into the discussions. Efforts by the EU to broaden the talks to include investment and competition policy were also resisted by the USA. The third Ministerial Conference, held in Seattle, Washington, USA, in November 1999, was severely disrupted by public demonstrations by a diverse range of interest groups concerned with the impact of WTO accords on the environment, workers' rights and developing countries. The differences between member states with regard to a formal agenda failed to be resolved during extensive negotiations, and the Conference was suspended. In February 2000 the General Council agreed to resume talks with regard to agriculture and services, and to consider difficulties in implementing the Uruguay Accord, which was a main concern of developing member states. The Council also urged industrialized nations to pursue an earlier initiative to grant duty-free access to the exports of LDCs. In May the Council resolved to initiate a series of Special Sessions to consider implementation of existing trade agreements, and approved more flexible provisions for implementation of TRIPS, as part of ongoing efforts to address the needs of developing member states and strengthen their confidence in the multilateral trading system.

In November 2001 the fourth Ministerial Conference, held in Doha, Qatar, adopted a final declaration providing a mandate for a three-year agenda for negotiations on a range of subjects. Most of the negotiations were initially scheduled to be concluded, on 1 January 2005, as a single undertaking, i.e. requiring universal agreement on all matters under consideration. (The deadline was subsequently advanced to end-2006, and in July 2006 was postponed indefinitely.) A new Trade Negotiations Committee (TNC) was established to supervise the process, referred to as the Doha Development Round. Several aspects of existing agreements were to be negotiated, while new issues included WTO rules, such as subsidies, regional trade agreements and anti-dumping measures, and market access. The Declaration incorporated a commitment to negotiate issues relating to trade and the environment, including fisheries subsidies, environmental labelling requirements, and the relationship between trade obligations of multilateral environment agreements and WTO rules. The Conference approved a separate decision on implementation-related issues, to address the concerns of developing countries in meeting their WTO commitments. A Doha Development Agenda Global Trust Fund was established in late 2001, with a core budget of 15m. Swiss francs, to help to finance technical support for trade liberalization in less developed member states. In September 2002 the WTO Director-General announced that, in support of the ongoing trade negotiations, the following four 'pillars' of the organization should be strengthened: beneficial use of the legal framework binding together the multilateral system; technical and capacity-building assistance to LDCs and developing states; greater coherence in international economic policy-making; and the WTO's functioning as an institution.

The fifth Ministerial Conference, convened in Cancún, Mexico, in September 2003 to advance the Doha Development Round, failed to achieve consensus on a number of issues, in particular investment and competition policy. Senior officials from member states met in December to discuss the future of the Doha Round, but no major breakthrough was achieved. Members did, however, indicate their willingness to recommence work in negotiating groups, which had been suspended after the Cancún conference. The General Council, meanwhile, was to continue working to explore the possibilities of agreements on a multilateral approach on trade facilitation and transparency in government procurement.

In July 2004 the General Council presented for consideration and revision by WTO member states a new draft Doha Agenda Work Programme (the so-called July Package of framework trade agreements) aimed at reviving the stalled Doha Development Round. Following intensive negotiations, the finalized July Package was adopted by the General Council at the beginning of August. The Package included an interim accord on agricultural subsidies that established guidelines for future Doha Round negotiations, entailing a key commitment by rich developed nations eventually to eliminate all agricultural export subsidies. The EU's subsidies to its milk and sugar producers and the USA's subsidies to its cotton farmers were withdrawn from the Package and were to be addressed by separate negotiations. Under the July Package all countries were to be required to reduce tariffs on agricultural imports, but the poorest countries would be set lower reduction targets and longer periods for their implementation.

The sixth Ministerial Conference, convened in Hong Kong, in December 2005, set a deadline of 30 April 2006 for finalizing details of the methods of reducing tariffs and subsidies (the 'modalities') in agriculture and industrial goods, with a view to concluding the Doha Round at the end of 2006. It was also agreed that duty- and quota-free access for at least 97% of LDCs' exports should be achieved by 2008. However, in July 2006 the Doha Development Round of negotiations was suspended across all sectors, with all related deadlines postponed, owing to failure by the participating countries to reach a satisfactory final agreement on agricultural trade, and, in particular, deadlock on the issues of reductions in market access restrictions and domestic support mechanisms in the agriculture sector. In February 2007 the Director-General announced that negotiations across all sectors had been resumed. In June discussions between the EU, the USA, India and Brazil, which were aimed at bridging the gaps in their negotiating positions and had been regarded as a basis for advancing the wider negotiations, failed to reach any agreement on the main areas of dispute i.e. farm subsidies and market access. In July 2008 a meeting of the TNC failed to reach agreement on the formal establishment of modalities in agriculture and non-agricultural market access.

The 2005 Ministerial Conference launched the Aid for Trade initiative, as a platform for developing countries to build the supply capacity and trade-related infrastructure necessary for implementing and benefiting from WTO agreements. In December 2011 the eighth Ministerial Conference determined to maintain, beyond 2011, Aid for Trade levels reflecting the average of the period 2006–08, and to pursue efforts with development banks to ensure the availability of trade finance to low-income states.

In October 2008 a task force was established within the WTO secretariat to address the effects of the ongoing global financial crisis. In January 2009 the WTO Director-General announced that the WTO was to issue periodic reports on trends in global trade, and was to organize future meetings on trade finance, in order to support members with dealing with the global situation. During that month the WTO launched a database on regional trade agreements; a database on non-reciprocal preferential schemes was launched in March 2012. The WTO, with the UN Conference on Trade and Development (UNCTAD), jointly lead an initiative on promoting trade—through combating protectionism, including through the conclusion of the Doha Round, and by strengthening aid-for-trade financing-for-trade initiatives—the third of nine activities that were launched in April 2009 by the UN System Chief Executives Board for Co-ordination, with the aim of alleviating the impact on poor and vulnerable populations of the global crisis. From early 2009 the WTO contributed, with the ILO, the IMF, the World Bank, and OECD (the co-ordinating agency), to the compilation of *A 'Global Charter'/'Legal Standard', Inventory of Possible Policy Instruments*, which aimed to stocktake the current range of financial policy instruments, as part of a united response to the financial crisis that involved establishing a shared 'global standard' of propriety and transparency for the future development of the global economic framework. In November–December 2009 the seventh WTO Ministerial Conference addressed the impact of the global financial crisis on LDCs (numbering 49 in 2014, of which 34 were WTO member states). In March 2012 the WTO and OECD agreed to develop statistics on trade in value added; accordingly, both organizations were to produce a publicly accessible database of trade flows estimated in value-added terms.

The seventh (Geneva) Ministerial Conference, held in November–December 2009, agreed that progress in the Doha Round should be assessed in the first quarter of 2010; accordingly, the TNC oversaw a phase of 'stocktaking' discussions in March. The eighth Ministerial Conference, held in Geneva in December 2011, acknowledged that, despite strong engagement to conclude the Doha Round, the negotiations remained at an impasse, and urged a refocusing of the discussions. In February 2012 the WTO Director-General urged the chairpersons of the various Doha negotiating groups to consult informally on small practical steps that might be taken to advance progress in each sector. In April the Director-General established a panel of WTO stakeholders who were instructed to analyse challenges to the global multilateral open trading system in the 21st century. In December the Director-General expressed support for the World Trade Agenda initiative, which was launched in 2011 by the International Chamber of Commerce with a view to re-animating the Doha negotiations. In October 2013 a meeting of multilateral financial institutions, with participation by the IMF, World Bank, African Development Bank, Asian Development Bank, European Bank for Reconstruction and Development, European Investment Bank, and Inter-American Development Bank, issued a statement urging WTO member states to conclude an agreement to facilitate multilateral trade that would deliver tangible economic benefits for developing and least developed countries.

In June 2013 an updated work programme was adopted for member LDCs, which aimed to mainstream into WTO's mandate the Istanbul Programme of Action for LDCs covering 2011–20, that was adopted, in May 2011, by the fourth UN Conference on the LDCs. The programme addressed, inter alia, capacity-building initiatives, trade-related technical assistance, market access, and the diversification of LDCs' exports.

In December 2013 intensive consultations during the ninth Ministerial Conference, convened in Bali, Indonesia, secured the adoption of a Bali Package of measures to advance the Doha Development Round. The Package included a Trade Facilitation Agreement to stimulate global trade through improved customs technology, training and procedures. The agreement was scheduled to be formally adopted by the General Council in July 2014. The Bali Package also included an interim agreement for developing countries to implement food security programmes without being liable to trade disputes, an agreement on tariff quota administration and a political statement to improve market access for cotton producers in least developing countries. The Conference instructed its negotiators to prepare, within the next 12 months, a clearly defined programme of work to conclude the Doha Round.

The WTO organizes an annual public forum, with participation by representatives of civil society, business, governments, parliaments, international agencies, the media, and academia; the 2013 event was held in October, in Geneva, on the theme 'Expanding Trade through Innovation and the Digital Economy'.

AGRICULTURE

The Final Act of the Uruguay Round extended previous GATT arrangements for trade in agricultural products through new rules and commitments to ensure more predictable and fair competition in the sector. All quantitive measures limiting market access for agricultural products were to be replaced by tariffs (i.e. a process of 'tariffication'), enabling more equal protection and access opportunities. All tariffs on agricultural items were to be reduced by 36% by developed countries, over a period of six years, and by 24% by developing countries (excluding least developed member states) over 10 years. A special treatment clause applied to 'sensitive' products (mainly rice) in four countries, for which limited import restrictions could be maintained. Efforts to reduce domestic support measures for agricultural products were to be based on calculations of total aggregate measurements of support (Total AMS) by each member state. A 20% reduction in Total AMS was required by developed countries over six years, and 13% over 10 years by developing countries. No reduction was required of LDCs. Developed member countries were required to reduce the value and quantity of direct export subsidies by 36% and 21%, respectively, (on 1986–90 levels) over six years. For developing countries these reductions were to be two-thirds of those of developed nations, over 10 years. A specific concern of LDCs and net food-importing developing countries, which previously had relied on subsidized food products, was to be addressed through other food aid mechanisms and assistance for agricultural development. The situation was to be monitored by WTO's Committee on Agriculture. Negotiations on the further liberalization of agricultural markets were part of the WTO 'built-in' programme for 2000 or earlier, but remained a major area of contention. In March 2000 negotiations on market access to the agricultural sector commenced, under an interim chairman owing to a disagreement among participating states. The Doha Declaration, approved in that month, established a timetable for further negotiations on agriculture, which were initially scheduled to be concluded as part of the single undertaking on 1 January 2005. (The deadline was subsequently postponed indefinitely.) A compromise agreement was reached with the EU to commit to a reduction in export subsidies, with a view to phasing them out (without a firm deadline for their elimination). Member states agreed to aim for further reductions in market access restrictions and domestic support mechanisms, and to incorporate non-trade concerns, including environmental protection, food security and rural development, into the negotiations. In December 2005 the sixth WTO ministerial conference agreed in principle that export subsidies on cotton should be eliminated, as well as trade-distorting domestic support for cotton exports, and that developed countries would permit the importation of cotton from LDCs duty- and quota-free. In December 2011 the seventh Conference reiterated these objectives. In December 2013 the ninth WTO ministerial conference agreed that, pending the conclusion of a long-term agreement on agriculture (scheduled to be negotiated over a further four-year time span), developing countries should be granted flexibility to implement—without risk of legal challenge, even when agreed limits of trade-distorting domestic support were breached—domestic food stockholding programmes for food security. A further interim measure was approved concerning the handling of persistently under-filled import tariff quotas.

TEXTILES AND CLOTHING

From 1974–94 the former Multi-Fibre Arrangement (MFA) provided the basis of international trade concerning textiles and clothing, enabling the major importers to establish quotas and protect their domestic industries, through bilateral agreements, against more competitive low-cost goods from developing countries. MFA restrictions that were in place on 31 December 1994 were carried over into a new transitional 10-year Agreement on Textiles and Clothing (ATC) and were phased out through integration into GATT 1994, in four planned stages: products accounting for 16% of the total volume of textiles and clothing imports (at 1990 levels) to be integrated from 1 January 1995; a further 17% on 1 January 1998; not less than a further 18% on 1 January 2002; and all remaining products by 1 January 2005. Since the expiry on that date of the ATC, international trade in clothing and textiles has, as envisaged, been governed by general rules and disciplines embodied in the multilateral trading system.

TRADE IN SERVICES

The General Agreement on Trade in Services (GATS)—negotiated during the GATT Uruguay Round—represents the first set of multilaterally agreed and legally enforceable rules and disciplines covering international trade in services. A Council for Trade in Services oversees the operation of the Agreement. The 29 articles of GATS include the following set of basic obligations: total coverage of all internationally traded services; national treatment, i.e. according services and service suppliers of other members no less favourable treatment than that accorded to domestic services and suppliers; MFN treatment, with any specific exemptions to be recorded prior to the implementation of the GATS, with a limit of 10 years' duration; transparency, requiring publication of all relevant national laws and legislations; bilateral agreements on recognition of standards and qualifications to be open to other members who wish to negotiate accession; no restrictions on international payments and transfers; progressive liberalization to be pursued; and market access and national treatment commitments to be bound and recorded in national schedules.

Annexes to the GATS cover the movement of natural persons, permitting governments to negotiate specific commitments regarding the temporary stay of people for the purpose of providing a service; the right of governments to take measures in order to ensure the integrity and stability of the financial system; the role of telecommunications as a distinct sector of economic activity and as a means of supplying other economic activities; and air transport services, excluding certain activities relating to traffic rights.

At the end of the Uruguay Round governments agreed to continue negotiations in basic telecommunications; maritime transport; movement of natural persons; and financial services. The Protocol to the GATS relating to movement of natural persons was concluded in July 1995. In May 1996 the USA withdrew from negotiations to conclude an agreement on maritime transport services. At the end of June the participating countries agreed to suspend the discussions and to recommence negotiations in 2000.

In July 1995 some 29 members signed an interim agreement to grant greater access to the banking, insurance, investment and securities sectors from August 1996. A final, full agreement was successfully concluded in December 1997, under which 102 countries endorsed the elimination of restrictions on access to the financial services sectors from 1 March 1999, and agreed to subject those services to legally binding rules and disciplines; entry into force of the agreement was, however, postponed. An agreement on trade in basic telecommunications (negotiated since May 1994) was concluded in February 1997. Accordingly the largest telecommunications markets, i.e. the USA, the EU and Japan, were to eliminate all remaining restrictions on domestic and foreign competition in the industry by 1 January 1998 (although delays were granted to Spain, until December 1998, Ireland, until 2000, and Greece and Portugal, until 2003). The majority of the signatories to the accord also agreed on common rules to ensure that fair competition could be enforced by the WTO dispute settlement mechanism, and pledged their commitment to establishing a regulatory system for the telecommunications sector and guaranteeing transparency in government licensing.

The negotiations to liberalize trade in services, suspended in 1996, were formally reopened in January 2000, with new guidelines and procedures for the negotiations approved in March 2001. The negotiations were incorporated into the Doha Agenda and were to be concluded as part of a single undertaking.

INTELLECTUAL PROPERTY RIGHTS

The WTO Agreement on Trade-Related Aspects of Intellectual Property Rights (TRIPS), which entered into force on 1 January 1995, recognizes that widely varying standards in the protection and enforcement of intellectual property rights and the lack of multilateral disciplines dealing with international trade in counterfeit goods have been a growing source of tension in international economic relations. The TRIPS agreement aims to ensure that nationals of member states receive equally favourable treatment with regard to the protection of intellectual property and that adequate standards of intellectual property protection exist in all WTO member countries. These standards are largely based on the obligations of the Paris and Berne Conventions of the World Intellectual Property Organization (WIPO), however, and the agreement aims to expand and enhance these where necessary, for example: computer programmes, to be protected as literary works for copyright purposes; definition of trade marks eligible for protection; stricter rules of geographical indications of consumer products; a 10-year protection period for industrial designs; a 20-year patent protection available for all inventions; tighter protection of layout design of integrated circuits; and protection for trade secrets and 'know-how' with a commercial value.

Under the agreement member governments are obliged to provide procedures and remedies to ensure the effective enforcement of intellectual property rights, such as injunctions, judicial authority to order the disposal of infringing goods, and criminal procedures and penalties, in particular for trademark counterfeiting and copyright piracy. A one-year period from TRIPS' entry into force was envisaged for developed countries to bring their legislation and practices into conformity with the agreement; developing countries were to do so in five years (or 10 years if an area of technology did not already have patent protection) and LDCs in 11 years. A Council for Trade-Related Property Rights monitors the compliance of governments with the agreement and its operation. In November 2001 the Doha Ministerial Conference extended the deadline for some of the poorest countries to apply provisions on pharmaceutical patents under TRIPS to 1 January 2016. In November 2005 the original deadline of 1 January 2006 for LDCs to bring their legislation and practices into conformity with TRIPS was extended by the Council for Trade-Related Property Rights to 1 July 2013; in June 2013—following a request to that effect submitted in November 2012 by Haiti, on behalf of all member LDCs—the deadline was extended further, until July 2021. In December 2013 the ninth ministerial conference agreed that member states should not bring before the Dispute Settlement Body so-called non-violation cases, in which—while a specific agreement may not have been violated—a country's actions are deemed to have deprived others of an expected benefit. Member states also agreed in December not to charge import duties on electronic transmissions.

LEGAL FRAMEWORK

In addition to the binding agreements mentioned above, the WTO aims to provide a comprehensive legal framework for the international trading system. Under GATT 1994 'anti-dumping' measures were permitted against imports of a product with an export price below its normal value, if these imports were likely to cause damage to a domestic industry. The WTO agreement provides for greater clarity and more detailed rules determining the application of these measures and determines settlement procedures in disputes relating to anti-dumping actions taken by WTO members. In general, anti-dumping measures were to be limited to five years. The WTO Agreement on Subsidies and Countervailing Measures is intended to expand on existing GATT agreements. It classifies subsidies into three categories: prohibited, which may be determined by the Dispute Settlement Body and must be immediately withdrawn; actionable, which must be withdrawn or altered if the subsidy is found to cause adverse effects on the interests of other members; and non-actionable, for example subsidies involving assistance to industrial research, assistance to disadvantaged regions or adaptation of facilities to meet new environmental requirements; non-actionable subsidies, however, were terminated in 1999. The Agreement also contains provisions on the use of duties to offset the effect of a subsidy (so-called countervailing measures) and establishes procedures for the initiation and conduct of investigations into this action. Countervailing measures must generally be terminated within five years of their imposition.

WTO members may take safeguard actions to protect a specific domestic industry from a damaging increase of imported products. However, the WTO agreement aims to clarify criteria for imposing safeguards, their duration (normally to be no longer than four years, which may be extended to eight years) and consultations on trade compensation for the exporting countries. Safeguard measures are not applicable to products from developing countries as long as their share of imports of the product concerned does not exceed 3%.

Further legal arrangements act to ensure the following: that technical regulations and standards (including testing and certification procedures) do not create unnecessary obstacles to trade; that import licensing procedures are transparent and predictable; that the valuation of goods for customs purposes are fair and uniform; that GATT principles and obligations apply to import preshipment inspection activities; the fair and transparent administration of rules of origin; and that no investment measures which may restrict or distort trade may be applied. A Working Group on Notification Obligations and Procedures aims to ensure that members fulfil their notification requirements, which facilitate the transparency and surveillance of the trading rules.

PLURILATERAL AGREEMENT

The majority of GATT agreements became multilateral obligations when the WTO became operational in 1995; however, four agreements, which had a selective group of signatories, remained in effect. These so-called plurilateral agreements, the Agreement on Trade in Civil Aircraft, the Agreement on Government Procurement, the International Dairy Agreement and the International Bovine Meat Agreement, aimed to increase international co-operation and fair and open trade and competition in these areas. The bovine meat and dairy agreements were terminated in 1997. The remaining two plurilateral agreements established their own management bodies, which are required to report to the General Council.

TRADE POLICY REVIEW MECHANISM

The mechanism, which was established provisionally in 1989, was subsequently given a permanent role in the WTO. Through regular monitoring and surveillance of national trade policies the mechanism aims to increase the transparency and understanding of trade policies and practices and to enable assessment of the effects of policies on the world trading system. In addition, it records efforts made by governments to bring domestic trade legislation into conformity with WTO provisions and to implement WTO commitments. Reviews are conducted in the Trade Policy Review Body on the basis of a policy statement of the government under review and an independent report prepared by the WTO Secretariat.

In February 1996 a Committee on Regional Trade Agreements was established. By 31 January 2014 some 583 regional trade agreements among WTO member states had been notified to the organization, and of these 377 were in force. The WTO maintains a database of regional trade agreements.

SETTLEMENT OF DISPUTES

A separate annex to the WTO agreement determines a unified set of rules and procedures to govern the settlement of all WTO disputes, substantially reinforcing the GATT procedures. WTO members are committed not to undertake unilateral action against perceived violations of the trade rules, but to seek recourse in the dispute settlement mechanism and abide by its findings.

The agreements that may be cited in the bilateral consultations (first stage, see below) of the disputes process relate to: Establishing the WTO (cited in 53 cases by April 2014); Agriculture (cited in 74 cases by April 2014); Anti-dumping (Article VI of GATT 1994) (102 cases); Civil Aircraft (no citations); Customs Valuation (Article VII of GATT 1994) (cited in 16 cases); Dispute Settlement Understanding (15 cases); GATT 1947 (one case); GATT 1994 (383 cases); Government Procurement (four cases); Import Licensing (41 cases); Intellectual Property (TRIPS) (34 cases); Preshipment Inspection (two cases); Rules of Origin (seven cases); Safeguards (43 cases); Sanitary and Phytosanitary Measures (SPS) (40 cases); Services (GATS) (23 cases); Subsidies and Countervailing Measures (102 cases); Technical Barriers to Trade (TBT) (49 cases); Textiles and Clothing (16 cases); Trade-Related Investment Measures (TRIMs) (39 cases); Protocol of Accession (26 cases).

The first stage of the process requires bilateral consultations between the members concerned in an attempt to conclude a mutually acceptable solution to the issue. These may be undertaken through the good offices and mediation efforts of the Director-General. Only after a consultation period of 60 days may the complainant ask the General Council, convened as the Dispute Settlement Body (DSB), to establish an independent panel to examine the case, which then does so within the terms of reference of the agreement cited. Each party to the dispute submits its arguments and then presents its case before the panel. Third parties which notify their interest in the dispute may also present views at the first substantive meeting of the panel. At this stage an expert review group may be appointed to provide specific scientific or technical advice. The panel submits sections and then a full interim report of its findings to the parties, who may then request a further review involving additional meetings. A final report should be submitted to the parties by the panel within six months of its establishment, or within three months in cases of urgency, including those related to perishable goods. Final reports are normally adopted by the DSB within 60 days of issuance. In the case of a measure being found to be inconsistent with the relevant WTO agreement, the panel recommends ways in which the member may bring the measure into conformity with the agreement. However, under the WTO mechanism either party has the right to appeal against the decision and must notify the DSB of its intentions before adoption of the final report. Appeal proceedings, which are limited to issues of law and the legal interpretation covered by the panel report, are undertaken by three members of the Appellate Body within a maximum period of 90 days. The report of the Appellate Body must be unconditionally accepted by the parties to the dispute (unless there is a consensus within the DSB against its adoption). If the recommendations of the panel or appeal report are not implemented immediately, or within a 'reasonable period' as determined by the DSB, the parties are obliged to negotiate mutually acceptable compensation pending full implementation. Failure to agree compensation may result in the DSB authorizing the complainant to suspend concessions or obligations against the other party. In any case the DSB monitors the implementation of adopted recommendations or rulings, while any outstanding cases remain on its agenda until the issue is resolved.

By April 2014 475 trade complaints had been notified to the DSB since 1995. Since the early 2000s a rising proportion of disputes have been filed by developing and emerging economies. In 2013 two appeals of panel reports were filed with the Appellate Body, which, during 1995–2013, circulated 119 final reports. The largest case yet to be raised in the dispute settlement system was filed in October 2004 by the USA, concerning subsidies provided by the EU to the aircraft manufacturer Airbus SAS; the EU, meanwhile, filed a similar case in June 2005 regarding US government assistance to Boeing. The Appellate Body adjudicated in May 2011 that some EU subsidies to Airbus had been illegal, and in March 2012 it ruled that subsidies granted to Boeing by the US Government were also illegitimate.

The Agreement on the Application of Sanitary and Phytosanitary Measures aims to regulate worldwide standards of food safety and animal and plant health in order to encourage the mutual recognition of standards and conformity, so as to facilitate trade in these products. The Agreement includes provisions on control inspection and approval procedures. In September 1997, in the first case to be brought under the Agreement, a dispute panel of the WTO ruled that the EU's ban on imports of hormone-treated beef and beef products from the USA and Canada was in breach of international trading rules. In January 1998 the Appellate Body upheld the panel's ruling, but expressed its support for restrictions to ensure food standards if there was adequate scientific evidence of risks to human health.

In December 2009 representatives of the EU and Latin American countries initialled the EU-Latin America Geneva Bananas Agreement, under which (with a view to ending a 15-year dispute) the EU was gradually to reduce its import tariff on bananas from Latin American countries, from €176 to €114 per metric ton, by 2017. Meanwhile, Latin American banana-producing countries undertook not to demand further tariff reductions, and to withdraw several related cases against the EU pending at the WTO. In response to the Agreement, the US authorities determined to settle a parallel dispute with the EU at the WTO relating to bananas. In November 2012, by which time the 2009 accord had been ratified and the EU had introduced several regulations to underpin its implementation, EU and Latin American representatives signed a final agreement confirming the new arrangements.

CO-OPERATION WITH OTHER ORGANIZATIONS

The WTO is mandated to pursue co-operation with the IMF and the World Bank, as well as with other multilateral organizations, in order to achieve greater coherence in global economic policy-making. In November 1994 the preparatory committee of the WTO resolved not to incorporate the new organization into the UN structure as a specialized agency. Instead, co-operation arrangements with the IMF and the World Bank were to be developed. In addition, efforts were pursued to enhance co-operation with UNCTAD in research, trade and technical issues. The Directors-General of the two organizations agreed to meet at least twice a year in order to develop the working relationship. In particular, co-operation was to be undertaken in the WTO's special programme of activities for Africa, which aimed to help African countries expand and diversify their trade and benefit from the global trading system. The WTO co-operates—with the IMF, the International Trade Centre, UNCTAD, the UN Development Programme and the World Bank—in the Enhanced Integrated Framework (EIF), a multi-donor programme which aims to support greater participation by LDCs in the global trading system; EIF funds are channelled through a dedicated EIF Trust Fund. The WTO, the IMF, the World Bank, UNCTAD and ECOSOC participate annually in high-level consultations.

From early 2009 WTO, the ILO, the IMF, the World Bank, and OECD entered into co-operation on the establishment of a new global standard for future economic development, in response to the ongoing global financial crisis; it was announced in April 2010 that the inter-agency collaboration would be intensified. In June 2009 the WTO and the UN Environment Programme jointly issued a report entitled *Trade and Climate Change*.

In July 2010 the WTO, WIPO and WHO organized a symposium to initiate a process of co-operation in addressing means of improving the access of poorer populations to necessary medicines.

With FAO and other agencies the WTO participates in the Agricultural Market Information System, founded in 2011 to improve market transparency and help to stabilize food price volatility.

International Trade Centre (ITC): Palais des Nations, 1211 Geneva 10, Switzerland; tel. 227300111; fax 227334439; e-mail itcreg@intracen.org; internet www.intracen.org; f. 1964 by GATT; jointly operated with the UN (through UNCTAD) since 1968; ITC works with developing countries in product and market development, the development of trade support services, trade information, human resource development, international purchasing and supply management, and needs assessment and programme design for trade promotion; in March 2014 the ITC signed a Memorandum of Understanding with UNCTAD on jointly assisting developing countries in the implementation of the Dec. 2013 WTO Trade Facilitation Agreement; allocated US $39.9m. under the proposed UN budget for 2014–15; publs *International Trade Forum* (quarterly), market studies, handbooks, etc.

Executive Director: ARANCHA GONZALEZ (Spain).

Finance

The WTO's 2013 budget amounted to 197m. Swiss francs, financed mainly by contributions from WTO member states, assessed in proportion to their share of the total volume of trading conducted by members.

Publications

Annual Report (2 volumes).
Annual Report of the Appellate Body.
International Trade Statistics (annually).
World Trade Report (annually).
World Trade Review (3 a year).
WTO Focus (monthly).

OTHER INTERNATIONAL ORGANIZATIONS

Agriculture, Food, Forestry and Fisheries

(For organizations concerned with agricultural commodities, see Commodities)

African Agricultural Technology Foundation: POB 30709, Nairobi 00100, Kenya; tel. (20) 4223700; fax (20) 4223701; e-mail aatf@aatf-africa.org; internet www.aatf-africa.org; f. 2003; aims to facilitate and promote public/private partnerships for the access and delivery of agricultural technologies for use by resource-poor smallholder farmers in sub-Saharan Africa; Exec. Dir DENIS T. TUMWESIGYE KYETERE (Uganda).

Arab Authority for Agricultural Investment and Development (AAAID): POB 2102, Khartoum, Sudan; tel. (18) 7096100; fax (18) 3772600; e-mail info@aaaid.org; internet www.aaaid.org; f. 1976 to accelerate agricultural devt in the Arab world and to ensure food security; acts principally by equity participation in agricultural projects in mem. countries; AAAID has adopted new programmes to help to raise productivity of food agricultural products and introduced zero-tillage farming technology for developing the rain-fed sector, which achieved a substantial increase in the yields of grown crops, including sorghum, cotton, sesame, and sunflower; mems: 21 countries; Pres. and Chair. MOHAMED BIN OBAID ALMAZROOEI (UAE); publs *Journal of Agricultural Investment* (English and Arabic), *Extension and Investment Bulletins*, *Annual Report* (Arabic and English), *AAAID Newsletter* (quarterly).

Association of Agricultural Research Institutions in the Near East and North Africa: POB 950764, 11195 Amman, Jordan; tel. (6) 5525750; fax (6) 5525930; e-mail i.hamdan@cgiar.org; internet www.aarinena.org; f. 1985; aims to strengthen co-operation among national, regional and international research institutions; operates the internet-based Near East and North Africa Rural and Agricultural Knowledge and Information Network; Exec. Sec. Dr MOHAMMAD MAHMOUD AJLOUNI (Jordan).

AVRDC—the World Vegetable Center: POB 42, Shanhua, Tainan 74199, Taiwan; tel. (6) 5837801; fax (6) 5830009; e-mail info@worldveg.org; internet www.avrdc.org; f. 1971 as the Asian Vegetable Research and Development Center; aims to enhance the nutritional well-being and raise the incomes of the poor in rural and urban areas of developing countries, through improved varieties and methods of vegetable production, marketing and distribution; runs an experimental farm, laboratories, genebank, greenhouses, quarantine house, insectarium, library and weather station; provides training for research and production specialists in tropical vegetables; exchanges and disseminates vegetable germplasm through regional offices in the developing world; serves as a clearinghouse for vegetable research information; and undertakes scientific publishing; mems: Japan, Republic of Korea, Philippines, Taiwan, Thailand, USA; Dir-Gen. Dr DYNO KEATINGE; publs *Annual Report*, *Technical Bulletin*, *Proceedings*.

CAB International (CABI): Nosworthy Way, Wallingford, Oxon, OX10 8DE, United Kingdom; tel. (1491) 832111; fax (149) 1833508; e-mail enquiries@cabi.org; internet www.cabi.org; f. 1929 as the Imperial Agricultural Bureaux (later Commonwealth Agricultural Bureaux), current name adopted in 1985; aims to improve human welfare worldwide through the generation, dissemination and application of scientific knowledge in support of sustainable devt; places particular emphasis on sustainable agriculture, forestry, human health and the management of natural resources, with priority given to the needs of developing countries; a separate microbiology centre, in Egham, Surrey (UK), undertakes research, consultancy, training, capacity building and institutional devt measures in sustainable pest management, biosystematics and molecular biology, ecological applications and environmental and industrial microbiology; compiles and publishes extensive information (in a variety of print and electronic forms) on aspects of agriculture, forestry, veterinary medicine, the environment and natural resources, and Third World rural devt; maintains regional centres in the People's Republic of China, India, Kenya, Malaysia, Pakistan, Switzerland, Trinidad and Tobago, and the USA; mems: 45 countries and territories; Chair. JOHN RIPLEY (United Kingdom); CEO Dr TREVOR NICHOLLS (United Kingdom).

Collaborative International Pesticides Analytical Council Ltd (CIPAC): c/o Dr Ralf Hänel, Referat 206, Messeweg 11/12, 38104 Braunschweig, Germany; tel. (531) 2993506; fax (531) 2993002; e-mail cipac@agroscope.admin.ch; internet www.cipac.org; f. 1957 to organize international collaborative work on methods of analysis for pesticides used in crop protection; 25 mems, 8 hon. life mems; Chair. Dr RALF HÄNEL (Germany); Sec. Dr LÁZLÓ BURA (Hungary).

Desert Locust Control Organization for Eastern Africa (DLCOEA): POB 4255, Addis Ababa, Ethiopia; tel. (1) 461477; fax (1) 460296; e-mail dlc@ethionet.et; internet www.dlcoea.org.et; f. 1962 to promote effective control of desert locust in the region and to conduct research into the locust's environment and behaviour; also assists mem. states in the monitoring, forecasting and extermination of other migratory pests; mems: Djibouti, Eritrea, Ethiopia, Kenya, Somalia, Sudan, Tanzania, Uganda; Dir GASPAR ATTMAN MALLYA; publs *Desert Locust Situation Reports* (monthly), *Annual Report*, technical reports.

European and Mediterranean Plant Protection Organization (EPPO): 21 blvd Richard Lenoir, 75011 Paris, France; tel. 1-45-20-77-94; fax 1-70-76-65-47; e-mail hq@eppo.int; internet www.eppo.int; f. 1951, present name adopted in 1955; aims to promote international co-operation between govt plant protection services to prevent the introduction and spread of pests and diseases of plants and plant products; mems: govts of 50 countries and territories; Chair. MARTIN WARD; publs *EPPO Bulletin*, *Data Sheets on Quarantine Organisms*, *Guidelines for the Efficacy Evaluation of Pesticides*, *Summary of the Phytosanitary Regulations of EPPO Member Countries*, *Reporting Service*, database on quarantine pests.

European Association for Animal Production (EAAP) (Fédération européenne de zootechnie): Via G. Tomassetti 3 A/1, 00161 Rome, Italy; tel. (06) 44202639; fax (06) 44266798; e-mail eaap@eaap.org; internet www.eaap.org; f. 1949 to help to improve the conditions of animal production and meet consumer demand; holds annual meetings; mems: asscns in 40 countries; Sec.-Gen. ANDREA ROSATI (Italy); publs *Epitheorisi Zootechnikis Epistimis* (Animal Science Review, with the Hellenic Society of Animal Production), *EAAP Newsletter*, and various scientific and technical reports.

European Association for Research on Plant Breeding (EUCARPIA): c/o Centre de Recherche Conthey, route des Vergers 18, 1964 Conthey, Switzerland; tel. 273453536; fax 273463017; e-mail eucarpia@art.admin.ch; internet www.eucarpia.org; f. 1956 to promote scientific and technical co-operation in the plant breeding field; mems: 1,100 individuals, 65 corp. mems; Pres. B. BOLLER (Switzerland); Sec.-Gen. JOSÉ VOUILLAMOZ (Switzerland); publ. *EUCARPIA Bulletin*.

European Grassland Federation (EGF): Dr Willy Kessler, c/o Agroscope, Reckenholzstrasse 191, 8046, Zürich, Switzerland; tel. 443777376; fax 443770201; e-mail fedsecretary@europeangrassland.org; internet www.europeangrassland.org; f. 1963 to facilitate and maintain liaison between European grassland orgs and to promote the interchange of scientific and practical knowledge and experience; holds General Meeting every two years and a Symposium in the intervening year; mems: 31 full and 8 corresponding mem. countries in Europe; Pres. Dr ATHOLE MARSHALL; Sec. Dr WILLY KESSLER (Switzerland); publ. *Grass and Forage Science*.

European Livestock and Meat Trading Union (UECBV): 81A rue de la Loi, 4th floor, 1040 Brussels, Belgium; tel. (2) 230-46-03; fax (2) 230-94-00; e-mail info@uecbv.eu; internet www.uecbv.eu; f. 1952 to study problems of the European livestock and meat trade and inform mems of all relevant legislation; acts as an international arbitration commission; conducts research on agricultural markets, quality of livestock, and veterinary regulations; incorporates the European Association of Livestock Markets and the Young European Meat Committee; mems: 55 nat. orgs in 33 countries, representing some 20,000 cos; Pres. PHILIPPE BORREMANS; Sec.-Gen. JEAN-LUC MÉRIAUX.

European Society for Sugar Technology (ESST): Lückhoffstr. 16, 14129 Berlin, Germany; tel. (30) 8035678; fax (30) 8032049; e-mail mail@esst-sugar.org; internet www.esst-sugar.org; Pres. DENIS BOURÉE (France); Sec. Dr JÜRGEN BRUHNS (Germany).

Global Foot-and-Mouth Disease Research Alliance (GFRA): 1400 Independence Ave, Washington, DC 20250, USA; tel. (202) 720-3656; fax (202) 720-5427; e-mail ars-gfra@ars.usda.gov; internet www.ars.usda.gov/gfra; f. 2003 as an asscn of animal health research orgs to work on measures for combating foot-and-mouth disease; operates through a global alliance of partners to share research and knowledge and develop strategic objectives to combat and eradicate the disease; mems: 14 animal and food health and safety asscns and institutes and 11 assoc. mems; Representatives Dr LUIS L. RODRIGUEZ, Dr CYRIL GAY.

Indian Ocean Tuna Commission (IOTC): POB 1011, Victoria, Mahé, Seychelles; tel. 4225494; fax 4224364; e-mail secretariat@iotc.org; internet www.iotc.org; f. 1996 as a regional fisheries org. with a mandate for the conservation and management of tuna and tuna-like species in the Indian Ocean; mems: Australia, Belize, People's Republic of China, the Comoros, European Union, Eritrea, France, Guinea, India, Indonesia, Iran, Japan, Kenya, Republic of Korea, Madagascar, Malaysia, Maldives, Mauritius, Mozambique, Oman, Pakistan, Philippines, Seychelles, Sierra Leone, Sudan, Sri Lanka, Tanzania, Thailand, United Kingdom, Vanuatu, Yemen; co-operating non-contracting parties: Senegal, South Africa; Exec. Sec. RONDOLPH PAYET (Seychelles).

Inter-American Tropical Tuna Commission (IATTC): 8604 La Jolla Shores Drive, La Jolla, CA 92037-1508, USA; tel. (858) 546-7100; fax (858) 546-7133; e-mail info@iattc.org; internet www.iattc.org; f. 1950; administers two programmes, the Tuna-Billfish Programme and the Tuna-Dolphin Programme; the principal responsibilities of the Tuna-Billfish Programme are to study the biology of the tunas and related species of the eastern Pacific Ocean to estimate the effects of fishing and natural factors on their abundance; to recommend appropriate conservation measures in order to maintain stocks at levels which will afford maximum sustainable catches; and to collect information on compliance with Commission resolutions; the principal functions of the Tuna-Dolphin Programme are to monitor the abundance of dolphins and their mortality incidental to purse-seine fishing in the eastern Pacific Ocean; to study the causes of mortality of dolphins during fishing operations and to promote the use of fishing techniques and equipment that minimize these mortalities; to study the effects of different fishing methods on the various fish and other animals of the pelagic ecosystem; and to provide a secretariat for the International Dolphin Conservation Programme; mems: Belize, Canada, People's Republic of China, Colombia, Costa Rica, Ecuador, El Salvador, European Union, France, Guatemala, Japan, Kiribati, Republic of Korea, Mexico, Nicaragua, Panama, Peru, Chinese Taipei (Taiwan), USA, Vanuatu, Venezuela; co-operating non-contracting parties: Bolivia, Cook Islands; Dir GUILLERMO A. COMPEÁN; publs *Bulletin* (irregular), *Annual Report*, *Fishery Status Report*, *Stock Assessment Report* (annually), *Special Report* (irregular).

International Association for Cereal Science and Technology (ICC): Marxergasse 2, 1030 Vienna, Austria; tel. (1) 707-72-020; fax (1) 707-72-040; e-mail office@icc.or.at; internet www.icc.or.at; f. 1955 (as the International Association for Cereal Chemistry, name changed 1986); aims to promote international co-operation in the field of cereal science and technology through the dissemination of information and the devt of standard methods of testing and analysing products; mems: 31 mem. and 6 observer mem. states; Pres. Dr JOEL ABECASSIS (France) (2013–14); Pres. Elect FENGCHENG WANG (China) (2014–15); Sec.-Gen. and CEO Dr ROLAND POMS (Austria).

International Association for Vegetation Science (IAVS): c/o Michael T. Lee, IAVS Administration, University of North Carolina, CB 3280, Chapel Hill 27599-3280, USA; e-mail admin@iavs.org; internet www.iavs.org; f. 1938; mems: 1,500 in 70 countries; Pres. MARTIN DIEKMANN (Germany); Sec. SUSAN WISER (New Zealand); publs *Journal of Vegetation Science*, *Applied Vegetation Science*.

International Association of Agricultural Economists (IAAE): 555 East Wells St, Suite 1100, Milwaukee, WI 53202, USA; tel. (414) 918-3199; fax (414) 276-3349; e-mail iaae@execinc.com; internet www.iaae-agecon.org; f. 1929 to foster devt of agricultural economic sciences; aims to further the application of research into agricultural processes; works to improve economic and social conditions for agricultural and rural life; mems: in 83 countries; Pres. Prof. JOHAN SWINNEN (Belgium); Sec. and Treas. WALTER J. ARMBRUSTER (USA); publs *Agricultural Economics* (8 a year), *IAAE Newsletter* (2 a year).

International Association of Agricultural Information Specialists: c/o Toni Greider, POB 63, Lexington, KY 40588-0063, USA; fax (859) 257-8379; e-mail info@iaald.org; internet www.iaald.org; f. 1955 to provide educational and networking opportunities for agricultural information professionals worldwide; aims to enable its mems to create, capture, access and disseminate information to achieve a more productive and sustainable use of the world's land, water, and renewable natural resources and to contribute to improved livelihoods of rural communities through educational programmes, confs, and networking opportunities; affiliated to INFITA; mems: 400 in 84 countries; Pres. FREDERICO SANCHO (Costa Rica); Sec.-Treas. TONI GREIDER (USA); publ. *Agricultural Information Worldwide*.

International Association of Horticultural Producers: Horticulture House, 19 High St, Theale, Reading, RG7 5AH, United Kingdom; tel. (118) 930-8956; e-mail sg@aiph.org; internet www.aiph.org; f. 1948; represents the common interests of commercial horticultural producers in the international field; authorizes international horticultural exhibitions; mems: nat. asscns in 19 countries; Pres. VIC KRAHN; Sec.-Gen. TIM BRIERCLIFFE (United Kingdom); publ. *Statistical Yearbook*.

International Bee Research Association (IBRA): Unit 6 Centre Court, Main Ave, Treforest, Rhondda Cynon Taff, CF37 5YR, United Kingdom; tel. (29) 2037-2409; fax (56) 0113-5640; e-mail mail@ibra.org.uk; internet www.ibra.org.uk; f. 1949 to further bee research and provide an information service for bee scientists and beekeepers worldwide; mems: 1,200 in 130 countries; Pres. Prof. OCTAAF VAN LAERE (Belgium); Sec. DAVID SMITH (United Kingdom); publs *Apicultural Abstracts* (quarterly), *Journal of Apicultural Research* (quarterly), *Bee World* (quarterly).

International Centre for Agricultural Research in the Dry Areas (ICARDA): POB 114, 5055 Beirut, Lebanon; tel. (1) 843472; fax (1) 804071; e-mail icarda@cgiar.org; internet www.icarda.org; f. 1977; aims to improve the production of lentils, barley and fava beans throughout the developing world; supports the improvement of on-farm water use efficiency, rangeland and small ruminant production in all dry-area developing countries; within the West and Central Asia and North Africa region promotes the improvement of bread and durum wheat and chickpea production and of farming systems; undertakes research, training and dissemination of information, in co-operation with national, regional and international research institutes, univs and ministries of agriculture, in order to enhance production, alleviate poverty and promote sustainable natural resource management practices; mem. of the network of 15 agricultural research centres supported by the Consultative Group on International Agricultural Research; Dir-Gen. Dr MAHMOUD MOHAMED BASHIR EL-SOLH; publs *Annual Report*, *Caravan Newsletter* (2 a year).

International Centre for Tropical Agriculture (Centro Internacional de Agricultura Tropical—CIAT): Apdo Aéreo 6713, Cali, Colombia; tel. (2) 445-0000; fax (2) 445-0073; e-mail ciat@cgiar.org; internet www.ciat.cgiar.org; f. 1967 to contribute to the alleviation of hunger and poverty in tropical developing countries by using new techniques in agriculture research and training; focuses on production problems in field beans, cassava, rice and tropical pastures in the tropics; Dir-Gen. RUBEN G. ECHEVERRÍA; publs *Annual Report*, *Growing Affinities* (2 a year), *Pasturas Tropicales* (3 a year), catalogue of publications.

International Commission for the Conservation of Atlantic Tunas (ICCAT): Calle Corazón de María 8, 28002 Madrid, Spain; tel. (91) 4165600; fax (91) 4152612; e-mail info@iccat.es; internet www.iccat.int; f. 1969 under the provisions of the International Convention for the Conservation of Atlantic Tunas (1966) to maintain the populations of tuna and tuna-like species in the Atlantic Ocean and adjacent seas at levels that permit the maximum sustainable catch; collects statistics; conducts studies; mems: 48 contracting parties; Chair. M. MIYAHARA (Japan); Exec. Sec. DRISS MESKI (Morocco); publs *ICCAT Biennial Report*, *ICCAT Collective Vol. of Scientific Papers*, *Statistical Bulletin* (annually), *Data Record* (annually).

International Committee for Animal Recording (ICAR): Via Tomassetti 3-1/A, 00161, Rome, Italy; tel. (06) 44202639; fax (06) 44266798; e-mail icar@icar.org; internet www.icar.org; f. 1951 to extend and improve the work of recording and to standardize methods; mems: 72 full mems, 35 assoc. mems; Pres. UFFE LAURITSEN (Denmark); Sec. MARCO WINTERS (United Kingdom).

International Crops Research Institute for the Semi-Arid Tropics (ICRISAT): Patancheru, Andhra Pradesh 502 324, India; tel. (40) 30713071; fax (40) 30713074; e-mail icrisat@cgiar.org; internet www.icrisat.org; f. 1972 to promote the genetic improvement of crops and for research on the management of resources in the world's semi-arid tropics, with the aim of reducing poverty and protecting the environment; research covers all physical and socio-economic aspects of improving farming systems on unirrigated land; maintains regional centres in Nairobi, Kenya (for Eastern and Southern Africa) and in Niamey, Niger (for Western and Central Africa); Dir-Gen. Dr WILLIAM D. DAR (Philippines); publs *ICRISAT Report* (annually), *Journal of Semi-Arid Tropical Agricultural Research* (2 a year), information and research bulletins.

International Dairy Federation (IDF): 70B blvd Auguste Reyers, 1030 Brussels, Belgium; tel. (2) 325-67-40; fax (2) 325-67-41; e-mail info@fil-idf.org; internet www.fil-idf.org; f. 1903 to link all dairy asscns, in order to encourage the solution of scientific, technical and economic problems affecting the dairy industry; holds annual World Dairy Summit (2013: Yokohama, Japan, in Oct.); mems: nat. cttees in 53 countries; Pres. JEREMY HILL; Dir-Gen. Dr NICO VAN BELZEN; publs *Bulletin of IDF*, *IDF-ISO Standard Methods of Analysis*.

International Federation of Beekeepers' Associations (APIMONDIA): Corso Vittorio Emanuele II 101, 00186 Rome, Italy; tel. (06) 6852286; fax (06) 6852287; e-mail apimondia@mclink.it; internet www.apimondia.com; f. 1949; collects and brings up to date documentation on international beekeeping; carries out studies into the particular problems of beekeeping; organizes international congresses, seminars, symposia and meetings; co-operates with other int. orgs interested in beekeeping, in particular, with FAO; mems: 112 asscns from 75 countries; Pres. GILLES RATIA (France); Sec.-Gen. RICCARDO JANNONI-SEBASTIANINI (Italy); publs *Dictionary of Beekeeping Terms*, *AGROVOC* (thesaurus of agricultural terms), studies.

International Food Policy Research Institute (IFPRI): 2033 K St, NW, Washington, DC 20006, USA; tel. (202) 862-5600; fax (202) 467-4439; e-mail ifpri@cgiar.org; internet www.ifpri.org; f. 1975; co-operates with academic and other institutions in further research; develops policies for cutting hunger and malnutrition; committed to increasing public awareness of food policies; participates in the Agricultural Market Information System (f. 2011); calculates an annual Global Hunger Index, measuring global, regional and national rates of hunger; Dir-Gen. SHENGGEN FAN (People's Republic of China).

International Hop Growers' Convention: Malgajeva 18, 3000 Celje, Slovenia; tel. (3) 712-16-00; fax (3) 712-16-20; e-mail martin.pavlovic@guest.arnes.si; internet www.ihgc.org; f. 1950; acts as a centre for the collection of national reports and global data on hop production and information management on the hop industry among mem. countries, estimates the world crop and promotes scientific research; mems: nat. hop producers' asscns and hop trading cos in 19 countries worldwide; Sec.-Gen. Dr MARTIN PAVLOVIČ.

International Institute for Beet Research (IIRB): 40 rue Washington, 1050 Brussels, Belgium; Holtenser Landstr. 77, 37079 Göttingen, Germany; tel. (551) 500-65-84; fax (551) 500-65-85; e-mail mail@iirb.org; internet www.iirb.org; f. 1932 to promote research and the exchange of information; organizes congresses and study group meetings; mems: 400 in 27 countries; Sec.-Gen. Dr STEPHANIE KLUTH (Germany).

International Institute of Tropical Agriculture (IITA): Oyo Rd, PMB 5320, Ibadan, Oyo State, Nigeria; tel. (2) 7517472; fax (2) 2412221; e-mail iita@cgiar.org; internet www.iita.org; f. 1967; principal financing arranged by the Consultative Group on International Agricultural Research and several non-governmental orgs for special projects; research programmes comprise crop management, improvement of crops and plant protection and health; conducts a training programme for researchers in tropical agriculture; maintains a virtual library and an image database; administers Research Stations, Research Sites, and Regional Administrative Hubs in 41 African countries; Dir-Gen. Dr NTERANYA SANGINGA (Democratic Republic of the Congo); publs *Annual Report*, *R4D Review*, *MTP Fact Sheets*, *BOT Newsletter* (quarterly), technical bulletins, research reports.

International Livestock Research Institute (ILRI): POB 30709, Nairobi 00100, Kenya; tel. (20) 4223000; fax (20) 4223001; e-mail ilri-kenya@cgiar.org; internet www.ilri.org; f. 1995 to supersede the International Laboratory for Research on Animal Diseases and the International Livestock Centre for Africa; conducts laboratory and field research on animal health and other livestock issues, focusing on the following global livestock devt challenges: developing vaccine and diagnostic technologies; conservation and reproductive technologies; adaptation to and mitigation of climate change; addressing emerging diseases; broadening market access for the poor; sustainable intensification of smallholder crop-livestock systems; reducing the vulnerability of marginal systems and communities; carries out training programmes for scientists and technicians; maintains a specialized science library; Dir-Gen. JIMMY SMITH (Guyana); publs *Annual Report*, *Livestock Research for Development* (newsletter, 2 a year).

International Maize and Wheat Improvement Centre (CIMMYT): Apdo Postal 6-641, 06600 México, DF, Mexico; tel. (55) 5804-2004; fax (55) 5804-7558; e-mail cimmyt@cgiar.org; internet www.cimmyt.org; conducts worldwide research programme for sustainable maize and wheat cropping systems to help the poor in developing countries; Dir-Gen. Dr THOMAS A. LUMPKIN (USA).

International Organization for Biological Control of Noxious Animals and Plants: c/o Dr Russell Messing, University of Hawaii, USA; e-mail messing@hawaii.edu; internet www.iobc-global.org; f. 1955 to promote and co-ordinate research on the more effective biological control of harmful organisms; reorganized in 1971 as a central council with worldwide affiliations and six largely autonomous regional sections; Pres. Dr BARBARA BARRATT (New Zealand); Gen. Sec. Dr RUSSELL MESSING (USA); publs *BioControl*, *Newsletter*.

International Organization of Citrus Virologists: c/o Dept of Plant Pathology, University of California, Riverside, CA 92521-0122, USA; tel. (909) 684-0934; fax (909) 684-4324; e-mail iocvsecretary@gmail.com; internet www.ivia.es/iocv/; f. 1957 to promote research on citrus virus diseases at international level by standardizing diagnostic techniques and exchanging information; mems: 250; Chair. MARK HILF; Sec. GIORGIOS VIDALAKIS.

International Red Locust Control Organization for Central and Southern Africa (IRLCO-CSA): POB 240252, Ndola, Zambia; tel. (2) 651251; fax (2) 650117; e-mail locust@zamnet.zm; f. 1971 to control locusts in Eastern, Central and Southern Africa; also assists in the control of African army-worm and quelea-quelea; mems: 6 countries; Dir MOSES M. OKHOBA; publs *Annual Report*, *Quarterly Report*, *Monthly Report*, scientific reports.

International Rice Research Institute (IRRI): Los Baños, Laguna, DAPO Box 7777, Metro Manila 1301, Philippines; tel. (2) 5805600; fax (2) 5805699; e-mail nfo@irri.org; internet www.irri.org; f. 1960; conducts research on rice, with the aim of developing technologies of environmental, social and economic benefit; works to enhance national rice research systems and offers training; operates Riceworld, a museum and learning centre about rice; maintains a library of technical rice literature; organizes international confs and workshops (third International Rice Congress held in Hanoi, Viet Nam, in Nov. 2010; sixth International Hybrid Rice Symposium: Sept. 2012, Hyderabad, India; seventh Rice Genetics Symposium: Nov. 2013, Philippines); Dir-Gen. Dr ROBERT S. ZEIGLER; publs *Rice Literature Update*, *Rice Today* (quarterly), *Hotline*, *Facts about IRRI*, *News about Rice and People*, *International Rice Research Notes*.

International Seed Testing Association (ISTA): Zürichstr. 50, 8303 Bassersdorf, Switzerland; tel. 448386000; fax 448386001; e-mail ista.office@ista.ch; internet www.seedtest.org; f. 1924 to promote uniformity and accurate methods of seed testing and evaluation in order to facilitate efficiency in production, processing, distribution and utilization of seeds; organizes meetings, workshops, symposia, training courses and triennial congresses; mems: 76 countries; Pres. JOËL LÉCHAPPÉ (France); Sec.-Gen. BENI KAUFMAN; publs *Seed Science and Technology* (3 a year), *Seed Testing International (ISTA News Bulletin)* (2 a year), *International Rules for Seed Testing* (annually).

International Sericultural Commission (ISC): 26 rue Bellecordière, 69002 Lyon, France; tel. 4-78-50-41-98; fax 4-78-86-09-57; e-mail info@inserco.org; internet www.inserco.org; f. 1948 to encourage the devt of silk production; mems: 13 states; Sec.-Gen. ISHITA ROY (India); publ. *Sericologia* (quarterly).

International Union for the Protection of New Varieties of Plant (Union internationale pour la protection des obtentions végétales—UPOV): 34 chemin des Colombettes, 1211 Geneva 20, Switzerland; tel. 223389111; fax 227330336; e-mail upov.mail@upov.int; internet www.upov.int; f. 1961 by the International Convention for the Protection of New Varieties of Plants (entered into force 1968, revised in 1972, 1978 and 1991); aims to encourage the devt of new plant varieties and provide an effective system of intellectual property protection for plant breeders; mems: 70 states; Pres. of the Council KITISRI SUKHAPINDI; Sec.-Gen. FRANCIS GURRY.

International Union of Forest Research Organizations (IUFRO): Marxergasse 2, 1030 Vienna, Austria; tel. (1) 877-01-51-0; fax (1) 877-01-51-50; e-mail office@iufro.org; internet www.iufro.org; f. 1892; aims to promote global co-operation in forest-related research and enhance the understanding of the ecological, economic and social aspects of forests and trees; disseminates scientific knowledge to stakeholders and decision-makers and aims to contribute to forest policy and on-the-ground forest management; mems: over 600 orgs in more than 100 countries, involving some 15,000 scientists; Pres. NIELS ELERS KOCH (Denmark); Exec. Dir Dr ALEXANDER BUCK (Austria); publs *Annual Report*, *IUFRO News* (10 a year, electronic format only), *IUFRO World Series*, *IUFRO Occasional Paper Series*, *IUFRO Research Series*.

International Whaling Commission (IWC): The Red House, 135 Station Rd, Impington, Cambridge, CB24 9NP, United Kingdom; tel. (1223) 233971; fax (1223) 232876; e-mail secretariat@iwcoffice.com; internet www.iwcoffice.org; f. 1946 under the International Convention for the Regulation of Whaling, for the conservation of world whale stocks; reviews the regulations covering whaling operations; encourages research; collects, analyses and disseminates statistical and other information on whaling. A ban on commercial whaling was passed by the Commission in July 1982, to take effect three years subsequently (in some cases, a phased reduction of commercial operations was not completed until 1988). A revised whale management procedure was adopted in 1994, to be implemented after the devt of a complete whale management scheme; mems: 89 countries; Sec. Dr SIMON BROCKINGTON; publs *Annual Report*, *Journal of Cetacean Research and Management*.

North Atlantic Salmon Conservation Organization (NASCO): 11 Rutland Sq., Edinburgh, EH1 2AS, United Kingdom; tel. (131) 228-2551; fax (131) 228-4384; e-mail hq@nasco.int; internet www.nasco.int; f. 1984; aims to conserve, restore and enhance Atlantic salmon through international co-operation; Chair. RAOUL BIERACH (Norway); Pres. MARY COLLIGAN (USA).

North Pacific Anadromous Fish Commission: 889 W. Pender St, Suite 502, Vancouver, BC V6C 3B2, Canada; tel. (604) 775-5550; fax (604) 775-5577; e-mail secretariat@npafc.org; internet www.npafc.org; f. 1993; aims to promote the conservation of anadromous stocks in the waters of the North Pacific Ocean and its adjacent seas; mems: Canada, Japan, Republic of Korea, Russia, USA; Pres. VLADIMIR

BELYAEV (Russia); Exec. Dir VLADIMIR RADCHENKO (Russia); publs *Annual Report*, *Newsletter* (2 a year), *Statistical Yearbook*, *Scientific Bulletin*, *Technical Report*.

Northwest Atlantic Fisheries Organization (NAFO): 2 Morris Drive, POB 638, Dartmouth, NS B2Y 3Y9, Canada; tel. (902) 468-5590; fax (902) 468-5538; e-mail info@nafo.int; internet www.nafo.int; f. 1979 (fmrly International Commission for the Northwest Atlantic Fisheries); aims at optimum use, management and conservation of resources; an amended Convention was adopted in 2007, and is being ratified by each Contracting Party; promotes research and compiles statistics in the Northwest Atlantic Ocean; Pres. VERONIKA VEITS; Exec. Sec. FRED KINGSTON; publs *Annual Report*, *Statistical Bulletin* (electronic format only), *Journal of Northwest Atlantic Fishery Science* (in electronic and print formats), *Scientific Council Reports*, *Scientific Council Studies*, *Meeting Proceedings*.

Western and Central Pacific Fisheries Commission: Kaselehie St, POB 2356, Kolonia, Pohnpei State 96941, Federated States of Micronesia; tel. 3201992; fax 3201108; e-mail wcpfc@wcpfc.int; internet www.wcpfc.int; f. 2004 under the Convention for the Conservation and Management of Highly Migratory Fish Stocks in the Western and Central Pacific, which entered into force in June of that year, six months after the deposit of the 13th ratification; inaugural session convened in Dec., in Pohnpei, Federated States of Micronesia; mems: 31 countries and the European Community; Exec. Dir Prof. GLENN HURRY; publs *Secretariat Quarterly Report*, *Newsletter*.

World Association for Animal Production (WAAP): Via Tomassetti 3A/1, 00161 Rome, Italy; tel. (06) 44202639; fax (06) 44266798; e-mail waap@waap.it; internet www.waap.it; f. 1965; holds world conf. on animal production every five years (11th World Conf.: Beijing, People's Republic of China, Oct. 2013); encourages, sponsors and participates in regional meetings, seminars and symposia; mems: 17 orgs; Pres. JAMES SARTIN (USA); Sec.-Gen. ANDREA ROSATI (Italy); publ. *WAAP Newsletter*.

WorldFish (International Centre for Living Aquatic Resources Management—ICLARM): Jalan Batu Maung, Batu Maung, 11960 Bayan Lepas, Penang, Malaysia; POB 500, GPO, 10670 Penang; tel. (4) 626-1606; fax (4) 626-5530; e-mail worldfishcenter@cgiar.org; internet www.worldfishcenter.org; f. 1973; became a mem. of the Consultative Group on International Agricultural Research (CGIAR) in 1992; aims to contribute to food security and poverty eradication in developing countries through the sustainable devt and use of living aquatic resources; carries out research and promotes partnerships; Dir-Gen. Dr STEPHEN J. HALL.

World Organisation of Animal Health: 12 rue de Prony, 75017 Paris, France; tel. 1-44-15-18-88; fax 1-42-67-09-87; e-mail oie@oie.int; internet www.oie.int; f. 1924 as Office International des Epizooties (OIE); objectives include promoting international transparency of animal diseases; collecting, analysing and disseminating scientific veterinary information; providing expertise and promoting international co-operation in the control of animal diseases; promoting veterinary services; providing new scientific guidelines on animal production, food safety and animal welfare; launched in May 2005, jointly with FAO and WHO, a Global Strategy for the Progressive Control of Highly Pathogenic Avian Influenza (H5N1), and, in partnership with other orgs, has convened confs on avian influenza; experts in a network of 156 collaborating centres and reference laboratories; mems: 178 countries; Dir-Gen. Dr BERNARD VALLAT (France); publs *Disease Information* (weekly), *World Animal Health* (annually), *Scientific and Technical Review* (3 a year), other manuals, codes, etc.

World Ploughing Organization (WPO): Fallaghmore, Athy, Co. Kildare, Ireland; tel. (59) 8625125; fax (59) 8625172; e-mail annamarie@npa.ie; internet www.worldploughing.org; f. 1952 to promote the World Ploughing Contest in a different country each year, to improve techniques and promote better understanding of soil cultivation practices through research and practical demonstrations; arranges tillage clinics worldwide; mems: affiliates in 33 countries; Gen. Sec. ANNA MARIE MCHUGH; publ. *WPO Handbook* (annually).

World Veterinary Association: ave de Tervueren, 1040 Brussels, Belgium; tel. (2) 533-70-20; fax (2) 537-28-28; e-mail secretariat@worldvet.org; internet www.worldvet.org; f. 1959 as a continuation of the International Veterinary Congresses (f. 1863); organizes congress every two years (2013: Prague, Czech Republic); mems: orgs in more than 80 countries, 15 orgs of veterinary specialists as assoc. mems; Pres. Dr FAOUZI KECHRID (Tunisia); Exec. Sec. JAN VAARTEN; publ. *WVA Newsletter* (every 2 months).

World's Poultry Science Association (WPSA): c/o Dr Roel Mulder, POB 31, 7360 AA Beekbergen, Netherlands; tel. 651519584; fax (20) 750-8941; e-mail roel.mulder@wpsa.com; internet www.wpsa.com; f. 1912 (as the International Association of Poultry Instructors); aims to advance and exchange knowledge relating to poultry science and the poultry industry; organizes World Poultry Congress every four years (2016: Beijing, China, in Sept.); mems: 8,000 individuals in more than 100 countries, branches in 77 countries; Pres. EDIR DA SILVA (Brazil); Sec. Dr ROEL MULDER (Netherlands); publ. *The World's Poultry Science Journal* (quarterly).

Arts and Culture

Culture Action Europe: 23 rue Ravenstein, 1000 Brussels, Belgium; tel. (2) 534-40-02; fax (2) 534-11-50; e-mail advocate@cultureactioneurope.org; internet www.cultureactioneurope.org; f. 1992 to unite artists, poets, scientists, philosophers and others through mutual interests and friendship in order to safeguard and improve the conditions required for creative activity; mems: 110 cultural orgs in 24 countries; Pres. MERCEDES GIOVINAZZO (Italy); Gen. Sec. LUCA BERGAMO.

Europa Nostra—Pan-European Federation for Cultural Heritage: Lange Voorhout 35, 2514 EC The Hague, Netherlands; tel. (70) 3024050; fax (70) 3617865; e-mail info@europanostra.org; internet www.europanostra.org; f. 1963; groups, orgs and individuals concerned with the protection and enhancement of the European architectural and natural heritage and of the European environment; has consultative status with the Council of Europe; mems: some 250 mem. orgs, around 170 supporting bodies, more than 1,200 individual mems; Exec. Pres. DENIS DE KERGORLAY (Spain); Sec.-Gen. SNESKA QUAEDVLIEG-MIHAILOVIĆ.

European Association of Conservatoires, Music Academies and Music High Schools: Ave des Celtes, Keltenlaan 20, 1040 Brussels, Belgium; tel. (2) 737-16-70; fax (2) 737-16-79; e-mail info@aec-music.eu; internet www.aec-music.eu; f. 1953; aims to establish and foster contacts and exchanges between and represent the interests of mems; initiates and supports international collaboration through research projects, congresses and seminars; mems: 294 institutions in 55 countries; Pres. PASCALE DE GROOTE; publs e-mail newsletters (2–3 a year), project newsletters (3 a year), conf. proceedings, research findings, various other publs and websites.

European Cultural Foundation: Jan van Goyenkade 5, 1075 HN Amsterdam, Netherlands; tel. (20) 5733868; fax (20) 6752231; e-mail eurocult@eurocult.org; internet www.culturalfoundation.eu; f. 1954 as a non-governmental organization, supported by private sources, to promote cultural co-operation in Europe; supports closer ties among European communities through joint artistic and cultural exploration; promotes good cultural policy-making that improves peoples' quality of life across Europe and its neighbouring regions; Chair. GÖRGÜN TANER; Dir KATHERINE WATSON; publs *Annual Report*, electronic newsletter (7 a year).

International Association of Art Critics: 32 rue Yves Toudic, 75010 Paris, France; tel. 1-47-70-17-42; e-mail aica.office@gmail.com; internet www.aica-int.org; f. 1949 to increase co-operation in plastic arts, promote international cultural exchanges and protect the interests of mems; mems: 4,600 in 70 countries; Pres. MAREK BARTELIK (USA); Gen. Sec. BRANE KOVIC (Slovenia); publs *Annuaire*, *Newsletter* (quarterly).

International Association of Bibliophiles: Réserve des livres rares, Quai François Mauriac, 75706 Cedex 13, France; tel. 1-53-79-54-52; fax 1-53-79-54-60; f. 1963 to create contacts between bibliophiles and encourage book-collecting in different countries; organizes and encourages congresses, meetings, exhibitions and the award of scholarships; mems: 450; Sec.-Gen. JEAN-MARC CHATELAIN (France); publs *Le Bulletin du Bibliophile* (2 a year), yearbooks.

International Association of Film and Television Schools (Centre international de liaison des écoles de cinéma et de television—CILECT): c/o Stanislav Semerdjiev, 1000 Sofia, ul. Rakosky 108A, Bulgaria; tel. (88) 7-64-63-70 (mobile); fax (2) 989-73-89; e-mail executive.director@cilect.org; internet www.cilect.org; f. 1955 to link higher teaching and research institutes and improve education of makers of films and television programmes; organizes confs and student film festivals; runs a training programme for developing countries; mems: 122 institutions in 56 countries; Pres. Dr MARIA DORA MOURÃO (Brazil); Exec. Dir Dr STANISLAV SEMERDJIEV (Bulgaria); publ. *Newsletter*.

International Board on Books for Young People (IBBY): Nonnenweg 12, Postfach, 4003 Basel, Switzerland; tel. 612722917; fax 612722757; e-mail ibby@ibby.org; internet www.ibby.org; f. 1953 to support and link bodies in all countries connected with the book work of young people; encourages the distribution of good children's and youth literature; promotes scientific investigation into problems of juvenile books; presents the Hans Christian Andersen Award every two years to a living author and a living illustrator whose work is an outstanding contribution to juvenile literature; presents the IBBY-Asahi Reading Promotion Award (every two years) to an org. that has made a significant contribution towards the encouragement of reading; sponsors International Children's Book Day (2 April); mems: nat. sections and individuals in more than 77 countries; Pres. AHMAD REDZA AHMAD KHAIRUDDIN (Malaysia); Exec. Dir LIZ PAGE

(Switzerland); publs *Bookbird* (quarterly, in English), *Congress Papers*, *IBBY Honour List* (every 2 years), special bibliographies.

International Centre for the Study of the Preservation and Restoration of Cultural Property (ICCROM): Via di San Michele 13, 00153 Rome, Italy; tel. (06) 585531; fax (06) 58553349; e-mail iccrom@iccrom.org; internet www.iccrom.org; f. 1959; assembles documents on the preservation and restoration of cultural property; stimulates research and proffers advice; organizes missions of experts; undertakes training of specialists; mems: 133 countries; Dir-Gen. STEFANO DE CARO (Italy); publ. *Newsletter* (annually, in English and French).

International Centre of Films for Children and Young People (Centre international du film pour l'enfance et la jeunesse—CIFEJ): CIFEJ, End of Seif St, phase 3, Shahrak-e Gharb, Tehran 1466893311, Iran; tel. (21) 88087870; fax (21) 88085847; e-mail info@cifej.com; internet www.cifej.com; f. 1955; serves as a clearing house for information about films for children and young people, the influence of films on the young, and the regulations in force for the protection and education of young people; promotes production and distribution of suitable films and their appreciation; awards the CIFEJ prize at selected film festivals; mems: 81 mems in 50 countries; Pres. FIRDOZE BULBULIA; Exec. Dir ELHAM SHIRVANI; publ. *CIFEJ Info* (every 3 months).

International Comparative Literature Association (ICLA) (Association Internationale de Littérature Comparée): Brigham Young University, 3168 JFSB, Provo, UT 84602, USA; tel. (801) 422-5598; e-mail ailc.icla@gmail.com; internet www.ailc-icla.org/site/; f. 1954 to work for the devt of the comparative study of literature in modern languages; mems: 35. asscns; Pres. HANS BERTENS (Netherlands).

International Confederation of Societies of Authors and Composers—World Copyright Summit: 20–26 blvd du Parc, 92200 Neuilly-sur-Seine, France; tel. 1-55-62-08-50; fax 1-55-62-08-60; e-mail cisac@cisac.org; internet www.cisac.org; f. 1926 to protect the rights of authors and composers; organizes biennial World Creators Summit; mems: 231 mem. socs from 121 countries; Pres. JEAN MICHEL JARRE (France); Dir-Gen. OLIVIER HINNEWINKEL.

International Council of Museums (ICOM): Maison de l'UNESCO, 1 rue Miollis, 75732 Paris Cedex 15, France; tel. 1-47-34-05-00; fax 1-43-06-78-62; e-mail secretariat@icom.museum; internet icom.museum; f. 1946; committed to the conservation and communication to society of the world's natural and cultural heritage; achieves its major objectives through its 30 international cttees, each devoted to the study of a particular type of museum or to a specific museum-related discipline; maintains with UNESCO the organization's documentation centre; mems: 26,000 individuals and institutions in 140 countries; Pres. HANS-MARTIN HINZ (Germany); Dir-Gen. Dr ANNE-CATHERINE ROBERT-HAUGLUSTAINE (from 1 May 2014); publ. *ICOM News—Nouvelles de l'ICOM—Noticias del ICOM* (quarterly).

International Committee of Museums and Collections of Arms and Military History (ICOMAM): Parc du Cinquantenaire 3, 1000 Brussels, Belgium; tel. (2) 737-79-00; e-mail secretary@icomam.icom.museum; internet www.icomam.icom.museum; f. 1957 as International Association of Museums of Arms and Military History (IAMAM); present name assumed in 2003; links museums and other scientific institutions with public collections of arms and armour and military equipment, uniforms, etc; holds annual confs and occasional specialist symposia; mems: over 250 institutions in more than 50 countries; Chair. EVA-SOFI ERNSTELL (Sweden); Sec.-Gen. MATHIEU WILLEMSEN (Netherlands); publ. *The Magazine* (online).

International Council on Monuments and Sites (ICOMOS): 49–51 rue de la Fédération, 75015 Paris, France; tel. 1-45-67-67-70; fax 1-45-66-06-22; e-mail secretariat@icomos.org; internet www.icomos.org; f. 1965 to promote the study and preservation of monuments and sites and to arouse and cultivate the interest of public authorities and people of every country in their cultural heritage; disseminates the results of research into the technical, social and administrative problems connected with the conservation of architectural heritage; holds triennial General Assembly and Symposium; mems: 24 int. cttees, 116 nat. cttees; Pres. GUSTAVO ARAOZ (USA); Sec.-Gen. KIRSTI KOVANEN (Finland); publs *ICOMOS Newsletter* (quarterly), *Scientific Journal* (quarterly).

International Dance Council (Conseil International de la Danse): 1 rue Miollis 75732 Paris, France; tel. 1-45-68-49-53; fax 1-45-68-49-31; e-mail execsec@cid-portal.org; internet www.cid-portal.org; f. 1973; serves as an umbrella body for international, national and local orgs active in all forms of dance; Pres. Dr ALKIS RAFTIS (Greece); Gen. Sec. Dr FLORENCE OUALID (France).

International Federation for Theatre Research (IFTR) (Fédération Internationale pour la Recherche Théâtrale): c/o Jan Clarke, School of Modern Languages and Culture, University of Durham, Durham, DH1 3JT, United Kingdom; e-mail jan.clarke@durham.ac.uk; internet www.firt-iftr.org; f. 1955 by 21 countries at the International Conference on Theatre History, London; Pres. CHRISTOPHER BALME (Germany); Jt Secs-Gen. Prof. JAN CLARKE (United Kingdom), PAUL MURPHY (United Kingdom).

International Federation of Film Archives (Fédération Internationale des Archives du Film—FIAF): 1 rue Defacqz, 1000 Brussels, Belgium; tel. (2) 538-30-65; fax (2) 534-47-74; e-mail info@fiafnet.org; internet www.fiafnet.org; f. 1938 to encourage the creation of audio-visual archives for the collection and conservation of the moving image heritage of every country; facilitates co-operation and exchanges between film archives; promotes public interest in the art of the cinema; aids and conducts research; compiles new documentation; holds annual congress; mems: c. 150 archives in 77 countries; Pres. ERIC LE ROY (France); Sec.-Gen. MICHAEL LOEBENSTEIN (Australia); publs *Journal of Film Preservation* (2 a year), *FIAF International Film Archive Database* (2 a year).

International Federation of Film Producers' Associations (Fédération Internationale des associations de Producteurs de Films—FIAPF): 9 rue de l'Echelle, 75001 Paris, France; tel. 1-44-77-97-50; fax 1-42-56-16-55; e-mail info@fiapf.org; internet www.fiapf.org; f. 1933 to represent film production internationally, to defend its general interests and promote its devt; studies all cultural, legal, economic, technical and social problems related to film production; mems: 32 producers' orgs in 28 countries; Pres. LUIS ALBERTO SCALELLA.

International Institute for Children's Literature and Reading Research (Internationales Institut für Jugendliteratur und Leseforschung): Mayerhofgasse 6, 1040 Vienna, Austria; tel. (1) 505-03-59; fax (1) 505-03-5917; e-mail office@jugendliteratur.net; internet www.jugendliteratur.net; f. 1965 as an international documentation, research and advisory centre of juvenile literature and reading; maintains specialized library; arranges confs and exhibitions; compiles recommendation lists; mems: individual and group mems in 28 countries; Pres. Prof. RENATE WELSH; Dir KARIN HALLER; publ. *1000 & 1 Buch* (quarterly).

International Institute for Conservation of Historic and Artistic Works: 3 Birdcage Walk, Westminster, London, SW1H 9JJ, United Kingdom; tel. (20) 7799-5500; fax (20) 7799-4961; e-mail iic@iiconservation.org; internet www.iiconservation.org; f. 1950; mems: 2,400 individual, 400 institutional mems; Pres. SARAH STANIFORTH (United Kingdom); Sec.-Gen. JOSEPHINE KIRBY; publs *Studies in Conservation*, *News in Conservation* (every 2 months), *Congress Preprints* (every 2 years).

International Music Council (IMC): Maison de l'UNESCO, 1 rue Miollis, 75732 Paris Cedex 15, France; tel. 1-45-68-48-50; fax 1-45-68-48-66; e-mail info@imc-cim.org; internet www.imc-cim.org; f. 1949; mems: reg. music councils, int. music orgs, nat. and specialized orgs in some 150 countries; Pres. FRANS DE RUITER; Sec.-Gen. SILJA FISCHER.

Mems of IMC include:

European Festivals Association: Kasteel Borluut, Kleine Gentstraat 46, 9051 Ghent, Belgium; tel. (9) 241-80-82; fax (9) 241-80-89; e-mail info@efa-aef.eu; internet www.efa-aef.eu; f. 1952 to maintain high artistic standards and the representative character of art festivals; holds annual General Assembly; mems: more than 100 regular int. performing arts festivals in 38 countries; Pres. DARKO BRLEK; Sec.-Gen. KATHRIN DEVENTER; publ. *Festivals* (annually).

International Association of Music Libraries, Archives and Documentation Centres (IAML): c/o Music and Drama Library, Göteborg University Library, POB 201, SE 405 30 Göteborg, Sweden; tel. (31) 786-40-57; fax (31) 786-40-59; e-mail secretary@iaml.info; internet www.iaml.info; f. 1951; mems: 1,800 institutions and individuals in 51 countries; Pres. BARBARA DOBBS MACKENZIE (USA); Sec.-Gen. PIA SHEKHTER (Sweden); publ. *Fontes artis musicae* (quarterly).

International Council for Traditional Music (ICTM): Dept of Musicology, Faculty of Arts, University of Ljubljana, 1000 Ljubljana, Slovenia; tel. (2) 6125-1449; e-mail secretariat@ictmusic.org; internet www.ictmusic.org; f. 1947 (as International Folk Music Council) to further the study, practice, documentation, preservation and dissemination of traditional music of all countries; holds ICTM World Conference every two years (2013: Shanghai, People's Republic of China, in July); mems: 1,885; Pres. Dr ADRIENNE L. KAEPPLER (USA); Sec.-Gen. Dr SVANIBOR PETTAN (Slovenia); publs *Yearbook for Traditional Music*, *ICTM Bulletin* (2 a year).

International Federation of Musicians: 21 bis rue Victor Massé, 75009 Paris, France; tel. 1-45-26-31-23; fax 1-76 70-14-18; e-mail office@fim-musicians.com; internet www.fim-musicians.com/; f. 1948 to promote and protect the interests of musicians in affiliated unions; mems: 75 unions in 64 countries; Pres. JOHN F. SMITH (United Kingdom); Gen. Sec. BENOÎT MACHUEL (France).

International Music and Media Centre (Internationales Musik + Medienzentrum): Stiftgasse 29, 1070 Vienna, Austria; tel. (1) 889 03-15; fax (1) 889 03-1577; e-mail office@imz.at; internet www.imz.at;

f. 1961 for the study and dissemination of music through technical media (film, television, radio, gramophone); organizes congresses, seminars and screenings on music in audio-visual media; holds courses and competitions designed to strengthen the relationship between performing artists and audio-visual media; mems: 180 ordinary mems and 30 assoc. mems in 35 countries, including 50 broadcasting orgs; Pres. ARILD ERIKSTAD (Norway); Sec.-Gen. FRANZ A. PATAY (Austria).

International Society for Contemporary Music (ISCM): c/o Gaudeamus Muziekweek, Loevenhoutsedijk 301, 3552 XE Utrecht, Netherlands; tel. (20) 3446062; e-mail info@iscm.org; internet www.iscm.org; f. 1922 to promote the devt of contemporary music; organizes annual World Music Day; mems: orgs in 50 countries; Pres. PETER SWINNEN; Sec.-Gen. ARTHUR VAN DER DRIFT.

Jeunesses Musicales International (JMI): 1 rue Defacqz, 1000 Brussels, Belgium; tel. (2) 513-97-74; fax (2) 514-47-55; e-mail mail@jmi.net; internet www.jmi.net; f. 1945 to enable young people to develop, through music, and to stimulate contacts between mem. countries; mems: orgs in 45 countries; Pres. PER EKEDAHL; Sec.-Gen. BLASKO SMILEVSKI; publ. *JMI News* (6 a year).

World Federation of International Music Competitions (WFIMC): 104 rue de Carouge, 1205 Geneva, Switzerland; tel. 223213620; fax 227811418; e-mail fmcim@fmcim.org; internet www.wfimc.org; f. 1957 to co-ordinate the arrangements for affiliated competitions and to exchange experience; holds General Assembly annually; mems: 129 int. music competitions; Pres. GLEN KWOK (USA); Sec.-Gen. MARIANNE GRANVIG.

International PEN (World Association of Writers): Brownlow House, 50–51 High Holborn, London, WC1V 6ER, United Kingdom; tel. (20) 7405-0338; fax (20) 7405-0339; e-mail info@pen-international.org; internet www.pen-international.org; f. 1921 to promote co-operation between writers; mems: 144 centres in 102 countries; International Pres. JOHN RALSTON SAUL; Treas. ERIC LAX; publ. *PEN International* (2 a year, in English, French and Spanish, with the assistance of UNESCO).

International Theatre Institute (ITI): Maison de l'UNESCO, 1 rue Miollis, 75732 Paris Cedex 15, France; tel. 1-45-68-48-80; fax 1-45-66-50-40; e-mail info@iti-worldwide.org; internet iti-worldwide.org; f. 1948 to facilitate cultural exchanges and international understanding in the domain of the theatre and performing arts; promotes performing arts/theatre on a national and international level and facilitates international collaboration; mems: around 100 nat. centres and co-operating mems worldwide; Pres. RAMENDU MAJUMDAR (Bangladesh); Dir-Gen. TOBIAS BIANCONE (Switzerland); publs *ITI News* (3 times a year in English and French), *The World of Theatre* (every 2 years).

Nordic Cultural Fund (Nordisk Kulturfond): Ved Stranden 18, 1061 Copenhagen K, Denmark; tel. 3396-0200; fax 3332-5636; e-mail kulturfonden@norden.org; internet www.nordiskkulturfond.org; f. 1967; aims to support a broad spectrum of Nordic cultural co-operation activities; awards around 28m. Danish kroner annually towards cultural projects being implemented in the Nordic Region, and Nordic projects being undertaken outside the region; projects are designated by the Fund as 'Nordic' if a minimum of three Nordic countries (Denmark, Iceland, Finland, Norway and Sweden) or self-governing areas (Faroe Islands, Greenland, and the Åland Islands) are involved, either as participants, organizers, or as the project subject area; CEO KAREN BUE.

Organization of World Heritage Cities: 835 Ave Wilfrid-Laurier, Québec, QC G1R 2L3, Canada; tel. (418) 692-0000; fax (418) 692-5558; e-mail secretariat@ovpm.org; internet www.ovpm.org; f. 1993 to assist cities inscribed on the UNESCO World Heritage List to implement the Convention concerning the Protection of the World Cultural and Natural Heritage (1972); promotes co-operation between city authorities, in particular in the management and sustainable devt of historic sites; holds a World Congress every two years (2013: Oaxaca, Mexico, in Nov.); mems: 250 cities worldwide; Sec.-Gen. DENIS RICARD; publ. *OWHC Newsletter* (2 a year, in English, French and Spanish).

Pan-African Writers' Association (PAWA): PAWA House, Roman Ridge, POB C456, Cantonments, Accra, Ghana; tel. (21) 773062; fax (21) 773042; e-mail pawahouse@gmail.com; internet http://www.panafricanwritersassociation.org.gh; f. 1989 to link African creative writers, defend the rights of authors and promote awareness of literature; mems: 52 nat. writers' asscns on the continent; Sec.-Gen. ATUKWEI OKAI (Ghana).

Royal Asiatic Society of Great Britain and Ireland: 14 Stephenson Way, London, NW1 2HD, United Kingdom; tel. (20) 7388-4539; fax (20) 7391-9429; e-mail cl@royalasiaticsociety.org; internet www.royalasiaticsociety.org; f. 1823 for the study of history and cultures of the East; mems: c. 700, branch socs in Asia; Pres. Prof. PETER ROBB; Dir ALISON OHTA; publ. *Journal* (quarterly).

World Crafts Council International (WCC): 98A Dr. Radhakrishnan Salai, Chennai 600004, India; tel. (44) 28478500; fax (44) 28478509; e-mail wcc.sect.in@gmail.com; internet www.worldcraftscouncil.org; f. 1964; aims to strengthen the status of crafts as a vital part of cultural and economic life, to link craftspeople around the world, and to foster wider recognition of their work; mems: nat. orgs in more than 89 countries; Pres. USHA KRISHNA (India).

Commodities

Africa Rice Center (AfricaRice): 01 BP 2031, Cotonou, Benin; tel. 64-18-13-13; fax 64-22-78-09; e-mail AfricaRice@cgiar.org; internet www.africarice.org/; f. 1971 (as the West Africa Rice Development Association, present name adopted in 2009); participates in the network of agricultural research centres supported by the Consultative Group on International Agricultural Research; aims to contribute to food security and poverty eradication in poor rural and urban populations, through research, partnerships, capacity strengthening and policy support on rice-based systems; promotes sustainable agricultural devt based on environmentally sound management of natural resources; maintains research stations in Nigeria and Senegal; provides training and consulting services; from 2007 expanded scope of membership and activities from West African to pan-African; mems: 25 African countries; Dir-Gen. Dr ADAMA TRAORÉ (Mali) (acting); publs *Program Report* (annually), *Participatory Varietal Selection* (annually), *Rice Interspecific Hybridization Project Research Highlights* (annually), *Inland Valley Newsletter*, *ROCARIZ Newsletter*, training series, proceedings, leaflets.

African Petroleum Producers' Association (APPA): POB 1097, Brazzaville, Republic of the Congo; tel. 665-38-57; fax 669-99-13; e-mail appa@appa.int; internet appa.int; f. 1987 by African petroleum-producing countries to reinforce co-operation among regional producers and to stabilize prices; council of ministers responsible for the hydrocarbons sector meets twice a year; holds regular African Petroleum Congress and Exhibition (CAPE): fifth CAPE held in Libreville, Gabon, in March 2013; mems: Algeria, Angola, Benin, Cameroon, Democratic Republic of the Congo, Republic of the Congo, Côte d'Ivoire, Egypt, Equatorial Guinea, Gabon, Libya, Nigeria; Exec. Sec. GABRIEL DANSOU LOKOSSOU; publ. *APPA Bulletin* (2 a year).

Alliance of Cocoa Producing Countries (COPAL): National Assembly Complex, Tafawa Balewa Sq., POB 1718, Lagos, Nigeria; tel. (9) 8141735; fax (9) 8141734; e-mail info@copal-cpa.org; internet www.copal-cpa.org; f. 1962 to exchange technical and scientific information, to discuss problems of mutual concern to producers, to ensure adequate supplies at remunerative prices and to promote consumption; organizes a Research Conference (Oct. 2012: Yaoundé, Cameroon); mems: Brazil, Cameroon, Côte d'Ivoire, Dominican Republic, Gabon, Ghana, Malaysia, Nigeria, São Tomé and Príncipe, Togo; Sec.-Gen. NANGA COULIBALY.

Asian and Pacific Coconut Community (APCC): Lina Bldg, 3rd Floor, Jalan H. R. Rasuna Said Kav. B7, Kuningan, Jakarta 12920, Indonesia; POB 1343, Jakarta 10013; tel. (21) 5221712; fax (21) 5221714; e-mail apcc@indo.net.id; internet www.apccsec.org; f. 1969 to promote and co-ordinate all activities of the coconut industry, to achieve higher production and better processing, marketing and research; organizes annual Coconut Technical Meeting (COCOTECH); mems: Fiji, India, Indonesia, Kiribati, Malaysia, Marshall Islands, Federated States of Micronesia, Papua New Guinea, Philippines, Samoa, Solomon Islands, Sri Lanka, Thailand, Vanuatu, Viet Nam, all accounting for over 90% of global coconut production; Exec. Dir ROMULO N. ARANCON, Jr; publs *Cocomunity* (monthly), *CORD* (2 a year), *CocoInfo International* (2 a year), *Coconut Statistical Yearbook*, guidelines and other ad hoc publications.

Association of Natural Rubber Producing Countries (ANRPC): Bangunan Getah Asli, 148 Jalan Ampang, 7th Floor, 50450 Kuala Lumpur, Malaysia; tel. (3) 21611900; fax (3) 21613014; e-mail secretariat@anrpc.org; internet www.anrpc.org; f. 1970 to co-ordinate the production and marketing of natural rubber, to promote technical co-operation among mems and to bring about fair and stable prices for natural rubber; holds seminars, meetings and training courses on technical and statistical subjects; a joint regional marketing system has been agreed in principle; mems: Cambodia, People's Republic of China, India, Indonesia, Malaysia, Papua New Guinea, Philippines, Singapore, Sri Lanka, Thailand, Viet Nam; Sec.-Gen. Dr KAMARUL BAHARAIN BIN BASIR; publs *NR Trends & Statistics* (monthly), *Quarterly NR Market Review, Market and Industry Update*.

Common Fund for Commodities (CFC): POB 74656, 1070 BR, Amsterdam, Netherlands; tel. (20) 5754949; fax (20) 6760231; e-mail managing.director@common-fund.org; internet www.common-fund.org; f. 1989 as the result of an UNCTAD negotiation conf.; finances commodity devt measures including research, marketing, productivity improvements and vertical diversification, with the aim of increasing the long-term competitiveness of particular commodities; paid-in cap. US $181m.; mems: 105 countries and 10 institutional mems; Chair. SIRAJUDDIN HAMID YOUSIF (Sudan); Man. Dir a.i. PARVINDAR SINGH.

European Aluminium Association (EAA): 12 ave de Broqueville, 1150 Brussels, Belgium; tel. (2) 775-63-63; fax (2) 779-05-31; e-mail eaa@aluminium.org; internet www.alueurope.eu; f. 1981 to encourage studies, research and technical co-operation, to make representations to int. bodies and to assist nat. asscns in dealing with nat. authorities; mems: individual producers of primary aluminium, 18 nat. groups for wrought producers, the Organization of European Aluminium Smelters, representing producers of recycled aluminium, and the European Aluminium Foil Association, representing foil rollers and converters; Pres. ROELAND BAAN; publs *Annual Report*, *EAA Quarterly Report*.

European Committee of Sugar Manufacturers (CEFS): 182 ave de Tervuren, 1150 Brussels, Belgium; tel. (2) 762-07-60; fax (2) 771-00-26; e-mail cefs@cefs.org; internet www.cefs.org; f. 1954 to collect statistics and information, conduct research and promote co-operation between national orgs; mems: nat. asscns in 19 European countries and other assoc. mems worldwide; Pres. JOHANN MARIHART; Dir-Gen. MARIE-CHRISTINE RIBERA.

Gas Exporting Countries Forum: POB 23753, Tornado Tower, 47-48th Floors, West Bay, Doha, Qatar; tel. 44048400; fax 44048415; e-mail gecfsg@gmail.com; internet www.gecf.org; f. 2001 to represent and promote the mutual interests of gas exporting countries; aims to increase the level of co-ordination among mem. countries and to promote dialogue between gas producers and consumers; a ministerial meeting is convened annually; the seventh ministerial meeting, convened in Moscow, Russia, in Dec. 2008, agreed on a charter and a permanent structure for the grouping; first meeting of heads of state convened in Doha, in 2011; second summit meeting held in Moscow, in July 2013; mems: Algeria, Bolivia, Egypt, Equatorial Guinea, Iran, Libya, Nigeria, Oman, Qatar, Russia, Trinidad and Tobago, UAE, Venezuela; observers: Iraq, Kazakhstan, Netherlands, Norway; Sec.-Gen. LEONID BOKHANOVSKIY.

Inter-African Coffee Organization (IACO) (Organisation Inter-Africaine du Café—OIAC): BP V210, Abidjan, Côte d'Ivoire; tel. 20-21-61-31; fax 20-21-62-12; e-mail sg@iaco-oiac.org; f. 1960 to adopt a common policy on the marketing and consumption of coffee; aims to foster greater collaboration in research technology transfer through the African Coffee Research Network; seeks to improve the quality of coffee exports, and implement poverty reduction programmes focusing on value added products and the manufacturing of green coffee; mems: 25 coffee-producing countries in Africa; Sec.-Gen. FREDERICK S. M. KAWUMA (Uganda).

International Cadmium Association: 168 ave de Tervueren, 1150 Brussels, Belgium; tel. (2) 776-00-73; fax (2) 776-00-92; e-mail contact@cadmium.org; internet www.cadmium.org; f. 1976; covers all aspects of the production and use of cadmium and its compounds; includes almost all producers and users of cadmium; Gen. Man. CHRISTIAN CANOO (Belgium).

International Cocoa Organization (ICCO): Westgate House, Ealing, London, W5 1YY, United Kingdom; tel. (20) 8991-6000; fax (20) 8997-4372; e-mail info@icco.org; internet www.icco.org; f. 1973 under the first International Cocoa Agreement, 1972; the ICCO supervises the implementation of the agreements, and provides mem. govts with up-to-date information on the world cocoa economy; the seventh International Cocoa Agreement (2010) entered into force in Oct. 2012; mems: 15 exporting countries and 30 importing countries, plus the European Union; Exec. Dir Dr JEAN-MARC ANGA (Côte d'Ivoire); publs *Quarterly Bulletin of Cocoa Statistics*, *Annual Report*, *World Cocoa Directory*, studies on the world cocoa economy.

International Coffee Organization (ICO): 22 Berners St, London, W1T 3DD, United Kingdom; tel. (20) 7612-0600; fax (20) 7612-0630; e-mail info@ico.org; internet www.ico.org; f. 1963 under the International Coffee Agreement, 1962, which was renegotiated in 1968, 1976, 1983, 1994 (extended in 1999), 2001 and 2007; aims to improve international co-operation and provide a forum for intergovernmental consultations on coffee matters; to facilitate international trade in coffee by the collection, analysis and dissemination of statistics; to act as a centre for the collection, exchange and publication of coffee information; to promote studies in the field of coffee; and to encourage an increase in coffee consumption; mems: 38 exporting countries and 6 importing countries, plus the European Union; Chair. of Council JAWAID AKHTAR (India); Exec. Dir ROBÉRIO OLIVEIRA SILVA (Brazil).

International Cotton Advisory Committee (ICAC): 1629 K St, NW, Suite 702, Washington, DC 20006-1636, USA; tel. (202) 463-6660; fax (202) 463-6950; e-mail secretariat@icac.org; internet www.icac.org; f. 1939 to observe devts in world cotton; to collect and disseminate statistics; to suggest measures for the furtherance of international collaboration in maintaining and developing a sound world cotton economy; and to provide a forum for international discussions on cotton prices; mems: 41 countries; Exec. Dir JOSÉ SETTE (Brazil); publs *Cotton This Week!* (internet/e-mail only), *Cotton This Month*, *Cotton: Review of the World Situation* (every 2 months), *Cotton: World Statistics* (annually), *The ICAC Recorder*, *World Textile Demand* (annually), other surveys, studies, trade analyses and technical publications.

International Diamond Manufacturers Association (IDMA): 22 Hoveniersstraat, 2018, Antwerp, Belgium; tel. (3) 233-11-29; fax (3) 227-46-30; e-mail idma.net@gmail.com; internet www.idma.co; f. 1946; committed to fostering and promoting best practice principles throughout the diamond industry worldwide; works to encourage fair and honourable practices and decent working conditions for those employed in the diamond industry; Pres. MAXIM SHKADOV (Russia); Sec.-Gen. RONNIE VANDERLINDEN (USA).

International Energy Forum (IEF): POB 94736, Diplomatic Quarter, Riyadh 11614, Saudi Arabia; tel. (1) 4810022; fax (1) 4810055; e-mail info@ief.org; internet www.ief.org; f. 1991; the IEF is an intergovernmental arrangement aimed at promoting dialogue on global energy matters among its membership; ministers responsible for energy affairs from states accounting for about 90% of global oil and gas supply and demand convene every two years; the gathering in recent years has been preceded by a meeting of the International Business Energy Forum (IEBF), comprising energy ministers and CEOs of leading energy cos; 13th IEF and fifth IEBF: March 2012, Kuwait; mems: 89 states, including the mems of OPEC and the International Energy Agency; Sec.-Gen. ALDO FLORES-QUIROGA.

International Gas Union (IGU): c/o Statoil, POB 3, 1330 Fornebu, Norway; tel. 51-99-00-00; fax 67-80-56-01; e-mail secrigu@statoil.com; internet www.igu.org; f. 1931; represents the gas industry worldwide; organizes World Gas Conference every three years (2012: Kuala Lumpur, Malaysia); mems: 81 Charter mems, 40 Assoc. mems in 81 countries; Pres. JÉRÔME FERRIER (France); Sec.-Gen. TORSTEIN INDREBØ (Norway).

International Grains Council (IGC): 1 Canada Sq., Canary Wharf, London, E14 5AE, United Kingdom; tel. (20) 7513-1122; fax (20) 7513-0630; e-mail igc@igc.int; internet www.igc.int; f. 1949 as International Wheat Council, present name adopted in 1995; responsible for the administration of the International Grains Agreement, 1995, comprising the Grains Trade Convention and the Food Aid Convention (under which donors pledge specified minimum annual amounts of food aid for developing countries in the form of grain and other eligible products); aims to further international co-operation in all aspects of trade in grains, to promote international trade in grains, and to achieve a free flow of this trade, particularly in developing mem. countries; seeks to contribute to the stability of the international grain market; acts as a forum for consultations between mems; provides comprehensive information on the international grain market (with effect from 1 July 2009 the definition of 'grain' was extended to include rice, and from 1 July 2013 it was expanded further, to include oilseeds); mems: 25 countries and the European Union; Exec. Dir ETSUO KITAHARA; publs *World Grain Statistics* (annually), *Grain Shipments* (annually), *Fiscal Year Reports* (annually), *Grain Market Report* (monthly), *IGC Grain Market Indicators* (weekly), *Rice Market Bulletin* (weekly).

International Jute Study Group (IJSG): 145 Monipuriparu, Tejgaon, Dhaka 1215, Bangladesh; tel. (2) 9125581; fax (2) 9125248; e-mail secy.gen@jute.org; internet www.jute.org; f. 2002 as successor to the International Jute Organization (f. 1984 in accordance with an agreement made by 48 producing and consuming countries in 1982, under the auspices of UNCTAD); aims to improve the jute economy and the quality of jute and jute products through research and devt projects and market promotion; Sec.-Gen BHUPENDRA SINGH (India).

International Lead and Zinc Study Group (ILZSG): Rua Almirante Barroso 38, 5th Floor, Lisbon 1000-013, Portugal; tel. (21) 3592420; fax (21) 3592429; e-mail root@ilzsg.org; internet www.ilzsg.org; f. 1959 for intergovernmental consultation on world trade in lead and zinc; conducts studies and provides information on trends in supply and demand; mems: 29 countries accounting for more than 85% of world production and usage of lead and zinc; Sec.-Gen. DON SMALE; publ. *Lead and Zinc Statistics* (monthly).

International Lead Association (also, International Lead Association—Europe): Bravington House, 2 Bravingtons Walk, London N1 9AF, United Kingdom; tel. (20) 7833-8090; fax (20) 7833-1611; e-mail enq@ila-lead.org; internet www.ila-lead.org; f. 1956 as Lead Development Association International; provides authoritative information on the use of lead and its compounds; financed by lead producers and users in the United Kingdom, Europe and elsewhere; Dir ANDY BUSH (United Kingdom).

International Molybdenum Association (IMOA): 4 Heathfield Terrace, London, W4 4JE, United Kingdom; tel. (20) 7871-1580; fax (2) 8994-6067; e-mail info@imoa.info; internet www.imoa.info; f. 1989; collates statistics; promotes the use of molybdenum; monitors health and environmental issues in the molybdenum industry; mems: 70; Sec.-Gen. TIM OUTTERIDGE.

International Olive Council: Príncipe de Vergara 154, 28002 Madrid, Spain; tel. (91) 5903638; fax (91) 5631263; e-mail iooc@internationaloliveoil.org; internet www.internationaloliveoil.org; f. 1959 to administer the International Agreement on Olive Oil and Table Olives, which aims to promote international co-operation in connection with problems of the world economy for olive products; works to prevent unfair competition, to encourage the production and consumption of olive products, and their international trade, and to reduce the disadvantages caused by fluctuations of supplies on the market; also takes action to foster a better understanding of the nutritional, therapeutic and other properties of olive products, to foster international co-operation for the integrated, sustainable devt of world olive growing, to encourage research and devt, to foster the transfer of technology and training activities in the olive products sector, and to improve the interaction between olive growing and the environment; mems: of the International Agreement on Olive Oil and Table Olives, 2005 (fifth Agreement, in force until 31 Dec. 2014): 14 countries, and the European Union; Exec. Dir JEAN-LOUIS BARJOL; publ. *OLIVAE* (2 a year, in Arabic, English, French, Italian and Spanish).

International Organisation of Vine and Wine (Organisation Internationale de la Vigne et du Vin—OIV): 18 rue d'Aguesseau, 75008 Paris, France; tel. 1-44-94-80-80; fax 1-42-66-90-63; e-mail contact@oiv.int; internet www.oiv.int; f. 2001 (agreement establishing an International Wine Office signed Nov. 1924, name changed to International Vine and Wine Office in 1958); researches vine and vine product issues in the scientific, technical, economic and social areas, disseminates knowledge, and facilitates contacts between researchers; mems: 45 countries; 10 orgs and 2 territories have observer status; Dir-Gen. JEAN-MARIE AURAND (France); publs *Bulletin de l'OIV* (every 2 months), *Lexique de la Vigne et du Vin*, *Recueil des méthodes internationales d'analyse des vins*, *Code international des Pratiques oenologiques*, *Codex oenologique international*, numerous scientific publs.

International Pepper Community (IPC): Lina Bldg, 4th Floor, Jalan H. R. Rasuna Said, Kav. B7, Kuningan, Jakarta 12920, Indonesia; tel. (21) 5224902; fax (21) 5224905; e-mail mail@ipcnet.org; internet www.ipcnet.org; f. 1972 for promoting, co-ordinating and harmonizing all activities relating to the pepper economy; holds an Annual Session and group meetings (Nov. 2013: 41st Session, Kuching, Sarawak, Malaysia); Brazil, India, Indonesia, Malaysia, Sri Lanka, Viet Nam are full mems, Papua New Guinea is an assoc. mem.; Exec. Dir SUBRAMANIAM KANNAN; publs *Directory of Pepper Exporters*, *Focus on Pepper*, *Weekly Prices Bulletin*, *Monthly Market Review*, *Pepper Statistical Yearbook*, *Pepper Production Guide*, *Good Agricultural Practices*, *Integrated Pests & Diseases Management*.

International Platinum Group Metals Association (IPA): Schiess-Staett-Str. 30, Munich, 80339 Germany; tel. (89) 51996770; fax (89) 51996719; e-mail info@ipa-news.com; internet www.ipa-news.com; links principal producers and fabricators of platinum; Pres. DEON CARTER; Man. Dir GABRIELE RANDLSHOFER.

International Rubber Research and Development Board (IRRDB): POB 10150, 50908 Kuala Lumpur, Malaysia; tel. (3) 42521612; fax (3) 42560487; e-mail sec_gen@theirrdb.org; internet www.irrdb.com; f. 1960 following the merger of International Rubber Regulation Committee (f. 1934) and International Rubber Research Board (f. 1937); mems: 19 natural rubber research institutes; Sec. Dr ABDUL AZIZ B. S. A. KADIR (Malaysia).

International Sugar Organization: 1 Canada Sq., Canary Wharf, London, E14 5AA, United Kingdom; tel. (20) 7513-1144; fax (20) 7513-1146; e-mail exdir@isosugar.org; internet www.isosugar.org; administers the International Sugar Agreement (1992), with the objectives of stimulating co-operation, facilitating trade and encouraging demand; aims to improve conditions in the sugar market through debate, analysis and studies; serves as a forum for discussion; holds annual seminars and workshops; sponsors projects from developing countries; mems: 87 countries producing some 86% of total world sugar; Exec. Dir JOSÉ ORIVE; publs *Sugar Year Book*, *Statistical Bulletin*, *Monthly Market Report*, *Quarterly Market Outlook*, seminar proceedings.

International Tea Committee Ltd (ITC): 1 Carlton House Terrace, London, SW1Y 5DB, United Kingdom; tel. (20) 7839-5090; e-mail info@inttea.com; internet www.inttea.com; f. 1933 to administer the International Tea Agreement; now serves as a statistical and information centre; in 1979 membership was extended to include consuming countries; producer mems: nat. tea boards or asscns in Bangladesh, People's Republic of China, India, Indonesia, Kenya, Malawi, Sri Lanka and Tanzania; consumer mems: Tea Association of the USA Inc., Irish Tea Trade Association, and the Tea Association of Canada; assoc. mems: Netherlands Ministry of Agriculture, Nature and Food Quality and United Kingdom Department for Environment Food and Rural Affairs, and nat. tea boards/asscns in 10 producing and 4 consuming countries; Chair. NORMAN KELLY; publs *Annual Bulletin of Statistics*, *Monthly Statistical Summary*.

International Tobacco Growers' Association (ITGA): Av. Gen. Humberto Delgado 30A, 6001-081 Castelo Branco, Portugal; tel. (272) 325901; fax (272) 325906; e-mail itga@tobaccoleaf.org; internet www.tobaccoleaf.org; f. 1984 to provide a forum for the exchange of views and information of interest to tobacco producers; holds annual meeting; mems: 23 countries producing over 80% of the world's internationally traded tobacco; Chief Exec. ANTÓNIO ABRUNHOSA (Portugal); publs *Tobacco Courier* (quarterly), *Tobacco Briefing*.

International Tropical Timber Organization (ITTO): International Organizations Center, 5th Floor, Pacifico-Yokohama, 1-1-1, Minato-Mirai, Nishi-ku, Yokohama 220-0012, Japan; tel. (45) 223-1110; fax (45) 223-1111; e-mail itto@itto.int; internet www.itto.int; f. 1985 under the International Tropical Timber Agreement (ITTA, 1983); subsequently, a new treaty, ITTA 1994, came into force in 1997, and this was replaced by ITTA 2006, which entered into force in Dec. 2011; provides a forum for consultation and co-operation between countries that produce and consume tropical timber, and is dedicated to the sustainable devt and conservation of tropical forests; facilitates progress towards 'Objective 2000', which aims to move as rapidly as possible towards achieving exports of tropical timber and timber products from sustainably managed resources; encourages, through policy and project work, forest management, conservation and restoration, the further processing of tropical timber in producing countries, and the gathering and analysis of market intelligence and economic information; mems: 28 producing and 37 consuming countries and the European Union; Exec. Dir EMMANUEL ZE MEKA (Cameroon); publs *Annual Review*, *Market Information Service* (every 2 weeks), *Tropical Forest Update* (quarterly).

International Tungsten Industry Association (ITIA): 4 Heathfield Terrace, London, W4 4JE, United Kingdom; tel. (20) 8996-2221; fax (20) 8994-8728; e-mail info@itia.info; internet www.itia.info; f. 1988 (fmrly Primary Tungsten Asscn, f. 1975); promotes use of tungsten; collates statistics; prepares market reports; monitors health and environmental issues in the tungsten industry; mems from 20 countries; Pres. CLAUDE LANNERS; Sec.-Gen. BURGHARD ZEILER.

International Zinc Association (IZA): 168 ave de Tervueren, Boîte 4, 1150 Brussels, Belgium; tel. (2) 776-00-70; fax (2) 776-00-89; e-mail contact@zinc.org; internet www.zinc.org; f. 1990 to represent the world zinc industry; provide a forum for senior executives to address global issues requiring industry-wide action; consider new applications for zinc and zinc products; foster understanding of zinc's role in the environment; build a sustainable devt policy; mems: 33 zinc-producing countries; Exec. Dir STEPHEN R. WILKINSON; publ. *Zinc Protects* (quarterly).

Kimberley Process: e-mail kpcs.chair@dmr.gov.za; internet www.kimberleyprocess.com; launched following a meeting of Southern African diamond-producing states, held in May 2000 in Kimberley, South Africa, to address means of halting the trade in 'conflict diamonds' and of ensuring that revenue derived from diamond sales would henceforth not be used to fund rebel movements aiming to undermine legitimate govts; in Dec. of that year a landmark UN General Assembly resolution was adopted supporting the creation of an international certification scheme for rough diamonds; accordingly, the Kimberley Process Certification Scheme (KPCS), detailing requirements for controlling production of and trade in 'conflict-free' rough diamonds, entered into force on 1 Jan. 2003; it was estimated in 2013 that participating states accounted for 99.8% of global rough diamond production; a review of the core objectives and definitions of the Process was being undertaken during 2012–13; participating countries, with industry and civil society observers, meet twice a year; working groups and cttees also convene frequently; implementation of the KPCS is monitored through 'review visits', annual reports, and through ongoing exchange and analysis of statistical data; mems: 54 participants representing 80 countries (the European Union is a single participating mem. representing its 27 mem. states); observers incl. the World Diamond Council; chaired, on a rotating basis, by participating states (2014: China).

Petrocaribe: e-mail info@petrocaribe.org; internet www.petrocaribe.org; f. June 2005; an initiative of the Venezuelan Govt to enhance the access of countries in the Caribbean region to petroleum on preferential payment terms; aims to co-ordinate the devt of energy policies and plans regarding natural resources among signatory countries; seventh summit held in Caracas, Venezuela, in May 2013, resolved to establish an economic zone, in collaboration with ALBA-TCP, to promote intra-regional devt projects, trade, food security and tourism; the proposal was reconfirmed by heads of state and govt meeting in Caracas, in Dec., along with plans to elaborate and co-ordinate the economic zone; efforts were to be made to incorporate mems of Mercosur into the new grouping; mems: Antigua and Barbuda, Bahamas, Belize, Cuba, Dominica, Dominican Republic, Grenada, Guyana, Haiti, Honduras, Jamaica, Nicaragua, Saint Christopher and Nevis, Saint Lucia, Saint Vincent and the Grenadines, Suriname, Venezuela.

Regional Association of Oil and Natural Gas Companies in Latin America and the Caribbean (Asociación Regional de Empresas de Petróleo y Gas Natural en Latinoamérica y el Caribe—ARPEL): Javier de Viana 1018, 11200 Montevideo, Uruguay; tel. 2410 6993; fax 2410 9207; e-mail info@arpel.org.uy; internet www.arpel.org; f. 1965 as the Mutual Assistance of the Latin American Oil Companies; aims to initiate and implement activities for the devt of the oil and natural gas industry in Latin America and the Caribbean; promotes the expansion of business opportunities and the improvement of the competitive advantages of its mems; promotes guidelines in support of competition in the sector; and supports the efficient and sustainable exploitation of hydrocarbon resources and the supply of products and services. Works in co-operation with int. orgs, govts, regulatory agencies, technical institutions, univs and non-governmental orgs; mems: 28 state-owned enterprises, representing more than 90% of regional operations, in Argentina, Bolivia, Brazil, Canada, Chile, Colombia, Costa Rica, Cuba, Ecuador, Jamaica, Mexico, Nicaragua, Paraguay, Peru, Suriname, Trinidad and Tobago, Uruguay, Venezuela; Exec. Sec. CÉSAR GONZALEZ NEWMAN; publ. *Boletín Técnico*.

World Association of Beet and Cane Growers: c/o IFAP, 60 rue St Lazare, 75009 Paris, France; tel. 1-45-26-05-53; fax 1-48-74-72-12; internet www.wabcg.org; f. 1983 (formal adoption of Constitution, 1984); groups national orgs of independent sugar beet and cane growers; aims to boost the economic, technical and social devt of the beet- and cane-growing sector; works to strengthen professional representation in int. and nat. fora; serves as a forum for discussion and exchange of information; mems: 33 orgs, representing 5m. cane growers and 650,000 beet growers in 29 countries; Pres. ROY SHARMA (South Africa); publs *World Sugar Farmer News* (quarterly), *World Sugar Farmer Fax Sheet*, *WABCG InfoFlash*, study reports.

World Diamond Council: 580 Fifth Ave, 28th Floor, New York, NY 10036, USA; tel. (212) 575-8848; fax (212) 840-0496; e-mail worlddiamondcouncil@gmail.com; internet www.worlddiamondcouncil.com; f. 2000, by a resolution passed at the World Diamond Congress, convened in July by the World Federation of Diamond Bourses, with the aim of promoting responsibility within the diamond industry towards its stakeholders; lobbied for the creation of a certification scheme to prevent trade in 'conflict diamonds', and became an observer of the ensuing Kimberley Process Certification Scheme, launched in Jan. 2003; has participated in review visits to Kimberley Process participating countries; in Oct. 2002 approved—and maintains—a voluntary System of Warranties, enabling dealers, jewellery manufacturers and retailers to pass on assurances that polished diamonds derive from certified 'conflict-free' rough diamonds, with the aim of extending the effectiveness of the Kimberley Process beyond the export and import phase; meets annually; mems: more than 50 diamond and jewellery industry orgs; Pres. ELI IZHAKOFF.

World Federation of Diamond Bourses (WFDB): 62 Pelikaanstraat, 2018 Antwerp, Belgium; tel. (3) 234-91-21; fax (3) 226-40-73; e-mail info@wfdb.com; internet www.wfdb.com; f. 1947 to protect the interests of affiliated bourses and their individual mems and to settle disputes through international arbitration; mems may display the WFDB Mark, a confirmation of compliance with the WFDB Code of Principles; holds bienniel World Diamond Congress (2014: Singapore); mems: 28 bourses worldwide; Pres. ERNEST BLOM (South Africa); Sec.-Gen. RONY UNTERMAN (Belgium).

World Gold Council (WGC): 10 Old Bailey, London, EC4M 7NG, United Kingdom; tel. (20) 7826-4700; fax (20) 7826-4799; e-mail info@gold.org; internet www.gold.org; f. 1987 as worldwide int. assen of gold producers, to promote the demand for gold; Chair. RANDALL OLIPHANT; Chief Exec. ARAM SHISHMANIAN.

World Petroleum Council (WPC): 1 Duchess St, 4th Floor, Suite 1, London, W1W 6AN, United Kingdom; tel. (20) 7637-4958; fax (20) 7637-4965; e-mail info@world-petroleum.org; internet www.world-petroleum.org; f. 1933 to serve as a forum for petroleum science, technology, economics and management; undertakes related information and liaison activities; 21st Congress: Moscow, Russia, June 2014; mems: Council includes 66 mem. countries; Pres. Dr RENATO BERTANI (Brazil); Dir-Gen. Dr PIERCE W. F. RIEMER (United Kingdom).

World Sugar Research Organisation (WSRO): 70 Collingwood House, Dolphin Sq., London, SW1V 3LX, United Kingdom; tel. (20) 7821-6800; fax (20) 7834-4137; e-mail info@wsro.org; internet www.wsro.org; an alliance of sugar producers, processors, marketers and users; monitors and communicates research on role of sugar and other carbohydrates in nutrition and health; organizes confs and symposia; operates a database of information; serves as a forum for exchange of views; mems: 32 orgs in 30 countries; Dir-Gen. Dr RICHARD COTTRELL; publs *WSRO Research Bulletin* (online, monthly), *WSRO Newsletter*, papers and conf. proceedings.

Development and Economic Co-operation

African Capacity Building Foundation (ACBF): 2 Fairbain Dr., Mount Pleasant, Harare, Zimbabwe; tel. (4) 304649; fax (4) 702915; e-mail root@acbf-pact.org; internet www.acbf-pact.org; f. 1991 by the World Bank, UNDP, the AfDB, African govts and bilateral donors; aims to build sustainable human and institutional capacity for sustainable growth, poverty reduction and good governance in Africa; mems: 44 African and non-African govts, the World Bank, UNDP, the AfDB, the IMF; Exec. Sec. Dr EMMANUEL NNADOZIE.

African Training and Research Centre in Administration for Development (Centre Africain de Formation et de Recherche Administratives pour le Développement—CAFRAD): POB 1796, Tangier, 90001 Morocco; tel. (539) 322707; fax (539) 325785; e-mail cafrad@cafrad.org; internet www.cafrad.org; f. 1964 by agreement between Morocco and UNESCO; undertakes research into administrative problems in Africa and documents results; provides a consultation service for govts and orgs; holds workshops to train senior civil servants; prepares the Biennial Pan-African Conference of Ministers of the Civil Service; mems: 37 African countries; Chair. MOHAMED BOUBDI; Dir-Gen. Dr SIMON MAMOSI LELO; publs *African Administrative Studies* (2 a year), *Research Studies*, *Newsletter* (internet), *Collection: Etudes et Documents*, *Répertoires des Consultants et des institutions de formation en Afrique*.

African-Asian Rural Development Organization (AARDO): No. 2, State Guest Houses Complex, Chanakyapuri, New Delhi 110 021, India; tel. (11) 24100475; fax (11) 24672045; e-mail aardohq@aardo.org; internet www.aardo.org; f. 1962 to act as a catalyst for the co-operative restructuring of rural life in Africa and Asia and to explore opportunities for the co-ordination of efforts to promote rural welfare and to eradicate hunger, thirst, disease, illiteracy and poverty; carries out collaborative research on devt issues; organizes training, study visits, deputation of experts; encourages the exchange of information; holds int. workshops and seminars; awards more than 300 individual training fellowships at 12 institutes in Bangladesh, Egypt, India, Republic of Korea, Malaysia, Nigeria, Pakistan, Taiwan and Zambia; mems: 15 African countries, 14 Asian countries, 1 African assoc.; Sec.-Gen. WASSFI HASSAN EL-SREIHIN (Jordan); publs *African-Asian Journal of Rural Development* (2 a year), *Annual Report*, *AARDO Newsletter* (2 a year).

Agadir Agreement: Fifth Circle, Hanna Qa'war St, Bldg 3, POB 830487, 11183 Amman, Jordan; tel. (6) 5935305; fax (6) 5935306; e-mail atu@agadiragreement.org; internet www.agadiragreement.org; a Declaration made in Agadir, in May 2001, by the govts of Egypt, Jordan, Morocco and Tunisia on the establishment of a common free trade area was followed, in Feb. 2004, by the adoption of the Agadir Agreement on the establishment of a Free Trade Zone between the Arabic Mediterranean Nations, as a means of implementing the Agadir Declaration; the Agadir Agreement entered into force in July 2006 and its implementation commenced in March 2007; a Technical Unit to follow-up implementation of the Agreement was established in April 2007; mems: Egypt, Jordan, Morocco, Tunisia; Technical Unit Exec. Pres. ELAID MAHSOUSSI.

Amazon Co-operation Treaty Organization: SHIS-QI 05, Conjunto 16, casa 21, Lago Sul, Brasília, DF 71615-160, Brazil; tel. (61) 3248-4119; fax (61) 3248-4238; internet www.otca.org.br; f. 1978, permanent secretariat established 1995; aims to promote the co-ordinated and sustainable devt of the Amazonian territories; there are regular meetings of ministers of foreign affairs; there are specialized co-ordinators of environment, health, science technology and education, infrastructure, tourism, transport and communications, and of indigenous affairs; mems: Bolivia, Brazil, Colombia, Ecuador, Guyana, Peru, Suriname, Venezuela; Sec.-Gen. ROBBY DEWNARAIN RAMLAKHAN (Brazil); Exec. Dir MAURICIO DORFLER.

Arctic Council: Fram Centre, 9296 Tromsø, Norway; tel. 77-75-01-40; fax 77-75-05-01; e-mail acs@arctic-council.org; internet www.arctic-council.org; f. 1996 to promote co-ordination of activities in the Arctic region, in particular in the areas of education, devt and environmental protection; permanent secretariat inaugurated in 2013; working groups, supported by scientific and technical expert groups, focus on the following six areas: action on Arctic contaminants; Arctic monitoring and assessment; conservation of Arctic flora and fauna; emergency prevention, preparedness and response; protection of the Arctic marine environment; and sustainable devt; ministerial meetings are normally convened at two-year intervals, 2013: Kiruna, Sweden, in May; Senior Arctic Officials meet annually; mems: Canada, Denmark, Finland, Iceland, Norway, Russia, Sweden, USA; observers: 11 observer mem. states, 9 intergovernmental orgs, 11 non-governmental orgs; in addition the following 6 orgs representing Arctic indigenous peoples have Permanent Participant status: the Arctic Athabaskan Council, Aleut International

Association, Gwich'in Council International, Inuit Circumpolar Council, Russian Arctic Indigenous Peoples of the North, and Saami Council, these are supported by an Indigenous People's Secretariat, based in Copenhagen, Denmark; chairmanship of the Council rotates on a 2-yearly basis (2013–15: Canada); Chair. of Senior Arctic Officials PATRICK BORBEY; Dir MAGNÚS JÓHANNESSON.

Association of Caribbean States (ACS): 5–7 Sweet Briar Rd, St Clair, POB 660, Port of Spain, Trinidad and Tobago; tel. 622-9575; fax 622-1653; e-mail mail@acs-aec.org; internet www.acs-aec.org; f. 1994 by the govts of the 13 CARICOM countries and Colombia, Costa Rica, Cuba, Dominican Republic, El Salvador, Guatemala, Haiti, Honduras, Mexico, Nicaragua, Suriname and Venezuela; aims to promote economic integration, sustainable devt and co-operation in the region; to preserve the environmental integrity of the Caribbean Sea which is regarded as the common patrimony of the peoples of the region; to undertake concerted action to protect the environment, particularly the Caribbean Sea; and to co-operate in the areas of trade, transport, sustainable tourism, and natural disasters. Policy is determined by a Ministerial Council and implemented by a Secretariat based in Port of Spain. The fourth ACS summit meeting of heads of state and govt was held in Panama, in July 2005. A final declaration included resolutions to strengthen co-operation mechanisms with the European Union and to promote a strategy for the Caribbean Sea Zone to be recognized as a special area for the purposes of sustainable devt programmes, support for a strengthened social agenda and efforts to achieve the Millennium Development Goals, and calls for mem. states to sign or ratify the following accords: an ACS Agreement for Regional Co-operation in the area of Natural Disasters; a Convention Establishing the Sustainable Tourism Zone of the Caribbean; and an ACS Air Transport Agreement. The fifth summit was held in Haiti, in April 2013. A final Plan of Action incorporated commitments to strengthen co-operation in sustainable tourism, the promotion of trade, transport, disaster risk reduction, and education, culture, science and technology; signed a Memorandum of Understanding with the UN World Tourism Organization in Feb. 2014 to strengthen collaboration in sustainable tourism; the sixth summit meeting was to be held in Mexico in late April; mems: 28 signatory states, 5 assoc. mems, 20 observers, 6 founding observer countries; Sec.-Gen. Dr ALFONSO MUÑERA CAVADÍA (Colombia).

Barents Euro-Arctic Council: International Secretariat, POB, 9915, Rådhusgt. 8, Kirkenes, Norway; tel. 78-97-08-70; fax 78-97-70-79; e-mail ibs@beac.st; internet www.beac.st; f. 1993 as a forum for Barents regional intergovernmental co-operation; mems: Denmark, Finland, Iceland, Norway, Russia, Sweden, European Commission; chairmanship of the Council rotates on a 2-yearly basis between the mem. states (2013–15: Finland); Head of Secretariat ARI SIRÉN.

Benelux Economic Union: 39 rue de la Régence, 1000 Brussels, Belgium; tel. (2) 519-38-11; fax (2) 513-42-06; e-mail info@benelux.int; internet www.benelux.int; f. 1960 to bring about the economic union of Belgium, Luxembourg and the Netherlands; in June 2008 a new Benelux Treaty was adopted to enter into force upon the expiry in 2010 of the treaty establishing the Union; under the new legal framework cross-border co-operation between the mem. states and co-operation within a broader European context were to be advanced and the name of the org. was to be changed to Benelux Union; the Union aims to introduce common policies in the field of cross-border co-operation and harmonize standards and intellectual property legislation; structure comprises: Committee of Ministers; Council; Court of Justice; Consultative Inter-Parliamentary Council; the Economic and Social Advisory Council; the General Secretariat; a Benelux Organisation for Intellectual Property was established in Sept. 2006; Sec.-Gen. Dr J. P. R. M. VAN LAARHOVEN (Netherlands); publs *Benelux Newsletter*, *Bulletin Benelux*.

BRICS: informal grouping of large emerging economies, comprising Brazil, Russia, India, the People's Republic of China, and South Africa (which together accounted for some 20% of global gross domestic product in 2011); known as BRIC prior to the accession of South Africa in Dec. 2010; convened an inaugural summit of heads of states and govt in June 2009, in Yekaterinburg, Russia, at which principles for future co-operation and devt were adopted; a second summit was held in April 2010, in Brasília, Brazil; and a third in Sanya, China, in April 2011, which adopted the Sanya Declaration, outlining the future deepening of co-operation in areas including trade, energy, finance and industry; a fourth summit, convened in New Delhi, India, in March 2012, directed mem. state ministers responsible for finance to examine the feasibility of establishing a new Development Bank to mobilize resources in support of infrastructure and sustainable development projects in BRICS economies, other emerging economies, and developing countries, with the aim of supplementing the existing efforts of multilateral and regional financial institutions; the establishment of the BRICS Development Bank was approved by the fifth summit, held in Durban, South Africa, in March 2013; the sixth summit was to be held in Fortaleza, Brazil, in July 2014; meetings of BRICS ministers responsible for foreign affairs are held every Sept. on the sidelines of the UN General Assembly; regular meetings are also convened of ministers responsible for finance and economics, security, agriculture, trade, and health; BRICS business forums, and meetings of officials of national statistics authorities, are held periodically; mems: Brazil, People's Republic of China, India, Russia, South Africa.

Caribbean-Britain Business Council: Temple Chambers, 3-7 Temple Ave, London, EC4Y 0HP, United Kingdom; tel. (20) 7583-8739; e-mail david.jessop@caribbean-council.org; internet www.caribbean-council.org; f. 2001; promotes trade and investment devt between the United Kingdom, the Caribbean and the European Union; Man. Dir DAVID JESSOP; publs *Caribbean Insight* (weekly), *Cuba Briefing* (weekly).

Central Asia Regional Economic Co-operation (CAREC): CAREC Unit, 6 ADB Ave, Mandaluyong City, 1550 Metro Manila, Philippines; tel. (2) 6325478; fax (2) 6362387; e-mail info@carecprogram.org; internet www.carecprogram.org; f. 1997; a sub-regional alliance supported by several multilateral institutions (the ADB, EBRD, the IMF, the IDB, UNDP, and the World Bank) to promote economic co-operation and devt; supports projects in the following priority areas: transport, energy, trade policy, trade facilitation; a Cross-Border Transport Agreement was signed by Kyrgyzstan and Tajikistan in Oct. 2010 (an accord for Afghanistan to accede to the Agreement was concluded in Aug. 2011); mems: Afghanistan, Azerbaijan, People's Republic of China, Kazakhstan, Kyrgyzstan, Mongolia, Pakistan, Tajikistan, Uzbekistan; Unit Head WANG HONG.

Central European Free Trade Association: 12–16 rue Joseph II, 1000 Brussels, Belgium; tel. (2) 229-10-11; fax (2) 229-10-19; e-mail cefta@cefta.int; internet www.cefta.int; f. 1992, Central European Free Trade Agreement (CEFTA) entered into force 1993; amended, enlarged CEFTA signed Dec. 2006, and entered into force in July 2007 for Albania, the former Yugoslav republic of Macedonia, Moldova, Montenegro and Kosovo (represented by the UN Interim Administration in Kosovo), in Aug. of that year for Croatia, Oct. for Serbia, and Nov. for Bosnia and Herzegovina; aims to expand trade and foster investment by monitoring regulation between parties concerned, establishing free trade areas with the recommendation of the European Union; mems: Albania, Bosnia and Herzegovina, Croatia, former Yugoslav republic of Macedonia, Moldova, Montenegro, Serbia, UNMIK/Kosovo; rotating chairmanship (2013: Bosnia and Herzegovina; 2014: Croatia); Dir RENATA VITEZ.

Centre on Integrated Rural Development for Asia and the Pacific (CIRDAP): Chameli House, 17 Topkhana Rd; GPO Box 2883, Dhaka 1000, Bangladesh; tel. (2) 9558751; fax (2) 9562035; e-mail infocom@cirdap.org; internet www.cirdap.org; f. 1979 to support integrated rural development; promotes reg. co-operation; mems: Afghanistan, Bangladesh, Fiji, India, Indonesia, Iran, Laos, Malaysia, Myanmar, Nepal, Pakistan, Philippines, Sri Lanka, Thailand, Viet Nam; Dir-Gen. Dr CECEP EFFENDI.

Coalition for Dialogue on Africa (CoDA): POB 3001, Addis Ababa, Ethiopia; tel. (11) 15445540; fax (11) 15443715; e-mail coda@uneca.org; internet www.uneca.org/coda; f. 2009; brings together African stakeholders and policy-makers; policy-oriented, working in collaboration with regional and international orgs to address issues relating to security, peace, governance and devt; sponsored by, but not a programme of, the AU Commission, the UN Economic Commission for Africa and the AfDB; Chair. FESTUS MOGAE.

Colombo Plan: POB 596, 31 Wijerama Rd, Colombo 7, Sri Lanka; tel. (11) 2684188; fax (11) 2684386; e-mail info@colomboplan.org; internet www.colombo-plan.org; f. 1950, as the Colombo Plan for Co-operative Economic and Social Development in Asia and the Pacific, by seven Commonwealth countries, to encourage economic and social devt in that region, based on principles of partnership and collective effort; the Plan comprises four training programmes: the Drug Advisory Programme, to enhance the capabilities of officials, in governmental and non-governmental orgs, involved in drug abuse prevention and control; the Programme for Public Administration, to develop human capital in the public sector; the Programme for Private Sector Development, which implements skills devt programmes in the area of small and medium-sized enterprises and related issues; and the Staff College for Technician Education (see below); all training programmes are voluntarily funded, while administrative costs of the org. are shared equally by all mem. countries; developing countries are encouraged to become donors and to participate in economic and technical co-operation activities; mems: 29 countries; Sec.-Gen. KINLEY DORJI (Bhutan) (from May 2014); publs *Annual Report*, *Colombo Plan Focus* (quarterly), *Consultative Committee Proceedings and Conclusions* (every 2 years).

Colombo Plan Staff College for Technician Education: blk C, DepEd Complex, Meralco Ave, Pasig City 1600, Metro Manila, Philippines; tel. (2) 6310991; fax (2) 6310996; e-mail cpsc@cpsctech.org; internet www.cpsctech.org; f. 1973 with the support of mem.

govts of the Colombo Plan; aims to enhance the devt of technician education systems in developing mem. countries; Dir MOHAMMAD NAIM BIN YAAKUB (Malaysia); publ. *CPSC Quarterly*.

COMESA-EAC-SADC Tripartite Secretariat: 1st Floor, Bldg 41, CSIR Campus, Meiring Naude Rd, Brummeria, Pretoria, 0001 South Africa; e-mail info@comesa-eac-sadc-tripartite.org; internet www.comesa-eac-sadc-tripartite.org; tripartite COMESA-EAC-SADC co-operation, aiming to advance regional integration through the harmonization of the trade and infrastructure devt programmes of these AU regional economic communities, was initiated in 2005 (a COMESA-SADC task force having been active during 2001–05); a Tripartite Task Force—led by the Secretaries-General of COMESA and the EAC, and the Executive Secretary of SADC—has convened regularly thereafter; a five-year Tripartite Programme on Climate Change Adaptation and Mitigation was adopted in July 2010; the first Tripartite Summit, organized in Oct. 2008, in Kampala, Uganda, approved a roadmap towards the formation of a single free trade area (FTA) and the eventual establishment of a single African Economic Community; at the second Tripartite summit, held in June 2011, in Johannesburg, South Africa, negotiations were initiated on the establishment of the proposed COMESA-EAC-SADC Tripartite FTA; in accordance with a Framework, Roadmap and Architecture for Fast Tracking the Establishment of a Continental FTA (referred to as CFTA), and an Action Plan for Boosting Intra-African Trade, adopted by AU leaders in Jan. 2012, the COMESA-EAC-SADC Tripartite FTA was to be finalized by 2014 and, during 2015–16, consolidated with other regional FTAs into the CFTA initiative, with the aim of establishing by 2017 an operational CFTA; a COMESA-EAC-SADC Tripartite Inter-regional Infrastructure Master Plan is under development.

Communauté Economique des Etats de l'Afrique Centrale (CEEAC) (Economic Community of Central African States): BP 2112, Libreville, Gabon; tel. (241) 44-47-31; fax (241) 44-47-32; e-mail secretariat@ceeac-eccas.org; internet www.ceeac-eccas.org; f. 1983, operational 1 Jan. 1985; aims to promote co-operation between mem. states by abolishing trade restrictions, establishing a common external customs tariff, linking commercial banks, and setting up a development fund; works to promote regional security; has since July 2008 deployed the Mission for the Consolidation of Peace in the CAR—MICOPAX; a CEEAC Parliament was inaugurated in Malabo, Equatorial Guinea, in April 2010; in June 2013 CEEAC participated, with ECOWAS and the Gulf of Guinea Commission, in a regional summit on maritime safety and security, convened in Yaoundé, Cameroon, which adopted a Code of Conduct concerning the Prevention and Repression of Piracy, Armed Robbery against Ships, and Illegal Maritime Activities in West and Central Africa; mems: 10 African countries; Sec.-Gen. ALLAM-MI AHMED.

Community of Sahel-Saharan States (Communauté des états Sahelo-Sahariens—CEN-SAD): Pl. d'Algeria, POB 4041, Tripoli, Libya; tel. (21) 361-4832; fax (21) 334-3670; e-mail info@cen-sad.bj; internet www.cen-sad.bj; f. 1998; fmrly known as COMESSA; aims to strengthen co-operation between signatory states in order to promote their economic, social and cultural integration and to facilitate conflict resolution and poverty alleviation; partnership agreements concluded with many orgs, including the AU, the UN and ECOWAS; extraordinary summit convened in Feb. 2013, in N'Djamena, Chad, to discuss regional security, with a particular focus on the ongoing situation in Mali; mems: Benin, Burkina Faso, Central African Republic, Chad, Côte d'Ivoire, Djibouti, Egypt, Eritrea, The Gambia, Ghana, Guinea-Bissau, Liberia, Libya, Mali, Morocco, Niger, Nigeria, Senegal, Sierra Leone, Somalia, Sudan, Togo, Tunisia; Sec.-Gen. Dr MOHAMMED AL-MADANI AL-AZHARI (Libya).

Conseil de l'Entente (Entente Council): 01 BP 3734, angle ave Verdier/rue de Tessières, Abidjan 01, Côte d'Ivoire; tel. 20-33-28-35; fax 20-33-11-49; e-mail fegece@conseil-entente.org; f. 1959 to promote economic development in the region; the Council's Mutual Aid and Loan Guarantee Fund (Fonds d' entraide et de garantie des emprunts) was created to finance devt projects, including agricultural projects, support for small and medium-sized enterprises, vocational training centres and research into new sources of energy; a Convention of Assistance and Co-operation was signed in Feb. 1996; holds annual summit; the 2012 summit, convened in Niamey, Niger, in Dec., considered the establishment of a new common solidarity and development fund; mems: Benin, Burkina Faso, Côte d'Ivoire, Niger, Togo; Exec. Dir PATRICE KOUAMÉ; publ. *Rapport d'activité* (annually).

Council of American Development Foundations (Consejo de Fundaciones Americanas de Desarrollo—SOLIDARIOS): Calle 6 No. 10 Paraíso, Apdo Postal 620, Santo Domingo, Dominican Republic; tel. 549-5111; fax 544-0550; e-mail solidarios@claro.net.do; internet www.redsolidarios.org; f. 1972; exchanges information and experience, arranges technical assistance, raises funds to organize training programmes and scholarships; administers devt fund to finance programmes carried out by mems through a loan guarantee programme; provides consultancy services. Mem. foundations provide technical and financial assistance to low-income groups for rural, housing and micro enterprise devt projects; mems: 18 institutional mems in 9 Latin American and Caribbean countries; Pres. MERCEDES CANALDA; Sec.-Gen. ZULEMA BREA DE VILLAMÁN; publs *Solidarios* (quarterly), *Annual Report*.

Developing Eight (D-8): Maya Aka Center, Kat 12 D, 50 Esentepe, 34390, Istanbul, Turkey; tel. (212) 3561823; fax (212) 3561829; e-mail secretariat@developing8.org; internet www.developing8.org; inaugurated at a meeting of heads of state in June 1997; aims to foster economic co-operation between mem. states and to strengthen the role of developing countries in the global economy; project areas include trade (with Egypt as the co-ordinating mem. state), agriculture (Pakistan), human resources (Indonesia), communication and information (Iran), rural devt (Bangladesh), finance and banking (Malaysia), energy (Nigeria), and industry, and health (Turkey); a roadmap of co-operation for the period 2008–18 envisaged the implementation of preferential trade agreement; ninth summit to be held in Turkey, in 2014; mems: Bangladesh, Egypt, Indonesia, Iran, Malaysia, Nigeria, Pakistan, Turkey; Sec.-Gen. Dr SEYED ALI MOHAMMAD MOUSAVI (Iran).

Earth Council Alliance: 1250 24th St, NW Suite 300, Washington, DC 20037, USA; tel. (202) 467-2786; e-mail contact@earthcouncil1.org; internet www.earthcouncilalliance.org; f. 1992, as the Earth Council, in preparation for the UN Conference on Environment and Development; supported the establishment of National Councils for Sustainable Development (NCSDs) and administers a programme to promote co-operation and dialogue and to facilitate capacity building and training, with NCSDs; works, with other partner orgs, to generate support for an Earth Charter (adopted in 2000); since 2002 supports other Earth Councils worldwide to promote and support sustainable devt; Chair. Dr DAVID J. JHIRAD (Canada); Pres. JAN A. HARTKE (Brazil).

East African Community (EAC): POB 1096, Arusha, Tanzania; tel. (27) 2162100; fax (27) 2162190; e-mail eac@eachq.org; internet www.eac.int; f. 2001, following the adoption of a treaty on political and economic integration (signed in Nov. 1999) by the heads of state of Kenya, Tanzania and Uganda, replacing the Permanent Tripartite Commission for East African Co-operation (f. 1993) and reviving the former East African Community (f. 1967, dissolved 1977); Rwanda and Burundi formally became mems of the Community on 1 July 2007; South Sudan (which achieved independence in July 2011) and Somalia have applied for membership; initial areas for co-operation were to be trade and industry, security, immigration, transport and communications, and promotion of investment; further objectives were the elimination of trade barriers and ensuring the free movement of people and capital within the grouping; a customs union came into effect on 1 Jan. 2005; an East African Legislative Assembly and an East African Court of Justice were both inaugurated in 2001; in April 2006 heads of state agreed that negotiations on a common market would commence in July; the Protocol on the Establishment of the EAC Common Market entered into force on 1 July 2010; negotiations on the establishment of an East African Monetary Union were initiated in 2011; in Sept. 2013 EAC dispatched an observer mission to monitor legislative elections in Rwanda; the 15th ordinary summit, held in Kampala, Uganda, in Nov., signed the protocol on the establishment of an East African Monetary Union which envisaged a single currency; in addition, the summit determined that the single customs territory should commence on 1 Jan. 2014 and all operational requirements be completed by June of that year; a roadmap and action plan for the establishment of an East African Federation were to be considered at an extraordinary summit meeting, to be held in April 2014; EAC has participated, since 2005, to advance regional co-operation through the COMESA-EAC-SADC Tripartite Secretariat, with a view to advancing regional co-operation; in March 2014 in March 2014 signed a Memorandum of Understanding with the Economic Community of the Great Lakes Countries to strengthen co-operation between the orgs and enhance regional integration; Sec.-Gen. RICHARD SEZIBERA (Rwanda).

Economic Community of the Great Lakes Countries (Communauté économique des pays des Grands Lacs—CEPGL): POB 58, Gisenyi, Rwanda; tel. 61309; fax 61319; f. 1976 main organs: annual Conference of Heads of State, Council of Ministers of Foreign Affairs, Permanent Executive Secretariat, Consultative Commission, Security Commission, three Specialized Technical Commissions; there are four specialized agencies: the Banque de Développement des Etats des Grands Lacs (BDEGL) at Goma, Democratic Republic of the Congo; an energy centre at Bujumbura, Burundi; the Institute of Agronomic and Zootechnical Research, Gitega, Burundi; and a regional electricity co (SINELAC) at Bukavu, Democratic Republic of the Congo; in March 2014 signed a Memorandum of Understanding with the East African Community to strengthen co-operation between the orgs and enhance regional integration; mems: Burundi, Democratic Republic of the Congo, Rwanda; Exec. Sec. HERMAN TUYAGA (Burundi); publs *Grands Lacs* (quarterly review), *Journal* (annually).

Eurasian Economic Community (EurAsEC): 105066 Moscow, 1-i Basmannyi per. 6/4, Russia; tel. (495) 223-90-00; fax (495) 223-90-23; e-mail evrazes@evrazes.ru; internet www.evrazes.com; f. 2000; formerly a Customs Union agreed between Belarus, Kazakhstan, Kyrgyzstan, Russia and Tajikistan in 1999; the merger of EurAsEC with the Central Asian Co-operation Organization (CACO) was agreed in Oct. 2005, and achieved in Jan. 2006 with the accession to EurAsEC of Uzbekistan, which had hitherto been the only mem. of CACO that did not also belong to EurAsEC; aims to create a Common Economic Space (CES) with a single currency; a free trade zone was established at the end of 2002; in Oct. 2007 EurAsEC leaders approved the legal basis for establishing a new customs union, initially to comprise Belarus, Kazakhstan and Russia, with Kyrgyzstan, Tajikistan and Uzbekistan expected to join subsequently; the customs union entered into formal existence on 1 Jan. 2010; in Dec. 2010 the heads of state of Belarus, Kazakhstan and Russia signed several agreements aimed at finalizing the establishment of the planned CES, and, in Nov. 2011, they signed a declaration on Eurasian economic integration and adopted a roadmap outlining integration processes aimed at creating a Eurasian Economic Union, to be established by 1 Jan. 2015, and to be based on the Customs Union and CES; in Jan. 2012 a EurAsEC Court, for the adjudication of economic disputes between mem. states, became operational; in March the Russian President urged the EurAsEC observer states to join the ongoing economic integration process; mems co-operate on issues including customs tariff harmonization, migration, border security and negotiating admission to the WTO; Uzbekistan announced the suspension of its membership of EurAsEC in Nov. 2008; Armenia, Moldova and Ukraine have observer status; Sec.-Gen. TAIR A. MANSUROV.

European Free Trade Association (EFTA): 9–11 rue de Varembé, 1211 Geneva 20, Switzerland; tel. 223322600; fax 223322677; e-mail mail.gva@efta.int; internet www.efta.int; f. 1960 to bring about free trade in industrial goods and to contribute to the liberalization and expansion of world trade; EFTA states (except Switzerland) participate in the European Economic Area with the 27 mem. countries of the European Union; has concluded free trade agreements with, inter alia, Albania, Canada, Chile, Colombia, Costa Rica, Croatia, Egypt, Gulf Cooperation Council (GCC), Hong Kong, Israel, Jordan, Republic of Korea, Lebanon, Macedonia, Mexico, Montenegro, Morocco, Palestinian Authority, Panama, Peru, Serbia, Singapore, Southern African Customs Union, Tunisia, Turkey and Ukraine; mems: Iceland, Liechtenstein, Norway, Switzerland; Sec.-Gen. KRISTINN F. ÁRNASON (Iceland); publs *EFTA Annual Report*, *EFTA Bulletin*.

Food Assistance Committee: c/o International Grains Council, 1 Canada Sq., Canary Wharf, London, E14 5AE, United Kingdom; tel. (20) 7513-1122; fax (20) 7513-0630; e-mail fac@foodassistanceconvention.org; internet www.foodassistanceconvention.org; the Food Assistance Convention, a constituent element of the International Grains Agreement (1995), came into effect on 1 Jan. 2013, replacing the previous Food Aid Convention (1999); aims to improve food security, and to enhance the nutritional status of the most vulnerable populations through the timely and efficient provision of food assistance, expanding the scope of the previous Food Aid Convention to include all forms of safe, nutritious food; Chair. KILIAN GRETER (Switzerland).

G-20 (Doha Round negotiating group): e-mail g-20@mre.gov.br; f. 2003 with the aim of defending the interests of developing countries in the negotiations on agriculture under the WTO's Doha Development Round and meets regularly to address WTO-related agricultural trade issues; now comprises 23 developing countries; mems: Argentina, Bolivia, Brazil, Chile, People's Republic of China, Cuba, Ecuador, Egypt, Guatemala, India, Indonesia, Mexico, Nigeria, Pakistan, Paraguay, Peru, Philippines, South Africa, Tanzania, Thailand, Uruguay, Venezuela, Zimbabwe.

Gambia River Basin Development Organization (Organisation pour la mise en valeur du fleuve Gambie—OMVG): BP 2353, 13 passage Leblanc, Dakar, Senegal; tel. 889-51-00; fax 822-59-26; e-mail omvg@omvg.sn; f. 1978 by Senegal and The Gambia; Guinea joined in 1981 and Guinea-Bissau in 1983. A masterplan for the integrated development of the Kayanga/Geba and Koliba/Corubal river basins has been developed, encompassing a projected natural resources management project; a hydraulic devt plan for the Gambia river was formulated during 1996–98; a pre-feasibility study on connecting the national electric grids of the four mem. states has been completed, and a feasibility study for the construction of the proposed Sambangalou hydroelectric dam, was undertaken in the early 2000s; maintains documentation centre; Exec. Sec. JUSTINO VIEIRA.

Group of Three (G-3): c/o Secretaría de Relaciones Exteriores, 1 Tlatelolco, Del. Cuauhtémoc, 06995 México, DF, Mexico; e-mail gtres@sre.gob.mx; f. 1990 by Colombia, Mexico and Venezuela to remove restrictions on trade between the three countries; in Nov. 2004 Panama joined the Group, which briefly became the Group of Four until Venezuela's withdrawal in Nov. 2006; the trade agreement covers market access, rules of origin, intellectual property, trade in services, and govt purchases, and entered into force in early 1994. Tariffs on trade between mem. states were to be removed on a phased basis. Co-operation was also envisaged in employment creation, the energy sector and the fight against cholera. The secretariat function rotates between the mem. countries on a two-yearly basis; mems: Colombia, Mexico and Panama.

Group of 15 (G15): G15 Technical Support Facility, 1 route des Morillons, CP 2100, 1218 Grand Saconnex, Geneva, Switzerland; tel. 227916701; fax 227916169; e-mail tsf@g15.org; internet www.g15.org; f. 1989 by 15 developing nations during the ninth summit of the Non-Aligned Movement; retains its original name although current membership totals 17; convenes biennial summits to address the global economic and political situation and to promote economic development through South-South co-operation and North-South dialogue; mems: Algeria, Argentina, Brazil, Chile, Egypt, India, Indonesia, Iran, Jamaica, Kenya, Malaysia, Mexico, Nigeria, Senegal, Sri Lanka, Venezuela, Zimbabwe; Head of Office SAURABH BHANDARI.

Group of 77 (G77): c/o UN Headquarters, Rm NL-2077, New York, NY 10017, USA; tel. (212) 963-4777; fax (212) 963-3515; e-mail secretariat@g77.org; internet www.g77.org; f. 1964 by the 77 signatory states of the Joint Declaration of the Seventy-Seven Countries (the G77 retains its original name, owing to its historic significance, although its membership has expanded since inception); first ministerial meeting, held in Algiers, Algeria, in Oct. 1967, adopted the Charter of Algiers as a basis for G77 co-operation; subsequently G77 Chapters were established with liaison offices in Geneva (UNCTAD), Nairobi (UNEP), Paris (UNESCO), Rome (FAO/IFAD), Vienna (UNIDO), and the Group of 24 (G24) in Washington, DC (IMF and World Bank); as the largest intergovernmental org. of developing states in the UN the G77 aims to enable developing nations to articulate and promote their collective economic interests and to improve their negotiating capacity with regard to global economic issues within the UN system; in Sept. 2006 G77 ministers of foreign affairs, and the People's Republic of China, endorsed the establishment of a new Consortium on Science, Technology and Innovation for the South; a chairperson, who also acts as spokesperson, co-ordinates the G77's activities in each Chapter; the chairmanship rotates on a regional basis between Africa, Asia, and Latin America and the Caribbean; the supreme decision-making body of the G77 is the South Summit, convened for the first time in Havana, Cuba, in April 2000, and then in Doha, Qatar, in June 2005; it is envisaged that the third Summit will be held in Africa; an annual meeting of G77 ministers of foreign affairs is convened at the start (in Sept.) of the regular session of the UN General Assembly; an Intergovernmental Follow-up and Coordination Committee on South-South Cooperation meets every two years; periodic sectoral ministerial meetings are organized in preparation for UNCTAD sessions and prior to the UNIDO and UNESCO General Conferences, and with the aim of promoting South-South co-operation; other special ministerial meetings are also convened from time to time; the first G77 Ministerial Forum on Water Resources was convened in Feb. 2009, in Muscat, Oman; mems: 133 countries.

Indian Ocean Commission (IOC) (Commission de l'Océan Indien—COI): Blue Tower, 3rd floor, rue de l'Institut, BP 7, Ebene, Mauritius; tel. 402-6100; fax 465-6798; e-mail secretariat@coi-ioc.org; internet www.coi-ioc.org; f. 1982 to promote regional co-operation, particularly in economic devt; projects include tuna-fishing devt, protection and management of environmental resources and strengthening of meteorological services; tariff reduction is also envisaged; in Oct. 2011 the Council of Ministers determined to establish an Anti-Piracy Unit within the secretariat; organizes an annual regional trade fair; mems: the Comoros, France (representing the French Overseas Department of Réunion), Madagascar, Mauritius, Seychelles; Sec.-Gen. JEAN-CLAUDE DE L'ESTRAC (Mauritius); publ. *La Lettre de l'Océan Indien*.

Indian Ocean Rim Association for Regional Co-operation (IOR–ARC): Nexteracom Tower 1, 3rd Floor, Ebene, Mauritius; tel. 454-1717; fax 468-1161; e-mail iorarcsec@iorarc.org; internet www.iorarc.org; the first intergovernmental meeting of countries in the region to promote an Indian Ocean Rim initiative was convened in March 1995; charter to establish the Asscn was signed at a ministerial meeting in March 1997; aims to promote the sustained growth and balanced devt of the region and of its mem. states and to create common ground for regional economic co-operation, inter alia through trade, investment, infrastructure, tourism, and science and technology; 14th meeting of the Working Group of Heads of Missions held in May 2013 (Pretoria, South Africa); mems: Australia, Bangladesh, Comoros, India, Indonesia, Iran, Kenya, Madagascar, Malaysia, Mauritius, Mozambique, Oman, Seychelles, Singapore, South Africa, Sri Lanka, Tanzania, Thailand, UAE and Yemen. Dialogue Partner countries: People's Republic of China, Egypt, France, Japan, United Kingdom, USA. Observers: Indian Ocean

Research Group Inc., Indian Ocean Tourism Org; Sec.-Gen. K. V. BHAGIRATH.

International Co-operation for Development and Solidarity (Co-opération Internationale pour le Développement et la Solidarité—CIDSE): 16 rue Stévin, 1000 Brussels, Belgium; tel. (2) 230-77-22; fax (2) 230-70-82; e-mail postmaster@cidse.org; internet www.cidse.org; f. 1967; an international alliance of Catholic devt agencies, whose mems share a common strategy in their efforts to eradicate poverty and establish global justice. CIDSE's advocacy work covers trade and food security, climate change, resources for devt, global governance, and European Union devt policy; promotes co-operation and the devt of common strategies on advocacy work, devt projects and programmes and devt education; mems: 17 Catholic agencies in 16 countries and territories; Pres. HEINZ HOEDL; Sec.-Gen. BERND NILLES.

Inuit Circumpolar Council: Aqqusinersuaq 3A, 1st Floor, POB 204, 3900 Nuuk Greenland; tel. 323632; fax 323001; e-mail iccgreenland@inuit.org; internet www.inuit.org; f. 1977 (as the Inuit Circumpolar Conference, name changed 2006) to protect the indigenous culture, environment and rights of the Inuit people, and to encourage co-operation among the Inuit; has adopted a Circumpolar Inuit Declaration on Sovereignty in the Arctic (in April 2009), and a Circumpolar Inuit Declaration on Resource Development Principles in Inuit Nunaat (May 2011); the Nuuk Declaration, adopted in June 2010 by the 11th General Assembly, directed the Council, inter alia, to implement a 2010–14 Circumpolar Inuit Health Strategy; to keep environmental stewardship of the Inuit homeland as a priority activity during 2010–14; to organize an Inuit leaders' summit on resource devt; to continue to participate in int. bodies to defend and promote the right of the Inuit to harvest marine mammals and to trade their products on a sustainable basis; and instructed the Council to organize a pan-Arctic Inuit leaders' summit during 2012; General Assemblies held every four years (2010: Nuuk, Greenland, in June); mems: Inuit communities in Canada, Greenland, Alaska and Russia; Chair. AQQALUK LYNGE; Exec. Dir ALFRED JAKOBSEN.

Lake Chad Basin Commission (LCBC): BP 727, N'Djamena, Chad; tel. 52-41-45; fax 52-41-37; e-mail lcbc@intnet.td; internet www.cblt.org; f. 1964 to encourage co-operation in developing the Lake Chad region and to promote the settlement of regional disputes; work programmes emphasize the regulation of the utilization of water and other natural resources in the basin; the co-ordination of natural resources devt projects and research; holds annual summit of heads of state; mems: Cameroon, Central African Republic, Chad, Niger, Nigeria; Exec. Sec. SANUSI IMRAN ABDULLAHI; publ. *Bibliographie générale de la CBLT* (2 a year).

Latin American Association of Development Financing Institutions (Asociación Latinoamericana de Instituciones Financieras para el Desarrollo—ALIDE): Apdo Postal 3988, Paseo de la República 3211, Lima 27, Peru; tel. (1) 4422400; fax (1) 4428105; e-mail sg@alide.org.pe; internet www.alide.org.pe; f. 1968 to promote co-operation among regional devt financing bodies; programmes: technical assistance; training; studies and research; technical meetings; information; projects and investment promotion; mems: more than 70 active, 3 assoc. and 5 collaborating (banks and financing institutions and devt orgs in 22 Latin American countries, Canada, Germany and Spain); Pres. FERNANDO CALLOIA RAFFO; Sec.-Gen. ROMMEL ACEVEDO FERNANDEZ DE PAREDES; publs *ALIDE Bulletin* (6 a year), *ALIDENOTICIAS Newsletter* (monthly), *Annual Report*, *Latin American Directory of Development Financing Institutions*.

Latin American Economic System (Sistema Económico Latinoamericano—SELA): Torre Europa, 4°, Urb. Campo Alegre, Avda Francisco de Miranda, Caracas 1060, Venezuela; Apdo 17035, Caracas 1010-A, Venezuela; tel. (212) 955-7111; fax (212) 951-5292; e-mail fguglielmelli@sela.org; internet www.sela.org; f. 1975 in accordance with the Panama Convention; aims to foster co-operation and integration among the countries of Latin America and the Caribbean, and to provide a permanent system of consultation and co-ordination in economic and social matters; conducts studies and other analysis and research; extends technical assistance to sub-regional and regional co-ordination bodies; provides library, information service and databases on regional co-operation. The Latin American Council, the principal decision-making body of the System, meets annually at ministerial level and high-level regional consultation and co-ordination meetings are held; acts as the Executive Secretariat of the Working Group on Trade and Competition in Latin America and the Caribbean; mems: 28 countries; Perm. Sec. Dr ROBERTO GUARNIERI (Venezuela); publs *Capítulos del SELA* (3 a year), *Bulletin on Latin America and Caribbean Integration* (monthly), *SELA Antenna in the United States* (quarterly).

Liptako-Gourma Integrated Development Authority (LGA): POB 619, ave M. Thevenond, Ouagadougou, Burkina Faso; tel. (3) 30-61-48; f. 1970; scope of activities includes water infrastructure, telecom munications and construction of roads and railways; in 1986 undertook study on devt of water resources in the basin of the Niger river (for hydroelectricity and irrigation); mems: Burkina Faso, Mali, Niger; Chair. SEYDOU BOUDA (Mali).

Mano River Union: Private Mail Bag 133, Delco House, Lightfoot Boston St, Freetown, Sierra Leone; tel. (22) 222811; f. 1973 to establish a customs and economic union between mem. states to accelerate devt via integration; a common external tariff was instituted in 1977. Intra-union free trade was officially introduced in May 1981, as the first stage in progress towards a customs union. A non-aggression treaty was signed by heads of state in 1986. The Union was inactive for three years until mid-1994, owing to regional conflict and disagreements regarding funding. In Jan. 1995 a Mano River Centre for Peace and Development was established, to provide a permanent mechanism for conflict prevention and resolution, and monitoring of human rights violations, and to promote sustainable peace and devt. A new security structure was approved in 2000. In Aug. 2001 ministers of foreign affairs, security, internal affairs, and justice, meeting as the Joint Security Committee, resolved to deploy joint border security and confidence-building units, and to work to re-establish the free movement of people and goods; implements programmes in the following areas: institutional revitalization, restructuring and devt; peace and security; economic devt and regional integration; and social devt; in June 2013 a high-level meeting, co-chaired, in Dakar, Senegal, by the Sec.-Gen. of the Union, the UN Special Representative for West Africa, and the President of the ECOWAS Commission, initiated the process of formulating a security strategy for the Union, as requested in recent resolutions of the UN Security Council; mems: Côte d'Ivoire, Guinea, Liberia, Sierra Leone; Sec.-Gen. Dr HADJA SARAN DARABA KABBA.

Mekong River Commission (MRC): POB 6101, Unit 18 Ban Sithane Neua, Sikhottabong District, Vientiane, Laos 01000; tel. (21) 263263; fax (21) 263264; e-mail mrcs@mrcmekong.org; internet www.mrcmekong.org; f. 1995 as successor to the Committee for Co-ordination of Investigations of the Lower Mekong Basin ('Mekong Committee' f. 1957); aims to promote and co-ordinate the sustainable devt and use of the water and related resources of the Mekong River Basin for navigational and non-navigational purposes, in order to assist the social and economic devt of mem. states and preserve the ecological balance of the basin; provides scientific information and policy advice; supports the implementation of strategic programmes and activities; organizes an annual donor consultative group meeting; maintains regular dialogue with Myanmar and the People's Republic of China; the first meeting of heads of govt was convened in Hua Hin, Thailand, in April 2010; mems: Cambodia, Laos, Thailand, Viet Nam; CEO HANS GUTTMAN; publs *Annual Report*, *Catch and Culture* (3 a year), *Mekong News* (quarterly).

Mesoamerican Integration and Development Project (Proyecto de Integración y Desarrollo de Mesoamérica): Edif. Torre Roble, Octavo nivel, Blvd. de los Héroes, San Salvador, El Salvador; tel. 2261-5444; fax 2260-9175; e-mail c.trinidad@proyectomesoamerica.org; internet www.proyectomesoamerica.org; f. 2001 as the Puebla-Panamá Plan (PPP); relaunched with formal institutionalized structure in 2004; current name and mandate approved in June 2008 by the Tuxtla summit meeting; aims to promote economic devt and reduce poverty in mem. countries; eight key areas of activity: energy, transport, telecommunications, tourism, trade environment and competitiveness, human devt, sustainable devt, prevention and mitigation of natural disasters; administers the Mesoamerica Biological Corridor initiative to enhance the management of the region's biodiversity; mems: Belize, Colombia, Costa Rica, El Salvador, Guatemala, Honduras, Mexico, Nicaragua, Panama; Exec. Dir ELAYNE WHYTE GÓMEZ.

Niger Basin Authority (Autorité du Bassin du Niger): BP 729, Niamey, Niger; tel. 20724395; fax 20724208; e-mail sec-executif@abn.ne; internet www.abn.ne; f. 1964 (as River Niger Commission; name changed 1980) to harmonize national programmes concerned with the River Niger Basin and to execute an integrated devt plan; compiles statistics; regulates navigation; runs projects on hydrological forecasting, environmental control; infrastructure and agro-pastoral development; mems: Benin, Burkina Faso, Cameroon, Chad, Côte d'Ivoire, Guinea, Mali, Niger, Nigeria; Exec. Sec. Maj.-Gen. COLLINS REMY UMUNAKWE IHEKIRE; publ. *NBA-INFO* (quarterly).

Nile Basin Initiative: POB 192, Entebbe, Uganda; tel. (41) 321424; fax (41) 320971; e-mail nbisec@nilebasin.org; internet www.nilebasin.org; f. 1999; aims to achieve sustainable socio-economic devt through the equitable use and benefits of the Nile Basin water resources and to create an enabling environment for the implementation of programmes with a shared vision. Highest authority is the Nile Basin Council of Ministers; other activities undertaken by a Nile Basin Technical Advisory Committee; mems: Burundi, Democratic Republic of the Congo, Egypt, Eritrea, Ethiopia, Kenya, Rwanda, South Sudan, Sudan, Tanzania, Uganda; Chair. JEMMA NUNU KUMBA (South Sudan).

Nordic Development Fund: Fabianinkatu 34, POB 185, 00171 Helsinki, Finland; tel. (10) 618-002; fax (9) 622-1491; e-mail info .ndf@ndf.fi; internet www.ndf.fi; f. 1989; supports activities by national administrations for overseas devt, with resources amounting to €330m. and a working capital of €1,000m; co-finances climate change investments in countries with low income; works with other multilateral devt finance institutions, including the African Development Bank Group, the Asian Development Bank, Inter-American Development Bank and Investment Corporation, the Multilateral Investment Fund and the World Bank; Chair. BILL FRANSSON; Man. Dir PASI HELLMAN.

Organization for the Development of the Senegal River (Organisation pour la mise en valeur du fleuve Sénégal—OMVS): c/o Haut-Commissariat, 46 rue Carnot, BP 3152, Dakar, Senegal; tel. 859-81-81; fax 864-01-63; e-mail omvssphc@omvs.org; internet www .omvs.org; f. 1972 to promote the use of the Senegal river for hydroelectricity, irrigation and navigation; the Djama dam in Senegal provides a barrage to prevent salt water from moving upstream, and the Manantali dam in Mali is intended to provide a reservoir for irrigation of about 375,000 ha of land and for production of hydroelectricity and provision of year-round navigation for ocean-going vessels. In 1997 two cos were formed to manage the dams: Société de gestion de l'énergie de Manantali and Société de gestion et d'exploitation du barrage de Djama; mems: Guinea, Mali, Mauritania, Senegal; High Commissioner KABINÉ KOMARA (Mauritania).

Organization for the Management and Development of the Kagera River Basin (Organisation pour l'aménagement et le développement du bassin de la rivière Kagera—OBK): BP 297, Kigali, Rwanda; tel. (7) 84665; fax (7) 82172; f. 1978; envisages joint devt and management of resources, including the construction of an 80-MW hydroelectric dam at Rusumo Falls, on the Rwanda-Tanzania border, a 2,000-km railway network between the four mem. countries, road construction (914 km), and a telecommunications network between mem. states; mems: Burundi, Rwanda, Tanzania, Uganda.

Organization of the Co-operatives of America (Organización de las Cooperativas de América): Apdo Postal 241263, Carrera 11, No 86-32, Of. 101, Bogotá, Colombia; tel. (1) 6103296; fax (1) 6101912; f. 1963 for improving socio-economic, cultural and moral conditions through the use of the co-operatives system; works in every country of the continent; regional offices sponsor plans and activities based on the most pressing needs and special conditions of individual countries; mems: nat. or local orgs in 23 countries and territories; publs *América Cooperativa* (monthly), *OCA News* (monthly).

Pacific Alliance (Alianza del Pacífico): internet www .alianzapacifico.net; f. June 2012 when Presidents of Chile, Colombia, Mexico and Peru, meeting in Antofagasta, Chile, signed a framework agreement establishing the Alliance; the inaugural meeting of the Alliance determined to finalize the establishment of a pan-Latin American stock exchange; to bring about the elimination of visa restrictions for citizens of mem. countries; to open joint export promotion offices in Asian countries; to establish a joint univ. system; and to seek to eliminate import duties and country-of-origin rules between mem. states; an agreement to eliminate trade tariffs was concluded at the 2013 presidential summit, held in Santiago de Cali, Colombia, in May; the meeting also resolved to establish a Pacific Alliance Partnership Fund; at the eighth summit meeting, held in Cartagena, Colombia, in Feb. 2014, heads of state signed an agreement to eliminate 92% of trade tariffs on goods and services; at the meeting Costa Rica signed a declaration of accession to the Alliance; mems: Chile, Colombia, Mexico, Peru; 26 observer states.

Pacific Basin Economic Council (PBEC): 2803–04, 28/F, Harbour Centre, 25 Harbour Rd, Wanchai, Hong Kong SAR; tel. 2815-6550; fax 2545-0499; e-mail info@pbec.org; internet www.pbec.org; f. 1967; an asscn of business representatives aiming to promote business opportunities in the region, in order to enhance overall economic devt; advises govts and serves as a liaison between business leaders and govt officials; encourages business relationships and co-operation among mems; holds business symposia; mems: 20 economies (Australia, Canada, Chile, People's Republic of China, Colombia, Ecuador, Hong Kong SAR, Indonesia, Japan, Republic of Korea, Malaysia, Mexico, New Zealand, Peru, Philippines, Russia, Singapore, Taiwan, Thailand, USA); Chair. WILFRED WONG YING-WAI; publs *PBEC Update* (quarterly), *Executive Summary* (annual conf. report).

Pacific Economic Cooperation Council (PECC): 29 Heng Mui Keng Terrace, Singapore 119620; tel. 67379823; fax 67379824; e-mail info@pecc.org; internet www.pecc.org; f. 1980; an independent, policy-orientated org. of senior research, govt and business representatives from 26 economies in the Asia-Pacific region; aims to foster economic devt in the region by providing a forum for discussion and co-operation in a wide range of economic areas; PECC is an official observer to APEC; holds a General Meeting annually; mems: Australia, Brunei, Canada, Chile, the People's Republic of China, Colombia, Ecuador, Hong Kong, Indonesia, Japan, the Republic of Korea, Malaysia, Mexico, Mongolia, New Zealand, Peru, Philippines, Singapore, Taiwan, Thailand, USA, Viet Nam and the Pacific Islands Forum; assoc. mem.: France (Pacific Territories); Sec.-Gen. EDUARDO PEDROSA; publs *Issues PECC* (quarterly), *Pacific Economic Outlook* (annually), *Pacific Food Outlook* (annually).

Pacific Islands Development Forum: 56 Domain Rd, Suva, Fiji; tel. 3309645; fax 3301741; e-mail secretariat@pidf.gov.fj; internet pacificidf.org; f. 2012; aims to advance South-South co-operation and establish multi-stakeholder partnerships to promote a 'green economy' approach to the sustainable devt of the region; the Forum is committed to participating in the processes of the UN High Level Political Forum, established to pursue the objectives of the UN Conference on Sustainable Development ('Rio +20'); the inaugural Forum meeting was convened in Nadi, Fiji, in Aug. 2013 on the theme of 'Leadership, Innovation and Partnership for Green/Blue Pacific Economies'; the second summit was scheduled to be convened in June 2014; a Governing Council, Senior Officials Committee and a Permanent Secretariat administer the org. during the periods between summit meetings; Sec.-Gen. a.i. FELETI TEO.

Pan-African Institute for Development (PAID): BP 1756, Ouagadougou 01, Burkina Faso; tel. 5036-4807; fax 5036-4730; e-mail ipdaos@fasonet.bf; internet www.ipd-aos.org; f. 1964; gives training to people from African countries involved with devt at grass-roots, intermediate and senior levels; emphasis is given to devt management and financing; agriculture and rural devt; issues of gender and devt; promotion of small and medium-sized enterprises; training policies and systems; environment, health and community devt; research, support and consultancy services; and specialized training. There are four regional institutes: Central Africa (Douala, Cameroon), Sahel (Ouagadougou, Burkina Faso), West Africa (Buéa, Cameroon), Eastern and Southern Africa (Kabwe, Zambia) and a European office in Geneva; publs *Newsletter* (2 a year), *Annual Progress Report*, *PAID Report* (quarterly).

Partners in Population and Development (PPD): IPH Bldg, 2nd Floor, Mohakhali, Dhaka 1212, Bangladesh; tel. (2) 988-1882; fax (2) 882-9387; e-mail partners@ppdsec.org; internet www .partners-popdev.org; f. 1994; aims to implement the decisions of the International Conference on Population and Development, held in Cairo, Egypt in 1994, in order to expand and improve South-South collaboration in the fields of family planning and reproductive health; administers a Visionary Leadership Programme, a Global Leadership Programme, and other training and technical advisory services; mems: 25 developing countries; Chair. GHULAM NABI AZAD.

Permanent Interstate Committee on Drought Control in the Sahel (Comité permanent inter-états de lutte contre la sécheresse au Sahel—CILSS): POB 7049, Ouagadougou 03, Burkina Faso; tel. 50-37-41-25; fax 50-37-41-32; e-mail cilss.se@cilss.bf; internet www .cilss.bf; f. 1973; works in co-operation with UNDP Drylands Development Centre; aims to combat the effects of chronic drought in the Sahel region, by improving irrigation and food production, halting deforestation and creating food reserves; initiated a series of projects to improve food security and to counter poverty, entitled Sahel 21; the heads of state of all mems have signed a convention for the establishment of a Fondation pour le Développement Durable du Sahel; maintains Institut du Sahel at Bamako (Mali) and centre at Niamey (Niger); mems: Burkina Faso, Cape Verde, Chad, The Gambia, Guinea-Bissau, Mali, Mauritania, Niger, Senegal; Pres. Dr DANGDÉ LAOUBELE DAMAYE; Exec. Sec. ALHOUSSEÏNI BRETAUDEAU (The Gambia); publ. *Reflets Sahéliens* (quarterly).

Population Council: 1 Dag Hammarskjöld Plaza, New York, NY 10017, USA; tel. (212) 339-0500; fax (212) 755-6052; e-mail pubinfo@ popcouncil.org; internet www.popcouncil.org; f. 1952; the council is organized into three programmes: HIV and AIDS; Poverty, Gender, and Youth; and Reproductive Health; aims to improve reproductive health and achieve a balance between people and resources; analyses demographic trends; conducts biomedical research to develop new contraceptives; works with private and public agencies to improve the quality and scope of family planning and reproductive health services; helps govts to design and implement population policies; communicates results of research. Four regional offices, in India, Mexico, Egypt and Ghana, and 18 country offices in the developing world, with programmes in more than 65 countries. Additional office in Washington, DC, USA, carries out worldwide operational research and activities for reproductive health and the prevention of HIV and AIDS; Pres. PETER J. DONALDSON; publs *Momentum* (2 a year), *Studies in Family Planning* (quarterly), *Population and Development Review* (quarterly), *Population Briefs* (3 a year).

Society for International Development: Via Ardeatina 802, 00178, Rome, Italy; tel. (06) 4872172; fax (06) 4872170; e-mail info@sidint.org; internet www.sidint.net; f. 1957; a global network of individuals and institutions wishing to promote participative, pluralistic and sustainable devt; builds partnerships with civil society groups and other sectors; fosters local initiatives and new forms of social experimentation; mems: 3,000 individual mems and 55 institutional mems in 125 countries, 65 local chapters; Pres.

JUMA V. MWAPACHU (Tanzania); Man. Dir STEFANO PRATO (Italy); publ. *Development* (quarterly).

South Centre: 17–19 Chemin du Champ-d'Anier, CP 228, 1211 Geneva 19, Switzerland; tel. 227918050; fax 227988531; e-mail south@southcentre.org; internet www.southcentre.org; f. 1990 as a follow-up mechanism of the South Commission (f. 1987); in 1995 established as an intergovernmental body to promote South-South solidarity and co-operation by generating ideas and action-oriented proposals on major policy issues; mems: 50 countries; Chair. BENJAMIN WILLIAM MKAPA (Tanzania); Exec. Dir MARTIN KHOR (Malaysia); publs *South Bulletin* (every 2 weeks), *Policy Brief* (monthly).

Southeast European Co-operative Initiative (SECI): Heldenplatz 1, Vienna 1010, Austria; tel. (1) 514-36-64-22; fax (1) 531-37-420; e-mail seci2@osce.org; f. 1996 in order to encourage co-operation among countries of South-East Europe and to facilitate their integration into European structures; received technical support from ECE and the OSCE; ad hoc Project Groups were established to undertake preparations for the following selected projects: commercial arbitration and mediation; co-operation between the Danube countries (particularly in the areas of policy harmonization, transport, energy, culture and education); electricity grids; energy efficiency; environmental recovery; combating organized crime; regional road transport; securities markets; trade and transport facilitation; and transport infrastructure; activities are overseen by a SECI Agenda Committee; established a SECI Business Advisory Council, based in Thessaloníki, Greece (which, in 2002, evolved into the Business Advisory Council for Southeast Europe), and a SECI Regional Centre for Combating Transborder Crime, based in Bucharest, Romania (reconstituted as the Southeast European Law Enforcement Center in 2011); SECI is actively involved with policy facilitation and cross-sectoral communication within the Danube Region, with a focus on stakeholder involvement, private sector devt, project implementation and policy co-ordination; mems: Albania, Bosnia and Herzegovina, Bulgaria, Croatia, Greece, Hungary, former Yugoslav republic of Macedonia, Moldova, Romania, Serbia, Slovenia, Turkey; Co-ordinator ERHARD BUSEK.

Trans-Pacific Strategic Economic Partnership Agreement (P4): c/o Coordinator, Trans-Pacific Partnership Free Trade Agreement Unit, Ministry of Foreign Affairs and Trade, Private Bag 18901, Wellington, New Zealand; tel. (4) 439-8765; e-mail tpp@mfat.govt.nz; f. 2006 upon entry into force of agreement signed by the four founding mems (the P4, i.e. Brunei, Chile, New Zealand, Singapore); eliminated some 90% of tariffs on trade between mems; negotiations on financial services and investment commenced in March 2008 with the participation of the USA; negotiations on an expanded Trans-Pacific Partnership agreement (TPP), to include, additionally, Australia, Malaysia, Peru and Viet Nam, commenced in March 2010; Canada and Mexico were invited to join the TPP negotiations in June 2012, and Japan joined in April 2013, taking part in negotiations for the first time at the 18th round of talks, held in Brunei, in July; TPP negotiating states' heads of state and govt convened on the sidelines of the APEC summit in Oct. to review progress in the negotiations and to reaffirm their commitment to the process; a ministerial meeting was convened in Singapore in Dec.

Union of the Arab Maghreb (Union du Maghreb arabe—UMA): 73 rue Tensift, Agdal, Rabat, Morocco; tel. (53) 7681371; fax (53) 7681377; e-mail sg.uma@maghrebarabe.org; internet www.maghrebarabe.org; f. 1989; aims to encourage joint ventures and to create a single market; structure comprises a council of heads of state (meeting annually), a council of ministers responsible for foreign affairs, a follow-up committee, a consultative council of 30 delegates from each country, a UMA judicial court, and four specialized ministerial commissions. Chairmanship rotates annually between heads of state. A Maghreb Investment and Foreign Trade Bank, funding joint agricultural and industrial projects, has been established and a customs union created; mems: Algeria, Libya, Mauritania, Morocco, Tunisia; Sec.-Gen. HABIB BEN YAHIA (Tunisia).

Vienna Institute for International Dialogue and Co-operation (Wiener Institut für internationalen Dialog und Zusammenarbeit): Möllwaldplatz 5/3, 1040 Vienna, Austria; tel. (1) 713-35-94; fax (1) 713-35-94-73; e-mail office@vidc.org; internet www.vidc.org; f. 1987 (as Vienna Institute for Development and Co-operation; fmrly Vienna Institute for Development, f. 1964); manages devt policy research on sectoral, regional and cross-cutting issues (for example, gender issues); arranges cultural exchanges between Austria and countries from Africa, Asia and Latin America; deals with conception and organization of anti-racist and integrative measures in sport, in particular football; Pres. BARBARA PRAMMER; Dir WALTER POSCH; publs *Report Series*, *Echo*.

World Economic Forum: 91–93 route de la Capite, 1223 Cologny/Geneva, Switzerland; tel. 228691212; fax 227862744; e-mail contact@weforum.org; internet www.weforum.org; f. 1971; the Forum comprises commercial interests gathered on a non-partisan basis, under the stewardship of the Swiss Government, with the aim of improving society through economic devt; convenes an annual meeting in Davos, Switzerland; organizes the following programmes: Technology Pioneers; Women Leaders; and Young Global Leaders; and aims to mobilize the resources of the global business community in the implementation of the following initiatives: the Global Health Initiative; the Disaster Relief Network; the West-Islamic World Dialogue; and the G20/International Monetary Reform Project; the Forum is governed by a guiding Foundation Board; an advisory International Business Council; and an administrative Managing Board; regular mems: representatives of 1,000 leading commercial cos in 56 countries worldwide; selected mem. cos taking a leading role in the movement's activities are known as 'partners'; Exec. Chair. KLAUS MARTIN SCHWAB.

Economics and Finance

African Insurance Organization (AIO): 30 ave de Gaulle, BP 5860, Douala, Cameroon; tel. 33-42-01-63; fax 33-43-20-08; e-mail info@africaninsurance.net; internet www.african-insurance.org; f. 1972 to promote the expansion of the insurance and reinsurance industry in Africa, and to increase regional co-operation; holds annual conf., periodic seminars and workshops, and arranges meetings for reinsurers, brokers, consultant and regulators in Africa; has established African insurance 'pools' for aviation, petroleum and fire risks, and created asscns of African insurance educators, supervisory authorities and insurance brokers and consultants; Sec.-Gen. P. M. G. SOARES; publ. *African Insurance Annual Review*.

African Reinsurance Corporation (Africa-Re): Africa Re House, Plot 1679, Karimu Kotun St, Victoria Island, PMB 12765, Lagos, Nigeria; tel. (1) 2800724; fax (1) 2800074; e-mail info@africa-re.com; internet www.africa-re.com; f. 1976; its purpose is to foster the devt of the insurance and reinsurance industry in Africa and to promote the growth of national and regional underwriting capacities; auth. cap. US $500m.; mems: 41 countries, 5 development finance institutions (the AfDB, IFC, DEG, PROPARCO, FMO), IRB-Brasil Re, and some 110 insurance and reinsurance cos; Chair. HASSAN BOUBRIK; Man. Dir and CEO CORNEILLE KAREKEZI; publs *The African Reinsurer* (annually), *Africa Re Newsletter* (quarterly), *Risk Watch* (quarterly).

African Rural and Agricultural Credit Association (AFRACA): ACK Garden House, 2nd Floor, POB 41378–00100, Nairobi, Kenya; tel. (20) 2717911; fax (20) 2710082; e-mail afraca@africaonline.co.ke; internet www.afraca.org; f. 1977 to develop the rural finance environment by adopting and promoting policy frameworks and assisting sustainable financial institutions to increase outreach; 86 mems in 27 African countries, including central, commercial and agricultural banks, microfinance institutions, and national programmes working in the area of agricultural and rural finance in the continent; Chair. MILLISON NARH; publs *Afraca Workshop Reports*, *Rural Finance Reports*.

Asian Clearing Union (ACU): No. 47, 7th Nagarestan Alley, Pasdaran Ave, POB 15875-7177, 47, 16646 Tehran, Iran; tel. (21) 22842076; fax (21) 22847677; e-mail acusecret@cbi.ir; internet www.asianclearingunion.org; f. 1974; provides a facility to settle payments, on a multilateral basis, for international transactions among participating central banks, thereby contributing to the expansion of trade and economic activity among ESCAP countries; the Central Bank of Iran is the agent for the Union; units of account are, with effect from 1 Jan. 2009, denominated as the ACU dollar and the ACU euro; mems: central banks of Bangladesh, Bhutan, India, Iran, Maldives, Myanmar, Nepal, Pakistan, Sri Lanka; Chair. YASEEN ANWAR; Sec.-Gen. LIDA BORHAN-AZAD; publs *Annual Report*, *Monthly Newsletter*.

Asian Reinsurance Corporation: Tower B, 17th Floor, Chamnan Phenjati Business Center, 65 Rama 9 Rd, Huaykwang, Bangkok 10320, Thailand; tel. (2) 245-2169; fax (2) 248-1377; e-mail asianre@asianrecorp.com; internet www.asianrecorp.com; f. 1979 under ESCAP auspices; aims to operate as a professional reinsurer serving the needs of the Asia-Pacific region; also aims to provide technical assistance to national insurance markets, 10 regional insurance/reinsurance cos; auth. cap. US $200m., cap. p.u. $50.9m. (April 2013); mems: Afghanistan, Bangladesh, Bhutan, People's Republic of China, India, Iran, Republic of Korea, Philippines, Sri Lanka, Thailand; Pres. and CEO S. A. KUMAR.

Association of African Central Banks (AACB): Ave Abdoulaye Fadiga, BP 3108, Dakar, Senegal; tel. 839-05-00; fax 839-08-01; e-mail akangni@bceao.int; internet www.aacb.org; f. 1968 to promote contacts in the monetary and financial sphere, in order to increase co-operation and trade among mem. states; aims to strengthen monetary and financial stability on the African continent; since 2002 administers an African Monetary Co-operation Programme;

mems: 40 African central banks representing 47 states; Chair. MOHAMMED LAKSACI (Algeria); Exec. Sec. SAMUEL MÉANGO.

Association of African Development Finance Institutions (AADFI): Immeuble AIAFD, blvd Latrille, rue J61, Cocody Deux Plateaux, 06 BP 321 Abidjan 06, Côte d'Ivoire; tel. 22-52-33-89; fax 22-52-25-84; e-mail info@adfi-ci.org; internet www.adfi-ci.org; f. 1975; aims to promote co-operation among financial institutions in the region in matters relating to economic and social devt, research, project design, financing and the exchange of information; mems: 92 in 43 African and non-African countries; Chair. PETER M. NONI; Sec.-Gen. JOSEPH AMIHERE; publs *Annual Report*, *AADFI Information Bulletin* (quarterly), *Finance and Development in Africa* (2 a year).

Association of Asian Confederation of Credit Unions (AACCU): U Tower Bldg 411, 8th Floor, Srinakarin Rd, Suanluang, Bangkok 10250, Thailand; tel. (2) 704-4253; fax (2) 704-4255; e-mail accumail@aaccu.coop; internet www.aaccu.asia; f. 1971; links and promotes credit unions and co-operatives in Asia, provides research facilities and training programmes; mems: in credit union leagues and feds in 24 Asian countries; CEO RANJITH HETTIARACHCHI (Thailand); publs *ACCU News* (every 3 months), *Annual Report*, *ACCU Directory*.

Association of European Institutes of Economic Research (AIECE) (Association d'instituts européens de conjoncture économique): 3 pl. Montesquieu, 1348 Louvain-la-Neuve, Belgium; tel. (10) 47-34-26; fax (10) 47-39-45; e-mail severine.dinjar@uclouvain.be; internet sites.uclouvain.be/aiece; f. 1957; provides a means of contact between mem. institutes; organizes two meetings annually, at which discussions are held on the economic situation and on a special theoretical subject; mems: 40 institutes in 20 European countries and 4 int. orgs; Admin. Sec. SEVERINE DINJAR.

Banco del Sur (South American Bank): Caracas, Venezuela; f. Dec. 2007; formal agreement establishing the bank signed in Sept. 2009; aims to provide financing for social and investment projects in South America; auth. cap. US $20,000m.; mems: Argentina, Brazil, Bolivia, Ecuador, Paraguay, Uruguay, Venezuela.

Centre for Latin American Monetary Studies (Centro de Estudios Monetarios Latinoamericanos—CEMLA): Durango 54, Col. Roma, Del. Cuauhtémoc, 06700 México, DF, Mexico; tel. (55) 5061-6640; fax (55) 5061-6695; e-mail cemla@cemla.org; internet www.cemla.org; f. 1952; organizes technical training programmes on monetary policy, devt finance, etc; runs applied research programmes on monetary and central banking policies and procedures; holds regional meetings of banking officials; mems: 30 assoc. mems (Central Banks of Latin America and the Caribbean), 23 co-operating mems (supervisory institutions of the region and non-Latin American Central Banks); Dir-Gen. FERNANDO TENJO GALARZA; publs *Bulletin* (every 2 months), *Monetaria* (quarterly), *Money Affairs* (2 a year).

East African Development Bank: 4 Nile Ave, POB 7128, Kampala, Uganda; tel. (417) 112900; fax (41) 4253585; e-mail inquiry@eadb.org; internet www.eadb.org; f. 1967 by the former East African Community to promote regional devt within Kenya, Tanzania and Uganda, which each hold 24.07% of the equity capital; Kenya, Tanzania and Uganda each hold 27.2% of the equity capital; the remaining equity is held by the AfDB (6.8%), Rwanda (4.3%) and other institutional investors; Dir-Gen. VIVIENNE YEDA APOPO.

Eastern Caribbean Central Bank (ECCB): POB 89, Basseterre, St Christopher and Nevis; tel. 465-2537; fax 465-9562; e-mail info@eccb-centralbank.org; internet www.eccb-centralbank.org; f. 1983 by OECS govts; maintains regional currency (Eastern Caribbean dollar) and advises on the economic devt of mem. states; mems: Anguilla, Antigua and Barbuda, Dominica, Grenada, Montserrat, Saint Christopher and Nevis, Saint Lucia, Saint Vincent and the Grenadines; Gov. Sir K. DWIGHT VENNER; Man. Dir JENNIFER NERO.

Econometric Society: Dept of Economics, New York University, 19 West Fourth St, 6th Floor, New York, NY 10012, USA; tel. (212) 998-3820; fax (212) 995-4487; e-mail sashi@econometricsociety.org; internet www.econometricsociety.org; f. 1930 to promote studies aiming at a unification of the theoretical-quantitative and the empirical-quantitative approaches to economic problems; mems: c. 7,000; Pres. JAMES J. HECKMAN; Exec. Vice-Pres. HYUNG SONG SHIN; publ. *Econometrica* (6 a year).

Equator Principles Association: tel. (1621) 853-900; fax (1621) 731-483; e-mail secretariat@equator-principles.com; internet www.equator-principles.com; f. July 2010; aims to administer and develop further the Equator Principles, first adopted in 2003, with the support of the International Finance Corporation, as a set of industry standards for the management of environmental and social risk in project financing; a Strategic Review conf. was convened in Beijing, People's Republic of China, in Dec. 2010; 77 signed-up Equator Principles Financial Institutions (EPFIs) and two assoc. mems; Administrators JOANNA CLARK, SAMANTHA HOSKINS.

Eurasian Development Bank: 050051 Almatı, ul. Dostık 51, Kazakhstan; tel. (727) 244-40-44; fax (727) 244-65-70; e-mail info@eabr.org; internet www.eabr.org; f. 2006; aims to facilitate the economic development of the region through investment and the promotion of trade; mems: Armenia, Belarus, Kazakhstan, Kyrgyzstan, Russia; Chair. IGOR FINOGENOV.

European Federation of Financial Analysts Societies (EFFAS): Mainzer Landstr. 47A, Frankfurt-am-Main, Germany; tel. (69) 264848300; fax (69) 264848335; e-mail claudia.stinnes@effas.com; internet www.effas.net; f. 1962 to co-ordinate the activities of European asscns of financial analysts; aims to raise the standard of financial analysis and improve the quality of information given to investors; encourages unification of national rules and draws up rules of profession; holds biennial congress; mems: asscns in 25 European countries; Chair. JESÚS LÓPEZ ZABALLOS; Gen. Sec. CLAUDIA STINNES.

European Financial Management and Marketing Association (EFMA): 8 rue Bayen, 75017 Paris, France; tel. 1-47-42-52-72; fax 1-47-42-56-76; e-mail info@efma.com; internet www.efma.com; f. 1971 to link financial institutions by organizing seminars, confs and training sessions and an annual Congress and World Convention, and by providing information services; mems: more than 3,000 financial institutions worldwide; Chair. HANS VAN DER NOORDAA; Sec.-Gen. PATRICK DESMARÈS; publ. *Newsletter*.

European Private Equity and Venture Capital Association (EVCA): Bastion Tower, 5 pl. du Champ de Mars, 1050 Brussels, Belgium; tel. (2) 715-00-20; fax (2) 725-07-04; e-mail info@evca.eu; internet www.evca.eu; f. 1983 to link private equity and venture capital cos within Europe; mems: over 950; Chair. GEORGE ANSON; Sec.-Gen. DÖRTE HÖPPNER (Germany); publs *Yearbook*, research and special papers, legal documents, industry guidelines.

Financial Action Task Force (FATF) (Groupe d'action financière—GAFI): 2 rue André-Pascal, 75775 Paris Cedex 16, France; tel. 1-45-24-90-90; fax 1-44-30-61-37; e-mail contact@fatf-gafi.org; internet www.fatf-gafi.org; f. 1989, on the recommendation of the Group of Seven (G7) industrialized nations, to develop and promote policies to combat money-laundering and the financing of terrorism; formulated a set of recommendations (40+9) for countries worldwide to implement; these are periodically revised (most recently in 2012); established partnerships with regional task forces in the Caribbean, Asia-Pacific, Central Asia, Europe, East and South Africa, the Middle East and North Africa and South America; mems: 36 state jurisdictions, the European Commission, and the Cooperation Council for the Arab States of the Gulf; there are also 8 regional assoc. mems; Pres. VLADIMIR NECHAEV (Russia); Exec. Sec. RICK MCDONELL; publs *Annual Report*, *News Alerts*.

Financial Stability Board: c/o BIS, Centralbahnplatz 2, 4002 Basel, Switzerland; tel. 612808298; fax 612809100; e-mail fsb@bis.org; internet www.financialstabilityboard.org; f. 1999 as the Financial Stability Forum, name changed in April 2009; brings together senior representatives of national financial authorities, international financial institutions, international regulatory and supervisory groupings and cttees of central bank experts and the European Central Bank; aims to promote international financial stability and to strengthen the functioning of the financial markets; in March 2009 agreed to expand its membership to include all Group of 20 (G20) economies, as well as Spain and the European Commission; in April 2009 the meeting of G20 heads of state and govt determined to re-establish the then Forum as the Financial Stability Board, strengthen its institutional structure (to include a plenary body, a steering cttee and three standing cttees concerned with Vulnerabilities Assessment; Supervisory and Regulatory Co-operation; and Standards Implementation) and expand its mandate to enhance its effectiveness as an international mechanism to promote financial stability; the Board was to strengthen its collaboration with the IMF, and conduct joint early warning exercises; in Dec. 2009 the Board initiated a peer review of implementation of the Principles and Standards for Sound Compensation Practices; in Nov. 2010 determined to establish six FSB regional consultative groups; Chair. MARK CARNEY (Canada).

Group of Seven (G7): f. 1975 as an informal framework of co-operation between major industrialized countries; despite the formation in 1998 of the Group of Eight (G8), incorporating Russia, and the inclusion of Russia in all G8 sectoral areas from 2003, the G7 remains a forum for regular discussion (at the level of ministers of finance and central bank governors) of devts in the global economy and of economic policy; a meeting was held in June 2012 with a focus on the sovereign debt crisis, and resolving banking instability, in the eurozone; meeting in May 2013 G7 ministers responsible for finance emphasized the importance of collective action in addressing tax evasion, and urged OECD to give consideration to issues surrounding the use by some multinational cos of transfer pricing rules to move profits into tax havens; the IMF Managing Director is normally invited to participate in G7 meetings; in March 2014 an emergency meeting of G7 heads of state reiterated its condemnation of Russia's actions in Ukraine and resolved to suspend Russia from the G8 process; mems: ministers responsible for finance and central bank governors of Canada, France, Germany, Italy, Japan, United Kingdom and the USA; European Union representation; the presidency rotates among the participating countries on an annual basis.

Group of 20 (G20): internet www.g20.org; f. Sept. 1999 as an informal deliberative forum of ministers responsible for finance and central bank governors representing both industrialized and 'systemically important' emerging market nations; aims to strengthen the international financial architecture and to foster sustainable economic growth and devt; in 2004 participating countries adopted the G20 Accord for Sustained Growth and stated a commitment to high standards of transparency and fiscal governance; the IMF Managing Director and IBRD President participate in G20 annual meetings; an extraordinary Summit on Financial Markets and the World Economy was convened in Washington, DC, USA, in Nov. 2008, attended by heads of state or govt of G20 mem. economies; a second summit meeting, held in London, United Kingdom, in April 2009, issued as its final communiqué a *Global Plan for Recovery and Reform* outlining commitments to restore economic confidence, growth and jobs, to strengthen financial supervision and regulation, to reform and strengthen global financial institutions, to promote global trade and investment and to ensure a fair and sustainable economic recovery; detailed declarations were also issued on measures agreed to deliver substantial resources (of some US $850,000m.) through international financial institutions and on reforms to be implemented in order to strengthen the financial system; as a follow-up to the London summit, G20 heads of state met in Pittsburgh, USA, in Sept. 2009; the meeting adopted a *Framework for Strong, Sustainable, and Balanced Growth* and resolved to expand the role of the G20 to be at the centre of future international economic policy-making; summit meetings were held in June 2010, in Canada (at the G8 summit), and in Seoul, Republic of Korea, in Nov. of that year; the sixth G20 summit, held in Cannes, France, in Nov. 2011, concluded an *Action Plan for Growth and Jobs* but was dominated by discussion of measures to secure financial stability in some countries using the euro; the seventh summit, convened in Los Cabos, Baja California Sur, Mexico, in June 2012, further considered means of stabilizing the eurozone, with a particular focus on reducing the borrowing costs of highly indebted mem. countries; the ongoing crisis in Syria was on the agenda of the eighth G20 summit of heads of state, which took place in Sept. 2013 in St Petersburg, Russia; 11 heads of state participating in the summit issued a statement condemning an alleged chemical attack perpetrated against civilians in Ghouta, Syria, on 21 Aug., and urging a strong international response; the heads of state also adopted a new Base Erosion and Profit Shifting Action Plan, developed by OECD with the aim of combating corp. tax avoidance globally; a parallel Business 20 summit, facilitating dialogue between prominent business asscns, is convened annually (2013: St Petersburg, in June); mems: Argentina, Australia, Brazil, Canada, People's Republic of China, France, Germany, India, Indonesia, Italy, Japan, Republic of Korea, Mexico, Russia, Saudi Arabia, South Africa, Turkey, United Kingdom, USA and the European Union; observers: Netherlands, Spain; the presidency rotates among the participating states on an annual basis (2013: Russia; 2014: Australia).

Insurance Europe: 51 rue Montoyer, 1000 Brussels, Belgium; tel. (2) 894-30-00; fax (2) 894-30-01; e-mail info@insuranceeurope.eu; internet www.insuranceeurope.eu; f. 1953 as the CEA (Comité Européen de Assurances) to represent the interests of European insurers, to encourage co-operation between mems, to allow the exchange of information and to conduct studies; mems: nat. insurance asscns of 34 full mems; Russia and Ukraine are partners; Pres. SERGIO BALBINOT (Italy); Dir-Gen. MICHAELA KOLLER (Germany); publs *European Insurance in Figures* (annually), *Indirect Taxation on Insurance Contracts* (annually).

Intergovernmental Group of 24 (G24) on International Monetary Affairs and Development: 700 19th St, NW, Rm 3-600 Washington, DC 20431, USA; tel. (202) 623-6101; fax (202) 623-6000; e-mail g24@g24.org; internet www.g24.org; f. 1971; aims to co-ordinate the position of developing countries on monetary and devt finance issues; operates at the political level of ministers of finance and governors of central banks, and also at the level of govt officials; mems (Africa): Algeria, Côte d'Ivoire, Democratic Republic of the Congo, Egypt, Ethiopia, Gabon, Ghana, Nigeria, South Africa; (Latin America and the Caribbean): Argentina, Brazil, Colombia, Guatemala, Mexico, Peru, Trinidad and Tobago and Venezuela; (Asia and the Middle East): India, Iran, Lebanon, Pakistan, Philippines, Sri Lanka and Syrian Arab Republic; the People's Republic of China has the status of special invitee at G24 meetings; G77 participant states may attend G24 meetings as observers.

International Accounting Standards Board (IASB): 30 Cannon St, London, EC4M 6XH, United Kingdom; tel. (20) 7246-6410; fax (20) 7246-6411; e-mail iasb@iasb.org.uk; internet www.iasb.org.uk; f. 1973 as International Accounting Standards Committee, reorganized and present name adopted 2001; aims to develop, in the public interest, a single set of high-quality, uniform, clear and enforceable global accounting standards requiring the submission of high-quality, transparent and comparable information in financial statements and other financial reporting, in order to assist participants in worldwide capital markets and other end users to make informed decisions on economic matters; aims also to promote the use and rigorous application of these global accounting standards, and to bring about the convergence of these with national accounting standards; Chair. and CEO HANS HOOGERVORST; publs *IASB Insight* (quarterly), *Bound Volume of International Accounting Standards* (annually), *Interpretations of International Accounting Standards*.

International Association for the Study of Insurance Economics (Geneva Association): Route de Malagnou 53, 1208 Geneva, Switzerland; tel. 227076600; fax 227367536; e-mail secretariat@genevaassociation.org; internet www.genevaassociation.org; f. 1973; aims to educate and develop understanding on the unique role and importance of insurance in economies; produces and distributes research and analysis on global strategic insurance and risk management issues; Chair. MICHAEL MCGAVICK (Ireland); Sec.-Gen. JOHN H. FITZPATRICK (USA).

International Association of Deposit Insurers: c/o BIS, Centralbahnplatz 2, 4002 Basel, Switzerland; tel. 612809933; fax 612809554; e-mail service.iadi@bis.org; internet www.iadi.org; f. 2002; aims to contribute to the stability of the international financial system by promoting co-operation among deposit insurers and establishing effective systems; mems: 67 orgs, 9 assoc. and 12 partners; Chair. JERZY PRUSKI; Sec.-Gen. GAIL L. VERLEY.

International Association of Insurance Supervisors: c/o BIS, Centralbahnplatz 2, 4002 Basel, Switzerland; tel. 612257300; fax 612809151; e-mail iais@bis.org; internet www.iaisweb.org; f. 1994 to improve supervision of the insurance industry and promote global financial stability; issues global insurance principles, standards and guidance; represents insurance supervisors from more than 200 jurisdictions, and has 130 observers; Sec.-Gen. YOSHIHIRO KAWAI.

International Bureau of Fiscal Documentation (IBFD): Rietlandpark 301, 1019 DW Amsterdam, Netherlands; tel. (20) 5540100; fax (20) 6228658; e-mail info@ibfd.org; internet www.ibfd.org; f. 1938 to supply information on fiscal law and its application; maintains library on international taxation; Chair. S. R. B. VAN DER FELTZ; publs *Bulletin for International Fiscal Documentation*, *Asia Pacific Tax Bulletin*, *Derivatives and Financial Instruments*, *European Taxation*, *International VAT Monitor*, *International Transfer Pricing Journal*, *Supplementary Service to European Taxation* (all monthly), *Tax News Service* (weekly); studies, databases, regional tax guides.

International Capital Market Association (ICMA): Talacker 29, 8001 Zürich, Switzerland; tel. 443634222; fax 443637772; e-mail thomas.hunziker@icmagroup.org; internet www.icma-group.org; f. 2005 by merger of International Primary Market Association and International Securities Association, f. 1969; maintains and develops an efficient and cost-effective market for capital; mems: 400 banks and major financial institutions in 47 countries; Pres. RENÉ KARSENTI; Chief Exec. MARTIN SCHECK; publs reports and market surveys.

International Economic Association: c/o Instituto de Análisis Económico, Campus de la UAB, 08193 Barcelona, Spain; tel. (93) 5806612; fax (93) 5805214; e-mail iea@iea-world.org; internet www.iea-world.com; f. 1949 to promote international collaboration for the advancement of economic knowledge and develop personal contacts between economists, and to encourage the provision of means for the dissemination of economic knowledge; mems: asscns in 59 countries; Pres. JOSEPH STIGLITZ; Sec.-Gen. OMAR LICANDRO.

International Federation of Accountants: 529 Fifth Ave, 6th Floor, New York, NY 10017, USA; tel. (212) 286-9344; fax (212) 286-9570; e-mail communications@ifac.org; internet www.ifac.org; f. 1977 to develop a co-ordinated worldwide accounting profession with harmonized standards; mems: 179 accountancy bodies in 130 countries; Pres. WARREN ALLEN (New Zealand); CEO FAYEZUL CHOUDHURY.

International Fiscal Association (IFA): World Trade Center, POB 30215, 3001 DE Rotterdam, Netherlands; tel. (10) 4052990; fax (10) 4055031; e-mail a.gensecr@ifa.nl; internet www.ifa.nl; f. 1938 to study international and comparative public finance and fiscal law, especially taxation; holds annual congresses; mems in 111 countries and branches in 66 countries; Pres. P. F. KAKA (India); Sec.-Gen. Prof. H. A. KOGELS (Netherlands); publs *Cahiers de Droit Fiscal International*, *Yearbook of the International Fiscal Association*, *IFA Congress Seminar Series*.

International Institute of Public Finance e.V.: POB 860446, 81631 Munich, Germany; tel. (89) 9224-1281; fax (89) 907795-2281; e-mail info@iipf.org; internet www.iipf.org; f. 1937; a private scientific org. aiming to establish contacts between people of every nationality, whose main or supplementary activity consists in the study of public finance; holds annual congress; mems: 800; Pres. MICHAEL P. DEVEREAUX (United Kingdom).

International Organization of Securities Commissions (IOSCO): Calle Oquendo 12, 28006 Madrid, Spain; tel. (91) 417-5549; fax (91) 555-9368; e-mail info@iosco.org; internet www.iosco.org; f. 1983 to facilitate co-operation between securities and derivatives regulatory bodies at international level; in 1998 adopted the Objectives and Principles of Securities Regulation (the IOSCO Principles); mems: 203 mems; Chair. GREG MEDCRAFT (Australia); Sec.-Gen. DAVID WRIGHT; publ. *Annual Report*.

International Union for Housing Finance (IUHF): 28 rue Jacques de Lalaing, 1040 Brussels, Belgium; tel. (2) 231-03-71; fax (2) 230-82-45; e-mail info@housingfinance.org; internet www.housingfinance.org; f. 1914 to foster worldwide interest in savings and home ownership and co-operation among mems; encourages comparative study of methods and practice in housing finance; promotes devt of appropriate legislation on housing finance; mems: 107 in over 45 countries; Sec.-Gen. Dr HARTWIG HAMM; publ. *Housing Finance International* (quarterly).

Islamic Financial Services Board: Sasana Kijang, Level 5, Bank Negara Malaysia, 2 Jalan Dato Onn, 50840 Kuala Lumpur, Malaysia; tel. (3) 91951400; fax (3) 91951405; e-mail ifsb_sec@ifsb.org; internet www.ifsb.org; f. 2002; aims to formulate standards and guiding principles for regulatory and supervisory agencies working within the Islamic financial services industry; mems: 185, incl. 58 regulatory and supervisory authorities, 8 orgs (including the World Bank, the IMF, the BIS, Islamic Development Bank, the Asian Development Bank), 112 financial institutions and professional firms, 7 self-regulatory orgs; Sec.-Gen. JASEEM AHMED.

Latin American Banking Federation (Federación Latinoamericana de Bancos—FELABAN): Cra 11A No. 93-67 Of. 202 A.A 091959, Bogotá, Colombia; tel. (1) 6215848; fax (1) 6217659; e-mail mangarita@felaban.com; internet www.felaban.com; f. 1965 to co-ordinate efforts towards wide and accelerated economic devt in Latin American countries; mems: 19 Latin American nat. banking asscns, representing more than 500 banks and financial institutions; Pres. JORGE HORACIO BRITO; Sec.-Gen. GIORGIO TRETTENERO CASTRO (Peru).

Nordic Investment Bank (NIB) (Nordiska Investeringsbanken): Fabianinkatu 34, POB 249, 00171 Helsinki, Finland; tel. (10) 618001; fax (10) 6180725; e-mail info@nib.int; internet www.nib.int; f. 1975; provides long-term loans and guarantees for both public and private projects in and outside its mem. countries; main business areas of the Bank are energy, environment, infrastructure, transport, telecommunications; industries, services; financial institutions and small and medium-sized enterprises; mems: govts of Denmark, Estonia, Finland, Iceland, Latvia, Lithuania, Norway and Sweden; Pres. and CEO HENRIK NORMANN.

Nordic Project Fund (Nopef): POB 241, 00171 Helsinki, Finland; tel. (9) 6840570; fax (9) 650113; e-mail brynhildur@kontakt.is; internet www.nopef.com; f. 1982; aims to strengthen the international competitiveness of Nordic exporting cos, and to promote industrial co-operation in international projects (e.g. in environmental protection); grants loans to Nordic cos for feasibility expenses relating to projects; with effect from 1 Jan. 2008 Nopef's geographical target area expanded to include Bulgaria, Romania and countries outside the European Union and EFTA; Chair. BRYNHILDUR BERGÞÓRSDÓTTIR; Man. Dir MIKAEL REIMS (acting).

South Asia Federation of Exchanges: W-96, Khyber Plaza, 2nd Floor, Fazal-ul-Haq Rd, Islamabad 44000, Pakistan; tel. (51) 2826763; fax (51) 2804215; e-mail farzin.khan@safe-asia.com; internet www.safe-asia.com; f. 2000 to promote the devt of securities markets in the region; aims to enhance mutual co-operation, and to establish a regional platform for South Asian stock exchanges; mems: 15 stock exchanges; Chair. AL MARUF KHAN.

Union of Arab Banks (UAB): POB 11-2416, Riad El-Solh 1107 2210, Beirut, Lebanon; tel. (1) 377800; fax (1) 364927; e-mail uab@uabonline.org; internet www.uabonline.org; f. 1974; aims to foster co-operation between Arab banks and to increase their efficiency; prepares feasibility studies for projects; organizes an annual International Arab Banking Summit (2014: Amman, Jordan, in April); mems: more than 330 Arab banks and financial institutions; Chair. MOHAMMED KAMEL EDDINE BARAKAT (Egypt); Sec.-Gen. WISSAM HASSAN FATTOUH (Lebanon).

World Council of Credit Unions (WOCCU): POB 2982, 5710 Mineral Point Rd, Madison, WI 53705-4493, USA; tel. (608) 395-2000; fax (608) 395-2001; e-mail mail@woccu.org; internet www.woccu.org; f. 1970 to link credit unions and similar co-operative financial institutions and assist them in expanding and improving their services; provides technical and financial assistance to credit union asscns in developing countries; mems: 55,952 credit unions in 101 countries; Pres. and CEO BRIAN BRANCH; publs *WOCCU Annual Report*, *Credit Union World* (3 a year), *Spotlights on Development*; technical monographs and brochures.

World Federation of Exchanges: 125 Old Broad St, London, EC2N 1AR, United Kingdom; tel. (20) 7151-4150; fax (20) 7151-4151; e-mail contact@secretariat@world-exchanges.org; internet www.world-exchanges.org; f. 1961; fmrly Fédération Internationale des Bourses de Valeurs—FIBV; central reference point for the securities industry; offers mem. exchanges guidance in business strategies, and improvement and harmonization of management practices; works with public financial authorities to promote increased use of regulated securities and derivatives exchanges; mems: 58 full mems, 2 assocs, 17 affiliates and 31 corresponding exchanges; Chair. ANDREAS PREUSS; CEO HÜSEYIN ERKAN.

World Savings Banks Institute: 11 rue Marie Thérèse, 1000 Brussels, Belgium; tel. (2) 211-11-11; fax (2) 211-11-99; e-mail info@savings-banks.com; internet www.wsbi.org; f. 1924 as International Savings Banks Institute, present name and structure adopted in 1994; promotes co-operation among mems and the devt of savings banks worldwide; mems: 104 banks and asscns in 86 countries; Pres. and Chair. HEINRICH HAASIS (Germany); Man. Dir CHRIS DE NOOSE; publs *Annual Report*, *International Savings Banks Directory*, *Perspectives* (4–5 a year).

Education

Agence Universitaire de la Francophonie (AUF): Case postale du Musée, CP 49714, Montréal, QC H3T 2A5, Canada; tel. (514) 343-6630; fax (514) 343-2107; e-mail rectorat@auf.org; internet www.auf.org; f. 1961; aims to develop a francophone univ. community, through building partnerships with students, teachers, institutions and govts; mems: 70 institutions in 40 countries; Pres. YVON FONTAINE (Canada); Exec. Dir BERNARD CERQUIGLINI; publ. *Le Français à l'Université* (quarterly).

AMSE-AMCE-WAER (Association mondiale des sciences de l'éducation) (Asociación mundial de ciencias de la educación) (World Association for Educational Research): c/o Gilles Baillat, University of Reims Champagne-Ardenne, 20 rue de l'Université, 51100 Reims, France; tel. 6-84-18-24-28; e-mail gilles.baillat@univ-reims.fr; internet www.univ-reims.fr/site/evenement/amse; f. 1953, present title adopted 2004; aims to encourage research in educational sciences by organizing congresses, issuing publications and supporting the exchange of information; mems: 27 research asscns; Pres. GILLES BAILLAT; publ. *Educational Research around the World*.

Asian Institute of Technology (AIT): POB 4, Klong Luang, Pathumthani 12120, Thailand; tel. (2) 524-5000; fax (2) 516-2126; e-mail president@ait.ac.th; internet www.ait.ac.th; f. 1959; master's, doctoral and diploma programmes are offered in four schools: Advanced Technologies, Civil Engineering, Environment, Resources and Development, and Management; specialized training is provided by the Center for Library and Information Resources (CLAIR), the Continuing Education Center, the Center for Language and Educational Technology, the Regional Computer Center, the AIT Center in Viet Nam (based in Hanoi) and the Swiss-AIT-Viet Nam Management Development Program (in Ho Chi Minh City); other research and outpost centres are the Asian Center for Engineering Computations and Software, the Asian Center for Research on Remote Sensing, the Regional Environmental Management Center, the Asian Center for Soil Improvement and Geosynthetics and the Urban Environmental Outreach Center; there are four specialized information centres (on ferro-cement, geotechnical engineering, renewable energy resources, environmental sanitation) under CLAIR; the Management of Technology Information Center conducts short-term courses in the management of technology and international business; Pres. Prof. WORSAK KANOK-NUKULCHAI (acting); publs *AIT Annual Report*, *Annual Report on Research and Activities*, *AIT Review* (3 a year), *Prospectus*, other specialized publs.

Asia South Pacific Association for Basic and Adult Education (ASPBAE): c/o MAAPL, Eucharistic Congress Bldg No. 3, 9th Floor, 5 Convent St, Colaba, Mumbai 400 039, India; tel. (22) 22021391; fax (22) 22832217; e-mail aspbae@gmail.com; internet www.aspbae.org; f. 1964, as Asian South Pacific Bureau of Adult Education, to assist non-formal education and adult literacy; organizes training courses and seminars; provides material and advice relating to adult education; mems in 32 countries; Pres. JOSE ROBERTO GUEVARA; Sec.-Gen. MARIA-LOURDES ALMAZAN-KHAN; publs *ASPBAE e-Bulletin*, *ASPBAE Ed-Lines* (3 a year).

Association for Childhood Education International: 1101 16th St., NW, Suite 300, Washington, DC 20036, USA; tel. (202) 372-9986; fax (202) 372-9989; e-mail headquarters@acei.org; internet www.acei.org; f. 1892 to work for the education of children (from infancy through early adolescence) by promoting desirable conditions in schools, raising the standard of teaching, co-operating with all groups concerned with children, informing the public of the needs of children; mems: 12,000; Pres. CARRIE WHALEY; Exec. Dir DIANE WHITEHEAD; publs *Childhood Education* (6 a year), *Professional Focus Newsletters*, *Journal of Research in Childhood Education* (quarterly), books on current educational subjects.

Association Montessori Internationale: Koninginneweg 161, 1075 CN Amsterdam, Netherlands; tel. (20) 6798932; fax (20) 6767341; e-mail info@montessori-ami.org; internet www.montessori-ami.org; f. 1929 to propagate the ideals and educational methods of Dr Maria Montessori on child devt, without racial, religious or political prejudice; organizes training courses for teachers in 26 countries; World Congress held every four years (2017: Prague, Czech Republic); Pres. ANDRÉ ROBERFROID (Belgium); Exec. Dir LYNNE LAWRENCE (United Kingdom); publs *AMI Journal* (2 a year), *AMI Bulletin*.

Association of African Universities (AAU) (Association des universités africaines): POB 5744, Accra-North, Ghana; tel. (21) 774495; fax (21) 774821; e-mail info@aau.org; internet www.aau.org; f. 1967 to promote exchanges, contact and co-operation among African univ. institutions and to collect and disseminate information on research and higher education in Africa; convenes a General Conference every four years (13th Conference: Libreville, Gabon, May 2013); mems: 282 in 46 countries; Pres. OLUSOLA OYEWOLE (Nigeria); Sec.-Gen. Prof. ETIENNE EHOUAN EHILE (Côte d'Ivoire); publs *AAU Newsletter* (3 a year), *Directory of African Universities* (every 2 years).

Association of Arab Universities: POB 2000, Amman, Jordan 13110; tel. (6) 5345131; fax (6) 5332994; e-mail secgen@aaru.edu.jo; internet www.aaru.edu.jo; f. 1964; a scientific conf. is held every three years; council meetings held annually; mems: 240 univs; Sec.-Gen. Prof. Dr SALEH HASHEM; publ. *AARU Bulletin* (annually and quarterly, in Arabic).

Association of Caribbean University and Research Institutional Libraries (ACURIL): Apdo postal 21609, San Juan 00931-1906, Puerto Rico; tel. 763-6199; e-mail executivesecretariat@acuril.org; internet www.acuril.uprrp.edu; f. 1968 to foster contact and collaboration between mem. univs and institutes; holds confs, meetings and seminars; circulates information through newsletters and bulletins; facilitates co-operation and the pooling of resources in research; encourages exchange of staff and students; mems: 250; Pres. CINDY JIMÉNEZ-VIRA; Exec.-Sec. LUISA VIGO-CEPEDA; publ. *Cybernotes*.

Association of South-East Asian Institutions of Higher Learning (ASAIHL): Secretariat, Rm 113, Jamjuree 1 Bldg, Chulalongkorn University, Phyathai Rd, Bangkok 10330, Thailand; tel. (2) 251-6966; fax (2) 253-7909; e-mail ninnat.o@chula.ac.th; internet www.seameo.org/asaihl; f. 1956 to promote the economic, cultural and social welfare of the people of South-East Asia by means of educational co-operation and research programmes; and to cultivate a sense of regional identity and interdependence; collects and disseminates information, organizes discussions; mems: 180 univ. institutions in 21 countries; Pres. IDRUS PATURUSI; Sec.-Gen. Dr NINNAT OLANVORAVUTH; publs *Newsletter*, *Handbook* (every 3 years).

Catholic International Education Office: 718 ave Houba de Strooper, 1020 Brussels, Belgium; tel. (2) 230-72-52; fax (2) 230-97-45; e-mail info@infoiec.org; internet www.infoiec.net; f. 1952 for the study of the problems of Catholic education throughout the world; co-ordinates the activities of mems; represents Catholic education at international bodies; mems: 102 countries, 18 assoc. mems, 13 collaborating mems, 6 corresponding mems; Pres. RODERICK SALAZAR; Sec.-Gen. ÁNGEL ASTORGANO; publs *OIEC Bulletin* (every 3 months, in English, French and Spanish), *OIEC Tracts on Education*.

Comparative Education Society in Europe (CESE): European University of Cyprus, POB 22006, 6 Diogenes Street, 1516 Nicosia, Cyprus; e-mail klerides.eleftherios@gmail.com; internet www.cese-europe.org; f. 1961 to promote teaching and research in comparative and international education; organizes confs and promotes literature; mems: in 49 countries; Pres. HANS-GEORG KOTTHOFF (Germany); Sec. and Treas. ELEFTHERIOS KLERIDES (Cyprus); publ. *Newsletter* (quarterly).

European Association for Education of Adults (EAEA): 40 rue d'Arlon, 1000 Brussels, Belgium; tel. (2) 234-37-63; fax (2) 235-05-39; e-mail eaea-info@eaea.org; internet www.eaea.org; f. 1953; aims to create a 'learning society' by encouraging demand for learning, particularly from women and excluded sectors of society; seeks to improve response of providers of learning opportunities and authorities and agencies; mems: 116 orgs in 43 countries; Pres. PER PALUDAN HANSEN; Sec.-Gen. GINA EBNER; publs *EAEA Monograph Series*, newsletter.

European Foundation for Management Development (EFMD): 88 rue Gachard, 1050 Brussels, Belgium; tel. (2) 629-08-10; fax (2) 629-08-11; e-mail info@efmd.org; internet www.efmd.org; f. 1971 through merger of European Association of Management Training Centres and International University Contact for Management Education; aims to help to improve the quality of management devt, disseminate information within the economic, social and cultural context of Europe and promote international co-operation; mems: over 750 institutions in 81 countries worldwide; Pres. ALAIN DOMINQUE PERRIN; Dir-Gen. ERIC CORNUEL; publs *Forum* (3 a year), *The Bulletin* (3 a year), *Guide to European Business Schools and Management Centres* (annually).

European University Association (EUA): 24 ave de l'Yser, 1040 Brussels, Belgium; tel. (2) 230-55-44; fax (2) 230-57-51; e-mail info@eua.be; internet www.eua.be; f. 2001 by merger of the Association of European Universities and the Confederation of EU Rectors' Conferences; represents European univs and national rectors' confs; promotes the devt of a coherent system of European higher education and research through projects and membership services; provides support and guidance to mems; mems: more than 850 in 47 countries; Pres. Prof. MARIA HELENA NAZARÉ; Sec.-Gen. LESLEY WILSON; publs *Thema*, *Directory*, *Annual Report*.

Graduate Institute of International and Development Studies (Institut universitaire de hautes études internationales—HEI): POB 136, 132 rue de Lausanne, 1211 Geneva 21, Switzerland; tel. 229085700; fax 229085710; e-mail webmaster@graduateinstitute.ch; internet graduateinstitute.ch; f. 1927, as the Graduate Institute of International Studies, to establish a centre for advanced studies in international relations of the present day; merged with the Graduate Institute of Development Studies in 2008; maintains a library of 147,000 vols; Dir Prof. PHILIPPE BURRIN.

Inter-American Centre for Research and Documentation on Vocational Training (Centro Interamericano de Investigación y Documentación sobre Formación Profesional—CINTERFOR): Avda Uruguay 1238, Casilla de correo 1761, Montevideo, Uruguay; tel. 2902 0557; fax 2902 1305; e-mail oitcinterfor@oitcinterfor.org; internet wwww.oitcinterfor.org; f. 1964 by the International Labour Organization for mutual help among the Latin American and Caribbean countries in planning vocational training; services are provided in documentation, research, exchange of experience; holds seminars and courses; Dir MARTHA PACHECA; publs *Bulletin CINTERFOR/OIT Heramientas para la transformación*, *Trazos de la formación*, studies, monographs and technical papers.

Inter-American Confederation for Catholic Education (Confederación Interamericana de Educación Católica—CIEC): Carrera 24, No. 34, Bogotá 37 DC, Colombia; tel. (1) 2871036; e-mail asistente@ciec.edu.co; internet www.ciec.edu.co; f. 1945 to defend and extend the principles and rules of Catholic education, freedom of education, and human rights; organizes congress every three years; Sec.-Gen. JOSÉ LEONARDO RINCÓN CONTRERAS (Colombia); publ. *Educación Hoy*.

Inter-American Organization for Higher Education (IOHE): Université de Montréal, 3744, Jean-Brillant, bureau 592, Québec H3T 1P1 6128, Canada; tel. (514) 343-6111; fax ((514) 343-6454; e-mail fbrown@oui-iohe.org; internet www.oui-iohe.org; f. 1980 to promote co-operation among univs of the Americas and the devt of higher education; mems: some 281 institutions and 35 nat. and reg. higher education asscns; Exec. Dir PATRICIA GUDIÑO.

International Anti-Corruption Academy (IACA): Münchendorfer Str. 2, 2361 Laxenburg, Austria; tel. (2236) 710-71-81-01; fax (2236) 710-71-83-11; e-mail mail@iaca.int; internet www.iaca.int; f. March 2011, as a joint initiative by the United Nations Office on Drugs and Crime (UNODC), the European Anti-Fraud Office (OLAF) and others; aims to expand existing knowledge and practice in the field of anti-corruption; Exec. Sec. MARTIN KREUTNER (Argentina).

International Association for Educational and Vocational Guidance (IAEVG): 119 Ross Ave, Suite 202, Ottawa, ON K1Y 0N6, Canada; tel. (613) 729-6164; fax (613) 729-3515; e-mail membership@iaevg.org; internet www.iaevg.org; f. 1951 to contribute to the devt of vocational guidance and promote contact between persons associated with it; mems: over 22,000 individuals; Pres. LESTER OAKES (New Zealand); Sec.-Gen. SUZANNE BULTHEEL (France); publs *IAEVG Journal* (2 a year), *Newsletter* (3 a year).

International Association of Educators for World Peace: POB 3282, Mastin Lake Station, Huntsville, AL 35810-0282, USA; tel. (256) 534-5501; fax (256) 536-1018; e-mail info@iaewp.org; internet www.iaewp.org; f. 1969 to develop education designed to contribute to the promotion of peaceful relations at personal, community and international levels; aims to communicate and clarify controversial views in order to achieve maximum understanding; organizes annual World Peace Congress; helps to put into practice the Universal Declaration of Human Rights; mems: 55,000 in 80 countries; Pres. Dr CHARLES MERCIECA (USA); Sec.-Gen. NENAD JAVORNIK (Croatia); publs *Diplomacy Journal* (every 3 months), *Peace Education Journal* (annually), other articles and irregular publications.

International Association of Papyrologists (Association Internationale de Papyrologues): Association Egyptologique Reine Elisabeth, Parc du Cinquantenaire 10, 1000 Brussels, Belgium; tel. (2) 741-73-64; e-mail amartin@ulb.ac.be; internet www.ulb.ac.be/assoc/aip; f. 1947; links all those interested in Graeco-Roman Egypt, especially Greek texts; mem. of the International Federation of the Societies of Classical Studies; mems: about 400; Pres. Prof. ANDREA JÖRDENS (Germany); Sec./Treas. Prof. ALAIN MARTIN (Belgium).

International Association of Physical Education in Higher Education (Association Internationale des Écoles Supérieures d'Éducation Physique—AIESEP): Department of Sport Sciences and Rehabilitation Sciences, University of Liège, Allée des Sports, 4 Bât B-21 B-4000 Liège, Belgium; tel. (4) 366-38-80; fax (4) 366-29-01; e-mail marc.cloes@ulg.ac.be; internet www.aiesep.org; f. 1962; organizes congresses, exchanges, and research in physical education; mems: institutions in 51 countries; Sec.-Gen. Dr MARC CLOES.

International Association of Universities (IAU): 1 rue Miollis, 75732 Paris Cedex 15, France; tel. 1-45-68-48-00; fax 1-47-34-76-05; e-mail iau@iau-aiu.net; internet www.iau-aiu.net; f. 1948 to allow co-operation at international level among univs and other institutions and orgs of higher education; provides clearing house services and operates the joint IAU/UNESCO Information Centre on Higher Education; brings together institutions and orgs from some 160 countries for reflection and action on common concerns, and collaborates with various international, regional and national bodies active in higher education; incorporates the International Universities Bureau; mems: more than 600 institutions of higher education and other orgs concerned with higher education in some 160 countries; Pres. DZULKIFLI ABDUL RAZAK (Malaysia); Sec.-Gen. and Exec. Dir EVA EGRON-POLAK; *Higher Education Policy* (quarterly), *IAU Horizons* (3 a year), *International Handbook of Universities* (annually), *World Higher Education Database (WHED) CD-ROM* (annually).

International Association of University Professors and Lecturers (IAUPL) (Association Internationale des Professeurs et Maîtres de Conférence Universitaires): c/o Prof. Michel Gay, 4 rue de Trévise, 75009, Paris, France; tel. 1-44-90-01-01; fax 1-46-59-01-23; e-mail migay@laposte.net; f. 1945 for the devt of academic fraternity among univ. teachers and research workers; the protection of independence and freedom of teaching and research; the furtherance of the interests of all univ. teachers; and the consideration of academic problems; mems: feds in 17 countries and territories.

International Baccalaureate Organization (IBO): 15 route des Morillons, Grand-Saconnex 1218, Geneva, Switzerland; tel. 223092540; fax 227882380; e-mail ibhq@ibo.org; internet www.ibo.org; f. 1968 to plan curricula and an international univ. entrance examination, the International Baccalaureate diploma, recognized by major univs worldwide; offers the Primary Years Programme for children aged 3–12, the Middle Years Programme for students in the 11–16 age range, and the Diploma Programme for 17–18-year-olds; mems: 3,676 participating schools in 146 countries; Chair. of Board of Governors CAROL BELLAMY (USA); Sec. KATY RICKS (United Kingdom).

International Catholic Federation for Physical and Sports Education (Fédération Internationale Catholique d'Education Physique et Sportive—FICEP): 22 rue Oberkampf, 75011 Paris, France; e-mail info@ficep.org; internet www.ficep.org; f. 1911 to group Catholic asscns for physical education and sport of different countries and to develop the principles and precepts of Christian morality by fostering meetings, study and int. co-operation; mems: 14 affiliated nat. feds representing about 3m. mems; Pres. GERHARD HAUER; Sec.-Gen. ANNE CORDIER.

International Centre for Minority Studies and Inter-Cultural Relations (IMIR) : 1303 Sofia, ul. I Antim 55, Bulgaria; tel. (2) 832-31-12; fax (2) 931-05-83; e-mail marko@imir-bg.org; internet www.imir-bg.org; f. 1992 to carry out scientific research and humanitarian work with minority communities in Bulgaria; works with experts in the study of ethnic relations and religious issues in the wider Balkan region; Chair. Dr ANTONINA ZHELYAZKOVA (Bulgaria); publs research, analyses, forecasts and policy recommendations.

International Council for Adult Education (ICAE): Ave 18 de Julio 2095/301, CP 11200, Montevideo, Uruguay; tel. and fax 2409 7982; e-mail secretariat@icae.org.uy; internet www.icae2.org; f. 1973 as a partnership of adult learners, teachers and orgs; General Assembly meets every four years; mems: 7 reg. orgs and over 700 literacy, adult and lifelong learning asscns in more than 50 countries; Pres. ALAN TUCKETT; Sec.-Gen. CELITA ECCHER; publs *Convergence*, *ICAE News*.

International Council for Open and Distance Education (ICDE): Lilleakerveien 23, 0283 Oslo, Norway; tel. 22-06-26-30; fax 22-06-26-31; e-mail icde@icde.no; internet www.icde.org; f. 1938 (name changed 1982); furthers distance education by promoting research, encouraging regional links, providing information and organizing confs; mems: institutions, corporations and individuals worldwide; Pres. TIAN BELAWATI (Indonesia); Sec.-Gen. GARD TITLESTAD (Norway); publ. *Open Praxis* (online, at www.openpraxis.com).

International Dance Teachers' Association (IDTA): International House, 76 Bennett Rd, Brighton, East Sussex, BN2 5JL, United Kingdom; tel. (1273) 685652; fax (1273) 674388; e-mail carol@idta.co.uk; internet www.idta.co.uk; f. 1967; aims to promote knowledge and foster the art of dance in all its forms; to offer a comprehensive range of professional qualifications in all dance genres; mems: over 7,000 in 55 countries; Pres. ANNA JONES; Exec. Dir KEITH HOLMES.

International Federation for Parent Education (IFPE) (Fédération internationale pour l'éducation des parents—FIEP): 1 ave Léon Journault, 92318 Sèvres Cedex, France; tel. 4-77-21-67-43; fax 1-46-26-69-27; e-mail marycrowleyjohnson@gmail.com; internet www.fiep-ifpe.fr; f. 1964 to gather in congresses and colloquia experts from different scientific fields and those responsible for family education in their own countries and to encourage the establishment of family education where it does not exist; mems: 60 nat. and local mem. orgs, 35 individual mems and 4 int. or reg. orgs; Sec.-Gen. MARTHA ILIESCU (Romania); publ. *Lettre de la FIEP* (2 a year).

International Federation of Catholic Universities (Fédération internationale d'universités catholiques—FIUC): 21 rue d'Assas, 75270 Paris Cedex 06, France; tel. 1-44-39-52-26; fax 1-44-39-52-28; e-mail sgfiuc@bureau.fiuc.org; internet www.fiuc.org; f. 1948; aims to ensure a strong bond of mutual assistance among all Catholic univs in the search for truth; to help to solve problems of growth and devt, and to co-operate with other int. orgs; mems: some 215 in 58 countries; Pres. PEDRO RUBENS FERREIRA OLIVEIRA; Sec.-Gen. GUY-RÉAL THIVIERGE (Canada); publ. *Monthly Newsletter*.

International Federation of Library Associations and Institutions (IFLA): POB 95312, 2509 CH The Hague, Netherlands; tel. (70) 3140884; fax (70) 3834827; e-mail ifla@ifla.org; internet www.ifla.org; f. 1927 to promote international co-operation in librarianship and bibliography; mems: over 1,450 in 140 countries; Pres. (2013–15) SINIKKA SIPILÄ (Finland); Sec.-Gen. JENNEFER NICHOLSON (Australia); publs *IFLA Annual Report*, *IFLA Directory*, *IFLA Journal*, *International Cataloguing and Bibliographic Control* (quarterly), *IFLA Professional Reports*.

International Federation of Physical Education (Fédération internationale d'éducation physique—FIEP): Foz do Iguaçu, PR, Brazil; tel. (45) 3574-1949; fax (45) 3525-1272; e-mail fiep.brasil@uol.com.br; internet www.fiep.net; f. 1923; studies physical education on scientific, pedagogic and aesthetic bases, with the aim of stimulating health, harmonious devt or preservation, healthy recreation, and the best adaptation of the individual to the general needs of social life; organizes int. congresses and courses; awards research prize; mems: from 112 countries; Pres. Prof. ALMIR GRUHN (Brazil); Sec. CLÁUDIO A. BOSHI (Brazil); publ. *FIEP Bulletin* (3 a year, in English, French and Spanish).

International Federation of Teachers of Modern Languages (Fédération des Professeurs de Langues Vivantes): POB 216, Belgrave 3160, Australia; tel. (6139) 754-4714; fax (6139) 416-9899; e-mail djc@netspace.net.au; internet www.fiplv.org; f. 1931; holds meetings on every aspect of foreign-language teaching; has consultative status with UNESCO; mems: 28 nat. and reg. language asscns and 9 int. unilingual asscns (teachers of Arabic, English, Esperanto, French, German, Portuguese, Russian); Pres. TERRY LAMB; Sec.-Gen. DENIS CUNNINGHAM.

International Federation of University Women (IFUW): 10 rue du Lac, 1207 Geneva, Switzerland; tel. 227312380; fax 227380440; e-mail ifuw@ifuw.org; internet www.ifuw.org; f. 1919; to promote lifelong learning; to work for improvement of the status of women and girls; to encourage and enable women as leaders and decision-makers; Affiliates: 63 nat. asscns and feds; Pres. CATHERINE BELL.

International Federation of Workers' Education Associations: c/o Labour Research Service, POB 376, Woodstock 7915, Cape Town, South Africa; tel. (21) 447-1677; fax (21) 447-9244; e-mail ifweasecretariat@lrs.org.za; internet www.ifwea.org; f. 1947 to promote co-operation between non-governmental bodies concerned with workers' education; organizes clearing house services; promotes exchange of information; holds international seminars, confs and summer schools; Pres. SUE SCHURMAN (USA); Gen. Sec. SAHRA RYKLIEF (South Africa); publ. *Worker's Education* (quarterly).

International Institute of Philosophy (IIP) (Institut international de philosophie): 96 blvd Raspail, 75006 Paris, France; tel. 1-43-36-39-11; e-mail inst.intern.philo@wanadoo.fr; internet www.i-i-p.org; f. 1937 to clarify fundamental issues of contemporary philosophy and to promote mutual understanding among thinkers of different backgrounds and traditions; mems: 107 in 45 countries; Pres. ENRICO BERTI (Italy); Sec.-Gen. BERNARD BOURGEOIS (France); publs *Bibliography of Philosophy* (quarterly), *Proceedings of annual meetings*, *Chroniques*, *Philosophy and World Community* (series), *Philosophical Problems Today*, *Open Problems*, *Philosophy of Education*.

International Reading Association: 800 Barksdale Rd, POB 8139, Newark, DE 19714-8139, USA; tel. (302) 731-1600; fax (302) 731-1057; e-mail pubinfo@reading.org; internet www.reading.org; f. 1956 to improve the quality of reading instruction at all levels, to promote the habit of lifelong reading, and to develop every reader's proficiency; mems: 85,000 in 118 countries; Pres. JILL LEWIS-SPECTOR (USA); Exec. Dir MARCIE CRAIG POST; publs *The Reading Teacher* (8 a year), *Journal of Adolescent and Adult Literacy* (8 a year), *Reading Research Quarterly*, *Lectura y Vida* (quarterly), *Reading Today* (6 a year).

International Schools Association (ISA): 10333 Diego Drive South, Boca Raton, FL 33428, USA; tel. (561) 883-3854; fax (561) 483-2004; e-mail info@isaschools.org; internet www.isaschools.org; f. 1951 to co-ordinate work in international schools and to promote their devt; convenes biennial Conferences and annual Youth Leadership Seminars on topics of global concern, and organizes specialist seminars on internationalism and international-mindedness; also issues self-study guides and certificates, and provides consultancy services and examination programmes in oral English; has consultative status at ECOSOC; mems: 100 schools worldwide; Chair. LUIS MARTINEZ ZORZO; Sec.-Gen. ANDREW MCEWEN.

International Society for Business Education (Société Internationale pour l'Enseignement Commercial—SIEC): 6302 Mineral Point Rd, 100 Madison, WI 53705, USA; tel. (608) 273-8467; e-mail secretary@siec-isbe.org; internet www.siec-isbe.org; f. 1901; encourages international exchange of information; organizes courses and congresses on business education; mems: 2,200 nat. orgs and individuals in 23 countries; Pres. PETRA BRAGADÓTTIR (Iceland); Gen. Sec. Dr JUDITH OLSON-SUTTON (USA); publ. *International Review for Business Education*.

International Society for Education through Art (INSEA): e-mail secretary@insea.org; internet www.insea.org; f. 1951 to unite art teachers throughout the world, to exchange information and to co-ordinate research into art education; organizes int. congresses and exhibitions of children's art; Pres. RITA IRWIN (Canada); Sec. GRAHAM NASH (Australia); publ. *International Journal for Education through Art* (3 a year).

International Society for Music Education (ISME): Suite 148, 45 Glenferrie Rd, Malvern, Victoria 3144, Australia; e-mail isme@isme.org; internet www.isme.org; f. 1953 to organize international confs, seminars and publications on matters pertaining to music education; acts as advisory body to UNESCO in matters of music education; organizes biennial World Conference (2014: Porto Alegre, Brazil); mems: nat. cttees and individuals in more than 70 countries; Pres. MARGARET BARRETT (Australia); Sec.-Gen. ANGELA RUGGLES (United Kingdom); publs *ISME Newsletter*, *International Journal of Music Education*.

International Society for the Study of Medieval Philosophy (SIEPM): Albert-Ludwigs-Universität Freiburg, Philosophisches Seminar, Platz der Universität 3, 79085 Freiburg, Germany; tel. (10) 47-48-07; fax (10) 47-82-85; internet www.siepm.uni-freiburg.de; f. 1958 to promote the study of medieval thought and the collaboration between individuals and institutions in this field; organizes International Congress of Medieval Philosophy every five years; mems: 800 in 45 countries; Sec. Prof. MAARTEN J. F. M. HOENEN; publ. *Bulletin de Philosophie Médiévale* (annually).

International Youth Library (Internationale Jugendbibliothek): Schloss Blutenburg, 81247 Munich, Germany; tel. (89) 8912110; fax (89) 8117553; e-mail info@ijb.de; internet www.ijb.de; f. 1949, since 1953 an associated project of UNESCO; promotes the international exchange of children's literature; provides study opportunities for specialists in childrens' books; maintains a library of 600,000 volumes in about 130 languages; Dir Dr CHRISTIANE RAABE; publs *The White Ravens*, *Das Bücherschloss*, catalogues.

Italian-Latin American Institute: Via Giovanni Paisiello 24, 00198 Rome, Italy; tel. (06) 684921; fax (06) 6872834; e-mail info@iila.org; internet www.iila.org; f. 1966; aims to promote Italian culture in Latin America; awarded observer status at the UN General Assembly in 2007; Dir-Gen. SIMONETTA CAVALIERI; Sec.-Gen. GIORGIO MALFATTI DI MONTE TRETTO.

LIBER (Association of European Research Libraries) (Ligue des Bibliothèques Européennes de Recherche): National Library of the Netherlands, POB 90407, 2509 LK The Hague, Netherlands; tel. (70) 3140767; fax (70) 3140197; e-mail liber@kb.nl; internet www.libereurope.eu; f. 1971 to encourage collaboration between the general research libraries of Europe, and national and univ. libraries in particular; gives assistance in finding practical ways of improving the quality of the services provided; mems: 400 libraries, library orgs and individuals in 40 countries; Pres. PAUL AYRIS; Sec.-Gen. ANN MATHESON; publ. *LIBER Quarterly*.

Organization of Ibero-American States for Education, Science and Culture (Organización de Estados Iberoamericanos para la Educación, la Ciencia y la Cultura—OEI): Centro de Recursos Documentales e Informáticos, Calle Bravo Murillo 38, 28015 Madrid, Spain; tel. (91) 5944382; fax (91) 5944622; internet www.oei.es; f. 1949 (as the Ibero-American Bureau of Education); promotes peace and solidarity between mem. countries, through education, science, technology and culture; provides information, encourages exchanges and organizes training courses; the General Assembly (at ministerial level) meets every four years; mems: govts of 20 countries; Sec.-Gen. ÁLVARO MARCHESI ULLASTRES; publ. *Revista Iberoamericana de Educación* (quarterly).

Organization of the Catholic Universities of Latin America (Organización de Universidades Católicas de América Latina—ODUCAL): Av. Libertador Bernardo O'Higgins 340, Of. 242, 2° piso, Santiago, Chile; tel. and fax (2) 354-1866; e-mail oducal@uc.cl; internet www.oducal.uc.cl; f. 1953 to assist the social, economic and cultural devt of Latin America through the promotion of Catholic higher education in the continent; mems: 43 Catholic univs in 15 countries; Pres. Dr PEDRO PABLO ROSSO; Sec.-Gen. ANTONIO DAHER HECHEM; publs *Anuario*, *Sapientia*, *Universitas*.

Pan-African Association for Literacy and Adult Education: Rue 10, Bldg 306, POB 21783, Ponty, Dakar, Senegal; tel. 825-48-50; fax 824-44-13; e-mail anafa@sentoo.sn; f. 2000 to succeed African Asscn for Literacy and Adult Education (f. 1984); Co-ordinator Dr LAMINE KANE.

Southeast Asian Ministers of Education Organization (SEAMEO): M. L. Pin Malakul Bldg, 920 Sukhumvit Rd, Bangkok 10110, Thailand; tel. (2) 391-0144; fax (2) 381-2587; e-mail secretariat@seameo.org; internet www.seameo.org; f. 1965 to promote co-operation among the South-East Asian nations through projects in education, science and culture; SEAMEO has 21 regional centres including: BIOTROP for tropical biology, in Bogor, Indonesia; INNOTECH for educational innovation and technology, in Philippines; SEAMOLEC, an open learning centre, in Indonesia; RECSAM for education in science and mathematics, in Penang, Malaysia; SEN for supporting the special educational needs of disabled and gifted children; RELC for languages, in Singapore; RIHED for higher education devt, in Bangkok, Thailand; SEARCA for graduate study and research in agriculture, in Los Baños, Philippines; SPAFA for archaeology and fine arts, in Bangkok, Thailand; TROPMED for tropical medicine and public health, with regional centres in Indonesia, Malaysia, Philippines and Thailand and a central office in Bangkok; VOCTECH for vocational and technical education; QITEPs, regional centres for quality improvement of teachers and education personnel, for language, based in Jakarta, Indonesia, for mathematics, in Yogyakarta, Indonesia, and for science, in Bandung, Indonesia; RETRAC, a training centre, in Ho Chi Minh City, Viet Nam; CELLL, promoting lifelong learning, in Ho Chi Minh City, Viet Nam; and the SEAMEO Regional Centre for History and Tradition (CHAT) in Yangon, Myanmar; mems: Brunei, Cambodia, Indonesia, Laos, Malaysia, Philippines, Singapore, Thailand, Timor-Leste and Viet Nam; assoc. mems: Australia, Canada, France, Germany, Netherlands, New Zealand, Norway, Spain and United Kingdom; Dir Dr WITAYA JERADECHAKUL (Thailand); publs *Annual Report*, *SEAMEO Education Agenda*; *Journal of Southeast Education*.

Union of Universities of Latin America and the Caribbean (Unión de Universidades de América Latina y el Caribe—UDUAL): Circuito Norponiente del Estadio Olímpico, Apartado Postal 70-232, Ciudad Universitaria, Del. Coyoacán, 04510 México, DF, Mexico; tel. (55) 5616-2383; fax (55) 5622-0092; e-mail enlace@udual.org; internet www.udual.org; f. 1949 to organize exchanges between professors, students, research fellows and graduates and generally encourage good relations between the Latin American univs; arranges confs; conducts statistical research; maintains centre for univ. documentation; mems: 240 univs and 8 univ. networks; Pres. JOSE TADEU JORGE (Brazil); Sec.-Gen. Dr ROBERTO ESCALANTE SEMERENA (Mexico); publs *Universidades* (2 a year), *Gaceta UDUAL* (quarterly), *Censo* (every 2 years).

Universal Esperanto Association (Universala Esperanto-Asocio): Nieuwe Binnenweg 176, 3015 BJ Rotterdam, Netherlands; tel. (10) 4361044; fax (10) 4361751; e-mail info@co.uea.org; internet www.uea.org; f. 1908 to assist the spread of the international language, Esperanto, and to facilitate the practical use of the language; organizes World Congresses (2014: Buenos Aires, Argentina, in July); mems: 71 affiliated national asscns and 15,800 individuals in 118 countries; Pres. MARK FETTES (Canada); Sec.-Gen. MARTIN SCHÄFFER (Mexico); publs *Esperanto* (monthly), *Kontakto* (every 2 months), *Jarlibro* (annually).

World Union of Catholic Teachers (Union mondiale des enseignants catholiques—UMEC): Clivo Monte del Gallo, 48, 00165 Rome, Italy; tel. (06) 634651; fax (06) 39375903; e-mail admin@wuct-umec.org; internet www.wuct-umec.info; f. 1951; encourages the grouping of Catholic teachers for the greater effectiveness of Catholic schools, distributes documentation on Catholic doctrine with regard to education, and facilitates personal contacts through congresses, and seminars, etc; nationally and internationally; mems: 32 orgs in 29 countries; Pres. GUY BOURDEAUD'HUI; publ. *Nouvelles de l'UMEC*.

Environmental Conservation

African Conservation Foundation: POB 189, Buéa, Cameroon; e-mail info@africanconservation.org; internet www

.africanconservation.org; f. 1999 as an Africa-wide network for information exchange and capacity building towards environmental conservation; aims to improve management and utilization of natural resources to reconcile devt needs in the region with biodiversity conservation; Dir AREND DE HAAS.

BirdLife International: Wellbrook Ct, Girton Rd, Cambridge, CB3 0NA, United Kingdom; tel. (1223) 277318; fax (1223) 277200; e-mail birdlife@birdlife.org; internet www.birdlife.org; f. 1922 as the International Council for Bird Preservation; a global partnership of organizations that determines status of bird species throughout the world and compiles data on all endangered species; identifies conservation problems and priorities; initiates and co-ordinates conservation projects and international conventions; mems: partners or representatives in more than 100 countries; Chair. KHALED ANIS IRANI (Jordan); Dir a.i. Dr HAZELL SHOKELLU THOMPSON (Sierra Leone); publs *Bird Red Data Book*, *World Birdwatch* (quarterly), *Bird Conservation Series*, study reports.

Coalition Clean Baltic (CCB): Östra Ågatan 53, SE-753 22 Uppsala, Sweden; tel. (18) 71-11-55; fax (18) 71-11-75; e-mail secretariat@ccb.se; internet www.ccb.se; f. 1990, network of environmental non-governmental orgs from countries bordering the Baltic Sea; Chair. JAKUB SKORUPSKI (Poland); Exec. Sec. GUNNAR NORÉN.

Commission for the Conservation of Antarctic Marine Living Resources (CCAMLR): POB 213, North Hobart, Tasmania 7002, Australia; tel. (3) 6210-1111; fax (3) 6224-8744; e-mail ccamlr@ccamlr.org; internet www.ccamlr.org; established under the 1982 Convention on the Conservation of Antarctic Marine Living Resources to manage marine resources in the Antarctic region; Exec. Sec. ANDREW WRIGHT.

Commission on the Protection of the Black Sea Against Pollution: Fatih Orman Kampüsü, Büyükdere Cad. 265, 34398 Maslak Şişli, İstanbul, Turkey; tel. (212) 2992940; fax (212) 2992944; e-mail secretariat@blacksea-commission.org; internet www.blacksea-commission.org; established under the 1992 Convention on the Protection of the Black Sea Against Pollution (Bucharest Convention) to implement the Convention and its Protocols; also oversees the 1996 Strategic Action Plan for the Rehabilitation and Protection of the Black Sea; Exec. Dir Prof. HALIL IBRAHIM SUR.

Consortium for Ocean Leadership: 1201 New York Ave, NW, Suite 420, Washington, DC 20005, USA; tel. (202) 232-3900; fax (202) 462-8754; e-mail info@oceanleadership.org; internet www.oceanleadership.org; f. 2007, following the merger of the Consortium for Oceanographic Research and Education (f. 1999) and the Joint Oceanographic Institutions; aims to promote, support and advance the science of oceanography; Pres. ROBERT B. GAGOSIAN.

Environment and Security Initiative (ENVSEC): c/o UNEP Regional Office for Europe, 11–13 chemin des Anémones, 1219 Châtelaine, Geneva, Switzerland; tel. 229178779; fax 229178024; e-mail marika.palosaari@unep.org; internet www.envsec.org; a partnership comprising UNEP, UNDP, the ECE, NATO, the OSCE, and the Regional Environment Centre for Central and Eastern Europe; the partner agencies aim to use their specialized and complementary mandates and expertise to strengthen co-operation to contribute to the reduction of environmental and security risks in Central Asia, Eastern Europe, Southern Caucasus, and South-Eastern Europe; the ENVSEC process involves assessing the situation on the ground and mapping problem areas ('hotspots'); drawing the attention of politicians to such hotspots; developing related work programmes and project portfolios; and supporting concrete actions to address security concerns on the ground; ENVSEC undertakes vulnerability assessments, and early warning and monitoring of environmental and security risks; supports national institutions in capacity building for strengthening environmental and security policies; provides technical expertise and mobilizes financial resources for environmental clean-up activities; and aims to raise awareness about linkages between environment and security risks; Chair. MARTA SZIGETI BONIFERT; Co-ordination Officer MARIKA PALOSAARI.

Forest Stewardship Council (FSC): Charles de Gaulle Str. 5, 53113 Bonn, Germany; tel. (228) 367660; fax (228) 3676630; e-mail fsc@fsc.org; internet www.fsc.org; f. 1994 to promote sustainable and socially aware practices in forest management while ensuring economic viability in the utilization of forest resources; certifies forest areas based on these criteria; mems: in 80 countries; Exec. Dir KIM CARSTENSEN (Denmark).

Framework Convention for the Protection of the Marine Environment of the Caspian Sea: Interim Secretariat, c/o UNEP Regional Office for Europe, 11 chemin des Anémones, 1219 Châtelaine, Geneva, Switzerland; tel. 229178696; e-mail tehranconvention@unep.ch; internet www.tehranconvention.org; the Framework Convention for the Protection of the Marine Environment of the Caspian Sea (Tehran Convention) was adopted in Nov. 2003 by the Governments of Azerbaijan, Iran, Kazakhstan, Russia and Turkmenistan; the Aktau Protocol Concerning Regional Preparedness, Response and Co-operation in Combating Oil Pollution Incidents was adopted in Aug. 2011; the fourth Conference of the Parties, convened in Moscow, Russia, in Dec. 2012, adopted a Protocol for the Protection of the Caspian Sea against Pollution from Land-based Sources and Activities; the Tehran Convention process is funded by the Global Environment Facility, the European Union and UNEP.

Friends of the Earth International: POB 19199, 1000 GD, Amsterdam, Netherlands; tel. (20) 6221369; fax (20) 6392181; internet www.foei.org; f. 1971 to promote the conservation, restoration and rational use of the environment and natural resources through public education and campaigning; mems: 76 nat. groups; Chair. JAGODA MUNIĆ (Croatia); International Co-ordinator DAVE HIRSCH (USA); publ. *Link* (quarterly).

Global Coral Reef Monitoring Network: c/o IUCN Conservation Centre, 28 Rue Mauverney, 1196 Gland, Switzerland; tel. 229990217; fax 229990025; e-mail coordinator@gcrmn.org; internet www.gcrmn.org; f. 1994, as an operating unit of the International Coral Reef Initiative; active in more than 80 countries; aims include improving the management and sustainable conservation of coral reefs, strengthening links between regional organizations and ecological and socio-economic monitoring networks, and disseminating information to assist the formulation of conservation plans; publ. *Status of Coral Reefs of the World*.

Global Wind Energy Council: Wind Power House, 80 rue d'Arlon, 1040 Brussels, Belgium; tel. (2) 213-18-97; fax (2) 213-18-90; e-mail info@gwec.net; internet www.gwec.net; represents the main national, regional and international institutions, cos and asscns related to wind power; aims to promote the devt and growth of wind as a major source of energy; organizes a Global Wind Power Conference every two years (2013: Chicago, USA, in May); Chair. KLAUS RAVE (Germany); Sec.-Gen. STEVE SAWYER (USA); publs *Global Wind Energy Outlook*, *Global Wind Report*, other reports, surveys.

Greencross International: 9–11 rue de Varembé, 1202 Geneva, Switzerland; tel. 227891662; fax 227891695; e-mail gcinternational@gci.ch; internet www.greencrossinternational.net; f. 1993; aims to promote Earth Charter, to mitigate the environmental legacy of conflicts, to deter conflict in water-stressed regions, to combat desertification, to promote new energy consumption patterns, and to promote international confs on and awareness of environmental issues; Chair. JAN KULCZYK (Poland); Pres. ALEXANDER LIKHOTAL (Russia).

Greenpeace International: Ottho Heldringstraat 5, 1066 AZ Amsterdam, Netherlands; tel. (20) 7182000; fax (20) 7182002; e-mail supporter.services.int@greenpeace.org; internet www.greenpeace.org; f. 1971 to campaign for the protection of the environment through non-violent direct action, and to offer solutions for positive change; aims to change attitudes and behaviour, to protect and conserve the environment, to promote peace by working for solutions for positive change; to maintain its independence Greenpeace does not accept donations from govts or corporations but relies on contributions from individual supporters and foundation grants; mems: representation in more than 40 countries across Europe, the Americas, Africa, Asia and the Pacific; Chair., Bd of Dirs ANA TONI (Brazil).

International Commission for the Protection of the Rhine: Postfach 200253, 56002 Koblenz, Germany; tel. (261) 94252; fax (261) 9425252; e-mail sekretariat@iksr.de; internet www.iksr.org; f. 1950; prepares and commissions research on the nature of the pollution of the Rhine; proposes protection, ecological rehabilitation and flood prevention measures; mems: 23 delegates from France, Germany, Luxembourg, Netherlands, Switzerland and the European Union; Chair. ANDRÉ WEIDENHAUPT; Sec.-Gen. BEN VAN DE WETERING; publ. *Annual Report*.

International Coral Reef Initiative: c/o Biodiversity Policy Div., Ministry of the Environment, 1-2-2 Kasumigaseki, Chiyoda-ku, 100-8975 Tokyo, Japan; e-mail icri@env.go.jp; internet www.icriforum.org; f. 1994 at the first Conference of the Parties of the Convention on Biological Diversity; a partnership of govts, international orgs and non-governmental orgs; aims to raise awareness at all levels on the degradation of coral reefs around the world; promotes sustainable management practices and supports the conservation of reefs and related marine ecosystems; the Secretariat is co-chaired by a developed and a developing country, on a rotational basis among mem. states (2014–15, Japan and Thailand); mems: 60 govts, int. and reg. orgs; Co-Chair. REIJI KAMEZAWA (Japan), NIPHON PHONGSUWAN (Thailand).

International Emissions Trading Association: 24 rue Merle d'Aubigné, 1207 Geneva, Switzerland; tel. 227370500; fax 227370508; e-mail secretariat@ieta.org; internet www.ieta.org; f. 1999 to establish a functional international framework for trading greenhouse gas emissions, in accordance with the objectives of the UN Framework Convention on Climate Change; serves as a specialized information centre on emissions trading and the greenhouse gas market; mems: 155 int. cos; Pres. and CEO DIRK FORRISTER.

International Fund for Saving the Aral Sea: 050020 Almatı, Dostyk Av. 280, Kazakhstan; tel. (727) 387-34-31; fax (727) 387-34-33; e-mail mail@ec-ifas.org; internet www.ec-ifas.org; f. 1993 by Central Asian heads of state; incorporates an Intergovernmental Sustainable Development Commission and an Interstate Commission for Water Co-ordination; granted observer status at the UN General Assembly in Nov. 2008; an international scientific conf. was held in May 2013 to commemorate the Fund's 20th anniversary; aims to incorporate the Syrdarya River Delta Wetlands into the Ramsar List of Wetlands of International Importance; mems: Kazakhstan, Kyrgyzstan, Tajikistan, Turkmenistan, Uzbekistan; Chair. SHAVKAT KHAMRAYEV (Uzbekistan).

International Renewable Energy Agency: C67 Office Bldg, Khalidiyah (32nd) St, POB 236, Abu Dhabi, United Arab Emirates; tel. (2) 4179000; internet www.irena.org; f. 2009 at a conf. held in Bonn, Germany; aims to promote the devt and application of renewable sources of energy; to act as a forum for the exchange of information and technology transfer; and to organize training seminars and other educational activities; inaugural Assembly convened in April 2011; mems: 119 mems (incl. the European Union); at Oct. 2013 a further 44 countries had signed but not yet ratified the founding agreement or had applied to become full mems; Dir-Gen. ADNAN Z. AMIN (Kenya).

IUCN—International Union for Conservation of Nature: 28 rue Mauverney, 1196 Gland, Switzerland; tel. 229990000; fax 229990002; e-mail mail@iucn.org; internet www.iucn.org; f. 1948, as the International Union for Conservation of Nature and Natural Resources; supports partnerships and practical field activities to promote the conservation of natural resources, to secure the conservation of biological diversity as an essential foundation for the future; to ensure the equitable and sustainable use of the Earth's natural resources; and to guide the devt of human communities towards ways of life in enduring harmony with other components of the biosphere, developing programmes to protect and sustain the most important and threatened species and eco-systems and assisting govts to devise and carry out national conservation strategies; incorporates the Species Survival Commission, a science-based network of volunteer experts aiming to ensure conservation of present levels of biodiversity; compiles annually updated Red List of Threatened Species (www.iucnredlist.org); the 2013 list, released in July of that year, comprised some 70,294 species, of which 20,934 were threatened with extinction; maintains a conservation library and documentation centre and units for monitoring traffic in wildlife; mems: more than 1,000 states, govt agencies, non-governmental orgs and affiliates in some 140 countries; Pres. ZHANG XINSHENG (People's Republic of China); publs *World Conservation Strategy*, *Caring for the Earth*, *Red List of Threatened Plants*, *Red List of Threatened Species*, *United Nations List of National Parks and Protected Areas*, *World Conservation* (quarterly), *IUCN Today*.

Nordic Environment Finance Corporation (NEFCO): Fabianinkatu 34, POB 249, 00171 Helsinki, Finland; tel. (10) 618003; fax (9) 630976; e-mail info@nefco.fi; internet www.nefco.org; f. 1990; finances environmentally beneficial projects in Central and Eastern Europe with transboundary effects that also benefit the Nordic region; Man. Dir MAGNUS RYSTEDT.

Permanent Commission of the South Pacific (Comisión Permanente del Pacífico Sur): Av. Carlos Julio Arosemena, Km 3 Edificio Inmaral, Guayaquil, Ecuador; tel. (4) 222-1202; fax (4) 222-1201; e-mail sgeneral@cpps-int.org; internet www.cpps-int.org; f. 1952 to consolidate the presence of the zonal coastal states; Sec.-Gen. HÉCTOR SOLDI SOLDI (Peru).

Secretariat of the Antarctic Treaty: Maipú 757, piso 4, Buenos Aires, Argentina; tel. (11) 4320-4250; fax (11) 4320-4253; e-mail ats@ats.aq; internet www.ats.aq; f. 2004 to administer the Antarctic Treaty (signed in 1959); has developed an Electronic Information Exchange System; organizes annual Consultative Meeting; mems: 50 states have ratified the Treaty; Exec. Sec. Dr MANFRED REINKE.

Secretariat of the Pacific Regional Environment Programme (SPREP): POB 240, Apia, Samoa; tel. 21929; fax 20231; e-mail sprep@sprep.org; internet www.sprep.org; f. 1978 by the South Pacific Commission (where it was based, now Pacific Community), the South Pacific (now Pacific Islands) Forum, ESCAP and UNEP; formally established as an independent institution in 1993; SPREP's mandate is to promote co-operation in the Pacific islands region and to provide assistance in order to protect and improve the environment and to ensure sustainable devt for present and future generations; has the following four strategic priorities: Biodiversity and Ecosystems Management, Climate Change, Environmental Monitoring and Governance, Waste Management and Pollution Control; convenes a biennial Pacific Climate Change Roundtable (2013: Nada, Fiji, in July); in March 2010 letters of agreement were signed relating to the transfer and integration to SPREP from the Pacific Islands Applied Geoscience Commission of the following functions: the Pacific Islands Global Ocean Observing System; the Islands Climate Update; the Climate and Meteorological Databases; and climate change-associated energy activities; mems: 21 Pacific islands, Australia, France, New Zealand, United Kingdom, USA; Dir-Gen. DAVID SHEPPARD (Australia).

SEED Initiative: POB 30552 00100 Nairobi, Kenya; tel. (20) 7621234; fax (20) 7624489; internet www.seedinit.org; f. 2002 by UNEP, UNDP and IUCN at the World Summit on Sustainable Development in Johannesburg, South Africa; aims to support local and small-scale entrepreneurships that integrate business practice with social and environmental sustainability; a mem. of the Green Economy Coalition; mems: projects active in Burkina Faso, Egypt, Ghana, Kenya, Rwanda, Senegal and South Africa; Exec. Dir HELEN MARQUARD.

South Asia Co-operative Environment Programme (SACEP): 10 Anderson Rd, Colombo 05, Sri Lanka; tel. (11) 2589787; fax (11) 2589369; e-mail info@sacep.org; internet www.sacep.org; f. 1982; aims to promote regional co-operation in the protection and management of the environment, in particular in the context of sustainable economic and social devt; works closely with governmental and non-governmental national, regional and international institutions in conservation and management efforts; Governing Council meets regularly; projects include a South Asia Coral Reef Task Force (SACRTF), the South Asia Environment and Natural Resource Centre, a South Asia Biodiversity Clearing House Mechanism and activities related to the conservation and integrated management of marine turtles and their habitats in the South Asia Seas region; reef-based corals management; accelerated penetration of cost-effective renewable energy technologies; the establishment of a Basel Convention Sub-regional Centre for South Asia; protected areas management of world heritage sites; and implementation of the Ramsar Strategic Plan at sub-regional level; mems: Afghanistan, Bangladesh, Bhutan, India, Maldives, Nepal, Pakistan, Sri Lanka; Dir-Gen. ANURA JAYATILAKE; publs *SACEP Newsletter*, *South Asia Environmental and Education Action Plan*, other reports.

Wetlands International: POB 471, 6700 AL Wageningen, Netherlands; tel. (318) 660910; fax (318) 660950; e-mail post@wetlands.org; internet www.wetlands.org; f. 1995 by merger of several regional wetlands orgs; aims to protect and restore wetlands, their resources and biodiversity through research, information exchange and conservation activities; promotes implementation of the 1971 Ramsar Convention on Wetlands; helped to organize the fifth European River Restoration Conference, held in Vienna, Austria, in Sept. 2013; Chair. JAN ERNST DE GROOT (Netherlands); CEO JANE MADGWICK.

World Association of Zoos and Aquariums (WAZA): IUCN Conservation Centre, 28 rue Mauverney, 1196 Gland, Switzerland; tel. 229990790; fax 229990791; e-mail secretariat@waza.org; internet www.waza.org; f. 1946, current name adopted 2000; aims to provide leadership and support for zoos and aquariums and to promote biodiversity, environmental education, and global sustainability; adopted WAZA Code of Ethics and Animal Welfare, and a Consensus Document on Responsible Reproductive Management, in 2003; in 2005 WAZA launched a World Zoo and Aquarium Conservation Strategy, adopted Research Guidelines, and participated for the first time in Conferences of the Parties to the Ramsar Convention and the Convention of Migratory Species; mems: leading zoos and aquariums and related reg. and nat. asscns; affiliate conservation orgs; Pres. LEE EHMKE; Exec. Dir GERALD DICK.

World Ocean Observatory: POB 1, Sedgwick, Maine 04676, USA; tel. (207) 563-3266; e-mail info@thew2o.net; internet www.worldoceanobservatory.org; f. 2004; recommendation of the final report of the Independent World Commission on the Oceans; serves as a focal point for ocean-related information from govts, non-governmental orgs and other networks; aims to enhance public awareness of the importance of oceans and to facilitate the dissemination of information; Dir PETER NEILL; publ. *World Ocean Observer* (monthly).

World Rainforest Movement (WRM): Maldonado 1858, Montevideo 11200, Uruguay; tel. 2413 2989; fax 2410 0985; e-mail wrm@wrm.org.uy; internet www.wrm.org.uy; f. 1986; aims to secure the lands and livelihoods of rainforest peoples and supports their efforts to defend rainforests from activities including commercial logging, mining, the construction of dams, the devt of plantations, and shrimp farming; issued the Penang Declaration in 1989 setting out the shared vision of an alternative model of rainforest devt based on securing the lands and livelihoods of forest inhabitants; released in 1998 the Montevideo Declaration, campaigning against large-scale monocrop plantations, for example of pulpwood, oil palm and rubber; and issued the Mount Tamalpais Declaration in 2000, urging govts not to include tree plantations as carbon sinks in international action against climate change; Co-ordinator WINFRIDUS OVERBEEK; publ. *WRM Bulletin* (monthly).

World Society for the Protection of Animals (WSPA): 222 Grays Inn Rd, London, WC1X 8HB, United Kingdom; tel. (20)

7239-0500; fax (20) 7239 0653; e-mail wspa@wspa-international.org; internet www.wspa-international.org; f. 1981, incorporating the World Federation for the Protection of Animals (f. 1950) and the International Society for the Protection of Animals (f. 1959); promotes animal welfare and conservation by humane education, practical field projects, international lobbying and legislative work; mems: over 850 mem. socs in 150 countries; Pres. MARK WATTS; Dir-Gen. MICHAEL BAKER.

World Water Council: Espace Gaymard, 2–4 pl. d'Arvieux, 13002 Marseille, France; tel. 4-91-99-41-00; fax 4-91-99-41-01; e-mail wwc@worldwatercouncil.org; internet www.worldwatercouncil.org; f. 1996; aims to facilitate the efficient conservation, protection, devt, planning, management and use of water resources on an environmentally sustainable basis; organizes a World Water Forum held every three years since 1997 (2012: Marseille, France, in March); Pres. BENEDITO BRAGA.

World Water Organization: 1866 United Nations Plaza, New York, NY 10017, USA; tel. (212) 759-1639; fax (646) 666-4349; e-mail info@theworldwater.org; internet www.theworldwater.org; organizes confs and special projects to highlight issues related to water security and to seek means of protecting the global water infrastructure; arranged High-Level Symposium on Water Security at UN headquarters, New York, in Oct. 2010; mems: experts from govt, business, medical and academic backgrounds; Chair. HAROLD OH; Exec. Dir Dr ELAINE VALDOV.

WWF International: 27 ave du Mont-Blanc, 1196 Gland, Switzerland; tel. 223649111; fax 223648836; e-mail info@wwfint.org; internet www.wwf.panda.org; f. 1961 (as World Wildlife Fund), name changed to World Wide Fund for Nature in 1986, current nomenclature adopted 2001; aims to stop the degradation of natural environments, conserve biodiversity, ensure the sustainable use of renewable resources, and promote the reduction of both pollution and wasteful consumption; addresses six priority issues: forests, freshwater, marine, species, climate change, and toxics; has identified, and focuses its activities in, 200 'ecoregions' (the 'Global 200'), believed to contain the best part of the world's remaining biological diversity; global initiatives being implemented in 2013 focused on climate and energy, forest and climate, smart fishing, tigers, and, geographically, on the Amazon, the Arctic, 'China for a Global Shift' (relating to the growing global influence of the People's Republic of China), Coastal East Africa, the Coral Triangle (a marine area in the Western Pacific), the Green Heart of Africa, the Heart of Borneo, and Living Himalayas; actively supports and operates conservation programmes in more than 90 countries; mems: 54 offices, 5 assoc. orgs, c. 5m. individual mems worldwide; Pres. YOLANDA KAKABADSE (Ecuador); Dir-Gen. MARCO LAMBERTINI (Italy) (from 1 May 2014); publs *Annual Report*, *Living Planet Report*.

Government and Politics

African Association for Public Administration and Management (AAPAM): 132 Fuchsia Close, POB 48677, 00100 GPO, Nairobi, Kenya; tel. (20) 2629650; fax (22) 310102; e-mail aapam@aapam.org; internet www.aapam.org; f. 1971 to promote good practices, excellence and professionalism in public administration through training, seminars, research, publications; convenes regular confs to share learning experiences among mems, and an annual Roundtable Conference; funded by membership contributions, govt and donor grants; mems: 500 individual, 50 corp.; Pres. ABDON AGAW JOK NHIAL (South Sudan); Sec.-Gen. GEORGE K. SCOTT (Uganda); publs *Newsletter* (quarterly), *Annual Seminar Report*, *African Journal of Public Administration and Management* (2 a year), books.

African Parliamentary Union: BP V314, Abidjan, Côte d'Ivoire; tel. 20-30-39-79; fax 20-30-44-05; e-mail upa1@aviso.ci; internet www.africanpu.org; f. 1976 (as Union of African Parliaments); holds annual conf. (2013: Libreville, Gabon, in Nov.); mems: 40 parliaments; Chair. ROSE MUKANTABANA (Rwanda); Sec.-Gen. N'ZI KOFFI.

Afro-Asian Peoples' Solidarity Organization (AAPSO): 89 Abdel Aziz Al-Saoud St, POB 11559-61 Manial El-Roda, Cairo, Egypt; tel. (2) 3636081; fax (2) 3637361; e-mail aapso@idsc.net.eg; internet www.aapsorg.org; f. 1958; acts among and for the peoples of Africa and Asia in their struggle for genuine independence, sovereignty, socio-economic development, peace and disarmament; mems: nat. cttees and affiliated orgs in 66 countries and territories, assoc. mems in 15 European countries; Sec.-Gen. NOURI ABDEL RAZZAK HUSSEIN (Iraq); publs *Solidarity Bulletin* (monthly), *Socio-Economic Development* (3 a year).

Agency for the Prohibition of Nuclear Weapons in Latin America and the Caribbean (Organismo para la Proscripción de las Armas Nucleares en la América Latina y el Caribe—OPANAL): Schiller 326, 5°, Col. Chapultepec Morales, 11570 México, DF, Mexico; tel. (55) 5255-2914; fax (55) 5255-3748; e-mail info@opanal.org; internet www.opanal.org; f. 1969 to ensure compliance with the Treaty for the Prohibition of Nuclear Weapons in Latin America (Treaty of Tlatelolco), 1967; to ensure the absence of all nuclear weapons in the application zone of the Treaty; to contribute to the movement against proliferation of nuclear weapons; to promote general and complete disarmament; to prohibit all testing, use, manufacture, acquisition, storage, installation and any form of possession, by any means, of nuclear weapons; the organs of the Agency comprise the General Conference, meeting every two years, the Council, meeting every two months, and the secretariat; mems: 33 states that have fully ratified the Treaty; the Treaty has two additional Protocols: the first signed and ratified by France, the Netherlands, the United Kingdom and the USA, the second signed and ratified by the People's Republic of China, the USA, France, the United Kingdom and Russia; Sec.-Gen. LUIZ FILIPE DE MACEDO SOARES GUIMARÃES (Brazil).

Bolivarian Alliance for the Peoples of our America-People's Trade Treaty (Alianza Bolivariana para los Pueblos de Nuestra América-Tratado de Comercio de los Pueblos—ALBA-TCP): Av. Francisco Solano, Esq. Calle San Gerónimo, Edif. Los Llanos, 8° Sabana Grande, Parroquia El Recreo, Caracas, Venezuela; tel. (212) 905-9384; fax (212) 761-1364; e-mail secretaria@alba-tcp.org; internet alba-tcp.org; f. 2002 (as the Bolivarian Alternative for the Americas) by the then President of Venezuela, Hugo Chávez, to promote an alternative model of political, economic and social co-operation and integration between Caribbean and Latin American countries sharing geographic, historical and cultural bonds; aims to reduce disparities in devt between countries in the region and to combat poverty and social exclusion; the so-called People's Trade Treaty (Tratado de Comercio de los Pueblos) was signed in April 2006 to formalize a process of complementarity; in June 2007 ministers of foreign affairs convened for the inaugural meeting of ALBA's Council of Ministers agreed to the establishment of joint enterprises, as an alternative to transnational corporations, a joint bank to finance projects supported by the grouping and to develop bilateral agreements; the establishment of a Bank of ALBA was endorsed at the sixth summit meeting of heads of state, convened in Jan. 2008; the use of a Unified System of Regional Compensation (Sistema Único de Compensación Regional—SUCRE) as a means of currency exchange for commercial transactions between mems was agreed in 2009 and first used in 2010; the agreement establishing SUCRE, signed in Oct. 2009, also envisaged the establishment of a Regional Monetary Council, a Central Clearing House, a regional reserve and emergency fund; in Feb. 2012 the Ecconomic Complementation Council agreed to establish an ALBA-TCP economic space ('ECOALBA'); in Aug. ALBA ministers of foreign affairs reaffirmed support for the sovereign right of the Ecuador Govt to grant asylum to the WikiLeaks founder Julian Assange, who was at that time accommodated in Ecuador's London embassy, and rejected perceived intimidation from the United Kingdom authorities concerning the territorial integrity of the Ecuador mission to London; in May 2013 mems agreed to strengthen co-operation with Petrocaribe through the establishment of a new economic zone to promote regional investment, trade, food security, tourism and devt projects; a second summit meeting between the two orgs, convened in Dec., reaffirmed support for the economic zone and agreed to develop mechanisms to support its establishment; Exec. Sec. BERNARDO ÁLVAREZ; mems: Antigua and Barbuda, Bolivia, Cuba, Dominica, Ecuador, Nicaragua, Saint Lucia, Saint Vincent and the Grenadines, Venezuela.

Alliance of Small Island States (AOSIS): c/o 800 Second Ave, Suite 400K, New York, NY 10017, USA; tel. (212) 599-0301; fax (212) 599-1540; e-mail grenada@un.int; internet www.aosis.info; f. 1990 as an ad hoc intergovernmental grouping to focus on the special problems of small islands and low-lying coastal developing states; mems: 44 island nations and observers; Chair. MARLENE MOSES (Nauru); publ. *Small Islands, Big Issues*.

ANZUS: c/o Dept of Foreign Affairs and Trade, R. G. Casey Bldg, John McEwen Crescent, Barton, ACT 0221, Australia; tel. (2) 6261-1111; fax (2) 6271-3111; internet www.dfat.gov.au; the ANZUS Security Treaty was signed in 1951 by Australia, New Zealand and the USA, and ratified in 1952 to co-ordinate partners' efforts for collective defence for the preservation of peace and security in the Pacific area, through the exchange of technical information and strategic intelligence, and a programme of exercises, exchanges and visits. In 1984 New Zealand refused to allow visits by US naval vessels that were either nuclear-propelled or potentially nuclear-armed, and this led to the cancellation of joint ANZUS military exercises: in 1986 the USA formally announced the suspension of its security commitment to New Zealand under ANZUS. Instead of the annual ANZUS Council meetings, ministerial consultations (AUSMIN) were subsequently held every year between Australia and the USA on policy and political-military issues. ANZUS continued to govern security relations between Australia and the USA, and between Australia and New Zealand; security relations between New Zealand and the USA were the only aspect of the treaty to be suspended. Senior-level contacts between New Zealand and the USA resumed in 1994. The Australian Govt invoked the ANZUS Security

Treaty for the first time following the international terrorist attacks against targets in the USA that were perpetrated in Sept. 2001; in Nov. 2011 the USA announced plans to deploy 2,500 troops to Darwin, Australia to conduct training exercises with Australian troops, with a provision also for the US Air Force to be granted increased access to airfields in the Northern Territory.

Association of Pacific Islands Legislatures (APIL): Carl Rose Bldg, Suite 207, 181 E. Marine Corps Drive, Hagatna, Guam; tel. (671) 477-2719; fax (671) 473-3004; e-mail apil@guam.net; internet www.apilpacific.com; f. 1981 to provide a permanent structure of mutual assistance for representatives of the people of the Pacific Islands; comprises legislative representatives from 12 Pacific Island Govts; Pres. JUDITH T. WON (Guam).

Association of Secretaries General of Parliaments: c/o Committee Office, House of Commons, London, SW1, United Kingdom; tel. (20) 7219-3253; fax (20) 7219-3690; e-mail asgp@parliament.uk; internet www.asgp.info; f. 1938; studies the law, practice and working methods of different Parliaments; proposes measures for improving those methods and for securing co-operation between the services of different Parliaments; operates as a consultative body to the Inter-Parliamentary Union, and assists the Union on subjects within the scope of the Association; mems: c. 200 representing 145 countries; 5 assoc. institutions; Pres. MARC BOSC (Canada); Jt Secs INÉS FAUCONNIER (France), EMILY COMMANDER (United Kingdom); publ. *Constitutional and Parliamentary Information* (2 a year).

Atlantic Treaty Association: Quartier Prince Albert, 20 rue des Petits Carmes, 1000 Brussels, Belgium; tel. (2) 502-31-60; fax (2) 502-48-77; e-mail jason.wiseman@ata-sec.org; internet www.ata-sec.org; f. 1954 to inform public opinion on the North Atlantic Alliance and to promote the solidarity of the peoples of the North Atlantic; holds annual assemblies, seminars, study confs for teachers and young politicians; mems: nat. asscns in 28 mem. countries of NATO; 12 assoc. mems from Central and Eastern Europe, 2 observer mems; Pres. Dr KARL A. LAMERS (Germany); Treas. JEAN-PAUL R. PREUMONT (Belgium).

Baltic Council: f. 1993 by the Baltic Assembly, comprising 60 parliamentarians from Estonia, Latvia and Lithuania; the Council of Ministers of the mem. countries co-ordinates policy in the areas of foreign policy, justice, the environment, education and science; Since 2003, the country holding the rotating presidency of the Baltic Assembly also presides over the Council, ensuring common priorities and organizational efficiency between both bodies.

Celtic League: c/o Mark Lockerby, 12 Magherdonnag, Ponyfields, Port Erin, IM9 6BY, United Kingdom; internet www.celticleague.net; f. 1961 to foster co-operation between the six Celtic nations (Ireland, Scotland, Isle of Man, Wales, Cornwall and Brittany), especially those actively working for political autonomy by non-violent means; campaigns politically on issues affecting the Celtic countries; monitors military activity in the Celtic countries; co-operates with national cultural organizations to promote the languages and culture of the Celts; mems: approx. 1,400 individuals in the Celtic communities and elsewhere; Gen. Sec. RHISIART TAL-E-BOT; publ. *Carn* (quarterly).

Central European Initiative (CEI): CEI Executive Secretariat, Via Genova 9, 34121 Trieste, Italy; tel. (040) 7786777; fax (040) 360640; e-mail cei@cei.int; internet www.cei.int; f. 1989 as 'Quadragonal' co-operation between Austria, Italy, Hungary and Yugoslavia, became 'Pentagonal' in 1990 with the admission of Czechoslovakia, and 'Hexagonal' with the admission of Poland in 1991, present name adopted in 1992, when Bosnia and Herzegovina, Croatia and Slovenia were admitted; the Czech Republic and Slovakia became separate mems in Jan. 1993, and Macedonia also joined in that year; Albania, Belarus, Bulgaria, Romania and Ukraine joined the CEI in 1995 and Moldova in 1996; the Federal Republic of Yugoslavia (now the separate sovereign states of Montenegro and Serbia) admitted in 2000; encourages regional political and economic co-operation with a focus on the following nine areas of activity: climate, environment and sustainable energy; enterprise development (incl. tourism); human resource devt; information society and media; intercultural co-operation (incl. minorities); multimodal transport; science and technology; sustainable agriculture; inter-regional and cross-border co-operation; economic forum held annually since 1998; Sec.-Gen. GIOVANNI CARACCIOLO DI VIETRI; publ. *Newsletter* (monthly).

Centrist Democrat International: 10 rue du Commerce, 1000 Brussels, Belgium; tel. (2) 285-41-45; fax (2) 300-80-13; e-mail info@idc-cdi.com; internet www.idc-cdi.com; f. 1961 (as Christian Democrat and Peoples' Parties International); serves as an asscn of political groups adhering to Christian humanist and democratic theology; mems: parties in 64 countries (of which 47 in Europe); Pres. PIER FERDINANDO CASINI (Italy); Exec. Sec. ANTONIO LÓPEZ ISTÚRIZ (Spain); publs *DC-Info* (quarterly), *Human Rights* (5 a year), *Documents* (quarterly).

Club of Madrid: Carrera de San Jerónimo 15, 3A planta, 28014 Madrid, Spain; tel. (91) 1548230; fax (91) 1548240; e-mail clubmadrid@clubmadrid.org; internet www.clubmadrid.org; f. 2001, following Conference on Democratic Transition and Consolidation; forum of former Presidents and Prime Ministers; aims to strengthen democratic values and leadership; maintains office in Brussels, Belgium; mems: 87 from 60 countries; Pres. VAIRA VIKE-FREIBERGA (Latvia); Sec.-Gen. CARLOS WESTENDORP (Spain).

Collective Security Treaty Organization (CSTO): 103012 Moscow, Varvarka 7, Russia; tel. (495) 606-97-71; fax (495) 625-76-20; e-mail odkb@gov.ru; internet www.dkb.gov.ru; f. 2003 by signatories to the Treaty on Collective Security (signed Tashkent, Uzbekistan, May 1992); aims to co-ordinate and strengthen military and political co-operation and to promote regional and national security; maintains a joint rapid deployment force; the Oct. 2007 leaders' summit endorsed documents enabling the establishment of CSTO joint peacekeeping forces and the creation of a co-ordination council for the heads of mem. states' emergency response agencies; the leaders' summit convened in Sept. 2008 issued a joint declaration stating that conflicts should be settled preferably through political and diplomatic means in line with international law and stating the following as immediate priorities: strengthening efforts to promote nuclear non-proliferation; to combat terrorism, drugs-trafficking and weapons-smuggling; to expand co-operation with international bodies; and to promote international efforts to establish 'anti-drug and financial security belts' around Afghanistan; the CSTO became an observer in the UN General Assembly in 2004; in April 2006 it signed a protocol with the UNODC to develop joint projects to combat drugs-trafficking, terrorism and transborder crime; in Feb. 2009 agreed to establish a rapid reaction force and conducted a joint military exercise (without the participation of Uzbekistan) in Aug.–Oct; in March 2010 the CSTO and UN Secretaries-General signed a declaration on co-operation, giving the CSTO full recognition as a regional security org; in Dec. CSTO ministers of defence and foreign affairs agreed to commit forces to collective peacekeeping activities in cases of emergency; in Sept. 2012 the CSTO and DPKO signed a Memorandum of Co-operation providing for the future expansion of collaboration on peacekeeping activities; the first CSTO peacekeeping training exercise (Undefeatable Brotherhood) was launched in Oct. in Kazakhstan; mems: Armenia, Belarus, Kazakhstan, Kyrgyzstan, Russia, Tajikistan, Uzbekistan (in June 2012 Uzbekistan announced the suspension of its membership); Sec.-Gen. NIKOLAY BORDYUZHA.

Community of Latin American and Caribbean States (CELAC) (Comunidad de Estados de América Latina y el Caribe): e-mail cumbre.calc@mppre.gob.ve; internet www.celac.gob.ve; f. 2010; heads of state of the Rio Group (f. 1987) and the Latin American and Caribbean Summit on Integration and Development agreed to establish CELAC as a pan-regional body to strengthen co-operation on political, cultural, social and economic issues; inaugural summit held in Dec. 2011; the first Ministerial Meeting on infrastructure for the physical integration of transport, telecommunications and frontiers was convened in Oct. 2012; second summit held in Jan. 2013, in Santiago, Chile, preceded by an inaugural CELAC-EU summit at which a revised Action Plan for bilateral relations was adopted; the first meetings of ministers responsible for education and for culture took place in Feb. and March, respectively; 33 Latin American and Caribbean states; Chair. RAÚL CASTRO (Cuba).

Comunidade dos Países de Língua Portuguesa (CPLP) (Community of Portuguese-Speaking Countries): rua de S. Mamede (ao Caldas) 21, 1100-533 Lisbon, Portugal; tel. (21) 392-8560; fax (21) 392-8588; e-mail comunicacao@cplp.org; internet www.cplp.org; f. 1996; aims to produce close political, economic, diplomatic and cultural links between Portuguese-speaking countries and to strengthen the influence of the Lusophone Commonwealth within the international community; in Nov. 2010 adopted, jointly with ECOWAS, the CPLP-ECOWAS roadmap on reform of the defence and security sector in Guinea-Bissau; mems: Angola, Brazil, Cape Verde, Guinea-Bissau, Mozambique, Portugal, São Tomé and Príncipe, Timor-Leste; assoc. observers: Equatorial Guinea, Mauritius, Senegal; Exec. Sec. MURADE ISAAC MIGUIGY MURARGY (Mozambique).

Conference on Interaction and Confidence-building Measures in Asia: 050000, Almatı, Aiteke Bi 65, Kazakhstan; tel. (727) 390-11-00; fax (727) 390-12-00; e-mail s-cica@s-cica.kz; internet www.s-cica.org; f. 1999 at first meeting of 16 Asian ministers of foreign affairs, convened in Almatı; aims to provide a structure to enhance co-operation, with the objectives of promoting peace, security and stability throughout the region; first meeting of heads of state held in June 2002, adopted the Almatı Act; a Secretariat was established in June 2006; activities focused on a catalogue of confidence-building measures grouped into five areas: economic dimension; environmental dimension; human dimension; fight against new challenges and threats (such as drugs-trafficking, terrorism, and money-laundering); and military-political dimension; a commemorative session was held in Astana, Kazakhstan, in Sept. 2012, to mark the 20th anniversary of the initiation of the conf. dialogue process; mems:

Afghanistan, Azerbaijan, Bahrain, Cambodia, People's Republic of China, Egypt, India, Iran, Israel, Jordan, Kazakhstan, Republic of Korea, Kyrgyzstan, Mongolia, Pakistan, Palestine, Russia, Tajikistan, Thailand, Turkey, UAE, Uzbekistan, Viet Nam; observers: Bangladesh, Indonesia, Japan, Malaysia, the Philippines, Qatar, Ukraine, USA, and the UN, the OSCE and the League of Arab States (Arab League); Exec. Dir ÇINAR ALDEMIR (Turkey).

Council for Security Co-operation in the Asia-Pacific: Institute of Strategic and International Studies (ISIS Malaysia), 1 Persiaran Sultan Salahuddin, POB 12424, 50778 Kuala Lumpur, Malaysia; tel. (3) 26939366; fax (3) 26939375; e-mail cscap@isis.org.my; internet www.cscap.org; f. 1993 to contribute to regional confidence-building efforts and to enhance regional security through dialogue, consultation and co-operation; aims to establish a focused and inclusive non-governmental process on Asia-Pacific security matters; headed by a Steering Committee led by two chairpersons, one representing an ASEAN mem. country and the other a non-ASEAN mem. country; mems: 20 full and 1 assoc. mem.; Co-Chair. LEELA PONAPPA (India), YEN HUONG NGUYEN THAI (Viet Nam).

Eastern Regional Organization for Public Administration (EROPA): National College of Public Administration, Univ. of the Philippines, Diliman, Quezon City 1101, Philippines; tel. and fax (2) 9297789; e-mail eropa.secretariat@gmail.com; internet www.eropa.org.ph; f. 1960 to promote regional co-operation in improving knowledge, systems and practices of governmental administration, to help to accelerate economic and social devt; organizes regional confs, seminars, special studies, surveys and training programmes; accredited, in 2000, as an online regional centre of the UN Public Administration Network for the Asia and Pacific region; there are three regional centres: Training Centre (New Delhi), Local Government Centre (Tokyo), Development Management Centre (Seoul); holds annual conf. (2013: Tachikawa City, Tokyo, Japan, in Oct.); mems: 10 countries, 63 groups, 266 individuals; Sec.-Gen. ORLANDO S. MERCADO (Philippines); publs *EROPA Bulletin* (quarterly), *Asian Review of Public Administration* (2 a year).

The Elders: c/o POB 67772, London, W14 4EH, United Kingdom; e-mail info@theelders.org; internet www.theelders.org; f. 2001; aims to alleviate human suffering worldwide by offering a catalyst for the peaceful resolution of conflicts, seeking new approaches to unresolved global issues, and sharing wisdom; comprises: Martti Ahtisaari (Finland), Kofi Annan (Ghana), Ela Bhatt (India), Lakhdar Brahimi (Algeria), Gro Brundtland (Norway), Fernando H. Cardoso (Brazil), Jimmy Carter (USA), Graça Machel (Mozambique), Mary Robinson (Ireland), Desmond Tutu (South Africa); CEO LESLEY-ANNE KNIGHT.

European Movement: 21 Rue Marie Thérese, B-1000 Brussels, Belgium; tel. (2) 508-30-88; fax (2) 508-30-89; e-mail secretariat@europeanmovement.eu; internet www.europeanmovement.eu; f. 1947 by a liaison cttee of representatives from European orgs, to study the political, economic and technical problems of a European Union and suggest how they could be solved and to inform and lead public opinion in the promotion of integration; confs have led to the creation of the Council of Europe, College of Europe, etc; mems: nat. councils and cttees in 39 European countries, and several int. social and economic orgs, 32 assoc. mems; Pres. JO LEINEN; Sec.-Gen. DIOGO PINTO.

European Union of Women (EUW): POB 52869, London, SW11 2UY, United Kingdom; tel. (20) 79244124; e-mail euw@euw-uk.co.uk; internet www.euw-uk.co.uk; f. 1953 to increase the influence of women in the political and civic life of their country and of Europe; mems: nat. orgs in 21 countries; Chair. Dr MARGARET STOCKHAM TURNER.

Group of Eight (G8): an informal meeting of developed nations, originally comprising France, Germany, Italy, Japan, United Kingdom and the USA, first convened in Nov. 1975, at Rambouillet, France, at the level of heads of state and govt; Canada became a permanent participant in 1976, forming the Group of Seven major industrialized countries—G7; from 1991 Russia was invited to participate in the then G7 summit outside the formal framework of co-operation; from 1994 Russia contributed more fully to the G7 political dialogue and from 1997 Russia became a participant in nearly all of the summit process scheduled meetings, excepting those related to finance and the global economy; from 1998 the name of the co-operation framework was changed to Group of Eight—G8, and since 2003 Russia has participated fully in all scheduled summit meetings, including those on the global economy; the European Union (EU) is also represented at G8 meetings, although it may not chair fora; G8 heads of govt and the President of the European Commission and President of the European Council convene an annual summit meeting, the chairmanship and venue of which are rotated in the following order: France, USA, the United Kingdom, Russia, Germany, Japan, Italy, Canada; G8 summit meetings address and seek consensus, published in a final declaration, on social and economic issues confronting the international community; heads of state or govt of non-mem. countries, and representatives of selected inter-governmental orgs, have been invited to participate in meetings; dialogue commenced in 2005 in the 'G8+5' format, including the leaders of the five largest emerging economies: Brazil, the People's Republic of China, India, Mexico and South Africa; G8 sectoral ministerial meetings (covering areas such as energy, environment, finance and foreign affairs) are held on the fringes of the annual summit, and further G8 sectoral ministerial meetings are convened through the year; the 2011 G8 summit meeting, convened in May, in Deauville, France, established the Deauville Partnership, aimed at supporting political and economic reforms being undertaken by several countries in North Africa and the Middle East; the 2012 summit meeting, held in May, at Camp David, Maryland, USA, without participation by the Russian President, reaffirmed the imperative of creating global growth and jobs, and—in response to the protracted eurozone sovereign debt crisis, exacerbated by recent inconclusive legislative elections in Greece amid a climate of popular resistance to the social impact of economic austerity measures—agreed on the relevance for global stability of promoting a strong eurozone, and welcomed ongoing discussion within the EU on means of stimulating economic growth while continuing to implement policies aimed at achieving fiscal consolidation; the participating G8 leaders also gave consideration to, *inter alia*, energy and climate change, Afghanistan's economic transition, food security, and the ongoing Deauville Partnership; and indicated readiness to request the International Energy Agency to release emergency petroleum stocks should international sanctions imposed on Iran result in disruption to global supply; meeting in April 2013, in London, United Kingdom, G8 ministers responsible for foreign affairs issued a Declaration on the Prevention of Sexual Violence in Conflict; the ministers at that time also considered an agenda that included security matters relating to the Democratic People's Republic of Korea and Syria; the 2013 summit, convened in June, in Lough Erne, Northern Ireland, agreed a 10-point plan to tighten regulations and transparency with regard to global corp. taxation; in March 2014 G7 countries announced that they would not participate in preparatory discussions for the scheduled G8 summit meeting in Sochi, Russia, in June, owing to Russia's intervention in Ukraine's domestic affairs and its subsequent recognition of Crimea (hitherto a Ukrainian autonomous territory) as a sovereign state; later in that month an emergency summit meeting of the G7 suspended Russia from the grouping, thus effectively making the format inactive; mems: Canada, France, Germany, Italy, Japan, Russia, United Kingdom and USA; EU representation.

Gulf of Guinea Commission (Commission du Golfe de Guinée—CGG): f. 2001 to promote co-operation among mem. countries, and the peaceful and sustainable devt of natural resources in the sub-region; mems: Angola, Cameroon, the Republic of the Congo, Equatorial Guinea, Gabon, Nigeria, São Tomé and Príncipe; in June 2013 the CGG participated, with ECOWAS and CEEAC, in a regional summit on maritime safety and security, convened in Yaoundé, Cameroon, which adopted a Code of Conduct concerning the Prevention and Repression of Piracy, Armed Robbery against Ships, and Illegal Maritime Activities in West and Central Africa; Exec. Sec. MIGUEL TROVOADA (São Tomé and Príncipe).

Hansard Society: 9 King St, 5th Floor, London, EC2V 8EA, United Kingdom; tel. (20) 7710-6070; fax (20) 7438-1229; e-mail contact@hansardsociety.org.uk; internet www.hansardsociety.org.uk; f. 1944 as Hansard Society for Parliamentary Government; aims to promote political education and research and the informed discussion of all aspects of modern parliamentary govt; presidency is held jointly by the incumbent Speakers of the United Kingdom House of Commons and House of Lords; Co-Pres JOHN BERCOW, Baroness FRANCES D'SOUZA; CEO FIONA BOOTH; publ. *Parliamentary Affairs* (quarterly).

Ibero-American General Secretariat (Secretaría General Iberoamericana—SEGIB): Paseo de Recoletos 8, 28001 Madrid, Spain; tel. (91) 5901980; fax (91) 5901984; e-mail info@segib.org; internet www.segib.org; f. 2003; aims to provide institutional and technical support to the annual Ibero-American summit meetings, to monitor programmes agreed at the meetings and to strengthen the Ibero-American community; meetings of Ibero-American heads of state and govt (the first of which was convened in Guadalajara, Mexico in 1991, and the 23rd was held in Oct. 2013, in Panama City, Panama) aim to promote political, economic and cultural co-operation among the 19 Spanish- and Portuguese-speaking Latin American countries and three European countries; Sec.-Gen. REBECA GRYNSPAN (Costa Rica).

International Alliance of Women (Alliance Internationale des Femmes): Aaloekken 11, 5250 Odense, Denmark; tel. 65-96-08-68; e-mail iawsec@womenalliance.org; internet www.womenalliance.org; f. 1904 to obtain equality for women in all fields and to encourage women to assume decision-making responsibilities at all levels of society; lobbies international orgs; mems: 58 nat. affiliates and associates; Pres. JOANNA MANGANARA (Greece); Sec.-Gen. MMABATHO RAMAGOSHI (South Africa); publs *International Women's News* (3 a year), electronic newsletter (monthly).

International Association for Community Development (IACD): The Stables, Falkland, Fife, KY15 7AF, United Kingdom; tel. (1337) 858808; fax (1337) 858120; e-mail info@iacdglobal.org; internet www.iacdglobal.org; f. 1953; promotes community development across international policies and programmes, supports community devt practitioners and encourages the exchange of research and information; membership open to individuals and orgs working in or supporting community development across eight world regions; organizes annual international colloquium for community-based orgs; Pres. Dr INGRID BURKETT; publs *IACD Newsletter* (2 a year), monthly e-bulletins.

International Commission for the History of Representative and Parliamentary Institutions (ICHRPI): c/o Prof. Dr Lothar Höbelt, Institut für Geschichte, Universität Wien, Universitaetsring 1, 1010 Vienna, Austria; fax (1) 4277 40821; e-mail lothar.hoebelt@univie.ac.at; internet www.ichrpi.com; f. 1936; promotes research into the origin and development of representative and parliamentary institutions worldwide; encourages wide and comparative study of such institutions, both current and historical; facilitates the exchange of information; 64th Conf. was held in Dublin, Ireland (Sept. 2013); mems: 300 individuals in 31 countries; Pres. MARIA SOFIA CORCIULO (Italy); Sec.-Gen. Prof. Dr LOTHAR HÖBELT (Austria); publs *Parliaments, Estates and Representation* (annually), studies.

International Conference on the Great Lakes Region, (ICGLR) (Conference Internationale sur la region des grands lacs): POB 7076, Bujumbura, Burundi; tel. 22256824; fax 22256828; e-mail secretariat@icglr.org; internet www.icglr.org; f. 2006 following the signing of the Security, Stability and Development Pact for the Great Lakes Region at the second summit meeting of the International Conference on the Great Lakes Region, held in Dec., in Nairobi, Kenya; the UN Security Council proposed in 2000 a Great Lakes Conference to initiate a process that would bring together regional leaders to pursue agreement on a set of principles and to articulate programmes of action to help end the cycle of regional conflict and establish durable peace, stability, security, democracy and devt in the whole region; the first summit meeting of the Conference was convened in Dar es Salaam, Tanzania, in Nov. 2004; the Executive Secretariat of the org. was inaugurated in May 2007; runs the Special Fund for Reconstruction and Development which is hosted and managed by the AfDB; in 2012–14 the Conference was working to mediate between govt and rebel forces fighting in eastern Democratic Republic of the Congo (DRC); following several high-level meetings and extraordinary summits a Military Assessment Team was dispatched to North Kivu Province in Sept. 2012 and agreement was reached, in early Nov., to establish an Expanded Joint Verification Mechanism, both with the aim of deploying an international force to counter rebel groups fighting in that region; in Nov. an emergency summit meeting was convened, in Kampala, Uganda, following the advance by the 23 March Movement (M23) grouping to take control of the provincial capital, Goma; leaders at that meeting demanded the withdrawal of M23 forces from Goma; in Feb. 2013 the leaders of 11 African countries signed the Peace, Security and Cooperation Framework for the DRC and the Region, which aimed to stabilize the Great Lakes region; with the UN, the African Union and SADC, the ICGLR was to act as a guarantor of the Framework; the signatories to the Framework committed to protect the future territorial sovereignty and the peace and stability of the DRC; an intervention brigade was mandated by the UN Security Council in the following month to target militias in eastern DRC; following the declaration by the M23, in early Nov., of the end of its rebellion in eastern DRC, a so-called Kampala dialogue was convened between the DRC Govt and the M23 leadership in Nov.–early Dec., culminating in the signing, under the auspices of the ICGLR and SADC, of final declarations by the parties, providing for, inter alia, an envisaged process of disarmament of former M23 combatants; sixth extraordinary summit meeting of the ICGLR convened in Nairobi, in July; mems: Angola, Burundi, Central African Republic, Democratic Republic of the Congo, Republic of the Congo, Kenya, Rwanda, Sudan, Tanzania, Uganda, Zambia; Exec. Sec. Prof. ALPHONSE LUMU NTUMBA LUABA.

International Democrat Union: POB 1536, Vika, 0117 Oslo, Norway; tel. 22-82-90-00; fax 22-82-90-80; e-mail secretariat@idu.org; internet www.idu.org; f. 1983 as a group of centre and centre-right political parties; facilitates the exchange of information and views; promotes networking; organizes campaigning seminars for politicians and party workers; holds Party Leaders' meetings every three years, also executive meetings and a Young Leaders' Forum; mems: political parties in some 60 countries, 46 assoc. mems in regions; Exec. Sec. EIRIK MOEN.

International Federation of Resistance Fighters (FIR): Franz-Mehring-Platz 1, 10243 Berlin, Germany; tel. (30) 29784174; fax (30) 29784179; e-mail office@fir.at; internet www.fir.at; f. 1951; supports the medical and social welfare of former victims of fascism; works for peace, disarmament and human rights, and against fascism and neo-fascism; mems: 76 nat. orgs; Pres. VILMOS HANTI (Hungary); Sec.-Gen. Dr ULRICH SCHNEIDER (Germany).

International Institute for Democracy and Electoral Assistance (IDEA): Strömsborg, 103 34 Stockholm, Sweden; tel. (8) 698-3700; fax (8) 20-2422; e-mail info@idea.int; internet www.idea.int; f. 1995; aims to promote sustainable democracy in new and established democracies; works with practitioners and institutions promoting democracy in Africa, Asia, Arab states and Latin America; mems: 28 mem. states and 1 observer; Sec.-Gen. YVES LETERME (Belgium) (from June 2014).

International Institute for Peace: Möllwaldplatz 5/2, 1040 Vienna, Austria; tel. (1) 504-64-37; fax (1) 505-32-36; e-mail secretariat@iip.at; internet www.iip.at; f. 1957; non-governmental org. with consultative status at ECOSOC and UNESCO; studies conflict prevention; new structures in international law; security issues in Europe and worldwide; mems: individuals and corp. bodies invited by the executive board; Pres. Dr PETER SCHIEDER (Austria); Dir PETER STANIA (Austria); publ. *Peace and Security* (quarterly).

International Institute for Strategic Studies (IISS): Arundel House, 13–15 Arundel St, London, WC2R 3DX, United Kingdom; tel. (20) 7379-7676; fax (20) 7836-3108; e-mail iiss@iiss.org; internet www.iiss.org; f. 1958 as an independent institution concerned with the study of the role of force in international relations, including problems of international strategy, the ethnic, political and social sources of conflict, disarmament and arms control, peacekeeping and intervention, defence economics, etc.; mems: c. 3,000; Chair. Prof. FRANÇOIS HEISBOURG (France); Dir-Gen. Dr JOHN M. W. CHIPMAN (United Kingdom); publs *Survival* (quarterly), *The Military Balance* (annually), *Strategic Survey* (annually), *Adelphi Papers* (10 a year), *Strategic Comments* (10 a year), *IISS Newsletter* (quarterly).

International Lesbian, Gay, Trans and Intersex Association (ILGA): 17 rue de la Charité, 1020 Brussels, Belgium; tel. and fax (2) 502-24-71; fax (2) 223-48-20; e-mail information@ilga.org; internet www.ilga.org; f. 1978; works to abolish legal, social and economic discrimination against homosexual and bisexual women and men, and transexuals, throughout the world; co-ordinates political action at an international level; co-operates with other supportive movements; 2012 world conf.: Stockholm. Sweden; mems: 1,000 nat. and reg. asscns in 110 countries; Co-Secs-Gen. GLORIA CAREAGA, AZUSA YAMASHITA; publs *ILGA State-Sponsored Homophobia Report*and a map on gay and lesbian rights worldwide.

International Peace Bureau (IPB): 41 rue de Zürich, 1201 Geneva, Switzerland; tel. 227316429; fax 227389419; e-mail mailbox@ipb.org; internet www.ipb.org; f. 1891; promotes international co-operation for general and complete disarmament and the non-violent solution of international conflicts; co-ordinates and represents peace movements at the UN; conducts projects on Disarmament for Development and the abolition of nuclear weapons; mems: 320 peace orgs and 150 individual mems in 70 countries; Co-Pres TOMAS MAGNUSSON, INGEBORG BREINES; Sec.-Gen. COLIN ARCHER (United Kingdom); publs *IPB News* (every 2 weeks, by e-mail), *IPB Geneva News*.

International Political Science Association (IPSA) (Association Internationale de Science Politique—AISP): c/o Concordia University, 331 ave Docteur Penfield, Montréal, QC H3G 1C5, Canada; tel. (514) 848-8717; fax (514) 848-4095; e-mail info@ipsa.org; internet www.ipsa.org; f. 1949; aims to promote the devt of political science; organizes International Congress of Political Science (2014: Montréal, Canada); mems: 53 national asscns, 100 institutions, 4,047 individual mems; Pres. HELEN MILNER (USA); Sec.-Gen. GUY LACHAPELLE (Canada); publs *Participation* (3 a year), *International Political Science Abstracts* (6 a year), *International Political Science Review* (quarterly).

Jewish Agency for Israel (JAFI): POB 92, 48 King George St, Jerusalem 91000 Israel; tel. (2) 6202251; fax (2) 6202577; e-mail barbaram@jafi.org; internet www.jafi.org.il; f. 1929; reconstituted 1971 as an instrument through which world Jewry can work to develop a national home; constituents are: World Zionist Organization, United Israel Appeal, Inc. (USA), and Keren Hayesod; Chair. Exec. NATAN SHARANSKY; Chair. of the Bd JAMES TISCH; Dir-Gen. ALAN HOFFMANN.

Latin American Parliament (Parlamento Latinoamericano): Casilla 1527, Edif. 1111-1113, Apdo 4, ave. Principal de Amador, Panama; tel. 201-9000; e-mail secgeneral@parlatino.org; internet www.parlatino.org; f. 1965; permanent democratic institution, representative of all existing political trends within the national legislative bodies of Latin America; aims to promote the movement towards economic, political and cultural integration of the Latin American republics, and to uphold human rights, peace and security; Pres. ELÍAS ARIEL CASTILLO GONZÁLEZ; Sec.-Gen. BLANCA ALCALA; publs *Acuerdos, Resoluciones de las Asambleas Ordinarias* (annually), *Parlamento Latinoamericano–Actividades de los Organos, Revista Patria Grande* (annually), statements and agreements.

Liberal International: 1 Whitehall Pl., London, SW1A 2HD, United Kingdom; tel. (20) 7839-5905; fax (20) 7925-2685; e-mail office@liberal-international.org; internet www.liberal-international.org; f. 1947; co-ordinates foreign policy work of mem. parties, and promotes freedom, tolerance, democracy, international understanding, protection of human rights and market-based economics; has consultative status at ECOSOC and the Council of Europe; mems: 101 mem. parties and 10 co-operating orgs in 63 countries; Pres. HANS VAN BAALEN; Sec.-Gen. EMIL KIRJAS; publ. *Liberal Aerogramme* (quarterly).

NATO Parliamentary Assembly: 3 pl. du Petit Sablon, 1000 Brussels, Belgium; tel. (2) 513-28-65; fax (2) 514-18-47; internet www.nato-pa.int; f. 1955 as the NATO Parliamentarians' Conference; name changed 1966 to North Atlantic Assembly; renamed as above 1999; the inter-parliamentary assembly of the North Atlantic Alliance; holds two plenary sessions a year and meetings of cttees (Political, Defence and Security, Economics and Security, Civil Dimension of Security, Science and Technology) to facilitate parliamentary awareness and understanding of key Alliance security issues, to provide the Alliance govts with a collective parliamentary voice, to contribute to a greater degree of transparency of NATO policies, and to strengthen the transatlantic dialogue; Pres. HUGH BAYLEY (United Kingdom); Sec.-Gen. DAVID HOBBS (United Kingdom).

Non-aligned Movement (NAM): c/o Imam Khomeini St, Tehran, Iran; tel. (21) 61151; fax (21) 66743149; e-mail matbuat@mfa.gov.ir; internet nam.gov.ir; f. 1961 by a meeting of 25 heads of state, with the aim of linking countries that had refused to adhere to the main East/West military and political blocs; co-ordination bureau established in 1973; works for the establishment of a new international economic order, and especially for better terms for countries producing raw materials; maintains special funds for agricultural devt, improvement of food production and the financing of buffer stocks; South Commission promotes co-operation between developing countries; seeks changes at the UN to give developing countries greater decision-making power; holds summit conf. every three years (17th summit: Caracas, Venezuela, in 2015); a 50th anniversary conf. was convened in Bali, Indonesia, in May 2011; in Sept. 2013 a ministerial meeting on Co-operation for the Rule of Law at the International Level was convened in New York, USA; mems: 120 countries, 17 observer countries and 10 observer orgs.

Nordic Council: Ved Stranden 18, 1061 Copenhagen, Denmark; tel. 33-96-04-00; fax 33-11-18-70; e-mail nordisk-rad@norden.org; internet www.norden.org; f. 1952 to facilitate co-operation between Nordic parliaments and govts; 87 elected mems; Pres. KARIN ÅSTRÖM (Sweden) (2014); Sec.-Gen. BRITT BOHLIN (Sweden) (until 31 Dec. 2018); publs *Norden the Top of Europe* (monthly newsletter in English and Russian), *Norden this Week* (weekly newsletter).

Nordic Council of Ministers: Ved Stranden 18, 1061, Copenhagen, Denmark; tel. 33-96-02-00; fax 33-96-02-02; e-mail nmr@norden.org; internet www.norden.org; the Nordic Council of Ministers coordinates the activities of the govts of the Nordic countries when decisions are to be implemented; co-operation with adjacent areas includes the Baltic States, where Nordic govts are committed to furthering democracy, security and sustainable devt, to contribute to peace, security and stability in Europe; the Nordic-Baltic Scholarship Scheme awards grants to students, teachers, scientists, civil servants and parliamentarians; Sec.-Gen. DAGFINN HØYBRÅTEN (Norway).

Northern Forum: 716 W 4th Ave, Office 100, Anchorage, Alaska, USA; tel. (907) 561-3280; fax (907) 561-6645; e-mail NForum@northernforum.org; internet www.northernforum.org; f. 1991; aims to improve the quality of life of northern peoples through support for sustainable development and socio-economic co-operation throughout the region; Exec. Dir VLADIMIR VASILIEV.

Organisation for the Prohibition of Chemical Weapons (OPCW): Johan de Wittlaan 32, 2517 JR The Hague, Netherlands; tel. (70) 4163300; fax (70) 3063535; e-mail media@opcw.org; internet www.opcw.org; f. April 1997, on the entry into force of the Chemical Weapons Convention (CWC)—an international, multilateral disarmament treaty banning the devt, production, stockpiling, transfer and use of chemical weapons—to oversee its implementation; verifies the irreversible destruction of declared chemical weapons stockpiles, as well as the elimination of all declared chemical weapons production facilities; OPCW mem. states undertake to provide protection and assistance if chemical weapons have been used against a state party, or if such weapons threaten a state party, and, together with OPCW inspectors, monitor the non-diversion of chemicals for activities prohibited under the CWC and verify the consistency of industrial chemical declarations; CWC states parties are obligated to declare any chemical weapons-related activities, to secure and destroy any stockpiles of chemical weapons within the stipulated deadlines, as well as to inactivate and eliminate any chemical weapons production capacity within their jurisdiction; the OPCW is a lead partner in the UN Counter-Terrorism Implementation Task Force's working group concerned with preventing and responding to weapons of mass destruction; in March 2013 the UN Secretary-General invited the OPCW to assist a UN fact-finding mission which was appointed at that time to investigate allegations relating to the use of chemical weapons by combatants in the ongoing conflict in Syria (which was not a signatory of the CWC); in Aug. the investigation team refocused its activities on the alleged use of chemical weapons in an attack in the Syrian capital Damascus; in mid-Sept. the mission's report confirmed that chemical weapons had been used in Syria; at that time the Syrian regime deposited its instrument of accession to the CWC (to enter into effect after 30 days) in accordance with a Russo–US agreement on a framework for the safeguarding and destruction of Syria's chemical weapons stockpiles; in Oct. the UN Security Council authorized the deployment of a joint OPCW-UN mission tasked with supervising the destruction by the Syrian authorities, by end-June 2014, of Syria's chemical weapons stockpiles and production facilities; OPCW was awarded the 2013 Nobel Peace Prize in Oct; mems: states parties to the Convention (190 at April 2014); 2013 budget: €69.8m.; Dir-Gen. AHMET ÜZÜMCÜ (Turkey).

Organisation Internationale de la Francophonie (La Francophonie): 19-21 ave Bosquet, 75007 Paris, France; tel. 1-44-37-33-00; fax 1-45-79-14-98; e-mail oif@francophonie.org; internet www.francophonie.org; f. 1970 as l'Agence de coopération culturelle et technique; promotes co-operation among French-speaking countries in the areas of education, culture, peace and democracy, and technology; implements decisions of the Sommet francophone; technical and financial assistance has been given to projects in every mem. country, mainly to aid rural people; mems: 57 states and govts (Mali's membership was suspended in March 2012, following a military coup, and in April 2013 the Central African Republic was similarly suspended); 20 countries with observer status; Sec.-Gen. ABDOU DIOUF (Senegal); publ. *Journal de l'Agence de la Francophonie* (quarterly).

Organisation of Eastern Caribbean States (OECS): Morne Fortune, POB 179, Castries, Saint Lucia; tel. 455-6327; fax 453-1628; e-mail oecss@oecs.org; internet www.oecs.org; f. 1981 by the seven states which formerly belonged to the West Indies Associated States (f. 1966); aims to promote the harmonized devt of trade and industry in mem. states; single market created on 1 Jan. 1988; principal institutions are the Authority of Heads of Government (the supreme policy-making body), the Foreign Affairs Committee, the Defence and Security Committee, and the Economic Affairs Committee; other functional divisions include an Export Development and Agricultural Diversification Unit (based in Dominica), a Pharmaceutical Procurement Service, a Regional Integration Unit, a Regional E-Government Unit and an HIV/AIDS Project Unit; an OECS Technical Mission to the World Trade Organization in Geneva, Switzerland, was inaugurated in June 2005; in Aug. 2008 heads of govt determined to achieve economic union by 2011 and political union by 2013; an agreement to establish an economic union was signed in Dec. 2009; a Revised Treaty of Basseterre Establishing the OECS Economic Union was signed by heads of govt of six mem. states (Antigua and Barbuda, Grenada, Dominica, Saint Christopher and Nevis, Saint Vincent and the Grenadines, and Saint Lucia) in June 2010; the Treaty envisaged a new governance structure, in which an OECS Commission was to be established as a supranational executive institution; the Revised Treaty entered into force in Feb. 2011, having been ratified by four of the signatory states; the inaugural session of the OECS Assembly was held in Aug. 2012, in Antigua and Barbuda; the inaugural meeting of an OECS Economic Affairs Council (EAC) was initially scheduled to be convened in late July 2013, later postponed to late Sept; mems: Antigua and Barbuda, Dominica, Grenada, Montserrat, Saint Christopher and Nevis, Saint Lucia, Saint Vincent and the Grenadines; assoc. mems: Anguilla, British Virgin Islands; Dir-Gen. Dr DIDACUS JULES (Saint Lucia) (from 1 May 2014).

Organization for Democracy and Economic Development (GUAM): 01001 Kyiv, str. Sofievska 2A, Ukraine; tel. (44) 2063737; fax (44) 2063006; e-mail secretariat@guam-organization.org; internet www.guam-organization.org; f. 1997 as a consultative alliance of Georgia, Ukraine, Azerbaijan and Moldova (GUAM); Uzbekistan joined the grouping in April 1999, when it became known as GUUAM, but withdrew in May 2005, causing the grouping's name to revert to GUAM; formally inaugurated as a full international org. and current name adopted by heads of state at a summit held in Kyiv in May 2006; objectives include the promotion of a regional space of democracy, security, and stable economic and social devt; strengthening relations with the European Union and NATO; developing a database on terrorism, organized crime, drugs-trafficking, and related activities; establishing a GUAM energy security council; creating the GUAM Free Trade Zone, in accordance with an agreement signed by heads of state at a meeting in Yalta, Ukraine, in July 2002; further economic devt, including the creation of an East–West trade corridor and transportation routes for petroleum; and participation in conflict resolution and peacekeeping activities, with the establishment of peacekeeping forces and civilian police units under consideration; Sec.-Gen. VALERI CHECHELASHVILI (Georgia).

Organization of Solidarity of the Peoples of Africa, Asia and Latin America (OSPAAAL) (Organización de Solidaridad de los Pueblos de Africa, Asia y América Latina): Calle C No 670 esq. 29, Vedado, Havana 10400, Cuba; tel. (7) 830-5510; fax (7) 830-5520; e-mail secretario.general@tricontinental.cu; internet www.tricontinental.cu; f. 1966 at the first Conference of Solidarity of the Peoples of Africa, Asia and Latin America, to unite, co-ordinate and encourage national liberation movements in the three continents, to oppose foreign intervention in the affairs of sovereign states, colonial and neo-colonial practices, and to fight against racialism and all forms of racial discrimination; favours the establishment of a new international economic order; mems: 76 orgs in 46 countries; Sec.-Gen. LOURDES CERVANTES; publ. *Tricontinental* (quarterly).

Parliamentary Association for Euro-Arab Co-operation (PAEAC) (Institut européen de recherche sur la coopération euro-arabe): 24 Sq. de Meeus, 5th Floor, 1000 Brussels, Belgium; tel. (2) 231-13-00; fax (2) 231-06-46; e-mail medea@medea.be; internet www.medea.be; f. 1974 as an asscn of 650 parliamentarians of all parties from the national parliaments of the Council of Europe countries and from the European Parliament, to promote friendship and co-operation between Europe and the Arab world; Executive Committee holds annual joint meetings with Arab Inter-Parliamentary Union; represented in Council of Europe and European Parliament; works for the progress of the Euro-Arab Dialogue and a settlement in the Middle East that takes into account the national rights of the Palestinian people; Pres. PIERRE COLOT; publs *Information Bulletin* (quarterly), *Euro-Arab and Mediterranean Political Fact Sheets* (2 a year), conf. notes.

Party of European Socialists (PES): 98 rue du Trône, 1050 Brussels, Belgium; tel. (2) 548-90-80; fax (2) 230-17-66; e-mail info@pes.eu; internet www.pes.eu; f. 1992 to replace the Confederation of the Socialist Parties of the EC (f. 1974); affiliated to Socialist International; mems: 32 parties, 11 assoc. parties and 10 observer parties; Pres. SERGEI STANISHEV; Sec.-Gen. ACHIM POST; publs various, including *The New Social Europe*, *The EU on the International Scene: Promoting Sustainable Peace*, statutes, manifestos and Congress documents.

Polynesian Leaders Group (PLG): c/o Govt of Samoa, POB L 1861, Apia, Samoa; tel. 24799; fax 26322; e-mail presssecretariat@samoa.ws; f. 2011 in Apia with the Memorandum of Understanding signed by eight states; to represent the collective interests of the Polynesian islands; third formal meeting scheduled to be held in Aug. 2014, in Niue; mems: American Samoa, Cook Islands, French Polynesia, Niue, Samoa, Tokelau, Tonga and Tuvalu; Chair. GASTON FLOSSE (French Polynesia).

Regional Co-operation Council: 71000 Sarajevo, Trg Bosne i Hercegovine 1/V, Bosnia and Herzegovina; tel. (33) 561700; fax (33) 561701; e-mail rcc@rcc.int; internet www.rcc.int; f. 2008, as successor to the Stability Pact for South Eastern Europe; serves as a focus for co-operation in the region; its six priority areas of activity cover: economic and social devt, energy and infrastructure, justice and home affairs, security co-operation, and building human capital, with parliamentary co-operation as an overarching theme; maintains a Liaison Office in Brussels, Belgium; 50 mem. countries and orgs; Sec.-Gen. GORAN SVILANOVIĆ (Serbia).

Shanghai Cooperation Organization (SCO): 7 Ritan Rd, Chaoyang District, Beijing, People's Republic of China; tel. (10) 65329807; fax (10) 65329808; e-mail sco@sectsco.org; internet www.sectsco.org; f. 2001, replacing the Shanghai Five (f. 1996 to address border disputes); aims to achieve security through mutual co-operation: promotes economic co-operation and measures to eliminate terrorism and drugs-trafficking; agreement on combating terrorism signed June 2001; a Convention on the Fight against Terrorism, Separatism and Extremism signed June 2002; Treaty on Long-term Good Neighbourliness, Friendship and Co-operation was signed Aug. 2007; maintains an SCO anti-terrorism centre in Tashkent, Uzbekistan; holds annual summit meeting (2013: Bishkek, Kyrgyzstan); mems: People's Republic of China, Kazakhstan, Kyrgyzstan, Russia, Tajikistan and Uzbekistan; observers: Afghanistan, India, Iran, Mongolia, Pakistan; dialogue partners: Belarus, Sri Lanka, Turkey; Sec.-Gen. DMITRII MEZENTSEV (Russia).

Socialist International: Maritime House, Clapham, London, SW4 0JW, United Kingdom; tel. (20) 7627-4449; fax (20) 7720-4448; e-mail secretariat@socialistinternational.org; internet www.socialistinternational.org; f. 1864; re-established in 1951; the world's oldest and largest asscn of political parties, grouping democratic socialist, labour and social democratic parties from every continent; provides a forum for political action, policy discussion and the exchange of ideas; works with many international orgs and trades unions (particularly mems of ITUC; established a Commission for a Sustainable World Society in Nov. 2006; holds Congress every three–four years (24th Congress: Cape Town, South Africa, Aug.–Sept. 2012); the Council meets twice a year, and regular confs and meetings of party leaders are also held; cttees and councils on a variety of subjects and in different regions meet frequently; mems: 162 parties and orgs worldwide; there are 3 fraternal orgs and 10 assoc. orgs, including the Party of European Socialists (PES), the Group of the PES at the European Parliament and the International Federation of the Socialist and Democratic Press; Pres. GEORGE A. PAPANDREOU (Greece); Gen. Sec. LUIS AYALA (Chile); publ. *Socialist Affairs* (quarterly).

International Falcon Movement—Socialist Educational International: 98 rue du Trône, 2nd Floor, 1050 Brussels, Belgium; tel. (2) 215-79-27; fax (2) 245-00-83; e-mail contact@ifm-sei.org; internet www.ifm-sei.org; f. 1924 to help children and adolescents to develop international understanding and a sense of social responsibility and to prepare them for democratic life; co-operates with several institutions concerned with children, youth and education; mems: 60 mems worldwide; Pres. ANA MARIA ALMARIO (Colombia); Sec.-Gen. CHRISTINE SUDBROCK (Germany); publs *IFM-SEI Newsletter* (quarterly), *IFM-SEI World News*, *EFN Newsletter* (6 a year), *Asian Regional Bulletin*, *Latin American Regional Bulletin*.

International Union of Socialist Youth (IUSY): Amtshausgasse 4, 1050 Vienna, Austria; tel. (1) 523-12-67; fax (1) 523-12-679; e-mail iusy@iusy.org; internet www.iusy.org; f. 1907 as Socialist Youth International (present name adopted 1946), to educate young people in the principles of free and democratic socialism and further the co-operation of democratic socialist youth orgs; conducts international meetings, symposia, etc; mems: 150 youth and student orgs in 100 countries; Pres. FELIPE JELDRES; Sec.-Gen. EVIN INCIR; publ. *IUSY Newsletter*.

Stockholm International Peace Research Institute (SIPRI): Signalistgatan 9, 169 70 Solna, Sweden; tel. (8) 655-97-00; fax (8) 655-97-33; e-mail sipri@sipri.org; internet www.sipri.org; f. 1966; researches regional and global security, armed conflict and conflict management, military spending, armaments, arms control, disarmament and non-proliferation; provides data, analysis and recommendations to policy-makers, researchers, the media and the interested public; has recently established programmes on China and Global Security and on Global Health and Security; maintains a number of databases on international arms transfers, military expenditure, multilateral peace operations, and international arms embargoes; mems: about 60 staff mems, about 40 of whom are researchers; Dir Prof. TILMAN BRÜCK (Germany); publs *SIPRI Yearbook: Armaments, Disarmament and International Security*, monographs and research reports.

Transparency International: Alt Moabit 96, 10559 Berlin, Germany; tel. (30) 3438200; fax (30) 34703912; e-mail ti@transparency.org; internet www.transparency.org; f. 1993; aims to promote governmental adoption of anti-corruption practices and accountability at all levels of the public sector; works to ensure that international business transactions are conducted with integrity and without resort to corrupt practices; raises awareness of the damaging effects of corruption; produces an annual Corruption Perceptions Index, a Bribe Payers Index, a Global Corruption Barometer and an annual Global Corruption Report; holds International Anti-Corruption Conference every two years (16th Congress: Tunis, Tunisia, in Oct. 2014); some 90 chapters worldwide; Chair. Dr HUGUETTE LABELLE (Canada); Man. Dir Dr COBUS DE SWARDT (South Africa).

Trilateral Commission: 1156 15th St, NW, Washington, DC 20005, USA; tel. (202) 467-5410; fax (202) 467-5415; e-mail contactus@trilateral.org; internet www.trilateral.org; also offices in Paris and Tokyo; f. 1973 by private citizens of Western Europe, Japan and North America, to encourage closer co-operation among these regions on matters of common concern; through analysis of major issues the Commission seeks to improve public understanding of problems, to develop and support proposals for handling them jointly, and to nurture the habit of working together in the 'trilateral' area. The Commission issues task force reports on such subjects as monetary affairs, political co-operation, trade issues, the energy crisis and reform of international institutions; holds annual meeting (2013: Berlin, Germany, in March; mems: about 335 individuals eminent in academic life, industry, finance, labour, etc.; those currently engaged as senior government officials are excluded; Chair. YASUCHIKA HASEGAWA, JOSEPH S. NYE, Jr, JEAN-CLAUDE TRICHET; Dirs MICHAEL J. O'NEIL, PAUL RÉVAY, KEN SHIBUSAWA; publs *Task Force Reports*, *Triangle Papers*.

Union for the Mediterranean Secretariat (UfMS): Palacio de Pedralbes, Pere Duran Farell, 11, 08034 Barcelona, Spain; tel. (93) 5214100; fax (93) 5214102; e-mail info@ufmsecretariat.org; internet www.ufmsecretariat.org; f. 2008 as a continuation of the Euro-Mediterranean Partnership (Barcelona Process), which had been launched in 1995; the statutes of the UfMS were adopted in March 2010; the UfMS's mandate is defined by the July 2008 Paris Declaration of the Euro-Mediterranean summit, and by the subsequent Marseilles Declaration, adopted in Nov. of that year; the Union was established as a framework for advancing relations (political, economic and social) between the European Union and countries of the Southern and Eastern Mediterranean, in accordance with the goals detailed in the 1995 Barcelona Declaration: i.e. working to create an area of stability and shared economic prosperity, underpinned by full respect for democratic principles, human rights and fundamental freedoms; mems: 28 European Union mem. states, the European Commission and 15 Mediterranean countries; Sec.-Gen. FATHALLAH SIJILMASSI (Morocco).

Union of International Associations (UIA): 40 rue Washington, 1050 Brussels, Belgium; tel. (2) 640-18-08; fax (2) 643-61-99; e-mail uia@uia.org; internet www.uia.org; f. 1907, present title adopted 1910; aims to facilitate the evolution of the activities of the worldwide network of non-profit orgs, especially non-governmental and voluntary asscns through training and networking opportunities; collects and disseminates information on such orgs; promotes research on the legal, administrative and other problems common to these asscns; mems: 101 individuals in 28 countries and 72 assoc. corp. bodies or individuals; Sec.-Gen. JACQUES DE MÉVIUS; publs *International Congress Calendar* (quarterly), *Yearbook of International Organizations*, *International Meetings Statistics ReportWorld of Associations News* (quarterly), *Encyclopedia of World Problems and Human Potential*, *International Association Statutes* series, *Who's Who in International Organizations*.

Union of South American Nations (UNASUR) (Unión de Naciones Suramericanas): Avda 6 de Diciembre, Quito, Ecuador; tel. (2) 4010400; e-mail secretaria.general@unasursg.org; internet www.unasursg.org; in April 2007, at the first South American Energy Summit, convened in Margarita Island, Venezuela, heads of state endorsed the establishment of UNASUR to replace the South America Community of Nations (SACN) as the lead org. for regional integration; a Constitutive Treaty, signed by heads of state in May 2008, entered into force in March 2011, having received the required nine ratifications; UNASUR convenes election observation missions with the aim of promoting regional co-operation and democratic participation; in Nov. 2012 UNASUR heads of state adopted the Declaration of Lima, comprising 16 actions aimed at promoting regional integration, 'building a South American citizenship', and the devt of a regional zone of peace; in April 2014, in response to the eruption in Venezuela from Feb. of violent protests against prevailing social and economic conditions, UNASUR mediated the start of a formal dialogue between representatives of the Venezuelan Government and opposition elements; mems: Argentina, Bolivia, Brazil, Chile, Colombia, Ecuador, Guyana, Paraguay, Peru, Suriname, Uruguay, Venezuela; Sec.-Gen. ALÍ RODRÍGUEZ ARAQUE (Venezuela).

United Cities and Local Governments (UCLG): Carrer Avinyó 15, 08002 Barcelona, Spain; tel. (93) 3428750; fax (93) 3428760; e-mail info@uclg.org; internet www.uclg.org; f. 2004 by merger of the Int. Union of Local Authorities and the World Federation of United Cities; aims to increase the role and influence of local govts, promotes democratic local governance, and facilitates partnerships and networks among cities and local authorities; initiated a Millennium Towns and Cities Campaign to encourage civic authorities to support implementation of the Millennium Development Goals; launched the Global Observatory on Local Democracy and Decentralisation to provide information on the situation and evolution of self-govt and local govt across the world; mems: 112 local govt asscns, more than 1,000 mem. cities in 95 countries; Pres. KADIR TOPBAS (Turkey); Sec.-Gen. JOSEP ROIG (Spain); publ. *Global Report on Decentralisation and Local Democracy*.

Uniting for Peace: 14 Cavell St, London E1 2HP, United Kingdom; tel. (20) 7790-1999; e-mail info@unitingforpeace.com; internet www.unitingforpeace.org; f. 2011 to promote peace, security and disarmament, human rights, international law, devt, and poverty reduction; Chair. VIJAY MEHTA; publ. *Newsletter*.

Unrepresented Nations and Peoples Organization (UNPO): Laan van Meerdervoort 70, 2517 AN The Hague, Netherlands; tel. (70) 3646504; fax (70) 3646608; e-mail unpo@unpo.org; internet www.unpo.org; f. 1991; an international, non-violent, and democratic membership org. representing indigenous peoples, minorities, and unrecognized or occupied territories united in the aim of protecting and promoting their human and cultural rights, preserving their environments, and finding non-violent solutions to conflicts that affect them; mems: 40 orgs representing occupied nations, indigenous peoples and minorities; Pres. NGAWANG CHOEPHEL; Gen. Sec. MARINO BUSDACHIN; publ. *UNPO Yearbook*.

War Resisters' International: 5 Caledonian Rd, London, N1 9DX, United Kingdom; tel. (20) 7278-4040; fax (20) 7278-0444; e-mail info@wri-irg.org; internet www.wri-irg.org; f. 1921; encourages refusal to participate in or support wars or military service, collaborates with movements that work for peace and non-violent social change; mems: approx. 150,000; Chair. HOWARD CLARK; publs *The Broken Rifle* (quarterly), *warprofiteers-news* (every 2 months) *co-update* (monthly).

Women's International Democratic Federation (WIDF): Guimarães Passos 422, Vila Mariana, São Paulo, SP, Brazil, 04107-031; tel. (11) 2892-3087; e-mail fdim.sec@terra.com.br; internet www.fdim-widf.org; f. 1945 to unite women regardless of nationality, race, religion or political opinion; to enable them to work together to win and defend their rights as citizens, mothers and workers; to protect children; and to ensure peace and progress, democracy and national independence; structure: Congress, Secretariat and Executive Committee; mems: 660 affiliated orgs in 160 countries; Pres. MARCIA CAMPOS (Brazil); publs *Women of the Whole World* (6 a year), *Newsletter*.

World Federalist Movement (WFM): 708 Third Ave, 24th Floor, New York, NY 10017, USA; tel. (212) 599-1320; fax (212) 599-1332; e-mail info@wfm-igp.org; internet www.wfm-igp.org; f. 1947; aims to acquire for the UN the authority to make and enforce laws for the peaceful settlement of disputes, and to raise revenue under limited taxing powers; to establish better international co-operation in the areas of environment, devt and disarmament; and to promote federalism throughout the world; an Institute for Global Policy was established in 1983 as the research and policy analysis mechanism of the WFM; Congress meetings held every five years (July 2012: Winnipeg, Canada); mems: 20 mem. orgs and 16 assoc. orgs; Pres. Dr LLOYD AXWORTHY; Exec. Dir WILLIAM R. PACE; publs *World Federalist News* (quarterly), *International Criminal Court Monitor* (quarterly).

World Federation of United Nations Associations (WFUNA) (Fédération Mondiale des Associations Pour les Nations Unies—FMANU): 1 United Nations Plaza, Rm 1177, New York, NY 10017, USA; tel. (212) 963-5610; e-mail info@wfuna.org; internet www.wfuna.org; f. 1946 to encourage popular interest and participation in UN programmes, discussion of the role and future of the UN, and education for international understanding; Plenary Assembly meets every three years; mems: nat. asscns in more than 100 countries; Pres. PARK SOO-GIL (Republic of Korea); Sec.-Gen. BONIAN GOLMOHAMMADI (Sweden); publ. *WFUNA News*.

World Peace Council: Othonos 10, Athens 10557, Greece; tel. (210) 331-6326; fax (210) 322-4302; e-mail info@wpc-in.org; internet www.wpc-in.org; f. 1950 at the Second World Peace Congress, Warsaw; principles: the prevention of nuclear war; the peaceful co-existence of the various socio-economic systems in the world; settlement of differences between nations by negotiation and agreement; complete disarmament; elimination of colonialism and racial discrimination; and respect for the right of peoples to sovereignty and independence; mems: representatives of nat. orgs, groups and individuals from 140 countries, and of 30 int. orgs; Executive Committee of 40 mems elected by world assembly held every 3 years; Pres. SOCORRO GOMES; Exec. Sec. IRAKLIS TSAVDARIDIS; publ. *Peace Courier* (monthly).

World Winter Cities Association for Mayors (WWCAM): Kita 1 Nishi 2, Chuo-ku, Sapporo 060-8611, Japan; tel. (11) 222-4894; fax (11) 221-4894; internet www.city.sapporo.jp/somu/kokusai/wwcam; f. 1981 as the Intercity Conference of Mayors, present name adopted in 2004; aims to promote close co-operation among northern cities and enable the sharing of information on city devt and winter technologies; holds a biennial Mayors Conference (2014: Hwacheon, Republic of Korea, in Jan.); mems: 19 cities from 9 countries; Pres. FUMIO UEDA.

Youth of the European People's Party (YEPP): 10 rue du Commerce, 1000 Brussels, Belgium; tel. (2) 285-41-63; fax (2) 285-41-65; e-mail yepp@epp.eu; internet youthepp.eu; f. 1997 to unite national youth orgs of mem. parties of European Young Christian Democrats and Democrat Youth Community of Europe; aims to develop contacts between youth movements and advance general political debate among young people; mems: 56 orgs in some 38 European countries; Pres. KONSTANTINOS KYRANAKIS (Greece); Sec.-Gen. COLM LAUDER (Ireland).

Industrial and Professional Relations

Association of Mutual Insurers and Insurance Co-operatives in Europe (AMICE): 98 rue de Trone, 1050 Brussels, Belgium; tel. (2) 503-38-78; fax (2) 503-30-55; e-mail secretariat@amice-eu.org; internet www.amice-eu.org; f. 2008 through the merger of the International Association of Mutual Insurance Companies (AISAM) and the Association of European Co-operative and Mutual Insurers (ACME), to raise the profile of the mutual and co-operative insurance sector in Europe; convenes congress every two years (2014: Nice, France, in June); mems: 100 direct mems and 1,600 indirect mems, representing one-third of the insurance cos in Europe; Pres. HILDE VERNAILLEN (Belgium); Sec.-Gen. GREGOR POZNIAK; publs *Annual Report*, *Newsletter*.

Business Africa (BA): c/o Federation of Kenya Employers (MEF), Waajiri House, 48311-00100 Nairobi, Kenya; tel. (20) 2721929; fax (20) 2720295; e-mail j.mugo@fke-kenya.org; f. 1986, as Pan-African Employers' Confederation (PEC); mems: representation in 42 countries on the continent; Sec.-Gen. JACQUELINE MUGO (Kenya).

European Association for People Management: c/o CIPD, 151 The Broadway, Wimbledon, London, SW19 1JQ, United Kingdom; tel. (20) 8612-6000; fax (20) 8612-6201; e-mail eapmsecretary@cipd.co.uk; internet www.eapm.org; f. 1962 to disseminate knowledge and information concerning the personnel function of management, to establish and maintain professional standards, to define the specific nature of personnel management within industry, commerce and the public services, and to assist in the devt of nat. asscns; mems: 27 nat. asscns; Pres. FILIPPO ABRAMO (Italy); Sec.-Gen. STEPHANIE BIRD (United Kingdom); publs *Newsletter*, *Annual Report*.

European Cities Marketing: 29D rue de Talant, 21000 Dijon, France; tel. 3-80-56-02-04; fax 3-80-56-02-05; e-mail headoffice@europeancitiesmarketing.com; internet www.europeancitiesmarketing.com; European Cities Marketing is the network of City Tourist Offices and Convention Bureaus; aims to strengthen city tourism by providing sales and marketing opportunities, communicating information, sharing knowledge and expertise, educating and working together on an operational level; Pres. IGNASI DE DELÀS.

European Civil Service Federation (ECSF) (Fédération de la Fonction Publique Européenne—FFPE): 200 rue de la Loi, L 102 6/14,1049 Brussels, Belgium; tel. (2) 295-00-12; fax (2) 298-17-21; e-mail secretariat.politique@ffpe.org; internet www.ffpe-bxl.eu; f. 1962 to foster the idea of a European civil service of staff of international orgs operating in Western Europe or pursuing regional objectives; upholds the interests of civil service mems; mems: local cttees in 12 European countries and individuals in 66 countries; Pres. BACRI PIERRE-PHILIPPE; Political Sec. TOSON MYRIAM; publ. *Eurechos*.

European Construction Industry Federation (Fédération de l'Industrie Européenne de la Construction—FIEC): 225 ave Louise, 1050 Brussels, Belgium; tel. (2) 514-55-35; fax (2) 511-02-76; e-mail info@fiec.eu; internet www.fiec.org; f. 1905 as International European Construction Federation, present name adopted 1999; mems: 33 nat. employers' orgs in 29 countries; Pres. THOMAS SCHLEICHER (Italy); Dir-Gen. ULRICH PAETZOLD; publs *FIEC News* (2 a year), *Annual Report*, *Construction Activity in Europe*.

European Industrial Research Management Association (EIRMA): 81A rue de la Loi, 1040 Brussels, Belgium; tel. (2) 233-11-80; fax (2) 231-08-35; e-mail info@eirma.org; internet www.eirma.org; f. 1966 under the auspices of OECD; a permanent body in which European science and technology firms meet to consider approaches to industrial innovation, support research and devt, and take joint action to improve performance in their various fields; mems: 120 in 20 countries; Pres. CARLOS HÄRTEL; Sec.-Gen. DANIEL MICHEL JUDKIEWICZ; publs *Annual Report*, *Conference Reports*, *Working Group Reports*, *Workshop Reports*.

European Trade Union Confederation (Conféderation européenne des syndicats): 5 blvd du Roi Albert II, 1210 Brussels, Belgium; tel. (2) 224-04-11; fax (2) 224-04-54; e-mail etuc@etuc.org; internet www.etuc.org; f. 1973; comprises 85 national trade union confeds and 10 European industrial feds in 36 European countries, representing 60m. workers; co-operates closely with the International Trade Union Confederation; Pres. IGNACIO FERNÁNDEZ TOXO (Spain); Gen. Sec. BERNADETTE SÉGOL; publ. *Newsletter*.

Federation of International Civil Servants' Associations (FICSA): Palais des Nations, Office BOC 74, 1211 Geneva 10, Switzerland; tel. 229173150; fax 229170660; e-mail ficsa@unog.ch; internet www.ficsa.org; f. 1952 to co-ordinate policies and activities of mem. asscns and unions, to represent staff interests before inter-agency and legislative organs of the UN and to promote the devt of an international civil service; mems: 30 asscns and unions consisting of staff of UN orgs, 9 assoc. mems from non-UN orgs, 16 consultative asscns and 21 inter-organizational feds with observer status; Pres. MAURO PACE; Gen. Sec. (vacant); publs *Annual Report*, *FICSA Newsletter*, *FICSA Update*, *FICSA circulars*.

INSOL International: 6–7 Queen St, London, EC4N 1SP, United Kingdom; tel. (20) 7248-3333; fax (20) 7248-3384; e-mail heather@insol.ision.co.uk; internet www.insol.org; f. 1982 as International Federation of Insolvency Professionals; comprises national asscns of accountants and lawyers specializing in corp. turnaround and insolvency; holds seminars, an annual conf. and congress every four years; mems: 43 asscns with approx. 9,000 professionals; Pres. JAMES H. M. SPRAYREGEN (USA); Exec. Dir CLAIRE BROUGHTON; publs *INSOL World* (quarterly newsletter), *International Insolvency Review* (2 a year).

International Association of Conference Interpreters: 46 ave Blanc, 1202 Geneva, Switzerland; tel. 229081540; fax 227324151; e-mail info@aiic.net; internet www.aiic.net; f. 1953 to represent professional conf. interpreters, ensure the highest possible standards and protect the legitimate interests of mems; establishes criteria designed to improve the standards of training; recognizes schools meeting the required standards; has consultative status with the UN and several of its agencies; mems: 3,000 in some 90 countries; Pres. LINDA FITCHETT; publs *Code of Professional Conduct*, *Yearbook* (listing interpreters), etc.

International Association of Conference Translators: 15 route des Morillons, 1218 Le Grand-Saconnex, Geneva, Switzerland; tel. 227910666; e-mail secretariat@aitc.ch; internet www.aitc.ch; f. 1962; represents revisers, translators, précis writers and editors working for international confs and orgs; aims to protect the interests of those in the profession and help to maintain high standards; establishes links with international orgs and conf. organizers; mems: c. 470 in 33 countries; Pres. MARY FRETZ; Exec. Sec. CORALIE GOURDON; publs *Directory*, *Bulletin*.

International Confederation of Energy Regulators: e-mail office@icer-regulators.net; internet www.icer-regulators.net; f. 2009; mems: 11 reg. energy regulatory asscns, representing more than 200 regulatory authorities worldwide; Interim Pres. JEAN-MICHEL GLACHANT.

International Federation of Actors (Fédération internationale des acteurs—FIA): 40 rue Joseph II B/04, 1000 Brussels, Belgium; tel. (2) 235-08-74; fax (2) 235-08-70; e-mail office@fia-actors.com; internet www.fia-actors.com; f. 1952; Exec. Cttee meets annually, Congress convened every four years; mems: 97 performers' unions in 71 countries; Pres. FERNE DOWNEY (Canada); Gen. Sec. DOMINICK LUQUER.

International Federation of Air Line Pilots' Associations (IFALPA): 485 rue McGill, Bureau 700, Montréal, QC H2Y 2H4, Canada; tel. (514) 419-1191; fax (514) 419-1195; e-mail ifalpa@ifalpa.org; internet www.ifalpa.org; f. 1948 to represent pilots worldwide; aims to promote the highest level of aviation safety worldwide and to provide services, support and representation to all its mem. asscns; mems: 102 asscns, representing more than 100,000 pilots; Pres. Capt. DON WYKOFF; publs *Interpilot* (6 a year), safety bulletins and news-sheets.

International Federation of Biomedical Laboratory Science (IFBLS): POB 2830, Hamilton, Ontario, ON L8N 3N8, Canada; tel. (905) 667-8695; fax (905) 528-4968; e-mail communications@ifbls.org; internet www.ifbls.org; f. 1954 to allow discussion of matters of common professional interest; fmrly the International Association of Medical Laboratory Technologists (f. 1954); aims to promote globally the highest standards in the delivery of care, of professional training, and ethical and professional practices; develops and promotes active professional partnerships in health care at the international level; promotes and encourages participation of mems in international activities; holds international congress every second year; mems: 180,000 in 37 countries; Pres. KYOKO KOMATSU (Japan); publ. *Biomedical Laboratory Science International* (quarterly).

International Federation of Business and Professional Women (BPW International): BPW International, POB 2042, Fitzroy, Victoria 3065, Australia; e-mail presidents.office@bpw-international.org; internet www.bpw-international.org; f. 1930 to promote interests of business and professional women and secure combined action by such women; mems: national feds, assoc. clubs and individual assocs, totalling more than 100,000 mems in over 100 countries; Pres. FREDA MIRIKLIS (Australia); Exec. Sec. Dr YASMIN DARWICH (Mexico); publ. *BPW News International* (every 2 months).

International Labour and Employment Relations Association (ILERA): c/o International Labour Office, 1211 Geneva 22, Switzerland; tel. 227997371; fax 227998749; e-mail ilera@ilo.org; internet www.ilo.org/ilera; f. 1966 as the International Industrial Relations Association; to encourage devt of national asscns of specialists, facilitate the spread of information, organize confs, and promote internationally planned research, through study groups and regional meetings; a World Congress is held every three years; mems: 39 asscns, 47 institutions and some 700 individuals; Pres. Prof. EVANCE R. KALULA (South Africa); Sec. MOUSSA OUMAROU (Niger); publs *IIRA Bulletin* (3 a year), *IIRA Membership Directory*.

International Organisation of Employers (IOE): 26 chemin de Joinville, BP 68, 1216 Cointrin/Geneva, Switzerland; tel. 229290000; fax 229290001; e-mail ioe@ioe-emp.org; internet www.ioe-emp.org; f. 1920; aims to establish and maintain contacts between mems and to represent their interests at international level; works to promote free enterprise; joined in 2008 the Green Jobs Initiative, a partnership launched in 2007 by UNEP, the ILO and the International Confederation of Trade Unions; and to assist the devt of employers' orgs; General Council meets annually; there is a Management Board and a General Secretariat; mems: 151 feds in 144 countries; Pres. Dato' AZMAN SHAH SERI HARON (Malaysia); Sec.-Gen. BRENT WILTON; publ. *IOE.net*.

International Public Relations Association (IPRA): POB 6945, London, W1A 6US, United Kingdom; tel. (1903) 744442; internet www.ipra.org; f. 1955 to provide an exchange of ideas, technical knowledge and professional experience among those engaged in public relations, and to foster the highest standards of professional competence; mems: 700 in 80 countries; Pres. ZEHRA GÜNGÖR (Turkey); Treas. NIGEL CHISM (United Kingdom); publs *Frontline* (every 2 months), *Directory of Members* (annually).

International Society of City and Regional Planners (ISOCARP): POB 983, 2501 CZ The Hague, Netherlands; tel. (70) 3462654; fax (70) 3617909; e-mail isocarp@isocarp.org; internet www.isocarp.org; f. 1965 to promote better planning practice through the exchange of professional knowledge; holds annual World Congress (Sept. 2014: Gdynia, Poland); mems: 653 in 87 countries; Pres. MILICA BAJIĆ-BRKOVIĆ (Serbia); Sec.-Gen. DIDIER VANCUTSEM (Germany); publs *ISoCaRP REVIEW* (annually), seminar and congress reports.

International Union of Architects (Union internationale des architectes—UIA): Tour Maine Montparnasse, BP 158, 33 ave du Maine, 75755 Paris Cedex 15, France; tel. 1-45-24-36-88; fax 1-45-24-02-78; e-mail uia@uia-architectes.org; internet www.uia-architectes.org; f. 1948; holds triennial congress (2013: Durban, South Africa); mems: professional orgs in 124 countries; Pres. ALBERT DUBLER (France); Gen. Sec. MICHEL BARMAKI (Lebanon); publ. *Lettre d'informations* (monthly).

Nordic Innovation (Nordisk Innovations Center): Stensberggt. 25, 0170 Oslo, Norway; tel. 47-61-44-00; fax 22-56-55-65; e-mail info@nordicinnovation.org; internet www.nordicinnovation.org; f. 1973; provides grants, subsidies and loans for industrial research and devt projects of interest to Nordic countries; Chair. KARIN WIKMAN; Man. Dir ROGER M. BJØRGAN.

Organisation of African Trade Union Unity (OATUU): POB M386, Accra, Ghana; tel. (21) 508855; fax (21) 508851; e-mail oatuu@ighmail.com; f. 1973 as a single continental trade union org., independent of international trade union orgs; has affiliates from all African trade unions. Congress, the supreme policy-making body, is composed of four delegates per country from affiliated national trade union centres, and meets at least every four years; the General Council, composed of one representative from each affiliated trade union, meets annually to implement Congress decisions and to approve the annual budget; mems: trade union movements in 53 independent African countries; Sec.-Gen. Gen. OWEI LAKEMFA; publ. *The African Worker*.

Society of European Affairs Professionals (SEAP): Brussels, Belgium; tel. 478996025; e-mail secretariat@seap.be; internet www.seap.be; f. 1997; aims to establish an open non-profit-making org. of European affairs professionals dealing with European institutions; Pres. SUSANNA DI FELICIANTONIO; Sec.-Gen. GARY HILLS.

World Federation of Scientific Workers (WFSW) (Fédération mondiale des travailleurs scientifiques—FMTS): Case 404, 263 rue de Paris, 93516 Montreuil Cedex, France; tel. 1-48-18-81-75; fax 1-48-18-80-03; e-mail fmts@fmts-wfsw.org; internet www.fmts-wfsw.org; f. 1946 to improve the position of science and scientists, to assist in promoting international scientific co-operation and to promote the use of science for beneficial ends; studies and publicizes problems of general, nuclear, biological and chemical disarmament; surveys the position and activities of scientists; mems: orgs in 28 countries; Pres. JEAN-PAUL LAINÉ (France); Sec.-Gen. SMATI ZOGHBI (Algeria).

World Movement of Christian Workers (WMCW): 124 blvd du Jubilé, 1080 Brussels, Belgium; tel. (2) 421-58-40; e-mail info@mmtc-infor.com; internet www.mmtc-infor.com; f. 1961 to unite national movements that advance the spiritual and collective well-being of workers; holds General Assembly every four years (2013: Haltern am See, Germany, in July); mems: more than 46 affiliated movements in 44 countries; Sec.-Gen. BETINA BEATE; publ. *INFOR*.

World Union of Professions (Union mondiale des professions libérales): 46 blvd de la Tour-Maubourg, 75007 Paris, France; tel. 1-44-05-90-15; fax 1-44-05-90-17; e-mail info@umpl.org; internet www.umpl.com; f. 1987 to represent and link mems of the liberal professions; mems: 27 nat. inter-professional orgs, 2 reg. groups and 12 int. feds; Chair. FRANCISCO ANTÔNIO FEIJO (Brazil).

Law

African Society of International and Comparative Law (ASICL): Private Bag 520, Kairaba Ave, KSMD, Banjul, The Gambia; tel. 375476; fax 375469; e-mail africansociety@aol.com; f. 1986; promotes public education on law and civil liberties; aims to provide a legal aid and advice system in each African country, and to facilitate the exchange of information on civil liberties in Africa; publs *Newsletter* (every 2 months), *African Journal of International and Comparative Law* (3 a year).

Asian-African Legal Consultative Organization (AALCO): 29-C, Rizal Marg, Diplomatic Enclave, Chanakyapuri, New Delhi 110057, India; tel. (11) 24197000; fax (11) 26117640; e-mail mail@aalco.int; internet www.aalco.int; f. 1956 to consider legal problems referred to it by mem. countries and to serve as a forum for Afro-Asian co-operation in international law, including international trade law, and economic relations; provides background material for confs, prepares standard/model contract forms suited to the needs of the region; promotes arbitration as a means of settling international commercial disputes; trains officers of mem. states; has permanent UN observer status; has established four International Commercial Arbitration Centres in Kuala Lumpur, Malaysia; Cairo, Egypt; Lagos, Nigeria; and Tehran, Iran; mems: 47 countries; Sec.-Gen. Prof. Dr RAHMAT BIN MOHAMAD (Malaysia).

Coalition for the International Criminal Court: Bezuidenhoutseweg 99A, 2594 AC The Hague, Netherlands; tel. (70) 3111080; fax (70) 3640259; e-mail cicc@coalitionfortheicc.org; internet www.iccnow.org; f. 1995 to support the activities of the International Criminal Court and to ensure that the Court functions fairly, transparently and independently; aims to promote stronger national laws to assist victims of war crimes, humanitarian conflict and genocide; mems: 2,500 civil society orgs in 150 countries; Convenor WILLIAM R. PACE.

Centre for International Environmental Law (CIEL): 1350 Connecticut Ave, NW, Suite 1100, Washington, DC 20036, USA; tel. (202) 785-8700; fax (202) 785-8701; e-mail info@ciel.org; internet www.ciel.org; f. 1989; aims to solve environmental problems and to promote sustainable societies through the use of law; works to strengthen international and comparative environmental law and policy and to incorporate fundamental ecological principles into international law; provides a range of environmental legal services; educates and trains environmental lawyers; Pres. and CEO CARROLL MUFFETT (USA).

Comité maritime international (CMI): Everdijstraat 43, 2000 Antwerp, Belgium; tel. (3) 203-45-00; fax (3) 203-45-01; e-mail info@comitemaritime.org; internet www.comitemaritime.org; f. 1897 to contribute to the unification of maritime law and to encourage the creation of national asscns; work includes drafting of conventions on collisions at sea, salvage and assistance at sea, limitation of shipowners' liability, maritime mortgages, etc; mems: nat. asscns in more than 59 countries; Pres. STUART HETHERINGTON (Australia); Sec.-Gen. JOHN HARE (South Africa); publs *CMI Newsletter*, *Year Book*.

Council of the Bars and Law Societies of Europe (CCBE): 40/8 rue Joseph II, 1000 Brussels, Belgium; tel. (2) 234-65-10; fax (2) 234-65-11; e-mail ccbe@ccbe.eu; internet www.ccbe.eu; f. 1960; the officially recognized representative org. for the legal profession in the European Union and European Economic Area; liaises between the bars and law societies of mem. states and represents them before the European institutions; also maintains contact with other international orgs of lawyers; principal objective is to study all questions affecting the legal profession in mem. states and to harmonize professional practice; mems: 32 delegations (representing some 1m. European lawyers) and observer/assoc. delegations from 11 countries; Pres. EVANGELOS TSOUROULIS; Sec.-Gen. JONATHAN GOLDSMITH.

East African Court of Justice: POB 1096, Arusha, Tanzania; tel. (27) 2506093; fax (27) 2509493; e-mail eacj@eachq.org; internet www.eacj.org/index.php; f. 2001; organ of the East African Community (EAC), established under the Treaty for the Establishment of the EAC with responsibility for ensuring compliance with the Treaty; Registrar Dr JOHN RUHANGISA.

East African Legislative Assembly: POB 1096, AICC Bldg, Arusha, Tanzania; tel. (27) 2504253; internet www.eala.org; f. 2001; established under the EAC's founding Treaty as the legislative organ of the Community; Speaker (2012–17) MARGARET NANTONGO ZZIWA (Uganda).

Eastern Caribbean Supreme Court: Heraldine Rock Bldg, Block B, Waterfront, POB 1093, Castries; tel. 457-3600; fax 457-3601; e-mail offices@eccourts.org; internet www.eccourts.org; f. 1967 as the West Indies Associated States Supreme Court, in 1974 as the Supreme Court of Grenada and the West Indies Associated States, present name adopted in 1979; composed of the High Court of Justice and the Court of Appeal, High Court is composed of the Chief Justice and 22 High Court Judges. The Court of Appeal is itinerant and presided over by the Chief Justice who is also President of the Court of Appeal, six other Justices of Appeal and three Masters; the Court is a superior court of record and has unlimited jurisdiction in the nine mem. states/territories of the OECS; jurisdiction of the Court extends to fundamental rights and freedoms, membership of the parliaments, and matters concerning the interpretation of constitutions; Chief Justice Dame JANICE MESADIS PEREIRA.

Hague Conference on Private International Law: Scheveningseweg 6, 2517 KT The Hague, Netherlands; tel. (70) 3633303; fax (70) 3604867; e-mail secretariat@hcch.net; internet www.hcch.net; f. 1893 to work for the unification of the rules of private international law; Permanent Bureau f. 1955; mems: 75 (incl. the European Union); Sec.-Gen. CHRISTOPHE BERNASCONI; publs *Proceedings of Diplomatic Sessions* (every 4 years), *Collection of Conventions*, *The Judges' Newsletter on International Child Protection*.

Institute of International Law (Institut de droit international): c/o IHEID, CP 136, 1211 Geneva 21, Switzerland; tel. 229085720; fax 229086277; e-mail joe.verhoeven@uclouvain.be; internet www.idi-iil

.org; f. 1873 to promote the devt of international law through the formulation of general principles, in accordance with civilized ethical standards; provides assistance for the gradual and progressive codification of international law; mems: limited to 132 mems and assocs worldwide; Pres. REIN MÜLLERSON; Sec.-Gen. JOE VERHOEVEN (Belgium); publ. *Annuaire de l'Institut de Droit international*.

Inter-American Bar Association (IABA): 1211 Connecticut Ave, NW, Suite 202, Washington, DC 20036, USA; tel. (202) 466-5944; fax (202) 466-5946; e-mail iaba@iaba.org; internet www.iaba.org; f. 1940 to promote the rule of law and to establish and maintain relations between asscns and orgs of lawyers in the Americas; mems: 90 asscns and 3,500 individuals in 27 countries; Pres. JOSE A. ALVAREZ (Panama); Sec.-Gen. HENRY DAHL; publs *Newsletter* (quarterly), *Conference Proceedings*.

International Association for the Protection of Industrial Property (AIPPI): Tödistr. 16, 8027 Zürich 27, Switzerland; tel. 442805880; fax 442805885; e-mail mail@aippi.org; internet www.aippi.org; f. 1897 to encourage the devt of legislation on the international protection of industrial property and the devt and extension of international conventions, and to make comparative studies of existing legislation with a view to its improvement and unification; holds triennial congress; mems: 8,200 (nat. and reg. groups and individual mems) in 108 countries; Pres. JOHN BOCHNOVIC; Sec.-Gen. STEPHAN FREISCHEM; publs *Yearbook*, reports.

International Association of Chiefs of Police (IACP): 515 North Washington St, Alexandria, VA, 22314, USA; tel. (703) 836-6767; fax (703) 836-4543; e-mail walkerg@theiacp.org; internet www.theiacp.org; f. 1893 to advance the science and art of police services; Pres. YOST ZAKHARY; Exec. Dir BART R. JOHNSON.

International Association of Democratic Lawyers: 21 rue Brialmont, 1210 Brussels, Belgium; tel. and fax (2) 223-33-10; e-mail oniikura@als.aoyama.ac.jp; internet www.iadllaw.org; f. 1946 to facilitate contacts and exchange between lawyers, encourage study of legal science and international law and support the democratic principles favourable to the maintenance of peace and co-operation between nations; promotes the preservation of the environment; conducts research on labour law, private international law, agrarian law, etc; has consultative status with the UN; mems: in 96 countries; Pres. JEANNE MIRER (USA); Sec.-Gen. OSAMU NIIKURA (Japan); publ. *International Review of Contemporary Law* (2 a year, in French, English and Spanish).

International Association of Law Libraries (IALL): University of Michigan Law Library, Ann Arbor, MI 48109-12103, USA; e-mail bvaccaro@umich.edu; internet www.iall.org; f. 1959 to encourage and facilitate the work of librarians and others concerned with the bibliographic processing and administration of legal materials; mems: over 600 from more than 50 countries (personal and institutional); Pres. JEROEN VERVLIET (Netherlands); Sec. BARBARA GARVAGLIA (USA); publ. *International Journal of Legal Information* (3 a year).

International Association of Legal Sciences (IALS) (Association internationale des sciences juridiques): c/o CISS, 1 rue Miollis, 75015 Paris, France; tel. 1-45-68-25-59; fax 1-45-66-76-03; e-mail info@aisj-ials.org; internet aisj-ials.org; f. 1950 to promote the mutual knowledge and understanding of nations and the increase of learning by encouraging throughout the world the study of foreign legal systems and the use of the comparative method in legal science; governed by a president and an executive committee of 11 mems known as the International Committee of Comparative Law; sponsored by UNESCO; mems: nat. cttees in 47 countries; Pres. Dr SYMEON C. SYMEONIDES (USA); Sec.-Gen. M. LEKER (Israel).

International Association of Penal Law: 12 rue Charles Fourier, 75013 Paris, France; tel. 1-79-25-45-76; fax 1-55-04-92-89; e-mail secretariat@penal.org; internet www.penal.org; f. 1924 to promote collaboration between those from different countries working in penal law, studying criminology, or promoting the theoretical and practical devt of international penal law; mems: 1,800; Pres. Prof. JOSÉ LUIS DE LA CUESTA (Spain); Sec.-Gen. KATALIN LIGETI (Luxembourg); publs *Revue Internationale de Droit Pénal* (2 a year), *Nouvelles Etudes Penales*.

International Association of Youth and Family Judges and Magistrates (IAYFJM): Lagergasse 6–8, 1030 Vienna, Austria; tel. (1) 713-18-25; e-mail nesrinlushta@yahoo.com; internet www.judgesandmagistrates.org; f. 1928 to support the protection of youth and family, and criminal behaviour and juvenile maladjustment; mems exercise functions as juvenile and family court judges or within professional services linked to youth and family justice and welfare; organizes study groups, meetings and an international congress every four years (April 2010: Tunis, Tunisia); mems: 12 nat. asscns and mems in more than 80 countries; Pres. JOSEPH MOYERSOEN (Italy); Sec.-Gen. EDUARDO REZENDE MELLO (Brazil).

International Bar Association (IBA): 10 St Bride St, London, EC4A 4AD, United Kingdom; tel. (20) 7842-0090; fax (20) 7842-0091; e-mail iba@int-bar.org; internet www.ibanet.org; f. 1947; a non-political fed. of national bar asscns and law socs; aims to discuss problems of professional organization and status; to advance the science of jurisprudence; to promote uniformity and definition in appropriate fields of law; to promote administration of justice under law among peoples of the world; to promote in their legal aspects the principles and aims of the UN; mems: 198 orgs in 194 countries, 30,000 individual mems; Pres. MICHAEL REYNOLDS (Belgium); Exec. Dir MARK ELLIS; publs *Business Law International* (3 a year), *International Bar News* (6 a year), *Competition Law International* (2 a year), *Journal of Energy and Natural Resources Law* (quarterly).

International Commission of Jurists (ICJ): POB 91, 33 rue des Bains, 1211 Geneva 8, Switzerland; tel. 229793800; fax 229793801; e-mail info@icj.org; internet www.icj.org; f. 1952 to promote the implementation of international law and principles that advance human rights; provides legal expertise to ensure that devts in international law adhere to human rights principles and that international standards are implemented at national level; disseminates reports and other legal documents through the ICJ Legal Resource Centre; maintains Centre for the Independence of Judges and Lawyers (f. 1978); in Oct. 2005 established an Eminent Jurists' Panel on Terrorism, Counter-terrorism and Human Rights; mems: 82 sections and affiliated orgs in 62 countries; Pres. Sir NIGEL RODLEY (Ireland); Sec.-Gen. WILDER TAYLER (Uruguay); publs special reports.

International Commission on Civil Status: 3 pl. Arnold, 67000 Strasbourg, France; tel. 3-88-61-18-62; fax 3-88-60-58-79; e-mail ciec-sg@ciec1.org; internet www.ciec1.org; f. 1950 for the establishment and presentation of legislative documentation relating to the rights of individuals; carries out research on means of simplifying the judicial and technical administration with respect to civil status; mems: govts of Belgium, Croatia, France, Germany, Greece, Hungary, Italy, Luxembourg, Mexico, Netherlands, Poland, Portugal, Spain, Switzerland, Turkey, United Kingdom; Pres. DUNCAN MACNIVEN; Sec.-Gen. WALTER PINTENS; publs *Guide pratique international de l'état civil* (available online), various studies on civil status.

International Council for Commercial Arbitration (ICCA): Peace Palace, Carnegieplein 2, The Hague, Netherlands; tel. (70) 3022834; fax (70) 3022837; e-mail secretariat@arbitration-icca.org; internet www.arbitration-icca.org; f. 1999; promotes international arbitration and other forms of dispute resolution; mems: 900 mems, 40 governing mems, 18 advisory mems; Pres. Prof. Dr ALBERT JAN VAN DEN BERG (Belgium); Sec.-Gen. KAP-YOU (KEVIN) KIM (Republic of Korea); publs *Yearbook on Commercial Arbitration*, *International Handbook on Commercial Arbitration*, *ICCA Congress Series*.

International Council of Environmental Law (ICEL): Godesberger Allee 108–112, 53175 Bonn, Germany; tel. (228) 2692-298; fax (228) 2692-251; e-mail icel@intlawpol.org; internet www.i-c-e-l.org; f. 1969 to promote the exchange of information and expertise on legal, administrative and policy aspects of environmental conservation and sustainable devt; mems: 300 elected mems; has consultative status with ECOSOC; Exec. Governors Dr WOLFGANG E. BURHENNE (Germany), AMADO TOLENTINO, Jr (Philippines); publs *Directory*, *References*, *Environmental Policy and Law*, *International Environmental Law—Multilateral Treaties*, etc.

International Criminal Police Organization (INTERPOL): 200 quai Charles de Gaulle, 69006 Lyon, France; tel. 4-72-44-70-00; fax 4-72-44-71-63; e-mail website@interpol.int; internet www.interpol.int; f. 1923, reconstituted 1946; aims to promote and ensure mutual assistance between police forces in different countries; co-ordinates activities of police authorities of mem. states in international affairs; works to establish and develop institutions with the aim of preventing transnational crimes; centralizes records and information on international criminals; operates a global police communications network linking all mem. countries; maintains a Global Database on Maritime Piracy; holds General Assembly annually; mems: 190 countries; Pres. MIREILLE BALLESTRAZZI; Sec.-Gen. RONALD K. NOBLE (USA); publ. *Annual Report*.

International Development Law Organization (IDLO): Viale Vaticano, 106 00165 Rome, Italy; tel. (06) 40403200; fax (06) 40403232; e-mail idlo@idlo.int; internet www.idlo.int; f. 1983; enables govts and empowers people to reform laws and strengthen institutions to promote peace, justice, sustainable devt and economic opportunities; provides technical legal assistance and capacity devt at national and local level; activities include Policy Dialogues, Technical Assistance, Global Network of Alumni and Partners, Training Programs, Research and Publications; maintains Country Offices for Afghanistan, Kenya, Kyrgyzstan, South Sudan, Somalia (based in Nairobi) and Tajikistan; mems: 27 mems (26 states and the OPEC Fund for International Development); Dir-Gen. IRENE KHAN.

International Federation for European Law (Fédération Internationale pour le Droit Européen—FIDE): 113 ave Louise, 1050 Brussels, Belgium; tel. (2) 534-71-63; fax (2) 534-28-58; e-mail general-secretary@fide2014.eu; internet www.fide-europe.eu; f. 1961 to advance studies on European law among mems of the European Community by co-ordinating activities of mem. societies;

organizes confs every two years (2014: Copenhagen, Denmark); mems: 12 nat. asscns; Pres. Dr ULLA NEERGAARD (Denmark); Gen. Sec. Dr CATHERINE JACQUESON (Denmark).

International Humanitarian Fact-Finding Commission (IHFFC): Fed. Palace North 3003 Bern, Switzerland; tel. 313244636; fax 313250767; e-mail info@ihffc.org; internet www.ihffc.org; f. 1992 in response to the First Additional Protocol (1977) of the Geneva Conventions, to establish an autonomous body to address the enforcement of international humanitarian law; operates through a declaration of recognition, signed by 75 states; first constitutional meeting convened in March 1992; organizes annual meetings; mems: 15 individuals elected by state parties; Pres. GISELA PERREN-KLINGLER.

International Institute for the Unification of Private Law (UNIDROIT): Via Panisperna 28, 00184 Rome, Italy; tel. (06) 696211; fax (06) 69941394; e-mail info@unidroit.org; internet www.unidroit.org; f. 1926 to undertake studies of comparative law, to prepare for the establishment of uniform legislation, to prepare drafts of international agreements on private law and to organize confs and publish works on such subjects; holds international congresses on private law and meetings of orgs concerned with the unification of law; maintains a library of 215,000 vols; mems: govts of 63 countries; Pres. Prof. ALBERTO MAZZONI; Sec.-Gen. JOSÉ ANGELO ESTRELLA FARIA; publs *Uniform Law Review* (quarterly), *Principles of International Commercial Contracts*, *Guide to International Master Franchise Arrangements*, etc.

International Institute of Space Law (IISL): 94 bis ave de Suffren, 75015 Paris, France; e-mail secretary@iislweb.org; internet www.iislweb.org; f. 1959 at the XI Congress of the International Astronautical Federation; organizes annual Space Law colloquium; studies juridical and sociological aspects of astronautics; Pres. TANJA MASSON-ZWAAN (New Zealand); publs *Proceedings of Annual Colloquium on Space Law*, *Survey of Teaching of Space Law in the World*.

International Juridical Institute (IJI): RJ Schimmelpenninck-laan 20–22, 2517 The Hague, Netherlands; tel. (70) 3460974; fax (70) 3625235; e-mail info@iji.nl; internet www.iji.nl; f. 1918 to supply information on any non-secret matter of international interest, respecting international, municipal and foreign law and the application thereof; Pres. E. M. WESSELING VAN GENT; Dir J. M. J. KELTJENS.

International Law Association (ILA): Charles Clore House, 17 Russell Sq., London, WC1B 5DR, United Kingdom; tel. (20) 7323-2978; fax (20) 7323-3580; e-mail info@ila-hq.org; internet www.ila-hq.org; f. 1873 for the study and advancement of international law, both public and private and the promotion of international understanding and goodwill; mems: 3,300 in 46 reg. branches; 25 int. cttees; Pres. Prof. ALEXANDER YANKOV (Bulgaria); Chair. Exec. Council Lord MANCE (United Kingdom); Sec.-Gen. DAVID J. C. WYLD (United Kingdom).

International Nuclear Law Association (INLA): 29 sq. de Meeûs, 1000 Brussels, Belgium; tel. (2) 547-58-41; fax (2) 503-04-40; e-mail info@aidn-inla.be; internet www.aidn-inla.be; f. 1972 to promote international studies of legal problems related to the peaceful use of nuclear energy; holds conf. every two years; mems: 600 in 40 countries; Sec.-Gen. PATRICK REYNERS; publ. *Congress reports*.

International Penal and Penitentiary Foundation (IPPF) (Fondation internationale pénale et pénitentiaire—FIPP): c/o Prof. P. H. van Kempen, Radboud University, 6500 Nijmegen, Netherlands; tel. (24) 3615538; fax (24) 3612185; e-mail info@InternationalPenalandPenitentiaryFoundation.org; internet fondationinternationalepenaleetpenitentiaire.org/; f. 1951 to encourage studies in the field of prevention of crime and treatment of delinquents; mems in 23 countries (membership limited to 3 people from each country) and corresponding mems and fellows in another 20 countries; Pres. PHILLIP RAPOZA (USA); Sec.-Gen. PIET HEIN VAN KEMPEN (Netherlands).

International Police Association (IPA): Arthur Troop House, 1 Fox Rd, West Bridgford, Nottingham, NG2 6AJ, United Kingdom; tel. (115) 945-5985; fax (115) 982-2578; e-mail isg@ipa-iac.org; internet www.ipa-iac.org; f. 1950 to permit the exchange of professional information, create ties of friendship between all sections of the police service and organize group travel and studies; mems: 400,000 in more than 64 countries; International Pres. PIERRE-MARTIN MOULIN (Switzerland); International Sec.-Gen. GEORGIOS KATSAROPOULOS (Greece).

International Society for Labour and Social Security Law (ISLSSL): CP 500, 1211 Geneva 22, Switzerland; tel. 227996961; fax 227998749; e-mail sidtss@ilo.org; internet www.asociacion.org.ar/ISLLSS; f. 1958 to encourage collaboration between labour law and social security specialists; holds World Congress every three years, as well as irregular regional congresses (Europe, Africa, Asia and the Americas); mems: 66 nat. asscns of labour law officers; Pres. ADRIAN GOLDIN (Argentina); Sec.-Gen. GIUSEPPE CASALE.

International Union of Latin Notaries (Union Internationale du Notariat Latin—UINL): Av. Las Heras 1833, 9°, Buenos Aires, Argentina; tel. (11) 4809-7161; fax (11) 4809-6851; e-mail onpiuinl@onpi.org.ar; internet www.uinl.org; f. 1948 to study and standardize notarial legislation and promote the progress, stability and advancement of the Latin notarial system; mems: orgs and individuals in 81 countries; Pres. DANIEL-SÉDAR SENGHOR (Senegal); publs *Revista Internacional del Notariado* (quarterly), *Notarius International*.

Law Association for Asia and the Pacific (LAWASIA): Suite 1101, 170 Phillip St, NSW 2000 Sydney, Australia; tel. (2) 9926-0165; fax (2) 9223-9652; e-mail lawasia@lawasia.asn.au; internet www.lawasia.asn.au; f. 1966; provides an international, professional network for lawyers to update, reform and develop law within the region; comprises six sections and 21 standing cttees in Business Law and General Practice areas, which organize speciality confs; also holds an annual conf. (2014: Bangkok, in Oct.); mems: nat. orgs in 25 countries; 1,500 mems in 55 countries; Pres. ISOMI SUZUKI; publs *Directory* (annually), *Journal* (annually), *LAWASIA Update* (3 a year).

Permanent Court of Arbitration: Peace Palace, Carnegieplein 2, 2517 KJ, The Hague, Netherlands; tel. (70) 3024165; fax (70) 3024167; e-mail bureau@pca-cpa.org; internet www.pca-cpa.org; f. 1899 (by the Convention for the Pacific Settlement of International Disputes); provides for the resolution of disputes involving combinations of states, private parties and intergovernmental orgs, under its own rules of procedure, by means of arbitration, conciliation and fact-finding; operates a secretariat, the International Bureau, which provides registry services and legal support to ad hoc tribunals and commissions; mems: govts of 115 countries; Sec.-Gen. HUGO SIBLESZ (Netherlands).

Society of Comparative Legislation: 28 rue Saint-Guillaume, 75007 Paris, France; tel. 1-44-39-86-23; fax 1-44-39-86-28; e-mail slc@legiscompare.com; internet www.legiscompare.com; f. 1869 to study and compare laws of different countries, and to investigate practical means of improving the various branches of legislation; mems: 750 in 40 countries; Pres. BÉNÉDICTE FAUVARQUE-COSSON (France); publ. *Revue Internationale de Droit Comparé* (quarterly).

Southeast European Law Enforcement Center (SELEC): calea 13 Septembrie 3–5, Sector 5, 050711 Bucharest, Romania; tel. (21) 303-60-09; fax (21) 303-60-77; internet www.secicenter.org; f. 2000 by the Southeast European Co-operative Initiative as the SECI Center, reconvened in Oct. 2011 under the terms of the new Convention signed in Dec. 2009; an operative collaboration of customs and police officials working under the guidance of recommendations and directives from INTERPOL and the World Customs Organization; Task Force on Illegal Human Beings Trafficking established May 2000, Task Force on Illegal Drugs Trafficking established July 2000, Task Force on Commercial Fraud established Feb. 2001; mems: Albania, Bosnia and Herzegovina, Bulgaria, Croatia, Greece, Hungary, former Yugoslav Republic of Macedonia, Moldova, Montenegro, Romania, Serbia, Slovenia, Turkey; Dir-Gen. GÜRBÜZ BAHADIR (Turkey).

Union Internationale des Avocats (International Association of Lawyers): 25 rue du Jour, 75001 Paris, France; tel. 1-33-88-55-66; fax 1-33-88-55-77; e-mail uiacentre@uianet.org; internet www.uianet.org; f. 1927 to promote the independence and freedom of lawyers, and defend their ethical and material interests on an international level; aims to contribute to the devt of international order based on law; mems: over 200 asscns and 3,000 lawyers in over 110 countries; Pres. STEPHEN L. DREYFUSS; Exec. Dir MARIE-PIERRE RICHARD.

World Jurist Association (WJA): 7910 Woodmont Ave, Suite 1440, Bethesda, MD 20814, USA; tel. (202) 466-5428; fax (202) 452-8540; e-mail wja@worldjurist.org; internet www.worldjurist.org; f. 1963; promotes the continued devt of international law and the legal maintenance of world order; holds biennial world confs, World Law Day and demonstration trials; organizes research programmes; mems: lawyers, jurists and legal scholars in 155 countries; Pres. ALEXANDER BĚLOHLÁVEK (Czech Republic); Exec. Vice-Pres. SONA PANCHOLY (USA); publs *The World Jurist* (6 a year), Research Reports, *Law and Judicial Systems of Nations*, 4th revised edn (directory), *World Legal Directory*, *Law / Technology* (quarterly), *World Law Review* Vols I–V (World Conference Proceedings), *The Chief Justices and Judges of the Supreme Courts of Nations* (directory), work papers, newsletters and journals.

World Association of Law Professors (WALP): 7910 Woodmont Ave, Suite 1440, Bethesda, MD 20814, USA; tel. (202) 466-5428; fax (202) 452-8540; e-mail wja@worldjurist.org; internet www.worldjurist.org; f. 1975 to improve scholarship and education in matters related to international law; Pres. KAREL KLIMA (Czech Republic).

World Association of Lawyers (WAL): 7910 Woodmont Ave, Suite 1440, Bethesda, MD 20814, USA; tel. (202) 466-5428; fax (202) 452-8540; e-mail wja@worldjurist.org; internet www.worldjurist.org;

f. 1975 to develop international law and improve lawyers' effectiveness in this field; Pres. ETHIA SIMHA (Israel).

Medicine and Health

Aerospace Medical Association (AsMA): 320 S. Henry St, Alexandria, VA 22314-3579, USA; tel. (703) 739-2240; fax (703) 739-9652; e-mail inquiries@asma.org; internet www.asma.org; f. 1929 as Aero Medical Association; aims to advance the science and art of aviation and space medicine; establishes and maintains co-operation between medical and allied sciences concerned with aerospace medicine; works to promote, protect, and maintain safety in aviation and astronautics; mems: more than 2,200 mems from over 70 countries; Pres. PHILIP J. SCARPA; Exec. Dir JEFFREY C. SVENTEK; publ. *Aviation Space and Environmental Medicine* (monthly).

Asia Pacific Academy of Ophthalmology (APAO): c/o Dept of Ophthalmology and Visual Sciences, Chinese University of Hong Kong, 4/F 147 K Argyle St, Kowloon, Hong Kong, SAR; tel. (852) 39435827; fax (852) 27159490; e-mail secretariat@apaophth.org; internet www.apaophth.org; f. 1956; aims to undertake activities promoting the prevention of blindness and restoration of sight through teaching, research, and service; and to foster co-operation between ophthalmological societies in different countries; holds Congress annually since 2006 (previously every two years); mems: mem. orgs in 20 countries, 5 sub-speciality soc. mems; Pres. RAJVARDHAN AZAD (India); Sec.-Gen. and CEO CLEMENT THAM (Hong Kong).

Asia Pacific Dental Federation (APDF): c/o 242 Tanjong Katong Rd, Singapore 437030; tel. 63453125; fax 63442116; e-mail droliver@singnet.com.sg; internet www.apdf.co; f. 1955 to establish closer relationships among dental asscns in Asia Pacific countries and to encourage research on dental health in the region; administers the International College of Continuing Dental Education; holds Congress every year (36th Congress: Dubai, UAE, in June 2014); mems: 28 nat. dental asscns; Pres. Dato' Dr A. RATNANESAN (Malaysia); Sec.-Gen. Dr OLIVER HENNEDIGE (Singapore).

Council for International Organizations of Medical Sciences (CIOMS): 1 Route des Morillons, Geneva, Switzerland; tel. 227916497; e-mail info@cioms.ch; internet www.cioms.ch; f. 1949 to serve the scientific interests of the international biomedical community; aims to facilitate and promote activities in biomedical sciences; runs long-term programmes on bioethics, health policy, ethics and values, drug devt and use, and the international nomenclature of diseases; maintains collaborative relations with the UN; holds a General Assembly every three years (21st: Geneva, Switzerland, Nov. 2013); mems: 17 int. orgs, 13 nat asscns and 23 assoc. mems; Pres. Prof. J. J. M. VAN DELDEN; Sec.-Gen. Dr GUNILLA SJÖLIN-FORSBERG; publs *Bioethics and Health Policy' Reports on Drug Development and Use, Proceedings of CIOMS Conferences, International Nomenclature of Diseases*.

Cystic Fibrosis Worldwide: 210 Park Ave, Suite 267, Worcester, MA 01609, USA; tel. (508) 762-4232; e-mail information@cfww.org; internet www.cfww.org; f. 2003 by merger of the International Association of Cystic Fibrosis Adults and International Cystic Fibrosis (Muscoviscidosis) Association (f. 1964); promotes the devt of lay organizations and the advancement of knowledge among medical, scientific and health professionals in underdeveloped areas; convenes annual conf; mems: 67 mem countries; Pres. TERRY STEWART (Australia); Treas. MITCH MESSER (Australia); publs *Annual Report, CFW Newsletter* (quarterly), *Joseph Levy Lecture,* booklet on physiotherapy.

European Association for Cancer Research (EACR): c/o Pharmacy School Bldg, University of Nottingham, University Park, Nottingham, NG7 2RD, United Kingdom; tel. (115) 9515116; fax (115) 9515115; e-mail eacr@nottingham.ac.uk; internet www.eacr.org; f. 1968 to facilitate contact between cancer research workers and to organize scientific meetings in Europe; operates a number of fellowship and award programmes; mems: more than 9,000 in over 80 countries worldwide, incl. 14 affiliated mem. socs in Belgium, Croatia, Denmark, France, Germany, Hungary, Ireland, Israel, Italy, Portugal, Spain, Turkey and United Kingdom; Pres. RICHARD MARAIS; Sec.-Gen. CLARE ISACKE (United Kingdom).

European Association for Paediatric Education (EAPE) (Association Européene pour l'Enseignement de la Pédatrie): c/o Dr Claude Billeaud, Dept Néonatal Médicine, Hôpital des Enfants-CHU Pellegrin, 33076 Bordeaux Cedex, France; tel. 5-56-79-56-35; fax 5-57-82-02-48; e-mail claude.billeaud@chu-bordeaux.fr; internet www.aeep.asso.fr; f. 1970 to promote research and practice in educational methodology in paediatrics; mems: 120 in 20 European countries; Pres. Dr CLAUDE BILLEAUD (France); Sec.-Gen. ELIE SALIBA (France).

European Association for Palliative Care (EAPC Onlus): National Cancer Institute Milano Via Venezian 1, 20133 Milan, Italy; e-mail amelia.giordano@istitutotumori.mi.it; internet www.eapcnet.eu; f. 1988; aims to promote palliative care in Europe and to act as a focus for all of those who work, or have an interest, in the field of palliative care at the scientific, clinical and social levels; 14th Congress: Lleida, Spain, in June 2014; mems: 54 nat. asscns in 32 countries, individual mems from 50 countries worldwide; Pres. SHEILA PAYNE (United Kingdom); Chief Exec. HEIDI BLUMHUBER; publs *European Journal of Palliative Care, Palliative Medicine*.

European Association for the Study of Diabetes (EASD): Rheindorfer Weg 3, 40591 Düsseldorf, Germany; tel. (211) 7584690; fax (211) 75846929; e-mail secretariat@easd.org; internet www.easd.org; f. 1965 to support research in the field of diabetes, to promote the rapid diffusion of acquired knowledge and its application; holds annual scientific meetings within Europe; mems: more than 7,000 individuals from over 110 countries; Pres. A. BOULTON (United Kingdom); Exec. Dir Dr VIKTOR JÖRGENS (Germany); publ. *Diabetologia* (13 a year).

European Brain and Behaviour Society (EBBS): Science Park 904, SILS-CNS, Amsterdam, 1098 XH, Netherlands; tel. (20) 5257621; fax (20) 5257934; e-mail vjb@st-and.ac.uk; internet www.ebbs-science.org; f. 1968; holds an annual conf. and organizes workshops; Pres. MARTINE. AMMASSARI-TEULE (Italy); Sec.-Gen. ANNE M MOULY (France); publ. *Newsletter* (annually).

European Federation of Internal Medicine (EFIM): Ave Tervueren 300, 1150 Brussels, Belgium; tel. (2) 643-20-40; fax (2) 743-15-50; e-mail info@efim.org; internet www.efim.org; f. 1969 as European Association of Internal Medicine (present name adopted 1996); aims to bring together European specialists, and establish communication between them, to promote internal medicine; organizes congresses and meetings; provides information; mems: 35 European socs of internal medicine; Pres. MARIA DOMENICA CAPPELLINI (Italy); Sec.-Gen. Dr PEDRO CONTHE (Spain); publ. *European Journal of Internal Medicine* (8 a year).

European Health Management Association (EHMA): 15–17 rue Belliar, 6th Floor, 1040 Brussels, Belgium; tel. (2) 502-65-25; fax (2) 503-10-05; internet www.ehma.org; f. 1966; aims to improve health care in Europe by raising standards of managerial performance in the health sector; fosters co-operation between managers, academia, policy-makers and educators to understand health management in different European contexts and to influence both service delivery and the policy agenda in Europe; mems: 170 mems across more than 30 countries; Pres. MARIANNE OLSSON; Dir JENNIFER BREMNER; publ. *Annual Report*.

European League against Rheumatism (EULAR): Seestr. 240, 8802 Kilchberg-Zürich, Switzerland; tel. 447163030; fax 447163039; e-mail eular@eular.org; internet www.eular.org; f. 1947 to co-ordinate research and treatment of rheumatic complaints; holds an annual Congress in Rheumatology; mems: in 45 countries; Pres. Prof. MAURIZIO CUTOLO (Italy); Exec. Dir HEINZ MARCHESI; publ. *Annals of the Rheumatic Diseases*.

European Organization for Caries Research (ORCA): c/o Academic Centre for Dentistry Amsterdam (ACTA), Gustav Mahlerlaan 3004, 1081 LA Amsterdam, Netherlands; tel. (20) 5980437; e-mail m.vd.veen@acta.nl; internet www.orca-caries-research.org; f. 1953 to promote and undertake research on dental health, encourage international contacts, and make the public aware of the importance of care of the teeth; mems: research workers in more than 30 countries; Pres. ANDREAS SCHULTE (Germany); Sec.-Gen. Dr M. H. VAN DER VEEN (Netherlands); publ. *Caries Research*.

European Orthodontic Society (EOS): 49 Hallam St, Flat 20, London, W1W 6JN, United Kingdom; tel. (20) 7637-0367; fax (20) 7323-0410; e-mail eoslondon@aol.com; internet www.eoseurope.org; f. 1907 (name changed in 1935), to advance the science of orthodontics and its relations with the collateral arts and sciences; mems: more than 3,000 in 91 countries; Pres. EWA CZOCHROWSKA (Poland); publ. *European Journal of Orthodontics* (6 a year).

European Society of Radiology: c/o ESR Office, Neutorgasse 9/2A, Vienna, Austria; tel. (1) 533-40-64-0; fax (1) 533-40-64-44-8; e-mail communications@myesr.org; internet www.myesr.org; f. 2005 by merger of European Society of Radiology (f. 1962) and European Congress of Radiology; aims to harmonize and improve training programmes throughout Europe and to develop a new research institute; organizes an Annual Congress; mems: some 55,657 individual mems; Pres. GUY FRIJA (France).

European Union of Medical Specialists (Union Européenne des Médecins Spécialistes—UEMS): 20 ave de la Couronne, Kroonlaan, 1050 Brussels, Belgium; tel. (2) 649-51-64; fax (2) 640-37-30; e-mail sg@uems.net; internet www.uems.net; f. 1958 to harmonize and improve the quality of medical specialist practices in the European Union and safeguard the interests of medical specialists; seeks formulation of common training policy; mems: 27 full mems, 7 assoc. mems; Pres. Prof. ROMUALD KRAJEWSKI (Poland); Sec.-Gen. Dr EDWIN BORMAN (United Kingdom).

Eurotransplant International Foundation: POB 2304, 2301 CH Leiden, Netherlands; tel. (71) 579-5700; fax (71) 579-0057; e-mail secretariat@eurotransplant.org; internet www.eurotransplant.org; f. 1967; co-ordinates the exchange of donor organs for transplants in Austria, Belgium, Croatia, Germany, Luxembourg, Netherlands and Slovenia; keeps register of c. 16,000 patients with all necessary information for matching with suitable donors in the shortest possible time; organizes transport and transplantation of the donor organ; collaborates with similar orgs in Western and Eastern Europe; Pres. Dr BRUNO MEISER; Medical Dir Dr AXEL RAHMEL.

FDI World Dental Federation: Tour de Cointrin, 84 ave Louis Casaï, CP 3, 1216 Geneva-Cointrin, Switzerland; tel. 225608150; fax 225608140; e-mail info@fdiworldental.org; internet www.fdiworldental.org; f. 1900; aims to bring together the world of dentistry, to represent the dental profession of the world and to stimulate and facilitate the exchange of information; mems: about 200 nat. dental asscns and groups; Pres. PATRICK HESCOT (France); Treas. KATHRYN KELL (USA); publs *International Dental Journal*, *Developing Dentistry*, *European Journal of Prosthodontics and Restorative Dentistry*.

Federation of Arab Medical Associations: 8-2 Gulberg Complex, Jail Rd, Lahore, Pakistan; tel. (42) 35716231; fax (42) 35715855; e-mail tanveer.zubairi@gmail.com; internet fimaweb.net; f. 1981; aims to foster the unity and welfare of Muslim medical and health care professionals, to promote Islamic medical activities including health services, education and research through co-operation and co-ordination among mem. orgs, to promote the understanding and the application of Islamic principles in the field of medicine, to mobilize professional and economic resources in order to provide medical care and relief to affected areas and communities, and to promote the exchange of medical information and technical expertise among mem. orgs; mems: 26 asscns, 5 observers; Sec. Dr TANVEER ZUBAIRI.

Federation of the European Dental Industry (Fédération de l'Industrie Dentaire en Europe—FIDE): Aachener Str. 1053–1055, 50858 Cologne, Germany; tel. (221) 50068723; fax (221) 50068721; e-mail m.heibach@fide-online.org; internet www.fide-online.org; f. 1957 to promote the interests of dental industry manufacturers; mems: almost 550 dental manufacturers and nat. asscns in 10 European countries; Pres. and Chair. Dr JÜRGEN EBERLEIN (Germany); Sec.-Gen. Dr MARKUS HEIBACH (Germany).

Global Fund to Fight AIDS, Tuberculosis and Malaria: 8 chemin de Blandonnet, 1214 Vernier-Geneva, Switzerland; tel. 587911700; fax 587911701; e-mail info@theglobalfund.org; internet www.theglobalfund.org; f. 2002; the Fund provides support for countries to implement prevention programmes, as well as for the treatment and care of people affected by the diseases; US $12,000m. was pledged by international donors at a conf. convened in Dec. 2013 to replenish the Fund during 2014–16; Exec. Dir MARK R. DYBUL (USA).

Inter-American Association of Sanitary and Environmental Engineering (Asociación Interamericana de Ingeniería Sanitaria y Ambiental—AIDIS): Av. Angélica 2355, 01227-200 São Paulo, SP, Brazil; tel. (11) 3812-4080; fax (11) 3814-2441; e-mail aidis@aidis.org.br; internet www.aidis.org.br; f. 1948 to assist in the devt of water supply and sanitation; aims to generate awareness on environmental, health and sanitary problems and assist in finding solutions; mems: 32 countries; Pres. JORGE TRIANA (Colombia); Treas. EVERTON DE OLIVEIRA (Brazil); publs *Revista Ingeniería Sanitaria* (2 a year), *Desafío* (quarterly).

International Academy of Aviation and Space Medicine (IAASM): c/o Dr C. Thibeault, 502-8500 rue St Charles, Brossard, QC J4X 2Z8, Canada; tel. (450) 923-6826; e-mail ctebo@videotron.ca; internet www.iaasm.org; f. 1955 to facilitate international co-operation in research and teaching in the fields of aviation and space medicine; mems: in 45 countries; Pres. Dr DANIEL B. LESTAGE (USA); Sec.-Gen. Dr CLAUDE THIBEAULT (Canada).

International Academy of Cytology: POB 1347, Burgunderstr. 1, 79013 Freiburg, Germany; tel. (761) 292-3801; fax (761) 292-3802; e-mail centraloffice@cytology-iac.org; internet www.cytology-iac.org; f. 1957 to facilitate the international exchange of information on specialized problems of clinical cytology, to stimulate research and to standardize terminology; mems: over 52 nat. socs of cytology worldwide; Pres. PHILIPPE VIELH (France); publs *Acta Cytologica*, *Analytical and Quantitative Cytology and Histology* (both every 2 months).

International Agency for the Prevention of Blindness (IAPB): c/o London School of Hygiene & Tropical Medicine, Keppel St, London, WC1E 7HT, United Kingdom; tel. (20) 7958-8394; e-mail communications@iapb.org; internet www.iapb.org; f. 1975; promotes advocacy and information sharing on the prevention of blindness; aims to encourage the formation of national prevention of blindness cttees and programmes; with WHO launched VISION 2020 initiative to eliminate the main causes of avoidable blindness by 2020; Pres. ROBERT MCMULLAN; Vice-Pres. JOHANNES TRIMMEL; publ. *IAPB Focus (newsletter)*.

International Association for Child and Adolescent Psychiatry and Allied Professions (IACAPAP): c/o Daniel Fung, Institute of Mental Health, Buangkok Green Medical Park, 10 Buangkok View, Singapore; tel. 63892309; fax 63895900; e-mail daniel_fung@imh.com.sg; internet www.iacapap.org; f. 1937; aims to promote the study, treatment, care and prevention of mental and emotional disorders and disabilities of children, adolescents and their families. The emphasis is on practice and research through collaboration between child psychiatrists and the allied professions of psychology, social work, pediatrics, public health, nursing, education, social sciences and other relevant fields; IACAPAP developed the guidelines and principles of Ethics in Child and Adolescent Mental Health; IACAPAP also develops and adopts other Declarations, Statements and Position Papers of help to mental health professionals in their work; mems: nat. asscns and individuals in 45 countries; Pres. Dr OLAYINKA OMIGBODUN (Nigeria); Sec.-Gen. Dr DANIEL FUNG (Singapore); publs *The Child in the Family* (Yearbook of the IACAPAP), *Newsletter (IACAPAP Bulletin)*, Monographs.

International Association for Dental Research (IADR): 1619 Duke St, Alexandria, VA 22314-3406, USA; tel. (703) 548-0066; fax (703) 548-1883; e-mail research@iadr.org; internet www.iadr.com; f. 1920; aims to advance research and increase knowledge for the improvement of oral health worldwide; holds annual meetings, triennial confs and divisional meetings; Pres. Dr HELEN WHELTON; Exec. Dir Dr CHRISTOPHER H. FOX.

International Association for Group Psychotherapy and Group Processes (IAGP): c/o Bonnie Buchele, 411 Nichols Rd, Suite 194, Kansas City, Missouri 64112 USA; tel. and fax (816) 531-2600; fax (816) 531-2754; e-mail office@iagp.com; internet www.iagp.com; f. 1973; holds a Congress every three years and regional congresses at more frequent intervals; mems: in 49 countries; Pres. DAVID GUTMANN (France); Sec. KATE BRADSHAW TAUVON (Sweden); publs *Forum* (annually), *Globeletter* (2 a year).

International Association for the Study of Obesity (IASO): Charles Darwin House, 12 Roger St, London, WCIN 2JU, United Kingdom; tel. (20) 7685-2580; fax (20) 7685-2581; e-mail enquiries@iaso.org; internet www.iaso.org; f. 1986; supports research into the prevention and management of obesity throughout the world and disseminates information regarding disease and accompanying health and social issues; incorporates the International Obesity Task Force; international congress every four years (2014: Kuala Lumpur, Malaysia, in March); mems: 53 asscns, representing 55 countries; Pres. PHILIP JAMES; Exec. Dir CHRISTINE TRIMMER.

International Association of Applied Psychology (IAAP): c/o Prof. José M. Prieto, Colegio Oficial de Psicólogos, Cuesta de San Vicente 4–5, 28008 Madrid, Spain; tel. (91) 3943236; fax (91) 3510091; internet www.iaapsy.org; f. 1920, present title adopted in 1955; aims to establish contacts between those carrying out scientific work on applied psychology, to promote research and to encourage the adoption of measures contributing to this work; organizes International Congress of Applied Psychology every four years (2014: Paris, France, in July) and co-sponsors International Congress of Psychology (2016: Yokohama, Japan, in July) and European Congress of Psychology (2013: Stockholm, Sweden, in July); mems: more than 1,500 from some 80 countries; Pres. Prof. JOSÉ MARIA PÉIRO (Spain); Sec.-Gen. Prof. MILTON D. HAKEL (USA); publ. *Applied Psychology: An International Review* (quarterly).

International Association of Asthmology (INTERASMA): (no permanent secretariat); internet www.interasma.org; f. 1954 to advance medical knowledge of bronchial asthma and allied disorders; mems: 1,100 in 54 countries; Pres. CARLOS E. BAENA-CAGNANI (Argentina); Sec.-Gen. CARLOS NUÑES (Portugal); publs *Interasma News*, *Journal of Investigative Allergology and Clinical Immunology* (every 2 months), *Allergy and Clinical Immunology International* (every 2 months).

International Association of Bioethics: POB 280, University of the Philippines, Diliman, Quezon City 1101, Philippines; tel. and fax (2) 426-9590; e-mail secretariat@bioethics-international.org; internet www.bioethics-international.org; f. 1992; aims to facilitate contact and to promote exchange of information among people working in the bioethics field; aims to promote the development of research and training in bioethics; organizes international confs every two years (12th World Congress of Bioethics: June 2014, Mexico City, Mexico); mems: over 1,000 individuals and institutions in more than 40 countries; Pres. Prof. ANGUS J. DAWSON (United Kingdom); Sec. Prof. ANGELA BALLANTYNE (New Zealand); publ. *Bioethics Journal*.

International Association of Gerontology and Geriatrics (IAGG): c/o Faculté de Médecine, Institut du Vieillissement, 37 Allées Jules Guesde, 31000 Toulouse, France; tel. 5-61-14-56-39; fax 5-61-14-56-40; e-mail contact@iagg.info; internet www.iagg.info; f. 1950 as the International Association of Gerontological Societies to promote research and training in all fields of gerontology and to protect the interests of gerontological societies and institutions; assumed current name in 2005, with the aim of promoting and developing Geriatrics as a medical specialism; holds World Congress every four years, (2013: Seoul, Korea); mems some 45,100 in over 65 countries; Pres. Prof. BRUNO VELLAS (France); Sec.-Gen./Vice-Pres. ALAIN FRANCO (France); publ. *IAGG Newsletter* (quarterly).

International Association of Logopedics and Phoniatrics (IALP): c/o Vanessa Borg, 32, Flat One, Francesco Buhagiar St, Birkirkara, BKR1154 Malta; tel. 21496370; fax 3330404; e-mail office@ialp.info; internet www.ialp.info; f. 1924 to promote standards of training and research in human communication disorders, to establish information centres and communicate with kindred organizations; 30th International Congress on Logopedics and Phoniatrics: Saggart, Ireland, in Aug. 2016; mems: 125,000 in 56 socs from 30 countries; Pres. HELLEN GRECH; publ. *Folia Phoniatrica et Logopedica* (6 a year).

International Association of Medicine and Biology of the Environment (IAMBE): 115 rue de la Pompe, 75116 Paris, France; tel. 1-45-53-45-04; fax 1-45-53-41-75; f. 1971 with assistance from UNEP; aims to contribute to the solution of problems caused by human influence on the environment; structure includes 13 technical commissions; mems: individuals and orgs in 79 countries; Pres. CÉLINE ABBOU.

International Association of Oral and Maxillofacial Surgeons (IAOMS): 5550 Meadowbrook Dr., Suite 210, Rolling Meadows, IL 60008, USA; tel. (224) 232-8737; fax (224) 735-2965; e-mail info@iaoms.org; internet www.iaoms.org; f. 1962 to advance the science and art of oral and maxillofacial surgery; organizes biennial international conf; mems: over 4,000; Pres. PIET E. HAERS (United Kingdom); Exec. Dir Dr BARBARA MORRISON (USA); publs *International Journal of Oral and Maxillofacial Surgery* (monthly), *Newsletter* (quarterly).

International Association of Rural Health and Medicine: c/o Japanese Association of Rural Medicine, JA Bldg, 1-3-1 Ohte-machi, Chiyoda-ku, Tokyo 100-6827, Japan; fax (2) 6782-7533; e-mail sakuscrt@valley.ne.jp; internet www.iaamrh.org; f. 1961 to study the problems of medicine in agriculture in all countries and to prevent the diseases caused by the conditions of work in agriculture; mems: 405 in 51 countries; Pres. Dr ASHOK PATIL (India); Gen. Sec. Dr SHUZO SHINTANI (Japan).

International Brain Research Organization (IBRO): 255 rue St Honoré, 75001 Paris, France; tel. 1-46-47-92-92; fax 1-46-47-42-50; e-mail stephanie@ibro.info; internet www.ibro.info; f. 1960 to further all aspects of brain research; Exec. Dir STEPHANIE DE LA ROCHEFOUCAULD; publs *IBRO News*, *Neuroscience* (every 2 months).

International Bronchoesophagological Society (IBES): BDB 563, 1530 3rd Ave, Univ. of Alabama at Birmingham, Birmingham, AL 35243-0012; tel. (205) 934-9765; fax (205) 934-399; e-mail inquiry@ibesociety.org; internet www.ibesociety.org; f. 1951 to promote the progress of bronchoesophagology and to provide a forum for discussion among bronchoesophagologists with various medical and surgical specialities; holds Congress every two years; mems: over 700 in 42 countries; Pres. PAUL F. CASTELLANOS.

International Bureau for Epilepsy (IBE): 11 Priory Hall, Stillorgan, Blackrock, Co Dublin, Ireland; tel. (1) 2108850; fax (1) 2108450; e-mail ibedublin@eircom.net; internet www.ibe-epilepsy.org; f. 1961; collects and disseminates information about social and medical care for people with epilepsy; organizes international and regional meetings; advises and answers questions on social aspects of epilepsy; has special consultative status with ECOSOC; mems: 126 nat. epilepsy orgs; Pres. ATHANASIOS COVANIS; Sec-Gen. SARI TERVONEN; publ. *International Epilepsy News* (quarterly).

International Catholic Committee of Nurses and Medico-Social Assistants (Comité International Catholique des Infirmières et Assistantes Médico-Sociales—CICIAMS): St Mary's Bloomfield Ave, Donnybrook, Dublin 4, Ireland; tel. and fax (1) 668-9150; e-mail ciciams@eircom.net; internet www.ciciams.org; f. 1933 to group professional Catholic nursing asscns; to represent Christian thought in the general professional field at international level; to co-operate in the general devt of the profession and to promote social welfare; mems: 34 full, 8 corresponding mems; Pres. Sister ANNE JOHN RJM; Gen. Sec. GERALDINE MCSWEENEY; publ. *Nouvelles/News/Nachrichten* (3 a year).

International Cell Research Organization (ICRO) (Organisation Internationale de Recherche sur la Cellule): c/o UNESCO, SC/BES/LSC, 1 rue Miollis, 75732 Paris, France; fax 1-45-68-58-16; e-mail icro@unesco.org; internet www.icro-unesco.org; f. 1962; organizes international laboratory courses on modern topics of cell and molecular biology and biotechnology for young research scientists.

International Centre for Diarrhoeal Disease Research, Bangladesh, B: Centre for Health and Population Research (ICDDR,B): GPO Box 128, Dhaka 1000, Bangladesh; tel. (2) 9827001; fax (2) 9827075; e-mail communications@icddrb.org; internet www.icddrb.org; f. 1960 as Pakistan-SEATO Cholera Research Laboratory, international health research institute since 1978; undertakes research, training and information dissemination on diarrhoeal diseases, child health, nutrition, emerging infectious diseases, environmental health, sexually transmitted diseases, HIV/AIDS, poverty and health, vaccine evaluation and case management, with particular reference to developing countries; supported by 55 govts and int. orgs; Exec. Dir Dr JOHN CLEMENS; publs *Annual Report*, *Journal of Health, Population and Nutrition* (quarterly), *Glimpse* (quarterly), *Shasthya Sanglap* (3 a year), *Health and Science Bulletin* (quarterly), *SUZY* (newsletter, 2 a year), scientific reports, working papers, monographs, special publications.

International Centre for Migration, Health and Development: 11 route du Nant-d'Avril, 1214 Geneva, Switzerland; tel. 227831080; fax 227831087; e-mail secretariat@icmhd.ch; internet www.icmhd.ch; f. 1995 (as International Centre for Migration and Health); aimed to respond to the growing needs for information, documentation, research, training and policy devt in migration health; has been designated as a WHO collaborating centre for health-related issues among people displaced by disasters and an implementing partner of UNFPA in reproductive health issues in situations of crisis; Pres. Dr EAMON KELLY; Exec. Dir Dr MANUEL CARBALLO.

International Chiropractors' Association: 6400 Arlington Blvd, Suite 800, Falls Church, VA 22042, USA; tel. (703) 528-5000; fax (703) 528-5023; e-mail chiro@chiropractic.org; internet www.chiropractic.org; f. 1926 to promote advancement of the art and science of chiropractors; mems: 7,000 individuals, and affiliated asscns; Pres. MICHAEL S. MCLEAN; Int. Dir PINCHAS NOYMAN; publs *International Review of Chiropractic* (every 2 months), *ICA Today* (every 2 months), *The Chiropractic Choice*.

International College of Angiology: 161 Morin Dr., Jay, VT 05859-9283, USA; tel. (802) 988-4065; fax (802) 988-4066; e-mail denisemrossignol@cs.com; internet www.intlcollegeofangiology.org; f. 1958, as an asscn of scientists working in the field of vascular medicine and surgery; aims to encourage, support and facilitate research and education in the problems of vascular disease; Chair. JOHN B. CHANG (USA); Exec. Dir DENISE M. ROSSIGNOL (USA); publ. *International Journal of Angiology*.

International College of Surgeons (ICS): 1516 N. Lake Shore Drive, Chicago, IL 60610, USA; tel. (312) 642-3555; fax (312) 787-1624; e-mail info@icsglobal.org; internet www.icsglobal.org; f. 1935, as a worldwide fed. of surgeons and surgical specialists for the advancement of the art and science of surgery; aims to create a common bond among the surgeons of all nations and promote the highest standards of surgery, without regard to nationality, creed, or colour; sends teams of surgeons to developing countries to teach local surgeons; provides research and scholarship grants, organizes surgical congresses around the world; manages the International Museum of Surgical Science in Chicago; mems: c. 8,000 in 100 countries and regions; Pres. Prof. YIK-HONG HO (Australia); Exec. Dir MAX C. DOWNHAM (USA); publ. *International Surgery* (every 2 months).

International Commission on Occupational Health (ICOH): Via Fontana Candida 1, 1-00040 Monteporzio Catone (Rome), Italy; tel. (06) 94181506; fax (06) 94181556; e-mail icoh@inail.it; internet www.icohweb.org; f. 1906, present name adopted 1985; aims to study and prevent pathological conditions arising from industrial work; arranges congresses on occupational medicine and the protection of workers' health; provides information for public authorities and learned socs; mems: 2,000 in 93 countries; Pres. Dr KAZUTAKA KOGI (Japan); Sec.-Gen. Dr SERGIO IAVICOLI (Italy); publ. *Newsletter* (electronic version).

International Commission on Radiological Protection (ICRP): 280 Slater St, Ottawa, ON K1P 5S9, Canada; tel. (613) 947-9750; fax (613) 944-1920; e-mail sci.sec@icrp.org; internet www.icrp.org; f. 1928 to provide technical guidance and promote international co-operation in the field of radiation protection; cttees on Radiation Effects, Doses from Radiation Exposure, Protection in Medicine, Application of Recommendations, and Radiological Protection of the Environment; mems: c. 85; Exec. Sec. LYNNE LEMAIRE; Scientific Sec. Dr CHRISTOPHER CLEMENT (Canada); publ. *Annals of the ICRP*.

International Committee of Military Medicine (ICMM) (Comité international de médecine militaire—CIMM): Hôpital Militaire Reine Astrid, rue Bruyn, 1120 Brussels, Belgium; tel. (2) 264-43-48; fax (2) 264-43-67; e-mail info@cimm-icmm.org; internet www.cimm-icmm.org; f. 1921 as Permanent Committee of the International Congresses of Military Medicine and Pharmacy; name changed 1990; aims to increase co-operation and promote activities in the field of military medicine; considers issues relating to mass medicine, dentistry, military pharmacy, veterinary sciences and the administration and organization of medical care missions, among others; mems: official delegates from 114 countries; Chair. Maj.-Gen. Dr S. MOHAMMED AL-ASMARY (Saudi Arabia); Sec.-Gen. Maj.-Gen. Dr ROGER VAN HOOF (Belgium); publ. *International Review of the Armed Forces Medical Services* (quarterly).

International Council for Laboratory Animal Science (ICLAS): 40 rue Washington, 1050 Brussels, Belgium; e-mail info@iclas.org; internet www.iclas.org; f. 1956; promotes the ethical care and use of laboratory animals in research, with the aim of advancing human and animal health; establishes standards and provides support resources; encourages international collaboration to develop knowledge; Pres. Dr PATRI VERGARA (Spain); Sec.-Gen. CYNTHIA PEKOW (USA) (acting).

International Council for Physical Activity and Fitness Research (ICPAFR): c/o Prof. F. G. Viviani, Faculty of Psychology, University of Padua, via Venezia 8, 35131 Padua, Italy; tel. (049) 880-4668; fax (049) 827-6600; e-mail franco.viviani@unipd.it; internet www.icpafr.com; f. 1964 to construct international standardized physical fitness tests, to encourage research based upon the standardized tests and to enhance participation in physical activity; organizes biennial symposiums on topics related to physical activity and fitness; mems: 34 countries; Pres. Prof. FRANCO G. VIVIANI (Italy); Sec./Treas. ZAIDA CORDERO-MACINTYRE; publs *International Guide to Fitness and Health*, biennial proceedings of seminars and symposia, other fitness and health publs.

International Council of Nurses (ICN): 3 pl. Jean-Marteau, 1201 Geneva, Switzerland; tel. 229080100; fax 229080101; e-mail icn@icn.ch; internet www.icn.ch; f. 1899 to allow national asscns of nurses to work together to develop the contribution of nursing to the promotion of health; holds quadrennial Congresses; mems: more than 130 national nurses' asscns; Pres. JUDITH SHAMIAN; CEO DAVID BENTON; publ. *The International Nursing Review* (quarterly).

International Council of Ophthalmology: 945 Green St, San Francisco, CA 94133, USA; tel. (415) 409-8410; fax (415) 409-8411; e-mail info@icoph.org; internet www.icoph.org; f. 1927; works to support and develop ophthalmology, especially in developing countries; carries out education and assessment programmes; promotes clinical standards; holds World Ophthalmology Congress every two years (2014: Tokyo, Japan, in April); Pres. Dr BRUCE E. SPIVEY; CEO WILLIAM C. FELCH,Jr .

International Diabetes Federation (IDF): 166 Chaussée de la Hulpe, 1170 Brussels, Belgium; tel. (2) 538-55-11; fax (2) 538-51-14; e-mail info@idf.org; internet www.idf.org; f. 1949 to help in the collection and dissemination of information on diabetes and to improve the welfare of people suffering from diabetes; mems: more than 200 asscns in more 160 countries; Pres. MICHAEL HIRST (United Kingdom); publs *Diabetes Voice*, *Bulletin of the IDF* (quarterly).

International Epidemiological Association (IEA): 1500 Sunday Dr., Suite 102, Raleigh, NC 27607, USA; tel. (919) 861-5586; fax (919) 787-4916; e-mail nshore@firstpointresources.com; internet www.ieaweb.org; f. 1954; mems: 1,500; promotes epidemiology and organizes international scientific meetings and region-specific meetings; Pres. Dr CESAR VICTORA (Brazil); Treas. Dr AHMED MANDIL; publ. *International Journal of Epidemiology* (6 a year).

International Federation for Psychotherapy: c/o Madeleine Hänggli, Dept of Clinical Psychology and Psychotherapy, University of Bern Gesellschaftsstr. 49, 3012 Bern, Switzerland; tel. 316315419; fax 6221565998; e-mail secretariat@ifp.name; internet www.ifp.name; f. 1934 (as International General Medical Society for Psychotherapy); aims to further research and teaching of psychotherapy; encourages and supports development within psychotherapy; organizes international congresses; mems: c. 6,000 psychotherapists from around 40 countries, 36 socs; Pres. Prof. FRANZ CASPAR (Switzerland); publ. *Newsletter*, *Psychotherapy and Psychosomatics*.

International Federation of Association of Anatomists: c/o Friedrich P. Paulsen, Dept of Anatomy II, Friedrich Alexander University Erlangen-Nuremberg, Universitätsstr. 19, 91054 Erlangen, Germany; e-mail friedrich.paulsen@anatomie2.med.uni-erlangen.de; internet www.ifaa.net; f. 1903 as the Federative International Anatomical Congress; 18th Conference: Beijing, People's Republic of China, 2014; Pres. BERNARD MOXHAM (United Kingdom); Sec.-Gen. FRIEDRICH P. PAULSEN (Germany); publ. *Plexus* (2 a year).

International Federation of Clinical Chemistry and Laboratory Medicine (IFCC): via Carlo Farini 81, 20159 Milan, Italy; tel. (02) 6680-9912; fax (02) 6078-1846; e-mail ifcc@ifcc.org; internet www.ifcc.org; f. 1952; mems: 88 nat. socs (about 35,000 individuals) and 53 corp. mems; Pres. Dr GRAHAM BEASTALL (United Kingdom); Sec. Dr SERGIO BERNARDINI (Italy); publs *IFCC eNews*, *eIFCC* (electronic journal), *Annual Report*.

International Federation of Clinical Neurophysiology: c/o Venue West Conference Services Ltd, 200–1168 Hamilton St, Vancouver, BC, Canada V6B 2S2; tel. (604) 681-5226; fax (604) 681-2503; e-mail sstevenson@venuewest.com; internet www.ifcn.info; f. 1949 to attain the highest level of knowledge in the field of electroencephalography and clinical neurophysiology in all the countries of the world; mems in 58 countries; Pres. Prof. PAOLO M. ROSSINI; Sec. Prof. DANIEL M. CIBILS (Uruguay); publs *Clinical Neurophysiology* (monthly), *Evoked Potentials* (every 2 months), *EMG and Motor Control* (every 2 months).

International Federation of Fertility Societies (IFFS): 19 Mantua Rd, Mount Royal, NJ 08061, USA; tel. (856) 423-7222; fax (856) 423-3420; e-mail secretariat@iffs-reproduction.org; internet www.iffs-reproduction.org; f. 1951 to study problems of fertility and sterility; mems: approx. 40,000 worldwide; Pres. Prof. JOE L. SIMPSON (USA); Sec.-Gen. GABRIEL DE CANDOLLE (Switzerland); publ. *Newsletter* (2 a year).

International Federation of Gynecology and Obstetrics (FIGO): FIGO House, Suite 3, Waterloo Court, 10 Theed St, London, SE1 8ST, United Kingdom; tel. (20) 7928-1166; fax (20) 7928-7099; e-mail figo@figo.org; internet www.figo.org; f. 1954; aims to improve standards in gynaecology and obstetrics, promote better health care for women, facilitate the exchange of information, and perfect methods of teaching; mems in 125 countries and territories; Pres. Prof. SABARATNAM ARULKUMARAN (United Kingdom); CEO Prof. HAMID RUSHWAN; publ. *International Journal of Obstetrics and Gynecology*.

International Federation of Oto-Rhino-Laryngological Societies (IFOS): Antolská 11, 851 07, Bratislava Slovakia; e-mail info@ifosworld.org; internet www.ifosworld.org; f. 1965 to initiate and support programmes to protect hearing and prevent hearing impairment; holds Congresses every four years; mems: socs in 120 countries; Pres. Dr CHONG-SUN KIM (Republic of Korea); Gen. Sec. MILAN PROFANT (Slovakia); publ. *IFOS Newsletter* (quarterly).

International Federation of Surgical Colleges: c/o ASGBI, 35–43 Lincoln's Inn Fields, London, WC2A 3PE, United Kingdom; tel. (20) 7304-4770; fax (20) 7430-9235; e-mail bhavnita@asgbi.org.uk; f. 1958 to encourage high standards in surgical training; worked in collaboration with WHO since 1960; a Memorandum of Agreement was signed with the College of Surgeons of East Central & Southern Africa in 2007 to help to promote standards of training and care in that region; mems: colleges or asscns in 77 countries; Pres. Prof. S. WILLIAM. A. GUNN (Switzerland); Sec.-Gen. ROBERT H. S. LANE.

International Hospital Federation (IHF) (Fédération Internationale des Hôpitaux—FIH): 151 route de Löex, 1233 Bern, Switzerland; tel. 228509420; fax 227571016; e-mail info@ihf-fih.org; internet www.ihf-fih.org; f. 1947 for information exchange and education in hospital and health service matters; represents institutional health care in discussions with WHO; conducts confs and courses on management and policy issues; mems: national hospital and health service orgs (33 full mems), assoc. mems, regional orgs and individual hospitals, (70 orgs); Pres. KWANG TAE KIM (South Korea); Treas. Dr JUAN CARLOS LINARES; publs *World Hospitals and Health Services Journal* (quarterly), *IHF e-Newsletter* (5 a year).

International League against Epilepsy (ILAE): 342 North Main St, West Hartford, CT 06117-2507, USA; tel. (860) 586-7547; fax (860) 586-7550; e-mail perucca@unipv.it; internet www.ilae.org; f. 1909 to link national professional asscns and to encourage research, including classification and the development of anti-epileptic drugs; collaborates with the International Bureau for Epilepsy and with WHO; mems: more than 15,000 mems in more than 100 countries; Pres. EMILIO PERUCCA; Sec.-Gen. HELEN CROSS.

International League of Associations for Rheumatology (ILAR): All India Institute of Medical Sciences, Ansari Nagar, New Delhi 110029, India; e-mail ilar@rheumatology.org; internet www.ilar.org; f. 1927 to promote international co-operation for the study and control of rheumatic diseases; to encourage the foundation of national leagues against rheumatism; to organize regular international congresses and to act as a connecting link between national leagues and international orgs; mems: 13,000; Chair. ROHINI HANDA (India); publs *Annals of the Rheumatic Diseases* (in the United Kingdom), *Revue du Rhumatisme* (in France), *Reumatismo* (in Italy), *Clinical Rheumatology*, *Arthritis and Rheumatism* (in the USA), etc.

International Leprosy Association (ILA): POB 3021, Bauru 17034-971, Brazil; e-mail :ila@ilsl.com; internet www.leprosy-ila.org; f. 1931 to promote international co-operation in work on leprosy; holds Congress every five years (2013: Brussels, Belgium); Pres. Dr MARCOS VIRMOND (Brazil); Sec. Dr INDIRA NATH (India); publ. *The International Journal of Leprosy and Other Mycobacterial Diseases* (quarterly).

International Narcotics Control Board (INCB): Vienna International Centre, Rm E-1339, 1400 Vienna, POB 500, Austria; tel. (1) 260-60-0; fax (1) 260-60-58-67; e-mail secretariat@incb.org; internet www.incb.org; f. 1961 by the Single Convention on Narcotic Drugs, to supervise the implementation of drug control treaties by govts; mems: 13 individuals; Pres. RAYMOND YANS; publ. *Annual Report* (with 3 technical supplements).

International Opticians' Association: c/o Association of British Dispensing Opticians, 199 Gloucester Terrace, London, W2 6LD, United Kingdom; tel. (20) 7298-5100; fax (20) 7298-5111; e-mail general@abdolondon.org.uk; internet www.abdo.org.uk; f. 1951 to promote the science of opthalmic dispensing, and to maintain and advance standards and effect co-operation in optical dispensing; Pres. KEVIN SIEW; Gen. Sec. Sir ANTHONY GARRETT.

International Organization for Medical Physics (IOMP): Fairmount House, 230 Tadcaster Rd, York, YO24 1ES, United Kingdom; tel. (0) 7787563913; e-mail sg.iomp@gmail.com; internet www.iomp.org; f. 1963; aims to advance medical physics practice worldwide by disseminating scientific and technical information, fostering the educational and professional devt of medical physicists, and promoting the highest quality medical services for patients; mems: represents more than 18,000 medical physicists worldwide and 80 adhering nat. orgs of medical physics; Pres. Dr KIN-YIN CHEUNG (Hong Kong); Sec.-Gen. Dr MADAN REHANI (Austria); publ. *Medical Physics World*.

International Pediatric Association (IPA): 141 Northwest Point Blvd, Elk Grove Village, IL 60007-1098, USA; e-mail adminoffice@ipa-world.org; internet www.ipa-world.org; f. 1912; holds triennial congresses and regional and national workshops; mems: nat. paediatric socs in 154 countries, 9 reg. affiliate socs, 11 paediatric specialty socs; Pres. ANDREAS KONSTANTOPOULOS (Greece); Exec. Dir Dr WILLIAM J. KEENAN (USA); publ. *International Child Health* (quarterly).

International Pharmaceutical Federation (Fédération Internationale Pharmaceutique—FIP): POB 84200, 2508 AE The Hague, Netherlands; tel. (70) 3021970; fax (70) 3021999; e-mail fip@fip.org; internet www.fip.org; f. 1912; aims to represent and serve pharmacy and pharmaceutical sciences worldwide and to improve access to medicines; holds World Congress of Pharmacy and Pharmaceutical Sciences annually; mems: 86 nat. pharmaceutical orgs in 62 countries, 55 assoc., supportive and collective mems, 4,000 individuals; Pres. Dr MICHEL BUCHMANN (Switzerland); Gen.-Sec. LUC BESANÇON; publ. *International Pharmacy Journal* (2 a year).

International Psychoanalytical Association (IPA): Broomhills, Woodside Lane, London, N12 8UD, United Kingdom; tel. (20) 8446-8324; fax (20) 8445-4729; e-mail ipa@ipa.org.uk; internet www.ipa.org.uk; f. 1908; aims to assure the continued vigour and development of psychoanalysis; acts as a forum for scientific discussions; controls and regulates training; contributes to the interdisciplinary area common to the behavioural sciences; mems: over 12,000; Pres. Dr STEFANO BOLOGNINI; Sec.-Gen. JUAN CARLOS WEISSMANN; publs *Bulletin*, *Newsletter*.

International Rhinologic Society: c/o Prof. Dr Metin Önerci, Hacettepe University Faculty of Medicine, Dept of Otorhinolaryngology, 06100 Hacettepe, Ankara, Turkey; tel. (532) 393-8668; fax (312) 468-6268; e-mail monerci@gmail.com; f. 1965; holds Congress every two years; Pres. DESIDERIO PASSALI; Gen. Sec. METIN ÖNERCI (Turkey); publ. *Rhinology*.

International Society for the Psychopathology of Expression and Art Therapy (SIPE): c/o Muriel Laharie, 10 rue du Fer à Cheval, 64000 Pau, France; tel. and fax 5-59-32-66-10; e-mail contact@sipe-art-therapy.com; internet www.sipe-art-therapy.com; f. 1959 to bring together specialists interested in the problems of expression and artistic activities in connection with psychiatric, sociological and psychological research; mems: 625; Chair. LAURENT SCHMITT (France); Sec.-Gen. JEAN-LUC SUDRES (France); publ. *Newsletter* (quarterly).

International Society for Vascular Surgery: 11 Scott Drive, Smithtown, NY 11787, USA; tel. (631) 979-3780; e-mail isvs@isvs.com; internet www.isvs.com; f. 1950 as the International Society for Cardiovascular Surgery to stimulate research on the diagnosis and therapy of cardiovascular diseases and to exchange ideas on an international basis; present name adopted in 2005; Pres. Dr CHRISTOS LIAPIS (Greece); Sec. Dr TIMUR SARAC (USA).

International Society of Audiology: 121 Anchor Drive, Halifax, Nova Scotia, B3N 3B9, Canada; tel. (902) 477-5360; internet www.isa-audiology.org; f. 1952 to facilitate the knowledge, protection and rehabilitation of human hearing and to represent the interests of audiology professionals and of the hearing-impaired; organizes biannual Congress and workshops and seminars; mems: 500 individuals; Pres. LINDA J. HOOD (USA); Gen. Sec. Prof. GEORGE TAVARTKILADZE; publ. *International Journal of Audiology* (monthly).

International Society of Blood Transfusion (ISBT): Marnixstraat 317, 1016 TB Amsterdam, Netherlands; tel. and fax (20) 7601760; fax (20) 7601761; e-mail office@isbtweb.org; internet www.isbtweb.org; f. 1935; mems: c. 1,400 in over 101 countries; Pres. PETER FLANAGAN (New Zealand); Sec.-Gen. GEOFF DANIELS; publs *Transfusion Today* (quarterly), *Vox Sanguinis* (8 a year).

International Society of Developmental Biologists (ISDB): c/o Marianne Bronner, Biology Div., California Institute of Technology, 1200 E. California Blvd, Pasadena, CA 91125, USA; tel. (626) 395-4952; fax (626) 449-0756; e-mail mbronner@caltech.edu; internet www.developmental-biology.org; f. 1911 as International Institute of Embryology; aims to promote the study of developmental biology and to encourage international co-operation among investigators in the field; mems: 850 in 33 countries; Pres. CLAUDIO STERN (United Kingdom); International Sec. MARIANNE BRONNER-FRASER (USA); publs *Mechanisms of Development* (monthly), *Gene Expression Patterns* (6 a year).

International Society of Internal Medicine (ISIM): Dept of Internal Medicine, RSZ-Bern Hospitals, Zieglerspital, Morillonstr. 75-91, 3001 Bern, Switzerland; tel. 319707178; fax 319707763; e-mail hanspeter.kohler@spitalnetzbern.ch; internet www.isim-online.org; f. 1948 to encourage research and education in internal medicine; mems: 61 nat. socs; Pres. Dr RODOLFO BADO (Argentina); Sec.-Gen. Prof. HANS-PETER KOHLER (Switzerland).

International Society of Lymphology: POB 245200, Tucson, AZ 85724-5200, USA; tel. (520) 626-6118; fax (520) 626-0822; e-mail lymph@u.arizona.edu; internet www.u.arizona.edu/~witte/ISL.htm; f. 1966 to further progress in lymphology through personal contacts and the exchange of ideas; mems: 375 in 42 countries; Pres. HAKAN BRORSON (Sweden); Sec.-Gen. MARYLS H. WITTE (USA); publ. *Lymphology* (quarterly).

International Society of Neuropathology: c/o David Hilton, Dept of Neuropathology, Derriford Hospital, Plymouth, PL6 8DH, United Kingdom; fax (175) 2763590; e-mail davidhilton@nhs.net; internet www.intsocneuropathol.com; f. 1950 as International Committee of Neuropathology; renamed as above in 1967; Pres. Dr HERBERT BUDKA (Austria); Sec.-Gen. Dr DAVID HILTON (United Kingdom); publ. *Brain Pathology* (quarterly).

International Society of Orthopaedic Surgery and Traumatology (Société Internationale de Chirurgie Orthopédique et de Traumatologie): Rue de la Loi 26, 1040 Brussels, Belgium; tel. (2) 648-68-23; fax (2) 649-86-01; e-mail hq@sicot.org; internet www.sicot.org; f. 1929; organizes Triennial World Congresses, Annual International Conferences and Trainees' Meetings; mems: 3,000 mems in 102 countries; Pres. Prof. MAURICE HINSENKAMP; Sec.-Gen. JOCHEN EULERT; publs. *International Orthopaedics* (scientific journal), *Newsletter* (quarterly), *e-Newsletter* (monthly).

International Society of Physical and Rehabilitation Medicine (ISPRM): c/o Kenes Associations Worldwide, 1-3 Rue de Chantepoulet, Geneva, Switzerland; tel. 229080483; fax 227322607; e-mail secretary@isprm.org; internet www.isprm.org; f. 1999 by merger of International Federation of Physical Medicine and Rehabilitation (f. 1952) and International Rehabilitation Medicine Association (f. 1968); eighth international congress: Cancún, Mexico (June 2014); mems: in 54 countries; Pres. MARTA IMAMURA; Sec. WALTER FRONTERA; publs *Newsletter*, *Disability and Rehabilitation*, Journal of Rehabilitation Medicine.

International Society of Radiology (ISR): 1891 Preston White Dr., Reston, VA 20191-4326, USA; tel. (703) 648-8360; fax (703) 648-8361; e-mail director@intsocradiology.org; internet www.isradiology.org; f. 1953 to promote radiology worldwide; International Commissions on Radiation Units and Measurements, on Radiation Protection, and on Radiological Education; organizes biannual International Congress of Radiology; collaborates with WHO and IAEA; mems: more than 80 nat. radiological socs; Pres. JAN LABASCAGNE (Australia); Sec.-Gen. LUIS DONOSO BACH (Spain); Exec. Dir THOMAS CALDWELL; publ. *Newsletter*.

International Society of Surgery (ISS): Seltisbergerstr. 16, 4419 Lupsingen, Switzerland; tel. 618159666; fax 618114775; e-mail surgery@iss-sic.ch; internet www.iss-sic.com; f. 1902 to promote understanding between surgical disciplines; groups surgeons to address issues of interest to all surgical specialists; supports general surgery as a training base for abdominal surgery, surgery with integuments and endocrine surgery; organizes congresses (2014 World Congress of Surgery: Montreal, Canada, in Aug.); mems: 4,000; Pres. NOPADOL WORA-URAI; Sec.-Gen. Prof. JEAN-CLAUDE GIVEL; publ. *World Journal of Surgery* (monthly).

International Society of Veterinary Dermatopathology (ISVD): c/o Sonja Bettenay, Tierdermatologie Deisenhofen, Schaeftlarner Weg 1A, Deisenhofen 82041, Germany; e-mail s-bettena@t-online.de; internet www.isvd.org; f. 1958; aims to advance veterinary and comparative dermatopathology, to group individuals with a professional interest in the histologic interpretation of animal skin diseases, to assist with and co-ordinate the adaptation and implementation of emerging technologies for the morphologic diagnosis of skin diseases in animals, and to provide an affiliation with physician dermatopathologists in order to exchange information on comparative dermatopathology; promotes professional training; Pres. Dr JUDITH NIMMO (Australia); Sec. SONJA BETTENAY (Germany).

International Spinal Cord Society (ISCoS): National Spinal Injuries Centre, Stoke Mandeville Hospital, Aylesbury, Bucks, HP21 8AL, United Kingdom; tel. (1296) 315866; fax (1296) 315870; e-mail admin@iscos.org.uk; internet www.iscos.org.uk; f. 1961; formerly the International Medical Society of Paraplegia (f. 1961); studies all problems relating to traumatic and non-traumatic lesions of the spinal cord, including causes, prevention, research and rehabilitation; promotes the exchange of information; assists in efforts to guide and co-ordinate research; Pres. Prof. DOUGLAS J. BROWN (Australia); Hon. Sec. SHINSUKE KATOH (Japan); publ. *Spinal Cord*.

International Union against Tuberculosis and Lung Disease (The Union): 68 blvd St Michel, 75006 Paris, France; tel. 1-44-32-03-60; fax 1-43-29-90-87; e-mail union@theunion.org; internet www.theunion.org; f. 1920 to co-ordinate the efforts of anti-tuberculosis and respiratory disease asscns, to mobilize public interest, to assist control programmes and research around the world, to collaborate with govts and WHO and to promote confs; mems: asscns in 145 countries, 10,000 individual mems; Pres. Dr JANE CARTER (USA); Sec.-Gen. Prof. GUY MARKS (Australia); publs *The International Journal of Tuberculosis and Lung Disease* (monthly), *Newsletter*.

International Union for Health Promotion and Education (IUHPE): 42 blvd de la Libération, 93203 St Denis Cedex, France; tel. 1-48-13-71-20; fax 1-48-09-17-67; e-mail iuhpe@iuhpe.org; internet www.iuhpe.org; f. 1951; provides an international network for the exchange of practical information on devts in health promotion and education; promotes research; encourages professional training for health workers, teachers, social workers and others; holds a World Conference on Health Promotion and Health Education every three years; organizes regional confs and seminars; mems: in more than 90 countries; Pres. MICHAEL SPARKS (Australia); Exec. Dir MARIE-CLAUDE LAMARRE (France); publ. *Global Health Promotion* (quarterly, in English, French and Spanish).

International Vaccine Institute (IVI): SNU Research Park, 1 Gwanak-ro, Gwanak-gu, Seoul 151-742, Republic of Korea; tel. (2) 872-2801; fax (2) 872-2803; e-mail iviinfo@ivi.int; internet www.ivi.int; f. 1997; concerned with designing, developing and evaluating vaccines; mems: 35 countries; Dir-Gen. Dr CHRISTIAN LOUCQ.

Medical Women's International Association (MWIA): 7555 Morley Drive, Burnaby, BC, V5E 3Y2, Canada; tel. and fax (604) 522-1960; e-mail secretariat@mwia.net; internet www.mwia.net; f. 1919 to facilitate contacts between women in medicine and to encourage co-operation in matters connected with international health problems; mems: nat. asscns in 48 countries, and individuals; Pres. KYUNG AH PARK (Korea); Sec.-Gen. Dr SHELLEY ROSS (Canada); publ. *MWIA UPDATE* (3 a year).

Multiple Sclerosis International Federation (MSIF): Skyline House, 3rd Floor, 200 Union St, London, SE1 0LX, United Kingdom; tel. (20) 7620-1911; fax (20) 7620-1922; e-mail info@msif.org; internet www.msif.org; f. 1967; promotes shared scientific research into multiple sclerosis and related neurological diseases; stimulates the active exchange of information; provides support for new and existing multiple sclerosis orgs; Pres. and Chair. WEYMAN JOHNSON (USA); Treas. ROB HUBBARD; publs *MSIF Annual Review*, *MS in Focus* (2 a year).

Organisation panafricaine de lutte contre le SIDA (OPALS): 15–21 rue de L'École de Médecine, 75006 Paris, France; tel. 1-43-26-72-28; fax 1-43-29-70-93; internet www.opals.asso.fr; f. 1988; disseminates information relating to the treatment and prevention of AIDS; provides training of medical personnel; promotes co-operation between African medical centres and specialized centres in the USA and Europe; Pres. Prof. MARC GENTILINI; Sec.-Gen. Prof. DOMINIQUE RICHARD-LENOBLE; publ. *OPALS Liaison*.

Organization for Co-ordination in the Struggle against Endemic Diseases in Central Africa (Organisation de coordination pour la lutte contre les endémies en Afrique Centrale—OCEAC): BP 288, Yaoundé, Cameroon; tel. 23-22-32; fax 23-00-61; e-mail contact@oceac.org; internet www.oceac.org; f. 1965 to standardize methods of controlling endemic diseases, to co-ordinate national action, and to negotiate programmes of assistance and training on a regional scale; mems: Cameroon, Central African Republic, Chad, Republic of the Congo, Equatorial Guinea, Gabon; Exec. Sec. Dr JEAN JACQUES MOKA; publ. *Bulletin de Liaison et de Documentation* (quarterly).

Pan-American Association of Ophthalmology (PAAO): 1301 South Bowen Rd, Suite 450, Arlington, TX 76013, USA; tel. (817) 275-7553; fax (817) 275-3961; e-mail info@paao.org; internet www.paao.org; f. 1939 to promote friendship within the profession and the dissemination of scientific information; holds Congress every two years (2013: Rio de Janeiro, Brazil); mems: nat. ophthalmological socs and other bodies in 39 countries; Pres. ANA LUISA HÖFLING-LIMA; Exec. Dir TERESA BRADSHAW; publ. *Vision Panamerica* (quarterly).

Rehabilitation International: 25 East 21st St, 4th Floor, New York, NY 10010, USA; tel. (212) 420-1500; fax (212) 505-0871; e-mail ri@riglobal.org; internet www.riglobal.org; f. 1922 to improve the lives of people with disabilities through the exchange of information and research on equipment and methods of assistance; functions as a global network of disabled people, service providers, researchers and government agencies; advocates promoting and implementing the rights, inclusion and rehabilitation of people with disabilities; organizes international confs and co-operates with UN agencies and other int. orgs; mems: 700 orgs in more than 90 countries; Pres. JAN A. MONSBAKKEN; Sec.-Gen. VENUS ILAGAN; publs *International Rehabilitation Review* (annually), *Rehabilitación* (bi-annually).

Société de neuro-chirurgie de langue française (Society of French-speaking Neuro-Surgeons): c/o Prof. B. George, Dept of Neurosurgery, Lariboisière Hospital, 2 rue Ambroise Paré, 75010 Paris, France; tel. 1-49-95-81-46; fax 1-49-95-81-55; e-mail bernard.george@lrb.aphp.fr; internet www.snclf.com; f. 1949; holds annual convention and congress; mems: 700; Pres. CHRISTIAN RAFTOPOULOS (Belgium); Sec.-Gen. DANIEL MAY; publ. *Neurochirurgie* (6 a year).

Transplantation Society (Société de Transplantation): 1255 University St, Suite 325, Montréal, QC H3B 3B4, Canada; tel. (514) 874-1717; fax (514) 874-1716; e-mail info@tts.org; internet www.tts.org; f. 1966; aims to provide a focus for development of the science and clinical practice of transplantations, scientific communication, education, and guidance on ethics; mems: more than 5,000 in 65 countries; Pres. FRANCIS DELMONICO.

Union for International Cancer Control (Union internationale contre le cancer—UICC): 62 route de Frontenex, 1207 Geneva, Switzerland; tel. 228091811; fax 228091810; e-mail info@uicc.org; internet www.uicc.org; f. 1933 to promote the campaign to prevent and control cancer on an international level; aims to connect, mobilize and support orgs, leading experts, key stakeholders and volunteers in a community working together to eliminate cancer as a life-threatening disease for future generations; works closely with its mem. orgs and partners to implement a comprehensive strategy that includes: organizing the World Cancer Congress; promoting the World Cancer Declaration; raising awareness through the World Cancer Campaign; co-ordinating World Cancer Day annually, on 4 Feb; reviewing and disseminating the TNM (tumour-node-metastasis) classification of malignant tumours; developing effective cancer control programmes especially in low- and middle-income countries; changing cancer-related beliefs and behaviour through information and education; creating special initiatives in prevention, early detection, access to treatment and supportive care; awarding international cancer fellowships; producing scientific publications; mems: more than 770 orgs in 155 countries; Pres. Dr MARY GOSPODAROWICZ (Canada); CEO CARY ADAMS (United Kingdom); publs *International Journal of Cancer* (24 a year), *UICC News* (quarterly).

World Allergy Organization (IAACI): 555 East Wells St, Suite 1100, Milwaukee, WI 53202-3823, USA; tel. (414) 276-1791; fax (414) 276-3349; e-mail info@worldallergy.org; internet www.worldallergy.org; f. 1945, as International Association of Allergology and Clinical Immunology, to further work in the educational, research and practical medical aspects of allergic and immunological diseases; World Congresses held every two years (June 2013: Milan, Italy); mems: 92 nat. and reg. socs; Pres. RUBY PAWANKAR (India/Japan); Sec.-Gen. Prof. MARIO SÁNCHEZ BORGES (Venezuela); publ. *Allergy and Clinical Immunology International* (6 a year).

World Association for Disaster and Emergency Medicine (WADEM): International Office, POB 55158, Madison, WI 53705-8958, USA; tel. (608) 819-6604; fax (608) 819-6055; e-mail info@wadem.org; internet www.wadem.org; f. 1976; aims to improve prehospital and emergency health care, public health, and disaster health and preparedness; became a full partner in the Global Health Cluster of the UN Inter-Agency Standing Committee in April 2008; mems: 600 in 55 countries; Pres. PAUL ARBON (Australia); Sec. ELAINE DAILY (USA); publs *International Disaster Nursing*, *Prehospital and Disaster Medicine* (6 a year).

World Confederation for Physical Therapy (WCPT): Victoria Charity Centre, 11 Belgrave Rd, London, SW1V 1RB, United Kingdom; tel. (20) 7931-6465; fax (20) 7931-6494; e-mail info@wcpt.org; internet www.wcpt.org; f. 1951; represents physical therapy internationally; encourages high standards of physical therapy education and practice; promotes exchange of information among mems, and the development of a scientific professional base through research; aims to contribute to the devt of informed public opinion regarding physical therapy; holds seminars and workshops and quadrennial scientific congress showcasing advancements in physical therapy research, practice and education (2015: Singapore, in May); mems: 106 nat. physical therapy orgs; Pres. MARILYN MOFFAT; Sec.-Gen. BRENDA J. MYERS; publ. *WCPT News* (quarterly).

World Council of Optometry (WCO): 42 Craven St, London, WC2N 5NG, United Kingdom; tel. (20) 7839-6000; fax (20) 7839-6800; e-mail enquiries@worldoptometry.org; internet www.worldoptometry.org; f. 1927 to co-ordinate efforts to provide a good standard of ophthalmic optical (optometric) care throughout the world; enables exchange of ideas between different countries; focuses on optometric education; gives advice on standards of qualification; considers optometry legislation throughout the world; mems: 94 optometric orgs in 49 countries; Pres. SUSAN COOPER (Canada).

World Federation for Medical Education (WFME) (Fédération mondiale pour l'enseignement de la medicine): University of Copenhagen, Faculty of Health Sciences, Blegdamsvej 3, 2200 Copenhagen N, Denmark; tel. (353) 27103; fax (353) 27070; e-mail wfme@wfme

.org; internet www.wfme.org; f. 1972; aims to promote and integrate medical education worldwide; links regional and international asscns; has official relations with WHO, UNICEF, UNESCO, UNDP and the World Bank; Pres. Prof. STEFAN LINDGREN; Sec. ANNA IVERSEN.

World Federation for Mental Health (WFMH): POB 807, Occoquan, VA 22125, USA; fax (703) 490-6926; e-mail info@wfmh.com; internet www.wfmh.org; f. 1948 to promote the highest standards of mental health; works with agencies of the UN in promoting global mental health needs; assists grass-roots efforts to improve mental health services, treatment and stigma; voting, affiliate and individual mems in more than 100 countries; Pres. DEBORAH WAN (Hong Kong SAR); Treas. HELEN MILLAR (United Kingdom); publs *Newsletter* (quarterly), *Annual Report*.

World Federation for Ultrasound in Medicine and Biology: 14750 Sweitzer Ln, Suite 100, Laurel, MD 20707-5906, USA; tel. (301) 498-4100; fax (301) 498-4150; e-mail admin@wfumb.org; internet www.wfumb.org; f. 1973; Pres. HASSEN GHARBI; Sec. DIETER NURENBERG; publs *Ultrasound in Medicine and Biology* (monthly), *Echoes* (2 a year).

World Federation of Associations of Paediatric Surgeons (WOFAPS): c/o Prof. Alastair Millar Capetown, South Africa; e-mail alastair.millar@uct.ac.za; internet www.wofaps.org; f. 1974; encourages high standards and ethical practice of paediatric surgery; aims to improve the standards of education for the training of paediatric surgeons; promotes paediatric surgical research. Conducts World Congress every three years (2013, Berlin, Germany); more than 120 countries; Pres. DEVENDRA GUPTA; Sec.-Gen./Treas. ALASTAIR MILLAR.

World Federation of Hydrotherapy and Climatotherapy: Cattedra di Terapia Med. E Medic. Termal, Università degli Studi, via Cicognara 7, 20129 Milan, Italy; tel. (02) 50318458; fax (02) 50318461; e-mail crbbmn@unimi.it; internet www.femteconline.org; f. 1947 as International Federation of Thermalism and Climatism; recognized by WHO in 1986; present name adopted 1999; mems: in 44 countries; Pres. M. NIKOLAI A. STOROZHENKO (Russia); Gen. Sec. Prof. UMBERTO SOLIMENE (Italy).

World Federation of Neurology (WFN): 1 Lyric Sq., London, W6 0NB, United Kingdom; tel. 9556(20) 3542–7857; fax (20) 3008–6161; e-mail info@wfneurology.org; internet www.wfneurology.org; f. 1955 as International Neurological Congress, present title adopted 1957; aims to assemble mems of various congresses associated with neurology and promote co-operation among neurological researchers; organizes Congress every two years; mems: 117 professional socs in 116 countries; Pres. RAAD SHAKIR (United Kingdom); Sec.-Treas. WOLFGANG GRISOLD (Austria); publs *Journal of the Neurological Sciences*, *World Neurology* (bimonthly).

World Federation of Neurosurgical Societies (WFNS): 5 rue du Marché, 1260 Nyon Vaud, Switzerland; tel. 223624303; fax 223624352; e-mail teresachen@wfns.ch; internet www.wfns.org; f. 1955 to assist in the devt of neurosurgery and to help the formation of asscns; facilitates the exchange of information and encourages research; mems: 124 socs; Pres. YONG KWANG TU; Sec. Dr BASANT MISRA.

World Federation of Occupational Therapists (WFOT): POB 30, Forrestfield, Western Australia 6058, Australia; fax (8) 9453-9746; e-mail admin@wfot.org.au; internet www.wfot.org; f. 1952 to further the rehabilitation of the physically and mentally disabled by promoting the development of occupational therapy in all countries; facilitates the exchange of information and publications; promotes research in occupational therapy; holds international congresses every four years; mems: 80 mem. orgs comprising some 378,000 individual mems; Pres. E. SHARON BRINTNELL (Canada); Exec. Dir MARILYN PATTISON (Australia); publ. *Bulletin* (2 a year).

World Federation of Public Health Associations: Office of the Secretariat, c/o Institute for Social and Preventive Medicine, University of Geneva CMU, 1 rue Michel Servet, 1211 Geneva 4, Switzerland; tel. 223970453; fax 223970452; e-mail secretariat@wfpha.org; internet www.wfpha.org; f. 1967; brings together researchers, teachers, health service providers and workers in a multidisciplinary environment of professional exchange, studies and action; endeavours to influence policies and to set priorities to prevent disease and promote health; holds a Congress every three years: 2015, Kolkata, India; mems: 79 nat. public health asscns; Pres. JAMES CHAUVIN (Canada); publs *WFPHA Report* (in English), occasional technical papers.

World Federation of Societies of Anaesthesiologists (WFSA): 21 Portland Pl., London, W1B 1PY, United Kingdom; tel. (20) 7631-8880; fax (20) 7631-8882; e-mail wfsahq@anaesthesiologists.org; internet www.anaesthesiologists.org; f. 1955; aims to make available the highest standards of anaesthesia, pain treatment, trauma management and resuscitation to all peoples of the world; mems: 122 nat. socs; Pres. Dr DAVID WILKINSON (United Kingdom); Sec. Dr GONZALO BARREIRO (Uruguay); publs *Update in Anaesthesia* (2 a year), *Annual Report*.

World Gastroenterology Organization (WGO): 555 East Wells St, Suite 1100, Milwaukee, WI 53202, USA; tel. (414) 918-9798; fax (414) 276-3349; e-mail info@worldgastroenterology.org; internet www.worldgastroenterology.org; f. 1958 as Organisation mondiale de gastro-entérologie, to promote clinical and academic gastroenterological practice throughout the world, and to ensure high ethical standards; focuses on the improvement of standards in gastroenterology training and education on a global scale; renamed as above in 2007; a WGO Foundation, incorporated in 2007, is dedicated to raising funds to support WGO educational programs and activities; organizes a World Congress every four years (2013: Shanghai, China, in Sept.); mems: some 50,000 individuals from over 100 nat. socs and asscns of gastroenterology; Pres. Prof. JAMES TOOULI (Australia); Sec.-Gen. Prof. CIHAN YURDAYDIN (Turkey).

World Heart Federation: 7 rue des Battoir, 1211 Geneva 4, Switzerland; tel. 228070320; fax 228070339; e-mail info@worldheart.org; internet www.world-heart-federation.org; f. 1978 as International Society and Federation of Cardiology, name changed as above 1998; aims to help people to achieve a longer and better life through prevention and control of heart disease and stroke, with a focus on low- and middle-income countries; mems: 197 orgs in more than 100 countries; Pres. Dr SRINATH REDDY; CEO JOHANNA RALSTON; publs *Nature Reviews Cardiology Journal*, *Global Heart*.

World Medical Association (WMA): 13 chemin du Levant, CIB-Bâtiment A, 01210 Ferney-Voltaire, France; tel. 4-50-40-75-75; fax 4-50-40-59-37; e-mail wma@wma.net; internet www.wma.net; f. 1947 to achieve the highest international standards in all aspects of medical education and practice, to promote closer ties among doctors and national medical asscns by personal contact and all other means, to study problems confronting the medical profession, and to present its views to appropriate bodies; holds an annual General Assembly; mems: 107 nat. medical asscns; Pres. Dr CECIL B. WILSON (Brazil); Sec.-Gen. Dr OTMAR KLOIBER (Germany); publ. *The World Medical Journal* (quarterly).

World Psychiatric Association (WPA): Psychiatric Hospital, 2 chemin du Petit-Bel-Air 1225, Chêne-Bourg, Switzerland; tel. 223055737; fax 223055735; e-mail wpasecretariat@wpanet.org; internet www.wpanet.org; f. 1961; aims to increase knowledge and skills necessary for work in the field of mental health and the care for the mentally ill; organizes World Psychiatric Congresses and regional and inter-regional scientific meetings; mems: 135 nat. psychiatric socs, representing some 200,000 psychiatrists, in 117 countries; Pres. PEDRO RUIZ (USA); Sec.-Gen. LEVENT KUEY (Turkey).

Posts and Telecommunications

Arab Permanent Postal Commission: c/o Arab League Bldg, Tahrir Sq., Cairo, Egypt; tel. (2) 5750511; fax (2) 5740331; f. 1952; aims to establish stricter postal relations between the Arab countries than those laid down by the Universal Postal Union, and to pursue the devt and modernization of postal services in mem. countries; publs *APU Bulletin* (monthly), *APU Review* (quarterly), *APU News* (annually).

Asia-Pacific Telecommunity (APT): No. 12/49, Soi 5, Chaengwattana Rd, Thungsonghong, Bangkok 10210, Thailand; tel. (2) 573-0044; fax (2) 573-7479; e-mail aptmail@apt.int; internet www.aptsec.org; f. 1979 to cover all matters relating to telecommunications in the region; serves as the focal organization for ICT in the Asia-Pacific region; contributes, through its various programmes and activities, to the growth of the ICT sector in the region and assists mems in their preparation for global telecommunications confs, as well as promoting regional harmonization for such events; mems: Afghanistan, Australia, Bangladesh, Bhutan, Brunei, Cambodia, People's Republic of China, Fiji, India, Indonesia, Iran, Japan, Kiribati, Democratic Republic of Korea, Republic of Korea, Laos, Malaysia, Maldives, Marshall Islands, Federated States of Micronesia, Mongolia, Myanmar, Nauru, Nepal, New Zealand, Pakistan, Palau, Papua New Guinea, Philippines, Samoa, Singapore, Solomon Islands, Sri Lanka, Thailand, Tonga, Tuvalu, Vanuatu, Viet Nam; assoc. mems: Cook Islands, Hong Kong, Macao, Niue; 132 affiliated mems; Sec.-Gen. TOSHIYUKI YAMADA.

Asian-Pacific Postal Union (APPU): APPU Bureau, POB 1, Laksi Post Office, 111 Chaeng Wattana Rd, Bangkok 10210, Thailand; tel. (2) 573-7282; fax (2) 573-1161; e-mail admin@appu-bureau.org; internet www.appu-bureau.org; f. 1962 to extend, facilitate and improve the postal relations between the mem. countries and to promote co-operation in the field of postal services; holds Congress every four years (2013: India); mems: postal administrations in 32 countries; Dir LIN HONGLIANG; publs *Annual Report*, *Exchange Program of Postal Officials*, *APPU Newsletter*.

European Conference of Postal and Telecommunications Administrations: Penblingehus, Nansensgade 19-3, 1366 Copenhagen, Denmark; tel. 33-89-63-00; fax 33-89-63-30; e-mail eco@eco.cept.org; internet www.cept.org; f. 1959 to strengthen relations between mem. administrations and to harmonize and improve their technical services; activities include co-operation on commercial, operational, regulatory and technical standardisation issues; supported by a separate European Communications Office; mems: 48 countries; Co-Pres Eric Fournier, Ulrich Dammann, Marcin Krasuski; Dir ECO Mark Thomas (United Kingdom); publ. *Bulletin*.

European Telecommunications Satellite Organization (EUTELSAT): 7 Tour Maine Montparnasse, 33 ave du Maine 75015 Paris, France; tel. 1-44-10-41-10; fax 1-44-10-41-11; e-mail secigo@eutelsat.fr; internet www.eutelsat.com; f. 1977 to operate satellites for fixed and mobile communications in Europe; EUTELSAT's in-orbit resource comprises 18 satellites; commercializes capacity in three satellites operated by other cos; mems: public and private telecommunications operations in 49 countries; Exec. Sec. Christian Roisse.

International Mobile Satellite Organization (IMSO): 99 City Rd, London, EC1Y 1AX, United Kingdom; tel. (20) 7728-1249; fax (20) 7728-1172; e-mail info@imso.org; internet www.imso.org; f. 1979, as the International Maritime Satellite Organization (name changed in 1994) to provide (from Feb. 1982) global communications for shipping via satellites on a commercial basis; in 1985 the operating agreement was amended to include aeronautical communications, and in 1988 amendments were approved which allowed provision of global land mobile communications; in April 1999 the commercial functions of the org. became the limited company INMARSAT Ltd (the first intergovernmental org. to be transferred to the private sector); IMSO was maintained, initially to monitor, under a Public Services Agreement adopted in 1999, INMARSAT Ltd's public service obligations in respect of the Global Maritime Distress and Safety System (GMDSS); following amendments adopted in 2008 to the IMSO Convention, IMSO's oversight functions were extended to all satellite operators approved to provide GMDSS services, and IMSO was also mandated to oversee long range tracking and identification of ships (LRIT); mems: 97 states parties to the founding Convention; Dir-Gen. Capt. Esteban Pacha-Vicente.

International Multinational Partnership against Cyber Threats (IMPACT): Jalan IMPACT, 63000 Cyberjaya, Malaysia; tel. (3) 83132020; fax (3) 83192020; e-mail contactus@impact-alliance.org; internet impact-alliance.org; f. 2008; aims to promote global collaboration in order to strengthen the capability of the international community and individual partner countries to prevent, defend against and respond to cyber threats; signed a Memorandum of Understanding with the ITU in Sept. 2008 to administer the Global Cyber Agenda; Chair. Datuk Mohd Noor Amin.

International Telecommunications Satellite Organization (ITSO): 3400 International Drive, NW, Washington, DC 20008-3006, USA; tel. (202) 243-5096; fax (202) 243-5018; internet www.itso.int; f. 1964 to establish a global commercial satellite communications system; Assembly of Parties attended by representatives of mem. govts, meets every two years to consider policy and long-term aims and matters of interest to mems as sovereign states; meeting of Signatories to the Operating Agreement held annually; 24 INTELSAT satellites in geosynchronous orbit provide a global communications service; provides most of the world's overseas traffic; in 1998 INTELSAT agreed to establish a private enterprise, incorporated in the Netherlands, to administer six satellite services; mems: 150 govts; Dir-Gen. José Toscano (USA).

Internet Corporation for Assigned Names and Numbers (ICANN): 12025 Waterfront Dr., Suite 300, Los Angeles, CA 90094-2536, USA; tel. (310) 301-5800; fax (310) 823-8649; e-mail icann@icann.org; internet www.icann.org; f. 1998; non-profit, private sector body; aims to co-ordinate the technical management and policy devt of the Internet in relation to addresses, domain names and protocol; supported by an At-Large Advisory Committee (representing individual users of the internet), a Country Code Names Supporting Organization, a Governmental Advisory Committee, a Generic Names Supporting Organization, and a Security and Stability Advisory Committee; through its Internet Assigned Numbers Authority department ICANN manages the global co-ordination of domain name system roots and internet protocol addressing; at 30 June 2011 there were 310 top-level domains (TLDs), 30 of which were in non-Latin scripts, and the most common of which were generic TLDs (gTLDs) (such as .org or .com) and country code TLDs (ccTLDs); in June 2011 ICANN adopted an expanded gTLD programme, under which, from 2012, applications were accepted from qualified orgs wishing to register domain names of their choosing; details of the first 1,930 filed applications were published in June 2012 ('app' being the most popular): the ensuing objections process was administered by the International Chamber of Commerce International Centre for Expertise; the expanded programme provides for Internationalized Domain Names (IDNs) incorporating non-Latin character sets (Arabic, Chinese and Cyrillic), with a view to making the internet more globally inclusive; launched in Oct. 2012, jointly with the African Regional Registry for Internet Number Resources, a three-year 'New Approach to Africa' initiative aimed at expanding activities in Africa; Pres. and CEO Fadi Chehadé (Lebanon).

Pacific Telecommunications Council (PTC): 914 Coolidge St, Honolulu, HI 96826-3085, USA; tel. (808) 941-3789; fax (808) 944-4874; e-mail info@ptc.org; internet www.ptc.org; f. 1978; mems: over 3,400 mem. representatives from more than 40 countries; Pres. Stephen Ho (Hong Kong, SAR); Sec. Susan J. Irwin (USA).

Postal Union of the Americas, Spain and Portugal (PUASP) (Unión Postal de las Américas, España y Portugal): Cebollatí 1468/70, 1°, Casilla de Correos 20.042, Montevideo, Uruguay; tel. 2410 0070; fax 2410 5046; e-mail secretaria@upaep.com.uy; internet www.upaep.com.uy; f. 1911 to extend, facilitate and study the postal relationships of mem. countries; mems: 27 countries; Sec.-Gen. Roberto Cavanna.

Press, Radio and Television

African Union of Broadcasting (AUB): 101 rue Carnot, BP 3237, Dakar, Senegal; tel. 821-16-25; fax 822-51-13; internet www.aub-uar.org; f. 1962 as Union of National Radio and Television Organizations of Africa (URTNA), new org. f. Nov. 2006; co-ordinates radio and television services, including monitoring and frequency allocation, the exchange of information and coverage of national and international events among African countries; mems: 48 orgs and 6 assoc. mems; Dir-Gen. Lawrence Addo-Yao Atiase (Ghana).

Asia-Pacific Broadcasting Union (ABU): IPPTAR Bldg, 2nd Floor, Angkasapuri, 50614 Kuala Lumpur Malaysia; tel. and fax (3) 22823592; e-mail info@abu.org.my; internet www.abu.org.my; f. 1964 to foster and co-ordinate the devt of broadcasting in the Asia-Pacific area, to develop means of establishing closer collaboration and co-operation among broadcasting orgs, and to serve the professional needs of broadcasters in Asia and the Pacific; holds annual General Assembly; mems: 255 in 63 countries and territories; Sec.-Gen. Dr Javad Mottaghi (Iran); publs *ABU News* (every 2 months), *ABU Technical Review* (every 2 months).

Association for the Promotion of International Circulation of the Press (DISTRIPRESS): Seefeldstr. 35, 8008 Zürich, Switzerland; tel. 442024121; fax 442021025; e-mail info@distripress.net; internet www.distripress.net; f. 1955 to assist in the promotion of the freedom of the press throughout the world, supporting and aiding UNESCO in promoting the free flow of ideas; organizes meetings of publishers and distributors of newspapers, periodicals and paperback books, to promote the exchange of information and experience among mems; mems: 397 in 91 countries; Pres. Tony Jashanmal (UAE); Man. Dir David Owen (United Kingdom); publs *Distripress Gazette*, *Who's Who*.

Association of European Journalists (AEJ): Chee de Stockel 8, 1200 Brussels, Belgium; tel. (478) 291985; e-mail tibor.macak@gmail.com; internet www.aej.org; f. 1963 to participate actively in the development of a European consciousness; to promote deeper knowledge of European problems and secure appreciation by the general public of the work of European institutions; to facilitate mems' access to sources of European information; and to defend freedom of the press; mems: 2,100 individuals and nat. asscns in 25 countries; Pres. Eileen Dunne (Ireland); Sec.-Gen. Tibor Macak (Slovakia).

Cable Europe: 41 ave des Arts, 1040 Brussels, Belgium; tel. (2) 521-17-63; fax (2) 521-79-76; e-mail jessica.fernandez@cable-europe.eu; internet www.cable-europe.eu; f. 1955 as European Cable Communications Associations (name changed in 2006); promotes the interests of the European cable industry and fosters co-operation among cos and national asscns; Pres. Manuel Kohnstamm (Netherlands).

Caribbean Broadcasting Union (CBU): Harbour Industrial Estate, St Michael 11145, Barbados; tel. 430-1006; fax 228-9524; e-mail sally.bynoe@caribsurf.com; internet www.caribunion.com; f. 1970; stimulating the flow of broadcast material among the radio and television systems in the Caribbean region; facilitates discussion and analysis that assist in policy formulation on major integration issues; mems: 29 mem. and 4 assoc. mem. countries; Pres. Shida Bolai (Trinidad and Tobago); Sec.-Gen. Sonia Gill (Jamaica).

European Alliance of News Agencies: Norrbackagatan 5, 11329 Stockholm, Sweden; tel. (8) 301-324; e-mail erik-n@telia.com; internet www.newsalliance.org; f. 1957 as European Alliance of Press Agencies (name changed 2002); aims to promote co-operation among mems and to study and protect their common interests; annual assembly; mems: in 30 countries; Pres. Peter Kropsch; Sec.-Gen. Erik Nylén.

European Broadcasting Union (EBU): CP 45, 17A Ancienne-Route, 1218 Grand-Saconnex, Geneva, Switzerland; tel. 227172111; fax 227474000; e-mail ebu@ebu.ch; internet www.ebu.ch; f. 1950 in succession to the International Broadcasting Union; a professional asscn of broadcasting orgs, supporting the interests of mems and assisting the devt of broadcasting in all its forms; activities include the Eurovision news and programme exchanges, co-productions including the annual Eurovision Song Contest, and the Euroradio music exchanges; mems: 85 active in 56 countries, 37 assoc. mems; Pres. JEAN-PAUL PHILIPPOT (Belgium); Dir-Gen. INGRID DELTENRE; publs *EBU Technical Review* (annually), *Dossiers* (2 a year).

Inter-American Press Association (IAPA) (Sociedad Interamericana de Prensa): Jules Dubois Bldg, 1801 SW 3rd Ave, Miami, FL 33129, USA; tel. (305) 634-2465; fax (305) 635-2272; e-mail info@sipiapa.org; internet www.sipiapa.org; f. 1942 to guard the freedom of the press in the Americas; to promote and maintain the dignity, rights and responsibilities of the profession of journalism; to foster a wider knowledge and greater interchange among the peoples of the Americas; mems: 1,400; Exec. Dir JULIO E. MUÑOZ; publ. *IAPA News* (monthly).

International Amateur Radio Union: POB 310905, Newington, CT 06131-0905, USA; tel. (860) 594-0200; fax (860) 594-0259; e-mail iaru@iaru.org; internet www.iaru.org; f. 1925 to link national amateur radio socs and represent the interests of two-way amateur radio communication; mems: 161 nat. amateur radio socs; Pres. TIMOTHY ELLAM (Canada); Sec. RODNEY STAFFORD.

International Association of Sound and Audiovisual Archives: c/o Lynn Johnson, e.tv (Pty) Ltd, POB 12124, Mill St Gdns, Cape Town 8010, South Africa; tel. (21) 481-4414; fax (21) 481-4660; e-mail secretary-general@iasa-web.org; internet www.iasa-web.org; f. 1969; supports the professional exchange of sound and audiovisual documents, and fosters international co-operation between audiovisual archives in all fields, in particular in the areas of acquisition, documentation, access, exploitation, copyright, and preservation; holds annual conf; mems: 400 individuals and institutions in 64 countries; Pres. JACQUELINE VON ARB (Norway) (2011–14); Sec.-Gen. LYNN JOHNSON (South Africa); publs *IASA Journal* (2 a year), *IASA Information Bulletin* (2 a year), *eBulletin* (2 a year).

International Association of Women in Radio and Television (IAWRT): South Gate Bldg, Mezzanine Floor, Rm 14, Mukoma Rd, South B, 45533-00100 Nairobi, Kenya; tel. and fax (20) 2689919; e-mail secretariat@iawrt.org; internet www.iawrt.org; f. 1951; Pres. RACHEAL NAKITARE (Kenya); Sec. VIOLET GONDA (Zimbabwe).

International Council for Film, Television and Audiovisual Communication (Conseil international du cinema de la television et de la communication audiovisuelle): 1 rue Miollis, 75732 Paris Cedex 15, France; tel. 1-45-68-48-55; fax 1-45-67-28-40; e-mail secretariat@cict-unesco.org; f. 1958 to support collaboration between UNESCO and professionals engaged in cinema, television and audiovisual communications; mems: 36 int. film and television orgs; Pres. HISANORI ISOMURA; Sec.-Gen. LOLA POGGI GOUJON; publ. *Letter of Information* (monthly).

International Council of French-speaking Radio and Television Organizations (Conseil international des radios-télévisions d'expression française): 52 blvd Auguste-Reyers, 1044 Brussels, Belgium; tel. (2) 732-45-85; fax (2) 732-62-40; e-mail cirtef@rtbf.be; internet www.cirtef.org; f. 1978 to establish links between French-speaking radio and television orgs; mems: 46 orgs; Sec.-Gen. GUILA THIAM (Senegal).

International Federation of Film Critics (Fédération Internationale de la Presse Cinématographique—FIPRESCI): Schleissheimerstr. 83, 80797 Munich, Germany; tel. (89) 182303; fax (89) 184766; e-mail info@fipresci.org; internet www.fipresci.org; f. 1930 to develop the cinematographic press and promote cinema as an art; organizes international meetings and juries in film festivals; mems: nat. orgs or corresponding mems in 68 countries; Pres. JEAN ROY (France); Gen. Sec. KLAUS EDER (Germany).

International Federation of Press Cutting Agencies (FIBEP) (Fédération Internationale des Bureaux D'Extraits de Presse): Chaussée de Wavre 1945, 1160 Brussels, Belgium; tel. (2) 508-17-17; fax (2) 513-82-18; internet www.fibep.info; f. 1953 to improve the standing of the profession, prevent infringements, illegal practices and unfair competition; and to develop business and friendly relations among press cutting agencies throughout the world; Congress held every 18 months (March 2014: Dubai, UAE); mems: 90 agencies in more than 40 countries; Pres. MAZEN NAHAWI (UAE); Gen. Sec. JOACHIM VON BEUST (Belgium).

International Federation of the Periodical Press (FIPP): 35 New Bridge St, Blackfriars, London, WC2A 3LJ, United Kingdom; tel. (20) 7404-4169; fax (20) 7404-4179; e-mail info@fipp.com; internet www.fipp.com; f. 1925; works for the benefit of magazine publishers around the world by promoting the common editorial, cultural and economic interests of consumer and business-to-business publishers, both in print and electronic media; fosters formal and informal alliances between magazine publishers and industry suppliers; mems: 52 nat. asscns, 470 publishing cos, 180 assoc. mems and 6 individual mems; Pres. and CEO CHRIS LLEWELYN; publ. *Magazine World* (quarterly).

International Institute of Communications: 2 Printers Yard, 90A The Broadway, London, SW19 1RD, United Kingdom; tel. (20) 8417-0600; fax (20) 8417-0800; e-mail enquiries@iicom.org; internet www.iicom.org; f. 1969 (as the International Broadcast Institute) to link all working in the field of communications, including policy makers, broadcasters, industrialists and engineers; holds local, regional and international meetings; undertakes research; mems: over 1,000 corp., institutional and individual; Pres. FABIO COLASANTI; Dir-Gen. ANDREA MILLWOOD HARGRAVE; publ. *Intermedia* (5 a year).

International Maritime Radio Association (CIRM): 202 Lambeth Road, London SE1 7JW, United Kingdom; tel. (20) (20) 3411-8345; fax (20) 7587-1436; e-mail office@cirm.org; internet www.cirm.org; f. 1928 to study and develop means of improving marine radio communications and radio aids to marine navigation; mems: some 75 orgs and cos from 21 maritime nations involved in marine electronics in the areas of radio communications and navigation; Pres. MICHAEL BERGMANN; Sec.-Gen. FRANCES BASKERVILLE.

International Press Institute (IPI): Spiegelgasse 2, 1010 Vienna, Austria; tel. (1) 5129011; fax (1) 5129014; e-mail ipi@freemedia.at; internet www.freemedia.at; f. 1951 as a non-governmental org. of editors, publishers and news broadcasters supporting the principles of a free and responsible press; aims to defend press freedom; conducts research; maintains a library; holds regional meetings and an annual World Congress; mems: about 2,000 from 120 countries; Chair. GALINA SIDOROVA (Russia); Exec. Dir ALISON BETHEL MCKENZIE (USA); publs *IPI Congress Report* (annually), *World Press Freedom Review* (annually).

International Press Telecommunications Council (IPTC): 25 Southampton Bldg,London WC2A 1AL, United Kingdom; tel. (20) 3178-4922; fax (20) 7664-7878; e-mail office@iptc.org; internet www.iptc.org; f. 1965 to safeguard the telecommunications interests of the world press; acts as the news industry's formal standards body; meets three times a year and maintains three cttees and four working parties; mems: 55 news agencies, newspapers, news websites and industry vendors; Chair. VINCENT BABY; Man. Dir MICHAEL STEIDL.

Organization of Asia-Pacific News Agencies (OANA): c/o Anadolu Ajansi, Gazi Mustafa Kemal Bulvari 128/C, Tandogan, Ankara, Turkey; tel. (312) 2317000; fax (312) 2312174; e-mail oana@aa.com.tr; internet www.oananews.org; f. 1961 to promote co-operation in professional matters and mutual exchange of news, features, etc. among the news agencies of Asia and the Pacific via the Asia-Pacific News Network; 15th General Assembly: Moscow, Russia, Sept. 2013; mems: 43 news agencies in 34 countries; Pres. KEMAL ÖZTÜRK (Turkey); Dir-Gen. ALTANTSETSEG SUKHBAATAR (Mongolia).

Pacific Islands News Association (PINA): Damodar Centre, 46 Gordon St, PMB, Suva, Fiji; tel. 3303623; fax 3317055; e-mail pina@connect.com.fj; internet www.pina.com.fj; f. 1991; regional press asscn; defends freedom of information and expression, promotes professional co-operation, provides training and education; mems: media orgs in 23 countries and territories; Man. MATAI AKAUOLA.

Pasifika Media Association (PasiMA): Apia, Samoa; internet www.pacific-media.org; f. 2010; Chair. SAVEA SANO MALIFA (Samoa); Sec./Treas. JOHN WOODS (New Zealand).

Reporters sans Frontières: 47 rue Vivienne, 75002 Paris, France; tel. 1-44-83-84-84; fax 1-45-23-11-51; e-mail administration@rsf.org; internet www.rsf.org; f. 1985 to defend press freedom throughout the world; generates awareness of violations of press freedoms and supports journalists under threat or imprisoned as a result of their work; mems in 150 countries; Sec.-Gen. CHRISTOPHE DELOIRE; publs *Annual Report*, *La Lettre de Reporters sans Frontières* (6 a year).

World Association for Christian Communication (WACC): 308 Main St, Toronto, ON M4C 4X7, Canada; tel. (416) 691-1999; fax (416) 691-1997; e-mail wacc@waccglobal.org; internet www.waccglobal.org; f. 1975 to promote human dignity, justice and peace through freedom of expression and the democratization of communication; offers professional guidance on communication policies; interprets devts in and the consequences of global communication methods; works towards the empowerment of women; assists the training of Christian communicators; mems: corp. and personal mems in 120 countries, organized in 8 reg. asscns; Pres. Dr DENNIS SMITH; Gen. Sec. Rev. Dr KARIN ACHTELSTETTER (Germany); publs *Action*, *Newsletter* (10 a year), *Media Development* (quarterly), *Communication Resource*, *Media and Gender Monitor* (both occasional).

World Association of Newspapers and News Publishers (WAN-IFRA): Washingtonplatz 1, 64287 Darmstadt, Germany; tel. (6151) 7336; fax (6151) 733800; e-mail info@wan-ifra.org; internet www.wan-ifra.org; f. 2009 by merger of World Association of Newspapers (f. 1948) and IFRA (f. 1961); WAN-IFRA is the worldwide service and representative org. of newspapers and the entire news publishing industry; aims to support this industry, as well as its technology and service; mems: more than 3,000 cos in 120 countries; Pres. TOMAS BRUNEGÅRD (Sweden); CEO VINCENT PEYRÈGNE (Germany); publ. *WAN-IFRA Magazine* (every 2 months, and online).

World Catholic Association for Communication (SIGNIS): 310 rue Royale, 1210 Brussels, Belgium; tel. (2) 734-97-08; fax (2) 734-70-18; e-mail sg@signis.net; internet www.signis.net; f. 2001; brings together professionals working in radio, television, cinema, video, media education, internet and new technology; Sec.-Gen. ALVITO DE SOUZA.

Religion

Agudath Israel World Organisation: Hacherut Sq., POB 326, Jerusalem 91002, Israel; tel. (2) 5384357; fax (2) 5383634; f. 1912 to help to solve the problems facing Jewish people all over the world in the spirit of the Jewish tradition; holds World Congress (every five years) and an annual Central Council; mems: over 500,000 in 25 countries; Sec. Rabbi MOSHE GEWIRTZ; publs *Hamodia* (Jerusalem, daily, in Hebrew; New York, daily, in English; Paris, weekly, in French), *Jedion* (Hebrew, monthly), *Jewish Tribune* (London, weekly), *Jewish Observer* (New York, monthly), *Dos Yiddishe Vort* (New York, monthly), *Coalition* (New York), *Perspectives* (Toronto, monthly), *La Voz Judia* (Buenos Aires, monthly), *Jüdische Stimme* (Zürich, weekly).

All Africa Conference of Churches (AACC): Waiyaki Way, POB 14205, 00800 Westlands, Nairobi, Kenya; tel. (20) 4441483; fax (20) 4443241; e-mail secretariat@aacc-ceta.org; internet www.aacc-ceta.org; f. 1963; an organ of co-operation and continuing fellowship among Protestant, Orthodox and independent churches and Christian Councils in Africa; 10th Assembly: Kampala, Uganda, in June 2013; mems: 173 churches and affiliated Christian councils in 40 African countries; Pres. Archbishop VALENTINE MOKIWA (Tanzania); Gen. Sec. Rev. Dr ANDRÉ KARAMAGA (Rwanda); publs *ACIS/APS Bulletin*, *Tam Tam*.

Anglican and Eastern Churches Association: c/o Rev. Dr William Taylor, St John's Vicarage, 25 Ladbroke Rd, London, W11 3PD, United Kingdom; tel. (20) 7727-3439; e-mail janet.laws@btopenworld.com; internet www.aeca.org.uk; f. 1864 to advance the Christian religion by encouraging mems of the Anglican and Eastern Church to learn more about each other, to facilitate scholarly discussion and mutual regard; functions under the patronage of the Ecumenical Patriarch and the Archbishop of Canterbury; organizes an annual Pilgrimage, an annual Constantinople Lecture, a summer Festival for mems; Cttee Chair. Rev. WILLIAM TAYLOR; Sec. JANET LAWS; publ. *Koinonia* (3 a year).

Bahá'í International Community: Bahá'í World Centre, POB 155, 31001 Haifa, Israel; tel. (4) 8358394; fax (4) 8313312; e-mail news@bahai.org; internet www.bahai.org; f. 1844; promotes and applies the principles of the Bahá'í faith, i.e. the abandonment of all forms of prejudice, the equality of women and men, recognition of the oneness of religion, the elimination of extremes of poverty and wealth, the realization of universal education and recognition that true religion is in harmony with reason and the pursuit of scientific knowledge, in order to contribute to the development of a peaceful, just, and sustainable society, and the resolution of the challenges currently facing humanity; Bahá'ís undertake to strengthen the moral and spiritual character of communities, for example by conducting classes that address the development of children and channel the energies of young people, and initiating study groups that enable people of varied backgrounds to explore the application of the Bahá'í teachings to their individual and collective lives; in some communities there is an annual election of a local council to administer affairs at that level; at national level there are elected governing councils; the head of the Bahá'í faith is the Universal House of Justice, a body of nine mems elected by the 186 National Spiritual Assemblies; has more than 5m. followers, living in more than 100,000 localities; 186 national governing councils; Sec.-Gen. JOSHUA LINCOLN (USA); publs *Bahá'í World News Service* (online), *One Country* (quarterly, in 6 languages).

Baptist World Alliance: 405 North Washington St, Falls Church, VA 22046, USA; tel. (703) 790-8980; fax (703) 893-5160; e-mail bwa@bwanet.org; internet www.bwanet.org; f. 1905; aims to unite Baptists, lead in evangelism, respond to people in need, defend human rights, and promote theological reflection; mems: 37m. individuals and more than 200 Baptist unions and conventions representing about 105m. people worldwide; Pres. JOHN UPTON (USA); Gen. Sec. NEVILLE CALLAM (Jamaica); publ. *The Baptist World* (quarterly).

Caribbean Conference of Churches: POB 876, Port of Spain, Trinidad and Tobago; tel. 662-3064; fax 662-1303; e-mail trinidad-headoffice@ccc-caribe.org; internet www.ccc-caribe.org; f. 1973; governed by a General Assembly which meets every five years and appoints a 15-mem. Continuation Committee (board of management) to establish policies and direct the work of the org. between Assemblies; maintains two sub-regional offices in Antigua, Jamaica and Trinidad with responsibility for programme implementation in various territories; mems: 33 churches in 34 territories in the Dutch-, English-, French- and Spanish-speaking territories of the region; Gen. Sec. GERARD GRANADO; publ. *Ecuscope Caribbean*.

Christian Conference of Asia (CCA): c/o Payap Univ. Muang, Chiang Mai 50000, Thailand; tel. (53) 243906; fax (53) 247303; e-mail cca@cca.org.hk; internet www.cca.org.hk; f. 1957 (present name adopted 1973) to promote co-operation and joint study in matters of common concern among the churches of the region and to encourage interaction with other regional confs and the World Council of Churches; mems: 100 national churches, and 17 national councils in 21 countries; Gen. Sec. HENRIETTE HUTABARAT LEBANG (Indonesia); publs *CCA News* (quarterly), *CTC Bulletin* (occasional).

Conference of European Churches (CEC): POB 2100, 150 route de Ferney, 1211 Geneva 2, Switzerland; tel. 227916111; fax 227916227; e-mail cec@cec-kek.org; internet www.ceceurope.org; f. 1959 as a regional ecumenical org. for Europe and a meeting-place for European churches, including mems and non-mems of the World Council of Churches; holds a General Assembly every five years; mems: 115 Protestant, Anglican, Orthodox and Old Catholic churches in all European countries; Gen. Sec. Rev. Dr GUY LIAGRE; publs *Monitor* (quarterly), CEC communiqués, reports.

Friends World Committee for Consultation: 173 Euston Rd, London, NW1 2AX, United Kingdom; tel. (20) 7663-1199; fax (20) 7663-1189; e-mail world@friendsworldoffice.org; internet www.fwccworld.org; f. 1937 to encourage and strengthen the spiritual life within the Religious Society of Friends (Quakers); to help Friends to a better understanding of their vocation in the world; and to promote consultation among Friends of all countries; representation at the UN as a non-governmental org. with general consultative status; mems: appointed representatives and individuals from 70 countries; Gen. Sec. GRETCHEN CASTLE; publs *Friends World News* (2 a year), *Calendar of Yearly Meetings* (annually), *Quakers around the World* (handbook).

Global Christian Forum: POB 306, 1290 Versoix, Switzerland; tel. 227554546; fax 227550108; e-mail gcforum@sunrise.ch; internet www.globalchristianforum.org; f. 1998 by the World Council of Churches, with an autonomous Continuation Committee, to provide opportunities for representatives of all the main Christian traditions to meet, foster mutual respect and address common challenges; a series of regional meetings was held during 2004–07 and the first Global Forum was convened in Nov. 2007 in Limuru, near Nairobi, Kenya; the second Forum was held in Manado, Indonesia, in Oct. 2011; Sec.-Gen. Rev. LARRY MILLER.

International Association for Religious Freedom (IARF): Essex Hall, 1-6 Essex St, London, WC2R 3HY, United Kingdom; e-mail hq@iarf.net; internet www.iarf.net; f. 1900 as a world community of religions, subscribing to the principle of openness and upholding the UN's Universal Declaration on freedom of religion or belief; conducts religious freedom programmes, focusing on inter-religious harmony; holds regional confs and a triennial congress; mems: 73 groups in 26 countries; Pres. MITSUO MIYAKE (Japan); Treas. JEFFREY TEAGLE (United Kingdom).

International Association of Buddhist Studies (IABS): c/o Prof. T. J. F. Tillemans, Section des langues et civilisations orientales, Université de Lausanne, 1015 Lausanne, Switzerland; fax 793561766; e-mail iabs.treasurer@unil.ch; internet www.iabsinfo.net; f. 1976; supports studies of Buddhist religion, philosophy and literature; holds international conf. every three or four years (17th Congress: Vienna, Austria, Aug. 2014); Pres. CRISTINA SCHERRER-SCHAUB (France); Gen. Sec. ULRICH PAGEL (Germany); publ. *Journal* (2 a year).

International Council of Christians and Jews (ICCJ): Martin Buber House, POB 1129, 64629 Heppenheim, Germany; tel. (6252) 6896810; fax (6252) 68331; e-mail info@iccj.org; internet www.iccj.org; f. 1947 to promote mutual respect and co-operation; holds annual international colloquium, seminars, meetings for young people and for women; maintains a forum for Jewish–Christian–Muslim relations; mems: 38 national councils worldwide; Pres. Dr DEBORAH WEISSMAN; publs *ICCJ History*, *ICCJ Brochure*, conf. documents.

International Council of Jewish Women: 5655 Silver Creek Valley Rd, 480 San Jose, CA 95138, USA; tel. (408) 274-8020; fax (408) 274-0807; e-mail president@icjw.org; internet www.icjw.org; f. 1912 to promote friendly relations and understanding among Jewish women throughout the world; campaigns for human and women's rights, exchanges information on community welfare activities, promotes volunteer leadership, sponsors field work in social welfare, co-sponsors the International Jewish Women's Human Rights Watch and fosters Jewish education; mems: over 2m. in 52 orgs across 47 countries; Pres. SHARON SCOTT GUSTAFSON;

Sec. VERA KRONENBERG; publs *Newsletter*, *Links around the World* (2 a year, English and Spanish), *International Jewish Women's Human Rights Watch* (2 a year).

International Fellowship of Reconciliation (IFOR): Spoorstraat 38, 1815 BK Alkmaar, Netherlands; tel. (72) 5123014; fax (72) 5151102; e-mail office@ifor.org; internet www.ifor.org; f. 1919; international, spiritually based movement committed to active non-violence as a way of life and as a means of building a culture of peace and non-violence; maintains over 81 branches, affiliates and groups in more than 48 countries; Pres. HANS ULRICH GERBER (Netherlands); Int. Co-ordinator FRANCESCO CANDELARI; publs *IFOR in Action* (quarterly), *Patterns in Reconciliation* (2 a year), *International Reconciliation* (3–4 times a year), *Cross the Lines* (3 a year, in Arabic, English, French, Russian and Spanish), occasional paper series.

International Humanist and Ethical Union (IHEU): 39 Moreland St, London, EC1V 8BB, United Kingdom; tel. (20) 7490-8468; fax (20) 7636-4797; e-mail office-iheu@iheu.org; internet www.iheu.org; f. 1952 to bring into asscn all those interested in promoting ethical and scientific humanism and human rights; mems: nat. orgs and individuals in 40 countries; Pres. SONJA EGGERICKX; Int. Dir BABU GOGINENI; publ. *International Humanist News* (quarterly).

Latin American Council of Churches (Consejo Latinoamericano de Iglesias—CLAI): Casilla 17-08-8522, Calle Inglaterra N.32–113 y Mariana de Jesús, Quito, Ecuador; tel. (2) 250-4377; fax (2) 256-8373; e-mail nilton@claiweb.org; internet www.claiweb.org; f. 1982; mems: some 150 churches in 21 countries; Pres. Pastor FELIPE ADOLF (Argentina); Gen. Sec. Rev. NILTON GUISE (Brazil); publs *Nuevo Siglo* (monthly, in Spanish), *Latin American Ecumenical News* (quarterly), *Signos de Vida* (quarterly), other newsletters.

Latin American Episcopal Council (Consejo Episcopal Latinoamericano—CELAM): Carrera 5A 118–31, Apartado Aéreo 51086, Bogotá, Colombia; tel. (1) 5879710; fax (1) 5879117; e-mail celam@celam.org; internet www.celam.org; f. 1955 to co-ordinate Church activities in and with the Latin American and the Caribbean Catholic Bishops' Conferences; mems: 22 Episcopal Conferences of Central and South America and the Caribbean; Pres. Archbishop CARLOS AGUIAR RETES (Mexico); publ. *Boletín* (6 a year).

Lutheran World Federation: 150 route de Ferney, POB 2100, 1211 Geneva 2, Switzerland; tel. 227916111; fax 227916630; e-mail info@lutheranworld.org; internet www.lutheranworld.org; f. 1947; provides inter-church aid and relief work in various areas of the globe; gives service to refugees, including resettlement; carries out theological research, advocates for human rights, organizes confs and exchanges; grants scholarship aid in various fields of church life; conducts inter-confessional dialogue and conversation with the Anglican, Baptist, Methodist, Orthodox, Reformed, Roman Catholic and Seventh-day Adventist churches; mems: 70.3m. worldwide; groups 142 Lutheran churches in 79 countries; Pres. Rev. MUNIB A. YOUNAN (Jordan); Gen. Sec. Rev. MARTIN JUNGE (Chile); publs *Lutheran World Information* (English and German, daily e-mail news service, online and monthly print edition), *LWF Annual Report*, *LWF Documentation* (in English and German).

Middle East Council of Churches: POB 5376, Beirut, Lebanon; tel. (1) 344896; fax (1) 344894; e-mail mecc@cyberia.net.lb; internet www.mecc.org; f. 1974; mems: 28 churches; Pres Catholicos ARAM I, Patriarch THEOPHILOS III, Archbishop BOULOS MATAR, Rev. Dr SAFWAT AL-BAYADI; Gen. Sec. GUIRGIS IBRAHIM SALEH; publs *MECC News Report* (monthly), *Al Montada News Bulletin* (quarterly, in Arabic), *Courrier oecuménique du Moyen-Orient* (quarterly), *MECC Perspectives* (3 a year).

Muslim World League (MWL) (Rabitat al-Alam al-Islami): POB 537, Makkah, Saudi Arabia; tel. (2) 5600919; fax (2) 5601319; e-mail info@themwl.org; internet www.themwl.org; f. 1962; aims to advance Islamic unity and solidarity, and to promote world peace and respect for human rights; provides financial assistance for education, medical care and relief work; has 45 offices throughout the world; Sec.-Gen. Prof. Dr ABDULLAH BIN ABDUL MOHSIN AL-TURKI; publs *Al-Aalam al Islami* (weekly, Arabic), *Dawat al-Haq* (monthly, Arabic), *Muslim World League Journal* (monthly, English), *Muslim World League Journal* (quarterly, Arabic).

Opus Dei (Prelature of the Holy Cross and Opus Dei): Viale Bruno Buozzi 73, 00197 Rome, Italy; tel. (06) 808961; e-mail info@opusdei.org; internet www.opusdei.org; f. 1928 by St Josemaría Escrivá de Balaguer to spread, at every level of society, an increased awareness of the universal call to sanctity and apostolate in the exercise of one's work; mems: 87,564 Catholic laypeople and 1,996 priests; Prelate Most Rev. JAVIER ECHEVARRÍA; publ. *Romana (Bulletin of the Prelature)* (2 a year).

Pacific Conference of Churches: POB 208, 4 Thurston St, Suva, Fiji; tel. 3311277; fax 3303205; e-mail pacific@pcc.org.fj; internet www.pcc.org.fj; f. 1961; organizes assembly every five years, as well as regular workshops, meetings and training seminars throughout the region; mems: 36 churches and councils; Programs Co-ordinator AISAKE CASIMIRA.

Pax Romana International Catholic Movement for Intellectual and Cultural Affairs (ICMICA); and International Movement of Catholic Students (IMCS): 3 rue de Varembé, 4th Floor, POB 161, 1211 Geneva 20, Switzerland; tel. 228230707; fax 228230708; e-mail international_secretariat@paxromana.org; internet www.icmica-miic.org; f. 1921 (IMCS), 1947 (ICMICA), to encourage in mems an awareness of their responsibilities as people and Christians in the student and intellectual milieux; to promote contacts between students and graduates throughout the world and co-ordinate the contribution of Catholic intellectual circles to international life; mems: 80 student and 60 intellectual orgs in 80 countries; Pres. JEAN N. LOKENGA (Democratic Repub. of Congo); Sec-Gen. PAUL ORTEGA.

Salvation Army: International HQ, 101 Queen Victoria St, London, EC4V 4EH, United Kingdom; tel. (20) 7332-0101; fax (20) 7236-4981; e-mail ihq-website@salvationarmy.org; internet www.salvationarmy.org; f. 1865 to spread the Christian gospel and relieve poverty; emphasis for mems is placed on the need for personal Christian discipleship; to enhance the effectiveness of its evangelism and non-discriminatory practical ministry it has adopted a quasi-military form of org; social, medical, educational and emergency relief activities are also performed in the 124 countries where the Army operates; Gen. ANDRÉ COX; Chief of Staff Commissioner WILLIAM ROBERTS; publs *All the World*, *Revive*, *The Officer*, *The Yearbook of the Salvation Army*, *Words of Life*, various other publs, including the Army's *Handbook of Doctrine*, are published under its Salvation Books label.

Theosophical Society: Adyar, Chennai 600 020, India; tel. (44) 24912474; fax (44) 4902706; e-mail intl.hq@ts-adyar.org; internet www.ts-adyar.org; f. 1875; aims at universal brotherhood, without distinction of race, creed, sex, caste or colour; study of comparative religion, philosophy and science; investigation of unexplained laws of nature and powers latent in man; mems: 32,000 in 70 countries; Pres. RADHA S. BURNIER; Int. Sec. MARY ANDERSON; publs *The Theosophist* (monthly), *Adyar News Letter* (quarterly), *Wake Up India* (quarterly).

United Bible Societies: World Service Centre, Reading Bridge House, Reading, RG1 8PJ, United Kingdom; tel. (118) 950-0200; fax (118) 950-0857; e-mail comms@ubs-wsc.org; internet www.unitedbiblesocieties.org; f. 1946; co-ordinates the translation, production and distribution of the Bible by Bible Societies worldwide; works with national Bible Societies to develop religious programmes; mems: 146 Bible Societies in more than 200 countries; Pres. Rev. Dr Robert CUNVILLE (India); Gen. Sec. MICHAEL PERREAU (United Kingdom); publs *The Bible Translator* (quarterly), *Publishing World* (3 a year), *Prayer Booklet* (annually).

Watch Tower Bible and Tract Society: 25 Columbia Heights, Brooklyn, NY 11201–2483, USA; tel. (718) 560-5000; internet www.jw.org; f. 1881; 98 branches; serves as legal agency for Jehovah's Witnesses; publ. *The Watchtower* (in 188 languages).

World Christian Life Community: Borgo Santo Spirito 4, 00193 Rome, Italy; tel. (06) 6869844; fax (06) 68132497; e-mail exsec@cvx-clc.net; internet www.cvx-clc.net; f. 1953 as World Federation of the Sodalities of our Lady (first group f. 1563) as a lay organization based on the teachings of Ignatius Loyola, to integrate Christian faith and daily living; mems: groups in 60 countries representing about 25,000 individuals; Pres. MAURICIO LOPEZ; Exec. Sec. FRANKLIN IBAÑEZ; publ. *Progressio* (in English, French and Spanish).

World Communion of Reformed Churches: Knochenhauerstr. 42, 30159 Hannover, Germany; tel. (511) 8973-8310; fax (511) 8973-8311; e-mail wcrc@wcrc.eu; internet wcrc.ch; f. 2010 by merger of World Alliance of Reformed Churches and the Reformed Ecumenical Council; mems: 216 churches in 108 countries; Pres. JERRY PILLAY (South Africa); Gen. Sec. Rev. Dr SETRI NYOMI (Ghana); publ. *Reformed World* (quarterly).

World Congress of Faiths: London Inter Faith Centre, 125 Salusbury Rd, London, NW6 6RG, United Kingdom; tel. (20) 8852-8377; fax (20) 8604-3052; e-mail enquiries@worldfaiths.org; internet www.worldfaiths.org; f. 1936 to promote a spirit of fellowship among mankind through an understanding of one another's religions, to bring together people of all nationalities, backgrounds and creeds in mutual respect and tolerance, to encourage the study and understanding of issues arising out of multi-faith socs, and to promote welfare and peace; sponsors lectures, confs, retreats, etc; works with other interfaith orgs; mems: about 400; Pres. Rev MARCUS BRAYBROOKE; Chair. Rev. ALAN RACE; publs *Interreligious Insight* (quarterly), *One Family*.

World Evangelical Alliance: Church St. Station, POB 3402, NY 10008-3402, USA; tel. (212) 233-3046; fax (646) 957-9218; e-mail wea@worldea.org; internet www.worldea.org; f. 1951 as World Evangelical Fellowship, on reorganization of World Evangelical Alliance (f. 1846), reverted to original name Jan. 2002; an international grouping of national and regional bodies of evangelical Christians; encourages the organization of national fellowships and assists national mems in planning their activities; mems: 7 reg.

asscns and 128 nat. evangelical asscns; CEO and Sec.-Gen. GEOFF TUNNICLIFFE; publs *Evangelical World* (monthly), *Evangelical Review of Theology* (quarterly).

World Fellowship of Buddhists (WFB): 616 Benjasiri Pk, Soi Medhinivet off Soi Sukhumvit 24, Bangkok 10110, Thailand; tel. (2) 661-1284-7; fax (2) 661-0555; e-mail webmaster@wfb-hq.org; internet www.wfbhq.org; f. 1950 to promote strict observance and practice of the teachings of the Buddha; holds General Conference every two years; 181 regional centres in 37 countries; Pres. PHAN WANNAMETHEE; Sec.-Gen. PHALLOP THAIARRY; publs *WFB Review* (quarterly), *WFB Newsletter* (monthly), documents, booklets.

World Hindu Federation: POB 20418, Kathmandu, Nepal; tel. (1) 4370322; fax (1) 4378551; e-mail whfintl@wlink.com.np; f. 1981 to promote and preserve Hindu philosophy and culture and to protect the rights of Hindus, particularly the right to worship; executive board meets annually; mems: in 45 countries and territories; Pres. HEM BAHADUR KARKI; Sec.-Gen. Dr BINOD RAJBHANDARI (Nepal); publ. *Vishwa Hindu* (monthly).

World Jewish Congress: 501 Madison Ave, New York, NY 10022, USA; tel. (212) 755-5770; fax (212) 755-5883; e-mail info@worldjewishcongress.org; internet www.worldjewishcongress.org; f. 1936 as a voluntary asscn of representative Jewish communities and orgs throughout the world; aims to foster the unity of the Jewish people and ensure the continuity and devt of their heritage; mems: Jewish communities in 100 countries; Pres. RONALD LAUDER (USA); publs *Dispatches*, *Jerusalem Review*, regular updates, policy studies.

World Methodist Council: International Headquarters, POB 518, Lake Junaluska, NC 28745, USA; tel. (828) 456-9432; fax (828) 456-9433; e-mail info@worldmethodistcouncil.org; internet www.worldmethodistcouncil.org; f. 1881 to deepen the fellowship of the Methodist peoples, encourage evangelism, foster Methodist participation in the ecumenical movement and promote the unity of Methodist witness and service; mems: 76 churches in 132 countries, comprising 38m. individuals; Gen. Sec. IVAN M. ABRAHAMS (USA); publ. *World Parish* (quarterly).

World Student Christian Federation (WSCF): Ecumenical Centre, POB 2100, 1211 Geneva 2, Switzerland; tel. 227916358; fax 227916152; e-mail wscf@wscf.ch; internet www.wscfglobal.org; f. 1895; aims to proclaim Jesus Christ as Lord and Saviour in the academic community, and to present students with the claims of the Christian faith over their whole life; has consultative status with the UN and advisory status at the World Council of Churches; holds General Assembly every four years; mems: more than 100 nat. Student Christian Movements, and 6 reg. officers; Chair. HORACIO MESONES (Uruguay); Gen. Sec. CHRISTINE HOUSEL (USA).

World Union for Progressive Judaism: 13 King David St, Jerusalem 94101, Israel; tel. (2) 6203447; fax (2) 6203525; e-mail wupjis@wupj.org.il; internet www.wupj.org; f. 1926; promotes and co-ordinates efforts of Reform, Liberal, Progressive and Reconstructionist congregations throughout the world; supports new congregations; assigns and employs rabbis; sponsors seminaries and schools; organizes international conf; maintains a youth section; mems: orgs and individuals in around 45 countries; Chair. MICHAEL GRABINER; Sec. Dr PHILIP BLISS; publs *News Updates*, *International Conference Reports*, *European Judaism*.

World Union of Catholic Women's Organisations: 76 rue des Saints-Pères, 75007 Paris, France; tel. 1-45-44-27-65; e-mail wucwoparis@wanadoo.fr; internet www.wucwo.org; f. 1910 to promote and co-ordinate the contribution of Catholic women in international life, in social, civic, cultural and religious matters; General Assembly held every four or five years (2014: Fátima, Portugal, in Oct.); mems: some 100 orgs representing 5m. women; Pres. MARIA GIOVANNA RUGGIERI (Italy); Sec.-Gen. MARIA LIA ZERVINO; publ. *Women's Voice* (quarterly, in 4 languages).

Science

Association for Tropical Biology and Conservation: e-mail andresen@cieco.unam.mx; internet www.tropicalbiology.org; f. 1963 as the Association for Tropical Biology (present name adopted in 2002), to promote research and to foster exchange of ideas among biologists working in tropical environments; holds annual Congress (July 2014: Cairns, Australia); Exec. Dir Dr ROBIN L. CHAZDON (USA); publ. *Biotropica* (2 a year).

Association of Academies and Societies of Sciences in Asia (AASA): 7-1, Gumi-dong, Bundang-gu, Seongnam 463-808, Republic of Korea; tel. (31) 710-4611; fax (31) 726-7909; e-mail aasa2@kast.or.kr; internet www.aasa-net.org; f. 2012 by merger of the Assoc. of Academies of Sciences in Asia (f. 1993) and the Federation of Asian Scientific Academies and Societies (f. 1984); provides a forum for the exchange of information and advice on issues related to science and technology research and the analysis of the role of technology in socio-economic devt; mems: 26 academies; Pres. PARK WON-HOON (Republic of Korea); Sec.-Gen. M. QASIM KHAN (Pakistan).

Association of Geoscientists for International Development (AGID): c/o Geological Survey of Bangladesh, Segunbagicha, Dhaka 1000, Bangladesh; tel. (2) 8358144; e-mail afia@dhaka.agni.com; internet www.bgs.ac.uk/agid; f. 1974 to encourage communication and the exchange of knowledge between those interested in the application of the geosciences to international devt; contributes to the funding of geoscience devt projects; provides postgraduate scholarships; mems: 500 individual and institutional mems in 70 countries; Pres. AFIA AKHTAR (Bangladesh); Sec. Dr A. J. REEDMAN (United Kingdom); publs *Geoscience and Development* (annually), *Geoscience Newsletter* (quarterly).

CIESM—The Mediterranean Science Commission (Commission internationale pour l'exploration scientifique de la mer Méditerranée): Villa Girasole, 16 blvd de Suisse, 98000 Monaco; tel. 93-30-38-79; fax 92-16-11-95; e-mail contact@ciesm.org; internet www.ciesm.org; f. 1919 for scientific exploration of the Mediterranean Sea; organizes multilateral research investigations, workshops, congresses; includes six permanent scientific cttees; mems: 22 countries, 4,300 scientists; Pres. HSH Prince ALBERT II of MONACO; Dir-Gen. Prof. FREDERIC BRIAND; publs White Papers, Congress reports.

Council for the International Congress of Entomology: c/o CSIRO Entomology, Private Bag No 5, PO Wembley, WA 6913, Australia; tel. (8) 9339-0762; e-mail james.ridsdill-smith@csiro.au; internet www.ice2016orlando.org; f. 1910 to act as a link between quadrennial congresses and to arrange the venue for each congress held every four years (2012: Daegou, Republic of Korea); the Council is also the entomology section of the International Union of Biological Sciences; Chair. Dr HARI SHARMA (India); Sec. JAMES RIDSDILL-SMITH (Australia).

European Association of Geoscientists and Engineers (EAGE): De Molen 42, POB 59, 3990 DB Houten, Netherlands; tel. (30) 6354055; fax (30) 6343524; e-mail eage@eage.org; internet www.eage.org; f. 1951; aims to promote the applications of geoscience and related subjects and to foster co-operation between those working or studying in the fields; organizes confs, workshops, education programmes and exhibitions; seeks global co-operation with orgs with similar objectives; mems: approx. 17,000 worldwide; Pres. GLADYS GONZALEZ; publs *Geophysical Prospecting* (6 a year), *First Break* (monthly), *Petroleum Geoscience* (quarterly).

European Atomic Forum (FORATOM): 56 ave des Arts, 1000 Brussels, Belgium; tel. (2) 502-45-95; fax (2) 502-39-02; e-mail foratom@foratom.org; internet www.foratom.org; f. 1960; promotes the peaceful use of nuclear energy; provides information on nuclear energy issues to the European Union (EU), the media and the public; represents the nuclear energy industry within the EU institutions; holds periodical confs; mems: nat. nuclear asscns in 16 countries; Pres. KEITH PARKER; Dir-Gen. JEAN-POL PONCELET.

European Molecular Biology Organization (EMBO): Meyerhofstr. 1, Postfach 1022.40, 69012 Heidelberg, Germany; tel. (6221) 8891-0; fax (6221) 8891-200; e-mail embo@embo.org; internet www.embo.org; f. 1964 to promote collaboration in the field of molecular biology and to establish fellowships for training and research; has established the European Molecular Biology Laboratory where a majority of the disciplines comprising the subject are represented; mems: approx. 1,500 elected mems in Europe and 100 assoc. mems worldwide; Dir MARIA LEPTIN; publs *Facts and Figures*, *The EMBO Journal* (24 a year), *EMBO Reports* (monthly), *EMBO Molecular Medicine*, *Molecular Systems Biology*, *EMBO Encounters*.

European Organization for Nuclear Research (CERN): 1211 Geneva 23, Switzerland; tel. 227678484; fax 227677676; e-mail press.office@cern.ch; internet www.cern.ch; f. 1954 to provide for collaboration among European states in nuclear research of a pure scientific and fundamental character, for peaceful purposes only; major experimental facilities: Proton Synchrotron (of 25–28 GeV), Super Proton Synchrotron (of 450 GeV), and Large Hadron Collider (of 14 TeV); in July 2012 preliminary results of the Compact Muon Solenoid (CMS) and ATLAS experiments indicated the discovery of the hitherto elusive Higgs particle; mems: 21 countries; observers: India, Japan, Russia, Turkey, USA, European Commission, UNESCO; Dir-Gen. ROLF-DIETER HEUER; publs *CERN Courier* (monthly), *Annual Report*, *Scientific Reports*.

European-Mediterranean Seismological Centre (EMSC): c/o CEA, Bât. BARD 1, Centre DAM, Ile de France, Bruyères le Châtel, 91297 Arpajon Cedex, France; fax 1-69-26-70-00; e-mail contact@emsc-csem.org; internet www.emsc-csem.org; f. 1976 for rapid determination of seismic hypocentres in the region; maintains database; mems: institutions in 45 countries; Pres. CHRIS BROWITT (United Kingdom); Sec.-Gen. RÉMY BOSSU (France); publ. *Newsletter* (2 a year).

Federation of European Biochemical Societies: c/o Dept of Immunology, The Weizmann Institute of Science, POB 26, Rehovot

76100, Israel; tel. (8) 9344019; fax (8) 9465264; e-mail febs@weizmann.ac.il; internet www.febs.org; f. 1964 to promote the science of biochemistry through meetings of European biochemists, advanced courses and the provision of fellowships; mems: approx. 40,000 in 36 socs; Chair. MIGUEL ANGEL DE LA ROSA (Spain); Sec.-Gen. ISRAEL PECHT (Israel); publs *The FEBS Journal*, *FEBS Open Bio*, *FEBS Letters*, *Molecular Oncology*.

Institute of General Semantics: 72-11 Austin St, 233 Forest Hills, NY 11375, USA; tel. ((212) 729-7973; fax (718) 793-2527; internet www.generalsemantics.org; f. 1943 as the International Society for General Semantics to advance knowledge of and inquiry into non-Aristotelian systems and general semantics; merged with Institute of General Semantics (f. 1938) in 2004; mems: approx. 700 (100 int.); Pres. MARTIN H. LEVINSON (USA); Sec. VANESSA BIARD-SCHAEFFER.

Interamerican Network of Academies of Sciences: Calle Cipreses s/n, Col. San Andrés Totoltepec, Tlalpan, 14400 Mexico City, DF, Mexico; tel. (55) 5849-4905; fax (55) 5849-5112; e-mail ianas@ianas.org; internet www.ianas.org; f. 2004 as a regional network of the Academies of the Sciences; aims to build and assist national scientific capacities through shared research and technical knowledge; provides a forum for co-operation and decision-making for the scientific communities of the region; mems: 18 nat. and reg. asscns; Co-Chair. JUAN PEDRO LACLETTE, MICHAEL T. CLEGG; publs. scientific research reports.

Intergovernmental Oceanographic Commission: UNESCO, 1 rue Miollis, 75732 Paris Cedex 15, France; tel. 1-45-68-39-84; fax 1-45-68-58-10; e-mail ioc.secretariat@unesco.org; internet ioc-unesco.org; f. 1960 to promote scientific investigation of the nature and resources of the oceans through the concerted action of its mems; mems: 129 govts; Chair. SANG-KYUNG BYUN (Korea); Exec. Sec. WENDY WATSON-WRIGHT; publs *IOC Technical Series* (irregular), IOC *Manuals* and *Guides* (irregular), *IOC Workshop Reports* (irregular) and *IOC Training Course Reports* (irregular), annual reports.

International Academy of Astronautics (IAA): 6 rue Galilee, POB 1268–16, 75766 Paris Cedex 16, France; tel. 1-47-23-82-15; fax 1-47-23-82-16; e-mail sgeneral@iaamail.org; internet iaaweb.org; f. 1960; fosters the devt of astronautics for peaceful purposes, holds scientific meetings and makes scientific studies, reports, awards and book awards; maintains 19 scientific cttees and a multilingual terminology database (20 languages); mems: in some 65 countries; Pres. Dr MADHAVAN G. NAIR (India); Sec.-Gen. Dr JEAN-MICHEL CONTANT (France); publ. *Acta Astronautica* (monthly).

International Association for Biologicals (IABS): 9 route des Jeunes, 1227 Carouge-Geneva Switzerland; tel. 223011036; fax 223011037; e-mail iabs@iabs.org; internet www.iabs.org; f. 1955 to connect producers and controllers of immunological products (sera, vaccines, etc.), for the study and devt of methods of standardization; supports international orgs in their efforts to solve problems of standardization; mems: approx 250 mems in some 50 countries; Pres. JOHN PETRICCIANI (USA); Sec. DANIEL GAUDRY (France); publs *Newsletter* (quarterly), *Biologicals* (6 a year).

International Association for Earthquake Engineering: Kenchiku-kaikan Bldg, 4th Floor, 5-26-20, Shiba, Minato-ku, Tokyo 108-0014, Japan; tel. (3) 3453-1281; fax (3) 5730-2830; e-mail secretary@iaee.or.jp; internet www.iaee.or.jp; f. 1963 to promote international co-operation among scientists and engineers in the field of earthquake engineering through exchange of knowledge, ideas and results of research and practical experience; mems: national delegates from 58 countries; Pres. Dr. SUDHIR K. JAIN (India); Sec.-Gen. MANABU YOSHIMURA (Japan).

International Association for Ecology (INTECOL): c/o College of Forest Science, Department of Forest Resources, Kookmin University, Songbuk-gu, Seoul 136-702, Republic of Korea; tel. (10) 3785-4814; fax (2) 910-4809; e-mail kimeuns@kookmin.ac.kr; internet www.intecol.net; f. 1967 to provide opportunities for communication among ecologists worldwide; to co-operate with orgs and individuals having related aims and interests; to encourage studies in the different fields of ecology; affiliated to the International Union of Biological Sciences; mems: 35 nat. and int. ecological socs, and 2,000 individuals; Pres. ALAN COVICH (USA); Sec.-Gen. EUN-SHIK KIM (Republic of Korea).

International Association for Mathematical Geology (IAMG): 5868 Westheimer Rd. Suite 537, Houston, TX 77057, USA; tel. (832) 380-8833; e-mail support@iamgmembers.org; internet www.iamg.org; f. 1968 for the preparation and elaboration of mathematical models of geological processes; the introduction of mathematical methods in geological sciences and technology; assistance in the devt of mathematical investigation in geological sciences; the organization of international collaboration in mathematical geology through various forums and publs; educational programmes for mathematical geology; affiliated to the International Union of Geological Sciences; mems: c. 750; Pres. QIUMING CHENG (Canada/People's Republic of China); Sec.-Gen. FRITS AGTERBERG (Canada); publs *Mathematical Geosciences*, *Computers and Geosciences* (10 a year), *Natural Resources Research* (quarterly), *Newsletter* (2 a year).

International Association for Mathematics and Computers in Simulation: c/o Free University of Brussels, 50 ave F. D. Roosevelt, 1050 Brussels, Belgium; e-mail emund@ulb.ac.be; internet metronu.ulb.ac.be/imacs-online.html; f. 1955 (as International Association for Analogue Computation, name changed as above 1976) to; aims to further the study of mathematical tools and computer software and hardware, analogue, digital or hybrid computers for simulation of soft or hard systems; regular confs and events are sponsored by some 25 Technical Cttees; holds a General Conference every three or four years (2013:; mems: 1,100 and 27 assoc. mems; Pres. ROSA MARIA SPITALERI (Italy); Gen. Sec. ERNEST MUND (Belgium).

International Association for Plant Taxonomy (IAPT): Institute of Botany, Slovak Academy of Sciences, 9 Dubravska cesta, 845-23 Bratislava, Slovakia; tel. (2) 59426-151; fax (2) 59426-150; e-mail office@iapt-taxon.org; internet www.iapt-taxon.org; f. 1950 to promote the devt of plant taxonomy and encourage contacts between people and institutes interested in this work; maintains the International Bureau for Plant Taxonomy and Nomenclature; affiliated to the International Union of Biological Sciences; mems: institutes and individuals in 85 countries; Pres. VICKI FUNK; Sec-Gen. KAROL MARHOLD; publs *Taxon* (quarterly), *Regnum vegetabile* (irregular).

International Association for the Physical Sciences of the Oceans (IAPSO): Johan Rodhe, POB 460, 40530 Göteborg, Sweden; e-mail johan.rodhe@gu.se; internet iapso.iugg.org; f. 1919 to promote the study of scientific problems relating to the oceans and interactions occurring at its boundaries, chiefly in so far as such study may be carried out by the aid of mathematics, physics and chemistry; to initiate, facilitate and co-ordinate oceanic research; and to provide for discussion, comparison and publication; affiliated to the International Union of Geodesy and Geophysics; mems: 65 states; Pres. Dr EUGENE MOROZOV; Sec.-Gen. Prof JOHAN RODHE (Sweden).

International Association for the Plant Protection Sciences (IAPPS): c/o Dept. of Entomology, University of Nebraska, Lincoln, NE 68583-0816, USA; tel. (402) 472-6011; fax (402) 472-4687; internet www.plantprotection.org; f. 1999 to address international crop protection issues; promotes an integrated approach to plant protection and the devt and implementation of ecologically sustainable plant protection practices; organizes an International Plant Protection Congress every four years (2015: Berlin, Germany, in Aug.); Sec.-Gen. Dr E. A. HEINRICHS.

International Association of Botanic Gardens (IABG): c/o Prof. J. E. Hernández-Bermejo, Córdoba Botanical Garden, Linnaeus Av. 14004 Córdoba, Spain; tel. (957) 203154; fax (957) 295333; e-mail jardinbotcord@retemail.es; internet www.bgci.org/; f. 1954 to promote co-operation between scientific collections of living plants, including the exchange of information and specimens; to promote the study of the taxonomy of cultivated plants; and to encourage the conservation of rare plants and their habitats; affiliated to the International Union of Biological Sciences; Pres. Prof. HE SHANAN (People's Republic of China); Sec. Prof. J. ESTEBAN HERNÁNDEZ-BERMEJO (Spain).

International Association of Geodesy: Deutsches Geodaetisches Forschungsinstitut (DGFI), Alfons-Goppel-Str. 11, 80539 Munich, Germany; tel. (89) 23031-1107; fax (89) 23031-1240; e-mail iag@dgfi.badw.de; internet www.iag-aig.org; f. 1922 to promote the study of all scientific problems of geodesy and encourage geodetic research; to promote and co-ordinate international co-operation in this field; to publish results; affiliated to the International Union of Geodesy and Geophysics; mems: national cttees in 65 countries; Pres. CHRIS RIZOS (Australia); Sec.-Gen. HERMANN DREWES (Germany); publs *Journal of Geodesy*, *Travaux de l'AIG*.

International Association of Geomagnetism and Aeronomy (IAGA): c/o Mioara Mandea, 2, Place Maurice Quentin, 75001 Paris, France; tel. 1-44-76-79-48; fax 1-57-27-84-82; e-mail iaga_sg@gfz-potsdam.de; internet www.iugg.org/IAGA; f. 1919 for the study of questions relating to geomagnetism and aeronomy and the encouragement of research; holds General and Scientific Assemblies every two years; affiliated to the International Union of Geodesy and Geophysics (IUGG); mems: countries that adhere to the IUGG; Pres. KATHRYN WHALER (United Kingdom); Sec.-Gen. MIOARA MANDEA (France); publs *IAGA Reporter Reviews*, *IAGA Newsletter*, *IAGA Guides*.

International Association of Hydrological Sciences: Agrocampus Ouest, 65 rue de Saint-Brieuc, 35042 Rennes, France; tel. 2-23-48-55-58; e-mail cudennec@agrocampus-ouest.fr; internet iahs.info; f. 1922 to promote co-operation in the study of hydrology and water resources; Pres. Prof. HUBERT SAVENIJE (Netherlands); Sec.-Gen. Prof. CHRISTOPHE CUDENNEC (France).

International Association of Meteorology and Atmospheric Sciences (IAMAS): Institut für Physik der Atmosphäre (IPA), Deutsches Zentrum für Luft und Raumfahrt, DLR-Oberpfaffenhofen, 82234 Wessling, Germany; tel. (8153) 282570; fax (8153) 281841; e-mail Hans.Volkert@dlr.de; internet www.iamas.org; f. 1919; maintains permanent commissions on atmospheric ozone, radiation, atmospheric chemistry and global pollution, dynamic meteorology, polar meteorology, clouds and precipitation, climate, atmospheric electricity, planetary atmospheres and their evolution, and meteorology of the upper atmosphere; holds general assemblies every four years, special assemblies between general assemblies; affiliated to the International Union of Geodesy and Geophysics; Pres. Dr ATHENA COUSTENIS (France); Sec.-Gen. Dr HANS VOLKERT (Germany).

International Association of Sedimentologists: c/o Prof. Vincenzo Pascucci, Dipartimento di Scienze della Natura e del Territorio, Università di Sassari, Via Piandanna 4, 07100 Sassari, Italy; tel. (079) 228685; fax (079) 233600; e-mail pascucci@uniss.it; internet www.sedimentologists.org; f. 1952; affiliated to the International Union of Geological Sciences; mems: 2,200; Pres. POPPE DE BOER (Netherlands); Gen. Sec. VINCENZO PASCUCCI (Italy); publ. *Sedimentology* (every 2 months).

International Association of Volcanology and Chemistry of the Earth's Interior (IAVCEI): Institute of Earth Sciences 'Jaume Almera', CSIC, Lluis Sole Sabaris s/n, 08028 Barcelona, Spain; tel. (93) 4095410; fax (93) 4110012; e-mail ageyertraver@gmail.com; internet www.iavcei.org; f. 1919 to examine scientifically all aspects of volcanology; affiliated to the International Union of Geodesy and Geophysics; Pres. Prof. RAY CAS (Australia); Sec.-Gen. Prof. JOAN MARTI (Spain); publs *Bulletin of Volcanology*, *Catalogue of the Active Volcanoes of the World*, *Proceedings in Volcanology*.

International Association of Wood Anatomists: c/o Netherlands Centre for Biodiversity Naturalis, POB 9514, 2300 RA Leiden, Netherlands; tel. (71) 5273570; fax (71) 5273511; e-mail eevn@euronet.nl; internet www.iawa-website.org; f. 1931 for the purpose of study, documentation and exchange of information on the structure of wood; holds annual conf; mems: 650 in 68 countries; Exec. Sec. FREDERIC LENS; publ. *IAWA Journal*.

International Astronautical Federation (IAF): 94 bis ave du Suffren, 75015 Paris, France; tel. 1-45-67-42-60; fax 1-42-73-21-20; e-mail secretariat.iaf@iafastro.org; internet www.iafastro.org; f. 1950; fosters the devt of astronautics for peaceful purposes at national and international level, encourages the advancement of knowledge about space and the devt and application of space assets for the benefit of humanity; organizes an annual International Astronautical Congress in conjunction with its associates, the International Academy of Astronautics and the International Institute of Space Law; mems: some 246 mems in 62 countries; Pres. KIYOSHI HIGUCHI; Exec. Dir CHRISTIAN FEICHTINGER.

International Astronomical Union (IAU): 98 bis blvd d'Arago, 75014 Paris, France; tel. 1-43-25-83-58; fax 1-43-25-26-16; e-mail iau@iap.fr; internet www.iau.org; f. 1919 to facilitate co-operation between the astronomers of various countries and to further the study of astronomy in all its branches; organizes colloquia every two months; mems: individual mems in 94 countries; Pres. SILVIA TORRES-PEIMBERT; Gen. Sec. THIERRY MONTMERLE; publs *IAU Colloquia*, *Symposia Series* (6 a year), *Highlights* (every 3 years).

International Biometric Society: International Business Office, 1444 I St, NW, Suite 700, Washington, DC 20005, USA; tel. (202) 712-9049; fax (202) 216-9646; e-mail ibs@biometricsociety.org; internet www.biometricsociety.org; f. 1947 for the advancement of quantitative biological science through the devt of quantitative theories and the application, devt and dissemination of effective mathematical and statistical techniques; the Society has 16 regional orgs and 17 national groups, is affiliated with the International Statistical Institute and WHO, and constitutes the Section of Biometry of the International Union of Biological Sciences; mems: over 6,000 in more than 80 countries; Pres. CLARICE DEMÉTRIO; Exec. Dir DEE ANN WALKER; publs *Biometrics* (quarterly), *Biometric Bulletin* (quarterly), *Journal of Agricultural, Biological and Environmental Statistics*, (quarterly).

International Botanical Congress: c/o Congress Secretariat, Shenzhen Fairy Lake, Botanical Garden, 160 Xianhu Rd, Liantang, Shenzhen 518004, People's Republic of China; tel. (3) 9682-0500; fax (3) 9682-0344; e-mail info@ibc2017.cn; internet www.ibc2017.cn; f. 1864 to inform botanists of recent progress in the plant sciences; the Nomenclature Section of the Congress attempts to provide a uniform terminology and methodology for the naming of plants; other Divisions deal with devtal, metabolic, structural, systematic and evolutionary, ecological botany; genetics and plant breeding; 2017 Congress: Shenzhen, People's Republic of China; affiliated to the International Union of Biological Sciences; Pres. LU RENFENG; Pres. Dr HONG DEYUAN.

International Bureau of Weights and Measures (Bureau international des poids et mesures—BIPM): Pavillon de Breteuil, 92312 Sèvres Cedex, France; tel. 1-45-07-70-70; fax 1-45-34-20-21; e-mail webmaster@bipm.org; internet www.bipm.org; f. 1875; works to ensure the international unification of measurements and their traceability to the International System of Unification; carries out research and calibration; organizes international comparisons of national measurement standards; mems: 51 mem. states and 10 assocs; Dir MARTIN J. T. MILTON (United Kingdom); publs *Le Système International d'Unités* (in English and French), *Metrologia* (6 a year), scientific articles, reports and monographs, committee reports.

International Cartographic Association (ICA) (Association Cartographique Internationale—ACI): c/o Eotvos University, Dept of Cartography and Geoinformatics, H-1117 Budapest, Pazmany Peter setany 1/A, Hungary; tel. (1) 372-2975; fax (1) 372-2951; e-mail lzentai@caesar.elte.hu; internet www.icaci.org; f. 1959 for the advancement, instigation and co-ordination of cartographic research involving co-operation between different nations; particularly concerned with furtherance of training in cartography, study of source material, compilation, graphic design, digital presentation of maps as artefacts communicating geographic information; organizes international confs, symposia, meetings, exhibitions; mems: 80 countries; Pres. GEORG GARTNER (Austria); Sec.-Gen./Treas. LASZLO ZENTAI (Hungary); publ. *ICA Newsletter* (2 a year).

International Centre of Insect Physiology and Ecology: POB 30772-00100, Nairobi, Kenya; tel. (20) 8632000; fax (20) 8632001; e-mail icipe@icipe.org; internet www.icipe.org; f. 1970; aims to alleviate poverty, ensure food security and improve the overall health status of peoples of the tropics through developing and extending tools and strategies for managing harmful and useful arthropods, while preserving the natural resource base through research and capacity building; Dir-Gen. Dr SEGENET KELEMU (Ethiopia); publs *International Journal of Tropical Insect Science* (quarterly), *Biennial Report*, training manuals, technical bulletins, newsletter.

International Commission for Optics (ICO): c/o Angela M. Guzman, Centre for Research and Education in Optics and Lasers, College of Optics and Photonics, University of Central Florida, 4000 Central Florida Blvd., Orlando, FL 32816-2700, USA; tel. (407) 823-6858; fax (407) 823-6880; e-mail angela.guzman@creol.ucf.edu; internet www.e-ico.org; f. 1948; aims to contribute, on an international basis, to the progress and diffusion of knowledge in the field of optics; co-ordinates the dissemination and advancement of scientific and technical knowledge relating to optics; holds Gen. Assembly every three years; mems: cttees in 53 territories, and 6 int. societies; Pres. Prof. DUNCAN T. MOORE; Sec.-Gen. Prof. ANGELA M. GUZMAN; publ. *ICO Newsletter*.

International Commission on Physics Education: e-mail leos.dvorak@mff.cuni.cz; internet web.phys.ksu.edu/icpe/; f. 1960 to encourage and develop international collaboration in the improvement and extension of the methods and scope of physics education at all levels; collaborates with UNESCO and organizes international confs; mems: appointed triennially by the International Union of Pure and Applied Physics; Chair. ROBERT LAMBOURNE; Sec. LEOS DVORAK.

International Commission on Radiation Units and Measurements, Inc (ICRU): 7910 Woodmont Ave, Suite 400, Bethesda, MD 20814-3095, USA; tel. (301) 657-2652; fax (301) 907-8768; e-mail icru@icru.org; internet www.icru.org; f. 1925 to develop internationally acceptable recommendations regarding quantities and units of radiation and radioactivity; procedures suitable for the measurement and application of these quantities in clinical radiology and radiobiology; and physical data needed in the application of these procedures; makes recommendations on quantities and units for radiation protection; mems: from about 18 countries; Chair. HANS-GEORG MENZEL; Exec. Sec. PATRICIA RUSSELL; publs reports.

International Commission on Zoological Nomenclature: c/o Natural History Museum, Cromwell Rd, London, SW7 5BD, United Kingdom; tel. (20) 7942-5653; e-mail iczn@nhm.ac.uk; internet www.iczn.org; f. 1895; has judicial powers to determine all matters relating to the interpretation of the International Code of Zoological Nomenclature and also plenary powers to suspend the operation of the Code where the strict application of the Code would lead to confusion and instability of nomenclature; also responsible for maintaining and developing the Official Lists and Official Indexes of Names and Works in Zoology; affiliated to the International Union of Biological Sciences; Pres. Dr JAN VAN TOL (Netherlands); Exec. Sec. Dr ELLINOR MICHEL (United Kingdom); publs *Bulletin of Zoological Nomenclature* (quarterly), *International Code of Zoological Nomenclature*, *Official Lists and Indexes of Names and Works in Zoology*, *Towards Stability in the Names of Animals*.

International Council for Science (ICSU): 5 rue Auguste Vacquerie, 75116 Paris, France; tel. 1-45-25-03-29; fax 1-42-88-94-31; e-mail secretariat@icsu.org; internet www.icsu.org; f. 1919 as International Research Council; present name adopted 1998; revised statutes adopted 2011; incorporates national scientific bodies and International Scientific Unions, as well as 19 Interdisciplinary Bodies (international scientific networks established to address specific areas of investigation); through its global network co-ordinates interdisciplinary research to address major issues of relevance to both science and society; advocates for freedom in the conduct of science, promotes equitable access to scientific data and information, and facilitates science education and capacity building;

General Assembly of representatives of national and scientific mems meets every three years to formulate policy. Interdisciplinary Bodies and Joint Initiatives: Future Earth; Urban Health and Well-being; Committee on Space Research; Scientific Committee on Antarctic Research; Scientific Committee on Oceanic Research; Scientific Committee on Solar-Terrestrial Physics; Integrated Research on Disaster Risk; Programme on Ecosystem Change and Society; DIVERSITAS; International Geosphere-Biosphere Programme; International Human Dimensions Programme on Global Environmental Change; World Climate Research Programme; Global Climate Observing System; Global Ocean Observing System; Global Terrestrial Observing System; Committee on Data for Science and Technology; International Network for the Availability of Scientific Publications; Scientific Committee on Frequency Allocations for Radio Astronomy and Space Science; World Data System; mems: 120 national mems from 140 countries, 31 Int. Scientific Unions; Pres. LEE YUAN-TSEH (Taiwan); publs *Insight* (quarterly), *Annual Report*.

International Council for the Exploration of the Sea (ICES): H. C. Andersens Blvd 44–46, 1553 Copenhagen V, Denmark; tel. 33-38-67-00; fax 33-93-42-15; e-mail info@ices.dk; internet www.ices.dk; f. 1902 to encourage and facilitate research on the utilization and conservation of living resources and the environment in the North Atlantic Ocean and its adjacent seas; publishes and disseminates results of marine research; advises mem. countries and regulatory commissions; mems: 20 mem. countries, partnership agreements with other int. orgs; Pres. PAUL CONNOLLY; Gen. Sec. ANNE CHRISTINE BRUSENDORFF; publs *ICES Journal of Marine Science*, *ICES Marine Science Symposia*, *ICES Cooperative Research Reports*, *ICES Insight*, *ICES Techniques in Marine Environmental Sciences*, *ICES Identification Leaflets for Plankton*, *ICES Identification Leaflets for Diseases and Parasites of Fish and Shellfish*, *ICES Survey Protocols*.

International Council of Psychologists: c/o Prof. Cecilia Cheng, Department of Psychology, University of Hong Kong, Pokfulam Rd, Hong Kong, SAR; e-mail ceci-cheng@hku.hk; internet icpweb.org; f. 1941 to advance psychology and the application of its scientific findings throughout the world; holds annual conventions; mems: 1,200 qualified psychologists; Pres. Dr TARA PIR (USA); Sec.-Gen. Prof. CECILIA CHENG (Hong Kong); publs *International Psychologist* (quarterly), *World Psychology* (quarterly).

International Council of the Aeronautical Sciences: c/o DGLR, Godesberger Al., 70 53175 Bonn, Germany; tel. (228) 3080519; fax (228) 3080524; e-mail icas@icas.org; internet www.icas.org; f. 1957 to encourage free interchange of information on aeronautical science and technology; holds biennial Congresses (2014: St Petersburg, Russia); mems: nat. asscns in more than 30 countries; Pres. MURRAY SCOTT (Australia); Exec. Sec. AXEL PROBST (Germany).

International Earth Rotation and Reference Systems Service: Central Bureau, c/o Bundesamt für Kartographie und Geodäsie (BKG), Richard-Strauss-Allee 11, 60598 Frankfurt am Main, Germany; tel. (69) 6333273; fax (69) 6333425; e-mail central_bureau@iers.org; internet www.iers.org; f. 1988 (fmrly International Polar Motion Service and Bureau International de l'Heure); maintained by the International Astronomical Union and the International Union of Geodesy and Geophysics; defines and maintains the international terrestrial and celestial reference systems; determines earth orientation parameters (terrestrial and celestial co-ordinates of the pole and universal time) connecting these systems; monitors global geophysical fluids; organizes collection, analysis and dissemination of data; Chair. of Directing Bd Dr BRIAN LUZUM; Dir DANIELLA THALLER (Germany).

International Federation of Cell Biology (IFCB): e-mail hern@unicamp.br; internet www.ifcbiol.org; f. 1972 to foster international co-operation, and organize confs; mems: some 30 full mem. socs, 20 assoc. and affiliated socs; Pres. Prof. NOBUTAKA HIROKAWA (Japan); Sec.-Gen. Prof. HERNANDES CARVALHO (Brazil); publs *Cell Biology International* (monthly), reports.

International Federation of Operational Research Societies (IFORS): c/o Mary Magrogan, 7240 Parkway Drive, Suite 300 Hanover, MD 21076, USA; tel. (443) 757-3534; fax (443) 757-3535; e-mail secretary@ifors.org; internet www.ifors.org; f. 1959 for devt of operational research as a unified science and its advancement in all nations of the world; mems: c. 30,000 individuals, 48 nat. socs, 5 kindred socs; Pres. NELSON DE MACULAN; Sec. MARY MAGROGAN; publs *International Abstracts in Operational Research*, *IFORS News*, *International Transactions in Operational Research*.

International Federation of Societies for Microscopy (IFSM): c/o Centre for Microscopy and Microanalysis, University of Western Australia, 35 Stirling Hwy, Perth, WA 6008, Australia; tel. (8) 6488-2739; fax (8) 6488-1087; e-mail Brendan.Griffin@uwa.edu.au; internet www.ifsm.info; f. 1955 to contribute to the advancement of all aspects of electron microscopy; promotes and co-ordinates research; sponsors meetings and confs; holds International Congress every four years; mems: representative orgs of 40 countries; Pres. Prof. C. BARRY CARTER (USA); Gen. Sec. BRENDAN GRIFFIN (Australia).

International Foundation of the High-Altitude Research Stations Jungfraujoch and Gornergrat: Sidlerstr. 5, 3012 Bern, Switzerland; tel. 316314052; fax 316314405; e-mail claudine.frieden@space.unibe.ch; internet www.ifjungo.ch; f. 1931; international research centre which enables scientists from many scientific fields to carry out experiments at high altitudes. Six countries contribute to support the station: Austria, Belgium, Germany, Italy, Switzerland, United Kingdom; Pres. Dr ERWIN FLÜCKIGER; Dir Prof. MARKUS LEUENBERGER.

International Geographical Union (IGU): University of Cape Town, Department of Geographical and Environmental Science, Rondebosch 7701, South Africa; tel. (21) 6502873; fax (21) 6503456; e-mail mmeadows@mweb.co.za; internet www.igu-online.org; f. 1922 to encourage the study of problems relating to geography, to promote and co-ordinate research requiring international co-operation, and to organize international congresses and commissions; mems: 83 countries, 11 assocs; Pres. VLADIMIR KOLOSSOV (Russia); Sec.-Gen. Prof. MICHAEL MEADOWS (South Africa); publ. *IGU Bulletin* (annually).

International Glaciological Society: Scott Polar Research Institute, Lensfield Rd, Cambridge, CB2 1ER, United Kingdom; tel. (1223) 355974; fax (1223) 354931; e-mail igsoc@igsoc.org; internet www.igsoc.org; f. 1936; aims to stimulate interest in and encourage research into the scientific and technical problems associated with snow and ice; mems: 950 in 30 countries; Pres. Dr D. R. MACAYEAL; Sec.-Gen. MAGNÚS MÁR MAGNÚSSON; publs *Journal of Glaciology* (6 a year), *ICE* (News Bulletin, 3 a year), *Annals of Glaciology* (3-4 a year).

International Hydrographic Organization (IHO): 4 Quai Antoine 1er, BP 445, 98000 Monaco; tel. 93-10-81-00; fax 93-10-81-40; e-mail info@iho.int; internet www.iho.int; f. 1921 to link the hydrographic offices of mem. govts and co-ordinate their work, with a view to rendering navigation easier and safer; seeks to obtain, as far as possible, uniformity in charts and hydrographic documents; fosters the devt of electronic chart navigation; encourages adoption of the best methods of conducting hydrographic surveys; encourages surveying in those parts of the world where accurate charts are lacking; provides IHO Data Centre for Digital Bathymetry; and organizes quinquennial conference; mems: 81 states; Directing Committee: Pres. ROBERT WARD (Australia); Dirs MUSTAFA IPTES (Turkey), GILLES BESSERO (France); publs *International Hydrographic Bulletin*, *IHO Yearbook*, other documents (available on the IHO website).

International Institute of Refrigeration: 177 blvd Malesherbes, 75017 Paris, France; tel. 1-42-27-32-35; fax 1-47-63-17-98; e-mail iif-iir@iifiir.org; internet www.iifiir.org; f. 1908 to further the science of refrigeration and its applications on a worldwide scale; to investigate, discuss and recommend any aspects leading to improvements in the field of refrigeration; mems: 60 nat., 1,200 assocs; Pres. E. JOACHIM FELIX ZIEGLER; Dir DIDIER COULOMB (France); publs *International Journal of Refrigeration* (8 a year), *Newsletter* (quarterly), books, proceedings, recommendations.

International Mathematical Union (IMU): Markgrafenstr. 32, 10117 Berlin, Germany; tel. (30) 20372-430; fax (30) 20372-439; e-mail office@mathunion.org; internet www.mathunion.org; f. 1952 to support and assist the International Congress of Mathematicians and other international scientific meetings or confs and to encourage and support other international mathematical activities considered likely to contribute to the devt of mathematical science—pure, applied or educational; mems: 80 countries; Pres. INGRID DAUBECHIES (USA); Sec.-Gen. MARTIN GRÖTSCHEL (Germany); publ. *IMU-Net Newsletter*.

International Mineralogical Association: c/o Richard Göd, Dept of Lithospheric Research, University of Vienna, 14 Althanstr., 1090 Vienna, Austria; tel. (1) 42775339-0; e-mail richard.goed@univie.ac.at; internet www.ima-mineralogy.org; f. 1958 to further international co-operation in the science of mineralogy; affiliated to the International Union of Geological Sciences; mems: nat. socs in 38 countries; Pres. Prof. WALTER MARESCH (Germany); Sec. RICHARD GÖD.

International Organization of Legal Metrology: 11 rue Turgot, 75009 Paris, France; tel. 1-48-78-12-82; fax 1-42-82-17-27; e-mail biml@oiml.org; internet www.oiml.org; f. 1955 to serve as documentation and information centre on the verification, checking, construction and use of measuring instruments, to determine characteristics and standards to which measuring instruments must conform for their use to be recommended internationally, and to determine the general principles of legal metrology; mems: govts of 59 countries; Pres. PETER MASON (United Kingdom); Dir STEPHEN PATORAY; publ. *Bulletin* (quarterly).

International Palaeontological Association: c/o Paleontological Institute, 1475 Jayhawk Blvd, Rm 121, Lindley Hall, University of Kansas, Lawrence, KS 66045, USA; tel. (785) 864-3338; fax (785) 864-5276; e-mail roger.thomas@fandm.edu; internet ipa.geo.ku.edu; f. 1933; affiliated to the International Union of Geological Sciences and the International Union of Biological Sciences; Pres. Dr MICHAEL BENTON (United Kingdom); Sec.-Gen. ROGER THOMAS (USA); publs *Lethaia* (quarterly), *Directory of Paleontologists of the World*, *Directory of Fossil Collectors of the World*.

International Peat Society: Kauppakatu 19 D 31, 40100 Jyväskylä, Finland; tel. (40) 4184075; e-mail ips@peatsociety.org; internet www.peatsociety.org; f. 1968 to encourage co-operation in the study and use of mires, peatlands, peat and related material, through international meetings, research groups and the exchange of information; mems: 18 National Cttees, research institutes and other orgs, and individuals from 42 countries; Pres. Prof. BJÖRN HÅNELL (Sweden); Sec.-Gen. JAAKKO SILPOLA (Finland); publs *Peat News* (monthly electronic newsletter), *International Peat Journal* (annually), *Peatlands International* (2 a year).

International Permafrost Association: c/o Dr Inga May, Alfred Wegener Institute, Helmholtz Centre for Polar and Marine Research, Telegrafenberg A43, 14473 Potsdam, Germany; tel. (331) 288-2162; fax (331) 288-2188; e-mail contact@ipa-permafrost.org; internet ipa.arcticportal.org; f. 1983; aims to foster dissemination and exchange of knowledge concerning permafrost and to promote co-operation among persons and orgs involved in scientific investigation and engineering work in permafrost; organizes the International Conference on Permafrost, held generally every five years (2016: Potsdam, Germany); mems: Adhering Bodies from 26 countries; Pres. Prof. ANTONI G. LEWKOWICZ; Exec. Dir Dr KARINA SCHOLLÄN; publs *Frozen Ground* (annually), conf. proceedings, other scientific reports and assessments, reports in *Permafrost and Periglacial Process* (2 a year).

International Phonetic Association: Dept of Linguistics, University of California, Los Angeles, CA 90095, USA; tel. (310) 794-6316; e-mail keating@humnet.ucla.edu; internet www.langsci.ucl.ac.uk/ipa/; f. 1886 to promote the scientific study of phonetics and its applications; organizes International Congress of Phonetic Sciences every four years (2015: Glasgow, UK, in Aug.); mems: 400; Prof. JOHN ESLING; Sec. Prof. PATRICIA KEATING; publs *Journal of the International Phonetic Association* (3 a year), *Handbook of the International Phonetic Association*.

International Phycological Society: c/o University of Adelaide School of Earth and Environmental Sciences, 112 Darling Bldg, Adelaide, SA 5005, Australia; tel. (8) 8222-9291; fax (8) 8222-9456; e-mail secretary@intphycsoc.org; internet www.intphycsoc.org; f. 1960 to promote the study of algae, the distribution of information, and international co-operation in this field; mems: about 1,000; Pres. JOE ZUCCARELLO (New Zealand); Sec. CARLOS F. GURGEL; publ. *Phycologia* (every 2 months).

International Primatological Society: c/o California State University San Marcos, San Marcos, CA 92096, USA; tel. (760) 750-4145; fax (760) 750-3418; e-mail ncaine@csusm.edu; internet www.internationalprimatologicalsociety.org; f. 1964 to promote primatological science in all fields; Congress held every two years (2014: Hanoi, Viet Nam); mems: about 1,500; Pres. TETSURO MATSUZAWA (Japan); Sec.-Gen. NANCY CAINE; publs *IPS Bulletin*, *International Journal of Primatology*, *Codes of Practice*.

International Radiation Protection Association (IRPA): c/o Bernard Le Guen, EDF Generation, Site Cap Ampère, 1 pl. Pleyel, 93282 Saint Denis, France; tel. 1-43-69-40-93; fax 1-43-69-27-40; e-mail exec.off@irpa.net; internet www.irpa.net; f. 1966 to link individuals and socs throughout the world concerned with protection against ionizing radiations and allied effects, and to represent doctors, health physicists, radiological protection officers and others engaged in radiological protection, radiation safety, nuclear safety, legal, medical and veterinary aspects and in radiation research and other allied activities; mems: 16,000 in 42 socs; Pres. RENATE CZARWINSKI (Germany); Exec. Officer BERNARD LE GUEN (France); publ. *IRPA Bulletin*.

International Society for Criminology (ISC) (Société internationale de criminologie): Hooverplein 10, 3000 Leuven, Belgium; tel. (16) 32-51-15; e-mail crim.sic@gmail.com; internet www.isc-sic.org; f. 1934 to promote the devt of the sciences in their application to the criminal phenomenon; mems: in 63 countries; Pres. Prof. SERGE BROCHU (Canada); Sec.-Gen. Prof. STEPHAN PARMENTIER (Belgium); publ. *Annales internationales de Criminologie*.

International Society for Human and Animal Mycology (ISHAM): c/o De Hoefkamp 1096, 6545 MD Nijmegen, Netherlands; tel. (24) 361-9987; e-mail p.donnelly@usa.net; internet www.isham.org; f. 1954 to pursue the study of fungi pathogenic for man and animals; holds congresses (2015: Melbourne, Australia); mems: 1,100 in 70 countries; Pres. Prof. NEIL GOW (United Kingdom); Gen. Sec. Dr PETER DONNELLY (Netherlands); publ. *Medical Mycology* (6 a year).

International Society for Rock Mechanics: c/o Laboratório Nacional de Engenharia Civil, 101 Av. do Brasil, 1700-066 Lisboa, Portugal; tel. (21) 8443419; fax (21) 8443021; e-mail secretariat.isrm@lnec.pt; internet www.isrm.net; f. 1962 to encourage and co-ordinate international co-operation in the science of rock mechanics; assists individuals and local orgs in forming national bodies; maintains liaisons with orgs representing related sciences, including geology, geophysics, soil mechanics, mining engineering, petroleum engineering and civil engineering; organizes international meetings; encourages the publication of research; mems: c. 7,500 mems and 53 nat. groups; Pres. Prof. XIA-TING FENG; Sec.-Gen. Dr LUÍS LAMAS; publ. *News Journal*.

International Society for Tropical Ecology: c/o Botany Dept, Banaras Hindu University, Varanasi, 221 005 India; tel. (542) 2368399; fax (542) 2368174; e-mail singh.js1@gmail.com; internet www.tropecol.com; f. 1956 to promote and develop the science of ecology in the tropics in the service of humanity; to publish a journal to aid ecologists in the tropics in communication of their findings; and to hold symposia from time to time to summarize the state of knowledge in particular or general fields of tropical ecology; mems: 500; Sec. Prof. J. S. SINGH (India); publ. *Tropical Ecology* (3 a year).

International Society of Biometeorology (ISB): c/o Dept of Geography, Bolton 410, POB 413, University of Wisconsin-Milwaukee, Milwaukee, WI 53201-0413, USA; tel. (414) 229-6611; fax (414) 229-3981; e-mail jmhanes@uwm.edu; internet www.biometeorology.org; f. 1956 to unite all biometeorologists working in the fields of agricultural, botanical, cosmic, entomological, forest, human, medical, veterinarian, zoological and other branches of biometeorology; mems: 250 individuals, nationals of 46 countries; Pres. GLENN MCGREGOR (New Zealand); Sec. JONATHAN M. HANES (USA); publs *Biometeorology* (Proceedings of the Congress of ISB), *International Journal of Biometeorology* (quarterly), *Biometeorology Bulletin*.

International Society of Limnology (Societas Internationalis Limnologiae—SIL): c/o Prof. Dr Tamar Zohary, Y. Allon Kinneret Limnological Laboratory, Israel Oceanographic & Limnological Research Ltd, POB 447, Migdal 14950, Israel; e-mail tamarz@ocean.org.il; internet www.limnology.org; f. 1922 (as the International Asscn of Theoretical and Applied Limnology, name changed 2007) for the study of physical, chemical and biological phenomena of lakes and rivers; affiliated to the International Union of Biological Sciences; mems: c. 3,200; Pres. Dr YVES PRAIRIE (Canada); Gen. Sec. and Treas. Prof. Dr TAMAR ZOHARY (Israel).

International Union for Physical and Engineering Sciences in Medicine (IUPESM): c/o Prof. James Goh, Division of Bioengineering, National University of Singapore, Block E3A, 04-15, 7 Engineering Dr., Singapore 117574; tel. 65165259; fax 68723069; e-mail dosgohj@nus.edu.sg; internet www.iupesm.org; f. 1980 by its two constituent orgs (International Federation for Medical and Biological Engineering, and International Organization for Medical Physics); promotes international co-operation in health care science and technology and represents the professional interests of mems; organizes seminars, workshops, scientific confs; holds World Congress every three years (2015: Toronto, Canada); Pres. Prof. HERBERT F. VOIGT (USA); Sec.-Gen. Prof. JAMES GOH (Singapore); publs *IUPESM Newsletter* (2 a year), Congress proceedings.

International Union for Pure and Applied Biophysics (IUPAB): Bosch Institute, Anderson Stuart F13, University of Sydney, Sydney, 2006 Australia; tel. (2) 9351-3209; fax (2) 9351-6546; e-mail dosremedios@iupab.org; internet www.iupab.org; f. 1961 to organize international co-operation in biophysics and promote communication between biophysics and allied subjects, to encourage national co-operation between biophysical socs, and to contribute to the advancement of biophysical knowledge; mems: 50 adhering bodies; Pres. GORDON ROBERTS (United Kingdom); Sec.-Gen. Prof. CRISTOBAL G. DOS REMEDIOS (Australia); publ. *Quarterly Reviews of Biophysics*.

International Union for Quaternary Research (INQUA): c/o Dr Julius Lejju, Dept of Biology, Mbarara University of Science & Technology, POB 1410, Mbarara, Uganda; tel. (782) 809814; fax (485) 20782; e-mail lejju2002@yahoo.co.uk; internet www.inqua.org; f. 1928 to co-ordinate research on the Quaternary geological era throughout the world; holds Congress every four years (2015: Nagoya, Japan); mems: in some 35 countries; Pres. Prof. MARGARET AVERY (South Africa); Sec.-Gen. Dr JULIUS LEIJU (Uganda); publs *Quarternary International*, *Quarternary Perspectives*.

International Union of Biochemistry and Molecular Biology (IUBMB): c/o Dept of Biochemistry & Molecular Biology, University of Calgary, Faculty of Medicine, 3330 Hospital Drive, NW Calgary, Alberta, T2N 4N1, Canada; tel. (403) 220-3021; fax (403) 270-2211; e-mail walsh@ucalgary.ca; internet www.iubmb.org; f. 1955 to sponsor the International Congresses of Biochemistry, to co-ordinate research and discussion, to organize co-operation between the societies of biochemistry and molecular biology, to promote high standards of biochemistry and molecular biology throughout the world and to contribute to the advancement of biochemistry and molecular biology in all its international aspects; mems: 77 bodies; Pres. Prof. GREGORY PETSKO (USA); Gen. Sec. Prof. MICHAEL WALSH (Canada).

International Union of Biological Sciences (IUBS): Bâtiment 442, Université Paris-Sud 11, 91405 Orsay Cedex, France; tel. 1-69-15-50-27; fax 1-69-15-79-47; e-mail nfomproix@iubs.org; internet www.iubs.org; f. 1919; serves as an international forum for the promotion of biology; administers scientific programmes on biodiversity, integrative biology (of ageing, bioenergy, and climate change), biological education, bioethics, bioenergy, and Darwin 200; carries out international collaborative research programmes; convenes General Assembly every three years; mems: 44 nat. bodies, 80 scientific bodies; Pres. NILS STENSETH (Norway); Exec. Dir Dr NATHALIE FOMPROIX; publs *Biology International* (quarterly), *IUBS Monographs*, *IUBS Methodology*, *Manual Series*.

International Union of Crystallography: c/o M. H. Dacombe, 2 Abbey Sq., Chester, CH1 2HU, United Kingdom; tel. (1244) 345431; fax (1244) 344843; e-mail execsec@iucr.org; internet www.iucr.org; f. 1947 to facilitate the international standardization of methods, units, nomenclature and symbols used in crystallography; and to form a focus for the relations of crystallography to other sciences; mems: in 40 countries; Pres. Prof. G. R. DESIRAJU (India); Gen. Sec. L. VAN MEERWELT (Belgium); publs *IUCR Newsletter*, *Acta Crystallographica*, *Journal of Applied Crystallography*, *Journal of Synchroton Radiation*, *International Tables for Crystallography*, *World Directory of Crystallographers*, *IUCr/OUP Crystallographic Symposia*, *IUCr/OUP Monographs on Crystallography*, *IUCr/OUP Texts on Crystallography*.

International Union of Geodesy and Geophysics (IUGG): IUGG Secretariat, Helmholtz Centre Potsdam, GFZ German Research Centre for Geosciences, Telegrafenberg A17, 14473 Potsdam, Germany; tel. (33)1 2881978; e-mail secretariat@iugg.org; internet www.iugg.org; f. 1919; fed. of eight asscns representing Cryospheric Sciences, Geodesy, Geomagnetism and Aeronomy, Hydrological Sciences, Meteorology and Atmospheric Physics, Seismology and Physics of the Earth's Interior, Physical Sciences of the Ocean, and Volcanology and Chemistry of the Earth's Interior, which meet in cttees and at the General Assemblies of the Union; organizes scientific meetings and sponsors various permanent services to collect, analyse and publish geophysical data; mems: 70 countries; Pres. Dr HARSH GUPTA (India); Sec.-Gen. Dr ALIK ISMAIL-ZADEH (Germany); publs *IUGG Yearbook*, *Journal of Geodesy* (quarterly), *IASPEI Newsletter* (irregular), *Bulletin of Volcanology* (8 a year), *Hydrological Sciences Journal* (6 a year), *IAMAS Newsletter* (irregular).

International Union of Geological Sciences (IUGS): c/o Li Zhijian, 26 Baiwanzhuang Rd, Xicheng District, Beijing, People's Republic of China; tel. (703) 648-6050; fax (703) 648-4227; e-mail iugs.beijing@gmail.com; internet www.iugs.org; f. 1961; aims to encourage the study of geoscientific problems, to facilitate international and interdisciplinary co-operation in geology and related sciences, and to support the quadrennial International Geological Congress; organizes international meetings and co-sponsors joint programmes, including the International Geological Correlation Programme (with UNESCO); mems: in 121 countries; Pres. Prof. ROLAND OBERHÄNSLI; Sec.-Gen. Dr IAN LAMBERT.

International Union of Immunological Societies (IUIS): IUIS Central Office, c/o Vienna Medical Academy, Alser Strasse 4, 1090 Vienna, Austria; tel. (1) 405-13-83-16; fax (1) 407-82-74; e-mail iuis-central-office@medacad.org; internet www.iuisonline.org; f. 1969; holds triennial international congress; mems: nat. socs in 65 countries and territories; Pres. JORGE KALIL (Brazil); Sec.-Gen. Dr SEPPO MERI (Finland); Asscn Man. NATALIE LANG.

International Union of Microbiological Societies (IUMS): c/o Dr Robert A. Samson, Centraalbureau voor Schimmelcultures Fungal Biodiversity Centre, POB 85167, 3508 AD, Utrecht, Netherlands; tel. (30) 2122600; fax (30) 2512097; e-mail samson@cbs.knaw.nl; internet www.iums.org; f. 1930; mems: 106 nat. microbiological socs; Pres. YUAN KUN LEE (Singapore); Sec.-Gen. ROBERT A. SAMSON (Netherlands); publs *International Journal of Systematic Bacteriology* (quarterly), *International Journal of Food Microbiology* (every 2 months), *Advances in Microbial Ecology* (annually), *Archives of Virology*.

International Union of Nutritional Sciences (IUNS): c/o Prof. Catherine Geissler, 155 Portland Road, London W11 4LR, United Kingdom; fax (523) 342187; e-mail iuns@kenes.com; internet www.iuns.org; f. 1946 to promote advancement in nutrition science, research and devt through international co-operation at global level; aims to encourage communication and collaboration among nutrition scientists as well as to disseminate information in nutritional sciences through modern communication technology; mems: 80 adhering bodies; Pres. Dr ANNA LARTEY (Ghana); Sec.-Gen. Prof. CATHERINE GEISSLER (UK); publs *Annual Report*, *IUNS Directory*, *Newsletter*.

International Union of Pharmacology: c/o Dr. S.J. Enna, Medical Center, University of Kansas, 3901 Rainbow Blvd, Kansas City, KN 66160, USA; tel. (913) 588-7533; fax (913) 588-7373; e-mail IUPHAR@kumc.edu; internet www.iuphar.org; f. 1963 to promote co-ordination of research, discussion and publication in the field of pharmacology, including clinical pharmacology, drug metabolism and toxicology; co-operates with WHO in all matters concerning drugs and drug research; holds int. congresses; mems: 54 nat. socs, 12 assoc. mem. socs, 3 corporate mems; Pres. Dr PATRICK DU SOUICH (Canada); Sec.-Gen. Dr S. J. ENNA; publ. *PI (Pharmacology International)*.

International Union of Photobiology: c/o Dept of Dermatology, Medical University of Vienna, AKH-E07 Waehringer Guertel 18–20, 1090 Vienna, Austria; tel. (1) 40400-7702; fax (1) 40400-7699; e-mail herbert.hoenigsmann@meduniwien.ac.at; internet www.iuphotobiology.com; f. 1928 (frmly International Photobiology Asscn); stimulation of scientific research concerning the physics, chemistry and climatology of non-ionizing radiations (ultra-violet, visible and infra-red) in relation to their biological effects and their applications in biology and medicine; 18 national cttees represented; affiliated to the International Union of Biological Sciences. International Congresses held every four years; Pres. HENRY LIM (USA); Sec.-Gen./Treas. HERBERT HÖNIGSMANN (Austria).

International Union of Physiological Sciences (IUPS): IUPS Secretariat, LGN, Bâtiment CERVI, Hôpital de la Pitié-Salpêtrière, 83 blvd de l'Hôpital, 75013 Paris, France; tel. 1-42-17-75-37; fax 1-42-17-75-75; e-mail iups@case.edu; internet www.iups.org; f. 1955; mems: 51 nat., 14 assoc., 4 reg., 2 affiliated mems; Pres. Prof. DENIS NOBLE; Sec.-Gen. WALTER BORON.

International Union of Psychological Science: Dept of Psychology, Univ. of Montreal, POB 6128, Succursale A, Downtown Station, Montréal, Quebec H3C 3J7, Canada; tel. (31) 261-8288; fax (31) 261-4566; e-mail secretariat@iupsys.org; internet www.iupsys.net; f. 1951 to contribute to the devt of intellectual exchange and scientific relations between psychologists of different countries; mems: 82 nat. and 20 affiliate orgs; Pres. Prof. SATHS COOPER (South Africa); Sec.-Gen. Dr ANN WATTS; publs *International Journal of Psychology* (quarterly), *The IUPsyS Directory* (irregular), *Psychological Resources Around the World (PRATWA)*.

International Union of Pure and Applied Chemistry (IUPAC): POB 13757, 104 T. W. Alexander Dr., Bldg 19, Research Triangle Park, NC 27709-3757, USA; tel. (919) 485-8700; fax (919) 485-8706; e-mail secretariat@iupac.org; internet www.iupac.org; f. 1919 to organize permanent co-operation between chemical asscns in the mem. countries, to study topics of international importance requiring standardization or codification, to co-operate with other international orgs in the field of chemistry and to contribute to the advancement of all aspects of chemistry; holds a biennial General Assembly; mems: in 60 countries; Pres. Prof. KAZUYUKI TATSUMI (Japan); Sec.-Gen. Prof. Dr RENÉ DEPLANQUE (Germany).

International Union of Pure and Applied Physics (IUPAP): c/o Institute of Physics, 76 Portland Pl., London, W1B 1NT, United Kingdom; tel. (20) 7470-4849; fax (20) 7470-4861; e-mail admin.iupap@iop.org; internet www.iupap.org; f. 1922 to promote and encourage international co-operation in physics and facilitate the worldwide devt of science; hosts a General Assembly every three years; mems: in 60 countries; Pres. CECILIA JARLSKOG (Sweden); Sec.-Gen. STUART PALMER (United Kingdom).

International Union of Radio Science: c/o INTEC, Ghent University, Sint-Pietersnieuwstraat 41, 9000 Ghent, Belgium; tel. (9) 264-3320; fax (9) 264-4288; e-mail info@ursi.org; internet www.ursi.org; f. 1919 to stimulate and co-ordinate, on an international basis, studies, research, applications, scientific exchange and communication in the field of radio science; aims to encourage the adoption of common methods of measurement and the standardization of measuring instruments used in scientific work; represents radio science at national and international level; mems: 44 nat. cttees; Pres. Dr PHIL WILKINSON (Australia); Sec.-Gen. Prof. PAUL LAGASSE (Belgium); publs *The Radio Science Bulletin* (quarterly), *URSI Newsletter* (every 2 months).

International Union of Soil Sciences: c/o Dept of Soil Science, University of Wisconsin-Madison, Madison, WI 53706, USA; tel. (608) 263-4947; e-mail hartemink@wisc.edu; internet www.iuss.org; f. 1924; mems: nat. academies or nat. soil science socs from 143 countries; Pres. Prof. JAE YANG (Republic of Korea); Sec.-Gen. Prof. ALFRED HARTEMINK (USA); publ. *Bulletin* (2 a year).

International Union of the History and Philosophy of Science: Division of the History of Science and Technology (DHST): National Hellenic Research Foundation, 48 Vas. Constantinou av., 11635 Athens, Greece; Division of the History of Logic, Methodology and Philosophy of Science (DLMPS): 161 rue Ada, 34392 Montpellier, France; e-mail e.nicolaidis@dhstweb.org; f. 1956 to promote research into the history and philosophy of science; DHST has 50 national cttees and DLMPS has 35 cttees; DHST: Pres. Prof. EFTHYMIOS NICOLAÏDES (Greece); Sec.-Gen. CATHERINE JAMI (France).

International Union of Theoretical and Applied Mechanics (IUTAM): IUTAM-Secretariat, Centre de Mathématiques et de Leurs Applications, Ecole Normale Supérieure de Cachan, 94235

Cachan, France; tel. 1-47-40-59-00; fax 1-47-40-59-01; e-mail frederic.dias@cmla.ens-cachan.fr; internet www.iutam.net; f. 1947 to form links between those engaged in scientific work (theoretical or experimental) in mechanics or related sciences; organizes international congresses of theoretical and applied mechanics, through a standing Congress Cttee, and other international meetings; engages in other activities designed to promote the devt of mechanics as a science; mems: from 49 countries; Pres. Prof. VIGGO TVERGAARD (Denmark); Sec.-Gen. Prof. FREDERIC DIAS (France); publs *Annual Report*, *Newsletter*.

International Union of Toxicology: IUTOX Headquarters, 1821 Michael Faraday Dr., Suite 300, Reston, VA 20190, USA; tel. (703) 438-3103; fax (703) 438-3113; e-mail iutoxhq@iutox.org; internet www.iutox.org; f. 1980 to foster international co-operation among toxicologists and promote worldwide acquisition, dissemination and utilization of knowledge in the field; sponsors International Congresses and other education programmes; mems: 61 nat. socs; Pres. Dr HERMAN AUTRUP; Sec.-Gen. Prof. ELAINE FAUSTMAN; publs *IUTOX Newsletter*, Congress proceedings.

International Water Association (IWA): Alliance House, 12 Caxton St, London, SW1H 0QS, United Kingdom; tel. (20) 7654-5500; fax (20) 7654-5555; e-mail water@iwahq.org.uk; internet www.iwahq.org; f. 1999 by merger of the International Water Services Association and the International Association on Water Quality; aims to encourage international communication, co-operative effort, and exchange of information on water quality management, through confs, electronic media and publication of research reports; mems: c. 9,000 in 130 countries; Pres. Dr GLEN DAIGGER; Exec. Dir GER BERGKAMP; publs *Water Research* (monthly), *Water Science and Technology* (24 a year), *Water 21* (6 a year), *Journal of Water and Health*, *Scientific and Technical Reports*.

Nuclear Threat Initiative: 1747 Pennsylvania Ave NW, 7th Floor, Washington, DC 20006, USA; tel. (202) 296-4810; fax (202) 296-4811; e-mail contact@nti.org; internet www.nti.org; f. 2001 to help to strengthen global security by reducing the risk of use of and preventing the spread of nuclear, biological and chemical weapons; promotes the objectives of the Nuclear Non-Proliferation Treaty; Pres. and COO JOAN ROHLFING; CEO SAM NUNN.

Pacific Science Association: 1525 Bernice St, Honolulu, HI 96817, USA; tel. (808) 848-4124; fax (808) 847-8252; e-mail info@pacificscience.org; internet www.pacificscience.org; f. 1920; a regional non-governmental org. that seeks to advance science, technology, and sustainable devt in and of the Asia-Pacific region, by actively promoting interdisciplinary and international research and collaboration; sponsors Pacific Science Congresses and Inter-Congresses and scientific working groups and facilitates research initiatives on critical emerging issues for the region; 12th Inter-Congress: Suva, Fiji, in July, on the theme: 'Human Security in the Pacific'; 22nd Congress: Kuala Lumpur, Malaysia, June 2011; mems: institutional representatives from 35 areas, scientific socs, individual scientists; Pres. Prof. NANCY D. LEWIS (USA); Sec-Gen. MAKOTO TSUCHIYA (Japan); publs *Pacific Science* (quarterly), *Information Bulletin* (2 a year).

Pugwash Conferences on Science and World Affairs: Ground Floor Flat, 63A Great Russell St, London, WC1B 3BJ, United Kingdom; tel. (20) 7405-6661; fax (20) 7831-5651; e-mail sandra@pugwash.org; internet www.pugwash.org; f. 1957 to organize international confs of scientists to discuss problems arising from the devt of science, particularly the dangers to mankind from weapons of mass destruction; mems: national Pugwash groups in 38 countries; Pres. JAYANTHA DHENAPALA; Sec.-Gen. Prof. PAOLO COTTA-RAMUSINO; publs *Pugwash Newsletter* (2 a year), occasional papers, monographs.

Unitas Malacologica (Malacological Union): c/o Dr Jackie Van Goethem, Royal Belgian Institute of Natural Sciences, Vautierstraat 29, 1000 Brussels, Belgium; tel. (2) 627-43-43; fax (2) 627-41-41; e-mail j.sigwart@qub.ac.uk; internet www.unitasmalacologica.org; f. 1962 to further the study of molluscs worldwide; affiliated to the International Union of Biological Sciences; holds triennial World Congress; mems: 400 in more than 35 countries; Pres. ANTÓNIO DE FRIAS MARTINS (Portugal); Sec. JESÚS TRONCOSO (Spain); publ. *UM Newsletter* (2 a year).

World Institute for Nuclear Security (WINS): Graben 19, Vienna, 1010 Austria; tel. (1) 230-606-083; fax (1) 230-606-089; e-mail info@wins.org; internet www.wins.org; f. 2008; aims to strengthen the physical protection and security of nuclear materials and facilities worldwide; Exec. Dir Dr ROGER HOWSLEY (United Kingdom).

World Organisation of Systems and Cybernetics (WOSC): c/o Prof Raul Espejo, 3 North Pl., 30 Nettleham Rd, Lincoln, LN2 1RE, United Kingdom; tel. and fax (1522) 589252; e-mail r.espejo@syncho.org; internet www.wosc.co; f. 1969 to act as a clearing house for all socs concerned with cybernetics and systems, to aim for the recognition of cybernetics as fundamental science, to organize and sponsor international exhibitions of automation and computer equipment, congresses and symposia, and to promote and co-ordinate research in systems and cybernetics; sponsors an honorary fellowship and awards a Norbert Wiener memorial gold medal; mems: dirs from 16 countries belonging to nat. and int. socs in 30 countries; Pres. Prof. R. VALLÉE (France); Dir-Gen. Prof. RAUL ESPEJO; publs *Kybernetes*, *International Journal of Cybernetics and Systems*.

Social Sciences

Arab Towns Organization (ATO): POB 68160, Kaifan 71962, Kuwait; tel. 24849705; fax 24849319; e-mail ato@ato.net; internet www.ato.net; f. 1967; works to preserve the identity and heritage of Arab towns; to support the devt and modernization of municipal and local authorities in mem. towns; to improve services and utilities in mem. towns; to support devt schemes in mem. towns through the provision of loans and other assistance; to support planning and the co-ordination of devt activities and services; to facilitate the exchange of service-related expertise among mem. towns; to co-ordinate efforts to modernize and standardize municipal regulations and codes among mem. towns; to promote co-operation in all matters related to Arab towns; manages the Arab Towns Development Fund, the Arab Institute for Urban Development, the Arab Towns Organization Award, the Arab Urban Environment Centre, the Arab Forum on Information Systems, and the Heritage and Arab Historic City Foundation; mems: 413 towns; Sec.-Gen. ABD AL-AZIZ Y. AL-ADASANI; publ. *Al-Madinah Al-Arabiyah* (every 2 months).

Association for the Study of the World Refugee Problem (AWR): POB 1241, 97201 Hoechberg, Germany; e-mail sibylle.wollenschlaeger@fhws.de; internet www.awr-int.de; f. 1951 to promote and co-ordinate scholarly research on refugee problems; Pres. Prof. ANDRZEJ SAKSON; Pres. of the Scientific Bd Prof. RALF ROSSKOPF; publs *AWR Bulletin* (quarterly, in English, French, Italian and German), treatises on refugee problems (17 vols).

Council for Research in Values and Philosophy (CRVP): 620 Michigan Ave, NE, Washington, DC 20064, USA; tel. and fax (202) 319-6089; e-mail cua-rvp@cua.edu; internet www.crvp.org; f. 1983; organizes 15 confs internationally and a 6-week seminar annually; mems: 70 teams from 60 countries; Pres. Prof. GEORGE F. MCLEAN (USA); Exec. Dir HU YEPING; publs *Cultural Heritage and Contemporary Change series* (300 titles).

Council for the Development of Social Science Research in Africa (CODESRIA): Ave Cheikh, Anta Diop X Canal IV, BP 3304, CP 18524, Dakar, Senegal; tel. 825-98-22; fax 825-12-89; internet www.codesria.org; f. 1973; promotes research, organizes confs, working groups and information services; mems: research institutes and university faculties and researchers in African countries; Exec. Sec. Dr EBRIMA SALL; publs *Africa Development* (quarterly), *CODESRIA Bulletin* (quarterly), *Index of African Social Science Periodical Articles* (annually), *African Journal of International Affairs* (2 a year), *African Sociological Review* (2 a year), *Afrika Zamani* (annually), *Identity, Culture and Politics* (2 a year), *Afro Arab Selections for Social Sciences* (annually), directories of research.

Eastern Regional Organisation for Planning and Human Settlements: Ministry of Housing and Local Government, Corp. Div., Room 26, Level 20, No. 51, Persiaran Perdana, Presint 4, 62100 Putrajaya, Malaysia; tel. and fax (3) 88930899; e-mail secretariat@earoph.info; internet www.earoph.info; f. 1956 to promote and co-ordinate the study and practice of housing and regional town and country planning; maintains offices in Japan, Republic of Korea, Australia, Malaysia and Indonesia; mems: 57 orgs and 213 individuals in 28 countries; Pres. PARK YANG HO (Republic of Korea); Sec.-Gen. NORLIZA HASHIM (Malaysia); publs *EAROPH News and Notes* (monthly), *Town and Country Planning* (bibliography).

English-Speaking Union: Dartmouth House, 37 Charles St, Berkeley Sq., London, W1J 5ED, United Kingdom; tel. (20) 7529-1550; fax (20) 7495-6108; e-mail esu@esu.org; internet www.esu.org; f. 1918 to promote international understanding through the use of the English language; mems: 37 United Kingdom branches; 50 int. affiliates; Chair. Dame MARY RICHARDSON; Dir-Gen. PETER KYLE.

European Association for Population Studies (EAPS): POB 11676, 2502 AR The Hague, Netherlands; tel. (70) 3565200; fax (70) 3647187; e-mail contact@eaps.nl; internet www.eaps.nl; f. 1983 to foster research and provide information on European population problems; organizes confs, seminars and workshops; mems: demographers from 40 countries; Pres. FRANCESO BILLARI (Italy); Exec. Dir NICO VAN NIMWEGEN (Netherlands); publ. *European Journal of Population/Revue Européenne de Démographie* (quarterly).

International African Institute (IAI): School of Oriental and African Studies, Thornhaugh St, Russell Sq., London, WC1H 0XG, United Kingdom; tel. (20) 7898-4420; fax (20) 7898-4419; e-mail iai@soas.ac.uk; internet www.internationalafricaninstitute.org; f. 1926 to promote the study of African peoples, their languages, cultures and social life in their traditional and modern settings; organizes an international seminar programme bringing together scholars from Africa and elsewhere; links scholars in order to facilitate research projects, especially in the social sciences; Chair. Prof. V. Y. MUDIMBE; Hon. Dir Prof. PHILIP BURNHAM; publs *Africa* (quarterly), *Africa Bibliography* (annually).

International Association for Media and Communication Research: c/o Fundación Comunica, Pablo de María 1036, Montevideo 11200, Uruguay; fax 339-8919; internet www.iamcr.org; f. 1957 (fmrly International Assen for Mass Communication Research) to stimulate interest in mass communication research and the dissemination of information about research and research needs, to improve communication practice, policy and research and training for journalism, and to provide a forum for researchers and others involved in mass communication to meet and exchange information; mems: over 2,300 in c. 70 countries; Pres. JANET WASKO (USA); publ. *Newsletter*.

International Association for the History of Religions (IAHR): c/o Prof. Tim Jensen, Institute of History, Dept of the Study of Religions, University of Southern Denmark, Odense, Campusvej 55, 5230 Odense M, Denmark; tel. 65-50-33-15; fax 65-50-26-68; e-mail t.jensen@sdu.dk; internet www.iahr.dk; f. 1950 to promote international collaboration of scholars, to organize congresses and to stimulate research; mems: 38 nat. and 6 reg. asscns; Pres. Prof. ROSALIND I. J. HACKETT; Gen. Sec. Prof. TIM JENSEN; publ. *Numen: International Review for the History of Religions* (annually).

International Association of Applied Linguistics (Association internationale de linguistique appliquée—AILA): Theaterstr. 15, 8401 Winterthur, Switzerland; tel. 589346060; fax 589357769; e-mail secretariat@aila.info; internet www.aila.info; f. 1964; organizes seminars on applied linguistics, and a World Congress every three years (2014: Brisbane, Australia, in Aug.); mems: more than 8,000; Pres. Prof. BERND RUESCHOFF (Germany); Sec.-Gen. Prof. DANIEL PERRIN (Switzerland); publ. *AILA Review* (annually).

International Committee for the History of Art: c/o Prof. Dr P. J. Schneemann, Institut für Kunstgeschichte, Hodlerstr. 8, 3011 Bern, Switzerland; tel. 316314741; fax 316318669; e-mail ciha@inha.fr; internet www.ciha-arthistory.org/index.html; f. 1930 by the 12th International Congress on the History of Art, for collaboration in the scientific study of the history of art; holds International Congress every four years, and at least two colloquia between Congresses; 33rd Congress: held in Nürnberg, Germany, in July 2012, themed 'The Challenge of the Object'; mems: National Committees in 34 countries; Pres. JAYNIE ANDERSON (Australia); Gen. Sec. THIERRY DUFRÊNE (France); Admin. Sec. Prof. Dr PETER JOHANNES SCHNEEMANN (Switzerland) (France); publ. *Bibliographie d'Histoire de l'Art—Bibliography of the History of Art* (quarterly).

International Committee of Historical Sciences (Comité International des Sciences Historiques—CISH): Centre d'histoire, Institut d'études politiques de Paris, 27 rue St Guillaume, 75007 Paris, France; e-mail pascal.cauchy@sciences-po.fr; internet www.cish.org; f. 1926 to work for the advancement of historical sciences by means of international co-ordination; holds international congress every five years, (2015: Jinan, China); mems: 53 national cttees, 28 affiliated int. orgs and 12 internal commissions; Pres. Prof. MARJATTA HIETALA (Finland); Sec.-Gen. Prof. PASCAL CAUCHY (France); publ. *Bulletin d'Information du CISH*.

International Council for Philosophy and Humanistic Studies (ICPHS): Maison de l'UNESCO, 1 rue Miollis, 75732 Paris Cedex 15, France; tel. 1-45-68-48-85; fax 1-40-65-94-80; e-mail cipsh@unesco.org; internet www.unesco.org/cipsh; f. 1949 under the auspices of UNESCO to encourage respect for cultural autonomy by the comparative study of civilization and to contribute towards international understanding through a better knowledge of humanity; works to develop international co-operation in philosophy, humanistic and kindred studies; encourages the setting up of international orgs; promotes the dissemination of information in these fields; sponsors works of learning, etc; mems: 13 orgs representing 145 countries; Pres. ADAMA SAMASSÉKOU; Sec.-Gen. MAURICE AYMARD; publs *Bulletin of Information* (biennially), *Diogenes* (quarterly).

International Council on Archives (ICA): 60 rue des Francs-Bourgeois, 75003 Paris, France; tel. 1-40-27-63-06; fax 1-42-72-20-65; e-mail ica@ica.org; internet www.ica.org; f. 1948 to develop relationships between archivists in different countries; aims to protect and enhance archives, to ensure preservation of archival heritage; facilitates training of archivists and conservators; promotes implementation of a professional code of conduct; encourages ease of access to archives; has 13 regional branches; mems: more than 1,465 in 198 countries; Pres. MARTIN BERENDSE (Netherlands); Sec.-Gen. DAVID LEITCH (France); publs *Comma* (2 a year), *Flash Newsletter* (2 a year), annual CD-Rom.

International Ergonomics Association (IEA): c/o Prof. Dr Eric Min-yang Wang, Dept of Industrial Engineering and Engineering Management, National Tsing Hua University, 101, Sec. 2, Guang Fu Rd, Hsinchu 30013, Taiwan; tel. (886) 35742649; fax (886) 35726153; e-mail mywangericl@gmail.com; internet www.iea.cc; f. 1957 to bring together orgs and persons interested in the scientific study of human work and its environment; to establish international contacts among those specializing in this field, to co-operate with employers' asscns and trade unions in order to encourage the practical application of ergonomic sciences in industries, and to promote scientific research in this field; mems: 47 fed. socs; Pres. Prof. Dr ERIC MIN-YANG WANG; Sec.-Gen. MARGO FRASER; publ. *Ergonomics* (monthly).

International Federation for Housing and Planning (IFHP): Binckhorstlaan 36, 2516 CG The Hague, Netherlands; tel. (70) 3244557; fax (70) 3282085; e-mail info@ifhp.org; internet www.ifhp.org; f. 1913 to study and promote the improvement of housing and the theory and practice of town planning; had four working groups in 2014, on climate-resilient cities, the spontaneous city, housing, and young planners; holds an annual World Congress (2014: Singapore, in May); mems: 200 orgs and 300 individuals in 65 countries; Pres. FLEMMING BORRESKOV (Denmark); CEO OLE STILLING (Denmark); publ. *Newsletter* (quarterly).

International Federation for Modern Languages and Literatures: c/o A. Pettersson, Gröna Gatan 37, 41454 Göteborg, Sweden; tel. (31) 16-2183; e-mail anders.pettersson@littvet.umu.se; internet www.fillm.ulg.ac.be; f. 1928 to establish permanent contact between historians of literature, to develop or perfect facilities for their work and to promote the study of modern languages and literature; holds Congress every three years; mems: 9 asscns; Pres. ROGER D. SELL (Finland); Sec.-Gen. ANDERS PETTERSSON (Sweden).

International Federation of Library Associations and Institutions—Metropolitan Libraries Section: Prins Willem-Alexanderhof 5, 2595 The Hague, Netherlands; tel. (70) 3140884; fax (70) 3834827; e-mail ifla@ifla.org; internet www.ifla.org/hq; f. 1966 as the International Association of Metropolitan Libraries (INTAMEL), became a round table in 1976, present name adopted 2004; serves as a platform for libraries in cities of over 400,000 inhabitants or serving a wide and diverse geographical area; promotes the exchange of ideas and information on a range of topics including library networks, automation, press relations and research; mems: 1,500 mems in approx. 150 countries; Chair. INGRID PARENT.

International Federation of Philosophical Societies (FISP): 1 rue Miollis, 75732 Paris Cedex 15, France; tel. 1-45-68-48-85; e-mail luca.scarantino@iulm.it; internet www.fisp.org; f. 1948 under the auspices of UNESCO, to encourage international co-operation in the field of philosophy; holds World Congress of Philosophy every five years (2013: Athens, Greece, in Aug.); mems: 86 socs from 56 countries; 42 int. socs; Pres. WILLIAM MCBRIDE (USA); Sec.-Gen. LUCA SCARANTINO (Italy); publs *Newsletter*, *International Bibliography of Philosophy*, *Chroniques de Philosophie*, *Contemporary Philosophy*, *Philosophical Problems Today*, *Philosophy and Cultural Development*, *Ideas Underlying World Problems*, *The Idea of Values*.

International Federation of Social Science Organizations (IFSSO): Faculty Center Rm 3055, University of the Philippines, Diliman, Quezon City, 1101 Metro Manila, Philippines; tel. and fax (2) 4261454; fax (2) 4261454; e-mail ifsso_secretariat@yahoo.com; internet www.ifsso.net; f. 1979 to assist research and teaching in the social sciences, and to facilitate co-operation and enlist mutual assistance in the planning and evaluation of programmes of major importance to mems; mems: 13 full and 4 assoc. mems; Pres. Dr NESTOR CASTRO; publs *IFSSO Newsletter* (quarterly), *International Directory of Social Science Organizations*.

International Federation of Societies of Classical Studies: c/o Prof. P. Schubert, 7 rue des Beaux-Arts, 2000 Neuchatel, Switzerland; tel. 223797035; fax 223797932; e-mail paul.schubert@unige.ch; internet www.fiecnet.org; f. 1948 under the auspices of UNESCO; mems: 80 socs in 44 countries; Pres. Dame AVERIL CAMERON (United Kingdom); Sec.-Gen. Prof. PAUL SCHUBERT (Switzerland); publs *L'Année Philologique*, *Thesaurus linguae Latinae*.

International Federation of Vexillological Associations (Fédération internationale des associations vexillologiques): 504 Branard St, Houston, TX 77006-5018, USA; tel. (713) 529-2545; e-mail sec.gen@fiav.org; internet www.fiav.org; f. 1969; unites associations and institutions throughout the world whose object is the pursuit of vexillology, i.e. the creation and devt of a body of knowledge about flags of all types, their forms and functions, and of scientific theories and principles based on that knowledge; sponsors International Congresses of Vexillology every two years (2013: Rotterdam, Netherlands; 2015: Sydney, Australia); mems: 59 institutions and asscns worldwide; Pres. Prof. MICHEL LUPANT (Belgium); Sec.-Gen. Hon. CHARLES A. SPAIN (USA); publs *Info FIAV* (annually), *Proceedings of the International Congresses of Vexillology* (every 2 years).

International Institute of Administrative Sciences (IIAS): 1 rue Defacqz, 1000 Brussels, Belgium; tel. (2) 536-08-80; fax (2) 537-97-02; e-mail info@iias-iisa.org; internet www.iias-iisa.org; f. 1930 for the comparative examination of administrative experience; carries out research and programmes designed to improve administrative law and practices; has consultative status with the UN, UNESCO and the ILO; organizes international congresses, annual confs, working groups; mems: 36 mem. states, 29 nat. sections, 4 int. governmental orgs, 60 corp. mems; Pres. GEERT BOUCKAERT (Belgium); Dir-Gen. ROLET LORETAN (Switzerland); publs *International Review of Administrative Sciences* (quarterly), *Newsletter* (3 a year).

International Institute of Sociology (IIS): c/o The Swedish Collegium for Advanced Study, Thunbergsvägen 2, 75238 Uppsala, Sweden; tel. (18) 55-70-85; e-mail info@iisoc.org; internet www.iisoc.org; f. 1893 to enable sociologists to meet and to study sociological questions; mems: c. 300 in 47 countries; Pres. BJÖRN WITTROCK (Sweden); Sec.-Gen. PETER HEDSTRÖM; publ. *The Annals of the IIS*.

International Musicological Society (IMS): POB 1561, 4001 Basel, Switzerland; tel. 449231022; fax 449231027; e-mail dorothea.baumann@ims-online.ch; internet www.ims-online.ch; f. 1927; holds international congresses every five years (2017: Tokyo, Japan); mems: c. 1,000 in 53 countries; Pres. DINKO FABRIS (Italy); Sec.-Gen. Dr DOROTHEA BAUMANN (Switzerland); publ. *Acta Musicologica* (2 a year).

International Numismatic Council (Conseil international de numismatique): Kunsthistorisches Museum, Coin Cabinet, Burgring 5, 1010 Vienna, Austria; tel. (1) 525-24-42-01; fax (1) 525-24-42-99; e-mail michael.alram@khm.at; internet www.inc-cin.org; f. 1934 as International Numismatic Commission; name changed to present in 2009; facilitates co-operation between scholars studying coins and medals; mems: 160 in 38 countries; Pres. Dr CARMEN ARNOLD-BIUCCHI; Sec. MICHAEL ALRAM.

International Peace Institute: 777 United Nations Plaza, New York, NY 10017-3521, USA; tel. (212) 687-4300; fax (212) 983-8246; e-mail ipi@ipinst.org; internet www.ipinst.org; f. 1970 (as the International Peace Academy) to promote the prevention and settlement of armed conflicts between and within states through policy research and devt; educates govt officials in the procedures needed for conflict resolution, peacekeeping, mediation and negotiation, through international training seminars and publications; off-the-record meetings are also conducted to gain complete understanding of a specific conflict; Chair. RITA E. HAUSER; Pres. TERJE ROD-LARSEN.

International Peace Research Association (IPRA): c/o Mie University, 1577 Kurimamachiya-cho, Tsu City, Mie 514-8507, Japan; tel. and fax (59) 231-5588; fax (16) 32-30-88; e-mail kkodama@human.mie-u.ac.jp; e-mail jake.lynch@usyd.edu.au; tel. ipra-peace.com; f. 1964 to encourage interdisciplinary research on the conditions of peace and the causes of war; mems: 150 corp., 5 reg. brs, 1,000 individuals, in 93 countries; Sec.-Gens KATAYA KODAMA (Japan), JAKE LYNCH (Australia); publ. *IPRA Newsletter* (quarterly).

International Social Science Council (ISSC): Maison de l'UNESCO, 1 rue Miollis, 75732 Paris Cedex 15, France; tel. 1-45-68-48-60; fax 1-45-68-48-62; e-mail issc@worldsocialscience.org; internet www.worldsocialscience.org; f. 1952; aims to promote the advancement of the social sciences throughout the world and their application to the major problems of the world; encourages co-operation at international level between specialists in the social sciences; comprises programmes on International Human Dimensions of Global Environmental Change, Gender, Globalization and Democratization, and Comparative Research on Poverty; mems: International Association of Legal Sciences, International Economic Association, International Federation of Social Science Organizations, International Geographical Union, International Institute of Administrative Sciences, International Peace Research Association, International Political Science Association, International Sociological Association, International Union for the Scientific Study of Population, International Union of Anthropological and Ethnological Sciences, International Union of Psychological Science, World Association for Public Opinion Research, World Federation for Mental Health; 28 nat. orgs; 16 assoc. mems; Pres. Dr OLIVE SHISHANA (South Africa); Exec. Dir Dr HEIDE HACKMANN (France).

International Society of Social Defence and Humane Criminal Policy (ISSD): c/o Centro nazionale di prevenzione e difesa sociale, Piazza Castello 3, 20121 Milan, Italy; tel. (02) 86460714; fax (02) 72008431; e-mail cnpds.ispac@cnpds.it; internet www.cnpds.it; f. 1945 to combat crime, to protect society and to prevent citizens from being tempted to commit criminal actions; mems: in 43 countries; Sec.-Gen. FRANCESCO VIGANÒ (Italy); publ. *Cahiers de défense sociale* (annually).

International Sociological Association: c/o Faculty of Political Sciences and Sociology, Universidad Complutense, 28223 Madrid, Spain; tel. (91) 3527650; fax (91) 3524945; e-mail isa@isa-sociology.org; internet www.isa-sociology.org; f. 1949 to promote sociological knowledge, facilitate contacts between sociologists, encourage the dissemination and exchange of information and facilities and stimulate research; has 55 research cttees on various aspects of sociology; holds World Congresses every four years (18th Congress: Yokohama, Japan, July 2014); Pres. MICHAEL BURAWOY; Exec. Sec. IZABELA BARLINSKA; publs *Current Sociology* (6 a year), *International Sociology* (6 a year), *Sage Studies in International Sociology* (based on World Congress).

International Statistical Institute (ISI): POB 24070, 2490 AB The Hague, Netherlands; tel. (70) 3375737; fax (70) 3860025; e-mail isi@cbs.nl; internet www.isi-web.org; f. 1885; devoted to the devt and improvement of statistical methods and their application throughout the world; executes international research programmes; mems: 2,000 ordinary mems, 11 hon. mems, 166 ex officio mems, 69 corp. mems, 45 affiliated orgs, 32 nat. statistical socs; Pres. VIJAY NAIR (USA); Dir Permanent Office ADA VAN KRIMPEN; publs *Bulletin of the International Statistical Institute* (proceedings of biennial sessions), *International Statistical Review* (3 a year), *Short Book Reviews* (3 a year), *Statistical Theory and Method Abstracts–Z* (available on CD-Rom and online).

International Studies Association (ISA): Social Science 324, Univ. of Arizona, Tucson, AZ 85721, USA; tel. (520) 621-7715; fax (520) 621-5780; e-mail isa@u.arizona.edu; internet www.isanet.org; f. 1959; links those whose professional concerns extend beyond their own national boundaries (govt officials, representatives of business and industry, and scholars); mems: 3,500 in 60 countries; Pres. HARVEY STARR (USA); Exec. Dir THOMAS J. VOLGY; publs *International Studies Quarterly*, *International Studies Perspectives*, *International Studies Review*, *ISA Newsletter*.

International Union for the Scientific Study of Population (IUSSP): 3–5 rue Nicolas, 75980 Paris Cedex 20, France; tel. 1-56-06-21-73; fax 1-56-06-22-04; e-mail iussp@iussp.org; internet www.iussp.org; f. 1928 to advance the progress of quantitative and qualitative demography as a science (reconstituted in 1947); organizes International Population Conference every four years (27th Conference: Busan, Republic of Korea, Aug. 2013); mems: 1,917 in 121 countries; Pres. PETER MCDONALD (Australia); Sec.-Gen./Treas. EMILY GRUNDY (United Kingdom); publs *IUSSP Bulletin* and books on population.

International Union of Academies (IUA) (Union académique internationale—UAI): Palais des Académies, 1 rue Ducale, 1000 Brussels, Belgium; tel. (2) 550-22-00; fax (2) 550-22-05; e-mail info@uai-iua.org; internet www.uai-iua.org; f. 1919 to promote international co-operation through collective research in philology, archaeology, art history, history and social sciences; mems: academic institutions in 66 countries; Sec.-Gen. HERVÉ HASQUIN.

International Union of Anthropological and Ethnological Sciences (IUAES): Dept of Anthropology, Faculty of Human Sciences, Osaka University, 1–2 Yamadaoka, Suita, Osaka 565-0871, Japan; tel. and fax (6) 6879-8085; e-mail iuaes@glocol.osaka-u.ac.jp; internet www.iuaes.org; f. 1948 under the auspices of UNESCO, to enhance exchange and communication between scientists and institutions in the fields of anthropology and ethnology; aims to promote harmony between nature and culture; organizes 24 international research commissions; 17th World Congress: Manchester, United Kingdom, Aug. 2013; mems: institutions and individuals in 80 countries; Pres. Dr PETER J. M. NAS (Netherlands); Sec.-Gen. JUNJI KOIZUMI (Japan); publ. *IUAES Newsletter* (3 a year).

International Union of Prehistoric and Protohistoric Sciences: GRI, Inst Politécnico de Tomar, ave Dr Cândido Madueira, 2300-531 Tomar, Portugal; tel. (249) 346363; fax (249) 346366; e-mail secretary@uispp.org; internet www.uispp.org; f. 1931 to promote congresses and scientific work in the fields of pre- and proto-history; mems: 120 countries; Pres. JEAN BOURGEOIS; Sec.-Gen. LUIZ OOSTERBEEK.

Mensa International: c/o British Mensa, St John's House, St. John's Sq., Wolverhampton, WV2 4AH, United Kingdom; tel. (1902) 772771; fax (1902) 392500; e-mail enquiries@mensa.org; internet www.mensa.org; f. 1946 to identify and foster intelligence for the benefit of humanity; mems: individuals who score higher than 98% of people in general in a recognized intelligence test may become mems; there are 100,000 mems worldwide; Exec. Dir MICHAEL FEENAN (United Kingdom); publ. *Mensa International Journal* (monthly).

Permanent International Committee of Linguists: Postbus 3023, 2301 DA Leiden, Netherlands; tel. (71) 5211552; e-mail pvansterkenburg@planet.nl; internet www.ciplnet.com; f. 1928; aims to further linguistic research, to co-ordinate activities undertaken for the advancement of linguistics, and to make the results of linguistic research known internationally; holds Congress every five years (19th Congress: Geneva, Switzerland, July 2013); mems: 40 linguistic orgs; Pres. N. VINCENT (UK); Sec.-Gen. P. G. J. VAN STERKENBURG (Netherlands); publ. *Linguistic Bibliography* (annually).

World Association for Public Opinion Research: c/o University of Nebraska-Lincoln, UNL Gallup Research Center, 201 N 13th St, Lincoln, NE 68588-0242, USA; tel. (402) 472-7720; fax (402) 472-

7727; e-mail renae@wapor.org; internet wapor.unl.edu; f. 1947 to establish and promote contacts between persons in the field of survey research on opinions, attitudes and behaviour of people in the various countries of the world; works to further the use of objective, scientific survey research in national and international affairs; mems: 600 mems from some 60 countries; Pres. Dr ALEJANDRO MORENO; Gen. Sec. Prof. Dr ALLAN MCCUTCHEON; publs *WAPOR Newsletter* (quarterly), *International Journal of Public Opinion* (quarterly).

World Society for Ekistics: c/o Athens Center of Ekistics, 23 Strat. Syndesmou St, 106 73 Athens, Greece; tel. (210) 3623216; fax (210) 3629337; e-mail ekistics@otenet.gr; internet www.ekistics.org; f. 1965; aims to promote knowledge and ideas concerning human settlements through research, publications and confs; encourages the devt and expansion of education in ekistics; aims to recognize the benefits and necessity of an interdisciplinary approach to the needs of human settlements; mems: 226 individuals; Pres. CALOGERO MUSCARA; Sec.-Gen. P. PSOMOPOULOS.

Social Welfare and Human Rights

African Commission on Human and Peoples' Rights: 31 Bijilo Annex Layout, POB 673, Banjul, The Gambia; tel. 4410505; fax 4410504; e-mail au-banjul@africa-union.org; internet www.achpr.org; f. 1987; monitors compliance with the African Charter on Human and People's Rights (ratified in 1986); investigates claims of human rights abuses perpetrated by govts that have ratified the Charter (claims may be brought by other African govts, the victims themselves, or by a third party); meets each year in March and Oct; mems: 11; Exec. Sec. Dr MARY MABOREKE.

Aid to Displaced Persons (L'Aide aux Personnes Déplacées): 33 rue du Marché, 4500 Huy, Belgium; tel. (85) 21-34-81; fax (85) 23-01-47; e-mail aidepersdepl.huy@skynet.be; internet www.aideauxpersonnesdeplacees.be; f. 1949; aims to provide aid and support for refugees; founder Fr. Georges Pire awarded the Nobel Prize for Peace in 1958.

Amnesty International: 1 Easton St, London, WC1X ODW, United Kingdom; tel. (20) 7413-5500; fax (20) 7956-1157; e-mail amnestyis@amnesty.org; internet www.amnesty.org; f. 1961; an independent, democratic, self-governing worldwide movement of people who campaign for internationally recognized human rights, such as those enshrined in the Universal Declaration of Human Rights; undertakes research and action focused on preventing and ending grave abuses of the rights to physical and mental integrity, freedom of conscience and expression, and freedom from discrimination, within the context of its work impartially to promote and protect all human rights; mems: more than 3m. represented by 7,800 local, youth, student and other specialist groups, in more than 150 countries and territories; nationally organized sections in 58 countries and pre-section co-ordinating structures in another 22 countries; major policy decisions are taken by an International Council comprising representatives from all national sections; financed by donations; no funds are sought or accepted from govts; Sec.-Gen. SALIL SHETTY (India); publs *International Newsletter* (monthly), *Annual Report*, country reports.

Anti-Slavery International: Thomas Clarkson House, The Stableyard, Broomgrove Rd, London, SW9 9TL, United Kingdom; tel. (20) 7501-8920; fax (20) 7738-4110; e-mail info@antislavery.org; internet www.antislavery.org; f. 1839; aims to eliminate all forms of slavery—bonded labour, child labour, human trafficking, early and forced marriage, slavery by descent—by exposing manifestations of it around the world and campaigning against it; supports initiatives by local orgs to release people from slavery, and develops rehabilitation programmes aimed at preventing people from re-entering slavery; pressures govts to implement international laws prohibiting slavery and to develop and enforce similar national legislation; maintains digital collection of 18th- and 19th-century documentation on the Transatlantic Slave Trade at www.recoveredhistories.org; mems: c. 2,000 worldwide; Dir AIDAN MCQUADE; publs *Annual Review*, *Reporter* (2 a year), special reports and research documentation.

Article 19: 60 Farringdon Rd, London, EC1R 3GA, United Kingdom; tel. (20) 7324-2500; e-mail info@article19.org; internet www.article19.org; f. 1987; an international human rights org., in particular dedicated to defending and promoting freedom of expression and of information; Exec. Dir Dr AGNÈS CALLAMARD.

Associated Country Women of the World (ACWW): Mary Sumner House, 24 Tufton St, London, SW1P 3RB, United Kingdom; tel. (20) 7799-3875; fax (20) 7340-9950; e-mail info@acww.org.uk; internet www.acww.org.uk; f. 1933; aims to aid the economic and social devt of countrywomen and home-makers of all nations, to promote international goodwill and understanding, to work to alleviate poverty, and promote good health and education; Pres MAY KIDD; Gen. Sec. JO ELLEN ALMOND; publ. *The Countrywoman* (quarterly).

Association Internationale de la Mutualité (AIM) (International Association of Mutual Health Funds): 50 rue d'Arlon, 5th Floor, 1000 Brussels, Belgium; tel. (2) 234-57-00; fax (2) 234-57-08; e-mail aim.secretariat@aim-mutual.org; internet www.aim-mutual.org; f. 1950 as a grouping of autonomous health insurance and social protection bodies; aims to promote and reinforce access to health care by developing the sound management of mutualities; serves as a forum for the exchange of information and debate; mems: 50 feds in 28 countries; Pres. JEAN-PHILIPPE HUCHET (France); publs *AIMS* (newsletter), reports on health issues.

Aviation sans Frontières (ASF): Orly Fret 768, 94398 Orly Aérogare Cedex, France; tel. 1-49-75-74-37; fax 1-49-75-74-33; e-mail asfparis@asf-fr.org; internet www.asf-fr.org; f. 1983 to make available the resources of the aviation industry to humanitarian orgs, for carrying supplies and equipment at minimum cost, both on long-distance flights and locally; Pres. HUGUES GENDRE; Gen. Sec. PATRICK SAUMONT.

Caritas Internationalis (International Confederation of Catholic Organizations for charitable and social action): Palazzo San Calisto, 00120 Città del Vaticano; tel. (06) 6987-9799; fax (06) 6988-7237; e-mail caritas.internationalis@caritas.va; internet www.caritas.org; f. 1950 to study problems arising from poverty, their causes and possible solutions; national mem. orgs undertake assistance and devt activities. The Confederation co-ordinates emergency relief and devt projects, and represents mems at international level; mems: 165 nat. orgs; Pres. Cardinal OSCAR RODRIGUEZ MARADIAGA (Honduras); Sec.-Gen. MICHEL ROY (France); publs *Caritas Matters* (quarterly), *Emergency Calling* (2 a year).

CISV International Ltd: Mea House, Ellison Pl., Newcastle upon Tyne, NE1 8XS, United Kingdom; tel. (191) 232-4998; fax (191) 261-4710; e-mail international@cisv.org; internet www.cisv.org; f. 1950 as the International Association of Children's International Summer Villages to promote peace, education and cross-cultural friendship; conducts International Camps for children and young people mainly between the ages of 11 and 19; mems: c. 49,000; Int. Pres. ARNE-CHRISTIAN HAUKELAND; Sec.-Gen. GABRIELLE MANDELL.

CIVICUS (World Alliance for Citizen Participation): POB 933, Southdale, Johannesburg 2135, South Africa; tel. (11) 833-5959; fax (11) 833-7997; e-mail info@civicus.org; internet www.civicus.org; f. 1993; aims to protect and strengthen citizen action and civil society throughout the world, in particular in areas where participatory democracy and citizen freedoms are threatened; convenes a World Assembly annually; over 1,000 mems in 120 countries; Sec.-Gen. DHANANJAYAN SRISKANDARAJAH.

Co-ordinating Committee for International Voluntary Service (CCIVS): Maison de l'UNESCO, 1 rue Miollis, 75732 Paris Cedex 15, France; tel. 1-45-68-49-36; fax 1-42-73-05-21; e-mail secretariat@ccivs.org; internet www.ccivs.org; f. 1948 to co-ordinate youth voluntary service orgs worldwide; organizes seminars and confs; publishes relevant literature; undertakes planning and execution of projects in collaboration with UNESCO, the UN, the European Union, etc; affiliated mems: 220 orgs in more than 100 countries; Pres. MATINA DELIGIANNI (France); Gen. Sec. ORIOL JOSA (Italy); publs *News from CCIVS* (3 a year), *The Volunteer's Handbook*, other guides, handbooks and directories.

Co-ordinator of the Indigenous Organizations of the Amazon Basin (COICA): Calle Sevilla 24–358 y Guipuzcoa, La Floresta, Quito, Ecuador; e-mail com@coica.org.ec; internet www.coica.org.ec; f. 1984; aims to co-ordinate the activities of national orgs concerned with the indigenous people and environment of the Amazon basin, and promotes respect for human rights and the self-determination of the indigenous populations; mems: 9 orgs; Co-ordinator-Gen. EDWIN VÁSQUEZ CAMPOS; publ. *Nuestra Amazonia* (quarterly, in English, Spanish, French and Portuguese).

EIRENE (International Christian Service for Peace): Engerser Str. 81, 56564 Neuwied, Germany; tel. (2631) 83790; fax (2631) 837990; e-mail eirene-int@eirene.org; internet www.eirene.org; f. 1957; undertakes professional training, apprenticeship programmes, and devt work in support of co-operatives in Africa and Latin America; conducts conflict resolution activities; runs volunteer programmes in co-operation with peace groups in Europe and the USA; Man. Dir Dr ANTHEA BETHGE.

European Federation of Older Persons (EURAG): Lečkova 1520, 149 00 Prague 4, Czech Republic; tel. 608552113; fax 272931248; e-mail dana_stein@volny.cz; internet www.eurageurope.org; f. 1962 as the European Federation for the Welfare of the Elderly (present name adopted 2002); serves as a forum for the exchange of experience and practical co-operation among mem. orgs; represents the interests of mem. before international orgs; promotes understanding and co-operation in matters of social welfare; draws attention to the problems of old age; mems in 28 countries; Pres. DIRK JARRÉ (Germany); Sec.-Gen. DANUSE STEINOVA (Czech Republic);

publ. (in English, French, German and Italian) *EURAG Information* (monthly).

Federation of Asia-Pacific Women's Associations (FAWA): 962 Josefa Llanes Escoda St, Ermita, Manila, Philippines; tel. (2) 741-1675; e-mail nfwcp@yahoo.com; internet fawainternational.org; f. 1959 to provide closer relations, and bring about joint efforts among Asians, particularly women, through mutual appreciation of cultural, moral and socio-economic values; mems: 415,000; Pres. Dr KIM JUNG-SOOK (Republic of Korea); Sec. REBECCA STEPHENSON (USA); publ. *FAWA News Bulletin* (quarterly).

Global Migration Group: 17 Route des Morillons, 1211, 19 Geneva, Switzerland; tel. 227179111; fax 227986150; internet www.globalmigrationgroup.org; f. 2003, as the Geneva Migration Group; renamed as above in 2006; mems: the ILO, IOM, UNCTAD, UNDP, United Nations Department of Economic and Social Affairs (UNDESA), UNESCO, UNICEF, UNFPA, UNITAR, OHCHR, UNHCR, UNODC, UN Women, the UN Regional Commissions, WHO and the World Bank; holds regular meetings to discuss issues relating to international migration, chaired by mem. orgs on a six-month rotational basis.

Inclusion Europe: Galeries de la Toison d'Or, 29 ch. d'Ixelles, bte 393/32, 1050 Brussels, Belgium; tel. (2) 502-28-15; fax (2) 502-80-10; e-mail secretariat@inclusion-europe.org; internet www.inclusion-europe.org; f. 1988 to advance the human rights and defend the interests of people with learning or intellectual disabilities, and their families, in Europe; mems: 46 socs in 34 European countries; Pres. MAUREEN PIGGOT (United Kingdom); publs *INCLUDE* (in English and French), *Information Letter* (weekly online, in English and French), *Human Rights Observer* (in English and French), *Enlargement Update* (online every 2 weeks, in English and French), other papers and publs.

Initiatives of Change International: 1 rue de Varembé, 1202 Geneva, Switzerland; tel. 227491620; fax 227330267; e-mail iofc-international@iofc.org; internet www.iofc.org; f. 1921; name changed from the Moral Rearmament Movement in 2001; an international network specializing in conflict resolution that is open to people of all cultures, nationalities, religions and beliefs, and works towards change, both locally and globally, commencing at personal level; has special consultative status with ECOSOC and participatory status with the Council of Europe; supports and publicizes the grass-roots work of the National Societies of Initiatives of Change; works in 60 countries; Pres. OMNIA MARZOUK; publs *Changer International* (French, 6 a year), *For a Change* (English, 6 a year), *Caux Information* (German, monthly).

Inter-American Conference on Social Security (Conferencia Interamericano de Seguridad Social—CISS): Calle San Ramón s/n Col. San Jeronimo Lidice Del. Magdalena Contreras, CP 10100, México, DF, Mexico; tel. (55) 5377-4700; fax (55) 5377-4716; e-mail ciss@ciss.org.mx; internet www.ciss.org.mx; f. 1942 to contribute to the devt of social security in the countries of the Americas and to co-operate with social security institutions; CISS bodies are: the General Assembly, the Permanent Inter-American Committee on Social Security, the Secretariat General, six American Commissions of Social Security and the Inter-American Center for Social Security Studies; mems: 66 social security institutions in 36 countries; Pres. Dr JOSÉ ANTONIO GONZÁLEZ ANAYA (Mexico); Sec.-Gen. JUAN LOZANO; publs *Social Security Journal / Seguridad Social* (every 2 months), *The Americas Social Security Report* (annually), *Social Security Bulletin* (monthly, online), monographs, study series.

International Association for Suicide Prevention: IASP Central Administrative Office, Sognsvannsveien 21, Bygg 12, 0372 Oslo, Norway; tel. 22-92-37-15; fax 22-92-39-58; e-mail office@iasp.info; internet www.iasp.info; f. 1960; serves as a common platform for interchange of acquired experience, literature and information about suicide; disseminates information; arranges special training; encourages and carries out research; organizes the Biennial International Congress for Suicide Prevention (Sept. 2013: Oslo, Norway); mems: 340 individuals and socs, in 55 countries of all continents; Pres. Dr LANNY BERMAN; publ. *Crisis* (quarterly).

International Association of Schools of Social Work: c/o A. Tasse, Graduate School of Social Work, University of Addis Ababa, POB 1176, Ethiopia; tel. (1) 231084; fax (1) 239768; e-mail abye.tasse@ids.fr; internet www.iassw-aiets.org; f. 1928 to provide international leadership and encourage high standards in social work education; mems: 1,600 schools of social work in 70 countries, and 25 nat. asscns of schools; Pres. VIMLA V. NADKARNI (India); publs *Newsletters* (in English, French and Spanish), *Directory of Schools of Social Work*, *Journal of International Social Work*, reports and case studies.

International Association of Social Educators (AIEJI): Galgebakken Soender 5-4, DK-2620 Albertslund, Denmark; tel. 72-48-68-62; e-mail bhd@sl.dk; internet www.aieji.net; f. 1951 (as International Asscn of Workers for Troubled Children and Youth); provides a centre of information about child welfare; encourages co-operation between mems; 2013 Congress: Luxembourg, in April; mems: 36 orgs; Pres. BENNY ANDERSEN (Denmark); Gen. Sec. LARS STEINOV (Denmark).

International Catholic Migration Commission (ICMC): POB 96, 1 rue de Varembé, 1211 Geneva, Switzerland; tel. 229191020; fax 229191048; e-mail info@icmc.net; internet www.icmc.net; f. 1951; serves and protects uprooted people (refugees, internationally displaced persons and migrants), regardless of faith, race, ethnicity or nationality; maintains staff and programmes in more than 40 countries; advocates for rights-based policies and durable solutions; Pres. JOHN KLINK (USA); Sec. H. E. Bishop PRECIOSO CANTILLAS (Philippines).

International Civil Defence Organization (ICDO) (Organisation internationale de protection civile—OIPC): POB 172, 10–12 chemin de Surville, 1213 Petit-Lancy 2, Geneva, Switzerland; tel. 228796969; fax 228796979; e-mail icdo@icdo.org; internet www.icdo.org; f. 1931, present statutes in force 1972; aims to contribute to the devt of structures ensuring the protection of populations and the safeguarding of property and the environment in the face of natural and man-made disasters; promotes co-operation between civil defence orgs in mem. countries; Sec.-Gen. VLADIMIR KUVSHINOV (Russia); publ. *International Civil Defence Journal* (quarterly, in Arabic, English, French, Russian and Chinese).

International Commission for the Prevention of Alcoholism and Drug Dependency: 12501 Old Columbia Pike, Silver Spring, MD 20904-6600, USA; tel. (301) 680-6719; fax (301) 680-6707; e-mail the_icpa@hotmail.com; internet icpaworld.org; f. 1952 to encourage scientific research on intoxication by alcohol, its physiological, mental and moral effects on the individual, and its effect on the community; mems: individuals in 120 countries; Exec. Dir Dr PETER N. LANDLESS; publ. *ICPA Reporter*.

International Council of Voluntary Agencies (ICVA): 26–28 ave Guiseppe Motta, 1202 Geneva, Switzerland; tel. 229509600; fax 229509609; e-mail secretariat@icvanetwork.org; internet www.icvanetwork.org; f. 1962 as a global network of human rights and humanitarian non-governmental orgs; focuses on information exchange and advocacy, primarily in the areas of humanitarian affairs and refugee issues; mems: 76 non-governmental orgs; Chair. PENNY LAWRENCE (United Kingdom); Exec. Dir NAN BUZARD; publ. *Talk Back* (newsletter, available online).

International Council of Women (ICW) (Conseil International des Femmes—CIF): 13 rue Caumartin, 75009 Paris, France; tel. 1-47-42-19-40; fax 1-42-66-26-23; e-mail office@icw-cif.com; internet www.icw-cif.com; f. 1888 to bring together in international affiliation National Councils of Women from all continents, for consultation and joint action; promotes equal rights for men and women and the integration of women in devt and decision-making; has five standing cttees; mems: 65 nat. councils; Pres. COSIMA SCHENK; publ. *Newsletter*.

International Council on Alcohol and Addictions (ICAA): CP 189, 1001 Lausanne, Switzerland; tel. 213209865; fax 213209817; e-mail secretariat@icaa.ch; internet www.icaa.ch; f. 1907; provides an international forum for all those concerned with the prevention of harm resulting from the use of alcohol and other drugs; offers advice and guidance in devt of policies and programmes; organizes training courses, congresses, symposia and seminars in different countries; mems: affiliated orgs in 74 countries, as well as individual mems; Pres. Dr PETER A. VAMOS (Canada); publs *ICAA Newsflash*, *Alcoholism* (2 a year), *President's Letter*.

International Council on Social Welfare (ICSW): Berkerly Lane, Plot 4, Entebbe, POB 28957, Kampala, Uganda; tel. (414) 32-1150; e-mail dcorrell@icsw.org; internet www.icsw.org; f. 1928 to provide an international forum for the discussion of social work and related issues and to promote interest in social welfare; holds international conf. every two years with the International Association of Schools of Social Work and the International Federation of Social Workers; provides documentation and information services; mems: 57 nat. cttees, 6 int. orgs, 34 other orgs in 87 countries; Pres. CHRISTIAN ROLLET; Exec. Dir DENYS CORRELL; publ. *Global Cooperation Newsletter Monthly*.

International Dachau Committee: 2 rue Chauchat, 75009 Paris, France; tel. 1-45-23-39-99; fax 1-48-00-06-13; e-mail info@comiteinternationaldachau.com; internet www.comiteinternationaldachau.com; f. 1958 to perpetuate the memory of the political prisoners of Dachau; to manifest the friendship and solidarity of former prisoners whatever their beliefs or nationality; to maintain the ideals of their resistance, liberty, tolerance and respect for persons and nations; and to maintain the former concentration camp at Dachau as a museum and international memorial; mems: nat. asscns in 20 countries; Pres. PIETER DIETZ DE LOOS; publ. *Bulletin Officiel du Comité International de Dachau* (2 a year).

International Federation for Human Rights Leagues (FIDH): 17 passage de la Main d'Or, 75011 Paris, France; tel. 1-43-55-25-18; fax 1-43-55-18-80; e-mail fidh@fidh.org; internet www.fidh.org; f. 1922; promotes the implementation of the Universal Declaration of Human Rights and other instruments of human rights protection; aims to raise awareness and alert public opinion to issues of human rights violations; undertakes investigation and observation missions; carries out training; uses its consultative and observer status to lobby international authorities; mems: 164 nat. leagues in over 100 countries; Pres. SOUHAYR BELHASSEN (Tunisia); Exec. Dir ANTOINE BERNARD; publs *Lettre* (2 a month), mission reports.

International Federation of Educative Communities (FICE): Hasengasse 60/14, 1100 Vienna, Austria; tel. (676) 6190871; e-mail bettinaterp@hotmail.com; internet www.fice-inter.net; f. 1948 under the auspices of UNESCO to co-ordinate the work of national asscns, and to promote the international exchange of knowledge and experience in the field of childcare; Congress held every two years (2013: Bern, Switzerland, in Oct.); mems: nat. asscns from 21 European countries, Canada, India, Israel, Morocco, South Africa and the USA; Pres. DASHENKA KRALEVA; publ. *Bulletin* (2 a year).

International Federation of Persons with Physical Disability (FIMITIC): Rákóczi út. 36, 2600 Vác, Hungary; tel. and fax (27) 502661; e-mail fimitic@invitel.hu; internet www.fimitic.org; f. 1953; an international, humanitarian, non-profit, politically and religiously neutral non-governmental umbrella fed. of persons with physical disability under the guidance of the disabled themselves; focuses activities on ensuring the equalization of opportunities and full participation of persons with physical disabilities in society and fights against any kind of discrimination against persons with disabilities; mems: nat. groups from 28 European countries; Pres. MIGUEL ANGEL GARCÍA OCA (Spain); publs *Bulletin*, *Nouvelles*.

International Federation of Social Workers (IFSW): POB 6875, Schwarztorstr. 22, 3001 Bern, Switzerland; tel. 225483625; fax 225181037; e-mail global@ifsw.org; internet www.ifsw.org; f. 1928 as International Permanent Secretariat of Social Workers; present name adopted 1956; aims to promote social work as a profession through international co-operation on standards, training, ethics and working conditions; organizes international confs; represents the profession at the UN and other international bodies; supports national asscns of social workers; mems: national asscns in 90 countries; Pres. GARY BAILEY (USA); Sec.-Gen, Dr RORY G. TRUELL (New Zealand); publs *IFSW update* (available online), policy statements and manifestos.

International Federation of the Blue Cross: Gesellschaftsstrasse 78, 3012 Bern, Switzerland; tel. 313019804; fax 313019805; e-mail office@ifbc.info; internet www.ifbc.info; f. 1877 to aid the victims of intemperance and drug addiction, and to take part in the general movement against alcoholism; mems: 43 orgs; Pres. ALBERT MOUKOLO; Sec.-Gen ANNE BABB.

International League against Racism and Antisemitism (La Ligue Internationale contre le Racisme et l'Antisémitisme—LICRA): 42 rue du Louvre, 75001 Paris, France; tel. 1-45-08-08-08; fax 1-45-08-18-18; e-mail licra@licra.org; internet www.licra.org; f. 1927; campaigns against all forms of racism in sport, culture, education, law, etc.; Pres. ALAIN JAKUBOWICZ.

International League for Human Rights: 352 Seventh Ave, Suite 1234, New York, NY 10001, USA; tel. (212) 661-0480; fax (212) 661-0416; e-mail info@ilhr.org; internet www.ilhr.org; f. 1942 to implement political, civil, social, economic and cultural rights contained in the Universal Declaration of Human Rights adopted by the UN and to support and protect defenders of human rights worldwide; maintains offices in Geneva, Switzerland, and in Freetown, Sierra Leone; mems: individuals, nat. affiliates and correspondents throughout the world; Pres. ROBERT ARSENAULT; Exec. Dir DAVID TAM-BARYOH; publs various human rights reports.

International Planned Parenthood Federation (IPPF): 4 Newhams Row, London, SE1 3UZ, United Kingdom; tel. (20) 7939-8200; fax (20) 7939-8300; e-mail info@ippf.org; internet www.ippf.org; f. 1952; aims to promote and support sexual and reproductive health rights and choices worldwide, with a particular focus on the needs of young people; works to bring relevant issues to the attention of the media, parliamentarians, academics, governmental and non-governmental orgs, and the general public; mobilizes financial resources to fund programmes and information materials; offers technical assistance and training; collaborates with other international orgs; the International Medical Panel of the IPPF formulates guidelines and statements on current medical and scientific advice and best practices; mems: independent family planning asscns in over 151 countries; Pres. Dr NAOMI SEBONI; Dir-Gen. TEWODROS MELESSE.

International Social Security Association (ISSA): 4 route des Morillons, CP 1, 1211 Geneva 22, Switzerland; tel. 227996617; fax 227998509; e-mail issa@ilo.org; internet www.issa.int; f. 1927 to promote the devt of social security throughout the world, mainly through the improvement of techniques and administration, in order to advance social and economic conditions on the basis of social justice; collects and disseminates information on social security programmes throughout the world; undertakes research and policy analysis on the social security issues and distributes their results; encourages mutual assistance between mem. orgs; facilitates good practice collection and exchange; co-operates with other international or regional orgs exercising activities related to the field; communicates with its constituency and media and promotes social security through advocacy and information; and forges partnerships between the ISSA and other international orgs active in the area of social security to advance common strategies, including the ILO, OECD and the World Bank; organizes a World Social Security Forum (2013: Doha, Qatar, in Nov.) and four Regional Social Security Forums (in Africa, the Americas, Asia-Pacific and Europe); convenes topic-related technical seminars in various regions; hosts international confs, for example on information and communication technology in social security, social security actuaries and statisticians, and international policy research; co-organizes the World Congress on Occupational Safety and Health every three years; mems: 340 institutions in 160 countries; Pres. ERROL FRANK STOOVÉ (Netherlands); Sec.-Gen. HANS-HORST KONKOLEWSKY; publs *International Social Security Review* (quarterly, in English, French, German, Spanish), *Social Security Observer* (quarterly, in English, French, German, Spanish), *Social Security Worldwide*, online Social Security Observatory and other databases.

International Social Service (Service social international—SSI): 32 quai du Seujet, 1201 Geneva, Switzerland; tel. 229067700; fax 229067701; e-mail info@iss-ssi.org; internet www.iss-ssi.org; f. 1921 to aid families and individuals whose problems require services beyond the boundaries of the country in which they live, and where the solution of these problems depends upon co-ordinated action on the part of social workers in two or more countries; studies from an international standpoint the conditions and consequences of emigration in their effect on individual, family, and social life; operates on a non-sectarian and non-political basis; runs the International Reference Centre for children deprived of family and analyses trends in national and international adoption; mems: 13 branches, 4 affiliated bureaux, and correspondents in more than 120 countries; Pres. a.i. DOUG LEWIS; Sec.-Gen. JEAN AYOUB.

International Union of Tenants: Box 7514, 10392 Stockholm, Sweden; tel. (8) 7910225; fax (8) 204344; e-mail info@iut.nu; internet www.iut.nu; f. 1955 to collaborate in safeguarding the interests of tenants; participates in activities of UN-Habitat; has working groups for EC matters, Eastern Europe, developing countries and for future devt; holds annual council meeting and triennial congress; mems: nat. tenant orgs in 29 European countries, and Australia, Benin, Canada, India, Japan, New Zealand, Nigeria, South Africa, Tanzania, Togo, Uganda, and USA; Chair. SVEN BERGENSTRÅHLE; Sec.-Gen. MAGNUS HAMMAR; publ. *The Global Tenant* (quarterly).

Inter-University European Institute on Social Welfare (IEISW): 179 rue du Débarcadère, 6001 Marcinelle, Belgium; tel. (71) 44-72-67; fax (71) 47-27-44; e-mail ieiasmayence@hotmail.com; f. 1970 to promote, carry out and publicize scientific research on social welfare and community work; Gen. Dir SERGE MAYENCE; publ. *COMM*.

Lions Clubs International: 300 West 22nd St, Oak Brook, IL 60523-8842, USA; tel. (630) 571-5466; fax (630) 571-8890; e-mail lions@lionsclubs.org; internet www.lionsclubs.org; f. 1917 to foster understanding among people of the world; to promote principles of good govt and citizenship and an interest in civic, cultural, social and moral welfare and to encourage service-minded people to serve their community without financial reward; mems: 1.35m. in over 46,000 clubs in 197 countries and geographic areas; Int. Pres. BARRY J. PALMER (Australia) (2014); publ. *The Lion* (10 a year, in 20 languages).

Médecins sans frontières (MSF): 78 rue de Lausanne, CP 116, 1211 Geneva 21, Switzerland; tel. 228498400; fax 228498404; internet www.msf.org; f. 1971; independent medical humanitarian org. composed of physicians and other mems of the medical profession; aims to provide medical assistance to victims of war and natural disasters; operates longer-term programmes of nutrition, immunization, sanitation, public health, and rehabilitation of hospitals and dispensaries; awarded the Nobel Peace Prize in 1999; mems: 23 asscns in more than 60 countries worldwide; Pres. Dr JOANNE LIU (Canada); Sec.-Gen. JÉRÔME OBERREIT; publ. *Activity Report* (annually).

Pacific Disability Forum: POB 18458, Suva, Fiji; tel. 3312008; fax 3310469; e-mail pdfsec@unwired.com.fj; internet www.pacificdisability.org; f. 2002 to foster regional co-operation in addressing issues related to disability for the benefit of affected persons; aims to build awareness and pool resources among regional orgs to work for the rights and dignity of people with disabilities; organizes a Pacific Disability Regional Conference (2013: Nouméa, New Caledonia); mems: 44 individuals and reg. orgs; CEO SETAREKI MACANAWAI.

Pan-Pacific and South East Asia Women's Association (PPSEAWA): POB 119, Nuku'alofa, Tonga; tel. 24003; fax 41404; e-mail info@ppseawa.org; internet www.ppseawa.org; f. 1928 to foster better understanding and friendship among women in the region, and to promote co-operation for the study and improvement of social conditions; holds international conf. every three years (2013: Suva, Fiji, in Aug.); mems: 22 nat. mem. orgs; Pres. TERESA A. HINTZKE; publ. *PPSEAWA Bulletin* (2 a year).

Relief International: 5455 Wilshire Blvd, Suite 1280 Los Angeles, CA 90036, USA; tel. (310) 478-1200; fax (310) 478-1212; e-mail info@ri.org; internet ri.org; f. 1990 to provide emergency relief, rehabilitation and devt assistance to people suffering as a result of social conflict or natural disaster; CEO and Pres. FARSHAD RASTEGAR.

Rotary International: 1560 Sherman Ave, Evanston, IL 60201, USA; tel. (847) 866-3000; fax (847) 328-3000; e-mail contact.center@rotary.org; internet www.rotary.org; f. 1905 to carry out activities for the service of humanity, to promote high ethical standards in business and professions and to further international understanding, goodwill and peace; mems: 1.2m. in more than 34,000 Rotary Clubs in more than 200 countries; Pres. SAKUJI TANAKA (Japan); Gen. Sec. JOHN HEWKO (USA); publs *The Rotarian* (monthly, English), *Rotary World* (5 a year, in 9 languages).

Service Civil International (SCI): Belgiëlei 37, 2018 Antwerp, Belgium; tel. (3) 226-57-27; fax (3) 232-03-44; e-mail info@sciint.org; internet www.sciint.org; f. 1920 to promote peace and understanding through voluntary service projects; more than 3,000 volunteers participate in SCI volunteer projects worldwide each year; SCI is also active in the field of peace education and organizes seminars, training activities and meetings; mems: 45 branches worldwide; Int. Pres. PAOLO PAGANO; Int. Coordinator SARA TURRA; publ. *Action* (quarterly).

Shack/Slum Dwellers International (SDI): Campground Centre, 1st Floor, Corner of Surrey and Raapenberg Rds, Mowbray, 7700 Cape Town, South Africa; tel. (21) 689-9408; fax (21) 689-3912; e-mail sdi@courc.co.za; internet www.sdinet.org; f. 1996; a transnational network of local shack/slum dweller orgs; mems: community-based orgs in 31 countries; Pres. ARPUTHAM JOCKIN.

Society of Saint Vincent de Paul: 6 rue du Londres, 75009 Paris, France; tel. 1-53-45-87-53; fax 1-42-61-72-56; e-mail cgi.information@ssvpglobal.org; internet www.ssvpglobal.org; f. 1833 to conduct charitable activities such as childcare, youth work, work with immigrants, adult literacy programmes, residential care for the sick, handicapped and elderly, social counselling and work with prisoners and the unemployed, through personal contact; mems: over 700,000 in 141 countries; Pres. MICHAEL THIO; Sec.-Gen. BRUNO MENARD; publ. *Confeder@tioNews* (quarterly, in English, French and Spanish).

SOLIDAR: 22 rue de Commerce, 1000 Brussels, Belgium; tel. (2) 500-10-20; fax (2) 500-10-30; e-mail solidar@solidar.org; internet www.solidar.org; f. 1948 (fmrly International Workers' Aid); network of non-governmental orgs working to advance social justice in Europe and worldwide; mems: 52 orgs based in 25 countries, operating in more than 90 countries; Sec.-Gen. CONNY REUTER.

Soroptimist International: 87 Glisson Rd, Cambridge, CB1 2HG, United Kingdom; tel. (1223) 311833; fax (1223) 467951; e-mail hq@soroptimistinternational.org; internet www.soroptimistinternational.org; f. 1921; unites professional and business women in promoting a world where women and girls may achieve their individual and collective potential, attain equality, and establish strong, peaceful communities worldwide; aims, through a global network of mems and international partnerships, to inspire action, and to create opportunities, that might transform the lives of women and girls; convention held every four years (2012: Porto Alegre, Brazil, in Jan., on the theme 'Capitalist Crisis, Social Justice and Environment'); mems: about 90,000 in 3,000 clubs in 124 countries and territories; International Pres. ANN GARVIE (United Kingdom) (2013–15); publ. *The International Soroptimist* (quarterly).

Terre des Hommes International Federation (TDHIF): 31 chemin Franck Thomas, 1223 Cologny/Geneva, Switzerland; tel. 227363372; fax 227361510; e-mail info@terredeshommes.org; internet www.terredeshommes.org; f. as an assoc. of child welfare orgs with a focus on community devt and the rights of the child; operates govt advocacy and public and political awareness programmes; co-ordinates the activities of orgs to develop and implement projects designed to improve the living conditions of disadvantaged children, their families and communities; granted consultative status with the UN, UNICEF, the ILO and the Council of Europe; has headquarters in Canada, Denmark, France, Germany, Italy, Luxembourg, the Netherlands, Spain and Switzerland (which hosts two orgs); mems: 10 Terre des Hommes orgs worldwide; Chair. RAFFAELE K. SALINARI.

Women for Women International: 2000 M Street, NW, Suite 200, Washington, DC 20008, USA; tel. (202) 737-7705; fax (202) 737-7709; e-mail general@womenforwomen.org; internet www.womenforwomen.org; f. 1993; aims to assist the recovery and rehabilitation of women in conflict and post-conflict environments, in order to promote sustainable and peaceful socs; Pres. and Chief Operating Officer AFSHAN KHAN.

Women's Global Network for Reproductive Rights: 13 Dao St, Project 3, Quezon City, 1102 Metro Manila, Philippines; tel. and fax (2) 9287785; e-mail office@wgnrr.org; internet www.wgnrr.org; f. 1984; aims to promote and work for sexual and reproductive health, rights and justice for women and all marginalized groups; Chair. FELISTAH MBITHE (Kenya).

World Blind Union: 1929 Bayview Ave, Toronto, ON M4G 3E8, Canada; tel. (416) 486-9698; fax (416) 486-8107; e-mail info@wbuoffice.org; internet www.worldblindunion.org; f. 1984 (amalgamating the World Council for the Welfare of the Blind and the International Federation of the Blind) to work for the prevention of blindness and the welfare of blind and visually impaired people; encourages devt of braille, talking book programmes and other media for the blind; organizes rehabilitation, training and employment; works on the prevention and cure of blindness in co-operation with the International Agency for the Prevention of Blindness; co-ordinates aid to the blind in developing countries; maintains the Louis Braille birthplace as an international museum; mems: in 190 countries; Pres. ARNT HOLTE (Norway); Sec.-Gen. RINA PRASARANI (Indonesia); publ. *E-Bulletin* (quarterly).

World Family Organization (WFO): 28 pl. Saint-Georges, 75009 Paris, France; tel. 1-48-78-07-59; fax 1-42-82-95-24; e-mail info@worldfamilyorganization.org; internet www.worldfamilyorganization.org; f. 1947 as the International Union of Family Organizations, to bring together all orgs throughout the world working for family welfare; present name adopted 1998; maintains commissions and working groups on issues including standards of living, housing, marriage guidance, rural families, etc; there are six regional orgs: the Pan-African Family Organisation (Rabat, Morocco), the North America org. (Montréal, Canada), the Arab Family Organisation (Tunis, Tunisia), the Asian Union of Family Organisations (New Delhi, India), the European regional org. (Bern, Switzerland) and the Latin American Secretariat (Curitiba, Brazil); mems: nat. asscns, groups and governmental departments in over 55 countries; Pres. Dr DEISI NOELI WEBER KUSZTRA (Brazil).

World Federation of the Deaf (WFD): POB 65, 00401 Helsinki, Finland; tel. (9) 5803573; fax (9) 5803572; e-mail Info@wfdeaf.org; internet www.wfdeaf.org; f. 1951 to serve the interests of deaf people and their national orgs and represent these in international fora; works towards the goal of full participation by deaf people in society; encourages deaf people to set up and run their own organizations; priority is given to the promotion of the recognition and use of national sign languages, the education of deaf people and deaf people in the developing world; mems: 133 mem. countries; Pres. COLIN ALLEN; publ. *WFD Newsletter* (6 a year).

World ORT: ORT House, 126 Albert St, London, NW1 7NE, United Kingdom; tel. (20) 7446-8500; fax (20) 7446-8650; e-mail wo@ort.org; internet www.ort.org; f. 1880 for the devt of industrial, agricultural and artisanal skills among Jewish people; conducts vocational training programmes for children and adults, including instructors' and teachers' education and apprenticeship training; implements technical assistance programmes in co-operation with interested govts; manages global network of schools, colleges, training centres and programmes; has assisted more than 3m. people; mems: cttees in more than 60 countries; Pres. JEAN DE GUNZBURG; Dir-Gen. ROBERT SINGER; publs *Annual Report*, *World ORT Times*.

World Social Forum (WSF): Support Office: Rua General Jardim 660, 7° andar, São Paulo, Brazil 01223-010; tel. (11) 3258-8914; fax (11) 3258-8469; e-mail fsminfo@forumsocialmundial.org.br; f. 2001 as an annual global meeting of civil society bodies; a Charter of Principles was adopted in June 2002; the WSF is a permanent global process which aims to pursue alternatives to neo-liberal policies and commercial globalization; its objectives include the devt and promotion of democratic international systems and institutions serving social justice, equality and the sovereignty of peoples, based on respect for the universal human rights of citizens of all nations and for the environment; the 13th edition of the WSF was held in Tunis, Tunisia, in March 2013; an International Council, comprising more than 150 civil soc. orgs and commissions, guides the Forum and considers general political questions and methodology; the Support Office in São Paulo, Brazil, provides administrative assistance to the Forum process, to the International Council and to the specific organizing cttees for each biannual event; mems: civil soc. orgs and movements worldwide.

World Veterans Federation: 17 rue Nicolo, 75116 Paris, France; tel. 1-40-72-61-00; fax 1-40-72-80-58; e-mail wvf@wvf-fmac.org; internet www.wvf-fmac.org; f. 1950 to maintain international peace and security by the application of the San Francisco Charter and work to help to implement the Universal Declaration of Human Rights and related international conventions; aims to defend the spiritual and material interests of war veterans and war victims; promotes practical international co-operation in disarmament, legislation concerning war veterans and war victims, and devt of international humanitarian law, etc; maintains regional cttees for Africa, Asia and the Pacific, and Europe and a Standing Committee on Women; mems: 173 nat. orgs in 90 countries, representing about 27m. war veterans and war victims; Pres. ABDUL HAMID IBRAHIM (Malaysia); Sec.-Gen. MOHAMMED BENJELLOUN (Morocco); publ. *WVF News*.

Zonta International: 1211 W 22nd St, Suite 900, Oak Brook, IL 60523, USA; tel. (630) 928-1400; fax (630) 928-1559; e-mail zontaintl@zonta.org; internet www.zonta.org; f. 1919; links executives in business and the professions, with the aim of advancing the status of women worldwide; carries out local and international projects; supports women's education and leadership; makes fellowship awards in various fields; mems: 30,000 in 63 countries and areas; Pres. LYNN MCKENZIE; Exec. Dir JASON FRISKE; publ. *The Zontian* (quarterly).

Sport and Recreations

Asian Football Confederation (AFC): Jalan 1/155B, Bukit Jalil, 57000 Kuala Lumpur, Malaysia; tel. (3) 89943388; fax (3) 89942689; e-mail media@the-afc.com; internet www.the-afc.com; f. 1954; responsible for regulating the game, drafting new laws to improve the sport, implementing the law, and conducting major competitions in Asia; mems: 46 mem. asscns and one assoc. mem. asscn; Pres. SHAIKH SALMAN BIN EBRAHIM AL KHALIFA; Gen. Sec. DATO' ALEX SOOSAY.

Badminton World Federation: Amoda Bldg, Level 17, 22 Jalan Imbi, 551000 Kuala Lumpur, Malaysia; tel. (3) 92837155; fax (3) 92847155; e-mail bwf@bwfbadminton.org; internet www.bwfbadminton.org; f. 1934, as International Badminton Federation, to oversee the sport of badminton worldwide; mems: affiliated nat. orgs in 164 countries and territories; Pres. POUL-ERIK HØYER; Chief Operating Officer THOMAS LUND; publs *World Badminton* (available online), *Statute Book* (annually).

Confederation of African Football (Confédération africaine de football—CFA): 3 Abdel Khalek Sarwat St, El Hay El Motamayez, POB 23, 6th October City, Egypt; tel. (2) 38371000; fax (2) 38370006; e-mail info@cafonline.com; internet www.cafonline.com; f. 1957; promotes football in Africa; organizes inter-club competitions and Cup of Nations (2013: held in South Africa, in Jan.–Feb.); General Assembly held every two years; mems: nat. asscns in 54 countries; Pres. ISSA HAYATOU (Cameroon); Sec.-Gen. HICHAM EL AMRANI (Morocco); publ. *CAF News* (quarterly).

Fédération Aéronautique Internationale (FAI) (World Air Sports Federation): 54 Av. de Rhodanie, 1007 Lausanne, Switzerland; tel. 213451070; fax 213451077; e-mail sec@fai.org; internet www.fai.org; f. 1905 to promote all aeronautical sports; sanctions world championships; develops rules through Air Sports Commissions; endorses world aeronautical and astronautical records; mems: in more than 100 countries and territories; Pres. Dr JOHN GRUBBSTROM; Sec.-Gen. JEAN-MARC BADAN (Switzerland).

Fédération Internationale de Philatélie (FIP): Biberlinstr. 6, 8032 Zürich, Switzerland; tel. 444223839; fax 444223843; e-mail ats@f-i-p.ch; internet www.f-i-p.ch; f. 1926 to promote philately internationally; also aims to establish and maintain close relations with the philatelic trade and postal administrations and to promote philatelic exhibitions; mems: 90 nat. feds, 3 assoc. mems (continental feds); Pres. TAY PENG HIAN (Singapore); Sec.-Gen. ANDRÉE TROMMER-SCHILTZ (Luxembourg); publ. quarterly journal.

International Amateur Athletic Federation: 17 rue Princesse Florestine, BP 359, 98007 Monte Carlo Cedex, Monaco; tel. 93-10-88-88; fax 93-15-95-15; e-mail info@iaaf.org; internet www.iaaf.org; f. 1912 to ensure co-operation and fairness and to combat discrimination in athletics; compiles athletic competition rules and organizes championships at all levels; frames regulations for the establishment of World, Olympic and other athletic records; settles disputes between mems; conducts a programme of devt consisting of coaching, judging courses, etc; and affiliates national governing bodies; mems: nat. asscns in 213 countries and territories; Pres. LAMINE DIACK (Senegal); publs *IAAF Handbook* (every 2 years), *IAAF Review* (quarterly), *IAAF Directory* (annually), *New Studies in Athletics* (quarterly).

International Automobile Federation (Fédération Internationale de l'Automobile—FIA): 8 pl. de la Concorde, 75008 Paris, France; tel. 1-43-12-44-55; fax 1-43-12-44-66; e-mail info@fiainstitute.com; internet www.fia.com; f. 1904; manages world motor sport and organizes international championships; mems: more than 230 nat. automobile clubs and asscns in 135 countries; Pres. JEAN TODT (France); Sec.-Gen. (Sport) PIERRE DE CONINCK; Sec.-Gen. (Mobility) SUSAN PIKRALLIDAS.

International Basketball Federation (Fédération Internationale de Basketball): 53 ave Louis Casai, 1216 Cointrin/Geneva, Switzerland; tel. 225450000; fax 225450099; e-mail info@fiba.com; internet www.fiba.com; f. 1932, as International Amateur Basketball Federation (present name adopted 1989); world governing body for basketball; mems: 213 affiliated nat. feds; Pres. YVAN MAININI (France); Sec.-Gen. PATRICK BAUMANN (Switzerland); publ. *FIBA Assist* (monthly).

International Boxing Association (AIBA): Maison du Sport International, 54 ave de Rhodanie, 1007 Lausanne, Switzerland; tel. 213212777; fax 213212772; e-mail info@aiba.org; internet www.aiba.org; f. 1946 as the world body controlling amateur boxing for the Olympic Games, continental, regional and inter-nation championships and tournaments in every part of the world; mems: 195 nat. asscns; Pres. Dr CHING-KUO WU (Republic of China); publ. *World Amateur Boxing Magazine* (quarterly).

International Canoe Federation (ICF): 54 ave de Rhodanie, 1007, Lausanne, Switzerland; tel. 216120290; fax 216120291; e-mail info@canoeicf.com; internet www.canoeicf.com; f. 1924; administers canoeing at the Olympic Games; promotes canoe/kayak activity in general; mems: 148 nat. feds; Pres. JOSÉ PERURENA LÓPEZ (Spain); Sec.-Gen. SIMON TOULSON (United Kingdom).

International Council for Health, Physical Education, Recreation, Sport and Dance (ICHPERSD): 1900 Association Drive, Reston, VA 20191, USA; tel. (800) 213-7193; e-mail ichper@aaperd.org; internet www.ichpersd.org; f. 1958 to encourage the devt of programmes in health, physical education, recreation, sport and dance throughout the world, by linking teaching professionals in these fields; Sec.-Gen. Dr ADEL M. ELNASHAR (Bahrain); Sec.-Gen. Dr MAGDA MOHAMED SALAH ALDIN AL-SHAZLY (Egypt); publ. *Journal* (quarterly).

International Cricket Council: POB 500070, St 69, Dubai Sports City, Emirates Rd, Dubai, UAE; tel. (4) 382-8800; fax (4) 382-8600; e-mail enquiry@icc-cricket.com; internet www.icc-cricket.com; f. 1909 as the governing body for international cricket; holds an annual conf; mems: Australia, Bangladesh, England, India, New Zealand, Pakistan, South Africa, Sri Lanka, West Indies, Zimbabwe, and 23 assoc. and 13 affiliated mems; Pres. ALAN ISAAC; CEO DAVID RICHARDSON.

International Cycling Union (UCI): 12 ch. de la Mêlée, 1860 Aigle, Switzerland; tel. 244685811; fax 244685812; e-mail admin@uci.ch; internet www.uci.ch; f. 1900 to develop, regulate and control all forms of cycling as a sport; mems: 160 feds; Pres. BRIAN COOKSON (United Kingdom); publs *International Calendar* (annually), *Velo World* (6 a year).

International Equestrian Federation (Fédération Equestre Internationale—FEI): 8 Chemin de la Joliette, 1006 Lausanne, Switzerland; tel. 213104747; fax 213104760; e-mail info@fei.org; internet www.fei.org; f. 1921; international governing body of equestrian sport recognized by the International Olympic Committee; establishes rules and regulations for conduct of international equestrian events, including on the health and welfare of horses; mems: 135 countries; Pres. HRH Princess HAYA BINT AL HUSSEIN (Jordan); Sec.-Gen. INGMAR DE VOS.

International Federation of Associated Wrestling Styles: 6 rue du Château, 1804 Corsier-sur-Vevey, Switzerland; tel. 213128426; fax 213236073; e-mail fila@fila-wrestling.com; internet www.fila-wrestling.com; f. 1912 to encourage the devt of amateur wrestling and promote the sport in countries where it is not yet practised and to further friendly relations between all mems; mems: 168 feds; Pres. NENAD LALOVIC (Serbia) (acting); Sec.-Gen. MICHEL DUSSON (France); publs *News Bulletin*, *Wrestling Revue*.

International Federation of Association Football (Fédération internationale de football association—FIFA): FIFA-Str. 20, POB 8044, Zürich, Switzerland; tel. 432227777; fax 432227878; e-mail media@fifa.org; internet www.fifa.com; f. 1904 to promote the game of association football and foster friendly relations among players and national asscns; to control football and uphold the laws of the game as laid down by the International Football Association Board; to prevent discrimination of any kind between players; and to provide arbitration in disputes between national asscns; organizes World Cup competition every four years (2014: Brazil); the FIFA Executive Committee—comprising the Federation's President, eight vice-presidents and 15 mems—meets at least twice a year; mems: 208 nat. asscns, 6 continental confeds; Pres. JOSEPH (SEPP) BLATTER (Switzerland); Sec.-Gen. JÉRÔME VALCKE (France); publs *FIFA News* (monthly), *FIFA Magazine* (every 2 months) (both in English, French, German and Spanish), *FIFA Directory* (annually), *Laws of the Game* (annually), *Competitions' Regulations* and *Technical Reports* (before and after FIFA competitions).

International Federation of Cheerleading (IFC): Aoyama Success Bldg, 7th Floor, Minami-Aoyama, Minato-ku, Tokyo 107-0062, Japan; tel. (3) 5770-5747; fax (3) 3404-2227; e-mail ifc@ifc-hdqrs.org; internet www.ifc-hdqrs.org; f. 1998; aims to promote cheerleading worldwide, to spread knowledge of cheerleading and to develop friendly sporting relations among the member asscns; mems: 47

mem. countries; Pres. SETSUO NAKAMURA; Gen.-Sec. DANNY YEN HO YIN.

International Federation of Park and Recreation Administration (IFPRA): Globe House, Crispin Close, Caversham, Reading, Berkshire, RG4 7JS, United Kingdom; tel. and fax (118) 946-1680; e-mail ifpraworld@aol.com; internet www.ifpra.org; f. 1957 to provide a world centre for mems of govt departments, local authorities, and all orgs concerned with recreational and environmental services to discuss relevant matters; mems: 550 in over 50 countries; Pres. TORGEIR SORENSEN; Gen. Sec. ALAN SMITH (United Kingdom); publ. *IFPRA World* (monthly).

International Fencing Federation (Fédération internationale d'escrime—FIE): Maison du Sport International, 54 ave de Rhodanie, 1007 Lausanne, Switzerland; tel. 213203115; fax 213203116; e-mail info@fie.ch; internet www.fie.ch; f. 1913; promotes devt and co-operation between amateur fencers; determines rules for international events; organizes World Championships; mems: 134 nat. feds; Pres. ALISHER USMANOV (Russia); Gen. Sec. FREDERIC PIETRUSZKA (France).

International Gymnastic Federation (Fédération internationale de Gymnastique—FIG): 12 ave de la Gare, 1003 Lausanne, Switzerland; tel. 213215510; fax 213215519; e-mail info@fig-gymnastics.org; internet www.fig-gymnastics.com; f. 1881 to promote the exchange of official documents and publications on gymnastics; mems: 127 affiliated feds and three assoc. feds; Pres. BRUNO GRANDI (Italy); Gen. Sec. ANDRÉ GUEISBUHLER (Switzerland); publs *FIG Bulletin* (3 a year), *World of Gymnastics* (3 a year).

International Hockey Federation: 61 rue du Valentin, Lausanne, Switzerland; tel. 216410606; fax 216410607; e-mail info@fih.ch; internet www.fih.ch; f. 1924; mems: 127 nat. asscns; Pres. LEANDRO NEGRE (Spain); CEO KELLY G. FAIRWEATHER (South Africa).

International Judo Federation: Maison du Sport International, 54 ave de Rhodanie, 1007 Lausanne, Switzerland; tel. 216017720; fax 216017727; e-mail office@ijf.org; internet www.ijf.org; f. 1951 to promote cordial and friendly relations between mems; to protect the interests of judo throughout the world; to organize World Championships and the judo events of the Olympic Games; to develop and spread the techniques and spirit of judo throughout the world; and to establish international judo regulations; Pres. MARIUS VIZER (Hungary); Gen. Sec. JEAN-LUC ROUGE (France).

International Kung Fu Federation: 1073 Baku, 529 Block, Metbuat Ave, Azerbaijan; tel. and fax (12) 370-14-65; e-mail office@internationalkungfu.com; internet www.internationalkungfu.com; f. 2003; governing authority of national and international kung fu and t'ai chi orgs worldwide; established internationally recognized rules and regulations and promotes regional and world championships; mems: 77 nat. asscns (at 2014 Hungary, Qatar, Saudi Arabia and UAE suspended by sanctions cttee); Pres. DAVUD MAHMUDZADEH (Azerbaijan).

International Modern Pentathlon Union (Union Internationale de Pentathlon Moderne—UIPM): Stade Louis II, Entreé E 13, ave des Castelans, 98000 Monte Carlo, Monaco; tel. 97-77 85-55; fax 97-77-85-50; internet www.pentathlon.org; f. 1948; administers and supports the devt and promotion of the modern pentathlon; mems: nat. asscns in more than 100 countries and territories; Sec.-Gen. SHINY FANG (People's Republic of China).

International Paralympic Committee (IPC): Adenauerallee 212–214, 53113 Bonn, Germany; tel. (228) 2097200; fax (228) 2097209; e-mail info@paralympic.org; internet www.paralympic.org; f. 1989 as the international governing body of the Paralympic Movement; supervises and co-ordinates the Paralympic Summer and Winter Games, and other multi-disability competitions, including the World and Regional Championships; promotes paralympic sports through the paralympic sport television channel (www.ParalympicSport.TV); mems: 160 Nat. Paralympic Committees and 4 disability-specific sport orgs and several int. sports feds; Pres. Sir PHILIP CRAVEN (United Kingdom); CEO XAVIER GONZALEZ (Spain); publs *The Paralympian* (quarterly), *IPC Newsflash* (monthly), *Annual Report*.

International Rowing Federation (Fédération internationale des sociétés d'aviron—FISA): MSI, 54 ave de Rhodanie, 1007 Lausanne, Switzerland; tel. 216178373; fax 216178375; e-mail info@fisa.org; internet www.worldrowing.com; f. 1892; serves as the world controlling body of the sport of rowing; mems: 128 nat. feds; Pres. DENIS OSWALD (Switzerland); Sec.-Gen. and Exec. Dir MATT SMITH (Switzerland/USA); publs *World Rowing Directory* (annually), *World Rowing E-Magazine* (quarterly), *FISA Bulletins* (annually).

International Rugby Board: Huguenot House, 35–38 St Stephen's Green, Dublin 2, Ireland; tel. (1) 240-9200; fax (1) 240-9201; e-mail irb@irb.com; internet www.irb.com; f. 1886; serves as the world governing and law-making body for the game of rugby union; supports education and devt of the game and promotes it through regional and world tournaments; since 1987 has organized a Rugby World Cup every four years (2011: New Zealand); holds General Assembly every two years; mems: 97 nat. unions as full mems, 20 assoc. mems and six reg. asscns; Chair. BERNARD LAPASSET; CEO BRETT GOSPER.

International Sailing Federation (ISAF): Ariadne House, Town Quay, Southampton, Hants, SO14 2AQ, United Kingdom; tel. (2380) 635111; fax (2380) 635789; e-mail secretariat@isaf.co.uk; internet www.sailing.org; f. 1907; world governing body for the sport of sailing; establishes and amends Racing Rules of Sailing; organizes the Olympic Sailing Regatta, the ISAF Sailing World Championships, the ISAF World Cup and other events; mems: 138 nat. authorities, 105 classes, 9 affiliated mems; Pres. CARLO CROCE (Italy); Sec.-Gen. JERÔME PELS (Netherlands); publ. *Making Waves* (weekly).

International Shooting Sport Federation (ISSF): 80336 Munich, Bavariaring 21, Germany; tel. (89) 5443550; fax (89) 54435544; e-mail munich@issf-sports.org; internet www.issf-sports.org; f. 1907 to promote and guide the devt of amateur shooting sports; organizes World Championships and controls the organization of continental and regional championships; supervises the shooting events of the Olympic and Continental Games under the auspices of the International Olympic Committee; mems: 157 nat. feds from 137 affiliated countries; Pres. OLEGARIO VÁZQUEZ RAÑA (Mexico); Sec.-Gen. FRANZ SCHREIBER (Germany); publs *ISSF News*, *International Shooting Sport* (6 a year).

International Skating Union (ISU): 2 chemin de Primerose, 1007 Lausanne, Switzerland; tel. 216126666; fax 216126677; e-mail info@isu.ch; internet www.isu.org; f. 1892; holds regular confs; mems: 78 nat. feds in 61 countries; Pres. OTTAVIO CINQUANTA (Italy); Gen. Sec. FREDI SCHMID; publs judges' manuals, referees' handbooks, general and special regulations.

International Ski Federation (Fédération Internationale de Ski—FIS): Marc Hodler House, Blochstr. 2, 3653 Oberhofen am Thunersee, Switzerland; tel. 332446161; fax 332446171; e-mail mail@fisski.ch; internet www.fis-ski.com; f. 1924 to further the sport of skiing; to prevent discrimination in skiing matters on racial, religious or political grounds; to organize World Ski Championships and regional championships and, as supreme international skiing authority, to establish the international competition calendar and rules for all ski competitions approved by the FIS, and to arbitrate in any disputes; mems: 108 nat. ski asscns; Pres. GIAN FRANCO KASPER (Switzerland); Sec.-Gen. SARAH LEWIS (United Kingdom); publs *Weekly Newsflash*, *FIS Bulletin* (2 a year).

International Swimming Federation (Fédération internationale de natation—FINA): POB 4, ave de l'Avant, 1005 Lausanne, Switzerland; tel. 213104710; fax 213126610; internet www.fina.org; f. 1908 to promote amateur swimming and swimming sports internationally; administers rules for swimming sports, competitions and for establishing records; organizes world championships and FINA events; runs a devt programme to increase the popularity and quality of aquatic sports; mems: 201 feds; Pres. JULIO C. MAGLIONE (Uruguay); Exec. Dir CORNEL MARCULESCU; publs *Handbook* (every 4 years), *FINA News* (monthly), *World of Swimming* (quarterly).

International Table Tennis Federation: 11 chemin de la Roche, 1020 Renens/Lausanne, Switzerland; tel. 213407090; fax 213407099; e-mail ittf@ittf.com; internet www.ittf.com; f. 1926; maintains the laws of the sport and regulations for international competitions; Pres. ADHAM SHARARA (Canada); CEO JUDIT FARAGO; publ. *Table Tennis Fascination*.

International Tennis Federation: Bank Lane, Roehampton, London, SW15 5XZ, United Kingdom; tel. (20) 8878-6464; fax (20) 8878-7799; e-mail communications@itftennis.com; internet www.itftennis.com; f. 1913 to govern the game of tennis throughout the world, promote its teaching and preserve its independence of outside authority; produces the Rules of Tennis; organizes and promotes the Davis Cup Competition for men, the Fed Cup for women, the Olympic Games Tennis Event, wheelchair tennis, 16 cups for veterans, the ITF Sunshine Cup and the ITF Continental Connelly Cup for players of 18 years old and under, the World Youth Cup for players of 16 years old and under, and the World Junior Tennis Tournament for players of 14 years old and under; organizes entry-level professional tournaments as well as junior and senior circuits, monitors equipment and technology and oversees the education and advancement of officials; mems: 145 full and 65 assoc.; Pres. FRANCESCO RICCI BITTI.

International Volleyball Federation (Fédération internationale de volleyball—FIVB): Château Les Tourelles, Edouard-Sandoz 2–4, Lausanne 1, Switzerland; tel. 213453535; fax 213453545; e-mail info@fivb.org; internet www.fivb.org; f. 1947 to encourage, organize and supervise the playing of volleyball, beach volleyball, and park volley; organizes biennial congress; mems: 220 nat. feds; Pres. Dr ARY DA SILVA GRAÇA FILHO (Brazil); publs *VolleyWorld* (every 2 months), *X-Press* (monthly).

International Weightlifting Federation (IWF): 1146 Budapest, Istvanmezei út 1–3, Hungary; tel. (1) 3530530; fax (1) 3530199; e-mail iwf@iwfnet.net; internet www.iwf.net; f. 1905 to control international weightlifting; draws up technical rules; trains referees; supervises World Championships, Olympic Games, regional games and international contests of all kinds; registers world records; mems: 189 nat. orgs; Pres. Dr TAMÁS AJAN (Hungary); Gen. Sec. MA WENGUANG (People's Republic of China); publs *IWF Constitution and Rules* (every 4 years), *World Weightlifting* (quarterly).

International World Games Association: 10 Lake Circle, Colorado Springs, CO 80906, USA; tel. (719) 471-8096; fax (719) 471-8105; e-mail info@theworldgames.org; internet www.theworldgames.org; f. 1980; organizes World Games every four years (2017: Wrocław, Poland), comprising 36 sports that are not included in the Olympic Games; Pres. RON FROEHLICH; CEO JOACHIM GOSSOW.

Olympic Council of Asia: POB 6706, Hawalli, 32042 Kuwait City, Kuwait; tel. 22274277; fax 22274280; e-mail info@ocasia.org; internet www.ocasia.org; f. 1982; organizes Asian Games and Asian Winter Games (held every four years), and Asian Indoor Games and Asian Beach Games (held every two years); mems: 45 nat. Olympic cttees; Dir-Gen. HUSAIN A. H. Z. AL-MUSALLAM.

SportAccord: Maison du Sport International, 54 ave de Rhodanie, 1007 Lausanne, Switzerland; tel. 216123070; fax 216123071; e-mail sportaccord@sportaccord.com; internet www.sportaccord.com; f. 1967 as the General Assembly of International Sports Federations (name changed in 1976 to General Association of International Sports Federations—GAISF, and in March 2009 renamed as above) to act as a forum for the exchange of ideas and discussion of common problems in sport; collects and circulates information; and provides secretarial, translation, documentation and consultancy services for mems; mems: 104 int. sports orgs; Pres. HEIN VERBRUGGEN (Netherlands); Dir VINCENT GAILLARD; publs *GAISF Calendar* (online), *Sports Insider* (weekly, electronic bulletin), *Sports Insider Magazine* (annually).

The Association For International Sport for All (TAFISA): Mainzer Landstrasse 153, D-60261 Frankfurt, Germany; tel. (69) 9739359920; fax (69) 9739359925; e-mail info@tafisa.net; internet www.tafisa.net; f. 1991; promotion of sports and physical activity; providing and coordinating programs and events; mems: over 200 mems from 130 countries; Pres. Prof. Dr JU-HO CHANG (Korea); Sec.-Gen. WOLFGANG BAUMANN (Germany).

Union of Arab Olympic Committees: POB 62997, Riyadh 11595, Saudi Arabia; tel. (1) 482-4927; fax (1) 482-1944; e-mail olympiccommittees@gmail.com; f. 1976 as Arab Sports Confederation to encourage regional co-operation in sport; mems: 22 Arab nat. Olympic Committees, 53 Arab sports feds; Sec.-Gen. SAUD ABD AL-AZIZ; publ. *Annual Report*.

Union of European Football Associations (UEFA): 46 route de Genève, 1260 Nyon 2, Switzerland; tel. 848002727; fax 848012727; e-mail info@uefa.com; internet www.uefa.com; f. 1954; works on behalf of Europe's national football asscns to promote football; aims to foster unity and solidarity between national asscns; mems: 54 nat. asscns; Pres. MICHEL PLATINI (France); Gen. Sec. GIANNI INFANTINO (Italy); publ. *Magazine* (available online).

World Archery Federation (Fédération mondiale de tir à l'arc): 54 ave de Rhodanie, 1007 Lausanne, Switzerland; tel. 216143050; fax 216143055; e-mail info@archery.org; internet www.worldarchery.org; f. 1931 to promote international archery; organizes world championships, world cup events and Olympic tournaments; holds Biennial Congress; mems: nat. asscns in 151 countries; Pres. UGUR ERDENER; Sec.-Gen. TOM DIELEN (Switzerland); publs *World Archery News* (monthly), *The Target* (2 a year).

World Boxing Organization: First Federal Bldg, 1056 Muñoz Rivera Ave, Suite 711–714, San Juan, PR 00927, Puerto Rico; tel. (787) 765-4444; fax (787) 758-9053; e-mail boxing@wbo-int.com; internet www.wboboxing.com; f. 1962; regulates professional boxing and sanctions World Championship bouts; Pres. FRANCISCO VALCARCEL; Sec. ARNALDO SANCHEZ-RECIO.

World Bridge Federation: Maison du Sport International, 54 Ave de Rhodanie, 1007 Lausanne, Switzerland; tel. 215447218; fax 216012315; internet www.worldbridge.org; e-mail secretariat@worldbridgefed.com; f. 1958 to promote the game of contract bridge throughout the world; federates national bridge asscns in all countries; conducts world championships competitions; establishes standard bridge laws; mems: 130 countries; Pres. GIANARRIGO RONA (Italy); Treas. MARC DE PAUW; publ. *World Bridge News* (annually).

World Chess Federation (Fédération internationale des echecs—FIDE): 9 Syggrou Ave, Athens 11743, Greece; tel. (210) 9212047; fax (210) 9212859; e-mail office@fide.com; internet www.fide.com; f. 1924; controls chess competitions of world importance and awards international chess titles; mems: nat. orgs in more than 160 countries; Pres. KIRSAN ILYUMZHINOV; publ. *International Rating List* (2 a year).

World Curling Federation: 74 Tay St, Perth, PN2 8NP, Scotland, United Kingdom; tel. (1738) 451630; fax (1738) 451641; e-mail info@worldcurling.org; internet www.worldcurling.org; f. 1991; mems: 53 mem. asscns; Sec.-Gen. COLIN GRAHAMSLAW.

World Squash Federation Ltd: 25 Russell St, Hastings, East Sussex, TN34 1QU, United Kingdom; tel. (1424) 447440; fax (1424) 430737; e-mail admin@worldsquash.org; internet www.worldsquash.org; f. 1966 to maintain quality and reputation of squash and increase its popularity; monitors rules and makes recommendations for change; trains, accredits and assesses international and world referees; sets standards for all technical aspects of squash; co-ordinates coaching training and awards; runs World Championships; mems: 147 nat. orgs; Pres. N. RAMACHANDRAN; CEO ANDREW SHELLEY.

World Underwater Federation: Viale Tiziano 74, 00196 Rome, Italy; tel. (06) 32110594; fax (06) 32110595; e-mail cmas@cmas.org; internet www.cmas.org; f. 1959 to develop underwater activities; to form bodies to instruct in the techniques of underwater diving; to perfect existing equipment, encourage inventions and experiment with newly marketed products; and to organize international competitions; mems: more than 130 affiliated feds; Pres. ANNA ARZHANOVA; Sec.-Gen. HASSEN BACCOUCHE; publs *International Year Book of CMAS*, *Scientific Diving: A Code of Practice*, manuals.

Technology

African Organization of Cartography and Remote Sensing: 5 route de Bedjarah, BP 102, Hussein Dey, Algiers, Algeria; tel. (21) 23-17-17; fax (21) 23-33-39; e-mail sg2@oact.dz; f. 1988 by amalgamation of African Association of Cartography and African Council for Remote Sensing; aims to encourage the devt of cartography and of remote sensing by satellites; organizes confs and other meetings, promotes establishment of training institutions; maintains four regional training centres (in Burkina Faso, Kenya, Nigeria and Tunisia); mems: nat. cartographic institutions of 24 African countries; Sec.-Gen. ANWER SIALA.

AIIM International: IT Centre 8, Lowesmoor Wharf, Worcester, WR1 2RR, United Kingdom; tel. (1905) 727606; fax (1905) 727609; e-mail training@aiim.org; internet www.aiim.org; f. 1999 by merger of the Association for Information and Image Management (f. 1943) and the International Information Management Congress (f. 1962); serves as the international body of the document technologies industry; Pres. JOHN F. MANCINI.

Bureau International de la Recupération et du Recyclage (Bureau of International Recycling): 24 ave Franklin Roosevelt, 1050 Brussels, Belgium; tel. (2) 627-57-70; fax (2) 627-57-73; e-mail bir@bir.org; internet www.bir.org; f. 1948 as the world federation of the reclamation and recycling industries; promotes international trade in scrap iron and steel, non-ferrous metals, paper, textiles, plastics and glass; mems: asscns in 70 countries; Pres. BJÖRN GRUFMAN (Sweden); Dir-Gen. ALEXANDRE DELACOUX (Belgium).

Ecma International: 114 rue de Rhône, 1204 Geneva, Switzerland; tel. 228496000; fax 228496001; e-mail istvan@ecma-international.org; internet www.ecma-international.org; f. 1961 to develop standards and technical reports, in co-operation with the appropriate national, European and international orgs, in order to facilitate and standardize the use of information processing and telecommunications systems; promulgates various standards applicable to the functional design and use of these systems; mems: 12 ordinary mems, 13 assoc. mems, 3 small and medium-sized enterprises, 4 single person co mems, 36 not-for-profit mems, 4 small private co mems; Sec.-Gen. Dr ISTVÁN SEBESTYÉN; publs *Ecma Standards*, *Ecma Memento*, *Ecma Technical Reports*.

EURELECTRIC (Union of the Electricity Industry): 66 blvd de l'Impératrice, BP 2, 1000 Brussels, Belgium; tel. (2) 515-10-00; fax (2) 515-10-10; e-mail htenberge@eurelectric.org; internet www.eurelectric.org; f. 1999 by merger of International Union of Producers and Distributors of Electrical Energy (f. 1925) and European Grouping of the Electricity Industry (f. 1989); a sector asscn representing the common interests of the electricity industry at pan-European level; contributes to the competitiveness of the electricity industry, provides effective representation for the sector in public affairs, promotes the role of electricity both in the advancement of society and in helping to provide solutions to the challenges of sustainable devt; Pres. FULVIO CONTI; Sec.-Gen. HANS TEN BERGE; publ. *Watt's New* (newsletter).

EUREKA: 107 rue Neerveld, bte 5, 1200 Brussels, Belgium; tel. (2) 777-09-50; fax (2) 770-74-95; e-mail info@eurekanetwork.org; internet www.eurekanetwork.org; f. 1985; aims to promote industrial collaboration between mem. countries on non-military research and devt activities; enables joint devt of technology; supports innovation and systematic use of standardization in new technology sectors; administers Eurostars programme, with European Commission, to fund and support collaborative research and innovation projects; mems: 40 countries and the EC; Dir PEDRO DE SAMPAIO NUNES; publs *Annual Report*, *Eureka News*.

European Convention for Constructional Steelwork (ECCS): 32 ave des Ombrages, bte 20, 1200 Brussels, Belgium; tel. (2) 762-04-29; fax (2) 762-09-35; e-mail eccs@steelconstruct.com; internet www

.steelconstruct.com; f. 1955 for the consideration of problems involved in metallic construction; mems: 20 full mems, 6 assoc. mems, 3 int. mems and 2 supporting mems; Sec.-Gen. VÉRONIQUE BAES-DEHAN; publs information sheets and documents, symposia reports, model codes.

European Federation of Chemical Engineering: c/o Institution of Chemical Engineers, Davis Bldg, 165–189 Railway Terrace, Rugby, Warwickshire, CV21 3HQ, United Kingdom; tel. (1788) 578214; fax (1788) 560833; e-mail dbrown@icheme.org.uk; internet www.efce.info; f. 1953 to encourage co-operation between non-profit-making scientific and technical socs, for the advancement of chemical engineering and its application in the processing industries; mems: 39 socs in 30 European countries, 15 corresponding socs in other countries; Pres. Prof. RICHARD DARTON.

European Federation of National Engineering Associations (Fédération européenne d'associations nationales d'ingénieurs—FEANI): 18 ave R. Vandendriessche, 1150 Brussels, Belgium; tel. (2) 639-03-90; fax (2) 639-03-99; e-mail dirk.bochar@feani.org; internet www.feani.org; f. 1951 to affirm the professional identity of the engineers of Europe and to strive for the unity of the engineering profession in Europe; mems: 32 mem. countries and 2 affiliated mems; Pres. RAFAEL ALLER (Spain); Sec.-Gen. DIRK BOCHAR; publs *FEANI News, Annual Report*,.

European Metal Union: 4 rue J. de Lalaing, 1040 Brussels, Belgium; tel. (2) 282-05-33; fax (2) 282-05-35; e-mail contact@emu-online.info; internet www.emu-online.info; f. 1954 as International Union of Metal; liaises between national craft orgs and small and medium-sized enterprises in the metal industry; represents members' interests at European level; provides for the exchange of information and ideas; mems: national feds from Austria, Belgium, Denmark, Germany, Italy, Hungary, Luxembourg, Netherlands and Switzerland representing around 70,000 enterprises and approximately 800,000 employees and 70,000 apprentices; Pres. ERWIN KOSTYRA; Sec. MARIETTE WENNMACHER (Belgium).

European Organisation for the Exploitation of Meteorological Satellites (EUMETSAT): 64295 Darmstadt, Eumetsat Allee 1, Germany; tel. (6151) 8077; fax (6151) 807555; e-mail ops@eumetsat.int; internet www.eumetsat.int; f. 1986; establishes, maintains and exploits European systems of operational meteorological satellites, supplying data to the national meteorological bodies of its mems and co-operating European states; projects include a second generation Meteosat programme for gathering weather data and satellite application facilities; mems: 29 European countries (pending ratification by Estonia and Lithuania) and 2 co-operating states; Dir-Gen. ALAIN RATIER; publs *Annual Report*, *IMAGE Newsletter* (2 a year), brochures, conf. and workshop proceedings.

European Organization for Civil Aviation Equipment (EURO-CAE): 102 rue Etienne Dolet, 4th Floor, 92240 Malakoff, France; tel. 1-40-92-79-30; fax 1-46-55-62-65; e-mail eurocae@eurocae.net; internet www.eurocae.net; f. 1963; studies and advises on problems related to the equipment used in aeronautics; assists international bodies in the establishment of international standards; mems: 92 manufacturers, and regulatory and research bodies; Sec.-Gen. ABDOULAYE N'DIAYE; publs reports, documents and specifications on civil aviation equipment.

Eurospace: 15–17 ave de Ségur, 75005 Paris, France; tel. 1-44-42-00-70; fax 1-44-42-00-79; e-mail letterbox@eurospace.org; internet www.eurospace.org; f. 1961 as an asscn of European aerospace industrial cos responsible for promotion of European Space activity; carries out studies on the legal, economic, technical and financial aspects of space activity; acts as an industrial adviser to the European Space Agency, in particular with regard to future space programmes and industrial policy matters; mems: 60 in 13 European countries; Pres. MARCO FUCHS; Sec.-Gen. JEAN-JACQUES TORTORA.

CIRP—International Academy for Production Engineering: 9 rue Mayran, 75009 Paris, France; tel. 1-45-26-21-80; fax 1-45-26-92-15; e-mail cirp@cirp.net; internet www.cirp.net; f. 1951, as International Institution for Production Engineering Research, to promote by scientific research the study of the mechanical processing of all solid materials; mems: 700 in 40 countries; Sec.-Gen. DIDIER DUMUR (France); publ. *Annals* (2 a year).

International Association for Bridge and Structural Engineering (IABSE): ETH—Hönggerberg, 8093 Zürich, Switzerland; tel. 446332647; fax 446331241; e-mail secretariat@iabse.org; internet www.iabse.org; f. 1929 to exchange knowledge and advance the practice of structural engineering worldwide; mems: 4,000 govt departments, local authorities, univs, institutes, firms and individuals in over 100 countries; Pres. PREDRAG POPOVIC (USA); Exec. Dir UELI BRUNNER; publs *Structural Engineering International* (quarterly), *Structural Engineering Documents*, *IABSE Report*, *e-newsletter*.

International Association for Hydraulic Engineering and Research (IAHR): Paseo Bajo Virgen del Puerto 3, 28005 Madrid, Spain; tel. (91) 3357908; fax (91) 3357935; e-mail iahr@iahr.org; internet www.iahr.org; f. 1935; promotes advancement and exchange of knowledge on hydraulic engineering; holds biennial congresses and symposia; mems: 3,030 individual, 300 corp.; Pres. Prof. ROGER FALCONER; Exec. Dir Dr CHRISTOPHER GEORGE; publs *The International Journal of River Basin Management*, *IAHR Newsletter*, *Hydrolink*, *Journal of Hydraulic Research*, *Proceedings of Biennial Conferences*, *Fluvial Processes Monograph*, *Fluvial Processes Solutions Manual*, *Hydraulicians in Europe 1800–2000*.

International Association of Marine Aids to Navigation and Lighthouse Authorities: 10 rue des Gaudines, 78100 St Germain en Laye, France; tel. 1-34-51-70-01; fax 1-34-51-82-05; e-mail contact@iala-aism.org; internet www.iala-aism.org; f. 1957; holds technical conf. every four years; working groups study special problems and formulate technical recommendations, guidelines and manuals; mems in 80 countries; Pres. DAVID GORDON; Sec.-Gen. GARY PROSSER; publ. *Bulletin* (quarterly).

International Association of Scientific and Technological University Libraries (IATUL): c/o Paul Sheehan, Dublin City University Library, Dublin 9, Ireland; e-mail paul.sheehan@dcu.ie; internet www.iatul.org; f. 1955 to promote co-operation between mem. libraries and stimulate research on library problems; mems: 238 univ. libraries in 41 countries; Pres. REINER KALLENBORN (Germany); Sec. ELISHA CHIWARE (South Africa); publs *IATUL Proceedings*, *IATUL Newsletter* (electronic version only).

International Bridge, Tunnel and Turnpike Association: 1146 19th St, NW, Suite 800, Washington, DC 20036-3725, USA; tel. (202) 659-4620; fax (202) 659-0500; e-mail info@ibtta.org; internet www.ibtta.org; f. 1932 to serve as a forum for sharing knowledge, with the aim of promoting toll-financed transportation services; mems: 250 in 23 countries; Exec. Dir and CEO ROBERT G. HORR; publ. *Tollways* (monthly).

International Cargo Handling Co-ordination Association (ICHCA): Suite 5, Meridian House, 62 Station Rd, London E4 7BA, United Kingdom; tel. (20) 33277560; fax (20) 85298236; e-mail info@ichca.com; internet www.ichca.com; f. 1952 to foster economy and efficiency in the movement of goods from origin to destination; mems: 2,000 in 90 countries; Int. Chair. DAVID BENDALL (Australia); Sec.-Gen. RACHAEL WHITE (United Kingdom).

International Commission of Agricultural and Biosystems Engineering (CIGR): Research Group of Bioproduction Engineering, Research Faculty of Agriculture, Hokkaido University, N–9, W–9, Kita-ku, Sapporo, Hokkaido 060-8589, Japan; tel. (11) 706-3885; fax (11) 706-4147; e-mail cigr_gs2010@bpe.agr.hokudai.ac.jp; internet www.cigr.org; f. 1930; aims to stimulate devt of science and technology in agricultural engineering; encourages education, training and mobility of professionals; facilitates exchange of research; represents profession at international level; mems: asscns from 92 countries; Pres. Prof. DA-WEN SUN; Sec.-Gen. Prof. TOSHINORI KIMURA (Japan); publs *Bulletin de la CIGR*, *Newsletter* (quarterly), technical reports.

International Commission on Glass: Nábrezná 5, 91101, Trençin, Slovakia; e-mail psimurka@stonline.sk; internet www.icglass.org; f. 1933 to co-ordinate research in glass and allied products, exchange information and organize confs; hosts an International Congress every three years (2013: Prague, Czech Republic, in July; 2016: China); mems: 37 nat. orgs; Pres. Prof. SHOU PENG (People's Republic of China); Exec. Sec. Dr PETER SIMURKA (Slovakia).

International Commission on Illumination (CIE) (Commission internationale de l'eclairage): Babenbergerstrasse 9/9A, 1010 Vienna, Austria; tel. (1) 714-31-87-0; e-mail ciecb@cie.co.at; internet www.cie.co.at; f. 1900 as International Commission on Photometry, present name adopted 1913; aims to provide an international forum for all matters relating to the science and art of light and lighting; serves as a forum for the exchange of information; develops and publishes international standards and provides guidance in their application; mems: 40 nat. cttees, 12 supportive; Pres. ANN WEBB; Gen. Sec. MARTINA PAUL; publs standards, technical reports, congress organization.

International Commission on Irrigation and Drainage (ICID) (Commission Internationale des Irrigations et du Drainage): 48 Nyaya Marg, Chanakyapuri, New Delhi 110 021, India; tel. (11) 26115679; fax (11) 26115962; e-mail icid@icid.org; internet www.icid.org; f. 1950; aims to enhance the worldwide supply of food and fibre by improving the productivity of irrigated and drained lands through the appropriate management of water and application of irrigation, drainage and flood management techniques; promotes the devt and application of the arts, sciences and techniques of engineering, agriculture, economics, ecological and social sciences in managing water and land resources for irrigation, drainage and flood management and for river training applications; holds triennial congresses; mems: 110 nat. cttees; Pres. GAO ZHANYI (People's Republic of China); Sec.-Gen. AVINASH C. TYAGI (India); publs *Annual Report*,

ICID News, *Multilingual Technical Dictionary*, *ICID Journal for Irrigation and Drainage*,, technical books.

International Commission on Large Dams (ICOLD): 61 ave Kléber, 75116 Paris, France; tel. 1-47-04-17-80; fax 1-53-75-18-22; e-mail secretaire.general@icold-cigb.org; internet www.icold-cigb .net; f. 1928; mems: in 94 countries; Pres. ADAMA NOMBRE (Burkina Faso); Sec.-Gen. MICHEL DE VIVO; publs *Technical Bulletin* (3 or 4 a year), *World Register of Dams*, *Technical Dictionary on Dams*, studies.

International Committee on Aeronautical Fatigue (ICAF): c/o Prof. Anders Blom, Swedish Defence Research Agency, 164 90 Stockholm, Sweden; tel. (6151) 7051; fax (6151) 705214; e-mail anders.blom@foi.se; f. 1951 for collaboration between aeronautical bodies and laboratories on questions of fatigue of aeronautical structures; organizes periodical confs (2013: Jerusalem, Israel, in June); mems: nat. centres in 13 countries; Gen. Sec. Prof. ANDERS BLOM (Sweden).

International Council for Research and Innovation in Building and Construction: Kruisplein 25G, 3014 DB Rotterdam, Netherlands; tel. (10) 4110240; fax (10) 4334372; e-mail secretariat@cibworld.nl; internet www.cibworld.nl; f. 1953 as the Conseil International du Bâtiment (International Council for Building); aims to facilitate co-operation in building research, studies and documentation in all aspects; mems: governmental and industrial orgs and qualified individuals in 70 countries; Pres. SHYAM SUNDER (USA); Treas. HELENA SOIMAKALLIO; publs *Information Bulletin* (every 2 months), conf. proceedings and technical, best practice and other reports.

International Council on Large High-Voltage Electric Systems (Conseil international des grands réseaux électriques—CIGRE): 21 rue d'Artois, 75008 Paris, France; tel. 1-53-89-12-95; fax 1-53-89-12-99; e-mail secretary-general@cigre.org; internet www .cigre.org; f. 1921 to facilitate and promote the exchange of technical knowledge and information in the general field of electrical generation and transmission at high voltages; holds general sessions (every two years) and symposia; mems: 12,000 in some 90 countries; Pres. ANDRÉ MERLIN (France); Sec.-Gen. FRANÇOIS MESLIER (France); publ. *Electra* (every 2 months).

International Electrotechnical Commission (IEC): 3 rue de Varembé, POB 131, 1211 Geneva 20, Switzerland; tel. 229190211; fax 229190300; e-mail info@iec.ch; internet www.iec.ch; f. 1906 as the authority for world standards for electrical and electronic engineering: its standards are used as the basis for regional and national standards, and are used in the preparation of specifications for international trade; mems: 82 full mems, 82 affiliate mems, representing all branches of electrical and electronic activities in 164 countries; Pres. KLAUS WUCHERER; Gen. Sec. and CEO FRANS VREESWIJK; publs *International Standards*, *Technical Specifications*, *Technical Reports*.

International Federation for Information Processing (IFIP): Hofstr. 3, 2361 Laxenburg, Austria; tel. (2236) 73616; fax (2236) 736169; e-mail ifip@ifip.org; internet www.ifip.org; f. 1960 to promote information science and technology; encourages research, devt and application of information processing in science and human activities; furthers the dissemination and exchange of information on information processing; mems: 46 full mems, 10 hon. mems, 4 assoc. mems and 3 ex officio mems; Pres. LEON STROUS (Netherlands); Sec. MARIA RAFFAI.

International Federation for the Promotion of Machine and Mechanism Science: Department of Mechano-Informatics, University of Tokyo, 7-3-1 Hongo, Bunkyo-ku, Tokyo 113-8656, Japan; tel. (3) 5841-6379; fax (3) 5841-7916; e-mail teresaz@meil.pw.edu.pl; internet www.iftomm.org; f. 1969 to study mechanisms, robots, manmachine systems, etc.; promotes research and devt in the field of machines and mechanisms by theoretical and experimental methods and practical application; Pres. YOSHIHIKO NAKAMURA; Sec.-Gen. TERESA ZIELINSKA; publs *Mechanism and Machine Theory*, *Problems of Mechanics*, *Journal of Gearing and Transmissions*, *Electronic Journal on Computational Kinematics*.

International Federation of Airworthiness (IFA): 14 Railway Approach, East Grinstead, West Sussex, RH19 1BP, United Kingdom; tel. (1342) 301788; fax (1342) 317808; e-mail sec@ifairworthy .com; internet www.ifairworthy.com; f. 1964 to provide a forum for the exchange of international experience in maintenance, design and operations; holds annual conf; awards international aviation scholarship annually; mems include 14 airlines, 6 regulatory authorities, 4 aerospace manufacturing cos, 8 service and repair orgs, 2 consultancies, 5 professional socs, 2 aviation insurance cos, 3 educational institutions, 1 aircraft leasing co, the Flight Safety Foundation (USA) and the Military Aviation Authority Netherlands (MAA-NLD); Exec. Dir JOHN W. SAULL (United Kingdom); publ. *IFA News* (quarterly).

International Federation of Automatic Control (IFAC): Schlosspl. 12, 2361 Laxenburg, Austria; tel. (2236) 71447; fax (2236) 72859; e-mail secretariat@ifac-control.org; internet www .ifac-control.org; f. 1957 to serve those concerned with the theory and application of automatic control and systems engineering; mems: 50 nat. asscns; Pres. IAN CRAIG; Sec. KURT SCHLACHER; publs *Annual Reviews in Control*, *Automatica*, *Control Engineering Practice*, *Journal of Process Control*, *Newsletter*, *Engineering Applications of AI*, IFAC journals and affiliated journals.

International Federation of Automotive Engineering Societies (Fédération Internationale des Sociétés d'Ingénieurs des Techniques de l'Automobile—FISITA): 30 Percy St, London, W1T 2DB, United Kingdom; tel. (20) 7299-6630; fax (20) 7299-6633; e-mail info@ fisita.com; internet www.fisita.com; f. 1948 to promote the technical and sustainable devt of all forms of automotive transportation; maintains electronic job centre for automotive engineers (www.fisitajobs.com); holds Congresses every two years (2014: Maastricht, Netherlands, in June); mems: nat. orgs in 38 countries; Pres. Dr LI JUN; Chief Exec. IAN DICKIE; publ. *Auto Technology*.

International Federation of Consulting Engineers (Fédération internationale des ingénieurs-conseils—FIDIC): POB 311, 1215 Geneva 15, Switzerland; tel. 227994900; fax 227994901; e-mail fidic@fidic.org; internet www.fidic.org; f. 1913 to encourage international co-operation and the establishment of standards for consulting engineers; organizes World Conference (Sept. 2014: Rio de Janeiro, Brazil); mems: 96 nat. asscns, representing more than 1m. professionals; Pres. PABLO BUENO; publs *FIDIC Report*, *Annual Survey*, *Annual Review*.

International Federation of Hospital Engineering: 2 Abingdon House, Cumberland Business Centre, Northumberland Rd, Portsmouth, PO5 1DS, United Kingdom; tel. (2392) 823186; fax (2392) 815927; e-mail ifhe@iheem.org.uk; internet www.ifhe.info; f. 1970 to promote internationally standards of hospital engineering and to provide for the exchange of knowledge and experience in the areas of hospital and health care facility design, construction, engineering, commissioning, maintenance and estate management; mems: 50 in more than 30 countries; Pres. OLE RIST (Norway); Gen. Sec. GUNNAR BAEKKEN (Norway); publ. *Hospital Engineering* (quarterly).

International Institute of Seismology and Earthquake Engineering (IISEE): Building Research Institute, 1 Tatehara, Tsukuba City, Ibaraki 305-0802, Japan; tel. (298) 79-0677; fax (298) 64-6777; e-mail iisee@kenken.go.jp; internet iisee.kenken.go.jp; f. 1962 to work on seismology and earthquake engineering for the purpose of reducing earthquake damage in the world; trains seismologists and earthquake engineers from the earthquake-prone countries; undertakes surveys, research, guidance and analysis of information on earthquakes and related matters; mems: 75 countries; Dir Dr TOSHIAKI YOKOI; publs *Bulletin* (annually), *Individual Studies* (annually).

International Institute of Welding: 90 rue des Vanesses, ZI Paris Nord II, 93420 Villepinte, France; tel. 1-49-90-36-08; fax 1-49-90-36-80; e-mail c.mayer@iiwelding.org; internet www.iiwelding.org; f. 1948; serves as the worldwide network for knowledge exchange of joining technologies; develops authorized education, training, qualification and certification programmes; mems: 56 mem. socs; Chief Exec. CÉCILE MAYER (France); publ. *Welding in the World* (6 a year).

International Measurement Confederation (IMEKO): Dalszínház utca 10, 1st floor No. 3, H-1061 Budapest, Hungary; tel. and fax (1) 353-1562; fax (1) 353-1562; e-mail imeko@t-online.hu; internet www.imeko.org; f. 1958 as a fed. of mem. orgs concerned with the advancement of measurement technology; aims to promote exchange of scientific and technical information in field of measurement and instrumentation and to enhance co-operation between scientists and engineers; holds World Congress every three years (2012: Busan, Republic of Korea, in Sept.); mems: 38 orgs; Pres. Prof. PASCALE DAPONTE (Italy); Sec.-Gen. ZOLTÁN ZELENKA (Hungary); publs *Acta IMEKO* (proceedings of World Congresses), *IMEKO TC Events Series*, *Measurement* (quarterly), *IMEKO Bulletin Newsletter*.

International Organization for Standardization: POB 56, 1 rue de de la Voie-Creuse, 1211 Geneva 20, Switzerland; tel. 227490111; fax 227333430; e-mail central@iso.org; internet www .iso.org; f. 1947 to reach international agreement on industrial and commercial standards; mems: nat. standards bodies of 163 countries; Pres. TERRY HILL (United Kingdom); Sec.-Gen. ROBERT STEELE (New Zealand); publs *ISO International Standards*, *ISO Memento* (annually), *ISO Management Systems* (6 a year), *ISO Focus* (11 a year), *ISO Catalogue* (annually, updated regularly online), *ISO Annual Report*.

International Research Group on Wood Protection: Drottning Kristinas väg 67A, Stockholm, Sweden; tel. (8) 10-14-53; fax (8) 10-80-81; e-mail irg@sp.se; internet www.irg-wp.org; f. 1965 as Wood Preservation Group by OECD; independent since 1969; consists of five sections; holds plenary annual meeting; mems: 335 in 54 countries; Pres. JACK NORTON (Australia); Sec.-Gen. JÖRAN JERMER (Sweden); publs technical documents.

International Society for Photogrammetry and Remote Sensing (ISPRS): c/o Hannover Institute of Photogrammetry and GeoInformation, Leibniz University, Nienburger Str. 1, D-30167 Hannover, Germany; tel. (511) 7622482; fax (511) 7622483; e-mail isprs-sg@ipi.uni-hannover.de; internet www.isprs.org; f. 1910; holds Congress every four years (2016: Prague, Czech Republic), and technical symposia; mems: 103 countries; Pres. CHEN JUN (People's Republic of China); Sec.-Gen. CHRISTIAN HEIPKE (Germany); publs *ISPRS Journal of Photogrammetry and Remote Sensing* (monthly), *ISPRS eBulletin International Archives of Photogrammetry and Remote Sensing and Spatial Information Sciences*, *ISPRS Annals of the Photogrammetry, Remote Sensing and Spatial Information Sciences*.

International Society for Soil Mechanics and Geotechnical Engineering: City University London, Northampton Sq., London, EC1V 0HB, United Kingdom; tel. (20) 7040-8154; fax (20) 7040-8832; e-mail secretariat@issmge.org; internet www.issmge.org; f. 1936 to promote international co-operation among scientists and engineers in the field of geotechnics and its engineering applications; maintains 30 technical cttees; holds quadrennial international conf., regional confs and specialist confs; mems: 19,000 individuals, 88 nat. socs, 48 corp. mems; Pres. Prof. ROGER FRANK; Sec.-Gen. Prof. R. N. TAYLOR; publs *ISSMGE Bulletin* (quarterly), *Lexicon of Soil Mechanics Terms* (in 8 languages).

International Solar Energy Society: Villa Tannheim, Wiesentalstr. 50, 79115 Freiburg, Germany; tel. (761) 459060; fax (761) 4590699; e-mail hq@ises.org; internet www.ises.org; f. 1954; addresses all aspects of renewable energy, including characteristics, effects and methods of use; undertakes projects in several countries on various aspects of renewable energy technology and implementation; organizes major international, regional and national congresses; mems: c. 30,000 in some 100 countries; Pres. DAVID RENNÉ (USA); publs *Solar Energy Journal* (monthly), *Renewable Energy Focus* (6 a year).

International Solid Waste Association (ISWA): Auerspergstr. 15, Top 41, 1080 Vienna, Austria; tel. 253-6001; fax 253-600199; e-mail iswa@iswa.org; internet www.iswa.org; f. 1970 to promote the exchange of information and experience in solid waste management, in order to protect human health and the environment; promotes research and devt activities; provides advice; organizes confs (World Congress, Sept. 2014: São Paolo, Brazil); Pres. DAVID NEWMAN; Man. Dir HERMANN KOLLER; publs *Waste Management World*, *Waste Management and Research* (monthly).

International Special Committee on Radio Interference (Comité International Spécial des Perturbations Radioélectriques—CISPR): 143 Jumping Brook Rd, Lincroft, NJ 07738-1442, USA; tel. (732) 741-7723; e-mail d.heirman@ieee.org; f. 1934; special committee of the IEC, promoting international agreement on the protection of radio reception from interference by equipment other than authorized transmitters; recommends limits of such interference and specifies equipment and methods of measurement; mems: 30 participating and 10 observer countries; Pres. DONALD N. HEIRMAN; Sec. STEPHEN COLCLOUGH.

International Union for Electricity Applications: c/o Consuel, Les Collines de l'Arche, Immeuble Concorde B – 1er étage, 76 route de la Demi-Lune, 92057 Paris la Défense (Nanterre) Cedex, France; tel. 1-41-26-56-48; fax 1-41-26-56-49; e-mail baake@ewh.uni-hannover.de; internet www.uie.org; f. 1953, present title adopted 1994; aims to study all questions relative to electricity applications, except commercial questions; links national groups and organizes international congresses on electricity applications (2017: Hannover, Germany); mems: 14 technical asscns; Pres. Prof. ING. EGBERT BAAKE; publ. *Electricity for More Efficiency: Electric Technologies and their Energy Savings Potential*.

International Union of Air Pollution Prevention and Environmental Protection Associations: Oakwood House, 11 Wingle Tye Rd, Burgess Hill, West Sussex RH15 9HR, United Kingdom; tel. (1444) 236848; e-mail secretariat@iuappa.org; internet www.iuappa.org; f. 1963; organizes triennial World Clean Air Congress (2016: Busan, Republic of Korea, in Sept.) and regional confs for developing countries (several a year); undertakes policy devt and research programmes on international environmental issues; Pres. HANLIE LIEBENBERG ENSLIN (South Africa); Dir-Gen. RICHARD MILLS; publ. *IUAPPA Newsletter*.

International Union of Laboratories and Experts in Construction Materials, Systems and Structures (Réunion Internationale des Laboratoires et Experts des Matériaux, systèmes de construction et ouvrages—RILEM): 157 rue des Blains, 92220 Bagneux, France; tel. 1-45-36-10-20; fax 1-45-36-63-20; e-mail sg@rilem.net; internet www.rilem.net; f. 1947 for the exchange of information and the promotion of co-operation on experimental research concerning structures and materials; promotes research with a view to improvement and standardization; mems: laboratories and individuals in 73 countries; Pres. Prof. MARK ALEXANDER; Sec.-Gen. PASCALE DUCORNET; publs *Materials and Structures* (10 a year), *RILEM Technical Recommendations*, conf. proceedings.

International Union of Scientific and Technical Associations and Organizations (Union internationale des associations et organismes techniques—UATI): UNESCO House, 1 rue Miollis, 75732 Paris Cedex 15, France; tel. 1-45-68-48-29; fax 1-43-06-29-27; e-mail uati@uati.info; internet www.uati.info; f. 1951 (fmrly Union of International Technical Associations) under the auspices of UNESCO; aims to promote and co-ordinate activities of mem. orgs and represent their interests; facilitates relations with international orgs, notably UN agencies; receives proposals and makes recommendations on the establishment of new international technical asscns; mems: 12 orgs; Pres. PHILIPPE AUSSOURD (France); Sec.-Gen. PHILIPPE VUILLEMIN; publ. *Convergence* (3 a year).

International Water Resources Association (IWRA): c/o Association Verseau Développement, 859 rue Jean-François Breton, 34093 Montpellier Cedex 5, France; tel. 4-4-67-61-29-45; fax 4-4-67-52-28-29; e-mail office@iwra.org; internet www.iwra.org; f. 1972 to promote collaboration in and support for international water resources programmes; holds confs; conducts training in water resources management; Pres. DOĞAN ALTINBILEK (Turkey); Exec. Dir TOM SOO; publ. *Water International* (every 2 weeks).

International Webmasters Association (IWA): Suite A, 119 E. Union St, Pasadena, California 91103, USA; tel. (626) 449-3709; fax (866) 607-1773; e-mail support@iwanet.org; internet iwanet.org; f. 1996; aims to maintain universal standards on ethical and professional practices for all web professionals and to provide and foster professional advancement opportunities; mems: 300,000 individual mems in 106 countries; Exec. Dir RICHARD BRINEGAR.

Latin-American Energy Organization (Organización Latinoamericana de Energía—OLADE): Avda Mariscal Antonio José de Sucre, No N58–63 y Fernándes Salvador, Edif. OLADE, Sector San Carlos, POB 17-11-6413 CCI, Quito, Ecuador; tel. (2) 2598-122; fax (2) 2531-691; e-mail oladel@olade.org.ec; internet www.olade.org; f. 1973 to act as an instrument of co-operation in using and conserving the energy resources of the region; mems: 26 Latin-American and Caribbean countries; Exec. Sec. VICTORIO OXILIA DAVALOS; publ. *Enerlac Magazine*.

Regional Centre for Mapping of Resources for Development (RCMRD): POB 632, 00618 Ruaraka, Nairobi, Kenya; tel. (20) 2680748; fax (20) 2680747; e-mail rcmrd@rcmrd.org; internet www.rcmrd.org; f. 1975; present name adopted 1997; provides services for the professional techniques of map-making and the application of satellite and remote sensing data in resource analysis and devt planning; undertakes research and provides advisory services to African govts; mems: 19 signatory govts; Dir-Gen. Dr HUSSEIN O. FARAH.

World Association of Industrial and Technological Research Organizations (WAITRO): c/o SIRIM Berhad, 1 Persiaran Dato' Menteri, Section 2, POB 7035, 40911 Shah Alam, Malaysia; tel. 55446635; fax 55446735; e-mail info@waitro.sirim.my; internet www.waitro.org; f. 1970 by UNIDO to organize co-operation in industrial and technological research; provides financial assistance for training and joint activities; arranges international seminars; facilitates the exchange of information; mems: 168 research institutes in 77 countries; Pres. Dr R. K. KHANDAL (India); publ. *WAITRO News* (quarterly).

World Association of Nuclear Operators (WANO): 25 Canada Sq., Level 35, Canary Wharf, London, E14 5LQ, United Kingdom; tel. (20) 7478-9200; fax (20) 7495-4502; internet www.wano.org.uk; f. 1989 by operators of nuclear power plants; aims to improve the safety and reliability of nuclear power plants through the exchange of information; in Sept. 2012 signed a Memorandum of Understanding with the IAEA to reflect enhanced co-operation in the aftermath of the March 2011 catastrophic nuclear accident at Fukushima Daiichi, Japan; operates four regional centres (in Paris, France; Tokyo, Japan; Moscow, Russia; and Atlanta, USA) and a Co-ordinating Centre in the United Kingdom; mems: in 35 countries; Pres. DUNCAN HAWTHORNE; Man. Dir KEN ELLIS.

World Bureau of Metal Statistics: 27A High St, Ware, Hertfordshire, SG12 9BA, United Kingdom; tel. (1920) 461274; fax (1920) 464258; e-mail enquiries@world-bureau.co.uk; internet www.world-bureau.com; f. 1947; produces statistics of production, consumption, stocks, prices and international trade in copper, lead, zinc, tin, nickel, aluminium and several other minor metals; publs *World Metal Statistics* (monthly), *World Tin Statistics* (monthly), *World Nickel Statistics* (monthly), *World Metal Statistics Yearbook*, *World Metal Statistics Quarterly Summary*, *Annual Stainless Steel Statistics* (annually), *Metallstatistik* (annually).

World Energy Council: 5th Floor, Regency House, 1–4 Warwick St, London, W1B 5LT, United Kingdom; tel. (20) 7734-5996; fax (20) 7734-5926; e-mail info@worldenergy.org; internet www.worldenergy.org; f. 1924 to link all branches of energy and resources technology and maintain liaison between world experts; holds

Congresses every three years; mems: cttees in over 90 countries; Chair. PIERRE GADONNEIX (France); Sec.-Gen. Dr CHRISTOPH FREI (Switzerland); publs energy supply and demand projections, resources surveys, technical assessments, reports.

World Federation of Engineering Organizations (WFEO): Maison de l'UNESCO, 1 rue Miollis, 75732 Paris, Cedex 15, France; tel. 1-45-68-48-47; fax 1-45-68-48-65; e-mail info@wfeo.net; internet www.wfeo.net; f. 1968 to advance engineering as a profession; fosters co-operation between engineering orgs throughout the world; undertakes special projects in co-operation with other international bodies; hosts a World Engineering Forum (Sept. 2012: Ljubljana, Slovenia); mems: 90 nat. mems, 9 int. mems; Pres. MARWAN ABDELHAMID (Kuwait); Exec. Dir TAHANI YOUSSEF (France); publ. *WFEO Newsletter* (2 a year).

World Foundry Organization (WFO): Winton House, Lyonshall, Kington, Herefordshire, HR5 3JP, United Kingdom; tel. (121) 601-6976; fax (1544) 340-332; e-mail secretary@thewfo.com; internet www.thewfo.com; f. 1927, as International Committee of Foundry Technical Associations; named changed to World Foundrymen Organization in 2000, and as above in 2010; Pres. XABIER GONZALES ASPIRI (Spain).

Tourism

African Tourism Organization: POB 605, Banjul, The Gambia; tel. 8806047; e-mail ato@african-tourism.org; internet www.african-tourism.org; f. 2002 in response to a World Tourism Consultative meeting in Dakar, Senegal; liaises with travel and tourism industries in Sub-Saharan Africa and a wide network of partners with a focus on responsible and sustainable tourism devt; aims to combat human trafficking, sex tourism and exploitation through advocacy networks, awareness-building activities, data collection and dissemination, and capacity building at national and regional level.

Caribbean Tourism Organization: Ground Floor, Baobab Tower, Warrens, St. Michael, Barbados; tel. 427-5242; fax 429-3065; e-mail ctobarbados@caribsurf.com; internet www.onecaribbean.org; f. 1989, by merger of the Caribbean Tourism Association (f. 1951) and the Caribbean Tourism Research and Development Centre (f. 1974); aims to encourage tourism in the Caribbean region; organizes annual Caribbean Tourism Conference, Sustainable Tourism Development Conference and Tourism Investment Conference; conducts training and other workshops on request; maintains offices in New York, Canada and London; mems: 32 Caribbean govts, 400 allied mems; Chair. BEVERLY NICHOLSON-DOTY; Sec.-Gen. HUGH RILEY; publs *Caribbean Tourism Statistical News* (quarterly), *Caribbean Tourism Statistical Report* (annually).

European Travel Commission: 61 rue du Marché aux Herbes, 1000 Brussels, Belgium; tel. (2) 548-90-00; fax (2) 514-18-43; e-mail info@visiteurope.com; internet www.etc-corporate.org; f. 1948; currently promotes and markets 'Destination Europe' around the world, through its operations groups in Canada, Brazil (for Latin America), China (for Asia), and the USA; mems: nat. tourist orgs in 33 European countries; Exec. Dir EDUARDO SANTANDER (Belgium).

International Association for Medical Assistance to Travellers: 67 Mowat Ave, Suite 036, Toronto, ON M6K 3E3, Canada; tel. (416) 652-0137; fax (416) 652-1983; e-mail info@iamat.org; internet www.iamat.org; f. 1960 to improve and provide easy accessibility to medical assistance for international travellers; aims to provide up-to-date and detailed information on travel health care in all countries, including advice on high-risk areas and prevention mechanisms; awards research grants and scholarships in the field of travel medicine; Chair. (Medical Advisory) Dr ELAINE C. JONG; Pres. M. ASSUNTA UFFER-MARCOLONGO; publishes an online Medical Directory.

International Association of Scientific Experts in Tourism: Dufourstr. 40A, 9000 St Gallen, Switzerland; tel. 712242530; fax 712242536; e-mail aiest@unisg.ch; internet www.aiest.org; f. 1949 to encourage scientific activity in tourism, to support tourist institutions of a scientific nature and to organize conventions; mems: 300 from more than 50 countries; Pres. Prof. Dr PETER KELLER (Switzerland); Gen. Sec. Prof. Dr CHRISTIAN LAESSER (Switzerland); publ. *The Tourism Review* (quarterly).

International Council of Tourism Partners: POB 208, Haleiwa, HI 96712, USA; e-mail supporters@tourismpartners.org; internet www.tourismpartners.org; f. 2012; aims to promote the sharing of resources and greater collaboration between mem. tourism destinations and their stakeholders; promotes the adoption of Green Growth strategies; mems: 178 in 40 countries; Pres. GEOFFREY LIPMAN.

International Hotel and Restaurant Association: 87 rue de Montbrillant, 1202 Geneva, Switzerland; tel. 227348041; fax 227348056; e-mail info@ih-ra.ch; internet www.ih-ra.com; f. 1869 to act as the authority on matters affecting the international hotel and restaurant industry, to promote its interests and to contribute to its growth, profitability and quality; membership extended to restaurants in 1996; mems: 130 nat. hospitality asscns, 200 nat. and int. hotel and restaurant chains; Pres. CASIMIR PLATZER (Switzerland); publs *Hotels* (monthly), *Yearbook and Directory* (annually).

International Tourism Trade Fairs Association: 1 Old Forge Cottage, Carrington Rd, Richmond, Surrey, TW10 5AA, United Kingdom; tel. (0777) 5571033; e-mail info@ittfa.org; internet www.ittfa.org; f. 1992 as European Tourism Trade Fairs Asscn; Chair. TOM NUTLEY (United Kingdom).

Latin-American Confederation of Tourist Organizations (Confederación de Organizaciones Turísticas de la América Latino—COTAL): Viamonte 640, 3°, 1053 Buenos Aires, Argentina; tel. (11) 4322-4003; fax (11) 5277-4176; e-mail cotal@cotal.org.ar; internet www.cotal.org.ar; f. 1957 to link Latin American national asscns of travel agents and their mems with other tourist bodies around the world; mems: in 21 countries; Pres. LUIS FELIPE AQUINO; Sec. MARIA JOSE MANCHEGO; publ. *Revista COTAL* (every 2 months).

Pacific Asia Travel Association (PATA): Siam Tower, 28th Floor, Unit B1, 989 Rama 1 Rd, Pratumwan, Bangkok 10330, Thailand; tel. (2) 658-2000; fax (2) 658-2010; e-mail patabkk@pata.org; internet www.pata.org; f. 1951; aims to enhance the growth, value and quality of Pacific Asia travel and tourism for the benefit of PATA mems; holds annual conf. and travel fair; divisional offices in Germany (Frankfurt), Australia (Sydney), USA (Oakland, CA) and the People's Republic of China (Beijing); mems: more than 1,200 govts, carriers, tour operators, travel agents and hotels; Chair. JOÃO MANUEL COSTA ANTUNES (Macau); Sec.-Gen. BILL CALDERWOOD (United Kingdom/Ireland); publs *PATA Compass* (every 2 months), *Statistical Report* (quarterly), *Forecasts Book*, research reports, directories, newsletters.

South Pacific Tourism Organization: POB 13119, Suva, Fiji; tel. 3304177; fax 3301995; e-mail tourism@spto.org; internet www.south-pacific.travel; fmrly the Tourism Council of the South Pacific; also known as south-pacific.travel; aims to foster regional co-operation in the devt, marketing and promotion of tourism in the island nations of the South Pacific; receives European Union funding and undertakes sustainable activities; mems: 13 govts in the South Pacific, more than 200 private sector mems in 25 countries worldwide; CEO ILISONI VUIDREKETI (Fiji); publ. *Weekly Newsletter*.

United Federation of Travel Agents' Associations (UFTAA): 19 ave des Castelans, Entrée C, 98000 Monaco; tel. 92-05-28-29; fax 92-05-29-87; e-mail uftaa@uftaa.org; internet www.uftaa.org; f. 1966 to unite travel agents' asscns; represents the interests of travel agents at international level; helps in international legal differences; issues literature on travel; mems: reg. feds representing some 80 nat. asscns; Pres. MARIO BEVACQUA.

World Association of Travel Agencies (WATA): Tranchepied 25, 1278 La Rippe, Switzerland; tel. 792397279; fax 223620753; e-mail wata@wata.net; internet www.wata.net; f. 1949 to foster the devt of tourism, to help the rational organization of tourism in all countries, to collect and disseminate information and to participate in commercial and financial operations to foster the development of tourism; mems: more than 100 individual travel agencies in some 50 countries; Pres. GIANCARLO CARRERA (Switzerland); publ. *WATA News* (online).

World Travel and Tourism Council (WTTC): 1–2 Queen Victoria Terrace, Sovereign Court, London, E1W 3HA, United Kingdom; tel. (20) 7481-8007; fax (20) 7488-1008; e-mail enquiries@wttc.org; internet www.wttc.org; f. 1989; promotes the devt of the travel/tourism industry; analyses impact of tourism on employment levels and local economies and promotes greater expenditure on tourism infrastructure; implements the Hotel Carbon Measurement Initiative to enable hotels to measure and report their carbon emissions; holds an annual summit (2014: in Hainan Province, China, in April); mems: reps from 100 cos worldwide; Pres. and CEO DAVID SCOWSILL; publs *WTTC Backgrounder*, *Travel and Tourism Review*, *Viewpoint* (quarterly), *Blueprint for New Tourism*, regional and country reports.

Trade and Industry

African Organization for Standardization (ARSO): POB 57363-00200, Nairobi, Kenya; tel. (20) 224561; fax (20) 218792; e-mail info@arso-oran.org; internet www.arso-oran.org; f. 1977 to promote standardization, quality control, certification and metrology in the African region, to formulate regional standards, and to co-ordinate participation in international standardization activities; mems: 27 African states; Pres. JOSEPH IKEMEFUNA ODUMODU (Nigeria); Sec.-Gen. HERMOGENE NSENGIMANA; publs *ARSO Bulletin*

(2 a year), *ARSO Catalogue of Regional Standards* (annually), *ARSO Annual Report*.

Arab Company for Drug Industries and Medical Appliances (ACDIMA): POB 925161, Amman 11190, Jordan; tel. (6) 5821618; fax (6) 5821649; e-mail acdima@go.com.jo; internet www.acdima.com; f. 1976.

Arab Federation for Oil and Gas Technologies: POB 954183, Amman 11954, Kindi St, Bldg 23, Jordan; tel. (6) 5511170; fax (6) 5541986; e-mail info@afogt.com; internet www.afoget.com; f. 2011 to facilitate regional co-operation and provide technical support in the oil and gas sector; works under the auspices of the Council of Arab Economic Unity; Sec.-Gen. Dr RAAD MUSLIH.

Arab Federation for Paper, Printing and Packaging Industries: POB 5456, Baghdad, Iraq; tel. (1) 717-6375; fax (1) 717-6374; e-mail info@afpppi.com; internet www.afpppi.com; f. 1977; mems: 250; Gen. Sec. FARES BAKR OMAR.

Arab Iron and Steel Union (AISU): BP 4, Chéraga, Algiers, Algeria; tel. (21) 36-27-04; fax (21) 37-19-75; e-mail relex@solbarab.com; internet www.arabsteel.info; f. 1972 to develop commercial and technical aspects of Arab steel production by helping mem. asscns to commercialize their production in Arab markets, guaranteeing them high-quality materials and intermediary products, informing them of recent devts in the industry and organizing training sessions; also arranges two annual symposia; mems: 80 cos in 15 Arab countries; Gen. Sec. MUHAMMAD LAID LACHGAR; publs *Arab Steel Review* (monthly), *Information Bulletin*, *News Steel World* (2 a month), *Directory* (annually).

Arab Mining Company: POB 20198, Amman 11118, Jordan; tel. (6) 5664175; fax (6) 5684114; e-mail armico@armico.com; internet www.armico.com; f. 1974 following a resolution adopted by the Council for Arab Economic Unity; promotes participation in investment and devt projects.

Arab Seaports Federation: 4 Ptolemy St, Alexandria, Egypt; tel. and fax 4818791; e-mail arabport@yahoo.com; internet www.aspf.org.eg; f. 1977; Sec.-Gen. Rear Adm. ESSAM EDDIN BADAWY.

Arab Union for Cement and Building Materials: POB 9015, Damascus, Syria; tel. (11) 6118598; fax (11) 6121731; e-mail aucbm@scs-net.org; internet www.aucbm.org; f. 1977; 22 mem. countries, 103 mem. cos; Sec.-Gen. AHMAD AL-ROUSAN; publ. *Cement and Building Materials Review* (quarterly).

Asian Productivity Organization: Leaf Square Hongo Building 2F, 1-24-1 Hongo, Bunkyo-ku, Tokyo 113–0033, Japan; tel. (3) 3830-0411; fax (3) 5840-5322; e-mail apo@apo-tokyo.org; internet www.apo-tokyo.org; f. 1961 as non-political, non-profit-making, non-discriminatory regional intergovernmental org. with the aim of contributing to the socio-economic devt of Asia and the Pacific through productivity promotion; activities cover industry, agriculture and service sectors, with the primary focus on human resources devt; five key areas are incorporated into its activities: knowledge management; green productivity; strengthening small and medium-sized enterprises; integrated community devt; and devt of national productivity orgs; serves its mems as a think tank, catalyst, regional adviser, institution builder and clearing house; mems: 20 countries; Sec.-Gen. RYUICHIRO YAMAZAKI (Japan); publs *APO News* (monthly), *Annual Report*, *APO Productivity Databook*, *Eco-products Directory*, other books and monographs.

Association of European Chambers of Commerce and Industry (EUROCHAMBRES): The Chamber House, 19A/D ave des Arts, 1000 Brussels, Belgium; tel. (2) 282-08-50; fax (2) 230-00-38; e-mail eurochambres@eurochambres.eu; internet www.eurochambres.eu; f. 1958 to promote the exchange of experience and information among its mems and to bring their joint opinions to the attention of the institutions of the European Union (EU); conducts studies and seminars; co-ordinates EU projects; mems: 45 nat. asscns of Chambers of Commerce and Industry and 1 transnational Chamber org, 2,000 reg. and local Chambers and 19m. mem. enterprises in Europe; Pres. ALESSANDRO BARBERIS (Italy); Sec.-Gen. ARNALDO ABRUZZINI (Italy).

Association of Gaming Equipment Manufacturers (AGEM): c/o Marcus Prater, POB 50049, Henderson, NV 89016-0049, USA; tel. (702) 812-6932; fax (702) 434-4597; e-mail agem.org@cox.net; internet www.agem.org; promotes and represents the interests and concerns of gaming manufacturers; mems: 126 mems in 18 countries; Pres. THOMAS A JINGOLI (USA); Exec. Dir MARCUS PRATER.

BusinessEurope: 168 ave de Cortenbergh, 1000 Brussels, Belgium; tel. (2) 237-65-11; fax (2) 231-14-45; e-mail main@businesseurope.eu; internet www.businesseurope.eu; f. 1958 as Union of Industrial and Employers' Confederations of Europe; name changed, as above, Jan. 2007; aims to ensure that European Union policy-making takes account of the views of European business; cttees and working groups develop joint positions in fields of interest to business and submit these to the Community institutions concerned; the Council of Presidents (of mem. feds) lays down general policy; the Executive Committee (of Directors-General of mem. feds) is the managing body; and the Committee of Permanent Delegates, consisting of fed. representatives in Brussels, ensures permanent liaison with mems; mems: 41 industrial and employers' feds from 35 countries; Pres. JÜRGEN THUMANN (Germany); Dir-Gen. MARKUS BEYRER (Austria); publ. *BusinessEurope Newsletter* (weekly).

CAEF—The European Foundry Association: Sohnstr. 70, 40237 Düsseldorf, Germany; tel. (211) 6871217; fax (211) 6871205; e-mail info@caef.eu; internet www.caef.eu; f. 1953 to safeguard the common interests of European foundry industries and to collect and exchange information; mems: asscns in 21 countries; Sec.-Gen. MAX SCHUMACHER; publ. *The European Foundry Industry* (annually).

Cairns Group: (no permanent secretariat); e-mail agriculture.negotiations@dfat.gov.au; internet www.cairnsgroup.org; f. 1986 by major agricultural exporting countries; aims to bring about reforms in international agricultural trade, including reductions in export subsidies, in barriers to access and in internal support measures; represents mems' interests in WTO negotiations; mems: Argentina, Australia, Bolivia, Brazil, Canada, Chile, Colombia, Costa Rica, Guatemala, Indonesia, Malaysia, New Zealand, Pakistan, Paraguay, Peru, Philippines, South Africa, Thailand, Uruguay.

Caribbean Association of Industry and Commerce (CAIC): 27A Saddle Rd, Ground Floor, Maraval, Trinidad and Tobago; tel. 628-9859; fax 622-7810; e-mail caic.admin@gmail.com; f. 1955; aims to encourage economic devt through the private sector; undertakes research and training and gives assistance to small enterprises; encourages export promotion; mems: Antigua and Barbuda, Bahamas, Barbados, Belize, British Virgin Islands, Cayman Islands, Dominica, Dominican Republic, Grenada, Guyana, Haiti, Jamaica, Saint Christopher and Nevis, Saint Lucia, Saint Vincent and the Grenadines, Suriname, Trinidad and Tobago; Pres. CAROL EVELYN (Saint Christopher and Nevis); publ. *Caribbean Investor* (quarterly).

CINOA—International Confederation of Art and Antique Dealers: 33 rue Ernest-Allard, 1000 Brussels, Belgium; tel. (2) 502-26-92; e-mail secretary@cinoa.org; internet www.cinoa.org; f. 1936; mems: 32 art and antique dealer asscns in 22 countries, representing 5,000 dealers; holds anuual conf. (June 2014: London, United Kingdom); Pres. PIETER HOOGENDIJK; Sec.-Gen. ERIKA BOCHEREAU.

Committee for European Construction Equipment (CECE): Diamant Bldg, 80 blvd Reyers, 1030 Brussels, Belgium; tel. (2) 706-82-26; fax (2) 706-82-10; e-mail info@cece.eu; internet www.cece.eu; f. 1959 to further contact between manufacturers, to improve market conditions and productivity and to conduct research into techniques; mems: representatives from 12 European countries; Pres. JOHANN SAILER (Germany); Sec.-Gen. RALF WEZEL.

Confederation of Asia-Pacific Chambers of Commerce and Industry (CACCI): 14/F, 3 11 Songgao Rd, Taipei 11073, Taiwan; tel. (2) 27255663; fax (2) 27255665; e-mail cacci@cacci.org.tw; internet www.cacci.org.tw; f. 1966; holds biennial confs to examine regional co-operation, and an annual Council meeting; liaises with govts to promote laws conducive to regional co-operation; serves as a centre for compiling and disseminating trade and business information; encourages contacts between businesses; conducts training and research; mems: 29 nat. chambers of commerce and industry from the region, also affiliated and special mems; Pres. BENEDICTO V. YUJUICO; Dir-Gen. DAVID LIU; publs *CACCI Profile* (monthly), *CACCI Journal of Commerce and Industry* (2 a year).

Consumers International: 24 Highbury Cres., London, N5 1RX, United Kingdom; tel. (20) 7226-6663; fax (20) 7354-0607; e-mail consint@consint.org; internet www.consumersinternational.org; f. 1960 as International Organization of Consumers' Unions; links consumer groups worldwide through information networks and international seminars; supports new consumer groups and represents consumers' interests at international level; maintains four regional offices; mems: over 220 orgs in 115 countries; Dir-Gen. AMANDA LONG; publs *World Consumer Rights Day Kit* (annually, English, French and Spanish), *Annual Report*, Policy Briefing Papers and issue-specific reports.

CropLife International: 326 ave Louise, POB 35, 1050 Brussels, Belgium; tel. (2) 542-04-10; fax (2) 542-04-19; e-mail croplife@croplife.org; internet www.croplife.org; f. 1960 as European Group of National Asscns of Pesticide Manufacturers, international body since 1967, present name adopted in 2001, evolving from Global Crop Protection Federation; represents the plant science industry, with the aim of promoting sustainable agricultural methods; aims to harmonize national and international regulations concerning crop protection products and agricultural biotechnology; promotes observation of the FAO Code of Conduct on the Distribution and Use of Pesticides; holds an annual General Assembly; mems: 8 cos, reg. bodies and nat. asscns in 91 countries; Pres. and CEO HOWARD MINIGH.

Energy Charter Conference: 56 blvd de la Woluwe, 1200 Brussels, Belgium; tel. (2) 775-98-00; fax (2) 775-98-01; e-mail info@encharter.org; internet www.encharter.org; f. 1995 under the provisions of the

Energy Charter Treaty (1994); provides a legal framework for promotion of trade and investment across Eurasia in the energy industries; mems: 53 states; Sec.-Gen. URBAN RUSNÁK (Slovakia); publs *Putting a Price on Energy: International Pricing Mechanisms for Oil and Gas*, *The Energy Charter Treaty—A Reader's Guide*, reports.

ESOMAR—World Association of Opinion and Marketing Research Professionals: Atlas Arena, Aziё Bldg, 5th Floor, Hoogoorddreef 5, 1101 BA, Amsterdam, Netherlands; tel. (20) 6642141; fax (20) 5897885; e-mail customerservice@esomar.org; internet www.esomar.org; f. 1948 (as European Society for Opinion and Marketing Research); aims to further professional interests and encourage high technical standards in the industry; creates and manages a comprehensive programme of industry-specific and thematic confs, publications and communications, as well as actively advocating self-regulation and the worldwide code of practice; mems: over 4,900 in 130 countries; Dir-Gen. FINN RABEN; publs *Research World* (monthly), *Global Market Research* (annually).

European Association of Communications Agencies (EACA): 152 blvd Brand Whitlock, 1200 Brussels, Belgium; tel. (2) 740-07-10; fax (2) 740-07-17; e-mail dominic.lyle@eaca.be; internet www.eaca.eu; f. 1959 (as European Association of Advertising Agencies) to maintain and raise the standards of service of all European advertising, media and sales promotions agencies; aims to promote honest, effective advertising, high professional standards, and awareness of the contribution of advertising in a free market economy and to encourage close co-operation between agencies, advertisers and media in European advertising bodies; mems: 29 nat. advertising agency asscns and 17 multinational agency networks; Pres. DAVID PATTON; Dir-Gen. DOMINIC LYLE.

European Brewery Convention: c/o The Brewers of Europe, 23–25 rue Caroly, 1050 Brussels, Belgium; tel. (2) 551-18-28; fax (2) 660-09-02; e-mail info@europeanbreweryconvention.org; internet www.europeanbreweryconvention.org; f. 1947; aims to promote scientific co-ordination in malting and brewing; mems: nat. asscns in 20 European countries; Pres. Dr STEFAN LUSTIG; publs *Analytica*, *Thesaurus*, *Dictionary of Brewing*, monographs, conf. proceedings, manuals of good practice.

European Chemical Industry Council: 4 ave E. van Nieuwenhuyse, Box 1, 1160 Brussels, Belgium; tel. (2) 676-72-11; fax (2) 676-73-00; e-mail apy@cefic.be; internet www.cefic.org; f. 1972; represents and defends the interests of the chemical industry in legal and trade policy, internal market, environmental and technical matters; liaises with intergovernmental orgs; provides secretariat for some 100 product sector groups; mems: 22 nat. feds; CEO GIORGIO SQUINZI; Dir-Gen. HUBERT MANDERY.

European Committee for Standardization (Comité européen de normalisation—CEN): 17 ave Marnix, 1000 Brussels, Belgium; tel. (2) 550-08-11; fax (2) 550-08-19; e-mail infodesk@cenorm.be; internet www.cenorm.be; f. 1961 to promote European standardization; works to eliminate obstacles caused by technical requirements, in order to facilitate the exchange of goods and services; mems: 32 nat. standards bodies, 8 assoc. and 5 affiliated bodies in Central and Eastern Europe and 7 partnership standardization bodies; Pres. FRIEDRICH SMAXWIL; Dir Gen. ELENA SANTIAGO CID; publs *Catalogue of European Standards* (2 a year), *CEN Networking* (newsletter, every 2 months), *Bulletin* (quarterly), *Directives and related standards* (in English, French and German), *Directions*, *European Standardization in a Global Context*, *The Benefits of Standards*, *Marking of Products and System Certification*.

European Committee of Associations of Manufacturers of Agricultural Machinery: Diamant Bldg, 80 blvd A. Reyers, 1030 Brussels, Belgium; tel. (2) 706-81-73; fax (2) 706-82-10; e-mail secretariat@cema-agri.org; internet www.cema-agri.org; f. 1959 to study economic and technical problems in the field of agricultural machinery manufacture, to protect mems' interests and to disseminate information; mems: 10 nat mem. asscns; Pres. GILLES DRYANCOUR; Sec.-Gen. ULRICH ADAM (Germany).

European Council for Motor Trades and Repairs (CECRA) (Conseil Européen du Commerce et de la Réparation Automobiles): Blvd de la Woluwe 42, Bte 6, 1200 Brussels, Belgium; tel. (2) 771-96-56; fax (2) 772-65-67; e-mail mail@cecra.org; internet www.cecra.eu; f. 1983; aims to promote the interests of its mems and to maintain a favourable European regulatory framework for the enterprises of motor trade and repair businesses it represents; 25 nat. professional asscns and 12 European dealer councils; Pres. JEAN-PAUL BAILLY; Dir Gen. BERNARD LYCKE.

European Council of Paint, Printing Ink and Artists' Colours Industry: 6 ave E. van Nieuwenhuyse, 1160 Brussels, Belgium; tel. (2) 676-74-80; fax (2) 676-74-90; e-mail secretariat@cepe.org; internet www.cepe.org; f. 1951 to study questions relating to the paint and printing ink industries, to take or recommend measures for the devt of these industries or to support their interests, and to exchange information; organizes an Annual Conference and General Assembly (Sept. 2013: Prague, Czech Rep.); mems: company mems of nat. asscns in 23 European countries; Chair. JOAO SERRENHO; Man. Dir JAN VAN DER MEULEN; publs *Annual Review*, guidance documents.

European Crop Protection Association (ECPA): 6 ave E. van Nieuwenhuyse, 1160 Brussels, Belgium; tel. (2) 663-15-50; fax (2) 663-15-60; e-mail ecpa@ecpa.eu; internet www.ecpa.eu; aims to harmonize national and international regulations concerning crop protection products, to support the devt of the industry and to promote observation of the FAO Code of Conduct on the Distribution and Use of Pesticides, forms part of Croplife International; mems: in 26 countries; Pres. VINCENT GROS; Dir-Gen. Dr FRIEDHELM SCHMIDER (Germany); publs *Annual Report*.

European Federation of Associations of Insulation Enterprises: c/o EiiF, 33 ave du Mont-Blanc, 1196 Gland, Switzerland; tel. 229950070; e-mail fesi@eiif.org; internet www.fesi.eu; f. 1970; groups orgs in Europe representing insulation firms; aims to facilitate contacts between mem. asscns; studies problems of interest to the profession; works to safeguard the interests of the profession and represent it in international fora; mems: professional orgs in 16 European countries; Pres. LORENZO BORSINI; Sec.-Gen. ANDREAS GÜRTLER.

European Federation of Associations of Market Research Organisations (EFAMRO): Bastion Tower, 20e étage, Pl. du Champ de Mars 5, 1050 Brussels, Belgium; tel. (2) 550-35-48; fax (2) 550-35-84; e-mail info@efamro.eu; internet www.efamro.eu; f. 1992; maintains specialist divisions on European chemical marketing research, European technological forecasting, paper and related industries, industrial materials, automotives, textiles, methodology, and information technology; mems: nat. asscns in 16 countries; Pres. ANDREW CANNON; publs *EFAMRO Monitoring Report* (weekly).

European Federation of Insurance Intermediaries (BIPAR): 40 ave Albert-Elisabeth, 1200 Brussels, Belgium; tel. (2) 735-60-48; fax (2) 732-14-18; e-mail bipar@skynet.be; internet www.bipar.eu; f. 1937; represents, promotes and defends the interests of national asscns of professional insurance agents and brokers at European and international level; works to co-ordinate mems' activities; mems: 48 asscns from 30 countries, representing approx. 250,000 brokers and agents; Chair. PAUL CARTY; Dir NIC DE MAESSCHALCK; publ. *BIPAR Press* (10 a year).

European Federation of Management Consultancies' Associations: 3–5 ave des Arts, 11e étage, 1210 Brussels, Belgium; tel. (2) 250-06-50; e-mail feaco@feaco.org; internet www.feaco.org; f. 1960; aims to promote networking within the management consultancy sector and its interests and promote a high standard of professional competence, by encouraging discussions of, and research into, problems of common professional interest; mems: 17 asscns; Chair. EZIO LATTANZIO (Italy); Sec.-Gen. DAVID IFRAH; publs *FEACO Newsletter* (quarterly), *Annual Survey of the European Management Consultancy Market*.

European Federation of Materials Handling and Storage Equipment: Diamant Bldg, 80 blvd A. Reyers, 1030 Brussels, Belgium; tel. (2) 706-82-37; fax (2) 706-82-53; e-mail olivier.janin@orgalime.org; internet www.fem-eur.com; f. 1953 to represent the technical, economic and political interests of one of the largest industrial sectors of the European mechanical engineering industry; mems: nat. orgs in 12 European countries; Pres. JAN VAN DER VELDEN; Sec.-Gen. OLIVIER JANIN.

European Furniture Manufacturers Federation (Union européenne de l'ameublement—UEA): 163 rue Royale, Koningsstraat, 1210 Brussels, Belgium; tel. (2) 218-18-89; fax (2) 219-27-01; e-mail secretariat@uea.be; internet www.ueanet.com; f. 1950 to determine and support the general interests of the European furniture industry and facilitate contacts between mems of the industry; mems: orgs in 25 European countries; Pres. MARTIN ČUDKA (Czech Republic); Sec.-Gen. BART DE TURCK; publs *UEA Newsletter* (every 2 months), *Focus on Issues*, *Strategy Survey*.

European General Galvanizers Association (EGGA): Maybrook House, Godstone Rd, Caterham, Surrey, CR3 6RE, United Kingdom; tel. (1883) 331277; fax (1883) 331287; e-mail mail@egga.com; internet www.egga.com; f. 1955 to promote co-operation between mems of the industry, especially in improving processes and finding new uses for galvanized products; mems: asscns in 16 European countries; Pres. ARNAUD ZEDET (France); Exec. Dir MURRAY COOKE.

European Organization for Packaging and the Environment (EUROPEN): Le Royal Tervuren, 6 ave de l'Armée, 1040 Brussels, Belgium; tel. (2) 736-36-00; fax (2) 736-35-21; e-mail packaging@europen-packaging-eu; internet www.europen-packaging.eu; provides policy support and a forum for the exchange of industry information related to packaging and the environment; mems: 42 corporate mems and 5 nat. orgs; Chair MARTIN REYNOLDS; Man. Dir VIRGINIA JANSSENS; publ. *EUROPEN Bulletin* (quarterly).

European Organization for Quality (EOQ): 36-38 rue Joseph II, 1000 Brussels, Belgium; tel. 474-24-08-00 (mobile); e-mail eoq@

eoq-org.eu; internet www.eoq.org; f. 1956 to encourage the use and application of quality management, with the aim of improving quality, lowering costs and increasing productivity; organizes the exchange of information and documentation; mems: orgs in 34 European countries; Pres. NIYAZI AKDAS; Dir-Gen. Dr ERIC JANSSENS.

European Panel Federation: 24 rue Montoyer, Box 20, 1000 Brussels, Belgium; tel. (2) 556-25-89; fax (2) 287-08-75; e-mail info@europanels.org; internet www.europanels.org; f. 1958 as European Federation of Associations of Particle Board Manufacturers; present name adopted 1999; works to develop and encourage international co-operation in the particle board and MDF industry; mems: in 23 countries; Pres. LADISLAUS DÖRY; Sec.-Gen. KRIS WIJNENDAELE (Belgium); publ. *Annual Report*.

European Patent Organisation (Office européen des brevets): Erhardtstr. 27, 80469 Munich, Germany; tel. (89) 2399-1101; fax (89) 2399-2891; e-mail council_secretary@epo.org; internet www.epo.org; f. 1977, in accordance with the European Patent Convention signed in Munich in 1973; conducts searches and examination of European patent applications; grants European patents; the Organisation comprises the European Patent Office and an Administrative Council; mems: 38 European countries; Pres BENOÎT BATTISTELLI (France); Dir YVES GRANDJEAN.

European Photovoltaic Industry Association: 63–67 rue d'Arlon, 1040 Brussels, Belgium; tel. (2) 465-38-84; fax (2) 400-10-10; internet www.epia.org; f. 1985; promotes and represents the European photovoltaics industry and advises mems in developing businesses within the European Union and internationally; organizes annual conf; mems: over 240 mems; Pres. Dr WINFRIED HOFFMANN; Sec.-Gen REINHOLD BUTTGEREIT; publs reports, research documents and policy recommendations.

European Steel Association (EUROFER): 172 ave de Cortenbergh, 1000 Brussels, Belgium; tel. (2) 738-79-37; fax (2) 738-79-60; e-mail a.katsiboubas@eurofer.be; internet www.eurofer.eu; f. 1976 as the European Confederation of Iron and Steel Industries, named changed in 2011; aims to foster co-operation between the mem. feds and cos and to represent their common interests to the European Union and other international orgs; mems: 60 nat. feds and cos in 23 European countries; Gen. Dir GORDON MOFFAT.

EUROGAS: 172 ave de Cortenbergh, Box 6, 1000 Brussels, Belgium; tel. (2) 894-48-48; fax (2) 894-48-00; e-mail eurogas@eurogas.org; internet www.eurogas.org; f. 1910; mems: 45 orgs, feds and cos in 25 European countries; Pres. JEAN-FRANÇOIS CIRELLI (France); Sec.-Gen. BEATE RAABE; publs *Activity Report*, annual statistical reports, brochures.

Fairtrade International: Bonner Talweg 177 53129 Bonn, Germany; tel. (228) 949230; fax (228) 2421713; e-mail info@fairtrade.net; internet www.fairtrade.net; f. 1997; co-ordinates Fairtrade labelling internationally, aims to set the strategic direction for Fairtrade, to produce the standards by which Fairtrade is conducted, and to support producers to gain Fairtrade certification and secure market opportunities; Producer Networks represent the interest of producers in the system while the Labelling Initiatives promote Fairtrade to business and consumers in the developed world; effective Dec. 2011, Fairtrade USA resigned its membership from the umbrella org; mems: 3 producer networks, 19 labelling initiatives, 3 marketing orgs in 27 countries; Chair. MOLLY HARRISS OLSON; CEO HARRIET LAMB.

Federación de Cámaras de Comercio del Istmo Centroamericano (Federation of Central American Chambers of Commerce): 9A avda Norte y 5, Calle Poniente 333, San Salvador, El Salvador; tel. 2231-3065; e-mail aechevarria@fecamco.com; internet www.fecamco.com; f. 1961; plans and co-ordinates industrial and commercial exchanges and exhibitions; mems: Chambers of Commerce in 11 countries; Pres. RAUL DELVALLE.

General Union of Chambers of Commerce, Industry and Agriculture for Arab Countries (GUCCIAAC): POB 11-2837, Beirut, Lebanon; tel. (1) 826020; fax (1) 826021; e-mail uac@uac.org.lb; internet www.uac.org.lb; f. 1951 to enhance Arab economic devt, integration and security through the co-ordination of industrial, agricultural and trade policies and legislation; mems: Chambers of Commerce, Industry and Agriculture in 22 Arab countries; Pres. ADNAN KASSAR; Sec.-Gen. Dr IMAD SHIHAB; publs *Arab Economic Report*, *Al-Omran Al-Arabi* (every 2 months), economic papers, proceedings.

Gulf Organization for Industrial Consulting (GOIC): POB 5114, Doha, Qatar; tel. 4858888; fax 4831465; e-mail goic@goic.org.qa; internet www.goic.org.qa; f. 1976 by the Gulf Arab states to encourage industrial co-operation among Gulf Arab states, to pool industrial expertise and to encourage joint devt of projects; undertakes feasibility studies, market diagnosis, assistance in policy-making, legal consultancies, project promotion, promotion of small and medium industrial investment profiles and technical training; maintains industrial data bank; mems: mem. states of the Cooperation Council for the Arab States of the Gulf; Sec.-Gen. ABDULAZIZ BIN HAMAD AL-AGEEL; publs *GOIC Monthly Bulletin* (in Arabic), *Al Ta'awon al Sina'e* (quarterly, in Arabic and English).

Instituto Centroamericano de Administración de Empresas (INCAE) (Central American Institute for Business Administration): Apdo 960, 4050 Alajuela, Costa Rica; tel. 2443-9908; fax 2433-9983; e-mail costarica@incae.edu; internet www.incae.edu; f. 1964; provides a postgraduate programme in business administration; runs executive training programmes; carries out management research and consulting; maintains a second campus in Nicaragua; libraries of 85,000 vols; Pres. Dr ARTURO CONDO; publs *Alumni Journal* (in Spanish), *Bulletin* (quarterly), books and case studies.

International Advertising Association Inc: World Service Center, 275 Madison Ave, Suite 2102, New York, NY 10016, USA; tel. (212) 557-1133; fax (212) 983-0455; e-mail iaa@iaaglobal.org; internet www.iaaglobal.org; f. 1938 as a global partnership of advertisers, agencies, the media and other marketing communications professionals; aims to protect freedom of commercial speech and consumer choice; holds World Congress every two years (2014: Cape Town, South Africa); mems: 4,000 individuals, 55 corp. mems and 30 orgs in 76 countries; Chair. and World Pres. FARIS ABOUHAMAD; publs electronic newsletters *IAA EU News*, *IAA Intelligence*, *IAA Network News*, *Annual Report*.

International Agricultural Trade Research Consortium (IATRC): World Service Center, 275 Madison Ave, Suite 2102, New York, NY 10016, USA; tel. (763) 755-9143; e-mail lbipes@umn.edu; internet www.iatrcweb.org; f. 1980 as an association of agricultural trade policy researchers, promoting policy formulation and industry knowledge; mems: 200 economists in 31 countries; Dir LAURA BIPES; publs. trade issues, commissioned papers and policy briefs.

International Association for Textile Professionals (American Association for Textile Chemists and Colourists): 1 Davis Dr., POB 12215, Research Triangle Park, NC 27709-2215, USA; tel. (919) 549-8141; fax (919) 549 8933; e-mail danielsj@aatcc.org; f. 1921 to establish industrial test methods, enable quality control and initiate networking between textile professionals globally; individual and corporate mems in 60 countries worldwide; Exec. Vice-Pres. JOHN. Y. DANIELS.

International Association of Department Stores: 11-13 rue Guersant, 75017 Paris, France; tel. 1-42-94-02-02; fax 1-42-94-02-04; e-mail iads@iads.org; internet www.iads.org; f. 1928 to conduct research and exchange information and statistics on management, organization and technical problems; maintains a documentation centre; mems: large-scale retail enterprises operating department stores in 16 countries; Pres. PAUL DELAOUTRE (France); Gen. Sec. MAARTEN DE GROOT VAN EMBDEN (Netherlands).

International Association of the Soap, Detergent and Maintenance Products Industry (AISE) (Association internationale de la savonnerie, de la détergence et des produits d'entretien): 15 A ave Herrmann Debroux, 3rd Floor, 1160 Brussels, Belgium; tel. (2) 679-62-60; fax (2) 679-62-79; e-mail aise.main@aise.eu; internet www.aise.eu; f. 1952; aims to promote the manufacture and use of a wide range of cleaning products, polishes, bleaches, disinfectants and insecticides; mems: 37 nat. asscns in 39 countries; Dir-Gen. SUSANNE ZÄNKER.

International Bureau for the Standardization of Man-Made Fibres (BISFA): 6 ave E. van Nieuwenhuyse, 1160 Brussels, Belgium; tel. (2) 676-74-55; fax (2) 676-74-54; e-mail secretariat@bisfa.org; internet www.bisfa.org; f. 1928 to examine and establish rules for the standardization, classification and naming of various categories of man-made fibres; mems: individual producers in 17 countries; Sec.-Gen. BERNARD DEFRAYE.

International Butchers' Confederation: Box 10, 4 rue Jacques de Lalaing, 1040 Brussels, Belgium; tel. (2) 230-38-76; fax (2) 230-34-51; e-mail info@cibc.be; internet www.cibc.be; f. 1907; aims to defend the interests of small and medium-sized enterprises in the meat-trading and catering industry; represents 16 asscns from the European Union and EFTA; Pres. JEAN-MARIE OSWALD (Luxembourg); Sec.-Gen. MARTIN FUCHS (Germany).

International Card Manufacturers Association (ICMA): 191 Clarksville Rd, Princeton Junction, New Jersey 08550, USA; tel. (609) 799-4900; fax (609) 799-7032; e-mail info@icma.com; internet www.icma.com; f. 1990; promotes the card industry and the value of its products and services; hosts a number of events and trade shows; mems: over 200 card manufacturers and suppliers in more than 40 countries; Pres. DEAN WARNER; Exec. Dir JEFFREY E. BARNHART.

International Centre for Trade and Sustainable Development (ICTSD): 7-9 chemin de Balexert, 1219 Geneva, Switzerland; tel. 229178492; fax 229178093; e-mail ictsd@ictsd.ch; internet www.ictsd.org; f. 1996 with the aim of promoting trade policy that encourages sustainable devt through information services, reporting and monitoring activities; CEO RICARDO MELÉNDEZ-ORTIZ.

International Confederation for Printing and Allied Industries (INTERGRAF): 7 pl. E. Flagey, Box 5, 1050 Brussels, Belgium; tel. (2) 230-86-46; fax (2) 231-14-64; e-mail intergraf@intergraf.eu; internet www.intergraf.org; f. 1983 to work for the common interests of the printing and related industries in mem. countries through its lobbying, informing and networking activities; mems: 22 feds in 20 countries; Pres. HÅVARD GRJOTHEIM (Norway); Sec.-Gen. BEATRICE KLOSE (Germany).

International Congress and Convention Association (ICCA): Toren A, De Entree 57, 1101 BH Amsterdam, Netherlands; tel. (20) 3981919; fax (20) 6990781; e-mail icca@icca.nl; internet www.iccaworld.com; f. 1963 to establish worldwide co-operation between all involved in organizing congresses, conventions and exhibitions; mems: some 950 in 88 countries and territories; Pres. ARNALDO NARDONE; CEO MARTIN SIRK; publs *ICCA Intelligence* (5 a year, electronic), *ICCA Statistics* (annually).

International Co-operative Alliance (ICA): 150 route de Ferney, 1211 Geneva 2, Switzerland; tel. 229298838; fax 227984122; e-mail ica@ica.coop; internet www.ica.coop; f. 1895 for the pursuit of co-operative aims; a General Assembly and four Regional Assemblies meet every two years, on an alternating basis; a 23-mem. ICA Board controls the affairs of the org. between meetings of the General Assembly; sectoral orgs and thematic cttees have been established to promote co-operative activities in the following fields: agriculture; banking; fisheries; consumer affairs; tourism; communications; co-operative research; health; human resource devt; housing; insurance; gender issues; and industrial, artisanal and worker co-operatives; mems: 271 affiliated nat. orgs, with a total membership of more than 1,000m. individuals in 96 countries, and 4 int. orgs; Pres. Dame PAULINE GREEN (United Kingdom); Dir-Gen. CHARLES (CHUCK) GOULD (USA); publs *Review of International Co-operation* (quarterly), *ICA Digest* (electronic newsletter, 2 a month), *Co-op Dialogue* (2 a year).

International Council of Communication Design (Icograda): 455 St Antoine Ouest, Suite SS 10, Montréal, QC H2Z 1J1, Canada; tel. (514) 448-4949; fax (514) 448-4948; e-mail info@icograda.org; internet www.icograda.org; f. 1963; aims to raise standards of communication design; promotes the exchange of information; organizes events; maintains archive; mems: 11 int. affiliated mems, 56 professional mems, 18 promotional mems, 86 educational mems, 5 corp. mems and 2 observers; Man. Dir JOVANA MILOVIC (Serbia); publs *Iridescent* (online) *Icograda eNews* (weekly), *Regulations and Guidelines governing International Design Competitions*, *Model Code of Professional Conduct*, other professional documents.

International Council of Societies of Industrial Design (ICSID): 455 St Antoine Ouest, Suite SS 10, Montréal, QC H2Z 1J1, Canada; tel. (514) 448-4949; fax (514) 448-4948; e-mail office@icsid.org; internet www.icsid.org; f. 1957 to encourage the devt of high standards in the practice of industrial design; works to improve and expand the contribution of industrial design throughout the world; mems: 8 assoc., 28 corp., 61 educational, 24 professional and 54 promotional mems; Pres. LEE SOON-IN (Republic of Korea); Sec.-Gen. DILKI DE SILVA; publs *ICSID News* (6 a year), *World Directory of Design Schools*.

International Council of Tanners: Leather Trade House, Kings Park Rd, Moulton Park, Northampton, NN3 6JD, United Kingdom; tel. (1604) 679917; fax (1604) 679998; e-mail sec@tannerscouncilict.org; internet www.tannerscouncilict.org; f. 1926 to study all questions relating to the leather industry and maintain contact with national asscns; mems: nat. tanners' orgs in 38 countries; Pres. WOLFGANG GOERLICH (Brazil).

International Council on Mining and Metals (ICMM): 35 Portman Sq., 6th Floor, London, W1H 6LR, United Kingdom; tel. (20) 7467-5070; fax (20) 7467-5071; e-mail info@icmm.com; internet www.icmm.com; f. 1991 (as the International Council on Metals and the Environment, present name adopted 2002); aims to promote sustainable devt practices and policies in the mining, use, recycling and disposal of minerals and metals; mems: 19 cos, 30 asscns; Chair. Dr R. ANTHONY (TONY) HODGE (Canada); publ. *ICMM Newsletter* (quarterly).

International Customs Tariffs Bureau: 15 rue des Petits Carmes, 1000 Brussels, Belgium; tel. (2) 501-87-74; fax (2) 501-31-47; e-mail dir@bitd.org; internet www.bitd.org; f. 1890; serves as the executive instrument of the International Union for the Publication of Customs Tariffs; translates and publishes all customs tariffs in five languages—English, French, German, Italian, Spanish; mems: 50 mem. countries; Pres. DIRK ACHTEN; Dir MICHEL GODFRIND; publs *International Customs Journal*, *Annual Report*.

International Exhibitions Bureau (Bureau International des Expositions): 34 ave d'Iéna, 75116 Paris, France; tel. 1-45-00-38-63; fax 1-45-00-96-15; e-mail info@bie-paris.org; internet www.bie-paris.org; f. 1931, revised by Protocol 1972, for the authorization and registration of international exhibitions falling under the 1928 Convention; mems: 163 states; Pres. FERDINAND NAGY; Sec.-Gen. VICENTE GONZALES LOSCERTALES; publ. *BIE Bulletin*.

International Federation of Pharmaceutical Manufacturers and Associations (IFPMA): 15 chemin Louis-Dunant, POB 195, 1211 Geneva 20, Switzerland; tel. 223383200; fax 223383299; e-mail info@ifpma.org; internet www.ifpma.org; f. 1968 for the exchange of information and international co-operation in all questions of interest to the pharmaceutical industry, particularly in the field of health legislation, science and research; represents the research-based pharmaceutical, biotech and vaccine sectors; develops ethical principles and practices and co-operates with national and international orgs; mems: 29 int. cos and 49 nat. and reg. industry asscns; Pres. JOHN LECHLEITER; Dir-Gen. EDUARDO PISANI (Italy); publs *IFPMA Code of Pharmaceutical Marketing Practices*, action papers, occasional publications.

International Federation of the Phonographic Industry (IFPI): 10 Piccadilly, London, W1J 0DD, United Kingdom; tel. (20) 7878-7900; fax (20) 7878-7950; e-mail info@ifpi.org; internet www.ifpi.org; f. 1933; represents the interests of record producers by campaigning for the introduction, improvement and enforcement of copyright and related rights legislation; co-ordinates the recording industry's anti-piracy activities; mems: around 1,400 in 66 countries and nat. groups in 55 countries; CEO FRANCES MOORE; publs *Digital Music Report* (annually), *Recording Industry in Numbers* (annually); reports on digital music and commercial piracy, world sales.

International Fertilizer Industry Association (IFA): 28 rue Marbeuf, 75008 Paris, France; tel. 1-53-93-05-00; fax 1-53-93-05-45; e-mail ifa@fertilizer.org; internet www.fertilizer.org; f. 1927; represents companies involved in all aspects of the global fertilizer industry, including the production and distribution of fertilizers, their raw materials and intermediates; also represents orgs involved in agronomic research and training with regard to crop nutrition; mems: some 540 in around 85 countries; Pres. ESIN METE; Dir-Gen. CHARLOTTE HEBEBRAND; publ. *Fertilizers and Agriculture*.

International Foodservice Distributors Association (IFDA): 1410 Spring Hill Rd, Suite 210, McLean, VA 22102, USA; tel. (703) 532-9400; fax (703) 538-4673; internet www.ifdaonline.org; f. 1906; mems: over 140 mems; Chair. THOMAS A ZATINA; Pres. and CEO MARK S. ALLEN.

International Fragrance Association (IFRA): Chemin de la Parfumerie 5, 1214 Vernier, Geneva, Switzerland; tel. 224318250; fax 224318806; e-mail secretariat@ifraorg.org; internet www.ifraorg.org; f. 1973 to develop and advance the fragrance industry, to collect and study scientific data on fragrance materials and to make recommendations on their safe use; mems: 6 multinational fragrance cos and 16 nat. asscns of fragrance manufacturers; Chair. MICHEL BONGI; Pres. PIERRE SIVAC; publs *Code of Practice*, *Information Letters*.

International Fur Trade Federation: POB 495, Weybridge, Surrey, KT12 8WD, United Kingdom; tel. (1932) 850020; e-mail info@iftf.com; internet www.iftf.com; f. 1949 to promote and organize joint action by fur trade orgs in order to develop and protect the trade in fur skins and the processing of skins; mems: 42 orgs in 35 countries; Chair. STEVEN HURWITZ.

International Meat Secretariat (Office international de la viande): 5 rue Lespagnol, 75020 Paris, France; tel. 1-45-26-68-97; fax 1-45-26-68-98; e-mail info@meat-ims.org; internet www.meat-ims.org; f. 1974; organizes World Meat Congress every two years (2014: Beijing, People's Republic of China, in June); mems: in more than 30 countries; Pres. ARTURO LLAVALLOL (Argentina); Sec.-Gen. HSIN HUANG; publs *Newsletter* (fortnightly), *IMS-GIRA World Meat Facts Book* (annually).

International Organization of Motor Vehicle Manufacturers (Organisation internationale des constructeurs d'automobiles—OICA): 4 rue de Berri, 75008 Paris, France; tel. 1-43-59-00-13; fax 1-45-63-84-41; e-mail oica@oica.net; internet www.oica.net; f. 1919 to co-ordinate and further the interests of the automobile industry, to promote the study of economic and other matters affecting automobile construction, and to control automobile manufacturers' participation in international exhibitions in Europe; mems: 37 nat. trade asscns; Pres. PATRICK BLAIN (USA); Gen. Sec. YVES VAN DER STRAATEN; publ. *Yearbook of the World's Motor Industry*.

International Organization of the Flavour Industry (IOFI): 6 ave des Arts, 1210 Brussels, Belgium; tel. (2) 214-20-50; fax (2) 214-20-69; e-mail secretariat@iofiorg.org; internet www.iofi.org; f. 1969 to support and promote the flavour industry; active in the fields of safety evaluation and regulation of flavouring substances; mems: nat. asscns in 24 countries; Exec. Dir JOS STELDER; publs *Documentation Bulletin*, *Information Letters*, *Code of Practice*.

International Publishers' Association: 23 ave de France, 1202 Geneva, Switzerland; tel. 227041820; fax 227041821; e-mail secretariat@internationalpublishers.org; internet www.internationalpublishers.org; f. 1896 to defend the freedom of publishers to publish, to defend publishers' interests, and to foster international co-operation; promotes the international trade in books and literacy as a step to economic and social devt; carries out work on international copyright; mems: 62 professional book publishers' orgs in 55 countries; Pres. YOUNGSUK CHI; Sec.-Gen. JENS BAMMEL.

International Rayon and Synthetic Fibres Committee (Comité international de la rayonne et des fibres synthétiques—CIRFS): 6 ave E. van Nieuwenhuyse, 1160 Brussels, Belgium; tel. (2) 676-74-55; fax (2) 676-74-54; e-mail info@cirfs.org; internet www.cirfs.org; f. 1950 to improve the quality and promote the use of man-made fibres and products made from fibres; mems: individual producers in 24 countries; Pres. GIULO BONAZZI; Dir-Gen. FRÉDÉRIC VAN HOUTE; publs *Statistical Booklet* (annually), market reports, technical test methods.

International Textile Manufacturers Federation (ITMF): Wiedingstr. 9, 8055 Zürich, Switzerland; tel. 442836380; fax 442836389; e-mail secretariat@itmf.org; internet www.itmf.org; f. 1904, present title adopted 1978; aims to protect and promote the interests of its mems, disseminate information, and encourage co-operation; mems: nat. textile trade asscns and cos in some 50 countries; Pres. JOSUÉ GOMES DA SILVA (Brazil); Dir-Gen. Dr CHRISTIAN P. SCHINDLER (Germany); publs *Annual Conference Report*, *Cotton Contamination Survey* (2 a year), *Country Statements* (annually), *International Textile Machinery Shipment Statistics* (annually), *International Cotton Industry Statistics* (annually), *International Production Cost Comparison* (2 a year), *State of Trade Report* (quarterly), *Directory*, various statistics, sectoral reports and guidelines.

International Union of Marine Insurance (IUMI): C. F. Meyer-Str. 14, POB 4288, 8022 Zürich, Switzerland; tel. 442082874; fax 442082800; e-mail simone.hirt@svv.ch; internet www.iumi.com; f. 1873 to collect and distribute information on marine insurance on a worldwide basis; mems: 54 asscns; organizes annual conf. (2013: London, United Kingdom, in Sept.); Pres. OLE WIKBORG (Norway); Sec.-Gen. LARS LANGE (Germany).

International Wool Textile Organisation (IWTO) (Fédération lanière internationale—FLI): 4 rue de l'Industrie, 1000 Brussels, Belgium; tel. (2) 505-40-10; fax (2) 503-47-85; e-mail info@iwto.org; internet www.iwto.org; f. 1929 to link wool textile orgs in mem. countries and represent their interests; holds annual Congress (2013: Biella, Italy, in June); mems: 21 nat. asscns, 27 assoc. mems; Pres. PETER ACKROYD (United Kingdom); Sec.-Gen. ELISABETH VAN DELDEN; publs *Wool Statistics* (annually), *Global Wool Supplies and Wool Textile Manufacturing Activity* (annually), *Blue Book*, *Red Book*.

International Wrought Copper Council: 55 Bryanston St, London, W1H 7AJ, United Kingdom; tel. (20) 7868-8930; fax (20) 7868-8819; e-mail iwcc@coppercouncil.org; internet www.coppercouncil.org; f. 1953 to link and represent copper fabricating industries and represent the views of copper consumers to raw material producers; organizes specialist activities on technical work and the devt of copper; mems: 16 nat. groups in Europe, Australia, Japan and Malaysia, 9 corporate mems; Chair. MASAYOSHI MATSUMOTO; Sec.-Gen. MARK LOVEITT; publs *Annual Report*, surveys.

Latin American Steel Association (Asociación Latinamericana del Acero—Alacero): Benjamín 2944, 5°, Las Condes, Santiago, Chile; tel. (2) 233-0545; fax (2) 233-0768; e-mail alacero@alacero.org; internet wwww.alacero.org; f. 1959 as the Latin American Iron and Steel Institute to help to achieve the harmonious devt of iron and steel production, manufacture and marketing in Latin America; conducts economic surveys on the steel sector; organizes technical conventions and meetings; disseminates industrial processes suited to regional conditions; prepares and maintains statistics on production, end uses, etc., of raw materials and steel products within this area; mems: 18 hon. mems, 49 active mems, 36 assoc. mems; Chair. BENJAMIN BAPTISTA FILHO (Brazil); Sec. ROBERTO DE ANDRACA BARBAS (Chile); publs *Industry Year Book*, *Latin American Steel Directory* (now electronic); also technical books, bulletins and manuals.

Orgalime (European Engineering Industries Association): Diamant Bldg, 5th Floor, 80 blvd A Reyers, 1030 Brussels, Belgium; tel. (2) 706-82-35; fax (2) 706-82-50; e-mail secretariat@orgalime.org; internet www.orgalime.org; f. 1954 to provide a permanent liaison between the mechanical, electrical and electronic engineering, and metalworking industries of mem. countries; mems: 33 nat. trade asscns in 22 European countries; Pres. SANDRO BONOMI; Dir-Gen. ADRIAN HARRIS.

Southern African Customs Union: Private Bag 13285, Windhoek, Namibia; tel. (61) 2958000; fax (61) 245611; e-mail info@sacu.int; internet www.sacu.int; f. 1910, later reconstituted by new SACU Agreements signed in 1969 and 2002; provides common pool of customs, excise and sales duties, according to the relative volume of trade and production in each country; goods are traded within the union free of duty and quotas, subject to certain protective measures for less developed mems; the South African rand is legal tender in Lesotho, Namibia and Swaziland; the Customs Union Commission meets quarterly in each of the mems' capital cities in turn; mems: Botswana, Lesotho, Namibia, South Africa, Swaziland; Exec. Sec. TSWELOPELE CORNELIA MOREMI.

UFI (Global Association of the Exhibition Industry): 17 rue Louise Michel, 92300 Levallois-Perret, France; tel. 1-46-39-75-00; fax 1-46-39-75-01; e-mail info@ufi.org; internet www.ufi.org; f. 1925 as Union des Foires Internationales; works to increase co-operation between international trade fairs/exhibitions, safeguard their interests and extend their operations; imposes exhibition quality criteria and defines standards; approves 805 events; mems: 628 in 85 countries; Pres. ARIE BRIENAN; Man. Dir PAUL WOODWARD.

Union of European Beverages Associations (UNESDA): 79 blvd St Michel, 1040 Brussels, Belgium; tel. (2) 743-40-50; fax (2) 732-51-02; e-mail mail@unesda.org; internet www.unesda.org; f. 1958, as Confederation of International Soft Drinks Associations; aims to promote co-operation among the national asscns of non-alcoholic drinks manufacturers on all industrial and commercial matters, to stimulate the sales and consumption of soft drinks, to deal with matters of interest to all mem. asscns and to represent the common interests of mem. asscns; holds a Congress every year; mems: 25 nat. asscns and 11 cos; Sec.-Gen. ALAIN BEAUMONT.

World Customs Organization (WCO): 30 rue du Marché, 1210 Brussels, Belgium; tel. (2) 209-92-11; fax (2) 209-92-62; e-mail communication@wcoomd.org; internet www.wcoomd.org; f. 1952 as Customs Co-operation Council; aims to enhance the effectiveness and efficiency of customs administrations by building capacity for more effective border enforcement, better application of international trade regulations, enhanced measures to protect society, and increased revenue security; mems: customs administrations of 179 countries and customs territories; Sec.-Gen. KUNIO MIKURIYA (Japan); publ. *WCO News* (3 a year).

World Fair Trade Organization: Prijssestraat 24, 4101 CR, Culemborg, Netherlands; tel. (34) 5535914; fax (84) 7474401; e-mail info@wfto.com; internet www.wfto.com; f. 1989 as the International Fair Trade Association; coalition of trading and producer orgs; prescribes 10 standards that fair trade orgs must follow in their day-to-day work and carries out monitoring to ensure that these principles are upheld; mems: 400 alternative trade orgs from 75 countries; Pres. RUDI DALVAI (USAItaly).

World Federation of Advertisers: 166 ave Louise, Box 6, 1050 Brussels, Belgium; tel. (2) 502-57-40; fax (2) 502-56-66; e-mail info@wfanet.org; internet www.wfanet.org; f. 1953; promotes and studies advertising and its related problems; mems: asscns in 56 countries and more than 70 int. cos; Pres. MARTIN RILEY; Man. Dir STEPHAN LOERKE; publ. *EU Brief* (weekly).

World Packaging Organisation: 1833 Centre Point Circle, Suite 123, Naperville IL 60563, USA; tel. (630) 596-9007; fax (630) 544-5055; e-mail wpo@kellencompany.com; internet www.worldpackaging.org; f. 1968 to provide a forum for the exchange of knowledge of packaging technology and, in general, to create conditions for the conservation, preservation and distribution of world food production; holds annual congress and competition; mems: Asian, North American, Latin American, European and African packaging feds; full mems in 44 countries, 7 affiliated mems; Pres. THOMAS SCHNEIDER (USA); Gen. Sec. KEITH PEARSON (South Africa).

World Steel Association: 120 rue Col Bourg, 1140 Brussels, Belgium; tel. (2) 702-89-00; fax (2) 702-88-99; e-mail info@worldsteel.org; internet www.worldsteel.org; f. 1967, as International Iron and Steel Institute, to promote the welfare and interests of the world's steel industries; name changed as above in 2008; undertakes research into all aspects of steel industries; serves as a forum for exchange of knowledge and discussion of problems relating to steel industries; collects, disseminates and maintains statistics and information; serves as a liaison body between international and national steel orgs; mems: in over 50 countries; Dir-Gen. EDWIN BASSON; publs *Worldsteel Newsletter*, policy statements and reports.

World Trade Centers Association: 420 Lexington Ave, Suite 518, New York, NY 10170, USA; tel. (212) 432-2626; fax (212) 488-0064; e-mail wtca@wtca.org; internet www.wtca.org; f. 1968 to promote trade through the establishment of world trade centres, including education facilities, information services and exhibition facilities; operates an electronic trading and communication system (WTC Online); mems: 322 trade centres, Chambers of Commerce and other orgs in more than 107 countries; Chair. GHAZI ABU NAHL; CEO ERIC DAHL; publs *WTCA News* (monthly), *Trade Center Profiles* (annually), *World Business Directory* (annually).

Transport

African Airlines Association: POB 20116, Nairobi 00200, Kenya; tel. (20) 2320144; fax (20) 6001173; e-mail afraa@afraa.org; internet www.afraa.org; f. 1968 to give African air companies expert advice in technical, financial, juridical and market matters; to improve air transport in Africa through inter-carrier co-operation; and to develop manpower resources; mems: 34 nat. carriers, representing 80% of African airlines; Pres. SIZA MZIMELA; Sec.-Gen. ELIJAH CHINGOSHO; publs *Newsletter*, reports.

Airports Council International (ACI): POB 302, 800 rue du Sq. Victoria, Montréal, QC H4Z 1G8, Canada; tel. (514) 373-1200; fax (514) 373-1201; e-mail aci@aci.aero; internet www.aci.aero; f. 1991, following merger of Airport Operators Council International and International Civil Airports Association; aims to represent and enhance co-operation among airports of the world and promote high standards in airport devt and management; organizes an annual General Assembly, Conference and Exhibition (June 2014: Durban, South Africa); mems: 591 mems operating over 1,861 airports in 177countries and territories; Chair. FREDRICK PICCOLO (USA); Dir-Gen. ANGELA GITTENS; publs *World Report* (6 a year), *Airport World Magazine*, *Policy Handbook*, reports.

Arab Air Carriers' Organization (AACO): POB 13-5468, Beirut, Lebanon; tel. (1) 861297; fax (1) 863168; e-mail info@aaco.org; internet www.aaco.org; f. 1965 to promote co-operation in the activities of Arab airline cos; mems: 27 Arab air carriers; Chair. GHAIDA ABDULLATIF; Sec.-Gen. ABDUL WAHAB TEFFAHA; publs bulletins, reports and research documents.

Arab Union of Railways: POB 6599, Aleppo, Syria; tel. (21) 2667270; fax (21) 2686000; e-mail uacf@scs-net.org; f. 1979.

Association of Asia Pacific Airlines: Level 27-1, Menara Prestige, 1 Jalan Pinang, 50450 Kuala Lumpur, Malaysia; tel. (3) 21621888; fax (3) 21626888; e-mail info@aapa.org.my; internet www .aapairlines.org; f. 1966 as Orient Airlines Asscn; present name adopted in 1997; as the trade asscn of the region's airlines, the AAPA aims to represent their interests and to provide a forum for all mems to exchange information and views on matters of common concern; maintains international representation in Brussels, Belgium, and in Washington, DC, USA; mems: 15 scheduled int. airlines (carrying approx. one-fifth of global passenger traffic and one-third of global cargo traffic); Dir-Gen. ANDREW HERDMAN; publs *Annual Report*, *Annual Statistical Report*, *Asia Pacific Perspectives*, *Orient Aviation* (10 a year).

Association of European Airlines: 350 ave Louise, 1050 Brussels, Belgium; tel. (2) 639-89-89; fax (2) 639-89-99; e-mail aea.secretariat@ aea.be; internet www.aea.be; f. 1954 to carry out research on political, commercial, economic and technical aspects of air transport; maintains statistical data bank; mems: 34 airlines; Chair. BERNARD GUSTIN; Sec.-Gen. ATHAR HUSAIN KHAN (acting).

Association of the European Rail Industry (UNIFE): 221 ave Louise, bte 11, 1050 Brussels, Belgium; tel. (2) 626-12-60; fax (2) 626-12-61; e-mail info@unife.org; internet www.unife.org; f. 1975 with the merger of Association internationale des constructeurs de matérial roulant, Association des fabricants européens d'equipements ferroviaires and Constructeurs européens des locomotives thermiques et electriques; represents cos concerned with the design, manufacture and maintenance of railway systems and equipment; mems: 60 cos and 18 nat. railway industry asscns in 14 countries; Chair. HENRI POUPART-LAFARGE; Dir-Gen. PHILIPPE CITROËN; publ. *Newsletter* (quarterly).

Baltic and International Maritime Council (BIMCO): Bagsvaerdvej 161, 2880 Bagsvaerd, Denmark; tel. 44-36-68-00; fax 44-36-68-68; e-mail mailbox@bimco.org; internet www.bimco.org; f. 1905 to unite shipowners and other persons and orgs connected with the shipping industry, to facilitate commercial operations by sharing information and training resources and to establish sound business practices; mems: 2,500 in 123 countries, representing over 65% of world merchant shipping by tonnage; Pres. JOHN DENHOLM (United Kingdom); Sec.-Gen. ANGUS R. FREW (United Kingdom); publs *BIMCO Review* (annually), *BIMCO Bulletin* (6 a year), *Vessel*, manuals.

Central Commission for the Navigation of the Rhine: Palais du Rhin, 2 Pl. de la République, 67082 Strasbourg, France; tel. 3-88-52-20-10; fax 3-88-32-10-72; e-mail ccnr@ccr-zkr.org; internet www .ccr-zkr.org; f. 1815 to ensure free movement of traffic and standard river facilities for ships of all nations; draws up navigational rules; standardizes customs regulations; arbitrates in disputes involving river traffic; approves plans for river maintenance work; there is an administrative centre for social security for boatmen; mems: Belgium, France, Germany, Netherlands, Switzerland; Sec.-Gen. HANS VAN DER WERF (Netherlands); publs guides, rules and directives (in French and German).

Danube Commission: Benczúr utca 25, 1068 Budapest, Hungary; tel. (1) 352-1835; fax (1) 352-1839; e-mail secretariat@ danubecom-intern.org; internet www.danubecommission.org; f. 1948; supervises implementation of the Belgrade Convention on the Regime of Navigation on the Danube; approves projects for river maintenance; supervises a uniform system of traffic regulations on the whole navigable portion of the Danube and on river inspection; mems: Austria, Bulgaria, Croatia, Germany, Hungary, Moldova, Romania, Russia, Serbia, Slovakia, Ukraine; Pres. BISERKA BANISHEVA; Dir-Gen. PETAR MARGIĆ; publs *Basic Regulations for Navigation on the Danube*, *Hydrological Yearbook*, *Statistical Yearbook*, proceedings of sessions.

European Civil Aviation Conference (ECAC): 3 bis Villa Emile-Bergerat, 92522 Neuilly-sur-Seine Cedex, France; tel. 1-46-41-85-44; fax 1-76-73-98-57; e-mail info@ecac-ceac.org; internet www .ecac-ceac.org; f. 1955; aims to promote the continued devt of a safe, efficient and sustainable European air transport system; mems: 44 European states; Pres. CATALIN RADU; Exec. Sec. SALVATORE SCIACCHITANO.

European Organisation for the Safety of Air Navigation (EUROCONTROL): 96 rue de la Fusée, 1130 Brussels, Belgium; tel. (2) 729-90-11; fax (2) 729-90-44; e-mail infocentre@eurocontrol .int; internet www.eurocontrol.int; f. 1960; aims to develop a coherent and co-ordinated air traffic control system in Europe. A revised Convention was signed in June 1997, incorporating the following institutional structure: a General Assembly (known as the Commission in the transitional period), a Council (known as the Provisional Council) and an Agency under the supervision of the Director-General; there are directorates, covering human resources and finance matters and a general secretariat. A special organizational structure covers the management of the European Air Traffic Management Programme. EUROCONTROL also operates the Experimental Centre (at Brétigny-sur-Orge, France), the Institute of Air Navigation Services (in Luxembourg), the Central Route Charges Office, the Central Flow Management Unit (both in Brussels) and the Upper Area Control Centre (in Maastricht, Netherlands); mems: 39 states and the European Community; Dir-Gen. FRANK BRENNER (Germany).

Forum Train Europe FTE: Mittelstr. 43, 3000 Bern 65, Switzerland; tel. 512202715; fax 512201242; e-mail mailbox@ forumtraineurope.org; internet www.forumtraineurope.org; f. 1923 as the European Passenger Train Time-Table Conference to arrange international passenger connections by rail and water; since 1997 concerned also with rail freight; mems: 98 mems from 35 European countries; Pres. STEPHAN PFUHL; Sec.-Gen. PETER JÄGGY.

Inland Waterways International: 20 Trinity Fields, Lower Beeding, Horsham, West Sussex, RH13 6PX, United Kingdom; e-mail info@inlandwaterwaysinternational.org; internet www .inlandwaterwaysinternational.org; f. 1995; promotes the use, conservation and devt of inland waterways worldwide; hosts the steering cttee to choose the venue of the annual World Canals Conference; mems: 18 countries; Pres. DAVID BALLINGER (Canada).

Intergovernmental Organization for International Carriage by Rail (OTIF): Gryphenhübeliweg 30, 3006 Bern, Switzerland; tel. 313591010; fax 313591011; e-mail info@otif.org; internet www.otif .org; f. 1893 as Central Office for International Carriage by Rail, present name adopted 1985; aims to establish and develop a uniform system of law governing the international carriage of passengers and goods by rail in mem. states, and to facilitate its application and devt; composed of a General Assembly, an Administrative Committee, a Revision Committee, a Committee of Experts on the Transport of Dangerous Goods, a Committee of Technical Experts and a Rail Facilitation Committee; mems: 47 states in Europe, the Middle East and North Africa, and 1 assoc. mem. (Jordan); Sec.-Gen. FRANÇOIS DAVENNE; publ. *Bulletin des Transports Internationaux ferroviaires* (quarterly, in English, French and German).

International Air Transport Association (IATA): 800 Pl. Victoria, POB 113, Montréal, Québec, QC H4Z 1M1, Canada; tel. (514) 874-0202; fax (514) 874-1753; e-mail iata@iata.org; internet www .iata.org; f. 1945 to represent, lead and serve the airline industry; priorities agreed by the Board of Governors in Dec. 2012 included improving global safety, especially in Africa; improving security at checkpoints; managing airline revenues securely and efficiently; rebalancing value chains; promoting sustainable growth of the airline industry; protecting mems from burdensome regulation; reducing industry costs; and improving customer service; maintains an executive office in Geneva, Switzerland; and regional offices in Amman, Beijing, Brussels, Johannesburg, Madrid, Miami, Moscow, Singapore, Washington, DC; holds an annual general meeting and World Air Transport Summit (2014: Doha, Qatar, in June); mems: c. 240 airlines in more than 115 countries; Chair. RICHARD H. ANDERSON (Chair. of Delta Air Lines); Dir-Gen. and CEO TONY TYLER; publ. *Airlines International* (every 2 months).

International Association for the Rhine Ships Register (IVR) (Internationale Vereniging het Rijnschepenregister): Vasteland 12E, 3011 BL Rotterdam (POB 23210, 3001 KE Rotterdam), Netherlands; tel. (10) 4116070; fax (10) 4129091; e-mail info@ivr.nl; internet www .ivr.nl; f. 1947 for the classification of Rhine ships, the organization and publication of a Rhine ships register, the unification of general average rules and the maintenance of European inland navigation law; provides a platform for experts in the field of shipping, insurance, maritime affairs and related sectors, and representatives of national govts; Gen. Sec. THERESIA K. HACKSTEINER; publs *IVR Report* (2 a year), *Registre de l'IVR* (annually).

International Association of Ports and Harbors (IAPH): 7F, New Pier Takeshiba South Tower, 1-16-1, Kaigan, Minato-ku, Tokyo 105-0022, Japan; tel. (3) 5403-2770; fax (3) 5403-7651; e-mail info@iaphworldports.org; internet www.iaphworldports.org; f. 1955 to increase the efficiency of ports and harbours through the dissemination of information on port organization, management, administration, operation, devt and promotion; encourages the growth of waterborne commerce; holds conf. every two years; mems: 350 in 90 states; Pres. GRANT GILFILLAN (Australia); Sec.-Gen. SUSUMU NARUSE (Japan); publs *Ports and Harbors* (6 a year), *Membership Directory* (annually).

International Association of Public Transport: 6 rue Sainte-Marie, Quai de Charbonnages, 1080 Brussels, Belgium; tel. (2) 673-61-00; fax (2) 660-10-72; e-mail info@uitp.org; internet www.uitp.org; f. 1885 to study all problems connected with the urban and regional public passenger transport industry; serves as an international network for public transport authorities and operators, policy decision-makers, scientific institutes and the public transport supply and service industry; mems: 3,500 in 87 countries; Pres. PETER HENDY; Sec.-Gen. ALAIN FLAUSCH; publs *Public Transport International* (every 2 months), *EU Express*, *Mobility News* (monthly, electronic), statistics reports.

International Bureau of Containers and Intermodal Transport (Bureau international des containers et du transport intermodal—BIC): 41 rue Réaumur, 75003 Paris, France; tel. 1-47-66-03-90; fax 1-47-66-08-91; e-mail bis@bic-code.org; internet www.bic-code.org; f. 1933 as Bureau International des Containers by the International Chamber of Commerce, present name adopted in 1948 on the assumption of intermodal activities; aims to bring together representatives of all means of transport and activities concerning containers, to promote combined door-to-door transport by the successive use of several means of transport, to examine and bring into effect advances in administrative, technical and customs practice, and to centralize data on behalf of mems; mems: 1,700; Chair. MICHEL HENNEMAND; Sec.-Gen. BERTRAND GEOFFRAY; publs *Containers Bulletin*, *Containers Bic-Code* (annually).

International Chamber of Shipping: 38 St Mary Axe, London, EC3A 8BH, United Kingdom; tel. (20) 7090-1460; e-mail info@ics-shipping.org; internet www.ics-shipping.org; f. 1921 to co-ordinate the views of the international shipping industry on matters of common interest, in the policy-making, technical and legal fields of shipping operations; mems: nat. asscns representing free enterprise shipowners and operators in 34 countries, representing about 80% of the world merchant fleet; Chair. MASAMICHI MOROOKA; Sec.-Gen. PETER HINCHLIFFE.

International Federation of Freight Forwarders Associations (FIATA): Schaffhauserstr. 104, 8152 Glattbrugg, Switzerland; tel. 432116500; fax 432116565; e-mail info@fiata.com; internet www.fiata.com; f. 1926 to represent the freight forwarding industry at an international level; has consultative status with ECOSOC (*inter alia* ECE, ESCAP, ESCWA), the United Nations Conference on Trade and Development and the United Nations Convention on International Trade Law; mems: 44,000 forwarding and logistics firms in 150 countries; Pres. STANLEY H. H. LIM (Singapore); Dir MARCO A. SANGALETTI; publ. *FIATA Review* (every 2 months).

International Rail Transport Committee (Comité international des transports ferroviaires—CIT): Weltpoststr. 20, 3015 Bern, Switzerland; tel. 313500190; fax 313500199; e-mail info@cit-rail.org; internet www.cit-rail.org; f. 1902 for the devt of international law relating to railway transport, on the basis of the Convention concerning International Carriage by Rail and its Appendices (CIV, CIM), and for the adoption of standard rules on other questions relating to international transport law; mems: 120 transport undertakings in 42 countries; Pres. JEAN-LUC DUFOURNAUD (France); Sec.-Gen. CESARE BRAND (Switzerland).

International Road Federation (IRF): Geneva Programme Centre: 2 chemin de Blandonnet 1214, Vernier, Geneva, Switzerland; tel. 655851503; e-mail info@irfnet.ch; internet www.irfnet.ch; f. 1948 to encourage the devt and improvement of highways and highway transportation; Programme Centres in Geneva, Switzerland, Brussels, Belgium and Washington, DC, USA; organizes IRF world and regional meetings; mems: 80 nat. road asscns and 500 individual firms and industrial asscns; Chair. KIRAN KAPILA; Deputy Dir-Gen. CAROLINE VISSER; publs *World Road Statistics* (annually), *World Highways* (8 a year).

International Road Safety Organization (La prevention routière internationale—PRI): Rietgors 1, 3755 GA Eemnes, Netherlands; tel. (65)5851503; fax ((35) 7850656; e-mail contact@lapri.info; internet www.lapri.info; f. 1959 for exchange of ideas and material on road safety, education, campaigns and advocacy; organizes international action and congresses; assists non-mem. countries; mems: 50 nat. orgs; Pres. JOOP GOOS; publs *Newsletter* (6 a year), also annual reports, news, brochures, booklets and manuals.

International Road Transport Union (IRU): Centre International, 3 rue de Varembé, BP 44, 1211 Geneva 20, Switzerland; tel. 229182700; fax 229182741; e-mail iru@iru.org; internet www.iru.org; f. 1948 to study all problems of road transport, to advocate harmonization and simplification of regulations relating to road transport, and to promote the use of road transport for passengers and goods; represents, promotes and upholds the interests of the road transport industry at international level; asscns and assoc. mems in 73 countries; Pres. JANUSZ LACNY; Sec.-Gen. UMBERTO DE PRETTO.

International Shipping Federation: 38 St Mary Axe, London, EC3A 8BH, United Kingdom; tel. (20) 7090-1460; e-mail info@ics-shipping.org; internet www.ics-shipping.org; f. 1909 to consider all personnel questions affecting the interests of shipowners; responsible for Shipowners' Group at confs of the ILO; represents shipowners at the IMO; mems: nat. shipowners' orgs in 32 countries; Sec.-Gen. PETER HINCHLIFFE; publs conf. papers, guidelines and training records.

International Transport Forum: 2 rue André Pascal, 75775 Paris Cedex 16, France; tel. 1-45-24-97-10; fax 1-45-24-97-42; e-mail itf.contact@oecd.org; internet www.internationaltransportforum.org; f. 2006 by a decision of the European Conference of Ministers of Transport (f. 1953) to broaden membership of the org; aims to create a safe, sustainable, efficient, integrated transport system; hosts an annual Forum in Liepzig, Germany (May 2013: 'Funding Transport'); organizes round-table discussions, seminars and symposia; shares Secretariat staff with OECD; mems: 54 countries; Sec.-Gen. JOSÉ VIEGAS (Portugal); publs *Annual Report*, various statistical publications and surveys.

International Union of Railways (Union internationale des chemins de fer—UIC): 16 rue Jean-Rey, 75015 Paris, France; tel. 1-44-49-20-20; fax 1-44-49-20-29; e-mail loubinoux@uic.org; internet www.uic.org; f. 1922 for the harmonization of railway operations and the devt of international rail transport; aims to ensure international interoperability of the rail system; compiles information on economic, management and technical aspects of railways; co-ordinates research and collaborates with industry and the European Union; organizes international confs; mems: 196 in 92 countries; Chair. VLADIMIR YAKUNIN; Dir-Gen. JEAN-PIERRE LOUBINOUX; publs *International Railway Statistics* (annually), *Activities Reports*, *UIC News* (newsletter).

Nordisk Defence Club (Nordisk Skibsrederforening): Kristinelundv. 22, POB 3033, Elisenberg, 0207 Oslo, Norway; tel. 22-13-56-00; fax 22-43-00-35; e-mail post@nordisk.no; internet www.nordisk.no; f. 1889 to assist mems in disputes over charter parties, contracts and sale and purchase; functions as a safeguard bearing the cost of all legal intervention while also providing commercial and strategic advice; mems: mainly Finnish, Swedish and Norwegian and some non-Scandinavian shipowners, representing about 2,150 ships and drilling rigs with gross tonnage of about 53m.; Man. Dir GEORGE SCHEEL; Chair. NILS P. DYVIK; publs *A Law Report of Scandinavian Maritime Cases* (annually), *Medlemsbladet (Membership Circular)* (2 a year), *Annual Report*.

Organisation for Co-operation Between Railways: Hozâ 63–67, 00681 Warsaw, Poland; tel. (22) 6573600; fax (22) 6219417; e-mail osjd@osjd.org.pl; internet www.osjd.org; f. 1956; aims to improve standards and co-operation in railway traffic between countries of Europe and Asia; promotes co-operation on issues relating to traffic policy and economic and environmental aspects of railway traffic; ensures enforcement of a number of rail agreements; aims to elaborate and standardize general principles for international transport law. Conference of Ministers of mem. countries meets annually; Conference of General Directors of Railways meets at least once a year; mems: ministries of transport of 27 countries worldwide; Chair. TADEUSZ SZOZDA; publs *OSShD Journal* (every 2 months, in Chinese, German and Russian), *Statistic Report on Railway Transport* (annually), *Report on OSJD Activities* (annually), *International Timetable EuroAsia Rail* (annually), *Information Guide* (2 a year).

Pan American Railway Congress Association (Asociación del Congreso Panamericano de Ferrocarriles): Av. Dr José María Ramos Mejía 1302, Planta Baja, 1104 Buenos Aires, Argentina; tel. (11) 4315-3445; fax (11) 4312-3834; e-mail acpf@acpf.com.ar; f. 1907, present title adopted 1941; aims to promote the devt and progress of railways in the American continent; holds Congresses every three years; mems: govt representatives, railway enterprises and individuals in 20 countries; Pres. LORENZO PEPE; Gen. Sec. JULIO SOSA; publ. *Boletín ACPF* (5 a year).

PIANC (World Association for Waterborne Transport Infrastructure): Bât Graaf de Ferraris, 11e étage, 20 blvd Roi Albert II, bte 3, 1000 Brussels, Belgium; tel. (2) 553-71-61; fax (2) 553-71-55; e-mail info@pianc.org; internet www.pianc.org; f. 1885; fmrly Permanent International Association of Navigation Congresses; fosters progress in the construction, maintenance and operation of inland and maritime waterways, of inland and maritime ports and of coastal areas; holds International Navigation Congress every four years (2014: San Francisco, USA, in June); mems: 33 govts, 3,400 others; Pres. GEOFFREY CAUDE; Sec.-Gen. LOUIS VAN SCHEL; publs *On Course* (quarterly), *Illustrated Technical Dictionary* (in 6 languages), *Sailing Ahead* (electronic newsletter), technical reports, Congress papers.

World Airlines Clubs Association (WACA): c/o IATA, 800 Pl. Victoria, POB 113, Montréal, Québec, QC H4Z 1M1, Canada; tel. (514) 874-0202; fax (514) 874-1753; e-mail info@waca.org; internet www.waca.org; f. 1966; holds a General Assembly annually, regional meetings, social programmes, international events and sports tournaments; mems: clubs in 35 countries; Pres. MAGA RAMASAMY; Sec.-Gen. ANGELA LERESCHE; publs *WACA Contact*, *WACA World News* (2 a year), *Annual Report*.

World Road Association (PIARC): La Grande Arche, Paroi Nord, Niveau 5, 92055 La Défense Cedex, France; tel. 1-47-96-81-21; fax 1-49-00-02-02; e-mail info@piarc.org; internet www.piarc.org; f. 1909 as the Permanent International Association of Road Congresses; aims to promote the construction, improvement, maintenance, use and economic devt of roads; organizes technical cttee and study sessions; mems: 120 govts; public bodies, orgs and private individuals in 142 countries; Pres. OSCAR DE BUEN RICHKARDAY (Mexico); Sec.-Gen. JEAN-FRANÇOIS CORTÉ (France); publs *Bulletin*, *Technical Dictionary*, *Lexicon*, technical reports.

Youth and Students

AIESEC International: Teilingerstraat 126, 3032 Rotterdam, Netherlands; tel. (10) 4434383; fax (10) 2651386; e-mail info@ai.aiesec.org; internet www.aiesec.org; f. 1948 as International Association of Students in Economics and Management; provides an international platform for young people to discover and develop their potential; enters into partnerships with selected orgs; mems: 86,000 students in more than 2,100 univs in c. 113 countries and territories; Pres. ROLF SCHMACTENBERG (Norway) (2013–14).

Commonwealth Youth Council (CYC): c/o Ahmed Adamu, Marlborough House, Pall Mall, London SW1Y 5HX, United Kingdom; e-mail info@commonwealthyouthcouncil.org; internet commonwealthyouthcouncil.org; f. 2013; aims to play an integral role in advancing the youth devt agenda and the co-ordination of activities and policies of the Commonwealth with a focus on youth devt; the first Commonwealth Youth Council General Assembly was held in Hambantota, Sri Lanka, in Nov. 2013; Chair. AHMED ADAMU (Nigeria).

Council on International Educational Exchange (CIEE): 300 Fore St, Portland, ME 04101, USA; tel. (207) 553-4000; fax (207) 553-4299; e-mail contact@ciee.org; internet www.ciee.org; f. 1947; issues International Student Identity Card entitling holders to discounts and basic insurance; arranges overseas work and study programmes for students; co-ordinates summer work programme in the USA for foreign students; administers programmes for teachers and other professionals and sponsors confs on educational exchange; operates a voluntary service programme; mems: over 350 colleges, univs and international educational orgs in 22 countries; Pres. and CEO ROBERT E. FALLON; publs *The Knowledge Series*, *Annual Report*, Occasional Papers in International Education.

European Students' Forum (Association des Etats Généraux des Etudiants de l'Europe—AEGEE): 55 rue du Noyer, 1000 Brussels, Belgium; tel. (2) 246-03-20; fax (2) 246-03-29; e-mail headoffice@aegee.org; internet www.aegee.org; f. 1985; promotes cross-border communication, co-operation and integration between students; fosters inter-cultural exchange; holds specialized confs; mems: 13,000 students in 200 univ. cities in 40 countries; Sec.-Gen. LUCILLE RIEUX.

European Youth Forum: 120 rue Joseph II, 1000 Brussels, Belgium; tel. (2) 230-64-90; fax (2) 230-21-23; e-mail youthforum@youthforum.org; internet www.youthforum.org; f. 1996; represents and advocates for the needs and interests of all young people in Europe; promotes their active participation in democratic processes, as well as understanding and respect for human rights; consults with international orgs and govts on issues relevant to young people; co-sponsors, with the Council of Europe's European Centre for Global Interdependence and Solidarity, the Spanish Govt, and other partners the University on Youth and Development, a youth event convened annually, since 2000, in Mollina, Spain; mems: 98 nat. youth councils and int. non-governmental youth orgs; Pres. PETER MATJAŠIČ; Sec.-Gen. GIUSEPPE PORCARO.

Hostelling International: Gate House, 2nd Floor, Fretherne Rd, Welwyn Garden City, Hertfordshire, AL8 6RD, United Kingdom; tel. (1707) 324170; fax (1707) 323980; e-mail info@hihostels.com; internet www.hihostels.com; f. 1932 as International Youth Hostel Federation, present name adopted 2006; facilitates international travel by members of the various youth hostel asscns; advises and helps in the formation of youth hostel asscns in countries where no such orgs exist; records over 35m. overnight stays annually in some 4,000 youth hostels; mems: 90 nat. asscns with over 3.2m. nat. mems and 1m. int. guest mems; 12 assoc. nat. orgs; CEO MIKAEL HANSSON; publs *Annual Report*, *Guidebook on World Hostels* (annually), *Manual*, *News Bulletin*.

International Association for the Exchange of Students for Technical Experience (IAESTE): 51 rue Albert Ier, 1117 Luxembourg; tel. (11) 303-1677; fax (11) 303-1675; e-mail board@iaeste.org; internet www.iaeste.org; f. 1948; operates an exchange programme between students and employers; launched a web-based alumni network in 2011, accessible at alumni.iaeste.org; mems: 88 nat. cttees and co-operating institutions in 85 countries; Pres. BERNARD BAEYENS (2014–16); publs *Activity Report*, *Annual Report*, *IAESTE Bulletin* (quarterly).

International Association of Dental Students (IADS): c/o FDI World Dental Federation, Tour de Cointrin, Ave Louis Casaï 84, CP 3, 1216 Genève-Cointrin, Switzerland; tel. 225608150; fax 225608140; e-mail info@fdiworldental.org; internet www.iads-web.org; f. 1951 to represent dental students and their opinions internationally, to promote dental student exchanges and international congresses; mems: 60,000 students in 45 countries, 15,000 corresponding mems; Pres. PAVEL SCARLAT (Moldova/Romania); Sec. Dr NADA UNCIANSCHI (Romania); publ. *IADS Newsletter* (2 a year).

International Federation of Medical Students' Associations (IFMSA): c/o WMA, BP 63, 01212 Ferney-Voltaire Cedex, France; fax 4-50-40-59-37; e-mail gs@ifmsa.org; internet www.ifmsa.org; f. 1951 to promote international co-operation in professional treatment and the achievement of humanitarian ideals; provides forum for medical students; maintains standing committees on professional and research exchange, medical education, public health, refugees and reproductive health, including AIDS; organizes annual General Assembly; mems: 94 asscns; Pres. ROOPA DHATT (USA); Gen. Sec. ALEXANDRE MOSER (Switzerland); publ. *IFMSA Newsletter* (quarterly).

International Law Students Association (ILSA): Suite OMB1051, 25 E. Jackson Blvd, Chicago, IL 60604, USA; tel. (312) 362-5025; fax (312) 362-5073; e-mail mszuminski@ilsa.org; internet www.ilsa.org; f. 1962; aims to educate students and lawyers around the world in the principles and purposes of international law, international orgs and institutions, and comparative legal systems; Exec. Dir LESLEY A. BENN.

International Pharmaceutical Students' Federation (IPSF): POB 84200, 2508 AE The Hague, Netherlands; tel. (70) 3021992; fax (70) 3021999; e-mail ipsf@ipsf.org; internet www.ipsf.org; f. 1949 to study and promote the interests of pharmaceutical students and to encourage international co-operation; mems: represents some 350,000 pharmacy students and recent graduates in 70 countries worldwide; Pres. RADOSLAW MITURA (Poland); Sec.-Gen. ANGELA SESTER (Germany); publ. *IPSF News Bulletin* (2 a year).

International Scout and Guide Fellowship (ISGF): 38 ave de la Porte de Hal, 1060 Brussels, Belgium; tel. and fax (2) 511-46-95; e-mail worldbureau@isgf.org; internet www.isgf.org; f. 1953 to help adult scouts and guides to keep alive the spirit of the Scout and Guide Promise and Laws in their own lives and to bring that spirit into the communities in which they live and work; promotes liaison and co-operation between national orgs for adult scouts and guides; encourages the founding of an org. in any country where no such org. exists; mems: 90,000 in 61 mem. states; Chair. of Cttee MIDÁ RODRIGUES; Sec.-Gen. CECILE BELLET.

International Young Christian Workers: 4 ave G. Rodenbach, 1030 Brussels, Belgium; tel. (2) 242-18-11; fax (2) 242-48-00; internet www.joci.org; f. 1925, on the inspiration of the Priest-Cardinal Joseph Cardijn; aims to educate young workers to take on present and future responsibilities in their commitment to the working class, and to gain personal fulfilment through their actions; Pres. LUDOVICUS MARDIYONO; publs *International INFO* (3 a year), *IYCW Bulletin* (quarterly).

International Young Democrat Union: e-mail iydu@iydu.com; internet www.iydu.org; f. 1991; a global alliance of centre-right political youth orgs; mems: 127 orgs from 81 countries; Chair. ARIS KALAFATIS (Greece); Treas. ZACH HOWELL (USA).

Junior Chamber International (JCI), Inc.: 15645 Olive Blvd, Chesterfield, MO 63017, USA; tel. (636) 449-3100; fax (636) 449-3107; e-mail news@jci.cc; internet www.jci.cc; f. 1944 to encourage and advance international understanding and goodwill; aims to solve civic problems by arousing civic consciousness; Junior Chamber orgs throughout the world provide opportunities for leadership training and for the discussion of social, economic and cultural questions; mems: 200,000 in more than 100 countries; Pres. SHINE BHASKARAN (India) (2014); publs *JCI News* (monthly in English, French and Spanish), *Leader Magazine* (2 a year).

Latin American and Caribbean Alliance of Young Men's Christian Associations (La Alianza Latinoamericana y del Caribe de Asociaciones Cristianas de Jóvenes): Rua N Pestana 125, 10° andar, Conj. 103, São Paulo 01303-010, Brazil; tel. (11) 3257-5867; fax (11) 3151-2573; e-mail secretariogeneral@lacaymca.org; internet www.lacaymca.org; f. 1914; aims to encourage the moral, spiritual, intellectual, social and physical devt of young men; to strengthen the work of national asscns and to sponsor the establishment of new asscns; mems: affiliated YMCAs in 94 countries; Pres. MAURO FONTICIELLA (Uruguay); Gen. Sec. MAURICIO DIAZ VANDORSEE (Brazil); publs *Diecisiete/21* (bulletin), *Carta Abierta*, *Brief*, technical articles and other studies.

Round Table International: e-mail secretary@rtinternational.org; internet www.rtinternational.org; f. 1947 to promote international fellowship and co-operation among national Round Table groupings aimed at young business people 18–40 years of age; mems: some 2,700 clubs in 65 countries; Pres. MOFFAT NYIRENDA (Zambia) (2013–14).

WFUNA Youth Network: c/o WFUNA, 1 United Nations Plaza, Room DC1-1177, New York, NY 10017, USA; tel. (212) 963-5610; fax (212) 963-0447; e-mail youth@wfuna.org; internet www.wfuna.org/youth; f. 1946 by the World Federation of United Nations Associations (WFUNA) as the International Youth and Student Movement for the United Nations, independent since 1949; an international non-governmental org. of students and young people dedicated especially to supporting the principles embodied in the United Nations Charter and Universal Declaration of Human Rights; encourages constructive action in building economic, social and cultural equality and in working for national independence, social justice and human rights on a worldwide scale; organizes periodic regional WFUNA International Model United Nations (WIMUN) confs; maintains regional offices in Switzerland and the USA; mems: asscns in over 100 mem. states of the UN.

World Alliance of Young Men's Christian Associations: 12 Clos. Belmont, 1208 Geneva, Switzerland; tel. 228495100; fax 228495110; e-mail office@ymca.int; internet www.ymca.int; f. 1855; organizes World Council every four years (2014: Estes Park, USA); mems: YMCAs in 119 countries; Pres. KEN COLLOTON (USA) (2010–14); Sec.-Gen. Rev. JOHAN VILHELM ELTVIK (Norway) (2010–14); publ. *YMCA World* (quarterly).

World Assembly of Youth: World Youth Complex, Lebuh Ayer Keroh, Ayer Keroh, 75450 Melaka, Malaysia; tel. (6) 2321871; fax (6) 2327271; e-mail info@way.org.my; internet www.way.org.my; f. 1949 as co-ordinating body for national youth councils and orgs; organizes confs, training courses and practical devt projects; has consultative status with ECOSOC; mems: 120 mem. orgs; Pres. Datuk Wira IDRIS HARON; Sec.-Gen. EDIOLA PASHOLLARI; publs *WAY Information* (every 2 months), *Youth Roundup* (every 2 months), *WAY Forum* (quarterly).

World Association of Girl Guides and Girl Scouts (WAGGGS): World Bureau, Olave Centre, 12c Lyndhurst Rd, London, NW3 5PQ, United Kingdom; tel. (20) 7794-1181; fax (20) 7431-3764; e-mail wagggs@wagggsworld.org; internet www.wagggsworld.org; f. 1928 to enable girls and young women to develop their full potential as responsible citizens, and to support friendship and mutual understanding among girls and young women worldwide; operates four 'World Centres': Pax Lodge (United Kingdom), Sangam (India), Cabaña (Mexico), and Chalet (Switzerland), which provide residential training programmes to enable girls and young women to develop leadership skills and friendships; World Conference meets every three years; mems: about 10m. individuals in 145 orgs; Chair. World Board NADINE EL-ACHY (Lebanon); Chief Exec. MARY MCPHAIL (Ireland); publs *Triennial Review*, *Annual Report*, *Trefoil Round the World* (every 3 years), *Our World News* (quarterly).

World Federation of Democratic Youth (WFDY): 1139 Budapest, Frangepán u. 16, Hungary; tel. (1) 350-2202; fax (1) 350-1204; e-mail wfdy@wfdy.org; internet www.wfdy.org; f. 1945; promotes the unity, co-operation, organized action, solidarity and exchange of information and experiences of work and struggle among the progressive youth forces; campaigns against imperialism, fascism, colonialism, exploitation and war and for peace, internationalist solidarity, social progress and youth rights under the slogans Youth unite! and Forward for lasting peace!; mems: 152 mems in 102 countries; publ. *World Youth*.

World Organization of the Scout Movement: CP 91, 1211 Geneva 4 Plainpalais, Switzerland; tel. 227051010; fax 227051020; e-mail worldbureau@world.scout.org; internet www.scout.org; f. 1922 to promote unity and understanding of scouting throughout the world; to develop good citizenship among young people by forming their characters for service, co-operation and leadership; and to provide aid and advice to mems and potential mem. asscns. The World Scout Bureau (Geneva) has regional offices in Egypt, Kenya, Panama, the Philippines, Russia, Senegal, South Africa and Ukraine (the European Region has its offices in Brussels and Geneva); mems: more than 30m. in 161 countries and territories; Sec.-Gen. SCOTT TEARE (USA); publs *Worldinfo*, *Triennial Report*.

World Union of Jewish Students (WUJS): POB 39359, Tel Aviv 61392, Israel; tel. (2) 6251682; fax (2) 6251688; e-mail info@wujs.org.il; internet www.wujs.org.il; f. 1924 (with Albert Einstein as its first President); promotes dialogue and co-operation among Jewish univ. students worldwide; divided into six regions; organizes Congress every year; mems: 52 nat. unions representing over 1.5m. students; Chair. OLIVER WORTH; publs *The Student Activist Yearbook*, *Heritage and History*, *Forum*, *WUJS Report*.

World Young Women's Christian Association (World YWCA): 16 Ancienne Route, 1218 Grand-Saconnex, Geneva, Switzerland; tel. 229296040; fax 229296044; e-mail worldoffice@worldywca.org; internet www.worldywca.org; f. 1894; global movement which aims to empower women and girls to change their lives and communities; works to achieve social and economic justice through grass-roots devt and global advocacy; addresses critical issues affecting women, such as HIV and AIDS and violence; promotes the sharing of human and financial resources among mem. asscns; mems: in 106 countries; Pres. DEBORAH THOMAS-AUSTIN (Trinidad and Tobago); Gen. Sec. NYARADZAYI GUMBONZVANDA (Zimbabwe); publs *Annual Report*, *Common Concern*, *Week of Prayer* (booklet), other reports.

PART TWO

Afghanistan–Jordan

AFGHANISTAN

Introductory Survey

LOCATION, CLIMATE, LANGUAGE, RELIGION, FLAG, CAPITAL

The Islamic Republic of Afghanistan is a landlocked country in south-western Asia. It is bordered by Turkmenistan, Uzbekistan and Tajikistan to the north, Iran to the west, the People's Republic of China to the north-east, and Pakistan to the east and south. The climate varies sharply between the highlands and lowlands; the temperature in the south-west in summer reaches 49°C (120°F), but in the winter, in the Hindu Kush mountains of the north-east, it falls to −26°C (−15°F). Of the many languages spoken in Afghanistan, the principal two are Pashto (Pakhto) and Dari (a dialect of Farsi or Iranian). The majority of Afghans are Muslims of the Sunni sect; there are also minority groups of Shi'a Muslims, Hindus, Sikhs and Jews. The state flag (proportions 1 by 2) has three equal vertical stripes from hoist to fly of black, red and green, bearing in the centre in white and red the state arms and an inscription reading 'There is no God but Allah, and Muhammad is his Prophet, and Allah is Great', in Arabic. The Islamic date 1298 appears under the inscription. The flag was first introduced in 1928, modified in 1964, and banned following the coup in 1978. The only difference featured in the current flag, which was introduced in June 2002 following the collapse of the Taliban regime, is the inscription bearing the word 'Afghanistan'. The capital is Kabul.

CONTEMPORARY POLITICAL HISTORY

Historical Context

The last King of Afghanistan, Mohammad Zahir Shah, reigned from 1933 to 1973. His country was neutral during both World Wars and became a staunch advocate of non-alignment. In 1953 the King's cousin, Lt-Gen. Sardar Mohammad Daoud Khan, was appointed Prime Minister and, securing aid from the USSR, initiated a series of economic plans for the modernization of the country. In 1963 Gen. Daoud resigned and Dr Mohammad Yusuf became the first Prime Minister not of royal birth. A new democratic Constitution, combining Western ideas with Islamic religious and political beliefs, was introduced in 1964; however, the King did not permit political parties to operate.

In July 1973, while King Zahir was in Italy, the monarchy was overthrown by a coup, in which the main figure was Gen. Daoud. The 1964 Constitution was abolished and Afghanistan was declared a republic. Daoud renounced his royal titles and took office as Head of State, Prime Minister, and Minister of Foreign Affairs and Defence. A Loya Jirga (Grand National Council) of tribal elders appointed by provincial governors was convened in January 1977 and adopted a new Constitution, providing for presidential government and a one-party state. Daoud was elected to continue as President for six years and the Loya Jirga was then dissolved. In March President Daoud formed a new civilian Government, nominally ending military rule.

Domestic Political Affairs

Communist/PDPA rule (1978–92)

During 1977 there was growing discontent with Daoud, especially within the armed forces, and in April 1978 a coup, known (from the month) as the 'Saur Revolution', ousted the President, who was killed with several members of his family. Nur Mohammad Taraki, the imprisoned leader of the formerly banned People's Democratic Party of Afghanistan (PDPA), was released and installed as President of the Revolutionary Council and Prime Minister. The country was renamed the Democratic Republic of Afghanistan, the year-old Constitution was abolished and all other political parties were banned. Afghanistan's already close relations with the USSR were further strengthened. However, opposition to the new regime led to armed insurrection, particularly by fiercely traditionalist Islamist tribesmen (known, collectively, as the *mujahidin*), and the flight of thousands of refugees to Pakistan and Iran. In September 1979 Taraki was ousted by Hafizullah Amin, an erstwhile Deputy Prime Minister and Minister of Foreign Affairs, whose subsequent imposition of rigorous communist policies proved unsuccessful and unpopular. In December Amin was killed in a coup, which was supported by the entry into Afghanistan of about 80,000 combat troops from the USSR. This incursion by Soviet armed forces into a traditionally non-aligned neighbouring country provoked worldwide condemnation. Babrak Karmal, a former Deputy Prime Minister under Taraki, returned from exile and was installed as the new head of state.

Riots, strikes and inter-factional strife and purges continued in 1980–81. In June 1981 Deputy Prime Minister Sultan Ali Keshtmand replaced Karmal as Prime Minister, and the regime launched the National Fatherland Front (NFF), incorporating the PDPA and other organizations, with the aim of promoting national unity. However, the PDPA regime struggled to gain widespread popular support. In an attempt to broaden the base of its support, in April 1985 the Government summoned a Loya Jirga, at which a new Constitution was ratified. Elections were held thereafter for new local government organs and several non-party members were appointed to high-ranking government posts.

In May 1986 Dr Mohammad Najibullah (the former head of the state security service, KHAD) succeeded Karmal as General Secretary of the PDPA and announced the formation of a collective leadership comprising himself, Karmal and Prime Minister Keshtmand. In November, however, Karmal was relieved of all party and government posts. Haji Muhammad Chamkani, formerly First Vice-President (and a non-PDPA member), became Acting President of the Revolutionary Council, pending the introduction of a new constitution and the establishment of a permanent legislature. In December an extraordinary plenum of the PDPA Central Committee approved a policy of national reconciliation, involving negotiations with opposition groups, and the proposed formation of a government of national unity. The NFF was renamed the National Front (NF), and became a separate organization from the PDPA. The new policy of reconciliation won some support from former opponents, but the seven-party *mujahidin* alliance (Ittehad-i-Islami Afghan Mujahidin, Islamic Union of Afghan Mujahidin—IUAM), which was based in Peshawar, Pakistan, refused to observe the ceasefire or to participate in negotiations, while continuing to demand an unconditional Soviet withdrawal from Afghanistan.

On 30 September 1987 Najibullah was unanimously elected as President of the Revolutionary Council, and Chamkani resumed his former post as First Vice-President. In order to strengthen his position, Najibullah ousted all the remaining supporters of former President Karmal from the Central Committee and Politburo of the PDPA in October. In November a Loya Jirga unanimously elected Najibullah as President of Afghanistan. In the same month a new Constitution was ratified, providing for, *inter alia*: the formation of a multi-party political system, under the auspices of the NF; the formation of a bicameral legislature, the Meli Shura (National Assembly), comprising a Sena (Senate) and a Wolesi Jirga (House of the People); the granting of a permanent constitutional status to the PDPA; the bestowal of unlimited power on the President, who was to hold office for seven years; and the reversion of the name of the country to the Republic of Afghanistan.

In April 1988 elections were held to both houses of the new National Assembly, which replaced the Revolutionary Council. Although the elections were boycotted by the *mujahidin*, the Government left vacant 50 of the 234 seats in the House of Representatives, and a small number of seats in the Senate, in the hope that the guerrillas would abandon their armed struggle and present their own representatives to participate in the new administration. The PDPA itself won only 46 seats in the House of Representatives, but was guaranteed support from the NF, which secured 45, and from the various newly recognized left-wing parties, which won a total of 24 seats. In May Dr Muhammad Hasan Sharq (a non-PDPA member and a Deputy Prime Minister since June 1987) replaced Keshtmand as Prime Minister, and in June a new Council of Ministers was appointed.

On 18 February 1989, following the completion of the withdrawal of Soviet troops from Afghanistan (see Soviet occupation and *mujahidin* resistance), Najibullah replaced all non-communist government ministers with loyal PDPA members. On the same day, Prime Minister Sharq (one of the main advocates of the national reconciliation policy) resigned from his post and was replaced by Keshtmand. On the following day Najibullah declared a state of emergency (citing allegations of repeated violations of the Geneva accords by Pakistan and the USA), and a PDPA-dominated 20-member Supreme Council for the Defence of the Homeland was established. The Council, which was headed by President Najibullah and was composed of ministers, members of the PDPA Politburo and high-ranking military figures, assumed full responsibility for the country's economic, political and military policies (although the Council of Ministers continued to function).

In March 1990 the Minister of Defence, Lt-Gen. Shahnawaz Tanay, with the alleged support of the air force and some divisions of the army, led an unsuccessful coup attempt against Najibullah's Government. Najibullah subsequently enacted thorough purges of PDPA and army leaders, and decided to revert rapidly to some form of constitutional civilian government. On 20 May the state of emergency was lifted; the Supreme Council for the Defence of the Homeland was disbanded; and a new Council of Ministers, under the premiership of Fazle Haq Khalikyar, was appointed. At the end of the month a Loya Jirga ratified constitutional amendments, greatly reducing Afghanistan's socialist orientation; ending the PDPA's and the NF's monopoly over executive power and paving the way for fully democratic elections; introducing greater political and press freedom; encouraging the development of the private sector and further foreign investment; and lessening the role of the State and affording greater prominence to Islam. However, the extensive powers of the presidency were retained. In June the PDPA changed its name to the Homeland Party (HP—Hizb-i Watan), and replaced the Politburo and the Central Committee with an Executive Board and a Central Council, respectively. Najibullah was unanimously elected as Chairman of the HP. An important factor in Najibullah's decision to focus on national reconciliation was the impending decline in material support for his regime from a Soviet administration that was beleaguered by its own internal problems.

Soviet occupation and mujahidin *resistance*

Fighting between the *mujahidin* and Afghan army units had begun in the eastern provinces after the 1978 coup and was aggravated by the implementation of unpopular social and economic reforms by the new administrations. The Afghan army relied heavily upon Soviet military aid in the form of weapons, equipment and expertise, but morale and resources were severely affected by defections to the rebels' ranks: numbers fell from around 80,000 men in 1978 to about 40,000 in 1985. During 1984–89 the guerrilla groups, which had been poorly armed at first, received ever-increasing military and financial support from abroad, notably from the USA, the United Kingdom and the People's Republic of China. Despite the Government's decision to seal the border with Pakistan in 1985, and the strong presence of Soviet forces there, foreign weapons continued to reach the guerrillas via Pakistan. Many of the guerrillas established bases in Pakistan's North-West Frontier Province (later renamed Khyber Pakhtoonkhwa), notably in the provincial capital, Peshawar. From 1985 the fighting intensified, especially in areas close to the Afghan–Pakistani border. There were many border violations, but the general pattern of the war remained the same: the regime held the main towns and a few strategic bases, and relied on bombing of both military and civilian targets, and occasional attacks in force, together with conciliatory measures such as the provision of funds for local development, while the rebel forces dominated rural areas and were able to cause serious disruption.

From 1980 extensive international negotiations took place to try to achieve the withdrawal of Soviet forces from Afghanistan. Between 1982 and 1987 seven rounds of indirect talks took place between the Afghan and Pakistani authorities in Geneva, Switzerland, under the auspices of the UN. In October 1986 the USSR made a token withdrawal of six regiments (6,000–8,000 men) from Afghanistan. As a result of the discussions in Geneva, an agreement was finally signed on 14 April 1988. The Geneva accords comprised detailed undertakings by Afghanistan and Pakistan, relating to non-intervention and non-interference in each other's affairs; international guarantees of Afghan neutrality (with the USA and the USSR as the principal guarantors); arrangements for the voluntary and safe return of Afghan refugees; and the establishment of a UN monitoring force, which was to oversee both the Soviet troop departures and the return of the refugees. The withdrawal of Soviet troops commenced on 15 May.

The Geneva accords did not incorporate any agreement regarding the composition of an interim coalition government in Afghanistan, or the cessation of Soviet aid to Najibullah's regime and US aid to the *mujahidin*. Therefore, despite the withdrawal of the Soviet troops, the supply of weapons to both sides was not halted, and the fighting continued. Nevertheless, the USSR, adhering to the condition specified in the Geneva accords, withdrew all of its troops from Afghanistan by February 1989.

Meanwhile, the *mujahidin* had intensified their military activities in mid-1988, attacking small provincial centres and launching missiles against major cities. In February 1989 the IUAM convened its own *shura* (council) in Rawalpindi, Pakistan, at which an interim government-in-exile (known as the Afghan Interim Government—AIG) was elected. However, the AIG was officially recognized by only four countries, and failed to gain any substantial support from the guerrilla commanders, who were beginning to establish their own unofficial alliances inside the country. In mid-1989 the unity of the *mujahidin* forces was seriously weakened by an increase in internecine violence, while the AIG was riven by disputes between moderates and fundamentalists. The USA, Saudi Arabia and Pakistan began to undertake the difficult task of delivering weapons and money directly to guerrilla commanders and tribal leaders inside Afghanistan. The *mujahidin* launched a series of military campaigns in the second half of 1990 in an apparent attempt to impress their international supporters, disrupt the return of refugees and obstruct contacts between the Government and moderate guerrillas. In March 1991 the south-eastern city of Khost was captured by the *mujahidin*, representing the most severe reversal sustained by the Government since the Soviet withdrawal.

In September 1991 the USA and the USSR announced that they would stop supplying arms to the warring factions, and would encourage other countries (namely Pakistan, Saudi Arabia and Iran) to do likewise. In February 1992 Pakistan announced that it was urging all guerrilla factions to support a proposed UN peace plan, effectively abandoning its insistence on the installation of a fundamentalist government in Kabul. There were growing fears, none the less, that the peace process might be placed in jeopardy by an increase in ethnic divisions within both the government forces and a number of *mujahidin* groups, between the majority Pashtuns and minority groups such as the Tajiks and Uzbeks. As a result of a mutiny staged by Uzbek militia forces in the Afghan army, under the command of Gen. Abdul Rashid Dostam, the northern town of Mazar-i-Sharif was captured by the *mujahidin* in March.

The mujahidin *in power (1992–96)*

On 16 April 1992 Najibullah was unexpectedly forced to resign by his own ruling party, following the capture of the strategically important Bagram air base and the nearby town of Charikar, about 50 km north of Kabul, by the Jamiat-i Islami guerrilla group under the command of the Tajik general Ahmad Shah Masoud. Najibullah went into hiding in the capital, under UN protection, while one of the Vice-Presidents, Abdul Rahim Hatif, assumed the post of acting President. Within a few days, every major town in Afghanistan was under the control of different coalitions of *mujahidin* groups co-operating with disaffected army commanders. On 25 April the forces of both Masoud and Gulbuddin Hekmatyar, the leader of a rival guerrilla group, the Pashtun-dominated Hizb-i Islami, entered Kabul. The army surrendered its key positions, and immediately the city was riven by *mujahidin* faction-fighting. The military council that had replaced the Government relinquished power to the *mujahidin*. Having discarded the UN's proposal to form a neutral ruling body, the guerrilla leaders in Peshawar agreed to establish a 51-member interim Islamic Jihad Council, composed of military and religious leaders, which was to assume power in Kabul. Prof. Sibghatullah Mojaddedi, leader of the moderate Jebha-i-Nejat-i-Melli (National Liberation Front), was to chair the Islamic Jihad Council for two months, after which period a 10-member Leadership Council, comprising *mujahidin* chiefs and presided over by the head of the Jamiat-i Islami, Prof. Burhanuddin Rabbani, would be set up for a period of four months. Within the six months a special council was to appoint an interim administration, which was to hold power for up to a year pending elections.

However, the Islamic Jihad Council was not supported by Hekmatyar, whose radical stance differed substantially from

Mojaddedi's more tolerant outlook. At the end of April 1992 Hekmatyar's forces lost control of their last stronghold in the centre of Kabul. Within a few weeks the Government of the newly proclaimed Islamic State of Afghanistan had won almost universal diplomatic recognition, and by May about one-half of the Islamic Jihad Council had arrived in the capital. An acting Council of Ministers was formed, in which Masoud was given the post of Minister of Defence and the premiership was set aside for Ustad Abdol Sabur Farid, a Tajik commander from the Hizb-i Islami (Hekmatyar declined to accept the post). As part of the process of 'Islamization', the death penalty was introduced, alcohol and narcotics were banned, and the wearing of strict Islamic dress by all women was enforced. Meanwhile, Hekmatyar's forces continued to bombard Kabul with artillery and indiscriminate rocket launches from various strongholds around the city, killing and wounding scores of citizens.

In June 1992, as agreed, Mojaddedi surrendered power to the Leadership Council, and Burhanuddin Rabbani assumed the presidency of the country and the concomitant responsibility for the interim Council of Ministers for four months. Rabbani announced the adoption of a new Islamic flag, the appointment of a constitutional commission, and the establishment of a council to address the country's severe economic problems. In July Farid assumed the premiership. In August the withdrawal from the Leadership Council of the members of the Hizb-i Islami faction led by Maulvi Muhammad Yunus Khalis revealed serious rifts within the Government, while inter-*mujahidin* violence escalated into a full-scale ground offensive launched by Hekmatyar's forces against Kabul, during which the airport was closed, hundreds of people were killed or wounded, and tens of thousands of civilians fled the city. In response, President Rabbani expelled Hekmatyar from the Leadership Council and dismissed Prime Minister Farid. Hekmatyar demanded the expulsion of the 75,000 Uzbek militia from Kabul as a precondition to peace talks, alleging that Gen. Dostam was still closely allied to former members of the communist regime. At the end of August a ceasefire agreement was reached between Rabbani and Hekmatyar. However, sporadic fighting involving various *mujahidin* and militia groups (notably Gen. Dostam's Uzbek forces) continued in Kabul and the provinces. In December a special advisory body, comprising 1,335 tribal leaders, elected Rabbani, the sole candidate, as national President for a further two-year period. In January 1993 200 members of the advisory council were selected to constitute the future membership of the country's legislature.

In March 1993 President Rabbani, Hekmatyar, Mojaddedi and leaders of other major *mujahidin* factions signed a peace accord in Islamabad, Pakistan, under the terms of which an interim government would hold power for 18 months; Rabbani would remain as head of state, and Hekmatyar (or his nominee) would assume the premiership of the acting Council of Ministers; an immediate ceasefire would be imposed; legislative elections would be held within six months; a 16-member defence commission, responsible for the establishment of a national army, would be formed; and all weaponry would be seized from the warring factions in an attempt to restore peace and order. The peace accord was officially approved by the Governments of Pakistan, Saudi Arabia and Iran.

In the new Council of Ministers presented by Hekmatyar in May 1993 each *mujahidin* faction was allocated two ministerial posts, with further positions left vacant for other representatives. Members of Gen. Dostam's group of predominantly Uzbek militiamen—known collectively as the National Islamic Movement (NIM—Jonbesh-i Melli-i Islami)—were offered two posts in July. Significantly, Hekmatyar removed Masoud, one of his most powerful rivals, from the crucial post of Minister of Defence. The new Prime Minister promised to hold a general election by October.

Despite the signing of the Islamabad peace accord, inter-*mujahidin* violence persisted. With Hekmatyar refusing to co-operate with Rabbani, the interim Government was disunited and ineffectual. Although preparations for a general election were taking place, fighting intensified in December, when Gen. Dostam transferred his allegiance to his hitherto arch-enemy, Hekmatyar, and the supporters of the two combined to confront the forces of Rabbani and Masoud. The violence spread throughout the provinces, resulting in large numbers of military and civilian casualties and the internal displacement of thousands of people. In June 1994 the Supreme Court ruled that Rabbani could retain the presidency for a further six months, but failed to grant a similar extension to Hekmatyar's premiership.

In the latter half of 1994 a new, hitherto unknown, militant grouping emerged in Afghanistan, known as the Taliban (the plural form of 'Talib', meaning 'seeker of religious knowledge'). The movement, which at the outset comprised an estimated 25,000 fighters (the majority of whom were reported to be young Pashtun graduates of fundamentalist Islamist schools established by Afghan refugees in Pakistan), advocated the adoption of extremist practices, including the complete seclusion of women from society. Although initially claiming that they had no interest in assuming power in Afghanistan, the Taliban, who were led by Mullah Mohammad Omar, captured the city of Qandahar from the forces of Hekmatyar in October. By February 1995 the Taliban had routed Hekmatyar's men from their headquarters in Charasiab and controlled 10 provinces, mostly in southern and south-eastern Afghanistan, but their attempted advance on Kabul was obstructed by President Rabbani's troops. Rabbani and his supporters subsequently gained an unprecedented level of authority and confidence in Kabul and its environs, reflected in Rabbani's reneging on his earlier promise of standing down from the presidency in March. However, the resurgence of the Taliban, which captured the key north-western city of Herat and the surrounding province from government forces in September, apparently provoked an attack on the Pakistani embassy in Kabul by hundreds of pro-Government demonstrators protesting against Pakistan's alleged support for the militia. The Taliban's constant bombardment of Kabul resulted in hundreds of civilian deaths in late 1995 and early 1996. In May 1996 President Rabbani persuaded Hekmatyar to rejoin the Government. Hekmatyar's forces arrived in the capital later that month to defend the city against the Taliban. In June Hekmatyar resumed the post of Prime Minister.

The Taliban seizes power

The political situation was radically altered in September 1996 when, as a culmination of two weeks of sweeping military advances (including the capture of the crucial eastern city of Jalalabad), the Taliban seized control of Kabul following fierce clashes with government troops, who fled northwards together with the deposed Government. Former President Najibullah and his brother were summarily executed in Kabul by the Taliban, who declared Afghanistan a 'complete' Islamic state and appointed an interim Council of Ministers, led by Mullah Mohammad Rabbani, to administer the country (of which it now controlled about two-thirds). Pakistan, which was widely suspected of actively aiding the Islamist militia, was the first of only three countries officially to recognize the new regime (Saudi Arabia and the United Arab Emirates being the others). The Taliban imposed a strict and intimidatory Islamic code: women were not permitted to enter employment or to be formally educated beyond the age of eight years; television, non-religious music and gambling were all banned; amputations and public stonings were enforced as forms of punishment; and compulsory attendance at mosques by all men was introduced.

In October 1996 a powerful military and logistical alliance was formed by Gen. Dostam, former Minister of Defence Masoud, who controlled six northern provinces, and Gen. Abdol Karim Khalili, leader of the Hizb-i Wahadat-i Islami (Islamic Unity Party—an alliance of eight Shi'a Afghan resistance groups). The grouping, whose leaders were now collectively known as the Supreme Council for the Defence of Afghanistan (the headquarters of which were situated in Gen. Dostam's stronghold of Mazar-i-Sharif), launched a concerted offensive against Kabul in the hope of ousting the Taliban. In January 1997, following the rapid collapse of UN-sponsored peace talks in Islamabad, the Taliban launched an unexpected offensive, advancing north and capturing Bagram air base and the provincial capital of Charikar. Following the defection of the Uzbek Gen. Abdul Malik and his men to the Taliban in May, the latter were able to capture the strategically important northern town of Mazar-i-Sharif. However, the alliance with Gen. Malik collapsed almost immediately and the Taliban were forced to retreat.

The anti-Taliban alliance was expanded and strengthened in June 1997 by the inclusion of the forces of Hekmatyar and of the Mahaz-i-Melli-i-Islami (National Islamic Front), led by Pir Sayed Ahmad Gailani. This new coalition—the United National Islamic Front for the Salvation of Afghanistan (commonly known as the United Front or the Northern Alliance)—superseded the Supreme Council for the Defence of Afghanistan and served as the military wing of the exiled Government, the 'Islamic State of Afghanistan'. By July the United Front forces were within firing range of Kabul, having recaptured Charikar and the air base at Bagram. In the same month the UN Security Council demanded a ceasefire and an end to all foreign intervention in Afghanistan; it was widely believed that the Taliban were supported by Pakistan and Saudi Arabia; on the opposing side, to various degrees, were Iran, India, the Central Asian states (which feared the encroachment of Taliban fundamentalism) and Russia.

In August 1997 the United Front appointed a new Government, based in Mazar-i-Sharif, with Rabbani continuing as President, Abdorrahim Ghafurzai as Prime Minister, Masoud as Minister of Defence and Gen. Malik as Minister of Foreign Affairs. However, a few days later Ghafurzai and six other members of the new Government (which Hekmatyar refused to recognize) were killed in an aeroplane crash. Abdolghaffur Rawanfarhadi was appointed Prime Minister later in August. Following his return from Turkey, to where he had reportedly fled earlier in the year, in October Gen. Dostam was re-elected as commander of the United Front forces and concurrently appointed Vice-President of the anti-Taliban administration. Dostam also resumed the leadership of the NIM militia, ousting Gen. Malik. Meanwhile, the Taliban unilaterally changed the country's name to the Islamic Emirate of Afghanistan and altered the state flag, provoking widespread condemnation.

Talks between the Taliban and the United Front in Islamabad broke down in May 1998, and fighting resumed to the north of Kabul. In August the Taliban captured the northern city of Shiberghan, Gen. Dostam's new headquarters, after a number of his Uzbek commanders allegedly accepted bribes from the Taliban and switched allegiance. Gen. Dostam was again reported to have fled to Turkey. The Taliban (who allegedly now included considerable numbers of extremist volunteers from various other Islamic countries, including Pakistan, Saudi Arabia, Algeria and Egypt) recaptured Mazar-i-Sharif later that month. In September Afghanistan and Iran appeared to be on the verge of open warfare, following the murder of nine Iranian nationals by members of the Taliban as they stormed Mazar-i-Sharif. (It was later reported that thousands of Shi'a Hazara civilians had been massacred by the guerrillas after recapturing the city.) Both Iran and Afghanistan amassed troops on the border, with 500,000 Iranian troops reportedly on full military alert. However, by the end of the year the Taliban had agreed to free all Iranian prisoners being held in Afghanistan and to punish those responsible for the killing of the nine Iranian diplomats; consequently, Iran scaled down its border forces and announced that it had no intention of invading Afghanistan.

The imposition of US and UN sanctions

In August 1998 the USA launched simultaneous air strikes against alleged terrorist bases in eastern Afghanistan and Sudan, reportedly operated by the Saudi-born militant leader of the al-Qa'ida organization, Osama bin Laden (who was supported by the Taliban), in retaliation for the bombing of two US embassies in East Africa earlier that month. Many aid agencies withdrew their remaining expatriate staff from Afghanistan, fearing terrorist acts of vengeance. In September the Taliban suffered a considerable setback when Saudi Arabia withdrew its support and recalled its envoy from Kabul in response to the reported brutality of the guerrilla authorities and to their sheltering of bin Laden. In the following month the Taliban stated that, although they were not willing to extradite the Saudi-born dissident, in the event of a lawsuit being filed against him, they would be prepared to place him on trial in Afghanistan. Evidence submitted by the US Government to the Afghan Supreme Court in November was deemed by the latter as inadequate grounds for bin Laden's arrest. In July 1999, following reports that bin Laden was being sheltered in eastern Afghanistan, the USA imposed financial and economic sanctions on the Taliban regime in a further attempt to persuade it to hand over the militant leader to stand trial in the USA. The Taliban claimed that the sanctions would have very little impact and again refused to extradite bin Laden.

Meanwhile, the Taliban captured the capital of Bamian province, a Shi'a stronghold, in September 1998, while Taliban advances in the north in late 1998 alarmed Russia and the Central Asian states, which feared the unsettling potential of a militant Islamist army along their southern borders.

At the 1999 session of the UN General Assembly (held in September–November) the UN again rejected the Taliban request to represent Afghanistan; the seat remained under the control of President Rabbani, the leader of the 'Islamic State of Afghanistan'. In October the UN Secretary-General's Special Envoy to Afghanistan, Lakhdar Brahimi, announced his withdrawal from his mission, owing to the lack of progress (and particularly to the alleged negative attitude of the Taliban). In November the UN Security Council imposed an embargo on all Taliban-controlled overseas assets and a ban on the international flights of the national airline, Ariana Afghan Airlines, as a result of the Afghan regime's continuing refusal to relinquish bin Laden. Following the imposition of the sanctions, large-scale demonstrations erupted throughout Afghanistan and international aid organizations again came under attack.

Heavy fighting between Taliban and United Front forces, concentrated in the north of Kabul, resumed in March 2000 and spread to northern and central Afghanistan. By September the Taliban had captured Taloqan, the capital of Takhar province and the headquarters of the United Front. In December the Taliban and the United Front entered into UN-mediated negotiations. In the same month the UN Security Council approved a resolution, which stated that, unless the Taliban surrendered bin Laden and closed down militant training camps by January 2001, the international community would impose an arms embargo, tighten an existing embargo on flights and the freeze on Taliban assets abroad, restrict the sale of chemicals used to produce heroin from poppies, and close Ariana Afghan Airlines offices abroad. The Taliban refused to concede to the demands, shut down the UN special mission to Afghanistan and cancelled planned peace negotiations. The UN sanctions were duly imposed, and in May 2001 all UN political staff were expelled from Afghanistan. In the following month the US ambassador to Pakistan issued a statement in which he warned the Taliban that they would be held accountable if bin Laden carried out an attack against US interests.

Despite widespread international condemnation, the destruction of much of Afghanistan's pre-Islamic cultural heritage was carried out, upon the order of the Taliban, in March 2001 (including the demolition of the world's tallest standing Buddhas in Bamian), although Hindu and Sikh statues, acknowledged as fundamental to the respective religious practices, were preserved. The order contravened a 1999 decree ordering the preservation of all ancient relics, thereby prompting speculation that members of bin Laden's al-Qa'ida had taken control of the Taliban by ousting the more moderate leaders. In July 2001 the Taliban issued another set of controversial edicts: the use of the internet was outlawed; women were banned from visiting picnic areas; and items such as tape recorders, musical instruments and lipstick were proscribed as non-Islamic. Meanwhile, in April the Taliban's Gen. Commander and Chairman of the interim Council of Ministers, Mullah Mohammad Rabbani, died in Pakistan and was subsequently replaced as Gen. Commander by his brother, Mullah Ahmed.

Meanwhile, following the coup in Pakistan in October 1999 (see the chapter on Pakistan), the new Pakistani leader, Gen. Pervez Musharraf, pledged to work for a 'truly representative government' in Afghanistan, and in the following month the State Bank of Pakistan complied with the UN sanctions in ordering a freeze on all Taliban financial assets in Pakistan. However, Pakistan continued to offer economic aid and support to the Taliban and condemned the UN sanctions against Afghanistan.

US-led military intervention and the fall of the Taliban

The situation in Afghanistan drastically changed as a result of the terrorist attacks on New York and Washington, DC, USA, on 11 September 2001. On 13 September the US Secretary of State publicly identified bin Laden and his al-Qa'ida organization as having been principally responsible for the attacks. On 16 September the UN imposed diplomatic sanctions on the Taliban, while the USA began to form an anti-terrorism coalition, with the assistance of the United Kingdom.

Pakistan came under considerable pressure to reverse its policy of supporting the Taliban and agreed to co-operate with the US-led coalition. On 17 September 2001 a Pakistani delegation issued Taliban leaders with an ultimatum to surrender bin Laden or face retaliation from the USA. A few days later a *shura* of Afghan clerics, under the leadership of Mullah Mohammad Omar, issued an edict for bin Laden to leave Afghanistan voluntarily, and also threatened to instigate a *jihad* (holy war) if the USA attacked Afghanistan. US officials, demanding unconditional surrender, considered the edict insufficient, and US President George W. Bush warned that the Taliban would also be targeted if they refused to extradite bin Laden and other al-Qa'ida members.

Meanwhile, on 15 September 2001 Ahmad Shah Masoud died of injuries sustained during a suicide bombing, allegedly orchestrated by al-Qa'ida, two days before the terrorist attacks on the USA; his deputy, Gen. (later Marshal) Muhammed Qasim Fahim, was subsequently appointed interim military leader of the United Front. In October there were reports that the USA was providing covert military aid to anti-Taliban groups within Afghanistan. The Taliban continued forcibly to conscript men to bolster their manpower, which in early October numbered an estimated 40,000 fighters. It was also reported that al-Qa'ida had provided the Taliban with several thousand troops.

The UN and other aid organizations began to withdraw their foreign staff from Afghanistan immediately after the September 2001 attacks, and an estimated 1.5m. Afghans were reported to have abandoned their homes in the latter half of September. Pakistan restricted entry at the border to those considered to be most in need of assistance, but thousands of refugees succeeded in entering Pakistan illegally. In October President Bush announced a humanitarian aid programme for Afghans, in an attempt to undermine the Taliban and to demonstrate to Muslim countries that the USA was planning war against terrorism and not Islam.

On 7 October 2001 US-led forces began the aerial bombardment of suspected al-Qa'ida camps and strategic Taliban positions in Afghanistan. In addition to military strikes, aircraft released food and medicine parcels to Afghan civilians near the southern border with Pakistan; leaflets were also dropped offering protection and a reward in return for information on the whereabouts of al-Qa'ida leaders. Mullah Mohammad Omar urged all Muslims to help defend Afghanistan, and as a result several thousand pupils of *madrassas* (mosque schools) in Pakistan and a number of Arab countries arrived in Afghanistan during October. A pre-recorded videotape of bin Laden's response to the military strikes was broadcast by the Qatar-based satellite television company Al-Jazeera. In the recording, bin Laden declared war on the 'infidels' and warned the USA that counter-attacks would continue until it withdrew from the Middle East; his comments were widely seen to be an implicit admission of al-Qa'ida's involvement in the September attacks.

The US-led military operation, named 'Operation Enduring Freedom', achieved rapid results. After 10 days President Bush announced that the Taliban regime's air defences had been destroyed. The nature of the attack changed when US and British ground forces, with Russian assistance, launched an assault on Afghanistan on 20 October 2001. Some three days later it was announced that all of the identified al-Qa'ida training camps had been destroyed by air strikes. However, evidence of civilian casualties adversely affected support for the military action. Saudi Arabia, which had hitherto remained silent about the military strikes, voiced its discontent in mid-October. In addition, tension mounted in Pakistan, and thousands of pro-Taliban fighters attempted to cross the border into Afghanistan.

Initially, the US-led coalition avoided targeting Kabul in order to prevent the fractious United Front from seizing the capital. There were fears that, while no alternative transitional government existed, the defeat of the Taliban in Kabul and other major cities would leave a power vacuum, resulting in anarchy. The USA, the United Kingdom, other UN Security Council members and countries neighbouring Afghanistan began discussions regarding the formation of a broad-based transitional government for Afghanistan. Meanwhile, the humanitarian situation worsened and in October 2001 the UN resumed the provision of food aid. At the same time, the number of Afghan refugees attempting to leave the country increased dramatically; in early November the Office of the UN High Commissioner for Refugees (UNHCR) estimated that 135,000 refugees had entered Pakistan since 11 September.

On 9 November 2001 the United Front captured Mazar-i-Sharif and proceeded to seize almost all of northern Afghanistan at a rapid pace. The USA, the United Kingdom and Pakistan advised the United Front not to enter Kabul until a leadership council was formed; however, on 12 November the Taliban fled the capital and, facing very little resistance, the United Front took control of Kabul on the following day. Although the United Front (which was mainly composed of Tajiks, Uzbeks and Hazaras) immediately requested assistance from the US-led coalition to create a transitional government, it was impossible to do so while the majority Pashtun ethnic group remained under-represented. The USA and Pakistan had hitherto failed to attract defectors from the Pashtun Taliban leadership to join the council; in addition, US-led forces had given little support to anti-Taliban Pashtun leaders attempting to seize control in southern Afghanistan. Within a short time, the various commanders of the United Front were in disagreement over the running of provinces in northern Afghanistan. Anti-Taliban forces from all ethnic backgrounds swiftly advanced on southern Afghanistan and by the end of November had captured the Taliban stronghold of Kunduz. Unlike the factions belonging to the United Front, these groups were not united under a political alliance.

On 27 November 2001 the UN hosted a conference of 28 Afghan leaders representing the United Front, the Rome Group led by former monarch Zahir Shah, the pro-Iranian Cyprus Process and the Pakistan-backed Peshawar Process (composed of Pashtun exiles and headed by the moderate religious leader Pir Sayed Ahmad Gailani), as well as other leading figures, in Bonn, Germany. On 5 December the leaders signed the Agreement on Provisional Arrangements in Afghanistan Pending the Re-establishment of Permanent Government Institutions, also known as the Bonn Agreement, stipulating the establishment of a 30-member multi-ethnic Interim Authority that was to preside over the country for six months from 22 December. Hamid Karzai, a Pashtun tribal chief, was named Chairman of the Interim Authority, which was to comprise 11 Pashtuns, eight Tajiks, five Hazaras, three Uzbeks and three members of smaller tribal and religious groups. The United Front received the most seats; three of the leading members, Gen. Fahim, Younis Qanooni and Dr Abdullah Abdullah, were allocated the defence, interior and foreign affairs portfolios, respectively. Two female doctors were also granted posts in the executive council. A number of leaders who were excluded from the government were dissatisfied with the outcome, including former President Rabbani.

The Taliban regime's sole official contact with the outside world ended in late November 2001, when Pakistan severed all diplomatic links with the Taliban and closed their last remaining embassy. On 7 December the Taliban finally surrendered Qandahar, thus marking the effective end of the Taliban regime. Meanwhile, following unconfirmed reports that bin Laden and Mullah Mohammad Omar were hiding in the Tora Bora caves with the remnants of the Islamist forces, the US-led coalition and United Front intensified the air and ground assault on the cave complex, to no avail. The World Food Programme began a massive aid distribution programme in Kabul, but poor weather conditions hampered the international relief campaign and most rural areas remained inaccessible, owing to safety concerns. Meanwhile, following the defeat of the Taliban regime, tens of thousands of refugees began to return to Afghanistan.

On 22 December 2001 the Interim Authority was inaugurated and Karzai was sworn in as Chairman. The new administration reinstated the Constitution of 1964, which combined *Shari'a* with Western concepts of justice. One of Karzai's first decisions was to appoint Gen. Dostam as Vice-Chairman and Deputy Minister of Defence. At the end of December, under the terms of the Bonn Agreement, the UN Security Council authorized the deployment of an International Security Assistance Force (ISAF), comprising 5,000 personnel from 19 countries and headed by the United Kingdom, to help maintain security in Kabul over the following six months.

In January 2002 the international community agreed to donate US $4,500m. over two-and-a-half years towards the reconstruction of Afghanistan. Deployment of ISAF began in mid-January and was initially confined to Kabul, despite Karzai's requests for troop increases and a geographical expansion of its mandate. The Force's mandate was subsequently extended on regular occasions, most recently in October 2013, until 31 December 2014 (in August 2003 the North Atlantic Treaty Organization—NATO—assumed formal control). ISAF participated in joint patrols with Afghan police and assisted in creating and training a new Afghan National Army (ANA). However, regional military commanders continued to reorganize their own armies, preventing resources from being sent to the ANA and making the onerous task of creating a multi-ethnic national army even more difficult. In February 2002 the Minister of Civil Aviation and Tourism, Abdul Rahman, was assassinated by a rival faction within the Interim Authority. The murder of Rahman, a staunch supporter of Zahir Shah, was evidently an attempt to deter the former monarch from returning to Afghanistan. Despite security concerns, Zahir Shah returned to Afghanistan as a 'private citizen' in April.

Internecine fighting escalated throughout Afghanistan as tribal commanders attempted to consolidate territorial and political influence in preparation for the Loya Jirga. Meanwhile, the US-led coalition continued its search for the leaders of al-Qa'ida and the Taliban. The search was often thwarted by the activities of regional Afghan (non-Taliban) military commanders, and complex tribal allegiances and enmities regularly dictated the type of information provided to US forces by tribal sources. Indeed, it was widely believed that bin Laden had been allowed to escape from Tora Bora in December 2001 (see above) by Afghans who claimed to be US allies. The USA's policy of hiring and arming local soldiers in the hope of capturing Islamist militants at times compounded the unstable political situation.

Transition to democracy

In January 2002 a Special Independent Commission for the Convening of the Emergency Loya Jirga (commonly known as the Loya Jirga Commission) was established under the auspices of the UN. The election of 1,051 delegates to attend the Emergency Loya Jirga by district representatives took place in May–June under the supervision of the Loya Jirga Commission. International aid agencies, universities and other organizations selected by the Commission appointed an additional 600 members to ensure that the assembly was balanced in terms of gender, geography, ethnicity and political beliefs. The Emergency Loya Jirga convened on 11 June. Karzai was elected President, with around 80% of the votes cast. Former monarch Zahir Shah and former President Rabbani had both renounced their respective candidatures, reportedly under pressure from the USA. On 19 June the Loya Jirga approved the Transitional Authority cabinet, retaining most of the incumbent members of the Interim Authority. Karzai announced the creation of a number of other commissions to address the issues of defence, human rights, internal security reform and a new constitution.

In July 2002 Karzai announced the establishment of a UN-supported security commission to disarm rebel troops and precipitate the creation of a national army. Despite commanding little control outside Kabul, Karzai warned military commanders that their powers would be removed unless they denounced factional fighting and joined the Government. In September Karzai escaped an assassination attempt in Qandahar; hours later a bomb explosion in Kabul killed 30 people and injured at least 160 others. Hekmatyar was reported to be responsible, having allegedly joined forces with remaining Taliban and al-Qa'ida members in southern and eastern Afghanistan. In November the President dismissed more than 20 senior regional officials—including Gen. Abdul Hamid, the military commander of Mazar-i-Sharif—in an attempt to consolidate the Transitional Authority's jurisdiction outside Kabul.

Meanwhile, reports indicated that less than one-third of the country's land was under cultivation in 2002, largely owing to a fourth successive year of drought and exacerbated by insufficient humanitarian assistance from the international donor community. The rapid return of refugees placed an even greater strain on the humanitarian programme. According to UNHCR, more than 1.5m. refugees returned from Pakistan (with an estimated 1.2m. remaining) and around 400,000 from Iran (with around 1.1.m. remaining) in 2002. Some 80% of the funds provided by the international agencies had been allocated to humanitarian aid, thus leaving only 20% available for the country's reconstruction programme.

In October 2003 a three-year programme of disarmament, demobilization and reintegration, drawn up by the Transitional Authority and the USA, was launched. Shortly before, the Government approved legislation legalizing the formation of political parties and a law proscribing the participation of military commanders and armed factions in political life.

A new draft constitution, which envisaged a strong presidential system of government and a bicameral legislature, provoked a wide range of reactions following its publication in November 2003, including concerns about inadequate protection of women's rights and religious freedoms. Following several weeks of intense negotiations, which were marred by ethnic divisions and arguments, Afghanistan's new Constitution was approved in January 2004, by consensus rather than an actual vote. In certain respects, the amended charter differed little from the earlier draft: it still provided for the introduction of a strongly presidential political system, despite a campaign by former *mujahidin* parties for the installation of a parliamentary state. However, the revised Constitution added a second vice-presidential post and gave the National Assembly powers of veto over major presidential appointments and policies. The charter also contained new human rights provisions and articulated the equal rights of men and women before the law. One of the most significant achievements was the ensuring of greater political representation for women: it was agreed that approximately 25% of seats in the Wolesi Jirga would be reserved for women; the President would appoint additional women to the Meshrano Jirga (House of Elders). However, concerns remained; *inter alia*, the failure to address adequately the role of *Shari'a*, and its relation to human rights safeguards, generated concerns that conservative elements in the judiciary would be able to implement interpretations of Islam that might violate human rights. In July it was announced that the presidential election would be held on 9 October 2004. However, legislative elections were to be deferred until 2005, owing to the ongoing unrest in the country.

Meanwhile, in May 2003 the US Secretary of Defense, Donald Rumsfeld, announced that major combat operations had ended in Afghanistan and that US forces had begun to concentrate on the stabilization and reconstruction of the country. Nevertheless, the security situation remained fragile, with an increase in attacks on the Afghan Transitional Authority and ISAF, as well as foreign aid workers and contractors. US-led forces launched major assaults on suspected Taliban and al-Qa'ida fighters in the south and east of Afghanistan and along its border with Pakistan, but drew condemnation for the deaths of children in miscalculated aerial attacks. In January 2004 ISAF assumed command of a Provincial Reconstruction Team (PRT) in Kunduz, as the pilot project for further expansion of the international security force. By the end of May 2005 ISAF controlled a total of nine PRTs—five in the north and four in the west of Afghanistan—allowing the US-led coalition to concentrate more on the volatile southern and eastern parts of the country.

Throughout 2004 violence and instability continued to affect significant areas of the country. In March the Minister of Civil Aviation and Tourism, Mirwais Sadiq, was killed in a reported grenade attack in Herat. Violent clashes ensued between rival forces in the province, and President Karzai subsequently deployed ANA troops to Herat in an attempt to restore order. In June the murder of 11 Chinese construction workers during an attack on a camp in the northern province of Kunduz, generally perceived to be one of the safer areas of the country, raised concerns regarding security for the forthcoming national elections. In the same month the killing of five Médecins Sans Frontières workers prompted the international aid organization to withdraw completely from Afghanistan. In an attempt to increase security in the country, and to ensure its expansion outside Kabul, NATO pledged to increase the size of ISAF from 6,500 to 10,000 troops. The Government expressed its concern that the additional forces would be deployed only in the north of the country, stressing that they were most urgently needed in the southern and eastern provinces.

In September 2004, in an apparent attempt to assert his jurisdiction outside Kabul in advance of the impending presidential election, President Karzai dismissed Ismail Khan, the powerful Governor of Herat province, and offered him the cabinet post of Minister of Mines and Industries. The dismissal provoked rioting in the province, and Khan subsequently rejected the ministerial portfolio. Shortly afterwards President Karzai survived an assassination attempt while on an official visit to the south-east of the country. The Taliban claimed responsibility for the attack.

Democratic elections; rising instability and violence

On 9 October 2004 Afghanistan held its first direct presidential election. Despite some sporadic violence on the day of the election, no widespread disturbances were reported. Shortly after polling had begun, all 15 opposition candidates launched a boycott of the vote and demanded that it be abandoned, owing to alleged widespread electoral fraud. However, following an inquiry, international observers concluded in November that alleged irregularities during the poll were insufficient to have altered the final result. Interim President Hamid Karzai was subsequently declared the winner, receiving 55.4% of the votes. Former Minister of Education Younis Qanooni came second, with 16.3% of the votes, followed by Mohammad Mohaqqeq, with 11.7%, and Gen. Dostam, with 10.0%. A reported 83.7% of the electorate participated in the poll. However, concerns were raised by the regional nature of Karzai's victory, which seemed largely confined to the Pashtun-majority provinces. President Karzai's new Cabinet retained Minister of Foreign Affairs Dr Abdullah Abdullah and Minister of Interior Affairs Ali Ahmad Jalali, but Marshal Fahim was replaced as Minister of Defence by Gen. Abdul Rahim Wardak, and Ismail Khan gained the energy and water portfolio. The Cabinet was dominated by Pashtuns, and several powerful regional commanders were excluded owing to a requirement that all cabinet ministers be university-educated.

On 18 September 2005 an estimated 5,800 candidates, including several former Taliban officials, contested elections to the 249-member Wolesi Jirga and 34 provincial legislatures. The polls constituted Afghanistan's first democratic legislative elections since 1969. The nationwide turnout was an estimated 53% of the electorate, with the figure decreasing to only 36% in Kabul—a significant decline compared with the level of participation at the 2004 presidential election. The widespread disruption that al-Qa'ida and the Taliban had threatened to orchestrate on polling day did not materialize. A delegation from the European Union (EU) initially described the elections as having been 'free, fair and transparent', but concerns were later expressed as to possible instances of fraud and intimidation of voters. The results, which were announced in November, showed that many of those who had been elected were powerful factional figures, not aligned with any particular party, leading to fears that the country's legislature would be less a unified mechanism through which the central Government could assert its authority, and more a conduit for the re-emergence of provincial 'warlordism'. The newly elected National Assembly convened for the first time in December. Younis Qanooni, who was widely perceived to be the most prominent opposition figure in the legislature, was subsequently elected Speaker of the Wolesi Jirga, and Sibghatullah Mojaddedi Speaker of the Meshrano Jirga.

In the mean time, in September 2005 Minister of Interior Affairs Ali Ahmad Jalali resigned; he was replaced by Zarar Ahmad Moqbel Osmani. In March 2006 Karzai announced an extensive reorganization of the Cabinet, including the replacement of Dr Abdullah Abdullah as Minister of Foreign Affairs by Dr Rangin Dadfar Spanta.

Provincial instability and violence, often co-ordinated by a resurgent Taliban, continued. More than 1,400 people were believed to have died in 2005 during fighting with Taliban insurgents, while a number of US and British soldiers were also killed. Violence escalated towards the end of the year, with a number of suicide bombings, hitherto a rarity in Afghanistan, taking place. The attacks were believed to have been instigated by al-Qa'ida and the Taliban and carried out by foreign militants. The security situation deteriorated further from 2006, with frequent suicide bombings and clashes between Taliban forces and coalition troops. Much of the conflict was centred on the southern and eastern provinces of the country, including Helmand and Qandahar. In July NATO announced the expansion of the mandate of its 18,000 troops into the southern provinces, assuming control from US-led coalition forces therein, and in October NATO forces, which had now increased to number approximately 30,000, also assumed military command of the eastern provinces; ISAF thus became responsible for international military operations throughout Afghanistan. At the end of 2006 a number of reports were published estimating that up to 3,700 fatalities (around one-quarter of which were civilians) had occurred in Afghanistan that year as a result of the ongoing conflict, a significant and alarming increase compared with the previous year.

Despite the deaths in 2007 of several senior figures within the Taliban, including Mullah Dadullah, who was believed to have been the group's foremost military commander, attacks on government officials continued: former Prime Minister Farid, a member of the Meshrano Jirga, was killed in May, and President Karzai survived another attempt on his life in June. According to the UN, an estimated 1,523 civilians died in 2007 as a result of military operations conducted by both coalition and insurgency forces; this was estimated to have increased by almost 40%, to 2,118, in 2008. Among the worst incidents was the reported bombing by US forces of a wedding party in Nangarhar province in July, which, according to the Afghan Government, killed 47 civilians, the majority of them women and children. During 2007–08 there were also several instances of hostage-taking by the Taliban, most notably the kidnapping in July 2007 of 23 Christian missionaries from the Republic of Korea (South Korea), who claimed to be involved in development projects rather than in work of a religious nature. Meanwhile, in May the Meshrano Jirga had adopted legislation aimed at opening lines of communication with the Taliban, and in September President Karzai expressed his willingness to enter into negotiations with the insurgents. The Taliban stipulated the withdrawal of foreign troops from Afghanistan as a precondition for the holding of bilateral talks, thereby stalling the nascent process indefinitely.

In 2007 Afghan government troops were reported to have carried out independent operations for the first time, and by May 2008 the strength of the ANA had reached more than 76,000 men. However, the Afghan Ministry of Defence had earlier stated that ideally the ANA should be expanded to 200,000 men in order to handle both external threats and the deteriorating security situation within Afghanistan itself. (The number of Afghan troops was increased to approximately 187,000 by August 2013; however, doubts remained as to the ANA's ability to function as an effective independent fighting force.)

In March 2007 a new political grouping entitled Jabhe-ye-Motahed-e-Milli (United National Front—UNF) was established, comprising senior government officials, members of parliament, and former members of the United Front (or Northern Alliance) and of communist parties. With former President Burhanuddin Rabbani as its Chairman and prominent figures such as Gen. Dostam, Marshal Fahim, Younis Qanooni and Vice-President Ahmad Zia Masoud within its ranks, the UNF was expected to have a significant impact on Afghan politics. Many of the Front's political objectives were reportedly in agreement with those of Karzai, but a number diverged considerably, including its advocacy of a parliamentary system of government. Former King Zahir Shah died in Kabul in July.

In February 2008 the assertion made by a senior US intelligence official that the Taliban controlled as much as 10% of Afghanistan while the Government was in charge of only 30% (with the remainder under the rule of tribal leaders) was greeted with disbelief in some quarters. Insurgents carried out a number of high-profile attacks throughout the year. The Deputy Governor of Helmand province, Haji Pir Mohammad, and the Governor of the eastern province of Loghar, Abdullah Wardak, were killed in separate bomb attacks, in January and September, respectively, and in April President Karzai was the target of another failed assassination attempt. Taliban forces executed a large-scale prison break in Qandahar in June, resulting in the escape of hundreds of Taliban detainees. Furthermore, in what was described as the worst attack to be carried out in Kabul since the defeat of the Taliban in 2001, a suicide bombing at the Indian embassy resulted in more than 40 fatalities in July 2008. In November President Karzai reportedly offered protection to Mullah Mohammad Omar in exchange for the commencement of peace negotiations; however, the Taliban again insisted on the withdrawal of foreign troops.

In October 2008, reportedly under pressure from the USA and its coalition partners to curb alleged endemic government corruption, President Karzai carried out further cabinet changes, including the replacement of Zarar Ahmad Moqbel Osmani as Minister of Interior Affairs by the incumbent Minister of Education, Dr Muhammad Hanif Atmar. Before the end of the year both the Minister of Transport and Aviation and the Minister of Commerce and Industry were dismissed on the grounds of suspected corruption.

Karzai returned to power; further escalation of unrest

Afghanistan's second direct presidential election, which was held on 20 August 2009 (four months later than scheduled), saw incumbent President Karzai run against 41 rivals (including his main opponent, the independent candidate Dr Abdullah Abdullah). Voting took place throughout the country with few violent incidents, although the proceedings were marred by numerous allegations of electoral fraud. After a two-month audit by the UN-backed Electoral Complaints Commission (ECC) invalidated votes from hundreds of polling stations, having found evidence of electoral fraud, Karzai's share of the vote fell from 54.6% (according to the initial uncertified results) to 49.7%, below the crucial 50% threshold required to avoid a run-off election. Accordingly, a second round of voting, between Karzai and Dr Abdullah, was scheduled to be held on 7 November, but the latter unexpectedly withdrew his candidacy on 1 November, claiming that the vote could be neither free nor fair. On the following day Karzai was officially declared the victor and was sworn in for his second term as President on 19 November, amid widespread concern about the validity of his victory. In his inauguration speech, Karzai pledged to work towards reconciliation with the Taliban, to hasten the transfer of responsibility for internal security to the ANA and police, and to tackle the problem of systematic government corruption. However, the Meli Shura rejected numerous ministerial nominations by Karzai, resulting in several long-term vacancies in the Cabinet. In January 2010 the Independent Election Commission of Afghanistan (IEC) announced the postponement of legislative elections from 22 May until 18 September, citing a lack of funds, logistical problems and security concerns. The IEC had attracted widespread criticism for its failure to control electoral irregularities during the presidential election.

Largely owing to the Taliban's increasing use of indiscriminate roadside bombs and suicide attacks, the UN estimated that at least 2,412 civilians were killed in Afghanistan in 2009 as a result of the continuing conflict (a rise of 14% compared with 2008); around 70% of these deaths were caused by insurgent activity. An additional 30,000 US troops had been dispatched to Afghanistan during the first few months of 2010 for the planned military 'surge', while NATO pledged that its other members would provide at least 5,000 more personnel to combat the Taliban. In February US officials reported the capture in Karachi, Pakistan, of the high-ranking Afghan Taliban military commander Mullah Abdul Ghani Baradar, who was widely believed to be second-in-command to Mullah Mohammad Omar. In the following week coalition forces and ANA troops launched 'Operation Moshtarak' in Helmand province, the largest offensive in Afghanistan since the ousting of the Taliban regime in 2001; one of the main aims was to seize control of the town of Marjah, the Taliban's last remaining stronghold in Helmand. A long-planned offensive in the Taliban stronghold of Qandahar commenced in June 2010, with reports that NATO troops had killed one of the Taliban's most senior commanders there providing an early boost for the coalition forces.

Meanwhile, an international conference on the future of Afghanistan was convened in London, United Kingdom, in January 2010 and was attended by officials from around 70 different countries and organizations, including President Karzai, UN Secretary-General Ban Ki-Moon and US Secretary of State Hillary Clinton. Key points covered included the proposed establishment of a substantial Peace and Reintegration Fund to encourage the more moderate members of the Taliban to cease fighting in exchange for employment, land and training; provisions for the gradual handover of security duties from the coalition forces to the ANA and Afghan police; the more effective channelling and utilization of foreign aid through the appropriate government ministries and departments rather than through aid agencies and foreign contractors; and the proposed creation of an independent anti-corruption body with the power to investigate government officials. Karzai stressed that the establishment of peace in Afghanistan would not be possible without the support of neighbouring countries (principally Pakistan) and of influential Muslim states (notably Saudi Arabia). In February officials confirmed that shortly before the conference in London clandestine peace talks had been held between representatives of the Afghan Government and the Taliban (including the son of the warlord Gulbuddin Hekmatyar) in the Maldives. Further peace talks were held in Kabul in March between government officials and a delegation from Hekmatyar's Hizb-i Islami. The representatives of the militant group reportedly offered to act as a bridge between the Government and the Taliban in return for the setting of definite dates for the withdrawal of foreign troops from Afghanistan and the establishment of an interim administration.

During a brief visit to Kabul in March 2010, US President Barack Obama (who had replaced Bush in January 2009) stressed the need for President Karzai to make further progress in tackling the corruption and cronyism that beset Afghan politics. In June Karzai staged a 'peace jirga' in Kabul, which, although boycotted by some Afghan leaders, was attended by more than 1,500 delegates, and constituted the first major public discussion within Afghanistan on the issue of how to bring an end to the conflict.

In July 2010 Gen. David Petraeus was appointed Commander of ISAF, replacing Gen. Stanley McChrystal, after negative comments about the Obama Administration had been attributed to McChrystal in a prominent US magazine. US-Afghan relations were compromised following the online release by WikiLeaks, an organization publishing leaked private and classified information, of a series of leaked US diplomatic cables in late 2010; one such communiqué, released in December, revealed US concerns about the political abilities of Karzai and widespread allegations of corruption among the Afghan authorities. On the following day President Obama made an unannounced second visit to Afghanistan; however, a planned visit to Kabul to meet with Karzai was cancelled, ostensibly owing to bad weather. Meanwhile, in August the Netherlands formally ended its military mission in Afghanistan after four years' deployment, despite requests from NATO for the mission to be extended.

The 2010 parliamentary elections

Following the widespread allegations of fraud during the 2009 presidential poll, the 2010 legislative elections, due to be held in September, were widely regarded by international observers as a critical test of President Karzai's commitment to democratic reform. Reports in mid-September of the apparent circulation of more than 1m. fraudulent voter registration cards did little to allay concerns of widespread fraud, and prompted calls for the elections to be postponed. Shortly thereafter the IEC announced that more than 1,000 polling stations (of a total of 6,835) across Afghanistan were to remain closed, following threats by the Taliban to target the election process. At least 19 people, including four electoral candidates, were reported to have been killed in election-related violence prior to the polls, while more than 30 candidates were disqualified in advance of the ballot, owing to suspected links with militia groups.

In the event, the elections were held as scheduled on 18 September 2010, and concerns regarding the possibility of large-scale, co-ordinated attacks were largely unrealized, although at least 14 people were reported to have been killed in numerous incidents. More than 2,500 candidates (including 406 women) contested the 249 seats in the Wolesi Jirga, primarily as independents; as in 2005, one-quarter of the legislative seats were reserved for female candidates. Turnout was low, at an estimated 40% of the registered electorate. In October the IEC announced that 1.3m. votes—nearly one-quarter of the total ballot—had been cancelled, owing to fraud or other irregularities, while more than 200 candidates were being investigated for alleged malpractice; the UN-backed ECC was reported to be investigating more than 4,000 official complaints, including numerous claims of voter intimidation. The ECC later disqualified 26 candidates on the grounds of alleged fraud. Final, certified results were released by the IEC later in November. Given that the vast majority of candidates had stood as independents, it was difficult to analyse the results in terms of political ramifications; however, Dr Abdullah, who had recently formed the Coalition for Change and Hope—subsequently renamed the National Coalition of Afghanistan, claimed that more than 90 of his supporters had secured seats in the Wolesi Jirga and would put pressure on the Government 'to bring reforms, positive changes, and to implement and strengthen the rule of law'. The majority Pashtun ethnic group saw its representation decrease to 88 seats, from 112 previously. While the IEC declared the election a success, the response of the international community to a vote that had, to most observers, appeared neither free nor fair was rather more muted; however, the UN security council did welcome the final results as constituting an 'important milestone' in Afghanistan's development.

The new parliament was sworn in on 26 January 2011. Hundreds of unsuccessful election candidates staged protests at the presidential palace, appealing for the election results to be annulled and for fresh, legitimate elections to be held. The fractious nature of the new parliament was exemplified by a one-month political impasse, during which the Wolesi Jirga failed on several occasions to elect a new Speaker. Abdul Rauf Ibrahimi, a little-known former Uzbek militia commander from Kunduz province, was finally elected Speaker of the lower house in February.

In June 2011 a special tribunal established by the Supreme Court to examine the widespread allegations of electoral fraud completed its investigations and ordered that 62 winning candidates—nearly one-quarter of the total—be removed from the legislature on account of electoral fraud, effectively overruling the IEC. The ruling prompted vociferous criticism from members of the IEC and of parliament, and the latter responded with a vote of no confidence in the Attorney-General, Muhammad Aloko. With the ongoing crisis severely undermining the legitimacy of both the executive and the legislative branches of the Afghan Government, in August Karzai issued a presidential decree that appeared to reinforce the status of the IEC as the ultimate authority on electoral proceedings, ordering the IEC to finalize the results of the election 'immediately'. Later in the month the IEC announced that nine of the 62 candidates identified for removal by the Supreme Court's special tribunal were to be replaced within the legislature by nine new candidates, all of whom had been among those disqualified for electoral fraud by the ECC in November 2010. However, the issue continued to divide the legislature, with many parliamentarians arguing against the constitutionality of the IEC's decision.

Meanwhile, in September 2010 Kabul Bank, the country's largest bank, was placed under the direct supervision of the

Central Bank following allegations of widespread fraud and mismanagement. It was reported that several hundred million dollars' worth of irregular loans had been issued to shareholders. Media reports in early 2011 identified several prominent politicians and businessmen with links to Karzai's Government, including the brothers of Karzai and of Vice-President Marshal Muhammed Qasim Fahim, as alleged beneficiaries in the scandal, which by January was reported to have resulted in losses of around US $900m. A commission of inquiry established by President Karzai to investigate the scandal published its findings in May, absolving the brothers of the President and the Vice-President of any wrongdoing; however, members of the Cabinet and of parliament were reported to be among the 207 borrowers found to have taken out undocumented loans. The revelations triggered the near-collapse of the bank and prompted the IMF to suspend its credit programme for Afghanistan. In June it was announced that a payment of $70m. due to have been disbursed to the Afghan Government by the World Bank's Afghanistan Reconstruction Trust Fund, as a reward for achieving stipulated standards in, *inter alia*, public administration reform, was to be withheld. In an attempt to persuade the IMF to resume its funding, in April the Government had proposed splitting the stricken bank into two units, one of which was to set up as a receivership to try to collect the irregular loans. This, together with a series of other government measures intended to shore up the financial sector resulted in the approval by the IMF, in November, of a new, three-year, $134m. credit programme for Afghanistan. However, the Fund cautioned that the Afghan Government would need to continue its efforts to recover assets and prosecute those responsible for the Kabul Bank scandal. In March 2013 the bank's founder, Sher Khan Fernod, and former chief executive, Haji Khalil Ferozi, were convicted of breach of trust (the more serious charges of money-laundering and embezzlement having been dropped unexpectedly at the last minute); they were ordered to repay a combined total of $808m. and were both sentenced to five years' imprisonment. Around 20 other former employees of the bank were convicted of having known of the fraud and were sentenced to prison terms of between two and five years. The apparent leniency of the sentences handed to Fernod and Ferozi, the main protagonists in the fraud, prompted concerns about the Karzai administration's commitment to tackling corruption.

The transition of security responsibilities to the Afghan authorities

In July 2010, during an international conference in Kabul on the security situation within Afghanistan, President Karzai announced ambitious plans for Afghan forces to have assumed control of all military and law enforcement operations throughout Afghanistan by 2014. The 60 or so foreign delegates in attendance, who included Ban Ki-Moon and US Secretary of State Clinton, adopted a statement endorsing the plan and urging the Afghan Government to accelerate reforms aimed at improving governance. In November 2010 the Afghan President and NATO leaders signed a long-term security partnership agreement pledging to transfer leadership of all security operations to Afghanistan by the end of 2014; however, NATO's Secretary-General stressed that the coalition would remain committed in Afghanistan in a training and supportive capacity indefinitely.

The killing of senior al-Qa'ida leader Abu Hafs al-Najdi (alias Abdul Ghani) in a NATO air strike in Kunar province in April 2011 was hailed as a significant success by ISAF. The killing in May of al-Qa'ida founder Osama bin Laden in the Pakistani town of Abbottabad, following his eventual discovery earlier in the year by US intelligence forces (see the chapter on Pakistan), provided further cause for celebration within the alliance. However, a steady deterioration in security conditions during 2010–11 appeared to run counter to any optimism, however cautious, regarding the prospects for peace and stability in Afghanistan. The year 2010 proved to be the most costly yet for the NATO alliance, with 711 NATO troops reported to have been killed (of which 499 were US soldiers). Although the number of NATO fatalities decreased in 2011, to 566 (of which 418 were US soldiers), this still represented the second highest number of deaths incurred by NATO personnel in a single year since the beginning of the campaign in 2001.

According to the UN, the number of civilian fatalities in Afghanistan increased to an estimated 2,792 in 2010 and further to 3,133 in 2011. In the latter year some 77% were attributed to insurgent activity, with almost 14% caused by pro-Government forces (including ISAF); the death toll included more than 430 civilians killed in suicide attacks by insurgents, an increase of some 80% compared with 2010. The high level of civilian casualties caused by NATO forces continued severely to undermine popular support for the alliance's mission in Afghanistan. In particular, the number of civilian casualties in 2011 resulting from NATO aerial attacks (187) and nocturnal search operations (63) was a source of growing tension between coalition officials and President Karzai. In April demonstrations against the foreign military presence were staged in towns throughout the country, several of which escalated into violent unrest and fatalities. Anger towards the US-led coalition was further exacerbated by the publication, in June, of a US military report revealing that almost 90% of those captured by US forces on suspicion of being members of the Taliban had, in fact, been civilians. Meanwhile, some 470 inmates, many of whom were reported to be Taliban insurgents, escaped from Qandahar prison in April. In June Taliban militants conducted an intensive raid on the heavily guarded Intercontinental Hotel in Kabul, which was regularly frequented by foreign and local officials and business people; 22 people, including nine insurgents, were killed during the incident.

Nevertheless, the first phase of the security transition commenced, as scheduled, in July 2011, and involved the handing over of seven NATO-held areas to Afghan control—Bamian and Panjshir provinces, the majority of Kabul province (excluding the restive Surobi district) and four provincial capitals (Herat, Lashkar Gah, Mazar-i-Sharif and Mehter Lam). Shortly before this, President Obama announced that 10,000 US forces were to leave Afghanistan by the end of the year, with a further 23,000 scheduled to depart by the end of 2012, with all remaining combat troops to withdraw in 2014. The pace of the announced withdrawal was quicker than had been generally anticipated, and Gen. Petraeus was reported to have recommended a more limited initial troop withdrawal. The new US Secretary of Defense, Leon Panetta, stressed that the US-led coalition would remain firmly committed to assisting the Afghan authorities in developing a skilled military, police force and local militias that would be sufficiently equipped to take over full responsibility for national security from 2014. The first stage in a phased withdrawal of French soldiers commenced in October 2011, and in January 2012 French President Nicolas Sarkozy, apparently in response to domestic political pressure, announced plans to accelerate the French withdrawal—the last of approximately 4,000 serving French troops left Afghanistan in November 2012. Canada, meanwhile, officially concluded its involvement in the NATO combat mission at the beginning of December 2011; a deployment of Canadian troops, numbering 650 in late 2013, was to provide training assistance in Kabul until March 2014.

Meanwhile, a wave of violent incidents served to underscore concerns about the deteriorating security situation amid the ongoing transition of responsibilities to the Afghan authorities. In July 2011 Ahmad Wali Karzai, the chairman of the Qandahar provincial council and a half-brother of President Karzai, was assassinated by the head of his own security team. Wali Karzai had done much to galvanize support for President Karzai in southern Afghanistan and, despite a contentious background, with widespread allegations that he had been involved in various criminal activities, Wali Karzai had also proven a key ally for the US-led coalition, serving as a stabilizing force by curbing, to a degree, simmering tribal tensions in the south. Two other prominent allies of President Karzai—Jan Mohammad Khan, a senior adviser to the President and former Governor of Uruzgan province, and Ghulam Haidar Hameedi, the mayor of Qandahar—were killed in separate attacks later in July. The Taliban claimed responsibility for all three incidents.

The assassination of former Afghan President Burhanuddin Rabbani, in a suicide bomb attack during a meeting with purported Taliban representatives at his Kabul home in September 2011, represented a severe setback to hopes of a negotiated settlement of the Afghan insurgency. Rabbani had been appointed as the head of the Afghan High Peace Council, an agency inaugurated by President Karzai in October 2010, which was charged with brokering an end to the war and opening up a dialogue with the Taliban and other insurgents. Three days of official mourning were proclaimed for Rabbani, and the Government broke off discussions with the Taliban as a result of the assassination. In April 2012 Rabbani's son, Salahuddin Rabbani, Afghanistan's ambassador to Turkey, was appointed to succeed his father as head of the High Peace Council.

In October 2011 'Operation Knife Edge' was launched by NATO and Afghan forces in south-eastern Afghanistan; the military operation was intended to target members of the Haqqani network (an influential, Taliban-affiliated insurgent group led by former *mujahidin* fighter Jalaluddin Haqqani and based in North Waziristan, Pakistan), which, the alliance alleged, was sheltering al-Qa'ida operatives in the Pakistani border region. In December a suicide bomb attack on a Shi'a mosque in Kabul killed at least 56 people, while, in an apparently co-ordinated attack, a second suicide bomber detonated explosives at a Shi'a mosque in Mazar-i-Sharif, claiming the lives of a further four people. Observers noted that the attacks, which coincided with the Shi'a festival of Ashura—the most important day in the Shi'a calendar—were of a sectarian nature unprecedented in recent Afghan history, prompting concerns that insurgents might be adopting a new strategy intended to foment further divisions within the country.

Despite the series of high-profile attacks and assassinations, the second phase of the transition of security responsibilities to the Afghan authorities was initiated in November 2011, following which local forces were afforded complete or partial control of approximately half of the country. Among the previously NATO-held areas handed over were: Balkh, Daikundi, Nimroz, Samangan and Takhar provinces, which were transferred to Afghan control in their entirety; seven provincial capitals, including Chaghcharan (Ghor province) Ghazni (Ghazni province), Jalalabad (Nangarhar province) and Maidanshahr (Wardak province); and more than 40 districts in provinces across the country, including the Marjah, Nadi Ali and Nawa districts of Helmand province, and Surobi, the final district in Kabul province to be handed over to the Afghan authorities. In the same month Gen. John Allen, who had replaced Gen. Petraeus as Commander of ISAF in July, wrote to President Karzai expressing his regret following a series of NATO air strikes in which Afghan civilians had been killed during the latter half of 2011, and informed the Afghan President that all ISAF units were to conduct retraining on methods of avoiding civilian casualties.

Amid heightened security arrangements, a meeting of the Loya Jirga in Kabul was attended by more than 2,300 tribal elders, local and regional leaders, and government officials in November 2011. President Karzai used the occasion to outline his vision for a long-term strategic partnership with the USA, which, he argued, remained in the best interests of Afghanistan; however, he stressed that any pact must respect Afghan sovereignty. Thus, while the Afghan Government was prepared to allow the USA to base military facilities within Afghanistan beyond 2014, Karzai demanded that foreign forces cease house searches and night raids, and that all foreign-run detention facilities within the country be shut down. Karzai also tendered implicit criticism of Pakistan and Iran for not doing more to curb insurgents. On the closing day of the four-day meeting, the Loya Jirga elected to support Karzai's outline for negotiating a strategic agreement with the USA. However, the second primary issue of debate—namely, how to reignite peace negotiations with the Taliban—was reported to have been largely inconclusive.

At an international conference held in Bonn in December 2011 on Afghanistan's development following the planned withdrawal in 2014 of all foreign troops, President Karzai stated that Afghanistan would require some US $10,000m. annually for the next 10 years to bolster its security and reconstruction efforts. Notably absent from the proceedings were any representatives from Pakistan, following the killing of 24 Pakistani soldiers during an ISAF air strike on the Afghan–Pakistani border in November. (The Pakistani Government subsequently severed communications and blocked ISAF's two supply routes running through Pakistan; the routes were reopened in July 2012 after US Secretary of State Clinton apologized for the incident.)

Preparations for the NATO withdrawal

In February 2012 Secretary of Defense Panetta stated that the US authorities aimed to conclude active combat operations in Afghanistan by the end of 2013, up to one year sooner than previously envisaged. US combat troops would, however, remain in Afghanistan in a supporting role during 2014. This apparent acceleration of US military disengagement in Afghanistan appeared to reflect the growing domestic unpopularity of the military campaign in the USA and other NATO countries, not least as a result of extensive coalition casualties and the apparently intractable security problems in Afghanistan. Moreover, the rise of 'insider attacks', in which members of the Afghan security forces attacked and killed NATO personnel, served further to erode popular support for the campaign. According to a US government report published in June 2013, some 15% of total US casualties from 'hostile action' in Afghanistan in 2012 were the result of insider attacks. A total of 61 NATO soldiers were reported to have been killed in such attacks in 2012, compared with just two in 2008.

Several events in early 2012 served to exacerbate tensions between ISAF and both the Afghan Government and the general populace. In January NATO officials issued an apology following the online release of video footage that appeared to show four US soldiers urinating on the corpses of Taliban fighters. On 21 February Secretary of Defense Panetta issued a further apology following reports that copies of the Koran, confiscated from Taliban prisoners, had inadvertently been burned and improperly disposed of at Bagram air base. The revelation provoked a wave of anti-US protests, violent unrest and attacks on Western military bases and diplomatic offices throughout the country. In an effort to calm tension, President Obama conveyed his 'deep apologies' in a letter to the Afghan President. However, within five days at least 30 people were reported to have been killed in the unrest. Following the killing of two NATO officials at the headquarters of the Ministry of the Interior in Kabul on 25 February, several NATO countries temporarily withdrew their civilian staff from Afghan government institutions. Further protests occurred following reports in March that 16 civilians, including nine children, were killed when a US soldier carried out a violent and apparently indiscriminate attack on villagers in Panjwai district, Qandahar province. President Karzai issued a demand that all NATO troops return to their main bases and cease operations in rural outposts in order to prevent further civilian casualties. Despite Afghan demands that the perpetrator be tried in an Afghan court, the chief suspect, Sergeant Robert Bales, was transported to a military base in the USA where he was charged with 16 counts of premeditated murder. (Bales pleaded guilty to the charges at a hearing in June 2013, and was sentenced to life in a military prison, with no chance of parole.) Another point of contention between the Afghan Government and US forces was the handover of US-controlled prisons in Afghanistan, a matter that was partially addressed in March 2012 when it was agreed that the controversial Bagram prison would be transferred to Afghan control. In April the outstanding issue of NATO night raids, which Karzai had repeatedly criticized, was resolved when the former agreed to allow Afghan security forces to take the leading role in such operations.

In March 2012 the long-running political impasse regarding President Karzai's ministerial nominees was finally resolved when the Wolesi Jirga voted to approve nine cabinet ministers nominated by the President; these included six nominees that had been rejected by parliament in early 2010 but who, in the mean time, had served as ministers in an acting capacity. However, several other important officials, including the Chief Justice and the Attorney-General, remained in their posts beyond the expiry of their tenure or without parliamentary approval. In August 2012 Minister of Defence Abdul Rahim Wardak and Minister of Interior Affairs Bismillah Khan Mohammadi were dismissed from the Cabinet after both lost votes of no confidence in the Wolesi Jirga, brought by parliamentarians critical of the ministers' performance on internal security. Moreover, claims of corruption had been raised against Wardak, as well as the Minister of Finance, Omar Zakhilwal. At the end of the month Afghanistan's intelligence chief, Rahmatullah Nabil, was dismissed by Karzai. Soon after, in early September, Mohammadi was allocated the defence portfolio, while Gen. Ghulam Mujtaba Patang was appointed to replace him as Minister of Interior Affairs. Asadullah Khalid, the erstwhile Minister of Border and Tribal Affairs, became Nabil's successor at the National Directorate of Security despite controversy over his alleged role in the torture of detainees during his time as Governor of Ghazni and Qandahar. A fourth nominee, Haji Din Mohammad, was prevented from assuming the position of Minister of Border and Tribal Affairs owing to an insufficient number of positive parliamentary votes. In an apparent response to continuing allegations of corruption and poor governance against the provincial leadership, Karzai then reassigned the governorships of ten provinces, dismissing several governors including the prominent, West-allied Governor of Helmand, Gulab Mangal.

In general, Afghanistan has experienced a relative lull in militant attacks during winter, as heavy snows render mountain passes along the border with Pakistan impassable; consequently, the spring thaw has often coincided with a period of renewed militant activity. In mid-April 2012 the Taliban signalled the commencement of its so-called 'spring offensive' by launching a dramatic series of co-ordinated gun and rocket attacks on foreign and government targets in Kabul and several other provincial towns. The assault in Kabul, which was even more extensive than similar attacks in September 2011, targeted the Afghan parliament, NATO's headquarters and foreign embassies. Following the attacks, which lasted for some 18 hours, it was reported that eight Afghan security personnel and 36 militants had been killed. The attacks served further to exacerbate concerns about the security situation amid the ongoing transition.

In late April 2012, after lengthy negotiations, it was reported that the Afghan Government had provisionally agreed on the conditions for a long-term strategic partnership with the USA, which would provide for a continued US military and civil presence in Afghanistan for a further 10 years after 2014. Under the agreement, it was anticipated that the US military would continue to support the Afghan security forces in a training and advisory capacity, but would also be permitted to mount counter-terrorism and intelligence-gathering operations within the country. The agreement also provided for ongoing US financial support for education and governance in Afghanistan. In early May Obama travelled to Afghanistan to sign the agreement with Karzai. Later that month the Chicago Summit Declaration on Afghanistan was approved, which reaffirmed the commitment of all countries contributing to ISAF to Afghan security and development beyond 2014; NATO forces would cease to lead combat operations in mid-2013, but would provide combat support to Afghan soldiers until the withdrawal of all combat troops by the end of 2014, after which only training units would remain. The cost of the 230,000-strong Afghan security forces was estimated at approximately US $4,100m. per year, initially to be raised by the USA and other countries, with the gradual assumption of the financial responsibility by the Afghan Government to be completed by 2024. In July, during a visit to Kabul, US Secretary of State Hillary Clinton announced that Afghanistan had been designated as a major non-NATO ally. In February 2013 Gen. Joseph Dunford, Jr took over from Gen. Allen as Commander of ISAF.

Meanwhile, in January 2012 the Taliban announced that it had reached a provisional agreement with the Qatari Government to open a political office in the Qatari capital, Doha, in a development that was interpreted by some observers as a precursor to the staging of peace talks between the Taliban and the US Administration. At the same time the Taliban demanded the release of prisoners from the US detention centre in Guantánamo Bay, Cuba. Secretary of State Clinton stated in response that the US Administration had not yet made any decisions regarding the potential release of Taliban prisoners, adding that reconciliation could only occur if the Taliban renounced violence, ceased its support of al-Qa'ida and recognized the Afghan Constitution. In March it was reported that the Taliban had suspended its involvement in nascent peace negotiations with the US authorities: the decision was thought mainly to be a result of the continued detention of the Taliban prisoners in question. The murder of another member of the High Peace Council, former Taliban minister Arsala Rahmani, in May, caused further uncertainty about the peace process. However, the Taliban denied responsibility for his shooting. In June members of the Afghan Government and the Taliban met in France and Japan, although the Islamist group was said to have attended only to clarify its position, rather than to negotiate. It was reported in September that the Taliban, while willing to negotiate with other parties such as the USA for a political solution to the insurgency, did not wish to deal with the Karzai administration. In December it was reported that, for the first time, members of the Afghan Government, the Taliban and the United National Front had convened in France to define their standpoints. As the NATO troop withdrawal loomed in 2014, a significant shift in policy seemed to have occurred, with increasing support for a negotiated settlement with the Taliban being offered by the USA and Pakistan, both vital to any long-term political settlement in Afghanistan. In late 2012 and early 2013 the Pakistani Government released some 26 Taliban prisoners to aid peace talks. While the Taliban remained officially intractable on its conditions for peace talks, including its refusal to negotiate with the High Peace Council, Pakistani involvement increased the momentum towards a settlement.

Impeachment proceedings were launched against 11 cabinet ministers in December 2012, including the Ministers of Interior Affairs, of Defence, and of Economy; the ministers were said to be responsible for a major under-spend on development projects. In April 2013 three of the ministers under scrutiny (those responsible for education, commerce and industry, and counter narcotics) won votes of confidence in the Wolesi Jirga and were confirmed in their posts. However, it was subsequently reported that up to 80 members of parliament had been implicated in bribery allegations relating to the parliamentary votes of confidence.

During a parliamentary session in May 2013, Minister of Finance Zakhilwal, having previously made general accusations about corruption in the Wolesi Jirga, disclosed the names of six parliamentarians whom he accused of smuggling and making illegal demands of the Government. All of those identified denied any wrongdoing and countered that Zakhilwal was using the revelations to deflect from allegations of corruption and misuse of authority that they had intended to bring against him. Zakhilwal survived a vote of no confidence later in May. In June a travel ban was imposed on five of the six accused parliamentarians, following their refusal to appear before prosecutors to discuss the allegations made by Zakhilwal. (Several refused to discuss the charges against them while Muhammad Aloko remained in office as Attorney-General, despite the vote of no confidence against him in 2011—see The 2010 parliamentary elections.) In July 2013 the Minister of Interior Affairs, Gen. Ghulam Mujtaba Patang, lost a vote of confidence in the Wolesi Jirga over his failure effectively to combat rising corruption and the worsening security situation. President Karzai initially challenged the legality of the decision; however, in September Patang was replaced by Muhammad Umar Daudzai, hitherto the Afghan ambassador to Pakistan.

Meanwhile, fatalities incurred by NATO personnel were estimated to have decreased by almost 30% in 2012, to 302. However, with the withdrawal of NATO troops continuing on schedule, the Afghan security forces assumed an increasingly high-profile role in efforts to combat insurgent groups; thus, while NATO casualties were moderating, Afghan casualties were on the increase. According to the Ministry of Interior Affairs, 1,792 Afghan police officers were killed and more than 2,500 others were injured between March and September 2013, more than twice the number of those killed or injured during the corresponding period of 2012. According to the Afghan Ministry of Defence, 1,170 Afghan soldiers were killed and some 3,000 wounded in the 12 months to March 2013.

According to the UN, in 2012 civilian deaths in Afghanistan had decreased for the first time in six years, by about 12% to 2,768. However, there was a marked increase in the number of civilian casualties incurred during the second half of the year, partly because of extreme winter conditions in early 2012. According to the UN, in 2013 civilian fatalities increased once again, by 7% to reach 2,959, while civilian injuries increased by 17% (to 5,656). Of the total number of casualties (deaths and injuries), 74% were attributed to insurgent activity (down from 81% in 2012). While improvised explosive devices continued to be the largest cause of civilian casualties in 2013, increased ground engagement between Afghan security forces and insurgents emerged as the second largest cause, representing a worrying new trend in the ongoing security crisis. Of the civilian casualties caused by pro-Government forces, some 57% were attributed to the Afghan security forces, 27% to ISAF and the remaining 16% to operations conducted jointly by the two. Of particular concern was a 36% increase in the total number of female civilian casualties (including 235 deaths) and a 34% increase in the total number of child casualties (including 561 fatalities).

Nevertheless, the final phase of the transition of security responsibilities was initiated in June 2013, with control of combat operations in the final 95 districts handed over by NATO to the Afghan authorities. However, a spate of deadly attacks on key installations in Kabul at this time, including a number within the so-called Ring of Steel (supposedly the most secure inner circle of the capital, responsibility for which had been formally handed over to the Afghan authorities in January), exacerbated widespread concerns about the ability of the ANA and Afghan police successfully to combat the threat posed to national security by insurgents. The Supreme Court building, Kabul International Airport, Bagram air base and a NATO supplier's compound were all targeted in June–July, and the ability of Taliban insurgents to wage a two-hour attack outside the presidential palace in late June, which included rocket-propelled grenade attacks on the nearby office of the USA's Central Intelligence Agency (CIA), was particularly troubling. More than 20 people were reported to have been killed, and dozens injured, in the attacks.

Increasing Afghan–US tension

Tension between the Afghan Government and the US Administration increased in 2013, not least as a result of Afghan allegations of widespread abuses of power by NATO forces and their local allies in Wardak Province. The situation was exacerbated by public statements made by President Karzai accusing the USA of collusion with the Taliban. The recently appointed US Secretary of State, John Kerry, held conciliatory talks with Karzai in Kabul in March, during which he confirmed the delayed handover to Afghan control of the prison at Bagram air base. However, tensions re-emerged soon after the opening of the Taliban's office in Qatar in June. Having previously cautiously welcomed the staging of talks with the Taliban, Karzai was angered by a television report that showed the Taliban's office displaying a rebel banner and describing itself as the 'political office of the Islamic Emirate of Afghanistan', a reference to the former name of Afghanistan prior to the Taliban's removal from government in 2001. Contesting that the office would be used to confer undue legitimacy upon the Taliban, Karzai announced that the Afghan Government would oppose any peace talks that were not 'Afghan-led', accused the Obama Administration of being duplicitous in its efforts to engage with the Taliban, and suspended talks with the USA on a bilateral security agreement, which would allow US troops to remain in Afghanistan beyond the final withdrawal scheduled for the end of 2014. In order to appease Karzai, the USA demanded that the Qatari authorities remove the banner and nameplate from the Taliban's office. Angered by this action, the Taliban promptly announced the temporary closure of its office in Qatar. The so-called Doha process remained stalled at early 2014.

In a statement issued in August 2013 to mark the festival of Id al-Fitr, Mullah Mohammad Omar stated that, following the withdrawal of foreign troops from Afghanistan by the end of 2014, the Taliban would try to form 'an inclusive government based on Islamic principles' but would not seek to monopolize power. The Taliban leader also rejected the validity of the forthcoming presidential election, due on 5 April 2014, and announced that the Taliban would, as in previous polls, boycott the process. In September 2013 the captured Taliban commander Mullah Abdul Ghani Baradar was released by the Pakistani authorities, apparently in response to a request by Karzai, in order to facilitate the revival of the stalled peace process. In November a senior Haqqani leader, Nasiruddin Haqqani, the son of the network's leader, Jalaluddin Haqqani, was reported to have been shot dead by unknown assailants in Islamabad.

An interview with Karzai broadcast by the British Broadcasting Corporation (BBC) in October 2013, in which the Afghan President strongly criticized NATO for bringing 'a lot of suffering, a lot of loss of life, and no gains because the country is not secure', did little to ameliorate relations between Afghanistan and its Western allies. Nevertheless, later that month President Karzai and his Pakistani counterpart, Asif Ali Zardari, attended talks in the United Kingdom with the British Prime Minister, David Cameron, during which the three leaders committed to accelerate the process of reconciliation in Afghanistan. (Trilateral talks had previously taken place in London in February 2013, in New York in September 2012 and in Kabul in July 2012.) Zardari agreed to facilitate a meeting in Pakistan between an Afghan High Peace Council delegation and Mullah Abdul Ghani Baradar, who it was hoped might be able to persuade the Taliban to enter into direct peace negotiations with the Afghan Government.

Following breakthrough negotiations between US Secretary of State Kerry and President Karzai in Kabul in mid-October 2013, whereupon agreement was reported to have been reached on a number of core issues, on 20 November the two sides announced that a final draft of the proposed bilateral security agreement had been agreed, pending approval by a Loya Jirga. Under the terms of the draft agreement, a small residual contingent of US troops (believed to number around 10,000) would be authorized to remain in Afghanistan beyond the end of 2014 to assist the Afghan security forces in a training and advisory capacity; full legal jurisdiction of the troops would be afforded to the USA, thus granting them immunity from Afghan law. The 2,500-member Loya Jirga overwhelmingly endorsed the draft on 24 November, and urged Karzai to sign the agreement by the end of 2013, on the explicit condition that authorization for the continued US troop presence be limited to 10 years. However, Karzai subsequently angered the Obama Administration by declaring that, while he believed the bilateral security agreement to be in the best interests of Afghanistan, he would not sign the accord until the USA had halted raids of Afghan civilian homes and helped to restart the moribund peace talks with the Taliban. An intensification of US efforts to exert pressure on Karzai to sign the agreement was evident in early 2014, including the threat that, if the agreement was not signed promptly, the Obama Administration would have no choice but to initiate planning for a complete withdrawal—the so-called 'zero option'—of US troops by the end of 2014 (around 34,000 US troops remained in Afghanistan in early 2014); Karzai dismissed such threats as US 'brinkmanship'.

Afghan–US tensions were further exacerbated in January 2014 by a US air strike targeting senior Taliban leaders in the northern province of Parvan (Parwan), during which 14 civilians, including three women and five children, were reported to have been killed. Three co-ordinated suicide bomb attacks on a Lebanese restaurant within Kabul's Ring of Steel two days later claimed the lives of at least 21 people, of whom 13 were foreign nationals—including four UN personnel and the IMF's residential representative in Afghanistan, Wabel Abdallah, a Lebanese national. Responsibility for the attacks was claimed by the Taliban, which stated that the blasts had been carried out as a reprisal for the US air strike in Parwan. On the same day as the attack, President Obama announced the establishment of a temporary Afghanistan and Pakistan Strategic Partnership Office, in order to facilitate the transition to a normalized US diplomatic presence in both countries and co-ordinate the final drawdown of the Department of State's civilian field operations and personnel in Afghanistan. In March NATO confirmed that at least five Afghan soldiers had been killed and eight others wounded by an ISAF air strike in Loghar province, and promised a full investigation into the circumstances behind the incident.

Recent developments: the 2014 presidential election

In October 2012 President Karzai announced that the election to choose his successor, which would bring about the first democratic transfer of power in Afghanistan's history, was to be held on 5 April 2014. However, there was considerable disagreement over his decision to exclude foreign representatives from the ECC, and further criticism was prompted by reports in December 2012 that the Cabinet had approved the transfer of the ECC's duties to a Supreme Court tribunal that was to be appointed directly by the President. Following months of heated debate, two new electoral laws were approved in July 2013, and were cautiously welcomed both within Afghanistan and among the wider international community. The ECC was to be retained after all, but international representatives were still to be excluded, a compromise measure adopted to secure Karzai's approval. Although the President would still select the composition of the five-member ECC, he would do so from a short list compiled by a selection panel including the head of the Supreme Court and the respective Speakers of the Wolesi Jirga and of the Meshrano Jirga. However, critics of the new legislation argued that the laws did not represent a genuine reform of the Afghan electoral system, and would not ensure the holding of a free and fair election.

Registration for candidates seeking to contest the presidential election commenced in September 2013. After a number of prospective candidates were disqualified for failing to meet all requirements of the newly adopted electoral legislation, a final list of 11 approved candidates, each with two vice-presidential running mates, was released in November. Among the leading candidates were National Council of Afghanistan leader Dr Abdullah Abdullah (Karzai's main opponent in 2009), Dr Zalmai Rassoul (who had resigned as Minister of Foreign Affairs in order to register as a candidate), Ashraf Ghani (a former Minister of Finance and World Bank official), and Qayum Karzai (the President's elder brother). Among the 22 vice-presidential running mates were three women.

In January 2014 President Karzai provoked US ire when he announced his Government's intention to release 72 high-level Taliban prisoners. Some analysts believed that the decision was intended, not as a genuine overture to the Taliban in order to facilitate the restarting of stalled peace talks with the Government, but rather as a means of pacifying local leaders whose relatives were in prison, in an attempt to secure their support in advance of the presidential election. Although Karzai was constitutionally barred from standing for a third term in office, and despite the President publicly maintaining that he would not be supporting any of the candidates, he was widely believed to be keen to influence the choice of his successor, with Zalmai Rassoul and Qayum Karzai—both of whose electoral campaigns appeared to represent a maintaining of the status quo—widely believed to be the preferred choices of the incumbent administration.

Interest in the election was heightened by intense campaigning, including the staging of three televised debates in February–March 2014, from which Dr Abdullah, Ashraf Ghani and Zalmai Rassoul, all of whom expressed their support for the bilateral security agreement with the USA, emerged as the frontrunners. Qayum Karzai withdrew his candidacy in early March, announcing that he would henceforth be supporting the candidacy of Rassoul. A few days later Vice-President Muhammed Qasim Fahim died of a heart attack; Yunus Qanooni's appointment as his replacement was confirmed in late March.

The Taliban, meanwhile, threatened to disrupt the election and to punish all who participated. The run-up to the poll was overshadowed by violence, with multiple attacks claiming the lives of dozens of people. In Kabul the offices of the IEC, the Ministry of Interior Affairs and a luxury hotel popular with foreigners were all targeted in mid-March–early April, while targets outside the capital included a police station in Jalalabad and an office of the National Directorate of Security in Qandahar. A Paraguayan election observer and a senior Afghan news reporter were among the nine civilians killed in the attack on the luxury hotel in Kabul, while on 4 April two female foreign journalists accompanying a convoy of election workers in Khost were shot (one fatally) by an Afghan police officer.

Amid heightened security, the presidential election was held as scheduled on 5 April 2014. A series of attacks across the country on the day was reported to have claimed the lives of around 20 people, including nine police officers and seven military personnel, with more than 40 others wounded. The authorities claimed to have foiled a number of attacks against polling stations, nearly 1,000 of which (around 10%) had been deemed unsafe to open to the public owing to security concerns. Despite the security threats a high level of voter participation was recorded throughout the country; the IEC reported that more than 7m. voters had turned out to cast their ballot (from a total registered electorate of approximately 12m.). Reports that some polling stations had run out of ballot papers were denied by the IEC. However, the ECC confirmed that it had received over 3,000 complaints, the majority of which pertained to a shortage of ballot papers. Among the other complaints were numerous allegations of fraud, including ballot-stuffing and the use of fraudulent voter cards, but there did not appear to have been the same level of fraud as that witnessed in 2009 and 2010, and the election was generally hailed by domestic and foreign observers as an overwhelming success. According to preliminary results issued by the IEC in late April, Dr Abdullah was the leading candidate, with an estimated 44.9% of the valid votes cast, Ashraf Ghani secured 31.5% and Zalmai Rassoul 11.1%. Of the other candidates, only three secured more than 1% of the vote: Abdul Rab Rassoul Sayyaf (7.1%), Qutbuddin Hilal (2.7%) and Shafiq Gul Agha Sherzai (1.6%). However, the preliminary results were subject to an audit by the ECC; it was reported that more than 230,000 votes had been invalidated by the IEC and more than 500 ballot boxes had been excluded from the vote count. None the less, it appeared likely that no candidate would secure more than 50% of the first-round vote and, assuming that remained the case, a run-off poll involving Abdullah and Ghani was scheduled to be held on 28 May.

Production of Illicit Drugs

In January 2002 the Interim Authority issued a decree banning poppy cultivation and the processing, trafficking and abuse of opiates. In April the Interim Authority introduced a radical programme whereby farmers would receive compensation for destroying their opium crops, and those who refused would have their land seized by the Government and risk prosecution. However, the offer of compensation did not compare well with the lucrative sale of opium, and farmers carried out violent demonstrations throughout the country against the initiative. Despite attempts by the Government and the UN to curb the drugs trade, the annual survey conducted by the UN Office on Drugs and Crime (UNODC), published in October, reported that, owing to the large-scale planting of poppies during the collapse of law and order in late 2001, Afghanistan had resumed its place as the world's largest producer of opium.

In an attempt to address Afghanistan's continuing problems with the widespread cultivation of opium, President Hamid Karzai, following his inauguration in December 2004, announced the formation of a Ministry of Counter Narcotics. According to the UN, in 2004 the total area under poppy cultivation had increased by 64%, compared with the previous year.

In 2008 there was a 6% decrease in opium production; further success was reported in 2009 when the area under poppy cultivation decreased to 123,000 ha, from 157,000 ha in 2008. In 2010 the area under poppy cultivation remained unchanged but opium production declined by about 50% year-on-year, mainly owing to a naturally occurring plant disease that had affected the crop. Owing to rising global opium prices, coupled with the declining price of wheat (one of Afghanistan's main crop alternatives to opium) and the deteriorating security situation, the area under poppy cultivation increased, by 7%, to 131,000 ha in 2011, while opium production increased by some 61%, rising from 3,600 metric tons to 5,800 tons. There was a further increase (of 18%) in the area under cultivation in 2012, but production declined by 36% owing to plant disease and adverse weather conditions affecting the crop. The area under cultivation increased by a further 36% in 2013, to reach a record high of 209,000 ha, while opium production increased by 49% to reach 5,500 tons. Furthermore, opium production was found to have resumed in Faryab and Balkh during 2013; both provinces had previously been declared poppy-free.

Meanwhile, a UNODC report published in April 2010 concluded that Afghanistan was also the world's largest producer of hashish resin, an illegal derivative of the cannabis plant, and stated that some two-thirds of cannabis farmers were also involved in the cultivation of opium. The report also noted that cultivation of both opium poppy and cannabis was concentrated in regions of instability and, through the levying of taxes on production and trafficking, served as an important source of revenue for militia groups. According to a UNODC report published in September 2013, the area under cultivation for cannabis in Afghanistan was estimated at 10,000 ha in 2012, representing a 17% decline from 2011. However, the total yield of cannabis resin was estimated to have increased by 8% in 2012 to 1,400 metric tons.

Foreign Affairs

On 22 December 2002 the Governments of Afghanistan, the People's Republic of China, Iran, Pakistan, Tajikistan, Turkmenistan and Uzbekistan signed the Kabul Declaration on Good-Neighbourly Relations, in which they pledged non-interference in each other's affairs. On paper, the agreement signalled a new era of regional co-operation, yet, in reality, the situation was somewhat different. Afghan officials claimed that Iranian Revolutionary Guards were continuing to provide financial and military assistance to Ismail Khan; Russia was reportedly supporting Marshal Fahim and his army; and certain Saudis had allegedly resumed sending financial assistance to the remnants of the Taliban in Pakistan. In addition, the Uzbekistani President had provided Uzbek Gen. Dostam with his own bodyguards. Publicly, the Pakistani President supported President Hamid Karzai and the USA's campaign against al-Qa'ida; however, at the same time, Pakistan's Inter-Services Intelligence (ISI) was reportedly giving sanctuary to senior Taliban members and other anti-Government military commanders, such as Gulbuddin Hekmatyar, leader of the Hizb-i Islami guerrilla group.

Despite repeated efforts to engender a lasting amelioration in bilateral ties, relations between Afghanistan and Pakistan encountered numerous setbacks during the early 2000s, and suffered a further deterioration from 2005 with President Karzai and his Pakistani counterpart engaging in protracted public recriminations over cross-border activities and the fight against the Taliban. Relations between the two countries appeared to improve with the holding of a joint 'peace jirga' in Kabul in August 2007; the four-day meeting was attended by some 650 tribal leaders from both countries, along with Karzai, Pakistani President Gen. Pervez Musharraf and other senior government officials. In March 2008 relations between Afghanistan and Pakistan deteriorated following the assertion by Karzai that Afghan troops had the right to enter Pakistani territory, which he claimed was being used as a base for cross-border attacks. The growing strength and influence of the Tehrik-e-Taliban Pakistan, or the so-called Pakistani Taliban—the stated objectives of which were resistance against the Pakistani state, enforcement of their version of *Shari'a* and support to the insurgency in Afghanistan—was a disturbing development for both Governments from 2008; despite a successful army offensive against the militants in the Swat valley in mid-2009, the Pakistani Taliban remained a tangible force.

However, a significant improvement in Afghan-Pakistani relations was apparent from 2009. In February the new US Secretary of State, Hillary Clinton, hosted a meeting with the foreign ministers of Pakistan and Afghanistan in Washington, DC, and announced that these trilateral negotiations would be held on a regular basis to discuss mutually strategic issues. In August an official meeting took place between President Karzai and the Pakistani Prime Minister, Yousaf Raza Gilani, during which the two leaders agreed to co-operate in combating terrorism and militancy. Subsequent Pakistani anti-insurgency efforts led to the arrest, in early 2010, of a number of high-ranking Afghan Taliban figures (including Mullah Abdul Ghani Baradar—see Domestic Political Affairs). In October 2010 a long-anticipated Afghanistan-Pakistan Trade Transit Agreement (APTTA) was signed between the two countries; the APTTA would, *inter alia*, allow Afghan trade vehicles to carry Afghan exports across Pakistan to the border with India, via the Pakistani port cities of Karachi and Gwadar; pending an improvement in the security situation in Afghanistan, Pakistani trade vehicles would also be granted right of passage through Afghanistan to trading partners in Central Asia.

In January 2011 representatives of the Afghan High Peace Council visited the Pakistani capital, Islamabad, to discuss Pakistan's involvement in the Afghan reconciliation process. During its visit, the Afghan delegation, which was led by former President Burhanuddin Rabbani, also held discussions with representatives of Hizb-i Islami. Following talks between President Karzai and Prime Minister Gilani in Kabul in April, the two leaders announced an agreement to establish a joint peace and reconciliation commission as part of efforts to end the Taliban insurgency. In June Karzai and the Pakistani President, Asif Ali Zardari, signed the so-called Islamabad Declaration, a 23-point agreement intended to bolster counter-terrorism co-operation and to facilitate a more general improvement in bilateral relations, including enhanced co-operation in the fields of communications, energy, infrastructure, and trade and commerce. Furthermore, the leaders announced the full implementation of the delayed APTTA. However, a series of cross-border attacks in July raised concerns that the apparent amelioration in bilateral relations would prove short-lived. Afghan officials claimed that Pakistani forces had fired hundreds of rockets into Afghan territory, killing dozens of border police and civilians; conversely, the Pakistani authorities contested that militants in the border regions of Afghanistan were launching frequent attacks on Pakistani border posts and villages. In November the Afghan and Pakistani Governments—meeting on the sidelines of a regional conference on the security situation in Afghanistan held in İstanbul, Turkey—announced an agreement jointly to investigate the assassination in September of Rabbani. In October Karzai had accused elements within the Pakistani establishment of supporting the insurgency within Afghanistan, claims that were adamantly denied by the Pakistani Government. At the İstanbul conference, a security agreement was signed by representatives of more than a dozen countries in South and Central Asia and the Middle East pledging to adhere to a policy of non-interference in Afghanistan's internal affairs.

President Karzai returned to Islamabad in February 2012 for further talks concerning regional security and Pakistan's potential role in facilitating direct negotiations between the Taliban and the Karzai administration. Following the bilateral discussions, trilateral talks on trade and security, involving President Mahmoud Ahmadinejad of Iran, took place. The summit was interpreted by many analysts as an attempt by the participants to reclaim a leading role in the search for a political solution in Afghanistan, following the initiation of exploratory negotiations, hosted by Qatar, between the Taliban and the USA (see Domestic Political Affairs). In late February, in what appeared to be a significant tactical shift, Prime Minister Gilani publicly urged the Taliban to enter direct peace negotiations with the Afghan Government. However, the Taliban continued to view the Karzai administration as an illegitimate entity and refused to engage in direct talks. In 2012 and early 2013 Pakistan took a more active role in promoting negotiations between the Taliban and the Afghan Government, engaging in a series of trilateral talks with Afghanistan and the United Kingdom and releasing numerous Taliban prisoners to further the peace process. However, tension mounted over shelling in the border province of Kunar in September 2012, which Pakistan blamed on the Pakistani Taliban, who were alleged to have established bases in Afghanistan. Nevertheless, in November the two countries began talks on a strategic partnership agreement, and in February 2013, during the third round of trilateral talks with the United Kingdom, held in London, United Kingdom, Presidents Karzai and Zardari reaffirmed their commitment to work towards such an agreement. In August Karzai met with new Pakistani Prime Minister Nawaz Sharif in Islamabad and declared that Pakistan's role in any long-term peace settlement remained crucial.

A summit on anti-terrorism and anti-narcotics efforts was held between Afghanistan, Pakistan, Russia and Tajikistan in the Russian capital, Moscow, in August 2010. The four states agreed to pursue joint economic projects in an attempt to introduce stability to the region. In January 2011 President Karzai visited Moscow, where he met with Russian Prime Minister Dmitrii Medvedev. Medvedev pledged Russian support for Afghan energy and infrastructure projects, including the long-running plan (first proposed in 1990 but subsequently delayed owing to security concerns) to construct a Turkmenistan–Afghanistan–Pakistan–India (TAPI) natural gas pipeline; Afghan, Pakistani and Indian officials had convened in Turkmenistan to sign a framework agreement on the pipeline project in December 2010. The Afghan Government pledged to commit about 7,000 troops to guard the pipeline during its construction; upon completion of the project, Afghanistan would receive an estimated 700m. cu ft of Turkmen natural gas via the pipeline annually. In late 2012 it was reported that the Afghan authorities had proposed to relinquish their share of gas from the pipeline in exchange for transit fees of up to US $450m. per year. In July 2013 Afghanistan and Turkmenistan signed an agreement providing for the supply of natural gas by Turkmenistan to Afghanistan through the pipeline, a corresponding agreement having been signed by Turkmenistan with India and Pakistan in May 2012. By early 2014 construction on the project had yet to commence; however, it was announced in January that the framework for the project was being fast-tracked by the four stakeholder nations, with completion of the project, culminating in the supply of gas to India, tentatively scheduled for 2017.

Meanwhile, in August 2005 Indian Prime Minister Manmohan Singh visited Afghanistan, the first such visit by an Indian premier since 1975. The Indian embassy in Kabul was targeted by a suicide bombing in July 2008, which resulted in more than 40 fatalities, and another in October 2009, which killed at least 17 people. During a visit to Kabul in May 2011, Singh announced the provision of US $500m. in aid to Afghanistan, taking the collective total pledged by India to some $2,000m.; priority was to be afforded to agriculture, infrastructure and social programmes. The two leaders signed a strategic partnership agreement in October, the first such partnership that Afghanistan had entered into in its history. Under the terms of the pact, Afghanistan and India agreed to deepen co-operation in the fields of trade, counter-terrorism, and political and cultural engagement, while India pledged to offer support in the form of training and equipment as Afghanistan prepared to assume full responsibility for its national security by the end of 2014. The deepening mistrust of Pakistan shared by both the Afghan and Indian Governments was widely believed to have accelerated the successful conclusion of negotiations on the partnership agreement. In November 2011 it was announced that the development rights for three blocks at the Hajigak iron ore concession in central Afghanistan had been awarded to the state-run Steel Authority of India; the Hajigak deposit contained an estimated 1,800m. metric tons of iron ore. In June 2012 India hosted an international investment summit on Afghanistan in Delhi. During subsequent visits to Delhi by Karzai, including, most latterly, in December 2013, Karzai appealed for further Indian investment in Afghanistan and a deepening of bilateral military ties.

In 2007 the state-owned China Metallurgical Group Corporation was awarded the rights to mine for copper in the Mes Aynak area of Loghar province; the region was reported to contain potentially the world's second largest reserves of copper. The Chinese committed to investing some US $3,500m. in the project (the largest single foreign investment in Afghanistan to date), which was to include the construction of a power plant and a 698-km railway from the Pakistan border to Kabul, passing through the Aynak mine. However, progress was hampered by persistent security threats and by the discovery of sensitive archaeological sites in the area. By early 2014 neither the extraction process nor construction of the railway line had commenced. Moreover, in 2013 it was reported that Chinese officials had proposed a renegotiation of the terms of the mining contract. Meanwhile, in March 2010 Karzai and his Chinese counterpart, President Hu Jintao, signed agreements on trade and economic co-operation aimed at supporting the recovery of the war-ravaged Afghan economy. In December 2011 the two countries concluded an oil agreement potentially worth an estimated US $7,000m. to Afghanistan over the course of a 25-year period. Under the terms of the agreement, the state-owned China National Petroleum Corporation (CNPC) was to develop three oilfields along the Amu Darya river in northern Afghanistan; the concession was believed to contain around 87m. barrels of oil. A China-Afghanistan Strategic and Co-operative Partnership, based on collaboration in political, economic, cultural and security affairs, as well as regional and international affairs, was concluded in June 2012. In October CNPC announced the commencement of oil production at the Amu Darya development. In May 2013 it was reported that, for the first time in Afghanistan's history, commercial oil production was to start later that year. However, in August CNPC suspended operations at the project, reportedly following a disagreement with the Afghan Government over the precise conditions attached to the transportation and refinement of the oil; Afghan officials claimed that operations would be resumed following the successful conclusion of an oil transit agreement with Uzbekistan. Earlier in August the Chinese embassy in Kabul had urged the Karzai administration to ensure the safety of Chinese nationals resident in Afghanistan, following the fatal shooting of three Chinese workers, together with an Afghan security guard, in an apartment in the Afghan capital; two others were abducted from the scene, one of whom was later found dead

Iran remains one of Afghanistan's most important sources of foreign aid and has been responsible for increasing levels of investment into the country. However, US officials have voiced concerns about perceived Iranian efforts to influence the Afghan political arena by means of bribery and collusion. In October 2010 the office of President Karzai admitted to having received sizeable monetary payments from Iran on a relatively regular basis; such payments were widely believed to be intended to promote Iranian interests within Afghanistan to the detriment of US and other Western interests. Senior US officials and NATO commanders have frequently alleged that Iran has sought to undermine the Western mission in Afghanistan through the supply of munitions and the facilitation of training camps for militants in south-western Afghanistan. The Iranian Government adamantly refutes such claims, dismissing the allegations as crude attempts to discredit its reputation. Meanwhile, the Iranian authorities have expressed concern regarding the expansion of US military facilities in Herat province, in close proximity to the border with Iran. In December 2012 Iran temporarily closed its consulate in Herat after attacks by Afghans protesting against the alleged execution of Afghan immigrants in Iran. The Iranian consulate was the scene of further unrest in September 2013, when hundreds of Afghan protesters gathered outside the building to protest against delays in the processing of visa applications; after protesters tried to storm the consulate, one person was killed and several others injured in clashes between police officers and the protesters. Meanwhile, following the signing of a bilateral security pact in August, a more broadly based long-term bilateral co-operation agreement—providing for enhanced political, security and economic co-operation—was signed in December.

CONSTITUTION AND GOVERNMENT

In December 2001 28 Afghan leaders signed the Agreement on Provisional Arrangements in Afghanistan Pending the Re-establishment of Permanent Government Institutions (also known as the Bonn Agreement), stipulating a timetable for the creation of a permanent constitution and the holding of free national elections. In accordance with the Agreement, Afghanistan temporarily reverted to the Constitution of 1964. In June 2002 an Emergency Loya Jirga (Grand National Council), comprising an estimated 1,650 delegates, appointed a head of state and the principal staff of a broad-based, gender-sensitive Transitional Authority. A new Constitution providing for a presidential system of government and a bicameral legislature, following eventual elections by universal suffrage, was approved by a Constitutional Loya Jirga in January 2004. Under the terms of the new charter, the President is elected for a five-year term, while the 249-member Wolesi Jirga (House of the People)—the lower house of the Meli Shura (National Assembly)—is elected on a provincial basis, with members also serving for five years; one-third of the 102-member Meshrano Jirga (House of Elders)—the upper house of the Meli Shura—is elected by the provincial councils, one-third by district councils, and the remaining members appointed by the President. The election of the President and the Meli Shura in October 2004 and September 2005, respectively, signified the end of the transitional period of government (the Bonn Process) that had been initiated in 2002.

Afghanistan is divided into 34 provinces. Each province is administered by a provincial council, which is headed by a governor and which is elected for a term of four years. The governor of each province is appointed by the President. Every village and town in the country also has a local council, with members serving for a three-year term.

REGIONAL AND INTERNATIONAL CO-OPERATION

Afghanistan is a member of the UN Economic and Social Commission for Asia and the Pacific (ESCAP, see p. 28), the Colombo Plan (see p. 449), which seeks to promote economic and social development in Asia and the Pacific, the Asian Development Bank (ADB, see p. 207) and the Economic Cooperation Organization (ECO, see p. 265). It was approved as a full member of the South Asian Association for Regional Cooperation (SAARC, see p. 420) in November 2005 and formally admitted as the eighth member of the regional organization in April 2007. Afghanistan was admitted as a member of the UN in November 1946. In April 2003 Afghanistan applied for membership to the World Trade Organization (WTO, see p. 434); the country formally initiated its accession process in November 2004, and the first Working Party meeting on its accession was convened in January 2011.

ECONOMIC AFFAIRS

In 2011, according to estimates by the World Bank, Afghanistan's gross national income (GNI), measured at average 2009–11 prices, was US $16,604m., equivalent to $570 per head (or $1,400 per head on an international purchasing-power parity basis). During 2003–12, it was estimated, the population increased at an average rate of 2.9% per year. According to the IMF, gross domestic product (GDP) per head increased, in real terms, at an average annual rate of 5.6% during 2003–12. In 2010/11, according to IMF estimates, Afghanistan's GDP, excluding the illegal cultivation of poppies and production of drugs, was $17,931m. This implied a per head GDP of $577. According to the IMF, GDP increased at an average annual rate of 9.1% during 2003–12. Growth was 6.1% in 2011 and 12.5% in 2012.

Agriculture (including hunting, forestry and fishing) contributed 26.4% of GDP in 2012/13, according to official estimates. According to FAO estimates, 58.6% of the economically active population were employed in the agricultural sector in mid-2013. Livestock plays an important role in the traditional Afghan economy and is normally a major source of income for the country's numerous nomadic groups. However, the total livestock population has been seriously depleted, owing to the many years of conflict and prolonged drought conditions. In 2008/09 ongoing drought in several regions of the country caused a major decline in the output of the agricultural sector; according to FAO estimates, cereal production decreased from 5.8m. tons in 2007 to around 3.7m. tons in 2008. Afghanistan thus continued to be dependent on food assistance. By 2010 the situation had improved markedly when cereal production recovered to 6.0m. tons. This was largely due to an increase in arable land devoted to wheat cultivation, favourable levels of rainfall, and the provision of seeds and fertilizers to farmers. Cereal production was again affected by drought in some areas in 2011 and production decreased to an estimated 4.7m. tons. However, the sector witnessed a strong recovery in 2012, with cereal production increasing to 6.5m. tons, including record wheat production of 5.0m. tons. Similar levels of production were maintained in 2013. According to Asian Development Bank (ADB) estimates, the GDP of the agricultural sector increased at an average annual rate of 1.9% during 2003–11; growth was 21.2% in 2007, but 2008 saw a decline of 11.7% owing to the severe drought conditions. In 2010/11 the GDP of the sector decreased again by 18.0% due to a significant decline in cereal production, but it increased by 4.7% in 2011/12 and by 3.3% in 2012/13.

The industrial sector (including mining, manufacturing, construction and power) contributed 21.3% of GDP in 2012/13, according to official estimates. The sector employed 6.2% of the economically active population in 2004/05, according to ADB figures. According to ADB estimates, sectoral GDP increased at an average annual rate of 9.9% between 2003 and 2011. The GDP of the sector grew by 7.8% in 2012/13.

Mining and quarrying, according to official figures, contributed 1.0% of GDP in 2012/13. Natural gas was previously the major mineral export (accounting for about 24% of total export earnings in 1988/89). However, production of natural gas decreased from a high of 8.2m. cu m per day in the mid-1980s to around 600,000 cu m per day in 2001. Gas reserves were estimated at 150,000m. cu m in 2002. Salt, hard coal, copper, lapis lazuli, emeralds, barytes and talc are also mined. In addition, Afghanistan has sizeable reserves of iron ore, notably at Hajigak, which, according to government estimates, contained some 1,800m. metric tons of iron ore; development rights for three blocks in the concession were awarded to the state-run Steel Authority of India in November 2011, in a contract worth US $10,300m., while rights for a fourth block were awarded to Kilo Goldmines of Canada. Afghanistan also has modest reserves of petroleum. In 2010 the Government claimed that Afghanistan's mineral wealth amounted to some US $3,000,000m. According to ADB estimates, mining GDP increased at an average annual rate of 40.2% during 2003–11. The sector increased by a massive 90.0% in 2011/12, but decreased by 1.1% in 2012/13.

Manufacturing, according to official estimates, contributed 12.5% of GDP in 2012/13. According to IMF estimates, the sector together with mining and utilities, employed about 4.9% of the labour force in 2002/03. Afghanistan's major manufacturing industries included food products, cotton textiles, chemical fertilizers, cement, leather and plastic goods. In 1999 only one of the four existing cement plants in Afghanistan and about 10% of the textile mills remained in operation (prior to the Soviet invasion in 1979 there were about 220 state-owned factories operating in Afghanistan). Although the Government has issued several licences for the construction of new private sector cement factories, by early 2014 the two Ghori cement plants remained the only functioning facilities in the country, and the country's construction sector continued to rely heavily on imports of cement, largely from Pakistan. The traditional handicraft sector has better survived the devastating effects of war, and carpets, leather, embroidery and fur products continue to be produced. According to ADB estimates, manufacturing GDP increased at an average annual rate of 3.7% during 2003–11. The GDP of the sector increased by 7.3% in 2012/13.

The construction sector contributed 7.8% of GDP in 2012/13, according to official estimates, and employed an estimated 1.3% of the economically active population in 2002/03. The sector has performed particularly well in recent years, owing to the extensive post-war reconstruction activity in the country. The GDP of the construction sector increased at an average annual rate of 19.8% during 2003–11, according to ADB figures. Sectoral growth was 8.9% in 2012/13.

Energy is derived principally from petroleum (which is imported from Iran and republics of the former USSR, notably Turkmenistan) and coal. It has been estimated that Afghanistan has some 73m. metric tons of coal reserves. Further work remains to be undertaken to assess petroleum reserves. The discovery in 2010 of an oilfield believed to contain an estimated 1,800m. barrels of oil, between Balkh and Jawzjan provinces in northern Afghanistan, represented a significant boon for the country's energy sector. In December 2011 the China National Petroleum Corporation was awarded a contract to develop three oilfields along the Amu Darya river, close to Afghanistan's border with Turkmenistan (see Foreign Affairs).

Services contributed 52.3% of GDP in 2012/13, according to official estimates. The sector employed an estimated 24.2% of the economically active population in 2004/05, according to ADB figures. According to the ADB, the GDP of the service sector increased at an average annual rate of 13.0% in 2003–11. The sector grew by 16.0% in 2012/13, according to official figures. Sectoral growth was mainly driven by the expansion of trade and financial activities.

In 2010/11 there was a surplus of an estimated US $618m. on the current account of the balance of payments. In the same year a merchandise trade deficit of $7,070m. was recorded. In 2012/13 the principal exports were carpets and handicrafts, dried and fresh fruit, and medicinal plants; the principal imports were household items and medicine, petroleum and petroleum products, food, machinery and equipment, metals, and building materials. In 2012/13, according to official estimates, the principal market for exports was Pakistan (which purchased an estimated 37.8% of the total), followed by India, Iran and Turkey. In that year the principal source of imports was Pakistan (providing an estimated 23.5% of the total), followed by United Arab Emirates, Iran, Uzbekistan, Turkmenistan, the People's Republic of China and Russia. These official statistics do not, however, include illegal trade and smuggling. According to estimates by the UN Office on Drugs and Crime (UNODC), exports of opiates from Afghanistan totalled $2,800m. in 2009; the value of opiate exports fell by 50%, to $1,400m., in 2010. This decline was due in part to falling production levels, owing to a naturally occurring plant disease, and stable cross-border prices. However, as anticipated, the value of opiate exports increased to some $2,400m. in 2011, before dropping slightly to about $1,940m. in 2012, equivalent to some 10% of the country's overall GDP. In 2012 UNODC estimated that opium production in Afghanistan accounted for about 64% of the global supply.

In the financial year ending 20 March 2013 there was a projected budgetary deficit of 66,800m. afghanis, which was expected to be covered by financial assistance. In 2012/13, according to budget projections, donor grants and loans totalled a projected 76,100m. afghanis and development assistance grants and loans totalled a projected 42,800m. afghanis. According to the ADB, the fiscal deficit of the central Government was equivalent to 1.8% of GDP in 2010/11, compared with 4.4% in 2007/08. Afghanistan's total external debt was US $2,623m. at the end of 2011, of which $2,023m. was public and publicly guaranteed debt. In 2009 the cost of debt-servicing was equivalent to 1.1% of earnings from the exports of goods, services and income. According to the ADB, the annual rate of inflation averaged 8.5% in 2004–12. Consumer prices in Afghanistan rose by 13.7% in 2011 and by 8.4% in 2012.

Following the US-led military intervention and the subsequent international reconstruction programme, from 2003 Afghanistan frequently recorded high levels of economic growth, with annual growth in GDP recorded at more than 10% on several occasions during 2003–12. However, growth has been volatile and heavily dependent on external aid and expenditure associated with the international military presence. Moreover, the economy was growing from a very low base. In particular, strong growth has been recorded in the services sector (including extensive development of telecommunications and transport services) and in construction during this period. Improvements in the domestic banking system have facilitated an increase in the levels of remittances from Afghans working abroad; according to one UN report, remittances totalled an estimated US $2,485m. in 2006. The opening in December 2011 of Afghanistan's first major rail link, between Mazar-i-Sharif and the Afghan–Uzbek border, constituted the initial phase of a project intended to link Afghanistan to the rail networks of its neighbouring countries. Further rail projects are planned and it is hoped that Afghanistan will eventually become an important regional trade and transportation hub. The mining sector has also been recognized as a potential major source of export revenue and economic growth, although foreign investment in the sector has been hindered by concerns over security and an inadequate regulatory framework. However, at early 2014 several serious risks to the economy remained. A high proportion of economic activity involved informal undertakings, including the illegal trade in arms and poppy cultivation, which greatly hampered the authorities' ability to regulate the economy and collect tax revenues. Unemployment (standing at around 40%) and endemic government corruption remained obstacles to economic stability. Moreover, following the transition of security responsibilities to the Afghan security forces and the concomitant withdrawal from Afghanistan of the international military presence by the end of 2014, the Afghan Government would have to assume the financial burden of activities previously funded by donors, including a greater proportion of national security spending. At a major donor conference held in Tokyo, Japan, in July 2012, countries including the USA, Japan, Germany and the United Kingdom promised to provide funds amounting to $16,000m. for the following four years, provided that the Afghan Government met a series of conditions concerning governance, corruption and human rights. Meanwhile, in November 2011 the IMF approved funding of $133.6m. under its Extended Credit Facility (ECF) to support Afghanistan's economic programme during 2011–14. The primary objectives of the ECF were: safeguarding the fragile financial sector; improving economic governance; and increasing domestic revenue collection. However, in October 2013 the World Bank reported that urgent measures, including the introduction of a planned value-added tax, were required to improve revenue collection, which had declined to 48,000m. afghanis during the first half of 2013, down from

54,000m. afghanis in the corresponding period of 2012. Revenues were expected to remain poor, at around 10% of GDP, during 2013–14. The ADB projected GDP growth of 3.7% for 2013, representing a significant decline from 2012, in part owing to increased uncertainty amid the ongoing security transition. Growth was forecast to increase to 5.3% in 2014, provided that ongoing political and security uncertainties were successfully resolved following the presidential election scheduled for April 2014 and the conclusion of a bilateral security agreement with the USA (see Contemporary Political History).

PUBLIC HOLIDAYS

The Afghan year 1393 runs from 21 March 2014 to 20 March 2015, and the year 1394 runs from 21 March 2015 to 19 March 2016.

2015: 2 January* (Roze-Maulud, Birth of Prophet Muhammad), 15 February (Liberation Day, commemoration of *mujahidin* struggle against Soviet occupation and withdrawal of Soviet troops in 1989), 21 March (Nauroz: New Year's Day, Iranian calendar), 28 April (Victory Day, commemoration of *mujahidin* victory over the communist regime in 1992), 1 May (Workers' Day), 17 June* (first day of Ramadan), 17 July* (Id al-Fitr, end of Ramadan), 19 August (Jeshen, Independence Day), 23 September* (Id al-Adha, Feast of the Sacrifice), 23 October* (Ashura, Martyrdom of Imam Husayn), 23 December* (Roze-Maulud, Birth of Prophet Muhammad).

* These holidays are dependent on the Islamic lunar calendar and may vary by one or two days from the dates given.

Statistical Survey

Sources (unless otherwise stated): Central Statistics Authority, Block 4, Microrayon, Kabul; tel. (93) 24883; Central Statistics Office, Ansari Wat, Kabul; e-mail info@cso.gov.af; internet www.cso.gov.af.

Area and Population

AREA, POPULATION AND DENSITY

Area (sq km)	652,864*
Population (census results)	
23 June 1979†	
Males	6,712,377
Females	6,338,981
Total	13,051,358
Population (official estimates of annual averages, year ending 20 March)‡	
2011/12	24,987,700
2012/13	25,500,100
2013/14§	26,023,100
Density (per sq km) at 2013/14	39.9

* 252,072 sq miles.

† Figures exclude nomadic population, estimated to total 2,500,000. The census data also exclude an adjustment for underenumeration, estimated to have been 5% for the urban population and 10% for the rural population.

‡ Figures are rounded to the nearest 100 persons and take no account of the nomadic population (estimated at 1.5m. in 2002) or emigration by refugees (at the end of December 2012 UNHCR estimated that the total Afghan refugee and 'refugee-like' population numbered 2.6m., of whom 1.6m. were located in Pakistan and 800,000 in Iran).

§ Males 13,312,400, females 12,710,700.

Mid-2014 (UN estimate): Total population 31,280,518 (Source: UN, *World Population Prospects: The 2012 Revision*).

POPULATION BY AGE AND SEX

(UN estimates at mid-2014)

	Males	Females	Total
0–14	7,329,881	7,000,093	14,329,974
15–64	8,189,876	8,009,052	16,198,928
65 and over	337,941	413,675	751,616
Total	15,857,698	15,422,820	31,280,518

Source: UN, *World Population Prospects: The 2012 Revision*.

PROVINCES

(year ending 20 March 2014, annual averages, official estimates of settled population)

	Area (sq km)	Population ('000)	Density (per sq km)	Capital
Kabul	4,524	4,086.5	903.3	Kabul
Kapisa	1,908	426.8	223.7	Mahmud-e-Iraqi
Parvan (Parwan)	5,715	642.3	112.4	Charikar
Wardak	10,348	577.1	55.8	Maidanshahr
Loghar (Logar)	4,568	379.4	83.1	Pul-i-Alam
Ghazni	22,461	1,188.6	52.9	Ghazni
Paktika	19,516	420.7	21.6	Sharan
Paktia (Paktya)	5,583	534.0	95.6	Gardez
Khost	4,235	556.0	131.3	Khost
Nangarhar	7,641	1,462.6	191.4	Jalalabad
Kunar (Kunarha)	4,926	436.0	88.5	Asadabad
Laghman	3,978	431.2	108.4	Mehter Lam
Nuristan (Nooristan)	9,267	143.2	15.5	Nuristan
Badakhshan	44,836	919.9	20.5	Faizabad
Takhar	12,458	950.1	76.3	Taloqan
Baghlan	18,255	879.0	48.2	Pul-e-Khomri
Kunduz	8,081	972.2	120.3	Kunduz
Samangan	13,438	375.1	27.9	Aybak
Balkh	16,186	1,271.3	78.5	Mazar-i-Sharif
Jawzjan (Juzjan)	11,292	521.4	46.2	Shiberghan
Sar-e Pol (Sar-e-Pul)	16,386	541.0	33.0	Sar-e Pol
Faryab	20,798	964.6	46.4	Maymana
Badghis	20,794	479.8	23.1	Qaleh-ye-Now
Herat	55,869	1,816.1	32.5	Herat
Farah	49,339	490.6	9.9	Farah
Nimroz	42,410	159.3	3.8	Zaranj
Helmand	58,305	894.2	15.3	Lashkar Gah
Qandahar (Kandahar)	54,845	1,175.8	21.4	Qandahar
Zabul	17,472	294.1	16.8	Qalat
Uruzgan (Urizan)	11,474	374.1	32.6	Tarin Kowt
Ghor	36,657	668.0	18.2	Chaghcharan
Bamian (Bamyan)	18,029	432.7	24.0	Bamian
Panjshir (Panjsher)	3,772	148.6	39.4	Bazarat
Daikundi (Daykundy)	17,501	410.8	23.5	Neli
Total	652,864	26,023.1	39.9	

Note: Totals may not be equal to the sum of components, owing to rounding.

PRINCIPAL TOWNS
(year ending 20 March 2014, annual averages, official estimates of settled population)

Kabul (capital)	3,414,100	Ghazni	160,800
Qandahar	505,300	Sar-e Pol	153,400
Herat	449,600	Khost	135,900
Mazar-i-Sharif	379,300	Chaghcharan	133,900
Kunduz	311,600	Mehter Lam	128,000
Taloqan	223,100	Farah	110,400
Jalalabad	212,900	Pul-i-Alam	104,500
Pul-e-Khomri	207,600	Aybak	102,400
Charikar	174,200	Lashkar Gah	102,000
Shiberghan	164,900	Tarin Kowt	101,500

Note: Figures are rounded to nearest 100 persons.

BIRTHS AND DEATHS
(annual averages, UN estimates)

	1995–2000	2000–05	2005–10
Birth rate (per 1,000)	51.1	47.9	41.7
Death rate (per 1,000)	13.1	11.5	9.6

Source: UN, *World Population Prospects: The 2012 Revision*.

Life expectancy (years at birth): 60.1 (males 58.8; females 61.4) in 2011 (Source: World Bank, World Development Indicators database).

ECONOMICALLY ACTIVE POPULATION*
(ISIC major divisions, '000 persons aged 15–59 years, year ending 20 March, estimates)

	2000/01	2001/02	2002/03
Agriculture, hunting, forestry and fishing	4,986.1	5,082.6	5,181.4
Mining, quarrying, manufacturing and utilities	348.6	355.3	362.2
Construction	94.9	96.7	98.6
Wholesale and retail trade	490.4	499.9	509.6
Transport, storage and communications	163.1	166.3	169.5
Other services	1,083.6	1,104.5	1,126.0
Total	7,166.6	7,305.4	7,447.3

* Figures refer to settled population only.

2004/05 (year ending 20 March, '000 persons): Agriculture 5,534; Industry 492; Services 1,203; Others 725; *Total employed* 7,954; Unemployed and unclassified 277; *Total labour force* 8,231 (Source: Asian Development Bank).

2012/13 (year ending 20 March, official estimates): Government employees 253,339; Contract workers 128,737.

Mid-2013 ('000 persons, FAO estimates): Agriculture, etc. 6,601; Total labour force 11,269 (Source: FAO).

Health and Welfare

KEY INDICATORS

Total fertility rate (children per woman, 2011)	6.2
Under-5 mortality rate (per 1,000 live births, 2011)	101
HIV/AIDS (% of persons aged 15–49, 2012)	<0.1
Physicians (per 1,000 head, 2005)	0.2
Hospital beds (per 1,000 head, 2010)	0.4
Health expenditure (2010): US $ per head (PPP)	52
Health expenditure (2010): % of GDP	10.4
Health expenditure (2010): public (% of total)	22.5
Total carbon dioxide emissions ('000 metric tons, 2010)	8,236.1
Carbon dioxide emissions per head (metric tons, 2010)	0.3
Access to water (% of persons, 2011)	61
Access to sanitation (% of persons, 2011)	28
Human Development Index (2012): ranking	175
Human Development Index (2012): value	0.374

For sources and definitions, see explanatory note on p. vi.

Agriculture

PRINCIPAL CROPS
('000 metric tons)

	2010	2011	2012
Wheat	4,532	3,388	5,050
Rice, paddy	672	672	746
Barley	437	306	336
Maize	301	300	322*
Millet	15	15*	15*
Potatoes	246	205	235†
Sesame seed*	32	32	32
Seed cotton	33	33	35†
Watermelons†	282	301	n.a.
Cantaloupes and other melons†	26	28	n.a.
Grapes	397*	411†	n.a.
Sugar cane	92	92	100†
Plums and sloes†	27	28	n.a.
Apricots†	46	56	n.a.

* Unofficial figure(s).
† FAO estimate(s).

Aggregate production ('000 metric tons, may include official, semi-official or estimated data): Total cereals 5,957 in 2010, 4,681 in 2011, 6,469 in 2012; Total roots and tubers 246 in 2010, 205 in 2011, 235 in 2012; Total pulses 53 in 2010, 67 in 2011, 50 in 2012; Total vegetables (incl. melons) 968 in 2010, 935 in 2011, n.a. in 2012; Total fruits (excl. melons) 746 in 2010, 774 in 2011, n.a. in 2012.

Source: FAO.

LIVESTOCK
('000 head)

	2010	2011	2012
Horses	197	181	178
Asses	1,405	1,466	1,423
Mules	24	25	24
Cattle	5,673	5,524	5,244
Camels	191	172	174
Sheep	13,286	14,262	13,820
Goats	6,789	7,635	7,311
Chickens	12,188	13,378	13,212

Source: FAO.

LIVESTOCK PRODUCTS
('000 metric tons)

	2010	2011	2012
Cattle meat	131	138	139
Sheep meat	113	115	111
Goat meat*	44	46	44
Chicken meat*	28	26	13
Cows' milk	1,401	1,403	1,508
Sheep's milk	200	212	211
Goats' milk	112	120	118
Hen eggs	16	17	18*
Wool, greasy*	16	17	18

* FAO estimate(s).

Source: FAO.

Forestry

ROUNDWOOD REMOVALS
('000 cubic metres, excl. bark, FAO estimates)

	2010	2011	2012
Sawlogs, veneer logs and logs for sleepers*	856	856	856
Other industrial wood†	904	904	904
Fuel wood	1,641	1,655	1,694
Total	3,401	3,415	3,454

* Assumed to be unchanged from 1976.
† Assumed to be unchanged from 1999.

Source: FAO.

SAWNWOOD PRODUCTION
('000 cubic metres, incl. railway sleepers, FAO estimates)

	1974	1975	1976
Coniferous (softwood)	360	310	380
Broadleaved (hardwood)	50	20	20
Total	410	330	400

1977–2012: Annual production as in 1976 (FAO estimates).

Source: FAO.

Fishing

(metric tons, live weight, FAO estimates)

	2002	2003	2004
Total catch (freshwater fishes)	900	900	1,000

2005–11: Catch assumed to be unchanged from 2004 (FAO estimates).

Source: FAO.

Mining

('000 metric tons unless otherwise indicated)

	2009	2010	2011*
Hard coal	500	725	750
Natural gas (million cu m)†	142	142	145
Salt (unrefined)	180	186	190
Gypsum (crude)	46	63	62

* Estimated production.
† Figures refer to gross output. Estimated marketed production was 140m. cu m per year in 2009–10 and 142m. cu m in 2011.

Source: US Geological Survey.

2011/12 (year ending 20 March, '000 metric tons, unless otherwise indicated): Coal 1,479.6; Natural gas (million cu m) 161.4; Salt 146.7; Marble 37.1.

2012/13 (year ending 20 March, '000 metric tons, unless otherwise indicated): Coal 1,239.9; Natural gas (million cu m) 160.3; Salt 145.3; Marble 55.5.

Industry

SELECTED PRODUCTS
(private sector only, year ending 20 March, '000 metric tons, unless otherwise indicated)

	2010/11	2011/12	2012/13
Bakery products	5.0	5.0	5.0
Confectionary	1.2	1.2	1.2
Soft drinks (million litres)	44	46	50
Vegetable oil	9.7	9.7	9.7
Ice	150	149	147
Cotton	1.7	1.6	n.a.
Woven woollen fabrics (million sq metres)	80	82	75
Metal profiles	9.1	9.1	9.0
Plastic footwear—incl. sandals (million pairs)	29.0	29.4	30.0
Cement*	35.6	35.7	70.8
Electric energy (million kWh)*	936.1	846.6	882.9

* Private and public sector estimates.

Finance

CURRENCY AND EXCHANGE RATES

Monetary Units:
100 puls (puli) = 2 krans = 1 afghani (Af).

Sterling, Dollar and Euro Equivalents (31 October 2013):
£1 sterling = 91.934 afghanis;
US $1 = 57.230 afghanis;
€1 = 78.067 afghanis;
1,000 afghanis = £10.88 = $17.47 = €12.81.

Average Exchange Rate (afghanis per US $):
2010 46.452
2011 46.747
2012 50.921

Note: The foregoing information refers to the official exchange rate.

OPERATING BUDGET
(million afghanis, year ending 20 March)

Revenue*	2010/11	2011/12†	2012/13‡
Tax revenue	66,400	71,800	88,600
Taxes on income, profits and capital gains	19,400	21,300	26,700
Taxes on international trade and transactions	27,700	30,100	35,600
Taxes on goods and services	16,300	17,100	22,100
Other taxes	3,000	3,200	4,200
Non-tax revenue	14,000	25,600	24,800
Total	80,400	97,300	113,500

Expenditure§	2010/11	2011/12†	2012/13‡
Wages and salaries	86,500	111,800	136,500
Purchase of goods and services	17,200	25,900	24,600
Transfers and subsidies	1,700	2,000	5,300
Pensions	3,400	7,100	9,500
Capital expenditure	1,600	2,700	3,400
Interest	100	800	900
Total	110,500	150,300	180,300

* Excluding donor assistance grants and loans (million afghanis): 54,500 in 2010/11; 70,300 in 2011/12 (estimate); 76,100 in 2012/13 (budget projection), and development assistance grants and loans: 25,600 in 2010/11; 30,800 in 2011/12 (estimate); 42,800 in 2012/13 (budget projection).
† Estimates.
‡ Budget projections.
§ Excluding development spending (million afghanis): 43,600 in 2010/11; 53,400 in 2011/12 (estimate); 65,900 in 2012/13 (budget projection).

Source: IMF, *Islamic Republic of Afghanistan: First Review Under the Extended Credit Facility Arrangement, Request for Waiver of Nonobservance of a Performance Criterion, Modification of Performance Criteria, and Rephasing of Disbursements Staff Report; Staff Supplement; Staff Statement; Press Release on the Executive Board Discussion; and Statement by the Executive Director for the Islamic Republic of Afghanistan* (August 2012).

INTERNATIONAL RESERVES
(US $ million at 31 December)

	2010	2011	2012
Gold (national valuation)	972	1,130	1,160
IMF special drawing rights	198	197	194
Foreign exchange	3,977	5,071	5,788
Total	5,147	6,398	7,142

Source: IMF, *International Financial Statistics*.

MONEY SUPPLY
(million afghanis at 31 December)

	2010	2011	2012
Currency outside depository corporations	116,952.9	141,245.3	142,761.1
Transferable deposits	123,304.3	149,476.6	176,403.0
Other deposits	16,469.5	20,711.2	19,675.5
Broad money	256,726.8	311,433.1	338,839.6

Source: IMF, *International Financial Statistics*.

COST OF LIVING
(Consumer Price Index; base: March 2004 = 100)

	2010	2011	2012
Food	155.7	177.4	191.2
Non-food	157.5	178.5	195.1
All items	156.4	177.8	192.7

Source: Asian Development Bank.

NATIONAL ACCOUNTS
(million afghanis at current prices, year ending 20 March)

Expenditure on the Gross Domestic Product

	2010/11	2011/12	2012/13*
Public consumption expenditure	104,639	109,884	131,176
Private consumption expenditure	727,195	819,180	913,196
Gross fixed capital investment	130,424	141,792	178,448
Total domestic expenditures	962,258	1,070,856	1,222,820
Exports of goods and services	73,164	52,298	58,551
Less Imports of goods and services	328,043	378,443	415,423
Statistical discrepancy	39,480	151,452	219,818
Gross domestic product (GDP) in market prices	746,859	896,163	1,085,766
GDP at constant 2002/03 prices	386,929	420,517	466,313

Gross Domestic Product by Economic Activity

	2010/11	2011/12	2012/13*
Agriculture, hunting, forestry and fishing	207,301	241,743	275,819
Mining and quarrying	4,473	10,396	10,066
Manufacturing	90,943	117,171	130,860
Electricity, gas and water	640	605	654
Construction	57,552	65,199	81,271
Trade, restaurants and hotels	59,679	71,640	95,296
Transport, storage and communications	145,913	174,419	242,580
Finance, insurance, real estate and business	16,259	9,719	10,592
Government services	84,473	111,704	132,607
Community, social and personal services	5,824	6,871	8,282
Ownership of dwellings	27,749	31,852	36,264
Other services	18,753	22,366	20,454
Sub-total	719,559	863,686	1,044,746
Taxes on imports	27,300	32,477	41,020
GDP at market prices	746,859	896,163	1,085,766

* Estimates.

BALANCE OF PAYMENTS
(US $ million, year ending 20 March)

	2008/09	2009/10	2010/11*
Exports of goods†	2,465	2,517	2,827
Imports of goods	–8,945	–8,872	–9,897
Trade balance	–6,480	–6,354	–7,070
Services and other income (net)	–240	–370	–403
Balance on goods, services and income	–6,720	–6,724	–7,473
Current transfers (net)	6,812	6,377	8,091
Current balance	92	–347	618
Capital and financial account (net)	338	–287	351
Net errors and omissions	541	190	–93
Overall balance	972	–445	876

* Preliminary.

† Excludes opium exports and flows associated with US Army and International Security Assistance Force activities.

Source: IMF, *Islamic Republic of Afghanistan: First Review Under the Extended Credit Facility Arrangement, Request for Waiver of Nonobservance of a Performance Criterion, Modification of Performance Criteria, and Rephasing of Disbursements Staff Report; Staff Supplement; Staff Statement; Press Release on the Executive Board Discussion; and Statement by the Executive Director for the Islamic Republic of Afghanistan* (August 2012).

OFFICIAL DEVELOPMENT ASSISTANCE
(disbursements, year ending 20 March, US $ million)

	2010/11	2011/12	2012/13
Bilateral	10,081	5,515	5,060
Multilateral	819	496	1,200
Total received	10,900	6,011	6,260

External Trade

PRINCIPAL COMMODITIES
(US $ million, year ending 20 March)

Imports c.i.f.	2010/11	2011/12	2012/13
Machinery and equipment	1,235	961	1,327
Petroleum and petroleum products	999	2,103	1,788
Metals	566	597	998
Chemical materials	57	53	135
Building material	270	247	484
Food	722	866	1,491
Fabrics, clothing and footwear	205	156	310
Household items and medicine	1,003	1,235	2,221
Total (incl. others)	5,154	6,390	8,932

Exports f.o.b.*	2010/11	2011/12	2012/13
Fresh fruits	28	9	13
Dried fruit	106	117	112
Medicinal plants	39	45	25
Animal skins	15	16	18
Carpets and handicrafts	156	170	210
Total (incl. others)	388	376	415

* Officially recorded transactions only.

PRINCIPAL TRADING PARTNERS
(US $ million, year ending 20 March)

Imports	2010/11	2011/12	2012/13
China, People's Republic	704	577	549
Germany	422	244	304
India	113	104	212
Iran	386	582	1,055
Japan	494	412	115
Kazakhstan	208	333	190
Korea, Republic	57	99	51
Malaysia	53	60	114
Pakistan	598	878	2,097
Russia	181	804	475
Saudi Arabia	54	51	15
Tajikistan	98	227	258
Turkey	109	138	203
Turkmenistan	117	353	634
United Arab Emirates	106	200	1,193
USA	78	91	126
Uzbekistan	1,088	732	709
Total (incl. others)	5,154	6,390	8,932

Exports*	2010/11	2011/12	2012/13
China, People's Republic	12	6	11
Egypt	4	1	1
Finland	3	6	6
India	65	70	92
Iran	32	20	29
Iraq	9	15	17
Netherlands	9	1	1
Pakistan	151	181	157
Russia	30	33	20
Tajikistan	7	5	12
Turkey	35	11	29
Turkmenistan	9	4	3
United Arab Emirates	6	3	18
USA	4	4	4
Total (incl. others)	388	376	415

* Officially recorded transactions only.

Transport

ROAD TRAFFIC
(year ending 20 March, motor vehicles in use)

	2010/11	2011/12	2012/13
Passenger cars	691,573	745,875	1,109,146
Lorries	184,799	210,601	288,936
Buses	74,834	77,946	95,027
Motorcycles	141,833	163,152	218,708
Rickshaws	10,647	11,635	12,646
Foreign vehicles	28,602	29,123	37,894

CIVIL AVIATION
(year ending 20 March, '000)

	2010/11	2011/12	2012/13
Kilometres flown	12,074	14,669	12,252
Passengers carried	1,159	1,081	1,132
Freight ton-km	21,561	16,222	11,212

Tourism

	1996	1997	1998
Tourist arrivals ('000)	4	4	4
Tourism receipts (US $ million)	1	1	1

Tourism receipts (US $ million, excl. passenger transport): 53 in 2010.

Source: World Tourism Organization.

Communications Media

	2010	2011	2012
Telephones ('000 main lines in use)	16.6	13.5	13.5
Mobile cellular telephones ('000 subscribers)	13,000.0	17,558.3	18,000.0
Broadband subscribers	1,500	n.a.	n.a.

Internet subscribers: 2,000 in 2009.

Sources: International Telecommunication Union.

Education

(2012/13, government schools only)

	Institutions	Teachers	Pupils
Pre-primary	348	2,422	26,326
Primary	6,411	52,874	6,118,138
Secondary*	8,064	131,168	2,525,806
Vocational schools	134	840	13,084
Higher	31	3,555	101,315

* Figures refer to general secondary education only, excluding vocational education and teacher training.

Sources: Ministries of Education, of Higher Education and of Labour, Social Affairs, Martyrs and the Disabled, Kabul, and UNICEF.

Pupil-teacher ratio (primary education, UNESCO estimate): 45.3 in 2010/11 (Source: UNESCO Institute for Statistics).

Adult literacy rate (UNESCO estimates): 28.0% (males 43.1%; females 12.6%) in 2000 (Source: UNESCO Institute for Statistics).

Directory

The Government

HEAD OF STATE

President: HAMID KARZAI (inaugurated as Chairman of Interim Authority 22 December 2001; elected as President of Transitional Authority by Loya Jirga 13 June 2002 and as President of the Islamic Republic of Afghanistan by direct popular vote 9 October 2004; sworn in as the country's President for a second term on 19 November 2009).

Vice-Presidents: KARIM KHALILI, YUNUS QANOONI.

CABINET
(April 2014)

Minister of Defence: BISMILLAH KHAN MOHAMMADI.

Minister of Foreign Affairs: ZARAR AHMAD MOQBEL OSMANI.

Minister of Finance: DR OMAR ZAKHILWAL.

Minister of Interior Affairs: MUHAMMAD UMAR DAUDZAI.

Minister of Economy: ABDUL HADI ARGHANDIWAL.

Minister of Information and Culture: DR SAYED MAKHDUM RAHEEN.

Minister of Public Works: NAJIBULLAH OZHAN.

Minister of Refugees and Repatriation: JAMAHIR ANWARI.

Minister of Border and Tribal Affairs: MUHAMMAD AKRAM KHPALWAK.

Minister of Commerce and Industries: MOHAMMAD SHAKIR KARGAR.

Minister of Mines and Petroleum: MOHAMMAD AKBAR BARAKZAI.

Minister of Agriculture, Irrigation and Livestock: Muhammad Asif Rahimi.

Minister of Justice: Habibullah Ghaleb.

Minister of Hajj and Islamic Affairs: Mohammad Yousuf Neyazi.

Minister of Labour, Social Affairs, Martyrs and the Disabled: Amina Afzali.

Minister of Education: Dr Ghulam Farooq Wardak.

Minister of Rural Rehabilitation and Development: Wais Ahmad Barmak.

Minister of Counter Narcotics: Din Mohammad Mobarez Rashidi.

Minister of Communications and Information Technology: Amirzai Sangin.

Minister of Public Health: Dr Suraya Dalil.

Minister of Higher Education: Obaidullah Obaid.

Minister of Urban Development Affairs: Hasan Abdullahi.

Minister of Women's Affairs: Hosna Banu Ghazanfar.

Minister of Transport and Civil Aviation: Daoud Ali Najafi.

Minister of Energy and Water: Mohammad Arif Noorzai.

MINISTRIES

Office of the President: Gul Khana Palace, Presidential Palace, Kabul; tel. (20) 2141135; e-mail aimal.faizi@arg.gov.af; internet www.president.gov.af.

Ministry of Agriculture, Irrigation and Livestock: Jamal Mena, Kart-i-Sakhi, Kabul; tel. 752034204 (mobile); e-mail info@mail.gov.af; internet www.mail.gov.af.

Ministry of Border and Tribal Affairs: Shah Mahmud Ghazi Wat, Kabul; tel. (20) 2101365; internet mob.gov.af/en.

Ministry of Commerce and Industries: Darulaman Wat, Kabul; tel. (20) 2500356; fax (20) 798013276; e-mail info@commerce.gov.af; internet moci.gov.af.

Ministry of Communications and Information Technology: 6th Floor, ICT Directorate, Mohammad Jan Khan Wat, Kabul; tel. (20) 2101113; fax (20) 2101708; e-mail jelani.waziri@mcit.gov.af; internet www.mcit.gov.af.

Ministry of Counter Narcotics: Kabul-Jalalabad Rd, Banaiey, Macroyan, Kabul; tel. 798242837 (mobile); e-mail spokesman@mcn.gov.af; internet www.mcn.gov.af.

Ministry of Defence: Shash Darak, Kabul; tel. (20) 2100451; fax (20) 2104172; internet www.mod.gov.af.

Ministry of Economy: Malik Asghar Sq., Kabul; tel. (20) 2100394; internet www.moec.gov.af.

Ministry of Education: Mohammad Jan Khan Wat, Kabul; tel. 798801066 (mobile); e-mail attaullah.wahidyar@moe.gov.af; internet www.moe.gov.af.

Ministry of Energy and Water: Darulaman Wat, Kabul; tel. 752004813 (mobile); e-mail mirzad.mir2007@gmail.com; internet mew.gov.af.

Ministry of Finance: Pashtunistan Wat, Kabul; tel. 752004199 (mobile); fax (20) 2103280; e-mail info@mof.gov.af; internet www.mof.gov.af.

Ministry of Foreign Affairs: Malek Asghar St, Kabul; tel. (20) 2100372; fax (20) 2100360; e-mail contact@mfa.gov.af; internet mfa.gov.af.

Ministry of Hajj and Islamic Affairs: nr District 10, Shir Pur, Shar-i-Nau, Kabul; tel. (20) 2201338; e-mail bakhshi1@hotmail.com; internet mohia.gov.af.

Ministry of Higher Education: Karte Char, Kabul; tel. (20) 2500363; e-mail info@mohe.gov.af; internet www.mohe.gov.af.

Ministry of Information and Culture: Mohammad Jan Khan Wat, Kabul; tel. (20) 2101301; fax (20) 2290088; e-mail znawabi2011@moic.gov.af; internet moic.gov.af.

Ministry of Interior Affairs: Shar-i-Nau, Kabul; tel. 799401540 (mobile); e-mail moiafghanistan@gmail.com; internet www.moi.gov.af.

Ministry of Justice: Pashtunistan Wat, Kabul; tel. (20) 2100325; e-mail info@moj.gov.af; internet www.moj.gov.af.

Ministry of Labour, Social Affairs, Martyrs and the Disabled: opp. First Makroryan Market, Kabul; tel. (20) 2300369; e-mail info@molsamd.gov.af; internet www.molsamd.gov.af.

Ministry of Mines and Petroleum: Pashtunistan Wat, Kabul; tel. (20) 2100309; e-mail info@mom.gov.af; internet www.mom.gov.af.

Ministry of Public Health: Wazir Akbar Khan, Sub-district 9, Kabul; tel. (20) 2301377; e-mail webmaster@moph.gov.af; internet www.moph.gov.af.

Ministry of Public Works: Microrayon 1, Kabul; tel. (20) 2301363; fax (20) 2301362; internet www.mopws.gov.af.

Ministry of Refugees and Repatriation: Jungaluk, off Darulaman Wat, Kabul; e-mail afgmorr@afgmorr.com; internet morr.gov.af.

Ministry of Rural Rehabilitation and Development: Shah Mahmud Ghazi Wat, Kabul; tel. 700280870 (mobile); e-mail daud.naemi@mrrd.gov.af; internet www.mrrd.gov.af.

Ministry of Transport and Civil Aviation: Ansari Wat, Kabul; tel. (20) 2103064; e-mail arasikh@motca.gov.af; internet motca.gov.af.

Ministry of Urban Development Affairs: Microrayon 3, Kabul; tel. 799682833 (mobile); e-mail info@moud.gov.af; internet www.muda.gov.af.

Ministry of Women's Affairs: beside Cinema Zainab, Shar-i-Nau, Kabul; tel. and fax (20) 2201378; fax 752004541; e-mail spokesman.mowa@gmail.com; internet www.mowa.gov.af.

President

Presidential Election (first round), 5 April 2014—preliminary results

Candidates	Votes	% of valid votes
Dr Abdullah Abdullah	2,973,706	44.9
Ashraf Ghani Ahmadzai	2,082,417	31.5
Zalmai Rassoul	759,540	11.5
Abdul Rab Rassoul Sayyaf	468,340	7.1
Qutbuddin Hilal	180,859	2.7
Shafiq Gul Agha Sherzai	106,673	1.6
Others	46,131	0.7
Invalid votes	275,150	—
Total	6,892,816	100.0

Note: The above results were subject to an audit by the Electoral Complaints Commission. In the event that no candidate secured more than 50% of the vote, a second round of voting, involving the two highest-polling candidates, was scheduled to be held on 28 May 2014.

Legislature

NATIONAL ASSEMBLY
(Meli Shura)

House of Elders
(Meshrano Jirga)

The Meshrano Jirga, the upper house of the Meli Shura, comprises 102 members (three times the number of provinces in Afghanistan). One-third are elected by provincial councils (for a four-year term), one-third by district councils (for a three-year term) and the remaining members are nominated by the President (for a five-year term). The Constitution requires that one-half of the members nominated by the President must be women.

Speaker: Fazal Hadi Muslimyar.

House of the People
(Wolesi Jirga)

The Wolesi Jirga, the lower house of the Meli Shura, comprises 249 directly elected members, all of whom serve a five-year term. Sixty-eight seats are reserved for women. The most recent election was held on 18 September 2010.

Speaker: Abdul Rauf Ibrahimi.

Election Commission

Independent Election Commission of Afghanistan (IEC): IEC Compound, Jalalabad Rd, Paktia Kot, POB 979, Kabul; tel. 752035203 (mobile); e-mail info@iec.org.af; internet iec.org.af; established by 2004 Constitution; assumed regulation and supervision of all election activities from 2006; appointed by the President; Chair. Muhammad Yosuf Nooristani; Chief Electoral Officer Zia ul-Haq Amarkhil.

There is, in addition, a five-member Electoral Complaints Commission (ECC—f. 2009). The ECC is an independent body that has the authority to resolve disputes or objections concerning the electoral process; its members are chosen by the President from a panel recommended by a selection committee (comprising representatives from the National Assembly, the judiciary and civil society). In its original form, the ECC included three foreign representatives nominated by the UN; however, from 2010 President Karzai rejected the inclusion of foreign commissioners.

Political Organizations

In September 2003 a new law allowing the formation of political parties was approved. In 2013 there were more than 80 parties registered with the Ministry of Justice, including the following:

Afghan Mellat (Afghan Social Democratic Party): National Bank Club, 3rd Floor, Nader Pashtoon Jadah, Kabul; tel. 70224793 (mobile); e-mail afghanmellat2@yahoo.com; f. 1966; Pres. Prof. Dr ANWAR-UL-HAQ AHADI; a breakaway faction, led by AJMAL SHAMS gained official recognition in 2007 (internet www.afghanmillat.org).

Da Afghanistan Da Solay Ghorzang Gond (Afghanistan Peace Movement): Kolola Poshta (adjacent to Dost Hotel), Kabul; tel. 799311523 (mobile); f. 1993; Leader SHAHNAWAZ TANAI.

Harakat-i Islami i Afghanistan (Islamic Movement of Afghanistan): St 4, Qala-i Fathullah, Shar-i-Nau, Kabul; tel. 799343998 (mobile); Leader SAYYED MOHAMMAD ALI JAWED.

Hizb-i Adalat-i Islami Afghanistan (Islamic Justice Party of Afghanistan): nr Aryub Cinema, Bagh-e-Bala, District 4, Kabul; tel. 799566386 (mobile); f. 2001; Leader MOHAMMAD KABIR MARZBAN.

Hizb-i Afghanistan-i Naweeen (New Afghanistan Party): 1st Rd, Khair Khana Phase One, Parwan Hotel Rd, District 11, Kabul; tel. 799342942 (mobile); f. 2005; Leader YOUNIS QANOONI.

Hizb-i Hambastagi-yi Melli-yi Jawanan-i Afghanistan (National Youth Solidarity Party of Afghanistan): House 2, St 3, Haji Yaqub Sq., towards Shaheed, Kabul; tel. 799424290 (mobile); f. 2004; Leader MOHAMMAD JAMIL KARZAI.

Hizb-i Haq wa Edalat (Right and Justice Party): Kabul; f. 2011; multi-ethnic; in mid-2012 the party was awaiting registration and was administered by a 53-mem. interim council.

Hizb-i Harakat-i-Islami Mardum-i Afghanistan (Islamic Movement Party of the People of Afghanistan): Rd 2–3, Qala-i-Fathullah, Kabul; tel. 799183484 (mobile); f. 2004; Leader Al-Hajj SAYYED HUSSAIN ANWARI.

Hizb-i Harakat-i-Melli Wahdat-i-Afghanistan (National Movement for the Unity of Afghanistan): Jamia Mosque, 6th Floor, Karte 4, District 3, Kabul; tel. 70204847 (mobile); f. 2004; Chair. MOHAMMAD NADIR ATASH.

Hizb-i Islami Afghanistan (Islamic Party of Afghanistan): Area A, Khushal Mena, Kabul; tel. 799421474 (mobile); Pashtun/Turkmen/Tajik; breakaway faction of Hizb-i Islami org., est. to participate in parliamentary politics; nature of relationship with Gulbuddin Hekmatyar's proscribed Hizb-i Islami org. is unclear; Chair. ABDUL HADI ARGHANDIWAL; Leader KHALID FAROOQI.

Hizb-i Isteqlal-i Afghanistan (Freedom Party of Afghanistan): Khair Khana, nr Al-Farooq Healthcare Clinic, Kabul; tel. 799333448 (mobile); f. 2004; Leader Dr GHULAM FAROOQ NAJRABI.

Hizb-i Jumhuri-i Khwahan-i Afghanistan (Republican Party of Afghanistan): Zainaba St, 6th Rd, Qala-i-Fathullah, Kabul; tel. 70275107 (mobile); f. 2003; supporter of presidential system of govt; Leader ADELA BAHRAM; c. 35,000 mems.

Hizb-i Junbesh-i Melli-i Islami (National Islamic Movement): St 4, Rd 15, Wazir Akbar Khan, Kabul; tel. 70511511 (mobile); f. 1992; formed mainly from troops of fmr Northern Command of the Afghan army; predominantly Uzbek/Tajik/Turkmen/Ismaili and Hazara Shi'a; Leader SAYED NOORULLAH; 65,000–150,000 supporters.

Hizb-i Kar wa Tawse'ah Afghanistan (Labour and Progress Party of Afghanistan): Karte 4, Rd 2, Kabul; tel. 799210998 (mobile); f. 1999 in Pakistan; fmrly known as the National Reconciliation Party; Leader ZULFIQAR OMID.

Hizb-i Nizat-i Azady Wa Demokrasi-ye Afghanistan (Movement for Democracy and Freedom in Afghanistan): Karte 4, adjacent to Suraya Lycee, Kabul; tel. 70281953 (mobile); f. 2004; Leader ABDUL RAQIB JAWED KOHESTANI.

Hizb-i Paiwand-e Melli-ye Afghanistan (National Solidarity Party of Afghanistan): Western Rd, Taimani Sq., Kabul; tel. 799182016 (mobile); predominantly Ismaili supporters; Leader SAYYED MANSUR NADERI.

Hizb-i Sahadat-i Mardum-i-Afghanistan (People's Welfare Party of Afghanistan): Apt 1, Block 13, Air Force Blocks, Kabul; tel. 70204847 (mobile); f. 1998; Leader MOHAMMAD ZUBAIR PAYROZ.

Hizb-i-Wahdat-i Islami Afghanistan (Islamic Unity Party of Afghanistan): opp. Hawzeh 3 Police, Karte 4, Kabul; tel. 796358868 (mobile); e-mail info@wahdat.net; internet www.wahdat.net; f. 1989; Leader MOHAMMAD KARIM KHALILI.

Hizb-i Wahdat-i Islami Mardum-i Afghanistan (People's Islamic Unity Party of Afghanistan): House 3, Mohammadia St, Tapa-i-Salaam, Karte Sakhi, Kabul; tel. 70278276 (mobile); represents Hazaras; advocate of equal rights, freedom and social justice; Leader Haji MUHAMMAD MOHAQEQ.

Hizb-i Wahdat-i Melli-i Afghanistan (National Unity Party of Afghanistan): Qaisar Market, 2nd Floor, adjacent to Gul-i-Surkh Hotel, Old Kolola Poshta Sq., Kabul; tel. 799210998 (mobile); Leader ABDUL RASHID JALILI.

Jamiat-i Islami (Islamic Society): Karte Parwan, Phase 2, Badaam Bagh, Kabul; tel. 70278950 (mobile); f. 1967; Turkmen/Uzbek/Tajik; Chair. SALAHUDDIN RABBANI (acting); Deputy Leaders AHMAD ZIA MASSOUD, KALIMULLAH NAQIBI; Pres. of the Exec. Council ATTA MUHAMMAD NUR; Chief Sec. WASIL NUR MOHMAND; c. 60,000 supporters.

Kangra-i Melli Afghanistan (National Congress Party of Afghanistan): House 207, Qala-e Mosa Pharmacy, District 10, Kabul; tel. 70290067 (mobile); e-mail mcnafghan@hotmail.com; internet mouv.national.afghan.free.fr; f. 2004; Leader ABDUL LATIF PEDRAM.

Mahaz-i-Melli-i-Islami (National Islamic Front): Malalai Wat, Interior Ministry Rd, Kabul; tel. 70204265 (mobile); Pashtun; Leader Pir SAYED AHMAD GAILANI; Dep. Leader HAMED GAILANI; c. 15,000 supporters.

Nizat-i Hambastagi Melli (National Solidarity Movement): St 6, Rd 2, Taimani, Kabul; tel. 799300045 (mobile); Chair. Pir SAYED ISHAQ GAILANI.

Nizat-i Melli-i Afghanistan (National Movement of Afghanistan): St 1, Taimani, Kabul; tel. 70277938 (mobile); f. 2002; Leader AHMAD WALI MASOUD.

Tanzim-i Dawat-i Islami (Organization for Invitation to Islam): Ansari Sq., Rd 1, District 4, Kabul; tel. 70277007 (mobile); Pashtun; fmrly Ittihad-i Islami; name changed as above 2005; Leader Prof. ABDUL RASSOUL SAYYAF.

There are, in addition, a number of influential opposition coalitions, including:

Jabhe-ye-Motahed-e-Milli (National Front of Afghanistan): internet www.jabhaemelli.com; f. 2007; informal political grouping incl. fmr mems of United Front; advocates parliamentary system of govt rather than presidential system; fmrly known as the United National Front; relaunched as above in late 2011 following the assassination of fmr Chair. Burhanuddin Rabbani; mems incl. Younis Qanooni, Gen. Abdul Rashid Dostam and Muhammad Mohaqeq; Chair. Prof. AHMAD ZIA MASOUD.

National Coalition of Afghanistan: Kabul; internet www.nca.af; f. 2010 as Omid wa Taghir (National Coalition of Hope and Change); expanded and renamed, as above, Dec. 2011; advocates transition to a fully parliamentary system of government; Leader Dr ABDULLAH ABDULLAH.

The following political organizations have been proscribed:

Hizb-i Islami Gulbuddin (Islamic Party Gulbuddin): originally est. as Hizb-i Islami in the mid-1970s to oppose the Soviet-backed communist regime; known as Hizb-i Islami Gulbuddin following a split in the org. around 1979; played a prominent role in the *mujahidin* guerrilla war against Soviet forces during 1980s, while based in North-West Frontier Province, Pakistan; engaged in violent power struggle between various *mujahidin* factions 1992–96; latterly, launched a campaign of violent opposition to the International Security Assistance Force and the Government of Hamid Karzai; has reportedly formed alliances with al-Qa'ida and the Taliban; promotes establishment of an Islamic state in accordance with Qu'ran, Sunnah and Shari'a doctrines; Leader GULBUDDIN HEKMATYAR.

Hizb-i Islami Khalis (Islamic Party Khalis): f. c. 1979, following a split in the Hizb-i Islami movt; Pashtun; Islamist; based in Nangarhar Province; est. by MAULVI MUHAMMAD YUNUS KHALIS (died 2006); Leader ANWAR UL-HAQ MUJAHID; current activities uncertain.

Taliban: emerged in 1994; Islamist fundamentalist; mainly Sunni Pashtuns; in power 1996–2001; also active in the Federally Administered Tribal Areas of Pakistan; Leader Mullah MOHAMMAD OMAR; c. 25,000 active supporters.

Diplomatic Representation

EMBASSIES IN AFGHANISTAN

Australia: Kabul; tel. 797248752 (mobile); e-mail nazer.nazir@dfat.gov.au; internet www.afghanistan.embassy.gov.au; Ambassador JONATHAN HUGH PHILIP; (the Australian mission operates from a number of locations that, due to security reasons, are not publicly disclosed).

Belgium: House 45–47, St 3, Chahar Rahi Haji Yaqoob, Shar-i-Nau, Kabul; tel. 700200135 (mobile); e-mail kabul@diplobel.fed.be; internet diplomatie.belgium.be/afghanistan; Ambassador ARNOUT PAUWELS.

Bulgaria: St 15, Wazir Akbar Khan, Kabul; tel. (20) 2311746; fax (20) 202311745; e-mail embassy.kabul@mfa.bg; internet www.mfa .bg/embassies/afghanistan; Ambassador NIKOLAY YANKOV.

Canada: House 256, St 15, Wazir Akbar Khan, POB 2052, Kabul; tel. 701108800 (mobile); fax 701108805 (mobile); e-mail kabul@ international.gc.ca; internet www.afghanistan.gc.ca/canada -afghanistan; Ambassador DEBORAH LYONS.

China, People's Republic: Sardar Shah Mahmoud Ghazi Wat, Kabul; tel. (20) 2102548; fax (20) 2102728; e-mail chinaemb_af@mfa .gov.cn; internet af.china-embassy.org; Ambassador DENG XIJUN.

Czech Republic: House 337, Rd 10, Wazir Akbar Khan, Kabul; tel. 798417418 (mobile); e-mail kabul@embassy.mzv.cz; internet www .mzv.cz/kabul; Ambassador MIROSLAV KOSEK.

Denmark: House 35–36, Rd 13, Lane 1, Wazir Akbar Khan, Kabul; tel. 796888100 (mobile); fax (20) 2302838; e-mail kblamb@um.dk; internet www.ambkabul.um.dk; Ambassador HENRIK BRAMSEN HAHN.

Egypt: House 48, Main Rd, Wazir Akbar Khan, Kabul; tel. 752021901 (mobile); fax 2104064; e-mail egypt_kabul@mfa.gov.eg; internet www.mfa.gov.eg/English/Embassies/Egyptian_Embassy _Kabul/Pages/default.aspx; Ambassador MAGED ABDUL REHMAN.

Finland: House 728, St 10, Lane 1, Wazir Akbar Khan, Kabul; tel. 793322924 (mobile); e-mail sanomat.kab@formin.fi; internet www .finland.org.af; Ambassador ARI MÄKI.

France: Cherpour Ave, Shar-i-Nau, POB 62, Kabul; tel. (20) 2105295; e-mail consul@ambafrance-af.org; internet www .ambafrance-af.org; Ambassador JEAN-MICHEL MARLAUD.

Germany: Zanbaq Sq., Wazir Akbar Khan, Mena 6, POB 83, Kabul; tel. (20) 2101512; fax (4930) 50007518 (Germany); e-mail info@kabul .diplo.de; internet www.kabul.diplo.de; Ambassador MARTIN JAEGER.

Hungary: c/o Embassy of the Federal Republic of Germany, Zanbaq Sq., Wazir Akbar Khan, Mena 6, POB 83, Kabul; tel. 797035375 (mobile); e-mail huembkbl@gmail.com; Ambassador ANTAL DRAGOS.

India: Malalai Wat, Shar-i-Nau, Kabul; tel. (20) 2200185; fax 763095561 (mobile); e-mail embassy@indembassy-kabul.com; internet meakabul.nic.in; Ambassador AMAR SINHA.

Indonesia: Interior Ministry St, Shar-i-Nau, POB 532, Kabul; tel. (20) 2201066; fax (20) 2201735; e-mail kbrikabul@neda.af; internet www.kemlu.go.id/kabul/Pages/default.aspx; Ambassador ANSHORY TADJUDIN.

Iran: Charahi Shir Pur, Kabul; tel. (20) 2101391; fax (20) 2101397; e-mail kabul@mfa.gov.ir; internet kabul.mfa.gov.ir; Ambassador MOHAMMAD REZA BAHRAMI.

Italy: Great Masoud Rd, Wazir Akbar Khan, Kabul; tel. and fax (20) 2103144; fax 700288942 (mobile); e-mail ambasciata.kabul@esteri .it; internet www.ambkabul.esteri.it; Ambassador LUCIANO PEZZOTTI.

Japan: House 83, St 15, Wazir Akbar Khan, Kabul; tel. 799363827 (mobile); fax 761218272 (mobile); e-mail plt1@eoj-af.org; internet www.afg.emb-japan.go.jp; Ambassador HIROSHI TAKAHASHI.

Kazakhstan: House 11, 1st Alley, Indira Gandhi St, Wazir Akbar Khan, Kabul; tel. (20) 70284296; e-mail kabul@mfa.kz; Ambassador OMIRTAY BITIMOV.

Korea, Republic: House 34, St 10, Wazir Akbar Khan, Kabul; tel. (20) 2102481; fax (20) 2102725; e-mail kabul@mofat.go.kr; internet afg.mofat.go.kr; Ambassador CHA YOUNG-CHEOL.

Netherlands: Malalai Wat, Interior Ministry Rd, Shar-i-Nau, Kabul; tel. 700286641 (mobile); e-mail kab@minbuza.nl; internet afghanistan.nlembassy.org/; Ambassador HAN P. M PETERS.

New Zealand: St 15 Roundabout, Wazir Akbar Khan, Kabul; tel. 700102000 (mobile); e-mail mea@mfat.govt.nz; Ambassador JOHN MATAIRA (designate).

Norway: St 15, Lane 4, Wazir Akbar Khan, Kabul; tel. 701105000 (mobile); fax 701105090 (mobile); e-mail emb.kabul@mfa.no; internet www.afghanistan.norway.info; Ambassador NILS HAUGSTVEIT.

Pakistan: Karte Parwan, Kabul; tel. (20) 2202745; fax (20) 2202871; e-mail parepkabul@yahoo.com; internet www.mofa.gov.pk/ afghanistan; Ambassador SYED ABRAR HUSSAIN.

Poland: Kart-e She, 10 Maghzan St, Kabul; tel. 796160392 (mobile); e-mail kabul.amb.sekretariat@msz.gov.pl; internet kabul.msz.gov .pl/en/; Ambassador PIOTR ŁUKASIEWICZ.

Russia: Darulaman Rd, Ayub Khan Mena, Kabul; tel. (20) 2500255; fax 762743497 (mobile); e-mail rusembafg@multinet.af; internet www.afghanistan.mid.ru/en; Ambassador ANDREI AVETISYAN.

Saudi Arabia: Shah Darak, Kabul; tel. (20) 2102064; fax (20) 2102063; e-mail ksa_kemb@hotmail.com; Ambassador MUSFER BIN ABDULRAHMAN AL-GHASEB.

Spain: Main St, Lane 3, Shir Pur, Kabul; tel. (20) 2310406; e-mail emb.kabul@maec.es; internet www.maec.es/subwebs/embajadas/ kabul; Ambassador JUAN JOSÉ RUBIO DE URQUÍA.

Sweden: MoI St, Opp. the MoI, Shar-i-Nau, Kabul; tel. (20) 2104912; fax (20) 2104913; e-mail ambassaden.kabul@gov.se; internet www .swedenabroad.com/kabul; Ambassador PETER SEMNEBY.

Tajikistan: House 41, St 15, Wazir Akbar Khan, Kabul; tel. (20) 2101080; fax (20) 2300392; e-mail kabultj@tojikistan.com; Ambassador IMOMOV SHAROFIDDIN.

Turkey: House 134, 13 Shah Mahmoud Ghazi Khan St, Kabul; tel. (20) 2101581; fax (20) 2101579; e-mail turkemb.kabul@mfa.gov.tr; internet kabul.emb.mfa.gov.tr; Ambassador ISMAYEL HERAMAS.

Turkmenistan: House 280, St 13, Lane 3, Wazir Akbar Khan, Kabul; tel. (20) 2302550; e-mail kabulemb@neda.af; Ambassador HEMRA TOGALAKOV.

United Arab Emirates: Charahi Zambak, Wazir Akbar Khan, Kabul; tel. (20) 2102389 (mobile); fax 777998877; e-mail kabul@ mofa.gov.ae; Chargé d'affaires a.i. YUSOUF SAIF KHAMES AL-ALI.

United Kingdom: St 15 Roundabout, Wazir Akbar Khan, POB 334, Kabul; tel. 700102000 (mobile); fax 700102250 (mobile); e-mail britishembassy.kabul@fco.gov.uk; internet ukinafghanistan.fco.gov .uk; Ambassador Sir RICHARD STAGG.

USA: Great Masoud Rd, Wazir Akbar Khan, Kabul; tel. 700108001 (mobile); fax (20) 2300546; e-mail usambassadorkabul@state.gov; internet kabul.usembassy.gov; Ambassador JAMES B. CUNNINGHAM.

Uzbekistan: House 14, St 13, Wazir Akbar Khan, Kabul; tel. (20) 2300124; e-mail mirnodir@hotmail.com; Ambassador YADGARKHOJA SHADMANOV.

Judicial System

The new Constitution that was introduced in early 2004 made no specific reference to the role of *Shari'a* but stated that Afghan laws should not contravene the main tenets of Islam. The Constitution made provision for the creation of a Supreme Court (Stera Mahkama) as the highest judicial organ in Afghanistan. The Court was inaugurated shortly after the Meli Shura (National Assembly) was officially opened on 19 December 2005.

The Supreme Court comprises nine members, including the Chief Justice, who are appointed by the President, subject to parliamentary approval.

Supreme Court: Masood Sq., Kabul; tel. (20) 2300359; e-mail info@ supremecourt.gov.af; internet www.supremecourt.gov.af.

Chief Justice: ABDUL SALAM AZIMI (acting).

Attorney-General's Office: District 10, Qala-i-Fatullah, Kabul; tel. (20) 2200017; e-mail ago.afg@gmail.com; internet ago.gov.af; Attorney-Gen. MUHAMMAD ISHAQ ALOKO (acting).

Religion

The official religion of Afghanistan is Islam. Muslims comprise some 99% of the population, an estimated 84% of them of the Sunni sect and the remainder of the Shi'ite sect. There are small minority groups of Hindus, Sikhs and Jews.

ISLAM

The High Council of Ulema and Clergy of Afghanistan: Kabul; f. 1980; 7,000 mems; Head Maulvi QIAMUDDIN KASHAF.

The Press

PRINCIPAL DAILIES

Anis (Friendship): 3rd Floor, Azadi Printing Press Bldg, Microrayon 2, Kabul; tel. (20) 2301342; e-mail anisdaily@yahoo.com; f. 1927; evening; Dari and Pashto; state-owned; news and literary articles; Editor-in-Chief MOHAMMAD QASIM SOROSH; circ. 5,000.

Arman-e Melli (Hope of the Nation): 4 Muslim St, Shar-i-Nau, Kabul; tel. 700282673 (mobile); internet www.armanemili.af; f. 2002 by the Afghan Interim Authority; now independent; Dari and Pashto; Editor-in-Chief MIR HAYDAR MOTAHAR; circ. 4,200.

Cheragh Daily (Light): 19 Shar-i-Nau, opp. District 10, Kabul; tel. 785693428 (mobile); e-mail cheragh_daily@yahoo.com; internet www.cheraghdaily.af; f. 2004; Dari, Pashto and English; independent; Editor-in-Chief KATHREEN WIDA; circ. 17,000.

The Daily Afghanistan: Karta-e-Seh, House 263, St 4, District 6, Kabul; tel. 777005019 (mobile); e-mail mail@outlookafghanistan .com; internet www.dailyafghanistan.com; f. 2006; owned by the Afghanistan Group of Newspapers; Dari and Pashto; Editor-in Chief MAHMOUD HAKIMI; circ. 7,000.

Daily Outlook Afghanistan: V-137, St 6, Phase 4, District 6, Shahrak Omeed Sabz, Kabul; tel. 799005019 (mobile); e-mail outlookafghanistan@gmail.com; internet outlookafghanistan.net; f. 2004; publ. of the Afghanistan Group of Newspapers; English, Dari, Pashto; Editor-in-Chief Dr HUSSAIN ALI YASA.

Erada (Intention): Nr Cinema Barikot, Dehmazang, District 2, Kabul; tel. 700244384 (mobile); e-mail eradadaily@hotmail.com; f. 2000 as weekly in Pakistan; relaunched as daily in Afghanistan 2002; independent; Dari and Pashto; Editor-in-Chief KHADEM AHMAD.

Eslah (Reform): Azadi Printing Press, 4th Floor, Microrayon Part II, Kabul; e-mail islahdaily@yahoo.com; f. 1921; Dari and Pashto; state-owned; Editor-in-Chief SHAMSOLHAQ ARIANFAR.

Hasht-e Subh (Daily 8 AM): House 384, St 5, Kartai Seh, Kabul; tel. 799037083 (mobile); e-mail afghanistan_8am@yahoo.com; internet www.8am.af; f. 2006; Dari and Pashto; publ. in Kabul, Mazar-i-Sharif, Herat, Bamian, Baghlan, Kunduz, Takkar, Badakshan, Jowzjan, Jalalabad and Ghazni; Publr SANJER SOHAIL.

Hewad (Homeland): Azadi Press Centre, Microrayon, District 16, Kabul; tel. (20) 2302130; f. 1949; Pashto and Dari; state-owned; Editor-in-Chief NAJIBULLAH SHINWARI; circ. 5,000.

Jahan-e-Naw (New World): Mazar-i-Sharif; Editor QAYOUM BAABAK.

Kabul Times: Macrorayon Azadi Printing Press, Kabul; tel. (20) 2301675; e-mail thekabultimes@yahoo.com; f. 1962 as Kabul Times, renamed Kabul New Times in 1980; ceased publication in 2001; revived in 2002 under new management; English; state-owned; Editor-in-Chief MOHAMMAD SHAFIQ AHMAD ZAI.

Mandegar Daily: tel. 799336075 (mobile); e-mail mandegardaily@gmail.com; internet mandegardaily.af; Dari; Editor-in-Chief NAZARI PARIANI.

Rah-e Nejat: Kabul; tel. 706747184 (mobile); e-mail info@rahenejat.com; internet www.rahenejatdaily.com; fmrly weekly, daily from 2005; Dari and Pashto; independent; Editor-in-Chief SAYED MOHAMMAD ALEMI.

Sarnavesht Daily: Kabul; Editor ASADULLAH WAHEEDI.

Tolo-e Afghan: Qandahar; e-mail afghan.tolo@yahoo.com; Pashto and Dari; Editor-in-Chief JANAN MOMIN.

Weesa Daily: House 11, St 9, Hesa-e-Du, Kartai Parwan, District 4, Kabul; tel. 799878224 (mobile); internet www.dailyweesa.com; f. 2006; Dari and Pashto; Editor-in-Chief FAZAL ELAHI SHAFIQI; 5,000.

PERIODICALS

Afghan Scene: House 3, St 12, Wazir Akbar Khan, Kabul; tel. 799306284 (mobile); e-mail info@afghanscene.com; internet www.afghanscene.com; f. 2005; monthly; English; free magazine; owned by MOBY Group; Editor SAAD MOHSENI.

Aina-e Zan (Women's Mirror): House 26, Muslim Wat, Shahr-i-Nau, District 10, Kabul; tel. 700281864 (mobile); e-mail womensmirror@hotmail.com; f. 2002; weekly; women's; Dari, Pashto and English; Chief Editor SHUKRIA BARAKZAI; circ. 3,000.

Eqtedar-e Melli: POB 4024, Kartai Char, University Rd, Kabul; tel. 799348791 (mobile); e-mail eqtedaremelli@yahoo.com; internet www.eqmweekly.com.af; f. 2002; weekly; Dari and Pashto; Editor SEYED MOHAMMAD ALI REZVANI.

Farda (Tomorrow): POB 1758, Kabul; tel. (20) 2100199; fax (20) 2100699; e-mail farda-news@yahoo.com; weekly; Publr ABDUL GHAFUR AITEQAD; circ. 4,000.

Killid (The Key): House 442, St 6, Chardehi Watt, Kabul; tel. (20) 2500717; fax (20) 2200574; e-mail info@tkg.af; internet www.tkg.af; weekly; current affairs; Editor LAL AQA SHIRIN; circ. 25,000.

Malalai: Afghan Visual Communication Institute, Malik Ashgar Crossroads, Kabul; internet www.ainaworld.org; f. 2002; monthly; women's; Dari, Pashto and English; publ. of Aïna humanitarian org.; Chief Editor JAMILA MUJAHID; circ. 3,000.

Mursal: House 442, St 6, Chardehi Watt, Kartai Seh, Kabul; tel. (20) 2500717; fax (20) 2200574; e-mail info@tkg.af; internet www.tkg.af/english/divisions/publishing/mursal-weekly; f. 2003; weekly; women's issues; Pashto and Dari; circ. 15,000.

Les Nouvelles de Kaboul (Kabul News): Afghan Visual Communication Institute, Malik Ashgar Crossroads, Kabul; tel. 70286215 (mobile); e-mail dimitri.beck@ainaworld.org; internet www.ainaworld.org; f. 2002; monthly; Dari, Pashto and French; publ. of Aïna humanitarian org.; Chief Editor DIMITRI BECK; Propr and Dir SHAFIQA HABIBI.

Parvaz (Flight): Afghan Visual Communication Institute, Malik Ashgar Crossroads, Kabul; e-mail communication@ainaworld.org; internet www.ainaworld.org; f. 2002; Dari and Pashto; every two months; children's; Editor CLAUDINE BOEGLIN; circ. 25,000.

Payam-e-Mujahid (Holy Warrior's Message): POB 5051, Kabul; e-mail payamemojahed@yahoo.com; internet www.payamemojahed.com; f. 1996; weekly; Dari and Pashto; sponsored by the Northern Alliance; Editor ABDUL HAFIZ MANSOOR.

Roz (The Day): Kabul; internet www.rozmagazine.com; f. 2002; monthly; women's; Dari, Pashto, French and English; Editor-in-Chief LAILOMA AHMADI.

Sada-e-Azadi: Kabul; e-mail newspaper@sada-e-azadi.net; internet sada-e-azadi.net; bi-weekly; run by the International Security Assistance Force; English, Dari and Pashto.

Takhassos (Experts): Jadai Baghi Azadi, Herat; tel. 70280258 (mobile); monthly; Dari; published by Council of Professionals.

Zanbil-e-Gham: Afghan Visual Communication Institute, Malik Ashgar Crossroads, Kabul; f. 1997; monthly; satirical; Editor OSMAN AKRAM; circ. 2,000.

NEWS AGENCIES

Afghan Islamic Press (AIP): POB 520, GPO, Peshawar, North-West Frontier Province, Pakistan; tel. (91) 5701100 (Peshawar); fax (91) 5842544 (Peshawar); e-mail info@afghanislamicpress.com; internet www.afghanislamicpress.com; f. 1982; English and Pashto.

Bakhtar News Agency (BNA): Ministry of Communications and Information Technology, Mohammad Jan Khan Wat, Kabul; tel. 700202282 (mobile); e-mail info@bakhtarnews.com.af; internet www.bakhtarnews.com.af; f. 1939; govt news agency; correspondents in 32 provinces; English, Dari and Pashto; Dir-Gen. KHALIL MENAVI.

Government Media and Information Centre (GMIC): Shah Mahmood Khan St, opp. the Ministry of Foreign Affairs, Kabul; e-mail info@gmic.gov.af; internet www.gmic.gov.af; f. 2007; co-ordinates govt communications and media activities; Exec. Dir Dr HAKIM ASHER.

Khaama Press: Qala-e-Fathullah, Kabul; e-mail info@khaama.com; internet www.khaama.com; f. 2010; news in English and Dari; Editor-in-Chief KHUSHNOOD NABIZADA.

Pajhwok Afghan News: House 130/138, St 8, Taimani, Kabul; tel. (20) 2201814; fax (20) 2201813; e-mail feedback@pajhwok.com; internet www.pajhwok.com; f. 2004; independent; eight regional bureaux incl. Mazar-i-Sharif, Qandahar, Herat and Jalalabad; news service provided in English, Pashto and Dari; Dir and Editor-in-Chief DANISH KAROKHEL; Man. Editor FARIDA NEKZAD.

Wakht News Agency: Darul Aman Rd, Kabul; internet www.wakht.af; f. 2008; private news agency; correspondents in 34 provinces; Dari, Pashto and English; Dir RAHIMULLAH SAMANDER.

PRESS ASSOCIATIONS

Afghanistan Independent Journalists' Association (AIJA): 6th District, Darulaman Wat, opposite Habibia High School, Karta Seh, Kabul; tel. 752001623 (mobile); f. 2003; Pres. ABDULHAMID MUBAREZ.

Afghanistan Journalists Center (AFJC): Bagh-e-Azadi, 2 Baghmorad St, Herat; tel. 798816124 (mobile); e-mail info@afjc.af; internet afjc.af; f. 2009; licensed by the Ministry of Information and Culture; fmrly known as Center for Support of Journalists of Afghanistan, renamed as above 2011; publishes statements and studies on the status of Afghan media, job opportunities and freedom of the press; Dir AHMAD QURAISHI.

Publishers

Afghanistan Today Publishers: c/o The Kabul Times, Ansari Wat, POB 983, Kabul; tel. (20) 61847; e-mail www.afghanistan-today.org; publicity materials; answers enquiries about Afghanistan.

Ariana Press: Poli Jarkhi, Kabul; under the supervision of the Ministry of Information and Culture; Dir ABDUL KADER.

Azady (Freedom) Press: Azady Printing Press Bldg, 2nd Microrayon, District 16, Kabul; tel. (20) 2100113; under supervision of the Ministry of Information and Culture; Dir MOHAMMAD RUSTAM ASHRAFI.

Beihagi Publishers: Azady Press Centre, Microrayon, District 9, Kabul; tel. (20) 2302361; f. 1964; books on Afghan culture; also prints information related to the Govt and its plans; Dir FAIZULLAH MUHTAJ.

Book Publishing Institute: Qandahar; f. 1970; supervised by Government Printing House; mainly books in Pashto language.

Danish Press: Milli Market, opp. Marwarid Hotel, Kolola Poshta St, Kabul; tel. 700639383 (mobile); e-mail danish2k2000@yahoo.com; internet www.danishpress.com; publishes dictionaries, translated works, guides and magazines; Dir ASADULLAH DANISH.

Educational Publications: Ministry of Education, Mohammad Jan Khan Wat, Kabul; tel. and fax (20) 200000; textbooks for primary and secondary schools in the Pashto and Dari languages; also 3 monthly magazines in Pashto and in Dari.

International Center for Pashto Studies: Kabul; f. 1975; research work on the Pashto language and literature and on the history and culture of the Pashtun people; Pres. and Assoc. Chief Researcher J. K. HEKMATY; publs *Pashto* (quarterly).

Kabul University Press: Kabul; tel. (20) 42433; f. 1950; textbooks; 2 quarterly scientific journals in Dari and in English, etc.

Research Center for Linguistics and Literary Studies: Afghanistan Academy of Sciences, Akbar Khan Mena, Kabul; tel. (20) 26912; f. 1978; research on Afghan languages (incl. Pashto, Dari, Balochi and Uzbek) and Afghan folklore; publs *Kabul* (Pashto), *Zeray* (Pashto, weekly) and *Khurasan* (Dari); Pres. Prof. MOHAMMED R. ELHAM.

Shah M. Book Co: 12 Charahi Sadarat, Kabul 111; tel. (20) 2101569; e-mail info@shahmbookco.com; internet www.shahmbookco.com; f. 1974; books on Afghan history, economics, sciences, fine arts, religion and various other topics; Man. Dir SHAH MUHAMMAD RAIS.

GOVERNMENT PUBLISHING HOUSE

Government Printing House: Kabul; tel. (93) 26851; f. 1870; under supervision of the Ministry of Communications and Information Technology; Dir SAID AHMAD RAHAA.

PUBLISHERS' ASSOCIATION

Afghan Libraries' and Publishers' Association: Chari Ansari, between Ansari Crossroads and Popo Lano Restaurant, Kabul.

Broadcasting and Communications

TELECOMMUNICATIONS

At the end of 2001 telecommunications services in Afghanistan were severely limited: outside the capital, Kabul, access to fixed-line services was negligible, while mobile telephone services were virtually non-existent throughout the country. The first mobile service provider, the Afghan Wireless Communication Co, was launched in 2002. In 2005 the Government approved the establishment of privately owned, independent telecommunications companies. By the end of 2013 there was a penetration rate of some 72% of the population for all telecommunications services and the mobile telephone market had expanded to 20.5m. subscribers. In 2011, according to International Telecommunication Union estimates, around 5% of the population were internet users.

Afghanistan Telecom Regulatory Authority (ATRA): Ministry of Communications and Information Technology, MOC Headquarters Tower, 10th Floor, Mohammad Jan Khan Wat, Kabul; tel. (20) 2101179; fax (20) 2103700; e-mail z.hamidy@atra.gov.af; internet www.atra.gov.af; succeeded Telecom Regulatory Board; Chair. ABDUL WAKIL SHIRGUL.

Afghan Telecom (AfghanTel): Post Parcel Bldg, 4th Floor, Mohammad Jan Khan Wat, Kabul; tel. 752012345 (mobile); e-mail info@afghantelecom.af; internet www.afghantelecom.af; f. 2004; state-owned; provides wireless and digital fixed-line services; 80% of shares offered for sale in March 2008; Dir AMIRZAI SANGIN.

Afghan Wireless Communication Co (AWCC): Khuja Mullah, nr Hajari Najari Bus Station, Darulaman Wat, Kabul; tel. and fax 70830830 (mobile); e-mail info@afghanwireless.com; internet www.afghan-wireless.com; f. 2002; jt venture between the Ministry of Communications and Information Technology (20% ownership) and Telephone Systems International, Inc of the USA (80% ownership); reconstruction of Afghanistan's national and international telecommunications network; covers 95 major cities and towns; 1.3m. subscribers (July 2007); Chair. EHSAN BAYAT.

Etisalat Afghanistan: Ehsan Plaza, Shar-i-Nau, POB 800, Kabul; tel. 786786786 (mobile); e-mail info@etisalat.af; internet www.etisalat.af; commenced operations in Afghanistan in 2007; GSM operator; from early 2012, licensed to provide 3G services; 100% owned by Etisalat UAE; 3m. subscribers (June 2010); CEO AHMED ALHOSANI.

MTN Afghanistan: House 35, Moslem St, Shar-i-Nau, POB 700, Central Post Office, Kabul; tel. 772222779 (mobile); internet www.mtn.com.af; fmrly Areeba, renamed as above in 2008; provides mobile telecommunications services; from mid-2012, licensed to provide 3G services; CEO HASSAN JABER.

Telecom Development Co Afghanistan Ltd (Roshan): Roshan Shop, St 13, off Main St, Wazir Akbar Khan, Kabul; tel. 799971333 (mobile); e-mail roshanca@roshan.af; internet www.roshan.af; f. 2002 by an international consortium comprising the Aga Khan Fund for Economic Development (AKFED), French cos Monaco Telecom International (MTI) and Alcatel, and US co MCT Corpn; 51% owned by AKFED, 36.75% by MTI and 12.25% by MCT Corpn; provides mobile telecommunications services; CEO KARIM KHOJA.

Wasel Telecom Co: House 33, Charahy Kamal Nabezada, Azizabad St, POB 06, Mazar-i-Sharif; tel. 750999888 (mobile); internet www.wasel.af; since 2007, licensed to provide voice and internet services in northern Afghanistan via CDMA technology; CEO MOHAMMAD GUL KHOLMI.

BROADCASTING

Radio

Radio-Television Afghanistan: St 10, Lane 2, Wazir Akbar Khan, POB 544, Kabul; tel. (20) 2101086; e-mail rta_afg@yahoo.com; internet rta.org.af; state broadcaster; revived in 2001; programmes in Dari, Pashto, Turkmen and Uzbek; Dir-Gen. MUHAMMAD ZAREEN ANZUR; Head of Radio GHULAM HASSAN HAZRATI.

Balkh Radio and TV: Mazar-i-Sharif; Pashto and Dari; Chair. ABDORRAB JAHED.

Radio Azadi: Kabul; c/o Radio Free Europe/Radio Liberty, Inc, Vinohradská 159A, 110 00 Prague 10, Czech Republic; internet pa.azadiradio.org; f. 1985 as Radio Free Afghanistan; service resumed and renamed as above 2002; outlet of Radio Free Europe/Radio Liberty (USA—based in the Czech Republic); Pashto, Dari; broadcasts 12 hours daily; Dir AKBAR AYAZI.

Radio Kabul: Ansari Wat, Kabul; tel. (20) 2101087; f. 1940; Dir GHULAM HASSAN HAZRATI.

Independent

Arman FM: POB 1045, Central Post Office, Kabul; tel. 799222229 (mobile); e-mail armanfm98.1@gmail.com; internet www.arman.fm; f. 2003; Afghanistan's first privately owned independent FM radio station; broadcasts in Kabul, Mazar-i-Sharif, Herat, Qandahar and Jalalabad; popular music and culture; Dari and Pashto; part of the Moby Media Group; Dir SAAD MOHSENI.

Radio Bakhtar: Kabul; e-mail info@bakhtarradio.com; internet bakhtarradio.com; live Afghan folk and alternative music.

Radio Killid: The Killid Group House 442, St 6, Chardehi Wat, nr Uzbekha Mosque, Karta Seh, Kabul; tel. (20) 2500717; fax (20) 2200574; e-mail info@tkg.af; internet www.tkg.af; f. 2003 by Development and Humanitarian Services for Afghanistan; broadcasts 24 hours daily; stations in Kabul, Mazar, Qandahar, Jelalabad, Ghazni, Khost and Herat; Chair. SHAHIR ZAHINE; Man. NAJIBA AYUBI.

Radio Rabia Balkhi: Mazar-i-Sharif; tel. 700656464 (mobile); e-mail info@rrb.af; internet rrb.af; f. 2003; broadcasts aimed at women in Balkh province; Head WAHEED SULTANI.

Radio Sahar: Herat; f. 2003; Dari; women's; broadcasts 12 hours daily; Dir HULAN KHATIBI; Station Man. HUMAIRA HABIB.

Radio Sharq: Jalalabad; e-mail info@sharq.radio-connect.af; internet www.sharq.radioconnect.af; f. 2003; broadcasts 12 hours daily.

Radio Tiraj Mir: Pol-e-Khomri; f. 2003; broadcasts 16 hours daily.

Voice of Afghan Women: Kabul; f. 2003; relaunched in 2005 following closure owing to lack of funds; dedicated to interests of women; Dir JAMILA MUJAHID.

Television

Radio-Television Afghanistan: see Radio.

Balkh Radio and TV: see Radio.

Herat TV: Herat; state-owned.

Independent

1 TV (Yak TV): 17 Wazir Akbar Khan, Kabul; e-mail info@1tvmedia.com/; internet www.1tvmedia.com; f. 2010; privately owned; entertainment-based programmes, hourly news broadcasts and periodicals on Islamic doctrine; Dari and Pashto; Dir FAHIM HASHIMI.

Afghan TV: Kabul; tel. (37) 99257750; e-mail afghantv1@gmail.com; internet www.afghantv.af; f. 2004; broadcasts 24 hours daily; CEO AHMED SHAH AFGHANZAI.

Ariana Radio and Television Network: 318 Darulaman Wat, Kabul; tel. 700111000 (mobile); e-mail feedback@arianatelevision.com; internet arianatelevision.com; broadcasts to 34 provinces in Afghanistan, as well as Europe, the USA, Canada and the Middle East; f. 2005; Chair. EHSANULLAH BAYAT.

Ayna (Mirror): Shebarghan; f. 2003; broadcasts to Jawzjan, Sar-e Pol and Balkh provinces and to the bordering areas of Turkmenistan and Uzbekistan; entertainment, news and political propaganda; mainly in Uzbek; Pres. ABDUL RASHID DOSTUM.

Lemar TV: House 3, St 12, Wazir Akbar Khan, Kabul 1000; tel. 799321010 (mobile); e-mail info@lemar.tv; internet www.lemar.tv; f. 2006; broadcasts in Pashto, Dari, English and Urdu; part of the Moby Media Group; Man. LAL AQA SHIRZAD.

Noorin TV: St 4, Silo, Kabul; tel. 786606010 (mobile); e-mail info@noorintv.net; internet www.noorintv.net; f. 2007; privately owned;

has coverage in 34 provinces; also operates a radio station; Dir MOHAMMAD ARIF NOORI.

Saba TV: House 47, St 2, Pul-e-Sorkh, Karte 3, POB 475, Kabul; tel. 752023756 (mobile); fax 752023757 (mobile); f. 2008; 2 channels; accessible through satellite, covering 11 provinces; Man. ZAINAB NADIRI.

Shamshad TV: Chaman Huzuri, nr Ghazi Stadium, Kabul; tel. 799322129 (mobile); internet www.shamshadtv.com; f. 2006; broadcasts 24 hours daily; mainly in Pashto; Dir FAZAL KARIM FAZAL.

Tamadon TV: St 1, Kartai Chahar, District 3, Kabul; tel. (20) 2500434; internet www.tamaddon.tv; live entertainment-based programmes.

Tolo TV: POB 225, Central Post Office, Kabul; tel. 799321010 (mobile); e-mail info@tolo.tv; internet tolo.tv; f. 2004; commercial station; broadcasts news, current affairs, entertainment, lifestyle and culture programmes in Dari and Pashto; launched Afghanistan's first 24-hour news satellite channel, Tolo News, in July 2010; part of the Moby Media Group; Dir SAAD MOHSENI; Head (Tolo News) MUJAHID KAKAR.

Zhwandoon TV (Life TV): Kabul; internet www.zhwandoon.tv; f. 2011; Pashto; Dir ISMAIL YOON.

Finance

(cap. = capital; res = reserves; dep. = deposits; m. = million; brs = branches; amounts in afghanis unless otherwise stated)

BANKING

In September 2003 the President approved a law allowing foreign banks to open branches in Afghanistan. By early 2014 there were 16 licensed commercial banks operating in Afghanistan, of which five were branches of foreign banks.

Central Bank

Da Afghanistan Bank (Central Bank of Afghanistan): Ibne Sina Wat, Kabul; tel. (20) 2104146; fax (20) 2100305; e-mail info@centralbank.gov.af; internet www.centralbank.gov.af; f. 1939; cap. and res 27,891m., dep. 82,950m. (March 2010); main functions: banknote issue, modernize the banking system, re-establish banking relations with international banks, create a financial market system, foreign exchange regulation, govt and private depository; granted complete independence in September 2003; Gov. NOORULLAH DILAWARI; 47 brs.

Other Banks

Afghan United Bank: Turabaz Khan Watt, Shar-i-Nau, POB 425, Kabul; tel. (20) 2203836; fax (20) 2203837; e-mail info@aub.af; internet www.afghanunitedbank.com; f. 2007; cap. 875.758m., dep. 7,937.5m. (Dec. 2011); Chair. FAZAL AHMAD JOYA; CEO SHAHZAD HAIDER YOUSAFZAI; 15 brs.

Afghanistan Commercial Bank: Tura Baz Khan St, Shar-i-Nau, Kabul; tel. (20) 2203871; fax (20) 2203870; e-mail info@afgcommercialbank.com; internet www.afgcommercialbank.com; f. 2012; Chair MUHAMMAD QURBAN HAQJO; CEO MOHAMMAD NAZRUL ISLAM.

Afghanistan International Bank: Haji Yaqoob Sq., Shahabudin Watt, Shar-i-Nau, POB 2074, Kabul; tel. (20) 2550255; fax (20) 2550256; e-mail info@aib.af; internet www.aib.af; f. 2004; established and managed by the ING Institutional and Government Advisory Group (Netherlands) on behalf of a consortium of Afghan and US investors; 75% owned by Afghan nationals, 25% owned by Asian Development Bank; cap. 1,465m., res –47.8m., dep 43,142.6m. (Dec. 2012); CEO KHALILULLAH SEDIQ; 23 brs.

Azizi Bank: Zambaq Sq., opp. Turkish Embassy, Main Rd, Kabul; tel. 799700900 (mobile); e-mail customercare@azizibank.af; internet www.azizibank.com; f. 2006; cap. US $64.2m., dep. US $437.5m. (Dec. 2011); Pres. and CEO INAYATULLAH FAZLI; Gov. MIRWAIS AZIZI; 63 brs.

Bakhtar Bank: Sher-Pur Sq., Shar-i-Nau, Kabul; tel. 776777000 (mobile); e-mail info@bakhtarbank.af; internet www.bakhtarbank.com; CEO ASHOKKUMAR VALECHHA.

Bank-e-Millie Afghan (Afghan National Bank): Jade Ibne Sina, POB 522, Kabul; tel. (20) 2102221; fax (20) 2101801; e-mail info@bma.com.af; internet www.bma.com.af; f. 1933 as private bank, nationalized in 1976; cap. 250m., res 807.2m., dep. 10,351.3m. (March 2011); Chair. MOHIBULLAH SAFI; 27 brs.

First Micro Finance Bank (FMFB): Plot No 174, Ashraf Watt, 2nd St, Ansari Sq., Shar-i-Nau, Kabul; tel. (20) 2201733; e-mail info@fmfb.com.af; f. 2004; cap. 292.6m., dep. 5,262.4m.; 51% owned by Aga Khan Agency for Microfinance, 32% by Kreditanstalt fur Wiederaufbau, 17% by International Finance Corpn; provides sustainable financial services to the poor in order to contribute to poverty alleviation and economic development; CEO MUSLIM UL-HAQ.

Ghazanfar Bank: 866/A, Wazir Akbar Khan, Kabul; tel. (20) 2101111; e-mail info@ghazanfarbank.com; internet ghazanfarbank.com; f. 2009; cap. 22.1m., dep. 101m. (Dec. 2012); conducts business under conventional and Islamic banking systems; CEO AHMED SIAR KHOREISHI; Dir HAJI MOHAMMED ISMAIL GHAZANFAR.

Maiwand Bank: Charahi Turabaz Khan, Shar-i-Nau, Kabul; tel. 752004000 (mobile); e-mail info@maiwandbank.com; internet www.maiwandbank.com; f. 2009; provides Islamic banking services; cap. 750m., dep. 8,046.3m. (Dec. 2011); Chair. and Man. Dir FRAIDOON NOORZAD; Pres. and CEO P. V. V. RAMA RAJU; 33 brs.

New Kabul Bank: 10–42 Turabaz Khan, Shar-i-Nau, Kabul; tel. 700222666 (mobile); e-mail info@newkabulbank.af; internet www.kabulbank.af; f. 2004 as Kabul Bank; in 2010 heavy losses and allegations of financial irregularities resulted in state intervention in the administration of the bank; restructured and renamed, as above, in 2011; cap. 27m., res 68m., dep. 976m. (Dec. 2009); CEO MASOOD KHAN MUSA GHAZI; 68 brs.

Pashtany Bank: Mohammad Jan Khan Watt, Kabul; tel. (20) 2105550; fax (20) 2102905; e-mail info@pashtanybank.com; internet www.pashtanybank.com; f. 1955 to provide short-term credits, forwarding facilities, opening letters of credit, purchase and sale of foreign exchange; nationalized in 1975; Pres. and CEO GUL MAQSOOD SABIT; 22 brs.

Banking Association

Afghanistan Banks Association (ABA): 718, St No 13, Lane 3, Wazir Akbar Khan, Kabul; tel. 799852497 (mobile); e-mail contact@aba.org.af; internet www.aba.org.af; f. 2004; Gen. Sec. NAJIBULLAH AMIRI.

INSURANCE

In mid-2006 the Afghanistan Insurance Authority was established by the Ministry of Finance; the Commission was to oversee the development of the insurance sector within Afghanistan.

Afghan National Insurance Co: Second Ave, Kartai Parwan, nr fmr British Embassy, POB 329, Kabul; tel. and fax (20) 2200189; fax (20) 2200189; e-mail insuranceafghan@yahoo.com; f. 1964; govt-owned; mem. of Asian Reinsurance Corpn; marine, aviation, fire, motor and accident insurance; Pres. FAHAD DAUD MOMAND; Claims Man. SHAH MOHAMMAD MOHAMMADZAI.

Afghan Global Insurance: Shar-i-Nau, Kabul; tel. 708744444 (mobile); e-mail info@afghanglobalinsurance.com; internet www.afghanglobalinsurance.com; f. 2010; Chair. and Man. Dir FRAIDOON NOORZAD; CEO MAHBOOB S. FROTAN.

Insurance Corporation of Afghanistan (ICA): Naser Khusraw Balkhi Bldg, Charrahi Sarsabai, Taimani, Kabul; tel. 798242455 (mobile); e-mail info@icaaf.com; internet www.icaaf.co; f. 2007; privately owned; aviation, banking, construction, mining and accident insurance; Chair. LEONARD DELUNAS; CEO SADAT M. NADERI.

Trade and Industry

GOVERNMENT AGENCIES

Afghanistan Investment Support Agency (AISA): Haji Yakub Sq. Computer Plaza St, House 24, Kabul; tel. (20) 2103404; fax (20) 2103402; e-mail invest@aisa.org.af; internet www.aisa.org.af; f. 2003; promotes and regulates domestic and foreign investment in the private sector; Pres. and CEO WAFIULLAH IFTIKHAR.

Afghanistan Reconstruction and Development Services (ARDS): 4th and 5th Floors, Ministry of Economy Bldg, Malik Asghar Sq, Kabul; tel. 799385712 (mobile); e-mail ards.procurement@ards.org.af; internet www.ards.gov.af; f. 2003; co-ordination of procurement activities and recruitment of technical staff for govt ministries.

Export Promotion Agency of Afghanistan (EPAA): off Karte Char 2nd St, Kabul; tel. (20) 2504837; e-mail info@epaa.org.af; internet www.epaa.org.af; f. 2006; provides guidance for traders, collects and disseminates trade information; CEO NAJILLA HABIBYAR.

DEVELOPMENT ORGANIZATION

Dehsabz-Barikab City Development Authority (DCDA): Qala-e-Fatehullah Khan, Kabul; tel. 752035153 (mobile); e-mail ms@dcda.gov.af; internet www.dcda.gov.af; est. for the expansion and devt of the capital, in particular Kabul New City, a major urban devt project to the north of the existing city; Chair. HEDAYAT AMIN ARSALA; CEO GHOLAM SACHI HASSANZADAH.

CHAMBERS OF COMMERCE AND INDUSTRY

Afghanistan Chamber of Commerce and Industries (ACCI): Chaman-e-Huzuri, next to Kabul Nendari, Kabul; tel. 776856824 (mobile); e-mail info@acci.org.af; internet www.acci.org.af; f. 1931; privately owned; merged with Afghanistan International Chamber of Commerce; Chair. ABDUL HOSSAIN FAHEEM; CEO MOHAMMAD QURBAN HAQJO.

Federation of Afghan Chambers of Commerce and Industry: Darulaman Wat, Kabul; f. 1923; includes chambers of commerce and industry in Ghazni, Qandahar, Kabul, Herat, Mazar-i-Sharif, Faryab, Jawzjan, Kunduz, Jalalabad and Andkhoy.

INDUSTRIAL AND TRADE ASSOCIATIONS

Afghan Carpet Exporters' Guild: POB 3159, Darulaman Wat, Kabul; tel. 70224575 (mobile); f. 1967; non-profit, independent organization of carpet manufacturers and exporters; Dir MOHAMMAD ZARIF YADGARI; c. 1,000 mems.

Afghanistan Builders Association: House 1310, Dehmazang, Kote-i-Sangi St, Karte-4, Kabul; tel. 700224822 (mobile); e-mail aba@aba.af; internet www.aba.af; f. 2004; Pres. NAEEM YASSIN.

Afghanistan Karakul Institute: Puli Charkhi, POB 506, Kabul; f. 1967; exporters of furs; Pres. G. M. BAHEER.

Animal Products Trading and Industrial Association: Ayub Khan Mina, South of Habibia High School, 2nd St, Darulaman Wat, Kabul; tel. and fax 752023490 (mobile); e-mail mohsin_ataie@yahoo.com; f. 1979; promotes and exports animal products, incl. wool and animal skins; Chief Officer M. MOHSIN ATAIE.

UTILITIES

Da Afghanistan Breshna Sherkat (DABS): Chaman Houzori, Kabul; tel. (75) 2024308; e-mail info@dabs.af; internet www.dabs.af; responsible for management and operation of national electric power assets since 2009; CEO ABDUL RAZIQUE SAMADI.

TRADE UNIONS

All Afghanistan Federation of Trade Unions (AAFTU): Karte Nau, First St, Kabul; tel. 799340196 (mobile); Chair. Dr LIAQUAT ADIL.

National Union of Afghanistan Employees (NUAE): POB 756, Kabul; tel. (20) 23040; internet www.nuae.info; f. 1978 as Central Council of Afghanistan Trade Unions, to establish and develop the trade union movement; name changed in 1990; composed of 7 vocational unions; 300,000 mems; Pres. of Cen. Council MOHAMMAD QASIM EHSAS; Vice-Pres. ASAD KHAN NACEIRY.

Transport

RAILWAYS

At the end of the 20th century there were no active railways in Afghanistan. Since 2002 the Afghan Government and its international partners have initiated various projects to develop a rail network, with the aim of establishing the country as a major regional transportation hub. However, owing to security concerns and political instability, implementation of several projects has been severely delayed. Plans for the construction of a 1,200-km northern rail link, from Herat to Sher Khan Bandar, on the border with Tajikistan, with assistance from the Asian Development Bank, are under development. In early 2012 cargo services commenced on a 75-km section of the project, connecting Mazar-i-Sharif with Hairatan, on the border with Uzbekistan. A further expansion of the network, to connect the Mazar-i-Sharif–Hairatan line with Kabul and Torkham, on the border with Pakistan, was also under consideration. After lengthy delays, construction of a 200-km railway line linking Herat with eastern Iran, funded by the Iranian Government, was reported to have resumed in mid-2012. In March 2013 a memorandum of understanding on the construction of a strategic rail link between Afghanistan, Turkmenistan and Tajikistan was signed. Construction on the Turkmen section commenced in June, although exact details of the route, which was to involve between 230 km and 350 km in northern Afghanistan (via Mazar-i-Sharif), had yet to be finalized. A 900-km Indian-funded rail link from Bamian province to Chabahar port in Iran via Herat province, which would facilitate exports of Afghan minerals, was under discussion from 2011.

ROADS

In 2006 there were an estimated 42,150 km of roads, of which more than 70% were unpaved. All-weather highways link Kabul with Qandahar and Herat in the south and west, Jalalabad in the east, and Mazar-i-Sharif and the Amu Darya (Oxus) river in the north. A massive reconstruction programme of the road system in Afghanistan began in 2002. Between 2002 and 2009 US funding for Afghan road projects totalled some US $1,800m. The Asian Development Bank (ADB) also provides substantial financing for the development of Afghanistan's transport networks; during 2002–11 ADB funding for Afghan road projects totalled $1,700m. In early 2011, through the Central Asia Regional Economic Cooperation (CAREC) initiative, the ADB provided $340m. to fund the construction of 233-km highway in north-western Afghanistan, which was to form the final part of a 2,700-km national ring-road system connecting major cities including Kabul, Qandahar, Herat and Mazar-i-Sharif.

Afghan Container Transport Company Ltd (ACTCO): House 43, St 2, Shar-i-Nau, POB 3165, Kabul; tel. 70214666 (mobile); e-mail kabul@afghancontainers.com; internet www.afghancontainers.com; f. 1974; Vice-Pres. ALI DAD BEIGH ZAD.

AFSOTR: Flower Street, Shar-i-Nau, Kabul; tel. (20) 2102358; e-mail afsotr@svt.ru; founded as Afghan Soviet Transportation Company; resumed operations in 1998; transport co.

Milli Bus Enterprise: Ministry of Transport and Civil Aviation, Ansari Wat, Kabul; tel. (20) 2101032; state-owned; 900 buses; Pres. Eng. AZIZ NAGHABAN.

INLAND WATERWAYS

There are 1,200 km of navigable inland waterways, including the Amu Darya (Oxus) river, which is capable of handling vessels of up to about 500 dwt. River ports on the Amu Darya are linked by road to Kabul.

CIVIL AVIATION

In early 2014 there were four international airports in Afghanistan, at Kabul, Qandahar, Mazar-i-Sharif and Herat (where international services commenced in late 2013), two major domestic airports, at Jalalabad and Kunduz, and numerous regional domestic airports. Plans were under way to relocate and upgrade the airport at Kabul and to upgrade the airport at Jalalabad to international standards. Plans for the construction of an international airport at Ghazni were announced in mid-2012.

Afghanistan Civil Aviation Authority: Kabul; tel. (20) 2311954; e-mail capt.hamidz@acaa.gov.af; internet acaa.gov.af; f. 2013; Dir-Gen. HAMID ZAHER.

Ariana Afghan Airlines: POB 76, Kabul; tel. 777071333 (mobile); e-mail info@flyariana.com; internet www.flyariana.com; f. 1955; merged with Bakhtar Afghan Airlines Co Ltd in 1985; state-owned; flights to India, Germany, the Middle East and Russia; CEO NASIR AHMAD HAKIMI.

East Horizon Airlines: St 11, Wazir Akbar Khan, Kabul; tel. 797717170 (mobile); e-mail info@flyeasthorizon.com; internet flyeasthorizon.com; f. 2011; cargo and passenger services on domestic routes; CEO Capt. JAHED AZIMI.

KamAir: Kabul Business Centre, Shar-i-Nau, Kabul; tel. (20) 2200447; e-mail info@flykamair.com; internet www.flykamair.com; f. 2003; privately owned; domestic and regional flights; Pres. ZAMARIA KAMGAR.

Safi Airways: Quai-e-Markaz, Shar-i-Nau, Kabul; tel. (20) 2222222; fax (20) 2202058; e-mail info@safiairways.aero; internet www.safiairways.aero; f. 2006; privately owned; international flights, scheduled and charter passenger services; Chair. GHULAM HAZRAT SAFI; Exec.-Dir HAMID SAFI.

Tourism

Afghanistan's potential tourism attractions include: Bamian, with its thousands of painted caves; Bandi Amir, with its suspended lakes; the Blue Mosque of Mazar; Herat, with its Grand Mosque and minarets; the towns of Qandahar and Girishk; Balkh (ancient Bactria), 'Mother of Cities', in the north; Bagram, Hadda and Surkh Kotal (of interest to archaeologists); and the high mountains of the Hindu Kush. Furthermore, ruins of a Buddhist city (known locally as Kaffir Got—'Fortress of the Infidels') dating from the second century were discovered in 2002 in southern Afghanistan. The restoration of cultural heritage, sponsored by UNESCO, began in 2002. In 1998 an estimated 4,000 tourists visited Afghanistan and receipts from tourism amounted to around US $1m.

Afghan Tour Organization (ATO): Asmaie Wat, next to National Gallery, Kabul; tel. 752016907 (mobile); e-mail jamalharoun@yahoo.fr; internet afghan-tours.com; f. 1958; Pres. MOHAMMAD ZAHER GHAUSS.

Defence

Following the defeat of the Taliban in late 2001, an International Security Assistance Force (ISAF) was deployed in Kabul and at Bagram airbase to help maintain security in the area. In August 2003 the North Atlantic Treaty Organization (NATO) assumed command of the force and in December NATO began to expand its presence in the country by assuming command of a number of Provincial Reconstruction Teams (PRTs) in the north and west of Afghanistan. By October 2006 ISAF, numbering some 30,000 troops from more than 35 countries, had assumed control of international military operations throughout Afghanistan. Meanwhile, the establishment of a new multi-ethnic Afghan National Army (ANA) and Afghan National Police (including a border police contingent and an élite national civil order unit) commenced from late 2002, under the direction of ISAF. In January 2010 the Joint Coordination and Monitoring Board, composed of representatives of the Afghan Government and various international bodies, stated that the Afghan authorities aimed to expand the country's security forces from the existing total of around 97,000 to 240,000 troops and 160,000 police officers by 2015. In July 2010 President Karzai announced that his Government aimed to restore full control of the country's security to the Afghan armed forces and police by 2014. The first phase of the transition of security responsibilities to the Afghan authorities commenced in July 2011, with the handover of seven NATO-held areas to Afghan control (the transition process was scheduled to be completed in five phases). Meanwhile, in June President Obama announced that 10,000 US forces were to leave Afghanistan by the end of the year, with all remaining foreign forces to withdraw by the end of 2014. The fifth and final phase of the security transition process commenced in June 2013. By February 2014 the ISAF contingent in Afghanistan totalled 52,686 troops; the number of US troops had been reduced to 33,600 (from a peak of about 100,000 in mid–2011).As assessed at November 2013, the ANA had 179,000 troops, while the Afghan Air Force numbered 6,800 personnel. In the same month, the strength of the Afghan National Police force was 152,350.

Defence Budget: Estimated at 152,000m. afghanis in 2013 (includes US military aid).

Chief of Staff of the Afghan National Army: Gen. SHER MOHAMMAD KARIMI.

Education

Before the Taliban rose to power in 1996, primary education began at seven years of age and lasted for six years. Secondary education, beginning at 13 years of age, lasted for a further six years. As a proportion of the school-age population, the total enrolment at primary and secondary schools was equivalent to 36% (males 49%; females 22%) in 1995. Following their seizure of power, the Taliban banned education for girls over the age of eight, closed all the women's institutes of higher education and drew up a new Islamic curriculum for boys' schools. UNICEF reported that by December 1998 about 90% of girls and 66% of boys were not enrolled in school.

After the Taliban regime was defeated in late 2001, the Afghan Government, with the help of foreign governments, UNICEF and humanitarian organizations, began to rehabilitate the education system. By 2003/04 the boy-girl ratio in education had returned to pre-Taliban levels. However, female attendance varied significantly throughout the country and the attendance of girls at schools in parts of southern and eastern Afghanistan remained very low. In the mid-2000s the Afghan Ministry of Education, assisted by UNICEF, launched an initiative to establish community-based education, in order to provide basic educational opportunities for those with no access to formal schools. By 2011 3,843 community-based schools had been created, attended by approximately 125,000 children. According to statistics issued by the Afghan Ministry of Education, in 2012/13 the number of children enrolled in primary and secondary levels of education had increased to some 8.6m., compared to about 1m. in 2001. During 2001–11 more than 9,000 new schools had been established. According to UNESCO, the total enrolment at primary and secondary schools in 2012 was equivalent to an estimated 82% (males 98%; females 65%) of children in the relevant age-groups; enrolment at secondary level only was equivalent to an estimated 54% (males 69%; females 38%) of children in the relevant age-group.

In 1991 there were six institutions of higher education (including Kabul University, which was founded in 1931) in Afghanistan. Kabul University reopened for men and women in 2002. By 2012/13 there were 31 institutions of higher education operating under the supervision of the Ministry of Higher Education, which were attended by an estimated 101,315 students. In 2011 there were 98 technical and vocational schools attended by an estimated 26,000 students (of whom 16% were females).

In 2003 UNESCO and the Afghan Transitional Authority launched a major project to boost literacy rates throughout Afghanistan. In that year an estimated 57% of men and 86% of women were illiterate in Afghanistan. According to UNICEF, in 2011 literacy rates in Afghanistan remained among the lowest in the world: 61% of all adults (aged 15 or older) and 87% of women were deemed illiterate.

ALBANIA

Introductory Survey

LOCATION, CLIMATE, LANGUAGE, RELIGION, FLAG, CAPITAL

The Republic of Albania lies in south-eastern Europe. It is bordered by Montenegro to the north, by Kosovo to the north-east, by the former Yugoslav republic of Macedonia (FYRM) to the east, by Greece to the south and by the Adriatic and Ionian Seas (parts of the Mediterranean Sea) to the west. The climate is Mediterranean throughout most of the country. The sea plays a moderating role, although frequent cyclones in the winter months make the weather unstable. The average temperature is 14°C (57°F) in the north-east and 18°C (64°F) in the south-west. The language is Albanian, the principal dialects being Gheg (north of the Shkumbin river) and Tosk, which is spoken in the south and has been the official dialect since 1952. Islam is the predominant faith, but there are small groups of Christians (mainly Catholic in the north and Eastern Orthodox in the south). The national flag (proportions 5 by 7) is red, with a two-headed black eagle in the centre. The capital is Tirana (Tiranë).

CONTEMPORARY POLITICAL HISTORY

Historical Context

On 28 November 1912, after more than 400 years of Turkish rule, Albania declared its independence under a provisional Government. Although the country was occupied by Italy in 1914, its independence was re-established in 1920. Albania was declared a republic in 1925 and Ahmet Beg Zogu was elected President; proclaimed King Zog I in 1928, he reigned until he was forced into exile by the Italian occupation of Albania in April 1939. Albania was united with Italy for four years, before being occupied by German forces during 1943–44.

The communist-led National Liberation Front (NLF), established in 1941, took power on 29 November 1944. Elections in December 1945 were contested by only communist candidates. The new regime was headed by Enver Hoxha, the leader of the Albanian Communist Party (PKSh). King Zog was declared deposed, and the People's Republic of Albania was proclaimed on 11 January 1946. The PKSh was renamed the Party of Labour of Albania (PLA) in 1948, the NLF having been succeeded by the Democratic Front of Albania (DFA) in 1945. Hoxha resigned as Head of Government in 1954, but retained effective national leadership as First Secretary of the PLA.

A new Constitution was adopted in December 1976, and the country was renamed the People's Socialist Republic of Albania. In December 1981 Mehmet Shehu, the Chairman of the Council of Ministers (Prime Minister) since 1954, was shot dead. Although he was officially reported to have committed suicide, suggestions of a leadership struggle with Hoxha, and allegations that he had been executed, ensued. A new Government, headed by Adil Çarçani, hitherto the First Deputy Chairman, was subsequently established. In November 1982 Ramiz Alia replaced Haxhi Lleshi as the head of state, as President of the Presidium of the Kuvendi Popullor (People's Assembly). A number of former state and PLA officials were reportedly executed in September 1983.

Hoxha died in April 1985, and was succeeded as First Secretary of the PLA by Alia. In March 1986 Hoxha's widow, Nexhmije, was elected to the chairmanship of the General Council of the DFA. Alia was re-elected as First Secretary of the PLA and as President of the Presidium of the People's Assembly in November 1986 and February 1987, respectively. In the latter month Çarçani was reappointed Chairman of the Council of Ministers.

In November 1989 an amnesty for certain prisoners (including some political prisoners) was declared. From December a number of anti-Government demonstrations were reportedly staged, particularly in the northern town of Shkodër. In January 1990 Alia announced proposals for limited political and economic reform, including the introduction of a system of multi-candidate elections. The judicial system was reorganized, the practice of religion (prohibited since 1967) again tolerated, and Albanians were granted the right to foreign travel. Following renewed unrest in July, more than 5,000 Albanians took refuge in foreign embassies, and were subsequently granted permission to leave the country. Meanwhile, both the Council of Ministers and the Political Bureau of the PLA had been reorganized. In December 1990 it was announced that the establishment of independent political parties was to be permitted, prior to elections to the People's Assembly. None the less, there was further unrest in several cities in mid-December. Nexhmije Hoxha resigned from the chairmanship of the General Council of the DFA, and was replaced by Çarçani (who was, in turn, replaced in mid-1991).

Domestic Political Affairs

On 20 February 1991, following widespread anti-Government demonstrations, Alia declared presidential rule. An eight-member Presidential Council and a provisional Council of Ministers was established. Çarçani was replaced as Chairman of the Council of Ministers by Fatos Nano, a liberal economist, who had been appointed Deputy Chairman in late January. In late February the unrest finally ended. In mid-March a general amnesty for all political prisoners was declared. The first round of multi-party legislative elections took place on 31 March, with second and third ballots on 7 and 14 April, respectively. The PLA and affiliated organizations won 169 of the 250 seats, while the Partia Demokratike e Shqipërisë (PDSh—Democratic Party of Albania) secured 75 seats and the Democratic Union of the Greek Minority (OMONIA) five seats. The victory of the PLA, amid allegations of electoral malpractice, prompted widespread protests, and in Shkodër security forces opened fire on demonstrators, killing four.

In April 1991 an interim Constitution replaced that of 1976, pending the drafting of a new constitution. The country was renamed the Republic of Albania, and the post of executive President, to be elected by two-thirds of the votes cast in the People's Assembly, was created. Alia was subsequently elected to the new post, defeating the only other candidate, Namik Dokle, also of the PLA. In May 1991 Nano was reappointed Chairman of the Council of Ministers. In accordance with the provisions of the interim Constitution, Alia resigned from the leadership of the PLA. In June a continuing general strike forced the resignation of Nano's administration. A subsequent Government of National Stability included representatives of the PLA, the PDSh, the Partia Republika e Shqipërisë (PRSh—the Republican Party of Albania), the Social Democratic Party (PDS) and the Agrarian Party of Albania (APA). Ylli Bufi became Chairman of the Council of Ministers, while Gramoz Pashko, a prominent member of the PDSh, was appointed Deputy Chairman and Minister of the Economy. Later in June the PLA was renamed the Partia Socialiste e Shqipërisë (PSSh—Socialist Party of Albania). In December the Chairman of the PDSh, Sali Berisha, announced the withdrawal of the seven party representatives from the coalition Government, which, following the dismissal of three PRSh ministers, forced the resignation of Bufi's administration. Pending elections, Alia appointed an interim Government of non-party 'technocrats', under a new Prime Minister, Vilson Ahmeti.

At a general election, conducted in two rounds on 22 and 29 March 1992, the PDSh secured 92 of the 140 seats in the People's Assembly, the PSSh 38, the PDS seven, the Partia Bashkimi për të Drejtat e Njeriut (PBDNj—Union for Human Rights Party, supported by the minority Greek and Macedonian communities) two and the PRSh one seat. (Under a new electoral law, organizations that represented ethnic minorities, such as OMONIA, were prohibited from contesting the election.) Following the resignation of Alia, the new People's Assembly elected Berisha to the presidency on 9 April. Berisha subsequently appointed a coalition Government dominated by the PDSh, with Aleksander Meksi, of that party, as Prime Minister. In July the PDSh secured 43% of the votes cast at multi-party local elections, while the PSSh received 41%. In September divisions within the PDSh resulted in the defection of a number of prominent party members, who formed the Partia Aleanca Demokratikë (PAD—Democratic Alliance Party).

During 1992–93 a number of former communist officials were arrested on charges of corruption and abuse of power. Nexhmije

Hoxha was imprisoned for nine years in January 1993, having been convicted of embezzling state funds. (She was released in January 1997.) In August Ahmeti was sentenced to two years' imprisonment. Despite an international campaign on his behalf, organized by the PSSh, in April 1994 Nano (by this time Chairman of the PSSh) was convicted of the misappropriation of state funds during his premiership in 1991, and was sentenced to 12 years' imprisonment. In July 1994 Alia was sentenced to nine years' imprisonment, but was released in 1995.

In October 1994 a draft Constitution was finally presented to Berisha, and was submitted for endorsement at a national referendum, after it failed to obtain the requisite two-thirds' majority approval in the People's Assembly. As a result of Berisha's support for the draft Constitution (which was to vest additional powers in the President), the referendum was widely perceived as a vote of confidence in his leadership. At the referendum, which took place on 6 November, with the participation of 84.4% of the electorate, the draft Constitution was rejected by 53.9% of voters. Despite an extensive reorganization of the Council of Ministers in December, the PRSh and the main faction of the PDS withdrew from the governing coalition. In March 1995 the Chairman of the PDSh, Eduard Selami, who had accused Berisha of abuse of power, was removed from his post.

In September 1995 the People's Assembly adopted legislation prohibiting those in power under the former communist regime from holding public office until 2002 (thereby banning a large number of prospective candidates, including incumbent PSSh deputies, from contesting legislative elections in 1996). In November 1995 a parliamentary commission initiated an inquiry, following the discovery of a mass grave near the border town of Shkodër. Families of the deceased urged the prosecution service to initiate charges against former members of the communist regime, including Alia, who had allegedly been responsible for the killing by border guards of nationals attempting to flee the country in 1990–92; Alia was detained in February 1996. Meanwhile, in December 1995 the People's Assembly approved legislation requiring senior civil servants to be investigated for their activities under the communist regime. In December 14 prominent former members of the communist regime were arrested on charges of involvement in the execution, internment and deportation of citizens. (In May 1996 three of the former officials received death sentences, which were later commuted to terms of imprisonment, while the remaining defendants received custodial sentences.)

The first round of the legislative elections took place on 26 May 1996. Following alleged electoral irregularities, the principal opposition parties, including the PSSh, the PDS and the PAD, withdrew from the poll. A subsequent demonstration by the PSSh was violently dispersed by the security forces. The second round of the elections took place on 2 June; as a result of opposition demands for a boycott, only 59% of the electorate participated in the poll (compared with 89% in the first round). According to official results, the PDSh secured 101 of the 115 directly elected seats (25 seats were to be allocated on the basis of proportional representation). However, international observers, who included representatives of the Organization for Security and Co-operation in Europe (OSCE, see p. 387), reported that widespread malpractice and intimidation of voters had been perpetrated, and urged the Government to conduct fresh elections, while PSSh deputies staged a hunger strike in protest at the results. Berisha rejected the allegations, but agreed to conduct further elections in 17 constituencies. With the principal opposition parties continuing their electoral boycott, the PDSh won all the seats contested in the partial elections, held on 16 June, and secured a total of 122 of the 140 elective seats. The PSSh won 10 of the remaining seats, while the PBDNj and the PRSh each secured three and the National Front two. (The PSSh, however, began a boycott of the new legislature.) In early July Meksi, who had been reappointed to the office of Prime Minister, formed a new Council of Ministers. In August the Government established a permanent Central Election Commission (CEC). In local government elections, which took place in October, the PDSh secured the highest number of votes in 58 of the 65 municipalities and in 267 of the 305 communes. Monitors from the Council of Europe (see p. 252) declared that, despite some irregularities, the elections had been conducted fairly.

Civil uprising

In January 1997 the collapse of several popular 'pyramid' financial investment schemes, resulting in huge losses of individual savings, prompted violent anti-Government demonstrations. It was widely believed that members of the Government were associated with the pyramid schemes, which had allegedly financed widespread illegal activities; legislation was subsequently adopted prohibiting the schemes. In late January the People's Assembly granted Berisha emergency powers to restore order. Several people were reported to have been killed in ensuing violent clashes between security forces and protesters. None the less, on 3 March Berisha was re-elected unopposed by the People's Assembly for a second five-year term.

After an escalation in hostilities between insurgents and government troops in the south of the country, Berisha declared a state of emergency in early March 1997. However, insurgent groups gained control of the southern towns of Vlorë, Sarandë and Gjirokastër. Following negotiations with representatives of nine opposition parties, Berisha signed an agreement providing for the installation of an interim coalition government, pending elections in June, and offered an amnesty to rebels who surrendered to the authorities. A former PSSh mayor of Gjirokastër, Bashkim Fino, was appointed as Prime Minister. Berisha subsequently formed a Government of National Reconciliation, which included representatives of eight opposition parties. None the less, the insurgency continued, reaching the northern town of Tropojë and Tirana. Those detained in Tirana central prison, including Nano and Alia, were released; Berisha subsequently granted Nano an official pardon. Extreme hardship prompted thousands of Albanians to flee to Italy. By late March government forces had regained control of Tirana, although insurgent groups held the south of the country. The Government requested military assistance in the restoration of civil order, and Fino appealed to the European Union (EU, see p. 273) for the establishment of a multinational force to supervise aid operations in Albania. At the end of March the UN Security Council endorsed an OSCE proposal that member states be authorized to contribute troops to the force. The 5,915-member Multinational Protection Force for Albania was established in April, with a three-month mandate to facilitate the distribution of humanitarian assistance.

In early April 1997 the PSSh ended its boycott of the legislature. Later in April the National Council of the PDSh endorsed Berisha's leadership of the party and removed a number of dissident members who had demanded his resignation. The son of King Zog I and claimant to the throne, Leka Zogu, returned to Albania in April, with the support of the monarchist Movement of Legality Party. In May the People's Assembly adopted legislation regulating the operation of pyramid investment schemes, and approved a proposal submitted by the PDSh on the introduction of a new electoral system, under which the number of legislative deputies was to be increased from 140 to 155. The PSSh and its allied parties agreed to participate in the elections, after Berisha complied with the stipulation that the CEC be appointed by the interim Government (rather than by himself).

The legislative elections of 1997: the PSSh gains power

Election campaigning was marred by violence, including several bomb explosions in Tirana. On 29 June 1997 the first round of voting in the legislative elections took place; a referendum on the restoration of the monarchy was conducted on the same day. Despite the presence of the Multinational Protection Force (the mandate of which had been extended to mid-August), three people were reportedly killed in violent incidents on polling day. A further ballot took place in 32 constituencies on 6 July. Observers from the OSCE subsequently declared the elections to have been conducted satisfactorily. Later in July the CEC announced that the PSSh had secured 101 seats in the People's Assembly, while the PDSh had won 29 seats; the PSSh and its allied parties (the PDS, the PAD, the APA and the PBDNj) thereby secured the requisite two-thirds' majority for the approval of constitutional amendments that they had proposed earlier in the month. At the referendum, 66.7% of the electorate voted in favour of retaining a republic. On 24 July, following Berisha's resignation as President, the People's Assembly elected the Secretary-General of the PSSh, Rexhep Mejdani, to that position. Parliamentary deputies also voted to end the state of emergency. The PSSh proposed Nano to the office of Prime Minister, and a new Council of Ministers, comprising representatives of the PSSh and its allied parties, was appointed. At the end of July the new Government's programme for the restoration of civil order and economic reconstruction received a legislative vote of confidence. The People's Assembly also voted in favour of auditing existing pyramid schemes and investigating those that had been dissolved. In August the Government dispatched troops to the south of the country, in an effort to restore order in major towns that were under the control of rebel forces. It was subsequently announced that Vlorë had been recaptured and a number of rebel forces arrested. By mid-August the Multinational Protection Force had left Albania.

In September 1997 the People's Assembly established a parliamentary commission to draft a new constitution, in accordance with the amendments proposed by the PSSh. In October Berisha was re-elected Chairman of the PDSh. Meanwhile, intermittent violent unrest continued, and in February 1998 an armed revolt by civilians and disaffected members of the local security forces in Shkodër was suppressed by government troops. In July a parliamentary commission into the unrest of 1997 recommended that several senior PDSh officials, including Berisha, be charged in connection with the deployment of the armed forces to suppress the protests.

In September 1998 Azem Hajdari, one of Berisha's deputies in the PDSh, was assassinated in Tirana. Berisha accused Nano of involvement in the killing, and the PDSh resumed its boycott of the legislature. The incident prompted violent protests by PDSh supporters, who seized government offices and occupied the state television and radio buildings. Government security forces regained control of the capital after clashes with protesters, in which about seven people were reported to have been killed. Although Berisha denied government claims that the uprising constituted a coup attempt, the People's Assembly voted to revoke Berisha's exemption (as a parliamentary deputy) from prosecution, allowing him to be charged with attempting to overthrow the Government. At the end of September the Minister of Public Order resigned, amid widespread criticism of the Government's failure to improve public security. Shortly afterwards Nano tendered his resignation, having failed to reach agreement with the government coalition on the composition of a new Council of Ministers. Mejdani subsequently requested that the Secretary-General of the PSSh, Pandeli Majko, form a new government. In October a new coalition Council of Ministers, headed by Majko, was installed. Later that month the People's Assembly approved the draft Constitution (with opposition deputies boycotting the vote). The new Constitution was submitted for endorsement at a national referendum, monitored by OSCE observers, on 22 November. The Government announced that 50.1% of the registered electorate had participated in the referendum, of whom 93.1% had voted in favour of adopting the draft. Berisha disputed the results of the referendum and announced that the PDSh would refuse to recognize the new Constitution. None the less, on 28 November the new Constitution was officially adopted. In July 1999 a PDSh congress voted in favour of ending the boycott of the legislature.

At a PSSh party congress in September 1999 Nano was re-elected as party Chairman, narrowly defeating Majko. In October Majko resigned as Prime Minister. Mejdani subsequently nominated Ilir Meta (hitherto Deputy Prime Minister) as Prime Minister. In early November the new Government was formally approved in the People's Assembly, despite a boycott by the PDSh.

Local government elections took place in two rounds in October 2000, following the preparation of a new voters' register, with assistance from the UN Development Programme (UNDP, see p. 54). Official results indicated that the PSSh had obtained control of a total of 252 communes and municipalities, while the PDSh had secured 118. In February 2001 the PDSh and the PSSh reached agreement on the adoption of a new electoral code. The first round of elections to the People's Assembly, which was conducted on 24 June, was judged by international observers to have been conducted satisfactorily. A second round took place on 8 July in 45 constituencies. Ballots were repeated in eight constituencies in July–August, after opposition complaints of irregularities were upheld by the Constitutional Court. According to the final results, which were announced by the CEC on 21 August, the PSSh won 73 seats and a PDSh-led coalition, the Union for Victory, won 46 seats in the People's Assembly (which had reverted to a total of 140 deputies).

Following Meta's reappointment as Prime Minister, a reorganized Council of Ministers, nominated by President Mejdani, was approved in September 2001. The new Government retained representatives of the PDS, notably the party Chairman, Skender Gjinushi, as Deputy Prime Minister and Minister of Labour and Social Affairs; Majko became Minister of Defence. (Deputies belonging to the Union for Victory boycotted the new People's Assembly, in continued protest at the outcome of the elections, which Berisha alleged had been characterized by widespread fraud.)

In December 2001 severe divisions emerged within the PSSh, after Nano publicly accused the Government of engaging in corrupt practices. In that month the Ministers of Finance and of the Public Economy and Privatization (both members of the PSSh) resigned from the Government, after being implicated in the corruption allegations. Two further PSSh members also resigned their ministerial portfolios. On 29 January 2002 Meta tendered his resignation, after the two PSSh factions failed to reach agreement on the appointment of new ministers to the vacant posts. Majko of the PSSh (a compromise candidate) was appointed as Prime Minister on 7 February. Following protracted negotiations between the two PSSh factions and allied parties, the People's Assembly approved a new Council of Ministers, in which portfolios were divided between supporters of Nano and Meta, on 22 February. The deputies of the Union for Victory subsequently agreed to resume participation in the People's Assembly.

As the end of Mejdani's term of office approached, it became apparent that Nano would be unable to secure majority support in the legislature, owing to strong opposition from Berisha. Following prolonged negotiations between the PSSh and the PDSh, Alfred Moisiu, a retired general who had served in the Berisha administration, was selected as a candidate. He was elected by 97 of the 140 legislative deputies on 24 June 2002, and was inaugurated on 24 July. On the following day Majko resigned as Prime Minister. Moisiu appointed Nano to the premiership, and a new administration, again including members of both PSSh factions, was approved at the end of the month, with Majko returning to his post as Minister of Defence; Meta became Deputy Prime Minister and Minister of Foreign Affairs. A new electoral code was adopted in June 2003. However, continuing dissension between the two PSSh factions culminated in Meta's resignation from the Government in mid-July, citing authoritarian behaviour by Nano. The Minister of State for Integration, an ally of Meta, also resigned.

Local government elections on 12 October 2003 prompted reports by OSCE observers of irregularities; the rate of participation by the electorate was reported to be less than 50%. Although the PSSh claimed to have secured control of 36 municipalities, the PDSh contested the results, accusing the authorities of malpractice. Later that month Nano removed the Minister of Public Order, Luan Rama. Meta declared that his faction would obstruct further ministerial appointments in the People's Assembly until Nano agreed to reorganize the Government. In mid-December Nano was re-elected as Chairman of the PSSh. Later that month, after initiating negotiations to secure the support of smaller parliamentary parties, Nano signed agreements with the leaders of the PDS, the PAD, the APA, the PBDNj, and a breakaway faction of the PDS, establishing the Coalition for Integration, and a government reorganization, which included the appointment of Namik Dokle as Deputy Prime Minister, was approved by the People's Assembly. Meanwhile, further municipal elections were conducted in parts of the country in December, after a court of appeal upheld PDSh allegations and declared the results in a number of districts to be invalid; OSCE monitors reported further irregularities at some ballots.

In early 2004 the PDSh organized large anti-Government protests in Tirana to demand Nano's resignation. In June, following protracted debate, the People's Assembly approved legislation on the restitution and compensation of property (providing for the payment of recompense to citizens whose property had been transferred to state ownership after the accession to power of the NLF in 1944).

The legislative elections of 2005: the PDSh returns to government

In September 2004 the ruling coalition was severely weakened by Meta's resignation from the PSSh, following continued disputes with Nano, and his establishment of a new political party, the Lëvizja Socialiste për Integrim (LSI—Socialist Movement for Integration). The PSSh subsequently lost its parliamentary majority following the defection of several deputies. Legislative elections took place on 3 July 2005, with the participation of some 56% of voters. A second round of voting was held in three constituencies on 21 August. According to the final results, announced in early September, the PDSh and its allies won 80 of the 140 seats in the People's Assembly, while the PSSh and allied parties secured 60 seats. Nano duly resigned as Chairman of the PSSh, but continued to dispute the results. The final report of the OSCE, which monitored the elections, concluded that the ballot only partly met international standards for democratic elections. On 2 September President Moisiu nominated Berisha as Prime Minister. On 10 September the People's Assembly approved the new PDSh-led, coalition Government in which the PRSh, the New Democratic Party (NDP), the APA and the PBDNj each received one portfolio. Notably, the Chairman of the PRSh, Fatmir Mediu, was appointed Minister of Defence. In October the Mayor of Tirana, Edi Rama, was elected as the new PSSh Chairman.

In January 2007 the main political parties agreed on the adoption of electoral reform legislation, designed to prevent malpractice. Moisiu rescheduled delayed local government elections for 18 February. The CEC announced that a number of irregularities were reported during the elections; an OSCE observer mission and the EU concluded that preparations for, and the conduct of, the elections had failed to meet international standards. According to official results, the ruling coalition secured some 51.1% of the votes cast, and the PSSh-led opposition alliance (known as Together for the Future) 42.9% (with about 48% of the registered electorate participating). Individually, however, the PSSh won the greatest proportion of votes, with 23.2%, while the PDSh received 20.6%. PSSh candidates secured control of several principal municipalities; notably, Edi Rama was re-elected as Mayor of Tirana, defeating PDSh candidate Sokol Olldashi, the Minister of the Interior. In March Berisha effected a number of government changes (among them the replacement of the Deputy Prime Minister). In mid-April Majko resigned as Secretary-General of the PSSh. Later that month the Minister of Foreign Affairs, Besnik Mustafaj, announced his resignation; he was replaced by Lulzim Basha. In May Rama was re-elected as Chairman of the PSSh.

In June 2007 the scheduled election by the People's Assembly of a new President, to succeed Moisiu on the expiry of his second term in office on 24 July, was postponed, owing to dissent between the parties. The PSSh objected to the PDSh's nomination, without consultation, of Bamir Topi as its presidential candidate, and boycotted three rounds of voting in the People's Assembly, in which Topi was unable to secure the support of the three-fifths of deputies required for election. At a fourth round of voting on 20 July five members of the PSSh voted for Topi, who narrowly obtained the required majority; he was inaugurated on 24 July.

In November 2007 the Minister of Justice, Ilir Rusmajli, tendered his resignation, shortly after that of the head of the prison service, who had made allegations of corruption involving Rusmajli's brother. Later that month Topi dismissed the Prosecutor-General, Theodhori Sollaku, who had been criticized for his perceived failure to address organized crime. He was succeeded by Ina Rama, who was the first woman to hold the post. In March 2008 Mediu resigned as Minister of Defence and three state officials were arrested, after 26 people were killed and some 300 injured in an explosion at an army munitions depot at Gërdec, near Tirana.

On 21 April 2008 the People's Assembly adopted significant constitutional amendments, which, notably, abolished the partial majority voting system in favour of proportional representation within each of the country's 12 administrative regions (counties), and revised parliamentary procedures for the election of the President. In June Topi dismissed the Chief of the General Staff, Lt-Gen. Luan Hoxha, after indications that the explosion at the Gërdec depot had been caused by negligence. In a government reorganization in July, Genc Pollo of the NDP, hitherto Minister of Education and Science, was appointed to the office of Deputy Prime Minister. Despite opposition from smaller parliamentary parties, which were expected to be disadvantaged by the new system of proportional representation, on 18 November a new electoral code was finally approved in the People's Assembly, with the support of the PSSh.

On 22 December 2008 a lustration law, which required all public officials to be investigated to determine whether they had co-operated with the secret police during the communist era, obtained parliamentary approval; however, in February 2010 the Constitutional Court ruled the lustration law, suspended in 2009, to be unconstitutional.

The disputed 2009 legislative elections

A number of violent incidents were reported prior to legislative elections in mid-2009, including the killing of a PSSh parliamentary deputy in May. The elections to the People's Assembly were conducted on 28 June. An OSCE observer mission report stated that the organization of the elections demonstrated improvements, but noted irregularities in the vote-counting process. The PSSh accused the authorities of malpractice in the counting of votes, particularly in the town of Fier and, following a recount there, gained an additional seat. According to the official results, announced in early August, the PDSh-led Alliance for Change secured a total of 70 seats (68 of which were obtained by the PDSh), with some 46.9% of the votes cast, while the PSSh-led Unification for Change coalition won 66 seats (65 of which were received by the PSSh), with about 45.3% of the votes. In early July it had been announced that the PDSh was to establish a coalition with the LSI, which won some 4.9% of the votes and four seats, in order to form a new government. The new People's Assembly was convened in early September; however, the PSSh began a parliamentary boycott, in protest against the rejection of its demands for an investigation into alleged electoral irregularities. On 9 September President Topi formally reappointed Berisha as Prime Minister. A new Government was established on 17 September; the PDSh received 12 portfolios, the LSI was allocated four and the PRSh obtained one ministerial post. Basha was appointed Minister of the Interior. Mediu (the PRSh representative) was returned to the Government as Minister of the Environment; the Supreme Court suspended legal proceedings against him in connection with the explosion at the Gërdec depot, owing to his consequent immunity from prosecution. The PSSh continued to organize demonstrations in Tirana, in protest against the election results, and in mid-November boycotted elections to fill five vacant seats. In January 2010 it was announced that the Parliamentary Assembly of the Council of Europe (PACE) was to assist Topi in mediating inter-party discussions with the aim of ending the ongoing PSSh boycott. In February the 65 PSSh deputies finally returned to the People's Assembly; however, dissent between the Government and the PSSh concerning the 2009 elections continued, with the former favouring the establishment of a parliamentary commission to investigate the allegations of malpractice and the latter insisting on a recount of the electoral ballots in disputed regions.

In April 2010 the PSSh organized a large anti-Government demonstration in Tirana. At the beginning of May some 22 PSSh parliamentary deputies and 180 supporters of the party commenced a hunger strike in protest against the Government's refusal to allow a recount of the votes cast in the legislative elections. The hunger strike ended on 19 May, following the intervention of the European Parliament. The PSSh subsequently resumed participation in parliamentary sessions, but, with a lack of progress in negotiations with the Government, continued to boycott votes on general and reform legislation. In September Meta (Deputy Prime Minister and Minister of Foreign Affairs since September 2009) was appointed as Deputy Prime Minister and Minister of Economy, Trade and Energy, replacing Dritan Prifti, who had resigned owing to corruption allegations. Edmond Haxhinasto was appointed as Minister of Foreign Affairs. In October 2010 the PSSh deputies again withdrew from a parliamentary session, and presented further conditions for their participation, demanding *inter alia* that the Government abandon plans to demolish the 'Pyramid' in Tirana (regarded as a symbol of the communist era). In November the PSSh resumed the organization of anti-Government protests.

Political impasse

In January 2011 Meta resigned from the Government, after a local television channel broadcast video footage in which he appeared to apply pressure on Prifti in an attempt to influence the outcome of a public tender for a hydroelectric plant. Haxhinasto became Deputy Prime Minister and Minister of Foreign Affairs. Edi Rama reiterated accusations of government corruption and demanded that Berisha's administration resign. On 21 January more than 20,000 people took part in an anti-Government demonstration in Tirana organized by the PSSh, which led to clashes between police and PSSh supporters; four protesters died, and several were injured. Berisha accused the opposition of attempting to overthrow his Government through violent means; meanwhile, EU officials condemned the excessive use of force, and urged a resumption of political dialogue. An arrest warrant issued by Prosecutor-General Ina Rama against six senior members of the Republican Guard, including its commander, in connection with the deaths was not implemented owing to alleged technical errors. Later in January former Slovakian Minister of Foreign Affairs Miroslav Lajčák, who had been appointed as the EU special envoy on the political crisis, began to mediate negotiations between the Government and the PSSh. In early February a parliamentary session ended in a violent altercation between deputies of the PDSh and the

PSSh (which temporarily withdrew from the People's Assembly). Later in February thousands of people attended a pro-Government rally in Tirana. In April, as part of a government reorganization, Bujar Nishani, hitherto the Minister of Justice, was appointed as Minister of the Interior, replacing Basha, who had resigned in order to stand as a mayoral candidate in forthcoming local elections. (In July Berisha appointed Eduard Halimi as Minister of Justice.)

Despite the continued unstable political environment, local government elections were conducted on 8 May 2011, as scheduled. The electoral campaign was marred by violence, with frequent clashes between supporters of rival political groups. A protracted dispute (owing to controversy over the validity of ballots that had not been cast in the designated boxes) ensued over the result of the mayoral election in Tirana, which initially indicated that PSSh Chairman and incumbent Mayor Edi Rama had won. In late June, however, after ruling that the disputed ballots be included, the CEC declared that PDSh candidate Basha had been elected as the new Mayor, defeating Rama. (The PSSh, which again boycotted the People's Assembly, nevertheless submitted a further challenge against Basha's election, which was rejected by the Electoral College—the highest election-related court in the country—on 8 July.) Overall, the PSSh-led coalition secured control of 35 municipalities (although winning about 48% of votes cast), and the PDSh-led coalition the remaining 30 (with some 52% of the votes). An OSCE report, issued in August, noted that acrimony between the two main political groupings, including disputes within the CEC, had adversely affected administration of the poll. Following an unfavourable progress report by the European Commission in October, in mid-November the PDSh and the PSSh, which had returned to the People's Assembly in the previous month, agreed to co-operate in meeting the Commission's requirements, and subsequently established a joint parliamentary committee for electoral reform. In January 2012 the Supreme Court dismissed the corruption charges brought against Meta in the previous year. In March 19 former officials received prison sentences in connection with the explosion at the Gërdec depot in March 2008. In May 2012 the Constitutional Court ruled that Mediu be charged with negligence, following appeals by two people injured in the explosion. (In February 2013 an appeals court in Tirana reduced the custodial terms of the three main officials convicted, to between six and 12 years' imprisonment, while Luan Hoxha's sentence of seven years for abuse of power was changed to six years.) Also in May the National Security Committee agreed to increased supervision of the Ministry of Defence, following media allegations of the involvement of defence officials in armaments trafficking and the illegal sale of army assets.

Election of a new President and electoral reform

Three unsuccessful attempts to elect a new President took place in the People's Assembly in late May and early June 2012, after which the PDSh candidate, Constitutional Court judge Xhezair Zaganjori, withdrew from the poll. He was replaced by the hitherto Minister of the Interior, Bujar Nishani, who was elected President in a fourth ballot on 11 June, securing 73 of the 76 votes cast (with PSSh deputies boycotting the vote). A government reorganization took place in late June; Nishani was succeeded as Minister of the Interior by Flamur Noka, while Haxhinasto was appointed as Deputy Prime Minister and Minister of Economy, Trade and Energy, and was replaced as Minister of Foreign Affairs by Edmond Panariti.

Meanwhile, in mid-July 2012 the PDSh and the PSSh reached agreement on the changes to the electoral code that had been demanded by the European Commission prior to the 2013 legislative elections, specifically relating to the selection of, and powers vested in, members of the CEC and the regulation of voter identification. On 19 July the electoral reforms were adopted by the People's Assembly, with 127 votes in favour. Nishani was inaugurated as President on 24 July. Owing to PSSh opposition, in early August the Government failed to secure parliamentary approval for legislation designed to restrict the right to immunity from prosecution by deputies and senior state officials, which had been cited as a precondition for Albania's admission to the EU. However, PSSh leader Rama subsequently announced that, in order to enable progress to be made in the EU integration process, the PSSh was to withdraw its objections, and on 19 September the legislation was finally adopted in the People's Assembly. Also in September some 20 communist-era political prisoners began hunger strikes in protest against the Government's refusal to award them adequate compensation; two prisoners set themselves on fire in early October, after which one died.

In April 2013 the LSI withdrew from the ruling coalition, after joining the PSSh-led alliance, in advance of the legislative elections scheduled for June. In the subsequent government reorganization, the Minister of Education and Science, Myqerem Tafaj, also became Deputy Prime Minister, Florion Mima was appointed as Minister of Economy, Trade and Energy, and Aldo Bumçi replaced Panariti as Minister of Foreign Affairs. Later in April the LSI-proposed member of the CEC was removed from the Commission by a parliamentary vote initiated by the PDSh. In response, the three remaining opposition members of the CEC resigned, their posts remaining vacant. In May legislation pertaining to the Supreme Court, public administration and parliamentary procedures was approved by the People's Assembly, in fulfilment of EU pre-requisites for Albania's eligibility for candidate status.

Recent developments: the 2013 legislative elections

Legislative elections, which were conducted on 23 June 2013, resulted in victory for the PSSh-led coalition, the Alliance for a European Albania, which won 57.7% of the votes cast and 84 seats in the 140-seat People's Assembly, while the Alliance for Employment, Prosperity and Integration coalition led by the incumbent PDSh took 39.4% of the votes and 56 seats. (The PSSh and the PDSh received 66 and 49 seats, respectively.) Despite violent disruption in the north-western town of Laç, in which an LSI member was shot dead, international observers considered the country to have made significant improvements to the electoral process. Later in June Berisha resigned as Chairman of the PDSh, in response to the party's poor electoral performance. It was subsequently announced that Berisha's Government was to remain in office until September, when a PSSh-led administration headed by Rama would be established. On 22 July Lulzim Basha was elected as the new PDSh Chairman, defeating Sokol Olldashi, who claimed that the result had been secured fraudulently. Meanwhile, Rama protested at the approval of important economic decisions and judicial appointments by Berisha's outgoing Government, despite its impending dissolution. Hostility subsequently intensified between Rama and Berisha, who in August accused the PSSh leader of taking bribes while in government and several other prospective members of the new administration of corrupt practices. Berisha refused to act as Speaker for the inaugural session of the People's Assembly on 10 September, again claiming that the PSSh under Rama had gained office through deception, including pre-election pledges that it was unable to fulfil; LSI leader Meta was elected as the new Speaker. On 15 September the People's Assembly approved the installation of a new Government, headed by Rama, and principally comprising representatives of the PSSh and the LSI; notably, a former mayor and senior PSSh official, Niko Peleshi, became Deputy Prime Minister.

In early December 2013 the Chief Justice of the Supreme Court, Xhezair Zaganjori, rejected allegations broadcast by an investigative television programme that he had accepted bribes to dismiss a case. The Office of the Prosecutor-General launched an investigation into the affair and suspended senior judicial officials from their posts. Meanwhile, Rama's Government asserted its intention to secure parliamentary approval of new anti-corruption legislation, which would, *inter alia*, grant new authorities to the Court and to the Prosecutor's Office for Serious Crimes, although the USA and the OSCE expressed concern about the authorities' lack of consultation in adopting the proposals. In the same month former Minister of Defence Arben Imami was charged with abuse of power, the embezzlement of state funds and holding illegal tenders; other ministry officials were also charged with corruption. Later in December three customs and two police officers were arrested in the northern border town of Kukës, on suspicion of involvement in the trafficking of illicit goods. In January 2014 the Government resumed official online publication of its decisions, in accordance with its stated commitment to full transparency. However, in February the PDSh organized an opposition rally in Tirana, in protest at the perceived failure of the PSSh-led Government to fulfil its electoral pledges.

Foreign Affairs

Regional relations

Albania's relations with Greece have frequently been strained. In August 1987 Greece formally ended the technical state of war with Albania that had been in existence since 1945. However, the status of the Greek minority in Albania, estimated to number some 300,000 by the Greek authorities, remained a sensitive issue. Relations between Albania and Greece became particularly tense in April 1994, following a border incident in which two Albanian guards were killed. In May six prominent members of the ethnic Greek organization OMONIA were arrested. Greece subsequently vetoed the provision of EU funds to Albania and increased the deportation of illegal Albanian immigrants. In September five of the OMONIA detainees were convicted on charges including espionage and the illegal possession of weapons, and received custodial sentences. Following the verdict, Greece and Albania both recalled their ambassadors. In addition, Greece submitted formal protests to the UN and the EU regarding Albania's perceived maltreatment of its ethnic Greek population and closed the Kakavija border crossing, which had hitherto been used by Albanian migrant workers. One of the OMONIA defendants was pardoned in December, after Greece withdrew its veto on EU aid to Albania in November. In February 1995 the four remaining prisoners were released, allowing a subsequent improvement in bilateral relations. In March 1996 a co-operation agreement was signed, with the aim of resolving outstanding issues of concern between the two nations. A new border crossing between Albania and Greece was opened in May 1999. In 2006 the Albanian and Greek authorities announced a joint plan for increased surveillance measures to combat cross-border trafficking. In November 2012 the Greek Minister of Foreign Affairs, Dimitris Avramopoulos, cancelled his planned attendance of celebrations to mark 100 years of Albanian independence, after Prime Minister Berisha made reference to 'Albanian' territories that form part of neighbouring states, including Preveza in north-western Greece. In August 2013 the Greek Ministry of Foreign Affairs condemned attacks by Albanian Muslims on Christian Orthodox churches in the southern towns of Përmet and Gjirokastër, which had substantial ethnic Greek communities. Berisha dismissed the Greek statement as interference in Albania's internal affairs, while urging dialogue to resolve the dispute over the ownership of property that had been appropriated by the state during the communist era. In December the Governments of Albania and Greece announced that they were willing to renegotiate demarcation of their Ionian Sea maritime border, following the rejection by Albania's Constitutional Court of a demarcation agreement signed in 2009.

Albania's relations with Serbia (then part of Yugoslavia) deteriorated sharply from 1989, when many ethnic Albanian demonstrators were killed during renewed unrest in the predominantly ethnic Albanian province of Kosovo. In early 1998 Albania condemned increased Serbian military activity against the ethnic Albanian majority in Kosovo, while clashes were reported on the Albanian border with that country between Serbian troops and members of the paramilitary Kosovo Liberation Army (KLA). The Albanian administration initiated measures to prevent the illicit transportation of armaments from northern Albania to KLA forces in Kosovo. By mid-1998 some 10,000 ethnic Albanian refugees had fled to northern Albania, following continued Serbian military reprisals against the ethnic Albanian population in Kosovo. The Albanian Government expressed support for the North Atlantic Treaty Organization (NATO, see p. 370) aerial bombardment of Serbia, which began in March 1999, and allowed Albania's air and sea facilities to be used for NATO operations. NATO troops (which later numbered about 8,000, and became known as AFOR) were dispatched to Albania to support humanitarian aid operations for the Kosovo refugee population. Following the deployment of a NATO-led peacekeeping Kosovo Force (KFOR) in the province, under the terms of a peace agreement in June, refugees began rapidly to return to Kosovo from Albania. In September NATO announced that AFOR, which had been gradually withdrawing from the country, was to be replaced by a 1,200-member contingent, Communications Zone West (COMMZ-W), which was mandated to maintain civil order in Albania and to support the KFOR mission in Kosovo. (In June 2002 COMMZ-W was officially dissolved, when a NATO headquarters was established at Tirana.) Following the removal from power of Yugoslav President Slobodan Milošević in late 2000, Albania and Yugoslavia formally restored diplomatic relations in January 2001. Bilateral diplomatic relations were upgraded to ambassadorial level in September 2002.

Albania officially recognized the former Yugoslav republic of Macedonia (FYRM) as an independent state in 1993. The Albanian Government remained concerned at the perceived oppression of the FYRM's ethnic Albanian minority, which constituted about 21% of the population. Conflict between government forces and ethnic Albanian rebels in the FYRM in February–August 2001 prompted large numbers of ethnic Albanian civilians to take refuge in Albania, and the region remained unstable thereafter. In November 2003 the Ministries of Defence of Albania, Greece and the FYRM pledged to increase military co-operation to address the issues of illegal immigration and cross-border organized crime. Albanian President Topi and other government officials visited the FYRM capital, Skopje, in April 2012, one week after the killing of five Macedonians in a nearby village, in an apparent further incidence of violence between ethnic Albanians and Macedonians in the country. The FYRM premier, Nikola Gruevski, visited Tirana in November, when an agreement was signed with Prime Minister Berisha on the opening of a new border crossing between the two countries.

The unilateral declaration of independence by a newly installed Kosovo Government on 17 February 2008 (which was rapidly approved by the USA and a number of EU member states) prompted public celebrations in Tirana, and Berisha announced that Albania officially recognized Kosovo as an independent and sovereign state. On 19 February the Council of Ministers approved the establishment of diplomatic relations with Kosovo at ambassadorial level. In November the President of Kosovo, Fatmir Sejdiu, made his first official visit to Albania. In October 2009 Berisha made an official visit to Kosovo's capital, Prishtina, where a number of bilateral co-operation agreements were signed, including protocols on customs and border policing. In January 2014 Prime Minister Rama and his Kosovo counterpart, Hashim Thaçi, signed an agreement in Prizren, Kosovo, on strategic co-operation and partnership, which sought to facilitate the EU integration process of the respective states.

In December 2010 Swiss senator and Council of Europe rapporteur Dick Marty presented a report (which was subsequently adopted by PACE) claiming that human-organ trafficking operations had occurred on Albanian territory during and after the 1999 conflict in Kosovo, and implicating the Kosovo Prime Minister, Hashim Thaçi. In July 2011 the Governments of Albania and Serbia approved an agreement to end visa requirements between the two states. In May 2012 the People's Assembly adopted legislation that granted the EU Rule of Law Mission in Kosovo powers to conduct investigations in Albania into the organ trafficking allegations (which the Albanian Government continued to dismiss vigorously).

Other external relations

The gradual relaxation of Albania's isolationist policies culminated in 1990 in a declaration of its intention to establish good relations with all countries, irrespective of their social system. In July of that year Albania and the USSR formally agreed to restore diplomatic relations (which had been suspended in 1961). Diplomatic relations between Albania and the USA (suspended since 1946) were re-established in March 1991.

Negotiations on the signature of a Stabilization and Association Agreement (SAA) with the EU officially commenced at the end of January 2003. Following a positive recommendation issued by the European Commission in March 2006, the SAA was officially signed between the Albanian Government and the EU on 12 June. The People's Assembly ratified the Agreement in late July. At a NATO summit meeting, convened in Bucharest, Romania, on 2 April 2008, it was announced that official invitations to begin accession negotiations were to be extended to Albania and Croatia. Albania acceded to membership of NATO on 1 April 2009. In that month the SAA with the EU entered into effect, and on 28 April Albania submitted a formal application for membership of the Union.

In November 2010 the European Commission issued a progress report stating that Albania had not fulfilled the criteria to receive official candidate status, citing high-level corruption, deficiencies in the judiciary, and organized crime as the continued main obstacles; however the Commission confirmed a recommendation by the European Parliament that visa requirements for Albanians entering the EU be removed (with effect from mid-December). Following a further critical report by the European Commission in 2011, the Albanian authorities adopted electoral and other reform legislation during 2012 (see Domestic Political Affairs), and in October of that year the Commission recommended that Albania be awarded EU candidate status, stipulating that this was conditional on the continued fulfilment of reform commitments. In December, however, the EU General Affairs Council failed to grant the country's candidate status, demanding further commitment to reforms and, in particular, the satisfactory conduct of legislative elections in June 2013. In October the European Commission reported that Albania had made further progress in fulfilling political criteria, including in the conduct of the elections, and again issued a recommendation that the country be granted candidate status, which was approved by a resolution of the European Parliament on 12 December. Meanwhile, in early December the Albanian Government signed a new co-operation agreement with the European Police Office (Europol), as part of its efforts to combat organized crime. However, following the opposition of several states, notably the Netherlands, on 17 December the EU General Affairs Council deferred the decision on Albania's candidate status to June 2014, citing the necessity of further judicial and public administration reforms.

CONSTITUTION AND GOVERNMENT

Under the Constitution adopted in November 1998, legislative power is vested in the unicameral Kuvendi Popullor (People's Assembly). The People's Assembly, which is elected for a term of four years, comprises 140 deputies, 100 of whom are directly elected in single-member constituencies. Parties receiving 2.5% or more of the votes cast, and party coalitions obtaining 4.0% or more in the first round of voting, are allocated further deputies in proportion to the number of votes secured, on the basis of multi-name lists of parties or party coalitions. The President of the Republic is head of state, and is elected by the People's Assembly for a term of five years. Executive authority is held by the Council of Ministers, which is led by the Prime Minister as head of government. The Prime Minister is appointed by the President and appoints a Council of Ministers, which is presented for approval to the People's Assembly. Judicial power is exercised by the High Court, as well as by the Courts of Appeal and the Courts of First Instance. The Chairman and members of the High Court are nominated by the President of the Republic, subject to the approval of the People's Assembly, for a term of nine years. For the purposes of local government, Albania is divided into 12 counties (*qarqe*—also called prefectures), 36 districts (*rrethe*), 65 municipalities and 309 communes. The representative organs of the basic units of local government are councils, which are elected by direct election for a period of three years. The Council of Ministers appoints a Prefect as its representative in each of the 12 counties.

REGIONAL AND INTERNATIONAL CO-OPERATION

Albania is a member of the European Bank for Reconstruction and Development (EBRD, see p. 267), the Organization for Security and Co-operation in Europe (OSCE, see p. 387), the Council of Europe (see p. 252) and the Organization of the Black Sea Economic Cooperation (see p. 401). Albania is also a member of the Organization of Islamic Cooperation (see p. 403).

Albania became a member of the UN in 1955, and was admitted to the World Trade Organization (see p. 434) in 2000. Albania acceded to the North Atlantic Treaty Organization (NATO, see p. 370) on 1 April 2009.

ECONOMIC AFFAIRS

In 2012, according to World Bank estimates, Albania's gross national income (GNI), measured at average 2010–12 prices, was US $12,923m., equivalent to $4,090 per head (or $9,390 on an international purchasing-power parity basis). During 2003–12, it was estimated, the population decreased by an annual average of 0.3%, while gross domestic product (GDP) per head increased, in real terms, by an average of 4.8% per year. According to World Bank estimates, overall GDP increased, in real terms, at an average annual rate of 4.5% in 2003–12; growth of 0.8% was recorded in 2012.

Agriculture contributed 19.5% of GDP in 2011, according to preliminary official figures. In 2012 the sector (including fishing) engaged 54.7% of the employed labour force. Increased private enterprise was permitted from 1990, and agricultural land was subsequently redistributed to private ownership. The principal crops are maize, wheat, watermelons, potatoes, tomatoes and grapes. Agricultural GDP increased at an average annual rate of 4.8%, in real terms, in 2005–12, according to official estimates; growth in the sector was 3.9% in 2011 and 7.2% in 2012.

Industry (comprising mining, manufacturing and construction) contributed 22.7% of GDP in 2011, according to preliminary official figures. In 2012 the sector (including utilities) engaged an estimated 10.6% of the employed labour force. Principal contributors to industrial output include mining, energy generation and food-processing. According to official estimates, industrial GDP increased at an average rate of 1.7% per year, in real terms, during 2005–12; the GDP of the sector increased by 0.1% in 2011, but decreased by 9.4% in 2012.

Mining and quarrying contributed 1.9% of GDP in 2011, according to preliminary official figures, and engaged some 1.0% of the employed labour force in 2012. Albania is one of the world's largest producers of chromite (chromium ore), possessing Europe's only significant reserves (an estimated 33m. metric tons of recoverable ore in 2008). Annual chromite production was estimated at 330,000 metric tons in 2012 (compared with 587,000 tons in 1991). Albania has petroleum resources and its own refining facilities, and since 1991 there has been considerable foreign interest in the exploration of both onshore and offshore reserves. Proven reserves of petroleum amounted to some 200m. barrels in 2012; production of crude petroleum increased to some 5.9m. barrels in 2012, compared with 5.0m. barrels in 2011.

The manufacturing sector contributed an estimated 10.1% of GDP in 2011, according to preliminary official figures. In 2012 the sector engaged some 5.2% of the employed labour force. The sector is based largely on the processing of building materials, agricultural products, minerals and chemicals. According to official figures, manufacturing GDP increased, in real terms, at an average annual rate of 2.1% during 2005–12; the GDP of the sector increased by 16.7% in 2010, but decreased by 8.2% in 2011 and by 4.1% in 2012.

The construction sector contributed 10.7% of GDP in 2011, according to preliminary official figures, and engaged an estimated 3.0% of the employed labour force in 2012. According to official estimates, construction GDP decreased at an average annual rate of 0.6% during 2005–12; sectoral GDP increased by 3.0% in 2011, but declined by 17.6% in 2012.

Electricity is produced from hydroelectric sources. In 2012 imports of mineral fuels and electricity accounted for 20.9% of the value of total merchandise imports. In 2011 a new, 97-MW thermal power plant opened some six km from the southern Albanian port of Vlorë.

Services contributed 57.8% of GDP in 2011, according to preliminary official figures. The sector engaged 34.8% of the employed labour force in 2012. The GDP of the services sector increased, in real terms, by an average of 5.2% per year during 2005–12; growth was 4.5% in 2012.

In 2012 Albania recorded a visible merchandise trade deficit of US $2,861.0m., and there was a deficit of $1,314.1m. on the current account of the balance of payments. In 2012 the principal source of imports (accounting for some 31.9% of the total) was Italy; other major suppliers were Greece, the People's Republic of China, Germany and Turkey. Italy was also the principal market for exports (accounting for 51.1% of the total); in addition, Spain, Kosovo and Turkey were important purchasers. The principal exports in 2012 were mineral fuels and electricity, textiles and footwear, construction materials and metals, and food, beverages and tobacco. The main imports in that year were mineral fuels and electricity, machinery equipment and spare parts, food, beverages and tobacco, construction materials and metals, chemical and plastic products, and textiles and footwear.

According to the Ministry of Finance, Albania's overall budget deficit in 2012 was estimated to be 49,538m. lekë, equivalent to 3.7% of GDP. Albania's general government gross debt was 828,275m. lekë in 2012, equivalent to 61.4% of GDP. Albania's total external debt in 2011 was US $5,938m., of which $3,198m. was public and publicly guaranteed debt. In that year, the cost of servicing long-term public and publicly guaranteed debt and repayments to the IMF was equivalent to 9.3% of the value of exports of goods, services and income (excluding workers' remittances). According to official figures, during 2003–12 the average annual rate of inflation was 2.8%; consumer prices increased by 1.9% in 2012. The rate of unemployment was 13.0% in 2012.

From the beginning of the 1990s Albania underwent an extensive transition to a more open market economy. Notably, in 2009 a Czech corporation, CEZ Group, signed an agreement with the Government for the purchase of a 76% stake in the state electricity distribution company OSSH; proceeds were allocated to funding the rehabilitation of the energy sector and addressing longstanding electricity supply difficulties. Following Albania's application for membership of the European Union (EU, see p. 273) in April 2009, dissension between the two main political parties (see Domestic Political Affairs) obstructed the adoption of reform legislation and the country's accession process. Although Albania was considered to have withstood the adverse affects of the global financial crisis from the late 2000s, GDP growth slowed (to only 0.8% in 2012), amid persistent difficulties in the eurozone. In December 2013 an IMF mission reached agreement with Albania on an economic programme that was to be supported by a three-year Extended Fund Facility (EFF); reduction of the public debt, which was estimated at nearly 70% of GDP at the end of that year, was identified as a priority, and reforms were to be focused on the improvement of property rights, tax administration and business registration procedures. As part of measures introduced under the 2014 budget to increase revenue, the Government replaced the existing 10% uniform rates of corporate and personal income tax with higher rates, and imposed excise duties on fuel. The EFF arrangement, totalling US $457.1m., and an immediate disbursement of $36.4m. were approved by the IMF at the end of February. Despite positive recommendations by the European Commission in response to progress in the adoption of political reforms during 2012–13, in December 2013 Albania again failed to secure confirmation of EU candidate status, with a final decision being deferred until mid-2014. With continued high levels of crime and malpractice in state management deemed to constitute the principal obstacles to Albania's aspirations for EU integration, the Government announced further measures to improve official transparency and to address corruption.

PUBLIC HOLIDAYS

2015: 1 January (New Year's Day), 20–22 March (Nevruz, Spring Holiday), 6 April (Catholic Easter), 13 April (Eastern Orthodox Easter), 1 May (International Labour Day), 17 July* (Small Bayram, end of Ramadan), 23 September* (Great Bayram, Feast of the Sacrifice), 19 October (Mother Theresa Day), 28 November (Independence and Liberation Day), 25 December (Christmas Day).

* These holidays are dependent on the Islamic lunar calendar and may vary by one or two days from the dates given.

Statistical Survey

Sources (unless otherwise indicated): Institute of Statistics (Instituti i Statistikës), POB 8194, Tirana; tel. (4) 2222411; fax (4) 2228300; e-mail root@instat.gov.al; internet www.instat.gov.al; Bank of Albania (Banka e Shqipërisë), Sheshi Skënderbej 1, Tirana; tel. (4) 2222152; fax (4) 2223558; e-mail public@bankofalbania.org; internet www.bankofalbania.org.

Area and Population

AREA, POPULATION AND DENSITY

Area (sq km)	
Land	27,398
Inland water	1,350
Total	28,748*
Population (census results)	
1 April 2001	3,069,275
1 October 2011	
Males	1,403,059
Females	1,397,079
Total	2,800,138
Population (official estimate at 1 January)	
2013	2,787,615
Density (per sq km) at 1 January 2013	97.0

* 11,100 sq miles.

POPULATION BY AGE AND SEX

(at 1 January 2013)

	Males	Females	Total
0–14	290,288	266,155	556,443
15–64	950,253	952,776	1,903,029
65 and over	156,929	171,214	328,143
Total	1,397,470	1,390,145	2,787,615

COUNTIES (PREFECTURES)

(population at 1 January 2013)

County	Area (sq km)	Population	Density (per sq km)	Capital
Berat	1,798	138,484	77.0	Berat
Dibër	2,586	132,876	51.4	Peshkopi
Durrës	766	266,823	348.3	Durrës
Elbasan	3,199	292,957	91.6	Elbasan
Fier	1,890	304,719	161.2	Fier
Gjirokastër	2,884	68,497	23.8	Gjirokastër
Korçë	3,711	216,429	58.3	Korçë
Kukës	2,374	83,276	35.1	Kukës
Lezhë	1,620	132,926	82.1	Lezhë
Shkodër	3,562	211,685	59.4	Shkodër
Tiranë	1,652	765,813	463.6	Tiranë
Vlorë	2,706	173,130	64.0	Vlorë
Total	28,748	2,787,615	97.0	

PRINCIPAL TOWNS

(population at 2011 census)

Tiranë (Tirana, the capital)	418,495	Paskuqan	37,349
Durrës (Durazzo)	113,249	Berat	36,496
Vlorë (Vlonë or Valona)	79,513	Lushnjë	31,105
Elbasan	78,703	Rrashbull	24,081
Shkodër (Scutari)	77,075	Farkë	22,633
Kamëz	66,841	Rrethinat	21,199
Fier	55,845	Pogradec	20,848
Korçë (Koritsa)	51,152	Kavajë	20,192
Kashar	43,353	Dajt	20,139

BIRTHS, MARRIAGES AND DEATHS

	Registered live births		Registered marriages		Registered deaths	
	Number	Rate (per 1,000)	Number	Rate (per 1,000)	Number	Rate (per 1,000)
2005	38,898	13.0	21,795	7.3	20,430	6.8
2006	35,891	12.1	21,332	7.2	20,852	7.0
2007	34,448	11.7	22,371	7.6	20,886	7.1
2008	33,445	11.5	21,290	7.3	20,749	7.1
2009	34,114	11.8	26,174	9.1	20,428	7.1
2010	34,061	11.9	25,428	8.9	20,107	7.0
2011	34,285	12.1	25,556	9.0	20,012	7.1
2012	35,295	12.6	22,891	8.1	20,849	7.4

Life expectancy (years at birth): 77.2 (males 74.2; females 80.3) in 2011 (Source: World Bank, World Development Indicators database).

ECONOMICALLY ACTIVE POPULATION
('000, official estimates)

	2010	2011	2012
Agriculture, hunting, forestry and fishing	507	507	522
Mining and quarrying	6	8	10
Manufacturing	53	63	50
Electricity, gas and water	26	21	12
Construction	39	35	29
Wholesale and retail trade	58	65	83
Hotels and restaurants	13	22	21
Transport, storage and communications	24	26	27
Education	42	41	42
Health and social work	27	28	27
Other activities	122	112	132
Total employed	916	928	955
Registered unemployed	143	142	143
Total labour force	1,059	1,070	1,098
Males	623	560	n.a.
Females	436	509	n.a.

Note: Totals may not be equal to the sum of components, owing to rounding.

Health and Welfare

KEY INDICATORS

Total fertility rate (children per woman, 2011)	1.5
Under-5 mortality rate (per 1,000 live births, 2011)	14
HIV/AIDS (% of persons aged 15–49, 2007)	<0.02
Physicians (per 1,000 head, 2011)	1.1
Hospital beds (per 1,000 head, 2009)	2.8
Health expenditure (2010): US $ per head (PPP)	515
Health expenditure (2010): % of GDP	6.0
Health expenditure (2010): public (% of total)	42.2
Access to water (% of total population, 2011)	95
Access to sanitation (% of total population, 2011)	94
Total carbon dioxide emissions ('000 metric tons, 2010)	4,283.1
Carbon dioxide emissions per head (metric tons, 2010)	1.4
Human Development Index (2012): ranking	70
Human Development Index (2012): value	0.749

For sources and definitions, see explanatory note on p. vi.

Agriculture

PRINCIPAL CROPS
('000 metric tons)

	2010	2011	2012
Wheat	294.9	292.8	300.0
Barley	7.3	8.7	7.0
Maize	362.0	366.4	360.0
Rye	2.3	3.4	3.4
Oats	27.3	29.9	27.0
Potatoes	208.0	230.1	233.0
Sugar beet	40.0*	40.0*	40.0†
Beans, dry	24.0	25.3	27.0
Olives	70.0	65.4	125.0
Sunflower seed	2.6	3.0	2.0
Tomatoes	199.3	200.0	205.0
Beans, green	9.3	8.2	8.4
Watermelons	199.4	231.2	237.3
Oranges	6.6	7.1	9.0
Apples	54.6	64.0	71.3
Pears	7.3	8.4	8.9
Sour (Morello) cherries	15.0†	17.0*	17.0†
Sweet cherries	12.5	14.4	14.6
Peaches and nectarines	11.5	13.1	14.6
—continued			
Plums and sloes	26.1	29.6	33.0
Grapes	184.9	195.2	197.0
Figs	18.4	19.6	27.3
Tobacco, unmanufactured	1.7	1.9	2.0

* Unofficial figure.
† FAO estimate.

Aggregate production ('000 metric tons, may include official, semi-official or estimated data): Total cereals 693.8 in 2010, 701.2 in 2011, 697.4 in 2012; Total roots and tubers 208.0 in 2010, 230.1 in 2011, 233.0 in 2012; Total vegetables (incl. melons) 868.7 in 2010, 936.8 in 2011, 957.2 in 2012; Total fruits (excl. melons) 370.2 in 2010, 397.9 in 2011, 426.9 in 2012.

Source: FAO.

LIVESTOCK
('000 head, year ending September)

	2010	2011	2012
Horses	35	36	34
Asses	55*	55†	55†
Cattle	493	492	498
Pigs	164	163	159
Sheep	1,806	1,758	1,809
Goats	775	775†	810
Chickens	5,245	6,558	5,938

* Unofficial figure.
† FAO estimate.

Source: FAO.

LIVESTOCK PRODUCTS
('000 metric tons)

	2010	2011	2012
Cattle meat*	40.8	41.2	41.4
Sheep meat*	13.4	13.7	16.4
Goat meat*	7.6	8.0	6.4
Pig meat*	12.5	13.1	13.3
Chicken meat	17.0	17.1	16.2
Cows' milk	930.0	955.0	956.7
Sheep's milk	77.0	79.0	80.6
Goats' milk	63.0	67.0	67.7
Hen eggs	31.3	31.8	32.8
Wool, greasy	3.3	3.4	3.0

* Unofficial figures.

Source: FAO.

Forestry

ROUNDWOOD REMOVALS
('000 cubic metres, excl. bark, FAO estimates)

	2009	2010	2011
Sawlogs, veneer logs and logs for sleepers	15	15	15
Other industrial wood	65	65	65
Fuel wood	350	350	1,100
Total	430	430	1,180

2012: Production assumed to be unchanged from 2011 (FAO estimates).

Source: FAO.

SAWNWOOD PRODUCTION
('000 cubic metres, incl. railway sleepers)

	2005*	2006*	2007†
Coniferous (softwood)	47	47	4
Broadleaved (hardwood)	50	50	4
Total	97	97	8

* FAO estimates.
† Unofficial figures.

2008–12: Figures assumed to be unchanged from 2007 (FAO estimates).

Source: FAO.

Fishing

(metric tons, live weight)

	2009	2010	2011
Capture	5,945	6,144	5,310
Common carp	214	670	450
Bleak	530	505	360
Crucian carp	208	458	230
Silver carp	183	165	180
Salmonoids	49	29	59
Common sole	69	120	68
European hake	336	280	286
Gilthead seabream	67	225	70
Bogue	154	80	88
Surmullets	187	113	132
Mullets	278	244	160
European pilchard (sardines)	120	104	125
Aquaculture	2,182	2,504	2,022
Mediterranean mussel	1,250	1,410	1,300
Rainbow trout	300	230	155
Gilthead seabream	370	467	375
Total catch	8,127	8,648	7,332

Note: Figures exclude Sardinia coral (metric tons): 1.0 in 2009; 1.2 in 2010–11.

Source: FAO.

Mining

('000 metric tons unless otherwise indicated)

	2010	2011	2012*
Lignite (brown coal)	2.5	1.2	1.2
Crude petroleum ('000 barrels)*	5,000	5,000	5,900
Natural gas (gross production, million cu m)*	8	8	8
Chromium ore (gross weight)	328	331	330
Kaolin	795	974	1,000

* Estimates.

2009: Dolomite 1,000 (estimate).

Source: US Geological Survey.

Industry

SELECTED PRODUCTS

('000 metric tons unless otherwise indicated)

	2007	2008	2009
Wheat flour	191	n.a.	129
Beer ('000 hectolitres)	366	n.a.	249
Wine ('000 hectolitres)	15	n.a.	25
Cement*	889	918	1,110
Petroleum bitumen (asphalt)*	69	92	80
Petroleum coke*	59	47	47
Ferro-chromium*	n.a.	12	8
Crude steel*	263	380	440
Kerosene	10	10	10
Gas-diesel (distillate fuel) oil	83	85	71
Residual fuel oils	32	30	25
Electric energy (million kWh)†	2,947	3,850	5,230

* Source: US Geological Survey.

† Source: Institute of Statistics, Tirana.

Source (unless otherwise indicated): UN Industrial Commodity Statistics Database.

Electric energy (million kWh): 7,715 in 2010; 4,057 in 2011; 4,288 in 2012.

2010 ('000 metric tons): Cement 1,300; Petroleum bitumen (asphalt) 33; Petroleum coke 20 (estimate); Ferro-chromium 23; Crude steel 390 (estimate) (Source: US Geological Survey).

2011 ('000 metric tons): Cement 1,800; Petroleum bitumen (asphalt) 44; Petroleum coke 20 (estimate); Ferro-chromium 29; Crude steel 464 (Source: US Geological Survey).

2012 ('000 metric tons): Cement 2,000 (estimate); Petroleum bitumen (asphalt) 44 (estimate); Petroleum coke 20 (estimate); Ferro-chromium 29 (estimate); Crude steel 500 (estimate) (Source: US Geological Survey).

Finance

CURRENCY AND EXCHANGE RATES

Monetary Units

100 qindarka (qintars) = 1 new lek.

Sterling, Dollar and Euro Equivalents (31 December 2013)

£1 sterling = 167.743 lekë;
US $1 = 101.860 lekë;
€1 = 140.475 lekë;
1,000 lekë = £5.96 = $9.82 = €7.12.

Average Exchange Rate (lekë per US $)

2011	100.895
2012	108.185
2013	105.669

CONSOLIDATED BUDGET

('000 million lekë)

Revenue*	2011	2012	2013†
Tax revenue	303.9	305.5	328.1
Tax revenue from Tax and Customs Directorate	235.5	235.9	255.2
Value-added tax	119.2	119.0	128.2
Profit tax	19.7	16.6	17.7
Excise taxes	40.4	36.5	42.5
Income tax	28.0	28.1	29.3
Customs duties	6.9	6.1	6.3
Other taxes	21.4	29.7	31.1
Property and local taxes	11.8	11.1	12.0
Social security contributions	56.6	58.5	60.9
Other revenue	22.7	23.2	20.6
Total	326.7	328.8	348.6

Expenditure	2011	2012	2013†
Current expenditure	305.5	313.2	336.5
Wages	67.4	69.2	71.9
Interest	41.1	42.2	51.0
Operational and maintenance	33.0	31.2	32.9
Subsidies	3.3	1.6	1.6
Social security	113.9	121.0	128.5
Local government expenditure	28.1	27.0	29.3
Social protection transfers	18.7	20.9	21.4
Reserve fund	0.1	4.4	2.2
Capital expenditure	70.6	64.7	70.9
Total	376.3	382.3	409.6

* Excluding grants received ('000 million lekë): 3.8 in 2011; 4.0 in 2012; 12.0 in 2013 (budget figures).

† Budget figures.

Source: Ministry of Finance, Tirana.

INTERNATIONAL RESERVES

(US $ million at 31 December)

	2010	2011	2012
Gold*	71.37	79.54	84.23
IMF special drawing rights	78.10	76.72	83.03
Reserve position in IMF	5.17	5.15	9.50
Foreign exchange	2,386.28	2,312.06	2,423.13
Total	2,540.92	2,473.47	2,599.88

* Valued at market-related prices.

Source: IMF, *International Financial Statistics*.

MONEY SUPPLY

('000 million lekë at 31 December)

	2010	2011	2012
Currency outside depository corporations	195.06	194.92	192.71
Transferable deposits	130.03	130.27	138.02
Other deposits	655.20	744.96	792.68
Broad money	980.28	1,070.15	1,123.41

Source: IMF, *International Financial Statistics*.

COST OF LIVING

(Consumer Price Index; annual averages; base: December 2007 = 100)

	2010	2011	2012
Food and non-alcoholic beverages	111.4	116.2	118.8
Alcoholic beverages and tobacco	109.9	122.8	125.5
Clothing and footwear	93.2	91.4	89.5
Rent, water, fuel and power	108.9	111.9	112.9
Household goods and maintenance	101.0	101.9	103.2
Medical care	111.3	119.9	123.1
Transport	107.3	113.7	118.4
Communication	81.1	81.3	81.3
Recreation and culture	110.9	112.1	113.9
Education	105.7	105.8	107.4
All items (incl. others)	107.1	110.8	112.9

NATIONAL ACCOUNTS

(million lekë at current prices)

Expenditure on the Gross Domestic Product

	2009	2010	2011
Final consumption expenditure	940,310	1,102,569	1,189,484
Households	818,580	974,974	1,060,136
General government	121,730	127,595	129,348
Gross capital formation	491,990	401,818	409,722
Total domestic expenditure	1,432,300	1,504,387	1,599,207
Exports of goods and services	333,133	396,027	438,291
Less Imports of goods and services	614,413	657,997	732,346
Statistical discrepancy	—	—	6,484
GDP in market prices	1,151,020	1,242,418	1,311,636

Source: UN, National Accounts Main Aggregates Database.

Gross Domestic Product by Economic Activity

	2009	2010*	2011*
Agriculture, hunting and forestry	192,263	211,346	226,599
Mining and quarrying	10,117	14,992	22,318
Manufacturing	93,829	113,512	117,498
Construction	146,044	119,973	124,127
Wholesale and retail trade, hotels and restaurants	213,840	229,767	253,163
Transport	56,362	67,568	71,235
Post and communications	39,368	36,411	37,510
Other services	276,696	301,066	309,886
Sub-total	1,028,519	1,094,635	1,162,335
Less Financial intermediation services indirectly measured	43,344	46,915	48,415
Gross value added in basic prices	985,175	1,047,720	1,113,920
Taxes on products	164,717	176,520	182,465
Less Subsidies on products	1,810	1,778	14,130
GDP in market prices	1,148,082	1,222,462	1,282,255

* Preliminary figures.

BALANCE OF PAYMENTS

(US$ million)

	2010	2011	2012
Exports of goods	736.9	962.1	1,122.8
Imports of goods	–3,775.1	–4,460.7	–3,983.8
Balance on goods	–3,038.1	–3,498.7	–2,861.0
Exports of services	2,587.2	2,814.4	2,411.6
Imports of services	–2,006.7	–2,248.4	–1,871.2
Balance on goods and services	–2,457.7	–2,932.6	–2,320.6
Primary income received	380.0	306.8	262.5
Primary income paid	–497.8	–275.8	–377.2
Balance on goods, services and primary income	–2,575.6	–2,901.6	–2,435.3
Secondary income received	1,427.3	1,398.2	1,310.0
Secondary income paid	–204.5	–146.5	–188.8
Current balance	–1,352.8	–1,649.8	–1,314.1

—continued	2010	2011	2012
Capital account (net)	112.3	118.3	104.0
Direct investment assets	–46.0	–371.2	–328.6
Direct investment liabilities	1,089.4	1,368.3	1,265.3
Portfolio investment assets	–110.5	–126.8	–113.0
Portfolio investment liabilities	430.7	105.6	81.6
Financial derivatives and employee stock options (net)	—	2.5	4.7
Other investment assets	–244.9	–413.4	–369.9
Other investment liabilities	–396.1	685.2	480.7
Net errors and omissions	442.3	253.4	289.8
Reserves and related items	–75.6	–27.9	100.4

Source: IMF, *International Financial Statistics*.

External Trade

PRINCIPAL COMMODITIES

(million lekë)

Imports c.i.f.	2010	2011	2012
Food, beverages and tobacco	87,090	91,954	93,177
Mineral fuels and electricity	73,522	102,269	110,476
Chemical and plastic products	56,301	60,994	66,015
Wood manufactures	20,432	20,419	18,100
Textiles and footwear	45,734	50,500	48,321
Construction materials and metals	76,426	82,101	68,066
Machinery equipment and spare parts	92,673	109,707	97,764
Total (incl. others)	477,768	544,004	528,478

Exports f.o.b.	2010	2011	2012
Food, beverages and tobacco	9,455	11,178	12,819
Mineral fuels and electricity	44,849	58,776	76,146
Chemical and plastic products	1,743	2,834	2,026
Wood manufactures	4,796	4,558	5,353
Textiles and footwear	55,646	64,106	62,092
Construction materials and metals	32,339	41,303	40,213
Machinery equipment and spare parts	6,730	7,750	7,639
Total (incl. others)	161,548	196,897	213,023

PRINCIPAL TRADING PARTNERS

(million lekë)*

Imports c.i.f.	2010	2011	2012
Austria	7,656	9,983	6,889
Brazil	4,440	4,402	4,881
Bulgaria	8,510	6,916	6,838
China, People's Republic	30,231	34,731	33,573
Czech Republic	6,754	8,070	5,553
Croatia	9,197	6,988	6,973
France	10,417	13,089	8,458
Germany	26,768	31,163	31,936
Greece	62,617	57,796	50,117
Italy	134,569	166,045	168,360
Macedonia, former Yugoslav republic	7,543	8,882	8,365
Netherlands	4,634	4,472	2,449
Poland	6,758	6,589	7,106
Romania	5,957	5,604	5,966
Russia	10,475	10,540	13,474
Serbia	17,707	19,607	23,321
Slovenia	5,158	4,205	3,692
Spain	7,375	11,441	10,362
Switzerland	7,291	14,183	15,407
Turkey	27,046	30,200	30,376
Turkmenistan	4,844	3,622	8,020
Ukraine	4,458	6,632	5,744
United Kingdom	6,980	5,975	5,322
USA	7,348	7,780	11,423
Total (incl. others)	477,768	544,004	528,478

Exports f.o.b.	2010	2011	2012
Austria	1,659	2,342	2,584
Bulgaria	1,636	2,438	2,763
China, People's Republic	8,867	4,903	5,744
Czech Republic	1,623	1,040	570
France	1,568	1,079	1,526
Germany	4,437	5,745	6,611
Greece	8,741	9,978	9,466
Italy	82,114	104,998	108,841
Kosovo	10,008	14,657	17,369
Macedonia, former Yugoslav republic	2,667	4,149	4,152
Serbia	1,951	3,597	1,647
Spain	5,589	7,010	19,693
Switzerland	6,692	5,279	2,041
Turkey	9,573	14,484	13,464
USA	2,379	2,006	1,037
Total (incl. others)	161,548	196,897	213,023

* Imports by country of origin; exports by country of destination.

Transport

RAILWAYS
(traffic)

	2010	2011	2012
Passengers carried ('000)	430	453	448
Passenger-km (million)	19	18	15
Freight carried ('000 metric tons)	403	317	448
Freight ton-km (million)	66	50	25

ROAD TRAFFIC
(motor vehicles in use at 31 December)

	2010	2011	2012
Passenger cars	294,729	300,974	297,370
Buses and coaches	7,032	6,698	5,250
Lorries and vans	84,314	71,278	60,165
Road tractors	1,997	761	509
Motorcycles and mopeds	24,022	24,009	25,492
Trailers	7,799	6,909	5,699

SHIPPING

Flag Registered Fleet
(31 December)

	2011	2012	2013
Number of vessels	52	52	57
Total displacement ('000 gross registered tons)	53.6	52.1	54.3

Source: Lloyd's List Intelligence (www.lloydslistintelligence.com).

International Sea-borne Freight Traffic
('000 metric tons)

	2003	2004	2005
Goods loaded	276	324	372
Goods unloaded	3,144	3,300	3,588

Source: UN, *Monthly Bulletin of Statistics*.

Goods loaded and unloaded ('000 metric tons): 4,170 in 2010; 4,067 in 2011; 3,985 in 2012.

CIVIL AVIATION
(traffic on scheduled services)

	2009	2010	2011
Passengers ('000):			
arrivals	687	752	896
departures	708	784	920
Freight (metric tons):			
loaded	1,217	249	468
unloaded	647	1,691	1,822

2012: Passengers carried ('000) 1,666; Freight (metric tons) 1,875.

Tourism

FOREIGN TOURIST ARRIVALS BY COUNTRY OF ORIGIN*

	2009	2010	2011
Germany	48,408	55,919	73,102
Greece	106,227	113,008	155,086
Italy	109,702	125,036	135,389
Macedonia, former Yugoslav republic	330,939	276,268	335,380
Montenegro	128,547	123,833	159,838
Serbia	40,873	43,940	48,029
United Kingdom	61,136	62,251	76,019
USA	48,599	49,537	55,950
Total (incl. others)	1,855,638	2,417,337	2,932,132

* Figures refer to arrivals at frontiers of visitors from abroad, and include same-day visitors.

Total tourist arrivals ('000): 3,514 in 2012.

Tourism receipts (US $ million, excl. passenger transport): 1,626 in 2010; 1,628 in 2011; 1,471 in 2012 (provisional).

Source: World Tourism Organization.

Communications Media

	2010	2011	2012
Telephones ('000 main lines in use)	333.1	338.8	312.0
Mobile cellular telephones ('000 subscribers)	2,692.4	3,100.0	3,500.0
Internet subscribers ('000)	112	140	n.a.
Broadband subscribers ('000)	105.5	128.2	160.0

Sources: International Telecommunication Union.

Education

(2011/12 unless otherwise indicated)

	Institutions	Teachers	Students
Pre-primary	1,774*	4,349	80,488†
Primary and lower secondary	1,605*	25,584	403,704
Upper secondary	502*	8,473	152,182
General	403‡	6,716	133,002
Vocational	89*	1,757	19,180
Higher education	26*	2,885*	158,963

* 2008/09.

† Figure includes enrolment in public schools only.

‡ 2006/07.

Source: mostly UNESCO Institute for Statistics.

Pupil-teacher ratio (primary education, UNESCO estimate): 19.5 in 2011/12 (Source: UNESCO Institute for Statistics).

Adult literacy rate (UNESCO estimates): 96.8% (males 98.0%; females 95.7%) in 2011 (Source: UNESCO Institute for Statistics).

Directory

The Government

HEAD OF STATE

President of the Republic: BUJAR NISHANI (elected by vote of the Kuvendi Popullor 11 June 2012; inaugurated 24 July 2012).

COUNCIL OF MINISTERS
(April 2014)

The Government comprises members of the Partia Socialiste e Shqipërisë (PSSh—Socialist Party of Albania) and the Lëvizja Socialiste për Integrim (LSI—Socialist Movement for Integration).

Prime Minister: EDI RAMA (PSSh).

Deputy Prime Minister: NIKO PELESHI (PSSh).

Minister of Defence: MIMI KODHELI (PSSh).

Minister of the Interior: SAIMIR TAHIRI (PSSh).

Minister of Foreign Affairs: DITMIR BUSHATI (PSSh).

Minister of European Integration: KLAJDA GJOSHA (LSI).

Minister of Finance: SHKËLQIM CANI (PSSh).

Minister of Transport and Infrastructure: EDMOND HAXHINASTO (LSI).

Minister of Urban Development and Tourism: EGLANTINA GJERMENI (PSSh).

Minister of Economic Development, Trade and Entrepreneurship: ARBEN AHMETAJ (PSSh).

Minister of Education and Sports: LINDITA NIKOLLA (PSSh).

Minister of Justice: NASIP NAÇO (LSI).

Minister of Culture: MIRELA KUMBARO (Independent).

Minister of Social Welfare and Youth: ERION VELIAJ (PSSh).

Minister of Public Administration and Innovation: MILENA HARITO (PSSh).

Minister of Health: ILIR BEQAJ (PSSh).

Minister of Energy and Industry: DAMIAN GJIKNURI (PSSh).

Minister of the Environment: LEFTER KOKA (LSI).

Minister of Agriculture, Rural Development and Water Management: EDMOND PANARITI (LSI).

Minister of State for Relations with the Parliament: ILIRJAN CELIBASHI (PSSh).

Minister of State for Local Government: BLEDI ÇUÇI (PSSh).

MINISTRIES

Office of the President: Bulevardi Dëshmorët e Kombit, Tirana; tel. (4) 2389811; e-mail info@president.al; internet www.president.al.

Office of the Prime Minister: Bulevardi Dëshmorët e Kombit 1, 1000 Tirana; tel. (4) 2277404; fax (4) 2237501; e-mail info@kryeministria.al; internet www.kryeministria.al.

Ministry of Agriculture, Rural Development and Water Management: Sheshi Skënderbej 2, 1001 Tirana; tel. and fax (4) 2226551; e-mail info@bujqesia.gov.al; internet www.bujqesia.gov.al.

Ministry of Culture: Rruga e Kavajës, Tirana; internet www.kultura.gov.al.

Ministry of Defence: Rruga e Dibrës, 1000 Tirana; tel. (4) 2226601; fax (4) 2228325; e-mail dmpi@mod.gov.al; internet www.mod.gov.al.

Ministry of Economic Development, Trade and Entrepreneurship: 1001 Tirana; tel. (4) 8001313; e-mail zmp@ekonomia.gov.al; internet www.ekonomia.gov.al.

Ministry of Education and Sports: Rruga Durrësit 23, 1001 Tirana; tel. (4) 2230289; e-mail info@arsimi.gov.al; internet www.mash.gov.al.

Ministry of Energy and Industry: Bulevardi Dëshmorët e Kombit, Tirana; tel. (4) 2227617; fax (4) 2234052; e-mail sekretaria@energjia.gov.al; internet www.energjia.gov.al.

Ministry of the Environment: Rruga Durrësit 27, Tirana; tel. (4) 2270630; fax (4) 2270627; e-mail kabineti@mjedisi.gov.al; internet www.mjedisi.gov.al.

Ministry of European Integration: Rruga Papa Gjon Pali II 3, POB 8302, Tirana; tel. and fax (4) 2228623; e-mail info@integrimi.gov.al; internet www.integrimi.gov.al.

Ministry of Finance: Bulevardi Dëshmorët e Kombit 1, 1001 Tirana; tel. (4) 2227937; e-mail dteliti@minfin.gov.al; internet www.financa.gov.al.

Ministry of Foreign Affairs: Bulevardi Gjergj Fishta 6, Tirana; tel. (4) 2364090; fax (4) 2362084; e-mail info@mfa.gov.al; internet www.mfa.gov.al.

Ministry of Health: Bulevardi Bajram Curri 1, Tirana; tel. and fax (4) 2364908; e-mail ministri@moh.gov.al; internet www.moh.gov.al.

Ministry of the Interior: Sheshi Skënderbej 3, Tirana; tel. (4) 2247155; e-mail minister@moi.gov.al; internet www.punetebrendshme.gov.al.

Ministry of Justice: Bulevardi Dëshmorët e Kombit, Tirana; tel. (4) 2259388; fax (4) 2228359; e-mail info@drejtesia.gov.al; internet www.drejtesia.gov.al.

Ministry of Public Administration and Innovation: Tirana; tel. (4) 2277355; e-mail info@inovacioni.gov.al; internet www.inovacioni.gov.al.

Ministry of Social Welfare and Youth: Rruga e Kavajës, 1001 Tirana; e-mail info@sociale.gov.al; internet www.sociale.gov.al.

Ministry of Transport and Infrastructure: Sheshi Skënderbej 5, Tirana; tel. and fax (4) 2380833; internet www.transporti.gov.al.

Ministry of Urban Development and Tourism: Rruga e Kavajës, Tirana; e-mail info@turizmi.gov.al; internet www.turizmi.gov.al.

President

On 11 June 2012 BUJAR NISHANI was elected President in a fourth round of voting in the Kuvendi Popullor (People's Assembly). Nishani was inaugurated on 24 July.

Legislature

People's Assembly (Kuvendi Popullor)

Bulevardi Dëshmorët e Kombit 4, Tirana; tel. (4) 2278262; e-mail llleshi@parlament.al; internet www.parlament.al.

Speaker: ILIR META.

General Election, 23 June 2013

	Votes	%	Seats
Alliance for a European Albania*	991,118	57.73	84
Alliance for Employment, Prosperity and Integration†	676,433	39.40	56
Other parties	40,025	2.33	—
Independent candidates	9,204	0.54	—
Total	1,716,780	100.00	140

* A coalition, led by the Partia Socialiste e Shqipërisë (Socialist Party of Albania, with 66 seats), and also including the Lëvizja Socialiste për Integrim (Socialist Movement for Integration, 16 seats), the Christian Democratic Party of Albania (one seat) and the Partia Bashkimi për të Drejtat e Njeriut (Union for Human Rights Party, one seat).

† A coalition, led by the Partia Demokratike e Shqipërisë (Democratic Party of Albania, with 49 seats), and also including the Partia Drejtesi Integrim dhe Unitet (Party for Justice, Integration and Unity, four seats) and the Partia Republika e Shqipërisë (Republican Party of Albania, three seats).

Election Commission

Komisioni Qendror i Zgjyedhjeve (KQZ) (Central Election Commission—CEC): Pallati i Kongreseve, Tirana; tel. and fax (4) 2281655; e-mail skendervrioni@cec.org.al; internet www.cec.org.al; f. 1996; seven members: two elected by the Kuvendi Popullor, two by the President and three by the High Council of Justice; Chair. LEFTERI LLESHI.

Political Organizations

The general election of 23 June 2013 was contested by two principal coalitions: the Alliance for a European Albania, comprising 37 parties led by the Partia Socialiste e Shqipërisë; and the Alliance for Employment, Prosperity and Integration, composed of 25 centrist and centre-right parties, led by the Partia Demokratike e Shqipërisë.

Fryma e Re Demokratike (FRD) (New Democratic Spirit—NDS): Rruga George W. Bush, Pallati i Kasmeve 15/1, Tirana; tel. and fax (4) 2242444; e-mail kontakt@frd.al; internet frd.al; f. 2012 by fmr mems of the DPA; Leader BAMIR TOPI.

Lëvizja Socialiste për Integrim (LSI) (Socialist Movement for Integration): Rruga Sami Frashëri, Godina 20/10, Tirana; tel. (4) 2270412; fax (4) 2270413; e-mail info@lsi.al; internet www.lsi.al; f. 2004 by fmr mems of the SPA; moderate socialist; contested 2013 legislative elections as mem. of Alliance for a European Albania; Chair. ILIR META; c. 40,000 mems (April 2005).

Partia Agrare Ambientaliste (PAA) (Environmentalist Agrarian Party—EAP): Rruga Budi 6, Tirana; tel. and fax (4) 2231904; e-mail lufterxhuveli@yahoo.com; f. 1991; contested the 2013 legislative elections as mem. of Alliance for Employment, Prosperity and Integration; Chair. LUFTER XHUVELI.

Partia Aleanca Demokratike (PAD) (Democratic Alliance Party—DAP): Tirana; tel. and fax (4) 2251971; e-mail aleancademokratikeal@yahoo.com; f. 1992 by fmr mems of the Partia Demokratike e Shqipërisë; contested 2013 legislative elections as mem. of Alliance for Employment, Prosperity and Integration; Chair. ARBEN DEMETI; Sec.-Gen. EDMOND DRAGOTI.

Partia Bashkimi Liberal Demokrat (PBLD) (Liberal Democratic Union Party—LDUP): Bulevardi Zhan D'Ark 16, Tirana; tel. and fax (4) 2251068; e-mail libdem@albmail.co; f. 1995; contested the 2013 legislative elections as mem. of Alliance for Employment, Prosperity and Integration; Chair. ARJAN STAROVA.

Partia Bashkimi për të Drejtat e Njeriut (PBDNj) (Union for Human Rights Party—UHRP): Bulevardi Bajram Curri 32, Tirana; tel. and fax (4) 2377921; e-mail contact@pbdnj.com; internet www.pbdnj.com; f. 1992; represents Greek and Macedonian minorities; contested 2013 legislative elections as mem. of the Alliance for a European Albania; Leader VANGJEL DULE.

Partia Demokracia Sociale (PDS) (Social Democracy Party): Bulevardi Dëshmorët e Kombit 4, Tirana; tel. and fax (4) 2228526; f. 2003 by breakaway faction of the SDP; contested the 2013 legislative elections as mem. of Alliance for a European Albania; Chair. Prof. Dr PASKAL MILO.

Partia Demokratike e Shqipërisë (PDSh) (Democratic Party of Albania—DPA): Rruga Punëtorët e Rilindjes 1, 1001 Tirana; tel. (4) 2228091; fax (4) 2223525; e-mail denonco@pd.al; internet www.perpara.al; f. 1990; centre-right, pro-democracy, pro-market; merged with the New Democratic Party (f. 2001 by fmr mems of the PDSh) in 2008; contested 2013 legislative elections as mem. of Alliance for Employment, Prosperity and Integration; Chair. LULZIM BASHA; Sec.-Gen. RIDVAN BODE.

Partia Drejtesi Integrim dhe Unitet (PDIU) (Party for Justice, Integration and Unity): Rruga e Elbasanit, Kati 3, Tirana; tel. (4) 2235449; e-mail info@pdiu.al; internet www.pdiu.al; f. 2011 by merger of the Party for Justice and Integration and the Party for Justice and Unity; centre-right; concerned with issues affecting the Cham minority, an ethnic group of Greek origin; contested 2013 legislative elections as mem. of Alliance for Employment, Prosperity and Integration; Chair. SHPËTIM IDRIZI.

Partia Gjelbërite e Shqipërisë (Albanian Green Party): Rruga Bajram Curri Pall. 31/1/4, Tirana; tel. (6) 62031303; e-mail office@pgj.al; f. 2001; ecologist; mem. of European Greens; contested 2013 legislative elections as mem. of Alliance for a European Albania; Chair. EDLIR PETANAJ.

Partia Lëvizja e Legalitetit (PLL) (Movement of Legality Party—MLP): Bulevardi Zog I, Tirana; tel. and fax (4) 2230076; e-mail levizja_legalitetit@yahoo.com; internet www.legaliteti.org; f. 1992; monarchist; contested the 2013 legislative elections as mem. of Alliance for Employment, Prosperity and Integration; Chair. EKREM SPAHIU; Sec.-Gen. ARTAN TUJANI.

Partia Republika e Shqipërisë (PRSh) (Republican Party of Albania—RPA): Rruga Abdi Toptani, Kati 3, 1000 Tirana; tel. (67) 2042251; internet www.prsh.al; f. 1991; contested 2013 legislative elections as mem. of Alliance for Employment, Prosperity and Integration; Chair. FATMIR MEDIU.

Partia Socialiste e Shqipërisë (PSSh) (Socialist Party of Albania—SPA): Sheshi Austria 19, Tirana; tel. (4) 2229428; fax (4) 2227417; e-mail info@ps.al; internet www.ps.al; f. 1941 as Albanian Communist Party; renamed Party of Labour of Albania in 1948, adopted present name in 1991; now rejects Marxism-Leninism and claims commitment to democratic socialism and a market economy; contested 2013 legislative elections as mem. of Alliance for a European Albania; Chair. EDI RAMA; 110,000 mems.

Diplomatic Representation

EMBASSIES IN ALBANIA

Austria: Rruga Frederik Shiroka 3, Tirana; tel. (4) 2274855; fax (4) 2233140; e-mail tirana-ob@bmeia.gv.al; Ambassador THOMAS SCHNÖLL.

Bulgaria: Rruga Skënderbej 12, Tirana; tel. (4) 2233155; fax (4) 2232272; e-mail embassy.tirana@mfa.bg; internet www.mfa.bg/embassies/albania; Ambassador DIMITAR ARNAUDOV.

China, People's Republic: Rruga Skënderbej 57, Tirana; tel. (4) 2232385; fax (4) 2233159; e-mail chinaemb_al@mfa.gov.cn; internet al.china-embassy.org; Ambassador YE HAO.

Croatia: Rruga A. Toptani, Torre Drin 4, Tirana; tel. (4) 2256948; fax (4) 2230578; e-mail croemb.tirana@mvpei.hr; Ambassador ALEKSANDER STIPETIĆ.

Czech Republic: Rruga Skënderbej 10, Tirana; tel. (4) 2234004; fax (4) 2232159; e-mail tirana@embassy.mzv.cz; internet www.mzv.cz/tirana; Ambassador BRONISLAVA TOMÁŠOVÁ.

Denmark: Rruga Nikolla Tupe 1/4, POB 1743, Tirana; tel. (4) 2280600; fax (4) 2280630; e-mail tiaamb@um.dk; internet www.albanien.um.dk; Ambassador MADS SANDAU-JENSEN.

Egypt: Rruga Skënderbej 1, Tirana; tel. (4) 2233022; fax (4) 2232295; e-mail egyemb@abcom.al; Ambassador AHMED HASSAN ABDELLAH.

France: Rruga Skënderbej 14, Tirana; tel. (4) 2389700; fax (4) 2389717; e-mail ambafrance.tr@adanet.com.al; internet www.ambafrance-al.org; Ambassador CHRISTINE MORO.

Germany: Rruga Skënderbej 8, Tirana; tel. (4) 2274505; fax (4) 2232050; e-mail info@tira.diplo.de; internet www.tirana.diplo.de; Ambassador HELMUT HOFFMAN.

Greece: Rruga Frederik Shiroka 3, Tirana; tel. (4) 2274670; fax (4) 2234290; e-mail gremb.tir@mfa.gr; internet www.mfa.gr/tirana; Ambassador LEONIDAS C. ROKANAS.

Holy See: Rruga e Durrësit 13, POB 8355, Tirana; tel. (4) 2233516; fax (4) 2232001; e-mail nunapal@icc-al.org; Apostolic Nuncio Most Rev. MOLINER INGLÉS RAMIRO (Titular Archbishop of Sardanensis).

Hungary: Rruga Skënderbej 16, Tirana; tel. (4) 2232238; fax (4) 2233211; e-mail mission.tia@mfa.gov.hu; internet www.mfa.gov.hu/kulkepviselet/al; Ambassador JÁNOS HUSZÁR.

Iran: Rruga Mustafa Matohiti 20, Tirana; tel. (4) 2255038; fax (4) 2254621; e-mail iranemb.tia@mfa.ir; internet www.tirana.mfa.ir; Ambassador ABDOLMAJID MOZAFFARI.

Italy: Rruga Papa Gjon Pali II 2, Tirana; tel. (4) 2275900; fax (4) 2250921; e-mail segramb.tirana@esteri.it; internet www.ambtirana.esteri.it; Ambassador MASSIMO GAIANI.

Kosovo: Rruga Donika Kastrioti, Vila nr 6, Tirana; tel. (4) 2261650; fax (4) 2225100; e-mail embassy.albania@rks-gov.net; internet www.ambasada-ks.net/al/?page=2,50; Ambassador SYLEJMAN SELIMI.

Kuwait: Rruga e Durrësit 134, Tirana; tel. (4) 2236800; fax (4) 2236501; e-mail kw.tirana@mofa.gov.kw; Ambassador NAJEEB ABDULRAHMAN AL-BADER.

Libya: Rruga e Elbasanit, përballë Pallatit të Brigadave 9, Tirana; tel. (4) 2347816; fax (4) 2343434; e-mail lib_emb_al@foreign.gov.ly; Chargé d'affaires ESSAM F. A. BEN GALIEL.

Macedonia, former Yugoslav republic: Rruga Kavajës 116, Tirana; tel. (4) 2230909; fax (4) 2232514; e-mail tirana@mfa.gov.mk; internet www.missions.gov.mk/tirana; Ambassador STOJAN KARAJANOV.

Montenegro: Rruga Abdi Toptani, Pallati Tore Drin, kati 8, Tirana; tel. (4) 2261309; fax (4) 2257406; e-mail mnembassy@albmail.com; Ambassador FERHAT DINOSHA.

Netherlands: Rruga Asim Zeneli 10, Tirana; tel. (4) 2240828; fax (4) 2232723; e-mail tir@minbuza.nl; internet www.mfa.nl/tir; Ambassador MARTIN DE LA BEIJ.

Poland: Rruga e Durrësit 123, Tirana; tel. (4) 4510020; fax (4) 2233364; e-mail tirana.amb.sekretariat@msz.gov.pl; internet www.tirana.polemb.net; Ambassador MAREK HENRYK JEZIORSKI.

Qatar: Rruga Skënderbej 116, Tirana; tel. (4) 2258772; fax (4) 2258773; e-mail tirana@mofa.gov.qa; Ambassador YOUSUF HASSEN AL-SAAI.

Romania: Rruga Pandeli Evangjeli 15, Tirana; tel. (4) 2303134; fax (4) 2303133; e-mail tirana@mae.ro; Ambassador VIOREL STANILĂ.

Russia: Rruga Donika Kastrioti 2, Tirana; tel. (4) 2256040; fax (4) 2256046; e-mail rusemb@albmail.com; Ambassador LEONID ABRAMOV.

Saudi Arabia: Rruga Kavaja 116, Tirana; tel. (4) 2248306; fax (4) 2229982; e-mail embsaudarab@albaniaonline.net; Ambassador ABDULLAH A. AL-ABDULKARIM.

Serbia: Rruga Donika Kastrioti 9/1, Tirana; tel. (4) 2232091; fax (4) 2232089; e-mail ambatira@icc-al.org; internet www.tirana.mfa.gov.rs; Ambassador MIROLJUB ZARIĆ.

Slovenia: Rruga Abdyl Frashëri, EGT Tower, 3rd Floor, Tirana; tel. (4) 2274858; fax (4) 2221311; e-mail vti@gov.si; Ambassador BOJAN BERTONCELJ.

Spain: Rruga Skënderbej 4, Tirana; tel. (4) 2274960; fax (4) 2225383; e-mail emb.tirana@maec.es; Ambassador RAFAEL TORMO PÉREZ.

Switzerland: Rruga Dëshmorët e 4 Shkurtit 3/1, Tirana; tel. (4) 2234888; fax (4) 2234889; e-mail tir.vertretung@eda.admin.ch; internet www.eda.admin.ch/tirana; Ambassador ALEXANDER WITTWER.

Turkey: Rruga e Elbasanit 65, Tirana; tel. (4) 2380350; fax (4) 2347767; e-mail embassy.tirana@mfa.gov.tr; internet www.tirana.emb.mfa.gov.tr; Ambassador HIDAYET BAYRAKTAR.

United Kingdom: Rruga Skënderbej 12, Tirana; tel. (4) 2234973; fax (4) 2247697; e-mail information.tiran@fco.gov.uk; internet www.ukinalbania.fco.gov.uk; Ambassador NICHOLAS CANNON.

USA: Rruga e Elbasanit 103, Tirana; tel. (4) 2247285; fax (4) 2232222; e-mail tirana-webcontact@usaid.gov; internet tirana.usembassy.gov; Ambassador Dr ALEXANDER A. ARVIZU.

Judicial System

The judicial structure comprises the Supreme Court, the Courts of Appeal and the Courts of First Instance. The Chairman and members of the Supreme Court are appointed by the President of the Republic, with the approval of the legislature, for a term of nine years. Other judges are appointed by the President upon the proposal of the High Council of Justice. The High Council of Justice comprises the President of the Republic (who is its Chairman), the Chief Justice of the Supreme Court, the Minister of Justice, three members elected by the legislature for a term of five years, and nine judges of all levels who are elected by a national judicial conference. The Supreme Court consists of 17 members, appointed to office by the President, with the approval of the legislature, for a single, nine-year term. The Constitutional Court arbitrates on constitutional issues, and determines, *inter alia*, the conformity of proposed legislation with the Constitution. It is empowered to prohibit the activities of political organizations on constitutional grounds, and also formulates legislation regarding the election of the President of the Republic. The Constitutional Court comprises nine members, who are appointed by the President, with the approval of the legislature, for a term of nine years.

High Council of Justice: Bulevardi Zogu I, Tirana; tel. (4) 2280804; fax (4) 2259822; e-mail kontakt@kld.al; internet www.kld.al; Chair. President of the Republic; Deputy Chair. ELVIS ÇEFA.

Supreme Court (Gjykata e Larte): Rruga Dëshmorët e 4 Shkurtit, Tirana; tel. (4) 2228327; fax (4) 2228837; e-mail supremecourt@gjykataelarte.gov.al; internet www.gjykataelarte.gov.al; Chief Justice XHEZAIR ZAGANJORI.

Constitutional Court (Gjykata Kushtetuese): Bulevardi Dëshmorët e Kombit, Tirana; tel. and fax (4) 22230924; e-mail kujtim.osmani@gjk.gov.al; internet www.gjk.gov.al; Pres. BASHKIM DEDJA.

Office of the Prosecutor-General (Zyra e Prokurorit te Pergjithshem): Rruga Qemal Stafa 1, Tirana; tel. (4) 2234850; fax (4) 2229085; e-mail denonco@pp.gov.al; internet www.pp.gov.al; Prosecutor-General ADRIATIK LLALLA.

Religion

In May 1990 a prohibition on religious activities, enforced since 1967, was revoked, religious services were permitted and, from 1991, mosques and churches began to be reopened. Under the Constitution of November 1998 Albania is a secular state, which respects freedom of religious belief. On the basis of declared affiliation in 1945, it is estimated that some 70% of the population are of Muslim background, of whom about 75% are associated with Sunni Islam; many of the remainder are associated with the Bektashi sect, a Sufi dervish order. Muslims are mainly concentrated in the middle and, to some extent, the south of the country. Some 20% of the population are of Eastern Orthodox Christian background (mainly in the south) and some 13% are associated with the Roman Catholic Church (mainly in the north).

ISLAM

Albanian Islamic Community (AIC) (Bashkesia Islame e Shqipërisë): Rruga Punëtorët e Rilindjes 50, Tirana; tel. and fax (22) 230492; e-mail icalb@yahoo.com; f. 1991 as Albanian Muslim Community; renamed as above in 2005; Chair. and Grand Mufti of Albania SELIM MUÇA.

Bektashi Sect

Albania is the world centre of the Bektashi sect.

World Council of Elders of the Bektashis (Kryegjyshata Boterore e Bektashinjve): Tirana; internet www.komunitetibektashi.org; f. 1991; Chair. Baba EDMOND BRAHIMAJ.

CHRISTIANITY

The Eastern Orthodox Church

Orthodox Autocephalous Church of Albania (Kisha Orthodhokse Autoqefale e Shqipërisë): Rruga e Kavajës 151, Tirana; tel. (4) 2234117; fax (4) 2232109; e-mail orthchal@orthodoxalbania.org; internet www.orthodoxalbania.org; the Albanian Orthodox Church was proclaimed autocephalous at the Congress of Berat in 1922, and it was recognized by the Ecumenical Patriarchate of Constantinople (İstanbul), Turkey, in 1937; Archbishop of Tirana, Durrës and all Albania ANASTASIOS YANNOULATOS.

The Roman Catholic Church

Many Roman Catholic churches have been reopened since 1990, and in September 1991 diplomatic relations were restored with the Holy See. Albania comprises two archdioceses, three dioceses and one apostolic administration. Some 12.8% of the population are Roman Catholics.

Bishops' Conference: Rruga Don Bosko 1, POB 2950, Tirana; tel. and fax (4) 2247159; e-mail cealbania@albmail.com; Pres. Most Rev. RROK K. MIRDITA (Archbishop of Tirana-Durrës).

Archbishop of Shkodër-Pult: Most Rev. ANGELO MASSAFRA, Sheshi Gjon Pali II, Shkodër; tel. (22) 242744; fax (22) 243673; e-mail curiashkoder@hotmail.com.

Archbishop of Tirana-Durrës: Most Rev. RROK K. MIRDITA, Bulevardi Zhan d'Ark, Tirana; tel. (4) 2232082; fax (4) 2230727; e-mail arq@icc.al.org.

The Press

PRINCIPAL NEWSPAPERS

Albanian Daily News: Rruga Dervish Hima 1, ADA Tower, Tirana; tel. (4) 5600610; fax (4) 5600618; e-mail editoradn@albnet.net; internet www.albaniannews.com; f. 1995; in English, subscription-based online edition updated daily, printed weekly newspaper; Editor-in-Chief GENC MLLOJA.

Gazeta 55 (Newspaper 55): Rruga Medar Shtylla; tel. (4) 2321364; fax (4) 2321365; e-mail info@gazeta55.net; internet www.gazeta55.net; f. 1997; independent; right-wing; English summary; Editor-in-Chief ILIR NIKOLLA.

Gazeta Ballkan: Rruga Durresit 61, Tirana; tel. and fax (4) 2229954; e-mail info@ballkan.com; internet www.ballkan.com; Editor-in-Chief ROMIR SARACI.

Gazeta Shqiptare (The Albanian Newspaper): Ish-Drejtoria e Uzines se AutoTraktoreve, Tirana; tel. (4) 2359104; fax (4) 2359116; e-mail redaksia@balkanweb.com; internet www.balkanweb.com; f. 1927; re-established 1993; independent; politics, economics, culture; local news section; Editor-in-Chief ERL MURATI.

Gazeta Start: Rruga Kajo Karafili, P. Bimbashi 4, Tirana; e-mail info@gazetastart.com; internet www.gazetastart.com; Editor-in-Chief SERVET GURA; circ. 10,000 (Jan. 2010).

Integrimi (Integration): Rruga Sami Frasheri 20/10, Tirana 1001; tel. (4) 2270413; fax (4) 2270412; e-mail gazetaintegrimi@europe.com; internet www.integrimi.com; organ of the Socialist Movement for Integration.

Koha Jonë (Our Time): Rruga Aleksandër Moisiu 1, Tirana; tel. (4) 2347805; fax (4) 2347808; e-mail edisonkurani@kohajone.com; internet www.kohajone.com; f. 1991; independent; Editor-in-Chief EDISON KURANI; circ. 400,000.

Korrieri (The Courier): Rruga Dervish Hima 1, Tirana; tel. (4) 2253574; fax (4) 2253575; e-mail posta@korrieri.com; internet www.korrieri.com; independent; Editor-in-Chief ALFRED PEZA.

Metropol: Rruga Dull Keta 5, Tirana; tel. (4) 2233991; fax (4) 2233998; e-mail gazetametropol@yahoo.com; internet www.gazetametropol.com; Editor-in-Chief BRAHIM SHIMA.

Panorama (Panorama): Rruga Panorama 3, prapa shkollës Harry Fultz, Pallati 1, Tirana; tel. (4) 2273207; fax (4) 2273206; e-mail info@panorama.com.al; internet www.panorama.com.al; independent; politics, economics, culture, sports, arts; Editor-in-Chief ROBERT RAKIPLLARI.

Rilindja Demokratike (Democratic Revival): Rruga Punëtorët e Rilindjes, pranë selisë së PD, Tirana; tel. (4) 2232355; fax (4) 2230329; e-mail gazetard@albaniaonline.net; internet www.rilindjademokratike.com; f. 1991; organ of the Partia Demokratike e Shqipërisë; Editor-in-Chief BLEDI KASMI; circ. 50,000.

Shekulli (Century): Rruga Ismail Qemali, Pallati Abissnet, Tirana; tel. (4) 2256025; fax (4) 2256016; e-mail info@shekulli.com.al; internet www.shekulli.com.al; independent; national and international politics, economics, culture; English summary; Editor-in-Chief ENED JANINA.

Sot News (News Today): Rruga Sitki Çiço; tel. (4) 2382019; fax (4) 2382020; e-mail gazeta@sot.com.al; internet www.sot.com.al; f. 2002; Albanian and English; current affairs; Editor-in-Chief ARJAN PRODANI.

Sporti Shqiptar (Albanian Sports): Rruga Ismail Qemali, ish-Blloku, Pallati Abissnet, Tirana; tel. (4) 4300731; fax (4) 2368322; e-mail gazetasportit@gmail.com; internet www.sportishqiptar.com .al; f. 1935; national and international sports; Publr KOÇO KOKËDHIMA; Editor BASHKIM TUFA; circ. 10,000.

Tema: Zayed Business Center, Rruga Sulejman Delvina, 3rd Floor, Tirana; tel. and fax (4) 2251073; e-mail info@tema.al; internet www .gazetatema.net; f. 1999; independent; liberal; Editor-in-Chief MERO BAZE.

Tirana Observer: Rruga Irfan Tomini, Pallati Biorn, Kati i 2-të, Tirana; tel. (4) 2419001; fax (4) 2419000; e-mail tiranaobserver@ gmail.com; internet www.tiranaobserver.al; f. 2005; Editor ALTIN SINANI.

Tirana Times: Rruga Dëshmorët e 4 Shkurtit 7/1, Tirana; tel. (4) 2274203; fax (4) 2274204; e-mail editor@tiranatimes.com; internet www.tiranatimes.com; f. 2005; weekly (hard copy), daily (online); in English; news, analysis, politics, business, culture; Editor-in-Chief ANDI BALA.

Zëri i Popullit (The Voice of the People): Bulevardi Zhan D'Ark, Tirana; tel. (4) 2233572; fax (4) 2233526; e-mail info@zeri-popullit .com; internet www.zeri-popullit.com; f. 1942; daily, except Mon.; organ of the Partia Socialiste e Shqipërisë; English summary; Editor-in-Chief ALDRIN DALIPI; circ. 105,000.

PERIODICALS

Albanian Journal of Natural and Technical Sciences (AJNTS): Akademia e Shkencave e Shqipërisë, Sheshi Fan S. Noli 7, Tirana; tel. (4) 2266548; fax (4) 2230305; e-mail sbushati@akad.edu.al; internet www.akad.edu.al; f. 1996; two a year; publ. by the Academy of Sciences of Albania Publishing House; in English; all fields of natural and technical sciences; Editor-in-Chief Prof. Dr SALVATORE BUSHATI.

Bujqesia Shqiptare (Albanian Agriculture): Ministria e Bujqësisë, Ushqimit dhe Mbrojtjes së Konsumatorit, Sheshi Skënderbej 2, Tirana; tel. (4) 2232796; fax (4) 2227924; e-mail gjana@hotmail .com; monthly; organ of the Ministry of Agriculture, Rural Development and Water Management; agriculture, cattle-breeding and gardening.

Fjala Review: Rruga M. Gjollesha 48, Tirana; tel. (4) 2273413; e-mail gazetafjala@hotmail.com; internet www.fjalareview.com; f. 2001; weekly; literature, culture, translation and anthropology; in Albanian; Editor-in-Chief ELVANA TUFA.

Gazeta Drita Islame: Rruga George W. Bush 50, Tirana; tel. (4) 2230492; e-mail info@dritaislame.al; internet www.dritaislame.al; monthly; owned by Islamic Community Organization of Albania; in Albanian; Editor HAXHI LIKA.

Iliria: Instituti i Arkeologjisë, Sheshi Nënë Tereza, Tirana; tel. and fax (4) 2240712; e-mail instark@albmail.com; f. 1971; two a year; publ. by the Archaeological Institute, Academy of Sciences of Albania Publishing House; concerned with archaeology studies in the fields of prehistory, antiquity and the early Middle Ages; in English and French, or in Albanian with English or French summaries; Editor-in-Chief Prof. Dr MUZAFER KORKUTI.

Jeta (Life): Rruga Gjergj Fishta, Pranë Ekspozites Shqiperia Sot, Tirana; tel. (4) 2270913; fax (4) 2270914; e-mail e.toni@ jetamediacompany.com; f. 2000; monthly; general interest; illustrated; Gen. Dir ESMERALDA T. ÇOMACKA; circ. 14,000 (2009).

Klan: Rruga Dervish Hima 1, Tirana; tel. (4) 2256111; fax (4) 2234424; e-mail info@revistaklan.com; internet www.revistaklan .com; f. 1997.

Kultura Popullore (Folk Culture Magazine): Instituti i Kultures Popullore, Rruga Kont Urani 3, Tirana; tel. (4) 2222323; e-mail ikp .alb@icc.al.org; f. 1980; annually; publ. by the Institute of Folk Culture, Academy of Sciences of Albania Publishing House; folk culture, anthropology; English summary; Editor-in-Chief Prof. Dr AFËRDITA ONUZI.

Mapo: Rruga Gjin Bue Shpata 9A; tel. (4) 2223110; e-mail info@ revistamapo.com; internet www.revistamapo.com; weekly; current affairs, economy, society, culture.

Mbrojtja (The Defence): Bulevardi Dëshmorët e Kombit, Tirana; tel. and fax (4) 2226701; f. 1931; monthly; publ. by the Ministry of Defence; Editor-in-Chief ALBERT HITOALIAJ; circ. 1,500.

Mesuesi (The Teacher): Rruga Durrësit, pranë Ministrise se Arsimit dhe Shkences, Tirana; tel. (4) 2227206; e-mail mesuesi@mash.gov.al; weekly; organ of the Ministry of Education and Sports; Editor-in-Chief ANDON ANTHONY.

Monitor: Media Union, bul. Zogu I, Pallati Edikom, Tirana; tel. (4) 2387000; fax (4) 2250654; e-mail revista@monitor.al; internet www .monitor.al; business and economic news; Editor-in-Chief ORNELA LIPERI.

Ngjallja (The Resurrection): Kisha Orthodhokse Autoqefale e Shqipërisë, Rruga e Kavajës 151, Tirana; tel. (4) 2234117; fax (4) 2232109; e-mail orthchal@orthodoxalbania.org; internet www .orthodoxalbania.org; f. 1992; monthly; organ of the Orthodox Autocephalous Church of Albania; Editor-in-Chief THOMA DHIMA.

Revista Pedagogjike (Institute of Educational Development): Rruga Naim Frashëri 37, Tirana; tel. (4) 2256440; fax (4) 2256441; e-mail sekretaria@izha.edu.al; internet www.izha.edu.al; f. 1945; twice a year; organ of the Institute i Studimeve Pedagogjike (Institute of Pedagogical Studies); educational development, psychology, pedagogy; Editor GERTI JANAQI; circ. 4,000.

Shqip: Bulevardi Zog I Pallati 13-katësh; e-mail info@shqip.al; internet www.shqip.al; f. 2009; monthly; information and culture; Editor NERITANA KRAJA.

Universi i Librit Shqiptar (Universe of the Albanian Book): Botimet Toena, Rruga Muhamet Gjollesha, POB 1420, Tirana; tel. (4) 2240116; fax (4) 2240117; e-mail toena@toena.com.al; internet www.toena.com.al; quarterly review of books publ. in Albanian and of foreign-language books about Albania, Albanian affairs, etc.; Editor-in-Chief IRENA TOÇI.

Ushtria (Army): Bulevardi Dëshmorët e Kombit, Tirana; tel. (4) 2226701; e-mail gazetaushtria@mod.gov.al; f. 1945; weekly; publ. by the Ministry of Defence; Editor-in-Chief MINA HYSA; circ. 3,200.

NEWS AGENCIES

Albanian Telegraphic Agency (ATA) (Agjencia Telegrafike Shqiptare—ATSh): Bulevardi Jeanne D'Ark 23, Tirana; tel. (4) 2251152; fax (4) 2234393; e-mail director@ata.gov.al; internet www.ata.gov.al; f. 1929; state-owned; domestic and foreign news; brs in provincial towns and in Kosovo; Dir-Gen. ANTONETA MALJA.

Alna (Albanian News Agency—Agjensi Private e pavarur Lajmesh në Shqiperi): Rruga Ismail Qemali, Tirana; tel. (4) 2257001; fax (4) 2256002; f. 2001.

TIR-FAX Albanian Independent News Agency (AINA TIR-FAX) (Agjensia e Lajmeve të Pavarura Shqiptare): Rruga 4 Dëshmorët Villa 80, Tirana; tel. (4) 2241727; fax (4) 2230094; e-mail aina@ abissnet.com.al; internet www.tirfaxnews.org; f. 1996; Albanian and English; Dir ZENEL ÇELIKU.

PRESS ASSOCIATIONS

Albanian Media Institute: Rruga Gjin Bue Shpata 8, Tirana; tel. and fax (4) 2229800; fax (4) 2267084; e-mail info@institutemedia.org; internet www.institutemedia.org; f. 1995; independent; produces books and publications on the Albanian and international media, incl. the *Albanian Media Newsletter* (monthly); Dir REMZI LANI.

Asscn of Professional Journalists of Albania: Rruga Dervish Hima 1, Tirana; e-mail ashkullaku@hotmail.com; affiliated to International Federation of Journalists (Brussels, Belgium); Pres. ARMAND SHKULLAKU.

League of Albanian Journalists: Bulevardi Dëshmorët e Kombit, Tirana; tel. and fax (4) 2228563; e-mail albania@albaniaonline.net; affiliated to International Federation of Journalists (Brussels, Belgium); Pres. YLLI RAKIPI.

Publishers

Academy of Sciences of Albania Publishing House (SHKENCA—Botime të Akademisë së Shkencave të RSH): Sheshi Fan S. Noli 7, Tirana; tel. and fax (4) 2230305; e-mail botimet_acad@ yahoo.com; publs include *Studia Albanica*, *Studime Filologjike* and *New and Technical Journal of Natural Sciences*; Chair. GUDAR BEQIRAJ.

Dituria: Rruga Frederik Shiroka 31, POB 1441, Tirana; tel. and fax (4) 2236635; e-mail dituria@icc.al.org; f. 1991; dictionaries, calendars, encyclopedias, social sciences, biographies, fiction and non-fiction; Gen. Dir PETRIT YMERI.

Dudaj: Rruga Sami Frashëri 41, Tirana; tel. and fax (4) 2250156; e-mail info@botimedudaj.com; internet www.botimedudaj.com; f. 2001; fiction and non-fiction; CEO ARLINDA HOVI DUDAJ.

Fan Noli: Rruga Bulev Shekip. Ere, Tirana; tel. (4) 2242739; f. 1991; Albanian and foreign literature; Pres. REXHEP HIDA.

Neraida: Rruga Myslym Shyri 54/4/1, Tirana; tel. (4) 2243310; fax (4) 2262312; e-mail neraida@albaniaonline.net; fiction and non-fiction; f. 1995; Dir JANI MALO.

Ombra GVG: Rruga Gjergj Fishta, Kompleksi Tirana 2000 4/2, Tirana; tel. (4) 2224173; fax (4) 2224986; e-mail info@ombragvg.com; internet www.ombragvg.com; f. 1998; Pres. GËZIM TAFA.

Omsca: Rruga Frederik Shiroka, Tirana; tel. (4) 2233648; fax (4) 360793; e-mail omsca@abissnet.al; fiction; Dir LUAN PENGILI.

Onufri: Rruga Sulejman Pasha, Tirana; tel. (4) 2270399; e-mail info@onufri.com; literary; Dir BUJAR HUDHRI.

Shtëpia Botuese e Librit Shkollor: Rruga Mine Peza 1/1, Tirana; tel. and fax (4) 2223633; e-mail info@shblsh.com; internet www.shblsh.com; f. 1967; educational books; Dir SHPËTIM BOZDO.

Shtëpia Botuese Naim Frashëri: Tirana; tel. (4) 2227906; f. 1950; fiction, poetry, drama, criticism, children's literature, translations; Dir GAQO BUSHAKA.

Skanderbeg Books: Rruga H. H. Dalliu, Pallat 184/9, Tirana; tel. and fax (4) 2260945; e-mail flutura@skanderbegbooks.com; internet www.skanderbegbooks.com; literary fiction and non-fiction in translation; Dir FLUTURA AÇKA.

Toena: Rruga Muhamet Gjollesha, POB 1420, Tirana; tel. (4) 2240116; fax (4) 2240117; e-mail toena@toena.com.al; internet www.toena.com.al; history, social sciences, humanities, fiction, linguistics; Pres. FATMIR TOÇI.

Uegen: Rruga Vaso Pasha, pall. Fratari kat. 3; tel. and fax (4) 2272858; e-mail uegen@pronet.com.al; internet www.uegen.com; f. 1992; fiction, history, psychology, philosophy, etc.; Dir XHEVAIR LLESHI.

PUBLISHERS' ASSOCIATION

Albanian Publishers' Asscn: Rruga Dervish Hima 32, Tirana; tel. (4) 2240116; fax (4) 2240117; e-mail toena@icc.al.org; f. 1992; Dir PETRIT YMERI.

Broadcasting and Communications

TELECOMMUNICATIONS

At January 2011 there were six main telecommunications operators in Albania.

Abissnet: Rruga Ismail Qemali 20, Tirana; tel. (4) 4300000; fax (4) 2256002; e-mail info@abissnet.al; internet www.abissnet.al; f. 1998; fixed-line telephone communications and internet services; Chair. of Bd ENDRI PUKA.

Albanian Mobile Communications (AMC): Rruga Gjergji Legisi, Laprakë, Tirana; tel. (4) 2275000; fax (4) 2275243; e-mail contact_us@amc.al; internet www.amc.al; f. 1996; 85% owned by Cosmote (Greece/Norway); operates mobile telephone network; Man. Dir DIMITRIS BLATSIOS.

Albtelecom: Rruga Myslym Shyri 42, Tirana; tel. (4) 2232169; fax (4) 2233323; e-mail corporatesales@albtelecom.al; internet www.albtelecom.al; 80% stake owned by consortium of Turk Telekom and Calik Enerji (both of Turkey); Chief Exec. ILIRIAN KUKA.

Eagle Mobile: Rruga Murat Toptani, Qendra e Biznesit 12 Katëshe, Kati 9-10, Tirana; tel. (4) 2290100; fax (4) 2290190; e-mail info@eaglemobile.al; internet www.eaglemobile.al; f. 2008; Dir-Gen. ALI TASKIN.

PLUS Communication: Rruga Dëshmorët e Shkurtit 4, Tirana; tel. (4) 4501500; fax (4) 44501538; e-mail info@plus.al; internet www.plus.al; f. 2009; mobile cellular telecommunications; CEO MONI BUCHNIK.

Vodafone Albania: Autostrada Tiranë-Durrës, Rruga Pavarësia 61, Kashar, Tirana; tel. (4) 2283072; fax (4) 2283333; e-mail ecaresupport.al@vodafone.com; internet www.vodafone.al; f. 2001; mobile cellular telecommunications; Gen. Dir THOMAS PAPASPYROU.

BROADCASTING

In 1991 state broadcasting was removed from political control and made subordinate to the Parliamentary Commission for the Media. In addition to the public national broadcasting service, in 2010 there were two national television stations, two satellite television channels, 71 local television stations, 83 cable television channels, two national radio stations and 46 local radio stations licensed by the National Council of Radio and Television.

Regulatory Authority

National Council of Radio and Television (NCRT) (Këshilli Kombëtar i Radios dhe Televizionit—KKRT): Rruga Abdi Toptani, Ish Hotel Drini, Tirana; tel. (4) 233599; fax (4) 226288; e-mail kkrt@kkrt.gov.al; internet www.kkrt.gov.al; f. 1999; Chair. ENDIRA BUSHATI.

Radio

Radio Televizioni Shqiptar: Rruga Ismail Qemali 11, Tirana; tel. and fax (4) 2222481; e-mail dushiulp@yahoo.com; internet www.rtsh.al; f. 1938 as Radio Tirana; two channels of domestic services (19 and five hours daily) and a third channel covering international broadcasting (two services in Albanian and seven in foreign languages); several local channels; 65% state-funded; 35% funded through commercial advertising and fees; Chair. KASTRIST CAUSBI; Dir-Gen. EDUARD MAZI; Dir of Radio MARTIN LEKA.

Plus 2 Radio: Rruga Aleksandër Moisiu Nr 76/1, Tirana; tel. (4) 4301016; internet www.plus2radio.com.al; f. 1998; popular music.

Top Albania Radio: Qendra Ndërkombëtare e Kulturës, Bulevardi Dëshmorët e Kombit, Tirana; tel. (4) 2247492; fax (4) 2247493; e-mail contact@topalbaniaradio.com; internet www.topalbaniaradio.com; Dir ENKELEJD JOTI.

Television

Radio Televizioni Shqiptar: Rruga Ismail Qemali 11, Tirana; tel. (4) 2256056; fax (4) 2256058; e-mail dushiulp@yahoo.com; internet www.rtsh.al; f. 1960; broadcasts range of television programmes; 65% state-funded; 35% funded through commercial advertising and fees; Chair. KASTRIST CAUSBI; Dir-Gen. EDUARD MAZI; Dir of Television VENA ISAK.

Albanian Satellite Television (ALSAT TV): Rruga Siri Kodra, Tirana; tel. and fax (4) 271738; e-mail news@albanianscreen.tv; internet www.alsat.tv; news satellite broadcasting in Albanian; from mid-2003 programmes also broadcast by local TV stations in Albania, the former Yugoslav republic of Macedonia and Kosovo.

Shijak TV: Rruga Kavajës, Sheshi Ataturk 5, Tirana; tel. (4) 2247135; fax (4) 2252619; e-mail shijaktv01@albaniaonline.net; internet www.shijaktv.com; f. 1995; local station; Pres. GËZIM ISMAILI.

Top Channel TV: Qendra Ndërkombëtare e Kulturës, Bulevardi Dëshmorët e Kombit, Tirana; tel. (4) 2253177; fax (4) 2253178; e-mail info@top-channel.tv; internet www.top-channel.tv; f. 2001; Dir ENKELEJD JOTI.

TVA—Televizioni Arbëria: Pall. i Kulturës, Kati III, Tirana; tel. (4) 2243932; fax (4) 8301466; e-mail tva@telearberia.tv; internet www.telearberia.tv; Dir ESTELA DASHI.

TV Klan: Rruga Aleksander Moisiu 97, Ish-Kinostudio, Tirana; tel. (4) 2347805; fax (4) 2347808; e-mail info@tvklan.tv; internet www.tvklan.tv; Dir-Gen. ALEKSANDER FRANGAJ.

Finance

(cap. = capital; res = reserves; dep. = deposits; m. = million; brs = branches; amounts in lekë, unless otherwise stated)

BANKING

There are 16 commercial banks operating in the country.

Central Bank

Bank of Albania (Banka e Shqipërisë): Sheshi Avni Rustemi, nr. 24 Tirana; tel. (4) 2419301; fax (4) 2419408; e-mail public@bankofalbania.org; internet www.bankofalbania.org; f. 1992; cap. 2,500m., res 30,048m., dep. 82,709m. (Dec. 2009); Gov. ARDIAN FULLANI; 5 brs.

Other Banks

Alpha Bank: Rruga e Kavajës, G-KAM Business Center, Tirana; tel. (4) 2278511; fax (4) 2237072; internet www.alphabank.al; owned by Alpha Bank (Greece); CEO PERIKLIS DROUGKAS.

Banka Credins: Rruga Ismail Qemali 21, Tirana; tel. (4) 2234096; fax (4) 2222916; e-mail info@bankacredins.com; internet www.bankacredins.com; f. 2003; cap. 4,742.9m., res 2,622.3m., dep. 79,158.6m. (Dec. 2012); Gen. Man. and Exec. Dir ARTAN SANTO.

Crédit Agricole Bank: Tirana Tower, Rruga e Kavajës 27, Tirana; tel. (4) 2258755; fax (4) 2240752; internet www.credit-agricole.al; owned by Crédit Agricole SA (France); cap. 6,807.2m., res 58.2m., dep. 17,051.6m. (Dec. 2012); CEO LUC BEISO.

Intesa Sanpaolo Bank Albania (Banka Amerikanë e Shqipërisë): Rruga Ismail Qemali 27, POB 8319, Tirana; tel. (4) 2276000; fax (4) 2248762; e-mail info@intesasanpaolobank.al; internet www.intesasanpaolobank.al; f. 1998; owned by Intesa Sanpaolo Gp; fmrly American Bank of Albania; name changed Oct. 2008, following merger with Banca Italo-Albanese; cap. 5,562.5m., res 3,717.8m., dep. 109,907.5m. (2012); Chair. MASSIMO PIERDICCHI; CEO ALEXANDER RESCH.

National Commercial Bank of Albania (Banka Kombëtare Tregtare ShA): Bulevardi Zhan D'Ark, Tirana; tel. (4) 2250955; fax (4) 2250956; e-mail info@bkt.com.al; internet www.bkt.com.al; f. 1993 by merger; privatized in 2000; cap. US $100.0m., res $10.7m., dep. $1,948.0m. (Dec. 2012); Chair. MEHMET USTA; 81 brs.

ProCredit Bank (Albania) (Banka ProCredit): Rruga Dritan Hoxha 92, Tirana; tel. (4) 2389389; fax (4) 2233918; e-mail info@procreditbank.com.al; internet www.procreditbank.com.al; f. 1995 as Foundation for Enterprise Finance and Development; name changed to Fedad Bank ShA in 1999, and as above in 2003; cap. 2,966m., res 592m., dep. 31,835m. (Dec. 2012); Chair. of Bd CLAUS-PETER ZEITINGER; 40 brs.

Raiffeisen Bank: European Trade Centre, 6th Floor, Tirana; tel. (4) 2381381; fax (4) 2275599; e-mail info@raiffeisen.al; internet www.raiffeisen.al; f. 1991 as Savings Bank of Albania; owned by Raiffeisen Zentralbank Österreich AG (Austria); cap. 14,179m., res 2,966m., dep. 286,337m. (Dec. 2012); CEO CHRISTIAN CANACARIS; 58 brs.

Société Générale Albania: Bulevardi Dëshmorët e Kombit, Twin Towers, Tower 1, 9th Floor, Tirana; tel. (4) 2280442; fax (4) 2280441; e-mail sgalb.info@socgen.com; internet www.societegenerale.al; f. 2004 as Banka Popullore; renamed in 2010 following acquisition by Société Générale, France; cap. 6,741m., res 68m., dep. 53,524m. (Dec. 2012); Chair. BERNARD DAVID; Man. FRÉDÉRIC BLANC; 43 brs.

Tirana Bank: Rruga Ibrahim Rugova 1, POB 2400/1, Tirana; tel. (4) 2277700; fax (4) 2277691; e-mail info@tiranabank.al; internet www.tiranabank.al; f. 1996; 96.71% owned by Piraeus Bank (Greece); cap. 10,954.0m., res 3,229.4m., dep. 72,889.0m. (Dec. 2012); Man. Dir and CEO SAVVAS THALASSINOS; 56 brs.

United Bank of Albania: Rruga e Durrësit (Zogu i zi), 14th Floor, POB 128, Tirana; tel. (4) 2228460; fax (4) 2404558; e-mail uba@albaniaonline.net; f. 1994; cap. 1,763.0m., res 64.1m., dep. 4,736.0m. (Dec. 2012); fmrly Arab-Albanian Islamic Bank, present name adopted 2003; 86.7% owned by Islamic Development Bank (Saudi Arabia); Chair. KAMIL GOKHAN BOZKURT; CEO EMINA ŠIŠIĆ; 6 brs.

STOCK EXCHANGE

Tirana Stock Exchange (Bursa e Tiranes): Rruga Dora D'Istria, Kutia Postare 274/1, Tirana; tel. and fax (4) 2265058; e-mail tseinfo@abcom-al.com; internet www.tse.com.al; f. 2002; CEO ANILA FUR-ERAJ.

INSURANCE

Albsig Insurance: Rruga Punëtorët e Rilindjes 10, Tirana; tel. (4) 2254764; fax (4) 2254664; e-mail info@albsig.com.al; internet www.albsig.com.al; f. 2004.

Atlantik: Rruga Themistokli Gërmenji 3/1, Tirana; tel. (4) 2230506; fax (4) 235088; e-mail info@atlantik.com.al; internet www.atlantik.com.al; f. 2001; Gen. Dir DRITAN ÇELAJ.

EUROSIG: Rruga Papa Gjon Pali i II, Tirana; tel. (4) 2238899; fax (4) 2223841; e-mail info@eurosig.al; internet www.eurosig.al; f. 2004; Exec. Dir MUHARREM BARDHOCI.

Health Insurance Institute (Instituti i Sigurimeve të Kujdesit Shëndetsor): Rruga Sami Frashëri 8, Tirana; tel. (4) 2230984; fax (4) 2274953; e-mail abeci@isksh.com.al; internet www.isksh.com.al; Dir ASTRIT BECI.

Insurance Institute of Albania (INSIG) (Instituti i Sigurimeve të Shqipërisë): Rruga e Dibrës 91, Tirana; tel. (4) 234170; fax (4) 223838; e-mail info@insig.com.al; internet www.insig.com.al; f. 1991; 61% owned by American Reserve Life Insurance (USA); the European Bank for Reconstruction and Development and the International Finance Corpn each acquired 19.5% stake in 2004; all types of insurance; Gen. Dir SAIMIR ZËMBLAKU; 12 brs.

INTERSIG: Rruga e Durrësit, Tirana; tel. (4) 2270576; fax (4) 2270577; e-mail info@intersig.al; internet www.intersig.al; f. 2001; non-life insurance; CEO FITNETE SULAJ.

Sigal: Bulevardi Zogu I 1, Tirana; tel. (4) 2233308; fax (4) 2250220; e-mail info@sigal.com.al; f. 1999; life, health, property, engineering, motor, marine, aviation, liability, accidents, banking, agriculture, credit; 68.64% owned by Uniqa Group (Austria), 13.30% owned by Albanian-American Enterprise Fund; CEO AVNI PONARI.

SIGMA: Rruga Komuna e Parisit, Pall. Lura, POB 1714, Tirana; tel. (4) 2258254; fax (4) 2258253; e-mail info@sigma-al.com; internet www.sigma-al.com; Gen. Dir QEMAL DISHA.

INSURERS' ASSOCIATION

Association of Albanian Insurers (Shoqata e Siguruesve të Shqipërisë): Rruga Gjergj Fishta, Pall. Edil–Al–It, Kati II, Tirana; tel. (4) 2254033; fax (4) 2267221; e-mail dritankastrati@insurers-al.org; internet www.insurers-al.org; f. 2003; Exec. Dir ANTONETA ÇELA.

Trade and Industry

PRIVATIZATION AGENCY

National Agency for Privatization (NAP) (Agjencia Kombetare e Privatizimit): Bulevardi Dëshmorët e Kombit, Tirana; tel. (4) 2257457; fax (4) 2227933; f. 1991; govt agency under the control of the Council of Ministers; prepares and proposes the legal framework concerning privatization procedures and implementation; Gen. Dir KOZETA FINO.

SUPERVISORY ORGANIZATIONS

Albkontroll: Rruga Skënderbej 45, Durrës; tel. (52) 223377; fax (52) 222791; f. 1962; brs throughout Albania; independent control body for inspection of goods for import and export, means of transport, etc.; Gen. Man. DILAVER MEZINI; 15 brs.

State Supreme Audit Control (Kontrolli i Larte i Shtetit): Bulevardi Dëshmorët e Kombit 3, Tirana; tel. (4) 2247294; fax (4) 2232491; e-mail klsh@klsh.org.al; internet www.klsh.org.al; Pres. BUJAR LESKAJ.

DEVELOPMENT ORGANIZATIONS

Albanian Business and Investment Agency (Albinvest): Bulevardi Gjergj Fishta, Pall. Shallvare, Tirana 1000; tel. (4) 2252886; fax (4) 2222341; e-mail info@albinvest.gov.al; internet www.albinvest.gov.al; Exec. Dir VIOLA PUCI.

Albanian Development Fund (Fondi Shqiptar i Zhvillimit): Rruga Sami Frashëri 10, Tirana; tel. (4) 2235597; fax (4) 2234885; e-mail adf@albaniandf.org; internet www.albaniandf.org; Exec. Dir BENET BECI.

Albanian Economic Development Agency (AEDA): Bulevardi Zhan D'Ark, Tirana 1000; tel. (4) 2230133; fax (4) 2228439; e-mail aeda@albnet.net; f. 1993; fmrly Albanian Centre for Foreign Investments Promotion; govt agency to promote foreign investment in Albania and to provide practical support to foreign investors; publ. *Ekonomia*; Chair. SELAMI XHEPA.

CHAMBERS OF COMMERCE

Union of Chambers of Commerce and Industry of Albania (Bashkimi i Dhomave të Tregtisë dhe Industrisë të Shqipërisë): Blvd Zhan D'Ark 23, Tirana; tel. and fax (4) 2247105; e-mail ilir.zhilla@uccial.al; internet www.uccial.al; f. 1958; Chair. ILIR ZHILLA; 15 mems (2012).

Dibër Chamber of Commerce and Industry: Bulevardi Elez Isufi, Peshkopi, Dibër; tel. and fax (218) 22645; e-mail ccidiber@gmail.com; Chair. ILIR BULKU.

Durrës Chamber of Commerce and Industry: Lagjja 11, Rruga A. Goga, POB 220, Durrës; tel. (52) 224440; fax (52) 222199; e-mail info@ccidr.al; internet www.ccidr.al; f. 1995; Chair. ANDREA XHAVARA.

Elbasan Chamber of Commerce and Industry (Dhoma e Tregtisë dhe ë Industrisë Elbasan): Godina e Prefekturës Elbasan, Kati 1, Elbasan; tel. (54) 255490; e-mail cciel@albmail.com; Chair. VELI KAZAZI.

Shkodër Chamber of Commerce and Industry (Dhoma ë Tregtisë dhe e Industrisë Shkodër): Shkodër; tel. (224) 22460; fax (224) 23656; e-mail ccish@abissnet.com.al; Chair. ANTON LEKA.

Tirana Chamber of Commerce and Industry (Dhoma e Tregtisë dhe Industrisë): 6 Rruga Kavaja, Tirana; tel. (4) 5800932; e-mail sekretaria@cci.al; internet www.cci.al; f. 1926; Chair. NIKOLIN JAKA.

Vlorë Chamber of Commerce and Industry (Dhoma e Tregtisë dhe Industrisë Vlorë): Pall. i Kulturës Liberia, Kati 1, Vlorë; tel. (33) 222111; fax (33) 225737; e-mail info@ccivlora.org; f. 1985; Chair. EDMOND LEKA; 1,800 mems.

There are also chambers of commerce in Berat, Fier, Gjirokastër, Korçë, Kukës and Lezhë.

UTILITIES

Electricity

State Electricity Corporation of Albania (KESH) (Korporata Elektroenergjetikë Shqiptarë): Biloky Vasil Shanto, Tirana; tel. (4) 2262947; fax (4) 2232046; e-mail mail@kesh.com.al; internet www.kesh.com.al; state corpn for the generation, transmission, distribution and export of electrical energy; govt-controlled; scheduled for transfer to private ownership; fmr distribution subsidiary OSSH was privatized in March 2009; Dir ENGJËLL ZEQO.

TRADE UNIONS

During 1991 independent trade unions were established. The most important of these was the Union of Independent Trade Unions of Albania. Other unions were established for workers in various sectors of the economy.

Alliance of Independent Trade Unions of Albania (Bashkimi i Sindikatave të Pavarura të Shqipërisë—BSPSh): Rruga Zogu i zi, Pall. i Kulturës Ali Kelmendi, Tirana; tel. and fax (4) 2232157; e-mail bspsh@albmail.com; f. 1991; Chair. GËZIM KALAJA; 85,000 mems (2010).

Confederation of Trade Unions of Albania (Konfederata e Sindikatave të Shqipërisë—KSSH): Sheshi Garibaldi 3, Pallati Tekstilisti, Kombinat, 1027 Tirana; tel. and fax (4) 2477284; e-mail kssh@kssh.org; internet www.kssh.org; f. 1991; includes 12 sectoral trade union federations; Chair. KOL NIKOLLAJ; 110,000 mems (2012).

Transport

RAILWAYS

In 2009 there were 423 km of railway track in Albania.

Albanian Railways (Hekurudha Shqiptare): Rruga Skënderbej, Durrës; tel. and fax (52) 222037; CEO SOKOL KAPIDANI.

ROADS

In 2002 the road network comprised an estimated 18,000 km of classified roads, including 3,220 km of main roads and 4,300 km of secondary roads; 39% of the total network was paved. In December 2002 a 23.5-km road linking Greece with southern Albania was opened. In 2003 the Albanian Government secured financing from the World Bank, the European Investment Bank and the European Bank for Reconstruction and Development for a number of road-maintenance projects. As part of the European Union's Transport Corridor Europe–Central Asia (TRACECA) programme, the construction of a west–east highway (Corridor VIII) from the port of Durrës to the Black Sea, via the former Yugoslav republic of Macedonia and Bulgaria, has been undertaken. Corridor X, another TRACECA project, runs north–south from Hani Hotit, at the border with Montenegro, to Tri Urat on the Greek frontier. A highway linking Tirana and Vlorë was completed in 2006. The construction of a major highway linking Durrës with Kosovo was completed in 2010.

SHIPPING

At December 2013 Albania's flag registered fleet had 57 vessels, totalling 54,272 grt. The chief ports are those in Durrës, Vlorë, Sarandë and Shëngjin. Ferry services have been established between Durrës and three Italian ports (Trieste, Bari and Ancona) and between Sarandë and the Greek island of Corfu. Services also connect Vlorë with the Italian ports of Bari and Brindisi. The World Bank, the European Union and the Organization of the Petroleum Exporting Countries Fund for International Development have financed projects to improve existing port facilities.

Adetare Shipping Agency: 1 Rruga Taulantia, Durrës; tel. (52) 232614; fax (52) 232614; e-mail adeag@albmail.com; f. 1991; Dir ARMAND GJERGJI.

Albanian State Shipping Enterprise: Durrës; tel. (52) 222233; fax (52) 229111.

Durrës Port Authority: Lagija 1, Rruga Tregtare, Durrës; tel. (52) 228636; fax (52) 223115; e-mail apd@apdurres.com.al; internet www.apdurres.com.al; state-owned; Gen. Dir EDUARD NDREU.

CIVIL AVIATION

There is a small international airport at Rinas, 17 km from Tirana. Reconstruction of the airport was undertaken in the late 1990s, and it was privatized in April 2005. A civil and military airport was constructed at Pish Poro, 29 km from Vlorë, under an agreement between Albania and Italy. The construction of a second international airport (Zayed International Airport) at the north-eastern town of Kukës, with funding from the Government of the United Arab Emirates, was completed in November 2005.

General Directorate of Civil Aviation: Rruga e Kavajës, Përballë Xhamise, POB 205, Tirana; tel. and fax (4) 2223969; e-mail dpac2@albanet.net; CEO AGRON DIBRA.

Tourism

In 2012, according to provisional figures, there were some 3.5m. international tourist arrivals, including same-day visitors. In that year receipts from tourism (excluding passenger transport) amounted to US $1,471m., according to provisional data. The main tourist centres include Tirana, Durrës, Sarandë, Shkodër and Pogradec. The Roman amphitheatre at Durrës is one of the largest in Europe. The ancient towns of Gjirokastër and Butrint are important archaeological sites, and there are many other towns of historic interest. However, expansion of tourism has been limited by the inadequacy of Albania's infrastructure and by a lack of foreign investment in the development of new facilities.

Albturist: Bulevardi Dëshmorët e Kombit 8, Hotel Dhajti, Tirana; tel. (4) 2251849; fax (4) 2234359; e-mail albturist@yahoo.com; brs in main towns and all tourist centres; 28 hotels throughout the country; Dir-Gen. BESNIK PELLUMBI.

Committee for Development and Tourism: Bulevardi Dëshmorët e Kombit 8, Tirana; tel. (4) 2258323; fax (4) 2258322; e-mail tdc@interalb.net; govt body.

Defence

As assessed at November 2013, the total strength of the Albanian armed forces was about 14,250, including a Joint Force Command of 8,150 and a Support Command of 4,300. There is a 500-member paramilitary force. From September 1999 a 2,400-member contingent, known as Communications Zone West (COMMZ-W), was deployed in Albania to maintain civil order and to support North Atlantic Treaty Organization (NATO) forces in neighbouring Kosovo. In June 2002 COMMZ-W was officially dissolved, and a NATO headquarters was established at Tirana. Under legislation adopted in August 2008, compulsory military service of 12 months ended officially at the end of 2010. NATO member states completed the process of ratifying Albania's accession protocol in February 2009; the country joined the Alliance on 1 April.

Defence Expenditure: Budgeted at 16,800m. lekë in 2014.

Chief of the General Staff: Maj-Gen. JERONIM BAZO.

Education

Education in Albania is free and compulsory for children between the ages of six and 14 years. Enrolment at pre-primary schools included 64% of children in the relevant age-group in 2011/12. In 2009/10 enrolment at primary schools included 80% of children in the relevant age-group (males 81%; females 80%), while, according to UNESCO estimates, secondary education enrolment was equivalent to 89% of children in the appropriate age-group (males 90%; females 88%). In 2011/12 a total of 158,963 students were enrolled at Albania's institutions of higher education. Spending on education accounted for some 10.6% of government expenditure in 2004 (equivalent to some 3.0% of GDP).

ALGERIA

Introductory Survey

LOCATION, CLIMATE, LANGUAGE, RELIGION, FLAG, CAPITAL

The People's Democratic Republic of Algeria lies in northern Africa, with the Mediterranean Sea to the north, Mali and Niger to the south, Tunisia and Libya to the east, and Morocco and Mauritania to the west. The climate on the Mediterranean coast is temperate, becoming more extreme in the Atlas mountains immediately to the south. Further south is part of the Sahara, a hot and arid desert. Temperatures in Algiers, on the coast, are generally between 9°C (48°F) and 29°C (84°F), while in the interior they may exceed 50°C (122°F). Arabic is the official language, but French is widely used. Tamazight, the principal language of Algeria's Berber community, was granted 'national' status in 2002. Islam is the state religion, and almost all Algerians are Muslims. The national flag (proportions 2 by 3) has two equal vertical stripes, of green and white, with a red crescent moon and a five-pointed red star superimposed in the centre. The capital is Algiers (el-Djezaïr).

CONTEMPORARY POLITICAL HISTORY

Historical Context

Algeria was conquered by French forces in the 1830s and annexed by France in 1842. The territory was colonized with French settlers, and many French citizens became permanent residents. Unlike most of France's overseas possessions, Algeria was not formally a colony but was 'attached' to metropolitan France. However, the indigenous Muslim majority were denied equal rights, and political and economic power within Algeria was largely held by the settler minority.

On 1 November 1954 the principal Algerian nationalist movement, the Front de Libération Nationale (FLN), began a war for national independence, in the course of which about 1m. Muslims were killed or wounded. The French Government agreed to a ceasefire in March 1962, and independence was declared on 3 July. In August the Algerian provisional Government transferred its functions to the Political Bureau of the FLN, and in September a National Constituent Assembly was elected (from a single list of FLN candidates) and a Republic proclaimed. A new Government was formed, with Ahmed Ben Bella, founder of the FLN, as Prime Minister.

A draft Constitution, providing for a presidential regime with the FLN as the sole party, was approved by popular referendum in September 1963. Ben Bella was elected President, although real power remained with the bureaucracy and the army. In June 1965 the Minister of Defence, Col Houari Boumedienne, deposed Ben Bella in a bloodless coup and took control of the country as President of a Council of the Revolution, composed chiefly of army officers. In 1975 Boumedienne announced a series of measures to consolidate the regime and enhance his personal power, including the holding of elections for a President and National People's Assembly. A newly drafted National Charter, which enshrined both the creation of a socialist system and the maintenance of Islam as the state religion, and Constitution were approved at referendums held in June and November 1976, respectively, and in December Boumedienne was elected President unopposed. In February 1977 FLN members were elected to the National People's Assembly.

President Boumedienne died in December 1978, and the Council of the Revolution took over the Government. In January 1979 the FLN elected a Central Committee that was envisaged as the highest policy-making body both of the party and of the nation as a whole. The Committee's choice of Col Ben Djedid Chadli, commander of Oran military district and new party Secretary-General, as the sole presidential candidate was endorsed by a referendum in February. Chadli appointed a Prime Minister, Col Muhammad Abd al-Ghani, anticipating constitutional changes approved by the National People's Assembly in June, which included the obligatory appointment of a premier. In mid-1980 the FLN authorized Chadli to form a smaller Political Bureau, with more limited responsibilities, thereby increasing the power of the President. Chadli was re-elected to the presidency in January 1984, and subsequently appointed Abd al-Hamid Brahimi as Prime Minister. Following a public debate on Boumedienne's National Charter in 1985, a revised Charter—which emphasized a state ideology based on the twin principles of socialism and Islam while encouraging the development of private enterprise—was approved by a referendum in January 1986.

During the second half of the 1980s opposition to the Government was increasingly manifest, and the security forces imprisoned a large number of both Berber and Islamist activists. From mid-1988 severe unemployment, high consumer prices and shortages of essential supplies provoked a series of strikes, and in October rioting in the capital, Algiers, spread to Oran and Annaba. In November constitutional amendments allowing non-FLN candidates to participate in elections and making the Prime Minister answerable to the National People's Assembly (rather than to the President) were approved in a referendum. In December Chadli was elected President for a third term of office.

In February 1989 a new Constitution, signifying the end of the one-party socialist state, was approved by referendum. The executive, legislative and judicial functions of the state were separated and made subject to the supervision of a Constitutional Council. In July legislation permitting the formation of political associations outside the FLN entered force: by mid-1991 a total of 47 political parties had been licensed by the Government, including a radical Islamist group, the Front Islamique du Salut (FIS), the Mouvement pour la Démocratie en Algérie (MDA), which had been founded by Ben Bella in 1984, the Parti d'Avant-Garde Socialiste (renamed Ettahaddi in 1993), the Parti Social-Démocrate (PSD) and the Berber Rassemblement pour la Culture et la Démocratie (RCD). Other legislation adopted in July 1989 further reduced state control of the economy, allowed the expansion of foreign investment and ended the state monopoly of the press (although the principal newspapers remained under FLN control). In September President Chadli appointed Mouloud Hamrouche as Prime Minister.

At local elections held in June 1990 the FIS received some 55% of total votes cast, while the FLN obtained about 32%. In July, following internal disagreement concerning the pace of economic and political reform, Hamrouche and four other ministers resigned from the FLN's Political Bureau. In December the National People's Assembly adopted a law whereby, from 1997, Arabic would be Algeria's only official language and the use of French and the Berber language, Tamazight, in schools and in official transactions would be punishable offences.

Domestic Political Affairs

In April 1991 President Chadli declared that Algeria's first multi-party general election would take place in late June. The FIS argued that a presidential election should be held simultaneously with, or shortly after, the general election, and in May organized an indefinite general strike and demonstrations to demand Chadli's resignation and changes in the electoral laws. Violent confrontations in June between Islamist activists and the security forces prompted Chadli to declare a state of emergency and postpone the general election; he also announced that he had accepted the resignation of the Prime Minister and his Government. Sid-Ahmad Ghozali was appointed premier, and he duly nominated a Council of Ministers consisting mainly of political independents.

Meanwhile, the FLN and the FIS reached a compromise whereby the strike was abandoned, and legislative and presidential elections were to be held before the end of 1991. In July, however, army units arrested some 700 Islamists and occupied the headquarters of the FIS. Among those arrested were the party's President, Abbassi Madani, who had threatened to launch a *jihad* ('holy war') if the state of emergency was not ended, and Vice-President, Ali Belhadj; both were charged with armed conspiracy against the state. The state of emergency was revoked in September.

Following revisions to the electoral code, the first round of the multi-party general election to the newly enlarged 430-seat legislature was held on 26 December 1991, with a second, run-off ballot scheduled for 16 January 1992. In all, 231 seats were won outright at the first round: the FIS took 188 seats (with 47.5% of the votes cast), the Front des Forces Socialistes (FFS) 25, the FLN just 15 and independents three. The FLN alleged widespread intimidation and electoral malpractice on the part of the FIS. On 11 January Chadli resigned as President, announcing that he had (one week earlier) dissolved the National People's Assembly. The following day the High Security Council (comprising the Prime Minister, three generals and two senior ministers) cancelled the second round of legislative voting, at which the FIS had been expected to consolidate its first-round victory.

On 14 January 1992 a five-member High Council of State (HCS) was appointed to act as a collegiate presidency until, at the latest, the expiry of Chadli's term of office in 1993; however, its constitutional legality was disputed by all the political parties. The HCS was chaired by Muhammad Boudiaf, a veteran of the war of independence, but its most influential figure was believed to be Maj.-Gen. Khaled Nezzar, the Minister of Defence. The HCS declared a 12-month state of emergency in February 1992, and detention centres were opened in the Sahara. The FIS, which was officially dissolved by the Government in March, claimed that 150 people had been killed, and as many as 30,000 detained, since the military-sponsored takeover. In April Boudiaf announced the creation of a 60-member National Consultative Council (NCC), which was to meet each month in the building of the suspended Assembly, although it was to have no legislative powers. In June Boudiaf promised a constitutional review, the dissolution of the FLN and a presidential election. Moreover, despite continuing violence, he ordered the release from detention of 2,000 FIS militants.

Boudiaf was assassinated on 29 June 1992, while making a speech in Annaba; the FIS denied all responsibility for his murder. Ali Kafi succeeded Boudiaf as Chairman of the HCS, and Redha Malek, the Chairman of the NCC, was appointed as a new member of the HCS. In early July Ghozali resigned in order to enable Kafi to appoint his own Prime Minister. He was replaced by Belaid Abd el-Salam, who appointed a new Council of Ministers later that month.

In July 1992 Madani and Belhadj were sentenced to 12 years' imprisonment for conspiracy against the state. Violent protests erupted in Algiers and quickly spread to other cities. As political manoeuvring and attempts at reconciliation continued against a background of escalating violence, in February 1993 the state of emergency was renewed for an indefinite period. In June the HCS announced that it would dissolve itself in December, asserting that a modern democracy and free market economy would be created within three years of that date.

The presidency of Liamine Zéroual

In July 1993 a retired general, Liamine Zéroual, succeeded Maj.-Gen. Nezzar as Minister of Defence. Redha Malek replaced Abd el-Salam as Prime Minister in August and subsequently appointed a new Council of Ministers. In October the HCS appointed a National Dialogue Commission (NDC) to prepare for the transition to an elected and democratic form of government. In December it was announced that the HCS would not be disbanded until a new presidential body had been elected at the NDC conference in January 1994. However, all the main political parties (with the exception of the moderate Islamist Hamas) boycotted the conference. Zéroual (who remained Minister of Defence) was inaugurated as President on 31 January for a three-year term.

An attack by Islamist militants on the high-security Tazoult prison, near Batna, in March 1994 resulted in the release of more than 1,000 political prisoners. Certain towns were virtually controlled by Islamist activists, and the deaths of a number of foreign nationals led several countries to advise their citizens to leave Algeria. In response to the rise in violence, the security forces intensified their campaign against armed Islamist groups, resorting to air attacks, punitive raids, torture and psychological warfare, and the killing of thousands of militants.

Malek resigned as Prime Minister in April 1994, and was replaced by Mokdad Sifi. In May the President inaugurated a National Transition Council (NTC), an interim legislature of 200 appointed members, the aim of which was to provide a forum for debate pending legislative elections. With the exception of Hamas, most of the 21 parties that agreed to participate in the NTC were virtually unknown, and the 22 seats that were allocated to other major parties remained vacant.

In August 1994 members of the FLN, the Parti du Renouveau Algérien (PRA), the MDA, Al-Nahda and Hamas engaged in a national dialogue with the Government; the meetings were boycotted by Ettahaddi, the FFS and the RCD. At further negotiations held in early September discussion focused on Abbassi Madani's purported offer of a 'truce'. Madani and Belhadj were released from prison in mid-September and placed under house arrest; however, the FIS declared that negotiations could take place only after the granting of a general amnesty, the rehabilitation of the FIS and the repeal of the state of emergency. The most prominent and radical Islamist militant group, the Groupe Islamique Armé (GIA), threatened reprisals if the FIS entered into dialogue with the regime, and intensified its campaign of violence against secular society by targeting educational institutions.

In November 1994 representatives of several major Algerian parties, including the FIS, the FLN, the FFS and the MDA, attended a conference in Rome, Italy, organized by the Sant' Egidio Roman Catholic community to foster discussion about the crisis in Algeria. The ensuing Sant' Egidio pact, endorsed by all the participants at a meeting in Rome in January 1995, rejected the use of violence to achieve or maintain power, and urged the Algerian regime to repeal the state of emergency and thereby facilitate negotiations between all parties. However, the pact was dismissed as a 'non-event' by the Government.

Despite an appeal by the FLN, the FFS and the FIS for voters to boycott the presidential election, official figures showed that some 75% of the electorate participated in the poll on 16 November 1995, at which Zéroual secured 61.0% of the valid votes cast. Zéroual was inaugurated for a five-year term on 27 November. Shortly afterwards the Government announced the closure of the last of seven detention centres opened since 1992, thereby releasing some 650 (mainly pro-Islamist) prisoners. In December 1995 Ahmed Ouyahia, a career diplomat, replaced Sifi as Prime Minister. Ouyahia's Government, named in January 1996, included two members of Hamas and a dissident leader of the FIS.

In May 1996 Zéroual announced his intention to hold legislative elections in early 1997. Prior to the elections, he proposed that a referendum be held on amendments to the Constitution: these included measures to increase the powers of the President while limiting his tenure to a maximum of two consecutive mandates; the creation of a second parliamentary chamber, the Council of the Nation (with one-third of members chosen by the President); the establishment of a State Council and a High State Court; and a ban on political parties that were based on religion, language, gender or regional differences. The proposed constitutional amendments were promulgated in December, having been approved by some 86% of the voters at a referendum held in November.

In January 1997 the Secretary-General of the FLN-affiliated Union Générale des Travailleurs Algériens (UGTA), Abd al-Hak Benhamouda, was shot dead in Algiers. Although an Islamist group claimed responsibility for the assassination, there was speculation that it may have been perpetrated by opponents within the regime. In February the NTC adopted restrictive legislation concerning political parties in accordance with the amended Constitution, as well as new electoral legislation replacing the majority system with proportional representation. Later that month Abdelkader Bensalah, the President of the NTC, formed a centrist grouping, the Rassemblement National Démocratique (RND), which received support from a wide range of organizations, including trade unions and anti-Islamist groups, and was closely linked with Zéroual and the Government. Several other political parties subsequently emerged, while certain existing parties changed their names to comply with the new legislation: notably, Hamas became the Mouvement de la Société pour la Paix (MSP).

Some 39 political parties contested the elections to the National People's Assembly, held on 5 June 1997, although the FIS and Ettahaddi urged a boycott of the polls. According to official results, the RND won 156 of the Assembly's 380 seats, followed by the MSP (69) and the FLN (62); Al-Nahda took 34 seats, the FFS 20 and the RCD 19. However, opposition leaders complained of irregularities, while international observers noted that the official rate of voter participation, at 65.5%, seemed unrealistically high. President Zéroual asked Ahmed Ouyahia to form a new Government, and later in June Ouyahia announced a new Council of Ministers, comprising members of the RND, the FLN and the MSP.

In September 1998 President Zéroual announced that a presidential election would be held in early 1999, nearly two years ahead of schedule. In December 1998 Ouyahia resigned; he was replaced as premier by Smaïl Hamdani.

The presidential election of 1999

A total of 47 candidates registered to contest the presidential election scheduled for 15 April 1999; however, the Constitutional Council declared only seven eligible to stand. Abdelaziz Bouteflika was believed to have the support of the military establishment, as well as that of the four main political parties and the UGTA. On the eve of the election Bouteflika's six rivals withdrew their candidacies after Zéroual refused to postpone the poll following allegations of massive electoral fraud in favour of Bouteflika. Voting papers were, nevertheless, distributed for all seven candidates, and no official boycott of the election was organized. However, the credibility of the poll was seriously diminished, and Bouteflika announced that he would accept the presidency only if there were both a high rate of voter participation and a large majority in his favour. According to official results, Bouteflika won 73.8% of the votes cast, while his closest rival, Ahmed Taleb Ibrahimi (a former Minister of Foreign Affairs who was now supported by the outlawed FIS), secured 12.5%. However, Bouteflika's overwhelming victory, together with the estimated official turnout of more than 60%, was immediately disputed by his opponents, who maintained that the actual turnout was around 23%. At his inauguration, on 27 April, Bouteflika emphasized the need for national reconciliation to end the civil conflict in Algeria, but pledged to continue the military campaign against terrorists.

Following clandestine negotiations between the Government and representatives of the FIS, in June 1999 the Armée Islamique du Salut (AIS, the armed wing of the FIS) announced the permanent cessation of its armed struggle against the Government. President Bouteflika's plans for a national reconciliation initiative were incorporated in a Law on Civil Concord, which provided for an amnesty for members of armed Islamist groups who surrendered within a six-month deadline and who were not implicated in mass killings, rape or bomb attacks on public places. The legislation was approved by 98.6% of those who voted in a national referendum in September. Meanwhile, Bouteflika exhibited unprecedented candour, admitting in August that the civil conflict of the past seven years had resulted in the deaths of at least 100,000 people (hitherto the authorities had put the number of deaths at 30,000). Bouteflika finally named his Council of Ministers in December, led by Ahmed Benbitour and comprising members of the FLN, the MSP, Al-Nahda, the RCD, the Alliance Nationale Républicaine (ANR), the RND and the PRA.

In early January 2000 the Government, army and the AIS reached an agreement whereby the AIS pledged to disband in return for the restoration of full civil and political rights to its former members. An estimated 1,500–3,000 rebels were to be granted a full pardon under the agreement, some of whom were to be temporarily enlisted in an auxiliary unit to assist the security forces in apprehending members of the GIA and of a breakaway group from the GIA, the Groupe Salafiste pour la Prédication et le Combat (GSPC, or Da'wa wal Djihad). In mid-January, following the expiry of the amnesty period specified under the Law on Civil Concord, the armed forces launched a concerted assault on rebel strongholds in the north-east and south-west of the country, in an attempt to eliminate remaining anti-Government factions. It was officially stated at this time that 80% of members of armed groups had surrendered. According to human rights' organizations there was a significant decline in violence and a clear improvement in the country's human rights situation, although the fate of an estimated 22,000 missing persons who had disappeared since 1992 remained unknown. Moreover, more than 1,300 deaths were reported as a result of continuing attacks involving armed Islamist groups between late 2000 and the holy month of Ramadan in 2001. Meanwhile, in August 2000 Benbitour resigned the premiership and was replaced by Ali Benflis, a former Minister of Justice who had directed Bouteflika's presidential campaign.

A total of 23 parties contested elections to the newly enlarged National People's Assembly held on 30 May 2002, although the polls were boycotted by the FFS and the RCD. According to official results, the FLN won 199 of the 389 available seats, while the RND's parliamentary representation was reduced to just 47. Sheikh Abdallah Djaballah's Mouvement El Islah took 43 seats, the MSP 38 and the Parti des Travailleurs (PT) 21. Independent candidates secured 30 seats. However, turnout was recorded at only 46.2% of eligible voters; participation rates of below 3% were recorded in Béjaïa and Tizi Ouzou, in the north-eastern region of Kabylia. The FFS and the RCD demanded an annulment of the results, claiming that real nationwide voter turnout had reached no more than 15%–20%. Bouteflika subsequently reappointed Benflis as Prime Minister, and a new coalition Government was named in June.

However, at the FLN party congress held in March 2003, Benflis announced his opposition to a number of Bouteflika's economic policies and withdrew the party's support for the President. Benflis, who was re-elected Secretary-General of the FLN for a further five-year term, was also granted considerably increased powers. In May 2003 Bouteflika dismissed Benflis as Prime Minister and appointed former premier Ahmed Ouyahia in his place. In September Bouteflika reorganized the Council of Ministers, dismissing a number of FLN ministers who had indicated their support for Benflis's rumoured ambition to stand as a candidate in the presidential election scheduled for April 2004. In October 2003 the remaining pro-Benflis FLN ministers withdrew from the Government. The following day, at an extraordinary congress of the FLN, 1,375 of the 1,500 members present approved Benflis's candidature, thus confirming him as the party's representative at the 2004 presidential election.

The two leaders of the proscribed FIS, Abbassi Madani and Ali Belhadj, were released in July 2003, after having completed their 12-year sentences. However, both men were issued with court orders prohibiting them from engaging in any political activity, among other restrictions. (Belhadj was rearrested in July 2005, after a statement broadcast by the Qatar-based satellite television channel Al Jazeera in support of the insurgency in Iraq.) According to official figures, fewer than 900 people were killed as a result of violence involving Islamists and the security forces in 2003, compared with almost 1,900 in 2001. The Government attributed this decline to the increased efficiency of the security forces, who had successfully dismantled many of the terrorists' support networks, and to divisions within the Islamist groups.

In December 2003 the administrative chamber of the Algiers Court suspended all activities of the FLN after the pro-Bouteflika faction of the party lodged a complaint maintaining that the party congress in March had been held illegally and that the results of the congress were 'null and void'. In January 2004 Benflis and 10 other leading politicians signed a statement demanding the formation of an interim government ahead of the presidential election—citing the lack of impartiality in the current Government—and an independent body to oversee the polls. Prime Minister Ouyahia (whose party, the RND, had already declared its support for President Bouteflika were he to stand for re-election) responded by affirming his intention to remain in office and pledging that the Government would organize a free and fair presidential election.

President Bouteflika's second term of office

In advance of the 2004 presidential election, Bouteflika declared that a committee would be established to ensure the fairness and transparency of the ballot, and invited representatives of international organizations to observe the electoral process. He dismissed claims that he was monopolizing state media and using state funds to assist his re-election campaign before the electoral race had officially begun. Bouteflika was joined in the presidential race by: Benflis; Sheikh Abdallah Djaballah, leader of the Islamist El Islah; Saïd Saâdi, President of the RCD; Louisa Hanoune, head of the PT; and Ali Fawzi Rebaïne, Secretary-General of the small nationalist party Ahd 54.

Bouteflika was decisively re-elected for a second term of office on 8 April 2004. He received 85.0% of the valid votes cast, while his nearest rival, Benflis, took 6.4%. The rate of turnout by eligible voters was reported to be 58.1%, although it was estimated to be as low as 18% in Kabylia. Bouteflika's rivals immediately accused the President of electoral malpractice; however, international observers declared the election to have been representative of popular will and free from any vote-rigging. Both Benflis and Saâdi boycotted Bouteflika's inauguration ceremony on 19 April, at which he vowed to: resolve the Berber crisis, improve the rights of women by readdressing the controversial family code of 1984, and continue his campaign for 'true national reconciliation'. On 26 April, having been reappointed as Prime Minister, Ouyahia named his new Council of Ministers; this consisted principally of FLN members and non-partisan supporters of Bouteflika, with some RND and MSP representation. Meanwhile, Benflis resigned as Secretary-General of the FLN; at a party congress held in January 2005 the Minister of State for Foreign Affairs, Abdelaziz Belkhadem, was elected to the post, while Bouteflika was elected honorary President of the FLN.

Meanwhile, violence between the GSPC and the Algerian military began to escalate, particularly in Kabylia. It was announced in October 2004 that Amari Saifi, the leader of one GSPC faction, had been intercepted by Libyan authorities and transferred to Algerian custody. Meanwhile, in June 2004 Nabil Sahraoui, the GSPC's leader since October 2003, was reportedly killed by the Algerian military in Kabylia during a gun battle that also killed his likely successor, Abdi Abdelaziz. The army subsequently announced that it had 'completely neutralized' the leadership of the GSPC and had seized many of its weapons and documents. In September 2004 Sahraoui was replaced as GSPC leader by Abdelmalek Droukdal (also known as Abu Musab Abd al-Wadud).

In January 2005 the Ministry of the Interior and Local Authorities announced that the GIA had been virtually destroyed following a military campaign during the latter part of 2004, in which they had arrested the group's leader, Noureddine Boudiafi, and later killed his replacement, Chabaâne Younès. The Ministry also confirmed that, despite reports to the contrary, former GIA leader Rachid Abou Tourab had been killed by members of his own group in July 2004. In April 2005 some 14 civilians were killed by suspected GIA militants in a roadside ambush in the Blida region; later that month the group's 'emir', Boulenouar Oukil, was arrested on suspicion of having planned the attack. In June the GSPC's Amari Saifi was sentenced *in absentia* to life imprisonment, having been found guilty of forming a terrorist group and of 'propagating terror'.

On 29 September 2005 a referendum was held to decide whether to grant a partial amnesty to Islamist rebels who had surrendered their weapons after the January 2000 deadline. The FFS and the RCD had appealed for a boycott of the poll on the grounds that an amnesty would 'consecrate impunity' for the crimes committed by the security forces during Algeria's civil war. The human rights organization Amnesty International also criticized the Charter for Peace and National Reconciliation, stating that it would simply 'obliterate crimes of the past'. However, a reported 79.8% of the electorate participated, with 97.4% of voters approving the partial amnesty.

The Government revealed the exact details of the partial amnesty in February 2006: those Islamist rebels who had not been involved in mass killings, rape or bomb attacks on public places would have six months to surrender to the authorities, while more than 2,000 armed Islamists imprisoned during the civil conflict would be pardoned and released by mid-March; a small number of detainees would have their sentences reduced. The release of the first group of prisoners, which included Belhadj and Abdelhak Layada, second-in-command of the GIA, took place in early March. Nevertheless, continuing attacks attributed to militants of the GSPC resulted in the deaths of a number of Algerian security officials in April. By the time that the six-month amnesty expired, in August, only some 250–300 militants had given up their weapons; it was estimated that up to 800 Islamist fighters, mostly of the GSPC, remained at large.

Meanwhile, in May 2006 Ouyahia resigned as Prime Minister. President Bouteflika subsequently appointed Abdelaziz Belkhadem, the FLN Secretary-General and, since May 2005, Minister of State and Special Representative of the President, to succeed him. Ouyahia had been strongly criticized for a perceived reluctance to use increased revenues from hydrocarbons exports to effect social reform, and a disagreement with Belkhadem over proposed constitutional reforms had precipitated rumours of a rift within the presidential alliance.

The emergence of the al-Qa'ida Organization in the Land of the Islamic Maghreb

It was reported in January 2007 that the GSPC had restyled itself as the al-Qa'ida Organization in the Land of the Islamic Maghreb (AQIM), having apparently joined the international al-Qa'ida organization led by the Saudi-born Islamist Osama bin Laden. There were widespread fears that an intensification of Islamist violence across North Africa was being co-ordinated by militant groups with an al-Qa'ida connection. Numerous civilians and security officers were killed in attacks by militants in March and April, including a bomb attack close to the Prime Minister's office in Algiers in early April that was believed to be the country's first suicide bombing. Later that month Algerian military officials announced that the second-in-command of AQIM, Samir Saioud (also known as Samir Moussaâb), had been shot dead during fighting to the east of the capital.

Elections to the National People's Assembly were held on 17 May 2007. The FFS again refused to participate, citing its lack of confidence in the country's parliamentary system as a means of bringing about real political change. The FLN retained its dominance of the legislature, winning 136 of the 389 seats and thus an overall majority. The RND again came second, with 62 seats, while the MSP and the PT also increased their representation, taking 51 and 26 seats, respectively. The RCD, which had boycotted the 2002 elections, secured 19 seats. In contrast, El Islah, which had been the principal opposition movement in the outgoing legislature, won only three seats. Independent candidates secured 33 seats. The rate of voter participation was reported to be a mere 36%. In June 2007 President Bouteflika appointed a new Council of Ministers, with Abdelaziz Belkhadem retaining the premiership and the Minister of Finance, Mourad Medelci, being appointed Minister of Foreign Affairs.

Two suicide bombings apparently carried out by AQIM in Batna and Algiers in September 2007 claimed up to 60 lives. These bomb attacks, the first of which was intended to assassinate President Bouteflika, resulted in an anti-violence demonstration being staged in the capital by thousands of Algerians. In October security forces claimed to have killed the deputy leader of AQIM, Hareg Zoheir (or Sofiane Abu Fasila), in Tizi Ouzou. Nevertheless, the violence being perpetrated by militant Islamists continued, with two suicide car bombings in Algiers in December resulting in a large number of fatalities. According to independent sources, an estimated 491 people were believed to have died as a result of political violence by the end of 2007. Car bomb attacks and suicide bombings continued in the Algiers region throughout 2008; in August 43 people were reportedly killed when a car bomb exploded at a gendarmerie academy.

In June 2008 President Bouteflika effected a reorganization of the Council of Ministers, which included the appointment of Ahmed Ouyahia to succeed Abdelaziz Belkhadem as Prime Minister. Ouyahia, who had served as premier in 1995–98 and 2003–06, was known for his firm stance against Islamist militants. In spite of concerns expressed by opposition parties, on 12 November 2008 both parliamentary chambers approved an amendment to the Constitution—which stipulated that a President could only renew his term of office once—in order to allow Bouteflika to seek a third term at the presidential election subsequently scheduled to take place in April 2009. The amending legislation also formally established the post of Prime Minister to replace that of Head of Government, allowed for the President to appoint several deputy prime ministers, and guaranteed a greater representation of women at all levels of Algerian politics.

Challenges confronting President Bouteflika in his third term

The candidates standing against Bouteflika in the presidential election of 9 April 2009 were: Hanoune; Rebaïne; Moussa Touati, President of the Front National Algérien (FNA); Muhammad Djahid Younsi, Secretary-General of El Islah; and Mohand Oussaïd Belaïd, a moderate Islamist independent. The incumbent President invited representatives from international organizations, including the League of Arab States (the Arab League, see p. 362), to observe the electoral process in an effort to appease demands by opposition parties for greater impartiality and transparency in the ballot. However, in the weeks preceding the poll opposition parties claimed that Bouteflika wielded excessive control over state media and had allocated state funds in favour of his re-election campaign, allegations which the President consistently denied.

Bouteflika was re-elected for a third term of office, having received 90.2% of the valid votes cast. His closest challenger, Hanoune, secured 4.5%, Touati 2.0%, Younsi 1.5%, and Belaïd and Rebaïne both took 0.9%. The rate of participation by eligible voters was reported to be 74.6%, although opposition parties disputed this figure. Indeed, several of Bouteflika's rivals questioned the legitimacy of the poll: both Hanoune (who intended to contest the results through the Constitutional Council) and Rebaïne boycotted the President's inauguration ceremony on 19 April. On 27 April Bouteflika reappointed Prime Minister Ouyahia and the entire Council of Ministers, with the exception of the Minister of State, Bougherra Soltani, who left the Government at his own request.

Islamist violence persisted in Algeria during 2009 and early 2010, although the security forces continued to issue reports of successful action against militants, particularly those belonging to AQIM. It was reported in mid-2009 that, further to a recent increase in violence, support was growing within the Algerian establishment for a new amnesty for Islamist militants, to include even the most senior AQIM members in the region. In October it was revealed that several militants had surrendered to the Algerian security forces in previous months, notably including the group's leader in the Zemmouri region, Nabil Touati. In April 2010 Algeria, Mali, Mauritania and Mali opened a joint military command and control centre in Tamanrasset, in southern Algeria; it was hoped that the centre would tackle the combined threats to the region of Islamist violence, kidnapping, and both weapons- and drugs-trafficking.

Meanwhile, on 29 December 2009 indirect elections took place to renew one-half of the 96 elected members of the Council of the Nation. The FLN won 22 seats, while the RND took 20. The MSP and the FNA each received two seats, and the RCD one; the remaining seat was won by a FLN-aligned independent candidate. The overall outcome of the election was to increase the representation of the presidential alliance (comprising the FLN, the RND and the MSP), the constituent parties having secured 45 of the 48 seats available. In January 2010 President Bouteflika nominated 16 members to replace the outgoing presidential appointees.

In May 2010 Bouteflika effected a limited reorganization of the Council of Ministers, with Ouyahia remaining as Prime Minister. The most high-profile change was the replacement of Chakib Khelil, the Minister of Energy and Mining since 1999, by Youcef Yousfi (who had previously held both the energy and foreign affairs portfolios). The decision to replace Khelil was believed to be linked to an ongoing investigation into allegations of corruption among senior officials of the state-owned oil and gas company, Sonatrach, with whom the former minister was reported to have been closely associated. Although the President and Director-General of Sonatrach, Muhammad Meziane, was dismissed and later imprisoned for his role in the scandal, Khelil (himself a former head of Sonatrach) was not formally questioned by police. Another notable appointment to the Government was that of Dahou Ould Kablia as Minister of the Interior and Local Authorities, replacing Noureddine Yazid Zerhouni, who assumed the newly created post of Vice-Prime Minister. In August 2010 the authorities announced their intention to create an anti-corruption agency, the Office Central de Répression de la Corruption; the new agency was formally established, under the supervision of the Ministry of Finance, in April 2013. Meanwhile, as the investigation continued into alleged corrupt practices at Sonatrach, in the same month the Government declared that it had frozen Khelil's assets. In August the authorities were reported to have issued an international arrest warrant for the former minister, together with his wife, two sons and five other officials suspected of wrongdoing. A second case involving alleged corruption at Sonatrach during the late 2000s, in relation to hydrocarbons contracts secured by the Italian company Eni and its subsidiary Saipem, was revealed in January 2013.

Despite an increase in security co-operation between Algeria and other Saharan countries, Islamist militants continued to wage a violent campaign against the Algerian defence establishment and other targets. In June 2010 AQIM claimed responsibility for the deaths of 11 paramilitary gendarmes in Tinzaoutine, close to the border with Mali. The Algerian military again offered militants the opportunity to surrender their weapons and renounce violence under the terms of the 2005 Charter for Peace and National Reconciliation, or be eliminated. According to various newspaper reports, on 9 December 2010 the army launched what was said to be the largest military offensive against AQIM in recent years in the Kabylia region, where the organization's 'northern command' (including its leader, Abdelmalek Droukdal) was thought to be based. By 30 December up to 50 suspected AQIM fighters were reported to have been killed, and military officials claimed that a significant plot to bomb the towns of Tizi Ouzou, Boumerdès and Bouira had been uncovered. In January 2011 a court in Boumerdès handed down a death sentence, *in absentia*, to Droukdal and 15 other militants. During the large-scale protests that were taking place across North Africa in that month, the AQIM leader urged Algerian and Tunisian protesters to seize the opportunity to overthrow their Governments and install Islamic states in both countries.

Following a series of strikes and protests during 2009–10, in early January 2011 significant demonstrations were held in Algiers in protest against a sharp increase in the price of basic food items, high levels of youth unemployment, inadequate housing and generally poor living standards. Two protesters were reported to have died during a confrontation with security forces in the Tipaza and M'Sila provinces, while other youths set fire to themselves as unrest spread across the country. In response, the authorities temporarily reduced taxes on certain foodstuffs, and President Bouteflika asked the Government to expand the provision of projects that would ease 'social distress', including improved housing. However, in late January several people were reportedly injured when riot police intervened to halt a renewed demonstration in Algiers by protesters demanding greater political rights. It appeared that disillusioned Algerians, who were now looting government buildings and private businesses, had been emboldened by recent developments in neighbouring Tunisia—where escalating protests had resulted in President Zine al-Abidine Ben Ali being forced into exile in Saudi Arabia. Government sources reported in late January that five people had been killed in the unrest earlier that month, 800 injured (most of whom were police officers) and some 1,100 arrests made by security forces. In an apparent attempt to placate the protesters, some of whom had begun to demand the ouster of the President (following the removal from office of Egypt's President Hosni Mubarak), in late February Bouteflika repealed the state of emergency originally imposed in 1992. However, new anti-terrorism laws were introduced, under which the army retained significant powers, and public demonstrations remained illegal in the capital.

In mid-April 2011, amid ongoing unrest, Bouteflika made a televised address, in which he promised to 'reinforce' democracy in Algeria through the introduction of constitutional reforms, as well as amendments to the country's electoral law, prior to the legislative elections scheduled for May 2012. In late May 2011 the Commission Nationale de Consultation sur les Réformes Politiques (CNCRP) was formally established, under the chairmanship of Abdelkader Bensalah (President of the Council of the Nation), to draft proposed amendments to the Constitution. The commission presented its final report to Bouteflika in late July, although no precise details were disclosed. The political dialogue had been opposed by many leading political figures, and several groups—such as the opposition FFS, RCD and Ahd 54—had declined to participate, claiming that the President's reforms did not go far enough and that a change of leadership was needed. In September Bouteflika announced that a new information law to be submitted to parliament would allow the establishment of private radio and television stations, create a new regulatory commission for the print media, and end the practice of imprisoning journalists convicted of libel.

As President Bouteflika was unveiling his proposed constitutional reforms in April 2011, suspected AQIM militants attacked a military post near Tizi Ouzou, killing 13 soldiers. In August two suicide bombers detonated their explosives at a military academy west of the capital. A reported 16 soldiers and two civilians were killed in the attack, which was again attributed to AQIM. Algerian security forces launched further operations to capture or kill suspected AQIM operatives, some of whom were believed to be benefiting from the state of civil war in neighbouring Libya. In October two Spanish and one Italian aid worker were kidnapped from a camp for Western Sahara refugees near Tindouf in western Algeria; the Mauritania-based militant group that claimed responsibility was later reported to have broken away from AQIM (the aid workers were released in July 2012). Nevertheless, despite the continuing violence, in January 2012 the Minister of the Interior and Local Authorities, Dahou Ould Kablia, declared that the security situation in Algeria was improving.

Recent developments: the May 2012 legislative elections and the 2014 presidential poll

In January 2012 legislation was promulgated that effectively allowed for the authorization of numerous new political organizations and increased the representation of women in elected bodies, including the National People's Assembly. In early January the MSP announced that it was withdrawing from the presidential alliance (which also comprised the FLN and the RND), in advance of legislative elections due to take place later that year. Leaders of the moderate Islamist party—which had four cabinet ministers and 51 parliamentary seats—cited differences with its former partners over the extent of the reforms proposed by Bouteflika in response to the serious rioting which had taken place in 2011. In the following month the MSP formed the Alliance de l'Algérie Verte (AAV—Green Alliance of Algeria) with Al-Nahda and El Islah. Meanwhile, the RCD announced a boycott of the forthcoming elections on account of its dissatisfaction with the political process. Furthermore, the MSP urged the President to appoint a government of technocrats to oversee the forthcoming polls. Renewed protests were reported at the start of 2012, as many Algerians complained that local authorities had not fulfilled pledges made in the aftermath of the previous year's unrest. In February Bouteflika announced that the legislative elections would take place on 10 May. The Council of Ministers also approved an increase in the number of seats in the Assembly from 389 to 462, arousing concerns that the opposition would be marginalized by the entry of various smaller parties. At the same time, the ruling FLN itself was reported to be experiencing factionalism in the run-up to the poll.

The elections to the National People's Assembly resulted in victory for the FLN, with 221 seats (albeit with only 17.3% of the valid votes cast). The RND took 70 seats, while the AAV secured just 47. An official turnout of 43.1% was recorded; however, this figure, which was significantly higher than in the previous legislative poll, was disputed by opposition parties. International election monitors declared the elections to have been largely free and fair, and there was a positive reaction internationally to the news that almost one-third of the elected representatives were women, as a result of the newly introduced parliamentary quota system. However, the AAV was quick to reject the official results and its newly elected deputies boycotted the first session of the Assembly. A further eight parties subsequently decided to boycott sessions of the Assembly in protest at alleged electoral irregularities. Furthermore, a national election-monitoring body concluded that the ballot 'lacked credibility and fairness'; the FLN, the RND and the FFS were reported to have refused to sign its report.

In early September 2012, following the conclusion of Ramadan in mid-August, a new Government was appointed by Bouteflika. Abdelmalek Sellal, the outgoing Minister of Water Resources and Bouteflika's former presidential campaign manager, was appointed as Prime Minister, heading a cabinet including Dahou Ould Kablia as Minister of Interior and Local Authorities, Mourad Medelci as Minister of Foreign Affairs and Karim Djoudi as Minister of Finance. Although many of the new ministers had no official political affiliation, members of the FLN, the RND and the MSP were also allocated portfolios. Soon after the appointment of the new Government, a new grouping led by Minister of Public Works Amar Ghoul, formerly of the MSP, was reported to have been established under the name of the Hope of Algeria Rally.

Elections to the Council of the Nation took place on 29 December 2012. Of the 48 seats contested, the RND won 21, giving it the largest representation in the chamber. The FLN took 17 seats and the FFS 2 seats. The remainder of the elective seats were allocated among a number of smaller parties. President Bouteflika nominated 30 new members to the Council in early January 2013. Also in that month, amid reports of significant disagreement within both the RND and the FLN, Ahmed Ouyahia resigned as Secretary-General of the RND, and Abdelaziz Belkhadem was removed as Secretary-General of the FLN, following a vote of the party's central committee. Ammar Saïdani was elected as FLN Secretary-General at the end of August.

Meanwhile, in 2012–13 the country experienced further unrest in the form of regular demonstrations, some violent, which highlighted continued frustration over social and economic issues. The Government's campaign against Islamist militants continued, with several arrests of AQIM members and reports of militant casualties in operations by security forces. In April 2012, following a military coup in Mali, the Algerian consul and six other Algerian diplomats were kidnapped by an armed militant group in the Malian town of Gao; three of the hostages were released in July, but in September it was reported that one of the four remaining captives had been murdered. Algeria was reported to be working closely with Niger, Mauritania and Burkina Faso towards a military solution to the problem of terrorism in the areas bordering eastern Mali. In October Boualem Bekai, the suspected second-in-command of AQIM, was reportedly killed by security forces in northern Algeria. In January 2013 Islamist militants attacked a gas plant near In Amenas, taking hostage numerous workers from countries around the world including Japan, Norway, France and the United Kingdom. The four-day siege that followed resulted in the deaths of at least 39 hostages and 29 militants, before Algerian forces took control of the plant. Responsibility for the attack was claimed by Mokhtar Belmokhtar, an Islamist militant who was rumoured to have led a breakaway faction of AQIM. According to official Algerian sources, the attackers originated from Algeria, Tunisia, Niger, Canada and Mauritania. In the aftermath of the crisis it was feared that the ongoing French-led military action against Islamist militants in Mali would precipitate an increase in the number of terrorist attacks in the Sahel-Sahara region. Algeria, while allowing French forces to use its airspace in order to launch air strikes, had appealed for dialogue between the relevant Malian groups. Despite reports that Belmokhtar had been killed by Chadian forces in northern Mali in early March, other sources claimed later in 2013 that the Islamist leader was still alive.

In mid-April 2013 a group of 12 opposition parties announced the formation of an electoral bloc that opposed Bouteflika seeking a fourth term of office at the presidential election due to be held in 2014; the parties also sought assurances from the Algerian military that it would remain neutral during the forthcoming election campaign. In late April 2013 the President underwent medical treatment in Paris, after reportedly having suffered a stroke. He did not return to Algeria until mid-July, prompting renewed speculation regarding his poor health and demands by some opposition politicians for an interim leader to be chosen pending the staging of an early presidential election (since, they claimed, Bouteflika was unable adequately to carry out his duties). Apparently in an effort to demonstrate his control over domestic affairs, in early September Bouteflika effected a reorganization of the Council of Ministers. Abdelmalek Sellal remained as Prime Minister, although several of the major portfolios were reallocated. The Chief of Staff of the armed forces, Lt-Gen. Ahmed Gaid Salah, joined the Government as Vice-Minister of National Defence, giving him effective responsibility for that ministry, though the President was nominally in charge of the portfolio. Tayeb Belaïz was appointed as Minister of State and Minister of the Interior and Local Authorities (replacing Kablia in the latter role), Ramtane Lamamra succeeded Medelci as Minister of Foreign Affairs, while Tayeb Louh became Minister of Justice and Attorney-General.

By January 2014 the Algerian Government was claiming some notable successes in its struggle against AQIM terrorism. During 2013 around 225 suspected Islamist militants were reported to have been killed by the security forces, while 27 militants renounced violence under the terms of the 2005 Charter for Peace and National Reconciliation. As Algerians marked the one-year anniversary of the siege that took place at the In Amenas gas plant, an estimated 50,000 security personnel were deployed in the south of Algeria, close to the country's borders with Libya, Mali and Niger, amid fears that terrorist groups might be planning to stage further attacks.

Shortly after returning from further medical tests in Paris, with government officials declaring the President's health to have improved, in mid-January 2014 Bouteflika announced that a presidential election would take place on 17 April. Bouteflika's long-time rival, former Prime Minister Ali Benflis, subsequently announced his candidacy, 10 years after he had withdrawn from political life in response to his defeat in the presidential poll of April 2004. A total of six candidacies were confirmed: Abdelaziz Belaïd, the President of the Front El-Moustakbel; Benflis; Bouteflika; Louisa Hanoune of the PT; Ali Fawzi Rebaïne of Ahd 54; and Moussa Touati of the FNA. According to preliminary results published by the Ministry of the Interior and Local Authorities on 8 April, Bouteflika won an overwhelming victory, securing 81.5% of valid votes cast. Benflis was placed second, winning 12.2%. Belaïd took 3.4% of the vote, Hanoune 1.4%, Rebaïne 1.0% and Touati 0.6%. Turnout was recorded at 51.7%. Following the poll, Benflis accused the authorities of 'fraud on a massive scale', while some observers claimed that the rate of participation had been exaggerated.

The Campaign for Cultural and Language Rights in Kabylia

In addition to the upheaval caused by Islamist violence in the mid-1990s, a campaign for enhanced cultural and language rights by Berber activists in Kabylia intensified in the wake of the Government's policy of 'Arabization'. In late 1994 the Berber RCD organized a general strike and urged a boycott of the start of the school year, in protest at the exclusion of the Berber language, Tamazight, from the syllabus and at the prospect of the FIS entering the national dialogue. In May 1995 the RCD welcomed the establishment of a government body to oversee the teaching of Tamazight in schools and universities from October, and to promote its use in the official media. However, protests were held in Kabylia in July 1998, when controversial legislation on the compulsory use of the Arabic language in public life came into effect; Berber activists demanded the recognition of Tamazight as an official language.

In April 2001 clashes broke out between protesters and security forces in several villages in Kabylia following the death of a secondary school student (who had been apprehended for allegedly committing an assault during a robbery) in police custody at Beni Douala near the regional capital, Tizi Ouzou. Thousands of local inhabitants joined demonstrations, demanding a full inquiry into the incident and the withdrawal of paramilitary gendarmes from Kabylia. The situation was further inflamed when three young Kabyles were assaulted by gendarmes near Béjaïa. The incidents coincided with demonstrations traditionally held to mark the anniversary of the so-called 'Berber Spring' protests of 1980, and although the two major political parties in Kabylia—the FFS and the RCD—appealed for calm, violence rapidly escalated throughout the area; as many as 80 people had reportedly died by the end of the month. President Abdelaziz Bouteflika announced the creation of a national commission of inquiry, to be headed by Mohand Issad, a lawyer originating from Kabylia, to investigate recent events in the region. Bouteflika also indicated that he planned revisions to the Constitution that would address the status of Tamazight, and revealed his intention to adopt a proposal making instruction in the Berber language compulsory in Tamazight-speaking areas. Furthermore, he accused unnamed groups both inside and outside the country of inciting extremism. The President's response to the crisis was strongly criticized by the main political groupings in Kabylia, and the RCD withdrew from the coalition Government. Increasingly violent demonstrations by Berbers took place during May and June 2001; in mid-June all protests in Algiers were prohibited.

By the end of June 2001 unrest had spread to the Aurès region, as well as to Annaba and Biskra. Official reports stated that 56 people had been killed, and 1,300 injured, since the violence first erupted. Despite repeated demands in the independent press for his resignation, Bouteflika declared that he would not relinquish the presidency. In July the Issad commission issued its preliminary report into the events in Kabylia, in which it blamed the gendarmerie for the rioting, since gendarmes had adopted a 'shoot-to-kill' policy and had acted in an illegal manner. However, the report failed to name those responsible for ordering the gendarmes' actions, and the commission complained of attempts, apparently on the part of vested interests within the security forces, to obstruct its investigations.

Security forces blocked roads in August 2001, in order to prevent a large number of Berbers from marching on the capital, where they intended to present a list of 15 demands at the presidential palace. This 'El-Kseur platform' (named after the Kabyle town in which it had been drawn up) notably requested: the granting of official status to Tamazight without the holding of a referendum; the removal of all paramilitary gendarmes from Kabylia; the annulment of legal proceedings against demonstrators; and the trial by civilian courts of all those who had ordered or perpetrated crimes and their dismissal from the security forces or the civil service.

In September 2001 President Bouteflika formally invited Berber community and tribal leaders, known as the *Aarouch*, to present their demands for social and political change, and designated Prime Minister Ali Benflis to act as interlocutor between the authorities and the Berbers. Although some Berber leaders were unwilling to enter into negotiations with the Government, a meeting reportedly took place in October between Benflis and moderate *Aarouch*, at which Benflis informed them that the President had decided to grant Tamazight the status of a national language in a forthcoming constitutional amendment. In January 2002 a series of resolutions were adopted, including proposals for the establishment of a special ministerial council to implement the creation of decentralized government councils in Kabylia at *wilaya* (department) level. The more radical *Aarouch* voiced their disapproval of the resolutions, stating that the El-Kseur platform was non-negotiable, and again insisted that the gendarmerie be withdrawn from Kabylia. However, this demand was consistently dismissed by Bouteflika as 'inconceivable'. In December the final report of the Issad commission was published, confirming the initial findings that the gendarmerie had been to blame for the repression in Kabylia, and also expressing deep pessimism about the immediate future of the region. Emphasizing the increasing authority of the military throughout the country since 1992, the report stated that the responsibilities of the civil and military authorities had become blurred, and denounced the subtle slide from 'a state of emergency to a state of siege'.

In a televised address in March 2002, Bouteflika officially announced that Tamazight would be recognized as a national language without the issue being put to a referendum. Accordingly, on 8 April the National People's Assembly voted almost unanimously in favour of amending the Constitution to grant Tamazight this status. Nevertheless, Kabyle leaders urged a boycott of the legislative elections scheduled for May (see Domestic Political Affairs), and the region was brought to a standstill by a series of strikes. Prior to local elections in October, the persistence of divisions within the Berber movement was highlighted when the RCD, supported by the Coordination des Aârchs, Daïras et Communes (CADC—also known as the Coordination des Comités de Villages Kabyles), announced that it would again boycott the polls. This was in direct contrast to the FFS, which was to present candidates in 40 of the country's 48 *wilayat*, maintaining that these would provide ordinary Kabyles with the possibility of attaining some form of political representation. At the elections the FLN won 668 of the 1,541 communes and thus secured control of 43 *wilayat*, although there were violent clashes in Kabylia, where demonstrators attempted to prevent voting from taking place.

The Government announced in July 2003 that it had agreed to reintroduce the use of Tamazight into Algeria's educational system, thereby fulfilling one of the demands of the El-Kseur platform. Moreover, in August the Government granted more than €23m. in 'overdue' development aid to Kabylia. In early January 2004 lengthy negotiations took place between the *Aarouch* and the Government, following which the authorities pledged to acquiesce to five of the six points deemed by the *Aarouch* to be 'prerequisites' to any further talks relating to the El-Kseur platform; these included the release of all remaining prisoners and the annulment of legal proceedings against demonstrators detained during the riots of April 2001. The sixth point, regarding the dissolution of municipal and regional councils elected in Kabylia in October 2002, was settled in late January 2004, when the Government agreed to remove any councillors who had been elected illegally in the contested polls. Days later the Algerian authorities released five Berber leaders who had been imprisoned for their role in the rioting, and Ouyahia stated that the meetings had provided a 'fundamental turning point' in the process between the two sides. However, the negotiations collapsed following the Government's assertion that the status of Tamazight should be decided in a national referendum, and further unrest ensued in Kabylia, while the FFS declared that it would not participate in the forthcoming presidential election. In January 2005, following a new round of talks, the Government and the *Aarouch* reached an agreement regarding implementation of the El-Kseur platform; two joint committees were established to implement and monitor the agreement.

In June 2010 the founder and leader of the separatist Mouvement pour l'Autonomie de la Kabylie, Ferhat Mehenni, announced that his movement had established a provisional 'government-in-exile' in Paris, France, with Mehenni leading a cabinet of nine ministers which would seek directly to challenge the Algerian leadership and to represent the Kabylia region at the international level. Although the formation of the Gouvernement Provisoire Kabyle was dismissed as insignificant by Ouyahia, there were reports that an arrest warrant had been issued for Mehenni.

Foreign Affairs

Relations with France

The Algerian military takeover in January 1992 was welcomed by the French Government, and French economic and political support for the Algerian regime increased in early 1993, following the appointment of Edouard Balladur as Prime Minister of France. In August 1994, following the killing of five French embassy employees in Algiers, 26 suspected Algerian extremists were interned in northern France; 20 of them were subsequently expelled to Burkina Faso. In September the French embassy in Algiers confirmed that entry visas would be issued to Algerians only in exceptional cases. By November the number of French nationals killed by Islamist militants in Algeria had reached 21 and the French Government urged its citizens to leave Algeria. An Air France aircraft was hijacked at Algiers airport in December by members of the GIA, resulting in the deaths of three passengers and, later, in the killing of the hijackers by French security forces when the aircraft landed in France. The GIA claimed responsibility for numerous bomb attacks across France between July and November 1995, in which seven people were killed and more than 160 injured. In August 1996 the success of a visit to Algeria by Hervé de Charette, the French Minister of Foreign Affairs, was marred by the assassination of the French Roman Catholic Bishop of Oran only hours after meeting de

Charette. In December four people were killed as the result of a bomb explosion on a passenger train in Paris, prompting speculation that the GIA had resumed its campaign of violence in France. In early 1998 a French court sentenced 36 Islamist militants to terms of imprisonment of up to 10 years for providing logistical support for the bomb attacks in France in 1995. A further 138 people stood trial in France in September 1998, accused of criminal association with Algerian terrorists.

In June 1999 the French National Assembly voted unanimously to abandon the official claim that the struggle between Algerian nationalists and French troops during 1954–62 had been no more than 'an operation for keeping order', and thus admitted that France had indeed fought in the Algerian war of independence. A meeting held in September 1999 between Bouteflika and the French President, Jacques Chirac, in New York, USA, was the first meeting between the leaders of the two countries since 1992. In June 2000 Bouteflika made a full state visit to France—the first of its kind by an Algerian head of state.

Algeria's relations with France were placed under strain from late 2000 by a series of revelations, mainly regarding occurrences during the war of independence. In November Gen. Jacques Massu, who had commanded French troops during the Battle of Algiers in 1957, asserted in an interview with the French daily *Le Monde* that France should admit and condemn the use of torture by its forces during the conflict. Moreover, a book published in May 2001 by a retired French general, Paul Aussarresses, contained allegations of Algerian army involvement in the torture and massacre of civilians since 1992. In August 2001 eight 'harkis'—Algerian Muslims who had served in the French army prior to independence—filed a formal complaint against the French Government for crimes and complicity in crimes against humanity. As many as 130,000 harkis were estimated to have been murdered by FLN troops following France's withdrawal from Algeria in 1962. In September 2001 President Chirac unveiled a plaque in Paris to commemorate those who were killed, and acknowledged his country's failure to halt the reprisals against the harkis. In November 2003 it was announced that Pierre Messmer, the French Minister of the Armed Forces during the latter stages of the war of independence, would face charges of committing 'crimes against humanity' for his role in the decision not to allow the harkis to settle in France.

Following a marked improvement in relations during 2002, in March 2003 Jacques Chirac became the first French President to make a full state visit to Algeria since 1962. Bouteflika and Chirac signed the 'Declaration of Algiers', whereby both countries pledged to rebuild bilateral relations by holding annual meetings of their heads of state as well as twice-yearly talks between their respective ministers responsible for foreign affairs. In June 2003 Air France resumed flights to Algeria, which had been suspended since the hijacking of one of its aircraft in December 1994. Furthermore, in August 2004 Bouteflika visited France to mark the 60th anniversary of the Algerian landings in Provence, which had opened up a new front against the Nazi German occupiers. However, in May 2005 Bouteflika again urged France to acknowledge that Algerians had been tortured and killed during French colonial rule and, specifically, to admit to the massacre of 45,000 Algerian protesters who were demanding independence at the end of the Second World War in May 1945. In May 2006 Bouteflika announced that the proposed treaty of friendship would remain on hold until France issued an apology to the Algerian people for 'crimes' committed under colonialism.

During a visit to Algiers in December 2007, the failure of the recently installed French President, Nicolas Sarkozy, to offer an explicit apology on behalf of the French nation for the era of colonial rule again angered some Algerian officials. Nevertheless, Sarkozy did acknowledge that France's colonization of Algeria had been 'profoundly unfair', and the two countries signed several important bilateral agreements in the fields of petroleum, gas and nuclear energy. Moreover, the French Government announced subsequently that it was to offer financial compensation to thousands of harkis. At the end of a visit by the French Prime Minister, François Fillon, to Algiers in June 2008, further agreements were signed concerning civil nuclear collaboration, military co-operation and bilateral financial matters. In May 2009 a visit to France by President Bouteflika scheduled for June was postponed indefinitely. The official reason given was a lack of sufficient time, although some commentators cited as possible reasons Algeria's displeasure at the French media's criticism of the conduct of the April 2009 presidential election and France's failure to provide a formal apology for its period of colonial rule. Algerians were also angered when, in January 2010, their country was named on a list of those whose citizens were perceived to threaten France's national security. In July, after a French aid worker was kidnapped by militant Islamists in Niger and subsequently murdered by his captors, Fillon declared his country to be 'at war' with AQIM across North Africa. France was expected to provide further assistance to the countries of the Sahel-Sahara region in training their armies to fight the militant group. However, the onset of civil war in Libya in early 2011 placed a further strain on relations between France and Algeria. The Algerian authorities opposed the North Atlantic Treaty Organization (NATO)-led intervention in the Libyan conflict from March onwards, while the French Government—which played a leading role in the NATO military action—accused Algeria of supporting the regime of Libyan leader Muammar al-Qaddafi.

In December 2012 the new French President, François Hollande, undertook a state visit to Algeria. Prior to the visit, Hollande had issued a statement acknowledging that the French police had been responsible for the deaths of up to 200 people during a protest in support of Algerian independence in Paris in 1961. However, although Hollande declared French colonial rule to have been 'profoundly unjust and brutal', he also failed to offer a formal apology for the wrongdoings of that period. Nevertheless, Hollande and Bouteflika signed the Declaration of Algiers, which committed both countries to greater co-operation in areas including the economy, defence and culture.

Regional relations

During the 1980s Algeria attempted to achieve a closer relationship with the other countries of the Maghreb region (Libya, Mauritania, Morocco and Tunisia). The Maghreb Fraternity and Co-operation Treaty, signed by Algeria and Tunisia in March 1983 and by Mauritania in December, established a basis for the creation of the long-discussed 'Great Arab Maghreb'. Although bilateral relations continued to be affected by the dispute over Western Sahara (see the chapter on Morocco), in May 1988 Algeria and Morocco restored diplomatic relations (severed in 1976) at ambassadorial level. Meeting in Algiers in June, the five heads of state of the Maghreb countries announced the formation of a Maghreb commission to examine areas of regional integration. In February 1989 the leaders signed a treaty establishing the Union du Maghreb Arabe (UMA, see p. 454), with the aim of encouraging economic co-operation and eventually establishing a full customs union. The Algerian army's intervention in January 1992 to prevent victory by the FIS in the general election provoked relief in Tunisia and Morocco that the establishment of a neighbouring fundamentalist state had been pre-empted.

Morocco imposed entry visas on Algerian nationals in August 1994, following the murder of two Spanish tourists in Morocco, allegedly by Algerian Islamist extremists. Algeria reciprocated by closing the border between the two countries and imposing entry visas on Moroccan nationals. Although in September Algeria announced the appointment of a new ambassador to Morocco, in December King Hassan II of Morocco expressed his disapproval at Algeria's alleged continuing support for the independence of Western Sahara, and demanded that UMA activities be suspended. A UMA summit meeting, scheduled for later that month, was subsequently postponed. Following his accession to the presidency in April 1999, Bouteflika initially attempted further to improve bilateral relations during a visit to the Moroccan capital to attend the funeral of King Hassan. However, the rapprochement was halted in August, on the day when the imminent reopening of the common border was announced, by the massacre by the GIA of 29 civilians in the border region of Béchar. Bouteflika's public allegation that Morocco was providing sanctuary for the perpetrators of the attack extended to accusations of drugs-trafficking and arms-dealing on the Algerian border. In September Bouteflika accused both Morocco and Tunisia of acting against the interests of the UMA by negotiating separate agreements with the European Union (EU, see p. 273).

In April 2000 Bouteflika met with the new Moroccan ruler, King Muhammad VI, at the Africa-EU summit held in Cairo, Egypt. The two leaders agreed to establish joint committees in an attempt to reduce the number of violent incidents on their mutual border, and joint military security operations began in May. In March 2001 a meeting in Algiers of the UMA's council of ministers responsible for foreign affairs ended acrimoniously following disagreements between the Moroccan and Algerian delegations. Relations were further strained after Algeria announced its opposition to UN proposals for a settlement to the Western Sahara issue, believing that the plans unduly favoured Morocco and would inevitably lead to the formal integration of the disputed territory into Morocco. In July 2004 talks on the future of Western Sahara between the Moroccan Minister of the Interior, Al Mustapha Sahel, and the Algerian Minister of State for the Interior and Local Authorities, Noureddine Yazid Zerhouni, recommenced in Algeria; senior French and Spanish representatives were also in attendance. However, Morocco continued to assert that the UN proposals jeopardized its sovereignty, and Morocco's ongoing dispute with Algeria over Western Sahara led to the eventual breakdown of the talks. A UMA summit meeting due to take place in Tripoli, Libya, in May 2005 was postponed indefinitely after King Muhammad announced that he would not be attending. In September, however, Sahel announced that the Moroccan Government was committed to improving relations with Algeria and negotiating a political end to the conflict.

At a summit meeting of UMA foreign ministers in Tripoli in December 2009, measures were put in place to facilitate the creation of the Maghreb Bank for Investment and Foreign Trade, which was intended to encourage the circulation of capital in the region and to fund common agricultural and industrial projects. There was subsequent evidence of an improvement in Algerian–Moroccan relations, particularly as far as economic co-operation was concerned. In late January 2012 Morocco's newly appointed Prime Minister, Abdelilah Benkirane, stated his Government's intention to seek rapprochement with fellow Maghreb countries. A visit by the Moroccan Minister of Foreign Affairs and Co-operation, Saâdeddine el-Othmani, to Algeria in that month was the first such visit since 2003. At a meeting attended by UMA foreign ministers, held in Algiers in July 2012, discussions were reported to have focused on the need for a common regional security agreement. Bilateral meetings held during 2013 were reported to have made progress as far as the long-awaited reopening of the Algerian–Moroccan border was concerned, although in July the Moroccan Government was angered by attempts by the Algerian Ministry of Foreign Affairs to link the normalization of bilateral relations to success in the ongoing talks on Western Sahara and a reduction in cross-border drugs-trafficking. Relations deteriorated further in October, after Bouteflika referred in a speech to the 'massive and systematic human rights abuses' being inflicted on the people of Western Sahara by the Moroccan authorities. Morocco recalled its ambassador to Algiers in protest against what it termed the Algerian President's 'deliberately provocative' remarks.

Algeria's relationship with Tunisia remained stable after President Zine al-Abidine was forced from office by Tunisian demonstrators in January 2011 (see Domestic Political Affairs). In July the Algerian and Tunisian Governments signed an accord finalizing the demarcation of their maritime borders. During 2012 and 2013 officials from the two countries worked closely in an effort to tighten security and thereby eliminate the threat posed by AQIM along their common border. A preferential trade agreement was signed during a visit by the Tunisian Prime Minister, Ali Laârayedh, to Algiers in April 2013.

In August 2011, following the fall of Tripoli to forces loyal to Libya's opposition National Transitional Council, it was revealed that the wife, daughter and two sons of Qaddafi had fled to Algeria. The authorities asserted that the fugitives had been permitted to enter Algeria 'on humanitarian grounds'. The Council demanded that the Algerian Government hand over Qaddafi's relatives to the interim Libyan authorities, and the country was the subject of considerable international criticism for harbouring them. Nevertheless, in September Algeria formally recognized the Council as 'the legitimate representatives of the Libyan people'. The Algerian authorities expressed concerns during 2011 that weapons employed during the Libyan civil war might be recovered by AQIM militants and used in future terrorist attacks in Algeria and other parts of the Sahel-Sahara region. In March 2012 the Minister of Foreign Affairs, Mourad Medelci, visited Libya for discussions with his Libyan counterpart, Ashour Ben Khayil, and the Chairman of the National Transitional Council, Mustafa Muhammad Abd al-Jalil, during which he called for a normalization of bilateral relations. Subsequent discussions between the Algerian and Libyan Governments focused on the need to maintain security in the border areas and in the wider Maghreb region. In December 2012 Libya had closed its borders with Algeria, Chad, Niger and Sudan, to enable the Government to administer its southern region as a military zone.

Other external relations

In December 1996 the EU and Algeria began negotiations on Algeria's participation in a Euro-Mediterranean free trade zone. In January 2001 the President of the European Commission, Romano Prodi, visited Algeria, where he signed the financing protocols for a number of joint projects. In December negotiations for the EU-Algeria Euro-Mediterranean Association Agreement were concluded, and both parties formally signed the agreement in April 2002. Following ratification by the European Parliament and requisite EU member states, it entered into effect on 1 September 2005.

In 2007 Nicolas Sarkozy proposed the idea of a Mediterranean Union as part of his election campaign for the French presidency. The initiative, which was intended to foster economic, political and cultural links between Mediterranean states, was described by Sarkozy as building upon the Barcelona Process launched by Euro-Mediterranean foreign ministers in November 1995. By the beginning of 2008 the project had been modified to encompass not just those nations bordering the Mediterranean Sea, but all EU member states. Despite expressing reservations about the project—namely that it would undermine the work of the Arab League and represent something of a return to colonial rule—Bouteflika was among the many heads of state of the 43 EU and Mediterranean member nations to be in attendance when the Union for the Mediterranean (as it had been renamed) was officially inaugurated at a summit meeting in Paris on 13 July. At the fifth meeting of the EU-Algeria Association Council in Luxembourg in June 2010, the Algerian Minister of Foreign Affairs, Mourad Medelci, urged member states to increase the level of direct EU investment in Algeria's economy. It was agreed to establish a sub-committee through which issues such as security and human rights could be discussed, while preparations for the creation of a free trade area in 2017 were also discussed. The seventh meeting of the EU-Algeria Association Council was held in Brussels, Belgium, in December 2012. The European Commission agreed on two financial assistance programmes to promote economic diversification and good governance in Algeria.

The Algerian Government was swift to condemn the suicide attacks on New York and Washington, DC, on 11 September 2001, for which the USA held the international al-Qa'ida network responsible, and to offer assistance for the USA's proposed 'coalition against terror'. Later that month the Algerian authorities handed the US authorities a list containing the profiles of some 350 Islamist militants it believed had links to bin Laden and al-Qa'ida. In December 2002 the US Administration announced that it had agreed to sell weaponry and other military equipment to Algeria as part of the USA's policy of intensifying bilateral security co-operation. In November 2010 the two countries concluded a three-year co-operation accord concerning the training of military personnel, holding of military exercises and sharing of vital technology in their joint struggle against terrorism in North Africa. Co-operation between Algeria and the USA on regional and international counter-terrorism efforts was increased during 2011–12. In October 2012 the US Secretary of State, Hillary Clinton, reportedly sought Bouteflika's support for plans to address the deteriorating security situation in northern Mali. During 2013 the US Administration continued to pursue close ties with the Algerian authorities in an attempt to minimize the threat from AQIM and other militant Islamist groups, especially in the aftermath of the attack on the gas plant near In Amenas in January of that year, in which three US citizens died.

Algeria has generally enjoyed strong bilateral relations with Russia since the era of the USSR, and in recent years Russia has provided the Bouteflika regime with both military and technical assistance. Following a visit by Russian President Vladimir Putin in March 2006, Russia pledged to forgive Soviet-era debt in exchange for Algeria's agreement to import a range of Russian products. In August the two countries' state-owned gas companies, Sonatrach and Gazprom, signed a memorandum of understanding according to which the Russian firm would assist in the development of Algeria's natural gas reserves. During a visit by President Dmitrii Medvedev to Algiers in October 2010, it was agreed that regular meetings at both presidential and ministerial level would be convened in order to strengthen bilateral co-operation, particularly in the fields of energy and transport. It was reported in January 2014 that Algerian and Russian officials were engaged in negotiations concerning the purchase by Algeria of 30 Russian-made unmanned aerial vehicles (or drones), at an estimated cost of AD 5,100m. The drones were to be used to conduct surveillance along Algeria's borders with neighbouring countries.

In early 2014 the People's Republic of China, with which Algeria had developed much closer political and economic relations since the early 2000s, was also expected to become a supplier of military drones to the Algerian Government. Chinese investment in Algeria during the decade to the end of 2012 was reported in April 2013 to have exceeded US $1,500m., and an estimated 30,000 Chinese workers were employed on various infrastructural projects in the country, including in the hydrocarbons, water and transport sectors.

CONSTITUTION AND GOVERNMENT

A new Constitution for the People's Democratic Republic of Algeria, approved by popular referendum, was promulgated on 22 November 1976. The Constitution was amended by the National People's Assembly on 30 June 1979 and, by referendum, on 3 November 1988, 23 February 1989 and 28 November 1996. On 8 April 2002 the Assembly approved an amendment that granted Tamazight, the principal language spoken by Algeria's Berber population, the status of a national language. On 12 November 2008 the Assembly endorsed an amendment to abolish the limit on the number of terms a President may serve.

Under the terms of the Constitution, Algeria is a multi-party state, with parties subject to approval by the Ministry of the Interior and Local Authorities. The head of state is the President of the Republic, who is elected by universal adult suffrage for a five-year term. The President presides over a Council of Ministers and a High Security Council. The President must appoint a Prime Minister as Head of Government, who appoints a Council of Ministers. The bicameral legislature consists of the 462-member National People's Assembly and the 144-member Council of the Nation. The members of the National People's Assembly are elected by universal, direct, secret suffrage for a five-year term. Two-thirds of the members of the Council of the Nation are elected by indirect, secret suffrage from regional and municipal authorities; the remainder are appointed by the President of the Republic. The Council's term of office is six years; one-half of its members are replaced every three years. Both the Head of Government and the parliamentary chambers may initiate legislation, which must be deliberated upon by the National People's Assembly and the Council of the Nation, respectively, before promulgation. The country is divided into 48 departments (*wilayat*), which are, in turn, sub-divided into communes. Each *wilaya* and commune has an elected assembly.

REGIONAL AND INTERNATIONAL CO-OPERATION

Algeria is a member of the Union of the Arab Maghreb (UMA, see p. 454), which aims to promote economic integration of member states. It is also a member of the African Union (AU, see p. 186) and the League of Arab States (the Arab League, see p. 362). A Euro-Mediterranean Association Agreement between Algeria and the European Union, signed in April 2002, entered into effect on 1 September 2005.

Having gained independence from France in May 1962, Algeria became a member of the UN on 8 October of that year. Algeria also participates in the Organization of the Petroleum Exporting Countries (OPEC, see p. 408) and the Group of 77 developing countries (G77, see p. 451). Negotiations concerning Algeria's accession to the World Trade Organization (WTO, see p. 434), which commenced in 1987, were still ongoing in early 2014.

ECONOMIC AFFAIRS

In 2011, according to estimates by the World Bank, Algeria's gross national income (GNI), measured at average 2009–11 prices, was US $155,105m., equivalent to $4,110 per head (or $7,550 on an international purchasing-power parity basis). During 2003–12, it was estimated, the population increased at an average annual rate of 1.7%, while gross domestic product (GDP) per head increased, in real terms, by an average of 1.4% per year. Overall GDP increased, in real terms, at an average annual rate of 3.2% in 2003–12; it grew by 2.5% in 2012.

According to provisional official figures, agriculture (including forestry and fishing) contributed 11.8% of GDP in 2012 and engaged 10.8% of the employed labour force in 2011. Domestic production of food crops is insufficient to meet the country's requirements. The principal crops are potatoes, wheat, onions and barley. Dates have traditionally been Algeria's principal non-hydrocarbon export; watermelons, citrus fruits and grapes are also grown, and wine has been an important export since the French colonial era. According to the World Bank, during 2003–10 agricultural GDP increased at an average annual rate of 2.2%; sectoral growth was 3.3% in 2010.

Industry (including mining, manufacturing, construction and power) contributed 61.7% of GDP in 2012, according to provisional official figures. The sector engaged 30.9% of the employed population in 2011. According to the World Bank, during 2003–10 industrial GDP increased at an average annual rate of 2.7%; it expanded by 3.3% in 2010.

The mining sector provides almost all of Algeria's export earnings, although it engaged only 2.0% of the employed population in 2011, according to official figures. Official figures also indicated that the sector contributed a provisional 43.9% of GDP in 2012, including petroleum and gas, which are overwhelmingly Algeria's principal exports (providing 98.4% of total export earnings in 2012). Algeria's proven reserves of petroleum were 12,200m. barrels at the end of 2012, sufficient to maintain output at that year's levels—which averaged 1.7m. barrels per day (b/d)—for 20.0 years. As a member of the Organization of the Petroleum Exporting Countries (OPEC), Algeria is subject to production quotas agreed by the Organization's Conference. Proven reserves of natural gas at the end of 2012 totalled 4,500,000m. cu m, sustainable at that year's production level (totalling 81,500m. cu m) for just over 55 years. Algeria currently transports natural gas through three pipelines—the Pedro Duran Farrell pipeline to Spain and Portugal via Morocco, the Enrico Mattei pipeline to Italy via Tunisia, and the Medgaz pipeline to Spain (which was inaugurated in 2011). Plans to construct a second pipeline (Galsi) linking Algeria to Italy via the island of Sardinia were also under way, although the project has experienced numerous delays. In May 2013 it was announced that a final decision on the Galsi project would be made in May 2014. Substantial reserves of iron ore, phosphates, barite (barytes), lead, zinc, mercury, salt, marble and industrial minerals are also mined.

Manufacturing provided 3.9% of GDP in 2011, according to the African Development Bank. According to official figures, the sector engaged 12.2% of the employed population in 2011. Measured by gross value of output, the principal branches of manufacturing are: food products, beverages and tobacco; metals, metal products, machinery and transport and scientific equipment; non-metallic mineral products; chemical, petroleum, coal, rubber and plastic products; wood, paper and products; and textiles and clothing. According to the World Bank, during 2003–10 the GDP of the manufacturing sector increased at an average annual rate of 0.6%; manufacturing GDP grew by 6.0% in 2009, but decreased by some 13.9% in 2010.

According to provisional official figures, the construction sector contributed 11.7% of GDP in 2012. The sector engaged 16.6% of the employed labour force in 2011.

Energy is derived principally from natural gas, which contributed 93.5% of total electricity output in 2011. Algeria is a net exporter of fuels, with imports of energy products comprising only an estimated 9.8% of the value of merchandise imports in 2012.

According to provisional official figures, services provided 26.5% of GDP in 2012. The sector engaged 58.4% of the employed labour force in 2011. According to the World Bank, during 2003–10 the combined GDP of the service sectors increased at an average annual rate of 5.2%; services GDP increased by 3.3% in 2010.

In 2012 Algeria recorded a visible trade surplus of US $20,049.3m., while there was a surplus of $11,944.1m. on the current account of the balance of payments. France was the principal source of imports in 2012 (providing 12.8% of the total); other important suppliers were the People's Republic of China, Italy, Spain and Germany. Italy was the principal market for exports (16.0%) in that year; other major purchasers were the USA, Spain, France, the Netherlands, Canada and the United Kingdom. The principal exports in 2012 were, overwhelmingly, mineral fuels and lubricants. The principal imports in that year were vehicles, machinery, iron and steel, electrical and electronic equipment, and cereals.

In 2011, according to the IMF, Algeria recorded an overall budget deficit of AD 63,000m., equivalent to 0.5% of GDP. Algeria's general government gross debt was AD 1,704.8m in 2012, equivalent to 10.5% of GDP. The country's total external debt at the end of 2011 amounted to US $6,072m., of which almost $2,213m. was public and publicly guaranteed debt. In that year, the cost of servicing long-term public and publicly guaranteed debt and repayments to the IMF was equivalent to

0.8% of the value of exports of goods, services and income (excluding workers' remittances). The annual rate of inflation averaged 4.3% in 2003–12, according to official figures. Consumer prices increased by an average of 8.9% in 2012. However, according to official figures, the average rate of inflation declined to 3.3% in 2013. According to official data, some 10.0% of the labour force were unemployed in 2011.

Algeria's economy remains reliant on hydrocarbons, which accounted for 98.4% of exports in 2012. In 2012 the country was the world's seventh largest exporter of liquefied natural gas, accounting for 4.6% of total global supply, and exporting chiefly to Europe. Algeria fared better than many other countries as far as the impact of the global economic slowdown from late 2008 was concerned. This was partly owing to a good grain harvest and strong performance in those parts of the economy targeted for increased public investment. In July 2010 President Bouteflika ratified a five-year investment plan worth US $286,000m., in an effort to reduce over-reliance on the hydrocarbons sector and to create some 3m. jobs by 2014. According to some analysts, the need for oil exploration was pressing as Algeria's reserves of oil for export were expected to be depleted within a decade. The international hostage crisis at the In Amenas gas plant in January 2013 (see Contemporary Political History) also prompted fears of negative repercussions for external investment in the wider economy. However, concerns were eased in July, when Algeria and the EU signed a memorandum of understanding concerning a strategic energy partnership; the deal confirmed the importance of Algeria as a provider of energy to the European market. Although the official rate of unemployment had declined considerably from 29.8% of the labour force in 2000 to 10.0% in 2011, the rates for young people and for women remained significantly higher, at 21.5% and 17%, respectively. Moreover, inflation had become a major concern: consumer prices increased by an average of 8.9% in 2012, almost double the rate of increase recorded for 2011, although a much smaller increase, of 3.3%, was recorded in 2013. Following growth of 2.5% in 2012, the IMF in November 2013 predicted that GDP would increase by 2.7% in that year. In the same report, the Fund commended the authorities for their success in reducing the large fiscal deficit created by increases in public expenditure following large-scale public protests from early 2011; a balanced budget was expected in 2013. In May 2013 it was announced that Algeria's state-owned banks were to fund the construction of more than 250,000 new homes by the end of 2014 in an effort to ease the country's severe housing crisis.

PUBLIC HOLIDAYS

2015: 1 January (New Year), 2 January* (Mouloud, Birth of Muhammad), 1 May (Labour Day), 15 May* (Leilat al-Meiraj, Ascension of Muhammad), 17 June* (Ramadan begins), 19 June (Ben Bella's Overthrow), 5 July (Independence Day), 17 July* (Id al-Fitr, end of Ramadan), 23 September* (Id al-Adha, Feast of the Sacrifice), 14 October* (Muharram, Islamic New Year), 23 October* (Ashoura), 1 November (Anniversary of the Revolution), 23 December* (Mouloud, Birth of Muhammad).

* These holidays are dependent on the Islamic lunar calendar and may differ by one or two days from the dates given.

Statistical Survey

Source (unless otherwise stated): Office National des Statistiques, 8 rue des Moussebilines, BP 202, Ferhat Boussad, Algiers; tel. (21) 63-99-74; fax (21) 63-79-55; e-mail ons@ons.dz; internet www.ons.dz.

Area and Population

AREA, POPULATION AND DENSITY

Area (sq km)	2,381,741*
Population (census results)	
25 June 1998	29,100,867
16 April 2008	
Males	17,232,747
Females	16,847,283
Total	34,080,030
Population (official estimates at mid-year)	
2011	36,717,000
2012	37,495,000
2013†	38,300,000
Density (per sq km) at mid-2013	16.1

* 919,595 sq miles.

† Provisional.

POPULATION BY AGE AND SEX

(UN estimates at mid-2014)

	Males	Females	Total
0–14	5,718,849	5,477,732	11,196,581
15–64	13,591,907	13,297,172	26,889,079
65 and over	872,293	970,995	1,843,288
Total	20,183,049	19,745,899	39,928,948

Source: UN, *World Population Prospects: The 2012 Revision*.

POPULATION BY WILAYA (ADMINISTRATIVE DISTRICT)

(2008 census)

	Area (sq km)	Population	Density (per sq km)
Adrar	439,700	399,714	0.9
Aïn Defla	4,897	766,013	156.4
Aïn Témouchent	2,379	371,239	156.0
Algiers (el-Djezaïr)	273	2,988,145	10,945.6
Annaba	1,439	609,499	423.6
Batna	12,192	1,119,791	91.8
el-Bayadh	78,870	228,624	2.9
Béchar	162,200	270,061	1.7
Béjaïa	3,268	912,577	279.2
Biskra (Beskra)	20,986	721,356	34.4
Blida (el-Boulaïda)	1,696	1,002,937	591.4
Borj Bou Arreridj	4,115	628,475	152.7
Bouira	4,439	695,583	156.7
Boumerdès	1,591	802,083	504.1
Chlef (el-Cheliff)	4,795	1,002,088	209.0
Constantine (Qacentina)	2,187	938,475	429.1
Djelfa	66,415	1,092,184	16.4
Ghardaïa	86,105	363,598	4.2
Guelma	4,101	482,430	117.6
Illizi	285,000	52,333	0.2
Jijel	2,577	636,948	247.2
Khenchela	9,811	386,683	39.4
Laghouat	25,057	455,602	18.2
Mascara (Mouaskar)	5,941	784,073	132.0
Médéa (Lemdiyya)	8,866	819,932	92.5
Mila	9,375	766,886	81.8
Mostaganem	2,175	737,118	338.9
M'Sila	18,718	990,591	52.9
Naâma	29,950	192,891	6.4
Oran (Ouahran)	2,121	1,454,078	685.6
Ouargla	211,980	558,558	2.6
el-Oued	54,573	647,548	11.9
Oum el-Bouaghi	6,768	621,612	91.8
Relizane (Ghilizane)	4,870	726,180	149.1
Saïda	6,764	330,641	48.9
Sétif (Stif)	6,504	1,489,979	229.1
Sidi-bel-Abbès	9,096	604,744	66.5
Skikda	4,026	898,680	223.2
Souk Ahras	4,541	438,127	96.5

—continued	Area (sq km)	Population	Density (per sq km)
Tamanrasset (Tamanghest)	556,200	176,637	0.3
el-Tarf	3,339	408,414	122.3
Tébessa (Tbessa)	14,227	648,703	45.6
Tiaret (Tihert)	20,673	846,823	41.0
Tindouf	159,000	49,149	0.3
Tipaza	2,166	591,010	272.9
Tissemsilt	3,152	294,476	93.4
Tizi Ouzou	3,568	1,127,607	316.0
Tlemcen	9,061	949,135	104.7
Total	2,381,741	34,080,030	14.3

PRINCIPAL TOWNS
(population at 1998 census)

Algiers (el-Djezaïr, capital)	1,519,570	Tébessa (Tbessa)	153,246
Oran (Ouahran)	655,852	Blida (el-Boulaïda)	153,083
Constantine (Qacentina)	462,187	Skikda	152,335
Batna	242,514	Béjaïa	147,076
Annaba	215,083	Tiaret (Tihert)	145,332
Sétif (Stif)	211,859	Chlef (el-Cheliff)	133,874
Sidi-bel-Abbès	180,260	el-Buni	133,471
Biskra (Beskra)	170,956	Béchar	131,010
Djelfa	154,265		

Mid-2011 ('000, incl. suburbs, UN estimate): Algiers 2,915.7 (Source: UN, *World Urbanization Prospects: The 2011 Revision*).

BIRTHS, MARRIAGES AND DEATHS*

	Registered live births†		Registered marriages		Registered deaths†	
	Number	Rate (per 1,000)	Number	Rate (per 1,000)	Number	Rate (per 1,000)
2005	703,000	21.4	279,548	8.5	147,000	4.5
2006	739,000	22.1	295,295	8.8	144,000	4.3
2007	783,000	23.0	325,485	9.6	149,000	4.4
2008	817,000	23.6	331,190	9.6	153,000	4.4
2009	849,000	24.1	341,321	9.7	159,000	4.5
2010	888,000	24.7	344,819	9.6	157,000	4.4
2011	910,000	24.8	369,031	10.1	162,000	4.4
2012	978,000	26.1	371,280	9.9	170,000	4.5

* Figures refer to the Algerian population only; including adjustment for underenumeration.

† Rounded estimates, excluding live-born infants dying before registration of birth.

Life expectancy (years at birth): 70.8 (males 69.2; females 72.4) in 2011 (Source: World Bank, World Development Indicators database).

ECONOMICALLY ACTIVE POPULATION
('000 persons aged 15 years and over at September)

	2003	2004
Agriculture, hunting, forestry and fishing	1,411.8	1,616.2
Mining and quarrying	82.9	135.1
Manufacturing	616.7	846.7
Electricity, gas and water	104.6	79.1
Construction	799.9	967.6
Trade; repair of motor vehicles, motorcycles and personal household goods	880.9	1,174.4
Hotels and restaurants	102.5	164.8
Transport, storage and communications	405.4	435.9
Financial intermediation	67.6	68.8
Real estate, renting and business activities	68.0	72.4
Public administration and defence; compulsory social security	1,071.2	1,104.1

—continued	2003	2004
Education	627.7	634.0
Health and social work	245.0	235.5
Other community, social and personal service activities	183.4	208.9
Households with employed persons	12.2	34.9
Extra-territorial organizations and bodies	2.9	3.9
Sub-total	6,682.7	7,782.2
Activities not adequately defined	1.4	16.2
Total employed	6,684.1	7,798.4
Unemployed	2,078.0	1,671.5
Total labour force	8,762.1	9,469.9

Source: ILO.

2011 (sample survey at July, '000 persons aged 15 years and over): Agriculture 1,034; Industry 2,962 (Mining and quarrying 192, Manufacturing 1,175; Construction 1,595); Services 5,603; *Total employed* 9,599 (males 8,038, females 1,561); Unemployed 1,063; *Total labour force* 10,662 (males 8,777, females 1,885).

Health and Welfare

KEY INDICATORS

Total fertility rate (children per woman, 2011)	2.2
Under-5 mortality rate (per 1,000 live births, 2011)	30
HIV/AIDS (% of persons aged 15–49, 2011)	0.1
Physicians (per 1,000 head, 2007)	1.2
Hospital beds (per 1,000 head, 2004)	1.7
Health expenditure (2010): US $ per head (PPP)	364
Health expenditure (2010): % of GDP	4.3
Health expenditure (2010): public (% of total)	79.9
Access to water (% of persons, 2011)	84
Access to sanitation (% of persons, 2011)	95
Total carbon dioxide emissions ('000 metric tons, 2010)	123,475.2
Carbon dioxide emissions per head (metric tons, 2010)	3.3
Human Development Index (2012): ranking	93
Human Development Index (2012): value	0.713

For sources and definitions, see explanatory note on p. vi.

Agriculture

PRINCIPAL CROPS
('000 metric tons)

	2010	2011	2012
Wheat	2,605	2,555	3,432
Barley	1,308	1,104	1,592
Oats	88	67	110
Potatoes	3,300	3,862	4,219
Broad beans, dry	37	38	41
Chick peas	23	24	28
Almonds	57	22	34
Olives	311	611	394
Rapeseed*	39	45	47
Cabbages	51	59	83
Artichokes	48	47	54
Tomatoes	718	772	797
Cauliflowers and broccoli	88	106	119
Pumpkins, squash and gourds	223	214	228
Cucumbers and gherkins	116	110	115
Aubergines (Eggplants)	91	95	92
Chillies and peppers, green	380	384	427
Onions, dry	1,001	1,144	1,183
Garlic	64	54	77
Beans, green	53	55	61
Peas, green	125	128	141
Carrots and turnips	324	342	354
Oranges	583	815	803
Tangerines, mandarins, clementines and satsumas	152	218	208
Lemons and limes	52	72	76

—continued	2010	2011	2012
Apples	379	404	398
Pears	234	233	211
Apricots	198	286	269
Peaches and nectarines	156	180	178
Plums and sloes	90	106	105
Grapes	561	403	543
Watermelons	1,224	1,285	1,495
Figs	124	120	110
Dates	645	725	789
Tobacco, unmanufactured	8	8	8

* FAO estimates.

Aggregate production ('000 metric tons, may include official, semi-official or estimated data): Total cereals 4,002 in 2010, 3,728 in 2011, 5,137 in 2012; Total roots and tubers 3,300 in 2010, 3,862 in 2011, 4,219 in 2012; Total vegetables (incl. melons) 5,216 in 2010, 5,579 in 2011, 6,044 in 2012; Total fruits (excl. melons) 3,307 in 2010, 3,678 in 2011, 3,837 in 2012.

Source: FAO.

LIVESTOCK
('000 head, year ending September, unless otherwise indicated)

	2010	2011	2012
Sheep	22,869	23,989	25,194
Goats	4,287	4,411	4,595
Cattle	1,748	1,790	1,844
Horses	44	44	46
Asses	141	147	139
Mules	35	34	33
Camels	314	319	340
Chickens (million)*	126	127	128

* FAO estimates.

Source: FAO.

LIVESTOCK PRODUCTS
('000 metric tons)

	2010	2011	2012
Cattle meat	126	125	136
Goat meat*	17	17	18
Chicken meat*	255	256	257
Rabbit meat*	8	8	8
Sheep meat	205	253	261
Cows' milk	2,071	2,387	2,377
Sheep's milk*	300	320	336
Goats' milk*	250	260	267
Hen eggs	260	266	309
Honey	5	5	5
Wool, greasy*	26	26	27

* FAO estimates.

Source: FAO.

Forestry

ROUNDWOOD REMOVALS
('000 cubic metres, excl. bark, FAO estimates)

	2010	2011	2012
Sawlogs, veneer logs and logs for sleepers	29	28	28
Pulpwood	64	59	59
Other industrial wood	52	52	52
Fuel wood	8,176	8,246	8,317
Total	8,321	8,385	8,456

Sawnwood production ('000 cubic metres, incl. railway sleepers, FAO estimates): 13 per year in 1975–2012.

Source: FAO.

Fishing

('000 metric tons, live weight)

	2009	2010	2011
Capture	127.5	93.6	101.8
Bogue	6.6	6.5	7.3
Jack and horse mackerels	18.5	11.1	11.3
Sardinellas	16.2	11.1	13.4
European pilchard (sardine)	55.3	31.2	34.0
European anchovy	3.2	2.0	2.7
Aquaculture*	2.2	1.8	2.2
Total catch*	130.0	95.4	104.0

* FAO estimates.

Source: FAO.

Mining

('000 metric tons unless otherwise indicated)

	2009	2010	2011
Crude petroleum*	77,200	74,122	73,538
Natural gas (dry basis, million cu m)*	79,550	80,412	82,700
Iron ore (gross weight)	1,307	1,469	1,400
Phosphate rock†	1,017	1,525	1,287
Barite (Barytes)	36	40	30
Salt (unrefined)	109	107	170
Gypsum (crude)	1,757	1,610	1,610

* Source: BP, *Statistical Review of World Energy*.
† Figures refer to gross weight. The estimated phosphoric acid content (in '000 metric tons, estimated) was 305 in 2009; 458 in 2010; 386 in 2011.

Mercury (kilograms): 73,451 in 2005.

2012: Crude petroleum 73,046,000 metric tons; Natural gas 81,500m. cu m (Source: BP, *Statistical Review of World Energy*).

Source (unless otherwise indicated): US Geological Survey.

Industry

SELECTED PRODUCTS
('000 metric tons unless otherwise indicated)

	2007	2008	2009
Olive oil (crude)	22	36	n.a.
Naphthas	3,698	3,641	4,913
Motor spirit (petrol)	2,100	2,780	2,417
Jet fuel	1,034	988	977
Gas-diesel (distillate fuel) oils	6,388	7,403	7,533
Residual fuel oils	5,518	6,009	5,581
Lubricating oils	143	89	140
Petroleum bitumen (asphalt)	331	315	310
Liquefied petroleum gas	9,183	9,240	8,869
Pig iron for steel-making	1,193	690	680
Crude steel (ingots)	1,278	646	543
Electric energy (million kWh)	37,196	40,236	38,195

2010 ('000 metric tons unless otherwise indicated): Motor spirit (petrol) 2,667; Jet fuel 1,409; Gas-diesel (distillate fuel) oils 7,806; Residual fuel oils 5,749; Petroleum bitumen (asphalt) 209; Liquefied petroleum gas 8,179; Electric energy (million kWh) 45,560.

Source: UN Industrial Commodities Statistics Database.

Finance

CURRENCY AND EXCHANGE RATES

Monetary Units
100 centimes = 1 Algerian dinar (AD).

Sterling, Dollar and Euro Equivalents (31 December 2013)
£1 sterling = 128.701 dinars;
US $1 = 78.152 dinars;
€1 = 107.780 dinars;
1,000 Algerian dinars = £7.77 = $12.80 = €9.28.

Average Exchange Rate (dinars per US $)
2011 72.938
2012 77.536
2013 79.368

GOVERNMENT FINANCE

(central government operations, '000 million AD)

Summary of Balances

	2009	2010	2011†
Revenue and grants	3,676	4,393	5,790
Less Expenditure	4,221	4,440	5,853
Budget balance	–545	–47	–63
Special accounts balance	508	11	26
Less Net lending by Treasury	642	184	153
Overall balance	–679	–220	–190

Revenue and Grants

	2009	2010	2011†
Hydrocarbon revenue	2,413	2,905	3,980
Sonatrach dividends	85	85	150
Other revenue	1,263	1,488	1,810
Tax revenue	1,147	1,298	1,527
Taxes on income and profits	462	562	685
Taxes on goods and services	478	515	573
Customs duties	170	182	222
Registration and stamps	36	40	47
Non-tax revenue	117	190	283
Total	3,676	4,393	5,790

Expenditure

Expenditure by economic type	2009	2010	2011†
Current expenditure	2,275	2,632	3,879
Personnel expenditure	880	1,193	1,740
War veterans' pensions	131	151	163
Material and supplies	113	122	130
Current transfers	1,114	1,130	1,808
Interest payments	37	36	38
Capital expenditure	1,946	1,808	1,974
Total	4,221	4,440	5,853

Sectoral allocation of capital expenditure*	2009	2010	2011†
Agriculture and fishery	25.8	22.4	17.6
Irrigation and waterworks	256.6	272.1	284.2
Industry and energy	0.1	0.2	0.2
Economic infrastructure	398.5	381.7	400.0
Housing	230.8	293.5	137.8
Education and professional training	144.9	153.5	127.6
Social infrastructure	68.5	71.2	77.7
Administrative infrastructure	85.7	113.7	116.3
Urban development	77.6	65.3	47.4
Unallocated	136.7	134.4	126.2
Total	1,425.5	1,508.6	1,335.1

* Commitment basis.
† Preliminary figures.

Source: IMF, *Algeria: Statistical Appendix* (February 2013).

CENTRAL BANK RESERVES

(US $ million at 31 December)

	2010	2011	2012
Gold*	301	300	300
IMF special drawing rights	1,653	1,649	1,651
Reserve position in IMF	394	599	636
Foreign exchange	160,568	180,574	189,010
Total	162,916	183,122	191,597

* National valuation.

Source: IMF, *International Financial Statistics*.

MONEY SUPPLY

('000 million AD at 31 December)

	2010	2011	2012
Currency outside depository corporations	2,098.63	2,571.48	2,952.34
Transferable deposits	2,804.41	3,591.19	3,519.54
Other deposits	2,524.28	2,732.49	3,192.53
Broad money	7,427.32	8,895.16	9,664.41

Source: IMF, *International Financial Statistics*.

COST OF LIVING

(Consumer Price Index; base: 2001 = 100)

	2010	2011	2012
Food and non-alcoholic beverages	144.9	151.0	169.4
Clothing and footwear	107.5	111.4	117.8
Furniture and household goods	113.6	117.5	122.1
Health	117.4	122.6	127.9
Transport and communications	145.3	149.7	156.4
Education, culture and recreation	118.9	119.6	123.0
Restaurants and hotels	131.7	133.5	139.6
All items (incl. others)	136.2	142.4	155.1

NATIONAL ACCOUNTS

('000 million AD at current prices)

Expenditure on the Gross Domestic Product

	2010	2011	2012*
Government final consumption expenditure	492.0	641.9	515.4
Private final consumption expenditure	4,102.2	4,534.9	5,197.5
Gross fixed capital formation	4,350.9	4,620.1	4,978.1
Changes in inventories	617.2	884.8	960.3
Total domestic expenditure	9,562.4	10,681.7	11,651.3
Exports of goods and services	4,610.1	5,624.4	5,894.0
Less Imports of goods and services	3,768.0	4,172.9	4,385.0
GDP at purchasers' values	10,404.5	12,133.2	13,160.4

Gross Domestic Product by Economic Activity

	2010	2011	2012*
Agriculture	1,015.3	1,183.2	1,421.7
Mining (including associated industries)	4,243.7	5,312.8	5,276.7
Construction	1,194.1	1,262.6	1,411.2
Other industry	617.4	663.8	728.6
Transport and communications	933.7	1,003.5	1,095.3
Trade	1,283.2	1,446.3	1,651.6
Other services	369.4	406.3	443.6
Sub-total	9,656.8	11,278.5	12,028.6
Taxes on products (net)	747.7	854.6	1,131.8
GDP at purchasers' values	10,404.5	12,133.2	13,160.4

* Provisional figures.

BALANCE OF PAYMENTS
(US $ million)

	2010	2011	2012
Exports of goods f.o.b.	57,090.0	72,779.5	71,558.2
Imports of goods f.o.b.	–38,792.0	–46,801.0	–51,508.9
Balance on goods	18,298.0	25,978.6	20,049.3
Exports of services	3,566.0	3,737.6	3,990.0
Imports of services	–12,000.0	–12,559.3	–11,083.5
Balance on goods and services	9,864.0	17,156.8	12,955.7
Primary income received	4,597.0	4,443.3	3,905.2
Primary income paid	–4,965.0	–6,556.9	–7,778.7
Balance on goods, services and primary income	9,496.0	15,043.2	9,082.2
Secondary income received	2,661.0	3,017.0	3,314.3
Secondary income paid	–325.0	–664.9	–452.4
Current balance	11,832.0	17,395.2	11,944.1
Capital account (net)	4.0	–1.3	–8.9
Direct investment assets	–287.0	–693.1	–75.9
Direct investment liabilities	2,331.0	2,720.5	1,601.6
Portfolio investment assets	1,435.0	8.3	—
Other investment assets	–316.0	609.4	29.8
Other investment liabilities	1,253.0	45.6	774.1
Net errors and omissions	–1,267.1	–185.0	–2,527.3
Reserves and related items	14,984.9	19,899.5	11,737.5

Source: IMF, *International Financial Statistics*.

External Trade

Note: Data exclude military goods. Exports include stores and bunkers for foreign ships and aircraft.

PRINCIPAL COMMODITIES
(distribution by HS, US $ million)

Imports c.i.f.	2010	2011	2012
Live animals and animal products	1,329.4	1,899.4	1,708.6
Dairy products, eggs, honey, edible animal products, etc.	994.0	1,543.3	1,268.7
Vegetables and vegetable products	2,836.7	5,238.8	4,564.2
Cereals	1,950.6	4,019.9	3,259.4
Wheat and meslin	1,251.6	2,846.9	2,129.0
Prepared foodstuffs; beverages, spirits, vinegar; tobacco and articles thereof	1,911.1	2,719.1	2,815.0
Mineral products	1,302.6	1,393.9	5,297.7
Mineral fuels, oils, distillation products, etc.	949.4	1,156.4	4,936.4
Petroleum oils, not crude	327.0	488.6	4,435.9
Chemicals and related products	3,321.6	3,931.8	4,436.6
Pharmaceutical products	1,673.1	1,961.4	2,240.7
Medicament mixtures	1,459.4	1,618.2	1,754.8
Plastics, rubber, and articles thereof	1,775.2	2,184.7	2,346.8
Plastics and plastic products	1,319.0	1,676.7	1,696.0
Iron and steel, other base metals and articles of base metal	7,603.0	6,913.9	6,222.9
Iron and steel	1,967.3	2,996.4	3,440.8
Bars of iron, etc.	1,094.0	1,816.2	2,098.4
Iron or steel products	4,797.7	2,901.4	1,722.8
Tubes, pipes and related products	2,015.7	701.5	308.5
Machinery and mechanical appliances; electrical equipment; parts thereof	11,855.5	11,696.9	9,714.9
Machinery, boilers, etc.	8,845.3	8,217.0	6,404.9
Electrical and electronic equipment	3,010.2	3,479.9	3,310.1
Vehicles, aircraft, vessels and associated transport equipment	4,884.9	5,968.2	7,949.6
Vehicles (other than railway and tramway)	4,083.8	5,034.4	7,739.2
Cars and station wagons	1,455.7	2,108.5	3,908.7
Trucks, motor vehicles for the transport of goods	1,303.6	1,568.1	2,205.5
Total (incl. others)	41,000.0	47,219.7	50,369.4

Exports f.o.b.	2010	2011	2012
Mineral products	56,147.9	72,367.7	70,879.9
Mineral fuels, lubricants, etc.	56,087.3	72,212.5	70,716.2
Crude petroleum oils, etc.	24,779.4	35,027.5	32,879.4
Petroleum gases	22,462.0	25,278.8	27,001.3
Petroleum oils, other than crude oil	8,282.0	11,070.6	9,921.6
Total (incl. others)	57,051.0	73,436.3	71,865.7

Source: Trade Map-Trade Competitiveness Map, International Trade Centre, www.intracen.org/marketanalysis.

PRINCIPAL TRADING PARTNERS
(US $ million)

Imports c.i.f.	2010	2011	2012
Argentina	1,230.7	1,782.4	1,802.7
Austria	313.8	347.0	352.6
Belgium	776.7	830.1	661.7
Brazil	902.4	1,758.8	1,343.8
Canada	329.7	258.2	523.6
China, People's Republic	4,605.1	4,737.3	5,964.8
Egypt	346.9	452.0	384.4
France (incl. Monaco)	6,119.7	7,115.4	6,433.3
Germany	2,382.0	2,558.0	2,591.2
Greece	420.1	576.3	526.8
India	777.5	1,092.6	1,107.6
Italy	4,114.1	4,675.3	5,191.1
Japan	1,570.2	1,072.9	929.7
Korea, Republic	1,987.8	1,615.1	1,291.0
Netherlands	481.0	701.6	964.3
Portugal	303.7	551.3	620.1
Romania	294.6	354.3	603.6
Russia	163.6	268.2	1,207.5
Spain	2,643.6	3,427.2	4,343.3
Sweden	393.0	462.4	533.0
Switzerland	588.2	600.8	540.6
Turkey	1,522.3	1,398.4	1,798.3
United Kingdom	767.6	1,011.6	1,283.3
Ukraine	150.5	251.3	331.9
USA	2,125.5	2,176.8	1,769.7
Total (incl. others)	41,000.0	47,219.7	50,369.4

Exports f.o.b.	2010	2011	2012
Belgium	1,920.0	2,119.2	1,922.6
Brazil	2,415.4	3,233.9	3,395.5
Canada	2,970.8	4,458.6	5,082.1
China, People's Republic	1,173.4	2,173.8	2,596.7
Egypt	427.0	650.9	764.9
France (incl. Monaco)	3,776.1	6,533.6	6,124.2
India	1,565.1	2,236.8	1,067.1
Ireland	0.5	150.1	766.9
Italy	8,779.3	10,440.8	11,512.6
Japan	126.0	235.7	854.5
Korea, Republic	1,157.5	257.0	357.9
Morocco	713.2	922.1	993.3
Netherlands	4,163.5	4,916.2	5,256.7
Portugal	1,014.6	1,848.5	1,711.0
Spain	5,908.6	7,186.1	7,809.4
Tunisia	536.3	650.3	1,018.7
Turkey	2,703.6	2,524.9	2,624.6
United Kingdom	1,290.0	2,855.0	3,668.1
USA	13,827.3	15,127.3	10,778.2
Total (incl. others)	57,051.0	73,436.3	71,865.7

Source: Trade Map-Trade Competitiveness Map, International Trade Centre, www.intracen.org/marketanalysis.

Transport

RAILWAYS
(traffic)

	2009	2010	2011
Passengers carried ('000)	27,843	27,299	27,416
Freight carried ('000 metric tons)	5,252	5,094	4,983
Passenger-km (million)	1,141	1,046	1,040
Freight ton-km (million)	1,184	1,281	1,248

Source: Société Nationale des Transports Ferroviaires.

ROAD TRAFFIC
(motor vehicles in use at 31 December)

	2009	2010
Passenger cars	2,593,310	2,691,075
Lorries and vans	1,247,300	1,282,970
Buses and coaches	70,070	72,538
Motorcycles and mopeds	10,978	12,109

Source: IRF, *World Road Statistics*.

SHIPPING
Flag Registered Fleet
(at 31 December)

	2011	2012	2013
Number of vessels	168	174	177
Total displacement ('000 grt)	815.1	787.4	788.0

Source: Lloyd's List Intelligence (www.lloydslistintelligence.com).

CIVIL AVIATION
(traffic on scheduled services)

	2010	2011
Kilometres flown (million)	53	53
Passengers carried ('000)	3,372	3,544
Passenger-km (million)	3,994	4,195
Total ton-km (million)	375	392

Source: UN, *Statistical Yearbook*.

Passengers carried ('000): 4,083 in 2012 (Source: World Bank, World Development Indicators database).

Tourism

FOREIGN TOURIST ARRIVALS BY COUNTRY OF ORIGIN*

	2009	2010	2011
France	171,314	140,129	112,241
Germany	12,148	9,244	9,492
Italy	18,824	16,886	19,127
Libya	16,359	19,313	28,615
Mali	23,907	30,648	34,478
Morocco	17,300	17,115	17,218
Spain	23,746	25,633	28,051
Tunisia	197,911	245,222	485,033
United Kingdom	9,375	8,024	7,992
Total (incl. others)	655,810	654,987	901,642

* Excluding arrivals of Algerian nationals resident abroad: 1,255,696 in 2009; 1,415,509 in 2010; 1,493,245 in 2011.

Tourism receipts (US $ million, excl. passenger transport): 267 in 2009; 219 in 2010; 209 in 2011.

Source: World Tourism Organization.

Communications Media

	2010	2011	2012
Telephones ('000 main lines in use)	2,922.7	3,059.3	3,202.0
Mobile cellular telephones ('000 subscribers)	32,780.2	35,615.9	37,692.0
Broadband subscribers ('000)	900	1,000	1,111

2009: Internet users ('000) 4,700.

Source: International Telecommunication Union.

Education

(2011/12 unless otherwise indicated)

	Institutions*	Teachers	Pupils
Pre-primary	n.a.	19,323†	490,035†
Primary	17,680	149,036	3,451,588
Secondary	6,529	176,375†	4,572,513†
Tertiary	n.a.	46,454	1,210,272

* 2009/10.
† 2010/11.

Sources: UNESCO, Institute for Statistics, and Ministère de l'Education Nationale.

1998/99 (Pre-primary and primary): 15,729 institutions; 170,562 teachers; 4,843,313 pupils.

Pupil-teacher ratio (primary education, UNESCO estimate): 23.2 in 2011/12 (Source: UNESCO Institute for Statistics).

Adult literacy rate (UNESCO estimates): 75.4% (males 84.3%; females 66.4%) in 2007 (Source: UNESCO Institute for Statistics).

Directory

The Government

HEAD OF STATE

President and Minister of National Defence: ABDELAZIZ BOUTEFLIKA (inaugurated 27 April 1999; re-elected 8 April 2004, 9 April 2009 and 17 April 2014).

COUNCIL OF MINISTERS
(April 2014)

Acting Prime Minister and Minister of Energy and Mining: YOUCEF YOUSFI.

Minister of State and Minister of the Interior and Local Authorities: TAYEB BELAÏZ.

Vice-Minister of National Defence and Chief of Staff of the People's National Army: Lt-Gen. AHMED GAID SALAH.

Minister of Foreign Affairs: RAMTANE LAMAMRA.

Minister of Justice and Attorney-General: TAYEB LOUH.

Minister of Finance: KARIM DJOUDI.

Minister of Industrial Development and Investment Promotion: AMARA BENYOUNES.

Minister of Agriculture and Rural Development: ABDELWAHAB NOURI.

Minister of Religious Affairs and Awqaf (Religious Endowments): BOUABDALLAH GHLAMALLAH.

Minister of War Veterans: MUHAMMAD CHÉRIF ABBES.

Minister of Water Resources: HOCINE NECIB.

Minister of Transport: AMAR GHOUL.

Minister of Public Works: FAROUK CHIALI.

Minister of Housing, Urban Planning and Towns: ABDELMADJID TEBBOUNE.

Minister of Territorial Planning and the Environment: DALILA BOUDJEMAÂ.

Minister of Communication: ABDELKADER MESSAHEL.

Minister of National Education: ABDELATIF BABA AHMED.

Minister of Higher Education and Scientific Research: MUHAMMAD MEBARKI.

Minister of Culture: KHALIDA TOUMI.

Minister of Vocational Training and Education: NOUREDINE BEDOUI.

Minister of National Solidarity, the Family and Women: SOUAD BENDJABALLAH.

Minister of Commerce: MUSTAPHA BENBADA.

Minister of Relations with Parliament: MAHMOUD KHEDRI.

Minister of Labour, Employment and Social Security: MUHAMMAD BENMERADI.

Minister of Health, Population and Hospital Reform: ABDELMALEK BOUDIAF.

Minister of Youth and Sports: MUHAMMAD TAHMI.

Minister of Postal Services and Information and Communications Technologies: ZOHRA DERDOURI.

Minister of Tourism and Handicrafts: MUHAMMAD AMINE HADJ SAID.

Minister of Fisheries and Marine Resources: SID AHMED FERROUKHI.

Minister-delegate to the Minister of Foreign Affairs, in charge of Maghreb and African Affairs: ABDELMADJID BOUGHERRA.

Minister-delegate to the Minister of Finance, in charge of the Budget: MUHAMMAD DJELLAB.

Secretary-General to the Government: AHMED NOUI.

MINISTRIES

Office of the President: Présidence de la République, el-Mouradia, Algiers; tel. (21) 69-15-15; fax (21) 69-15-95; e-mail president@el-mouradia.dz; internet www.el-mouradia.dz.

Office of the Prime Minister: rue Docteur Saâdane, Algiers; tel. (21) 73-12-00; fax (21) 71-79-29; internet www.cg.gov.dz.

Ministry of Agriculture and Rural Development: 12 ave Col Amirouche, Algiers; tel. (23) 50-32-38; fax (23) 50-31-17; internet www.minagri.dz.

Ministry of Commerce: Cité Zerhouni Mokhtar les El Mohamadia, Algiers; tel. (21) 89-00-74; fax (21) 89-00-34; e-mail info@mincommerce.gov.dz; internet www.mincommerce.gov.dz.

Ministry of Culture: BP 100, Palais de la Culture 'Moufdi Zakaria', Plateau des Annassers, Kouba, Algiers; tel. (21) 29-10-10; fax (21) 29-20-89; e-mail contact@m-culture.gov.dz; internet www.m-culture.gov.dz.

Ministry of Energy and Mining: BP 677, Tower A, Val d'Hydra, Alger-Gare, Algiers; tel. (21) 48-85-26; fax (21) 48-85-57; e-mail info@memalgeria.org; internet www.mem-algeria.org.

Ministry of Finance: Immeuble Ahmed Francis, Ben Aknoun, Algiers; tel. (21) 59-51-51; e-mail mfmail@mf.gov.dz; internet www.mf.gov.dz.

Ministry of Fisheries and Marine Resources: route des Quatre Canons, Algiers; tel. (21) 43-39-47; fax (21) 43-31-68; e-mail info@mpeche.gov.dz; internet www.mpeche.gov.dz.

Ministry of Foreign Affairs: place Mohamed Seddik Benyahia, el-Mouradia, Algiers; tel. (21) 29-12-12; fax (21) 50-43-63; internet www.mae.dz.

Ministry of Future Planning and Statistics: Algiers.

Ministry of Health, Population and Hospital Reform: 125 rue Abderrahmane Laâla, el-Madania, Algiers; tel. (21) 67-53-15; fax (21) 65-36-46; internet www.sante.gov.dz.

Ministry of Higher Education and Scientific Research: 11 chemin Doudou Mokhtar, Ben Aknoun, Algiers; tel. (21) 91-23-23; fax (21) 91-17-17; e-mail webmaster@mesrs.dz; internet www.mesrs.dz.

Ministry of Housing and Urban Planning: 135 rue Mourad Didouche, Algiers; tel. (21) 74-07-22; e-mail mhabitat@wissal.dz; internet www.mhu.gov.dz.

Ministry of Industry, Small and Medium-sized Enterprises and Investment Promotion: Immeuble de la Colisée, 2 rue Ahmed Bey, el-Biar, Algiers; tel. (21) 23-91-43; fax (21) 23-94-88; internet www.mipi.dz.

Ministry of Information: Algiers.

Ministry of the Interior and Local Authorities: 18 rue Docteur Saâdane, Algiers; tel. (21) 73-23-40; fax (21) 73-61-06.

Ministry of Justice: 8 place Bir Hakem, el-Biar, Algiers; tel. (21) 92-41-83; fax (21) 92-17-01; e-mail contact@mjustice.dz; internet www.mjustice.dz.

Ministry of Labour, Employment and Social Security: 44 rue Muhammad Belouizdad, 16600 Algiers; tel. (21) 65-99-99; fax (21) 66-12-92; e-mail informa@mtess.gov.dz; internet www.mtess.gov.dz.

Ministry of National Defence: Les Tagarins, el-Biar, Algiers; tel. (21) 71-15-15; fax (21) 64-67-26; internet www.mdn.dz.

Ministry of National Education: 8 rue de Pékin, el-Mouradia, Algiers; tel. (21) 60-55-60; fax (21) 60-67-02; e-mail education@men.dz.

Ministry of National Solidarity and Family: BP 31, route nationale no 1, Les Vergers, Bir Khadem, Algiers; tel. (21) 44-99-46; fax (21) 44-96-64; e-mail cellulemassn@massn.gov.dz; internet www.massn.gov.dz.

Ministry of Postal Services and Information and Communications Technologies: 4 blvd Krim Belkacem, Algiers 16027; tel. (21) 71-12-20; fax (21) 73-00-47; e-mail contact@mptic.dz; internet www.mptic.dz.

Ministry of Public Works: 6 rue Moustafa Khalef, Ben Aknoun, Algiers; tel. (21) 91-49-47; fax (21) 91-35-85; e-mail info@mtp-dz.com; internet www.mtp.gov.dz.

Ministry of Religious Affairs and Awqaf (Religious Endowments): 4 rue de Timgad, Hydra, Algiers; tel. (21) 60-88-20; fax (21) 69-15-69.

Ministry of Territorial Planning, the Environment and Towns: rue des Quatre Canons, Bab-el-Oued, Algiers; tel. (21) 43-28-01; fax (21) 43-28-90; e-mail deeai@ifrance.com; internet www.mate.gov.dz.

Ministry of Tourism and Handicrafts: 119 rue Didouche Mourad, Algiers; tel. (21) 71-45-45; e-mail contact@mta.gov.dz; internet www.mta.gov.dz.

Ministry of Transport: 1 chemin ibn Badis el-Mouiz (ex Poirson), el-Biar, 16300 Algiers; tel. (21) 92-98-85; fax (21) 92-98-94; internet www.ministere-transports.gov.dz.

Ministry of Vocational Training and Education: rue des Frères Aîssou, Ben Aknoun, Algiers; tel. (21) 91-15-03; fax (21) 91-22-66; e-mail contacts@mfep.gov.dz; internet www.mfep.gov.dz.

Ministry of War Veterans: 2 ave du Lt Muhammad Benarfa, el-Biar, Algiers; tel. (21) 92-23-55; fax (21) 92-35-16; e-mail sinformatique@m-moudjahidine.dz; internet www.m-moudjahidine.dz.

Ministry of Water Resources: 3 rue du Caire, Kouba, Algiers; tel. (21) 68-95-00; e-mail deah@mre.gov.dz; internet www.mre.gov.dz.

Ministry of Youth and Sports: 3 rue Muhammad Belouizdad, Algiers; tel. (21) 65-55-55; fax (21) 65-71-74; e-mail contact@mjs.dz; internet www.mjs.dz.

President

Presidential Election, 17 April 2014*

Candidate	Votes	% of votes
Abdelaziz Bouteflika	8,332,598	81.53
Ali Benflis	1,244,918	12.18
Abdelaziz Belaïd	343,624	3.36
Louisa Hanoune	140,253	1.37
Ali Fawzi Rebaïne	101,046	0.99
Moussa Touati	57,590	0.56
Total	10,220,029†	100.00

* Preliminary results.
† Excluding 1,087,449 invalid votes.

Legislature

NATIONAL PEOPLE'S ASSEMBLY

National People's Assembly: 18 blvd Zighout Youcef, 16000 Algiers; tel. (21) 73-86-00; internet www.apn-dz.org.

President: Dr MUHAMMAD LARBI OULD KHELIFA.

General Election, 10 May 2012

	Seats
Front de Libération Nationale (FLN)	221
Rassemblement National Démocratique (RND)	70
Alliance de l'Algérie Verte (AAV)	47
Front des Forces Socialistes (FFS)	21
Parti des Travailleurs (PT)	17
Front National Algérien (FNA)	9
Front pour la Justice et le Développement (FJD-El-Addala)	7
Mouvement Populaire Algérien (MPA)	6
Parti el-Fedjr el-Jadid (PFJ)	5
Parti National pour la Solidarité et le Développement (PNSD)	4
Front du Changement (FC)	4
Ahd 54	3
Alliance Nationale Républicaine (ANR)	3
Front National pour la Justice Sociale (FNJS)	3
Union des Forces Démocratiques et Sociales (UFDS-El-Ittihad)	3
Rassemblement Algérien (RA)	2
Rassemblement Patriotique Républicain (RPR)	2
Mouvement National de l'Espérance (MNE)	2
Front El-Moustakbel (FM)	2
Parti El-Karama (PK)	2
Mouvement des Citoyens Libres (MCL)	2
Parti des Jeunes (PJ)	2
Parti Ennour el-Djazairi (PED)	2
Others	4
Independents	19
Total	**462**

COUNCIL OF THE NATION

Council of the Nation: 7 blvd Zighout Youcef, 16000 Algiers; tel. (21) 74-60-85; fax (21) 74-60-79; e-mail hamrani@majliselouma.dz; internet www.majliselouma.dz.

President: ABDELKADER BENSALAH.

Elections, 29 December 2009 and 29 December 2012*

	Seats
Rassemblement National Démocratique (RND)	44
Front de Libération Nationale (FLN)	40
Front des Forces Socialistes (FFS)	2
Mouvement de la Société pour la Paix (MSP)	2
Ahd 54	1
Front El-Moustakbel (FM)	1
Front National Algérien (FNA)	1
Mouvement Populaire Algérien (MPA)	1
Rassemblement pour la Culture et la Démocratie (RCD)	1
Independents	3
Appointed by the President†	48
Total	**144**

* Deputies of the 144-member Council of the Nation serve a six-year term; one-half of its members are replaced every three years. Elected representatives are selected by indirect, secret suffrage from regional and municipal authorities.

† 30 new members were appointed by the President on 6 January 2013.

Political Organizations

Until 1989 the FLN was the only legal party in Algeria. Amendments to the Constitution in February of that year permitted the formation of other political associations, with some restrictions. The right to establish political parties was guaranteed by constitutional amendments in November 1996; however, political associations based on differences in religion, language, race, gender or region were proscribed. Some 27 political parties contested the legislative elections of May 2012. The most prominent political organizations are listed below.

Ahd 54 (Oath 54): 53 rue Larbi Ben M'Hedi, Algiers; tel. (21) 73-00-83; fax (21) 73-00-82; e-mail info@ahd54.com; internet www.ahd54.com; f. 1991; small nationalist party; Pres. ALI FAWZI REBAÏNE.

Alliance de l'Algérie Verte (AAV): Algiers; f. 2012; electoral alliance including three Islamist parties: Mouvement de la Société pour la Paix (MSP), Mouvement de la Renaissance Islamique (Al-Nahda) and Mouvement pour la Réforme Nationale; Leader BOUGHERRA SOLTANI.

Alliance Nationale Républicaine (ANR): 202 blvd Bougara, el-Biar, Algiers; tel. (21) 91-69-30; fax (21) 91-48-34; e-mail contact@anr.dz; f. 1995; anti-Islamist; Leader REDHA MALEK; Sec.-Gen. BELKACEM SAHLI.

Front de Libération Nationale (FLN): 7 rue du Stade, 16405 Hydra, Algiers; tel. (21) 69-42-81; fax (21) 69-47-07; e-mail contact@pfln.dz; internet www.pfln.dz; f. 1954; sole legal party until 1989; socialist in outlook, the party is organized into a Secretariat, a National Council, an Executive Committee, Federations, Kasmas and cells; under the aegis of the FLN are various mass political orgs, incl. the Union Nationale de la Jeunesse Algérienne and the Union Nationale des Femmes Algériennes; Pres. ABDELAZIZ BOUTEFLIKA; Sec.-Gen. AMMAR SAÏDANI.

Front Démocratique Libre (FDL) (Free Democratic Front): Algiers; f. 2012; Pres. BRAHMI RABAH.

Front des Forces Socialistes (FFS): 56 ave Souidani Boudjemaâ, el-Mouradia, 16000 Algiers; tel. (21) 69-41-41; fax (21) 69-41-42; e-mail ffscomdz@gmail.com; internet www.ffs-dz.net; f. 1963; revived 1989; seeks greater autonomy for Berber-dominated regions and official recognition of the Berber language; Leader HOCINE AÏT AHMED; Sec.-Gen. AHMAD BETATACHE.

Front du Changement (FC): Algiers; Chair. ABDELMADJID MENASRA.

Front El-Moustakbel (FM): Algiers; internet www.frontelmoustakbel.dz; f. 2012; Pres. ABDELAZIZ BELAÏD.

Front National Algérien (FNA): 18 rue Chaib Ahmed, 16100 Algiers; tel. (21) 73-07-88; fax (21) 73-30-96; e-mail touatimoussa@yahoo.fr; f. 1999; advocates eradication of poverty and supports the Govt's peace initiative; Pres. MOUSSA TOUATI.

Front National Démocratique (FND): Algiers; Pres. MABROUK SASSI.

Front National des Indépendants pour la Concorde (FNIC): Algiers; Pres. Dr LEKAL YACINE.

Front National pour la Justice Sociale (FNJS): Algiers; f. 2012; Pres. KHALED BOUNEDJMA.

Front pour la Justice et le Développement (FJD—El-Addala): Algiers; f. 2012; Leader ABDELLAH DJABALLAH.

Mouvement des Citoyens Libres (MCL): Algiers; f. 2012; Pres. MUSTAPHA BOUDINA.

Mouvement El-Infitah (ME): Algiers; f. 1997; Pres. OMAR BOUACHA.

Mouvement pour l'Autonomie de la Kabylie (MAK): Tizi Ouzou; e-mail info@makabylie.info; internet mak.makabylie.info; f. 2001; advocates autonomy for the north-eastern region of Kabylia within a federal Algerian state; Pres. BOUAZIZ AÏT-CHEBIB.

Mouvement Démocratique et Social (MDS): 67 blvd Krim Belkacem, 16200 Algiers; tel. (21) 63-86-05; fax (21) 63-89-12; e-mail mds-algerie@orange.fr; f. 1998 by fmr mems of Ettahaddi; left-wing party; 4,000 mems; Sec.-Gen. YACINE TEGUIA.

Mouvement El Islah (MRN) (Mouvement de la Réforme Nationale): Algiers; internet www.elislah.net; f. 1998; radical Islamist party; contested May 2012 legislative elections as part of Alliance de l'Algérie Verte; Sec.-Gen. MUHAMMAD DJAHID YOUNSI.

Mouvement Populaire Algérien (MPA): 53 Coopérative des Médecins, Ben Aknoun, Algiers; tel. (21) 94-67-07; fax (21) 94-67-27; internet mouvementpopulairealgerien.org; Sec.-Gen. AMARA BENYOUNES.

Mouvement de la Renaissance Islamique (Al-Nahda) (Harakat al-Nahda al-Islamiyya): blvd des Martyrs, 16100 Algiers; tel. (21) 74-85-14; fundamentalist Islamist group; contested May 2012 legislative elections as part of Alliance de l'Algérie Verte; Leader FATEH REBAI.

Mouvement de la Société pour la Paix (MSP) (Harakat Mujtamaa al-Silm): 63 rue Ali Haddad, Algiers; e-mail info@hmsalgeria.net; internet hmsalgeria.net; fmrly known as Hamas; adopted current name in 1997; moderate Islamist party, favouring the gradual introduction of an Islamic state; contested May 2012 legislative elections as part of Alliance de l'Algérie Verte; Pres. ABDERREZAK MOKRI.

Parti Algérien Vert pour le Développement (PAVD) (Algerian Green Party for Development): Algiers; f. 2012; Sec.-Gen. AMARA ALI.

Parti des Fidèles à la Patrie (PFP) (Party of Patriots): Algiers; f. 2012; Pres. MUSTAPHA KAMEL.

Parti des Jeunes (PJ): Algiers; f. 2012; Gen. Co-ordinator HAMANA BOUCHERMA.

Parti des Travailleurs (PT): 2 rue Belkheir Hassan Badi, el-Harrach, 16000 Algiers; tel. (21) 52-62-45; fax (21) 52-89-90; e-mail contact@pt-dz.com; internet www.pt-dz.com; workers' party; Leader LOUISA HANOUNE.

Parti du Renouveau Algérien (PRA): 8 ave de Pékin, 16209 el-Mouradia, Algiers; tel. (21) 59-43-00; Sec.-Gen. KAMEL BENSALEM; Leader NOUREDDINE BOUKROUH.

Parti El-Karama (PK): Algiers; f. 2012; Pres. MUHAMMAD BENHAMOU.

Parti Ennour el-Djazairi (PED): Algiers; Sec.-Gen. BADREDDINE BELBA.

Parti National pour la Solidarité et le Développement (PNSD): BP 110, Staouéli, Algiers; tel. and fax (21) 39-40-42; e-mail cherif_taleb@yahoo.fr; f. 1989 as Parti Social Démocrate; Leader MUHAMMAD CHÉRIF TALEB.

Rassemblement Algérien (RA): cité Ahcène Mahiouz, BP 158, Ben Aknoun, 16000 Algiers; e-mail info@rassemblement-algerien.com; internet www.rassemblement-algerien.com; f. 2008; Pres. Dr ALI ZEGHDOUD.

Rassemblement National Démocratique (RND): BP 10, Cité des Asphodèles, Ben Aknoun, Algiers; tel. (21) 91-64-10; fax (21) 91-47-40; e-mail contact@rnd-dz.com; internet www.rnd-dz.com; f. 1997; centrist party; Sec.-Gen. ABDELKADER BENSALAH.

Rassemblement Patriotique Républicain (RPR): Algiers; Pres. ABDELKADER MERBAH.

Union des Forces Démocratiques et Sociales (UFDS-El-Ittihad): Algiers; internet www.ufds-algerie.com; Sec.-Gen. NOUREDDINE BAHBOUH.

The following groups are in armed conflict with the Government:

Al-Qa'ida Organization in the Land of the Islamic Maghreb (AQIM): f. 1998 as the Groupe Salafiste pour la Prédication et le Combat (GSPC), a breakaway faction from the Groupe Islamique Armé; adopted current name in Jan. 2007, when it aligned itself with the militant Islamist al-Qa'ida network; particularly active to the east of Algiers and in Kabylia; as the GSPC, traditionally responded to preaching by Ali Belhadj, the second most prominent member of the proscribed Front Islamique du Salut; Leader ABDELMALEK DROUKDAL (also known as ABU MUSAB ABD AL-WADUD).

Groupe Islamique Armé (GIA): f. 1992; was the most prominent and radical Islamist militant group in the mid-1990s, but has reportedly split into several factions that do not all adhere to one leader.

Diplomatic Representation

EMBASSIES IN ALGERIA

Angola: 12 rue Mohamed Khoudi, el-Biar, Algiers; tel. (21) 92-21-43; fax (21) 92-04-18; e-mail ngolamd@wissal.dz; Ambassador JOSÉ ANTONIO CONDESA DE CARVALHO.

Argentina: Lotissement el-Feth, Villa 68, el-Biar, 16030 Algiers; tel. (21) 92-31-18; fax (21) 92-31-08; e-mail earge@mrecic.gov.ar; Ambassador ERNESTO SANTIAGO MARTÍNEZ GONDRA.

Austria: 17 chemin Abdelkader Gadouche, 16035 Hydra, Algiers; tel. (21) 69-11-34; fax (21) 69-12-32; e-mail algier-ob@bmeia.gv.at; internet www.aussenministerium.at/algier; Ambassador ALOISIA WÖRGETTER.

Bahrain: 24 chemin Abdelkader Gadouche, Hydra, Algiers; tel. (21) 69-11-97; fax (21) 69-24-49; e-mail algiers.mission@mofa.gov.bh; internet www.mofa.gov.bh/algiers; Ambassador HAMAD MUHAMMAD AL-ASFOOR.

Belgium: BP 341, 16030 el-Biar, Algiers; tel. (21) 92-26-20; fax (21) 92-50-36; e-mail algiers@diplobel.fed.be; internet www.diplomatie.be/algiersfr; Ambassador FRÉDÉRIC MEURICE.

Benin: BP 103, 16 Lot du Stade Birkhadem, Algiers; tel. (21) 56-52-71; Ambassador LEONARD ADJIN.

Brazil: 55 Bis, chemin Cheikh Bachir el-Ibrahimi, el-Biar, 16030 Algiers; tel. (21) 92-44-37; fax (21) 92-41-25; e-mail brasemb.argel@itamaraty.gov.br; internet argel.itamaraty.gov.br/fr; Ambassador EDUARDO BOTELHO BARBOSA.

Bulgaria: 13 blvd Col Bougara, el-Biar, Algiers; tel. (21) 23-00-14; fax (21) 23-05-33; e-mail Embassy.Algiers@mfa.bg; internet www.mfa.bg/embassies/algeria; Chargé d'affaires a.i. MAXIM BLAGOEV.

Burkina Faso: BP 212, 23 Lot el-Feth, chemin ibn Badis el-Mouiz (ex Poirson), el-Biar, Didouche Mourad, Algiers; tel. (21) 92-33-39; fax (21) 92-73-90; e-mail abfalger@yahoo.fr; Ambassador DOMINIQUE DJINDJÉRÉ.

Cameroon: 15 lotissement el-Feth, 16134 el-Biar, Algiers; tel. (21) 92-11-24; fax (21) 92-11-25; e-mail ambacamalger@yahoo.fr; Ambassador CLAUDE JOSEPH MBAFOU.

Canada: BP 464, 18 rue Mustapha Khalef, Ben Aknoun, 16306 Algiers; tel. (770) 08-30-00; fax (770) 08-30-40; e-mail alger@international.gc.ca; internet www.international.gc.ca/world/embassies/algeria; Ambassador GENEVIÈVE DES RIVIÈRES.

Chad: Villa 18, Cité DNC, chemin Ahmed Kara, Hydra, Algiers; tel. (21) 69-26-62; fax (21) 69-26-63; Ambassador OUSMANE MATAR BREME.

Chile: 8 rue F. les Crêtes, Hydra, Algiers; tel. (21) 48-31-63; fax (21) 60-71-85; e-mail embachileargelia@gmail.com; Ambassador PABLO MUÑOZ ROMERO.

China, People's Republic: 34 blvd des Martyrs, Algiers; tel. (21) 69-27-24; fax (21) 69-30-56; e-mail chinaemb_dz@mfa.gov.cn; internet dz.chineseembassy.org; Ambassador LIU YUHE.

Congo, Republic: 13 rue Rabah Noel, Algiers; tel. (21) 58-06-13; Ambassador JEAN-PIERRE LOUYEBO.

Côte d'Ivoire: BP 260, Immeuble 'Le Bosquet', Parc Paradou, Hydra, Algiers; tel. (21) 69-23-78; fax (21) 69-28-28; Ambassador SIA BI SEI.

Croatia: 26 bis, rue Hadj Ahmed Mohamed, Hydra, 16405 Algiers; tel. (21) 48-49-07; fax (21) 48-48-98; e-mail croemb.algeria@mvep.hr; Ambassador MARIN ANDRIJAŠEVIĆ.

Cuba: 22 rue Larbi Allik, Hydra, Algiers; tel. (21) 69-21-48; fax (21) 69-32-81; e-mail embacubargelia@assila.net; Ambassador EUMELIO CABALLERO RODRÍGUEZ.

Czech Republic: BP 358, Villa Koudia, 3 chemin Ziryab, Alger-Telemly, Algiers; tel. (21) 23-00-56; fax (21) 23-01-33; e-mail algiers@embassy.mzv.cz; internet www.mzv.cz/algiers; Ambassador PAVEL KLUCKÝ.

Egypt: BP 297, 8 chemin Abdelkader Gadouche, 16300 Hydra, Algiers; tel. (21) 69-16-73; fax (21) 69-29-52; Ambassador EZZ EL-DIN FAHMI MAHMOUD.

Finland: 10 rue des Cèdres, el-Mouradia, Algiers; tel. (21) 69-29-25; fax (21) 69-16-37; e-mail sanomat.alg@formin.fi; internet www.finlandalgeria.org; Ambassador HANNELE VOIONMAA.

France: 25 chemin Abdelkader Gadouche, 16035 Hydra, Algiers; tel. (21) 98-17-17; fax (21) 98-17-09; e-mail contact@ambafrance-dz.org; internet www.ambafrance-dz.org; Ambassador ANDRÉ PARANT.

Gabon: BP 125, Rostomia, 21 rue Hadj Ahmed Mohamed, Hydra, Algiers; tel. (21) 69-24-00; fax (21) 60-25-46; Ambassador YVES ONGOLLO.

Germany: BP 664, 165 chemin Sfindja, Alger-Gare, 16000 Algiers; tel. (21) 74-19-56; fax (21) 74-05-21; e-mail zreg@algi.diplo.de; internet www.algier.diplo.de; Ambassador GÖTZ LINGENTHAL.

Ghana: 62 rue des Frères Benali Abdellah, Hydra, Algiers; tel. (21) 60-64-44; fax (21) 69-28-56; Ambassador ADOLPHUS KINGSLEY ARTHUR.

Greece: 60 blvd Col Bougara, 16030 el-Biar, Algiers; tel. (21) 92-34-91; fax (21) 92-34-90; e-mail gremb.alg@mfa.gr; internet www.mfa.gr/algiers; Ambassador VASILIOS MOUTSOGLOU.

Guinea: 43 blvd Central Saïd Hamdine, Hydra, Algiers; tel. (21) 69-36-11; fax (21) 69-34-68; e-mail ambaga49@yahoo.fr; Ambassador OUSMANE DIAO BALDÉ.

Guinea-Bissau: BP 32, 17 rue Ahmad Kara, Colonne Volrol, Hydra, Algiers; tel. (21) 60-01-51; fax (21) 60-97-25; Ambassador IBRAIMA SANO.

Holy See: 1 rue Noureddine Mekiri, 16021 Bologhine, Algiers (Apostolic Nunciature); tel. (21) 95-45-20; fax (21) 95-40-95; e-mail nuntiusalger2@yahoo.fr; Apostolic Nuncio Most Rev. THOMAS YEH SHENG-NAN (Titular Archbishop of Leptis Magna).

Hungary: BP 68, 18 ave des Fréres Oughlis, el-Mouradia, Algiers; tel. (21) 69-79-75; fax (21) 69-81-86; e-mail alg.missions@kum.hu; Ambassador JÓZSEF HAJGATÓ.

India: BP 108, 14 rue des Abassides, 16030 el-Biar, Algiers; tel. (21) 92-32-88; fax (21) 92-40-11; e-mail amb.algiers@mea.gov.in; internet www.indianalg.org; Ambassador Dr KULDEEP SINGH BHARDWAJ.

Indonesia: BP 62, 17 chemin Abdelkader Gadouche, 16070 el-Mouradia, Algiers; tel. (21) 69-49-15; fax (21) 69-49-10; e-mail kbrialger@indonesia-dz.org; internet algiers.kemlu.go.id; Ambassador AHMAD NI'AM SALIM.

Iraq: BP 249, 4 rue Abri Arezki, Hydra, Algiers; tel. (21) 69-31-25; fax (21) 69-10-97; e-mail algemb@iraqmofamail.com; Ambassador ABDULLAH AL-KHAIRALLAH.

Italy: 18 rue Muhammad Ouidir Amellal, 16030 el-Biar, Algiers; tel. (21) 92-23-30; fax (21) 92-59-86; e-mail segretaria.algeri@esteri.it; internet www.ambalgeri.esteri.it; Ambassador MICHELE GIACOMELLI.

Japan: BP 80, 1 chemin el-Bakri (ex Macklay), Ben Aknoun, el-Biar, Algiers; tel. (21) 91-20-04; fax (21) 91-20-46; internet www.dz.emb-japan.go.jp; Ambassador TSUKASA KAWADA.

Jordan: 47 rue Ammani Belkalem, Hydra, Algiers; tel. (21) 69-20-31; fax (21) 69-15-54; e-mail jordan@wissal.dz; Ambassador MUHAMMAD SALAMAH NUEIMAT.

Korea, Democratic People's Republic: Algiers; tel. (21) 62-39-27; Ambassador PAK HO IL.

Korea, Republic: 23 chemin de la Madeleine Chekiken, Hydra, Algiers; tel. (21) 54-65-55; fax (21) 54-65-70; e-mail koemal@mofa.go.kr; internet dza.mofat.go.kr/kor/af/dza/main/index.jsp; Ambassador KIM JONG-HOON.

Kuwait: chemin Abdelkader Gadouche, Hydra, Algiers; tel. (21) 59-31-57; Ambassador SAUD FAISAL SAUD AL-DAWEESH.

Lebanon: 9 rue Kaïd Ahmad, el-Biar, Algiers; tel. (21) 78-20-94; Ambassador BASSAM ALI TARABAH.

Libya: 15 chemin Cheikh Bachir el-Ibrahimi, Algiers; tel. (21) 92-15-02; fax (21) 92-46-87; Ambassador ABD AL-MOULA EL-GHADHBANE.

Madagascar: BP 65, 22 rue Abd al-Kader Aouis, 16090 Bologhine, Algiers; tel. (21) 95-03-74; fax (21) 95-17-76; e-mail ambamadalg@yahoo.fr; Ambassador VOLA DIEUDONNÉ RAZAFINDRALAMBO.

Mali: Villa 15, Cité DNC/ANP, chemin Ahmed Kara, Hydra, Algiers; tel. (21) 69-13-51; fax (21) 69-20-82; Ambassador BOUBACAR KARAMOKO COULIBALY.

Mauritania: 107 Lot Baranès, Aire de France, Bouzaréah, Algiers; tel. (21) 79-21-39; fax (21) 78-42-74; Ambassador BOULAH OULD MOGUEYE.

Mexico: BP 329, 25 chemin El-Bakri, Ben Aknoun, 16306 Algiers; tel. (21) 91-46-00; fax (21) 91-46-01; e-mail embamexargelia@gmail.com; internet embamex.sre.gob.mx/argelia; Ambassador JUAN JOSÉ GONZÁLEZ MIJARES.

Morocco: 8 rue Abd al-Kader Azil, el-Mouradia, Algiers; tel. (21) 60-57-07; fax (21) 60-50-47; e-mail ambmaroc-alg@maec.gov.ma; Ambassador ABDELLAH BELKEZIZ.

Netherlands: BP 72, 23/27 chemin Cheikh Bachir el-Ibrahimi, el-Biar, Algiers; tel. (21) 92-28-28; fax (21) 92-29-47; e-mail alg@minbuza.nl; internet alger.nlambassade.org; Ambassador FRANCISCUS GIJSBERTUS (FRANS) BIJVOET.

Niger: 54 rue Vercors Rostamia, Bouzaréah, Algiers; tel. (21) 78-89-21; fax (21) 78-97-13; Ambassador MAHAMIDOU ELHADJI YAHAYA.

Nigeria: BP 629, 27 bis rue Blaise Pascal, Algiers; tel. (21) 69-18-49; fax (21) 69-11-75; Ambassador HARUNA GINSAU.

Norway: 7 chemin Doudou Mokhtar, Ben Aknoun, 16035 Algiers; tel. (21) 94-65-65; fax (21) 94-64-65; e-mail emb.alger@mfa.no; internet www.norvege-algerie.org; Ambassador ARILD RETVEDT ØYEN.

Oman: BP 201, 52 rue Djamel Eddine, el-Afghani, Bouzaréah, Algiers; tel. (21) 91-28-35; fax (21) 91-47-37; e-mail algeria@mofa.gov.om; Ambassador ALI ABDULLAH AL-ALAWI.

Pakistan: BP 395, Villa no 18, rue des Idrissides, el-Biar, Algiers; tel. (21) 79-37-56; fax (21) 79-37-58; e-mail pakembagiers@yahoo.com; internet www.mofa.gov.pk/algeria; Ambassador SYED QASIM RAZA MUTTAQI (designate).

Peru: 2 et 4 Capitaine Salah Moghni, El Biar, 16406 Algiers; tel. (21) 92-38-54; fax (21) 92-38-56; e-mail ambaperou@yahoo.fr; Ambassador LUIS FELIPE GÁLVEZ VILLARROEL.

Poland: rue Olof Palme, Nouveau-Paradou, Hydra-Algiers; tel. (21) 60-99-50; fax (21) 60-99-59; e-mail algier.amb.sekretariat@msz.gov.pl; internet algier.msz.gov.pl; Ambassador MICHAŁ RADLICKI.

Portugal: 4 rue Mohamed Khoudi, el-Biar, Algiers; tel. (21) 92-55-82; fax (21) 92-53-13; e-mail embportdz@yahoo.fr; internet www.embaixadaportugalargel.com; Ambassador ANTÓNIO GAMITO.

Qatar: BP 35, Quartier Diplomatique, Dely Ibrahim, Algiers; tel. (21) 91-08-84; fax (21) 91-09-44; e-mail algeria@mofa.gov.qa; Ambassador ABDULLAH NASSER ABDULLAH AL-HUMAIDI.

Romania: 24 rue Abri Arezki, Hydra, 16035, Algiers; tel. (21) 60-08-71; fax (21) 69-36-42; e-mail alger@mae.ro; internet alger.mae.ro; Ambassador MARCEL ALEXANDRU.

Russia: 7 chemin du Prince d'Annam, el-Biar, Algiers; tel. (21) 92-31-39; fax (21) 92-28-82; e-mail ambrussie@yandex.ru; internet www.algerie.mid.ru; Ambassador ALEKSANDR Y. ZOLOTOV.

Saudi Arabia: BP 256, 5 chemin Doudou Mokhtar, Ben Aknoun, el-Biar, Algiers; tel. (21) 60-35-18; e-mail dzemb@mofa.gov.sa; Ambassador Dr SAMI IBN ABDULLAH IBN OTHMAN AL-SALEH.

Senegal: 1 chemin Mohamed Drarni, Hydra, Algiers; tel. (21) 54-90-90; fax (21) 54-90-94; e-mail senegal@wissal.dz; Ambassador PAPA OUSMANE SEYE.

Serbia: BP 366, 7 rue des Frères Ben-hafid, 16035 Hydra, Algiers; tel. (21) 69-12-18; fax (21) 69-34-72; e-mail ambasada@ambserbie-alger.com; internet www.ambserbie-alger.com; Ambassador MIROSLAV SESTOVIĆ.

South Africa: 21 rue du Stade, Hydra, Algiers; tel. (21) 48-44-18; fax (21) 48-44-19; e-mail teffahim@foreign.gov.za; internet www.saealgiers.com; Ambassador JOSEPH KOTANE.

Spain: BP 142, 46 bis, rue Muhammad Chabane, el-Biar, Algiers; tel. (21) 92-27-13; fax (21) 92-27-19; e-mail emb.argel@mae.es; Ambassador GABRIEL BUSQUETS APARICIO.

Sudan: Algiers; tel. (21) 56-66-23; fax (21) 69-30-19; Ambassador MADJI MUHAMMAD TAHA EL-HASSAN.

Sweden: BP 263, rue Olof Palme, Nouveau Paradou, Hydra, Algiers; tel. (21) 54-83-33; fax (21) 54-83-34; e-mail ambassaden.alger@gov.se; internet www.swedenabroad.se/algersv; Ambassador CARIN WALL.

Switzerland: Villa 5, rue no 4, Parc du Paradou, 16035 Hydra, Algiers; tel. (21) 98-10-00; fax (21) 98-10-29; e-mail alg.vertretung@eda.admin.ch; internet www.eda.admin.ch/alger; Ambassador JEAN-CLAUDE RICHARD.

Syria: Domaine Tamzali, 11 chemin Abdelkader Gadouche, Hydra, Algiers; tel. (21) 91-20-26; fax (21) 91-20-30; Ambassador NAMIR WAHIB GHANEM.

Tunisia: 5 rue du Bois, Hydra, 16405 Algiers; tel. (21) 60-13-88; fax (21) 69-23-16; e-mail ambassade@ambtunisie-dz.com; Ambassador MUHAMMAD EL-FADHAL KHALIL.

Turkey: 21 Villa Dar el-Oued, chemin de la Rochelle, blvd Col Bougara, 16000 Algiers; tel. (21) 23-00-64; fax (21) 23-01-12; e-mail ambassade.alger@mfa.gov.tr; internet www.algiers.emb.mfa.gov.tr; Ambassador ADNAN KEÇECI.

Ukraine: 19 rue des Frères Benhafid, Hydra, Algiers; tel. (21) 69-13-87; fax (21) 69-48-87; e-mail emb_dz@mfa.gov.ua; internet algeria.mfa.gov.ua; Ambassador VALERIY KIRDODA.

United Arab Emirates: BP 165, Alger-Gare, 14 rue Muhammad Drarini, Hydra, Algiers; tel. (21) 54-96-99; fax (21) 54-96-66; e-mail algeria@mofa.gov.ae; internet uae-embassy.ae/Embassies/dz; Ambassador MUHAMMAD ALI NASSER AL-WALI AL-MAZROUEI.

United Kingdom: 3 chemin Capitaine Hocine Slimane, Hydra, Algiers; tel. (770) 08-50-00; fax (770) 08-50-99; e-mail britishembassy.algiers@fco.gov.uk; internet ukinalgeria.fco.gov.uk; Ambassador MARTYN ROPER.

USA: BP 549, 5 chemin Cheikh Bachir el-Ibrahimi, el-Biar, 16030 Algiers; tel. (770) 08-20-00; fax (770) 08-20-64; e-mail algiers_webmaster@state.gov; internet algiers.usembassy.gov; Ambassador HENRY S. ENSHER.

Venezuela: BP 297, 3 impasse Ahmed Kara, Hydra, Algiers; tel. (21) 54-74-14; fax (21) 54-73-96; e-mail hector.mujica@mre.gob.ve; Ambassador HECTOR MICHEL MUJICA.

Viet Nam: 30 rue de Chenoua, Hydra, Algiers; tel. (21) 60-88-43; fax (21) 69-37-78; e-mail sqvnalgerie@yahoo.com.vn; internet www.vietnamembassy-algerie.org; Ambassador TRONG CUONG DO.

Yemen: 18 chemin Mahmoud Drarnine, Hydra, Algiers; tel. (21) 54-89-50; fax (21) 54-87-40; Ambassador JAMAL AWADH NASSER.

Judicial System

Justice is exercised through 183 courts (Tribunaux) and 31 appeal courts (Cours d'Appel), grouped on a regional basis. The highest court of justice is the Supreme Court (Cour Suprême). Legislation promulgated in March 1997 provided for the eventual establishment of 214 courts and 48 appeal courts. The Court of Accounts (Cour des Comptes) was established in 1979. Algeria adopted a penal code in 1966, retaining the death penalty. In February 1993 three special courts were established to try suspects accused of terrorist offences; however, the courts were abolished in February 1995. Constitutional amendments introduced in November 1996 provided for the establishment of a High State Court (empowered to judge the President of the Republic in cases of high treason, and the Head of Government for crimes and offences), and a State Council to regulate the administrative judiciary. In addition, a Conflicts Tribunal has been established to adjudicate in disputes between the Supreme Court and the State Council.

Supreme Court: rue du 11 décembre 1960, Ben Aknoun, Algiers; tel. (21) 92-58-52; fax (21) 92-96-44; e-mail coursupreme@mjustice.dz; internet www.coursupreme.dz; f. 1963; comprises 150 judges; Pres. SLIMANE BOUDI.

Minister of Justice and Attorney-General: TAYEB LOUH.

Religion

ISLAM

Islam is the official religion, and the vast majority of Algerians are Muslims.

High Islamic Council

16 rue du 11 décembre 1960, Ben Aknoun, 16030 Algiers; tel. (21) 91-54-10; fax (21) 91-54-09; e-mail hci@hci.dz; internet www.hci.dz.

President of the High Islamic Council: Dr CHEIKH BOUAMRANE.

CHRISTIANITY

The majority of the European inhabitants, and a few Arabs, are Christians.

The Roman Catholic Church

Algeria comprises one archdiocese and three dioceses (including one directly responsible to the Holy See). The Bishops' Conference of North Africa (Conférence des Evêques de la Région Nord de l'Afrique—CERNA) moved from Algiers to Tunis, Tunisia, in 2004.

Archbishop of Algiers: Most Rev. GHALEB ABDULLAH MOUSSA, 22 chemin d'Hydra, 16030 el-Biar, Algiers; tel. (21) 92-56-67; fax (21) 92-55-76; e-mail evechealger@yahoo.fr.

Protestant Church

Eglise Réformée d'Alger: 31 rue Reda Houhou, 16110 Alger-HBB, Algiers; tel. and fax (21) 71-62-38; e-mail protestants_alger@yahoo.com; 38 parishes; 7,000 mems; Pres. MOUSTAFA KRIM.

The Press

In 2008 there were an estimated 290 newspapers in circulation, including more than 60 dailies.

DAILIES

El Acil: 1 rue Kamel Ben Djelit, Constantine; tel. and fax (31) 92-46-13; e-mail elacilquotidien@yahoo.fr; f. 1993; French; Dir GHALIB DJABBOUR.

Akher Sâa: Intersection Bougandoura Miloud et Sakhri Abdelhamid, Annaba; tel. (38) 86-02-41; fax (38) 86-47-19; e-mail saidbel@hotmail.com; internet www.akhersaa-dz.com; Arabic; Dir SAÏD BELHADJOUDJA.

L'Authentique: 4 rue Abane Ramdane, Algiers; tel. (17) 06-13-80; fax (21) 74-27-15; e-mail lauthentiqueredaction@yahoo.fr; French; Editorial Dir TAHAR AKEZOUH.

Ech-Cha'ab (The People): 1 ave Pasteur, 16000 Algiers; tel. (21) 60-70-40; fax (21) 60-67-93; e-mail webmaster@ech-chaab.com; internet www.ech-chaab.com; f. 1962; Arabic; journal of the Front de Libération Nationale; Dir AZZEDINE BOUKERDOUSSE; circ. 24,000.

Echorouk El-Youmi: Maison de la presse Abdelkader Safir, Kouba, Algiers; tel. and fax (21) 29-89-41; e-mail contact@echoroukonline.com; internet www.echoroukonline.com; f. 2000; Arabic; Dir ALI FOUDIL.

Le Courier d'Algérie: Maison de la presse Abdelkader Kouba, Algiers; tel. (21) 46-25-12; fax (21) 46-25-13; e-mail redactioncourrier@yahoo.fr; internet www.lecourrier-dalgerie.com; f. 2003; French; Dir AHMED TOUMIAT.

La Dépêche de Kabylie: Maison de la presse Tahar Djaout, place du 1er mai, 16016 Algiers; tel. (21) 66-38-05; fax (21) 66-37-87; e-mail info@depechedekabylie.com; internet www.depechedekabylie.com; f. 2001; Dir IDIR BENYOUNÈS.

Djazair News: Maison de la presse Tahar Djaout, place du 1er mai, 16016 Algiers; tel. (21) 66-36-93; fax (21) 66-36-93; e-mail djazairnews@gmail.com; internet www.djazairnews.info; f. 2003; Arabic; Man. Dir HMIDA AYACHI.

L'Expression: Maison de la presse Abdelkader Safir, Kouba, Algiers; tel. (21) 68-94-55; fax (21) 28-02-29; e-mail laredaction@lexpressiondz.com; internet www.lexpressiondz.com; f. 2000; French; Editor AHMED FATTANI; circ. 70,000.

Al-Fedjr: Maison de la presse Tahar Djaout, place du 1er mai, 16016 Algiers; tel. and fax (21) 65-76-60; e-mail fadjr@al-fadjr.com; internet www.al-fadjr.com; f. 2000; Arabic; Dir ABDA HADDA HAZEM.

Horizons: 20 rue de la Liberté, Algiers; tel. (21) 73-67-24; fax (21) 73-61-34; e-mail administration@horizons-dz.com; internet www.horizons-dz.com; f. 1985; evening; French; Dir NAÂMA ABBAS; circ. 35,000.

Le Jeune Indépendant: Maison de la presse Tahar Djaout, 1 rue Bachir Attar, place du 1er mai, 16016 Algiers; tel. (21) 67-07-48; fax (21) 67-07-46; e-mail redaction@jeune-independant.net; internet www.jeune-independant.net; f. 1990; French; Man. Dir ALI MECHERI; Editor NAÏMA NEFLA; circ. 60,000.

El-Joumhouria (The Republic): 6 rue Bensenouci Hamida, Oran; tel. (41) 39-04-97; fax (41) 39-10-39; e-mail djoumhouria@yahoo.fr; internet www.eldjoumhouria.dz; f. 1963; Arabic; Dir BOUZIANE BEN ACHOUR; circ. 20,000.

El Khabar: 32 rue El Feth Ibn Khlakane, Hydra, Algiers; tel. (21) 48-44-37; fax (21) 48-44-31; e-mail cherif_dz@hotmail.com; internet www.elkhabar.com; f. 1990; Arabic; Dir-Gen. CHERIF REZKI; circ. 470,000.

Liberté: BP 178, 37 rue Larbi Ben M'Hidi, Alger-Gare, Algiers; tel. (21) 64-34-25; fax (21) 64-34-29; e-mail infos@liberte-algerie.com; internet www.liberte-algerie.com; f. 1992; French; independent; Dir ALI OUAFEK; Editors SALIM TAMANI, AMAR OUALI; circ. 20,000.

El-Massa: Maison de la presse Abdelkader Safir, Kouba, 16000 Algiers; tel. (21) 74-57-99; fax (21) 74-57-90; e-mail info@el-massa.com; internet www.el-massa.com; f. 1977; evening; Arabic; Dir ABDERRAHMANE TIGANE; circ. 45,000.

Le Matin: Maison de la Presse Tahar Djaout, 1 rue Bachir Attar, place du 1er mai, 16016 Algiers; tel. (21) 66-07-08; fax (21) 66-20-97; e-mail redactionlematin@gmail.com; internet www.lematindz.net; French; Dir MUHAMMAD BENCHICOU.

El-Moudjahid (The Fighter): 20 rue de la Liberté, Algiers; tel. (21) 73-70-81; fax (21) 73-56-70; e-mail elmoudja@elmoudjahid.com; internet www.elmoudjahid.com; f. 1965; govt journal in French and Arabic; Dir ABDELMADJID CHERBAL; circ. 392,000.

An-Nasr (The Victory): BP 388, Zone Industrielle, La Palma, Constantine; tel. (31) 66-82-61; fax (31) 66-81-45; e-mail contact@annasronline.com; internet www.annasronline.com; f. 1963; Arabic; Dir LARBI OUANOUGHI; circ. 340,000.

La Nouvelle République: Maison de la presse Tahar Djaout, 1 rue Bachir Attar, place du 1er mai, 16016 Algiers; tel. (21) 67-10-44; fax (21) 67-10-75; e-mail inr98@yahoo.fr; internet www.lanouvellerepublique.com; French; Dir ABDELWAHAB DJAKOUNE; Editor MEHENNA HAMADOUCHE.

Ouest Tribune: 13 Cité Djamel, 31007 Oran; tel. (41) 45-31-30; fax (41) 45-34-62; e-mail redaction@ouestribune-dz.com; internet www.ouestribune-dz.com; French; Dir ABDELMADJID BLIDI.

Le Quotidien d'Oran: BP 110, 63 ave de l'ANP, 1 rue Laid Ould Tayeb, Oran; tel. (41) 32-63-09; fax (41) 32-51-36; e-mail infos@lequotidien-oran.com; internet www.lequotidien-oran.com; French; Dir-Gen. MUHAMMAD ABDOU BENABBOU.

Sawt al-Ahrar: 6 ave Pasteur, Algiers; tel. (21) 73-47-76; fax (21) 73-47-65; e-mail sawtalahrar@hotmail.com; internet www.sawt-alahrar.net; Arabic; Dir MUHAMMAD NADIR BOULAGROUNE.

Le Soir d'Algérie: Maison de la presse Tahar Djaout, 1 rue Bachir Attar, place du 1er mai, 16016 Algiers; tel. (21) 67-06-58; fax (21) 67-06-76; e-mail info@lesoirdalgerie.com; internet www.lesoirdalgerie.com; f. 1990; evening; independent information journal in French; Dir FOUAD BOUGHANEM; Editor NACER BELHADJOUDJA; circ. 80,000.

La Tribune: Maison de la presse Tahar Djaout, 1 rue Bachir Attar, place du 1er mai, 16016 Algiers; tel. (21) 68-54-21; fax (21) 68-54-22; e-mail latribun@latribune-online.com; internet www.latribune-online.com; f. 1994; current affairs journal in French; Dir HASSAN BACHIR-CHERIF; Editorial Dir ABDELKRIM GHEZALI.

La Voix de l'Oranie: 3 rue Rouis Rayah, Haï Oussama, 31000 Oran; tel. (41) 32-22-18; fax (41) 35-18-01; e-mail contact@voix-oranie.com; internet www.voix-oranie.com; French; Dir RAFIK CHARRAK.

El Watan: Maison de la presse, 1 rue Bachir Attar, place du 1er mai, 16016 Algiers; tel. (21) 68-21-83; fax (21) 68-21-87; e-mail admin@elwatan.com; internet www.elwatan.com; f. 1990; French; Dir OMAR BELHOUCHET; circ. 140,000.

El-Youm: Maison de la presse Tahar Djaout, 1 rue Bachir Attar, place du 1er mai, 16016 Algiers; tel. (21) 66-70-82; fax (21) 67-57-05; e-mail pubelyoum@yahoo.fr; internet www.elyawm.com; Arabic; Dirs MAHFOUD HADJI, AMINA HADJI; Editor KHALED LAKHDARI; circ. 54,000.

WEEKLIES

Les Débats: 2 blvd Muhammad V, Algiers; tel. (21) 63-73-05; fax (21) 63-70-05; e-mail lesdebats@hotmail.com; internet www.lesdebats.com; French; Dir AÏSSA KHELLADI.

Al-Mohakik Assiri (The Secret Enquirer): 2 ave Nafaâ Hafaf, Algiers; tel. (21) 71-05-58; e-mail almohakik@yahoo.fr; internet www.almohakik.com; f. 2006; Arabic; Dir HABET HANNACHI.

La Nation: 33 rue Larbi Ben M'hidi, Algiers; tel. (21) 43-21-76; f. 1992; French; Dir ATTIA OMAR; Editor SALIMA GHEZALI; circ. 35,000.

Révolution Africaine: Algiers; tel. (21) 59-77-91; fax (21) 59-77-92; current affairs journal in French; socialist; Dir FERRAH ABDELLALI; circ. 50,000.

OTHER PERIODICALS

Al-Acala: 4 rue Timgad, Hydra, Algiers; tel. (21) 60-85-55; fax (21) 60-09-36; f. 1970; publ. by the Ministry of Religious Affairs and Awqaf (Religious Endowments); fortnightly; Arabic; Editor MUHAMMAD AL-MAHDI.

Algérie Médicale: Algiers; f. 1964; publ. of the Union Médicale Algérienne; 2 a year; French; circ. 3,000.

Alouan (Colours): 119 rue Didouche Mourad, Algiers; f. 1973; cultural review; monthly; Arabic.

L'Auto Marché: 139 blvd Krim Belkacem; tel. (21) 74-44-59; fax (21) 74-14-63; e-mail contact@lautomarche.com; internet www

.lautomarche.com; f. 1998; fortnightly; French; motoring; Dir MOURAD CHEBOUB.

Bibliographie de l'Algérie: Bibliothèque Nationale d'Algérie, BP 127, Hamma el-Annasser, 16000 Algiers; tel. (21) 67-57-81; fax (21) 67-23-00; e-mail contact@biblionat.dz; internet www.biblionat.dz; f. 1963; lists books, theses, pamphlets and periodicals publ. in Algeria; bi-annual; Arabic and French; Dir-Gen. MUHAMMAD AÏSSA OUMOUSSA.

Le Buteur: Maison de la presse Tahar Djaout, 1 rue Bachir Attar, place du 1er mai, 16016 Algiers; tel. (21) 73-25-76; fax (21) 73-99-71; e-mail contact@lebuteur.com; internet www.lebuteur.com; Mon., Thur. and Sat.; French; sports; Dir BOUSAÂD KAHEL.

Al-Cha'ab al-Thakafi (Cultural People): Algiers; f. 1972; cultural monthly; Arabic.

Al-Chabab (Youth): Algiers; journal of the Union Nationale de la Jeunesse Algérienne; bi-monthly; Arabic and French.

Al-Djeich (The Army): Office de l'Armée Nationale Populaire, Algiers; f. 1963; monthly; Arabic and French; Algerian army review; circ. 10,000.

IT Mag: 5è groupe, Bat J, 1er Mai, Algiers; tel. (21) 66-29-92; fax (21) 65-03-28; e-mail info@itmag-dz.com; internet www.itmag.dz; f. 2002; French; telecommunications and IT in North Africa; Dir ABDERRAFIQ KHENIFSA.

Journal Officiel de la République Algérienne Démocratique et Populaire: pl. Seddik Ben Yahia, el-Mouradia, Algiers; tel. (21) 68-65-50; internet www.joradp.dz; f. 1962; Arabic and French.

Révolution et Travail: Maison du Peuple, 1 rue Abdelkader Benbarek, place du 1er mai, Algiers; tel. (21) 66-73-53; journal of the Union Générale des Travailleurs Algériens (central trade union) with Arabic and French edns; monthly; Editor-in-Chief RACHIB AÏT ALI.

Revue Algérienne du Travail: 28 rue Hassiba Bouali, Algiers; f. 1964; labour publ; quarterly; French; Dir A. DJAMAL.

Al-Thakafa (Culture): 2 place Cheikh Ben Badis, Algiers; tel. (21) 62-20-73; f. 1971; every 2 months; cultural review; Editor-in-Chief CHEBOUB OTHMANE; circ. 10,000.

NEWS AGENCIES

Agence Algérienne d'Information (AAI): Maison de la presse Tahar Djaout, 1 rue Bachir Attar, place du 1er mai, 16016 Algiers; tel. (21) 67-07-44; fax (21) 67-07-32; e-mail aai@aai-online.com; f. 1999; Dir HOURIA AÏT KACI.

Algérie Presse Service (APS): BP 444, 58 ave des Frères Bouadou, Bir Mourad Raïs, 16300 Algiers; tel. (21) 56-44-44; fax (21) 44-03-12; e-mail aps@aps.dz; internet www.aps.dz; f. 1961; provides news reports in Arabic, English and French.

Publishers

BERTI Editions: Lot el-Nadjah no 24, 16320 Dely Ibrahim, Algiers; tel. (21) 33-50-75; fax (21) 33-53-65; e-mail berti@berti-editions.com; internet www.berti-editions.com; f. 1995; publishes books on medicine, law, finance and IT; Dir MUHAMMAD GACI.

Casbah Editions: Lot Saïd Hamdine, Hydra, 16012 Algiers; tel. (21) 54-79-10; fax (21) 54-72-77; f. 1995; literature, essays, memoirs, textbooks and children's literature; Dir-Gen. SMAÏN AMZIANE.

CHIHAB Diffusion (CHIDIF): BP 74/4, Zone industriel de Reghaia, 16000 Algiers; tel. (21) 84-87-02; fax (21) 85-83-25; e-mail chidif@chihab.com; internet www.chihab.com; f. 1989; publishes educational textbooks.

Editions Bouchène: 4 rue de l'oasis, Algiers; tel. (21) 59-69-23; e-mail edbouchene@wanadoo.fr; internet www.bouchene.com; f. 1998; publishes books on the Maghreb region.

Editions Dahlab: 18 rue d'Auzia, Hydra, Algiers; tel. and fax (21) 69-40-06; e-mail editiondahlab@yahoo.fr; internet editions-dahlab .com; history, social sciences, economics; Dir ABDELLAH CHEGHNANE.

Editions du Tell: 3 rue des Frères Yacoub Torki, 09000 Blida; tel. (25) 31-10-35; fax (25) 31-10-36; e-mail contact@editions-du-tell.com; internet www.editions-du-tell.com; f. 2002; publishes books on literature, history, economics and social sciences.

Entreprise Nationale des Arts Graphiques (ENAG): BP 75, Zone industriel de Réghaia, Algiers; tel. (21) 84-86-11; fax (21) 84-80-08; e-mail edition@enag.dz; internet www.enag.dz; f. 1983; art, literature, social sciences, economics, science, religion, lifestyle and textbooks; Dir-Gen. HAMIDOU MESSAOUDI.

Maison d'Édition El Amel: Cité 600, Logement EPLF 53, 15000 Tizi Ouzou; tel. (26) 21-96-55; fax (26) 21-07-21; law and political science publishers.

Office des Publications Universitaires (OPU): 1 place Centrale de Ben Aknoun, 16306 Algiers; tel. (21) 91-23-14; fax (21) 91-21-81; e-mail info@opu-dz.com; internet www.opu-dz.com; publishes university textbooks; Dir-Gen. NOUREDDINE LACHEB.

Sedia: Cité les Mandariniers, Lot 293, al-Mohammadia, 16211 Algiers; tel. 770973861 (mobile); fax (21) 21-90-16; e-mail sedia@sedia-dz.com; internet www.sedia-dz.com; f. 2000; literature and educational textbooks; Pres. and Dir-Gen. BRAHIM DJELMAMI-HANI.

Broadcasting and Communications

TELECOMMUNICATIONS

New legislation approved by the National People's Assembly in August 2000 removed the state's monopoly over the telecommunications sector and redefined its role to that of a supervisory authority. Under the legislation, an independent regulator for the sector was created, and both the fixed-line and mobile sectors were opened to foreign competition.

Algérie Télécom: route Nationale 5, Cinq Maisons, Mohammadia, 16130 Algiers; tel. (21) 82-38-38; fax (21) 82-38-39; e-mail contact@algerietelecom.dz; internet www.algerietelecom.dz; f. 2001 to manage and develop telecommunications infrastructure; Pres. and Dir-Gen. AZOUAOU MEHMEL.

Mobilis: Site Sider, 7 rue Belkacem Amani, Paradou, Hydra, Algiers; tel. (21) 54-71-63; fax (21) 54-72-72; e-mail commercial@mobilis.dz; internet www.mobilis.dz; f. 2003; subsidiary of Algérie Télécom; Pres. and Dir-Gen. SAÂD DAMMA.

AnwarNet SPA: 11 rue Ahmad Ouaked, Dely Ibrahim, Algiers; tel. (21) 91-71-10; fax (21) 91-04-77; e-mail infos@anwarnet.dz; internet www.anwarnet.dz; internet and VOIP service provider; Dir-Gen. MUHAMMAD FADI GOUASMIA.

Djezzy GSM: Orascom Telecom Algérie, rue Mouloud Feraoun, Lot no. 8A, el-Beida, Algiers; tel. (70) 85-00-00; fax (70) 85-70-85; e-mail djezzy.entreprises@otalgerie.com; internet www.djezzy.com; f. 2002; operates mobile cellular telephone network; some 17m. subscribers (2013); Exec. Pres. VINCENZO NESCI.

Wataniya Telecom Algérie (Nedjma): BP 74, Algiers; e-mail mtouati@wta.dz; internet www.nedjma.dz; f. 2004; owned by Nat. Mobile Telecommunications Co KSC (Kuwait); offers mobile cellular telecommunications services under brand name Nedjma; Dir-Gen. JOSEPH GED.

Regulatory Authority

Autorité de Régulation de la Poste et des Télécommunications (ARPT): 1 rue Kaddour Rahim, Hussein Dey, 16008 Algiers; tel. (21) 47-02-05; fax (21) 47-01-97; e-mail info@arpt.dz; internet www.arpt.dz; f. 2001; Pres. MUHAMMAD TOUFIK BESSAI; Dir-Gen. MUHAMMAD AMGHAR.

BROADCASTING

Radio

Radiodiffusion Algérienne (ENRS): 21 blvd des Martyrs, Algiers; tel. (21) 48-37-90; fax (21) 23-08-23; e-mail info@algerian-radio.dz; internet www.radioalgerie.dz; govt-controlled; operates 30 local radio stations; Dir-Gen. CHABANE LOUNAKEL.

Arabic Network: transmitters at Adrar, Aïn Beïda, Algiers, Béchar, Béni Abbès, Djanet, El Goléa, Ghardaïa, Hassi Messaoud, In Aménas, In Salah, Laghouat, Les Trembles, Ouargla, Reggane, Tamanrasset, Timimoun, Tindouf.

French Network: transmitters at Algiers, Constantine, Oran and Tipaza.

Kabyle Network: transmitter at Algiers.

Television

The principal transmitters are at Algiers, Batna, Sidi-Bel-Abbès, Constantine, Souk-Ahras and Tlemcen. Television plays a major role in the national education programme.

Télédiffusion d'Algérie: BP 50, Algiers; tel. (21) 90-17-17; fax (21) 90-15-22; e-mail contact@tda.dz; internet www.tda.dz; f. 1991; govt-controlled; Dir-Gen ABD AL-MALEK HOUYOU.

Télévision Algérienne (ENTV): BP 16070, 21 blvd des Martyrs, Algiers; tel. (21) 60-23-00; fax (21) 60-19-22; e-mail alger-contact@entv.dz; internet www.entv.dz; f. 1986; govt-controlled; Dir-Gen. TEWFIK KHELLADI.

Finance

(cap. = capital; res = reserves; dep. = deposits; brs = branches; m. = million; amounts in Algerian dinars)

BANKING

Central Bank

Banque d'Algérie: Immeuble Joly, 38 ave Franklin Roosevelt, 16000 Algiers; tel. (21) 23-00-23; fax (21) 23-03-71; e-mail ba@bank-of-algeria.dz; internet www.bank-of-algeria.dz; f. 1962 as Banque Centrale d'Algérie; present name adopted 1990; bank of issue; cap. 40m., res 74,367.5m. (March 2006); Gov. MUHAMMAD LAKSACI; 48 brs.

Nationalized Banks

Banque Al-Baraka d'Algérie: Haï Bouteldja Houidef, Villa 1, Ben Aknoun, Algiers; tel. (21) 91-27-67; fax (21) 91-64-57; e-mail info@albaraka-bank.com; internet www.albaraka-bank.com; f. 1991; Algeria's first Islamic financial institution; owned by the Saudi Arabia-based Al-Baraka Investment and Devt Co (56%) and the local Banque de l'Agriculture et du Développement Rural (44%); cap. 10,000m., res 3,912m., dep. 86,396m. (Dec. 2012); Chair. ADNANE AHMAD YOUCEF; Gen. Man. HAFID MUHAMMAD SEDDIK; 18 brs.

Banque Extérieure d'Algérie (BEA): 48 rue des Trois Frères Bouadou, Bir Mourad Raïs, Algiers; tel. (21) 44-90-25; fax (21) 56-17-40; e-mail dtm-direction@bea.dz; internet www.bea.dz; f. 1967; chiefly concerned with energy and maritime transport sectors; cap. 76,000m., res 77,029m., dep. 1,902,350m. (Dec. 2012); Pres. and Dir-Gen. MUHAMMAD LOUKAL; 80 domestic brs, 1 abroad.

Banque du Maghreb Arabe pour l'Investissement et le Commerce (BAMIC): 7 rue Dubois, Hydra, Algiers; tel. (21) 69-45-43; fax (21) 60-19-54; e-mail bamic@bamic-dz.com; internet www.bamic-dz.com; f. 1988; owned by Libyan Arab Foreign Bank (50%) and by Banque Extérieure d'Algérie, Banque Nationale d'Algérie, Banque de l'Agriculture et du Développement Rural and Crédit Populaire d'Algérie (12.5% each); cap. 50m., res 16.2m. (Dec. 2005); Pres. MUHAMMAD DJELLAB; Dir-Gen. TAHER NEFFATI.

Crédit Populaire d'Algérie (CPA): BP 411, 2 blvd Col Amirouche, 16000 Algiers; tel. (23) 50-32-62; fax (23) 50-32-64; e-mail info@cpa-bank.com; internet www.cpa-bank.dz; f. 1966; specializes in light industry, construction and tourism; cap. 48,000m., res 42,782m., dep. 958,566m. (Dec. 2012); Pres. and Dir-Gen. MUHAMMAD DJELLAB; 128 brs.

Development Banks

Banque de l'Agriculture et du Développement Rural (BADR): BP 484, 17 blvd Col Amirouche, 16000 Algiers; tel. (21) 63-49-22; fax (21) 63-51-46; e-mail dcm@badr-bank.net; internet www.badr-bank.net; f. 1982; wholly state-owned; finance for the agricultural sector; cap. 33,000m., res 10,148m., dep. 711,222m. (Dec. 2010); Pres. and Dir-Gen. BOUALEM DJEBBAR; 270 brs.

Banque de Développement Local (BDL): 5 rue Gaci Amar, Staouéli, 16000 Algiers; tel. (21) 39-28-20; fax (21) 39-37-57; e-mail clientele@bdl.dz; internet www.bdl.dz; f. 1985; regional devt bank; cap. 15,800m., res 11,775m., dep. 296,702m. (Dec. 2012); CEO MUHAMMAD ARSLANE BACHTARZI; 150 brs.

Caisse Nationale d'Epargne et de Prévoyance (CNEP-Banque): 42 rue Khélifa Boukhalfa, Algiers; tel. (21) 71-33-53; fax (21) 71-70-22; e-mail infos@cnepbanque.dz; internet www.cnepbanque.dz; f. 1964; savings and housing bank; cap. and res 22.6m., total assets 443,239.6m. (Dec. 2001); Pres. and Dir-Gen. DJAMEL BESSA.

Fonds National d'Investissement (FNI): 21 blvd Zighout Youcef, Algiers; tel. (21) 73-99-04; fax (21) 55-55-20; e-mail bad@ist.cerist.dz; f. 1963; fmrly, Banque Algérienne de Développement, name changed as above in 2009; a public establishment with fiscal sovereignty; aims to contribute to Algerian economic devt through long-term investment programmes; cap. and res 7,125.4m., total assets 132,842.3m. (Dec. 2003); Dir-Gen. SADEK ALILAT; 4 brs.

Private Banks

Arab Banking Corporation-Algeria (ABC Bank): BP 367, 54 ave des Trois Frères Bouadou, Algiers; tel. (21) 54-15-37; fax (21) 54-16-04; e-mail abc.general_management@arabbanking.com.dz; internet www.arabbanking.dz; f. 1998; cap. 10,000m., res 1,775m., dep. 30,860m. (Dec. 2012); Chair. Dr MUHAMMAD ABD EL-SALAM SHOKRI.

Arab Leasing Corpn: 3, rue Ahmed Ouaked, Dély Ibrahim, Algiers; tel. (21) 33-63-93; fax (21) 33-63-90; e-mail Contact@arableasing-dz.com; internet www.arableasing-dz.com; f. 2001; owned by Arab Banking Corpn (41%), The Arab Investment Co (25%), CNEP (27%) and other small shareholders; cap. and res 758m., total assets 801.6m. (Dec. 2002); Dir-Gen. ABDENOUR HOUAOUI.

BNP Paribas El-Djazair: 8 rue de Cirta, 16405 Hydra, Algiers; tel. (21) 60-39-42; fax (21) 60-39-29; e-mail mounir.belaidene@bnpparibas.com; internet www.bnpparibas.dz; f. 2001; cap. 10,000m., res 3,493m., dep. 156,429m. (Dec. 2012); Dir-Gen. LAURENT DUPUCH.

Gulf Bank Algeria: BP 26, route de Chérage, Dély Ibrahim, Algiers; tel. (21) 91-00-31; fax (21) 91-02-37; e-mail agbank_dz@hotmail.com; internet www.ag-bank.com; f. 2004; owned by United Gulf Bank, Bahrain (60%), Tunis Int. Bank (30%) and Jordan Kuwait Bank (10%); cap. 10,000m., res 397m., dep. 73,253m. (Dec. 2012); Pres. ABDELKRIM AL-KABARITY; Man. Dir MUHAMMAD LOUAB.

Trust Bank Algeria: 70 chemin Larbi Allik, Hydra, Algiers; tel. (21) 54-97-55; fax (21) 54-97-50; e-mail direction@trust-bank-algeria.com; internet www.trust-bank-algeria.com; f. 2002; cap. 13,000m., res 3,142m., dep. 14,724m. (Dec. 2012); Dir-Gen. SENOUCI OULD KABLIA; 3 brs.

Banking Association

Association des Banques et des Etablissements Financiers (ABEF): 03 chemin Romain, Val d'Hydra, el-Biar, Algiers; tel. (21) 91-55-77; fax (21) 91-56-08; e-mail abenkhalfa@gmail.com; f. 1995; serves and promotes the interests of banks and financial institutions in Algeria; Del.-Gen. ABDERREZAK TRABELSI.

STOCK EXCHANGE

Bourse d'Alger (Algiers Stock Exchange): 27 blvd Col Amirouche, 16000 Algiers; tel. and fax (21) 63-47-99; e-mail sgbv-email@sgbv.dz; internet www.sgbv.dz; f. 1999; Pres. MILOUD GHOLLAM; Dir-Gen. MUSTAPHA FERFERA.

Commission d'Organisation et de Surveillance des Opérations de Bourse (COSOB): 17 Campagne Chkiken, 16045 Hydra, Algiers; tel. and fax (21) 59-10-13; e-mail contact@cosob.org; internet www.cosob.org; f. 1993; Pres. ABD EL-HAKIM BERRAH.

INSURANCE

The insurance sector is dominated by the state; however, in 1997 regulations were drafted to permit private companies to enter the Algerian insurance market.

L'Algérienne des Assurances (2a): 1 rue de Tripoli, Hussein-Dey, Algiers; tel. (21) 47-68-72; fax (21) 47-65-78; e-mail info@assurances-2a.com; internet www.assurances-2a.com; f. 1999; general; Pres. ABDELWAHAB RAHIM; Dir-Gen. TAHAR BALA.

Caisse Nationale de Mutualité Agricole (CNMA): 24 blvd Victor Hugo, Algiers; tel. (21) 74-33-28; fax (21) 73-34-79; e-mail cnma@cnma.dz; internet www.cnma.dz; f. 1972; Dir-Gen. KAMEL ARBA; 62 brs.

Cie Algérienne d'Assurance et de Réassurance (CAAR): 48 rue Didouche Mourad, 16000 Algiers; tel. (21) 63-20-72; fax (21) 63-13-77; e-mail caaralg@caar.com.dz; internet www.caar.com.dz; f. 1963 as a public corpn; partial privatization pending; Pres. and Dir-Gen. BRAHIM DJAMEL KASSALI.

Cie Algérienne d'Assurances (CAAT): 52 rue des Frères Bouaddou, Bir Mourad Raïs, Algiers; tel. (21) 44-90-75; fax (21) 44-92-03; e-mail info@caat.dz; internet www.caat.dz; f. 1985; general; majority state ownership; Pres. and Dir-Gen. ABDELKRIM DJAFRI.

Cie Centrale de Réassurance (CCR): Lot Saïd Hamdine, Bir Mourad Raïs, 16012 Algiers; tel. (21) 54-70-33; fax (21) 54-75-06; e-mail contact@ccr.dz; internet www.ccr.dz; f. 1973; general; Pres. and Dir-Gen. HADJ MUHAMMAD SEBA.

Société Nationale d'Assurances (SAA): 5 blvd Ernesto Ché Guévara, Algiers; tel. (21) 71-47-60; fax (21) 71-22-16; internet www.saa.dz; f. 1963; state-sponsored co; Pres. and Dir-Gen. AMARA LATROUS.

Trust Algeria Assurances-Réassurance: 70 chemin Larbi Allik, 16405 Hydra, Algiers; tel. (21) 54-88-00; fax (21) 54-71-36; e-mail secretariat@trustalgerians.com; f. 1987; 60% owned by Trust Insurance Co (Bahrain), 17.5% owned by CAAR; Pres. and Dir-Gen. ABD AL-SALAM ABU NAHL.

Trade and Industry

GOVERNMENT AGENCIES AND DEVELOPMENT ORGANIZATIONS

Agence Algérienne de Promotion du Commerce Extérieur (ALGEX): 5 rue Nationale, Algiers; tel. (21) 52-12-10; fax (21) 52-11-26; e-mail info@algex.dz; internet www.algex.dz; f. 2004; Dir-Gen. MUHAMMAD BENNINI.

Agence Nationale de l'Aménagement du Territoire (ANAT): 30 ave Muhammad Fellah, Kouba, Algiers; tel. (21) 68-78-16; fax (21)

68-85-03; e-mail anat@anat.dz; f. 1980; Dir-Gen. MUHAMMAD MEKKAOUI.

Agence Nationale de Développement de l'Investissement (ANDI): 27 rue Muhammad Merbouche, Hussein-Dey, Algiers; tel. (21) 77-32-62; fax (21) 77-32-57; e-mail dg@andi.dz; internet www.andi.dz; Dir-Gen. ABDELKARIM MANSOURI.

Institut National de la Productivité et du Développement Industriel (INPED): 35000 Boumerdès; tel. (24) 81-77-50; fax (24) 81-59-14; e-mail dg@inped.edu.dz; internet www.inped.edu.dz; f. 1967; Dir-Gen. ABDERRAHMANE MOUFEK.

Office National de Recherche Géologique et Minière (ORGM): BP 102, Cité Ibn Khaldoun, 35000 Boumerdès; tel. (24) 81-75-99; fax (24) 81-83-79; e-mail orgm-dg@orgm.com.dz; f. 1992; mining, cartography, geophysical exploration; Dir-Gen. ESSAID AOULI.

CHAMBERS OF COMMERCE

Chambre Algérienne de Commerce et d'Industrie (CACI): BP 100, Palais Consulaire, 6 blvd Amilcar Cabral, place des Martyres, 16003 Algiers; tel. (21) 96-77-77; fax (21) 96-70-70; e-mail infos@caci.dz; internet www.caci.dz; f. 1980; Pres. TAHER KELLIL; Dir-Gen. YAHIA SAHRAOUI.

Chambre Française de Commerce et d'Industrie en Algérie (CFCIA): Villa Clarac, 3 rue des Cèdres, 16070 el-Mouradia, Algiers; tel. (21) 48-08-00; fax (21) 60-95-09; e-mail jf.heugas@cfcia.org; internet www.cfcia.org; f. 1975; c. 24,500 mems; Pres. JEAN MARIE PINEL.

INDUSTRIAL ASSOCIATIONS

Centre d'Etudes et de Services Technologiques de l'Industrie des Matériaux de Construction (CETIM): BP 93, Cité Ibn Khaldoun, 35000 Boumerdès; tel. (24) 81-99-72; fax (24) 81-72-97; e-mail contact@cetim-dz.com; f. 1982; CEO ABDENNOUR ADJTOUTAH.

Institut National Algérien de la Propriété Industrielle (INAPI): 42 rue Larbi Ben M'hidi, 16000 Algiers; tel. (21) 73-01-42; fax (21) 73-55-81; e-mail info@inapi.org; internet www.inapi.org; f. 1973; Dir-Gen. ABD EL-HAFID BELMEHDI.

Institut National des Industries Manufacturières (INIM): 35000 Boumerdès; tel. (21) 81-62-71; fax (21) 82-56-62; f. 1973; Dir-Gen. YOUSUF OUSLIMANI.

STATE TRADING ORGANIZATIONS

Since 1970 all international trading has been carried out by state organizations, of which the following are the most important:

Entreprise Nationale d'Approvisionnement en Outillage et Produits de Quincaillerie Générale (ENAOQ): 5 rue Amar Semaous, Hussein-Dey, Algiers; tel. (21) 23-31-83; fax (21) 47-83-33; tools and general hardware; Dir-Gen. SMATI BAHIDJ FARID.

Entreprise Nationale de Produits Alimentaires (ENAPAL): 29 rue Larbi Ben M'hidi, Algiers; tel. (21) 76-10-11; f. 1983; monopoly of import, export and bulk trade in basic foodstuffs; brs in more than 40 towns; Chair. LAÏD SABRI; Man. Dir BRAHIM DOUAOURI.

Office Algérien Interprofessionnel des Céréales (OAIC): 5 rue Ferhat-Boussaad, Algiers; tel. (21) 23-73-04; fax (21) 23-70-83; e-mail oaic@ist.cerist.dz; f. 1962; responsible for the regulation, distribution and control of the national market and the importation of cereals and vegetables; Dir-Gen. MUHAMMAD KACEM.

Office National de Commercialisation des Produits Viti-Vinicoles (ONCV): 112 Quai Sud, Algiers; tel. (21) 73-82-59; fax (21) 73-72-97; e-mail info@oncv-dz.com; internet www.oncv-groupe.com; f. 1968; monopoly of importing and exporting products of the wine industry; Man. Dir MAJID AMZIANI.

Société des Emballages Fer Blanc et Fûts (EMB-FBF): BP 245, Kouba, route de Baraki, Gué de Constantine, Algiers; tel. (21) 83-94-23; fax (21) 83-05-29; e-mail info@emb-fbf.com; internet www.emb-fbf.com; Dir-Gen. HAMID ZITOUN.

UTILITIES

Regulatory Authority

Commission de Régulation de l'Electricité et du Gaz (CREG): Immeuble du Ministère de l'Energie et des Mines, Tour B, Val d'Hydra, Algiers; tel. (21) 48-81-48; fax (21) 48-84-00; e-mail contact@creg.mem.gov.dz; internet www.creg.gov.dz; f. 2005; Pres. NADJIB OTMANE.

Electricity and Gas

Linde Gas Algérie SpA (GI): BP 247, 23 ave de l'ALN, Hussein-Dey, Kouba, Algiers; tel. (21) 49-85-99; fax (21) 49-71-94; internet www.gaz-industriels.com.dz; f. 1972 as Entreprise Nationale des Gaz Industriels; production, distribution and commercialization of industrial and medical gas; Pres. and Dir-Gen. LAHOCINE BOUCHERIT.

New Energy Algeria (NEAL): 15 Haouche Kaouche, Dely Ibrahim, 16302 Algiers; tel. (21) 37-28-83; fax (21) 37-28-84; e-mail info@neal-dz.net; internet www.neal-dz.net; a jt venture between Sonatrach and Sonelgaz; promotion and development of new and renewable energy sources, and the completion of related projects.

Société Algérienne de l'Electricité et du Gaz (Sonelgaz SpA): 2 blvd Col Krim Belkacem, Algiers; tel. (21) 72-31-00; fax (21) 71-26-90; e-mail n.boutarfa@sonelgaz.dz; internet www.sonelgaz.dz; f. 1969; production, distribution and transportation of electricity, and transportation and distribution of natural gas; Chair. and CEO NOUREDDINE BOUTARFA.

Société de Travaux d'Electrification (KAHRIF): Villa Nour, Aïn d'Heb, Médéa; tel. (25) 58-51-67; fax (25) 61-31-14; e-mail djellouli.yazid@kahrif.com; internet www.kahrif.com; f. 1982; planning and maintenance of electrical infrastructure; Pres. and Dir-Gen. YAZID DJELLOULI.

Water

L'Algérienne des Eaux (ADE): BP 548, 3 rue du Caire, Kouba, 16016 Algiers; tel. (21) 28-28-07; fax (21) 28-10-06; internet www.ade.dz; f. 1985 as Agence Nationale de l'Eau Potable et Industrielle et de l'Assainissement; state-owned co; Dir-Gen. ABDELKRIM MECHIA.

STATE HYDROCARBONS AGENCIES AND COMPANIES

Agence Nationale pour la Valorisation des Ressources en Hydrocarbures (Alnaft): Ministère de l'Energie et des Mines, Tour B, Val d'Hydra, Algiers; tel. (21) 48-82-67; fax (21) 48-82-76; e-mail firstender-alnaft@alnaft.mem.gov.dz; f. 2005; Dir SID ALI BETATA.

Autorité de Régulation des Hydrocarbures (ARH): Ministère de l'Energie et des Mines, Tour B, Val d'Hydra, Algiers; tel. (21) 48-81-67; fax (21) 48-83-15; e-mail arh@arh.mem.gov.dz; internet www.arh.gov.dz; f. 2005; Dir NOUREDDINE CHEROUATI.

Société Nationale pour la Recherche, la Production, le Transport, la Transformation et la Commercialisation des Hydrocarbures (Sonatrach): Djenane el-Malik, Hydra, Algiers; tel. (21) 54-70-00; fax (21) 54-77-00; e-mail sonatrach@sonatrach.dz; internet www.sonatrach-dz.com; f. 1963; exploration, exploitation, transport and marketing of petroleum, natural gas and their products; Pres. and Dir-Gen. ABDELHAMID ZERGUINE; Gen. Sec. ABDELMALEK ZITOUNI.

The following companies are wholly owned subsidiaries of Sonatrach:

Entreprise Nationale de Canalisation (ENAC): 132 rue Tripoli, Algiers; tel. (21) 77-04-63; fax (21) 53-85-53; internet www.enac-dz.com; piping; Vice-Pres. HOCINE CHEKIRED.

Entreprise Nationale de Forage (ENAFOR): BP 211, Hassi Messaoud, W. Ouargla; tel. (29) 73-81-85; fax (29) 73-21-70; e-mail zoubir@enafor.dz; internet www.enafor.dz; f. 1981; drilling; CEO ABDELKADER ZOUBIRI.

Entreprise Nationale de Géophysique (ENAGEO): BP 140, 30500 Hassi Messaoud, Ouargla; tel. (29) 73-77-00; fax (29) 73-72-12; e-mail engeoh1@wissal.dz; internet www.enageo.com; f. 1981; seismic acquisition, geophysics; Dir-Gen. RÉDA RAHAL.

Entreprise Nationale des Grands Travaux Pétroliers (ENGTP): BP 09, Zone Industrielle, Reghaïa, Boumerdès; tel. (21) 84-86-26; fax (21) 84-80-34; e-mail engtpcommunication@engtp.com; internet www.engtp.com; f. 1980; major industrial projects; Dir-Gen. MUHAMMAD SEGHIR LAOUISSI.

Entreprise Nationale des Services aux Puits (ENSP): BP 83, 30500 Hassi Messaoud, Ouargla; tel. (29) 73-73-33; e-mail info@enspgroup.com; internet www.enspgroup.com; f. 1981; oil-well services; Pres. and Dir-Gen. ABDELWAHAB OUBIRA.

Entreprise Nationale des Travaux aux Puits (ENTP): BP 206–207, Base du 20 août 1955, 30500 Hassi Messaoud, Ouargla; tel. (29) 73-88-50; fax (29) 73-84-06; e-mail contact@entp-dz.com; internet www.entp-dz.com; f. 1981; oil-well construction; Pres. and Dir-Gen. BACHIR BEN AMOR.

Société Nationale de Commercialisation et de Distribution des Produits Pétroliers (NAFTAL, SpA): BP 73, route des Dûnes, Chéraga, Algiers; tel. (21) 38-13-13; fax (21) 38-19-19; e-mail webmaster@naftal.dz; internet www.naftal.dz; f. 1987; international marketing and distribution of petroleum products; Pres. and Dir-Gen. SAÏD AKRETCHE.

Société Nationale de Génie Civil et Bâtiment (GCB, SpA): BP 110, blvd de l'ALN, Boumerdès-Ville; tel. (24) 41-41-50; fax (24) 81-38-80; e-mail contact@gcb.dz; internet www.gcb.dz; civil engineering.

Société Nationale de la Pétrochimie (ENIP): BP 215, Zone industrielle, 21000 Skikda; tel. (38) 74-52-94; fax (38) 74-52-80; e-mail inr@enip-dz.com; f. 1984; design and construction for petroleum-processing industry; Dir-Gen. N. KOURDACHE.

TRADE UNIONS

Syndicat National des Journalistes (Algerian Journalists' Union): Maison de la presse Tahar Djaout, 1 rue Bachir Attar, place du 1er mai, 16016 Algiers; tel. and fax (21) 67-36-61; e-mail snjalgerie2006@yahoo.fr; f. 2001; Sec.-Gen. KAMEL AMARNI.

Union Générale des Entrepreneurs Algériens (UGEA): Villa 28, Quartier Aïn Soltane, les Oliviers, Birkhadem, Algiers; tel. and fax (21) 54-10-82; e-mail contact@ugea-dz.com; internet www.ugea-dz.com; f. 1989; Pres. Dr ABDELMADJID DENNOUNI.

Union Générale des Travailleurs Algériens (UGTA): Maison du Peuple, place du 1er mai, Algiers; tel. (21) 65-07-36; e-mail sgeneral@ugta.dz; internet www.ugta.dz; f. 1956; there are 10 national 'professional sectors' affiliated to the UGTA; Sec.-Gen. ABDELMADJID SIDI SAÏD.

Union Nationale des Paysans Algériens (UNPA): f. 1973; 700,000 mems; Sec.-Gen. MUHAMMAD ALIOUI.

Transport

RAILWAYS

In 2010 the total length of Algerian railways was 3,512 km.

Entreprise du Métro d'Alger (EMA): 170 rue Hassiba Ben Bouali, Algiers; tel. (21) 66-17-47; fax (21) 66-17-57; e-mail contact@metroalger-dz.com; internet metroalger-dz.com; initial 9-km section (10 stations) commenced operations Nov. 2011; construction of a second line currently underway, as well as extensions to line 1; Pres. and Dir-Gen. OMAR HADBI.

Infrafer (Entreprise Publique Economique de Réalisation des Infrastructures Ferroviaires): BP 208, 15 rue Col Amirouche, 35300 Rouiba; tel. (21) 85-67-02; fax (21) 85-49-62; e-mail info@infrafer.com; internet www.infrafer.com; f. 1986; responsible for construction and maintenance of track; Dir-Gen. ABDERAHMANE AKTOUF.

Société Nationale des Transports Ferroviaires (SNTF): 21–23 blvd Muhammad V, Algiers; tel. (21) 71-15-10; fax (21) 63-32-98; e-mail dg-sntf@sntf.dz; internet www.sntf.dz; f. 1976 to replace Société Nationale des Chemins de Fer Algériens; daily passenger services from Algiers to the principal provincial cities and services to Tunisia and Morocco; Dir-Gen. OMAR BENAMEUR.

ROADS

In 2010 there were an estimated 113,655 km of roads, including 29,468 km of highways, main or national roads, 24,108 km of secondary, regional roads and 60,079 km of other roads. The French administration built a good road system (partly for military purposes), which, since independence, has been allowed to deteriorate in places. New roads have been built linking the Sahara oilfields with the coast, and the Trans-Sahara highway is a major project. Construction of the 1,216-km East–West motorway, linking el-Tarf with Tlemcen, at an estimated cost of more than US $11,000m., was scheduled for completion by the end of 2010. However, by early 2012 only around 1,000 km of the route was open to traffic. It was subsequently reported that the remaining sections would not open until late 2013.

Agence Nationale des Autoroutes (ANA): BP 72M Mohammadia, El Harrach, Algiers; tel. (21) 53-09-63; fax (21) 53-09-62; e-mail dgana@ana.org.dz; internet www.ana.org.dz; f. 2005 to manage the construction and maintenance of the motorway network; Dir-Gen. MUHAMMAD ZIANI.

Société Nationale des Transports Routiers (SNTR): 27 rue des Trois Frères Bouadou, Bir Mourad Raïs, Algiers; tel. (21) 54-06-00; fax (21) 54-05-35; e-mail dg-sntr@sntr-groupe.com; internet www.sntr-groupe.com; f. 1967; goods transport by road; maintainance of industrial vehicles; Pres. and Dir-Gen. ABDELLAH BENMAÂROUF.

Société Nationale des Transports des Voyageurs (SNTV): Algiers; tel. (21) 66-00-52; f. 1967; long-distance passenger transport by road; Man. Dir MUHAMMAD DIB.

SHIPPING

Algiers is the main port, with anchorage of between 23 m and 29 m in the Bay of Algiers, and anchorage for the largest vessels in Agha Bay. The port has a total quay length of 8,610 m. In November 2008 United Arab Emirates-based DP World signed a 30-year contract with the Algerian Government to manage and redevelop the ports at Algiers and Djen-Djen. The proposed redevelopment at Algiers port included an expansion of capacity from 500,000 20-ft equivalent units (TEUs) to 800,000 TEUs. DP World officially commenced operations at Algiers in March 2009 and at Djen-Djen in June. There are also important ports at Annaba, Arzew, Béjaïa, Djidjelli, Ghazaouet, Mostaganem, Oran, Skikda and Ténès. Petroleum and liquefied gas are exported through Arzew, Béjaïa and Skikda. Algerian crude petroleum is also exported through the Tunisian port of La Skhirra. At 31 December 2013 Algeria's flag-registered fleet totalled 177 vessels, with an aggregate displacement of 788,023 grt. Of those vessels, four were bulk carriers, seven were fish carriers, 11 were gas tankers and 10 were general cargo ships.

Port Authorities

Entreprise Portuaire d'Alger (EPAL): BP 259, 2 rue d'Angkor, Alger-Gare, Algiers; tel. (21) 42-36-14; fax (21) 42-36-03; e-mail epal@portalger.com.dz; internet www.portalger.com.dz; f. 1982; responsible for management and growth of port facilities and sea pilotage; Dir-Gen. ABDELAZIZ GUERRAH.

Entreprise Portuaire d'Annaba (EPAN): BP 1232, Môle Cigogne, quai Nord, 23000 Annaba; tel. (38) 86-31-31; fax (38) 86-54-15; e-mail epan@annaba-port.com; internet www.annaba-port.com; Pres. and Dir-Gen. DJILANI SALHI.

Entreprise Portuaire d'Arzew (EPA): BP 46, 7 rue Larbi Tebessi, 31200 Arzew; tel. and fax (41) 47-21-27; e-mail contact@arzew-ports.com; internet www.arzewports.com; Pres. and Dir-Gen. NOUREDDINE HADJIOUI.

Entreprise Portuaire de Béjaïa (EPB): BP 94, 13 ave des frères Amrani, 06000 Béjaïa; tel. (34) 21-18-07; fax (34) 20-14-88; e-mail portbj@portdebejaia.dz; internet www.portdebejaia.dz; Dir-Gen. DJELLOUL ACHOUR.

Entreprise Portuaire de Djen-Djen (EPJ): BP 87, El Achouat Taher-Wilaya de JIJEL, 18000 Jijel; tel. (34) 44-21-64; fax (34) 44-21-60; e-mail contact@djendjen-port.com; internet www.djendjen-port.com; f. 1984; Dir-Gen. ABDERREZAK SELLAMI.

Entreprise Portuaire de Ghazaouet (EPG): BP 217, Wilaya de Tlemcen, 13400 Ghazaouet; tel. (43) 32-32-37; fax (43) 32-32-55; e-mail contact@portdeghazaouet.com; internet www.portdeghazaouet.com; f. 1982; Pres. and Dir-Gen. BRAHIM ABDELMALEK.

Entreprise Portuaire de Mostaganem (EPM): BP 131, quai du Maghreb, 27000 Mostaganem; tel. (45) 21-14-11; fax (45) 21-78-05; e-mail epm@port-mostaganem.dz; internet www.port-mostaganem.dz; Pres. and Dir-Gen. MOKHTAR CHERIF.

Entreprise Portuaire d'Oran (EPO): 1 rue du 20 août, 31000 Oran; tel. (41) 33-24-49; fax (41) 33-24-98; e-mail pdg@port-oran.dz; internet www.port-oran.dz; Dir-Gen. MUHAMMAD BOUTOUIL (acting).

Entreprise Portuaire de Skikda (EPS): BP 65, 46 ave Rezki Rahal, 21000 Skikda; tel. (38) 75-68-50; fax (38) 75-20-15; e-mail epskikda@skikda-port.com; internet www.skikda-port.com; Man. Dir LAÏDI LEMRABET.

Entreprise Portuaire de Ténès (EPT): BP 18, Wilaya de Chlef, 02200 Ténès; tel. (27) 76-61-96; fax (27) 76-61-77; e-mail porttenes@yahoo.fr; internet www.portdetenes.dz; f. 1985; Man. Dir ALI ASSENOUNI.

Principal Shipping Companies

Cie Algéro-Libyenne de Transport Maritime (CALTRAM): 19 rue des Trois Frères Bouadou, Bir Mourad Raïs, Algiers; tel. (21) 54-17-00; fax (21) 54-21-04; e-mail caltram@wissal.dz; f. 1974; Man. Dir A. KERAMANE.

Cie Nationale de Navigation (CNAN Group): BP 280, 2 quai no 9, Nouvelle Gare Maritime, Algiers; tel. (21) 42-33-89; fax (21) 42-31-28; f. 2003 as part of restructuring of the Société Nationale de Transports Maritimes/Compagnie Nationale Algérienne de Navigation (SNTM/CNAN); state-owned; fleet of 12 freight ships; includes CNAN Maghreb Lines; rep. offices in Marseille (France) and La Spezia (Italy), and rep. agencies in Antwerp (Belgium), Barcelona (Spain), Hamburg (Germany) and the principal ports in many other countries; Dir-Gen. ALI BOUMBAR.

Entreprise Nationale de Réparation Navale (ERENAV): quai no 12, Algiers; tel. (21) 42-37-83; fax (21) 42-30-39; e-mail azzedine.bourouga@erenav.com; f. 1987; ship repairs; Pres. and Dir-Gen. A. BOUROUGA.

Entreprise Nationale de Transport Maritime de Voyageurs—Algérie Ferries (ENTMV): BP 467, 5–6 rue Jawharlal Nehru, 16001 Algiers; tel. (21) 42-46-50; fax (21) 42-98-74; e-mail entmv@algerieferries.com; internet www.algerieferries.com; f. 1987 as part of restructuring of SNTM-CNAN; responsible for passenger transport; operates car ferry services between Algiers, Annaba, Skikda, Alicante (Spain), Marseille (France) and Oran; Dir-Gen. AHCÈNE GRAÏRIA.

HYPROC Shipping Co (HYPROC SC): BP 7200, Zone des Sièges 'ZHUN-USTO', el-Seddikia, 31025 Oran; tel. (41) 42-62-62; fax (41) 42-32-75; e-mail hyproc@hyproc.com; internet www.hyproc.com; f. 1982 as Société Nationale de Transports Maritimes des Hydrocarbures et des Produits Chimiques; name changed as above in 2003; wholly owned subsidiary of Sonatrach; Pres. and Dir-Gen. MOSTEFA MUHAMMADI.

Société Générale Maritime (GEMA): BP 368, 2 rue Jawharlal Nehru, 16100 Algiers; tel. (21) 74-73-00; fax (21) 74-76-73; e-mail gemadg@gema-groupe.com; internet www.gema-groupe.com; f. 1987 as part of restructuring of SNTM/CNAN; shipping, ship-handling and forwarding; Pres. and Dir-Gen. ALI LARBI CHÉRIF.

CIVIL AVIATION

Algeria's principal international airport, Houari Boumedienne, is situated 20 km from Algiers. Other international airports are situated at Constantine, Annaba, Tlemcen and Oran. There are, in addition, 65 aerodromes, of which 20 are public, and a further 135 airstrips connected with the petroleum industry.

Air Algérie (Entreprise Nationale d'Exploitation des Services Aériens): BP 858, 1 place Maurice Audin, Immeuble el-Djazair, Algiers; tel. (21) 74-24-28; fax (21) 61-05-53; e-mail contacts@airalgerie.dz; internet www.airalgerie.dz; f. 1953 by merger; state-owned from 1972; internal services and extensive services to Europe, North and West Africa, and the Middle East; flies to more than 70 destinations; Dir-Gen. and CEO MUHAMMAD SALAH BOULTIF.

Tassili Airlines: BP 301, blvd Mustapha Ben Boulaïd, 30500 Hassi Messaoud; tel. (29) 73-80-25; fax (29) 73-84-24; internet www.tassiliairlines.dz; f. 1997; wholly owned by Sonatrach; domestic passenger services; Chair. and Man. Dir FAIÇAL KHELIL.

Tourism

Algeria's tourist attractions include the Mediterranean coast, the Atlas mountains and the Sahara desert. According to provisional data, in 2011 there were 1.5m. visitors to Algeria. Receipts from tourism totalled US $209m. in 2011. It was announced in early 2007 that the Government was investing some $1,000m. in the tourism sector; the construction of 42 new resorts was scheduled to be completed by 2015.

Agence Nationale de Développement Touristique (ANDT): BP 78, Sidi Fredj Staoueli, Algiers; tourism promotion; Dir-Gen. NOUREDDINE NEDRI.

Office National du Tourisme (ONT): 2 rue Ismail Kerrar, 16000 Algiers; tel. (21) 43-80-60; fax (21) 43-80-59; e-mail ont@ont-dz.org; internet www.ont-dz.org; f. 1988; state institution; oversees tourism promotion policy; Dir-Gen. HADJ SAÏD MUHAMMAD AMINE.

ONAT (Entreprise Nationale Algérienne de Tourisme): 126 bis A, rue Didouche Mourad, 16000 Algiers; tel. (21) 74-44-48; fax (21) 74-32-14; e-mail direction-marketing@onatalgerie.com; internet www.onatalgerie.com; f. 1983; Dir-Gen. SELATNIA MUHAMMAD CHÉRIF.

Touring Club d'Algérie (TCA): 30 rue Hassène Benaâmane, Les Vergers, Bir Mourad Raïs, Algiers; tel. (21) 54-13-13; fax (21) 54-15-11; e-mail sg_touring@algeriatouring.dz; internet www.algeriatouring.dz; f. 1963; Pres. ABDERRAHMANE ABDEDAÏM.

Touring Voyages Algérie: Centre commercial 'el-Hammadia', Bouzaréah, Algiers; tel. (21) 54-13-13; fax (21) 94-26-87; e-mail contact@touring-algerie.com; internet www.touringvoyagesalgerie.dz; f. 1995 to manage the commercial activities of Touring Club d'Algérie; 89% owned by Touring Club d'Algérie; Pres. and Dir-Gen. TAHAR SAHRI.

Defence

Chief of Staff of the People's National Army: Lt-Gen. AHMED GAID SALAH.

Commander of the Land Force: Maj.-Gen. AHCÈNE TAFER.

Commander of the Air Force: Maj.-Gen. ABDELKADER LOUNES.

Commander of the Naval Forces: Maj.-Gen. MALEK NECIB.

Commander of the Territory Air Defence Forces: Maj.-Gen. AMAR AMRANI.

Commander of the National Gendarmerie: Maj.-Gen. AHMED BOUSTEILA.

Commander of the Republican Guard: Maj.-Gen. AHMED MOULAY MILIANI.

Defence Budget (2013): AD 826,000m.

Military Service: 18 months (army only).

Total Armed Forces (as assessed at November 2013): 130,000: army 110,000 (75,000 conscripts); navy est. 6,000; air force 14,000. Reserves 150,000.

Paramilitary Forces (as assessed at November 2013): est. 187,200 (National Security Forces 16,000; Republican Guards 1,200; an est. 150,000 self-defence militia and communal guards, and a gendarmerie of 20,000).

Education

Education, in the national language (Arabic), is officially compulsory for a period of nine years, for children between six and 15 years of age. Primary education begins at the age of six and lasts for five years. Secondary education begins at 11 years of age and lasts for up to seven years, comprising first cycle of four years and a second of three years. In 2012 the total enrolment at primary schools included 97% of children in the relevant age-group. The comparable ratio for secondary enrolment in 2011 was equivalent to 98% of students in the relevant age-group. In 2012 the Algerian Government allocated AD 821,000m. to education (equivalent to 20% of the national budget).

There were some 490,035 pupils at pre-primary schools in 2011/12, while in 2010/11 some 3,451,588 pupils attended primary schools (compared with about 800,000 in 1962). In 2010/11 some 4,572,513 pupils attended secondary schools. Most education at primary level is in Arabic, but at higher levels French is still widely used. In mid-2003 the Government agreed to permit the use of the Berber language, Tamazight, as a language of instruction in Algerian schools. The majority of foreign teachers in Algeria come from Egypt, Syria, Tunisia and other Arab countries.

In 2010/11 the number of students receiving higher education (including post-graduate) was 1,210,272. In addition to the 27 main universities, there are 16 other *centres universitaires* and a number of technical colleges. Several thousand students go abroad to study. Efforts have been made to combat adult illiteracy by means of a large-scale campaign in which instruction is sometimes given by young people who have only recently left school, and in which the broadcasting services are widely used.

ANDORRA

Introductory Survey

LOCATION, CLIMATE, LANGUAGE, RELIGION, FLAG, CAPITAL

The Principality of Andorra lies in the eastern Pyrenees, bounded by France and Spain, and is situated roughly midway between Barcelona and Toulouse. The climate is alpine, with frequent snow in winter and a warm summer. The average minimum temperature is −2°C (28°F), while the average maximum temperature is 24°C (76°F); however, temperatures vary significantly between low-lying and mountainous regions. Average annual precipitation is between 700 mm and 1,100 mm. The official language is Catalan, but French and Spanish are also widely spoken. Most of the inhabitants profess Christianity and more than 90% are Roman Catholics. The civil flag (proportions 2 by 3) has three equal vertical stripes, of blue, yellow and red. The state flag has, in addition, the state coat of arms (a quartered shield above the motto *Virtus unita fortior*) in the centre of the yellow stripe. The capital is Andorra la Vella.

CONTEMPORARY POLITICAL HISTORY

Historical Context

Andorra effectively gained its independence in 1278, when the Spanish Bishop of Urgell and the French Count of Foix settled their territorial dispute by agreeing to become joint overlords, or Co-Princes (Coprínceps). Sovereignty eventually passed from the Count of Foix to the King of France and, subsequently, to the President of the French Republic, but the system of government remained largely unchanged until 1993. Owing to the lack of distinction between the authority of the Co-Princes and the General Council (Consell General), founded in 1419, the Andorrans encountered many difficulties in their attempts to gain international status for their country and control over its essential services.

Until 1970 the franchise was granted only to third-generation Andorran males over the age of 25 years. Thereafter, women, persons aged between 21 and 25 years, and second-generation Andorrans were allowed to vote in elections to the General Council. In 1977 the franchise was extended to include all first-generation Andorrans of foreign parentage who were aged 28 years and over. The electorate remained small, however, in proportion to the size of the population, and Andorra's foreign residents increased their demands for political and nationality rights.

Prior to 1993 political parties were not directly represented in the General Council, but there were loose groupings with liberal or conservative sympathies. The country's only political organization, the Partit Democràtic d'Andorra (PDA—Andorran Democratic Party), was technically illegal and in the 1981 elections to the General Council the party urged its supporters to cast blank votes.

Domestic Political Affairs

In 1980, during discussions on institutional reform, representatives of the Co-Princes and the General Council agreed that an executive council should be formed and that a referendum should be held on changes to the electoral system. In early 1981 the Co-Princes formally requested the General Council to prepare plans for reform, in accordance with these proposals. Following the December elections to the General Council, in January 1982 the new legislature elected Oscar Ribas Reig as Head of Government (Cap de Govern). Ribas appointed an executive of six ministers, who expressed their determination to provide Andorra with a written constitution. The formation of the Government (Govern) constituted the separation of powers between an executive and a legislature.

In August 1983 the General Council approved a proposal to introduce income tax, in order to alleviate Andorra's budget deficit. The decision proved deeply unpopular, however, and the Government was unable to implement it successfully. Subsequent proposals to introduce a range of indirect taxes encountered strong opposition from financial and tourism concerns, and prompted the Government's resignation in April 1984. Josep Pintat Solans was elected unopposed by the General Council as Head of Government in May. At the December 1985 elections to the General Council the electorate was increased by about 27%, as a result of the newly introduced lower minimum voting age of 18 years. The Council re-elected Pintat as Head of Government in January 1986.

Elections to the General Council took place in December 1989, following which the reformist Ribas was elected as Head of Government. In June 1990 the Council voted unanimously to establish a special commission to draft a constitution. In April 1991 representatives of the Co-Princes agreed to recognize popular sovereignty in Andorra and to permit the drafting of a constitution, which would be subject to approval by referendum. In September, however, Ribas was threatened with a vote of no confidence by traditionalist members of the Council, who were opposed to the proposed constitution, which would effectively legalize political parties and trade unions. There followed a period of political impasse, during which no official budget was authorized for the principality. In January 1992, following small, but unprecedented, public demonstrations in protest against the political deadlock, Ribas and the General Council resigned. The result of a general election in April was inconclusive, necessitating a second round of voting one week later, following which supporters of Ribas secured a narrow majority. Accordingly, Ribas was re-elected as Head of Government.

At a referendum held in March 1993, in which 75.7% of the electorate participated, 74.2% of those who voted approved the draft Constitution. The document was signed by the Co-Princes in April, and was promulgated on 4 May. Under its provisions, the Co-Princes remained as Heads of State, but with greatly reduced powers, while Andorran nationals were afforded full sovereignty and (together with foreigners who had lived in Andorra for at least 20 years) were authorized to form and to join political parties and trade unions. The Constitution also provided for the establishment of an independent judiciary and permitted the principality to formulate its own foreign policy and to join international organizations. The Co-Princes were to retain a right of veto over treaties with France and Spain that affected Andorra's borders or security.

The first general election under the terms of the new Constitution took place in December 1993. One of the constitutional provisions was the implementation of a new system of partial proportional representation—one-half of the General Council's 28 members were directly elected from a single national constituency by a system of proportional representation, the remainder being elected by Andorra's seven parishes (two for each parish). Ribas's Agrupament Nacional Democràtic (AND—National Democratic Grouping), the successor to the PDA, won the largest number of seats, and in January 1994 Ribas was re-elected Head of Government. However, opposition to Ribas's proposed budget and tax legislation led in November to the adoption of a motion of no confidence in the Government. Ribas immediately submitted his resignation; Marc Forné Molné, the leader of the Unió Liberal (UL), was subsequently elected Head of Government.

Forné's Government lacked an overall majority in the General Council; however, the support of councillors from regional political organizations enabled the administration to adopt more than 30 bills between December 1994 and July 1996—including controversial legislation allowing certain foreign nationals to become 'nominal residents', for the purpose of avoiding taxation, on payment of an annual levy. After being censured twice in one year by the General Council, Forné was obliged to announce an early general election, which took place in February 1997. The UL won an overall majority, and in April Forné announced the formation of a new, expanded Government. The UL was subsequently renamed the Partit Liberal d'Andorra (PLA—Andorran Liberal Party). In 2000 the AND split into two parties—the Partit Socialdemòcrata (PS—Social Democratic Party) and the Partit Democràta (PD—Democratic Party).

Elections to the General Council took place in March 2001, attracting a turnout of 81.6% of the registered electorate; however, the number of citizens eligible to vote represented only 20.7% of Andorra's total population. The PLA won 15 of the 28 seats, six seats were secured by the PS, the PD took five seats and the two remaining seats went to independent candidates. Forné was re-elected Head of Government.

In May 2003 Joan Enric Vives i Sicília succeeded Joan Martí Alanis as the Bishop of Urgell and therefore as *ex officio* Episcopal Co-Prince of Andorra. In September 2004 the PLA selected the former Minister of Foreign Affairs, Albert Pintat Santolària, as its candidate for Head of Government in the forthcoming general election, following Forné's decision not to seek a new term of office. Polling took place in April 2005; the PLA won 14 seats in the General Council, the PS secured 11, a coalition of two smaller centrist parties, the Centre Demòcrata Andorrà (CDA—Andorran Democratic Centre, the successor to the PD) and Segle 21 (21st Century), took two seats and the Renovació Democràtica (RD—Democratic Renewal) secured one seat. Pintat was elected Head of Government in May. Since no party had won an absolute majority, the PLA began negotiations with the CDA/Segle 21 coalition on the formation of a government. However, as no agreement on the division of portfolios was reached, CDA/Segle 21 agreed to support only part of the PLA's programme.

As a result of the global financial crisis in 2008–09, international resolve to prevent tax evasion in the 'offshore' banking sector was strengthened. Many jurisdictions, including Andorra, which was listed by the Organisation for Economic Co-operation and Development (OECD, see p. 379) as an 'unco-operative tax haven', were subject to pressure from world leaders prior to the meeting of the Group of 20 leading industrialized and developing nations (G20) in London, United Kingdom, in April 2009. In March Andorra agreed to amend its secrecy laws to allow for greater transparency and to comply with OECD rules on the sharing of bank data to combat tax evasion. As a result, in May Andorra was removed from the OECD's list of 'unco-operative tax havens' (along with Liechtenstein and Monaco, the only two remaining countries listed).

At elections to the General Council held in April 2009, which attracted a participation rate of 75.3%, the PS won 14 of the 28 seats, thus ending 14 years of dominance in the legislature by the PLA. The newly formed Coalició Reformista (CR—Reformist Coalition), which was led by the PLA, took 11 seats and Andorra pel Canvi (ApC—Andorra for Change), which was supported by the RD, secured three. The leader of the PS, Jaume Bartumeu Cassany, was elected Head of Government in June. The new Government expressed its commitment to introducing new forms of taxation, including income tax and value-added tax (VAT), and to accelerating the introduction of legislation to address banking secrecy. Accordingly, in September the General Council approved legislation allowing for the exchange of financial information with foreign jurisdictions, providing bilateral agreements for this purpose (tax information exchange agreements—TIEAs) were in place. By March 2012 Andorra had signed a total of 21 TIEAs and a further eight were under negotiation.

In December 2009 the Government failed to gain the support of the ApC members of the General Council for the proposed budget for 2010, and was therefore obliged to operate using the equivalent of one-twelfth of the previous year's budgeted expenditure for each month. Furthermore, in October 2010 it was announced that the PS had not reached agreement with the ApC councillors on adopting a budget for 2011: Bartumeu stated that, if no consensus could be reached, an early general election would be held in 2011, as the Constitution does not allow a Government to operate with an unapproved budget for two consecutive years. In December 2010 the General Council adopted legislation introducing three new forms of direct taxation: income tax for non-residents, a modest corporate tax and a tax on economic activities.

The Government's failure, once again, to agree the budget, led Bartumeu, on 15 February 2011, to dissolve the General Council and to announce that legislative elections would take place on 3 April. A major cause of disagreement within the General Council had been the proposal by the PS to introduce income tax for residents, a policy which was opposed by all the other major political groups in Andorra. The opposition formed a centre-right alliance styled Demòcrates per Andorra (DA—Democrats for Andorra), replacing the CR, in order to contest the elections. The DA, which was led by Antoni Martí Petit and which included the recently established Partit Reformista d'Andorra (PRA—Reformist Party of Andorra) and the PLA, won a decisive victory at the elections with 20 of the 28 seats in the legislature, while the PS took only six seats. The Unió Laurediana, a local conservative grouping which supported the DA's programme, secured the two remaining seats. Turnout was some 74.1% of eligible voters. Martí was inaugurated as Head of Government of a seven-member executive on 12 May. In July Albert Esteve Garcia was appointed to the new position of Minister of Culture. In July 2012 the Minister of Justice and the Interior, Marc Vila Amigó, resigned from his post and was replaced by Xavier Espot Zamora. During 2011–13 the Government introduced a number of new taxes (both direct and indirect) as part of its aim to align the Andorran tax system more closely with those of the European Union (EU, see p. 273) member states. Following the replacement of the sales tax regime by a full VAT system in January 2013, in June, under increasing pressure from the EU to tackle tax evasion, the Government published details of a draft bill to introduce a tax on the incomes of the principality's residents (together with a general capital gains tax) from 1 January 2015. The passage of this legislation would effectively end Andorra's unofficial status as a tax haven.

Foreign Affairs

Following the referendum of March 1993, Andorra formally applied for membership of the Council of Europe (see p. 252), gaining entry in November 1994. In June 1993 the Andorran Government signed a treaty of co-operation with France and Spain which explicitly recognized the sovereignty of Andorra. In July Andorra became the 184th member of the UN. Andorra has enjoyed 'most favoured nation' status with the European Union (EU, see p. 273) since 1991. In 2003 Forné announced plans for Andorra to join the EU within 15 years. In June 2004 the Charter of Fundamental Social Rights of Workers (commonly known as the Social Charter) of the EU was ratified by the General Council; however, certain articles of the Charter, relating to employment rights, were omitted. A co-operation agreement with the EU—covering the environment, communications, information, culture, transport, regional and cross-border co-operation, and social issues—came into effect on 1 July 2005, together with an agreement on the effective taxation of savings held in the principality by EU residents. Following delays in the negotiating procedure (which had begun in 2004), a monetary agreement with the EU was concluded in February 2011 and signed on 30 June. Under the agreement (which came into effect on 1 April 2012) the euro was to become Andorra's official currency; in turn, Andorra agreed to adopt EU legislation on financial supervision and the prevention of fraud and money-laundering. Prior to the enactment of this monetary agreement, the euro, while holding no legal status in Andorra, had de facto replaced the Spanish peseta and the French franc from the beginning of 2000 (although these two currencies remained legal tender until the end of 2002). Following delays in the adoption of the requisite legislation, in December 2013 the Government stated that it hoped that the country would commence minting its own euro coins in March/April 2014.

In December 2012 the European Commission published a report outlining options for the further integration of the European microstates, Andorra, Monaco and San Marino, into the EU. The report dismissed EU membership for the three states in the near future, but recommended either membership of the European Economic Area (EEA) or the drawing up of a comprehensive, multilateral Framework Association Agreement (FAA) with each of the states. Following consultations with the relevant parties, in November 2013 the Commission published another report which concluded that EEA membership was not currently a viable option for the microstates, while maintaining that their participation in the EU internal market could feasibly be achieved through the negotiation of one or several FAA(s), preferably covering all three states.

CONSTITUTION AND GOVERNMENT

According to the Constitution promulgated in May 1993, Andorra is a parliamentary co-principality, in which the Co-Princes—the President of the French Republic and the Spanish Bishop of Urgell—serve jointly as head of state.

The General Council (Consell General) currently comprises 28 councillors (although the number can be between 28 and 42), who are elected by universal suffrage for a four-year period. Two councillors are directly elected by each of the seven parishes of Andorra, and the remainder are elected from a single national constituency by a system of proportional representation. At its opening session the Council elects as its head the Speaker (Síndic General) and the Deputy Speaker (Subsíndic General), who cease to be members of the Council on their election. The General Council elects the Head of Government (Cap de Govern), who, in turn, appoints ministers to the executive body, the Govern.

Andorra is divided into seven parishes, each of which is administered by a communal council. Communal councillors are elected for a four-year term by direct universal suffrage. At its opening session each communal council elects two consuls, who preside over it.

REGIONAL AND INTERNATIONAL CO-OPERATION

In 1990 Andorra approved a trade agreement with the European Community (EC, now the European Union—EU), which was effective from July 1991, allowing for the establishment of a customs union with the EC and enabling Andorran companies to sell non-agricultural goods to the EU market without being subject to the external tariffs levied on third countries. Andorra benefits from duty-free transit for goods imported via EU countries. A monetary agreement with the EU was signed in June 2011. Andorra was admitted to the Council of Europe (see p. 252) in 1994, and is also a member of the Organization for Security and Co-operation in Europe (OSCE).

Andorra joined the UN in 1993, following the country's accession to full sovereignty. Andorra is an observer at the World Trade Organization (WTO, see p. 434).

ECONOMIC AFFAIRS

In 2011, according to UN estimates, Andorra's gross national income (GNI), measured at average 2009–11 prices, totalled US $3,577m., equivalent to $41,517 per head. According to World Bank estimates, during 2003–12, the population grew at an average rate of 0.4% per year, while gross domestic product (GDP) per head increased, in real terms, by an average of 3.7% per year during 2003–08. According to official estimates, overall GDP decreased, in real terms, at an average annual rate of 0.3% in 2003–12; GDP declined by 1.6% in 2012.

Arable land accounts for only around 2% of the total area of Andorra. The contribution of agriculture (including hunting, forestry and fishing) to GDP was a mere 0.6% in 2012. Andorra's principal crop is tobacco (although production has decreased considerably since the late 1990s owing to a decline in demand); livestock-rearing, particularly sheep and cattle, is also of some importance. The agricultural sector (including forestry and hunting) accounted for only 0.5% of total employment (excluding unclassified occupations) in 2012 and Andorra is dependent on imports of foodstuffs to satisfy domestic requirements. According to UN estimates, the GDP of the agricultural sector increased, in real terms, at an average annual rate of 2.5% in 2003–11; agricultural GDP declined by 3.3% in 2011.

Industry in Andorra includes the production of foodstuffs and beverages, wood products, graphic arts, and the manufacture of cigars and cigarettes. In addition to forested timber, natural resources include iron, lead, alum and stone. Industry contributed 12.7% of GDP in 2012. Including manufacturing, construction and the production and distribution of electricity, industry provided 14.2% of total employment (excluding unclassified occupations) in 2012. According to UN estimates, industrial GDP increased, in real terms, at an average annual rate of 0.8% in 2003–11; industrial GDP declined by 2.4% in 2011.

Manufacturing (and utilities) contributed 5.2% of GDP in 2012; the manufacturing sector engaged 4.2% of the employed labour force in the same year (excluding unclassified occupations). According to UN estimates, the GDP of the manufacturing sector increased, in real terms, at an average annual rate of 0.6% in 2003–11; manufacturing GDP declined by 2.8% in 2011.

Construction contributed 7.6% of GDP in 2012 and provided 9.5% of total employment in that year. During 2003–11, according to UN estimates, the GDP of the construction sector increased, in real terms, at an average annual rate of 1.1%; sectoral GDP declined by 2.3% in 2011.

Andorra is dependent on imports of electricity and other fuels from France and Spain. The country's hydroelectric power plant supplied only 13.5% of domestic needs in 2011. In 2012 fuel imports accounted for 14.4% of total merchandise imports. In 2006 a project to extend the production capacity of the hydroelectric plant commenced as part of a government strategic energy plan for 2006–15. The generation of electricity from the combustion of urban waste also began in 2006 and contributed 2.1% of Andorra's domestic requirements in 2011. Andorra's total electricity consumption in 2011 amounted to 587 GWh.

In 2012 the services sector accounted for 85.3% of total employment (excluding unclassified occupations) and contributed 86.7% of GDP. Tourism and tourist-related commerce are the principal contributors to GDP. Andorra attracts visitors owing to its well-developed facilities for winter sports and also the availability of low-duty consumer items. A total of 2.2m. tourists and 5.7m. excursionists (mostly from Spain and France) visited Andorra in 2012. The hotel industry provided 13.5% of total employment (excluding unclassified occupations) in 2012. Over the years, the absence of income tax, inheritance tax or capital transfer tax, in addition to the laws on secrecy governing the country's banks, favoured the development of Andorra as a tax haven. The banking and insurance sectors make a significant contribution to the economy. According to UN estimates, the GDP of the services sector increased, in real terms, at an average annual rate of 0.3% in 2003–11; sectoral GDP declined by 3.2% in 2011.

Andorra's external trade is dominated by the import of consumer goods destined for sale, with low rates of duty, to visitors. In 2012 imports were valued at €1,085.6m. and exports at only €53.2m. Spain and France are Andorra's principal trading partners, respectively providing 61.4% and 17.5% of imports and taking 53.0% and 20.5% of exports in 2012. The European Union (EU, see p. 273) as a whole provided 90.9% of imports and received 96.3% of exports in 2006.

In 2013, according to official estimates, there was a budgetary surplus of €82m. Prior to 2013, in the absence of direct taxation (although a capital gains tax was introduced in 2007, a tax on the income of non-resident companies and individuals in 2011 and a business tax in 2012), the Government derived most of its revenue from levies on imports and on financial institutions, indirect taxes on petrol and other items, stamp duty and the sale of postage stamps. However, on 1 January 2013 the Government replaced its sales tax regime with a value-added tax (VAT) system (levied at the standard rate of 4.5%). Total general government debt was equivalent to an estimated 41.1% of GDP in 2012. There is no recorded unemployment in Andorra: the restricted size of the indigenous labour force necessitates high levels of immigration. Consumer prices increased by an average of 2.3% per year in 2003–12. The annual rate of inflation was 1.1% in 2012.

Andorra has a small, open, prosperous economy, which is narrowly focused on the services sector, principally tourism, tourism-related commerce and banking. Despite enjoying one of the highest per caput incomes in the world, the prosperity of the principality is highly vulnerable to economic conditions in France and Spain. Economic growth during most of the 2000s was robust; however, GDP contracted by 2.9% in 2009, by 1.2% in 2010 and by 2.8% in 2011, partly owing to a considerable decline in tourist arrivals, but predominantly as a result of the global economic crisis and, more specifically, the ongoing eurozone sovereign debt crisis, which has had a particularly severe impact on Spain. Notably, the resultant decrease in the prices of consumer goods in Spain undercut duty-free shopping in Andorra. In an attempt to increase foreign investment and encourage economic diversification, in 2008 the Government introduced reforms increasing the maximum investment for non-Andorrans from 33% to 49% of a business in key areas, such as ski resorts and property, and to 100% in other industries. Foreign direct investment was further liberalized in 2012 with the passage of new legislation. In the latter half of the 20th century the principality's favourable tax regime and banking secrecy fostered the development of a large financial sector, although increased scrutiny of tax evasion by the Organisation for Economic Co-operation and Development (OECD, see p. 379) and individual national governments led to the withdrawal of some foreign funds from 'offshore' accounts. In 2009 Andorra agreed to amend banking secrecy laws ensuring greater transparency and compliance with OECD rules; by March 2012 Andorra had signed bilateral tax information exchange agreements with 21 jurisdictions. Government spending was constrained by the failure of the legislature to reach agreement on a budget for both 2010 and 2011. The victory of the centre-right Demòcrates per Andorra (DA—Democrats for Andorra) alliance in the general election of April 2011 promised a period of political stability and the introduction of a range of measures aimed at strengthening the tourism sector and increasing employment in the country. The new Government oversaw further major restructuring of Andorra's tax system: a new corporate income tax came into effect on 1 January 2012 and VAT replaced the existing consumption taxes on 1 January 2013. Under increasing pressure from the EU, which was demanding greater transparency throughout Europe regarding income data in a bid more effectively to tackle tax evasion, in June 2013 the Andorran Government announced details of a draft bill providing for the introduction in 2016 of a tax on the incomes of the principality's residents (at a flat rate of 10%). Despite a 14.9% year-on-year increase in the number of tourist arrivals in 2012, annual GDP contracted once again, by 1.6%.

PUBLIC HOLIDAYS

2015: 1 January (New Year's Day), 6 January (Epiphany), 16 February (Carnival), 14 March (Constitution Day), 3 April (Good Friday), 6 April (Easter Monday), 1 May (Labour Day), 25 May (Whit Monday), 15 August (Assumption), 8 September (National Day), 1 November (All Saints' Day), 8 December (Immaculate Conception), 25 December (Christmas Day), 26 December (St Stephen's Day).

Each parish also holds its own annual festival, which is taken as a public holiday, usually lasting for three days, in July, August or September.

Statistical Survey

Source (unless otherwise stated): Servei d'Estudis, Ministeri de Finances, Carrer Prat de la Creu 62–64, Andorra la Vella AD500; tel. 865714; fax 829218; e-mail servest@andorra.ad; internet www.estadistica.ad.

AREA AND POPULATION

Area: 467.8 sq km (180.6 sq miles).

Population: 65,844 (males 34,268, females 31,576) at census of 31 December 2000; 76,246, comprising: Andorrans 34,417, Spanish 20,320, Portuguese 11,229, French 3,794 and others 6,486 at 31 December 2012. Source: partly UN, *Population and Vital Statistics Report*.

Density (31 December 2012): 163.0 per sq km.

Population by Age and Sex (persons at 31 December 2012): *0–14:* 11,841 (males 6,089, females 5,752); *15–64:* 54,801 (males 28,151, females 26,650); *65 and over:* 9,604 (males 4,598, females 5,006); *Total* 76,246 (males 38,838, females 37,408).

Parishes (population at 31 December 2012): Andorra la Vella (capital) 22,398; Escaldes-Engordany 14,282; Encamp 12,051; La Massana 9,902; Sant Julià de Lòria 9,063; Canillo 4,133; Ordino 4,417.

Births, Marriages and Deaths (2012): Registered live births 737 (birth rate 9.7 per 1,000); Registered marriages 288 (marriage rate 3.8 per 1,000); Registered deaths 303 (death rate 4.0 per 1,000).

Life Expectancy (years at birth, WHO estimates): 82 (males 79; females 85) in 2011. Source: WHO, *World Health Statistics*.

Employment (2012): Agriculture, forestry and hunting 167; Mining 2; Construction 3,258; Manufacturing 1,460; Production and distribution of electricity 164; Repair and sale of motor vehicles 9,042; Hotels 4,667; Real estate 3,931; Administration 4,337; Finance and insurance 1,711; Transport and storage 1,084; Education 546; Other services 4,098; *Sub-total* 34,467; Unclassified occupations 1,565; *Total* 36,032 (males 18,334, females 17,698).

HEALTH AND WELFARE

Key Indicators

Total Fertility Rate (children per woman, 2011): 1.4.

Under-5 Mortality Rate (per 1,000 live births, 2011): 3.

Physicians (per 1,000 head, 2009): 3.9.

Hospital Beds (per 1,000 head, 2009): 2.5.

Health Expenditure (2010): US $ per head (PPP): 3,122.

Health Expenditure (2010): % of GDP: 7.2.

Health Expenditure (2010): public (% of total): 73.4.

Total Carbon Dioxide Emissions ('000 metric tons, 2010): 517.0.

Total Carbon Dioxide Emissions Per Head (metric tons, 2010): 6.6.

Human Development Index (2012): ranking: 33.

Human Development Index (2012): value: 0.846.

For sources and definitions, see explanatory note on p. vi.

AGRICULTURE

Principal Crop (metric tons, 2012): Tobacco 235.8.

Livestock (head, 2012): Cattle 1,552; Sheep 2,656; Horses 853; Goats 364.

FINANCE

Currency and Exchange Rates: 100 cent = 1 euro (€). *Sterling and Dollar Equivalents* (31 December 2013): £1 sterling = €1.194; US $1 = €0.725; €10 = £8.37 = US $13.79. *Average Exchange Rate* (euros per US dollar): 0.7194 in 2011; 0.7779 in 2012; 0.7532 in 2013. Note: French and Spanish currencies were formerly in use. From the introduction of the euro, with French and Spanish participation, on 1 January 1999, fixed exchange rates of €1 = 6.55957 francs and €1 = 166.386 pesetas were in operation. Euro notes and coins were introduced on 1 January 2002. The euro and local currencies circulated alongside each other until 17 February (francs) and 28 February (pesetas), after which the euro became the sole legal tender.

Budget (€ million, 2013, estimates): *Revenue:* Direct taxes 72.2; Indirect taxes 262.2; Property income 8.9; Other taxes and income 20.5; Current transfers 0.0; Assets 0.0; Liabilities 608.8; Total 972.7. *Expenditure:* Current expenditure 321.2 (Personnel emoluments 98.0, Goods and services 47.8, Interest payments 33.9, Current transfers 141.6); Capital expenditure 215.9 (Fixed capital investment 168.8, Capital transfers 47.1); Assets 4.8; Liabilities 349.2; Total 891.0.

Cost of Living (Consumer Price Index at December; base: 2001 = 100): All items 127.2 in 2010; 130.4 in 2011; 131.8 in 2012.

Gross Domestic Product (€ million at current prices): 2,571.9 in 2010; 2,521.9 in 2011; 2,507.9 in 2012.

Gross Domestic Product by Economic Activity (€ million at current prices, 2012): Agriculture 13.9; Manufacturing and utilities 113.5; Construction 166.4; Wholesale and retail trade 386.2; Hotels and restaurants 198.7; Transport and communications 126.8; Financial activities 403.3; Real estate and housing 354.3; Public administration, education and health services 311.6; Other services 128.7; *Gross value added in basic prices* 2,203.5; Taxes, *less* subsidies, on products 304.4; *GDP in purchasers' values* 2,507.9.

EXTERNAL TRADE

Principal Commodities (€ million, 2012): *Imports:* Live animals and animal products 59.0; Prepared foodstuffs, beverages, spirits and tobacco products 174.3 (Alcoholic drinks and vinegars 63.8; Tobacco and tobacco substitutes 31.2); Mineral products 160.9 (Flammable minerals, oils, petroleum 156.3); Chemical products 124.6 (Essential oils, perfume and toiletries 72.3); Textiles and textile articles 103.8 (Clothes and clothing accessories, not knitted 66.6); Machinery and mechanical appliances, electrical equipment 127.5 (Boilers and mechanical engines 54.2; Electric machines, tools and materials 73.2); Vehicles, transport equipment 68.6 (Automobile vehicles, tractors, motorcycles 66.8); Miscellaneous manufactured articles 43.5; Total (incl. others) 1,085.6. *Exports:* Chemical products 2.7 (Essential oils, perfumes and toiletries 2.6); Pulp of wood, paper and paperboard 3.3; Textiles and textile articles 7.2 (Clothes and clothing accessories, knitted 3.5; Clothes and clothing accessories, not knitted 3.4); Fine pearls, gems, gemstones and precious metals 7.1; Base metals and articles 3.5 (Iron and steel 1.6); Machinery and mechanical appliances, electrical equipment 6.8 (Boilers and mechanical engines 3.0; Electric machines, tools and materials 3.8); Automobile vehicles, tractors, motorcycles 10.1; Miscellaneous manufactured articles 2.4; Total (incl. others) 53.2.

Principal Trading Partners (€ million, 2012): *Imports c.i.f.:* China, People's Republic 40.8; France 189.9; Germany 39.3; Italy 25.4; Netherlands 10.9; Portugal 12.4; Spain 666.1; Switzerland 15.4; United Kingdom 18.2; Total (incl. others) 1,085.6. *Exports f.o.b.:* France 10.9; Germany 1.9; Hong Kong 3.2; Italy 2.0; Netherlands 0.7; Spain 28.2; Switzerland 3.6; Total (incl. others) 53.2.

TRANSPORT

Road Traffic (registered motor vehicles, 2012): Passenger cars 52,038; Buses and coaches 206; Trucks (lorries) and vans 5,075; Tractors 354; Motorcycles 10,572.

TOURISM

Tourist Arrivals (country of residence, 2011): Spain 1,507,111; France 327,250; Total (incl. others) 1,947,531. Note: Figures exclude excursionists, numbering 6,413,612 in 2011. *2012:* Total arrivals 2,237,939.

COMMUNICATIONS MEDIA

Telephones (main lines in use, 2012): 38,320.

Mobile Cellular Telephones (subscribers, 2012): 65,000.

Internet Subscribers (2011): 26,000.

Broadband Subscribers (2012): 27,100.

Source: partly International Telecommunication Union and Servei de Telecomunicacions d'Andorra.

EDUCATION

Pre-primary Enrolment (2012/13): 2,432 (Andorran schools 891, French schools 919, Spanish schools* 622).

Primary Enrolment (2012/13): 4,031 (Andorran schools 1,765, French schools 1,034, Spanish schools* 1,232).

Secondary Enrolment (2012/13): 3,998 (Andorran schools 1,511; French schools 1,235; Spanish schools* 1,252).

Non-university Higher Education Enrolment (2012/13): 364 (Andorran institutions 173, French institutions 191).

University Enrolment (2005/06): Andorra 431 (males 205, females 226); France 131 (males 53, females 78); Spain 503 (males 204, females 299); Total (incl. others) 1,066 (males 462, females 604).

* Including congregational schools.

Pupil-teacher Ratio (primary education, UNESCO estimate): 9.6 in 2011/12 (Source: UNESCO Institute for Statistics).

Directory

The Government

HEAD OF STATE

Episcopal Co-Prince: JOAN ENRIC VIVES I SICÍLIA (Bishop of Urgell).

French Co-Prince: FRANÇOIS HOLLANDE (President of the French Republic).

GOVERN
(April 2014)

The executive is formed by the Demòcrates per Andorra (Democrats for Andorra).

Head of Government (Cap de Govern): ANTONI MARTÍ PETIT.

Minister of Finance and Public Service: JORDI CINCA MATEOS.

Minister of Economy and Territorial Planning: JORDI ALCOBÉ FONT.

Minister of Foreign Affairs: GILBERT SABOYA SUNYÉ.

Minister of Justice and the Interior: XAVIER ESPOT ZAMORA.

Minister of Health and Welfare: CRISTINA RODRÍGUEZ GALAN.

Minister of Education and Youth: ROSER SUÑÉ PASCUET.

Minister of Tourism and the Environment: FRANCESC CAMP TORRES.

Minister of Culture: ALBERT ESTEVE GARCIA.

Minister of the Presidency: ANTONI RIBERAYGUA SASPLUGAS.

MINISTRIES

Office of the Head of Government: Govern d'Andorra, Carrer Prat de la Creu 62–64, Edif. Administratiu, Andorra la Vella AD500; tel. 875700; e-mail portal@govern.ad; internet www.govern.ad.

Ministry of Culture: Carrer Prat de la Creu 62–64, Edif. Administratiu, Andorra la Vella AD500; tel. 875700; fax 826707.

Ministry of Economy and Territorial Planning: Carrer Prat de la Creu 62–64, Edif. Administratiu, Andorra la Vella AD500; tel. 875701; fax 875757; e-mail muot@andorra.ad.

Ministry of Education and Youth: Prada Casadet, Andorra la Vella AD500; tel. 829456; fax 743310; internet www.educacio.ad; www.joventut.ad.

Ministry of Finance and Public Service: Carrer Prat de la Creu 62–64, Edif. Administratiu, Andorra la Vella AD500; tel. 875700; fax 860962; e-mail finances.gov@andorra.ad; internet www.finances.ad.

Ministry of Foreign Affairs: Carrer Prat de la Creu 62–64, Edif. Administratiu, Andorra la Vella AD500; tel. 875704; fax 869559; e-mail exteriors@govern.ad; internet www.mae.ad.

Ministry of Health and Welfare: Avinguda Príncep Benlloch 30, Edif. Clara Rabassa, 4°, Andorra la Vella AD500; tel. 874800; fax 829347; e-mail salut@govern.ad; internet www.salut.ad.

Ministry of Justice and the Interior: Carretera de l'OBAC, Edif. Administratiu de l'OBAC, Escaldes-Engordany AD700; tel. 872080; fax 869250.

Ministry of the Presidency: Carrer Prat de la Creu 62–64, Edif. Administratiu, Andorra la Vella AD500; tel. 875700.

Ministry of Tourism and the Environment: Camí de la Grau, Edif. Prat del Rull, Andorra la Vella AD500; tel. 875702; fax 860184; internet www.turisme.ad; www.mediambient.ad.

Legislature

GENERAL COUNCIL
(Consell General)

General Council (Consell General): Casa de la Vall 9–13, Andorra la Vella AD500; tel. 877877; fax 869863; e-mail consell_general@parlament.ad; internet www.consell.ad.

Speaker (Síndic General): VICENÇ MATEU ZAMORA.

Deputy Speaker (Subsíndica General): MÒNICA BONELL TUSET.

General Election, 3 April 2011

Party	Votes cast*	% of votes*	Seats†
Demòcrates per Andorra	8,553	55.15	20
Partit Socialdemòcrata	5,397	34.80	6
Andorra pel Canvi	1,040	6.71	—
Els Verds d'Andorra	520	3.35	—
Unió Laurediana	—	—	2
Total	15,510	100.00	28

* Figures refer to votes cast in the national constituency, from which 14 candidates were elected by proportional representation. In addition, two candidates were elected from each of the seven parishes.

† Figures refer to both the national and parochial lists. The Unió Laurediana only contested one parish constituency, Sant Julià de Lòria.

Election Commission

Junta Electoral: Carrer Prat de la Creu 62–64, Edif. Administratiu, Andorra la Vella AD500; tel. 875700; e-mail portal@govern.ad; internet www.eleccions.ad; govt agency; Pres. DAVID MOYNAT ROSSELL.

Political Organizations

The establishment of political parties was sanctioned under the Constitution that was promulgated in May 1993.

Andorra pel Canvi (ApC) (Andorra for Change): Baixada del Molí 3–5, Edif. Molí Parc, Andorra la Vella AD500; internet www.apc.ad; f. 2008; Parliamentary Leader EUSEBI NOMEN.

Demòcrates per Andorra (DA) (Democrats for Andorra): Passatge Antonia Font Caminal 1, Edif. Prat de les Orques, despatx 403, Andorra la Vella AD700; tel. 805777; e-mail democrates@democrates.ad; internet www.democrates.ad; f. February 2011 to contest the election in April; alliance, including the PLA, the PRA and Nou Centre; Leader ANTONI MARTÍ PETIT.

Nou Centre (New Centre): Andorra la Vella AD500; f. 2005 by the merger of Segle 21 and the Centre Demòcrata Andorrà; contested the 2011 general election as part of the Demòcrates per Andorra.

Partit Reformista d'Andorra (PRA) (Reform Party of Andorra): Andorra; f. 2010; Spokesman GILBERT SABOYA.

Partit Socialdemòcrata (PS) (Social Democratic Party): Carrer Verge del Pilar 5, 3°, Andorra la Vella AD500; tel. 805260; fax 821740; e-mail psdandorra@gmail.com; internet www.psa.ad; f. 2000; Pres. VICENÇ ALAY; First Sec. PERE LÓPEZ.

Unió Nacional de Progrés (UNP) (National Union for Progress): Avinguda Carlemany 36, Hotel Eureka, Escaldes-Engordany AD700; tel. and fax 821149; e-mail unp@unionacionaldeprogres.com; internet www.unionacionaldeprogres.com; f. 2007; Parliamentary Leader TOMAS PASCUAL CASABOSCH.

Els Verds d'Andorra (The Andorran Greens): Apartat de Correus 2136, Andorra la Vella AD500; tel. 671271; e-mail verds@verds.ad; internet www.verds.ad; f. 2004; Spokespersons JULI FERNÀNDEZ, ISABEL LOZANO.

Other parties exist at the parish level.

Diplomatic Representation

EMBASSIES IN ANDORRA

France: Carrer les Canals 38–40, POB 155, Andorra la Vella AD500; tel. 736700; fax 736701; e-mail info@ambafrance-ad.org; internet www.ambafrance-ad.org; Ambassador ZAÏR KEDADOUCHE.

Spain: Carrer Prat de la Creu 34, Andorra la Vella AD500; tel. 800030; fax 868500; e-mail embaesp@andorra.ad; internet www.maec.es/embajadas/andorra; Ambassador ALBERTO MORENO.

Judicial System

Judicial power is vested, in the first instance, in the Magistrates' Courts (Batllia) and in the Judges' Tribunal (Tribunal de Batlles), the criminal law courts (Tribunal de Corts) and the Higher Court of Justice (Tribunal Superior de la Justícia). The judiciary is represented, directed and administered by the Higher Council of Justice (Consell Superior de la Justícia), whose five members are appointed for single terms of six years. Final jurisdiction, in constitutional matters, is vested in the Constitutional Court (Tribunal Constitucional), whose four members hold office for no more than two consecutive eight-year terms.

The 1993 Constitution guarantees the independence of the judiciary.

Higher Council of Justice (Consell Superior de la Justícia): Edif. les columnes, Andorra la Vella AD500; tel. 807390; fax 868778; e-mail csj@justicia.ad; internet www.justicia.ad; Pres. CASADEVALL MEDRANO.

Religion

More than 90% of the population of Andorra are Roman Catholic. Andorra forms part of the Spanish diocese of Urgell.

The Press

Bondia: Carrer Maria Pla 28, 1°, Andorra la Vella AD500; tel. 808888; fax 828888; e-mail bondia@bondia.ad; internet www.bondia.ad; f. 2004; daily; distributed free of charge; edn in Lleida, Spain; Dir MARC SEGALÉS.

Butlletí Oficial del Principat d'Andorra: Carrer Dr Vilanova 15, Andorra la Vella AD500; tel. 729410; fax 724300; e-mail atencio.public.bopa@govern.ad; internet www.bopa.ad; weekly; official govt gazette.

Diari d'Andorra: Carrer Bonaventura Riberaygua 39, 5°, Andorra la Vella AD500; tel. 877477; fax 863800; e-mail info@diariandorra.ad; internet www.diariandorra.ad; f. 1991; daily; local issues; Pres. MARC VILA AMIGÓ; Dir-Gen. IGNASI DE PLANELL; circ. 17,165.

El Periòdic d'Andorra: Avinguda Fiter i Rossell 4, Escaldes-Engordany AD700; tel. 736200; fax 736210; e-mail redaccio@elperiodicdandorra.ad; internet www.elperiodicdandorra.ad; daily; local issues; Propr Grupo Zeta, SA (Spain); Dir JOAN RAMON BAIGES; Editor-in-Chief EVA ARASA.

Broadcasting and Communications

TELECOMMUNICATIONS

Andorra Telecom: Carrer Mossen Lluis Pujol 8–14, Santa Coloma AD500; tel. 875105; fax 725003; internet www.andorratelecom.ad; f. 1975 as Servei de Telecomunicacions d'Andorra; provides national and international telecommunications and internet services under the SOM brand; manages the radio and television broadcasting infrastructure; Dir-Gen. JAUME SALVAT FONT.

BROADCASTING

In 2010 one television station was active in Andorra; it was possible to receive broadcasts from television stations in neighbouring countries. Analogue broadcasting was phased out in September 2007.

Radio

Ràdio i Televisió d'Andorra, SA—Ràdio Nacional Andorra (RTVA): Baixada del Molí 24, Andorra la Vella AD500; tel. 873777; fax 863242; e-mail rtva@rtva.ad; internet www.rtva.ad; f. 1990 as an Andorran-owned commercial public broadcasting service; adopted present name in 2000; Ràdio Nacional Andorra (RNA) is the national radio station; Dir-Gen. FRANCESC ROBERT RIBES.

R7P Ràdio: Avinguda Príncep Benlloch 24, Encamp AD200; tel. 732000; fax 831901; e-mail administracio@cadenapirenaica.com; internet www.cadenapirenaica.com; commercial broadcasting service, aimed at people aged 25–45 years; owned by Cadena Pirenaica de Ràdio i Televisió; Man. Dir EDUARD NAVARRO ISCLA.

Ràdio Valira: Avinguda Príncep Benlloch 24, Encamp AD200; tel. 732000; fax 831901; e-mail administracio@cadenapirenaica.com; internet www.cadenapirenaica.com; f. 1986; commercial broadcasting service, aimed at people aged 40–65 years; owned by Cadena Pirenaica de Ràdio i Televisió; Man. Dir EDUARD NAVARRO ISCLA.

Television

Ràdio i Televisió d'Andorra, SA—Andorra Televisió (RTVA): Baixada del Molí 24, Andorra la Vella AD500; tel. 873777; fax 864232; e-mail rtva@rtva.ad; internet www.rtva.ad; f. 1995 as an Andorran-owned commercial public broadcasting service; Andorra Televisió (ATV) is the national television channel; Dir-Gen. FRANCESC ROBERT.

Finance

(cap. = capital; res = reserves; dep. = deposits; m. = million; brs = branches; amounts in euros)

REGULATORY AUTHORITY

Institut Nacional Andorrà de Finances (INAF): Carrer Bonaventura Armengol, Edif. Montclar 10, bloc 2, 4°A, Andorra la Vella AD500; tel. 808898; fax 865977; e-mail inaf.sc@inaf.ad; internet www.inaf.ad; f. 1993; Chair. RAÜL GONZÁLEZ FERNÁNDEZ; CEO MARIA COSAN CANUT.

BANKS

In 2013 five banking groups were operating in Andorra.

Andbanc: Carrer Manuel Cerqueda i Escaler 6, Escaldes-Engordany AD700; tel. 873333; fax 873353; e-mail corporate@andbanc.com; internet www.andbanc.com; f. 2001 as Andorra Banc Agrícol Reig by merger of Banca Reig and Banc Agrícol i Comercial d'Andorra; cap. 78.1m., res 330.1m., dep. 2,581.8m. (Dec. 2012); Chair. MANEL CERQUERDA DONADEU; Gen. Man. JORDI COMAS PLANAS; 12 brs.

BancSabadell d'Andorra: Avinguda del Fener 7, Andorra la Vella AD500; tel. 735600; fax 735601; e-mail operacions@bsa.ad; internet www.bsandorra.com; cap. 30.1m., res 23.5m., dep. 525.4m. (Dec. 2012); Chair. ROBERT CASSANY I VILA; Gen. Man. MIQUEL ALABERN I COMAS; 7 brs.

BPA (Banca Privada d'Andorra SA): Avinguda Carlemany 119, POB 25, Escaldes-Engordany AD700; tel. 873501; fax 873515; e-mail bpa@bpa.ad; internet www.bpa.ad; f. 1962 as Banca Cassany SA; name changed to Banca Privada d'Andorra in 1994; cap. 70.0m., res 149.7m., dep. 2,363.5m. (Dec. 2012); Pres HIGINI CIERCO NOGUER, RAMON CIERCO NOGUER; Gen. Man. JOAN PAU MIQUEL PRATS; 8 brs.

Crèdit Andorrà: Avinguda Meritxell 80, Andorra la Vella AD500; tel. 888600; fax 888601; e-mail comunicacio@creditandorra.ad; internet www.creditandorra.ad; f. 1949; merged with CaixaBank SA in 2007; cap. 70.0m., res 405.2m., dep. 5,006.1m. (Dec. 2012); Chair. ANTONI PINTAT; CEO JOSEP PERALBA; 17 brs.

MoraBanc: Avinguda Meritxell 96, Andorra la Vella AD500; tel. 884488; fax 884499; e-mail morabanc@morabanc.ad; internet www.morabanc.ad; f. 1958 as Banc International; known as BIBM until 2011; cap. 42.4m., res 197.6m., dep. 1,735.6m. (Dec. 2012); Chair. FRANCESC MORA SAGUÉS; Chief Exec. GILLES SERRA; 11 brs.

Banking Association

Associació de Bancs Andorrans (Association of Andorran Banks—ABA): Carrer Ciutat de Consuegra 16, Edif. L'Illa, Escala A-2°, Andorra la Vella AD500; tel. 807110; fax 866847; e-mail aba@aba.ad; internet www.aba.ad; f. 1960; Dir ANTONI ARMENGOL.

INSURANCE

In 2013 there were 15 Andorran insurance companies registered, while a further 14 foreign companies were also authorized to operate in Andorra.

Assegur: Calle Pau Casals 10, planta 2, AD500 Andorra la Vella; tel. 876555; fax 860759; e-mail atencioclient@assegur.com; internet www.assegur.com.

Assegurances Generals Andorra, SA: Carrer Sant Salvador 7, Edif. Rosella, Andorra la Vella AD500; tel. 877677; fax 860093; e-mail aga@andorra.ad; internet www.assegurancesgenerals.com; Pres. AMADEU CALVÓ CASAL.

BPA Assegurances, SA: Avinguda Carlemany 119, Escaldes-Engordany AD700; tel. 873500; fax 873515; e-mail atencioclient@bpa.ad; internet www.bpa.ad; savings, life and health; insurance division of Banca Privada d'Andorra; Pres HIGINI C. NOGUER, RAMON C. NOGUER.

Financera d'Assegurances, SA: Carrer Babot Camp 11, Andorra la Vella AD500; tel. 890300; fax 864717; e-mail info@e-financera.com; internet www.e-financera.com; non-life.

Trade and Industry

GOVERNMENT AGENCY

Andorra Desenvolupament i Inversió (ADI) (Andorra Development and Investment): Camí de la Grau, Edif. Prat del Rull, Andorra la Vella AD500; tel. 812020; fax 812021; e-mail info@adi.ad; internet www.adi.ad; f. 2009; fmrly Oficina d'Innovació Empresarial; promotes economic development and foreign investment; Dir CARLES ALEIX.

CHAMBER OF COMMERCE

Cambra de Comerç, Indústria i Serveis d'Andorra (Chamber of Commerce, Industry and Services of Andorra): Carrer Prat de la Creu 8, Edif. Le Mans, Despatx 204–207, Andorra la Vella AD500; tel. 809292; fax 809293; e-mail ccis@andorra.ad; internet www.ccis.ad; Pres. MARC PANTEBRE PALMITJAVILA; Dir PILAR ESCALER PENELLA.

UTILITIES

Electricity

The Forces Elèctriques d'Andorra (FEDA) distributes 69% of energy used in Andorra, while four smaller companies, supplied by FEDA, distribute the rest of the electricity used.

Forces Elèctriques d'Andorra (FEDA): Avinguda de la Barta s/n, Encamp AD200; tel. 739100; fax 739118; e-mail feda@feda.ad; internet www.feda.ad; f. 1988; imports, generates and distributes electricity; state-owned; Pres. JORDI CINCA MATEOS (Minister of Finance and Public Service); Dir-Gen. ALBERT MOLES BETRIU.

EMPLOYERS' ORGANIZATIONS

Associació Empresa Familiar Andorrana (EFA): Carrer Bonaventura Armengol 15, Edif. OCCESA, 6è, Andorra la Vella AD500; tel. 808136; fax 826174; e-mail efa@andorra.ad; internet www.efa.ad; f. 2002; family-owned businesses; c. 50 mems.

Associació de la Micro, Petita i Mitjana Empresa d'Andorra (PIME): Carrer de les Escoles 28, Escalades-Engordany AD700; tel. 824344; fax 855750; e-mail info@pimeandorra.com; internet www.pimeandorra.com; f. 2005; small and medium-sized enterprises; Pres. MARC ALEIX TUGÁS; c. 150 mems.

Club de Marketing d'Andorra: Avinguda Meritxell 105, 5°, Andorra La Vella AD500; tel. 327757; fax 863737; e-mail retroferran@gmail.com; internet www.clubmarketingandorra.com; Pres. CARLES NAUDI.

Confederació Empresarial Andorrana (CEA): Carrer Prat de la Creu 59–65, Escala B, 2on, Andorra la Vella AD500; tel. 800020; fax 800024; e-mail info@cea.ad; internet www.cea.ad; f. 2006; Pres. XAVIER ALTIMIR PLANES.

TRADE UNIONS

Sindicat Andorrà de Treballadors (SAT): Carretera de l'Adosa, Edif. Busquets, Anyós, La Massana; tel. 826085; internet www.sitca.org; Pres. CRISTIAN ASENSIO.

Sindicat de l'Ensenyament Públic (SEP): Carrer de les Escoles 3, La Massana AD400; tel. 379630; e-mail contacte@sep.ad; internet www.sep.ad; f. 2007; Sec.-Gen. SANTI RODRÍGUEZ.

Unió Sindical d'Andorra (USdA): Carrer de les Boïgues s/n, Edif. Pic Blanc, Andorra la Vella AD500; tel. 356270; fax 826770; e-mail usda@andorra.ad; internet www.usda.ad; Sec.-Gen. GABRIEL UBACH.

Transport

RAILWAYS

There are no railways in Andorra. The nearest stations are Ax-les-Thermes, L'Hospitalet and La Tour de Carol, in France (with trains from Toulouse and Perpignan), and Puigcerdà, in Spain, on the line from Barcelona. There is a connecting bus service from all four stations to Andorra.

ROADS

A good road connects the Spanish and French frontiers, passing through Andorra la Vella. The Envalira tunnel, between Andorra and France, was opened in September 2002. The Dos Valires tunnel to link Encamp and La Massana opened in 2012. Two companies, Cooperativa Interurbana Andorrana and Hispano Andorrana, operate bus services within Andorra.

CIVIL AVIATION

The Pirineus-La Seu airport at La Seu d'Urgell, located in Spanish territory 10 km from the border with Andorra, reopened in June 2010 following a redevelopment programme financed jointly by the Andorran, Spanish and Catalan administrations.

Tourism

Andorra has attractive mountain scenery, and winter sports facilities are available at five skiing centres. Tourists are also attracted by Andorra's duty-free shopping facilities. A total of 2.2m. tourists visited Andorra in 2012, mainly from Spain and France. In 2004 the valley of Madriu was declared a UNESCO World Heritage Site.

Andorra Turisme, SAU: Carrer Prat de la Creu 59–65, Andorra la Vella AD500; tel. 891189; fax 828123; e-mail info@visitandorra.com; internet visitandorra.com; f. 2008; Man. BETIM BUDZAKU.

Ski Andorra: Avinguda Tarragona 58–70, Despatx 14, Andorra la Vella AD500; tel. 805200; fax 865910; e-mail skiandorra@skiandorra.ad; internet www.skiandorra.ad; association of ski stations; Dir MARTA ROTÉS.

Unió Hotelera d'Andorra (Hotel Association of Andorra): Antic Carrer Major 18, Andorra la Vella AD500; tel. 809602; fax 861539; e-mail uhotelera@uha.ad; internet www.uha.ad; f. 1961; Pres. ALEX ARMENGOL; Sec.-Gen. ELISABETH ROSSELL; 200 mems.

Each parish has its own tourist office.

Defence

Andorra has no defence budget.

Education

Education is compulsory for children of between six and 16 years of age, and is provided free of charge by Catalan-, French- and Spanish-language schools. (Children educated under the French or Spanish state systems are required to study some Catalan.) Six years of primary education are followed by four years of secondary schooling. University education is undertaken either at the University of Andorra or abroad, mostly in Spain and France. The University of Andorra offers degrees in business administration, education science, nursing and computer science. According to UNESCO figures, in 2011/12 85% of the relevant age-group were enrolled in pre-primary education, 75% in primary and 73% in secondary education. In 2012/13 there were a total of 10,461 pupils enrolled at Andorra's schools. Of these, 4,167 were under the Andorran education system (where Catalan is the teaching medium), 3,188 were attending French-speaking schools and 3,106 were being educated under the Spanish system (secular and congregational). In 2005/06 1,066 students were in higher education; 431 students were studying in Andorra, 131 in France and 503 in Spain. A new baccalaureate examination, which was intended to facilitate direct access for students in the Andorran education system to universities in other European countries, was introduced in 2008. In 2010 public spending on education equalled 2.9% of gross domestic product.

ANGOLA

Introductory Survey

LOCATION, CLIMATE, LANGUAGE, RELIGION, FLAG, CAPITAL

The Republic of Angola lies on the west coast of Africa. The province of Cabinda is separated from the rest of the country by the estuary of the River Congo and territory of the Democratic Republic of the Congo (DRC—formerly Zaire), with the Republic of the Congo lying to its north. Angola is bordered by the DRC to the north, Zambia to the east and Namibia to the south. The climate is tropical, locally tempered by altitude. There are two distinct seasons (wet and dry) but little seasonal variation in temperature. It is very hot and rainy in the coastal lowlands but temperatures are lower inland. The official language is Portuguese, but African languages (the most widely spoken being Umbundu, Lunda, Kikongo, Chokwe and Kwanyama) are also in common use. Much of the population follows traditional African beliefs, although a majority profess to be Christians, mainly Roman Catholics. The flag (proportions 2 by 3) has two equal horizontal stripes, of red and black; superimposed in the centre, in gold, are a five-pointed star, half a cog-wheel and a machete. The capital is Luanda.

CONTEMPORARY POLITICAL HISTORY

Historical Context

Formerly a Portuguese colony, Angola became an overseas province in 1951. African nationalist groups began to form in the 1950s and 1960s, including the Movimento Popular de Libertação de Angola (MPLA) in 1956, the Frente Nacional de Libertação de Angola (FNLA) in 1962 and the União Nacional para a Independência Total de Angola (UNITA) in 1966. Severe repression followed an unsuccessful nationalist rebellion in 1961, but, after a new wave of fighting in 1966, nationalist guerrilla groups were able to establish military and political control in large parts of eastern Angola and to press westward. Following the April 1974 coup in Portugal, Angola's right to independence was recognized.

In January 1975 a transitional Government was established, comprising representatives of the MPLA, the FNLA, UNITA and the Portuguese Government. However, following violent clashes between the MPLA and the FNLA, by the second half of 1975 control of Angola was effectively divided between the three major nationalist groups, each aided by foreign powers. The MPLA (which held the capital) was supported by the USSR and Cuba, the FNLA by Zaire and Western powers (including the USA), while UNITA was backed by South African forces. The FNLA and UNITA formed a united front to fight the MPLA.

The Portuguese Government proclaimed Angola independent from 11 November 1975, transferring sovereignty to 'the Angolan people' rather than to any of the liberation movements. The MPLA proclaimed the People's Republic of Angola in Luanda under the presidency of Dr Agostinho Neto. The FNLA and UNITA proclaimed the Democratic People's Republic of Angola, based in Nova Lisboa (renamed Huambo). By the end of February 1976, however, the MPLA, aided by Cuban technical and military expertise, had effectively gained control of the whole country.

Domestic Political Affairs

Neto died in September 1979, and José Eduardo dos Santos, hitherto the Minister of Planning, was elected party leader and President by the Central Committee of the Movimento Popular de Libertação de Angola—Partido do Trabalho (MPLA—PT, as the MPLA had been renamed in December 1977). Elections to the Assembleia Popular (People's Assembly), which replaced the Conselho da Revolução (Council of the Revolution), were first held in 1980.

The MPLA—PT Government's recovery programme was continually hindered by security problems and UNITA conducted sustained and disruptive guerrilla activities, mainly in southern and central Angola, throughout the 1980s. In addition, forces from South Africa, which was providing UNITA with considerable military aid, made numerous armed incursions over the Angolan border with Namibia, ostensibly in pursuit of guerrilla forces belonging to the South West Africa People's Organization (SWAPO), which was supported by the Angolan Government. UNITA was excluded from a series of major peace negotiations, between Angola, Cuba and South Africa (with the unofficial mediation of the USA), which commenced in May 1988. By July the participants had agreed to a document containing the principles for a peace settlement that provided for independence for Namibia, the discontinuation of South African military support for UNITA and the withdrawal of Cuban troops from Angola. Following the conclusion of the New York accords on Angola and Namibia in December, the UN Security Council established the UN Angola Verification Mission (UNAVEM) to verify the phased withdrawal of Cuban troops from Angola, which was completed in May 1991.

In October 1990 the Central Committee of the MPLA—PT proposed a general programme of reform, including the replacement of the party's official Marxist-Leninist ideology with a commitment to 'democratic socialism', the legalization of political parties, the transformation of the army from a party institution to a state institution, the introduction of a market economy, a revision of the Constitution and the holding of multi-party elections in 1994, following a population census. In March 1991 the People's Assembly approved legislation permitting the formation of political parties.

On 1 May 1991 the Government and UNITA concluded a peace agreement in Estoril, Portugal, which provided for a ceasefire from 15 May. A new national army of 50,000 men was to be established, comprising equal numbers of government and UNITA soldiers. Free and democratic elections were to be held by the end of 1992. On 31 May the Government and UNITA signed a formal agreement in Lisbon, Portugal, ratifying the Estoril agreement. The UN Security Council agreed to establish UNAVEM II, with a mandate to ensure implementation of the peace accord.

Representatives of the Government and 26 political parties met in Luanda in January 1992 to discuss the transition to multi-party democracy. It was agreed in February that the elections, which were to take place in September, would be conducted on the basis of proportional representation, with the President elected for a five-year term, renewable for a maximum of three terms. The legislature would be a national assembly, elected for a four-year term. In April the People's Assembly adopted electoral legislation incorporating these decisions and providing for the creation of an Assembleia Nacional (National Assembly) comprising 223 members (90 to be elected in 18 provincial constituencies and the remainder from national lists).

In April 1992 the Tribunal da Relação (Court of Appeal) approved UNITA's registration as a political party. In May the MPLA—PT removed the suffix Partido do Trabalho from the organization's official name. In August the legislature approved a further revision of the Constitution, removing the remnants of the country's former Marxist ideology, and deleting the words 'People's' and 'Popular' from the Constitution and from the names of official institutions. The name of the country was changed from the People's Republic of Angola to the Republic of Angola.

In early September 1992 in Cabinda province, the enclave that provides most of Angola's petroleum revenue, secessionist groups, notably the Frente para a Libertação do Enclave de Cabinda (FLEC), intensified attacks on government troops. Later that month the government Forças Armadas Populares de Libertação de Angola (FAPLA) and the UNITA forces were formally disbanded, and the new national army, the Forças Armadas de Angola (FAA), was established.

Presidential and legislative elections were held, as scheduled, on 29 and 30 September 1992. When preliminary results indicated victory for the MPLA in the elections to the new National Assembly, the leader of UNITA, Dr Jonas Savimbi, accused the Government of electoral fraud, withdrew his troops from the FAA, and demanded the suspension of the official announcement of the election results until an inquiry into the alleged irregularities had been conducted. A second round of the presidential election was required to be held between dos Santos and Savimbi, as neither candidate had secured 50% of the votes cast in the first round. Savimbi agreed to participate in this second round on the condition that it be conducted by the UN, while the Government insisted that the election should not take place until UNITA had satisfied the conditions of the Estoril peace agreement by transferring its troops to assembly points or to the FAA.

Post-election conflict

By the end of October 1992, following the release of the official election results, hostilities had spread throughout Angola, with the majority of UNITA's demobilized soldiers returning to arms. In November Savimbi agreed to abide by the results of the September elections, although he maintained that the ballot had been fraudulent. Subsequently dos Santos announced that the National Assembly would be inaugurated on 26 November. On that day delegations from the Government and UNITA issued a joint communiqué, declaring full acceptance of the validity of the Estoril peace agreement and the intention to implement immediately a nationwide ceasefire. However, UNITA's 70 elected deputies failed to attend the inauguration of the Assembly. On 27 November 1992 dos Santos announced the appointment of Marcolino José Carlos Moco, the Secretary-General of the MPLA, as Prime Minister. At the end of November, however, hostilities broke out in the north of the country.

In December 1993 an agreement was reportedly reached between UNITA and the Government on issues concerning the demobilization of UNITA troops and the integration of UNITA generals into the FAA. An agreement was also reached in Lusaka, Zambia, on the formation, under UN supervision, of a national police force of 26,700 members, of which UNITA was to provide 5,500, while in June 1994 an 18-point document on national reconciliation was signed, and acceptance of the September 1992 election results by both sides was reaffirmed.

In September 1994, following successive extensions, the UN Security Council further extended the mandate of UNAVEM II until 31 October. Talks continued throughout October, concentrating on the issue of Savimbi's security and the replacement of the joint political and military commission with a new joint commission, which was to be chaired by the UN Secretary-General's special representative and was to comprise representatives of the Government and UNITA and observers from the USA, Russia and Portugal. A peace accord was finally initialled on 31 October and formally signed on 20 November. However, hostilities continued beyond 22 November, when a permanent ceasefire was to have come into force, notably in Huambo and in Bié province. In February 1995 the UN Security Council adopted a resolution creating UNAVEM III, but deployment of the new peacekeeping mission remained conditional on the cessation of hostilities and the disengagement of government and UNITA forces.

In May 1995 dos Santos and Savimbi met in Lusaka for direct talks, which concluded with the ratification of the Lusaka peace accord. Savimbi recognized the status of dos Santos as President of Angola and pledged his full co-operation in the reconstruction of the nation.

In July 1995 the Assembly approved the creation of two new vice-presidential positions, of which one was to be offered to Savimbi, conditional upon the prior disbanding of UNITA forces. The other post was to be assumed by Fernando José França Van-Dúnem, the President of the National Assembly. Savimbi, who had publicly expressed his intention to accept the vice-presidency, had in June declared the war in Angola to be at an end. In July the UN announced that the deployment of UNAVEM III personnel would be completed by the end of August.

In March 1996 discussions between dos Santos and Savimbi, conducted in Libreville, Gabon, resulted in agreement on the establishment of a government of national unity, in accordance with the provisions of the Lusaka accord. Savimbi proposed UNITA governmental nominees, while dos Santos formally invited Savimbi to assume the vice-presidency. Agreement was also reached in Libreville on the formation of a unified national army, which, it was envisaged, would be concluded in June. In May the Government and a Cabinda secessionist faction, FLEC—Forças Armadas Cabindesas (FLEC—FAC), signed an agreement outlining the principles of a ceasefire. However, following renewed fighting later that month between government troops and the secessionists, the leader of FLEC—FAC, N'zita Henriques Tiago, declared that a definitive ceasefire would only follow the withdrawal of the FAA from Cabinda. A separate ceasefire had been signed with FLEC—Renovada (FLEC—R) in September 1995.

In November 1996 the National Assembly adopted a constitutional revision extending its mandate, which was due to expire that month, for a period of between two and four years, pending the establishment of suitable conditions for the conduct of free and fair elections. In April 1997 an agreement was reached to accord Savimbi the special status of official 'leader of the opposition'. Following the arrival of the full contingent of UNITA deputies and government nominees in Luanda, on 11 April the new Government of National Unity and Reconciliation was inaugurated. As envisaged, UNITA assumed a number of ministerial and deputy ministerial portfolios.

On 30 June 1997 the UN Security Council unanimously approved the discontinuation of UNAVEM III and its replacement by a scaled-down observer mission, the UN Observer Mission in Angola (MONUA), with a seven-month mandate to oversee the implementation of the remaining provisions of the Lusaka accord.

Protracted peace attempts

On 31 October 1997, as a result of UNITA's continued failure to meet its obligations under the peace accord, the UN Security Council ordered the implementation of additional sanctions against the movement. In November UNITA expressed its intention to continue to pursue a peaceful settlement, and during the ensuing months ceded further territory to state administration, including the important Cuango valley diamond mines in Lunda-Norte province.

In January 1998 a new schedule was agreed for the implementation of the Lusaka protocol. In early March UNITA announced the disbandment of its remaining forces, following which it received official recognition as a legally constituted party. However, allegations persisted of preparations by UNITA for a resumption of hostilities. By June fighting had spread to 14 of the country's 18 provinces, displacing some 150,000 people. In August UNITA accused the observer countries in the joint commission of bias in the Government's favour and declared that it would no longer negotiate with them. On 31 August the Government suspended UNITA's government and parliamentary representatives from office.

In September 1998 a group of five UNITA moderates issued a manifesto declaring the suspension of Savimbi and the introduction of an interim UNITA leadership, pending a general congress of the party. Although the group, which styled itself UNITA—Renovada (UNITA—R), commanded very limited support among UNITA's leaders in Luanda, the Government welcomed the development, recognizing UNITA—R as the sole and legitimate representative of UNITA in negotiations concerning the implementation of the Lusaka peace process. The UN Security Council continued to seek a dialogue between dos Santos and Savimbi as the only solution to the conflict. In late September the Government revoked the suspension of UNITA's representatives in the Government and legislature, and in October the National Assembly revoked Savimbi's special status. In that month UNITA—R failed to impose its candidate to lead the UNITA parliamentary group when Abel Chivukuvuku was overwhelmingly re-elected as its Chairman. Chivukuvuku, while no longer claiming allegiance to Savimbi, was opposed to UNITA—R and subsequently formed his own wing of UNITA.

Following increasingly frequent outbreaks of fighting, in January 1999, in an effort to address the prevailing military and economic crisis, dos Santos assumed the role of Prime Minister. In February the UN Security Council voted unanimously to end MONUA's mandate and withdraw its operatives by 20 March, on the grounds that conditions had deteriorated to such an extent that UN personnel were no longer able to function. In October the UN and the Government formally agreed on the establishment of a 30-member 'follow-up' mission, the UN Office in Angola (UNOA), which was to focus on issues concerning humanitarian assistance and human rights.

During 1999 the UN increased its efforts to impose sanctions on UNITA. A UN report published in June disclosed the contravention of UN sanctions by a number of African heads of state, who were apparently involved in the trading of arms for UNITA-mined diamonds. In October the South African diamond company De Beers, which controls the majority of the international trade in diamonds, announced that it had placed a worldwide embargo on the purchase of all diamonds from Angola, except those whose acquisition was already under contract. The Angolan Government also attempted to stem the flow of illegal diamonds by introducing a strict regime of stone certification. In early 2000 the Angolan Government announced the establishment of a state-owned company, which was to be responsible for centralizing and regulating the country's diamond trade. All marketing was transferred to the newly created Angolan Selling Corporation.

In February 2002 Savimbi was killed during an ambush by FAA soldiers in Moxico province. In March the Government halted military offensives against UNITA, and at the end of that month both parties signed a memorandum of understanding, aimed at ending the civil war. On 4 April a ceasefire agreement was ratified, in which UNITA accepted the Lusaka protocol and agreed to the cantonment of its soldiers. Some 5,000 UNITA soldiers were to be integrated into the FAA, and UNITA representatives were to take up positions in central, provincial and local government.

By the end of July 2002 some 85,000 UNITA soldiers and an estimated 300,000 family members had registered in quartering camps, and in early August UNITA announced that its military wing had been disbanded, following the integration of its soldiers into the FAA. Also in August, the UN Security Council established the UN Mission in Angola (UNMA) to succeed UNOA until 15 February 2003. On 23 August 2002 the Government and UNITA set a 45-day deadline for the full implementation of the Lusaka protocol, which was to be monitored by a UN-led joint commission, comprising representatives of the Government, UNITA and observer countries (Portugal, Russia and the USA). In October the inauguration of a new national political commission for UNITA, including former members of UNITA—R, marked the official reunification of the party.

The FAA maintained forces in Cabinda throughout 2003, and by the middle of that year it was believed that the province had been largely pacified. In September 2004 the merger was announced of FLEC—FAC and FLEC—R. The new grouping, which adopted the name FLEC, was led by Tiago, while António Bento Bembe, previously the President of FLEC—R, became Secretary-General of the movement. A political wing, styling itself FLEC—Conselho Superior Alargado (FLEC—CSA), with the stated aim of achieving independence through political means, was subsequently established under the leadership of Liberal Nuno.

Towards constitutional reform

In December 2002 Fernando (Nando) da Piedade Dias dos Santos, hitherto Minister of the Interior, was appointed as Prime Minister, a post that President dos Santos had held since January 1999. The Council of Ministers was subsequently reorganized, with the inclusion of the four UNITA representatives. Shortly afterwards the UN Security Council voted to lift all remaining sanctions on UNITA, having previously removed travel restrictions on officials of the former rebel group. Meanwhile, a Constitutional Commission (which had been established by the National Assembly in 1998) was considering proposals for a new draft constitution. Agreement was reached on a major point of contention in January 2003, when the Commission decided that the President of the Republic would remain Head of Government, as favoured by MPLA deputies; UNITA had advocated the devolvement of executive power to the Prime Minister. In February UNMA withdrew from Angola, as scheduled. The demobilization of former UNITA soldiers continued throughout 2003. The Government closed the 35 quartering camps in June, and by November around 80,000 soldiers, along with their families, had been demobilized.

In January 2004 the Constitutional Commission was presented with a draft constitution and in mid-2004 the Government, which had identified 14 'key tasks' it wished to accomplish before calling concurrent legislative and presidential elections—including constitutional reform and the compiling of an electoral register—stated that polls would not take place until late 2006. However, several opposition parties, including UNITA, insisted that elections could take place in 2005 without constitutional reform and withdrew from the Commission in May 2004 in protest. In November the Commission was dissolved, after a draft constitutional bill had been presented to the National Assembly. In July 2005 the Court of Appeal ruled that President dos Santos was eligible to stand for re-election, and in August, following approval by that body, dos Santos signed into law legislation providing for the creation of a Comissão Nacional Eleitoral (CNE—National Electoral Commission).

In August 2006 a peace agreement was signed with FLEC, recognizing Cabinda as part of Angola but granting it special status, with a greater degree of autonomy than other provinces. Human rights organizations alleged that this deal had been imposed by force, and members of the Fórum Cabindês para o Diálogo (FCD) claimed that Bembe, with whom the agreement had been reached, was not a valid spokesman (as did members of FLEC). In August 2007 President dos Santos announced further steps to consolidate peace, including the appointment of a number of FCD members to positions in government.

The 2008 legislative elections

A total of 14 political parties contested the first legislative elections to take place in Angola for 16 years, which were held on 5–6 September 2008. Some 7.2m. Angolans (representing 87.4% of those eligible to vote) participated in the polls, at which the ruling MPLA secured 81.6% of the valid votes cast, equating to 191 of the 220 seats in the National Assembly. UNITA became the second largest party in the legislature, taking 10.4% of the total votes cast and winning 16 seats. The remaining seats were taken by the Partido de Renovação Social (PRS—eight), the FNLA (three) and the Nova Democracia—União Eleitoral (two). Observers from the European Union (EU, see p. 273) noted organizational problems and declared, that owing to state control of the media, the election fell short of international standards. None the less, the head of the EU mission stated that the election still marked an 'advance for democracy'. In late September António Paulo Kassoma, a member of the MPLA politburo and hitherto the Governor of Huambo province, was appointed Prime Minister, and early the following month a new 35-member Government, which included 17 new ministers, was named. The two most senior members of the outgoing administration, the Minister of National Defence, Gen. Kundi Paihama, and the Minister of the Interior, Gen. Roberto Leal Monteiro, retained their posts.

A new Constitution

In October 2009 three different draft versions of the proposed text of the new constitution were made available for a public consultation process. While opposition parties favoured the insertion of a clause providing for the direct popular election of the President, the ruling MPLA was expected to be able to secure its preferred constitutional document (which advocated the selection of the President by the largest party in the legislature) owing to the overwhelming majority of its members in both the National Assembly and the Tribunal Constitucional (Constitutional Court).

In late January 2010 the National Assembly approved the text of the new constitution and, after minor amendments were made by the Constitutional Court, on 5 February President dos Santos officially promulgated the new basic law. According to the Constitution, the presidency was henceforth to be assumed by the leader of the political party, or coalition of political parties, obtaining the majority of votes in legislative elections, and the President, who was to be both Head of State and Head of Government, was eligible to serve a maximum of two five-year terms. The 223 members of the National Assembly were also to serve five-year terms concurrent with that of the President (hitherto they had served four-year terms that had run to a different schedule). The position of Prime Minister was abolished and a Vice-President (the deputy leader of the ruling party) was to be appointed. The new Constitution also outlawed the death penalty. On 6 February dos Santos announced the formation of a new Government, in accordance with the provisions of the new Constitution. Former Prime Minister Nando dos Santos became Vice-President. Monteiro and the ministers responsible for the economy and foreign affairs portfolios in the outgoing administration were all reappointed; however, Cândido Pereira dos Santos Van-Dúnem replaced Gen. Paihama as Minister of National Defence.

In September 2010 Monteiro was dismissed from his post amid claims that the interior ministry had illegally detained and extradited (to Angola) a Portuguese citizen resident in São Tomé and Príncipe; Jorge Manuel dos Santos Oliveira was to be tried in Angola for fraud against an Angolan company. Sebastião José António Martins was subsequently named as Monteiro's replacement. Further ministerial changes were effected in November; most notably, George Rebelo Chicoty, hitherto Secretary of State for Foreign Affairs, was appointed Minister of Foreign Affairs, replacing Assunção Afonso dos Anjos.

Recent developments: the 2012 legislative elections

Inspired by the pro-democracy demonstrations that had erupted across the Middle East and North Africa during early 2011, a small group of online activists attempted to stage its own anti-Government rally in Luanda in March to demand the resignation of the dos Santos regime. However, the authorities pre-emptively disbanded the march and briefly detained 15 demonstrators and journalists, attracting criticism from human rights organizations. The Government had earlier organized multiple pro-MPLA rallies, attended by some 20,000 people, and had issued threats against potential protesters. Further arrests were made in May, when a small-scale protest against poverty was dispersed by the Luandan police, and in September, following violent clashes in the capital between police and demonstrators. As a result of the latter incident, 18 anti-regime protesters received short gaol sentences (which were subsequently rescinded by the Tribunal Supremo—Supreme Court) and demonstrations in central Luanda were proscribed. Another small, youth-led demonstration was halted by the police in late September, and several journalists were reportedly attacked by unknown assailants. The MPLA repeatedly accused UNITA of orchestrating the protests, a charge denied by the opposition party. Sporadic anti-Government demonstrations continued during 2012–13, and further arrests and violence were reported.

Although dos Santos had been shaken by this unprecedented popular challenge to his authority, it was confirmed in June 2012 that he would lead the MPLA in the upcoming legislative elections, which were scheduled to be held in August. Minister of State for Economic Co-ordination Manuel Vicente, who was widely regarded as a potential successor to the 69-year-old President, was named as the ruling party's vice-presidential nominee.

Meanwhile, controversy was aroused in January 2012 when the MPLA-dominated legislature designated Suzana Inglês, a high-profile figure within the ruling party, as President of the CNE. Opposition parties argued that her appointment would undermine the legitimacy of the upcoming polls and demanded that, in accordance with new electoral regulations approved during the previous month, she be replaced by an independent candidate. Following opposition threats of large-scale protests and an electoral boycott, in May the Supreme Court ruled that Inglês' appointment had been unlawful; she was succeeded by André da Silva Neto in June.

The legislative elections took place as scheduled on 31 August 2012. The MPLA retained its position as the dominant political force, winning 71.9% of the valid votes cast and 175 seats in the National Assembly. As leader of the victorious party, dos Santos was awarded the presidency for a further five years, although there was media speculation that he would stand down before serving his full term in office. UNITA obtained 18.7% of the ballot and 32 seats, while the recently formed Convergência Ampla de Salvação de Angola-Coligação Eleitoral (CASA-CE) won eight seats, the PRS three and the FNLA two. Parties that had failed to attract 0.5% of the vote were to be formally disbanded. Turnout was recorded at 62.8%, and African Union monitors, while acknowledging some deficiencies, endorsed the results. UNITA, the CASA-CE and the PRS asserted that the election had been fraudulent, citing numerous alleged irregularities, but their appeals were dismissed by the CNE and the Constitutional Court in mid-September. Dos Santos and Vicente were inaugurated later that month. The President announced a largely unchanged Council of Ministers shortly afterwards, the most notable appointment being Ângelo de Barros Veiga Tavares as Minister of the Interior. Armando Manuel received the finance portfolio in May 2013, leaving vacant his former position as head of the national sovereign wealth fund. In the following month it was announced that the President's son, José Filomeno de Sousa dos Santos, had been appointed to this post, prompting allegations of nepotism.

Details emerged in November 2013 implicating the security services in the suspected murder of two activists who had disappeared during the previous year. UNITA organized a large-scale demonstration in Luanda in response to this revelation, and approximately 300 protesters were arrested amid violent clashes with the police. Tensions had been exacerbated by the killing of a CASA-CE activist by the security forces shortly before the start of the rally. Opposition deputies staged a walk-out protest in the National Assembly later that month to register their disapproval of the security response to the demonstration. UNITA and the CASA-CE pledged to organize further anti-Government protest action.

Refugees

Between late 2002 and late 2003 the Angolan Government and the office of the UN High Commissioner for Refugees (UNHCR) established separate tripartite commissions with Zambia, the Democratic Republic of the Congo (DRC), Namibia, Botswana, the Republic of the Congo and South Africa, with the aim of facilitating the repatriation of Angolan refugees from these countries. In mid-2012 there were approximately 120,000 Angolan refugees in the region, including 81,000 in the DRC and 23,000 in Zambia. This was a significant reduction from figures from early 2003, at which time UNHCR had estimated that there were some 470,000 Angolan refugees in the region. UNHCR resumed its Angolan refugee repatriation scheme in November 2011, while continuing to seek co-operation from governments in the country of asylum in finding alternative solutions for refugees, including naturalization or local integration with permanent residency. In June 2012 UNHCR declared that Angolan exiles who had fled from the various conflicts in the country since 1965 would no longer be considered refugees, owing to the relative stability of the political climate in Angola and the availability of repatriation options. Efforts were ongoing in early 2014 to normalize the status of the remaining former Angolan refugees (numbering 108,000 at mid-2013) or to encourage their return to Angola.

Foreign Affairs

Regional relations

Following the internal uprising in August 1998 against the regime of Laurent-Désiré Kabila in the DRC, the Angolan Government moved swiftly to provide Kabila with military support against the rebels. In October, as the conflict escalated in the east of the DRC, Angola, in alliance with Namibia and Zimbabwe, stated that it would continue supporting Kabila until the rebels were defeated. Following the assassination of Kabila in January 2001, the Angolan Government announced its intention to allow its troops stationed in the DRC to remain there until further notice; moreover, several thousand additional Angolan troops were moved into that country later in January. However, by the end of October 2002 Angola, Namibia and Zimbabwe had completed the withdrawal of their troops from the DRC. Between December 2003 and August 2004 the Angolan authorities were reported to have expelled an estimated 120,000 illegal diamond workers, mostly DRC nationals, from northern Angola. During 2008 and 2009 the Angolan and Congolese authorities engaged in mutual expulsions of refugees from their respective territories. In 2009 it was estimated that some 160,000 Congolese had been expelled from Angola, while at least 30,000 Angolans had been forcibly removed from the DRC. Although the two countries had agreed in October 2009 to cease these activities, during 2010–13 Angola continued to expel large numbers of DRC nationals, many of whom were reportedly beaten, tortured or sexually assaulted. It was widely believed that the forced repatriations (which often affected illegal diamond miners from the DRC) reflected bilateral tensions over the control of natural resources in the proximity of their shared border, the delineation of which was in dispute. Recurrent Angolan incursions into the DRC (and the Republic of the Congo), ostensibly to monitor FLEC rebels, were also a source of discord.

In March 2011, following discussions with the Guinea-Bissau Government, Angola dispatched some 200 military personnel to the West African country as part of the Angolan Armed Forces Security Mission in Guinea-Bissau (MISSANG). The Angolan advisers were deployed to support the Guinea-Bissau authorities in their efforts to restructure the country's military, which was alleged to be heavily involved in the illegal drugs trade. MISSANG was viewed with deep suspicion by senior Guinea-Bissau officers since the reforms would reduce their power and privileges. Tensions escalated sharply in December when elements within the Guinea-Bissau military staged an abortive coup against the pro-Angolan Government of Prime Minister Carlos Gomes Júnior, who was forced to take temporary shelter in the Angolan Embassy. On 9 April 2012 Gomes Júnior blocked an attempt by Guinea-Bissau's military leadership unilaterally to terminate MISSANG's mandate, precipitating a renewed crisis. Although the Angolan Government agreed to the replacement of MISSANG by a multinational mission, on 12 April the Guinea-Bissau military deposed Gomes Júnior and interim President Raimundo Pereira. The military junta that assumed power claimed that the coup had been necessary to prevent Angola from dismantling Guinea-Bissau's armed forces. A settlement on the restoration of constitutional order was subsequently concluded following mediation by the Economic Community of West African States (ECOWAS), which established a new mission to replace MISSANG, thus curtailing Angola's influence in Guinea-Bissau. All MISSANG troops were withdrawn by June.

Other external relations

In 2000 a French judicial inquiry was instigated into alleged arms-trafficking to Angola by a French company, Brenco International, and a French businessman, Pierre Falcone. The company, along with a number of prominent French politicians, was alleged to have engaged in money-laundering and the unauthorized sales of arms worth some US $600m. to the dos Santos Government in 1993–94. Falcone was placed under provisional detention in France in December 2000, but was released after one year, the maximum term allowed for temporary detention. Falcone's appointment, in June 2003, as a plenipotentiary minister at the Angolan permanent delegation to UNESCO, entitling him to diplomatic immunity, provoked considerable international controversy and condemnation from Angolan opposition parties and civil society organizations. None the less, in April 2007 it was reported that 42 people, including Falcone and the Russian-Israeli businessman Arkadi Gaydamak (who was to be tried *in absentia*), would face charges ranging from arms-trafficking to tax evasion. Other notable defendants in the trial, which began in Paris in October 2008, were former French Minister of the Interior Charles Pasqua, and Jean-Christophe Mitterrand, son of former French President François Mitterrand. Of the 42 charged none were Angolan nationals, although prosecutors claimed that many officials in that country, including dos Santos, had received tens of millions of dollars in illegal payments. In October 2009 guilty verdicts were handed down to Gaydamak and Falcone, who were each sentenced to six years' imprisonment. Pasqua was jailed for three years, two of which were suspended, and was fined €100,000, while Jean-Christophe Mitterrand was given a two-year suspended prison sentence and fined €375,000. Following an appeal, in April 2011 a French court acquitted Pasqua and reduced the prison sentences imposed upon Falcone and Gaydamak to two-and-a-half years and three years, respectively.

The Vice-President of the People's Republic of China, Xi Jinping, met with officials from Angola in November 2010 to discuss co-operation between the two countries. The delegations agreed that the two nations were strategic partners and pledged to improve dialogue, realign their institutional mechanisms and raise the level of trade and economic co-operation. This joint declaration was regarded as an attempt to build on the foundations established in 2008 when the Angolan and Chinese Governments signed a Framework Agreement on Co-operation.

CONSTITUTION AND GOVERNMENT

According to the Constitution promulgated on 5 February 2010, legislative power is vested in the Assembleia Nacional (National Assembly), with 223 members elected for five years on the basis of proportional representation. Executive power is held by the President, who serves a term of five years (renewable for a maximum of two terms). The leader of the political party, or coalition of political parties, obtaining the majority of votes in legislative elections shall be named President of the Republic and shall be assisted by a Vice-President; the position of Vice-President shall be filled by the deputy leader of the ruling party. As Head of State and Commander-in-Chief of the armed forces, the President governs with the assistance of an appointed Council of Ministers.

For the purposes of local government, the country is divided into 18 provinces, each administered by an appointed Governor.

REGIONAL AND INTERNATIONAL CO-OPERATION

Angola is a member of the African Union (AU, see p. 186), of the Common Market for Eastern and Southern Africa (COMESA, see p. 233), of the Southern African Development Community (SADC, see p. 424), and of the Gulf of Guinea Commission (Commission du Golfe de Guinée—CGG, see p. 465). The CGG's headquarters were established in Luanda in 2006.

Angola became a member of the UN in 1976, and was admitted to the World Trade Organization (WTO, see p. 434) in 1996. In 2007 Angola joined the Organization of the Petroleum Exporting Countries (see p. 408). Angola is also a member of the Comunidade dos Países de Língua Portuguesa (see p. 464), a Portuguese-speaking commonwealth.

ECONOMIC AFFAIRS

In 2012, according to estimates by the World Bank, Angola's gross national income (GNI), measured at average 2010–12 prices, was US $95,389m., equivalent to $4,580 per head (or $5,490 per head on an international purchasing-power parity basis). During 2003–2012, it was estimated, Angola's population grew at an average annual rate of 3.4%, while gross domestic product (GDP) per head increased, in real terms, by an average of 7.6% per year. Overall GDP increased, in real terms, at an average annual rate of 11.2% in 2003–2012; growth in 2012 was 6.8%.

According to the African Development Bank (AfDB), agriculture contributed an estimated 10.2% of GDP in 2012. An estimated 68.2% of the total working population were employed in the agricultural sector in 2014, according to FAO figures. Coffee is the principal cash crop. The main subsistence crops are cassava, potatoes, sweet potatoes, sugar cane and maize. The widespread presence of unexploded anti-personnel mines continued to be an obstacle to the successful redevelopment of the agricultural sector. From 2005 the Government commenced a programme of investment in the formerly flourishing fisheries sector, which held much potential for redevelopment. During 2003–11, according to the World Bank, agricultural GDP increased at an average annual rate of 13.7%. According to the AfDB, agricultural GDP grew by 13.9% in 2012.

Industry (including mining, manufacturing, construction and power) provided an estimated 61.5% of GDP in 2012, according to the AfDB, and employed an estimated 10.5% of the labour force in 1991. The economic recovery in the country, as well as increased petroleum production and earnings, and Chinese sponsorship, led to strong expansion in the construction sector in 2005–08, with investment in the redevelopment of infrastructure. According to the World Bank, industrial GDP increased, in real terms, at an average annual rate of 9.9% in 2003–11; industrial GDP grew by 0.1% in 2010, but contracted by 1.4% in 2011.

Mining contributed an estimated 47.0% of GDP in 2012, according to the AfDB. Angola's principal mineral exports are petroleum and diamonds. In addition, there are reserves of iron ore, copper, lead, zinc, gold, manganese, phosphates, salt and uranium. At the end of 2012 Angola had estimated petroleum reserves of 12,700m. barrels, sufficient to sustain production at current levels for some 19 years. As a member of the Organization of the Petroleum Exporting Countries (OPEC, see p. 408), Angola is subject to production quotas agreed by the Organization's Conference. The GDP of the mining sector grew by 7.3% in 2012, according to the AfDB.

The manufacturing sector provided an estimated 6.6% of GDP in 2012, according to the AfDB. The principal branch of manufacturing is petroleum-refining. Other manufacturing activities include food-processing, brewing, textiles and construction materials. The GDP of the manufacturing sector increased at an average annual rate of 18.8% in 2003–11. According to the AfDB, manufacturing GDP grew by 6.0% in 2012.

Construction provided 7.8% of GDP in 2012, according to the AfDB. The GDP of the construction sector grew by 4.5% in 2012.

Energy is derived mainly from hydroelectric power, which, according to the World Bank, provided 70.9% of Angola's electricity production in 2011, while petroleum accounted for 29.1%. Angola's power potential exceeds its requirements; however, power supply is erratic and the country lacks a national grid.

According to the AfDB, services accounted for an estimated 28.4% of GDP in 2012, and engaged an estimated 20.1% of the labour force in 1991. In real terms, the GDP of the services sector increased at an average annual rate of 15.3% in 2003–11. Services GDP increased by 13.5% in 2011.

In 2012 Angola recorded an estimated visible merchandise trade surplus of US $47,374m. and there was a surplus of $13,851m. on the current account of the balance of payments. In 2012 the principal source of imports was Portugal (18.7%); other major suppliers were the People's Republic of China, the USA, South Africa and Brazil. The principal market for exports in 2012 was China (47.6%); India, the USA, Taiwan and Canada were also significant purchasers of Angola's exports. The principal imports in 2012 were machinery and mechanical appliances, electrical equipment and parts, vehicles, aircraft, vessels and associated transport equipment, iron and steel, other base metals and articles of base metal, mineral products, prepared foodstuffs, live animals and animal products, chemicals and related products, and mineral products. The principal exports in 2012 were mineral products, accounting for an estimated 98.1% of total export earnings, while pearls, precious or semi-precious stones, precious metals, and articles thereof contributed 1.8%.

In 2012 there was a budget surplus of 395,333.1m. kwanza, equivalent to 10.8% of GDP in that year. Angola's general government gross debt was 3,319,640m. kwanza in 2012, equivalent to 29.8% of GDP. Angola's total external debt at the end of

2011 was US $21,115m., of which $17,518m. was public and publicly guaranteed debt. In that year the cost of servicing long-term public and publicly guaranteed debt and repayments to the IMF was equivalent to 4.2% of the value of exports of goods, services and income (excluding workers' remittances). In 2010 a Public Debt Management Unit was established to improve the mechanisms in place for monitoring and controlling the country's debt. In 2003–12 the average annual rate of inflation was 17.0%, according to the International Labour Organization. Consumer prices increased by an average of 10.3% in 2012.

Following the ratification of a ceasefire agreement in April 2002 which brought an end to the civil war, Angola experienced dramatic economic growth, led largely by developments in the petroleum sector. By 2012, according to the BP Statistical Review of World Energy, total national output of crude petroleum had reached 1.8m. barrels per day, and Angola was the second largest oil producer in Africa after Nigeria. However, the benefits of the economic boom did not filter through to the majority of the Angolan people; some two-thirds of the population continued to subsist on less than US $2 per day, while the rate of unemployment stood at around 25% in the early 2010s. The global financial crisis and the resultant decrease in international oil prices precipitated a sharp deceleration in real GDP growth in 2009 and left the country unable to service its debts. Hence, in November the IMF approved a 27-month Stand-By Arrangement totalling $1,320m., and the Government, in return, agreed to implement a fiscal reform programme, which involved significantly decreasing public expenditure. As a result of these measures and a subsequent rise in the price of oil, by late 2011 Angola's financial position had improved markedly. However, owing to technical issues in the petroleum sector, real GDP growth remained relatively subdued during 2010–11. Nevertheless, with the production problems resolved and the international economic climate improving, Angola achieved real GDP growth of 5.2% in 2012 and 5.6% in 2013, and the IMF projected further economic expansion, of 6.3%, in 2014. The prospects for the hydrocarbons industry appeared favourable: major petroleum discoveries continued to be announced and the Government was committed to boosting output significantly over the medium term. In addition, exports of liquefied natural gas had commenced in mid-2013. However, Angola's heavy reliance on hydrocarbons left it vulnerable to market fluctuations. Efforts at diversification were focused on the agricultural, services and extractive sectors, with the expansion of diamond-mining, in particular, regarded as a potential driver of future growth. The development of the country's infrastructural networks, the improvement of the business environment and the implementation of a more inclusive growth strategy were also priorities for the Government.

PUBLIC HOLIDAYS

2015: 1 January (New Year's Day), 4 January (Martyrs' Day), 4 February (Anniversary of the outbreak of the armed struggle against Portuguese colonialism), 17 February (Carnival Day), 4 March (International Women's Day), 27 March (Victory Day)*, 3 April (Good Friday), 4 April (Peace and National Reconciliation Day), 14 April (Youth Day)*, 1 May (Workers' Day), 25 May (Africa Day), 1 June (International Children's Day), 1 August (Armed Forces' Day)*, 17 September (National Hero's Day, birthday of Dr Agostinho Neto), 2 November (All Souls' Day), 11 November (Independence Day), 1 December (Pioneers' Day)*, 10 December (Foundation of the MPLA Day)*, 25 December (Christmas Day and Family Day).

* Although not officially recognized as public holidays, these days are popularly treated as such.

Statistical Survey

Sources (unless otherwise stated): Instituto Nacional de Estatística, Av. Ho Chi Minh, CP 1215, Luanda; tel. 938217557; e-mail info@ine.gov.ao; internet www.ine.gov.ao; Ministério do Planeamento, Largo do Palácio do Povo, Rua 17 de Setembro, Luanda; tel. 222390188; fax 222339586; e-mail geral@minplan.gov.ao; internet www.minplan.gov.ao.

Area and Population

AREA, POPULATION AND DENSITY

Area (sq km)	1,246,700*
Population (census results)	
30 December 1960	4,480,719
15 December 1970	
Males	2,943,974
Females	2,702,192
Total	5,646,166
Population (UN estimates at mid-year)†	
2012	20,820.525
2013	21,471,617
2014	22,137,263
Density (per sq km) at mid-2014	17.8

* 481,354 sq miles.

† Source: UN, *World Population Prospects: The 2012 Revision*.

POPULATION BY AGE AND SEX

(UN estimates at mid-2014)

	Males	Females	Total
0–14	5,246,551	5,205,976	10,452,527
15–64	5,495,754	5,658,260	11,154,014
65 and over	236,863	293,859	530,722
Total	10,979,168	11,158,095	22,137,263

Source: UN, *World Population Prospects: The 2012 Revision*.

PROVINCES

(population estimates, 2008)

	Area (sq km)	Population ('000)	Density (per sq km)
Luanda	2,416	2,893	1,197.4
Huambo	34,274	2,475	72.2
Bié	70,314	1,832	26.1
Malanje	97,600	1,461	15.0
Huíla	75,002	1,370	18.3
Uíge	58,696	1,409	24.0
Benguela	31,788	1,028	32.3
Kwanza-Sul	55,658	1,016	18.3
Kwanza-Norte	24,190	629	26.0
Moxico	223,023	514	2.3
Lunda-Norte	102,782	459	4.5
Zaire	40,129	375	9.3
Cunene	89,342	366	4.1
Cabinda	7,283	286	39.3
Bengo	31,370	272	8.7
Lunda-Sul	45,647	236	5.2
Kuando Kubango	199,049	200	1.0
Namibe	58,137	219	3.8
Total	1,246,700	17,040	13.7

PRINCIPAL TOWNS

(population at 1970 census)

Luanda (capital)	480,613	Benguela	40,996
Huambo (Nova Lisboa)	61,885	Lubango (Sá da Bandeira)	31,674
Lobito	59,258	Malange	31,559

Source: Direcção dos Serviços de Estatística.

Mid-2011 ('000, incl. suburbs, UN estimate): Luanda 5,068 (Source: UN, *World Urbanization Prospects: The 2011 Revision*).

BIRTHS AND DEATHS
(annual averages, UN estimates)

	1995–2000	2000–05	2005–10
Birth rate (per 1,000)	51.0	49.8	48.2
Death rate (per 1,000)	21.1	17.7	15.8

Source: UN, *World Population Prospects: The 2012 Revision*.

2008 (official figures): Live births 21,285; marriages 2,690; registered deaths 12,089.

Life expectancy (years at birth): 51.1 (males 49.6; females 52.6) in 2011 (Source: World Bank, World Development Indicators database).

ECONOMICALLY ACTIVE POPULATION
('000 persons, 1991, estimates)

	Males	Females	Total
Agriculture, etc.	1,518	1,374	2,892
Industry	405	33	438
Services	644	192	836
Total labour force	2,567	1,599	4,166

Source: UN Economic Commission for Africa, *African Statistical Yearbook*.

Mid-2014 (estimates in '000): Agriculture, etc. 6,508; Total (incl. others) 9,543 (Source: FAO).

Health and Welfare

KEY INDICATORS

Total fertility rate (children per woman, 2011)	5.3
Under-5 mortality rate (per 1,000 live births, 2011)	158
HIV/AIDS (% of persons aged 15–49, 2012)	2.3
Physicians (per 1,000 head, 2009)	0.17
Hospital beds (per 1,000 head, 2005)	0.8
Health expenditure (2010): US $ per head (PPP)	194
Health expenditure (2010): % of GDP	3.4
Health expenditure (2010): public (% of total)	61.0
Access to water (% of persons, 2011)	53
Access to sanitation (% of persons, 2011)	59
Total carbon dioxide emissions ('000 metric tons, 2010)	30,417.8
Carbon dioxide emissions per head (metric tons, 2010)	1.6
Human Development Index (2012): ranking	148
Human Development Index (2012): value	0.508

For sources and definitions, see explanatory note on p. vi.

Agriculture

PRINCIPAL CROPS
('000 metric tons)

	2010	2011	2012
Wheat	4*	4*	4†
Rice, paddy	18	23	21
Maize	1,073	1,262	454
Millet	41	61	18
Potatoes	841	841	654
Sweet potatoes	987	1,045	645
Cassava (Manioc)	13,859	14,334	10,636
Sugar cane†	500	510	520
Beans, dry	250	304	96
Groundnuts, with shell	115	161	67
Palm oil*	57	50	48
Sunflower seed†	11	12	12
Oil palm fruit†	280	280	280
Cottonseed†	2	3	3
Tomatoes†	16	16	17
Onions and shallots, green†	24	24	26
Bananas	2,048	2,646	2,991
Citrus fruit	248	267	200
Pineapples	313	326	281
Coffee, green	46	49	50†

* Unofficial figure(s).
† FAO estimate(s).

Aggregate production ('000 metric tons, may include official, semi-official or estimated data): Total cereals 1,135 in 2010, 1,351 in 2011, 498 in 2012; Total roots and tubers 15,687 in 2010, 16,220 in 2011, 11,935 in 2012; Total vegetables (incl. melons) 365 in 2010, 377 in 2011, 402 in 2012; Total fruits (excl. melons) 2,641 in 2010, 3,279 in 2011, 3,512 in 2012.

Source: FAO.

LIVESTOCK
('000 head, year ending September)

	2010	2011	2012
Cattle	4,488	4,587	4,687
Pigs	1,935	2,136	2,358
Sheep	983	1,010	1,037
Goats	3,845	3,949	4,055
Chickens	17,119	19,977	23,314

Source: FAO.

LIVESTOCK PRODUCTS
('000 metric tons, FAO estimates)

	2010	2011	2012
Cattle meat	98.6	100.3	102.0
Goat meat	17.3	17.8	10.7
Pig meat	68.9	76.4	78.0
Chicken meat	19.3	22.5	23.4
Game meat	8.9	8.9	8.9
Sheep meat	3.7	3.8	2.6
Cows' milk	183.8	184.0	185.5
Hen eggs	4.5	4.5	4.5
Honey	22.9	22.9	23.0

Source: FAO.

Forestry

ROUNDWOOD REMOVALS
('000 cubic metres, excluding bark, FAO estimates)

	2010	2011	2012
Sawlogs, veneer logs and logs for sleepers	46	46	46
Other industrial wood	1,050	1,050	1,050
Fuel wood	4,009	4,101	4,194
Total	5,105	5,196	5,290

Source: FAO.

SAWNWOOD PRODUCTION
('000 cubic metres, including railway sleepers, FAO estimates)

	1983	1984	1985
Total	6	2	5

1986–2012: Annual production as in 1985 (FAO estimates).

Source: FAO.

Fishing

('000 metric tons, live weight)

	2009	2010	2011
Capture	268.4	263.0*	262.5*
Freshwater fishes	5.8	10.0*	10.0*
West coast sole	0.8	0.8*	0.8*
West African croakers	19.1	18.4*	18.4*
Dentex	33.8	30.0*	29.0*
Cunene horse mackerel	13.8	15.0*	15.0*
Pilchards and sardinellas	74.2	74.0	74.0
Chub mackerel	10.1	9.7*	9.7*
Aquaculture*	0.3	0.3	0.4
Total catch (incl. others)*	268.7	263.3*	262.9

* FAO estimate(s).

Source: FAO.

Mining

('000 metric tons unless otherwise indicated)

	2009	2010	2011
Crude petroleum ('000 42-gallon barrels)	665,760	687,295	637,290
Salt (unrefined)	35	50	40
Diamonds ('000 carats)*	13,828	8,362	8,329

* Reported figures, based on estimates of 10% of production at industrial grade.

Source: US Geological Survey.

Industry

SELECTED PRODUCTS
('000 metric tons unless otherwise indicated)

	2008	2009	2010
Cement*	1,780	1,800	1,500
Jet fuels	325	356	303
Motor gasoline (petrol)	68	42	65
Naphthas	118	133	n.a.
Kerosene	1	0	0
Distillate fuel oils	527	509	n.a.
Residual fuel oils	680	671	620
Electric energy (million kWh)	3,930	4,172	n.a.

* Data from US Geological Survey.

Source: mainly UN Industrial Commodity Statistics Database.

Cement ('000 metric tons): 1,500 in 2011 (Source: US Geological Survey).

Finance

CURRENCY AND EXCHANGE RATES

Monetary Units
100 lwei = 1 kwanza.

Sterling, Dollar and Euro Equivalents (31 December 2013)
£1 sterling = 160.665 kwanza;
US $1 = 97.562 kwanza;
€1 = 134.548 kwanza;
1,000 kwanza = £6.22 = $10.25 = €7.43.

Average Exchange Rate (kwanza per US $)
2011 93.935
2012 95.468
2013 96.518

Note: In April 1994 the introduction of a new method of setting exchange rates resulted in an effective devaluation of the new kwanza, to US $1 = 68,297 new kwanza, and provided for an end to the system of multiple exchange rates. Further substantial devaluations followed, and in July 1995 a 'readjusted' kwanza, equivalent to 1,000 new kwanza, was introduced. The currency, however, continued to depreciate. Between July 1997 and June 1998 a fixed official rate of US $1 = 262,376 readjusted kwanza was in operation. In May 1999 the Central Bank announced its decision to abolish the existing dual currency exchange rate system. In December 1999 the readjusted kwanza was replaced by a new currency, the kwanza, equivalent to 1m. readjusted kwanza.

BUDGET
('000 million kwanza)

Revenue*	2010	2011†	2012‡
Tax revenue	3,094	4,528	4,695
Petroleum	2,500	3,817	3,753
Non-petroleum	594	711	943
Non-tax revenue	199	246	196
Total	3,293	4,774	4,892

Expenditure	2010	2011†	2012‡
Current	2,142	2,928	3,242
Wages and salaries	714	877	1,061
Goods and services	619	1,031	1,153
Interest payments	90	95	111
Domestic	27	56	70
External	63	38	41
Transfers	720	926	917
Capital	733	846	981
Domestic financed	580	660	714
Foreign financed	154	186	266
Total	2,875	3,775	4,223

* Excluding grants received ('000 million kwanza): 2 in 2010; 2 in 2011 (estimate); 0 in 2012 (projection).

† Estimates.

‡ Projections.

Source: IMF, *Angola: Staff Report for the 2012 Article IV Consultation and Post Program Monitoring* (August 2012).

2012 (revised forecasts, '000 million kwanza): *Revenue:* Current revenue 2,630.4 (Petroleum 1,970.9, Diamonds 9.2, Other current revenue 650.4); Capital revenue 191.8 (Transfers 1.1, Financial revenue 190.7); Total 2,822.2. *Expenditure:* Current expenditure 1,365.7 (Wages and salaries 670.4, Goods 148.3, Services 293.0, Interest payments 68.9 Other transfers 185.1); Capital expenditure 1,061.2 (Investment 482.9, Capital transfers 8.2, Financial expenditure 570.0); Total 2,426.9 (Source: Ministry of Finance, Luanda).

INTERNATIONAL RESERVES
(US $ million at 31 December)

	2010	2011	2012
IMF special drawing rights	410.13	393.11	379.97
Foreign exchange	19,339.35	28,393.10	33,034.81
Total	19,749.47	28,786.21	33,414.77

Source: IMF, *International Financial Statistics*.

MONEY SUPPLY
(million kwanza at 31 December)

	2010	2011	2012
Currency outside banks	171,631	208,740	244,630
Demand deposits at banking institutions	693,352	952,981	1,037,096
Total (incl. others)	869,391	1,161,747	1,281,727

Source: IMF, *International Financial Statistics*.

COST OF LIVING
(Consumer Price Index for Luanda at December; base: 1994 average = 100)

	1999	2000	2001
Food	3,551.1	11,211.2	22,494.2
Clothing	5,189.4	21,449.2	45,733.9
Rent, fuel and light	28,392.7	157,756.4	434,224.6
All items (incl. others)	5,083.6	18,723.6	40,456.1

Source: IMF, *Angola: Selected Issues and Statistical Appendix* (September 2003).

All items (Consumer Price Index for Luanda; base: 2000 = 100): 3,437.5 in 2010; 3,901.1 in 2011; 4,302.1 in 2012 (Source: ILO).

NATIONAL ACCOUNTS
(million kwanza at current prices)

Expenditure on the Gross Domestic Product

	2010	2011	2012*
Government final consumption expenditure	1,825,639	2,355,674	2,648,440
Private final consumption expenditure	3,082,798	3,471,417	4,010,940
Gross fixed capital formation	1,162,277	1,499,719	1,686,106
Increase in stocks	60,769	78,412	88,157
Total domestic expenditure	6,131,483	7,405,222	8,433,643
Exports of goods and services	4,719,996	6,898,341	7,755,675
Less Imports of goods and services	3,271,931	4,523,458	5,085,639
GDP in purchasers' values	7,579,547	9,780,104	11,103,679

Gross Domestic Product by Economic Activity

	2010	2011	2012*
Agriculture, forestry and fishing	745,993	977,838	1,100,778
Mining and quarrying	3,467,054	4,525,273	5,094,217
Manufacturing	473,735	636,602	716,640
Construction	601,642	752,155	846,721
Wholesale and retail trade; restaurants and hotels	1,229,626	1,535,377	1,728,414
Transport and communications	325,503	411,250	462,954
Public administration and defence	548,198	697,137	878,746
GDP at factor cost	7,391,751	9,535,632	10,828,469
Indirect taxes on products	187,796	244,473	275,209
GDP in purchasers' values	7,579,547	9,780,104	11,103,679

* Provisional.

Source: African Development Bank.

BALANCE OF PAYMENTS
(US $ million)

	2010	2011	2012
Exports of goods	50,594.9	67,310.3	71,091.2
Imports of goods	–16,666.9	–20,228.5	–23,716.9
Balance on goods	33,928.0	47,081.8	47,374.3
Exports of services	856.9	732.3	780.0
Imports of services	–18,754.4	–23,669.8	–22,119.2
Balance on goods and services	16,030.5	24,144.2	26,035.1
Primary income received	134.0	209.8	259.8
Primary income paid	–8,220.9	–9,907.1	–10,681.6
Balance on goods, services and primary income	7,943.6	14,446.9	15,613.4
Secondary income received	58.4	115.6	66.9
Secondary income paid	–496.1	–1,477.8	–1,829.0

—continued	2010	2011	2012
Current balance	7,506.0	13,084.6	13,851.2
Capital account (net)	0.9	2.3	0.2
Direct investment assets	–1,340.4	–2,092.6	–2,740.8
Direct investment liabilities	–3,227.2	–3,023.8	–6,898.0
Portfolio investment assets	–273.5	–52.2	–200.0
Portfolio investment liabilities	3.0	—	—
Other investment assets	–158.6	–2,543.4	–2,608.6
Other investment liabilities	3,335.4	3,419.4	3,038.5
Net errors and omissions	–645.9	–345.4	–77.7
Reserves and related items	5,199.7	8,448.9	4,364.9

Source: IMF, *International Financial Statistics*.

External Trade

SELECTED COMMODITIES
(distribution by HS, US $ million)

Imports	2011	2012
Live animals and animal products	1,140.9	1,741.9
Vegetables and vegetable products	874.4	1,231.7
Prepared foodstuffs; beverages, spirits, vinegar; tobacco and articles thereof	1,536.0	2,318.7
Mineral products	2,622.0	1,460.9
Chemicals and related products	1,043.6	1,710.4
Plastics, rubber, and articles thereof	623.5	1,074.7
Iron and steel, other base metals and articles of base metal	2,030.5	3,508.0
Machinery and mechanical appliances; electrical equipment; parts thereof	4,327.9	6,811.9
Vehicles, aircraft, vessels and associated transport equipment	4,069.6	5,260.0
Total (incl. others)	20,791.2	28,916.3

Exports	2011	2012
Live animals and animal products	25.7	44.7
Mineral products	65,192.5	69,708.1
Pearls, precious or semi-precious stones, precious metals, and articles thereof	1,209.2	1,110.2
Total (incl. others)	66,427.4	70,863.1

PRINCIPAL TRADING PARTNERS
(US $ million)

Imports c.i.f.	2011	2012
Belgium	633.1	1,037.9
Brazil	940.2	1,480.3
China, People's Republic	1,837.1	3,527.2
France	851.9	1,107.8
Germany	336.2	422.8
India	341.0	707.3
Italy	235.2	369.4
Japan	396.3	797.9
Namibia	186.6	353.0
Netherlands	1,816.6	608.5
Portugal	3,455.5	5,398.5
South Africa	949.6	1,542.6
United Arab Emirates	421.1	995.1
United Kingdom	789.2	1,138.3
USA	1,747.6	2,067.4
Total (incl. others)	20,791.2	28,916.3

Exports f.o.b.	2011	2012
Canada	5,849.7	3,520.0
China, People's Republic	24,360.8	33,710.0
France	2,187.0	1,176.7
India	6,842.0	6,932.1
Israel	390.3	163.4
Italy	2,270.2	1,090.1
Netherlands	1,676.0	1,086.3
South Africa	1,697.6	3,001.3
Spain	650.1	1,627.7
Taiwan	5,386.5	4,699.8
USA	10,625.3	6,594.5
Total (incl. others)	66,427.4	70,863.1

Transport

GOODS TRANSPORT
(million metric tons)

	2002	2003	2004
Air	646.4	248.6	21,745.0
Road	7,505.7	4,635.5	19,031.0
Railway	253.6	129.3	54.0
Water	3,523.8	4,259.7	1,189.0

Source: Portais Governo de Angola.

PASSENGER TRANSPORT
(million passenger-km)

	2002	2003	2004
Air	804.9	978.4	21,229.0
Road	235,208.0	1,112,272.0	1,188,063.0
Railway	2,975.2	3,708.4	192.0
Water	—	—	1,522.0

Source: Portais Governo de Angola.

ROAD TRAFFIC
(motor vehicles in use at 31 December, estimates)

	1997	1998	1999
Passenger cars	103,400	107,100	117,200
Lorries and vans	107,600	110,500	118,300
Total	211,000	217,600	235,500

2000–02: data assumed to be unchanged from 1999 (estimates).

Source: UN, *Statistical Yearbook*.

2007 (motor vehicles in use at 31 December): Total 671,060 (Source: IRF, *World Road Statistics*).

SHIPPING

Flag Registered Fleet
(at 31 December)

	2011	2012	2013
Number of vessels	84	87	94
Total displacement (grt)	187,881	190,353	191,073

Source: Lloyd's List Intelligence (www.lloydslistintelligence.com).

International Sea-borne Freight Traffic
(estimates, '000 metric tons)

	1989	1990	1991
Goods loaded	19,980	21,102	23,288
Goods unloaded	1,235	1,242	1,261

Source: UN Economic Commission for Africa, *African Statistical Yearbook*.

CIVIL AVIATION
(traffic on scheduled services)

	2010	2011
Kilometres flown (million)	34	20
Passengers carried ('000)	1,010	988
Passenger-km (million)	2,706	2,533
Total ton-km (million)	291	279

Source: UN, *Statistical Yearbook*.

Passengers carried ('000): 1,116 in 2012 (Source: World Bank, World Development Indicators database).

Tourism

FOREIGN TOURIST ARRIVALS

Country of origin	2009	2010	2011
Belgium	1,650	1,472	1,458
Brazil	46,866	45,848	29,738
China, People's Republic	51,900	60,577	69,907
France	21,760	18,243	20,884
Germany	3,361	2,334	2,254
Italy	4,259	3,854	4,133
Namibia	1,225	3,506	37,834
Philippines	6,096	8,414	7,452
Portugal	86,330	100,645	84,755
Russia	2,694	1,484	1,737
South Africa	25,803	29,217	62,380
Spain	5,007	4,052	4,138
United Kingdom	15,870	18,766	31,932
USA	15,140	20,313	17,170
Total (incl. others)	365,784	424,919	481,207

Tourism receipts (US $ million, excl. passenger transport): 719 in 2010; 647 in 2011.

Source: World Tourism Organization.

Communications Media

	2010	2011	2012
Telephones ('000 main lines in use)	303.2	303.2	303.0
Mobile cellular telephones ('000 subscribers)	8,909.2	9,491.0	9,801.0
Broadband subscribers ('000)	20.0	25.0	31.3

Internet subscribers ('000): 320 in 2010.

Source: International Telecommunication Union.

Education

(2010/11)

	Teachers	Students		
		Males	Females	Total
Pre-primary	18,894	242,317	353,621	595,938
Primary	93,379*	3,070,771	1,956,032	5,026,803
Secondary:				
general	18,557	266,738	217,979	484,717
vocational	13,722	269,318	130,947	400,265
Higher	7,863	11,851	130,947	142,798

* 2009/10 figure.

Source: UNESCO Institute for Statistics.

Pupil-teacher ratio (primary education, UNESCO estimate): 45.6 in 2009/10 (Source: UNESCO Institute for Statistics).

Adult literacy rate (UNESCO estimates): 70.4% (males 82.6%; females 58.6%) in 2011 (Source: UNESCO Institute for Statistics).

Directory

The Government

HEAD OF STATE

President: José Eduardo dos Santos.

Vice-President: Manuel Domingos Vicente.

COUNCIL OF MINISTERS
(April 2014)

President: José Eduardo dos Santos.

Vice-President: Manuel Domingos Vicente.

Minister of State and Head of Civil Staff: Edeltrude Maurício Fernandes Gaspar da Costa.

Minister of State and Head of Military Staff: Gen. Manuel Hélder Vieira Dias, Jr.

Minister of National Defence: Joño Manuel Gonçalves Lourenço.

Minister of the Interior: Ângelo de Barros Veiga Tavares.

Minister of Foreign Affairs: George Rebelo Pinto Chicoty.

Minister of the Economy: Abrahão Pio dos Santos Gourgel.

Minister of Finance: Armando Manuel.

Minister of Planning and Territorial Development: Job Graça.

Minister of Territorial Administration: Bornito de Sousa Baltazar Diogo.

Minister of Public Administration, Labour and Social Security: Dr António Domingos Pitra da Costa Neto.

Minister of Justice and Human Rights: Rui Jorge Carneiro Mangueira.

Minister of Former Combatants and War Veterans: Gen. Cândido Pereira dos Santos Van-Dúnem.

Minister of Agriculture: Afonso Pedro Canga.

Minister of Fisheries: Vitória Francisco Lapas Cristóvão de Barros Neto.

Minister of Industry: Bernarda Gonçalves Martins Henriques da Silva.

Minister of Petroleum: José Maria Botelho de Vasconcelos.

Minister of Geology and Mines: Manuel Francisco Queirós.

Minister of Commerce: Rosa Pedro Pacavira de Matos.

Minister of Hotels and Tourism: Pedro Mutindi.

Minister of Construction: Waldemar Pires Alexandre.

Minister of Town Planning and Housing: José António da Conceição e Silva.

Minister of Energy and Water: João Baptista Borges.

Minister of Transport: Augusto da Silva Tomás.

Minister of the Environment: Maria de Fátima Monteiro Jardim.

Minister of Telecommunications and Information Technology: José Carvalho da Rocha.

Minister of Science and Technology: Maria Cândida Pereira Teixeira.

Minister of Social Communication: José Luís de Matos.

Minister of Health: José Viera Dias Van-Dúnem.

Minister of Education: M'Pinda Simão.

Minister of Higher Education: Adão do Nascimento.

Minister of Culture: Rosa Maria Martins da Cruz e Silva.

Minister of Social Assistance and Reintegration: João Baptista Kussumua.

Minister of Family and the Promotion of Women: Maria Filomena Lobão Telo Delgado.

Minister of Youth and Sports: Gonçalves Manuel Muandumba.

Minister of Parliamentary Affairs: Rosa Luís de Sousa Micolo.

MINISTRIES

Office of the President: Rua 17 de Setembro, Palácio do Povo, Luanda; tel. 222332939; fax 222339855; internet www.pr.ao.

Office of the Vice-President: Largo 17 de Setembro, Luanda; tel. 222396501; fax 222397071; internet www.vicepresidencia.gov.ao.

Ministry of Agriculture: Largo António Jacinto, CP 527, Luanda; tel. 222322377; fax 222320553; e-mail geral@minagri.gov.ao; internet www.minagri.gov.ao.

Ministry of Commerce: Palácio de Vidro, Largo 4 de Fevereiro 3, CP 1242, Luanda; tel. 222311191; fax 222310335; e-mail gamaarte63@yahoo.com.br; internet www.minco.gov.ao.

Ministry of Construction: Luanda; internet www.mincons.gov.ao.

Ministry of Culture: Edif. Ministerial, 1° andar, Largo António Jacinto, Luanda; tel. and fax 222322070; e-mail geral@mincult.gov.ao; internet www.mincult.gov.ao.

Ministry of the Economy: Luanda; e-mail geral@minec.gov.ao; internet www.minec.gov.ao.

Ministry of Education: Largo António Jacinto, CP 1281, Luanda; tel. 222321236; fax 222321592; e-mail geral@med.gov.ao; internet www.med.gov.ao.

Ministry of Energy and Water: Rua Cónego Manuel das Neves 234, CP 2229, Luanda; tel. 222393681; fax 222393684; e-mail geral@minen.gov.ao; internet www.minerg.gov.ao.

Ministry of the Environment: Rua Frederico Engels 94, 8º andar, Luanda; tel. 222334761; fax 222394758; e-mail geral@minam.gov.ao; internet www.minam.gov.ao.

Ministry of Family and the Promotion of Women: Palácio de Vidro, 2° andar, Largo 4 de Fevereiro, Luanda; tel. and fax 222311728; e-mail geral@minfamu.gov.ao; internet www.minfamu.gov.ao.

Ministry of Finance: Largo da Mutamba, Luanda; tel. and fax 222338548; e-mail geral@minfin.gov.ao; internet www.minfin.gv.ao.

Ministry of Fisheries: Luanda.

Ministry of Foreign Affairs: Rua Major Kanhangulo, Luanda; tel. 222394827; fax 222393246; e-mail geral@mirex.gov.ao; internet www.mirex.gov.ao.

Ministry of Former Combatants and War Veterans: Av. Comandante Gika 2, CP 3828, Luanda; tel. 222321648; fax 222320876; e-mail geral@macvg.gov.ao; internet www.macvg.gov.ao.

Ministry of Geology and Mines: Av. Comandante Gika, CP 1260, Luanda; tel. 222322905; fax 222321655; e-mail geral@mgm.gov.ao; internet www.mgm.gov.ao.

Ministry of Health: Rua 17 de Setembro, CP 1201, Luanda; tel. and fax 222391641; e-mail geral@minsa.gov.ao; internet www.minsa.gov.ao.

Ministry of Higher Education: Av. Lenine 106/108, Maianga, Luanda; tel. 222330218; fax 222338210; e-mail geral@mct.gov.ao; internet www.mct.gov.ao.

Ministry of Hotels and Tourism: Luanda; internet www.minhotur.gov.ao.

Ministry of Industry: Rua Cerqeira Lukoki 25, Luanda; tel. 222334700; e-mail contactos@mind.gov.ao; internet www.mind.gov.ao.

Ministry of the Interior: Largo do Palácio de Vidro, Rua 25 de Abril 1 R/C, CP 2723, Luanda; tel. 222335976; fax 222395133; e-mail geral@minint.gov.ao; internet www.minint.gov.ao.

Ministry of Justice and Human Rights: Rua 17 de Setembro, CP 2250, Luanda; tel. and fax 222336045; e-mail geral@minjus.gov.ao; internet www.minjus.gov.ao.

Ministry of National Defence: Rua 17 de Setembro, Luanda; tel. 222330354; fax 222334276; e-mail geral@minden.gov.ao; internet www.minden.gov.ao.

Ministry of Parliamentary Affairs: Luanda.

Ministry of Petroleum: Av. 4 de Fevereiro 105, CP 1279, Luanda; tel. and fax 222385847; e-mail geral@minpet.gov.ao; internet www.minpet.gov.ao.

Ministry of Planning and Territorial Development: Largo do Palácio do Povo, Rua 17 de Setembro, Luanda; tel. 222390188; fax 222339586; e-mail geral@minplan.gov.ao; internet www.minplan.gov.ao.

Ministry of Public Administration, Labour and Social Security: Rua do 1° Congresso do MPLA 5, Luanda; tel. 222399506; fax 222399507; e-mail geral@mapess.gov.ao; internet www.mapess.gov.ao.

Ministry of Science and Technology: Luanda; internet www.minct.gov.ao.

Ministry of Social Assistance and Reintegration: Av. Hoji Ya Henda 117, CP 102, Luanda; tel. 222440370; fax 222342988; e-mail geral@minars.gov.ao; internet www.minars.gov.ao.

Ministry of Social Communication: Av. Comandante Valódia 206, 1° e 2° andares, CP 2608, Luanda; tel. and fax 222443495; e-mail geral@mcs.gov.ao; internet www.mcs.gov.ao.

Ministry of Telecommunications and Information Technology: Av. 4 de Fevereiro, Rua das Alfândegas 10, Luanda; tel. and fax 222390895; e-mail geral@mtti.gov.ao; internet www.mtti.gov.ao.

Ministry of Territorial Administration: Av. Comandante Gika 8, Luanda; tel. 222321072; fax 222323272; internet www.mat.gov.ao.

Ministry of Town Planning and Housing: Av. 4 de Fevereiro, Luanda; tel. 222334429; e-mail geral@minuh.gov.ao; internet www.minuh.gov.ao.

Ministry of Transport: Av. 4 de Fevereiro 42, CP 1250-C, Luanda; tel. 222311303; fax 222311582; e-mail geral@mintrans.gov.ao; internet www.mintrans.gov.ao.

Ministry of Youth and Sports: Av. Comandante Valódia 299, 4° andar, Luanda; tel. and fax 222443521; e-mail geral@minjud.gov.ao; internet www.minjud.gov.ao.

PROVINCIAL GOVERNORS

(April 2014)

All Provincial Governors are ex officio members of the Government.

Bengo: JOÃO BERNARDO DE MIRANDA.

Benguela: ISAAC FRANCISCO MARIA DOS ANJO.

Bié: ÁLVARO MANUEL DE BOAVIDA NETO.

Cabinda: ALBINA MATILDE BARROS DA LOMBA.

Cunene: ANTÓNIO DIDALELWA.

Huambo: FERNANDO FAUSTINO MUTEKA.

Huíla: JOÃO MARCELINO TYIPINGE.

Kuando Kubango: FRANCISCO HIGINO LOPES CARNEIRO.

Kwanza-Norte: HENRIQUE ANDRÉ JÚNIOR.

Kwanza-Sul: EUSÉBIO DE BRITO TEIXEIRA.

Luanda: BENTO SEBASTIÃO FRANCISCO BENTO.

Lunda-Norte: ERNESTO MUANGALA.

Lunda-Sul: CÂNDIDA MARIA GUILHERME NARCISO.

Malanje: NORBERTO FERNANDES DOS SANTOS.

Moxico: JOÃO ERNESTO DOS SANTOS.

Namibe: RUI LUÍS FALCÃO PINTO DE ANDRADE.

Uíge: PAULO POMBOLO.

Zaire: JOSÉ JOANES ANDRÉ.

President

Under the terms of the Constitution, the leader of the political party, or coalition of political parties, obtaining a majority vote in the legislative elections shall be named President of the Republic.

Legislature

National Assembly: CP 1204, Luanda; tel. 222334021; fax 222331118; e-mail assembleianacional@parlamento.ebonet.net; internet www.parlamento.ao.

President: FERNANDO DA PIEDADE DIAS DOS SANTOS.

General Election, 31 August 2012

Party	Votes	% of valid votes	Seats
MPLA	4,135,503	71.85	175
UNITA	1,074,565	18.67	32
CASA-CE	345,589	6.00	8
PRS	98,233	1.71	3
FNLA	65,163	1.13	2
Others	36,951	0.64	—
Total	5,756,004	100.00	220

Election Commission

Comissão Nacional Eleitoral (CNE): Av. Amílcar Cabral, 30–31, Luanda; tel. 222393825; internet www.cne.ao; f. 2005; govt agency; Pres. ANDRÉ DA SILVA NETO.

Political Organizations

In August 2012 there were 78 legally recognized political parties in Angola, many of which formed part of the 10 recognized coalitions.

Angola Democrática—Coligação (AD): e-mail info@ad-coligacao.org; internet www.ad-coligacao.org; Pres. KENGELE JORGE (acting).

Bloco Democrático: 4° andar, 74 C, Av. de Portugal, Luanda; tel. 222397482; fax 222440556; Pres. JUSTINO PINTO DE ANDRADE; Sec.-Gen. Dr FILOMENO VIEIRA LOPES.

Convergência Ampla de Salvação de Angola-Coligação Eleitoral (CASA-CE): Sagrada Família, Rua Cabral Moncada 179, Junto ao INE Garcia Neto, Luanda; e-mail casa.inform@yahoo.com; f. 2011; Leader ABEL CHIVUKUVUKU.

Fórum Fraternal Angolano Coligação (FOFAC): Luanda; f. 1997; Leader ARTUR QUIXONA FINDA.

Frente Nacional de Libertação de Angola (FNLA): Av. Hoji Va Henda (ex Av. do Brasil) 91/306, CP 151, Luanda; e-mail contact@fnla.net; internet www.fnla.net; f. 1962; Pres. LUCAS NGONDA; Sec.-Gen. BENJAMIM MANUEL DA SILVA.

Movimento Popular de Libertação de Angola (MPLA) (People's Movement for the Liberation of Angola): Luanda; e-mail sede@mpla-angola.org; f. 1956; in 1961–74 conducted guerrilla operations against Portuguese rule; governing party since 1975; known as Movimento Popular de Libertação de Angola—Partido do Trabalho (MPLA—PT) (People's Movement for the Liberation of Angola—Workers' Party) 1977–92; in Dec. 1990 replaced Marxist-Leninist ideology with commitment to 'democratic socialism'; absorbed the Fórum Democrático Angolano (FDA) in 2002; Chair. JOSÉ EDUARDO DOS SANTOS; Sec.-Gen. JULIÃO MATEUS PAULO.

Nova Democracia—União Eleitoral: f. 2006; a splinter group from the Partidos de Oposição Civil comprising the Frente Unida para Liberdade Democratica (FULD), the Movimento para Democracia de Angola (MPDA), the Partido Angolano Republicano (PAR), the Partido Social Independente de Angola (PSIA), the Partido Socialista Liberal (PSL) and the União Nacional para Democracia (UND); Sec.-Gen. QUINTINO DE MOREIRA.

Partido Democrático para o Progresso de Aliança Nacional Angolana (PDP—ANA): Rua n° 6, Casa n° 73, Quarterão 6, Bairro Palanca, Municipio de Kilamba Kiaxi; tel. 926013905 (mobile); e-mail pdpana@pdp-ana.org; f. 1991; Pres. SEDIANGANI MBIMBI.

Partido Democrático de Renovação Social: Luanda; f. 2009; Leader LINDO BERNARDO TITO.

Partido de Renovação Social (PRS): Rua n°1, Martires de Kifangondo n° 33D; tel. 222326293; fax 222323037; e-mail sede@prs-angola.com; internet www.prs-angola.com; Pres. EDUARDO KWANGANA; Sec.-Gen. JOÃO BAPTISTA NGANDAJINA.

Partido Renovador Democrático (PRD): internet prd-angola.org; Leader LUÍS DA SILVA DOS PASSOS.

Plataforma Política Eleitoral (PPE): nine-party coalition; Leader JOSÉ MANUEL.

União Nacional para a Independência Total de Angola (UNITA): Rua 28 de Maio, 1A Travessa 2, Maianga, Luanda; tel. and fax 222331215; e-mail info@unitaangola.org; internet www.unitaangola.com; f. 1966 to secure independence from Portugal; later received Portuguese support to oppose the MPLA; UNITA and the Frente Nacional de Libertação de Angola conducted guerrilla campaign against the MPLA Govt with aid from some Western countries, 1975–76; supported by South Africa until 1984 and in 1987–88, and by USA after 1986; obtained legal status in March 1998, but hostilities between govt and UNITA forces resumed later that year; signed ceasefire agreement with the MPLA Govt in April 2002; joined the Govt in Dec. 2002; support drawn mainly from Ovimbundu ethnic group; Pres. ISAÍAS HENRIQUE GOLA SAMAKUVA.

Other parties include:

Forças de Libertação do Estado de Cabinda/Posição Militar (FLEC/PM): f. 2003; a breakaway faction of FLEC seeking the secession of Cabinda province; Sec.-Gen. RODRIGUES MINGAS.

Frente para a Libertação do Enclave de Cabinda (FLEC): f. 1963; comprises several factions, claiming total forces of c. 5,000 guerrillas, seeking the secession of Cabinda province; in Sept. 2004 the Frente para a Libertação do Enclave de Cabinda—Forças Armadas Cabindesas (FLEC—FAC) and the Frente para a Libertação do Enclave de Cabinda—Renovada (FLEC—R) merged under the above name; Leader N'ZITA HENRIQUES TIAGO; Sec.-Gen. ANTÓNIO BENTO BEMBE.

Frente para a Libertação do Enclave de Cabinda—Conselho Superior Alargado (FLEC—CSA): f. 2004; political wing of FLEC; supports Cabindan independence through negotiation.

The **Fórum Cabindês para o Diálogo (FCD)** was formed in 2004 to provide a united platform for Cabindan separatists and civil-society leaders through which to negotiate with the Government. Its leader was ANTÓNIO BENTO BEMBE.

Diplomatic Representation

EMBASSIES IN ANGOLA

Algeria: Edif. Siccal, Rua Rainha Ginga, CP 1389, Luanda; tel. 222332881; fax 222334785; e-mail ambalg@netangola.com; Ambassador KAMEL BOUGHABA.

Argentina: Rua Comandante Nicolau Gomes Spencer 62, Bairro Maculusso, Luanda; tel. 222325098; fax 222324095; Ambassador JÚLIO LASCANO Y VEDIA.

Belgium: Rua Houari Boumedienne 100, CP 1203, Luanda; tel. 222449396; fax 222449178; e-mail luanda@diplobel.fed.be; internet diplomatie.belgium.be/angola; Ambassador CHARLES DELOGNE.

Brazil: Rua Houari Boumedienne 132, Miramar, CP 5428, Luanda; tel. 222441307; fax 222444913; e-mail bras.secretariado@netcabo.co.ao; internet luanda.itamaraty.gov.br; Ambassador ANA LUCY GENTIL CABRAL PETERSEN.

Cape Verde: Rua Oliveira Martins 3, Luanda; tel. 222321765; fax 222320832; Ambassador FRANCISCO PEREIRA DA VEIGA.

China, People's Republic: Rua Houari Boumedienne 196, Miramar, CP 52, Luanda; tel. 222441683; fax 222444185; internet ao.chineseembassy.org; Ambassador GAO KOTIANG.

Congo, Democratic Republic: Rua Cesário Verde 24, Luanda; tel. 222361953; Ambassador MUNDINDI DIDI KILENGO.

Congo, Republic: Av. 4 de Fevereiro 3, Luanda; tel. 222310293; Ambassador CHRISTIAN GILBERT BEMBET.

Côte d'Ivoire: Rua Eng. Armindo de Andrade 75, Miramar, CP 432, Luanda; tel. 222440878; fax 222440907; e-mail aciao@ambaci-angola.org; internet www.ambaci-angola.org; Ambassador ASSAMOI B. DÉSIRÉ.

Cuba: Rua Eduardo Mondlane 121, Maianga, Luanda; tel. 222339171; fax 222339165; e-mail embcuba.ang@supernet.ao; internet www.cubadiplomatica.cu/angola; Ambassador GISELA GARCIA RIVERA.

Egypt: Rua Comandante Stona 247, Alvalade, CP 3704, Luanda; tel. 222321591; fax 222323285; e-mail embegipto@ebonet.net; Ambassador GAMAL ABDEL METWALY.

Equatorial Guinea: Luanda; Ambassador JOSE MICHA AKENG.

France: Rua Reverendo Pedro Agostinho Neto 31–33, CP 584, Luanda; tel. 222334841; fax 222391949; e-mail cad.luanda-amba@diplomatie.gouv.fr; internet www.ambafrance-ao.org; Ambassador JEAN-CLAUDE MOYRET.

Gabon: Av. 4 de Fevereiro 95, Luanda; tel. 222372614; Ambassador FRANÇOIS MOUELY-KOUMBA.

Germany: Av. 4 de Fevereiro 120, CP 1295, Luanda; tel. 222334773; fax 222372551; e-mail info@luanda.diplo.de; internet www.luanda.diplo.de; Ambassador JÖRG-WERNER WOLFGANG MARQUARDT.

Ghana: Rua Cirilo da Conceição E Silva 5, 1A, CP 1012, Luanda; tel. 222338239; fax 222338235; e-mail embassyghana@ebonet.net; Ambassador MARTIN ACHIAMPONG QUANSAH.

Holy See: Rua Luther King 123, CP 1030, Luanda; tel. 222330532; fax 222332378; Apostolic Nuncio Most Rev. NOVATUS RUGAMBWA.

India: Rua Marquês das Minas 18A, Macalusso, CP 6040, Luanda; tel. 222392281; fax 222371094; e-mail indembluanda@netcabo.co.ao; internet www.indembangola.org; Ambassador (vacant).

Israel: Edif. Siccal, 11° andar, Rua Rainha Ginga 34, Luanda; tel. 222395295; fax 222396366; e-mail info@luanda.mfa.gov.il; internet luanda.mfa.gov.il; Ambassador RAPHAEL SHLOMO SINGER.

Italy: Rua Américo Boavida 51, Ingombotas, CP 6220, Luanda; tel. 222331245; fax 222333743; e-mail segreteria.luanda@esteri.it; internet www.ambluanda.esteri.it; Ambassador GUISEPPE MISTRELLA.

Japan: Rua Armindo de Andrade 183–185, Miramar, Luanda; tel. 222442007; fax 222449888; internet www.angola.emb-japan.go.jp; Ambassador RYOZO MYOI.

Korea, Republic: Chalet A 101, Centro de Convenções, Talatona, Luanda; tel. 222006067; fax 222006066; internet ago.mofa.go.kr; Ambassador KIM HYON-IL.

Mali: Rua Alfredo Felner 5, Nelito Souares 11, Luanda; e-mail ambamali@netangola.com; Ambassador FAROUK CAMARA.

Morocco: Edif. Siccal, 10° andar, Rua Rainha Ginga, CP 20, Luanda; tel. 222393708; fax 222338847; e-mail aluanda@supernet.ao; Ambassador EL GHALLAOUI SIDATI.

Mozambique: Rua Salvador Alende 55, Luanda; tel. and fax 222334871; e-mail embamoc.angola@minec.gov.mz; Ambassador DOMINGOS FERNANDES.

Namibia: Rua dos Coqueiros 37, CP 953, Luanda; tel. 222395483; fax 222339234; e-mail embnam@netangola.com; Ambassador CLAUDIA NDADALEKA USHONA.

Netherlands: Empreendimento CdTe, Gika, Torre B Piso 8, Travessa Ho Chi Minh, Alvalade, CP 3624, Luanda; tel. 924068802 (mobile); fax 847300850; e-mail lua@minbuza.nl; Ambassador SUSANNA TERSTAL.

Nigeria: Rua Houari Boumedienne 120, Miramar, CP 479, Luanda; tel. and fax 222340089; Ambassador FOLORUNSO OLUKAYODE OTUKOYA.

Norway: Rua de Benguela 17, Bairro Patrice Lumumba, CP 3835, Luanda; tel. 222449936; fax 222446248; e-mail emb.luanda@mfa.no; internet www.noruega.ao; Ambassador INGRID OFSTAD.

Poland: Rua Damião de Góis 64, Alvalade, CP 1340, Luanda; tel. 222327199; fax 222321829; e-mail luanda.amb.sekretariat@msz.gov.pl; internet luanda.msz.gov.pl; Ambassador (vacant).

Portugal: Av. de Portugal 50, CP 1346, Luanda; tel. 222333027; fax 222390392; e-mail embaixada.portugal@netcabo.co.ao; internet www.embaixadadeportugal-luanda.com.pt; Ambassador JOÃO DA CAMARA.

Romania: Rua Ramalho Ortigão 30, Alvalade, Luanda; tel. and fax 222321076; e-mail ambromania@ebonet.net; Ambassador VALERIU NICOLAE.

Russia: Rua Houari Boumedienne 170, CP 3141, Luanda; tel. 222445028; fax 222445320; e-mail rusemb@netangola.com; Ambassador DIMITRI LUBACH.

São Tomé and Príncipe: Rua Armindo de Andrade 173–175, Luanda; tel. 222345677; Ambassador DAMIÃO VAZ DE ALMEIDA.

Serbia: Rua Comandante N'zagi 25–27, Alvalade, CP 3278, Luanda; tel. 222321421; fax 222321724; e-mail serbiaemb@snet.co.ao; Ambassador DRAGAN MARKOVIĆ.

South Africa: Edif. Maianga, 1° e 2° andares, Rua Kwamme Nkrumah 31, Largo da Maianga, CP 6212, Luanda; tel. 222334187; fax 222398730; e-mail saemb.ang@netangola.com; internet www.sambangola.info; Ambassador GODFREY NGWENYA.

Spain: Av. 4 de Fevereiro 95, 1° andar, CP 3061, Luanda; tel. 222391166; fax 222332884; e-mail emb.luanda@maec.es; Ambassador JÚLIA ALICIA OLMO Y ROMERO.

Sweden: Rua Houari Boumedienne 96, CP 3835, Miramar, Luanda; tel. 928013310; fax 222443460; e-mail ambassaden.luanda@foreign.ministry.se; internet www.swedenabroad.com/luanda; Ambassador LENA SUNDH.

Switzerland: Rua Agostinho Tomé das Neves 8, Bairro Maianga, Luanda; tel. 222353710; fax 222353689; e-mail lua.vertretung@eda.admin.ch; Ambassador BENEDICT GUBLER.

Turkey: Hotel Colinas do Sol, Talatona, Luanda; tel. 914522800 (mobile); fax 222393330; e-mail embassy.luanda@mfa.gov.tr; Ambassador AHMET IHSAN KIZILTAN.

Ukraine: Rua Companhia de Jesus 35, Miramar, Luanda; tel. 912340926; fax 222448467; e-mail emb_ao@mfa.gov.ua; Ambassador OLEKSANDR NYKONENKO.

United Kingdom: Rua 17 de Setembro, CP 1244, Luanda; tel. 222334583; fax 222333331; e-mail postmaster.luand@fco.gov.uk; internet www.gov.uk/government/world/organisations/british-embassy-luanda; Ambassador JOHN DAVID DENNIS.

USA: Rua Houari Boumedienne 32, Miramar, CP 6468, Luanda; tel. 222641000; fax 222641232; e-mail ConsularLuanda@state.gov; internet angola.usembassy.gov; Chargé d'affaires a.i. HEATHER C. MERRITT.

Venezuela: Luanda; Ambassador LOURDES ELENA PÉREZ MARTINEZ.

Viet Nam: Rua Alexandre Peres 4, Maianga, CP 1774, Luanda; tel. 222010697; fax 222010696; e-mail vnemb.angola@mofa.gov.vn; internet www.vietnamembassy-angola.org; Ambassador PHAM TIEN NHIEN.

Zambia: Rua Rei Katyavala 106–108, CP 1496, Luanda; tel. 222331145; Ambassador BARBARA CHILANGWA.

Zimbabwe: Edif. Secil, Av. 4 de Fevereiro 42, CP 428, Luanda; tel. and fax 222311528; e-mail embzimbabwe@ebonet.net; Ambassador NGONI FRANCIS SENGWE.

Judicial System

The country's highest judicial body is the Constitutional Court (Tribunal Constitucional), while there is also a Supreme Court (Tribunal Supremo), an Audit Court (Tribunal de Contas) and a Supreme Military Court (Supremo Tribunal Militar). There are also civil and criminal courts at the provincial level.

Constitutional Court (Tribunal Constitucional): Palácio da Justiça, Av. 1º Congresso, Luanda; tel. 222330687; e-mail geral@tribunalconstitucional.ao; internet www.tribunalconstitucional.ao; f. 2008; 7 judges; Pres. Dr RUI CONSTANTINO DA CRUZ FERREIRA.

Supreme Court (Tribunal Supremo): Rua 17 de Setembro, Luanda; fax 222335411; internet www.tribunalsupremo.ao; Pres. Dr CRISTIANO AUGUSTO ANDRÉ.

Audit Court (Tribunal de Contas): Cidade Alta, Rua 17 de Setembro, Luanda; tel. 222371920; e-mail tcontas@tcontas.ao; internet www.tcontas.ao; Pres. JULIÃO ANTÓNIO.

Office of the Attorney-General: Rua 17 de Setembro, Luanda; tel. 222333171; fax 222333172; Attorney-General JOÃO MARIA DE SOUSA.

Religion

In 1998 it was estimated that 47% of the population followed indigenous beliefs, with 53% professing to be Christians, mainly Roman Catholic. There is a small Muslim community, which comprises less than 1% of the population.

CHRISTIANITY

In early 2005 some 85 Christian denominations were registered in Angola.

Conselho de Igrejas Cristãs em Angola (CICA) (Council of Christian Churches in Angola): Rua 15 24, Bairro Cassenda, CP 1301/1659, Luanda; tel. 222354838; fax 222356144; e-mail info@cicaangola.org; f. 1977 as Conselho Angolano de Igrejas Evangélicas; 14 mem. churches; 5 assoc. mems; 1 observer; Pres. Rev. ALVARO RODRIGUES; Gen. Sec. Rev. DEOLINDA TECA.

Protestant Churches

Igreja Evangélica Congregacional em Angola (Evangelical Congregational Church in Angola—IECA): CP 1552, Luanda; tel. 222355108; fax 222350868; e-mail iecageral@snet.co.ao; f. 1880; 900,000 mems; Gen. Sec. Rev. AUGUSTO CHIPESSE.

Igreja Evangélica Lutherana de Angola (Evangelical Lutheran Church of Angola): CP 222, Lubango; tel. 22228428; e-mail iela_lubango@yahoo.com.br; 40,000 mems (2010); Pres. Rev. TOMÀS NDAWANAPO.

Igreja Evangélica Unida de Angola (United Evangelical Church of Angola): CP 122, Uíge; 11,000 mems; Gen. Sec. Rev. A. L. DOMINGOS.

Missão Evangélica Pentecostal de Angola (Evangelical Pentecostal Church of Angola): CP 219, Porto Amboim; 13,600 mems; Sec. Rev. JOSÉ DOMINGOS CAETANO.

Other active denominations include the African Apostolic Church, the Church of Apostolic Faith in Angola, the Church of Our Lord Jesus Christ in the World, the Evangelical Baptist Church, the Evangelical Church in Angola, the Evangelical Church of the Apostles of Jerusalem, the Evangelical Reformed Church of Angola, the Kimbanguist Church in Angola, the Maná Church and the United Methodist Church.

The Roman Catholic Church

Angola comprises five archdioceses and 14 dioceses. An estimated 52% of the population are Roman Catholics.

Bishops' Conference: Conferência Episcopal de Angola e São Tomé (CEAST), CP 3579, Luanda; tel. 222443686; fax 222445504; e-mail ceast@snet.co.ao; internet www.ceastangola.org; f. 1967; Pres. Most Rev. GABRIEL MBILINGI (Archbishop of Lubango).

Archbishop of Huambo: Most Rev. JOSÉ DE QUEIRÓS ALVES, Arcebispado, CP 10, Huambo; tel. 241220130; fax 241220133; e-mail bispado.huambo@asat.signis.net.

Archbishop of Luanda: Most Rev. DAMIÃO ANTÓNIO FRANKLIN, Arcebispado, Largo do Palácio 9, CP 87, 1230-C, Luanda; tel. 222331481; fax 222334433; e-mail spastoral@snet.com.ao.

Archbishop of Lubango: Most Rev. GABRIEL MBILINGI, Arcebispado, CP 231, Lubango; tel. and fax 261230140; e-mail arquidiocese.lubango@netangola.com.

Archbishop of Malanje: Most Rev. DOM BENEDITO ROBERTO, CP 192, Malanje; tel. 2038421708.

Archbishop of Saurimo: Most Rev. JOSÉ MANUEL IMBAMBA, CP 52, Saurimo; tel. 761572551 (mobile); fax 761572553 (mobile).

The Press

DAILIES

Diário da República: CP 1306, Luanda; tel. 217810870; fax 213945750; e-mail dre@incm.pt; internet www.dre.pt; official govt bulletin.

O Jornal de Angola: Rua Rainha Ginga 18–24, CP 1312, Luanda; tel. 222335531; fax 222333342; e-mail jornaldeangola@nexus.ao; internet jornaldeangola.sapo.ao; f. 1975; state-owned; Dir JOSÉ RIBEIRO; mornings and Sun.; circ. 41,000.

PERIODICALS

Angolense: Rua Cónego Manuel das Neves 83B, Luanda; tel. 222445753; fax 222340549; e-mail angolense@netangola.com; internet www.jornalangolense.com; f. 1998; weekly; Dir AMÉRICO GONÇALVES; Editor-in-Chief SUZANA MENDES.

O Apostolado: Rua Comandante Bula 118, São Paulo, CP 3579, Luanda; tel. 222432641; fax 222440628; e-mail redaccao@apostolado-angola.org; internet www.apostolado-angola.org; f. 1935; current and religious affairs; Dir MAURÍCIO AGOSTINHO CAMUTO.

A Capital: Rua Canego Manuel das Neves, Prédio 5, 1º andar, Luanda; tel. 222440549; e-mail info@semanarioacapital.com; internet semanarioacapital.com; f. 2003; weekly; Dir TANDALA FRANCISCO.

Chocolate: Rua Augusto Tadeu de Bastos 52, Maianga, Luanda; tel. 222398565; e-mail revistachocolate@visao.co.ao; internet www.revistachocolate.com; publ. by Media Nova; monthly; lifestyle; circ. 10,000.

Eme: Luanda; tel. 222321130; f. 1996; fortnightly; MPLA publ; Dir FERNANDO FATI.

EXAME Angola: Zona Residencial ZR6-B, Lote 32, Sector de Talatona, Luanda Sul; tel. 222003275; fax 222003289; e-mail exameangola@gmail.com; internet www.exameangola.com; publ. by Media Nova; Editor JAIME FIDALGO.

Folha 8: Rua Conselheiro Júlio de Vilhena 24, 5° andar, CP 6527, Luanda; tel. 222391943; fax 222392289; e-mail folha8@ebonet.net; internet folha8online.com; f. 1994; 2 a week; Editor WILLIAM TONET.

Jornal dos Desportos: Rua Rainha Ginga 18–24, CP 1312, Luanda; tel. 222335531; fax 222335481; e-mail jornaldosdesportos@hotmail.com; internet jornaldosdesportos.sapo.ao; f. 1994; bi-weekly; Dir MATIAS ADRIANO; Editorial Dir POLICARPO DA ROSA; circ. 5,000.

Lavra & Oficina: CP 2767-C, Luanda; tel. 222322421; fax 222323205; e-mail uea@uea-angola.org; internet www.uea-angola.org; f. 1975; journal of the União dos Escritores Angolanos (Union of Angolan Writers); monthly; circ. 5,000.

O País: Condomínio Alfa, Edifício nº6, Talatona, Luanda; tel. 222003268; fax 222007754; e-mail info@opais.co.ao; internet www.opais.net; f. 2008; publ. by Media Nova; weekly; Editor-in-Chief JOSÉ KALIENGUE.

Semanário Angolense: Rua António Feliciano de Castilho 103, Luanda; tel. 222264915; fax 222263506; e-mail info@semanarioangolense.net; internet www.semanarioangolense.net; f. 2003; independent; current affairs; Dir FELIZBERTO GRAÇA CAMPOS; weekly.

Semanário Económico: Luanda; f. 2009; publ. by Media Nova; weekly; Editor PEDRO NARCISO.

Vida: Condomínio Alfa, Edifício nº 6, Talatona, Luanda Sul; tel. 222003268; fax 222007754; e-mail info@opais.co.ao; internet www.vida.opais.net; publ. by Media Nova; Editor JOSÉ KALIENGUE.

NEWS AGENCIES

In early 2006 legislation was passed by the National Assembly ending the governmental monopoly over news agencies.

Agência Angola Press (ANGOP): Rua Rei Katyavala 120, CP 2181, Luanda; tel. 222447343; fax 222447342; e-mail angop@netangola.com; internet www.angolapress-angop.ao; f. 1975; Dir-Gen. MANUEL DA CONCEIÇÃO.

Centro de Imprensa Anibal de Melo (CIAM): Rua Cerqueira Lukoki 124, CP 2805, Luanda; tel. 222393341; fax 222393445; govt press centre; Dir Dr OLYMPIO DE SOUSA E SILVA.

Publishers

Chá de Caxinde: Av. do 1° Congresso do MPLA 20–24, CP 5731, Luanda; tel. 222390936; fax 222332876; e-mail geral@chadecaxinde.net; internet chadecaxinde.net; f. 1999; Dir JAQUES ARLINDO DOS SANTOS.

Editorial Kilombelombe: Luanda; Dir MATEUS VOLÓDIA.

Editorial Nzila: Rua Comandante Valódia 1, ao Largo do Kinaxixi, Luanda; tel. 222447137; e-mail edinzila@hotmail.com.

Plural Editores: Rua Lucrécia Paim 16A, Bairro do Maculusso, Luanda; tel. 924351990 (mobile); fax 222339107; e-mail plural@pluraleditores.co.ao; internet www.pluraleditores.co.ao; f. 2005; 100% owned by Porto Editora (Portugal); technical and educational; CEO ALEXANDRE ALVES.

Ponto Um Indústria Gráfica: Rua Sebastião Desta Vez 55, Luanda; tel. 222448315; fax 222449424.

União dos Escritores Angolanos (UEA): Av. Ho-Chi-Min, Largo das Escolas 1º de Maio, CP 2767, Luanda; tel. and fax 222322421; fax 222323205; e-mail contacto@ueangola.com; internet www.ueangola.com.

GOVERNMENT PUBLISHING HOUSE

Imprensa Nacional, UEE: Rua Henrique de Carvalho 2, Cidade Alta, Ingombota, CP 1306, Luanda; tel. 222336139; fax 222337270; e-mail secretaria.geral@imprensanacional.gov.ao; internet www.imprensanacional.gov.ao; f. 1845; Gen. Man. ANA MARÍA SOUSA E SILVA.

Broadcasting and Communications

TELECOMMUNICATIONS

Angola Telecom (AT): Rua das Quipacas 186, CP 625, Luanda; tel. 222395990; fax 222391688; internet www.angolatelecom.com; state telecommunications co; Pres. FELICIANO ANTÓNIO.

Movicel Telecomunicações, Lda: Rua Mãe Isabel 1, Luanda; tel. 222692000; fax 222692090; internet www.movicel.co.ao; f. 2002; mobile cellular telephone operator; Chair. MANUEL AVELINO; Exec. Dir CARLOS BRITO.

Mundo StarTel: Rua Ndunduma 188, São Paulo, Município de Sambizanga, Luanda; tel. 222432417; fax 222446972; e-mail sede@startel.co.ao; internet www.startel.co.ao; f. 2004; 44% owned by Telecom Namibia; Dir-Gen. PAULO ANTÓNIO DA MOTTA GARCIA.

Nexus Telecomunicações e Serviços SARL: Rua dos Enganos 1, 1° andar, Luanda; tel. 228740041; fax 228740741; e-mail nexus@nexus.ao; internet www.nexus.ao; began operations mid-2004; fixed-line operator.

Unitel SARL: Talatona Sector 22, Via C3, Luanda Sul; tel. 923192222 (mobile); fax 222013624; e-mail unitel@unitel.co.ao; internet www.unitel.ao; f. 1998; 25% owned by Portugal Telecom; private mobile telephone operator; Dir-Gen. MIGUEL F. VEIGA MARTINS; 5.7m. subscribers.

Regulatory Authority

Instituto Angolano das Comunicações (INACOM): Av. de Portugal 92, 7° andar, CP 1459, Luanda; tel. 222338352; fax 222339356; e-mail inacom.dg@netangola.com; internet www.inacom.og.ao; f. 1999; monitoring and regulatory authority; Dir-Gen. DOMINGOS PEDRO ANTÓNIO.

BROADCASTING

Radio

A decree on the regulation of radio broadcasting was approved in 1997. Since that time private operators have reportedly experienced difficulty in gaining permission to broadcast, although several private stations were operating in Luanda in the early 2010s.

Rádio Nacional de Angola: Av. Comandante Gika, CP 1329, Luanda; tel. 222320192; fax 222324647; e-mail dgeral@rna.ao; internet www.rna.ao; state-controlled; operates Canal A, Radio 5, Radio FM Estério, Radio Luanda and Radio N'gola Yetu; broadcasts in Portuguese, English, French, Spanish and vernacular languages (Chokwe, Kikongo, Kimbundu, Kwanyama, Fiote, Ngangela, Luvale, Songu, Umbundu); Dir-Gen. ALBERTO DE SOUSA.

Luanda Antena Comercial (LAC): Rua Luther King 5, CP 3521, Luanda; tel. 222394989; fax 222396229; e-mail lac@ebonet.net; internet www.nexus.ao/lac; popular music.

Radio CEFOJOR: Rua Luther King 123/4, Luanda; tel. 222336140; f. 2003; commercial station, provides journalistic training; Dir-Gen. JOAQUIM PAULO DA CONCEIÇÃO.

Rádio Ecclésia—Emissora Católica de Angola: Rua Comandante Bula 118, São Paulo, CP 3579, Luanda; tel. 222447153; fax 222446346; e-mail info@radioecclesia.org; internet www.radioecclesia.org; f. 1955; broadcasts mainly restricted to Luanda; coverage of politics and current affairs; Dir-Gen. MUANAMOSSI MATUMONA.

Radio Escola: Rua Luther King 123/124, Luanda; tel. 222337409; fax 222446346; educational.

Rádio Mais: Edifício Laranja, Projecto Nova Vida, Rua 40, Luanda; tel. 928818316 (mobile); e-mail info@radiomais.co.ao; internet www.radiomais.co.ao; Dir-Gen. JOSÉ MARQUES VIEIRA.

Rádio Morena Comercial, Lda: Rua Comandante Kassanji, CP 537, Benguela; tel. 272232525; fax 272234242.

The Voice of America (internet www.ebonet.net/voa) also broadcasts from Luanda.

Television

In early 2006 legislation was passed by the National Assembly ending the Government's monopoly over television and simplifying the radio licensing process. A digital television system, TV Cabo Angola, began broadcasting in early 2006.

Televisão Pública de Angola (TPA): Av. Ho Chi Minh, CP 2604, Luanda; tel. 222320026; fax 222323027; e-mail gabinetedg@tpa.ao; internet www.tpa.ao; f. 1976; state-controlled; 2 channels; Co-ordinator of the Executive Committee HÉLDER BÁRBER.

TV Cabo Angola: Rua Comandante Che Guevara 87/89, Bairro do Maculusso, Ingombota, Luanda; tel. 222680000; fax 222680001; e-mail tvcabo@tvcabo.co.ao; internet www.tvcabo.co.ao; provider of digital television and internet services.

TV Zimbo: Av. do Talatona, Luanda Sul; tel. 222004201; e-mail info@tvzimbo.co.ao; internet www.tvzimbo.net; Dir-Gen. FILIPE CORREIA DE SÁ.

Finance

(cap. = capital; res = reserves; dep. = deposits; m. = million; brs = branches; amounts in kwanza (equivalent to 1m. readjusted kwanza), unless otherwise indicated)

BANKING

All banks were nationalized in 1975. In 1995 the Government authorized the formation of private banks. In 2011 there were 23 banks licensed to operate in Angola.

Central Bank

Banco Nacional de Angola: Av. 4 de Fevereiro 151, CP 1298, Luanda; tel. and fax 222333717; e-mail bna.cri@ebonet.net; internet www.bna.ao; f. 1976; bank of issue; cap. 5m., res –39,106m., dep. 1,291,174m. (Dec. 2008); Gov. JOSÉ DE LIMA MASSANO; 6 brs.

Commercial Banks

Banco Angolano de Negócios e Comércios SA: Travessa da Sorte nº 12, Maianga, Luanda; tel. 222395026; fax 222391059; e-mail servicosgerais@banc.ws; internet www.banc.co.ao; f. 2007; cap. 1,750.0m., res 644.2m., dep. 9,170.9m. (Dec. 2011); Chair. JOSÉ AIRES.

Banco BIC SA: Rua Major Kanhangulo 212, Luanda; tel. 222371227; fax 222395099; e-mail bancobic@bancobic.ao; internet www.bancobic.ao; f. 2005; 25% owned by Fidel Kiluange Assis Araujo; 20% owned by Fernando Mendes Teles; cap. 2,414.5m., res 48,194.1m., dep. 525,785.3m. (Dec. 2012); Chair. FERNANDO MENDES TELES.

Banco Comercial Angolano SARL (BCA): Av. Comandante Valódia 83A, CP 6900, Luanda; tel. 222449548; fax 222449516; internet www.bca.co.ao; f. 1997; 50% owned by Absa; cap. 1,308.7m., res 2,621.0m., dep. 30,811.5m. (Dec. 2012); Pres. FRANCISCO DA SILVA CRISTOVÃO; CEO MATEUS FILIPE MARTINS; 4 brs (2005).

Banco de Fomento Angola—BFA: Rua Amílcar Cabral 58, Maianga, Luanda; tel. 222638900; fax 222638925; internet www.bfa.ao; f. 1993 as Banco Fomento Exterior; name changed to above in 2001; 50.1% owned by Banco BPI, SA, Portugal; cap. 3,521.9m., res 48,624.5m., dep. 668,113.3m. (Dec. 2012); CEO EMIDIO PINHEIRO; 38 brs (2005).

Banco Millennium Angola SA: 59 Av. Lenine, Luanda; tel. 222632100; fax 222632494; e-mail comunicacao@millenniumangola.ao; internet www.millenniumangola.ao; f. 2006; 52.7% owned by Banco Comercial Português SA, 31.5% owned by Sonangol, 15.8% owned by Banco Privado Atlântico; cap. 4,009.8m., res 18,876.7m., dep. 117,955.8m. (Dec. 2012); Pres. and CEO Eng. JOSÉ REINO DA COSTA.

Banco de Poupança e Crédito SARL (BPC): Largo Saydi Mingas, CP 1343, Luanda; tel. and fax 222372529; e-mail bpc@bpc.ao; internet www.bpc.ao; f. 1956 as Banco Comercial de Angola; 99% state-owned, 1% owned by the Instituto Nacional de Segurança Social; cap. 31,671.6m., res 35,553.9m., dep. 587,212.7m. (Dec. 2012); Chair. PAIXÃO ANTÓNIO JÚNIOR.

Banco Regional do Keve SARL: Edif. Robert Hudson, Rua Rainha Ginga 77, CP 1804, Luanda; tel. 222394100; fax 222395101; e-mail sedecentral@bancokeve.ao; internet www.bancokeve.ao; f. 2003; cap. 4,000.0m., res 3,471.6m., dep. 70,630.3m. (Dec. 2012); Pres. AMILCAR AZEVEDO DA SILVA.

Banco Sol: Rua Rei Katyavala 110–112, Maculusso, Zona 8, Ingombotas, CP 814, Luanda; tel. 222394717; fax 222440226; e-mail banco.sol@ebonet.net; internet www.bancosol.ao; f. 2000; 55% owned by SANSUL; cap. 1,377.5m., res 1,266.4m., dep. 119,149.3m. (Dec. 2012); Pres. COUTINHO NOBRE MIGUEL.

Development Banks

Banco de Comércio e Indústria SARL: Rua Rainha Ginga, Largo do Atlético 73–83, POB 1395, Luanda; tel. 222330209; fax 222334924; e-mail falfredo@bci.ebonet.net; internet www.bci.ao; f. 1991; 91% state-owned; privatization pending; provides loans to businesses in all sectors; cap. 2,531.8m., res 6,618.6m., dep. 44,329.6m. (Dec. 2010); Chair. ADRIANO RAFAEL PASCOAL; 5 brs.

Banco de Desenvolvimento de Angola (BDA): Av. 4 de Fevereiro 113, Luanda; tel. 222692800; fax 222396901; e-mail bancobda@bda.ao; internet www.bda.ao; f. 2006; Pres. FRANCO PAIXÃO.

Investment Bank

Banco Angolano de Investimentos SARL (BAI): Rua Major Kanhangulo 34, CP 6022, Luanda; tel. 222693800; fax 222335486; e-mail baised@bancobai.co.ao; internet www.bancobai.ao; f. 1997; fmrly Banco Africano de Investimentos SARL; name changed as above in 2011; 8.95% owned by BAI Treasury Stock; 8.5% owned by SONANGOL; cap. 14,786.7m., res 66,779.2m., dep. 815,203.6m. (Dec. 2012); Chair. Dr JOSÉ CARLOS DE CASTRO PAIVA; 45 brs.

Foreign Banks

Banco Comercial Português—Atlântico SA: Rua Rainha Ginga 83, CP 5726, Luanda; tel. 222397922; fax 222397397; Gen. Man. MARIA NAZARÉ FRANCISCO DANG.

Banco Espírito Santo Angola SARL (BESA): Rua 1, Congresso No. 27, Ingombotas, Luanda; tel. 222693600; fax 222693697; internet www.besa.ao; f. 2002; 9.96% owned by Banco Espírito Santo SA (Portugal); cap. US $162.9m., res $24.4m., dep. $5,958.6m. (Dec. 2009); Pres. and Chair. ÁLVARO DE OLIVEIRA MADALENO SOBRINAO.

Banco Totta de Angola SARL: Av. 4 de Fevereiro 99, CP 1231, Luanda; tel. 222332729; fax 222333233; e-mail tottango@ebonet.net; 99.98% owned by Banco Santander Totta; cap. €15.5m. (Dec. 2003); Man. Dir Dr MÁRIO NELSON MAXIMINO; 7 brs.

NovoBanco: Rua Ndunduma 253/257, Bairro Miramar, Município Sambizanga, Luanda; tel. 222430040; fax 222430074; e-mail secretariado@novobanco.ao; internet www.novobanco.net; f. 2004; Pres. MARIO A. BARBER.

STOCK EXCHANGE

Bolsa de Valores e Derivativos do Angola (BVDA): Mutamba, Luanda; f. 2006; Pres. JOSÉ PEDRO DE MORAIS.

INSURANCE

AAA Seguros e Pensões SA: Rua Lenine 58, Ingombota, Luanda; tel. 222691200; fax 222691342; e-mail carlos.vicente@aaa.co.ao; internet www.aaa.co.ao; f. 2000; life and non-life; Pres. Dr CARLOS MANUEL DE SÃO VICENTE.

ENSA Seguros de Angola (Empresa Nacional de Seguros e Resseguros de Angola, UEE): Av. 4 de Fevereiro 93, CP 5778, Luanda; tel. 222332990; fax 222332946; e-mail geral@ensa.co.ao; internet www.ensaangola.com; f. 1978; state-owned; to be privatized; Chair. MANUEL JOAQUIM GONÇALVES; Pres. and Dir-Gen. ALEIXO AUGUSTO.

GA Angola Seguros (Global Alliance Insurance Angola): Av. 4 de Fevereiro 79, 1° andar, Luanda; tel. 222330368; fax 222398815; e-mail blara@globalalliance.co.ao; internet www.globalalliance.co.ao; f. 2005; owned by Global Alliance Group (United Kingdom); CEO ROBERT LEWIS.

Nova Sociedade de Seguros de Angola S.A. (Nossa Seguros): Av. 4 de Fevereiro 111, Luanda; tel. 222399909; fax 222399153; e-mail info@nossaseguros.com; internet www.nossaseguros.ao; Man. Dir CARLOS ARMÉNIO DE ALMEIDA DUARTE.

Trade and Industry

GOVERNMENT AGENCIES

Agência Nacional para o Investimento Privado (ANIP): Edificio do Ministerio da Industria, 9º andar, Rua Cerqueira Lukoki No. 25, CP 5465, Luanda; tel. 222391434; fax 222332965; e-mail geral@anip.co.ao; internet www.anip.co.ao; f. 2003; Co-ordinator MARIA LUÍSA ABRANTES.

Gabinete de Obras Especiais: Luanda; Dir MANUEL FERREIRA CLEMENTE JÚNIOR.

Gabinete de Reconstrução Nacional: Luanda; f. 2004; monitors economic and social reconstruction programmes; Dir ANTÓNIO TEIXEIRA FLOR.

Gabinete de Redimensionamento Empresarial: Rua Cerqueira Lukoki 25, 9° andar, CP 594, Luanda; tel. 222390496; fax 222392987; internet www.gare-minfin.org; privatization agency.

Instituto Angolano da Propriedade Industrial: Rua Cerqueira Lukoki 25, 6º andar, CP 3840, Luanda; tel. 222004991; fax 222336428; e-mail prudencia.iapi@hotmail.com; Dir BARROS BEBIANO JOSÉ LICENÇA.

Instituto de Desenvolvimento Agrário: Rua Comandante Gika, CP 2109, Luanda; tel. and fax 222323651; e-mail ida.canga@netangola.com; promotes agricultural devt; Dir MARCOS NHUNGA.

Instituto de Desenvolvimento Industrial de Angola (IDIA): Rua Cerqueira Lukoki 25, 8° andar, CP 594, Luanda; tel. and fax 222338492; e-mail idiadg@netangola.com; f. 1995; promotes industrial devt; Dir BENJAMIM DO ROSÁRIO DOMBOLO.

Instituto de Investimento Estrangeiro (IIE): Rua Cerqueira Lukoki 25, 9º andar, CP 594, Luanda; tel. 222392620; fax 222393381; foreign investment agency.

Instituto Nacional de Cereais (INCER): Av. 4 de Fevereiro 101, CP 1105, Luanda; tel. and fax 222331611; promotes cereal crops; Dir-Gen. BENJAMIM ALVARO CASTELO.

CHAMBER OF COMMERCE

Câmara de Comércio e Indústria de Angola (CCIA) (Angolan Chamber of Commerce and Industry): Largo do Kinaxixi 14, 1° andar, CP 92, Luanda; tel. 222444506; fax 222444629; e-mail ccira@ebonet.net; internet www.ccia.ebonet.net; Pres. ANTÓNIO JOÃO DOS SANTOS; Sec.-Gen. ANTÓNIO TIAGO GOMES.

INDUSTRIAL AND TRADE ASSOCIATIONS

Associação Comercial de Benguela: Rua Sacadura Cabral 104, CP 347, Benguela; tel. 272232441; fax 272233022; e-mail acbenguela@netangola.com; internet www.netangola.com/acb; f. 1907; Pres. AIRES PIRES ROQUE.

Associação Comercial e Industrial da Ilha de Luanda (ACIL): Largo do Kinaxixi 9, Luanda; tel. 222341866; fax 222349677; Pres. PEDRO GODHINO DOMINGOS.

Associação Industrial de Angola (AIA): Rua Manuel Fernando Caldeira 6, CP 61227, Luanda; tel. 222330624; fax 222338650; e-mail contactos@aiangola.net; internet aiangola.net; Pres. JOSÉ SEVERINO.

Associação de Mulheres Empresárias: Largo do Kinaxixi 14, 3° andar, Luanda; tel. 222346742; fax 222343088; f. 1990; asscn of business women; Sec.-Gen. HENRIQUETA DE CARVALHO.

Rede Angolana do Sector Micro-Empresarial (RASME): Luanda; asscn of small businesses; Exec. Co-ordinator BAY KANGUDI.

STATE TRADING ORGANIZATIONS

Angolan Selling Corporation (ASCORP): Edif. Soleil B, Rua Tipografia Mama Tita, Ingombotas, CP 3978, Luanda; tel. 222396465; fax 222397615; e-mail ascorpadmin@ebonet.net; f. 1999; 51% state-owned diamond-trading co; Pres. NOE BALTAZAR.

Direcção dos Serviços de Comércio (DNCI) (Dept of Trade): Palácio de Vidro, 3° andar, Largo 4 de Fevereiro 7, CP 1337, Luanda; tel. and fax 222310658; e-mail minco.dnci.gc@netangola.com; internet www.dnci.net; f. 1970; brs throughout Angola; Dir GOMES CARDOSO.

Exportang, UEE (Empresa de Exportações de Angola): Rua dos Enganos 1A, CP 1000, Luanda; tel. 222332363; co-ordinates exports.

Importang, UEE (Empresa de Importações de Angola): Calçada do Município 10, CP 1003, Luanda; tel. 222337994; f. 1977; co-ordinates majority of imports; Dir-Gen. SIMÃO DIOGO DA CRUZ.

Nova Angomédica, UEE: Rua do Sanatório, Bairro Palanca, CP 2698, Luanda; tel. 222261366; fax 222260010; f. 1981; production and distribution of pharmaceutical goods; Gen. Dir JOSÉ LUÍS PASCOAL.

Sociedade de Comercialização de Diamantes de Angola SARL (SODIAM): Edif. Endiama/De Beers, Rua Rainha Ginga 87, CP 1072, Luanda; tel. 222370217; fax 222370423; e-mail sodiamadmin@ebonet.net; f. 2000; part of the ENDIAMA group; diamond-trading org.; Man. Dir MANUEL ARNALDO DE SOUSA CALADO.

STATE INDUSTRIAL ENTERPRISES

Empresa de Obras Especiais (EMPROE): Rua Ngola Kiluange 183–185, Luanda; tel. 222382142; fax 222382143; building and civil engineering; Dir-Gen. SILVA NETO.

Empresa de Rebenefício e Exportação do Café de Angola, UEE (CAFANGOL): Rua Robert Shields 4–6, CP 342, Luanda; tel. 222337916; fax 222332840; e-mail cafangol@nexus.ao; f. 1983; nat. coffee-processing and trade org.; Dir-Gen. ISAIAS DOMINGOS DE MENEZES.

Empresa dos Tabacos de Angola: Rua Major Kanyangulu, 220, CP 1238, Luanda; tel. 222332760; fax 222331091; e-mail eta@nexus.ao; manufacture of tobacco products; Gen. Man. K. BITTENCOURT.

Empresa Nacional de Cimento, UEE (ENCIME): CP 157, Lobito; tel. 272212325; cement production.

Empresa Nacional de Diamantes de Angola (ENDIAMA), UEE: Rua Major Kanhangulo 100, CP 1247, Luanda; tel. and fax 222332718; fax 222337216; internet www.endiama.co.ao; f. 1981; commenced operations 1986; diamond-mining; a number of subsidiary cos undergoing privatization; Pres. Dr MANUEL ARNALDO DE SOUSA CALADO.

Empresa Nacional de Ferro de Angola (FERRANGOL): Rua João de Barros 26, CP 2692, Luanda; tel. 222373800; iron production; Chair. DIAMANTINO PEDRO DE AZEVEDO; Dir ARMANDO DE SOUSA.

Empresa Nacional de Manutenção, UEE (MANUTECNICA): Rua 7, Av. do Cazenga 10, CP 3508, Luanda; tel. 222383646; assembly of machines and specialized equipment for industry.

Sociedade Nacional de Combustíveis de Angola (SONANGOL): Rua Rainha Ginga 22, CP 1316, Luanda; tel. 226643342; fax 222391782; e-mail hld.gci@sonangol.co.ao; internet www.sonangol.co.ao; f. 1976; exploration, production and refining of crude petroleum, and marketing and distribution of petroleum products; sole concessionary in Angola, supervises on- and offshore operations of foreign petroleum cos; 17 subsidiaries, incl. shipping cos; holds majority interest in jt ventures with Cabinda Gulf Oil Co (CABGOC), Fina Petróleos de Angola and Texaco Petróleos de Angola; CEO FRANCISCO DE LEMOS JOSE MARIA; c. 7,000 employees.

Sonangalp, Lda: Rua Manuel Fernando Caldeira 25, 1725 Luanda; tel. 222334527; fax 222339802; e-mail geral@sonangalp.co.ao; internet www.sonangalp.co.ao; f. 1994; 51% owned by SONANGOL, 49% owned by Petrogal Angola (Portugal); fuel distribution; Pres. ANTÓNIO SILVESTRE.

UTILITIES

Electricity

Empresa Nacional de Construções Eléctricas, UEE (ENCEL): Rua Comandante Che Guevara 185–187, CP 5230, Luanda; tel. 222446712; fax 222446759; e-mail encel@encel.co.ao; internet www.encel.co.ao; f. 1982; supplier of electromechanical equipment; Dir-Gen. DANIEL SIMAS.

Empresa Nacional de Electricidade, EP (ENE): Edif. Geominas 6°–7° andar, CP 772, Luanda; tel. 222321499; fax 222323382; e-mail enepdg@netangola.com; internet www.ene.co.ao; f. 1980; production and distribution of electricity; Pres. and Dir-Gen. Eng. FERNANDO BARROS C. GONGA.

Water

Empresa Provincial de Água de Luanda (EPAL): Rua Frederich Engels 3, CP 1387, Luanda; tel. 222335001; fax 222330380; e-mail epalsdg@snet.co.ao; state-owned; Pres. LEONÍDIO GUSTAVO FERREIRA DE CEITA.

TRADE UNION

União Nacional dos Trabalhadores Angolanos (UNTA) (National Union of Angolan Workers): Av. 4 de Fevereiro 210, CP 28, Luanda; tel. 222334670; fax 222393590; e-mail untadis@netangola.com; f. 1960; Sec.-Gen. MANUEL AUGUSTO VIAGE; c. 160,000 mems (2007).

Transport

The transport infrastructure was severely dislocated by the civil war that ended in 2002. Subsequently, major rebuilding and upgrading projects were undertaken.

RAILWAYS

There are three main railway lines in Angola: the Benguela railway, which runs from the coast to the Zambian border; the Luanda–Malange line; and the Moçâmedes line, which connects Namibe and Kuando Kubango. In 2004 only 850 km, out of a total of almost 3,000 km, of track were operational. A plan introduced in late 2004 to rehabilitate and extend the rail network was expected to take 11 years and to cost US $4,000m. In mid-2005 a project for rebuilding and upgrading the railway system was approved by the Southern African Development Community (SADC). The 424-km Luanda–Malange line was completed in mid-2010; passenger services resumed in January 2011 and goods transport (between Luanda and Dondo) in May 2013. The Benguela line—a significant export route—reopened in 2011, following demining and reconstruction work by Chinese workers. The Moçâmedes line was reopened in mid-2012. More than 100 new railway stations were opened during 2013.

Direcção Nacional dos Caminhos de Ferro: Rua Major Kanhangulo, CP 1250, Luanda; tel. 222370091; f. 1975; nat. network operating 4 fmrly independent systems covering 2,952 track-km; Dir JULIO BANGO.

Benguela Railway (Caminho de Ferro de Benguela—Empresa Pública): Praça 11 Novembro 3, CP 32, Lobito, Benguela; tel. 272222645; fax 272225133; e-mail cfbeng@ebonet.net; owned by Govt of Angola; line carrying passenger and freight traffic from the port of Lobito across Angola, via Huambo and Luena, to the border of the Democratic Republic of the Congo (DRC, fmrly Zaire); 1,301 track-km; in 2004 a consortium from China (People's Republic) agreed to rehabilitate the line to the DRC; CEO JOSÉ CARLOS GOMES; 1,700 employees.

Caminho de Ferro de Moçâmedes (CFM): CP 130, Lubango; tel. 261221752; fax 261224442; e-mail gab.dir.cfm@netangola.com; f. 1905; main line from Namibe to Menongue, via Lubango; br. lines to Chibia and iron ore mines at Cassinga; 838 track-km; Chair. DANIEL KIPAXE; CEO JÚLIO BANGO JOAQUIM.

Luanda Railway (Empresa de Caminho de Ferro de Luanda, UEE): CP 1250-C, Luanda; tel. 222370061; f. 1886; serves an iron-, cotton- and sisal-producing region between Luanda and Malange; 536 track-km; CEO OSVALDO LOBO DO NASCIMENTO.

ROADS

In 2001 Angola had 51,429 km of roads, of which 7,944 km were main roads and 13,278 km were secondary roads. About 10.4% of roads were paved. It was estimated that 80% of the country's road network was in disrepair. In 2005–06 contracts were awarded to various foreign companies to upgrade the road network, including the main north–south coastal road. A government programme to rebuild some 14,000 km of the road network commenced in the late 2000s.

Direcção Nacional dos Transportes Rodoviárias: Rua Rainha Ginga 74, 1° andar, Luanda; tel. 222339390; fax 222334427.

Instituto Nacional de Estradas de Angola (INEA): Rua Amílcar Cabral 35, 3° andar, CP 5667, Luanda; tel. 222332828; fax 222335754; Dir-Gen. JOAQUIM SEBASTIÃO.

SHIPPING

The main harbours are at Lobito, Luanda and Namibe. In December 2013 Angola's flag registered fleet comprised 94 vessels, totalling 191,073 grt.

Instituto Marítimo e Portuário de Angola (IMPA): Rua Rainha Ginga 74, 4° andar, Luanda; tel. and fax 222390034; Dir-Gen. VICTOR DE CARVALHO.

Agenang, UEE: Rua Engracia Fragoso 47–49, CP 485, Luanda; tel. 222393988; fax 222391444; state shipping co; scheduled for privatization.

Cabotang—Cabotagem Nacional Angolana, UEE: Av. 4 de Fevereiro 83A, Luanda; tel. 222373133; operates off the coasts of Angola and Mozambique; Dir-Gen. JOÃO OCTAVIO VAN-DÚNEM.

Empresa Portuária do Lobito, UEE: Av. da Independência 16, Lobito, Benguela; tel. 272222645; fax 272222865; e-mail dop@portodolobito.com; long-distance sea transport; CEO BENTO PAIXÃO DOS SANTOS.

Empresa Portuária de Luanda: Av. 4 de Fevereiro, CP 1229, Porto de Luanda; tel. 222311753; fax 222311178; e-mail geral@portoluanda.co.ao; internet www.portoluanda.co.ao; CEO FRANCISCO VENÂNCIO.

Empresa Portuária de Moçâmedes—Namibe, UEE: Rua Pedro Benje 10A e C, CP 49, Namibe; tel. 264260643; long-distance sea transport; CEO JOAQUIM DOMINGOS NETO.

Orey Angola, Lda: Largo 4 de Fevereiro 3, 3° andar, CP 583, Luanda; tel. 222311454; fax 222310882; e-mail orey@oreylad.ebonet.net; internet www.orey-angola.com; int. shipping, especially to Portugal; Dir JOÃO TEIGA.

Sécil Marítima SARL, UEE: Edif. Secil, Av. 4 de Fevereiro 42, 1° andar, CP 5910, Luanda; tel. 222311334; fax 222311784; e-mail secilmaritima@msn.com; operates ports at Lobito, Luanda and Namibe; Gen. Man. MARIA AMÉLIA RITA.

CIVIL AVIATION

Angola's airport system is well developed, but suffered some damage in the later years of the civil war. The 4 de Fevereiro international airport in Luanda underwent modernization in the late 2000s, while a new international airport, at Lubango was opened in January 2010. During the late 2000s airports at Luanda, Lobito, Soyo, Namibe, Saurimo, Uíge, Huambo and Bié also underwent rehabilitation. In August 2012 a new international airport, built at a cost of US $250m., was inaugurated at Catumbela, Benguela province. Another new international airport, in the town of Bom Jesus in Luanda province, was not expected to open until 2015 at the earliest (owing to financing problems).

Direcção Nacional da Aviação Civil: Rua Frederich Engels 92, 6° andar, CP 569, Luanda; tel. 222339412.

Instituto Nacional da Aviação Civil: Rua Miguel de Melo 96, 6º andar, Luanda; tel. 222335936; fax 222390529; internet www.inavic.gv.ao; Dir-Gen. Dr GASPAR FRANCISCO DOS SANTOS.

Empresa Nacional de Aeroportos e Navegação Aerea (ENANA): Av. Amílcar Cabral 110, CP 841, Luanda; tel. and fax 222351267; e-mail cai_enana@snet.co.ao; administers airports; Chair. MANUEL FERREIRA DE CEITA.

Air Nacoia: Rua Comandante Che Guevara 67, 1° andar, Luanda; tel. and fax 222395477; f. 1993; Pres. SALVADOR SILVA.

SONAIR SARL: Aeroporto Internacional 4 de Fevereiro, Luanda; tel. 222633502; fax 222321572; e-mail commercial.sonair@sonangol.co.ao; internet www.sonairsarl.com; f. 1998; subsidiary of SONANGOL; operates direct flights between Luanda and Houston, USA; Chair. MANUEL D. VICENTE; CEO JOÃO ALVES ANDRADE.

TAAG—Linhas Aéreas de Angola: Rua da Missão 123, CP 79, Luanda; tel. 222332338; fax 222390396; e-mail gci_taag@ebonet.net; internet www.nexus.ao/taag; f. 1938; internal scheduled passenger and cargo services, and services from Luanda to destinations within Africa and to Europe and South America; Chair. Dr ANTÓNIO LUIS PIMENTEL DE ARAÚJO.

Angola Air Charter: Aeroporto Internacional 4 de Fevereiro, CP 3010, Luanda; tel. 222321290; fax 222320105; e-mail aacharter@independente.net; f. 1992; subsidiary of TAAG; CEO A. DE MATOS.

Transafrik International Ltd: Aeroporto Internacional 4 de Fevereiro, Luanda; tel. 222353714; fax 222354183; e-mail info@transafrik.com; internet www.transafrik.com; f. 1986; operates int. contract cargo services; CEO BJÖRN NÄF; Chief Financial Officer STEPHAN BRANDT.

Tourism

Angola's tourism industry is undeveloped as a result of the years of civil war, although its potential for development is great. Tourist arrivals totalled 481,207 in 2011 and receipts from tourism in that year amounted to US $647m. (excluding passenger transport).

National Tourist Agency: Palácio de Vidro, Largo 4 de Fevereiro, CP 1240, Luanda; tel. 222372750.

Defence

As assessed at November 2013, the Forças Armadas de Angola had an estimated total strength of 107,000: army 100,000, navy 1,000 and air force 6,000. In addition, there was a paramilitary force numbering an estimated 10,000.

Defence Expenditure: Budgeted at 588,000m. kwanza for 2013.

Chief of General Staff of the Armed Forces: Gen. GERALDO SACHIPENGO NUNDA.

Chief of General Staff of the Army: Gen. JORGE BARROS NGUTÓ.

Chief of General Staff of the National Air Force: Gen. FRANCISCO GONÇALVES AFONSO.

Chief of General Staff of the Navy: Adm. AUGUSTO DA SILVA CUNHA.

Education

Education is officially compulsory for eight years, between seven and 15 years of age, and is provided free of charge by the Government. Primary education begins at seven years of age and lasts for four years. Secondary education, beginning at the age of 11, lasts for up to six years, comprising two cycles of three years each. As a proportion of the school-age population, the total enrolment at primary and secondary schools was equivalent to 83% in 2009/10. According to UNESCO estimates, enrolment at primary schools in 2010/11 included 86% of children in the relevant age-group (boys 97%; girls 74%), while secondary enrolment in 2009/10 included 13% of children in the relevant age-group (boys 15%; girls 12%). In 2010/11 a total of 142,798 students were enrolled in higher education. In November 2002 the Government announced plans for the construction of seven provincial universities, five science and technology institutes, three medical schools and a nutrition research centre. There are also four private universities. Much education is now conducted in vernacular languages rather than Portuguese. In 2004 the Government recruited 29,000 new teachers, to be trained by the UN Children's Fund (UNICEF). The 2006 budget allocated an estimated 83,500m. kwanza to education.

ANTARCTICA

INTRODUCTION

The continent of Antarctica is estimated to cover 13,661,000 sq km. There are no indigenous inhabitants, but a number of permanent research stations have been established. W. S. Bruce, of the Scottish National Antarctic Expedition (1902–04), established a meteorological station on Laurie Island, South Orkney Islands, in 1903. After the expedition, this was transferred to the Argentine authorities (the British Government having declined to operate the station), who have maintained the observatory since 1904 (see Orcadas, below). The next permanent stations were established in 1944 by the United Kingdom, and then subsequently by other countries.

RESEARCH

Scientific Committee on Antarctic Research (SCAR): Secretariat: Scott Polar Research Institute, Lensfield Rd, Cambridge, CB2 1ER, United Kingdom; tel. (1223) 336550; fax (1223) 336549; e-mail info@scar.org; internet www.scar.org; f. 1958 to initiate, promote and co-ordinate scientific research in the Antarctic, and to provide scientific advice to the Antarctic Treaty System; an inter-disciplinary cttee of the International Council for Science (ICSU); 31 Full Mems; 9 ICSU Scientific Unions Mems; 7 Assoc. Mems

President: Prof. Jerónimo López-Martínez (Spain).

Vice-Presidents: Prof. Dr Sergio A. Marenssi (Argentina), Dr Yeadong Kim (Republic of Korea), Prof. Dr Karin Lochte (Germany), Prof. Bryan Storey (New Zealand).

Executive Director: Dr Mike Sparrow.

WINTERING STATIONS

(The following list includes wintering stations south of latitude 60° occupied during austral winter 2013)

	Latitude	Longitude
ARGENTINA		
Belgrano II, Bertrab Nunatak, Luitpold Coast	77° 52' S	34° 38 'W
Esperanza, Hope Bay	63° 24' S	57° 00' W
Carlini, King George Island	62° 14' S	58° 40' W
Marambio, Seymour Island	64° 15' S	56° 37' W
Orcadas, South Orkney Islands	60° 44' S	44° 44' W
San Martín, Barry Island	68° 08' S	67° 06' W
AUSTRALIA		
Casey, Vincennes Bay, Budd Coast	66° 17' S	110° 32' E
Davis, Ingrid Christensen Coast	68° 35' S	77° 58' E
Mawson, Mac. Robertson Land	67° 36' S	62° 52' E
BRAZIL		
Comandante Ferraz, King George Island*	62° 05' S	58° 24' W
CHILE		
Eduardo Frei Montalva, King George Island	62° 12' S	58° 58' W
Bernardo O'Higgins Riquelme, Cape Legoupil	63° 19' S	57° 54' W
Arturo Prat, Greenwich Island	62° 29' S	59° 40' W
PEOPLE'S REPUBLIC OF CHINA		
Chang Cheng (Great Wall), King George Island	62° 13' S	58° 58' W
Zhongshan, Princess Elizabeth Land	69° 22' S	76° 22' E
FRANCE		
Dumont d'Urville, Terre Adélie	66° 40' S	140° 00' E
FRANCE-ITALY†		
Concordia, Dome Circe	75° 06' S	123° 20' E
GERMANY		
Neumayer, Ekstrømisen	70° 41' S	08° 16' W
INDIA		
Maitri, Schirmacheroasen	70° 46' S	11° 44' E
Bharati, Larsemann Hills	69° 24' S	76° 11' E
JAPAN		
Syowa, Ongul	69° 00' S	39° 35' E
REPUBLIC OF KOREA		
King Sejong, King George Island	62° 13' S	58° 47' W
NEW ZEALAND		
Scott Base, Ross Island	77° 51' S	166° 46' E
NORWAY		
Troll	72° 01' S	02° 32' E
POLAND		
Arctowski, King George Island	62° 10' S	58° 28' W
RUSSIA		
Bellingshausen, King George Island	62° 12' S	58° 58' W
Mirny, Queen Mary Land	66° 33' S	93° 00' E
Novolazarevskaya, Prinsesse Astrid Kyst	70° 47' S	11° 49' E
Progress 2, Princess Elizabeth Land	69° 23' S	76° 23' E
Vostok, Wilkes Land	78° 28' S	106° 50' E
SOUTH AFRICA		
SANAE IV, Vesleskarvet	71° 40' S	02° 50' W
UKRAINE		
Vernadsky, Argentine Islands	65° 15' S	64° 15' W
UNITED KINGDOM		
Halley, Brunt Ice Shelf, Caird Coast	75° 35' S	26° 44' W
Rothera, Adelaide Island	67° 34' S	68° 07' W
USA		
McMurdo, Ross Island	77° 51' S	166° 40' E
Palmer, Anvers Island	64° 46' S	64° 03' W
Amundsen-Scott	South Pole‡	
URUGUAY		
Artigas, King George Island	62° 11' S	58° 54' W

* The station was destroyed by fire in 2012; following rebuilding work, the station was expected to be operational by March 2015.

† The Concordia research station is a joint venture between France and Italy.

‡ The precise co-ordinates of the location of this station are: 89° 59′ 51″ S, 139° 16′ 22″ E.

TERRITORIAL CLAIMS

Territory	Claimant State
Antártida Argentina	Argentina
Australian Antarctic Territory	Australia
British Antarctic Territory	United Kingdom
Dronning Maud Land	Norway
Ross Dependency	New Zealand
Terre Adélie	France
Territorio Chileno Antártico	Chile

These claims are not recognized by the USA or Russia. No claims in the sector of the Antarctic continent between 90° W and 150° W have been defined by governments. However, Peter I Øy (68° 47'S, 90° 35'W) is claimed as Norwegian territory.

Article 4, Clause 2 of the Antarctic Treaty (see below) states that, 'No acts or activities taking place while the present Treaty is in force shall constitute a basis for asserting, supporting or denying a claim to territorial sovereignty in Antarctica or create any rights of sovereignty in Antarctica. No new claim, or enlargement of an existing claim, to territorial sovereignty in Antarctica shall be asserted while the present Treaty is in force.'

THE ANTARCTIC TREATY

The Antarctic Treaty was signed in Washington, DC, USA, on 1 December 1959 by the 12 nations co-operating in the Antarctic during the International Geophysical Year (1957–58), and entered into force on 23 June 1961. The Treaty made provision for a review of its terms 30 years after ratification; however, no signatory to the Treaty has requested such a review.

The full original text of the Antarctic Treaty is reproduced by the Antarctic Treaty Secretariat at www.ats.aq/documents/ats/treaty_original.pdf.

Signatories

The Original Signatories to the Antarctic Treaty are Argentina, Australia, Belgium, Chile, France, Japan, New Zealand, Norway, Russia (as successor to the former USSR), South Africa, the United Kingdom and the USA. Each holds the status of Consultative Party.

By virtue of their scientific activity in Antarctica, Brazil, Bulgaria, the People's Republic of China, Ecuador, Finland, Germany, India, Italy, the Republic of Korea, the Netherlands, Peru, Poland, Spain, Sweden, Ukraine and Uruguay have the status of Consultative Party under the Treaty. Austria, Belarus, Canada, Colombia, Cuba, the Czech Republic, Denmark, Estonia, Greece, Guatemala, Hungary, the Democratic People's Republic of Korea, Malaysia, Monaco, Pakistan, Papua New Guinea, Portugal, Romania, Slovakia, Switzerland, Turkey and Venezuela are Acceding States but do not have Consultative Party status.

Antarctic Treaty Secretariat: Maipú 757, 4°, C1006ACI Buenos Aires, Argentina; tel. (11) 4320-4250; fax (11) 4320-4253; e-mail ats@ats.aq; internet www.ats.aq; f. 2004; Exec. Sec. Dr MANFRED REINKE.

Commission for the Conservation of Antarctic Marine Living Resources (CCAMLR): 181 Macquarie St, Hobart, Tas 7000, Australia; tel. (3) 6210-1111; fax (3) 6224-8744; e-mail ccamlr@ccamlr.org; internet www.ccamlr.org; f. 1982 to conserve Antarctic marine life in response to increasing commercial interest in Antarctic krill resources; ecosystem-based management approach; observer at Antarctic Treaty meetings; Chair. LESZEK DYBIEC (Poland); Exec. Sec. ANDREW WRIGHT; 25 mems, 11 acceding states.

Council of Managers of National Antarctic Programmes (COMNAP): c/o Gateway Antarctica, University of Canterbury, Private Bag 4800, Christchurch, New Zealand 8140; tel. (3) 364-2273; fax (3) 364-2907; e-mail info@comnap.aq; internet www.comnap.aq; f. 1988; comprises the Managers of the National Antarctic Programmes; supports scientific research in the Antarctic Treaty Area and provides technical advice to the Antarctic Treaty System; observer at Antarctic Treaty meetings; Chair. HEINZ MILLER (Germany); Exec. Sec. MICHELLE ROGAN-FINNEMORE; 29 mems.

Antarctic Treaty Consultative Meetings

Meetings of representatives of the original signatory nations of the Antarctic Treaty and acceding nations accorded consultative status are held annually to discuss scientific, environmental and political matters. The 37th meeting was scheduled to take place in Brasília, Brazil, in May 2014.

Among the numerous measures that have been agreed and implemented by the Consultative Parties are several designed to protect the Antarctic environment and wildlife. These include the designation of Specially Protected Areas and Sites of Special Scientific Interest, a Convention for the Conservation of Antarctic Seals, and a Convention on the Conservation of Antarctic Marine Living Resources.

The Protocol on Environmental Protection to the Antarctic Treaty was adopted by the original signatory nations in October 1991. It entered into force in January 1998, having been ratified by all 26 of the then Consultative Parties. Under Article 7, any activity relating to mineral resources, other than scientific research, is prohibited. Article 25, on modification or amendment, states that a conference shall be held as soon as practicable if, after the expiration of 50 years from the date of entry into force of the Protocol, any of the Antarctic Treaty Consultative Parties so requests; it further specifies that, in respect of Article 7, any proposed modification to the prohibition on mining activity shall be considered only if a regulatory regime is in place. The first four annexes to the Protocol, providing for environmental impact assessment, conservation of fauna and flora, waste disposal, and monitoring of marine pollution, entered into force with the Protocol; a fifth annex, on area protection and management, incorporating all the existing Specially Protected Areas and Sites of Special Scientific Interest as Antarctic Specially Protected Areas, entered into effect in May 2002. A sixth annex, on liability arising from environmental emergencies, was adopted in June 2005, and was to take effect upon ratification by all Consultative Parties to the Protocol. The Protocol effectively superseded the provisions of the 1964 Agreed Measures for the Conservation of Antarctic Fauna and Flora, including area protection in Antarctica. A Committee for Environmental Protection (CEP) was established in 1998, under the provisions of the Protocol on Environmental Protection. The CEP meets at the location of the annual Antarctic Treaty Consultative Meeting.

Committee for Environmental Protection (CEP): e-mail cep@cep.aq; internet www.cep.aq; f. 1998; Chair. Dr YVES FRENOT.

RECENT DEVELOPMENTS

The World Meteorological Organization (WMO) reported that the hole in the ozone layer formed over Antarctica in 2006 was the most serious on record, at 29.5m. sq km at its maximum point. Furthermore, the greatest mass deficit was also recorded in 2006—of 40.8m. metric tons—with the effect that the mass of ozone over Antarctica was lower than that ever previously recorded. WMO data for 2007 showed that the ozone hole area, at a maximum of 25m. sq km, was somewhat weaker, as was the mass deficit, which reached 28m. tons. WMO stated that the relatively smaller size of the ozone hole was not a sign of recovery, but was instead related to mild temperatures in the Antarctic stratosphere during the 2007 austral winter. In 2008 the ozone hole area reached 27m. sq km, and the mass deficit 35m. tons: each was the fourth largest recorded since 1999. The daily maximum ozone hole area in 2009 was 24.0m. sq km. For 2010 the ozone hole reached a peak daily maximum of 22.6m. sq km in September. In 2011 the daily maximum ozone hole area reached 26.1m. sq km and in 2012 the daily maximum ozone hole was 21.1m. sq km in September. The mass deficit stood at 22.0m. tons in the same month. By September 2013 the daily maximum ozone hole had increased to 24.0m. sq km, more than in 2012 and 2010, but less than in 2011. The mass deficit averaged 19.6m. tons.

A comprehensive study of glaciers in the Antarctic Pensinsula, published by researchers of the British Antarctic Survey in 2005, showed that 87% of glaciers there were retreating, and that the rate of retreat had increased markedly since 2000. The survey analysed data back to the 1950s, when a majority of glaciers were stable or advancing. Research published in 2006, led by the University of Colorado, USA, gave evidence of the significant decline of the total mass balance of the Antarctic ice sheet. Satellite data indicated that the volume of ice being lost was raising global sea levels by some 0.4 mm per year. Research published by an international team of scientists in 2008 estimated that 132,000m. metric tons of ice had been lost from West Antarctica in 2006, compared with 83,000m. tons in 1996. Loss was concentrated at narrow glacier outlets with accelerating ice flow, suggesting that the mass balance of the entire ice sheet had been altered by glacier flow. (Previous simulation had suggested that the ice mass would increase in response to future climate change during the 21st century, owing to increased snowfall.) While recorded loss to the East Antarctic ice sheet was near zero in 1996–2006, the thinning of maritime sectors suggested that this may change in the near future. Analysis published in 2009 by scientists at the University of Texas at Austin, USA, suggested that the East Antarctic ice sheet was losing mass, mainly in coastal areas, at an estimated rate of some 57,000m. tons annually. The same study confirmed annual ice loss from West Antarctica of 132,000m. tons. A study of changes in polar ice mass and trends in acceleration in polar ice loss, published in the journal *Geophysical Research Letters* in 2011, based on analysis of data from 1992–2009, found that loss from the Antarctic ice sheet was increasing by an average of 14,500m. metric tons per year. In November 2012 a study co-ordinated jointly by the European Space Agency and NASA concluded that current ice losses in Antarctica were three times higher than in the 1990s, equivalent to 0.95 mm of sea level rise per year, although this was still within the average sea level rises predicted by the 2007 *Fourth Assessment Report* of the Intergovernmental Panel on Climate Change (IPCC). A 2013 NASA study concluded that Antarctic ice sheet losses were caused by warmer seas more than icebergs breaking away from glaciers. The IPCC's *Fifth Assessment Report*, published in 2013, concluded that the contribution of Antarctic ice sheets to sea level change had increased since the 1990s. Meanwhile, a study, led by US academics, of trends in Antarctic surface temperatures during 1957–2006, results of which were released in 2009, suggested that the continent was warming by an average of about 0.1°C per decade, with the strongest warming trends being in winter and spring and over West Antarctica. The report's authors concluded that while natural climatic cycles probably influenced the warming, it was difficult to explain the warming trend without considering the near-certain impact of increased concentrations of greenhouse gases.

TOURISM AND MARITIME SAFETY

Tourism is co-ordinated by the International Association of Antarctica Tour Operators (IAATO). The number of tourists visiting Antarctica in 2012/13 totalled 34,354 (compared with 4,700 in 1990/91), including 25,284 landed passengers. Increases in tourist numbers led to expressions of concern by the early 2000s regarding the environmental impact of the industry on the region. In 2009 signatories to the Antarctic Treaty agreed, subject to ratification, to prevent vessels carrying more than 500 passengers from landing in Antarctica, and to allow no more than 100 passengers on permitted vessels to land at any one time. A mandatory safety code for vessels operating in the Antarctic region was also adopted. The International Maritime Organization (IMO) adopted guidelines for ships operating in polar waters; the guidelines formed the basis of a planned mandatory Polar Code, intended to address the risks specific to shipping operations in polar waters, taking into account the extreme environmental conditions and remoteness of operation, as well as comprehensively to address the possible impact on the environment of shipping activity. Under amendments to the IMO International Convention for the Prevention of Pollution from Ships (MARPOL), the use of heavy fuel oils by passenger and cargo ships in Antarctic waters was prohibited with effect from August 2011. In January 2013 a Boeing 737 aircraft landed successfully for the first time at the Norwegian Troll wintering station.

ANTIGUA AND BARBUDA

Introductory Survey

LOCATION, CLIMATE, LANGUAGE, RELIGION, FLAG, CAPITAL

The country comprises three islands: Antigua (280 sq km—108 sq miles), Barbuda (161 sq km—62 sq miles) and the uninhabited rocky islet of Redonda (1.6 sq km—0.6 sq mile). They lie along the outer edge of the Leeward Islands chain in the West Indies. Barbuda is the most northerly (40 km—25 miles north of Antigua), and Redonda is 40 km south-west of Antigua. The French island of Guadeloupe lies to the south of the country, the United Kingdom Overseas Territory of Montserrat to the south-west and Saint Christopher and Nevis to the west. The climate is tropical, although tempered by constant sea breezes and the trade winds, and the mean annual rainfall of 1,000 mm (40 ins) is slight for the region. The temperature averages 27°C (81°F), but can rise to 33°C (93°F) during the hot season between May and October. English is the official language, but an English patois is commonly used. The majority of the inhabitants profess Christianity, and are mainly adherents of the Anglican Communion. The national flag consists of an inverted triangle centred on a red field; the triangle is divided horizontally into three unequal bands, of black, blue and white, with the black stripe bearing a symbol of the rising sun in gold. The capital is St John's, on Antigua.

CONTEMPORARY POLITICAL HISTORY

Historical Context

The British colonized Antigua in the 17th century. The island of Barbuda, formerly a slave stud farm for the Codrington family, was annexed to the territory in 1860. Until December 1959 Antigua and other nearby British territories were administered, under a federal system, as the Leeward Islands. The first elections under universal adult suffrage were held in 1951. The colony participated in the West Indies Federation, formed in 1958 but dissolved in 1962.

Attempts to form a smaller East Caribbean Federation failed, and most of the eligible colonies subsequently became Associated States in an arrangement that gave them full internal self-government while the United Kingdom retained responsibility for defence and foreign affairs. Antigua attained associated status in February 1967. A House of Representatives replaced the Legislative Council, the Administrator became Governor and the Chief Minister was restyled Premier.

Domestic Political Affairs

In the first general election under associated status, held in February 1971, the Progressive Labour Movement (PLM) ousted the Antigua Labour Party (ALP), which had held power since 1946. George Walter, leader of the PLM, replaced Vere C. Bird, Sr, as Premier. However, a general election in February 1976 was won by the ALP. Vere Bird, the ALP's leader, again became Premier, while Lester Bird, one of his sons, became Deputy Premier.

In 1975 the Associated States agreed to seek independence separately. In the 1976 elections the PLM campaigned for early independence while the ALP opposed it. In September 1978, however, the ALP Government declared that the economic foundation for independence had been laid, and a premature general election was held in April 1980, when the ALP was re-elected. There was strong opposition in Barbuda to gaining independence as part of Antigua, and at local elections in March 1981 the Barbuda People's Movement (BPM), which continued to campaign for secession from Antigua, won all the seats on the Barbuda Council. However, the territory finally became independent, as Antigua and Barbuda, on 1 November 1981, remaining within the Commonwealth. The grievances of the Barbudans concerning control of land and devolution of power were unresolved, although the ALP Government had conceded a certain degree of internal autonomy to the Barbuda Council. The Governor, Sir Wilfred Jacobs, became Governor-General, while the Premier, Vere Bird, Sr, became the country's first Prime Minister.

In April 1984, at the first general election since independence, divisions within the opposition allowed the ALP to win all of the 16 seats that it contested. The remaining seat, representing Barbuda, was retained by an unopposed independent.

Controversy surrounding a rehabilitation scheme at the international airport on Antigua in 1986 led to an official inquiry, which concluded that Vere Bird, Jr (a senior minister and the eldest son of the Prime Minister), had acted inappropriately by awarding part of the contract to a company with which he was personally involved. The affair divided the ALP, with eight ministers (including Lester Bird, the Deputy Prime Minister) demanding the resignation of Vere Bird, Jr, and Prime Minister Bird refusing to dismiss him. The ALP remained the ruling party at a general election in 1989.

In April 1990 the Government of Antigua and Barbuda received a diplomatic note of protest from the Government of Colombia regarding the sale of weapons to the Medellín cartel of drugs-traffickers in Colombia. The weapons had originally been sold by Israel to Antigua and Barbuda, but, contrary to regulation, were then immediately shipped on to Colombia in April 1989. The communication from the Colombian Government implicated Vere Bird, Jr, and the Prime Minister eventually agreed to establish a judicial inquiry. In November 1990 the Government dismissed Vere Bird, Jr, and banned him for life from holding office in the Government.

In 1992 further reports of corruption involving Vere Bird, Sr, provoked public unrest and demands for his resignation. In April the Antigua Caribbean Liberation Movement, the PLM and the United National Democratic Party consolidated their opposition to the Government by merging to form the United Progressive Party (UPP). In August further controversy arose when proposed anti-corruption legislation was withdrawn as a result of legal intervention by the Prime Minister.

The Government of Lester Bird, 1994–2004

At a general election in March 1994 the ALP remained the ruling party, although with a reduced majority; Lester Bird assumed the premiership.

An ALP activist, Leonard Aaron, was charged in February 1995 with threatening to murder Tim Hector, editor of an opposition newspaper, *The Outlet*. It was reported that Hector's house had been burgled on several occasions, when material containing allegedly incriminating information relating to members of the Government had been stolen. Aaron was subsequently released following the intervention of the Prime Minister. In May the Prime Minister's brother, Ivor, was arrested following an incident in which he collected luggage at V. C. Bird International Airport, from a Barbadian citizen from Venezuela, that contained 12 kg of cocaine. *The Outlet* claimed that such an exchange had occurred on at least three previous occasions. Ivor Bird's subsequent release from police custody, upon payment of a fine, attracted considerable criticism. A report published by the US Government in early 1998 found Antigua and Barbuda to be 'of primary concern' with regard to drugs-trafficking and money-laundering.

In May 1996 Vere Bird, Jr, who had been declared unfit for public office in 1990, was controversially appointed to the post of Special Adviser to the Prime Minister. In September Molwyn Joseph resigned as Minister of Finance over allegations of corruption. A demonstration took place at the end of the month at which some 10,000 people demanded a full inquiry into the affair and an early general election. In December 1997, however, Joseph was reinstated in the Cabinet, an appointment that was vehemently condemned by the opposition.

In March 1997 the opposition BPM defeated the ALP's ally, the New Barbuda Development Movement, in elections to the Barbuda Council, winning all five of the contested seats and thus gaining control of the nine-member Council. In the same month the High Court upheld a constitutional motion presented by UPP leader Baldwin Spencer seeking the right of expression for the opposition on state-owned radio and television (denied during the 1994 electoral campaign).

Meanwhile, in August 1997 *The Outlet* published further allegations regarding government-supported drugs-trafficking, including a claim that a Colombian drugs cartel had contributed US $1m. to the ALP's election campaign in 1994. In response, Prime Minister Lester Bird obtained a High Court injunction in

September prohibiting the newspaper from publishing further allegations. In November the printing presses of *The Outlet* were destroyed by fire, two days after Tim Hector had publicly alleged that a large consignment of 'sophisticated' weaponry had entered Antigua. The Government denied allegations that it was responsible for the fire, and stated that a shipment of 'basic' arms had been imported for police use.

At a general election held in March 1999, the ALP increased its representation in the 17-seat House of Representatives at the expense of the UPP. Lester Bird was reappointed Prime Minister, and his new Cabinet again controversially included Vere Bird, Jr. Independent observers declared the election to have been free, although they expressed reservations concerning its fairness, owing to the ALP's large-scale expenditure and use of the media during its electoral campaign.

Also in March 1999 the US Government published a report that claimed that recent Antiguan financial legislation had weakened regulations concerning money-laundering and 'offshore' banks. It advised US banks to scrutinize all financial dealings with Antigua and Barbuda, which was described as a potential 'haven for money-laundering'. In April the United Kingdom issued a similar financial advisory to its banks. In response, in July Antigua and Barbuda became the first Eastern Caribbean country to bring into force a treaty with the USA on extradition and mutual legal assistance and in September established an independent body, the International Financial Sector Regulatory Authority, to regulate 'offshore' banking. Although in 2000 Antigua and Barbuda's financial system was criticized by the Organisation for Economic Co-operation and Development (OECD, see p. 379) and by the Financial Action Task Force (FATF, see p. 455), in 2001 the FATF recognized the state as a 'fully co-operative jurisdiction against money-laundering'. The USA and the United Kingdom also both withdrew their financial advisory notices. In December the Government signed a tax information exchange agreement with the USA. In 2003 the Government strongly criticized OECD and the FATF for protecting the financial regimes of powerful states at the expense of smaller nations.

In November 2003 a UPP request for a motion of no confidence in two government ministers, Molwyn Joseph and Gaston Browne, was denied by the Speaker; the opposition party alleged that both men received substantial sums of money from Allen Stanford, a US businessman and Chairman of the Bank of Antigua, during the negotiation of a real-estate transaction between the Government and the bank.

The Governments of Baldwin Spencer, 2004–

At a general election on 23 March 2004 the opposition UPP, led by Baldwin Spencer, secured 12 out of the 17 parliamentary seats, thereby removing from government the ALP, which had held power since 1976. The ALP, which had been weakened by personal allegations surrounding Lester Bird and by a damaging contraction in the crucial tourism sector, secured only four seats. An extremely high rate of participation—91.2% of the electorate—was interpreted as a strong indication of public resentment towards the Bird regime. The BPM narrowly retained its seat. In advance of the general election a completely new electoral register was prepared for the first time since 1975. Elimination of deceased and non-resident names reduced the list by more than one-fifth, while voters were issued with identity cards. Spencer was sworn in as Prime Minister on 24 March.

The Antigua Public Utilities Authority filed a lawsuit against five ex-cabinet ministers, including Bird, in June 2007, seeking to recover an estimated US $34m. allegedly misappropriated from the company and used to finance several projects around the country.

Louise Lake-Tack was sworn in as Governor-General in July 2007, becoming the first woman in the country's history to assume the role.

At a general election on 12 March 2009 the incumbent UPP secured 51.1% of the vote, winning nine of the 17 seats, while the ALP gained 47.0% of total votes and seven seats. The BPM secured one seat. Some 79.9% of eligible voters participated in the poll. Spencer subsequently announced a reorganization of his Cabinet and a reduction in the number of ministries. Errol Cort, the previous Minister of Finance, who had lost his parliamentary seat in the election, returned in the newly created post of Minister of National Security, while Spencer himself assumed responsibility for foreign affairs and utilities.

Following complaints by the ALP regarding the conduct of the general election, in March 2010 the High Court of Justice invalidated the election of Spencer and two members of his Cabinet owing to delays in the opening of polling stations in their constituencies, necessitating by-elections or another general election. The Government initiated an appeal against the decision with the Eastern Caribbean Court of Appeal (ECCA), and in October the ECCA overturned the High Court's ruling, arguing that it was highly unlikely that the late opening times had distorted the election results. Lester Bird criticized the ECCA judgment, accusing the Court of 'political decision-making', while Spencer denounced the ALP for generating a climate of uncertainty that discouraged foreign investment. In a related development, in June the Speaker of the House of Representatives controversially suspended ALP deputy Gaston Browne for the remainder of the parliamentary session for initiating a disruptive protest in the legislature, in which he demanded that the Prime Minister resign and new elections be held.

The replacement of Sir Gerald Watt as Chairman of the Antigua and Barbuda Electoral Commission (ABEC) with Juno Samuel in January 2011 prompted further controversy. Watt had been suspended in July 2010 along with two other electoral commissioners over alleged breaches of electoral procedure in the 2009 election, including the delays in opening certain polling stations. A tribunal in December 2010 had cleared Watt of any wrongdoing. The ALP condemned the appointment as politically motivated while Watt appealed to the High Court. In November 2011 Lester Bird and several other ALP deputies walked out of the House of Representatives in protest during a debate over controversial legislation to restructure the ABEC. Nevertheless, the amendments, which transferred some of the powers of the Chief Elections Officer to an expanded body of commissioners, were approved later that month. The Government argued that a larger, more decentralized commission would hinder potential attempts to interfere in its operations and eliminate the procedural problems experienced in the 2009 poll. However, the ALP and Watt contended that these measures were in contravention of the Constitution and that the commissioners would be appointed by the Government, thereby jeopardizing the independence of the ABEC. In January 2012 the High Court ruled that Watt's dismissal had been illegal. Spencer appealed against this judgment in February, but in May 2013 the ECCA upheld the High Court's ruling; a further appeal, which had been submitted to the Privy Council in the United Kingdom (Antigua and Barbuda's final appellate court), was pending in early 2014.

Meanwhile, in April 2011 Hilroy Humphreys, a former ALP Minister of Agriculture, was fined after being convicted of defrauding the Medical Benefits Scheme. Humphreys appealed against a further conviction in September, following a court ruling that declared him guilty of involvement in a fraudulent land deal.

Gaston Browne was elected as leader of the ALP in November 2012, defeating Lester Bird, whose family had been in control of the party for 66 years. Browne was inaugurated as Leader of the Opposition in Parliament in the following month. In elections to the Barbuda Council in March 2013, the ALP secured a majority of the contested seats, thereby ending the BPM's longstanding dominance of the island legislature.

An ALP appeal against the proposed restructuring of electoral boundaries was rejected by the High Court in December 2013. The opposition party claimed that the planned alterations were tantamount to gerrymandering, while the UPP-dominated Constituencies Boundaries Commission argued that redelineation was necessary to rebalance the number of voters in each constituency. A second ALP appeal, concerning the alleged disenfranchisement of some voters following a recently completed re-registration exercise, was also dismissed by the High Court later that month. The ALP responded to these defeats by petitioning the ECCA. A general election was constitutionally due in 2014.

Crime

An increase in the number of reported murders in the country (16 in 2009, compared to just three in 2005) was attributed to a rise in the number of criminal deportees from the USA. In 2007 the Government undertook a series of discussions with the US Department of Homeland Security, aimed at increasing co-operation between the two countries on this matter. The police force was also strengthened by 120 new officers in 2009, and there was a 23% budget increase intended to improve the force's criminal database and forensic capabilities. The number of murders declined sharply in 2010, to just six, but rose to nine in 2011 and 2012, and to 13 in 2013.

The Stanford affair

Parliament, which had been suspended in early February 2009 in preparation for a general election in the following month, was hastily reconvened on 26 February, following a crisis that threatened the economic stability of the islands and made them the focus of international attention. Revelations concerning the business practices of Sir Allen Stanford (as he had become) led to the US Securities and Exchange Commission (SEC) issuing charges of fraud against him totalling some US $8,000m. Companies owned by Stanford were Antigua's second largest employer after the civil service. Parliament approved the compulsory acquisition of land owned by Stanford and his extensive assets, both in Antigua and Barbuda and throughout the region, were frozen by the US authorities, pending further investigation. The revelations came only months after Antigua's Financial Services Regulatory Commission (FSRC, as the International Financial Sector Regulatory Authority had become) had declared Stanford International Bank to be operating satisfactorily. In June, following the issuing of criminal charges against Stanford, the millionaire businessman surrendered to US authorities. Stanford's trial commenced in January 2012 and in March he was convicted of 13 of the 14 charges of fraud against him. Stanford received a 110-year prison sentence for these crimes in June.

In June 2009, following an extradition request from the USA, the Chairman of the FSRC, Leroy King, was dismissed from his post. King had been charged by the SEC with accepting bribes in return for ignoring fraudulent practices by Stanford-owned companies. Antigua's Chief Magistrate ruled in favour of King's extradition to the USA in April 2010, and this judgment was endorsed by the High Court in February 2012. King unsuccessfully petitioned the ECCA in March, and in the following month Spencer finally authorized his extradition. In early 2014 King was still appealing against this decision.

Recent developments: Citizenship by Investment

In October 2012 the Government confirmed that it was planning to introduce a Citizenship by Investment Programme (CIP) in the country. The proposals generated considerable controversy since comparable 'economic citizenship' schemes in neighbouring Caribbean states had attracted interest from foreign criminal elements. The Government emphasized that appropriate measures would be implemented to prevent undesirable candidates from acquiring Antiguan citizenship and argued that the initiative would lead to greater investment inflows. CIP legislation was adopted by Parliament in March 2013: citizenship could be obtained by either investing US $400,000 in real estate, making a $250,000 contribution to the National Development Fund, or by investing at least $1.5m. in a business project. The programme was officially inaugurated in October, and was expected to generate $11.8m. in its first year of operation, according to government estimates.

Foreign Affairs

Regional relations

In foreign relations Antigua and Barbuda has traditionally followed a policy of non-alignment, although it has strong links with the USA.

In 2003 the Government challenged US restrictions on 'offshore' internet gambling, a significant industry in Antigua and Barbuda, through the structures of the World Trade Organization (WTO), and in April 2005 received a ruling that was interpreted as partly in its favour. However, the dispute continued unabated throughout 2006, aggravated by the successful passage of an 'Unlawful Internet Gambling Enforcement Act' in the US Congress on 30 September. In March 2007 the WTO Dispute Settlement Body ruled that the US ban was illegal, and in May the USA announced that it would withdraw from any commitments relating to gambling under the General Agreement on Trade in Services. In June the Government of Antigua and Barbuda filed formal trade sanctions against the USA, demanding US $3,400m. in compensation; however, the USA contended that the terms it had originally negotiated under the Agreement did not explicitly refer to internet gambling, thus rendering it exempt from the payment of such compensation. WTO arbitrators ruled in December that Antigua be awarded the right to levy $21m. per year in sanctions from the USA, although the Government declined to exercise this option, preferring instead to continue to seek a negotiated settlement. However, with the issue still unresolved, in July 2010 Spencer, speaking at a Caribbean Community and Common Market (CARICOM, see p. 223) Heads of Government meeting in Jamaica, threatened to impose these sanctions upon the USA. CARICOM supported this position and expressed its concern that an agreement had yet to be concluded despite the efforts of the Antiguan Government. In April 2011 the Government strongly criticized US legal action against an Antiguan gambling website used by, *inter alia*, US citizens. Harold Lovell, the Minister of Finance, Economy and Public Administration, declared that the prosecution of non-US internet gambling companies was 'in clear contravention of international law'. In March 2013, after Spencer had again threatened to invoke the sanctions against the USA, the Antiguan Government entered into negotiations with US trade officials in an effort to settle the dispute, while in June Spencer also held discussions on the matter with US Vice-President Joseph Biden. Ultimately, however, no substantive progress was made, and the talks appeared to have collapsed by November. In 2011 and 2012 the Antiguan Government signed co-operation agreements with Guadeloupe and Martinique, respectively.

Other external relations

At the annual meeting of the International Whaling Commission in 2006, Antigua and Barbuda voted, along with other members of the Organisation of Eastern Caribbean States (OECS, see p. 467), in favour of an end to a 20-year commercial whaling moratorium. The Government's apparent pro-whaling stance provoked allegations that Japanese financial assistance had amounted to bribery (Japan was in favour of ending the ban). At the 2007 meeting of the Commission Antigua and Barbuda was among several OECS countries to confirm their concurrence with a request, issued by Saint Vincent and the Grenadines, for an increase to those islands' commercial whaling quotas. An appeal for the protection of the indigenous and coastal population's rights to preserve their traditional fishing practices—and for acknowledgement of earlier recommendations, by Saint Kitts and Nevis, that a policy of appropriate management of marine resources be adopted as opposed to a complete ban—was presented to the Commission.

Spencer held discussions with a delegation of officials from the People's Republic of China in January 2011, and several trade and technology accords were concluded. Furthermore, an agreement was reached regarding the construction of an additional terminal at V. C. Bird International Airport, to be financed by a US $45m. Chinese loan. The terminal was scheduled for completion in 2014. In March 2012 China pledged financial support of over $10m. to fund a variety of infrastructural and developmental projects in Antigua.

CONSTITUTION AND GOVERNMENT

Antigua and Barbuda is a constitutional monarchy. The Constitution came into force at independence, on 1 November 1981. Executive power is vested in the British sovereign, as Head of State, and exercised by the Governor-General, who represents the sovereign locally and is appointed on the advice of the Antiguan Prime Minister. Legislative power is vested in Parliament, comprising the sovereign, a 17-member Senate and a 17-member House of Representatives. Members of the House are elected from single-member constituencies for up to five years by universal adult suffrage. The Senate is composed of 11 members (of whom one must be an inhabitant of Barbuda) appointed on the advice of the Prime Minister, four appointed on the advice of the Leader of the Opposition, one appointed at the Governor-General's discretion and one appointed on the advice of the Barbuda Council. Government is effectively by the Cabinet. The Governor-General appoints the Prime Minister and, on the latter's recommendation, selects the other ministers. The Prime Minister must be able to command the support of a majority of the House, to which the Cabinet is responsible. The Barbuda Council has nine seats, with partial elections held every two years.

REGIONAL AND INTERNATIONAL CO-OPERATION

Antigua and Barbuda is a member of the Caribbean Community and Common Market (CARICOM, see p. 223), the Association of Caribbean States (see p. 449), the Organisation of Eastern Caribbean States (OECS, see p. 467), the Organization of American States (see p. 394), and of the Community of Latin American and Caribbean States (see p. 464), which was formally inaugurated in December 2011. In July 2007 the country joined the single market component of CARICOM's Single Market and Economy, full implementation of which was expected by 2015. Antigua and Barbuda is also a member of the Eastern Caribbean Central Bank (see p. 455) and the Eastern Caribbean Securities

Exchange (both based in Saint Christopher and Nevis). In June 2010 Antigua and Barbuda was a signatory to the Revised Treaty of Basseterre, establishing an Economic Union among member states. The Economic Union, which involved the removal of barriers to trade and the movement of labour as a step towards a single financial and economic market, came into effect on 21 January 2011. Freedom of movement between the signatory states was granted to OECS nationals on 1 August. The OECS Regional Assembly, which held its first session in August 2012, is situated in Antigua. The country joined the Venezuelan-led Bolivarian Alliance for the Peoples of our America-People's Trade Treaty (Alianza Bolivariana para los Pueblos de Nuestra América-Tratado de Comercio de los Pueblos—ALBA-TCP, see p. 463) in 2009 and has been benefiting from ALBA-TCP's Petrocaribe programme, which provides Venezuelan petroleum at preferential prices, since 2005.

Antigua and Barbuda became a member of the UN upon independence in 1981. As a contracting party to the General Agreement on Tariffs and Trade, Antigua and Barbuda joined the World Trade Organization (see p. 434) on its establishment in 1995. The country is a member of the Commonwealth (see p. 236) and is a signatory of the Cotonou Agreement (the successor agreement to the Lomé Conventions) with the European Union (EU, see p. 273). In 2006 the country was admitted to the Non-aligned Movement (see p. 467). Antigua became a member of the International Organization for Migration (see p. 345) in 2011.

ECONOMIC AFFAIRS

In 2012, according to estimates by the World Bank, Antigua and Barbuda's gross national income (GNI), measured at average 2010–12 prices, was US $1,126m., equivalent to $12,640 per head (or $19,260 per head on an international purchasing-power parity basis). During 2003–12, it was estimated, the population increased at an average rate of 1.1% per year while gross domestic product (GDP) per head increased, in real terms, by an average of 0.2% per year. According to Eastern Caribbean Central Bank (ECCB) estimates, overall GDP increased, in real terms, at an average annual rate of 1.7% in 2003–12; real GDP decreased by 2.0% in 2011, but increased by 3.3% in 2012.

Agriculture (including forestry and fishing) engaged an estimated 2.8% of the active labour force in 2008. According to ECCB estimates, the sector contributed 1.9% of GDP in 2012. Agricultural GDP decreased, in real terms, at an average annual rate of 0.6% per year in 2003–12. The sector's GDP increased by 4.1% in 2011, but decreased by 2.3% in 2012. The principal crops are cucumbers, pumpkins, sweet potatoes, mangoes, coconuts, limes, melons and the speciality Antigua Black pineapple. Lobster, shrimp and crab farms are also in operation.

Industry (comprising mining, manufacturing, construction and utilities) employed an estimated 15.6% of the active labour force in 2008. According to ECCB estimates, the sector provided 16.2% of GDP in 2012. Industrial GDP increased, in real terms, at an average rate of 1.2% per year during 2003–12; the sector contracted by 13.2% in 2011, but expanded by 3.0% in 2012.

Mining and quarrying employed only some 0.3% of the active labour force in 2008. According to ECCB estimates, the sector contributed 0.8% of GDP in 2012. The real GDP of the mining sector decreased at an average rate of 4.8% per year during 2003–12. The sector decreased by 19.3% in 2011, but increased by 6.3% in 2012.

The manufacturing sector consists of some light industries producing garments, paper, paint, furniture and food and beverage products, and the assembly of household appliances and electrical components for export. Manufacturing contributed 2.4% of GDP in 2012, and employed an estimated 4.6% of the active labour force in 2008. In real terms, the GDP of the manufacturing sector increased at an average rate of 1.2% per year during 2003–12. Manufacturing GDP increased by 2.8% in 2011, but decreased by 12.4% in 2012.

The construction sector contributed 9.2% to GDP in 2012, and employed an estimated 9.2% of the employed labour force in 2008. In real terms, the GDP of the construction sector increased at an average rate of 0.6% per year in 2003–12. Construction GDP decreased by 24.4% in 2011, but increased by 10.0% in 2012.

Most of the country's energy production is derived from imported fuel. Imports of mineral fuels, lubricants and related materials accounted for 36.8% of total imports in 2012. Antigua and Barbuda was signatory to the Petrocaribe accord, under which the country could purchase petroleum from Venezuela at reduced prices. In 2011 a new 30-MW power plant on Antigua came into operation. The plant, commissioned to combat the worsening power shortages on the islands, was financed by a US $47m. loan from the Export and Import Bank of China (China Exim Bank).

Services provided 81.6% of employment in 2008 and 81.9% of GDP in 2012. The combined GDP of the service sectors increased, in real terms, at an average rate of 1.3% per year during 2003–12. The sector expanded by just 0.3% in 2011 and by 2.4% in 2012. The islands' economy is heavily dependent on the tourism industry, which is particularly vulnerable to external factors, such as the behaviour of the world economy and the movement of tropical storms. Visitor arrivals fluctuated throughout the 2000s. Numbers fell to 812,859 in 2010, recovered to 870,240 in 2011, before falling back to 842,693 in 2012. Receipts from the sector fell to EC $803.9m. in 2010 before registering improvment in 2011 and 2012, to EC $841.8m. and EC $861.3m., respectively. Construction of a new terminal at V. C. Bird International Airport, also financed by a China Exim Bank loan, was scheduled for completion in 2014. A significant number (37.7% in 2012) of stop-over tourists are from the USA, followed by the United Kingdom (27.8% in 2012). The real GDP of the hotels and restaurants sector increased in 2012, by 2.2%, when its contribution to GDP stood at 12.8%.

Antigua and Barbuda recorded a visible merchandise trade deficit in 2012 of EC $280.50m. and a deficit of $317.77m. on the current account of the balance of payments. The country's principal trading partners are the other members of the Caribbean Community and Common Market (CARICOM, see p. 223), the USA, the United Kingdom and the People's Republic of China. In 2012 the USA provided 50.1% of total imports and 21.6% of total exports. The principal imports in 2012 were vehicles, aircraft, vessels and associated transport equipment, vegetables and vegetable products, and electrical and electronic equipment. The major exports in 2012 included textile articles, sets and worn clothing and machinery and electrical equipment.

In 2012 there was a budgetary deficit of EC $43.6m., equivalent to 1.4% of GDP. Antigua and Barbuda's general government gross debt was EC $2,830m. in 2012, equivalent to 89.14% of GDP. By the end of 2009, according to IMF estimates, total public external debt amounted to EC $1,352m., and the cost of servicing long-term public and publicly guaranteed debt and repayments to the IMF was equivalent to 3.9% of the value of exports of goods, services and income (excluding workers' remittances). According to ECCB estimates, the annual average rate of inflation was 2.5% in 2003–12. Consumer prices rose by 1.9% in 2012. The rate of unemployment in 2001 was reported to be 8.1% of the labour force.

Despite some efforts at diversification, for example, the development of 'offshore' financial services, the economy of Antigua and Barbuda is dominated by tourism. The World Travel and Tourism Council estimated that in 2013 the tourism industry directly provided 19.2% of total employment and 19% of GDP. The economy contracted in 2009–11, largely owing to the impact of the global economic and financial crisis on the tourism and construction sectors. In 2010 the IMF concluded a stand-by arrangement for Antigua and Barbuda, worth SDR 81m. over three years, the first tranche of which was disbursed in October. Under the terms of the arrangement, the Government would reduce public spending, implement measures to increase tax revenues and discuss debt-restructuring with its creditors. The 'Paris Club' of creditors agreed to reschedule US $117m. of Antiguan debt in September, and further restructuring plans were subsequently finalized with France, Japan and the OPEC Fund for International Development. The success of the Government's fiscal consolidation programme was acknowledged by the IMF upon the expiration of the stand-by arrangement in mid-2013. The Fund estimated that real GDP rose by 1.6% in 2012 (compared to the ECCB's estimate of 3.3%), driven by a recovery in stay-over tourist arrivals and increased construction activity (primarily owing to the building, with Chinese funding, of a new airport terminal, which was expected to be in operation by September 2014). In spite of a decline in visitor numbers during 2013, the buoyant construction sector supported further economic expansion of 1.7% in that year, and the IMF projected that real GDP would grow by 3.2% in 2014 (although the ECCB put growth slightly lower, at 1.5%).

PUBLIC HOLIDAYS

2015: 1 January (New Year's Day), 3 April (Good Friday), 6 April (Easter Monday), 4 May (Labour Day), 25 May (Whit Monday), 3 August (Carnival Monday—J'Ouvert), 4 August (Carnival Tuesday—Last Lap), 2 November (for Independence Day), 9 December (National Heroes' Day), 25–26 December (Christmas).

Statistical Survey

Source (unless otherwise stated): Ministry of Finance, Economy and Public Administration, Coolidge Business Complex, Sir George Walter Highway, St John's; tel. 468-4600; e-mail minfinance@antigua.gov.ag; internet www.ab.gov.ag.

AREA AND POPULATION

Area: 441.6 sq km (170.5 sq miles).

Population: 76,886 at census of 28 May 2001; 86,295 (males 41,481, females 44,814) at census of 28 May 2011 (preliminary). *Mid-2014* (UN estimate): 90,905 (Source: UN, *World Population Prospects: The 2012 Revision*).

Density (at mid-2014): 205.9 per sq km.

Population by Age and Sex (UN estimates at mid-2014): *0–14:* 22,315 (males 11,191, females 11,124); *15–64:* 62,126 (males 29,519, females 32,607); *65 and over:* 6,464 (males 2,731, females 3,733); *Total* 90,905 (males 43,441, females 47,464). Source: UN, *World Population Prospects: The 2012 Revision*.

Principal Town: St John's (capital), population 22,193 at 2011 census (preliminary).

Births, Marriages and Deaths (2007 unless otherwise indicated): Live births 1,240 (birth rate 14.44 per 1,000); Marriages 1,863; Deaths 504 (death rate 5.87 per 1,000). *2008:* Birth rate 16.8 per 1,000; Death rate 6.1 per 1,000. *2012:* Birth rate 16.2 per 1,000; Death rate 5.7 per 1,000 (Source: Pan American Health Organization).

Life Expectancy (years at birth): 75.5 (males 73.2; females 78.0) in 2011. Source: World Bank, World Development Indicators database.

Employment (persons aged 15 years and over, official estimates, 2008): Agriculture, hunting and forestry 789; Fishing 290; Mining and quarrying 121; Manufacturing 1,754; Electricity, gas and water supply 585; Construction 3,557; Wholesale and retail trade 5,516; Hotels and restaurants 5,783; Transport, storage and communications 3,203; Financial intermediation 1,195; Real estate, renting and business activities 1,665; Public administration and defence 4,986; Education 1,956; Health and social work 1,955; Other community, social and personal service activities 3,057; Households with employed persons 1,485; Extra-territorial organizations and bodies 572; Total employed 38,470 (males 19,321, females 19,149). Source: ILO.

HEALTH AND WELFARE

Key Indicators

Total Fertility Rate (children per woman, 2011): 2.1.

Under-5 Mortality Rate (per 1,000 live births, 2011): 8.

Physicians (per 1,000 head, 1999): 0.2.

Hospital Beds (per 1,000 head, 2009): 2.2.

Health Expenditure (2010): US $ per head (PPP): 981.

Health Expenditure (2010): % of GDP: 5.9.

Health Expenditure (2010): public (% of total): 70.8.

Access to Water (% of persons, 2011): 98.

Access to Sanitation (% of persons, 2011): 91.

Total Carbon Dioxide Emissions ('000 metric tons, 2010): 513.4.

Total Carbon Dioxide Emissions Per Head (metric tons, 2010): 5.9.

Human Development Index (2012): ranking: 67.

Human Development Index (2012): value: 0.760.

For sources and definitions, see explanatory note on p. vi.

AGRICULTURE, ETC.

Principal Crops ('000 metric tons, 2012, FAO estimates): Cantaloupes and other melons 1.0; Vegetables (incl. melons) 3.3; Guavas, mangoes and mangosteens 1.2; Fruits (excl. melons) 10.0.

Livestock ('000 head, 2012, FAO estimates): Asses 1.7; Cattle 15.0; Pigs 3.0; Sheep 23.0; Goats 37.0; Poultry 150.0.

Livestock Products ('000 metric tons, 2012, FAO estimates): Cattle meat 0.6; Cows' milk 6.0; Hen eggs 0.3.

Fishing (metric tons, live weight, 2011, estimates): Groupers and seabasses 243; Snappers and jobfishes 296; Grunts and sweetlips 190; Parrotfishes 169; Surgeonfishes 119; Triggerfishes and durgons 44; Caribbean spiny lobster 175; Stromboid conchs 764; Total catch (incl. others) 2,300.

Source: FAO.

INDUSTRY

Production (1988 estimates unless otherwise indicated): Rum 4,000 hectolitres; Wines and vodka 2,000 hectolitres; Electric energy (2009) 119m. kWh. Source: partly UN Industrial Commodity Statistics Database and Yearbook.

FINANCE

Currency and Exchange Rates: 100 cents = 1 Eastern Caribbean dollar (EC $). *Sterling, US Dollar and Euro Equivalents* (31 December 2013): £1 sterling = EC $4.446; US $1 = EC $2.700; €1 = EC $3.724; EC $100 = £22.49 = US $37.04 = €26.86. *Exchange rate:* Fixed at US $1 = EC $2.700 since July 1976.

Budget (EC $ million, 2012): *Revenue:* Tax revenue 604.2; Other current revenue 42.4; Capital revenue 2.2; Total 648.8 (excl. grants 0.0). *Expenditure:* Current expenditure 671.5 (Wages and salaries 273.8, Goods and services 113.8, Interest payments 80.0, Pensions 70.7, Transfers and subsidies 133.2); Capital expenditure 20.9; Total 692.4. Source: Eastern Caribbean Central Bank.

International Reserves (US $ million at 31 December 2012): IMF special drawing rights 0.71; Reserve position in IMF 0.08; Foreign exchange 161.25; Total 162.05. Source: IMF, *International Financial Statistics*.

Money Supply (EC $ million at 31 December 2012): Currency outside depository corporations 121.73; Transferable deposits 842.96; Other deposits 2,177.32; *Broad money* 3,142.02. Source: IMF, *International Financial Statistics*.

Cost of Living (Consumer Price Index; base: January 2001 = 100): 123.9 in 2010; 128.9 in 2011; 131.3 in 2012. Source: Eastern Caribbean Central Bank.

Expenditure on the Gross Domestic Product (EC $ million at current prices, 2012): Government final consumption expenditure 566.87; Private final consumption expenditure 2,334.88; Gross capital formation 716.45; *Total domestic expenditure* 3,618.20; Exports of goods and services 1,462.18; *Less* Imports of goods and services 1,856.59; *GDP at market prices* 3,223.79. Source: Eastern Caribbean Central Bank.

Gross Domestic Product by Economic Activity (EC $ million at current prices, 2012): Agriculture, hunting, forestry and fishing 53.97; Mining and quarrying 21.62; Manufacturing 68.93; Electricity and water 107.84; Construction 260.27; Trade 411.24; Restaurants and hotels 362.27; Transport and communications 358.61; Finance, insurance, real estate and business services 655.44; Government services 246.01; Education 137.59; Health and social work 80.10; Other community, social and personal service activities 52.62; Activities of private households as employers 14.61; *Sub-total* 2,831.10; *Less* Financial intermediation services indirectly measured 84.93; *Gross value added in basic prices* 2,746.17; Taxes, less subsidies, on products 477.61; *GDP in market prices* 3,223.79. Source: Eastern Caribbean Central Bank.

Balance of Payments (EC $ million, 2012): Goods (net) –1,011.34; Services (net) 730.84; *Balance on goods and services* –280.50; Income (net) –106.57; *Balance on goods, services and income* –387.07; Current transfers (net) 69.30; *Current balance* –317.77; Capital account (net) 32.86; Direct investment (net) 175.93; Portfolio investment (net) 27.39; Other investments (net) 184.40; Net errors and omissions –72.68; *Overall balance* 30.14. Source: Eastern Caribbean Central Bank.

EXTERNAL TRADE

Total Trade (EC $ million): *Imports f.o.b.:* 1,353.32 in 2010; 1,271.96 in 2011; 1,437.43 in 2012. *Exports f.o.b.:* (incl. re-exports): 94.04 in 2010; 78.38 in 2011; 78.32 in 2012. Source: Eastern Caribbean Central Bank.

Principal Commodities (US $ million, 2012): *Imports:* Live animals and animal products 35.3 (Meat and edible meat offal 19.9); Vegetables and vegetable products 21.3; Prepared foodstuffs; beverages, spirits, vinegar; tobacco and articles thereof 67.6 (Beverages, spirits and vinegar 23.9; Miscellaneous edible preparations 12.1); Chemicals and related products 30.6; Plastics, rubber, and articles thereof 12.6; Pulp of wood, paper and paperboard, and articles thereof 12.1; Textiles and textile articles 17.2; Iron and steel, other base metals and articles of base metal 20.2; Machinery and mechanical appliances; electrical equipment; parts thereof 40.9 (Machinery, boilers, etc. 19.6; Electrical, electronic equipment 21.3); Vehicles, aircraft, vessels and associated transport equipment 21.4 (Vehicles other than railway, tramway 18.3); Miscellaneous manufactured articles 12.0; Total (incl. others) 339.5. *Exports:* Live animals and animal products 1.2 (Fish, crustaceans, molluscs, aquatic invertebrates 1.0); Prepared foodstuffs; beverages, spirits, vinegar; tobacco and articles thereof 1.6 (Beverages, spirits and vinegar 1.4); Textiles and textile articles 8.3 (Textile articles, sets, worn clothing etc. 7.6); Articles of stone, plaster, cement, asbestos; ceramic and glass products 1.0; Pearls, precious stones, metals, coins, etc. 1.2; Iron and steel, other base metals and articles of base metal 3.1 (Articles of iron or steel 2.0); Machinery and mechanical appliances; electrical equipment; parts thereof 7.1; (Machinery, boilers, etc. 3.3; Electrical, electronic equipment 3.8); Vehicles, aircraft, vessels and associated transport equipment 2.5 (Vehicles other than railway, tramway 1.1); Total (incl. others) 29.0. Source: Trade Map-Trade Competitiveness Map, International Trade Centre, www.intracen.org/marketanalysis.

Principal Trading Partners (US $ million, 2012): *Imports:* Barbados 5.2; Brazil 6.1; Canada 7.7; China, People's Republic 19.2; Dominican Republic 4.5; France 4.4; Guyana 3.5; Jamaica 5.7; Japan 8.5; Mexico 3.7; former Netherlands Antilles 4.0; Saint Vincent and the Grenadines 5.4; Switzerland 4.8; Trinidad and Tobago 18.8; United Kingdom 20.7; USA 170.1; Total (incl. others) 339.5. *Exports:* Barbados 2.8; British Virgin Islands 0.4; Canada 0.5; Dominica 0.3; Dominican Republic 1.4; France (incl. Monaco) 1.0; Italy 0.6; Jamaica 0.1; Montserrat 0.5; former Netherlands Antilles 0.4; New Zealand 0.6; Saint Christopher and Nevis 1.0; Saint Vincent and the Grenadines 0.9; Spain 0.7; Thailand 0.5; Trinidad and Tobago 0.9; United Kingdom 5.4; USA 6.3; Total (incl. others) 29.1. Source: Trade Map-Trade Competitiveness Map, International Trade Centre, www.intracen.org/marketanalysis.

TRANSPORT

Road Traffic (registered vehicles, 1998): Passenger motor cars and commercial vehicles 24,000. Source: UN, *Statistical Yearbook*.

Shipping (international freight traffic, '000 metric tons, 1990): Goods loaded 28; Goods unloaded 113 (Source: UN, *Monthly Bulletin of Statistics*). *Flag Registered Fleet* (at 31 December): 1,225 vessels (total displacement 10,120,815 grt) in 2013 (Source: Lloyd's List Intelligence—www.lloydslistintelligence.com).

Civil Aviation (traffic on scheduled services, 2009): Kilometres flown (million) 6; Passengers carried ('000) 748; Passenger-km (million) 123; Total ton-km (million) 11 (Source: UN, *Statistical Yearbook*). *2012* ('000): Passengers carried 1,310 (Source: World Bank, World Development Indicators database).

TOURISM

Visitor Arrivals: 812,859 (229,943 stop-over visitors, 25,886 yacht passengers, 557,030 cruise ship passengers) in 2010; 870,240 (241,331 stop-over visitors, 24,403 yacht passengers, 604,506 cruise ship passengers) in 2011; 842,693 (246,926 stop-over visitors, 28,060 yacht passengers, 567,707 cruise ship passengers) in 2012.

Tourism Receipts (EC $ million): 803.9 in 2010; 841.8 in 2011; 861.3 in 2012.

Source: Eastern Caribbean Central Bank.

COMMUNICATIONS MEDIA

Telephones (2012): 35,000 main lines in use.

Mobile Cellular Telephones (2012): 179,800 subscribers.

Internet Subscribers (2011): 14,600.

Broadband Subscribers (2012): 5,100.

Source: International Telecommunication Union.

EDUCATION

Pre-primary (2010/11 unless otherwise indicated): 31 schools; 165 teachers; 2,438 pupils.

Primary (2011/12 unless otherwise indicated): 55 schools (2000/01); 794 teachers (males 66, females 728, 2010/11); 10,855 students (males 5,680, females 5,175).

Secondary (2010/11 unless otherwise indicated): 14 schools (2000/01); 637 teachers (males 201, females 436, 2010/11); 8,449 students (males 4,212, females 4,237).

Special (2011/12 unless otherwise indicated): 2 schools (2000/01); 15 teachers (2000/01); 104 students (males 61, females 43).

Tertiary (2009/10 unless otherwise indicated): 2 colleges (1986); 173 teachers (males 66, females 107); 1,068 students (males 342, females 726). Source: UNESCO Institute for Statistics.

Pupil-teacher ratio (primary education, UNESCO estimate): 14.5 in 2010/11. Source: UNESCO Institute for Statistics.

Adult Literacy Rate: 99.0% (males 98.4, females 99.4) in 2011. Source: UNESCO Institute for Statistics.

Directory

The Government

HEAD OF STATE

Queen: HM Queen ELIZABETH II.

Governor-General: LOUISE LAKE-TACK (took office on 17 July 2007).

CABINET

(April 2014)

The Cabinet comprised members of the United Progressive Party.

Prime Minister and Minister of Foreign Affairs: WINSTON BALDWIN SPENCER.

Minister of Health, Social Transformation and Consumer Affairs: WILMOTH STAFFORD DANIEL.

Minister of National Security: Sen. Dr ERROL CORT.

Minister of Agriculture, Lands, Housing and the Environment: HILSON BAPTISTE.

Minister of Tourism, Civil Aviation and Culture: JOHN HERBERT MAGINLEY.

Minister of Finance, Economy and Public Administration: HAROLD LOVELL.

Minister of Public Works and Transport: TREVOR MYKE WALKER.

Minister of Education, Sports, Youth and Gender Affairs: Dr JACQUI QUINN-LEANDRO.

Attorney-General and Minister of Legal Affairs: JUSTIN L. SIMON.

Minister of State in the Ministry of Legal Affairs: Sen. JOANNE MAUREEN MASSIAH.

Minister of State in the Ministry of Education, Sports and Youth Affairs: WINSTON VINCENT WILLIAMS.

Minister of State in the Ministry of Tourism, Civil Aviation and Culture: ELESTON MONTGOMERY ADAMS.

Minister of State in the Ministry of Agriculture, Lands, Housing and the Environment: CHANLAH CODRINGTON.

Minister of State in the Ministry of Public Works and Transport: ELMORE CHARLES.

Minister of State in the Office of the Prime Minister (with responsibility for Information and Broadcasting): Dr EDMOND MANSOOR.

Minister of State in the Office of the Prime Minister: WINSTON VINCENT WILLIAMS.

MINISTRIES

Office of the Prime Minister: Queen Elizabeth Hwy, St John's; tel. 462-4610; fax 462-3225; internet www.antigua.gov.ag.

Ministry of Agriculture, Lands, Housing and the Environment: Queen Elizabeth Hwy, St John's; tel. 462-1213; fax 462-6104; e-mail minagri@antigua.gov.ag; internet agricultureantiguabarbuda.com.

Ministry of Education, Sports and Youth Affairs: Govt Office Complex, Queen Elizabeth Hwy, St John's; tel. 462-4959; fax 462-4970; e-mail mineducation.edwards3@gmail.com; internet www.education.gov.ag.

Ministry of Finance, Economy and Public Administration: Govt Office Complex, Parliament Dr., St John's; tel. 462-2922; fax 462-4860; e-mail ps.finance2011@gmail.com.

Ministry of Foreign Affairs: Queen Elizabeth Hwy, St John's; tel. 462-1052; fax 462-2482; e-mail foreignaffairs@ab.gov.ag; internet www.foreignaffairs.gov.ag.

Ministry of Health, Social Transformation and Consumer Affairs: Popeshead St, St John's; tel. 562-6640; e-mail socialtransformationantigua@gmail.com.

Ministry of Legal Affairs: New Government Office Complex, Parliament Dr., St John's; tel. 462-0017; fax 462-2465; e-mail legalaffairs@antigua.gov.ag.

Ministry of National Security: Long and Thames St, St John's; tel. 561-6141; e-mail mnsanugov@gmail.com.

Ministry of Public Works and Transport: St John's St, St John's; tel. 462-2953; e-mail publicworks@antigua.gov.ag.

Ministry of Tourism, Civil Aviation and Culture: Government Office Complex, Bldg 1, Queen Elizabeth Hwy, St John's; tel. 462-0480; fax 462-2483; e-mail mililetteambrose@hotmail.com.

Legislature

PARLIAMENT

Senate

President: HAZELYN MASON-FRANCIS.

There are 17 nominated members.

House of Representatives

Speaker: D. GISELLE ISAAC-ARRINDELL.

General Election, 12 March 2009

Party	Votes cast	%	Seats
United Progressive Party	21,205	51.1	9
Antigua Labour Party	19,460	47.0	7
Barbuda People's Movement	474	1.1	1
Independents	194	0.5	—
Organisation for National Development	119	0.3	—
Total	41,452	100.0	17

The Attorney-General is also an ex-officio member of the House of Representatives.

Election Commission

Antigua and Barbuda Electoral Commission (ABEC): Queen Elizabeth Hwy, POB 664, St John's; tel. 562-4196; fax 562-4331; e-mail eleccom@candw.ag; internet www.abec.gov.ag; f. 2001; Chief Elections Officer LORNA SIMON.

Political Organizations

Antigua Labour Party (ALP): Market St, ANU, St John's; tel. 562-5401; e-mail voteablp@gmail.com; f. 1946; Leader GASTON BROWNE.

Barbuda People's Movement (BPM): Codrington; campaigns for separate status for Barbuda; allied to United Progressive Party; Leader THOMAS HILBOURNE FRANK.

Barbuda People's Movement for Change (BPMC): Codrington; f. 2004; effectively replaced Organisation for National Reconstruction, which was f. 1983 and re-f. 1988 as Barbuda Independence Movt; advocates self-govt for Barbuda; supports the Antigua Labour Party; Pres. ARTHUR SHABAZZ-NIBBS.

Barbudans for a Better Barbuda: Codrington; f. 2004 by fmr Gen. Sec. of Barbuda People's Movt for Change; Leader ORDRICK SAMUEL.

National Movement for Change (NMC): St John's; f. 2003; Leader ALISTAIR THOMAS.

Organisation for National Development: Upper St Mary's St, St John's; f. 2003 by breakaway faction of the United Progressive Party; Leader MELFORD NICHOLAS.

United Progressive Party (UPP): UPP Headquarters Bldg, Upper Nevis St, POB 2379, St John's; tel. 481-3888; fax 481-3877; e-mail info@uppantigua.com; internet www.uppantigua.com; f. 1992 by merger of the Antigua Caribbean Liberation Movt (f. 1979), the Progressive Labour Movt (f. 1970) and the United National Democratic Party (f. 1986); Leader BALDWIN SPENCER; Deputy Leader HAROLD E. E. LOVELL; Chair. LEON (CHAKU) SYMISTER.

Diplomatic Representation

EMBASSIES IN ANTIGUA AND BARBUDA

Brazil: Price Waterhouse Bldg, Old Parham Rd, St John's; tel. 562-7532; fax 562-7537; e-mail michael.neele@itamaraty.gov.br; Ambassador RAUL CAMPOS E CASTRO.

China, People's Republic: Cedar Valley, POB 1446, St John's; tel. 462-1125; fax 462-6425; e-mail chinaemb_ag@mfa.gov.cn; internet ag.chineseembassy.org/eng; Ambassador REN GONGPING.

Cuba: Coral Villas 6 Crosbies, St John's; tel. 562-5865; fax 562-5867; e-mail cubanembassy@candw.ag; internet www.cubadiplomatica.cu/antiguaybarbuda; Ambassador JOSÉ MANUEL INCLÁN EMBADE.

Venezuela: ALBA CARIBE Bldg, Old Parham Rd, POB 1201, St John's; tel. 462-1574; fax 462-1570; e-mail embaveneantigua@yahoo.es; Ambassador CARLOS AMADOR PÉREZ SILVA.

Judicial System

Justice is administered by the Eastern Caribbean Supreme Court (ECSC), based in Saint Lucia, which consists of a High Court of Justice and a Court of Appeal. Three of the Court's High Court Judges are resident in and responsible for Antigua and Barbuda, and preside over the Court of Summary Jurisdiction on the islands. One of two ECSC Masters, chiefly responsible for procedural and interlocutory matters, is also resident in Antigua. Magistrates' Courts in the territory administer lesser cases.

High Court Judges: CLARE HENRY, BRIAN COTTLE, KEITH THOM.

Registrar: CECILE HILL.

Attorney-General: JUSTIN L. SIMON.

Religion

The majority of the inhabitants profess Christianity, and the largest denomination is the Church in the Province of the West Indies (Anglican Communion).

CHRISTIANITY

Antigua Christian Council: POB 863, St Mary's St, St John's; tel. 461-1135; fax 462-2383; f. 1964; five mem. churches; Pres. Bishop KENNETH RICHARDS; Treas. MARY-ROSE KNIGHT.

The Anglican Communion

Anglicans in Antigua and Barbuda are adherents of the Church in the Province of the West Indies. The diocese of the North Eastern Caribbean and Aruba comprises 12 islands: Antigua, St Kitts, Nevis, Anguilla, Barbuda, Montserrat, Dominica, Saba, St-Martin/St Maarten, Aruba, St-Barthélemy and St Eustatius. The Bishop is resident in St John's, Antigua and Barbuda. According to the 2001 census, some 26% of the population are Anglicans.

Bishop of the North Eastern Caribbean and Aruba: Rt Rev. LEROY ERROL BROOKS, Bishop's Lodge, POB 23, St John's; tel. 462-0151; fax 462-2090; e-mail dioceseofneca@hotmail.com; internet www.dioneca.org.

The Roman Catholic Church

The diocese of St John's-Basseterre, suffragan to the archdiocese of Castries (Saint Lucia), includes Anguilla, Antigua and Barbuda, the British Virgin Islands, Montserrat and Saint Christopher and Nevis. The Bishop participates in the Antilles Episcopal Conference (whose Secretariat is based in Trinidad and Tobago). Some 10% of the population are Roman Catholics, according to the 2001 census.

Bishop of St John's-Basseterre: Mgr KENNETH DAVID OSWIN RICHARDS, Chancery Offices, POB 836, St John's; tel. 461-1135; fax 462-2383; e-mail diocesesjb@gmail.com.

Other Christian Churches

According to the 2001 census, some 12% of the population are Seventh-day Adventists, 11% are Pentecostalists, 10% are Moravians, 8% are Methodists and 5% are Baptists.

East Caribbean Baptist Mission: POB 2678, St John's; tel. 462-2894; fax 462-6029; e-mail admin@baptistantigua.org; internet www.baptistantigua.org; f. 1991; mem. congregation of the Baptist Circuit of Churches in the East Caribbean Baptist Mission; Presiding Elder Dr HENSWORTH W. C. JONAS.

Methodist Church: Methodist Manse, Hodges Bay, POB 69, St John's; tel. 764-5998; fax 560-5922; e-mail novjosiah@hotmail.com; internet www.lidmethodist.org; Supt Rev. NOVELLE C. JOSIAH.

St John's Church of Christ: Golden Grove, Main Rd, St John's; tel. and fax 461-6732; e-mail stjcoclectureship2013@hotmail.com;

internet www.stjohnscoc.com; Contact Evangelist CORNELIUS GEORGE.

St John's Evangelical Lutheran Church: Woods Centre, POB W77, St John's; tel. and fax 462-2896; e-mail sjluther@candw.ag; Principal ANDREW JOHNSTON; Pastors Rev. ANDREW JOHNSTON, Rev. JOSHUA STERNHAGEN, Rev. JASON RICHARDS, Rev. PAUL WORKENTINE.

The Press

Business Focus: Bryson's Office Complex, Suite 5A, Friar's Hill Rd, POB 180, St John's; tel. 481-7680; fax 481-7685; e-mail info@businessfocusantigua.com; internet www.businessfocusantigua.com; 6 a year; Man. Dir and Editor LOKESH SINGH.

Daily Observer: 15 Pavilion Dr., Coolidge, POB 1318, St John's; tel. 480-1750; fax 480-1757; e-mail editor@antiguaobserver.com; internet www.antiguaobserver.com; f. 1999; owned by the Observer Media Group; Gen. Man. CECILIA DERRICK; Editors CHERISSE CONSTANT, JULIET BENJAMIN; circ. 5,000.

Paradise Antigua and Barbuda: Bryson's Office Complex, Suite 5A, Friar's Hill Rd, POB 180, St John's; tel. 481-7680; fax 481-7685; e-mail info@paradiseantiguabarbuda.com; internet paradiseantiguabarbuda.com; annual tourism guide; Man. Dir and Editor LOKESH SINGH.

The Worker's Voice: Emancipation Hall, 46 North St, POB 3, St John's; tel. 462-0090; fax 462-4056; f. 1943; 2 a week; official organ of the Antigua Labour Party and the Antigua Trades and Labour Union; Editor NOEL THOMAS; circ. 6,000.

Publishers

Antigua Printing and Publishing Ltd: Factory Rd, POB 670, St John's; tel. 481-1500; fax 481-1515; e-mail antprint@candw.ag.

The Best of Books Ltd: Lower St Mary's St, St John's; tel. 562-3198; fax 562-3198; e-mail bestofbooks@yahoo.com; textbooks; authorized distributor of Macmillan Caribbean and Nelson Thornes books.

Caribbean Publishing Co Ltd: Ryan's Pl., Suite 1B, High St, POB 1451, St John's; tel. 462-2215; fax 462-0962; e-mail lan-sales@caribpub.com.

Regional Publications Ltd: Bryson's Office Complex, Suite 5A, Friar's Hill Rd, POB 180, St John's; tel. 481-7680; fax 481-7685; e-mail info@regionalpub.com; internet regionalpub.com; f. 2006; publishes the business periodical *Business Focus*, the local Yellow Pages and the annual tourist magazine *Paradise Antigua and Barbuda*; Man. Dir LOKESH SINGH.

Treasure Island Publishing Ltd: Anchorage Dockyard Dr., POB W283, Woods Centre, St John's; tel. and fax 463-7414; e-mail colettif@candw.ag; internet www.thetreasureislands.com; Publr and Editor FRANCESCA COLETTI.

West Indies Publishing Ltd: Wood's Centre, POB W883, St John's; tel. 461-0565; fax 461-9750; e-mail wip@candw.ag; internet www.westindiespublishing.com; f. 1992; Publr BERTEL DEJOIE; Gen. Man. and Editor ALISON ARCHER.

Broadcasting and Communications

TELECOMMUNICATIONS

Antigua Computer Technology Ltd (ACT): Old Parham Rd, St John's; tel. 480-5228; e-mail act@actol.net; internet www.act2000.net; f. 1989 as computer sales and repair service; internet provider since 2001.

Digicel Antigua and Barbuda: Antigua Wireless Ventures Ltd, POB W32, St John's; tel. 480-2050; fax 480-2060; e-mail customercareantiguaandbarbuda@digicelgroup.com; internet www.digicelantiguaandbarbuda.com; acquired Cingular Wireless' Caribbean operations and licences in 2005; owned by an Irish consortium; Chair. DENIS O'BRIEN; Group CEO and Dir COLM DELVES.

I-Mobile: Cassada Gardens, POB 416, St John's; tel. 480-7000; fax 480-7476; internet www.apua.ag; f. 2000 as PCS, relaunched in 2011 under present name; owned by Antigua Public Utilities Authority (see Trade and Industry—Utilities); digital mobile cellular telephone network; controls less than 20% of market; Chair. CLARVIS JOSEPH; Man. (Telecommunications) DALMA HILL.

LIME: Cable & Wireless, Wireless Rd, Clare Hall, St John's; tel. 480-4000; e-mail customerservice@lime.com; internet www.lime.com/ag; fmrly Cable & Wireless (Antigua and Barbuda) Ltd; name changed as above in 2008; fixed line, mobile telecommunications and internet services provider; monopoly ended in 2012; CEO (Caribbean) TONY RICE.

Regulatory Body

Telecommunications Division: part of the Office of the Prime Minister; see The Government—Ministries.

BROADCASTING

Radio

ABS Radio: POB 590, St John's; tel. 464-9376; fax 463-4525; e-mail davelpayne@hotmail.com; internet www.abstvradio.com; f. 1956; state-owned; Station Man. DAVE LESTER PAYNE.

Abundant Life Radio: Codrington Village, Barbuda; tel. 562-4821; e-mail afternoonpraise@gmail.com; internet www.abundantliferadio.com; f. 2001; began broadcasting in Antigua in 2003; Christian station; daily, 24-hour broadcasts; Man. Dir Rt Rev. CLIFTON FRANCOIS.

Caribbean Radio Lighthouse: POB 1057, St John's; tel. 462-1454; fax 462-7420; e-mail info@radiolighthouse.org; internet www.radiolighthouse.org; f. 1975; religious broadcasts in Spanish and English; operated by Baptist Int. Mission Inc (USA); Station Man. JERRY BAKER.

Crusader Radio: Redcliffe St, POB 2379, St John's; tel. 562-4610; fax 481-3892; e-mail crusaderradio@candw.ag; internet www.crusaderradio.com; f. 2003; Crusader Publishing & Broadcasting Ltd; official station of the UPP; Station Man. CONRAD POLE.

Gem Radio Network: Tristan's Crescent Cedar Valley, POB W939, St John's; tel. 744-7768; fax 720-7017; e-mail gemfmstereo@gmail.com.

Observer Radio: POB 1318, St John's; tel. 460-0911; e-mail voice@antiguaobserver.com; internet www.antiguaobserver.com; f. 2001; owned by the Observer Media Group; Chair. (vacant).

ZDK Liberty Radio International (Radio ZDK): Grenville Radio Ltd, Bryant Pasture, Bird Rd, Ottos, POB 1100, St John's; tel. 462-1116; fax 462-1101; e-mail mail@radiozdk.com; internet www.radiozdk.com; f. 1970; commercial; also operates SUN Radio; Man. Dir IVOR GRENVILLE BIRD.

Television

ABS Television: POB 1280, St John's; tel. 462-0010; fax 462-1622; f. 1964; state-run.

CTV Entertainment Systems: POB 1536, St John's; tel. 462-4224; fax 462-4211; internet ctv.ag; cable television co; transmits 33 channels of US television 24 hours per day to subscribers; Programme Dir K. BIRD.

Finance

(cap. = capital; res = reserves; dep. = deposits; m. = millions; brs = branches)

BANKING

The Eastern Caribbean Central Bank, based in Saint Christopher, is the central issuing and monetary authority for Antigua and Barbuda.

ABI Bank Ltd (ABIB): ABI Financial Center, 156 Redcliffe St, POB 1679, St John's; tel. 480-2700; fax 480-2750; e-mail afaisal@abibank.com.ag; internet www.abibank.com.ag; f. 1990 as Antigua Barbuda Investment Bank Ltd; part of the ABI Financial Group; taken over by the Govt and the Eastern Caribbean Central Bank in 2011, review process still under way in 2014; cap. EC $21.2m., res EC $38.0m., dep. EC $997.7m. (Sept. 2008); Chair. SYLVIA O'MARD; Man. ALOUSIA FAISAL (acting); 3 brs.

Antigua and Barbuda Development Bank: 27 St Mary's St, POB 1279, St John's; tel. 462-0838; fax 462-0839; f. 1974; Gen. Man. S. ALEX OSBORNE.

Antigua Commercial Bank: St Mary's and Thames Sts, POB 95, Loans, St John's; tel. 481-4200; fax 481-4229; e-mail acb@acbonline.com; internet www.acbonline.com; f. 1955; auth. cap. EC $5m.; Chair. DAVIDSON CHARLES; Man. GLADSTON S. JOSEPH; 2 brs.

Caribbean Union Bank Ltd: Friar's Hill Rd, POB W2010, St John's; tel. 481-8278; fax 481-8290; e-mail customerservice@cub.ag; internet www.caribbeanunionbank.com; f. 2005; total assets US $42.4m. (Sept. 2007); Chair. CLEMENT BIRD; Gen. Man. GREGORY GILPIN-PAYNE; 2 brs.

CIBC FirstCaribbean International Bank: High and Market Sts, POB 225, St John's; tel. 480-5000; fax 462-4910; internet www.cibcfcib.com; f. 2002 as FirstCaribbean International Bank following merger of Caribbean operations of CIBC and Barclays Bank PLC; Barclays relinquished its stake in 2006; adopted current name in 2011; Exec. Chair. MICHAEL MANSOOR; CEO RIK PARKHILL; 2 brs.

Eastern Caribbean Amalgamated Bank (ECAB): 1000 Airport Blvd, Pavilion Dr., POB 315, Coolidge; tel. 480-5300; fax 480-5433;

e-mail info@ecabank.com; internet www.ecabank.com; f. 1981 as Bank of Antigua; name changed in 2010 following purchase by Eastern Caribbean Amalgamated Financial Co Ltd in 2009; total assets EC $487m. (Sep. 2012); Chair. CRAIG J. WALTER (acting); Gen. Man. HENRY HAZEL; 3 brs.

Global Bank of Commerce Ltd (GBC): Global Commerce Centre, Old Parham Rd, POB W1803, St John's; tel. 480-2240; fax 462-1831; e-mail customer.service@gbc.ag; internet www.globalbank.ag; f. 1983; int. financial services operator; total assets US $74.4m.; shareholder equity US $8.1m.; Chair. and CEO BRIAN STUART-YOUNG; Gen. Man. WINSTON ST AGATHE; 1 br.

RBC Royal Bank (Barbados) Ltd: 45 High St, POB 1324, St John's; tel. 462-4217; fax 462-5040; internet www.rbtt.com; Chair. PETER JULY; Man. ALAN HAMEL-SMITH; 117 brs.

Scotiabank Antigua (Canada): High and Market Sts, POB 342, St John's; tel. 480-1500; fax 480-1554; e-mail bns.antigua@scotiabank.com; internet www.antigua.scotiabank.com; f. 1961; subsidiary of Bank of Nova Scotia, Canada; Country Man. GORDON JULIEN; Operations Man. PASCAL HUGHES; 2 brs.

Regulatory Body

Financial Services Regulatory Commission (FSRC): Royal Palm Pl., Friar's Hill Rd, POB 2674, St John's; tel. 481-3300; fax 463-0422; e-mail anuifsa@candw.ag; internet www.fsrc.gov.ag; fmrly known as International Financial Sector Regulatory Authority, adopted current name in 2002; Chair. ALTHEA CRICK; Administrator and CEO JOHN BENJAMIN.

STOCK EXCHANGE

Eastern Caribbean Securities Exchange: tel. (869) 466-7192; fax (869) 465-3798; e-mail info@ecseonline.com; internet www.ecseonline.com; based in Basseterre, Saint Christopher and Nevis; f. 2001; regional securities market designed to facilitate the buying and selling of financial products for the 8 mem. territories—Anguilla, Antigua and Barbuda, Dominica, Grenada, Montserrat, St Kitts and Nevis, St Lucia and St Vincent and the Grenadines; Chair. Sir K. DWIGHT VENNER; Gen. Man. TREVOR E. BLAKE.

INSURANCE

Several foreign companies have offices in Antigua. Local insurance companies include the following:

ABI Insurance Co Ltd (ABII): ABI Financial Center, 156 Redcliffe St, POB 2386, St John's; tel. 480-2825; fax 480-2834; e-mail abii@abifinancial.com; internet www.abifinancial.com/abii; f. 1999; subsidiary of the ABI Financial Group; Chair. BRADLEY LEWIS.

Antigua Insurance Co Ltd (ANICOL): Long St, POB 511, St John's; tel. 480-9000; fax 480-9035; e-mail anicol@candw.ag; internet www.anicolinsurance.com.

Brysons Insurance Agency: Friars Hill Rd, POB 162, St. John's; tel. 480-1220; fax 462-0320; e-mail office@brysonsinsurance.com; internet www.brysonsantigua.com; f. 1835; Gen. Man. MAJORIE PARCHMENT.

General Insurance Co Ltd: Upper Redcliffe St, POB 340, St John's; tel. 462-2346; fax 462-4482; e-mail info@gicantigua.com; internet www.gicantigua.com; Man. Dir PETER BLANCHARD.

Sagicor Life Inc: Sagicor Financial Centre, 9 Factory Rd, St. John's; tel. 480-5500; fax 480-5520; e-mail info_antigua@sagicor.com; internet www.sagicorlife.com; f. 1863; Man. Dr TREVOR VIGO.

Selkridge Insurance Agency Ltd: 7 Woods Centre, Friar's Hill Rd, POB W306, St John's; tel. 462-2042; fax 462-2466; e-mail selkins@candw.ag; internet www.selkridgeinsuranceantigua.com; f. 1961; agents for American Life Insurance Co (ALICO) and Island Heritage Insurance Co; Man. CHARLENE SELKRIDGE.

State Insurance Co Ltd: Redcliffe St, POB 290, St John's; tel. 481-7804; fax 481-7860; e-mail stateins@candw.ag; f. 1977; fmrly State Insurance Corpn; privatized in March 2011; Chair. Dr VINCENT RICHARDS; Gen. Man. LYNDELL BUTLER.

Trade and Industry

DEVELOPMENT ORGANIZATIONS

Antigua and Barbuda Investment Authority: Sagicor Financial Centre, POB 80, St John's; tel. 481-1000; fax 481-1020; e-mail abia@antigua.gov.ag; internet www.investantiguabarbuda.org; f. 2007; Exec. Dir LESTROY SAMUEL.

Citizenship by Investment Unit: 3rd Floor, ABI Financial Centre, Redcliffe St, POB W2074, St John's; tel. 562-8427; fax 562-8431; e-mail info@cip.gov.ag; internet cip.gov.ag; f. 2013; responsible for processing applications to the economic citizenship programme; Chair. DONALD MYATT.

Development Control Authority: Cecil Charles Bldg, 1st Floor, Cross St, POB 895, St John's; tel. 462-2038; fax 462-6426; developing lands, regulating construction; Chair. LEON (CHAKU) SYMISTER.

St John's Development Corpn: Thames St, POB 1473, St John's; tel. 462-3925; fax 462-3931; e-mail info@stjohnsdevelopment.com; internet www.stjohnsdevelopment.com; f. 1986; manages the Heritage Quay Duty Free Shopping Complex, Vendors' Mall, Public Market and Cultural and Exhibition Complex; Chair. SYLVESTER BROWNE; Exec. Dir (vacant).

CHAMBER OF COMMERCE

Antigua and Barbuda Chamber of Commerce and Industry Ltd: Cnr of North and Popeshead Sts, POB 774, St John's; tel. 462-0743; fax 462-4575; e-mail chamcom@candw.ag; f. 1944 as Antigua Chamber of Commerce Ltd; name changed as above in 1991; Pres. ERROL SAMUEL; Exec. Dir HOLLY PETERS.

INDUSTRIAL AND TRADE ASSOCIATIONS

Antigua and Barbuda Manufacturers' Association (ABMA): POB 115, St John's; tel. 462-1536; fax 462-1912.

Antigua and Barbuda Marine Association (ABMA): English Harbour, St John's; tel. 562-5085; e-mail info@abma.ag; internet www.abma.ag; protection and improvement of marine industry; Pres. FRANKLYN BRAITHWAITE.

EMPLOYERS' ORGANIZATIONS

Antigua and Barbuda Employers' Federation: Upper High St, POB 298, St John's; tel. 462-0247; fax 462-0449; e-mail aempfed@candw.ag; internet abef-anu.org; f. 1950; affiliated to the International Organization of Employers and the Caribbean Employers' Confederation; 135 mems; Pres. ACRES STOWE.

Antigua and Barbuda Small Business Association Ltd (ABSBA): Cross and Tanner Sts, POB 1401, St John's; tel. and fax 461-5741; Pres. LAWRENCE KING.

UTILITIES

Antigua Public Utilities Authority (APUA): Cnr Independence Ave and High St, POB 416, St John's; tel. 480-7000; fax 462-4131; e-mail support@apua.ag; internet www.apua.ag; f. 1973; state-owned; generation, transmission and distribution of electricity; telecommunications; colln, treatment, storage and distribution of water; Chair. CLARVIS JOSEPH; Gen. Man. ESWORTH MARTIN.

Antigua Power Co Limited (APC): Old Parham Rd, POB 10, St John's; tel. 460-9461; fax 460-9462; e-mail cmills@candw.ag; electricity provider; Owner FRANCIS HADEED; Gen. Man. CALID HASSAD.

Sembcorp (Antigua) Water: St John's; internet www.sembcorp.com; fmrly known as Eneserve; water supplier; Group Pres. and CEO TANG KIN FEI; Operations Man. RICKY BUCKLEY.

TRADE UNION

Antigua and Barbuda Trades Union Congress (ABTUC): c/o Antigua and Barbuda Workers' Union, Freedom Hall, Newgate St, POB 940, St John's; tel. 462-0442; fax 462-5220; e-mail awu@candw.ag; Pres. KIM BURDON; Gen. Sec. NATASHA MUSSINGTON.

Transport

ROADS

There are 384 km (239 miles) of main roads and 781 km (485 miles) of secondary dry-weather roads. Of the total 1,165 km (724 miles) of roads, only 33% are paved.

SHIPPING

The port of St John's has three operating harbours. The Deep Water Harbour handles cargo and is the main commercial pier. The other two harbours, Nevis Pier and Heritage Quay, are used by cruise ships and a number of foreign shipping lines. There are regular cargo and passenger services internationally and regionally. The other harbours in Antigua include Falmouth, English and Jolly on the south-eastern and southern parts of the island. In December 2013 Antigua and Barbuda's flag registered fleet comprised 1,225 vessels, with an aggregate displacement of some 10,120,815 grt.

Antigua and Barbuda Port Authority: Terminal Bldg, Deep Water Harbour, POB 1052, St John's; tel. 484-3400; fax 462-4243; e-mail abpa@port.gov.ag; internet www.port.gov.ag; f. 1968; responsible to Ministry of Public Works and Transport; Chair. GREGG WALTER; Port Man. AGATHA C. DUBLIN.

Barbuda Express: POB 958, St John's; tel. 560-7989; fax 460-0059; e-mail info@barbudaexpress.com; internet www.barbudaexpress

.com; f. 2004; ferry services between the islands of Antigua and Barbuda; Owner GREG URLWIN; Man. FREDERIQUE BONFILS.

Brysons Shipping: Friar's Hill Rd, POB 162, St John's; tel. 480-1240; fax 462-0170; internet www.brysonsantigua.com; f. 1835; all shipping services; represents major cruise line; local agent for CMA-CGM Group; Gen. Man. NATHAN DUNDAS.

Consolidated Maritime Services: CMS Enterprise Complex, Old Parham Rd, POB 2478, St John's; tel. 462-1224; fax 462-1227; e-mail caribms@candw.ag; shipping agents for Crowley Corpn and Navivan Corpn; liner and freight services; Gen. Man. TERRENCE D'ORNELLAS.

Geest Line: Francis Trading Agency Ltd, High St, POB 194, St John's; tel. 462-0854; fax 462-0849; e-mail quotes@geestline.com; internet www.geestline.com; operates between Europe and the Windward and Leeward islands; Man. Dir PETER DIXON.

Tropical Shipping: Antigua Maritime Agencies Ltd, Milburn House, Old Parham Rd, POB W1310, St John's; tel. 562-2934; fax 562-2935; internet www.tropical.com; f. 1992; operates between Canada, the USA and the Caribbean; Pres. MIKE PELLICCI.

Vernon Edwards Shipping Co: Thames St, POB 82, St John's; tel. 462-2034; fax 462-2035; e-mail vedwards@candw.ag; cargo service to and from San Juan, Puerto Rico; Man. Dir VERNON G. EDWARDS, Jr.

CIVIL AVIATION

Antigua's V. C. Bird (formerly Coolidge) International Airport, 9 km (5.6 miles) north-east of St John's, is modern and accommodates jet-engined aircraft. There is a small airstrip at Codrington on Barbuda. Antigua and Barbuda Airlines, a nominal company, controls international routes, but services to Europe and North America are operated by foreign airlines. Antigua and Barbuda is a shareholder in, and the headquarters of, the regional airline LIAT. Other regional services are operated by Caribbean Airlines (Trinidad and Tobago) and Air BVI (British Virgin Islands). In November 2011 construction of a new airport terminal at the V. C. Bird International Airport began, with Chinese financing. The new terminal was scheduled to open in September 2014.

LIAT Airlines: V. C. Bird Int. Airport, POB 819, St John's; tel. 480-5713; fax 480-5717; e-mail customerrelations@liatairline.com; internet www.liatairline.com; f. 1956 as Leeward Islands Air Transport Services; privatized in 1995; shares are held by the Govts of Antigua and Barbuda, Montserrat, Grenada, Barbados, Trinidad and Tobago, Jamaica, Guyana, Dominica, Saint Lucia, Saint Vincent and the Grenadines and Saint Christopher and Nevis (30.8%), Caribbean Airlines (29.2%), LIAT employees (13.3%) and private investors (26.7%); acquired Caribbean Star Airlines in 2007; scheduled passenger and cargo services to 19 destinations in the Caribbean; charter flights are also undertaken; Chair. Dr JEAN HOLDER; CEO DAVID EVANS.

Tourism

Tourism is the country's main industry. Antigua offers a reputed 365 beaches, an annual international sailing regatta and Carnival week, and the historic Nelson's Dockyard in English Harbour (a national park since 1985). Barbuda is less developed, but is noted for its beauty, wildlife and beaches of pink sand. In 2012 there were 246,926 stop-over visitors and 567,707 cruise ship passengers. Tourism receipts totalled EC $861.3m. in the same year.

Antigua & Barbuda Cruise Tourism Association (ABCTA): POB 2208, St John's; tel. 562-1746; fax 562-2858; e-mail abcta@candw.ag; internet www.abc-ta.com; f. 1995; Pres. NATHAN DUNDAS; 42 mems.

Antigua and Barbuda Department of Tourism: c/o Ministry of Tourism, Civil Aviation and Culture, Govt Complex, Queen Elizabeth Hwy, POB 363, St John's; tel. 462-0480; fax 462-2483; e-mail deptourism@antigua.gov.ag; internet www.antigua-barbuda.org; Dir-Gen. CORTHWRIGHT MARSHALL.

Antigua Hotels and Tourist Association (AHTA): Island House, Newgate St, POB 454, St John's; tel. 462-0374; fax 462-3702; e-mail ahta@candw.ag; internet www.antiguahotels.org; Exec. Dir NEIL FORRESTER.

Defence

There is a small defence force of 180 men (army 130, navy 50). There were also joint reserves numbering 80. The US Government leases two military bases on Antigua. Antigua and Barbuda participates in the US-sponsored Regional Security System. In 2014 Antigua and Barbuda signed a framework agreement on defence and security. The defence budget in 2013 was estimated at EC $70m.

Education

Education is compulsory for 11 years between five and 16 years of age. Primary education begins at the age of five and normally lasts for seven years. Secondary education, beginning at 12 years of age, lasts for five years, comprising a first cycle of three years and a second cycle of two years. In 2009/10 there were 63 primary and 20 secondary schools; the majority of schools are administered by the Government. According to UNESCO estimates, in 2012 enrolment at primary schools included 85% of the pupils in their relevant age-groups while that of secondary schools included 78% of pupils in their relevant age-groups. An estimated 72% of children in the appropriate age-group were enrolled in pre-primary education in 2012. Teacher training and technical training are available at the Antigua State College in St John's. An extra-mural department of the University of the West Indies offers several foundation courses leading to higher study at branches elsewhere. There are 11 other tertiary educational institutes. Government expenditure on the Ministry of Education, Sports and Youth Affairs in 2013 was projected at EC $84.4m. In late 2013 the Caribbean Development Bank provided a US $13.4m. loan to improve secondary education in the country.

ARGENTINA

Introductory Survey

LOCATION, CLIMATE, LANGUAGE, RELIGION, FLAG, CAPITAL

The Argentine Republic occupies almost the whole of South America south of the Tropic of Capricorn and east of the Andes. It has a long Atlantic coastline stretching from Uruguay and the River Plate to Tierra del Fuego. To the west lie Chile and the Andes mountains, while to the north are Bolivia, Paraguay and Brazil. Argentina also claims the Falkland Islands (known in Argentina as the Islas Malvinas), South Georgia, the South Sandwich Islands and part of Antarctica. The climate varies from sub-tropical in the Chaco region of the north to sub-arctic in Patagonia, generally with moderate summer rainfall. Temperatures in Buenos Aires are usually between 5°C (41°F) and 29°C (84°F). The language is Spanish. The majority of the population profess Christianity: about 76% are Roman Catholics and about 2% Protestants. The national flag (proportions 14 by 9) has three equal horizontal stripes, of light blue (celeste), above white, above light blue. The state flag (proportions 1 by 2) has the same design with, in addition, a gold 'Sun of May' in the centre of the white stripe. The capital is Buenos Aires.

CONTEMPORARY POLITICAL HISTORY

Historical Context

During the greater part of the 20th century, government in Argentina tended to alternate between military and civilian rule. In 1930 Hipólito Yrigoyen, a member of the reformist Unión Cívica Radical (UCR), who in 1916 had become Argentina's first President to be freely elected by popular vote, was overthrown by an army coup, and the country's first military regime was established. Civilian rule was restored in 1932, only to be supplanted by further military intervention in 1943. A leading figure in the new military regime, Col (later Gen.) Juan Domingo Perón Sosa, won a presidential election in 1946. He established the Peronista party in 1948 and pursued a policy of extreme nationalism and social improvement, aided by his second wife, Eva ('Evita') Duarte de Perón, whose popularity greatly enhanced his position and contributed to his re-election as President in 1951. In 1954, however, his promotion of secularization and the legalization of divorce brought him into conflict with the Roman Catholic Church. In September 1955 President Perón was deposed by a revolt of the armed forces. He went into exile, eventually settling in Spain, from where he continued to direct the Peronist movement.

Following the overthrow of Perón, Argentina entered another lengthy period of political instability. Political control continued to pass between civilian (mainly Radical) and military regimes during the late 1950s and the 1960s. Congressional and presidential elections were conducted in March 1973. The Frente Justicialista de Liberación, a Peronist coalition, secured control of the Congreso Nacional (National Congress), while the presidential election was won by the party's candidate, Dr Héctor Cámpora. However, Cámpora resigned in July, to enable Gen. Perón, who had returned to Argentina, to contest a fresh presidential election. In September Perón was returned to power, with more than 60% of the votes.

Domestic Political Affairs

Military rule

Gen. Perón died in July 1974 and was succeeded as President by his widow, María Estela ('Isabelita') Martínez de Perón, hitherto Vice-President. The Government's economic austerity programme and the soaring rate of inflation led to widespread strike action and demands for the President's resignation. In March 1976 the armed forces, led by Gen. Jorge Videla, overthrew the President and installed a three-man junta: Gen. Videla was sworn in as head of state. The junta substantially altered the Constitution, dissolved the National Congress, suspended political and trade union activity and removed most government officials from their posts. Several hundred people were arrested, while 'Isabelita' Perón was detained and later went into exile. The military regime launched a ferocious offensive against left-wing guerrillas and opposition forces. The imprisonment, torture and murder of suspected left-wing activists by the armed forces provoked domestic and international protests. Repression eased in 1978, after all armed opposition had been eliminated.

In March 1981 Gen. Roberto Viola, a former junta member, succeeded President Videla and made known his intention to extend dialogue with political parties as a prelude to an eventual return to democracy. Owing to ill health, he was replaced in December by Lt-Gen. Leopoldo Galtieri, the Commander-in-Chief of the Army, who attempted to cultivate popular support by continuing this process of political liberalization.

In April 1982, in order to distract attention from an increasingly unstable domestic situation, and following unsuccessful negotiations with the United Kingdom in February over Argentina's long-standing sovereignty claim, President Galtieri ordered the invasion of the Falkland Islands (Islas Malvinas—see chapter on the Falkland Islands). The United Kingdom recovered the islands after a short conflict, in the course of which about 750 Argentine lives were lost. Argentine forces surrendered in June, but no formal cessation of hostilities was declared until October 1989. Humiliated by the defeat, Galtieri was forced to resign, and the members of the junta were replaced. The army installed a retired general, Reynaldo Bignone, as President in July 1982. The armed forces were held responsible for the disastrous economic situation, and the transfer of power to a civilian government was accelerated. Moreover, in 1983 a Military Commission of Inquiry into the Falklands conflict concluded in its report that the main responsibility for Argentina's defeat lay with members of the former junta. Galtieri was sentenced to imprisonment, while several other officers were put on trial for corruption, murder and insulting the honour of the armed forces. In the same year the regime approved the Ley de Pacificación Nacional, an amnesty law which granted retrospective immunity to the police, the armed forces and others for political crimes that had been committed over the previous 10 years.

Civilian rule

General and presidential elections were held in October 1983, in which the UCR defeated the Peronist Partido Justicialista (PJ), attracting the votes of many former Peronist supporters. Dr Raúl Alfonsín, the UCR candidate, took office as President on 10 December. He announced a radical reform of the armed forces, repealed the Ley de Pacificación Nacional and ordered the court martial of the first three military juntas to rule Argentina after the 1976 coup, for offences including abduction, torture and murder. Public opposition to the former military regime was reinforced by the discovery and exhumation of hundreds of bodies from unmarked graves throughout the country. (It was believed that 15,000–30,000 people 'disappeared' during the so-called 'dirty war' between the former military regime and its opponents in 1976–83.) President Alfonsín also announced the formation of the National Commission on the Disappearance of Persons to investigate the events of the 'dirty war'. The trial of the former leaders began in April 1985. In December four of the accused were acquitted, but sentences were imposed on five others, including sentences of life imprisonment for Gen. Videla and Adm. Eduardo Massera (they were released in 1990). In May 1986 all three members of the junta that had held power during the Falklands conflict were found guilty of negligence and received prison sentences, including a term of 12 years for Galtieri.

In December 1986 the National Congress approved the Punto Final ('Full Stop') law, whereby civil and military courts were to begin new judicial proceedings against members of the armed forces accused of violations of human rights, within a 60-day period. However, in May 1987, following a series of minor rebellions at army garrisons, the Government announced new legislation, known as the Obediencia Debida ('Due Obedience') law, whereby an amnesty was to be declared for all but senior ranks of the police and armed forces. Therefore, of the 350–370 officers hitherto due to be prosecuted for alleged violations of human rights, only 30–50 senior officers were now to be tried.

A return to Peronismo

In the May 1989 elections, the Frente Justicialista de Unidad Popular (FREJUPO) electoral alliance, headed by Carlos Saúl Menem and comprising his own PJ grouping, the Partido Demócrata Cristiano (PDC) and the Partido Intransigente (PI), secured 49% of the votes cast in the presidential ballot and 310 of the 600 seats in the electoral college. The Peronists were also victorious in the election for 127 seats (one-half of the total) in the Cámara de Diputados (Chamber of Deputies). The worsening economic situation compelled Alfonsín to resign five months early, and Menem assumed the presidency on 8 July.

In early 1990 the Government introduced a radical economic readjustment plan, incorporating the expansion of existing plans for the transfer to private ownership of many state-owned companies and the restructuring of the nation's financial systems. However, public disaffection with the Government's economic policy was widespread. Failure to contain the threat of hyperinflation led to a loss in purchasing power, and unrest became more frequent. In January 1991 Antonio Erman González was forced to resign as Minister of the Economy following a sudden decline in the value of the austral in relation to the US dollar. He was succeeded by Domingo Cavallo.

In October 1989 the Government pardoned 210 officers and soldiers who had been involved in the 'dirty war', as well as the governing junta during the Falklands conflict (including Gen. Galtieri) and leaders of three recent military uprisings (including Lt-Col Rico and Col Seineldín). Public concern at the apparent impunity of military personnel further increased after a second round of presidential pardons in late 1990.

Peronist success in gubernatorial and congressional elections held during 1991 was widely attributed to the popularity of Domingo Cavallo, who implemented the 'Convertibility Plan', which linked the austral to the US dollar, at a fixed rate of exchange. This Plan led to a reduction in inflation, and impressed international finance organizations sufficiently to secure the negotiation of substantial loan agreements. In October the President ordered the removal of almost all of the remaining bureaucratic apparatus of state regulation of the economy, and in November the Government announced plans to accelerate the transfer to private ownership of the remaining public sector concerns. Agreements for the renegotiation of repayment of outstanding debts with the Government's leading creditor banks and with the 'Paris Club' of Western creditor governments followed in 1992. The October 1993 elections to renew 127 seats in the Chamber of Deputies were won convincingly by the PJ.

In late 1993 the President and the UCR agreed on a framework for constitutional reform, which included the possibility of re-election of the President for one consecutive term, a reduction in the presidential term (to four years), the abolition of the presidential electoral college, the delegation of some presidential powers to a Chief of Cabinet, an increase in the number of seats in the Senado (Senate) and a reduction in the length of the mandate of all senators, a reform of the procedure for judicial appointments, the removal of religious stipulations from the terms of eligibility for presidential candidates, and the abolition of the President's power to appoint the mayor of the federal capital. The need for constitutional reform was approved by the Congress in December. Following the convening of a Constituent Assembly in May 1994, a new Constitution was promulgated in August.

Menem's campaign for re-election in 1995 concentrated on the economic success of his previous administration and, despite the increasingly precarious condition of the economy, he secured 50% of the votes at the presidential election in May, thereby avoiding a second ballot. José Octavio Bordón, the candidate of the Frente del País Solidario (Frepaso—a centre-left alliance of socialist, communist, Christian Democrat and dissident Peronist groups), was second with 29% of the votes, ahead of the UCR candidate, Horacio Massaccesi, who received 17%. However, Frepaso won the largest share of the 130 contested seats in the Chamber of Deputies at concurrent legislative elections and significantly increased its representation in the Senate (as did the Peronists), largely at the expense of the UCR.

Meanwhile, the Government's ongoing programme of economic austerity provoked violent opposition, particularly from the public sector. In March 1995 the Government presented an economic consolidation programme aimed at protecting the Argentine currency against devaluation and supporting the ailing banking sector, which had been adversely affected by the financial crisis in Mexico in late 1994.

In 1996 public disaffection with the Government was reflected in the PJ's poor performance in the first direct elections for the Head of Government of the Autonomous City of Buenos Aires, as well as in concurrent elections to a Constituent Assembly charged with drafting a constitution for the capital. In July Cavallo was dismissed as Minister of the Economy following months of bitter dispute with the President and other cabinet members. Roque Fernández, hitherto President of the Central Bank, assumed the economy portfolio. Cavallo became increasingly vociferous in his attacks against the integrity of certain cabinet members.

Industrial and social unrest increased in 1996–97, owing to discontent with proposed labour reforms, as well as reductions in public expenditure and high levels of unemployment. General strikes, organized by the Confederación General de Trabajo (CGT), the Central de los Trabajadores Argentinos (CTA) and the Movimiento de Trabajadores Argentinos (MTA), received widespread support in August and September 1996. In October relations between the Government and the trade unions deteriorated following the submission to the Congress of controversial labour reform legislation. In December Menem introduced part of the reforms by decree, although a court declared the decrees to be unconstitutional in the following month. In May 1997 police clashed with thousands of anti-Government demonstrators who had occupied government buildings and blockaded roads and bridges. In July some 30,000 people demonstrated in the capital to protest at the high level of unemployment, then estimated at more than 17%. A general strike in August, organized by the MTA and the CTA, was only partially observed, however.

At the mid-term congressional elections in October 1997 the UCR and Frepaso (united in the Alianza por el Trabajo, la Justicia y la Educación—ATJE) increased their representation while the PJ lost its overall majority in the Chamber of Deputies.

Economic crisis

A presidential election was held on 24 October 1999. The ATJE candidate, Fernando de la Rúa, ended 10 years of Peronist rule, winning 49% of the votes cast. The ATJE also performed well in concurrent congressional elections. De la Rúa took office as President on 10 December. Later that month the National Congress approved an austerity budget that reduced public expenditure by US $1,400m., as well as a major tax-reform programme and a federal revenue-sharing scheme.

In April 2000 the Senate approved a controversial revision of employment law. The legislation led to mass demonstrations by public sector workers and, subsequently, to two 24-hour national strikes organized by the CGT. Later that year the Government came under intense pressure after it was alleged that some senators had received bribes from government officials to approve the employment legislation. In September the Senate voted to end the immunity that protected law-makers, judges and government ministers from criminal investigation in order to allow an inquiry into the corruption allegations. The political crisis intensified on 6 October when Carlos Alvarez resigned as Vice-President, one day after a cabinet reorganization in which two ministers implicated in the bribery scandal were not removed. One of these, former labour minister Alberto Flamarique, who was appointed presidential Chief of Staff in the reshuffle, resigned later the same day. The other, Fernando de Santibáñez, head of the state intelligence service, resigned in late October. Earlier that month the President of the Senate, José Genoud, also resigned after he too was implicated in the bribery allegations. (In August 2012 de la Rúa went on trial accused of bribing the senators in 2000; he denied the charges, claiming that they were politically motivated.)

The economic situation continued to deteriorate in 2000–01. In November 2000 thousands of unemployed workers blocked roads throughout the country in protest at the worsening economic conditions and a 36-hour national strike was organized in response to the Government's proposed introduction of an IMF-backed economic recovery package that included a five-year freeze on federal and provincial spending, a reform of the pension system and an increase in the female retirement age. In December, following the approval of the reforms by the Congress, the IMF agreed a package, worth an estimated US $20,000m., to meet Argentina's external debt obligations for 2001.

The resignation of the Minister of the Economy, José Luis Machinea, precipitated another political crisis in March 2001. The announcement by his successor, Ricardo López Murphy, of major reductions in public expenditure resulted in several cabinet resignations. As a consequence, in late March a second reshuffle occurred, in which Domingo Cavallo was reappointed

Minister of the Economy. In June Cavallo announced a series of measures designed to ease the country's financial situation. The most controversial of these was the introduction of a complex trade tariff system that created multiple exchange rates (based on the average of a euro and a US dollar); this was, in effect, a devaluation of the peso for external trade, although the dollar peg remained in operation for domestic transactions. As Argentina's debt crisis intensified and fears of a default increased, a further emergency package, the seventh in 19 months, was implemented in July. A policy of 'zero deficit' was announced, whereby neither the federal Government nor any province would be allowed to spend more than it collected in taxes. In order to achieve this, state salaries and pensions were to be reduced by 13%. Despite mass protests and a one-day national strike, the measures were approved by the Congress at the end of July. In the legislative elections of October 2001 the PJ won control of the Chamber of Deputies and increased its majority in the Senate.

In December 2001, as the economic situation deteriorated and the possibility of a default on the country's debt increased considerably, owing to the IMF's refusal to disburse more funds to Argentina, the Government introduced restrictions on bank account withdrawals and appropriated private pension funds. These measures provoked two days of rioting and demonstrations nationwide, in which at least 27 people died. On 20 December Cavallo resigned as Minister of the Economy and de la Rúa stepped down as President. Because Alvarez had resigned as Vice-President in the previous year, the newly appointed head of the Senate, Ramón Puerta, became acting President, but was succeeded two days later by the Peronist Adolfo Rodríguez Saá. He, in turn, resigned one week later after protests against his proposed economic reforms (including the introduction of a new currency and the suspension of debt repayments) resulted in further unrest. (Due to Puerta's resignation as President of the Senate, Eduardo Camaño, the head of the Chamber of Deputies, briefly became acting President.) On 1 January 2002 the former Peronist presidential candidate and recently elected senator for the Province of Buenos Aires, Eduardo Alberto Duhalde, was elected President by the Congress. On 3 January Argentina officially defaulted on its loan repayments, reportedly the largest ever debt default, and three days later the Senate authorized the Government to set the exchange rate, thus officially ending the 10-year-old parity between the US dollar and the peso. In February the Government initiated the compulsory conversion to pesos of US dollar bank deposits in order to prevent capital flight. This process of 'pesofication' led to many lawsuits being brought by depositors against financial institutions in an attempt to recover their losses. However, in October 2004 the Supreme Court ruled that the 'pesofication' was not unconstitutional.

Nevertheless, in February 2002 the Supreme Court ruled that the restrictions imposed on bank withdrawals (the *corralito*) were unconstitutional. In order to forestall the complete collapse of the financial system, the Government imposed a six-month ban on legal challenges to the remainder of the bank withdrawal regime. Numerous bank holidays were also decreed to prevent another run on the banks and a further devaluation of the currency. Later that month the Government signed a new tax-sharing pact with the provincial Governors, linking the monthly amount distributed to the provinces to tax collections, as recommended by the IMF. However, in April Jorge Remes Lenicov resigned as Minister of the Economy following the Senate's refusal to support an emergency plan to exchange frozen bank deposits for government bonds. He was replaced by Roberto Lavagna.

The economy achieved mixed progress during 2002. While the number of deposits in Argentine banks increased, Argentina still defaulted on a US $805m. loan instalment to the World Bank in November, thus jeopardizing the country's last remaining source of external finance. Public anger against the Government and at the state of the economy did not subside.

Kirchnerismo

At a presidential election on 27 April 2003 Menem, one of three Peronist candidates, obtained the largest share of the popular vote, with 24%, followed by Néstor Carlos Kirchner (representing the Frente para la Victoria—FPV—faction of the PJ), with 22%. Ricardo López Murphy of the centre-right Movimiento Federal para Recrear el Crecimiento alliance came third, with 16% of the ballot. Faced with the very likely possibility of a decisive protest vote against him, Menem withdrew his candidacy from a planned run-off ballot. Kirchner was thus elected by default. He was sworn in as President on 25 May.

Upon taking office, the new President sought to strengthen his relatively weak popular mandate. Having pledged to put the needs of the Argentine people before the demands of the IMF, Kirchner immediately announced a series of popular measures, including the replacement of several high-ranking military and police commanders, the opening of an investigation into allegedly corrupt practices by several Supreme Court Justices (which prompted the resignation of the President of the Supreme Court in June) and increases in pensions and minimum wages. He also announced a programme of investment in infrastructure, particularly housing, intended to lower the high unemployment rate.

President Kirchner's increasing popularity translated into significant gains for the PJ in the legislative elections that were held during the latter half of 2003, which resulted in a working majority for the PJ and its allies in both the Chamber of Deputies and the Senate. Moreover, the corruption inquiry within the Supreme Court resulted in the removal of four Justices considered to be hostile to Kirchner. Nevertheless, frequent demonstrations against high levels of crime and unemployment continued to cause disruption. Loosely organized groups of protesters, known as *piqueteros*, became increasingly radical, erecting roadblocks and occupying both private and public institutions to demand jobs, redistribution of money and an end to a perceived culture of impunity.

At mid-term elections to the Congress, held in October 2005, President Kirchner's FPV faction of the PJ secured a resounding victory over the faction of the party led by former President Duhalde, Peronismo Federal. Following the ballot, the FPV controlled 118 of the 257 seats in the Chamber of Deputies, compared with 31 held by Peronismo Federal, while the PJ bloc as a whole had 33 of the 72 senatorial seats. The UCR controlled 36 seats in the lower house and 11 in the Senate. President Kirchner effected a major cabinet reorganization in November. Notably, Lavagna resigned as Minister of Economy and Production and was replaced by Felisa Miceli.

The Government of Cristina Fernández de Kirchner

Factional division in both the PJ and the UCR characterized the elections of October 2007. Following several months of speculation concerning President Kirchner's intention to seek re-election, in July it was announced that his wife, Cristina Elisabet Fernández de Kirchner, a senator for the Province of Buenos Aires, would instead stand as the FPV presidential candidate. Her bid was supported by a significant section of the UCR, known as the 'K Radicals', whereas another faction of that party—the so-called 'L Radicals'—endorsed the candidacy of Lavagna, who also received support from Peronists opposed to President Kirchner's policies. Alberto Rodríguez Saá (brother of Adolfo Rodríguez Saá) entered the contest representing another anti-Kirchner faction of the PJ. Fernández's campaign was damaged to some extent by a number of allegations of corruption that affected the Government in 2007, including Miceli's resignation as Minister of Economy and Production in July following judicial investigations into the discovery of a large quantity of cash in her office. (Miceli was replaced by Miguel Peirano, and was sentenced to four years' imprisonment in December 2012.) In August 2007 a further scandal surrounded the discovery of nearly US $800,000 in cash in the suitcase of Guido Antonini Wilson, a Venezuelan businessman who was travelling from Venezuela to Argentina on an aircraft chartered by a state-owned company. Opposition parties accused the Government of illegally importing the money in order to fund Fernández's election campaign.

In spite of these obstacles, Fernández won a decisive victory in the presidential election held on 28 October 2007, securing 41.8% of the votes cast. No candidate succeeded in unifying the opposition: Elisa Carrió of the Afirmación para una República Igualitaria, who stood as part of the Coalición Cívica alliance, obtained 21.3% of the vote, while Lavagna received 15.6% of votes cast and Rodríguez Saá took just 7.1%. Fernández's margin of victory was thus considerably in excess of the 10 percentage points below which a run-off ballot would have been required. The participation rate was 76.2%. Following the concurrent partial elections to the Congress, the FPV legislative bloc emerged with 120 seats in the Chamber of Deputies and 42 seats in the Senate, thereby gaining an overall majority in the upper chamber, while the UCR's representation was reduced to 24 and eight seats, respectively. President Fernández was sworn in on 10 December. Her Cabinet retained seven members of the outgoing administration.

In March 2008 the four main agricultural unions began strike action in protest at sharp increases in tariffs on the export of soybeans, sunflower products and other foodstuffs. Despite causing serious food shortages, the protests attracted widespread popular support. The Government defended the tax rises as necessary to control inflation resulting from substantial rises in grain prices on international markets, as well as to guarantee domestic supplies. A 30-day truce was called by the unions in April to allow for negotiations with the Government; however, strikes resumed in May after talks failed. In response to the public exhortation of Vice-President Julio César Cleto Cobos, President Fernández agreed to allow the Congress to ratify the tariff increases in June. (The farmers' fourth and final strike ended two days later.) The ensuing draft legislation was narrowly approved by the Chamber of Deputies, but was defeated in the Senate in mid-July by the casting vote of Cobos, the chamber's President. The decree that had introduced the tariff increases was subsequently revoked. The Government's defeat in the legislature, which occurred despite the FPV's dominance of both chambers, resulted in the resignation of the Cabinet Chief, Alberto Fernández. He was replaced by Sergio Massa.

In October 2008 the Government announced plans to assume state control of Argentina's 10 private pension funds (Administradoras de Fondos de Jubilaciones y Pensiones—AFJPs). President Fernández declared that nationalization would protect workers' investments from the decline in the value of the funds caused by turmoil in worldwide financial markets, but the opposition claimed that the Government intended to use the AFJPs' assets (worth some US $30,000m.) to meet its rising debt-servicing obligations. None the less, the take-over received congressional approval in November and took effect in January 2009.

The Government performed badly in mid-term congressional elections held in June 2009 (four months early), losing its majority in both legislative houses. Following the ballot, the FPV's representation was reduced from 116 to 87 in the 257-seat lower house and from 38 to 30 in the Senate. Notably, the list of candidates headed by former President Kirchner in the Province of Buenos Aires secured fewer seats in the Chamber of Deputies than that led by Francisco de Narváez of the centre-right Unión PRO alliance; immediately after the ballot Kirchner resigned as President of the PJ (although the party leadership committee voted to reject his resignation in November, and he reassumed the PJ presidency in March 2010). Nevertheless, the fragmented nature of the opposition meant that the FPV remained the largest congressional bloc. The UCR held 43 of the seats in the Chamber of Deputies, although it was allied to the Partido Socialista (PS) and the Coalición Cívica, among others, bringing its total support to around 70. The Unión PRO, comprising the Propuesta Republicana (PRO) and various dissident Peronist factions, could count on the support of some 47 deputies in the lower house.

Following the elections, both Carlos Fernández, the Minister of Economy and Public Finance, and Cabinet Chief Massa resigned. Amado Boudou, who had presided over the nationalization of the AFJPs in 2008, was appointed to the public finance ministry, while Aníbal Domingo Fernández, hitherto justice and security minister, became Cabinet Chief. In August 2009 the Congress approved a further year's extension to the law allowing certain legislative powers to be delegated to the executive. The original legislation, which notably allowed the Government to set the agricultural export tariffs, the raising of which had prompted the ongoing dispute with the farming unions, had been approved during the 2001–02 financial crisis. In the same month Fernández used her presidential veto to overturn another law temporarily suspending grain export duties and granting emergency aid to the agricultural sector. The Government claimed that income from the tariffs would fund anti-poverty initiatives.

The Government succeeded in gaining legislative approval for a controversial reform of the media in October 2009. The new law provided for a reduction in the number of television or radio licences that broadcasting companies were allowed to own, from 24 to 10, and the establishment of a federal body to oversee the broadcast media. Critics of the legislation claimed that it gave the Government too much control over the sector. In December the Government also secured congressional approval for major political reforms, forcing political parties to hold simultaneous open primaries to select their presidential candidates, banning the private financing of radio and television advertising in electoral campaigns, reducing the length of political campaigns and establishing a minimum level of membership for parties. A legal challenge against the media law, initiated by the Clarín media group, had some success in October 2010, when the Supreme Court upheld an earlier ruling by a lower court that, pending a final verdict on the constitutionality of the legislation, suspended the requirement that companies with more than 10 broadcast licences should sell off their excess operations within one year of the law's enactment. In May 2012 the Supreme Court ruled that the injunction suspending this requirement would expire on 7 December. On 6 December, however, with the Government preparing to auction off the excess licences of companies that had not yet voluntarily submitted divestiture plans, a court granted a last-minute extension of the injunction preventing the full enforcement of the media law, pending the still-awaited judgment on its constitutionality. A week later Clarín's legal challenge against the legislation was rejected, but the group lodged an appeal against this verdict; the injunction was to remain in force until this appeal had been considered. Finally, on 29 October 2013, the Supreme Court ruled that all clauses of the legislation were constitutional and should come into effect immediately. Clarín acknowledged the ruling and on 4 November announced plans to break up the company into six separate units, although its directors pledged to pursue international legal avenues to overturn the decision.

A presidential decree providing for the use of some US $6,600m. of central bank reserves to guarantee debt payments provoked tensions between the Government and other state institutions in early 2010. Opposition figures maintained that the use of the reserves required congressional authorization, while the refusal of the Governor of the Central Bank, Martín Redrado, to disburse the funds led to his dismissal by President Fernández on 7 January. Redrado insisted that only the legislature was empowered to remove him from office, a stance supported on the following day by a federal court judge, who reinstated Redrado to his post and suspended the decree on the proposed use of federal reserves. However, Redrado resigned in late January, a few days before a specially convened congressional commission voted in support of his dismissal. The congressional commission also recommended the continued suspension of the decree on the use of the reserves, pending the consideration of its legitimacy by the Congress. When the Congress returned from recess in March, however, Fernández announced the annulment of this decree and the introduction of two new ones establishing funds to which central bank reserves would be transferred to service debt payments to multilateral lending institutions and to repay private creditors. Subsequent opposition attempts to challenge the new decrees ultimately failed.

Héctor Timerman, ambassador to the USA, was appointed as Minister of Foreign Affairs, International Trade and Worship in June 2010, following the resignation of the incumbent Jorge Taiana, reportedly over policy differences and alleged leaks to the media regarding efforts to resolve the pulp mill dispute between Argentina and Uruguay (see Foreign Affairs). In December the illegal occupation of land in the Parque Indoamericano, in the south of Buenos Aires, by thousands of people demanding housing and social assistance led to violence in which at least three squatters were killed. A new Ministry of Security was created in response to the unrest. Nilda Garré, hitherto Minister of Defence, was appointed as Minister of Security, being replaced at the Ministry of Defence by Arturo Puricelli. The Parque Indoamericano was eventually cleared after the federal and city Governments agreed to fund a joint housing plan. Members of the four main agricultural unions halted the sale of wheat and other cereals for one week in January 2011 in a renewed protest against the system of export tariffs and quotas (see above), although the strike action received less support than in 2008.

Fernández's second term

Speculation regarding the presidential election due in October 2011 intensified following the sudden death, in October 2010, of former President Kirchner, who had been widely expected to be the FPV candidate. President Fernández did not confirm her intention to seek re-election until a few days before the deadline for registration in June 2011, her popularity having risen in the preceding months, according to opinion polls, amid public sympathy following her husband's death and robust economic growth. Opposition to Fernández was largely divided. The UCR, the PS and the Coalición Cívica did not renew their alliance from the 2009 mid-term elections, the first two instead joining with more minor parties to form new coalitions, namely the

Unión para el Desarrollo Social (Udeso) and the Frente Amplio Progresista (FAP). Ricardo Alfonsín, son of former President Alfonsín, was the candidate of the UCR-led Udeso, while Hermes Binner, the outgoing Governor of Santa Fe, represented the centre-left FAP, and Elisa Carrió, the leader of the Coalición Cívica, was to stand for a third time. Following a failed attempt by the Peronismo Federal faction of the PJ to select a presidential candidate in a primary election conducted earlier in the year, the two main challengers for the nomination, former President Duhalde and Alberto Rodríguez Saá, the outgoing Governor of San Luis, opted to contest the presidency separately, for two newly formed Peronist coalitions: the Frente Popular and the Alianza Compromiso Federal, respectively.

In accordance with the political reforms adopted in December 2009, mandatory primary elections to select presidential candidates took place on 14 August 2011. However, with all political parties and alliances having chosen to field single candidates, the poll was effectively a dry run for the actual contest in October. Of the 10 candidates in the primary election, Fernández received by far the strongest support, obtaining 50.2% of the vote nationwide and winning in every province with the exception of San Luis, where Governor Rodríguez Saá was favoured. Rodríguez Saá was placed fifth overall, however, with 8.2% of the vote, after Alfonsín (12.2%), Duhalde (12.1%) and Binner (10.2%). Only two other candidates exceeded the 1.5% share of the vote required to proceed to the general election on 23 October: Carrió and Jorge Altamira, representing the Alianza Frente de Izquierda y de los Trabajadores.

As expected, Fernández achieved an outright and convincing victory in the presidential election on 23 October 2011, securing re-election with 54.0% of the valid votes cast, the most emphatic win since the return to civilian rule in 1983. The opposition vote remained split, although Binner improved on his performance in the primary elections, to come second with 16.9% of the vote, followed by Alfonsín, with 11.2%, Rodríguez Saá, with 8.0%, and Duhalde, with 5.9%. A participation rate of 78.9% was recorded. In addition to achieving a third consecutive term in presidential office for the PJ, the FPV and its allies also regained control of both legislative chambers in the concurrent partial congressional elections, increasing their combined representation to some 134 seats in the Chamber of Deputies (of which the FPV itself held 115) and to 38 seats in the Senate. The UCR retained its position as the largest opposition party, with 38 and 14 seats in the lower and upper chambers, respectively.

President Fernández was sworn in to serve her second term of office on 10 December 2011. Her Cabinet was largely unchanged, only the three ministers who had left office to contest seats in the general election in October being replaced. Hernán Lorenzino, who as Secretary of Finance had managed the second phase of negotiations to restructure Argentina's debt in 2009–10, succeeded Amado Boudou, the new Vice-President, as Minister of Economy and Public Finance.

With its congressional majority restored, the Government moved swiftly to secure approval of several bills in a number of special legislative sessions in December 2011. Most controversial was legislation that, deeming the production, sale and distribution of newsprint to be of national interest, granted the Government the power to determine the price of newsprint and the operating capacity of the country's sole newsprint producer, Papel Prensa. The Clarín and La Nación media groups, which together owned a majority stake in Papel Prensa, strongly opposed the new law, which would allow the Government to seize control of the company if it failed to meet production targets. Also provoking criticism was an anti-terrorism law that some claimed could be used to prosecute participants in social protests and anti-Government demonstrations, for example, owing to its ambiguity. Meanwhile, tensions between the Government and trade union leaders, particularly Hugo Moyano, the Secretary-General of the CGT and a former ally of Presidents Kirchner and Fernández, mounted, as the Government sought to reduce state subsidies for utilities and other services and to curb wage rises, despite high inflation (this issue being further complicated by the wide disparity between official inflation figures and private estimates). Moyano resigned his posts in the PJ, as a national Vice-President and as President of the Buenos Aires branch of the party, in December, and the CGT joined the opposition in condemning the repression by police of protests against open-pit mining in Catamarca province in February 2012, urging the authorities to employ dialogue to resolve social disputes.

The Secretary of Transport, Juan Pablo Schiavi, resigned in March 2012, citing ill health, although he had been criticized in the aftermath of a train crash in Buenos Aires two weeks earlier that had killed 51 people. Alejandro Ramos replaced Schiavi, and in June ministerial responsibility for the transport sector was transferred from Julio de Vido, the long-standing Minister of Federal Planning, Public Investment and Services, to the Minister of the Interior, Aníbal Randazzo, prompting speculation that the latter was being considered as a possible presidential candidate in the 2015 election. The Government was further damaged in May 2012, when a criminal investigation was initiated into corruption allegations against Vice-President Boudou, who was accused of having assisted a printing company to avoid bankruptcy in 2010 and subsequently to secure government contracts, including one to print the Argentine currency. Formal charges were brought against Boudou in February 2014.

Only four days after Fernández's re-election in October 2011, the Government implemented a series of economic measures aimed at stabilizing the exchange rate of the peso and at curbing capital flight, amid rising demand for US dollars resulting from fears of a devaluation of the national currency (see Economic Affairs). However, the Government's actions prompted concerns regarding the country's balance of payments position, and restrictions on imports followed in early 2012, leading to tensions with trading partners (see Foreign Affairs).

A deceleration in the rate of economic growth and the introduction of further measures aimed at stemming capital flight, notably increased restrictions on the purchase of US dollars, contributed to a continued decline in the Fernández administration's poll ratings in 2012. At the end of June the CGT organized a 24-hour strike in support of demands for an increase in the threshold for income tax payments, amid continued high inflation (estimated at more than 20% by private agencies, compared with an official rate of some 10%). Fiscal difficulties provoked a dispute between the federal Government and the administration of the Province of Buenos Aires that month, when Fernández only partially acceded to a request from the provincial Governor, the PJ's Daniel Scioli, for additional funds to finance mid-year bonuses to public sector workers. In response, Scioli announced major austerity measures in the province and a plan to pay the bonuses in four instalments, prompting several provincial trade union branches to undertake strike action. In May Scioli, who had served as Kirchner's Vice-President, had confirmed his ambition to contest the presidential election due in 2015, with the proviso that he would not stand against Fernández if she chose to seek re-election. A third consecutive mandate for Fernández would necessitate constitutional reform, which was reportedly being mooted by her supporters within the FPV. However, the establishment of a constituent assembly to effect such change would require the approval of a two-thirds' majority in both chambers of the Congress, the achievement of which would depend on a strong performance by the FPV at the mid-term congressional elections due to be conducted in October 2013. Meanwhile, the FPV Governor of the Province of Santa Cruz, Daniel Peralta, also came into conflict with the federal Government over his economic and financial plans, accusing the Fernández administration of attempting to remove him from office in September 2012.

A series of nationwide anti-Government protests took place on 13 September 2012. Organized by a group of civil society organizations and private citizens rather than by the political opposition, the demonstrations were the largest to be held since the President took office in 2007, attended by more than 200,000 people, who expressed discontent at rising inflation, crime levels, the restrictions on the purchase of US dollars and public corruption, among other issues. The Government also came under external pressure that month, when the IMF criticized Argentina for making insufficient progress in improving the accuracy of its official inflation and growth figures. In early October a decree amending pay scales for the paramilitary security forces, which effectively entailed substantial salary reductions, prompted major protests by members of the forces, which resulted in the reversal of the measure and the resignation of the heads of the national gendarmerie and the naval prefecture. The Chief of Staff of the Navy, Adm. Carlos Alberto Paz, was also forced to leave office in October, following the detention of the naval vessel *Libertad* while on a routine visit to Ghana (see Foreign Affairs).

At the end of October 2012 the Congress approved legislation lowering the voting age from 18 to 16 with the stated aim of expanding democratic rights; however, critics claimed that the move was an attempt to improve the ruling party's performance at the 2013 mid-term elections, as President Fernández had achieved strong support among young people in previous votes. Further major anti-Government protests took place nationwide on 8 November, with participation exceeding that of the September demonstrations. Again the demands of the protesters were wide-ranging, but the Government claimed that they were mainly middle-class and upper-class citizens who opposed policies supporting the poor. A 24-hour general strike organized by the CGT and the CTA followed on 20 November, which was widely observed, severely disrupting economic activity in much of the country, as some 160 roadblocks were reportedly erected. In late December a wave of looting in several towns and cities resulted in four deaths and at least 500 arrests.

A further nationwide anti-Government demonstration took place on 18 April 2013, this time mainly in protest at the Government's proposed reforms to the judiciary, five out of six of which had received senate approval one day earlier. Opponents of the legislation, which, *inter alia*, would introduce elections to the council of magistrates that appoints judges, accused President Fernández of attempting to politicize the judiciary. In mid-June the Supreme Court ruled, by a majority of six to one, that the reforms were unconstitutional.

In late May 2013 Arturo Puricelli replaced Nilda Garré as the Minister of Security. Puricelli was succeeded by Agustín Rossi as Minister of Defence.

Recent developments: the 2013 mid-term elections

In advance of mid-term congressional elections that were scheduled to be held in October 2013, on 11 August all political parties held 'open, simultaneous and obligatory' primary elections to select their candidates for legislative seats. Although FPV candidates attracted about 26.0% of the votes cast nationwide, this was the lowest percentage polled by the ruling party since 2003. The dissident Peronist candidate Sergio Massa, a former Cabinet Chief under President Fernández, who left the FPV to form his own party, Frente Renovador (FR), in 2013, performed well in the densely populated province of Buenos Aires (home to 37% of the national electorate), defeating rival FPV candidates. Dissident Peronist candidates also secured candidacies in the second most highly populated province, Córdoba, while in the next three most populous provinces—Santa Fe, Buenos Aires City and Mendoza—non-FPV left-allied parties emerged victorious. The prospect of the FPV gaining enough seats in the legislative elections to form a two-thirds' majority—necessary to attempt to revise the Constitution to allow Fernández to seek a third term in office in 2015—seemed highly unlikely. Instead, in the weeks preceding the vote on 27 October, the FPV and its allies concentrated on retaining a simple majority in both houses in order to facilitate its legislative agenda. The FPV suffered a further setback three weeks before the elections proper, when on 5 October Fernández was diagnosed with a subdural haematoma and forced to take 30 days' medical leave. Then, on 19 October, a train crash in Buenos Aires, injuring 99 commuters, again highlighted the Government's failure to improve rail safety (following the March 2012 train crash at the same station that had killed 51 people). The Minister of the Interior and Transport, Aníbal Randazzo, responded by nationalizing the Sarmiento railway line.

One-half of the lower house's 257 seats and one-third (24) of the Senate's seats were contested on 27 October 2013. As expected, the FPV and its allies failed to secure a large enough majority in either house to make constitutional amendments. However, the ruling faction did increase its majority in the Chamber of Deputies to 132 (from 129 before the election) and although its senatorial representation fell by three seats, the FPV and its allies still held 40 of the 72 seats. The UCR, allied with the FAP and other centre-left partners, held 54 seats in the Chamber of Deputies and 19 seats in the Senate following the elections. The dissident Peronist FR again performed well in the electorally important Buenos Aires province, attracting almost 44% of all votes cast there, well ahead of the FPV. Although the support did not translate into congressional seats for the Frente (dissident Peronist factions held 37 lower house seats and seven upper house seats), it left its leader Sergio Massa well-placed for the Peronist presidential nomination in 2015.

President Fernández returned from medical leave on 18 November 2013 and immediately implemented a reallocation of cabinet portfolios. Jorge Capitanich, who had secured re-election to the governorship of Chaco in October, was appointed Cabinet Chief, replacing Juan Abal Medina. Axel Kicillof, hitherto a deputy economy minister, was promoted to Minister of Economy and Public Finance, while his predecessor, Hernán Lorenzino, was appointed head of a team on foreign debt negotiations. Notably, Guillermo Moreno, the secretary for domestic trade and communications within the economy ministry since 2005, resigned. Moreno was believed to have been responsible for the Government's interventionist policies, including the enforcement of price controls. The Minister of Agriculture, Livestock and Fisheries, Norberto Yahuar, was dismissed and replaced by Carlos Casamiquela. Fernández also sacked the head of the central bank, Mercedes Marco del Pont, appointing Juan Carlos Fábrega in her stead. In December the President made a further cabinet change, dismissing Arturo Puricelli as Minister of Security and replacing him with María Cecilia Rodríguez.

Rioting and looting broke out in Córdoba on 3 December 2013 following an announcement that the provincial police had gone on strike. The police force there were demanding a 52% increase in wages, necessary, it was argued, to combat spiralling inflation (although the official inflation rate stood at 9.4% in November, the real rate was estimated to be three times as much). The violence was contained after the Governor of Córdoba, José de la Sota, agreed to a 33% increase in police salaries, and the strike was ended. The federal Government distanced itself from the social unrest, with Cabinet Chief Jorge Capitanich insisting it was a provincial matter; however, looting occurred in seven other provinces in the days that followed, and some 10,000 federal troops were deployed across the country in anticipation of further violence.

Further strains on the economy became evident in January 2014 after the Government eased its strict controls on foreign exchange, in an attempt to increase foreign reserves, following a fall in the value of the peso. Henceforth, citizens meeting certain criteria would be allowed to purchase up to US $2,000 per month, and deposit the funds in Argentine banks, rather than buying them on the 'black' market and storing them in foreign accounts or at home, as was common practice. The Government's economic difficulties worsened in March when teachers' unions across the country began industrial action in support of salary increases of at least 30%. The teachers returned to work at the end of the month after an agreement on pay was reached, but other industrial sectors were expected to demand similar wage rises in the face of continuing high inflation rates.

Human Rights and the 'Dirty War'

Despite public expressions of regret (in 1995 and 2004) by the heads of the navy, the army and the air force for crimes committed by the armed forces during 1976–83, issues concerning the 'dirty war' remained politically sensitive in the early 21st century. In 2003 President Kirchner revoked a decree that had prevented the extradition of Argentine citizens suspected of human rights violations. Courts in Spain, France, Germany and Sweden all subsequently sought the extradition of former Argentine military personnel for crimes committed against their citizens. Alfredo Astiz, a former naval captain, was the subject of extradition requests by the Italian, French and Swedish Governments. In 2010 an Argentine court refused a French extradition request for Astiz, who was standing trial in Buenos Aires (see below). (In 1990 Astiz had been convicted in France, *in absentia*, and sentenced to life imprisonment for murder, and in 2007 he was convicted of the same crime in an Italian court.) In 2001 former President Videla was ordered to stand trial for the abduction of 72 foreigners under 'Plan Condor', an alleged scheme among right-wing dictators in Argentina, Chile, Uruguay and Bolivia to eradicate leftist political opponents living in exile during the 1970s. In 2002 former dictator Gen. Galtieri was arrested, along with at least 30 others, on charges relating to the torture and murder of 20 members of the left-wing Montoneros guerrilla group in 1980. He remained under house arrest until his death in January 2003.

In August 2003 the Senate approved legislation that would allow the annulment of the Punto Final and Obediencia Debida laws (adopted in 1986 and 1987, respectively), and ratified a UN Convention that ostensibly removed all constitutional limitations on human rights prosecutions. Both laws were repealed by the Supreme Court in June 2005.

In 2005 Adolfo Scilingo, a former military official, was convicted in Spain of crimes against humanity during the 'dirty war'; he was sentenced to 640 years' imprisonment. In 2006 Miguel Etchecolatz, a former senior police officer, was sentenced to life imprisonment after being convicted of murder, torture and kidnapping during the 'dirty war'; he received an additional life sentence in December 2012. In April 2010 former President Bignone and six other former officials were convicted of charges related to the abduction, torture and killing of 56 government opponents during the 'dirty war'; Bignone was sentenced to 25 years' imprisonment, receiving a life sentence for murder in a separate case in 2011. In December 2010, moreover, Videla and several co-defendants received life sentences for their involvement in the murder in 1976 of 31 political prisoners. In October 2011, following a 22-month trial, Alfredo Astiz was among 12 former military officials sentenced to life imprisonment after being found guilty of perpetrating torture and forced disappearance at a naval school (the Escuela de Mecánica de la Armada—ESMA) that was used as a secret detention facility during the dictatorship. Videla and Bignone were further convicted in July 2012 on charges related to the abduction and illegal adoption of 34 children whose parents had died or disappeared during the dictatorship, being sentenced to additional prison terms of 50 years and 15 years, respectively; seven other defendants were also found guilty. At least 400 infants born in special holding centres during the 'dirty war' were believed to have been abducted by the military and police, and in November 2009 the Congress had approved a law compelling those thought to have been illegally adopted to undergo DNA tests in order to establish their true parentage. The largest trial to date of crimes committed during the 'dirty war' commenced in November 2012, with 68 former officials, including Astiz, charged with nearly 800 counts of kidnapping, torture and murder associated with the ESMA detention centre. In the following month Jaime Smart, a former interior minister for Buenos Aires province, became the first civilian to be sentenced for crimes against humanity perpetrated during the 1976–83 period, receiving a life sentence; 22 other defendants were also convicted in the trial, including Etchecolatz (see above). In September 2013 Chile extradited Otilo Romano, a former judge accused of human rights violations during the military regime.

Foreign Affairs

Regional relations

Argentina and Chile reached a settlement in 1991 regarding claims to territory in the Antarctic region; however, the sovereignty of the territory remained under dispute, necessitating the signing of an additional protocol in 1996. In 1998 the Presidents of the two countries signed a new agreement on the border demarcation of the contested 'continental glaciers' territory in the Antarctic region (despite the 1991 treaty). In February 1999 President Menem and his Chilean counterpart signed a significant defence agreement and issued a joint declaration on both countries' commitment to the consolidation of their friendship. Relations between the two countries were strained in 2004, however, following President Kirchner's decision to reduce exports of gas to Chile by some 25% in order to meet a shortfall in stocks for domestic consumption. Following the inauguration of Michelle Bachelet as Chilean President in 2006, a bilateral group was established to resolve any future disagreements over energy matters. Tensions arose in August 2013 after LAN Argentina, a subsidiary of the Chilean carrier LAN Airlines, was ordered to leave Aeroparque Jorge Newbery airport in Buenos Aires. Although the eviction was overturned by a court, the move was interpreted by many as a government attempt to reduce competition to benefit the state carrier Aerolíneas Argentinas.

Argentina was a founder member of the Southern Common Market, Mercosur (Mercado Común del Sur, see p. 429), which came into effect on 1 January 1995. Mercosur, comprising Argentina, Brazil, Paraguay and Uruguay (joined by Venezuela in 2012), removed customs barriers on 80%–85% of mutually exchanged goods, and was intended to lead to the eventual introduction of a common external tariff. Following a series of trade disputes within Mercosur, particularly between Argentina and Brazil, the two largest members, a document, known as the 'Buenos Aires Consensus', was signed in 2003 by President Kirchner and his Brazilian counterpart, Lula da Silva. The agreement was to study the creation of common institutions for resolving trade disputes, in addition to the eventual establishment of a Mercosur legislature. A tribunal responsible for ruling on disputes duly commenced operations in 2004, while the Mercosur parliament, Parlasur, was inaugurated in 2007. Mercosur heads of state agreed on a new common customs code at a summit meeting held in San Juan, in August 2010. None the less, measures implemented by Argentina's Government to protect the country's own trade interests continued to provoke tension with its Mercosur partners.

From 2005 relations between Argentina and Uruguay were strained owing to the latter's decision to allow the construction of two pulp mills on the Uruguayan side of the River Uruguay by Botnia of Finland and Ence of Spain. The Argentine Government opposed the project on environmental grounds, although a World Bank study released in April 2006 concluded that the mills posed no threat to the environment. Argentina, however, demanded an independent assessment (the mills were partly financed by the World Bank) and ecological groups from Argentina erected roadblocks across bridges spanning the river. Following the failure of bilateral negotiations in April, Argentina filed a complaint with the International Court of Justice (ICJ) in The Hague, Netherlands, claiming that the mills violated the Statute of the River Uruguay signed by both countries in 1975. An initial finding by the ICJ in July 2006 dismissed Argentina's demand that the construction be halted, ruling that it would not cause irreversible damage to the environment. In September, however, the ongoing dispute prompted Ence to cancel its plans for a mill. Also in September, a three-member Mercosur arbitration panel ruled that Argentina had failed to adhere to the trade agreement's free trade clauses by not preventing the ongoing roadblocks, although it also ruled that it had not done so intentionally. A final ruling by the World Bank, stating that the project met all international environmental standards, was dismissed by Argentina in October, and prompted further roadblocks across the bridges. The inauguration of the Botnia mill in September 2007 provoked large-scale demonstrations by Argentine protesters, and the roadblocks remained in place following the start of operations at the plant in November. The ICJ issued its ruling on the dispute in April 2010, concluding that Uruguay had breached its procedural obligations under the Statute of the River Uruguay by failing to inform Argentina of its plans for the construction of the mills, but had not violated its environmental obligations. The Court rejected Argentina's request for the dismantling of the plant in operation (now owned by UPM of Finland) and for compensation for alleged damage to its economy. In July President Fernández and Uruguayan President José Mujica signed an agreement on the establishment of a bilateral scientific committee to monitor the environmental impact of all industrial and agricultural operations on the banks of the River Uruguay. A further technical agreement, on the details of the joint monitoring programme, was signed in November. At a meeting in Buenos Aires in August 2011, Fernández and Mujica signed a series of bilateral agreements aimed at strengthening relations in a number of areas, including transport infrastructure and the business sector. However, friction arose during 2012, with the Uruguayan Government notably critical of the Argentine Government's restrictions on imports, including those from Mercosur members, and of its continued apparent reluctance to proceed with a joint project to deepen the binational Martín García canal that would benefit Uruguayan ports. In October 2013 Mujica announced he had approved a request by UPM to increase production at the mill by 100,000 metric tons per year, contingent on meeting certain environmental standards. The Argentine Minister of Foreign Affairs, International Trade and Worship, Héctor Timerman, immediately declared his country's intention to refer the matter back to the ICJ. In the following month the Argentine Government imposed retaliatory restrictions on the transshipment of goods bound for Argentina via Uruguayan ports. In January 2014 both sides agreed to reopen dialogue on the dispute.

Other external relations

Full diplomatic relations were restored with the United Kingdom in February 1990. In November Argentina and the United Kingdom concluded an agreement for the joint administration of a comprehensive protection programme for the lucrative South Atlantic fishing region. The question of sovereignty over the disputed Falkland Islands was not resolved. The results of seismic investigations in 1993, which indicated rich petroleum deposits in the region, further complicated the issue. In 1998 relations with the United Kingdom were strained by the presentation of draft legislation to the Congress on the imposition of sanctions on petroleum companies and fishing vessels operating in Falkland Island waters without Argentine authorization. Although a comprehensive agreement on exploration was signed by both countries in September 1995, negotiations on fishing rights in the region remained tense. Relations between Argentina and the United Kingdom improved in 1997 when the two countries agreed to resume negotiations on a long-term fisheries accord. Moreover, in October 1998 President Menem made an official visit to the United Kingdom, during which he held talks with the British Prime Minister, Tony Blair, on a range of issues. In late 1998 the United Kingdom partially lifted its arms embargo against Argentina. In July 1999 an agreement was reached providing for an end to the ban on Argentine citizens visiting the Falkland Islands and for the restoration of air links between the islands and South America, with stop-overs in Argentina to be introduced. An understanding on co-operation against illegal fishing in the South Atlantic was reached in September.

Relations between the two countries deteriorated in March 2007, when Argentina withdrew from the 1995 agreement on petroleum exploration, and again in May 2008, when the Argentine Government accused the United Kingdom of illegitimately issuing licences for hydrocarbon exploration around the Falkland Islands. In February 2010, as oil companies prepared to commence drilling in the waters around the islands, President Fernández decreed that ships entering Argentine waters en route to the Falklands would be required to obtain prior permission. The foreign minister, Jorge Taiana, formally requested the UN to initiate negotiations with the United Kingdom over the sovereignty of the islands. The United Kingdom's announcement in October that it was to conduct military exercises, including the firing of missiles, off the coast of the Falklands provoked strong protests from the Argentine Government. Meanwhile, Argentina's Mercosur partners demonstrated their support for Argentine sovereignty over the Falklands, with Uruguay and Brazil refusing to allow British naval vessels to refuel at their ports en route to the islands in 2010 and 2011, respectively. In December 2011, moreover, Mercosur heads of state agreed to prevent vessels flying the flag of the Falkland Islands from entering their ports. Fernández reiterated demands for talks on the status of the islands, but the British Government maintained its stance that negotiations would not take place without the agreement of the inhabitants of the islands. Bilateral tensions mounted in early 2012, as the 30th anniversary of the Falklands conflict approached. The British Prime Minister, David Cameron, compared Argentina's sovereignty claims to a form of colonialism in January, prompting an angry response from Argentinian government ministers, and in February Argentina's Government made an official complaint to the UN alleging that the United Kingdom was militarizing the South Atlantic with the planned deployment of an advanced naval destroyer to the area. The British Government insisted that its defences in the region remained unchanged. However, the Argentine Government continued to exert pressure on the United Kingdom. In February the Minister of Industry, Débora Giorgi, reportedly encouraged major Argentinian companies to find other sources for goods currently imported from the United Kingdom, and in the following month Héctor Timerman, the Minister of Foreign Affairs, International Trade and Worship, threatened to take legal action against companies involved in oil exploration around the Falklands. On 2 April, the anniversary of the invasion of the Falkland Islands, several hundred protesters participated in a violent demonstration outside the British embassy in Buenos Aires. Later that month the United Kingdom halted British exports to the Argentinian armed forces with the stated aim of ensuring that such exports could not be used by Argentina in the imposition of an 'economic blockade' on the islands. In June Fernández addressed the UN Special Committee on Decolonization, reasserting Argentina's claim to sovereignty of the Falklands and again demanding talks with the United Kingdom. Furthermore, in an open letter published in British newspapers on 3 January 2013, on which date in 1833 she claimed that Argentina had been 'forcibly stripped of the Malvinas', Fernández urged Cameron to abide by a resolution adopted by the UN General Assembly in 1965 that had invited both countries to negotiate a peaceful solution to their dispute. The Argentine Government rejected the result of the referendum held in the Falkland Islands in March 2013, in which 99.8% of participating islanders voted in favour of retaining the political status quo. President Fernández insisted that the plebiscite had no legal validity, as discussions on the territory's status should involve only Argentina and the United Kingdom. In November Timerman made good his threat to prosecute any company involved in oil exploration in Falkland Island waters when the Chamber of Deputies approved legislation imposing a fine, equivalent to 1.5m. barrels of petroleum, on any company doing so without the consent of the Government. Firms would also be prohibited from operating in Argentina and their directors could face prison sentences of up to 15 years.

Argentina's increasingly nationalistic economic policies damaged its external relations during 2012, most notably with Spain and the USA, its two most important foreign investors. Tensions with Spain arose in April, when President Fernández issued a decree ordering the expropriation of 51% of the Spanish company Repsol's shares in the formerly state-run oil firm Repsol YPF, citing a lack of investment by Repsol as justification for the takeover. The Spanish Government condemned the seizure of YPF, swiftly retaliating by announcing measures to restrict imports of biodiesel from Argentina, while Repsol lodged a complaint against Argentina with the World Bank's International Centre for Settlement of Investment Disputes (ICSID), in which it demanded compensation amounting to US $10,500m. Following more than a year of stalemate, in February 2014 Repsol and the Argentine Government reached a resolution of the dispute in which Argentina would pay Repsol some $5,000m. in compensation. The agreement came after a change in stance by the Government that followed the appointment of Axel Kicillof as economy minister, and after the intervention of the Mexican state oil company Petróleos de México (PEMEX).

In May 2012 the European Union (see p. 273) complained to the World Trade Organization (WTO) that Argentina was seeking to restrict imports in contravention of international trade rules; the USA and several other countries subsequently filed similar disputes with the WTO against Argentina. In March, meanwhile, the USA had suspended Argentina from eligibility for trade benefits under its Generalized System of Preferences for developing countries, following the latter's failure to pay compensation to two US companies in compliance with rulings issued by the ICSID in 2005–06.

The seizure of the Argentine naval training ship *Libertad* when it was docked in Tema, Ghana, in October 2012 provoked a lengthy diplomatic dispute. The vessel was detained at the request of an investment company attempting to recover funds still owed to it after Argentina's 2002 debt default; although more than 90% of the defaulted debt had been restructured, several creditors were seeking the full recovery of their assets. The dispute escalated in November, when the port authorities cut off water and electricity supplies to the frigate and attempted to board it in what Argentina's Minister of Defence, Arturo Puricelli, described as a 'flagrant attack on our sovereignty'. In December the UN's International Tribunal on the Law of the Sea ordered Ghana to release the ship on the grounds that as a military vessel it was protected by diplomatic immunity. Meanwhile, however, in November a US court, ruling in a case initiated by the same company, ordered Argentina to give equal treatment to holders of both defaulted and restructured debt. Argentina appealed against the ruling, which required it to deposit US $1,330m. in an escrow account to ensure payment of creditors demanding full repayment of defaulted debt. In September 2013 both houses of Congress approved a decision by the Government to offer those creditors with whom it was yet to agree terms an unlimited 'debt swap'; nevertheless, in November the original court decision was upheld. Argentina was to appeal the decision in the US Supreme Court, with a ruling expected in mid-2014.

CONSTITUTION AND GOVERNMENT

A new Constitution was introduced in 1994. Executive power is vested in the President, who is elected directly for a four-year term, renewable only once. Legislative power is vested in the bicameral Congreso (Congress): the Cámara de Diputados (Chamber of Deputies) has 257 members, elected by universal adult suffrage for a term of four years (with approximately one-half of the seats renewable every two years); the Senado (Senate) has 72 members, with three members drawn from each of the 23 provinces and the City of Buenos Aires. Senators are elected for a six-year term (with one-third of the seats renewable every two years). Each province has its own elected Governor and legislature, concerned with all matters not delegated to the federal Government. Judicial power is exercised by the Supreme Court and all other competent tribunals.

For administrative purposes Argentina comprises 23 provinces together with the Autonomous City (formerly the Federal District) of Buenos Aires. The provinces are generally subdivided into departments and municipalities.

REGIONAL AND INTERNATIONAL CO-OPERATION

Argentina is a member of the Organization of American States (see p. 394), the Inter-American Development Bank (see p. 331), the Latin American Integration Association (ALADI, see p. 361) and of Mercosur (Mercado Común del Sur, see p. 429). In December 2004 Argentina was one of 12 countries that were signatories to the agreement, signed in Cusco, Peru, creating the South American Community of Nations (Comunidad Sudamericana de Naciones, which was renamed the Union of South American Nations—Unión de Naciones Suramericanas, UNASUR, see p. 469, in 2007), intended to promote greater regional economic integration. The country is also a member of the Community of Latin American and Caribbean States (see p. 464), which was formally inaugurated in December 2011.

Argentina was a founder member of the UN in 1945, and commenced a two-year mandate as a non-permanent member of the UN Security Council on 1 January 2013. As a contracting party to the General Agreement on Tariffs and Trade, Argentina joined the World Trade Organization (see p. 434) on its establishment in 1995. The country is a member of the Group of 15 (G15, see p. 451) and the Group of 20 (G20, see p. 456).

ECONOMIC AFFAIRS

In 2011, according to estimates by the World Bank, Argentina's gross national income (GNI), measured at average 2009–11 prices, was US $397,190m., equivalent to $9,740 per head (or $17,250 on an international purchasing-power parity basis). During 2003–12, it was estimated, Argentina's population increased at an average rate of 0.9% per year, while gross domestic product (GDP) per head increased, in real terms, by an average of 6.8% per year during 2002–11. According to official estimates, overall GDP increased, in real terms, at an average annual rate of 7.0% in 2003–12; growth was 1.9% in 2012, according to preliminary government figures.

Agriculture (including forestry and fishing) contributed 9.0% of GDP in 2012. The sector engaged 6.9% of the total labour force in mid-2014, according to FAO estimates. The principal cash crops are wheat, maize, sugar cane and soybeans. Beef production is also important. During 2003–12, according to official preliminary figures, agricultural GDP increased at an average annual rate of 1.3%. The sector recovered well from drought in 2009, expanding by 28.0% in 2010; but the sector declined in 2011, by 2.2%, and further in 2012, by 11.1%.

Industry (including mining, manufacturing, construction and power) contributed an estimated 30.2% of GDP in 2012 and engaged 23.7% of the employed labour force in 2006. During 2003–12, according to official preliminary figures, industrial GDP increased, in real terms, at an average annual rate of 6.5%; sectoral GDP increased by 9.2% in 2011, but declined by 0.4% in 2012.

Mining contributed an estimated 3.8% of GDP in 2012, and engaged 0.4% of the employed labour force in 2006. Petroleum reserves totalled 2,500m. barrels in 2012 and production stood at 664,000 barrels per day in the same year. Natural gas production was 37,700m. cu m and proven gas reserves totalled 300,000m. cu m in 2012. According to official government estimates, the GDP of the mining sector declined by 0.3% during 2003–12; the sector's GDP decreased by 3.5% in 2011, but increased by 0.9% in 2012.

Manufacturing contributed an estimated 19.5% of GDP in 2012, and employed 14.0% of the working population in 2006. During 2003–12, according to official preliminary figures, manufacturing GDP increased, in real terms, at an average annual rate of 6.6%; manufacturing GDP increased by 11.0% in 2011, but declined by 0.4% in 2012.

The construction sector contributed an estimated 5.9% of GDP in 2012, and engaged 8.8% of the employed labour force in 2006. During 2003–12, according to official government estimates, the GDP of the sector increased at an average annual rate of 9.4%; construction GDP increased by 9.1% in 2011, but declined by 2.6% in 2012.

Energy is derived principally from thermal power (largely fuelled by natural gas), responsible for an estimated 51.4% of national production in 2011. Hydroelectricity accounted for an estimated 24.4% and petroleum for 15.1% of Argentina's total energy production in the same year, while the country's two nuclear power stations produced 4.9% of energy in 2011. A third nuclear reactor was scheduled to begin operations in 2014. In 2012 imports of mineral fuels comprised an estimated 13.0% of the country's total imports.

Services accounted for an estimated 60.8% of GDP in 2012 and engaged 75.2% of the employed labour force in 2006. According to official preliminary figures, the combined GDP of the service sectors increased, in real terms, at an average rate of 7.1% per year during 2003–12; sectoral GDP increased by 4.2% in 2012.

In 2012 Argentina recorded a visible merchandise trade surplus of US $15,372m., and there was a deficit of $57m. on the current account of the balance of payments. In 2012, according to provisional figures, the principal source of imports was Brazil (26.1%), followed by the People's Republic of China, the USA and Germany. Brazil was also the principal recipient of exports, accounting for 20.4% of total exports in that year, followed by Chile, China, and the USA. The principal exports in 2012, according to provisional figures, were residues from the food industries and prepared animal feed, followed by vehicles, cereals, fats and oils, and mineral fuels and lubricants. The principal imports in 2012 were vehicles, nuclear reactors, boilers, machines and mechanical appliances, mineral fuels and lubricants, and electrical machinery.

In 2013 a consolidated general government budgetary surplus of 1,002.4m. new pesos was forecast. Argentina's general government gross debt was 1,032,340m. new pesos in 2012, equivalent to 47.7% of GDP. Argentina's total external debt in 2011 was US $114,704m., of which $68,285m. was public and publicly guaranteed debt. In that year, the cost of servicing long-term public and publicly guaranteed debt and repayments to the IMF was equivalent to 15.3% of the value of exports of goods, services and income (excluding workers' remittances). The annual rate of inflation averaged 9.5% in 2004–13; consumer prices increased by 10.6% in 2013. According to labour force survey figures, the national unemployment rate was 7.9% in the first quarter of 2013.

Following the restructuring in 2009 of 92.6% of outstanding defaulted debt owed to creditors, robust economic growth was recorded in 2010 and 2011, of 9.2% and 8.9%, respectively. This was attributed to a strong performance by the agricultural sector, in addition to growing demand from Brazil and China, Argentina's principal trading partners. Nevertheless, amid rising inflationary pressures and concern regarding the risk of further capital flight, in October 2011 the Government implemented economic measures aimed at stabilizing the exchange rate and at curbing the outflow of capital, imposing restrictions on foreign exchange transactions and forcing mining and energy companies to repatriate their export revenues. Import restrictions followed in early 2012, together with measures intended further to control the use and purchase of foreign currency. The Government's expropriation of the majority of shares in the formerly state-run oil company Repsol YPF in April represented a further deterrent to foreign investment. Weaker global economic conditions and reduced agricultural output resulting from drought contributed to a significant deceleration in GDP growth in 2012, to some 1.9%. The deteriorating fiscal position, as well as the accuracy of official inflation and GDP figures, continued to be of concern in 2013; in December the IMF urged Argentina to improve the quality of its statistics by March 2014 or risk expulsion from the Fund. Fears of a second default on Argentina's sovereign debt were renewed in November after a US court upheld an earlier ruling that Argentina had acted illegally by discriminating against creditors who had refused to agree to the 2009 debt restructuring. If these creditors, owed the 7.4% of outstanding debt, were ultimately successful, the Government faced a bill of US $1,330m. The resolution of the dispute with Repsol in February 2014 removed a significant obstacle to much-needed foreign investment in the lucrative Vaca Muerta oil and gas fields in Patagonia. Exploitation of these shale gas reserves would, it was hoped, redress Argentina's energy deficit and improve the country's economic prospects. Nevertheless, in early 2014 the Government was forced to ease the strict foreign exchange controls imposed in 2011 in an attempt to ward off further falls in the value of the peso. In 2013 the Government put economic growth at 3.0%, below the forecast figure of 5.1%, although an improvement on 2012.

PUBLIC HOLIDAYS

2015: 1 January (New Year's Day), 24 March (Truth and Justice Memorial Day), 2 April (Veterans' Day and Tribute to the Fallen of the Falklands (Malvinas) War), 3 April (Good Friday), 1 May (Labour Day), 25 May (Anniversary of the 1810 Revolution), 15 June (Death of Gen. Manuel Belgrano), 9 July (Independence Day), 17 August (Death of Gen. José de San Martín), 12 October (Columbus Day), 8 December (Immaculate Conception), 25 December (Christmas).

Statistical Survey

Sources (unless otherwise stated): Instituto Nacional de Estadística y Censos, Avda Julio A. Roca 609, C1067AAB Buenos Aires; tel. (11) 4349-9200; fax (11) 4349-9601; e-mail ces@indec.mecon.gov.ar; internet www.indec.mecon.ar; Banco Central de la República Argentina, Reconquista 266, C1003ABF Buenos Aires; tel. (11) 4348-3500; fax (11) 4348-3955; e-mail sistema@bcra.gov.ar; internet www.bcra.gov.ar.

Area and Population

AREA, POPULATION AND DENSITY

Area (sq km)	2,780,403*
Population (census results)†	
17–18 November 2001	36,260,130
27 October 2010	
Males	19,523,766
Females	20,593,330
Total	40,117,096
Population (official estimates at mid-year)‡	
2012	41,281,631
2013	41,660,417
2014	42,034,884
Density (per sq km) at mid-2014	15.1

* 1,073,519 sq miles. The figure excludes the Falkland Islands (Islas Malvinas) and Antarctic territory claimed by Argentina.

† Figures exclude adjustment for underenumeration.

‡ Estimates not adjusted to take account of the results of the 2010 census.

POPULATION BY AGE AND SEX
(at 2010 census)

	Males	Females	Total
0–14	5,195,096	5,027,221	10,222,317
15–64	12,654,528	13,135,603	25,790,131
65 and over	1,674,142	2,430,506	4,104,648
Total	19,523,766	20,593,330	40,117,096

ADMINISTRATIVE DIVISIONS
(official estimates at mid-2014)

	Area (sq km)	Population	Density (per sq km)	Capital
Buenos Aires—City	203	3,085,275	15,198.4	—
Buenos Aires—Province	307,571	15,820,456	51.4	La Plata
Catamarca	102,602	436,628	4.3	San Fernando del Valle de Catamarca
Chaco	99,633	1,109,995	11.1	Resistencia
Chubut	224,686	490,227	2.2	Rawson
Córdoba	165,321	3,505,797	21.2	Córdoba
Corrientes	88,199	1,080,717	12.3	Corrientes
Entre Ríos	78,781	1,333,027	16.9	Paraná
Formosa	72,066	588,921	8.2	Formosa
Jujuy	53,219	735,459	13.8	San Salvador de Jujuy
La Pampa	143,440	356,926	2.5	Santa Rosa
La Rioja	89,680	384,315	4.3	La Rioja
Mendoza	148,827	1,835,326	12.3	Mendoza
Misiones	29,801	1,180,382	39.6	Posadas
Neuquén	94,078	599,683	6.4	Neuquén
Río Negro	203,013	614,846	3.0	Viedma
Salta	155,488	1,356,558	8.7	Salta
San Juan	89,651	753,418	8.4	San Juan
San Luis	76,748	495,864	6.5	San Luis
Santa Cruz	243,943	250,519	1.0	Río Gallegos
Santa Fe	133,007	3,366,801	25.3	Santa Fe
Santiago del Estero	136,351	921,020	6.8	Santiago del Estero
Tierra del Fuego	21,571	149,054	6.9	Ushuaia
Tucumán	22,524	1,583,670	70.3	San Miguel de Tucumán
Total	2,780,403	42,034,884	15.1	—

Note: Estimates not adjusted to take account of the 2010 census.

PRINCIPAL TOWNS
(population at 2001 census)*

Buenos Aires (capital)	2,776,138	Malvinas Argentinas†	290,691
Córdoba	1,267,521	Berazategui†	287,913
La Matanza†	1,255,288	Bahía Blanca†	284,776
Rosario	908,163	Resistencia	274,490
Lomas de Zamora†	591,345	Vicente López†	274,082
La Plata†	574,369	San Miguel†	253,086
General Pueyrredón†	564,056	Posadas	252,981
San Miguel de Tucumán	527,150	Esteban Echeverría†	243,974
Quilmes†	518,788	Paraná	235,967
Almirante Brown†	515,556	Pilar†	232,463
Merlo†	469,985	San Salvador de Jujuy	231,229
Salta	462,051	Santiago del Estero	230,614
Lanús†	453,082	José C. Paz†	230,208
General San Martín†	403,107	Guaymallén	223,365
Moreno†	380,503	Neuquén	201,868
Santa Fe	368,668	Formosa	198,074
Florencio Varela†	348,970	Godoy Cruz	182,563
Tres de Febrero†	336,467	Escobar†	178,155
Avellaneda†	328,980	Hurlingham†	172,245
Corrientes	314,546	Las Heras	169,248
Morón†	309,380	Ituzaingó	158,121
Tigre†	301,223	San Luis	153,322
San Isidro†	291,505	San Fernando†	151,131

* In each case, the figure refers to the city proper. At the 2001 census the population of the Buenos Aires agglomeration was 12,045,921.

† Settlement within the Province of Buenos Aires.

2010 census (population of capital and settlements within the Province of Buenos Aires at 27 October): Buenos Aires (capital) 2,890,151; La Matanza 1,775,816; La Plata 654,324; General Pueyrredón 618,989; Lomas de Zamora 616,279; Quilmes 582,943; Almirante Brown 552,902; Merlo 528,494; Lanús 459,263; Moreno 452,505; Florencio Varela 426,005; General San Martín 414,196; Tigre 376,381; Avellaneda 342,677; Tres de Febrero 340,071; Berazategui 324,244; Malvinas Argentinas 322,375; Morón 321,109; Bahía Blanca 301,572; Esteban Echeverría 300,959; Pilar 299,077; San Isidro 292,878; San Miguel 276,190; Vicente López 269,420; José C. Paz 268,981; Escobar 213,619; Hurlingham 181,241; San Fernando 163,240.

BIRTHS, MARRIAGES AND DEATHS

	Registered live births		Marriages		Registered deaths	
	Number	Rate (per 1,000)	Number	Rate (per 1,000)	Number	Rate (per 1,000)
2004	736,261	19.3	128,212	3.4	294,051	7.7
2005	712,220	18.5	132,720	3.4	293,529	7.6
2006	696,451	17.9	134,496	3.5	292,313	7.5
2007	700,792	17.8	136,437	3.5	315,852	8.0
2008	746,460	18.8	133,060	3.3	302,133	7.6
2009	745,336	18.6	126,081	3.1	304,525	7.6
2010	756,176	18.7	123,208	3.0	318,602	7.9
2011	758,042	18.5	128,797	3.1	319,059	7.8

Sources: Dirección de Estadísticas e Información en Salud (DEIS) and UN, *Demographic Yearbook* and *Population and Vital Statistics Report*.

Life expectancy (years at birth): 75.8 (males 72.2; females 79.6) in 2011 (Source: World Bank, World Development Indicators database).

ECONOMICALLY ACTIVE POPULATION

(labour force survey of 31 urban agglomerations, persons aged 10 years and over, 2006)

	Males	Females	Total
Agriculture, hunting and forestry	59,242	13,640	72,882
Fishing	8,215	821	9,036
Mining and quarrying	34,127	5,687	39,814
Manufacturing	988,343	422,321	1,410,664
Electricity, gas and water	38,066	5,991	44,057
Construction	854,764	29,917	884,681
Wholesale and retail trade; repair of motor vehicles, motorcycles and personal and household goods	1,263,477	755,160	2,018,637
Hotels and restaurants	213,854	166,975	380,829
Transport, storage and communications	557,431	86,613	644,044
Financial intermediation	95,938	93,497	189,435
Real estate, renting and business activities	528,349	281,460	809,809
Public administration and defence; compulsory social security	444,379	324,337	768,716
Education	185,900	620,900	806,800
Health and social work	163,470	426,735	590,205
Other community, social and personal services	317,127	229,607	546,734
Private households with employed persons	18,151	778,801	796,952
Extra-territorial organizations and bodies	2,031	164	2,195
Sub-total	5,772,864	4,242,626	10,015,490
Activities not adequately described	13,854	11,161	25,015
Total employed	5,786,718	4,253,787	10,040,505
Unemployed	488,935	560,263	1,049,198
Total labour force	6,275,653	4,814,050	11,089,703

2011 (labour force survey of 31 agglomerations at January–March, '000 persons aged 10 years and over): Total employed 10,605; Unemployed 846; Total labour force 11,451.

2012 (labour force survey of 31 agglomerations at January–March, '000 persons aged 10 years and over): Total employed 10,664; Unemployed 820; Total labour force 11,485.

2013 (labour force survey of 31 agglomerations at January–March, '000 persons aged 10 years and over): Total employed 10,748; Unemployed 925; Total labour force 11,673.

Health and Welfare

KEY INDICATORS

Total fertility rate (children per woman, 2011)	2.2
Under-5 mortality rate (per 1,000 live births, 2011)	14
HIV (% of persons aged 15–49, 2012)	0.4
Physicians (per 1,000 head, 2004)	3.2
Hospital beds (per 1,000 head, 2010)	4.5
Health expenditure (2010): US $ per head (PPP)	1,321
Health expenditure (2010): % of GDP	8.3
Health expenditure (2010): public (% of total)	64.4
Access to water (% of persons, 2011)	99
Access to sanitation (% of persons, 2011)	96
Total carbon dioxide emissions ('000 metric tons, 2010)	180,511.7
Carbon dioxide emissions per head (metric tons, 2010)	4.5
Human Development Index (2012): ranking	45
Human Development Index (2012): value	0.811

For sources and definitions, see explanatory note on p. vi.

Agriculture

PRINCIPAL CROPS

('000 metric tons)

	2010	2011	2012
Wheat	15,876	14,501	8,198
Rice, paddy	1,243	1,748	1,568
Barley	2,964	4,086	5,158
Maize	22,677	23,800	21,196
Rye	44	43	40
Oats	660	415	496
Sorghum	3,629	4,458	4,252
Potatoes*	1,996	2,127	2,200
Sweet potatoes*	353	390	400
Cassava (Manioc)*	182	185	187
Sugar cane*	25,960	26,960	25,000
Beans, dry	338	333	350*
Soybeans (Soya beans)	52,677	48,879	40,100
Groundnuts, with shell	611	702	686
Olives*	165	170	
Sunflower seed	2,221	3,672	3,341
Artichokes*	85	101	106
Tomatoes*	721	699	715
Pumpkins, squash and gourds*	327	338	345
Chillies and peppers, green*	145	133	138
Onions, dry*	723	718	726
Garlic*	129	120	135
Carrots and turnips*	227	244	260
Watermelons*	122	124	127
Cantaloupes and other melons*	77	77	80
Bananas*	171	172	175
Oranges	833	877*	900*
Tangerines, mandarins, clementines and satsumas	424	401*	415*
Lemons and limes	1,113	1,229*	1,300*
Grapefruit and pomelos	189	189*	200*
Apples*	1,050	1,116	1,250
Pears*	704	691	700
Peaches and nectarines*	318	285	290
Plums and sloes*	150	148	150
Grapes	2,617	2,890†	2,800*
Tea	89	97	100*
Mate	250	273*	290*
Tobacco, unmanufactured*	137	145	148

* FAO estimate(s).

† Unofficial figure.

Aggregate production ('000 metric tons, may include official, semi-official or estimated data): Total cereals 47,149 in 2010, 49,101 in 2011, 40,964 in 2012; Total roots and tubers 2,531 in 2010, 2,701 in 2011, 2,787 in 2012; Total vegetables (incl. melons) 3,351 in 2010, 3,464 in 2011, 3,557 in 2012; Total fruits (excl. melons) 7,645 in 2010, 8,070 in 2011, 8,260 in 2012.

Source: FAO.

LIVESTOCK

('000 head, year ending September)

	2010	2011	2012
Horses*	3,600	3,590	3,650
Asses*	98	98	98
Mules*	185	185	185
Cattle	48,950	46,000*	47,500
Pigs*	2,300	2,350	2,400
Sheep	15,025	14,731	16,300*
Goats*	4,250	4,280	4,350
Chickens*	98,000	100,000	105,000
Ducks*	2,500	2,550	2,600
Geese*	160	165	167
Turkeys	3,000	3,050	3,070

* FAO estimate(s).

Source: FAO.

LIVESTOCK PRODUCTS
('000 metric tons)

	2010	2011	2012
Cattle meat	2,630	2,497*	2,500†
Sheep meat†	44	47	49
Pig meat	281	301	305†
Horse meat	32	29	30†
Chicken meat†	1,597	1,648	1,664
Cows' milk	10,502	11,206	11,815*
Butter and ghee†	48	51	52
Cheese†	580	580	
Hen eggs	554*	591*	600†
Honey	59	74†	75†
Wool, greasy	54	54†	55†

* Unofficial figure.
† FAO estimate(s).

Source: FAO.

Forestry

ROUNDWOOD REMOVALS
('000 cubic metres, excl. bark)

	2009	2010	2011
Sawlogs, veneer logs and logs for sleepers*	4,289	4,403	4,403
Pulpwood	5,250	5,874	5,874
Other industrial wood	283	358	363
Fuel wood	4,267	4,375	4,547*
Total*	14,089	15,010	15,187

* FAO estimate(s).

2012: Production assumed to be unchanged from 2011 (FAO estimates).

Source: FAO.

SAWNWOOD PRODUCTION
('000 cubic metres, incl. railway sleepers)

	2008	2009	2010
Coniferous (softwood)	470	1,115	761
Broadleaved (hardwood)	485	1,036	1,398
Total	955	2,151	2,159

2011–12: Production assumed to be unchanged from 2010 (FAO estimates).

Source: FAO.

Fishing

('000 metric tons, live weight)

	2009	2010	2011
Capture	862.0	811.7	792.5
Southern blue whiting	21.7	11.6	3.5
Argentine hake	280.7	281.8	287.8
Patagonian grenadier	110.7	82.7	70.9
Argentine red shrimp	53.7	72.1	82.9
Patagonian scallop	80.8	50.9	47.8
Argentine shortfin squid	71.4	86.0	76.6
Aquaculture*	2.6	2.7	3.2
Total catch*	864.6	814.4	795.7

* FAO estimates.

Note: The data exclude aquatic animals, recorded by number rather than by weight. The number of dolphins and toothed whales caught was 112 in 2009; 121 in 2010; 180 in 2011. The number of broad-nosed and spectacled caimans caught was 10,546 in 2009; 6,292 in 2010; 6,132 in 2011.

Source: FAO.

Mining

('000 metric tons unless otherwise indicated)

	2009	2010	2011
Crude petroleum ('000 barrels)	230,885	224,077	214,142
Natural gas (million cu metres)	36,708	35,625	34,060
Lead ore*	24.8	22.6	26.1
Zinc ore*	31.9	32.6	34.0
Aluminium (primary)	410.2	412.8	432.0
Lithium:			
carbonate (metric tons)	8,574	11,178	10,000†
chloride (metric tons)	4,279	6,644	4,480†
Silver ore (kg)*	532,823	723,238	747,449
Copper ore*	143.1	140.0	116.7
Gold ore (kg)*	46,588	63,138	59,140
Fluorspar (metric tons)	13,424	17,657	25,099
Boron (crude)	506.0	623.0	648.8
Gypsum (crude)	1,355.3	1,346.5	1,452.8
Clay (common)	6,941.7	7,313.4	8,323.9
Salt	1,477.5	1,532.1	1,884.9
Sand:			
for construction	27,183.5	31,345.8	33,455.2
Silica (glass) sand	364.2	531.2	516.8
Limestone	15,746.7	17,309.8	19,782.4
Stone (various crushed)	19,663.4	22,237.9	22,638.7
Rhodochrosite (kg)	122,117	122,839	120,673
Quartzite (crushed)	946.7	1,164.4	1,292.5
Gemstones (kg)	119,650	45,054	45,000†

* Figures refer to the metal content of ores and concentrates.
† Estimate.

Source: US Geological Survey.

2012 (estimates): Crude petroleum 31.5m. metric tons; Natural gas 37,729m. cu metres (Source: BP, *Statistical review of World Energy*).

Industry

SELECTED PRODUCTS
('000 metric tons unless otherwise indicated)

	2010	2011	2012
Wheat flour	4,901	4,843	4,635
Beer (sales, '000 hectolitres)*	19,860	21,433	20,408
Wine (sales, '000 hectolitres)	9,753	9,810	10,016†
Cigarettes (sales, million packets)	2,102	2,188	2,173
Paper (excl. newspaper)	1,614	1,623	1,607
Aluminium	417	416	413
Iron (primary)	4,098	4,471	3,683
Crude steel	5,138	5,611	4,996
Portland cement	10,423	11,592	10,716
Refined petroleum ('000 cu m)†	36,205	36,087	37,668
Ethylene	640	655	680
Urea	942	1,159	1,179
Ammonia	590	759	757
Washing machines ('000 units)	1,103	1,242	1,445
Home refrigerators ('000 units)	750	822	897
Air conditioning units (domestic, '000)	1,138	1,685	1,529
Motor vehicles ('000)	508	577	497
Electric energy (million kWh)	120,011	124,901	n.a.

* Estimates.
† Provisional figure(s).

Finance

CURRENCY AND EXCHANGE RATES

Monetary Units

100 centavos = 1 nuevo peso argentino (new Argentine peso).

Sterling, Dollar and Euro Equivalents (31 December 2013)

£1 sterling = 10.706 new pesos;
US $1 = 6.501 new pesos;
€1 = 8.966 new pesos;
100 new pesos = £9.34 = $15.38 = €11.15.

Average Exchange Rate (new pesos per US $)

2011	4.110
2012	4.537
2013	5.459

Note: From April 1996 to December 2001 the official exchange rate was fixed at US $1 = 99.95 centavos. In January 2002 the Government abandoned this exchange rate and devalued the peso: initially there was a fixed official exchange rate of US $1 = 1.40 new pesos for trade and financial transactions, while a free market rate was applicable to other transactions. In February, however, a unified 'floating' exchange rate system, with the rate to be determined by market conditions, was introduced.

GENERAL GOVERNMENT BUDGET

(public sector accounts, million new pesos, forecasts)

Revenue	2012	2013	2014
Current revenue	553,522.7	685,376.0	786,362.4
Tax revenue	329,163.1	406,549.5	464,647.1
Social security contributions	174,893.8	212,494.3	245,035.8
Sale of public goods and services	2,020.2	2,567.2	3,208.9
Property income	29,795.0	40,652.5	45,505.4
Current transfers	611.4	803.8	820.7
Other current revenue	3,671.3	4,165.5	4,870.8
Capital revenue	1,133.7	1,375.4	1,472.4
Total	554,656.4	686,751.4	787,834.8

Expenditure	2012	2013	2014
Current expenditure	525,965.8	610,948.1	701,111.8
Consumption expenditure	108,077.7	122,908.8	126,294.1
Property income	47,204.5	58,174.3	82,302.0
Social security benefits	198,203.5	241,722.7	287,673.1
Current transfers	149,852.3	165,744.4	178,475.7
Capital expenditure	64,328.6	74,800.9	83,783.6
Direct investment	31,467.9	36,786.0	40,110.4
Capital transfers	31,813.7	37,007.6	42,616.0
Financial investment	1,047.0	1,007.3	1,057.2
Total	590,294.4	685,749.0	784,895.4

Note: Budget figures refer to the consolidated accounts of the central and local governments and state-owned companies and entities.

Source: Oficina Nacional de Presupuesto, Secretaría de Hacienda, Ministerio de Economía, Buenos Aires.

INTERNATIONAL RESERVES

(US $ million at 31 December)

	2010	2011	2012
Gold (national valuation)	2,497	3,127	3,326
IMF special drawing rights	3,114	3,152	3,155
Foreign exchange	46,619	40,075	36,765
Total	52,230	46,354	43,246

Source: IMF, *International Financial Statistics*.

MONEY SUPPLY

(million new pesos at 31 December)

	2010	2011	2012
Currency outside banks	113,554	151,282	209,979
Demand deposits at commercial banks	59,247	64,001	111,504
Total money	172,801	215,283	321,483

Source: IMF, *International Financial Statistics*.

COST OF LIVING

(Consumer Price Index for Buenos Aires metropolitan area; annual averages; base: April 2008 = 100)

	2011	2012	2013
Food and beverages	127.9	141.0	151.7
Housing and basic services	116.5	124.9	136.1
Clothing	159.2	172.9	186.0
Furnishings and fittings	131.5	146.5	165.3
Health	140.8	158.6	179.6
Education	151.0	170.5	194.3
Transport and communications	127.4	139.3	164.0
Recreation and culture	137.2	155.5	178.4
Miscellaneous goods and services	117.3	127.8	138.1
All items	130.2	143.3	158.5

NATIONAL ACCOUNTS

(million new pesos at current prices, preliminary)

Expenditure on the Gross Domestic Product

	2010	2011	2012
Government final consumption expenditure	215,278	278,961	359,628
Private final consumption expenditure	826,794	1,039,072	1,235,401
Increase in stocks*	35,468	65,934	47,852
Gross fixed capital formation	317,417	415,836	471,364
Total domestic expenditure	1,394,957	1,799,803	2,114,245
Exports of goods and services	313,150	401,992	426,670
Less Imports of goods and services	265,451	359,774	376,669
Gross domestic product (GDP) in market prices	1,442,655	1,842,022	2,164,246
GDP at constant 1993 prices	422,130	459,571	468,301

* Including statistical discrepancy.

Gross Domestic Product by Economic Activity

	2010	2011	2012
Agriculture, forestry and hunting	129,882	176,071	174,405
Fishing	2,484	2,675	2,976
Mining and quarrying	47,727	57,585	74,593
Manufacturing	271,665	347,309	383,965
Electricity, gas and water supply	15,716	17,902	20,080
Construction	74,212	96,770	116,776
Wholesale and retail trade	161,325	213,362	263,818
Hotels and restaurants	33,543	40,241	46,205
Transport, storage and communications	107,326	134,288	155,930
Financial intermediation	76,646	95,514	126,495
Real estate, renting and business activities	140,273	167,997	189,538
Public administration and defence*	91,606	119,635	153,281
Education, health and social work	115,803	150,509	187,508
Other community, social and personal service activities†	54,991	64,762	76,723
Sub-total	1,323,199	1,684,619	1,972,292
Value-added tax	120,152	157,333	195,723
Import duties	11,428	14,593	16,501
Less Financial intermediation services indirectly measured	12,124	14,523	20,270
GDP in market prices	1,442,655	1,842,022	2,164,246

* Including extra-territorial organizations and bodies.

† Including private households with employed persons.

BALANCE OF PAYMENTS
(US $ million)

	2010	2011	2012
Exports of goods f.o.b.	68,134	84,051	80,927
Imports of goods f.o.b.	–53,868	–71,126	–65,556
Trade balance	14,266	12,925	15,372
Exports of services	13,648	15,670	15,076
Imports of services	–14,808	–17,804	–18,657
Balance on goods and services	13,106	10,791	11,790
Other income received (net)	–11,341	–12,400	–11,452
Balance on goods, services and income	1,765	–1,609	338
Current transfers (net)	–405	–565	–395
Current balance	1,360	–2,173	–57
Capital account (net)	89	62	49
Net investment in banking sector	–2,679	6,900	–1,649
Net investment in public sector	2,459	–2,250	–3,950
Net investment in private sector	3,536	–4,356	3,921
Net errors and omissions	–606	–4,291	–1,618
Overall balance	4,157	–6,108	–3,305

External Trade

PRINCIPAL COMMODITIES
(US $ million)

Imports c.i.f.	2010	2011	2012*
Mineral fuels, lubricants and related products	4,479	9,402	8,878
Paper and cardboard	1,010	1,152	1,044
Rubber and manufactures of rubber	1,183	1,494	1,284
Organic chemicals and related products	2,660	3,089	3,034
Pharmaceutical products	1,566	1,790	2,092
Plastic and manufactures of laminate	2,428	3,034	2,845
Metalliferous ore	1,423	1,547	1,385
Electrical machinery	6,980	8,316	7,707
Boilers, machines and mechanical appliances, etc.	8,540	11,050	9,897
Vehicles	10,125	12,880	12,054
Optical instruments and apparatus, etc.	1,227	1,637	1,615
Total (incl. others)	56,793	74,319	68,508

* Provisional figures.

Exports f.o.b.	2010	2011	2012*
Meat and meat products	1,694	1,905	1,802
Fish	1,307	1,438	1,306
Residues from the food industries and prepared animal feed	8,783	10,774	11,669
Fats and oils	5,192	7,034	5,929
Cereals	4,622	8,382	9,530
Oil seeds and oleaginous fruits	5,338	5,995	3,796
Milk and milk products	1,059	1,717	1,059
Skins and leathers	1,001	927	832
Mineral fuels, lubricants and related materials	5,388	4,956	4,962
Mineral by-products	1,820	1,889	2,116
Chemical products	1,925	2,856	2,542
Plastic and manufactures of laminate	1,346	1,536	1,388
Pearls, stones, metals and articles thereof	2,258	2,734	2,575
Metalliferous ore	1,201	1,494	1,391
Boilers and mechanical appliances, etc.	1,691	1,891	1,873
Vehicles	7,973	9,974	9,557
Total (incl. others)	68,187	84,051	80,927

* Provisional figures.

PRINCIPAL TRADING PARTNERS
(US $ million)*

Imports c.i.f.	2010	2011	2012†
Bolivia	350	629	1,416
Brazil‡	17,950	22,181	17,907
Chile‡	885	1,093	1,011
China, People's Republic§	7,678	10,573	9,952
France (incl. Monaco)	1,529	1,634	1,599
Germany	3,215	3,646	3,713
Italy	1,297	1,482	1,457
Japan	1,191	1,415	1,509
Korea, Republic	968	1,420	1,140
Mexico	1,817	2,533	2,251
Netherlands	394	435	1,130
Russia	397	792	1,125
Spain	1,024	1,396	1,320
Thailand	640	696	872
Trinidad and Tobago	511	1,275	1,905
USA	6,125	7,700	8,388
Uruguay‡	587	606	520
Total (incl. others)	56,793	74,319	68,508

Exports f.o.b.	2010	2011	2012†
Algeria	1,010	1,699	1,503
Brazil‡	14,425	17,347	16,495
Canada	1,402	4,845	2,194
Chile‡	4,490	4,845	5,065
China, People's Republic§	6,117	6,232	5,021
Colombia	1,302	1,806	2,067
Germany	1,832	2,486	1,981
Egypt	979	1,746	1,013
India	1,321	1,087	1,183
Indonesia	852	1,542	1,634
Iran	1,453	1,092	984
Italy	1,586	2,018	1,172
Japan	855	843	1,223
Korea, Republic	780	981	1,379
Malaysia	813	706	870
Netherlands	2,367	2,627	2,236
Peru	1,121	1,808	1,924
South Africa	879	1,131	1,050
Spain	2,242	3,089	2,650
USA	3,656	4,248	4,089
Uruguay‡	1,554	1,996	1,983
Venezuela	1,424	1,867	2,225
Total (incl. others)	68,187	84,051	80,927

* Imports by country of origin; exports by country of destination.
† Provisional figures.
‡ Including free trade zones.
§ Including Hong Kong and Macao.

Transport

RAILWAYS
(traffic)

	2009	2010	2011
Passengers carried ('000)	433,420	421,392	346,225
Freight carried ('000 tons)	20,731	23,551	24,194
Passenger-km (million)	8,810	8,588	7,083
Freight ton-km (million)	10,649	12,112	12,198

ROAD TRAFFIC
('000 motor vehicles in use)

	2003	2004	2005
Passenger cars	4,668	4,926	5,230
Commercial vehicles	1,198	1,684	1,775

Source: UN, *Statistical Yearbook*.

2007 ('000 motor vehicles in use at 31 December): Total vehicles 12,399.9 (Source: IRF, *World Road Statistics*).

SHIPPING

Flag Registered Fleet
(at 31 December)

	2011	2012	2013
Number of vessels	395	398	409
Total displacement ('000 grt)	826.2	759.9	732.6

Source: Lloyd's List Intelligence (www.lloydslistintelligence.com).

International Sea-borne Freight Traffic
('000 metric tons)

	1996	1997	1998
Goods loaded	52,068	58,512	69,372
Goods unloaded	16,728	19,116	19,536

Goods unloaded: 23,736 in 2010; 30,204 in 2011; 25,272 in 2012.

Source: UN, *Monthly Bulletin of Statistics*.

Total maritime freight handled ('000 metric tons): 133,001 in 2009; 163,764 in 2010; 175,539 in 2011 (Source: Dirección Nacional de Puertos).

CIVIL AVIATION

	2010	2011	2012
Passengers carried ('000)	17,212	17,664	19,009
Total freight carried ('000 metric tons)	256	234	256

2009 (million): Kilometres flown 190; Passenger-km 21,286.

Tourism

TOURIST ARRIVALS BY REGION
('000 arrivals at Jorge Newbery and Ezeiza airports)

	2010	2011	2012
Europe	581.0	560.8	533.8
North America	310.3	289.9	277.2
South America	1,609.3	1,690.3	1,603.9
Brazil	863.5	886.8	817.2
Chile	215.0	220.0	220.6
Total (incl. others)	2,648.0	2,692.1	2,568.2

Spending by tourists (arrivals at Jorge Newbery and Ezeiza airports, US $ million): 3,369.4 in 2010; 3,514.0 in 2011; 3,426.9 in 2012.

Total tourist arrivals ('000 arrivals at frontiers, excl. excursionists): 5,325 in 2010; 5,705 in 2011; 5,599 in 2012 (provisional) (Source: World Tourism Organization).

Total tourism receipts (US $ million): 4,942 in 2010; 5,354 in 2011; 4,895 in 2012 (provisional) (Source: World Tourism Organization).

Communications Media

	2010	2011	2012
Telephones ('000 main lines in use)	9,800.0	9,900.0	9,997.0
Mobile cellular telephones ('000 handsets in use)	57,300.0	55,000.0	58,599.4
Internet subscribers ('000)	3,995.3	n.a.	n.a.
Broadband subscribers ('000)	3,862.4	4,220.5	4,475.4

Source: International Telecommunication Union.

Education

(2012 unless otherwise indicated)

	Institutions	Teachers	Students
Pre-primary	18,035	115,515	1,610,845
Primary	22,256	340,015	4,603,422
Secondary	21,281*	141,389*	3,813,545
Basic	14,155*	44,210*	2,330,757
Specialized	7,126*	97,179*	1,482,788
Higher			
University†	37	n.a.	1,273,156
Non-university	2,164	24,679	767,698

* 2007.

† 2004.

Source: partly Red Federal de Información Educativa, *Relevamiento*.

Pupil-teacher ratio (primary education, UNESCO estimate): 16.3 in 2007/08 (Source: UNESCO Institute for Statistics).

Adult literacy rate (UNESCO estimates): 97.9% (males 97.8%; females 97.9%) in 2011 (Source: UNESCO Institute for Statistics).

Directory

The Government

HEAD OF STATE

President of the Nation: CRISTINA ELISABET FERNÁNDEZ DE KIRCHNER (took office 10 December 2007, re-elected 23 October 2011).

Vice-President: AMADO BOUDOU.

CABINET
(April 2014)

The Cabinet is composed of members of the Frente para la Victoria alliance.

Cabinet Chief: JORGE MILTON CAPITANICH.

Minister of the Interior and Transport: ANÍBAL FLORENCIO RANDAZZO.

Minister of Foreign Affairs, International Trade and Worship: HÉCTOR MARCOS TIMERMAN.

Minister of Defence: AGUSTÍN ROSSI.

Minister of Economy and Public Finance: AXEL KICILLOF.

Minister of Industry: DÉBORA ADRIANA GIORGI.

Minister of Tourism: CARLOS ENRIQUE MEYER.

Minister of Education: ALBERTO ESTANISLAO SILEONI.

Minister of Science, Technology and Productive Innovation: LINO BARAÑAO.

Minister of Labour, Employment and Social Security: CARLOS ALFONSO TOMADA.

Minister of Federal Planning, Public Investment and Services: JULIO MIGUEL DE VIDO.

Minister of Health: JUAN LUIS MANZUR.

Minister of Security: MARÍA CECILIA RODRÍGUEZ.

Minister of Justice and Human Rights: JULIO CÉSAR ALAK.

Minister of Social Development: ALICIA MARGARITA KIRCHNER.

Minister of Agriculture, Livestock and Fisheries: CARLOS HORACIO CASAMIQUELA.

MINISTRIES

General Secretariat to the Presidency: Balcarce 50, C1064AAB Buenos Aires; tel. and fax (11) 4344-3600; e-mail secretariageneral@presidencia.gov.ar; internet www.secretariageneral.gov.ar.

Office of the Cabinet Chief: Avda Julio Argentino Roca 782, C1067ABP Buenos Aires; tel. (11) 4331-1951; e-mail privada@jgm.gov.ar; internet www.jgm.gov.ar.

Ministry of Agriculture, Livestock and Fisheries: Avda Paseo Colón 982, C1063ACW Buenos Aires; tel. (11) 4349-2000; fax (11) 4349-2589; e-mail prensa1@minagri.gob.ar; internet www.minagri.gob.ar.

Ministry of Defence: Azopardo 250, C1328ADB Buenos Aires; tel. (11) 4346-8800; e-mail mindef@mindef.gov.ar; internet www.mindef.gov.ar.

Ministry of Economy and Public Finance: Hipólito Yrigoyen 250, C1086AAB Buenos Aires; tel. (11) 4349-5000; e-mail ciudadano@mecon.gov.ar; internet www.mecon.gov.ar.

Ministry of Education: Pizzurno 935, C1020ACA Buenos Aires; tel. (11) 4129-1000; fax (11) 4129-1180; e-mail prensa@me.gov.ar; internet www.me.gov.ar.

Ministry of Federal Planning, Public Investment and Services: Hipólito Yrigoyen 250, 11°, Of. 1112, C1086AAB Buenos Aires; tel. (11) 4349-5000; internet www.minplan.gov.ar.

Ministry of Foreign Affairs, International Trade and Worship: Esmeralda 1212, C1007ABR Buenos Aires; tel. (11) 4819-7000; e-mail info@cancilleria.gob.ar; internet www.cancilleria.gov.ar.

Ministry of Health: 9 de Julio 1925, C1073ABA Buenos Aires; tel. (11) 4379-9000; fax (11) 4381-2182; e-mail prensa@msal.gov.ar; internet www.msal.gov.ar.

Ministry of Industry: Hipólito Yrigoyen 250, C1086AAB Buenos Aires; tel. (11) 4349-3000; e-mail prensa@industria.gob.ar; internet www.minprod.gob.ar.

Ministry of the Interior and Transport: 25 de Mayo 101/145, C1002ABC Buenos Aires; tel. (11) 4339-0800; fax (11) 4331-6376; e-mail info@mininterior.gov.ar; internet www.mininterior.gov.ar.

Ministry of Justice and Human Rights: Sarmiento 329, C1041AAG Buenos Aires; tel. (11) 5300-4000; e-mail prensa@jus.gov.ar; internet www.jus.gov.ar.

Ministry of Labour, Employment and Social Security: Avda Leandro N. Alem 650, C1001AAO Buenos Aires; tel. (11) 4311-2913; fax (11) 4312-7860; e-mail cfederal@trabajo.gov.ar; internet www.trabajo.gov.ar.

Ministry of Science, Technology and Productive Innovation: Avda Godoy Cruz 2320, C1425FQD Buenos Aires; tel. (11) 4899-5000; fax (11) 4312-8364; e-mail info@mincyt.gov.ar; internet www.mincyt.gov.ar.

Ministry of Security: Gelly y Obes 2289, C1425EMA Buenos Aires; internet www.minseg.gob.ar.

Ministry of Social Development: 9 de Julio 1925, 19°, C1073ABA Buenos Aires; tel. (11) 4379-3648; e-mail privadaministro@desarrollosocial.gov.ar; internet www.desarrollosocial.gov.ar.

Ministry of Tourism: Buenos Aires; e-mail info@turismo.gov.ar; internet www.turismo.gov.ar.

President and Legislature

PRESIDENT

Election, 23 October 2011

Candidates	Votes	% of valid votes cast
Cristina E. Fernández de Kirchner (Frente para la Victoria)	11,593,023	53.96
Hermes Juan Binner (Frente Amplio Progresista)	3,624,518	16.87
Ricardo Luis Alfonsín (Unión para el Desarrollo Social)	2,395,056	11.15
Alberto J. Rodríguez Saá (Alianza Compromiso Federal)	1,714,385	7.98
Eduardo Duhalde (Frente Popular)	1,264,609	5.89
Jorge Altamira (Frente de Izquierda y de los Trabajadores)	497,082	2.31
Elisa M. A. Carrió (Coalición Cívica Afirmación para una República Igualitaria)	396,171	1.84
Total valid votes*	21,484,844	100.00

* In addition, there were 678,724 blank and 206,030 spoiled ballots. There were also a further 23,921 contested votes.

CONGRESS

Chamber of Deputies

President: JULIÁN ANDRES DOMÍNGUEZ.

The Chamber of Deputies has 257 members, who hold office for a four-year term, with approximately one-half of the seats renewable every two years. The last election was held on 27 October 2013.

Distribution of Seats by Legislative Bloc, December 2013

	Seats
Frente para la Victoria	118
Unión Cívica Radical	41
Dissident Peronists*	33
Propuesta Republicana	20
Frente Amplio Progresista	15
Frente Cívico por Santiago	7
Nuevo Encuentro	4
Coalición Cívica ARI/UNEN	3
Frente de Izquierda y de los Trabajadores	3
Movimiento Popular Neuquino	3
Unidad Popular	3
Others	7
Total	257

* Including the Frente Renovador.

Senate

President: BEATRIZ ROJKÉS.

The Senate has 72 directly elected members, three from each province. One-third of these seats are renewable every two years. The last election was held on 27 October 2013, in which, according to preliminary results, the FPV won 11 seats, the PRO, Frente Cívico por Santiago and the MPN two seats each, and the UNEN, Unión por Chaco, Alianza Unión por Entre Ríos, Frente Popular Salteño, Frente Popular, Alianza Frente Progresista and the Movimiento Popular Fueguino each won one seat.

Distribution of Seats by Legislative Bloc, December 2013

	Seats
Frente para la Victoria and allies	40
Unión Cívica Radical/Frente Amplio Progresista	19
Frente Renovador and allies	7
Propuesta Republicana and allies	3
Others	3
Total	72

Provincial Administrators

(April 2014)

Head of Government of the Autonomous City of Buenos Aires: MAURICIO MACRI (PRO).

Governor of the Province of Buenos Aires: DANIEL OSVALDO SCIOLI (FPV).

Governor of the Province of Catamarca: LUCÍA CORPACCI (FPV).

Governor of the Province of Chaco: JUAN CARLOS BACILEFF IVANOFF (acting).

Governor of the Province of Chubut: MARTÍN BUZZI (Modelo Chubut).

Governor of the Province of Córdoba: JOSÉ MANUEL DE LA SOTA (PJ).

Governor of the Province of Corrientes: RICARDO COLOMBI (UCR).

Governor of the Province of Entre Ríos: SERGIO DANIEL URRIBARRI (FPV).

Governor of the Province of Formosa: Dr GILDO INSFRÁN (PJ).

Governor of the Province of Jujuy: EDUARDO ALFREDO FELLNER (PJ).

Governor of the Province of La Pampa: OSCAR MARIO JORGE (PJ).

Governor of the Province of La Rioja: LUIS BEDER HERRERA (PJ).

Governor of the Province of Mendoza: FRANCISCO PÉREZ (FPV).

Governor of the Province of Misiones: MAURICE FABIÁN CLOSS (Frente Renovador de la Concordia).

Governor of the Province of Neuquén: JORGE AUGUSTO SAPAG (MPN).

Governor of the Province of Río Negro: ALBERTO WERETILNECK (FPV).

Governor of the Province of Salta: JUAN MANUEL URTUBEY (FPV).

Governor of the Province of San Juan: Dr JOSÉ LUIS GIOJA (FPV).

Governor of the Province of San Luis: CLAUDIO POGGI (Alianza Compromiso Federal).

Governor of the Province of Santa Cruz: DANIEL ROMAN PERALTA (FPV).

Governor of the Province of Santa Fe: ANTONIO BONFATTI (PS).

Governor of the Province of Santiago del Estero: CLAUDIA DE ZAMORA (FPV/Frente Cívico por Santiago).

Governor of the Province of Tierra del Fuego, Antártida e Islas del Atlántico Sur: MARÍA FABIANA RÍOS (CCARI).

Governor of the Province of Tucumán: JOSÉ JORGE ALPEROVICH (PJ).

Election Commission

Dirección Nacional Electoral: 25 de Mayo 101, 3°, Of. 346, C1002ABC Buenos Aires; tel. (11) 4346-1683; fax (11) 4346-1634; e-mail elecciones@mininterior.gov.ar; internet www.elecciones.gov.ar; part of the Ministry of the Interior and Transport; Dir ALEJANDRO TULLIO.

Political Organizations

Coalición Cívica ARI (Coalición Cívica Afirmación para una República Igualitaria—CCARI): Rivadavia 1475, C1022AAB Buenos Aires; tel. (11) 4384-1268; e-mail prensa@coalicioncivicaari.org.ar; internet coalicioncivicaari.org.ar; f. 2001 as Alternativa por una República de Iguales; progressive party; contested the 2013 legislative elections as mem. of the UNEN coalition, which forms a parliamentary bloc with the UCR; Sec.-Gen. PABLO JAVKIN; 48,000 mems.

Frente Amplio Progresista (FAP): f. 2011; centre-left; Leader HERMES JUAN BINNER; contested the 2011 presidential election with Partido Nuevo and the following parties:

Generación para un Encuentro Nacional (GEN): Riobamba 67, 1°, C1025ABA Buenos Aires; tel. (11) 4951-9503; e-mail gen@partidogen.com.ar; internet www.partidogen.com.ar; f. 2007; Leader MARGARITA ROSA STOLBIZER; Sec.-Gen. JUAN CARLOS JUÁREZ.

Movimiento Libres del Sur: Humberto I 542, San Telmo, C1103ACL Buenos Aires; tel. (11) 4307-3724; e-mail contacto@libresdelsur.org.ar; internet www.libresdelsur.org.ar; Leader HUMBERTO TUMINI.

Partido Socialista (PS): Entre Ríos 488, 2°, Buenos Aires; tel. (11) 4383-2395; e-mail pscen@ar.inter.net; internet www.partidosocialista.org.ar; f. 2002 following merger of the Partido Socialista Democrático and the Partido Socialista Popular; Pres. HERMES JUAN BINNER; Sec.-Gen. ALFREDO LAZZERETTI; 115,000 mems.

Unidad Popular: Rivadavia 2515, C1034ACE Buenos Aires; tel. (11) 2055-7778; e-mail info@corrienteup.org; internet corrienteup.org; comprises the Unidad Popular, Unión de los Neuquinos (UNE), Buenos Aires para Todos, Participación, Ética y Solidaridad (PARES) and Cruzada Renovadora de San Juan; Leader LILIANA PARADA.

Frente Cívico—Córdoba: Córdoba; regional party.

Frente Cívico por Santiago: Santiago del Estero; f. 2005; regional party; Leader GERARDO ZAMORA.

Frente de Izquierda y de los Trabajadores (FIT): La Rioja 853, C1221ACG Buenos Aires; tel. (11) 4932-9297; e-mail laverdadobrera@pts.org.ar; internet www.frentedeizquierda.org; f. 2011; left-wing; Pres. JORGE ALTAMIRA; comprises the following parties:

Partido Obrero: Ayacucho 444/8, C1026AAB Buenos Aires; tel. (11) 4953-3824; fax (11) 4954-5829; e-mail secretariaprensapo@gmail.com; internet www.po.org.ar; f. 1982; Trotskyist; Leader JORGE ALTAMIRA; 26,000 mems.

Partido de los Trabajadores Socialistas (PTS): La Rioja 853, C1221ACG Buenos Aires; tel. (11) 4932-9297; e-mail pts@pts.org.ar; internet www.pts.org.ar; f. 1988 as a schism of Movimiento al Socialismo; Trotskyist; Pres. CHRISTIAN CASTILLO.

Movimiento de Integración y Desarrollo (MID): Ayacucho 49, C1025AAA Buenos Aires; tel. (11) 4954-0817; e-mail midcapital@midnacional.com.ar; internet midnacional.com.ar; f. 1963; mem. of the Unidos por la Libertad y el Trabajo alliance formed to contest the 2013 elections; Leader EFRAÍN GUSTAVO PUYÓ PEÑA; 51,000 mems.

Movimiento Popular Neuquino (MPN): Neuquén; internet www.mpn.org.ar; f. 1961; provincial party; Pres. JORGE OMAR SOBISCH; 112,000 mems.

Movimiento Proyecto Sur: Sarandí 56, C1088AAI Buenos Aires; tel. (11) 4952-3103; e-mail sur@proyecto-sur.com.ar; internet www.proyecto-sur.com.ar; f. 2001 as an alliance comprising Partido Socialista Auténtico, Partido Proyecto Sur and Buenos Aires para Todos; contested the 2013 legislative elections as part of the UNEN coalition, which forms a parliamentary bloc with the UCR; Pres. FERNANDO 'PINO' SOLANAS.

Movimiento Socialista de los Trabajadores (MST): San Nicolás, Peru 439, Buenos Aires; tel. (11) 4342-7520; e-mail webmaster@mst.org.ar; internet www.mst.org.ar; f. 1944; Leader VILMA RIPOLL.

Nuevo Encuentro: Hipólito Yrigoyen 1189, 1°, Buenos Aires; tel. (11) 4381-0286; internet www.partidoencuentro.org.ar; f. 2009; centre-left; Leader MARTÍN SABBATELLA.

Partido del Campo Popular (PCP): Alicia Moreau de Justo 1150, Rosario; e-mail partidocampopopular@gmail.com; internet www.pcp.org.ar; f. 1991 as Movimiento por la Dignidad y la Independencia (Modin); present name adopted in 2008; nationalist; Pres. JOSÉ ALEJANDRO BONACCI; Sec. LUIS FERNANDO RETO; 15,000 mems.

Partido Comunista de Argentina: Entre Ríos 1039, C1080ABQ Buenos Aires; tel. and fax (11) 4304-0066; e-mail info@pca.org.ar; internet www.pca.org.ar; f. 1918; Leader PATRICIO ECHEGARAY.

Partido Demócrata Cristiano (PDC): Combate de los Pozos 1055, C1222AAK Buenos Aires; tel. (11) 4305-1229; fax (11) 4306-8242; e-mail pdcblog@fibertel.com.ar; internet www.democraciacristiana.org.ar; f. 1954; mem. of the Unidos por la Libertad y el Trabajo alliance formed to contest the 2013 elections; Pres. Dr JUAN BRUGGE; 51,000 mems.

Partido Demócrata Progresista (PDP): Entre Ríos 1443, Rosario; tel. (341) 440-0777; e-mail prensapdpsantafe@gmail.com; internet www.pdp.org.ar; f. 1914; Gen. Sec. CARLOS FAVARI; 36,000 mems.

Partido Federal: Avda de Mayo 962, 1°, Buenos Aires; tel. (11) 4338-3071; e-mail partido@federal.org.ar; internet www.federal.org.ar; f. 1983; mem. of the Unidos por la Libertad y el Trabajo alliance formed to contest the 2013 elections.

Partido Justicialista (PJ): Domingo Matheu 128/130, C1082ABD Buenos Aires; tel. (11) 4954-2450; fax (11) 4954-2421; e-mail contacto@pj.org.ar; internet www.pj.org.ar; f. 1945; broad grouping of Peronist parties; Pres. (vacant); Vice-Pres. DANIEL OSVALDO SCIOLI; Sec.-Gen. JOSÉ LUIS GIOJA; 3.6m. mems; includes the following factions:

Frente para la Victoria (FPV): e-mail webmaster@diarioelsol.com.ar; internet www.frenteparalavictoria.org; f. 2003; centre-left; ruling faction of the PJ; Leader CRISTINA FERNÁNDEZ DE KIRCHNER.

Partido Conservador Popular: Rivadavia 1645, (Entre EP°), C1033AAG Buenos Aires; tel. (11) 4372-3791; internet www.atalayaweb.com.ar/pcp; f. 1958; Pres. GUILLERMO DURAND CORNEJO.

Partido Frente Grande: Junín 156, entre Bartolomé Mitre y Perón, Buenos Aires; tel. (11) 3970-6480; e-mail info@frentegrande.org.ar; internet www.frentegrande.org.ar; f. 1993 as an electoral front; Pres. ADRIANA PUIGGRÓS; Sec.-Gen. DANIEL SAN CRISTOBAL.

Partido Humanista: San Juan 1828, C1232AAN Buenos Aires; tel. (11) 6176-4132; e-mail phumanistaprensa@gmail.com; internet www.partidohumanista.org.ar; f. 1984; Gen. Sec. ESTHER SOSA.

Partido Intransigente: Riobamba 482, C1025ABJ Buenos Aires; tel. (11) 4954-2283; e-mail nacional@pi.org.ar; internet www.pi.org.ar; f. 1957; left-wing; Pres. Dr ENRIQUE GUSTAVO CARDESA; Sec. AMERICO PARODI; 57,000 mems.

Frente Renovador (FR): Buenos Aires; internet www.frenterenovador.org.ar; dissident Peronist party; Leader SERGIO MASSA.

Partido Socialista Auténtico: Sarandí 56, C1081ACB Buenos Aires; tel. and fax (11) 4952-3103; e-mail consultas@psa.org.ar; internet www.psa.org.ar; Sec.-Gen. MARIO MAZZITELLI; 13,000 mems.

Política Abierta para la Integridad Social (PAIS): Corrientes 2141, Of. 10, C1043AAL Buenos Aires; tel. (11) 4383-6350; e-mail info@partidopais.com.ar; internet www.partidopais.com.ar; f. 1994 following split with the PJ; contested the 2011 elections as a mem. of the Alianza Compromiso Federal; Pres. FÉLIX MARIANO ACEVEDO.

Propuesta Republicana (PRO): Alsina 1325, C1088AAI Buenos Aires; e-mail info@pro.com.ar; internet www.pro.com.ar; f. 2005; centre-right; Leader MAURICIO MACRI.

Unión Celeste y Blanco: tel. (11) 4779-6418; e-mail union@celesteyblanco.com; internet www.unioncelesteyblanco.com; mem. of the Unidos por la Libertad y el Trabajo alliance formed to contest the 2013 elections; Leader FRANCISCO DE NARVÁEZ.

Unión del Centro Democrático (UCeDé): Hipólito Yrigoyen 636, 6°B Buenos Aires; tel. (11) 4381-3763; internet ucedenacional.blogspot.com; f. 1980; contested the 2011 elections as a mem. of the Alianza Compromiso Federal; Pres. JORGE PEREYRA DE OLAZÁBAL; Sec.-Gen. HUGO EDUARDO BONTEMPO; 77,000 mems.

Unión Cívica Radical (UCR): Alsina 1786, C1088AAR Buenos Aires; tel. and fax (11) 5199-0600; e-mail webmaster@ucr.org.ar; internet www.ucr.org.ar; f. 1890; moderate; contested the 2011 elections as mem. of the Unión para el Desarrollo Social coalition; Pres. LILIA PUIG DE STUBRIN; Gen. Sec. JUAN MANUEL CASELLA; 2.5m. mems.

Unión por Córdoba: Córdoba; Leader FRANCISCO J. FORTUNA.

Unión Popular: Maipú 3685, 1702, Buenos Aires; tel. (11) 4488-3279; e-mail pdounionpopular@yahoo.com.ar; internet www.partidounionpopular.org; mem. of the Unidos por la Libertad y el Trabajo alliance formed to contest the 2013 elections; Nat. Pres. Dr MARCELO D'ALESSANDRO; 16,000 mems.

OTHER ORGANIZATIONS

Asociación Madres de Plaza de Mayo: Hipólito Yrigoyen 1584, C1089AAD Buenos Aires; tel. (11) 4383-0377; fax (11) 4954-0381; e-mail madres@madres.org; internet www.madres.org; f. 1979; formed by mothers of those who 'disappeared' during the years of military rule, it has since become a broad-based anti-poverty grouping with socialist aims; Founder and Leader HEBE MARÍA PASTOR DE BONAFINI.

Diplomatic Representation

EMBASSIES IN ARGENTINA

Albania: Juez Tedín 3036, 4°, C1425CWH Buenos Aires; tel. (11) 48093574; fax (11) 48078767; e-mail embassy.buenosaires@mfa.gov.al; Ambassador REZAR BREGU.

Algeria: Montevideo 1889, C1021AAE Buenos Aires; tel. (11) 4815-1271; fax (11) 4815-8837; e-mail embajadaargelia@fibertel.com.ar; Ambassador BENAOUDA HAMEL.

Angola: La Pampa 3452-56, C1430BXD Buenos Aires; tel. (11) 4554-8383; fax (11) 4554-8998; Ambassador HERMÍNIO JOAQUIM ESCÓRCIO.

Armenia: José Andrés Pacheco de Melo 1922, C1126AAD Buenos Aires; tel. (11) 4816-8710; fax (11) 4812-2803; e-mail armenia@fibertel.com.ar; Ambassador VAHAGN MELIKYAN.

Australia: Villanueva 1400, C1426BMJ Buenos Aires; tel. (11) 4779-3500; fax (11) 4779-3581; e-mail info.ba.general@dfat.gov.au; internet www.argentina.embassy.gov.au; Ambassador PATRICIA ANN HOLMES.

Austria: French 3671, C1425AXC Buenos Aires; tel. (11) 4807-9185; fax (11) 4805-4016; e-mail buenos-aires-ob@bmeia.gv.at; internet www.bmeia.gv.at/botschaft/buenos-aires.html; Ambassador KARIN PROIDL.

Azerbaijan: Gorostiaga 2176, C1426BMC Buenos Aires; tel. (11) 4777-3655; fax (11) 4777-8928; e-mail buenosaires@azembassy.com.ar; internet www.azembassy.com.ar; Ambassador MAMMAD AHAMDZADA.

Belarus: Cazadores 2166, C1428AVH Buenos Aires; tel. (11) 4788-9394; fax (11) 4788-2322; e-mail argentina@mfa.gov.by; internet www.argentina.mfa.gov.by; Ambassador VICTOR KOZINTEV.

Belgium: Defensa 113, 8°, C1065AAA Buenos Aires; tel. (11) 4331-0066; fax (11) 4331-0814; e-mail BuenosAires@diplobel.fed.be; internet www.diplomatie.be/buenosaires; Ambassador PATRICK RENAULT.

Bolivia: Corrientes 545, 2°, C1043AAF Buenos Aires; tel. (11) 4394-1463; fax (11) 4394-0460; e-mail embolivia-baires@ree.gov.bo; internet www.embajadadebolivia.com.ar; Ambassador LIBORIO FLORES ENRIQUEZ.

Brazil: Cerrito 1350, C1010ABB Buenos Aires; tel. (11) 4515-2400; fax (11) 4515-2401; e-mail info@embrasil.org.ar; internet www.brasil.org.ar; Ambassador EVERTON VIEIRA VARGAS.

Bulgaria: Mariscal A. J. de Sucre 1568, C1428DUT Buenos Aires; tel. (11) 4781-8644; fax (11) 4781-1214; e-mail embular@uolsinectis.com.ar; internet www.mfa.bg/embassies/argentina; Ambassador MAXIM GAYTANDJIEV.

Canada: Tagle 2828, C1425EEH Buenos Aires; tel. (11) 4808-1000; fax (11) 4808-1111; e-mail bairs-webmail@international.gc.ca; internet www.canadainternational.gc.ca/argentina-argentine; Ambassador GWYNETH A. KUTZ.

Chile: Tagle 2762, C1425EEF Buenos Aires; tel. (11) 4808-8600; fax (11) 4804-5927; e-mail echile.argentina@minrel.gov.cl; internet chileabroad.gov.cl/argentina; Ambassador MARCELO DÍAZ.

China, People's Republic: Crisólogo Larralde 5349, C1431APM Buenos Aires; tel. (11) 4547-8100; fax (11) 4545-1141; e-mail chinaemb_ar@mfa.gov.cn; internet ar.chineseembassy.org/esp; Ambassador YIN HENGMIN.

Colombia: Carlos Pellegrini 1363, 3°, C1011AAA Buenos Aires; tel. (11) 4325-0258; fax (11) 4322-9370; e-mail ebaires@cancilleria.gov.co; internet argentina.embajada.gov.co; Ambassador CARLOS ENRIQUE RODADO NORIEGA.

Congo, Democratic Republic: Arcos 2340, 2°, Depto G, C1428EON Buenos Aires; tel. (11) 4896-4963; e-mail rdcbuenos@hotmail.com; Chargé d'affaires a.i. YEMBA LOHAKA.

Costa Rica: Pacheco de Melo 1833, 5°, C1126AAD Buenos Aires; tel. (11) 4802-5983; fax (11) 4801-3222; e-mail embarica@fibertel.com.ar; Ambassador LUIS ALBERTO CORDERO ARIAS.

Croatia: Gorostiaga 2104, C1426CTN Buenos Aires; tel. (11) 4777-6409; fax (11) 4777-9159; e-mail croemb.ar@mvpei.hr; Ambassador ŽELJKO BELAJ.

Cuba: Virrey del Pino 1810, Belgrano, C1426EGF Buenos Aires; tel. (11) 4782-9049; fax (11) 4786-7713; e-mail oficinaembajador@ar.embacuba.cu; internet www.cubadiplomatica.cu/argentina; Ambassador JORGE NÉSTOR LAMADRID MASCARÓ.

Czech Republic: Junín 1461, C1113AAM Buenos Aires; tel. (11) 4807-3107; fax (11) 4800-1088; e-mail buenosaires@embassy.mzv.cz; internet www.mzv.cz/buenosaires; Ambassador PETR KOPŘIVA.

Denmark: Avda Leandro N. Alem 1074, 9°, C1001AAS Buenos Aires; tel. (11) 4312-6901; fax (11) 4312-7857; e-mail bueamb@um.dk; internet www.buenosaires.um.dk; Chargé d'affaires a.i. LARS BO KIRKETERP LUND.

Dominican Republic: Juncal 802, 6°, C1062ABF Buenos Aires; tel. (11) 4312-9378; fax (11) 4894-2078; e-mail embajadadombaires@fibertel.com.ar; Ambassador GUILLERMO EDUARDO PIÑA-CONTRERAS.

Ecuador: Quintana 585, 9°, C1129ABB Buenos Aires; tel. (11) 4804-0073; fax (11) 4804-0074; e-mail embecuador@embecuador.com.ar; Ambassador GLORIA PIEDAD VIDAL ILLINGWORTH.

Egypt: Virrey del Pino 3140, C1426EHF Buenos Aires; tel. (11) 4553-3311; fax (11) 4553-0067; e-mail embegypt@fibertel.com.ar; Ambassador REDA HABIB ZAKI.

El Salvador: Rodriguez Peña 1627 3°, C1011ACD Buenos Aires; tel. (11) 4813-2525; fax (11) 4812-9353; e-mail elsalvador@fibertel.com.ar; internet www.embajadaelsalvador.com.ar; Ambassador OSCAR ERNESTO MENJIBAR CHÁVEZ.

Finland: Santa Fe 846, 5°, C1059ABP Buenos Aires; tel. (11) 4312-0600; fax (11) 4312-0670; e-mail sanomat.bue@formin.fi; internet www.finlandia.org.ar; Ambassador JUKKA SIUKOSAARI.

France: Cerrito 1399, C1010ABA Buenos Aires; tel. (11) 4515-2930; fax (11) 4515-0120; e-mail ambafr@abaconet.com.ar; internet www.embafrancia-argentina.org; Ambassador JEAN-MICHEL CASA.

Georgia: 14 de Julio 1656, C1430END Buenos Aires; tel. (11) 4554-5176; e-mail buenosaires.emb@mfa.gov.ge; Ambassador GUELA SEKHNIACHVILI.

Germany: Villanueva 1055, C1426BMC Buenos Aires; tel. (11) 4778-2500; fax (11) 4778-2550; e-mail info@buenos-aires.diplo.de; internet www.buenos-aires.diplo.de; Ambassador BERNHARD GRAF VON WALDERSEE.

Greece: Mariscal Ramón Castilla 2952, C1425DZF Buenos Aires; tel. (11) 4805-1100; fax (11) 4806-4686; e-mail gremb.bay@mfa.gr; internet www.mfa.gr/buenosaires; Ambassador ELENI LEIVADITOU.

Guatemala: Juncal 802, 3° H, C1062ABF Buenos Aires; tel. (11) 4313-9180; fax (11) 4313-9181; e-mail embajadaguatemala@fibertel.com.ar; Ambassador CARLOS RAMIRO MARTÍNEZ ALVARADO.

Haiti: Avda Figueroa Alcorta 3297, C1425CKL Buenos Aires; tel. (11) 4802-0211; fax (11) 4802-3984; e-mail embajadahaiti@fibertel.com.ar; Chargé d'affaires a.i. JEANÇOIS JOSEPH.

Holy See: Marcelo T. de Alvear 1605, C1014AAD Buenos Aires; tel. (11) 4813-9697; fax (11) 4815-4097; e-mail nunciaturaapostolica@speedy.com.ar; Apostolic Nuncio Most Rev. EMIL PAUL TSCHERRIG (Titular Archbishop of Voli).

Honduras: Avda Callao 1564, 2°, C1024AAO Buenos Aires; tel. (11) 5199-7080; fax (11) 4804-1875; e-mail embajada@embajadadehonduras.com.ar; Chargé d'affaires a.i. DIMAS ALEXI ESCOBAR GUILLEN.

Hungary: Plaza 1726, C1430DGF Buenos Aires; tel. (11) 4553-4646; fax (11) 4555-6859; e-mail mission.bue@kum.hu; internet www.mfa.gov.hu/emb/buenosaires; Ambassador PÁL VARGA KORITÁR.

India: Torre Madero, 19°, Avda Eduardo Madero 942, C1106ACW Buenos Aires; tel. (11) 4393-4001; fax (11) 4393-4063; e-mail indemb@indembarg.org.ar; internet www.indembarg.org.ar; Ambassador Dr AMARENDRA KHATUA.

Indonesia: Mariscal Ramón Castilla 2901, C1425DZE Buenos Aires; tel. (11) 4807-2211; fax (11) 4802-4448; e-mail emindo@tournet.com.ar; internet www.indonesianembassy.org.ar; Ambassador NURMALA KARTINI PANDJAITAN SJAHRIR.

Iran: Avda Figueroa Alcorta 3229, C1425CKL Buenos Aires; tel. (11) 4802-1470; fax (11) 4805-4409; e-mail embajadairan@fibertel.com.ar; Chargé d'affaires HAHMAD REZA KHEIRMAND.

Ireland: Avda del Libertador 1068, Edif. Bluesky, 6°, Recoleta, C1112ABN Buenos Aires; tel. (11) 5787-0801; fax (11) 5787-0802; e-mail info@irlanda.org.ar; internet www.embassyofireland.org.ar; Ambassador JAMES MCINTYRE.

Israel: Avda de Mayo 701, 10°, C1084AAC Buenos Aires; tel. (11) 4338-2500; fax (11) 4338-2624; e-mail info@buenosaires.mfa.gov.il; internet buenosaires.mfa.gov.il; Ambassador DORIT SHAVIT.

Italy: Billinghurst 2577, C1425DTY Buenos Aires; tel. (11) 4011-2100; fax (11) 4011-2159; e-mail segreteria.buenosaires@esteri.it; internet www.ambbuenosaires.esteri.it; Ambassador TERESA CASTALDO.

Japan: Bouchard 547, 17°, C1106ABG Buenos Aires; tel. (11) 4318-8200; fax (11) 4318-8210; e-mail taishikan@japan.org.ar; internet www.ar.emb-japan.go.jp; Ambassador MASASHI MIZUKAMI.

Korea, Republic: Avda del Libertador 2395, C1425AAJ Buenos Aires; tel. (11) 4802-9665; fax (11) 4803-6993; e-mail argentina@mofa.go.kr; Ambassador BYUNG-KIL HAN.

Kuwait: Uruguay 739, C1015ABO Buenos Aires; tel. (11) 4374-7202; fax (11) 4374-0489; e-mail info@embajadadekuwait.com.ar; internet www.embajadadekuwait.com.ar; Ambassador SALAH MUBARAK AL-MUTAIRI.

Lebanon: Avda del Libertador 2354, C1425AAW Buenos Aires; tel. (11) 4802-0466; fax (11) 4802-0929; e-mail embajada@ellibano.com.ar; internet www.ellibano.com.ar; Ambassador ANTONIO NASER ANDARY.

Libya: Virrey del Pino 3432, C1426EHL Buenos Aires; tel. (11) 4553-4669; fax (11) 4551-6187; e-mail embajadadelibia@hotmail.com.ar; Chargé d'affaires a.i. MATOUG S. S. ABORAWI.

Malaysia: Villanueva 1040, C1426BMD Buenos Aires; tel. (11) 4776-2553; fax (11) 4776-0604; e-mail malbnaires@kln.gov.my; internet www.kln.gov.my/perwakilan/buenosaires; Chargé d'affaires a.i. AHMAD KAMRIZAMIL BIN MOHD RIZA.

Mexico: Arcos 1650, C1426BGL Buenos Aires; tel. (11) 4118-8800; fax (11) 4118-8837; e-mail info@embamex.int.ar; internet embamex.sre.gob.mx/argentina; Chargé d'affaires a.i. MARÍA TERESA MERCADO PÉREZ.

Morocco: Castex 3461, C1425CDG Buenos Aires; tel. (11) 4801-8154; fax (11) 4802-0136; e-mail sifamarruecos@fibertel.com.ar; Ambassador FOUAD YAZOURH.

Netherlands: Edif. Porteño II, Olga Cossettini 831, 3°, C1107CDC Buenos Aires; tel. (11) 4338-0050; fax (11) 4338-0060; e-mail bue@minbuza.nl; internet www.embajadaholanda.int.ar; Ambassador HEIN DE VRIES.

New Zealand: Carlos Pellegrini 1427, 5°, C1011AAC Buenos Aires; tel. (11) 4328-0747; fax (11) 4328-0757; e-mail kiwiarg@speedy.com.ar; internet www.nzembassy.com/argentina; Ambassador HAYDEN MONTGOMERY.

Nicaragua: Santa Fe 1845, 7°, Of. B, C1123AAA Buenos Aires; tel. (11) 4811-0973; fax (11) 4811-0973; e-mail zmasis@cancilleria.gob.ni; Ambassador NORMA MORENO SILVA.

Nigeria: Juez Estrada 2746, Palermo, C1425CPD Buenos Aires; tel. (11) 4328-8717; fax (11) 4807-1782; e-mail info@nigerianembassy.org; internet www.nigerianembassy.org.ar; Ambassador CHIVE KAAVE.

Norway: Carlos Pelegrini 1427, 2°, C1011AAC Buenos Aires; tel. (11) 3724-1200; fax (11) 4328-9048; e-mail emb.buenosaires@mfa.no; internet www.noruega.org.ar; Ambassador JANNE JULSRUD.

Pakistan: Gorostiaga 2176, C1426CTN Buenos Aires; tel. (11) 4775-1294; fax (11) 4776-1186; e-mail parepbaires@fibertel.com.ar; internet www.embassypakistan.com.ar; Ambassador IMTIAZ AHMAD.

Panama: Santa Fe 1461, 1°, C1060ABA Buenos Aires; tel. (11) 4811-1254; fax (11) 4814-0450; e-mail epar@fibertel.com.ar; internet www.embajadadepanama.com.ar; Ambassador MARIO ANTONIO BOYD GALINDO.

Paraguay: Las Heras 2545, C1425ASC Buenos Aires; tel. (11) 4802-3826; fax (11) 4807-7600; e-mail embaparba@fibertel.com.ar; Ambassador NICANOR DUARTE FRUTOS.

Peru: Avda del Libertador 1720, C1425AAQ Buenos Aires; tel. (11) 4802-2000; fax (11) 4802-5887; e-mail contacto@embajadadelperu.int.ar; internet www.embajadadelperu.int.ar; Ambassador JOSÉ LUIS NÉSTOR PÉREZ SÁNCHEZ-CERRO.

Philippines: Zapiola 1701, C1426AUI Buenos Aires; tel. (11) 4554-4015; fax (11) 4554-9194; e-mail pheba@fibertel.com.ar; internet www.buenosairespe.com.ar; Ambassador REY A. CARANDANG.

Poland: Alejandro María de Aguado 2870, C1425CEB Buenos Aires; tel. (11) 4808-1700; fax (11) 4808-1701; e-mail secretaria.buenosaires@msz.gov.pl; internet www.buenosaires.polemb.net; Ambassador JACEK BAZAŃSKI.

Portugal: Maipú 942, 17°, C1006ACN Buenos Aires; tel. (11) 4312-3524; fax (11) 4311-2586; e-mail embpor@buenosaires.dgaccp.pt; internet www.embaixadaportugal.com.ar; Ambassador HENRIQUE SILVEIRA BORGES.

Qatar: Buenos Aires; tel. (11) 4318-9198; Ambassador FAHAD BIN IBRAHIM AL HAMAD AL MANA.

Romania: Arroyo 962–970, C1007AAD Buenos Aires; tel. (11) 4326-5888; fax (11) 4322-2630; e-mail embarombue@rumania.org.ar; internet www.rumania.org.ar; Chargé d'affaires a.i. SENA LATIF.

Russia: Rodríguez Peña 1741, C1021ABK Buenos Aires; tel. (11) 4813-1552; fax (11) 4815-6293; e-mail embrusia@gmail.com; internet www.argentina.mid.ru; Ambassador VICTOR KORONELLI.

Saudi Arabia: Alejandro María de Aguado 2881, C1425CEA Buenos Aires; tel. (11) 4802-0760; fax (11) 4806-1581; e-mail aremb@mofa.gov.sa; Ambassador TURKI M. A. AL-MADI.

Serbia: Marcelo T. de Alvear 1705, C1060AAG Buenos Aires; tel. (11) 4813-3446; fax (11) 4812-1070; e-mail serbembaires@ciudad.com.ar; internet www.buenosaires.mfa.gov.rs; Chargé d'affaires a.i. MARIJA PETROVIC.

Slovakia: Figueroa Alcorta 3240, C1425CKY Buenos Aires; tel. (11) 4801-3917; fax (11) 4801-4654; e-mail emb.buenosaires@mzv.sk; Ambassador PAVEL ŠÍPKA.

Slovenia: Santa Fe 846, 6°, C1059ABP Buenos Aires; tel. (11) 4894-0621; fax (11) 4312-8410; e-mail vba@gov.si; internet www.buenosaires.veleposlanistvo.si; Ambassador TOMAŽ MENCIN.

South Africa: Marcelo T. de Alvear 590, 8°, C1058AAF Buenos Aires; tel. (11) 4317-2900; fax (11) 4311-8993; e-mail embajador.argentina@foreign.gov.za; internet www.sudafrica.org.ar; Ambassador ZENANI MANDELA-DLAMINI.

Spain: Avda Figueroa Alcorta 3102, C1425CKX Buenos Aires; tel. (11) 4809-4900; fax (11) 4809-4919; e-mail emb.buenosaires@maec.es; internet www.maec.es/embajadas/buenosaires; Ambassador ESTANISLAO DE GRANDES PASCUAL.

Sweden: Tacuari 147, 6°, C1071AAC Buenos Aires; tel. (11) 4329-0800; fax (11) 4342-1697; e-mail ambassaden.buenos-aires@foreign.ministery.se; internet www.swedenabroad.com/buenosaires; Ambassador GUFRAN AL-NADAF.

Switzerland: Santa Fe 846, 12°, C1059ABP Buenos Aires; tel. (11) 4311-6491; fax (11) 4313-2998; e-mail bue.vertretung@eda.admin.ch; internet www.eda.admin.ch/buenosaires; Ambassador JOHANN STEPHAN MATYASSY.

Syria: Callao 956, C1023AAP Buenos Aires; tel. (11) 4813-2113; fax (11) 4814-3211; Chargé d'affaires a.i. HAMZEH DAWALIBI.

Thailand: Vuelta de Obligado 1947, 12°, C1428ADC Buenos Aires; tel. (11) 4780-0555; fax (11) 4782-1616; e-mail thaiembargen@fibertel.com.ar; internet www.thaiembargen.org; Ambassador MEDHA PROMTHEP.

Tunisia: Ciudad de la Paz 3086, C1429ACD Buenos Aires; tel. (11) 4544-2618; fax (11) 4545-6369; e-mail atbuenosaires@infovia.com.ar; Ambassador HICHEM BAYOUDH.

Turkey: 11 de Septiembre 1382, C1426BKN Buenos Aires; tel. (11) 4788-3239; fax (11) 4784-9179; e-mail embajada.buenosaires@mfa.gov.tr; internet buenosaires.be.mfa.gov.tr; Ambassador TANER KARAKAS.

Ukraine: Conde 1763, C1426AZI Buenos Aires; tel. (11) 4552-0657; fax (11) 4552-6771; e-mail embucra@embucra.com.ar; internet www.mfa.gov.ua/argentina; Ambassador YURII DIUDIN.

United Arab Emirates: Olleros 2021, C1426BRK Buenos Aires; tel. (11) 4771-9716; fax (11) 4772-5169; Ambassador ABDULKHALEQ ALI SABED BIN DHAEER ALYAFEI.

United Kingdom: Dr Luis Agote 2412, C1425EOF Buenos Aires; tel. (11) 4808-2200; fax (11) 4808-2274; e-mail askinformation.baires@fco.gov.uk; internet ukinargentina.fco.gov.uk; Ambassador JOHN FREEMAN.

USA: Avda Colombia 4300, C1425GMN Buenos Aires; tel. (11) 5777-4533; fax (11) 5777-4240; internet argentina.usembassy.gov; Chargé d'affaires a.i. KEVIN K. SULLIVAN.

Uruguay: Las Heras 1907, C1127AAB Buenos Aires; tel. (11) 4807-3040; fax (11) 4807-3050; e-mail urubaires@embajadadeluruguay.com.ar; internet www.embajadadeluruguay.com.ar; Ambassador GUILLERMO JOSÉ POMI BARRIOLA.

Venezuela: Virrey Loreto 2035, C1426DXK Buenos Aires; tel. (11) 4788-4944; fax (11) 4784-4311; e-mail embaven@arnet.com.ar; Ambassador CARLOS EDUARDO MARTÍNEZ MENDOZA.

Viet Nam: 11 de Septiembre 1442, C1426BKP Buenos Aires; tel. (11) 4783-1802; fax (11) 4782-0078; e-mail sqvnartn@fibertel.com.ar; Ambassador THAO NGUYEN DINH.

Judicial System

SUPREME COURT

Corte Suprema: Talcahuano 550, 4°, C1013AAL Buenos Aires; tel. (11) 4370-4600; fax (11) 4340-2270; e-mail consultas@cjsn.gov.ar; internet www.csjn.gov.ar; mems of the Supreme Court are appointed by the President with the agreement of at least two-thirds of the Senate; mems can be dismissed by impeachment; Pres. RICARDO LUIS LORENZETTI; Vice-Pres. ELENA I. HIGHTON DE NOLASCO.

OTHER COURTS

Judges of the lower, national or further lower courts are appointed by the President, with the agreement of the Senate, and can be dismissed by impeachment. Judges retire on reaching 75 years of age.

The Federal Court of Appeal in Buenos Aires has three courts: civil and commercial, criminal, and administrative. There are six other courts of appeal in Buenos Aires: civil, commercial, criminal, peace, labour, and penal-economic. There are also federal appeal courts in La Plata, Bahía Blanca, Paraná, Rosario, Córdoba, Mendoza, Tucumán and Resistencia. In 1994 the Office of the Attorney-General was established and in 1997 a Council of Magistrates was created.

The provincial courts each have their own Supreme Court and a system of subsidiary courts. They deal with cases originating within and confined to the provinces.

Consejo de la Magistratura de la Nación: Avda Libertad 731, 2°, 1017 Buenos Aires; tel. (11) 4124-5394; fax (11) 4124-5394; e-mail propuestas@pjn.gov.ar; internet www.consejomagistratura.gov.ar; responsible for the selection of judges, of suspending or deposing them, and the administration of the judiciary; consists of 13 mems; six legislators, three national judges, two federal lawyers, one academic and a govt representative; Pres. Dr MARIO S. FERA; Sec.-Gen. Dr MARÍA SUSANA BERTERREIX.

Attorney-General: ALEJANDRA GILS CARBÓ.

Religion

CHRISTIANITY

The Roman Catholic Church

Some 76% of the population are Roman Catholics.

Argentina comprises 14 archdioceses, 51 dioceses (including one each for Uniate Catholics of the Ukrainian rite, of the Maronite rite and of the Armenian rite), four territorial prelatures and an apostolic exarchate for Catholics of the Melkite rite. The Bishop of San Gregorio de Narek en Buenos Aires is also the Apostolic Exarch of Latin America and Mexico for Catholics of the Armenian rite, and the Archbishop of Buenos Aires is also the Ordinary for Catholics of other Oriental rites.

Bishops' Conference (Conferencia Episcopal Argentina): Suipacha 1034, C1008AAV Buenos Aires; tel. (11) 4328-0993; fax (11) 4328-9570; e-mail seccea@cea.org.ar; internet www.episcopado.org; f. 1959; Pres. JOSÉ MARÍA ARANCEDO (Archbishop of Santa Fe de la Vera Cruz).

Armenian Rite

Bishop of San Gregorio de Narek en Buenos Aires: VARTÁN WALDIR BOGHOSSIAN, Charcas 3529, C1425BMU Buenos Aires; tel. (11) 4824-1613; fax (11) 4827-1975; e-mail exarmal@pcn.net; f. 1989.

Latin Rite

Archbishop of Bahía Blanca: GUILLERMO JOSÉ GARLATTI, Avda Colón 164, B8000FTO Bahía Blanca; tel. (291) 455-0707; fax (291) 452-2070; e-mail arzobis@arzobispadobahia.org.ar; internet www.arzobispadobahia.org.ar.

Archbishop of Buenos Aires: Cardinal MARIO AURELIO POLI, Rivadavia 415, C1002AAC Buenos Aires; tel. (11) 4343-0812; fax (11) 4334-8373; e-mail arzobispado@arzbaires.org.ar; internet www.arzbaires.org.ar.

Archbishop of Córdoba: CARLOS JOSÉ ÑAÑEZ, Hipólito Irigoyen 98, X5000JHN Córdoba; tel. and fax (351) 422-1015; e-mail comunicacionpastoral@arzobispado.org.ar; internet www.arzobispadocba.org.ar.

Archbishop of Corrientes: ANDRÉS STANOVNIK, 9 de Julio 1543, W3400AZA Corrientes; tel. and fax (3783) 422436; e-mail arzobispadodecorrientes@gmail.com; internet www.arzcorrientes.com.ar.

Archbishop of La Plata: HÉCTOR RUBÉN AGUER, Calle 14 Centro 1009, B1900DVQ La Plata; tel. (221) 425-1656; e-mail arzobispadodelaplata@speedy.com.ar; internet www.arzolap.org.ar.

Archbishop of Mendoza: CARLOS MARÍA FRANZINI, Catamarca 98, M5500CKB Mendoza; tel. (261) 423-3862; fax (261) 429-5415; e-mail arzobispadomza@supernet.com.ar; internet www.arquimendoza.org.ar.

Archbishop of Mercedes-Luján: AGUSTÍN ROBERTO RADRIZZANI, Calle 22 745, B6600HDU Mercedes; tel. (2324) 432-412; fax (2324) 432-104; e-mail arzomerce.informacion@gmail.com; internet arquimercedes-lujan.com.ar.

Archbishop of Paraná: JUAN ALBERTO PUIGGARI, Monte Caseros 77, E3100ACA Paraná; tel. (343) 431-1440; fax (343) 423-0372; e-mail prensa@arzparan.org.ar; internet www.arzparan.org.ar.

Archbishop of Resistencia: FABRICIANO SIGAMPA, Bartolomé Mitre 363, Casilla 35, H3500BLG Resistencia; tel. and fax (3722) 441908; e-mail arzobrcia@arnet.com.ar.

Archbishop of Rosario: JOSÉ LUIS MOLLAGHAN, Córdoba 1677, S2000AWY Rosario; tel. (341) 425-1298; fax (341) 425-1207; e-mail arzobros@uolsinectis.com.ar; internet www.delrosario.org.ar.

Archbishop of Salta: MARIO ANTONIO CARGNELLO, España 596, A4400ANL Salta; tel. (387) 421-4306; fax (387) 421-3101; e-mail prensaarzobispado@ucasal.net; internet www.arquidiocesissalta.org.ar.

Archbishop of San Juan de Cuyo: ALFONSO ROGELIO DELGADO EVERS, Bartolomé Mitre 250 Oeste, J5402CXF San Juan; tel. (264) 422-2578; fax (264) 427-3530; e-mail arzobispadosanjuan@infovia.com.ar; internet www.iglesiasanjuancuyo.org.ar.

Archbishop of Santa Fe de la Vera Cruz: JOSÉ MARÍA ARANCEDO, Avda Brig.-Gen. E. López 2720, S3000DCJ Santa Fe; tel. (342) 459-1780; fax (342) 459-4491; e-mail curia@arquisantafe.org.ar; internet www.arquisantafe.org.ar.

Archbishop of Tucumán: ALFREDO ZECCA, Avda Sarmiento 895, T4000GTI San Miguel de Tucumán; tel. (381) 431-0617; e-mail arztuc@arnet.com.ar; internet www.arztucuman.org.ar.

Maronite Rite

Bishop of San Charbel en Buenos Aires: CHARBEL GEORGES MERHI, Eparquía Maronita, Colegio San Marón, Paraguay 834, C1057AAL Buenos Aires; tel. (11) 4311-7299; fax (11) 4312-8348; e-mail sanmaron@misionlibanesa.com; internet www.misionlibanesa.com.ar.

Melkite Rite

Apostolic Exarch: ABDO ARBACH, Exarcado Apostólico Greco-Melquita, Corrientes 276, X5000ANF Córdoba; tel. (351) 421-0625; e-mail catedralmelquitasanjorge@gmail.com; internet www.exarcadoapostolicogreco-melkitacatolicoenargentina.com.

Ukrainian Rite

Bishop of Santa María del Patrocinio en Buenos Aires: Rt Rev. DANIEL KOZELINSKI NETTO, Ramón L. Falcón 3950, Casilla 28, C1407GSN Buenos Aires; tel. (11) 4671-4192; fax (11) 4671-7265; e-mail pokrov@ciudad.com.ar.

The Anglican Communion

The Iglesia Anglicana del Cono Sur de América (Anglican Church of the Southern Cone of America) comprises seven dioceses: Argentina, Northern Argentina, Chile, Paraguay, Peru, Bolivia and Uruguay.

Bishop of Argentina: Rt Rev. GREGORY JAMES VENABLES, 25 de Mayo 282, C1002ABF Buenos Aires; tel. (11) 4342-4618; fax (11) 4784-1277; e-mail diocesisanglibue@fibertel.com.ar; internet www.anglicanaargentina.org.ar.

Bishop of Northern Argentina: Rt Rev. NICHOLAS JAMES QUESTED DRAYSON, Iglesia Anglicana, Casilla 187, A4400ANL Salta; tel. (387) 431-1718; fax (371) 142-0100; e-mail nicobispo@gmail.com; jurisdiction extends to Jujuy, Salta, Tucumán, Catamarca, Santiago del Estero, Formosa and Chaco.

Other Christian Churches

Church of Jesus Christ of Latter-Day Saints (Mormons): Autopista Richieri y Puente 13, Ciudad Evita, B1778DUA Buenos Aires; tel. (11) 4487-1848; internet www.lds.org; 412,095 mems.

Convención Evangélica Bautista Argentina (Baptist Evangelical Convention): Virrey Liniers 42, C1174ACB Buenos Aires; tel. and fax (11) 4864-2711; e-mail administracion@confeba.org.ar; internet www.confeba.org.ar; f. 1908; Pres. NÉSTOR GOLLUSCIO.

Federación Argentina de Iglesias Evangélicas (Argentine Federation of Evangelical Churches): Condarco 321, C1604AFE Buenos Aires; tel. and fax (11) 4611-1437; e-mail presidencia@faie.org.ar; internet www.faie.org.ar; f. 1938; 21 mem. churches; Pres. KARIN KRUG; Sec. Dr ALBERTO ROLDÁN.

Iglesia Evangélica Luterana Argentina (Evangelical Lutheran Church of Argentina): Ing. Silveyra 1639-41, B1607BQM Villa Adelina, Buenos Aires; tel. (11) 4735-4155; fax (11) 4766-7948;

e-mail ielapresidente@arnet.com.ar; internet www.iela.org.ar; f. 1905; 30,000 mems; Pres. CARLOS NAGEL.

Iglesia Evangélica Luterana Unida (United Evangelical Lutheran Church): Marcos Sastre 2891, C1417FYE Buenos Aires; tel. (11) 4501-3925; fax 4504-7358; e-mail contacto@ielu.org; internet www.ielu.org; 11,000 mems; Pres. Rev. GUSTAVO GÓMEZ PASCUA.

Iglesia Evangélica Metodista Argentina (Methodist Church of Argentina): Rivadavia 4044, 3°, C1205AAN Buenos Aires; tel. (11) 4981-4474; fax (11) 4981-0885; e-mail secretariaadministracion@iglesiametodista.org.ar; internet www.iglesiametodista.org.ar; f. 1836; Bishop FRANK DE NULLY BROWN.

Iglesia Evangélica del Río de la Plata (Evangelical Church of the Plate River): Mariscal Sucre 2855, C1428DVY Buenos Aires; tel. (11) 4787-0436; fax (11) 4787-0335; e-mail presidente@ierp.org.ar; internet www.iglesiaevangelica.org; f. 1899; 27,500 mems; Pres. CARLOS ALFREDO DUARTE VOELKER; Gen. Sec. SONIA SKUPCH.

JUDAISM

There are about 230,000 Jews in Argentina, mostly in Buenos Aires.

Delegación de Asociaciones Israelitas Argentinas (DAIA) (Delegation of Argentine Jewish Associations): Pasteur 633, 7°, C1028AAM Buenos Aires; tel. and fax (11) 4378-3200; e-mail daia@daia.org.ar; internet www.daia.org.ar; f. 1935; Pres. JULIO SCHLOSSER; Exec. Dir VÍCTOR GARELIK.

The Press

PRINCIPAL DAILIES

Buenos Aires

Ambito Financiero: Paseo Colón 1196, C1063ACY Buenos Aires; tel. (11) 4349-1500; fax (11) 4349-1505; e-mail editor@ambito.com.ar; internet www.ambito.com; f. 1976; morning (Mon.–Fri.); business; Dir ORLANDO MARIO VIGNATTI; circ. 115,000.

Boletín Oficial de la República Argentina: Suipacha 767, C1008AAO Buenos Aires; tel. and fax (11) 5218-8400; e-mail dnro@boletinoficial.gov.ar; internet www.boletinoficial.gov.ar; f. 1893; morning (Mon.–Fri.); official records publ; Dir Dr JORGE EDUARDO FEIJOÓ; circ. 15,000.

Buenos Aires Herald: AvdaSan Juan 141, C1064AEB Buenos Aires; tel. and fax (11) 4349-1524; e-mail info@buenosairesherald.com; internet www.buenosairesherald.com; f. 1876; English; independent; morning; Editor-in-Chief SEBASTIÁN LACUNZA; circ. 20,000.

Clarín: Piedras 1743, C1140ABK Buenos Aires; tel. (11) 4309-7500; fax (11) 4309-7559; e-mail cartas@claringlobal.com.ar; internet www.clarin.com; f. 1945; morning; Dir ERNESTINA HERRERA DE NOBLE; Editor RICARDO KIRSCHBAUM; circ. 342,749 (daily), 686,287 (Sun.).

Crónica: Avda Juan de Garay 130, C1063ABN Buenos Aires; tel. (11) 5550-8608; fax (11) 4361-4237; e-mail info@cronica.com.ar; internet www.cronica.com.ar; f. 1963; morning and evening; Dir ALEJANDRO OLMOS; circ. 330,000 (morning), 190,000 (evening), 450,000 (Sun.).

El Cronista Comercial: Paseo Colón 740/6, 1°, C1063ACU Buenos Aires; tel. (11) 4121-9300; fax (11) 4121-9301; e-mail publicidad@cronista.com; internet www.cronista.com; f. 1908; morning; Dir FERNANDO GONZÁLEZ; Editor WALTER BROWN; circ. 65,000.

La Nación: Bouchard 557, C1106ABG Buenos Aires; tel. (11) 4319-1600; fax (11) 4319-1969; e-mail cescribano@lanacion.com.ar; internet www.lanacion.com.ar; f. 1870; morning; independent; Pres. JULIO SAGUIER; Editor-in-Chief JORGE LIOTTI; circ. 170,782 (2012).

Página 12: Solís 1525, C1134ADG Buenos Aires; tel. (11) 6772-4444; fax (11) 6772-4428; e-mail publicidad@pagina12.com.ar; internet www.pagina12.com.ar; f. 1987; morning; independent; Dir ERNESTO TIFFENBERG; Pres. FERNANDO SOKOLOWICZ; circ. 280,000.

La Prensa: Azopardo 715, C1107ADK Buenos Aires; tel. (11) 4349-1000; e-mail informaciongeneral@laprensa.com.ar; internet www.laprensa.com.ar; f. 1869; morning; independent; Dir FLORENCIO ALDREY IGLESIAS; circ. 100,000.

La Razón: Río Cuarto 1242, C1168AFF Buenos Aires; tel. and fax (11) 4309-6000; e-mail lectores@larazon.com.ar; internet www.larazon.com.ar; f. 1992; evening; Dir LUIS VINKER; circ. 62,000.

PRINCIPAL PROVINCIAL DAILIES

Catamarca

El Ancasti: Sarmiento 526, 1°, K4700EML Catamarca; tel. (3833) 431385; fax (3833) 453995; e-mail mzitelli@durhone.com.ar; internet www.elancasti.com.ar; f. 1988; morning; Dir MARCELO SOSA; circ. 9,000.

Chaco

Norte: Carlos Pellegrini 744, H3500CDP Resistencia; tel. (362) 445-1222; fax (362) 442-6047; e-mail webchaco@diarionorte.com; internet www.diarionorte.com; f. 1968; Dir MIGUEL ANGEL FERNÁNDEZ; circ. 16,500.

Chubut

Crónica: Namuncurá 122, U9000BVD Comodoro Rivadavia; tel. (297) 447-0117; fax (297) 447-1780; e-mail diariocronica@diariocronica.com.ar; internet www.diariocronica.com.ar; f. 1962; morning; Dir DANIEL CÉSAR ZAMIT; circ. 15,000.

Córdoba

Comercio y Justicia: Félix Paz 310, Alto Alberdi, X5002IGQ Córdoba; tel. and fax (351) 488-0088; e-mail redaccion@comercioyjusticia.info; internet www.comercioyjusticia.info; f. 1939; morning; economic and legal news with periodic supplements on architecture and administration; Dir JOSÉ MARÍA LAS HERAS; Editor-in-Chief ADOLFO RUIZ; circ. 5,800.

La Voz del Interior: Monseñor P. Cabrera 6080, X5008HKJ Córdoba; tel. (351) 475-7135; fax (351) 475-7282; e-mail atencionalcliente@lavozdelinterior.com.ar; internet www.lavozdelinterior.com.ar; f. 1904; morning; independent; Dir Dr CARLOS HUGO JORNET; circ. 50,340 (2012).

Corrientes

El Litoral: Hipólito Yrigoyen 990, W3400AST Corrientes; tel. and fax (379) 4410150; e-mail redaccion@ellitoral.com.ar; internet www.ellitoral.com.ar; f. 1960; morning; Dir CARLOS A. ROMERO FERIS; circ. 14,973 (2012).

Entre Ríos

El Diario: Buenos Aires y Urquiza, E2823XBC Paraná; tel. (343) 400-1000; fax (343) 431-9104; e-mail institucional@eldiario.com.ar; internet www.eldiario.com.ar; f. 1914; morning; Dir SEBASTIÁN ETCHEVEHERE; circ. 4,274.

El Heraldo: Quintana 42, E3200XAE Concordia; tel. (345) 421-5304; fax (345) 421-1397; e-mail redaccion@elheraldo.com.ar; internet www.elheraldo.com.ar; f. 1915; evening; Editor ROBERTO W. CAMINOS; circ. 10,000.

Mendoza

Los Andes: San Martín 1049, M5500AAK Mendoza; tel. (261) 449-1200; fax (261) 420-2011; e-mail aguardiola@losandes.com.ar; internet www.losandes.com.ar; f. 1982; morning; Dir ARTURO GUARDIOLA; circ. 30,400.

Misiones

El Territorio: Quaranta No 4307, N3301GAC Posadas; tel. and fax (3752) 451844; e-mail info@territoriodigital.com; internet www.territoriodigital.com.ar; f. 1925; Dir GONZALO PELTZER; Editor-in-Chief ROBERTO MAACK; circ. 4,707 (2012).

Provincia de Buenos Aires

El Atlántico: Bolívar 2975, B7600GDO Mar del Plata; e-mail cronicadelacosta@cronica.com.ar; internet www.cronicadelacosta.com; f. 1938; morning; Dir OSCAR ORTIZ; circ. 20,000.

La Capital: Avda Marcelino Champagnat 2551, B7604GXA Mar del Plata; tel. (223) 478-8490; e-mail contacto@lacapitalmdq.com.ar; internet www.lacapitalmdp.com; f. 1905; Editor-in-Chief OSCAR LARDIZÁBAL; circ. 32,000.

El Día: Avda A, Diagonal 80 815, B1900CCI La Plata; tel. (221) 425-0101; fax (221) 423-2996; e-mail lectores@eldia.com; internet www.eldia.com.ar; f. 1884; morning; independent; Dir RAÚL E. KRAISELBURD; circ. 35,292 (2012).

Ecos Diarios: Calle 62, No. 2486, B7630XAF Necochea; tel. and fax (2262) 430754; e-mail redaccion@ecosdiarios.com; internet www.ecosdiariosweb.com.ar; f. 1921; morning; independent; Dir MARÍA JOSEFINA IGNACIO; circ. 2,233 (2012).

La Nueva Provincia: Rodríguez 55, B8000HSA Bahía Blanca; tel. (291) 459-0000; fax (291) 459-0001; e-mail abel@lanueva.com; internet www.lanueva.com; f. 1898; morning; independent; Gen. Editor ABEL ESCUDERO ZADRAYEC; circ. 12,402 (2012).

El Nuevo Cronista: 5 Calle 619, B8000XAV Mercedes; tel. and fax (2324) 400111; e-mail redaccion@nuevocronista.com.ar; internet www.nuevocronista.com.ar; f. 1987; Dir CLAUDIO GUEVARA.

El Popular: Vicente López 2626, B7400CRH Olavarría; tel. and fax (22) 8442-0502; e-mail diario@elpopular.com.ar; internet elpopular.com.ar; f. 1899; morning; Dir JORGE GABRIEL BOTTA; circ. 5,086 (2012).

El Sol: Hipólito Yrigoyen 122, B1878FND Quilmes; tel. and fax (11) 4257-6325; e-mail elsol@elsolquilmes.com.ar; internet www.elsolquilmes.com.ar; f. 1927; Dir CARLOS E. BOTTASO; circ. 25,000.

La Voz del Pueblo: San Martín 991, B7500IKJ Tres Arroyos; tel. (2983) 430680; fax (2938) 430684; e-mail avisos@lavozdelpueblo.com.ar; internet www.lavozdelpueblo.com.ar; f. 1902; morning; independent; Dir MARIA RAMONA MACIEL; circ. 3,400.

Río Negro

Río Negro: 9 de Julio 733, R8332AAO General Roca; tel. (2941) 439300; fax (2941) 439638; e-mail publicidadonline@rionegro.com.ar; internet www.rionegro.com.ar; f. 1912; morning; Dir JULIO RAJNERI; Co-Dir NÉLIDA RAJNERI; circ. 30,000.

Salta

El Tribuno: Avda Ex Combatientes de Malvinas 3890, A4412BYA Salta; tel. (387) 424-6200; fax (387) 424-6240; e-mail gpublicidad@eltribuno.com.ar; internet www.eltribuno.info/salta; f. 1949; morning; Dir SERGIO ROMERO; circ. 20,000.

San Juan

Diario de Cuyo: Mendoza 380 Sur, J5402GUH San Juan; tel. (264) 429-0038; fax (264) 429-0063; e-mail comercialdc@diariodecuyo.com.ar; internet www.diariodecuyo.com.ar; f. 1947; morning; independent; Dir FRANCISCO B. MONTES; circ. 14,450.

San Luis

El Diario de La República: Lafinur 924, D5700ASO San Luis; tel. and fax (2623) 422037; e-mail redaccion@eldiariodelarepublica.com; internet www.eldiariodelarepublica.com; f. 1966; Dir ALBERTO RODRIGUEZ SAÁ; circ. 7,650.

Santa Fe

La Capital: Sarmiento 763, S2000CMK Rosario; tel. (341) 420-1100; fax (341) 420-1114; internet www.lacapital.com.ar; f. 1867; morning; independent; Dirs ORLANDO MARIO VIGNATTI, DANIEL EDUARDO VILA; circ. 40,000.

El Litoral: 25 de Mayo 3536, S3000DPJ Santa Fe; tel. (342) 450-2500; fax (342) 450-2530; e-mail publicidad@ellitoral.com; internet www.litoral.com.ar; f. 1918; morning; independent; Dir GUSTAVO VÍTTORI; circ. 14,973 (2012).

Santiago del Estero

El Liberal: Libertad 263, G4200CZC Santiago del Estero; tel. (385) 422-4400; fax (385) 422-4538; e-mail redaccion@elliberal.com.ar; internet www.elliberal.com.ar; f. 1898; morning; Dir GUSTAVO EDUARDO ICK; circ. 25,008 (2012).

Tucumán

La Gaceta: Mendoza 654, T4000DAN San Miguel de Tucumán; tel. (381) 484-2200; fax (381) 431-1597; e-mail redaccion@lagaceta.com.ar; internet www.lagaceta.com.ar; f. 1912; morning; independent; Dir DANIEL DESSEIN; circ. 53,219 (2012).

WEEKLY NEWSPAPER

Perfil: Chacabuco 271, 8°, C1069AAE Buenos Aires; tel. (11) 4341-9000; fax (11) 4341-8988; e-mail gangeli@perfil.com.ar; internet www.perfil.com; f. 2005; Saturday and Sunday; Gen. Editor GERMÁN ANGELI; circ. 38,600.

PERIODICALS

Aeroespacio (Revista Nacional Aeronáutica y Espacial): Avda Rafael Obligado 2580, C1425COA Buenos Aires; tel. and fax (11) 4514-1561; e-mail director@aeroespacio.com.ar; internet www.aeroespacio.com.ar; f. 1941; every 2 months; aeronautics; Dir ALEJANDRO BALLESPÍN; circ. 12,000.

Billiken: Azopardo 565, C1307ADG Buenos Aires; tel. (11) 4346-0107; fax (11) 4343-7040; e-mail billiken@atlantida.com.ar; internet www.billiken.com.ar; f. 1919; weekly; children's magazine; Dir JUAN CARLOS PORRAS; circ. 54,000.

Caras: Chacabuco 271, 8°, C1069AAE Buenos Aires; tel. (11) 4341-9000; fax (11) 4341-8988; e-mail correocaras@perfil.com.ar; internet www.caras.perfil.com; f. 1992; weekly; celebrities; Dir LILIANA CASTAÑO; circ. 41,000.

Chacra: The New Farm Company, SA, Paseo Colón 728, 7°B, C1063ACU Buenos Aires; tel. (11) 4342-4390; fax (11) 4343-0576; e-mail ventas@nfco.com.ar; internet www.revistachacra.com.ar; f. 1930; monthly; agriculture magazine; Dir RUBÉN BARTOLOMÉ; circ. 12,000.

El Economista: Paraguay 776, 8º, C1057AAJ Buenos Aires; tel. (11) 4312-3529; fax (11) 4314-7680; e-mail pperez@eleconomista.com.ar; internet www.eleconomista.com.ar; f. 1951; weekly; financial; Dir PATRICIA S. PÉREZ; circ. 37,800.

El Federal: Cap. General R. Freire 948, C1426AVT Buenos Aires; tel. (11) 4556-2900; fax (11) 4556-2990; e-mail eraies@infomedia.com.ar; internet revistaelfederal.com; weekly; farming and countryside; Editor ESTEBAN RAIES; circ. 18,900.

Gente: Azopardo 565, C1307ADG Buenos Aires; tel. (11) 4346-0240; e-mail genteonline@atlantida.com.ar; internet www.gente.com.ar; f. 1965; weekly; celebrities; Dir JORGE DE LUJÁN GUTIÉRREZ; circ. 45,000.

El Gráfico: Balcarce 510, 1064 Buenos Aires; tel. (11) 5235-5100; e-mail elgrafico@elgrafico.com.ar; internet www.elgrafico.com.ar; f. 1919; monthly; sport; Editor MARTIN MAZUR; circ. 40,000.

Mercado: Bartolomé Mitre 648, 8°, CP, Buenos Aires; tel. (11) 5254-9400; fax (11) 4343-7880; e-mail info@mercado.com.ar; internet www.mercado.com.ar; f. 1969; monthly; business; Dir MIGUEL ANGEL DIEZ; circ. 28,000.

Mundo Israelita, SA: Corrientes 4006, 4°, Of. 35, C1194ABS Buenos Aires; tel. (11) 4861-2224; fax (11) 4861-8434; e-mail mundoeditor@hotmail.com; internet www.mundoisraelita.com.ar; f. 1923; owned by Mundo Editor, SA; fortnightly; Jewish interest; Editor-Dir Dr CORINA SCHVARTZAPEL; circ. 2,000.

Noticias de la Semana: Chacabuco 271, 8°, C1069AAE Buenos Aires; tel. (11) 4341-9000; fax (11) 4341-8988; e-mail correonoticias@perfil.com; internet noticias.perfil.com; f. 1977; weekly; news and current affairs; Editor GUSTAVO GONZÁLEZ; circ. 63,000.

Para Ti: Azopardo 565, C1107ADG Buenos Aires; tel. (11) 4331-4591; fax (11) 4331-3272; e-mail parationline@atlantida.com.ar; internet www.parati.com.ar; f. 1922; weekly; women's interest; Dir JUAN CARLOS PORRAS; circ. 35,000.

La Prensa Médica Argentina: Junín 917, 2°D, C1113AAA Buenos Aires; tel. and fax (11) 4961-9213; e-mail presmedarg@hotmail.com; internet www.prensamedica.com.ar; f. 1914; monthly; medical; Editor Dr PABLO A. LÓPEZ; circ. 8,000.

Prensa Obrera: Ayacucho 444, C1026AAB Buenos Aires; tel. (11) 4953-3824; fax (11) 4953-7164; e-mail info@po.org.ar; internet www.po.org.ar; f. 1982; weekly; publ. of Partido Obrero; Editor J. CHRISTIAN RATH; circ. 16,000.

Saber Vivir: Magallanes 1315, C1288ABA Buenos Aires; tel. (11) 4303-2305; e-mail sabervivir@gentille.biz; internet www.sabervivir.com.ar; f. 1999; fortnightly; health; Dir RICARDO GENTILLE; circ. 81,000.

Veintitrés: Serrano 1650, C1414CHX Buenos Aires; tel. (11) 4775-0300; e-mail lectores@veintitres.com; internet www.veintitres.com; f. 1998; weekly; political and cultural; Dir JORGE CICUTTIN; circ. 35,000.

NEWS AGENCIES

Diarios y Noticias (DYN): Julio A. Roca 636, 8°, C1067ABO Buenos Aires; tel. (11) 4342-3040; fax (11) 4342-3043; e-mail editor@dyn.com.ar; internet www.dyn.com.ar; f. 1982; Chair. JOSÉ POCHAT; Dir HUGO E. GRIMALDI.

Noticias Argentinas, SA (NA): Moreno 769, 3º, C1091AAO Buenos Aires; tel. and fax (11) 4331-3850; e-mail infogral@noticiasargentinas.com; internet www.noticiasargentinas.com; f. 1973; Pres. FRANCISCO FASCETTO; Dir GABRIEL PROFITI.

Télam, SE: Bolívar 531, C1066AAK Buenos Aires; tel. (11) 4339-0330; fax (11) 4339-0353; e-mail telam@telam.com.ar; internet www.telam.com.ar; f. 1945; state-owned; Pres. SANTIAGO ALVAREZ; Gen. Man. Dr ESTEBAN ORESTES CARELLA.

PRESS ASSOCIATIONS

Asociación de Diarios del Interior de la República Argentina (ADIRA): Chacabuco 314, 4º, C1069AAH Buenos Aires; tel. (11) 4342-7003; e-mail adira@adira.org.ar; internet www.adira.org.ar; f. 1975; association for regional newspapers and periodicals; Pres. SEBASTIAN ZUELGARAY; Sec. NAHUEL CAPUTTO.

Asociación de Entidades Periodísticas Argentinas (ADEPA): Chacabuco 314, 3°, C1069AAH Buenos Aires; tel. and fax (11) 4331-1500; e-mail adepa@adepa.org.ar; internet www.adepa.org.ar; f. 1962; Pres. CARLOS JORNET; Sec.-Gen. CARLOS RAGO.

Publishers

Aguilar, Altea, Alfaguara, Taurus, SA de Ediciones: Leandro N. Alem 720, C1001AAP Buenos Aires; tel. (11) 4119-5000; fax (11) 4119-5021; e-mail info@alfaguara.com.ar; internet www.alfaguara.com.ar; f. 1946; part of Grupo Editorial Santillana Argentina; general, literature, children's books; Pres. EMILIANO MARTINEZ; Dir-Gen. ARMANDO COLLAZOS.

Aique Grupo Editor, SA: Francisco Acuña de Figueroa 352, C1180AAF Buenos Aires; tel. (11) 4867-7000; e-mail centrodocente@aique.com.ar; internet www.aique.com.ar; f. 1976; educational; Dir-Gen. MARÍA PÍA GAGLIARDI.

Amorrortu Editores, SA: Paraguay 1225, 7°, C1057AAS Buenos Aires; tel. (11) 4816-5812; fax (11) 4816-3321; e-mail info@amorrortueditores.com; internet www.amorrortueditores.com; f. 1967; academic, social sciences and humanities; Man. Dir HORACIO DE AMORRORTU.

A–Z Editora, SA: Paraguay 2351, C1121ABK Buenos Aires; tel. (11) 4961-4036; fax (11) 4961-0089; e-mail contacto@az.com.ar; internet www.az.com.ar; f. 1976; educational, children's, literature, social sciences, medicine, law; Pres. RAMIRO VILLALBA GARIBALDI.

Biblioteca Nacional de Maestros: c/o Ministerio de Educación, Pizzurno 935, planta baja, C1020ACA Buenos Aires; tel. (11) 4129-1272; fax (11) 4129-1268; e-mail bnminfo@me.gov.ar; internet www.bnm.me.gov.ar; f. 1884; Dir GRACIELA TERESA PERRONE.

Cosmopolita, SRL: Piedras 744, C1070AAP Buenos Aires; tel. (11) 4361-8925; fax (11) 4361-8049; e-mail cosmopolita09@yahoo.com.ar; internet www.ed-cosmopolita.com.ar; f. 1940; science and technology; Man. Dir RUTH F. DE RAPP.

Crecer Creando Editorial: Viamonte 2052, C1056ABF Buenos Aires; tel. (11) 4372-4165; fax (11) 4371-9351; e-mail info@crecercreando.com.ar; internet www.crecercreando.com.ar; educational; Pres. CARLOS RIVERA.

De Los Cuatro Vientos Editorial: Venezuela 726, C1096ABD Buenos Aires; tel. and fax (11) 4331-4542; e-mail info@deloscuatrovientos.com.ar; internet www.deloscuatrovientos.com.ar; f. 2000; Dir PABLO GABRIEL ALBORNOZ; Editor MARIELA FERNANDA AQUILANO.

Edebé, SA: Don Bosco 4069, C1206ABM Buenos Aires; tel. (11) 4883-0111; fax (11) 4883-0115; tel. info@edebe.com.ar; internet www.edebe.com.ar; f. 1996; religious and educational literature for children; Gen. Man. NORA WAGNER.

Ediciones de la Flor SRL: Gorriti 3695, C1172ACE Buenos Aires; tel. (11) 4963-7950; fax (11) 4963-5616; e-mail edic-flor@datamarkets.com.ar; internet www.edicionesdelaflor.com.ar; f. 1966; fiction, poetry, theatre, juvenile, humour and scholarly; Co-Dirs ANA MARÍA MILER, DANIEL DIVINSKY.

Ediciones Gránica: Lavalle 1634, 3° G, C1048AAN Buenos Aires; tel. (11) 4374-1456; fax (11) 4373-0669; e-mail granica.ar@granicaeditor.com; internet www.granicaeditor.com; management, reference; Gen. Man. CLAUDIO IANNINI.

Ediciones Macchi, SA: Pacheco 3190, C1431FJN Buenos Aires; tel. and fax (11) 4542-7835; e-mail info@macchi.com; internet www.macchi.com; f. 1946; economic sciences; Pres. RAÚL LUIS MACCHI.

Ediciones Manantial, SRL: Avda de Mayo 1365, 6º, Of. 28, C1085ABD Buenos Aires; tel. (11) 4383-6059; fax (11) 4383-7350; e-mail info@emanantial.com.ar; internet www.emanantial.com.ar; f. 1984; social science, education and psychoanalysis; Gen. Man. CARLOS A. DE SANTOS.

Ediciones Nueva Visión, SAIC: Tucumán 3748, C1189AAV Buenos Aires; tel. (11) 4864-5050; fax (11) 4863-5980; e-mail ednuevavision@ciudad.com.ar; f. 1954; psychology, education, social sciences, linguistics; Man. Dir HAYDÉE P. DE GIACONE.

Ediciones del Signo: Julián Alvarez 2844, 1° A, C1425DHT Buenos Aires; tel. (11) 4804-4147; fax (11) 4782-1836; e-mail info@edicionesdelsigno.com.ar; internet www.edicionesdelsigno.com.ar; f. 1995; philosophy, psychoanalysis, politics and scholarly; Man. MICAELA GERCMAN.

Editorial Albatros, SACI: Torre Las Plazas, J. Salguero 2745, 5°, Of. 51, C1425DEL Buenos Aires; tel. (11) 4807-2030; fax (11) 4807-2010; e-mail info@albatros.com.ar; internet www.albatros.com.ar; f. 1945; technical, non-fiction, social sciences, sport, children's books, medicine and agriculture; Man. Dir ANDREA INÉS CANEVARO.

Editorial Argenta Sarlep, SA: Avda Corrientes 1250, 3°, Of. F, C1043AAZ Buenos Aires; tel. (11) 4382-9085; fax (11) 4381-6100; e-mail info@editorialargenta.com; internet www.editorialargenta.com; f. 1970; literature, poetry, theatre and reference; Man. ALEXANDER ERNST RENNES.

Editorial Bonum, SACI: Avda Corrientes 6687, C1427BPE Buenos Aires; tel. and fax (11) 4554-1414; e-mail marina@editorialbonum.com.ar; internet www.editorialbonum.com.ar; f. 1960; religious, educational and self-help; Pres. MARTÍN GREMMELSPACHER.

Editorial Catálogos, SRL: Avda Independencia 1860, C1225AAN Buenos Aires; tel. and fax (11) 4381-5708; e-mail catalogos@ciudad.com.ar; internet www.catalogossrl.com.ar; religion, literature, academic, general interest and self-help; Co-Dirs HORACIO GARCÍA, LEONARDO PÉREZ.

Editorial Claretiana: Lima 1360, C1138ACD Buenos Aires; tel. (11) 4305-9597; fax (11) 4305-6552; e-mail contacto@editorialclaretiana.com.ar; internet www.editorialclaretiana.com.ar; f. 1956; Catholicism; Man. Dir P. GUSTAVO M. LARRAZÁBAL.

Editorial Claridad, Heliasta, unaLuna, SA: Juncal 3451, C1425AYT Buenos Aires; tel. and fax (11) 4804-0472; e-mail editorial@editorialclaridad.com.ar; internet www.heliasta.com.ar; f. 1922; literature, biographies, social science, politics, reference, dictionaries; Co-Dirs Dra ANA MARÍA CABANELLAS DE LAS CUEVAS, GUILLERMO CABANELLAS DE LAS CUEVAS.

Editorial Errepar: Paraná 725, C1017AAO Buenos Aires; tel. (11) 4370-2002; fax (11) 4383-2202; e-mail clientes@errepar.com; internet www.errepar.com; encyclopaedias, technical and legal texts; Pres. RICARDO PARADA; Dir FRANCISCO CAÑADA.

Editorial Grupo Cero: Mansilla 2686, planta baja 1 y 2, C1425BPD Buenos Aires; tel. (11) 4966-1710; fax (11) 4966-1713; e-mail pedidos@editorialgrupocero.com; internet www.editorialgrupocero.com; fiction, poetry and psychoanalysis; Dir MARÍA NORMA MENASSA.

Editorial Guadalupe: Mansilla 3865, C1425BQA Buenos Aires; tel. and fax (11) 4826-8587; e-mail gerencia@editorialguadalupe.com.ar; internet www.editorialguadalupe.com.ar; f. 1895; social sciences, religion, anthropology, children's books and pedagogy; Man. Dir P. LUIS O. LIBERTI; Man. Editor LILIANA FERREIRÓS.

Editorial Hispano-Americana, SA (HASA): Rincón 686, C1227ACD Buenos Aires; tel. (11) 4943-7111; fax (11) 4943-7061; e-mail info@hasa.com.ar; internet www.hasa.com.ar; f. 1934; science and technology; Pres. Prof. HÉCTOR ALBERTO ALGARRA.

Editorial Inter-Médica, SAICI: Junín 917, 1°A, C1113AAC Buenos Aires; tel. (11) 4961-9234; fax (11) 4961-5572; e-mail info@inter-medica.com.ar; internet www.inter-medica.com.ar; f. 1959; medicine and veterinary; Pres. JORGE MODYEIEVSKY.

Editorial Juris: Moreno 1580, S2000DLF Rosario, Santa Fe; tel. (341) 426-7301; e-mail editorial@editorialjuris.com; internet www.editorialjuris.com; f. 1952; legal texts; Dir LUIS MAESANO.

Editorial Kier, SACIFI: Avda Santa Fe 1260, C1059ABT Buenos Aires; tel. (11) 4811-0507; fax (11) 4811-3395; e-mail info@kier.com.ar; internet www.kier.com.ar; f. 1907; Eastern doctrines and religions, astrology, parapsychology, tarot, I Ching, occultism, cabbala, freemasonry and natural medicine; Pres. HÉCTOR S. PIBERNUS; Dirs CRISTINA GRIGNA, OSVALDO PIBERNUS.

Editorial Losada, SA: Avda Corrientes 1551, C1042AAB Buenos Aires; tel. (11) 4375-5001; fax (11) 4373-4006; e-mail losada@editoriallosada.com; internet www.editoriallosada.com; f. 1938; general; Pres. JOSÉ JUAN FERNÁNDEZ REGUERA; Editor GONZALO LOSADA.

Editorial Médica Panamericana, SA: Marcelo T. de Alvear 2145, C1122AAG Buenos Aires; tel. (11) 4821-5520; fax (11) 4825-1214; e-mail info@medicapanamericana.com; internet www.medicapanamericana.com.ar; f. 1962; medicine and health sciences; Pres. HUGO BRIK.

Editorial Mercosur: Dean Funes 923, C1231ABI Buenos Aires; tel. (11) 4956-2297; e-mail info@editorialmercosur.com; internet www.editorialmercosur.com; self-help and general interest.

Editorial del Nuevo Extremo: Angel J. Carranza 1852, C1414COV Buenos Aires; tel. (11) 4773-3228; fax (11) 4773-8445; e-mail info@delnuevoextremo.com; internet www.delnuevoextremo.com; general interest; Pres. MIGUEL ANGEL LAMBRÉ; Dir TOMÁS LAMBRÉ.

Editorial Planeta Argentina, SAIC: Avda Independencia 1668, C1100ABQ Buenos Aires; tel. (11) 4124-9100; fax (11) 4124-9190; e-mail info@eplaneta.com.ar; internet www.editorialplaneta.com.ar; f. 1939; fiction, non-fiction, biographies, history, art, essays; subsidiary of Grupo Planeta, Spain; Editorial Dir ALBERTO DÍAZ.

Editorial Sigmar, SACI: Avda Belgrano 1580, 7°, C1093AAQ Buenos Aires; tel. (11) 4381-2510; fax (11) 4383-5633; e-mail editorial@sigmar.com.ar; internet www.sigmar.com.ar; f. 1941; children's books; Man. Dir ROBERTO CHWAT.

Editorial Stella: Viamonte 1984, C1056ABD Buenos Aires; tel. (11) 4374-0346; fax (11) 4374-8719; e-mail ventas@editorialstella.com.ar; internet www.editorialstella.com.ar; f. 1941; general non-fiction and textbooks; owned by Asociación Educacionista Argentina; Dir TELMO MEIRONE; Editor ADOLFO GARCÍA SÁEZ.

Editorial Troquel, SA: Olleros 1818, 4° I, C1426CRH Buenos Aires; tel. and fax (11) 4779-9444; e-mail info@troquel.com.ar; internet www.troquel.com.ar; f. 1954; general literature, religion, philosophy and education; Pres. GUSTAVO A. RESSIA.

Editorial Zeus, SRL: San Lorenzo 1329, S2000DNP Rosario, Santa Fe; tel. (341) 449-5585; fax (341) 425-4259; e-mail zeus@zeus.com.ar; internet www.editorial-zeus.com.ar; legal texts; Editor and Dir GUSTAVO L. CAVIGLIA.

EUDEBA (Editorial Universitaria de Buenos Aires): Avda Rivadavia 1573, C1033AAF Buenos Aires; tel. (11) 4383-8025; fax (11) 4383-2202; e-mail info@eudeba.com.ar; internet www.eudeba.com.ar; f. 1958; university textbooks and general interest publs; Pres. GONZALO ALVAREZ; Gen. Man. LUIS QUEVEDO.

Galerna: Lambaré 893, C1185ABA Buenos Aires; tel. (11) 4867-1661; fax (11) 4862-5031; e-mail contacto@galerna.net; internet www.galernalibros.com; fiction, theatre, poetry and scholarly; Pres. MATÍAS SANABRIA; Dir HUGO LEVÍN.

Gram Editora: Cochabamba 1652, C1148ABF Buenos Aires; tel. (11) 4304-4833; fax (11) 4304-5692; e-mail grameditora@infovia.com.ar; internet www.grameditora.com.ar; f. 1990; education; Man. MANUEL HERRERO MONTES.

Grupo Editorial Lumen, SRL: Montevideo 604,2°, C1019ABN, Buenos Aires; tel. (11) 4373-1414; fax (11) 4375-0453; e-mail contacto@lumen.com.ar; internet www.edlumen.net; f. 1958; imprints include Lumen (religion, spirituality, etc.), Magisterio (educational), Lumen-Hvmanitas (social sciences) and Lohlé-Lumen (politics, philosophy, literature); Man.Dir ALEJANDRO MARKER.

Grupo Santillana Argentina: Avda Leandro N. Alem 720, C1001AAP Buenos Aires; tel. (11) 4119-5000; e-mail info@santillana.com.ar; internet www.santillana.com.ar; f. 1963; part of Grupo Editorial Santillana (Spain); education; Dir-Gen. DAVID DELGADO DE ROBLES.

Kapelusz Editora, SA: San José 831, C1076AAQ Buenos Aires; tel. (11) 5236-5000; fax (11) 5236-5051; e-mail jvergara@kapelusz.com.ar; internet www.kapelusznorma.com.ar; f. 1905; textbooks, psychology, pedagogy, children's books; Vice-Pres. RAFAEL PASCUAL ROBLES.

LexisNexis Argentina: Carlos Pellegrini 887, 3°, C1013AAQ Buenos Aires; tel. (11) 5236-8800; fax (11) 5236-8811; e-mail info@lexisnexis.com.ar; internet www.lexisnexis.com.ar; f. 1999 upon acquisition of Depalma and Abeledo-Perrot; periodicals and books covering law, politics, sociology, philosophy, history and economics; Gen. Man. CAROLINA TRONGE.

Random House Mondadori: Humberto Primo 545, 1°, C1103ACK Buenos Aires; tel. (11) 5235-4400; fax (11) 4362-7364; e-mail info@rhm.com.ar; internet www.megustaleer.com.ar; f. 1939; general fiction and non-fiction; Man. Dir JUAN IGNACIO BOIDO.

Siglo Veintiuno Editores: Guatemala 4824, C1425BUP Buenos Aires; tel. and fax (11) 4770-9090; e-mail info@sigloxxieditores.com.ar; internet www.sigloxxieditores.com.ar; social science, history, economics, art; Editorial Dir CARLOS E. DIEZ.

PUBLISHERS' ASSOCIATIONS

Cámara Argentina del Libro: Avda Belgrano 1580, 4°, C1093AAQ Buenos Aires; tel. (11) 4381-8383; fax (11) 4381-9253; e-mail cal@editores.org.ar; internet www.editores.org.ar; f. 1938; Pres. ISAAC RUBINZAL; Exec. Dir DIANA SEGOVIA.

Cámara Argentina de Publicaciones: Lavalle 437, 5°, Of. A, C1047AAI Buenos Aires; tel. (11) 5218-9707; e-mail info@publicaciones.org.ar; internet www.publicaciones.org.ar; f. 1970; Pres. HÉCTOR DI MARCO; Sec. MARÍA PÍA GAGLIARDI.

Broadcasting and Communications

TELECOMMUNICATIONS

AT&T Argentina: Alicia Moreau de Justo 400, C1107AAH Buenos Aires; tel. (11) 4310-8700; fax (11) 4310-8706; e-mail info_Argentina@cla.att.com; internet www.att.com; Vice-Pres. (Canada, Caribbean and Latin America) MARY E. LIVINGSTON; Country Pres. ALEJANDRO ROSSI.

Claro Argentina, SA (AMX Argentina, SA): Edif. Corporativo, Avda de Mayo 878, C1084AAQ Buenos Aires; tel. (11) 4109-8888; e-mail nscocimarro@claro.com.ar; internet argentina.claro.com.ar; f. 1994 as CTI Móvil; wholly owned subsidiary of América Móvil, SA de CV (Mexico) since 2003; mobile cellular telephone services; CEO JULIO CARLOS PORRAS ZADIK.

Ericsson, SACI: Güemes 676, 1°, Vicente López PCIA, B1638CJF Buenos Aires; tel. (11) 4319-5500; fax (11) 4315-0629; e-mail infocom@cea.ericsson.se; internet www.ericsson.com; Head (Latin America) SERGIO QUIROGA DA CUNHA; Exec. Vice-Pres. (Argentina) DANIEL CARUSO.

Movistar: Avda Corrientes 655, 3°, C1043AAG Buenos Aires; tel. (11) 5321-0000; fax (11) 5321-1604; internet www.movistar.com.ar; 98% owned by Telefónicas Móviles, SA (Spain); operates mobile telephone network; Dir (Products and Services) LEANDRO MUSCIANO.

Nextel Communications Argentina, SRL: Olga Cossettini 363, Dique 4, C1107CCG Buenos Aires; tel. (11) 5359-0000; e-mail prensa@nextel.com.ar; internet www.nextel.com.ar; f. 1998; Pres. RUBEN BUTVILOFSKY.

Telcosur, SA: Don Bosco 3672, 5°, C1206ABF Buenos Aires; tel. (11) 4865-9060; e-mail telcosur@telcosur.com.ar; internet www.telcosur.com.ar; f. 1998; 99% owned by Transportador de Gas del Sur (TGS); Operations Man. EDUARDO VIGILANTE.

Telecom Argentina, SA: Alicia Moreau de Justo 50, 10°, C1107AAB Buenos Aires; tel. (11) 4968-4000; fax (11) 4968-1420; e-mail contactos@telecompersonal.com.ar; internet www.telecom.com.ar; provision of telecommunication services in the north of Argentina; provides wireless services under the brand *Telecom Personal*; Exec. Dir STEFANO DE ANGELIS; Gen. Sec. MARÍA D. CARRERA SALA.

Regulatory Body

Comisión Nacional de Comunicaciones (CNC): Perú 103, 1°, C1067AAC Buenos Aires; tel. (11) 4347-9501; fax (11) 4347-9897; internet www.cnc.gov.ar; f. 1996; Insp. CEFERINO NAMUNCURÁ.

BROADCASTING

Radio

Radio Nacional Argentina (RNA): Maipú 555, C1006ACE Buenos Aires; tel. (11) 4325-9100; fax (11) 4325-4313; e-mail direccionlra1@radionacional.gov.ar; internet www.radionacional.gov.ar; f. 1937; state-controlled, part of Radio y Televisión Argentina, SE; six national radio stations: AM 870; Nacional Folklórica; Nacional Clásica; Nacional Rock; Fútbol; and Radiodifusión Argentina al Exterior (f. 1947); 49 provincial stations; Exec. Dir MARÍA SEOANE.

Asociación de Radiodifusoras Privadas Argentinas (ARPA): Juan D. Perón 1561, 3°, C1037ACC Buenos Aires; tel. (11) 4371-5999; fax 4382-4483; e-mail arpaorg@arpa.org.ar; internet www.arpa.org.ar; f. 1958; asscn of privately owned commercial stations; Pres. Dr EDMUNDO O. RÉBORA; Exec. Dir HECTOR J. PARREIRA.

Television

América TV: Fitzroy 1650, C1414CHX Buenos Aires; tel. (11) 5032-2222; e-mail americanoticias@america2.com.ar; internet www.america2.com.ar; Pres. DANIEL VILA; CEO GUSTAVO CAPUA.

Canal 9 (Telearte, SA): Dorrego 1782, C1414CKZ Buenos Aires; tel. (11) 3220-9999; e-mail webmaster@canal9.com.ar; internet www.canal9.com.ar; f. 1960; private channel; Pres. CARLOS E. LOREFICE LYNCH; Dir-Gen. ENRIQUE TABOADA.

Canal 13: Lima 1261, C1138ACA Buenos Aires; tel. (11) 4305-0013; fax (11) 4331-8573; e-mail eltrecetv@artear.com; internet www.eltrecetv.com.ar; f. 1989; part of Arte Radiotelevisivo Argentino, SA; leased to a private concession in 1992; Gen. Man. DANIEL ZANARDI; Programme Man. PABLO CODEVILLA.

Telefé (Canal 11): Pavón 2444, C1248AAT Buenos Aires; tel. (11) 4941-9549; fax (11) 4942-6773; e-mail prensa@telefe.com.ar; internet www.telefe.com.ar; private channel; Pres. JUAN WAEHNER; Programme Man. CLAUDIO VILLARRUEL.

TV Pública Canal Siete: Avda Figueroa Alcorta 2977, C1425CKI Buenos Aires; tel. (11) 4808-2500; e-mail contacto@tvpublica.com.ar; internet www.tvpublica.com.ar; f. 1951; state-controlled, part of Radio y Televisión Argentina, SE; Pres. TRISTÁN BAUER; Exec. Dir MARTÍN BONAVETTI.

Asociación de Teleradiodifusoras Argentinas (ATA): Avda Córdoba 323, 6°, C1054AAC Buenos Aires; tel. (11) 4312-4208; fax (11) 4315-4681; e-mail info@ata.org.ar; internet www.ata.org.ar; f. 1959; asscn of 23 private television channels; Pres. RICARDO NOSIGLIA; Sec. PABLO CASEY.

Regulatory Bodies

Autoridad Federal de Servicios de Comunicación Audiovisual (AFSCA): Suipacha 765, 9°, C1008AAO Buenos Aires; tel. (11) 4320-4900; fax (11) 4394-6866; e-mail prensa@afsca.gob.ar; internet www.afsca.gov.ar; f. 1972 as Comisión Nacional de Radio y Televisión (CONART); name changed to Comité Federal de Radiodifusión (COMFER) in 1981; reorg. as a decentralized regulatory authority and adopted present name in 2009; controls various technical aspects of broadcasting and transmission of programmes; Pres. MARTÍN SABATELLA.

Secretaría de Comunicaciones: Sarmiento 151, 4°, C1041AAC Buenos Aires; tel. (11) 4318-9410; fax (11) 4318-9432; internet www.secom.gov.ar; co-ordinates 30 stations and the international service; Sec. CARLOS LISANDRO SALAS.

Finance

(cap. = capital; res = reserves; dep. = deposits; m. = million; br(s) = branch(es); amounts in nuevos pesos argentinos)

BANKING

Central Bank

Banco Central de la República Argentina: Reconquista 266, C1003ABF Buenos Aires; tel. (11) 4348-3500; fax (11) 4348-3955; e-mail sistema@bcra.gov.ar; internet www.bcra.gov.ar; f. 1935 as a central reserve bank; bank of issue; all capital is held by the state; cap. 14,604.7m., res 34,972.1m., dep. 108,855.3m. (Dec. 2009); Pres. JUAN CARLOS FÁBREGA.

Government-owned Commercial Banks

Banco del Chubut: Rivadavia 615, Rawson, U9103ANG Chubut; tel. (2965) 482505; fax (2965) 484196; e-mail contacto@chubutbank.com.ar; internet www.bancochubut.com.ar; cap. 198.6m., res 44.6m., dep. 2,312.3m. (June 2011); Pres. DR RUBÉN FELIPE BAMBACI; Gen. Man. HUGO GARNERO.

Banco de la Ciudad de Buenos Aires: Sarmiento 630, C1005AAH Buenos Aires; tel. (11) 4329-8600; fax (11) 4329-8729; e-mail Exterior@bancociudad.com.ar; internet www.bancociudad.com.ar; municipal bank; f. 1878; cap. 985.7m., res 726.6m., dep. 16,573.5m. (Dec. 2011); Chair. and Pres. FEDERICO ADOLFO STURZENEGGER; Gen. Man. GUILLERMO ANTONINO CASCIO; 65 brs.

Banco de Inversión y Comercio Exterior, SA (BICE): 25 de Mayo 526/532, C1002ABL Buenos Aires; tel. (11) 4317-6900; fax (11) 4311-5596; e-mail info@bice.com.ar; internet www.bice.com.ar; f. 1991; cap. 489.2m., res 743.1m., dep. 476.7m. (Dec. 2010); Pres. MAURO ALEM; Gen. Man. JORGE GIACOMOTTI.

Banco de la Nación Argentina: Bartolomé Mitre 326, Capital Federal Of. 235, C1036AAF Buenos Aires; tel. (11) 4347-6000; fax (11) 4347-6316; e-mail prensabna@bna.com.ar; internet www.bna.com.ar; f. 1891; national bank; cap. 2,510.2m. (Dec. 2010), res 11,516.8m., dep. 132,611.1m. (Dec. 2011); Pres. JUAN IGNACIO FORLÓN; Gen. Man. RAÚL DUZEVIC; 645 brs.

Banco de la Pampa SEM: Carlos Pellegrini 255, L6300DRE Santa Rosa; tel. (295) 445-1000; e-mail cexterior@blp.com.ar; internet www.blp.com.ar; f. 1958; cap. 128.5m., res 89.2m., dep. 3,215.7m. (Dec. 2011); Chair. LAURA AZUCENA GALLUCCIO; Gen. Man. CARLOS DESINANO; 51 brs.

Banco de la Provincia de Buenos Aires: San Martín 137, 9°, C1004AAC, Buenos Aires; tel. (11) 4347-0000; fax (11) 4347-0299; e-mail gerenciageneral@bpba.com.ar; internet www.bapro.com.ar; f. 1822; provincial govt-owned bank; cap. 2,764.8m., dep. 38,107.4m. (Dec. 2011), res 1,904.4m. (Dec. 2009); Pres. GUSTAVO M. MARANGONI; Gen. Man. MARCELO H. GARCÍA; 343 brs.

Banco de la Provincia de Córdoba: San Jerónimo 110, esq. Buenos Aires, CP 5000, X5000AGD Córdoba; tel. (351) 420-7507; fax (351) 420-5905; e-mail contgral@bancor.com.ar; internet www.bancor.com.ar; f. 1873; provincial bank; cap. 210.2m., res 16.8m., dep. 7,398.7m. (Dec. 2010); Pres. FABIÁN MAIDANA; Exec. Dir JOSÉ LUIS DOMINGUEZ; 143 brs.

Banco Provincia del Neuquén: Avda Argentina 61, 1°, Q8300AYA Neuquén; tel. (299) 449-6618; fax (299) 449-6622; e-mail institucional@bpn.com.ar; internet www.bpn.com.ar; f. 1960; cap. 141.8m., res 25.2m., dep. 1,687m. (Dec. 2010); Pres. MARCOS GABRIEL KOOPMANN IRIZAR; Gen. Man. ADRIANA VELASCO; 22 brs.

Banco de Tierra del Fuego: Maipú 897, V9410BJQ Ushuaia; tel. (2901) 441600; fax (2901) 441601; e-mail info@bancotdf.com.ar; internet www.bancotdf.com.ar; national bank; cap. and res 173.9m., dep. 979.3m. (Dec. 2011); Pres. RICARDO IGLESIAS; Gen. Man. MIGUEL LANDERRECHE; 8 brs.

Nuevo Banco de la Rioja, SA: Rivadavia 702, F5300ACU La Rioja; tel. (3822) 430575; fax (3822) 430618; e-mail nblrsa@nblr.com.ar; internet www.nblr.com.ar; f. 1994; provincial bank; cap. 21m., res 37m., dep. 496.6m. (Dec. 2011); Pres. JORGE RODOLFO GONZALEZ; Gen. Man. JUAN JOSÉ MANUEL LOBATO; 13 brs.

Nuevo Banco de Santa Fe, SA: Tucumán 2545, S3000FTS Santa Fe; tel. (342) 450-4700; e-mail contactobc@bancobsf.com.ar; internet www.bancobsf.com.ar; f. 1847 as Banco Provincial de Santa Fe, adopted current name in 1998; provincial bank; cap. 91.1m., res 460.5m., dep. 9,661.5m. (Dec. 2011); Chair. ENRIQUE ESKINAZI; Exec. Dir MARCELO BUIL; 105 brs.

Private Commercial Banks

Banco BI Creditanstalt, SA: Bouchard 547, 24° y 25°, C1106ABG Buenos Aires; tel. (11) 4319-8400; fax (11) 4319-8230; e-mail info@bicreditanstalt.com.ar; internet www.bicreditanstalt.com.ar; f. 1971 as Banco Interfinanzas; adopted current name 1997; cap. and res 444.8m., dep. 8.7m. (Dec. 2009); Pres. DR DIEGO MIGUEL MARÍA ANGELINO; Gen. Man. RICARDO RIVERO HAEDO.

Banco CMF, SA: Macacha Güemes 150, Puerto Madero, C1106BKD Buenos Aires; tel. (11) 4318-6800; fax (11) 4318-6859; e-mail contacto@cmfb.com.ar; internet www.bancocmf.com.ar; f. 1978 as Corporación Metropolitana de Finanzas, SA; adopted current name in 1999; cap. 145.9m., res 65.9m., dep. 1,951.2m. (Dec. 2011); Pres. and Chair. JOSÉ ALBERTO BENEGAS LYNCH; Gen. Man. MARCOS PRIETO.

Banco COMAFI: Roque S. Peña 660, C1035AAO Buenos Aires; tel. (11) 4347-0400; fax (11) 4347-0404; e-mail contactenos@comafi.com.ar; internet www.comafi.com.ar; f. 1984; assumed control of 65% of Scotiabank Quilmes in April 2002; cap. 36.7m., res 126m., dep. 4,364.4m. (June 2012); Pres. GUILLERMO CERVIÑO; Vice-Pres. EDUARDO MASCHWITZ; 56 brs.

Banco de Corrientes: 9 de Julio 1002, esq. San Juan, W3400AYQ Corrientes; tel. (3783) 479300; fax (3783) 479372; e-mail bcteservicios@bcoctes.com.ar; internet www.bancodecorrientes.com.ar; f. 1951; est. as Banco de la República de Corrientes; adopted current name in 1993, after transfer to private ownership; cap. 124.1m., dep. 1,780.1m. (Dec. 2011); Pres. DR ALEJANDRO ABRAHAM; Gen. Man. CARLOS GUSTAVO MACORATTI; 33 brs.

Banco Finansur, SA: Sarmiento 700, esq. Maipú, Buenos Aires; tel. (11) 4324-3400; fax (11) 4322-4687; e-mail bafin@bancofinansur.com.ar; internet www.bancofinansur.com.ar; f. 1973; est. as Finansur Compañía Financiera, SA; adopted current name in 1993; cap. 32.7m., res 10.9m., dep. 585m. (Dec. 2011); Pres. JORGE SÁNCHEZ CÓRDOVA; 4 brs.

Banco de Galicia y Buenos Aires, SA: Juan D. Perón 407, Casilla 86, C1038AAI Buenos Aires; tel. (11) 6329-0000; fax (11) 6329-6100; e-mail bancogalicia@bancogalicia.com.ar; internet www.bancogalicia.com.ar; f. 1905; cap. 562.3m., res 1,360.6m., dep. 30,149.2m. (Dec. 2011); Chair. ANTONIO R. GARCÉS; Gen. Man. DANIEL LLAMBÍAS; 236 brs.

Banco Industrial: San Martín 549, Azul 7300, Buenos Aires; tel. (2281) 431779; e-mail atencionalcliente@bancoindustrial.com.ar; internet www.bancoindustrial.com.ar; f. 1971; cap. 172.7m., res 100.3m., dep. 2,549.2m. (Dec. 2011); Pres. CARLOTA EVELINA DURST; Gen. Man. LUIS LARA; 30 brs.

Banco Itaú Argentina, SA: Calle Cerrito 740, 19°, 1309 Buenos Aires; tel. (11) 4378-8400; fax (11) 4394-1057; e-mail contactenos@itau.com.ar; internet www.itau.com.ar; fmrly Banco Itaú Argentina, SA; renamed as above following purchase of Banco del Buen Ayre, SA, in 1998; subsidiary of Banco Itaú, SA (Brazil); cap. 426.4m., res 204.1m., dep. 5,926.2m. (Dec. 2011); Pres. RICARDO VILLELA MARINO; Gen. Man. SERGIO SALOMON FELDMAN; 117 brs.

Banco Macro, SA: Sarmiento 447, 4°, C1041AAI Buenos Aires; tel. (11) 5222-6500; fax (11) 5222-6624; e-mail relacionesinstitucionales@macro.com.ar; internet www.macro.com.ar; f. 1995 as Banco Bansud by merger; merged with Banco Macro in 2002; adopted current name 2006; cap. 594.5m., res 1,369.7m., dep. 29,167.1m. (Dec. 2011); Pres. JORGE HORACIO BRITO; 400 brs.

Banco Mariva, SA: Sarmiento 500, C1041AAJ Buenos Aires; tel. (11) 4321-2200; fax (11) 4321-2292; e-mail info@mariva.com.ar; internet www.mariva.com.ar; f. 1980; cap. 67.1m., res 32.4m., dep. 566.5m. (Dec. 2011); Pres. JOSÉ LUIS PARDO.

Banco Patagonia, SA: Juan D. Perón 500, C1038AAJ Buenos Aires; tel. (11) 4132-6300; fax (11) 4132-6059; e-mail international@bancopatagonia.com.ar; internet www.bancopatagonia.com.ar; f. 1912; fmrly Banco Sudameris; adopted current name in 2004 following merger with Banco Patagonia; cap. 719.3m., res 653m., dep. 13,825.2m. (Dec. 2009); Chair. JORGE GUILLERMO STUART MILNE.

Banco de San Juan: Ignacio de la Roza 85, J5402DCA San Juan; tel. (264) 429-1000; fax (264) 421-4126; internet www.bancosanjuan.com; f. 1943; 20% owned by provincial govt of San Juan; 80% privately owned; cap. and res 266.7m., dep. 1,294.1m. (Dec. 2009); Pres. ENRIQUE ESKENAZI; Gen. Man. MARIA SILVINA BELLANTIG TARDIO; 8 brs.

Banco Santander Río, SA: Bartolomé Mitre 480, 2°, C1036AAH Buenos Aires; tel. (11) 4341-1000; fax (11) 4341-1020; e-mail sgalvan@santanderrio.com.ar; internet www.santanderrio.com.ar; f. 1908 as Banco Río de la Plata; adopted current name 2007; owned by Banco Santander (Spain); cap. 3,062.1m., dep. 33,142m. (Dec. 2011); Pres. JOSÉ LUIS ENRIQUE CRISTOFANI; 276 brs.

Banco Santiago del Estero: Belgrano 529 Sur, G4200AAF Santiago del Estero; tel. (385) 450-2300; fax (385) 450-2316; e-mail cgelid@bse.com.ar; internet www.bse.com.ar; Pres. NÉSTOR CARLOS ICK; Gen. Man. ALDO RENÉ MAZZOLENI.

Banco Supervielle, SA: Bartolomé Mitre 434, C1036AAH Buenos Aires; tel. (11) 4324-8000; fax (11) 4324-8090; e-mail informes@ar.socgen.com; internet www.supervielle.com.ar; f. 1887; owned by Grupo Supervielle; took over Banco Regional de Cuyo in Oct. 2010; cap. 356.1m., res 82.3m., dep. 7,258.1m. (Dec. 2011); Pres. PATRICIO SUPERVIELLE; Gen. Man. JOSÉ LUÍS PANERO; 165 brs.

Banco de Valores, SA: Sarmiento 310, C1041AAH Buenos Aires; tel. (11) 4323-6900; fax (11) 4323-6942; e-mail info@banval.sba.com.ar; internet www.bancodevalores.com; f. 1978; cap. 75m., res 99.6m., dep. 912.1m. (Dec. 2010); Pres. HÉCTOR JORGE BACQUÉ; Exec. Dir HÉCTOR NORBERTO FERNÁNDEZ SAAVEDRA; 1 br.

BBVA Banco Francés, SA: Reconquista 199, C1003ABC Buenos Aires; tel. (11) 4346-4000; fax (11) 4346-4320; e-mail mensajes@bancofrances.com.ar; internet www.bancofrances.com; f. 1886 as Banco Francés del Río de la Plata, SA; changed name to Banco Francés, SA, in 1998 following merger with Banco de Crédito Argentino; adopted current name in 2000; cap. 536.9m., res 495.5m., dep. 29,165.7m. (Dec. 2011); Pres. JORGE CARLOS BLEDEL; Gen. Man. ANTONIO MARTÍNEZ JORQUERA; 308 brs.

HSBC Bank Argentina, SA: Florida 201, 27°, C1005AAE Buenos Aires; tel. (11) 4320-2800; fax (11) 4132-2409; e-mail contactenos@hsbc.com.ar; internet www.hsbc.com.ar; f. 1978 as Banco Roberts, SA; name changed to HSBC Banco Roberts, SA, in 1998; adopted current name in 1999; cap. 1,244.1m., res 390.7m., dep. 18,531.8m. (June 2011); Pres. and CEO GABRIEL MARTINO; 68 brs.

Nuevo Banco de Entre Ríos, SA: Monte Caseros 128, E3100ACD Paraná; tel. (343) 420-1200; fax (343) 421-1221; e-mail info@nuevobersa.com.ar; internet www.nuevobersa.com.ar; f. 1935 as Banco Entrerriano; provincial bank; transferred to private ownership in 1995; adopted present name in 2002; cap. 172m., res 53m., dep. 2,793.7m. (Dec. 2010); Pres. ENRIQUE ESKENAZI; Gen. Man. LUIS ROBERTO NÚÑEZ; 73 brs.

Standard Bank Argentina: Della Paolera 265, 13°, C1001ABA Buenos Aires; tel. (11) 4820-9200; fax (11) 4820-2050; e-mail lavozdelcliente@standardbank.com.ar; internet www.standardbank.com.ar; f. 2005; cap. 847.1m., res 234.3m., dep. 12,291.1m. (Dec. 2011); Pres. MYLES JOHN DENNIS RUCK; Gen. Man. ALEJANDRO LEDESMA; 98 brs.

Co-operative Bank

Banco Credicoop Cooperativo Ltdo: Reconquista 484, C1003ABJ Buenos Aires; tel. (11) 4320-5000; fax (11) 4324-5891; e-mail credicoop@bancocredicoop.coop; internet www.bancocredicoop.coop; f. 1979; cap. 1m., res 1,362.2m., dep. 20,103.7m. (June 2012); Chair., Pres. and CEO CARLOS HELLER; Gen. Man. GERARDO GALMÉS; 249 brs.

Bankers' Associations

Asociación de Bancos Argentinos (ADEBA): Juan D. Perón 564, 6°, C1038AAL Buenos Aires; tel. and fax (11) 5238-7790; e-mail info@adebaargentina.com.ar; internet www.adeba.com.ar; f. 1972; Pres. JORGE HORACIO BRITO; Exec. Dir NORBERTO PERUZZOTTI; 28 mems.

Asociación de Bancos de la Argentina (ABA): San Martín 229, 10°, 1004 Buenos Aires; tel. (11) 4394-1836; fax (11) 4394-6340; e-mail webmaster@aba-argentina.com; internet www.aba-argentina.com; f. 1999 by merger of Asociación de Bancos de la República Argentina (f. 1919) and Asociación de Bancos Argentinos (f. 1972); Pres. CLAUDIO CESARIO; Sec. SEBASTIÁN REYNAL; 27 mems.

Asociación de Bancos Públicos y Privados de la República Argentina (ABAPPRA): Florida 470, 1°, C1005AAJ Buenos Aires; tel. and fax (11) 4322-5342; e-mail info@abappra.com.ar; internet www.abappra.com; f. 1959; Pres. JUAN IGNACIO FORLÓN; Exec. Dir DEMETRIO BRAVO AGUILAR; 31 mems.

STOCK EXCHANGES

Bolsa de Comercio de Buenos Aires (BCBA): Sarmiento 299, 1°, C1041AAE Buenos Aires; tel. (11) 4316-7000; fax (11) 4316-7011; e-mail info@bcba.sba.com.ar; internet www.bcba.sba.com.ar; f. 1854; Pres. ADELMO GABBI.

Mercado de Valores de Buenos Aires, SA: 25 de Mayo 367, 8°–10°, C1002ABG Buenos Aires; tel. and fax (11) 4316-6000; e-mail merval@merval.sba.com.ar; internet www.merval.sba.com.ar; f. 1929; Pres. MARIO BAGNARDI.

There are also stock exchanges at Córdoba, Rosario, Mendoza and La Plata.

Supervisory Authority

Comisión Nacional de Valores (CNV): 25 de Mayo 175, C1002ABC Buenos Aires; tel. (11) 4329-4600; fax (11) 4331-0639; e-mail webadm@cnv.gov.ar; internet www.cnv.gob.ar; monitors capital markets; Pres. ALEJANDRO VANOLI; Gen. Man. RODOLFO CLAUDIO IRIBARREN.

INSURANCE

There were 180 insurance companies operating in Argentina in 2011, of which 101 were general insurance companies. The following is a list of those offering all classes or a specialized service.

Supervisory Authority

Superintendencia de Seguros de la Nación: Julio A. Roca 721, 5°, C1067ABC Buenos Aires; tel. (11) 4338-4000; fax (11) 4331-9821; e-mail consultasydenuncias@ssn.gov.ar; internet www.ssn.gov.ar; f. 1938; Supt JUAN A. BONTEMPO.

Major Companies

Allianz Argentina, Cía de Seguros, SA: Avda Corrientes 299, C1043AAC, Buenos Aires; tel. 4222-3443; fax 4320-7143; e-mail atencionalcliente@allianz.com.ar; internet www.allianz.com.ar; f. 1988; fmrly AGF Allianz Argentina; changed name as above 2007; CEO EDWARD HENRY LANGE.

Aseguradora de Créditos y Garantías, SA (ACG): Maipú 71, 4°, C1084ABA Buenos Aires; tel. (11) 4320-7200; fax (11) 4320-7277; e-mail infoacg@bristolgroup.com.ar; internet www.bristolgroup.com.ar/ACG; f. 1965; part of the Bristol Group; Pres. HORACIO G. SCAPPARONE.

Aseguradores de Cauciones, SA: Paraguay 580, C1057AAF Buenos Aires; tel. (11) 5235-3700; fax (11) 5235-3784; e-mail consultas@caucion.com.ar; internet www.caucion.com.ar; f. 1968; all classes; Pres. JOSÉ DE VEDIA.

Berkley International Argentina, SA: Avda Carlos Pellegrini 1023, 1009, Buenos Aires; tel. (11) 4378-8100; e-mail comercial@berkley.com.ar; internet www.berkley.com.ar; f. 1908; part of Berkley International Latinoamérica; Pres. EDUARDO I. LLOBET.

Caja de Seguros, SA: Fitz Roy 957, C1414CHI Buenos Aires; tel. (11) 4857-8118; fax (11) 4857-8001; e-mail suc_villacrespo@lacaja.com.ar; internet www.lacaja.com.ar; f. 1992; Pres. GERARDO WERTHEIN.

CESCE Argentina—Seguro de Crédito y Garantías, SA: Corrientes 345, 7°, C1043AAD Buenos Aires; tel. (11) 4313-4303; fax (11) 4313-2919; e-mail info@casce.com.ar; internet www.casce.com.ar; f. 1967 as Cía Argentina de Seguros de Créditos a la Exportación; part of Grupo CESCE Internacional; covers credit and extraordinary and political risks for Argentine exports; Pres. EDUARDO ANGEL FORNS; Gen. Man. LUIS IMEDIO SERRANO.

Chiltington Internacional, SA: Reconquista 559, 8°, C1003ABK Buenos Aires; tel. (11) 4312-8600; fax (11) 4312-8884; e-mail msmith@chiltington.com.ar; internet chiltington.com; f. 1982; Regional Head MARTIN SMITH.

Cía. de Seguros La Mercantil Andina, SA: Avda Eduardo Madero 942, 18°, C1106ACW Buenos Aires; tel. 4310-5400; internet www.mercantilandina.com.ar; f. 1923; part of Grupo Pescarmona since 1978; Gen. Man. PEDRO MIRANTE.

El Comercio Seguros, SA: Maipú 71, baja, C1084ABA Buenos Aires; tel. (11) 4324-1300; fax (11) 4393-1311; e-mail gguerrero@bristolgroup.com.ar; internet www.bristolgroup.com.ar/ec; f. 1889; all classes; part of the Bristol Group; Exec. Dirs CLAUDIO LANDA, JORGE DURBANO.

Generali Argentina, Cía de Seguros, SA: Reconquista 458, 3°, C1003ABJ, Buenos Aires; tel. 4857-7942; fax 4857-7946; e-mail infogenerali@generali.com.ar; internet www.generali.com.ar; f. 1948 as Assicurazioni Generali; changed name as above 1998; Gen. Man. CLAUDIO MELE.

HDI Seguros Argentina, SAC: Tte Gral D. Perón 650, 5°, C1038AAN Buenos Aires; tel. (11) 5300-3300; fax (11) 5811-0744; e-mail hdi@hdi.com.ar; internet www.hdi.com.ar; f. 1896 as L'Union IARD, known as L'UNION de Paris Compañía Argentina de Seguros in 2004–11; part of HDI Seguros group; general.

Liberty Seguros Argentina, SA: Avda Paseo Colón 357, C1063ACD Buenos Aires; tel. 4104-0000; fax 4346-0400; e-mail centrodecontacto@libertyseguros.com.ar; internet www.libertyseguros.com.ar; f. 1995; Pres. SUSANA AUGUSTÍN.

Mapfre Argentina: Juana Manso 205, C1107CBE Buenos Aires; tel. (11) 4320-9439; fax (11) 4320-9444; e-mail comunicacion@mapfre.com.ar; internet www.mapfre.com.ar; all classes; Exec. Pres. DIEGO SERGIO SOBRINI.

Prudential Seguros, SA: Avda Leandro N. Alem 855, 5°, C1001AAD Buenos Aires; tel. (11) 4891-5000; fax 4314-3435; e-mail atencionalcliente@prudential.com; internet www.prudentialseguros.com.ar; f. 2000; Pres. MAURICIO ZANATTA.

RSA Argentina (United Kingdom): Lima 653, Buenos Aires; tel. (11) 4339-0000; fax (11) 4331-1453; e-mail atencion.cliente@rsagroup.com; internet www.rsagroup.com.ar; fmrly known as Royal & Sun Alliance Seguros; life and general; Pres. FERRARO ROBERTO PASCUAL.

Victoria Seguros, SA: Florida 556, C1005AAL Buenos Aires; tel. (11) 4322-1100; fax (11) 4325-9016; e-mail seguros@victoria.com.ar; internet www.victoria.com.ar; f. 1921; Pres. SEBASTIÁN BAGÓ; Vice-Pres. and Exec. Dir DANIEL RICARDO SALAZAR.

Zurich Argentina Cía de Seguros, SA: Cerrito 1010, C1010AAV Buenos Aires; tel. (11) 4819-1010; e-mail servicioalcliente@zurich.com; internet www.zurich.com.ar; f. 1947; all classes; Pres. JOSÉ MARÍA ORLANDO POTT.

Insurance Association

Asociación Argentina de Cías de Seguros (AACS): 25 de Mayo 565, 2°, C1002ABK Buenos Aires; tel. (11) 4312-7790; fax (11) 4312-6300; e-mail info@aacs.org.ar; internet www.aacs.org.ar; f. 1894; 27 mems; Pres. FRANCISCO M. ASTELARRA.

Trade and Industry

GOVERNMENT AGENCIES

Consejo Federal de Inversiones: San Martín 871, C1004AAQ Buenos Aires; tel. (11) 4317-0700; fax (11) 4315-1238; e-mail administrator@cfired.org.ar; internet www.cfired.org.ar; f. 1959; federal board to co-ordinate domestic and foreign investment and provide technological aid for the provinces; Sec.-Gen. JUAN JOSÉ CIÁCERA.

Dirección de Forestación (DF): 982, Anexo Jardín, C1063ACW Buenos Aires; tel. (11) 4349-2131; fax (11) 4349-2102; e-mail solivero@minagri.gob.ar; internet www.forestacion.gov.ar; assumed the responsibilities of the national forestry commission (Instituto Forestal Nacional—IFONA) in 1991, following its dissolution; supervised by the Secretaría de Agricultura, Ganadería, Pesca y Alimentos; maintains the Centro de Documentación e Información Forestal; Dir MIRTA ROSA LARRIEU.

Instituto de Desarrollo Económico y Social (IDES): Aráoz 2838, C1425DGT Buenos Aires; tel. (11) 4804-4949; fax (11) 4804-5856; e-mail ides@ides.org.ar; internet www.ides.org.ar; f. 1960; investigation into social sciences and promotion of social and economic devt; 1,100 mems; Pres. SERGIO VISACOVSKY.

Instituto Nacional de Tecnología Agropecuaria (INTA): Rivadavia 1439, C1033AAE Buenos Aires; tel. (11) 4338-4600; internet inta.gob.ar; f. 1956; research and support for technological advances in agriculture; Pres. FRANCISCO JUAN OSCAR ANGLESIO.

Oficina Nacional de Control Comercial Agropecuario (ONCCA): Paseo Colón 922, C1063ACW Buenos Aires; tel. (11) 4349-2492; fax (11) 4349-2005; e-mail web@oncca.gov.ar; internet www.oncca.gov.ar; oversees the agricultural sector; supervised by the Secretaría de Agricultura, Ganadería, Pesca y Alimentos; Pres. JUAN MANUEL CAMPILLO.

Organismo Nacional de Administración de Bienes (ONABE): José Ramos Mejía 1302, 3°, Of. 300, C1104AJN Buenos Aires; tel. (11) 4318-3658; e-mail consultas@onabe.gov.ar; internet www.onabe.gov.ar; f. 2000; responsible for administration of state property; supervised by the Ministry of Federal Planning, Public Investment and Services; Exec. Dir Dr ANTONIO ALBERTO VULCANO; Gen. Man. MARTÍN REIBEL MAIER.

Subsecretaría de Desarrollo de Inversiones y Promoción Comercial: Esmeralda 1212, 6°, C1005AAG Buenos Aires; tel. (11) 4819-7488; fax (11) 4819-7269; e-mail info@inversiones.gob.ar; internet www.inversiones.gob.ar; fmrly Agencia Nacional de Desarrollo de Inversiones (ProsperAr); promotion of investment in Argentina; Dir CARLOS BIANCO.

DEVELOPMENT ORGANIZATIONS

Instituto Argentino del Petróleo y Gas: Maipú 639, C1006ACG Buenos Aires; tel. (11) 5277-4274; fax (11) 5277-4263; e-mail informa@iapg.org.ar; internet www.iapg.org.ar; f. 1957; promotes the devt of petroleum exploration and research; Pres. ERNESTO LÓPEZ ANADÓN.

Instituto para el Desarrollo Social Argentino (IDESA): Montevideo 451, 11°, Of. 33, C1019ABI Buenos Aires; tel. (11) 4374-7660; e-mail atorres@idesa.org; internet www.idesa.org; centre for research in public policies related to social devt; Pres. OSVALDO GIORDANO; Exec. Dir ALEJANDRA TORRES.

Sociedad Rural Argentina: Florida 460, C1005AAJ Buenos Aires; tel. (11) 4324-4700; e-mail acciongremial@sra.org.ar; internet www.sra.org.ar; f. 1866; private org. to promote the devt of agriculture; Pres. Dr HUGO LUIS BIOLCATI; 9,400 mems.

CHAMBERS OF COMMERCE

Cámara Argentina de Comercio: Leandro N. Alem 36, C1003AAN Buenos Aires; tel. (11) 5300-9000; fax (11) 5300-9058; e-mail difusion2@cac.com.ar; internet www.cac.com.ar; f. 1927; Pres. CARLOS RAÚL DE LA VEGA; Sec. ALBERTO O. DRAGOTTO.

Cámara de Comercio Argentino Brasileña: Montevideo 770, 12°, C1019ABP Buenos Aires; tel. (11) 4811-4503; e-mail cambras@cambras.org.ar; internet www.cambras.org.ar; Pres. JORGE RODRÍGUEZ APARICIO.

Cámara de Comercio de los Estados Unidos en la República Argentina (AMCHAM): Viamonte 1133, 8°, C1053ABW Buenos Aires; tel. (11) 4371-4500; fax (11) 4371-8400; e-mail amcham@amchamar.com.ar; internet www.amchamar.com.ar; f. 1918; US Chamber of Commerce; Pres. ALEJANDRO BOTTAN; CEO ALEJANDRO DÍAZ.

Cámara de Comercio Exterior de Rosario: Córdoba 1868, Rosario, S2000AXD Santa Fe; tel. and fax (341) 425-7147; e-mail consultas@commerce.com.ar; internet www.commerce.com.ar; f. 1958; deals with imports and exports; Pres. JUAN CARLOS RETAMERO; Vice-Pres. GUILLERMO BECCANI; 150 mems.

Cámara de Comercio, Industria y Producción de la República Argentina: Florida 1, 4°, C1005AAA Buenos Aires; tel. (11) 4342-8252; fax (11) 4331-9116; e-mail correo@cacipra.org.ar; internet www.cacipra.org.ar; f. 1913; Pres. Dr CARLOS A. CANTA YOY; 1,500 mems.

Cámara de Comercio Italiana de Rosario: Córdoba 1868, 1°, S2000AXD, Rosario; tel. and fax (341) 426-6789; e-mail info@italrosario.com; internet www.ccir.com.ar; f. 1985; promotes Argentine–Italian trade; Pres. EDUARDO ROMAGNOLI; Sec.-Gen. GUSTAVO MICATROTTA; 104 mems.

Cámara de Exportadores de la República Argentina: Roque Sáenz Peña 740, 1°, C1035AAP Buenos Aires; tel. and fax (11) 4394-4482; e-mail contacto@cera.org.ar; internet www.cera.org.ar; f. 1943; export promotion; 700 mems; Pres. Dr ENRIQUE S. MANTILLA; Gen. Man. RUBÉN E. GIORDANO.

Similar chambers are located in most of the larger centres, and there are many other foreign chambers of commerce.

INDUSTRIAL AND TRADE ASSOCIATIONS

Asociación Argentina de Productores Porcinos: Florida 520, 2°, Of. 205, C1005AAL Buenos Aires; internet www.porcinos.org.ar; f. 1922; promotion of pork products; Pres. JUAN LUIS UCCELLI.

Asociación de Importadores y Exportadores de la República Argentina: Manuel Belgrano 124, 1°, C1092AAO Buenos Aires; tel. (11) 4342-0010; fax (11) 4342-1312; e-mail aiera@aiera.org.ar; internet www.aiera.org; f. 1966; Pres. DANIEL SOLDA; Man. ADRIANO A. DE FINA.

Bodegas de Argentina: Thames 2334, 16A, C1425FIH Buenos Aires; tel. (11) 5786-1220; fax (11) 5786-1266; e-mail info@bodegasdeargentinaac.com; internet www.bodegasdeargentina.org; f. 2001 following merger between Centro de Bodegueros de Mendoza and Asociación Vitivinícola Argentina; wine industry; Pres. ÁNGEL VESPA.

Cámara de la Industria Aceitera de la República Argentina—Centro de Exportadores de Cereales: Bouchard 454, 7°, C1106ABS Buenos Aires; tel. (11) 4311-4477; fax (11) 4311-3899; internet www.ciaracec.com.ar; f. 1980; vegetable oil producers and grain exporters; 49 mems; Pres. ALBERTO RODRIGUEZ.

Cámara de la Industria Química y Petroquímica (CIQyP): Avda Córdoba 629, 4°, C1054AAF Buenos Aires; tel. (11) 4313-1000; fax (11) 4313-1059; e-mail informacion@ciqyp.org.ar; internet www.ciqyp.org.ar; Pres. ALBERTO CANCIO; Exec. Dir JOSÉ MARÍA FUMAGALLI.

Cámara de Informática y Comunicaciones de la República Argentina (CICOMRA): Avda Córdoba 744, 2° D, C1054AAT Buenos Aires; tel. (11) 4325-8839; fax (11) 4325-9604; e-mail gerente@cicomra.org.ar; internet www.cicomra.org.ar; f. 1985; represents enterprises in the communications sector; Pres. NORBERTO CAPELLÁN; Exec. Dir ALFREDO BALLARINO.

Confederación Argentina de la Mediana Empresa (CAME): Florida 15, 3°, C1005AAA Buenos Aires; tel. (11) 5556-5556; fax (11) 5556-5502; e-mail info@came.org.ar; internet www.came.org.ar; f. 1956; fmrly Coordinadora de Actividades Mercantiles Empresarias; adopted current name 2006; small and medium enterprises; Pres. OSVALDO CORNIDE.

Confederación Intercooperativa Agropecuaria Ltda (CONINAGRO): Lavalle 348, 4°, C1047AAH Buenos Aires; tel. (11) 4311-4664; fax (11) 4311-0623; internet www.coninagro.org.ar; f. 1958; farming co-operative; Pres. CARLOS ALBERTO GARETTO; Gen. Man. DANIEL EDUARDO ASSEFF.

Confederaciones Rurales Argentinas (CRA): México 628, 2°, C1097AAN Buenos Aires; tel. (11) 4300-4451; fax (11) 4300-4471; internet www.cra.org.ar; f. 1943; promotion and devt of agricultural activities; 14 federations comprising over 300 mem. orgs, representing 109,000 farmers; Pres. Dr RUBÉN FERRERO.

Consorcio de Exportadores de Carnes Argentinas (ABC): San Martín 575, 5°B, C1004AAK Buenos Aires; tel. (11) 4394-9734; fax (11) 4394-9658; e-mail gerencia@abc-consorcio.com.ar; internet www.abc-consorcio.com.ar; f. 2002 following the merger between the Asociación de Industrias Argentinas de Carnes and several meat exporters; meat industry; refrigerated and canned beef and mutton; Pres. MARIO DARÍO RAVETTINO.

Federación Agraria Argentina (FAA): Alfonsina Storni 745, S2000DYA Rosario, Santa Fe; tel. (341) 512-2000; fax (341) 512-2001; e-mail comunicacion@faa.com.ar; internet www.faa.com.ar; f. 1912; oversees the interests of small and medium-sized grain producers; Pres. EDUARDO BUZZI.

Federación Lanera Argentina: 25 de Mayo 516, 4°, C1002ABL Buenos Aires; tel. (11) 5199-5617; e-mail info@flasite.com; internet www.flasite.com; f. 1929; wool industry; Pres. RAÚL ERNESTO ZAMBONI; Sec. JUAN PABLO LEFEBVRE; 40 mems.

EMPLOYERS' ORGANIZATION

Unión Industrial Argentina (UIA): Avda de Mayo 1147/57, C1085ABB Buenos Aires; tel. (11) 4124-2300; fax (11) 4124-2301; e-mail uia@uia.org.ar; internet www.uia.org.ar; f. 1887; re-established in 1974 with the fusion of the Confederación Industrial Argentina (CINA) and the Confederación General de la Industria; following the dissolution of the CINA in 1977, the UIA was formed in 1979; asscn of manufacturers, representing industrial corpns; Pres. Dr JOSÉ IGNACIO DE MENDIGUREN; Sec. MIGUEL ALBERTO ACEVEDO.

STATE HYDROCARBON COMPANY

YPF, SA: Macacha Güemes 515, CP 1364, C1106BKK Buenos Aires; tel. (11) 4329-2000; fax (11) 4329-5717; e-mail federico.etiennot@ypf.com; internet www.ypf.com; f. 1922 as Yacimientos Petrolíferos Fiscales, a state-owned company; bought by Repsol (Spain) and changed name as Repsol YPF, SA 1992; in April 2012 the Govt announced it was expropriating 51% of Repsol's shares in YPF; petroleum and gas exploration and production; CEO MIGUEL MATÍAS GALUCCIO; 9,750 employees.

YPF Tecnología, SA: La Plata; f. 2012; 51% owned by YPF and 49% owned by Consejo Nacional de Investigaciones Científicas y Técnicas; devt of oil and gas exploration and exploitation techniques.

UTILITIES

Regulatory Authorities

Compañía Administradora del Mercado Mayorista Eléctrico, SA (CAMMESA): Avda Madero 942, 1°, C1106ACW Buenos Aires; tel. (11) 4319-3700; e-mail agentes@cammesa.com.ar; internet portalweb.cammesa.com; f. 1992; responsible for administering the wholesale electricity market; 20% state-owned, 80% by electricity companies; Pres. JULIO MIGUEL DE VIDO (Minister of Federal Planning, Public Investment and Services).

Ente Nacional Regulador de la Electricidad (ENRE): Avda Eduardo Madero 1020, 10°, C1106ACX Buenos Aires; tel. (11) 4510-4600; fax (11) 4510-4210; internet www.enre.gov.ar; f. 1993; agency for regulation and control of electricity generation, transmission and distribution; Pres. MARIO DE CASAS.

Ente Nacional Regulador del Gas (ENARGAS): Suipacha 636, 10°, C1008AAN Buenos Aires; tel. (11) 4325-2500; fax (11) 4348-0550; internet www.enargas.gov.ar; regulates and monitors gas utilities; brought under govt control in 2007; Insp. ANTONIO LUIS PRONSATO.

Electricity

Central Puerto, SA (CEPU): Tomás Edison 2701, Dársena E, Puerto de Buenos Aires, C1104BAB Buenos Aires; tel. (11) 4317-5000; fax (11) 4317-5099; e-mail info@centralpuerto.com; internet www.centralpuerto.com; electricity generating co; Pres. JOSÉ MARÍA VÁZQUEZ.

Comisión Nacional de Energía Atómica (CNEA): Avda del Libertador 8250, C1429BNP Buenos Aires; tel. (11) 4704-1000; fax (11) 4704-1154; e-mail comunicacion@cnea.gov.ar; internet www.cnea.gov.ar; f. 1950; nuclear energy science and technology; operates three nuclear power stations for research purposes; Pres. NORMA LUISA BOERO.

Comisión Técnica Mixta de Salto Grande (CTMSG): Leandro N. Alem 449, C1003AAE Buenos Aires; tel. (11) 5554-3400; fax (11) 5554-3402; e-mail secgral@saltogrande.org; internet www.saltogrande.org; operates Salto Grande hydroelectric station, which has an installed capacity of 650 MW; jt Argentine-Uruguayan project; Pres., Argentine delegation JUAN CARLOS CRESTO; Gen. Mans CARLOS MASCIMO (Argentina), HUGO MAQUEIRA (Uruguay).

Dirección Provincial de Energía: Calle 55, 629, e/7 y 8, La Plata, B1900BGY Buenos Aires; tel. and fax (221) 427-1185; e-mail dpe@dpe.mosp.gba.gov.ar; internet www.dpe.mosp.gba.gov.ar; f. 1957 as Dirección de Energía de la Provincia de Buenos Aires; name changed as above in 2000; electricity co for province of Buenos Aires; Dir NÉSTOR CALLEGARI.

Empresa Distribuidora y Comercializadora Norte, SA (EDENOR): Avda del Libertador 6363, C1428ARG Buenos Aires; tel. (11) 4346-8400; fax (11) 4346-5441; e-mail ofitel@edenor.com.ar; internet www.edenor.com.ar; f. 1992; distribution of electricity; Pres. RICARDO TORRES; Dir-Gen. EDGARDO VOLOSIN.

Empresa Distribuidora Sur, SA (EDESUR): San José 140, C1076AAD Buenos Aires; tel. (11) 4381-8981; fax (11) 4383-3699; e-mail prensa@edesur.com.ar; internet www.edesur.com.ar; f. 1992; distribution of electricity; Gen. Man. ANTONIO JEREZ AGUDO.

Endesa Costanera, SA (CECCO): España 3301, C1107ANA Buenos Aires; tel. (11) 4307-3040; fax (11) 4300-4168; e-mail comercialweb@ccostanera.com.ar; internet www.endesacostanera.com; subsidiary of Endesa (Spain); generation, transmission, distribution and sale of thermal electric energy; Pres. JOSEPH M. HIDALGO MARTÍN-MATEOS; Gen. Man. JOSÉ MIGUEL GRANGED BRUÑEN.

Energía Argentina, SA (ENARSA): Avda Libertador 1068, 2°, C1112ABN Buenos Aires; tel. and fax (11) 4801-9325; e-mail contacto@enarsa.com.ar; internet www.enarsa.com.ar; f. 2004; state-owned; generation and distribution of electricity, especially from renewable sources; exploration, extraction and distribution of natural gas and petroleum; Pres. JOSÉ GRANERO.

Entidad Binacional Yacyretá: Eduardo Madero 942, 21°, C1106ACW Buenos Aires; tel. (11) 4510-7500; e-mail rrpp@eby.org.ar; internet www.eby.org.ar; operates the hydroelectric dam at Yacyretá on the Paraná river; owned jtly by Argentina and Paraguay; completed in 1998, it is one of the world's largest hydroelectric complexes, consisting of 20 generators with a total generating capacity of 3,200 MW; 14,673 GWh of electricity produced in 2007; Exec. Dir OSCAR ALFREDO THOMAS.

Hidronor Ingeniería y Servicios, SA (HISSA): Hipólito Yrigoyen 1530, 6°B, C1089AAD Buenos Aires; tel. (11) 4382-6316; fax (11) 4382-5111; e-mail hidronor@ciudad.com.ar; internet www.hissa.com; f. 1967; fmrly HIDRONOR, SA, the largest producer of electricity in Argentina; responsible for developing the hydroelectric potential of the Limay and neighbouring rivers; Pres. CARLOS ALBERTO ROCCA; transferred to private ownership in 1992 and divided into the following companies.

Central Hidroeléctrica Alicurá, SA: Leandro N. Alem 712, 7°, C1001AAP Buenos Aires.

Central Hidroeléctrica Cerros Colorados, SA: Leandro N. Alem 690, 12°, C1001AAO Buenos Aires.

Central Hidroeléctrica El Chocón, SA: Suipacha 268, 9°, Of. A, C1008AAF Buenos Aires.

Hidroeléctrica Piedra del Aguila, SA: Ruta Nacional 237 km, 1450.5, Piedra del Aguila 16, CP 8315 Neuquén; tel. (2942) 493-152; fax (2942) 493-166; f. 1993; owned by Hidroneuquén, SA; generation and distribution in the provinces of Neuquén and Río Negro; Pres. GONZALO PÉRÈS MOORE; Gen. Man. HORACIO TURRI.

Transener, SA: Paseo Colón 728, 6°, C1063ACU Buenos Aires; tel. (11) 4342-6925; fax (11) 4342-7147; e-mail info-trans@transx.com.ar; internet www.transener.com.ar; energy transmission co; Gen. Man. ANDRÉS G. COLOMBO.

Petrobrás Energía, SA: Maipú 1, 22°, C1084ABA Buenos Aires; tel. (11) 4344-6000; fax (11) 4344-6315; internet www.petrobras.com.ar; f. 1946 as Pérez Companc, SA; petroleum interests acquired by Petrobrás of Brazil in 2003; operates the hydroelectric dam at Pichi Picún Leufu; Exec. Dir CARLOS ALBERTO DA COSTA.

Gas

Asociación de Distribuidores de Gas (ADIGAS): Avda Poniente Roque Saenz Peña 740, 5° B, C1035AAP Buenos Aires; tel. (11) 4328-1729; fax (11) 4393-8294; e-mail adigas@adigas.com.ar; internet www.adigas.com.ar; f. 1993 to represent newly privatized gas companies; Gen. Man. CARLOS ALBERTO ALFARO.

Distribuidora de Gas del Centro, SA: Ituzaingó 774, Córdoba; tel. (351) 468-8108; fax (351) 468-1568; e-mail clientescentro@ecogas.com.ar; internet www.ecogas.com.ar/appweb/leo/centro/centro.php; state-owned co; distributes natural gas in Córdoba, Catamarca and La Rioja; Gen. Man. DONALDO SLOOG.

Distribuidora de Gas Cuyana, SA: Ituzaingó 774, Córdoba; tel. (351) 468-8108; fax (351) 468-1568; e-mail clientescuyo@ecogas.com.ar; internet www.ecogas.com.ar/appweb/leo/cuyo/cuyo.php; state-owned co; distributes natural gas in Mendoza, San Juan, San Luis; Pres. EDUARDO A. HURTADO.

Energía Argentina, SA (ENARSA): see Electricity.

Gas Natural Fenosa, SA: Isabel la Católica 939, C1268ACS Buenos Aires; tel. (11) 4754-1137; e-mail comercial@gasnaturalban.com.ar; internet www.gasnaturalban.com.ar; f. 1992 as Gas Natural BAN; changed name as above 2011; distribution of natural gas; Pres. HORACIO CRISTIANI.

Metrogás, SA: Gregorio Aráoz de Lamadrid 1360, C1267AAB Buenos Aires; tel. (11) 4309-1000; fax (11) 4309-1025; e-mail atencionclientes@metrogas.com.ar; internet www.metrogas.com.ar; f. 1992; 70% state-owned; gas distribution, mainly in Buenos Aires region; Dir-Gen. ANDRÉS CORDERO.

Transportadora de Gas del Norte, SA: Don Bosco 3672, 3°, C1206ABF Buenos Aires; tel. (11) 4008-2000; fax (11) 4008-2242; internet www.tgn.com.ar; f. 1992; distributes natural gas; Pres. EDUARDO OJEA QUINTANA; Gen. Man. FREDDY CAMEO.

Transportadora de Gas del Sur, SA (TGS): Don Bosco 3672, 6°, C1206ABF Buenos Aires; tel. (11) 4865-9050; fax (11) 4865-9059; e-mail totgs@tgs.com.ar; internet www.tgs.com.ar; f. 1992; processing and transport of natural gas; Pres. RICARDO ISIDRO MONGE; Dir-Gen. CARLOS SEIJO.

Water

Agua y Saneamientos Argentinos, SA (AySA): Tucumán 752, C1049APP Buenos Aires; tel. (11) 6319-0000; fax (11) 6139-2460; e-mail prensa@aysa.com.ar; internet www.aysa.com.ar; f. 2006; 90% state-owned; distribution of water in the Buenos Aires metropolitan area; Dir-Gen. Dr CARLOS HUMBERTO BEN.

TRADE UNIONS

Central de Trabajadores de la Argentinos (CTA): Piedras 1065, C1070AAU Buenos Aires; tel. (11) 4307-3829; fax (11) 4300-1015; e-mail prensacentral@cta.org.ar; internet www.cta.org.ar; f. 1992; dissident trade union confederation; Gen. Sec. HUGO YASKY.

CGT Azul y Blanca: Avda Belgrano 1280, C1093AAN Buenos Aires; f. 2008 by dissident faction of CGT comprising c. 60 unions; Sec.-Gen. LUIS BARRIONUEVO.

Confederación General del Trabajo (CGT) (General Confederation of Labour): Azopardo 802, C1107ADN Buenos Aires; tel. (11) 4334-0596; fax (11) 4334-0599; e-mail secgral@cgtra.org.ar; internet www.cgtra.org.ar; f. 1930; Peronist; represents approx. 90% of Argentina's 1,100 trade unions; Sec.-Gen. HUGO ANTONIO MOYANO.

Transport

Comisión Nacional de Regulación del Transporte (CNRT): Maipú 88, Apdo 129, C1000WAB Buenos Aires; tel. (11) 4819-3000; e-mail cnrt@miv.gov.ar; internet www.cnrt.gov.ar; f. 1996; regulates domestic and international transport services; Pres. EDUARDO SÍCARO.

Secretaría de Transporte de la Nación: Hipólito Yrigoyen 250, 12°, C1086AAB Buenos Aires; tel. (11) 4349-7254; fax (11) 4349-7201; e-mail transporte@minplan.gov.ar; internet www.transporte.gov.ar; Sec. ALEJANDRO RAMOS.

RAILWAYS

There are direct rail links with the Bolivian Railways network to Santa Cruz de la Sierra and La Paz; with Chile, through the Las Cuevas–Caracoles tunnel (across the Andes) and between Salta and Antofagasta; with Brazil, across the Paso de los Libres and Uruguayana bridge; with Paraguay (between Posadas and Encarnación by ferry-boat); and with Uruguay (between Concordia and Salto). In 2012 there were 25,023 km of tracks.

Following privatization in the early 1990s the state-run Ferrocarriles Argentinos was replaced by Ente Nacional de Administración de Bienes Ferroviarios (which was subsumed by the Organismo Nacional de Administración de Bienes in 2000), which assumed responsibility for railway infrastructure and the rolling stock not already sold off. The Buenos Aires commuter system was divided into eight concerns (one of which incorporates the underground railway system) and sold to private operators as 10- or 20-year (subsidized) concessions. In 2013 the Government of Buenos Aires took control of the metro network from the federal Government. The railway network is regulated by the Comisión Nacional de Regulación del Transporte (CNRT—see above). Construction of a 710-km high-speed railway linking Buenos Aires, Rosario and Córdoba was planned, although by 2014 the project remained stalled.

ALL Central: Santa Fe 4636, 3°, C1425BHV Buenos Aires; tel. (11) 4778-2425; fax (11) 4778-2493; internet en.all-logistica.com; f. 1993 as Ferrocarril Buenos Aires al Pacífico San Martín; bought by Brazil's América Latina Logística (ALL), SA, in 1999; nationalized in 2013; operates freight services on the San Martín line.

ALL Mesopotámica: Santa Fe 4636, 3°, C1425BHV Buenos Aires; tel. (11) 4778-2425; fax (11) 4778-2493; internet en.all-logistica.com; f. 1993 as Ferrocarril Mesopotámico; bought by Brazil's América Latina Logística (ALL), SA, in 1999; nationalized in 2013; operates freight services on the Urquiza lines; 2,704 km of track.

Cámara de Industriales Ferroviarios: Alsina 1609, 1°, C1088AAO Buenos Aires; tel. (11) 4382-0598; e-mail cifra@argentina.com; private org. to promote the devt of Argentine railway industries; Pres. ANA MARÍA GHIBAUDI.

Ferrobaires: Gen. Hornos 11, 4°, C1154ACA Buenos Aires; tel. (11) 4305-5174; fax (11) 4305-5933; e-mail calidadservicio@ferrobaires.gba.gov.ar; internet www.ferrobaires.gba.gov.ar; f. 1993; owned by the govt of the Province of Buenos Aires; local services; Gen. Man. Dr JOSÉ PUCCIARELLI.

Ferroexpreso Pampeano, SA (FEPSA): Conesa 1073, C1426AQU Buenos Aires; tel. (11) 4510-4900; e-mail feppau@fepsa.com.ar; operates services on the Rosario–Bahía Blanca grain lines; 5,094 km of track; Man. PABLO AUTILLO.

Ferrosur Roca (FR): Bouchard 680, 8°, C1106ABJ Buenos Aires; tel. (11) 4319-3900; fax (11) 4319-3901; e-mail ferrosur@elsitio.net; internet www.ferrosur.com.ar; f. 1993; operator of freight services on the Roca lines; Gen. Man. PABLO TERRADAS; 3,000 km of track.

Ferrovías: Avda Dr Ramos Mejía 1430, C1104AJO Buenos Aires; tel. (11) 4314-1444; fax (11) 3311-1181; internet www.ferrovias.com.ar; f. 1994; operates northern commuter line (Belgrano Norte) in Buenos Aires; Pres. GABRIEL ROMERO.

Metrovías (MV): Bartolomé Mitre 3342, C1201AAL Buenos Aires; tel. (11) 4959-6800; fax (11) 4866-3037; e-mail info@metrovias.com.ar; internet www.metrovias.com.ar; f. 1994; operates Subterráneos de Buenos Aires (Subte, although govt of Buenos Aires responsible for network), a light rail line (Premetro) and Urquiza commuter line; Pres. ALDO ROGGIO.

Nuevo Central Argentino, SA (NCA): Avda Alberdi 50, Rosario; tel. (3411) 437-6561; e-mail sac@nca.com.ar; internet www.nca.com.ar; f. 1993; operates freight services on the Bartolomé Mitre lines; Pres. MIGUEL ALBERTO ACEVEDO; Gen. Man. HORACIO DÍAZ HERMELO; 5,011 km of track.

Subterráneos de Buenos Aires (Subte): Bartolomé Mitre 3342, C1201AAL Buenos Aires; tel. (11) 4862-6844; fax (11) 4864-0633; internet www.sbase.com.ar; f. 1913; completely state-owned in 1951–93, responsibility for operations was transferred in 1993 to a private consortium, Metrovías, with control returned to the Municipalidad de la Ciudad de Buenos Aires (from the federal authorities) from 2012; six underground lines totalling 53.7 km, 74 stations, and a 7.4 km light rail line (Premetro) with 17 stations; three additional lines planned; Pres. JUAN PABLO PICCARDO.

Unidad de Gestión Operativa Ferroviaria de Emergencia, SA (UGOFE): internet www.ugofe.com.ar; f. 2005; consortium of Ferrovías, Metrovías and now defunct Trenes de Buenos Aires formed to assume control of three lines (Belgrano Sur, Roca and San Martín) following termination of concession held by Metropolitano (f. 1995); 304-km network; Pres. ROBERTO LATTANZI.

ROADS

In 2010 the intercity road network comprised 231,374 km of roads, of which 30% were paved. Of the total, 38,313 km were under the national road network and 191,812 km formed the provincial road network. In the national network, 87% of roads are paved, whereas only 20% of provincial roads are paved. Four branches of the Pan-American highway run from Buenos Aires to the borders of Chile, Bolivia, Paraguay and Brazil. In 2006 the Inter-American Development Bank financed road development in the Norte Grande region with US $1,200m. A further US $300m. for the second phase of the project was approved in 2012.

Asociación Argentina de Empresarios Transporte Automotor (AAETA): Bernardo de Irigoyen 330, 6°, C1072AAH Buenos Aires; tel. (11) 4334-3254; fax (11) 4334-6513; e-mail info@aaeta.org.ar; internet www.aaeta.org.ar; f. 1941; Pres. Dr JUAN ZUNINO; Gen. Man. MARCELO GONZALVEZ.

Autobuses Sudamericanos, SA: Tres Arroyos 287, C1414EAC Buenos Aires; tel. (11) 4857-3065; fax (11) 4307-1956; f. 1928; international bus services; car and bus rentals; charter bus services; Pres. ARMANDO SCHLECKER HIRSCH; Gen. Man. MIGUEL ANGEL RUGGIERO.

Dirección Nacional de Vialidad: Julio A. Roca 783, C1067ABC Buenos Aires; tel. (11) 4343-8520; internet www.vialidad.gov.ar; controlled by the Secretaría de Transportes; Gen. Man. NELSON GUILLERMO PERIOTTI.

Federación Argentina de Entidades Empresarias de Autotransporte de Cargas (FADEEAC): Sánchez de Bustamante 54, C1173AAB Buenos Aires; tel. (11) 4860-7700; fax (11) 4383-7870; e-mail fadeeac@fadeeac.org.ar; internet www.fadeeac.org.ar; Pres. LUIS A. MORALES.

INLAND WATERWAYS

There is considerable traffic in coastal and river shipping, mainly carrying petroleum and its derivatives.

Dirección Nacional de Vías Navegables: Avda España 221, 4°, Buenos Aires; tel. (11) 4361-5964; e-mail amparadela@yahoo.com.ar; internet www.sspyvn.gov.ar; part of the Ministry of Federal Planning, Public Investment and Services, Transport Secretariat; responsible for the maintenance and improvement of waterways and dredging operations; Dir Dr JOSÉ BENI.

SHIPPING

There are more than 100 ports, of which the most important are Buenos Aires, Quequén and Bahía Blanca. There are specialized terminals at Ensenada, Comodoro Rivadavia, San Lorenzo and Campana (petroleum); Bahía Blanca, Rosario, Santa Fe, Villa Concepción, Mar del Plata and Quequén (cereals); and San Nicolás and San Fernando (raw and construction materials). In 2013 Argentina's flag registered fleet totalled 409 vessels, totalling 732,587 grt.

Administración General de Puertos: Avda Ing. Huergo 431, 1°, C1107AOE Buenos Aires; tel. (11) 4342-1727; fax (11) 4342-6836;

e-mail institucionales@puertobuenosaires.gov.ar; internet www.puertobuenosaires.gov.ar; f. 1956 as a state enterprise for administration of all national sea- and river-ports; following privatization of much of its activity in the mid-1990s, operates the port of Buenos Aires; Gen. Man. Dr JORGE FRANCISCO CHOLVIS.

Consorcio de Gestión del Puerto de Bahía Blanca: Dr Mario M. Guido s/n, 8103 Provincia de Buenos Aires; internet www.puertobahiablanca.com; Pres. HUGO ANTONIO BORELLI; Gen. Man. VALENTÍN D. MORAN.

Terminales Río de la Plata: Avda Ramón Castillo y Avda Cdre Py, Puerto Nuevo, Buenos Aires; tel. (11) 4319-9500; e-mail info@trp.com.ar; internet www.trp.com.ar; operates one of five cargo and container terminals in the port of Buenos Aires; Gen. Man. GUSTAVO FIGUEROLA.

CIVIL AVIATION

Argentina has 10 international airports (Aeroparque Jorge Newbery, Córdoba, Corrientes, El Plumerillo, Ezeiza, Jujuy, Resistencia, Río Gallegos, Salta and San Carlos de Bariloche). Ezeiza, 22 km from Buenos Aires, is one of the most important air terminals in Latin America.

Aerolíneas Argentinas: Bouchard 547, 9°, C1106ABG Buenos Aires; tel. (11) 4317-3000; fax (11) 4320-2116; internet www.aerolineas.com.ar; f. 1950; bought by Grupo Marsans (Spain) in 2001; renationalized in 2008; services to North and Central America, Europe, the Far East, New Zealand, South Africa and destinations throughout South America; the internal network covers the whole country; passengers, mail and freight are carried; Gen. Man. MARIANO RECALDE.

Austral Líneas Aéreas: Corrientes 485, 9°, C1043AAE Buenos Aires; tel. (11) 4317-3600; fax (11) 4317-3777; internet www.austral.com.ar; f. 1971; domestic flights.

Líneas Aéreas del Estado (LADE): Perú 710, San Telmo, C1068AAF Buenos Aires; tel. (11) 5353-2387; fax (11) 4362-4899; e-mail informes@lade.com.ar; internet www.lade.com.ar; f. 1940; domestic flights.

Sol Líneas Aéreas: Aeropuerto Internacional Rosario, Entre Ríos 986, S2000CRR Rosario; tel. (11) 6091-0032; e-mail contacto@sol.com.ar; internet www.sol.com.ar; f. 2005; services between Argentina and Uruguay.

Tourism

Argentina's superb tourist attractions include the Andes mountains, the lake district centred on Bariloche (where there is a National Park), Patagonia, the Atlantic beaches and Mar del Plata, the Iguazú falls, the Pampas and Tierra del Fuego. Tourism receipts totalled a provisional US $4,895m. in 2012, when visitor arrivals totalled an estimated 5.6m.

Asociación Argentina de Agencias de Viajes y Turismo (AAAVYT): Viamonte 640, 10°, B6015XAA Buenos Aires; tel. (11) 4325-4691; fax (11) 4322-9641; e-mail secretaria@aaavyt.org.ar; internet www.aaavyt.org.ar; f. 1951; Pres. FABRICIO DI GIAMBATTISTA; Exec. Dir GERARDO BELIO.

Instituto Nacional de Promoción Turística (INPROTUR): Paraguay 866, 8°, C1057AAL Buenos Aires; tel. (11) 4850-1400; fax (11) 4313-6834; e-mail inprotur@turismo.gov.ar; internet www.argentina.travel; f. 2005; Pres. ENRIQUE MEYER; Exec. Sec. LEONARDO BOTO.

Defence

As assessed at November 2013, Argentina's Armed Forces numbered an estimated 73,100: Army 38,500, Navy 20,000 (including Naval Air Force), Air Force 14,600. There were also paramilitary forces numbering 31,250. Conscription was ended in 1995 and a professional (voluntary) military service was created in its place.

Defence Budget: An estimated 26,300m. new pesos in 2013.

Chair. of the Joint Chiefs of Staff: Gen. LUIS MARÍA CARENA.

Chief of Staff (Army): Gen. CÉSAR SANTOS GERARDO DEL CORAZÓN DE JESÚS MILANI.

Chief of Staff (Navy): Rear-Adm. GASTÓN FERNANDO ERICE.

Chief of Staff (Air Force): Brig. MARIO MIGUEL CALLEJO.

Education

Education from pre-school to university level is available free of charge. Education is officially compulsory for all children at primary level, between the ages of six and 14 years. Secondary education lasts for between five and six years, depending on the type of course: the normal certificate of education (bachillerato) takes five years, a course leading to a commercial bachillerato lasts five years, and one leading to a technical or agricultural bachillerato takes six years. Technical education is supervised by the Consejo Nacional de Educación Técnica. Non-university higher education, usually leading to a teaching qualification, is for three or four years, while university courses last for four years or more. There were three main categories of universities: national, which are supported by the federal budget; provincial (or state), supported by the provincial governments; and private, supported entirely by private initiative, but authorized to function by the Ministry of Education. Enrolment at primary schools in 2005 included 99% of the relevant age-group, while enrolment at secondary schools in 2011 included 85% of pupils in the relevant age-group. Government expenditure on education in 2013 was 34,462.3m. new pesos, equivalent to 5.5% of government expenditure.

ARMENIA

Introductory Survey

LOCATION, CLIMATE, LANGUAGE, RELIGION, FLAG, CAPITAL

The Republic of Armenia is situated in the western South Caucasus. It borders Turkey to the south-west, Iran to the south, Azerbaijan to the east, and Georgia to the north. Naxçıvan, an exclave of Azerbaijan, is situated to the south. The climate is typically continental: dry, with wide temperature variations. The average January temperature in Yerevan is −3°C (26°F), while August temperatures average 25°C (77°F), although high altitude moderates the heat in much of the country. The official language is Armenian, the sole member of a distinct Indo-European language group, written in the Armenian script. Most of the population are adherents of Christianity, the largest denomination being the Armenian Apostolic Church. There are also Islamic and Yazidi communities. The national flag (approximate proportions 2 by 3) consists of three equal horizontal stripes, of red, blue and orange. The capital is Yerevan.

CONTEMPORARY POLITICAL HISTORY

Historical Context

Although Armenia was an important power in ancient times, and formed the first Christian state around AD 300, for much of its history it was ruled by foreign powers. In 1639 Armenia was partitioned, with the larger, western part being annexed by the Osmanlı (Ottoman) Empire and the eastern region becoming part of the Persian Empire. In 1828 eastern Armenia was ceded to the Russian Empire. At the beginning of the 20th century Armenians living in western, Anatolian, Armenia were subject to severe persecution by the Ottoman Turks. As a result of massacres and deportations, the Anatolian lands were largely emptied of their Armenian population, and it was estimated that some 1.5m. perished during 1915–23. After the collapse of Russian imperial power in 1917, eastern, Caucasian, Armenia joined the anti-Bolshevik Transcaucasian Federation in April 1918, with Georgia and Azerbaijan. This collapsed when threatened by Turkish forces, and on 28 May Armenia was proclaimed an independent state, which was recognized by the Allied Powers and by Turkey in the Treaty of Sèvres, signed in August 1920. However, the new Turkish regime led by Mustafa Kemal rejected the treaty and in September attacked Armenia, but was prevented from establishing control over the territory by a Bolshevik invasion, and the founding, on 29 November, of a Soviet Republic of Armenia. In December 1922 the republic was absorbed into the Transcaucasian Soviet Federative Socialist Republic (TSFSR) as a constituent republic of the USSR. In 1936 the TSFSR was dissolved, and the Armenian Soviet Socialist Republic (SSR) was formed. The Soviet authorities implemented a policy of agricultural collectivization and industrialization, and thousands of Armenians were deported, executed or imprisoned during the 1930s.

From late 1987 the status of the largely Armenian-populated Nagornyi Karabakh autonomous oblast (region) within neighbouring Azerbaijan gained increasing significance (q.v., see p. 770). In February 1988 some 1m. people took part in demonstrations in Yerevan, the Armenian capital, led by the outlawed Karabakh Committee, in support of demands from inhabitants of Nagornyi Karabakh for the incorporation of the territory into Armenia. As ethnic tensions intensified, Azeris began to leave Armenia, while anti-Armenian riots in Sumqayıt, Azerbaijan, in late February, resulted in the deaths of 26 Armenians. The Presidium of the USSR's Supreme Soviet (legislature) ruled that Nagornyi Karabakh should remain under Azerbaijani jurisdiction, provoking further Armenian anger. In May, as unrest continued, the First Secretary of the ruling Communist Party of Armenia (HKK) was dismissed. Inter-ethnic violence resulted in the killing of numerous Azeris in and near Gugark, in northern Armenia, in late November. In December a severe earthquake killed some 25,000 people in northern Armenia; members of the Karabakh Committee were subsequently arrested, ostensibly for interfering in relief work. Following huge demonstrations, they were released in May 1989. Meanwhile, in January a Special Administration Committee (SAC) of the USSR Council of Ministers was formed to preside over Nagornyi Karabakh. In September Azerbaijan announced the closure of its borders with Armenia. In November the SAC was disbanded. The USSR Supreme Soviet ruled as unconstitutional a pronouncement of the Armenian Supreme Soviet that Nagornyi Karabakh formed part of a 'unified Armenian Republic'.

The Pan-Armenian National Movement (HHSh), the successor to the Karabakh Committee, won 35% of the seats at elections held to the Armenian Supreme Soviet, in May–July 1990. A leader of the Movement, Levon Ter-Petrosyan, was elected to the chairmanship of the Supreme Soviet. Another HHSh leader, Vazgen Manukyan, was appointed Prime Minister. On 23 August the legislature adopted a declaration of sovereignty, and demanded international recognition of the Turkish massacres of Armenians in 1915 as an act of genocide.

Domestic Political Affairs

The Armenian Government refused to enter into negotiations on a new treaty of union between Soviet republics, and boycotted the referendum on the renewal of the USSR, which was held in March 1991 in nine republics. Instead, the legislature resolved that a referendum on secession from the USSR would take place in September. The attempted coup by conservative communists in the Soviet and Russian capital, Moscow, in August, further strengthened the position of those demanding Armenian independence. According to the official results of the referendum held on 21 September, 99.3% of those participating (some 94.4% of the electorate) supported Armenia's reconstitution as an independent, democratic state. On 23 September the Supreme Soviet declared Armenia to be a fully independent state, and a congress of the HKK voted to dissolve the party. Six candidates contested an election to the post of republican President held on 16 October; Ter-Petrosyan won, with some 87% of the votes cast. Armenia joined the Commonwealth of Independent States (CIS, see p. 243), signing the founding Almatı (Alma-Ata) Declaration on 21 December. In early 1992 the country was admitted to the Conference on Security and Co-operation in Europe (CSCE—now the Organization for Security and Co-operation in Europe—OSCE, see p. 387) and the UN.

In 1992 economic conditions deteriorated, and the situation was exacerbated by the influx of refugees resulting from the continuing conflict in Nagornyi Karabakh, the closure of borders with Azerbaijan, and fighting in neighbouring Georgia (which impeded supplies to Armenia). In February Ter-Petrosyan dismissed the Prime Minister, Harutiunyan, and a new Council of Ministers was announced, headed by Hrant Bagratyan. The assassination in December of a former mayor of Yerevan prompted the Government to suspend the leading opposition party, the Armenian Revolutionary Federation—Dashnaktsutiun (HYD or the Dashnaks).

Legislative elections to the new 190-member Azgayin Zhoghov (National Assembly) were held in July 1995, contested by 13 parties and organizations, while nine parties were barred from participation. The Republican bloc, an alliance of six groups led by the HHSh, won 119 seats, and 45 independent candidates were elected. In late July Ter-Petrosyan appointed a new Government, again led by Bagratyan. In a referendum held concurrently with the general election, 68% of those who voted (56% of the electorate) endorsed a new Constitution, which granted wide-ranging executive authority to the President and provided for a smaller, 131-member National Assembly.

A presidential election was held on 22 September 1996. Ter-Petrosyan was the candidate of the Republican bloc, while five opposition parties united to support Manukyan, now the Chairman of the National Democratic Union. Although preliminary results indicated that Ter-Petrosyan had been re-elected, the opposition made allegations of widespread electoral malpractice, and staged protest rallies in Yerevan. According to the final results, Ter-Petrosyan received 51.8% of the votes cast, and Manukyan secured 41.3%. Bagratyan resigned as Prime Minister in November; he was replaced by Armen Sargsyan, who, in turn, resigned in March 1997 on grounds of ill health. In what was regarded as an attempt to appease opposition nationalist groups, Ter-Petrosyan appointed Robert Kocharyan, hitherto the self-styled President of the unrecognized 'Republic of Nagornyi Karabakh', as Prime Minister.

The presidency of Robert Kocharyan, 1998–2008

President Ter-Petrosyan resigned on 3 February 1998, after his support for an OSCE plan concerning Nagornyi Karabakh had generated accusations that he was insufficiently protective of Armenian interests. Kocharyan, who campaigned on a nationalist platform, was elected as President in a second round of voting on 30 March, defeating the former HKK leader, Karen Demirchyan. Kocharyan was inaugurated as President on 9 April. One day later he appointed Armen Darbinyan as Prime Minister. In May two members of the relegalized HYD were appointed to the Government.

In the legislative elections held on 30 May 1999, the Unity bloc, an alliance of the Republican Party of Armenia (HHK) and the People's Party of Armenia (HZhK), won 55 of the 131 seats; 32 independent candidates were elected. The HKK (which had been permitted to reform) secured 11 seats and the HYD obtained nine. On 11 June Vazgen Sargsyan, the unofficial leader of the HHK and hitherto Minister of Defence, succeeded Darbinyan (who became Minister of the Economy) as Prime Minister. Meanwhile, Demirchyan, the leader of the HZhK, was elected legislative Chairman.

On 27 October 1999 five gunmen staged an attack in the National Assembly, killing eight people, including Prime Minister Sargsyan, Demirchyan and his two deputies, and a cabinet minister. The gunmen, who claimed no political affiliation, announced that they were seeking revenge against the 'corrupt political élite'. On their surrender the assailants were charged with murder and terrorist offences. In the aftermath of the attack, the Ministers of the Interior and of National Security tendered their resignations. In November Armen Khachatryan of the HZhK was elected parliamentary Chairman. (Demirchyan's son, Stepan, replaced him as leader of the HZhK.) Aram Sargsyan, the younger brother of the assassinated premier, was subsequently appointed Prime Minister. In May 2000 Kocharyan appointed Andranik Margaryan, the leader of the HHK, as Prime Minister, prior to a government reorganization.

In October 2001 the HZhK (which had left the Unity bloc shortly before), together with the recently formed Republic grouping and the National Unity Party, organized a rally to demand the impeachment of President Kocharyan, whom they accused of precipitating an economic crisis, acting in contravention of the Constitution and condoning terrorism. In April 2002 legislation abolishing the death penalty was adopted, although the new law was not to apply retroactively to those found guilty of perpetrating terrorist offences. However, in September 2003 the Government removed this stipulation, after the Council of Europe (see p. 252) threatened to expel Armenia unless it abolished capital punishment fully.

Nine candidates participated in the presidential election of 19 February 2003. In a second round, held on 5 March, Kocharyan was re-elected President with 67.5% of the votes cast, defeating Stepan Demirchyan. Monitors from the OSCE and the Council of Europe recorded procedural irregularities, and large protests were staged against the results, which the Constitutional Court, none the less, endorsed.

At legislative elections held on 25 May 2003, the HHK won 32 seats, the Law-Governed Country Party of Armenia (OYeK) 18 seats, the Justice bloc (led by Demirchyan) 15 and the HYD 11. International observers and opposition parties again reported incidences of electoral malpractice. A concurrent referendum on proposed constitutional amendments failed to win the approval of the requisite one-third of registered voters. On 11 June the HHK, the OYeK and the HYD formed a coalition Government, again led by Margaryan. The Chairman of the OYeK, Artur Baghdasaryan, was appointed Chairman of the National Assembly. Members of the Justice bloc boycotted parliamentary sessions until September, in protest at the election results.

In November 2003 Armen Sargsyan, brother of the former premiers Vazgen and Aram Sargsyan, was sentenced to 15 years' imprisonment, having been found guilty of organizing the killing of the Chairman of the Board of Armenian Public Television and Radio, Tigran Naghdalyan, in December 2002. In December 2003 six men were sentenced to life imprisonment for their involvement in the 1999 attack on the National Assembly (one other defendant was imprisoned for 14 years).

The Justice bloc resumed its legislative boycott in February 2004, after the National Assembly refused to debate proposed constitutional amendments permitting a referendum of confidence in the President (the boycott continued on a selective basis for the following two years). From mid-2004 the Justice bloc parties also organized demonstrations in Yerevan, urging Kocharyan's resignation. Two of the three ministerial representatives of the OYeK left office during that year.

Following negotiations with the Council of Europe, in September 2005 the National Assembly approved draft constitutional amendments that (subject to approval by referendum) would limit presidential powers and enhance those of the judiciary. In the constitutional referendum, held on 27 November, with the participation of 65.3% of the electorate, some 94.5% of the valid votes supported the amendments. Meanwhile, in December 2005 a prominent businessman and legislative deputy, Gagik Tsarukyan, founded a new party, Prosperous Armenia (BHK).

In May 2006 Baghdasaryan resigned the chairmanship of the National Assembly and withdrew the OYeK from the governing coalition. Some members of the party defected to other political blocs in response to Baghdasaryan's actions. The United Labour Party agreed to co-operate with the remaining members of the coalition and was allocated one ministerial portfolio and other senior official posts. Tigran Torosyan of the HHK was elected Chairman of the National Assembly in June. In July the Minister of Defence, Serzh Sargsyan, joined the ruling HHK.

On 25 March 2007 Prime Minister Margaryan died, having suffered a heart attack; he was succeeded on 4 April, by Sargsyan, who had also been appointed acting President of the HHK. Sargsyan was replaced as Minister of Defence by the hitherto Armed Forces Chief of General Staff, Col-Gen. Mikael Harutyunyan. At legislative elections, conducted on 12 May, the HHK obtained 64 seats, with 33.9% of the votes cast, while its allies, BHK and the HYD, were placed second and third, with 25 seats (15.1% of the ballot) and 16 seats (13.2%), respectively. Two opposition parties also secured parliamentary representation: the OYeK, with nine seats (7.1% of the votes cast), and the Heritage Party, with seven seats (6.0%). A joint group of OSCE and Council of Europe observers assessed that the elections were conducted largely in accordance with international standards, but observed numerous irregularities. The HHK and three other opposition parties unsuccessfully filed appeals against the results at the Constitutional Court. Despite having secured an outright parliamentary majority, the HHK agreed to form a coalition administration with BHK and the HYD; the three parties together controlled 105 of the 131 legislative seats. Sargsyan was reappointed Prime Minister, and in the new Government, announced in June 2007, 11 portfolios were allocated to the HHK, and three each to BHK and the HYD. In November it was announced that the next presidential election was to be held on 19 February 2008, by which time former President Ter-Petrosyan had established himself as the principal challenger to Sargsyan.

The presidency of Serge Sargsyan

The presidential poll was conducted, as scheduled, on 19 February 2008; according to official results, Serge Sargsyan secured 52.8% of the votes cast and Ter-Petrosyan 21.5%. Ter-Petrosyan (and other opposition candidates) immediately attributed the results to widespread falsification and demanded that the ballot be repeated, prompting his followers to stage mass protests. On 1 March at least eight demonstrators were killed and some 200 people injured in Yerevan during the violent suppression of opposition protests by special police units and interior ministry forces, following which President Kocharyan announced the imposition of a state of emergency for of 20 days. More than 100 associates of Ter-Petrosyan and opposition members were arrested on charges of instigating the violence. On 8 March the Constitutional Court upheld the final official election results. Sargsyan was officially inaugurated as President one day later; he immediately nominated Tigran Sargsyan, hitherto the Governor of the Central Bank, as Prime Minister. Later that month a new administration, in which 10 of the incumbent ministers were retained, was formed.

In April 2008 PACE adopted a resolution that demanded the conduct of an independent inquiry into the violence of 1 March, the immediate release of opposition supporters detained in its aftermath, and the annulment of restrictions on the right to stage public rallies and demonstrations. On 11 June the National Assembly voted in favour of lifting the restrictions. An opposition demonstration in support of Ter-Petrosyan, who demanded that Kocharyan stand trial for crimes against the Armenian people, was subsequently conducted in Yerevan. In August, at a further rally in Yerevan, Ter-Petrosyan officially announced the establishment of an opposition alliance, the Armenian National Congress (HAK), comprising 16 parties and public organizations. In September Torosyan tendered his resignation as Chairman of the National Assembly, following pressure from the HHK leadership to cede the post to Hovik Abrahamyan, a long-term supporter of both Kocharyan and President Sargsyan; Torosyan subsequently left the HHK. Abrahamyan was elected as the new parliamentary Chairman later in September.

In December 2008 the PACE Monitoring Committee criticized the trial of opposition members, whom it described as political prisoners, and recommended the imposition of sanctions against Armenia, in response to the failure of the authorities to comply with its April resolution. However, after the Government pledged to amend two articles of the criminal code that allowed the trial of the opposition supporters, PACE, convening in January 2009, significantly modified the resolution of the Monitoring Committee. The post-election campaign of demonstrations in support of Ter-Petrosyan (which had been suspended in October 2008) was resumed in early 2009; the HAK organized a rally in Yerevan on 1 March to mark the anniversary of the violently suppressed demonstrations of 2008.

In May 2009 the HYD announced its withdrawal from the governing coalition, expressing discontent at the Government's continuing policy of rapprochement with Turkey (see Foreign Affairs). On 31 May municipal elections were held in Yerevan, representing the first occasion on which the Mayor (hitherto a presidential appointment) was elected by the 65-member city assembly. At the elections to the assembly, the HHK were the most successful party, obtaining 47.4% of the votes cast and 35 representatives, ahead of BHK, with 22.7% of the votes cast and 17 representatives and the HAK (which had nominated Ter-Petrosyan as its mayoral candidate), with 17.6% of the votes cast and 13 representatives. Therefore, the HHK nominee, Gagik Beglaryan, who had been appointed Mayor by President Sargsyan in early March, remained in office.

In June 2009 the Government granted a general amnesty covering those detained during the 2008 protest, which was accompanied by the cessation of operations of the commission investigating the deaths resulting from clashes between police and protesters. A prominent opposition journalist, Nikol Pashinyan, the editor of the daily newspaper *Haykakan Zhamanak*, who had been in hiding since March 2008, surrendered himself to police under the terms of the amnesty. (Pashinyan's trial, on charges of inciting and organizing mass disorder during the post-election protests, commenced in October 2009; he was sentenced to seven years' imprisonment in January 2010.)

In March 2010 Baghdasaryan announced that he was to replace two of the three OYeK government ministers, and subsequently appointed two close associates to the Government. In June the National Assembly approved legislation allowing private foreign-language schools to operate, despite widespread public opposition. A civic pressure group that had been formed to campaign against the legislation (which was regarded as providing for greater use of the Russian language in the education sector) received the support of the main opposition parties and prominent pro-establishment politicians. In September the HAK resumed the organization of regular protests in Yerevan, led by Ter-Petrosyan, who reiterated demands for the immediate release of HAK members remaining in detention, Sargsyan's resignation, and early elections.

Anti-Government protests

In early December 2010 Beglaryan was obliged to resign as Mayor of Yerevan, after physically assaulting a presidential aide. Shortly afterwards, the Minister of Justice was dismissed from the Government, after failing to discipline the head of a ministry agency for allegedly assaulting an employee. Later that month the Minister of the Economy, Nerses Yetitsian, was also dismissed, and succeeded by Tigran Davtyan (hitherto Minister of Finance), while severe food shortages and sharp price increases prompted the replacement of the Minister of Agriculture, amid increasing public discontent. In the same month the Azgayin Zhoghov rejected a motion proposed by the Heritage Party providing for recognition of the independence of Nagornyi Karabakh. In February 2011 the head of the National Security Service opposed draft amendments to state legislation regulating the right to public assembly, which had been proposed by the newly appointed Minister of Justice, Hrayr Tovmasyan, in compliance with Council of Europe standards. An announcement by Sargsyan of proposals to create a second chamber in the Armenian legislature, in which elected representatives of the diaspora would participate, prompted public controversy, although Abrahamyan subsequently announced that the required constitutional amendments would not be considered until after the next elections to the Azgayin Zhoghov. In the same month the BHK, together with the OYeK, signed a joint declaration with the HHK pledging to support Sargsyan's candidacy in the 2013 presidential election.

Meanwhile, the HAK increased its campaign of anti-Government protests and on 1 March 2011, to mark the anniversary of the violent suppression of the March 2008 demonstrations, convened a large-scale opposition rally in Yerevan, when Ter-Petrosyan issued an ultimatum for the Government to accede to his political and economic demands, including the holding of new parliamentary and presidential elections. Despite an official prohibition of the holding of protests in the capital's Liberty Square, imposed after the violence of 2008, on 15 March 2011 the Chairman of the Heritage Party, Raffi Hovhannisyan, began a hunger strike in the Square in support of a number of demands, including an end to official corruption, the rescission of the accords with Turkey (which remained unratified), and the recognition of the statehood of the 'Republic of Nagornyi Karabakh'. On 17 March police officers permitted an estimated 10,000 demonstrators (who were attending an authorized protest march led by the HAK) to enter the Square and conduct a rally. Later in the month several Heritage Party parliamentary deputies, gathering in Liberty Square, also demanded the holding of early elections, and the adoption of reforms to the electoral code. In April, despite the continuing official ban, some 12,000 people attended a further HAK rally, led by Ter-Petrosyan, in Liberty Square. The prohibition on demonstrating in the square was formally rescinded shortly before a further large opposition demonstration, which was staged, as planned, on 28 April. On 26 May the National Assembly adopted legislation acceding to several of the demands of the HAK, including the release of some 396 prisoners (among them Pashinyan and a number of other opposition activists convicted of involvement in the violent protests of 2008), and the reduction in sentences of 379 others, while the investigation into the deaths that occurred during the clashes was to be reopened. Nevertheless, at the end of May, and in subsequent months, the HAK organized mass rallies demanding early presidential and parliamentary elections.

The 2012 legislative elections

In November 2011 Abrahamyan announced his resignation as Chairman of the National Assembly, in order to lead the HHK campaign for the forthcoming legislative elections; he was succeeded by Samvel Nikoyan. The removal of two senior state officials by President Sargsyan was widely attributed to their connections with former President Kocharyan, who had recently indicated that he envisaged a return to political life. In January 2012 the HYD and the Heritage Party submitted proposals in the National Assembly for the amendment of the electoral system so that all parliamentary seats would be contested on a party-list basis in the forthcoming elections; the HAK subsequently organized further demonstrations in support of these demands (which were rejected by HHK officials).

Attacks on opposition candidates and activists were reported during the election campaign period in April 2012. At the elections to the National Assembly on 6 May, the HHK strengthened its parliamentary representation, securing 69 seats, with 42.2% of the votes cast on the basis of party lists. The BHK also increased its representation, to 37 seats, its share of the vote rising to 28.9%. The HAK won seven seats (6.8%), while the HYD obtained only six seats (5.4%), the OYeK also six seats (5.3%) and the Heritage Party five seats (5.5%). Despite opposition claims of irregularities, OSCE observers generally endorsed the conduct of the elections, although again reporting a number of shortcomings. On 2 June President Sargsyan reappointed Tigran Sargsyan as Prime Minister. The HHK established a new ruling coalition with the OYeK (which BHK declined to join), and a reorganized Government with three new OYeK ministers was formed on 16 June. Meanwhile, Abrahamyan was re-elected Chairman of the National Assembly.

On 2 October 2012 the National Assembly voted to remove the parliamentary immunity of Vardan Oskanyan, a BHK deputy and former Minister of Foreign Affairs, who was subsequently charged with the misappropriation of funds donated to his Civilitas Foundation, a research organization that had become increasingly critical of the Government. Oskanyan and his supporters claimed that the charges were politically motivated, in the context of pressure on BHK leaders not to oppose President Sargsyan's candidacy in the forthcoming presidential election.

Recent developments: the 2013 presidential election

In January 2013 eight candidates successfully registered to contest the presidential poll (although one later withdrew); they included incumbent President Sargsyan, former premier Bagratyan of Freedom, and Hovhannisyan of the Heritage Party. However, two of the most prominent opponents of Sargsyan, Ter-Petrosyan and Tsarukyan, had announced that they would not participate in the presidential election, and the HYD also announced a boycott of the poll, principally owing to expectations that it would not be conducted fairly. Later in the month presidential candidate Andrias Ghukasyan, the head of private radio station Radio Hay, staged a hunger strike, after his appeal for President Sargsyan to be declared ineligible to seek re-election was rejected by the Central Electoral Commission. At the end of January another candidate, Paruyr Hayrikyan, the leader of a small party, the Union for National Self-Determination, was shot and injured; he presented but subsequently withdrew an application that the presidential poll be postponed.

At the presidential election, which proceeded on 18 February 2013 as scheduled, Sargsyan secured 58.6% of votes cast, according to official results, while Hovhannisyan received 36.8% and Bagratyan only 2.2%. Hovhannisyan immediately attributed Sargsyan's victory to malpractice, and began a campaign of mass protests in Yerevan and other major towns. Although OSCE observers, in addition to criticizing a lack of democratic competition in the poll, noted inconsistencies in the official results, EU and other international leaders issued congratulatory statements to Sargsyan on his re-election. In early March the independent presidential candidate and poet, Vardan Sedrakyan, was detained in connection with the attempt to kill Hayrikyan (following the arrest of two alleged perpetrators who were reportedly acquainted with him). On 10 March Hovhannisyan began a hunger strike in Liberty Square to demand the resignation of Sargsyan. Nevertheless, on 14 March the Constitutional Court upheld the final election results, rejecting complaints of violations by Hovhannisyan and Ghukasyan. Hovhannisyan ended his hunger strike at the end of March, but pledged to continue the organization of opposition protests. Sargsyan was inaugurated for a second presidential term on 9 April, when Hovhannisyan staged a parallel ceremony at a rally in Liberty Square. (However, support for opposition rallies organized by Hovhannisyan subsequently declined.) A government reorganization was effected in May: notably, Vahran Avanesyan became Minister of the Economy, succeeding Davtyan, while the hitherto Government Chief of Staff, David Sargsyan, became Minister of Finance, exchanging posts with Vache Gabrielyan.

In September 2013 a government commission to draft constitutional amendments was established, following President Sargsyan's expressed interest in changing the Constitution to transfer significant presidential powers to the legislature (with the possible intention of remaining in power as Prime Minister after the end of his second term). At the end of September Sargsyan granted amnesty to several hundred prisoners, including opposition activists. Meanwhile, an announcement by the Armenian Government early that month that the country would join the Russian-led customs union (see below), thereby effectively suspending its EU integration process, prompted criticism and resulted in protests in Yerevan; President Sargsyan issued official denials that the decision (which was widely believed to have been prompted by pressure from Russian President Vladimir Putin) would preclude future dialogue and co-operation with the EU. In October supporters of the Armenian Apostolic Church, and other institutions demonstrated in Yerevan and submitted a petition against proposed government legislation that purported to further the cause of what was termed gender equality (and which demonstrators alleged could eventually bring about the legal recognition of single-sex marriage). An anti-Government protest in early November resulted in clashes between demonstrators and police in central Yerevan, and several arrests. A further small protest in Yerevan (attended by an estimated 500 people) was staged in early December to coincide with a visit by Putin.

In January 2014 a planned pension reform involving a compulsory savings plan for citizens (see Economic Affairs) provoked public protests; following an appeal by civil society activists and the country's main opposition parties, the Constitutional Court ruled later that month that introduction of the measure would be postponed pending a review of its legality in March. In early February the National Security Service announced that a former senior police official had been detained on charges of spying for the Azerbaijani secret services. A businessman who was arrested in February on suspicion of fraud involving a diamond-processing concern was alleged to have connections with President Sargsyan and a former Armenian Apostolic archbishop.

On 3 April 2014 Tigran Sargsyan resigned as Prime Minister. The hitherto Chairman of the National Assembly, Abrahamyan, was appointed as his successor on 13 April; in accordance with the Constitution, a new Government was to be formed within 20 days.

Foreign Affairs

Regional relations

In September 1991 the disputed territory of Nagornyi Karabakh (in Azerbaijan, but with a predominantly ethnically Armenian population) declared itself an independent republic (q.v., see p. 770). Violence intensified following the dissolution of the USSR in December. International efforts to negotiate a peace settlement foundered, owing to Azerbaijan's insistence that the conflict was a domestic problem. In May 1992 the Nagornyi Karabakh 'self-defence forces' (which the Armenian Government continued to claim were operating without its military support) gained complete control of the territory. With the capture of the Laçin valley, the ethnic Armenian militia succeeded in opening a 'corridor' linking Nagornyi Karabakh with Armenia. Following an Azerbaijani counter-offensive in August, a state defence committee, in close alignment with the Ter-Petrosyan administration of Armenia, replaced the Government of Nagornyi Karabakh. With the capture of the Kälbäcär district in April 1993, a second corridor linking the territory with Armenia was established. The seizure of Azerbaijani territory outside the oblast prompted international condemnation. UN Security Council Resolutions 822 and 853, which demanded the withdrawal of occupying and local Armenian forces from Azerbaijan, went unheeded; hostilities intensified further, and more than 20% of Azerbaijan's total territory was reported to have been captured by the Nagornyi Karabakh forces; Azerbaijani forces recaptured some territory in a counter-offensive launched in December. In February 1994 it was reported that as many as 18,000 people had been killed since 1988. More than 500,000 Azeris were believed to have been displaced.

In May 1994 a new ceasefire agreement was signed by the Ministers of Defence of Armenia and Azerbaijan and representatives of Nagornyi Karabakh. Ter-Petrosyan held talks with the President of Azerbaijan, Heydär Äliyev, in Moscow, in September, but Äliyev stated that his willingness to negotiate a peace accord depended on the unconditional withdrawal of Armenian forces from Azerbaijani territory. Negotiations were held during 1995, under the aegis of the OSCE's 11-nation Minsk Group, but produced only limited progress towards a political settlement. Direct discussions between Armenia and Azerbaijan were initiated in December.

In December 1996 Ter-Petrosyan and Äliyev attended an OSCE summit meeting in Lisbon, Portugal. The OSCE Chairman subsequently issued a statement recommending three principles that would form the basis of a future settlement: the territorial integrity of Armenia and Azerbaijan; the status of Nagornyi Karabakh as a broadly autonomous region within Azerbaijan; and security guarantees for its population. Armenia refused to accept these terms, however. In late 1997 the recently elected 'President' of Nagornyi Karabakh, Arkadi Ghukasyan, rejected the proposed OSCE peace settlement on the grounds that the proposals presupposed Azerbaijan's sovereignty over the territory. A subsequent statement by President Ter-Petrosyan that Nagornyi Karabakh could hope neither to gain full independence, nor to be united with Armenia, appeared to indicate a significant change in policy, but widespread criticism of this stance in Armenia led to his resignation in February 1998 and his subsequent replacement by former Nagornyi Karabakh 'President' Robert Kocharyan. Several meetings between the Armenian and Azerbaijani Presidents in 1999–2002, produced no substantive progress towards a resolution of the dispute. Negotiations resumed, after İlham Äliyev succeeded his father as President of Azerbaijan in late 2003. In January 2005 PACE approved a resolution, expressing concern at large-scale ethnic expulsions resulting from the Nagornyi Karabakh conflict. In July 2006 the Minsk Group publicized for the first time the details of its fundamental criteria for an agreement between the two countries. On 10 December 2006 the territory held an internationally unrecognized referendum, which affirmed the population's desire for independence from Azerbaijan. In July

2007 Bako Sahakyan, a former head of Nagornyi Karabakh's security service, was elected as 'President' of the territory.

In March 2008, after several people had been killed in renewed clashes in Nagornyi Karabakh, a non-binding resolution, submitted by Azerbaijan, reaffirming its territorial integrity and demanding the withdrawal of all occupying forces, was adopted by the UN General Assembly, by 39 votes in favour and seven opposing (and 100 abstentions); in addition to Armenia, countries that rejected the resolution included France, Russia and the USA. In June Sargsyan met President Äliyev of Azerbaijan for discussions on the occasion of a CIS summit meeting in St Petersburg, Russia.

Meeting near Moscow on 2 November 2008, Sargsyan and Äliyev, together with Russian President Dmitrii Medvedev, in the capacity of mediator, signed a declaration reaffirming their commitment to reach a political resolution to the Nagornyi Karabakh conflict. Three further such trilateral meetings took place during 2009. President Medvedev convened meetings between Sargsyan and Äliyev in Sochi, Russia, in January and during the St Petersburg Economic Forum in June. However, shortly afterwards, in June, one Azerbaijani and four Armenian soldiers were killed in what Armenia claimed was an attack by Azerbaijani forces at the 'line of contact' in Nagornyi Karabakh. Later that month the Presidents of Russia, the USA and France (the states co-chairing the OSCE Minsk Group) issued a joint statement urging Armenia and Azerbaijan to finalize the drafting of a peace agreement. In September three Armenian and two Azerbaijani soldiers were killed in a further clash at the enclave's border. Further discussions between Sargsyan and Äliyev, convened by Medvedev in Astrakhan, Russia, in October, resulted in a formal agreement on a mutual exchange of prisoners of war and the return of the remains of those killed in clashes, but no significant concessions.

Discussions between Sargsyan, Äliyev and Medvedev, convened in Sochi in March 2011, resulted only in a joint declaration urging the full implementation of the agreement reached the previous October. Further trilateral discussions took place in the Russian city of Kazan in June 2011, and in Sochi in January 2012. Hopes that planned Armenian participation in the annual European festival of popular music, the Eurovision Song Contest, which was to be held in Baku, the Azerbaijani capital, in May 2012, would serve as a demonstration of improved relations (and provide a rare opportunity on which Armenian citizens would be permitted to visit Azerbaijan) were thwarted when, in March, it was announced that Armenia would not participate. The withdrawal was precipitated by an incident in which an Armenian conscript soldier had been killed in February, although initial reports that the death had been attributed to Azerbaijani sniper fire were withdrawn after it became apparent that the shooting had been perpetrated by another Armenian soldier. In June 2012 at least three Armenian and five Azerbaijani soldiers were killed in a further series of clashes near the Armenian border, which coincided with a visit to the region by US Secretary of State Hillary Clinton.

In August 2012, at the request of President Äliyev, the Hungarian Government approved the extradition to Azerbaijan of Ramil Säfärov, an Azerbaijani soldier who had murdered an Armenian fellow participant during a NATO 'Partnership for Peace' course in Budapest, Hungary, in 2004. Säfärov's release and subsequent pardon in Azerbaijan prompted widespread outrage in Armenia (which suspended diplomatic relations with Hungary), and protests were staged in Yerevan and internationally. The OSCE also criticized the development as having damaged peace efforts. In October the Armenian armed forces conducted military exercises that simulated an attack on Azerbaijani facilities, while a senior Armenian military official stated publicly that Armenia was prepared to use long-range missiles, acquired from Russia, against Azerbaijan. In January 2013 the Armenian and Azerbaijani Ministers of Foreign Affairs met for mediated discussions in Paris, France. A meeting between Sargsyan and Äliyev (the first since January 2012) in the Austrian capital, Vienna, on 19 November 2013 resulted in agreement to continue regular meetings, and was followed by further discussions between the two Ministers of Foreign Affairs in Kyiv, Ukraine, in early December. Later in December, however, the Armenian Government informed Minsk Group representatives visiting Yerevan that numerous ceasefire violations, which it attributed to Azerbaijani forces, were impeding progress towards a settlement; an estimated 20 soldiers and officers had been killed on each side during 2013. An escalation in military skirmishes at the 'line of contact', after which the Azerbaijani authorities claimed to have repelled an incursion by Armenian troops, preceded a further mediated meeting of the Ministers of Foreign Affairs in Paris in January 2014.

In 1997 the Armenian legislature ratified a 1995 treaty allowing Russia to maintain military bases in Armenia for 25 years, and several bilateral agreements were concluded in 2000. A further, 10-year economic co-operation agreement was signed in 2001. In August 2010, a bilateral defence agreement amending the 1995 treaty was signed, allowing Russia's military presence in the country to be extended until 2044 and the mission of some 4,000 Russian troops based in the town of Gyumri (hitherto confined to protecting Russian interests) to be upgraded to defending Armenia's security in co-operation with the Armenian army. Russia also committed to supply Armenia with modern armaments. In February 2011 President Sargsyan met Medvedev for discussions in St Petersburg. Amid the increased tensions with Azerbaijan, the Collective Security Treaty Organization (CSTO, see p. 464) conducted large-scale military exercises in Armenia in September. On 4 October the Armenian legislature ratified a CSTO protocol under which member states were not permitted to host foreign military forces or bases without the consent of the body.

After his re-election in February 2013, President Sargsyan met Vladmir Putin (who had returned to the Russian presidency in the previous year) near Moscow. In an unexpected development that followed his further visit to Moscow in early September, Sargsyan announced that Armenia was to join the Russian-led customs union (also comprising Belarus and Kazakhstan). In December Putin made a state visit to Yerevan, when he agreed with Sargsyan an arrangement for Armenia's purchase of Russian natural gas at the reduced price of US $189 per cu m. Putin also reaffirmed that Russia would continue to supply Armenia with armaments and military equipment. In January 2014 the Armenian Government approved a timetable for membership of the customs union. In the same month an agreement was signed under which the Russian state-owned corporation Gazprom acquired the remaining 20% share that it did not already own in Armenia's sole natural gas producer ArmRosGazProm (which was to be renamed Gazprom Armenia).

Armenia's relations with Georgia were generally relatively cordial in the post-Soviet period, although concerns were expressed regarding the condition or treatment of historic Armenian sites within Georgia. The Armenian Government reacted with caution to Russian military operations in Georgia, taken in support of separatists in South Ossetia (see Georgia), in August 2008. (Despite Russian pressure, Sargsyan subsequently declared that his country would not recognize the independence of South Ossetia and Abkhazia while the status of Nagornyi Karabakh remained unresolved.) In January 2009 the arrest in Georgia, in the region of Samtskhe-Javakheti, predominantly inhabited by ethnic Armenians, of two ethnic Armenians on charges of espionage and of attempting to establish a paramilitary grouping, prompted public outrage in Armenia. In March the two men were released on bail, having pleaded guilty to espionage. In January 2013 the newly installed Georgian Prime Minister, Bidzina Ivanishvili, made an official visit to Armenia, where he signed two co-operation agreements with President Sargsyan. In the same month the Georgian Government announced the release from prison (under a general amnesty) of Vahagn Chakhalyan, an advocate of ethnic Armenian rights in Georgia.

Meanwhile, relations with Turkey (which controlled large areas of historic Armenia, including Mount Ararat, regarded as a national symbol by many Armenians) remained uneasy, particularly after Turkey closed its borders with Armenia in 1993, as an expression of support for Azerbaijan in the conflict over Nagornyi Karabakh. In December 2004, following an appeal from President Kocharyan, the European Parliament issued a statement that Turkey should recognize that the killings of Armenians in 1915 constituted an act of genocide, and open its borders; in September 2005 the European Parliament issued a further non-binding resolution, which indicated that Turkey's refusal to recognize the killings as genocide could adversely affect its efforts to secure membership of the European Union (EU, see p. 273). Both Armenia's campaign to secure recognition by other states of the killings as genocide and its continuing conflict with Azerbaijan remained serious obstacles to the development of closer relations with Turkey. The murder of a prominent ethnic-Armenian Turkish journalist in Turkey in January 2007 further heightened the sensitivity of relations between the two countries.

Hopes of a rapprochement between Armenia and Turkey, after President Sargsyan's installation in April 2008, increased significantly when Turkish President Abdullah Gül accepted an invitation from President Sargsyan to attend the first football match between the national teams, in Yerevan on 6 September (the first visit by a Turkish Head of State to Armenia). The Armenian Government additionally waived visa requirements to allow Turkish football fans to travel to Armenia. The announcement followed confirmation by Turkish foreign ministry officials in July of media speculation that Turkish and Armenian delegations had met in Switzerland for informal discussions on bilateral relations. In September the Ministers of Foreign Affairs of Turkey, Armenia and Azerbaijan met in New York, USA, to conduct discussions on Nagornyi Karabakh. In January 2009 Sargsyan met Turkish Prime Minister Recep Tayyip Erdoğan during the Davos World Economic Forum, and conducted discussions with the Turkish Minister of Foreign Affairs at the Munich Security Conference, in Germany, in early February. In April the ministries of foreign affairs of the two countries announced that further Swiss-brokered discussions had resulted in the drawing-up of a comprehensive framework for normalization of relations. In August the two ministries issued a joint statement announcing that they had agreed to conduct internal political consultations on two protocols: one establishing diplomatic relations and the other developing bilateral ties, which would then be signed and submitted to their respective legislatures for ratification. On 10 October the Ministers of Foreign Affairs of Turkey and Armenia, meeting in Geneva, Switzerland, signed an agreement providing for the normalization of relations between their two countries, which would take effect following its ratification by the legislature of each country.

Progress towards ratification of the treaty subsequently halted, however. A ruling by the Armenian Constitutional Court, on 12 January 2010, that the treaty was constitutionally legitimate, precipitated controversy among some Turkish nationalists. In February the Armenian legislature approved a Law on International Treaties, which provided for an expedited process by which the Government could suspend or rescind international agreements. In April President Sargsyan suspended ratification of the Armenian-Turkish treaty, after Turkey made ratification conditional on progress towards a resolution of the Nagornyi Karabakh conflict. In September some 1,000 Armenian Christians travelled to the Turkish island of Akhtamar, in Lake Van in eastern Anatolia, to attend the first religious services to be held in a 10th-century Armenian church since 1915, after the Turkish Government had restored the church and had agreed that an act of worship could be held there once a year (although the Armenian Government criticized the failure of the Turkish authorities to place a cross on the church). In early October an extreme nationalist Turkish party organized an Islamic religious ceremony, with official permission, in an 11th century Armenian church in the abandoned historic town (and former Armenian capital) of Ani, in Anatolia; the ceremony was strongly condemned by the Armenian Apostolic Church and representatives of the Armenian diaspora. In August 2011 Sargsyan reiterated warnings that Armenia would withdraw from the treaty with Turkey unless the Turkish Government unconditionally ratified the protocols. In April 2013 the first ever scheduled flights between Turkey and Armenia by a Turkish airline, which were to have linked Yerevan with the eastern Turkish city of Van, and which were scheduled to begin early that month, were cancelled shortly beforehand by the Turkish civil aviation authority, reportedly owing to pressure from Azerbaijan. (In the same month the principal Armenian airline, Armavia, which had operated flights between Yerevan and Turkey for several years, suspended operations, after it entered into bankruptcy proceedings.) During an Eastern Partnership summit meeting in Vilnius, Lithuania, in November, Sargsyan urged EU member states to request that Turkey acknowledge the 1915 killings as genocide and reopen the border with Armenia. However, in December, the Turkish Minister of Foreign Affairs, attending a meeting of Organization of the Black Sea Economic Co-operation (see p. 401) in Yerevan, met his Armenian counterpart for discussions, prompting hopes of some improvement in bilateral relations.

Armenia generally enjoyed cordial relations with Iran, and a permanent bridge between the two countries was opened in 1995. In September 2004 President Muhammad Khatami of Iran made an official visit to Armenia, signing seven bilateral agreements with President Kocharyan, which, *inter alia*, were to promote enhanced co-operation in energy and transport. In May 2009 Armenia began to import natural gas from Iran through a new pipeline. In July 2010 it was announced that construction of a new Armenian–Iranian power transmission line was to begin, prior to planned exports of Armenian electricity to Iran. A bilateral agreement, approved by the Armenian Government in September, provided for the construction of two large hydro-electric plants near the border with Iran and of a 365-km oil pipeline linking the two countries (work on the pipeline was subsequently scheduled for completion in 2014).

Other external relations

In June 2000 PACE voted to admit both Armenia and Azerbaijan to the Council of Europe; they became full members in January 2001. In June 2004 Armenia, Azerbaijan and Georgia were included in the EU's new European Neighbourhood Policy and in November 2006 a five-year action plan for co-operation was adopted. With the aim of strengthening relations and addressing integration aspirations, in December 2008 the European Commission presented an Eastern Partnership proposal for Armenia (together with other regional states); the new programme, offering further economic integration and envisaging enhanced free trade and visa arrangements, was officially established at an EU summit meeting in May 2009. On 19 July 2010 Armenia and the EU began negotiations on the signature of an Association Agreement within the framework of the Eastern Partnership. After the European Commission assessed that Armenia had made sufficient progress in preparatory reforms, the opening of negotiations on an envisaged free trade area was approved on 20 February 2012. On 17 December the EU signed a visa facilitation agreement with Armenia. Negotiations to determine the basis for the free trade agreement with the EU were completed in July 2013. However, the Armenian Government's decision, announced in September, to join the Russian-led customs union (see above) prevented the expected initialling of the Association Agreement at an Eastern Partnership Summit meeting in Vilnius in November. EU officials subsequently indicated that other co-operation mechanisms with Armenia would be considered.

CONSTITUTION AND GOVERNMENT

Under the Constitution of 1995, the President of the Republic is Head of State and Supreme Commander-in-Chief of the armed forces, but also holds broad executive powers. The President is directly elected for a term of five years (and for no more than two consecutive terms of office). The President appoints the Prime Minister (upon the approval of the majority of members of the Azgayin Zhoghov—National Assembly) and, on the Prime Minister's recommendation, the members of the Government. Legislative power is vested in the 131-member National Assembly, which is elected by universal adult suffrage for a term of five years. Judicial power is exercised by the Court of Cassation (the members of which are appointed by the President, for life), and appellate courts. For administrative purposes, Armenia is divided into 11 regions (*marzer*), including the capital, Yerevan.

REGIONAL AND INTERNATIONAL CO-OPERATION

Armenia is a founder member of the Commonwealth of Independent States (CIS, see p. 243) and was admitted to the Conference on Security and Co-operation in Europe (CSCE—now the Organization for Security and Co-operation in Europe—OSCE, see p. 387) in 1992. It is also a member of the Organization of the Black Sea Economic Co-operation (BSEC, see p. 401).

Armenia joined the UN in 1992 and was admitted to the World Trade Organization (WTO, see p. 434) in 2003.

ECONOMIC AFFAIRS

In 2012, according to estimates by the World Bank, Armenia's gross national income (GNI), measured at average 2010–12 prices, was US $11,058m., equivalent to $3,720 per head (or $6,990 on an international purchasing-power parity basis). In 2003–12, it was estimated, the population decreased by an annual average of 0.2%, while gross domestic product (GDP) per head increased, in real terms, by an annual average rate of 6.4%. In 2003–12 Armenia's overall GDP increased, in real terms, by an annual average rate of 6.1%. Real GDP increased by 7.1% in 2012. According to the Asian Development Bank (ADB, see p. 207), real GDP increased by 3.5% in 2013

According to official figures, agriculture, hunting, forestry and fishing contributed 20.9% of GDP and employed 37.3% of the workforce in 2012. (However, FAO estimated that just 8.4% of the workforce were employed in agriculture.) The principal crops are potatoes and other vegetables, cereals, and fruit, primarily grapes. In 2003–11, according to estimates by the World Bank, agricultural GDP increased, in real terms, at an average annual rate of 4.0%. The GDP of the sector declined by 15.8% in 2010 but increased by 5.6% in 2011, according to the World Bank. According to the ADB, agriculture grew by 8.1% in 2013.

According to official figures, industry (including mining, manufacturing, construction and utilities) contributed 32.2% of GDP and employed 17.7% of the workforce in 2012. World Bank estimates indicated that in 2003–11 real industrial GDP increased at an annual average rate of 4.2%. According to World Bank figures, the GDP of the sector declined substantially, by some 30.8% in 2009, partly because of a downturn in construction activity, in 2009; it increased by 6.5%, in 2010 and by 7.5% in 2011. According to the ADB, industry grew by 5.4% in 2012, but declined by 1.8% in 2013

The mining sector has not been extensively developed. According to official figures, the sector contributed 3.2% of GDP and employed 0.9% of the labour force in 2012. Copper, molybdenum, gold, silver and iron are extracted on a small scale, and there are reserves of lead and zinc. There are also substantial, but largely unexploited, reserves of mineral salt, calcium oxide and carbon. Gold production increased in the early 2000s, from 600 kg of gold ore in 2000 to 2,100 kg in 2004, although output declined to 1,400 kg in 2005, but reached 2,000 kg in 2010. According to official figures, production in the mining sector increased by an annual average rate of 8.0% in 2000–08.

According to official figures, the manufacturing sector provided 10.9% of GDP and employed 8.0% of the workforce in 2012. According to the World Bank, in 2003–11 the GDP of the manufacturing sector increased, in real terms, at an average annual rate of 4.1%. Real sectoral GDP increased by 7.0% in 2011.

In 2012, according to official figures, the construction sector provided 13.4% of GDP and employed 5.9% of the workforce. According to the ADB, in 2001–10 the GDP of the sector increased, in real terms, at an average annual rate of 20.6%. Real sectoral GDP decreased by 38.6% in 2009 but increased by 20.6% in 2010.

Armenia is heavily dependent on imported energy, much of which is supplied by Russia (petroleum and derivatives) and Turkmenistan (natural gas). In 2007 a natural gas pipeline connecting the pipeline networks of Armenia and Iran, to provide Armenia with supplies of gas from Iran (although this was likely to be sourced from Turkmenistan) was inaugurated. By 1999 Armenia had a surplus of electricity, some of which was exported to Georgia; a new high-voltage electricity line opened between the two countries in 2000, and two high-voltage lines were subsequently opened to permit exports of electric energy to Iran. In 2005 Armenia, Georgia and Iran pursued plans to integrate their electricity networks. In 2007 the Government approved a plan for the closure of Armenia's sole nuclear power station, at Medzamor, although no specific date for the closure was given. In 2009 the Government decided that a new nuclear power station would be constructed in Armenia, with Russian assistance. Although it had initially been anticipated that construction would commence in 2011, the project was significantly delayed. The construction of some 15 small hydroelectric power stations was initiated in 2004, and the construction of two joint Armenian-Iranian hydroelectric plants on the River Araks commenced in 2012. In 2012 nuclear power contributed 34.3% of the country's electricity output, hydroelectric power provided 33.5% and natural gas produced 32.2% of the total. Imports of mineral fuels comprised 21.2% of the value of merchandise imports in 2012. In that year Armenia produced a total of 8,036m. kWh of electric energy.

According to official figures, the services sector contributed 46.8% of GDP and engaged 45.0% of the employed labour force in 2012. According to the World Bank, in 2003–11 the GDP of the sector increased by an average annual rate of 7.5%, in real terms. Real sectoral GDP increased by 4.5% in 2010 but declined by 0.1% in 2011. According to the ADB, the services sector grew by 5.9% in 2013

In 2012 Armenia recorded a visible merchandise trade deficit of US $2,111.1m., while the deficit on the current account of the balance of payments was $1,107.9m. In 2012 the principal sources of imports were Russia (which supplied 24.8% of total imports), the People's Republic of China, Germany, Iran, Ukraine and Turkey. Armenia's principal export partner in that year was Russia (taking 20.2% of total exports). Other important purchasers were Bulgaria, Belgium, Iran, Germany, the USA, Canada, the Netherlands, Switzerland and Georgia. The principal exports in 2012 were manufactured goods, crude materials (except fuels), beverages and tobacco, mineral fuels, food and live animals, and non-monetary gold. The principal imports in that year were mineral fuels, machinery and transport equipment, manufactured goods, food and live animals, chemical products, and miscellaneous manufactured articles.

In 2012 there was a budgetary deficit of 61,661.6m. drams (equivalent to 1.5% of GDP). Armenia's general government gross debt was 1,549,053m. drams in 2012, equivalent to 38.9% of GDP. At the end of 2011 Armenia's gross external debt was US $7,383m., of which $2,736m. was public and publicly guaranteed debt. In that year, the cost of debt-servicing long-term public and publicly guaranteed debt and repayments to the IMF was equivalent to 25.4% of the value of exports of goods, services and income (excluding workers' remittances). According to the International Labour Organization (ILO), consumer prices increased at an average annual rate of 5.0% in 2003–12. According to the ADB, consumer prices increased by 5.8% in 2012. The official rate of unemployment was 17.3% in 2012.

An extensive programme of market-based reforms was initiated in the 1990s, and after 2001 steady GDP growth was recorded. In June 2010 the IMF approved a new three-year Extended Fund Facility (EFF) and Extended Credit Facility (ECF) arrangement totalling US $395m. Armenia and seven other member states of the Commonwealth of Independent States (CIS, see p. 243) signed a free trade agreement in October 2011 (although its implementation was subsequently delayed pending ratification by all the signatory states). Nevertheless, and despite concerns that Armenia's adherence to this agreement would not be compatible with closer trade integration with Europe, after the European Commission assessed that Armenia had made sufficient progress in preparatory measures, the opening of negotiations on the eventual establishment of a free trade area with the EU, within the framework of the Union's Eastern Partnership scheme, was approved in February 2012. The European Bank for Reconstruction and Development commended government reform efforts in areas such as business regulations and property rights, and the adoption of a new mining code. The negotiations to determine the basis for the free trade agreement with the EU were completed in July 2013. However, the Armenian Government's decision, announced in September, to join a Russian-led customs union (then also comprising Belarus and Kazakhstan—which was to be expanded into an Eurasian Economic Union), prevented the expected initialling of the Association Agreement at a summit in November. In December it was officially agreed that Armenia would purchase Russian natural gas at a reduced price of US $189 per cu m; other prospective financial benefits included Russian funding for a north–south railway in Armenia (scheduled for completion by 2017), a discount on the price of Russian diamonds for Armenia's diamond-processing industry, and a $100m. loan from the Eurasian Economic Community (EURASEC, see p. 451). Growth was estimated to have slowed to 4% during 2013 (from more than 7% in 2012). In January 2014 a planned pensions reform, under which 5% of the monthly salaries of younger citizens would be withheld and placed in a pension fund, prompted considerable controversy; introduction of the measure was postponed, pending a constitutional review.

PUBLIC HOLIDAYS

2015: 1–2 January (New Year), 6 January (Christmas), 28 January (Army Day), 8 March (Women's Day), 3–5 April (Easter), 24 April (Armenian Genocide Commemoration Day), 1 May (Labour Day), 9 May (Victory and Peace Day), 28 May (Declaration of the First Armenian Republic Day), 5 July (Constitution Day), 21 September (Independence Day).

Statistical Survey

Principal source: National Statistical Service of the Republic of Armenia, 0010 Yerevan, Republic Sq., Government House 3; tel. (10) 52-42-13; fax (10) 52-19-21; e-mail info@armstat.am; internet www.armstat.am.

Area and Population

AREA, POPULATION AND DENSITY

Area (sq km)	29,743*
Population (census results)†	
10 October 2001	3,002,594
12 October 2011 (preliminary)	
Males	1,346,729
Females	1,525,042
Total	2,871,771
Population (official estimates at 1 January)	
2012	3,021,376
2013	3,026,879
Density (per sq km) at 1 January 2013	101.8

* 11,484 sq miles (including inland water, totalling 1,278 sq km).
† Figures refer to de facto populations; the *de jure* total population for 2001 was 3,213,011, and for 2011 was 3,018,854.

POPULATION BY AGE AND SEX
(official estimates at 1 January 2013)

	Males	Females	Total
0–14	305,001	265,680	570,681
15–64	1,018,982	1,117,718	2,136,700
65 and over	127,663	191,835	319,498
Total	1,451,646	1,575,233	3,026,879

POPULATION BY ETHNIC GROUP*
(permanent inhabitants, 2001 census)

	Number	%
Armenian	3,145,354	97.89
Yazidi	40,620	1.26
Others	27,037	0.84
Total	3,213,011	100.00

* According to official declaration of nationality; figures refer to *de jure* population.

MARZER (PROVINCES)
(population estimates at 1 January 2013)

Marz (Province)	Area (sq km)	Population	Density (per sq km)	Capital
Yerevan City	227	1,066,264	4,697.2	Yerevan
Aragatsotn	2,753	133,070	48.3	Ashtarak
Ararat	2,096	261,335	124.7	Artashat
Armavir	1,242	267,101	215.1	Armavir
Gegharkunik	5,348	235,587	44.1	Gavar
Kotayk	2,089	255,353	122.2	Hrazdan
Lori	3,789	234,663	61.9	Vanadzor
Shirak	2,681	251,267	93.7	Gyumri
Syunik	4,506	141,645	31.4	Kapan
Tavush	2,704	128,342	47.5	Ijevan
Vayots Dzor	2,308	52,252	22.6	Yeghegnadzor
Total	29,743	3,026,879	101.8	—

PRINCIPAL TOWNS
(population estimates at 1 January 2013)

Yerevan (capital)	1,066,264	Etchmiadzin	46,710
Gyumri	121,342	Kapan	43,184
Vanadzor	85,673	Hrazdan	42,010

BIRTHS, MARRIAGES AND DEATHS

	Registered live births		Registered marriages		Registered deaths	
	Number	Rate (per 1,000)	Number	Rate (per 1,000)	Number	Rate (per 1,000)
2005	37,499	11.7	16,624	5.2	26,379	8.2
2006	37,639	11.7	16,887	5.2	27,202	8.5
2007	40,105	12.4	18,145	5.6	26,830	8.3
2008	41,185	12.7	18,465	5.7	27,412	8.5
2009	44,413	13.7	18,773	5.8	27,528	8.5
2010	44,825	13.8	17,984	5.5	27,921	8.6
2011	43,340	13.3	19,706	6.0	27,963	8.6
2012	42,480	14.0	19,063	6.3	27,599	9.1

Life expectancy (years at birth): 74.3 (males 71.1; females 77.8) in 2011 (Source: World Bank, World Development Indicators database).

ECONOMICALLY ACTIVE POPULATION
(annual averages, '000 persons)

	2010	2011	2012
Agriculture, hunting, forestry and fishing	457.4	457.4	437.2
Mining and quarrying	11.0	15.5	10.0
Manufacturing	68.0	79.3	93.7
Electricity, gas and water supply	41.7	34.0	34.7
Construction	85.8	67.4	69.1
Wholesale and retail trade; repair of motor vehicles, motorcycles and personal household goods	109.8	111.1	113.7
Hotels and restaurants	18.6	12.8	16.2
Transport, storage and communications	70.6	65.8	73.9
Financial intermediation	12.5	9.0	10.1
Real estate, renting and business activities	30.9	31.8	24.3
Public administration and defence; compulsory social security	75.2	77.1	78.0
Education	107.2	111.4	105.3
Health and social work	52.5	54.1	54.7
Other community, social and personal service activities	43.9	48.4	51.9
Total employed	1,185.2	1,175.1	1,172.8
Registered unemployed	278.2	265.7	245.5
Total labour force	1,463.3	1,440.9	1,418.3
Males	777.2	739.0	724.4
Females	686.1	701.8	693.8

Health and Welfare

KEY INDICATORS

Total fertility rate (children per woman, 2011)	1.7
Under-five mortality rate (per 1,000 live births, 2011)	18
HIV (% of persons aged 15–49, 2012)	0.2
Physicians (per 1,000 head, 2011)	2.8
Hospital beds (per 1,000 head, 2009)	3.7
Health expenditure (2010): US $ per head (PPP)	240
Health expenditure (2010): % of GDP	4.5
Health expenditure (2010): public (% of total)	40.5
Access to water (% of persons, 2011)	99
Access to sanitation (% of persons, 2011)	90
Total carbon dioxide emissions ('000 metric tons, 2010)	4,220.7
Carbon dioxide emissions per head (metric tons, 2010)	1.4
Human Development Index (2012): ranking	87
Human Development Index (2012): value	0.729

For sources and definitions, see explanatory note on p. vi.

Agriculture

PRINCIPAL CROPS
('000 metric tons)

	2010	2011	2012
Wheat	183.5	224.1	243.1
Barley	118.6	178.2	170.1
Maize	12.8	19.1	19.1
Potatoes	482.0	557.3	647.2
Cabbages and brassicas	114.3	128.5	131.8
Tomatoes	251.9	275.5	265.2
Cauliflowers and broccoli	9.9	10.1	12.4
Cucumbers and gherkins	63.3	73.7	74.5
Onions, dry	38.3	40.6	44.5
Garlic	8.8	10.6	12.3
Carrots and turnips	20.4	23.9	22.9
Watermelons	132.5	180.9	205.1
Apples	56.5	77.6	110.3
Pears	16.6	23.0	23.1
Apricots	7.7	4.9	7.6
Peaches and nectarines	23.8	43.8	63.5
Plums and sloes	4.0	12.4	18.7
Grapes	222.9	229.6	241.4

Aggregate production ('000 metric tons, may include official, semi-official or estimated data): Total cereals 322.0 in 2010, 435.5 in 2011, 451.0 in 2012; Total roots and tubers 482.0 in 2010, 557.3 in 2011, 647.2 in 2012; Total pulses 4.5 in 2010, 5.2 in 2011, 5.1 in 2012; Total vegetables (incl. melons) 840.1 in 2010, 968.0 in 2011, 1,054.1 in 2012; Total fruits (excl. melons) 351.4 in 2010, 420.8 in 2011, 504.7 in 2012.

Source: FAO.

LIVESTOCK
('000 head, year ending September)

	2010	2011	2012
Horses	11	10	10
Asses*	6	6	6
Mules*	0.3	0.3	0.3
Cattle	571	571	599
Pigs	113	115	108
Sheep	511	504	562
Goats	30	29	29
Chickens†	3,910	3,274	3,800
Turkeys†	225	189	223

* FAO estimates.
† Unofficial figures.

Source: FAO.

LIVESTOCK PRODUCTS
('000 metric tons)

	2010	2011	2012
Cattle meat	48	48	48
Sheep meat*	8	8	9
Pig meat	8	9	10
Chicken meat	5	6	7
Cows' milk	557	558	575
Sheep's milk	41	41	40
Hen eggs†	38	35	36
Wool: greasy	1	1	1

* FAO estimates.
† Unofficial figures.

Source: FAO.

Forestry

ROUNDWOOD REMOVALS
('000 cu m, excluding bark)

	2009	2010	2011
Sawlogs, veneer logs and logs for sleepers	2	1	1
Fuel wood*	1,500	1,750	2,074
Total*	1,502	1,751	2,075

* FAO estimates.

2012: Annual production assumed to be unchanged from 2011 (FAO estimates).

Source: FAO.

SAWNWOOD PRODUCTION
('000 cu m, incl. railway sleepers)

	2007	2008	2009
Total (all broadleaved)	0.9	0.2	1.0

2010–12: Production assumed to be unchanged from 2009 (FAO estimate).

Source: FAO.

Fishing

(metric tons, live weight)

	2009*	2010*	2011
Capture	619	617	795
Common carp	58	58	75
Crucian carp	85	85	110
Other freshwater fishes	71	70	90
Trouts	80	80	105
Whitefishes	44	44	55
Danube crayfish	266	266	340
Aquaculture	5,240	5,000	6,300*
Common carp	620	560	650*
Crucian carp	120	120	120*
Silver carp	600	550	600*
Trouts	3,400	3,100	4,000*
Total catch	5,859	5,617	7,095*

* FAO estimate(s).

Source: FAO.

Mining

	2009	2010	2011
Copper concentrates (metric tons)*	23,233	31,062	33,597
Molybdenum concentrates (metric tons)*	4,365	4,335	4,817
Silver (kg)	52,876	68,428	73,000†
Gold ores (kg)*	944	974	1,266
Salt ('000 metric tons)	29	29	36

* Figures refer to the metal content of ores and concentrates.
† Estimate.

Source: US Geological Survey.

Industry

SELECTED PRODUCTS
('000 metric tons unless otherwise indicated)

	2010	2011	2012
Wheat flour	156	164	235
Wine ('000 hl)	58	62	57
Beer ('000 hl)	154	147	137
Soft drinks ('000 hl)	383	412	567
Cigarettes (million)	4,127	3,361	6,155
Cotton fabrics ('000 sq m)	14	5	26
Carpets ('000 sq m)	14	17	10
Cement	488	422	438
Electric energy (million kWh)	6,491	7,433	8,036

Woollen fabrics ('000 sq metres): 2 in 2006.

Finance

CURRENCY AND EXCHANGE RATES

Monetary Units
100 louma = 1 dram.

Sterling, Dollar and Euro Equivalents (31 December 2013)
£1 sterling = 668.008 drams;
US $1 = 405.640 drams;
€1 = 559.418 drams;
1,000 drams = £1.50 = $2.47 = €1.79.

Average Exchange Rate (drams per US $)
2011 372.501
2012 401.764
2013 409.626

STATE BUDGET
(million drams)

Revenue	2010	2011	2012
Tax revenue	574,066.8	631,595.4	725,496.9
Value-added tax	301,730.5	328,482.8	369,661.6
Enterprise profits tax	98,912.9	125,466.2	156,944.4
Income tax	73,939.8	81,210.6	91,667.3
Excises	48,140.5	39,404.5	49,323.8
Customs duties	29,366.7	36,289.4	43,040.1
Fixed payments	21,976.4	20,741.8	14,859.7
Financial duties	20,034.6	22,367.0	23,826.0
Compulsory social security contributions	105,335.9	123,449.6	129,058.6
Transfers	6,056.2	27,122.5	12,250.0
Other revenue	50,339.6	43,562.7	48,756.7
Total	755,833.0	848,097.1	939,388.1

Expense by economic type	2010	2011	2012
Current expenditure	750,570.5	800,377.5	865,405.5
Wages	73,141.9	78,898.2	80,891.2
Compulsory social security payments	5,281.2	5,934.9	5,546.5
Purchase of goods and services	160,018.8	171,481.6	204,784.9
Interest	30,190.0	35,231.3	40,208.0
Grants	17,854.5	19,751.0	21,092.9
Current transfers	94,481.4	99,406.4	112,030.0
Social benefits and pensions	244,039.7	256,445.4	288,995.9
Other current expenditure	125,562.9	133,228.7	111,856.1
Capital expenditure	106,248.0	114,388.3	86,327.3
Additional expenditure	72,173.2	42,679.8	49,316.9
Total	928,991.7	957,445.6	1,001,049.7

Outlays by function of government	2010	2011	2012
General public services	141,795.7	152,062.2	157,661.0
Defence	147,585.5	145,557.9	152,864.9
Public order, security and justice	65,172.5	70,293.7	75,646.8
Economic affairs	38,886.6	34,929.4	39,729.7
Environmental protection	2,388.7	4,436.8	3,802.4
Housing and community services	31,180.1	31,768.7	6,151.3
Health	52,694.6	61,182.2	61,899.2
Recreation, culture and religion	16,030.4	17,603.4	19,382.9
Education	95,262.8	104,028.5	100,903.5
Social protection	244,063.5	256,093.4	291,761.6
Other expenditures (incl. reserve funds)	21,758.2	36,809.6	41,929.6
Total	856,818.5	914,765.8	951,732.8

INTERNATIONAL RESERVES
(US $ million at 31 December)

	2010	2011	2012
IMF special drawing rights	33.48	57.03	31.72
Foreign exchange	1,832.34	1,875.44	1,767.65
Total	1,865.82	1,932.47	1,799.37

Source: IMF, *International Financial Statistics*.

MONEY SUPPLY
(million drams at 31 December)

	2010	2011	2012
Currency outside depository corporations	304,543	349,407	384,065
Transferable deposits	246,884	287,294	310,242
Other deposits	359,776	490,277	652,057
Broad money	911,203	1,126,978	1,346,365

Source: IMF, *International Financial Statistics*.

COST OF LIVING
(Consumer Price Index; base: 2000 = 100)

	2010	2011	2012
Food (incl. non-alcoholic beverages)	169.7	189.1	192.8
All items (incl. others)	154.2	165.2	169.5

Source: ILO.

NATIONAL ACCOUNTS
('000 million drams at current prices)

Expenditure on the Gross Domestic Product

	2010	2011	2012
Government final consumption expenditure	452.3	488.4	517.9
Private final consumption expenditure	2,837.3	3,161.0	3,536.1
Increase in stocks	−19.4	44.8	3.9
Gross fixed capital formation	1,156.7	985.9	946.4
Total domestic expenditure	4,426.9	4,680.0	5,004.4
Exports of goods and services	720.8	897.5	983.2
Less Imports of goods and services	1,568.1	1,789.0	1,974.2
Statistical discrepancy*	−119.4	−10.6	−15.7
GDP in market prices	3,460.2	3,777.9	3,997.6

* Referring to the difference between the sum of the expenditure components and official estimates of GDP, compiled from the production approach.

Gross Domestic Product by Economic Activity

	2010	2011	2012
Agriculture, hunting, forestry and fishing	588.2	767.9	764.0
Construction	599.5	491.1	489.0
Manufacturing	335.1	399.3	396.8
Mining and quarrying	89.3	102.8	116.9
Electricity, gas and water supply	113.4	145.7	173.7
Wholesale and retail trade; repair of motor vehicles, motorcycles and personal and household goods	444.7	476.7	517.0
Hotels and restaurants	24.5	27.0	37.6
Transport, storage and communications	249.7	252.7	269.3
Financial intermediation	126.3	151.9	181.1
Real estate, renting and business activities	153.9	183.6	199.6
Public administration and defence	127.9	141.8	150.7
Education	120.2	120.7	119.8
Health and social work	111.2	138.7	151.3
Other community, social and personal service activities	51.5	61.8	81.9
Sub-total	3,135.3	3,461.8	3,648.8
Less Financial intermediation services indirectly measured	64.2	96.2	109.3
Gross value added in basic prices	3,071.1	3,365.6	3,539.5
Taxes, *less* subsidies on products	389.1	412.3	458.1
GDP in market prices	3,460.2	3,777.9	3,997.6

Note: Totals may not be equal to the sum of components, owing to rounding.

BALANCE OF PAYMENTS
(US $ million)

	2010	2011	2012
Exports of goods	1,173.9	1,455.9	1,537.8
Imports of goods	–3,207.7	–3,561.3	–3,648.9
Balance on goods	–2,033.8	–2,105.4	–2,111.1
Exports of services	762.8	920.9	886.9
Imports of services	–1,003.8	–1,229.7	–1,235.4
Balance on goods and services	–2,274.8	–2,414.2	–2,459.7
Primary income received	959.8	1,261.8	1,323.9
Primary income paid	–621.1	–706.3	–695.4
Balance on goods, services and primary income	–1,936.1	–1,858.6	–1,831.2
Secondary income received	783.7	969.1	983.2
Secondary income paid	–220.8	–246.9	–260.0
Current balance	–1,373.2	–1,136.4	–1,107.9
Capital account (net)	107.9	94.4	108.0
Direct investment assets	–8.3	–216.0	–15.8
Direct investment liabilities	570.1	663.5	489.4
Portfolio investment assets	–1.5	0.4	–1.1
Portfolio investment liabilities	12.2	–10.8	2.0
Other investment assets	–245.6	–88.1	–62.6
Other investment liabilities	647.2	734.7	436.2
Net errors and omissions	17.6	0.4	156.2
Reserves and related items	–273.5	42.1	4.3

Source: IMF, *International Financial Statistics*.

External Trade

PRINCIPAL COMMODITIES
(distribution by SITC, US $ million)

Imports c.i.f.	2010	2011	2012
Food and live animals	486.1	595.3	618.0
Cereals and cereal preparations	126.6	142.4	176.0
Meat and meat preparation	74.0	94.7	91.6
Vegetables and fruits	70.9	87.3	70.9
Sugar, honey and sugar preparations	43.1	66.1	62.7
Coffee, tea, spices and manufactures thereof	72.6	82.0	80.5
Beverages and tobacco	131.6	120.5	126.0
Tobacco and tobacco manufactures	80.2	74.8	74.4
Mineral fuels, etc.	648.7	806.1	902.4
Petroleum and petroleum products	316.2	384.5	378.0
Gas, natural and manufactured	320.1	411.7	520.4
Chemicals and related products	352.9	395.5	413.1
Medical and pharmaceutical products	92.2	110.3	110.9
Essential oils, perfume materials, polishing and cleaning preparations	82.1	87.2	87.3
Manufactured goods classified chiefly by material	726.1	773.4	727.3
Non-metallic mineral manufactures	173.1	211.5	177.3
Iron and steel	152.3	132.4	125.1
Non-ferrous metals	109.1	92.1	82.1
Machinery and transport equipment	832.5	774.8	776.7
Telecommunications, sound-recording and -reproducing equipment	111.1	112.7	95.9
Electrical machinery, apparatus and appliances and parts thereof	199.9	143.8	145.6
Road vehicles	134.1	150.1	165.4
Miscellaneous manufactured articles	291.8	315.1	321.4
Commodities and transactions not classified elsewhere	60.2	78.4	74.0
Gold (non-monetary, unwrought, in powder or semi-manufactured)	60.1	78.4	74.0
Total (incl. others)	3,749.0	4,145.3	4,261.2

Exports f.o.b.	2010	2011	2012
Food and live animals	39.3	59.9	86.4
Beverages and tobacco	117.0	163.0	226.8
Beverages	108.7	146.7	185.0
Crude materials (inedible) except fuels	265.0	315.2	311.4
Metalliferous ores and metal scrap	251.6	310.2	303.5
Mineral fuels, etc.	71.1	106.8	109.8
Manufactured goods classified chiefly by material	422.9	484.6	429.1
Non-metallic mineral manufactures	108.5	138.8	108.0
Iron and steel	120.2	122.3	107.0
Non-ferrous metals	187.4	217.1	206.2
Machinery and transport equipment	32.6	57.3	44.8
Miscellaneous manufactured articles	32.9	42.2	62.7
Commodities and transactions not classified elsewhere	28.6	67.4	77.6
Gold (non-monetary, unwrought, in powder or semi-manufactured)	28.6	67.4	77.6
Total (incl. others)	1,041.1	1,334.3	1,380.2

PRINCIPAL TRADING PARTNERS
(US $ million)

Imports c.i.f.	2010	2011	2012
Austria	56.6	47.7	39.8
Belgium	71.4	64.6	73.8
Brazil	51.8	83.3	93.1
Bulgaria	112.4	102.2	86.5
China, People's Republic	404.0	404.2	399.7
France (incl. Monaco)	76.7	82.5	67.5
Georgia	54.3	60.2	48.9
Germany	210.7	245.1	265.2
Greece	50.9	60.7	28.9
India	46.7	68.7	69.6
Iran	199.9	216.8	219.4
Israel	14.0	27.4	57.9
Italy	122.2	169.6	168.8
Japan	83.3	72.4	98.7
Korea, Republic	72.8	57.6	50.5
Romania	85.7	105.0	87.8
Russia	835.3	890.9	1,057.4
Spain	24.6	40.3	48.4
Switzerland-Liechtenstein	69.4	78.3	87.0
Turkey	210.4	240.2	213.5
Ukraine	229.9	232.4	215.6
United Arab Emirates	37.3	50.1	48.6
United Kingdom	37.8	47.0	39.8
USA	110.8	147.4	143.1
Total (incl. others)	3,749.0	4,145.3	4,261.2

Exports f.o.b.	2010	2011	2012
Belgium	72.5	70.5	127.2
Bulgaria	156.6	152.2	129.3
Canada	29.6	70.4	85.1
China, People's Republic	30.9	16.3	31.3
Georgia	49.0	61.9	70.9
Germany	132.6	158.0	104.4
Iran	84.8	106.3	108.5
Netherlands	98.6	117.2	79.7
Poland	30.3	35.5	0.6
Russia	160.5	222.3	279.1
Spain	15.2	82.5	30.1
Switzerland-Liechtenstein	16.9	33.7	71.4
Ukraine	12.1	11.1	14.5
USA	82.7	100.7	87.5
Total (incl. others)	1,041.1	1,334.3	1,380.2

Transport

RAILWAYS
(traffic)

	2010	2011	2012
Passenger journeys ('000)	844.4	586.5	551.4
Passenger-km (million)	50.1	49.5	53.0
Freight carried ('000 metric tons)	3,063.3	3,269.4	3,460.2
Freight ton-km (million)	743.2	815.9	867.3

CIVIL AVIATION
(traffic)

	2010	2011	2012
Passengers carried ('000)	1,664.4	1,674.5	1,763.4
Passengers-km (million)	1,278.6	951.2	725.5
Freight carried ('000 metric tons)	8.8	10.0	12.3
Cargo ton-km ('000)	9.7	9.2	11.2

Tourism

ARRIVALS BY NATIONALITY

	2009	2010	2011
Argentina	26,600	24,350	26,414
Brazil	10,500	10,490	11,203
Canada	30,200	30,350	32,807
CIS countries*	208,328	228,810	239,978
France	24,100	24,250	24,735
Germany	18,970	19,120	22,193
Iran	55,243	120,863	154,278
Japan	11,900	11,730	12,973
Lebanon	23,100	23,330	24,171
Syria	21,000	21,340	23,001
USA	63,100	65,760	68,916
Total (incl. others)	575,284	683,979	757,935

* Comprising Azerbaijan, Belarus, Georgia, Kazakhstan, Kyrgyzstan, Moldova, Russia, Tajikistan, Turkmenistan, Ukraine and Uzbekistan.

Total arrivals: 843,330 in 2012.

Tourism receipts (US $ million, excl. passenger transport): 408 in 2010; 446 in 2011; 451 in 2012 (provisional).

Source: mainly World Tourism Organization.

Communications Media

	2010	2011	2012
Telephones ('000 main lines in use)	592.3	577.5	584.2
Mobile cellular telephones ('000 subscribers)	3,865.4	3,210.8	3,322.8
Internet subscribers ('000)	96.6	163.7	n.a.
Broadband subscribers ('000)	85.2	154.5	206.4

Source: International Telecommunication Union.

Education

(2012/13 unless otherwise indicated, public institutions)

	Institutions	Teachers	Students
Pre-primary	683	7,585*	69,965
General	1,435	40,830	368,708
Gymnasia and lyceums	44†	313‡	10,400†
Specialized secondary schools	99	2,958	29,307
Higher schools (incl. universities)	65	8,356	90,145

* 1998/99.
† 2008/09.
‡ 2004/05.

Pupil-teacher ratio (primary education, UNESCO estimate): 19.3 in 2006/07 (Source: UNESCO Institute for Statistics).

Adult literacy rate (UNESCO estimates): 99.5% (males 99.5%; females 99.5%) in 2011 (Source: UNESCO Institute for Statistics).

Directory

The Government

HEAD OF STATE

President: SERZH SARGSYAN (elected 19 February 2008, inaugurated 9 April; re-elected 18 February 2013, inaugurated 9 April).

GOVERNMENT

(April 2014)

A coalition, principally comprising members of the Republican Party of Armenia (HHK) and the Law-Governed Country Party of Armenia (OYeK).

Prime Minister: HOVIK ABRAHAMYAN (HHK).

Deputy Prime Minister and Minister of Territorial Administration: ARMEN GEVORGYAN (acting) (Independent).

Minister of Agriculture: SERGO KARAPETYAN (OYeK).

Minister of Culture: HASMIK POGHOSYAN (Independent).

Minister of Defence: SEYRAN OHANYAN (Independent).

Minister of the Diaspora: HRANUSH HAKOBYAN (HHK).

Minister of the Economy: KAREN CHSHMARITYAN (HHK).

Minister of Education and Science: ARMEN ASHOTYAN (HHK).

Minister of Emergency Situations: ARMEN YERITSYAN (OYeK).

Minister of Energy and Natural Resources: ARMEN MOVSISYAN (acting) (HHK).

Minister of Environmental Protection: ARAM HARUTYUNYAN (acting) (HHK).

Minister of Finance: GAGIK KHACHATRYAN (Independent).

Minister of Foreign Affairs: EDVARD NALBANDYAN (Independent).

Minister of Health: ARMEN MURADYAN (Independent).

Minister of Justice: HRAYR TOVMASYAN (acting) (HHK).

Minister of Labour and Social Affairs: ARTEM ASATRYAN (HHK).

Minister of Sport and Youth Affairs: YURI VARDANYAN (acting) (Independent).

Minister of Transport and Communications: GAGIK BEGLARYAN (HHK).

Minister of Urban Development: NAREK TARGSYAN (Independent).

Government Chief of Staff: DAVIT HARUTYUNYAN (HHK).

MINISTRIES

Office of the President: 0077 Yerevan, Marshal Baghramyan poghota 26; tel. and fax (10) 58-87-12; e-mail press@president.am; internet www.president.am.

Office of the Prime Minister: 0010 Yerevan, Hanrapetutyun Hraparak, Govt Bldg 1; tel. (10) 51-57-03; fax (10) 15-10-35; e-mail hotline@gov.am; internet www.gov.am.

Ministry of Agriculture: 0010 Yerevan, Hanrapetutyun Hraparak, Govt Bldg 3; tel. and fax (10) 52-46-41; e-mail agro@minagro.am; internet www.minagro.am.

Ministry of Culture: 0010 Yerevan, Hanrapetutyun Hraparak, Govt Bldg 3; tel. (10) 52-93-49; fax (10) 52-39-22; e-mail admin@mincult.am; internet www.mincult.am.

Ministry of Defence: 0044 Yerevan, Bagrevand poghots 5; tel. (10) 29-46-99; fax (10) 29-45-31; e-mail modpress@mil.am; internet www.mil.am.

Ministry of the Diaspora: 0010 Yerevan, V. Sarkgsyan poghots 26/1; tel. and fax (10) 58-56-02; e-mail contact@mindiaspora.am; internet www.mindiaspora.am.

Ministry of the Economy: 0010 Yerevan, M. Mkrtchyan poghots 5; tel. (10) 59-72-05; fax (10) 52-65-77; e-mail secretariat@mineconomy.am; internet www.mineconomy.am.

Ministry of Education and Science: 0010 Yerevan, Hanrapetutyun Hraparak, Govt Bldg 3; tel. and fax (10) 52-73-43; e-mail info@edu.am; internet www.edu.am.

Ministry of Emergency Situations: 0054 Yerevan, Mikoyan poghots 109/8; tel. (10) 36-20-15; fax (10) 36-34-50; e-mail mes@ema.am; internet www.mes.am.

Ministry of Energy and Natural Resources: 0010 Yerevan, Hanrapetutyun Hraparak, Govt Bldg 2; tel. (10) 52-19-64; fax (10) 52-63-65; e-mail minenergy@minenergy.am; internet www.minenergy.am.

Ministry of Environmental Protection: 0079 Yerevan, Hanrapetutyun Hraparak, Govt Bldg 3; tel. (10) 51-91-82; fax (10) 54-08-57; e-mail min_ecology@mnp.am; internet www.mnp.am.

Ministry of Finance: 0010 Yerevan, M. Adamyan poghots 1; tel. (10) 59-53-59; fax (10) 52-42-82; e-mail secretariat@minfin.am; internet www.minfin.am.

Ministry of Foreign Affairs: 0010 Yerevan, Hanrapetutyun Hraparak, Govt Bldg 2; tel. (10) 62-00-00; fax (10) 62-00-62; e-mail info@mfa.am; internet www.mfa.am.

Ministry of Health: 0010 Yerevan, Hanrapetutyun Hraparak, Govt Bldg 3; tel. (10) 52-88-72; fax (10) 15-10-97; e-mail info@moh.am; internet www.moh.am.

Ministry of Justice: 0079 Yerevan, Halabyan poghots 41A; tel. (10) 35-83-99; fax (10) 38-03-89; e-mail info@moj.am; internet www.moj.am.

Ministry of Labour and Social Affairs: 0010 Yerevan, Hanrapetutyun Hraparak, Govt Bldg 3; tel. and fax (10) 52-08-30; e-mail hasmik.khachatryan@mss.am; internet www.mss.am.

Ministry of Sport and Youth Affairs: 0001 Yerevan, Abovyan poghots 9; tel. (10) 52-99-28; fax (10) 52-65-29; e-mail msy@msy.am; internet www.minsportyouth.am.

Ministry of Territorial Administration: 0010 Yerevan, Hanrapetutyun Hraparak, Govt Bldg 2; tel. (10) 51-13-02; fax (10) 51-13-32; e-mail mta@mta.gov.am; internet www.mta.gov.am.

Ministry of Transport and Communications: 0010 Yerevan, Nalbandyan poghots 28; tel. (10) 59-00-17; e-mail info@mtc.am; internet www.mtc.am.

Ministry of Urban Development: 0010 Yerevan, Hanrapetutyun Hraparak, Govt Bldg 3; tel. (10) 62-17-42; fax (10) 52-32-00; e-mail info@mud.am; internet www.mud.am.

President

Presidential Election, 18 February 2013

Candidates	Votes	% of votes
Serzh Sargsyan	861,155	58.64
Raffi Hovhannisyan	539,691	36.75
Hrant Bagratyan	31,643	2.15
Paruyr Hayrikyan	18,096	1.23
Others	18,055	1.23
Total	1,468,640	100.00

Legislature

National Assembly (Azgayin Zhoghov)

0095 Yerevan, Marshal Baghramyan poghota 19; tel. (10) 52-05-15; fax (10) 52-96-95; e-mail abrahamyan@parliament.am; internet www.parliament.am.

Chairman: GALUST SAHAKYAN.

General Election, 6 May 2012

		Seats		
Parties	%*	A†	B†	Total
Republican Party of Armenia	42.24	40	29	69
Prosperous Armenia Party	28.90	28	9	37
Armenian National Congress	6.80	7	—	7
Armenian Revolutionary Federation—Dashnaktsutiun	5.44	5	1	6
Law-Governed Country Party of Armenia	5.28	5	1	6
Heritage Party	5.53	5	—	5
Independent	—	—	1	1
Others	2.39	—	—	—
Total	100.00‡	90	41	131

* Percentage refers to the share of the vote cast for seats awarded on the basis of party lists.

† Of the 131 seats in the National Assembly, 90 (A) are awarded according to proportional representation on the basis of party lists and 41 (B) are elected in single-member districts.

‡ Including invalid votes (representing 3.42% of the total).

Election Commission

Central Electoral Commission (CEC): 0009 Yerevan, G. Kochar poghots 21A; tel. and fax (10) 54-35-23; e-mail cec@elections.am; internet www.elections.am; Chair. TIGRAN MUKUCHIAN.

Political Organizations

At February 2010 there were 74 registered political parties.

Armenian Democratic Party (HDK) (Hayastani Demokratakan Kusaktsutyun): 0009 Yerevan, Koryuni poghots 14; tel. and fax (10) 53-90-24; e-mail democracy@armenia.com; f. 1992 by elements of Communist Party of Armenia; Chair. ARAM SARGSYAN.

Armenian National Congress (HAK) (Hay Azgayin Kongres): 0010 Yerevan, Koryuni poghots 19 A; tel. (10) 52-09-74; e-mail info@anc.am; internet www.anc.am; f. 2008; coalition of movements opposed to regime of Pres. Sargsyan; Pres. LEVON TER-PETROSYAN.

Armenian Revolutionary Federation—Dashnaktsutiun (HYD) (Hay Yeghapokhakan—Dashnaktsutiun): 0010 Yerevan, M. Mkrtchyan poghots 30, POB 123; tel. (10) 52-18-90; fax (10) 52-14-53; e-mail intsec@arf.am; internet www.arfd.am; f. 1890; formed the ruling party in independent Armenia, 1918–20; prohibited under Soviet rule, but continued its activities in other countries; permitted to operate legally in Armenia from 1991; suspended in December 1994; legally reinstated 1998; Chair. HRANT MARKARYAN.

Freedom (Azatutyun Kusaktsutyun): Yerevan; f. 1996; Chair. HRANT BAGRANTYAN.

Heritage Party (Zharangutyun Kusaktsutyun): 0002 Yerevan, Moskovyan poghots 31; tel. (10) 53-69-13; fax (10) 53-26-97; e-mail office@heritage.am; internet www.heritage.am; f. 2002; liberal nationalist party; Chair. RAFFI HOVHANNISYAN.

Law-Governed Country Party of Armenia (OYeK) (Orinats Yerkir Kusaktsutyun): 0009 Yerevan, Abovyan poghots 43; tel. (10) 56-65-05; fax (10) 56-99-69; e-mail info@oek.am; internet www.oek.am; f. 1998; centrist; Head ARTUR BAGHDASARYAN.

Liberal Democratic Party (Armenia) (RAK—H) (Ramvakar Azatakan Kusaltsutyun—Hayastan): Yerevan; f. 2012 on basis of merger of Democratic Liberal Party of Armenia and Armenakan-Democratic Liberal Party; Chair. HAKOB AVETIKYAN.

Mighty Fatherland Party (Hzor Hayrenik Kusaktsutyun): 0010 Yerevan, Tigran Mets poghota 9; tel. (10) 52-92-15; fax (10) 52-25-45; e-mail hzor_hayrenik@xter.net; f. 1997; Chair. VARDAN VARDAPETYAN.

National Democratic Party (AZhK) (Azgayin Zhoghovrdavarakan Kusaktsutyun): 0015 Yerevan, Paronyan poghots 11/4; tel. and fax (10) 56-21-50; internet www.ajk.am; f. 2001 following the division of the National Democratic Union; Leader SHAVARSH KOCHARYAN.

National Democratic Union (Azgayin Zhoghovrdavarakan Miutyun): 0001 Yerevan, Abovyan poghots 12; tel. (10) 52-34-12; fax (10) 56-31-88; f. 1991; Chair. VAZGEN MANUKYAN; 2,600 mems (Jan. 2011).

National Unity Party (AMK) (Azgayin Miabanutyun Kusaktsutyan): 0002 Yerevan, Moskovyan poghots 33A; tel. (10) 53-36-32; fax (10) 53-03-31; e-mail amiab@yandex.ru; internet www.amiab.am; f. 1998; Chair. ARTASHES GEGHAMYAN.

New Times Party (NZhK) (Nor Zhamanakner Kusaktsutyun): 0001 Yerevan, Mamikonyants poghots 58; tel. (10) 56-83-17; fax (10) 56-83-39; e-mail nor_jamanakner@yahoo.com; f. 2003; Chair. ARAM KARAPETYAN.

People's Party of Armenia (HzhK) (Hayastani Zhoghovrdakan Kusaktsutyun): 0002 Yerevan, Parpetsi poghots; tel. (10) 53-15-01; fax (10) 53-77-01; f. 1998; Chair. STEPAN DEMIRCHYAN.

Prosperous Armenia Party (BHK) (Bargavach Hayastani Kusaktsutyun): 0015 Yerevan, Chovakal Isakovi poghota; tel. (10) 52-02-81; e-mail info@bhk.am; internet www.bhk.am; f. 2004; Pres. GAGIK TSARUKYAN.

Republic Party (Hanrapetutyun Kusaktsutyun): 0002 Yerevan, Mashtots poghota 37/30; tel. (10) 53-86-34; e-mail republic@arminco.com; f. 2001 by members of the Yerkrapah Union of Volunteers and fmr members of the Republican Party of Armenia; Chair. ARAM SARGSYA.

Republican Party of Armenia (HHK) (Hayastani Hanrapetakan Kusaktsutyun): 0010 Yerevan, M. Adamyan poghots 2; tel. (10) 58-00-31; fax (10) 50-12-59; e-mail hhk@hhk.am; internet www.hhk.am; f. 1990; national conservative party; Chair. SERZH SARGSYAN; 140,000 mems (2011).

Diplomatic Representation

EMBASSIES IN ARMENIA

Argentina: Yerevan, Aygestan poghots 12/6; tel. (10) 57-64-51; fax (10) 57-71-51; e-mail earme@mrecic.gov.ar; internet www.earme.mrecic.gov.ar; Ambassador DIEGO ERNESTO ÁLVAREZ RIVERA.

Belarus: 0028 Yerevan, N. Dumani poghots 12–14; tel. (10) 22-02-69; fax (10) 26-03-84; e-mail armenia@mfa.gov.by; internet www.armenia.mfa.gov.by; Ambassador STEPAN SUKHORENKO.

Brazil: 0010 Yerevan, S. Yerevantsi poghots 57; tel. (10) 50-02-10; fax (10) 50-02-11; e-mail embassy@brasil.am; internet www.brasil.am; Ambassador EDMON MARINU DUARTE MONTEIRU.

Bulgaria: Yerevan, Nor Aresh, Sofiayi poghots 16; tel. and fax (10) 45-82-33; e-mail embassy.yerevan@mfa.bg; internet www.mfa.bg/embassies/armenia; Ambassador GEORGI KARASTAMATOV.

China, People's Republic: 0019 Yerevan, Marshal Baghramyan poghota 12; tel. (10) 56-00-67; fax (10) 54-57-61; e-mail chinaemb-am@mfa.gov.cn; internet am.chineseembassy.org; Ambassador TIAN CHANGCHUN.

Egypt: 0028 Yerevan, Sepuhi poghots 6A; tel. (10) 22-01-17; fax (10) 22-64-25; e-mail egyemb@arminco.com; Ambassador MUHAMMAD ALA ELDIN SAAD EL LEIS.

France: 0015 Yerevan, G.Lusavorchi poghots 8; tel. (10) 59-19-50; fax (10) 59-19-70; e-mail cad.erevan-amba@diplomatie.gouv.fr; internet www.ambafrance-am.org; Ambassador HENRI REYNAUD.

Georgia: 0010 Yerevan, Babayan poghots 2/10; tel. and fax (10) 20-07-38; e-mail yerevan.emb@mfa.gov.ge; internet www.armenia.mfa.gov.ge; Ambassador TENGIZ SHARMANASHVILI.

Germany: 0025 Yerevan, Charentsi poghots 29; tel. (10) 52-32-79; fax (10) 52-47-81; e-mail info@eriw.diplo.de; internet www.eriwan.diplo.de; Ambassador RAINER MORELL.

Greece: 0002 Yerevan, Demirchyan poghots 6; tel. (10) 53-00-51; fax (10) 53-00-49; e-mail gremb.ere@mfa.gr; Ambassador IOANNIS TAGHIS.

India: 0019 Yerevan, Dzorapi poghots 50/2; tel. (10) 53-91-73; fax (10) 53-39-84; e-mail ambassador@embassyofindia.am; internet www.indianembassy.am; Ambassador T. SURESH BABU.

Iran: Yerevan, Budaghyan poghots 1; tel. (10) 28-04-57; fax (10) 23-00-52; e-mail info@iranembassy.am; internet www.iranembassy.am; Ambassador MOHAMMAD RAIESI.

Italy: 0010 Yerevan, Italiayi poghots 5; tel. (10) 54-23-35; fax (10) 54-23-41; e-mail ambitaly@arminco.com; internet www.ambjerevan.esteri.it; Ambassador GIOVANNI RICCIULLI.

Kazakhstan: 0019 Yerevan, Armenakyan poghots 153; tel. (10) 65-20-01; fax (10) 65-03-40; e-mail erevan@mfa.kz; internet www.kazembassy.am; Ambassador AIYMDOS YE. BOZZHIGITOV.

Kuwait: 0070 Yerevan, H. Kochar poghots 7/3; tel. (60) 50-80-50; fax (60) 50-06-22; e-mail kuwaitembassyyerevan@gmail.com; Ambassador BASSAM MUHAMMAD ALQABANDI.

Lebanon: 0010 Yerevan, Joragyugh poghots 13/14; tel. (10) 50-13-03; fax (10) 50-13-01; e-mail libanarm@gmail.com; Ambassador JEAN MAKARON.

Lithuania: 0037 Yerevan, Babayan poghots 2/13; tel. (10) 29-76-80; fax (10) 29-76-81; e-mail amb.am@urm.lt; internet am.mfa.lt; Ambassador ERIKAS PETRIKAS.

Poland: 0010 Yerevan, Hanrapetutiun poghots 44A; tel. (10) 54-24-91; fax (10) 54-24-98; e-mail erewan.amb.sekretariat@msz.gov.pl; internet www.erywan.msz.gov.pl; Ambassador ZDZISŁAW RACZYŃSKI.

Romania: Yerevan, Barbusse poghots 15; tel. (10) 27-53-32; fax (10) 22-75-47; e-mail ambrom@netsys.am; Ambassador SORIN VASILE.

Russia: 0015 Yerevan, G. Lusavorchi poghots 13A; tel. (10) 56-74-27; fax (10) 56-71-97; e-mail info@rusembassy.am; internet www.armenia.mid.ru; Ambassador IVAN VOLYNKIN.

Syria: 0019 Yerevan, Marshal Baghramyan poghota 14; tel. (10) 52-40-36; fax (10) 54-52-19; e-mail syrem_ar@intertel.am; Chargé d'affaires a.i. ESSAM NAYYAL.

Turkmenistan: 0033 Yerevan, Yerznkyan poghots 52; tel. (10) 22-10-29; fax (10) 22-66-56; e-mail tmembassy@netsys.am; internet www.turkmenistanembassy.am; Ambassador GURBANNAZAR NAZAROV.

Ukraine: 0037 Yerevan, Arabkir poghots 29/5/1; tel. (10) 22-97-27; fax (10) 27-12-14; e-mail emb_am@mfa.gov.ua; internet www.mfa.gov.ua/armenia; Ambassador IVAN P. KUKHTA.

United Kingdom: 0019 Yerevan, Marshal Baghramyan poghota 34; tel. (10) 26-43-01; fax (10) 26-43-18; e-mail enquiries.yerevan@fco.gov.uk; internet www.ukinarmenia.fco.gov.uk; Ambassador JONATHAN AVES, KATHERINE LEACH.

USA: 0082 Yerevan, Amerikan poghota 1; tel. (10) 46-47-00; fax (10) 46-47-42; e-mail usinfo@usa.am; internet yerevan.usembassy.gov; Ambassador JOHN A. HEFFERN.

Judicial System

A new judicial and legal system came into force in January 1999. Members of the Court of Cassation, the highest court of appeal, were appointed by the President, for life. A constitutional referendum, held in November 2005, provided for the President to cede the chairmanship of the Council of Justice to the Chairman of the Court of Cassation; the Azgayin Zhoghov (National Assembly) was henceforth to appoint the Prosecutor-General; and the Council of Justice was to nominate the chairmen of all courts (including the Court of Cassation) and to draw up a list of proposed judges for approval by the President.

Constitutional Court: 0019 Yerevan, Marshal Baghramyan poghota10; tel. (10) 58-81-30; fax (10) 52-99-91; e-mail armlaw@concourt.am; internet www.concourt.am; f. 1996; Chair. GAGIK HAROUTUNIAN.

Court of Cassation: 0010 Yerevan, V. Sargsyan poghots 5; tel. (10) 51-17-45; fax (10) 56-31-73; internet www.court.am; Chair. ARMAN MKRTUMYAN.

Office of the Prosecutor-General: 0010 Yerevan, V. Sargsyan poghots 5; tel. (10) 51-16-50; fax (10) 51-16-46; e-mail info@genpro.am; internet www.genproc.am; Prosecutor-General GEVORG KOSTANYAN.

Religion

The major religion is Christianity. The Armenian Apostolic Church is the leading denomination and was widely identified with the movement for national independence. There are also Russian Orthodox and Islamic communities, although the latter lost adherents as a result of the departure of large numbers of Muslim Azeris from the republic. Most Kurds are also adherents of Islam, although some are Yazidis. In 2006 10 religious organizations were registered in Armenia. (The Jehovah's Witness community was estimated to number 12,000, but failed to qualify for registration as its statutes were deemed to be in contravention of the Constitution.)

ADVISORY COUNCIL

Religious Council: Yerevan, c/o Department for National Minorities and Religious Affairs; tel. (10) 58-16-63; f. 2002 as consultative council to advise the Govt on religious affairs; was to comprise representatives of the Govt, the Office of the Prosecutor-General, the Armenian Apostolic Church, and the Catholic and Protestant Churches.

CHRISTIANITY

Armenian Apostolic Church: 1101 Etchmiadzin, Monastery of St Etchmiadzin; tel. (10) 51-71-10; fax (10) 51-73-01; e-mail divanatun@etchmiadzin.am; internet www.armenianchurch.org; eight dioceses in Armenia, 22 dioceses and bishoprics in the rest of the world; Supreme Patriarch KAREKIN II (Catholicos of All Armenians).

The Roman Catholic Church

Armenian Rite

Armenian Catholics in Eastern Europe are under the jurisdiction of an Ordinary. At 31 December 2007 there were an estimated 540,000 adherents within this jurisdiction.

Ordinary of Eastern Europe of Catholics of the Armenian Rite: Most Rev. RAPHAËL FRANÇOIS MINASSIAN (Titular Archbishop of Cesarea di Cappadocia of the Armenian Rite), Yerevan, Tbilisi poghots 1/3; e-mail ordiarm@mail.ru.

Latin Rite

The Apostolic Administrator of Latin Rite Catholics of the Caucasus is resident in Tbilisi, Georgia.

JUDAISM

In the early 2000s the Jewish community numbered around 1,000 and was located principally in Yerevan.

Mordechay Navi Jewish Religious Community of Armenia: 0018 Yerevan, Nar-Dosi poghots 23; tel. (10) 57-19-68; fax (10) 55-41-32; e-mail mordechay@netsys.am; internet www.yehudim.am; f. 1992; Chief Rabbi of Armenia GERSH MEIR BURSHTEIN; Chair. of the Jewish Community in Armenia RIMMA VARJAPETYAN.

The Press

PRINCIPAL NEWSPAPERS

In 2005 177 newspaper titles were published in Armenia. In 2011 there were 11 daily newspapers in the country. Those listed below are in Armenian except where otherwise stated.

168 zham (168 Hours): 0010 Yerevan, Pushkin poghots 3A, 2nd Floor; tel. (10) 58-48-31; fax (10) 52-29-58; e-mail info@168.am; internet www.168.am; f. 1994; 3 a week; opposition; news; also online edn in Armenian and English; Editor-in-Chief SATIK SEIRANIAN.

Aravot (The Morning): 0023 Yerevan, Arshakunyats poghota 2, 15 hark; tel. (10) 56-89-68; fax (10) 52-87-52; e-mail news@aravot.am; internet www.aravot.am; f. 1994; daily; Editor ARAM ABRAMIAN; circ. 5,000.

Azg (The Nation): 0010 Yerevan, Hanrapetutean poghots 47; tel. (10) 52-93-53; fax (10) 56-28-63; e-mail azg@azg.am; internet www.azg.am; f. 1991; daily; also daily online edition in Armenian, Russian, Turkish and English; Editor-in-Chief HAGOP AVETIKIAN; circ. 3,000 (2009).

Delovoi Ekspress (Business Express): 0005 Yerevan, Tigran Mets poghota 67A; tel. (10) 57-33-05; fax (10) 57-31-25; e-mail delovoy@express.am; internet www.express.am; f. 1992; weekly; economic; in Russian; Editor EDUARD NAGDALIAN.

Golos Armenii (The Voice of Armenia): 0023 Yerevan, Arshakunyats poghota 2, hark 7; tel. (10) 52-77-23; fax (10) 52-89-08; e-mail info@golosarmenii.am; internet www.golos.am; f. 1934 as *Kommunist*; current name adopted in 1991; 3 a week; in Russian; Chief Editor FLORA NAKHSHKARIAN.

Grakan Tert (Literary Paper): 0019 Yerevan, Marshal Baghramyan poghota 3; tel. (10) 52-05-94; e-mail gr_tert@free.am; f. 1932; weekly; organ of the Union of Writers; Editor SAMUEL KOSIAN.

Haiastani Hanrapetutiun (Republic of Armenia): 0023 Yerevan, Arshakunyats poghota 2; tel. (10) 52-69-74; fax (10) 54-86-11; e-mail hh@press.aic.net; internet www.hhpress.am; f. 1990; daily; Editor-in-Chief TIGRAN FARMANIAN; circ. 6,000.

Haikakan Zhamanak (Armenian Times): 0016 Yerevan, Israelyan poghots 37; tel. (10) 58-11-75; e-mail editor@armtimes.com; internet www.armtimes.com; f. 1999; daily; Editor-in-Chief NIKOL PASHINYAN; circ. 6,000.

Haiots Ashkhar (Armenian World): 0001 Yerevan, Tumanyan poghots 38; tel. (10) 53-88-65; fax (10) 53-32-21; e-mail hayashkh@arminco.com; internet www.armworld.am; f. 1997; daily; Editor GAGIK MKRTCHYAN; circ. 3,500.

Iravunk (Right): 0002 Yerevan, Koghbatsu 50, hark 2; tel. (10) 53-27-30; fax (10) 53-41-92; e-mail iskakan@mail.ru; internet www.iravunk.com; f. 1989; two a week; opposition newspaper; Editor HOVHANNES GALAJYAN; circ. 17,000.

Lusantsk: 0023 Yerevan, Arshakunyats poghota 2/13; tel. (10) 52-38-75; e-mail lusantsk@list.ru; f. 2007; weekly; Editor-in-Chief SUREN GEKAMYAN.

Novoye Vremya (New Times): 0023 Yerevan, Arshakunyats poghota 2, hark 3; tel. (10) 52-29-61; fax (10) 52-73-97; e-mail nv@nv.am; internet www.nv.am; f. 1992; 3 a week; in Russian; Editor RUBEN SATYAN; circ. 5,000 (2009).

Respublika Armenia (Republic of Armenia): 0023 Yerevan, Arshakunyats poghota 2, hark 9; tel. and fax (10) 54-57-00; e-mail ra@arminco.com; internet www.ra.am; f. 1990; state-owned; two a week; in Russian; Editor YELENA KURDIYAN; circ. 3,000.

Taregir: 0025 Yerevan, Tigran Mets poghota 49; tel. (10) 57-39-03; e-mail taregir@hotmail.com; internet www.taregir.am; f. 2007; two a week; politics and current affairs; in Armenian; Editor-in-Chief VASAK DARBINIAN.

Yeter: 0025 Yerevan, A. Manukyan poghots 5; tel. (10) 55-34-13; fax (10) 55-17-13; e-mail editor@eter.am; internet www.eter.am; weekly; independent; television and radio programme information; in Armenian with Russian supplement; Editor GOR KAZARYAN.

Zhamanak (The Times): 0010 Yerevan, Hanrapetutean poghots 76/3; tel. (10) 52-04-60; e-mail zhamanakyerevan@gmail.com; internet www.zhamanak.com; f. 2003; in Armenian; also online edn in English; daily; Editor-in-Chief ARMAN BABAZHANYAN.

Zhamanaki Mitk (Thoughts of The Times): Yerevan; tel. and fax (10) 35-73-54; weekly; Editor-in-Chief SIMON SARKISSIAN; circ. 3,000.

PRINCIPAL PERIODICALS

In 2005 some 120 periodicals were published.

Agrogitutiun/ Agronauka (Agricultural Science): 0010 Yerevan, Hanrapetutean Hraparak, Govt Bldg 3; tel. (10) 23-20-17; fax (10) 232441; e-mail agrpress@arminco.com; every two months; agriculture and forestry; in Armenian and Russian; publ. by Ministry of Agriculture; Editor ARMEN KHOJOYAN; circ. 500 (2009).

Armenia: Finance and Economy: 0023 Yerevan, Arshakunyats poghota 2A, 10th Floor; tel. (10) 54-48-97; e-mail armef@arminco.com; f. 1999; Editor-in-Chief MHER DAVOYAN.

Armenia Now: 0002 Yerevan, Parpetsi poghots 26/9; tel. (10) 53-24-22; e-mail info@armenianow.com; internet www.armenianow.com; f. 2002; online only; weekly; in Armenian, Russian and English; Editor-in-Chief JOHN HUGHES.

Aroghchapoutiun (Health): 0036 Yerevan, Halabyan poghots 46; tel. (10) 39-65-36; e-mail mharut@dmc.am; f. 1956; quarterly; theoretical, scientific-methodological, organizational and practical journal of the Ministry of Health; Editor M. A. MURADYAN; circ. 2,000–5,000.

Bazis (Basis): 1000 Yerevan; tel. (10) 50-10-48; e-mail basis@anfas.am; 10 a year; economics; in Russian; Chief Editor ASHOT ARAMYAN.

De Facto: 0010 Yerevan, Amiryan poghots 3/20; tel. (10) 56-43-64; fax (10) 54-77-80; e-mail spdefacto@yahoo.com; internet www.hayastan.com/defacto; politics and society; in Armenian; monthly; Editor-in-Chief MENUA HARUTYUNYAN.

EL Style (Elite Life Style): 0010 Yerevan, Vardants poghots 15/29; tel. (10) 54-88-91; e-mail editor@el.am; internet www.el.am; fashion, culture, travel; f. 2004; 10 a year; Editor MAYA POGHOSSYAN.

Garun (Spring): 0015 Yerevan, G. Lusavorchi poghots 15; tel. (10) 56-29-56; fax (10) 56-29-06; e-mail garinfo@freenet.am; f. 1967; monthly; independent; fiction, poetry and socio-political issues; Editor V. S. AYVAZYAN; circ. 1,500.

Gitutiun ev Tekhnika (Science and Technology): 0048 Yerevan, Komitas poghota 49/3; tel. (10) 23-37-27; e-mail giteknik@rambler.ru; f. 1963; monthly; journal of the Research Institute of Scientific-Technical Information and of Technological and Economic Research; Dir S. AGAJANIAN; Editor H. R. KHACHATRYAN; circ. 1,000.

Literaturnaya Armeniya (Literary Armenia): 0019 Yerevan, Marshal Baghramyan poghota 3; tel. (10) 56-35-57; fax (10) 56-36-66; f. 1958; quarterly; journal of the Union of Writers; fiction; in Russian; Editor ALBERT NALBANDYAN.

Sobesednik Armenii (Armenian Interlocutor): Yerevan, Moskovyan poghots 31; tel. (10) 53-65-09; fax (10) 53-65-89; e-mail info@sobesednik.am; internet www.sobesednik.am; f. 2007; weekly; in Russian; politics, society, the arts; Editor-in-Chief GENOFIA MARTIROSYAN.

TV-Mol/ TV-Man: 0037 Yerevan, Shosse Yegvardi 1; tel. (10) 36-83-31; e-mail best@tvmall.am; f. 2004; Armenian and Russian edns; weekly; Editor-in-Chief ARTASHES KHACHATRYAN; total circ. 45,000.

Yerkir (The Country): 0010 Yerevan, Hanrapetutean poghots 30; tel. (10) 52-15-01; fax (10) 52-04-26; e-mail news@yerkir.am; internet www.yerkir.am; f. 1991; weekly; organ of the ARF; also published in Lebanon; Editor-in-Chief SPARTAK SEYRANIAN; circ. 2,500.

NEWS AGENCIES

Arka News Agency: 0010 Yerevan, Pavstos Byuzand poghots 1/3; tel. (10) 52-21-52; fax (10) 52-40-80; e-mail arka@arminco.com; internet www.arka.am; f. 1996; economic, financial and political news; Russian and English; Dir KONSTANTIN PETROSSOV.

Armenia Today: Yerevan; tel. (91) 40-35-56; e-mail editor@armtoday.info; internet www.armtoday.info; f. 2007; Editor ARGISHTI KIVIRYAN.

Armenpress (Armenian News Agency): 0009 Yerevan, Isaahakyan poghots 28, 4th Floor; tel. (10) 52-67-02; fax (10) 52-67-82; e-mail info@armenpress.am; internet www.armenpress.am; f. 1918 as state information agency, transformed into state joint-stock company in 1997; Armenian, English and Russian; Dir HRAYR ZORYAN.

Arminfo: 0009 Yerevan, Isaahakyan poghots 28, hark 2; tel. (10) 54-31-74; fax (10) 54-31-72; e-mail news@arminfo.am; internet www.arminfo.info; f. 1991; Dir EMMANUIL MKRTCHYAN.

De Facto: 0023 Yerevan, Arshakunyats poghota 2A, hark 9; tel. (10) 54-57-99; fax (10) 54-53-89; e-mail info@defacto.am; internet www.defacto.am; f. 2000; Chair. KAREN ZAKHARYAN.

Noyan Tapan (Noah's Ark): 0009 Yerevan, Isaahakyan poghots 28, hark 3; tel. (60) 27-64-62; fax (60) 27-64-61; e-mail info@nt.am; internet www.nt.am; f. 1991; Dir TIGRAN HAROUTUNYAN.

Panarmenian.net: 0025 Yerevan, A. Manukyan poghots 5; tel. (10) 55-36-23; e-mail editorial@panarmenian.net; internet www.panarmenian.net; f. 2000; Dir ARMEN AZARYAN.

Panorama: 0018 Yerevan, Khorenatsi poghots 34B; tel. (10) 54-72-75; e-mail info@panorama.am; internet www.panorama.am; f. 2005; Exec. Dir TAMARA AVANESOVA.

Tert.am: 0023 Yerevan, Arshakunyats poghota 2; tel. (10) 52–17–75; e-mail editor@tert.am; internet www.tert.am; f. 2008; Dir NARINE HOVHANNISYAN.

Publishers

Academy of Sciences Publishing House: 0019 Yerevan, Marshal Baghramyan poghota 24G; tel. (10) 52-70-31; fax (10) 56-92-81; Dir KH. H. BARSEGHYAN.

Arevik Publishing House: 0009 Yerevan, Teryan poghots 91; tel. (10) 52-45-61; fax (10) 52-05-36; e-mail smbatg@mail.ru; f. 1986; political, scientific, fiction for children, textbooks; Pres. DAVID HOVHANNES; Dir ASTGHIK STEPANIAN.

Haikakan Hanragitaran Hratarakchutioun (Armenian Encyclopedia Publishing House): 1015 Yerevan, G. Lusavorchi poghots 15; tel. (10) 52-13-50; fax (10) 52-43-41; e-mail encyclop@sci.am; internet www.encyclopedia.am; f. 1967; encyclopedias and other reference books; Editor-in-Chief HOVHANNES M. AIVAZIAN.

Hayastan (Armenia Publishing House): 0009 Yerevan, Isaahakyan poghots 28; tel. (10) 52-85-20; fax (10) 52-57-62; f. 1921; science, social sciences, fiction and children's books; Dir VAHAGN SARGSYAN.

Louys Publishing Co: 0009 Yerevan, Isaahakyan poghots 28; tel. (10) 52-53-13; fax (10) 56-55-07; e-mail louys@arminco.com; f. 1955; textbooks; Dir HOVHANNES Z. HAROUTUNYAN.

Tigran Mets (Tigran the Great) Publishing House: 0023 Yerevan, Arshakunyats poghota 2; tel. (10) 52-17-75; e-mail info@tigran-mets.am; internet www.tigran-mets.am; fiction, poetry, science and children's books; Dir VREZH MARKOSYAN.

Yerevan State University Publishing House: 0025 Yerevan, A. Manukyan poghots 1; tel. (10) 55-52-40; fax (10) 55-46-41; e-mail pr-int@ysu.am; internet www.ysu.am; f. 1919; textbooks and reference books, history, literary criticism, science, and fiction; Dir PERCH STEPANYAN.

Zangak-97: 0051 Yerevan, Komitasi poghots 49/2; tel. (10) 23-25-28; fax (10) 23-25-95; e-mail info@zangak.am; internet www.zangak.am; f. 2000; scientific works, school teaching manuals, literature for children, translations of foreign authors; Pres. SOKRAT MKRTCHYAN.

PUBLISHERS' ASSOCIATION

National Union of Armenian Publishers: 0009 Yerevan, G. Lusavorchi poghots 15; tel. (10) 58-21-72; fax (10) 22-34-34; e-mail armnpa@netsys.am; f. 1999; Pres. VAHAN KHACHATRYAN.

Broadcasting and Communications

TELECOMMUNICATIONS

By 2011 Armenia's telecommunications sector was 100% privately owned. In 2012 there were 584,200 fixed telephone lines, while there were 3.9m. subscriptions to mobile telephone services in the country in 2013.

Armenia Telephone Co (ArmenTel): 0037 Yerevan, Azatutiun poghota 24; tel. (10) 54-91-00; fax (10) 28-98-88; e-mail pr@beeline.am; internet www.beeline.am; f. 1995; 100% owned by VimpelCom (Russia); fixed-line and mobile telecommunications operator; Dir-Gen. ANDREY PYATAKHIN.

Orange Armenia: 0015 Yerevan, G. Lusavorchi poghots 9; tel. (10) 51-35-51; fax (10) 56-06-19; e-mail contact-centre@orangearmenia.am; internet www.orangearmenia.am; f. 2009; mobile telecommunications and internet service provider; subsidiary of France Telecom; Dir FRANCIS GELIBTER.

VivaCell: 0015 Yerevan, Argisti poghots 4/1; tel. (10) 56-87-77; fax (10) 56-92-22; e-mail info@mts.am; internet www.vivacell.am; f. 2004; mobile telecommunications provider; operated by K Telecom CJSC; Man. Dir RALF YIRIKIAN.

BROADCASTING

In addition to the publicly owned national broadcast network, Armenian Public Radio, and the two public television stations, the country has 20 major private radio stations and 40 major private television stations.

National Commission for Television and Radio (NCTR) (HRAH): 0002 Yerevan, Isahakyan poghots 28; tel. (10) 52-83-70; fax (10) 52-83-71; e-mail nctr@tvradio.am; internet www.tvradio.am; Dir GRIGOR AMALYAN.

Radio

Armenian Public Radio: 0025 Yerevan, A. Manukyan poghots 5; tel. (10) 55-11-43; fax (10) 55-46-00; e-mail info@armradio.am; internet www.armradio.am; domestic broadcasts in Armenian, Russian and Kurdish; external broadcasts in Armenian, Russian, Kurdish, Azerbaijani, Arabic, English, French, German, Spanish and Farsi; Dir-Gen. ARMEN AMIRYAN.

Radio Hay: 0010 Yerevan, Pavstos Byuzandi 1/3; tel. (10) 56-00-00; fax (10) 52-98-68; internet www.radiohay.am; Dir ANDRIAS GHUKASYAN.

Television

Armenian Public Television—First Channel: 0047 Yerevan, G. Hovsepyan poghots 26; tel. (10) 65-00-15; fax (10) 65-05-23; e-mail support@armtv.com; internet www.1tv.am; f. 1956; state jt-stock co; Chair. of Council ALEKSAN HAROUTUNIAN; Exec. Dir MARGARITA GRIGORYAN.

Armenia TV: 0054 Yerevan, Yeghvardi poghota 1; tel. (10) 36-93-44; fax (10) 36-68-52; e-mail site@armeniatv.am; internet www.armeniatv.am; f. 1999; largest private television company in Armenia; transmits programming terrestrially, by cable and by satellite; Dir BAGRAT SARGSYAN.

H2 (Armenian Second TV Channel): 0088 Yerevan, Ajapnyak, Nazarbekyan Distr., G. 3, Bl. 3/1; tel. (10) 39-88-31; fax (10) 39-25-36; e-mail info@tv.am; internet www.tv.am; f. 2001; present name adopted 2005; Dir SAMVEL A. MAYRAPETYAN.

Hrazdan TV: 2301 Kotayk Marz, Hrazdan, hark 7; tel. (223) 20-292; e-mail hrazdantv@mail.ru; internet www.hrazdantv.am; f. 1990; privately owned; Exec. Dir MNATSAKAN HARUTYUNYAN.

Shant TV: 0028 Yerevan, Kievyan poghots 16, hark 10; tel. (10) 27-76-68; fax (10) 26-16-88; e-mail info@shanttv.am; internet www.shanttv.com; f. 1994; private, independent; Pres. ARTYOM YERKANYAN.

Finance

(cap. = capital; res = reserves; dep. = deposits; m. = million; brs = branches; amounts in drams)

BANKING

Central Bank

Central Bank of the Republic of Armenia: 0010 Yerevan, V. Sargsyan poghots 6; tel. (10) 58-38-41; fax (10) 52-38-52; e-mail mcba@cba.am; internet www.cba.am; f. 1993; state-owned; cap. 100.0m., res 95,641.7m., dep. 382,380.9m. (Dec. 2009); Chair. ARTHUR JAVADYAN.

Selected Banks

At the end of June 2010 there were 21 commercial banks, with total assets amounting to 1,329,200m. drams, in operation in Armenia.

ACBA-Credit Agricole Bank CJSC: 0009 Yerevan, Bayroni poghots 1; tel. (10) 56-58-58; fax (10) 54-34-85; e-mail acba@acba.am; internet www.acba.am; f. 1996 as Agricultural Co-operative Bank of Armenia; name changed as above Sept. 2006; cap. 30,000m., res 6,987m., dep. 69,588m. (Dec. 2012); Gen. Man. STEPAN GISHYAN; 36 brs.

Ameriabank: 0015 Yerevan, G. Lusavorchi poghots 9; tel. (10) 56-11-11; fax (10) 51-31-33; e-mail office@ameriabank.am; internet www.ameriabank.am; f. 2008; owned by Ameria Group Ltd, Limassol (Cyprus); cap. 25,447.6m., res 71.0m., dep. 134,726.0m. (Dec. 2012); Gen. Dir ARTAK HANESYAN; 5 brs.

Ardshininvestbank (ASHIB) (Bank for Industry, Construction and Investment): 0015 Yerevan, G. Lusavorchi poghots 13; tel. (10) 59-05-01; fax (10) 56-74-86; e-mail office@ashib.am; internet www.ashib.am; f. 2003 with acquisition of banking business of Ardshinbank and partially acquired the assets of Armagrobank; 97% owned by Business Investments Centre Ltd; cap. 13,802.4m., res 4,629.0m., dep. 114,441.0m. (Dec. 2012); Chair. of Man. Bd MHER GRIGORYAN; 38 brs.

Armbusinessbank (ABB): 0010 Yerevan, Nalbandyan poghots 48; tel. (10) 59-20-00; fax (10) 59-20-64; e-mail info@armbusinessbank.am; internet www.armbusinessbank.am; f. 1991; owned by Chrystie Management Inc; cap. 17,500.0m., res 507.3m., dep. 93,392.2m. (Dec. 2012); Chair. ARSEN MIKAYELYAN.

Armenian Economy Development Bank (Armeconombank) (AEB): 0002 Yerevan, Amiryan poghots 23/1; tel. (10) 56-33-32; fax (10) 53-89-04; e-mail bank@aeb.am; internet www.aeb.am; f. 1988; jt-stock co; corporate banking; cap. 2,333.3m., res 5,585.0m., dep. 37,921.1m. (Dec. 2012); 25% owned by the European Bank for Reconstruction and Development (United Kingdom); Chair. SARIBEK SUGIASYAN; CEO ARMEN NALZHYAN; 29 brs.

Artsakhbank: 0028 Yerevan, Kievyan poghots 3; tel. (10) 27-77-19; fax (10) 27-77-49; e-mail artsakhbank@ktsurf.net; internet www.artsakhbank.am; f. 1996; cap. 6,561.2m., res 1,541.3m., dep. 50,119.3m. (Dec. 2012); Chair. of Bd of Dirs HRATCH KAPRIELYAN; Chair. of Bd KAMO NERSISYAN; 6 brs.

Converse Bank: 0010 Yerevan, V. Sargsyan poghots 26/1; tel. (10) 51-12-00; fax (10) 51-12-12; e-mail post@conversebank.am; internet www.conversebank.am; f. 1993; 95% owned by Advanced Global Investments (USA); cap. 1,233.1m., res 3,939.0m., dep. 87,237.4m. (Dec. 2012); Exec. Dir TIGRAN DAVTYAN; 18 brs (2012).

HSBC Bank Armenia: 0009 Yerevan, Teryan poghots 66; tel. (10) 51-50-00; fax (10) 51-50-01; e-mail hsbc.armenia@hsbc.com; internet www.hsbc.am; f. 1996; 70% owned by HSBC Europe BV (Netherlands), 30% by Wings Establishment (Liechtenstein); cap. 18,434.4m., res 338.0m., dep. 137,585.1m. (Dec. 2012); Pres. WATCHE MANOUKYAN; Chief Exec. THIES CLEMENZ; 4 brs.

InecoBank: 0001 Yerevan, Tumanyan poghots 17; tel. (10) 51-05-10; fax (10) 51-05-73; e-mail inecobank@inecobank.am; internet www.inecobank.am; f. 1996; cap. 6,926.5m., res 4,080.1m., dep. 34,074.0m. (Dec. 2012); Chair. ASHOT AVETISSYAN; CEO AVETIS BALOIAN; 9 brs.

Mellat Bank: 0010 Yerevan, Amiryan poghots 6, POB 24; tel. (10) 58-17-91; fax (10) 54-08-85; e-mail mellat@mellatbank.am; internet www.mellatbank.am; f. 1995; wholly owned by Bank Mellat (Iran); cap. 6,850.0m. (Dec. 2009); Chair. and Gen. Dir TOURAJ MEHRDAD.

VTB Bank (Armenia): 0010 Yerevan, Nalbandyan poghots 46; tel. (10) 58-04-51; fax (10) 56-55-78; e-mail info@vtb.ru; internet www.vtb.am; f. 1923 under the name Armsavingsbank; present name adopted 2006; owned by Bank VTB (Russia); cap. 13,775.7m., res 3,242.0m., dep. 157,502.3m. (Dec. 2012); Chair. YURII V. GUSEV; 81 brs.

Banking Union

Union of Banks of Armenia: 0009 Yerevan, Koryuni poghots 19A; tel. and fax (10) 52-77-31; e-mail uba@uba.am; internet www.uba.am; f. 1995; oversees banking activity; Chair. ASHOT OSIPIAN; Exec. Dir SEYRAN SARGSYAN.

COMMODITY AND STOCK EXCHANGES

NASDAQ OMX Armenia: 0010 Yerevan, M. Mkrtchyan poghots 5B, hark 3-4,; tel. (10) 54-33-21; fax (10) 54-33-24; e-mail info@nasdaqomx.am; internet www.nasdaqomx.am; f. 1997 as Armenian Securities Market Members Asscn; renamed as Armenian Stock Exchange in Nov. 2000, and as above in Jan. 2009; CEO KONSTANTIN SAROYAN.

Yerevan Adamand Commodity and Raw Materials Exchange: 0010 Yerevan, Agatangeghos poghots 6/1; tel. and fax (10) 56-52-28; fax (10) 56-31-07; e-mail info@yercomex.am; internet www.yercomex.am; f. 1990; Dir GRIGOR VARDIKYAN.

INSURANCE

In 2013 there were nine licensed insurance companies in Armenia.

AHA Royal Insurance: 0010 Yerevan, Nalbandyan poghots 17; tel. and fax (10) 52-80-62; e-mail aharoyal@insurer.am; internet www.insurer.am; f. 2004; insurance and reinsurance; Gen. Dir HRACHA I. KARAPETYAN.

Cascade Insurance (CIN): 0033 Yerevan, H. Kochari poghots 5/1; tel. (10) 22-21-11; fax (10) 27-82-21; e-mail info@cin.am; f. 2004; 35% owned by the European Bank for Reconstruction and Development; CEO GARNIK TONOYAN.

Garant-Limence Insurance: Yerevan, Shirvan poghots 17; tel. (10) 23-60-68; fax (10) 23-03-81; e-mail info@glinsurance.am; f. 2000; all types of insurance; Exec. Dir ARTAK MARTIROSYAN.

Ingo Armenia: 0010 Yerevan, Hanrapetutyan poghots 51; tel. (10) 59–21-21; fax (10) 54-75-06; e-mail info@ingoarmenia.am; internet www.ingoarmenia.am; f. 1997; Exec. Dir LEVON ALTUNYAN.

ISG Insurance: Yerevan, Belyakov poghots 5/4; tel. (10) 54-68-60; fax (10) 56-03-92; e-mail isg@isg.am; f. 2007; general insurance; Chair. NAVASARD KHACHATRYAN.

Nairi Insurance: 1101 Yerevan, V. Sargsyan poghots 10/110; tel. (10) 54-35-91; fax (10) 54-35-94; e-mail nairi@nairi-insurance.am; internet www.nairi-insurance.am; f. 1996; non-life insurance; Chair. VAHAN GABRIELYAN.

RESO Insurance: 0014 Yerevan, Komitasi poghots 62; internet (60) 27-57-57; e-mail info@reso.am; internet www.reso.am; f. 2008 as UniRESO; renamed as above in Oct. 2009; life and general insurance; Gen. Man. SAMVEL GRIGORYAN.

Rosgosstrakh Armenia: 0001 Yerevan, Hyusisayin poghota 1; tel. (10) 59-10-10; e-mail info@rgs-armenia.am; internet www.rgs.am; f. 2008; Dir GAGIK GRIGORYAN; 18 brs.

Sil Insurance Co: 0018 Yerevan, Tigran Mets poghota 39; tel. (10) 58-00-00; fax (10) 50-55-88; e-mail info@silinsurance.am; internet www.silinsurance.am; f. 2000; Exec. Dir HAYK BAGHRAMYAN.

State Insurance Armenia (Gosstrakh-Armenia): 0001 Yerevan, Hanrapetutyan poghots 76/3; tel. and fax (10) 56-06-89; f. 2001; Russian-Armenian joint venture; insurance and reinsurance; Man. Dir VAHAN H. AVETISSYAN.

Trade and Industry

GOVERNMENT AGENCY

Armenian Development Agency (ADA): 0010 Yerevan, M. Mkrtchyan St 5; tel. and fax (10) 57-01-70; e-mail info@ada.am; internet www.ada.am; f. 1998; foreign investment and export development; Gen. Dir Dr ROBERT HARUTYUNYAN.

CHAMBER OF COMMERCE

Chamber of Commerce and Industry of the Republic of Armenia: 0010 Yerevan, Khanjyan St 11; tel. (10) 56-01-84; fax (10) 58-78-71; e-mail armcci@arminco.com; internet www.armcci.am; f. 1959; Chair. MARTIN G. SARGSYAN.

EMPLOYERS' ORGANIZATION

Armenian Union of Manufacturers and Businessmen (Employers) of Armenia—UMB(E)A: 0018 Yerevan, Tigran Mets Ave 20/2, 2nd Floor; tel. and fax (10) 54-07-15; e-mail umba@arminco.com; internet www.umba.info.am; f. 1996; Chair. ARSEN KHAZARIAN.

TRADE ASSOCIATION

Union of Merchants of Armenia: 0037 Yerevan, Azatutioun Ave 1/1; tel. (10) 25-28-54; fax (10) 25-91-76; e-mail merchants@netsys.am; f. 1993; reorganized 1999; Pres. TSOLVARD GEVORGYAN.

UTILITIES

Public Services Regulatory Commission of Armenia (PSRC): 0002 Yerevan, Saryan St 22; tel. (10) 52-25-22; fax (10) 52-55-63; e-mail psrc@psrc.am; internet www.psrc.am; f. 1997; fmrly Energy Commission of Armenia; Chair. ROBERT NAZARYAN.

Electricity

Armenian Energy Power Operator: 0009 Yerevan, Abovyan St 27; tel. (10) 52-47-25; fax (10) 54-73-17; e-mail office@energyoperator.am; internet www.energyoperator.am; f. 2003; assumed part of the function of former state monopoly Armenergo; Dir-Gen. MNATSAKAN MNATSAKANYAN.

Electricity Networks of Armenia (ArmElNet—ENA): 0047 Yerevan, Armenakyan St 127; tel. (10) 59-12-27; fax (10) 65-16-64; e-mail office@ena.am; internet www.ena.am; f. 2002; owned by Inter RAO (Russia); national electricity distributor comprising the four former regional electricity networks; Gen. Dir YEVGENY BIBIN; 12 brs.

Gas

ArmRosGazProm—ARG: 0091 Yerevan, Tbilisi Shosse 43; tel. (10) 29-49-33; fax (10) 29-47-28; e-mail inbox@armrusgasprom.am; internet www.armrusgasprom.am; f. 1997; 100% owned by Gazprom (Russia) (q.v.); sole natural gas producer in Armenia; Exec. Dir VARDAN R. ARUTIUNYAN.

Water

Yerevan Djur—Veolia Armenia (YD): 0025 Yerevan, Abovyan St 66A; tel. (10) 56-13-26; fax (10) 56-93-57; e-mail office@yerevandjur.am; internet www.veoliadjur.am; f. 2005; contracted to provide water and sewerage services to Yerevan municipality for the period 2006–16; subsidiary of Veolia Environnement (France); Gen. Man. GOR GRIGORYAN; 1,450 employees (2011).

TRADE UNIONS

At 1 January 2006 some 743 trade union organizations were registered with the Ministry of Justice.

Confederation of Trade Unions of Armenia: 0010 Yerevan, V. Sargsyan St 26/3; tel. (10) 54-52-37; fax (10) 58-34-66; e-mail hamk@xar.am; internet www.hamk.am; Chair. EDWARD TUMASYAN; 24 mem. unions.

Transport

RAILWAYS

In 2012 there were 780 km of railway track in Armenia, of which 98% was electrified, and 71 railway stations. There are international lines to Iran and Georgia, although passenger services are very limited.

South Caucasus Railway (SCR): 0005 Yerevan, Tigran Mets poghota 50; tel. (10) 57-50-02; fax (10) 57-36-30; e-mail ukzhdpressoffice@inbox.ru; internet www.ukzhd.am; f. 1998; managed by Russian Railways (q.v.); Dir-Gen. VIKTOR REBETS.

Yerevan Metro: 0033 Yerevan, Marshal Baghramyan poghota 78; tel. and fax (10) 27-30-81; e-mail mmetro.arm@gmail.com; f. 1981; govt-owned; 12.1 km, with 10 stations (2005); Dir PAILAK YAILOYAN.

ROADS

In 2008 the total length of the road network was estimated at 7,704 km, of which 90.5% was paved.

CIVIL AVIATION

Zvartnots International Airport, 15 km west of Yerevan, is the main national airport; there are also international airports in Gyumri and Yerebuni.

Civil Aviation Department: 0042 Yerevan, Zvartnots Airport; tel. (10) 59-30-03; fax (10) 28-53-45; e-mail artiom.movsesyan@aviation.am; internet www.aviation.am; f. 1933; Dir-Gen. ARTYOM MOVSESYAN.

Air Armenia: 0009 Yerevan, G. Kochar poghots 21; tel. (10) 54-79-99; fax (10) 58-35-08; e-mail info@airarmenia.net; internet www.air.am; f. 2003 as cargo airline; scheduled passenger flights between Yerevan and destinations in Russia, commenced 2013, flights to France and Greece expected to commence in 2014; Chair. ARSEN AVETISYAN.

Tourism

According to the World Tourism Organization, tourism receipts (excluding passenger transport) amounted to a provisional US $451m. in 2012. In that year Armenia received 843,330 tourist arrivals, compared with 382,136 in 2006.

Armenian Tourism Development Agency (ATDA): 0010 Yerevan, Nalbandyan poghots 3; tel. (10) 54-23-03; fax (10) 54-47-92; e-mail info@armeniainfo.am; internet www.armeniainfo.am; f. 2001; Dir NINA HOVNANYAN.

Defence

Following the dissolution of the USSR in December 1991, Armenia became a member of the Commonwealth of Independent States and its collective security system, which was formally transformed into a regional defence organization, the Collective Security Treaty Organization (CSTO), in April 2003. The country also began to establish its own armed forces. The armed forces numbered 44,800, as assessed at November 2013, comprising an army of 41,850 (including 18,950 conscripts), joint air and air defence aviation forces of 1,100 and other air defence forces of 1,850. There was also a paramilitary force of 4,300. Military service is compulsory and lasts for two years (a law adopted in 2002 provided for a 42-month alternative civilian service). There were an estimated 3,303 Russian troops on Armenian territory at November 2013. In 1994 Armenia joined the North Atlantic Treaty Organization's 'Partnership for Peace' programme of military co-operation. In December 2005 Armenia's 'individual partnership action plan' with that body was approved, envisaging large-scale military reforms.

Defence Expenditure: Budgeted at 188,000m. drams in 2013.

Chief of General Staff of the Armed Forces: Col-Gen. YURI G. KHACHATUROV.

Education

Education is free and compulsory at primary and secondary levels. Until the early 1990s the general education system conformed to that of the centralized Soviet system. Extensive changes were subsequently made, with greater emphasis placed on Armenian history and culture. Armenia adopted an 11-year system of schooling in 2001/02. In 2006 it was announced that this would be extended to 12 years. In 2012 total enrolment at pre-school establishments was equivalent to 51% of those in the relevant age-group. Secondary enrolment in 2012 included 83% of children in the relevant age-group. Most instruction is in Armenian, although Russian is widely learnt as a second language. In 2007/08 some 98.6% of students in general education schools were taught in Armenian, while for 1.2% Russian was the main language of instruction. In 2012/13 90,145 students were enrolled at 65 higher schools (including universities). State expenditure on education was 100,903.5m. drams in 2012 (10.6% of total state expenditure).

AUSTRALIA

Introductory Survey

LOCATION, CLIMATE, LANGUAGE, RELIGION, FLAG, CAPITAL

The Commonwealth of Australia occupies the whole of the island continent of Australia, lying between the Indian and Pacific Oceans, and its offshore islands, principally Tasmania to the south-east. Australia's nearest neighbours are Timor-Leste (formerly East Timor) and Papua New Guinea, to the north. In the summer (November–February) there are tropical monsoons in the northern part of the continent (except for the Queensland coast), but the winters (July–August) are dry. Both the north-west and north-east coasts are liable to experience tropical cyclones between December and April. In the southern half of the country, winter is the wet season; rainfall decreases rapidly inland. Very high temperatures, sometimes exceeding 50°C (122°F), are experienced during the summer months over the arid interior and for some distance to the south, as well as during the pre-monsoon months in the north. The official language is English; 170 indigenous languages are spoken by Aboriginal and Torres Strait Islander peoples, who comprised 2.5% of the population at the census of August 2011. The majority of the population profess Christianity (of whom 25.3% were Roman Catholics and 17.1% Anglicans at the 2011 census). The national flag (proportions 1 by 2) is blue, with a representation of the United Kingdom flag in the upper hoist, a large seven-pointed white star in the lower hoist and five smaller white stars, in the form of the Southern Cross constellation, in the fly. The capital, Canberra, lies in one of two enclaves of federal territory known as the Australian Capital Territory (ACT).

CONTEMPORARY POLITICAL HISTORY

Historical Context

The Commonwealth of Australia was established in 1901, having been colonized by European settlers, who originally included many convicts transported from the United Kingdom. The abolition of the 'White Australia' policy after 1945 resulted in the arrival of large numbers of non-European immigrants. After the signing of a security treaty in 1951 and the establishment of ANZUS (see p. 463), Australia co-operated more closely with the USA. Australia subsequently began to acknowledge the strategic importance of the Asia-Pacific region, strengthening its relations with Indonesia, Japan and the People's Republic of China.

Domestic Political Affairs

At the election of December 1949 the ruling Australian Labor Party (ALP) was defeated by the recently established Liberal Party, in coalition with the Country Party. In January 1966 Sir Robert Menzies resigned after 16 years as Prime Minister, and was succeeded by Harold Holt, who was returned to office at elections in December of that year. However, Holt died in December 1967. His successor, Senator John Gorton, took office in January 1968 but resigned, after losing a parliamentary vote of confidence, in March 1971. William McMahon was Prime Minister from March 1971 until December 1972, when, after 23 years in office, the Liberal-Country Party coalition was defeated at a general election. The ALP, led by Gough Whitlam, won 67 of the 125 seats in the House of Representatives. Following conflict between the Whitlam Government and the Senate, both Houses of Parliament were dissolved in April 1974, and a general election was held in May. The ALP was returned to power, although with a reduced majority in the House of Representatives. However, the Government failed to secure a majority in the Senate, and in October 1975 the Opposition in the Senate obstructed approval of budget proposals. The Government was not willing to consent to a general election over the issue, but in November the Governor-General, Sir John Kerr, intervened and took the unprecedented action of dismissing the Government. An interim administration was installed under Malcolm Fraser, the Liberal leader, who formed a coalition Government with the Country Party. This coalition secured large majorities in both Houses of Parliament at a general election in December 1975, but the majorities were progressively reduced at elections in December 1977 and October 1980.

Fraser's coalition Government was defeated by the ALP at a general election in March 1983. Bob Hawke, the Labor leader, became the new Prime Minister and immediately organized a meeting of representatives of government, employers and trade unions to reach agreement on a prices and incomes policy (the 'Accord') that would allow economic recovery. At an early general election held in December 1984, the ALP was returned to power with a reduced majority in the House of Representatives. The opposition coalition between the Liberal Party and the National Party (formerly the Country Party) disintegrated in April 1987, when 12 National Party Members of Parliament (MPs) withdrew from the agreement and formed the New National Party (led by the right-wing Sir Johannes Bjelke-Petersen, the Premier of Queensland); the remaining 14 National Party MPs continued to support their leader, Ian Sinclair, who wished to remain within the alliance. At an early general election held in July, the ALP was returned to office with an increased majority, securing 86 of the 148 seats in the House of Representatives. The Liberal and National Parties renewed their opposition alliance in August. Four months later Bjelke-Petersen was forced to resign as Premier of Queensland, under pressure from National Party officials.

During 1988 the Hawke Government suffered several defeats at by-elections, seemingly as a result of its unpopular policy of wage restraint. The ALP narrowly retained power at state elections in Victoria, but was defeated in New South Wales, where it had held power for 12 years. In May 1989 the leader of the Liberal Party, John Howard, was replaced by Andrew Peacock, and Charles Blunt succeeded Ian Sinclair as leader of the National Party. In July a commission of inquiry into alleged corruption in Queensland published its findings. The report documented several instances of official corruption and electoral malpractice by the Queensland Government, particularly during the administration of Bjelke-Petersen. In December the ALP defeated the National Party in the state election. By the end of 1991 four former members of the Queensland Cabinet and the former chief of the state's police force had received custodial sentences for corruption. The trial of Bjelke-Petersen, initially on charges of perjury and corruption but subsequently of perjury alone, resulted in dismissal of the case, when the jury failed to reach a verdict. Meanwhile, the Government's position was further strengthened by the removal of an unpopular Labor leadership in Western Australia and its replacement by the country's first female state Premier, Dr Carmen Lawrence, who took office in February 1990.

Parliamentary elections were held in March 1990. Although the opposition parties won the majority of the first-preference votes in the election for the House of Representatives, the endorsement of environmental groups delivered a block of second-preference votes to the ALP, which was thus returned to power, albeit with a reduced majority, securing 78 of the 148 seats. Peacock immediately resigned as leader of the Liberal Party and was replaced by Dr John Hewson, a former professor of economics. Blunt lost his seat in the election and was succeeded as leader of the National Party by Timothy Fischer.

In September 1990 senior ALP members endorsed government proposals to initiate a controversial programme of privatization, effectively ending almost 100 years of the ALP's stance against private ownership. Plans for constitutional and structural reform envisaged the creation of national standards in regulations and services, and measures to alleviate the financial dependence of the states and territories on the Federal Government. Despite strong opposition from sections of the public services, the trade unions and the business community, in July 1991 the leaders of the federal and state Governments finally agreed to reforms to the country's systems of marketing, transport, trade and taxation.

In June 1991 Hawke narrowly defeated a challenge to his leadership from Paul Keating, the Deputy Prime Minister and Treasurer, who then resigned. In December 1991 Hawke dismissed John Kerin, Keating's replacement as Treasurer, following a series of political and economic crises. Hawke called another leadership election, but this time he was defeated by

Keating, who accordingly became Prime Minister. A major reorganization of the Cabinet was implemented.

Following the ALP's defeat in state elections in Tasmania, the party encountered further embarrassment in April 1992, when a by-election in Melbourne to fill the parliamentary seat vacated by Bob Hawke was won by a local football club coach, standing as an independent candidate. Meanwhile, Brian Burke, the former Labor Premier of Western Australia, was arrested, after it was alleged that, during his term of office, he had misused a parliamentary expense account. In October 1992 the conclusions of the inquiry into the ALP's alleged involvement in corrupt practices in Western Australia were released. The Royal Commission was highly critical of the improper transactions between successive governments of Western Australia and business entrepreneurs. In July 1994 Burke received a prison sentence of two years upon conviction on four charges of fraud; he was released in February 1995, but was sentenced to three years' imprisonment in February 1997 for theft from ALP funds. In February 1995, furthermore, Ray O'Connor, Premier of Western Australia between 1982 and 1983, received a short prison sentence, having been found guilty of the theft in 1984 of a donation to the Liberal Party.

In September 1992 John Bannon, the ALP Premier of South Australia, became the seventh state Premier since 1982 to leave office in disgrace. His resignation was due to a scandal relating to attempts to offset the heavy financial losses incurred by the State Bank of South Australia. At state elections in Queensland in mid-September, the ALP administration of Wayne Goss was returned to power. In the following month, however, the ruling ALP was defeated in state elections in Victoria. Furthermore, in November a new financial scandal emerged: the federal Treasurer was alleged to have suppressed information pertaining to the former ALP Government of Victoria, which, in a clandestine manner prior to the state elections, was believed to have exceeded its borrowing limits. At state elections in Western Australia in February 1993, the incumbent Labor Government was defeated. Dr Carmen Lawrence was replaced as Premier by Richard Court of the Liberal-National coalition.

At the general election held in March 1993 the ALP was unexpectedly returned to office for a fifth consecutive term, having secured 80 of the 147 seats in the House of Representatives. In early 1994 two ministers resigned in connection with separate financial scandals. In May Dr John Hewson was replaced as leader of the Liberal Party by Alexander Downer, a supporter of the monarchy. In January 1995, however, Downer resigned and was replaced by John Howard, also a monarchist.

At state elections in New South Wales in March 1995 the ALP defeated the ruling Liberal-National coalition. Robert (Bob) Carr was appointed Premier. However, at a federal by-election in Canberra the ALP suffered a serious reverse when, for the first time in 15 years, the seat was taken by the Liberal Party. In July, at state elections in Queensland, the ALP Government of Wayne Goss was narrowly returned to office, only to be ousted following a by-election defeat in February 1996. In June 1995, meanwhile, the Deputy Prime Minister, Brian Howe, announced his resignation from the Cabinet. He was replaced by the Minister for Finance, Kim Beazley.

The Howard administration, 1996–2007

At the general election held in March 1996 the Liberal-National coalition achieved a decisive victory, securing a total of 94 of the 148 seats in the House of Representatives. The ALP won only 49 seats. In the Senate the minor parties and independent members retained the balance of power. John Howard of the Liberal Party became Prime Minister, and immediately promised to give priority to the issues of industrial relations, the transfer to partial private ownership of the state telecommunications company, Telstra, and to expanding relations with Asia. The leader of the National Party, Tim Fischer, was appointed Deputy Prime Minister and Minister for Trade. Paul Keating was replaced as leader of the ALP by Kim Beazley.

Meanwhile, fears for Australia's tradition of racial tolerance continued to grow. In October 1996 Pauline Hanson, a former member of the Liberal Party and a newly elected independent member of the House of Representatives, aroused much controversy when, in a speech envisaging 'civil war', she reiterated her demands for the ending of immigration from Asia and for the elimination of special funding for Aboriginal people. In March 1997 Hanson established the One Nation party, which rapidly attracted support. In subsequent months, however, large protests against her policies took place. In August the Government issued a document on foreign policy, in which Hanson's views were strongly repudiated and in which Australia's commitment to racial equality was reiterated. In December the New One Nation Party was established by former supporters of Hanson who had become disillusioned with her autocratic style of leadership. In June 1998, at state elections in Queensland, One Nation won 23% of first-preference votes, thus securing 11 of the 89 seats in the legislature.

At the early federal election held in October 1998, the Liberal-National coalition was narrowly returned to office, winning a total of 80 of the 148 seats in the House of Representatives. The ALP increased its representation to 67 seats. Contrary to expectations, the One Nation party failed to win any representation in the lower house, the controversial Hanson losing her Queensland seat, and secured one seat in the Senate. In a referendum held on the same day, the electorate of the Northern Territory unexpectedly rejected a proposal for the territory's elevation to full statehood.

In February 1999 Hanson was re-elected leader of One Nation, despite a series of defections, including the departure from the party of several of the 11 One Nation members of the Queensland legislature. At state elections in New South Wales in March, at which the ALP was returned to power, One Nation won two seats in the 42-member upper chamber. In January 2000 police officers in Queensland and New South Wales seized hundreds of documents from party premises. In April the Queensland Electoral Commission ruled that the party had been fraudulently registered, owing to the falsification of significant sections of its 200-name membership list. As the sole signatory on the registration papers, Hanson found herself personally responsible for the repayment of $A0.5m. of public funding to the party. Hanson repaid the funds after a successful appeal for public donations, and she re-registered the One Nation party in January 2001 to contest the forthcoming Queensland state elections (see below). Following state elections in Victoria in September 1999, meanwhile, the Liberal-National Premier, Jeffrey Kennett, was replaced by Stephen Bracks of the ALP.

A marked increase in the number of asylum seekers attempting to enter Australia by sea prompted the introduction of new legislation empowering Australian police to board vessels in international waters. In 1999 almost 2,000 asylum seekers were intercepted by the authorities and transferred to detention centres in Australia, while many others were believed to have died at sea. The issue of alleged maltreatment of asylum seekers detained in Australia was highlighted by a series of protests at a privately managed detention centre in Woomera, South Australia. Moreover, in November the Government ordered an inquiry into allegations that children at the centre had been subjected to systematic sexual abuse. Campaigners claimed that the Government had suppressed evidence of abuse at Woomera and other detention centres.

Australia's handling of immigration issues provoked international condemnation in August 2001 when the Prime Minister refused to admit 433 refugees, stranded on a Norwegian cargo ship off Christmas Island, onto the Australian mainland. The Government swiftly enacted new legislation empowering the navy to prevent migrants coming ashore and excluding remote Australian island territories from the definition of official landfall. The situation was eventually resolved when New Zealand, Nauru and Papua New Guinea agreed to accommodate the asylum seekers while their applications for asylum were processed. In the interim, however, traffic in asylum seekers attempting to reach Australia's outlying territories (the majority via Indonesia) continued to increase. The Government proposed a 'Pacific solution', whereby neighbouring South Pacific nations could agree to host asylum seekers during their processing in exchange for substantial aid. Nauru signed an agreement to take up to 1,200 refugees at any one time.

A state election in Western Australia in February 2001 resulted in defeat for the governing Liberal-National coalition and the replacement of Premier Richard Court by the state's Labor leader, Geoffrey Gallop. Ongoing anxieties regarding illegal immigration were reflected in the unexpected success of One Nation, which secured almost 10% of the vote at the poll. At the state election in Queensland in the same month, the ALP Government, led by Peter Beattie, was decisively re-elected. One Nation garnered 9% of the total vote.

A federal election took place in November 2001. The Liberal-National coalition won 82 of the 150 seats in the House of Representatives, thereby narrowly securing a third consecutive term of office. Despite its successes at state and territorial elections in Western Australia and the Northern Territory earlier in the year, the ALP won 65 seats, two fewer than at the previous federal election. Many political commentators attributed the coalition's apparent recovery to Howard's stance on immigration. Kim Beazley resigned as leader of the ALP and was replaced by Simon Crean. One Nation won no seats in either the House of Representatives or the Senate. (In December Pauline Hanson resigned as leader of the party to concentrate on contesting charges of electoral fraud brought against her in July 2001.)

John Howard announced the composition of his third Government in late November 2001, appointing six new cabinet ministers. Changes included the incorporation of the Department of Reconciliation and Aboriginal and Torres Strait Islander Affairs into the new portfolio of Immigration and Multicultural and Indigenous Affairs. At a state election in South Australia in February 2002 the ruling Liberal-National coalition was defeated. Mike Rann of the ALP was appointed Premier.

In February 2002, after it emerged that government claims that refugees in a ship intercepted by the Australian navy had thrown their children into the sea were false, John Howard withstood a parliamentary motion of censure. In November the ruling ALP, led by Stephen Bracks, won a state election in Victoria. The Labor Government in New South Wales was re-elected in March 2003 for an unprecedented third term; Bob Carr was reappointed Premier. Meanwhile, in February the Senate approved a motion of no confidence in Howard over the Government's decision to deploy troops to the Middle East in preparation for the likelihood of a US-led military campaign to remove the regime of Saddam Hussain in Iraq. Public demonstrations against Australia's anticipated involvement in the campaign followed. Public support for Howard rose substantially from May, largely owing to the apparent swift end to the immediate conflict in Iraq and the absence of Australian casualties. In July, however, a former UN weapons inspector, Richard Butler, claimed that the Government had misled the public about Iraq's supposed programme to develop weapons of mass destruction. A former senior intelligence analyst, who had resigned in protest over Australia's involvement in Iraq, informed a parliamentary inquiry in August that the Government had exaggerated and fabricated intelligence used to justify the case for war. Meanwhile, in July Australia committed 870 troops to assist in the rehabilitation of Iraq. In February 2005 the Government announced that it would send 450 additional troops to Iraq.

Protesters against the Government's mandatory detention of all asylum seekers stormed the Woomera detention centre in March 2002. Most of the approximately 50 asylum seekers who managed to escape were recaptured. In April riots occurred at detention centres in Curtin and Port Hedland, Western Australia. The Government offered financial incentives to Afghan asylum seekers to return to their homeland, but by mid-July only 76 out of 1,000 Afghans had accepted the offer. In June concerns about the alleged maltreatment of asylum seekers were raised again after supporters helped 34 detainees to escape from the Woomera detention centre. More than 120 inmates began a hunger strike to protest against their living conditions and processing delays. In December the Minister for Immigration and Multicultural and Indigenous Affairs, Philip Ruddock, announced plans to expand a programme to allow women and child asylum seekers to live in the community rather than in the detention camps. The authorities strengthened security measures at detention centres following further riots in December.

In March 2003 it was announced that the Woomera and Christmas Island detention centres were to be closed. In April the Federal Court issued a ruling that the Government had no right to detain asylum seekers indefinitely prior to deportation, even if the asylum seeker had been refused permission to enter another country. The Government lodged an appeal at the High Court, which in August 2003 upheld the ruling and rebuked the Government. The Family Court ordered the Government to release from custody five children who had been detained as illegal immigrants since January 2002. The Government came under heavy criticism again in November 2003 when, in response to the arrival of an Indonesian boat carrying 14 Turkish Kurdish asylum seekers at Melville Island, the Government immediately separated the island and 4,000 other small islands from the Australian migration zone. It then ordered an Australian warship to tow the boat to the Indonesian island of Yamdena. The UN High Commissioner for Refugees stated that Australia's exclusion of the islands was 'meaningless', since its obligations as a signatory to the UN refugee convention applied to its entire territory. The Indonesian Government insisted that its agreement to the Kurds' expulsion had neither been requested nor given. In May 2004 Australia's Human Rights and Equal Opportunities Commission issued a report describing the country's immigration detention system as 'cruel, inhumane and degrading', and urged the Government to release all child detainees within a month. In July it was announced that 9,500 asylum seekers who had been released from detention centres since 1999 on temporary protection visas (renewable every three years) would be entitled to apply for permanent settlement in Australia.

In June 2003 John Howard ended months of speculation by announcing that he intended to seek a fourth term of office. Although the leader of the opposition ALP, Simon Crean, won a leadership challenge mounted against him by his predecessor, Kim Beazley, he subsequently failed to reunite the party and resigned as leader in November. In December the republican Mark Latham was elected ALP leader, defeating Beazley. Meanwhile, in August Richard Butler was appointed Governor of Tasmania, replacing Sir Guy Green. In the same month Pauline Hanson was convicted of electoral fraud and sentenced to a three-year prison term; however, her conviction was overruled by a court of appeal in November. In September the Cabinet was reorganized. Changes included the transfer of the controversial Minister for Immigration and Multicultural and Indigenous Affairs, Philip Ruddock, to the post of Attorney-General; Senator Amanda Vanstone was allocated the immigration portfolio. At a state election in Queensland in February 2004, the ruling ALP was re-elected for a third term; Peter Beattie was reappointed Premier. In mid-February riots broke out in the predominantly Aboriginal district of Redfern in Sydney in protest against the death of an Aboriginal youth in an apparent cycling accident while, it was claimed, being pursued by police. More than 30 police officers were injured during Sydney's worst violence in many years; three separate inquiries into the death of the youth and into the riots were instigated. In August the New South Wales state coroner deemed the youth's death to have been an accident.

In March 2004 the parliamentary committee on intelligence on Iraq's weapons of mass destruction published its report, largely exonerating the Government from claims that it had manipulated the intelligence used to justify Australia's involvement in the military campaign in Iraq. In July an independent inquiry into the performance of the intelligence agencies concluded that there had been an overall serious failure of intelligence relating to Iraq's alleged weapons of mass destruction, but that the Australian agencies' assessment of the available material had been more measured than that of their counterparts in the United Kingdom and the USA.

In August 2004 the Governor of Tasmania, Richard Butler, stood down after four senior members of his staff tendered their resignations; he was replaced by William Cox, hitherto Chief Justice of Tasmania. The Liberal-National coalition increased its majority in the House of Representatives at the federal election on 9 October, securing 86 of the 150 seats, and gained an outright majority in the Senate. Prime Minister John Howard was thus returned to office for a fourth consecutive term. The ALP won 60 seats in the lower chamber, five fewer than at the 2001 election, surprising many political analysts, who had predicted a much closer result. The coalition's victory was widely attributed to the continued strong performance of the economy.

In January 2005 Mark Latham, leader of the ALP, resigned from the party leadership and the legislature for health reasons. Kim Beazley was elected to succeed him as ALP leader later in that month, thus resuming the position. In March Australia's asylum policy came under scrutiny once again, following a ruling by the High Court that the country was obliged to accept refugees fleeing persecution in their homeland. John Anderson was succeeded by Mark Vaile as both Deputy Prime Minister and National Party leader following his resignation in June for health reasons. Meanwhile, at elections to the 25-seat Northern Territory legislature in June, the ALP increased its majority, winning 19 seats. In July Bob Carr, the long-serving Premier of New South Wales, announced his resignation; he was succeeded in August by Morris Iemma.

Racially motivated rioting, believed to have been co-ordinated by right-wing extremists, broke out in the Sydney suburb of Cronulla in December 2005. As the disturbances continued, the New South Wales legislature approved emergency legislation to prevent civil unrest.

In January 2006 the Premier of Western Australia, Geoffrey Gallop, resigned on the grounds of ill health. He was replaced by Alan Carpenter. In the same month Dr Ken Michael succeeded

Lt-Gen. John Murray Sanderson as Governor of the state. Also in January Robert Hill resigned as federal Minister for Defence, prompting a minor cabinet reorganization, in which he was succeeded by Dr Brendan Nelson, hitherto Minister for Education, Science and Training. In April Prof. David de Kretser was sworn in as Governor of Victoria. Federal cabinet members Mark Vaile and Warren Truss exchanged portfolios in September 2006: Mark Vaile remained Deputy Prime Minister but also assumed responsibility for the transport and regional services portfolio, while Warren Truss became Minister for Trade. In December Kevin Rudd, the foreign affairs spokesman of the ALP, mounted a successful leadership challenge against Kim Beazley to become the federal Leader of the Opposition. Prime Minister Howard effected a ministerial reorganization in January 2007: among the appointees were Malcolm Turnbull as Minister for the Environment and Water Resources and Kevin Andrews as Minister for Immigration and Citizenship.

In March 2006, meanwhile, the ALP was returned to power at state elections in both South Australia and Tasmania. In September Peter Beattie of the ALP gained a fourth consecutive term as Premier of Queensland at state elections. The ALP's dominance of state politics continued with its victory at elections in Victoria in November, thus ensuring a third term for Premier Stephen Bracks; however, Bracks resigned in July 2007 and was replaced by John Brumby. The ALP also prevailed at elections in New South Wales in March 2007, returning Premier Morris Iemma to office. In September Queensland Premier Peter Beattie resigned and was succeeded by Anna Bligh, who was returned to the post at state elections in March 2009. In July 2008, meanwhile, the Queensland branches of the Liberal and National Parties merged to form the Liberal National Party of Queensland (LNP).

The findings of the so-called Cole Inquiry were published in November 2006. Led by retired judge Terence Cole, the inquiry had been established at the end of 2005 in order to investigate allegations of misconduct or unlawful actions by Australian companies in connection with the UN's oil-for-food programme in Iraq (whereby the Government of Saddam Hussain had been permitted to use revenue from oil exports to purchase food and medicines). The inquiry found that, in contravention of UN regulations, between 1999 and 2003 irregular payments totalling $A300m. had been made by the Australian Wheat Board (AWB) to the Government of Iraq in order to secure lucrative contracts under the oil-for-food programme. The Cole report exonerated the Australian Government, but recommended that 11 former AWB executives answer charges of corruption.

The Rudd administration, 2007–10

At the federal election held on 24 November 2007, the ALP secured a majority in the House of Representatives, winning 83 of the 150 seats. The Liberal Party won only 55 seats, while the National Party, its coalition partner, took 10 seats. The Liberal-National coalition also lost its majority in the upper chamber. Prime Minister Howard suffered a humiliating personal defeat in his long-held constituency of Bennelong. He was succeeded as Federal Parliamentary Leader of the Liberal Party by the erstwhile Minister of Defence, Dr Brendan Nelson. Kevin Rudd was sworn in as Prime Minister in early December, along with a Cabinet that included Julia Gillard as Deputy Prime Minister, Stephen Smith as Minister for Foreign Affairs and Wayne Swan as Treasurer. Fulfilling his election pledge, Rudd's first undertaking as Prime Minister was to ratify the Kyoto Protocol (negotiated in Japan in 1997), thereby committing Australia to reducing its emissions of carbon dioxide and other greenhouse gases. Among other commitments, he reiterated his intention to withdraw Australian troops from Iraq and to reverse the previous Government's position on a formal apology to the Aboriginal peoples (see Other Aboriginal Issues).

In April 2008 Prime Minister Rudd hosted the so-called Australia 2020 Summit. More than 1,000 invited delegates, including representatives of the business community, academics and opposition politicians, participated in discussions on 10 long-term national policy challenges. A final report outlined the principal recommendations submitted during the conference, which included constitutional reform (see below), formal legal recognition for Aboriginal and Torres Strait Islander people, the promotion of sustainable energy and a revision of the taxation system.

In May 2008 the Labor Premier of Tasmania, Paul Lennon, whose administration had been marred by various scandals and who had recently been criticized for his support of plans for the construction of a controversial timber pulp mill, announced his resignation and departure from politics. He was succeeded by the Deputy Premier, David Bartlett.

In the Northern Territory election of August 2008 the incumbent Labor Chief Minister, Paul Henderson, was returned to office by only a narrow margin, after a substantial transfer of support to the Liberal Party. In September Morris Iemma, the Labor Premier of New South Wales, unexpectedly resigned, following a revolt by party members who had refused to endorse his proposed removal of several cabinet ministers, precipitated by the resignation of the state's Deputy Premier. Nathan Rees was selected as Iemma's successor. Also in September the ALP lost its parliamentary majority at state elections in Western Australia. Colin Barnett of the Liberal Party replaced Alan Carpenter as the state's Premier, heading a Liberal-National administration.

In September 2008 the Liberal Party elected Malcolm Turnbull, a former leader of the Australian Republican Movement and erstwhile Minister for the Environment and Water Resources, as Federal Parliamentary Leader, in place of Dr Brendan Nelson, who had served as Leader of the Opposition for less than 10 months.

In December 2008 the Prime Minister announced various new measures intended to curb Australia's greenhouse gas emissions: he undertook to reduce emissions by at least 5% by 2020 in comparison with the levels of 2000, and by as much as 15% in the 'unlikely' event of international agreement on such a percentage decrease being reached by developed nations. A carbon trading scheme, applicable to 75% of Australia's emissions, was to be introduced by 2010. However, environmentalists immediately denounced these targets as inadequate. In January and February 2009 unusually severe bush fires in the state of Victoria, following a prolonged drought and record high temperatures, led to the deaths of more than 170 people, and stimulated debate on whether climate change was exacerbating extreme weather conditions. In May, under pressure from the business sector, the Government postponed the introduction of the emissions trading scheme to July 2011, citing deteriorating global economic conditions. Having been endorsed by the House of Representatives, the legislation failed to secure approval in the opposition-controlled Senate in August 2009. Attempts to reach a compromise with the Liberal-National coalition prior to the next vote in the Senate in November dismayed environmental groups and exposed divisions within the opposition, with a number of senior party members emerging as strongly opposed to the scheme. In December Malcolm Turnbull, a supporter of carbon emissions trading, was narrowly defeated in a ballot for the Liberal Party leadership by Tony Abbott, a 'climate change sceptic' and erstwhile Minister for Health. The new Leader of the Opposition immediately stated his intention to oppose the Government's emissions trading legislation. The previously agreed compromise was thus abandoned. The proposed legislation was once again rejected by the Senate.

From late 2008 the number of boats carrying asylum seekers to Australia began to increase rapidly, partly as a result of the worsening conflicts in Sri Lanka and Afghanistan. The Government was therefore obliged to review its policy with regard to the use of the Christmas Island detention centre, which had been commissioned by the Howard administration but remained unused. In December, therefore, the new facility received the first asylum seekers. An amendment to the Migration Act, which sought to end the much-criticized policy of charging asylum seekers for the cost of their detention, was approved by the House of Representatives in June 2009 and by the Senate in September. Also in June the Minister for Defence, Joel Fitzgibbon, resigned following reports of a number of discrepancies in his declarations of interest, and was replaced by Senator John Faulkner in a limited cabinet reorganization.

In state politics, in December 2009 the Labor Premier of New South Wales, Nathan Rees, was defeated in a party leadership ballot by the state's Minister for Planning, Kristina Keneally, amid reports of factional divisions. Keneally promptly reorganized the Cabinet, which had undergone numerous changes during the previous 12 months. At state elections in South Australia in March 2010 Labor Premier Mike Rann was returned to office for a third consecutive term. In the same month some controversy followed state elections in Tasmania, where neither of the two main political parties secured a majority. Although his party had received fewer votes than the Liberal Party, the incumbent Labor Premier, David Bartlett, was invited by the Tasmanian Governor, Peter Underwood (who had replaced William Cox in

April 2008), to form a minority government. The Labor administration was thus reinstalled, in coalition with the Greens.

In April 2010 the newly created federal post of Minister for Population was given to Tony Burke, in addition to his responsibilities for agriculture, fisheries and forestry. In the same month the Government announced that the processing of applications for visas for asylum seekers from Afghanistan and Sri Lanka was to be suspended with immediate effect: those arriving by boat would still be taken to the Christmas Island detention centre, but would not be permitted to apply for asylum in Australia. Also in April, Rudd announced that the introduction of the emissions trading scheme was to be further postponed, until after the expiry in 2012 of the Kyoto Protocol (see above): he thereby incurred criticism for having apparently abandoned an important principle. In May 2010 the Government announced the imposition of a tax of 40% on the profits of mining companies, on the grounds that royalties paid by mining companies to the state administrations had not increased in proportion to the industry's considerable profits during the past 10 years. Rudd argued that, since the mining companies were often partly or largely foreign-owned, an unfair share of the country's wealth was being transferred overseas. The mining companies, in response, claimed that their contribution to the economy had helped Australia to avoid the recession that had affected most other developed countries in 2008/09, and argued that the new tax would deter investment, reduce the competitiveness of the Australian mining industry and create unemployment.

Controversy over the postponement of the emissions trading scheme and the debate regarding the proposed mining tax appeared to lead to a rapid decline in popular support for the Prime Minister in May 2010. In addition, there was reportedly criticism within the ALP of his abrasive style of leadership. In June Rudd was challenged for the leadership of the party by the Deputy Prime Minister, Julia Gillard. Acknowledging his likely defeat, Rudd resigned before the proposed party ballot. On 24 June Gillard became the Federal Parliamentary Leader of the ALP and was sworn in as the country's first female Prime Minister. Wayne Swan, the federal Treasurer, was elected unopposed as deputy party leader and assumed the post of Deputy Prime Minister.

The Gillard and Rudd administrations 2010–13

Upon taking office in June 2010 Julia Gillard made few initial ministerial changes: the portfolios previously held by Gillard, namely education, employment, workplace relations and social inclusion, were given to Simon Crean; the latter's former post of Minister for Trade was allocated to Stephen Smith, who remained Minister for Foreign Affairs. In July the new Government announced that the controversial additional resource tax on mines, proposed by its predecessor, would apply to coal and iron ore mines only, and would exclude those companies earning annual profits of less than $A50m., while the rate of taxation was to be reduced from 40% to 30% of the profits.

The general election that had been due to take place before the end of 2010 was brought forward to 21 August, when the ALP narrowly avoided being ejected from office, winning 72 seats in the 150-member House of Representatives, while the Liberal-National coalition also won 72 (with one member of the National Party of Western Australia declaring himself an independent); the Australian Greens won a federal seat for the first time. It was announced on 7 September that the ALP would form a minority Government (the first since 1940), relying on the support of the single Greens representative and of three independents. In simultaneous elections to 40 of the 76 seats in the Senate, the Greens won six seats in addition to the three that they already held, thus acquiring a powerful position in the upper house (with effect from 1 July 2011, when most of the new senators were to assume their seats). Julia Gillard's new administration included the previous Prime Minister, Kevin Rudd, as Minister for Foreign Affairs, while Stephen Smith became Minister for Defence and Wayne Swan remained as Deputy Prime Minister and Treasurer.

In July 2010 Gillard had proposed that a regional processing centre for asylum seekers be established in Timor-Leste, but this was rejected by the legislature of that country. In October the Government announced that two new detention centres for asylum seekers were to be established within Australia, while family groups were to be given community-based accommodation so as to avoid confining children in detention. In November legislation was approved on the creation of a high-speed national broadband network to improve telecommunications, particularly in rural areas; the promised introduction of the network had been a major factor in securing the support of independent members of the House of Representatives for the ALP (the opposition favoured a less expensive but less technically advanced network).

From 2003 onwards much of Australia had been afflicted by severe drought, necessitating emergency state assistance for many farmers. In December 2010 and January 2011, however, heavy rains, believed to be caused by the recurrent weather phenomenon known as La Niña, resulted in severe flooding in Queensland, and to a lesser extent in Victoria. At least 35 people lost their lives, and there was extensive damage to property, crops, infrastructure and the region's important coal mines. In January Gillard announced the imposition of a new tax to help meet the cost of reconstruction, which was initially estimated to require $A5,600m. in federal spending: the levy was to be imposed for 12 months, with effect from 1 July, on individuals earning more than $A50,000 per year. Reductions in previously planned expenditure were also announced (including infrastructure projects and several environmental measures intended to reduce carbon emissions) in order to finance reconstruction projects. In early February further serious damage was caused in northern Queensland by Cyclone Yasi.

At state elections in Victoria in November 2010 the ruling Labor administration was defeated by the Liberal-National coalition after 11 years in office, and Ted Baillieu replaced John Brumby as Premier. In January 2011 the Labor Premier of Tasmania, David Bartlett, resigned, citing the needs of his family, and was replaced by Lara Giddings, who retained her previous posts as state Treasurer and Minister for the Arts. At state elections in New South Wales in March, the Labor administration of Kristina Keneally was heavily defeated. Barry O'Farrell of the Liberal Party was subsequently appointed as the state's Premier. In April Alex Chernov, Chancellor of the University of Melbourne, replaced Prof. David de Kretser as Governor of Victoria. In October Sally Thomas became Administrator of the Northern Territory, replacing Tom Pauling.

In July 2011 the federal Government announced the introduction of a Clean Energy Bill, which would impose a 'carbon price' on some 500 Australian companies that were causing the most pollution in the form of carbon dioxide emissions: according to the proposed legislation, such companies were to pay $A23 per metric ton of emissions over a three-year period, with effect from July 2012, and from July 2015 this arrangement would be replaced by a market-based carbon emissions trading scheme. Despite the inclusion of measures to compensate households for resultant higher electricity costs, and to assist industries to adopt the use of less polluting energy sources, the plan encountered vociferous opposition, particularly since, before the 2010 election, Gillard had undertaken not to introduce such a tax (she had been obliged to reverse this undertaking by her Government's dependence on the Australian Greens for support). Following its adoption by a small majority in the House of Representatives in October 2011, and by the Senate in November, the legislation duly entered into force on 1 July 2012. The controversial tax on mining companies (see above) was also approved by the lower house in November 2011, and by the Senate in March 2012, becoming effective, likewise, from 1 July; the tax was expected to raise some $A10,600m. over the next three years, but revenue from the tax amounted to only $A126m. in the first six months following its introduction.

In December 2010 some 50 asylum seekers died when their unseaworthy boat was wrecked off Christmas Island. The Government attempted to respond to domestic concerns about border security in July 2011 by concluding an agreement with the Malaysian Government that was intended to deter asylum seekers from arriving by boat, usually under dangerous conditions, and to prevent their exploitation by people-smugglers. These so-called irregular maritime arrivals (IMAs) were reported to number 6,535 in 2010 and 2,183 in the first eight months of 2011; in late August 2011 there were about 4,400 IMAs in detention on the mainland, and some 800 more on Christmas Island. According to the agreement, over a four-year period Australia would dispatch 800 asylum seekers to Malaysia for processing, while Malaysia would send to Australia 4,000 refugees whose status had been approved. In August, however, the Australian High Court declared the agreement unlawful, because Malaysia was not a signatory to the UN Convention relating to the Status of Refugees and therefore did not provide adequate legal protection for asylum seekers. An agreement concluded earlier in that month to reopen an assessment centre in Papua New Guinea for asylum seekers arriving in Australia was brought into question by the same ruling. In October the Government's attempt to amend legislation in order to reverse the High Court's judgment was defeated. In November the Government began to allocate 'bridging visas' to some asylum seekers whose refugee status had not yet been determined, thus ending the policy of mandatory detention for all arriving without visas.

The ALP administration's precarious status in the House of Representatives improved slightly in November 2011 when the Speaker, Harry Jenkins, an ALP member, unexpectedly resigned from his post, citing a desire to return to party politics, and was thus enabled to vote in the legislature; he was replaced by Peter Slipper, a reportedly disaffected member of the Liberal Party, which thus lost one of its voting members. Slipper's appointment was criticized as underhand by the opposition.

A ministerial reorganization was effected in December 2011. Among other changes, Nicola Roxon, hitherto Minister for Health and Ageing, was appointed as Attorney-General, replacing Robert McClelland, who became Minister for Housing, for Homelessness and for Emergency Management. Three existing Ministers were promoted to an expanded Cabinet: Tanya Plibersek as Minister for Health, Bill Shorten as Minister for Employment and Workplace Relations and for Financial Services and Superannuation, and Mark Butler as Minister for Mental Health and Ageing, and for Social Inclusion.

Following months of speculation that Kevin Rudd intended to force a leadership election within the ALP, Rudd announced his resignation as Minister for Foreign Affairs in February 2012, during an official visit to the USA. On 27 February, following a bitter campaign that exposed the deep divisions within the party, Gillard defeated Rudd in a parliamentary ballot for the ALP leadership, which she had organized, by 71 votes to 31. As part of a ministerial reorganization announced in early March, the former Premier of New South Wales, Bob Carr, replaced Rudd as Minister for Foreign Affairs and was allocated a seat in the Senate, while Robert McClelland, an ally of Rudd, left the Government (although several other ministers who had supported Rudd in the leadership election retained their posts).

Diminishing support for the ALP was demonstrated at state elections in 2012. The party was heavily defeated by the LNP at state elections in Queensland in March: Campbell Newman of the LNP replaced Anna Bligh as Premier of Queensland. In August the ALP suffered a further defeat at an election to the legislative assembly of the Northern Territory, whereupon Terry Mills (Liberal) replaced Paul Henderson as Chief Minister of the territory. In October, at an election in the Australian Capital Territory, the ALP narrowly secured a fourth term of office, but only with the support of the sole representative of the Greens. In April, meanwhile, the Parliamentary Leader of the Australian Greens, Bob Brown, retired, and was replaced by his deputy, Christine Milne. The Speaker of the House of Representatives, Peter Slipper, resigned in October after winning a parliamentary motion of confidence by only one vote, following an investigation into allegations that he had submitted false expenses claims and sent inappropriate text messages to an adviser.

In June 2012 two unseaworthy boats, carrying some 300 asylum seekers, capsized off Christmas Island with considerable loss of life. In the same month Gillard appointed an independent panel of experts to identify possible solutions to the continuing dilemma over illegal immigration, after the Senate had rejected legislative proposals that would have permitted the reopening of a processing camp in Nauru and the sending of asylum seekers to Malaysia while their applications were being reviewed. The panel's report, issued in August, recommended the reopening of processing centres in both Nauru and Manus Island (Papua New Guinea), and the negotiation of an agreement with Malaysia on providing a temporary base for asylum seekers. These proposals were approved by the legislature in the same month, and the first groups of asylum seekers were flown to Nauru in September and to Manus Island in November. In November conditions at the Nauru camp were criticized by the UN High Commissioner for Human Rights and by the human rights organization Amnesty International.

Australia experienced its hottest year on record in 2013. In January there were severe bush fires in Tasmania, New South Wales and Victoria, with widespread damage to property, although only two deaths were reported. The Climate Commission (established by the Government in 2011) responded by warning of an increasing likelihood of extreme temperatures, which it attributed to climate change, and predicted that the risk of bush fires would also rise in the coming years. Also in January 2013 a tropical cyclone again caused serious flooding in Queensland. Further severe fires devastated parts of New South Wales in October.

At the end of January 2013 Gillard announced that the general election due to take place by November of that year would be conducted on 14 September. A few days later, in early February, two senior government ministers, Nicola Roxon and Senator Chris Evans, resigned from office, citing personal reasons. Among the changes in the ensuing reorganization, Mark Dreyfus, hitherto Cabinet Secretary, was promoted to Roxon's former post as Attorney-General and Minister for Emergency Management, while Chris Bowen succeeded Evans as Minister for Tertiary Education, Skills, Science and Research, also assuming responsibility for the small business portfolio. Senator Stephen Conroy, the Minister for Broadband, Communications and the Digital Economy, was elected unopposed to succeed Evans as Leader of the Government in the Senate.

At a state election in Western Australia on 9 March 2013 the ruling Liberal-National coalition, led by Colin Barnett, was returned to power with an increased majority. In the same month the Liberal Premier of Victoria, Ted Baillieu, resigned following a scandal over the release of recordings of conversations that suggested that a senior aide had made payments, and offered help in finding a new post, to a former ministerial adviser who had been accused of campaigning to remove the former chief commissioner of police; Baillieu was replaced as state party leader and Premier by a ministerial colleague, Denis Napthine. Also in March the Chief Minister of the Northern Territory, Terry Mills, was informed (while abroad) that he had lost the support of the local Liberal Party, and was removed from office, to be replaced by Adam Giles (the first indigenous person to hold the principal political office in any state or territory).

Gillard encountered a renewed threat to her leadership of the ALP on 21 March 2013, when Simon Crean, the Minister for Regional Australia, Regional Development and Local Government, and for the Arts, urged her to organize a leadership election, announcing his support for Kevin Rudd's return to the post. However, Gillard was re-elected unopposed to the ALP leadership later that day, following a last-minute decision by Rudd not to challenge her, when it became apparent that he lacked sufficient support within the parliamentary party to win the ballot. Gillard subsequently effected a cabinet reorganization, in which Crean, Bowen and a number of other supporters of Rudd were replaced and several portfolios were combined. Although he had supported Rudd's candidacy, Anthony Albanese retained the post of Minister for Infrastructure and Transport, and was additionally allocated the regional development and local government portfolio. In June, after public opinion polls had consistently predicted an electoral defeat for the ALP if Gillard remained at its head, Rudd's supporters within the parliamentary party again petitioned for a ballot on the leadership, and this duly took place. In the ballot Rudd received 57 votes and Gillard 45. Gillard thereupon resigned as Prime Minister, and announced her retirement from political life; her deputy, Wayne Swan, and five other ministers also resigned from office. Rudd was sworn in as Prime Minister on 27 June. He appointed Anthony Albanese as Deputy Prime Minister and Minister for Broadband, Communications and the Digital Economy, while Chris Bowen became Treasurer. The ministers hitherto responsible for foreign affairs, defence and home affairs remained in place.

Although Rudd himself enjoyed greater public support than his predecessor, there was little time available to improve the low popularity ratings of the ALP before the general election, which, as Rudd announced in early August 2013, was to be brought forward by one week to 7 September. It was announced in July that (if re-elected) the Government would replace the controversial carbon tax by an emissions trading scheme in 2014, a year earlier than originally planned (see above). Also in July Rudd announced that asylum seekers arriving illegally by boat would henceforth be resettled in Papua New Guinea, which, under a new agreement, was to receive additional aid in compensation (see Foreign Affairs). Within the ALP, new rules were announced making it more difficult to mount the recurrent leadership challenges that had caused such damage to the party's reputation in recent years. During the election campaign the opposition leader, Tony Abbott, undertook to give priority (if successful) to the immediate abolition of the carbon tax, a reduction in foreign aid in favour of spending on domestic infrastructure, and the deployment of the armed forces to prevent illegal immigration.

Recent developments: the Abbott administration 2013–

At the federal election on 7 September 2013 the Liberal-National coalition regained power after six years in opposition, winning 90 of the 150 seats in the House of Representatives, while the ALP won 55. In the concurrent partial election to the Senate, the Liberal-National coalition won 17 of the 40 contested seats, the ALP 12, the Greens four, and minor parties seven: a result which indicated that the new Government would need to rely on minor parties in order to have legislation approved by the upper house. Tony Abbott was sworn in as Prime Minister on 18 September. His Cabinet included Warren Truss (the parliamentary leader of the National Party) as Deputy Prime Minister and Minister for Infrastructure and Regional Development, Julie Bishop (the only woman in the Cabinet) as Minister for Foreign Affairs, Joe Hockey as Treasurer and Andrew Robb as Minister for Trade and Investment.

Immediately following his party's electoral defeat, Kevin Rudd resigned as leader of the ALP, and he retired from politics altogether in November 2013. In October Bill Shorten (who had been Minister for Education and for Workplace Relations in the brief Rudd administration) defeated Anthony Albanese in an election to the ALP leadership, in which, for the first time, the entire party membership, not just the ALP members of the legislature, participated.

In November 2013, at the first session of the newly elected Parliament, the Government introduced a bill, as promised, to abolish the carbon tax and replace it by the direct granting of subsidies to encourage businesses to reduce their emissions of carbon dioxide; it also introduced legislation to abolish the tax on mineral resources introduced by the ALP administration. It was expected that adoption of both measures would be delayed in the Senate. Also in November the Government encountered strong opposition in the legislature when it proposed increasing the current limit on government debt from $A300,000m. to $A500,000m. in order to avoid making reductions in expenditure, but in December, with the support of the Greens, the debt limit was abolished altogether, with the proviso that the Government would make a statement to Parliament whenever the debt increased by a further $A50,000m. In that month the Treasurer, Joe Hockey, warned that the country's fiscal position was unsustainable and that urgent remedial action would be needed to reduce the budget deficit.

In January 2014 Abbott announced that Peter Cosgrove, a retired general and Chief of the Defence Force in 2002–05, was to succeed Quentin Bryce as Governor-General of Australia after the expiry of the latter's term of office in March. Prior to Cosgrove being sworn in, Abbott controversially reintroduced the titles of knight and dame into the Australian honours system (which had been abolished under a Labor Government in 1986) and conferred them on Cosgrove and Bryce. All future holders of the office of Governor-General were to receive the honour.

At state elections in South Australia in March 2014 neither the ALP (which won 23 of the 47 seats) nor the Liberal Party (22 seats) had sufficient seats to form a majority government. The independent Geoff Brock subsequently lent his support to the formation of a minority Labor Government with Jay Weatherill as Premier. Meanwhile, in concurrent elections in Tasmania the Liberal Party won a convincing victory, taking 15 of the 25 seats in the legislature, defeating the ruling alliance of the ALP and the Greens; William Hodgman assumed office as Premier. In April the Premier of New South Wales, Barry O'Farrell resigned after wrongly denying accepting a gift to an inquiry; he was replaced by Mike Baird.

Aboriginal Land Rights

The sensitive issue of Aboriginal land rights was addressed by the Government in August 1985, when it formulated proposals for legislation that would give Aboriginal people inalienable freehold title to national parks, vacant Crown land and former Aboriginal reserves, in spite of widespread opposition from state governments (which had previously been responsible for their own land policies), from mining companies and from the Aboriginal people themselves, who were angered by the Government's withdrawal of its earlier support for the Aboriginal right to veto mineral exploitation. In October Uluru (also known as Ayers Rock, the main tourist attraction of the Northern Territory) was officially transferred to the Mutijulu Aboriginal community, on condition that continuing access to the site be guaranteed. In 1986, however, the Government abandoned its pledge to impose such federal legislation on unwilling state governments, and this led to further protests from Aboriginal leaders. In June 1991 the Government imposed a permanent ban on mining at a traditional Aboriginal site in the Northern Territory.

An important precedent was established in June 1992, when the High Court overruled the concept of *terra nullius* (unoccupied land) by recognizing the existence of land titles that predated European settlement in 1788 in cases where a close association with the land in question had been continued; however, land titles legally acquired since 1788 were to remain intact. As a result of the 'Mabo' decision of 1992 (named after the Aboriginal claimant, Eddie Mabo), in December 1993 Parliament approved the Native Title Act, historic legislation granting Aboriginal people the right to claim title to their traditional lands. The legislation aroused much controversy, particularly in Western Australia (vast areas of the state being vacant Crown land), where rival legislation to replace native title rights with lesser rights to traditional land usage, such as access for ceremonial purposes only, had been enacted. In March 1995 the High Court declared the Native Title Act to be valid, rejecting as unconstitutional Western Australia's own legislation.

In October 1996, following protracted delays in the development of a valuable zinc mine in Queensland owing to Aboriginal land claims, the Howard Government announced proposals to amend the Native Title Act to permit federal ministers to overrule Aboriginal concerns if a project of 'major economic benefit' to Australia were threatened. In December the Larrakia people of the Northern Territory presented a claim under the Native Title Act, the first such claim to encompass a provincial capital, namely Darwin. Meanwhile, in October the federal High Court upheld an appeal by two Aboriginal communities in Queensland (including the Wik people of Cape York) against an earlier ruling that prevented them from submitting a claim to land leased by the state government to cattle and sheep farmers. The Court's decision, known as the Wik judgment, was expected to encourage similar challenges to 'pastoral' leases.

In April 1997 the first native title deed to be granted on mainland Australia was awarded to the Dunghutti people of New South Wales. In the same month the Prime Minister announced the introduction of legislation to clarify the issue of land tenure; a 10-point plan was to be drawn up in consultation with state governments and with representatives of the Aboriginal community. In September the Government introduced the Wik Native Title Bill, which was subsequently approved by the House of Representatives. In November, however, the Senate questioned the constitutional validity of the proposed legislation, whereby pastoralists' rights and activities would prevail over, but not extinguish (as had been assumed), the Aboriginal people's rights to native title. Finally, in July 1998, following a protracted and acrimonious debate, the Senate narrowly approved the Native Title Amendment Bill, thereby restricting the Aboriginal people's rights to claim access to Crown land leased to farmers. The approval of the controversial legislation was immediately denounced by Aboriginal leaders. In the same month, however, at a session in Darwin the Federal Court granted communal (but not exclusive or commercial) native title to the waters and sea-bed around Croker Island in the Northern Territory to five Aboriginal groups. With about 140 similar claims over Australian waters pending, the historic ruling represented the first recognition of native title rights over the sea. However, the area's traditional owners launched an appeal against the decision, insisting on the commercial right to negotiate on fishing and pearling activities.

In August 2002 the High Court in Canberra rejected a claim by the Miriuwung-Gajerrong people to territory in Western Australia and the Northern Territory that contained the Argyle diamond mine, owned by the Anglo-Australian mining company Rio Tinto. In September, however, Rio Tinto offered to close the Jabiluka uranium mine in the Northern Territory, following opposition to the project from the indigenous Mirrar people (the owners of the land) and environmental groups. The Government of the Northern Territory approved a plan to fill in the mine in August 2003. Meanwhile, in September 2002 the Federal Court awarded native title over 136,000 sq km of Western Australia (the largest area so far determined) to the Martu people. A ruling by the Federal Court in September 2006 granted the Noongar people native title over more than 6,000 sq km of land in Western Australia, around and including Perth. The Government of Western Australia appealed against the decision, and the federal Government also contested the ruling in order to clarify questions arising, including the issue of public access to vacant Crown land. In April 2008 parts of the appeal were upheld by the Federal Court. In December 2009 the Western Australia

Government and the South West Aboriginal Land and Sea Council agreed to try to resolve the native title claims by negotiation rather than by lengthy and costly court procedures. By mid-2013 agreement in principle had been reached, subject to consideration by meetings of the estimated 35,000 Noongar people: the agreement, if accepted, would involve the surrender of all native title rights, but would include official recognition by an act of the state Parliament of the traditional ownership of Noongar country; customary rights of access to land for traditional purposes; the designation of 320,000 ha of land as Noongar Land Estate; contributions by the state Government of $A50m. per year for 12 years to a 'Future Fund' for the benefit of the Noongar people, and $A10m. per year for 12 years for the operation of six regional Noongar corporations and a supporting central services corporation; and extensive community development and conservation measures.

In December 2008, citing a lack of due process, the Federal Court ruled against Xstrata, an Anglo-Swiss mining corporation, which in 2006 had been permitted by the Government to proceed with the expansion of a controversial zinc mine in the Northern Territory. Also opposed by environmentalists owing to the risk of pollution, the project had involved the diversion of a river, which Aboriginal leaders now demanded be restored to its original course. The ruling was regarded as a major setback for the country's mining industry.

In July 2010 a court in Queensland awarded native title rights over 40,000 sq km of sea to the Torres Strait Islanders, who had first submitted the claim in 2001: this represented the largest maritime claim made so far. In June 2011 Rio Tinto announced that it had concluded agreements with five Aboriginal groups in the Pilbara region of Western Australia, allowing the company to expand its iron mining operations on their land over a period of 40 years, in return for a share of the profits and an undertaking by the company to ensure that at least 14% of its employees would comprise Aboriginal workers. In May 2012 the Federal Court awarded native title to the Arabana people over an area of some 70,000 sq km in South Australia, including Lake Eyre, the country's largest lake when at full capacity.

Other Aboriginal Issues

In August 1988 a UN report accused Australia of violating international human rights in its treatment of Aboriginal people. In October an unofficial study indicated that Aboriginal people, although accounting for only 1% of the total population of Australia, comprised more than 20% of persons in prison. In May 1991 the report of the Royal Commission into Aboriginal Deaths in Custody was published: it gave evidence of racial prejudice in the police force and included more than 300 recommendations for changes in policies relating to Aboriginal people. In March 1992 radical plans for judicial, economic and social reforms, with the objective of improving the lives of Aboriginal people, were announced; a total of $A500m. was to be made available over the next 10 years. In February 1993 the human rights organization Amnesty International issued a highly critical report on the prison conditions of Aboriginal people, and in March 1996 it claimed that Australia had made little progress with regard to its treatment of Aboriginal prisoners. In March 2000 the UN Committee on Elimination of Racial Discrimination issued a report denouncing Australia's treatment of its indigenous people. The report was particularly critical of the mandatory prison sentences for minor property offences in force in the Northern Territory and Western Australia, which appeared to target juvenile Aboriginal people.

In July 1996 the Roman Catholic Church issued an apology for its role in the forcible removal from their parents of tens of thousands of Aboriginal and part-Aboriginal children, in a controversial practice of placement in institutions and white foster homes, where many were abused. Some received little or no education, with girls being employed as domestic servants and boys as stockmen. This policy of so-called assimilation had continued until the late 1960s. In May 1997 the publication of the findings of a two-year inquiry into the removal of as many as 100,000 Aboriginal children from their families had profound political repercussions: the Prime Minister made an unexpected personal apology to the 'stolen generations', but the Government rejected recommendations that compensation be paid to victims, and refused to issue a formal apology. However, a $A63m. programme to help reunite divided Aboriginal families was announced. During 1997 successive state governments also made apologies to the 'stolen generations'. In February 1998 the Anglican Church apologized unreservedly for its part in the removal of Aboriginal children from their families.

Two separate UN reports, released in March and July 2000, were highly critical of Australia's treatment of the Aboriginal population; their findings were strongly rejected by the Australian Government. In August, at the conclusion of a test case brought in the Northern Territory by two members of the 'stolen generations' who hoped to win compensation for the trauma occasioned by their removal from their families, the Federal Court ruled that the Government was not obliged to pay punitive damages to the two Aboriginal claimants, on the grounds of insufficient evidence. As many as 30,000 similar cases had been pending. During 2000–01 the Government rejected recommendations by a Senate committee and by various indigenous and legal groups for the establishment of a reparations tribunal, insisting that its own programme of 'practical' assistance was sufficient.

In April 2004 Prime Minister Howard announced controversial plans to abolish the elected Aboriginal and Torres Strait Islander Commission (ATSIC), claiming that it had failed to improve conditions for the indigenous community since commencing operations in 1990. In response, the first national party for Aboriginal people, Your Voice, was launched in May 2004. In December a new government-appointed advisory body on Aboriginal affairs, the 14-member National Indigenous Council, held its first meeting. In March 2005, following a senate committee report, legislation to abolish ATSIC was approved.

In October 2006 the first official compensation scheme for the 'stolen generations' was initiated when the Government of Tasmania announced that $A5m. was to be made available for the state's victims. In August 2007 compensation was granted to an individual for the first time when a South Australian court awarded compensation to Bruce Trevorrow, an Aboriginal man who had been forcibly separated from his family as a child; in March 2010 the South Australian Government lost an appeal against the court's decision.

In June 2007 the Howard Government announced plans to ban alcohol and the most offensive types of pornography in Aboriginal communities in the Northern Territory, along with other federal measures formulated in response to reports of widespread child abuse and the prevalence of poor health and social conditions in the area. Amid much controversy, the House of Representatives approved the relevant legislation in August. In order to permit the implementation of the intervention measures in the Northern Territory, the Racial Discrimination Act of 1975 was suspended.

In February 2008 the new Prime Minister, Kevin Rudd, issued a long-awaited formal apology for the 'profound grief, suffering and loss' inflicted upon indigenous people by successive governments. The motion received unanimous parliamentary approval, although some Liberal members were reported to have boycotted the historic opening session. Although they remained unrepresented in the legislature, the ceremony was attended by 100 delegates from the Aboriginal community and members of the 'stolen generations'. While Rudd's initiative was generally welcomed, his decision not to grant federal compensation to those affected by the policies of previous governments drew some criticism; instead, the Government reiterated its intention to give priority to the improvement of health and educational services in Aboriginal areas. Rudd declared his commitment to raising Aboriginal life expectancy to a level comparable to that of other Australians within a generation and also his intention to halve the indigenous infant mortality rate within a decade. In July funding of $A550m., to be provided for various projects over a five-year period, was agreed. In April 2009, in a reversal of the previous Government's policy, the Rudd administration adopted the UN Declaration on the Rights of Indigenous Peoples.

In July 2009 a national report into Aboriginal disadvantage found little improvement in social and economic conditions among indigenous communities. In August the UN Special Rapporteur on human rights and indigenous peoples visited Aboriginal communities and described the Australian Government's controversial intervention in the Northern Territory (see above) as a discriminatory act that infringed upon Aboriginal people's rights and self-determination. He expressed particular concern with regard to the suspension of the Racial Discrimination Act. The process of income management, whereby one-half of welfare payments to indigenous people was 'quarantined' for food and other necessities, was regarded as a particular source of humiliation for Aboriginal people. In June 2010 the Racial Discrimination Act was reinstated, and the policy of income management was extended to non-indigenous recipients of welfare payments.

A new representative body, the National Congress of Australia's First Peoples, was formed in May 2010: it was to comprise 120 members elected by Aboriginal people and Torres Strait Islanders. At the general election in August an Aboriginal member of the Liberal Party was elected to the House of Representatives: this was the first time that the indigenous community had been represented in the lower house of the legislature (although there had previously been two Aboriginal senators). In November the Government established a panel of experts to prepare for a referendum, to be conducted within the next three years, on an amendment to the Constitution that would explicitly recognize Aboriginal people and Torres Strait Islanders: to this end the Aboriginal and Torres Strait Islanders Peoples Recognition Bill was introduced in November 2012. Meanwhile, a new Aboriginal grouping, First Nations Political Party, led by Maurie Japarta Ryan, was registered with the Australian Electoral Commission in early 2011.

The new Liberal-National Government, elected in September 2013, identified indigenous affairs as a 'significant priority', and in that month responsibility for most indigenous policy programmes was transferred to the Department of the Prime Minister and Cabinet, instead of being divided among different government departments. The new Minister for Aboriginal Affairs, Nigel Scullion, stated that one of his principal aims was to improve school attendance among Aboriginal children. In October Adam Giles, the new Chief Minister of the Northern Territory, became the first indigenous Australian to lead a state government.

International Terrorism

In 2002 Australia was for the first time obliged directly to address the issue of international terrorism. On 12 October 88 Australians were among the 202 people killed in a bomb explosion in a night-club on the Indonesian island of Bali. The Islamist militant group Jemaah Islamiah (JI) was held principally responsible for the attack. The Australian Government proscribed the organization, which was suspected of having links with the al-Qa'ida network, and successfully led a campaign to have JI listed as a terrorist organization by the UN. A further seven militant Islamist groups were banned in March and April 2003, and in May the Government decided to create a new counter-terrorist unit from the country's volunteer military reserve force. One month later the Senate approved anti-terrorism legislation giving significant new powers to the Australian Security Intelligence Organisation, including the power to detain suspects for up to seven days without charge. In February 2004 Australia and Indonesia co-hosted a counter-terrorism conference held on Bali. A bomb exploded outside the Australian embassy in the Indonesian capital of Jakarta in September, killing at least nine people, mostly Indonesians, and injuring more than 180 others. JI was suspected of being responsible for the attack. In October 2005 four Australian citizens were among 20 people killed in three suicide bombings on Bali.

In September 2005 Prime Minister John Howard announced a series of proposals intended to strengthen Australia's anti-terrorism laws, including plans to make the incitement of terrorist acts a criminal offence and to detain suspects for up to 14 days without charge. In November it was reported that Australian police had averted a potential terrorist attack by Islamist extremists upon an unspecified target in the country, arresting a number of suspects in operations in Sydney and Melbourne. Meanwhile, the Senate had approved amendments to existing anti-terrorism legislation, enabling police to intervene at any stage of terrorist planning, and to charge suspects without evidence of a specific terrorist act.

In September 2008 the Supreme Court of Victoria convicted Abdul Nacer Benbrika, a Muslim cleric of Algerian origin, and six of his followers on charges of membership of a terrorist organization, which in 2005 had plotted attacks against sporting events in Melbourne in an attempt to effect the withdrawal of Australian troops from Iraq. The convictions were the culmination of Australia's largest and most protracted trial on terrorism-related charges to date, with the proceedings representing a significant test case in the so-called 'war on terror' (see below). In February 2009 Benbrika was sentenced to a prison term of 15 years.

In Melbourne in August 2009 five men were arrested in a counter-terrorism operation by the police and charged with planning a suicide attack on an army barracks in Sydney, apparently motivated by opposition to Australia's military involvement in Iraq and Afghanistan. Three of the accused were found guilty in December 2010, and in December 2011 they were sentenced to 18 years' imprisonment. In another terrorism-related trial in Sydney five Islamists, who had been arrested in September 2005, were convicted in October 2009 of conspiring to commit a terrorist act. In February 2010 the men received maximum prison sentences.

Relations with the United Kingdom

In March 1986 Australia's constitutional links with the United Kingdom were reduced by the Australia Act, which abolished the British Parliament's residual legislative, executive and judicial controls over Australian state law. In February 1992, shortly after a visit by Queen Elizabeth II, Prime Minister Keating caused a furore by accusing the United Kingdom of abandoning Australia to the Japanese threat during the Second World War. In September 1993 Keating announced that, subject to approval by referendum, Australia was to become a republic by 2001. Although John Howard personally favoured the retention of the monarchy, in 1996 the new Prime Minister announced plans for a constitutional convention, which met in February 1998 and endorsed proposals to adopt a republican system and to replace the British monarch as head of state; however, delegates were divided over the method of election of a future head of state. At the subsequent referendum on the issue, conducted in November 1999, 55% of voters supported the retention of the monarchy (although opinion polls had indicated that more than two-thirds of Australians would support the introduction of a republican system of government if the President were to be directly elected). Moreover, 61% of voters expressed opposition to a proposal to include a preamble to the Constitution, recognizing Aboriginals as 'the nation's first people'.

In June 2001 the Anglican Archbishop of Brisbane, Peter Hollingworth, was sworn in as Governor-General, succeeding Sir William Deane. In May 2003, however, Hollingworth resigned, after criticism that he had deliberately concealed alleged cases of child abuse by the clergy in Queensland. The former Governor of Western Australia, Maj.-Gen. Michael Jeffery, was sworn in as the country's new Governor-General in August.

In December 2003 the High Court ruled that long-term British residents without Australian citizenship who committed a crime in Australia could be deported to the United Kingdom. The judgment overruled the special status held by British residents, according to which they did not have to take Australian citizenship, and declared that any non-citizen who had arrived in the country after 26 January 1949 would henceforth be considered a foreign alien for immigration purposes.

At the Australia 2020 Summit convened in April 2008 (see The Rudd administration, 2007–10) proposals for a popular consultation on the establishment of a republic were renewed, with a further referendum on the issue being envisaged. On 5 September Quentin Bryce was formally inaugurated as Governor-General, replacing Maj.-Gen. Jeffery. Bryce, who had previously served as Governor of Queensland, was the first woman to occupy the post since its inception in 1901. Debate over whether Australia should become a republic was revived in January 2010 with the visit of Prince William, second-in-line to the British throne, to Australia. In October 2011 Queen Elizabeth paid an 11-day visit to Australia, the 16th of her reign, during which she opened a meeting of Commonwealth heads of government in Perth.

In February 2010, following the issue of an apology to the 'forgotten Australians' by the Australian Prime Minister in November of the previous year, the United Kingdom formally apologized for its role in the dispatch of thousands of children to Australia under the Child Migrants Programme, a policy of white emigration that had operated until the late 1960s. Taken from British orphanages or poor families, many children had been subjected to mental and physical abuse in Australian institutions, often being deprived of adequate education.

Foreign Affairs

While retaining strong links with the United Kingdom and the USA, from the 1980s Australia placed increasing emphasis on its relations with Asia. The Australian Government initiated the creation of Asia-Pacific Economic Cooperation (APEC, see p. 201), a forum to facilitate the exchange of services, tourism and direct foreign investment in the region. The inaugural APEC conference took place in Canberra in November 1989, and numerous APEC meetings of ministers and officials occur each year. From 2010 11 of the 21 members of APEC (Australia, Brunei, Canada, Chile, Malaysia, Mexico, New Zealand, Peru, Singapore, the USA and Viet Nam) conducted negotiations on a Trans-Pacific Partnership with the aim of eventually forming a free trade area. Negotiations were stalled in early 2014 as the USA and Japan were unable to reach an agreement over agricultural products and vehicles. In October 2012 a consultative body commissioned by the Australian Government issued a document entitled 'Australia in the Asian Century', examining the potential for expanding Australia's regional role and building on its relations with Asian countries, through economic links and collaboration in the fields of science, technology, energy, education and culture.

Relations with South-East Asia

In November 2004 it was announced that Australia, New Zealand and the members of the Association of Southeast Asian Nations (ASEAN, see p. 211) were to commence negotiations on a free trade agreement. In December, however, Australia provoked tensions with South-East Asia when it proposed the creation of a coastal security zone extending five times as far as its territorial waters. Under this counter-terrorist measure, which took effect in March 2005, all ships entering the 1,000-nautical mile zone would be monitored, with Australian naval and customs ships given powers to intercept and board all vessels suspected of constituting a terrorist threat. Nevertheless, in December 2005 Australia acceded to ASEAN's Treaty of Amity and Co-operation. The free trade agreement was signed in February 2009.

Australian relations with Indonesia, which had been strained since the Indonesian annexation of the former Portuguese colony of East Timor in 1976, improved in August 1985, when Prime Minister Hawke made a statement recognizing Indonesian sovereignty over the territory. In December 1989 Australia and Indonesia signed an accord regarding joint exploration for petroleum and gas reserves in the Timor Gap (an area of sea forming a disputed boundary between the two countries). In April 1992 Prime Minister Paul Keating's visit to Indonesia aroused controversy, owing to the repercussions of the massacre of unarmed civilians in Dili, East Timor, by Indonesian troops in November 1991. In July 1995, as a result of strong opposition in Australia, Indonesia was obliged to withdraw the appointment as ambassador to Canberra of a former Chief of the General Staff of the Armed Forces. Nevertheless, in December Australia and Indonesia unexpectedly signed a joint security treaty. In March 1997 the two countries signed a treaty defining their seabed and 'economic zone' boundaries.

Meanwhile, the investigation into the deaths of six Australia-based journalists in East Timor in 1975 had been reopened, and in June 1996 a government report concluded that they had been murdered by Indonesian soldiers. In August 1998 the International Commission of Jurists, the Geneva-based human rights organization, reported that five of the six journalists had been murdered in an East Timorese village in October 1975 in an attempt to conceal the invasion of the territory, while the sixth man was killed in Dili in December of that year. Furthermore, it was claimed that the Australian embassy in Jakarta had been aware of the forthcoming invasion of East Timor but had failed to give adequate warning to the journalists. In late 1998 Australia announced that its judicial inquiry was to be reopened. Government documents declassified in late 2000 proved conclusively that Australian officials had prior knowledge of Indonesia's plans to invade East Timor. In September 2009 the Australian police opened a war crimes investigation into the killings of the five journalists in 1975.

In January 1999, in a significant shift in its policy, Australia announced that henceforth it would support eventual self-determination for East Timor. A rapid escalation of violence followed a referendum held in August, when the territory's people voted overwhelmingly in favour of independence. Thousands of refugees were airlifted to safety in northern Australia. With a commitment of 4,500 troops in its largest operation since the Viet Nam War, Australia took a leading role in the deployment of a multinational peacekeeping force in East Timor. In November 2000 the Australian Government agreed to help create an East Timor defence force, contributing some US $26m. over five years and providing training for police officers and border guards.

East Timor became independent, as Timor-Leste, in May 2002. In December Timor-Leste's Parliament ratified a treaty with Australia on production, profit-sharing and royalty and tax distribution from oil and gas reserves. However, relations were made difficult by disagreements over the maritime boundaries in the Timor Sea. In January 2006 the two countries finally signed an agreement to share the revenue from the Greater Sunrise oil and gas field equally between them, but the accord was criticized for including a condition that a final decision regarding the disputed maritime boundaries be postponed for at least 50 years. In October the two Governments agreed to ensure bilateral co-operation in security operations in the Joint Petroleum Development Area.

In May 2006, following looting and violence in Dili, Australia responded to a request for assistance from the Timorese Government by leading an International Stabilisation Force (ISF), comprising approximately 2,500 troops, drawn from Australia (its contingent numbering 1,800), New Zealand, Malaysia and Portugal. In August the UN Integrated Mission in Timor-Leste (UNMIT) was established. Also in August, the Australian Government announced the expansion of its army and police force in order to deal with security issues in South-East Asia and the Pacific region. In November 2012 it was announced that the ISF was concluding its operations, and was to be fully withdrawn by April 2013, but the Australian Government undertook to continue a programme of defence co-operation with Timor-Leste and to provide support for the country's police force. UNMIT completed its mandate at the end of 2012.

In December 2013 a hearing began at the Permanent Court of Arbitration in The Hague, Netherlands, concerning Timor-Leste's claim that its agreement with Australia on sharing resources (see above) had been invalidated by the actions of the Australian intelligence service: it was alleged that in 2004 Australian agents had placed listening devices in the Timor-Leste government offices, thereby obtaining an unfair commercial advantage for Australia in negotiations. In December 2013 the Timor-Leste Government demanded an explanation for a raid on the office of the lawyer representing Timor-Leste by members of the Australian intelligence service, who allegedly seized documents and data pertaining to the case. In March 2014 the court ruled that Australia should cease spying on communications between Timor-Leste officials and its legal advisers and banned it from using the documents obtained in December 201, which were ordered to be kept 'under seal'.

Meanwhile, the increasing numbers of asylum seekers attempting to enter Australia by boat via Indonesia became a contentious issue. At an international forum on the issue of people-smuggling in February 2002, delegates agreed to pursue a 12-month programme, which included imposing stricter law enforcement and better information and intelligence-sharing, to combat smuggling and illegal immigration. Officials from Australia, Indonesia and Timor-Leste held the first trilateral discussions on future co-operation on the Indonesian island of Bali.

In November 2006 the Australian Minister for Foreign Affairs, Alexander Downer, and his Indonesian counterpart signed a treaty informally known as the Lombok Agreement, providing for the strengthening of bilateral relations and increased security co-operation. The treaty succeeded the bilateral defence pact of 1995 and entered into force in February 2008.

In 2009, as the number of asylum seekers entering Australian waters via Indonesia continued to increase, discussions between the two countries took place on how best to co-operate in apprehending people-smugglers. Relations were tested in October when a group of Tamil asylum seekers from Sri Lanka was rescued from a sinking vessel in Indonesian waters by an Australian ship and taken to the Indonesian island of Bintan, where they refused to disembark, demanding to be taken to Australia for processing. After four weeks the Tamils finally agreed to be transferred to an Indonesian detention centre. All 78 asylum seekers were subsequently found to be genuine refugees, and were resettled in Australia and elsewhere.

In November 2010 the recently appointed Australian Prime Minister, Julia Gillard, paid a visit to Indonesia, during which she undertook to provide $A500m. for education in Indonesia over the next five years, and the two Governments agreed to begin negotiations on a Comprehensive Economic Partnership Agreement (CEPA), to cover trade, economic co-operation and investment: formal negotiations on the CEPA began in September 2012. In January 2012, meanwhile, the agreement on free trade between ASEAN members, Australia and New Zealand (see above) entered into force for Indonesia. Under the accord, 92% of Australian exports to Indonesia and 99% of Indonesian exports to Australia would eventually be tariff-free.

Despite an undertaking by the Australian Government to provide extra assistance for search and rescue operations in Indonesian waters, the number of 'irregular maritime arrivals' in Australia, mostly via Indonesia, increased from 69 boats carrying 4,565 passengers in 2011 to 278 boats carrying 17,202 passengers in 2012, with 218 such boats, carrying

15,182 passengers, arriving between January and mid-July 2013, while unknown numbers of lives were lost when vessels capsized en route. The new Australian Government which took office in September 2013, led by Tony Abbott, undertook to implement a stricter deterrent policy, 'Operation Sovereign Borders', including the use of the Australian navy to enforce the return of intercepted boats to Indonesia. The Indonesian Government expressed concern that such actions could violate its own national sovereignty. In November the Indonesian Government demanded an explanation for reports that Australian embassies had been used for US espionage activities in Asia, and in the same month Indonesia recalled its ambassador and suspended military co-operation following allegations that (in 2009) the Australian intelligence services had intercepted telephone calls made by President Yudhoyono, his wife and senior ministers. Abbott declined to apologize or comment on intelligence matters, but emphasized the importance of Australia's relationship with Indonesia. In January 2014 the Australian Government apologized for inadvertently violating Indonesian sovereignty when Australian naval vessels entered Indonesian waters during operations to turn back asylum seekers.

A bilateral trade and investment agreement with Malaysia took effect in January 1998. During 1999 Australia was critical of the continued detention and the trials of Anwar Ibrahim, the former Deputy Prime Minister and Minister of Finance. After Prime Minister Howard stated in December 2002 that he would be prepared to conduct pre-emptive strikes on militant organizations in neighbouring countries suspected of planning terrorist attacks on Australia, Malaysia warned that any incursion into its territory would be considered as an act of war. Relations with Malaysia appeared to improve following the succession of Abdullah Ahmad Badawi to the premiership of that country in October. In June 2004, during a visit to Malaysia by the Australian Minister for Foreign Affairs, agreement was reached to hold formal annual talks with his Malaysian counterpart. In April 2005 Prime Minister Abdullah Badawi visited Australia, the first visit to the country by a Malaysian leader in more than 20 years, and the two Governments agreed to begin negotiations on a bilateral free trade agreement. Australia's increasing involvement in regional affairs was emphasized by its attendance at the inaugural East Asia Summit meeting, held in Kuala Lumpur, Malaysia, in December. A bilateral agreement concluded in July 2011, under which Australia would send asylum seekers to Malaysia for processing in return for accepting refugees from Malaysia, provoked considerable controversy and was ruled unlawful by the Australian High Court in August (see The Gillard and Rudd administrations 2010–13). The bilateral free trade agreement was concluded in May 2012 and entered into force in January 2013, whereupon Australia eliminated tariffs on all imports from Malaysia, while Malaysia abolished tariffs on 97.6% of goods imported from Australia (increasing to 99% by 2017). In November 2013 Malaysia made an official protest to Australia following reports that Australian diplomatic missions in Asia had been used by the US security services for intercepting data.

Restrictions on travel and financial transactions by members of Myanmar's ruling bodies were imposed by Australia in 1990, owing to concerns about democracy and human rights in that country. In October 2002 the Australian Minister for Foreign Affairs met Myanma government officials and the opposition leader, Aung Sang Suu Kyi, for discussions, during the first visit to Myanmar by an Australian minister for nearly 20 years. In October 2009 the Australian chargé d'affaires in Myanmar, along with diplomats from the United Kingdom and the USA, was permitted to hold discussions with Suu Kyi in Yangon, Myanmar, in the first such meeting between an Australian representative and the opposition leader since February 2003. The Australian Government expressed serious reservations about the circumstances that surrounded the holding of elections in Myanmar in November 2010. However, following progress towards democratic reform in Myanmar, in June 2012 it was announced that Australia was to end its sanctions (while retaining an embargo on the supply of arms) and to increase its annual aid to Myanmar to $A100m. by 2015. During an official visit to Australia by the Myanma head of state, President Thein Sein, in March 2013, the Australian Government undertook to reduce restrictions on defence co-operation (although not on weapons supply) and to provide finance for strengthening democratic institutions.

Relations with East Asia

By the early 21st century China had become one of Australia's most important trading partners, overtaking Japan in 2009 as the country's principal market for exports (chiefly iron ore and coal). Following his election in 2013, Prime Minister Abbott declared his intention to sign bilateral trade deals with China, the Republic of Korea (South Korea) and Japan in 2014.

In June 2010 the Chinese Vice-President, Xi Jinping, paid an official visit to Australia, during which agreements were concluded on Chinese investment in major Australian mining projects, and Xi reaffirmed China's commitment to the future conclusion of a free trade agreement with Australia, which had first been mooted in 2005. The Chinese Government gave a guarded response to the announcement in November that US military personnel were to be stationed in northern Australia (see below), declaring that their deployment might not be 'appropriate'. In March 2012 the central banks of Australia and China concluded a currency swap agreement, permitting the exchange of the two currencies up to the value of $A30,000m. over a three-year period, in order to facilitate bilateral trade and investment. In November 2013 the Australian Government officially expressed its disapproval of China's recent declaration of an air defence identification zone affecting flights over an area of the East China Sea that is claimed by both China and Japan.

Japan is another major trading partner, Australia's second largest export market (after China) since 2009. In April 2014 negotiations on a bilateral trade agreement that had begun in 2007 were completed. Australia agreed to lower tariffs on electronic products, vehicles and white goods, while Japan was to reduce tariffs on Australian beef and raise the duty-free quota for dairy products. The deal was expected to be signed later in the year.

Australia's relations with Japan were strained in the late 1990s by a fishing dispute relating to the latter's failure to curb its catches of the endangered southern bluefin tuna, as agreed in a treaty of 1993, to which New Zealand was also a signatory. In August 1999, however, an international tribunal ruled in favour of Australia and New Zealand. Another cause of contention was Japan's continued hunting of whales in the Southern Ocean, ostensibly for scientific purposes, as permitted by an agreement imposing a moratorium on commercial whaling, which had been concluded by the members of the International Whaling Commission (IWC) in 1982. A serious confrontation in Australian territorial waters between an anti-whaling organization, Sea Shepherd, and the Japanese whaling fleet occurred in January 2010, when Japanese whaling officials denied accusations that a speedboat belonging to Sea Shepherd had been deliberately rammed by a patrol vessel. At a meeting of the IWC in June the Australian delegation successfully argued against a proposal to reverse the ban on commercial whaling, and the Australian Government announced that it would apply to the International Court of Justice (ICJ) to prevent Japan from hunting whales for the purposes of scientific research. In January 2013 the Australian Government officially protested to Japan after a Japanese whaling vessel entered Australian waters in the Southern Ocean; further confrontations took place in February between Australian-registered Sea Shepherd vessels and Japanese whaling ships. Public hearings on the case before the ICJ commenced in June. At the end of March 2014 the ICJ ruled that Japan should halt its whaling programme in the Antarctic as it had not sufficiently justified that the quotas it set were necessary for the purposes of scientific research. Japan agreed to comply with the ruling.

In May 2000 diplomatic relations between Australia and the Democratic People's Republic of Korea (DPRK—North Korea), which had been severed in 1975, were restored. Discussions between the two nations, initiated by the North Korean Government in April 1999, had been dominated by the International Atomic Energy Agency's concerns over nuclear facilities and long-range missile testing. Plans to open an embassy in North Korea were deferred in late 2002, however, owing to North Korea's efforts to reactivate its nuclear weapons programme. Australian development assistance to the DPRK was suspended in 2002, except for humanitarian assistance provided through multilateral organizations. In October 2006 North Korea's announcement that it had conducted its first test of a nuclear weapon prompted Australia to impose sanctions against the DPRK, including the prohibition of access to assets by designated individuals, and to ban North Korean ships from its ports. In early 2008 the North Korean embassy in Canberra was closed, apparently for financial reasons: a request to reopen it was received by the Australian Government in January 2013, but following a further nuclear test by North Korea in February discussions on the reopening were suspended.

South Korea is among Australia's principal trading partners. During her official visit to East Asia in April 2011, Prime Minister Gillard's discussions with the South Korean leadership emphasized the importance of a proposed bilateral free trade agreement: negotiations on the agreement reached a conclusion in December 2013 and the Australia Korea Free Trade Agreement, which included the removal of tariffs on primary products, was signed in April 2014. The two countries' navies conducted an inaugural bilateral maritime exercise in May 2012.

Relations with New Zealand and the Pacific islands

The relationship between the Governments of Australia and New Zealand is close, with frequent meetings of ministers and exchanges of officials. In addition to defence links under the ANZUS treaty (see below), the two countries conduct bilateral free trade in goods and services under the Australia-New Zealand Closer Economic Relations Trade Agreement, which entered into force in 1983.

Australia plays an important role among the developing Pacific island nations in terms of development assistance, trade and security co-operation. Its relations with neighbouring Pacific island states have none the less been intermittently strained. At a meeting of the South Pacific Forum (now Pacific Islands Forum, see p. 416) in September 1997, the member countries failed to reach agreement on a common policy regarding mandatory targets for the reduction of emissions of greenhouse gases. The low-lying nation of Tuvalu was particularly critical of Australia's refusal to compromise, the Australian Prime Minister declaring that the Pacific islands' concerns over rising sea levels were exaggerated.

Australia's relations with Papua New Guinea were strained in early 1997 as a result of the latter's decision to engage the services of a group of foreign mercenaries in the Government's operations against secessionists on the island of Bougainville. In early 1998 a permanent ceasefire agreement between the Papua New Guinea Government and the Bougainville secessionists was signed in New Zealand. Australia reaffirmed its commitment to the provision of a peace-monitoring force. Since 1998 both Canberra and Townsville, in Queensland, had provided a neutral venue for negotiations regarding the Bougainville issue, and in August 2001 the Minister for Foreign Affairs, Alexander Downer, signed the Bougainville Peace Agreement as a witness. In October the Government concluded an agreement with Papua New Guinea for that country to accommodate 223 asylum seekers in exchange for $A1m. In December 2003 the Australian Government announced its intention to send around 300 police officers and civil servants to Papua New Guinea as part of a five-year operation to counter crime and corruption. In July 2004 the National Parliament of Papua New Guinea approved legislation allowing the deployment of the Australian police officers and officials; the first contingent of police officers arrived in Bougainville in September. However, in May 2005, following a ruling by the Papua New Guinea Supreme Court that the deployment violated the Constitution, the police officers were withdrawn from the country.

In March 2008 Kevin Rudd visited Papua New Guinea for discussions with Sir Michael Somare. The two Prime Ministers committed themselves to a partnership to reduce carbon emissions resulting from deforestation. The Australian Prime Minister announced a $A38m. increase in aid to Papua New Guinea (in addition to the annual allocation of more than $A355m.). Rudd also announced a new policy for the development of the Pacific islands, embodied in the Port Moresby Declaration. This manifesto of 20 objectives confirmed the Australian Government's commitment to developing partnerships in the region and its assistance in addressing the challenges confronting the Pacific islands in areas such as governance, public services, economic development and climate change. In September 2012 the Governments of Australia and Papua New Guinea signed a memorandum of understanding on the establishment of a regional processing centre for asylum seekers on Manus Island, in Papua New Guinea, with the first group of asylum seekers arriving from Australia in November; a similar agreement was reached with Nauru. In July 2013 a 'Regional Settlement Arrangement' was concluded by the two Governments, whereby asylum seekers were to be both processed and (if found to be genuinely eligible) permanently resettled in Papua New Guinea, which was to receive additional Australian aid in exchange. The UN High Commissioner for Refugees expressed concern at the agreement, citing a lack of relevant expertise in Papua New Guinea's legal system and inadequate physical conditions.

Australia played a leading role in the aftermath of a coup in Solomon Islands in June 2000. The Australian navy dispatched a warship to assist in the evacuation of Australian and other nationals from the islands, while a similar ship anchored off shore served as a venue for negotiations between the two warring ethnic militias. The Australian Minister for Foreign Affairs led an international delegation with the aim of facilitating discussions between the factions. In October a peace agreement was signed in Townsville, which ended the two-year conflict; it was qualified and complemented by the Marau Peace Agreement, signed in February 2001. The Australian Government subsequently led an International Peace Monitoring Team. Australia provided financial and technical support for democratic elections held in December 2001. In July 2003 an Australian-led regional peacekeeping force was deployed in Solomon Islands to restore law and order. The Regional Assistance Mission to Solomon Islands (RAMSI) was welcomed by the islanders, and at the end of the year the operation was judged to have been a success. In 2006, however, following a dispute concerning the Solomon Islands Attorney-General, Julian Moti, who was due to answer criminal charges in Australia, Prime Minister Manasseh Sogavare of Solomon Islands warned Australia that repeated extradition requests might lead to the expulsion of Australian peacekeepers from the country. Relations deteriorated further when Australian peacekeepers forcibly entered Sogavare's office in search of evidence relating to the Moti affair. At the Pacific Islands Forum meeting soon afterwards, Sogavare acted to diminish Australia's role in RAMSI; the Forum decided instead to establish a task force to evaluate its operations. In September 2007 Australia's extradition request for Julian Moti was formally rejected by the Solomon Islands Government. However, following Sogavare's removal from office in December and his replacement by Derek Sikua, Moti was dismissed as Attorney-General, and the extradition request was subsequently granted. In December 2011, however, the Australian High Court granted a permanent stay of proceedings in the case against Moti, ruling that correct procedures had not been followed during the extradition process.

In March 2008 Prime Minister Rudd visited Solomon Islands and expressed gratitude for Prime Minister Sikua's continued support for the RAMSI peacekeeping force, announcing additional Australian aid of $A14m. for the purposes of rural development. Sikua welcomed the Australian Prime Minister's announcement of the Port Moresby Declaration on his recent visit to Papua New Guinea (see above). In August 2010 Australia provided a group of observers, under the auspices of the Pacific Islands Forum, to monitor the general election in Solomon Islands. In February 2011 the Australian Government firmly denied allegations made by the office of the recently appointed Prime Minister of Solomon Islands, Danny Philip, that Australia had supported efforts by the country's opposition to eject him from his post. As a result of the improved security situation, the military element of RAMSI, the Australian-led Combined Task Force, was gradually withdrawn between July and September 2013.

In November 2006 pro-democracy protests in the Tongan capital, Nuku'alofa, led to serious rioting and the destruction of numerous buildings; several people were killed in the violence. In response to an appeal from the Tongan Government, Australian and New Zealand security forces, including 50 soldiers and 35 police officers from Australia, were deployed in Tonga to restore stability. As well as ongoing development assistance, Australia provided technical and financial support for the elections held in Tonga in November 2010; it also provides patrol vessels for the Tonga Defence Services, and supports a police development programme.

The Australian Government responded to the military coup in Fiji in December 2006 by suspending military co-operation with the country and by banning those associated with the leader of the coup, Cdre Frank Bainimarama, from travelling to and via Australia. The Government's sanctions against Fiji were extended to incorporate a suspension of aid to several sectors, excluding health and education. Following the abrogation of the Constitution by the Fijian President in April 2009, Australia demonstrated support for the country's suspension from the Commonwealth. In November 2009 Fiji expelled the envoys of Australia and New Zealand; in response, their Fijian counterparts were also expelled. The Australian Government expressed deep disappointment at Fiji's actions. In July 2010 Fiji expelled

Australia's acting high commissioner, claiming that Australia had used its influence to persuade Vanuatu to cancel a meeting of the Melanesian Spearhead Group, at which Bainimarama had been expected to assume the chair of the regional organization. In July 2012, acknowledging that Fiji was making progress towards the restoration of democracy, Australia agreed to resume full diplomatic relations.

In October 2010 the Australian Government affirmed its commitment to the liberalization of regional trade through the Pacific Agreement on Closer Economic Relations (PACER), being negotiated by members of the Pacific Islands Forum. The initiative is known as PACER Plus. Negotiations, which were ongoing in early 2014, covered not only trade in goods and services, but also labour mobility, development assistance, rules of origin, customs procedures, sanitary and phytosanitary measures, and investment. Australia provided support for small island nations participating in the negotiations, such as training officials and providing funding for them to attend PACER Plus meetings.

Other external relations

The ANZUS Security Treaty was signed in 1951 and entered into force in 1952, linking Australia, New Zealand and the USA. The treaty's viability was disputed by the US Government following the New Zealand Government's declaration in July 1984 that vessels believed to be powered by nuclear energy, or to be carrying nuclear weapons, would be barred from the country's ports. Prime Minister Hawke did not support the New Zealand initiative, and Australia continued to participate with the USA in joint military exercises from which New Zealand had been excluded. In February 1994 the USA announced its decision to resume senior-level contacts with New Zealand. Prime Minister John Howard condemned the terrorist attacks against the USA in September 2001 and subsequently expressed his support for the USA's 'war on terror'. Australia subsequently became the largest contributor among nations not belonging to the North Atlantic Treaty Organization (NATO) to the NATO-led International Security Assistance Force (ISAF) in Afghanistan. In early 2003 some 2,000 Australian troops were deployed to the Middle East in preparation for the US-led military campaign to oust the regime of Saddam Hussain in Iraq. Australia's full, formal withdrawal from Iraq took place at the end of July 2009 under Prime Minister Rudd, in accordance with his 2007 electoral pledge.

The Australian military involvement in Afghanistan continued, with 1,094 personnel deployed there in December 2012 (compared with 1,550 in January), including task forces for mentoring and reconstruction. The withdrawal of Australian members of ISAF was completed by the end of 2013. By that time 40 members of the Australian armed forces had lost their lives in Afghanistan and 261 had been seriously injured. About 400 military personnel were to remain in Afghanistan in training and support roles. Australia was to contribute US $100m. annually for three years from 2015 towards the costs of the Afghan security forces, as well as providing support for economic development.

Annual joint consultations take place between the Australian and US ministers responsible for foreign affairs and defence. During a visit to Australia by the US President, Barack Obama, in November 2011, to celebrate the 60th anniversary of the ANZUS pact, it was announced that 2,500 US military personnel were to be permanently stationed in Darwin, in the Northern Territory, as part of the expansion of the USA's role as a 'Pacific power'. The first contingent of US military personnel arrived in Darwin in April 2012. In November it was announced that the proposed joint space monitoring centre would be established in Western Australia by 2014.

Owing to Australian opposition to French testing of nuclear weapons at Mururoa Atoll (French Polynesia) in the South Pacific Ocean, a ban on uranium sales to France was introduced in 1983. However, in August 1986 the Government announced its decision to resume uranium exports. In December Australia ratified a treaty declaring the South Pacific area a nuclear-free zone. France's decision, in April 1992, to suspend its nuclear-testing programme was welcomed by Australia. In June 1995, however, the French President's announcement that the programme was to be resumed provoked outrage throughout the Pacific region. The Australian ambassador to France was recalled, and the French consulate in Perth was destroyed in an arson attack. Further widespread protests followed the first of the new series of tests in September. Australia's relations with the United Kingdom were strained by the British Government's refusal to join the condemnation of France's policy. The final test was conducted in January 1996. A ban on new contracts for the supply of uranium to France, imposed in September 1995, was removed in October 1996. Meanwhile, Australia remained committed to achieving the elimination of all nuclear testing. In August, following a veto of the draft text by India and Iran at the UN Conference on Disarmament in Geneva, Switzerland, Australia took the initiative in leading an international effort to secure the passage of the Comprehensive Test Ban Treaty, approved by the UN General Assembly in September.

In January 2008 the new Australian Government reinstated the ban on sales of uranium to India, owing to that country's continued refusal to sign the Treaty on the Non-Proliferation of Nuclear Weapons (NPT). Australia's long-standing ban had been removed by the Howard administration in August of the previous year. In December 2011 the Australian Government agreed to remove the ban on uranium exports to India on the grounds that, although not a signatory of the NPT, India had undertaken to observe limits on the use of nuclear power similar to those imposed by the treaty. In July 2012 it was reported that India had superseded China and the United Kingdom as the principal source of permanent migration to Australia during the year to June, accounting for 15.7% (or about 29,000) of the total number of immigrants.

CONSTITUTION AND GOVERNMENT

Australia comprises six states and three territories. Executive power is vested in the British monarch and exercised by the monarch's appointed representative, the Governor-General, who normally acts on the advice of the Federal Executive Council (the Ministry), led by the Prime Minister. The Governor-General officially appoints the Prime Minister and, on the latter's recommendation, other Ministers.

Legislative power is vested in the Federal Parliament. This consists of the monarch, represented by the Governor-General, and two chambers elected by universal adult suffrage (voting is compulsory). The Senate has 76 members (12 from each state and two each from the Northern Territory and the Australian Capital Territory), who are elected by a system of proportional representation for six years when representing a state, with half the seats renewable every three years, and for a term of three years when representing a territory. The House of Representatives has 150 members, elected for three years (subject to dissolution) from single-member constituencies. The Federal Executive Council is responsible to Parliament.

Each state has a Governor, representing the monarch, and its own legislative, executive and judicial system. The state governments are essentially autonomous, but certain powers are placed under the jurisdiction of the Federal Government. All states except Queensland have an upper house (the Legislative Council) and a lower house (the Legislative Assembly or House of Assembly). The chief ministers of the states are known as Premiers, as distinct from the Federal Prime Minister. The Northern Territory (self-governing since 1978) and the Australian Capital Territory (self-governing since 1988) have unicameral legislatures, and each has a government led by a Chief Minister. The Jervis Bay Territory is not self-governing.

REGIONAL AND INTERNATIONAL CO-OPERATION

Australia is a member of the Asian Development Bank (ADB, see p. 207), the Pacific Islands Forum (see p. 416), the Pacific Community (see p. 412) and the Colombo Plan (see p. 449). In 1989 Australia played a major role in the creation of Asia-Pacific Economic Cooperation (APEC, see p. 201), a grouping that aimed to promote economic development in the region. Australia is a member of the UN's Economic and Social Commission for Asia and the Pacific (ESCAP, see p. 28).

Australia was a founder member of the UN in 1945, and commenced a two-year mandate as a non-permanent member of the UN Security Council on 1 January 2013. As a contracting party to the General Agreement on Tariffs and Trade, Australia joined the World Trade Organization (WTO, see p. 434) on its establishment in 1995. The country participates in the Group of 20 (G20, see p. 456) major industrialized and systemically important emerging market nations. Australia's presidency of the G20 was to extend from 1 December 2013 to 30 November 2014. Australia is also a member of the Organisation for Economic Co-operation and Development (OECD, see p. 379), the Cairns Group (see p. 505) of agricultural exporters and the International Grains Council (see p. 446).

ECONOMIC AFFAIRS

In 2012, according to estimates by the World Bank, Australia's gross national income (GNI), measured at average 2010–12 prices, was US $1,351,246m., equivalent to US $59,570 per head (or US $43,300 per head on an international purchasing-power parity basis). During 2003–12, it was estimated, the population increased at an average annual rate of 1.5%, while gross domestic product (GDP) per head increased, in real terms, by an average of 1.6%. Overall GDP increased, in real terms, at an average annual rate of 3.1% in 2003–12, according to the World Bank; GDP increased by 3.4% in 2012. In 2012/13, according to chain linked methodologies, GDP rose by 2.6%.

Agriculture (including forestry, hunting and fishing) contributed 2.4% of GDP in 2012/13. The sector engaged 2.8% of the employed labour force in November 2012. In the first decade of the 21st century agricultural production was severely affected by drought conditions, although rainfall in most of the country was significantly above average in 2010–11, with flooding causing damage to crops. The principal crops are wheat, fruit, sugar and cotton. Wheat production reached 29.9m. metric tons in 2012. Australia is the world's leading producer of wool. Export earnings from wool and sheepskins totalled $A2,869m. in 2012/13. Australia has become one of the world's largest exporters of wine. The value of wine exports was $A1,852m. in the 12 months to December 2012. Meat production is also important; beef is Australia's leading meat export. According to World Bank estimates, agricultural GDP increased at an average annual rate of 5.4% in 2003–12, rising by 7.4% in 2012. According to chain linked methodologies, sectoral GDP increased by 1.0% in 2011/12, but declined by 5.5% in 2012/13.

Industry (comprising mining, manufacturing, construction and utilities) employed 20.6% of the working population in November 2012, and provided 27.1% of GDP in 2012/13. Industrial GDP increased at an average rate of 2.5% per year between 2003 and 2012, according to World Bank estimates, rising by 2.8% in 2012.

The mining sector employed 2.3% of the working population in November 2012, and contributed 8.6% of GDP in 2012/13. Australia is one of the world's leading exporters of coal. Production of black coal reached 468m. metric tons in 2011. Earnings from coal, coke and briquettes in 2012/13 reached $A38,911m., accounting for 15.6% of total export receipts in that year. Other principal minerals extracted are iron ore, gold, silver and magnesite. Bauxite, zinc, copper, titanium, nickel, tin, lead, zirconium and diamonds are also mined. Production of crude petroleum reached 22,808m. litres in 2010/11. The Gorgon gas project, off the north-western coast, is being developed in collaboration with various overseas companies. Upon completion, the liquefied natural gas (LNG) plant was expected to reach an annual production capacity of 15m. tons of LNG. In 2002–11, according to the UN, the GDP of the mining sector combined with that of utilities increased at an average annual rate of 2.9%. According to chain linked methodologies, the sector's GDP grew by 9.2% in 2012/13.

Manufacturing contributed 7.1% of GDP in 2012/13. The sector employed 8.4% of the working population in November 2012. The principal branches of manufacturing include food, beverages and tobacco, equipment and machinery, chemical products and metal products. According to World Bank estimates, the manufacturing sector's GDP declined at an average annual rate of 0.1% between 2003 and 2012; manufacturing GDP increased by 0.04% in 2011, but declined by 1.1% in 2012. In 2012/13, according to chain linked methodologies, the GDP of the manufacturing sector declined by 1.2%.

Construction contributed 8.3% of GDP in 2012/13. The sector employed 8.7% of the working population in November 2012. In 2002–11, according to the UN, the GDP of the construction sector increased at an average annual rate of 5.1%. According to chain linked methodologies, the GDP of the construction sector grew by 10.7% in 2011/12, but by only 0.5% in 2012/13.

Energy is derived principally from coal and natural gas. Coal accounted for 69.7% and natural gas for 19.4% of electricity production in 2012. Imports of fuels accounted for 17.3% of total import costs in 2012.

The services sector provided 70.5% of GDP in 2012/13, and engaged 76.6% of the employed labour force in November 2012. The tourism industry has become a major source of foreign exchange earnings. The number of visitor arrivals increased by 4.6% in 2012, to 6,145,500. Receipts from international tourism reached an estimated $A25,547m. in 2011/12. According to World Bank estimates, the GDP of the services sector increased at an average annual rate of 3.3% between 2003 and 2012, and rose by 3.3% in 2012.

In 2012 Australia recorded a visible merchandise trade deficit of US $5,212m., and there was a deficit of US $57,037m. on the current account of the balance of payments. In 2012 the People's Republic of China remained the principal source of imports, supplying 18.4%, followed by the USA, Japan and Singapore. China was also the principal market for exports in 2012 (purchasing 29.6% of the total). Other major export markets were Japan, the Republic of Korea and India. The principal exports in 2012 included mineral products, pearls, precious or semi-precious stones, precious metals, and articles thereof (gold in unwrought or semi-manufactured forms), vegetables and vegetable products, iron and steel, other base metals and articles of base metal, and chemicals and related products. The principal imports included machinery and mechanical appliances, electrical equipment parts, mineral products, vehicles, and chemicals and related products.

For the fifth consecutive year a budgetary shortfall was recorded in 2012/13, when the fiscal deficit (including net capital investment) amounted to $A22,484m., equivalent to 1.5% of GDP. General government gross debt totalled $A414.654m. in 2012, equivalent to 27.9% of GDP. At the end of 2012/13 Australia's net foreign debt stood at $A762,173m. (equivalent to 50.1% of GDP), some 73.6% of which was incurred by the private sector. The rate of unemployment was estimated at 6.0% of the labour force in February 2014. According to International Labour Organization estimates, the annual rate of inflation averaged 2.8% in 2003–12. Consumer prices rose by 3.4% in 2011 and by 1.7% in 2012.

The Australian economy proved able to withstand the effects of the global financial crisis that afflicted most developed countries from 2008, and avoided recession. A significant factor was sustained demand from China, a major purchaser of Australian mineral commodities, particularly coal and iron ore. The unprecedented mining 'boom' contrasted, however, with less favourable conditions for the manufacturing sector, exports from which were made less competitive by the continuing strength of the Australian dollar. The Reserve Bank of Australia, the central bank, made successive reductions in the official interest rate from November 2011 onwards, to a record low level of 2.5% in August 2013 (remaining unchanged in March 2014), with the aim of stimulating economic growth by encouraging domestic spending, while still intending to limit inflation to a level of 2%–3%. During 2012 and 2013 unemployment remained relatively low, at less than 6%, and a shortage of skilled labour exerted pressure on wage costs. During the financial year ending 30 June 2012 there was a budgetary deficit for the period equivalent to 3.0% of GDP, owing to a decline in tax receipts from the mining industry and other sectors, while extra expenditure was incurred as compensation for natural disasters and to offset the increased energy costs resulting from carbon pricing. The federal budget for 2012/13 failed to achieve a return to surplus, with the newly introduced and controversial minerals revenue tax (see Domestic Political Affairs) proving much less lucrative than expected, as slowing demand in China and other Asian markets adversely affected income from mining. In December 2013 the recently appointed Government undertook to reduce public spending in order to mitigate what it described as an unsustainable fiscal position. Australia's public debt remained relatively low in proportion to GDP (at less than 30%), compared with that of other developed countries, and its credit rating remained at the highest level. The IMF predicted annual GDP growth increasing from around 2.5% in 2013 to 3% in 2016. With its continuing dependence on the resources sector, however, Australia remained vulnerable to the decrease in the rate of growth in China, the principal market for its minerals, and although the Australian currency depreciated by some 12% in 2013 against the US dollar, a further weakening of the currency was seen as desirable to stimulate exports.

PUBLIC HOLIDAYS*

2015: 1 January (New Year's Day), 26 January (for Australia Day), 3–6 April (Easter), 25 April (Anzac Day), 8 June (Queen's Official Birthday, except Western Australia), 25–26 December (Christmas).

* National holidays only. Some states observe these holidays on different days. There are also numerous individual state holidays.

Statistical Survey

Source (unless otherwise stated): Australian Bureau of Statistics, POB 10, Belconnen, ACT 2616; tel. (2) 6252-7983; fax (2) 6251-6009; internet www.abs.gov.au.

Area and Population

AREA, POPULATION AND DENSITY

Area (sq km)	7,692,024*
Population (census results)†	
8 August 2006	19,855,288
9 August 2011	
Males	10,634,013
Females	10,873,706
Total	21,507,719
Population (official estimate at mid-year)	
2012	22,721,995
Density (per sq km) at mid-2012	3.0

* 2,969,907 sq miles; including Jervis Bay Territory.

† Population is *de jure*; including Jervis Bay Territory, Christmas Island and the Cocos (Keeling) Islands.

POPULATION BY AGE AND SEX

(population at mid-2012)

	Males	Females	Total
0–14	2,206,722	2,093,156	4,299,878
15–64	7,616,949	7,587,113	15,204,062
65 and over	1,486,220	1,731,835	3,218,055
Total	11,309,891	11,412,104	22,721,995

STATES AND TERRITORIES

(official population estimates at mid-2012)

	Area (sq km)	Population	Density (per sq km)
New South Wales (NSW)	800,642	7,305,882	9.1
Victoria	227,416	5,630,855	24.8
Queensland	1,730,648	4,568,414	2.6
South Australia	983,482	1,656,454	1.7
Western Australia	2,529,875	2,434,738	1.0
Tasmania	68,401	512,199	7.5
Northern Territory	1,349,129	235,233	0.2
Australian Capital Territory (ACT)	2,358	375,076	159.1
Other territories*	73	3,144	—
Total	7,692,024	22,721,995	3.0

* Area refers to Jervis Bay Territory only, but population also includes data for Christmas Island and the Cocos (Keeling) Islands.

PRINCIPAL TOWNS

(estimated population mid-2012)*

Sydney (capital of NSW)	4,293,416	Sunshine Coast	286,497
Melbourne (capital of Victoria)	4,086,734	Wollongong	283,243
Brisbane (capital of Queensland)	2,099,328	Hobart (capital of Tasmania)	205,557
Perth (capital of W. Australia)	1,834,184	Geelong	179,689
Adelaide (capital of S. Australia)	1,250,795	Townsville	171,824
Gold Coast-Tweed	592,389	Cairns	142,124
Newcastle	420,850	Darwin (capital of N. Territory)	116,215
Canberra (national capital)	412,049	Toowoomba	110,855

* Figures refer to metropolitan areas, each of which normally comprises a municipality and contiguous urban areas.

BIRTHS, MARRIAGES AND DEATHS*

	Registered live births		Registered marriages		Registered deaths	
	Number	Rate (per 1,000)	Number	Rate (per 1,000)	Number	Rate (per 1,000)
2005	259,791	12.7	109,323	5.4	130,714	6.0
2006	265,949	12.8	114,222	5.5	133,739	6.0
2007	285,213	13.6	116,322	5.5	137,854	6.0
2008	296,621	13.8	118,756	5.5	143,946	6.1
2009	295,738	13.5	120,118	5.5	140,760	5.8
2010	297,903	13.4	121,176	5.4	143,473	5.7
2011	301,617	13.3	121,752	5.4	146,932	5.6
2012	309,582	13.6	n.a.	n.a.	147,098	6.5

* Data are tabulated by year of registration rather than by year of occurrence.

Life expectancy (years at birth): 81.8 (males 79.7; females 84.1) in 2011 (Source: World Bank, World Development Indicators database).

IMMIGRATION AND EMIGRATION

(year ending 30 June)*

	2010/11	2011/12	2012/13
Permanent immigrants	127,470	158,950	152,410
Permanent emigrants	88,470	87,500	91,770

* Figures refer to persons intending to settle in Australia, or Australian residents intending to settle abroad.

EMPLOYMENT

(labour force survey at November, '000 persons aged 15 years and over, excluding armed forces)

	2010	2011	2012
Agriculture, hunting, forestry and fishing	354.0	327.9	320.7
Mining and quarrying	200.8	243.1	259.6
Manufacturing	983.5	950.6	966.5
Electricity, gas and water	144.2	162.7	141.5
Construction	1,042.5	1,033.8	997.4
Wholesale and retail trade	1,652.0	1,650.4	1,654.1
Hotels and restaurants	752.8	751.8	768.1
Transport, storage and communications	800.2	768.0	821.3
Financial intermediation	386.8	413.1	413.1
Real estate, renting and business activities	1,066.0	1,050.4	1,091.8
Administrative and support services	429.8	393.8	395.2
Public administration and defence; compulsory social security	685.0	738.0	690.3
Education	877.2	859.1	912.4
Health and social work	1,286.0	1,350.1	1,386.5
Arts and recreation services	195.8	203.9	205.3
Other services	466.7	456.8	445.4
Total employed	11,323.2	11,353.4	11,469.3

Unemployment (annual averages, '000 persons aged 15 years and over, excluding armed forces): 636.4 in 2010; 610.5 in 2011; 617.3 in 2012.

Health and Welfare

KEY INDICATORS

Total fertility rate (children per woman, 2011)	2.0
Under-5 mortality rate (per 1,000 live births, 2011)	5
HIV/AIDS (% of persons aged 15–49, 2011)	0.2
Physicians (per 1,000 head, 2010)	3.9
Hospital beds (per 1,000 head, 2009)	3.8
Health expenditure (2010): US $ per head (PPP)	3,685
Health expenditure (2010): % of GDP	9.0
Health expenditure (2010): public (% of total)	68.5
Total carbon dioxide emissions ('000 metric tons, 2010)	373,080.6
Carbon dioxide emissions per head (metric tons, 2010)	16.9
Human Development Index (2012): ranking	2
Human Development Index (2012): value	0.938

For sources and definitions, see explanatory note on p. vi.

Agriculture

PRINCIPAL CROPS

('000 metric tons)

	2010	2011	2012
Wheat	22,138.0	27,410.1	29,905.0
Rice, paddy	196.7	723.3	918.7
Barley	7,294.0	7,994.7	8,220.9
Maize	328.0	356.9	450.5
Oats	1,374.0	1,127.7	1,262.0
Millet*	36.9	44.0	45.0
Sorghum	1,598.0	1,934.5	2,238.9
Triticale (wheat-rye hybrid)	502.0	355.1	284.6
Potatoes	1,278.1	1,128.2	1,288.2
Sugar cane	31,457.0	25,181.8	25,957.1
Beans, dry	43.5	65.2	50.0*
Broad beans, dry	250.0*	350.0	425.0†
Peas, dry	280.0	394.7	342.5
Chick peas	602.0	513.3	673.4
Lentils	140.0	379.7	463.0†
Lupins	629.0	807.7	981.5
Soybeans (Soya beans)	59.6	29.8	86.1
Sunflower seed	41.0	42.5	47.0
Rapeseed	2,180.6*	2,358.7	3,427.3
Seed cotton	939.0	2,154.4	2,870.3†
Lettuce and chicory	166.1*	144.6	114.7
Tomatoes	471.9	301.7	371.5
Cauliflower and broccoli	70.9*	66.9	70.0*
Pumpkins, squash and gourds	98.0*	102.9	103.0
Onions, dry	259.9	330.8	346.6
Peas, green	41.9*	30.3	38.0
Carrots and turnips	267.4	224.6	319.2
Watermelons	132.3*	135.6†	140.0*
Cantaloupes and other melons	76.3*	76.3†	80.0*
Bananas	302.2	202.8	285.5
Oranges	391.3	291.2	389.8
Tangerines, mandarins, clementines and satsumas	91.0	97.9	85.1
Apples	264.4	299.8	289.1
Pears	95.1	123.3	119.3
Peaches and nectarines	113.7*	97.5	100.5
Grapes	1,684.4	1,715.7	1,656.6
Pineapples	125.0*	83.2	90.0*

* FAO estimate(s).

† Unofficial figure.

Aggregate production ('000 metric tons, may include official, semi-official or estimated data): Total cereals 33,505.7 in 2010, 39,991.8 in 2011, 43,371.7 in 2012; Total roots and tubers 1,324.1 in 2010, 1,168.7 in 2011, 1,330.2 in 2012; Total vegetables (incl. melons) 1,947.8 in 2010, 1,804.4 in 2011, 1,973.0 in 2012; Total fruits (excl. melons) 3,283.2 in 2010, 3,117.3 in 2011, 3,243.7 in 2012.

Source: FAO.

LIVESTOCK

('000 head at 30 June)

	2010	2011	2012
Horses	258.0*	259.5	265.0*
Cattle	26,733.0	28,506.2	28,418.4
Pigs	2,289.3	2,285.2	2,137.9
Sheep	68,085.5	73,098.8	74,721.6
Goats*	3,500.0	3,500.0	3,550.0
Chickens	83,024	90,744	100,996
Ducks	1,200*	1,000	1,100*
Turkeys	1,200*	1,203	1,205*

* FAO estimate(s).

Source: FAO.

LIVESTOCK PRODUCTS

('000 metric tons)

	2010	2011	2012
Cattle meat	2,108.3	2,109.9	2,125.4
Sheep meat	555.2	512.2	556.4
Goat meat*	25.0	25.0	25.8
Pig meat	335.8	343.4	350.4
Horse meat*	25.8	26.3	26.3
Chicken meat	882.0	1,016.2	1,038.4
Duck meat*	16.8	15.8	15.8
Turkey meat*	22.4	21.7	22.5
Cows' milk	9,023.0	9,101.0	9,480.1
Hen eggs	174.0	205.2	214.7†
Honey	16.2*	10.0†	10.5*
Wool, greasy	352.7	368.3	362.1

* FAO estimate(s).

† Unofficial figure.

Note: Figures for meat and milk refer to the 12 months ending 30 June of the year stated.

Source: FAO.

Forestry

ROUNDWOOD REMOVALS

('000 cubic metres, excl. bark)

	2010	2011	2012
Sawlogs, veneer logs and logs for sleepers	12,160	11,277	10,602
Pulpwood	12,789	14,663	12,482
Other industrial wood	628	627	675
Fuel wood	4,853	4,862	4,745
Total	30,430	31,429	28,504

Source: FAO.

SAWNWOOD PRODUCTION

('000 cubic metres, incl. railway sleepers)

	2009	2010	2011
Coniferous (softwood)	3,740	4,201	3,826
Broadleaved (hardwood)	990	878	730
Total	4,730	5,079	4,556

2012: Production assumed to be unchanged from 2011 (FAO estimates).

Source: FAO.

Fishing

('000 metric tons, live weight, year ending 30 June)

	2008/09	2009/10	2010/11
Capture	171.6	173.2	163.3
Blue grenadier	4.0	3.5	4.0
Clupeoids	31.7	39.7	38.2
Australian spiny lobster	7.6	7.3	6.5
Penaeus shrimps	10.2	7.3	7.2
Scallops	7.6	7.6	6.2
Aquaculture	65.1	71.4*	71.4*
Atlantic salmon	29.9	31.8	35.2
Total catch	236.7	244.6*	234.7*

* FAO estimate.

Note: Figures exclude aquatic plants ('000 metric tons, capture only): 1.6 in 2008/09; 1.9 in 2009/10; 0.4 in 2010/11. Also excluded are crocodiles, recorded by number rather than by weight. The number of estuarine crocodiles caught was: 20,929 in 2008/09; 30,518 in 2009/10; 32,117 in 20110/11. Also excluded are whales, recorded by number rather than weight. The number of Baleen whales caught was: 2 in 2008/09; nil in 2009/10; 1 in 2010/11. The number of toothed whales (incl. dolphins) caught was: 32 in 2008/09; 37 in 2009/10; 40 in 2010/11. Also excluded are pearl oyster shells (metric tons, estimates): 200 each year in 2008/09–2010/11.

Source: FAO.

Mining

(year ending 30 June, '000 metric tons, unless otherwise indicated)

	2007/08	2008/09	2009/10
Black coal	421,181	446,174	471,089
Brown coal*	66,000	68,000	69,000
Crude petroleum (million litres)	25,789	26,950	25,572
Natural gas (million cu m)	39,283	41,499	43,767
Iron ore: gross weight*	324,693	353,163	423,393
Copper ore*†	863	890	819
Nickel ore*†	190	185	160
Bauxite: gross weight	63,463	64,055	67,810
Bauxite: alumina content	19,359	19,597	20,057
Lead ore*†	641	596	617
Zinc ore*†	1,571	1,411	1,362
Tin ore (metric tons)*†	1,631	4,045	19,829
Manganese ore (metallurgical): gross weight*	5,412	3,730	5,795
Ilmenite*	2,208	1,932	1,394
Leucoxene*	157	117	123
Rutile*	327	285	361
Zirconium concentrates*	562	485	408
Silver (metric tons)*†	1,867	1,764	1,809
Uranium (metric tons)†	10,114	10,311	7,156
Gold (metric tons)*†	230	218	240
Salt (unrefined)*†‡	11,243	11,311	11,745
Diamonds ('000 carats, unsorted)	16,528	15,169	11,138

* Estimated production.

† Figures refer to the metal content of ores and concentrates.

‡ Excludes production in Victoria.

Source: Australian Bureau of Agricultural and Resource Economics, *Australian Mineral Statistics* and *Australian Commodity Statistics*.

2011 ('000 metric tons unless otherwise indicated): Black coal 468,000; Brown coal 65,000; Crude petroleum ('000 barrels) 143,456; Natural gas (million cu m) 51,253; Iron ore: gross weight 488,000; Copper ore 958; Nickel ore 212; Bauxite: gross weight 69,976; Bauxite: alumina content 19,399; Lead ore 621; Zinc ore 1,515; Manganese ore (metallurgical): gross weight 6,963; Ilmenite 1,277; Leucoxene 224; Rutile 474; Zirconium concentrates 762; Silver (metric tons) 1,725; Uranium (metric tons) 6,942; Gold (metric tons) 260; Salt (unrefined) 11,744; Diamonds ('000 carats, unsorted) 7,586 (Source: US Geological Survey).

Industry

SELECTED PRODUCTS

(year ending 30 June, '000 metric tons, unless otherwise indicated)

	2007/08	2008/09	2009/10
Raw steel	8,151	5,568	6,886
Aluminium—unwrought*	1,964	1,974	1,920
Copper—unwrought*	444	499	395
Lead—unwrought*	203	213	189
Zinc—unwrought*	507	506	515
Pig iron	6,329	4,352	5,929
Automotive gasoline (million litres)	17,079	17,159	16,771
Fuel oil (million litres)	979	872	846
Diesel-automotive oil (million litres)	12,177	12,231	11,720
Aviation turbine fuel (million litres)	5,182	5,494	5,341

* Primary refined metal only.

Tin (unwrought, '000 metric tons): 321 in 2006/07.

Sources: mainly Australian Bureau of Agricultural and Resource Economics, *Australian Mineral Statistics*, *Australian Commodity Statistics* and *Energy in Australia*.

2011 ('000 metric tons unless otherwise indicated): Raw steel 6,538; Aluminium—unwrought 1,945; Copper—unwrought 477; Lead—unwrought 187; Zinc—unwrought 507; Pig iron 6,400 (estimate) (Source: US Geological Survey).

Finance

CURRENCY AND EXCHANGE RATES

Monetary Units

100 cents = 1 Australian dollar ($A).

Sterling, US Dollar and Euro Equivalents (31 December 2013)

£1 sterling = $A1.858;
US $1 = $A1.128;
€1 = $A1.556;
$A100 = £53.84 = US $88.65 = €64.28.

Average Exchange Rate (Australian dollars per US $)

2011 0.9695
2012 0.9658
2013 1.0358

COMMONWEALTH GOVERNMENT BUDGET

($A million, year ending 30 June)

Revenue	2011/12	2012/13*	2013/14*
Tax revenue	316,779	338,727	366,664
Income taxes	231,268	242,412	265,539
Individuals	151,433	160,850	175,350
Taxes on fringe benefits	3,964	3,890	4,320
Superannuation taxation	7,852	7,800	8,480
Companies	66,726	68,132	73,969
Petroleum resource rent tax	1,293	1,740	3,420
Sales taxes	50,004	51,380	54,260
Excise and customs	32,585	34,060	34,880
Excise duty revenue	25,480	25,590	26,050
Carbon pricing mechanism	—	7,540	8,340
Other taxes	2,922	3,335	3,646
Non-tax revenue	21,330	21,234	21,085
Total	338,109	359,961	387,749

Expenditure	2011/12	2012/13*	2013/14*
Defence	21,692	21,122	22,045
Education	29,050	28,411	29,742
Health	62,012	62,249	64,636
Social security and welfare	126,747	132,388	138,145
Other services	44,833	40,974	47,150
General purpose inter-governmental transactions	49,940	51,160	52,397
General public services	23,153	25,555	23,023
Public-debt interest	11,421	12,209	12,456
Total (incl. others)	377,739	381,439	398,301

* Budget estimates.

2012/13 (revised figures): *Revenue:* Tax revenue 337,323 (Income taxes 242,238, Sales taxes 51,462, Excise and customs 33,882, Carbon pricing mechanism 6,535, Other taxes 3,206); Non tax revenue 22,836; Total 360,160. *Expenditure:* Defence 21,146; Education 28,468; Health 61,302; Social security and welfare 131,901; Other services 35,166; General purpose inter-governmental transactions 51,160; General public services 25,955; Public-debt interest 12,521; Total (incl. others) 382,644.

Source: Government of Australia.

INTERNATIONAL RESERVES

(US $ million at 31 December)

	2010	2011	2012
Gold (national valuation)	3,608	4,042	4,281
IMF special drawing rights	4,764	4,633	4,536
Reserve position in IMF	1,102	2,147	2,485
Foreign exchange	32,793	36,003	37,922
Total	42,267	46,825	49,224

Source: IMF, *International Financial Statistics*.

MONEY SUPPLY

($A million at 31 December)

	2010	2011	2012
Currency outside banks	47,901	50,804	53,754
Demand deposits at trading and savings banks	367,023	433,892	459,987
Total money (incl. others)	414,973	484,735	513,953

Source: IMF, *International Financial Statistics*.

COST OF LIVING

(Consumer Price Index*; base 2000 = 100)

	2009	2010	2011
Food	143.6	145.8	152.9
Clothing	101.9	98.5	99.5
Rent†	141.3	147.4	154.3
Electricity, gas and other fuels	165.6	187.7	206.8
All items (incl. others)	130.7	134.4	139.0

* Weighted average of eight capital cities.

† Including expenditure on maintenance and repairs of dwellings; excluding mortgage interest charges and including house purchase and utilities.

2012: Food 150.4; All items (incl. others) 141.4.

Source: ILO.

NATIONAL ACCOUNTS

($A million, current prices, year ending 30 June)

National Income and Product

	2010/11	2011/12	2012/13
Compensation of employees	666,411	714,894	740,840
Gross operating surplus	488,082	513,533	509,303
Gross mixed income	116,878	119,803	120,696
Total factor incomes	1,271,371	1,348,230	1,370,839
Taxes, less subsidies, on production and imports	135,300	137,841	150,477
Statistical discrepancy	—	—	-153
GDP in market prices	1,406,671	1,486,071	1,521,163
Net primary incomes from abroad	-53,900	-42,441	-35,620
Statistical discrepancy	—	—	153
Gross national income	1,352,771	1,443,630	1,485,696
Current taxes on income, wealth, etc.	991	1,027	944
Other current transfers (net)	-2,769	-3,089	-2,945
Gross disposable income	1,350,993	1,441,568	1,483,695

Expenditure on the Gross Domestic Product

	2010/11	2011/12	2012/13
Government final consumption expenditure	251,218	265,770	272,074
Private final consumption expenditure	759,051	799,137	838,686
Gross fixed capital formation	376,205	417,656	428,454
Change in inventories	6,223	6,582	2,276
Total domestic expenditure	1,392,697	1,489,145	1,541,490
Exports of goods and services	297,321	315,638	301,597
Less Imports of goods and services	283,348	318,710	319,145
Statistical discrepancy	—	—	-2,778
GDP in market prices	1,406,671	1,486,071	1,521,163
GDP in chain-linked prices	1,434,226	1,486,071	1,524,674

Gross Domestic Product by Economic Activity

	2010/11	2011/12	2012/13
Agriculture, hunting, forestry and fishing	32,356	33,725	34,190
Mining and quarrying	131,719	134,119	122,028
Manufacturing	104,625	104,892	101,427
Electricity, gas and water	33,892	38,008	44,531
Construction	103,914	114,785	117,588
Wholesale and retail trade	122,151	128,688	130,997
Hotels and restaurants	32,791	34,920	34,779
Transport, storage and communications	106,667	113,219	115,714
Finance and insurance	112,709	117,656	123,695
Rental, hiring and real estate services	33,190	37,662	38,156
Professional, scientific and technical services	87,618	97,303	103,191
Ownership of dwellings	112,479	120,208	126,631
Public administration and defence	73,294	77,644	79,576
Education	61,491	66,807	69,935
Health and community services	86,577	90,840	97,760
Cultural and recreational services	11,304	11,858	12,199
Administrative and support services	41,124	42,547	43,801
Personal and other services	25,347	27,763	26,983
Gross value added at basic prices	1,313,248	1,392,644	1,423,181
Taxes, less subsidies, on products	93,423	93,427	98,135
Statistical discrepancy	—	—	-153
GDP in market prices	1,406,671	1,486,071	1,521,163

BALANCE OF PAYMENTS
(US $ million)

	2010	2011	2012
Exports of goods	213,782	271,677	257,754
Imports of goods	−196,303	−242,915	−262,966
Balance on goods	17,479	28,763	−5,212
Exports of services	46,968	51,852	52,672
Imports of services	−51,313	−60,994	−64,389
Balance on goods and services	13,134	19,621	−16,928
Primary income received	35,711	42,965	42,097
Primary income paid	−84,646	−94,689	−80,778
Balance on goods, services and primary income	−35,800	−32,103	−55,610
Secondary income received	5,813	7,389	7,357
Secondary income paid	−7,189	−8,920	−8,783
Current balance	−37,176	−33,634	−57,037
Capital account (net)	−393	−830	−1,145
Direct investment assets	−24,804	−13,906	−13,528
Direct investment liabilities	37,098	66,271	56,595
Portfolio investment assets	−45,191	−42,029	−42,269
Portfolio investment liabilities	114,193	73,332	54,343
Financial derivatives and employee stock options (net)	−1,180	−26,926	−12,707
Other investment assets	−14,190	−27,776	−12,619
Other investment liabilities	−29,063	8,654	29,675
Net errors and omissions	1,135	1,389	1,227
Reserves and related items	430	4,546	2,536

Source: IMF, *International Financial Statistics*.

External Trade

PRINCIPAL COMMODITIES
(distribution by HS, US $ million)

Imports c.i.f.	2010	2011	2012
Prepared foodstuffs; beverages, spirits, vinegar; tobacco and articles thereof	6,183	7,605	8,065
Mineral products	26,768	40,766	43,441
Mineral fuels, oils, distillation products, etc.	25,926	39,514	42,333
Crude petroleum oils	14,576	21,496	22,349
Petroleum oils, not crude	8,962	14,766	16,440
Chemicals and related products	18,194	22,286	22,516
Pharmaceutical products	8,280	10,440	10,276
Medicament mixtures	7,072	8,740	8,397
Plastics, rubber, and articles thereof	7,286	9,186	9,757
Textiles and textile articles	6,696	8,000	8,243
Pearls, precious or semi-precious stones, precious metals, and articles thereof	8,043	9,617	8,153
Gold, unwrought, or in semi-manufactured forms	6,330	6,527	5,940
Iron and steel, other base metals and articles of base metal	10,021	12,264	13,653
Machinery and mechanical appliances; electrical equipment; parts thereof	48,369	57,759	63,017
Boilers, machinery, etc.	28,104	33,804	38,575
Automatic data-processing machines; optical readers, etc.	5,862	6,794	6,968
Electrical, electronic equipment	20,265	23,955	24,442
Vehicles, aircraft, vessels and associated transport equipment	26,066	29,395	36,255
Vehicles other than railway, tramway	24,028	25,967	32,131
Cars (incl. station wagons)	14,300	14,611	17,518
Trucks, motor vehicles for the transport of goods	5,352	6,260	8,689
Optical, medical apparatus, etc.; clocks and watches; musical instruments; parts thereof	7,030	8,290	8,870
Optical, photo, technical, medical, etc. apparatus	6,557	7,706	8,257
Total (incl. others)	188,741	234,206	250,465

Exports f.o.b.	2010	2011	2012
Live animals and animal products	9,847	11,768	11,784
Vegetables and vegetable products	7,511	12,339	14,000
Cereals	4,600	8,065	8,620
Mineral products	115,920	158,020	145,694
Ores, slag and ash	55,840	81,769	72,358
Iron ores and concentrates; including roasted iron pyrites	44,290	66,217	56,727
Mineral fuels, oils, distillation products, etc.	59,753	75,819	72,891
Coal; briquettes, ovoids and similar solid fuels manufactured from coal	38,572	48,235	42,699
Crude petroleum oils	9,385	11,830	11,318
Petroleum gases	9,452	12,445	15,166
Chemicals and related products	11,008	12,662	13,017
Pearls, precious or semi-precious stones, precious metals, and articles thereof	13,909	16,866	17,345
Gold, unwrought, or in semi-manufactured forms	12,816	15,441	16,034
Iron and steel, other base metals and articles of base metal	12,740	15,877	13,801
Machinery and mechanical appliances; electrical equipment; parts thereof	7,458	8,798	8,984
Total (incl. others)	206,705	269,423	256,243

Source: Trade Map-Trade Competitiveness Map, International Trade Centre, www.intracen.org/marketanalysis.

PRINCIPAL TRADING PARTNERS
(US $ million)

Imports c.i.f.	2010	2011	2012
China, People's Republic	35,261	43,447	45,996
France	3,434	3,868	3,946
Germany	9,424	10,952	11,628
India	1,767	2,297	2,677
Indonesia	4,773	6,099	6,555
Ireland	2,075	2,188	1,641
Italy	4,395	5,181	5,536
Japan	16,327	18,578	19,713
Korea, Republic	6,416	7,353	10,201
Malaysia	8,196	8,780	9,928
New Zealand	6,469	7,830	7,528
Papua New Guinea	2,711	3,792	3,548
Singapore	9,597	14,596	15,011
Sweden	1,967	2,586	2,508
Switzerland	1,978	3,066	2,990
Taiwan	3,252	3,897	3,872
Thailand	9,887	8,710	10,534
United Arab Emirates	2,003	4,267	3,152
United Kingdom	5,213	6,939	6,953
USA	20,947	26,798	29,386
Viet Nam	2,808	2,916	3,263
Total (incl. others)	188,741	234,206	250,465

Exports f.o.b.	2010	2011	2012
China, People's Republic	52,314	73,804	75,836
Hong Kong	2,824	3,086	2,651
India	14,694	15,750	12,612
Indonesia	4,021	5,566	4,953
Japan	39,137	52,088	49,680
Korea, Republic	18,329	24,009	20,541
Malaysia	3,263	4,639	5,256
Netherlands	2,343	3,602	3,003
New Zealand	7,179	7,927	7,666
Singapore	4,331	6,580	7,374
Taiwan	7,501	9,420	8,249
Thailand	5,250	6,991	5,043
United Arab Emirates	1,913	2,303	2,118
United Kingdom	7,456	7,785	6,931
USA	8,232	9,845	9,516
Total (incl. others)	206,705	269,423	256,243

Source: Trade Map-Trade Competitiveness Map, International Trade Centre, www.intracen.org/marketanalysis.

Transport

RAILWAYS
(traffic)*

	1997/98	1998/99	1999/2000
Passengers carried (million)	587.7	595.2	629.2
Freight carried (million metric tons)	487.5	492.0	508.0
Freight ton-km ('000 million)	125.2	127.4	134.2

* Traffic on government railways only.

Passengers carried (million): 610 in 2003/04; 616 in 2004/05.

Freight carried (million metric tons): 557.3 in 2001/02; 589.1 in 2002/03.

Freight ton-km ('000 million): 150.7 in 2001/02; 161.8 in 2002/03.

ROAD TRAFFIC
('000 vehicles, registered at 31 January)

	2011	2012	2013
Passenger vehicles	12,474	12,714	13,000
Light commercial vehicles	2,531	2,618	2,718
Trucks*	597	610	625
Buses	88	91	93
Motorcycles	679	709	744

* Including camper vans, previously classified as passenger vehicles.

SHIPPING

Flag Registered Fleet
(at 31 December)

	2011	2012	2013
Number of vessels	628	688	733
Total displacement ('000 grt)	1,846.8	2,018.4	2,047.1

Source: Lloyd's List Intelligence (www.lloydslistintelligence.com).

International Sea-borne Traffic
('000 metric tons)

	2010	2011	2012
Goods loaded	887,364	912,720	1,015,224
Goods unloaded	88,956	93,456	96,876

Source: UN, *Monthly Bulletin of Statistics*.

CIVIL AVIATION
(traffic)*

	2008	2009	2010
International services ('000):			
passenger arrivals	11,881.1	n.a.	13,430.4
passenger departures	11,584.1	n.a.	13,361.5
Domestic services:			
passengers carried ('000)	49,857	49,848	53,341
passenger-km (million)	54,132	54,079	57,623

* Includes estimates for regional airline data.

Passengers carried ('000): 62,538 in 2011; 65,158 in 2012 (Source: World Bank, World Development Indicators database).

Tourism

VISITOR ARRIVALS BY COUNTRY OF ORIGIN
('000)*

	2010	2011	2012
Canada	121.9	117.7	120.0
China, People's Republic	453.8	542.0	626.4
France	97.3	94.0	97.6
Germany	160.1	153.9	154.8
Hong Kong	163.9	166.3	176.6
India	138.7	148.2	159.2
Indonesia	124.0	140.4	145.6
Ireland	53.1	58.8	61.3
Japan	398.1	332.7	353.9
Korea, Republic	214.0	198.0	196.8
Malaysia	236.9	241.2	262.7

—*continued*	2010	2011	2012
New Zealand	1,161.8	1,172.7	1,201.0
Singapore	308.0	318.5	343.6
Taiwan	87.1	84.4	94.7
Thailand	84.1	85.4	83.9
United Kingdom	646.7	608.3	593.6
USA	472.2	456.2	478.9
Total (incl. others)	5,885.0	5,875.3	6,145.5

* Visitors intending to stay for less than one year.

Receipts from tourism (US $ million, excl. passenger transport): 29,107 in 2010; 31,473 in 2011; 31,534 in 2012 (provisional) (Source: World Tourism Organization).

Communications Media

	2010	2011	2012
Telephones ('000 main lines in use)	10,590	10,573	10,471
Mobile cellular telephones ('000 subscribers)	22,500	24,490	24,338
Internet subscribers ('000)	6,092	5,970	n.a.
Broadband subscribers ('000)	5,165	5,498	5,743

Source: International Telecommunication Union.

Education

(August 2012 unless otherwise indicated)

	Institutions	Teaching staff*	Students
Government schools	6,697	167,152	2,321,217†
Non-government schools	2,730	91,834	1,245,848†
Universities‡	39	86,624	1,066,095

* Full-time teaching staff and full-time equivalent of part-time teaching staff.

† Primary and secondary students. In 2011 the total at both government and non-government schools comprised 2,037,148 primary and 1,482,384 secondary students.

‡ 2008 (Source: Department of Education, Science and Training).

Directory

The Government

Queen: HM Queen ELIZABETH II (succeeded to the throne 6 February 1952).

Governor-General: Sir PETER COSGROVE (assumed office 28 March 2014).

THE MINISTRY

(April 2014)

The Government is formed by the Liberal-National Coalition.

Cabinet Ministers

Prime Minister: TONY ABBOTT (Liberal Party).

Deputy Prime Minister and Minister for Infrastructure and Regional Development: WARREN TRUSS (National Party).

Minister for Foreign Affairs: Senator JULIE BISHOP (Liberal Party).

Minister for Trade and Investment: ANDREW ROBB (Liberal Party).

Minister for Employment and Minister Assisting the Prime Minister on Public Service: Senator ERIC ABETZ (Liberal Party).

Attorney-General and Minister for the Arts: Senator GEORGE BRANDIS (Liberal Party).

Treasurer: JOE HOCKEY (Liberal Party).

Minister for Small Business: BRUCE BILLSON (Liberal Party).

Minister for Agriculture: BARNABY JOYCE (National Party).

Minister for Education: CHRISTOPHER PYNE (Liberal Party).

Minister for Indigenous Affairs: NIGEL SCULLION (Liberal Party).

Minister for Industry: IAN MACFARLANE (Liberal Party).

Minister for Social Services: KEVIN ANDREWS (Liberal Party).

Minister for Communications: MALCOLM TURNBULL (Liberal Party).

Minister for Health and for Sport: PETER DUTTON (Liberal Party).

Minister for Defence: Senator DAVID JOHNSTON (Liberal Party).

Minister for Veteran's Affairs, Minister Assisting the Prime Minister for the Centenary of ANZAC and Special Minister of State: Senator MICHAEL RONALDSON (Liberal Party).

Minister for the Environment: GREG HUNT (Liberal Party).

Minister for Immigration and Border Protection: SCOTT MORRISON (Liberal Party).

Minister for Finance: Senator MATHIAS CORMANN (Liberal Party).

DEPARTMENTS

Department of the Prime Minister and Cabinet: 1 National Circuit, Barton, ACT 2600; tel. (2) 6271-5111; fax (2) 6271-5414; internet www.dpmc.gov.au.

Department of Agriculture: GPOB 858, Canberra, ACT 2601; tel. (2) 6272-3933; fax (2) 6272-3008; internet www.daff.gov.au.

Attorney-General's Department: Central Office, 3–5 National Circuit, Barton, ACT 2600; tel. (2) 6141-6666; fax (2) 6141-2553; internet www.ag.gov.au.

Department of Communications: GPOB 2154, Canberra, ACT 2601; tel. (2) 6271-1000; fax (2) 6271-1901; e-mail media@dbcde.gov.au; internet www.dbcde.gov.au.

Department of Defence: Russell Offices, Russell Dr., Campbell, Canberra, ACT 2600; tel. (2) 6265-9111; e-mail public.enquiries@defence.gov.au; internet www.defence.gov.au.

Department of Education: GPOB 9880, Canberra, ACT 2601; tel. (2) 6121-6000; fax (2) 6240-8571; e-mail feedback@deewr.gov.au; internet www.deewr.gov.au.

Department of Employment: GPOB 9880, Canberra, ACT 2601; tel. (2) 6121-6000; fax (2) 6240-8571; e-mail feedback@deewr.gov.au; internet www.deewr.gov.au.

Department of the Environment: GPOB 787, Canberra, ACT 2601; tel. (2) 6274-1111; fax (2) 6274-1123; internet www.environment.gov.au.

Department of Finance: John Gorton Bldg, King Edward Terrace, Parkes, ACT 2600; tel. (2) 6215-1783; fax (2) 6273-3021; e-mail feedback@finance.gov.au; internet www.finance.gov.au.

Department of Foreign Affairs and Trade: R. G. Casey Bldg, John McEwen Cres., Barton, ACT 0221; tel. (2) 6261-1111; fax (2) 6261-3111; internet www.dfat.gov.au.

Department of Health: GPOB 9848, Canberra, ACT 2601; tel. (2) 6289-1555; e-mail enquiries@health.gov.au; internet www.health.gov.au.

Department of Immigration and Border Protection: POB 25, Belconnen, ACT 2616; tel. (2) 6264-1111; fax (2) 6225-6970; internet www.immi.gov.au.

Department of Industry: GPOB 9839, Canberra, ACT 2601; tel. (2) 6213-6000; fax (2) 6213-7000; e-mail enquiries@innovation.gov.au; internet www.innovation.gov.au.

Department of Infrastructure and Regional Development: GPOB 594, Canberra, ACT 2601; tel. (2) 6274-7111; fax (2) 6257-2505; e-mail publicaffairs@infrastructure.gov.au; internet www.infrastructure.gov.au.

Department of Social Services: Tuggeranong Office Park, Soward Way (cnr Athllon Drive), Greenway, ACT 2900; POB 7576, Canberra Business Centre, ACT 2610; tel. (2) 6146-0001; e-mail dssfeedback@dss.gov.au; internet www.dss.gov.au.

Department of the Treasury: Langton Cres., Parkes, ACT 2600; tel. (2) 6263-2111; fax (2) 6273-2614; e-mail department@treasury.gov.au; internet www.treasury.gov.au.

Department of Veterans' Affairs: Lovett Tower, 13 Keltie St, POB 9998, Woden, ACT 2606; tel. (2) 6225-4620; fax (2) 6289-6257; e-mail generalenquiries@dva.gov.au; internet www.dva.gov.au.

Legislature

FEDERAL PARLIAMENT

Senate

President: JOHN HOGG.

Distribution of seats following election, 7 September 2013

Party	Seats*
Liberal-National Coalition	33
Australian Labor Party	25
Australian Greens	10
Others	8
Total	76

* The election was for 36 of the 72 seats held by state senators, who serve a six-year term, and for the two senators representing the Northern Territory and the two representing the Australian Capital Territory. The newly elected senators were to take office on 1 July 2014, with the exception of the four territory representatives, whose three-year term of office commenced on election.

House of Representatives

Speaker: BRONWYN BISHOP.

Distribution of seats following election, 7 September 2013

Party	Seats
Liberal-National Coalition	90
Liberal Party of Australia	59
Liberal National Party of Queensland	21
National Party of Australia	9
Country Liberals	1
Australian Labor Party	55
Australian Greens	1
Katter's Australian Party	1
Palmer United Party	1
Independents	2
Total	150

State and Territory Governments

(April 2014)

NEW SOUTH WALES

Governor: Prof. MARIE BASHIR, Level 3, Chief Secretary's Bldg, 121 Macquarie St, Sydney, NSW 2000; tel. (2) 9242-4200; fax (2) 9242-4266; e-mail ootgenquiries@governor.nsw.gov.au; internet www.governor.nsw.gov.au.

Premier: MIKE BAIRD (Liberal), GPOB 5341, Sydney, NSW 2001; tel. (2) 9228-5239; fax (2) 9228-3935; e-mail office@premier.nsw.gov.au; internet www.premier.nsw.gov.au.

State Legislative Council: Parliament House, Macquarie St, Sydney, NSW 2000; tel. (2) 9230-2111; fax (2) 9230-2876; internet www.parliament.nsw.gov.au; upper house of Parliament, with one-half of the members elected every four years for an eight-year term; following the election of 26 March 2011 the composition of the chamber was as follows: Australian Labor Party 14; Liberal Party of Australia 12; National Party of Australia 7; Greens New South Wales 5; Others 4; Total 42 seats; Pres. DON HARWIN.

State Legislative Assembly: Parliament House, Macquarie St, Sydney, NSW 2000; tel. (2) 9230-2111; fax (2) 9230-2876; internet www.parliament.nsw.gov.au; lower house of Parliament with members directly elected for four years; last election 26 March 2011: Liberal-National Coalition 69; Australian Labor Party 20; Total 89 seats; Speaker SHELLEY HANCOCK.

VICTORIA

Governor: ALEX CHERNOV, Government House, Melbourne, Vic 3004; tel. (3) 9655-4211; fax (3) 9650-9050; internet www.governor.vic.gov.au.

Premier: Dr DENIS NAPTHINE (Liberal), 1 Treasury Place, Melbourne, Vic 3002; tel. (3) 9651-5000; fax (3) 9651-5054; e-mail premier@dpc.vic.gov.au; internet www.premier.vic.gov.au.

State Legislative Council: Parliament House, Spring St, East Melbourne, Vic 3002; tel. (3) 9651-8911; fax (3) 9654-5284; e-mail info@parliament.vic.gov.au; internet www.parliament.vic.gov.au; upper house of Parliament; last election 27 November 2010: Liberal-National Coalition 21; Australian Labor Party 16; Victorian Greens 3; Total 40 seats; Pres. BRUCE ATKINSON.

State Legislative Assembly: Parliament House, Spring St, East Melbourne, Vic 3002; tel. (3) 9651-8911; fax (3) 9654-5284; e-mail info@parliament.vic.gov.au; internet www.parliament.vic.gov.au; lower house of Parliament; last election 27 November 2010: Liberal-National Coalition 45; Australian Labor Party 43; Total 88 seats; Speaker CHRISTINE FYFFE.

QUEENSLAND

Governor: PENELOPE WENSLEY, GPOB 434, Brisbane, Qld 4001; tel. (7) 3858-5700; fax (7) 3858-5701; e-mail govhouse@govhouse.qld.gov.au; internet www.govhouse.qld.gov.au.

Premier: CAMPBELL NEWMAN (LNP), POB 15185, City East, Qld 4002; tel. (7) 3224-4500; fax (7) 3229-2900; e-mail thepremier@premiers.qld.gov.au; internet www.thepremier.qld.gov.au.

State Legislative Assembly: Parliament House, George St, Brisbane, Qld 4000; tel. (7) 3406-7111; fax (7) 3221-7475; internet www.parliament.qld.gov.au; last election 24 March 2012: Liberal National Party of Queensland 78; Australian Labor Party 7; Katter's Australian Party 2; Others 2; Total 89 seats; Speaker FIONA SIMPSON.

SOUTH AUSTRALIA

Governor: Rear Adm. KEVIN SCARCE, GPOB 2373, Adelaide, SA 5001; tel. (8) 8203-9800; fax (8) 8203-9899; e-mail governors.office@sa.gov.au; internet www.governor.sa.gov.au.

Premier: JAY WEATHERILL (Labor), GPOB 2343, Adelaide, SA 5001; tel. (8) 8463-3166; fax (8) 8463-3168; e-mail premier@dpc.sa.gov.au; internet www.premier.sa.gov.au.

State Legislative Council: GPOB 572, Adelaide, SA 5001; tel. (8) 8237-9100; fax (8)8237-9482; e-mail assembly@parliament.sa.gov.au; internet www.parliament.sa.gov.au; upper chamber of Parliament; 22 seats; following the election of 15 March 2014 the composition of the chamber was as follows: Liberal Party of Australia 8; Australian Labor Party 7; Greens South Australia 2; Others 5; Total 22 seats; Pres. (vacant).

State Legislative Assembly: GPOB 572, Adelaide, SA 5001; tel. (8) 8237-9100; fax (8)8237-9482; e-mail assembly@parliament.sa.gov.au; internet www.parliament.sa.gov.au; lower chamber of Parliament; 47 seats; last election 15 March 2014: Australian Labor Party 23; Liberal Party of Australia 22; Independents 2; Total 47 seats; Speaker MICHAEL ATKINSON.

WESTERN AUSTRALIA

Governor: MALCOLM MCCUSKER, Government House, St George's Terrace, Perth, WA 6000; tel. (8) 9429-9199; fax (8) 9325-4476; e-mail enquiries@govhouse.wa.gov.au; internet www.govhouse.wa.gov.au.

Premier: COLIN BARNETT (Liberal), 24th Floor, Gov. Stirling Tower, 197 St George's Terrace, Perth, WA 6000; tel. (8) 6552-5000; fax (8) 6552-5001; e-mail wa-government@dpc.wa.gov.au; internet www.premier.wa.gov.au.

State Legislative Council: Parliament House, Harvest Terrace, Perth, WA 6000; tel. (8) 9222 7466; fax (8) 9486 1274; e-mail LCAdmin@parliament.wa.gov.au; internet www.parliament.wa.gov.au; upper house of Parliament; following the election of 9 March 2013 the composition of the chamber was as follows: Liberal Party of Australia 17; Australian Labor Party 11; National Party of Western Australia 5; Others 3; Total 36 seats; Pres. BARRY HOUSE.

State Legislative Assembly: Parliament House, Harvest Terrace, Perth, WA 6000; tel. (8) 9222 7390; fax (8) 9222 7803; e-mail laquery@parliament.wa.gov.au; internet www.parliament.wa.gov.au; lower house of Parliament; last election 9 March 2013: Liberal Party of Australia 31; Australian Labor Party 21; National Party of Western Australia 7; Total 59 seats; Speaker MICHAEL SUTHERLAND.

TASMANIA

Governor: PETER UNDERWOOD, Government House, Lower Domain Rd, Hobart, Tas 7000; tel. (3) 6234-2611; fax (3) 6234-2556; e-mail admin@govhouse.tas.gov.au; internet www.govhouse.tas.gov.au.

Premier: WILLIAM HODGMAN (Liberal), Executive Bldg, Level 11, 15 Murray St, Hobart, Tas 7000; tel. (3) 6233-3464; fax (3) 6234-1572; e-mail lara.giddings@dpac.tas.gov.au; internet www.premier.tas.gov.au.

State Legislative Council: Parliament House, Hobart, Tas 7000; tel. (3) 6212-2300; fax (8) 6231-1849; e-mail council@parliament.tas.gov.au; internet www.parliament.tas.gov.au; upper house of Parliament; 15 seats; 15 single-member electorates with members elected for a six-year term; elections are held every year in May for two to three seats; Pres. JAMES SCOTT WILKINSON.

State Legislative Assembly: Parliament House Hobart, Tas 7000; tel. (3) 6212-2200; fax (3) 6223-3803; e-mail assembly@parliament.tas.gov.au; internet www.parliament.tas.gov.au; lower house of Parliament; last election 15 March 2014: Liberal Party of Australia 15; Australian Labor Party 7; Tasmanian Greens 3; Total 25 seats; Speaker MICHAEL ROBERT POLLEY.

NORTHERN TERRITORY

Administrator: SALLY THOMAS, GPOB 497, Darwin, NT 0801; tel. (8) 8999-7103; fax (8) 8999-5521; e-mail governmenthouse.darwin@nt.gov.au; internet www.nt.gov.au/administrator.

Chief Minister: ADAM GILES (Liberal), GPOB 3146, Darwin, NT 0801; tel. (8) 8928-6500; fax (8) 8928-6621; e-mail chiefminister@nt.gov.au; internet chiefminister.nt.gov.au.

State Legislative Assembly: Parliament House, Mitchell St, Darwin, NT 0800; tel. (8) 8946-1512; fax (8) 8941-2558; e-mail latableoffice@nt.gov.au; internet www.nt.gov.au; last election 25 August 2012: Liberal Party 16; Australian Labor Party 8; Total 25 seats; Speaker KEZIA PURICK.

AUSTRALIAN CAPITAL TERRITORY

Chief Minister: KATY GALLAGHER (Labor), GPOB 158, Canberra, ACT 2601; tel. (2) 6207-5883; fax (2) 6205-3030; e-mail gallagher@act.gov.au; internet www.cmd.act.gov.au.

State Legislative Assembly: GPOB 1020, Canberra, ACT 2601; tel. (2) 6205-0439; fax (2) 6205-3109; e-mail ola@parliament.act.gov.au; internet www.parliament.act.gov.au; last election 20 October 2012: Australian Labor Party 8; Liberal Party 8; ACT Greens 1; Total 17; Speaker VICKI DUNNE.

Election Commission

Australian Electoral Commission (AEC): West Block Offices, Queen Victoria Terrace, Parkes, ACT 2600; POB 6172, Kingston, ACT 2604; tel. (2) 6215-9999; fax (2) 6271-4558; e-mail info@aec.gov.au; internet www.aec.gov.au; f. 1984; statutory body; administers federal elections and referendums; Chair. PETER HEEREY; Electoral Commr ED KILLESTEYN.

Political Organizations

Australians for Constitutional Monarchy (ACM): GPOB 9841, Sydney, NSW 2001; tel. (2) 9251-2500; fax (2) 9261-5033; e-mail acmhq@norepublic.com.au; internet www.norepublic.com.au; f. 1992; also known as No Republic; Nat. Convener Prof. DAVID FLINT.

Australian Democrats Party: Suite 328, 2 Endeavour House, Captain Cook Cres., Manuka, ACT 2603; tel. and fax (2) 6171-0707; e-mail info@australiandemocrats.org.au; internet www.australiandemocrats.org.au; f. 1977; comprises the fmr Liberal Movement and the Australia Party; Nat. Pres. HAYDEN OSTROM BROWN; Nat. Sec. STUART HORREX.

Australian Greens (The Greens): GPOB 1108, Canberra, ACT 2601; tel. (2) 6140-3217; fax (2) 6247-6455; e-mail greens@greens.org.au; internet www.greens.org.au; f. 1992; Parl. Leader Senator CHRISTINE MILNE; Dep. Parl. Leader ADAM BANDT.

Australian Labor Party (ALP): POB 6222, Kingston, ACT 2604; tel. (2) 6120-0800; fax (2) 6120-0801; e-mail info@cbr.alp.org.au; internet www.alp.org.au; f. 1891; advocates social democracy; trade unions form part of its structure; Fed. Parl. Leader BILL SHORTEN; Deputy Fed. Parl. Leader TANYA PLIBERSEK; Nat. Pres. JENNY MCALLISTER; Nat. Sec. GEORGE WRIGHT.

Australian Republican Movement (ARM): POB 7188, Watson LPO, Watson, ACT 2602; tel. (2) 6257-3705; fax (2) 6241-2194; e-mail media@ourrepublic.org.au; internet www.ouridentity.org.au; f. 1991; Chair. Prof. GEOFF GALLOP; Nat. Dir DAVID MORRIS.

Communist Party of Australia: 74 Buckingham St, Surry Hills, NSW 2010; tel. (2) 9699-8844; fax (2) 9699-9833; e-mail cpa@cpa.org.au; internet www.cpa.org.au; f. 1971; fmrly Socialist Party; advocates public ownership of the means of production, working-class political power; Pres. DR VINNIE MOLINA; Gen. Sec. BOB BRITON.

Country Liberals: 229 McMillans Rd, Jingili, POB 4194, Darwin, NT 0801; tel. (8) 8948-1744; fax (8) 8948-0656; e-mail info@countryliberals.org.au; internet www.countryliberals.org.au; Leader ADAM GILES.

First Nations Political Party (FNPP): e-mail firstnationspoliticalparty@hotmail.com; f. 2010; represents interests of Aboriginal people; Leader MAURIE JAPARTA RYAN.

Katter's Australian Party: POB 386, Banyo, Qld 4014; tel. (7) 3267-7799; fax (7) 3267-0650; e-mail myausparty@ausparty.org.au; internet www.ausparty.org.au; f. 2011; socially conservative; Parl. Leader BOB KATTER; Pres. ROBBIE KATTER.

Liberal National Party of Queensland (LNP): POB 940, Spring Hill, Qld 4004; tel. (7) 3844-0666; fax (7) 3844-0388; e-mail info@lnp.org.au; internet lnp.org.au; f. 2008; formed by merger of the Queensland divisions of the Liberal Party of Australia and the National Party of Australia; aims to provide prosperity and security for Queensland; Pres. BRUCE MCIVER; Vice-Pres. GARY SPENCE.

Liberal Party of Australia: POB 6004, Kingston, ACT 2604; tel. (2) 6273-2564; fax (2) 6273-1534; e-mail libadm@liberal.org.au; internet www.liberal.org.au; f. 1944; advocates private enterprise, social justice, individual liberty and initiative; committed to national devt, prosperity and security; Fed. Dir BRIAN LOUGHNANE; Fed. Parl. Leader TONY ABBOTT; Fed. Pres. ALAN STOCKDALE.

National Party of Australia: POB 6190, Kingston, ACT 2604; tel. (2) 6273-3822; fax (2) 6273-1745; e-mail federal.nationals@nationals.org.au; internet www.nationals.org.au; f. 1916 as the Country Party of Australia; adopted present name in 1982; advocates balanced national devt based on free enterprise, with special emphasis on the needs of people outside the major metropolitan areas; Fed. Pres. CHRISTINE FERGUSON; Fed. Parl. Leader WARREN TRUSS; Fed. Dir SCOTT MITCHELL.

Palmer United Party: 380 Queen St, POB 3138, Brisbane, Qld 4001; tel. (7) 3233-0888; fax (7) 3036-6666; e-mail Admin@PalmerUnited.com; internet palmerunited.com; Leader CLIVE PALMER.

WikiLeaks Party: POB 434, Surry Hills, NSW 2010; tel. 405-222-251; e-mail contact@wikileaksparty.org.au; internet www.wikileaksparty.org.au; f. 2013; Founder and Editor-in-Chief JULIAN ASSANGE.

Diplomatic Representation

EMBASSIES AND HIGH COMMISSIONS IN AUSTRALIA

Afghanistan: 4 Beale Cres., Deakin West, ACT 2600; tel. (2) 6282-7377; fax (2) 6282-7322; e-mail ambassador@afghanembassy.net; internet www.afghanembassy.net; Ambassador NASIR AHMAD ANDISHA.

Algeria: 29 Cobbadah St, O'Malley, ACT 2606; tel. (2) 6286-7355; fax (2) 6286-7037; e-mail info@algeriaemb.org.au; internet www.algeriaemb.org.au; Ambassador HADI BROURI.

Argentina: 7 National Circuit, Level 2, Barton, ACT 2600; tel. (2) 6273-9111; fax (2) 6273-0500; e-mail info@argentina.org.au; internet www.eaust.mrecic.gov.ar; Ambassador PEDRO VILLAGRA DELGADO.

Austria: POB 3375, Manuka, ACT 2603; tel. (2) 6295-1533; fax (2) 6239-6751; e-mail canberra-ob@bmeia.gv.at; internet www.austria.org.au; Ambassador Dr HELMUT BÖCK.

Bangladesh: 57 Culgoa Circuit, O'Malley, ACT 2606; tel. (2) 6290-0511; fax (2) 6290-0544; e-mail hoc@bhcanberra.com; internet www.bhcanberra.com; High Commissioner Lt-Gen. MASUD UDDIN CHOWDHURY.

Belgium: 19 Arkana St, Yarralumla, ACT 2600; tel. (2) 6273-2501; fax (2) 6273-3392; e-mail canberra@diplobel.fed.be; internet www.diplomatie.be/canberra; Ambassador JEAN-LUC BODSON.

Bosnia and Herzegovina: 5 Beale Cres., Deakin, ACT 2600; tel. (2) 6232-4646; fax (2) 6232-5554; e-mail embassy@bih.org.au; internet www.bih.org.au; Ambassador (vacant).

Botswana: 130 Denison St, Deakin, ACT 2600; tel. (2) 6234-7500; fax (2) 6282-4140; e-mail botaus-info@gov.bw; internet www.botswanahighcom.org.au; High Commissioner MOLOSIWA SELEPENG.

Brazil: 19 Forster Cres., Yarralumia, ACT 2600; tel. (2) 6273-2372; fax (2) 6273-2375; e-mail consular.camberra@itamaraty.gov.br; internet camberra.itamaraty.gov.br; Ambassador RUBEM CORRÊA BARBOSA.

Brunei: 10 Beale Cres., Deakin, ACT 2600; tel. (2) 6285-4500; fax (2) 6285-4545; e-mail bruneihc@brunei.org.au; internet brunei.org.au; High Commissioner ZAKARIA AHMAD.

Bulgaria: POB 6096, Mawson, ACT 2607; tel. (2) 6286-9711; fax (2) 6286-9600; e-mail embassy.canberra@mfa.bg; internet www.mfa.bg/embassies/australia; Ambassador KRASSIMIR STEFANOV.

Cambodia: 5 Canterbury Cres., Deakin, ACT 2600; tel. (2) 6273-1154; fax (2) 6273-1053; e-mail cambodianembassy@ozemail.com.au; internet www.embassyofcambodia.org.nz/au.htm; Ambassador CHUM SOUNRY.

Canada: Commonwealth Ave, Canberra, ACT 2600; tel. (2) 6270-4000; fax (2) 6270-4081; e-mail cnbra@international.gc.ca; internet www.australia.gc.ca; High Commissioner MICHAEL SMALL.

Chile: 10 Culgoa St, O'Malley, Canberra, ACT 2606; tel. (2) 6286-2430; fax (2) 6286-1289; e-mail embassy@chile.net.au; internet chileabroad.gov.cl/australia/en/; Ambassador PEDRO PABLO DÍAZ HERRERA.

China, People's Republic: 15 Coronation Dr., Yarralumla, ACT 2600; tel. (2) 6273-4780; fax (2) 6273-5848; e-mail chinaemb_au@mfa.gov.cn; internet au.china-embassy.org/eng; Ambassador MA ZHAOXU.

Colombia: Level 2, 40 Macquarie St, Barton, Canberra, ACT 2600; tel. (2) 6273–2090; fax (2) 6273–2092; e-mail australia@cancilleria.gov.co; internet australia.embajada.gov.co; Ambassador CLEMENCIA FORERO-UCROS.

Croatia: 14 Jindalee Cres., O'Malley, ACT 2600; tel. (2) 6286-6988; fax (2) 6286-3544; e-mail croemb.canberra@mvpei.hr; Ambassador Dr DAMIR KUSEN.

Cuba: 1 Gerogery Place, O'Malley, ACT 2606; tel. (2) 6290-2151; fax (2) 6286-9354; e-mail embajada@cubaus.net; internet www.cubadiplomatica.cu/australia; Ambassador PEDRO MONZÓN BARATA.

Cyprus: 30 Beale Cres., Deakin, ACT 2600; tel. (2) 6281-0832; fax (2) 6281-0860; e-mail info@cyprus.org.au; internet www.mfa.gov.cy/highcomcanberra; High Commissioner YANNIS IACOVOU.

Czech Republic: 8 Culgoa Circuit, O'Malley, ACT 2606; tel. (2) 6290-1386; fax (2) 6290-0006; e-mail canberra@embassy.mzv.cz; internet www.mzv.cz/canberra; Chargé d'affaires a.i. MARTIN POHL.

Denmark: 15 Hunter St, Yarralumla, ACT 2600; tel. (2) 6270-5333; fax (2) 6270-5324; e-mail cbramb@um.dk; internet www.australien.um.dk; Ambassador BØRGE PETERSEN.

Ecuador: 6 Pindari Cres., O'Malley, ACT 2606; tel. (2) 6286-4021; fax (2) 6286-1231; e-mail embassy@ecuador-au.org; internet www.ecuador-au.org; Ambassador RAÚL GANGOTENA RIVADENEIRA.

Egypt: 1 Darwin Ave, Yarralumla, ACT 2600; tel. (2) 6273-4437; fax (2) 6273-4279; e-mail embassy.canberra@mfa.gov.eg; Ambassador HASSAN HANAFY EL-LAITHY.

Fiji: POB 159, Deakin West, ACT 2600; tel. (2) 6260-5115; fax (2) 6260-5105; e-mail admin@aus-fhc.org; internet www.fijihighcom.com; Chargé d'affaires a.i. CHERYL BROWN-IRAVA.

Finland: 12 Darwin Ave, Yarralumla, ACT 2600; tel. (2) 6273-3800; fax (2) 6273-3603; e-mail sanomat.can@formin.fi; internet www.finland.org.au; Ambassador PASI PATOKALLIO.

France: 6 Perth Ave, Yarralumla, ACT 2600; tel. (2) 6216-0100; fax (2) 6216-0132; e-mail secretariat.canberra-amba@diplomatie.gouv.fr; internet www.ambafrance-au.org; Ambassador STÉPHANE ROMATET.

Georgia: 28 Kareelah Vista, O'Malley, ACT 2606; tel. (2) 6162-0126; e-mail canberra.emb@mfa.gov.ge; Ambassador VLADIMER KONSTANTINIDI.

Germany: 119 Empire Circuit, Yarralumla, ACT 2600; tel. (2) 6270-1911; fax (2) 6270-1951; e-mail info@canberra.diplo.de; internet www.canberra.diplo.de; Ambassador Dr CHRISTOPH MUELLER.

Ghana: 52 Culgoa Circuit, O'Malley, ACT 2606; tel. (2) 6290-2110; fax (2) 6290-2115; e-mail gh57391@bigpond.net.au; internet www.ghanahighcom.org.au; High Commissioner RASHEED SEIDU INUSAH.

Greece: 9 Turrana St, Yarralumla, ACT 2600; tel. (2) 710100; fax (2) 732620; e-mail gremb.can@mfa.gr; internet www.mfa.gr/australia; Ambassador CHARALAMPOS DAFARANOS.

Holy See: POB 3633, Manuka, ACT 2603 (Apostolic Nunciature); tel. (2) 6295-3876; fax (2) 6295-3690; e-mail nuntius@cyberone.com.au; Apostolic Nuncio Most Rev. PAUL RICHARD GALLAGHER (Titular Archbishop of Hodelm).

Hungary: 17 Beale Cres., Deakin, ACT 2600; tel. (2) 6282-3226; fax (2) 6285-3012; e-mail mission.cbr@mfa.gov.hu; internet www.mfa.gov.hu/kulkepviselet/au; Ambassador ANNA SIKÓ.

India: 3–5 Moonah Pl., Yarralumla, ACT 2600; tel. (2) 6273-3999; fax (2) 6273-1308; e-mail hco@hcindia-au.org; internet www.hcindia-au.org; High Commissioner BIREN NANDA.

Indonesia: 8 Darwin Ave, Yarralumla, ACT 2600; tel. (2) 6250-8600; fax (2) 6273-6017; e-mail indonemb@kbri-canberra.org.au; internet www.kemlu.go.id/canberra; Ambassador NADJIB RIPHAT KESOEMA.

Iran: POB 705, Mawson, ACT 2607; tel. (2) 6290-7000; fax (2) 6290-2825; e-mail amb.office@iranembassy.org.au; internet www.iranembassy.org.au; Ambassador MAHMOUD BABAEE.

Iraq: 48 Culgoa Circuit, O'Malley, ACT 2606; tel. (2) 6286-2744; fax (2) 6290-2993; e-mail iraq.embassy@iceiraq.org; internet www.iceiraq.org; Ambassador MOUAYED SALEH.

Ireland: 20 Arkana St, Yarralumla, ACT 2600; tel. (2) 6214-0000; fax (2) 6273-3741; e-mail canberraembassy@dfa.ie; internet www.embassyofireland.au.com; Ambassador NOEL WHITE.

Israel: 6 Turrana St, Yarralumla, ACT 2600; tel. (2) 6215-4500; fax (2) 6215-4555; e-mail info@canberra.mfa.gov.il; internet canberra.mfa.gov.il; Ambassador SHMUEL BEN-SHMUEL.

Italy: 12 Grey St, Deakin, ACT 2600; tel. (2) 6273-3333; fax (2) 6273-4223; e-mail ambasciata.canberra@esteri.it; internet www.ambcanberra.esteri.it; Ambassador PIER FRANCESCO ZAZO.

Japan: 112 Empire Circuit, Yarralumla, ACT 2600; tel. (2) 6273-3244; fax (2) 6273-1848; e-mail cultural@cb.mofa.go.jp; internet www.au.emb-japan.go.jp; Ambassador YOSHITAKA AKIMOTO.

Jordan: 17 Cobbadah St, O'Malley, ACT 2606; tel. (2) 6295-9951; fax (2) 6239-7236; e-mail jordan@jordanembassy.org.au; internet www.jordanembassy.org.au; Ambassador RIMA AHMAD ALAADEEN.

Kenya: GPOB 1990, Canberra, ACT 2601; tel. (2) 6247-4788; fax (2) 6257-6613; e-mail khc-canberra@kenya.asn.au; internet www.kenya.asn.au; High Commissioner YVONNE WAMALWA (acting).

Korea, Republic: 113 Empire Circuit, Yarralumla, ACT 2600; tel. (2) 6270-4100; fax (2) 6273-4839; e-mail australia@mofa.go.kr; internet australia@mofat.go.kr; Ambassador BONGHYUN KIM.

Kuwait: POB 26, Woden, ACT 2606; tel. (2) 6286-7777; fax (2) 6286-3733; e-mail kuwaitcan_2002@yahoo.com.au; internet www.kuwaitemb-australia.com; Ambassador KHALED AL-SHAIBANI.

Laos: 1 Dalman Cres., O'Malley, ACT 2606; tel. (2) 6286-4595; fax (2) 6290-1910; e-mail laoemb@bigpond.net.au; internet www.laosembassy.net; Ambassador PHOMMA KHAMMANICHANH.

Lebanon: 27 Endeavour St, Red Hill, ACT 2603; tel. (2) 6295-7378; fax (2) 6239-7024; e-mail lebanemb@tpg.com.au; internet www.lebanemb.org.au; Ambassador JEAN DANIEL.

Libya: 50 Culgoa Circuit, O'Malley, ACT 2606; tel. (2) 6290-7900; fax (2) 6286-4522; e-mail info@libyanembassy.org.au; Ambassador MUSBAH A. A. ALLAFI.

Macedonia, former Yugoslav republic: 25 Cobbadah St, O'Malley, ACT 2606; tel. (2) 6282-6220; fax (2) 6282-6229; e-mail macedonia@grapevine.com.au; internet www.missions.gov.mk/canberra; Ambassador VELE TRPEVSKI.

Malaysia: 7 Perth Ave, Yarralumla, ACT 2600; tel. (2) 6120-0300; fax (2) 6273-2496; e-mail malcanberra@malaysia.org.au; internet www.malaysia.org.au; High Commissioner Datuk ZAINAL ABIDIN AHMAD.

Malta: 38 Culgoa Circuit, O'Malley, ACT 2606; tel. (2) 6290-1724; fax (2) 6290-2453; e-mail highcommission.canberra@gov.mt; internet www.foreign.gov.mt/australia; High Commissioner CHARLES MUSCAT.

Mauritius: 2 Beale Cres., Deakin, ACT 2600; tel. (2) 6281-1203; fax (2) 6282-3235; e-mail canberrahc@mail.gov.mu; High Commissioner MARIE FRANCE LISIANNE MIRELLA CHAUVIN.

Mexico: 14 Perth Ave, Yarralumla, ACT 2600; tel. (2) 6273-3963; fax (2) 6273-1190; e-mail embamex@mexico.org.au; internet embamex.sre.gob.mx/australia; Ambassador MARÍA LUISA BEATRIZ LÓPEZ GARGALLO.

Mongolia: 23 Culgoa Circuit, O'Malley, ACT 2606; tel. (2) 6286-2947; fax (2) 6286-6381; e-mail canberra@mfat.gov.mn; internet www.mongolianembassy.org.au; Ambassador RAVDANGIIN BOLD.

Morocco: 17 Terrigal Crescent, O'Malley, ACT 2606; tel. (2) 6290-0755; fax (2) 6290-0744; e-mail sifmacan@moroccoembassy.org.au; internet www.moroccoembassy.org.au; Ambassador MOHAMED MAEL-AININ.

Myanmar: 22 Arkana St, Yarralumla, ACT 2600; tel. (2) 6273-3811; fax (2) 6273-3181; e-mail mecanberra@bigpond.com; internet mecanberra.com.au; Ambassador MIN THEIN.

Nepal: POB 1070, Mawson, ACT 2607; tel. (2) 6286-9978; fax (2) 6162-1557; e-mail info@necan.gov.np; internet www.necan.gov.np; Ambassador RUDRA KUMAR NEPAL.

Netherlands: 120 Empire Circuit, Yarralumla, ACT 2600; tel. (2) 6220-9400; fax (2) 6273-3206; e-mail can@minbuza.nl; internet www.mfa.nl/can; Ambassador ANNEMIEKE RUIGROK.

New Zealand: Commonwealth Ave, Canberra, ACT 2600; tel. (2) 6270-4211; fax (2) 6273-3194; e-mail nzhccba@bigpond.net.au; internet www.nzembassy.com/australia; High Commissioner CHRIS SEED.

Nigeria: 26 Guilfoyle St, Yarralumla, ACT 2600; tel. 0424757698 (mobile); fax (2) 6282-8471; e-mail chancery@nigeria-can.org.au; High Commissioner AYOOLA LAWRENCE OLUKANNI.

Norway: 17 Hunter St, Yarralumla, ACT 2600; tel. (2) 6270-5700; fax (2) 6270-5701; e-mail emb.canberra@mfa.no; internet www.norway.org.au; Ambassador SIREN GJERME ERIKSEN.

Pakistan: POB 684, Mawson, ACT 2607; tel. (2) 6290-1676; fax (2) 6290-1073; e-mail hcparepcanberra@internode.on.net; internet www.pakistan.org.au; High Commissioner ABDUL MALIK ABDULLAH.

Papua New Guinea: POB E6317, Kingston, ACT 2604; tel. (2) 6273-3322; fax (2) 6273-3732; e-mail kundu@pngcanberra.org; internet www.pngcanberra.org; High Commissioner CHARLES W. LEPANI.

Peru: POB 106, Red Hill, ACT 2603; tel. (2) 6273-7351; fax (2) 6273-7354; e-mail embassy@embaperu.org.au; internet www.embaperu.org.au; Ambassador LUIS FELIPE QUESADA INCHAUSTEGUI.

Philippines: 1 Moonah Pl., Yarralumla, ACT 2600; tel. (2) 6273-2535; fax (2) 6273-3984; e-mail cbrpe@philembassy.org.au; internet www.philembassy.org.au; Ambassador BELEN F. ANOTA.

Poland: 7 Turrana St, Yarralumla, ACT 2600; tel. (2) 6272-1000; fax (2) 6273-3184; e-mail canberra.amb.sekretariat@msz.gov.pl; internet www.canberra.msz.gov.pl; Ambassador PAWEL MILEWSKI.

Portugal: Suites 8 and 9, Stephen House, 32 Thesiger Court, Deakin, ACT 2600; tel. (2) 6260-4970; fax (2) 6282-4387; e-mail embportcanb@internode.on.net; internet www.secomunidades.pt/web/camberra; Ambassador PAULO CUNHA-ALVES.

Qatar: 10 Akame Circuit, O'Malley, ACT 2606; tel. (2) 6269-8309; fax (2) 6269-8387; e-mail canberra@mofa.gov.qa; Ambassador YOUSEF ALI AL-KHATER.

Romania: 4 Dalman Cres., O'Malley, ACT 2606; tel. (2) 6286-2343; fax (2) 6286-2433; e-mail embassy@roemb.com.au; internet www.canberra.mae.ro; Ambassador NINETA BARBULESCU.

Russia: 78 Canberra Ave, Griffith, ACT 2603; tel. (2) 6295-9033; fax (2) 6295-1847; e-mail rusembassy.australia@rambler.ru; internet www.australia.mid.ru; Ambassador VLADIMIR MOROZOV.

Samoa: 13 Culgoa Circuit, O'Malley, ACT 2606; tel. (2) 6286-5505; fax (2) 6286-5678; e-mail samoahcaussi@netspeed.com.au; High Commissioner (vacant).

Saudi Arabia: 38 Guilfoyle St, Yarralumla, ACT 2600; tel. (2) 6250-7000; fax (2) 6282-8911; e-mail auemb@mofa.gov.sa; internet www.mofa.gov.sa; Ambassador NABEEL BIN MOHAMMED AL-SALEH.

Serbia: 4 Bulwarra Close, O'Malley, ACT 2606; tel. (2) 6290-2630; internet www.canberra.mfa.gov.rs; fax (2) 6290-2631; e-mail serbembau@optusnet.com.au; Charge d'affaires a.i. ZORAN MARINKOVIC.

Singapore: 17 Forster Cres., Yarralumla, ACT 2600; tel. (2) 6271-2000; fax (2) 6273-9823; e-mail singhc_cbr@sgmfa.gov.sg; internet www.mfa.gov.sg/canberra; High Commissioner MICHAEL TEO.

Slovakia: 47 Culgoa Circuit, O'Malley, ACT 2606; tel. (2) 6290-1516; fax (2) 6290-1755; e-mail emb.canberra@mzv.sk; internet www.mzv.sk/canberra; Ambassador IGOR BARTHO.

Slovenia: 26 Akame Circuit, O'Malley, ACT 2606; tel. (2) 6290-0000; fax (2) 6290-0619; e-mail vca@gov.si; internet canberra.veleposlanistvo.si; Ambassador MILAN BALAŽIC.

Solomon Islands: POB 256, Deakin West, ACT 2600; tel. (2) 6282-7030; fax (2) 6282-7040; e-mail info@solomonemb.org.au; High Commissioner BERAKI JINO.

South Africa: cnr State Circle and Rhodes Place, Yarralumla, ACT 2600; tel. (2) 6272-7300; fax (2) 6273-1033; e-mail info.canberra@dirco.gov.za; internet www.sahc.org.au; High Commissioner KOLEKA ANITA MQULWANA.

Spain: 15 Arkana St, Yarralumla, ACT 2600; tel. (2) 6273-3555; fax (2) 6273-3918; e-mail emb.canberra@maec.es; internet www.maec.es/embajadas/canberra; Ambassador ENRIQUE VIGUERA RUBIO.

Sri Lanka: 61 Hampton Circuit, Yarralumla, Canberra, ACT 2600; tel. (2) 6198-3756; fax (2) 6198-3760; e-mail admin@slhcaust.org; internet www.slhcaust.org; High Commissioner LAKSHMAN HULUGALLE (designate).

Sweden: 5 Turrana St, Yarralumla, ACT 2600; tel. (2) 6270-2700; fax (2) 6270-2755; e-mail ambassaden.canberra@gov.se; internet www.swedenabroad.com/canberra; Ambassador SVEN-OLOF PETERSSON.

Switzerland: 7 Melbourne Ave, Forrest, ACT 2603; tel. (2) 6162-8400; fax (2) 6273-3428; e-mail can.vertretung@eda.admin.ch; internet www.eda.admin.ch/australia; Ambassador MARCEL STUTZ.

Thailand: 111 Empire Circuit, Yarralumla, ACT 2600; tel. (2) 6206-0100; fax (2) 6206-0123; e-mail thaican@mfa.go.th; internet canberra.thaiembassy.org; Ambassador MARIS SANGIAMPONGSA.

Timor-Leste: 7 Beale Cres., Deakin, ACT 2600; tel. (2) 6260-4833; fax (2) 6232-4075; e-mail timor.embassy@bigpond.com; Ambassador ABEL GUTERRES.

Tonga: 7 Newdegate St, Deakin, ACT 2600; tel. (2) 6232-4806; fax (2) 6232-4807; e-mail info@tongahighcom.com.au; High Commissioner HRH Princess ANGELIKA TUKU'AHO.

Tunisia: Level 5, 221 London Circuit, Canberra, ACT 2600; tel. (2) 6246-0300; fax (2) 6257-1603; e-mail canberra@embassytunisia.com; Ambassador NABIL LAKHAL.

Turkey: 6 Moonah Place, Yarralumla, ACT 2600; tel. (2) 6234-0000; fax (2) 6273-4402; e-mail embassy.canberra@mfa.gov.tr; internet kanberra.be.mfa.gov.tr; Ambassador REHA KESKINTEPE.

Uganda: 7 Dunoon St, O'Malley, Canberra ACT 2606; tel. (2) 6286-1234; fax (2) 6286-1243; e-mail ugandahc@velocitynet.com.au; internet www.ugandahighcommission.org; High Commissioner ENOCH NKURUHO.

Ukraine: Level 12, St George Centre, 60 Marcus Clarke St, Canberra, ACT 2601; tel. (2) 6247-2182; fax (2) 6230-7298; e-mail emb_au@mfa.gov.ua; internet www.mfa.gov.ua/australia; Chargé d'affaires a.i. STANISHEV STASHEVSKYI.

United Arab Emirates: 12 Bulwarra Close, O'Malley, ACT 2606; tel. (2) 6286-8802; fax (2) 6286-8804; e-mail uaeembassy@bigpond.com; internet www.uaeembassy.org.au; Ambassador ABDUL RAHIM AL-SIDDIQ.

United Kingdom: Commonwealth Ave, Canberra, ACT 2600; tel. (2) 6270-6666; fax (2) 6273-3236; e-mail canberra.enquiries@fconet.fco.gov.uk; internet ukinaustralia.fco.gov.uk; High Commissioner PAUL MADDEN.

Uruguay: Suite 2, Level 4, 24 Brisbane Ave, Barton, ACT 2600; tel. (2) 6273-9100; fax (2) 6273-9099; e-mail uruaustralia@mrree.gub.uy; Ambassador RICARDO JAVIER VARELA FERNANDEZ.

USA: Moonah Place, Yarralumla, ACT 2600; tel. (2) 6214-5600; fax (2) 6214-5930; e-mail canberrausaembassy@state.gov; internet canberra.usembassy.gov; Ambassador JOHN BERRY.

Vanuatu: POB 281, Deakin West, ACT 2600; tel. (2) 6282-9931; e-mail kkaloris@vanuatu.gov.vu; High Commissioner KALVAU KALORIS.

Venezuela: 7 Culgoa Circuit, O'Malley, 2606; tel. (2) 6290-2968; fax (2) 6290-2911; e-mail despacho.australia@mppre.gob.ve; internet australia.embajada.gob.ve; Ambassador NELSÓN DÁVILA-LAMEDA.

Viet Nam: 6 Timbarra Cres., O'Malley, ACT 2606; tel. (2) 6286-6059; fax (2) 6286-4534; e-mail vembassy@webone.com.au; internet www.vietnamembassy.org.au; Ambassador LUONG THANH NGHI.

Zimbabwe: 7 Timbarra Cres., O'Malley, ACT 2606; tel. (2) 6286-2700; fax (2) 6290-1680; e-mail consular@zimembassycanberra.org.au; internet www.zimembassycanberra.org.au; Ambassador JACQUELINE NOMHLE ZWAMBILA.

Judicial System

The judicial power of the Commonwealth of Australia is vested in the High Court of Australia, in such other Federal Courts as the Federal Parliament creates, and in such other courts as it invests with Federal jurisdiction.

In March 1986 all remaining categories of appeal from Australian courts to the Queen's Privy Council in the United Kingdom were abolished by the Australia Act.

High Court of Australia: POB 6309, Kingston, Canberra, ACT 2604; tel. (2) 6270-6811; fax (2) 6270-6868; e-mail enquiries@hcourt.gov.au; internet www.hcourt.gov.au; the High Court's original jurisdiction extends to all matters arising under any treaty, affecting representatives of other countries, in which the Commonwealth of Australia or its representative is a party, between states or between residents of different states or between a state and a resident of another state, and in which a writ of mandamus, or prohibition, or an injunction is sought against an officer of the Commonwealth of Australia; it also extends to matters arising under the Australian Constitution or involving its interpretation, and to many matters arising under Commonwealth laws; the Court's appellate jurisdiction has, since June 1984, been discretionary; appeals from the Federal Court, the Family Court and the territorial and state Supreme Courts can only be brought if special leave is granted, in the event of a legal question of general public importance, or of there being differences of opinion between intermediate appellate courts as to the state of the law; the Court comprises a Chief Justice and six other Justices having both original and appellate jurisdiction, each appointed by the Governor-General in Council; Chief Justice ROBERT S. FRENCH.

Federal Court of Australia: Law Courts Bldg, Level 17, Queens Sq., NSW 2000; tel. (2) 9230-8567; fax (2) 9230-8535; e-mail query@fedcourt.gov.au; internet www.fedcourt.gov.au; 47 judges; Chief Justice JAMES LESLIE BAIN ALLSOP.

Family Court of Australia: GPOB 9991, Parramatta, NSW 2150; tel. (2) 8892-8590; fax (2) 8892-8585; e-mail enquiries@familylawcourts.gov.au; internet www.familylawcourts.gov.au; Chief Justice DIANA BRYANT.

Federal Circuit Court of Australia: Level 17, Queens Square, Sydney, NSW 2000; tel. (2) 9230-8567; fax (2) 9230-8295; e-mail customer.service@federalcircuitcourt.gov.au; internet www.federalcircuitcourt.gov.au; fmrly the Federal Magistrates Court of Australia, present name adopted April 2013; the Court is constituted by the Chief Judge (fmrly Chief Federal Magistrate) and other appointed judges; Chief Judge JOHN PASCOE.

Religion

CHRISTIANITY

According to the results of the population census of August 2011, Christians numbered 13,150,600 (rounded figure), representing 61.1% of the total population.

National Council of Churches in Australia: Locked Bag 199, Sydney, NSW 1230; tel. (2) 9299-2215; fax (2) 9262-4514; e-mail secretariat@ncca.org.au; internet www.ncca.org.au; f. 1946; est. as Australian Council of Churches; assumed present name in 1994; 19 mem. churches; Pres. Rev. Dr MIKE SEMMLER; Gen. Sec. Rev. TARA CURLEWIS.

The Anglican Communion

The constitution of the Church of England in Australia, which rendered the church an autonomous member of the Anglican Communion, came into force in January 1962. The body was renamed the Anglican Church of Australia in August 1981. The Church comprises five provinces (together containing 22 dioceses) and the extra-provincial diocese of Tasmania. According to the 2011 population census, there were 3,679,907 adherents (17.1% of the total population).

Anglican Church of Australia—General Synod Office: Suite 2, Level 9, 51 Druitt St, Sydney, NSW 2000; tel. (2) 8267-2700; fax (2) 8267-2727; e-mail reception@anglican.org.au; internet www.anglican.org.au; Primate Most Rev. Dr PHILLIP ASPINALL; Gen. Sec. MARTIN DREVIKOVSKY.

Archbishop of Adelaide and Metropolitan of South Australia: Most Rev. JEFFREY DRIVER, 18 King William Rd, North Adelaide, SA 5006; tel. (8) 8305-9350; fax (8) 8305-9399; e-mail diocesanoffice@adelaide.anglican.com.au; internet www.adelaide.anglican.com.au.

Archbishop of Brisbane and Metropolitan of Queensland, Primate of Australia: Most Rev. Dr PHILLIP JOHN ASPINALL, Bishopsbourne, GPOB 421, Brisbane, Qld 4001; tel. (7) 3835-2222; fax (7) 3832-5030; e-mail info@anglicanbrisbane.org.au; internet www.anglicanbrisbane.org.au.

Archbishop of Melbourne and Metropolitan of Victoria: Most Rev. Dr PHILIP FREIER, The Anglican Centre, 209 Flinders Lane, Melbourne, Vic 3000; tel. (3) 9653-4220; fax (3) 9653-4268; e-mail archbishop@melbourne.anglican.com.au; internet www.melbourne.anglican.com.au.

Archbishop of Perth and Metropolitan of Western Australia: Most Rev. ROGER ADRIAN HERFT, GPOB W2067, Perth, WA 6846; tel. (8) 9325-7455; fax (8) 9221-4118; e-mail diocese@perth.anglican.org; internet www.perth.anglican.org; also has jurisdiction over Christmas Island and the Cocos (Keeling) Islands.

Archbishop of Sydney and Metropolitan of New South Wales: Most Rev. Dr PETER F. JENSEN, POB Q190, QVB PO, Sydney, NSW 1230; tel. (2) 9265-1555; fax (2) 9261-4485; e-mail reception@sydney.anglican.asn.au; internet www.sydneyanglicans.net.

The Roman Catholic Church

Australia comprises five metropolitan archdioceses, two archdioceses directly responsible to the Holy See and 24 dioceses, including one diocese each for Catholics of the Maronite and Melkite rites, and one military ordinariate. According to the 2011 population census, there were 5,439,268 adherents (25.3% of the total population).

Australian Catholic Bishops' Conference: GPOB 368, Canberra, ACT 2601; tel. (2) 6201-9845; fax (2) 6247-6083; e-mail gensec@catholic.org.au; internet www.acbc.catholic.org.au; f. 1979; Pres. Most Rev. PHILIP WILSON (Archbishop of Adelaide); Sec. Rev. BRIAN LUCAS.

Archbishop of Adelaide: Most Rev. PHILIP WILSON, GPOB 1364, Adelaide, SA 5001; tel. (8) 8210-8108; fax (8) 8223-2307; e-mail archbishop3@adelaide.catholic.org.au; internet www.adelaide.catholic.org.au.

Archbishop of Brisbane: Most Rev. MARK BENEDICT COLERIDGE, 790 Brunswick St, New Farm, Brisbane, Qld 4005; tel. (7) 3336-9361; fax (7) 3358-1357; e-mail archbishop@bne.catholic.net.au; internet www.bne.catholic.net.au.

Archbishop of Canberra and Goulburn: Most Rev. MARK BENEDICT COLERIDGE, GPOB 3089, Canberra, ACT 2601; tel. (2) 6201-9800; fax (2) 6257-7410; e-mail archbishop@cg.catholic.org.au; internet www.cg.catholic.org.au.

Archbishop of Hobart: Most Rev. ADRIAN DOYLE, GPOB 62, Hobart, Tas 7001; tel. (3) 6208-6222; fax (3) 6208-6292; e-mail vicar.general@aohtas.org.au; internet www.hobart.catholic.org.au.

Archbishop of Melbourne: Most Rev. DENIS JAMES HART, POB 146, East Melbourne, Vic 3002; tel. (3) 9926-5677; fax (3) 9926-5617; e-mail info@cam.org.au; internet www.cam.org.au.

Archbishop of Perth: Most Rev. TIMOTHY COSTELLOE, Catholic Church Office, 25 Victoria Ave, Perth, WA 6000; tel. (8) 9223-1351; fax (8) 9221-1716; e-mail enquiries@perthcatholic.org.au; internet www.perthcatholic.org.au.

Archbishop of Sydney: Cardinal GEORGE PELL, Polding Centre, 133 Liverpool St, Sydney, NSW 2000; tel. (2) 9390-5100; fax (2) 9261-8312; e-mail chancery@sydneycatholic.org; internet www.sydney.catholic.org.au.

Orthodox Churches

Greek Orthodox Archdiocese of Australia: 242 Cleveland St, Redfern, Sydney, NSW 2016; tel. (2) 9690-6100; fax (2) 9698-5368; e-mail webmaster@greekorthodox.org.au; internet www.greekorthodox.org.au; f. 1924; 700,000 mems; Primate Archbishop STYLIANOS HARKIANAKIS.

The Antiochian, Coptic, Romanian, Serbian and Syrian Orthodox Churches are also represented.

Other Christian Churches

Baptist Union of Australia: 1 Francis Ave, Broadview, SA 5083; tel. (8) 8261-1844; e-mail bua@baptist.org.au; internet www.baptist.org.au; f. 1926; 61,409 mems; 868 churches; Nat. Dir Rev. Dr JOHN BEASY.

Churches of Christ in Australia: 1st Floor, 582 Heidelberg Rd, Fairfield, Vic 3078; tel. (3) 9488-8800; fax (3) 9481-8543; e-mail andrew.ball@freshhope.org.au; internet cofcaustralia.org; 40,000 mems; Chair. ANDREW BALL.

Lutheran Church of Australia: National Office, 197 Archer St, North Adelaide, SA 5006; tel. (8) 8267-7300; fax (8) 8267-7310; e-mail admin@lca.org.au; internet www.lca.org.au; f. 1966; 70,000 mems; Bishop Rev. JOHN HENDERSON.

United Pentecostal Church of Australia: POB 60, Woden, ACT 2606; tel. and fax (2) 6281-2330; fax (2) 6281-2241; e-mail contact@upca.org.au; internet www.upca.org.au; f. 1953; over 3,500 adherents in 2013; associated with United Pentecostal Church Int. in North America; Gen. Superintendent JOHN DOWNS.

Uniting Church in Australia: POB A2266, Sydney South, NSW 1235; tel. (2) 8267-4428; fax (2) 8267-4222; e-mail enquiries@nat.uca.org.au; internet uca.org.au; f. 1977; est. as a union of Methodist, Presbyterian and Congregational Churches; 300,000 mems; Pres. Rev. ANDREW DUTNEY; Gen. Sec. Rev. TERENCE CORKIN.

ISLAM

At the census of August 2011, the Muslim community numbered 476,291.

Australian Federation of Islamic Councils: 932 Bourke St, Zetland, Sydney, NSW 2017; tel. (2) 9319-6733; fax (2) 9319-0159; e-mail admin@afic.com.au; internet www.afic.com.au; Pres. IKEBAL PATEL; Vice-Pres. HAFEZ KASSEM.

JUDAISM

The Jewish community numbered 97,335 at the census of August 2011.

Great Synagogue: 166 Castlereagh St, Sydney, NSW; tel. (2) 9267-2477; fax (2) 9264-8871; e-mail admin@greatsynagogue.org.au; internet www.greatsynagogue.org.au; f. 1878; Sr Rabbi JEREMY LAWRENCE; Pres. MICHAEL GOLD.

OTHER FAITHS

According to the August 2011 census, Buddhists numbered 528,977 and Hindus 275,534.

The Press

The total circulation of Australia's daily newspapers is relatively high, but in the more remote parts of the country weekly papers are even more popular. Most of Australia's newspapers are published in sparsely populated rural areas where the demand for local news is strong.

APN News and Media Ltd: Level 4, 100 William St, Sydney, NSW 2011; tel. (2) 9333-4999; fax (2) 9333-4900; e-mail info@apn.com.au; internet www.apn.com.au; publishes 14 daily newspapers, incl. *The Chronicle*, *Daily Mercury*, *Northern Star* and over 75 community publs; Dep. Chair. ALBERT E. HARRIS; Chair. (vacant); Chief Exec. MICHAEL MILLER.

Bauer Media Group: 54–58 Park St, Sydney, NSW 2000; tel. (2) 9282-8000; fax (2) 9126-3769; internet www.bauer-media.com.au; publishes over 80 magazines, incl. *The Australian Women's Weekly*, *Cleo*, *Cosmopolitan*, *Woman's Day*, *Dolly*, *Australian Gourmet Traveller*, *Top Gear Australia* and *Wheels*; CEO MATTHEW STANTON.

Fairfax Media: GPO 506, Sydney, NSW 2001; tel. (2) 9282-2833; fax (2) 9282-3133; internet www.fxj.com.au; f. 1987; fmrly known as John Fairfax Holdings Ltd; merged with Rural Press Ltd 2007; Chair. ROGER CORBETT; Chief Exec. and Man. Dir GREG HYWOOD; publs include *The Sydney Morning Herald*, *Australian Financial Review* and *Sun-Herald* (NSW), *The Age* and *BRW Publications* (Victoria), and *The Canberra Times*; also provides online and interactive services.

News Ltd: GPOB 4245, Sydney, NSW 2001; tel. (2) 9288-3000; fax (2) 9288-2300; e-mail news@news.com.au; internet www.news.com.au; Australian subsidiary of US News Corpn; Chair. and CEO JULIAN CLARKE; controls *The Australian* and *The Weekend Australian* (national), *The Daily Telegraph*, *Sunday Telegraph* (NSW), *Herald Sun* and *Sunday Herald Sun* (Victoria), *Northern Territory News* (Darwin), *Sunday Times* (WA), *Townsville Bulletin*, *The Courier-Mail*, *The Sunday Mail* (Queensland), *Mercury* (Tasmania), *The Advertiser*, *Sunday Mail* (South Australia).

West Australian Newspapers Holdings Ltd: Newspaper House, 50 Hasler Rd, Osborne Park, WA 6017; tel. (8) 9482-9047; fax (8) 9482-9051; e-mail westinfo@wanews.com.au; internet www.thewest.com.au; Chair. KERRY STOKES; CEO CHRIS WHARTON.

NEWSPAPERS

Australian Capital Territory

The Canberra Times: POB 7155, Canberra Mail Centre, ACT 2610; tel. (2) 6280-2122; fax (2) 6280-2282; e-mail letters.editor@canberratimes.com.au; internet www.canberratimes.com.au; f. 1926; daily and Sun.; morning; Editor-in-Chief JACK WATERFORD; Editor ROD QUINN; circ. 34,000 (Mon.–Fri.), 56,000 (Sat.), 35,000 (Sun.).

New South Wales

Dailies

The Australian: POB 4245, Sydney, NSW 2001; tel. (2) 9288-3000; fax (2) 9288-2250; e-mail letters@theaustralian.com.au; internet www.theaustralian.com.au; f. 1964; distributed nationally; edited in Sydney, simultaneous edns in Sydney, Melbourne, Perth, Townsville, Adelaide and Brisbane; Editor-in-Chief CHRIS MITCHELL; Editor CLIVE MATHIESON; circ. 122,428 (Mon.–Fri.); *The Weekend Australian* (Sat.) 266,696.

The Daily Telegraph: News Ltd, 2 Holt St, Surry Hills, NSW 2010; tel. (2) 9288-3000; fax (2) 9288-2300; e-mail news@dailytelegraph.com.au; internet www.dailytelegraph.com.au; f. 1879; merged in 1990 with *Daily Mirror* (f. 1941); 24-hour tabloid; Editor PAUL WHITTAKER; circ. 333,424 (Mon.–Fri.), 320,505 (Sat.).

The Manly Daily: 26 Sydney Rd, Manly, NSW 2095; tel. (2) 9689-5500; fax (2) 9977-1203; e-mail editor@manlydaily.com.au; internet www.manlydaily.com.au; f. 1906; Tue.–Sat.; Editor LUKE McILVEEN; circ. 91,816.

The Newcastle Herald: 28–30 Bolton St, Newcastle, NSW 2300; tel. (2) 4979-5000; fax (2) 4979-5588; e-mail news@theherald.com.au; internet www.theherald.com.au; f. 1858; morning; 6 a week; Editor CHAD WATSON; Gen. Man. JULIE AINSWORTH; circ. 48,000.

The Sydney Morning Herald: GPOB 506, Sydney, NSW 2001; tel. (2) 9282-2833; fax (2) 9282-3253; e-mail newsdesk@smh.com.au; internet www.smh.com.au; f. 1831; morning; Editor-in-Chief GARRY LINNELL (acting); circ. 157,931 (Mon.–Fri.), 272,849 (Sat.).

Weeklies

Bankstown Canterbury Torch: 47 Allingham St, Condell Park, NSW 2200; tel. (2) 9795-0000; fax (2) 9795-0096; e-mail torch@torchpublishing.com.au; internet www.torchpublishing.com.au; f. 1920; Wed.; owned by Torch Publishing Co Pty Ltd; Editor MARK KIRKLAND; circ. over 90,000 copies per week.

Northern District Times: Suite 2, 3 Carlingford Rd, Epping, NSW 2121; tel. (2) 9024-8718; fax (2) 9024-8788; e-mail editor@northerndistricttimes.com.au; internet www.northerndistricttimes.com.au; f. 1921; Wed.; Editor COLIN KERR; circ. 58,140.

The Parramatta Advertiser: 142–154 Macquarie St, Parramatta, NSW 2150; tel. (2) 9689-5323; fax (2) 9689-5388; e-mail editor@parramattaadvertiser.com.au; internet www.parramattaadvertiser.com.au; f. 1933; Wed.; Editor RICK ALLEN; circ. 83,110.

St George and Sutherland Shire Leader: 13A, Montgomery St, Kogarah, NSW 2217; tel. (2) 9588-8888; fax (2) 9588-8887; e-mail leaderenquiries@fairfaxmedia.com.au; internet www.theleader.com.au; f. 1960; Tue. and Thur.; Editor ALBERT MARTINEZ; circ. 150,000.

Sun-Herald: GPOB 506, Sydney, NSW 2001; tel. (2) 9282-2833; fax (2) 9282-2151; e-mail newsdesk@smh.com.au; internet www.smh.com.au; f. 1953; Sun.; Editor RICK FENELEY; circ. 290,174.

Sunday Telegraph: 2 Holt St, Surry Hills, NSW 2010; tel. (2) 9288-3000; fax (2) 9288-2300; e-mail letters@sundaytelegraph.com.au; f. 1938; Editor MICK CARROLL MICK CARROLL; circ. 559,026.

Northern Territory

Daily

Northern Territory News: Printers Place, GPOB 1300, Darwin, NT 0801; tel. (8) 8944-9900; fax (8) 8981-6045; e-mail ntnmail@ntnews.com.au; internet www.ntnews.com.au; f. 1952; morning; Editor-in-Chief JULIAN RICCI; Gen. Man. EVAN HANNAH; circ. 16,539 (Mon.–Fri.), 26,163 (Sat.); *The Sunday Territorian*, circ. 18,620.

Weekly

Centralian Advocate: 2 Gap Rd, Alice Springs, NT 0871; tel. (8) 8950-9777; fax (8) 8950-9740; e-mail ceneditorial@aliceadvocate.com.au; f. 1947; Tue. and Thur.; Editor DALLAS FRAKKING; circ. 18,000.

Queensland

Dailies

The Courier-Mail: Cnr Mayne Rd and Campbell St, Bowen Hills, Qld 4001; tel. (7) 3666-6775; fax (7) 3666-6696; e-mail crutcherm@gnp.newsltd.com.au; internet www.thecouriermail.com.au; f. 1933; morning; Editor MICHAEL CRUTCHER; Man. Editor ANNA REYNOLDS; circ. 172,801 (Mon.–Fri.), 228,650 (Sat.).

Gold Coast Bulletin: 12-14 Marine Parade Southport, Qld 4214; tel. (7) 5584-2000; internet www.goldcoast.com.au; f. 1885; 6 a week; Editor DEAN GOULD; circ. 29,952 (Mon.–Fri.), 43,509 (Sat.).

Weekly

The Sunday Mail: cnr Mayne Rd and Campbell St, Bowen Hills, Qld 4006; tel. (7) 3666-6775; fax (7) 3666-6696; e-mail karen.lewis@news.com.au; internet www.thesundaymail.com.au; f. 1923; owned by News Limited; Editor PETER GLEESON; circ. 966,000.

South Australia

Daily

The Advertiser: 31 Waymouth St, Adelaide, SA 5000; tel. (8) 8206-2300; fax (8) 8206-3669; e-mail tiser@adv.newsltd.com.au; internet www.adelaidenow.com.au; f. 1858; morning; Editor SAM WEIR; circ. 160,842 (Mon.–Fri.), 213,378 (Sat.).

Weekly

Sunday Mail: Level 2, 31 Waymouth St, GPOB 339, Adelaide, SA 5000; tel. (8) 8206-2767; fax (8) 8206-3646; e-mail mailedit@sundaymail.com.au; internet www.advertiser.com.au; f. 1912; Editor DAVID PENBERTHY; circ. 294,930.

Tasmania

Dailies

The Advocate: POB 63, Burnie, Tas 7320; tel. (3) 6440-7409; fax (3) 6440-7461; e-mail news@theadvocate.com.au; internet www.theadvocate.com.au; f. 1890; morning; Editor JASON PURDIE; circ. 22,786.

Examiner: 71–75 Paterson St, POB 99, Launceston, Tas 7250; tel. (3) 6336-7111; fax (3) 6331-4858; e-mail admin@examiner.com.au; internet www.examiner.com.au; f. 1842; 6 a week; Editor MARTIN GILMOUR; Gen. Man. PHIL LEERSEN; circ. over 50,000.

Mercury: 93 Macquarie St, Hobart, Tas 7000; tel. (3) 6230-0622; fax (3) 6230-0711; e-mail mercury.news@dbl.newsltd.com.au; internet www.themercury.com.au; f. 1854; morning; Man. Dir REX GARDNER; Editor GARRY BAILEY; circ. 40,638 (Mon.–Fri.), 64,469 (Sat.); *Sunday Tasmanian*, circ. 51,617.

Weekly

Sunday Examiner: 71–75 Paterson St, Launceston, Tas 7250; tel. (3) 6336-7320; fax (3) 6334-7328; e-mail mail@examiner.com.au; internet www.examiner.com.au; f. 1924; Editor MARTIN GILMOUR; circ. 38,826.

Victoria

Dailies

The Age: 655 Collins St, Docklands, Melbourne, Vic 3008; tel. (3) 8667-2250; e-mail newsdesk@theage.com.au; internet www.theage.com.au; f. 1854; daily; Editor-in-Chief ANDREW HOLDEN; circ. 144,277 (Mon.–Fri.), 219,696 (Sat.).

Australian Financial Review: GPOB 55, Melbourne, Vic 3001; tel. (2) 9282-1547; e-mail afreditor@afr.com.au; internet www.afr.com; f. 1951; distributed nationally; Publr/Editor-in-Chief MICHAEL GILL; Editor PAUL BAILEY; circ. 64,861 (Mon.–Fri.), 81,606 (Sat.).

Geelong Advertiser: 191–195 Ryrie St, Geelong, Vic 3220; tel. (3) 5227-4300; fax (3) 5227-4451; internet www.geelongadvertiser.com.au; f. 1840; morning; Editor NICK PAPPS; circ. 27,463 (Mon.–Fri.), 45,987 (Sat.).

Herald Sun: HWT Tower, 40 City Rd, Southbank, Vic 3006; tel. (3) 9292-2000; fax (3) 9292-2112; e-mail news@heraldsun.com.au; internet www.heraldsun.com.au; f. 1840; Editor-in-Chief PETER BLUNDEN; Editor DAMON JOHNSTON; circ. 425,253 (Mon.–Fri.), 433,365 (Sat.).

Weeklies

The Sunday Age: 655 Collins St, Docklands, Melbourne, Vic 3008; tel. (3) 8667-2250; e-mail newsdesk@theage.com.au; internet www.theage.com.au; f. 1989; Editor GAY ALCORN; circ. 178,141.

Sunday Herald Sun: HWT Tower, 40 City Rd, Southbank, Vic 3006; tel. (3) 9292-2963; fax (3) 9292-2080; e-mail sundayhs@heraldsun.com.au; internet www.heraldsun.com.au; f. 1991; Editor DAMON JOHNSTON; circ. 501,642.

Western Australia

Daily

The West Australian: GPOB D162, Perth, WA 6840; tel. (8) 9482-3111; fax (8) 9482-9080; internet www.thewest.com.au; f. 1833; morning; Editor BRETT MCCARTHY; circ. 192,230 (Mon.–Fri.), 316,062 (Sat.).

Weekly

Sunday Times: 34 Stirling St, Perth, WA 6000; tel. (8) 9326-9000; fax (8) 9221-1121; e-mail online@perthnow.com.au; internet www.perthnow.com.au; f. 1897; Man. Dir DAVID MAGUIRE; Editor ROD SAVAGE; circ. 293,136.

PRINCIPAL PERIODICALS

Weeklies and Fortnightlies

Business Review Weekly (BRW): GPOB 55, Melbourne, Vic 3001; tel. (2) 9282-1111; fax (2) 9282-1779; e-mail brweditor@brw.fairfax.com.au; internet www.brw.com.au; f. 1981; Editor JAMES THOMSON; circ. 38,550.

Computerworld Australia: POB 1753, North Sydney, NSW 2059; tel. (2) 9902-2700; fax (2) 9439-5512; e-mail editor@idg.com.au; internet www.computerworld.com.au; weekly; information technology news; Editor ROHAN PEARCE.

The Countryman: GPOB D162, Perth, WA 6840; tel. (8) 9482-3111; fax (8) 9482-3324; e-mail countryman@countryman.com.au; internet www.countryman.com.au; f. 1885; Thur.; farming; Editor LARA LADYMAN; circ. 10,500.

The Medical Journal of Australia: Locked Bag 3030, Strawberry Hills, NSW 2012; tel. (2) 9562-6666; fax (2) 9562-6699; e-mail medjaust@ampco.com.au; internet www.mja.com.au; f. 1914; fortnightly; Editor-in-Chief STEPHEN LEEDER; circ. 28,576.

New Idea: 35–51 Mitchell St, McMahons Point, NSW 2060; tel. (2) 9464-3200; fax (2) 9464-3203; e-mail letters@newidea.com.au; internet www.newidea.com.au; weekly; women's; Editor KIM WILSON; Publr SUZANNE MONKS; circ. 41,715.

News Weekly: 35 Whitehorse Rd, POB 251, Balwyn, Vic 3103; tel. (3) 9816-0800; fax (3) 9816-0899; e-mail nw@newsweekly.com.au; internet www.newsweekly.com.au; f. 1943; publ. by Nat. Civic Council; fortnightly; Sat.; political, social, educational and trade union affairs; Editor PETER WESTMORE; circ. 9,000.

NW: 54 Park St, Sydney, NSW 2000; tel. (2) 9282-2000; e-mail nw@acp.com.au; internet www.nwonline.com.au; weekly; entertainment news; Editor LISA SINCLAIR; circ. 143,302.

People: Level 18, 66–68 Goulburn St, Sydney, NSW 2000; tel. (2) 9282-8388; fax (2) 9283-7923; e-mail mvine@acpmagazines.com.au; internet www.acpmagazines.com.au/people.htm; fortnightly; men's interest; Editor JAMES COONEY; circ. 40,045.

Picture: GPOB 5201, Sydney, NSW 2001; tel. (2) 9288-9686; fax (2) 9267-4372; e-mail picture@bauer-media.com.au; internet www.picturemag.com; weekly; men's interest; Editor JAMES COONEY; circ. 56,559.

Queensland Country Life: cnr Finucane Rd and Delancey St, Ormiston, Qld 4160; tel. (7) 3826-8200; fax (7) 3821-1226; e-mail editorialsec.qcl@ruralpress.com; internet qcl.farmonline.com.au; f. 1935; Thur.; Editor BRAD COOPER; Gen. Man. JOHN WARLTERS; circ. 34,990.

Stock and Land: 655 Collins St, Docklands, Vic 3008; tel. (3) 8667-1200; fax (3) 9338-1044; e-mail stockandland@fairfaxmedia.com.au; internet www.stockandland.com.au; f. 1914; weekly; agricultural and rural news; Editor ALISHA FOGDEN; circ. 8,400.

Take 5: 54–58 Park St, Sydney, NSW 2000; tel. (2) 9282-8000; fax (2) 9267-4361; e-mail take5@acpmagazines.com.au; internet www.take5mag.com.au; weekly; Editor PAUL MERRILL; circ. 174,816.

That's Life!: 35–51 Mitchell St, McMahons Point, NSW 2060; tel. (2) 9464-3300; fax (2) 9464-3480; e-mail thatslife@pacificmags.com.au; internet www.thatslife.com.au; f. 1994; weekly; features; Editor LINDA SMITH; circ. 309,076.

Time South Pacific: Level 10, 32 Walker St, North Sydney, NSW 2060; tel. (2) 9925-2500; fax (2) 9954-0828; e-mail letters@time.com; internet www.time.com/time/magazine/pacific; weekly; current affairs; Editor STEVE WATERSON; circ. 136,762.

TV Week: 54 Park St, Sydney, NSW 2000; tel. (2) 9288-9611; fax (2) 9283-4849; e-mail tvweek@acp.com.au; internet www.tvweek.ninemsn.com.au; f. 1957; Wed.; colour national; Editor EMMA NOLAN; circ. 158,518.

The Weekly Times: POB 14999, Melbourne, Vic 8001; tel. (3) 9292-2672; fax (3) 9292-2697; e-mail wtimes@theweeklytimes.com.au; internet www.weeklytimesnow.com.au; f. 1869; farming, regional issues, country life; Wed.; Editor ED GANNON; circ. 60,951.

Woman's Day: POB 5245, Sydney, NSW 2001; tel. (2) 9282-8000; fax (2) 9267-4360; e-mail womansday@acp.com.au; internet womansday.ninemsn.com.au; weekly; circulates throughout Australia and NZ; Editor FIONA CONNOLLY; circ. 345,356.

Monthlies and Others

Architectural Product News: Architecture Media Pty Ltd, Level 6, 163 Eastern Rd, South Melbourne, Vic 3205; tel. (3) 8699-1000; fax (3) 9696-2617; e-mail apn@archmedia.com.au; internet www.architecturemedia.com; 6 a year; Editorial Dir CAMERON BRUHN; Editor MARY MANN; circ. 24,584.

Australian Geographic: 54 Park St, Sydney, NSW 2000; tel. (2) 9263-9813; fax (2) 9263-9810; e-mail editorial@ausgeo.com.au; internet www.australiangeographic.com.au; f. 1986; bi-monthly; Man. Dir RORY SCOTT; Editor-in-Chief CHRISSIE GOLDRICK; circ. 79,053.

Australian Good Taste: Locked Bag 5030, Alexandria, NSW 2015; tel. (2) 9353-6666; fax (2) 9353-6699; e-mail goodtaste@newsmagazines.com.au; internet www.taste.com.au/good+taste; monthly; food and lifestyle; Editor BRODEE MYERS-COOKE; circ. 160,511.

Australian Gourmet Traveller: GPOB 4088, Sydney, NSW 2001; tel. (2) 9282-8758; fax (2) 9264-3621; e-mail askgourmet@bauer-media.com.au; internet gourmettraveller.com.au; monthly; food and travel; Editor ANTHEA LOUCAS; circ. 68,018.

Australian Home Beautiful: 35–51 Mitchell St, McMahons Point, NSW 2060; tel. (2) 9394-2388; fax (2) 9394-2406; e-mail homebeautiful@pacificmags.com.au; internet www.homebeautiful.com.au; f. 1925; monthly; Editor-in-Chief WENDY MOORE; circ. 72,296.

Australian House and Garden: 54 Park St, Sydney, NSW 2000; tel. (2) 9282-8456; fax (2) 9267-4912; internet www.houseandgarden.com.au; f. 1948; monthly; design, decorating, renovating, gardens, food, travel, health and beauty; Editor-in-Chief LISA GREEN; circ. 113,569.

Australian Journal of Mining: Informa Australia Pty Ltd, Level 2, 120 Sussex St, Sydney, NSW 2000; tel. (2) 9080-4300; fax (2) 9299-4622; e-mail charles.macdonald@informa.com.au; internet www.theajmonline.com.au; f. 1986; bi-monthly; mining and exploration throughout Australia and South Pacific; Editor CHARLES MACDONALD; circ. 5,204.

Australian Journal of Pharmacy: Level 5, 8 Thomas St, Chatswood, NSW 2067; tel. (2) 8117-9542; fax (2) 8117-9511; e-mail david.weston@appco.com.au; internet www.ajp.com.au; f. 1886; monthly; journal for pharmacists and pharmaceutical industry; Publishing Dir DAVID WESTON; Editor MATTHEW ETON; circ. 16,553.

Australian Law Journal: 100 Harris St, Pyrmont, NSW 2009; tel. (2) 8587-7000; fax (2) 8587-7104; e-mail lta.alj@thomsonreuters.com; internet www.thomsonreuters.com.au; f. 1927; monthly; Gen. Editor Justice P. W. YOUNG; circ 4,500.

Australian Photography: 17–21 Bellevue St, Surry Hills, NSW 2010; tel. (2) 9281-2333; fax (2) 9281-2750; e-mail jodiereid@yaffa.com.au; internet www.australianphotography.com; f. 1950; monthly; Editor JAMES OSTINGA; circ. 9,099.

The Australian Women's Weekly: 54–58 Park St, Sydney, NSW 2000; tel. (2) 9282-8000; fax (2) 9267-4459; e-mail womensweekly@acpmagazines.com.au; internet www.aww.com.au; f. 1933; monthly; Editor-in-Chief HELEN MCCABE; circ. 459,175.

Belle: 54 Park St, Sydney, NSW 2000; tel. (2) 9282-8000; fax (2) 9267-8037; e-mail belle@acp.com.au; internet www.acpmagazines.com.au/belle.htm; f. 1975; every 2 months; interior design and architecture; Editor-in-Chief NEALE WHITAKER; circ. 44,534.

Better Homes and Gardens: 35–51 Mitchell St, McMahon's Point, NSW 2060; e-mail bhgmagenquiries@pacificmags.com.au; internet au.lifestyle.yahoo.com/better-homes-gardens; f. 1978; 13 a year; Editor JULIA ZAETTA; circ. 362,150.

Cleo: 54 Park St, Sydney, NSW 2000; tel. (2) 9282-8617; fax (2) 9267-4368; internet www.cleo.com.au; f. 1972; women's monthly; Editor LUCY COUSINS; circ. 76,63; f. 0.

Cosmopolitan: 54 Park St, Sydney, NSW 2000; tel. (2) 9282-8039; fax (2) 9267-4457; e-mail cosmo@acp.com.au; internet www.cosmopolitan.com.au; f. 1973; monthly; women's lifestyle; Editor BRONWYN MCCAHON; circ. 98,294.

Delicious: Locked Bag 5030, Alexandria, NSW 2015; tel. (2) 9353-6666; fax (2) 9353-6699; e-mail delicious@newsmagazines.com.au; internet www.taste.com.au/delicious; 11 a year; food and lifestyle; Editor TRUDI JENKINS; circ. 129,626.

Dolly: 54–58 Park St, Sydney, NSW 2000; tel. (2) 9282-8437; fax (2) 9126-3715; internet dolly.ninemsn.com.au/dolly; f. 1970; monthly; youth lifestyle; Editor LUCY COUSINS; circ. 80,315.

Family Circle: Pacific Magazines, Media City, 8 Central Ave, Eveleigh, NSW 2015; tel. (2) 9394-2000; fax (2) 9394-2481; internet www.pacificmagazines.com.au; 2 a year; Editor MARA LEE; circ. 61,600.

FHM: EMAP Australia, Level 6, 187 Thomas St, Haymarket, Sydney, NSW 2000; tel. (2) 9581-9400; fax (2) 9581-9570; e-mail incoming@emap.com.au; internet www.fhm.com.au; monthly; men's interest; Editor GUY MOSEL; circ. 27,352.

Financial Review Smart Investor: 201 Sussex St, GPOB 506, Sydney, NSW 2000; tel. (2) 8667-3844; fax (2) 8667-3898; e-mail smartinvestor@afr.com.au; internet www.afrsmartinvestor.com; monthly; Editor JAMES FROST.

Gardening Australia: POB 199, Alexandria, NSW 1435; tel. (2) 9353-6666; fax (2) 9317-4615; e-mail ga@newsmagazines.com.au; internet www.gardeningaustralia.com.au; f. 1991; monthly; Editor DEBBIE MCDONALD; circ. 94,868.

Girlfriend: Media City, 8 Central Ave, Eveleigh, NSW 2015; tel. (2) 9394-2000; fax (2) 9394-2903; e-mail girlfriend@pacificmags.com.au; internet www.girlfriend.com.au; monthly; for teenage girls; Editor SARAH TARCA; circ. 70,002.

Good Health and Medicine: 54 Park St, Sydney, NSW 2000; tel. (2) 9282-8000; fax (2) 9267-4361; internet health.ninemsn.com.au/goodmedicine/goodmedicine.aspx; monthly; fmrly *Good Medicine*; health and beauty; Editor CATHERINE MARSHALL; circ. 66,115.

Houses: Architecture Media Pty Ltd, Level 6, 163 Eastern Rd, South Melbourne, Vic 3205; tel. (3) 8699-1000; fax (3) 9696-2617; e-mail houses@archmedia.com.au; internet www.architecturemedia.com/houses; f. 1989; 6 a year; Publisher/Editorial Dir SUE HARRIS; Editorial Dir KATELIN BUTLER; circ. 20,000.

K-Zone: Media City, 8 Central Ave, Eveleigh, NSW 2015; tel. (2) 9394-2760; fax (2) 9464-3483; e-mail kzone@pacificmags.com.au; internet www.kzone.com.au; monthly; gaming and entertainment; Editor DANIEL FINDLAY; circ. 40,004.

Marie Claire: Media City, 8 Central Ave, Eveleigh, NSW 2015; tel. (2) 9394-2372; e-mail marieclaire@pacificmags.com.au; internet www.marieclaire.com.au; f. 1995; owned by Pacific Magazines Pty Ltd; monthly; fashion and lifestyle; Editor and Publr JACKIE FRANK; circ. 90,092.

Motor: POB 4088, Sydney, NSW 2001; tel. (2) 9288-9172; fax (2) 9263-9777; e-mail motor@acpmagazines.com.au; f. 1954; monthly; Editor IAIN KELLY; circ. 22,221.

Open Road: NRMA Publishing, Level 1, 9 George St, North Strathfield, NSW 2137; tel. (2) 8741-6675; fax (2) 8741-6697; e-mail jo@openroad.com.au; internet www.openroad.com.au; f. 1927; every 2 months; journal of Nat. Roads and Motorists' Asscn (NRMA); Publr BERNADETTE BRENNAN; Editor-in-Chief SUZANNE MONKS; circ. 1,465,056.

Ralph: 54–58 Park St, Sydney, NSW 2000; tel. (2) 9282-8000; fax (2) 9267-4361; internet ralph.ninemsn.com.au; monthly; men's lifestyle; Editor SANTI PINTADO; circ. 68,061.

Reader's Digest: GPOB 5030, Sydney, NSW 2001; tel. (2) 9690-6111; fax (2) 9690-6211; e-mail editors.au@readersdigest.com; internet www.readersdigest.au.com; monthly; Editor-in-Chief SUE CARNEY; circ. 400,000.

Street Machine: Locked Bag 756, Epping, NSW 2121; tel. (2) 9868-4832; fax (2) 9869-7390; e-mail streetmachine@acpaction.com.au; internet www.acpmagazines.com.au/street_machine.htm; monthly; motoring magazine; Editor GEOFF SEDDON; circ. 39,072.

Super Food Ideas: Locked Bag 5030, Alexandria, NSW 2015; tel. (2) 9353-6666; fax (2) 9353-6699; e-mail superfoodideas@newsmagazines.com.au; internet www.taste.com.au/super+food+ideas; 11 a year; Editor REBECCA COX; circ. 170,396.

TV Soap: Level 6, 207 Pacific Highway, St Leonards, NSW 2065; tel. (2) 9901-6132; fax (2) 9901-6116; e-mail tvsoap@next.com.au; internet www.tvsoap.com.au; f. 1983; monthly; Editor VESNA PETROPOULOS; circ. 108,319.

Vogue Australia: 180 Bourke Rd, Alexandria, NSW 2015; tel. (2) 9353-6666; fax (2) 9353-0935; e-mail vogue@vogue.com.au; internet www.vogue.com.au; f. 1959; monthly; fashion; Editor-in-Chief EDWINA MCCANN; circ. 51,305.

Wheels: GPOB 4088, Sydney, NSW 2001; tel. (2) 9263-9732; fax (2) 9263-9702; e-mail wheels@acp.com.au; internet motoring.ninemsn.com.au/wheelsmag; f. 1953; monthly; international motoring magazine; Editor GED BULMER; circ. 45,864.

Your Garden: Media City 8, Cen. Ave, Eveleigh, NSW 2015; tel. (2) 9394-2381; fax (2) 9394-4206; e-mail yg@pacificmags.com.au; internet pacificmagazines.com.au/pages/magazines; f. 1947; every three months; owned by Pacific Magazines; Editor GEOFFREY BURNIE; circ. 53,824.

NEWS AGENCY

AAP: 3 Rider Blvd, Rhodes Waterside, Rhodes, NSW 2138; tel. (2) 9322-8000; fax (2) 9322-8888; e-mail newswire@aap.com.au; internet www.aap.com.au; f. 1983; owned by major daily newspapers of Australia; Chair. MICHAEL GILL; CEO BRUCE DAVIDSON.

PRESS ASSOCIATIONS

Australian Press Council: Suite 10.02, 117 York St, Sydney, NSW 2000; tel. (2) 9261-1930; fax (2) 9267-6826; e-mail info@presscouncil.org.au; internet www.presscouncil.org.au; Chair. Prof. JULIAN DISNEY.

Community Newspapers of Australia Pty Ltd: POB 234, Auburn, NSW 1835; tel. (2) 8789-7362; fax (2) 8789-7387; e-mail kim@cna.org.au; internet www.cna.org.au; Chair. PAUL THOMAS; Coordinator KIM KOHEN.

Country Press Association of SA Inc: 198 Greenhill Rd, Eastwood, SA 5063; tel. (8) 8373-6533; fax (8) 8373-6544; e-mail countrypsa@bigpond.com; internet www.sacountrypress.com.au; f. 1912; represents South Australian country newspapers; Pres. T. MCAULIFFE; Admin. Officer MARILYN MCAULIFFE.

Country Press Australia: 163 Epsom Rd, Flemington, Vic 3031; tel. (3) 8387-5580; fax (3) 9372-2427; e-mail mpolla@countrypress.net.au; internet www.countrypress.net.au; f. 1906; 420 mems.

Queensland Country Press Association: POB 229, Kelvin Grove DC, Qld 4059; tel. (7) 3356-0033; fax (7) 3356-0027; e-mail nmclary@qcpa.com.au; internet www.qcpa.com.au; Pres. JOHN HUGHES; Exec. Dir NEAL MCLARY; 25 mems.

Tasmanian Press Association Pty Ltd: 71–75 Paterson St, Launceston, Tas 7250; tel. (3) 6336-7111; Sec. TOM O'MEARA.

Victorian Country Press Association Ltd: 1st Floor, 163 Epsom Rd, Flemington, Vic 3031; tel. (3) 8387-5500; fax (3) 9371-2792; internet www.vcpa.com.au; f. 1910; Chair. MICHAEL GILES; Exec. Dir PAUL MCEVEY; 110 mems.

Publishers

Allen and Unwin Pty Ltd: 83 Alexander St, Crows Nest, NSW 2065; tel. (2) 8425-0100; fax (2) 9906-2218; e-mail info@allenandunwin.com; internet www.allenandunwin.com; fiction, trade, academic, children's; Exec. Chair. and Publishing Dir PATRICK A. GALLAGHER; Man. Dir PAUL DONOVAN.

Australasian Medical Publishing Co Pty Ltd: AMPCo House, 277 Clarence St, Sydney, NSW 2000; tel. (2) 9562-6666; fax (2) 9562-6699; e-mail ampco@ampco.com.au; internet www.ampco.com.au; f. 1913; scientific, medical and educational; Gen. Man. JACKIE GAMBRELL.

Black Inc: 37–39 Langridge St, Collingwood, Vic 3066; tel. (3) 9654-0288; fax (3) 9654-0244; e-mail enquiries@blackincbooks.com; internet www.blackincbooks.com; f. 2000; literary fiction and non-fiction; an imprint of Schwartz Publishing; Man. Dir SOPHY WILLIAMS.

Cambridge University Press (Australia): 477 Williamstown Rd, PB 31, Port Melbourne, Vic 3207; tel. (3) 8671-1411; fax (3) 9676-9966; e-mail enquiries@cambridge.edu.au; internet www.cambridge.org/aus; scholarly and educational; Chief Exec. STEPHEN BOURNE.

Cengage Learning Australia Pty Ltd: Level 7, 80 Dorcas St, South Melbourne, Vic 3205; tel. (3) 9685-4111; fax (3) 9685-4199; e-mail anz.customerservice@cengage.com; internet www.cengage.com.au; fmrly Thomson Learning Australia, name changed as above 2007; educational; Gen. Man. PAUL PETRULIS.

Commonwealth Scientific and Industrial Research Organisation (CSIRO Publishing): 150 Oxford St, POB 1139, Collingwood, Vic 3066; tel. (3) 9662-7500; fax (3) 9662-7555; e-mail publishing@csiro.au; internet www.publish.csiro.au; f. 1926; scientific and technical journals, books, magazines, videos, CD-ROMs; Dir A. M. STAMMER.

Elsevier Australia: Level 12, Tower 1, 475 Victoria Ave, Chatswood, NSW 2067; tel. (2) 9422-8500; fax (2) 9422-8501; e-mail customerserviceau@elsevier.com; internet www.elsevier.com.au; a division of Reed Int. Books Australia Pty Ltd; health sciences, science and medicine; Man. Dir ROB KOLKMAN.

Encyclopaedia Britannica Australia Ltd: POB 5608, Chatswood West, NSW 1515; tel. (2) 9915-8800; fax (2) 9419-5247; e-mail feedback@britannica.com.au; internet www.britannica.com.au; reference, education, art, science and commerce; Man. Dir JAMES BUCKLE.

Harlequin Enterprises (Australia) Pty Ltd: Locked Bag 7002, Chatswood, NSW 2067; tel. (2) 9415-9200; fax (2) 9415-9292; internet www.eharlequin.com.au; Man. Dir MICHELLE LAFOREST.

Hyland House Publishing Pty Ltd: POB 1116, Carlton, Vic 3053; tel. (3) 9818-5700; fax (3) 9818-5044; e-mail info@hylandhouse.com.au; internet www.hylandhouse.com.au; f. 1977; Aboriginal and children's literature, gardening, pet care; Rep. MICHAEL SCHOO.

Lansdowne Publishing: POB 1669, Crows Nest, NSW 1585; tel. and fax (2) 9436-2974; e-mail info@lansdownepublishing.com.au; internet www.lansdownepublishing.com.au; cookery, new age, interior design, gardening, health, history, spirituality; Chief Exec. STEVEN MORRIS.

LexisNexis: Tower 2, 475–495 Victoria Ave, Chatswood, NSW 2067; tel. (2) 9422-2174; fax (2) 9422-2405; e-mail customer.relations@lexisnexis.com.au; internet www.lexisnexis.com.au; f. 1910; div. of Reed Elsevier; legal and commercial; CEO T. J. VILJOEN.

McGraw-Hill Australia Pty Ltd: Level 2, The Everglade Bldg, 82 Waterloo Rd, North Ryde, NSW 2113; tel. (2) 9900-1800; fax (2) 9900-1980; e-mail cservice_sydney@mcgraw-hill.com; internet www.mcgraw-hill.com.au; f. 1964; educational, professional and technical; Man. Dir MURRAY ST LEGER.

Melbourne University Publishing Ltd: 187 Grattan St, Carlton, Vic 3053; tel. (3) 9342-0300; fax (3) 9342-0399; e-mail mup-info@unimelb.edu.au; internet www.mup.com.au; f. 1922; scholarly non-fiction, Australian history and biography; CEO LOUISE ADLER.

Murdoch Books: GPOB 4115, Sydney, NSW 2001; tel. (2) 8220-2000; fax (2) 8220-2558; e-mail inquiry@murdochbooks.com.au; internet www.murdochbooks.com.au; cooking, gardening, DIY, craft, gift, general leisure and lifestyle, narrative, history, non-fiction, travel memoirs and business; CEO MATT HANDBURY; Publishing Dir CHRIS RENNIE.

National Library of Australia: Parkes Place, Canberra, ACT 2600; tel. (2) 6262-1111; fax (2) 6257-1703; e-mail media@nla.gov.au; internet www.nla.gov.au; f. 1968; produces trade and library-related publs; Chair. JAMES J. SPIGELMAN.

Oxford University Press: 253 Normanby Rd, South Melbourne, Vic 3205; tel. (3) 9934-9123; fax (3) 9934-9100; e-mail cs.au@oup.com; internet www.oup.com.au; f. 1908; general non-fiction and educational; Man. Dir MAREK PALKA.

Pan Macmillan Australia Pty Ltd: Level 25, BT Tower, 1 Market St, Sydney NSW 2000; tel. (2) 9285-9100; fax (2) 9285-9190; e-mail pansyd@macmillan.com.au; internet www.panmacmillan.com.au; general, reference, children's, fiction, non-fiction; Chair. R. GIBB.

Pearson Education Australia Pty Ltd: Unit 4, Level 3, 14 Aquatic Dr., Frenchs Forest, NSW 2086; tel. (2) 9454-2200; fax (2) 9453-0089; e-mail customer.service@pearson.com.au; internet www.pearson.com.au; f. 1957; mainly educational, academic, computer, some general; CEO MARJORIE SCARDINO.

Penguin Group (Australia): POB 701, Hawthorn, Vic 3122; tel. (3) 9811-2400; fax (3) 9811-2620; internet www.penguin.com.au; f. 1946; general; Man. Dir GABRIELLE COYNE; Publishing Dir ROBERT SESSIONS.

Random House Australia Pty Ltd: Level 3, 100 Pacific Highway, North Sydney, NSW 2060; tel. (2) 9954-9966; fax (2) 9954-4562; e-mail random@randomhouse.com.au; internet www.randomhouse.com.au; fiction, non-fiction and children's; Man. Dir MARGARET SEALE.

Reader's Digest (Australia) Pty Ltd: GPOB 5030, Sydney, NSW 2001; tel. (2) 9018-6000; fax (2) 9018-7000; e-mail customerservice.au@readersdigest.com; internet www.readersdigest.com.au; general; Man. Dir PAUL HEATH.

Scholastic Australia Pty Ltd: 76–80 Railway Cres., Lisarow, NSW 2250; tel. (2) 4328-3555; fax (2) 4323-3827; e-mail customer_service@scholastic.com.au; internet www.scholastic.com.au; f. 1968; educational and children's; Man. Dir DAVID PEAGRAM.

Schwartz Publishing (Victoria) Pty Ltd: 37–39 Langridge St, Melbourne, Vic 3000; tel. (3) 9486-0288; fax (3) 9486-0244; e-mail admin@blackincbooks.com; internet www.blackincbooks.com; non-fiction; Dir MORRY SCHWARTZ.

Simon and Schuster (Australia) Pty Ltd: Suite 19A, Level 1, Bldg C, 450 Miller St, Cammeray, NSW 2062; tel. (2) 9983-6600; fax (2) 9988-4232; e-mail cservice@simonandschuster.com.au; internet www.simonandschuster.com.au; non-fiction incl. anthropology, cooking, gardening, house and home, craft, parenting, health, history, travel, biography, motivation and management; Man. Dir LOU JOHNSON.

Thames and Hudson Australia Pty Ltd: 11 Central Boulevard, Portside Business Park, Fishermans Bend, Vic 3207; tel. (3) 9646-7788; fax (3) 9646-8790; e-mail enquiries@thaust.com.au; internet www.thamesandhudson.com.au; art, history, archaeology, architecture, photography, design, fashion, textiles, lifestyle; Man. Dir JAMIE CAMPLIN.

Thomson Reuters Australia Ltd: Level 5, 100 Harris St, Pyrmont, NSW 2009; tel. (2) 8587-7980; fax (2) 8587-7981; e-mail lta.service@thomsonreuters.com; internet www.thomsonreuters.com.au; legal, professional, tax and accounting; CEO TONY KINNEAR.

Thorpe-Bowker: Level 1, 607 St Kilda Rd, Melbourne, Vic 3004; tel. (3) 8517-8333; fax (3) 8517-8399; e-mail yoursay@thorpe.com.au; internet www.thorpe.com.au; bibliographic, library and book trade reference; Gen. Man. GARY PENGELLY.

UNSW Press Ltd: University of New South Wales, Sydney, NSW 2052; tel. (2) 9664-0900; fax (2) 9664-5420; e-mail enquiries@newsouthpublishing.com.au; internet www.unswpress.com.au; f. 1962; scholarly, general and tertiary texts; Chief Exec. KATHY BAIL.

University of Queensland Press: POB 6042, St Lucia, Qld 4067; tel. (7) 3365-7244; fax (7) 3365-7579; e-mail uqp@uqp.uq.edu.au; internet www.uqp.uq.edu.au; f. 1948; scholarly and general cultural interest, incl. Black Australian writers, adult and children's fiction; Gen. Man. GREG BAIN.

University of Western Australia Publishing: M419, 35 Stirling Highway, Crawley, WA 6009; tel. (8) 6488-3670; fax (8) 6488-1027; e-mail admin-uwap@uwa.edu.au; internet uwap.com.au; f. 1935; literary fiction, natural history, history, literary studies, Australiana, general non-fiction; Dir Assoc. Prof. TERRI-ANN WHITE.

John Wiley & Sons Australia, Ltd: POB 3065, Stafford BC, Qld 4053; tel. (7) 3859-9755; fax (7) 3859-9715; e-mail brisbane@wiley.com; internet au.wiley.com; f. 1954; educational, reference and trade; Pres. and CEO STEPHEN SMITH.

PUBLISHERS' ASSOCIATION

Australian Publishers Association Ltd: 60/89 Jones St, Ultimo, NSW 2007; tel. (2) 9281-9788; fax (2) 9281-1073; e-mail apa@publishers.asn.au; internet www.publishers.asn.au; f. 1948; over 210 mems; Pres. STEPHEN MAY; Chief Exec. MAREE MCCASKILL.

Broadcasting and Communications

REGULATORY AUTHORITY

Australian Communications and Media Authority (ACMA): POB 13112, Law Courts, Melbourne, Vic 8010; tel. (3) 9963-6800; fax (3) 9963-6899; e-mail candinfo@acma.gov.au; internet www.acma.gov.au; f. 2005; Commonwealth regulator for telecommunications, broadcasting, internet and radiocommunications; Chair. CHRIS CHAPMAN.

TELECOMMUNICATIONS

In 2012 189 licensed telecommunications carriers were in operation.

AAPT Ltd: 680 George St, Sydney, NSW 2000; tel. (2) 9009-9009; fax (2) 9009-9999; internet www.aapt.com.au; f. 1991; part of Telecom New Zealand Group; long-distance telecommunications carrier; CEO DAVID YUILE.

Hutchison Telecoms Australia: Level 7, 40 Mount St, NSW 2060; tel. (2) 8579-8888; fax (2) 8904-0457; e-mail investors@hutchison.com.au; internet www.hutchison.com.au; f. 2003; mobile services; owns 50% share in Vodafone Hutchison Australia; Chair. CANNING FOK KIN-NING.

IiNet Ltd: Locked Bag 16, Cloisters Sq., WA 6850; tel. (8) 9214-2207; e-mail cosec@staff.iinet.net.au; internet www.iinet.net.au; f. 1993; internet services; Chair. MICHAEL SMITH; Man. Dir MICHAEL MALONE.

Optus Ltd: POB 1, North Sydney, NSW 2059; tel. (2) 9342-7800; fax (2) 9342-7100; internet www.optus.com.au; f. 1992; division of Singapore Telecommunications Ltd; general and mobile telecommunications, data and internet services, pay-TV; Chair. Sir RALPH ROBINS; Chief Exec. PAUL O'SULLIVAN.

Telstra Corpn Ltd: Level 41, 242 Exhibition St, Melbourne, Vic 3000; tel. (3) 9634-6400; e-mail companysecretary@team.telstra.com; internet www.telstra.com.au; general and mobile telecommunication services; Chair. CATHERINE LIVINGSTONE; CEO DAVID THODEY.

Vodafone Hutchison Australia: Level 7, 40 Mount St, NSW 2060; tel. (2) 8579-8888; fax (2) 8904-0457; internet www.three.com.au; third generation (3G) mobile services; est. following merger between Hutchison Whampoa and Vodafone Australia Ltd in 2009; CEO IÑAKI BERROETA.

BROADCASTING

Many programmes are provided by the non-commercial statutory corporation, the Australian Broadcasting Corporation (ABC). Commercial radio and television services are provided by stations operated by companies under licences granted and renewed by the Australian Communications and Media Authority (ACMA). They rely for their income on the broadcasting of advertisements. In late 2011 there were about 273 commercial radio stations in operation, and 69 commercial television stations.

Australian Broadcasting Corporation (ABC): 700 Harris St, Ultimo, POB 9994, Sydney, NSW 2001; tel. (2) 8333-1500; fax (2) 8333-5344; internet www.abc.net.au; f. 1932; est. as Australian Broadcasting Comm; became corpn in 1983; one national television network operating on about 961 transmitters, one international television service broadcasting via satellite to Asia and the Pacific, and nine radio networks operating on more than 6,000 transmitters; Chair. JAMES SPIGELMAN; Man. Dir MARK SCOTT.

Radio Australia: GPOB 428, Melbourne 3001; tel. (3) 9626-1500; fax (3) 9626-1899; internet www.radioaustralia.net.au; international service broadcast by short wave and satellite in English, Burmese, French, Indonesian, Standard Chinese, Khmer, Tok Pisin and Vietnamese; CEO MIKE MCCLUSKEY.

Radio

Commercial Radio Australia Ltd: Level 5, 88 Foveaux St, Surry Hills, NSW 2010; tel. (2) 9281-6577; fax (2) 9281-6599; e-mail mail@commercialradio.com.au; internet www.commercialradio.com.au; f. 1930; represents the interests of Australia's commercial radio broadcasters; CEO JOAN WARNER.

Major Commercial Broadcasting Station Licensees

Associated Communications Enterprises (ACE) Radio Broadcasters Pty Ltd: Level 8C, 18 Albert Rd, South Melbourne, Vic 3205; tel. (3) 9645-9877; fax (3) 9645-9866; e-mail headoffice@aceradio.com.au; internet www.aceradio.com.au; operates six stations; Chair. ROWLY PATERSON; Man. Dir S. EVERETT.

Austereo Pty Ltd: Ground Level, 180 St Kilda Rd, St Kilda, Vic 3182; tel. (3) 9230-1051; fax (3) 9593-9007; e-mail guy.dobson@austereo.com.au; internet www.austereo.com.au; operates 15 stations; CEO GUY POBSON.

Australian Radio Network Pty Ltd: 3 Byfield St, North Ryde, NSW 2113; tel. (2) 8899-9999; fax (2) 8899-9811; e-mail webmaster@arn.com.au; internet www.arn.com.au; operates 12 stations; jt venture between APN News & Media and Clear Channel Communications Inc, Texas; CEO CIARAN DAVIS.

Capital Radio Network: POB 1206, Mitchell, ACT 2911; tel. (2) 6452-1521; fax (2) 6452-1006; operates seven stations; Man. Dir KEVIN BLYTON.

DMG Radio Australia: Level 5, 33 Saunders Street, Pyrmont, NSW 2009; tel. (2) 9564-9999; e-mail enquiries@dmgradio.com.au; internet www.dmgradio.com.au; operates 11 stations; Chair. LACHLAN MURDOCH; CEO CATHY O'CONNOR.

Grant Broadcasting Pty Ltd: Suite 303, 10–12 Clarke St, Crows Nest, NSW 2065; tel. (2) 9437-8888; fax (2) 9437-8881; e-mail corporate@grantbroadcasters.com.au; internet www.grantbroadcasters.com.au; operates 31 stations; Man. Dir JANET CAMERON.

Greater Cairns Radio Ltd: Virginia House, Abbott St, Cairns, Qld 4870; tel. (7) 4050-0800; fax (7) 4051-8060; e-mail cnssales@dmgradio.com.au; Gen. Man. ROD COUTTS.

Macquarie Radio Network: Level 1, Bldg C, 33–35 Saunders St, Pyrmont, NSW 2009; tel. (2) 8570-0000; fax (2) 8570-0219; internet www.mrn.com.au; operates two stations; Chair. RUSSELL TATE.

Prime Radio: N. A. B. Bldg, 17 Carnaby St, Maroochydore, Qld 4558; tel. (7) 5475-1911; fax (7) 5475-1961; e-mail info@primeradio.com.au; internet www.primeradio.com.au; operates 10 stations; Group Gen. Man. BRYCE NIELSEN.

Regional Broadcasters (Australia) Pty: McDowal St, Roma, Qld 4455; tel. (7) 4622-1800; fax (7) 4622-3697; Chair. G. MCVEAN.

Rural Press Ltd: 159 Bells Line of Rd, North Richmond, NSW 2754; tel. (2) 4570-4444; fax (2) 4570-4663; internet www.ruralpress.com; f. 1911; operates six stations; Man. Dir and CEO B. K. MCCARTHY.

Southern Cross Media Pty Ltd: Level 2, 257 Clarendon St, South Melbourne, Vic 3205; tel. (3) 9252-1019; fax (3) 9252-1270; e-mail corporate@scmedia.com.au; internet www.scmediagroup.com.au; operates 68 stations; Exec. Chair. MAX MOORE-WILTON; CEO RHYS HOLLERAN.

RadioWest: 89 Egan St, Kalgoorlie, WA 6430; tel. (8) 9021-2666; fax (8) 9091-2209; e-mail rhutchinson@radiowest.com.au; internet theradio.com.au; f. 1931; operates 10 stations along with HOT FM in Western Australia.

SEA FM Pty Ltd: Level 2, Oracle East, 3 Oracle Blvd, Broadbeach, Qld 4218; tel. (7) 5591-5000; fax (7) 5591-6080; e-mail paul.bartlett@sca.com.au; internet www.seafm.com.au; operates 28 stations.

Super Radio Network: POB 1269, Pyrmont, NSW 2009; owned by Broadcast Operations Pty Ltd; operates 33 stations; Chair. BILL CARALIS.

Radio 2SM Gold 1269: Level 3, 8 Jones Bay Rd, Pyrmont, NSW 2009; tel. (2) 9660-1269; fax (2) 9552-2979; e-mail admin@2sm.com.au; internet www.2sm.com.au; f. 1931.

Tamworth Radio Development Company Pty Ltd: POB 497, Tamworth, NSW 2340; tel. (2) 6765-7055; fax (2) 6762-0008; e-mail traffic@2tn.com.au; operates two stations; acquired by Super Radio Network in 1993; Man. W. A. MORRISON.

Tasmanian Broadcasting Network (TBN): POB 665G, Launceston, Tas 7250; tel. (3) 6431-2555; fax (3) 6431-3188; operates three stations; Chair. K. FINDLAY.

Tasmanian Radio Network: 109 York St, Launceston, Tas 7250; tel. (3) 6331-4844; fax (3) 6334-5858; internet www.bestmusicmix.com.au; operates six radio stations and part of Macquarie Regional Radioworks; Man. MATT RUSSELL.

Television

Free TV Australia: 44 Avenue Rd, Mosman, NSW 2088; tel. (2) 8968-7100; fax (2) 9969-3520; e-mail contact@freetv.com.au; internet www.freetv.com.au; f. 1960; fmrly Commercial Television Australia; represents all commercial free-to-air broadcasters in Australia; CEO JULIE FLYNN.

Commercial Television Station Licensees

Channel 9 South Australia Pty Ltd: 202 Tynte St, North Adelaide, SA 5006; tel. (8) 8267-0111; fax (8) 8267-3996; e-mail news@nws9.com.au; internet www.nws9.com.au; f. 1959; Gen. Man. GRAEME GILBERTSON.

General Television Corporation Pty Ltd: 22–46 Bendigo St, POB 100, Richmond, Vic 3121; tel. (3) 9429-0201; fax (3) 9429-3670; e-mail customer.service@ninemsn.com.au; internet www.ninemsn.com.au; f. 1957; operates one station; Man. Dir GRAEME YARWOOD.

Golden West Network Pty Ltd: Roberts Cres., Bunbury, WA 6230; tel. (8) 9721-4466; fax (8) 9792-2932; e-mail gwn.bunbury@gwn.com.au; internet www.gwn.com.au; f. 1967; subsidiary of Prime Television Ltd; operates three stations (SSW10, VEW and WAW); CEO W. FENWICK.

Imparja Television Pty Ltd: POB 52, Alice Springs, NT 0871; tel. (8) 8950-1411; fax (8) 8950-1422; e-mail imparja@imparja.com.au; internet www.imparja.com; CEO ALISTAIR FEEHAN.

NBN Television Ltd: 11–17 Mosbri Cres., Newcastle, NSW 2300; tel. (2) 4929-2933; fax (2) 4926-2936; internet www.nbntv.com.au; f. 1962; operates one station; Man. Dir DENIS LEDBURY.

Network Ten Ltd: GPOB 10, Sydney, NSW 2000; tel. (2) 9650-1010; fax (2) 9650-1111; e-mail tenwebsite@ten.com.au; internet www.ten.com.au; f. 1964; operates Australian TV network and commercial stations in Sydney, Melbourne, Brisbane, Perth and Adelaide; Exec. Chair. BRIAN LONG; CEO (vacant).

Nine Network Australia Pty Ltd: Level 7, Tower Bldg, Australia Sq., 264–278 George St, Sydney, NSW 2000; tel. (2) 9383-6000; fax (2) 9383-6100; e-mail customer.service@ninemsn.com.au; internet www.ninemsn.com.au; f. 1956; division of Publishing and Broadcasting Ltd; operates three stations: TCN Channel Nine Pty Ltd (Sydney), Queensland Television Ltd (Brisbane) and General Television Corpn Ltd (Melbourne); CEO MARK BRITT.

Prime Television (Holdings) Pty Ltd: POB 878, Dickson, ACT 2602; tel. (2) 6242-3700; fax (2) 6242-3889; e-mail primetv@primetv.com.au; internet www.primemedia.com.au; part of Prime Media Group Ltd; Chair. PAUL RAMSAY; CEO IAN AUDSLEY.

Queensland Television Ltd: GPOB 72, Brisbane, Qld 4001; tel. (7) 3214-9999; fax (7) 3369-3512; f. 1959; operated by Nine Network Australia Pty Ltd; Gen. Man. CHRIS TAYLOR.

Seven Network Ltd: 38-42 Pirrama Rd, Pyrmont, NSW 2009; tel. (2) 8777-7777; internet www.sevencorporate.com.au; owns Amalgamated Television Services Pty Ltd (Sydney), Brisbane TV Ltd (Brisbane), HSV Channel 7 Pty Ltd (Melbourne), South Australian Telecasters Ltd (Adelaide) and TVW Enterprises Ltd (Perth); Exec. Chair. KERRY STOKES; CEO DAVID JOHN LECKIE.

Channel Seven Adelaide Pty Ltd: 40 Port Rd, Hindmarsh, SA 5007; tel. (8) 8342-7777; fax (8) 8342-7717; f. 1965; mem. of Seven Network; Man. Dir TONY DAVISON.

Channel Seven Brisbane Pty Ltd: Sir Samuel Griffith Dr., Mt Coot-tha, Qld 4006; tel. (7) 3369-7777; fax (7) 3368-7410; f. 1959; operates one station; mem. of Seven Network; Man. Dir MAX WALTERS.

Channel Seven Melbourne Pty Ltd: 160 Harbour Esplanade, Docklands Melbourne, Vic 3008; tel. (3) 9697-7777; fax (3) 9697-7747; e-mail daspinall@seven.com.au; f. 1956; operates one station; Gen. Man. LEWIS MARTIN.

Channel Seven Perth Pty Ltd: POB 77, Tuart Hill, WA 6939; tel. (8) 9344-0777; fax (8) 9344-0670; e-mail traffic@7perth.com.au; internet www.7perth.com.au; f. 1959; Man. Dir MARIO D'ORAZIO.

Channel Seven Queensland Pty Ltd: 140–142 Horton Parade, Maroochydore, Qld 4558; tel. (7) 5430-1777; fax (7) 5430-1760; f. 1965; fmrly Sunshine Television Network Ltd.

Southern Cross Media Pty Ltd: (see above) operates two stations: Southern Cross Ten and Southern Cross Television.

Special Broadcasting Service (SBS): Locked Bag 028, Crows Nest, NSW 1585; tel. (2) 9430-2828; fax (2) 9430-3047; e-mail comments@sbs.com.au; internet www.sbs.com.au; f. 1980; national multicultural broadcaster of TV and radio; Chair. JOSEPH SKRZYNSKI; Man. Dir MICHAEL EBEID.

Spencer Gulf Telecasters Ltd: 76 Wandearah Rd, Port Pirie, SA 5540; tel. (8) 8632-2555; fax (8) 8633-0984; e-mail dweston@centralonline.com.au; f. 1968; operates two stations; Chair. P. M. STURROCK.

Swan Television & Radio Broadcasters Pty Ltd: POB 99, Tuart Hill, WA 6939; tel. (8) 9449-9999; fax (8) 9449-9900; Gen. Man. P. BOWEN.

Territory Television Pty Ltd: POB 1764, Darwin, NT 0801; tel. (8) 8981-8888; fax (8) 8981-6802; f. 1971; operates one station; Gen. Man. A. G. BRUYN.

WIN Corpn Pty Ltd: Television Ave, Mt St Thomas, NSW 2500; tel. (2) 4227-3682; fax (2) 4223-4199; internet www.wintv.com.au; f. 1962; Owner BRUCE GORDON.

Satellite, Cable and Digital Television

Digital television became available in metropolitan areas in January 2001 and was available in all major regional areas by 2004.

Austar United Communications Ltd: Locked Mailbag A3940, Sydney South, NSW 1235; tel. (2) 9251-6999; fax (2) 9251-0134; e-mail corporate@austar.com.au; internet www.austarunited.com.au; began operations in 1995; 750,000 subscribers (2011); Chair. MICHAEL T. FRIES; CEO JOHN C. PORTER.

Australia Network: GPOB 9994, Sydney, NSW 2001; tel. (2) 8333-5598; fax (2) 8333-1558; internet australianetwork.com; f. 2001; international satellite service; broadcasts to countries and territories in Asia and the Pacific; owned by Australian Broadcasting Corpn; Chief Exec. BRUCE DOVER.

Foxtel: 5 Thomas Holt Dr., North Ryde, NSW 2113; tel. (2) 9813-6000; fax (2) 9813-7303; e-mail corporateaffairs@foxtel.com.au; internet www.foxtel.com.au; owned by News Corpn and Telstra Corpn; over 2,300,000 subscribers; Chair. ROBERT NASON; CEO RICHARD FRUEDENSTEIN.

Optus Television: Tower B, Level 15, 16 Zenith Centre, 821–841 Pacific Highway, Chatswood, NSW 2067; provides Foxtel cable television under the Optus brand as part of its broader services.

Finance

(cap. = capital; p.u. = paid up; res = reserves; dep. = deposits; m. = million; brs = branches; amounts in Australian dollars)

Australian Prudential Regulation Authority (APRA): GPOB 9836, Sydney, NSW 2001; tel. (2) 9210-3000; fax (2) 9210-3411; internet www.apra.gov.au; f. 1998; responsible for regulation of banks, insurance cos, superannuation funds, credit unions, building societies and friendly societies; Chair. Dr JOHN LAKER.

BANKING

Central Bank

Reserve Bank of Australia: GPOB 3947, Sydney, NSW 2001; tel. (2) 9551-8111; fax (2) 9551-8000; e-mail rbainfo@rba.gov.au; internet www.rba.gov.au; f. 1911; est. as Commonwealth Bank of Australia; assumed functions of central bank in 1959; responsible for monetary policy, financial system stability, payment system development; cap. 40m., res 41,000m., dep. 17,504m., total assets 75,313m. (June 2011); Chair. and Gov. GLENN STEVENS.

Development Bank

Rabobank Australia Ltd: GPOB 4577, Sydney, NSW 2001; tel. (2) 8115-4000; e-mail sydney.webmaster@rabobank.com; internet www.rabobank.com.au; f. 1978 as Primary Industry Bank of Australia Ltd; name changed as above 2003; Chair. WILLIAM P. GURRY; CEO THEODORUS GIESKES; 219 brs.

Trading Banks

Arab Bank Australia Ltd: POB N645, Grosvenor Place, Sydney, NSW 1220; tel. (2) 9377-8900; fax (2) 9221-5428; e-mail service@arabbank.com.au; internet www.arabbank.com.au; cap. 62.5m., res 5,791m., dep. 987.7m. (Dec. 2012); Chair. GEOFFREY WILD; Man. Dir and CEO JOSEPH RIZK.

Australia and New Zealand Banking Group Ltd: ANZ Centre, 833 Collins St, Docklands, Vic 3008; tel. (3) 9683-9999; fax (3) 8654-9977; e-mail investor.relations@anz.com; internet www.anz.com; f. 1835; present name adopted in 1970; cap. 23,941m., res –2,498m., dep. 426,388m. (Sept. 2012); Chair. JOHN MORSCHEL; CEO MICHAEL SMITH; 748 domestic brs, 204 overseas brs.

Bank of Queensland Ltd: GPOB 898, Brisbane, Qld 4001; tel. (7) 3212-3463; fax (7) 3212-3399; internet www.boq.com.au; f. 1874; cap. 2,660.1m., res 106.2m., dep. 31,349.7m. (Aug. 2012); Chair. NEIL SUMMERSON; Man. Dir and CEO STUART GRIMSHAW; 162 brs.

Bank of Tokyo-Mitsubishi UFJ Ltd: Level 25, Gateway, 1 Macquarie Pl., Sydney, NSW 2000; tel. (2) 9296-1111; fax (2) 9247-4266; f. 1985; Gen. Man. K. TSUSHIMA.

Bankers' Trust Financial Group: GPOB 2675, Sydney, NSW 2001; tel. (2) 9274-5780; fax (2) 9274-5786; e-mail customer.relations@btfinancialgroup.com; internet www.bt.com.au; f. 1986; wealth management division of Westpac Banking Corpn; CEO BRAD COOPER.

Bankwest: GPOB E237, Perth, WA 6841; tel. (8) 9449-2840; fax (8) 9449-2570; internet www.bankwest.com.au; f. 1895; est. as Agricultural Bank of Western Australia; renamed Bank of Western Australia Ltd (BankWest) in 1994; present name adopted in 2012; wholly owned subsidiary of Commonwealth Bank; Chair. HARVEY COLLINS; Man. Dir ROB DE LUCA; 139 brs.

Bendigo and Adelaide Bank Ltd: The Bendigo Centre, POB 480, Bendigo, Vic 3552; tel. (3) 5485-7911; fax (3) 5485-7000; e-mail customercontactandcaremailbox@bendigoadelaide.com.au; internet www.bendigobank.com.au; f. 1995; cap. 3,870.3m., res 50.9m., dep. 44,899.9m. (June 2012); Chair. ROBERT N. JOHANSON; Man. Dir MIKE HIRST; 373 brs.

Citigroup Australia: 2 Park St, Sydney, NSW 2000; tel. (2) 8225-1000; fax (2) 8225-5208; internet www.citibank.com.au; f. 1954; fmrly Citibank Pty Ltd, name changed as above in 2005; cap. 460.0m, res 677.4m., dep. 13,744.7m. (Dec. 2011); Group CEO MICHAEL CORBAT; CEO (Citi Australia) STEPHEN ROBERTS; 13 brs.

Commonwealth Bank of Australia: Ground Floor, Tower 1, 201 Sussex St, Sydney, NSW 2000; tel. (2) 9378-2000; fax (2) 9118-7192; internet www.commbank.com.au; f. 1912; merged with Colonial Ltd in 2000; cap. 25,175m., res 2,510m., dep. 508,734m. (June 2012); Chair. DAVID TURNER; CEO and Man. Dir IAN NAREV; more than 1,200 brs world-wide.

HSBC Bank Australia Ltd: Level 32, HSBC Centre, 580 George St, Sydney, NSW 2000; tel. (2) 9006-5888; fax (2) 9006-5440; e-mail pr@hsbc.com.au; internet www.hsbc.com.au; f. 1985; fmrly Hongkong Bank of Australia; cap. 811.0m., res 17.0m., dep. 19,813.3m. (Dec. 2012); Chair. GRAHAM BRADLEY; CEO PAULO MAIA; 35 brs.

ING DIRECT (Australia) Ltd: 140 Sussex St, Sydney, NSW 2001; tel. (2) 9028-4077; fax (2) 9028-4708; internet www.ingdirect.com.au; f. 1994; fmrly known as ING Bank; name changed as above 2007; cap. 1,334m., res 17.4m., dep. 32,315.2m. (Dec. 2011); CEO VAUGHN RICHTER.

Investec Bank (Australia) Ltd: Level 23, Chifley Tower, 2 Chifley Sq., Phillip St, Sydney, NSW 2000; tel. (2) 9323-2000; fax (2) 9323-2002; e-mail australia@investec.com.au; internet www.investec.com.au; fmrly N. M. Rothschild & Sons; acquired by Investec Bank in July 2006; cap. 291.7m., res 11,100.0m., dep. 2,465.5m. (March 2013); Chair. DAVID GONSKI; CEO STEPHEN KOSEFF; 5 brs.

JPMorgan Australia: Level 32, Grosvenor Place, 225 George St, Sydney, NSW 2000; tel. (2) 9250-4111; internet www.jpmorgan.com/australia; formed through merger of Ord Minnett, Chase Manhattan Bank, JPMorgan and Bank One; CEO (Australia and New Zealand) ROB PRIESTLEY.

Macquarie Bank Ltd: 1 Martin Place, Sydney, NSW 2000; tel. (2) 8232-3333; fax (2) 8232-3350; internet www.macquarie.com.au; f. 1969 as Hill Samuel Australia Ltd; present name adopted in 1985; cap. 7,969m., res –509m., dep. 44,335m. (March 2012); Chair. KEVIN MCCANN; Exec. Dir and CEO NICHOLAS MOORE; 4 brs.

Merrill Lynch (Australia) Pty Ltd: Level 38, Gov. Phillip Tower, 1 Farrer Pl., Sydney, NSW 2000; tel. (2) 9225-6500; fax (2) 9221-1023; internet www.ml.com; f. 1964; Man. Dir JOHN LILES.

National Australia Bank Ltd (NAB): 800 Bourke St, Melbourne, Vic 3008; tel. (3) 8641-9083; fax (3) 8641-4912; e-mail feedback@nab.com.au; internet www.nab.com.au; f. 1858; cap. 23,042m., res 2,319m., dep. 430,249m. (Sept. 2012); Chair. MICHAEL A. CHANEY; Group CEO CAMERON CLYNE; 2,349 brs.

RBS Group (Australia) Pty Ltd: RBS Tower, 88 Phillip St, Sydney, NSW 2000; tel. (2) 8259-5000; fax (2) 8259-5444; e-mail mailbox.au@rbs.com; internet www.rbs.com.au; f. 1971; fmrly ABN AMRO Australia Pty Ltd, rebranded as above in 2009; CEO ANDREW CHICK.

SG Australia Ltd: Level 23, 400 George St, Sydney, NSW 2000; tel. (2) 9210-8000; fax (2) 9231-2196; internet www.sgcib.com.au; f. 1981; fmrly Société Générale Australia Ltd; Chief Officer ANDRE GOURRET.

St George Bank Ltd: Locked Bag 1, St George House, 4–16 Montgomery St, Kogarah, NSW 2217; tel. (2) 9236-1111; fax (2) 9952-1000; e-mail stgeorge@stgeorge.com.au; internet www.stgeorge.com.au; f. 1937 as building society; purchased by Westpac Group in Dec. 2008; CEO GEORGE FRAZIS; 409 brs.

Standard Chartered Bank Australia Ltd: Level 1, 345 George St, Sydney, NSW 2000; tel. (2) 9232-9333; fax (2) 9232-9334; internet www.standardchartered.com/au; f. 1986; Chair. JOHN PEACE; CEO (Asia) JASPAL SINGH BINDRA.

Westpac Banking Corporation: 275 Kent St, Sydney, NSW 2000; tel. (2) 9293-9270; fax (2) 8253-4128; e-mail online@westpac.com.au; internet www.westpac.com.au; f. 1817; merged with St George Bank Ltd in Dec. 2008; cap. 26,355m., res 766m., dep. 427,543m. (Sept. 2012); Chair. LINDSAY MAXSTED; Man. Dir and CEO GAIL KELLY; 825 domestic brs, 197 brs in New Zealand, 48 other brs.

STOCK EXCHANGES

Asia Pacific Stock Exchange (APX): Level 16, Central Sq., 323 Castlereagh St, Sydney, NSW 2000; tel. 9217-2723; fax 9215-2833; e-mail info@apx.com.au; internet www.apx.com.au; securities exchange, notably offering Chinese market participants an alternative listing from the Shanghai and Shenzhen stock exchanges; Chair. RAYMOND JOHN SCHOER; CEO DAVID LAWRENCE.

Australian Securities Exchange (ASX): Level 7, 20 Bridge St, Sydney, NSW 2000; tel. (2) 9227-0000; fax (2) 9347-0005; e-mail info@asx.com.au; internet www.asx.com.au; Australian Stock Exchange f. 1987 by merger of the stock exchanges in Sydney, Adelaide, Brisbane, Hobart, Melbourne and Perth, to replace the fmr Australian Associated Stock Exchanges; demutualized and listed Oct. 1998; Australian Securities Exchange formed through merger of Australian Stock Exchange and Sydney Futures Exchange July 2006; ASX group operates under the brand Australian Securities Exchange; spans markets for corporate control, capital formation and price discovery; operator, supervisor, central counter-party clearer and payments system facilitator; Chair. RODERIC HOLLIDAY-SMITH; Man. Dir and CEO ELMER FUNKE KUPPER.

Chi-X: Level 23, Gov. Phillip Tower, 1 Farrer Pl., Sydney, NSW 2000; tel. (2) 8078-1701; e-mail support-cxa@chi-x.com; internet www.chi-x.com/australia; f. 2011; wholly owned subsidiary of Chi-X Global Inc; COO PETER FOWLER.

Supervisory Body

Australian Securities and Investments Commission (ASIC): GPOB 9827, Sydney, NSW 2001; tel. (2) 9911-2000; fax (2) 9911-2414; internet www.asic.gov.au; f. 1990; corpns and financial products regulator; Chair. TODO D'ALOISIO.

PRINCIPAL INSURANCE COMPANIES

Allianz Australia Ltd: GPOB 4049, Sydney, NSW 2001; tel. (7) 3023-9322; e-mail corporate_communications@allianz.com.au; internet www.allianz.com.au; f. 1914; workers' compensation; fire, general accident, motor and marine; Chair. J. S. CURTIS; Man. Dir T. TOWELL.

AMP Ltd: 750 Collins St, Melbourne, Vic 3008; tel. (3) 8688-3911; fax (3) 9614-2240; e-mail amp_investor_relations@amp.com.au; internet www.amp.com.au; f. 1849; AMP Ltd merged with AXA Asia Pacific Holdings Ltd in 2011; financial advice, funds management, superannuation, retirement and savings products, life and trauma insurance, income protection; Chair. PETER MASON; CEO CRAIG MELLER.

Calliden Insurance Ltd: Level 7, 100 Arthur St, North Sydney, NSW 2060; tel. (2) 9551-1111; fax (2) 9551-1155; e-mail feedback@calliden.com.au; internet www.calliden.com.au; general insurance products; CEO NICHOLAS KIRK.

Catholic Church Insurance Ltd: Level 8, 485 La Trobe St, Melbourne, Vic 3001; tel. (3) 9934-3000; fax (3) 9934-3464; e-mail reception@ccinsurance.org.au; internet www.ccinsurance.org.au; f. 1911; Chair. PAUL A. GALLAGHER; CEO PETER RUSH.

General Reinsurance Australia Ltd: Level 24, 123 Pitt St, Sydney, NSW 2000; tel. (2) 8236-6100; fax (2) 9222-1540; e-mail lifesydney@genre.com; f. 1961; reinsurance, life and health, fire, accident, marine; Chair. F. A. McDONALD; Man. Dir C. J. CROWDER.

GIO Australia Holdings Ltd: GPOB 1453, Brisbane, Qld 4001; tel. (3) 8650-4196; fax (3) 8650-4552; e-mail emailus@gio.com.au; internet www.gio.com.au; f. 1926; CEO PETER CORRIGAN.

Guild Insurance Ltd: 5 Burwood Rd, Hawthorn, Vic 3122; tel. (3) 9810-9820; fax (3) 9810-9810; internet www.guildinsurance.com.au; f. 1963; Chair. JOHN BARRINGTON; CEO MARIO J. PIRONE.

Insurance Australia Group Ltd: Level 26, 388 George St, Sydney, NSW 2000; tel. (2) 9292-9222; fax (2) 9292-8485; e-mail investor.relations@iag.com.au; internet www.iag.com.au; f. 1926; fmrly NRMA Insurance Ltd; name changed as above 2002; Chair. BRIAN SCHWARTZ; CEO MIKE WILKINS.

Lumley General Insurance Ltd: Level 9, Lumley House, 309 Kent St, Sydney, NSW 2000; tel. (2) 9248-1111; fax (2) 9248-1122; e-mail general@lumley.com.au; internet www.lumley.com.au; owned by Westfarmers General Insurance Ltd; Man. Dir ROBERT SCOTT.

MLC Wealth Management Ltd: POB 200, North Sydney, NSW 2059; tel. (3) 8634-4721; fax (3) 9964-3334; e-mail contactmlc@mlc.com.au; internet www.mlc.com.au; f. 2000; est. as CGNU following merger of CGU and Norwich Union, renamed as Aviva Australia Holdings Ltd in 2003; renamed as above after acquisition by National Australia Bank in 2009; CEO STEVE TUCKER.

QBE Insurance Group Ltd: Level 2, 82 Pitt St, Sydney, NSW 2000; tel. (2) 9375-4193; fax (2) 9231-6104; e-mail corporate@qbe.com; internet www.qbe.com; f. 1886; general insurance; Chair. BELINDA HUTCHINSON; CEO JOHN NEAL.

RAC Insurance Pty Ltd: 228 Adelaide Terrace, Perth, WA 6000; tel. (8) 9436-4444; fax (8) 9421-4593; internet rac.com.au; f. 1947; Chair. ALDEN HALSE.

RACQ Insurance: POB 4, Springwood, Qld 4127; tel. (7) 3361-2444; fax (7) 3361-2140; e-mail racq@racq.com.au; internet www.racq.com.au; f. 1971; Chair. RICHARD PIETSCH; CEO IAN GILLESPIE.

Suncorp Ltd: Level 18, 36 Wickham Tce, Brisbane, Qld 4000; tel. (7) 3362-1222; fax (7) 3836-1190; e-mail direct@suncorp.co.au; internet www.suncorp.com.au; f. 1996; Chair. JOHN STORY; CEO PATRICK SNOWBALL.

Swiss Reinsurance Co Ltd: Level 29, 363 George St, Sydney, NSW 2000; tel. (2) 8295-9500; fax (2) 8295-9600; internet www.swissre.com; f. 1956; Head of Australia and New Zealand operations MARK SENKEVICS.

Vero Insurance Ltd: GPOB 3999, Sydney, NSW 2001; tel. (8) 8205-5878; e-mail veroinformation@vero.com.au; internet www.vero.com.au; fmrly RSA Insurance Australia Ltd; name changed as above 2003; CEO ANTHONY DAY.

Wesfarmers Insurance Ltd (WFI): 184 Railway Parade, Bassendean, WA 6054; tel. (8) 9273-5333; fax (8) 9378-2172; e-mail info@wfi.com.au; internet www.wfi.com.au; Man. Dir ROBERT SCOTT.

Westpac Life Insurance Services Ltd: 275 Kent St, Sydney, NSW 2000; tel. (2) 9293-9270; fax (2) 8253-4128; e-mail online@westpac.com.au; internet www.westpac.com.au; f. 1986; CEO GAIL KELLY.

Zurich Financial Services Australia Ltd: 5 Blue St, North Sydney, NSW 2060; tel. (2) 9995-1111; fax (2) 9995-3797; e-mail client.service@zurich.com.au; internet www.zurich.com.au; Chair. TERENCE JOHN PARADINE; CEO DAVID SMITH.

Insurance Associations

Australian and New Zealand Institute of Insurance and Finance: Level 8, 600 Bourke St, Melbourne, Vic 3000; tel. (3) 9613-7280; fax (3) 9642-4166; e-mail customerservice@theinstitute.com.au; internet www.theinstitute.com.au; f. 1884; provider of education, training and professional devt courses across the region; 15,000 mems; 8,500 students; Pres. and Chair. of the Bd DUNCAN WEST; CEO JOAN FITZPATRICK.

Financial Services Council (FSC): Level 24, 44 Market St, Sydney, NSW 2000; tel. (2) 9299-3022; fax (2) 9299-3198; e-mail info@fsc.org.au; internet www.fsc.org.au; f. 1997; est. following merger of Australian Investment Managers' Asscn, Investment Funds Asscn, and Life, Investment and Superannuation Asscn of Australia Inc; fmrly Investment and Financial Services Association (IFSA); non-profit org.; Chair. GREG COOPER; CEO JOHN BROGDEN.

Insurance Council of Australia Ltd: Level 4, 56 Pitt St, Sydney, NSW 2000; tel. (2) 9253-5100; fax (2) 9253-5111; e-mail comms@insurancecouncil.com.au; internet www.insurancecouncil.com.au; f. 1975; Pres. MARK MILINER; CEO ROBERT W. WHELAN.

Trade and Industry

GOVERNMENT AGENCY

Austrade: Level 23, Aon Tower, 201 Kent St, Sydney, NSW 2000; tel. (2) 9390-2000; fax (2) 9390-2024; e-mail info@austrade.gov.au; internet www.austrade.gov.au; f. 1931; export promotion agency; CEO BRUCE GOSPER.

CHAMBERS OF COMMERCE

Australian Chamber of Commerce and Industry (ACCI): POB 6005, Kingston, ACT 2604; tel. (2) 6273-2311; fax (2) 6273-3286; e-mail info@acci.asn.au; internet www.acci.asn.au; Pres. DAVID MICHAELIS; CEO PETER ANDERSON.

Chamber of Commerce and Industry of Western Australia (CCIWA): POB 6209, East Perth, WA 6892; tel. (8) 9365-7627; fax (8) 9365-7550; e-mail info@cciwa.com; internet www.cciwa.com; f. 1890; 5,200 mems; Chief Exec. PETER HOOD; Pres. Dr PENNY FLETT.

Commerce Queensland: Industry House, 375 Wickham Terrace, Brisbane, Qld 4000; tel. (7) 3842-2244; fax (7) 3832-3195; internet www.cciq.com.au; f. 1868; operates World Trade Centre, Brisbane; 5,500 mems; Pres. DAVID GOODWIN; Gen. Man. NICK WILLIS.

South Australian Employers' Chamber of Commerce and Industry Inc: Enterprise House, 136 Greenhill Rd, Unley, SA 5061; tel. (8) 8300-0103; fax (8) 8300-0204; e-mail enquiries@business-sa.com; internet www.business-sa.com; f. 1839; 4,700 mems; Pres. VINCENT TREMAINE; CEO PETER VAUGHAN.

Sydney Chamber of Commerce: Level 12, 83 Clarence St, Sydney, NSW 2000; tel. (2) 9350-8100; fax (2) 9350-8199; e-mail enquiries@thechamber.com.au; internet www.thechamber.com.au; f. 1825; offers advice to and represents over 70,000 businesses; Pres. ROGER HOOD; Exec. Dir PATRICIA FORSYTHE.

Tasmanian Chamber of Commerce and Industry: GPOB 793, Hobart, Tas 7001; tel. (3) 6236-3600; fax (3) 6231-1278; e-mail admin@tcci.com.au; internet www.tcci.com.au; Chair. TROY HARPER; CEO ROBERT WALLACE.

Victorian Employers' Chamber of Commerce and Industry: Industry House, 486 Albert St, Melbourne, Vic 3002; tel. (3) 8662-5333; fax (3) 8662-5462; e-mail vecci@vecci.org.au; internet www.vecci.org.au; f. 1851; Pres. PETER McMULLIN; CEO WAYNE KAYLER-THOMSON.

AGRICULTURAL, INDUSTRIAL AND TRADE ASSOCIATIONS

Australian Business Ltd: Locked Bag 938, North Sydney, NSW 2059; tel. (2) 9458-7500; fax (2) 9923-1166; e-mail customerservice@australianbusiness.com.au; internet www.australianbusiness.com.au; f. 1885; fmrly Chamber of Manufactures of NSW; Man. Dir and CEO KEVIN MACDONALD.

Australian Coal Association: POB 9115, Deakin, ACT 2600; tel. (2) 6120-0200; fax (2) 6120-0222; e-mail info@australiancoal.com.au; internet www.australiancoal.com.au; mems include coal producers and processors; Chair. JOHN PEGLER; CEO Dr NIKKI WILLIAMS.

Australian Manufacturers' Export Council: POB E14, Queen Victoria Terrace, ACT 2600; tel. (2) 6273-2311; fax (2) 6273-3196; f. 1955; Exec. Dir G. CHALKER.

Australian Wool Innovation Ltd: Level 30, HSBC Centre, 580 George St, Sydney, NSW 2000; tel. (2) 8295-3100; fax (2) 8295-4100; e-mail info@wool.com; internet www.wool.com; f. 2001; est. following privatization of Australian Wool Research and Promotion Org; owner of The Woolmark Co; Chair. WALTER B. MERRIMAN; CEO STUART McCULLOGH.

Business Council of Australia (BCA): GPOB 1472, Melbourne, Vic 3001; tel. (3) 8664-2664; fax (3) 8664-2666; e-mail info@bca.com.au; internet www.bca.com.au; public policy research and advocacy; governing council comprises chief execs of Australia's major cos; Pres. TONY SHEPHERD; Chief Exec. JENNIFER WESTACOTT.

Cotton Australia: 247 Coward St, Suite 4.01, Mascot, NSW 2020; tel. (2) 9669-5222; fax (2) 9669-5511; e-mail talktous@cottonaustralia.com.au; internet www.cottonaustralia.com.au; Chair. ANDREW WATSON; CEO ADAM KAY.

Meat and Livestock Australia: Level 1, 165 Walker St, North Sydney, NSW 2060; tel. (2) 9463-9333; fax (2) 9463-9393; e-mail info@mla.com.au; internet www.mla.com.au; producer-owned co; represents, promotes, protects and furthers interests of industry in both the marketing of meat and livestock and industry-based research and devt activities; Chair. ARTHUR (DON) HEATLEY; Man. Dir DAVID PALMER.

National Farmers' Federation: POB E10, Kingston, ACT 2604; tel. (2) 6269-5666; fax (2) 6273-2331; e-mail nff@nff.org.au; internet www.nff.org.au; Pres. JOCK LAURIE; CEO MATT LINNEGAR.

Standing Council on Primary Industries (SCoPI): GPOB 858, Canberra, ACT 2601; tel. (2) 6272-4995; e-mail scopi@daff.gov.au; internet www.mincos.gov.au; f. 2011; replaced Primary Industries Ministerial Council and the Natural Resource Management Ministerial Council; promotes development and sustainability of agriculture, fisheries and forestry industries and Australia's natural resources; supervises and monitors the primary production sectors; mems comprise the state/territory and New Zealand govt agencies responsible for primary industries; Chair. Dr CONALL O'CONNELL.

Wine Australia Corporation (WAC): POB 2733, Kent Town Business Centre, Kent Town, SA 5071; tel. (8) 8228-2000; fax (8) 8228-2022; e-mail enquiries@wineaustralia.com; internet www.wineaustralia.com; f. 1981; Chair. GEORGE WAHBY; Chief Exec. ANDREAS CLARK (acting).

Winemakers' Federation of Australia (WFA): National Wine Centre, Botanic Rd, POB 2414, Kent Town, SA 5071; tel. (8) 8133-4300; fax (8) 8133-4366; e-mail wfa@wfa.org.au; internet www.wfa.org.au; f. 1990; Pres. TONY D'ALOISIO; Chief Exec. PAUL EVANS.

WoolProducers Australia: POB E10, Kingston, Canberra, ACT 2604; tel. (2) 6273-2531; fax (2) 6273-1120; e-mail woolproducers@nff.org.au; internet www.woolproducers.com.au; f. 2001; fmrly Wool Council Australia; represents wool-growers in dealings with the Federal Govt and industry; Pres. DONALD HAMBLIN.

EMPLOYERS' ORGANIZATIONS

Australian Industry Group: 51 Walker St, North Sydney, NSW 2060; tel. (2) 9466-5566; fax (2) 9466-5599; e-mail helpdesk@aigroup.asn.au; internet www.aigroup.asn.au; f. 1998 through merger of Metal Trades Industry Association and Australian Chamber of Manufacturers; 11,500 mems; Nat. Pres. LUCIO DI BARTOLOMEO; CEO HEATHER RIDOUT.

Australian Meat Industry Council: Level 2, 460 Pacific Hwy, St Leonard's, NSW 2065; tel. (2) 9086-2200; fax (2) 9086-2201; e-mail admin@amic.org.au; internet www.amic.org.au; f. 1928; represents meat retailers, processors and small goods mfrs; Chair. FRANK HERD; CEO KEVIN COTTRILL.

NSW Farmers' Association: GPOB 1068, Sydney, NSW 2001; tel. (2) 8251-1700; fax (2) 8251-1750; e-mail emailus@nswfarmers.org.au; internet www.nswfarmers.org.au; f. 1978; Pres. CHARLES ARMSTRONG; CEO MATT BRAND.

UTILITIES

Australian Institute of Energy: POB 193, Surry Hills, Vic 3127; fax (3) 9898-0249; e-mail aie@aie.org.au; internet www.aie.org.au; f. 1977; Pres. BRIAN TRUMAN.

Australian Water Association: POB 222, St Leonards, NSW 1590; tel. (2) 9436-0055; fax (2) 9436-0155; e-mail info@awa.asn.au; internet www.awa.asn.au; f. 1962; c. 5,500 mems; Pres. LUCIA CADE; CEO TOM MOLLENKOPF.

Energy Supply Association of Australia: GPOB 1823, Melbourne, Vic 3001; tel. (3) 9670-0188; fax (3) 9670-1069; e-mail info@esaa.com.au; internet www.esaa.com.au; Chair. IAN STIRLING; CEO MATTHEW WARREN.

Electricity Companies

Delta Electricity: Level 20, 175 Liverpool St, Sydney, NSW 2000; tel. (2) 9285-2700; fax (2) 9285-2777; e-mail info@de.com.au; internet www.de.com.au; f. 1996; Chair. HELEN GARNETT; Chief Exec. GREGORY EVERETT.

ENERGEX: GPOB 1461, Brisbane, Qld 4001; tel. (7) 3664-4000; fax (7) 3025-8301; e-mail custserve@energex.com.au; internet www.energex.com.au; spans Queensland and New South Wales; Chair. SHANE STONE; Gen. Man. TERRY EFFENEY.

EnergyAustralia: Locked Bag 14-060, Melbourne, Vic 8001; tel. (2) 9269-4200; fax (2) 9269-2830; internet www.energyaustralia.com.au; supplies customers in NSW; acquired by TRUenergy in 2011 to form one entity; owned by CLP Power Asia; Man. Dir RICHARD McINDOE.

Ergon Energy: POB 308, Rockhampton, Qld 4700; tel. (7) 4921-6001; fax (7) 3228-8118; e-mail customerservice@ergon.com.au; internet www.ergon.com.au; electricity supplier serving Qld; Chair. MALCOLM HALL-BROWN; Chief Exec. IAN McLEOD.

Essential Energy: POB 718, Queanbeyan, NSW 2620; tel. (2) 6338-3628; fax (2) 6589-8695; internet www.essentialenergy.com.au; f. 2011; est. from Country Energy following its privatization and acquisition by Origin Energy; state-owned; electricity and gas distributor; Chair. ROGER MASSY-GREENE; Man. Dir VINCE GRAHAM.

Power and Water Corpn: Mitchell Centre, Level 2, 55 Mitchell St, Darwin, NT 0800; tel. (8) 8923-4681; fax (8) 8924-7730; e-mail customerservice@powerwater.com.au; internet www.powerwater.com.au; state-owned; supplier of electricity, water and sewerage services in NT; Chair. MICHAEL HANNON; Man. Dir ANDREW MACRIDES.

Powercor Australia Ltd: Locked Bag 14-090, Melbourne, Vic 8001; fax (3) 9683-4499; e-mail info@powercor.com.au; internet www.powercor.com.au; Chair. PETER TULLOCH; CEO SHANE BREHENY.

Snowy Hydro Ltd: AMP Centre, Level 37, 50 Bridge St, Sydney, NSW 2000; tel. (2) 9278-1888; fax (2) 9278-1879; e-mail info@snowyhydro.com.au; internet www.snowyhydro.com.au; Chair. BRUCE HOGAN; Man. Dir TERRY V. CHARLTON.

United Energy Ltd: Locked Bag 7000, Mount Waverley, Vic 3149; tel. (3) 8544-9000; internet www.ue.com.au; f. 1994; est. following division of State Electricity Comm. of Victoria; transferred to private sector; distributor of electricity and gas; CEO HUGH GLEESON.

Western Power Corpn: 363 Wellington St, Perth, WA 6000; tel. (8) 9326-4911; fax (8) 9326-4595; e-mail info@westernpower.com.au; internet www.westernpower.com.au; f. 1995; principal supplier of electricity in WA; Chair. ALAN MULGREW; CEO PAUL ITALIANO.

Gas Companies

APA Group: HSBC Bldg, Level 19, 580 George St, Sydney, NSW 2000; tel. (2) 9693-0000; fax (2) 9693-0093; e-mail apawebsitefeedback@apa.com.au; internet www.apa.com.au; f. 2000; Chair. LEONARD BLEASEL; CEO MICHAEL MCCORMACK.

ATCO Gas Australia: Locked Bag 2507, Perth, WA 6849; tel. (8) 6218-1700; e-mail info@wng.com.au; internet www.atcogas.com.au; owned by the ATCO Group; acquired Western Australian Gas Networks in 2011; Chair. STEVEN LANDRY; Pres. BRIAN HAHN.

Australian Gas Light Co: AGL Centre, Level 22, 101 Miller St, North Sydney, NSW 2060; tel. (2) 9921-2999; fax (2) 9957-3671; e-mail aglmail@agl.com.au; internet www.agl.com.au; f. 1837; Chair. JEREMY MAYCOCK; Man. Dir and CEO MICHAEL FRASER.

Envestra: 10th Floor, 81 Flinders St, Adelaide, SA 5000; tel. (8) 8227-1500; fax (8) 8277-1511; e-mail envestra@envestra.com.au; internet www.envestra.com.au; f. 1997; est. by merger of South Australian Gas Co, Gas Corpn of Queensland and Centre Gas Pty Ltd; purchased Victorian Gas Network in 1999; Chair. JOHN GEOFFREY ALLPASS; Man. Dir IAN BRUCE LITTLE.

Epic Energy: Level 8, 60 Collins St, Melbourne, Vic 3000; tel. (3) 8626-8400; fax (3) 8626-8454; internet www.epicenergy.com.au; f. 1996; privately owned gas transmission co; Chair. BRUCE MCKAY; Man. Dir and CEO MATT BRASSINGTON.

Origin Energy: Level 45, Australia Sq., 264–278 George St, Sydney, NSW 2000; tel. (2) 8345-5000; fax (2) 9252-9244; e-mail enquiry@originenergy.com.au; internet www.originenergy.com.au; Chair. H. KEVIN MCCANN; Man. Dir GRANT KING.

Water Companies

Melbourne Water Corpn: 990 LaTrobe St, Docklands, Vic 3008; tel. (3) 9235-7100; fax (3) 9235-7200; internet www.melbournewater.com.au; state-owned; Chair. PAUL CLARKE; Man. Dir SHAUN COX.

Power and Water Corpn: see Electricity, above.

South Australian Water Corpn: SA Water House, Ground Floor, 250 Victoria Sq., Adelaide, SA 5000; tel. (8) 8204-1000; fax (8) 7003-3329; e-mail customerservice@sawater.com.au; internet www.sawater.com.au; state-owned; Chair. LEWIS OWENS; Chief Exec. JOHN RINGHAM.

South East Water Ltd: Locked Bag 1, Moorabbin, Vic 3189; tel. (3) 9552-3000; fax (3) 9552-3001; e-mail info@sewl.com.au; internet www.southeastwater.com.au; f. 1995; state-owned; Chair. DOUG SHIRREFS; Man. Dir KEVIN HUTCHINGS.

Sydney Water Corpn: POB 399, Parramatta, NSW 2124; internet www.sydneywater.com.au; state-owned; Chair. Dr THOMAS PARRY; Man. Dir KEVIN YOUNG.

Water Corpn: 629 Newcastle St, Leederville, WA 6007; tel. (8) 9420-2420; fax (8) 9423-7722; e-mail customer@watercorporation.com.au; internet www.watercorporation.com.au; state-owned; Chair. EVA SKIRA; CEO SUE MURPHY.

Yarra Valley Water Ltd: Private Bag 1, Mitcham, Vic 3132; tel. (3) 9874-2122; fax (3) 9872-1353; e-mail enquiry@yvw.com.au; internet www.yvw.com.au; f. 1995; state-owned; Chair. PETER WILSON; Man. Dir TONY KELLY.

TRADE UNIONS

Australian Council of Trade Unions (ACTU): Level 6, 365 Queen St, Melbourne, Vic 3000; tel. (3) 9664-7333; fax (3) 9600-0050; e-mail help@actu.org.au; internet www.actu.org.au; f. 1927; br. in each state, generally known as a Trades and Labour Council; 45 affiliated trade unions; Pres. GED KEARNEY; Sec. DAVE OLIVER.

Transport

Standing Council on Transport and Infrastructure: GPOB 594, Canberra, ACT 2601; tel. (2) 6274-7333; e-mail mike.mrdak@infrastructure.gov.au; internet www.scoti.gov.au; f. 1993, fmrly the Australian Transport Council, est. as above in 2011; mems include Australian and New Zealand ministers responsible for transport; Chair. MIKE MRDAK.

Adelaide Metro: Dept of Planning, Transport and Infrastructure, GPOB 1533, Adelaide, SA 5001; fax (8) 8343-2222; e-mail dpti.enquiriesadministrator@sa.gov.au; internet www.adelaidemetro.com.au; f. 1999; operates metropolitan bus, train and tram services; CEO (vacant).

State Transit Authority of New South Wales: 219–241 Cleveland St, Strawberry Hills, NSW 2010; tel. (2) 9508-2900; e-mail info@sydneybuses.nsw.gov.au; internet www.statetransit.info; operates government buses and ferries in Sydney and the Greater Newcastle metropolitan areas; Chair. BARRIE UNSWORTH; CEO PETER ROWLEY.

RAILWAYS

In June 2012 there were 41,980 km of railways in Australia. In 2003 the construction of a 1,400-km railway between Alice Springs and Darwin was completed. The development of a high-speed network for the country's east coast remained under consideration in 2014.

Pacific National: Level 6, 15 Blue St, North Sydney, NSW 2060; tel. (2) 8484-8000; fax (2) 8484-8151; e-mail communication@pacificnational.com.au; internet www.pacificnational.com.au; freight; fmrly Nat. Rail Corpn Ltd; CEO JOHN MULLEN.

QR (Queensland Rail): GPOB 1429, Brisbane, Qld 4001; tel. (7) 3235-2180; fax (7) 3072-2222; internet www.queenslandrail.com.au; f. 1863; passenger commuter and long-distance services, freight and logistic services, track access and rail-specific expert services; Chair. GLEN DAWE; CEO JIM BENSTEAD.

RailCorp: POB K349, Haymarket, NSW 1238; tel. (2) 8202-2000; fax (2) 8202-2111; internet www.railcorp.info; f. 1980; responsible for passenger rail and associated coach services in NSW; CEO ROB MASON.

Victorian Rail Track (VicTrack): Level 8, 1010 LaTrobe St, Docklands, Vic 3008; tel. (3) 9619-1111; fax (3) 9619-8851; e-mail victrack@victrack.com.au; internet www.victrack.com.au; f. 1997; Chair. BOB ANNELLS; Gen. Man CYNTHIA LAHIFF.

ROADS

In 2010 there were 825,500 km of roads in Australia.

Austroads: Suite 2, Level 9, 287 Elizabeth St, Sydney, NSW 2000; tel. (2) 9264-7088; fax (2) 9264-1657; e-mail austroads@austroads.com.au; internet www.austroads.com.au; f. 1989; asscn of road transport and traffic authorities; Chair. ANDY MILAZZO; Chief Exec. MURRAY KIDNIE.

SHIPPING

In December 2013 the Australian flag registered fleet comprised 733 vessels, with a total displacement of 2,047,137 grt.

ANL Ltd (Australian National Line): GPOB 2238, Melbourne, Vic 3001; tel. (3) 8842-5555; fax (3) 9257-0619; e-mail marketing@anl.com.au; internet www.anl.com.au; f. 1998; shipping agents; coastal and overseas container shipping and coastal bulk shipping; container management services; overseas container services to Asia; extensive transshipment services; Chair. JACQUES SAADE; Man. Dir JOHN LINES.

Svitzer Australia: Level 25, 66 Goulburn St, Sydney, NSW 2000; tel. (2) 9369-9200; fax (2) 9369-9277; e-mail info.australasia@svitzer.com; internet www.svitzer.com; f. 1875; fmrly Adelaide Steamship Co; later known as Adsteam Marine Ltd, until acquisition by Svitzer (Denmark); Man. Dir MARK MALONE.

CIVIL AVIATION

Cobham Aviation Services: National Dr., Adelaide Airport, SA 5950; tel. (8) 8154-7000; fax (8) 8154-7019; internet www.nationaljet.com.au; f. 1989, fmrly National Jet Systems; chartered flights; CEO JOHN DEVANEY; Group CEO BOB MURPHY.

Jetstar Airways Pty Ltd: POB 635, Sunshine, Vic 3020; tel. (3) 9347-0091; internet www.jetstar.com.au; f. 2004; owned by Qantas Airways Ltd; low-cost domestic passenger services and flights to New Zealand, Fiji, Singapore, Indonesia, Japan and other Asia-Pacific destinations; Chief Exec. JAYNE HRDLICKA.

Qantas Airways Ltd: Qantas Centre, 203 Coward St, Mascot, NSW 2020; tel. (2) 9691-3636; fax (2) 9691-3339; internet www.qantas.com; f. 1920; est. as Queensland and Northern Territory Aerial Services; Australian Govt became sole owner in 1947; merged with Australian Airlines in Sept. 1992; British Airways purchased 25% in March 1993; remaining 75% transferred to private sector in 1995;

services throughout Australia and to 36 countries, including destinations in Europe, Africa, the USA, Canada, South America, Asia, the Pacific and New Zealand; subsidiary QantasLink operates regional services; Chair. LEIGH CLIFFORD; CEO ALAN JOYCE.

Virgin Australia: 56 Edmondstone Rd, Bowen Hills, QLD 4006; tel. (7) 3295-3000; e-mail corporatecommunications@virginaustralia.com; internet www.virginaustralia.com; f. 2000 as Virgin Blue; renamed as above in 2011; domestic and international services; CEO JOHN BORGHETTI.

Tourism

The main attractions are the cosmopolitan cities, the Great Barrier Reef, the Blue Mountains, water sports and also winter sports in the Australian Alps, notably the Snowy Mountains. The town of Alice Springs, the Aboriginal culture and the sandstone monolith of Uluru (also known as Ayers Rock) are among the attractions of the desert interior. Much of Australia's wildlife is unique to the country. Australia received 6.5m. foreign visitors in 2013, an increase of 5.5% in comparison with 2012. New Zealand, the People's Republic of China, the United Kingdom, the USA, Japan and Singapore are the principal sources of visitors. Receipts from international tourism totalled an estimated US $31,534m. in 2012. Tourist accommodation facilities comprised 227,015 rooms in September 2012.

Tourism Australia: GPOB 2721, Sydney, NSW 1006; tel. (2) 9360-1111; fax (2) 9331-6469; e-mail corpaffairs@tourism.australia.com; internet www.tourism.australia.com; f. 2004; govt authority responsible for marketing of international and domestic tourism; Chair. GEOFF DIXON.

Defence

As assessed at November 2013, Australia's active armed forces numbered 56,200: army 28,600, navy 13,550, air force 14,050. There were also reserve forces of 28,550. Military service is voluntary. All restrictions on the deployment of women in combat roles were ended in September 2011. Australia is a member of the ANZUS Security Treaty (with New Zealand and the USA), and of the Five Power Defence Arrangements (with Singapore, Malaysia, the United Kingdom and New Zealand). The withdrawal from Afghanistan of Australian members of the NATO-led International Security Assistance Force (ISAF) was completed by the end of 2013.

Defence Budget: Estimated at $A22,045m. for 2013/14.

Chief of the Defence Force: Gen. DAVID HURLEY; Air Marshal Mark Binskin to replace Gen. Hurley in July 2014.

Chief of Navy: Vice-Adm. RAY GRIGGS.

Chief of Army: Lt-Gen. DAVID MORRISON.

Chief of Air Force: Air Marshal GEOFFREY BROWN.

Education

Education is the responsibility of each of the states and the Federal Government. It is free of charge and compulsory for all children from the ages of six to at least 16 years (in most states) or 17 if not going into training. Primary education generally begins with a preparatory year commencing at five years of age, followed by six or seven years of schooling. Secondary education, beginning at the age of 12, usually lasts for five or six years. In 2010/11 enrolment at primary schools included 96% of children in the relevant age-group, while enrolment at secondary schools included 86% of children in the relevant age-group. In August 2011 there were 2,037,148 children enrolled in primary schools (including those attending non-government schools, the majority being Catholic institutions) and 1,482,384 in secondary schools. A total of 1,066,095 students were attending 39 universities in 2008. Public expenditure on education under the federal budget for the financial year 2013/14 was projected at $A29,742m.

AUSTRALIAN EXTERNAL TERRITORIES

CHRISTMAS ISLAND

Introductory Survey

LOCATION, CLIMATE, LANGUAGE, RELIGION, FLAG, CAPITAL

Christmas Island lies 360 km south of Java Head (Indonesia) in the Indian Ocean. The nearest point on the Australian coast is North West Cape, 1,408 km to the south-east. Christmas Island has no indigenous population. The climate is equable, with temperatures varying between 26°C (79°F) and 28°C (83°F), and rainfall of 2,000 mm per year. A variety of languages are spoken (two or more languages were spoken in 59% of households in 2011), but English is the official language. The Christmas Island flag (proportions 1 by 2) is divided diagonally from the upper hoist to the lower fly: the upper portion displays a Golden Bosun bird in silhouette on a green background, the lower portion has five white five-pointed stars, in the form of the Southern Cross constellation, on a blue background, and in the centre is a golden circle containing the shape of the island in green. The predominant religious affiliations are Buddhist (16.9% in 2011), Christian (16.4%) and Muslim (14.9%). The principal settlement and only anchorage is Flying Fish Cove (Kampong).

CONTEMPORARY POLITICAL HISTORY

Historical Context

Following annexation by the United Kingdom in 1888, Christmas Island was incorporated for administrative purposes with the Straits Settlements (now Singapore and part of Malaysia) in 1900. Japanese forces occupied the island from March 1942 until the end of the Second World War, and in 1946 Christmas Island became a dependency of Singapore. Administration was transferred to the United Kingdom on 1 January 1958, pending final transfer to Australia, effected on 1 October 1958. The Australian Government appointed Official Representatives to the territory until 1968, when new legislation provided for an Administrator, appointed by the Governor-General. Responsibility for the island's administration lies with the Minister for Infrastructure and Regional Development. In 1980 an Advisory Council was established for the Administrator to consult. In 1984 the Christmas Island Services Corporation was created to perform those functions that are normally the responsibility of municipal government. This body was placed under the direction of the Christmas Island Assembly, the first elections to which took place in September 1985. Nine members were elected for one-year terms. In November 1987 the Assembly was dissolved, and the Administrator empowered to perform its functions. The Corporation was superseded by the Christmas Island Shire Council in 1992.

Domestic Political Affairs

In May 1994 an unofficial referendum on the island's status was held concurrently with local government elections. At the poll, sponsored by the Union of Christmas Island Workers, the islanders rejected an option to secede from Australia, but more than 85% of voters favoured increased local government control. The referendum was prompted, in part, by the Australian Government's plans to abolish the island's duty-free status (which had become a considerable source of revenue).

Since 1981 all residents of the island have been eligible to acquire Australian citizenship. In 1984 the Australian Government extended social security, health and education benefits to the island, and enfranchised Australian citizens resident there. Full income-tax liability was introduced in the late 1980s. The Territories Law Reform Act 2010 (see Norfolk Island) included provision for the comprehensive application of the laws of Western Australia to Christmas Island.

Asylum Seekers and Detention Arrangements

From the late 1990s an increasing number of illegal immigrants travelling to Australia landed on Christmas Island. International attention was focused on Christmas Island in August 2001 when the *MV Tampa*, a Norwegian container ship carrying 433 refugees whom it had rescued from a sinking Indonesian fishing boat, was refused permission to land on the island. As the humanitarian crisis escalated, the Australian Government's steadfast refusal to admit the mostly Afghan refugees prompted international condemnation and led to a serious diplomatic dispute between Australia and Norway. Hundreds of Christmas Island residents attended a rally urging the Australian Government to reconsider its uncompromising stance. In September the refugees were transferred to Nauru, where their applications for asylum were to be processed. In the same month the Senate in Canberra approved new legislation, which excised Christmas Island and other outlying territories from Australia's official migration zone. The new legislation also imposed stricter criteria for the processing of asylum seekers and the removal of their right to recourse to the Australian court system. Meanwhile, increasing numbers of asylum seekers continued to attempt to reach Christmas Island via Indonesia.

In March 2002 the Government announced plans to establish a permanent detention centre (with a capacity of 1,200 people) on the island, at a projected cost of more than $A150m., in order to accommodate the growing number of asylum seekers. Following an unexpected decline in the number of boat arrivals on the island in the early 2000s, however, the Government scaled down its plans and the construction of a 800-bed detention centre began in February 2005. By late 2007 the estimated cost of the project had reportedly increased to $A396m. Although the centre was completed in early 2008, it was—initially at least—unused, in accordance with the new Australian Government's policy of opposition to its construction. Kevin Rudd's Labor administration relaxed Australia's policy on the treatment of refugees in July, when it announced that the automatic incarceration of asylum seekers upon arrival was to be ended. However, in December the Government announced that a group of suspected asylum seekers from Afghanistan and Iran found in a boat off the north-west coast of Australia was to be taken to the Christmas Island detention centre. In January 2009 28 of these refugees (including 10 children) became the first beneficiaries of the Rudd Government's 'more humane' approach to the asylum issue when they were granted permanent residency in Australia.

In 2009 the number of asylum seekers arriving in Australian waters increased dramatically, reportedly owing to the deteriorating security situation in countries such as Afghanistan and Sri Lanka. These asylum seekers were taken to Christmas Island for processing, and in October the Government announced plans to increase the detention centre's capacity beyond 1,400, in order to accommodate the growing numbers. Representatives of the human rights organization Amnesty International were permitted to visit the detention centre in August 2008 and again in December 2009, when it reiterated its concerns with regard to the facilities and described the Australian Government's policy as 'unviable and inhumane'. By January 2010, according to the Australian Department of Immigration, the detention centre held a total of 1,628 asylum seekers. In February, with numbers at the centre again approaching capacity, the Government announced plans for a further extension of the facility, to hold 2,200–2,300 inmates. In June, in an attempt to ease the overcrowding, the authorities commenced the transfer of dozens of asylum seekers from the centre to a disused mining camp on the mainland, located at Leonora in Western Australia. Meanwhile, asylum seekers on Christmas Island continued to be processed and resettled in mainland Australia. In April, however, the Government imposed moratoriums of six and of three months, respectively, on processing the claims of applicants who had travelled from Afghanistan and from Sri Lanka, in response to 'changing conditions' in those countries.

In November 2010, in a unanimous ruling that was expected to have extensive implications for government policy, the Australian High Court found in favour of two unsuccessful Sri Lankan asylum seekers. The two Tamil migrants had been detained on Christmas Island and had argued that legislation that prevented them from appealing against the rejection of their asylum claims was unfair. The dispute centred on the official distinction made between asylum seekers who arrived by sea and those who had travelled by air: the latter category was not subject to automatic detention and had the right of appeal in the event of the rejection of a claim for asylum.

In a major incident in rough seas in December 2010 some 50 asylum seekers, mainly from Iraq and Iran, perished when their wooden vessel disintegrated on rocks off Christmas Island. A parliamentary inquiry into the disaster held in Australia concluded in June 2011 that the response of the authorities to the disaster had been as effective as possible under the prevailing weather conditions. In January that year three Indonesian members of the ship's crew were indicted on charges of illegally transporting people to Australia. Also, Ali Khorram Heydarkhani, an Australian citizen of Iranian descent, was arrested in Indonesia in connection with various allegations of immigration offences, including arrangements for the dispatch of the boat that had foundered off Christmas Island in the previous month. In May, following his deportation from Indonesia, Heydarkhani appeared in court in the Australian city of Sydney, whereupon he was charged with people-smuggling. In September 2012 the three crew members were each sentenced to more than five years' imprisonment and in the following month Heydarkhani received a sentence of 14 years' imprisonment. Meanwhile, at least 90 further lives were lost in June, when two boats carrying asylum seekers from Indonesia to Christmas Island sank en route. Those rescued were transferred to Christmas Island. It was hoped that the offshore processing of asylum seekers, which recommenced in Nauru in September and in Papua New Guinea in November, following the approval of the necessary legislation by the Australian Parliament in August, would deter asylum seekers from making the often perilous journey to Christmas Island.

In March 2011 about 170 asylum seekers were recaptured following a mass escape from the detention centre. Furthermore, in a protest against the slow processing of their applications for asylum, detainees were reported to have set fire to the facility and to have assaulted security personnel. The authorities resorted to the use of tear gas to quell the disturbances. In June riot police were drafted in to curb further protests, and there was renewed unrest in July when as many as 100 inmates were involved in a confrontation during which medical records were destroyed. At 31 May 2013 there were 1,238 detainees in the centre; a further 1,533 people, of whom 627 were children, were in alternative places of detention on Christmas Island and the Cocos (Keeling) Islands.

In July 2013, in an attempt to curb the number of boat arrivals, which had sharply increased in 2012 and the first half of 2013, the Australian Government signed a new offshore resettlement agreement with Papua New Guinea according to which asylum seekers arriving by boat in Australia would be sent to Manus Island, Papua New Guinea, for processing and, if their applications were successful, would be permanently resettled in Papua New Guinea (rather than in Australia); a similar agreement was signed with Nauru in August. Within only a few months, a significant fall in the number of boat arrivals and a decrease in the number of inmates at the detention centre on Christmas Island appeared to indicate the efficacy of the controversial new policy. The new, conservative Government headed by Tony Abbott which came to power in September vowed further to discourage people smuggling—partly through assigning greater control over such operations to the military, and in January 2014 there were reports that Australian naval vessels had violated Indonesian sovereignty while forcing boats carrying asylum seekers back towards Indonesia.

ECONOMIC AFFAIRS

Despite its auspicious climate, Christmas Island does not possess a significant agricultural sector. The predominance of tropical forest (much of which has been granted national park status) has discouraged commercial farming activities and the territory relies, for the most part, on food imports from mainland Australia. Abundant marine resources exist in the island's surrounding waters, although without proper regulation opportunities for commercial fishing have remained limited. Islanders who participate in subsistence and recreational fishing activities do so without licences, and therefore no official data exist relating to the volume of activity in this sector.

The recovery of phosphates has been the principal economic activity on Christmas Island. In November 1987 the Australian Government announced the closure of the phosphate mine, owing to industrial unrest, and mining activity ceased in December of that year. However, in 1990 the Government allowed private operators to recommence phosphate extraction, subject to certain conditions. A new, 21-year lease, drawn up by the Government and the owner of the mine, Phosphate Resources Ltd, took effect in February 1998. The agreement incorporated environmental safeguards and provided for a conservation levy, based on the tonnage of phosphate shipped, which was to finance a programme of rainforest rehabilitation. At the census of 2011, 16.7% of Christmas Island's employed population were engaged in the mining sector.

The services sector engaged 71.0% of the employed labour force at the census of 2011. Efforts have been made to develop the island's considerable potential for tourism. In 1989, in an attempt to protect the natural environment and many rare species of flora and fauna (including the Abbott's Booby and the Christmas frigate bird), the National Park was extended to cover some 63% of the island. A large hotel and casino complex was opened in November 1993, and revenue from the development totalled $A500m. in 1994. In April 1998, however, the complex was closed down, and some 350 employees were made redundant. In 2003 receipts from Christmas Island's tourism, hospitality and retail sector were estimated at between $A3m. and $A5m.

Between 1992 and 1999 the Australian Government invested an estimated $A110m. in the development of Christmas Island's infrastructure as part of the Christmas Island Rebuilding Programme. The main areas of expenditure under this programme were a new hospital, the upgrading of port facilities, school extensions, the construction of housing, power, water supply and sewerage, and the repair and construction of roads. In 2000 further improvements to marine facilities and water supply were carried out, in addition to the construction of new housing to relocate islanders away from a major rockfall risk area. In 2001 the Australian Government pledged a total of more than $A50m. for further developments, including improvements to the airport and the road network, as well as an alternative port. The proposed additional port was to be constructed on the east coast of the island, allowing for the handling of sea freight and the launching of emergency vessels at times when the existing port at Flying Fish Cove is closed owing to north-west swells. These closures, which most commonly occur between December and March, result in inflated costs for shipping companies and inconvenience for Christmas Islanders. The Australian Government provided $A2.5m. to fund a new mobile telephone network for the territory, which replaced the old analogue network in February 2005. In 2004 the Australian Government created a funding programme to support economic development in its Indian Ocean territories; in 2012/13 total funding of up to $A150,000 was available for projects in Christmas Island.

The cost of the island's imports from Australia decreased from $A17m. in 1999/2000 to $A5m. in 2006/07, when the territory's exports to that country earned $A26m. Exports to New Zealand in 2006/07 were worth $NZ9m. The 2013/14 budget envisaged operating revenue of $A13.8m. and operating expenditure of $A11.6m. Capital expenditure was $A5.6m. The 2011 census recorded 0.4% of the total labour force as being unemployed.

The closure of the casino resort in 1998 had serious economic and social repercussions for Christmas Island. A project to develop a communications satellite launching facility on the island received government approval in 2000, but the scheme was subsequently postponed indefinitely. A major issue for the local population has been the substantial rise in the cost of living on the island, largely owing to the presence of around 2,500 mainland personnel, including immigration officials, security guards and medical staff. Furthermore, prospects for the development of eco-tourism have been curtailed by the negative publicity surrounding the detention centre. Christmas Island possesses more than 20 species of crab. These include the robber (or coconut) crab, the largest land invertebrate in the world. In 2010, however, local reports suggested that increasing numbers of this protected native species were being killed by road vehicles driven at undue speed by personnel from the mainland. Although the establishment of the detention centre has had a number of negative consequences for the island, a government report issued in October 2013 intimated that, if the facility were to be closed (as seemed possible given the potential impact of the new asylum/resettlement policies), the economy of Christmas Island would be in danger of collapse. Accordingly, it appeared even more imperative that the tourism sector of the island be strengthened in an attempt to counter such a situation.

PUBLIC HOLIDAYS

2015: 1 January (New Year's Day), 26 January (Australia Day), 19–22 February (Chinese New Year), 24 March (Labour Day), 3 April (Good Friday), 25 April (Anzac Day), 18 July (Hari Raya Puasa), 24 September (Hari Raya Haji), 6 October (Territory Day), 25–26 December (Christmas).

Statistical Survey

AREA AND POPULATION

Area: 136.7 sq km (52.8 sq miles).

Population: 1,347 at census of 8 August 2006; 2,072 (males 1,465, females 607) at census of 9 August 2011.

Density (at 2011 census): 15.2 per sq km.

Population by Age and Sex (2011 census): *0–14:* 264 (males 134, females 130); *15–64:* 1,730 (males 1,277, females 453); *65 and over:* 78 (males 53, females 25); *Total* 2,072 (males 1,465, females 607).

Country of Birth (2011 census): Afghanistan 112; Australia 648; Iraq 93; Malaysia 372; Singapore 45; Other 804.

Births, Marriages and Deaths (1985 unless otherwise indicated): Registered live births 36 (birth rate 15.8 per 1,000); Registered marriages 519 (2011); Registered deaths 2.

Economically Active Population (persons aged 15 years and over, excl. overseas visitors, 2011 census): Mining 135; Manufacturing 6; Electricity, gas and water 21; Construction 52; Wholesale and retail trade, restaurants, and hotels 91; Transport, storage and communications 42; Financing, insurance, real estate and business services 28; Government administration and defence 263; Community, social and personal services 150; Activities not stated or not adequately defined 21; *Total employed* 809 (males 482, females 327); Unemployed 3 (males 3); *Total labour force* 812 (males 485, females 327).

MINING

Natural Phosphates ('000 metric tons, official estimates): 285 in 1994; 220 in 1995. Note: By 2007 it was estimated that 600,000 metric tons of phosphates were being mined each year.

FINANCE

Currency and Exchange Rates: Australian currency is used.

Budget ($A, year ending 30 June 2014, budget figures): Operating revenue 13,845,676 (General purpose funding 5,593,074; Welfare 692,200; Community amenities 1,501,000; Recreation and culture 1,603,704; Transport 4,253,953); Operating expenditure 11,619,908 (Governance 740,731; Law and order and public safety 259,799; Health 126,553; Welfare 685,011; Housing 189,856; Community amenities 2,167,123; Recreation and culture 2,930,802; Transport 4,110,010); Capital expenditure 5,633,000 (Community amenities 398,000; Recreation and culture 634,000; Transport 3,775,000).

EXTERNAL TRADE

Exports: An estimated 600,000 metric tons of phosphates are exported each year to mainland Australia and markets in South-East Asia.

Principal Trading Partners (phosphate exports, '000 metric tons, year ending 30 June 1984): Australia 463; New Zealand 332; Total (incl. others) 1,136.

2006/07 ($A million): *Imports:* Australia 5. *Exports:* Australia 26. Source: Australian Bureau of Statistics, *Year Book Australia*.

2006/07 ($NZ million): *Exports:* New Zealand 9. Source: Ministry of Foreign Affairs and Trade, New Zealand.

TRANSPORT

International Sea-borne Shipping (estimated freight traffic, '000 metric tons, 1990): Goods loaded 1,290; Goods unloaded 68. Source: UN, *Monthly Bulletin of Statistics*.

TOURISM

Visitor Arrivals and Departures by Air: 2,712 in 1998. Source: *Year Book Australia*.

COMMUNICATIONS MEDIA

Personal Computers (home users, 2001 census): 506.

Internet Users (2006 census): 480.

EDUCATION

Pre-primary (2011): 29 pupils.

Primary (2011): 106 pupils.

Secondary (2011): 66 pupils.

Tertiary (2011): 19 pupils.

Source: Education Department of Western Australia.

Directory

The Government

The Administrator, appointed by the Governor-General of Australia and responsible to the Minister for Infrastructure and Regional Development, is the senior government representative on the island.

Administrator: JON STANHOPE.

Office of the Administrator: POB 868, Christmas Island 6798, Indian Ocean; tel. (8) 9164-7960; fax (8) 9164-7961.

Shire of Christmas Island: George Fam Centre, 2 Murray Rd, POB 863, Christmas Island 6798, Indian Ocean; tel. (8) 9164-8300; fax (8) 9164-8304; e-mail kelvin@shire.gov.cx; internet www.shire.gov.cx; CEO KELVIN MATTHEWS; Pres. GORDON THOMSON.

Judicial System

Judicial services on Christmas Island are provided through the Western Australian Department of the Attorney-General. Western Australian Court Services provides a Magistrate's Court, District Court, Supreme Court, Family Court, Children's Court and Coroner's Court.

Managing Registrar: JEFFREY LOW, c/o Dept of Regional Australia, Local Government, Arts and Sport, POB 868, Christmas Island 6798, Indian Ocean; tel. (8) 9164-7901; fax (8) 9164-8530; e-mail jeffrey.low@dotars.gov.cx.

Religion

According to the census of 2011, a total of 350 Christmas Island residents were Buddhists (about 16.9%), 340 (16.4%) were Christians, of whom 146 were Roman Catholics and 74 were Anglicans, and 308 (14.9%) were Muslims; 41% chose not to state their religious affiliation. Within the Christian churches, Christmas Island lies in the jurisdiction of both the Anglican and Roman Catholic Archbishops of Perth, in Western Australia.

The Press

The Islander: Shire of Christmas Island, George Fam Centre, 2 Murray Rd, POB 863, Christmas Island 6798, Indian Ocean; tel. (8) 9164-8300; fax (8) 9164-8304; e-mail chong@shire.gov.cx; internet www.christmas.shire.gov.cx; newsletter; fortnightly; Editor KELVIN MATTHEWS.

Broadcasting and Communications

BROADCASTING

Radio

Christmas Island Community Radio Service: f. 1967; operated by the Administration since 1991; daily broadcasting service by Radio VLU-2 on 1422 KHz and 102 MHz FM, in English, Malay, Cantonese and Mandarin; Station Man. WILLIAM TAYLOR.

Christmas Island Radio VLU2–FM: POB 474, Christmas Island 6798, Indian Ocean; tel. (8) 9164-8316; fax (8) 9164-8315; daily broadcasts on 102.1FM and 105.3FM in English, Malay, Cantonese and Mandarin; Chair. and Station Man. TONY SMITH.

Television

Christmas Island Television: POB AAA, Christmas Island 6798, Indian Ocean.

Finance

BANKING

Commercial Bank

Westpac Banking Corpn (Australia): Canberra Pl., Christmas Island 6798, Indian Ocean; tel. (8) 9164-8221; fax (8) 9164-8241; e-mail dpoyner@westpac.com.au; Man. DONNA POYNER.

Trade and Industry

Administration of Christmas Island: POB 868, Christmas Island 6798, Indian Ocean; tel. (8) 9164-7901; fax (8) 9164-8245; operates power, public housing, local courts; Dir of Finance JEFFERY TAN.

Christmas Island Chamber of Commerce: POB 510, Christmas Island 6798, Indian Ocean; tel. (8) 9164-8856; fax (8) 9164-8322; e-mail info@cicommerce.org.cx; Pres. JOHN RICHARDSON; Vice-Pres. PHILLIP OAKLEY.

Shire of Christmas Island: see The Government.

Union of Christmas Island Workers (UCIW): Poon Saan Rd, POB 84, Christmas Island 6798, Indian Ocean; tel. (8) 9164-8472; fax (8) 9164-8470; e-mail uciw@pulau.cx; Pres. FOO KEE HENG; Gen. Sec. GORDON THOMSON.

Transport

There are good roads in the developed areas. Virgin Australia operates an air service between Perth and Christmas Island, and Christmas Island Air operates a weekly Malaysia Airlines flight connecting the Malaysian capital, Kuala Lumpur, to the island. The Australian National Line (ANL) operates ships to the Australian mainland. Cargo vessels from Fremantle, Western Australia, deliver regular supplies to the island. The Joint Island Supply System, established in 1989, provides a shipping service for Christmas Island and the Cocos (Keeling) Islands. The only anchorage is at Flying Fish Cove.

Tourism

Tourism has the potential to be an important sector of the island's economy. Much of the unique flora and fauna is found in the national park, which covers about 70% of the island and contains large tracts of rainforest. Other attractions are the waterfalls, beaches, coves and excellent conditions for scuba-diving and game-fishing.

Christmas Island Tourism Association/Christmas Island Visitor Information Centre: POB 63, Christmas Island 6798, Indian Ocean; tel. (8) 9164-8382; fax (8) 9164-8080; e-mail cita@christmas.net.au; internet www.christmas.net.au.

Christmas Island Travel: Christmas Island 6798, Indian Ocean; tel. (8) 9164-7168; fax (8) 9164-7169; e-mail xch@citravel.com.au; internet www.citravel.com.au; Dir TAN SIM KIAT.

Parks Australia: POB 867, Christmas Island 6798, Indian Ocean; tel. (8) 9164-8700; fax (8) 9164-8755; internet www.environment.gov.au/parks/christmas/index.html.

Education

The Christmas Island District High School, operated by the Western Australia Ministry of Education, provides education from pre-school level up to Australian 'Year 12'. In 2011 enrolment totalled 29 at pre-primary, 106 at primary and 66 at secondary level.

COCOS (KEELING) ISLANDS

Introductory Survey

LOCATION, CLIMATE, LANGUAGE, RELIGION, FLAG, CAPITAL

The Cocos (Keeling) Islands are 27 in number and lie 2,768 km north-west of Perth, in the Indian Ocean. The islands, with a combined area of 14.1 sq km (5.4 sq miles), form two low-lying coral atolls, densely covered with coconut palms. The climate is equable, with temperatures varying from 21°C (69°F) to 32°C (88°F), and rainfall of 2,000 mm per year. English is the official language, but Cocos Malay and Malay are also widely spoken. Most of the inhabitants are Muslims (around 76% in 2011). The flag of the Cocos Islands (proportions 1 by 2) is green, with a palm tree on a gold disc in the upper hoist, a gold crescent in the centre and five gold five-pointed stars, in the form of the Southern Cross constellation, in the fly. The Cocos Malay community is based on Home Island. The only other inhabited island is West Island, where most of the European community lives and where the administration is based.

CONTEMPORARY POLITICAL HISTORY

Historical Context

The Cocos Islands were declared a British possession in 1857 and came successively under the authority of the Governors of Ceylon (now Sri Lanka), from 1878, and the Straits Settlements (now Singapore and part of Malaysia), from 1886. In 1946, when the islands became a dependency of the Colony of Singapore, a resident administrator, responsible to the Governor of Singapore, was appointed. Administration of the islands was transferred to the Commonwealth of Australia on 23 November 1955. The agent of the Australian Government was known as the Official Representative until 1975, when an Administrator was appointed. The Minister for Infrastructure and Regional Development is responsible for the governance of the islands. The territory is part of the Northern Territory Electoral District.

Domestic Political Affairs

In June 1977 the Australian Government announced new policies concerning the islands, which resulted in its purchase from landowner John Clunies-Ross of the whole of his interests in the islands, with the exception of his residence and associated buildings. Although in 1886 the Clunies-Ross family had been granted all land above the high-water mark in perpetuity by the British Crown, the Australian Government's purchase for $A6.5m. took effect on 1 September 1978. An attempt by the Australian Government to acquire Clunies-Ross' remaining property was deemed by the Australian High Court in October 1984 to be unconstitutional.

In July 1979 the Cocos (Keeling) Islands Council was established, with a wide range of functions in the Home Island village area (which the Government transferred to the Council on trust for the benefit of the Cocos Malay community) and, from September 1984, in most of the rest of the territory.

On 6 April 1984 a referendum to decide the future political status of the islands was held by the Australian Government, with UN observers present. A large majority voted in favour of integration with Australia. As a result, the islanders were to acquire the rights, privileges and obligations of all Australian citizens. In July 1992 the Cocos (Keeling) Islands Council was replaced by the Cocos (Keeling) Islands Shire Council, composed of seven members and modelled on the local government and state law of Western Australia. The first Shire Council was elected in 1993. The Clunies-Ross family was declared bankrupt in mid-1993, following unsuccessful investment in a shipping venture, and the Australian Government took possession of its property.

In September 2001, following an increase in the numbers of illegal immigrants reaching Australian waters (see Christmas Island), legislation was enacted removing the Cocos Islands and other territories from Australia's official migration zone. In October of that year the Australian Government sent contingency supplies to the islands as a precaution, should it be necessary to accommodate more asylum seekers. This development provoked concern among many Cocos residents that the former quarantine station used as a detention centre might become a permanent asylum-processing facility under the order of the Australian Government. In December 123 Sri Lankan and Vietnamese asylum seekers were housed at the station, which was built to accommodate only 40. They were transferred to Christmas Island in February 2002.

In July 2009 an edict reportedly issued by the Shire Council banning employees and students from speaking Cocos Malay caused considerable consternation among the Malay residents. Those found speaking languages other than English in the workplace or at school were liable to penalties. The ban exacerbated the growing tensions between the majority Cocos Malay population and Australian public servants, deployed from the mainland, with regard to pay claims and cultural attitudes.

The Territories Law Reform Act 2010 (see Norfolk Island) included provision for the comprehensive application of the laws of Western Australia to the Cocos Islands.

A report in *The Washington Post* in March 2012 claimed that, as part of an agreement on closer military co-operation between Australia and the USA, it was planned to base US surveillance aircraft on the Cocos Islands. However, the Australian Minister of Defence, Stephen Smith, insisted that, although the use of the Cocos Islands had been mooted, this was very much a 'long-term prospect', which would notably require a $A75m.–$A100m. upgrade of the territory's runway, and no decision had yet been made.

ECONOMIC AFFAIRS

The Cocos Islands possess substantial marine resources, and opportunities for local fishing are plentiful. In 2006 the Australian Department of Fisheries introduced a basic regulatory framework for recreational fishing in the territory, with the aim of fostering greater sustainability. A clam farm, established in 2000, was one of the first commercial ventures on the islands. Coconuts, grown throughout the islands, have been the sole cash crop: total output was an estimated 7,600 metric tons in 2006, with copra production being estimated at 1,000 tons. Although some livestock is kept, and domestic gardens provide vegetables, bananas and papayas (pawpaws), the islands are not self-sufficient, and foodstuffs are imported from mainland Australia. According to the 2006 census, agriculture, together with forestry and fishing, provided 1.6% of the employed population with work, but by the 2011 census no islanders identified themselves as being employed in the agricultural sector.

Industrial activity also remains limited on the islands, with all those working in this area being engaged either in construction or the utilities sector. The construction sector engaged 7.3% of the employed labour force at the 2011 census, while activities related to the production of electricity, gas and water accounted for a further 4.1%.

The islands have a small tourism industry. During August, September and October 2003, for example, there were a total of 76 non-resident arrivals, of whom 28 were travelling on business and 19 were visiting relatives. In 1995 a national park was designated on North Keeling Island. Some controversy arose in July 2004 when it was revealed that the Australian Government had drawn up plans to develop a resort on the Cocos Islands without having undertaken any consultation with the islanders. A Cocos postal service (including a philatelic bureau) came into operation in September 1979, and revenue from the service is used for the benefit of the community. In early 2000 the islands' internet domain name suffix, '.cc', was sold to Clear Channel, a US radio group, thus providing additional revenue. According to census data, the services sector engaged 86.7% of the employed population in 2011.

The cost of the islands' imports from Australia increased from $A6m. in 2006/07 to $A10m. in 2012/13. Exports to Australia totalled

US $231,000 in 2012. In 2004 the Australian Government created a funding programme to support economic development initiatives in its Indian Ocean territories; in 2012/13 total funding of up to $A150,000 was available for projects in the Cocos Islands. At the 2011 census 6.7% of the total labour force were unemployed. The Shire Council and the Co-operative Society are the principal employers.

PUBLIC HOLIDAYS

2015: 1 January (New Year's Day), 3 January (Hari Maulad Nabi), 26 January (Australia Day), 3 April (Good Friday), 6 April (Easter Monday), 7 April (Act of Self Determination Day), 25 April (Anzac Day), 18 July (Hari Raya Puasa), 24 September (Hari Raya Haji), 15 October (Islamic New Year), 25–26 December (Christmas).

Statistical Survey

AREA AND POPULATION

Area: 14.1 sq km (5.4 sq miles).

Population: 572 at census of 8 August 2006; 550 (males 283, females 267) at census of 9 August 2011.

Density (at 2011 census): 39.0 per sq km.

Population by Age and Sex (2011 census): *0–14:* 128 (males 63, females 65); *15–64:* 368 (males 182, females 186); *65 and over:* 54 (males 38, females 16); *Total* 550 (males 283, females 267).

Country of Birth (2011 census): Australia (incl. Cocos Islands) 465; Malaysia 26; New Zealand 3; Singapore 10; South Africa 3; United Kingdom 6; USA 3; Other 34.

Births and Deaths (1986): Registered live births 12 (birth rate 19.8 per 1,000); Registered deaths 2.

Economically Active Population (persons aged 15 years and over, excl. overseas visitors, 2011 census): Electricity, gas and water 9; Construction 16; Wholesale and retail trade, restaurants, and hotels 51; Transport, storage and communications 20; Real estate, renting and business activities 28; Government administration, defence and social security 84; Community, social and personal services 6; Activities not stated or not adequately defined 4; *Total employed* 218 (males 131, females 87).

AGRICULTURE

Production (metric tons, 2006, FAO estimate): Coconuts 7,600. Source: FAO.

INDUSTRY

Production (metric tons, 2006, FAO estimates): Copra 1,000; Coconut (copra) oil 650. Source: FAO.

FINANCE

Currency and Exchange Rates: Australian currency is used.

EXTERNAL TRADE

2012 (US $ '000): *Exports* (to Australia): 231. *Imports* (from Australia): 19,688 (Source: Trade Map-Trade Competitiveness Map, International Trade Centre, www.intracen.org/marketanalysis).

COMMUNICATIONS MEDIA

Radio Receivers (1992): 300 in use.

Personal Computers (home users, 2001 census): 142.

Internet Users (2001 census): 171.

EDUCATION

Pre-primary (August 2008): 15 pupils.

Primary (August 2008): 83 pupils.

Secondary (August 2008): 31 pupils.

Teaching Staff (2004): 17 (10 primary, 7 secondary).

Source: Education Department of Western Australia.

Directory

The Government

The Administrator, appointed by the Governor-General of Australia and responsible to the Minister for Infrastructure and Regional Development, is the senior government representative in the islands.

Administrator: JON STANHOPE (non-resident).

Administrative Offices: Lot 256, Jalan Melati, Home Island, Cocos (Keeling) Islands 6799, Indian Ocean; tel. (8) 9162-6649; fax (8) 9162-6668.

Cocos (Keeling) Islands Shire Council: POB 1094, Home Island, Cocos (Keeling) Islands 6799, Indian Ocean; tel. (8) 9162-6649; fax (8) 9162-6668; e-mail info@cocos.wa.gov.au; internet www.shire.cc; f. 1992 by Territories Law Reform Act; Pres. AINDIL MINKOM; CEO PETER CLARKE.

Judicial System

Judicial services in the Cocos (Keeling) Islands are provided through the Western Australian Department of the Attorney-General. Western Australian Court Services provide a Magistrates Court, District Court, Supreme Court, Family Court, Children's Court and Coroner's Court.

Court Services: c/o Australian Federal Police, Cocos (Keeling) Islands 6799, Indian Ocean; tel. (8) 9162-6600; fax (8) 9162-6691; e-mail cocosadmin@afp.gov.au.

Religion

According to the census of 2011, of the 550 residents, 419 (some 76%) were Muslims and 62 (11%) Christians. The majority of Muslims live on Home Island, while most Christians are West Island residents. The Cocos Islands lie within both the Anglican and the Roman Catholic archdioceses of Perth (Western Australia).

Broadcasting and Communications

BROADCASTING

Radio

As well as a local radio station, Radio 6CKI (see below), the Cocos (Keeling) Islands receive daily broadcasts from ABC regional radio and the Western Australian station Red FM.

Radio 6CKI Voice of the Cocos (Keeling) Islands: POB 1084, Cocos (Keeling) Islands 6799, Indian Ocean; tel. and fax (8) 9162-6666; e-mail 6cki@cki.cc; non-commercial, run by volunteers; daily broadcasting service in Cocos Malay and English; Chair. DENISE MASON.

Television

Four television stations, ABC, SBS, WIN and GWN, are broadcast from Western Australia via satellite.

Industry

Cocos (Keeling) Islands Co-operative Society Ltd: POB 1058, Home Island, Cocos (Keeling) Islands 6799, Indian Ocean; tel. (8) 9162-6708; fax (8) 9162-6764; e-mail admin@cocoscoop.com; internet www.cocoscoop.com; f. 1979; conducts the business enterprises of the Cocos Islanders; activities include boat construction and repairs, copra and coconut production, sail-making, stevedoring, and airport operation; owns and operates a supermarket and tourist accommodation; Chair. MOHAMMED SAID CHONGKIN; Gen. Man. RONALD TAYLOR.

Transport

An airport is located on West Island. Virgin Australia operates a thrice-weekly service from Perth (Western Australia), via Christmas Island, with a return service departing West Island for Perth once a week. Cargo vessels from Singapore and Perth deliver regular supplies. The islands have a total of 10 km of sealed and 12 km of unsealed roads.

Zentner Shipping Pty Ltd: POB 49, Cocos (Keeling) Islands 6799, Indian Ocean; tel. (8) 9337-5911; e-mail shipping@zentnershipping.com.au; operates sea freight service from Fremantle (WA) every 4–6 weeks.

Tourism

Tourism is relatively undeveloped. However, the Cocos Islands possess unique flora and fauna, along with pristine beaches and coral reefs that offer excellent opportunities for scuba-diving and snorkelling. In 2009 there was one 28-room hotel on West Island, as well as several self-catering villas.

Cocos Island Tourism Association: Admiralty House, POB 1030, Cocos (Keeling) Islands 6799, Indian Ocean; tel. (8) 9162-6790; fax (8) 9162-7708; e-mail info@cocoskeelingislands.com.au; internet www.cocoskeelingislands.com.au.

Parks Australia: POB 1043, Cocos (Keeling) Islands 6798, Indian Ocean; tel. (8) 9162-6678; fax (8) 9162-6680; internet www.environment.gov.au/parks/cocos/index.html.

Education

Pre-primary and primary education is provided at the schools on Home and West Islands. Secondary education is provided to the age of 16 years on West Island. In August 2008 pre-primary pupils totalled 15. Primary pupils numbered 83, and there were 31 secondary students. A bursary scheme enables Cocos Malay children to continue their education on the Australian mainland.

NORFOLK ISLAND

Introductory Survey

LOCATION, CLIMATE, LANGUAGE, RELIGION, FLAG, CAPITAL

Norfolk Island lies off the eastern coast of Australia, about 1,400 km east of Brisbane, to the south of New Caledonia and 640 km north of New Zealand. The territory also comprises the uninhabited Phillip Island and Nepean Island, 7 km and 1 km south of the main island, respectively. Norfolk Island is hilly and fertile, with a coastline of cliffs and an area of 34.6 sq km (13.4 sq miles). It is about 8 km long and 4.8 km wide. The climate is mild and subtropical, with temperatures varying between 18°C (64°F) and 25°C (77°F), and the average annual rainfall is 1,350 mm, most of which occurs between May and August. English and Norfuk, which combines elements of a local Polynesian dialect (related to Pitcairnese) and 18th-century English, are the official languages. Most of the population (62% at the 2011 census) adhere to the Christian religion. The island's flag (proportions 1 by 2) has three vertical stripes (proportions 7:9:7) of green, white and green, with a Norfolk Island pine in green silhouette on the centre stripe. The capital of the territory is Kingston.

CONTEMPORARY POLITICAL HISTORY

Historical Context

The island was uninhabited when discovered in 1774 by a British expedition, led by Capt. James Cook. Norfolk Island was used as a penal settlement from 1788 to 1814 and again from 1825 to 1855, when it was abandoned. In 1856 it was resettled by 194 emigrants from Pitcairn Island, which had become overpopulated. Norfolk Island was administered as a separate colony until 1897, when it became a dependency of New South Wales. In 1913 control was transferred to the Australian Government.

Domestic Political Affairs

Under the Commonwealth Norfolk Island Act 1979, Norfolk Island was to progress to responsible legislative and executive government, enabling the territory to administer its own affairs to the greatest practicable extent. Wide powers were to be exercised henceforth by the nine-member Legislative Assembly and by the Executive Council, comprising the executive members of the Legislative Assembly who were given ministerial-type responsibilities. The Act preserved the Australian Government's responsibility for Norfolk Island as a territory under its authority. The Act indicated that consideration would be given within five years to an extension of the powers of the Legislative Assembly and the political and administrative institutions of Norfolk Island. In 1985 legislative and executive responsibility was assumed by the Norfolk Island Government for public works and services, civil defence, betting and gaming, territorial archives and matters relating to the exercise of executive authority. In 1988 further amendments empowered the Legislative Assembly to select a Norfolk Island government auditor (territorial accounts were previously audited by the Commonwealth Auditor-General). The office of Chief Minister was replaced by that of the President of the Legislative Assembly. David Buffett was reappointed to this post following the May 1992 general election.

A lack of consensus among members of the Executive Council on several major issues prompted early legislative elections in April 1994. The newly elected Legislative Assembly was notable for its inclusion of three female members. Following elections in April 1997, in which 22 candidates contested the nine seats, George Smith was appointed President (subsequently reverting to the title of Chief Minister) of the Legislative Assembly. Later that year the Legislative Assembly debated the issue of increased self-determination for the island.

In August 1998 a referendum proposing that the Norfolk Island electoral system be integrated more closely with that of mainland Australia (initiated in Canberra by the Minister for Regional Development, Territories and Local Government) was rejected by 78% of the territory's electorate. A similar referendum in May 1999 was opposed by 73% of voters. Frustration with the Australian Government's perceived reluctance to facilitate the transfer of greater powers to the territory (as outlined in the Norfolk Island Act of 1979, see above) led the island's Legislative Assembly in mid-1999 to vote in favour of full internal self-government. Negotiations regarding the administration of Crown land on the island, which continued in 2000, were seen as indicative of the islanders' determination to pursue greater independence from Australia.

At legislative elections in February 2000 three new members were elected to the Assembly, and Ronald Nobbs was subsequently appointed Chief Minister. Geoffrey Gardner, hitherto Minister for Health, replaced Nobbs as Chief Minister following the elections of November 2001. The incoming Assembly included four new members.

Legislation was approved in March 2003 to amend the requirements for voting in Norfolk Island elections. Under the new system Australian, New Zealand and British citizens were to be allowed to vote after a residency period of 12 months (reduced from 900 days). The amendments, which followed a series of occasionally acrimonious discussions with the Australian Government, provoked concern among islanders who feared that succumbing to Australian pressure to reform the Norfolk Island Act would result in the effective removal of authority over electoral matters from island control. Moreover, a report by an Australian parliamentary committee published in July 2003 was critical of Norfolk Island's Government and public services. Many residents believed that the report constituted a further attempt by Australia to undermine their autonomy. The Chief Minister rejected the committee's claims. A further report by the Australian Government published later in the year alleged that officials on the island used intimidation to achieve political and financial gain and recommended that Norfolk Island's elections, government and financial matters be overseen by the federal authorities.

The inhabitants of Norfolk Island were profoundly shocked when the Deputy Chief Minister, Ivens Buffett, was shot dead in his office in July 2004. Leith Buffett, the politician's son, was arrested on suspicion of murder but, owing to severe mental illness, was found to be incompetent to stand trial.

A total of 14 candidates contested the legislative election held on 20 October 2004. Geoffrey Gardner, the Chief Minister, retained his seat in the nine-member Legislative Assembly, as did Speaker David Buffett. However, two long-serving members were defeated in the poll.

In early 2005 the Legislative Assembly declared Norfuk, the local creole spoken by around one-half of the island's population and described as a hybrid of Tahitian and 18th-century English, as an official language alongside English. The legislature's action was prompted by reports of a decline in the use of the language among islanders. Norfuk was subsequently introduced into the school curriculum on Norfolk Island, its usage having previously been forbidden in schools. In August 2007 the UN placed Norfuk on its list of endangered languages.

In February 2006 the Australian Government unexpectedly announced that it was to resume responsibility for matters such as immigration, customs and quarantine, claiming that the existing arrangements under the Norfolk Island Act of 1979 had become too complex and costly for a community of the island's size to sustain. Two main alternative options were to be considered: a form of modified self-government that would allow greater powers for involvement by the Australian Government; and a model of local government whereby Australia might assume responsibility for state-type functions. Other options under consideration included the possibility of an island territory government with the power to legislate on local responsibilities. The island's revenue-raising capacities were also to be reviewed, along with the provision of basic services such as health and education. In December 2006, however, following the conclusion of this comprehensive review, it was declared that no restructuring of the system of governance was necessary, an announcement that brought mixed reactions from the people of Norfolk Island. While many in the territory wished to retain a degree of autonomy, concerns remained over the future sustainability of the island's economy.

In November 2006 a group of Norfolk Islanders challenged the introduction of new electoral laws requiring voters to be citizens of Australia. The group claimed that this did not take into consideration the fact that a proportion of Norfolk Island's adult population did not have Australian citizenship. However, lawyers for the Australian Government dismissed the argument. The group's claim that Norfolk Islanders represented a distinct community, and thus should be considered separately from Australia, was also dismissed as unfounded.

Following the legislative election of 21 March 2007, Andre Nobbs replaced David Buffett as the island's Chief Minister (David Buffett having taken over as Chief Minister from Geoffrey Gardner in June 2006). Neville Christian was replaced as Speaker of the Legislative Assembly by Lisle Snell, but remained as Minister for Finance. Christopher Magri was appointed to the new post of Minister for Commerce and Industry. In October 2007, following Grant Tambling's departure from the post, Owen Walsh was appointed Administrator.

In August 2008 the Government of Norfolk Island issued its response to an Australian Senate Committee inquiry into the financial management of the island. The local Government claimed that the existing arrangements remained viable, reiterating its commitment to the continued improvement of the delivery of services on the island. The Government expressed particular concern in relation to its repeated obligation to divert the island's scarce human and financial resources to the task of responding to what was perceived to be constant scrutiny by external committees and consultants, often with regard to issues that it believed to have been adequately addressed on previous occasions. In October Bob Debus, the Australian Minister for Home Affairs (whose remit included responsibility for Australian territories) warned that Norfolk Island was in danger of becoming a 'failed state'. The Minister subsequently visited Norfolk Island, where he had discussions with Chief Minister Andre Nobbs. In December the island's Government submitted its formal response to the concerns raised by Debus, in which it disputed the Minister's claims that the current governance arrangements were operating 'to the disadvantage of many on Norfolk Island'. The local Government reiterated the view that, while the island might benefit from minor modifications to the legislation of 1979, the implementation of radical changes was unnecessary. Meanwhile, the Government had commissioned an independent review of the Norfolk Island Act of 1979, following which detailed proposals for the simplification and modernization of the prevailing legislation were presented to Debus. The retention of the role of Administrator was envisaged. Throughout 2009 Norfolk Island government officials had discussions about governance reforms with Debus and, following the latter's retirement, with the new Minister for Home Affairs, Brendan O'Connor. By the end of 2009 no substantive progress had been achieved, although it had been agreed that more regular meetings to discuss self-governing arrangements, particularly financial matters and accountability, would take place.

Following the legislative elections in March 2010, which were contested by 28 candidates, David Buffett was reappointed to the post of Chief Minister, replacing Andre Nobbs, who became Minister for Tourism, Industry and Development. The other portfolios were similarly rearranged: Craig Anderson was appointed as Attorney-General and Minister for Finance, and Timothy Sheridan was allocated the portfolio of community services. The incoming Legislative Assembly included several new members. Robin Adams replaced Lisle Snell as Speaker, the latter becoming Deputy Speaker.

On the same day as the island's legislative elections the Territories Law Reform Bill 2010 was introduced into the House of Representatives in Canberra. While the Norfolk Island Government again acknowledged the need for reform, it regarded the draft legislation as inappropriate and raised numerous concerns, particularly in relation to the proposed reduction in local powers. The parliamentary debate was subsequently adjourned. The Australian Senate referred the draft law to the Joint Standing Committee on the National Capital and External Territories, which was required to conduct an inquiry and compile its report by May. In that month the Committee concluded that the proposed reforms would lead to improvements in the accountability and transparency of Norfolk Island's governance, recommending that the changes be adopted. It was envisaged that the Governor-General of Australia and the federal minister responsible for Norfolk Island would play a more active role in the drafting and enactment of legislation. The radical reforms were to include provision for the removal of the Chief Minister by the island's Administrator in 'exceptional circumstances'.

In October 2010 it was reported that, in collaboration with an Australian university, the world's first trial of a personal carbon trading programme was to commence on Norfolk Island in 2011. In addition to reducing greenhouse gas emissions, it was hoped that the three-year trial would reduce obesity and improve the health of islanders. Residents and visitors to the island were to be offered a carbon credit card, to be used initially when purchasing petrol or power. Frugal users would be able to exchange the remaining units of their annual quota for cash. Researchers hoped to add foodstuffs to the scheme in 2012, ranking products in terms of health as well as carbon costs.

In November 2010, as the island's financial situation continued to deteriorate, it was announced that, in exchange for federal funding and access to welfare facilities and other services, the local Government had agreed in principle to the implementation of the Territories Law Reform Bill. The Bill was duly enacted as the Territories Law Reform Act 2010 in December, following its approval by the Australian legislature. The stringent conditions attached to the Australian Government's provision of emergency funding included the introduction of federal law in areas such as privacy and freedom of information. Under an initial funding agreement concluded in December, the federal Government was to provide $A3.8m. in emergency financial support for Norfolk Island for the remainder of the 2010/11 financial year; the provision of a further $A1.8m. for that year was agreed in April 2011. Meanwhile, in March the federal and local Governments published a 'roadmap' outlining a five-year plan for wide-ranging reforms in Norfolk Island aimed at strengthening governance, the economy, social cohesion, and heritage and environment. Also in that month Craig Anderson resigned as Attorney-General and Minister for Finance, although he remained a member of the Legislative Assembly. His ministerial duties were redistributed between the remaining three members of the Executive Council, with Chief Minister David Buffett notably assuming responsibility for most financial matters and justice. In September a funding agreement for 2011/12 was signed: in return for federal funding of up to $A2.9m., the local Government was to implement further reforms, including the gradual removal of immigration restrictions on Australian citizens moving to Norfolk Island and the reduction of barriers to competition for businesses.

Neil Pope was sworn in as Administrator, replacing Owen Walsh, on 1 April 2012.

Federal funding of $A2.9m. was allocated to Norfolk Island for 2012/13 to continue the reform process. However, further financial assistance was required to ensure the provision of essential government services. Consequently, in December 2012 a funding agreement was signed under which the local Government would receive up to $A4.5m. during the remainder of the financial year, in return for a series of conditions being met on reforms involving, *inter alia*, immigration and taxation arrangements, the licensing of tourist accommodation, health care and other public services, and the liberalization of the telecommunications sector. Norfolk Island's immigration regulations were accordingly amended in May 2013, permitting Australian and New Zealand citizens to visit without a permit and facilitating procedures for them to become residents of the territory.

Elections to the Legislative Assembly were held on 13 March 2013 and were contested by a total of 15 candidates. Lisle Snell, hitherto Deputy Speaker of the Assembly, was appointed to the post of Chief Minister on 20 March, replacing David Buffett, who was elected Speaker; Ronald Nobbs replaced Snell as Deputy Speaker. Timothy Sheridan remained in the Executive Council, being allocated the finance portfolio, while former Speaker Robin Adams was appointed Minister for Cultural Heritage and Community Services, and Ronald Ward became Minister for the Environment.

ECONOMIC AFFAIRS

Despite Norfolk Island's natural fertility, agriculture is no longer the principal economic activity. Agriculture (including forestry and fishing) accounted for only 3.7% of employment according to the census of 2011. About 400 ha of land are arable. The main crops are Kentia palm seeds, cereals, vegetables and fruit. Cattle and pigs are farmed for domestic consumption. Development of a fisheries industry is restricted by the lack of a harbour. Some flowers and plants are grown commercially. Exports of Kentia palm seeds and sprouts earned $A620,000 in 2010/11, the principal market being European countries. The administration is increasing the area devoted to Norfolk Island pine and hardwoods. Seed and seedlings of the Norfolk Island pine are exported. Potential oil- and gas-bearing sites in the island's waters may provide a possible future source of revenue.

The Government is the most important employer, and 124 people were engaged in government and public administration in 2011. Tourism is the island's main industry. In the mid-1980s the Governments of Australia and Norfolk Island jointly established the

465-ha Norfolk Island National Park. In 2006 some 26.3% of the employed labour force were engaged in tourism and recreation. A re-export industry has been developed to serve the island's tourism industry. The resurfacing of the island's main runway in 2006 allowed the airport to accommodate larger aircraft and would, it was hoped, improve the potential for an increase in tourist arrivals. However, the cessation of operations by Norfolk Jet Express, the airline linking Norfolk Island with Australia, in June 2005 and the initial uncertainty surrounding the establishment of a replacement service illustrated the island's reliance on overseas airlines for the success of its tourism industry. Tourist arrivals decreased by 16% in 2005/06, to 28,219, as a result of the failure of Norfolk Jet Express, but recovered to reach 34,318 in 2006/07, following the establishment of Norfolk Air by the Government. However, tourist arrivals saw another decline in the early 2010s, falling from 25,133 in 2011/12 to 22,684 in 2012/13. The revival of the tourism industry was a principal aim of the 'roadmap' of reforms developed by the federal and local Governments in early 2011 (see Contemporary Political History); efforts to improve access to the island, to reduce the costs of travel and to facilitate visits by cruise ships were planned. After the government-operated Norfolk Air ceased operations in February 2012, Air New Zealand began to operate flights between Norfolk Island and the Australian mainland, in addition to its existing service to New Zealand.

The island's imports are purchased mainly from Australia and New Zealand. In 2012 imports from Australia cost $A8.8m. and those from New Zealand totalled $NZ8.0m. Exports to those countries earned only $A79,000 (in 2012) and $NZ50,000 (in 2010), respectively.

In 2011/12 revenue amounted to $A59.9m., of which $A32.9m. was derived from charges for goods and services, $A10.0m. from taxation receipts (including $A7.6m. from the goods-and-services tax and $A2.0m. from customs duties) and $A14.3m. from Australian government grants. Expenditure in that year totalled around $A63.0m., of which $A44.8m. was allocated to purchasing supplies and services and $A8.6m. to the payment of salaries and other employee benefits. The goods-and-services tax originated in December 2005, when, in order to raise funds for road projects and health services, the Norfolk Sustainability Levy (NSL), a 1% tax on goods and services, was implemented for an initial six-month trial period, which was subsequently extended. In April 2007 it was announced that the NSL, along with various other taxes such as the accommodation levy, was to be replaced by a broader tax on goods and services, which was to be imposed at a rate of 9% with effect from January 2007. Following a major review (see Contemporary Political History), in December 2006 it was confirmed that Norfolk Island was to remain exempt from federal income taxes. Although the territory would thus retain its attraction as a tax haven for wealthy individuals, many islanders expressed disappointment at the decision, as they had hoped that this potential source of government revenue might provide support in meeting the high costs of education and health care.

The global economic downturn of 2008/09 had a significant impact on Norfolk Island, particularly in terms of tourism revenue. In November 2009 the Government reported a decrease in its revenue of $A3.9m. in 2008/09, in comparison with the previous financial year. This decline was attributed to a 15% reduction in tourist arrivals and to a rise in public expenditure of $A1.1m., which was due mainly to a general wage increase awarded by the Norfolk Island Public Sector Remuneration Tribunal. Government measures to alleviate the economic situation included, *inter alia*, the sale of surplus government assets and land, a freeze on discretionary spending and tax increases. The Australian Government deferred Norfolk Island's repayments on an interest-free loan of $A12m., used in 2005–06 for the purposes of upgrading the airport. Norfolk Air recorded a loss of more than $A1m. in the first three months of 2009/10. An audit conducted at mid-2010 revealed that the island's reserves stood at only $A220,000. Bills were no longer being paid by the Government, and creditors were being deferred. Furthermore, 11 retail outlets were reported to have closed, with attendant job losses, while other businesses began to retrench. Although the goods-and-services tax was now levied at 12% (up from the original 9%), islanders had remained exempt from income tax. However, following the approval of the Territories Law Reform Act in late 2010 (see Contemporary Political History), the integration of Norfolk Island into the federal taxation system from 2013/14 was envisaged, while federal health and social security benefits would be extended to residents of the island. Barriers to business investment were also to be removed. Meanwhile, the Australian Government agreed to provide financial support for the provision of essential services in 2010/11–2012/13, pending the negotiation of longer-term arrangements with Norfolk Island. Despite the federal bailout, the island's economy continued to founder largely as a result of the downward trend in tourist arrivals. An independent report commissioned by the Australian Government on the future economic development of Norfolk Island, which was published in March 2012, described the severity of the economic downturn on Norfolk Island—with the island being declared officially insolvent—and emphasized the continued importance of the tourism sector in driving growth. The report notably recommended the privatization of government business enterprises and the allocation of 75% of the revenue from such divestments to investment in infrastructure. In 2013 the implementation of the provisions of the 2010 Territories Law Reform Act, including the introduction of much-needed social security services and unemployment benefits for the islanders in return for joining the federal tax system, was put on hold. The federal authorities claimed that the island's Government was not sufficiently committed to the key reform issues of the 2011 'roadmap'. In the federal budget for 2013/14 $A4.4m. was allocated to Norfolk Island to allow for the provision of essential services; an additional $A1m. was also provided to enable the island's authorities to continue the reform agenda regarding improved governance measures.

PUBLIC HOLIDAYS

2015: 1 January (New Year's Day), 26 January (Australia Day), 6 March (Foundation Day), 3 April (Good Friday), 6 April (Easter Monday), 25 April (Anzac Day), 8 June (Bounty Day), 8 June (Queen's Official Birthday), 25 November (Thanksgiving), 25–26 December (Christmas).

Statistical Survey

Source: The Administration of Norfolk Island, Administration Offices, Kingston, Norfolk Island 2899; tel. 22001; fax 23177; internet www.norfolk.gov.nf.

AREA AND POPULATION

Area: 34.6 sq km (13.4 sq miles).

Population: 2,523, comprising 1,863 'ordinarily resident' and 660 visitors, at census of 8 August 2006; 2,302 (males 1,082, females 1,220), comprising 1,795 'ordinarily resident' and 507 visitors, at census of 9 August 2011.

Density (2011 census): 66.5 per sq km.

Population by Age and Sex (2011 census): *0–14:* 361 (males 185, females 176); *15–64:* 1,388 (males 632, females 756); *65 and over:* 553 (males 265, females 288); *Total* 2,302 (males 1,082, females 1,220).

Births, Marriages and Deaths (2010/11): Live births 4; Marriages 31; Deaths 20.

Employment ('ordinarily resident' population aged 15 years and over, 2011 census): Agriculture, forestry and fishing 47; Industry 153; Wholesale and retail trade 258; Transport, storage and communication 66; Restaurants, hotels, accommodation and clubs 255; Finance, property and business services 32; Public administration and defence 124; Health and social work 41; Education 42; Other community and personal services 195; *Sub-total* 1,213; Activities not stated or not adequately described 57; *Total* 1,270 (males 591, females 679).

FINANCE

Currency and Exchange Rates: Australian currency is used.

Budget ($A, year ending 30 June 2012): Revenue 49,275,700 (Tax revenue 10,548,000, Other revenue 38,727,700); Expenditure 58,274,500 (Wages and salaries 11,671,700, Other current expenditure 45,920,600, Capital expenditure 682,200).

Cost of Living (Retail Price Index, average of quarterly figures; base: October–December 1990 = 100): All items 159.7 in 2004; 168.6 in 2005; 181.1 in 2006.

EXTERNAL TRADE

Trade with Australia ($A '000, 2012): *Imports:* 8,750. *Exports:* 79.

Trade with New Zealand ($NZ '000): *Imports* (2012): 8,000. *Exports* (2010): 50.

TOURISM

Visitors (year ending 30 June): 24,268 in 2010/11; 25,133 in 2011/12; 22,684 in 2012/13.

COMMUNICATIONS MEDIA

Telephones (2010/11): 1,601 main lines in use.

Internet Users (2002/03): 494.

Non-daily Newspaper (2002): 1 (estimated circulation 1,400).

EDUCATION

Institution (2003): 1 state school incorporating infant, primary and secondary levels.

Teachers (2004/05): Primary 8; Secondary 12.

Students (1999/2000): Infants 79; Primary 116; Secondary 119.

Directory

The Government

The Administrator, who is the senior representative of the Commonwealth Government, is appointed by the Governor-General of Australia and is accountable to a minister of the federal Cabinet. A form of responsible legislative and executive government was extended to the island in 1979.

Administrator: NEIL POPE.

EXECUTIVE COUNCIL

(April 2014)

Chief Minister and Minister for Tourism: LISLE SNELL.

Minister for Finance: TIMOTHY SHERIDAN.

Minister for Cultural Heritage and Community Services: ROBIN ADAMS.

Minister for the Environment: RONALD WARD.

MINISTRIES

All Ministries are located at:

Old Military Barracks, Quality Row, Kingston, Norfolk Island 2899; tel. 22003; fax 22624; e-mail executives@assembly.gov.nf; internet www.norfolkislandgovernment.com.

GOVERNMENT OFFICES

Office of the Administrator: POB 201, New Military Barracks, Norfolk Island 2899; tel. 22152; fax 22681.

Administration of Norfolk Island: Administration Offices, Kingston, Norfolk Island 2899; tel. 22001; fax 23177; e-mail records@admin.gov.nf; internet www.norfolkislandgovernment.com; all govt depts; CEO JONATHAN GIBBONS.

Legislature

LEGISLATIVE ASSEMBLY

Nine candidates are elected for not less than three years but no more than four years. The most recent general election was held on 13 March 2013.

Speaker: DAVID BUFFETT.

Deputy Speaker: RONALD NOBBS.

Other Members: LISLE SNELL, ROBIN ADAMS, RONALD WARD, TIMOTHY SHERIDAN, MELISSA WARD, DAVID PORTER, HADYN EVANS.

Judicial System

Supreme Court of Norfolk Island: Kingston; tel. 323691; fax 323403; e-mail registry@admin.gov.nf; appeals lie to the Federal Court of Australia; Chief Justice WARREN DONALD; Registrar ALLEN BATAILLE.

Religion

The majority of the resident population professes Christianity (62%, according to the census of 2011), with the principal denominations being the Church of England (34%), the Uniting Church (13%) and the Roman Catholic Church (12%). At the 2011 census 24% of the resident population professed no religious affiliation.

The Press

Norfolk Island Government Gazette: Kingston, Norfolk Island 2899; tel. 22001; fax 23177; internet www.info.gov.nf; weekly.

Norfolk Islander: Greenways Press, POB 248, Norfolk Island 2899; tel. 22159; fax 22948; e-mail news@islander.nf; internet www.norfolkislander.com; f. 1965; weekly; Co-Editors TOM LLOYD, JONATHAN SNELL; circ. 1,350.

Broadcasting and Communications

TELECOMMUNICATIONS

Norfolk Telecom: New Cascade Rd, POB 469, Kingston; tel. 322244; fax 322499; e-mail webmaster@ni.net.nf; internet www.ni.net.nf; mobile services introduced in 2007; Man. KIM DAVIES.

BROADCASTING

Radio

Norfolk Island Broadcasting Service: New Cascade Rd, POB 456, Norfolk Island 2899; tel. 22137; fax 23298; e-mail manager@radio.gov.nf; internet www.radio.gov.nf; govt-owned; non-commercial; broadcasts 7 days per week; relays television and radio programmes from Australia and New Zealand; Broadcast Man. LOUCI REYNOLDS (acting).

Radio Norfolk: New Cascade Rd, POB 456, Norfolk Island 2899; tel. 22137; fax 23298; e-mail manager@radio.gov.nf; internet www.radio.gov.nf; f. 1950s; govt-owned; Man. LOUCI REYNOLDS.

Television

Norfolk Island Broadcasting Service: see Radio.

Norfolk Island Television Service: f. 1987; govt-owned; relays programmes of Australian Broadcasting Corpn, Special Broadcasting Service Corpn and Central Seven TV by satellite.

TV Norfolk (TVN): locally operated service featuring programmes of local events and information for tourists.

Finance

BANKING

Commonwealth Bank of Australia (Australia): Taylors Rd, Norfolk Island 2899; tel. 22144; fax 22805.

Westpac Banking Corpn Savings Bank Ltd (Australia): Burnt Pine, Norfolk Island 2899; tel. 22120; fax 22808.

Trade

Norfolk Island Chamber of Commerce Inc: POB 370, Norfolk Island 2899; tel. 22317; fax 23221; e-mail photopress@ni.net.nf; f. 1966; affiliated to the Australian Chamber of Commerce and Industry; 60 mems; Pres. GARY ROBERTSON; Sec. MARK MCGUIRE.

Norfolk Island Gaming Authority: POB 882, Norfolk Island 2899; tel. 22002; fax 22499; e-mail secgameauth@norfolk.net.nf; internet www.gamingauthority.nlk.nf; Dir RODERICK MCALPINE.

Transport

ROADS

At March 2012 there were 67 km of sealed roads and 9 km of unsealed roads. In addition, within the National Park there are 3 km of sealed roads leading to the Captain Cook Monument and Mount Pitt.

SHIPPING

Norfolk Island is served by three shipping lines, Neptune Shipping, Pacific Direct Line and Roslyndale Shipping Company Pty Ltd. A small tanker from Nouméa (New Caledonia) delivers petroleum products to the island and another from Australia delivers liquid propane gas.

CIVIL AVIATION

Norfolk Island's airport has two runways and is capable of taking jet-engined aircraft. Work to resurface the main runway, in order to accommodate larger aircraft, was completed in 2006. Norfolk Air, which was operated by the Norfolk Island Government and provided services to the Australian cities of Brisbane, Sydney, Melbourne and Newcastle, ceased operations in February 2012. Air New Zealand, which already provided a service from Auckland, began to operate flights between Norfolk Island and the Australian mainland from March, with twice-weekly services to Brisbane and Sydney.

Tourism

Visitor arrivals totalled 22,684 in 2012/13, the majority of whom came from Australia. In 2012 tourist accommodation totalled 1,649 beds.

Norfolk Island Tourism: Taylors Rd, Burnt Pine, POB 211, Norfolk Island 2899; tel. 22147; fax 22708; e-mail info@nigtb.gov.nf; internet www.norfolkisland.com.au; Gen. Man. GLEN BUFFETT.

Education

Education is free and compulsory for all children between the ages of six and at least 15. Pupils attend the one government school from infant to secondary level. In 2002/03 a total of 187 pupils were enrolled at infant and primary levels and 118 at secondary levels. Students wishing to follow higher education in Australia are eligible for bursaries and scholarships. The budgetary allocation for education was more than $A2.4m. in 2006/07.

Other Australian Territories

Ashmore and Cartier Islands

The Ashmore Islands (known as West, Middle and East Islands) and Cartier Island are situated in the Timor Sea, about 850 km and 790 km west of Darwin, respectively. The Ashmore Islands cover some 93 ha of land and Cartier Island covers 0.4 ha. The islands are small and uninhabited, consisting of sand and coral, surrounded by shoals and reefs. Grass is the main vegetation. Maximum elevation is about 2.5 m above sea level. The islands abound in birdlife, sea cucumbers (*bêches-de-mer*) and, seasonally, turtles.

The United Kingdom took formal possession of the Ashmore Islands in 1878, and Cartier Island was annexed in 1909. The islands were placed under the authority of the Commonwealth of Australia in 1931. They were annexed to, and deemed to form part of, the Northern Territory of Australia in 1938. On 1 July 1978 the Australian Government assumed direct responsibility for the administration of the islands; this rests with a parliamentary secretary appointed by the Minister for Infrastructure and Regional Development. Periodic visits are made to the islands by the Royal Australian Navy and the Royal Australian Air Force, and the Navy and the Australian Customs and Border Protection Service undertake patrols of the islands and neighbouring waters to ensure their protection against illegal foreign fishing. The oilfields of Jabiru and Challis are located in waters adjacent to the territory.

In August 1983 Ashmore Reef was declared a National Nature Reserve, while Cartier Island Marine Reserve was established in June 2000. In November 2012, as part of a major expansion and reorganization of Australia's marine reserves, the Ashmore and Cartier reserves were renamed Ashmore Reef Commonwealth Marine Reserve and Cartier Island Commonwealth Marine Reserve, respectively, with both forming part of the North-west Commonwealth Marine Reserves Network. An agreement between Australia and Indonesia permits Indonesian traditional fishermen to continue fishing in the territorial waters and to land on West Island to obtain supplies of fresh water. In 1985 the Australian Government extended the laws of the Northern Territory to apply in Ashmore and Cartier.

From 2000 increasing numbers of asylum seekers attempted to land at Ashmore Reef, hoping to gain residency in Australia. The majority had travelled from the Middle East via Indonesia, where the illegal transport of people was widespread. Consequently, in late 2000 a vessel with the capacity to transport up to 150 people was chartered to ferry unauthorized arrivals to the Australian mainland. In September 2001 Ashmore and Cartier Islands were excised from Australia's migration zone. However, in March 2004 a group of nine women and six men, believed to be seeking asylum in Australia, was discovered on Ashmore Reef. A government spokesperson reiterated the territory's exclusion from Australia's migration zone, stating that this would preclude the group from seeking any form of residency in the country. In December 2008 it was reported that a vessel carrying suspected asylum seekers had been apprehended by the Australian authorities in the vicinity of the Ashmore Islands. A total of 35 passengers and five crew members were taken into custody, pending the processing of their claims. Such interceptions by the authorities occurred periodically thereafter. In a major incident off Ashmore Reef in April 2009, five people were killed when a boat carrying 47 Afghan asylum seekers, which had been intercepted by the Australian Navy, caught fire and sank following an explosion.

In April 2005 the Australian Government invited petroleum exploration companies to bid for a number of leases that it had made available in an area covering some 920 sq km near the islands. In mid-2006 two permits were granted for exploration to take place in the territory's Bonaparte Basin. Two more offshore petroleum exploration permits were issued in April 2007, with further permits being granted subsequently. Petroleum extraction activities adjacent to the islands are administered by the Department of Mines and Energy of the Northern Territory.

Australian Antarctic Territory

The Australian Antarctic Territory was established by Order in Council in February 1933 and proclaimed in August 1936, subsequent to the Australian Antarctic Territory Acceptance Act (1933). It consists of the portion of Antarctica (divided by the French territory of Terre Adélie) lying between 45°E and 136°E, and between 142°E and 160°E. The Australian Antarctic Division (AAD) of the Department of the Environment, Sport and Territories (currently the Department of the Environment) was established in 1948 as a permanent agency, and to administer and provide support for the Australian National Antarctic Research Expeditions (ANARE), which maintains three permanent scientific stations (Mawson, Davis and Casey) in the territory. The area of the territory is estimated to be 5,896,500 sq km (2,276,650 sq miles), and there are no permanent inhabitants, although there is a permanent presence of scientific personnel, which increases from around 70 in winter to some 200 in summer. Environmentalists expressed alarm at proposals in the late 1990s to encourage tourism in the territory, which, they claimed, could damage the area's sensitive ecology. In November 2001 an international team of scientists commenced Australia's largest ever scientific expedition, to gather data on the influence of the Southern Ocean on the world's climate and the global carbon cycle. In January 2002 Australia attempted to expel Japanese whaling ships from the 200-nautical-mile exclusive economic zone (EEZ) it claimed to be under the jurisdiction of the Australian Antarctic Territory. (The EEZ was included in the areas covered by the Australian Whale Sanctuary, which was established in 1999.) However, the Government was severely criticized in mid-2005 for its failure to protect whales in its Antarctic territorial waters. Its reluctance to intercept Japanese whaling vessels in its territorial waters for 'diplomatic reasons' was blamed for the slaughter of more than 400 whales since 2000. In January 2008 the Australian Federal Court ruled that Japanese whaling activities within the Antarctic EEZ were illegal and issued an injunction against them. However, according to international law, the ruling remained effectively unenforceable since Japan did not recognize Australian claims to Antarctic land and sea territory. Australia is a signatory to the Antarctic Treaty (see p. 616). As part of the Australian Government's commitment to the establishment of regular flights to the territory, a trial runway was constructed in the 2005/06 Antarctic summer season at the Wilkins Aerodrome, located 75 km from Casey. A full runway was opened in December 2007, with regular flights between the Tasmanian capital of Hobart and Antarctica becoming operational during the 2007/08 Antarctic summer season. The 2012/13 budget allocated funding of $A29.8m. over a two-year period to maintaining shipping and aviation support for research and expedition activities in the Antarctic, as well $A11.2m. for the operations of the scientific stations.

Coral Sea Islands Territory

The Coral Sea Islands became a territory of the Commonwealth of Australia under the Coral Sea Islands Act of 1969. The territory lies east of Queensland, between the Great Barrier Reef and longitude 156° 06'E, and between latitude 12°S and 24°S, and comprises several islands and reefs. The islands are composed largely of sand and coral, and have no permanent fresh water supply, but some have a cover of grass and scrub. The area has been a notorious hazard to shipping since the 19th century, the danger of the reefs being compounded by shifting sand cays and occasional tropical cyclones. The Coral Sea Islands have been acquired by Australia by numerous acts of sovereignty since the early years of the 20th century.

Extending over a sea area of approximately 780,000 sq km (300,000 sq miles), all the islands and reefs in the territory are very small, totalling only a few sq km of land area. They include Cato Island, Chilcott Islet in the Coringa Group, and the Willis Group. In 1997 the Coral Sea Islands Act was amended to include Elizabeth and Middleton Reefs. A meteorological station, operated by the Commonwealth Bureau of Meteorology and with a staff of four, has provided a service on one of the Willis Group since 1921. The other islands are uninhabited. There are eight automatic weather stations (on Cato Island, Flinders Reef, Frederick Reef, Holmes Reef, Lihou Reef, Creal Reef, Marion Reef and Gannet Cay) and several navigation aids distributed throughout the territory.

The Governor-General of Australia is empowered to make ordinances for the peace, order and good government of the territory and, by ordinance, the laws of the Australian Capital Territory apply. The Supreme Court of Norfolk Island exercises criminal jurisdiction in the territory. The territory is administered by a parliamentary secretary, who is appointed by the Minister for Infrastructure and Regional Development. The Royal Australian Navy and the Australian Customs and Border Protection Service conduct sea and aerial surveillance of the area.

The Act constituting the territory provides means of controlling the activities of those who visit it. Officers of the Australian Department of the Environment make regular visits to the Coral Sea Islands. The Lihou Reef and Coringa-Herald National Nature

Reserves were established in 1982 to provide protection for the wide variety of terrestrial and marine wildlife, which include rare species of birds and sea turtles (one of which is the largest, and among the most endangered, of the world's species of sea turtle). Middleton and Elizabeth Reefs were declared Marine National Nature Reserves in 1987 (prior to their inclusion in the territory). In November 2012 the Coral Sea Commonwealth Marine Reserve, covering 989,842 sq km and encompassing the former Lihou Reef and Coringa-Herald National Nature Reserves and the former Coral Sea Conservation Zone, was established, formally protecting the area from over-fishing, and from petroleum and gas exploration.

Heard Island and the McDonald Islands

These islands are situated about 4,000 km (2,500 miles) south-west of Perth, Western Australia. The territory, consisting of Heard Island, Shag Island (8 km north of Heard) and the McDonald Islands, is almost entirely covered in ice and has a total area of 369 sq km (142 sq miles). Sovereignty was transferred from the United Kingdom to the Commonwealth of Australia on 26 December 1947, following the establishment of a scientific research station on Heard Island (which functioned until March 1955). The islands are administered by the Antarctic Division of the Australian Department of the Environment. There are no permanent inhabitants. However, in 1991 evidence emerged of a Polynesian community on Heard Island some 700 years before the territory's discovery by European explorers. The island is of considerable scientific interest, as it is believed to be one of the few Antarctic habitats uncontaminated by introduced organisms. Heard Island is about 44 km long and 20 km wide and possesses an active volcano, named Big Ben. In January 1991 an international team of scientists travelled to Heard Island to conduct research involving the transmission of sound waves, beneath the surface of the ocean, in order to monitor any evidence of the greenhouse effect (melting of polar ice and the rise in sea level as a consequence of pollution). The pulses of sound, which travel at a speed largely influenced by temperature, were to be received at various places around the world, with international co-operation. Heard Island was chosen for the experiment because of its unique location, from which direct paths to the five principal oceans extend. The McDonald Islands, with an area of about 1 sq km (0.4 sq miles), lie some 42 km west of Heard Island. Only two successful landings by boat have been recorded since the discovery of the McDonald Islands in the late 19th century. In late 1997 Heard Island and the McDonald Islands were accorded World Heritage status by UNESCO in recognition of their outstanding universal significance as a natural landmark.

In 1999 concern was expressed that stocks of the Patagonian toothfish in the waters around the islands were becoming depleted as a result of over-exploitation, mainly by illegal operators. (The popularity of the fish in Japan and the USA, where it is known as Chilean sea bass, increased significantly during the early 21st century.) This problem was highlighted in August 2003 when a Uruguayan fishing vessel was seized, following a 20-day pursuit over 7,400 km by Australian, South African and British patrol boats. The trawler had been fishing illegally in waters near Heard and McDonald Islands and had a full cargo of Patagonian toothfish worth some US $1.5m. In December the Australian Government announced that it was to send an ice-breaking patrol vessel with deck-mounted machine guns to police the waters around Heard and McDonald Islands with the aim of deterring illegal fishing activity, much of which was believed to involve international criminal organizations. However, many vessels continued fishing in protected waters, including operations on the Banzare Bank, a plateau in the Southern Ocean, which in February 2005 was closed to fishing by the Convention for the Conservation of Arctic Marine Living Resources Commission. (An anomaly of international law meant that vessels flying flags of non-member countries of the Commission could not be evicted by Australian forces.) In August the Australian customs department announced that it was to train commandos to patrol the protected waters around Heard and McDonald for vessels fishing illegally. Following such efforts to eliminate illegal fishing and the implementation of measures to conserve stocks, in March 2012 the Marine Stewardship Council certified Heard Island and McDonald Islands fishery as being sustainable and well managed. In 2012 the three Australian operated vessels permitted to operate in the area landed 1,935 metric tons of Patagonian toothfish (the total allowable catch being set at 2,730 tons).

In 2001 the Australian Government's Antarctic Division conducted a five-month scientific expedition to Heard Island. It claimed that glacial cover had retreated by 12% since 1947 as a result of global warming. In October 2002 the Australian Government declared the establishment of the Heard Island and McDonald Islands Marine Reserve. Covering 6.5m. ha, the marine reserve was to be one of the largest in the world, strengthening existing conservation measures and imposing an official ban on all fishing and petroleum and mineral exploitation. Among the many species of plant, bird and mammal to be protected by the reserve were the southern elephant seal, the sub-Antarctic fur seal and two species of albatross. Limited scientific research and environmental monitoring were to be allowed. The Marine Reserve Management Plan for 2005–12 introduced measures further to restrict human activity on the islands, in an attempt to protect their unique flora and fauna from damage and from introduced organisms. A new Management Plan was being drafted in early 2014. The islands remain the only unmodified example of a sub-Antarctic island ecosystem in the world.

AUSTRIA

Introductory Survey

LOCATION, CLIMATE, LANGUAGE, RELIGION, FLAG, CAPITAL

The Republic of Austria lies in central Europe, bordered by Germany and the Czech Republic to the north, by Slovakia and Hungary to the east, by Italy and Slovenia to the south, and by Switzerland and Liechtenstein to the west. The mean annual temperature lies between 7°C and 9°C (45°F and 48°F). The population is 99% German-speaking, with small Croat- and Slovene-speaking minorities. The majority of the inhabitants profess Christianity: more than two-thirds are Roman Catholics and about 5% are Protestants. The national flag (proportions 2 by 3) consists of three equal horizontal stripes, of red, white and red. The state flag has, in addition, the coat of arms (a small shield, with horizontal stripes of red separated by a white stripe, superimposed on a black eagle, wearing a golden crown and holding a sickle and a hammer in its feet, with a broken chain between its legs) in the centre. The capital is Vienna (Wien).

CONTEMPORARY POLITICAL HISTORY

Historical Context

Austria was formerly the centre of the Austrian (later Austro-Hungarian) Empire, which comprised a large part of central Europe. The Empire, under the Habsburg dynasty, was dissolved in 1918, at the end of the First World War, and Austria proper became a republic. The first post-war Council of Ministers was a coalition led by Dr Karl Renner, who remained Chancellor until 1920, when a new Constitution introduced a federal form of government. Many of Austria's inhabitants favoured union with Germany, but this was forbidden by the post-war peace treaties. In March 1938, however, Austria was occupied by Nazi Germany's armed forces and incorporated into the German Reich, led by the Austrian-born Adolf Hitler.

After Hitler's defeat in Austria, a provisional Government, under Renner, was established in April 1945. In July, following Germany's surrender to the Allied forces, Austria was divided into four zones, occupied respectively by forces of the USA, the USSR, the United Kingdom and France. Following the first post-war elections to the 165-seat National Council (Nationalrat), held in November 1945, the conservative Österreichische Volkspartei (ÖVP—Austrian People's Party) and the Sozialistische Partei Österreichs (SPÖ—Socialist Party of Austria) formed a coalition Government. In December Renner became the first Federal President of the second Austrian Republic, holding office until his death in December 1950. However, it was not until May 1955 that the four powers signed a State Treaty with Austria, recognizing Austrian independence, effective from 27 July; occupation forces left in October.

Domestic Political Affairs

More than 20 years of coalition government came to an end in April 1966 with the formation of a Council of Ministers by the ÖVP alone, under Dr Josef Klaus, the Federal Chancellor since April 1964. The SPÖ won a plurality of seats in the March 1970 general election and formed a minority Government, with Dr Bruno Kreisky as Chancellor. In April 1971 the incumbent President, Franz Jonas of the SPÖ, was re-elected, defeating the ÖVP candidate, Dr Kurt Waldheim (who subsequently served two five-year terms as UN Secretary-General, beginning in January 1972). The SPÖ won an absolute majority of seats in the National Council at general elections in October 1971 (when the number of seats was increased to 183) and October 1975. Following the death of Jonas in April 1974, a presidential election held in June was won by Dr Rudolf Kirchschläger, hitherto Federal Minister of Foreign Affairs. He was re-elected for a second term in 1980.

At the general election in May 1979 the SPÖ increased its majority in the National Council. The general election of April 1983, however, marked the end of the 13-year era of one-party government: the SPÖ lost its absolute majority in the National Council and Kreisky, unwilling to participate in a coalition, resigned as Chancellor. Kreisky's successor, Dr Fred Sinowatz (the former Vice-Chancellor and Federal Minister of Education), took office in May, leading a coalition of the SPÖ and the right-of-centre Freiheitliche Partei Österreichs (FPÖ—Freedom Party of Austria).

The presidential election held in May 1986 was won by Waldheim, who stood independently, although with the support of the ÖVP. The campaign was dominated by allegations that Waldheim, a former officer in the army of Nazi Germany, had been implicated in atrocities committed by the Nazis in the Balkans during 1942–45. The defeat of the SPÖ presidential candidate, Dr Kurt Steyrer (the Federal Minister of Health and Environment), prompted Chancellor Sinowatz and four of his ministers to resign. Dr Franz Vranitzky, hitherto Federal Minister of Finance, became the new Chancellor. Waldheim's election to the presidency was controversial both domestically and internationally, straining Austria's relations with Israel and the USA, in particular. In February 1988 a specially appointed international commission of historians concluded that Waldheim must have been aware of the atrocities that had been committed. Waldheim refused to resign, but in June 1991 he announced that he would not seek a second presidential term.

In September 1986 the FPÖ elected a controversial new leader, Dr Jörg Haider, who represented the far-right wing of his party. This precipitated the end of the governing coalition, and the general election for the National Council was brought forward to November 1986. No party won an absolute majority: the SPÖ won 80 seats, the ÖVP 77, the FPÖ 18 and an alliance of three environmentalist parties eight.

SPÖ-ÖVP 'grand coalitions': 1987–2000

A 'grand coalition' of the SPÖ and the ÖVP, with Vranitzky as Chancellor, was formed in January 1987, and presided over a period of economic expansion from 1988. However, it was beset by numerous scandals, including large-scale tax evasion by senior SPÖ officials and revelations from a parliamentary inquiry established to investigate the sinking in 1977 of a freighter, the *Lucona*, in which six crew members died. Two SPÖ ministers who were implicated in hindering investigations into the incident, which had formed part of a fraudulent insurance claim, were forced to resign in January 1989.

At the general election held in October 1990 the SPÖ increased its number of seats to 81, while the ÖVP obtained only 60; the FPÖ's representation rose to 33 seats, its success being largely attributed to its support for restrictions on immigration. The Grüne Alternative Liste (GAL, Green Alternative List), an electoral alliance comprising Die Grüne Alternative (The Green Alternative) and the Vereinte Grüne Österreichs (United Green Party of Austria), increased the representation of environmentalist parties to nine. In December the SPÖ and the ÖVP again formed a coalition government under Vranitzky.

In June 1991 the SPÖ reverted to its original name, the Sozialdemokratische Partei Österreichs (SPÖ—Social Democratic Party of Austria). In the same month Haider was dismissed as Governor of Carinthia (Kärnten) after publicly praising Hitler's employment policies. In December the National Council approved legislation whereby Austria became the only country in Europe able to reject asylum requests from individuals without identity papers. Following the imprisonment in January 1992 of a prominent right-wing activist for demanding the restoration of the Nazi party, and the subsequent fire-bombing of a refugee hostel by neo-Nazis in northern Austria, the National Council voted unanimously in February to amend anti-Nazi legislation. The minimum prison sentence for Nazi agitation was reduced from five years to one year (in order to increase the number of successful prosecutions) and denial of the Nazi Holocaust was made a criminal offence.

At the presidential election in April 1992 the two main candidates were Dr Rudolf Streicher for the SPÖ (hitherto the Federal Minister of Public Economy and Transport) and Dr Thomas Klestil (a former ambassador to the USA), representing the ÖVP. In a run-off ballot, held in May, Klestil received almost 57% of the votes cast; he assumed the presidency in July.

In January 1993 the FPÖ organized a national petition seeking to require the National Council to debate the introduction of legislation that would halt immigration into Austria and impose stricter controls on foreign residents in the country. Some 417,000 people signed the petition (the constitutional requirement to force parliamentary debate was 100,000). The initiative was strongly opposed by a broad coalition of politicians, church leaders and intellectuals. In February five FPÖ deputies in the National Council (including the party's Vice-President) left the party and formed the Liberales Forum (LiF, Liberal Forum).

At the general election in October 1994 the ruling coalition lost its two-thirds' majority in the National Council. The SPÖ won 66 seats, the ÖVP 52 and the FPÖ 42 (an increase of nine seats on the 1990 election). Die Grünen (the Greens) also made gains, winning 13 seats, while the LiF took 10. The success of the FPÖ's populist campaign, which had concentrated on countering corruption and immigration and had advocated referendum-based rather than parliamentary-based governance, unsettled the Austrian political establishment after years of relative consensus. In November the SPÖ and ÖVP agreed to form a new coalition Government, with Vranitzky remaining as Chancellor.

The new SPÖ-ÖVP coalition was beleaguered by disagreements, mainly concerning differences in approach to the urgent need to reduce the budget deficit, in compliance with Austria's commitment, following its accession to the European Union (EU) in January 1995, to future Economic and Monetary Union (EMU). In early 1995 five ministers, including the Vice-Chancellor, Dr Erhard Busek, resigned. Busek was replaced as Chairman of the ÖVP by Dr Wolfgang Schüssel. In October the rift between the SPÖ and ÖVP regarding the budget deficit precipitated the collapse of the coalition. At a general election held in December the SPÖ won 71 legislative seats, the ÖVP 53, the FPÖ 40, the LiF 10 and the Greens nine. In March 1996, following lengthy negotiations, the SPÖ and ÖVP agreed an economic programme and formed a new coalition Government, again under Vranitzky. However, in January 1997 Vranitzky unexpectedly resigned from the chancellorship. Viktor Klima, hitherto the Federal Minister of Finance, replaced Vranitzky as Chancellor and as Chairman of the SPÖ.

At the presidential election in April 1998 Klestil was re-elected, winning 63.5% of the votes cast. The FPÖ made significant gains at regional elections in March 1999, becoming the dominant party in Carinthia; Haider was subsequently elected Governor of Carinthia (having been dismissed from that post in 1991). The general election in October 1999 resulted in unprecedented success for the FPÖ, which narrowly took second place ahead of the ÖVP. The SPÖ won 65 seats in the National Council, while the FPÖ and ÖVP both secured 52 and the Greens 14. The FPÖ had campaigned on a programme that advocated a halt to immigration, the obstruction of EU expansion, and the introduction of a uniform low rate of income tax and of increased child allowances for Austrian citizens. During the election campaign Haider allegedly revived nationalist terminology previously employed by the Nazi regime, although he consistently denied embracing neo-Nazi ideology. The election result was widely regarded as a protest against the 'grand coalition', which had acquired a reputation for unwieldy bureaucracy and for sanctioning politically motivated appointments to public companies. In February 2000 Klima was succeeded as Chairman of the SPÖ by Dr Alfred Gusenbauer.

ÖVP-FPÖ coalition Government: 2000–02

Following the failure of negotiations aimed at renewing the outgoing coalition, in February 2000 President Klestil reluctantly presided over the inauguration of an ÖVP-FPÖ coalition Government, with Schüssel as Chancellor. Haider elected not to participate directly in the new administration, which included an FPÖ Vice-Chancellor, Dr Susanne Riess-Passer, and five FPÖ ministers. Although the new coalition had adopted a relatively moderate political programme, the FPÖ's participation in government provoked strong opposition both within Austria and abroad. Israel and the USA immediately recalled their ambassadors from Vienna, while Austria's fellow EU member states each suspended bilateral political co-operation, maintaining diplomatic relations at a 'technical' level, pending the removal of the FPÖ from the coalition. In late February Haider announced that he was to resign as FPÖ leader, while remaining Governor of Carinthia; few people, however, doubted that he would retain significant influence within the party. An EU delegation that visited Austria in July recommended in its subsequent report that the diplomatic sanctions be lifted. While criticizing the FPÖ, the report confirmed that Austria's treatment of minorities was superior to that of some other EU member states. The EU lifted its sanctions in September, but warned that it would continue to monitor closely the influence of the FPÖ, and Haider, upon government policies.

By the end of 2000 the FPÖ's influence and popularity was in decline. In October a number of senior party members (including the Federal Minister for Justice, Dr Dieter Böhmdorfer) were accused of using illicitly obtained police files to discredit opponents. In that month Böhmdorfer survived a third vote of no confidence against him. By November the number of FPÖ members under investigation had risen to 67. The party fared badly in two provincial elections and, in November, the Federal Minister of Science and Transport, Michael Schmid, became the third FPÖ minister to resign since the formation of the Government, citing the FPÖ's poor electoral performances. Schmid subsequently resigned from the FPÖ.

In September 2001, purportedly as part of a plan to combat international terrorism following the devastating Islamist terrorist attacks in the USA, Haider asserted that refugees from continents other than Europe seeking asylum within the EU should no longer be granted residence in Europe while their requests were being processed. The FPÖ also suggested the introduction of 'biometric' identification methods, a fortnightly 'control' of all asylum seekers and the immediate expulsion of any foreigners suspected of being involved in criminal activities. Furthermore, the FPÖ proposed the introduction of a so-called Integrationsvertrag (integration contract) for immigrant workers and their families, including those who were already living in the country. Under this contract, immigrants would be obliged to attend courses and pass tests on both the German language and citizenship; those who did not comply within four years would have their social security benefits gradually reduced, and, in extreme cases, would face expulsion from the country. The proposals provoked fierce criticism both within Austria and throughout the EU. Despite initial reservations, in October the ÖVP endorsed the FPÖ's recommendations regarding asylum seekers and immigrants (with the exception of the proposal to deny those seeking asylum the right of temporary residence). The measures were approved by the legislature and came into force on 1 January 2003.

An internal power struggle within the FPÖ led to the resignation in September 2002 of a number of moderate FPÖ ministers, including Vice-Chancellor Riess-Passer. Hitherto, Schüssel's strategy of persuading these ministers to eschew the more extremist elements of their party's credo, while himself adopting some of the FPÖ's more reasonable policies, had contributed to a loss of support for the FPÖ. In late September the instability within the junior coalition partner led Schüssel to dissolve the legislature. At an early general election held on 24 November the ÖVP received 42.3% of the votes cast (the party's largest single share of the votes in more than 30 years), securing 79 seats, mainly at the expense of the FPÖ, which obtained only 10.0% of the votes cast (18 seats), compared with 26.9% in 1999. The SPÖ won 69 seats and the Greens 17.

Second ÖVP-FPÖ coalition Government: 2003–06

In February 2003, following the reluctance of the SPÖ and the Greens to enter into coalition talks, Schüssel invited the FPÖ, now led by Herbert Haupt, to form another coalition administration with the ÖVP. The new Government included only three ministers from the FPÖ.

The FPÖ suffered heavy losses in regional elections in September 2003. The following month Haupt resigned as Vice-Chancellor, but retained his ministerial position. He remained as the nominal leader of the FPÖ pending party elections in 2004, but under the supervision of the party's new Managing Chairwoman, Haider's sister, Ursula Haubner. Many observers viewed the latter's appointment as evidence that Haider had again assumed control of the FPÖ. In March 2004 forecasts of an SPÖ victory in elections in Carinthia were confounded when the FPÖ won 42.4% of the votes cast, compared with 38.4% for the SPÖ and only 11.6% for the ÖVP. Haider, therefore, retained the governorship.

In October 2003 the National Council approved amendments to Austria's asylum legislation that were intended to accelerate the asylum process; the office of the UN High Commissioner for Refugees, however, described the amendments as 'among the most restrictive pieces of legislation' within the EU. The changes included measures such as deporting some asylum seekers while their appeals were under review, demanding full statements from asylum seekers within 72 hours of their arrival in Austria, and medically certifying cases involving traumatized people.

At a presidential election in April 2004, Dr Heinz Fischer of the SPÖ defeated Dr Benita Ferrero-Waldner of the ÖVP with 52.4%

of the votes cast. On 5 July, just three days before the end of his term of office, President Klestil suffered a heart attack: he died the following day. Chancellor Schüssel assumed charge of Klestil's duties until Fischer was sworn in as the new President on 8 July.

As a result of the continuing decline in support for the FPÖ, Haider left the party in early April 2005 to form Bündnis Zukunft Österreich (BZÖ—Alliance for the Future of Austria). The FPÖ government ministers, several FPÖ members of Parliament (Parlament) and the party Chairwoman, Haubner (who had been elected unopposed in July 2004), all defected to the BZÖ. The party replaced the FPÖ in the ruling coalition and the ministers retained their posts in the Government. Haider was elected as leader of the BZÖ, while Heinz-Christian Strache was elected to the chairmanship of the FPÖ. In mid-April Siegfried Kampl, a BZÖ member from Carinthia, who was due to assume the rotating presidency of the Federal Council (Bundesrat) in July, provoked considerable controversy when he denounced deserters from Austria's Nazi-era armed forces and deplored what he called the 'brutal persecution' of Austrian Nazis following the Second World War. Amid the ensuing furore, he resigned from the BZÖ but stated his intention to take up the presidency of the Federal Council as planned. However, a constitutional amendment adopted in June with the support of all parties allowed Carinthia to withdraw Kampl's nomination and to designate Peter Mitterer as President of the Federal Council for the last six months of 2005.

Following a strong performance by the SPÖ at elections in three provinces in October 2005, the ruling ÖVP-BZÖ coalition lost its majority in the Federal Council. In May 2006 Haider resigned as leader of the BZÖ; he was replaced by Peter Westenthaler in June.

Political activity in 2006 was dominated by a financial scandal surrounding the Bank für Arbeit und Wirtschaft AG PSK (BAWAG PSK), which was owned by the Österreichischer Gewerkschaftsbund (ÖGB—Austrian Trade Union Federation) and had links to the SPÖ. BAWAG was revealed to have accumulated huge debts and to have used the ÖGB strike fund to conceal the losses. The Federal Government intervened to prevent the collapse of the bank, which was sold to a US-based company in December. At the general election in October the SPÖ won 68 seats in the legislature (one fewer than in 2002), while the ÖVP secured 66 seats, compared with 79 in 2002. The Greens and the FPÖ obtained 21 seats apiece, while the BZÖ won seven.

Return to 'grand coalition': Gusenbauer 2007–08

Following the 2006 election, the SPÖ began talks with the ÖVP over the formation of a 'grand coalition'. Negotiations foundered after the SPÖ allied itself at the first meeting of the new National Council with the Greens and the FPÖ to initiate a parliamentary inquiry into a controversial purchase agreement entered into by the Government in 2002 for 18 Eurofighter aircraft.

In January 2007 the SPÖ and ÖVP finally formed a 'grand coalition', giving the Government control of 134 of the 183 seats in the National Council. The new Council of Ministers comprised seven ministers each from the SPÖ and ÖVP. Gusenbauer became Chancellor and Wilhelm Molterer of the ÖVP was appointed Vice-Chancellor and Federal Minister of Finance. The new coalition's programme included austerity measures aimed at eradicating the budget deficit by 2010, with savings to be achieved largely by administrative reform, but also incorporated increased spending on education and social issues and a rise in personal contributions to the health system. Molterer was officially elected as ÖVP Chairman at the party congress in April 2007, while Schüssel, who had resigned following the party's relatively poor electoral performance, assumed the leadership of the ÖVP parliamentary group.

Relations between the coalition partners were strained in June 2007 by an announcement from the SPÖ Federal Minister of Defence, Norbert Darabos, that he had signed a new contract with the manufacturers of the Eurofighter jets, reducing the number of aircraft involved from 18 to 15, before the parliamentary inquiry into the purchase had published its findings. The committee closed its inquiry in July, concluding that although evidence of wrongdoing in the circumstances surrounding the awarding of the original contract in 2002 potentially justified a complete withdrawal from the deal, the probability of exposure to lengthy judicial proceedings, owing to a lack of conclusive proof of bribery, made such a course inadvisable.

Relations between the two governing parties became increasingly acrimonious in March 2008, following the SPÖ's decision to support an opposition motion in the National Council to establish a parliamentary commission of inquiry into abuses of office in the Federal Ministry of the Interior under the control of the ÖVP. The inquiry was prompted by accusations by a former federal police chief, Herwig Haidinger, that errors in a child kidnapping case in 1998 had been suppressed in 2006 by the Federal Minister of the Interior in order to avoid a political scandal shortly before the general election in October, and that in the same year the Ministry of the Interior had instructed Haidinger to pass findings from investigations into the BAWAG scandal to the ÖVP in an attempt to find information to discredit the SPÖ during the election campaign.

By mid-2008 relations between the coalition parties had deteriorated significantly. In early June leading figures from both the ÖVP and the SPÖ, including the Federal Minister of Agriculture, Forestry, the Environment and Water Management, Josef Pröll of the ÖVP, and former Chancellor Vranitzky, issued public statements criticizing Gusenbauer's leadership. The SPÖ's poor performance in provincial elections in Tyrol on 8 June, at which it received just 15.6% of the vote, provoked further discontent within the party. Later that month Gusenbauer was replaced as Chairman of the SPÖ on an interim basis by the Federal Minister for Transport, Innovation and Technology, Werner Faymann.

Following the accession of Faymann to the leadership of the SPÖ, the party sought to recover its standing in the opinion polls by adopting a more populist policy with regard to the EU. In July 2008 the influential Eurosceptic daily newspaper the *Kronen Zeitung* published an open letter co-authored by Faymann and Gusenbauer, in which they indicated that any future EU treaties or amendments to treaties requiring ratification, as well as any decision on Turkish accession to the Union, would be submitted to a referendum. The change in policy on the part of the SPÖ led to the withdrawal of the largely pro-EU ÖVP from the 'grand coalition', the dissolution of the legislature and the scheduling of an early general election. Gusenbauer subsequently nominated Faymann as the SPÖ's candidate for the role of Chancellor. Faymann was elected as Chairman of the SPÖ in August. Later that month Haider was re-elected as leader of the BZÖ, replacing Westenthaler, following the latter's conviction for perjury during a trial in which his bodyguard was accused of assault.

At the general election, which took place on 28 September 2008, the SPÖ retained its position as the largest party in the legislature, winning 57 seats, while the ÖVP lost support, securing just 51 seats. By contrast, large gains were made by the two right-wing populist parties: the FPÖ won 34 seats, while the BZÖ tripled its representation, securing 21 seats. The Greens lost support, winning just 20 seats. In accordance with reforms promulgated in June 2007, the parliamentary term was extended to five years following the election. The following day Molterer resigned as Chairman of the ÖVP. Pröll was appointed as his successor on an interim basis. Despite the electoral success of the FPÖ and the BZÖ, both the SPÖ and the ÖVP ruled out forming a coalition with the two right-wing parties and subsequently began talks over the formation of a new 'grand coalition' government.

The 'grand coalition' under Faymann

In late November 2008 the SPÖ and the ÖVP agreed to form a new 'grand coalition'. Ursula Plassnik of the ÖVP, hitherto the Federal Minister of European and International Affairs, announced that she would not accept a position in the new Council of Ministers owing to Faymann's refusal to include in the terms of the coalition agreement a guarantee that future EU treaties or amendments to treaties would be ratified through Parliament, rather than by referendum. The new Council of Ministers was sworn in at the beginning of December. Faymann was appointed Chancellor, while Pröll replaced Molterer as Vice-Chancellor and Federal Minister of Finance.

Meanwhile, in October 2008 Haider was killed in a road traffic accident near Klagenfurt, while driving under the influence of alcohol. His deputy, Stefan Petzner, was nominated to succeed him as leader of the BZÖ, while Gerhard Dörfler, hitherto the Deputy Governor of Carinthia, replaced him as Governor of that province. However, Petzner's suitability to lead the party was questioned, following an emotional radio interview in which he made indiscreet remarks regarding his personal relationship with Haider. In November Petzner resigned as interim party leader and was replaced by a former FPÖ Federal Minister of Defence, Herbert Scheibner.

At provincial elections in March 2009 in Carinthia and Salzburg the BZÖ and the FPÖ both made gains at the expense of the

SPÖ. In Carinthia, with a campaign that emphasized the legacy of Haider, the BZÖ won 45.5% of the vote, the SPÖ 28.8% and the ÖVP 16.8%. Dörfler retained the post of provincial Governor. The following month the BZÖ elected its Parliamentary Spokesman, Josef Bucher, to serve concurrently as party leader. The SPÖ's fortunes continued to decline, at elections to the European Parliament in June and again at regional elections in Vorarlberg and Upper Austria (Oberösterreich) in September. The FPÖ's controversial campaign for the European parliamentary elections centred around warnings of a growing 'Islamization' of Austria and Europe, and used images of a cross and the slogan 'The West in Christian hands'. Advertisements also warned of the possibility of Israel and Turkey entering the EU. The campaign was condemned by church leaders, politicians, and Islamic and Jewish groups; none the less, at the polls the FPÖ secured 12.7% of votes, compared with 6.3% in 2004.

President Fischer was re-elected to a second and final term of office at a presidential election held on 25 April 2010, securing 79.3% of the votes cast, with the support of the Greens, as well as his own party, the SPÖ. His closest rival, Barbara Rosenkranz of the FPÖ, won 15.2% of the votes. Rosenkranz's candidacy attracted substantial media attention during the electoral campaign: following considerable controversy surrounding her vague responses in interviews to questions regarding her views on the Holocaust, she signed a public statement pledging never to contest anti-Nazi legislation. An historically low turnout of 53.6% was attributed, in part, to the decision of the ÖVP neither to nominate nor to endorse a candidate.

At provincial elections held in Burgenland in May 2010, the FPÖ made gains at the expense of both the SPÖ and the ÖVP, although the former retained the governorship. The FPÖ also performed well in the Styria (Steiermark) and Vienna provincial elections held in September and October, respectively, with the share of the votes won by the two federal coalition parties again declining. In the elections in Vienna, the FPÖ made substantial gains, replacing the ÖVP, which recorded its poorest ever result in the capital, as the second largest party in the provincial assembly after the SPÖ, which lost its absolute majority in the provincial legislature. Christine Marek, the ÖVP's leader in Vienna, resigned as State Secretary in the Federal Ministry of Economy, Family and Youth in November; she was replaced by Verena Remler.

In April 2011 a reorganization of the Federal Government was necessitated by the resignation of Pröll as Vice-Chancellor and Federal Minister of Finance, on the grounds of ill health. Pröll also resigned as the leader of the ÖVP; he was replaced as party leader and thus as Vice-Chancellor by Dr Michael Spindelegger, who retained his position as the Federal Minister of European and International Affairs. Among other notable changes to ÖVP portfolios, Dr Maria Fekter was allocated the finance portfolio, Dr Beatrix Karl took over the Federal Ministry of Justice and Johanna Mikl-Leitner became Federal Minister of the Interior.

Austrian politicians were subject to a series of corruption allegations in 2011. Two ÖVP members of the European Parliament, Ernst Strasser and Hella Ranner, resigned from office in March, following accusations, which both refuted, that the former had accepted bribes in return for proposing amendments to European legislation and that the latter had intended to use her parliamentary expense account to repay a business debt. (Strasser was convicted of bribe-taking and sentenced to four years' imprisonment in January 2013.) In August 2011, moreover, Uwe Scheuch, the Deputy Governor of Carinthia and Chairman of Die Freiheitlichen in Kärnten (FPK, Freedom Party in Carinthia, which was the Carinthian branch of the BZÖ until December 2009, when it disassociated from the federal BZÖ to co-operate with the FPÖ at federal level as an independent party), was sentenced to a short term of imprisonment, after being found guilty of offering, in 2009, to assist a Russian entrepreneur to gain Austrian citizenship in return for a donation to the BZÖ, the party to which he then belonged; Scheuch resigned from political office in August 2012. Meanwhile, further scandals emerged in 2011 in which several former government ministers from the ÖVP-FPÖ/BZÖ coalition administrations in office in 2000–07 were implicated. Strasser, who had served as Federal Minister of the Interior in 2000–04, and two former FPÖ ministers, Hubert Gorbach and Mathias Reichhold, were accused of receiving illicit payments from Telekom Austria or lobbyists co-operating with the partially state-owned telecommunications provider. In addition, the role of former Federal Minister of Finance Karl-Heinz Grasser in the controversial privatization of the real estate company Die Bauen und Wohnen GmbH (BUWOG) was under investigation, as was alleged impropriety by the former Federal Minister of Defence, Herbert Scheibner, in relation to the purchase of Eurofighter aircraft. Although he had not personally been accused of corruption, former Chancellor Schüssel resigned as a member of Parliament in early September 2011, claiming that he was retiring from politics in order to facilitate the investigations into his former ministers. Later that month Parliament agreed to establish a committee of inquiry to probe the various corruption allegations.

Economic concerns came to the fore from late 2011. In the context of the sovereign debt crisis affecting the wider eurozone, the Government sought to avert a threatened downgrading of the AAA credit status assigned to Austria's debt by rating agencies, amid fears that the heavy exposure of the Austrian banking sector to financially stricken Central and Eastern European economies, particularly Hungary, had made it vulnerable. In November the Government pledged to accelerate reductions in public expenditure and to introduce a constitutional amendment that would commit the Government to lowering the ratio of public debt to gross domestic product to 60% by 2020 (from some 72% in 2011). However, differences of opinion between the governing SPÖ and the ÖVP on what austerity measures to implement hindered subsequent negotiations, while the support of at least one opposition party was required to achieve the two-thirds' parliamentary majority needed to revise the Constitution. In early December the opposition parties refused to support the coalition Government's draft constitutional amendment on the debt limit, prompting the SPÖ and the ÖVP to adopt the proposal as a regular law with a simple majority. In January 2012, none the less, the credit rating agency Standard & Poor's downgraded Austria's credit rating; however, the two other major rating agencies, Moody's and Fitch, had recently confirmed Austria's AAA rating. A detailed austerity plan was approved by Parliament in March (see Economic Affairs).

Amid the ongoing investigations into political corruption, in June 2012 Parliament adopted legislation aimed at increasing transparency in the financing of political parties and electoral campaigning. Further details of a scandal surrounding Carinthian-based banking group Hypo Group Alpe Adria (HGAA) emerged in the following month, during the trial of Dietrich Birnbacher, a tax consultant hired by Haider and the leader of the ÖVP in Carinthia, Josef Martinz, at the time of the sale by the Carinthian authorities of a majority stake in the banking group in 2007. Birnbacher testified that, under his contract with Haider and Martinz, part of his excessively large fee had been used illicitly to fund the two politicians' respective parties. Martinz admitted the allegations and resigned as ÖVP leader in Carinthia as a result; he was sentenced to five-and-a-half years' imprisonment in October 2012. (In mid-2010 prosecutors investigating the near collapse, in December 2009, of HGAA, which had necessitated its nationalization by the Federal Government, had reportedly discovered several secret bank accounts in Liechtenstein in which the late Haider had allegedly deposited up to US $45m.)

Recent developments: new political parties and legislative elections

There were signs of public dissatisfaction with the coalition parties during 2012, with support for the ÖVP, in particular, declining and being equalled or surpassed for much of the year, according to opinion polls, by that for the FPÖ, with the latter's opposition to EU financial assistance for heavily indebted eurozone members such as Greece and Portugal proving popular with sections of the electorate. Disillusionment with the traditional parties was evident in the modest success of the minor Piratenpartei Österreichs (Pirate Party of Austria) in municipal elections in April in Innsbruck and in November in Graz, where a strong performance was also recorded by the non-parliamentary Kommunistische Partei Österreichs (Communist Party of Austria), which came second in the vote. Yet more significant, meanwhile, was the establishment in September of a new party by Austro-Canadian businessman Frank Stronach. Team Stronach für Österreich (Team Stronach for Austria), which notably was sceptical about Austria's continued membership of the eurozone and advocated the introduction of a 25% flat tax on incomes, gained parliamentary status in November, when five members of other parties represented in the National Council defected to the new organization. Another new party, Das Neue Österreich (NEOS—The New Austria), led by Dr Matthias Stolz, was formally launched in October.

Public disenchantment with the SPÖ and the ÖVP could be partly attributed to continued disagreement between the two parties on government policy, an example of which was their differing views on defence, with the ÖVP strongly rejecting an SPÖ proposal to abolish compulsory military service in favour of creating a professional army. In September 2012 the Government decided to resolve this issue by consulting the electorate in a national referendum. At the plebiscite (Austria's first ever such poll), which was conducted on 20 January 2013, 59.7% of participants voted in favour of retaining conscription. Meanwhile, the governing parties provoked widespread criticism, including from President Fischer, in September 2012, when it was announced that the activities of the committee of inquiry established a year earlier to examine corruption allegations would be curtailed. Critics of the move claimed that the parties were concerned that a protracted focus on political graft would damage their prospects in the provincial and federal elections due to take place in 2013.

The Federal Minister of Defence and Sports, Norbert Darabos, resigned in March 2013 to take up the position of National Secretary of the SPÖ in the run-up to the legislative elections and was replaced by Gerald Klug.

An early provincial election in Carinthia in March 2013 saw a drastic reduction in support for the Austrian far right (from some 45% of the vote—as achieved by the BZÖ in 2009—to only around 17% for the FPK), which lost control of its erstwhile stronghold to the SPÖ. The FPK merged with the FPÖ in June, becoming the latter's state section in Carinthia. Despite substantial losses incurred by the two federal ruling parties in the provincial election in Salzburg in May (in the case of the SPÖ, largely as a result of a financial scandal), the general election, which was held on 29 September, saw the 'grand coalition' potentially returned to power, albeit with a reduced majority—the SPÖ securing 52 seats and the ÖVP 47. The number of seats won by the FPÖ rose from the total of 34 achieved in the 2008 election to 40, while the BZÖ lost all of its representation in the National Council. The Greens increased their tally from 20 seats to 24, while Team Stronach and NEOS performed well, winning 11 seats and nine seats, respectively. The election attracted a turnout of 74.4%. As widely predicted, the SPÖ and the ÖVP renewed their coalition, and a new Federal Government under Faymann was sworn in on 16 December. Klug and Mikl-Leitner retained their respective portfolios, of defence and the interior, while Spindelegger was transferred to head the Federal Ministry of Finance, handing over responsibility for the Federal Ministry of European and International Affairs to Sebastian Kurz (whose post was restyled as Federal Minister for Europe, Integration and Foreign Affairs in March 2014).

Foreign Affairs

Regional relations

Austria was formally admitted to the European Union (EU, see p. 273) on 1 January 1995, following a national referendum in June 1994, at which 66.4% of those who voted supported Austria's accession to the Union. Austria participated in the introduction of the European single currency, the euro, on 1 January 1999. In May 2005 the Austrian Parliament ratified the EU's Treaty establishing a Constitution for Europe. However, the treaty was rejected at referendums held in France and the Netherlands. In April 2008 Parliament ratified the Treaty of Lisbon, which replaced the rejected constitutional treaty and which came into effect in December 2009. During 2010–12 the Austrian Government supported EU efforts to improve the financial stability of the eurozone, including agreements on the establishment of the European Financial Stability Facility in June 2010, on the European Stability Mechanism (ESM) in October of that year and on a Treaty on Stability, Co-ordination and Governance in the Economic and Monetary Union (the so-called fiscal compact), providing for new, stricter fiscal arrangements, in March 2012. In July 2012 the Austrian Parliament approved the establishment of the ESM and the ratification of the fiscal compact (which had been signed by all EU states with the exception of the Czech Republic and the United Kingdom), with the opposition Greens joining the governing SPÖ and ÖVP to provide the constitutionally required two-thirds' majority in favour.

In October 2005 a demand by Austria that a 'privileged partnership' with the EU be offered to Turkey rather than full membership threatened to delay the official launch of accession talks with that country. Austria was finally persuaded to withdraw this demand, and negotiations commenced. Observers suggested that Austria's concession on Turkey was linked to the decision to proceed with previously suspended talks with Croatia, whose bid for membership of the EU the Austrian Government supported. Relations with Turkey were again strained prior to the European Parliament elections in June 2009, with both the ÖVP and the FPÖ campaigning on a platform of opposition to full EU membership for Turkey. Criticism of Austria's treatment of immigrants from Turkey made by the Turkish ambassador to Austria, Kadri Ecvet Tezcan, in a newspaper interview provoked further diplomatic tensions in November 2010; Tezcan was replaced as ambassador a year later. Meanwhile, in May 2011 Turkey's President, Abdullah Gül, sought to strengthen bilateral relations, particularly economic ties, during the first Turkish presidential visit to Austria for 13 years. During the visit, however, Chancellor Faymann reiterated his position that Austria would conduct a national referendum on Turkey's membership of the EU, whatever the outcome of negotiations between the EU and the Turkish Government on Turkish accession. In June tensions were further heightened when Turkey vetoed an application by the former Austrian Federal Minister of European and International Affairs, Ursula Plassnik, for the position of Secretary-General of the Organization for Security and Co-operation in Europe owing to her opposition to Turkish membership of the EU.

The activation in October 2000 of a Soviet-designed nuclear power installation at Temelín in the Czech Republic, 48 km from the border with Austria, prompted protests from environmental activists and claims by both Austria and Germany that the plant was dangerously flawed: Austria subsequently suspended imports of Czech electricity. Following negotiations between the Austrian and Czech authorities, an agreement was signed by the two countries in December under which the plant was not to operate at commercial capacity until a full evaluation of its safety and environmental impact had been completed by a joint Austro-Czech safety body under the supervision of the European Commission. In August 2001 the Czech authorities reconnected the plant with the national power network, citing the findings of a report by the European Commission; however, the Austrian and German Governments continued to express concern over the safety of the plant. Later that year Chancellor Schüssel threatened to veto the Czech Republic's accession to the EU unless the matter were satisfactorily resolved. Further safety issues were subsequently agreed, and in April 2003 the Temelín installation commenced production at full capacity for an 18-month trial period, prior to entering into commercial operations by the end of 2004. Relations between Austria and the Czech Republic were further marred by the latter's refusal to abolish the so-called Beneš Decrees—legislation enacted at the end of the Second World War, providing for the expulsion of about 2.5m. ethnic Sudeten Germans from the Czech Republic without recourse to compensation. Austria repeatedly threatened to block the Czech Republic's anticipated accession to the EU in 2004 unless the Decrees were annulled; the EU authorities, however, did not regard their abolition as a prerequisite for entry, and Austria did not ultimately carry out its threats. Following the Czech Republic's accession to the EU in May 2004, relations between the two countries improved. None the less, the Czech Republic's plan to commence construction of an additional two nuclear rectors at its Temelín installation in 2013 (subsequently put on hold until mid-2014 at the earliest) was opposed by the Austrian Government, which advocated that European countries abandon the production and use of nuclear energy. In July 2013, despite EU opposition, the Austrian Parliament passed legislation banning imports of nuclear power.

The heads of government of Austria, Hungary and Slovakia met on several occasions during the late 1990s in order to pursue co-operation on security and economic issues. In September 1999, however, Austria threatened to hinder Slovakia's entry into the EU, in protest at the alleged inadequacy of that country's nuclear safety standards. Following diplomatic pressure from Austria, the terms of Slovakia's accession treaty included a commitment to decommission two Soviet-era nuclear reactors at Jaslovské Bohunice, some 40 km from the border with Austria, by the end of 2008; the first reactor was duly disconnected in late 2006 and the second on 31 December 2008. Meanwhile, however, work on the expansion of Slovakia's Mochovce nuclear power station proceeded in 2008, despite Austrian opposition, with completion envisaged for 2014–15.

The implementation in December 2007 of the Schengen Agreement on border controls by nine Central and Eastern European countries included four countries that share a border with

Austria. In order to assuage public fears of mass migration, the Government promised temporarily to mount a guard on its eastern borders, provoking anger in the Czech Republic and Hungary. Relations with Hungary were already strained following an attempt by the Austrian oil and gas company OMV to take over its Hungarian counterpart, MOL. The border patrols were initially scheduled to end in 2009; however, in December the SPÖ Federal Minister of Defence and Sports, Norbert Darabos, announced that the patrols would continue indefinitely. Meanwhile, in October 2009 the Federal Minister of the Interior, Dr Maria Fekter, expressed the Austrian Government's support for Bulgaria and Romania's entry into the Schengen Agreement in 2011, although their entry was delayed in the event, owing to Finnish and Dutch concerns regarding corruption and organized crime in the two countries. From May 2011 Austria and Germany opened their labour markets to citizens of the eight Central and Eastern European countries that joined the EU in May 2004 (the Czech Republic, Estonia, Hungary, Latvia, Lithuania, Poland, Slovenia and Slovakia), having imposed the longest period of restrictions on workers from these countries of the 15 longer-standing EU members.

Other external relations

In March 1998, following months of debate, the Government announced that Austria would not apply to join the North Atlantic Treaty Organization (NATO, see p. 370), and would thereby preserve its traditional neutrality. Nevertheless, in April 1999 Austria, in conjunction with the three other officially neutral EU member countries, signed an EU declaration stating that the ongoing bombing of Serbia by NATO forces was, although regrettable, 'both necessary and warranted'. During the 1990s, in its capacity as a participant of NATO's Partnership for Peace programme (which it had joined in 1995), Austria took an active role in the aftermath of the wars and ethnic conflicts in the Balkans, participating in UN-authorized peacekeeping operations in Bosnia and Herzegovina in 1996–2001 and providing substantial humanitarian aid. Austria also contributed troops to an EU peacekeeping mission in eastern Chad in 2008–09 and to a NATO-led peacekeeping force that was deployed in Kosovo from June 1999, its contingent numbering 383 in November 2013. In June 2013, following an escalation in the civil conflict in Syria, Austria began withdrawing its 377 peacekeeping troops from the Golan Heights, where they had formed part of the UN Disengagement Observer Force (UNDOF) monitoring the demilitarized zone between Syria and Israel.

Austria's relationship with the USA was, on the whole, free from tension, notwithstanding the strain caused by the election of Dr Kurt Waldheim in 1986, and the formation of the coalition Government between the ÖVP and FPÖ in 2000. The Austrian Government deployed 93 troops on a three-month mission to Afghanistan to assist in stabilizing the country prior to elections in 2005, although, under their mandate of neutrality, the troops did not engage in combat. In 2009 the US President, Barack Obama, sought more international assistance in the ongoing campaign against the Taliban in Afghanistan. However, in December of that year the Austrian Federal Minister of Defence and Sports, Norbert Darabos, reportedly stated that, despite pressure from the USA and also the United Kingdom, Austria would not commit more troops. In May 2012 the Austrian Government announced that it would provide funding of €18m. for police training in Afghanistan in 2014–16, following the planned withdrawal of foreign troops from that country. At October 2013 Austria's contribution to NATO's International Security Assistance Force (ISAF) in Afghanistan was only three military personnel.

Austria's reliance on natural gas supplies from Russia left the nation vulnerable to ongoing disputes over prices and supply between Russia and Ukraine, a key transit country. According to figures from the European Council on Foreign Relations, Russia supplied more than 60% of Austria's gas supplies in 2006; securing another source was thus a major issue for the nation. In 2002 Austria participated in discussions with Bulgaria, Hungary, Romania and Turkey regarding the construction of a gas pipeline. The impetus to reach agreement on an alternative gas supply route was intensified, following an incident in January 2009 when Russia shut down its main pipeline to Europe for two weeks in a price dispute with Ukraine, leaving houses and businesses throughout Europe without energy. An agreement to build the 'Nabucco' pipeline was signed by the countries' respective leaders at a ceremony in July 2009. The pipeline, which was to run from Erzurum, Turkey, through Bulgaria, Romania and Hungary to Baumgarten an der March, Austria, had formal backing from the EU and USA. (In May 2012 the project was modified, as the Nabucco-West pipeline, which was to run from Strandzha in Bulgaria, on the border with Turkey, westwards to Austria.) Austria was also involved in the Russian-led 'South Stream' pipeline project, which was to carry Russian gas under the Black Sea to the Austrian border town of Arnoldstein via Bulgaria, Serbia and Hungary. Austria's participation in 'South Stream' was confirmed in April 2010, during a visit to Vienna by the Russian Prime Minister, Vladimir Putin, with the signature of an agreement on the construction of the Austrian section of the pipeline. Building work on the pipeline commenced in December 2012 and the first commercial deliveries were scheduled for late 2015.

CONSTITUTION AND GOVERNMENT

The Austrian Constitution of 1920, as amended in 1929, was restored on 1 May 1945. Austria is a federal republic, divided into nine provinces, each with its own provincial assembly and government. The head of state, the Federal President (Bundespräsident), is elected by popular vote for a six-year term. The President is eligible for re-election only once in succession. Legislative power is held by the bicameral Parliament (Parlament). The first chamber, the National Council (Nationalrat), has 183 members, elected by universal, direct adult suffrage for four years (subject to dissolution) on the basis of proportional representation. In 2007 the National Council approved legislation extending the maximum parliamentary term from four to five years. The reform entered into effect following the early legislative elections on 28 September 2008. The second chamber, the Federal Council (Bundesrat), has 62 members, elected for varying terms by the provincial assemblies. The Federal Assembly (Bundesversammlung—a joint meeting of the National Council and the Federal Council) is convened for certain matters of special importance, for example to witness the swearing-in of the Federal President. The Federal Government consists of the Federal Chancellor, the Vice-Chancellor and the other ministers and state secretaries, who may vary in number. The Chancellor is chosen by the President, usually from the party with the strongest representation in the newly elected National Council, and the other ministers are then selected by the President on the advice of the Chancellor. The Federal President normally acts on the advice of the Council of Ministers, which is responsible to the National Council.

REGIONAL AND INTERNATIONAL CO-OPERATION

Austria joined the European Union (EU, see p. 273) in January 1995 and participated in the introduction of the European single currency, the euro, on 1 January 1999. Austria is also a member of the Council of Europe (see p. 252) and the Central European Initiative (see p. 464). The Secretariat of the Organization for Security and Co-operation in Europe (OSCE, see p. 387), in which Austria participates, is based in Vienna.

Austria joined the UN in 1955 and hosts the third headquarters of the organization. As a contracting party to the General Agreement on Tariffs and Trade, Austria joined the World Trade Organization (WTO, see p. 434) on its establishment in 1995. The country is also a member of the Organisation for Economic Co-operation and Development (OECD, see p. 379). Austria participates in the Partnership for Peace framework of the North Atlantic Treaty Organization (NATO, see p. 370). Austria hosts the International Atomic Energy Agency (IAEA, see p. 117) and the Organization of Petroleum Exporting Countries (OPEC, see p. 408).

ECONOMIC AFFAIRS

In 2012, according to estimates by the World Bank, Austria's gross national income (GNI), measured at average 2010–12 prices, was US $407,585m., equivalent to $48,160 per head (or $44,100 per head on an international purchasing-power parity basis). During 2003–12 the population grew at an estimated average rate of only 0.5% per year, while gross domestic product (GDP) per head increased, in real terms, at an average annual rate of 1.2%. According to the World Bank, overall GDP grew, in real terms, at an average annual rate of 1.7% in 2003–12; in 2012 GDP increased by 0.8%, measured at constant prices and according to chain-linked methodologies.

The contribution of agriculture (including hunting, forestry and fishing) to GDP was 1.6% in 2012. In that year, according to official data, 4.9% of the employed labour force were engaged in the agricultural sector. The principal crops are sugar beet, maize, wheat and barley. According to World Bank estimates, the GDP of the agricultural sector increased, in real terms, at an average annual rate of 2.3% in 2003–10; agricultural GDP declined by 4.3% in 2009, but increased, by 0.1%, in 2010. According to chain-linked methodologies, agricultural GDP increased by 13.9% in 2011, but decreased by 8.0% in 2012.

Industry (including mining and quarrying, manufacturing, construction and power) contributed 28.6% of GDP in 2012; in that year, according to official data, 26.2% of the employed labour force worked in industry (including manufacturing, mining and quarrying, electricity, water supply, sewerage and waste management and construction). According to World Bank estimates, industrial GDP increased, in real terms, at an average annual rate of 1.6% in 2003–10; it declined by 10.6% in 2009, but increased by 2.9% in 2010.

In 2009 mining and quarrying contributed 0.4% of GDP. According to official data, the sector employed 0.2% of the employed labour force in 2012. The most important indigenous mineral resource is iron ore (2.1m. metric tons were mined in 2011). Austria also has deposits of petroleum, natural gas, magnesite and tungsten. Austria is one of the world's leading producers of sand and gravel. According to UN estimates, the GDP of the mining sector (including power) increased, in real terms, at an average annual rate of 2.5% in 2002–11; GDP of the sector increased by 8.2% in 2011.

In 2012 manufacturing (including mining and quarrying) contributed 18.7% of GDP and, according to official data, engaged 15.8% of the employed labour force. According to World Bank estimates, the GDP of the manufacturing sector increased, in real terms, at an average annual rate of 2.6% during 2003–10; it declined by 14.3% in 2009, but expanded by 6.7% in 2010. In 2012, according to chain-linked methodologies, manufacturing and mining and quarrying GDP increased by 1.1%.

Construction contributed 6.8% of GDP in 2012. According to official data, the sector engaged 9.1% of the employed labour force in that year. According to UN estimates, the GDP of the construction sector decreased, in real terms, at an average annual rate of 0.1% in 2002–11; it declined by 2.5% in 2010, but increased by 3.5% in 2011. In 2012, according to chain-linked methodologies, construction GDP increased by 0.8%.

Hydroelectric power resources provide the major domestic source of energy, accounting for 61.4% of total electricity production in 2012, followed by gas (15.0%), coal (9.7%) and petroleum (1.2%). Austria is heavily dependent on imports of energy, mainly from Eastern Europe. Fuel imports accounted for 12.3% of the total cost of imports in 2011.

The services sector contributed 69.8% of GDP in 2012. In that year, according to official data, the sector engaged 68.9% of the employed labour force. Tourism has traditionally been a leading source of revenue, providing receipts of an estimated US $18,894m. in 2012 (excluding passenger transport). Real estate and business services accounted for 18.9% of GDP in 2012, while wholesale and retail trade contributed 12.6%. According to World Bank estimates, the GDP of the services sector increased, in real terms, at an average annual rate of 1.8% in 2003–10; it fell by 1.3% in 2009, but grew by 1.9% in 2010.

In 2012, according to the IMF, Austria recorded a visible merchandise trade deficit of US $4,196m., while there was a surplus of $6,394m. on the current account of the balance of payments. According to official figures, in 2012 the principal source of imports was Germany (37.6%); other major suppliers were Italy, Switzerland (including Liechtenstein) and the People's Republic of China. Principal markets for exports were Germany (30.6%), Italy, the USA and Switzerland (including Liechtenstein). The principal exports in 2012 were machinery and transport equipment, basic manufactures, miscellaneous manufactured articles, chemicals and related products, and food and live animals. In the same year, the principal imports were machinery and transport equipment, basic manufactures, miscellaneous manufactured articles, mineral fuels, chemicals and related products, food and live animals, and crude materials.

In 2012 there was a general government deficit of €7,818m., equivalent to 2.5% of GDP. Austria's general government gross debt was €227,431m. in 2012, equivalent to 74.1% of GDP. The average annual rate of inflation was 2.1% in 2005–12. Consumer prices increased by 2.5% in 2012. In 2012 4.3% of the labour force were unemployed.

Austria is a small, wealthy country with an open economy, which is largely dependent on the export of manufactured products and is closely integrated with the German industry sector (particularly the machinery and automotive sector). Following strong GDP growth in 2004–07, Austria's economic performance was adversely affected from late 2008 by the global economic crisis. Austrian banks suffered from a lack of availability of credit and their exposure to the economies of Central and Eastern Europe, where the impact of the international downturn had been particularly severe. Despite the introduction of stimulatory measures, GDP contracted by 3.8% in 2009, representing the worst performance since the Second World War, largely owing to a decline in exports. Fiscal measures had a severely detrimental effect on state finances. The budget deficit, which had been equivalent to 0.9% of GDP in 2008, increased to 4.1% in 2009, while public debt, which had declined to 60.2% of GDP in 2007, close to the EU limit of 60%, rose to 69.2% in 2009. The economy returned to growth in 2010, of 2.1%, primarily owing to a recovery in exports. However, public debt and the budget deficit rose further, to 72.0% and 4.5% of GDP, respectively. Austerity measures led to a significant narrowing in the budget deficit in 2011, to 2.5% of GDP, but public debt increased to 72.3% of GDP. GDP growth rose to 2.7% in 2011, according to chain-linked methodologies, despite slowing in the second half of the year owing to weaker external demand. In November 2011 the central bank announced stricter capital requirements for banks and a limit on the loan-to-deposit ratio of 110% for lending in Central and Eastern Europe. Nevertheless, in January 2012, amid continued concerns regarding the sovereign debt crisis in the eurozone, Austria's credit rating was downgraded by the agency Standard & Poor's. In March Parliament adopted an austerity plan, aimed at achieving a balanced budget by 2016, which envisaged reductions in expenditure, notably affecting civil service pay, public pensions and state-run companies, as well as new taxation measures and savings through social welfare reform. Furthermore, as a result of an agreement concluded with Switzerland in the following month, the Austrian Government generated significant additional revenue in 2013 by levying a withholding tax on funds held by Austrian citizens in undeclared Swiss bank accounts; a similar accord with Liechtenstein was signed in January 2013 and came into force in January 2014. Although public debt rose to 74.1% of GDP in 2012 and GDP growth was estimated to have decelerated to 0.8% in 2012 and further to only 0.4% in 2013, Austria's economic performance remained relatively strong compared with other eurozone countries, with unemployment—although rising slightly to 4.7% in 2013—staying the lowest in the EU. It was predicted that GDP growth would recover to reach some 1.8% in 2014, with expectations of a strengthening of exports and domestic consumption and a decrease in inflation (helped by falling fuel prices) and unemployment. Moreover, with increased tax revenue and a disciplined approach to public expenditure, the Government looked set to achieve its goal of returning to a balanced budget by 2016.

PUBLIC HOLIDAYS

2015: 1 January (New Year's Day), 6 January (Epiphany), 6 April (Easter Monday), 1 May (Labour Day), 14 May (Ascension Day), 25 May (Whit Monday), 4 June (Corpus Christi), 15 August (Assumption), 26 October (National Holiday), 1 November (All Saints' Day), 8 December (Immaculate Conception), 25 December (Christmas Day), 26 December (St Stephen's Day).

Statistical Survey

Sources (unless otherwise stated): Statistik Austria, Hintere Zollamtsstr. 2B, 1033 Vienna; tel. (1) 711-28-76-55; fax (1) 711-28-77-28; e-mail info@statistik.gv.at; internet www.statistik.at; Austrian National Bank, Postfach 61, Otto-Wagner-Pl. 3, 1090 Vienna; tel. (1) 404-20-0; fax (1) 404-20-66-96; e-mail oenb.info@oenb.co.at; internet www.oenb.at.

Area and Population

AREA, POPULATION AND DENSITY

Area (sq km)	83,871*
Population (census results)†	
15 May 2001	8,032,926
31 October 2011	
Males	4,093,938
Females	4,308,002
Total	8,401,940
Population (official estimates at 1 January)	
2012	8,408,121
2013	8,451,860
Density (per sq km) at 1 January 2013	100.8

* 32,383 sq miles.
† Figures include all foreign workers.

POPULATION BY AGE AND SEX
(official estimates at 1 January 2013)

	Males	Females	Total
0–14	625,531	593,832	1,219,363
15–64	2,853,680	2,851,560	5,705,240
65 and over	644,411	882,846	1,527,257
Total	4,123,622	4,328,238	8,451,860

PROVINCES
(official population estimates at 1 January 2013)

	Area (sq km)	Population	Density (per sq km)	Capital (with population)
Burgenland	3,965.5	286,691	72.3	Eisenstadt (13,351)
Kärnten (Carinthia)	9,536.0	555,473	58.3	Klagenfurt (95,450)
Niederösterreich (Lower Austria)	19,177.8	1,618,592	84.4	Sankt Pölten (51,926)
Oberösterreich (Upper Austria)	11,981.9	1,418,498	118.4	Linz (191,501)
Salzburg	7,154.2	531,898	74.3	Salzburg (145,871)
Steiermark (Styria)	16,391.9	1,210,971	73.9	Graz (265,778)
Tirol (Tyrol)	12,647.7	715,888	56.6	Innsbruck (122,458)
Vorarlberg	2,601.5	372,603	143.2	Bregenz (127,676)
Wien (Vienna)	414.7	1,741,246	4,198.8	—
Total	83,871.1	8,451,860	100.8	—

PRINCIPAL TOWNS
(official population estimates at 1 January 2013)

Wien (Vienna, the capital)	1,741,246	Klagenfurt	95,450
Graz	265,778	Villach	59,646
Linz	191,501	Wels	58,882
Salzburg	145,871	Sankt Pölten	51,926
Innsbruck	122,458	Dornbirn	46,425

BIRTHS, MARRIAGES AND DEATHS

	Registered live births		Registered marriages		Registered deaths	
	Number	Rate (per 1,000)	Number	Rate (per 1,000)	Number	Rate (per 1,000)
2005	78,190	9.5	39,153	4.8	75,189	9.1
2006	77,914	9.4	36,923	4.5	74,295	9.0
2007	76,250	9.2	35,996	4.3	74,625	9.0
2008	77,752	9.3	35,223	4.2	75,083	9.0
2009	76,344	9.1	35,469	4.2	77,381	9.3
2010	78,742	9.4	37,545	4.5	77,199	9.2
2011	78,109	9.3	36,426	4.3	76,479	9.1
2012	78,952	9.4	38,592	4.6	79,436	9.4

Life expectancy (years at birth): 81.0 (males 78.3; females 83.9) in 2011 (Source: World Bank, World Development Indicators database).

IMMIGRATION AND EMIGRATION

Immigrants from:	2010	2011	2012
Europe	96,168	104,697	116,637
Bosnia and Herzegovina	2,526	3,872	4,133
Croatia	1,894	1,908	2,008
Germany	17,966	17,410	17,774
Hungary	6,412	9,250	13,066
Poland	4,037	6,428	7,105
Romania	11,344	12,907	13,362
Serbia and Montenegro*	7,210	6,145	6,833
Slovakia	3,997	5,314	5,957
Turkey	4,258	3,812	4,088
Africa	3,135	3,685	3,808
Americas	3,330	3,627	3,704
Asia	9,566	12,104	15,705
China, People's Republic	1,297	1,403	1,521
Iran	1,627	1,349	2,409
Oceania	300	334	306
Stateless, undeclared or unknown	192	172	198
Total	112,691	124,619	140,358

Emigrants to:	2010	2011	2012
Europe	77,489	81,128	83,688
Bosnia and Herzegovina	1,996	2,650	2,597
Croatia	1,876	1,678	1,547
Germany	10,331	11,230	11,545
Hungary	4,249	5,310	6,457
Poland	2,994	3,263	3,686
Romania	6,358	7,707	8,004
Serbia and Montenegro*	5,714	5,877	5,046
Slovakia	3,089	3,430	3,538
Turkey	3,137	3,258	3,151
Africa	2,916	2,604	2,428
Americas	2,812	2,878	2,967
Asia	7,659	6,841	7,003
Oceania	271	268	280
Stateless, undeclared or unknown	228	195	195
Total	91,375	93,914	96,561

* Although the federation of Serbia and Montenegro was dissolved in 2006, official reporting of Austrian immigration and emigration data with the successor states has continued to be aggregated.

Note: Totals for immigration include Austrian nationals returning from permanent residence abroad: 15,795 in 2010; 14,698 in 2011; 14,753 in 2012.

ECONOMICALLY ACTIVE POPULATION
('000 persons aged 15 years and over)

	2010	2011	2012
Agriculture, hunting, forestry and fishing	214.6	219.3	204.6
Mining and quarrying	10.0	10.9	9.2
Manufacturing	624.5	653.9	660.1
Electricity, gas and water supply	45.4	48.7	44.3
Construction	340.7	363.8	381.0
Wholesale and retail trade; repair of motor vehicles, motorcycles and personal and household goods	624.9	629.1	626.0
Hotels and restaurants	253.2	251.1	265.0
Transport, storage and communications	306.6	308.9	315.4
Financial intermediation	148.6	151.3	148.4
Real estate, renting and business activities	395.1	399.3	399.5
Public administration and defence; compulsory social security	278.4	274.3	275.1
Education	261.0	256.5	263.4
Health and social work	395.1	385.4	395.0
Other community, social and personal service activities	179.4	176.0	180.6
Private households with employed persons	10.8	9.2	10.5
Extra-territorial organizations and bodies	8.4	6.2	5.8
Total employed	4,096.5	4,143.9	4,183.8
Unemployed	188.2	179.0	189.1
Total labour force	4,284.7	4,322.9	4,372.9
Males	2,302.2	2,320.8	2,341.9
Females	1,982.5	2,002.1	2,031.0

Health and Welfare

KEY INDICATORS

Total fertility rate (children per woman, 2011)	1.4
Under-5 mortality rate (per 1,000 live births, 2011)	4
HIV/AIDS (% of persons aged 15–49, 2011)	0.4
Physicians (per 1,000 head, 2010)	4.9
Hospital beds (per 1,000 head, 2009)	7.7
Health expenditure (2010): US $ per head (PPP)	4,398
Health expenditure (2010): % of GDP	11.0
Health expenditure (2010): public (% of total)	76.2
Total carbon dioxide emissions ('000 metric tons, 2010)	66,897.1
Carbon dioxide emissions per head (metric tons, 2010)	8.0
Human Development Index (2012): ranking	18
Human Development Index (2012): value	0.895

For sources and definitions, see explanatory note on p. vi.

Agriculture

PRINCIPAL CROPS
('000 metric tons)

	2010	2011	2012
Wheat	1,517.8	1,781.8	1,275.5
Barley	778.0	859.4	662.5
Maize	2,168.8	2,453.1	2,351.4
Rye	163.6	202.1	204.7
Oats	97.9	109.8	93.5
Triticale (wheat-rye hybrid)	230.5	228.1	220.1
Potatoes	671.7	816.1	665.4
Sugar beet	3,131.7	3,456.2	3,133.2
Peas, dry	32.8	36.4	14.6
Sunflower seed	66.5	73.7	53.1
Rapeseed	170.6	179.7	148.9
Cabbages and other brassicas	91.9	102.3	93.3
Lettuce	47.6	47.4	54.0
Onions, dry	154.1	200.5	135.4
Carrots and turnips	85.6	109.0	98.3
Apples*	489.0	546.7	471.4
Pears*	120.7	244.0	193.9
Plums	78.3*	103.2*	71.9
Grapes	231.7	375.3	287.3

* Unofficial figure(s).

Aggregate production ('000 metric tons, may include official, semi-official or estimated data): Total cereals 5,035.6 in 2010, 5,704.7 in 2011, 4,877.3 in 2012; Total roots and tubers 671.7 in 2010, 816.1 in 2011, 665.4 in 2012; Total vegetables (incl. melons) 591.3 in 2010, 705.8 in 2011; 617.9 in 2012; Total fruits (excl. melons) 1,030.4 in 2010, 1,419.9 in 2011; 1,116.6 in 2012.

Source: FAO.

LIVESTOCK
('000 head at December)

	2010	2011	2012
Horses*	83.0	86.0	86.5
Cattle	2,026.3	2,013.3	1,976.5
Pigs	3,137.0	3,134.2	3,004.9
Sheep	344.7	358.4	361.2
Goats	68.2	71.8	72.4
Chickens	15,650†	16,000†	16,250*
Ducks	79†	80†	82*
Geese	24†	20†	20*
Turkeys	616†	606†	600*

* FAO estimates.
† Unofficial figure.

LIVESTOCK PRODUCTS
('000 metric tons)

	2010	2011	2012
Cattle meat	226.7	222.2	222.2
Sheep meat	6.1	6.6	6.6
Pig meat	545.8	544.2	530.3
Chicken meat	107.2	112.3	108.5
Cows' milk	3,257.7	3,307.1	3,382.1
Sheep's milk	9.5	10.6	10.6
Goats' milk	18.7	19.3	20.3
Hen eggs	94.6	102.7	106.0
Honey	4.7	6.0	5.0

Source: FAO.

Forestry

ROUNDWOOD REMOVALS
('000 cubic metres, excl. bark)

	2010	2011	2012
Sawlogs, veneer logs and logs for sleepers	10,167	10,386	9,654
Pitprops (mine timber), pulpwood, and other industrial wood	3,114	3,245	3,178
Fuel wood	4,550	5,065	5,189
Total	17,831	18,696	18,021

Source: FAO.

SAWNWOOD PRODUCTION
('000 cubic metres, incl. railway sleepers)

	2010	2011	2012
Coniferous (softwood)	9,445	9,485	8,793
Broadleaved (hardwood)	158	151	159
Total	9,603	9,636	8,952

Source: FAO.

Fishing

(metric tons, live weight)

	2009	2010	2011*
Capture	350	350	350
Freshwater fishes	350	350	350
Aquaculture	2,141	2,167	2,160
Common carp	345	348	350
Rainbow trout	1,246	1,211	1,200
Brook trout	244	256	260
Total catch	2,491	2,517	2,510

* FAO estimates.

Source: FAO.

Mining

('000 metric tons unless otherwise indicated)

	2009	2010	2011
Crude petroleum ('000 barrels)	6,371	6,167	6,000*
Iron ore:			
gross weight	2,002	2,069	2,050*
Magnesite (crude)	545	757	800*
Tungsten, concentrate (metric tons)†	345	430	424
Gypsum and anhydrite (crude)	911	872	900*
Kaolin (crude)	84	59	60*
Basalt	1,744	1,473	1,500*
Dolomite	3,967	3,915	3,900*
Limestone and marble	22,074	21,190	22,000*
Quartz and quartzite	377	294	300*
Natural gas (million cu metres)	1,559	1,713	1,750

* Estimate.

† Figures refer to metal content.

Source: US Geological Survey.

Industry

SELECTED PRODUCTS
('000 metric tons unless otherwise indicated)

	2008	2009	2010
Wheat flour	573	573	n.a.
Mechanical wood pulp	380	303	359
Chemical and semi-chemical wood pulp	1,335	1,235	1,344
Newsprint	420	299	406
Other printing and writing paper	2,648	2,248	2,368
Other paper and paperboard	2,085	2,058	2,235
Motor spirit (petrol)	1,595	1,652	1,353
Jet fuel	472	313	476
Distillate fuel oils	3,945	3,567	n.a.
Residual fuel oils	769	852	n.a.
Cement*	5,309	4,646	4,254
Crude steel*	7,594	5,662	7,206
Refined copper—unwrought: secondary*	107	96	114
Passenger motor cars (number)	125,836	56,913	86,310
Electric energy (million kWh)	66,877	69,088	71,127

* Data from the US Geological Survey.

Sources: FAO; UN Industrial Commodity Statistics Database; IRF, *World Road Statistics*.

2011 ('000 metric tons): Mechanical wood pulp 380; Chemical and semi-chemical wood pulp 1,336; Newsprint 421; Other printing and writing paper 2,284; Other paper and paperboard 2,196; Cement 4,427; Crude steel 7,474; Refined copper—unwrought: secondary 112.5 (Sources: FAO; US Geological Survey).

2012 ('000 metric tons): Mechanical wood pulp 390; Chemical and semi-chemical wood pulp 1,337; Newsprint 391; Other printing and writing paper 2,422; Other paper and paperboard 2,190 (Source: FAO).

Finance

CURRENCY AND EXCHANGE RATES

Monetary Units
100 cent = 1 euro (€).

Sterling and Dollar Equivalents (31 December 2013)
£1 sterling = 1.194 euros;
US $1 = 0.0.725 euros;
€10 = £8.37 = $13.79.

Average Exchange Rate (euros per US $)

2011	0.7194
2012	0.7783
2013	0.7532

Note: The national currency was formerly the Schilling. From the introduction of the euro, with Austrian participation, on 1 January 1999, a fixed exchange rate of €1 = 13.7603 Schilling was in operation. Euro notes and coins were introduced on 1 January 2002. The euro and local currency circulated alongside each other until 28 February, after which the euro became the sole legal tender.

GENERAL GOVERNMENT BUDGET
(€ '000 million)

Revenue	2010	2011	2012
Taxes	77,830	82,119	86,033
Taxes on income, profits and capital gains	36,441	39,049	41,191
Taxes on production and imports	42,069	43,842	45,580
Social contributions	46,588	48,659	50,901
Other current transfers	3,932	3,959	3,973
Capital transfers	179	257	220
Other revenue	9,236	9,586	9,791
Total	137,765	144,579	150,917

Expenditure	2010	2011	2012
General public services	19,518	19,914	20,566
Defence	2,122	2,155	2,124
Public order and safety	4,335	4,418	4,593
Economic affairs	16,349	15,963	17,946
Environmental protection	1,692	1,529	1,645
Housing and community amenities	1,800	1,776	1,833
Health	23,323	23,278	24,358
Recreation, culture and religion	2,906	2,923	2,992
Education	16,332	16,733	17,088
Social protection	62,216	63,191	65,590
Total	150,593	151,881	158,735

INTERNATIONAL RESERVES
(US $ million at 31 December)

	2010	2011	2012
Gold*	12,695	14,174	14,979
IMF special drawing rights	2,691	2,594	2,570
Reserve position in IMF	723	1,322	1,691
Foreign exchange	6,175	7,071	7,972
Total	22,284	25,161	27,212

* Eurosystem valuation.

Source: IMF, *International Financial Statistics*.

MONEY SUPPLY
(incl. shares, depository corporations, national residency criteria, € '000 million at 31 December)

	2010	2011	2012
Currency issued	22.76	24.04	24.75
Oesterreichische Nationalbank	–2.16	–8.76	–17.20
Demand deposits	109.50	112.38	128.77
Other deposits	167.77	173.32	162.54
Securities other than shares	252.07	250.01	228.36
Money market fund shares	2.34	1.22	0.42
Other items (net)	55.65	58.90	78.99
Total	610.10	619.88	623.84

Source: IMF, *International Financial Statistics*.

COST OF LIVING
(Consumer Price Index; base: 2005 = 100)

	2010	2011	2012
Food and non-alcoholic beverages	113.6	118.4	122.2
Alcoholic beverages, tobacco	111.1	115.7	118.5
Housing, water, energy	117.1	120.9	124.8
Communication	87.7	88.5	88.4
Household goods/furnishings and operations	108.2	109.9	112.5
Clothing and footwear	106.2	109.4	110.8
Recreation and culture	100.1	102.1	103.1
Health	108.5	110.7	112.4
Education	93.4	97.2	101.4
Restaurants and hotels	112.4	116.3	119.5
Transport	107.4	113.4	116.3
Other goods and services	113.8	117.4	120.7
All items	109.5	113.1	115.9

NATIONAL ACCOUNTS
(€ '000 million at current prices)

National Income and Product

	2010	2011	2012
Compensation of employees	142.62	148.15	154.25
Gross operating surplus and mixed income	111.58	118.69	119.32
Gross domestic product (GDP) at factor cost	254.21	266.84	273.57
Taxes, less subsidies, on production and imports	30.96	32.40	33.43
GDP in market prices	285.17	299.24	307.00
Net primary incomes from abroad	0.21	–2.03	–1.89
Gross national income (GNI)	285.37	297.21	305.11
Less Consumption of fixed capital	45.73	47.39	49.42
Net national income	239.64	249.82	255.69
Net current transfers from abroad	–2.39	–2.36	2.52
Net national disposable income	237.25	247.46	258.20

Expenditure on the Gross Domestic Product

	2010	2011	2012
Private final consumption expenditure	156.91	163.88	169.02
Government final consumption expenditure	55.53	56.77	58.36
Gross capital formation	60.03	68.87	69.62
Total domestic expenditure	272.47	289.52	297.00
Exports of goods and services	155.09	171.47	175.59
Less Imports of goods and services	142.63	162.52	165.72
Statistical discrepancy	0.24	0.77	0.13
GDP in market prices	285.17	299.24	307.00
GDP in chain linked prices	106.7	109.8	110.7

Gross Domestic Product by Economic Activity

	2010	2011	2012
Agriculture, hunting, forestry and fishing	3.89	4.53	4.43
Mining and quarrying and manufacturing	48.36	51.44	52.02
Electricity, gas and water	8.16	8.48	8.42
Construction	17.35	17.81	18.88
Wholesale and retail trade; repair of motor vehicles, motorcycles and personal and household goods	33.81	34.94	34.95
Restaurants and hotels	12.59	13.23	13.87
Transport, storage and communications	19.71	21.32	22.05
Finance and insurance	12.63	13.70	13.52
Real estate and business services*	47.74	50.46	52.52
Public administration and defence	15.39	15.61	16.01
Other services	38.02	39.17	40.91
Sub-total	257.65	270.69	277.59
Taxes, less subsidies, on products	27.51	28.55	29.42
GDP in market prices	285.17	299.24	307.00

* Including imputed rents of owner-occupied dwellings.

BALANCE OF PAYMENTS
(US $ million)

	2010	2011	2012
Exports of goods	145,518	169,901	159,224
Imports of goods	–145505	–175,433	–163,420
Balance on goods	14	–5,532	–4,196
Exports of services	53,328	59,263	58,143
Imports of services	–39,867	–45,313	–44,971
Balance on goods and services	13,475	8,418	8,975
Primary income received	39,344	49,182	38,757
Primary income paid	–37,251	–48,237	–38,629
Balance on goods, services and primary income	15,568	9,362	9,103
Secondary income received	4,660	5,118	5,002
Secondary income paid	–7,078	–7,870	–7,711

—continued	2010	2011	2012
Current balance	13,149	6,610	6,394
Capital account (net)	277	–542	–550
Direct investment assets	15,334	–38,000	–17,574
Direct investment liabilities	–25,304	23,676	4,144
Portfolio investment assets	–8,821	11,478	14,406
Portfolio investment liabilities	–1,059	11,051	–6,766
Financial derivatives and employee stock options (net)	–178	1,057	3,366
Other investment assets	22,965	–32,933	1,950
Other investment liabilities	–6,371	20,086	–4,518
Net errors and omissions	–8,557	–1,478	391
Reserves and related items	1,435	1,005	1,244

Source: IMF, *International Financial Statistics*.

External Trade

Note: Austria's customs territory excludes Mittelberg im Kleinen Walsertal (in Vorarlberg) and Jungholz (in Tyrol). The figures also exclude trade in silver specie and monetary gold.

SELECTED COMMODITIES
(distribution by SITC, € million)

Imports c.i.f.	2010	2011	2012
Food and live animals	6,679	7,422	7,914
Crude materials (inedible) except fuels	5,811	6,708	6,308
Metalliferous ores and metal scrap	2,583	3,148	2,868
Mineral fuels, lubricants, etc.	12,167	15,660	17,297
Crude petroleum and bituminous oils	7,716	9,725	10,919
Gas, natural and manufactured	2,923	3,785	4,399
Chemicals and related products	14,441	16,163	16,448
Medicinal and pharmaceutical products	5,476	6,008	6,386
Basic manufactures	18,060	21,516	20,310
Iron and steel	3,359	4,189	3,799
Metal manufactures	3,238	4,389	3,594
Machinery and transport equipment	36,958	41,714	42,068
General industrial machinery and equipment	5,923	6,598	6,606
Electrical machinery, apparatus and appliances, etc.	6,677	7,294	7,472
Road vehicles	10,761	12,840	12,543
Miscellaneous manufactured articles	16,499	18,056	18,108
Total (incl. others)	113,652	131,008	131,982

Exports f.o.b.	2010	2011	2012
Food and live animals	5,671	6,358	6,677
Crude materials (inedible) except fuels	3,692	3,988	3,833
Mineral fuels, lubricants, etc.	3,511	4,112	4,524
Chemicals and related products	14,167	15,617	16,456
Medicinal and pharmaceutical products	6,207	6,573	7,286
Basic manufactures	25,162	28,515	28,198
Paper, paperboard and articles thereof	3,747	4,031	4,191
Iron and steel	6,083	7,372	7,105
Metal manufactures	5,443	6,291	6,420
Machinery and transport equipment	41,365	46,072	46,963
Power-generating machinery and equipment	6,016	6,693	6,448
Machinery specialized for particular industries	5,651	6,672	7,101
General industrial machinery and equipment	6,648	7,372	7,825
Electrical machinery, apparatus and appliances, etc.	7,967	8,699	8,402
Road vehicles	8,711	10,264	10,201
Miscellaneous manufactured articles	12,924	13,970	13,834
Total (incl. others)	109,373	121,774	123,544

PRINCIPAL TRADING PARTNERS
(€ million)*

Imports c.i.f.	2010	2011	2012
Belgium-Luxembourg	2,017	2,279	2,241
China, People's Republic	5,428	6,394	6,751
Czech Republic	4,186	4,879	4,894
France	3,234	3,760	3,727
Germany	44,851	50,050	49,587
Hungary	3,132	3,654	3,761
Italy	7,690	8,527	8,209
Japan	1,777	1,954	1,780
Kazakhstan	873	1,401	1,434
Netherlands	3,231	3,670	3,591
Poland	1,896	2,433	2,643
Russia	2,317	3,333	4,094
Slovakia	2,630	3,240	3,179
Slovenia	1,256	1,619	1,741
Spain	1,772	2,018	2,032
Sweden	1,247	1,391	1,403
Switzerland-Liechtenstein	5,941	7,234	7,063
United Kingdom	1,728	2,018	2,183
USA	3,261	3,764	4,114
Total (incl. others)	113,652	131,008	131,982

Exports f.o.b.	2010	2011	2012
Belgium-Luxembourg	1,632	1,707	1,885
China, People's Republic	2,807	2,919	3,031
Czech Republic	4,145	4,763	4,471
France	4,557	4,975	5,642
Germany	34,530	38,042	37,843
Hungary	3,345	3,775	3,688
Italy	8,576	9,345	8,447
Japan	1,023	1,294	1,313
Netherlands	1,719	1,905	1,869
Poland	2,745	3,409	3,440
Romania	1,691	1,865	1,948
Russia	2,547	2,936	3,185
Slovakia	2,276	2,431	2,660
Slovenia	2,221	2,292	2,295
Spain	2,003	1,958	1,862
Sweden	1,191	1,405	1,296
Switzerland-Liechtenstein	5,199	6,503	6,693
Turkey	1,062	1,248	1,226
United Kingdom	3,319	3,553	3,406
USA	4,958	6,389	6,932
Total (incl. others)	109,373	121,774	123,544

* Imports by country of production; exports by country of consumption.

Transport

RAILWAYS
(traffic, Federal Railways only)

	2010	2011	2012
Number of passengers carried ('000)	242,100	243,981	262,891
Passenger-km (millions)	10,737	10,962	11,323
Domestic freight gross ton-km (millions)	19,833	20,345	19,499
Freight tons carried ('000)	107,670	107,587	100,452

ROAD TRAFFIC
(motor vehicles in use at 31 December)

	2010	2011	2012
Passenger cars	4,441,027	4,513,421	4,584,202
Buses and coaches	9,648	9,602	9,546
Goods vehicles	379,965	390,704	400,203
Motorcycles	406,822	425,079	446,347
Mopeds and motor scooters	321,030	318,350	316,045

SHIPPING

Flag Registered Fleet
(at 31 December)

	2011	2012	2013
Number of vessels	9	9	10
Total displacement ('000 grt)	5.9	5.9	2.2

Source: Lloyd's List Intelligence (www.lloydslistintelligence.com).

International Freight Traffic on the Danube
('000 metric tons, excl. transit traffic)

	2010	2011	2012
Goods loaded	1,667.8	1,545.7	1,623.7
Goods unloaded	6,199.9	5,564.2	5,438.8

CIVIL AVIATION
(traffic, millions)

	2010	2011
Kilometres flown	159	172
Passengers carried	13.5	17.2
Passenger-km	17,528	19,745
Total ton-km	2,135	2,366

Source: UN, *Statistical Yearbook*.

Passengers carried ('000): 15,560 in 2012 (Source: World Bank, World Development Indicators database).

Tourism

FOREIGN TOURIST ARRIVALS
(by country of origin, '000)*

	2010	2011	2012
Belgium	461.8	488.8	494.0
Czech Republic	569.3	603.6	619.3
France (incl. Monaco)	499.9	522.0	519.5
Germany	10,706.2	10,929.7	11,411.6
Hungary	442.2	466.9	472.8
Italy	1,067.7	1,087.0	1,060.1
Netherlands	1,617.7	1,644.6	1,714.5
Switzerland-Liechtenstein	1,053.6	1,199.0	1,275.6
United Kingdom	731.4	709.2	741.0
USA	505.4	496.1	531.5
Total (incl. others)	22,004.3	23,012.0	24,150.8

* Arrivals at accommodation establishments.

Tourism receipts (US $ million, excl. passenger transport): 18,596 in 2010; 19,860 in 2011; 18,894 in 2012 (provisional) (Source: World Tourism Organization).

Communications Media

	2010	2011	2012
Radio licences issued	3,440,910	3,482,711	3,515,038
Television licences issued	3,251,697	3,264,478	3,331,030
Telephones ('000 main lines in use)	3,398	3,388	3,342
Mobile cellular telephones ('000 subscribers)	12,241	13,023	13,588
Internet subscribers ('000)	2,305	2,461	n.a.
Broadband subscribers ('000)	2,076	2,139	2,127
Daily newspapers:			
titles	29	29	29
circulation ('000)	5,231	5,213	5,224
Weekly newspapers	230	262	259

Source: partly International Telecommunication Union.

Education

(2011/12 unless otherwise indicated)

	Institutions	Staff	Students
Pre-primary*	8,322	51,656†	326,444
General primary and secondary	6,120	124,972	1,153,912
Compulsory vocational	158	5,087	134,282
Secondary technical and vocational	794	22,819	215,201
Teacher training:			
second level	39	1,705	14,824
third level‡	28	2,799	11,535
Universities §	22	20,393	272,061
Tertiary vocational‡§	205	3,942	28,426

* 2012/13 figures; including crèches and day care centres.
† Including non-teaching staff.
‡ 2006/07 figures.
§ Excluding private institutions.

Pupil-teacher ratio (primary education, UNESCO estimate): 10.9 in 2010/11 (Source: UNESCO Institute for Statistics).

Directory

The Government

HEAD OF STATE

Federal President: Dr HEINZ FISCHER (sworn in 8 July 2004; re-elected 25 April 2010).

FEDERAL GOVERNMENT
(April 2014)

A coalition of the Sozialdemokratische Partei Österreichs (SPÖ—Social Democratic Party of Austria) and the Österreichische Volkspartei (ÖVP—Austrian People's Party).

Federal Chancellor: WERNER FAYMANN (SPÖ).

Vice-Chancellor and Federal Minister of Finance: Dr MICHAEL SPINDELEGGER (ÖVP).

Chancellery Minister: JOSEF OSTERMAYER (SPÖ).

Federal Minister of Agriculture, Forestry, Environment and Water Management: ANDRÄ RUPPRECHTER (ÖVP).

Federal Minister of Defence and Sports: GERALD KLUG (SPÖ).

Federal Minister of Science, Research and Economy: Dr REINHOLD MITTERLEHNER (ÖVP).

Federal Minister for Education and Women's Affairs: GABRIELE HEINISCH-HOSEK (SPÖ).

Federal Minister for Europe, Integration and Foreign Affairs: SEBASTIAN KURZ (ÖVP).

Federal Minister of Health: ALOIS STÖGER (SPÖ).

Federal Minister for Justice: Dr WOLFGANG BRANDSTETTER (Ind.).

Federal Minister of the Interior: JOHANNA MIKL-LEITNER (ÖVP).

Federal Minister of Labour, Social Affairs and Consumer Protection: RUDOLF HUNDSTORFER (SPÖ).

Federal Minister for Transport, Innovation and Technology: DORIS BURES (SPÖ).

Federal Minister for Family and Youth: Dr SOPHIE KARMASIN (ÖVP).

MINISTRIES

Office of the Federal President: Hofburg, Ballhauspl. 1014, Vienna; tel. (1) 534-22; fax (1) 535-65-12; e-mail heinz.fischer@hofburg.at; internet www.hofburg.at.

Office of the Federal Chancellor: Ballhauspl. 2, 1014 Vienna; tel. (1) 531-15-0; fax (1) 535-03-38-0; e-mail post@bka.gv.at; internet www.bka.gv.at.

Federal Ministry of Agriculture, Forestry, Environment and Water Management: Stubenring 1, 1012 Vienna; tel. (1) 711-00-21-27; fax (1) 513-16-79-99-00; e-mail service@lebensministerium.at; internet www.lebensministerium.at.

Federal Ministry of Defence and Sports: Rossauer Lände 1, 1090 Vienna; tel. (1) 502-01-0; fax (1) 502-01-10-17-041; e-mail presse@bmlvs.gv.at; internet www.bmlv.gv.at.

Federal Ministry of Family and Youth: Hintere Zollamtsstr. 2B, 1030 Vienna; tel. (1) 711-00; e-mail service@bmfj.gv.at; internet www.bmfj.gv.at.

Federal Ministry of Education and Women's Affairs: Minoritenpl. 5, 1014 Vienna; tel. (1) 531-20-0; fax (1) 531-20-30-99; e-mail ministerium@bmbf.gv.at; internet www.bmbf.gv.at.

Federal Ministry for Europe, Integration and Foreign Affairs: Minoritenpl. 8, 1014 Vienna; tel. (5) 011-50-0; fax (5) 011-59-0; e-mail abtvi8@bmeia.gv.at; internet www.bmeia.gv.at.

Federal Ministry of Finance: Johannesgasse 5, 1010 Vienna; tel. (1) 514-33-0; fax (1) 514-33-50-70-87; e-mail buergerservice@bmf.gv.at; internet www.bmf.gv.at.

Federal Ministry of Health: Radetzkystr. 2, 1030 Vienna; tel. (1) 711-00-0; fax (1) 711-00-14-30-0; e-mail buergerservice@bmg.gv.at; internet www.bmg.gv.at.

Federal Ministry of the Interior: Herrengasse 7, Postfach 100, 1014 Vienna; tel. (1) 531-26-0; fax (1) 531-26-10-86-13; e-mail post@bmi.gv.at; internet www.bmi.gv.at.

Federal Ministry of Justice: Museumstr. 7, 1070 Vienna; tel. (1) 521-52-0; fax (1) 521-52-27-30; internet www.bmj.gv.at.

Federal Ministry of Labour, Social Affairs and Consumer Protection: Stubenring 1, 1010 Vienna; tel. (1) 711-00-0; fax (1) 711-00-14-26-6; e-mail post@bmask.gv.at; internet www.bmask.gv.at.

Federal Ministry of Science, Research and Economy: Stubenring 1, 1011 Vienna; tel. (1) 711-00-0; fax (1) 531-20-90-99; e-mail presseabteilung@bmwfw.gv.at; internet www.bmwfw.gv.at.

Federal Ministry for Transport, Innovation and Technology: Radetzkystr. 2, Postfach 3000, 1030 Vienna; tel. (1) 711-62-65-0; fax (1) 711-62-65-74-98; e-mail info@bmvit.gv.at; internet www.bmvit.gv.at.

President and Legislature

PRESIDENT

Presidential Election, 25 April 2010

Candidates	Votes	% of votes
Dr Heinz Fischer	2,508,373	79.33
Barbara Rosenkranz	481,923	15.24
Dr Rudolf Gehring	171,668	5.43
Total	3,161,964	100.00

PARLIAMENT
(Parlament)

Dr Karl Renner-Ring 3, 1017 Vienna; tel. and fax (1) 401-10-0; e-mail services@parlament.gv.at; internet www.parlament.gv.at

National Council
(Nationalrat)

President of the National Council: BARBARA PRAMMER (SPÖ).

General Election, 29 September 2013

Party	Votes	% of votes	Seats
Sozialdemokratische Partei Österreichs (SPÖ)	1,258,605	26.82	52
Österreichische Volkspartei (ÖVP)	1,125,876	23.99	47
Freiheitliche Partei Österreichs (FPÖ)	962,313	20.51	40
Die Grünen	582,657	12.42	24
Team Stronach	268,679	5.73	11
Das Neue Österreich (NEOS)	232,946	4.96	9
Bündnis Zukunft Österreich (BZÖ)	165,746	3.53	—
Kommunistische Partei Österreichs (KPÖ)	48,175	1.02	—
Piratenpartei Österreichs (PPÖ)	36,265	0.77	—
Christliche Partei Österreichs (CPÖ)	6,647	0.14	—
Others	4,998	0.11	—
Total	4,692,907	100.00	183

Federal Council
(Bundesrat)
(April 2014)

President of the Federal Council: MICHAEL LAMPEL (SPÖ) (Jan. 2014–July 2015).

Provinces	ÖVP	SPÖ	FPÖ	Die Grünen	Other	Total seats
Burgenland	1	2	—	—	—	3
Carinthia (Kärnten)	1	2	1	—	—	4
Lower Austria (Niederösterreich)	7	3	1	—	1	12
Upper Austria (Oberösterreich)	5	3	1	1	—	10
Salzburg	1	1	1	1	—	4
Styria (Steiermark)	4	4	1	—	—	9
Tyrol (Tirol)	3	1	—	1	—	5
Vorarlberg	2	—	1	—	—	3
Vienna (Wien)	1	6	3	1	—	11
Total	25	22	9	4	1	61

Governments of the Federal Provinces

BURGENLAND

Governor: HANS NIESSL (SPÖ).

President of the Provincial Assembly (Landtag): GERHARD STEIER (SPÖ).

Burgenländischer Landtag: Europapl. 1, 7000 Eisenstadt; tel. (57) 600-20-00; fax 600-20-50; e-mail post@bgld-landtag.at; internet www.bgld.gv.at/politik-verwaltung/landtag.

Election, 30 May 2010

Party	Seats
SPÖ	18
ÖVP	13
FPÖ	3
Die Grünen	1
Liste Burgenland	1
Total	**36**

CARINTHIA (KÄRNTEN)

Governor: Dr PETER KAISER (SPÖ).

President of the Provincial Assembly (Landtag): REINHART ROHR (SPÖ).

Kärntner Landtag: Landhaus, 9020 Klagenfurt; tel. (463) 577-57-20-1; fax (463) 577-57-20-0; e-mail post.landtagsamt@ktn.gv.at; internet www.kaerntner-landtag.ktn.gv.at.

Election, 3 March 2013

Party	Seats
SPÖ	14
FPK*	6
Die Grünen	5
ÖVP	5
Team Stronach	4
BZÖ	2
Total	**36**

* Die Freiheitlichen in Kärnten (FPK—fmrly the provincial branch of the BZÖ, which seceded from the federal party in January 2010). The FPK merged with the Freiheitliche Partei Österreichs (FPÖ) in June 2013 to become the FPÖ's branch in Carinthia.

LOWER AUSTRIA (NIEDERÖSTERREICH)

Governor: Dr ERWIN PRÖLL (ÖVP).

President of the Provincial Assembly (Landtag): HANS PENZ (ÖVP).

Landtag Niederösterreich: Landhauspl. 1, 3109 St. Pölten; tel. (2742) 900-51-24-31; fax (2742) 900-51-34-30; e-mail post.landtagsdirektion@noel.gv.at; internet www.landtag-noe.at.

Election, 3 March 2013

Party	Seats
ÖVP	30
SPÖ	13
Team Stronach	5
FPÖ	4
Die Grünen	4
Total	**56**

SALZBURG

Governor: WILFRIED HASLAUER (SPÖ).

President of the Provincial Assembly (Landtag): Dr BRIGITTA PALLAUF (ÖVP).

Salzburger Landtag: Chiemseehof, 5010 Salzburg; tel. (662) 804-22-23-8; fax (662) 804-22-91-0; internet www.salzburg.gv.at/pol/landtag.

Election, 5 May 2013

Party	Seats
ÖVP	11
SPÖ	9
Die Grünen	7
FPÖ	6
Team Stronach	3
Total	**36**

STYRIA (STEIERMARK)

Governor: FRANZ VOVES (SPÖ).

President of the Provincial Assembly (Landtag): FRANZ MAJCEN (ÖVP).

Landtag Steiermark: Herrengasse 16, 8010 Graz; tel. (316) 877-22-16; fax (316) 877-21-98; e-mail ltd@stmk.gv.at; internet www.landtag.steiermark.at.

Election, 26 September 2010

Party	Seats
SPÖ	23
ÖVP	22
FPÖ	6
Die Grünen	3
KPÖ	2
Total	**56**

TYROL (TIROL)

Governor: GÜNTHER PLATTER (ÖVP).

President of the Provincial Assembly (Landtag): THOMAS WIDMANN (ÖVP).

Tiroler Landtag: Eduard-Wallnöfer-Pl. 3, 6020 Innsbruck; tel. (512) 508-30-00; fax (512) 508-30-05; e-mail herwig.vanstaa@tirol.gv.at; internet www.tirol.gv.at/landtag.

Election, 28 April 2013

Party	Seats
ÖVP	16
Die Grünen	5
SPÖ	5
FPÖ	4
Vorwärts Tirol	4
Liste Fritz Dinkhauser—Bürgerforum Tirol	2
Total	**36**

UPPER AUSTRIA (OBERÖSTERREICH)

Governor: Dr JOSEF PÜHRINGER (ÖVP).

President of the Provincial Assembly (Landtag): VIKTOR SIGL (ÖVP).

Oberösterreichischer Landtag: Landhauspl. 1, 4021 Linz; tel. (732) 772-01-11-71; fax (732) 772-02-11-71-3; e-mail ltdion.post@ooe.gv.at; internet www.landtag.ooe.gv.at.

Election, 27 September 2009

Party	Seats
ÖVP	28
SPÖ	14
FPÖ	9
Die Grünen	5
Total	**56**

VIENNA (WIEN)

Bürgermeister (Mayor) and Governor: Dr MICHAEL HÄUPL (SPÖ).

President of the Provincial Assembly (Landtag): Prof. HARRY KOPIETZ (SPÖ).

Wiener Landtag: Rathaus, 1082 Vienna; e-mail post-ltg@mdgb.wien.gv.at; internet www.wien.gv.at/politik/landtag.

Election, 10 October 2010

Party	Seats
SPÖ	49
FPÖ	27
ÖVP	13
Die Grünen	11
Total	100

VORARLBERG

Governor: MARKUS WALLNER (ÖVP).

President of the Provincial Assembly (Landtag): Dr GABRIELE NUSSBAUMER (ÖVP).

Vorarlberger Landtag: Landhaus, 6901 Bregenz; tel. (5574) 511-30-00-5; fax (5574) 511-30-09-5; e-mail landtag@vorarlberg.at; internet www.vorarlberg.at/landtag.

Election, 20 September 2009

Party	Seats
ÖVP	20
FPÖ	9
Die Grünen	4
SPÖ	3
Total	36

Election Commission

Bundeswahlbehörde (Federal Election Board): Bundesministerium für Inneres, Abteilung III/6, Postfach 100, 1014 Vienna; tel. (1) 53126-2160; fax (1) 53126-2110; e-mail wahl@bmi.gv.at; internet www.bmi.gv.at/wahlen; comprises 17 Beisitzer (assessors); 15 of the assessors are nominated by the political orgs represented in the Nationalrat; the remaining 2 are members of the judiciary; Chair. JOHANNA MIKL-LEITNER (Minister of the Interior).

Political Organizations

Bündnis Zukunft Österreich (BZÖ) (Alliance for the Future of Austria): Volksgartenstr. 3/5, 1010 Vienna; tel. (1) 513-28-38; fax (1) 513-28-38-30; e-mail office@bzoe.at; internet www.bzoe.at; f. 2005 by split from Freiheitliche Partei Österreichs (FPÖ); proponent of social market economy, controlled immigration and protection of Austria's cultural identity; Leader and Parliamentary Spokesman GERALD GROSZ.

Christliche Partei Österreichs (CPÖ) (Christian Party of Austria): Kunschak-Gasse 6, 2380 Perchtoldsdorf; tel. (676) 331-46-86; e-mail gehring@cpoe.or.at; internet www.cpoe.or.at; f. 2007; Leader Dr RUDOLF GEHRING.

Freiheitliche Partei Österreichs (FPÖ/Die Freiheitlichen) (Freedom Party of Austria): Friedrich Schmidt-Pl. 4/3A, 1080 Vienna; tel. and fax (1) 512-35-35-0; fax (1) 512-35-35-9; e-mail bgst@fpoe.at; internet www.fpoe.at; f. 1955; partially succeeded the Verband der Unabhängigen (League of Independents, f. 1949); popularly known as Die Freiheitlichen; populist right-wing party advocating the participation of workers in management, stricter immigration controls and deregulation in the business sector; opposes Austria's membership of the EU; Chair. and Parliamentary Spokesperson HEINZ-CHRISTIAN STRACHE.

Die Grünen (Greens): Rooseveltpl. 4–5, 1090 Vienna; tel. (1) 236-39-98-0; fax (1) 526-91-10; e-mail bundesbuero@gruene.at; internet www.gruene.at; f. 1986; campaigns for environmental protection, peace and social justice; Chair. and Parliamentary Spokesperson Dr EVA GLAWISCHNIG-PIESCZEK.

Junge Liberale Österreich (JuLis) (Young Liberals Austria): Neustiftgasse 73–75/7, 1070 Vienna; e-mail office@julis.at; internet www.julis.at; f. 2009; contested the 2013 general election in alliance with Das Neue Österreich (NEOS) and Liberales Forum (LiF); Leader NIKOLAUS SCHERAK.

Kommunistische Partei Österreichs (KPÖ) (Communist Party of Austria): Drechslergasse 42, 1140 Vienna; tel. (1) 503-65-80-0; fax (1) 503-65-80-49-9; e-mail bundesvorstand@kpoe.at; internet www.kpoe.at; f. 1918; strongest in the industrial centres and trade unions; advocates a policy of strict neutrality; mem. party of European Left; Chair. and Parliamentary Spokesperson Dr MIRKO MESSNER.

Liste Fritz Dinkhauser—Bürgerforum Tirol (Fritz Dinkhauser List—Tyrol Residents' Forum): Maximilianstr. 2, 6020 Innsbruck; tel. (512) 561-16-60; fax (512) 561-16-688; e-mail office@liste-fritz.at; internet www.listefritz.at; f. 2008 to contest elections to the Tyrol provincial parliament; contested Sept. 2008 federal election as Bürgerforum Österreich—Liste Fritz Dinkhauser; campaigns for political and economic reform; Chair. FRITZ DINKHAUSER.

Das Neue Österreich und Liberales Forum (NEOS) (The New Austria): Neustiftgasse 73–75/7, 1070 Vienna; e-mail kontakt@neos.eu; internet neos.eu; f. 2012 as Das Neue Österreich; contested the 2013 general election in collaboration with Junge Liberale Österreich and Liberales Forum; renamed as present in 2014; Chair. Dr MATTHIAS STROLZ.

Österreichische Volkspartei (ÖVP) (Austrian People's Party): Lichtenfelsgasse 7, 1010 Vienna; tel. (1) 401-26-0; fax (1) 401-26-10-9; e-mail email@oevp.at; internet www.oevp.at; f. 1945; Christian Democratic party; advocates an ecologically orientated social market economy; Chair. MICHAEL SPINDELEGGER; Parliamentary Spokesman Dr REINHOLD LOPATKA; Sec.-Gen. GERNOT BLÜMEL.

Piratenpartei Österreichs (PPÖ) (Pirate Party of Austria): Birkengasse 55, 3100 St Pölten; e-mail bv@piratenpartei.at; internet www.piratenpartei.at; f. 2006; Federal Bd CHRISTOPHER CLAY, LUKAS DANIEL KLAUSNER, NORA WALCHSHOFER, BERNHARD HAYDEN, MARCUS HOHENECKER.

Sozialdemokratische Partei Österreichs (SPÖ) (Social Democratic Party of Austria): Löwelstr. 18, 1014 Vienna; tel. (1) 534-27; fax (1) 535-96-83; e-mail direkt@spoe.at; internet www.spoe.at; f. as the Social Democratic Party in 1889, subsequently renamed the Socialist Party, reverted to its original name in 1991; advocates democratic socialism and Austria's permanent neutrality; Chair. WERNER FAYMANN; Parliamentary Spokesperson REINHARD TODT; Nat. Sec. NORBERT DARABOS.

Team Stronach für Österreich (Team Stronach) (Team Stronach for Austria): Reichsratsstr. 3, 1010 Vienna; tel. (1) 919-50-00; e-mail info@teamstronach.at; internet www.teamstronach.at; f. 2012; populist, economically liberal; Leader FRANK STRONACH.

Vorwärts Tirol: Valiergasse 15, 6020 Innsbruck; tel. (512) 327-97-90; e-mail info@vorwaerts-tirol.at; internet www.vorwaerts-tirol.at; f. 2013; Chair. HANSJÖRG PEER.

Diplomatic Representation

EMBASSIES IN AUSTRIA

Afghanistan: Lackierergasse 9/9, 1090 Vienna; tel. (1) 524-78-06; fax (1) 406-02-19; e-mail afg.emb.vie@chello.at; internet www.afghanistan-vienna.org; Ambassador AYUB M. IRFANI.

Albania: Prinz-Eugen-Str. 18/1/5, 1040 Vienna; tel. (1) 328-86-56; fax (1) 328-86-58; e-mail embassy.vienna@mfa.gov.al; Ambassador ROLAND BIMO.

Algeria: Rudolfinergasse 18, 1190 Vienna; tel. (1) 369-88-53; fax (1) 369-88-56; e-mail office@algerische-botschaft.at; internet www.algerische-botschaft.at; Ambassador MOHAMED BENHOCINE.

Andorra: Kärntner Ring 2A/13, 1010 Vienna; tel. (1) 961-09-09; fax (1) 961-09-09-50; e-mail office@ambaixada-andorra.at; Chargé d'affaires a.i. GEMMA CANÓ BERNE.

Angola: Seilerstätte 15/10, 1010 Vienna; tel. (1) 718-74-88; fax (1) 718-74-86; e-mail embangola.viena@embangola.at; internet www.embangola.at; Ambassador Dr MARIA DE JESUS DOS REIS FERREIRA.

Argentina: Goldschmiedgasse 2/1, 1010 Vienna; tel. (1) 533-84-63; fax (1) 533-87-97; e-mail embargviena@embargviena.at; Ambassador RAFAEL MARIANO GROSSI.

Armenia: Hadikgasse 28, 1140 Vienna; tel. (1) 522-74-79; fax (1) 522-74-81; e-mail armenia@armembassy.at; Ambassador ARMAN KIRAKOSSIAN.

Australia: Mattiellistr. 2–4, 1040 Vienna; tel. (1) 506-74-0; fax (1) 504-11-78; e-mail austemb@aon.at; internet www.austria.embassy.gov.au; Ambassador DAVID GORDON STUART.

Azerbaijan: Hügelgasse 2, 1130 Vienna; tel. (1) 403-13-22; fax (1) 403-13-23; e-mail vienna@mission.mfa.gov.az; Ambassador GALIB M. ISRAFILOV.

Belarus: Hüttelbergstr. 6, 1140 Vienna; tel. (1) 419-96-30; fax (1) 416-96-30-30; e-mail mail@byembassy.at; internet austria.mfa.gov.by; Ambassador Dr VALERY I. VORONETSKY.

Belgium: Wohllebengasse 6, 1040 Vienna; tel. (1) 502-07-0; fax (1) 502-07-0; e-mail vienna@diplobel.fed.be; internet www.diplomatie.be/vienna; Ambassador FRANK RECKER.

Belize: Franz Josefs Kai 13/5/16, Postfach 982, 1011 Vienna; tel. (1) 533-76-63; fax (1) 533-81-14; e-mail belizeembassy@utanet.at; Ambassador ALEXANDER PILETSKY.

Bolivia: Waaggasse 10/8, 1040 Vienna; tel. (1) 587-46-75; fax (1) 586-68-80; e-mail embolaustria@of-viena.at; Chargé d'affaires a.i. Dr RICARDO JAVIER MARTÍNEZ COVARRUBIAS.

Bosnia and Herzegovina: Tivoligasse 54, 1120 Vienna; tel. (1) 811-85-55; fax (1) 811-85-69; e-mail bhbotschaft@bhbotschaft.at; internet www.bhbotschaft.at; Ambassador TANJA MARTINOVIĆ.

Brazil: Pestalozzigasse 4, 1010 Vienna; tel. (1) 512-06-31; fax (1) 513-83-74; e-mail mail@brasilemb.at; internet www.brasilemb.at; Ambassador EVANDRO DE SAMPAIO DIDONET.

Bulgaria: Schwindgasse 8, 1040 Vienna; tel. (1) 505-31-13; fax (1) 505-14-23; e-mail amboffice@embassybulgaria.at; Ambassador ELENA RADKOVA SHEKERLETOVA.

Burkina Faso: Strohgasse 14C, 1030 Vienna; tel. (1) 503-82-64-0; fax (1) 503-82-64-20; e-mail s.r@abfvienne.at; internet www.abfvienne.at; Ambassador PAUL ROBERT TIENDREBEOGO.

Canada: Laurenzerberg 2, 3rd Floor, 1010 Vienna; tel. (1) 531-38-30-00; fax (1) 531-38-33-21; e-mail vienn@international.gc.ca; internet www.canadainternational.gc.ca/austria-autriche; Ambassador MARK BAILEY.

Chile: Lugeck 1/3/10, 1010 Vienna; tel. (1) 512-92-08; fax (1) 512-92-08-33; e-mail echile.austria@minrel.gov.cl; internet www.chileabroad.gov.cl/austria; Ambassador ALFREDO LABBÉ VILLA.

China, People's Republic: Metternichgasse 4, 1030 Vienna; tel. (1) 714-31-49; fax (1) 713-68-16; e-mail chinaemb_at@mfa.gov.cn; internet www.chinaembassy.at; Ambassador BIN ZHAO.

Colombia: Stadiongasse 6–8/15, 1010 Vienna; tel. (1) 405-42-49; fax (1) 408-83-03; e-mail eaustria@cancilleria.gov.co; internet austria.embajada.gov.co; Ambassador JAIME ALBERTO CABAL SANCLEMENTE (designate).

Costa Rica: Wagramerstr. 23/1/1 Top 2 and 3, 1220 Vienna; tel. (1) 263-38-24; fax (1) 263-38-24-5; e-mail embajadaaustria_costa.rica@chello.at; Ambassador ANA TERESA DENGO BENAVIDES.

Côte d'Ivoire: Neulinggasse 29/6/20, 1030 Vienna; tel. (1) 581-00-76; fax (1) 581-00-76-31; e-mail office@ambaciaut.org; Ambassador LARGATON GILBERT OUATTARA.

Croatia: Heuberggasse 10, 1170 Vienna; tel. (1) 485-95-24; fax (1) 480-29-42; e-mail croemb.bec@mvep.hr; internet at.mfa.hr; Ambassador GORDAN BAKOTA.

Cuba: Kaiserstr. 84/1/1, 1070 Vienna; tel. (1) 877-81-98; fax (1) 877-81-98-20; e-mail secembajador@ecuaustria.at; internet www.cubadiplomatica.cu/austria; Ambassador JUAN CARLOS MARSAN AGUILERA.

Cyprus: Parkring 20, 1010 Vienna; tel. (1) 513-06-30; fax (1) 513-06-32; e-mail office@cyprusembassy.at; Ambassador COSTAS A. PAPADEMAS.

Czech Republic: Penzingerstr. 11-13, 1140 Vienna; tel. (1) 899-58-111; fax (1) 894-12-00; e-mail vienna@embassy.mzv.cz; internet www.mzv.cz/vienna; Ambassador DR JAN SECHTER.

Denmark: Führichgasse 6, Postfach 19, 1015 Vienna; tel. (1) 512-79-04; fax (1) 513-81-20; e-mail vieamb@um.dk; internet www.ambwien.um.dk; Ambassador LISELOTTE K. PLESNER.

Dominican Republic: Prinz-Eugen-Str. 18, 1040 Vienna; tel. (1) 505-85-55; fax (1) 505-85-55-20; e-mail mprdoiv@yahoo.com; Ambassador RAMÓN ANDRÉS QUIÑONES RODRÍGUEZ.

Ecuador: Goldschmiedgasse 10/2/205, 1010 Vienna; tel. (1) 535-32-08; fax (1) 535-08-97; e-mail mecaustria@chello.at; Ambassador WILSON MARCELO PASTOR MORRIS.

Egypt: Hohe Warte 50–54, 1190 Vienna; tel. (1) 370-81-04; fax (1) 370-81-04-27; e-mail egyptembassyvienna@egyptembassyvienna.at; internet www.egyptembassyvienna.at; Ambassador KHALED ABD AL-RAHMAN ABD AL-LATIF SHAMAA.

El Salvador: Prinz-Eugen-Str. 72/2/1, 1040 Vienna; tel. (1) 505-38-74; fax (1) 505-38-76; e-mail elsalvador@embasal.at; Ambassador MARIO ANTONIO RIVERA MORA.

Estonia: Wohllebengasse 9/13, 1040 Vienna; tel. (1) 503-77-61; fax (1) 503-77-61-20; e-mail embassy@estwien.at; internet www.estemb.at; Ambassador EVE-KÜLLI KALA.

Ethiopia: Wagramerstr. 14/1/2, 1220 Vienna; tel. (1) 710-21-68; fax (1) 710-21-71; e-mail office@ethiopianembassy.at; Ambassador MINELIK ALEMU GETAHUN.

Finland: Gonzagagasse 16, 1010 Vienna; tel. (1) 531-59-0; fax (1) 535-57-03; e-mail sanomat.wie@formin.fi; internet www.finnland.at; Ambassador ANU IRENE LAAMANEN.

France: Technikerstr. 2, 1040 Vienna; tel. (1) 502-75-0; fax (1) 502-75-16-8; e-mail contact@ambafrance-at.org; internet www.ambafrance-at.org; Ambassador STÉPHANE GOMPERTZ.

Georgia: Doblhoffgasse 5/5, 1010 Vienna; tel. (1) 403-98-48; fax (1) 403-98-48-20; e-mail vienna@geomission.at; internet www.austria.mfa.gov.ge; Ambassador KONSTANTIN ZALDASTANISHVILI.

Germany: Metternichgasse 3, 1030 Vienna; tel. (1) 711-54-0; fax (1) 713-83-66; e-mail info@wien.diplo.de; internet www.wien.diplo.de; Ambassador DETLEV RÜNGER.

Greece: Argentinierstr. 14, 1040 Vienna; tel. (1) 506-15; fax (1) 505-62-17; e-mail gremb@griechischebotschaft.at; internet www.griechische-botschaft.at; Ambassador CHRYSSOULA ALIFERI (designate).

Guatemala: Landstr. Hauptstr. 21/Top 9, 1030 Vienna; tel. (1) 714-35-70; fax (1) 714-35-70-15; e-mail embajada@embaguate.co.at; Ambassador ANTONIO ROBERTO CASTELLANOS LÓPEZ.

Holy See: Theresianumgasse 31, 1040 Vienna; tel. (1) 505-13-27; fax (1) 505-61-40; e-mail nuntius@nuntiatur.at; internet www.nuntiatur.at; Apostolic Nuncio Most Rev. PETER STEPHAN ZURBRIGGEN (Titular Archbishop of Glastonia).

Hungary: Bankgasse 4–6, 1010 Vienna; tel. (1) 537-80-30-0; fax (1) 535-99-40; e-mail kom@kum.hu; internet www.mfa.gov.hu/emb/vienna; Ambassador VINCE SZALAY-BOBROVNICZKY.

Iceland: Naglergasse 2/3/8, 1010 Vienna; tel. (1) 533-27-71; fax (1) 533-27-74; e-mail emb.vienna@mfa.is; internet www.iceland.org/at; Ambassador AUDUNN ATLASON.

India: Kärntner Ring 2, 2nd Floor, 1010 Vienna; tel. (1) 505-86-66; fax (1) 505-92-19; e-mail indemb@eoivien.vienna.at; internet www.indianembassy.at; Ambassador RAJIV MISRA.

Indonesia: Gustav-Tschermak-Gasse 5–7, 1180 Vienna; tel. (1) 476-23-0; fax (1) 479-05-57; e-mail unitkom@kbriwina.at; internet www.kbriwina.at; Ambassador RACHMAT BUDIMAN.

Iran: Jaurèsgasse 9, 1030 Vienna; tel. (1) 712-26-57; fax (1) 713-57-33; e-mail public@iranembassy-wien.at; internet www.iranembassy-wien.at; Ambassador HASSAN TAJIK.

Iraq: Laurenzerbergstraße 2, 1A, Postfach 599, 1010 Vienna; tel. (1) 713-81-95; fax (1) 713-82-08; e-mail office@iraqembassy.at; Ambassador SUROOD R. NAJIB NAJIB.

Ireland: Rotenturmstr. 16–18, 5th Floor, 1010 Vienna; tel. (1) 715-42-46; fax (1) 713-60-04; e-mail vienna@dfa.ie; internet www.embassyofireland.at; Ambassador JAMES BRENNAN.

Israel: Anton-Frank-Gasse 20, 1180 Vienna; tel. (1) 476-46-0; fax (1) 476-46-57-5; e-mail info-assistant@vienna.mfa.gov.il; internet embassies.gov.il/vienna; Ambassador ZVI HEIFETZ.

Italy: Rennweg 27, 1030 Vienna; tel. (1) 712-51-21; fax (1) 713-97-19; e-mail ambasciata.vienna@esteri.it; internet www.ambvienna.esteri.it; Ambassador GIORGIO MARRAPODI.

Japan: Hessgasse 6, 1010 Vienna; tel. (1) 531-92-0; fax (1) 532-05-90; e-mail info@embjp.at; internet www.at.emb-japan.go.jp; Ambassador MAKOTO TAKETOSHI.

Jordan: Rennweg 17/4, 1030 Vienna; tel. (1) 405-10-25-26; fax (1) 405-10-31; e-mail info@jordanembassy.at; internet www.jordanembassy.at; Ambassador HUSSAM ABDULLAH AL-HUSSEINI.

Kazakhstan: Wipplingerstr. 35, 1010 Vienna; tel. (1) 890-80-08-10; fax (1) 890-80-08-20; e-mail embassy@kazakhstan.at; internet www.kazakhstan.at; Ambassador KAIRAT SARYBAY.

Kenya: Neulinggasse 29/8, 1030 Vienna; tel. (1) 712-39-19; fax (1) 712-39-22; e-mail kenyarep-vienna@aon.at; internet kenyaembassyvienna.at; Ambassador MICHAEL A. O. OYUGI.

Korea, Democratic People's Republic: Beckmanngasse 10–12, 1140 Vienna; tel. (1) 894-23-13; fax (1) 894-31-74; e-mail d.v.r.korea.botschaft@chello.at; Ambassador KIM GWANG SOP.

Korea, Republic: Gregor-Mendel-Str. 25, 1180 Vienna; tel. (1) 478-19-91; fax (1) 478-10-13; e-mail mail@koreaemb.at; internet aut.mofat.go.kr; Ambassador CHO HYUN.

Kosovo: Goldeggasse 2/14, 1040 Vienna; tel. (1) 503-11-77; fax (1) 503-11-77-20; e-mail embassy.austria@rks-gov.net; internet www.ambasada-ks.net/at; Chargé d'affaires a.i. BLERIM CANAJ.

Kuwait: Strassergasse 32, 1190 Vienna; tel. (1) 405-56-46; fax (1) 405-56-46-13; e-mail kuwait.embassy.vienna@speed.at; Ambassador SADIQ MARAFI.

Kyrgyzstan: Invalidenstr. 3/8, 1030 Vienna; tel. (1) 535-03-79; fax (1) 535-03-79-13; e-mail kyremb@inode.at; internet www.kyremb.at; Ambassador LYDIA IMANALIEVA.

Latvia: Stefan-Esders-Pl. 4, 1190 Vienna; tel. (1) 403-31-12; fax (1) 403-31-12-27; e-mail embassy.austria@mfa.gov.lv; Ambassador EDGARS SKUJA.

Lebanon: Oppolzergasse 6/3, 1010 Vienna; tel. (1) 533-88-21; fax (1) 533-49-84; e-mail embassy.lebanon@inode.at; Ambassador ISHAYA AL-KHOURY.

Libya: Blaasstr. 33, 1190 Vienna; tel. (1) 367-76-39; fax (1) 367-76-01; e-mail office@libyanembassyvienna.at; Ambassaor IBRAHIM A. S. ALBESBAS.

Liechtenstein: Löwelstr. 8/7, 1010 Vienna; tel. (1) 535-92-11; fax (1) 535-92-11-4; e-mail info@vie.llv.li; internet www.liechtenstein.li/fl-aussenstelle-wien; Ambassador Princess MARIA-PIA KOTHBAUER of Liechtenstein.

Lithuania: Löwengasse 47/4, 1030 Vienna; tel. (1) 718-54-67; fax (1) 718-54-69; e-mail amb.at@urm.lt; internet at.mfa.lt; Chargé d'affaires a.i. EDVILAS RAUDONIKIS.

Luxembourg: Sternwartestr. 81, 1180 Vienna; tel. (1) 478-21-42; fax (1) 478-21-44; e-mail vienne.amb@mae.etat.lu; internet vienne.mae.lu/ge; Ambassador HUBERT WURTH.

Macedonia, former Yugoslav republic: Kinderspitalgasse 5, 1090 Vienna; tel. (1) 524-87-56; fax (1) 524-87-53; e-mail botschaft@makedonien.co.at; Ambassador Prof. Dr GJORGJI FILIPOV.

Malaysia: Floridsdorfer Hauptstr. 1–7, Florido Tower, 24th Floor, 1210 Vienna; tel. (1) 505-10-42; fax (1) 505-79-42; e-mail embassy@embassymalaysia.at; Ambassador SELWYN VIJAYARAJAN DAS.

Malta: Opernring 5/1, 1010 Vienna; tel. (1) 586-50-10; fax (1) 586-50-10-9; e-mail maltaembassy.vienna@gov.mt; internet www.mfa.gov.mt/austria; Ambassador KEITH AZZOPARDI.

Mexico: Operngasse 21/10, 1040 Vienna; tel. (1) 310-73-83; fax (1) 310-73-87; e-mail embamex@embamex.or.at; internet www.sre.gob.mx/austria; Ambassador LUIS ALFONSO DE ALBA GÓNGORA.

Moldova: Löwengasse 47/10, 1030 Vienna; tel. (1) 961-10-30; fax (1) 961-10-30-34; e-mail viena@mfo.md; internet www.austria.mfa.md; Chargé d'affaires a.i. ANGELA PONOMARIOV.

Mongolia: Fasangartengasse 45, 1130 Vienna; tel. (1) 535-28-07-12; fax (1) 535-28-07-20; e-mail office@embassymon.at; internet www.embassymon.at; Ambassador GUNAAJAV BATJARGAL.

Montenegro: Nibelungengasse 13, 1010 Vienna; tel. (1) 715-31-02; fax (1) 715-31-02-20; e-mail diplomat-mn@me-austria.eu; Ambassador SLAVICA MILAČIĆ.

Morocco: Hasenauerstr. 57, 1180 Vienna; tel. (1) 586-66-51; fax (1) 586-76-67; e-mail emb-pmissionvienna@morocco.at; Ambassador ALI EL MHAMDI.

Namibia: Zuckerkandlgasse 2, 1190 Vienna; tel. (1) 402-93-71; fax (1) 402-93-70; e-mail nam.emb.vienna@speed.at; internet www.embnamibia.at; Ambassador SIMON MADJUMO MARUTA.

Netherlands: Opernring 5, 7th Floor, Postfach 190, 1015 Vienna; tel. (1) 589-39-0; fax (1) 589-39-26-5; e-mail wen-public@minbuza.nl; internet www.mfa.nl/wen; Ambassador PETER PAUL VAN WULFFTEN PALTHE.

New Zealand: Mattiellistr. 2–4/3, 1040 Vienna; tel. (1) 505-30-21; fax (1) 505-30-20; e-mail nzpm@aon.at; internet www.nzembassy.com/austria; Ambassador DEBORAH GEELS.

Nicaragua: Ebendorferstr. 10/3/12, 1010 Vienna; tel. (1) 403-18-38; fax (1) 403-27-52; e-mail embanicviena@aon.at; Ambassador ALVARO JOSÉ ROBELO GONZÁLEZ.

Nigeria: Rennweg 25, Postfach 183, 1030 Vienna; tel. (1) 712-66-85; fax (1) 714-14-02; e-mail info@nigeriaembassyvienna.com; internet www.nigeriaembassyvienna.com; Ambassador ADELAKUN ABEL AYOKO.

Norway: Reisnerstr. 55–57, 1030 Vienna; tel. (1) 716-60; fax (1) 716-60-99; e-mail emb.vienna@mfa.no; internet www.norwegen.or.at; Ambassador JAN PETERSEN.

Oman: Währingerstr. 2–4/24–25, 1090 Vienna; tel. (1) 310-86-43; fax (1) 310-72-68; e-mail vienna@omanembassy.at; Ambassador Dr BADR MOHAMED ZAHIR AL-HINAI.

Pakistan: Hofzeile 13, 1190 Vienna; tel. (1) 368-73-81-82; fax (1) 368-73-76; e-mail parepvienna@gmail.com; internet www.mofa.gov.pk/austria; Ambassador AYESHA RIYAZ.

Panama: Goldschmiedgasse 10/403, 1010 Vienna; tel. (1) 587-23-47; fax (1) 586-30-80; e-mail mail@empanvienna.co.at; Ambassador RICARDO VALLARINO PÉREZ.

Paraguay: Prinz-Eugen-Str. 18/1/2/7, 1040 Vienna; tel. (1) 505-46-74; fax (1) 941-98-98; e-mail embaparviena@chello.at; Ambassador Dr HORACIO NOGUÉS ZUBIZARRETA.

Peru: Mahlerstrasse 7/22, 2nd Floor, 1010, Vienna; tel. (1) 713-43-77; fax (1) 712-77-04; Ambassador ANTONIO JAVIER ALEJANDRO GARCÍA REVILLA.

Philippines: Laurenzerberg 2, 1010 Vienna; tel. (1) 533-24-01; fax (1) 533-24-01-24; e-mail office@philippine-embassy.at; internet www.philippine-embassy.at; Ambassador LOURDES O. YPARRAGUIRRE.

Poland: Hietzinger Hauptstr. 42C, 1130 Vienna; tel. (1) 870-15-10-0; fax (1) 870-15-22-2; e-mail wieden.amb.sekretariat@msz.gov.pl; internet www.wien.polemb.net; Ambassador ARTUR LORKOWSKI.

Portugal: Opernring 3, 1010 Vienna; tel. (1) 586-75-36; fax (1) 586-75-36-99; e-mail viena@mne.pt; internet www.embaixadaportugalaustria.mne.pt; Ambassador PEDRO LUIS BAPTISTA MOITINHO DE ALMEIDA.

Qatar: Schottenring 10, Top 7A,B, C, 1010 Vienna; tel. (1) 310-49-50; fax (1) 319-08-97; e-mail botschaft@katarbotschaft.at; Ambassador ALI KHALFAN A. K. AL-MANSOURI.

Romania: Prinz-Eugen-Str. 60, 1040 Vienna; tel. (1) 505-32-27; fax (1) 504-14-62; e-mail ambromviena@ambrom.at; internet viena.mae.ro; Ambassador SILVIA DAVIDOIU.

Russia: Reisnerstr. 45–47, 1030 Vienna; tel. (1) 712-12-29; fax (1) 712-33-88; e-mail info@rusemb.at; internet www.austria.mid.ru; Ambassador SERGEI NECHAYEV.

San Marino: Prinz-Eugen-Str. 16/1/5A, 1040 Vienna; tel. (1) 941-59-69; fax (1) 941-59-75; e-mail rsmvienna@gmail.com; Ambassador Dr ELENA MOLARONI BERGUIDO.

Saudi Arabia: Formanekgasse 38, 1190 Vienna; tel. (1) 367-25-31; fax (1) 367-25-40; e-mail saudiembassy@saudiembassy.at; Ambassador MOHAMMED AL SALLOUM.

Serbia: Ölzeltgasse 3, Top 7, 1030 Vienna; tel. (1) 713-25-95; fax (1) 713-25-97; e-mail embassy.vienna@mfa.rs; internet www.vienna.mfa.gov.rs; Ambassador PERO JANKOVIĆ.

Slovakia: Armbrustergasse 24, 1190 Vienna; tel. (1) 318-90-55-20-0; fax (1) 318-90-55-20-8; e-mail emb.vieden@mzv.sk; internet www.vienna.mfa.sk; Ambassador Dr JURAJ MACHÁČ.

Slovenia: Kolingasse 12, 1090 Vienna; tel. (1) 319-11-60; fax (1) 586-12-65; e-mail vdu@gov.si; internet www.vienna.embassy.si; Ambassador ANDREJ RAHTEN.

South Africa: Sandgasse 33, 1190 Vienna; tel. (1) 320-64-93; fax (1) 320-64-93-51; e-mail vienna.ambassador@foreign.gov.za; internet www.dirco.gov.za/vienna; Ambassador TEBOGO JOSEPH SEOKOLO.

Spain: Argentinierstr. 34, 1040 Vienna; tel. (1) 505-57-88; fax (1) 505-57-88-125; e-mail emb.viena@maec.es; internet www.maec.es/embajadas/viena/es; Ambassador ALBERTO CARNERO FERNÁNDEZ.

Sri Lanka: Weyringergasse 33–35, 4th Floor, 1040 Vienna; tel. (1) 503-79-88; fax (1) 503-79-93; e-mail embassy@srilankaembassy.at; internet www.srilankaembassy.at; Ambassador A. L. ABDUL AZEEZ.

Sudan: Reisnerstr. 29/5, 1030 Vienna; tel. (1) 710-23-43; fax (1) 710-23-46; e-mail sudanivienna@prioritytelecom.biz; Chargé d'affaires a.i. YOUSIF AHMED EL-TAYEB YOUSIF EL-KORDOFANI.

Sweden: Obere Donaustr. 49–51, Postfach 18, 1020 Vienna; tel. (1) 217-53-0; fax (1) 217-53-370; e-mail ambassaden.wien@gov.se; internet www.swedenabroad.com/wien; Ambassador NILS DAAG.

Switzerland: Kärntner Ring 12, 1030 Vienna; tel. (1) 795-05; fax (1) 795-05-21; e-mail vie.vertretung@eda.admin.ch; internet www.eda.admin.ch/wien; Ambassador Dr URS BREITER.

Syria: Daffingerstr. 4, 1030 Vienna; tel. (1) 533-46-33; fax (1) 533-46-32; e-mail syrianembassyvienna@utanet.at; Ambassador BASSAM SABBAGH.

Tajikistan: Universitätsstr. 8/1A, 1090 Vienna; tel. and fax (1) 409-82-66; fax (1) 409-82-66-14; e-mail info@tajikembassy.at; internet tajikembassy.at; Ambassador ISMATULLO NASREDINOV.

Thailand: Cottagegasse 48, 1180 Vienna; tel. (1) 478-33-35; fax (1) 478-29-07; e-mail embassy@thaivienna.at; internet www.thaiembassy.at; Ambassador Princess BAJRAKITIYABHA.

Tunisia: Sieveringerstr. 187, 1190 Vienna; tel. (1) 581-52-81-82; fax (1) 581-55-92; e-mail at.vienne@aon.at; Ambassador MUHAMMAD SAMIR KOUBAA.

Turkey: Prinz-Eugen-Str. 40, 1040 Vienna; tel. (1) 505-73-38-0; fax (1) 505-36-60; e-mail tuerkische-botschaft@chello.at; Ambassador MEHMET HASAN GÖGÜS.

Turkmenistan: Argentinierstr. 22/II/EG, 1040 Vienna; tel. (1) 503-64-70; fax (1) 503-64-73; e-mail info@botschaft-turkmenistan.at; internet www.botschaft-turkmenistan.at; Ambassador SILAPBERDI NURBERDIEV.

Ukraine: Naaffgasse 23, 1180 Vienna; tel. (1) 479-71-72-11; fax (1) 479-71-72-47; e-mail info@ukremb.at; internet www.mfa.gov.ua/austria; Ambassador ANDRIY BEREZNYI.

United Arab Emirates: Peter-Jordan-Str. 66, 1190 Vienna; tel. (1) 368-14-55; fax (1) 368-44-85; e-mail emirates@aon.at; Ambassador ABDUL HADI ABDUL WAHID AL-KHAJA.

United Kingdom: Jaurèsgasse 12, 1030 Vienna; tel. (1) 716-13-0; fax (1) 716-13-29-99; e-mail press@britishembassy.at; internet ukinaustria.fco.gov.uk; Ambassador SUSAN LE JEUNE D'ALLEGEERSHECQUE.

USA: Boltzmanngasse 16, 1090 Vienna; tel. (1) 313-39-0; fax (1) 310-06-82; e-mail embassy@usembassy.at; internet austria.usembassy.gov; Ambassador ALEXA L. WESNER.

Uruguay: Palais Esterhazy, Wallnerstr. 4/3/17, 1010 Vienna; tel. (1) 535-66-36; fax (1) 535-66-18; e-mail uruaustria@mrree.gub.uy; Ambassador CARLOS ALEJANDRO BARROS OREIRO.

Uzbekistan: Poetzleinsdorferstr. 49, 1180 Vienna; tel. (1) 315-39-94; fax (1) 315-39-93; e-mail embassy@usbekistan.at; internet www.usbekistan.at; Chargé d'affaires a.i. RAVSHENBAK DUSCHANOV.

Venezuela: Prinz-Eugen-Str. 72/1.OG/Steige 1/Top1.1, 1040 Vienna; tel. (1) 712-26-38; fax (1) 715-32-19; e-mail embajada@

austria.gob.ve; internet www.austria.gob.ve; Ambassador ALÍ DE JESÚS UZCATEGUI DUQUE.

Viet Nam: Félix-Mottl-Str. 20, 1190 Vienna; tel. (1) 368-07-55-10; fax (1) 368-07-54; e-mail office@vietnamembassy.at; internet www.vietnamembassy.at; Ambassador THIEP NGUYEN.

Yemen: Reisnerstr. 18–20, 1st Floor, Top 3–4, 1030 Vienna; tel. (1) 503-29-30; fax (1) 505-31-59; e-mail yemenembassy.vienna@aon.at; Ambassador ABD AL-HAKIM ABD AL-RAHMAN YAHYA AL-ERYANI.

Zimbabwe: Neustift am Walde 91, 1190 Vienna; tel. (1) 407-92-36-37; fax (1) 407-92-38; e-mail z.vien@chello.at; Ambassador GRACE TSITSI MUTANDIRO.

Judicial System

The Austrian legal system is based on the principle of a division between legislative, administrative and judicial power. There are three supreme courts (Verfassungsgerichtshof, Verwaltungsgerichtshof and Oberster Gerichtshof). The judicial courts are organized into 141 local courts (Bezirksgerichte), 20 provincial and district courts (Landesgerichte), and four higher provincial courts (Oberlandesgerichte) in Vienna, Graz, Innsbruck and Linz.

SUPREME ADMINISTRATIVE COURTS

Verfassungsgerichtshof (Constitutional Court): Freyung 8, 1010 Vienna; tel. (1) 531-22-0; fax (1) 531-22-49-9; e-mail vfgh@vfgh.gv.at; internet www.vfgh.gv.at; f. 1919; deals with matters affecting the Constitution, examines the constitutionality of legislation and administration; Pres. Dr GERHART HOLZINGER; Vice-Pres. Dr BRIGITTE BIERLEIN.

Verwaltungsgerichtshof (Administrative Court): Judenpl. 11, Postfach 73, 1014 Vienna; tel. (1) 531-89-21; fax (1) 531-11-50-8; e-mail office@vwgh.gv.at; internet www.vwgh.gv.at; deals with matters affecting the legality of administration; Pres. Prof. Dr RUDOLF THIENEL; Vice-Pres. Dr ANNA SPORRER.

SUPREME JUDICIAL COURT

Oberster Gerichtshof: Schmerlingpl. 11, 1011 Vienna; tel. (1) 521-52-0; fax (1) 521-52-37-10; e-mail ogh.praesidium@justiz.gv.at; internet www.ogh.gv.at; Pres. Prof. Dr ECKART RATZ; Vice-Pres. Dr ILSE HUBER, Dr BRIGITTE SCHENK.

Religion

At the 2001 census, professed membership in major religions was as follows: Roman Catholic Church 74.0% of the population; Lutheran and Presbyterian churches (Evangelical Church, Augsburg and Helvetic confessions) 4.7%; Islam 4.2%; Judaism 0.1%; Eastern Orthodox (Russian, Greek, Serbian, Romanian and Bulgarian) 2.2%; other Christian churches 0.9%; other non-Christian religious groups 0.2%. Atheists accounted for 12% of respondents, while 2% did not indicate a religious affiliation. The vast majority of groups termed 'sects' by the Government are small organizations with fewer than 100 members. Among the larger groups are the Church of Scientology, with between 5,000 and 6,000 members, and the Unification Church, with approximately 700 adherents.

CHRISTIANITY

Ökumenischer Rat der Kirchen in Österreich (Ecumenical Council of Churches in Austria): Severin-Schreiber-Gasse 3, 1180 Vienna; tel. (1) 479-15-23-30-0; fax (1) 479-15-23-33-0; e-mail oerkoe@kirchen.at; internet www.oekumene.at; f. 1948; 16 mem. Churches, 9 observers; Pres. Supt Dr LOTHAR PÖLL (Methodist Church); Vice-Pres Bishop Dr MANFRED SCHEUER (Roman Catholic Church), Archbishop Dr ARSENIOS KARDAMAKIS (Greek Orthodox Church); Sec. Mag. ERIKA TUPPY (Protestant Church of the Helvetic Confession).

The Roman Catholic Church

Austria comprises two archdioceses, seven dioceses and the territorial abbacy of Wettingen-Mehrerau (directly responsible to the Holy See). The Archbishop of Vienna is also the Ordinary for Catholics of the Byzantine rite in Austria (totalling an estimated 8,000). At 31 December 2006 there were an estimated 5,633,552 adherents (68.8% of the population).

Bishops' Conference: Österreichische Bischofskonferenz, Wollzeile 2, 1010 Vienna; tel. (1) 516-11-0; fax (1) 516-11-34-36; e-mail sekretariat@bischofskonferenz.at; internet www.bischofskonferenz.at; f. 1849; Pres. Cardinal CHRISTOPH SCHÖNBORN (Archbishop of Vienna); Gen. Sec. Mgr Dr PETER SCHIPKA.

Archbishop of Salzburg: Most Rev. FRANZ LACKNER, Kapitelpl. 2, 5020 Salzburg; tel. (662) 80-47-0; fax (662) 80-47-20-29; e-mail office@kommunikation.kirchen.net; internet www.kirchen.net.

Archbishop of Vienna: Cardinal CHRISTOPH SCHÖNBORN, Wollzeile 2, 1010 Vienna; tel. (1) 515-52-0; fax (1) 515-52-37-28; internet stephanscom.at.

The Anglican Communion

Within the Church of England, Austria forms part of the diocese of Gibraltar in Europe. The Bishop is resident in London, United Kingdom.

Archdeacon of the Eastern Archdeaconry: Ven. PATRICK CURRAN, Christ Church, Jaurèsgasse 12, 1030 Vienna; tel. and fax (1) 714-89-00; e-mail office@christchurchvienna.org; internet www.christchurchvienna.org.

Protestant Churches

Bund der Baptistengemeinden in Österreich (Fed. of Baptist Communities): Krummgasse 7/4, 1030 Vienna; tel. (1) 713-68-28; fax (1) 713-68-28-11; e-mail bund@baptisten.at; internet www.baptisten.at; Gen. Sec. WALTER KLIMT.

Evangelische Kirche Augsburgischen Bekenntnisses in Österreich (Protestant Church of the Augsburg Confession): Severin-Schreiber-Gasse 3, 1180 Vienna; tel. (1) 479-15-23; fax (1) 479-15-23-44-0; e-mail office@okr-evang.at; internet www.evang.at; 319,752 mems (2011); Bishop Dr MICHAEL BÜNKER.

Evangelische Kirche HB (Helvetischen Bekenntnisses) (Protestant Church of the Helvetic Confession): Dorotheergasse 16, 1010 Vienna; tel. (1) 513-65-64; fax (1) 512-44-90; e-mail kirche-hb@evang.at; internet www.reformiertekirche.at; 13,784 mems (2010); Landessuperintendent Pfarrer THOMAS HENNEFELD.

Evangelisch-methodistische Kirche (United Methodist Church): Sechshauserstr. 56, 1150 Vienna; tel. (1) 604-53-47; fax (1) 89-75-87-6; e-mail superintendent@emk.at; internet www.emk.at; Superintendent Pastor LOTHAR PÖLL.

Orthodox Churches

The Armenian Apostolic Church and the Bulgarian, Coptic, Greek, Romanian, Russian, Serbian and Syrian Orthodox Churches are active in Austria.

Other Christian Churches

Altkatholische Kirche Österreichs (Old Catholic Church in Austria): Schottenring 17/1/3/12, 1010 Vienna; tel. (1) 317-83-94; fax (1) 317-83-94-9; e-mail kilei@altkatholiken.at; internet www.altkatholiken.at; c. 10,000 mems; Bishop JOHN OKORO.

ISLAM

In 2001 there were 338,988 Muslims in Austria.

Islamische Glaubensgemeinschaft in Österreich (Official Islamic Religious Community in Austria—IGGIÖ): Bernardgasse 5, 1070 Vienna; tel. (1) 526-31-22; fax (1) 526-31-22-4; e-mail info@derislam.at; internet www.derislam.at; Pres. Dr FUAT SANAC.

JUDAISM

There are five Jewish communities in Austria, the largest of which is in Vienna. At the end of 2004 there were 6,890 Jews in Vienna, and a combined total of 400 in Graz, Innsbruck, Linz and Salzburg.

Israelitische Kultusgemeinde Graz (Jewish Community in Graz): David-Herzog-Pl. 1, 8020 Graz; tel. (316) 712-46-8; fax (316) 720-43-3; e-mail office@ikg-graz.at; internet www.ikg-graz.at; Pres. Dr RUTH YU-SZAMMER.

Israelitische Kultusgemeinde Salzburg (Jewish Community in Salzburg): Lasserstr. 8, 5020 Salzburg; tel. (662) 872-22-8; e-mail office@ikg-salzburg.at; internet www.ikg-salzburg.at.

Israelitische Kultusgemeinde für Tirol und Vorarlberg (Jewish Community in Tyrol and Vorarlberg): Sillgasse 15, 6020 Innsbruck; tel. and fax (512) 586-89-2; e-mail office@ikg-innsbruck.at; internet www.ikg-innsbruck.at; Pres. Dr ESTHER FRITSCH.

Israelitische Kultusgemeinde Wien (Jewish Community in Vienna): Seitenstettengasse 4, 1010 Vienna; tel. (1) 531-04-10-3; fax (1) 531-04-10-8; e-mail office@ikg-wien.at; internet www.ikg-wien.at; Pres. OSKAR DEUTSCH; Gen. Sec. RAIMUND FASTENBAUER.

The Press

Austria's first newspaper was published in 1605. *Wiener Zeitung*, founded in 1703, is one of the world's oldest daily newspapers still in circulation. Restrictions on press freedom are permissible only within the framework of Article 10 (2) of the European Convention on Human Rights.

Vienna is the focus of newspaper and periodical publishing, although there is also a strong press in some provinces.

In 2011 there were 18 daily newspapers, three of which were distributed without charge.

PRINCIPAL DAILIES

(Average net circulation figures, for January–June 2011, unless otherwise stated)

Bregenz

NEUE Vorarlberger Tageszeitung: Gutenbergstr. 1, 6858 Schwarzach; tel. (5572) 501-850; fax (5572) 501-860; e-mail neue-redaktion@neue.at; internet www.neue.at; f. 1972; morning, Tue.–Sun.; independent; Editor-in-Chief FRANK ANDRES; circ. 12,318.

Vorarlberger Nachrichten: Gutenbergstr. 1, 6858 Schwarzach; tel. (5572) 501-993; fax (5572) 501-227; e-mail redaktion@vn.vol.at; internet www.vn.vol.at; morning; Editor-in-Chief Dr CHRISTIAN ORTNER; circ. Mon.–Sat. 68,780.

Graz

Kleine Zeitung: Schönaugasse 64, 8010 Graz; tel. (316) 875-0; fax (316) 875-40-34; e-mail redaktion@kleinezeitung.at; internet www.kleinezeitung.at; f. 1904; independent; Editor-in-Chief HUBERT PATTERER; circ. Mon.–Sat. 208,731.

Innsbruck

Tiroler Tageszeitung: Ing.-Etzel-Str. 30, 6020 Innsbruck; tel. (512) 53-54-0; fax (512) 53-54-38-99; e-mail redaktion@tt.com; internet www.tt.com; morning; independent; Editors-in-Chief ALOIS VAHRNER, MARIO ZENHÄUSERN; circ. Mon.–Sat. 106,427.

Klagenfurt

Kärntner Tageszeitung: Viktringer Ring 28, 9010 Klagenfurt; tel. (463) 51-20-00; fax (463) 38-15-0; e-mail redaktion@ktz.at; internet www.ktz.at; f. 1946; morning except Mon.; socialist; Editor-in-Chief RALF MOSSER; circ. 32,000 (2007).

Kleine Zeitung: Funderstr. 1A, 9020 Klagenfurt; tel. (463) 58-00-0; fax (463) 58-00-31-3; e-mail redaktion@kleinezeitung.at; internet www.kleinezeitung.at; independent; Editor-in-Chief REINHOLD DOTTOLO; circ. Mon.–Sat. 102,621.

Linz

Neues Volksblatt: Hafenstr. 1–3, 4010 Linz; tel. (732) 76-06-78-2; fax (732) 76-06-70-7; e-mail verlagsleitung@volksblatt.at; internet www.volksblatt.at; f. 1869; organ of Austrian People's Party; Editor-in-Chief Dr WERNER ROHRHOFER.

Oberösterreichische Nachrichten: Promenade 23, 4010 Linz; tel. (732) 78-05-0; fax (732) 78-05-73-1; e-mail redaktion@nachrichten.at; internet www.nachrichten.at; f. 1865; morning; independent; Editor-in-Chief GERALD MANDLBAUER; circ. Mon.–Sat. 133,354.

Salzburg

Salzburger Nachrichten: Karolingerstr. 40, 5021 Salzburg; tel. (662) 83-73-0; fax (662) 83-73-39-9; e-mail redakt@salzburg.com; internet www.salzburg.com; f. 1945; morning; independent; Editor-in-Chief MANFRED PERTERER; circ. Mon.–Sat. 88,963.

Salzburger Volkszeitung: Schrannengasse 6, 5020 Salzburg; tel. (662) 87-94-91; fax (662) 87-94-91-13; e-mail redaktion@svz.at; internet www.svz.at; f. 1945; fmrly organ of the Austrian People's Party; acquired by Aistenleitner Holding in 2005; Editor-in-Chief KONNIE AISTLEITNER; circ. weekdays 12,030 (2007).

Wien
(Vienna)

Heute: Heiligenstädter Lände 29/Top 6, 1190 Vienna; tel. (50) 950-12-20-0; fax (50) 950-12-22-2; e-mail redaktion@heute.at; internet www.heute.at; distributed free of charge; Editor-in-Chief WOLFGANG AINETTER; circ. weekdays 396,171.

Kronen Zeitung: Muthgasse 2, 1190 Vienna; tel. (1) 360-11-0; fax (1) 369-83-85; e-mail lokales@kronenzeitung.at; internet www.krone.at; f. 1900; independent; Editor and Publr HANS DICHAND; circ. weekdays 894,493 (2009), Sun. 1,346,712 (2009).

Kurier: Lindengasse 48–52, 1070 Vienna; tel. (1) 521-00-0; fax (1) 521-00-22-57; e-mail leser@kurier.at; internet www.kurier.at; f. 1954; independent; Editor-in-Chief CHRISTOPH KOTANKO; circ. weekdays 208,276 (2009), Sun. 417,370 (2009).

Die Presse: Hainburgerstr. 33, 1030 Vienna; tel. (1) 514-14-0; fax (1) 514-14-71; e-mail chefredaktion@diepresse.com; internet www.diepresse.com; f. 1848; morning; independent; Editor-in-Chief MANUEL REINARTZ; circ. Mon.–Sat. 96,189.

Der Standard: Wallnerstr. 8, 1010 Vienna; tel. (1) 531-70-70-0; fax (1) 531-70-13-1; e-mail redaktion@derstandard.at; internet derstandard.at; f. 1988; independent; Editor-in-Chief ALEXANDRA FÖDEL-SCHMID; circ. Mon.–Sat. 109,932.

Wiener Zeitung: Wiedner Gürtel 10, 1040 Vienna; tel. and fax (1) 206-99-0; fax (1) 206-99-10-0; e-mail redaktion@wienerzeitung.at; internet www.wienerzeitung.at; f. 1703; morning; official govt paper; Editor-in-Chief REINHARD GÖWEIL; circ. 20,020 (2006).

WirtschaftsBlatt: Hainburgerstr. 33, 1030 Vienna; tel. (1) 601-17-0; fax (1) 601-17-25-9; e-mail redaktion@wirtschaftsblatt.at; internet www.wirtschaftsblatt.at; Mon.–Fri.; business and economics; independent; Editor-in-Chief Dr WOLFGANG UNTERHUBER; circ. weekdays 34,084.

PRINCIPAL WEEKLIES

(Average net circulation figures, for January–June 2011, unless otherwise stated)

Die Furche: Lobkowitzpl. 1, 1010 Vienna; tel. (1) 512-52-61-0; fax (1) 512-82-15; e-mail furche@furche.at; internet www.furche.at; f. 1945; Editor-in-Chief CLAUS REITAN; circ. 18,694.

Kärntner Nachrichten: Kohldorferstr. 98, 1st Floor, 9020 Klagenfurt; tel. (463) 51-15-15; fax (463) 51-15-15-51; e-mail office@abc-werbeagentur.at; internet www.abc-werbeagentur.at; f. 1954; Wed.; Editor Dr HELMUT PRASCH.

KirchenZeitung Diözese Linz: Kapuzinerstr. 84, 4020 Linz; tel. (732) 761-03-94-4; fax (732) 761-03-93-9; e-mail office@kirchenzeitung.at; internet www.kirchenzeitung.at; f. 1945; publ. by Diocese of Linz; Editor-in-Chief MATTHÄUS FELLINGER; circ. 37,439.

Neue Wochenschau: J. N. Bergerstr. 2, 7210 Mattersburg; tel. and fax (2622) 67-47-3; e-mail redaktion@wochenschau.at; internet www.wochenschau.at; f. 1908; Publr and Editor-in-Chief HELMUT WALTER.

NFZ (Neue Freie Zeitung): Friedrich-Schmidt-Pl. 4, 1080 Vienna; tel. (1) 512-35-35-0; fax (1) 512-35-35-9; internet www.fpoe.at; f. 1949; organ of Freedom Party; Man. Editor ANDREAS RUTTINGER.

Niederösterreichische Nachrichten: Gutenbergstr. 12, 3100 St Pölten; tel. (2742) 802-13-18; fax (2742) 802-14-80; e-mail chefredaktion@noen.at; internet www.noen.at; Editor-in-Chief HARALD KNABL; circ. 132,078 (2007).

Oberösterreichische Rundschau: Hafenstr. 1–3, 4020 Linz; tel. (732) 76-16-0; fax (732) 76-16-30-2; e-mail linz@bezirksrundschau.com; internet www.rundschau.co.at; Editor-in-Chief Dr THOMAS WINKLER.

Österreichische Bauernzeitung: Brucknerstr. 6, 1040 Vienna; tel. (1) 533-14-48; fax (1) 533-14-48-33; e-mail demuth@bauernzeitung.at; internet www.bauernzeitung.at; Thur.; f. 2001; publ. by Österreichischer Bauernbund; Editorial Co-ordinator CHRISTINE DEMUTH.

Rupertusblatt: Kaigasse 8, 5020 Salzburg; tel. (662) 87-22-23-0; fax (662) 87-22-23-13; e-mail rupertusblatt@kommunikation.kirchen.net; internet www.kirchen.net/rupertusblatt; publ. by Archdiocese of Salzburg; Editor-in-Chief KARL ROITHINGER; circ. 14,490.

Der Sonntag: Stephanspl. 4/VI/DG, Postfach 152, 1014 Vienna; tel. (1) 512-60-63-39-71; fax (1) 512-60-63-39-70; e-mail redaktion@dersonntag.at; internet www.dersonntag.at; f. 1848 as the *Wiener Kirchenzeitung*; present name adopted in 2004; publ. by the Archdiocese of Vienna; Editor-in-Chief ELVIRA GROISS; circ. 23,000.

POPULAR PERIODICALS

Alles Auto: Beckgasse 24, 1130 Vienna; tel. (1) 877-97-11; fax (1) 877-97-11-4; e-mail redaktion@allesauto.at; internet www.allesauto.at; f. 1992; 10 a year; motoring; Publr WALTHER KÖCK; Editor-in-Chief ENRICO FALCHETTO; circ. 55,600 (July–Dec. 2012).

Auto Touring: ÖAMTC Verlag GmbH, Schubertring 1–3, 1010 Vienna; tel. (1) 711-99-22-70-1; fax (1) 711-99-22-72-1; e-mail office@oeamtc.at; internet www.autotouring.at; f. 1947; monthly; official journal of the Austrian Automobile Organization; Editor-in-Chief PETER PISECKER; circ. 1,573,579.

Format: Taborstr. 1–3, 1020 Vienna; tel. (1) 213-12-0; fax (1) 213-12-56-00; e-mail redaktion@news.at; internet www.format.at; f. 1998; weekly, Fri.; business; independent; Editors-in-Chief ANDREAS LAMPL, ANDREAS WEBER; circ. 53,824 (July–Dec. 2012).

Die Ganze Woche: Heiligenstädter Str. 121, 1190 Vienna; tel. (1) 290-97-30; fax (1) 290-97-30-30; e-mail redaktion@dgw.at; internet www.ganzewoche.at; f. 1985; circ. 396,428 (July–Dec. 2012).

Gewinn: Stiftgasse 31, 1071 Vienna; tel. (1) 521-24-0; fax 521-24-40; e-mail gewinn@gewinn.com; internet www.gewinn.com; monthly; business, economics, personal finances; Editor-in-Chief Prof. Dr GEORG WAILAND; circ. 73,300 (July–Dec. 2012).

Gusto: Ferdinandstr. 4, 1020 Vienna; tel. (1) 863-31-53-01; fax (1) 863-31-56-10; e-mail redaktion@gusto.at; internet www.gusto.at;

f. 1983; monthly; food and drink; Editor-in-Chief Wolfgang Schlüter; circ. 63,383 (July–Dec. 2012).

Maxima: Fockygasse 29–31, 1120 Vienna; tel. and fax (2236) 600-67-30; e-mail redaktion@maxima.co.at; internet www.maxima.at; f. 1996; 11 a year; women's magazine; Editor-in-Chief Brigitte B. Fuchs; circ. 25,913 (July–Dec. 2012).

NEWS: Taborrstr. 1–3, 1020 Vienna; tel. (1) 213-12-0; fax (1) 213-12-666-1; e-mail redaktion@news.at; internet www.news.at; f. 1992; weekly, Thur.; illustrated; Editor-in-Chief Peter Pelinka; circ. 175,184 (July–Dec. 2012).

ORF nachlese: Würzburggasse 30, 1136 Vienna; tel. (1) 870-77-15-00-0; fax (1) 870-77-14-82-4; e-mail enterprise@orf.at; internet www.enterprise.orf.at; f. 1979; monthly; programme guide to television and radio broadcasts; Editor-in-Chief Katja Zinggl-Pokorny; circ. 114,667 (July–Dec. 2012).

Profil: Taborstr. 1-3, 1020 Vienna; tel. (1) 534-70-35-02; fax (1) 534-70-35-00; e-mail redaktion@profil.at; internet www.profil.at; f. 1970; weekly, Mon.; political, general; independent; Editor-in-Chief and Publr Dr Christian Rainer; circ. 63,140 (Jan.–June 2010).

Seitenblicke: Heinrich-Collin Str. 1/Top 1, 1140 Vienna; tel. (1) 90-221-0; fax (1) 90-27-93-0; e-mail redaktion@seitenblicke.at; internet www.seitenblicke.at; weekly; lifestyle, celebrity news; Editor-in-Chief Andreas Wollinger; circ. 74,874 (July–Dec. 2012).

Ski Austria: Olympiastr. 10, 6010 Innsbruck; tel. (512) 335-01-0; fax (512) 361-99-8; e-mail schmid@oesv.at; internet www.oesv.at; 7 a year; official journal of Austrian Skiing Asscn; Editor Josef Schmid.

Sportzeitung: Linke Wienzeile 40/2/22, 1060 Vienna; tel. and fax (1) 585-57-57-41-5; e-mail sportzeitung@lwmedia.at; internet www.sportzeitung.at; f. 1949; weekly sports illustrated; Editors-in-Chief Horst Hötsch, Gerhard Weber; circ. 25,464 (July–Dec. 2012).

TOPIC: Königsklostergasse 7/15, 1060 Vienna; tel. (1) 535-57-83; e-mail topic@topmedia.at; internet www.mytopic.at; 11 a year; politics, economics and culture for young people; publ. by Austrian Youth Red Cross and Austrian Youth Book Club; Dir Dr Eva Lingens; circ. 145,000 (July–Dec. 2012).

Trend: Taborstr. 1–3, 1020 Vienna; tel. (1) 213-12-0; fax (1) 213-12-56-00; e-mail redaktion@trend.at; internet www.trend.at; monthly; economics; Editors-in-Chief Andreas Lampl; Andreas Weber; circ. 56,083 (July–Dec. 2012).

TV-Media: Taborstr. 1–3, 1020 Vienna; tel. (1) 213-12-0; fax (1) 213-12-56-00; e-mail redaktion@tv-media.at; internet www.tv-media.at; f. 1995; weekly, Wed.; illustrated; Editor-in-Chief Hadubrand Schreibershofen; circ. 233,704 (July–Dec. 2012).

Welt der Frau: Dametzstr. 1–5, 4020 Linz; tel. (732) 77-00-01-11; fax (732) 77-00-01-24; e-mail info@welt-der-frau.at; internet www.welt-der-frau.at; women's monthly; Editor-in-Chief Dr Christine Haiden; circ. 59,002 (July–Dec. 2012).

Wienerin: Geiselbergstr. 15, 1100 Vienna; tel. (1) 601-17-0; fax (1) 601-17-19-1; e-mail wienerin@wienerin.at; internet www.wienerin.at; monthly; women's interest; Editor-in-Chief Sylvia Margret Steinitz; circ. 94,592 (July–Dec. 2012).

Woman: Taborstr. 1-3, 1020 Vienna; tel. (1) 213-12-0; fax (1) 213-12-56-00; e-mail kindl.gabriele@woman.at; internet www.woman.at; fortnightly; women's interest; Editor-in-Chief Euke Frank; circ. 190,000 (July–Dec. 2012).

SPECIALIST PERIODICALS

FSG Direkt: Verlag des ÖGB GmbH, Johann-Böhm-Pl. 1, 1020 Vienna; tel. (1) 662-32-96-39-74-4; fax (1) 662-32-96-39-79-3; e-mail christoph.hoellriegl@fsg.at; internet www.fsg.or.at; monthly; organ of the Fraktion Sozialdemokratischer GewerkschafterInnen (FSG—Social Democratic movement within the Austrian Trade Union Fed.); Editor-in-Chief Christoph Höllriegl; circ 47,500.

ITM praktiker: Apollogasse 22, Postfach 36, 1072 Vienna; tel. (1) 526-46-68-0; fax (810) 95-54-29-83-37; e-mail redaktion@praktiker.at; internet www.praktiker.at; f. 1945; technical hobbies, photography; Editor-in-Chief Felix Wessely; circ. 10,500.

Juristische Blätter (with 'Wirtschaftsrechtliche Blätter'): Springer Verlag, Sachsenpl. 4, Postfach 89, 1201 Vienna; tel. (1) 330-24-15-0; fax (1) 330-24-26; internet www.springer.at/jbl; f. 1872; monthly; law; Editor M. Lukas; circ. 6,500.

Die Landwirtschaft: Wiener Str. 64, 3100 St Pölten; e-mail office@lk-noe.at; internet www.lk-noe.at; f. 1922; monthly; Editor-in-Chief Ulrike Raser; circ. 42,000.

Literatur und Kritik: Otto-Müller-Verlag, Ernest-Thun-Str. 11, 5020 Salzburg; tel. (662) 88-19-74; fax (662) 87-23-87; e-mail info@omvs.at; internet www.omvs.at; f. 1966; 5 a year; Austrian and European literature and criticism; Editor Karl-Markus Gauss.

MEDIZIN Populär: Nibelungengasse 13, 1010 Vienna; tel. (1) 512-44-86-0; fax (1) 512-44-86-24; e-mail k.kirschbichler@aerzteverlagshaus.at; internet www.medizinpopulaer.at; monthly; health and fitness; Editor-in-Chief Karin Kirschbichler; circ.77,600 (July–Dec. 2012).

Öffentliche Sicherheit: Postfach 100, Herrengasse 7, 1014 Vienna; tel. (1) 531-26-23-07; fax (1) 531-26-25-04; e-mail redaktion.sicherheit@gmail.com; internet www.bmi.gv.at/oeffentlsicherheit; 6 a year; published by the Federal Ministry of the Interior; Editor-in-Chief Werner Sabitzer; circ. 15,000.

onrail: Leberstr. 122, 1110 Vienna; tel. (1) 740-95-0; fax (1) 740-95-18-3; e-mail christina.dany@bohmann.at; internet www.onrail.at; every 2 months; travel, culture, lifestyle; Editor-in-Chief Christina Dany; circ. 85,000.

Österreichische Ärztezeitung: Nibelungengasse 13, 1010 Vienna; tel. (1) 512-44-86-0; fax (1) 512-44-86-24; e-mail office@aerzteverlagshaus.at; internet www.aerztezeitung.at; f. 1945; 20 a year; organ of the Austrian Medical Board; Editor-in-Chief Dr Agnes M. Mühlgassner; circ. 42,606 (July–Dec. 2012).

Österreichische Ingenieur- und Architekten-Zeitschrift (ÖIAZ): Eschenbachgasse 9, 1010 Vienna; tel. (1) 587-35-36; fax (1) 370-58-06-33-3; e-mail office@oiav.at; internet www.oiav.at; f. 1849; 6 a year; Editor Peter Reichel; circ. 2,200.

Österreichische Monatshefte: Rathausstr. 10, 1010 Vienna; tel. (1) 409-55-37-0; fax (1) 409-55-37-36-9; e-mail redaktion.omh@alpha-medien.at; internet www.alpha-medien.at; f. 1945; 6 a year; organ of Österreichische Volkspartei; Editor-in-Chief Andreas Kratschmar.

Österreichische Musikzeitschrift: Hanuschgasse 1/3/3/6, 1010 Vienna; tel. (1) 664-186-386-8; e-mail redaktion@oemz.at; internet www.oemz.at; f. 1946; bi-monthly; music; Editor Dr Daniel Ender; circ. 5,000.

Reichsbund-Aktuell mit SPORT: Laudongasse 16, 1080 Vienna; tel. and fax (1) 729-19-55; e-mail info@amateurfussball.at; internet www.amateurfussball.at; f. 1917; monthly; Catholic; organ of Reichsbund, Bewegung für christliche Gesellschaftspolitik und Sport; Editor Walter Raming; circ. 12,000.

SPÖ-Aktuell: Löwelstr. 18, 1014 Vienna; tel. (1) 534-27-27-5; fax (1) 534-27-28-2; e-mail spoe.aktuell@spoe.at; internet aktuell.spoe.at; weekly; organ of Social Democratic Party; Editor-in-Chief Peter Slawik.

Wiener Klinische Wochenschrift: Sachsenpl. 4–6, 1200 Vienna; tel. (1) 330-24-15-31-3; fax (1) 330-24-26-26-0; e-mail wkw-office@springer.at; internet www.springer.at/wkw; f. 1888; medical bi-weekly; Editor-in-Chief M. Köller.

NEWS AGENCY

APA (Austria Presse Agentur): Laimgrubengasse 10, 1060 Vienna; tel. (1) 360-60-0; fax (1) 360-60-30-99; e-mail apa@apa.at; internet www.apa.at; f. 1946; co-operative agency of the Austrian Newspapers and Broadcasting Co (private co, incl. 15 daily newspapers and Österreichische Rundfunk); CEO Peter Kropsch; Editor-in-Chief Michael Lang.

PRESS ASSOCIATIONS

Österreichischer Zeitschriften- und Fachmedienverband (Austrian Magazine Publishers Asscn): Wipplingerstr. 15/5, 1010 Vienna; tel. and fax (1) 319-70-01; e-mail office@oezv.or.at; internet www.oezv.or.at; f. 1946; 146 mems; Man. Dir Gerald Grünberger.

Verband Österreichischer Zeitungen (Austrian Newspaper Asscn): Wipplingerstr. 15, Postfach 65, 1013 Vienna; tel. (1) 533-79-79; fax (1) 533-79-79-42-2; e-mail office@voez.at; internet www.voez.at; f. 1946; 61 mems; mems include 16 daily newspapers and 45 other newspapers and periodicals; Pres. Thomas Kralinger; Man. Dir Gerald Grünberger.

Publishers

Akademische Druck- und Verlagsanstalt (ADEVA): St Peter Hauptstr. 98, 8010 Graz; tel. (316) 46-30-03; fax (316) 46-30-03-24; e-mail info@adeva.com; internet www.adeva.com; f. 1949; scholarly reprints and new works, facsimile editions of codices, fine art facsimile editions, music books and facsimile editions; Man. Dr Paul Struzl.

Amalthea Signum Verlag: Am Heumarkt 19, 1030 Vienna; tel. (1) 712-35-60; fax (1) 713-89-95; e-mail verlag@amalthea.at; internet www.amalthea.at; f. 2002 by merger of Amalthea Verlag (f. 1917) and Buchverlags Signum (f. 1978); politics, economics; Man. Dir Dr Herbert Fleissner.

Böhlau Verlag GmbH & Co KG: Wiesingerstr. 1, 1010 Vienna; tel. (1) 330-24-27-0; fax (1) 330-24-32; e-mail info@boehlau-verlag.com; internet www.boehlau.at; f. 1947; history, law, philology, the arts, sociology, social sciences; Dir Dr Peter Rauch.

Christian Brandstätter Verlag GmbH & Co KG: Wickenburggasse 26, 1080 Vienna; tel. (1) 512-15-43-0; fax (1) 512-15-43-23-1; e-mail info@cbv.at; internet www.cbv.at; f. 1982; the arts, lifestyle; Publrs Dr CHRISTIAN BRANDSTÄTTER, NIKOLAUS BRANDSTÄTTER.

Wilhelm Braumüller Universitäts Verlagsbuchhandlung GmbH: Servitengasse 5, 1090 Vienna; tel. (1) 319-11-59; fax (1) 310-28-05; e-mail office@braumueller.at; internet www.braumueller.at; f. 1783; politics, law, ethnology, literature and theatre, linguistics, history, journalism, sociology, philosophy, psychology, communications; university publrs; Dirs BERNHARD BOROVANSKY, KONSTANZE BOROVANSKY.

Verlag Brüder Hollinek und Co GmbH: Luisenstr. 20, 3002 Purkersdorf; tel. and fax (2231) 673-65; fax (2231) 673-65-24; e-mail office@hollinek.at; internet www.hollinek.at; f. 1872; science, law and administration, printing, reference works, dictionaries; Dir RICHARD HOLLINEK.

Czernin Verlags GmbH: Kupkagasse 4, 1080 Vienna; tel. (1) 403-35-63; fax (1) 403-35-63-15; e-mail office@czernin-verlag.com; internet www.czernin-verlag.com; f. 1999; philosophy, politics, literature, the arts; Dir BENEDICT FÖGER.

Edition und Atelier Koenigstein: Anzengrubergasse 50, 3400 Klosterneuburg; tel. (2243) 26-04-6; e-mail office@koenigsteinkunst.com; internet www.koenigsteinkunst.com; f. 1987; stories, fairy tales, poetry; Publr GEORG KOENIGSTEIN.

Facultas Verlags- und Buchhandels AG: Stolberggasse 26, 1050 Vienna; tel. (1) 310-53-56; fax (1) 319-70-50; e-mail office@facultas.at; internet www.facultas.at; f. 2001 by merger of WUV Universitätsverlags GmbH and Servicebetriebe GmbH an der Wirtschaftsuniversität Wien; imprint: facultas.wuv; science, medicine, law, social sciences; Dir THOMAS STAUFFER.

Wilhelm Maudrich KG: Spitalgasse 21A, 1090 Vienna; tel. (1) 402-47-12-27; fax (1) 402-47-12-40; e-mail sortiment@maudrich.com; internet www.facultas.at/maudrich; f. 1909; medical.

Folio Verlagsgesellschaft mbH: Schönbrunner Str. 31, 1050 Vienna; tel. (1) 581-37-08-0; fax (1) 581-37-08-20; e-mail office@folioverlag.com; internet www.folioverlag.com; literature, contemporary art, non-fiction; Dirs Dr LUDWIG PAULMICHL, HERMANN GUMMERER.

Freytag-Berndt u. Artaria KG: Brunner Str. 69, 1231 Vienna; tel. (1) 869-90-90-0; fax (1) 869-90-90-61; e-mail office@freytagberndt.at; internet www.freytagberndt.at; f. 1879; cartography, geography, atlases, maps, guides, geographical data; Dir Dr CHRISTIAN HALBWACHS.

Haymon Verlag GesmbH: Erlerstr. 10, 6020 Innsbruck; tel. (512) 57-63-00; fax (512) 57-63-00-14; e-mail office@haymonverlag.at; internet www.haymonverlag.at; f. 1982; fiction, non-fiction; Dir MARKUS HATZER.

Jugend & Volk Gesellschaft GmbH: Hainburger Str. 33, 1016 Vienna; tel. (1) 407-27-07; fax (1) 407-27-07-31; e-mail service@jugendvolk.at; internet www.jugendvolk.at; f. 1921; pedagogics, textbooks; Dir IRIS BLATTERER.

Verlag Kremayr & Scheriau KG: Währinger Str. 76/8, 1090 Vienna; tel. (1) 713-87-70-0; fax (1) 713-87-70-20; e-mail office@kremayr-scheriau.at; internet www.kremayr-scheriau.at; f. 1951; non-fiction, history, lifestyle; Dir MARTIN SCHERIAU.

Kunstverlag Wolfrum: Augustinerstr. 10, 1010 Vienna; tel. (1) 512-53-98-0; fax (1) 512-53-98-57; e-mail wolfrum@wolfrum.at; internet www.wolfrum.at; f. 1919; art; Publr HUBERT WOLFRUM.

Leykam Buchverlagsgesellschaft mbH Nfg & Co KG: Dreihackengasse 20, 8020 Graz; tel. (316) 80-95-58-1; fax (501) 80-95-58-5; e-mail office@leykamverlag.at; internet www.leykamverlag.at; f. 1585; art, literature, academic, law; Dir Dr WOLFGANG HÖLZL.

LexisNexis Verlag ARD ORAC GmbH & Co KG: Marxergasse 25, 1030 Vienna; tel. (1) 534-52-0; fax (1) 534-52-14-1; e-mail verlag@lexisnexis.at; internet www.lexisnexis.at; f. 1946; legal books, periodicals and online databases; subsidiary of Reed Elsevier Group PLC (UK); CEO PETER J. DAVIES; Dir Dr GERIT KANDUTSCH.

Linde Verlag GmbH: Scheydgasse 24, 1211 Vienna; tel. (1) 246-30-0; fax (1) 246-30-23; e-mail office@lindeverlag.at; internet www.lindeverlag.at; f. 1925; business, economics, law; Dirs ANDREAS JENTZSCH, Dr EDUARD MÜLLER, Dr OSKAR MENNEL, EDUARD MÜLLER.

Literaturverlag Droschl GmbH: Stenggstr. 33, 8043 Graz; tel. (316) 32-64-04; fax (316) 32-40-71; e-mail office@droschl.com; internet www.droschl.com; f. 1978; contemporary literature.

MANZ'sche Verlags- und Universitätsbuchhandlung GmbH: Johannesgasse 23, 1010 Vienna; tel. (1) 531-61-0; fax (1) 531-61-18-1; e-mail verlag@manz.at; internet www.manz.at; f. 1849; law, tax and economic sciences; textbooks and school books; Man. Dir SUSANNE STEIN-DICHTL; Publr Dr WOLFGANG PICHLER.

Otto Müller Verlag: Ernest-Thun-Str. 11, 5020 Salzburg; tel. (662) 88-19-74-0; fax (662) 87-23-87; e-mail info@omvs.at; internet www.omvs.at; f. 1937; general; Man. ARNO KLEIBEL.

Musikverlag Doblinger: Dorotheergasse 10, 1010 Vienna; tel. (1) 515-03-0; fax (1) 515-03-51; e-mail music@doblinger.at; internet www.doblinger-musikverlag.at; f. 1876; music; Dir PETER PANY.

Niederösterreichisches Pressehaus Druck- und Verlagsgesellschaft mbH (Residenz Verlag): Gutenbergstr. 12, 3100 St Pölten; tel. (2742) 802-16-12; fax (2742) 802-14-31; e-mail info@residenzverlag.at; internet www.residenzverlag.at; f. 1956; literature, children's, non-fiction; Dir CLAUDIA ROMEDER.

Verlag Österreich GmbH: Bäckerstr. 1, 1010 Vienna; tel. (1) 610-77-0; fax (1) 610-77-41-9; e-mail office@verlagoesterreich.at; internet www.verlagoesterreich.at; f. 1804; fmrly state-owned; acquired by Wissenschaftlichen Verlags GmbH (Germany) in 2008; law, CD-ROMs; Dir ANDRÉ CARO.

Österreichischer Bundesverlag Schulbuch GmbH & Co KG: Frankgasse 4, 1090 Vienna; tel. (1) 401-36-0; fax (1) 401-36-18-5; e-mail office@oebv.at; internet www.oebv.at; educational books, dictionaries; Dir Dr RAINER STAHL.

Picus Verlag GmbH: Friedrich-Schmidt-Pl. 4, 1080 Vienna; tel. (1) 408-18-21; fax (1) 408-18-21-6; e-mail info@picus.at; internet www.picus.at; f. 1984; children's books, literature, travel; Dirs DOROTHEA LÖCKER, Dr ALEXANDER POTYKA.

Springer-Verlag GmbH: Sachsenpl. 4–6, 1201 Vienna; tel. (1) 330-24-15-55-2; fax (1) 330-24-26-44-4; e-mail springer@springer.at; internet www.springer.at; f. 1924; medicine, natural sciences, technology, architecture, art, periodicals; Man. Dir ALOIS SILLABER.

Leopold Stocker Verlag GmbH: Hofgasse 5, Postfach 438, 8011 Graz; tel. (316) 82-16-36; fax (316) 83-56-12; e-mail stocker-verlag@stocker-verlag.com; internet www.stocker-verlag.com; f. 1917; history, nature, hunting, fiction, agriculture, textbooks; Dir WOLFGANG DVORAK-STOCKER.

Verlagsgruppe Styria GmbH & Co KG: Lobkowitzpl. 1, 1010 Vienna; tel. (1) 512-88-08-0; fax (1) 512-88-08-75; e-mail office@styriabooks.at; internet www.verlagsgruppestyria.at; f. 2003 by merger of Styria Verlag and Pichler Verlag; biographies, theology, religion, philosophy; imprints: Styria Verlag, Pichler Verlag, Molden Verlag, Kneipp Verlag, Edition Styria; Man. Dir GERDA SCHAFFELHOFER.

Tyrolia Buchverlag: Exlgasse 20, Postfach 220, 6020 Innsbruck; tel. (512) 223-32-02; fax (512) 223-32-06; e-mail buchverlag@tyrolia.at; internet www.tyrolia-verlag.at; f. 1888; subsidiary of Verlagsanstalt Tyrolia GmbH; geography, history, science, children's, religion, fiction; Chair. Dr GOTTFRIED KOMPATSCHER.

Verlag Carl Ueberreuter GmbH: Alserstr. 24, 1090 Vienna; tel. (1) 404-44-17-1; fax (1) 404-44-5; e-mail office@ueberreuter.at; internet www.ueberreuter.at; f. 1946; non-fiction, children's, literature; imprints: Annette Betz and Tosa; Man. Dir Dr KLAUS KÄMPFE-BURGHARDT.

Universal Edition AG: Karlspl. 6, 1010 Vienna; tel. (1) 337-23-0; fax (1) 337-23-40-0; e-mail office@universaledition.com; internet www.universaledition.com; f. 1901; music; Dirs JOHANN JURANEK, ASTRID KOBLANCK, STEFAN RAGG.

VERITAS Verlags- und Buchhandelsgesellschaft mbH & Co OHG: Hafenstr. 2A, 4010 Linz; tel. (732) 77-64-51-0; fax (732) 77-64-51-22-39; e-mail kundenberatung@veritas.at; internet www.veritas.at; f. 1945; acquired Oldenbourg Schulbuch-Verlag in 2006; training materials, educational books; Dir MANFRED MERANER.

Paul Zsolnay Verlag Deuticke GmbH: Prinz-Eugen-Str. 30, 1041 Vienna; tel. (1) 505-76-61-0; fax (1) 505-76-61-10; e-mail info@zsolnay.at; internet www.zsolnay.at; f. 1923; fiction, non-fiction; incl. Deuticke Verlag; Dir MICHAEL KRÜGER.

PUBLISHERS' ASSOCIATION

Hauptverband des Österreichischen Buchhandels (Asscn of Austrian Publrs and Booksellers): Grünangergasse 4, 1010 Vienna; tel. (1) 512-15-35; fax (1) 512-84-82; e-mail sekretariat@hvb.at; internet www.buecher.at; f. 1859; Pres. Dr GERALD SCHANTIN; Man. Dir Dr INGE KRALUPPER; 530 mems.

Broadcasting and Communications

REGULATORY BODIES

Rundfunk und Telekom Regulierungs GmbH (Austrian Regulatory Authority for Broadcasting and Telecommunications—RTR): Mariahilfer Str. 77–79, 1060 Vienna; tel. (1) 580-58-0; fax (1) 580-58-91-91; e-mail rtr@rtr.at; internet www.rtr.at; f. 2001; comprises 2 divisions: broadcasting and telecommunications; provides operational support to KommAustria and Telekom-Control Kommission; CEO Telecommunications Dr GEORG SERENTSCHY; CEO Broadcasting Dr ALFRED GRINSCHGL.

Kommunikationsbehörde Austria (KommAustria) (Austrian Communications Authority): Mariahilferstr. 77–79, 1060

Vienna; tel. (1) 580-58-0; fax (1) 580-58-91-91; e-mail rtr@rtr.at; internet www.rtr.at/de/rtr/organekommaustria; f. 2001; regulatory authority for the Austrian broadcasting industry (responsible for activities such as issuing licenses to private television and radio stations, managing broadcasting frequencies, handling the legal supervision of private broadcasters, as well as preparing and launching digital broadcasting in Austria); Chair. MICHAEL OGRIS.

Telekom-Control-Kommission (TKK): Mariahilferstr. 77–79, 1060 Vienna; tel. (1) 580-58-0; fax (1) 580-58-91-91; e-mail rtr@rtr.at; internet www.rtr.at/en/rtr/OrganeTKK; f. 1997; regulates competition in the telecommunications market, as well as postal services; Chair. Dr ELFRIEDE SOLÉ.

TELECOMMUNICATIONS

A1 Telekom Austria: Postfach 1001, 1011 Vienna; tel. 506-64-0; internet www.a1telekom.at; f. 2010 following the merger of Telekom Austria AG and mobilkom austria; fixed-line telecommunications and broadband internet access; part of Telekom Austria Group; CEO Dr HANNES AMETSREITER.

Hutchison 3G Austria GmbH (3 AT): Gasometer C, Guglgasse 12/10/3, 1110 Vienna; tel. (5) 066-00; fax (5) 066-30-30-31; e-mail 3serviceteam@drei.at; internet www.drei.at; f. 2002; mobile cellular telecommunications; subsidiary of Hutchison Whampoa Ltd (Hong Kong); CEO JAN TRIONOW.

Orange Austria Telecommunication GmbH: Brünner Str. 52, 1210 Vienna; tel. (1) 277-28-0; fax (0) 699-70-77-0; e-mail info@orange.co.at; internet www.orange.at; f. 1998; fmrly ONE GmbH; present name adopted 2008; mobile cellular telecommunications; acquired by Hutchison 3G Austria GmbH in 2012; CEO MICHAEL KRAMMER.

Tele2 Telecommunication GmbH: Donau-City-Str. 11, 1220 Vienna; tel. (5) 050-0; fax (5) 050-03-79-4; e-mail kundenservice@at.tele2.com; internet www.tele2.at; f. 1998; owned by Tele2 AB (Sweden); fixed-line telecommunications and broadband internet access; Man. Dir Dr ALFRED PUFITSCH.

tele.ring: Rennweg 97–99, Postfach 1012, 1030 Vienna; tel. (1) 795-85-60-30; fax (1) 795-85-65-86; e-mail info@telering.co.at; internet www.telering.at; mobile cellular telecommunications; wholly owned by T-Mobile Austria GmbH; Chair. ROBERT CHVÁTAL.

T-Mobile Austria GmbH: Rennweg 97–99, 1030 Vienna; tel. (1) 795-85-0; fax (1) 795-85-65-86; e-mail presse@t-mobile.at; internet www.t-mobile.at; f. 1996 as max.mobil; present name adopted 2002; subsidiary of T-Mobile International AG & Co KG (Germany); CEO ROBERT CHVÁTAL.

UPC Austria GmbH: Wolfganggasse 58-60, 1120 Vienna; tel. (1) 960-60-60-0; fax (1) 960-60-96-0; e-mail info.wien@upc.at; internet www.upc.at; fixed-line telecommunications, broadband internet access (under brand name Chello), and digital cable television; also owns internet service provider, Inode; owned by Liberty Global, Inc. (USA); Man. Dir THOMAS HINTZE.

BROADCASTING

Radio

The state-owned Österreichischer Rundfunk (ORF) provides three national and nine regional radio channels, as well as an overseas service. The provision of radio services was liberalized in 1998.

Österreichischer Rundfunk (ORF) (Austrian Broadcasting Company): Würzburggasse 30, 1136 Vienna; tel. (1) 870-70-30; fax (1) 878-70-33-0; e-mail kundendienst@orf.at; internet orf.at; f. 1924; state-owned; operates 3 national radio stations: Ö1, Hitradio Ö3 and FM4; 9 regional radio stations (Ö2): Radio Burgenland, Radio Kärnten, Radio Niederösterreich, Radio Oberösterreich, Radio Salzburg, Radio Steiermark, Radio Tirol, Radio Vorarlberg, Radio Wien; 7 foreign-language programmes for minorities in Austria; 1 international radio station: Radio Österreich 1 International; 1 internet-based radio station: oe1campus; 4 television channels: ORF1, ORF2, ORF III and ORF SPORT +; operates satellite television channel, 3 Sat, in conjunction with ARD (Germany), SRG (Switzerland) and ZDF (Germany); also distributes content via teletext and internet; Dir-Gen. Dr ALEXANDER WRABETZ; Dirs KARL AMON (Radio), KATHRIN ZECHNER (Television), MICHAEL GÖTZHABER (Technics, Online and New Media).

Private and Commercial Radio Operators

Antenne Kärnten Regionalradio GmbH & Co KG: Hasnerstr. 2, 9020 Klagenfurt; tel. (463) 458-88-0; fax (463) 458-88-90-9; e-mail servicektn@antenne.net; internet www.antennekaernten.at; 1 FM station, Antenne Kärnten; broadcasts in Carinthia; Mans GOTTFRIED BICHLER, RUDOLF KUZMICKI, Dr KLAUS SCHWEIGHOFER.

Antenne Oberösterreich GmbH: Durisolstr. 7/Top22A, 4600 Wels; tel. and fax (7242) 351-29-9; e-mail info@antennewels.at; internet www.antennewels.at; 1 FM station, Antenne Wels 98.3; broadcasts in Oberösterreich; Man. Dr CHRISTOPH LEON.

Antenne Österreich GmbH (Niederlassung Salzburg): Friedensstr. 14A, 5020 Salzburg; tel. (662) 40-80-0; fax (662) 40-80-70; e-mail info@antennesalzburg.at; internet www.antennesalzburg.at; 1 FM station, Antenne Salzburg; broadcasts in Salzburg and Lienz; Dir SYLVIA BUCHHAMMER; Station Man. MATTHIAS NIESWANDT.

Antenne Österreich GmbH (Niederlassung Tirol): Maria-Theresien-Str. 8, 6020 Innsbruck; tel. (512) 574-12-72-3; fax (512) 574-12-75-0; e-mail info@antennetirol.at; internet www.antennetirol.at; 2 FM stations, Antenne Tirol (Innsbruck) and Antenne Tirol (Unterland); broadcasts in Tyrol; Dir SYLVIA BUCHHAMMER; Station Man. MATTHIAS NIESWANDT.

Antenne Österreich GmbH (Niederlassung Wien): Makartgasse 3, 1010 Vienna; tel. (1) 217-00-0; fax (1) 217-00-77-09; e-mail office@antennewien.at; internet www.antennewien.at; 1 FM station, Antenne Wien 102.5; broadcasts in Vienna; Dir SYLVIA BUCHHAMMER.

Antenne Steiermark Regionalradio GmbH & Co KG: Am Sendergrund 15, 8143 Dobl; tel. (3136) 505-0; fax (3136) 505-11-1; e-mail info@antenne.net; internet www.antenne.net; 1 FM station, Antenne Steiermark; broadcasts in Styria; Mans GOTTFRIED BICHLER, RUDOLF KUZMICKI, Dr KLAUS SCHWEIGHOFER.

KRONEHIT: KRONEHIT Radiobetriebs GmbH, Daumegasse 1, 1100 Vienna; tel. (1) 600-61-00; e-mail office@kronehit.at; internet www.kronehit.at; Austria's sole national, private radio operator; popular music; Man. Dr ERNST SWOBODA.

Radio Arabella GmbH: Alser Str. 4, Hof 1, Altes AKH, 1090 Vienna; tel. (1) 492-99-29-20-2; fax (1) 492-99-29-20-1; e-mail office@radioarabella.at; internet www.radioarabella.at; 5 radio stations in Austria: Radio Arabella Mostviertel-St. Pölten, Radio Arabella Oberösterreich, Radio Arabella Salzburg, Radio Arabella Tulln-Krems and Radio Arabella Wien; sister station broadcasts in Munich, Germany; Man. Dir WOLFGANG STRUBER.

88.6—wir spielen was wir wollen: Radio Eins Privatradio GmbH, Heiligenstädter Lände 29, 1190 Vienna; tel. (1) 360-88-0; fax (1) 360-88-30-9; e-mail webmaster@radio886.at; internet www.radio886.at; broadcasts in Vienna, Burgenland and Lower Austria; popular music; Mans OLIVER BÖHM, HOLGER WILLOH.

Television

The state-owned Österreichischer Rundfunk (ORF) retained a monopoly over television broadcasting in Austria until 2001. It operates two terrestrial television channels and a satellite station in conjunction with German and Swiss companies. Digital television services, comprising three television channels, ORF1, ORF2 and a commercial service, ATV, were launched in October 2006. Analogue broadcasting was discontinued in 2011.

Österreichischer Rundfunk: see Radio.

Private and Commercial Television Operators

ATV Privat TV GmbH & Co KG: Aspernbrückengasse 2, 1020 Vienna; tel. (1) 213-64-0; fax (1) 213-64-99-9; e-mail atv@atv.at; internet www.atv.at; f. 2003; CEO LUDWIG BAUER.

Austria 9 TV GmbH: Rosenhügel Filmstudios, Speisinger Str. 121–127, 1230 Vienna; tel. (1) 888-04-03; fax (1) 888-04-03-99; e-mail office@austria9.at; internet www.austria9.at; f. 2007; free-to-air digital satellite and cable channel; owned by Hubert Burda Media AG & Co KG (Germany); Man. Dir Dr CONRAD HEBERLING.

Puls4 TV GmbH & Co KG: Mariahilfer Str. 2, 1070 Vienna; tel. (1) 999-88-0; fax (1) 999-88-88-88; e-mail office@puls4.com; internet www.puls4.com; f. 2004 as Puls TV; commercial channel (Puls4), broadcast via digital satellite and cable; acquired by ProSiebenSat1. Media AG (Germany) in 2007; Man. Dir MARKUS BREITENECKER.

Sky Österreich GmbH: Schönbrunne Str. 297/2, 1120 Vienna; tel. (1) 166-20-0; e-mail service@sky.at; internet www.sky.at; f. 2003 as Premiere Fernsehen GmbH; adopted current name in 2009; satellite operator offering films, sport and adult programming; wholly owned by Sky Deutschland AG; Man. Dirs CARSTEN SCHMIDT, KAI MITTERLECHNER.

Finance

(cap. = capital; res = reserves; dep. = deposits; m. = million; brs = branches; amounts in euros)

BANKS

Banks in Austria, apart from the National Bank, belong to one of five categories: banks that are organized as corporations (i.e. joint-stock and private banks), and special-purpose credit institutions; savings banks; and co-operative banks. Co-operative banks include rural credit co-operatives (Raiffeisenbanken) and industrial credit co-operatives (Volksbanken). The remaining two categories comprise the mortgage banks of the various Austrian federal provinces, and the building societies. The majority of Austrian banks (with the exception of the building societies) operate on the basis of universal banking, although certain categories have specialized. Banking operations are governed by the Banking Act of 1993 Bankwesengesetz.

At the end of 2012 there were 809 banks and credit organizations in Austria.

Central Bank

Oesterreichische Nationalbank (OeNB) (Austrian National Bank): Otto-Wagner-Pl. 3, 1090 Vienna; tel. (1) 404-20-0; fax (1) 404-20-04-23-99; e-mail oenb.info@oenb.co.at; internet www.oenb.at; f. 1922; 100% state-owned; cap. 12m., res 4,136.6m., dep. 35,168.6m. (Dec. 2009); Pres. Dr CLAUS J. RAIDL; Gov. Prof. Dr EWALD NOWOTNY; brs in Graz, Innsbruck and Linz.

Commercial Banks

Adria Bank AG: Gonzagagasse 16, 1010 Vienna; tel. (1) 514-09-0; fax (1) 514-09-43; e-mail headoffice@adriabank.at; internet www.adriabank.at; f. 1980; 50.54% owned by Nova Kreditna Banka Maribor and 28.46% by Nova Ljubljanska Banka (both Slovenia), 21% by Beogradska Banka (Serbia); cap. 8.7m., res 21.9m., dep. 149.6m. (Dec. 2012); Chair. GREGOR KAISER.

Alpenbank AG: Kaiserjägerstr. 9, 6020 Innsbruck; tel. (512) 599-77; fax (512) 562-01-5; e-mail private-banking@alpenbank.com; internet www.alpenbank.at; f. 1983 as Save Rössler Bank AG; name changed as above in 1991; cap. 10.2m., res 5.1m., dep. 126.6m. (Dec. 2012); Chair. REINHARD MAYR; CEO MARTIN STERZINGER.

Bank Gutmann AG: Schwarzenbergpl. 16, 1010 Vienna; tel. (1) 502-20-0; fax (1) 502-202-249; e-mail mail@gutmann.at; internet www.gutmann.at; f. 1970 as Bank Gebrüd AG; present name adopted 1995; 83% owned by Gutmann Holding AG, 17% owned by partners; cap. 12.2m., res 27.7m., dep. 710.3m. (Dec. 2012); Chair. Dr FRANK W. LIPPITT.

Bank Winter & Co AG: Singerstr. 10, POB 878, 1010 Vienna; tel. (1) 515-04-0; fax (1) 515-04-20-0; e-mail contact@bankwinter.com; internet www.bankwinter.com; f. 1892; re-established 1959; present name adopted 1986; cap. 35m., res 36.1m., dep. 612.5m. (June 2013); Chair. and CEO THOMAS MOSKOVICS.

Bankhaus Carl Spängler und Co AG: Postfach 41, 5024 Salzburg; Schwarzstr. 1, 5020 Salzburg; tel. (662) 86-86-0; fax (662) 86-86-15-8; e-mail bankhaus@spaengler.at; internet www.spaengler.at; f. 1828; cap. 15m., res 53.4m., dep. 940.2m. (Dec. 2012); Chair., Management Bd Dr HELMUT GERLICH; 9 brs.

Bankhaus Krentschker und Co AG: Am Eisernen Tor 3, 8010 Graz; tel. (316) 80-30-0; fax (316) 80-30-86-90; e-mail mail@krentschker.at; internet www.krentschker.at; f. 1924; 92.58% owned by Steiermärkische Bank und Sparkassen AG, 7.34% by Kärntner Sparkasse AG, and 0.08% by private shareholders; cap. 13.8m., res 47.7m., dep. 845.4m. (Dec. 2012); Chair., Management Bd Dr GEORG WOLF-SCHÖNACH; 3 brs.

Bankhaus Schelhammer & Schattera AG: Postfach 618, 1011 Vienna; Goldschmiedgasse 3, 1010 Vienna; tel. (1) 534-34-0; fax (1) 534-34-80-65; e-mail bank.office@schelhammer.at; internet www.schelhammer.at; f. 1832; cap. 50m., res 22m., dep. 543.6m. (Dec. 2012); Chair. MICHAEL MARTINEK; 1 br.

BAWAG PSK Bank für Arbeit und Wirtschaft und Österreichische Postsparkasse AG (BAWAG PSK): Georg-Coch-Pl. 2, 1018 Vienna; tel. (1) 599-05; fax (1) 534-53-22-84-0; e-mail kundenservice@bawagpsk.com; internet www.bawag.com; f. 1922 as Bank für Arbeit und Wirtschaft AG; acquired by Cerberus Capital Management (USA) in 2006; cap. 250m., res 2,169.5m., dep. 27,477m. (Dec. 2012); Chair., Management Bd BYRON HAYNES; 150 brs.

Capital Bank-Grawe Gruppe AG: Burgring 16, 8010 Graz; tel. (316) 807-20; fax (316) 807-23-90; e-mail office.graz@capitalbank.at; internet www.capitalbank.at; f. 1922 as Gewerbe- und Handelsbank; present name adopted 2001; wholly owned by Hypo-Bank Burgenland AG (Austria); cap. 10m., res 111.6m., dep. 341.4m. (Dec. 2012); CEO CHRISTIAN JAUK.

DenizBank AG: Thomas-Klestil-Pl. 1, 1030 Vienna; tel. (1) 505-10-52-02-0; fax (1) 505-10-52-02-9; e-mail service@denizbank.at; internet www.denizbank.at; f. 1996 as ESBANK AG; present name adopted 2003; 64.06% owned by DenizBank AS (Turkey), 35.93% by Deniz Leasing AS (Turkey); cap. 95.8m., res 170.7m., dep. 3,812.8m. (Dec. 2012); Chair., Supervisory Bd HAKAN ATES.

Kathrein Privatbank AG: Postfach 174, Wipplingerstr. 25, 1013 Vienna; tel. (1) 534-51-26-9; fax (1) 534-51-23-3; e-mail anita.ilic@kathrein.at; internet www.kathrein.at; f. 1924 as Kathrein Privatbank; present name adopted in 1998; owned by Raiffeisen Zentralbank Österreich AG; cap. 20m., res 7.1m., dep. 453.6m. (Dec. 2012); Chair. Dr SUSANNE HÖLLINGER.

Meinl Bank AG: Postfach 99, Bauernmarkt 2, 1010 Vienna; tel. (1) 531-88-0; fax (1) 531-88-44-0; e-mail servicecenter@meinlbank.com; internet www.meinlbank.com; f. 1923; cap. 9m., res 28.1m., dep. 249.7m. (Dec. 2012); Dir PETER WEINZIERL; 2 brs.

Österreichische Volksbanken-Aktiengesellschaft: Kolingasse 14-16, POB 95, 1090 Vienna; tel. (1) 313-40-0; fax (1) 531-35-98-3; e-mail invest@investkredit.at; internet www.volksbank.com/investkredit; f. 1957; cap. 885.6m., res –0.08m., dep. 14,903.1m. (Dec. 2012); Chair. HANS JÖRG SCHELLING; CEO STEPHAN KOREN.

Schoellerbank AG: Palais Rothschild, Renngasse 3, 1010 Vienna; tel. (1) 534-71-0; fax (1) 534-71-655; e-mail info@schoellerbank.at; internet www.schoellerbank.at; f. 1998 by merger of Schoellerbank AG (f. 1833) and Salzburger Kredit- und Wechsel-Bank AG (f. 1922); owned by UniCredit Bank Austria AG; cap. 20m., res 53.9m., dep. 2,736.8m. (Dec. 2012); Chair., Management Bd HELMUT BERNKOPF.

Unicredit Bank Austria AG: Schottengasse 6–8, 1010 Vienna; tel. (0) 505-05-25; fax (0) 505-05-56155; e-mail info@unicreditgroup.at; internet www.bankaustria.at; f. 1991; name changed as above in 2008; 96.3% owned by UniCredito Italiano, SpA; cap. 1,681m., res 5,176m., dep. 125,645m. (Dec. 2012); Chair., Supervisory Bd ERICH HAMPEL; CEO WILLIBALD CERNKO; 276 brs.

VakifBank International AG: Kärntner Ring 18, 1010 Vienna; tel. (1) 512-35-20; fax (1) 512-35-20-20; e-mail info@vakifbank.at; internet www.vakifbank.at; f. 1999 as Vakifbank International (Wien) AG; present name adopted 2002; 90% owned by Türkiye Vakifar Bankası TAO, 10% owned by Pension Fund of Türkiye Vakifar Bankası TAO; cap. 41m., res 50.9m., dep. 635.7m. (Dec. 2012); Chair. SÜLEYMAN KALKAN; Dep. Chair. VEDAT PAKDIL; 3 brs in Austria.

Valartis Bank (Austria) AG: Postfach 306, Rathausstr. 20, 1011 Vienna; tel. (0) 577-89-100; fax (0) 577-89-200; e-mail info@valartis.at; internet www.valartis.at; f. 1890 as Bankhaus Rosenfeld; present name adopted 2009; 80.1% owned by Valartis (Austria) GmbH, 19.9% by Valartis (Wien) GmbH; cap. 6.6m., res 56.3m., dep. 783.2m. (Dec. 2012); Chair., Management Bd Dr ERWIN W. HERI; Chair., Supervisory Bd MONIKA JUNG.

VTB Bank (Austria) AG: Postfach 560, Parkring 6, 1011 Vienna; tel. (1) 515-35; fax (1) 515-35-29-7; e-mail general@vtb-bank.at; internet www.vtb-bank.at; f. 1974 as Donau-Bank AG; present name adopted 2006; owned by Bank for Foreign Trade (Russia); cap. 212.7m., res 297.3m., dep. 10,003.2m. (Dec. 2012); CEO IGOR STREHL.

Regional Banks

Allgemeine Sparkasse Oberösterreich Bank AG (Sparkasse Oberösterreich): Postfach 92, Promenade 11–13, 4041 Linz; tel. (0) 50100-40000; fax (0) 50100-940000; e-mail info@sparkasse-ooe.at; internet www.sparkasse.at/oberoesterreich; f. 1849 as Allgemeine Sparkasse; present name adopted 1991; cap. 64.4m., res 113.2m., dep. 9,326.1m. (Dec. 2012); CEO and Chair. Dr MARKUS LIMBERGER; 140 brs.

Bank für Tirol und Vorarlberg AG (BTV): Postfach 573, Stadtforum, 6020 Innsbruck; tel. (512) 53-33-0; fax (512) 533-31-14-08; e-mail btv@btv.at; internet www.btv.at; f. 1904; mem. of 3 Banken Gruppe; cap. 50m., res 160.7m., dep. 7,458.9m. (Dec. 2012); Chair. Dr FRANZ GASSELSBERGER; 35 brs.

BKS Bank AG: St. Veiter Ring 43, 9020 Klagenfurt; tel. (463) 58-58-0; fax (463) 58-58-32-9; e-mail bks@bks.at; internet www.bks.at; f. 1922; fmrly Bank für Kärnten und Steiermark AG, present name adopted 2005; mem. of 3 Banken Gruppe; cap. 65.5m., res 111.9m., dep. 5,113.8m. (Dec. 2012); Dir-Gen. Dr HEIMO PENKER; 51 brs.

Hypo Alpe-Adria-Bank AG: Postfach 517, Alpen-Adria-Pl. 1, 9020 Klagenfurt; tel. (0) 502-02-0; fax (0) 502-02-30-00; e-mail austria@hypo-alpe-adria.com; internet www.hypo-alpe-adria.com; f. 1896 as Kärntner Landes- und Hypothekenbank AG; present name adopted 1999; 100% state-owned following the nationalization of Hypo Group Alpe Adria in Dec. 2009; cap. 30m., res 119.8m., dep. 3,587.1m. (Dec. 2012); Chair., Exec. Bd Dr GOTTWALD KRANEBITTER; 17 brs.

Hypo Alpe-Adria-Bank International AG: Alpen-Adria-Pl. 1, 9020 Klagenfurt; tel. (0) 502-02-0; fax (0) 502-02-3000; e-mail international@hypo-alpe-adria.com; internet www.hypo-alpe-adria.com; f. 1896 as Kaerntner Landes-und Hypothekenbank AG; reorganized structure in 2004 to form above; operates in 11 other European countries; 100% state-owned following the nationalization of Hypo Group Alpe Adria in Dec. 2009; cap. 1,308.6m., res –138.8m., dep. 12,888m. (Dec. 2012); Chair., Supervisory Bd Dr JOHANNES DITZ; Chair., Management Bd Dr GOTTWALD KRANEBITTER.

HYPO NOE Gruppe Bank AG: Kremsergasse 20, 3100 St Pölten; tel. (2742) 49-20-0; e-mail office@hypoinvest.at; internet www.hypoinvest.at; f. 1888 as Landes-Hypothekenbank Niederösterreich; present name adopted 2010; cap. 52m., res 158.2m, dep. 4,171.7m. (Dec. 2012); Chair., Supervisory Bd Dr BURKHARD HOFER; Chair., Management Bd Dr PETER HAROLD; 26 brs.

Hypo Tirol Bank AG: Meranerstr. 8, 6020 Innsbruck; tel. (512) 50-70-0; fax (512) 50-70-04-10-00; e-mail office@hypotirol.com; internet www.hypotirol.at; f. 1901 as Landes-Hypothekenbank Tirol AG;

present name adopted 2000; owned by federal province of Tyrol; cap. 50m., res 310.6m., dep. 3,640.3m. (Dec. 2012); CEO Dr MARKUS JOCHUM; 20 brs in Austria.

Oberbank AG: Untere Donaulände 28, 4020 Linz; tel. (732) 78-02-0; fax (732) 78-02-21-40; e-mail office@oberbank.at; internet www.oberbank.at; f. 1869 as Bank für Oberösterreich und Salzburg; present name adopted 1998; mem. of 3 Banken Gruppe; cap. 86.1m., res 217.3m., dep. 13,634.5m. (Dec. 2012); Chair., Supervisory Bd Dr HERMANN BELL; Chair. and CEO Dr FRANZ GASSELSBERGER; 149 brs and sub-brs.

Oberösterreichische Landesbank AG (Hypo Oberösterreich): Landstr. 38, 4010 Linz; tel. (70) 76-39-0; fax (70) 76-39-37-3; e-mail vorstand@hypo-ooe.at; internet www.hypo.at; f. 1891 as Oberösterreichische Landes-Hypothekenanstalt; present name adopted 1988; 50.57% owned by federal province of Upper Austria, 48.59% by Hypo Holding GmbH, 0.84% by employees; cap. 13.7m., res 19.2m., dep. 3,328.7m. (Dec. 2012); Pres. Dr WOLFGANG STAMPFL; Chair. Dr ANDREAS MITTERLEHNER; 18 brs.

Salzburger Landes-Hypothekenbank AG: Postfach 136, Residenzpl. 7, 5020 Salzburg; tel. (662) 804-6; fax (662) 804-64-64-6; e-mail office@hyposalzburg.at; internet www.hyposalzburg.at; f. 1909 as bank of the Government of Salzburg; present name adopted 1992; 50.03% owned by Hypo Holding GmbH, 25% owned by Oberösterreichische Landesbank AG, 14.97% owned by Raiffeisenlandesbank Oberösterreich AG, 10% owned by Salzburger Landesholding; cap. 15m., res 37.6m., dep. 2,066.2m. (Dec. 2012); Gen. Man. Dr REINHARD SALHOFER; 24 brs.

Steiermärkische Bank und Sparkassen AG (Steiermärkische Sparkasse): Postfach 844, Am Sparkassenpl. 4, 8010 Graz; tel. (0) 50100-36000; fax (0) 50100-936000; e-mail international@steiermaerkische.com; internet www.sparkasse.at/steiermaerkische; f. 1825 as Steiermärkischer Sparkasse Graz; present name adopted 1992 following merger; 73% owned by Steiermärkische Verwaltungssparkasse, 25% by Erste Bank der oesterreichischen Sparkassen AG, 2% by employees; cap. 55.5m., res 118.4m., dep. 12,124.7m. (Dec. 2012); CEO Dr GERHARD FABISCH; 188 brs.

Tiroler Sparkasse Bankaktiengesellschaft Innsbruck (Tiroler Sparkasse): Postfach 245, Sparkassenpl. 1, 6020 Innsbruck; tel. (512) 59-10-07-00-00; fax (512) 50-10-09-70-00-0; e-mail sparkasse@tirolersparkasse.at; internet www.sparkasse.at/tirolersparkasse; f. 1822 as Sparkasse der Stadt Innsbruck; present name adopted 1990, following merger in 1975; 97.6% owned by AVS Beteiligungs GmbH, 1.8% owned by Erste Bank der oesterreichischen Sparkassen AG; cap. 66m., res 136.4m., dep. 3,193m. (Dec. 2012); Dirs WOLFGANG HECHENBERGER, Dr HANS UNTERDORFER, KARL OBERNOSTERER; 49 brs.

Volkskreditbank AG (VKB Bank): Postfach 116, Rudigierstr. 5–7, 4010 Linz; tel. (732) 76-37-0; fax (732) 76-37-13-92; e-mail international@vkb-bank.at; internet www.vkb-bank.at; f. 1872; wholly owned by Volkskredit Verwaltungsgenossenschaft; cap. 5.5m., res 296.6m., dep. 2,371.3m. (Dec. 2012); Chair., Supervisory Bd Dr RUDOLF TRAUNER; CEO Dr ALBERT WAGNER; 40 brs.

Vorarlberger Landes- und Hypothekenbank AG: Hypo-Passage 1, 6900 Bregenz; tel. (50) 414-10-00; fax (50) 414-10-50; e-mail info@hypovbg.at; internet www.hypovbg.at; f. 1899 as Hypothekenbank des Landes Vorarlberg; name changed to Vorarlberger Landes- und Hypothekenbank 1990; status changed as above 1996; cap. 165.5m., res 54.8m., dep. 5,152.1m. (Dec. 2012); Chair. Dr KURT RUPP; Chair., Management Bd Dr MICHAEL GRAHAMMER; 25 brs.

Specialized Banks

European American Investment Bank AG (Euram Bank): Palais Esterházy, Wallnerstr. 4, 1010 Vienna; tel. (1) 512-38-80-0; fax (1) 512-388-08-88; e-mail office@eurambank.com; internet www.eurambank.com; f. 1999; cap. 10m., res 5.2m., dep. 158.7m. (June 2013); CEO VIKTOR POPOVIC.

Kommunalkredit Austria AG: Türkenstr. 9, 1092 Vienna; tel. (1) 316-31-0; fax (1) 316-31-105; e-mail kommunal@kommunalkredit.at; internet www.kommunalkredit.at; f. 1958; 99.78% stake acquired by federal Govt in Nov. 2008; cap. 225.3m., res 116.9m., dep. 4,627.2m. (Dec. 2012); Chair., Supervisory Bd Dr KLAUS LIEBSCHER; CEO and Chair., Exec. Bd ALOIS STEINBICHLER.

Oesterreichische Kontrollbank AG (OeKB): Postfach 70, Am Hof 4 & Strauchgasse 1–3, 1011 Vienna; tel. (1) 531-27-24-41; fax (1) 531-27-56-98; e-mail corporate.communications@oekb.at; internet www.oekb.at; f. 1946; administration of guarantees, export financing, stock exchange clearing, organization and administration of domestic bond issues, central depository for securities and settlement of off-floor transactions, money market operations; cap. 130m., res 445.4m., dep. 11,711.4m. (Dec. 2012); Mans Dr JOHANNES ATTEMS, Dr RUDOLF SCHOLTEN.

Zürcher Kantonalbank Österreich AG: Griesgasse 11, 5020 Salzburg; tel. (662) 80-48-0; fax (662) 80-48-33-3; e-mail info@zkb-oe.at; internet www.zkb-oe.at; f. 1885 as Bankhaus Daghofer & Co AG; present name adopted 2011; 100% owned by Zürcher Kantonalbank, Switzerland; cap. 6m., res 7.7m., dep. 76.2m. (Dec. 2012); Man. Dirs ADRIAN KOHLER, HERMANN WONNEBAUER, MICHAEL WALTERSPIEL; 2 brs.

Savings Banks

Dornbirner Sparkasse Bank AG: Postfach 199, Bahnhofstr. 2, 6850 Dornbirn; tel. (50100) 740-00; fax (50100) 741-80; e-mail service@dornbirn.sparkasse.at; internet www.sparkasse.at/dornbirn; f. 1867 as Dornbirner Sparkasse; name changed as above in 2002; 74% owned by Dornbirner Anteilsverwaltungssparkasse, 26% owned by DOSPA Aktienverwaltung GmbH; cap. 10m., res 219.9m., dep. 2,398.9m. (Dec. 2012); Chair. WALTER MARTIN; Gen. Man. WERNER BÖHLER; 15 brs.

Erste Bank der oesterreichischen Sparkassen AG (Erste Bank): Postfach 162, Graben 21, 1010 Vienna; tel. (1) 501-00-0; fax (1) 501-00-9; e-mail service.center@erstebank.at; internet www.sparkasse.at/erstebank; f. 1819; present name adopted 1997; cap. 2,547m., res 6,181.3m., dep. 147,464.9m. (Dec. 2012); Pres. ANDREAS TREICHL; CEO THOMAS UHER; 996 brs in Austria.

Kärntner Sparkasse AG: Neuer Pl. 14, 9020 Klagenfurt; tel. (0) 50100-20706; fax (0) 50100-30000; e-mail info@kaerntnersparkasse.co.at; internet www.sparkasse.at/kaernten; f. 1835; 75% owned by private foundation Die Kärntner Sparkasse AG, 25% owned by Erste Group Bank AG; cap. 30.1m., res 153.1m., dep. 3,884.4m. (Dec. 2012); Pres. HEINZ WOLSCHNER; Chair. OTTO UMLAUFT; 56 brs.

Salzburger Sparkasse Bank AG: Postfach 180, Alter Markt 3, 5021 Salzburg; tel. (0) 50100-20404; fax (0) 50100-941000; e-mail info@salzburg.sparkasse.at; internet www.sparkasse.at/salzburg; f. 1855 as Salzburger Sparkasse; present name adopted 1991; absorbed ALPHA-Beteiligungs GmbH in 1997; 95.7% owned by Erste Group Bank AG; cap. 34m., res 155.4m., dep. 3,822.6m. (Dec. 2012); Chair. Dr PETER BOSEK; Gen. Dir REGINA OVESNY-STRAKA; 79 brs.

Co-operative Banks

Österreichische Volksbanken-AG (VBAG): Kolingasse 14–16, 1090 Vienna; tel. (1) 504-00-40; fax (1) 504-004-36-83; e-mail mail@volksbank.com; internet www.volksbank.com; f. 1922 as Österreichische Zentralgenossenschaftskasse rGmbH; present name adopted 1974; cap. 885.6m., res –0.08m., dep. 14,903.1m. (Dec. 2012); Chair. HANS JÖRG SCHELLING; CEO Dr STEPHAN KOREN.

Raiffeisen Centrobank AG: Tegetthoffstr. 1, 1015 Vienna; tel. (1) 515-20-0; fax (1) 513-43-96; e-mail office@rcb.at; internet www.rcb.at; f. 1973 as Centro International Handelsbank; present name adopted 2001; 99.99% owned by RZB IB Beteiligungs GmbH, 0.01% owned by Raiffeisen-Invest-Gesellschaft mbH; cap. 47.6m., res 6.7m., dep. 149.6m. (Dec. 2012); Chair. Dr EVA MARCHART.

Raiffeisen-Landesbank Steiermark AG: Kaiserfeldgasse 5–7, 8010 Graz; tel. (316) 80-36-0; fax (316) 80-36-24-37; e-mail info@rlb-stmk.raiffeisen.at; internet www.rlbstmk.at; f. 1927; cap. 135.3m., res 502.6m., dep. 6,451.8m. (Dec. 2012); Chair., Management Bd MARKUS MAIR; 86 mem. banks, with 323 brs.

Raiffeisen-Landesbank Tirol AG (RLB Tirol AG): Adamgasse 1–7, 6020 Innsbruck; tel. (512) 530-50; fax (512) 530-05-35-49; e-mail andrea.zankl@rlb-tirol.at; internet www.rlb-tirol.at; f. 1894; cap. 85m., res 277.9m., dep. 5,121.5m. (Dec. 2012); Chair. JOSEF GRABER; 82 mem. banks, with 272 brs.

Raiffeisenlandesbank Kärnten-Rechenzentrum und Revisionsverband rGmbH: Raiffeisenpl. 1, 9020 Klagenfurt; tel. (463) 99300-0; fax (463) 99300-27-37; e-mail rlb-ktn@rbgk.raiffeisen.at; internet www.rlb-bank.at; f. 1900 as Spar- und Darlehensverband Kärnten; present name adopted 1996; cap. 7m., res 167.2m., dep. 2,129.8m. (Dec. 2012); Exec. Dirs PETER GAUPER, GEORG MESSNER, GERT SPANZ.

Raiffeisenlandesbank Niederösterreich-Wien AG: Friedrich-Wilhelm-Raiffeisen-Pl. 1, Raiffeisenhaus, 1020 Vienna; tel. (1) 517-00-90-0; e-mail info@raiffeisenbank.at; internet www.raiffeisenbank.at; f. 1898; cap. 291m., res 432.7m., dep. 19,925.8m. (Dec. 2012); Chair., Supervisory Bd Dr JOHANNES SCHUSTER; Chair., Management Bd and CEO Dr MICHAEL KLAR, WALTER MÖSENBACHER, ELFRIEDE MARIA SCHIEFERMAIR.

Raiffeisenlandesbank Oberösterreich AG: Postfach 455, Europapl. 1A, 4020 Linz; tel. (732) 65-96-0; fax (732) 65-96-22-0-22; e-mail internet@rlbooe.at; internet www.rlbooe.at; f. 1900 as Oberösterreichische Raiffeisen-Zentralkasse rGmbH; name changed as above in 2004; cap. 253m., res 996.6m., dep. 14,860.9m. (Dec. 2012); Chair. Dr HEINRICH SCHALLER; 100 mem. banks, with 451 brs.

Raiffeisenlandesbank Vorarlberg Waren-und Revisions Verband rGmbH: Rheinstr. 11, 6900 Bregenz; tel. (5574) 405-0; fax (5574) 405-33-1; e-mail info@raiba.at; internet www.raiba.at; f. 1895 as Verband der Spar-und Darlehenskassenvereine; name changed as above in 1995; cap. 28.4m., res 190.1m., dep. 4,876.8m. (Dec. 2012);

Chair., Supervisory Bd Dr WALTER HÖRBURGER; Chair., Management Bd WILFRIED HOPFNER; 23 mem. banks, with 94 brs.

Raiffeisenverband Salzburg eGen: Schwarzstr. 13–15, Postfach 6, 5024 Salzburg; tel. (662) 88-86-0; fax (662) 88-86-13-80-9; e-mail friedrich.buchmueller@rvs.at; internet www.rvs.at; f. 1905 as Salzburgische Genossenschafts-Zentralkasse; present name adopted 1949; cap. 54.2m., res 353.7m., dep. 5,987.6m. (Dec. 2012); Chair., Management Bd Dr GÜNTHER REIBERSDORFER; 66 mem. banks, with 135 brs.

Raiffeisen Zentralbank Österreich AG (RZB-Austria): Am Stadtpark 9, 1030 Vienna; tel. (1) 717-07-0; fax (1) 717-07-17-15; internet www.rzb.at; f. 1927; cap. 492.5m., res 1,834.8m., dep. 96,827.7m. (Dec. 2012); central institute of the Austrian Raiffeisen banking group; Chair., Supervisory Bd ERWIN HAMESEDER; Chair., Management Bd Dr WALTER ROTHENSTEINER.

Volksbank Linz-Wels-Mühlviertel AG: Postfach 234, Pfarrgasse 5, 4601 Wels; tel. (7242) 495-0; fax (7242) 495-97; e-mail office@volksbank-wels.at; internet www.volksbank-wels.at; f. 1912 as Welser Handels- und Gewerbekasse rGmhH; present name adopted 2010 following merger with Volksbank Linz-Mühlviertel rGmbH; cap. 6.7m., res 33.4m., dep. 663.5m. (Dec. 2012); Gen. Mans ANDREAS PIRKLBAUER, CHRISTIAN MAYR, PETER HOHENSINNER; 16 brs.

Bankers' Organization

Verband Österreichischer Banken und Bankiers (Austrian Bankers' Asscn): Börsegasse 11, 1010 Vienna; tel. (1) 535-17-71-0; fax (1) 535-17-71-38; e-mail bv@bankenverband.at; internet www.bankenverband.at; f. 1946; Pres. WILLIBALD CERNKO; CEO and Chair. Dr FRANZ GASSELSBERGER; Gen. Sec. MARIA GEYER; 64 mems and 17 extraordinary mems (Jan. 2010).

STOCK EXCHANGE

Wiener Börse (Vienna Stock Exchange): Wallnerstr. 8, 1014 Vienna; tel. (1) 531-65-0; fax (1) 532-97-40; e-mail info@wienerborse.at; internet www.wienerborse.at; f. 1771; 2 sections: Stock Exchange, Commodity Exchange; absorbed equity and futures exchanges in 1997; CEO BIRGIT KURAS, MICHAEL BUHL.

INSURANCE COMPANIES

In 2012 there were 60 insurance companies in Austria, with total assets of €103,742m.

Allianz Elementar Lebensversicherung-AG: Hietzinger Kai 101–105, 1130 Vienna; tel. (5) 900-90; fax (5) 900-970-000; e-mail feedback@allianz.at; internet www.allianz.at; life insurance; Chair., Supervisory Bd Dr WERNER ZEDELIUS; Chair., Management Bd Dr WOLFRAM LITTICH.

Allianz Elementar Versicherungs-AG: Hietzinger Kai 101–105, 1130 Vienna; tel. (5) 900-90; fax (5) 900-970-000; e-mail feedback@allianz.at; internet www.allianz.at; f. 1860; owned by Allianz SE; all classes except life insurance; Chair., Supervisory Bd Dr WERNER ZEDELIUS; Chair., Management Bd Dr WOLFRAM LITTICH.

Bank Austria Versicherung: Modecenterstr. 17, 1110 Vienna; tel. (1) 313-83-0; fax (1) 313-83-60-30; e-mail office@ba-v.at; internet www.ba-versicherung.at; f. 1911; life insurance; Dir-Gen. JOSEF ADELMANN.

Donau Versicherung AG: Argentinierstr. 22, 1040 Vienna; tel. (0) 503-307-01-10; fax (0) 503-309-970-110; e-mail wien@donauversicherung.at; internet www.donauversicherung.at; f. 1867; all classes; mem. of Vienna Insurance Group; Gen. Dir ANDREW GLASER.

FinanceLife Lebensversicherung AG: Postfach 150, Untere Donaustr. 21, 1029 Vienna; tel. (1) 214-54-01; fax (1) 214-54-01-37-80; e-mail service@financelife.com; internet www.financelife.com; life insurance; fmrly MLP-Lebensversicherung AG Wien; mem. of UNIQA Group; Chair., Management Bd HARTWIG LÖGER.

Generali Versicherung AG: Landskrongasse 1–3, 1011 Vienna; tel. (1) 534-01-0; fax (1) 532 09-49-11-011; e-mail headoffice@generali.at; internet www.generali.at; f. 1882 as Erste Österreichische Allgemeine Unfall-Versicherungs-Gesellschaft; CEO PETER THIRRING.

Grazer Wechselseitige Versicherung AG (GRAWE): Herrengasse 18–20, 8011 Graz; tel. (316) 80-37-62-22; fax (316) 80-37-64-90; e-mail service@grawe.at; internet www.grawe.at; f. 1828; all classes; Gen. Dir Dr OTHMAR EDERER.

Oberösterreichische: Gruberstr. 32, 4020 Linz; tel. (0) 578-9170; fax (0) 578-917-15-66; e-mail office@ooev.at; internet www.keinesorgen.at; f. 1811; life and non-life; Exec. Dir OTHMAR NAGL.

Raiffeisen-Versicherung AG: Untere Donaustr. 21, 1029 Vienna; tel. (1) 202-55-88; fax (1) 211-19-14-19; e-mail service@raiffeisen-versicherung.at; internet www.raiffeisen-versicherung.at; f. 1970; mem. of UNIQA Group; life and non-life; CEO Dr KLAUS PEKAREK.

Sparkassen Versicherung AG: Wipplingerstr. 36–38, 1011 Vienna; tel. (501) 007-54-00; fax (501) 009-754-00; e-mail sag@s-versicherung.co.at; internet www.s-versicherung.co.at; f. 1985; mem. of VIG; all classes; Dirs ERWIN HAMMERBACHER, MANFRED RAPF, HEINZ SCHUSTER.

UNIQA Versicherungen AG: Untere Donaustr. 21, 1029 Vienna; tel. (1) 211-75-0; fax (1) 214-33-36; e-mail info@uniqa.at; internet www.uniqagroup.com; f. 1999; CEO Dr ANDREAS BRANDSTETTER.

VIG (Vienna Insurance Group): Schottenring 30, 1010 Vienna; tel. (0) 503-902-20-00; fax (0) 503-909-922-000; e-mail info@vig.com; internet www.vig.com; f. 1824; life and non-life; CEO PETER HAGEN.

Wiener Städtische Versicherung AG: Schottenring 30, 1010 Vienna; tel. (0) 503-502-00-00; fax (0) 503-509-920-000; e-mail kundenservice@staedtische.co.at; internet www.wienerstaedtische.at; f. 1824; all classes; mem. of VIG; Dir-Gen. ROBERT LASSHOFER.

Wüstenrot Versicherungs-AG: Alpenstr. 61, 5033 Salzburg; tel. (570) 701-00; fax (570) 701-09; e-mail versicherung@wuestenrot.at; internet www.wuestenrot.at; life and non-life; Dirs Dr SUSANNE RIESS, Prof. ANDREAS GRÜNBICHLER, FRANZ MEINGAST.

Zürich Versicherungs AG: Schwarzenbergpl. 15, 1010 Vienna; tel. (1) 801-303-190; fax (1) 801-302-138; e-mail service@zurich.at; internet www.zurich.at; f. 1872; all classes; Chair. and CEO GERHARD MATSCHNIG.

Insurance Organization

Verband der Versicherungsunternehmen Österreichs (Asscn of Austrian Insurance Cos): Schwarzenbergpl. 7, 1030 Vienna; tel. (1) 711-56-0; fax (1) 711-56-27-0; e-mail vvo@vvo.at; internet www.vvo.at; f. 1945; Pres. Dr LOUIS NORMAN AUDENHOVE; 136 mems.

Trade and Industry

GOVERNMENT AGENCIES

ABA—Invest in Austria: Opernring 3, 1010 Vienna; tel. (1) 588-58-0; fax (1) 586-86-59; e-mail office@aba.gv.at; internet www.investinaustria.at; f. 1982; promotes foreign investment in Austria; state-owned; Man. Dir RENÉ SIEGL.

Österreichische Industrieholding AG (ÖIAG): Dresdner Str. 87, 1201 Vienna; tel. (1) 711-14-0; fax (1) 711-14-24-5; e-mail kommunikation@oiag.at; internet www.oiag.at; f. 1946; Chair., Supervisory Bd Dr PETER MITTERBAUER; Man. Dir Dr MARKUS BEYRER.

CHAMBERS OF COMMERCE

All Austrian enterprises must by law be members of the Economic Chambers. The Federal Economic Chamber promotes international contacts and represents the economic interests of trade and industry at a federal level.

Wirtschaftskammer Österreich (Austrian Federal Economic Chamber): Wiedner Hauptstr. 63, 1045 Vienna; tel. (0) 590-90-0; fax (0) 590-90-02-50; e-mail office@wko.at; internet www.wko.at; f. 1946; 7 divisions: Banking and Insurance, Commerce, Crafts and Trades, Industry, Information and Consulting, Tourism and Leisure, Transport and Communications; these divisions are subdivided into branch asscns; Regional Economic Chambers with divisions and branch asscns in each of the 9 federal provinces; Pres. Dr CHRISTOPH LEITL; Sec.-Gen. ANNA-MARIA HOCHHAUSER; c. 370,000 mems.

INDUSTRIAL AND TRADE ASSOCIATIONS

Wirtschaftskammer Österreich—Bundessparte Industrie: Wiedner Hauptstr. 63, 1045 Vienna; tel. (0) 590900-3417; fax (0) 590900-273; internet www.wko.at/industrie; f. 1896 as Zentralverband der Industrie Österreichs (Central Fed. of Austrian Industry), merged into present org. 1947; Pres. CHRISTOPH LEITL; Sec.-Gen. ANNA MARIA HOCHHAUSER; comprises the following industrial feds:

Fachverband der Bauindustrie (Building): Schaumburgergasse 20/8, 1040 Vienna; tel. (1) 718-37-37-0; fax (1) 718-37-37-22; e-mail office@bau.or.at; internet www.wk.or.at/fvbi; Pres. THOMAS BIRTEL; Gen. Dir MANFRED KATZENSCHLAGER; 150 mems.

Fachverband Bergwerke und Stahl (Mining and Steel Production): Wiedner Haupstr. 63, 1045 Vienna; tel. (1) 590900-3311; e-mail roman.stiftner@wko.at; internet www.bergbaustahl.at; Pres. HEIMO STIX; Gen. Dir ROMAN STIFTNER; 35 mems.

Fachverband der Chemischen Industrie (Chemicals): Wiedner Hauptstr. 63, 1045 Vienna; tel. (0) 590900-3340; fax (0) 590900-280; e-mail office@fcio.wko.at; internet www.fcio.at; Pres. PETER UNTERSPERGER; Gen. Dir Dr SYLVIA HOFINGER; 530 mems.

Fachverband der Elektro- und Elektronikindustrie—FEEI (Electrical): Mariahilfer Str. 37–39, 1060 Vienna; tel. (1) 588-39-0;

fax (1) 586-69-71; e-mail info@feei.at; internet www.feei.at; Pres. ALBERT HOCHLEITNER; Man. Dir Dr LOTHAR ROITNER; c. 300 mems.

Fachverband der Fahrzeugindustrie (Vehicles): Wiedner Hauptstr. 63, 1045 Vienna; tel. (0) 590900-4800; fax (0) 590900-289; e-mail kfz@wko.at; internet www.fahrzeugindustrie.at; Pres. BRUNO KRAINZ; Gen. Sec. WALTER LINSZBAUER; c. 170 mems (2010).

Fachverband der Film- und Musikindustrie Österreichs (Film and Music): Wiedner Hauptstr. 63, Postfach 327, 1045 Vienna; tel. (0) 590900-3012; fax (0) 590900-276; e-mail mueller@fama.or.at; internet www.fama.or.at; Pres. DANIEL KRAUSZ; Man. Dir Dr WERNER MÜLLER; 4,044 mem. cos (2012).

Fachverband der Gas- und Wärmeversorgungsunternehmungen (Gas and Heating): Schubertring 14, 1010 Vienna; tel. (1) 513-15-88-0; fax (1) 513-15-88-25; e-mail office@gaswaerme.at; internet www.gaswaerme.at; f. 1947; Pres. HELMUT MIKSITS; Gen. Dir MICHAEL MOCK; c. 660 mems.

Fachverband der Giessereiindustrie (Foundries): Wiedner Hauptstr. 63, Postfach 339, 1045 Vienna; tel. and fax (0) 590-90-0; e-mail giesserei@wko.at; internet www.diegiesserei.at; Pres. PETER MAIWALD; Dir ADOLF KERBL; 47 mems.

Fachverband der Glasindustrie (Glass): Wiedner Hauptstr. 63, 1045 Vienna; tel. (0) 590-900-3428; fax (0) 590-900-281; e-mail office@fvglas.at; internet www.fvglas.at; Dir ALEXANDER KRISSMANEK; 66 mems.

Fachverband der Holzindustrie (Wood): Schwarzenbergpl. 4, Postfach 123, 1037 Vienna; tel. (1) 712-26-01; fax (1) 713-03-09; e-mail office@holzindustrie.at; internet www.holzindustrie.at; f. 1947 as Fachverband der Sägeindustrie Österreichs; present name adopted 2000; Pres. Dr ERICH WIESNER; Dir Dr CLAUDIUS KOLLMANN; c. 1,500 mems.

Fachverband der Ledererzeugenden Industrie (Leather Production): Postfach 312, Wiedner Hauptstr. 63, 1045 Vienna; tel. (0) 590900-3453; fax (0) 590900-278; e-mail schuh-leder@wko.at; internet www.leather-industry.at; f. 1945; Pres. ULRICH SCHMIDT; Dir ANDREA SCHREDER-BINDER; 7 mems.

Fachverband Maschinen & Metallwaren Industrie (Machinery and Metalware Industries): Wiedner Hauptstr. 63, 1045 Vienna; tel. (0) 590900-3482; fax (0) 150-51-02-0; e-mail office@fmmi.at; internet www.fmmi.at; Pres. Dr CLEMENS MALINA-ALTZINGER; Man. Dir Dr BERNDT-THOMAS KRAFFT.

Fachverband der Mineralölindustrie (Petroleum): Wiedner Hauptstr. 63, 1045 Vienna; tel. (0) 590900-4892; fax (0) 590900-4895; e-mail office@oil-gas.at; internet www.oil-gas.at; f. 1947; Pres. and CEO GERHARD ROISS; Man. Dir CHRISTOPH CAPEK; 25 mems (2014).

Fachverband der Nahrungs- und Genussmittelindustrie (Provisions): Zaunergasse 1–3, 1030 Vienna; tel. (1) 712-21-21; fax (1) 712-21-21-35; e-mail fiaa@dielebensmittel.at; internet www.dielebensmittel.at; Pres. JOHANN MARIHART; Dir KATHARINA KOSSDORFF; 422 mems.

Fachverband der NE-Metallindustrie Österreichs (Austrian Non-Ferrous Metals Federation): Wiedner Hauptstr. 63, 1045 Vienna; tel. (0) 590900-3310; fax (0) 590900-3378; e-mail office@nemetall.at; internet www.nemetall.at; f. 1946; Pres. ALFRED HINTRINGER; Man. Dir ROMAN STIFTNER; 58 mems.

Fachverband der Papier und Pappe verarbeitenden Industrie (Paper and Board Processing): Brucknerstr. 8, 1041 Vienna; tel. (1) 505-53-82-0; fax (1) 505-90-18; e-mail office@ppv.at; internet www.ppv.at; Pres. GEORG DIETER FISCHER; Gen. Dir MARTIN WILDERMANN; 98 mems.

Fachverband der Papierindustrie (Paper): Gumpendorferstr. 6, 1061 Vienna; tel. (1) 588-86-20-5; fax (1) 588-86-22-2; e-mail austropapier@austropapier.at; internet www.austropapier.at; Pres. THOMAS M. SALZER; Man. Dir WERNER AURACHER; 24 mems.

Fachverband der Stein- und keramischen Industrie (Building Materials and Ceramics): Wiedner Hauptstr. 63, Postfach 329, 1045 Vienna; tel. (0) 590900-3531; fax (1) 505-62-40; e-mail steine@wko.at; internet www.baustoffindustrie.at; f. 1947; Pres. MANFRED ASAMER; Gen. Dir Dr ANDREAS PFEILER; 400 mems.

Fachverband der Textil-, Bekleidungs-, Schuh- und Lederindustrie (Clothing, Shoe and Leather): Wiedner Hauptstr. 63, 1040 Vienna; tel. (0) 590900-5417; fax (0) 590900-5416; e-mail tbsl@wko.at; internet www.tbsl.at; Man. Dir Dr WOLFGANG ZEYRINGER; 550 mems.

UTILITIES

Electricity

Burgenländische Elektrizitätswirtschafts-AG (BEWAG): Kasernenstr. 9, 7000 Eisenstadt; tel. (2682) 900-0; fax (2682) 900-01-90-0; e-mail info@bewag.at; internet www.bewag.at; f. 1958; owned by federal province of Burgenland (51%) and Burgenland Holding AG (49%); CEO MICHAEL GERBAVSITS.

Energie AG Oberösterreich: Böhmerwaldstr. 3, Postfach 298, 4021 Linz; tel. (732) 9000-0; fax (732) 90-00-36-00; e-mail service@energieag.at; internet www.energieag.at; fmrly Oberösterreichische Kraftwerke AG; subsidiaries active in Germany, the Czech Republic, Hungary and Slovakia; 52.50% owned by federal province of Upper Austria; Chair. and Man. Dir Dr LEOPOLD WINDTNER.

Energie Steiermark AG: Leonhardgürtel 10, 8010 Graz; tel. (316) 900-0; fax (316) 900-02-29-09; e-mail office@e-steiermark.com; internet www.estag.com; f. 1996 as holding co. for Steirische Wasserkraft- und Elektrizitäts-AG, Steirische Fernwärme and Steirische Ferngas; 75% owned by federal province of Steiermark; Chair. JOSEF MÜLNER.

Energie-Versorgung-Niederösterreich AG (EVN): EVN Pl., 2344 Maria Enzersdorf; tel. (2236) 200-0; fax (2236) 200-20-30; e-mail info@evn.at; internet www.evn.at; f. 1987; Chair., Supervisory Bd BURKHARD HOFER.

Kärntner Elektrizitäts-AG (KELAG): Arnulfpl. 2, Postfach 176, 9010 Klagenfurt; tel. (463) 525-0; fax (463) 525-15-96; e-mail office@kelag.at; internet www.kelag.at; f. 1923; 51% owned by federal province of Carinthia, 49% owned by RWE Energy AG; Pres Dr HERMANN EGGER, ARMIN WIERSMA, HARALD KOGLAR.

Österreichische Elektrizitätswirtschafts-AG (Verbund): Am Hof 6A, 1010 Vienna; tel. (1) 503-13-0; fax (1) 503-13-54-19-1; e-mail information@verbund.com; internet www.verbund.at; f. 1947; federal electricity authority; operates national grid, sells electricity wholesale to the 9 regional operators; Chair., Supervisory Bd Dr GILBERT FRIZBERG; Chair., Management Bd WOLFGANG ANZENGRUBER.

Salzburg AG für Energie, Verkehr und Telekommunikation: Bayerhamerstr. 16, 5020 Salzburg; tel. (662) 88-84-0; fax (662) 88-84-17-0; e-mail office@salzburg-ag.at; internet www.salzburg-ag.at; f. 2000 by merger of SAFE and Salzburger Stadtwerke; 42.56% owned by federal province of Salzburg, 31.31% by city of Salzburg and 26.13% by Energie Oberösterreich Service- und Beteiligungsverwaltungs-GmbH; Chair., Supervisory Bd DAVID BRENNER; Mans Dr ARNO GASTEIGER, AUGUST HIRSCHBICHLER.

Tiroler Wasserkraftwerke AG (TIWAG): Eduard-Wallnöfer-Pl. 2, 6020 Innsbruck; tel. 50607-27060; fax 50607-21126; e-mail office@tiwag.at; internet www.tiwag.at; f. 1924; Chair., Management Bd Dr BRUNO WALLNÖFER.

Vorarlberger Kraftwerke AG (VKW): Weidachstr. 6, 6900 Bregenz; tel. (5574) 601-72-60-0; fax (5574) 601-78-50-6; e-mail unternehmen@vkw.at; internet www.vkw.at; f. 1901; Chair. Dr LUDWIG SUMMER.

Wien Energie GmbH: Thomas-Klestil-Pl. 14, 1030 Vienna; tel. (1) 531-23-0; fax (1) 531-23-73-90-8; e-mail office@wienenergie.at; internet www.wienenergie.at; Mans ROBERT GRÜNEIS, THOMAS IRSCHIK.

Gas

BEGAS (Burgenländische Erdgasversorgungs AG): Kasernenstr. 10, 7000 Eisenstadt; tel. (2682) 709-0; fax (2682) 709-174; e-mail office@begas.at; internet www.begas.at; Exec. Dirs MICHAEL GERBAVSITS, LEOPOLD BUCHMAYER.

Oberösterreichische Ferngas-AG: Neubauzeile 99, Postfach 1, 4030 Linz; tel. (732) 38-83-0; fax (732) 38-83-93-00; e-mail ferngas@ooefg.co.at; internet www.ooeferngas.at; 65% owned by Energie AG Oberösterreich, 28% by Linz AG and 7% by Elektrizitätswerk Wels; Chair. Dr JOHANN GRÜNBERGER.

Steirische Gas-Wärme GmbH: Leonhardgürtel 10 8010 Graz; tel. (316) 900-0; fax (316) 900-02-80-00; e-mail gaswaerme@e-steiermark.com; internet www.e-steiermark.com; f. 2003 by merger of Steirische Fernwärme GmbH with Steirische Ferngas GmbH; part of Energie Steiermark AG; Man. Dir OLAF KIESER.

Water

Water is supplied to 90% of the population by municipalities, either directly or through private companies in which they retain a majority stake. The remaining 10% of the population accesses water from private wells or small facilities organized as co-operative societies.

Österreichischer Wasser- und Abfallwirtschaftsverband (ÖWAV) (Austrian Water and Waste Management Asscn): Marc-Aurel-Str. 5, 1010 Vienna; tel. (1) 535-57-20; fax (1) 535-40-64; e-mail buero@oewav.at; internet www.oewav.at; f. 1909; Man. Dir MANFRED ASSMANN.

Association

Österreichische Vereinigung für das Gas- und Wasserfach (ÖVGW) (Austrian Association for Gas and Water): Schubertring 14, 1010 Vienna; tel. (1) 513-15-88-0; fax (1)513-15-88-25; e-mail office@ovgw.at; internet www.ovgw.at; f. 1881; independent, non-profit-making body, representing the technical, scientific and economic interests of gas and water; Man. MICHAEL MOCK.

TRADE UNIONS

National Federation

Österreichischer Gewerkschaftsbund (ÖGB) (Austrian Trade Union Fed.): Johann-Böhm-Pl. 1, 1020 Vienna; tel. (1) 534-44-39; e-mail oegb@oegb.at; internet www.oegb.at; f. 1945; non-party union org. with voluntary membership; affiliated with ITUC and the ETUC; 8 affiliated unions; Pres. ERICH FOGLAR; 1.2m. mems.

Transport

RAILWAYS

ÖBB-Konzern (Austrian Federal Railways) operates more than 90% of all the railway routes in Austria. At December 2012 the total length of operated railway lines stood at 5,566 km, of which 3,852 km of lines were electrified. There are also several private railway companies.

ÖBB-Konzern (Austrian Federal Railways): Wienerbergstr. 11, 1100 Vienna; tel. (1) 930-00-0; e-mail holding@oebb.at; internet www.oebb.at; f. 2004 following reorg. of Östereichische Bundesbahnen (ÖBB) in 2003; Chair., Management Bd CHRISTIAN KERN; consists of ÖBB Holding AG (management) and the following orgs:

ÖBB-Infrastruktur AG: Praterstern 3, 1020 Vienna; tel. (1) 930-00-0; e-mail infra.kundenservice@oebb.at; internet www.oebb.at/infrastruktur; responsible for construction and maintenance of the rail infrastructure; provides power and telecommunications for the network; Chair., Management Bd ANDREAS MATTHÄ.

ÖBB-Personenverkehr AG: Wagramer Str. 17–19, 1220 Vienna; tel. (1) 930-00-0; e-mail service@pv.oebb.at; internet www.oebb.at/pv; passenger transport; jointly responsible, with Rail Cargo Austria AG (q.v.), for ÖBB-Produktion GmbH (locomotives) and ÖBB-Technische Services GmbH (technical services); subsidiary: ÖBB-Postbus GmbH; Chair., Management Bd GABRIELE LUTTER.

Rail Cargo Austria AG: Erdberger Lände 40–48, 1030 Vienna; tel. (1) 577-50; fax (1) 577-50-70-0; e-mail info@railcargo.at; internet www.railcargo.at; freight and logistics; jointly responsible, with ÖBB-Personenverkehr AG (q.v.), for ÖBB-Produktion GmbH (locomotives) and ÖBB-Technische Services GmbH (technical services); Chair., Management Bd CHRISTIAN KERN.

ROADS

In 2010 Austria had some 110,206 km of classified roads, of which 1,696 km were motorways. There are 145 tunnels with a total length of 340 km. The Autobahnen- und Schnellstrassen-Finanzierungs-Aktiengesellschaft (ASFiNAG) regulates the planning, financing and maintaining of expressways and other roads.

Autobahnen- und Schnellstrassen-Finanzierungs-Aktiengesellschaft (AFSiNAG): Rotenturmstr. 5–9, Postfach 983, 1011 Vienna; tel. (50) 108-10-00-0; fax (50) 108-10-02-0; e-mail office@asfinag.at; internet www.asfinag.at; f. 1982; planning, financing and maintaining of expressways and other roads; wholly owned by the Austrian Government; Chair. Dr KLAUS SCHIERHACKL.

INLAND WATERWAYS

The Danube (Donau) is Austria's only navigable river. It enters Austria from Germany at Passau and flows into Slovakia near Hainburg. The length of the Austrian section of the river is 350 km. Danube barges carry up to 1,800 metric tons, but loading depends on the water level, which varies considerably throughout the year. Cargoes are chiefly petroleum and derivatives, coal, coke, iron ore, iron, steel, timber and grain. The Rhine–Main–Danube Canal opened in 1992. A passenger service is maintained on the Upper Danube and between Vienna and the Black Sea. Passenger services are also provided on Bodensee (Lake Constance) and Wolfgangsee by Austrian Federal Railways, and on all the larger Austrian lakes.

CIVIL AVIATION

Civil aviation is regulated by the Federal Ministry of Transport, Innovation and Technology, as well as Austro Control GmbH (Austrian air traffic control), Österreichischer Aeroclub (the Austrian Aeroclub), provincial governors and district administrative authorities. The main international airport is located at Schwechat, near Vienna. There are also international flights from Graz, Innsbruck, Klagenfurt, Linz and Salzburg, and internal flights between these cities.

Principal Airlines

Austrian Airlines Group (Österreichische Luftverkehrs AG): Office Park 2, Postfach 100, 1300 Vienna Airport; tel. (1) 517-66-10-00; e-mail customer.relations@austrian.com; internet www.austrian.com; f. 1957; 95.4% owned by Deutsche Lufthansa AG, following a takeover in 2009; serves 130 cities in 66 countries worldwide; Chair., Supervisory Bd STEFAN LAUER; CEO JAAN ALBRECHT.

Tyrolean Airways: Postfach 98, Fürstenweg 176, 6020 Innsbruck; tel. (517) 66-10-00; fax (512) 28-66-46; e-mail austrianinternet@austrian.com; internet www.tyrolean.at; f. 1978 as Aircraft Innsbruck; renamed Tiroler Luftfahrt GmbH 1980; operates scheduled services and charter flights within Austria and to other European countries; Man. Dir CHRISTIAN FITZ.

Tourism

Tourism plays an important part in the Austrian economy. In 2012 Austria received 24.2m. foreign visitors at accommodation establishments. Receipts from the tourism sector were provisionally estimated at US $18,894m. in 2012. The country's mountain scenery attracts visitors in both summer and winter, while Vienna and Salzburg, hosts to a number of internationally renowned arts festivals, are important cultural centres.

Österreich Werbung (Austrian National Tourist Office): Vordere Zollamtsstr. 13, 1030 Vienna; tel. (1) 588-66-0; fax (1) 588-66-20; e-mail urlaub@austria.info; internet www.austria.info; f. 1955; Pres. Dr REINHOLD MITTERLEHNER (Federal Minister of Economy, Family and Youth); CEO Dr PETRA STOLBA.

Defence

After the ratification of the State Treaty in 1955, Austria declared its permanent neutrality. To protect its independence, the armed forces were instituted. In 1995 Austria joined the Partnership for Peace programme of the North Atlantic Treaty Organization (NATO), but reaffirmed its neutrality in March 1998, having evaluated and discounted the possibility of becoming a full member of NATO. Military service is compulsory for male citizens and normally consists of six months' initial training, after which men remain liable for conscription until 50 years of age (65 years for officers, non-commissioned officers and specialists). In January 2013 a non-binding referendum on the abolishment of conscription in favour of a professional army was defeated by 59.7% of votes. As assessed at November 2013, the total armed forces numbered some 22,800. The air force (numbering 2,700), is an integral part of the armed forces. Total reserves in November 2013 numbered 171,400. In November 2004 the European Union (EU) ministers responsible for defence agreed to create a number of 'battlegroups' (each numbering about 1,500 men), which could be deployed at short notice to crisis areas around the world. The EU battlegroups, two of which were to be ready for deployment at any one time, following a rotational schedule, reached full operational capacity from 1 January 2007.

Defence Expenditure: Budgeted at €2,430m. for 2013.

Commander-in-Chief of the Armed Forces: Federal President Dr HEINZ FISCHER.

Chief of the Defence Staff: Gen. EDMUND ENTACHER.

Education

The central controlling body is the Federal Ministry of Education, Arts and Culture. Provincial boards (Landesschulräte) supervise school education in each of the nine federal provinces. Expenditure on education was budgeted at €17,088m. in 2012 (equivalent to 10.8% of total spending).

Education is free and compulsory for nine years between the ages of six and 15 years. Pre-primary education at a Kindergarten between the ages of three and six years is optional. Primary education at a Volksschule lasts for four years between the ages of six and 10 years. For the first four years of secondary education, most students attend a general secondary school (Hauptschule) or an academic secondary school (Allgemeinbildende höhere Schule). After four years the Hauptschule may be followed by one of a variety of schools offering technical, vocational and other specialized training. The Allgemeinbildende höhere Schule, to which admission is gained through achievement at primary level or by entrance examination, provides an eight-year general education, divided into two four-year cycles, covering a wide range of subjects. After the lower secondary cycle the student may remain at the Allgemeinbildende höhere Schule or enrol at a higher technical and vocational college (Berufsbildende höhere Schule). Both these routes culminate in the school-leaving certificate (Reifeprüfung or Matura), which gives access to Austrian universities. A new comprehensive system of New Secondary Schools (Neue Mittelschulen) to cater for all children aged between 10 and 14 years was introduced on a trial basis in five provinces from September 2008; it was announced in 2011 that this system was to replace the Hauptschule nationally by 2018/19.

Enrolment at pre-primary level included 84% of all children aged three to five years in 2011/12. In 2010, according to the OECD, 78% of pupils aged 15 to 19 years were in education. In 2010/11 some 10% of pupils attended private schools.

At tertiary level there are universities, universities of applied sciences (Fachhochschulen), private universities and colleges of teacher education, as well as vocational institutions. Institutes of adult education, Volkshochschulen, of which there were 205 in 2010/11, are found in all provinces, as are other centres operated by public authorities, church organizations and the Austrian Trade Union Federation. In addition, all Austrian citizens over the age of 24 years, and with professional experience, may attend certain university courses in connection with their professional career or trade.

AZERBAIJAN

Introductory Survey

LOCATION, CLIMATE, LANGUAGE, RELIGION, FLAG, CAPITAL

The Republic of Azerbaijan is situated in the eastern South Caucasus, on the western coast of the Caspian Sea. To the south it borders Iran, to the west Armenia, to the north-west Georgia, and to the north the Republic of Dagestan, in Russia. The Autonomous Republic of Naxçıvan is part of Azerbaijan, although it is separated from the rest of Azerbaijan by Armenian territory, and borders Iran to the south. Azerbaijan also includes the territory of the self-proclaimed 'Republic of Nagornyi Karabakh' (Dağlik Karabağ), which is largely populated by Armenians. The Kura plain has a dry, temperate climate with an average July temperature of 27°C (80°F) and an average January temperature of 1°C (34°F). Average annual rainfall on the lowlands is 200 mm–300 mm, but the Lankaran plain normally receives between 1,000 mm and 1,750 mm. The official language is Azerbaijani, a South Turkic language. Religious adherence corresponds largely to ethnic origins: almost all ethnic Azerbaijanis (Azeris) are Muslims, some 70% being Shi'ite and 30% Sunni. There are also small Christian communities. The national flag (proportions 1 by 2) consists of three equal horizontal stripes, of pale blue, red and green, with a white crescent moon framing a white eight-pointed star on the red stripe. The capital is Baku (Bakı).

CONTEMPORARY POLITICAL HISTORY

Historical Context

An independent state in ancient times, Azerbaijan was dominated for much of its subsequent history by foreign powers. Under the Treaty of Turkmanchai of 1828, Azerbaijan was divided between Persia (now Iran) and Russia. After the October Revolution of 1917 in Russia, there was a short period of pro-Bolshevik rule in Baku before a nationalist Government took power and established an independent state on 28 May 1918, with Gäncä (formerly Elisavetpol, but renamed Kirovabad in 1935–89) as the capital. After occupying troops of both the Allied and Central Powers withdrew from independent Azerbaijan, the Red Army invaded, and on 28 April 1920 a Soviet Republic of Azerbaijan was established, and many nationalist and Islamic activists were killed. In December 1922 the republic became a member of the Transcaucasian Soviet Federative Socialist Republic (TSFSR), within the newly formed Union of Soviet Socialist Republics (USSR). The TSFSR was disbanded in 1936, and the Azerbaijani Soviet Socialist Republic (SSR) was formed. The purges of 1937–38, under the Soviet leader, Stalin (Iosif V. Dzhugashvili), involved the execution or imprisonment of many prominent members of the Communist Party of Azerbaijan (AKP). In 1945 the Soviet Government attempted to unite the Azeri population of northern Iran with the Azerbaijan SSR, by providing military support for a local 'puppet' government in Iran; Soviet troops were forced to withdraw from Iran in 1946 by US-British opposition.

In 1982 Heydär Äliyev, First Secretary of the AKP since 1969, was promoted to First Deputy Chairman of the USSR Council of Ministers, while retaining his republican office; he remained influential at all-Union level until his dismissal from the Politburo in October 1987.

Domestic Political Affairs

From 1988, a principal focus of political debate concerned the status of Nagornyi Karabakh (a nominally autonomous oblast, or region, within Azerbaijan, which had a majority of ethnic Armenians among its population—see the separate section on Nagornyi Karabakh). In February the Soviet and Azerbaijani authorities rejected a request by the Nagornyi Karabakh regional soviet (council) for the transfer of the territory to Armenia. Following rising inter-ethnic tensions, 32 people, 26 of whom were Armenians, were killed in anti-Armenian violence in the Azerbaijani town of Sumqayıt. Disturbances continued, leading to a large-scale migration of refugees from both Armenia and Azerbaijan.

In 1989 the Azerbaijan Popular Front Party (AXCP) was established. The party organized a national strike in September and demanded discussion on the issues of sovereignty, Nagornyi Karabakh, the release of political prisoners and official recognition of the party. The Azerbaijan Supreme Soviet (Supreme Council) agreed concessions to the AXCP, including official recognition, and on 23 September adopted a 'Constitutional Law on the Sovereignty of the Azerbaijan SSR'. Azerbaijan closed its borders and prohibited all trade with Armenia. In November the Soviet Government transferred control of Nagornyi Karabakh from a Special Administrative Committee established in January and directly answerable to the USSR Council of Ministers to an Organizing Committee dominated by Azeris. In response, the Armenian Supreme Soviet declared Nagornyi Karabakh to be part of a 'unified Armenian republic', prompting further outbreaks of violence.

In January 1990 radical members of the AXCP led assaults on AKP and government buildings in Baku, Naxçıvan and along the Soviet–Iranian border. Following renewed anti-Armenian violence, with some 60 people killed in rioting in Baku, the remaining non-Azeris were evacuated from the city. On 19 January a state of emergency was declared in Azerbaijan, and Soviet troops were ordered into Baku, where the AXCP was in control. According to official reports, 131 people were killed during the Soviet intervention. Äbdürrähman Väzirov was dismissed as First Secretary of the AKP; he was replaced by Ayaz Mütällibov. Continuing unrest caused the scheduled elections to Azerbaijan's Supreme Soviet to be postponed until September–October 1990, and the continuing state of emergency severely disrupted campaigning by the opposition. When the new Supreme Soviet convened in February 1991, some 80% of its deputies were members of the AKP. The small group of opposition deputies united as the Democratic Bloc of Azerbaijan.

Unlike neighbouring Armenia and Georgia, Azerbaijan declared its willingness to sign a new Union Treaty, and participated in the March 1991 all-Union referendum on the preservation of the USSR. In Azerbaijan 75.1% of the electorate participated, of whom 93.3% voted for a 'renewed federation'. In Naxçıvan, however, only 20% of voters supported the proposal. In August, following the attempted seizure of power in Moscow, the Russian and Soviet capital, by the conservative communist 'State Committee for the State of Emergency', Mütällibov issued a statement that appeared to demonstrate support for the coup. Large demonstrations took place, demanding: his resignation, the declaration of Azerbaijan's independence; the repeal of the state of emergency; and the postponement of the presidential election, scheduled for 8 September. The opposition was supported by Heydär Äliyev, now Chairman of the Supreme Soviet of Naxçıvan. Mütällibov subsequently ended the state of emergency and resigned as First Secretary of the AKP; on 30 August the Azerbaijani Supreme Soviet voted to restore Azerbaijani independence. The opposition boycotted the presidential election, with the result that Mütällibov was the only candidate, officially winning 84% of the votes cast. The AKP agreed to dissolve itself at a congress held later in September.

Independence

Independence was formally declared on 18 October 1991. In that month the Supreme Soviet voted to establish a standing legislature, the National Council, comprising 20% of the members of the Supreme Soviet. On 21 December Azerbaijan joined the Commonwealth of Independent States (CIS, see p. 243), signing the Almatı (Alma-Ata) Declaration. Following the dissolution of the USSR, hostilities intensified in Nagornyi Karabakh. In March 1992 Mütällibov resigned as President, owing to military reverses. He was replaced, on an interim basis, by Yaqub Mämmädov, the Chairman of the Milli Mäclis, or National Assembly (which had replaced the National Council), although, following further military defeats, the Supreme Soviet reinstated Mütällibov in May; however, his declaration of a further state of emergency and his cancellation of the presidential election outraged the AXCP, which organized a protest rally in Baku. One day later, demonstrators occupied the parliamentary building and the presidential palace, deposing Mütällibov, who took refuge in Russia; the Supreme Soviet was abolished. In June the leader of the AXCP, Äbülfäz Elçibäy, was elected President of Azerbaijan, defeating four other candidates by a substantial margin.

Military defeats in and around Nagornyi Karabakh and continuing economic decline severely undermined the Government and led to divisions within the AXCP. In June 1993 a rebel army led by Col Surät Hüseynov seized the city of Gäncä and advanced towards Baku. In an attempt to bolster his leadership, Elçibäy summoned Heydär Äliyev to Baku. In mid-June Äliyev was elected Chairman of the National Assembly. Following Elçibäy's flight from the capital, later in the month the National Assembly, having impeached Elçibäy, transferred virtually all presidential powers to Äliyev. Hüseynov was appointed Prime Minister, with control over the security services. A referendum of confidence in Elçibäy (who had taken refuge in Naxçıvan and still laid claim to the presidency) was held in August; of the 92% of the electorate that participated, 97.5% voted against him. The National Assembly endorsed the result and announced a direct presidential election. Äliyev was elected President on 3 October, with 98.8% of the votes cast. The AXCP boycotted the election.

During 1994 opponents of Äliyev and his New Azerbaijan Party (YAP) were subject to increasing harassment. The signature, in May, of a ceasefire agreement in Nagornyi Karabakh (effectively acknowledging that Azerbaijan had lost control of both the territory itself and a number of adjacent regions) led to further unrest, and the AXCP organized large anti-Government demonstrations in Baku in May and September. In September the Deputy Chairman of the National Assembly and Äliyev's security chief were assassinated; three members of the special militia, OPON, attached to the Ministry of Internal Affairs, were subsequently arrested. In early October 100 OPON troops, led by Col Rövşän Cavadov, stormed the office of the Procurator-General, taking him and his officials hostage and securing the release of the three OPON members in custody. Äliyev declared a state of emergency in Baku and Gäncä. Other forces subsequently mutinied in Baku and elsewhere in Azerbaijan. Äliyev dismissed Hüseynov as Prime Minister, replacing him, on an acting basis, by Fuad Quliyev. However, Äliyev stated that he would head the Government for the immediate future, and dismissed several senior officials. In October the National Assembly voted unanimously to remove Hüseynov's parliamentary immunity from prosecution (he had, however, fled to Russia).

Further political turmoil arose in March 1995, after the Government issued a decree to disband OPON. In response, OPON forces seized government and police buildings, and many casualties were reported. The rebellion was crushed when government troops stormed the OPON headquarters; Cavadov and many of his men were killed, and some 160 rebels were arrested. Äliyev accused Elçibäy and Hüseynov of collusion in the attempted coup. The AXCP was also accused of involvement, and the party was banned. In April Äliyev extended the state of emergency in Baku until June, although that in Gäncä was lifted. In May Quliyev was confirmed as Prime Minister.

Elections to an expanded, 125-member National Assembly took place under a mixed system on 12 November 1995. Of Azerbaijan's 31 officially registered parties, only eight were permitted to participate, including two opposition parties: the recently relegalized AXCP and the Azerbaijan National Independence Party (AMIP). Almost 600 nominally independent candidates were barred from participation. Äliyev's YAP won 19 of the 25 seats filled by proportional representation on the basis of party lists, with the AXCP and the AMIP each receiving three seats. The YAP and independent candidates supporting Äliyev won most of the 100 seats filled by majority voting in single-member constituencies. Further rounds of voting were held on 26 November and in February 1996. Concurrently with the legislative elections, a national referendum overwhelmingly approved Azerbaijan's new Constitution, which provided for extensive presidential powers.

In early 1996 supporters of Hüseynov and Elçibäy received lengthy custodial sentences for their involvement in the coup attempts of October 1994 and March 1995. In February 1996 two former government members were sentenced to death on charges of treason. Several others were sentenced to death on conspiracy charges in the following months. Mütällibov, whom Äliyev had accused of conspiring with Cavadov, was arrested in Russia in April, although the Russian authorities refused to extradite him. In July Fuad Quliyev resigned as Prime Minister; he was succeeded by Artur Rasizadä. In September the Chairman of the National Assembly, Räsul Quliyev, resigned. Murtuz Äläsgärov was elected in his place. In January 1997 the authorities announced that an abortive coup in October 1996 had been organized by, among others, Mütällibov and Hüseynov. Charges were subsequently brought against some 40 alleged conspirators, and in early 1997 many people received prison sentences for their part in the attempted coups of 1994 and 1995. Hüseynov was extradited from Russia in March 1997 and was sentenced to life imprisonment in February 1999. (He received a presidential pardon in March 2004.) In January 1998 the Azerbaijani authorities accused Räsul Quliyev (who was now resident in the USA) of organizing a conspiracy to depose President Äliyev. In April Quliyev was charged *in absentia* with alleged abuses of power; however, government efforts to secure his extradition failed.

Heydär Äliyev re-elected as President

Legislation regulating presidential elections, which required candidates to collect 50,000 signatures in order to stand, was approved in June 1998; the initially announced minimum level of voter participation of 50% was reduced to 25% in July, precipitating opposition protests. At the election held on 11 October, Äliyev was re-elected with 77.6% of the votes cast. Five other candidates contested the election, which was criticized by the Organization for Security and Co-operation in Europe (OSCE, see p. 387) and the Council of Europe (see p. 252) for failing to meet democratic standards.

Widespread electoral violations were reported in the country's first municipal elections, held in December 1999. In April 2000 the Democratic Congress (including members of the AXCP and the Civic Solidarity Party—VHP) organized a large demonstration demanding the introduction of measures to ensure that the legislative elections due to be held in November would be free and fair. Many arrests were made, and the security forces were accused of using excessive force. The death, in August, of Elçibäy prompted the division of the AXCP into 'traditionalist' and 'reformist' factions; the Central Electoral Commission recognized only the reformist wing, led by Äli Kärimli.

The legislative elections, held on 5 November 2000, prompted criticism from the OSCE for the falsification of results and intimidatory practices, and country-wide protests followed. Of the 25 seats filled by proportional representation, 17 were obtained by the YAP and four by the AXCP, while the KPA and the VHP each secured two seats. Of the 99 seats contested in single-mandate constituencies, 62 were obtained by the YAP and 26 by independent candidates. The election results were invalidated in 11 constituencies, where polls were repeated on 7 January 2001. Later that year Äliyev was re-elected Chairman of the YAP, while his son İlham (the Deputy Chairman of the State Oil Company of the Azerbaijan Republic—SOCAR) was elected First Deputy Chairman of the party.

On 24 August 2002 a referendum was held on extensive constitutional amendments, including the proposal that the outcome of the presidential election be determined by a simple majority, rather than by two-thirds, of votes cast. According to official figures, 96% of votes (cast by 84% of the electorate) approved the constitutional amendments, although demonstrations followed, after reports of electoral fraud. Protest rallies and demonstrations to demand the President's resignation continued in early 2003.

In April 2003 President Äliyev collapsed while delivering a speech; in subsequent months he travelled abroad for medical treatment. On 4 August an emergency session of the National Assembly approved İlham Äliyev's appointment as Prime Minister. Two days later, Rasizadä became acting premier, to allow İlham Äliyev to campaign for the presidential election. In early October it was announced that Heydär Äliyev was to withdraw his candidacy, in favour of that of his son.

The Presidency of İlham Äliyev

İlham Äliyev secured 79.5% of the votes cast in the presidential election, held on 15 October 2003.0 The second-placed candidate, the Chairman of the Equality Party (Müsavat), İsa Qämbär, obtained 12.1% of the votes. The opposition refused to recognize the results, and a number of deaths were reported as the authorities violently suppressed opposition protests. İlham Äliyev was inaugurated as President in late October. The National Assembly approved the nomination of Rasizadä as premier on 4 November. Heydär Äliyev died on 12 December. In April 2004 İlham Äliyev appointed a new Minister of Foreign Affairs, Elmar Mämmädyarov, and in July he dismissed the longstanding Minister of National Security, Namiq Abbasov. By

January 2005 some 50 people had received custodial sentences for their involvement in the 2003 post-election protests.

Municipal elections on 17 December 2004, in which the YAP won 64.7% of seats and independent candidates received 31.1%, were criticized by the OSCE for failing to meet democratic standards. The AMIP was the only major opposition party to participate; Etibar Mämmädov resigned as Chairman of the party shortly after the elections.

Prior to legislative elections scheduled for late 2005, the only groups to submit a sufficient number of candidates to be entitled to campaign in the broadcast media were the ruling YAP, the Azerbaijan Liberal Party, the Freedom bloc (Azadlıq—comprising Müsavat, the AXCP and the Azerbaijan Democratic Party—ADP) and the New Policy bloc, which included the AMIP. Meanwhile, several opposition leaders, detained on charges of inciting violence following the 2003 election, were released, under an amnesty, in March 2005, and public demonstrations in Baku, prohibited since October 2003, were again authorized.

In October 2005 Räsul Quliyev, who remained in exile as leader of the ADP, was detained in Simferopol, Ukraine, after his aircraft was prevented from landing in Baku, where he had been intending to return in order to participate in the elections. Allegations emerged that a former Minister of Finance, Fikrät Yusifov, had facilitated the transfer of funds from Quliyev to the Minister of Economic Development, Färhad Äliyev, in order to finance a coup attempt. Färhad Äliyev and the Minister of Public Health, Äli Insanov, were subsequently dismissed from their government posts and arrested. (In October 2007 Färhad Äliyev was sentenced to 10 years' imprisonment on charges of corruption and abuse of power, together with his brother, Rafiq, previously President of the Azpetrol Group, who received a term of nine years.)

The legislative elections (the first to be contested wholly on a basis of single-mandate seats) were held on 6 November 2005. Observers from the OSCE and the Council of Europe stated that the polls again failed to meet democratic standards, while opposition parties held a number of large-scale protests. In late November the security forces violently dispersed a demonstration organized by the Azadlıq bloc, and further rallies were prohibited. On 1 December the Constitutional Court annulled the results in 10 constituencies (including two in which opposition candidates had been elected). After elections were repeated in those constituencies on 13 May 2006, the YAP held a total of 61 seats, the Azadlıq bloc six seats, and there were 46 independent deputies (mainly supporters of the Government).

The new National Assembly convened on 2 December 2005, when Oktai Äsädov of the YAP replaced Äläsgärov as its Chairman. Following the elections, President Äliyev effected several personnel changes, including the appointment in early December of Natiq Äliyev, hitherto the President of SOCAR, as Minister of Industry and Energy, and the dismissal in April 2006 of the longstanding Minister of Finance, Avaz Alekperov, who was suceeded by Samir Şarifov, hitherto the head of the State Oil Fund. In May Abbas Abbasov, who had served as First Deputy Prime Minister since 1992, tendered his resignation.

Meanwhile, the opposition again fragmented. While the ADP and the reformist wing of the AXCP announced their intention to boycott the new legislature, in February 2006 Müsavat (which had won four seats) confirmed that it would participate in the National Assembly and withdrew from the Azadlıq bloc. Meanwhile, in January the AMIP divided into two rival factions, one supporting the party's Chairman, Äli Äliyev, and the other supporting the founder of the party, honorary party leader Etibar Mämmädov.

Serious irregularities were again observed during the municipal elections held on 6 October 2006. Meanwhile, the repression of independent media intensified. In January 2007 the European Court of Human Rights (ECHR) ruled in favour of Särdar Jalaloğlu of the ADP, who stated that his treatment by the authorities following the presidential election of 2003 constituted torture. In April 2007 a prominent journalist critical of the Government, Eynulla Fätullayev, was imprisoned for two-and-a-half years, on charges of libel relating to an internet article that suggested that both Azerbaijanis and Armenian forces were responsible for a massacre of hundreds of Azeri civilians during the conflict in Nagornyi Karabakh; in October he was sentenced to eight-and-a-half years' imprisonment on charges of terrorism, inciting ethnic hatred and tax evasion.

In response to the approval, in June 2008, by the National Assembly of amendments to the electoral code, the main opposition parties announced a boycott of the forthcoming presidential election (although six minor opposition leaders did register to contest the poll). On 15 October İlham Äliyev was elected to a second term of office, obtaining 88.7% of the votes cast, according to official results, with a 75.6% rate of participation. An International Election Observation Mission stated that there had been significant improvements in the conduct of the election, while noting that it had nevertheless failed to meet international democratic standards, particularly with regard to media bias. The US Administration issued a statement welcoming perceived progress in the organization of the election. On 24 October Äliyev was inaugurated for a second presidential term.

The abolition of presidential term limits

Shortly after İlham Äliyev's re-election in October 2008, the Executive Secretary of the YAP, Äli Ahmedov, proposed that the constitutional stipulation restricting the President to two terms of office be removed. In December the National Assembly voted overwhelmingly in favour of conducting a national referendum on proposed legislation (strongly contested by opposition groups) to amend the Constitution accordingly. The Constitutional Court ruled in favour of the legality of the referendum, although opposition leaders urged a boycott of the plebiscite. The referendum, held on 18 March 2009, resulted in the overwhelming approval of amendments to 29 articles of the Constitution. Opposition parties disputed the results and the official rate of participation of 70.8%, while the Council of Europe stated that adoption of the amendments violated government commitments to democratic principles. On 2 April Äliyev signed a decree incorporating the new amendments removing the limit on presidential terms into the Constitution. Meanwhile, in March the National Assembly adopted a number of controversial amendments to media regulations, notably allowing the suspension of media outlets for 'abuse of power'. In June the National Assembly approved legislation placing new restrictions on the operations of non-governmental organizations (NGOs).

At the elections to the National Assembly, held on 7 November 2010, the YAP secured 72 of the 125 seats, while two electoral alliances formed by parties loyal to the Government, the Democratic Bloc and Reform Bloc, took four and three seats, respectively; nominally independent candidates received 41 seats. Although all the opposition parties contested the elections, the main opposition alliance, the AXCP-Müsavat bloc, failed to obtain representation. International observers suggested that the low voter turnout, of 50.1%, reflected public disaffection following the failure of many prospective opposition electoral candidates to secure registration. The Government rejected opposition demands that the legislative elections be repeated; however, observers from the OSCE, the Parliamentary Assembly of the Council of Europe (PACE) and the European Parliament reported a lack of democracy.

Anti-Government protests

A government ban on the wearing of the *hijab* (headscarf) by female students in state educational institutions, which had been announced by the Minister of Education in November 2010, prompted a series of protests by Muslim activists. In January 2011 the leader of the proscribed Azerbaijan Islamic Party (AIP), Mövsüm Sämädov, was arrested on charges of conspiring to overthrow the Government, after a video of a speech he had made denouncing President Äliyev was published online. In February a revived opposition grouping known as Public Chamber urged a campaign of anti-Government demonstrations. During March about 50 people were detained after unauthorized protests in Baku, led by youth groups and co-ordinated through social networking websites. On 2 April some 200 arrests were reported during an unauthorized opposition demonstration termed a 'day of rage' in Baku; the OSCE condemned violent measures employed by the security forces against the protesters. Further anti-Government demonstrations were organized by Public Chamber in Baku during May and June, and were again accompanied by the arrest of large numbers of participants. In late May Fätullayev was released from prison under a presidential amnesty. Later in the year a number of opposition leaders arrested during the demonstrations received custodial terms. In August six prominent members of Public Chamber were sentenced to three years' imprisonment for participation in the unauthorized 2 April protest; later in August a three-year sentence was imposed on a human rights activist, Vidadi Iskandarov, for offences committed during the 2010 parliamentary election campaign.

In July 2011 the AIP, which had organized a number of protests against the ban on the *hijab* concurrently with the

Public Chamber campaign, was refused authorization by the authorities to conduct a rally in Baku. The party's Deputy Chairman, Arif Qaniyev, and two other prominent party members were arrested in August, following suspicions that they had engaged in subversive activities in collaboration with the Iranian authorities. In early October Sämädov was convicted and sentenced to 12 years' imprisonment on charges of possession of armaments, planning to seize power and preparing a terrorist act; six other prominent AIP members received custodial terms of between 10 and 12 years. Also in October a further seven opposition activists were sentenced to terms of between two and three years for participation in the 2 April demonstration. In November the National Assembly adopted legislation imposing severe restrictions on the distribution of religious literature, and participation in religious activities.

In January 2012 the Ministry of National Security announced that it had discovered a conspiracy by an Iranian-sponsored group of militants to assassinate a number of public figures in Baku, including the Israeli ambassador to Azerbaijan. On 1 March riots erupted in the north-eastern town of Quba, and the house of the regional governor (who was reported to have made derogatory remarks about the residents of the region) was set alight, before the protesters were forcibly dispersed. One day later President Äliyev dismissed the governor. Also in March an Azerbaijani journalist working for Radio Free Europe/Radio Liberty, Khadija Ismayilova, announced that she had received threats that a sexually explicit video of her would be published online if she continued investigations into incidents of corruption allegedly carried out by the family and associates of President Äliyev. The subsequent release of the video prompted condemnation from local and international human rights organizations.

The staging of the international popular music competition the Eurovision Song Contest in Baku in May 2012 focused international attention on Azerbaijan's human rights situation; however, plans by Public Chamber to stage concurrent protests were thwarted by a large-scale security operation by the authorities. In June the National Assembly approved legislation that provided life-long immunity from prosecution to former Presidents and their close relatives. Former President Mütällibov returned to Azerbaijan from Russia in the following month. Qaniyev was released from detention in June 2012, while Äliyev formally pardoned 64 prisoners. Also in June, however, a prominent human rights activist, Hilal Mämmädov was arrested and subsequently charged with possession of illegal drugs, spying for Iran and inciting ethnic hatred. (In September 2013 he was sentenced to five years' imprisonment.)

On 9 October 2012 some 22 suspects were sentenced to between 10 and 15 years' imprisonment by a Baku court for planning terrorist attacks against US and Israeli targets on behalf of the Iranian secret services. Meanwhile, in early October some 200 Muslim men demonstrating in Baku against the ban on the *hijab* resisted efforts by the police to suppress the protest; it was reported that some 20 police officers had been injured, while 65 demonstrators had been arrested. Later that month youth elements of Public Chamber staged an unauthorized demonstration in Baku to demand new legislative elections, with 110 arrests ensuing. In early December four Islamists with Iranian connections received custodial sentences of between 12 and 14 years for planning bomb attacks on the occasion of the Eurovision Song Contest. Later that month two journalists and a number of opposition activists were pardoned by the Government. In January 2013 youth activists staged a rally in the outskirts of the capital, in protest at alleged abuses within the military following the non-combat death of an army conscript.

On 23 January 2013 a private dispute in the north-western town of İsmayıllı escalated into violent rioting directed at the local authorities; some 3,000 protesters, who complained of economic hardship and demanded the resignation of the regional governor, were violently dispersed by police. A subsequent demonstration staged by about 100 activists in Baku in support of the İsmayıllı protest was also suppressed by police. In early February two prominent opposition leaders—İlqar Mämmädov, the Chairman of the Republican Alternative movement, and Tofiq Yaqublu, the Deputy Chairman of Müsavat—were arrested and charged with the organization of mass disorder in association with the protests in İsmayıllı. (Their trial began in November; in March 2014 Mämmädov was sentenced to seven years' imprisonment, while Yaqublu received a gaol sentence of five years.) Later in the month the National Assembly approved legislation imposing tight restrictions on the terms under which donations could be made to political parties, religious organizations and NGOs, prompting speculation that the measures would be used to inhibit support for opposition movements in advance of the presidential election scheduled to take place on 16 October. Meanwhile, in February President Äliyev's removal of state honours and a state pension from an author, Äkräm Äylisli, who had published a novel depicting violence committed by Azeris against Armenians in the early 1990s, and which was regarded as presenting Armenians sympathetically, provoked controversy nationally and internationally; a presidential spokesman called for 'public hatred' to be expressed towards Äylisli. In April the authorities closed an independent, US-funded, educational institution known as the 'Free Thought University', on the grounds that it had failed to comply with official registration requirements.

Recent developments: the 2013 presidential election

In June 2013 an opposition grouping, the National Council of Democratic Forces (DQMS), which comprised Müsavat, the AXCP and numerous smaller groups, nominated a prominent former Soviet and Azerbaijani film writer, Rustam Ibragimbekov, as its candidate in the forthcoming presidential election. Ten candidates, including Äliyev, were subsequently registered to contest the presidential election, which was scheduled for 9 October; however, five opposition candidates were ruled ineligible for registration, among them Ibragimbekov (who held dual Russian citizenship), who was excluded on the grounds that he had not principally resided in Azerbaijan during the previous 10 years. The DQMS consequently nominated a historian, Cämil Häsänli, as its presidential candidate.

According to official results, Äliyev was overwhelmingly re-elected as President on 9 October 2013, obtaining 84.6% of the votes cast; Häsänli was placed second, with 5.5%. Although a report issued by observers from PACE and the European Parliament described the election as 'free, fair and transparent', OSCE monitors recorded widespread electoral irregularities, including incidents of intimidation and attacks on journalists. The DQMS subsequently organized a rally in Baku in protest at the results. Following his re-election, Äliyev signed a decree pardoning 20 prisoners, including former minister Färhad Äliyev and his brother. (In November 2010 the ECHR had upheld an appeal by Färhad Äliyev against his October 2007 conviction.) Äliyev was inaugurated to a third presidential term of office on 19 October 2013. Later that month he reorganized the Government, notably replacing the long-serving Minister of Defence, Safar Abiyev, with Zakir Häsänov, hitherto the Minister of the Interior, who was reported to favour a more aggressive stance with regard to the Nagornyi Karabakh conflict.

In November 2013 a further 29 people were convicted of planning terrorist attacks on the occasion of the Eurovision Song Contest; three were sentenced to life imprisonment, while the remainder received prison terms of between nine and 15 years. Increased intimidation of opposition journalists was reported following the presidential election, and in December the head of an independent election monitoring group that had criticized the conduct of the poll was placed in detention on suspicion of tax evasion. In mid-December the DQMS organized a further anti-Government demonstration in Baku to protest at increasing food and fuel prices, and to demand President Äliyev's resignation. However, in the following month Müsavat announced its withdrawal from the DQMS alliance, citing the need for different tactics in combating the authorities. In December, meanwhile, a veteran of the Nagornyi Karabakh conflict died after setting himself on fire outside government offices in protest at treatment of him by the state; by late February 2014 at least eight further cases of self-immolation by anti-Government protestors had been reported. In February journalist Ismayilova was questioned by the Office of the Prosecutor-General, following allegations in the pro-Government media that she had leaked state secrets to visiting US officials.

Naxçıvan

The Autonomous Republic of Naxçıvan lies to the west of metropolitan Azerbaijan, separated from it by Armenian territory. Although Azerbaijan apparently surrendered its claims to Naxçıvan (which then had a substantial ethnically Armenian population) in 1920, it never became part of Soviet Armenia. In 1921 it was recognized as part of Azerbaijan. This fact, and a substantial decline in the numbers of the ethnic Armenian population under Soviet rule (to around 5% of the population at the 1989 census), rendered renewed Armenian claims to the republic in the late 1980s and early 1990s largely rhetorical. However, the subsequent Azerbaijani economic blockade on Armenia meant that

Naxçıvan had to rely on air links with metropolitan Azerbaijan or on road routes through Iran.

Naxçıvan provided a source of strong support both for the nationalists who emerged in the late 1980s and for Heydär Äliyev, leader of Azerbaijan in 1969–87 and in 1993–2003. In 1990 nationalist demonstrators seized buildings of the ruling Communist Party in Naxçıvan and attempted to declare the republic's secession from the USSR. In March 1991 Azerbaijan participated in the Soviet referendum on the renewal of the USSR; some 93.3% of those who voted favoured remaining in the Union, but in Naxçıvan support was only some 20%. The leader of the nationalist AXCP, Äbülfäz Elçibäy, was a native of Naxçıvan, as was Heydär Äliyev, who had retired to the region after his dismissal in 1987. Äliyev formed the YAP in Naxçıvan, and in September 1991 was elected Chairman of the local Supreme Soviet. He again became involved in national politics in 1993, replacing Elçibäy as President of Azerbaijan in that year. Elçibäy, meanwhile, took refuge in the exclave, and remained in effective internal exile until 1997 (he died in 2000). The Azerbaijani National Assembly approved a revised Constitution for Naxçıvan in December 1998, which was endorsed by the republic's legislature, defining the exclave as an 'autonomous state' within Azerbaijan. The highest official in the republic is the Chairman of the Ali Mäclis (Supreme Assembly), which position has been held by Vasif Talıbov since 1993 (in succession to Heydär Äliyev). The post of Prime Minister of the Autonomous Republic has been held by Älövset Baxşıyev since 2000.

During the 2000s and early 2010s concerns about alleged human rights abuses in Naxçıvan were expressed both domestically and internationally. In 2007 a pro-opposition journalist, Hakim Mehdiyev, was reported to have been subjected to torture while in detention; in the same year an AXCP activist was reported to have been detained in a psychiatric institution. (The threat or practice of detaining political opponents or those who made complaints about police behaviour was reported on further occasions.) In February 2011 an observer for an opposition candidate at the parliamentary elections held in November 2010 claimed that he had been tortured by the republican Minister of the Interior, Ahmad Ahmadov, after he had alleged that electoral fraud had occurred. In August 2011 it was reported that a man who had been accused of participating in espionage for Iran had been found dead, allegedly as the result of a beating, at offices of the Ministry of the Interior in Naxçıvan. Reports also emerged of an apparently systematic campaign, from the late 1990s onwards, to remove evidence of Armenian settlement or heritage, from the territory of Naxçıvan, including, most notably, the destruction of an Armenian cemetery, parts of which dated to the 10th century, at Culfa (Julfa, Djulfa, Jugha), near the border with Iran. Despite the existence of video and photographic evidence that purported to document the destruction of at least 2,000 Armenian gravestones and monuments, the Azerbaijani authorities denied that any such destruction had occurred, although international observers, including a delegation from the European Parliament in 2006, and successive US ambassadors, in 2011 and 2012, were prohibited from visiting the site on numerous occasions. Amid continued tensions in the territory of Nagornyi Karabakh, in July 2013 Azerbaijani and Turkish troops staged joint military exercises in Naxçıvan and Baku; these were followed by Armenian exercises along the border with Naxçıvan in September.

Foreign Affairs

Regional relations

Although Azerbaijan signed the Almatı Declaration that established the CIS in December 1991, in October 1992 the National Assembly voted against the country's participation in the organization. With the overthrow of the AXCP Government and the accession to power of Heydär Äliyev, this stance was reversed, and in September 1993 Azerbaijan was formally admitted to full membership of the body. Azerbaijan withdrew from the CIS Collective Security Treaty in 1999, owing to the continued occupation of Nagornyi Karabakh by ethnic Armenian troops, and in protest against Russia's supply of armaments to Armenia. However, a visit to Azerbaijan by Russian President Vladimir Putin in January 2001, and the signature of a number of co-operation agreements, appeared to signal a new stage in relations between the two countries. President Heydär Äliyev visited Russia in January 2002, when a 10-year economic co-operation plan was agreed. Furthermore, in September a bilateral agreement was signed on the delimitation of the Caspian Sea, according to which the seabed would be divided into national sectors, and the surface be used in common. A similar agreement had already been reached with Kazakhstan, and a trilateral agreement was signed in May 2003. In February 2004 President İlham Äliyev undertook an official visit to Russia, during which a declaration was signed, reaffirming previous bilateral agreements; a further visit followed in 2005. However, in December 2006 Azerbaijan suspended imports of natural gas from Russia, after the Russian state-controlled natural gas monopoly Gazprom sharply increased the price.

Relations with Russia strengthened, amid rival Russian and European Union—EU (see p. 273) plans for prospective gas pipeline networks to supply fuel from the Caspian to Europe; in 2009 SOCAR and Gazprom signed an agreement, whereby Russia was to purchase an initial 500m. cu m of natural gas annually from Azerbaijan. Following a defence co-operation accord reached between Russia and Armenia in August 2012, in September Russian President Dmitrii Medvedev visited Azerbaijan, where he provided assurances that Russia's neutrality with regard to Nagornyi Karabakh remained unchanged; an agreement was also signed, under which the volume of natural gas exported to Russia by Azerbaijan was to increase significantly from 2011. In December 2012, however, Azerbaijan announced that Russia's lease of the Qabala radar installation, in the north-east of the country, had expired, after Azerbaijan had increased the annual fee from US $7m. to a reported $300m.; the withdrawal of the Russian contingent at the base was completed in October 2013.

During a visit by Putin (who had returned to the Russian presidency) to Baku in August 2013, the heads of SOCAR and the Russian state petroleum company Rosneft signed an agreement on the establishment of a joint venture to develop projects in Azerbaijan. In October, however, nationalist rioting in Moscow that followed the killing of a Russian citizen by an Azerbaijani migrant, Orkhan Zeynalov, provoked strong anti-Russian sentiment in Azerbaijan and strained bilateral relations. The Azerbaijani Government formally protested to the Russian ambassador in Baku at the alleged mistreatment of Zeynalov in detention and demanded that a full investigation into the incident be conducted. Furthermore, it was reported that, prior to the October presidential election in Azerbaijan (see above), an unofficial grouping of ethnically Azeri oligarchs which had been formed in Russia had established links with Azerbaijani opposition movements. The Azerbaijani authorities also displayed consternation at Armenia's decision, announced in September to join the Russian-led customs union, and at subsequent concessions granted by Putin to Armenia in December.

The strengthening of relations with Turkey continued throughout the 1990s and 2000s. Turkey supported Azerbaijan in the conflict over Nagornyi Karabakh, providing humanitarian and other aid and reinforcing Armenia's international isolation by closing its borders and prohibiting trade with that country. A pipeline connecting Azerbaijani petroleum fields with the Turkish port of Ceyhan, via Tbilisi, Georgia, became fully operational in 2006. Construction of a rail transport connection between Turkey, Georgia and Azerbaijan began in November 2007, when the Turkish President, Abdullah Gül, made an official visit to Azerbaijan. In October 2009 Turkey and Armenia signed an agreement on the normalization of relations; however, continued pressure from the Azerbaijani Government was instrumental in the Turkish legislature's subsequent failure to ratify the agreement and the formal suspension of the process by Armenia in April 2010. In May Azerbaijan and Turkey established a Strategic Partnership Council, which was intended to strengthen political, economic and cultural links. At the 10th summit meeting of Turkic-speaking countries in İstanbul, Turkey, in September, the Heads of State of Turkey, Azerbaijan, Kyrgyzstan, Kazakhstan and Turkmenistan finalized the formation of a Co-operation Council of Turkic-Speaking Countries.

In October 2011, at a ceremony in İzmir, Turkey, attended by President Äliyev and Prime Minister Erdoğan, agreements establishing the terms for gas transit from Azerbaijan to Europe via Turkey, and for Azerbaijani gas supplies to Turkey, were signed. In June 2012 Azerbaijan and Turkey signed an agreement formalizing a project comprising the construction of a Trans-Anatolia Gas Pipeline (TANAP), which was to be principally supplied by the Şah Deniz gas field in the Caspian. Äliyev made an official visit to Turkey in November 2013, when further energy co-operation was under discussion.

In late 2011 the Azerbaijani Government accused Iran of supporting subversive activities by militant Islamists within Azerbaijan, and in January 2012 claimed that it had thwarted an

Iranian conspiracy to assassinate the Israeli ambassador in Baku. In February Azerbaijan, in turn, strongly denied that it was assisting Israeli intelligence agents operating against Iranian targets on Azerbaijani territory, following a formal protest from the Iranian Government. In May Iran temporarily withdrew its ambassador from Azerbaijan, owing to objections regarding the hosting of the Eurovision Song Contest (see above) in the capital. In July it was announced that an Azerbaijani human rights activist was to be charged with spying for Iran (see Domestic Political Affairs), while two Azerbaijani poets, who had been arrested by Iranian security forces in early May, were brought to trial in the Iranian city of Tabriz in August on charges of entering Iran illegally, drugs-trafficking, and espionage on behalf of the Azerbaijani secret services. In September, however, the two poets were released. In October and December a number of suspects were convicted of planing terrorist attacks in Azerbaijan in collaboration with the Iranian authorities (see Domestic Political Affairs). In October 2013 a court in Baku sentenced a former Iranian intelligence officer, Bahram Feyzi, to 15 years' imprisonment, after convicting him on charges of espionage and terrorism related to an attempt to attack the Israeli embassy in Baku; the Iranian Ministry of Foreign Affairs subsequently issued demands for his release. Following a number of reported incidents at the border with Iran, in December an Azerbaijani border official was killed in an exchange of fire. (Despite the deterioration in relations, the Azerbaijan-Iran Intergovernmental Commission on bilateral co-operation was convened in Baku in that month and a further meeting was scheduled for February 2014.)

In 2007 the Presidents of the Caspian littoral states (Azerbaijan, Iran, Kazakhstan, Russia and Turkmenistan) signed a security co-operation agreement at a Caspian summit meeting in Baku. However, in 2012 the longstanding dispute over the Kyapaz (Serdar) oilfield in the Sea was revived, when Azerbaijan protested officially against exploration work undertaken by Turkmenistan in the area. In April 2013 Azerbaijan claimed that Turkmenistan's naval forces had fired on Azerbaijani offshore oil facilities. Meetings between representatives of the five littoral states on a draft Convention on the Legal Status of the Caspian Sea continued and a fourth Caspian summit was planned for late 2014.

Other external relations

In 2001 the USA agreed to halt the provision of financial assistance to separatists in Nagornyi Karabakh and commit funds to Azerbaijan, through the temporary suspension of Amendment 907 to the Freedom Support Act of 1992 (establishing a foreign assistance programme to the countries of the former USSR), which prevented the donation of aid to Azerbaijan while that country's closure of the Armenian border remained in place. The waiver was subsequently renewed annually. In 2005 Azerbaijan confirmed that two new, US-funded radar stations were under construction close to the Iranian and Russian borders, respectively. In April 2006 President İlham Äliyev made his first official visit to the USA. From 2008 Azerbaijan's relations with the USA were adversely affected by US support for the rapprochement between Armenia and Turkey. In July 2010 US Secretary of State Hillary Clinton met Äliyev for discussions in Baku. In September two members of the US Senate indefinitely blocked the nomination of Matthew Bryza as the new US ambassador to Azerbaijan (a post that had remained vacant since July 2009), in response to the allegedly close associations of Bryza with elements of the Azerbaijani state. In December 2010 President Obama appointed Bryza directly as ambassador on an interim basis, although he remained in the post for only one year, following the continued failure of the Senate to confirm his appointment. Richard Morningstar, formerly the US Special Envoy for Eurasian Energy, was finally appointed as the new US ambassador to Azerbaijan in mid-2012. In June US Secretary of State Clinton again visited Azerbaijan.

From 2009 the diversification of gas supply away from Russia became a priority for the EU, reinforcing Azerbaijan's importance as a source of energy. In January Azerbaijan agreed to begin exports of gas to Greece and Bulgaria (pending transit agreements). In May President Äliyev, along with his Georgian and Turkish counterparts, and the Egyptian Minister of Petroleum, signed an agreement with the EU intended to result in the establishment of a 'Southern Corridor' of gas supplies from the Caspian to the Mediterranean region. In July 2010 Azerbaijan and the EU began negotiations on the signature of an Association Agreement in the framework of the Eastern Partnership established in the previous year. During a meeting in September in Baku, Presidents Äliyev, Saakashvili of Georgia, and Traian Băsescu of Romania, together with Prime Minister Viktor Orbán of Hungary, announced the launching of a liquefied natural gas project (the Azerbaijan–Georgia–Romania Interconnector) which was to import natural gas from Azerbaijan to Romania and Hungary. The Azerbaijani Government's commitment to providing large volumes of gas for the EU's planned Nabucco project (which would supply gas from the Caspian region to Western and Central Europe) was deemed essential for construction of the pipeline to proceed. In January 2011 Äliyev and European Commission President José Manuel Barroso signed a declaration on development of the 'Southern Corridor' to Europe, which was believed to be preparatory to investment decisions for the second phase of production at the Şah Deniz gas field in the Caspian Sea. In August 2012 a funding agreement was signed for the construction of a Trans-Adriatic Pipeline (TAP), which was to connect with the TANAP and deliver gas to Western Europe via Greece, Albania and Italy. The Şah Deniz consortium (in which BP, SOCAR and Statoil of Norway were the major enterprises) announced in June 2013 that the TAP project was its chosen export route, effectively ending the viability of the planned Nabucco pipeline. (A final investment decision by the consortium in December endorsed construction of the TANAP and TAP projects.) At an Eastern Partnership summit meeting in Vilnius, Lithuania, in November, Azerbaijan signed an agreement with the EU that relaxed mutual visa requirements; a joint declaration stated that the EU was prepared to begin negotiations on a free trade agreement after Azerbaijan had acceded to the World Trade Organization (see p. 434).

In September 2012 international controversy surrounded the decision of President Äliyev to grant a pardon to an Azerbaijani army officer, Lt Ramil Säfärov, who, in 2006, had been sentenced to life imprisonment for the killing of an Armenian officer while both were attending a military training course in Budapest, Hungary; Säfärov had been released from prison in Hungary and extradited at the request of Äliyev at the end of August (receiving a popular welcome upon his return to Azerbaijan). The release and pardoning of Säfärov (in addition to increasing tensions with Armenia) drew international criticism, including from the USA, Russia and the European Parliament. In December it was announced that Azerbaijan was to host the first European Olympic Games (a newly created event) in 2015, having been the only state to submit an application to do so.

CONSTITUTION AND GOVERNMENT

Under the 1995 Constitution, the President of the Republic of Azerbaijan is Head of State and Commander-in-Chief of the armed forces. The President, who is directly elected for a five-year term of office, holds supreme executive authority in conjunction with the Cabinet of Ministers, which is appointed by the President and is headed by the Prime Minister. Supreme legislative power is vested in the 125-member Milli Mäclis (National Assembly), which is directly elected for a five-year term. Judicial power is exercised by the Supreme Court, the Economic Court, the Court on Grave Crimes, the Court of Appeal and local courts. Naxçıvan has its own Supreme Court. Azerbaijan is divided into 74 administrative districts (rayons), of which eight are located within the Autonomous Republic of Naxçıvan. The former autonomous oblast (region) of Nagornyi Karabakh and seven rayons located between Nagornyi Karabakh and Armenia are governed by internationally unrecognized authorities.

REGIONAL AND INTERNATIONAL CO-OPERATION

Azerbaijan is a member of the Commonwealth of Independent States (CIS, see p. 243) and the Organization for Security and Co-operation in Europe (OSCE, see p. 387). It is also a member of the Council of Europe (see p. 252), the Economic Cooperation Organization (ECO, see p. 265), the Organization of the Black Sea Economic Cooperation (BSEC, see p. 401), the Organization for Democracy and Economic Development (GUAM, see p. 467) and the Organization of Islamic Cooperation (OIC, see p. 403).

Azerbaijan joined the UN in 1992. The country joined the 'Partnership for Peace' programme of the North Atlantic Treaty Organization (NATO, see p. 373) in May 1994, and was awarded observer status at the Alliance in June 1999.

ECONOMIC AFFAIRS

In 2012, according to World Bank estimates, Azerbaijan's gross national income (GNI), measured at average 2010–12 prices, was US $56,096m., equivalent to $6,030 per head (or $9,200 per head on an international purchasing-power parity basis). During

2003–12, it was estimated, the population increased at an average rate of 1.4% per year, while gross domestic product (GDP) per head increased, in real terms, at an average annual rate of 12.0%. Overall GDP increased, in real terms, at an average annual rate of 13.6% in 2003–12. According to the Asian Development Bank (ADB, see p. 183), real GDP increased by 5.8% in 2013.

Agriculture (including fishing) contributed 5.5% of GDP in 2012, when some 37.7% of the employed labour force were employed in the sector, according to official figures. The principal crops are grain, potatoes, barley, tomatoes, watermelons, apples and sugar beet. By 2001 all collective farms had been privatized. During 2003–11, according to World Bank estimates, agricultural GDP increased, in real terms, at an average annual rate of 4.3%. According to the ADB, agricultural GDP increased by 4.9% in 2013.

Industry (including mining, manufacturing, construction and power) contributed 62.8% of GDP in 2012 and employed 14.3% of the employed labour force, according to official sources. According to the World Bank, during 2003–11 industrial GDP increased, in real terms, at an average annual rate of 18.7%. Industrial growth was driven principally by the mining sector. Real sectoral GDP decreased by 0.6% in 2012, but increased by 4.9% in 2013, according to the ADB.

Mining accounted for 46.6% of GDP in 2012 and employed just 0.9% of the employed labour force, according to official figures. Azerbaijan is richly endowed with mineral resources. The country's proven reserves of petroleum were estimated to total 1,000m. metric tons at the end of 2012, mainly located in offshore Caspian fields; production in that year was 43.4m. tons. In September 1994 the Azerbaijani Government and a consortium of international petroleum companies, the Azerbaijan International Operating Company (AIOC), concluded an agreement to develop the offshore oilfields, despite an unresolved maritime border dispute with Turkmenistan. By 2000 the Azerbaijani state-owned oil company SOCAR had signed more than 20 production-sharing agreements with international partners. In October 2000 the Government signed an agreement with SOCAR and a consortium of petroleum companies on the construction of a pipeline from Baku, via Tbilisi (Georgia), to Ceyhan in Turkey (the BTC pipeline). Deliveries through the pipeline commenced in 2006. Azerbaijan has substantial reserves of natural gas (mostly off shore), but a lack of suitable infrastructure meant that until 2006 the country was a net importer of gas. A pipeline, constructed to transport gas to Erzurum (Turkey), via Tbilisi, running parallel with the BTC pipeline, known as the BTE or South Caucasus Pipeline commenced operations in 2006. Output of natural gas in 2012 amounted to 15,602m. cu m. Other minerals extracted include gold, silver, iron ore, copper concentrates, alunite (alum-stone), iron pyrites, barytes, cobalt and molybdenum.

According to official figures, manufacturing accounted for 4.4% of GDP and engaged 4.9% of the employed labour force in 2012. The GDP of the sector increased, in real terms, at an average annual rate of 6.4% in 2003–10, according to the World Bank. Sectoral growth was 6.8% in 2010.

In 2012 the construction sector provided 9.8% of GDP and engaged 7.2% of the employed labour force, according to official figures. During 2003–12, according to UN figures, the GDP of the sector increased at an average annual rate of 15.8%. Construction GDP increased by 18.0% in 2012.

In 2011 85.1% of Azerbaijan's supply of primary energy was provided by natural gas, compared with 19.8% in 2000. In 2006 Azerbaijan drastically reduced its imports of Russian gas, after the Russian state-controlled Gazprom corporation increased prices, and in 2007 SOCAR's petroleum exports via the Baku–Novorossiisk pipeline were suspended. In November 2006 a memorandum on energy co-operation was signed between Azerbaijan and the European Union (EU, see p. 273). Mineral fuels accounted for only 3.2% of merchandise imports in 2012.

In 2012 the services sector provided 31.7% of GDP and engaged 48.1% of the employed labour force, according to official figures. During 2003–11 the GDP of the services sector increased, in real terms, at an average annual rate of 13.7%. Growth of 7.2% was recorded in 2013, according to the ADB.

In 2012 Azerbaijan recorded a visible merchandise trade surplus of US $21,913.6m., and there was a surplus of $14,976.0m. on the current account of the balance of payments. In that year the principal source of imports was Turkey (supplying 15.8% of the total). Other major sources of imports were Russia, Germany, the USA, the People's Republic of China, Ukraine and the United Kingdom. Italy was the largest export market in 2012, accounting for 23.2% of total exports. Other important purchasers were India, France, Indonesia, Israel and the USA. The principal exports in 2012 were mineral products, which accounted for 93.2% of all exports. The principal imports were machinery and electrical equipment, base metals and articles thereof, vehicles and transportation equipment, prepared foodstuffs, plastic goods and vegetable products.

Azerbaijan's projected budgetary surplus for 2013 was 1,634m. manats. Azerbaijan's general government gross debt was 6,260m. manats in 2012, equivalent to 11.6% of GDP. At the end of 2011 the country's total external debt was US $8,427m., of which $4,655m. was public and publicly guaranteed debt. In that year, the cost of servicing long-term public and publicly guaranteed debt and repayments to the IMF was equivalent to 4.9% of the value of exports of goods, services and income (excluding workers' remittances). According to official figures, consumer price inflation increased at an annual average rate of 8.7% during 2006–12. Consumer prices increased by 2.4% in 2013, according to the ADB. According to official figures, 5.2% of the total labour force were registered as unemployed in 2012.

The economic prospects of Azerbaijan have remained favourable, owing to its substantial mineral wealth and strategic geopolitical location. Rapid economic growth was recorded in 2005–07, following the launch of the BTC pipeline, while state revenue increased, owing to the expiry of the preferential tax arrangements enjoyed by foreign petroleum companies developing the Caspian oilfields. In July 2010 Azerbaijan began negotiations with the EU on the signature of an Association Agreement in the framework of its Eastern Partnership, with objectives including the eventual establishment of a free trade area. In September 2011 the Azerbaijani authorities announced the discovery of significant new natural gas reserves at an offshore field, near the Abşeron peninsula, increasing estimated reserves to 350,000m. cu m of gas. In June 2012 Azerbaijan and Turkey signed an agreement for the construction of a Trans-Anatolia Gas Pipeline, and in August a funding agreement was reached for the construction of a Trans-Adriatic Pipeline (TAP, see Other external relations); both projects were to constitute a 'Southern Corridor' of gas supplies to Western Europe. Meanwhile, under a 2009 accord, Azerbaijan, previously an importer of Russian fuel, had committed to export gas to Russia (by 2012 the volume of supplies had increased to a reported 3,000m. cu m), while in August 2013 the heads of SOCAR and Russian state petroleum company Rosneft signed an agreement on the establishment of a joint venture to develop projects in Azerbaijan. Nevertheless, in June an investment decision by the enterprise consortium controlling the Şah Deniz gas field in the Caspian Sea, in favour of the TAP export route, confirmed Azerbaijan's orientation towards Western European markets. The EU declared in November that it was prepared to commence discussions with Azerbaijan on a free trade agreement after the country had joined the World Trade Organization (see p. 434) (following ongoing accession negotiations since 2004). According to government figures, GDP growth rose to 6.0% in 2013, following a slowdown in 2011–12 owing to falling oil output; however, the IMF continued to urge diversification, as well as recommending the introduction of banking supervision measures. In December 2013 anti-Government protests were staged, after a rise in fuel prices was announced.

PUBLIC HOLIDAYS

2015: 1–4 January (New Year), 8 March (International Women's Day), 20–21 March (Novruz Bayramy, Spring Holiday), 9 May (Victory Day), 28 May (Republic Day), 15 June (Gayidish, Day of Liberation of the Azerbaijani People), 26 June (Day of the Foundation of the Army), 17 July* (Ramazan Bayramy, end of Ramadan), 23 September* (Kurban Bayramy, Feast of the Sacrifice), 18 October (Day of Statehood), 12 November (Constitution Day), 17 November (Day of National Revival), 31 December (Day of Azerbaijani Solidarity Worldwide).

* These holidays are dependent on the Islamic lunar calendar and may vary by one or two days from the dates given.

Statistical Survey

Source (unless otherwise stated): State Statistical Committee of the Republic of Azerbaijan, 1136 Baku, İnşaatçılar pr.; tel. (12) 438-64-98; fax (12) 438-24-42; e-mail sc@azstat.org; internet www.azstat.org.

Area and Population

AREA, POPULATION AND DENSITY

Area (sq km)	86,600*
Population (census results)†	
27 January 1999	7,953,438
13 April 2009 (rounded figure)	8,922,400
Population (official estimates at 1 January)	
2011	9,111,100
2012	9,235,100
2013	9,356,500
Males	4,648,800
Females	4,707,700
Density (per sq km) at 1 January 2013	108.0

* 33,400 sq miles.
† Figures refer to *de jure* population.

POPULATION BY AGE AND SEX
(UN estimates at mid-2014)

	Males	Females	Total
0–14	1,128,364	981,988	2,110,352
15–64	3,384,696	3,489,578	6,874,274
65 and over	217,136	313,123	530,259
Total	4,730,196	4,784,689	9,514,885

Source: UN, *World Population Prospects: The 2012 Revision*.

Population by Age ('000, official estimates at 1 January 2013): *0–14:* 2,087.1; *15–64:* 6,731.2; *65 and over:* 538.2; *Total* 9,356.5.

ETHNIC GROUPS
(permanent inhabitants, 2009 census)

	Number ('000)	%
Azeri	8,172.8	91.6
Lazs (Lezghi)	180.3	2.0
Russian	120.3	1.3
Armenian	119.3	1.3
Talish	112.0	1.3
Others	217.7	2.5
Total	8,922.4	100.0

ECONOMIC REGIONS
(estimated population at 1 January 2013)

	Area ('000 sq km)	Population (rounded)	Density (per sq km)
Bakı şahari (Baku city)	2.15	2,150,800	1,000.4
Abşeron	3.34	538,400	161.2
Gäncä-Qazax	12.48	1,216,100	97.4
Şäki-Zaqatala	8.83	587,700	66.6
Länkäran	6.07	868,100	143.0
Quba-Xaçmaz	7.03	511,700	72.8
Aran	21.45	1,887,300	88.0
Yuxarı Qarabağ*	7.25	636,900	87.8
Kälbäcär-Laçın*	6.40	236,400	36.9
Dağlıq Şirvan	6.06	295,900	48.8
Naxçıvan†	5.56	427,200	76.8
Total	86.60	9,356,500	108.0

* The economic region of Yuxarı Qarabağ, and much of the economic region of Kälbäcär-Laçın, remained outside central government control in mid-2013, being controlled by the forces of the unrecognized 'Republic of Nagornyi Karabakh'.
† Autonomous republic.

Note: The secessionist 'Republic of Nagornyi Karabakh', estimated to occupy some 11,458 sq km of the territory of the Republic of Azerbaijan, reported a total population of 137,747 at 1 January 2007.

PRINCIPAL TOWNS
(official population estimates at 1 January 2013)

Bakı (Baku, the capital)	2,150,800	Şirvan*	80,900
Sumqayıt	325,200	Yevlax	59,000
Gäncä	323,000	Xankändi (Stepanakert)	55,400
Mingäçevir	99,700	Länkäran	51,100
Naxçıvan	88,000		

* Known as Äli-Bayramlı between 1938 and 2008.

BIRTHS, MARRIAGES AND DEATHS

	Registered live births		Registered marriages		Registered deaths	
	Number	Rate (per 1,000)	Number	Rate (per 1,000)	Number	Rate (per 1,000)
2005	141,901	17.2	71,643	8.7	51,962	6.3
2006	148,946	17.8	79,443	9.5	52,248	6.2
2007	151,963	18.0	81,758	9.7	53,655	6.3
2008	152,086	17.8	79,964	9.3	52,710	6.2
2009	152,139	17.2	78,072	8.8	52,514	5.9
2010	165,643	18.5	79,172	8.9	53,580	6.0
2011	176,072	19.4	88,145	9.7	53,762	5.9
2012	174,469	19.0	79,065	8.6	55,017	6.0

Life expectancy (years at birth, official estimates): 73.9 (males 71.3; females 76.6) in 2012.

ECONOMICALLY ACTIVE POPULATION
(ISIC major divisions, annual average, '000 persons)

	2010	2011	2012
Agriculture, hunting, forestry and fishing	1,655.0	1,657.4	1,673.8
Mining and quarrying	41.5	41.2	41.8
Manufacturing	208.9	210.3	215.6
Electricity, gas and water supply	55.8	55.4	55.9
Construction	287.5	308.9	321.8
Wholesale and retail trade; repair of motor vehicles, motorcycles and household goods	626.7	635.4	646.8
Hotels and restaurants	46.9	48.1	48.9
Transport, storage and communications	234.9	239.8	241.4
Financial intermediation	24.4	26.3	26.9
Real estate, renting and business activities	161.7	165.3	178.6
Public administration and defence; compulsory social security	279.1	281.0	281.7
Education	349.8	349.9	349.0
Health and social work	170.3	165.2	165.4
Other community, social and personal service activities	186.6	191.0	197.7
Total employed	4,329.1	4,375.2	4,445.3
Unemployed	258.3	250.9	243.1
Total labour force	4,587.4	4,626.1	4,688.4

Health and Welfare

KEY INDICATORS

Total fertility rate (children per woman, 2011)	2.2
Under-five mortality rate (per 1,000 live births, 2011)	45
HIV (% of persons aged 15–49, 2012)	0.2
Physicians (per 1,000 head, 2011)	3.4
Hospital beds (per 1,000 head, 2009)	7.7
Health expenditure (2010): US $ per head (PPP)	520
Health expenditure (2010): % of GDP	5.3
Health expenditure (2010): public (% of total)	21.9
Access to water (% of persons, 2011)	80
Access to sanitation (% of persons, 2011)	82
Total carbon dioxide emissions ('000 metric tons, 2010)	45,731.2
Carbon dioxide emissions per head (metric tons, 2010)	5.1
Human Development Index (2012): ranking	82
Human Development Index (2012): value	0.734

For sources and definitions, see explanatory note on p. vi.

Agriculture

PRINCIPAL CROPS
('000 metric tons)

	2010	2011	2012
Wheat	1,272.3	1,594.4	1,797.0
Rice, paddy	3.9	3.7	3.7
Barley	513.3	616.4	721.2
Maize	136.1	152.3	181.9
Potatoes	953.7	938.5	968.5
Sugar beet	251.9	252.9	173.8
Hazelnuts	29.5	32.9	29.6
Cotton seed*	25.2	43.8	37.6
Cabbages and other brassicas	94.1	100.1	110.6
Tomatoes	434.0	463.2	471.6
Cucumbers and gherkins	217.0	212.1	210.2
Onions, dry	171.6	182.4	166.2
Garlic	21.1	19.5	20.7
Watermelons	328.8	357.8	312.3
Oranges	0.8	0.8	1.1
Apples	211.7	223.1	234.8
Pears	35.5	36.6	39.2
Apricots	19.2	18.7	24.0
Peaches and nectarines	16.7	18.0	23.6
Plums	20.4	22.1	24.7
Grapes	129.5	137.0	151.0
Tobacco (leaves)	3.2	3.6	4.3
Cotton (lint)*	12.6	22.0	18.8

* Unofficial figures.

Aggregate production ('000 metric tons, may include official, semi-official or estimated data): Total cereals 1,928.8 in 2010, 2,370.8 in 2011, 2,706.9 in 2012; Total nuts 42.0 in 2010, 46.3 in 2011, 43.2 in 2012; Total pulses 21.7 in 2010, 24.0 in 2011, 24.8 in 2012; Total roots and tubers 953.7 in 2010, 938.5 in 2011, 968.5 in 2012; Total vegetables (incl. melons) 1,627.0 in 2010, 1,696.6 in 2011, 1,647.9 in 2012; Total fruits (excl. melons) 815.1 in 2010, 854.9 in 2011, 916.5 in 2012.

Source: FAO.

LIVESTOCK
('000 head, year ending September)

	2010	2011	2012
Horses	76	77	77
Asses	46	46	44
Cattle	2,369	2,412	2,447
Buffaloes	277	270	266
Pigs	6	6	6
Sheep	7,871	7,932	8,020
Goats	621	627	645
Chickens	22,432	23,162	24,581
Turkeys	892*	912*	942

* Unofficial figure.

Source: FAO.

LIVESTOCK PRODUCTS
('000 metric tons)

	2010	2011	2012
Cattle meat	114.2	117.0	119.5
Sheep meat	74.3	74.4	76.0
Pig meat	0.8	0.7	0.7
Chicken meat	64.5	71.6	89.3
Cows' milk	1,507.4	1,566.8	1,683.4
Hen eggs	71.0	60.9	73.9
Wool, greasy	15.6	16.2	16.5

Source: FAO.

Forestry

ROUNDWOOD REMOVALS
('000 cu m, excl. bark)

	2001	2002	2003
Total	13,500*	52,800†	6,500†

* FAO estimate.
† Unofficial figure.

2004–12: Total production assumed to be unchanged from 2003 (FAO estimates).

Source: FAO.

Fishing

(metric tons, live weight)

	2009	2010	2011
Capture	1,206	1,081	1,061
Azov sea sprat	839	708	485
Aquaculture*	1,000	1,000	517
Total catch*	2,206	2,081	1,578

* FAO estimates.

Source: FAO.

Mining

	2010	2011	2012
Crude petroleum ('000 metric tons)	50,838	45,626	43,375
Natural gas (million cu m)	15,088	14,807	15,602

Source: BP, *Statistical Review of World Energy*.

Industry

SELECTED PRODUCTS
('000 metric tons unless otherwise indicated)

	2007	2008	2009
Wheat flour	1,421	1,313	1,315
Wine ('000 hectolitres)	64	86	59
Beer ('000 hectolitres)	328	325	344
Mineral water ('000 hectolitres)	1,122	765	839
Soft drinks ('000 hectolitres)	2,182	2,235	1,877
Cigarettes (million units)	3,789	2,773	2,316
Cotton yarn—pure and mixed (metric tons)	377	382	450
Woven cotton fabrics ('000 sq m)	1,690	1,052	900
Footwear, excluding rubber ('000 pairs)	302	360	292
Cement	1,687	1,587	1,288
Caustic soda (Sodium hydroxide)	17	22	5
Jet fuels	761	731	603
Motor spirit (petrol)	1,129	1,320	1,235
Gas-diesel (distillate fuel) oil	2,109	2,526	2,367
Lubricants	55	66	46
Residual fuel oil (Mazout)	2,340	1,276	287
Electric energy (million kWh)	21,847	21,643	18,868

2010: Jet fuels 600; Motor spirit (petrol) 1,249; Lubricants 87; Residual fuel oil (Mazout) 231; Electric energy (million kWh) 18,710.

Source: UN Industrial Commodity Statistics Database.

2010 ('000 metric tons unless otherwise indicated): Cement 1,279; Kerosene 600; Gas-diesel (distillate fuel) oil 2,488; Finished cotton fabrics ('000 sq m) 1,104.

2011 ('000 metric tons unless otherwise indicated): Cement 1,425; Motor spirit (petrol) 1,296; Kerosene 622; Gas-diesel (distillate fuel) oil 2,483; Residual fuel oil (Mazout) 235; Finished cotton fabrics ('000 sq m) 822; Electric energy ('000 million kWh) 20.3.

2012 ('000 metric tons unless otherwise indicated): Cement 1,965; Motor spirit (petrol) 1,297; Kerosene 627; Gas-diesel (distillate fuel) oil 2,369; Residual fuel oil (Mazout) 274; Finished cotton fabrics ('000 sq m) 209; Electric energy ('000 million kWh) 21.6.

Finance

CURRENCY AND EXCHANGE RATES

Monetary Units

100 gopik = 1 new Azerbaijani manat.

Sterling, Dollar and Euro Equivalents (31 December 2013)

£1 sterling = 1.292 new manats;
US $1 = 0.785 new manats;
€1 = 1.082 new manats;
10 new manats = £7.74 = $12.75 = €9.24.

Average Exchange Rate (Azerbaijani manats per US $)

2011 0.790
2012 0.786
2013 0.785

Note: The Azerbaijani manat was introduced in August 1992, initially to circulate alongside the Russian (formerly Soviet) rouble, with an exchange rate of 1 manat = 10 roubles. In December 1993 Azerbaijan left the rouble zone, and the manat became the country's sole currency. The manat was redenominated from 1 January 2006, with 1 new unit of currency (new manat) equivalent to 5,000 of the old currency. Figures in this survey are given in terms of the new manat, where possible. In 1993 the Armenian dram was introduced as the prevailing currency in the self-declared 'Republic of Nagornyi Karabakh'.

STATE BUDGET
(million new manats)

Revenue*	2010	2011†	2012†
Tax revenue	5,834	7,016	7,651
Value-added tax	2,082	2,223	2,355
Excises	515	480	569
Taxes on income	2,020	2,850	3,104
Taxes on international trade	292	440	402
Social security contributions	697	744	902
Other	227	280	318
Non-tax revenue	13,549	16,269	14,281
Total	19,383	23,285	21,932

Expenditure	2010	2011†	2012†
Current expenditure	8,157	9,305	11,442
Wages and salaries	1,884	1,934	2,716
Goods and services	3,540	3,870	4,272
Transfers to households	2,328	2,747	3,635
Subsidies	239	210	232
Oil fund operating expenditures	14	203	205
Other purposes	113	131	144
Interest	39	210	238
Investment expenditure and net lending	5,293	8,209	8,814
Total	13,450	17,514	20,256

* Excluding grants received (million new manats): 3 in 2010; 7 in 2011 (preliminary); 8 in 2012 (preliminary).

† Preliminary figures.

2013 (projected figures): *Revenue:* Tax revenue 8,540; Non-tax revenue 13,400; Total (excl. grants received) 21,940. *Grants received:* 9. *Expenditure:* Current expenditure 12,939; Investment expenditure and net lending 10,626; Total 23,565.

Source: IMF, *Republic of Azerbaijan: 2013 Article IV Consultation* (June 2013).

INTERNATIONAL RESERVES
(excl. gold, US $ million at 31 December)

	2010	2011	2012
IMF special drawing rights	236.59	235.92	237.02
Reserve position in IMF	0.21	0.21	0.21
Foreign exchange	6,172.17	10,037.70	11,040.01
Total	6,408.97	10,273.83	11,277.24

Source: IMF, *International Financial Statistics*.

MONEY SUPPLY
(million new manats at 31 December)

	2010	2011	2012
Currency outside depository corporations	5,455.78	7,158.16	9,256.54
Transferable deposits	1,825.50	2,446.48	2,668.21
Other deposits	3,227.28	4,246.36	4,776.21
Securities other than shares	18.92	52.19	74.24
Broad money	10,527.49	13,903.18	16,775.20

Source: IMF, *International Financial Statistics*.

COST OF LIVING
(Consumer Price Index; base: 2005 = 100)

	2010	2011	2012
Food	176.7	195.1	196.8
All items (incl. others)	163.8	176.7	178.6

NATIONAL ACCOUNTS

(million new manats at current prices)

Expenditure on the Gross Domestic Product

	2010	2011	2012
Government final consumption expenditure	2,845.9	3,309.0	3,574.4
Private final consumption expenditure	18,490.2	21,370.7	23,410.2
Changes in stocks	–45.5	47.0	56.0
Gross fixed capital formation	7,714.5	10,508.9	11,798.0
Total domestic expenditure	29,005.1	35,235.6	38,838.6
Exports of goods and services	23,060.5	29,388.3	29,000.3
Less Imports of goods and services	8,782.3	12,541.9	13,843.9
Statistical discrepancy	–818.3	—	—
GDP in purchasers' values	42,465.0	52,082.0	53,995.0

Gross Domestic Product by Economic Activity

	2010	2011	2012
Agriculture and fishing	2,354.5	2,644.2	2,783.1
Mining	19,485.8	24,980.2	23,689.4
Manufacturing	2,041.8	2,077.2	2,219.2
Electricity, gas and water	456.4	953.6	1,049.2
Construction	3,492.8	4,140.9	4,993.9
Transport and communications	3,180.4	3,487.4	3,868.6
Trade	2,772.7	3,283.8	3,631.4
Hotels and restaurants	450.0	757.3	971.8
Finance	505.5	714.9	767.1
Real estate, renting and business activities	807.9	1,235.8	1,595.8
Public administration	854.1	1,162.2	1,440.2
Other services	3,411.4	3,792.0	3,868.5
Sub-total	39,813.3	49,229.5	50,878.2
Less Financial intermediation services indirectly measured	224.8	203.4	203.2
Indirect taxes *less* subsidies	2,876.5	3,055.9	3,320.0
GDP in purchasers' values	42,465.0	52,082.0	53,995.0

BALANCE OF PAYMENTS

(US $ million)

	2010	2011	2012
Exports of goods	25,741.1	33,996.3	31,877.1
Imports of goods	–6,306.9	–9,867.9	–9,963.5
Balance on goods	19,434.2	24,128.4	21,913.6
Exports of services	2,493.6	3,042.5	4,808.7
Imports of services	–3,929.5	–5,839.5	–7,429.6
Balance on goods and services	17,998.4	21,331.4	19,292.8
Primary income received	675.5	1,018.7	1,151.6
Primary income paid	–4,142.6	–5,878.6	–5,418.4
Balance on goods, services and primary income	14,531.3	16,471.6	15,026.0
Secondary income received	1,420.4	1,882.3	1,953.1
Secondary income paid	–911.3	–1,209.0	–2,003.1
Current balance	15,040.4	17,144.9	14,976.0
Capital account (net)	14.3	18.7	12.5
Direct investment assets	–3,021.8	–3,552.5	–4,480.8
Direct investment liabilities	3,353.0	4,485.1	5,293.3
Portfolio investment assets	–163.3	–344.8	–253.1
Portfolio investment liabilities	24.5	27.9	521.3
Other investment assets	–14,698.0	–15,487.8	–14,282.6
Other investment liabilities	1,810.6	1,325.0	1,258.3
Net errors and omissions	–989.7	569.0	–1,938.9
Reserves and related items	1,370.0	4,185.5	1,105.9

Source: IMF, *International Financial Statistics*.

External Trade

PRINCIPAL COMMODITIES

(US $ million)

Imports c.i.f.	2010	2011	2012
Vegetables and products	437.4	519.6	500.1
Cereals	315.9	315.4	373.9
Prepared foodstuffs, beverages, spirits and vinegars; tobacco and manufactured substitutes	616.4	659.8	721.3
Sugars and sugar confectionery	208.3	197.1	202.8
Tobacco and manufactured tobacco substitutes	228.1	248.7	303.6
Mineral products	208.2	237.8	307.7
Products of chemical or allied industries	437.9	625.7	662.5
Plastic, rubber and articles thereof	225.5	358.2	427.3
Plastic and articles thereof	179.5	292.3	361.0
Articles of stone, plaster, cement, asbestos, mica; glass and glassware	201.7	215.3	235.9
Base metals and articles thereof	925.2	1,331.6	1,467.5
Iron and steel	227.0	416.0	440.2
Articles of iron and steel	560.2	755.9	870.3
Machinery and mechanical appliances; electrical equipment; sound and television apparatus	1,903.2	3,035.4	2,629.3
Boilers, machinery and mechanical appliances and parts thereof	1,413.8	2,139.5	1,872.6
Electrical machinery and equipment; apparatus parts thereof	489.4	896.0	756.7
Vehicles, aircraft, vessels and associated transportation equipment	796.9	1,689.8	1,414.9
Vehicles other than railway or tramway rolling-stock and parts thereof	626.2	695.2	1,001.1
Aircraft, spacecraft and parts thereof	71.9	927.6	362.2
Optical, photographic, checking, medical instruments and apparatus; clocks and watches; musical instruments	174.7	198.7	344.2
Optical, photographic, checking, medical instruments and apparatus	170.0	193.8	336.5
Total (incl. others)	6,600.6	9,756.0	9,652.9

Exports f.o.b.	2010	2011	2012
Vegetables and vegetable products	190.3	268.8	308.1
Mineral products	20,119.9	25,112.5	22,281.1
Mineral fuels, mineral oils and products	20,110.2	25,089.3	22,259.2
Products of the chemical industry	47.9	120.1	174.6
Base metals and articles thereof	126.2	231.6	218.4
Vehicles, aircraft, vessels and associated transportation equipment	181.1	6.8	42.4
Total (incl. others)	21,360.2	26,570.9	23,908.0

PRINCIPAL TRADING PARTNERS
(US $ million)

Imports c.i.f.	2010	2011	2012
Austria	87.6	93.6	124.6
Belarus	112.5	64.5	68.0
Brazil	161.6	175.9	183.3
China, People's Republic	587.6	628.3	631.9
Czech Republic	37.8	102.7	98.2
France	136.1	608.9	185.8
Georgia	50.4	89.5	129.9
Germany	607.1	845.3	780.0
Iran	118.2	160.5	176.4
Italy	118.3	254.6	261.6
Japan	146.3	174.9	243.1
Kazakhstan	293.6	217.3	340.6
Korea, Republic	157.3	203.8	242.8
Netherlands	46.4	141.2	150.1
Poland	25.7	119.5	45.3
Russia	1,145.0	1,641.1	1,378.4
Singapore	173.9	16.0	19.8
Switzerland	96.9	180.7	133.7
Turkey	771.4	1,302.4	1,520.4
Ukraine	465.6	557.8	539.1
United Arab Emirates	56.6	95.2	101.6
United Kingdom	302.8	485.7	496.2
USA	206.3	630.5	715.7
Total (incl. others)	6,600.6	9,756.0	9,652.9

Exports f.o.b.	2010	2011	2012
Belarus	7.2	666.8	11.7
Bulgaria	136.5	410.4	597.6
Canada	317.1	—	8.5
China, People's Republic	338.9	39.0	183.8
Croatia	787.2	347.7	330.6
Czech Republic	—	203.9	511.8
France	1,856.5	4,036.7	1,775.6
Georgia	411.0	535.3	570.7
Germany	9.9	523.4	964.8
Greece	255.0	208.1	833.8
India	299.6	366.8	1,890.7
Indonesia	782.2	913.2	1,757.3
Iraq	31.3	99.1	418.4
Israel	1,744.8	817.6	1,666.6
Italy	7,044.2	9,341.0	5,548.0
Korea, Republic	218.4	444.2	1.1
Malaysia	740.8	664.0	370.7
Malta	116.5	268.6	51.7
Portugal	224.6	324.9	243.1
Russia	773.6	1,187.4	959.8
Singapore	510.9	—	250.4
Spain	178.5	283.8	66.9
Taiwan	294.6	—	650.1
Thailand	194.4	135.4	343.7
Tunisia	2.1	—	247.2
Turkey	170.9	455.8	600.0
Ukraine	888.6	909.3	86.2
United Kingdom	6.4	15.9	326.7
USA	1,623.0	1,804.6	1,600.8
US Virgin Islands	78.6	469.9	—
Total (incl. others)	21,360.2	26,570.9	23,908.0

Transport

RAILWAYS

	2010	2011	2012
Passengers carried ('000)	4,803	3,451	2,668
Passenger-km (million)	917	660	591
Freight carried (million metric tons)	22.3	22.2	23.1
Freight ton-km (million)	8,250	7,845	8,212

ROAD TRAFFIC
(vehicles in use at 31 December)

	2010	2011	2012
Passenger cars	815,683	871,449	958,594
Buses	29,569	29,189	29,647
Lorries and vans	118,460	122,182	130,019
Motorcycles	1,643	1,647	2,067

SHIPPING

Flag Registered Fleet
(at 31 December)

	2011	2012	2013
Number of vessels	329	346	351
Total displacement ('000 grt)	812.4	855.4	890.3

Source: Lloyd's List Intelligence (www.lloydslistintelligence.com).

International Sea-borne Freight Traffic
('000 metric tons)

	2010	2011	2012
Goods loaded	10,764	11,880	11,993
Goods unloaded	60	72	83

Source: UN, *Monthly Bulletin of Statistics*.

CIVIL AVIATION
(traffic on scheduled services)

	2010	2011	2012
Passengers carried ('000)	1,017	1,394	1,599
Passenger-km (million)	1,613	2,106	2,476
Freight carried ('000 metric tons)	40	51	82
Total ton-km (million)	139	224	357

Tourism

FOREIGN TOURIST ARRIVALS

Country of residence	2009	2010	2011
Georgia	529,613	491,942	573,063
Iran	329,913	349,960	407,576
Russia	598,894	701,110	786,684
Turkey	177,308	214,594	242,606
Total (incl. others)	1,830,367	1,962,906	2,239,141

Total arrivals ('000): 1,986 in 2012 (provisional).

Tourism receipts (excl. passenger transport, US $ million): 657 in 2010; 1,287 in 2011; 2,433 in 2012 (provisional).

Source: World Tourism Organization.

Communications Media

	2010	2011	2012
Telephones ('000 main lines in use)	1,506.6	1,683.9	1,733.6
Mobile cellular telephones ('000 subscribers)	9,100.1	10,120.1	10,125.2
Internet subscribers ('000)	870.6	1,318.3	n.a.
Broadband subscribers ('000)	460.0	998.3	1,300.0

Personal computers: 698,424 (80.5 per 1,000 persons) in 2008.

Source: International Telecommunication Union.

Education

(2012/13 unless otherwise indicated)

	Institutions	Teachers	Students
Pre-primary	1,677	10,947*	111,090
General (primary and secondary)	4,508	163,500	1,284,900
Specialized secondary education institutions	59	6,260	55,954
Higher	52†	15,069	145,584

* State institutions only, 2004/05.

† Including specialized higher educational schools.

Pupil-teacher ratio (primary education, UNESCO estimate): 11.9 in 2011/12 (Source: UNESCO Institute for Statistics).

Adult literacy rate (UNESCO estimates): 99.8% (males 99.8%; females 99.4%) in 2009 (Source: UNESCO Institute for Statistics).

Directory

The Government

HEAD OF STATE

President: İLHAM ÄLIYEV (elected 15 October 2003, inaugurated 31 October; re-elected 15 October 2008, inaugurated 24 October; re-elected 9 October 2013, inaugurated 19 October).

CABINET OF MINISTERS

(April 2014)

Prime Minister: ARTUR RASIZADÄ.

First Deputy Prime Minister: YAQUB EYYUBOV.

Deputy Prime Minister: ELÇIN ÄFÄNDIYEV.

Deputy Prime Minister, Chairman of the State Committee for Refugees and Internally Displaced Persons: ÄLI HÄSÄNOV.

Deputy Prime Minister: ABID ŞARIFOV.

Deputy Prime Minister: ÄLI ÄHMÄDOV.

Deputy Prime Minister: İSMÄT ABASOV.

Minister of Foreign Affairs: ELMAR MÄMMÄDYAROV.

Minister of Internal Affairs: Col RAMIL USUBOV.

Minister of National Security: Lt-Gen. ELDAR MAHMUDOV.

Minister of Defence: Col-Gen. ZAKIR HÄSÄNOV.

Minister of Justice: FIKRÄT MÄMMÄDOV.

Minister of Defence Industries: YAVÄR CAMALOV.

Minister of Finance: SAMIR ŞÄRIFOV.

Minister of Taxation: FAZIL MÄMMÄDOV.

Minister of Economic Development: ŞAHIN MUSTAFAYEV.

Minister of Emergency Situations: Col-Gen. KÄMALÄDDIN HEYDÄROV.

Minister of Labour and Social Protection: SÄLIM MÜSLÜMOV.

Minister of Agriculture: HEYDÄR ÄSÄDOV.

Minister of Culture and Tourism: ÄBÜLFÄZ QARAYEV.

Minister of Education: MIKAYIL CABBAROV.

Minister of Health: OQTAY ŞIRÄLIYEV.

Minister of Communications and Information Technology: ÄLI ABBASOV.

Minister of Industry and Energy: NATIQ ÄLIYEV.

Minister of Youth and Sport: AZAD RÄHIMOV.

Minister of Ecology and Natural Resources: HÜSEYNQULU BAĞIROV.

Minister of Transport: ZIYA MÄMMÄDOV.

Note: The Chairmen of State Committees and Agencies are also members of the Cabinet of Ministers.

MINISTRIES

Office of the President: 1066 Baku, İstiqlaliyyät küç. 19; tel. (12) 492-53-81; fax (12) 492-35-43; e-mail office@pa.gov.az; internet www.president.az.

Office of the Prime Minister: 1066 Baku, Lermontov küç. 68; tel. (12) 492-84-19; fax (12) 492-91-79; e-mail nk@cabmin.gov.az; internet www.cabmin.gov.az.

Ministry of Agriculture: 1000 Baku, U. Hacıbayov küç., 40 Hökümat House; tel. and fax (12) 498-64-49; e-mail agro@azerin.com; internet agro.gov.az.

Ministry of Communications and Information Technology: 1000 Baku, Zarifa Äliyeva küç. 33; tel. (12) 498-58-38; fax (12) 498-79-12; e-mail mincom@mincom.gov.az; internet www.mincom.gov.az.

Ministry of Culture and Tourism: 1000 Baku, Azadlıq meydanı 1, 3rd Floor; tel. (12) 493-43-98; fax (12) 493-56-05; e-mail mct@mct.gov.az; internet www.mct.gov.az.

Ministry of Defence: 1139 Baku, Azärbaycan pr.; tel. (12) 439-41-89; fax (12) 492-92-50.

Ministry of Defence Industries: 1141 Baku, Matbuät pr. 40; tel. (12) 539-24-53; fax (12) 510-63-47; e-mail info@mdi.gov.az; internet www.mdi.gov.az.

Ministry of Ecology and Natural Resources: 1073 Baku, Bahram Ağayev küç. 100A; tel. (12) 538-04-81; fax (12) 592-59-07; e-mail ekologiya.nazirliyi@gmail.com; internet eco.gov.az.

Ministry of Economic Development: 1000 Baku, Uzeyir Hacibeyov küç. 40, Government House; tel. (12) 493-88-67; fax (12) 492-58-95; e-mail office@economy.gov.az; internet www.economy.gov.az.

Ministry of Education: 1008 Baku, Xatai pr. 49; tel. (12) 496-34-00; fax (12) 496-34-83; e-mail office@edu.gov.az; internet edu.gov.az.

Ministry of Emergency Situations: 1073 Baku, M. Müşfiq küç. 501; tel. (12) 512-00-61; fax (12) 512-00-46; e-mail info@fhn.gov.az; internet www.fhn.gov.az.

Ministry of Finance: 1022 Baku, S. Vurğun küç. 83; tel. (12) 404-46-99; fax (12) 404-47-20; e-mail office@maliyye.gov.az; internet maliyye.gov.az.

Ministry of Foreign Affairs: 1009 Baku, S. Qurbanov küç. 4; tel. (12) 596-90-00; fax (12) 596-90-01; e-mail katiblik@mfa.gov.az; internet www.mfa.gov.az.

Ministry of Health: 1022 Baku, M. Mirqasımov küç. 1A; tel. (12) 598-50-94; fax (12) 493-06-95; e-mail office@health.gov.az; internet sehiyye.gov.az.

Ministry of Industry and Energy: 1000 Baku, U. Hacibeyov küç. 40, Hökumat House; tel. (12) 598-16-75; fax (12) 598-16-78; e-mail mie@mie.gov.az; internet www.mie.gov.az.

Ministry of Internal Affairs: 1005 Baku, Azerbaycan pr. 7; tel. (12) 590-92-22; fax (12) 492-45-90; e-mail info@mia.gov.az; internet mia.gov.az.

Ministry of Justice: 1000 Baku, İnşaatçılar pr. 1; tel. (12) 430-09-77; fax (12) 430-06-81; e-mail contact@justice.gov.az; internet www.justice.gov.az.

Ministry of Labour and Social Protection: 1009 Baku, S. Asgarov küç. 85; tel. (12) 596-50-33; fax (12) 596-50-34; e-mail info@mlspp.gov.az; internet www.mlspp.gov.az.

Ministry of National Security: 1006 Baku, Parlament pr. 2; tel. and fax (12) 493-76-22; e-mail cpr@mns.gov.az; internet mns.gov.az.

Ministry of Taxation: 1073 Baku, Landau küç. 16; tel. (12) 403-89-70; fax (12) 403-89-71; e-mail office@taxes.gov.az; internet www.taxes.gov.az.

Ministry of Transport: 1122 Baku, Tbilisi pr. 1054; tel. (12) 430-99-41; fax (12) 430-99-42; e-mail ziyamamedov@mintrans.az; internet mot.gov.az.

Ministry of Youth and Sport: 1072 Baku, Olimpiya küç. 4; tel. (12) 465-84-21; fax (12) 465-64-38; e-mail mys@mys.gov.az; internet mys.gov.az.

President

Presidential Election, 9 October 2013

Candidates	Votes	% of votes
İlham Äliyev (New Azerbaijan Party)	3,126,113	84.54
Cämil Häsänli (National Council of Democratic Forces)	204,642	5.53
İqbal Ağazadä (Azerbaijan Hope Party)	88,723	2.40
Qüdrät Häsänquliyev (Azerbaijan Popular Front Party)	73,702	1.99
Zahid Oruj (Independent)	53,839	1.46
Ilyas Ismayılov (Justice Party)	39,722	1.07
Others	111,229	3.01
Total	3,697,970	100.00

Legislature

National Assembly
(Milli Mäclis)

1152 Baku, Parlament pr. 1; tel. (12) 498-97-48; fax (12) 498-97-22; e-mail azmm@meclis.gov.az; internet www.meclis.gov.az.

Chairman: OKTAY ÄSÄDOV.

General Election, 7 November 2010

Parties and blocs	Seats
New Azerbaijan Party	72*
Democratic Bloc	4†
Reform Bloc	3‡
Fatherland Party	2
Others	44§
Total	125

* Including one party member who contested the elections as an independent candidate.

† Comprising three members of the Civic Solidarity Party and one member of the Azerbaijan Democratic Reforms Party.

‡ Comprising one member of the United Azerbaijan Popular Front Party, one member of the Great Creation Party and one member of the Justice Party.

§ Comprising 35 independent candidates, three members of non-partisan initiative groups, three candidates who did not state any party membership, and one member each of the Azerbaijan Hope Party, the Azerbaijan Social Welfare Party and the Civic Unity Party.

Election Commission

Central Electoral Commission: 1000 Baku, Rasul Rza küç. 3; tel. (12) 493-60-08; fax (12) 562-70-09; e-mail office@cec.gov.az; internet www.cec.gov.az; f. 1998; Chair. MAZAHIR PANAHOV.

Political Organizations

Azerbaijan Democratic Party (ADP) (Azärbaycan Demokrat Partiyası): 1008 Baku, Sabail rayonu, Acad. A. Älizadä küç. 13; tel. (12) 496-07-22; fax (12) 496-18-61; e-mail adp2005@mail.ru; internet adp-muxalifet.blogspot.com; f. 1991; Chair. SÄRDAR CALALOĞLU MÄMMÄDOV.

Azerbaijan Democratic Reforms Party (Azärbaycan Demokratik İslahatlar Partiyası): 1078 Baku, Sabit Rähman 7; tel. (12) 437-15-76; fax (12) 437-15-77; e-mail demreforms@party.az; internet www.demreforms.org; f. 2005; contested 2010 legislative elections as mem. of the Democratic Bloc; Chair. ASIM MOLLAZADÄ.

Azerbaijan Hope Party (Azärbaycan Ümid Partiyası): 1000 Baku, Qanub küç. 19/29; tel. (12) 496-66-59; e-mail umid2004@box.az; f. 1993; contested 2010 legislative elections as mem. of the Karabakh Bloc; Chair. İQBAL AĞAZADÄ.

Azerbaijan National Independence Party (AMIP) (Azärbaycan Milli İstiqlal Partiyası): 1000 Baku, Näsimi rayonu, Mirqasımov küç. 4; tel. (12) 444-55-66; e-mail info@amip.az; internet www.amip.az; f. 1992; economically and politically liberal; Chair. ETIBAR MÄMMÄDOV.

Azerbaijan Popular Front Party (AXCP) (Azärbaycan Xalq Cabhasi Partiyası): Baku; tel. (12) 498-07-94; e-mail faiq73@mail.ru; internet www.axcp.az; f. 1989; formed part of the National Council of Democratic Forces in advance of 2013 presidential election; Chair. ÄLI KÄRIMLI.

Civic Solidarity Party (VHP) (Vätändaş Hämräylıyı Partiyası): 1025 Baku, Xatai rayonu, Xäqani Rüstamov küç. 1210; tel. (12) 490-66-22; fax (12) 493-71-45; e-mail vhp.1992@gmail.com; internet www.vhp.az; f. 1992; contested 2010 legislative elections as mem. of the Democratic Bloc; Chair. SABIR RÜSTAMXANLI.

Equality Party (Müsavat) (Müsavat Partiyası): 1025 Baku, Därnägül qäsäbäsi 30/97; tel. (12) 448-23-82; fax (12) 448-23-81; e-mail info@musavat.org; f. 1992 as revival of party founded in 1911 and in exile from 1920; formed part of the National Council of Democratic Forces in advance of 2013 presidential election; Chair. ISA QÄMBÄR.

Fatherland Party (AVP) (Ana Vätän Partiyası): 1000 Baku, Aziz Äliyev küç. 3; tel. (12) 493-82-92; f. 1992; supports administration of Pres. İlham Äliyev; represents interests of Naxçıvan Autonomous Republic in Azerbaijan; Leader FAZAIL AGAMÄLIYEV.

Great Creation Party (Böyük Quruluş Partiyası): Baku, Şövkät Mämmädova küç. 3; tel. and fax (12) 490-39-59; e-mail info@bqp.az; internet www.bqp.az; f. 2003; nationalist; contested 2010 legislative elections as mem. of the Reform Bloc; Leader FAZIL MUSTAFA.

Justice Party (Ädalät) (Adalat Partiyası): 1000 Baku, Näsimi rayonu, Ceyhun Hacıbäyli küç. 2; tel. (12) 440-85-23; e-mail adalat@azinternet.com; f. 2001; mem. of the Democratic Azerbaijan alliance; contested 2010 legislative elections as mem. of the Reform Bloc; Leader İLYAS İSMAYILOV; 21,000 mems.

Modern Equality Party (Müasir Müsavat Partiyası): 1000 Baku; supports administration of Pres. İlham Äliyev; Leader HAFIZ HACIYEV.

New Azerbaijan Party (YAP) (Yeni Azärbaycan Partiyası): 1000 Baku, Bül-Bül pr. 13; tel. (12) 493-84-25; fax (12) 498-59-71; e-mail secretariat@yap.org.az; internet www.yap.org.az; f. 1992; Chair. İLHAM ÄLIYEV; 557,805 mems (2011).

United Azerbaijan Popular Front Party (BAXCP) (Bütöv Azärbaycan Xalq Cabhasi Partiyası): 1000 Baku, 12-ci Aşırım küç. 70A; tel. (12) 492-96-23; fax (12) 461-29-42; e-mail qudrat@hasanquliyev.com; internet www.xalqcebhesi.az; f. 2003 by fmr mems of AXCP (q.v.); contested 2010 legislative elections as mem. of Reform Bloc; Leader QÜDRÄT HÄSÄNQULIYEV.

Note: the **Azerbaijan Islamic Party (AİP)**, which was founded in 1991 and proscribed in 1995, remains influential, although its leader MOVSUM SAMADOV, along with other senior members of the party, was imprisoned in 2011 having been convicted of attempting to overthrow the Government.

Diplomatic Representation

Argentina: Baku, Ü. Hacıbäyov; tel. (55) 504-98-57; Ambassador CARLOS DANTE RIVA.

Austria: 1010 Baku, Nizami küç. 90A, 7th Floor; tel. (12) 465-99-33; fax (12) 465-99-94; e-mail baku-ob@bmeia.gv.at; internet www.bmeia.gv.at/baku; Ambassador SYLVIA MEIER-KAJBIC.

Belarus: 1069 Baku, Gänclik, Kral Huseyn küç. 64; tel. (12) 436-46-38; fax (12) 436-46-37; e-mail azerbaijan@mfa.gov.by; internet www.azerbaijan.mfa.gov.by; Ambassador NIKOLAI Y. PATSKEVICH.

Belgium: 1073 Baku, S. Dadaşev küç. 19; tel. (12) 437-37-70; fax (12) 437-37-71; e-mail embassy.baku@diplobel.fed.be; internet www.diplomatie.be/baku; Ambassador CARINE PETIT.

Brazil: 1069 Baku, Haci Murad küç. 23A; tel. (12) 598-20-46; fax (12) 598-2-03; Ambassador SANTIAGO LUIS BENTO FERNÁNDEZ ALCÁZAR.

Bulgaria: 1073 Baku, H. Cavid küç. 13; tel. (12) 538-69-71; fax (12) 598-31-42; e-mail embassy.baku@mfa.bg; internet www.mfa.bg/embassies/azerbaidzan; Ambassador MAYA HRISTOVA.

China, People's Republic: 1010 Baku, Xaqani küç. 67; tel. (12) 498-62-57; fax (12) 498-00-10; e-mail chinaemb_az@mfa.gov.cn; internet az.china-embassy.org; Ambassador HONG JIUYIN.

Cuba: 1000 Baku, Cafar Xandan 10C; tel. (12) 596-24-74; fax (12) 568-07-21; e-mail embajada@az.embacuba.cu; internet www.cubadiplomatica.cu/azerbaijan; Ambassador OMAR MEDINA QUINTERO.

Czech Republic: 1065 Baku, C. Cabbarlı küç. 44, Caspian Plaza, 16th Floor; tel. (12) 436-85-55; fax (12) 436-85-57; e-mail baku@embassy.mzv.cz; internet www.mzv.cz/baku; Ambassador VITĚZSLAV PIVOŇKA.

Egypt: 1078 Baku, H. Äliyev küç. 7; tel. (12) 498-79-06; fax (12) 498-79-54; e-mail emb.egypt@azeuro.net; Ambassador TAREK AHMED ABOU SENNA.

France: 1000 Baku, Rasul Rza küç. 7, POB 36; tel. (12) 490-81-00; fax (12) 490-81-28; e-mail presse.bakou-amba@diplomatie.gouv.fr; internet www.ambafrance-az.org; Ambassador PASCAL MEUNIER.

Georgia: 1069 Baku, Yaşar Huseynov küç. 15; tel. (12) 497-45-60; fax (12) 497-45-61; e-mail baku@geoemb.az; internet www.azerbaijan.mfa.gov.ge; Ambassador TEIMURAZ SHARASHENIDZE.

Germany: 1005 Baku, Nizami küç. 69, ISR Plaza; tel. (12) 465-41-00; fax (12) 465-41-28; e-mail info@baku.diplo.de; internet www.baku.diplo.de; Ambassador HEIDRUN TEMPEL.

Greece: 1065 Baku, C. Cabbarlı küç. 44, Caspian Plaza, 9th Floor; tel. (12) 492-01-19; fax (12) 492-48-35; e-mail gremb.bak@mfa.gr; internet www.mfa.gr/baku; Ambassador DIMITRIOS TSOUNGAS.

Hungary: 1004 Baku, Mirza Mansur küç. 72; tel. (12) 492-86-26; fax (12) 492-12-73; e-mail mission.bku@kum.hu; internet www.mfa.gov.hu/emb/baku; Ambassador ZSOLT CSUTORA.

India: 1069 Baku, Gänclik, Oqtay Karimov küç. 31/39; tel. (12) 447-25-62; fax (12) 447-25-72; e-mail amb.baku@indianembassybaku.org; internet www.indianembassybaku.org; Ambassador VINOD KUMAR.

Iran: 1000 Baku, B. Sardarov küç. 4; tel. (12) 492-44-07; fax (12) 498-07-33; e-mail press@iranembassyaz.org; Ambassador MOHSEN PAK-AEEN.

Iraq: 1000 Baku, Qizil sherq küç. 5; tel. (12) 538-17-34; fax (12) 538-17-35; e-mail bakemb@mofaml.gov.iq; internet www.mofamission.gov.iq/aze/ab/articles.aspx; Ambassador HEYDAR SHIYA GUBEYSHI AL-BERRAKI.

Israel: 1033 Baku, İzmir küç. 1033, Hyatt Tower III, 7th Floor; tel. (12) 490-78-81; fax (12) 490-78-92; e-mail info@baku.mfa.gov.il; internet baku.mfa.gov.il; Ambassador RAFAEL HARPAZ.

Italy: 1004 Baku, İçeri Şahar, Kiçik Qala küç. 44; tel. (12) 497-51-33; fax (12) 497-52-02; e-mail ambasciata.baku@esteri.it; internet www.ambbaku.esteri.it; Ambassador GIAMPAOLO CUTILLO.

Japan: 1065 Baku, İzmir küç. 1033, Hyatt Tower III, 6th Floor; tel. (12) 490-78-18; fax (12) 490-78-20; e-mail info@bk.mofa.go.jp; internet www.az.emb-japan.go.jp; Ambassador TSUGUO TAKAHASHI.

Jordan: 1065 Baku, C. Cabbarlı küç. 44; tel. (12) 437-31-21; fax (12) 437-31-23; e-mail baku@fm.gov.jo; Chargé d'affaires a.i. FAREEDAH MOHAMMAD SAID OUDEH.

Kazakhstan: 1078 Baku, X. Äliyev küç. 882/82; tel. (12) 465-62-48; fax (12) 465-62-49; e-mail embassyk@azdata.net; Ambassador AMANGELDY ZHUMABAEV.

Korea, Republic: 1078 Baku, X. Äliyev küç. 1/12; tel. (12) 596-79-01; fax (12) 596-79-04; e-mail azeremb@mofat.go.kr; internet aze.mofat.go.kr; Ambassador CHOI SUK-INN.

Kuwait: 1000 Baku, C. Cabbarlı küç. 44, Caspian Plaza 2, 15th Floor; tel. (12) 596-81-72; fax (12) 596-81-75; e-mail baku@mofa.gov.kw; Ambassador SAUD ABDULAZIZ AL-RUMI.

Latvia: 1065 Baku, C. Cabbarlı küç. 44; tel. (12) 436-67-78; fax (12) 436-67-79; e-mail embassy.azerbaijan@mfa.gov.lv; Ambassador HARDIJS BAUMANIS.

Lithuania: 1073 Baku, S. Dadaşev küç. 35/523; tel. (12) 539-22-95; fax (12) 539-22-97; e-mail amb.az@urm.lt; internet www.az.mfa.lt; Chargé d'affaires a.i. ŠARŪNĖ KUBILIŪTĖ.

Moldova: 1073 Baku, H. Cavid pr. 520/12; tel. (12) 510-15-38; fax (12) 403-52-91; e-mail baku@mfa.md; Ambassador IGOR BODYU.

Morocco: 1078 Baku, H. Äliyev küç. 2; tel. (12) 596-51-30; fax (12) 480-25-42; Ambassador HASSAN HAMI.

Netherlands: 1010 Baku, Nizami küç. 96, Landmark Bldg I/3; tel. (12) 465-99-22; fax (12) 465-99-72; e-mail bak@minbuza.nl; internet azerbaijan.nlembassy.org; Ambassador ROBBERT GABRIËLSE.

Norway: 1000 Baku, Nizami küç. 340, ISR Plaza, 11th Floor; tel. (12) 497-43-25; fax (12) 497-37-98; e-mail emb.baku@mfa.no; internet www.norway.az; Ambassador ERLING SKJØNSBERG.

Pakistan: 1000 Baku, Atatürk pr. 30; tel. (12) 436-08-39; fax (12) 436-08-41; e-mail parepbaku@yahoo.com; internet www.mofa.gov.pk/azerbaijan; Ambassador KHALID USMAN.

Poland: 1000 Baku, Içari Şahar, Kiçik Qala küç. 2; tel. (12) 492-01-14; fax (12) 492-02-14; e-mail baku.amb.sekretariat@msz.gov.pl; internet www.baku.msz.gov.pl; Ambassador MICHAŁ ŁABENDA.

Qatar: 1000 Baku, Temyur Äliyev küç. 70; tel. (12) 564-58-24; fax (12) 564-58-25; e-mail baku@mofa.gov.qa; Ambassador MUBARAK BIN FAHD AL THANI.

Romania: 1000 Baku, Gänclik, Häsän Äliyev küç. 125A; tel. (12) 465-63-78; fax (12) 456-60-76; e-mail romania@ultel.net; Ambassador DANIEL CRISTIAN CIOBANU.

Russia: 1022 Baku, Bakıxanov küç. 17; tel. (12) 597-08-70; fax (12) 597-16-73; e-mail embrus@embrus-az.com; internet www.embrus-az.com; Ambassador VLADIMIR DOROKHIN.

Saudi Arabia: 1073 Baku, S. Dadaşev küç. 44/2; tel. (12) 497-23-05; fax (12) 497-23-02; e-mail azemb@mofa.gov.sa; Ambassador MUSAED AL-SALEM.

Serbia: 1004 Baku, Gesr side küç. 1; tel. (12) 492-50-80; fax (12) 492-51-72; e-mail serbianembassy.baku@azeurotel.com; internet www.serbianembassy-baku.org; Ambassador (vacant).

Switzerland: 1004 Baku, Böyük Qala küç. 9; tel. (12) 437-38-50; fax (12) 437-38-51; e-mail baku.vertretung@eda.admin.ch; internet www.eda.admin.ch/baku; Ambassador PASCALE AEBISCHER.

Tajikistan: 1000 Baku, Badamdar, Baghlar küç. 20; tel. and fax (12) 502-14-32; e-mail embassy.rtra@gmail.com; Ambassador ZOHIR SAIDOV.

Turkey: 1000 Baku, Samad Vurghun küç. 94; tel. (12) 444-73-20; fax (12) 444-73-55; e-mail embassy.baku@mfa.gov.tr; internet www.baku.emb.mfa.gov.tr; Ambassador İSMAIL ALPER COŞKUN.

Turkmenistan: 1000 Baku, D. Mammedquluzadeh küç. 85; tel. and fax (12) 496-35-27; e-mail turkmen.embaz@gmail.com; Ambassador TOYLI KOMEKOV.

Ukraine: 1069 Baku, Yusif Vazirov küç. 49; tel. (12) 449-40-95; fax (12) 449-40-96; e-mail ukremb@azdata.net; internet www.mfa.gov.ua/azerbaijan; Ambassador OLEKSANDR P. MISHCHENKO.

United Arab Emirates: Baku, Y. Safarov küç. 23A; e-mail uaeembassy.baku@yahoo.com; Ambassador SALEM KHALIFA ALEGH-FELI.

United Kingdom: 1010 Baku, Xaqani küç. 45; tel. (12) 437-78-78; fax (12) 492-27-39; e-mail generalenquiries.baku@fco.gov.uk; internet www.gov.uk/government/world/azerbaijan; Ambassador IRFAN SIDDIQ.

USA: 1007 Baku, Azadlıq pr. 83; tel. (12) 498-03-36; fax (12) 465-66-71; internet azerbaijan.usembassy.gov; Ambassador RICHARD MORNINGSTAR.

Uzbekistan: 1021 Baku, Patamdart, 1 şosse, 9 dönga, 437; tel. (12) 497-25-49; fax (12) 497-25-48; e-mail office@uzembassy.az; internet www.uzembassy.az; Ambassador SHERZOD M. FAYZIYEV.

Judicial System

The judicial system in Azerbaijan is implemented by the following courts: regional (municipal) courts; the Court on Grave Crimes; the Military Court on Grave Crimes; local economic courts; the Economic Court on Disputes arising from International Agreements; the Supreme Court of Naxçıvan Autonomous Republic; the Court of Appeal; the Economic Court; and the Supreme Court.

Supreme Court (Azärbaycan Respublikası Ali Mähkämäsi): 1193 Baku, Yusif Säfärov küç. 14; tel. (12) 489-07-07; e-mail contact@supremecourt.gov.az; internet www.supremecourt.gov.az; the highest judicial body in civil, criminal, administrative and other cases, referring to the activity of the general courts; judges are nominated by the President of the Republic and confirmed in office by the National Assembly; Pres. RAMIZ RZAYEV.

Office of the Prosecutor-General (Baş Prokurorluğu): 1001 Baku, Nigar Räfibäyli küç. 7; tel. (12) 492-97-03; e-mail contact@prosecutor.gov.az; internet www.genprosecutor.gov.az; Prosecutor-General ZAKIR QARALOV.

Constitutional Court (Azärbaycan Republıkasi Konstıtusıya Mähkamäsı): 1005 Baku, Gänclär meydanı 1; tel. (12) 492-96-68; fax (12) 492-36-78; e-mail inter.dept@constcourt.gov.az; internet www.constcourt.gov.az; f. 1998; comprises a Chairman and eight judges, who are nominated by the President and confirmed in office by the National Assembly for a term of office of 15 years; only the President, the National Assembly, the Cabinet of Ministers, the Procurator-General, the Supreme Court and the Supreme Assembly of the Naxçıvan Autonomous Republic are permitted to submit cases to the Constitutional Court; Chair. FÄRHAD ABDULLAYEV.

Religion

ISLAM

The majority (some 70%) of Azerbaijanis are Shi'ite Muslims; most of the remainder are Sunni (Hanafi school). The Chairman of the Spiritual Board of the Muslims of the Caucasus, which is based in Baku, is normally a Shi'ite, while the Deputy Chairman is usually a Sunni.

Spiritual Board of Muslims of the Caucasus: 1000 Baku; Chair. Sheikh ul-Islam Haci ALLAŞUKUR PASHEZADÄ.

CHRISTIANITY

The Roman Catholic Church

A Mission was established in 2000. There were an estimated 320 adherents at 31 December 2007.

Superior: Fr VLADIMIR FEKETE, 1069 Baku, Teimur Äliyev küç. 69B/1; tel. (12) 562-22-55; fax (12) 436-09-43; e-mail admin@catholic.az; internet www.catholic.az.

The Russian Orthodox Church (Moscow Patriarchate)

Bishop of Baku and the Caspian Region: ALEKSANDR, 1010 Baku, Ş. Azizbekova küç. 205; tel. (12) 440-43-52; fax (12) 440-04-43; e-mail baku@eparchia.ru.

The Press

PRINCIPAL NEWSPAPERS AND PERIODICALS

In Azerbaijani, except where otherwise stated.

525-ci Qazet: 1033 Baku, Ş. Mustafayev küç. 27/121; tel. (12) 466-67-98; fax (12) 466-25-20; e-mail info@525.az; internet www.525.az; f. 1992; 5 a week; in Azerbaijani, also online edns in English and Russian; Editor-in-Chief RASHAD MAJID.

Adabiyyat qazeti (Literary Gazette): 1146 Baku, Matbuät pr. 529; tel. (12) 439-50-37; internet www.edebiyyatqazeti.com; f. 1934; every two weeks; publ. by Union of Writers; Chief Editor AYAZ VAFALI.

Ädalät (Justice): Baku; tel. (12) 438-51-49; fax (12) 465-10-64; e-mail aqilabbas@rambler.ru; internet www.adalet-az.com; f. 1990; 5 a week; publ. of Office of the Prosecutor-General; Editor AGIL ABBAS.

Ayna/Zerkalo (Mirror): 1138 Baku, Sharifzadeh küç. 1; tel. (12) 497-51-68; fax (12) 497-71-23; e-mail gazeta@zerkalo.az; internet www.ayna.az; internet www.zerkalo.az; f. 1990; daily; independent; Azerbaijani and Russian edns; Editor-in-Chief ELCIN SIXLINSKI; circ. 4,500 (daily).

Azadlıq (Freedom): 1000 Baku, Xaqani küç. 33; tel. (12) 498-90-81; fax (12) 498-78-18; e-mail mail@azadliq.com; internet www.azadliq.info; f. 1989; weekly; independent; organ of the Azerbaijan Popular Front Party (q.v.); Editor-in-Chief GANIMAT ZAKHIDOV.

Azärbaycan (Azerbaijan): 1073 Baku, Matbuät pr. 529/4; tel. (12) 438-20-87; fax (12) 439-43-23; e-mail azerbaijan_newspaper@azeronline.com; internet www.azerbaijan-news.az; f. 1991; 5 a week; publ. by the Milli Mäclis; Editor-in-Chief BAKHTIYAR SADIGOV.

Azernews: 1130 Baku, Darnagul Sähär 3097, 4th Floor; tel. (12) 561-01-42; fax (12) 562-06-45; e-mail azernews@azeurotel.com; internet www.azernews.net; f. 1997; weekly; in Azerbaijani, Russian and English; Editor-in-Chief FAZIL ABBASOV; circ. 5,000–6,000.

Bakı Xäbär (Baku News): 1000 Baku, Matbuät pr. 529; tel. (12) 510-87-40; internet www.baki-xeber.com; f. 2003; newspaper of the Azerbaijan Democratic Party; 6 a week; Editor-in-Chief AYDIN QULIYEV; circ. 5,000 (2007).

Bakinskii Rabochii (The Baku Worker): 1073 Baku, Matbuät pr. 529; tel. (12) 438-00-29; fax (12) 438-78-49; e-mail bakrab1906@gmail.com; internet www.br.az; f. 1906; 5 a week; govt newspaper; in Russian; Chief Editor AGABEK ASKEROV.

Bizim Yol (Our Way): Baku, H. Z. Tağıyev küç. 15/3; tel. (12) 418-91-79; e-mail info@bizimyol.az; internet bizimyol.az; f. 2003; independent; weekly; associated with the Azerbaijan Popular Front Party (q.v.); Editor-in-Chief BAHADDIN HAZIYEV.

Day: 1000 Baku; e-mail editor@day.az; internet www.day.az; online only; in Russian and English.

Ekho (Echo): 1138 Baku, Şärifzadä küç. 1; tel. (12) 497-50-31; fax (12) 447-41-50; e-mail gazeta@echo-az.com; internet www.echo-az.com; daily; in Russian; Editor-in-Chief RAUF TALISHINSKYI; circ. 10,000.

Ekspress (The Express): 1000 Baku, Xaqani küç. 20B/43; tel. (12) 498-08-63; internet www.ekspress.az; Editor QAZANFAR BAYRAMOV.

İki Sahil: 1025 Baku, Zardabi 88A; tel. (12) 530-26-46; fax (12) 430-87-47; e-mail ikisahil@azdata.net; internet www.ikisahil.com; f. 1965; 5 a week; organ of SOCAR; Editor-in-Chief VÜQAR RÄHIMZADÄ; circ. 7,500.

İstiqlal (Independence): 1014 Baku, 28 May küç. 3–11; tel. (12) 493-33-78; fax (12) 498-75-55; e-mail istiklal@ngonet.baku.az; 4 a month; organ of the Azerbaijan Social Democratic Party; Editor ZARDUSHT ÄLIZÄDE; circ. 5,000.

Respublıka (Republic): 1146 Baku, Matbuät pr. 529; tel. (12) 493-59-08; fax (12) 493-50-87; e-mail resp@azdata.net; internet www.respublica-news.az; f. 1996; daily; govt newspaper; Editor-in-Chief T. AHMÄDOV; circ. 5,500.

Şarq (The East): 1000 Baku, Matbuät pr. 529; tel. (12) 447-37-80; fax (12) 447-37-80; e-mail sharq@azerin.com; internet www.sherg.az; Editor AKIF ISHIGLI.

Vyshka—Oil (Oil Derrick): 1073 Baku, Matbuät pr. 529; tel. and fax (12) 439-96-97; e-mail medina@vyshka.com; internet vyshka.com; f. 1928; weekly; independent; in Russian; Editor MEDINA HÄSÄNOV.

Xalq Cäbhäsi (Popular Front): Baku; internet www.xalqcebhesi.az; 5 a week.

Xalq Qazetı (Popular Gazette): 1000 Baku, Bül-Bül pr. 18; tel. (12) 493-59-03; fax (12) 493-02-80; e-mail info@xalqqazeti.com; internet www.xalqqazeti.com; f. 1919; fmrly *Kommunist*; 6 a week; in Azerbaijani; also online edns in Russian and English; organ of the Office of the President; Editor HÄSÄN HÄSÄNOV.

Yeni Azärbaycan (A New Azerbaijan): 1095 Baku, Uzeyir Hacibeyov küç. 32; tel. (12) 498-81-24; fax (12) 497-53-04; e-mail yeniazerbaycan@azdata.net; internet www.yeniazerbaycan.com; f. 1993; 5 a week; organ of the New Azerbaijan Party; Editor ALGYSH MUSAYEV; circ. 2,493.

Yeni Müsavat (A New Equality): 1000 Baku; tel. (12) 498-00-61; e-mail ymusavat@azeronline.com; internet www.musavat.com; independent; pro-opposition; Chief Editor RAUF ARIFOĞLU.

NEWS AGENCIES

Azadinform Information Agency: 1146 Baku, Matbuät pr. 529; tel. (12) 510-70-43; fax (12) 498-47-60; e-mail info@azadinform.az; internet azadinform.az; f. 1998; independent information agency; Chief Editor ASAF HAJIYEV.

AzarTAc—Azärbaycan Dövlat Teleqraf Agentlıyı (Azerbaijan State Telegraph Agency—AzerTAg): 1000 Baku, Bül-Bül pr. 18; tel. (12) 493-59-29; fax (12) 493-62-65; e-mail azertac@azdata.net; internet www.azertag.gov.az; f. 1920; provides information in Azerbaijani, Russian and English; Dir-Gen. ASLAN ASLANOV.

Azeri Press Agency (APA): 1000 Baku, Zarifa Äliyeva küç. 27; tel. (12) 596-33-57; fax (12) 596-31-94; e-mail apa@azeurotel.com; internet www.apa.az; f. 2004; in Azerbaijani, Russian and English; Dir-Gen. VUSALA MAHIRGIZI.

Trend Information-Analytical Agency: 1141 Baku, Firudin Agayev küç. 14; tel. (12) 497-31-72; fax (12) 497-30-89; e-mail agency@trendaz.com; internet trend.az; f. 1995; in Azerbaijani, Russian, Farsi, Arabic and English; Dir-Gen. ILGAR HUSEYNOV.

Turan İnformasıya Agentlıyı: 1000 Baku, Xaqani küç. 20/56; tel. (12) 498-42-26; fax (12) 498-38-17; e-mail agency@turan.az; internet www.turan.az; f. 1990; independent news agency; in Azerbaijani, Russian and English; Dir MEHMAN ÄLIYEV.

PRESS ASSOCIATION

Azerbaijan Press Council (Azärbaycan Metbuät Şurası): 1010 Baku, Zarifa Äliyeva küç. 27; tel. (12) 488-35-42; fax (12) 488-35-79; e-mail apa@azeurotel.com; internet www.az.apa.az; f. 2004; mediates disputes between the media and the authorities; acts as a self-regulatory body for the print media; Dir-Gen. VUSALA MAHIRGIZI.

Publishers

Azärbaycan Ensiklopediyası (Azerbaijan Encyclopedia): 1004 Baku, Böyük Qala küç. 41; tel. (12) 492-87-11; fax (12) 492-77-83; e-mail azenciklop@ctc.net.az; f. 1965; encyclopedias and dictionaries; Gen. Dir I. O. VELIYEV.

Azarneshr State Publishing House: 1005 Baku, Gusi Haciyev küç. 4; tel. (12) 492-50-15; f. 1924; Dirs A. MUSTAFAZADE, AGABEK ASKEROV.

Elm Azerbaijani Academy of Sciences Publishing House: 1141 Baku, F. Agayev küç. 9; scientific books and journals.

Khazar University Press (KUP): 1096 Baku, Mehseti küç. 11; tel. (12) 421-79-27; fax (12) 498-93-79; e-mail contact@khazar.org; internet www.khazar.org/general/publication.htm; f. 1995; textbooks, reference books and journals.

Broadcasting and Communications

TELECOMMUNICATIONS

Azerbaijan's fixed-line telephone sector is dominated by the state operator, and in 2011 there were four providers of mobile cellular communications services. In 2012 there were 1.7m. subscriptions to fixed-line telephone services and 10.1m. subscriptions to mobile telephone services.

Azercell Telecom: 1139 Baku, Tbilisi pr. 61A; tel. (12) 496-70-07; fax (12) 430-05-68; e-mail customercare@azercell.com; internet www.azercell.com; f. 1996; jt venture between the Ministry of Communications and Information Technology and Fintur Holdings B.V. (Netherlands); Chair. KIRIL QABURIÇI.

Azerfon: 1029 Baku, Heydär Äliyev pr. 106; tel. (12) 444-07-30; fax (12) 444-07-31; e-mail corpcom@azerfon.az; internet www.narmobile.az; f. 2007; provides mobile cellular communications under the Narmobile brand name; CEO KENT MCNELEY.

AzTelecom Production Assen: 1122 Baku, Tbilisi pr. 187; tel. (12) 344-00-00; fax (12) 493-17-87; e-mail aztelekom@aztelekom.net; internet www.aztelekom.net; national monopoly fixed-line telecommunications operator; f. 1992; owned by the Ministry of Communications and Information Technology; privatization pending; Dir MUHAMMAD MAMEDOV.

Bakcell: 1010 Baku, Neftçilär pr. 153; tel. (12) 498-89-89; fax (12) 464-04-00; e-mail info@bakcell.com; internet www.bakcell.com; f. 1994; mobile telecommunications service provider; wholly owned by GTIB (Israel); CEO RICHARD SHEARER.

Delta Telecom: 1139 Baku, Şärifzadä küç. 241; tel. (12) 431-14-20; fax (12) 431-00-65; e-mail office@delta-telecom.net; internet www.delta-telecom.net; f. 2000; internet service provider; Pres. RAMAZAN VÄLIYEV.

RADIO AND TELEVISION

Regulatory Authority

National Television and Radio Council (Milli Televiziya vä Radio Şurası): 1000 Baku, Nizami küç. 105; tel. (12) 598-36-59; fax (12) 498-76-68; e-mail office@ntrc.gov.az; internet www.ntrc.gov.az; f. 2002; regulatory body, comprising nine mems, six of whom are presidential appointees; Chair. NUSHIRAVAN MAGERRAMLI.

Broadcasters

ANS Independent Broadcasting and Media Co (Azerbaijan News Service): 1073 Baku, Matbuät pr. 28/11; tel. (12) 497-72-67; fax (12) 498-94-98; e-mail ans@ans.az; internet www.ansgroup.ws; f. 1999; independent; broadcasts ANS-TV (f. 1990) and NAS-CHM Radio (f. 1994); Pres. VAHID MUSTAFAYEV.

Azerbaijan Television and Radio Broadcasting Co: 1011 Baku, Mehti Hussein küç. 1; tel. (12) 492-38-07; fax (12) 497-20-20; e-mail webmaster@aztv.az; internet www.aztv.az; f. 1956; closed jt-stock co; Chair. ARIF ALIŞANOV.

Lider TV and Radio: 1141 Baku, A. Alekperov küç. 83/23; tel. (12) 497-29-24; fax (12) 497-87-77; e-mail support@h2h.az; internet www.lidertv.com; f. 2000.

Public Television and Radio Broadcasting Co (İctimiai Televizya vä Radiyo Yayımları Şirkati—ITV): 1012 Baku, Şärifzadä küç. 241; tel. (12) 430-23-04; e-mail info@itv.az; internet www.itv.az; f. 2005; Gen. Dir CÄMIL QULIYEV.

Radio Antenn: 1130 Baku, Azadlıq pr. 189; tel. (12) 565-31-01; e-mail info@antenn.az; internet www.antenn.az; f. 1998.

Finance

(cap. = capital; res = reserves; dep. = deposits; m. = million; brs = branches; amounts in new manats, unless otherwise stated)

BANKING

The banking sector in Azerbaijan is dominated by the state-owned International Bank of Azerbaijan, which accounts for around one-half of all banking assets in the country.

Central Bank

Central Bank of the Republic of Azerbaijan: 1014 Baku, R. Behbutov küç. 32; tel. (12) 493-11-22; fax (12) 493-55-41; e-mail mail@cbar.az; internet www.cbar.az; f. 1992 as National Bank of Azerbaijan; renamed as above in 2009; central bank and supervisory authority; cap. 10.0m., res 209.5m., dep. 1,382.0m. (Dec. 2009); Chair. Dr ELMAN RUSTAMOV.

State-owned Bank

International Bank of Azerbaijan (Azärbaycan Beynälxalq Banki): 1005 Baku, Nizami küç. 67; tel. (12) 493-00-91; fax (12) 493-40-91; e-mail ibar@ibar.az; internet www.ibar.az; f. 1992 to succeed br. of USSR Vneshekonombank; 50.2% owned by the Ministry of Finance (q.v.), 11.2% by other state entities; f. 1992; provides all banking services; cap. 331.0m., res 25.0m., dep. 4,313.4m. (Dec. 2012); Chair. of Bd CAHANGIR F. HACIYEV; 48 brs.

Other Banks

In 2010 there were a total of 46 commercial banks operating in Azerbaijan, 23 of which included foreign capital.

Amrahbank: 1025 Baku, Y. Säfärov küç. 10; tel. (12) 497-88-60; fax (12) 497-88-63; e-mail info@amrahbank.com; internet www.amrahbank.com; f. 1993; 49% owned by International Investment Bank (Bahrain); cap. 17.3m., res 5.1m., dep. 75.2m. (Dec. 2012); Pres. YUNUS ILDIRIMZADÄ; Chair. EMIL HÄSÄNOV (acting); 7 brs.

AtaBank: 1010 Baku, Ş. Badalbäyli küç. 102; tel. (12) 497-87-00; fax (12) 498-74-47; e-mail atabank@atabank.com; internet www.atabank.com; f. 1994; cap. 25m., res 4m., dep. 159m. (Dec. 2011); Exec. Chair. ILTIFAT AGAEV; 11 brs.

Azärbaycan Sänaye Banki (ASB) (Azerbaijan Industry Bank): 1005 Baku, Zarifä Äliyeva küç. 3; tel. (12) 493-14-16; fax (12) 493-84-50; e-mail info@asb.az; internet www.asb.az; f. 1996; present name adopted 2006; 94% owned by Anadolu Investment Kompani; cap. 28.0m., res –0.2 m., dep. 63.4m. (Dec. 2012); Pres. ZEYNAB KONYAR; CEO HUSEIN OZMEN; 4 brs.

Azerigazbank: 1073 Baku, Landau küç. 16; tel. (12) 497-50-17; fax (12) 498-96-15; e-mail info@agbank.az; internet www.azerigazbank.com; f. 1992; jt-stock investment bank; cap. 20.0m., res 9.4m., dep. 254.0m. (Dec. 2012); Chair. AZER F. MOVSUMOV; 6 brs.

Bank of Baku: 1069 Baku, Atatürk pr. 40/42; tel. (12) 447-00-55; fax (12) 498-82-78; e-mail fsalizade@bankofbaku.com; internet www.bankofbaku.com; f. 1994; 40% owned by NAB DIS Ticarat (Turkey), 28.9% owned by Azpetrol Holding; cap. 53.0m., res 8.0m., dep. 351.1m. (Dec. 2012); Chair. of Bd FARID ALIZADA; 16 brs.

Bank Respublika: 1095 Baku, Xaqani küç. 21; tel. (12) 598-08-00; fax (12) 598-08-80; e-mail info@bankrespublika.az; internet www.bankrespublika.az; f. 1992; cap. 37.5m., res 7.0m., dep. 263.5m. (Dec. 2012); Chair. of Exec. Bd KHADIJA HÄSÄNOVA; 22 brs.

DämirBank (DemirBank): 1008 Baku, Qarabağ küç. 31; tel. (12) 444-71-71; fax (12) 441-19-76; e-mail info@demirbank.az; internet www.demirbank.az; f. 1992; present name adopted 2009; 25% owned by European Bank for Reconstruction and Development (United Kingdom), 10% by Netherlands Development Finance Company (The Netherlands); cap. 21.0m., res 8.8m., dep. 186.5m. (Dec. 2012); Chair. of Bd ROMAN AMIRJANOV; 30 brs.

Rabitäbank: 1010 Baku, Ü. Hacıbayov küç. 33/35; tel. (12) 492-57-61; fax (12) 497-11-01; e-mail rb@rabitabank.com; internet www.rabitabank.com; f. 1993; cap. 30.0m., res 4.0m., dep. 93.3m. (Dec. 2012); Exec. Chair. NIKOLOZ ŞURGAIA; 15 brs.

Unibank Commercial Bank: 1022 Baku, Raşid Behbudov küç. 55; tel. (12) 498-22-44; fax (12) 498-09-53; e-mail bank@unibank.az; internet www.unibank.az; f. 2002 by merger; cap. 62.0m., res 0.5m., dep. 338.0m. (Dec. 2012); Chair. FAIG HUSEYNOV; 24 brs.

Association

Association of Banks of Azerbaijan (Azärbaycan Banklar Asossiasiyası): 1073 Baku, S. Dadaşov küç. 29; tel. (12) 497-61-69; fax (12) 497-15-15; e-mail aba@aba.az; internet www.aba.az; f. 1990; co-ordinates banking activity; Pres. ELDAR ISMAYLOV; 47 mems.

STOCK EXCHANGE

Baku Stock Exchange (Bakı Fond Birjasi): 1000 Baku, Bül-Bül pr. 19; tel. (12) 498-98-20; fax (12) 493-77-93; e-mail info@bse.az; internet www.bse.az; f. 2000; Pres. ANAR AKHUNDOV.

INSURANCE

At January 2013 there were 27 insurance companies operating in Azerbaijan.

Ataşgah Insurance Co: Baku, Näsib bäy Yusifbäyli küç. 75B; tel. and fax (12) 497-81-82; e-mail ateshgah@ateshgah.com; internet www.ateshgah.com; f. 1996; 30% owned by State Oil Co of Azerbaijan, 30% owned by Atlantic Reinsurance Co, 19% owned by LUKoil Azerbaijan; Pres. RUSLAN ÄLIYEV.

AXA MBASK Insurance Co: 1095 Baku, Azi Aslanov küç. 90/9; tel. (12) 498-91-90; fax (12) 498-10-62; e-mail office@mbask.com; internet www.axambask.az; f. 1992; present name adopted 2010; 83% owned by AXA Seguros Generales (Spain); 7 brs; Chair. of Bd of Dirs (vacant).

Azärqarant Sığorta (Azergarant Sigorta): 1072 Baku, May küç. 28; tel. (12) 498-68-42; fax (12) 493-85-38; e-mail azergarant@rambler.ru; internet www.azergarant.az; f. 1993; Pres. RÄŞAD ÄHLIMAN MÄMMÄDOV; Gen. Dir FAIG HUSSEINOV.

Azersiğorta: 1108 Baku, Dadaşov 60; tel. (12) 561-24-11; fax (12) 495-94-69; e-mail azersigorta@azeuro.net; internet www.azersigorta-az.com; state-owned; Dir MÄMMÄD MÄMMÄDOV.

AzSığorta: 1073 Baku, Qutqaşınlı küç. 99/1; tel. (12) 505-66-66; fax (12) 497-89-59; e-mail info@azinsurance.eu; internet www.azsigorta.az; f. 2007; Chair. ELXAN HÄŞIMOV.

Beynälxalq Sığorta Şirkäti (International Insurance Co—IIC): 1065 Baku, C. Cabbarlı küç. 40C, IIC Bldg; tel. (12) 596-22-02; fax (12) 596-22-12; e-mail iic@iic.az; internet www.iic.az; f. 2002; universal insurance co; wholly owned subsidiary of the International Bank of Azerbaijan; Chair. of Bd CÄMIL HÜSEYN SULTANOV.

İpäk Yolu Sığorta—Silk Way Insurance: 1010 Baku, Z. Äliyeva küç. 55; tel. (12) 598-38-50; fax (12) 598-38-02; e-mail contact@

silkwayinsurance.com; internet www.azalsigorta.com; f. 1995; life and non-life; Dir ELŞAD RÜSTÄMOV.

Mega Siğorta: 1052 Baku, Ä. Räcäbli küç. 19A; tel. (12) 565-32-32; fax (12) 565-45-05; internet www.meqasigorta.az; life and non-life; Dir YAŞAR QURBANOV.

Paşa Sığorta: 1000 Baku, Tolstoy küç. 170; tel. (12) 598-18-03; fax (12) 598-18-07; e-mail office@pasha-insurance.az; internet www.pasha-insurance.az; f. 2006; Man. Dir MIR CAMAL PAŞAYEV.

Qala Heyat Siğorta: 1122 Baku, Tbilisi küç. 1058; tel. and fax (12) 404-77-74; internet www.qala.az; f. 2010; life; Chair. of Bd ÄSGÄR ÄLÄKBÄROV.

Xalq Sığorta: 1006 Baku, İnşaatçılar küç. 22L; tel. (12) 598-00-66; fax (12) 404-43-08; e-mail mail@xalqsigorta.az; internet www.xalqsigorta.az; f. 2005; life and non-life; Chair. of Bd ROMAN QURBANOV.

Trade and Industry

GOVERNMENT AGENCY

Azerbaijan Export and Investment Promotion Foundation: 1001 Baku, Häsän Abdullayev küç. 11; tel. (12) 598-01-47; fax (12) 598-01-52; e-mail office@azpromo.org; internet www.azpromo.org; internet www.azerinvest.az; f. 2003; Pres. ADIL MÄMMÄDOV.

CHAMBER OF COMMERCE

Chamber of Commerce and Industry: 1001 Baku, İstiqlaliyyät küç. 31/33; tel. (12) 492-89-12; fax (12) 497-19-97; e-mail expo@chamber.baku.az; Pres. SÜLEYMAN TATLIYEV.

INDUSTRIAL AND TRADE ASSOCIATIONS

National Confederation of Entrepreneurs' (Employers') Organizations of Azerbaijan (Azärbaycan Respublikasi Sahibkarlar—İşägötüränlär—Täşkilatları Milli Konfederasiyası—ASK): 1110 Baku, Häsän Äliyev küç. 57; tel. (12) 465-72-42; fax (12) 465-72-43; e-mail office@ask.org.az; internet www.ask.org.az; f. 1999; Pres. MAMMAD MUSAEV.

UTILITIES

Electricity

Azärenerji: 1005 Baku, A. Älizäde küç. 10; tel. (12) 492-31-09; fax (12) 492-63-55; e-mail azerenerji@azerenerji.com; internet www.azerenerji.gov.az; f. 1962; state-owned jt-stock co; power generation and transmission company; Pres. ETIBAR S. PIRVERDIEV.

Bakı Electrikşebeke (Baku Electricity Network): 1065 Baku, Bakıxanov 13; tel. (12) 440-39-93; fax (12) 565-05-72; e-mail info@bes.az; internet www.bes.az; f. 2001.

Bayva-Enerji: 2000 Gäncä, Ruzigar Qasimov küç. 10; tel. and fax (22) 56-97-40; e-mail bayva-qerbenerji@mail.ru; f. 2002 as Gäncäelektrikşebeke; comprising the Azerbaijani electricity distribution network's western zone; managed by Bakı Yüksakgarginlikli Elektroavadanliq (BYGEA—Baku High Voltage Electrical Equipment Co); Gen. Dir RAMIZ AGAMÄLIYEV.

Gas

Azäriqaz (AzeriGaz): 1025 Baku, Yusif Säfärov küç. 23; tel. (12) 490-43-34; fax (12) 490-42-92; e-mail info@azerigaz.com; f. 1992; transport, distribution, sale, compression and storage of natural gas; acquired by State Oil Co of the Azerbaijan Republic (SOCAR) (q.v.) in 2010; Chair. AKBAR HAJIYEV; 13,000 employees.

TRADE UNIONS

Confederation of Azerbaijan Trade Unions (AHIK): 1000 Baku, Gänclär meydanı 3; tel. (12) 492-66-59; fax (12) 492-72-68; e-mail ahik@azerin.com; internet www.ahik.org; Chair. SATTAR MEHBÄLIEV; 1.3m. mems.

Transport

RAILWAYS

In 2010 there were 2,079 km of railway track, of which 1,241 km were electrified. An international line links Naxçıvan with Tabriz (Iran). In 2007 construction began on a new 258-km railway line, linking Kars, in Turkey, with Tbilisi (via Akhalkalaki, Georgia) and Baku; the project was scheduled for completion in 2015. There is an underground railway in Baku.

Azerbaijani Railways (ADDY): 1010 Baku, Dilara Äliyeva küç. 230; tel. (12) 499-44-99; fax (12) 499-65-84; e-mail info@addy.gov.az; internet addy.gov.az; f. 1992; Chair. ARIF ASKEROV.

Baku Metro (Bakı Metropoliteni): 1073 Baku, H. Cavid pr. 33A; tel. (12) 490-02-64; fax (12) 497-53-96; e-mail press@metro.gov.az; internet www.metro.gov.az; f. 1967; 23 stations on two lines (34.6 km); further expansion of network underway in 2014; Gen. Man. TAGI M. AKHMEDOV.

ROADS

In 2006 the total length of roads in Azerbaijan was 52,942 km, of which 50.60% were paved.

SHIPPING

At 31 December 2013 the Azerbaijani flag registered fleet comprised 351 vessels, with a combined displacement of 890,254 grt.

Baku International Sea Trade Port: 1010 Baku, U. Hacibeyov küç. 72; tel. (12) 493-02-68; fax (12) 493-36-72; e-mail office@bakuseaport.az; internet www.bakuseaport.az; Gen. Dir ELÇIN MIRZAYEV.

Shipowning Company

Azerbaijani State Caspian Shipping Co (CASPAR) (Azärbaycan Dövlat Xazar Daniz Gamiçiliyi—ADXDG): 1005 Baku, M. Rasulzadä küç. 5; tel. (12) 493-20-58; fax (12) 493-53-39; e-mail adxdg@caspar.az; operates cargo and passenger ferries; state-owned; Pres. AYDIN BAŞIROV.

CIVIL AVIATION

There are five airports in Azerbaijan, of which Heydär Äliyev Airport at Baku is the largest.

State Civil Aviation Administration: 1000 Baku, Azadlıq pr. 11; tel. and fax (12) 598-51-91; e-mail hq@caa.gov.az; internet www.caa.gov.az; f. 2006; Dir FUAD QULIYEV.

Azerbaijan Airlines (AZAL) (Azärbaycan Hava Yollari): 1010 Baku, Nizami küç. 84; tel. (12) 497-85-09; fax (12) 598-52-37; e-mail ftl@azal.az; internet azal.az; f. 1992; state airline; domestic and international passenger and cargo services; Gen. Dir CAHANGIR ASKEROV.

Tourism

Tourism is not widely developed. There were 2,239,141 tourist arrivals in 2011; according to provisional figures, receipts from tourism in 2012 (excluding passenger transport) amounted to US $2,433m.

Dept of Tourism of the Ministry of Culture and Tourism: 1004 Baku, Neftçilär pr. 65; tel. (12) 492-87-13; fax (12) 492-98-41; e-mail tourism@myst.co-az.net; internet www.mct.gov.az; Head TEYMUR MEHDIYEV.

Defence

As assessed at November 2012 the Azerbaijani military numbered 66,950: an army of 56,850, a navy of 2,200 and an air force of 7,900. Reserves number some 300,000. Military service is for 17 months (but may be extended for ground forces). The Ministry of Internal Affairs controls a militia of some 10,000 and a border guard of an estimated 5,000. In May 1994 Azerbaijan joined the North Atlantic Treaty Organization's 'Partnership for Peace' programme.

Defence Expenditure: Budgeted at 1,640m. new manats in 2014.

Chief of the General Staff: Col-Gen. NÄCMÄDDIN SADIQOV.

Commander of Air Forces: Lt. Gen. VAHID ÄLIYEV.

Commander of the Navy: Capt. YUNUS MÄMMÄDOV.

Education

Education is compulsory between the ages of six and 17 years. Primary education begins at the age of six years. Secondary education comprises a first cycle of five years and a second cycle of two years. In 2011/12 total enrolment at pre-school establishments included 21% of children of the relevant age-group. In the same year enrolment at primary schools included 89% of the relevant age-group; the comparable ratio for secondary enrolment was 87%. In 2012/13 there were 52 institutions of higher education and 145,584 students in higher education. Government expenditure on education was estimated at 723m. new manats in 2007, representing 12.1% of total state spending.

AZERBAIJANI SECESSIONIST TERRITORY

The self-proclaimed 'Republic of Nagornyi Karabakh', which has a predominately ethnically Armenian population, is located in the south-west of Azerbaijan, and borders Armenia to the south-west. The regional assembly of the Nagorno-Karabakh Autonomous Oblast (which comprised a smaller territory, and did not share a border with Armenia) proclaimed a 'Republic of Nagornyi Karabakh' on 2 September 1991. Following the dissolution of the USSR at the end of that year, the territory declared its independence from Azerbaijan on 6 January 1992. All such pronouncements were declared invalid by the Azerbaijani authorities, and military conflict ensued, in which the separatists obtained control of other areas of Azerbaijan, until a ceasefire entered into effect in May 1994. Although a political solution remained elusive, local forces secured a de facto independence. While the separatist authorities have enjoyed de facto political and military support from Armenia, the self-proclaimed 'Republic' is not formally recognized by any state.

NAGORNYI KARABAKH

Introductory Survey

LOCATION, CLIMATE, LANGUAGE, RELIGION, FLAG, CAPITAL

Nagornyi Karabakh, Upper or Mountainous Karabakh (Dağlıq Qarabağ in Azerbaijani, Artsakh in Armenian), is on the north-eastern slopes of the Lesser Caucasus. The region lies in the south-west of Azerbaijan, and the territory claimed by the 'Republic of Nagornyi Karabakh' (unlike the Soviet-era Autonomous Oblast) has a south-western border with Armenia. The climate is mild and mostly subtropical. Average temperatures range from −1°C (30°F) in January to 22°C (72°F) in July, although the climate in lowland areas is markedly warmer than in the mountain ranges. Precipitation averages 410 mm–480 mm per year in the lowlands, but in the highlands amounts to 560 mm–840mm. The population principally speak Armenian, the sole member of a distinct Indo-European language group, written in the Armenian script. Most of the population are adherents of Christianity, the largest denomination being the Armenian Apostolic Church. The separatist authorities use a flag (proportions 1 by 2) based upon that of Armenia, comprising three equal horizontal stripes, of red, blue and orange, with each stripe being divided, towards the fly, by a white zig-zag chevron. The principal city and capital of the self-proclaimed 'Republic' is Stepanakert (known in Azerbaijani as Xankändi).

CONTEMPORARY POLITICAL HISTORY

Historical Context

After the collapse of the Russian Empire in 1917, and the subsequent proclamation of independent Armenian and Azerbaijani republics, Nagornyi Karabakh was disputed by both states. Following the Soviet conquest of the region, in June 1921 the Bolshevik Bureau for Caucasian Affairs (Kavburo) voted to unite Nagornyi Karabakh with Armenia. However, following intervention by Stalin (Iosif Dzhugashvili), the decision was reversed, and in 1923 the territory was declared an autonomous oblast within Azerbaijan.

Following a revival of nationalism, in February 1988 the Soviet and Azerbaijani authorities rejected a request by the Nagornyi Karabakh regional soviet (council) for the transfer of the territory to Armenia, provoking huge demonstrations by Armenians in both Nagornyi Karabakh and Yerevan, the capital of Armenia, while outbreaks of inter-ethnic violence, in both Armenia and Azerbaijan, brought about a large-scale migration of refugees between both countries.

Domestic Political Affairs

In January 1989 the Soviet Government suspended the activities of the Nagornyi Karabakh authorities and established a Special Administration Committee (SAC), responsible to the USSR Council of Ministers. The dispatch of some 5,000 Soviet troops failed to reduce tensions within Nagornyi Karabakh, and in November the SAC was disbanded. Upon the USSR's disintegration in 1991, the leadership of Nagornyi Karabakh declared the enclave to be an independent republic. In January 1992 the President of Azerbaijan, Ayaz Mutällibov, placed the region under direct presidential rule; in the same month Azerbaijani forces surrounded and attacked Stepanakert (Xankändi), the capital of Nagornyi Karabakh, while Armenian forces laid siege to Shushi (Şuşha), a town with a mainly Azeri population. In May the Nagornyi Karabakh 'self-defence forces' (which the Armenian Government continued to claim were operating without its military support) captured Shushi, gaining complete control of the territory. With the capture of the Laçin valley, the ethnic Armenian militia succeeded in opening a 'corridor' linking Nagornyi Karabakh with Armenia. In June Azerbaijani forces launched a sustained counter-offensive in Nagornyi Karabakh. In August Azerbaijani forces resumed the bombardment of Stepanakert. In response, a state defence committee, in close alignment with the Armenian administration of President Levon Ter-Petrosyan, replaced the Government of Nagornyi Karabakh. In December Azerbaijani forces launched a new counter-offensive. International efforts to halt the conflict continued, led by the 11-nation Minsk Group of the Conference on Security and Co-operation in Europe (CSCE—later Organization for Security and Co-operation in Europe—OSCE, see p. 387). In April 1993 ethnic Armenian forces had formed a second corridor linking Nagornyi Karabakh with Armenia, by capturing the Kälbäcär district, and by June they had secured full control of Nagornyi Karabakh. The seizure of Azerbaijani territory outside the oblast prompted international condemnation. The UN Security Council issued Resolutions 822 and 853 demanding the withdrawal of occupying and local Armenian forces from Azerbaijan, which went unheeded; hostilities intensified further, and more than 20% of Azerbaijan's total territory was captured by the Nagornyi Karabakh forces (although Azerbaijani forces recaptured some territory in a counter-offensive launched in December). In February 1994 it was reported that as many as 18,000 people had been killed since 1988, with a further 25,000 wounded.

In May 1994 Azerbaijan signed the so-called Bishkek Protocol, which had been adopted by the Inter-Parliamentary Assembly of the Commonwealth of Independent States (CIS), with the approval of representatives of both Armenia and the self-styled 'Republic of Nagornyi Karabakh'. On 8 May the Nagornyi Karabakh leadership ordered its forces to cease hostilities, in accordance with the Protocol. Although violations were subsequently reported, the ceasefire remained in force.

In December 1994 Robert Kocharyan, hitherto Chairman of the State Defence Committee and premier, was elected by the Nagornyi Karabakh Supreme Soviet as the (internationally unrecognized) 'President' of Nagornyi Karabakh. In April–June a new, 33-seat legislature, the Azgayin Zhoghov (National Assembly), was elected in Nagornyi Karabakh—replacing the 81-member Supreme Soviet. In November 1996 Kocharyan was re-elected by popular vote, with more than 86% of the votes cast. In December President Heydär Äliyev and his Armenian counterpart, Ter-Petrosyan, attended a summit meeting of the OSCE, in Lisbon, Portugal. Following demands by Azerbaijan, a statement was released by the OSCE Chairman, recommending three principles that would form the basis of a political settlement to the conflict: the territorial integrity of Armenia and Azerbaijan; legal status for Nagornyi Karabakh, which would be granted self-government within Azerbaijan; and security guarantees for the population of Nagornyi Karabakh. However, Armenia refused to accept the terms of the statement.

The election of Arkadi Ghukasyan as 'President' of Nagornyi Karabakh in September 1997 threatened to hamper further progress on reaching a settlement, owing to his rejection of the OSCE proposals. In an apparently significant change in Armenian policy, Ter-Petrosyan publicly admitted that Nagornyi Karabakh could expect neither to gain full independence, nor to be united with Armenia. However, ensuing public criticism in Armenia led to his resignation in February 1998; he was replaced by Kocharyan. In November the Armenian Government announced that it accepted the latest proposals put forward by the Minsk Group, which were based on the principle of a 'common state' (comprising Azerbaijan and Nagornyi Karabakh). The Azerbaijani Government, however, rejected the proposals, claiming that they threatened the country's territorial integrity.

Following an assassination attempt against Ghukasyan in March 2000, the former 'Minister of Defence' of Nagornyi Karabakh, Samvel Babayan, was charged with organizing the attack, as part of a purported coup. (He was sentenced to 14 years' imprisonment in February 2001, but was released in September 2004.) Legislative elections were held in Nagornyi Karabakh on 18 June 2000. On 11 August 2002 Ghukasyan was re-elected 'President', receiving 88.4% of the votes cast. Meanwhile, direct negotiations between the Armenian and Azerbaijani Presidents continued in 1999–2002, but with little progress. Negotiations resumed in 2004, under the administration of the new Azerbaijani President, İlham Äliyev.

On 25 January 2005 the Parliamentary Assembly of the Council of Europe adopted a resolution describing the occupation of Azerbaijani territory by ethnic Armenian forces as a 'grave violation' and stating that aspects of the conflict resembled 'ethnic cleansing'. The resolution also urged Azerbaijani leaders to establish contacts with the secessionist leaders (which they had hitherto refused to do) and refrain from the use of force. (Internationally unrecognized) legislative elections were held in Nagornyi Karabakh in June 2006. A referendum was held on 10 December, in which some 84% of eligible voters participated; a 'Constitution' defining the territory as an independent and sovereign state was approved by some 98.6% of the votes cast. At an election to the 'presidency' of Nagornyi Karabakh, which was conducted on 19 July 2007, Bako Sahakyan, a former head of the territory's security service, secured a decisive victory, with 85.1% of the votes cast. Sahakyan was installed on 7 September. His nomination of Arayik Harutyunyan, the leader of the Free Fatherland party, as 'Prime Minister' was approved on 3 September, and a new 'Government' was formed later that month. In November the Minsk Group presented a draft of 10 basic principles for resolving the conflict.

In March 2008 clashes between ethnic Armenian forces and Azerbaijani military units erupted at the 'line of contact' separating the two sides; five members of the Azerbaijani armed forces were confirmed to have been killed, while Azerbaijan claimed that a number of Armenian soldiers had also died. On 14 March a non-binding resolution, submitted by Azerbaijan, reaffirming its territorial integrity and demanding the withdrawal of all Armenian forces, was adopted by the UN General Assembly, with 39 votes in favour and seven opposing (with 100 abstentions); in addition to Armenia, countries that rejected the resolution included France, Russia and the USA. In June Äliyev met the recently installed Armenian President, Serzh Sargsyan (who had previously played a senior role in organizing the Nagornyi Karabakh military forces), for discussions in St Petersburg, Russia; the two heads of state agreed that negotiations on the situation in Nagornyi Karabakh continue on the basis of the 2007 proposals submitted by the Minsk Group. Negotiations continued throughout 2009, with three trilateral meetings between Äliyev, Sargsyan and Russian President Dmitrii Medvedev, in the capacity of mediator.

Following legislative elections in Nagornyi Karabakh on 23 May 2010, Free Fatherland emerged as the largest party in the new National Assembly, with 14 of the 33 seats. The Democratic Party of Artsakh obtained seven seats, while the local branch of the Armenian Revolutionary Federation—Dashnaktsutiun (Dashnaks) obtained six seats. Meanwhile, President Medvedev convened further meetings between Sargsyan and Äliyev in January and in June. However, shortly afterwards in June one Azerbaijani and four Armenian soldiers were killed, in what Armenia claimed was an attack by Azerbaijani forces at the 'line of contact' separating the two sides. In September it was reported that three Armenian and two Azerbaijani soldiers had been killed in a further clash. Further discussions between Sargsyan and Äliyev, convened by Medvedev in the Russian city of Astrakhan on 27 October, produced an agreement on a mutual exchange of prisoners of war and the return of the remains of those killed in clashes. Further discussions between Sargsyan, Äliyev and Medvedev, convened in the Russian city of Sochi in March 2011, resulted only in a joint declaration urging the full implementation of the agreement reached the previous October, and further trilateral negotiations were held in Kazan, Russia, in June. In September it was announced that, with the approval of the Azerbaijani Government, work had commenced on the construction of a wall, which was officially described as constituting 'protection from Armenian snipers', to separate Azerbaijani-inhabited centres of population from territory controlled by the Nagornyi Karabakh authorities. Another meeting between the Armenian and Azerbaijani Presidents took place in Sochi in January 2012. In June, however, further clashes, in which three Armenian and five Azerbaijani soldiers were killed, erupted at the 'line of contact'.

Recent developments: Sahakyan's re-election to a second term

In an internationally unrecognized poll on 19 July 2012, Sahakyan was decisively re-elected to a second term of office, securing 64.7% of the votes cast, defeating former deputy minister Vitaly Balasanyan, who received 31.5% of the votes, and another candidate. On 14 September Sahakyan's nomination to return Harutyunyan to the post of 'Prime Minister' was approved in the National Assembly.

Meanwhile, in August 2012 tensions between Armenia and Azerbaijan were exacerbated by the decision of President Äliyev to grant a pardon to an Azerbaijani army officer Lt Ramil Säfärov, who had been sentenced to life imprisonment, in 2006, for the killing of an Armenian officer while both were attending a military training course in Budapest, Hungary. Following outrage in Armenia, legislation providing for Armenia's official recognition of Nagornyi Karabakh was proposed by the opposition in the Armenian parliament in early September 2012, although the proposals were rejected by the ruling coalition. On 22 September Harutyunyan appointed a new 'Government' of the secessionist republic. Reports in the Armenian media, in late September, that flights would soon resume (after repeated delays) from a newly reconstructed airport near Stepanakert further antagonized the Azerbaijani Government, which threatened to shoot down any planes that entered the airspace over Nagornyi Karabakh. (The resumption of flights to and from the airport was further postponed.) In October a statement by a senior Armenian military official that Armenia was prepared to use long-range missiles, acquired from Russia from December 2010, to attack Azerbaijani facilities increased international concerns of an escalation in the conflict. In January 2013 the Azerbaijani Minister of Foreign Affairs, Elmar Mämmädyarov, and his Armenian counterpart met for mediated discussions in Paris, France, in an attempt to advance the peace process. A meeting between Presidents Sargsyan and Äliyev in the Austrian capital, Vienna, on 19 November (the first since January 2012) resulted in agreement to continue regular meetings, and was followed by further discussions between the two Ministers of Foreign Affairs in Kyiv, Ukraine, in early December 2013. However, mutual accusations regarding numerous ceasefire violations continued; an estimated 20 soldiers and officers had been killed on each side during 2013. An escalation in military activity at the 'line of contact' was reported prior to a further meeting in Paris of the Ministers of Foreign Affairs in January 2014: Azerbaijani planes entered the airspace of Nagornyi Karabakh, while the Azerbaijani authorities claimed to have repelled an incursion by Armenian troops. Following a visit to the region, in early February the Minsk Group co-chairs announced that the Governments of Armenia and Azerbaijan had stated their intention to strengthen observance of the ceasefire. Meanwhile, in January the Azerbaijan authorities issued official figures, according to which a total of 11,557 Azerbaijani soldiers had been killed in the conflict (fewer than previously claimed); the Armenian Government estimated Armenian and Nagornyi Karabakh troop fatalities of 6,500. In mid-March the Ministry of Foreign Affairs of Nagornyi Karabakh issued a statement describing the referendum held on 16 March, under Russian military occupation, in the Ukrainian territory of Crimea on the unification of that territory with Russia as constituting a 'manifestation of realization of the right of people to self-determination', while expressing the wish that the future status of Crimea be determined by solely peaceful and legal means.

PUBLIC HOLIDAYS

2015: 1–2 January (New Year), 6 January (Christmas), 8 March (Women's Day), 24 April (Armenian Genocide Commemoration Day), 1 May (Labour Day), 9 May (Victory Day and Liberation of Shushi Day), 28 May (Declaration of the First Armenian Republic Day), 2 September (Independence Day), 31 December (New Year's Eve).

Directory: Nagornyi Karabakh

The Government of the 'Republic of Nagornyi Karabakh'

Note: the territories proclaimed as, or administered by, the 'Republic of Nagornyi Karabakh' officially form part of the following districts (rayons) of Azerbaijan: Cäbrayıl; Füzuli; Kälbäcär; Laçın; Qubadlı; Şuşa; Xankändi; Xocalı; Xocavänd; and Zängilan.

HEAD OF STATE

President: BAKO SAHAKYAN.

COUNCIL OF MINISTERS

(April 2014)

Prime Minister: ARAYIK HARUTYUNYAN.

Deputy Prime Minister: ARTUR AGHABEKYAN.

Minister of Agriculture: ANDRANIK KHACHTRYAN.

Minister of Culture and Youth Affairs: NARINE AGHABALYAN.

Minister of Defence: MOVSES HAKOBYAN.

Minister of Education and Science: SLAVIK ASRYAN.

Minister of Finance and the Economy: SPARTAK TEVOSYAN.

Minister of Foreign Affairs: KAREN MIRZOYAN.

Minister of Health: HARUTYUN KUSHKYAN.

Minister of Industrial Infrastructure: HAKOB GHAHRAMANYAN.

Minister of Justice: ARARAT DANIELYAN.

Minister of Labour and Social Welfare: SAMVEL AVANESYAN.

Minister of Urban Planning: KAREN SHAHRAMANYAN.

MINISTRIES

Office of the President: 374430 Stepanakert, Petrvari 20 poghots 3; tel. and fax (47) 94-52-22; e-mail ps@president.nkr.am; internet www.president.nkr.am.

Office of the Prime Minister: 374430 Stepanakert, Petrvari 20 poghots 1; tel. and fax (47) 94-32-14; e-mail info@gov.nkr.am; internet gov.nkr.am.

Ministry of Agriculture: 375000 Stepanakert, Petrvari 20 poghots 1; tel. (47) 94-35-88; fax (47) 97-11-49; e-mail agro@minagro.nkr.am; internet www.minagro.nkr.am.

Ministry of Culture and Youth Affairs: Shushi, Hakhumyan 28; tel. and fax (47) 73-23-06; e-mail mcartsakh@mc.am; internet www.mc.am.

Ministry of Defence: 374430 Stepanakert; tel. and fax (47) 94-22-86; e-mail info@nkrmil.am; internet www.nkrmil.am.

Ministry of Education and Science: 374430 Stepanakert; tel. and fax (47) 94-22-86.

Ministry of Finance and the Economy: 374430 Stepanakert; tel. and fax (47) 94-22-86; internet www.minfin.nkr.am.

Ministry of Foreign Affairs: 374430 Stepanakert, Azatmartikneri poghota 28; tel. (47) 94-40-87; fax (47) 97-15-51; internet www.nkr.am.

Ministry of Health: 374430 Stepanakert, Petrvari 20 poghots 1; tel. (47) 97-12-57; e-mail moh@health.nkr.am; internet moh.nkr.am.

Ministry of Industrial Infrastructure: 374430 Stepanakert; tel. and fax (47) 94-22-86.

Ministry of Justice: 374430 Stepanakert, Petrvari 20 poghots; tel. and fax (47) 94-22-86; e-mail info@minjustnkr.am; internet minjustnkr.am.

Ministry of Labour and Social Welfare: 374430 Stepanakert, Azatmartikneri poghota 54; tel. and fax (47) 94-54-43; e-mail info@mss.nkr.am; internet www.mss.nkr.am.

Ministry of Urban Planning: 374430 Stepanakert; tel. and fax (47) 94-22-86.

President

Presidential Election, 19 July 2012

Candidates	Votes	% of votes
Bako Sahakyan	47,085	64.65
Vitaly Balasanyan	22,966	31.53
Arkadi Soghomonyan	594	0.82
Total*	72,833	100.00

* Including 2,188 invalid votes (representing 3.00% of the total).

Legislature

Azgayin Zhoghov
(National Assembly)

374430 Stepanakert; e-mail parlpress@ktsurf.net; internet www.nkrusa.org/country_profile/national_assembly.shtml.

Chairman: ASHOT GHULYAN.

General Election, 23 May 2010

Parties and blocs	Seats A*	Seats B*	Seats Total
Free Motherland	8	6	14
Democratic Party of Artsakh	5	2	7
Armenian Revolutionary Federation—Dashnaktsutyun	4	2	6
Independents	—	6	6
Total	17	16	33

* Of the 33 seats in the Azgayin Zhoghov, 17 (A) are awarded according to proportional representation on the basis of party lists, and 16 (B) are elected in single-mandate constituencies.

Election Commission

Central Election Commission: Stepanakert; Chair. RASHID PETROSYAN.

Political Organizations

The following are among the principal political parties operating in the 'Republic of Nagornyi Karabakh'.

Armenian Revolutionary Federation—Dashnaktsutiun (HYD) (Hay Yeghapokhakan—Dashnaktsutiun): c/o 374430 Stepanakert, National Assembly; local branch of HYD, headquartered in Yerevan, Armenia (q.v.).

Communist Party of Artsakh (Artsakhi Komunistakan Kusaktsutyun): Stepanakert; Chair. HRANT MELKUMYAN.

Democratic Party of Artsakh (Artsakhi Demokratakan Kusaktsutyun) (AZhK): c/o 374430 Stepanakert, National Assembly; fmrly Democratic Artsakh Union; Chair. ASHOT GHULYAN.

Free Fatherland (Azat Hayrenik Kusaktsutyun) (AHK): c/o 374430 Stepanakert, National Assembly; Chair. ARAYIK HARUTYUNYAN.

The Press

PRINCIPAL NEWSPAPER

Azat Artsakh (Free Artsakh): Stepanakert, Tumanyan poghots 63; tel. (47) 94-33-32; e-mail artsakhtert@gmail.com; internet www.artsakhtert.com; f. 1923 as *Geghtchouk (Villager)*; later renamed, in turn, *Khorherdayin (Soviet) Karabakh*, *Artsakh*, and *Nagornyi Karabakh Republic*; state-owned; Editor-in-Chief LEONID M. MARTIROSYAN.

PERIODICAL

Analyticon: Stepanakert; internet www.theanalyticon.com; f. 2008; monthly; political analysis, international relations; published with funding from the European Union; in Armenian, selection of articles is published online in Russian and English; Editor-in-Chief GEGAM BAGDASARYAN; circ. 500 (June 2011).

THE BAHAMAS

Introductory Survey

LOCATION, CLIMATE, LANGUAGE, RELIGION, FLAG, CAPITAL

The Commonwealth of the Bahamas consists of about 700 islands and more than 2,000 cays and rocks, extending from east of the Florida coast of the USA to just north of Cuba and Haiti, in the West Indies. The main islands are New Providence, Grand Bahama, Andros, Eleuthera and Great Abaco. Almost 70% of the population reside on the island of New Providence. The remaining members of the group are known as the 'Family Islands'. A total of 29 of the islands are inhabited. The climate is mild and sub-tropical, with average temperatures of about 30°C (86°F) in summer and 20°C (68°F) in winter. The average annual rainfall is about 1,000 mm (39 ins). The official language is English. Most of the inhabitants profess Christianity, the largest denominations being the Anglican, Baptist, Roman Catholic and Methodist Churches. The national flag (proportions 1 by 2) comprises three equal horizontal stripes, of blue, gold and blue, with a black triangle at the hoist, extending across one-half of the width. The capital is Nassau, on the island of New Providence.

CONTEMPORARY POLITICAL HISTORY

Historical Context

A former British colonial territory, the Bahamas attained internal self-government in January 1964, although the parliamentary system dates back to 1729. The first elections under universal adult suffrage were held in January 1967 for an enlarged House of Assembly. The Progressive Liberal Party (PLP), supported mainly by Bahamians of African origin and led by Lynden (later Sir Lynden) Pindling, formed a Government and Pindling became Premier. At the next elections, in April 1968, the PLP increased its majority at the expense of the United Bahamian Party (UBP), dominated by those of European origin.

In the elections of September 1972, which were dominated by the issue of independence, the PLP maintained its majority. Following a constitutional conference in December 1972, the Bahamas became an independent nation, within the Commonwealth, on 10 July 1973.

Domestic Political Affairs

The PLP increased its majority in the elections of July 1977 and was again returned to power in the June 1982 elections, with 32 of the 43 seats in the House of Assembly. The remaining 11 seats were won by the Free National Movement (FNM), which had reunited for the elections after splitting into several factions over the previous five years.

Trading in illicit drugs, mainly for the US market, became a major problem for the country, since many of the small islands and cays were used by drugs-traffickers in their smuggling activities. In 1983 allegations of widespread corruption, and the abuse of Bahamian bank secrecy laws by drugs-traffickers and US tax evaders, led Pindling to appoint a Royal Commission to investigate thoroughly the drugs trade in the Bahamas. The Commission's hearings revealed the extent to which money deriving from this trade had permeated Bahamian social and economic affairs. Evidence presented to the Commission led to the resignation of two cabinet ministers, and by the end of 1985 a total of 51 suspects had been indicted, including the assistant police commissioner. The Commission also revealed that Pindling had received several million dollars in gifts and loans from business executives, although it found no evidence of a link to the drugs trade. Despite this, the PLP was returned to power for a fifth consecutive term in June 1987.

The FNM won the August 1992 general election. Hubert Ingraham, the FNM leader, replaced Pindling as Prime Minister, and announced a programme of measures aimed at increasing the accountability of government ministers, combating corruption and revitalizing the economy.

A marked increase in violent crime in parts of New Providence led the Government to announce the creation, in March 1995, of a special police unit to address the problem. Meanwhile, the trade in illegal drugs remained widespread in the country. In October the Prime Minister introduced further legislation that aimed to prevent the abuse of Bahamian banks by drugs-traffickers, and thus improve the reputation of the country's financial sector, particularly in the USA.

The FNM increased its majority at a general election held in March 1997. Its win was attributed both to the Prime Minister's success in reversing the economic decline and the involvement of the PLP in various financial scandals. Most notably, Pindling was implicated in February in the findings of a public inquiry to investigate alleged corruption and misappropriation of funds in the three principal state corporations. Following the election, Pindling resigned as leader of the PLP and was replaced by Perry Christie.

In April 1998 the Government signed a convention drawn up by the Organization of American States (OAS, see p. 394) to ban illegal guns, amid a disturbing increase in gun-related crime. In September, following the murders of several tourists, the Prime Minister increased security in tourist areas, and announced plans to limit the right of appeal against death sentences. The hanging in October of two convicted murderers caused international controversy, despite growing public demand for execution as a deterrent against crime. (In March 2006 the Privy Council in the United Kingdom banned the mandatory death penalty for murder.)

The PLP takes power

At the general election held in May 2002 the PLP unexpectedly secured an overwhelming victory over the FNM, winning 29 of the 40 seats in the House of Assembly. The FNM retained seven seats and independent candidates won the remaining four seats.

Significant disruption was caused within the Bahamas' judicial system in November 2006 when a supreme court ruling concluded that the Cabinet had acted illegally in failing to appoint a commission to review judicial salaries and, consequently, had compromised the independence of the judiciary. Despite the furore, on 18 December a contingent of Law Lords from the Privy Council sat in the Court of Appeal in Nassau, the first instance of the country's final appellate court operating outside the United Kingdom. The Bahamas retained the Privy Council as its ultimate court of appeal, in contrast to several other Caribbean countries that had accepted the jurisdiction of the Caribbean Court of Justice following its inauguration in April 2005.

In December 2006 a National Health Insurance Act was approved by the House of Assembly. The new legislation allowed private sector participation in the national health care system in an effort to improve the quality of public health care. Doctors, employers and trade unions opposed the reform on the grounds that the scheme, which was to cost an estimated US $235m. per year, was not financially viable.

The return of the FNM

The PLP was defeated at the general election of 2 May 2007, retaining 18 seats in the 41-seat House of Assembly, while the FNM won 23 seats. Some 91.3% of eligible voters participated in the poll. The FNM formed a new Government, with party leader Hubert Ingraham sworn in as Prime Minister. Ingraham also assumed the portfolio for finance. The FNM had its majority in the House of Assembly increased to seven seats in January 2009 when former opposition deputy Kenyatta Gibson joined the party.

In July 2008 Ingraham reorganized his Cabinet following the resignation of Sidney Collie as Minister of Lands and Local Government after widespread criticism regarding his failure to act within electoral law in the recent local government elections.

In August 2009 the Minister of Legal Affairs and Attorney-General, Michael Barnett, resigned from his post in order to be sworn in as the Bahamas' new Chief Justice. The appointment of Barnett was criticized by members of the newly formed National Development Party for overtly politicizing the judiciary. Meanwhile, Sir Arthur Foulkes, one of the founders of the FNM, was inaugurated as Governor-General on 14 April 2010.

Following the announcement in early December 2010 by Cable & Wireless Communications of the United Kingdom that it had reached agreement with the Government to purchase a majority stake in the Bahamas Telecommunications Co (BTC), public sector trade unions threatened a nationwide strike in protest against the privatization. Tensions increased after a violent demonstration on 15 December in which union supporters clashed with police officers. The opposition PLP also raised objections to the sale. In January 2011 several communications workers unions lodged an appeal against the sale with the Supreme Court, but it was turned down in early February. Further clashes between protesters and police occurred later that month in front of the House of Assembly, which, nevertheless, adopted legislation in March approving the privatization. The Government claimed that the divestment was 'essential for the advancement of the Bahamian economy'.

A record 94 murders were committed in the Bahamas in 2010, raising fears of a violent crime epidemic. Ingraham stated that the illegal drugs trade was a major factor in the rising murder rate. A special court was established in January 2011 to expedite cases involving firearms offences, a particular concern given the high proportion of murders committed with such weapons. To complement this initiative, an illegal firearms task force was created at the same time, and earlier that month the police had announced the commencement of Operation Rapid Strike, which was to target violent crime. Other measures included the installation of security cameras in high crime areas and the introduction of an electronic system to monitor individuals granted bail. In May structural reforms within the judicial system were implemented in an attempt to streamline criminal trials, and a series of 10 anti-crime bills was approved later that year. In spite of the authorities' efforts, official data for 2011 indicated that rates of violent crime had risen by 9% and that the number of reported murders had reached a record 127.

The Government defended legislation, approved in November 2011 in preparation for the upcoming legislative elections, that reduced the number of constituencies in the country. The PLP claimed that this restructuring of electoral boundaries amounted to gerrymandering, although proponents maintained that the process had been unprejudiced and had been implemented to rebalance the number of voters in each constituency and to reduce public expenditure.

Recent developments: the PLP returns to government

The opposition PLP triumphed in the general election that was held on 7 May 2012, winning 48.6% of the votes cast and 29 of the 38 seats (reduced from 41 seats) in the House of Assembly. With 42.1% of the ballot, the FNM retained the remaining nine seats. The rate of participation by the electorate was 90.5%. Perry Christie, who had served as Prime Minister during 2002–07, once again assumed the premiership and also assigned himself the finance portfolio. Christie pledged to introduce an urban renewal scheme to address the islands' rising crime and unemployment rates, both of which had been prominent issues during the election campaign. Hubert Minnis was elected as FNM leader on 9 May 2012 after Ingraham had announced his retirement from public life. The PLP won control of Ingraham's vacated seat in a by-election in October.

In accordance with a pre-election pledge, the new Government opened negotiations with Cable & Wireless in late 2012 in an effort to regain a controlling stake in the BTC. However, Cable & Wireless expressed no interest in ceding majority control to the Government, and the talks were suspended in December. Christie conceded in February 2013 that the attempted renationalization had failed.

A proposal to create a national lottery and to legalise non-casino gambling operations, known locally as 'web shops', was rejected by the electorate in a referendum on 28 January 2013. A further plebiscite, concerning offshore petroleum production, was also expected to be conducted during 2015. Oil-drilling was a controversial issue in the Bahamas owing to the inherent risk of environmental damage, which could undermine the vital tourism sector.

The prevalence of violent crime and gang-related activity remained a serious concern. In September 2013 the Government announced that the Royal Bahamas Defence Force (RBDF) would be partially mobilized to provide the police with extra personnel, while the units responsible for investigating firearms offences, homicides and the illegal drugs trade were also to be strengthened. Additional proposals, publicized by the Christie administration in December, most notably included the expansion of police patrols, the creation of an anti-gang division and the introduction of new bail restrictions. Also in that month, Deputy Prime Minister Philip Davis was subjected to an armed robbery at his home, further increasing the perception that crime on the islands was out of control. The number of recorded murders rose from 111 in 2012 to 120 in 2013.

Foreign Affairs

Regional relations

The Bahamas' traditionally close relationship with the USA has been strained in recent years by the increasingly uncompromising attitude of the US authorities towards bank secrecy laws and drugs-smuggling in the islands. Relations with the USA, however, improved in 2004 after the Bahamian Government amended the country's extradition laws to give the state increased rights of appeal against the release of a suspect by the courts. These rights were exercised in September 2006 when leading drugs-trafficker Samuel Knowles was extradited to the USA. In 2008, as part of the implementation of the USA's Proliferation Security Initiative, an agreement was signed that would allow US officials to board and inspect Bahamian-registered ships if they were suspected of carrying weapons of mass destruction. In 2010 the two countries reached agreement on joint efforts to address drugs-trafficking and other organized crime. The USA contributed US $1.85m. to transnational crime prevention in the Bahamas in February 2014. The Bahamas and the USA held preliminary discussions in 2012 on the delimitation of their shared maritime boundary.

Meanwhile, relations with the Bahamas' other neighbours, Haiti and Cuba, were strained by the influx, and subsequent deportation, of large numbers of illegal immigrants from both countries. In 2003 the human rights organization Amnesty International released a report that accused the Bahamas of mistreating asylum-seekers from Cuba and Haiti, a charge denied by the Christie Government. In June 2007 the Narcotics Joint Task Force, comprising government representatives from the Bahamas, Turks and Caicos Islands and the USA, identified increased cocaine traffic from Hispaniola as an immediate threat and resolved to work towards a more comprehensive integration of their respective law enforcement agencies' efforts to combat the illegal transshipment of migrants and drugs in the region. In 2008 the country was again criticized in a report by Amnesty International for beatings and unlawful killings allegedly carried out by security forces, as well as for the continued deportation and reported ill-treatment of migrants. Following the earthquake that devastated Haiti in January 2010, the Government of the Bahamas suspended the deportation of Haitian refugees on humanitarian grounds; however, repatriation proceedings resumed in September. After many years of discussions, in October 2011 the Bahamas and Cuba finally delimited their shared border. The agreement was expected to precipitate petroleum exploration operations in Bahamian waters. Cuban activists organized a series of demonstrations outside the Bahamian consulate in Florida, USA, during mid-2013 in protest against alleged abuses perpetrated by the RBDF against Cuban asylum-seekers, as well as the Bahamian Government's policy of forced repatriation. A video recording apparently showing RBDF marines beating Cuban detainees was leaked to the media in June and brought the Bahamas' strict immigration regime under international scrutiny. An official investigation into the incident was ordered by the Christie administration, and an RBDF legal hearing was ongoing in early 2014.

Other external relations

Relations with China were strengthened in February 2009 by the signing of an agricultural agreement, which would see the Bahamas benefit from Chinese production and farming technology. These ties were reinforced by the visit of Wu Bangguo, Chairman of the Standing Committee of the National People's Congress of the People's Republic of China, to the Bahamas in September. As a result of the visit, a 20-year concessionary loan for the construction of a new four-lane highway and a grant for the National Stadium were agreed. Further co-operation agreements were signed in 2011 and 2013, pledging Chinese assistance in the construction and funding of various infrastructural schemes on the islands.

In 2000 the Bahamas was listed by the Financial Action Task Force (FATF, see p. 455) as a 'non-co-operative' jurisdiction, and by the Organisation for Economic Co-operation and Development (OECD, see p. 379) as a tax haven. The Bahamas also remained classified as a 'Country of Primary Concern' in the US International Narcotics Control Strategy Report, partly because of its banking secrecy laws and the size of its 'offshore' financial sector. The Government responded by establishing a Financial

Intelligence Unit and by adopting legislation intended to encourage transparency in the sector. As a result, in 2001 the FATF removed the Bahamas from its 'black list'. In January 2002 an agreement to share information on tax matters with the USA was signed, while in March OECD accepted the Bahamas' commitment to improve the transparency of its financial sector. However, in 2005 a US Department of State report on global money-laundering and drugs-trafficking listed the Bahamas as a 'major money laundering country'. In 2009 OECD placed the Bahamas on its 'grey list' of nations that had failed to sign a sufficient number of tax information exchange agreements with other states. The country was removed from the list in 2010, after signing 18 such agreements, and received positive assessments from the organization during 2011–13.

CONSTITUTION AND GOVERNMENT

Although a representative House of Assembly was first established in 1729, universal adult suffrage was not introduced until 1962. A new Constitution for the Commonwealth of the Bahamas came into force at independence, in 1973. Legislative power is vested in the bicameral Parliament. The Senate has 16 members, of whom nine are appointed by the Governor-General on the advice of the Prime Minister, four by the Leader of the Opposition and three after consultation with the Prime Minister. The House of Assembly has 38 members, elected for five years (subject to dissolution) by universal adult suffrage. Executive power is vested in the British monarch, represented by a Governor-General, who is appointed on the Prime Minister's recommendation and who acts, in almost all matters, on the advice of the Cabinet. The Governor-General appoints the Prime Minister and, on the latter's recommendation, selects the other ministers. The Cabinet is responsible to the House of Assembly. The Constitution provides for a Supreme Court and a Court of Appeal, with further appeals allowed to the Privy Council in the United Kingdom.

REGIONAL AND INTERNATIONAL CO-OPERATION

The Bahamas is a member of the Caribbean Community (CARICOM—although it is not a member of CARICOM's Common Market, see p. 223), of the Organization of American States (OAS, see p. 394), of the Inter-American Development Bank (IDB, see p. 331), of the Association of Caribbean States (see p. 449), and of the Community of Latin American and Caribbean States (see p. 464), which was formally inaugurated in December 2011. The Bahamas became a member of the UN following independence, in 1973. The Government applied for membership of the World Trade Organization (see p. 434) in 2001, and accession talks began in 2010; negotiations were progressing slowly in 2014. The Bahamas is a member of the Commonwealth (see p. 236) and is a signatory of the Cotonou Agreement (see p. 324) with the European Union (see p. 273).

ECONOMIC AFFAIRS

In 2011, according to estimates by the World Bank, the Bahamas' gross national income (GNI), measured at average 2009–11 prices, was US $7,795m., equivalent to US $21,280 per head (or $29,740 per head on an international purchasing-power parity basis). During 2003–12 it was estimated that the population increased at an average annual rate of 1.8%. In 2003–11 gross domestic product (GDP) per head decreased, in real terms, at an average annual rate of 1.2%. According to official estimates, overall GDP increased, in real terms, at an average annual rate of 0.7% in 2003–12; GDP increased by a preliminary 1.8% in 2012.

Agriculture, hunting, forestry and fishing together accounted for only 1.9% of GDP and engaged an estimated 3.0% of the employed labour force in 2012. Crops grown for export included cucumbers, tomatoes, pineapples, papayas, avocados, mangoes, limes and other citrus fruits. The development of commercial fishing in recent years has concentrated on conchs and crustaceans. In 2011 exports of Caribbean spiny lobster (crawfish) accounted for 17.9% of total domestic exports. There is also some exploitation of pine forests in the northern Bahamas. According to official estimates, in 2003–12 agricultural GDP decreased at an average annual rate of 4.5%; sectoral GDP for agriculture decreased by an estimated 9.0% in 2012.

Industry (comprising mining, manufacturing, construction and utilities) employed an estimated 12.5% of the working population and provided 16.6% of GDP in 2012. According to official estimates, in 2003–12 industrial GDP increased at an average annual rate of 3.0%; sectoral GDP decreased by an estimated 3.3% in 2011, but increased by a preliminary 14.9% in 2012.

Mining and quarrying contributed only 0.6% of GDP in 2012. The sector (including utilities) provided an estimated 1.9% of employment in the same year. The islands' principal mineral resource is salt. Minerals provided 38.6% of total export earnings in 2012. According to official estimates, in 2003–12 mining GDP remained constant; sectoral GDP decreased by an estimated 20.7% in 2011 and by a preliminary 8.4% in 2012.

The manufacturing sector contributed some 4.2% of GDP and employed 4.3% of the working population in 2012. According to official estimates, in 2003–12 manufacturing GDP increased at an average annual rate of 1.0%; sectoral GDP declined by an estimated 1.8% in 2011, but increased by a preliminary 16.4% in 2012. The principal branches of manufacturing were chemicals, beverages, and printing and publishing.

Construction contributed some 9.8% to the GDP and employed 6.3% of the employed labour force in 2012. Activity in the construction sector fluctuated; according to official estimates, in 2003–12 construction GDP increased at an average annual rate of 4.9%. After a decrease of 3.6% in 2011, sectoral GDP increased by a preliminary 24.3% in 2012.

Most of the energy requirements of the Bahamas are fulfilled by the petroleum that Venezuela and Mexico provide. Under the Petrocaribe agreement with Venezuela, the Bahamas was allowed to purchase petroleum at reduced prices. Imports of mineral products accounted for 24.0% of the total value of imports in 2012.

Service industries constitute the principal sectors of the economy, providing some 81.5% of GDP and about 84.5% of total employment in 2012. According to official estimates, in 2003–11 services GDP increased at an average annual rate of 2.7%; sectoral GDP increased by a preliminary 0.2% in 2012. In 2012 a total of 1,531 vessels were registered under the Bahamian flag. With a combined displacement of 56.1m. grt, the fleet is the sixth largest in the world. Banking is the second most important economic activity in the Bahamas, and there is a large 'offshore' financial sector. A stock exchange was trading the shares of 28 local companies in February 2014. Tourism is the predominant sector of the economy, directly and indirectly accounting for almost one-half of GDP and employing about one-third of the working population. The majority of stop-over visitors come from the USA (some 80.5% in 2008), although attempts were made to attract visitors from other countries following amendments in 2007 to the Western Hemisphere Travel Initiative requiring all US citizens travelling to and from the Caribbean to hold a valid passport. Visitor arrivals increased from 5.59m. in 2011 to 5.94m. in 2012. The global economic downturn, particularly in the USA, had an impact on the tourism sector; however, receipts recovered from 2010, reaching a provisional $2,367m. in 2012. The Bahamas receives more cruise ship arrivals annually than any other Caribbean destination.

According to preliminary official figures, in 2012 the Bahamas recorded a visible merchandise trade deficit of B $2,401.5m., and there was a deficit of $1,457.7m. on the current account of the balance of payments. The USA is the principal trading partner of the Bahamas, providing 87.1% of non-petroleum imports and taking 63.8% of non-petroleum exports in 2012. The principal imports in 2012 were mineral products, machinery and transport equipment, manufactured goods classified chiefly by materials, food and live animals, products of chemical or allied industries, and miscellaneous manufactured articles. In that year the principal exports were mineral products, products of chemical or allied industries, food and live animals, and machinery and transport equipment.

According to preliminary official figures, in 2013/14 there was a budgetary deficit of B $377.3m. The Bahamas' general government gross debt was B $4,100m. in 2012, equivalent to 51.2% of GDP. In 2011 the external debt of the central Government was some $798.5m. In 2005, the cost of servicing long-term debt and repayments to the IMF was equivalent to 3.3% of the value of exports of goods, services and income (excluding workers' remittances). The annual rate of inflation averaged 2.6% in 2005–12; consumer prices increased by 1.2% in 2012. The rate of unemployment stood at some 16.2% of the labour force in May 2013.

The Bahamian economy is heavily reliant upon tourism and the financial services industry, particularly the 'offshore' banking sector. In February 2011 construction began of a US $2,600m. resort on Nassau, the Baha Mar, to be financed, in part, by the Export-Import Bank of China. The project had been criticized for its recruitment of foreign, mostly Chinese, workers, rather than utilizing Bahamians, although proponents argued that up to 7,000 full-time jobs would be created for local workers once the resort was built. The economy contracted sharply in 2009 owing to the impact of the global financial crisis, and only negligible growth was recorded in the following year. Nevertheless, a gradual recovery in the tourism sector, rising foreign direct investment and the commencement of work on the Baha Mar resort resulted in real GDP expansion of 1.7% in 2011, 1.8% in 2012 and an estimated 1.9% in 2013, according to the IMF. However, the economic crisis had weakened the Government's financial position considerably, and the fiscal deficit and debt-to-GDP ratio had increased to unsustainable levels by 2012. The IMF and international credit rating agencies expressed concern about the country's deteriorating fiscal situation, prompting the Government to announce plans to reduce public spending. Moreover, the taxation system was restructured in mid-2013 and a value-added tax was due to be introduced in mid-2014. Despite what the IMF termed the 'painfully slow pace' of economic recovery, GDP growth of 2.1% was forecast in 2014, driven by the ongoing tourism recovery and the expected inauguration of the Baha Mar resort.

PUBLIC HOLIDAYS

2015: 1 January (New Year's Day), 3 April (Good Friday), 6 April (Easter Monday), 25 May (Whit Monday), 5 June (Labour Day), 10 July (Independence Day), 3 August (Emancipation Day), 12 October (Discovery Day/Columbus Day/National Heroes Day), 25–26 December (Christmas).

Statistical Survey

Source (unless otherwise stated): Department of Statistics, Clarence A. Bain Bldg, Thompson Blvd, POB N-3904, Nassau; tel. 302-2400; fax 325-5149; e-mail dpsdp@bahamas.gov.bs; internet statistics.bahamas.gov.bs/index.php; The Central Bank of the Bahamas, Frederick St, POB N-4868, Nassau; tel. 322-2193; fax 322-4321; e-mail cbob@centralbankbahamas.com; internet www.centralbankbahamas.com.

AREA AND POPULATION

Area: 13,939 sq km (5,382 sq miles).

Population: 303,611 at census of 1 May 2000; 351,461 (males 170,257, females 181,204) at census of 3 May 2010; 364,000 at mid-2014 (official estimate). *By Island* (census of 2010): New Providence 246,329; Grand Bahama 51,368; Eleuthera 8,202; Andros 7,490; Others 38,072.

Density (at mid-2014): 26.1 per sq km.

Population by Age and Sex ('000, official estimates at mid-2014): *0–14:* 87.0 (males 44.8, females 42.2); *15–64:* 252.6 (males 122.8, females 129.8); *65 and over:* 24.4 (males 10.2, females 14.2); *Total* 364.0 (males 177.8, females 186.2).

Principal Town (incl. suburbs, UN estimate): Nassau (capital) 250,000 in mid-2011. Source: UN, *World Urbanization Prospects: The 2011 Revision*.

Births, Marriages and Deaths (2011, provisional): Registered live births 4,670 (birth rate 13.3 per 1,000); Registered deaths 2,127 (death rate 6.1 per 1,000); Registered marriages 3,915 (marriage rate 11.2 per 1,000).

Life Expectancy (years at birth): 74.8 (males 71.8; females 77.9) in 2011. Source: World Bank, World Development Indicators database.

Economically Active Population (persons aged 15 years and over, excl. armed forces, 2012): Agriculture, hunting, forestry and fishing 4,955; Mining, quarrying, electricity, gas and water 3,095; Manufacturing 7,150; Construction 10,400; Wholesale and retail trade 26,975; Hotels and restaurants 24,480; Transport, storage and communications 13,945; Finance, insurance, real estate and other business services 25,370; Community, social and personal services 48,885; *Total employed* 165,255 (males 82,065, females 83,190); Unemployed 26,950 (males 13,440, females 13,510); *Total labour force* 192,205 (males 95,505, females 96,700). *Mid-2013:* Total employed 163,995 (males 83,160, females 80,835); Unemployed 31,665 (males 15,965, females 15,700); Total labour force 195,660 (males 99,125, females 96,535).

HEALTH AND WELFARE

Key Indicators

Total Fertility Rate (children per woman, 2011): 1.9.

Under-5 Mortality Rate (per 1,000 live births, 2011): 16.

HIV/AIDS (estimated % of persons aged 15–49, 2011): 2.8.

Physicians (per 1,000 head, 1998): 1.1.

Hospital Beds (per 1,000 head, 2009): 3.1.

Health Expenditure (2010): US $ per head (PPP): 2,348.

Health Expenditure (2010): % of GDP: 7.5.

Health Expenditure (2010): public (% of total): 46.8.

Access to Water (% of persons, 2011): 96.

Total Carbon Dioxide Emissions ('000 metric tons, 2010): 2,464.2.

Total Carbon Dioxide Emissions Per Head (metric tons, 2010): 6.8.

Human Development Index (2012): ranking: 49.

Human Development Index (2012): value: 0.794.

For sources and definitions, see explanatory note on p. vi.

AGRICULTURE, ETC.

Principal Crops ('000 metric tons, 2012 unless otherwise indicated): Sweet potatoes 0.8 (FAO estimate); Sugar cane 57.5 (FAO estimate); Bananas 9.5; Lemons and limes 3.1; Grapefruit and pomelos 20.4; Vegetables (incl. melons) 29.4; Fruits (excl. melons) 48.3.

Livestock ('000 head, year ending September 2012, FAO estimates): Cattle 0.8; Pigs 5.0; Sheep 6.6; Goats 15.0; Poultry 3,000.

Livestock Products ('000 metric tons, 2012, FAO estimates): Chicken meat 6.6; Cows' milk 0.8; Goat's milk 2.0; Hen eggs 1.3.

Forestry ('000 cubic metres, 2012, FAO estimates): *Roundwood Removals (excl. bark):* Sawlogs and veneer logs 17 (output assumed to be unchanged since 1992); *Sawnwood Production (incl. railway sleepers):* Coniferous (softwood) 1.4 (output assumed to be unchanged since 1970).

Fishing (metric tons, live weight, 2011): Nassau grouper 123; Snappers 537; Caribbean spiny lobster 8,504; Stromboid conchs 750; Total catch (all capture) 10,223.

Source: FAO.

MINING

Production ('000 metric tons, 2011, preliminary figures): Unrefined salt 1,000.0; Aragonite 1.5. Source: US Geological Survey.

INDUSTRY

Production (million kWh, 2009): Electric energy 2,068.7.

FINANCE

Currency and Exchange Rates: 100 cents = 1 Bahamian dollar (B $). *Sterling, US Dollar and Euro Equivalents* (31 December 2013): £1 sterling = B $1.647; US $1 = B $1.000; €1 = B $1.379; B $100 = £60.72 = US $100.00 = €72.51. *Exchange Rate:* Since February 1970 the official exchange rate, applicable to most transactions, has been US $1 = B $1, i.e. the Bahamian dollar has been at par with the US dollar. There is also an investment currency rate, applicable to certain capital transactions between residents and non-residents and to direct investments outside the Bahamas. Since 1987 this exchange rate has been fixed at US $1 = B $1.225.

General Budget (B $ million, 2013/14, budget, preliminary): *Revenue:* Taxation 1,325.8 (Taxes on international trade and transactions 660.2; Taxes on property 110.6; Taxes on companies 180.0); Other current revenue 159.4; Capital revenue 0.0; Grants 8.0; Total 1,493.2. *Expenditure:* Current expenditure 1,635.2 (Wages and salaries 649.6; Goods and services 314.5; Interest payments 229.4; Subsidies and transfers 441.7); Capital expenditure and net lending 235.3; Total 1,870.5.

International Reserves (B $ million at 31 December 2012): IMF special drawing rights 28.4; Reserve position in IMF 9.6; Foreign exchange 808.9; Total 846.9. Source: IMF, *International Financial Statistics*.

Money Supply (B $ million at 31 December 2012): Currency outside banks 217; Demand deposits at deposit money banks 1,311; Total money (incl. others) 1,537. Source: IMF, *International Financial Statistics*.

Cost of Living (Consumer Price Index; base: 2005 = 100): All items 113.4 in 2010; 118.0 in 2011; 119.4 in 2012. Source: IMF, *International Financial Statistics*.

Gross Domestic Product (B $ million at current prices): 7,888.1 in 2010; 7,872.6 in 2011; 8,149.0 in 2012 (preliminary).

Expenditure on the Gross Domestic Product (B $ million at current prices, 2012, preliminary): Government final consumption expenditure 1,214.8; Private final consumption expenditure 5,709.6; Change in stocks 102.2; Gross fixed capital formation 2,597.6; *Total domestic expenditure* 9,624.2; Exports of goods and services 3,649.8; *Less* Imports of goods and services 5,125.0; *GDP in purchasers' values* 8,149.0.

Gross Domestic Product by Economic Activity (B $ million at current prices, 2012, preliminary): Agriculture, hunting, forestry and fishing 156.4; Mining and quarrying 51.1; Manufacturing 337.9; Electricity and water 158.5; Construction 788.7; Wholesale and retail trade 828.9; Restaurants and hotels 983.1; Transport, storage and communications 698.8; Finance, insurance, real estate and business services 2,536.6; Government services 438.3; Education 320.4; Health 293.2; Other community, social and personal services 481.5; *Sub-total* 8,073.4; *Less* Financial intermediation services indirectly measured 615.9; *Gross value added in basic prices* 7,457.4; Net indirect taxes 691.6; *GDP in purchasers' values* 8,149.0.

Balance of Payments (B $ million, 2012, preliminary): Exports of goods f.o.b. 984.0; Imports of goods f.o.b. –3,385.5; *Trade balance* –2,401.5; Services (net) 1,203.0; *Balance on goods and services* –1,198.5; Other income (net) –269.7; *Balance on goods, services and income* –1,468.2; Current transfers (net) 10.5; *Current balance* –1,457.7; Capital account (net) –7.3; Financial account (net) 1,141.4; Net errors and omissions 248.7; *Overall balance* –74.7.

EXTERNAL TRADE

Principal Commodities (B $ million, 2012, distribution according to HS): *Imports c.i.f.:* Food and live animals 483.7; Beverages and tobacco 83.6; Crude materials, inedible, excl. fuels 68.0; Mineral products 874.8; Products of chemical or allied industries 398.3; Manufactured goods classified chiefly by material 524.3; Machinery and transport equipment 688.0; Miscellaneous manufactured articles 382.2; Total (incl. others) 3,647.0. *Exports (incl. re-exports) f.o.b.:* Food and live animals 81.7; Mineral products 319.7; Products of chemical or allied industries 281.6; Machinery and transport equipment 63.8; Total (incl. others) 827.7.

Principal Trading Partners (non-petroleum transactions, B $ million, 2012): *Imports c.i.f.:* Canada 19.9; United Kingdom 17.5; USA 2,414.3; Total (incl. others) 2,772.2. *Exports f.o.b.:* Canada 25.9; United Kingdom 12.4; USA 357.1; Total (incl. others) 559.9.

TRANSPORT

Road Traffic (vehicles in use, '000): Passenger cars 90 (2002); Commercial vehicles 25 (2001); Total 27,058 (2007). Sources: IRF, *World Road Statistics*; Auto and Truck International (Illinois), *World Automotive Market Report*.

Shipping: *Flag Registered Fleet* (at 31 December 2013): Number 1,493; Displacement ('000 grt) 56,663 (Source: Lloyd's List Intelligence—www.lloydslistintelligence.com). *International Sea-borne Freight Traffic* (estimates, '000 metric tons, 1990): Goods loaded 5,920; Goods unloaded 5,705 (Source: UN, *Monthly Bulletin of Statistics*).

Civil Aviation (2009): Kilometres flown (million) 8; Passengers carried ('000) 979; Passenger-km (million) 276; Total ton-km of freight (million) 25 (Source: UN, *Statistical Yearbook*). *Passengers carried* ('000): 968 in 2010; 1,056 in 2011; 1,048 in 2012 (Source: World Bank, World Development Indicators database).

TOURISM

Visitor Arrivals ('000): 5,255 (1,295 by air, 3,960 by sea) in 2010; 5,588 (1,268 by air, 4,320 by sea) in 2011; 5,940 (1,357 by air, 4,583 by sea) in 2012.

Tourism Receipts (B $ million, excl. passenger transport): 2,147 in 2010; 2,254 in 2011; 2,367 in 2012 (provisional) (Source: partly World Tourism Organization).

COMMUNICATIONS MEDIA

Telephones: 137,000 main lines in use in 2012.

Mobile Cellular Telephones: 254,000 subscribers in 2012.

Internet Subscribers: 24,700 in 2010.

Broadband Subscribers: 9,700 in 2012.

Source: International Telecommunication Union.

EDUCATION

Pre-primary (2002/03, unless otherwise indicated): 20 schools (1996/97); 338 teachers (all females); 3,771 pupils (males 1,931, females 1,840).

Primary (2009/10 unless otherwise indicated): 113 schools (1996/97); 2,402 teachers (males 192, females 2,210); 33,977 pupils (males 17,139 females 16,838).

Secondary (2009/10 unless otherwise indicated): 37 junior/senior high schools (1990); 2,837 teachers (males 669, females 2,168); 34,406 students (males 16,917, females 17,489).

Tertiary (1987): 249 teachers; 5,305 students. In 2002 there were 3,463 students registered at the College of the Bahamas.

Pupil-teacher Ratio (primary education, UNESCO estimate): 14.1 in 2009/10.

Sources: UNESCO, *Statistical Yearbook*; UN, Economic Commission for Latin America and the Caribbean, *Statistical Yearbook*; Caribbean Development Bank, *Social and Economic Indicators 2001*.

Adult Literacy Rate (UNESCO estimates): 95.0% (males 95.0%; females 95.0%) in 2003. Source: UN Development Programme, *Human Development Report*.

Directory

The Government

HEAD OF STATE

Queen: HM Queen ELIZABETH II.

Governor-General: Sir ARTHUR FOULKES (took office 14 April 2010).

THE CABINET
(April 2014)

The Cabinet is formed by the Progressive Liberal Party.

Prime Minister and Minister of Finance: PERRY GLADSTONE CHRISTIE.

Deputy Prime Minister and Minister of Works and Urban Development: PHILIP EDWARD BRAVE DAVIS.

Minister of Foreign Affairs and Immigration: FREDERICK MITCHELL.

Minister of National Security: Dr BERNARD J. NOTTAGE.

Minister of Tourism: OBEDIAH WILCHCOMBE.

Minister of Agriculture, Marine Resources and Local Government: ALFRED GRAY.

Minister of Education, Science and Technology: JEROME FITZGERALD.

Minister of Financial Services: RYAN PINDER.

Minister of Health: Dr PERRY GOMEZ.

Minister of Transport and Aviation: GLENYS HANNA MARTIN.

Minister of Environment and Housing: KENDRED DORSETT.

Attorney-General and Minister of Legal Affairs: ALLYSON MAYNARD GIBSON.

Minister of Labour and National Insurance: SHANE GIBSON.

Minister of Youth, Sports and Culture: DANIEL JOHNSON.

Minister of Social Services and Community Development: MELANIE GRIFFIN.

Minister of Grand Bahama Affairs: Dr MICHAEL DARVILLE.

Minister of State in the Ministry of Finance: MICHAEL HALKITIS.

Minister of State in the Ministry of National Security: KEITH BELL.

Minister of State in the Ministry of Legal Affairs: DAMIAN GOMEZ.

Minister of State in the Ministry of Transport and Aviation: HOPE STRACHAN.

Minister in the Office of the Prime Minister with responsibility for Investments: KHAALIS ROLLE.

MINISTRIES

Attorney-General's Office and Ministry of Legal Affairs: Post Office Bldg, 7th Floor, East Hill St, POB N-3007, Nassau; tel. 322-1141; fax 322-2255; e-mail attorneygeneral@bahamas.gov.bs.

Office of the Prime Minister: Sir Cecil Wallace-Whitfield Centre, West Bay St, POB CB-10980, Nassau; tel. 327-5826; fax 327-5806; e-mail primeminister@bahamas.gov.bs.

Office of the Deputy Prime Minister: John F. Kennedy Dr., POB N-8156, Nassau; tel. 322-4830; fax 326-7344.

Ministry of Agriculture, Marine Resources and Local Government: Levy Bldg, East Bay St, POB N-3028, Nassau; tel. 328-27002; fax 322-8632; e-mail minagriculturemarine@bahamas.gov.bs.

Ministry of Education, Science and Technology: Thompson Blvd, POB N-3913, Nassau; tel. 502-2700; fax 322-8491; e-mail info@bahamaseducation.com; internet www.bahamaseducation.com.

Ministry of Environment and Housing: Charlotte House, Charlotte St, POB N-275, Nassau; tel. 322-6005; fax 326-2650.

Ministry of Finance: Sir Cecil Wallace-Whitfield Centre, West Bay St, POB N-3017, Nassau; tel. 327-1530; fax 327-1618; e-mail mofgeneral@bahamas.gov.bs; internet www.bahamas.gov.bs/finance.

Ministry of Foreign Affairs and Immigration: Goodman's Bay Corporate Centre, West Bay St, POB N-3746, Nassau; tel. 322-7624; fax 356-3967; e-mail mofa@bahamas.gov.bs.

Ministry of Health: Poinciana Bldg, Meeting and Augusta Sts, POB N-3730, Nassau; tel. 502-4700; fax 502-4711; internet www.bahamas.gov.bs/health.

Ministry of National Security: Churchill Bldg, 3rd Floor, Rawson Sq., POB N-3217, Nassau; tel. 356-6792; fax 356-6087; e-mail nationalsecurity@bahamas.gov.bs.

Ministry of Public Service: Poinciana Hill, Meeting and Augusta Sts, POB N-3915, Nassau; tel. 502-7200; fax 326-6929.

Ministry of Social Services and Community Development: Post Office, East Hill St, Nassau; tel. 325-2261; fax 356-6228.

Ministry of Tourism: Bolam House, George St, POB N-3701, Nassau; tel. 302-2000; fax 302-2098; e-mail tourism@bahamas.com; internet www.bahamas.com.

Ministry of Transport and Aviation: Manx Bldg, West Bay St, Nassau; tel. 328-2701; fax 328-1324; e-mail admin@mowt.bs.

Ministry of Works and Urban Development: John F. Kennedy Dr., POB N-8156, Nassau; tel. 322-4830; fax 326-7344; e-mail publicworks@bahamas.gov.bs.

Ministry of Youth, Sports and Culture: Thompson Blvd, POB N-4891, Nassau; tel. 502-0600; fax 326-0085; internet youthmysc@bahamas.gov.bs.

Legislature

PARLIAMENT

Senate

President: SHARON WILSON.

There are 16 nominated members.

House of Assembly

Speaker: KENDAL MAJOR.

General Election, 7 May 2012

Party	% of votes	Seats
Progressive Liberal Party (PLP)	48.62	29
Free National Movement (FNM)	42.09	9
Democratic National Alliance (DNA)	8.48	—
Independent	0.75	—
Total valid votes	100.00	38

Election Commission

Office of the Parliamentary Commissioner: c/o Ministry of National Security, Farrington Rd, POB N-1653, Nassau; tel. 397-2000; fax 322-1637; e-mail errolbethel@hotmail.com; internet www.bahamas.gov.bs/parliamentary; Commr ERROL W. BETHEL.

Political Organizations

Bahamas Constitution Party (BCP): Nassau; internet hope4bahamalandbcp.blogspot.in; conservative, Christian; Leader S. ALI MCINTOSH.

Democratic National Alliance (DNA): Prince Charles Dr. Shopping Center (Above KFC), Prince Charles Dr., POB AP59217, Nassau; tel. 326-9362; e-mail info@mydnaparty.org; internet www.mydnaparty.org; f. 2011; Leader BRANVILLE MCCARTNEY.

Free National Movement (FNM): 144 Mackey St, POB N-10713, Nassau; tel. 393-7853; fax 393-7914; e-mail info@fnm2012.org; internet www.fnm2012.org; f. 1972; incorporated Bahamas Democratic Movt (f. 2000) in 2011; Leader Dr HUBERT MINNIS.

Progressive Liberal Party (PLP): Sir Lynden Pindling Centre, PLP House, Farrington Rd, POB N-547, Nassau; tel. 326-9688; fax 328-0808; internet www.myplp.com; f. 1953; centrist party; Chair. BRADLEY ROBERTS; Leader PERRY G. CHRISTIE.

Diplomatic Representation

EMBASSIES IN THE BAHAMAS

Brazil: Sandringham House, 83 Shirley St, POB SS-6265, Nassau; tel. 356-7613; fax 356-7617; e-mail brasembnassau@yahoo.com.br; Chargé d'affaires a.i. ALEXANDRE DE AZEVEDO SILVEIRA.

China, People's Republic: East Shirley St, POB SS-6389, Nassau; tel. 393-1415; fax 393-0733; e-mail chinaemb_bs@mfa.gov.cn; internet bs.china-embassy.org; Ambassador YUAN GUISEN.

Cuba: Miller House, 61 Collins Ave, POB EE-15679, Nassau; tel. 356-3473; fax 356-3472; e-mail cubanembassy@coralwave.com; internet www.cubadiplomatica.cu/bahamas; Ambassador ENERSTO SOBERÓN GUZMÁN.

Haiti: Sears House, Shirley St and Sears Rd, POB N-3036, Nassau; tel. 326-0325; fax 322-7712; Ambassador ANTONIO RODRIGUE.

San Marino: 291, The Office of the Old Fort Bay, Bldg 2, Western Rd, POB N-7776, Nassau; tel. 362-4382; fax 362-4669; e-mail smembassy@coralwave.com; Ambassador GIULIA GHIRARDI BORGHESE.

USA: Mosmar Bldg, Queen St, POB N-8197, Nassau; tel. 322-1181; fax 328-7838; e-mail embassynassau@state.gov; internet nassau.usembassy.gov; Chargé d'affaires a.i. JOHN DINKELMAN.

Judicial System

The Judicial Committee of the Privy Council (based in the United Kingdom), the Bahamas Court of Appeal, the Supreme Court and the Magistrates' Courts are the main courts of the Bahamian judicial system.

All courts have both a criminal and civil jurisdiction. The Magistrates' Courts are presided over by professionally qualified Stipendiary and Circuit Magistrates in New Providence and Grand Bahama, and by Island Administrators sitting as Magistrates in the Family Islands.

Whereas all magistrates are empowered to try offences that may be tried summarily, a Stipendiary and Circuit Magistrate may, with the consent of the accused, also try certain less serious indictable offences. Magistrates also hear inquests, although their jurisdiction is limited by law.

The Supreme Court consists of the Chief Justice, two Senior Justices and six Justices. The Supreme Court also sits in Freeport, with two Justices.

Appeals in almost all matters lie from the Supreme Court to the Court of Appeal, with further appeal in certain instances to the Judicial Committee of the Privy Council.

Supreme Court of the Bahamas: Bank Lane, POB N-167, Nassau; tel. 322-3315; fax 323-6463; e-mail registrar@courts.gov.bs; internet www.courts.gov.bs; Chief Justice MICHAEL L. BARNETT.

Court of Appeal: Claughton House, 3rd Floor, POB N-3209, Nassau; tel. 328-5400; fax 323-4659; e-mail info@courtofappeal.org.bs; internet www.courtofappeal.org.bs; Pres. ANITA ALLEN.

Office of the Registrar-General: Shirley House, 50 Shirley St, POB N-532, Nassau; tel. 397-8954; e-mail registrargeneral@

bahamas.gov.bs; internet www.bahamas.gov.bs/rgd; Registrar-Gen. JACINDA P. BUTLER.

Religion

Most of the population profess Christianity, but there are also small communities of Jews and Muslims.

CHRISTIANITY

Bahamas Christian Council: POB N-3103, Nassau; tel. 326-7114; f. 1948; 27 mem. churches; Pres. Rev. RANFORD PATTERSON.

The Baptist Church

According to the latest available census figures, some 35% of the population are Baptists.

Bahamas National Baptist Missionary and Educational Convention: Blue Hill Rd, POB N-4435, Nassau; tel. 325-0729; fax 326-5473; internet bahamasbaptist.com; mem. of the Baptist World Alliance; 270 churches and c. 75,000 mems; Pres. Dr ANTHONY CARROLL.

The Roman Catholic Church

The Bahamas comprises the single archdiocese of Nassau. According to the latest available census figures (2000), some 14% of the population are Roman Catholics. The Archbishop participates in the Antilles Episcopal Conference (whose Secretariat is based in Port of Spain, Trinidad). The Turks and Caicos Islands are also under the jurisdiction of the Archbishop of Nassau.

Archbishop of Nassau: Most Rev. PATRICK PINDER, Archdiocesan Pastoral Centre, West St North, POB N-8187, Nassau; tel. 322-8919; fax 322-2599; e-mail rcchancery@batelnet.bs; internet www.archdioceseofnassau.org.

The Anglican Communion

Anglicans in the Bahamas, who account for some 15% of the population, according to the 2000 census, are adherents of the Church in the Province of the West Indies, comprising eight dioceses. The Archbishop of the Province currently is the Bishop of Barbados. The diocese of the Bahamas also includes the Turks and Caicos Islands.

Bishop of the Bahamas and the Turks and Caicos Islands: Rt Rev. LAISH Z. BOYD, Bishop's Lodge, Sands Rd, POB N-656, Nassau; tel. 322-3015; fax 322-7943; e-mail media@bahamasanglicans.org; internet www.bahamasanglicans.org.

Other Christian Churches

According to the latest available census figures (2000), 8% of the population are Pentecostalists, 5% belong to the Church of God, 4% are Methodists and 4% are Seventh-day Adventists.

Bahamas Conference of the Methodist Church: Baltic Ave, Off Mackey St, POB SS-5103, Nassau; tel. 393-3726; fax 393-8135; e-mail bcmc@bahamasmethodist.org; internet bahamasmethodist.org; 34 mem. churches; Pres. CHRISTOPHER NEELY.

Bahamas Conference of Seventh-day Adventists: Tonique Williams-Darling Hwy, POB N-356, Nassau; tel. 341-4021; fax 341-4088; e-mail southbahamasconference@gmail.com; internet www.southbahamasconference.org; Pres. PAUL A. SCAVELLA.

Greek Orthodox Church: Church of the Annunciation, West St, POB N-823, Nassau; tel. 326-0850; fax 326-0851; e-mail officemanager.agoc@gmail.com; internet www.orthodoxbahamas.com; f. 1928; part of the Archdiocese of North and South America, based in New York (USA); Priest Rev. THEODORE ROUPAS.

Other denominations include African Methodist Episcopal, the Assemblies of Brethren, Christian Science, Church of the Latter Day Saints (Mormons), the Jehovah's Witnesses, the Salvation Army, Presbyterian and Lutheran churches.

OTHER RELIGIONS

Bahá'í Faith

Bahá'í National Spiritual Assembly: POB N-7105, Nassau; tel. 326-0607; e-mail nsabaha@mail.com; internet www.bahai.org; Sec. PATRICIA JOSEY.

Islam

There is a small community of Muslims, numbering 292 at the 2000 census.

Islamic Centre: Carmichael Rd, POB N-10711, Nassau; tel. 341-6612; fax 364-6233; e-mail questions@jamaa-ahlussunnah-bahamas.com; internet www.jamaa-ahlussunnah-bahamas.com; fmrly Jamaat ul-Islam of the Commonwealth of the Bahamas.

Judaism

Most of the Bahamian Jewish community, numbering 228 at the 2000 census, are based on Grand Bahama.

Freeport Hebrew Congregation (Luis de Torres Synagogue): East Sunrise Hwy, POB F-41761, Freeport; tel. 373-9457; fax 373-2130; e-mail jberlind@coralwave.com; Pres. TONY GEE; Sec. JEAN BERLIND.

Nassau Jewish Congregation: POB N-95, Nassau; tel. 325-8416; e-mail gangieval@coralwave.com.

The Press

NEWSPAPERS

The Abaconian: Marsh Harbour, POB AB-20551, Abaco; tel. 367-3200; fax 367-3677; e-mail abaconiannews@gmail.com; internet abaconian.com; f. 1993; privately owned; local news; Editor BRADLEY ALBURY.

The Bahama Journal: Media House, East St North, POB N-8610, Nassau; tel. 325-3082; fax 325-3996; internet www.jonesbahamas.com; f. 1987; daily; Publr WENDALL JONES; circ. 5,000.

Bahamas Press: Nassau; e-mail media@bahamaspress.com; internet www.bahamaspress.com; online newspaper; f. 2007; Editor ALEXANDER JAMES.

The Eleutheran: Cupid's Cay, POB EL-25046, Governor's Harbour, Eleuthera; tel. 422-9350; fax 332-2993; e-mail editor@theeleutheran.com; internet www.eleutheranews.com; Man. Editor ELIZABETH BRYAN.

The Freeport News: Cedar St, POB F-40007, Freeport; tel. 352-8321; fax 351-3449; e-mail tfneditor@nasguard.com; internet freeport.nassauguardian.net; f. 1961; owned by *The Nassau Guardian*; daily; Publr ANTHONY FERGUSON; Man. Editor JOHN FLEET; circ. 5,000.

The Nassau Guardian: 4 Carter St, Oakes Field, POB N-3011, Nassau; tel. 302-2300; fax 328-8943; e-mail editor@nasguard.com; internet www.thenassauguardian.com; f. 1844; daily; Pres. ANTHONY FERGUSON; Man. Editor ERICA WELLS; circ. 15,000.

The Tribune: Shirley St, POB N-3207, Nassau; tel. 322-1986; fax 328-2398; e-mail tips@tribunemedia.net; internet www.tribune242.com; f. 1903; daily; Publr and Editor EILEEN CARRON; circ. 15,000.

PERIODICALS

The Bahamas Financial Digest and Business Today: Miramar House, 2nd Floor, Bay and Christie Sts, POB N-4271, Nassau; tel. 356-2981; fax 326-2849; e-mail info@smgbahamas.com; f. 1973; 4 a year; business and investment; Publr and Editor MICHAEL A. SYMONETTE; circ. 15,890.

Ca Mari: POB N-3672, Nassau; tel. 565-9069; e-mail camari@camariinc.com; internet www.camariinc.com; lifestyle magazine for women; Editor-in-Chief CAMILLE KENNY.

Insitu Arch: West Bay St, SP-60785, Nassau; tel. 376-4600; fax 327-8931; e-mail info@insitumag.com; internet www.insitumag.com; architecture; quarterly; CEO MARCUS LAING.

Nu Woman: Freddie Munnings Manor, Harbour Bay, CB-13236, Nassau; tel. 676-7908; fax 479-2318; e-mail info@nuwomanmagazine.com; internet www.nuwomanmagazine.com; f. 2007; lifestyle magazine for women; quarterly; Publr and Editor-in-Chief ERICA MEUS-SAUNDERS.

What's On Bahamas: Woodes Rogers Wharf, POB CB-11713, Nassau; tel. 323-2323; fax 322-3428; e-mail info@whatsonbahamas.com; internet www.whatsonbahamas.com; monthly; Publr NEIL ABERLE.

Publishers

Aberland Publications Ltd: Woodes Rodger's Wharf, CB-11713, Nassau; tel. 323-2323; fax 322-3428; e-mail submissions@whatsonbahamas.com; internet www.whatsonbahamas.com; Publr ANDREW BERLANDA.

Dupuch Publications Ltd: 51 Hawthorne Rd, Oakes Field, POB N-7513, Nassau; tel. 323-5665; fax 323-5728; e-mail info@dupuch.com; internet www.dupuch.com; f. 1959; publishes *Bahamas Handbook*, *The Bahamas Investor*, *Trailblazer* maps, *What To Do* magazines, *Welcome Bahamas* and *Dining and Entertainment Guide*; Publr ETIENNE DUPUCH, Jr.

Guanima Press Ltd: East Bay St, POB CB-13151, Nassau; tel. and fax 393-3221; e-mail : bookstore@guanimapress.com; internet www.guanima.com; f. 1992; Owner P. MEICHOLAS.

Media Enterprises Ltd: 31 Shirley Park Ave, POB N-9240, Nassau; tel. 325-8210; fax 325-8065; e-mail info@bahamasmedia.com; internet www.bahamasmedia.com; f. 1984; educational and other non-fiction books; authorized representative for Macmillan Caribbean, Oxford University Press and Nelson Thornes; Pres. and Gen. Man. LARRY A. SMITH; Publishing Dir NEIL E. SEALEY.

Broadcasting and Communications

REGULATORY AUTHORITY

Utilities Regulation and Competition Authority (URCA): UBS Annex Bldg, East Bay St, POB N-4860, Nassau; tel. 393-0234; fax 393-0153; e-mail info@urcabahamas.bs; internet www.urcabahamas.bs; f. 2009; replaced both the Public Utilities Commission and the Television Regulatory Authority; regulatory authority for electronic communications and broadcasting (including cable television); Chair. RANDOL DORSETT; CEO KATHLEEN RIVIERE-SMITH.

TELECOMMUNICATIONS

Bahamas Telecommunications Co (BTC): John F. Kennedy Dr., POB N-3048, Nassau; tel. 302-7008; fax 326-8423; e-mail help@batelnet.bs; internet www.btcbahamas.com; f. 1966, fmrly known as BaTelCo; 51% stake acquired by Cable and Wireless (United Kingdom) in 2011; Chair. MARTIN JOOS (acting); CEO GEOFF HOUSTON.

Cable Bahamas Ltd: Robinson Rd at Marathon, POB CB-13050, Nassau; tel. 356-8940; fax 356-8997; e-mail info@cablebahamas.com; internet www.cablebahamas.com; f. 1995; provides cable television and internet services; Chair. PHILIP KEEPING; Pres. and CEO ANTHONY BUTLER.

BROADCASTING

Radio

Broadcasting Corporation of the Bahamas: Harcourt 'Rusty' Bethel Dr., 3rd Terrace, Centreville, POB N-1347, Nassau; tel. 502-3800; fax 322-6598; e-mail info@znsbahamas.com; internet www.znsbahamas.com; f. 1936; govt-owned; operates the ZNS radio and television network; Chair. Rev. Dr WILLIAM L. THOMPSON; Gen. Man. EDWIN LIGHTBOURNE.

Radio ZNS Bahamas: internet www.znsbahamas.com; f. 1936; broadcasts 24 hours per day on 4 stations: the main Radio Bahamas ZNS1, Radio New Providence ZNS2, which are both based in Nassau, Radio Power 104.5 FM, and the Northern Service (ZNS3—Freeport); Station Man. ANTHONY FORSTER.

Cool 96 FM: Yellow Pine St, POB F-40773, Freeport, Grand Bahama; tel. 351-2665; fax 352-8709; e-mail cool96@coralwave.com; internet cool96fm.com; f. 1995; opened office in Nassau in Jan. 2005; Pres. and Gen. Man. ANDREA GOTTLIEB.

Gems Radio: 51 Sears Hill, POB SS-6094, Nassau; tel. 326-4381; fax 326-4371; e-mail shenac@gemsbahamas.com; internet gemsbahamas.com; f. 2006; subsidiary of Bartlett-McWeeney Communications Ltd; Programming Dir SHENA CARROL.

Island FM: EdMark House, Dowdeswell St, POB N-1807, Nassau; tel. 322-8826; fax 356-4515; internet www.islandfmonline.com; Owner EDDIE CARTER.

Love 97 FM: Bahamas Media House, East St North, POB N-3909, Nassau; tel. 356-4960; fax 356-7256; e-mail twilliams@jonescommunications.com; internet www.jonesbahamas.com; operated by Jones Communications Ltd.

More 94 FM: Carmichael Rd, POB CR-54245, Nassau; tel. 361-2447; fax 361-2448; e-mail media@more94fm.com; internet www.more94fm.com.

One Hundred JAMZ: Shirley and Deveaux St, POB N-3207, Nassau; tel. 677-0950; fax 356-5343; e-mail michelle@100jamz.com; internet www.100jamz.com; operated by *The Tribune* newspaper; Gen. Man. STEPHEN HAUGHEY; Programme Dir ERIC WARD.

Television

Broadcasting Corporation of the Bahamas: see Radio**JCN Channel 14:** East St North 99999, New Providence, Nassau; tel. 356-9071; fax 356-9073; internet www.jonesbahamas.com; subsidiary of the Jones Communications Network; CEO WENDALL JONES.

US television programmes and some satellite programmes can be received. Most islands have a cable television service.

Finance

The Bahamas has developed into one of the world's foremost financial centres (there are no corporation, income, capital gains or withholding taxes or estate duties), and finance has become a significant feature of the economy. In 2012 there were 268 'offshore' banks and trust companies in operation in the islands.

BANKING

(cap. = capital; res = reserves; dep. = deposits; m. = million; brs = branches)

Central Bank

The Central Bank of the Bahamas: Frederick St, POB N-4868, Nassau; tel. 302-2600; fax 322-4321; e-mail queries@centralbankbahamas.com; internet www.centralbankbahamas.com; f. 1974; bank of issue; cap. B $3.0m., res B $127.1m., dep. B $411.4m. (Dec. 2009); Gov. and Chair. WENDY M. CRAIGG.

Development Bank

The Bahamas Development Bank: Cable Beach, West Bay St, POB N-3034, Nassau; tel. 702-5700; fax 327-5047; internet bahamasdevelopmentbank.com; f. 1978 to fund approved projects and channel funds into appropriate investments; total assets B $58.3m. (Dec. 2004); Chair. DARRON B. CASH; Man. Dir ANTHONY WOODSIDE (acting); 1 br.

Principal Banks

Bank of the Bahamas Ltd (Bank of the Bahamas International): Claughton House, Shirley and Charlotte Sts, POB N-7118, Nassau; tel. 326-2560; fax 325-2762; e-mail info.bob@bankbahamas.com; internet www.bankbahamasonline.com; f. 1970; est. as Bank of Montreal (Bahamas and Caribbean); name changed as above in 2002; 50% owned by Govt, 50% owned by c. 4,000 Bahamian shareholders; cap. B $50.0m., res B $32.6m., dep. B $649.3m. (Jan. 2013); Chair. MACGREGOR ROBERTSON; Man. Dir PAUL JOSEPH MCWEENEY; 13 brs.

Banque Privée Edmond de Rothschild Ltd (Switzerland): Lyford Financial Centre, Lyford Cay 2, West Bay St, POB SP-63948, Nassau; tel. 702-8000; fax 702-8008; e-mail dswaby@bper.ch; internet www.edmond-de-rothschild.bs; f. 1997; owned by Banque Privée Edmond de Rothschild SA (Switzerland); cap. 15.0m. Swiss francs, res 23.9m. Swiss francs, dep. 442.9m. Swiss francs (Jan. 2013); Chair. MANUEL LEUTHOLD; CEO GIAN FADRI PINOESCH.

BSI Overseas (Bahamas) Ltd (Italy): Goodman's Bay Corporate Centre, West Bay St, Sea View Dr., POB N-7130, Nassau; tel. 502-2200; fax 502-2230; e-mail info@bsibank.com; internet www.bs.bsibank.com; f. 1969 as Banca della Svizzera Italiana (Overseas) Ltd; name changed as above 1990; wholly owned subsidiary of BSI SA Lugano; cap. US $10.0m., res US $18.2m., dep. US $3,857.8m. (Jan. 2013); Pres. ALFREDO GYSI; CEO STEFANO CODURI.

Canadian Imperial Bank of Commerce (CIBC) (Canada): Goodman's Bay Corporate Centre, West Bay St, POB 3933, Nassau; tel. 356-1800; fax 322-3692; e-mail privatebanking@cibc.com; internet www.cibc.com; Pres. and CEO GERALD T. MCCAUGHEY; Area Man. TERRY HILTS; 9 brs.

Citibank NA (USA): Citibank Bldg, 4th Floor, Thompson Blvd, Oakes Field, POB N-8158, Nassau; tel. 302-8500; fax 323-3088; internet www.citibank.com; CEO MICHAEL CORBAT; 2 brs.

Commonwealth Bank Ltd: The Plaza, Mackey St, POB SS 5541, Nassau; tel. 502-6200; fax 394-5807; e-mail cbinquiry@combankltd.com; internet www.combankltd.com; f. 1960; cap. B $86.9m., res B $37.1m., dep. B $1,203.0m. (Jan. 2013); Chair. WILLIAM BATEMAN SANDS, Jr; Pres. IAN ANDREW JENNINGS; 11 brs.

Crédit Agricole Suisse Bank & Trust (Bahamas) Ltd: Goodman's Bay Corporate Centre, Ground Floor, West Bay St, POB N-3015, Nassau; tel. 502-8100; fax 502-8166; internet www.ca-suisse.bs; f. 1978; 100% owned by Crédit Agricole (Suisse) SA, Geneva (Switzerland); fmrly National Bank of Canada (International) Ltd; name changed as above 2008; Pres. ANTOINE CANDIOTTI.

Crédit Suisse (Bahamas) Ltd (Switzerland): Bahamas Financial Centre, 4th Floor, Shirley and Charlotte Sts, POB N-4928, Nassau; tel. 356-8100; fax 326-6589; internet www.credit-suisse.com/bs; f. 1968; subsidiary of Crédit Suisse Zurich; portfolio and asset management, 'offshore' company management, trustee services, foreign exchange; CEO BRADY W. DOUGAN.

FirstCaribbean International Bank (Bahamas) Ltd: Bahamas International Banking Centre, Shirley St, POB N-8350, Nassau; tel. 322-8455; fax 326-6552; internet www.firstcaribbeanbank.com; f. 2002 following merger of Caribbean operations of Barclays Bank PLC and CIBC; Barclays Bank relinquished its stake to CIBC in 2006; cap. B $12.0m., res B $430.4m., dep. B $2,767.3m. (Oct. 2010); Exec. Chair. MICHAEL MANSOOR; CEO RIK PARKHILL; Country Man. MARIE RODLAND-ALLEN; 16 brs.

Guaranty Trust Bank Ltd: Lyford Manor Ltd, Lyford Cay, POB N-4918, Nassau; tel. 362-7200; fax 362-7210; e-mail info@

guarantybahamas.com; internet www.guarantybahamas.com; f. 1962; cap. US $21.0m., res US $0.2m., dep. US $73.9m. (Dec. 2010); Chair. Sir WILLIAM C. ALLEN; Man. Dir JAMES P. COYLE.

Pictet Bank and Trust Ltd (Switzerland): Bldg No. 1, Bayside Executive Park, West Bay St and Blake Rd, POB N-4837, Nassau; tel. 302-2222; fax 327-6610; e-mail pbtbah@bahamas.net.bs; internet www.pictet.com; f. 1978; cap. US $1.0m., res US $10.0m., dep. US $126.2m. (Dec. 1995); Pres., Dir and Gen. Man. YVES LOURDIN.

Private Investment Bank Ltd: Devonshire House, Queen St, POB N-3918, Nassau; tel. 302-5950; fax 302-5970; e-mail valerio.zanchi@pib.bs; internet www.bfsb-bahamas.com; f. 1984; est. as Bank Worms and Co International Ltd; renamed in 1990, 1996 and 1998; in 2000 merged with Geneva Private Bank and Trust (Bahamas) Ltd; wholly owned by Banque de Patrimoines Privés Genève BPG SA (Switzerland); cap. US $3.0m., res US $12.0m., dep. US $163.6m. (Dec. 2009); Gen. Man VALERIO ZANCHI.

Royal Bank of Canada Ltd (Canada): 323 Bay St, POB N-7549, Nassau; tel. 322-8700; fax 328-7145; e-mail banks@rbc.com; internet www.rbc.com; f. 1869; Chair. DAVID P. O'BRIEN; Pres. and CEO GORDON M. NIXON; 25 brs.

Scotiabank (Bahamas) Ltd (Canada): Scotiabank Bldg, Rawson Sq., POB N-7518, Nassau; tel. 356-1697; fax 356-1689; e-mail scotiabank.bs@scotiabank.com; internet www.bahamas.scotiabank.com; f. 1956; Chair. ANTHONY C. ALLEN; Man. Dir SEAN ALBERT; 20 brs.

SG Hambros Bank and Trust (Bahamas) Ltd (United Kingdom): Lyford Cay House, West Bay St, POB N-7785, Nassau; tel. 302-5000; fax 326-6709; e-mail renaud.vielfaure@socgen.com; internet www.privatebanking.societegenerale.com; f. 1936; above name adopted in 1998; cap. B $2.0m., res –B $3.2m., dep. B $435.2m. (Dec. 2008); Chair. JEAN-PIERRE FLAIS.

UBS (Bahamas) Ltd (Switzerland): UBS House, East Bay St, POB N-7757, Nassau; tel. 394-9300; fax 394-9333; internet www.ubs.com/bahamas; f. 1968; est. as Swiss Bank Corpn (Overseas) Ltd, name changed as above 1998; wholly owned by UBS AG (Switzerland); cap. US $4.0m., dep. US $420.2m. (Dec. 1997); Chair. KASPAR VILLIGER; Group CEO SERGIO P. ERMOTTI.

Principal Bahamian Trust Companies

Ansbacher (Bahamas) Ltd: 308 East Bay St, POB N-7768, Nassau; tel. 322-1161; fax 326-5020; e-mail info@ansbacher.bs; internet www.ansbacher.bs; f. 1957; offers bank and trust services; total assets US $128m. (2012); Man. Dir CARLTON MORTIER.

Bank of Nova Scotia Trust Co (Bahamas) Ltd: Scotia House, 404 East Bay St, POB N-3016, Nassau; tel. 502-5700; fax 393-0582; e-mail scotiatrust@coralwave.com; internet www.bahamas.scotiabank.com; wholly owned by the Bank of Nova Scotia; Vice-Pres. and Head JAMES STOOKE.

Winterbotham Trust Co Ltd: Winterbotham Pl., Marlborough and Queen Sts, POB N-3026, Nassau; tel. 356-5454; fax 356-9432; e-mail ihooper@winterbotham.com; internet www.winterbotham.com; total assets US $14.1m. (Dec. 2007); CEO IVAN HOOPER; 2 brs.

Bankers' Organizations

Association of International Banks and Trust Companies in the Bahamas: Montague Sterling Centre, 2nd Floor, East Bay St, POB N-7880, Nassau; tel. 393-5500; fax 393-5501; e-mail info@aibt-bahamas.com; internet www.aibt-bahamas.com; f. 1976; Chair. ANTOINETTE RUSSELL.

Bahamas Financial Services Board (BFSB): Montague Sterling Centre, East Bay St, POB N-1764, Nassau; tel. 393-7001; fax 393-7712; e-mail info@bfsb-bahamas.com; internet www.bfsb-bahamas.com; f. 1998; jt govt/private initiative responsible for industry promotion and overseas marketing of financial services; CEO and Exec. Dir ALIYA ALLEN; Chair. PRINCE RAHMING.

Bahamas Institute of Financial Services (BIFS): Verandah House, Market St and Trinity Pl., POB N-3202, Nassau; tel. 325-4921; fax 325-5674; e-mail info@bifs-bahamas.com; internet www.bifs-bahamas.com; f. 1974 as Bahamas Institute of Bankers, name changed as above 2003; Pres. TANYA MCCARTNEY; Exec. Dir KIM W. BODIE.

STOCK EXCHANGE

Bahamas International Securities Exchange (BISX): Fort Nassau Centre, 2nd Floor, British Colonial Hilton, Bay St, POB EE-15672, Nassau; tel. 323-2330; fax 323-2320; e-mail info@bisxbahamas.com; internet www.bisxbahamas.com; f. 1999; 28 primary listings and 24 mutual funds in Feb. 2014; Chair. IAN FAIR; CEO KEITH DAVIES.

INSURANCE

BAF Financial: Independence Dr., POB N-4815, Nassau; tel. 461-1000; fax 361-2524; e-mail info@mybafsolutions.com; internet bahamas.mybafsolutions.com; f. 1920; est. as British American Insurance Co; name changed to British American Financial in 2007 when comprehensive range of financial services added; rebranded as above in 2010; owned by local consortium, BAB Holdings Ltd, since 2007; Chair. BASIL L. SANDS; Pres. and CEO CHESTER COOPER.

Bahamas First General Insurance Co Ltd: Bahamas First Centre, 32 Collins Ave, POB SS-6238, Nassau; tel. 302-3900; fax 302-3901; e-mail info@bahamasfirst.com; internet www.bahamasfirst.com; f. 1983; Chair. IAN D. FAIR; Pres. and CEO PATRICK G. W. WARD.

Colina Insurance Ltd: 308 Bay St, POB N-4728, Nassau; tel. 396-2100; fax 393-1710; internet www.colina.com; fmrly known as Colina Imperial Insurance Ltd; Colina Insurance Co merged with Global Life Assurance Bahamas in 2002; operates under above name; fully owned subsidiary of Colina Holdings Bahamas Ltd; Chair. TERENCE HILTS; Exec. Vice-Chair. and CEO EMANUEL M. ALEXIOU.

Family Guardian Insurance Co Ltd (FamGuard): East Bay & Shirley St, POB SS-6232, Nassau; tel. 396-4000; fax 393-1100; e-mail info@familyguardian.com; internet www.familyguardian.com; f. 1965; life and health; fully owned subsidiary of FamGuard Corpn Ltd; Pres. and CEO PATRICIA A. HERMANNS.

RoyalStar Assurance: Second Terrace West, Collins Ave, POB N-4391, Nassau; tel. 328-7888; fax 325-3151; internet www.rsabahamas.com; Man. Dir ANTON A. SAUNDERS.

Summit Insurance Co Ltd: 42 Montrose Ave, Sears Hill, POB SS-19028, Nassau; tel. 677-7878; fax 677-7873; e-mail info@summitbahamas.com; internet www.summitbahamas.com; f. 1994; Chair. CEDRIC A. SAUNDERS; Gen. Man. and Dir TIMOTHY N. INGRAHAM.

Association

Bahamas Insurance Association (BIA): Royal Palm Mall, Unit 8, Mackey St, POB N-860, Nassau; tel. 394-6625; fax 394-6626; e-mail bgia@coralwave.com; internet www.bahamasinsurance.org; Chair. HOWARD KNOWLES; Co-ordinator Dr RHONDA CHIPMAN-JOHNSON; 29 mems.

Trade and Industry

DEVELOPMENT ORGANIZATIONS

Bahamas Agricultural and Industrial Corpn (BAIC): BAIC Bldg, East Bay St, POB N-4940, Nassau; tel. 322-3740; fax 322-2123; e-mail baic@bahamas.gov.bs; internet www.bahamas.gov.bs/baic; f. 1981; an amalgamation of Bahamas Development Corpn and Bahamas Agricultural Corpn for the promotion of greater co-operation between tourism and other sectors of the economy through the development of small and medium-sized enterprises; Chair. ARNOLD FORBES; Gen. Man. BENJAMIN RAHMING.

Bahamas Investment Authority: Sir Cecil Wallace-Whitfield Centre, West Bay St, POB CB-10990, Nassau; tel. 327-5826; fax 327-5806; e-mail bia@bahamas.gov.bs; govt-owned; operates from the Office of the Prime Minister; Dir of Investments JOY JIBRILU.

Nassau Paradise Island Promotion Board: Hotel Center, S. G. Hambros Bldg, West Bay St, Nassau; tel. 322-8381; fax 326-5346; e-mail michael@npipb.com; internet www.nassauparadiseisland.com; f. 1973; Chair. GEORGE R. MYERS; Vice-Chair. GEORGE MARKANTONIS; 17 mems.

CHAMBERS OF COMMERCE

Bahamas Chamber of Commerce and Employers Confederation (BCCEC): Shirley St and Collins Ave, POB N-665, Nassau; tel. 322-2145; fax 322-4649; e-mail info@thebahamaschamber.com; internet www.thebahamaschamber.com; f. 1935 as Bahamas Chamber of Commerce; changed name as above after merger with Bahamas Employers Conf.; Pres. CHESTER COOPER; Exec. Dir KESHELLE KERR; over 500 mems.

Grand Bahama Chamber of Commerce: 5 Mall Dr., POB F-40808, Freeport, Grand Bahama; tel. 352-8329; fax 352-3280; e-mail gbchamberofcommerceassistant@hotmail.com; internet www.gbchamber.org; Pres. BARRY MALCOLM; Exec. Dir MERCYNTH FERGUSON; 264 mems.

EMPLOYERS' ASSOCIATIONS

Bahamian Contractors' Association: POB N-9286, Nassau; tel. 322-2145; fax 322-4649; e-mail info@bahamiancontractors.org; internet www.bahamascontractors.org; f. 1959; Pres. GODFREY FORBES; Sec. ROBYN OGILVIE.

Bahamas Hotel Employers' Association: SG Hambros Bldg, West Bay, POB N-7799, Nassau; tel. 322-2262; fax 502-4221; e-mail bhea4mcr@hotmail.com; f. 1958; Pres. J. BARRIE FARRINGTON; Exec. Vice-Pres. MICHAEL C. RECKLEY; 16 mems.

Bahamas Institute of Chartered Accountants: Maritima House, 2nd Floor, Frederick St, POB N-7037, Nassau; tel. 326-6619; fax 326-6618; e-mail secbica@batelnet.bs; internet www.bica.bs; f. 1971; Pres. JASMINE DAVIS.

Bahamas Motor Dealers' Association (BMDA): POB SS-6213, Nassau; tel. 302-1030; internet www.bmda.bs; 16 mem. cos.

Bahamas Real Estate Association: Dowdeswell St, POB N-8860, Nassau; tel. 356-4578; fax 356-4501; e-mail info@bahamasrealestateassociation.com; internet www.bahamasrealestateassociation.com; f. 1959; Pres. FRANON WILSON; Sec. DONNA JONES; 400 mems.

Professional Engineers Board (PEB): 3 21st Century Rd, POB N-3817, Nassau; tel. 328-3574; e-mail info@pebahamas.org; internet www.pebahamas.org; f. 2004; Chair. ROBERT DEAL.

UTILITIES

Electricity

Bahamas Electricity Corpn (BEC): Big Pond and Tucker Rds, POB N-7509, Nassau; tel. 302-1000; fax 323-6852; e-mail customercare@bahamaselectricity.com; internet www.bahamaselectricity.com; f. 1956; state-owned, scheduled for privatization; provides electricity to approx. 100,000 customers; Exec. Chair. LESLIE MILLER; Gen. Man. KEVIN A. BASDEN.

Grand Bahama Power Co (GBPC): Pioneers Way & East Mall Dr., POB F-40888, Freeport; tel. 350-9000; fax 351-8008; e-mail customerservice@gb-power.com; internet www.gb-power.com; f. 1962 as Freeport Power Co Ltd; 80% owned by Emera (Canada); Pres. and CEO SARAH MACDONALD.

Gas

Tropigas: Gladstone Rd, POB SS-5833, Nassau; tel. 361-2695; fax 341-4875.

Water

Bahamas Water and Sewerage Corpn (WSC): 87 Thompson Blvd, POB N-3905, Nassau; tel. 322-5500; fax 328-3896; e-mail wccomplaints@wsc.com.bs; internet www.wsc.com.bs; f. 1976; state-run; Chair. BRADLEY B. ROBERTS; Gen. Man. GLEN LAVILLE.

TRADE UNIONS

Confederations

Commonwealth of the Bahamas Trade Union Congress: 3 Warwick St, POB N-3399, Nassau; tel. 394-6301; fax 394-7401; e-mail tuc@bahamas.net.bs; Pres. OBIE FERGUSON, Jr; Gen. Sec. TIMOTHY MOORE; 12,500 mems.

National Congress of Trade Unions (NCTUB): Horseshoe Dr., POB GT-2887, Nassau; tel. 356-7459; fax 356-7457; e-mail ncongress@hotmail.com; internet nctu-bahamas.org; f. 1995; Pres. JENNIFER ISAACS-DOTSON; Gen. Sec. ROBERT FARQUHARSON; 20,000 mems.

Transport

ROADS

There are about 1,600 km (994 miles) of roads in New Providence and 1,368 km (850 miles) in the Family Islands, mainly on Grand Bahama, Cat Island, Eleuthera, Exuma and Long Island. In 2001 57.4% of roads were paved.

SHIPPING

The principal seaport is at Nassau (New Providence), which can accommodate the very largest cruise ships. Passenger arrivals exceed 2m. annually. The other main ports are at Freeport (Grand Bahama), where a container terminal opened in 1997, and Matthew Town (Inagua). There are also modern berthing facilities for cruise ships at Potters Cay (New Providence), Governor's Harbour (Eleuthera), Morgan's Bluff (North Andros) and George Town (Exuma). In 2012 plans were approved for construction of a new port in northern Abaco, financed by the Export-Import Bank of China at the cost of US $39m. Construction of the 35-acre project was expected to begin in 2014 and take two years.

The Bahamas converted to free flag status in 1976. In December 2013 the fleet comprised 1,493 vessels, totalling 56,663,130 grt (the third largest national fleet in the world).

There is a weekly cargo and passenger service to all the Family Islands.

Bahamas Maritime Authority: Shirlaw House, 87 Shirley St, POB N-4679, Nassau; tel. 356-5772; fax 356-5889; e-mail nassau@bahamasmaritime.com; internet www.bahamasmaritime.com; f. 1995; promotes ship registration and co-ordinates maritime administration; state-owned; CEO and Man. Dir Cdre DAVY F. ROLLE.

Freeport Harbour Co Ltd: POB F-42465, Freeport; tel. 350-8000; fax 350-8044; internet www.freeportcontainerport.com; owned by Hutchison Port Holdings (HPH), Hong Kong; CEO GARY GILBERT; Dir ORLANDO FORBES.

Grand Bahama Port Authority (GBPA): Pioneer's Way and East Mall Dr., POB F-42666, Freeport; tel. 350-9002; fax 352-6184; e-mail fstubbs@gbpa.com; internet www.gbpa.com; f. 1955; receivers were appointed to operate co in Nov. 2006 pending outcome of contested ownership trial, which was resolved in 2010; Chair. HANNES BABAK; Pres. IAN ROLLE.

Principal Shipping Companies

Bahamas Ferries: Potters Cay West, Nassau; tel. 323-2166; fax 393-7451; e-mail customerservice@bahamasferries.com; internet www.bahamasferries.com; f. 1999; services Spanish Wells, Harbour Island, Current Island and Governors Harbour in Eleuthera, Morgan's Bluff and Fresh Creek in Andros, Sandy Point in Abaco and George Town in Exuma; Gen. Man. ALAN BAX.

Dean's Shipping Co: 11 Parkgate, POB EE17318, Nassau; tel. 394-0245; fax 394-0253; e-mail deansshippingco@gmail.com; internet www.deanshipping.com; Man. TWEED DEAN.

Dockendale Shipping Co Ltd: Dockendale House, 3rd Floor, West Bay St, POB N-3033, Nassau; tel. 325-0448; fax 328-1542; e-mail dscopr@dockendale.com; internet www.dockendale.com; f. 1973; ship management; Man. Dirs LESLIE J. FERNANDES, KAMMANA VALLURI.

Freeport Ship Services: 8 Logwood Rd, POB F-40423, Freeport; tel. 351-4343; fax 351-4332; e-mail info@freeportshipservices.com; internet www.freeportshipservices.com; f. 2003; privately owned co; affiliated to United Shipping Co Ltd; agents, customs brokers, logistics providers, chandlers; Pres. JEREMY CAFFERATA; Gen. Man. JOHN LANE.

Tropical Shipping Co Ltd: Container Terminals Ltd, John Alfred Dock, Bay St, POB N-8183, Nassau; tel. 322-1012; fax 323-7566; internet www.tropical.com; Pres. MIKE PELLICCI.

United Abaco Shipping Co Ltd: Marsh Harbour, POB AB-20737, Abaco; tel. 367-2091; fax 367-2235; e-mail unitedabacoshippingco@coralwave.com; internet www.unitedabacoshipping.com; Man. SIDNEY ALBURY.

United Shipping Co (Nassau) Ltd: Centreville House, 5th Floor, Terrace 2, West Centreville, POB N-4005, Nassau; tel. 322-1341; fax 323-8779; e-mail operations@unitedshippingnassau.com; internet www.uscbahamas.com; sister co of Freeport Ship Services; Chair. TERRY MUNDAY; Gen. Man. RICH RYAN.

CIVIL AVIATION

Lynden Pindling International Airport (formerly Nassau International Airport) (15 km—9 miles—outside the capital), Freeport International Airport (5 km—3 miles—outside the city, on Grand Bahama) and Marsh Harbour International Airport (on Abaco Island) are the main terminals for international and internal services. There are also important airports at West End (Grand Bahama) and Rock Sound (Eleuthera) and some 50 smaller airports and landing strips throughout the islands. An estimated US $200m. development of Lynden Pindling International Airport was completed in late 2013.

Bahamasair Holdings Ltd: Windsor Field, POB N-4881, Nassau; tel. 702-4100; fax 702-4180; e-mail astuart@bahamasair.com; internet bahamasair.com; f. 1973; state-owned, proposed privatization plans shelved indefinitely by 2009; scheduled services between Nassau, Freeport, Cuba, Jamaica, Dominican Republic, Turks and Caicos Islands, destinations within the USA and 20 locations within the Family Islands; Chair. VALENTINE GRIMES; Man. Dir HENRY WOODS.

Western Air Limited: San Andros International Airport, POB AP 532900, North Andros, Nassau; tel. 329-4000; fax 329-4013; e-mail westernairltd@gmail.com; internet www.westernairbahamas.com; f. 2001; private, wholly Bahamian-owned company; scheduled services between Nassau, Freeport, San Andros and Bimini, and to Cuba, and on-demand charter flights throughout the Bahamas, the Caribbean and Central and South America; Pres. and CEO REX ROLLE.

Tourism

The mild climate and beautiful beaches attract many tourists. In 2012 tourist arrivals totalled some 5,940,000, including 4,583,000 visitors by sea. The majority of stop-over arrivals (83% in 2007) were from the USA. Receipts from the tourism industry stood at a provisional B $2,367m. in 2012.

Bahamas Hotel Association: Serenity House, East Bay St, POB N-7799, Nassau; tel. 322-8381; fax 502-4246; e-mail bha@bahamashotels.org; internet www.bhahotels.com; Pres. STUART BOWE; Exec. Vice-Pres. FRANK COMITO.

Hotel Corporation of the Bahamas: Marlborough St and Navy Lion Rd, POB N-9520, Nassau; tel. 356-4571; fax 356-4846; operates from Office of the Prime Minister; Chair. MICHAEL SCOTT.

Nassau Tourism Development Board: POB N-4740, Nassau; tel. 326-0992; fax 323-2998; e-mail linkages@batelnet.bs; f. 1995; Chair. CHARLES KLONARIS.

Defence

The Royal Bahamian Defence Force, a paramilitary coastguard, is the only security force in the Bahamas, and numbered 850, as assessed at November 2013. Increasing concerns over rising crime levels in the Caribbean region prompted the recruitment of an additional 100 personnel to the Royal Bahamas Defence Force and 200 officers to the Royal Bahamas Police Force in 2007.

Defence Budget: an estimated B $87m. in 2014.

Commodore: RODERICK BOWE.

Education

Education is compulsory between the ages of five and 16 years, and is provided free of charge in government schools. There are several private and denominational schools. Primary education begins at five years of age and lasts for six years. Secondary education, beginning at the age of 11, also lasts for six years and is divided into two equal cycles. In 2010 some 98% of children in the relevant age-group were enrolled at primary level, while 86% of children in the relevant age-group were enrolled at secondary level. The University of the West Indies has an extra-mural department in Nassau, offering degree courses in hotel management and tourism. Ross University School of Medicine, which has a 126-acre campus on Grand Bahama for overseas medical students, began teaching activities in 2009. Technical, teacher-training and professional qualifications can be obtained at the three campuses of the College of the Bahamas.

In 2013/14 the estimated recurrent expenditure allocated to the Ministry of Education, Science and Technology was B $199.6m., equivalent to 11.4% of total recurrent expenditure.

BAHRAIN

Introductory Survey

LOCATION, CLIMATE, LANGUAGE, RELIGION, FLAG, CAPITAL

The Kingdom of Bahrain consists of a group of some 36 islands, situated midway along the Persian (Arabian) Gulf, approximately 24 km (15 miles) from the east coast of Saudi Arabia (to which it is linked by a causeway), and 28 km from the west coast of Qatar. There are six principal islands in the archipelago, the largest of these being Bahrain itself, which is about 50 km long, and between 13 km and 25 km wide. To the north-east of Bahrain island, and linked to it by a causeway and road, lies Muharraq island, which is approximately 6 km long. Another causeway links Bahrain island with Sitra island. The climate is temperate from December to the end of March, with temperatures ranging from 19°C to 25°C, but becomes very hot and humid during the summer months. In August and September temperatures can rise to 40°C. The official language is Arabic, but English is also widely spoken. According to the 2010 census, some 99.8% of Bahraini citizens are Muslims, divided into two sects: Shi'a (almost 60%) and Sunnis (more than 40%). Non-Bahrainis comprised 54.0% of the total population. The national flag (proportions 3 by 5) is red, with a vertical white stripe at the hoist, the two colours being separated by a serrated line forming five white triangles. The capital is Manama, on Bahrain island.

CONTEMPORARY POLITICAL HISTORY

Historical Context

Bahrain, a traditional Arab monarchy, became a British Protected State in the 19th century. Under this arrangement, government was shared between the ruling Sheikh and his British adviser. Following a series of territorial disputes in the 19th century, Persia (renamed Iran in 1935) made renewed claims to Bahrain in 1928. This disagreement remained unresolved until May 1970, when Iran accepted the findings of a UN-commissioned report showing that the inhabitants of Bahrain overwhelmingly favoured complete independence, rather than union with Iran.

Sheikh Sulman bin Hamad Al Khalifa, ruler of Bahrain since 1942, was succeeded upon his death in November 1961 by his eldest son, Sheikh Isa bin Sulman Al Khalifa. Extensive administrative and political reforms were implemented in January 1970, when a supreme executive authority, the 12-member Council of State, was established, representing the first formal derogation of the ruler's powers. Sheikh Khalifa bin Sulman Al Khalifa, the ruler's eldest brother, was appointed President of the Council.

Meanwhile, in January 1968 the United Kingdom had announced its intention to withdraw British military forces from the area by 1971. Plans to create a fully independent, federal state to be comprised of Bahrain, Qatar and the Trucial States (now United Arab Emirates—UAE) proved unworkable, and Bahrain became a separate independent state on 15 August 1971. Sheikh Isa took the title of Amir, while the Council of State became the Cabinet, with Sheikh Khalifa as Prime Minister. A Constituent Assembly, convened in December 1972, formulated a new Constitution, which came into force on 6 December 1973. Elections to a new National Assembly, composed of 14 cabinet ministers and 30 elected members, were conducted the following day. In the absence of political parties, candidates sought election as independents. However, in August 1975 the Assembly was dissolved by Amiri decree, following complaints from the Prime Minister that its members were obstructing the Government's legislative programme. New elections were to be held following minor changes to the Constitution and the electoral law, but the National Assembly was not reconvened; thus, the ruling family continued to exercise near-absolute power.

On 16 January 1993 a 30-member Majlis al-Shura (Consultative Council)—appointed by the ruling authorities and comprising a large number of business executives and some members of the old National Assembly—held its inaugural meeting. The Council was to act in a purely advisory capacity, with no legislative powers.

Domestic Political Affairs

For many years there have been indications of tension between Shi'a and Sunni Muslims. (The former comprise a majority of the population of Bahrain, while the royal family belongs to the latter sect.) During the 1980s two plots to overthrow the Government and a plan to sabotage Bahrain's petroleum installations were uncovered, all of which were alleged to have Iranian support. In December 1993 the human rights organization Amnesty International published a report criticizing the Bahraini Government's treatment of Shi'a Muslims, some of whom had been forcibly exiled. In March 1994 the Amir issued a decree pardoning 64 Bahrainis who had been in exile since the 1980s and permitting them to return to Bahrain. In December 1994, however, Sheikh Ali Salman Ahmad Salman, a Shi'a Muslim cleric, was arrested following his criticism of the Government and his public appeal for reform, particularly the restoration of the National Assembly. Widespread rioting ensued, especially in Shi'a districts, and large-scale demonstrations were held in Manama in support of Sheikh Ali Salman's demands and to petition for his release. Civil unrest continued despite the Amir's pledge to extend the powers of the Consultative Council; 12 people died and some 2,500 demonstrators were arrested in clashes with the security forces during December and January 1995. Sheikh Ali Salman was deported and sought asylum in the United Kingdom (a request that was granted in July 1998). The unprecedented scale of the protests was widely attributed to a marked deterioration in socio-economic conditions in Bahrain, and in particular to a high level of unemployment.

There were further anti-Government demonstrations in Shi'a districts in March and April 1995, following a police search of the property of an influential Shi'a cleric, Sheikh Abd al-Amir al-Jamri, who was subsequently placed under house arrest and later imprisoned. In June, in an apparent attempt to appease Shi'a opposition leaders, the Prime Minister announced the first major government reorganization for 20 years; the new Cabinet included five Shi'a ministers, although many strategic portfolios remained unchanged.

In August 1995 the Government initiated talks with Shi'a opposition leaders in an effort to foster reconciliation, while the Amir pardoned 150 people detained since the unrest. However, a report issued by Amnesty International in September indicated that as many as 1,500 demonstrators remained in detention, and that two prisoners had died in police custody following torture. The talks collapsed in mid-September, although more than 40 political prisoners, among them Sheikh al-Jamri, were released later in the month. In October al-Jamri and six other opposition figures began a hunger strike in protest at the Government's refusal to concede to their demands, which included the release of all political prisoners and the restoration of the National Assembly. Following a large demonstration to mark the end of the hunger strike, the Government announced in November that it would take 'necessary action' to prevent future 'illegal' gatherings. In December the Amir declared an amnesty for nearly 150 prisoners, most of whom had been arrested during the recent disturbances.

There were large-scale demonstrations in December and January 1996, in protest at the heavy deployment of security forces in Shi'a districts and at the closure of two mosques. In mid-January eight opposition leaders, including al-Jamri, were arrested on charges of inciting unrest. In February Ahmad al-Shamlan, a noted lawyer and writer, became the first prominent Sunni to be detained in connection with the disturbances, after he accused the Government of authoritarianism. A number of bomb explosions in February and March culminated in an arson attack on a restaurant in Sitra, in which seven Bangladeshi workers died. Also in March jurisdiction with regard to a number of criminal offences was transferred from ordinary courts to the High Court of Appeal, acting in the capacity of State Security Court. This move effectively accelerated the pace of court proceedings, while removing the right of appeal and limiting the role of the defence. In late March Isa Ahmad Hassan Qambar was executed by firing squad, having been condemned to death for killing a police officer during the unrest of March 1995. The execution—the first to take place in Bahrain since 1977—provoked mass protests by Bahrainis, while international human rights organizations challenged the validity of Qambar's confession and trial.

Civil tensions were exacerbated by the creation, in April 1996, of a Higher Council of Islamic Affairs (to be appointed by the Prime Minister and headed by the Minister of Justice and Islamic Affairs) to supervise all religious activity (including that of the Shi'a community) in Bahrain. As the Amir sought to placate opponents of his reforms, a new Consultative Council—expanded from 30 to 40 members—was appointed in September. Meanwhile, in July the State Security Court imposed death sentences on three of the eight Bahrainis convicted of the arson attack in Sitra, while four men were sentenced to life imprisonment. The death sentences were commuted to life imprisonment in December 2000.

In January 1997 a National Guard was created, to provide support for the Bahrain Defence Force (BDF) and the security forces of the Ministry of the Interior. The Amir's son, Crown Prince Sheikh Hamad bin Isa Al Khalifa, was appointed to command the new force, prompting speculation that its primary duty would be to protect the ruling family. In March a week of anti-Government protests marked the first anniversary of the execution of Isa Qambar. It was reported that since the outbreak of civil unrest at the end of 1994 some 28 people had been killed and 220 imprisoned in connection with the protests. In November 1997 the trial *in absentia* of eight prominent exiled activists (including Sheikh Ali Salman) on charges including the attempted overthrow of the regime resulted in the imposition of prison sentences of between five and 15 years. Meanwhile, during 1997 publishing restrictions were relaxed, and in December the Amir announced plans to allow greater media coverage of the activities of the Consultative Council.

The accession of Sheikh Hamad and constitutional change

Sheikh Isa died on 6 March 1999. He was succeeded as Amir by Sheikh Hamad, whose eldest son, Sheikh Salman bin Hamad Al Khalifa, became Crown Prince and also assumed Hamad's military command. Initially, opposition groups welcomed Sheikh Hamad's accession, which raised expectations of political change. In his first months in office Sheikh Hamad permitted Shi'a to join the armed forces, allowed an investigation by Amnesty International into alleged brutality by the security forces and released more than 300 Shi'a prisoners being held on security-related charges. However, the opposition claimed that 1,200–1,500 political prisoners remained in detention. In July al-Jamri, who was brought to trial in February, was sentenced to 10 years' imprisonment for espionage and inciting anti-Government unrest; a substantial fine was also imposed. Following intense international pressure, Sheikh Hamad granted al-Jamri an official pardon the following day, although he remained effectively under house arrest. In October 1999 the Amir issued a decree ordering the Consultative Council to establish a human rights committee, and in November–December he released some 345 detainees.

In May 2000 the Prime Minister stated that municipal elections, on the basis of universal suffrage, would be held in early 2001 and that parliamentary elections would take place in 2004. In September 2000 four women, as well as a number of non-Muslims, were appointed for the first time to the Consultative Council. The Amir announced in November that a 46-member Supreme National Committee (SNC) had been formed to prepare a National Action Charter (NAC), which would outline the further reform of Bahrain's political system. Among the SNC's recommendations, submitted in December, were that there should be a transition from an emirate to a constitutional monarchy, comprising a directly elected bicameral parliament (with women permitted both to vote and to seek election), a consultative chamber that would be appointed by the Government from all sections of society and an independent judiciary. Critics of the Bahrain regime dismissed the proposed transition to a monarchy as a pretext for the continuation of autocratic rule.

The new Charter was submitted for approval in a national referendum held on 14–15 February 2001 (at which Bahraini women were permitted to vote for the first time), and was duly endorsed by 98.4% of participating voters. Two committees were formed by Sheikh Hamad later that month: the first, headed by the Crown Prince, was asked to implement the NAC and to define the respective roles of the legislature and the monarchy; the second, chaired by the Minister of Justice and Islamic Affairs, was to oversee amendments to the Constitution. The Decree Law on State Security Measures and the State Security Court were both abolished. Following the removal of travel restrictions for members of the opposition, by March 2001 at least 100 political exiles had returned to Bahrain, among them Sheikh Ali Salman. In the same month the Government granted a licence to the independent Bahrain Human Rights Society (BHRS).

On 14 February 2002 Sheikh Hamad announced the establishment of a constitutional monarchy in Bahrain, proclaiming himself King. The new monarch approved the amendments to the Constitution outlined in the NAC and dissolved the Consultative Council. Municipal elections were held on 9 May (with run-off voting one week later); however, female candidates—for the first time permitted to stand for public office—failed to win any seats on the five new regional councils.

The 2002 and 2006 legislative elections

In early 2002 it was announced that Bahrain's first legislative election for 27 years would take place on 24 October. However, opposition activists expressed strong concern that the unelected Consultative Council would have the same rights as the elected Majlis al-Nuab (Council of Representatives) in the bicameral parliament, and stated that they would boycott the polls. In July 2002 the King ordered the establishment of an independent financial auditing court, with far-reaching powers to monitor state spending. The creation of a Constitutional Court was also approved by the Government: this became operational in April 2005.

At the election, held on 24 October 2002, 21 of the 40 seats were won by independents and 'moderate' Sunni candidates, with the remaining 19 seats taken by more radical Islamists. The rate of participation by voters was recorded as 53.2% of the registered electorate. Reformists claimed that the newly elected legislature did not reflect the structure of Bahraini society, since a large proportion of the Shi'a majority had boycotted the elections and female candidates had failed to win any seats (there had been eight women among a total of 174 candidates). Moreover, there was considerable criticism of the policy of political naturalization adopted by the King (whereby Sunnis from the Eastern Province of Saudi Arabia were granted full voting rights), which was interpreted as a deliberate attempt to reduce the size of the Shi'a majority. On 17 November the new Consultative Council was sworn in by the King; as in 2000, four women were appointed to the Council. Earlier in November 2002 King Hamad named an expanded Cabinet: the changes included the appointment of two Shi'a, Dr Majid bin Hassan al-Alawi and Jawad bin Salem al-Arrayed, as Minister of Labour and Social Affairs and Minister of Justice, respectively. Meanwhile, legislation permitting the establishment of independent trade unions was ratified in November.

In April 2004 Dr Nada Haffadh was appointed as Minister of Health, thereby becoming the first woman to attain cabinet rank in Bahrain. In May King Hamad dismissed the long-serving Minister of the Interior, Sheikh Muhammad bin Khalifa Al Khalifa, following clashes between Bahraini police and mainly Shi'a protesters who were demonstrating against US military operations in two Shi'a holy cities in Iraq. Lt-Gen. Sheikh Rashid bin Abdullah bin Ahmad Al Khalifa was named as his successor. In a government reorganization in September 2005, Sheikh Khalid bin Ahmad Al Khalifa, the former Bahraini ambassador to the United Kingdom, was appointed as Minister of Foreign Affairs, replacing Sheikh Muhammad bin Mubarak Al Khalifa, who remained one of three Deputy Prime Ministers and assumed additional responsibility for ministerial committees. Another notable change was the dissolution of the Ministry of Oil, the functions of which were transferred to a newly established National Oil and Gas Authority.

In late 2005 the King's reform strategy was tested by the progress of the draft political societies law that would oblige political groupings to agree to certain conditions, such as a pledge to work within the existing Constitution and the refusal of funding from foreign benefactors, in order to receive a licence (in effect granting a group political party status) from the Ministry of Justice. Al-Wefaq National Islamic Society (or the Islamic National Accord Association), the largest Shi'a group, which had boycotted the 2002 parliamentary election, agreed to register under the proposed regulations. The group, however, was reported to have split into two factions over the issue; the smaller of the two groups—now called Al-Haq (Movement for Liberty and Democracy)—declined to compete in the 2006 legislative elections, for which a date of 25 November had since been designated.

In an effort to minimize fears of an undemocratic ballot, and to preserve the political neutrality of the military sector, the Ministry of the Interior prohibited military staff from participating in election campaigns and appointed the BHRS as an independent election monitor. However, a report compiled by Dr Salah al-Bandar, Chancellor of Strategic Planning in the Ministry of Cabinet Affairs, and released in September 2006, accused several government officials of deliberately exacerbating sectarianism and of contriving unfairly to influence the elections. Dr al-Bandar, a Sudanese-born British citizen, was deported to the United Kingdom, and Bahrain's Higher Criminal Court issued an edict prohibiting any press coverage or comment relating to the affair. The Government's policy of incremental naturalization also provoked protests: the announcement that 5,000 non-Bahraini citizens of other Cooperation Council for the Arab States of the Gulf (or Gulf Cooperation Council—GCC, see p. 246) states would be permitted voting rights was also interpreted as an effort to increase the number of Sunni voters.

Elections to the Council of Representatives were held on 25 November 2006 (with a run-off ballot on 2 December); municipal elections were held concurrently. Following both rounds of voting, the Shi'a opposition Al-Wefaq, led by Sheikh Ali Salman, effectively held 18 seats in the Council (with one of these being an aligned independent). However, Sunni candidates—comprising 12 Sunni Islamists and 10 independent Sunnis—achieved a majority, winning 22 seats. (Only one seat was attained by a liberal candidate.) Latifa al-Qouood became the first female parliamentarian in the Gulf states when her constituency seat remained unopposed. The overall participation of registered voters in both polls was reported as 71%.

On 5 December 2006 King Hamad announced the appointment of the new Consultative Council, which included 10 female members and just two religious personalities (compared with 30 elected to the lower house); the selection was widely regarded as a counterbalancing measure to achieve a more representative parliament. Sheikh Khalifa presented his new Cabinet on 11 December, notably appointing Jawad bin Salem al-Arrayed as one of three Deputy Prime Ministers. The Cabinet instituted one new portfolio pertaining to Oil and Gas Affairs, which was awarded to the head of the National Oil and Gas Authority, Dr Abd al-Hussain bin Ali Mirza, and also introduced the post of Minister of State for Defence Affairs. Members of Al-Wefaq boycotted parliament's inauguration on 15 December, protesting that the composition of the new Cabinet effectively marginalized the Shi'a majority.

Civil unrest

Hundreds of demonstrators were reportedly injured in sporadic riots in Shi'a villages during the latter part of 2007. In mid-December, when Shi'a demonstrators gathered in Manama to commemorate those killed in the riots of December 1994 and to protest against human rights violations, police were reported to have used tear-gas and rubber bullets to disperse the crowds, injuring dozens of people, while one man was reported to have been killed. As clashes between the demonstrators and police intensified in subsequent days, dozens of people were arrested, a number of whom claimed to have been tortured while in police custody. This prompted the independent BHRS to apply to the authorities in late December 2007 for permission to visit the inmates; however, it was denied access, with the authorities stating that medical tests 'proved' that no acts of torture had been committed. The trial of 15 of the detainees took place in July, with 11 receiving sentences of between one and seven years and four being acquitted owing to insufficient evidence. The perceived harshness of the sentences led to sporadic outbreaks of violent unrest in Shi'a areas throughout 2008. A report published by Human Rights Watch in February 2010 concluded that, since late 2007, security forces in Bahrain had resumed the use of torture against detainees. The Minister of Foreign Affairs, Sheikh Khalid, subsequently announced that the Government would conduct an internal inquiry into the allegations.

Meanwhile, in a development that was seen as an attempt to strengthen royal control over the military, in January 2008 King Hamad announced the disbandment of the Ministry of Defence and the appointment of Crown Prince Sheikh Salman bin Hamad Al Khalifa as Deputy Commander-in-Chief of the BDF. The outgoing Minister of Defence, Maj.-Gen. Sheikh Khalifa bin Ahmad Al Khalifa, was appointed as BDF Commander-in-Chief, and the administration of matters pertaining to the military was henceforth to be managed by the Minister of State for Defence Affairs. The transfer of military authority from a government ministry to the direct control of the King, in his capacity as Supreme Commander of the BDF, rendered the military, according to the terms of the Constitution, immune to scrutiny by the legislature.

In mid-December 2008 security forces made a number of arrests in Shi'a villages outside Manama. The authorities announced that they had uncovered a plot to launch a series of co-ordinated terrorist attacks on police, government and commercial targets in the capital to coincide with Bahrain's National Day, 16 December. At least 14 suspects were detained, and on 28 December Bahrain Television broadcast a series of alleged confessions, in which prisoners apparently admitted to having received directions from Bahraini nationals resident in the United Kingdom, and to having travelled to Syria to obtain weapons training. In January 2009 police arrested a further three Shi'a political activists in connection with the National Day plot. Hassan Mesheima, Secretary-General of Al-Haq, Dr Abd al-Jalil al-Singace, an Al-Haq spokesperson, and Muhammad al-Moqdad, a Shi'a cleric, were charged variously with aiding and financing a terrorist organization and plotting to overthrow the Government; all three denied the charges. Al-Singace was released shortly thereafter, whereas the other two activists remained in custody. The arrests provoked clashes between protesters and police in various Shi'a areas. Following intensive pressure from international human rights organizations, a royal pardon was granted to 178 political prisoners, including Mesheima and al-Moqdad, in April.

The 2009/10 budget and labour market reforms

Following a protracted impasse concerning the 2009/10 budget, in early March 2009 the Council of Representatives voted to reject the budget; however, it was finally approved later that month following the intervention of King Hamad, who instructed the Government to allocate an additional BD 100m. to fund a monthly anti-inflation subsidy for poorer families. None the less, the relationship between the legislature and the executive remained tense. In May members of parliament rejected the closing budget statements for 2006 and 2007, claiming that the Government had withheld some details of spending on defence and on the Royal Court. The closing budget statement for 2008 was similarly rejected in January 2010.

Meanwhile, in April 2009 the Minister of Labour, Majid bin Hassan al-Alawi, announced the introduction, from August, of a Labour Market Reform Law. This guaranteed freedom of movement in the labour market for expatriate workers, thus ending the controversial sponsorship system that gave employers complete control over foreign workers. Under the new legislation, expatriates could apply for government-issued work permits and would be entitled to seek new employment without the permission of their current employer. A limited system of unemployment benefits for Bahraini citizens was also introduced.

The 2010 legislative elections

Direct elections to the Council of Representatives took place on 23 October 2010 (with run-off elections held in nine districts on 30 October). The elections were held against a backdrop of escalating tensions between the country's Shi'a and Sunni communities, following the detention of a number of Shi'a opposition figures and political activists, including the re-arrest in August of Mesheima and al-Singace of the Al-Haq movement (see Civil unrest); Mesheima and al-Singace were among 23 people charged in September with 'conducting a wide-ranging propaganda campaign against the Kingdom and seeking to overthrow the regime by force'. Several opposition alliances, including Al-Haq and the Islamic Action Society, boycotted the polls in protest both against the arrests and against claims that the Government had manipulated electoral boundaries in order to prevent the Shi'a opposition from securing a parliamentary majority. Critics of the Government and international human rights organizations cited numerous examples of alleged government repression of Shi'a in advance of the polls, while the Government's continued refusal to allow foreign observers to monitor elections elicited further criticism.

Despite the elevated tensions, the poll passed off without major incident, and voter turnout was reported at about 67%. Following both rounds of voting, Al-Wefaq had secured 18 seats, while five seats were won by Sunni Islamist candidates (three from Al-Asala Islamic Society, two from Al-Menbar Islamic Society); the remaining 17 seats were won by pro-Government Sunni independents, affording supporters of the Government a narrow majority in the 40-seat lower chamber. A new 40-seat Consultative Council was appointed by King Hamad on 25 November 2010. A minor government reorganization had been announced earlier that month, in which former Minister of Justice and Islamic Affairs Sheikh Khalid bin Abdullah Al Khalifa was appointed as a fourth Deputy Prime Minister. Meanwhile, in March Al-Wefaq had called for the cabinet to be selected by the Council of Representatives, rather than being appointed directly by the King, adding that the power-sharing arrangement envisaged in Bahrain's 2002 amended Constitution had not yet been satisfactorily implemented.

Anti-Government protests of 2011

In mid-February 2011 a number of demonstrations by protesters demanding democratic reforms—including greater powers for parliament and anti-corruption measures—and the release of Shi'a activists from custody took place in villages surrounding Manama, and in the capital itself. These were seemingly inspired by the recent anti-Government protests which had led to the removal from office of the Tunisian and Egyptian Presidents. On 15 February large crowds initiated protests at the Pearl roundabout in central Manama. During 14–15 February two protesters were shot dead in the capital during clashes with the police; King Hamad subsequently apologized for the conduct of the police. However, on 17 February security forces entered the area surrounding the roundabout in an attempt to disperse protesters who had been camping there, allegedly firing tear-gas and rubber bullets into the encampment; four people were reported to have been killed during the raid. The crackdown prompted vehement criticism from opposition groups, including Al-Wefaq, while the US Secretary of State, Hillary Clinton, and other foreign government officials urged the Bahraini authorities to exercise restraint in their response to the demonstrations.

Nevertheless, violent confrontations continued in the capital until 21 February 2011, when the armed forces withdrew from the Pearl roundabout, thus allowing protesters to reoccupy the area. In a concession to one of the protesters' key demands, on 23 February some 50 people—including the Shi'a political activists charged in September 2010—were released from gaol, while Mesheima and al-Singace were granted official pardons by King Hamad. Opponents of the Government were also being urged to participate in a 'National Dialogue', to be led by Crown Prince Sheikh Salman bin Hamad Al Khalifa. However, on 27 February 2011 Al-Wefaq announced that its 18 parliamentarians had submitted letters of resignation in protest against the deaths of seven anti-Government demonstrators earlier that month. Meanwhile, on 26 February the King issued a decree reallocating several cabinet portfolios, notably including those of housing and of labour. A new Ministry of Energy was also created, to be led by the former Minister of Oil and Gas Affairs, Dr Ali Mirza. However, the protesters demanded the removal from office of Prime Minister Sheikh Khalifa bin Sulman Al Khalifa and the replacement of the Cabinet with a government elected by the Council of Representatives.

On 13 March 2011 anti-Government demonstrators asserted control of parts of Manama, including the Financial Harbour district, following clashes with police. The following day around 1,500 troops and police officers from Saudi Arabia, the UAE and Qatar arrived in Bahrain as part of a GCC 'Peninsula Shield' force, ostensibly to assist the Bahraini security forces in protecting strategic buildings and facilities; their arrival was denounced by members of Al-Wefaq as an 'overt occupation'. (The GCC had earlier that week agreed to provide some US $10,000m. of aid to the Bahraini Government in support of the National Dialogue process.) Later the same day at least five people were reportedly killed amid attempts by government forces to disperse protesters gathered at locations in central Manama, including the Pearl roundabout and the Salmaniya hospital, bringing the total number of deaths since the protests began to 12.

King Hamad issued a decree on 15 March 2011 announcing a three-month state of 'national safety', according to which the BDF implemented curfews in parts of the capital previously occupied by protesters. Fears of a sectarian conflict increased thereafter, as the Bahraini authorities accused the Iranian Government and the Lebanese Shi'a militant organization Hezbollah of fomenting sectarian unrest. On 17 March six people, including Mesheima, al-Singace and Ibrahim Sharif (of the secular Al-Waad party), were arrested on charges including 'communicating with foreign countries' and 'inciting murder and the destruction of property'; by early April it was estimated that up to 400 people had been arrested in connection with the protests. On 8 May Mesheima, al-Singace and Sharif were among 21 opposition activists charged with attempting to overthrow the monarchy with the aid of a foreign terrorist organization. On 22 June, having been convicted of the charges, Mesheima, al-Singace and six other leading Shi'a campaigners were sentenced to life imprisonment. The remaining 13 defendants were given gaol terms of up to 15 years, including Sharif, who received a five-year term; seven of these were sentenced *in absentia*. Meanwhile, on 18 March the monument at the symbolic Pearl roundabout was destroyed by the authorities and the area renamed Al-Farooq Junction. A further cabinet reorganization was announced in late March, following the resignations of the recently appointed Ministers of Health and of Housing in protest against the Government's treatment of demonstrators. In mid-June a new Ministry of Human Rights and Social Development was created.

In response to further pro-democracy protests during April 2011, hundreds of demonstrators, opposition politicians, human rights campaigners and lawyers, doctors and nurses were arrested and put on trial for their involvement in the demonstrations. Human rights groups claimed that some of those in detention were being tortured, and four protesters died in police custody in early April. In mid-April it was reported that at least 100 public sector workers had been dismissed from their posts for participating in the demonstrations. (In July the General Federation of Bahrain Trade Unions claimed that some 2,500 workers had been removed, although some of these had later been allowed to return to work.) In mid-April the Government declared that it was seeking legal authority to dissolve Al-Wefaq and the Islamic Action Society because, it claimed, the Shi'a parties had 'violated' the Constitution and damaged 'social peace and national unity'. However, after receiving criticism from the US Administration, the authorities agreed to delay the imposition of such a ban until after the events surrounding the political unrest had been investigated. At the end of April four Shi'a protesters were sentenced to death by a military court in Manama, while three others were sentenced to life imprisonment, having been convicted of the murder of two police officers during recent clashes.

On 3 May 2011 the Ministry of Justice and Islamic Affairs charged 47 Shi'a medical workers (23 doctors and 24 nurses) who had treated wounded anti-Government demonstrators with crimes including acting against the state and failing to treat injured Sunnis during the recent protests; their trial began on 6 June. By mid-2011 more than 32 people were reported to have died as a result of the political violence. However, amid an apparent restoration of calm, on 1 June—two weeks earlier than originally stipulated—King Hamad declared an end to the three-month state of national safety. At the end of the month a partial withdrawal of the GCC troops was announced and in mid-June the ban imposed on the Al-Waad party in April was lifted, in preparation for the country's National Dialogue. However, heightened security measures remained in place, particularly in Shi'a villages. On 29 June King Hamad issued a decree establishing the Bahrain Independent Commission of Inquiry (BICI)—an independent, international commission of judicial and human rights experts—to investigate both the causes of the recent unrest and allegations of human rights violations arising from the state of national safety. These were to include any violent acts perpetrated by the police, demonstrators or foreign forces deployed in Bahrain. The five-member commission, led by former UN human rights lawyer Prof. Cherif Bassiouni, was asked to report its findings by the end of October.

The King's National Dialogue process was inaugurated on 2 July 2011, under the chairmanship of parliamentary Speaker Khalifa bin Ahmad al-Dhahrani. Some 300 representatives of Bahrain's political parties, civil society and expatriate groups, human rights organizations and other leading figures participated in discussions concerning political, legal, social and economic issues affecting the country's future. However, although Al-Wefaq agreed to participate in the dialogue, in mid-July the party reportedly declined to attend the meetings concerning economic and social issues, citing excessive government control of the talks. The discussions ended on 25 July, and three days later King Hamad unveiled plans to expand the legislative and monitoring powers of the Council of Representatives and henceforth to stipulate that cabinet members would require parliamentary approval prior to assuming their posts. The King granted a number of concessions to opposition parties in August, such as lifting the charges against some of those arrested since the recent unrest, instituting labour market and pensions reforms, and raising food subsidies.

Parliamentary by-elections, boycotted by Al-Wefaq and Al-Waad, were held on 24 September 2011 to elect representatives in 14 of the 18 seats vacated by Al-Wefaq in February, with candidates in the remaining four being returned unopposed. A run-off ballot was held on 1 October for nine seats where no candidate had secured 50% of the vote. Turnout during the first round of voting was reported at only 17%, owing to the widespread opposition boycott; however, a higher rate was reported at the second round. The majority of those elected were said to be pro-Government, although some described themselves as independents. Two female candidates were elected to the Council of Representatives in the second round of voting, bringing the total number of women in the chamber to four. On 29 September eight doctors and 12 other medical personnel—all Shi'a employed at the Salmaniya hospital—were found guilty by a military court in Manama of 'incitement to overthrow the Government' during the recent protests; they were convicted of refusing to treat wounded Sunnis and using ambulances to supply weapons to the protesters, and were sentenced to prison terms of between five and 15 years. A number of the medical practitioners alleged that they had been tortured by security forces while in detention. The verdicts were met with international condemnation, notably from Bahrain's allies such as the USA and the United Kingdom, and in late October, following an intervention by King Hamad, the Government announced that all 20 defendants would be retried in a civilian court.

Continuing tensions following publication of the BICI report

The Government admitted on 21 November 2011, prior to the release of the BICI's report, that its security forces had been guilty of 'excessive force and mistreatment of detainees', and affirmed that 20 security officials would face criminal proceedings as a result of such violations. On 23 November—the date that the commission officially published its findings—the BICI found that a 'culture of impunity' had developed among Bahrain's security forces, and that they had been involved in the illegal detention and systematic torture of detained protesters. Of the 35 deaths recorded during the period under investigation by the BICI (14 February–15 April), security forces were found to have been responsible for 19; five of these were as a result of torture. Five of those 35 people killed were members of Bahrain's security forces, while the remainder were civilians. A total of 46 deaths (mostly of protesters) were linked to the political unrest between February and October. It was also noted that Sunnis had been attacked by members of the majority Shi'a population. The report found 'no discernible evidence' of Iranian involvement in the protests and no evidence that any GCC troops had committed human rights abuses. It also criticized the unlawful dismissal of public sector workers and the biased and provocative reporting of events by Bahrain's state media.

King Hamad announced his acceptance of the Commission's findings, although he continued to insist that Iran had been responsible for provoking sectarian tensions. The King declared that a National Commission would be established (including Sunni and Shi'a representatives) to oversee implementation of the BICI's recommendations and to suggest possible legislative reforms by February 2012, and that civilians would no longer be tried by military courts. However, there were renewed clashes between police and protesters that month, as opposition parties demanded the Government's resignation; Al-Wefaq and Al-Waad declared that they would boycott further reconciliation talks. On 29 November Sheikh Khalifa bin Abdullah Al Khalifa, head of the National Security Agency (NSA), which—together with the Ministry of the Interior—was accused of having tortured protesters, was replaced in an acting capacity by Adel bin Khalifa al-Fadhel. As the BICI had recommended, the NSA had its powers to arrest suspects withdrawn.

On 1 January 2012 the Chairman of the Consultative Council, Ali bin Saleh al-Saleh, resigned as Chairman of the National Commission, after he was accused of 'irregularities' concerning the reinstatement of four Council members. On 10 January thousands of demonstrators held a peaceful protest outside the UN offices in Manama, demanding the removal from office of the Prime Minister. On 15 January King Hamad announced a series of constitutional reforms that granted, *inter alia*, additional powers to the Council of Representatives to approve new royally appointed cabinets, and to scrutinize the Government and question ministers suspected of wrongdoing. The Government also pledged to rebuild Shi'a mosques that had been destroyed by the authorities. However, although the constitutional amendments were ratified by the King on 3 May, opposition politicians claimed that the reforms were not sufficiently far-reaching, since parliament would still not be able to question or remove the Prime Minister.

It was announced on 6 February 2012 that a new, independent political grouping had been formed to encourage discussion among Bahrain's various moderate political societies and ease the sectarian tensions exacerbated by the recent political unrest. The Patriotic Independent Gathering, which counted among its leaders former government minister Dr Ali Fakhro, proposed a number of reforms—based on a seven-point plan outlined in early 2011 by Crown Prince Sheikh Salman—on which it suggested that pro-Government and opposition groups could agree. These included an increase in the powers of parliament, and changes to ensure a fairer balance of power between Bahrain's Sunni and Shi'a communities. On 8 February 2012 the prominent activist and co-founder of the proscribed Bahrain Centre for Human Rights (BCHR), Abd al-Hadi al-Khawaja, who was serving a term of life imprisonment, began a hunger strike to protest against his incarceration and that of 13 other pro-democracy campaigners from the Shi'a community (seven of whom were also facing life terms); these included Ibrahim Sharif of Al-Waad. Several members of al-Khawaja's family had also staged hunger strikes since his arrest in April 2011 and conviction by a military court, in June, on charges of 'plotting against the state'. However, al-Khawaja ended his hunger strike on 28 May 2012, after the ruling, by the Court of Cassation on 30 April, that the activist and 20 other Shi'a political prisoners should face a retrial in a civilian court. The retrial commenced on 8 May, with seven of the activists being charged *in absentia*; at its conclusion on 4 September, the court upheld all the defendants' convictions. The verdicts were subsequently reaffirmed by the Court of Cassation on 7 January 2013, prompting renewed protests. Meanwhile, King Hamad implemented changes to the composition of the Cabinet in mid-February and late April 2012, although the principal portfolios remained unchanged.

On 14 February 2012 efforts by opposition activists to mark the first anniversary of the security forces' crackdown on demonstrations at the former Pearl roundabout were largely prevented by a heavy security presence in Manama; a large number of people—both police and demonstrators—were, nevertheless, reported to have been injured in clashes, and several arrests were made. On 9 March a largely peaceful demonstration was held in the capital, at which protesters called for King Hamad to step down and for the Government to release all political prisoners. The rally—which, according to activists, was attended by at least 200,000 people (the authorities estimated 100,000)—had been instigated by leading Shi'a cleric Sheikh Isa Qassim. Some violence was reported when demonstrators attempted to access the site of the former Pearl roundabout and were prevented from doing so by riot police. On 11 March, following their retrial, 15 of the 20 medical workers at the Salmaniya hospital convicted in September 2011 of 'incitement to overthrow the Government' had their convictions revoked by the civilian court. Four days later the remaining medics were informed that their convictions had been upheld. On 17 March the Government proposed draft amendments to the law on political associations, which included a ban on any overt religious activity and on any action that risked provoking sectarian tensions. On 9 April a number of police officers were wounded in a bomb explosion in the Shi'a village of Akar, leading to acts of vengeance by Sunni youths. Further anti-Government protests were held amid the international focus on Bahrain during the Formula One Grand Prix (see Recent developments) on 20–22 April 2012, and continued into the following month. Some of the focus of protesters in mid-2012 was the proposed union between Saudi Arabia and Bahrain—in anticipation of a wider union of GCC states (see Foreign Affairs)—which was vehemently opposed by many Bahrainis.

The Ministry of Justice and Islamic Affairs initiated legal proceedings to seek to dissolve the Islamic Action Society in early June 2012. On 12 June the Bahrain Foundation for Reconciliation and Civil Discourse, a new grouping intended to promote reconciliation between Bahrain's diverse communities by encouraging dialogue and facilitating mutual understanding, was launched as part of the Ministry of Social Development. Two days later, following their retrial in a civilian court, nine of the 20 medical personnel were acquitted, while nine were given reduced prison terms ranging from one month to five years; they announced that they would appeal the sentences. Two doctors believed to be living abroad or in hiding had not appealed against their 15-year prison terms. On 26 June, in response to the BICI's recommendations, the Government agreed to pay some US $2.6m. in compensation to the relatives of 17 protesters who had died during the previous year's violent clashes with the security forces. Amid continued protests against King Hamad and the Cabinet, in July the Government was forced to instigate an inquiry into claims being circulated by foreign media organizations in Manama that the police and security personnel were still engaged in the torture of demonstrators. It was reported in that month that more than 80 people had been killed in Bahrain since the start of the political unrest in February 2011.

On 16 August 2012, the influential co-founder and President of the BCHR, Nabeel Rajab, was sentenced to three years in prison, having been convicted by a Manama court of various charges relating to his role in organizing unauthorized anti-Government demonstrations and marches. Rajab's most recent arrest followed the publication by the BCHR of a report detailing a series of human rights violations that had allegedly been committed by the Bahraini authorities since the BICI published its recommendations in November 2011.

On 1 October 2012 the Court of Cassation upheld the convictions of the nine Shi'a medical workers whose prison terms had been announced in June; five of them subsequently began a hunger strike to protest against their sentences. On 30 October the Minister of the Interior, Lt-Gen. Sheikh Rashid bin Abdullah bin Ahmad Al Khalifa, declared an official ban on all demonstrations, claiming that the continuing opposition protests represented a serious threat to public safety. The new measure followed a further series of rallies by largely Shi'a demonstrators in Manama and other towns, which had resulted in clashes with security forces, and in which two police officers had recently died. Representatives of Al-Wefaq declared that the group would refuse to adhere to the ban, describing it as an infringement of their human rights and in contravention of international law. On 21 November Amnesty International joined local and international human rights groups in criticizing the Bahraini Government for the lack of progress made since the issuing of the BICI report one year previously. The human rights organization described the 'spiralling repression' in the kingdom, citing in particular the recent revocation of the citizenship of 31 activists, the ban on public demonstrations and continuing instances of torture being used against detained protesters.

Recent developments: the National Dialogue resumes

On 10 February 2013 the National Dialogue between opposition parties and representatives of the Government and of pro-Government groups was reconvened, raising hopes of an agreement on measures to end the unrest. (Despite some disagreement regarding the opposition's demand that a member of the royal family attend the talks, a preliminary agenda was finally set on 31 March.) On 14 February a teenage activist was killed during clashes between protesters and the security forces in Manama, while a police officer was reportedly killed in a separate incident. The following week another protester, who was identified as a relative of the teenager, died of wounds allegedly sustained after being hit with a tear-gas canister fired by a member of the security forces. Meanwhile, also on 14 February the authorities claimed that an explosive device had been discovered on the King Fahd Causeway linking Bahrain to Saudi Arabia; several days later the arrest was announced of eight members of Jaish al-Imam, a terrorist grouping allegedly led by a member of Iran's Islamic Revolutionary Guards Corps (IRGC). In early March Crown Prince Salman was appointed as First Deputy Prime Minister, with particular responsibility for improving the performance of the country's executive bodies. Later that month the convictions of some 21 of the medical workers arrested in 2011 were overturned by a court in Manama. It was subsequently reported that all those medical workers acquitted were to be reinstated by the Ministry of Health.

Protests continued into April 2013, when the Coalition of February 14 Youth (an opposition group formed in 2011) claimed responsibility for four minor explosions aimed as a protest against the Formula One Grand Prix which was held in Bahrain that month. The event passed peacefully, although security forces claimed to have discovered caches of weapons in the run-up. Meanwhile, the US State Department published a report which referred to 'significant' violations of human rights in Bahrain, including torture in detention, while the UN Special Rapporteur on Torture expressed his disappointment that a planned visit to the kingdom had been postponed indefinitely. Also that month, the Government supported a proposal to increase to five years' imprisonment the penalty for insulting the King. In May the Al-Asala Islamic Society withdrew from the National Dialogue, citing differences within the pro-Government (Al-Fateh) coalition. On 17 May security forces raided the home of Sheikh Isa Qassim, prompting a protest rally by his supporters and harsh criticism from the Iranian Government.

In late May 2013 the Minister of Justice and Islamic Affairs, Sheikh Khalid bin Ali Al Khalifa, banned all political societies in Bahrain from contacts with Hezbollah, which he termed a 'terrorist organization'. Meanwhile, Jaish al-Imam appeared to be gaining in influence; several members were among those arrested on terrorism charges in mid-June, while on 25 June the authorities claimed that they had foiled an attempt by eight members of the organization to storm a pre-trial detention centre. (Six detainees from the centre suspected of attacks against the security forces had escaped on their way to court the previous month; two were recaptured in late July.) The killing of a 19-year-old policeman by a homemade bomb in an attempted attack on a police station in Sitra on 7 July resulted in condemnation from Germany, the United Kingdom and the USA, as well as locally. Following the explosion of a car bomb outside a Sunni mosque close to the Royal Court on 18 July, the Government sought to ban a protest march scheduled for the following day. Hundreds of protesters none the less gathered in several Shi'a villages west of Manama, after a call issued by the Coalition of February 14 Youth; several people were reportedly wounded, including one policeman.

On 28 July 2013, the day after an explosive device wounded three policemen, an emergency session of parliament was held to discuss the rising number of bombings in Bahrain. Measures proposed included revoking the citizenship of those convicted of involvement in such acts and banning protest rallies in Manama. There were also calls for the implementation of an emergency law in the run-up to a demonstration scheduled for 14 August (which date marked the 42nd anniversary of Bahrain's independence). The following day King Hamad endorsed parliament's recommendations, despite criticism from the international human rights organizations. The demonstration was to take place in front of the US embassy in Manama. It had been organized by the Bahrain Tamarod movement (a loose association of opposition activists) and was modelled on the Egyptian protests of mid-2013 that had resulted in the removal of President Muhammad Mursi. Although the rally in Manama was prevented from taking place, a series of clashes took place in Shi'a villages close to the capital; these continued for several days.

Despite the implementation of several recommendations of the BICI in mid-2013, including the installation of a police ombudsman and the establishment of an independent commission on the rights of prisoners and detainees, the Bahraini Government continued to impose restrictions on opposition activists. On 3 September a ruling was imposed whereby political societies planning to meet foreign diplomats were obliged to notify the Ministry of Foreign Affairs no less than three working days in advance. Meanwhile, Al-Wefaq withdrew from the National Dialogue after the arrest of Khalil al-Marzouq, a prominent former member of parliament. While the Government denied that al-Marzouq had been detained for political reasons, Iran condemned his arrest as a 'baseless excuse'. At the end of September large protests were held in villages west of Manama to demand his release. Al-Marzouq was subsequently accused of inciting terrorist crimes; he was released from detention at the end of October, but the following month was banned from leaving the country.

At the end of September 2013 it was reported that a total of at least 89 people had died since the beginning of the conflict in Bahrain in February 2011. On 29 September 2013 50 people were sentenced to up to 15 years' imprisonment for forming the Coalition of February 14 Youth, several *in absentia*. Some of the defendants were also accused of spying for Iran. On 3 November a further 10 Shi'a were gaoled for their alleged role in forming Jaish al-Imam, as well as for espionage, bringing to 138 the number of Shi'a convicted following the demand by King Hamad at the end of September for stricter penalties for those found guilty of acts of terror. On the same day Sheikh Ali Salman, leader of Al-Wefaq, was summoned for questioning, but was later released from custody. The cleric was questioned again by police at the end of December on allegations of incitement; he was not detained, but was barred from travelling abroad. On 8 January 2014 the Al-Fateh coalition withdrew from the National Dialogue, allegedly owing to Al-Wefaq's continued boycott of the talks and the Government's apparent unwillingness to discuss certain items on the agenda; the Government subsequently officially suspended the talks. However, the following week Crown Prince

Salman intervened directly in the dialogue process, meeting with representatives of Al-Wefaq—including Sheikh Ali Salman and Khalil al-Marzouq—and other opposition groups. During the talks the Crown Prince was reported to have expressed his commitment to solving the political crisis in the kingdom. In early February King Hamad approved legislation that stipulated a sentence of seven years' imprisonment and a fine of BD 10,000 for anyone convicted of insulting the monarch.

Foreign Affairs

Regional relations

Although relations between Bahrain and Iran were upgraded to ambassadorial level in late 1990, bilateral tensions increased in the mid-1990s. While there was sufficient evidence to suggest largely domestic motivation for the recent increase in popular disaffection, the Bahraini authorities continued to imply that the disturbances were fomented by Iranian-backed militant Shi'a fundamentalists seeking to destabilize the country. In June 1996 the Bahraini Government announced that it had uncovered details of a plot, initiated in 1993 with support from Shi'a fundamentalist groups in Iran, to oust the Government and ruling family in Bahrain and replace them with a pro-Iranian administration. It was claimed that a previously unknown Shi'a group, Hezbollah Bahrain, had been established and financed by Iran's IRGC. Young Bahraini Shi'a were alleged to have received military training in Iran and at guerrilla bases in Lebanon, in preparation for a terrorist offensive in Bahrain, which had culminated in the unrest of the previous 18 months. Within days of the Government's announcement more than 50 Bahrainis had been arrested in connection with the alleged plot, many of whom admitted membership of Hezbollah Bahrain. Although the Iranian authorities denied any involvement in the planned insurrection, the two countries' respective ambassadors were withdrawn, and diplomatic relations were downgraded. During 1996 and early 1997 more than 60 Bahrainis received prison sentences of between one and 15 years from the State Security Court for offences connected to the disturbances.

There was a period of *détente* in relations between most countries of the GCC and Iran following the election of Muhammad Khatami to the Iranian presidency in May 1997, and in December 1999 relations at ambassadorial level were formally restored between Bahrain and Iran. However, relations deteriorated in 2005, following the publication in the Bahraini daily *Al-Ayam* of a cartoon that Iranians considered insulting to their Supreme Leader, Ayatollah Ali Khamenei. Moreover, Bahrain took umbrage at the display of pictures of Iranian religious leaders during the country's own Ashoura festival.

In July 2007 an editorial published in a conservative Iranian newspaper, in which its author revived claims that Bahrain was rightfully an Iranian province, provoked protests outside the Iranian embassy in Manama. Distancing itself from the comments, the Iranian Government dispatched the Minister of Foreign Affairs, Manouchehr Mottaki, to meet with his counterpart in Manama and convey a public message of 'peace and friendship' to the Bahraini Government. Sheikh Khalid, Bahrain's Minister of Foreign Affairs, asserted that the editorial had not compromised their 'strong' bilateral relations, which had improved during 2006. In November 2007, during a visit to Manama by Iranian President Mahmoud Ahmadinejad (who had assumed office in August 2005), a memorandum of understanding (MOU) pertaining to oil and gas was signed. In March 2008 the Bahraini Prime Minister, Sheikh Khalifa, publicly endorsed Iran's right to develop nuclear technology for peaceful purposes, and a framework agreement concerning the import of large quantities of Iranian gas was signed by the two countries in October. Sheikh Khalid visited the Iranian capital, Tehran, in December, holding talks with both Ahmadinejad and Mottaki, which led to the signing of an extended security agreement, covering drugs-trafficking and counter-terrorism, as well as plans for the establishment of a joint security committee.

The positive trend in relations with Iran was jeopardized in February 2009, following reports that Ali Akbar Nateq Nouri, a senior political figure, had described Bahrain as a former province of Iran, in a speech marking the 30th anniversary of the establishment of the Islamic Republic. The remark, which was interpreted by many as an attack on Bahrain's sovereignty, provoked vociferous condemnation from numerous regional and international leaders. Negotiations over the planned gas import agreement were suspended as a result of the controversy. However, the Iranian authorities acted quickly to defuse the crisis: Sadeq Mahsouli, Iran's Minister of the Interior, visited Manama in late February and, following a visit by Sheikh Khalid to Tehran in March, the diplomatic row was officially ended and trade negotiations were resumed; the gas import negotiations, nevertheless, remained stalled. In June the Bahraini Ministry of Culture and Information suspended publication of the prominent daily newspaper *Akhbar al-Khaleej*, following its inclusion of an article written by a member of the Consultative Council, Sameera Rajab, in which she criticized the Iranian authorities and the conduct of the disputed presidential election in Iran. After the Bahraini authorities had, in October 2009, agreed to resume the gas import negotiations, in September 2010 Iran's Deputy Minister of Petroleum, Javad Oji, announced that discussions had been held in Tehran concerning proposals to construct a natural gas pipeline which would transfer some 1,000m. cu m of Iranian gas to Bahrain, and to establish a joint commission intended to increase co-operation in the sector.

Meanwhile, in January 2010 a Bahraini delegation led by the Speaker of the Council of Representatives, Khalifa al-Dhahrani, travelled to Tehran. During the visit President Ahmadinejad declared that relations between the two countries were based on mutual respect and recognition of sovereignty, and invited King Hamad to visit Tehran. In August Sheikh Khalid insisted that Bahrain would not allow the USA to launch an attack on Iran from its military bases in Bahrain, stating that Bahrain's military agreements with the USA were purely for defence. However, relations were compromised following the publication by the WikiLeaks organization of a series of classified US diplomatic cables in late 2010; in one such communiqué, King Hamad was reported to have identified Iran as the cause of the ongoing violence in Iraq and Afghanistan (q.v.) and to have argued vehemently in favour of forceful action to terminate Iran's nuclear programme. Ongoing contention between the USA (among other countries) and Iran over the latter's nuclear programme was regarded by some observers as a potential threat to Bahrain's security: in the event of conflict, the US Fifth Fleet military base in Manama was considered a likely target for Iranian military action. In early 2011 relations deteriorated again after the Bahraini authorities accused Iran of influencing anti-Government demonstrations which erupted in Manama from mid-February. In March Bahrain's ambassador in Tehran, Rashid bin Saad al-Dosari, was withdrawn, and later that month the Iranian chargé d'affaires in Manama was expelled from the country, owing to alleged links to Bahraini opposition groups. However, in mid-August al-Dosari returned to Tehran to resume his post. In early 2013 the Bahraini authorities uncovered a militant group with alleged links to Iran's IRGC (see Domestic Political Affairs). Bilateral relations came under further strain in September, when Iran condemned the arrest of a prominent member of the Shi'a opposition, Khalil al-Marzouq. However, later that month the ministers responsible for foreign affairs of both countries stressed the importance of bilateral relations and of mutual respect for sovereignty.

In common with other Gulf states, Bahrain consistently expressed support for Iraq at the time of the Iran–Iraq War (1980–88). However, following the Iraqi invasion of Kuwait in August 1990, the Government firmly supported the implementation of UN economic sanctions against Iraq and permitted the stationing of US troops and combat aircraft in Bahrain. (Military co-operation with the USA had been close for many years.) In June 1991, following the liberation of Kuwait in February, it was confirmed that Bahrain would remain a regional support base for the USA, and later in the year the two countries signed a defence co-operation agreement. In January 1994 Bahrain signed further accords of military co-operation with the USA and the United Kingdom. Relations with Iraq remained strained, and in October hopes of improved relations receded when Iraqi forces were again deployed in the Iraq–Kuwait border area. In response, Bahrain deployed combat aircraft and naval units to join GCC and US forces in the defence of Kuwait. In June 1998, as part of a wider US effort to reduce its military presence in the region, US military aircraft were withdrawn from Bahrain. A further US-led military campaign against Iraq centred in Manama in December was supported by the Bahraini authorities, although Bahrain refrained from any public endorsement of the air strikes.

Bahrain joined the other GCC states in condemning the suicide attacks on New York and Washington, DC, USA, on 11 September 2001, and pledged to co-operate with the USA's attempts to forge an international 'coalition against terror', notably by freezing the financial assets of individuals or organizations allegedly linked to the militant Islamist al-Qa'ida network of Osama bin Laden, held by the USA to be principally responsible for the attacks. Nevertheless, as the momentum grew towards a US-led military campaign to oust the regime of Saddam Hussain in Iraq, anti-war riots became increasingly frequent in Bahrain, and in February 2003 police opened fire on a 2,000-strong violent demonstration outside the US embassy in Manama. Although King Hamad expressed hope that a diplomatic solution to the crisis might be found, Bahrain announced that it would contribute a frigate and an unspecified number of troops to the defence of Kuwait from possible Iraqi retaliation should the US-led campaign proceed.

Following the commencement, later in March 2003, of US-led military action in Iraq, in April Bahrain ordered the expulsion of an Iraqi diplomat who was alleged to be linked to an explosion outside the Fifth Fleet base. Sporadic violent incidents and threats, believed to be related to the continued presence of the US military in Bahrain, continued throughout 2003–04. The bombing of the al-Askari Mosque (or Golden Mosque) in Samarra, one of the holiest Shi‘a shrines in Iraq, by insurgents in February 2006 prompted the largest demonstration in Bahrain for many years. In an effort to combat terrorism, King Hamad presented a 'Protecting Society from Terrorist Acts' bill to parliament in July; despite protestations of human rights contravention by the UN and Amnesty International (among others), the legislation was ratified in August. In October 2007 three Bahraini nationals became the first people to go on trial under the remit of the controversial new legislation after they were charged with belonging to a terrorist cell plotting attacks on US interests in Manama, and of supporting insurgents loyal to the deposed Taliban regime in Afghanistan; a fourth Bahraini man and a Qatari citizen were tried *in absentia*. In January 2008 all five were convicted and sentenced to six months' imprisonment.

After more than three years without a senior diplomatic representative in Iraq, Bahrain appointed Salah al-Maliki as its ambassador in October 2008—the chargé d'affaires, Hassan Ansari, had been withdrawn after narrowly escaping an assassination attempt in 2005. Minister of Foreign Affairs Sheikh Khalid visited Baghdad in October 2008, declaring his country's support for the Iraqi Government. Following the intervention of GCC troops in the unrest in Bahrain of early 2011, Iraqi Prime Minister Nuri al-Maliki warned that the intervention of foreign forces might lead to renewed sectarian conflict across the Middle East. The Bahraini Government threatened to boycott the League of Arab States (Arab League) summit held in March 2012 in Baghdad, accusing the Iraqi authorities of interference through their apparent support for the anti-Government protest movement and amid widespread animosity among Arab states towards Iraq's Shi‘a-led, Iranian-backed Government. However, in the event senior Bahraini delegates did attend the summit.

In April 1986 Qatari military forces raided the island of Fasht al-Dibal, which had been artificially constructed on a coral reef (submerged at high tide), situated midway between Bahrain and Qatar; both countries claimed sovereignty over the island. Following GCC mediation, in May the two Governments agreed to destroy the island. Other areas of dispute between the two states were Zubarah (which was part of Bahraini territory until the early 20th century), in mainland Qatar, and the Hawar islands, which were believed to contain potentially valuable reserves of petroleum and natural gas. In July 1991 Qatar instituted proceedings at the International Court of Justice (ICJ) in The Hague, Netherlands, regarding the islands (in 1939 a British judgment had awarded them to Bahrain), Fasht al-Dibal and Qit‘at Jaradah (over which the British Government had recognized Bahrain's 'sovereign rights' in 1947), together with the delimitation of the maritime border between Qatar and Bahrain. The question of sovereignty was further confused in April 1992, when the Qatari Government issued a decree redefining its maritime borders to include territorial waters claimed by Bahrain, and tensions were exacerbated by Qatar's unilateral application to the ICJ. Moreover, Bahrain had reportedly attempted to widen the issue to include its claim to the Zubarah region. In December 1996 Bahrain boycotted the GCC annual summit convened in Doha, Qatar, at which it was decided to establish a quadripartite committee (comprising those GCC members not involved in the dispute) to facilitate a solution. Following senior-level ministerial meetings between Bahrain and Qatar in London, United Kingdom, and in Manama in early 1997, it was announced that bilateral diplomatic relations at ambassadorial level were to be established. Qatar, however, was alone in nominating its diplomatic representative shortly afterwards.

At the end of 1999 the Amir of Qatar made his first official visit to Manama, during which it was agreed that a joint committee, headed by the Crown Princes of Bahrain and Qatar, would be established to encourage bilateral co-operation. Qatar also agreed to withdraw its petition from the ICJ in the event of the joint committee's reaching a solution to the territorial disputes. In January 2000 the new Amir of Bahrain, Sheikh Hamad, visited Qatar, and the two countries agreed to hasten the opening of embassies in Manama and Doha. In February, following the first meeting of the Bahrain-Qatar Supreme Joint Committee, it was announced that the possibility of constructing a causeway (to be named the Friendship Bridge) to link the two states was to be investigated; Qatar officially named its ambassador to Bahrain on the same day. In May, however, Bahrain unilaterally suspended the Supreme Joint Committee pending the ruling of the ICJ. A verdict was issued in March 2001, whereby Bahrain was found to have sovereignty over the Hawar islands and Qit‘at Jaradah, while Qatar held sovereignty over Zubarah, Janan island and the low-tide elevation of Fasht al-Dibal; the Court drew a single maritime boundary between the two states. Both Bahrain and Qatar accepted the ICJ ruling. Later in March, following a high-profile visit by Sheikh Hamad to Doha, the two sides announced that meetings of the Supreme Joint Committee would resume.

From early 2002 international oil companies were invited to submit bids to drill for petroleum and gas off the Hawar islands, which the newly enthroned King Hamad intended to transform into a major tourist resort. Approval for the construction of the causeway linking Bahrain to Qatar was finally given in May 2004, and a public commission to oversee the project was appointed in February 2005. In May 2008 the contract to design and build the causeway was awarded to a French-led consortium. Construction was expected to begin in 2010 and to be completed in 2014–15. However, in early 2011 the project, then estimated to cost some US $5,500m., stalled amid heightened bilateral tensions. Relations had been damaged in May 2010 when a Bahraini fisherman was seriously injured by Qatari coastguards in a 'naval incident', which had resulted in a resumption of hostilities over ownership of the Hawar islands. Tensions were further exacerbated later that month following the airing by the Qatar-based satellite broadcaster Al Jazeera of a television programme on poverty and the treatment of foreign labourers in Bahrain. The Bahraini Government promptly announced a suspension of the local operations of Al Jazeera, citing a 'breach of press and publishing regulations'. Work on the causeway had yet to commence by early 2014; it was revealed in December 2012 that the growing cost of the project meant that completion was unlikely much in advance of Qatar's hosting of the Fédération Internationale de Football Association (FIFA) World Cup in 2022. Meanwhile, in October 2013 the new Amir of Qatar, Sheikh Tamim bin Hamad Al Thani, made his first official visit to Bahrain.

Prior to the GCC summit meeting held in Riyadh, Saudi Arabia, in May 2012, King Hamad expressed his support for the creation of a 'Gulf Union', which would require member states to develop a common foreign and defence policy, and to increase their level of political and economic co-operation. The proposal, which was being strongly advocated by King Abdullah of Saudi Arabia, was seen as the Gulf states' response to Iran's growing influence in the region. Following the meeting some Bahraini news sources reported that an initial union between Bahrain and Saudi Arabia was imminent, and further discussions—particularly concerning closer security co-operation—were held at the GCC summit held in Manama in late December. In December 2013 Prime Minister Sheikh Khalifa reiterated his full support for the proposed Gulf Union, despite opposition from Oman and other member states.

Other external relations

In September 2004 Bahrain signed a free trade agreement with the USA. In response, the Saudi Government, which claimed that the accord contravened the GCC's external tariff agreement, threatened to impose customs duties on foreign goods imported duty-free through GCC countries, a move that would affect US goods imported to Bahrain under the bilateral agreement. In December Crown Prince Abdullah of Saudi Arabia declined to attend the GCC annual summit in Manama, and, in another apparently punitive measure, the Saudi authorities reduced petroleum transfers by withdrawing the extra output resulting from the doubling of capacity at the jointly owned Abu Saafa oilfield. Nevertheless, in May 2005 GCC ministers responsible for finance reportedly decided to allow bilateral commercial accords between individual member states and the USA, and the Bahraini-US agreement was duly implemented following US congressional approval in December; it became effective in August 2006.

George W. Bush became the first US President to embark upon an official visit to Bahrain when he travelled to the Gulf state in January 2008 during a wider regional tour. King Hamad welcomed President Bush's visit as a reflection of the burgeoning relationship enjoyed by the two allies, and proposed further bilateral military co-operation, while Bush was unreserved in his praise of King Hamad and the Bahraini Government's efforts to create significant political change in the Gulf state. In March the King paid an official visit to the USA, during which he signed an MOU on civil nuclear co-operation with the US Administration. In May Houda Nonoo, a female member of the Consultative Council, was appointed as Bahrain's ambassador to the USA, thereby becoming the first Jewish envoy from the Arab world to occupy such a post.

Despite maintaining extremely close ties with the kingdom, the US Administration under President Barack Obama expressed concern at the Bahraini Government's crackdown on pro-democracy protesters in early 2011. In May President Obama urged the Government to improve its human rights record and to release imprisoned opposition leaders, and in June Bahrain was listed among a group of countries which the USA considered should be placed under the scrutiny of the UN Human Rights Council. In May 2012 the US Administration announced that it would resume the sale of weapons to Bahrain, which had been put on hold following the start of the Government's crackdown on protesters in 2011; however, specific measures were outlined to ensure that US weapons were used to defend Bahrain against external threats, rather than in operations against internal opponents. In September 2012 US officials were critical of the pace of reform in Bahrain, demanding further accountability as far as the security forces were concerned (despite recent prison sentences being given to three security officials) and urging the release from detention of human rights activists; their concerns were reiterated in April 2013 in the form of a highly critical State Department report on human rights in the kingdom (see Domestic Political Affairs).

In December 2008 King Hamad paid his first ever official visit to Russia, during which he held talks with Russian President Dmitrii Medvedev. During the summit the King voiced his support for Russia's involvement in the Middle East peace process. The two countries also signed an MOU on civil nuclear co-operation. In February 2009 French President Nicolas Sarkozy paid an official visit to Bahrain, during which both a military co-operation agreement and a joint declaration on civil nuclear energy projects were signed. Although the European Union joined the USA in criticizing the Bahraini authorities for their harsh response to the anti-Government demonstrations from early 2011, France continued to enjoy largely favourable relations with the kingdom. In mid-2011 Crown Prince Salman and other senior Bahraini officials visited a number of Bahrain's traditional allies, including the USA, the United Kingdom and France, to seek to reinforce relations and to secure those countries' support for the newly instituted National Dialogue process (see Domestic Political Affairs).

CONSTITUTION AND GOVERNMENT

The 108-article Constitution that came into force on 6 December 1973 stated that 'all citizens shall be equal before the law' and guaranteed freedom of speech, of the press, of conscience and of religious beliefs. Other provisions included compulsory free primary education and free medical care. The Constitution also provided for a National Assembly, composed of 14 members of the Cabinet and 30 members elected by popular vote, although this was dissolved in August 1975. A National Action Charter, drafted in late 2000 by a Supreme National Committee and approved in a national referendum held in February 2001, recommended the transition from an emirate to a constitutional monarchy. The Amir proclaimed himself King in February 2002, when the amended Constitution was promulgated. Subsequently, a bicameral legislature, comprising a directly elected legislative body and a royally appointed consultative chamber, was instituted; each body was to serve a four-year term. Elections to a 40-member Council of Representatives took place in October 2002, and a new Consultative Council, comprising 40 appointed members, was sworn in by the King in November. Further legislative polls held in November 2006 resulted in a narrow Sunni Islamist parliamentary majority, a majority that was maintained following Bahrain's third direct legislative elections in October 2010.

REGIONAL AND INTERNATIONAL CO-OPERATION

Bahrain is a member of the Cooperation Council for the Arab States of the Gulf (or Gulf Cooperation Council—GCC, see p. 246), the six members of which established a unified regional customs tariff in 2003. The economic convergence criteria for the proposed introduction of a single market and currency were agreed at a heads of state meeting in Abu Dhabi, the UAE, in 2005, and in January 2008 the GCC launched its common market. A monetary union agreement, signed by four member states including Bahrain, in Riyadh, Saudi Arabia, in June 2009, defined the characteristics of the planned unified currency and monetary institutions. In addition, Bahrain is a participant in the League of Arab States (Arab League, see p. 362) and the Organization of Arab Petroleum Exporting Countries (OAPEC, see p. 400).

Bahrain became a member of the UN in 1971 and, as a contracting party to the General Agreement on Tariffs and Trade, joined the World Trade Organization (WTO, see p. 434) on its establishment in 1995. The country also participates in the Organization of Islamic Cooperation (OIC, see p. 403).

ECONOMIC AFFAIRS

In 2010, according to estimates by the World Bank, Bahrain's gross national income (GNI), measured at average 2008–10 prices, was US $18,552m., equivalent to $14,820 per head (or $19,080 per head on an international purchasing-power parity basis). During 2003–12, it was estimated, the population increased at an average annual rate of 6.1%, while gross domestic product (GDP) per head declined, in real terms, by an average of 0.8%. According to provisional official figures, overall GDP increased, in real terms, at an average annual rate of 4.5% per year in 2006–12; growth was 3.4% in 2012.

According to FAO, agriculture (including hunting, forestry and fishing) engaged 0.6% of the labour force in mid-2014. According to provisional official figures, the sector contributed 0.3% of GDP in 2012. The principal crops are dates, tomatoes, and lemons and limes. Livestock production is also important. Agricultural GDP increased by an average annual rate of 1.5% in 2006–12; the GDP of the sector increased by 6.9% in 2012.

Industry (comprising mining, manufacturing, construction and utilities) engaged 28.0% of the employed labour force in 2001, and provided 48.1% of GDP in 2012, according to provisional figures. During 2006–12 industrial GDP increased by an average of 2.2% per year; the sector increased by some 1.5% in 2011, but declined by 1.7% in 2012.

Mining and quarrying engaged 1.0% of the employed labour force in 2001, and, according to provisional figures, contributed 25.5% of GDP in 2012. The major mining activities are the exploitation of petroleum and natural gas, production of which accounted for 24.9% of GDP in that year. At the beginning of 2013 Bahrain's proven published reserves of crude petroleum were estimated at just 120m. barrels. Including output from the Abu Saafa oilfield (situated between Bahrain and Saudi Arabia), all revenue from which was, until the field was expanded in 2004, allocated to Bahrain, total crude oil production for 2012 was recorded at 63.3m. barrels. Excluding output from Abu Saafa, Bahrain produced an estimated 16.6m. barrels of crude oil in the same year. Bahrain's reserves of natural gas at the end of 2012 were put at 200,000m. cu m, sufficient to maintain production (at 2012 levels) for just 14 years. According to provisional official figures, mining GDP declined at an average annual rate of 0.5% in 2006–12; the sector's GDP increased by 3.5% in 2011, but declined by 8.1% in 2012.

In 2001 manufacturing engaged 17.2% of the employed labour force, and the sector provided 15.2% of GDP in 2012, according to provisional figures. Important industries include the petroleum refinery at Sitra, aluminium (Bahrain is the region's largest producer) and aluminium-related enterprises, shipbuilding, iron and steel, and chemicals. Since the mid-1980s the Government has encouraged the development of light industry. During 2006–12 manufacturing GDP increased at an average annual rate of 4.7%; the sector's GDP increased by 4.7% in 2012.

The construction sector engaged 9.1% of the employed labour force in 2001. According to provisional official figures, the sector contributed 6.1% of GDP in 2012. During 2006–12 the GDP of the sector increased at an average annual rate of 3.8%; the sector contracted by 7.9% in 2011, before expanding by 4.1% in 2012.

Industrial expansion has resulted in energy demand that in the past threatened to exceed the country's total installed generating capacity (estimated at 3,800 MW in mid-2012). However, the largely state-owned Aluminium Bahrain (ALBA) smelter plant has supplemented domestic power generation in an attempt to accommodate the energy deficit, and by 2008 the Al-Ezzal independent power project provided some 30% of the country's generating capacity. As part of the Electricity and Water Authority's strategic plan for the electricity sector up to 2020, several new power stations have been built since 2007 in order to extend Bahrain's distribution network. (Fuel imports amounted to 2.8% of total merchandise imports in 2011, compared with 38.0% in 2010.) The initial phase of a regional electricity 'inter-exchange' grid, connecting members of the Cooperation Council for the Arab States of the Gulf (or Gulf Cooperation Council—GCC, see p. 246) (linking Qatar, Bahrain, Saudi Arabia and Kuwait) was formally launched in 2009. Interconnection with the United Arab Emirates (UAE) was achieved in 2011, and the network was ultimately to achieve regional self-sufficiency in electricity generation to 2058.

The services sector engaged 70.4% of the employed labour force in 2001, and contributed 51.6% of GDP in 2012, according to provisional figures. The financial services industry, notably the operation of 'offshore' banking units (OBUs), is a major source of Bahrain's prosperity. Bahrain has also developed as a principal centre for Islamic banking and finance. The first International Islamic Financial Market, with a liquidity management centre and Islamic ratings agency based in Bahrain, was inaugurated in 2002. The Bahrain Financial Harbour project was completed in 2009: this redeveloped the Manama port area to provide a home for the 'offshore' financial sector and protect Bahrain's status as a leading financial centre in the Gulf. However, the financial services sector has been damaged by the instability arising from the political unrest which began in early 2011. According to provisional official figures, during 2006–12 the services sector showed an average GDP increase of 6.4% per year; the GDP of the sector increased by 7.1% in 2012.

In 2012 Bahrain recorded a visible merchandise trade surplus of US $6,528.7m., and there was a surplus of some $2,938.0m. on the current account of the balance of payments. According to provisional figures, in 2011 the principal source of imports was the People's Republic of China (accounting for 13.4% of the total). Among the member states of the GCC, Saudi Arabia (17.9% of the total) was the principal customer for Bahrain's non-petroleum exports in that year, followed by Oman, Qatar and the UAE. Outside of the GCC countries, India was the principal customer for non-petroleum exports (accounting for 6.9% of the total). The principal exports in 2010 were basic manufactures, non-ferrous metals, metalliferous ore and metal scrap and crude materials. The principal imports were machinery and transport equipment, crude materials, basic manufactures, and food and live animals.

According to official figures, a budgetary deficit of BD 1,028.6m. was recorded in 2012. Bahrain's general government gross debt was BD 3,429m. in 2012, equivalent to 33.6% of GDP. The annual rate of inflation averaged 2.3% in 2006–12; consumer prices decreased by an annual average of 0.4% in 2011, but increased by 2.8% in 2012. Some 75.8% of the employed labour force were non-Bahrainis in 2008. The official rate of unemployment was 5.5% in 2001, but unofficial sources estimated unemployment to be at around 20% in 2005. According to figures published by the Central Informatics Organization, by the end of 2012 the unemployment rate had increased to 3.7%, although some observers contended that the actual figure remained significantly higher.

As a result of substantial financial aid from the GCC following the anti-Government protests of 2011 and subsequent political unrest, by 2013 a number of major infrastructure projects were under way, including several road schemes, improvements to the King Fahd Causeway and the international airport, and a rail link to Saudi Arabia. However, a long-anticipated project to build a road and rail causeway linking Bahrain with Qatar, construction of which had been expected to commence in 2010, stalled in 2011 and by early 2014 remained suspended. Despite some diversification of Bahrain's industrial base and attempts to attract more foreign investment, in an effort to reduce the country's dependence on petroleum and gas production, this sector remained by far the largest contributor to the economy, accounting for some 85% of government revenues in 2012. Expansion of Bahrain's energy supplies and the upgrade of existing facilities were regarded as essential in promoting industrial growth; in May 2012 the Government unveiled plans to increase petroleum refining capacity from 260,000 b/d to 450,000 b/d by 2019. However, in October 2012 it was announced that plans to commence production of nuclear power by 2017 were to be delayed, for both cost and safety reasons. There was evidence by late 2011 that financial institutions were being forced to adapt in response to lenders' fears regarding the country's stability, prompted by the anti-Government protests that had erupted earlier that year. After Bahrain's sovereign credit rating was downgraded by three international ratings agencies there were fears that, in the event of further unrest, investors would favour neighbouring territories such as Qatar and Dubai (UAE). The Government, therefore, made concerted efforts to reaffirm Bahrain's position as a stable country in which to invest; by 2013 it appeared that most foreign firms would remain and that the banking sector had largely avoided the potential negative effects of the unrest. In early 2013 the Central Bank of Bahrain announced the introduction of a series of tough regulatory requirements in order to strengthen the banking system against future crises. GDP growth in 2011 was just 1.9%, compared with 4.5% in 2010. However, the following year the economy showed signs of recovery with an increase in GDP of 3.4% for 2012, a rate that was slightly below that originally forecast, owing to maintenance work at the country's main oilfield. In December 2013 the Economic Development Board estimated an increase in GDP of 4.8% for that year.

PUBLIC HOLIDAYS

2015: 1 January (New Year's Day), 2 January* (Mouloud, Birth of the Prophet), 1 May (Labour Day), 17 July* (Id al-Fitr, end of Ramadan), 23 September* (Id al-Adha, Feast of the Sacrifice), 14 October* (Muharram, Islamic New Year), 23 October* (Ashoura), 16 December (National Day), 23 December (Mouloud, Birth of the Prophet).

* These holidays are dependent on the Islamic lunar calendar and may vary by one or two days from the dates given.

Statistical Survey

Sources (unless otherwise stated): Central Informatics Organization (formerly Central Statistics Organization), POB 33305, Manama; tel. 17727722; e-mail ciohelpdesk@cio.gov.bh; internet www.cio.gov.bh; Central Bank of Bahrain, POB 27, Bldg 96, Block 317, Rd 1702, Manama; tel. 17547777; fax 17530399; e-mail info@cbb.gov.bh; internet www.cbb.gov.bh; Ministry of Finance, POB 333, Diplomatic Area, Manama; tel. 17575000; fax 17532713; e-mail mofne@batelco.com.bh; internet www.mofne.gov.bh.

Area and Population

AREA, POPULATION AND DENSITY

Area (sq km)	767.3*
Population (census results)	
7 April 2001	650,604
27 April 2010	
Males	768,414
Females	466,157
Total	1,234,571
Bahrainis	568,399
Non-Bahrainis	666,172
Population (official estimates at mid-year)	
2011	1,195,020
2012†	1,226,090
Density (per sq km) at mid-2012	1,597.9

* 296.2 sq miles.

† Provisional.

POPULATION BY AGE AND SEX
(official estimates at mid-2011)

	Males	Females	Total
0–14	127,890	122,147	250,037
15–64	600,312	317,904	918,216
65 and over	13,281	13,486	26,767
Total	741,483	453,537	1,195,020

GOVERNORATES
(official population estimates at mid-2011)

	Area (sq km)	Population	Density (per sq km)
Capital	38.4	296,427	7,725.5
Central	84.9	314,719	3,706.5
Muharraq	61.8	188,597	3,050.7
Northern	143.2	273,105	1,907.2
Southern	438.9	100,388	228.7
Total	767.3	1,195,020*	1,557.4

* Total population also includes 21,784 nationals not permanently resident in one location.

PRINCIPAL TOWNS
(at 2001 census)

Manama (capital)	153,395	Hamad Town	52,718
Muharraq	91,939	Jidd Hafs	52,450
Rifa'a	79,985		

Mid-2011 (incl. suburbs, UN estimate): Manama 261,782 (Source: UN, *World Urbanization Prospects: The 2011 Revision*).

BIRTHS, MARRIAGES AND DEATHS

	Registered live births		Registered marriages		Registered deaths	
	Number	Rate (per 1,000)	Number	Rate (per 1,000)	Number	Rate (per 1,000)
2002	13,576	19.1	4,909	7.3	2,035	2.9
2003	14,560	19.0	5,373	7.8	2,114	2.8
2004	14,968	18.2	4,929	7.0	2,215	2.7
2005	15,198	17.1	4,669	6.4	2,222	2.5
2006	15,053	15.7	4,724	6.4	2,317	2.4
2007	16,062	15.4	4,914	4.8	2,270	2.2
2008	17,022	15.4	4,896	4.4	2,390	2.2
2009	n.a.	n.a.	5,067	4.3	2,314	2.0

Registered marriages: 4,960 in 2010; 6,769 in 2011; 7,559 in 2012.

Marriage rate (per 1,000): 4.0 in 2010; 5.7 in 2011.

Life expectancy (years at birth): 76.4 (males 75.6; females 77.2) in 2011 (Source: World Bank, World Development Indicators database).

ECONOMICALLY ACTIVE POPULATION
(persons aged 15 years and over, at 2010 census)

	Males	Females	Total
Agriculture, fishing and animal husbandry	7,479	72	7,551
Mining and quarrying	1,678	58	1,736
Manufacturing	77,137	7,237	84,374
Electricity, gas and water	1,109	60	1,169
Construction	155,042	5,666	160,708
Trade and repairs	95,771	13,723	109,494
Restaurants and hotels	29,318	6,194	35,512
Transport, storage and communications	19,961	4,080	24,041
Banks, insurance and finance	12,330	5,023	17,353
Real estate and business	34,624	6,733	41,357
Government, defence, social affairs and security	67,824	15,233	83,057
Education	10,710	13,563	24,273
Health	1,427	1,989	3,416
Community, social and personal services	11,723	4,098	15,821
Households with employed persons	24,666	59,737	84,403
Sub-total	550,799	143,466	694,265
Activities not adequately defined	7,145	1,797	8,942
Total employed	557,944	145,263	703,207
Unemployed	2,466	5,557	8,023
Total labour force	560,410	150,820	711,230

Mid-2014 (estimates in '000): Agriculture and animal husbandry 4; Total labour force 685 (Source: FAO).

Health and Welfare

KEY INDICATORS

Total fertility rate (children per woman, 2011)	2.5
Under-5 mortality rate (per 1,000 live births, 2011)	10
HIV/AIDS (% of persons aged 15–49, 2003)	0.2
Physicians (per 1,000 head, 2010)	2.6
Hospital beds (per 1,000 head, 2010)	2.1
Health expenditure (2010): US $ per head (PPP)	937
Health expenditure (2010): % of GDP	4.3
Health expenditure (2010): public (% of total)	71.1
Total carbon dioxide emissions ('000 metric tons, 2010)	24,202.2
Carbon dioxide emissions per head (metric tons, 2010)	19.3
Human Development Index (2012): ranking	48
Human Development Index (2012): value	0.796

For sources and definitions, see explanatory note on p. vi.

Agriculture

PRINCIPAL CROPS
('000 metric tons, FAO estimates)

	2010	2011	2012
Lettuce	0.7	0.7	0.7
Tomatoes	3.9	3.8	4.0
Onions, dry	0.7	0.8	0.8
Bananas	0.9	0.9	1.0
Lemons and limes	1.1	1.1	1.1
Dates	14.2	14.6	15.0

Aggregate production ('000 metric tons, may include official, semi-official or estimated data): Total vegetables (incl. melons) 16.5 in 2010, 18.4 in 2011, 19.1 in 2012; Total fruits (excl. melons) 20.7 in 2010, 21.8 in 2011, 22.4 in 2012.

Source: FAO.

LIVESTOCK
('000 head, year ending September)

	2010	2011*	2012*
Cattle	10*	10	10
Sheep	40†	40	41
Goats	19†	19	19
Chickens	530*	540	550

* FAO estimate(s).
† Unofficial figure.

Source: FAO.

LIVESTOCK PRODUCTS
('000 metric tons, FAO estimates)

	2010	2011	2012
Cattle meat	1.0	1.0	1.0
Sheep meat	16.6	16.8	16.9
Goat meat	0.2	0.2	0.2
Chicken meat	6.3	6.3	6.5
Cows' milk	9.3	9.5	10.0

Source: FAO.

Fishing

('000 metric tons, live weight)

	2009	2010	2011
Capture	16.4	13.5	9.9
Spangled emperor	0.5	0.3	0.2
Spinefeet (Rabbitfishes)	1.4	1.7	1.1
Blue swimming crab	4.1	3.9	3.0
Green tiger prawn	3.4	4.6	2.5
Aquaculture	0.0	0.0	0.0
Total catch	16.4	13.5	9.9

Source: FAO.

Mining

	2010	2011	2012
Crude petroleum ('000 barrels)*	66,376	69,452	63,302
Natural gas ('000 million cu ft)	556.6	552.1	542.5

* Including a share of production from the Abu Saafa offshore oilfield, shared with Saudi Arabia (54,741,000 barrels in 2010, 53,936,000 barrels in 2011 and 46,726,000 barrels in 2012).

Industry

SELECTED PRODUCTS
('000 barrels unless otherwise indicated)

	2009	2010	2011
Liquefied petroleum gas	365	548	584
Butane	907	908	908
Propane	953	990	990
Naphtha	1,730	1,760	1,760
Motor spirit (petrol)	7,600	7,600	6,205
Kerosene and jet fuel	1,716	1,606	1,168
Distillate fuel oil	32,120	31,755	28,470
Residual fuel oil*	15,330	15,330	16,279
Aluminium (unwrought, metric tons)	847,738	850,700	881,310
Electric energy (million kWh)	12,120	13,757	13,826

* Estimates.

2012: Electric energy (million kWh) 14,104.

Source: mainly US Geological Survey.

Finance

CURRENCY AND EXCHANGE RATES

Monetary Units
1,000 fils = 1 Bahraini dinar (BD).

Sterling, Dollar and Euro Equivalents (31 December 2013)
£1 sterling = 619 fils;
US $1 = 376 fils;
€1 = 519 fils;
10 Bahraini dinars = £16.15 = $26.60= €19.28.

Average Exchange Rate
Note: This has been fixed at US $1 = 376 fils (BD 1 = $2.6596) since November 1980.

BUDGET
(BD million)

Revenue	2010	2011	2012
Petroleum and gas	1,852.1	1,930.7	2,133.1
Taxation and fees	179.0	238.0	269.2
Government goods and services	52.0	33.6	35.6
Investments and government properties	19.4	12.9	12.2
Grants	28.6	37.6	37.6
Sale of capital assets	0.4	0.4	0.4
Fines, penalties and miscellaneous	44.1	42.1	34.9
Total	2,175.6	2,295.4	2,523.0

Expenditure	2010	2011	2012
Recurrent expenditure	1,868.0	2,585.5	2,666.6
Manpower	868.1	984.6	1,105.1
Services	130.5	138.4	139.8
Consumption	79.7	87.2	89.8
Assets	20.8	20.7	21.5
Maintenance	44.4	51.2	54.0
Transfers	529.4	1,000.2	832.1
Grants and subsidies	195.1	303.2	424.4
Projects	767.4	635.0	885.0
Total	2,635.4	3,220.5	3,551.6

INTERNATIONAL RESERVES
(US $ million at 31 December)

	2010	2011	2012
Gold (national valuation)	6.6	6.6	6.6
IMF special drawing rights	196.8	196.7	197.6
Reserve position in IMF	109.7	109.3	109.4
Foreign exchange (central bank)*	4,782.2	4,238.6	4,897.6
Total*	5,095.2	4,551.1	5,211.2

* Excluding foreign exchange reserves held by government.

Source: IMF, *International Financial Statistics*.

MONEY SUPPLY
(BD million at 31 December)

	2010	2011	2012
Currency outside banks	349.6	402.2	421.4
Demand deposits at commercial banks	1,954.3	2,234.7	2,189.7
Total money	2,303.9	2,636.9	2,611.1

Source: IMF, *International Financial Statistics*.

COST OF LIVING
(Consumer Price Index; base: 2006 = 100)

	2010	2011	2012
Food and non-alcoholic beverages	132.5	135.5	140.7
Alcoholic beverages and tobacco	117.5	124.5	139.7
Clothing	106.4	108.7	111.0
House-related expenses, water, electricity, gas and other fuels	108.2	94.8	91.7
Goods for home service	113.2	115.4	121.1
Transport	105.7	107.3	111.9
Education	112.7	114.8	116.9
Health	105.9	109.2	110.3
Culture, entertainment and recreation	105.4	112.8	135.9
Communication	94.3	92.3	88.5
Other goods and services	117.5	131.2	135.9
All items	112.1	111.6	114.7

NATIONAL ACCOUNTS
(BD million at current prices)

National Income and Product

	2010	2011	2012*
Compensation of employees	2,785.8	2,955.8	3,172.3
Operating surplus	6,022.5	7,035.9	7,294.7
Domestic factor incomes	8,808.3	9,991.7	10,467.0
Consumption of fixed capital	540.9	617.8	628.7
Gross domestic product (GDP) at factor cost	9,349.2	10,609.5	11,095.7
Indirect taxes, less subsidies	319.0	311.0	320.4
GDP in purchasers' values	9,668.2	10,920.6	11,416.1
Primary income (net)	−892.3	−1,415.5	−1,442.8
Gross national income	8,775.9	9,505.1	9,973.3
Less Consumption of fixed capital	540.9	617.8	628.7
Net national income	8,235.0	8,887.3	9,344.6
Current transfers (net)	−617.3	−770.8	−780.0
Net national disposable income	7,617.7	8,116.5	8,564.6

* Provisional figures.

Expenditure on the Gross Domestic Product

	2010	2011	2012*
Government final consumption expenditure	1,249.9	1,501.1	1,667.0
Private final consumption expenditure	3,981.7	4,226.4	4,372.2
Gross fixed capital formation	2,518.1	1,706.4	2,225.9
Change in stocks	120.0	79.7	92.7
Total domestic expenditure	7,869.7	7,513.6	8,357.8
Exports of goods and services	6,723.0	8,627.5	8,592.8
Less Imports of goods and services	4,924.5	5,220.5	5,534.5
GDP in purchasers' values	9,668.2	10,920.6	11,416.1
GDP at constant 2010 prices	9,668.2	9,871.2	10,206.8

* Provisional figures.

Gross Domestic Product by Economic Activity

	2010	2011	2012*
Agriculture and fishing	28.8	31.5	36.7
Mining	2,099.8	3,012.02	2,874.8
Petroleum and gas	2,041.5	2,954.6	2,811.0
Manufacturing	1,400.2	1,628.1	1,717.8
Electricity and water	128.7	137.5	143.9
Construction	719.8	669.0	692.9
Transport and communications	647.1	661.4	726.8
Trade	451.9	449.4	477.4
Hotels and restaurants	260.6	201.7	247.1
Real estate and business activities	598.4	562.7	586.5
Finance and insurance	1,696.3	1,712.9	1,796.2
Government services	1,014.3	1,180.2	1,326.3
Education	232.7	258.3	269.4
Health	127.8	138.5	145.9
Other social and personal services	442.3	499.3	583.3
Private non-profit institutions serving households	3.4	4.0	4.4
Households with employed persons	75.7	78.6	81.6
Sub-total	9,567.2	10,828.4	11,295.8
Import duties	101.0	92.1	120.2
GDP in purchasers' values	9,668.2	10,920.5	11,416.1

* Provisional figures.

BALANCE OF PAYMENTS
(US $ million)

	2010	2011	2012
Exports of goods	13,647.1	19,650.3	19,768.1
Imports of goods	–11,190.4	–12,105.9	–13,239.4
Balance on goods	2,456.6	7,544.4	6,528.7
Exports of services	4,233.2	3,295.7	3,085.1
Imports of services	–1,905.1	–1,778.5	–1,480.1
Balance on goods and services	4,784.8	9,061.7	8,133.8
Primary income received	1,467.6	6,821.8	1,835.1
Primary income paid	–3,840.6	–10,586.2	–4,956.4
Balance on goods, services and primary income	2,411.8	5,297.3	5,012.5
Secondary income (net)	–1,641.8	–2,050.0	–2,074.5
Current balance	770.1	3,247.3	2,938.0
Capital account (net)	50.0	76.1	100.0
Direct investment assets	–334.0	–893.6	–922.3
Direct investment liabilities	155.8	780.9	891.2
Portfolio investment assets	2,051.6	5,164.1	2,741.2
Portfolio investment liabilities	2,704.2	419.1	1,101.6
Other investment assets	2,739.7	17,327.4	2,809.6
Other investment liabilities	–6,964.8	–26,780.1	–8,388.0
Net errors and omissions	107.1	71.5	–598.5
Overall balance	1,279.5	–587.3	672.8

Source: IMF, *International Financial Statistics*.

External Trade

PRINCIPAL COMMODITIES
(distribution by SITC, US $ million)

Imports f.o.b	2008	2009	2010*
Food and live animals	965.3	879.9	1,010.4
Crude materials, except fuels	1,226.6	818.8	2,375.9
Metalliferous ore and metal scrap	1,076.4	668.6	2,243.6
Mineral fuels, lubricants and related materials	8,166.4	5,384.6	223.7
Petroleum and related materials	8,151.6	5,378.2	215.2
Crude petroleum	7,850.7	5,147.4	0.1
Chemicals and related products	700.2	640.6	682.8
Basic manufactures	2,190.6	1,375.0	1,337.2
Iron and steel	965.7	306.2	373.1
Machinery and transport equipment	4,028.2	3,251.9	3,593.5
Road vehicles	1,461.1	1,099.9	1,158.8
Miscellaneous manufactured articles	881.7	733.3	715.8
Total (incl. others)	18,414.6	13,260.0	10,142.9

Exports (incl. re-exports) f.o.b.	2008	2009	2010*
Food and live animals	263.4	266.0	283.2
Crude materials, except fuels	657.5	280.7	1,239.1
Metalliferous ore and metal scrap	652.4	275.1	1,231.2
Mineral fuels, lubricants and related materials	8,685.8	5,425.8	n.a.
Petroleum and related materials	8,676.9	5,425.4	n.a.
Non-crude petroleum	8,636.2	5,372.4	n.a.
Chemicals and related products	593.1	312.5	111.0
Basic manufactures	2,136.0	1,390.4	2,115.1
Non-ferrous metals	1,494.9	934.8	1,574.4
Machinery and transport equipment	535.9	517.4	539.4
Road vehicles	226.9	194.0	226.9
Miscellaneous manufactured articles	188.8	151.8	215.6
Total (incl. others)	13,083.0	8,365.2	4,554.4

* Full data for petroleum imports and exports were not available.

Source: UN, *International Trade Statistics Yearbook*.

2011 (excluding petroleum, BD million, provisional): Total imports 3,825.8; Total exports 2,295.5; Total re-exports 342.3.

PRINCIPAL TRADING PARTNERS
(excluding petroleum, BD million)

Imports	2009	2010*	2011*
Australia	228.6	234.9	158.7
Brazil	106.9	687.5	473.0
Canada	24.6	18.0	40.3
China, People's Republic	307.6	442.9	514.0
France	74.4	101.7	90.9
Germany	134.1	202.6	188.0
India	96.5	130.1	149.1
Italy	70.5	90.5	117.7
Japan	218.2	283.5	221.5
Korea, Republic	78.2	136.8	10.6
Kuwait	51.2	33.6	34.2
Malaysia	35.9	42.8	39.2
Netherlands	38.1	53.6	49.8
Pakistan	28.1	32.1	33.3
Russian Federation	2.2	0.7	49.8
Saudi Arabia	227.4	181.8	233.7
Spain	26.5	35.1	65.7
Switzerland	58.2	63.0	61.1
Thailand	44.9	47.3	70.1
Turkey	34.3	79.3	55.4
United Arab Emirates	137.9	140.9	217.0
United Kingdom	98.5	142.8	116.1
USA	176.6	269.7	314.1
Total (incl. others)	2,574.1	3,813.9	3,825.8

Exports	2009	2010*	2011*
Algeria	9.6	20.7	22.5
Australia	20.2	30.8	40.8
China, People's Republic	21.5	65.6	98.3
Egypt	23.4	47.2	29.4
France	10.7	19.6	13.9
Germany	6.5	21.3	16.6
India	81.9	210.1	182.4
Indonesia	2.1	18.3	35.1
Italy	16.2	45.0	59.2
Jordan	21.6	16.7	16.9
Kuwait	30.5	38.2	41.3
Malaysia	1.5	16.8	24.7
Morocco	12.1	28.6	36.7

Exports—*continued*	2009	2010*	2011*
Netherlands	16.0	31.1	50.9
Oman	30.6	71.9	283.9
Peru	3.3	1.6	38.5
Qatar	78.1	235.9	279.5
Saudi Arabia	280.2	361.8	476.7
Syria	15.2	18.6	23.0
Taiwan	1.8	11.8	34.2
United Arab Emirates	101.4	124.9	192.0
USA	75.8	103.9	101.1
Total (incl. others)	1,112.1	1,956.5	2,637.8

* Provisional figures.

Transport

ROAD TRAFFIC
(motor vehicles in use at 31 December, estimates)

	2010	2011	2012
Passenger cars	328,536	342,218	357,355
Buses and coaches	10,134	10,621	11,133
Lorries and vans	58,622	61,571	65,013
Motorcycles and mopeds	7,136	8,120	9,586

SHIPPING

Flag Registered Fleet
(at 31 December)

	2011	2012	2013
Number of vessels	321	343	367
Total displacement ('000 grt)	781.8	757.7	741.4

Source: Lloyd's List Intelligence (www.lloydslistintelligence.com).

International Sea-borne Freight Traffic ('000 metric tons, 1990): *Goods loaded:* Dry cargo 1,145; Petroleum products 12,140. *Goods unloaded:* Dry cargo 3,380; Petroleum products 132 (Source: UN, *Monthly Bulletin of Statistics*).

CIVIL AVIATION
(traffic on scheduled services)

	2010	2011
Kilometres flown (million)	98	103
Passengers carried ('000)	6,029	5,591
Passenger-km (million)	12,691	11,960
Total ton-km (million)	1,590	1,446

Source: UN, *Statistical Yearbook*.

2012: Passengers carried ('000) 5,862 (Source: World Bank, World Development Indicators database).

Tourism

FOREIGN VISITOR ARRIVALS BY NATIONALITY
('000)

	2005	2006	2007
India	466.8	590.2	718.4
Kuwait	239.5	298.6	309.3
Philippines	143.6	198.3	225.6
Saudi Arabia	3,864.6	4,225.6	4,366.6
United Kingdom	210.1	245.1	263.7
USA	137.3	168.4	187.2
Total (incl. others)	6,313.2	7,288.7	7,833.6

2011 ('000): India 837.5; Kuwait 275.9; Philippines 175.8; Saudi Arabia 3,320.2; United Kingdom 250.6; USA 206.4; Total (incl. others) 6,732.0.

Receipts from tourism (US $ million, incl. passenger transport): 1,873 in 2009; 1,362 in 2010; 1,035 in 2011.

Source: World Tourism Organization.

Communications Media

	2010	2011	2012
Telephones ('000 main lines in use)	228.0	276.5	290.0
Mobile cellular telephones ('000 subscribers)	1,567.0	1,693.6	2,123.9
Internet subscribers ('000)	67.6	183.0	n.a.
Broadband subscribers ('000)	67.6	183.0	173.2

Source: International Telecommunication Union.

Education

(state schools only, 2009/10 unless otherwise indicated)

	Institutions	Teachers	Students
Primary	109	4,788	54,433
Primary/Intermediate	21	1,165	13,429
Intermediate	36	2,141	24,496
Intermediate/Secondary	2	218	2,306
Secondary	30	3,385	29,059
Religious institutes	3	167	1,880
University level*	16	1,240	29,678

* 2005/06 figures.

2012/13 (state schools): *Students:* 63,648 in primary education; 31,921 in intermediate education; 31,167 in secondary education; 2,005 in religious institutes.

Private education (2009/10): *Pre-primary:* 143 schools; 1,084 teachers; 16,593 infants. *Other:* 65 schools; 3,768 teachers; 56,078 students.

Pupil-teacher ratio (primary education, UNESCO estimate): 11.8 in 2011/12 (Source: UNESCO Institute for Statistics).

Adult literacy rate (UNESCO estimates): 94.6% (males 96.1%; females 91.6%) in 2010 (Source: UNESCO Institute for Statistics).

Directory

The Government

HEAD OF STATE

King and Supreme Commander of the Bahrain Defence Force: HM Sheikh HAMAD BIN ISA AL KHALIFA (acceded as Amir 6 March 1999; proclaimed King 14 February 2002).

CABINET
(April 2014)

Prime Minister: Sheikh KHALIFA BIN SULMAN AL KHALIFA.

First Deputy Prime Minister: Crown Prince Sheikh SALMAN BIN HAMAD AL KHALIFA.

Deputy Prime Ministers: Sheikh MUHAMMAD BIN MUBARAK AL KHALIFA, Sheikh ALI BIN KHALIFA AL KHALIFA, Sheikh KHALID BIN ABDULLAH AL KHALIFA, JAWAD BIN SALEM AL-ARRAYED.

Minister of Foreign Affairs: Sheikh KHALID BIN AHMAD AL KHALIFA.

Minister of the Interior: Lt-Gen. Sheikh RASHID BIN ABDULLAH BIN AHMAD AL KHALIFA.

Minister of Justice and Islamic Affairs: Sheikh KHALID BIN ALI AL KHALIFA.

Minister of the Royal Court: Sheikh KHALID BIN AHMAD BIN SALMAN AL KHALIFA.

Minister of the Royal Court for Follow-up Affairs: Sheikh AHMAD BIN ATIYATALLAH AL KHALIFA.

Minister of Royal Court Affairs: Sheikh ALI BIN ISA AL KHALIFA.

Minister of Municipal Affairs and Urban Planning: Dr JUMA AL-KA'ABI.

Minister of Energy and Minister of State for Electricity and Water Affairs: Dr ABD AL-HUSSAIN BIN ALI MIRZA.

Minister of Works: ISAM BIN ABDULLAH KHALAF.

Minister of Housing: BASSEM BIN YACOUB AL-HAMER.

Minister of Finance and Minister of Oil and Gas Affairs: Sheikh AHMAD BIN MUHAMMAD AL KHALIFA.

Minister of Culture: SHEIKA MAI BINT MUHAMMAD AL KHALIFA.

Minister of Industry and Commerce: Dr HASSAN BIN ABDULLAH FAKHRO.

Minister of Education: Dr MAJID BIN ALI AL-NO'AIMI.

Minister of Labour: JAMIL HUMAIDAN.

Minister of Social Development: Dr FATIMA MUHAMMAD AL-BLUSHI.

Minister of Health: SADIQ BIN ABD AL-KARIM AL-SHEHABI.

Minister of Transportation: KAMAL BIN AHMAD MUHAMMAD.

Minister of Shura Council and Parliament Affairs: ABD AL-AZIZ BIN MUHAMMAD AL-FADHIL.

Minister of State for Interior Affairs: Maj.-Gen. ADEL BIN KHALIFA AL-FADHUL.

Minister of State for Foreign Affairs: GHANEM FADHUL AL-BUAINAIN.

Minister of State for Human Rights Affairs: SALAH ALI.

Minister of State for Information Affairs: SAMEERA RAJAB.

Minister of State for Defence Affairs: Lt.-Gen. Dr SHEIKH MUHAMMAD BIN ABDULLAH AL KHALIFA.

Minister of State for Follow-up Affairs: MUHAMMAD BIN IBRAHIM AL-MUTAWA.

Minister of State for Telecommunications Affairs: Sheikh FAWAZ BIN MUHAMMAD AL KHALIFA.

MINISTRIES

Royal Court: POB 555, Riffa Palace, Manama; tel. 17666666; fax 17663070.

Prime Minister's Court: POB 1000, Government House, Government Rd, Manama; tel. 17253361; fax 17533033.

Ministry of Culture: POB 2199, Manama; tel. 17298777; fax 17293873; e-mail webmaster@moc.gov.bh; internet www.moc.gov.bh.

Ministry of Education: POB 43, Manama; tel. 17278409; fax 17273656; e-mail moe@moe.gov.bh; internet www.moe.gov.bh.

Ministry of Energy: Manama.

Ministry of Finance: POB 333, Diplomatic Area, Manama; tel. 17575000; fax 17532853; e-mail mofne@batelco.com.bh; internet www.mofne.gov.bh.

Ministry of Foreign Affairs: POB 547, Government House, Government Rd, Manama; tel. 17227555; fax 17212603; e-mail info@mofa.gov.bh; internet www.mofa.gov.bh.

Ministry of Health: POB 12, Bldg 1228, Rd 4025, Juffair 340, Manama; tel. 17288888; fax 17286691; e-mail webmaster@health.gov.bh; internet www.moh.gov.bh.

Ministry of Housing: POB 5802, Manama; tel. 17533000; fax 17534116; internet www.housing.gov.bh.

Ministry of Industry and Commerce: POB 5479, Diplomatic Area, Manama; tel. 17574777; fax 17530151; e-mail info@moic.gov.bh; internet www.moic.gov.bh.

Ministry of the Interior: POB 13, Police Fort Compound, Manama; tel. 17572222; e-mail info@interior.gov.bh; internet www.interior.gov.bh.

Ministry of Justice and Islamic Affairs: POB 450, Diplomatic Area, Manama; tel. 175313000; fax 17536343; internet www.moj.gov.bh.

Ministry of Labour: POB 32333, Isa Town; tel. 17873777; fax 17686954; e-mail web.contain@mol.gov.bh.

Ministry of Municipal Affairs and Urban Planning: POB 53, Manama; tel. 17501501; fax 17211767; e-mail prinfo@mun.gov.bh; internet www.mun.gov.bh.

Ministry of Oil and Gas Affairs: Manama.

Ministry of Social Development: POB 32868, Isa Town; tel. 17873999; fax 17682248; e-mail info@social.gov.bh; internet www.social.gov.bh.

Ministry of Transportation: POB 10325, Diplomatic Area, Manama; tel. 17534534; fax 17534041; internet www.transportation.gov.bh.

Ministry of Works: POB 5, Manama; tel. 17545555; fax 17545608; e-mail info@works.gov.bh; internet www.works.gov.bh.

Legislature

CONSULTATIVE COUNCIL

The new 40-seat Consultative Council was appointed by King Hamad on 25 November 2010.

Consultative Council: POB 2991, Manama; tel. 17748888; fax 17714583; e-mail info@shura.bh; internet www.shura.bh.

Chairman: ALI BIN SALEH AL-SALEH.

COUNCIL OF REPRESENTATIVES

Council of Representatives: POB 54040, Manama; tel. 17748444; fax 17748445; e-mail fshehabi@almajlis.gov.bh; internet www.nuwab.gov.bh.

Speaker: KHALIFA BIN AHMAD AL-DHAHRANI.

Election, 23 and 30 October 2010

Groups	Seats
Al-Wefaq National Islamic Society	18
Al-Asala Islamic Society	3
Al-Menbar Islamic Society	2
Independents	17
Total	40

Political Organizations

Political parties are still prohibited in Bahrain. However, several political and civic societies (many of which were previously in exile) are now active in the country, and a number of new groups have been established since 2001. Restrictions on campaigning by political groups were revoked prior to the first elections to the new Council of Representatives, held in October 2002. By mid-2009 it was reported that there were 18 political alliances or blocs functioning in Bahrain. Organizations currently represented in the Majlis include:

Al-Asala Islamic Society: Manama; Sunni Islamist; promotes the implementation of strict Salafi principles in society and law; Pres. GHANEM FADHUL AL-BUAINAIN.

Al-Menbar Islamic Society (Islamic National Tribune Society): Bldg 30, Sheikh Salman St, Muharraq; tel. 17324996; fax 17324997; internet www.almenber.bh; Sunni Islamist; political wing of the al-Islah Soc., affiliated with the Muslim Brotherhood; Sec.-Gen. Dr ALI AHMED ABDULLAH.

Al-Wefaq National Islamic Society (Islamic National Accord Association): POB 1553, Manama; tel. 17406020; fax 17406024; e-mail info@alwefaq.org; internet www.alwefaq.org; f. 2001; Shi'a Islamist; mems of the soc. won 18 out of 40 seats in the 2010 elections; Sec.-Gen. SHEIKH ALI SALMAN AHMAD SALMAN.

Other prominent groups include Al-Adala (National Justice Movement—a secular, liberal society established in 2006), Al-Haq (Movement for Liberty and Democracy—a radical breakaway faction of Al-Wefaq, opposed to participation in parliamentary politics), the Islamic Action Society (Shi'a Islamist), Al-Meethaq (liberal, pro-democracy) and Al-Waad (National Democratic Action—secular, left-wing).

Diplomatic Representation

EMBASSIES IN BAHRAIN

Algeria: Villa 1220, Rd 3324, Blk 333, Umm al-Hassam, Manama; tel. 17740659; fax 17740652; e-mail algerian.embassy@gmail.com; Ambassador NADJIB SENOUSSI.

Bangladesh: POB 26718, Bldg 71, Rd 56, Blk 356, al-Qufool, Manama; tel. 17233925; fax 17233683; e-mail bangla@batelco.com.bh; internet www.bdembassy.org.bh; Ambassador MUHAMMAD ALI AKBAR.

Brunei: POB 15700, Bldg 892, Rd 3218, Blk 332, al-Mahooz, Manama; tel. 17720222; fax 17741757; e-mail kbbhhom@batelco.com.bh; Ambassador Haji AHMAD Haji JUMAAT.

China, People's Republic: POB 3150, Bldg 158, Rd 4156, Blk 341, Juffair Ave, Manama; tel. 17723800; fax 17727304; e-mail chinaemb_bh@mfa.gov.cn; internet bh.china-embassy.org; Ambassador LEE CHEN.

Egypt: POB 818, Villa 18, Rd 33, Blk 332, al-Mahooz, Manama; tel. 17720005; fax 17721518; e-mail egyembbh@batelco.com.bh; Ambassador ESSAM SALEH AWAD MUSTAPHA.

France: POB 11134, Bldg 51A, Rd 1901, Blk 319, Diplomatic Area, Manama; tel. 17298660; fax 17298607; e-mail chancellerie.manama-amba@diplomatie.gouv.fr; internet www.ambafrance-bh.org; Ambassador CHRISTIAN TESTOT.

Germany: POB 10306, Bldg 39, Rd 322, Blk 327, Salmaniya Ave, Manama; tel. 17745277; fax 17714314; e-mail info@manama.diplo.de; internet www.manama.diplo.de; Ambassador SABINE TAUFMANN.

India: POB 26106, Bldg 182, Rd 2608, Blk 326, Adliya, Manama; tel. 17712785; fax 17715527; e-mail indemb@batelco.com.bh; internet indianembassybahrain.com; Ambassador Dr MOHAN KUMAR.

Indonesia: Villa 2113, Rd 2432, Blk 324, Juffair, Manama; tel. 17400164; fax 17400267; e-mail indonesia.manama@batelco.com.bh; internet www.kemlu.go.id/manama; Ambassador CHILMAN ARISMAN.

Iran: POB 26365, Bldg 1034, Rd 3221, Blk 332, al-Mahooz, Manama; tel. 17722880; fax 17722101; internet bahrain.mfa.ir; Chargé d'affaires MUHAMMAD HADI ROUHANI SARVESTANI.

Iraq: POB 26477, Bldg 396, Rd 3207, Blk 332, al-Mahooz, Manama; tel. 17741472; fax 17720756; e-mail bhremb@iraqmofamail.com; Ambassador AHMAD NAIF RASHID AL-DULAIMI.

Italy: POB 347, Villa 1554, Rd 5647, Blk 356, Manama; tel. 17252424; fax 17277060; e-mail segreteriaambasciatore.manama@esteri.it; internet www.ambmanama.esteri.it; Ambassador ALBERTO VECCHI.

Japan: POB 23720, Bldg 55, Blk 327, Salmaniya Ave, Manama; tel. 17716565; fax 17715059; e-mail japan@bh.mofa.go.jp; internet www.bh.emb-japan.go.jp; Ambassador SHIGEKI SUMI.

Jordan: POB 5242, Bldg 43, Rd 1901, Blk 319, Manama; tel. 17291109; fax 17291980; e-mail jordemb@batelco.com.bh; Ambassador MUHAMMED ALI ABD AL-HAMID SIRAJ.

Korea, Republic: POB 20554, Rd 915, Villa 401, Blk 309, Salmaniya, Manama; tel. 17531120; fax 17530577; e-mail koreanembassy.bahrain@gmail.com; internet nma.mofa.go.kr/english; Ambassador YU JOON-HA.

Kuwait: POB 786, Rd 1703, Blk 317, Manama; tel. 17534040; fax 17536475; e-mail almanama@mofa.gov.kw; Ambassador Sheikh AZZAM MUBARAK AL-SABAH.

Lebanon: POB 32474, Villa 1556, Rd 5647, Blk 356, al-Barhama, al-Salihia, Manama; tel. 17579001; fax 17232535; e-mail lebembassy@gmail.com; Chargé d'affaires a.i. IBRAHIM ELIAS AASAF.

Libya: POB 26015, Villa 787, Rd 3315, Blk 333, Umm al-Hassam, Manama; tel. 17722252; fax 17722911; e-mail libyan_bbb@hotmail.com; Ambassador FAWZI EL-TAHIR AHMAD ABD AL-A'ALI.

Malaysia: POB 18292, Bldg 2305, Rd 2835, Blk 428, al-Seef District, Manama; tel. 17564551; fax 17564552; e-mail malmnama@kln.gov.my; internet www.kln.gov.my/perwakilan/manama; Ambassador Dato' AHMAD SHAHIZAN ABD SAMAD.

Morocco: POB 26229, Villa 2743, Rd 2771, Blk 327, Manama; tel. 17180444; fax 17180555; e-mail sifamana@batelco.com; Ambassador AHMAD RASHID KHATTABI.

Nepal: Manama; Ambassador Dr DURGA BAHADUR SUBEDI.

Oman: POB 26414, Bldg 37, Rd 1901, Blk 319, Diplomatic Area, Manama; tel. 17293663; fax 17293540; e-mail oman@batelco.com.bh; Ambassador ABDULLAH BIN RASHID AL-MADAILWI.

Pakistan: POB 563, Bldg 35, Rd 1901, Blk 319, Manama; tel. 17244113; fax 17255960; e-mail parepbah@batelco.com.bh; Ambassador MUHAMMAD SAEED (designate).

Philippines: POB 26681, Villa 939, Rd 3220, Blk 332, al-Mahooz, Manama; tel. 17721234; fax 17720827; e-mail manamape@batelco.com.bh; internet philembassy-bahrain.com; Ambassador CORAZON YAP-BAHJIN.

Qatar: POB 15105, Villa 814, Rd 3315, Blk 333, al-Mahooz, Manama; tel. 17722922; fax 17740662; Ambassador Sheikh JASSIM BIN MUHAMMAD BIN SAUD AL THANI.

Russia: POB 26612, Villa 877, Rd 3119, Blk 331, Zinj, Manama; tel. 17725222; fax 17725921; fax 17725921; e-mail bahrain@mid.ru; internet www.bahrain.mid.ru; Ambassador VICTOR YU. SMIRNOV.

Saudi Arabia: POB 1085, Bldg 82, Rd 1702, Blk 317, Diplomatic Area, Manama; tel. 17537722; fax 17533261; e-mail bhemb@mofa.gov.sa; internet embassies.mofa.gov.sa/sites/bahrain; Ambassador ABDULLAH IBN ABD AL-MALIK AL-SHEIKH.

Senegal: Villa 25, Rd 33, Blk 333, Umm-Shoom Ave, al-Mahooz, Manama; tel. 17821060; fax 17721650; e-mail sengemb@batelco.com.bh; Ambassador ABDOU LAHAT SOURANG.

Sudan: POB 5438, Villa 423, Rd 3614, Blk 336, al-Adliya, Manama; tel. 17717959; fax 17710113; e-mail norabousen@hotmail.com; Ambassador ABDULLA AHMED OSMAN.

Syria: POB 11585, Villa 867, Rd 3315, Blk 333, al-Mahooz, Manama; tel. 17722484; fax 17740380; e-mail syremb@batelco.com.bh; Chargé d'affaires a.i. FAYZEH ISKANDAR AHMAD.

Thailand: POB 26475, Villa 132, Rd 66, Blk 360, Zinj, Manama; tel. 17246242; fax 17272714; e-mail thaimnm@mfa.go.th; internet www.thaiembassy.org/manama; Ambassador VICHAI VARASIRIKUL.

Tunisia: POB 26911, Villa 54, Rd 3601, Blk 336, Adliya, Manama; tel. 17714149; fax 17715702; e-mail atmanama@batelco.bh; Ambassador MUHAMMAD BEN YOUSSEF.

Turkey: POB 10821, Suhail Centre, 5th Floor, Bldg 81, Rd 1702, Blk 317, Manama; tel. 17533448; fax 17536557; e-mail turkemb.manama@mfa.gov.tr; internet www.manama.emb.mfa.gov.tr; Ambassador HATUN DEMIRER.

United Arab Emirates: POB 26505, Villa 270, Rd 2510, Blk 325, Manama; tel. 17748333; fax 17717724; e-mail uaeembassybahrain@hotmail.com; Ambassador MUHAMMAD SULTAN SAIF AL-SUWEIDI.

United Kingdom: POB 114, Blk 306, 21 Govt Ave, Manama; tel. 17574100; fax 17574101; e-mail british.embassy@batelco.com.bh; internet ukinbahrain.fco.gov.uk; Ambassador IAIN LINDSAY.

USA: POB 26431, Bldg 979, Rd 3119, Blk 331, Zinj, Manama; tel. 17242700; fax 17270547; e-mail manamaconsular@state.gov; internet bahrain.usembassy.gov; Ambassador THOMAS C. KRAJESKI.

Yemen: POB 26193, Villa 442, Rd 3512, Blk 335, Umm al-Hassam, Manama; tel. 17822110; fax 17822078; e-mail yemenmb@batelco.com.bh; Chargé d'affaires HAMID SHEIKH HUSSAIN.

Judicial System

Since the termination of British legal jurisdiction in 1971, intensive work has been undertaken on the legislative requirements of Bahrain. All nationalities are subject to the jurisdiction of the Bahraini courts, which guarantee equality before the law irrespective of nationality or creed. The 1974 Decree Law on State Security Measures and the State Security Court were both abolished in February 2001. The adoption of the amended Constitution in 2002 provided for the establishment of an independent judiciary; however, all judges are appointed by royal decree. The Criminal Law is at present contained in various Codes, Ordinances and Regulations; a new Code of Criminal Procedure was introduced in 2002.

Constitutional Court: POB 18380, Manama; tel. 17578181; fax 17224475; e-mail info@constitutional-court.bh; internet www.ccb.bh; f. 2002 to undertake review of, and to settle disputes concerning the constitutionality of laws and regulations; consists of seven members appointed by the King; Pres. Sheikh KHALIFA BIN RASHID BIN ABDULLAH AL KHALIFA.

Court of Cassation: f. 1990; serves as the final court of appeal for all civil and criminal cases; Pres. Sheikh SALIM BIN MUHAMMAD AL-KUWARI.

Civil Law Courts: All civil and commercial cases, including disputes relating to the personal affairs of non-Muslims, are settled in the Civil Law Courts, which comprise the Higher Civil Appeals Court, Higher Civil Court and Lesser Civil Courts.

Criminal Law Courts: Higher Criminal Court, presided over by three judges, rules on felonies; Lower Criminal Courts, presided over by one judge, rule on misdemeanours.

Religious Courts: *Shari'a* Judiciary Courts operate according to Islamic principles of jurisprudence and have jurisdiction in all disputes relating to the personal affairs of Muslims, including marriage contracts and inheritances. They are structured according to the following hierarchy: Higher *Shari'a* Appeals Court, Greater *Shari'a* Court, Lesser *Shari'a* Court; each court has separate Sunni and Shi'a departments.

Supreme Judicial Council: Founded in 2000, and further regulated by law decree in 2002, the Supreme Judicial Council, headed by the King, is made up of the most senior figures from each branch of the judiciary. The Council supervises the performance of the courts and recommends candidates for judicial appointments and promotions; Pres. Sheikh SALIM BIN MUHAMMAD AL-KUWARI.

Attorney-General: Dr ALI BIN FADHUL AL-BUAINAIN.

Religion

At the 2010 census the total population was recorded at 1,234,571, of whom 866,888 were Muslims. According to the census data, Bahraini citizens totalled some 568,399, of whom some 99.8% were Muslims. Of the 666,172 non-Bahrainis resident in the country, 55.0% were classified as adhering to religions other than Islam.

ISLAM

Muslims are divided between the Sunni and Shi'a sects. The ruling family is Sunni, although the majority of the Bahraini Muslim population are Shi'a.

CHRISTIANITY

The Anglican Communion

Within the Episcopal Church in Jerusalem and the Middle East, Bahrain forms part of the diocese of Cyprus and the Gulf. There are two Anglican churches in Bahrain: St Christopher's Cathedral in Manama and the Community Church in Awali. The congregations are entirely expatriate. The Dean of St Christopher's Cathedral is the Archdeacon in the Gulf, while the Bishop in Cyprus and the Gulf is resident in Cyprus.

Archdeacon in the Gulf: Very Rev. ALAN HAYDAY, St Christopher's Cathedral, POB 36, al-Mutanabi Ave, Manama; tel. 17253866; fax 17246436; e-mail cathedra@batelco.com.bh; internet www.stchcathedral.org.bh.

Roman Catholic Church

A small number of adherents, mainly expatriates, form part of the Apostolic Vicariate of Northern Arabia.

The Press

DAILIES

Akhbar al-Khaleej (Gulf News): POB 5300, Manama; tel. 17620111; fax 17621566; e-mail editor@aaknews.com; internet www.aaknews.com; f. 1976; Arabic; Chair. and Editor-in-Chief ANWAR ABD AL-RAHMAN; circ. 32,000.

Al-Ayam (The Days): POB 3232, Manama; tel. 17617777; fax 17617111; e-mail alayam@batelco.com.bh; internet www.alayam.com; f. 1989; Arabic; publ. by Al-Ayam Establishment for Press and Publications; Editor-in-Chief ISA AL-SHAIJI; circ. 36,000.

Bahrain Tribune: POB 3232, Manama; tel. 17827111; fax 17827222; e-mail tribune@batelco.com.bh; internet www.bahraintribune.com; f. 1997; English; Editor-in-Chief JALIL OMAR; circ. 13,000.

Gulf Daily News: POB 5300, Manama; tel. 17620222; fax 17622141; e-mail gdn1@batelco.com.bh; internet www.gulf-daily-news.com; f. 1978; English; publ. by Al-Hilal Publishing and Marketing Group; Chair. ANWAR ABD AL-RAHMAN; Editor-in-Chief GEORGE WILLIAMS; circ. 11,000.

Khaleej Times: POB 26707, City Centre Bldg, Suite 403, 4th Floor, Government Ave, Manama; tel. 17213911; fax 17211819; e-mail ktimesbn@batelco.com.bh; internet www.khaleejtimes.com; f. 1978; English; based in Dubai (United Arab Emirates); circ. 72,565.

Al-Meethaq: Manama; tel. 17877777; fax 17784118; f. 2004; Arabic; supports the Govt's reform programme; publ. by Al-Meethaq Media and Publishing House; Editor-in-Chief MUHAMMAD HASSAN AL-SATRI; circ. 35,000.

Al-Wasat: Dar al-Wasat for Publishing and Distribution, POB 31110, Manama; tel. 17596999; fax 17596900; e-mail news@alwasatnews.com; internet www.alwasatnews.com; Editor-in-Chief MANSOOR AL-JAMRI.

Al-Watan: Rifa'a; tel. 17496666; fax 17496667; e-mail malaradi@alwatannews.net; internet www.alwatannews.net; f. 2005; Arabic; Editor-in-Chief YUSSEF AL-BINKHALIL.

WEEKLIES

Al-Adhwaa' (Lights): POB 250, Old Exhibition Rd, Manama; tel. 17290942; fax 17293166; f. 1965; Arabic; publ. by Arab Printing and Publishing House; Chair. RAID MAHMOUD AL-MARDI; Editor-in-Chief MUHAMMAD QASSIM SHIRAWI; circ. 7,000.

The Gulf: POB 224, Manama; tel. 17293131; fax 17293400; e-mail editorial@thegulfonline.com; internet www.thegulfonline.com; f. 2008; English; business and current affairs; publ. by Al-Hilal Publishing and Marketing Group; Editor DIGBY LIDSTONE; circ. 7,500.

Gulf Weekly: POB 5300, Manama; tel. 17293131; fax 17293400; e-mail editor@gulfweekly.com; internet www.gulfweekly.com; f. 2002; English; publ. by Al-Hilal Publishing and Marketing Group; Editor STAN SZECOWKA; circ. 13,000.

Huna al-Bahrain (Here is Bahrain): POB 26005, Isa Town; tel. 17870166; fax 17686600; e-mail bahrainmag@info.gov.bh; internet www.moci.gov.bh/en/PressandPublications/; f. 1957; Arabic; publ. by the Ministry of Culture; Editor ABD AL-QADER AQIL; circ. 3,000.

Al-Mawakif (Attitudes): POB 1083, Manama; tel. 17231231; fax 17271720; e-mail mwmradhi@batelco.com.bh; f. 1973; Arabic; general interest; Editor-in-Chief MANSOOR M. RADHI; circ. 6,000.

Oil and Gas News: POB 224, Bldg 149, Exhibition Ave, Manama; tel. 17293131; fax 17293400; e-mail editor@oilandgasnewsworldwide.com; internet www.oilandgasnewsworldwide.com; f. 1983; English; publ. by Al-Hilal Publishing and Marketing Group; Editor-in-Chief CLIVE JACQUES; circ. 5,000.

Sada al-Usbou (Weekly Echo): POB 549, Manama; tel. 17291234; fax 17290507; f. 1969; Arabic; Owner and Editor-in-Chief ALI ABDULLAH SAYYAR; circ. 40,000 (in various Gulf states).

OTHER PERIODICALS

Arab Agriculture: POB 10131, Bahrain Tower, 8th Floor, Manama; tel. 17213900; fax 17211765; e-mail fanar@batelco.com.bh; f. 1984; annually; English and Arabic; publ. by Fanar Publishing WLL; Editor-in-Chief ABD AL-WAHED ALWANI; circ. 13,000.

Arab World Agribusiness: POB 10131, Bahrain Tower, 8th Floor, Manama; tel. 17213900; fax 17211765; e-mail fanar@batelco.com.bh; internet www.fanarpublishing.com; f. 1985; 9 per year; English and Arabic; publ. by Fanar Publishing WLL; Editor-in-Chief ABD AL-WAHED ALWANI; circ. 18,000.

Bahrain Telegraph: POB 55055, Manama; tel. 17530535; fax 17530353; e-mail info@bahraintelegraph.com; internet www.bahraintelegraph.com; f. 2009; monthly; English; news, business and politics; Editor-in-Chief SOMAN BABY.

Al-Bahrain ath-Thaqafia: POB 2199, Manama; tel. 17290210; fax 17292678; internet www.moc.gov.bh; quarterly; Arabic; publ. by the Ministry of Culture; Editor ABD AL-QADER AQIL.

Bahrain This Month: POB 20461, Manama; tel. 17813777; fax 17813700; e-mail redhouse@batelco.com.bh; internet www.bahrainthismonth.com; f. 1997; monthly; English; publ. by Red House Marketing; Publr and Chair. GEORGE F. MIDDLETON; circ. 13,750.

Gulf Construction: POB 224, Exhibition Ave, Manama; tel. 17293131; fax 17293400; e-mail editor@gulfconstructionworldwide.com; internet www.gulfconstructionworldwide.com; f. 1980; monthly; English; publ. by Al-Hilal Publishing and Marketing Group; Editor BINA PRABHU GOVEAS; circ. 26,539.

Gulf Industry: POB 224, Manama; tel. 17293131; fax 17293400; e-mail editor@gulfindustryworldwide.com; internet www.gulfindustryworldwide.com; English; industry and transport; publ. by Al-Hilal Publishing and Marketing Group; Editor SALVADOR ALMEIDA; circ. 10,924.

Al-Hayat at-Tijariya (Commerce Review): POB 248, Manama; tel. 17229555; fax 17224985; e-mail bcci@bcci.bh; monthly; English and Arabic; publ. by Bahrain Chamber of Commerce and Industry; Editor KHALIL YOUSUF; circ. 7,500.

Al-Hidayah (Guidance): POB 450, Manama; tel. 17727100; fax 17729819; f. 1978; monthly; Arabic; publ. by Ministry of Justice and Islamic Affairs; Editor-in-Chief ABD AL-RAHMAN BIN MUHAMMAD RASHID AL KHALIFA; circ. 5,000.

Al-Mohandis (The Engineer): POB 835, Manama; tel. 17727100; fax 17729819; e-mail mohandis@batelco.com.bh; internet www.mohandis.org; f. 1972; quarterly; Arabic and English; publ. by Bahrain Society of Engineers; Editor SHAHRABAN SHARIF.

Al-Musafir al-Arabi (Arab Traveller): POB 10131, Bahrain Tower, 8th Floor, Manama; tel. 17213900; fax 17211765; e-mail fanar@batelco.com.bh; internet www.fanarpublishing.com; f. 1985; 6 per year; Arabic; publ. by Fanar Publishing WLL; Editor-in-Chief ABD AL-WAHED ALWANI; circ. 36,000.

Al-Quwwa (The Force): POB 245, Manama; tel. 17291331; fax 17659596; e-mail dgcdf@gmail.com; internet www.bdf.gov.bh; f. 1977; monthly; Arabic; publ. by Bahrain Defence Force; Editor-in-Chief Maj. AHMAD MAHMOUD AL-SUWAIDI.

Travel and Tourism News Middle East: POB 224, Exhibition Ave, Manama; tel. 17293131; fax 17293400; e-mail editor@ttnworldwide.com; internet www.ttnworldwide.com; f. 1983; monthly; English; travel trade; publ. by Al-Hilal Publishing and Marketing Group; Publishing Dir KIM THOMPSON; circ. 12,370.

Woman This Month: POB 20461, Manama; tel. 17813777; fax 17813700; e-mail editor@womanthismonth.com; internet www.womanthismonth.com; f. 2003; English; monthly; publ. by Red House Marketing; Editor KIRSTY EDWARDS-HARRIS; Publr and Man. Dir GEORGE F. MIDDLETON.

NEWS AGENCY

Bahrain News Agency (BNA): Information Affairs Authority, POB 5421, Manama; tel. 17871602; fax 17681874; e-mail info@bna.bh; internet www.bna.bh; f. 2001 to cover local and foreign news; replaced Gulf News Agency as national news agency; Dir MUHANNAD SULEIMAN.

PRESS ASSOCIATION

Bahrain Journalists' Association (BJA): 2057, Rd 4156, Block 0341, Juffair, Manama 332; tel. 17811770; e-mail bja@batelco.com .bh; internet www.bja-bh.org; f. 2000; Chair. ISA AL-SHAIJI; Sec.-Gen. JAWAD ABD AL-WAHAB; 250 mems.

Publishers

Arabian Magazines Group: POB 26810, Villa 910, Rd 3316, Opp. Qatar Embassy, Blk 333, Mahooz, Manama; tel. 17822388; fax 17721722; e-mail info@arabianmagazines.com; internet www .arabianmagazines.com; f. 2001; publs include *Bahrain Confidential*, *Areej*, *Gulf Insider*, *Shout Confidential*; CEO NICHOLAS COOKSEY.

Fanar Publishing WLL: POB 10131, Manama; tel. 17213900; fax 17211765; e-mail fanar@batelco.com.bh; internet www .fanarpublishing.com; f. 1985; Editor-in-Chief ABD AL-WAHED ALWANI.

Al-Hilal Publishing and Marketing Group: POB 1100, Manama; tel. 17293131; fax 17293400; e-mail hilalad@tradearabia.net; internet www.alhilalgroup.com; f. 1978; specialist magazines, newspapers and websites of commercial interest, incl. *Gulf Daily News*, *Gulf Weekly*, *Gulf Construction*, *Gulf Industry*, *Travel & Tourism News*, etc.; Man. Dir RONNIE MIDDLETON.

Al-Maseerah Printing & Publishing House Co WLL: POB 5981, Manama; tel. 17258882; fax 17276178; e-mail info@ almaseerahprintings.com; internet www.almaseerahprintings.com; f. 1981.

Primedia International BSC: POB 2738, Manama; tel. 17490000; fax 17490001; e-mail info@primediaintl.com; internet www .primedia.com.bh; f. 1977; fmrly Tele-Gulf Directory Publications WLL; publrs of, *inter alia*, annual *Gulf Directory* and *Arab Banking and Finance*, as well as *Bahrain Telephone Directory with Yellow Pages*, *Qatar Telephone Directory with Yellow Pages* and *Banks in Bahrain*; CEO MIKE ORLOV.

Red House Marketing: POB 20461, Manama; tel. 17813777; fax 17813700; e-mail redhouse@batelco.com.bh; internet www .redhousemarketing.com; British-owned; publs include *Bahrain This Month*, *Woman This Month*, *Bahrain Hotel & Restaurant Guide*, maps, tourist guides and various specialist trade publs; Man. Dir and Publr GEORGE F. MIDDLETON.

GOVERNMENT PUBLISHING HOUSE

Directorate of Press and Publications: POB 253, Manama; tel. 17717525; e-mail jamaldawood@hotmail.com; internet www.info .gov.bh/en/PressandPublications; publs include *Official Gazette* and *Huna Al-Bahrayn Magazine*; Dir JAMAL DAWOOD AL-JLAHMA.

Broadcasting and Communications

TELECOMMUNICATIONS

The telecommunications sector in Bahrain was fully opened to private sector competition in 2002. Since liberalization of the sector Bahrain has been at the forefront of the development of new infrastructure and technologies in the region. Several companies provide fixed-line services. Three providers have been awarded mobile telecommunications licences; the third mobile licence was awarded to Saudi Telecom (STC) in January 2009.

Bahrain Telecommunications Co BSC (BATELCO): POB 14, Manama; tel. 17881881; fax 17311120; e-mail batelco@btc.com.bh; internet www.batelco.com.bh; f. 1981; cap. BD 120m.; 100% owned by Govt of Bahrain, financial institutions and public of Bahrain; launched mobile cellular telecommunications service, Sim Sim, in 1999; provides fixed-line and mobile telephone services, broadband internet and data services; Chair. Sheikh HAMAD BIN ABDULLAH BIN MUHAMMAD AL KHALIFA; CEO (vacant).

Nuetel Communications: POB 50960, Amwaj Islands; tel. 16033000; fax 16033001; e-mail info@nue-tel.com; internet www .nue-tel.com; f. 2006; provides fixed-line telephone, broadband internet, internet telephony and data services; CEO MARK NIXON.

2Connect Bahrain WLL: POB 18057, 12th Floor, NBB Tower, Government Ave, Manama; tel. 16500110; fax 16500109; e-mail info@2connectbahrain.com; internet www.2connectbahrain.com; f. 2004; provides fixed-line telephone, broadband internet and data-hosting services; Man. Dir FAHAD SHIRAWI.

VIVA Bahrain: Bldg 15, Blk 428, Seef, Manama; internet www.viva .com.bh; f. 2010; subsidiary of Saudi Telecommunications Co—Saudi Telecom; mobile telephone and broadband internet services; CEO ULAIYAN AL-WETAID.

Zain Bahrain: POB 266, Manama; tel. 36107107; e-mail customercare@bh.zain.com; internet www.bh.zain.com; f. 2003 under the name MTC Vodafone Bahrain; present name adopted 2007; acquired Celtel International (Netherlands) in 2005; 60% owned by Mobile Telecommunications Co (Kuwait), 40% by Bahraini Govt; provides mobile telephone services; Group CEO Dr SCOTT GEGENHEIMER; Gen. Man. MUHAMMAD ZAIN AL-ABDEEN.

Regulatory Authority

Telecommunications Regulatory Authority (TRA): POB 10353, Taib Tower, 7th Floor, Diplomatic Area, Manama; tel. 17520000; fax 17532125; e-mail contact@tra.org.bh; internet www .tra.org.bh; f. 2002; Chair. Dr MUHAMMAD AHMAD AL-AMER; Gen. Dir MUHAMMAD HAMAD BUBSHAIT.

BROADCASTING

Radio

Bahrain Radio and Television Corpn: POB 702, Manama; tel. 17871405; fax 17681622; e-mail ceobrtc@batelco.com.bh; internet www.bahraintv.com; f. 1955; state-owned; two 10-kW transmitters; programmes are in Arabic and English, and include news, drama and discussions; CEO Sheikh RASHID BIN ABD AL-RAHMAN AL KHALIFA.

Radio Bahrain: POB 702, Manama; tel. 17871585; fax 17780911; e-mail info@radiobahrain.fm; internet www.radiobahrain.fm; f. 1977; English-language commercial radio station; Head of Station SALAH KHALID.

Television

Bahrain Radio and Television Corpn: POB 1075, Manama; tel. 17686000; fax 17681544; e-mail ceobrtc@batelco.bh; internet www .bahraintv.com; commenced colour broadcasting in 1973; broadcasts on 5 channels, of which the main Arabic and the main English channel accept advertising; offers a 24-hour Arabic news and documentary channel; covers Bahrain, eastern Saudi Arabia, Qatar and the United Arab Emirates; an Amiri decree in early 1993 established the independence of the Corpn, which was to be controlled by a committee; CEO Sheikh RASHID BIN ABD AL-RAHMAN AL KHALIFA.

Finance

(cap. = capital; res = reserves; dep. = deposits; m. = million; br.(s) = branch(es); amounts in Bahraini dinars unless otherwise stated)

BANKING

Central Bank

Central Bank of Bahrain (CBB): POB 27, Bldg 96, Block 317, Rd 1702, Diplomatic Area, Manama; tel. 17547777; fax 17530399; e-mail info@cbb.gov.bh; internet www.cbb.gov.bh; f. 1973 as Bahrain Monetary Agency; in operation from Jan. 1975; name changed as above Sept. 2006; controls issue of currency, regulates exchange control and credit policy, organization and control of banking and insurance systems, bank credit and stock exchange; cap. 200m., res 276m., dep. 1,156m. (Dec. 2009); Chair. QASSIM MUHAMMAD FAKHRO; Gov. RASHID MUHAMMAD AL-MARAJ.

Locally Incorporated Commercial Banks

Ahli United Bank BSC (AUB): POB 2424, Bldg 2495, Rd 2832, al-Seef District 428, Manama; tel. 17585858; fax 17580569; e-mail info@ ahliunited.com; internet www.ahliunited.com; f. 2001 by merger of Al-Ahli Commercial Bank and Commercial Bank of Bahrain; cap. US $1,428m., res $992m., dep. $23,376m. (Dec. 2012); Chair. FAHAD AL-RAJAAN; Group CEO and Man. Dir ADEL EL-LABBAN; 21 brs.

Awal Bank BSC: POB 1735, Manama; tel. 17203333; fax 17203355; e-mail info@awal-bank.com; internet www.awal-bank.com; f. 2004; owned by Saad Group (Saudi Arabia); placed into administration July 2009; cap. US $2,000m., res $72.2m., dep. $4,861.2m. (Dec. 2008); Chair. MAAN A. AL-SANEA; CEO and Dir ALISTAIR MACLEOD (acting).

Bahrain Islamic Bank BSC: POB 5240, Al-Salam Tower, Diplomatic Area, Manama; tel. 17515151; fax 17535808; e-mail contactcenter@bisb.com; internet www.bisb.com; f. 1979; cap. 93m., res 11m., dep. 748m. (Dec. 2012); Chair. ABD AL-RAZAK ABDULLA AL-QASSIM; CEO MUHAMMAD EBRAHIM MUHAMMAD; 13 brs.

BBK BSC: POB 579, 43 Government Ave, Area 305, Manama; tel. 17223388; fax 17229822; e-mail swar@bbkonline.com; internet www .bbkonline.com; f. 1971 as Bank of Bahrain and Kuwait BSC; name changed as above 2005; cap. 85m., res 154m., dep. 2,459m. (Dec. 2012); Chair. MURAD ALI MURAD; Chief Exec. ABD AL-KARIM AHMAD BUCHEERY; 20 brs.

Future Bank BSC: POB 785, Government Rd, Manama; tel. 17505000; fax 17224402; e-mail info@futurebank.com.bh; internet www.futurebank.com.bh; f. 2004; owned by Ahli United Bank BSC, Bank Melli Iran and Bank Saderat Iran; cap. 83m., res 7m., dep. 394m. (Dec. 2013); Chair. ABD AL-NASER HEMMATI; CEO and Man. Dir GHOLAM SOURI; 3 brs.

Ithmaar Bank BSC: POB 2820, 10th Floor, Addax Tower, Manama; tel. 17584000; fax 17584017; e-mail info@ithmaarbank.com; internet www.ithmaarbank.com; f. 1984 as Faisal Investment Bank of Bahrain EC, a wholly owned subsidiary of Shamil Bank of Bahrain BSC; acquired by Dar al-Maal al-Islami and assumed name as above in 2003; merged with Shamil Bank of Bahrain in April 2010; cap. US $252m., res. $105m., dep. $1,663m. (Dec 2012); Chair. Prince AMR MUHAMMAD AL-FAISAL; CEO AHMAD ABD AL-RAHIM; 11 brs.

National Bank of Bahrain BSC (NBB): POB 106, Government Ave, Manama; tel. 17228800; fax 17228998; e-mail nbb@nbbonline.com; internet www.nbbonline.com; f. 1957; 49% govt-owned; cap. 85m., res 126m., dep. 2,246m. (Dec. 2012); Chair. FAROUK YOUSUF AL-MOAYYED; CEO and Dir ABD AL-RAZAK A. HASSAN AL-QASSIM; 25 brs.

Al-Salam Bank Bahrain BSC: POB 18282, Bldg 22, Ave 58, al-Seef District, Manama; tel. 17560000; fax 17560003; internet www.alsalambahrain.com; f. 2006; acquired Bahraini Saudi Bank in July 2009; Islamic bank; cap. 149m., res 18m., dep. 714m. (Dec 2012); Chair. Sheikha HESSA BINT KHALIFA BIN HAMAD AL KHALIFA; CEO and Dir YOUSUF ABDULLAH TAQI; 7 brs.

Specialized Financial Institutions

Bahrain Development Bank (BDB): POB 20501, Manama; tel. 17511111; fax 17530116; internet www.bdb-bh.com; f. 1992; invests in manufacturing, agribusiness and services; cap. 50m., res 754,000, dep. 60m. (Dec. 2011); Chair. Sheikh MUHAMMAD BIN ISSA BIN MUHAMMAD AL KHALIFA; CEO NEDHAL S. AL-AUJAN.

First Energy Bank BSC: POB 209, Manama; tel. 17100001; fax 17170170; internet www.1stenergybank.com; f. 2008; owned by Gulf Finance House BSC and other Gulf shareholders; Islamic wholesale bank providing investment and advice for energy projects; cap. US $1,000m., res. $2m., dep. $59m. (Dec. 2012); CEO MUHAMMAD SHUKRI GHANEM; Chair. KHADEM ABDULLAH AL-QUBAISI.

'Offshore' Banking Units

Bahrain has been encouraging the establishment of 'offshore' banking units (OBUs) since 1975. An OBU is not permitted to provide local banking services, but is allowed to accept deposits from governments and large financial organizations in the area and make medium-term loans for local and regional capital projects. In late 2006 there were 49 OBUs in operation in Bahrain.

ABC Islamic Bank EC: POB 2808, ABC Tower, Diplomatic Area, Manama; tel. 17543000; fax 17533163; e-mail webmaster@arabbanking.com; internet www.arabbanking.com; f. 1987 as ABC Investment and Services Co (EC); name changed as above in 1998 when converted into Islamic bank; 100% owned by Arab Banking Corpn BSC; cap. US $132m., res $15m. (Dec. 2012), dep. $1,133m. (Dec. 2009); Man. Dir NAVEED KHAN; Chair. KHALID KAWAN.

Alubaf Arab International Bank BSC: POB 11529, Sheraton Tower 13F, Manama; tel. 17517722; fax 17517721; e-mail info@alubafbank.com; internet www.alubafbank.com; f. 1982; 99.5% owned by Libyan Foreign Bank; cap. US $250m., res $29m., dep. $807m. (Dec. 2012); Chair. MORAJA GAITH SULAYMAN; CEO HASAN ABULHASAN.

Arab Bank PLC (Jordan): POB 813, Manama; tel. 17549000; fax 17541116; e-mail arabbank@batelco.com.bh; internet www.arabbank.bh; f. 1930; Chair. SABIH AL-MASRI.

Arab Banking Corpn BSC: POB 5698, ABC Tower, Diplomatic Area, Manama; tel. 17543000; fax 17533062; e-mail webmaster@arabbanking.com; internet www.arabbanking.com; f. 1980; cap. US $3,110m., res $275m., dep. $18,314m. (Dec. 2013); Chair. SADDEK AL-KABER; Pres. and Chief Exec. KHALED KAWAN.

Arab Investment Co SAA (Saudi Arabia): POB 5559, Bldg 2309, Rd 2830, al-Seef District 428, Manama; tel. 17588888; fax 17588885; e-mail taic@taicobu.com; internet www.taic.com; f. 1974; cap. US $700m., res $158m., dep. $1,206m. (Dec. 2012); Chair. YOUSEF BIN IBRAHIM AL-BASSAM; CEO IBRAHIM H. AL-MAZYAD.

BNP Paribas (France): POB 5253, Bahrain Financial Harbour, West Tower, Manama; tel. 17866607; fax 17866601; e-mail souad.hindawi@bnpparibas.com; internet www.bahrain.bnpparibas.com; f. 1975; Regional Man. JEAN-CHRISTOPHE DURAND.

Gulf International Bank BSC (GIB): POB 1017, Al-Duwali Bldg, 3 Palace Ave, Area 317, Manama; tel. 17534000; fax 17522633; e-mail info@gibbah.com; internet www.gibonline.com; f. 1975; cap. US $2,500m., res $374m., dep. $15,197m. (Dec. 2013); Chair. Sheikh JAMMAZ BIN ABDULLAH AL-SUHAIMI; CEO YAHYA AL-YAHYA.

Korea Exchange Bank (Repub. of Korea): POB 5767, Yateem Centre Bldg, 5th Floor, Manama; tel. 17229333; fax 17225327; e-mail bahrain@keb.co.kr; internet www.keb.co.kr; f. 1977; Pres. and CEO YUN YONG-RO.

MCB Bank Ltd (MCB) (Pakistan): POB 10164, Diplomatic Area, Manama; tel. 17533306; fax 17533308; e-mail mcbobubh@batelco.com.bh; internet www.mcb.com.pk; f. 1947 as Muslim Commercial Bank Ltd, name changed as above in 2005; Chair. MUHAMMAD MANSHA.

National Bank of Abu Dhabi (UAE): POB 5886, Manama 304; tel. 17560870; fax 17583281; e-mail hassan.bahzad@nbad.com; internet www.nbad.com; f. 1977; Regional Man. HASSAN BAHZAD.

National Bank of Kuwait SAK: POB 5290, Bahrain BMB Centre, Diplomatic Area, Manama; tel. 17583333; fax 17587111; e-mail nbkbah@batelco.com.bh; f. 1977; Gen. Man. ALI Y. FARDAN.

Standard Chartered Bank (United Kingdom): POB 29, Manama; tel. 17223636; fax 17225001; internet www.standardchartered.com/bh; f. 1976; cap. US $1,207m., res $17,594m., dep. $488,567m. (Dec. 2012); CEO HASSAN JARRAR.

State Bank of India: POB 5466, GBCorp Tower, Bahrain Financial Harbour, Manama; tel. 17505177; fax 17224692; e-mail opns.wbbbah@statebank.com; internet www.sbibahrain.com; f. 1977; Country Head and CEO ASHWINI KUMAR SHUKLA.

Yapi ve Kredi Bankasi AS (Turkey): POB 10615, c/o Bahrain Development Bank, Diplomatic Area, Manama; tel. 17530313; fax 17530311; internet www.yapikredi.com; f. 1982; Chair. MUSTAFA V. KOÇ.

Investment Banks

Bahrain Middle East Bank BSC (BMB Investment Bank): POB 797, BMB Centre, Diplomatic Area, Manama; tel. 17532345; fax 17530526; e-mail requests@bmb.com.bh; internet www.bmb.com.bh; f. 1982; fmrly Bahrain Middle East Bank EC; cap. US $60m., res $18m., dep. $11m. (Dec. 2012); Chair. WILSON S. BENJAMIN; CEO RITCHIE SKELDING; 1 br.

Al-Baraka Islamic Bank BSC (EC): POB 1882, Diplomatic Area, Manama; tel. 17535300; fax 17533993; e-mail baraka@batelco.com.bh; internet www.albaraka.bh; f. 1984 as Al-Baraka Islamic Investment Bank BSC (EC); current name adopted 1998; owned by Al-Baraka Banking Group BSC; cap. 122m., res 18m., dep. 1,216m. (Dec. 2012); Chair. KHALID RASHID AL-ZAYANI; CEO MUHAMMAD AL-MUTAWEH; 400 brs.

First Investment Bank: 7th Floor, Euro Tower, al-Seef District, POB 10016, Manama; tel. 17389089; fax 17556621; e-mail info@first-ibank.com; internet www.first-ibank.com; f. 2007; Islamic investment bank; jt venture between 8 Gulf investors; cap. US $200m.; Chair. MUHAMMAD A. AL-ALLOUSH; Dep. CEO YOUSIF AL-THAWADI.

Global Banking Corpn (GBCORP): POB 1486, GBCORP Tower, Bahrain Financial Harbour, Manama; tel. 17200200; fax 17200300; e-mail info@gbcorponline.com; internet www.gbcorponline.com; f. 2007; Islamic investment bank; cap. 200m., res 5m., dep. 3m. (Dec. 2012); Chair. TALAL MUHAMMAD AL-MUTAWA; CEO Dr ZAKARIA AHMAD AL-JASMI.

Gulf Finance House BSC: POB 10006, Bahrain Financial Harbour, Manama; tel. 17538538; fax 17540006; e-mail info@gfh.com; internet www.gfhouse.com; f. 1999 as Gulf Finance House EC, name changed as above in 2004; cap. US $595m., res $77m., dep. $128m. (Dec. 2012); Chair. Dr AHMAD AL-MUTAWA; CEO HISHAM AHMAD AL-RAYES.

Ibdar Bank: POB 1001, Manama; tel. 17510000; fax 17510051; e-mail info@ibdarbank.com; internet www.ibdarbank.com; f. 2013 by merger of Capital Management House, Capinvest and Elaf Bank; Islamic investment bank; cap. 300m., res 36m., dep. 39m. (Dec. 2012); Chair. PAUL ANDREW MERCER; CEO SAMEEH ABDULLA AL-KHAN.

INVESTCORP Bank BSC: POB 5340, Investcorp House, Diplomatic Area, Manama; tel. 17532000; fax 17530816; e-mail info@investcorp.com; internet www.investcorp.com; f. 1982 as Arabian Investment Banking Corpn (Investcorp) EC, current name adopted in 1990; cap. US $711m., res $141m., dep. $361m. (June 2013); Exec. Chair. and CEO NEMIR A. KIRDAR.

Nomura Investment Banking (Middle East) EC: POB 26893, BMB Centre, 7th Floor, Diplomatic Area, Manama; tel. 17530531; fax 17530365; f. 1982; cap. US $25.0m., res $46.3m., dep. $0.3m. (Dec. 2007); Chair. TAKUYA FURUYA.

TAIB Bank BSC: POB 20485, TAIB Tower, 79 Rd 1702, Diplomatic Area, Manama 317; tel. 17549494; fax 17533174; e-mail taibprivatebank@taib.com; internet www.taibdirect.com; f. 1979 as Trans-Arabian Investment Bank EC, renamed TAIB Bank EC in 1994, current name adopted in 2004; cap. US $112m., res $11m., dep. $133m. (Dec. 2011); Chair. ABD AL-RAHMAN HAREB RASHED AL-HAREB; Dir ABD AL-RAHMAN ABDULLAH MUHAMMAD.

United Gulf Bank BSC: POB 5964, UGB Tower, Diplomatic Area, Manama; tel. 17533233; fax 17533137; e-mail info@ugbbah.com;

internet www.ugbbah.com; f. 1980; cap. US $208m., res $193m., dep. $239m. (Dec. 2012); Chair. MASAUD M. J. HAYAT; CEO RABIH SOUKARIEH.

Venture Capital Bank BSC: POB 11755, Manama; tel. 17518888; fax 17518880; e-mail info@vc-bank.com; internet www.vc-bank.com; f. 2005; Islamic investment bank; cap. US $250m., res $21m., dep. 13m. (Dec. 2011); Chair. Dr GHASSAN AHMED AL-SULAIMAN; CEO ABD AL-LATIF MUHAMMAD JANAHI.

Other investment banks operating in Bahrain include Al-Amin Bank, Amex (Middle East) EC, Capital Union EC, Daiwa Securities SMBC Europe Ltd (Middle East), Global Banking Corpn BSC, Investors Bank EC, Al-Khaleej Islamic Investment Bank (BSC) EC and Merrill Lynch Int. Bank Ltd.

STOCK EXCHANGES

Bahrain Bourse: POB 3203, Manama; tel. 17261260; fax 17256362; e-mail info@bahrainbourse.com.bh; internet www.bahrainbourse .com.bh; f. 1989; 51 listed cos at Dec. 2008; scheduled for privatization; Chair. YOUSUF ABDULLA HUMOOD; Dir FOUAD A. RAHMAN RASHID.

Bahrain Financial Exchange (BFX): POB 1936, 12th Floor, East Tower, Bahrain Financial Harbour, Manama; tel. 16511511; fax 16511599; e-mail info@bfx.bh; internet www.bfx.bh; f. 2009; trading in securities, derivatives, commodities, foreign exchange and *Shari'a*-compliant financial products; owned by Financial Technologies Group (India); Chair. JIGNESH SHAH; Man. Dir and CEO ARSHAD KHAN.

INSURANCE

In 2009 there were 25 locally incorporated insurance firms operating in Bahrain, including:

Al-Ahlia Insurance Co BSC: POB 5282, Chamber of Commerce Bldg, 4th Floor, King Faisal Rd, Manama; tel. 17225860; fax 17224870; e-mail alahlia@alahlia.com; internet www.alahlia.com; f. 1976; Chair. HUSSAIN ALI SAJWANI; Gen. Man. TAWFIQ SHEHAB.

Arab Insurance Group BSC (ARIG): POB 26992, Arig House, Diplomatic Area, Manama; tel. 17544444; fax 17531155; e-mail info@arig.com.bh; internet www.arig.net; f. 1980; owned by Govts of Kuwait, Libya and the United Arab Emirates (49.5%), and other shareholders; reinsurance and insurance; Chair. KHALID ALI AL-BUSTANI; CEO YASSIR ALBAHARNA.

Bahrain Kuwait Insurance Co BSC: POB 10166, Diplomatic Area, Manama; tel. 17119999; fax 17921111; e-mail info@bkic.com; internet www.bkic.com; f. 1975; CEO IBRAHIM SHARIF AL-RAYES; Chair. ABDULLAH HASSAN BUHINDI.

Bahrain National Holding Co BSC (BNH): POB 843, BNH Tower, al-Seef District; tel. 17587300; fax 17583099; e-mail bnh@bnhgroup.com; internet www.bnhgroup.com; f. 1999 by merger of Bahrain Insurance Co and Nat. Insurance Co; all classes incl. life insurance; Chair. FAROUK Y. AL-MOAYYED; Chief Exec. SAMEER AL-WAZZAN.

Gulf Union Insurance and Reinsurance Co: POB 10949, Manama Centre, Ground Floor, Manama; tel. 17215622; fax 17215421; e-mail guirco@batelco.com.bh; internet www.thyra.com/Sites/gulfunion; Chair. Sheikh IBRAHIM BIN HAMAD AL KHALIFA.

Solidarity Insurance Co: POB 18668, Seef Tower, 11th Floor, al-Seef District, Manama; tel. 17585222; fax 17585200; e-mail mail@solidarity.cc; internet www.solidarity.cc; f. 2004 by Qatar Islamic Bank; Chair. KHALID ABDULLAH JANAHI; CEO ASHRAF BSEISU.

Takaful International Co: POB 3230, B680 R2811, al-Seef District 428, Manama; tel. 17565656; fax 17582688; internet www .takafulweb.com; f. 1989 as Bahrain Islamic Insurance Co; restructured and renamed as above in 1998; Chair. BARA'A ABD AL-AZIZ AL-QENAEI; CEO YOUNIS J. AL-SAYED.

Insurance Association

Bahrain Insurance Association (BIA): POB 2851, Manama; tel. 17532555; fax 17536006; e-mail biabah@batelco.com.bh; internet www.bia-bh.com; f. 1993; 43 mems; Chair. YOUNIS JAMAL AL-SAYED.

Trade and Industry

GOVERNMENT AGENCIES

Economic Development Board (EDB): POB 11299, Manama; tel. 17589999; fax 17589900; e-mail info@bahrainedb.com; internet www .bahrainedb.com; f. 2000; assumed duties of Bahrain Promotions and Marketing Board (f. 1993) and Supreme Council for Economic Devt (f. 2000) in 2001; provides national focus for Bahraini marketing initiatives; attracts inward investment; encourages devt and expansion of Bahraini exports; Chair. Sheikh SALMAN BIN HAMAD AL KHALIFA; CEO Sheikh MUHAMMAD BIN ISSA AL KHALIFA.

National Oil and Gas Authority (NOGA): POB 1435, Manama; tel. 17312644; fax 17293007; e-mail info@noga.gov.bh; internet www .noga.gov.bh; f. 2005 for the regulation and devt of oil- and gas-related industries in the kingdom; Chair. Sheikh AHMAD BIN MUHAMMAD AL KHALIFA (Minister of Finance and Minister of Oil and Gas Affairs); Sec.-Gen. AHMAD AL-SHARYAN.

CHAMBER OF COMMERCE

Bahrain Chamber of Commerce and Industry: POB 248, Bldg 122, Rd 1605, Block 216, Manama; tel. 17576666; fax 17576600; e-mail bcci@bcci.bh; internet www.bcci.bh; f. 1939; 12,023 mems (Jan. 2007); Chair. Dr ESSAM ABDULLAH YOUSUF FAKHRO; CEO NABIL ABD AL-RAHMAN AL-MAHMOOD (acting).

STATE HYDROCARBONS COMPANIES

Bahrain National Gas Co BSC (BANAGAS): POB 29099, Rifa'a; tel. 17756222; fax 17756991; e-mail bng@banagas.com.bh; internet www.banagas.com.bh; f. 1979; responsible for extraction, processing and sale of hydrocarbon liquids from associated gas derived from onshore Bahraini fields; 75% owned by Govt of Bahrain, 12.5% by Caltex and 12.5% by Boubyan Petrochemical Co; produces approx. 2,900 barrels per day (b/d) of propane, 2,700 b/d of butane and 5,200 b/d of naphtha; Chair. ALI BIN MUHAMMAD AL-JALAHMA; Chief Exec. Dr Sheikh MUHAMMAD BIN KHALIFA AL KHALIFA.

Bahrain Petroleum Co BSC (BAPCO): POB 25555, Awali; tel. 17704040; fax 17704070; e-mail info@bapco.net; internet www.bapco .com.bh; f. 1999 by merger of Bahrain Nat. Oil Co (f. 1976) and Bahrain Petroleum Co (f. 1980); 100% govt-owned; fully integrated co responsible for exploration, drilling and production of oil and gas; supply of gas to power-generating plants and industries, refining crude petroleum, international marketing of crude petroleum and refined petroleum products, supply and sale of aviation fuel at Bahrain International Airport, and local distribution and marketing of petroleum products; Chair. Dr ABD AL-HUSSAIN BIN ALI MIRZA (Minister of Energy); CEO FAISAL MUHAMMAD AL-MAHROOS.

Gulf Petrochemical Industries Co BSC (GPIC): POB 26730, Manama; tel. 17731777; fax 17731047; e-mail gpic@gpic.com; internet www.gpic.com; f. 1979 as jt venture between the Govts of Bahrain, Kuwait and Saudi Arabia, each with one-third equity participation; a petrochemical complex at Sitra, inaugurated in 1981; produces 1,200 metric tons of both methanol and ammonia per day; Chair. Sheikh ISA BIN ALI AL KHALIFA; Pres. ABD AL-RAHMAN A. HUSSEIN JAWAHERI.

UTILITIES

Electricity and Water Authority: POB 2, King Faisal Rd, Manama; tel. 17996330; fax 17546669; e-mail publicrelations@ewa.bh; internet www.mew.gov.bh; f. 2007; privatization of electricity production was approved in December 2003; CEO Sheikh NAWAF BIN IBRAHIM AL KHALIFA.

TRADE UNIONS

In November 2002 legislation was ratified to permit the establishment of independent trade unions. There were reported to be more than 50 trade unions operating within Bahrain by early 2007. In July 2012 the Bahrain Labour Union Free Federation (now Bahrain Free Labour Unions Federation) was launched, following disagreement within the General Federation of Bahrain Trade Unions over its alleged political activities.

Bahrain Free Labour Unions Federation: POB 32806, Villa 3776, Rd 915, Blk 809, Isa, Manama; tel. 17226522; fax 17226422; e-mail bflufbh@bflufbh.com; internet www.bflufbh.com; f. 2012; Chair. YAQOOB MUHAMMAD YOUSIF.

General Federation of Bahrain Trade Unions (GFBTU): Manama; tel. 17727333; fax 17729599; internet www.gfbtu.org; f. 2002; Sec.-Gen. SALMAN JAFFAR AL-MAHFOUD.

Transport

RAILWAYS

There are no railways in Bahrain. In early 2011 a detailed feasibility study began into plans for a 184-km domestic rail network, to be constructed in three phases by 2030. The Bahraini project was expected to form part of a planned regional rail network, connecting Bahrain with member countries of the Cooperation Council for the Arab States of the Gulf (or Gulf Cooperation Council—GCC). In early 2013 a feasibility study into plans for a railway connecting Bahrain and Saudi Arabia was also under way, and was due to be completed by 2014.

ROADS

In 2011 Bahrain had 4,147 km of roads, including 576 km of highways, main or national roads, 585 km of secondary or regional roads and 2,256 km of other roads; 82.4% of roads were paved. The King Fahd Causeway, a 25-km causeway link with Saudi Arabia, was opened in 1986. A three-lane dual carriageway links the causeway to Manama. Other causeways link Bahrain with Muharraq island and with Sitra island. The Strategic Roads Masterplan 2021, launched by the Ministry of Works in 2005, outlined plans for the modernization of Bahrain's road network in anticipation of significant increases in road traffic volume. Approval for the construction of a causeway linking Askar in eastern Bahrain with Ras Ishairij in Qatar (the Friendship Bridge) was given in 2004. The project was to be supervised by a committee established in February 2005 by the Governments of both countries. After protracted discussions and numerous delays, in May 2008 the contract to design and build the causeway, at a cost of some US $3,000m., was awarded to a France-based consortium. The decision, in late 2008, to incorporate a dual railway line into the project necessitated substantial design revisions that were expected to add up to $1,000m. to the cost of the causeway. Construction work had been expected to begin in early 2009, with a projected completion date of 2013; however, following further delays as a result of financial difficulties, by early 2014 construction work had yet to commence.

Responsibility for the management and development of Bahrain's roads is divided between the Ministry of Works (Roads Projects and Maintenance Directorate, and Roads, Planning and Design Directorate) and the Ministry of the Interior (Directorate of Traffic).

SHIPPING

Numerous shipping services link Bahrain and the Gulf with Europe, the USA, Pakistan, India, the Far East and Australia.

The deep-water harbour of Mina Salman was opened in 1962. However, following the opening of Khalifa bin Salman port in 2009 (see below), commercial operations at Mina Salman were phased out and plans for an expanded US Navy base at the port were under discussion.

In 1999 work began on the construction of a new port and industrial zone at Hidd, on Muharraq island. Incorporating the Bahrain Gateway Terminal, the new port, Khalifa bin Salman, which became operational in April 2009 (at an estimated cost of over US $350m.), has an annual handling capacity of 1.1m. 20-foot equivalent units (TEUs). The port, which has 1,800 m of quayside walls and a quayside depth of 12.8 m (due to be increased to 15 m), includes a general cargo berth and two container berths with roll-on roll-off facilities. Khalifa bin Salman is managed and operated by APM Terminals Bahrain, under the terms of a 25-year contract awarded in 2007. At 31 December 2013 Bahrain's flag registered fleet totalled 367 vessels, with an aggregate displacement of 741,459 grt. Of those vessels, three were bulk carriers, one was a fish carrier and three were general cargo ships.

Port and Regulatory Authorities

APM Terminals Bahrain BSC: PO Box 50490, Khalifa bin Salman Port, Hidd; tel. 17365500; fax 17365505; e-mail bahapmtcom@apmterminals.com; internet www.apmterminals.com/africa-mideast/bahrain; f. 2006; 80% owned by APM Terminals Management BV, 20% by Yusuf bin Ahmad Kanoo Holdings; management and operation of Bahrain's commercial port; Man. Dir STEEN DAVIDSEN.

General Organization of Sea Ports: POB 75315, Manama; tel. 17359595; fax 17359359; e-mail info@gop.gov.bh; internet www.gop.bh; responsible for regulation, devt and promotion of maritime and logistics zones; Chair. Sheikh DAIJ BIN SALMAN BIN DAIJ AL KHALIFA; Dir-Gen. HASSAN ALI AL-MAJID.

Principal Shipping Companies

Alsharif Group WLL: POB 1322, Manama; tel. 17515055; fax 17537637; e-mail alsharif@batelco.com.bh; internet www.alsharifbahrain.com; f. 1957; shipping agency; Man. Dir ALI ABD AL-RASOOL AL-SHARIF; Gen. Man. BALAJI ARDHANARI.

Arab Shipbuilding and Repair Yard Co (ASRY): POB 50110, Hidd; tel. 17671111; fax 17670236; e-mail asryco@batelco.com.bh; internet www.asry.net; f. 1974 by OAPEC mems; 500,000-ton dry dock opened 1977; 2 floating docks in operation since 1992; new twin slipway completed 2008; repaired 139 ships in 2006; Chair. Sheikh DAIJ BIN SALMAN BIN DAIJ AL KHALIFA; Chief Exec. CHRIS POTTER.

The Gulf Agency Co (Bahrain) WLL: POB 412, Rd 20, 224 Muharraq Area, GLS Premises, Manama; tel. 17339777; fax 17320498; e-mail bahrain@gac.com; internet www.gacworld.com/bahrain; f. 1957; shipping agency; operates at Sitra, Mina Salman and Hidd ports; Man. Dir MIKAEL LEIJONBERG.

Al-Jazeera Shipping Co WLL: POB 302, Mina Salman Industrial Area, Manama; tel. 17728837; fax 17728217; e-mail almelaha@batelco.com.bh; internet www.ajsco.com; operates a fleet of tugboats and barges; Man. Dir ALI HASSAN MAHMOUD.

Kanoo Shipping: POB 45, Al Khalifa Ave, Manama; tel. 17220220; fax 17229122; e-mail kanoomgt@batelco.com.bh; internet www.ybakanoo.com; f. 1890; owned by Yusuf bin Ahmad Kanoo Group; air and shipping cargo services, commercial and holiday services; Chair. MUBARAK JASIM KANOO; Shipping Man. DON BANNERMAN.

Nass Marine Services: POB 669, Manama; tel. 17467722; fax 17467773; e-mail nassmarine@batelco.com.bh; internet www.nassgroup.com; f. 2006; part of Nass Group; shipbuilding and ship-repair; Chair. ABDULLAH AHMAD NASS.

UCO Marine Contracting WLL: POB 1074, Manama; tel. 17730816; fax 17732131; e-mail ucomarin@batelco.com.bh; owns and operates a fleet of bulk carriers, tugboats, barges and dredgers; Man. Dir ALI AL-MUSALAM.

CIVIL AVIATION

Bahrain International Airport (BIA) has a first-class runway, capable of taking the largest aircraft in use. In 2012 BIA handled some 8.5m. passengers. Plans for a two-phase project to expand the airport's capacity through the construction of two new passenger terminals, at an estimated total cost of US $4,700m., were finalized in late 2009. However, in 2011 it was announced that plans for a second terminal had been abandoned. The project to expand the existing terminal to accommodate up to 13.5m. passengers per year was to continue and was due to be completed by 2015.

Department of Civil Aviation Affairs: POB 586, Manama; tel. 17321110; fax 17339066; e-mail prelation@caa.gov.bh; internet www.caa.gov.bh; Under-Sec. Capt. ABD AL-RAHMAN MUHAMMAD AL-GAOUD.

Gulf Air: POB 138, Manama; tel. 17339339; fax 17224494; e-mail gfpr@batelco.com.bh; internet www.gulfair.com; f. 1950 as Gulf Aviation Co; name changed 1974; wholly owned by the Govt of Bahrain; services to the Middle East, South-East Asia, the Far East, Australia, Africa and Europe; Chair. Sheikh KHALID BIN ABDULLAH AL KHALIFA (Deputy Prime Minister); CEO MAHER SALMAN JABER AL-MUSALLAM (acting).

Tourism

There are several archaeological sites of importance in Bahrain, which is the site of the ancient trading civilization of Dilmun. Qal'at al-Bahrain, the ancient capital of Dilmun, was designated a UNESCO World Heritage Site in 2005. In early 2014 major hotel and resort developments were ongoing at Bahrain Bay, City Centre Mall, Al-Areen, the Amwaj Islands and Durrat al-Bahrain. The Government is currently promoting Bahrain as a destination for sports and leisure activities. The Bahrain Grand Prix, held annually since 2004, was the first Formula One event to be held in the Middle East. In 2011 the event was cancelled owing to unrest in the country, but in 2012 and 2013 the Grand Prix took place as scheduled, despite continued protests within Bahrain and international criticism. In 2011 Bahrain received 6.7m. foreign visitors. Income from tourism (excluding passenger transport) totalled US $1,035m. in 2011.

Bahrain Exhibition and Convention Authority: POB 11644, Manama; tel. 17558800; fax 17555513; e-mail info@bahrainexhibitions.com; internet www.bahrainexhibitions.com; Chair. Dr HASSAN BIN ABDULLAH FAKHRO (Minister of Industry and Commerce); CEO HASSAN JAFFAR MUHAMMAD.

Bahrain Tourism Co (BTC): POB 5831, Manama; tel. 17530530; fax 17530867; e-mail btc@alseyaha.com; internet www.alseyaha.com; f. 1974; Chair. QASSIM MUHAMMAD FAKHROO; CEO ABD AL-NABI DAYLAMI.

Tourism Affairs: Ministry of Culture, POB 26613, Manama; tel. 17201244; fax 17211717; e-mail azizisherida@info.gov.bh; internet www.moc.gov.bh/en/TourismAffairs; Asst Under-Sec. for Tourism SHAFIQA SHAHIN.

Defence

Supreme Commander of the Bahrain Defence Force: HM Sheikh HAMAD BIN ISA AL KHALIFA.

Commander-in-Chief of the Bahrain Defence Force: Field Marshal Sheikh KHALIFA BIN AHMAD AL KHALIFA.

Chief of Staff of the Bahrain Defence Force: Maj.-Gen. Sheikh DUAIJ BIN SALMAN BIN AHMAD AL KHALIFA.

Commander of the Royal Bahraini Navy: Cdre Sheikh KHALIFA BIN ABDULLAH AL KHALIFA.

Commander of the Royal Bahraini Air Force: Maj.-Gen. Sheikh HAMAD BIN ABDULLAH AL KHALIFA.

Defence Budget (2013): BD 524m.

Military Service: voluntary.

Total Armed Forces (as assessed at November 2013): 8,200 (army 6,000; navy 700; air force 1,500).

Paramilitary Forces (as assessed at November 2013): est. 11,260 (police 9,000; national guard est. 2,000; coastguard some 260).

Education

Although education is not compulsory, it is provided free of charge up to secondary level. Basic education, from the ages of six to 14, is divided into two levels: children attend primary school from six to 11 years of age and intermediate school from 12 to 14. Secondary education, beginning at the age of 15, lasts for three years; students choose to follow a general (science or literary), commercial, technical or vocational curriculum. In 1996 enrolment at primary, intermediate and secondary levels was 97.8%, 96.0% and 95.0% of the relevant age-groups, respectively. According to UNESCO, in 2008/09 the total enrolment at primary schools included 97% of children in the relevant age-group, while the comparable ratio for secondary enrolment in 2012 was 86%. Private and religious education are also available. In 2011 recurrent expenditure by the Ministry of Education totalled BD 245.8m. (equivalent to 10.2% of total recurrent government expenditure).

The University of Bahrain, established by Amiri decree in 1986, comprises nine Colleges: of Engineering, Arts, Science, Information Technology, Law, Applied Studies, Business Administration, Bahrain Teachers College and the Academy of Physical Education and Physiotherapy. Some 18,137 students were enrolled at the University in 2012/13. Higher education is also provided by the College of Health Sciences. The Arabian Gulf University (AGU), funded by seven Arab Governments, also provides higher education. The AGU comprises the College of Medicine and Medical Sciences, and the College of Graduate Studies. The Royal College of Surgeons in Ireland Medical University of Bahrain was founded in 2004, and construction of a new campus at Muharraq was completed in 2008, at an estimated cost of US $78.9m. In addition, ambitious plans to establish a Higher Education City, at a projected cost of $1,000m., were finalized in December 2006; the development was to include a full branch of a leading US university, an international research centre and a specialist academy.

BANGLADESH

Introductory Survey

LOCATION, CLIMATE, LANGUAGE, RELIGION, FLAG, CAPITAL

The People's Republic of Bangladesh lies in southern Asia, surrounded by Indian territory except for a short south-eastern frontier with Myanmar (formerly Burma) and a southern coast fronting the Bay of Bengal. The country has a tropical monsoon climate and suffers from periodic cyclones. The average temperature is 19°C (67°F) from October to March, rising to 29°C (84°F) between May and September. The average annual rainfall in Dhaka is 188 cm (74 in), of which about three-quarters occurs between June and September. About 95% of the population speak Bengali, the state language, while the remainder use mostly tribal dialects. Around 90% of the people are Muslims, Islam being the state religion, and there are small minorities of Hindus, Buddhists and Christians. The national flag (proportions 3 by 5) is dark green, with a red disc slightly off-centre towards the hoist. The capital is Dhaka (Dacca).

CONTEMPORARY POLITICAL HISTORY

Historical Context

Present-day Bangladesh was formerly East Pakistan, one of the five provinces into which Pakistan was divided at its initial creation, when Britain's former Indian Empire was partitioned in August 1947. East Pakistan and the four western provinces were separated by about 1,000 miles (1,600 km) of Indian territory. East Pakistan was created from the former Indian province of East Bengal and the Sylhet district of Assam. Although the East was more populous, government was based in West Pakistan. Dissatisfaction in East Pakistan at its dependence on a remote central government flared up in 1952, when Urdu was declared Pakistan's official language. Bengali, the main language of East Pakistan, was finally admitted as the joint official language in 1954, and in 1955 Pakistan was reorganized into two wings, east and west, with equal representation in the central legislative assembly. However, discontent continued in the eastern wing, particularly as the region was under-represented in the administration and armed forces, and received a disproportionately small share of Pakistan's development expenditure. The leading political party in East Pakistan was the Awami League (AL), led by Sheikh Mujibur (Mujib) Rahman, who demanded autonomy for the East. A general election in December 1970 gave the AL an overwhelming victory in the East, and thus a majority in Pakistan's National Assembly. Sheikh Mujib should therefore have been appointed Prime Minister, but Pakistan's President, Gen. Yahya Khan, would not accept this, and negotiations on a possible constitutional compromise broke down. The convening of the new National Assembly was postponed indefinitely in March 1971, leading to violent protests in East Pakistan. The AL decided that the province should unilaterally secede from Pakistan, and on 26 March Sheikh Mujib proclaimed the independence of the People's Republic of Bangladesh ('Bengal Nation').

Civil war immediately broke out. President Yahya Khan outlawed the AL and arrested its leaders. By April 1971 the Pakistan army dominated the eastern province. In August Sheikh Mujib was secretly put on trial in West Pakistan. However, resistance continued from the Liberation Army of East Bengal (the Mukhti Bahini), which launched a major offensive in November. As a result of the conflict, an estimated 9.5m. refugees crossed into India. On 4 December India declared war on Pakistan, with Indian forces intervening in support of the Mukhti Bahini. Pakistan surrendered on 16 December, and Bangladesh became independent. Pakistan was thus confined to its former western wing. In January 1972 Sheikh Mujib was freed by Pakistan's new President, Zulfiqar Ali Bhutto, and became Prime Minister of Bangladesh. Under a provisional Constitution, Bangladesh was declared to be a secular state and a parliamentary democracy. The new nation quickly achieved international recognition, causing Pakistan to withdraw from the Commonwealth in January 1972. Bangladesh joined the Commonwealth in April. The members who had been elected from the former East Pakistan for the Pakistan National Assembly and the Provincial Assembly in December 1970 formed the Bangladesh Constituent Assembly. A new Constitution was approved by this Assembly in November 1972 and came into effect in December. A general election for the country's first Jatiya Sangsad (Parliament) was held in March 1973. The AL received 73% of the total votes and won 292 of the 300 directly elective seats in the legislature. Bangladesh was finally recognized by Pakistan in February 1974. Internal stability, however, was threatened by opposition groups which resorted to terrorism and included extremists such as Islamist fundamentalists and Maoists. In December a state of emergency was declared and constitutional rights were suspended. In January 1975 parliamentary government was replaced by a presidential form of government. Sheikh Mujib became President, assuming absolute power, and created the Bangladesh Peasants' and Workers' Awami League. In February Bangladesh became a one-party state.

Domestic Political Affairs

Gen. Zia in power (1975–81)

In August 1975 Sheikh Mujib and his family were assassinated in a right-wing coup, led by a group of Islamist army officers. Khandakar Mushtaq Ahmed, the former Minister of Commerce, was installed as President; martial law was declared, and political parties were banned. A counter-coup on 3 November brought to power Brig. Khalid Musharaf, the pro-Indian commander of the Dhaka garrison, who was appointed Chief of Army Staff; on 7 November a third coup overthrew Brig. Musharaf's short-lived regime, and power was assumed jointly by the three service chiefs, under a non-political President, Abusadet Mohammed Sayem, the Chief Justice of the Supreme Court. A neutral non-party Government was formed, in which the reinstated Chief of Army Staff, Major-Gen. Ziaur Rahman (Gen. Zia), took precedence over his colleagues. Political parties were legalized again in July 1976.

An early return to representative government was promised, but in November 1976 elections were postponed indefinitely and, in a major shift of power, Gen. Zia took over the role of Chief Martial Law Administrator from President Sayem, assuming the presidency also in April 1977. In a national referendum held in May, 99% of voters affirmed their confidence in President Zia's policies, and in June 1978 the country's first direct presidential election resulted in a clear victory for Zia, who formed a Council of Ministers to replace his Council of Advisers. Parliamentary elections followed in February 1979: in an attempt to persuade opposition parties to participate in the elections, Zia met some of their demands by repealing a number of 'undemocratic' constitutional amendments, releasing political prisoners and withdrawing press censorship. Consequently, 29 parties contested the elections, in which Zia's Bangladesh Jatiyatabadi Dal (Bangladesh Nationalist Party—BNP) received 49% of the total votes and won 207 of the 300 contested seats in Parliament. In April 1979 a new Prime Minister was appointed, and martial law was repealed. As part of Zia's bid to give Islam a greater role in political life (in contrast to the AL's secular approach), the Fifth Amendment of the Constitution, which was approved by Parliament in April 1979, replaced secularism with Islam as one of the state's four fundamental principles. The Fifth Amendment also granted constitutional legitimacy to all proclamations made during the period of martial law. The state of emergency was revoked in November.

Political instability recurred, however, when Gen. Zia was assassinated on 30 May 1981 during an attempted military coup, allegedly led by Maj.-Gen. Mohammad Abdul Manzur, an army divisional commander who was himself later killed in unclear circumstances. The Vice-President, Justice Abdus Sattar, assumed the role of acting President, prior to securing an overwhelming victory at the presidential election held in November. President Sattar announced his intention of continuing the policies of the late Gen. Zia.

Ershad in power (1982–90)

On 24 March 1982 the Chief of Army Staff, Lt-Gen. Hossain Mohammad Ershad, seized power in a bloodless coup, claiming that political corruption and economic mismanagement had become intolerable. The country was placed under martial law, with Ershad as Chief Martial Law Administrator (redesignated Prime Minister in October), aided by a mainly military Council of Advisers. Ershad nominated a retired judge, Justice Abul Chowdhury, as President. Political activities were banned, and several former ministers were later tried and imprisoned on charges of corruption.

Although the Government's economic policies achieved some success and gained a measure of popular support for Ershad, there were increasing demands in 1983 for a return to democratic government. The two principal opposition groups that emerged were an eight-party alliance headed by the AL under Sheikh Hasina Wajed (daughter of the late Sheikh Mujib), and a seven-party group led by the BNP under former President Sattar (who died in 1985) and Begum Khaleda Zia (widow of Gen. Zia). In September 1983 the two groups formed an alliance, the Movement for the Restoration of Democracy (MRD), and jointly issued demands for an end to martial law, for the release of political prisoners and for the holding of parliamentary elections before any other polls. In November the resumption of political activity was permitted, and the Jana Dal (People's Party) was formed to support Ershad as a presidential candidate. Following demonstrations demanding civilian government, the ban on political activity was reimposed at the beginning of December, only two weeks after it had been rescinded, and leading political figures were detained. On 11 December Ershad declared himself President.

Strikes and political demonstrations occurred frequently during 1984. Local elections, planned for March, were postponed, as the opposition objected to their taking place prior to the presidential and parliamentary elections, claiming that Ershad was trying to strengthen his power base. The presidential and parliamentary elections, scheduled for May, were also postponed, until December, in response to persistent opposition demands for the repeal of martial law and for the formation of an interim neutral government to oversee fair elections. In October an offer by Ershad to repeal martial law if the opposition would participate in the elections was met with an appeal for a campaign of civil disobedience, which led to the indefinite postponement of the elections.

In January 1985 it was announced that parliamentary elections would be held in April, to be preceded by a partial relaxation of martial law: the Constitution was to be fully restored after the elections. The announcement was followed by the formation of a new Council of Ministers, composed entirely of military officers and excluding all members of the Jana Dal, in response to demands by the opposition parties for a neutral government during the pre-election period. Once more, the opposition threatened to boycott the elections, as President Ershad would not relinquish power to an interim government, and in March the elections were abandoned and political activity was again banned. This was immediately followed by a referendum, held in support of the presidency, in which Ershad reportedly received 94% of the total votes. Local elections were held in May, without the participation of the opposition; Ershad claimed that 85% of the elected council chairmen were his supporters, although not necessarily members of his party. In September a new five-party political alliance, the National Front (comprising the Jana Dal, the United People's Party, the Gonotantrik Party, the Bangladesh Muslim League and a breakaway section of the BNP), was established to promote government policies.

In January 1986 the 10-month ban on political activity was ended. The five components of the National Front formally became a single pro-Government entity, named the Jatiya Party (JP—National Party). In March President Ershad announced that parliamentary elections were to be held at the end of April; he relaxed martial law by removing all army commanders from important civil posts and abolishing more than 150 military courts and the martial law offices. These concessions fulfilled some of the opposition's demands, and candidates from the AL alliance (including Sheikh Hasina herself), the Islamist Jamaat-e-Islami Bangladesh and other smaller opposition parties consequently participated in the parliamentary elections—which eventually proceeded in May. However, the BNP alliance, led by Khaleda Zia, boycotted the polls, which were characterized by allegations of extensive fraud, violence and intimidation. The JP won 153 of the 300 directly elective seats in Parliament, as well as the 30 seats reserved for women. In July a predominantly civilian Council of Ministers was sworn in. Mizanur Rahman Chowdhury, former General Secretary of the JP, was appointed Prime Minister.

In order to be eligible to stand as a candidate in the forthcoming presidential election, Ershad retired as Chief of Army Staff in August 1986, while remaining Chief Martial Law Administrator and Commander-in-Chief of the Armed Forces. In September Ershad officially joined the JP, whereupon he was elected as Chairman of the party and nominated as its presidential candidate. The presidential election, held in October, was boycotted by both the BNP and the AL, and resulted in an overwhelming victory for Ershad over his 11 opponents.

In November 1986 Parliament approved indemnity legislation, effectively legitimizing the military regime's actions since March 1982. Ershad repealed martial law and restored the 1972 Constitution. The opposition alliances criticized the indemnity law, stating that they would continue to campaign for the dissolution of Parliament and the overthrow of the Ershad Government. In December 1986, in an attempt to curb increasing dissent, President Ershad formed a new Council of Ministers, including four AL legislators. The Minister of Justice, Justice A. K. M. Nurul Islam, was appointed Vice-President.

Anti-Government strikes and demonstrations continued during 1987, often with the support of trade unions and student groups. In November, in a renewed effort to oust President Ershad, opposition groups combined forces and organized further large-scale protests, during which thousands of activists were detained. In an attempt to forestall another general strike, President Ershad declared a nationwide state of emergency, suspending political activity and civil rights, imposing curfews in the main towns and banning all anti-Government protests. In December, with about 6,000 activists remaining in detention, 12 opposition members withdrew from Parliament and the 73 AL members agreed to do likewise, prompting Ershad to dissolve Parliament. In January 1988 the President announced that parliamentary elections would be held on 28 February, but leaders of the main opposition parties declared a boycott of the poll. Local elections, held throughout Bangladesh in February, although not boycotted by the opposition, were marred by serious outbreaks of violence. The parliamentary elections (postponed until 3 March) were also characterized by widespread violence, as well as alleged fraud and malpractice. The actual level of participation by the electorate appeared to have been considerably lower than the Government's estimate of 50%. As expected, the JP won a large majority of the seats.

Following the parliamentary elections, Moudud Ahmed (a long-time political ally of Ershad and hitherto Deputy Prime Minister and Minister of Industry) was appointed Prime Minister, in place of Mizanur Rahman Chowdhury. In response to an abatement in the opposition's anti-Government campaign, Ershad repealed the state of emergency in April 1988. Despite strong condemnation by the political opposition and sections of the public, a constitutional amendment (the Eighth Amendment) formally establishing Islam as Bangladesh's state religion was approved by an overall majority in Parliament in June.

In July 1989 Parliament approved legislation limiting the tenure of the presidency to two electoral terms of five years each and creating the post of a directly elected Vice-President. (However, in the event of the vice-presidency being vacated, the President could make a new appointment with the prior approval of Parliament.) In August Ershad appointed Prime Minister Moudud Ahmed as Vice-President to replace Justice A. K. M. Nurul Islam, who had been dismissed following charges of inefficiency. Kazi Zafar Ahmed, formerly Deputy Prime Minister and Minister of Information, was in turn promoted to the post of Prime Minister. Local elections held in March 1990 were officially boycotted by the opposition parties, although many members participated on an individual basis.

Opposition groups, with the support of thousands of students, co-operated to intensify their anti-Government campaign in late 1990. On 27 November President Ershad proclaimed a nationwide state of emergency for the second time in three years. On the following day, however, army units were summoned to impose order in the capital as thousands of protesters defied the curfew and attacked police. Under increasing pressure from the opposition groups, Ershad resigned on 4 December and declared that parliamentary elections would be held before the presidential election scheduled for mid-1991; the state of emergency was revoked, and Parliament was dissolved. Following his nomination by the opposition, Justice Shahabuddin Ahmed, the Chief

Justice of the Supreme Court, was appointed Vice-President. He assumed the responsibilities of acting President and was appointed to lead a neutral interim Government pending the elections. Shahabuddin Ahmed removed Ershad's appointees from important posts in financial institutions, local government and the civil service. The opposition parties welcomed these developments and abandoned their protest campaigns. They also demanded that Ershad be tried for alleged corruption and abuse of power. Ershad was placed under house arrest, and was later sentenced to 20 years' imprisonment for illegal possession of firearms and other offences.

The end of presidential rule: Khaleda Zia and the Bangladesh Nationalist Party in power (1991–96)

The BNP won the largest number of votes at parliamentary elections held in February 1991. Following discussions with Jamaat-e-Islami Bangladesh, as a result of which the BNP was ensured a small working majority in Parliament, Khaleda Zia assumed office as Prime Minister. In August Parliament approved a constitutional amendment (endorsed by national referendum in the following month) ending 16 years of presidential rule and restoring the Prime Minister as executive leader; the role of the President, who was to be elected by Parliament for a five-year term, was reduced to that of a titular head of state. Accordingly, a new President, BNP nominee and former parliamentary Speaker Abdur Rahman Biswas, was elected in October. Meanwhile, by September the BNP had secured an absolute majority in Parliament as a result of a number of by-election victories.

The opposition initiated an anti-Government campaign involving mass demonstrations and a boycott of parliamentary proceedings and culminating in the resignation of all opposition members from Parliament in December 1994. With the opposition parties refusing to take part in forthcoming by-elections, Parliament was dissolved in November 1995, pending the holding of a general election in early 1996. Despite opposition demands for a neutral interim government to oversee the election, the President requested that Khaleda Zia's administration continue in office in an acting capacity. The main opposition parties boycotted the general election, which was held in mid-February, and the Election Commission estimated the turnout at less than 27% of the electorate (independent estimates ranged from as low as 10% to 21% of voters). Of the 207 legislative seats declared by the end of February, the BNP had won 205 (a partial re-poll had been ordered in most of the 93 remaining constituencies where violence had disrupted the electoral process). The opposition rejected the legitimacy of the polls, and announced the launch of a 'non-co-operation' movement against the Government. Renewed street protests rendered the country virtually ungovernable, and Khaleda Zia eventually agreed to the holding of fresh elections under neutral auspices. The Prime Minister and her Government duly resigned on 30 March, and Parliament was dissolved. President Biswas appointed former Chief Justice Muhammad Habibur Rahman as acting Prime Minister; another general election was to be held within three months.

The Awami League takes power under Sheikh Hasina (1996–2001)

At the general election, held on 12 June 1996, the AL won 146 of the 300 elective seats in Parliament, the BNP 116, the JP 32 and Jamaat-e-Islami Bangladesh three. An understanding was rapidly reached between the AL and the JP, the latter's major interest being the release of Ershad, who had secured a legislative seat from within prison. (The former President was released on bail in January 1997.) Sheikh Hasina was sworn in as Prime Minister on 23 June 1996. On 23 July the AL's presidential nominee, retired Chief Justice and former acting President Shahabuddin Ahmed, was elected unopposed as head of state. In the same month the AL was allocated 27 of the 30 nominated women's parliamentary seats, thereby gaining an absolute parliamentary majority.

On assuming power, Sheikh Hasina had vowed to bring to justice those responsible for the assassination of her father, Sheikh Mujibur Rahman, in 1975. In November 1996 Parliament voted unanimously to repeal the indemnity law enacted in 1975 to protect the perpetrators of the military coup in that year; the BNP and Jamaat-e-Islami Bangladesh, however, boycotted the vote. The trial of 19 people accused of direct involvement in Sheikh Mujib's assassination began in March 1997, with 14 of the defendants being tried *in absentia*. (In November 2009 the Supreme Court rejected the appeals against the convictions and death sentences imposed on five former army officers in November 1998 for the murder of Sheikh Mujib, and the convicted men were executed in January 2010.)

Like that of her predecessor, Sheikh Hasina's tenure was marred by persistent civil and political instability, as the BNP in conjunction with Islamist and right-wing groups staged strikes and demonstrations, and BNP deputies regularly boycotted parliamentary proceedings. The BNP's foremost demand was the holding of fresh elections, replicating the AL's earlier campaign. However, the AL strengthened its position through a series of by-election victories, and the departure of the JP from the coalition in March 1998 had little effect on the ruling party's hold on power.

In June 2001 Sheikh Hasina became the first Prime Minister in the history of Bangladesh to complete a five-year term of office. The following month the Government resigned, and Parliament was dissolved in order to allow an interim neutral administration to prepare for a general election, to be held within three months (in accordance with Bangladesh's unique caretaker electoral system, as first used in 1991). The interim administration was established shortly afterwards under the leadership of former Chief Justice Latifur Rehman. The election campaign was reportedly the most violent in the country's history, and Rehman ordered the deployment of more than 50,000 troops to curb the unrest.

The BNP returns to power (2001–06)

The general election proceeded on 1 October 2001, although voting was postponed in several constituencies owing to violent incidents. The AL claimed that voting had been manipulated as it became clear that the opposition alliance, led by the BNP, had won an overwhelming majority in Parliament; however, international monitors declared the poll to be free and fair. Following elections on 9 October in 15 of those constituencies where voting had been delayed, the BNP-led alliance controlled a total of 214 of the 300 directly elective seats, the AL 62 and the JP 14. On 10 October Khaleda Zia was sworn in as Prime Minister. At the end of October newly elected members of Parliament representing the AL took the oath of office, but refused to join the opening session of the Parliament, in continuing protest against what they considered a rigged election; the opposition party also demanded that the Government demonstrate a greater commitment to curbing the violence allegedly perpetrated by the BNP-led alliance and its supporters against AL members, religious minority groups and women. Reports of attacks, particularly against the Hindu minority, increased markedly after the victory of the BNP-led coalition.

In November 2001 the BNP's presidential candidate, Prof. A. Q. M. Badruddoza Chowdhury, a former Minister of Foreign Affairs, was declared President after his sole nominated opponent withdrew his candidacy. The AL (which had refused to participate in the presidential election) boycotted the oath-taking ceremony. In December Parliament repealed the Father of the Nation Family Security Act, which had been approved in June under the AL administration and had guaranteed lifelong security for Sheikh Hasina and her sister, the daughters of Sheikh Mujib (the 'father of the nation', according to the AL), because several convicted assassins of the latter remained at large. The Act had been strongly criticized by the BNP, which considered its own founder, Gen. Zia, to be the 'father of the nation'.

AL legislators continued their boycott of Parliament until June 2002. The party also refused to take part in civic elections in April and carried out a policy of agitation, organizing a series of strikes in protest against higher taxes, crime and rises in fuel prices. In response, the Government filed two corruption charges against Sheikh Hasina and other AL members in December 2001, in relation to a weapons contract with Russia signed in 1999.

In a move considered unconstitutional by many observers, in June 2002 the President yielded to pressure from the BNP to resign after failing to visit Gen. Zia's grave on the anniversary of the latter's assassination. Two days later Khaleda Zia appointed her son, Tarique Rahman, to the post of Secretary-General of the BNP, prompting claims that the Prime Minister intended eventually to relinquish power to Rahman. In September the BNP candidate, Iajuddin Ahmed, was declared President by the Election Commission after it was established that the nomination papers of the two other candidates were invalid.

In September 2002 bomb explosions in the south-western town of Satkhira were reported to have killed at least 10 people. Islamist militant groups were suspected of having carried out the attack, although none claimed responsibility. In October the

Government launched a campaign to curb crime; some 40,000 members of the armed forces had been enlisted to assist the police. The AL claimed that the Government was using this campaign as a guise for the harassment of opposition members. By the end of the month almost 3,500 people had been arrested, including two former AL ministers. Concerns were raised over the unusually high number of people who had died in army custody, but the armed forces were later granted legal immunity for any actions carried out during the three-month operation. Meanwhile, in December multiple bomb explosions in the town of Mymensingh were reported to have killed at least 18 people. The Prime Minister rejected suggestions that the Islamist militant al-Qa'ida organization was involved in the attack. However, it was claimed that since 1999 Bangladeshi Islamist militant groups had collaborated with South-East Asian Islamist groups connected with al-Qa'ida.

A report published by the Bureau of Human Rights Bangladesh in September 2003 stated that nearly 3,000 people had been killed in separate violent occurrences throughout Bangladesh between January and September. In January 2004 a bomb explosion at the Muslim Hazrat Shah Jalal shrine in Sylhet killed five people. In May a grenade attack at the shrine resulted in the deaths of three more people and injuries to at least a further 100, including the British High Commissioner to Bangladesh. By the end of that month more than 100 people had been arrested in connection with the attack. Also in May, an AL legislator, was shot dead in his constituency. While the AL accused the Government of having ordered the shooting, the Government blamed factional fighting within the AL. In June the AL announced the end of the parliamentary boycott that it had reinstated one year previously.

In May 2004 Parliament approved a bill of constitutional amendments providing for the existing 300-member legislature to be enlarged to 345 members—45 seats were to be reserved for women (the constitutional provision for women to hold 30 seats in the legislature had lapsed in 2001). The 14th Amendment to the Constitution was formally introduced in December 2004.

In August 2004 a grenade attack on an AL rally in Dhaka resulted in the deaths of 20 people, including senior AL offícals. Widespread rioting subsequently took place in Dhaka and other towns, and the AL called a series of general strikes in protest. Later in that month a previously unknown group, Hikmatul Zihad, claimed responsibility for the attack. In January 2005 an explosion at an AL rally in Habiganj, in the north-east of the country, killed five party activists, including former Minister of Finance Shah Kibria. The worsening security situation in Bangladesh provoked increasing international disquiet, owing largely to the Government's persistent failure to bring to justice the perpetrators of many of the violent incidents.

In February 2005 the Government acknowledged, for the first time, that fundamentalist Islamist groups were operating in the country and officially banned two such organizations, Jamatul Mujahideen Bangladesh (JMB) and Jagrata Muslim Janata Bangladesh (JMJB), which were believed to have been responsible for several bomb attacks. In March 10 people were charged with involvement in the January attack that had resulted in the death of Shah Kibria. It was reported that eight of those accused were district officials or members of the BNP, lending credence to opposition accusations that the ruling party, acting through its coalition partner, Jamaat-e-Islami Bangladesh, was covertly encouraging the activities of Islamist militant groups in the country. On 17 August approximately 500 small bombs exploded virtually simultaneously at around 300 locations across Bangladesh, killing two people. The JMB claimed responsibility for the attacks, and the AL alleged that the BNP had, once again, been complicit. In October another Islamist militant group, Harakat-ul-Jihad-i-Islami (HJI), was outlawed by the Government. Media reports suggested that the HJI had 'merged' with other militant groups in the country, including the JMB and the JMJB, in order to conduct a concerted terrorist campaign intended to effect the transformation of Bangladesh into an Islamic state. In November two bomb attacks on courthouses in Gazipur and Chittagong, which were believed to be the country's first suicide bombings, resulted in the deaths of nine people. Approximately 800 alleged members of the JMB had been arrested by the end of 2005, as the Government attempted to bring the deteriorating security situation under control. In February 2006 21 people received death sentences for carrying out bomb attacks in Jhenidah district in August 2005 (part of the large-scale bombing campaign mentioned above). In March 2006 Siddiqul Islam and Abdur Rahman, who were alleged to be senior figures in the JMB, were sentenced to death, along with five others, on murder charges arising from the November 2005 courthouse bombings. In August 2006 Ataur Rahman, who was reported to be the leader of the JMB's military wing, and two others were sentenced to death for their role in recent bomb attacks. It was reported in March 2007 that six militants, including Islam and Abdur Rahman, had been executed.

Meanwhile, in February 2006 the AL ended its latest parliamentary boycott (which had commenced one year previously), while continuing to co-ordinate a campaign of civil disobedience against the Government. Political and civil unrest continued throughout 2006, a year characterized by regular strikes, demonstrations, and clashes between government and opposition supporters. In May protests by garment workers demanding increased wages and a reduction in working hours erupted into violence. In August at least six people were killed in demonstrations against plans for the development of an open-cast coal mine in Phulbari. The controversial project, which would have necessitated the relocation of around 50,000 people, was subsequently cancelled by the Government. In October several members of the BNP defected to form the Liberal Democratic Party, with former President Prof. A. Q. M. Badruddoza Chowdhury and Col (retd) Oli Ahmed as its leaders.

Bangladesh under a caretaker government (2006–08)

Prime Minister Khaleda Zia and her Government duly stepped down at the end of their term in office in October 2006, but the transition was marked by widespread protests and sporadic violence. The AL coalition demanded a non-partisan caretaker government and election officials, as well as a revision of the electoral roll, and threatened an electoral boycott over the nominee for Chief Adviser (the head of the caretaker government that was to oversee the election process). President Iajuddin Ahmed then announced that he himself would assume the additional role of Chief Adviser in an attempt to curb the unrest. However, protests and transport blockades called by the opposition coalition continued to cause widespread disruption. In November the scheduled January 2007 general election date was rejected by the AL-led coalition, which argued that it did not allow sufficient time for the necessary reforms to be enacted. President Ahmed attempted to control opposition protests by deploying army troops in December 2006. In the same month it was reported that the former President and the Chairman of the JP, Lt-Gen. Ershad, who earlier in the year had been acquitted of several corruption charges dating back to the previous decade, had joined the opposition coalition.

On 3 January 2007 the AL coalition announced a boycott of the elections and appealed for another transport blockade. The interim Government stood firm, stressing that, according to constitutional stipulations, it was required to hold elections within 90 days of assuming power. Thousands of protesters took to the streets in Dhaka as the nationwide transport blockade was implemented. On 11 January President Ahmed stepped down as Chief Adviser, postponed the elections and declared a state of emergency; Dr Fakhruddin Ahmed was sworn in as Chief Adviser on 12 January, and 10 new advisers were subsequently appointed. On 21 January Justice M. A. Aziz stood down as Chief Election Commissioner, followed by five other election commissioners. Under emergency rules, a ban on political activity came into effect, along with curbs on media reporting. The electoral roll that had been released prior to the postponed elections was subsequently invalidated by the High Court.

The interim Government embarked on a large-scale campaign against corruption, apparently as part of a wider attempt to overhaul the political system and prepare the country for free and fair elections to be held by the end of 2008. A new Chairman, former Chief of Army Staff Lt-Gen. (retd) Hasan Mashhud Chowdhury, was appointed to head the reconstituted Anti-Corruption Commission (ACC). Large numbers of prominent BNP and AL politicians and businessmen were detained, and several (including a number of former government ministers) were subsequently charged and convicted of corruption or other crimes. Most noteworthy were the arrests of the two dominant figures in Bangladeshi politics: Sheikh Hasina was detained in July 2007 on charges of extortion, and her erstwhile rival Khaleda Zia was arrested in September on corruption charges. Both were denied bail. Meanwhile, there was growing discontent over the perceived severity of the emergency measures and the curtailment of civil rights. The Government announced a partial suspension of its ban on political activity in the following month. Iajuddin Ahmed's term as President, which expired in September, was extended in light of the delayed legislative elections. In

November the lengthy process of transferring power over the judiciary away from the executive arm of government appeared to be complete, with the announcement that judges and magistrates would henceforth be selected by the Supreme Court.

In May 2008 it was announced that legislative elections would be held in December, although the AL and the BNP expressed reluctance to participate in the process, citing the continuing detention of their respective leaders. In June thousands were arrested as part of a major government 'clean-up' campaign; although the arrests were carried out ostensibly to ensure free and fair elections, political organizations claimed that many of the detainees were from their ranks. It was reported in July that a 'Truth and Accountability Commission' had been established to tackle corruption. In the same month the Bangladesh Election Commission completed the revision of the electoral register and implemented a number of electoral reforms, including the limiting of constituencies to three per candidate and an increase in the maximum permitted amount of campaign funding. Local elections were held in August, with candidates supported by the AL securing the majority of positions.

The Awami League returns to power (2008–)

The AL secured a decisive victory over the BNP in the legislative elections held on 29 December 2008, winning 230 of the 300 elective parliamentary seats; the BNP secured a mere 29 seats. Turnout was high, at an estimated 70% of the electorate, and the election process was generally deemed to have been free and fair. Sheikh Hasina was sworn in as Prime Minister in January 2009, assuming responsibility for the defence portfolio and heading a new Council of Ministers that included Dipu Moni as Minister of Foreign Affairs and Sahara Khatun as Minister of Home Affairs. In February the AL's candidate, Zillur Rahman, was elected unopposed as President.

In February 2009 a revolt by a unit of the Bangladesh Rifles (BDR—paramilitary forces responsible for patrolling the border) led to violent clashes in Dhaka and elsewhere. Members of the BDR, whose demands for increased salaries, improved conditions and other changes had been rejected by the army, seized their headquarters in Pilkhana, in the Dhaka district, taking hostages and fighting with army troops in the capital and at bases around the country. The mutiny resulted in some 74 deaths (mostly senior army officers, including the commandant). In December 2010, following a reorganization of its command structure, the BDR was renamed the Border Guard Bangladesh. By October 2012 nearly 6,000 soldiers accused of involvement in the rebellion had been sentenced by military courts to prison terms ranging from four months to the maximum seven years for mutiny. Moreover, by the end of July 2011 more than 840 soldiers had also been indicted by civilian courts on charges of murder, rape, arson, looting and other serious offences. The mass trials conducted by the civilian authorities attracted criticism from human rights groups, and there were allegations of the use of torture to extract confessions and witness testimony. While the torture allegations were adamantly denied by the authorities, the Government did acknowledge that more than 50 soldiers had died in police custody following their arrest for alleged involvement in the revolt. In November 2013 152 of the defendants were sentenced to death, 161 were given life sentences, 256 received sentences of between three and 10 years, and more than 270 were acquitted.

Meanwhile, in May 2010 the corruption charges against Sheikh Hasina were dismissed by the High Court. In July the Supreme Court repealed the majority of the constitutional amendments introduced in 1979; *inter alia*, the Court's ruling stated that henceforth Islamist parties would not be able to use religion in politics, and declared the 1975–90 period of military rule to have been illegal. The discovery of a large weapons and explosives cache in a residential property in Dhaka in late July 2010, which the authorities stated had been intended for use in a large-scale terrorist attack in the capital, prompted an escalation in efforts to apprehend suspected Islamist militants.

In March 2010 the Government established an International Crimes Tribunal (ICT) to prosecute those accused of committing war crimes (including collaborating with Pakistan) during Bangladesh's war of independence in 1971. In July 2010 Motiur Rahman Nizami and Ali Ahsan Mohammad Mojaheed, Chairman and Secretary-General, respectively, of Bangladesh Jamaat-e-Islami (BJI), and three other senior leaders of the Islamist party, Delwar Hossain Sayedee, Mohammad Kamaruzzaman and Abdul Quader Mollah, were detained on suspicion of committing mass atrocities during the conflict. (BJI, formerly Jamaat-e-Islami Bangladesh, was renamed in 2008 following a revision of its constitution effected in order to comply with Election Commission regulations.) In December Salauddin Quader Chowdhury, a prominent member of the BNP, was arrested on suspicion of crimes against humanity. The authorities denied claims by human rights organization Amnesty International that Chowdhury had been tortured during his interrogation by the police. In March 2011 Abdul Alim, a former BNP minister, was also detained on suspicion of crimes against humanity, having allegedly been involved in the killing of more than 10,000 people in 1971.

Delwar Hossain Sayedee became the first person to be formally charged by the ICT, in October 2011, when he was accused of, *inter alia*, genocide, rape, torture and religious persecution. His trial—the tribunal's first—opened in late November. By the end of the year similar charges had been formally submitted against Salauddin Quader Chowdhury, Nizami, Mojaheed and Kamaruzzaman. All of those charged denied the allegations against them, declaring them to be politically motivated.

Meanwhile, in October 2010 Khaleda Zia was evicted from the house allocated to her on humanitarian grounds following the assassination of her husband Gen. Zia in the 1981 abortive military coup. In response the BNP staged a nationwide general strike in protest at Zia's treatment. Further strikes were organized by the BNP in late 2010, in protest against perceived government misrule and 'harassment' of the opposition. Compounding the sense of unrest in the country, in December textile workers staged protests in Dhaka, Chittagong and the northern district of Gazipur, demanding improved working conditions and the immediate implementation of a promised increase in the minimum monthly wage. Three people were reported to have been killed during the protests, with dozens more injured, as police forcibly dispersed the crowds.

In a firm indication of the ruling party's declining popularity, BNP-backed candidates performed strongly in local elections held in January 2011, mainly at the expense of the AL. Later that month a report published by Human Rights Watch claimed that the Bangladeshi Government had not ended 'systematic human rights abuses', including torture and extrajudicial killings by the security forces, and urged the Government to establish an impartial inquiry into each death and hold to account those found to be responsible.

In March 2011 the Council of Ministers approved a new National Women's Development Policy (NWDP), which set out the Government's commitment to safeguarding and promoting equal rights for women with regard to employment, education, health, inheritance and ownership of property. Islamist groups staged protests, claiming that legislation based on the NWDP would violate Koranic principles, notably the granting of equal inheritance rights to women; hitherto, inheritance in Bangladesh had been governed by *Shari'a* principles, under which female heirs normally received only half as much as their male counterparts.

The 15th Amendment to the Constitution

In June 2011 Parliament approved a bill of constitutional amendments (the 15th Amendment to the Constitution), in a motion that was boycotted by the BNP. The Amendment restored secularism as one of the four fundamental principles of the state, while retaining Islam as the state religion and rescinding the ban on religion-based politics. It also provided for the abolition of the existing electoral system (officially introduced in 1996) whereby, upon completion of a government's term, power was transferred to an interim neutral administration, which was responsible for overseeing new parliamentary elections, to be held within 90 days. (In May 2011 the Supreme Court had ruled that the interim system of government was illegal—overturning a previous decision by the High Court, which had upheld the constitutionality of the provision in 2004—but had decreed that the system could remain in place for the next two parliamentary terms, for the sake of national stability. Later in May 2011 the Supreme Court upheld a previous High Court ruling outlawing the Truth and Accountability Commission established by the interim Government in 2008.) The BNP was vehemently opposed to the abolition of the interim government system, arguing that without it incumbent governments could manipulate the staging of future elections, and boycotted parliamentary sessions from May in protest at the proposal.

The 15th Amendment provided for a number of other changes to the charter, including an increase in the number of parliamentary seats reserved for women, from 45 to 50. Another provision decreed that rulings issued by the ICT could not be appealed in any court, thereby rendering the tribunal as the highest judicial authority for charges pertaining to atrocities committed during Bangladesh's 1971 war of independence.

Twelve Islamist political parties staged a 30-hour nationwide strike in early July 2011 in protest at the restoration of secularism within the Constitution. A few days later the BNP, together with the BJI, the JP, Islami Oikya Jote (an alliance of hardline Islamist groups), Khelafat Majlis and a number of smaller parties, staged a 48-hour, nationwide general strike—the seventh general strike to be called by the BNP since the 2008 parliamentary elections—in protest at the abolition of the caretaker government system, insisting that elections overseen by the incumbent Government would be neither free nor fair. The BNP claimed that during the strike nearly 550 people were injured in police action and more than 400 protesters were arrested. Later in 2011 the BNP and its allies staged two mass 'road marches', to underscore the opposition's demands for the reintroduction of the caretaker government system.

Responsibility for a series of minor bomb explosions in Dhaka, which killed one person, on 17–19 December 2011 was attributed by the authorities to supporters of the BNP. Four bombs exploded on 17 December in Jessore district along the border with West Bengal, India, during a demonstration staged by the BNP in protest at the killing, by unidentified assailants, of a local party leader. Several bomb explosions occurred in the capital during clashes between BNP supporters and police officers on 18 December. Another eight bombs were detonated on 19 December, near the BNP headquarters. The arrest of more than 200 BNP members in the aftermath of the explosions prompted further violent protests by the opposition.

In January 2012 the Bangladeshi army announced that it had foiled a conspiracy intended to overthrow the Government, claiming that the alleged plot had involved a group of up to 16 Islamist military officers and had been orchestrated by expatriate Bangladeshi nationals. Some observers suggested that the increasing secularization of the Bangladeshi state, as a result of the 2011 constitutional amendments, was a primary motivating factor behind the alleged coup plot.

The perceived persecution by the authorities of former premier Khaleda Zia appeared to intensify from mid-2011. In June Zia's younger son, Arafat Rahman, was convicted *in absentia* of money-laundering during Zia's tenure as Prime Minister; he was imprisoned for six years and fined US $5.2m. In July a warrant was issued for the arrest of Zia's elder son, Tarique Rahman, who was accused of orchestrating the grenade attack on an AL rally in Dhaka in August 2004—see The BNP returns to power (2001–06). Tarique Rahman was reported to have been living in exile in the United Kingdom since 2008 and at early 2014 it remained unclear whether he would return to Bangladesh to face trial. Tarique Rahman was also charged by the ACC in August 2011 of money-laundering. Khaleda Zia herself was charged with abuse of power by the ACC in January 2012; the agency claimed to have found evidence of funding irregularities in a land purchase deal in 2005 on behalf of a charitable trust established by Zia. The BNP adamantly denied all of the allegations against Khaleda Zia and her sons, insisting that the charges were politically motivated. In March 2012 Tarique Rahman and 29 others, primarily BNP members, were formally indicted on charges relating to the 2004 grenade attack.

Meanwhile, in 2011–12 Human Rights Watch and Amnesty International continued to accuse Bangladesh's special police force, the Rapid Action Battalion (RAB), of extrajudicial killings and other human rights violations (including torture in custody). In August 2011 Amnesty claimed that the RAB had been implicated in the unlawful killing of more than 700 people since its establishment in 2004, and urged the Government to honour previous pledges to end extrajudicial killings.

An investigation was initiated in September 2011 into corruption allegations pertaining to a US $2,900m. project to build a bridge over the Padma river, which was intended to connect the north-west of Bangladesh with Dhaka and Chittagong Port, and which was described as the nation's most ambitious infrastructure project to date. It was claimed that Bangladeshi officials, including the Minister of Communications, Syed Abul Hossain, had been offered bribes by employees of a Canadian construction company during the bidding process. The corruption allegations prompted the World Bank to suspend pledged funding of $1,200m. for the project. Hossain was transferred from the Communications ministry in early December in a government reorganization apparently effected to salvage the bridge project. (Other notable appointments included that of Suranjit Sengupta as head of the newly created Ministry of Railways.) However, in June 2012 the World Bank announced an official cancellation of funding for the bridge project, citing an 'unsatisfactory' response from the Bangladeshi Government to the corruption allegations. Sheikh Hasina was critical of the World Bank's decision, and in February 2013 Bangladesh formally withdrew its World Bank funding application, a decision that ultimately led to the withdrawal of the project's other major funders, including the Asian Development Bank and the Japan International Co-operation Agency. Nevertheless, the Government subsequently vowed to wholly finance the project with public funds and insisted that construction would commence during 2014. Meanwhile, in April 2012 the Government was undermined by a further corruption scandal, following the discovery of a large quantity of cash in a vehicle carrying officials from the Ministry of Railways and Bangladesh Railway. Investigations into the incident were launched by both the ministry and the ACC. Despite denying any involvement in the alleged corruption, Sengupta resigned from his post in mid-April.

Rising political and social unrest

The BNP-led opposition's high-profile campaign for the restoration of the caretaker government system continued with a major rally in Dhaka in March 2012, the largest event of its kind since the 2008 elections. In April, in a further effort to bolster the opposition movement, Khaleda Zia announced the formation of an 18-party opposition alliance, comprising the BNP, the BJI and 16 smaller parties. In the same week, the disappearance of a BNP official from Sylhet provoked allegations by the opposition that government agents had abducted the official. The opposition initiated a series of general strikes throughout the country and violent confrontations between police and opposition supporters were reported in Sylhet and Dhaka.

Meanwhile, the BNP's absence at parliamentary sessions continued to hamper proceedings, and the opposition threatened to boycott the forthcoming parliamentary elections. In June 2012 Lt-Gen. Ershad announced that the JP—currently part of the ruling alliance—would contest the elections on its own, criticizing both the AL and the BNP for failing to effect progress; according to Ershad, the JP represented a viable 'third force' in politics. In July Sheikh Hasina proposed the formation of an interim cabinet including the BNP to oversee elections, but she was rebuffed by Khaleda Zia, who insisted on a non-party caretaker government. There was significant resistance to the Government's plan to hold elections without dissolving Parliament, and in September Sheikh Hasina declared that Parliament would indeed be dissolved in advance of elections scheduled for early 2014; however, she dismissed opposition demands for a caretaker administration. Also in September, Sheikh Hasina effected a reorganization of the Council of Ministers, the most notable change being the replacement of the controversial Minister of Home Affairs, Sahara Khatun, with Mohiuddin Khan Alamgir. The new Minister of Information, Hasanul Haq Inu of the Jatiya Samajtantrik Dal, was the only non-AL member to be appointed. The ongoing protests and strikes staged by the BNP and the Jamaat-e-Islami in late 2012 contributed to significant concerns over the breakdown of the democratic process in Bangladesh.

Proceedings at the ICT also served to heighten tensions between the Government and the opposition in 2012–13. In March 2012 a second tribunal, known as ICT-2, was established. In May Ghulam Azam, who had been Chairman of the BJI during 1969–2000, was charged with murder and torture, among other crimes against humanity. Later that month the presiding Chairman of the same party, Motiur Rahman Nizami, faced 16 charges, including genocide, murder and rape. In August the party's acting Secretary-General, A. T. M. Azharul Islam, was arrested on similar charges. The BJI denounced the charges as politically motivated and its campaign of street agitation intensified, with strikes and protests descending into violence around the country. In December Nizamul Haq, the ICT's presiding judge, resigned amid media reports of his consultations with an outside legal expert. The ICT's first verdict was reached in January 2013, when Abul Kalam Azad, a former BJI leader who was believed to be hiding in Pakistan, was convicted *in absentia* of various war crimes; he was sentenced to death. Violent demonstrations ensued in Dhaka, and a few days later two deaths were reported in the city of Bogra in fighting between supporters of the Government and the opposition. In early February one of the detained BJI leaders, Abdul Quader Mollah, was convicted of war crimes and sentenced to life imprisonment. Further violent protests by supporters of the Islamist party erupted in the capital and several other cities in response to the verdict; seven people reportedly died in the unrest. Conversely, the conviction of Quader Mollah also sparked an unprecedented series of mass demonstrations by opponents of the BJI, demanding a ban on the Islamist party and calling for the death penalty to be issued for all war crimes convictions at the ICT. The protest movement, which was centred on Dhaka's Shahbhag Square, lasted for several weeks and was notable for the large-scale participation of students and young people. In mid-February, apparently in response to the Shahbhag Square protests, Parliament approved amendments to the ICT legislation enabling the state to appeal against sentences issued by the court and giving the ICT the power to prosecute any organization or political party that had allegedly been involved in war crimes. At the end of February the ICT issued its third verdict, convicting Delwar Hossain Sayedee on eight charges of war crimes, including mass killing, rape and the forceful conversion of non-Muslims; Sayedee was sentenced to death. The verdict provoked renewed violent unrest across the country, as supporters of the BJI clashed with security forces and with demonstrators celebrating the sentence. The situation became even more febrile in early May when the ICT sentenced Mohammad Kamaruzzaman to death for various wartime atrocities committed in 1971. The following week another senior member of the BJI, the veteran politician A. K. M. Yusuf, was arrested for alleged war crimes. In July the party's former long-standing Chairman, Ghulam Azam, was sentenced to 90 years' imprisonment for his involvement in mass killings and rape during the war of independence; it was reported that Azam, who was viewed by many as the spiritual leader of the Islamist party, was spared the death sentence only owing to his advanced age. A few days later the Secretary-General of the BJI, Ali Ahsan Mohammad Mojaheed, received a death sentence from the ICT for a catalogue of war crimes. Following an appeal by the Government for a harsher sentence, in September the earlier life term imposed on Quader Mollah was increased to a death sentence. The convictions of these senior Islamist politicians prompted numerous outbreaks of violent unrest and angry protests throughout the country (as well as demonstrations celebrating the rulings); by September more than 100 people had been killed as a result of the violence. On 1 October one of the two BNP detainees, Salauddin Quader Chowdhury, who was an incumbent member of parliament, was also sentenced to death by the ICT on war-crime charges. The following week, the other BNP defendant, Abdul Alim, was handed a life sentence by the ICT, having been found guilty of similar charges (his ill health reportedly spared him the death sentence). The response of the BNP and its allies was to stage crippling strikes and road and rail blockades throughout the country. Following the dismissal by the Supreme Court of his final appeal and despite objections by human rights organizations, which continued to claim that the ICT did not conform with international standards, Quader Mollah was executed on 12 December. This appeared a risky move on the part of the authorities, given the fact that, despite protests by the opposition, the Government had scheduled the general election to be held in early January 2014; however, the public unrest following the hanging proved relatively muted and short-lived. In late January 2014 the Chairman of the BJI, Motiur Rahman Nizami, who was facing separate charges of war crimes, was sentenced (together with 13 other individuals) to death for smuggling arms to separatists in India.

Communal violence also contributed to instability in 2012–13: in September 2012 rioters in the area of Cox's Bazar destroyed 12 Buddhist temples and attacked numerous Buddhist homes. The riots were said to have been precipitated by online photographs of a desecrated Koran, allegedly posted by a Buddhist, who denied responsibility. A subsequent government investigation found that members of the BJI, the BNP and the AL were involved in the violence, which, it was suspected, had been pre-planned. In 2013 the country's minority Buddhist and Hindu communities often bore the brunt of the violent attacks launched by BJI supporters following the convictions of their party leaders by the ICT. During a mass rally in Dhaka in April, attended by hundreds of thousands of supporters of a recently formed umbrella organization of Islamist groups, the Hefajat-e-Islam Bangladesh, the protesters demanded the introduction of an anti-blasphemy law to punish those who defamed Islam; the demand was firmly rebuffed by Prime Minister Sheikh Hasina. The following month it was reported that at least 27 people were killed in the capital as a result of clashes between the police and members of the Hefajat-e-Islam Bangladesh.

Elsewhere, the garment industry witnessed large-scale strikes in June 2012, with hundreds of thousands of workers demanding salary increases. In November a fire at a garment factory near Dhaka resulted in some 112 fatalities; the ensuing government inquiry found evidence of sabotage, but also recommended that the factory owner face unrelated criminal charges, having prevented workers from leaving the factory despite the sounding of the fire alarm. Working conditions in the Bangladeshi garment industry attracted intense international attention in late April 2013, following the collapse in the capital of an eight-storey building (the Rana Plaza) housing five garment factories, producing clothing mainly for Western retailers; more than 1,100 people were killed in the disaster, which prompted several days of violent protests in Dhaka demanding that those responsible be severely punished (many called for the death penalty) and that factory conditions be made safer. By the end of the month eight people, including the owner of the building, had been arrested for alleged negligence, illegal construction and for persuading the workers to enter a dangerous building. In response to continuing unrest among garment workers, the Government launched an official inquiry into what was Bangladesh's worst ever industrial accident, and established a panel of trade union representatives and factory owners to discuss raising the minimum wage in the garments industry. In addition, in mid-May the Government amended the 2006 Labour Act by lifting restrictions on the formation of unions within the majority of industries. By late July 2013 more than 70 major clothing retailers, mainly from Europe, had agreed to sign a legally-binding agreement drawn up by global unions to conduct safety inspections at factories in Bangladesh from which their products were sourced. In November the government-appointed wage panel proposed raising the minimum salary for garment workers by 77%; under pressure from the Prime Minister herself, the country's factory owners reluctantly agreed to the increase.

Following a lengthy illness, President Zillur Rahman died in March 2013. Mohammed Abdul Hamid, hitherto Speaker of Parliament, was elected unopposed as Bangladesh's new President in April.

Recent developments: the general election of January 2014

The BJI suffered a setback in August 2013 when the Supreme Court ruled that the registration of the party in 2009 had been illegal (on the grounds that its charter breached the secular Constitution) and that the party would therefore be unable to field candidates in the forthcoming legislative elections. Throughout the latter half of the year the BNP continued to demand that the AL-led Government stand down and that a neutral caretaker administration be appointed to oversee the elections (as was the practice during 1996–2008, prior to the constitutional amendment of 2011). In September the Prime Minister announced that, contrary to a government declaration made a year earlier, Parliament would not be dissolved prior to the holding of the general election. Sheikh Hasina's proposal in October to form a cross-party interim cabinet to supervise the poll was rejected by the BNP-led opposition alliance, which staged protests and strikes throughout the country in an attempt to force the Government to resign. Following the Government's announcement in late November that the general election would be held on 5 January 2014, the opposition intensified its protest action by organizing a nationwide transport blockade. As the tension escalated the protests became more violent and more than 100 people were killed in attacks by activists and in clashes with the security forces. In an effort to contain the unrest and enable the elections to proceed, the Government deployed the army across the country.

Despite being boycotted by the opposition alliance and thereby, according to some observers, lacking any real credibility, the general election was held as scheduled on 5 January 2014. BNP leader Khaleda Zia described the poll, during which at least 18 people died in violent incidents, as a 'scandalous farce'. As a result of the boycott 153 seats were uncontested, and members of the AL or its allies were accordingly declared elected unopposed in those constituencies. The AL obtained a total of 231 seats and the JP 33. The electoral turnout was reported to be very low, at just over 20% (compared with about 70% in 2008). On 12 January Sheikh Hasina was sworn in for her third term as Prime Minister, at the head of an AL-dominated coalition Government; three members of the JP also joined the Council of Ministers, including Ershad as Special Envoy to the Prime Minister, and one member each from the Workers' Party, and the Jatiya Samajtantrik Dal. In mid-February Abul Hasan Mahmood Ali of the AL was appointed Minister of Foreign Affairs.

In early 2014 the opposition parties decided to challenge the AL by participating in sub-district council (*upazila parishad*) elections, which commenced in February. Candidates supported by the BNP performed strongly in the first phase of the local government polls, securing the chairmanship of 43 out of 97 sub-districts; the AL won 34 sub-districts and the BJI secured 13. (Officially, local government elections are held on a non-party political basis; however, in practice the candidates' political affiliations are clearly recognized, thus enabling the BJI, which had been de-registered in August 2013, to test its popularity in the polls.) By late March, after a fifth phase of local elections, the AL was reported to have won control of 231 out of 459 sub-districts contested thus far, while the BNP had taken 161 sub-districts and the BJI controlled 35. The polls were conducted amid sporadic outbreaks of violence and regular allegations by the opposition of vote rigging by the AL. A final phase of voting was scheduled for late May. Meanwhile, in mid-March the Minister of Liberation War Affairs, A. K. M. Mozammel Huq, announced that the Government was planning to enforce a complete ban on the BJI by mid-2014.

The Chittagong Hill Tracts

In 1989 the Government attempted to suppress the insurgency in the Chittagong Hill Tracts, in south-eastern Bangladesh, where Buddhist tribal rebels, the Shanti Bahini, had waged a lengthy guerrilla campaign against the Bangladeshi police and Bengali settlers, by introducing concessions providing limited autonomy to the region in the form of three new semi-autonomous hill districts. Power was vested in district councils in order to give the tribals sufficient authority to regulate any further influx of Bengali settlers to the districts (the chief complaint of the tribals since Bengalis were settled in the Chittagong Hill Tracts, as plantation workers and clerks, by the British administration in the 19th century). Council elections took place relatively peacefully in June, despite attempts at disruption by the Shanti Bahini, who continued to demand total autonomy for the tribals. Violence continued unabated, and tribal refugees continued to flee across the border into India (the number of refugees living in camps in the Indian state of Tripura reached about 56,000). Following successful negotiations between Bangladesh and India, a process of phased repatriation of the refugees commenced in early 1994. In December 1997 the Bangladeshi Government signed a peace agreement with the political wing of the Shanti Bahini. The treaty offered the rebels a general amnesty in return for the surrender of their weapons and gave the tribal people greater powers of self-governance through the establishment of three new elected district councils (to control the area's land management and policing) and a regional council (the chairman of which was to enjoy the rank of a state minister). The peace agreement, which was strongly criticized by the opposition for representing a 'sell-out' of the area to India and a threat to Bangladesh's sovereignty, served to accelerate the process of repatriating the remaining refugees from Tripura (who totalled about 31,000 at the end of 1997). By the end of 2000 most of the tribal refugees had been repatriated, the district and regional councils were in operation, and a land commission had been established. However, rioting in the Chittagong area in mid-2001 and the accession to power of the BNP-led alliance in October of that year prompted thousands of members of Buddhist, Christian and Hindu minorities to flee to Tripura. In December 2003 and January 2004 protesters in the south-eastern Hill Tracts succeeded in cutting off the region from the rest of the country as they demanded the full implementation of the 1997 peace agreement. In December 2005 the Government and the United Nations Development Programme (UNDP) announced investment of US $50m. in the Hill Tracts, in order to assist with implementation of the 1997 agreement by strengthening the local economy. In July 2009 the Government announced plans to carry out a large-scale withdrawal of troops from the Hill Tracts over the following few months (the most substantive withdrawal since the signing of the peace agreement in 1997). However, in February 2010 violence again erupted in the Hill Tracts with a series of clashes between Bengali settlers and tribal people. A number of buildings, including two Buddhist temples, were burnt down, allegedly by Bengali settlers, and the severity of the incidents (with several people reportedly being killed) necessitated the redeployment of troops to the region. In June 2013 Amnesty International's annual report highlighted continuing discord between the two groups, claiming that the government-appointed Land Commission had failed to restore traditional lands to the tribal people (as stipulated in the 1997 peace accord).

Foreign Affairs

Regional relations

In foreign affairs, Bangladesh has traditionally maintained a policy of non-alignment. Relations with Pakistan improved in 1976: ambassadors were exchanged, and trade and communications links were resumed. In 1991 Pakistan finally agreed to accept and rehabilitate some 250,000 Urdu-speaking Bihari Muslims (who openly supported Pakistan in Bangladesh's war of liberation in 1971) still remaining in refugee camps in Bangladesh. The first group of Bihari refugees migrated to Pakistan from Bangladesh in 1993, but the repatriation process proved very slow. In May 2008 the Dhaka High Court concluded that approximately 150,000 Biharis (those who had been minors in 1971 or who had been born in the intervening years) could become citizens of Bangladesh. In July 2002 Pakistani President Pervez Musharraf paid a visit to Bangladesh, during which he expressed regret for the atrocities committed by Pakistani troops during the 1971 war. In February 2006 Prime Minister Khaleda Zia visited Pakistan to hold talks with her Pakistani counterpart, Shaukat Aziz; the latter hailed the visit, during which the two sides signed four memoranda of understanding on trade, agriculture, tourism, and standardization and quality control, as a turning point in bilateral relations. At a fifth round of Bangladesh-Pakistan bilateral consultations, held in Islamabad, the Pakistani capital, in November 2010, the Bangladeshi delegation requested a formal apology from Pakistan for the war of liberation; other issues reportedly discussed included repatriation of Pakistani refugees stranded in Bangladesh, the division of state assets pertaining to the pre-separation period and war reparations. While Pakistani officials affirmed their willingness 'to continue discussion on these [issues] at all levels', no tangible progress towards resolution of the chief issues was reported. In November 2012 the Pakistani Minister of Foreign Affairs, Hina Rabbani Khar, travelled to Dhaka to invite Sheikh Hasina to a forthcoming summit of the Developing Eight (D-8) group of countries in Islamabad. Although a formal apology was again sought by her Bangladeshi counterpart, Dipu Moni, Rabbani Khar was reported to have recommended moving forward instead of dwelling on the past. Sheikh Hasina subsequently cancelled her visit to Pakistan. Relations between the two countries became more tense following the adoption by the Pakistani National Assembly in December 2013 of a resolution condemning as 'judicial murder' the execution of the BJI leader Abdul Quader Mollah for war crimes committed in the 1971 war of independence. The Bangladesh Government accused Pakistan of interfering in its internal affairs.

Relations with India have been strained over the questions of cross-border terrorism (especially around the area of the Chittagong Hill Tracts—q.v.) and of the Farakka barrage, which was constructed by India on the Ganges (Ganga) river in 1975, so depriving Bangladesh of water for irrigation and river transport during the dry season. In December 1996, however, Indo-Bangladeshi relations were given a major boost following the signing of an historic 30-year water-sharing agreement covering the Ganges river. In January 1997 Indian Prime Minister H. D. Deve Gowda paid an official visit to Bangladesh, the first Indian premier to do so for 20 years. In June 1999, during a visit to Dhaka to celebrate the inauguration of the first direct passenger bus service between Bangladesh and India, Indian Prime Minister Atal Bihari Vajpayee promised Bangladesh greater access to Indian markets and announced that India would give its neighbour substantial financial aid to help develop its transport and industrial infrastructure.

In June 1992 the Indian Government, under the provisions of an accord signed with Bangladesh in 1974, formally leased the Tin Bigha Corridor (a small strip of land covering an area of only 1.5 ha) to Bangladesh for 999 years. India maintained sovereignty over the corridor, but the lease gave Bangladesh access to its enclaves of Dahagram and Angarpota. In September 1997 India granted Nepal a transit route through Indian territory joining Nepal and Bangladesh, thus facilitating trade between those two countries. The issue of territorial rights along the irregular border remained a source of dispute, and resulted in intermittent clashes between border guards. Notably, in April 2001 three members of the Bangladesh Rifles (BDR) and 16 members of the Indian Border Security Forces (BSF) were killed during skirmishes on the Bangladeshi border with the Indian state of Meghalaya. Tension mounted following further border clashes in 2004–05; the problem was exacerbated by India's continued construction of a border fence in contravention of its obligations under a 1974 treaty. The Indian Government claimed that the fence was intended to prevent illegal immigrants and insurgents from crossing the border.

In March 2006 Khaleda Zia, during her first official visit to India as Prime Minister, held talks with her Indian counterpart, Dr Manmohan Singh, and other senior officials. The two countries signed agreements on trade and anti-drugs-trafficking measures, and stressed their commitment to working together on security issues. Security, however, remained a point of contention between Bangladesh and India throughout 2006. The Bangladeshi Government vehemently denied reports in the Indian media that the explosives used in the Mumbai bomb attacks in July (see the chapter on India) originated in Bangladesh. The BDR, meanwhile, denied repeated BSF claims that Assamese rebels were based in Bangladesh. In February 2007, after a series of high-level bilateral talks in Dhaka, the two countries agreed to increase co-operation in their respective fights against terrorism. Military officials from Bangladesh and India held talks in Dhaka in October to work towards a resolution of border issues, with the two sides agreeing to greater co-operation in order to combat militant and criminal activity in border areas. A direct train link between Dhaka and Kolkata (Calcutta), India, began operating in April 2008.

Observers have noted that Bangladesh has generally enjoyed a closer relationship with India during periods of AL rule. Bilateral relations were boosted by the Bangladeshi authorities' arrest and transfer into Indian custody of several leaders of the United Liberation Front of Assam (ULFA) during 2009–10, and, in October 2010, of Rajkumar Meghen, the leader of the United National Liberation Front, a prominent separatist group in the north-eastern Indian state of Manipur. Following a visit to New Delhi made by the Bangladeshi Prime Minister, Sheikh Hasina, in January 2010, it was reported that Bangladesh and India aimed to remove all barriers to mutual trade in an effort to improve bilateral economic co-operation. In August the two countries announced an agreement providing for a US $1,000m. Indian loan to fund infrastructural development and improve road and rail connectivity in Bangladesh. Border talks resumed in November, following a five-year hiatus, which was interpreted by some observers as a tacit acknowledgement from India of the importance of ensuring continued growth and development in Bangladesh in order to safeguard the development and security of India's north-eastern states. A joint border survey of disputed frontier areas was concluded in early 2011. In August Bangladesh and India began the process of approving border maps, officially recognizing their 4,156-km frontier; however, a 6.5-km stretch of the border had yet to be demarcated and remained disputed.

A water-sharing agreement on the Teesta river, which is crucial to agricultural production in north-western Bangladesh, was one of several significant deals that had been expected to be finalized during Indian Prime Minister Manmohan Singh's first official visit to Dhaka—the first state visit to Bangladesh by an Indian premier in 12 years—which took place in September 2011. However, reportedly owing to objections from the Chief Minister of West Bengal, Singh withdrew the deal. The two countries also failed to reach agreement on a land transit accord that would have granted India overland access to its landlocked north-eastern states through Bangladeshi territory. (Bangladesh had insisted that the latter agreement was dependent upon a successful conclusion to the water-sharing deal.) Nevertheless, a land border agreement, resolving demarcation of the remaining 6.5-km stretch on the bilateral frontier, and an agreement providing for the exchange of 111 Indian enclaves within Bangladesh and 51 Bangladeshi enclaves within India, were signed, formally concluding a dispute dating back to 1947. Other agreements signed included the granting of tax concessions by India on Bangladeshi textile exports, which was seen as another step towards the conclusion of a bilateral free trade agreement. In spite of several rounds of senior-level talks between Bangladeshi and Indian officials, a water-sharing agreement on the Teesta river had yet to be reached in early 2014. However, the generally positive trend in bilateral relations was reinforced by a three-day official visit to Bangladesh by India's President, Pranab Mukherjee, in March 2013.

The question of settlers has been the prevalent issue in Bangladesh's relations with its eastern neighbour Myanmar. While the 320-km border itself was finally demarcated in 1985, in accordance with a 1979 agreement, during 1991–92 about 270,000 Rohingya Muslims, a Myanma ethnic minority who live in the western Arakan region, crossed into Bangladesh, claiming persecution by the Myanma authorities. In 1992 an agreement was signed between the Governments of Bangladesh and Myanmar to allow for voluntary repatriation. The official deadline for the repatriation of the Rohingya refugees expired in August 1997, by which time about 230,000 refugees were reported to have returned to Myanmar. Smaller-scale repatriations resumed in late 1998 following intervention by the office of the UN High Commissioner for Refugees (UNHCR).

In January 2001 Bangladeshi and Myanma border guards exchanged fire, amid rising tension over a controversial dam project on the Naaf river, which Bangladesh claimed would cause flooding in its territory. In February, following border negotiations between the two countries, Myanmar agreed permanently to halt construction of the dam. The official visit of the Myanma ruler, Gen. Than Shwe, to Bangladesh in December 2002 indicated an apparent improvement in relations despite the ongoing Rohingya issue. In December 2009 it was announced that Myanmar had agreed to repatriate about 9,000 Rohingyas living in Bangladeshi camps. In June 2012 Bangladesh refused entry to thousands of Rohingyas fleeing renewed violence in Myanmar, prompting criticism from human rights organizations. Further criticism followed the Government's decision to block the aid programmes of three international non-governmental organizations (NGOs) to unregistered Rohingya refugees on the grounds that this increased refugee numbers. At early 2013 an estimated 30,000 Rohingyas with official refugee status remained in the two camps run by UNHCR, the rate of repatriation having slowed considerably; in addition, there were an estimated 200,000 stateless Rohingyas living in squalid unregistered camps around Cox's Bazar (already one of the most impoverished areas of Bangladesh).

In December 2009 Bangladesh initiated proceedings with the UN International Tribunal for the Law of the Sea (ITLOS) concerning delimitation of the maritime boundary with Myanmar, which had been the subject of a long-running dispute. In March 2012 ITLOS upheld Bangladesh's claim to a full 200-nautical-mile exclusive economic zone in the Bay of Bengal and awarded Bangladesh control of a 12-nautical-mile zone surrounding St Martin's Island (which is located in the Bay of Bengal, less than 10 km from both Bangladeshi and Myanma territory). Moreover, the Tribunal recognized Bangladesh's right to a proportional share of the outer continental shelf, beyond the 200-nautical-mile zone. It was anticipated that the settlement would enable significant development of Bangladesh's offshore hydrocarbon projects.

Bangladesh is a member of the South Asian Association for Regional Cooperation (SAARC, see p. 420), formally constituted in 1985, with Bhutan, India, the Maldives, Nepal, Pakistan and Sri Lanka. Included in SAARC's charter are pledges of non-interference by members in each other's internal affairs and a joint effort to avoid 'contentious' issues whenever the association meets. The SAARC Preferential Trading Arrangement (SAPTA) was signed in April 1993 and came into effect in December 1995. At the 12th SAARC summit meeting held in Islamabad, Pakistan, in January 2004, members signed an agreement providing for the establishment of a South Asian Free Trade Area (SAFTA—which came into force on 1 January 2006, although its phased implementation was not due to be fully effected until 2016). At a SAFTA Working Group meeting in September 2011, the Bangladeshi Government announced that, pending approval by the Bangladeshi Council of Ministers, it was to eliminate import tariffs on 248 products from India, Pakistan and Sri Lanka, and 246 products from Afghanistan, Bhutan, the Maldives and Nepal, in exchange for similar measures by the seven other SAFTA signatories. It was hoped that the tariff concessions would help to boost interregional trade.

Other external relations

Relations with China had uncertain beginnings, with China initially refusing to recognize Bangladesh's sovereignty upon the latter's accession to independence in 1971. However, following the establishment of bilateral relations in 1975, they have steadily gained in importance in recent years, with the East Asian country increasingly establishing itself as a significant challenger for India's position as the main trading superpower within the South Asian region. During a visit to the Chinese capital, Beijing, by Prime Minister Sheikh Hasina in March 2010, the two countries signed a series of agreements, including, most notably, a Closer Comprehensive Partnership of Co-operation, which formalized the signatories' commitment to expanding mutually beneficial co-operation; a memorandum of understanding providing for enhanced bilateral co-operation in the oil and gas sector was also signed. The Chinese Vice-President, Xi Jinping, made a state visit to Dhaka in June, during which the two countries signed an economic co-operation agreement providing for substantial Chinese investment in Bangladeshi infrastructure and industrial projects. In the following month, in a development that was thought likely to have caused irritation to the Indian Government, China announced the elimination of tariffs on exports from Bangladesh and Nepal, effective from the start of that month. An agreement signed between Bangladesh and the Export and Import Bank of China in June 2011 provided for a Chinese loan of US $211m., to be disbursed on the upgrading of Bangladesh's telecommunications network. During a visit to Beijing in September, Bangladesh's Chief of Army Staff held discussions with the Chinese Minister of National Defence, during which they agreed to enhance bilateral military co-operation. The proposed creation of a Bangladesh-China-India-Myanmar (BCIM) Economic Corridor, which had been under discussion for around a decade, moved one step closer to reality in December 2013, following the first working-group meeting of the four involved countries, held in the Chinese city of Kunming; a joint research plan on constructing the corridor was signed by the four participants.

In March 2000 Bill Clinton became the first US President to make a state visit to Bangladesh. In September 2001 Bangladesh's interim administration agreed, with the support of the AL and BNP, to offer the USA use of Bangladeshi airspace and ports in the event of military action against Afghanistan, where the Taliban leadership was believed to be harbouring Osama bin Laden and other members of al-Qa'ida—held principally responsible by the USA for that month's suicide attacks against New York and Washington, DC. However, the US-led military campaign to oust the regime of Saddam Hussain in Iraq from 2003 provoked anti-US and anti-British demonstrations in Dhaka. In June 2004 US Secretary of Defense Donald Rumsfeld visited Bangladesh and held talks with Prime Minister Khaleda Zia. There were protests against his visit, as it was believed that he intended to request that Bangladesh contribute troops to assist the US-led coalition in Iraq. Although Bangladesh had been a regular contributor of personnel to UN peacekeeping operations throughout the world, the Bangladeshi Minister of Foreign Affairs stressed that no troops would be sent to Iraq without a UN mandate. In April 2012 Bangladeshi officials participated in the inaugural US-Bangladeshi Dialogue on Security Issues in Dhaka. The forum aimed to promote bilateral co-operation on a range of military and security initiatives, including joint military exercises, peacekeeping missions and maritime security. The positive trend in bilateral relations was further underlined by the staging of the first US-Bangladeshi Partnership Dialogue in Washington, DC, in September, during which a broad range of bilateral and regional issues were discussed. A strategic partnership agreement had been signed by the two sides during a visit to Dhaka in May by US Secretary of State Hillary Clinton, who had held talks with both Sheikh Hasina and Khaleda Zia. However, in June 2013 the Bangladesh Government criticized a decision by the US Administration to suspend trade privileges for Bangladesh under the generalized system of preferences scheme in the wake of the recent Rana Plaza disaster (see Domestic Political Affairs); the USA demanded that Bangladesh improve safety conditions and labour rights within the clothing industry.

As of January 2014 an estimated 7,933 Bangladeshi military and police personnel were deployed overseas on UN peacekeeping operations, a total contribution exceeded only by Pakistan (8,232).

CONSTITUTION AND GOVERNMENT

The People's Republic of Bangladesh was established following the secession of East Pakistan from Pakistan in 1971. The members who were returned from East Pakistan for the Pakistan National Assembly and the Provincial Assembly in the December 1970 elections formed the Bangladesh Constituent Assembly. A new Constitution for the People's Republic of Bangladesh was approved by this Assembly and came into effect in December 1972. Following the military coup of March 1982, the Constitution was suspended, and the country was placed under martial law. In November 1986 martial law was repealed and the suspended Constitution was revived. The Constitution was initially based on the fundamental principles of nationalism, socialism, democracy and secularism, but in 1977 an amendment replaced secularism with Islam. A further amendment in 1988 formally established Islam as the state religion. Under the 15th Amendment to the Constitution of 2011, secularism was restored as a fundamental principle of the state, while Islam was retained as the state religion.

The role of the President, who is elected by the Parliament (Jatiya Sangsad, or House of the Nation) for a five-year term, is essentially that of a titular head of state. Executive power is held by the Prime Minister, who heads the Council of Ministers. The President appoints the Prime Minister and, on the latter's recommendation, other ministers. The Jatiya Sangsad serves a five-year term, subject to dissolution, and comprises 350 members: 300 of whom are elected by universal suffrage and an additional 50 female members who are appointed by the elective members on the basis of proportional representation.

For purposes of local government, the country is divided into seven administrative divisions (each named after their respective divisional headquarters), which are themselves subdivided into 64 administrative districts—*zila* (each of which is further subdivided into sub-districts—*upazila*).

REGIONAL AND INTERNATIONAL CO-OPERATION

Bangladesh is a member of the Asian Development Bank (ADB, see p. 207), of the South Asian Association for Regional Cooperation (SAARC, see p. 420) and of the Colombo Plan (see p. 449). Having joined the UN in 1974, Bangladesh is a member of the UN Economic and Social Commission for Asia and the Pacific (ESCAP, see p. 28).

As a contracting party to the General Agreement on Tariffs and Trade (GATT), Bangladesh became a member of the World Trade Organization (WTO) on its establishment in 1995. In 1997 eight of the world's major Muslim states, including Bangladesh, established the Developing Eight (D-8), with a view to furthering economic and political co-operation among the member countries.

ECONOMIC AFFAIRS

In 2012, according to estimates by the World Bank, Bangladesh's gross national income (GNI), measured at average 2010–12 prices, was US $129,188m., equivalent to $840 per head (or $2,070 per head on an international purchasing-power parity basis). During 2003–12, it was estimated, the population increased at an average annual rate of 1.2%, while gross domestic product (GDP) per head increased, in real terms, by an average of 5.0% per year. Overall GDP increased at an average annual rate of 6.3% in 2003–12. According to the Asian Development Bank (ADB), GDP grew by 4.7% in the fiscal year ending 30 June 2013.

Agriculture (including hunting, forestry and fishing) contributed an estimated 17.2% of total GDP in 2012/13, according to provisional figures. In 2010 47.5% of the total employed labour force was engaged in that sector. The principal sources of revenue in the agricultural sector are jute, tea, shrimps and fish. Raw jute and jute goods accounted for 3.8% of total export earnings in 2012/13, according to provisional figures. Despite severe flooding in 2000, Bangladesh achieved self-sufficiency in basic foods for the first time in 2000/01, mainly owing to increased rice production. Agricultural GDP expanded at an average annual rate of 4.1% in 2003–12. According to the ADB, the GDP of the agricultural sector increased by 2.2% in the fiscal year ending 30 June 2013.

Industry (including mining, manufacturing, power and construction) employed 17.6% of the working population in 2010. The industrial sector contributed an estimated 28.9% of total GDP in 2012/13, according to provisional figures. During 2003–12, according to the ADB, industrial GDP increased at an average annual rate of 7.9%; growth in the industrial sector was 9.0% in the fiscal year ending 30 June 2013.

Recent discoveries of large reserves of natural gas appear to offer opportunities both in terms of domestic fuel self-sufficiency and, in the longer term, export potential. Bangladesh's proven reserves of natural gas totalled 184,000m. cu m at the end of 2012. According to the US Geological Survey, production of natural gas increased from 19,919m. cu m in 2008/09 to 20,100m. cu m in 2010/11. In 2004 the US company Unocal (acquired by Chevron Corpn in 2005) signed an agreement with the state-owned Petrobangla corporation to develop the country's most extensive gas field, at Bibiyana. Production at Bibiyana commenced in 2007, and an expansion project was launched in 2011. Bangladesh possesses substantial deposits of coal (estimated at more than 1,000m. metric tons, although difficulties of exploitation continue to make coal imports necessary) and petroleum.

Manufacturing contributed an estimated 17.6% of GDP in 2012/13, according to provisional official figures. The sector employed 12.4% of the working population in 2010. The principal branches of the manufacturing sector include textiles, food products, garments and chemicals. During 2003–12, according to the ADB, manufacturing GDP increased at an average annual rate of 8.3%. The GDP of the manufacturing sector grew by 9.3% in 2012/13, according to provisional official figures.

The construction sector contributed 9.0% of GDP in 2012/13, according to provisional figures, and engaged 4.8% of the employed labour force in 2010. During 2003–12, according to the ADB, the GDP of the sector increased at an average annual rate of 7.0%. Sectoral GDP grew by 8.1% in 2012/13, according to provisional official figures.

Energy is derived principally from natural gas (which contributed 91.5% of total electricity output in 2011). Imports of petroleum products comprised 10.7% of the cost of total imports in 2012/13, according to official provisional figures. Economic growth has been undermined by inadequate and unreliable electricity production, although a major expansion of generation capacity is under way. As of October 2011 Bangladesh had total installed generating capacity of 7,119 MW per day, although actual dependable capacity was estimated at just over 5,000 MW, against peak demand of approximately 6,000 MW per day. By November 2013 total installed generating capacity had increased to over 10,000 MW. In early 2012 the Bangladesh Power Development Board signed a joint venture agreement with the National Thermal Power Corporation of India for the construction of a 1,320-MW coal-fired power plant, at an estimated cost of US $1,500m.; despite environmental concerns, work on the Rampal power plant commenced in October 2013.

The services sector accounted for an estimated 53.9% of total GDP in 2012/13, according to provisional figures. In 2010 35.1% of the employed labour force was engaged in the sector. According to the ADB, the GDP of the services sector increased at an average annual rate of 6.3% during 2003–12; the sector's GDP expanded by 5.7% in the fiscal year ending 30 June 2013.

In 2012, according to the IMF, Bangladesh recorded a visible merchandise trade deficit of US $7,373.8m., while there was a surplus of $2,647.6m. on the current account of the balance of payments. In 2012, according to the ADB, the principal sources of imports were the People's Republic of China (which contributed 19.5% of the total) and India, while the USA was the principal market for exports (accounting for 16.7% of the total). Other major trading partners were Germany, the United Kingdom and France. The principal exports in 2012/13 were ready-made garments, and knitwear and hosiery products (together accounting for an estimated 79.6% of total export revenue). The principal imports were petroleum products, textiles, iron and steel, cotton and capital machinery.

In 2012/13, according to the ADB, the overall fiscal deficit of the central Government amounted to the equivalent of 4.5% of GDP. According to ADB figures, Bangladesh's total external debt was US $23,319m. at the end of 2013. In 2013, the cost of debt-servicing long-term public and publicly guaranteed debt and repayments to the IMF was equivalent to 2.5% of the value of goods, services and income (excluding workers' remittances). The annual rate of inflation averaged 7.9% in 2003–12, according to the International Labour Organization. According to the Bangladesh Bank, consumer prices increased by an average of 10.6% in 2011/12 and 7.7% in 2012/13. According to the ADB, about 2.1% of the total labour force was unemployed in 2012.

The problems confronting developing Bangladesh include political instability, widespread poverty, severe infrastructural deficiencies and the economy's heavy dependence on foreign aid. Limited success in diversifying the national export base has been achieved, particularly within the information and communications technology industry. In an attempt to address the country's chronic power shortages, government expenditure of some 223,650m. taka was allocated to the power and energy sectors in 2012/13, and in 2012 the ADB and the Japan Bank for International Co-operation announced that they would provide substantial loans to develop Bangladesh's power sector. In October 2013 work commenced on the establishment of the first of two nuclear power plants, which were to be funded largely by Russian loans and were to be built by the Russian state nuclear energy corporation, Rosatom. The new plants—both of which were to have a capacity of 1,000 MW—were due to be fully completed by 2022. Plans for the construction of a combined road and rail bridge over the Padma river, which was to link south-western Bangladesh with the northern and eastern regions, were delayed after the World Bank suspended funding in October 2011 owing to corruption allegations (see Contemporary Political History). The Government subsequently announced that the project would proceed without foreign funding; construction work was scheduled to commence in mid-2014. Another major infrastructure project under discussion at early 2014 was a proposed metro rail system in Dhaka; the Japan International Co-operation Agency pledged in February 2013 to provide around three-quarters of the total estimated cost of 220,000m. taka in the form of a soft loan for the construction of the 20.1-km railway. Building work was expected to commence in 2016 and be fully completed—in three phases—by 2022. A new Country Partnership Strategy for Bangladesh covering the period 2011–15 was approved by the ADB in 2011, and included a US $4,500m. investment programme intended to address, *inter alia*, infrastructural deficits, a shortage of skilled labour and the effects of rapid urbanization; the programme was to prioritize agriculture, education, energy, finance, transport and urban development. In 2012 the IMF announced a new three-year Extended Credit Facility (ECF) worth $987m., which was intended to elevate Bangladesh to a higher growth trajectory and achieve the status of a middle-income country by the 2020s. The IMF noted the need for a strong policy response to macroeconomic and structural challenges posed by the recent weakening in the global economic environment and rising oil imports and subsidy costs, and for further efforts to tighten monetary and fiscal policy (including modernization of the tax system). Meanwhile, annual growth in foreign remittances decreased from a peak of 32.4% in 2007/08 to 6.0% in 2010/11, primarily owing to a general downward trend in labour migration rates; however, remittances increased by 10.2% in 2011/12 as a result of a rise that year in the number of Bangladeshi workers going to the Middle East, improved banking services and a depreciation in the taka. According to the ADB, GDP growth stood at 6.3% in 2011/12, but slowed to 4.7% in 2012/13. Inflation declined from 10.6% in 2011/12 to 7.7% in 2012/13, as a result of a fall in food prices and the implementation of more stringent monetary policies. The country's economic performance in 2014 was widely forecast to be adversely affected by continuing political instability and unrest, although a rise in consumer demand (both domestic and external) was also predicted.

PUBLIC HOLIDAYS

2015: 2 January* (Eid-i-Milad-un-Nabi, Birth of the Prophet), 21 February (Shaheed Day and International Mother Language Day), 17 March (Birth of the Father of the Nation), 26 March (Independence Day), 15 April (Bengali New Year), 1 May (May Day), May* (Buddha Purnima), 3 June (Shab-i Bharat), 6 July (Bank Holiday), 10 July* (Jumatul Wida), 13 July* (Shab-i Qadr), 17 July* (Id al-Fitr, end of Ramadan), 15 August (National Mourning Day), 5 September* (Janmashtami), 23 September* (Id al-Adha, Feast of the Sacrifice), 11 October* (Ashoura), 22 October* (Durga Puja), 16 December (Victory Day), 25 December (Christmas Day), 31 December (Bank Holiday).

* Dates of certain religious holidays are subject to the sighting of the moon, and there are also optional holidays for different religious groups.

Statistical Survey

Source (unless otherwise stated): Bangladesh Bureau of Statistics, Statistics Division, Ministry of Planning, E-27/A, Agargaon, Sher-e-Bangla Nagar, Dhaka 1207; tel. (2) 9118045; fax (2) 9111064; e-mail ndbp@bangla.net; internet www.bbs.gov.bd.

Area and Population

AREA, POPULATION AND DENSITY

Area (sq km)	147,570*
Population (census results)†	
22 January 2001	124,355,263
15 March 2011	
Males	74,980,386
Females	74,791,978
Total	149,772,364
Population (UN estimates at mid-year)‡	
2012	154,695,370
2013	156,594,964
2014	158,512,571
Density (per sq km) at mid-2014	1,074.2

* 56,977 sq miles.

† Including adjustment for underenumeration, estimated to have been 4.95% in 2001 and 5.24% in 2011.

‡ Source: UN, *World Population Prospects: The 2012 Revision*.

POPULATION BY AGE AND SEX
(UN estimates at mid-2014)

	Males	Females	Total
0–14	23,910,754	22,836,812	46,747,566
15–64	52,334,592	51,808,254	104,142,846
65 and over	3,904,254	3,717,905	7,622,159
Total	80,149,600	78,362,971	158,512,571

Source: UN, *World Population Prospects: The 2012 Revision*.

ADMINISTRATIVE DIVISIONS
('000 population at 2011 census)

Division	Area (sq km)	Population*	Density (per sq km)
Barisal	13,225	8,326	629.6
Chittagong	33,909	28,423	838.2
Dhaka	31,178	47,424	1,521.1
Khulna	22,284	15,688	704.0
Rajshahi	18,153	18,485	1,018.3
Rangpur	16,185	15,788	975.5
Sylhet	12,636	9,910	784.3
Total	147,570	144,044	976.1

* Excluding adjustment for underenumeration; the adjusted total was 149,772,364.

PRINCIPAL TOWNS
(population at 2001 census)*

Dhaka (capital)	5,327,306	Nawabganj	152,223
Chittagong	2,023,489	Sylhet	146,247
Khulna	770,498	Brahmanbaria	129,278
Rajshahi	388,811	Tangail	128,785
Tongi (Tungi)	283,099	Kadamrasul (Bandar)	128,561
Narayanganj	241,393	Sirajganj	128,144
Rangpur	241,310	Sabhar (Savar)	127,540
Mymensingh (Nasirabad)	227,204	Narsingdi	124,204
Barisal (Bakerganj)	192,810	Naogaon	124,046
Jessore	176,655	Gazipur	122,801
Comilla	166,519	Jamalpur	120,955
Dinajpur	157,914	Pabna	116,305
Bogra	154,807	Saidpur	112,609

* Figures in each case refer to the city corporations.

Mid-2008 (official estimates): *City Corporations:* Dhaka 7,000,940; Chittagong 2,579,107; Khulna 855,650; Rajshahi 472,775; Sylhet 463,198; Barisal 210,374. *Statistical Metropolitan Areas (SMA):* Dhaka 12,797,394; Chittagong 3,858,093; Khulna 1,388,425; Rajshahi 775,495.

Mid-2011 (incl. suburbs, UN estimate): Dhaka 15,390,900 (Source: UN, *World Urbanization Prospects: The 2011 Revision*).

BIRTHS, MARRIAGES AND DEATHS*
(crude rates per 1,000 persons)

	Live births	Marriages	Deaths
2003	20.9	10.4	5.9
2004	20.8	12.4	5.8
2005	20.7	13.0	5.8
2006	20.6	12.5	5.6
2007	20.9	12.5	6.2
2008	20.5	11.6	6.0
2009	19.4	13.2	5.8
2010	19.2	12.7	5.6
2011	19.2	13.4	5.5

* Estimates based on sample vital registration system (SVRS). According to UN estimates, the average annual rates per 1,000 for births and deaths were: Births 27.7 in 1995–2000, 25.1 in 2000–05, 22.8 in 2005–10; Deaths 7.8 in 1995–2000, 6.8 in 2000–05, 6.2 in 2005–10 (Source: UN, *World Population Prospects: The 2012 Revision*).

2010 (provisional): Registered live births 2,868,494; Registered deaths 842,095 (Source: UN, *Population and Vital Statistics Report*).

2011 (provisional): Registered live births 2,891,000; Registered deaths 828,000 (Source: UN, *Population and Vital Statistics Report*).

Marriages: 1,181,000 in 1997 (Source: UN, *Demographic Yearbook*).

Life expectancy (years at birth): 69.9 (males 69.2; females 70.7) in 2011 (Source: World Bank, World Development Indicators database).

ECONOMICALLY ACTIVE POPULATION*
(sample survey, '000 persons aged 15 years and over, year ending June 2000)

	Males	Females	Total
Agriculture, hunting, forestry and fishing	17,256	14,914	32,171
Mining and quarrying	107	188	295
Manufacturing	2,346	1,436	3,783
Electricity, gas and water	116	18	134
Construction	999	100	1,099
Trade, restaurants and hotels	5,769	506	6,275
Transport, storage and communications	2,432	77	2,509
Financing, insurance, real estate and business services	357	46	403
Community, social and personal services	1,243	1,726	2,969
Sub-total	30,625	19,011	49,638
Activities not adequately defined	1,744	384	2,126
Total employed	32,369	19,395	51,764
Unemployed	1,083	666	1,750
Total labour force	33,452	20,061	53,514

* Figures exclude members of the armed forces.

Note: Totals may not be equal to sum of components, owing to rounding.

Source: ILO.

2010 (labour force survey, million persons aged 15 years and over, year ending 30 June): Agriculture, forestry and fishing 25.7; Mining and quarrying 0.1; Manufacturing 6.7; Electricity, gas and water 0.1; Construction 2.6; Trade, hotels and restaurants 8.3; Transport, storage and communications 4.0; Finance, real estate and business services 1.0; Health, education, public administration and defence 2.3; Community and personal services 3.4; *Total employed* 54.1; Unemployed 2.6; *Total labour force* 56.7.

Health and Welfare

KEY INDICATORS

Total fertility rate (children per woman, 2011)	2.2
Under-five mortality rate (per 1,000 live births, 2011)	46
HIV/AIDS (% of persons aged 15–49, 2012)	<0.1
Physicians (per 1,000 head, 2011)	0.4
Hospital beds (per 1,000 head, 2005)	0.4
Health expenditure (2010): US $ per head (PPP)	61
Health expenditure (2010): % of GDP	3.7
Health expenditure (2010): public (% of total)	36.5
Access to water (% of persons, 2011)	83
Access to sanitation (% of persons, 2011)	55
Total carbon dioxide emissions ('000 metric tons, 2010)	56,152.8
Carbon dioxide emissions per head (metric tons, 2010)	0.4
Human Development Index (2012): ranking	146
Human Development Index (2012): value	0.515

For sources and definitions, see explanatory note on p. vi.

Agriculture

PRINCIPAL CROPS
('000 metric tons, year ending 30 June)

	2009/10	2010/11	2011/12
Wheat	901	972	995
Maize	887	1,018	1,298
Rice, paddy	50,061	50,627	33,890
Millet	12	11*	12*
Potatoes	7,930	8,326	8,205
Sweet potatoes	307	298	253
Sugar cane	4,491	4,671	4,603
Other sugar crops	315	322	327*
Beans, dry	48	52*	55*
Lentils	71	80	80
Groundnuts, with shell	53	54	52
Areca nuts (betel)	92	106	108*
Coconuts	81†	80†	82*
Rapeseed	222	230†	230†
Sesame seed†	32	33	34
Linseed	7	7	6
Seed cotton	43†	52†	57*
Cabbages and other brassicas	220	207	213
Lettuce and chicory	35	35	37*
Spinach	45	43	45*
Tomatoes	190	232	255
Cauliflowers and broccoli	160	168	166
Pumpkins, squash and gourds	352	355	365*
Onions, dry	872	1,052	1,159
Garlic	164	209	234
Beans, green	89	95	94
Cantaloupes and other melons	216	205	212*
Guavas, mangoes and mangosteens	1,048	889	945
Pineapples	234	219	181
Bananas	818	801	746
Papayas	113	125	120
Tea	60	61	62*
Tobacco, unmanufactured	55	79	85
Ginger	75	74	72
Jute	923	1,523	1,452

* FAO estimate.
† Unofficial figure(s).

Aggregate production ('000 metric tons, may include official, semi-official or estimated data): Total cereals 51,863 in 2009/10, 52,629 in 2010/11, 36,195 in 2011/12; Total roots and tubers 8,237 in 2009/10, 8,624 in 2010/11, 8,458 in 2011/12; Total vegetables (incl. melons) 3,689 in 2009/10, 3,969 in 2010/11, 4,155 in 2011/12; Total pulses 220 in 2009/10, 235 in 2010/11, 315 in 2011/12; Total fruits (excl. melons) 3,907 in 2009/10, 3,689 in 2010/11, 3,656 in 2011/12.

Source: FAO.

LIVESTOCK
('000 head, year ending September)

	2010	2011	2012
Cattle	23,051	23,121	23,150*
Buffaloes	1,349	1,394	1,443
Sheep*	1,820	1,860	1,890
Goats*	51,400	53,400	55,000
Chickens	228,035	234,686	240,000*
Ducks	42,677	44,120	45,000*

* FAO estimate(s).

Source: FAO.

LIVESTOCK PRODUCTS
('000 metric tons, FAO estimates)

	2010	2011	2012
Cattle meat	189	192	195
Buffalo meat	6.0	6.0	6.4
Sheep meat	3.9	4.1	4.1
Goat meat	191	199	200
Chicken meat	162	164	165
Duck meat	41.5	44.0	44.0
Cows' milk	830	832	835
Buffalo milk	36	37	38
Sheep's milk	36.4	37.1	37.8
Goats' milk	2,496	2,592	2,608
Hen eggs (in shell)	188	199	205
Other poultry eggs (in shell)	80.3	85.0	86.5

Source: FAO.

Forestry

ROUNDWOOD REMOVALS
('000 cubic metres, excl. bark, FAO estimates)

	2010	2011	2012
Sawlogs, veneer logs and logs for sleepers*	174	174	174
Pulpwood	18	18	18
Other industrial wood	90	90	90
Fuel wood	27,287	27,128	26,971
Total	27,569	27,410	27,253

* Annual output assumed to be unchanged since 1996.

Source: FAO.

SAWNWOOD PRODUCTION
('000 cubic metres, incl. railway sleepers)

	2001	2002	2003
Total (all broadleaved)	79*	255	388

* FAO estimate.

2004–12: Production assumed to be unchanged from 2003 (FAO estimates).

Source: FAO.

Fishing

('000 metric tons, live weight)

	2009	2010	2011
Capture	1,821.6	1,726.6	1,600.9
Freshwater fishes	1,028.0	869.6	884.9
Hilsa shad	298.9	313.8	339.8
Marine fishes	259.5	266.1	171.5
Aquaculture	1,064.3	1,308.5	1,523.8
Roho labeo	227.0	254.3	276.8
Catla	178.9	196.4	215.3
Silver carp	172.5	195.6	138.9
Penaeus shrimps	8.1	2.1	8.0
Total catch	2,885.9	3,035.1	3,124.7

Source: FAO.

Mining

(million cubic metres, year ending 30 June)

	2008/09	2009/10	2010/11
Natural gas	19,919	20,075	20,100

Source: US Geological Survey.

Industry

SELECTED PRODUCTS
('000 metric tons unless otherwise indicated; year ending 30 June)

	2010/11	2011/12	2012/13
Refined sugar	101.0	63.3	107.1
Cigarettes (million)	23,451	31,505	26,262
Cotton yarn ('000 bales)*	1,030	955	970
Woven cotton fabrics ('000 metres)	56,181	56,546	56,949
Paper	20.2	20.7	17.8
Fertilizers	1,011.9	1,036.9	1,074.8

* 1 bale = 180 kg.

Jute goods ('000 metric tons): 295.3 in 2007/08.

Cement ('000 metric tons): 2,195.6 in 2005/06.

Electric energy (million kWh): 22,741 in 2005/06.

Source: Bangladesh Bank.

Finance

CURRENCY AND EXCHANGE RATES

Monetary Units:
100 poisha = 1 taka.

Sterling, Dollar and Euro Equivalents (31 December 2013):
£1 sterling = 128.039 taka;
US $1 = 77.750 taka;
€1 = 107.225 taka;
1,000 taka = £7.81 = $12.86 = €9.33.

Average Exchange Rate (taka per US $):
2011 74.152
2012 81.863
2013 78.103

BUDGET
(million taka, year ending 30 June)

Revenue*	2011/12	2012/13†	2013/14‡
Taxation	952,280	1,168,240	1,412,190
Import duties	119,830	145,280	146,290
Income and profit taxes	281,580	353,000	482,970
Excise duties	6,640	9,970	13,100
Value-added tax	343,040	404,660	499,560
Other revenue	194,670	228,460	262,400
Total	1,146,950	1,396,700	1,674,590

Expenditure§	2011/12	2012/13†	2013/14‡
General public services	102,980	110,400	300,280
Local government and rural development	19,370	24,590	22,850
Defence	119,780	132,880	142,290
Public order and safety	81,570	89,710	95,660
Education and technology	147,190	150,990	170,220
Health	50,550	55,070	58,680
Social security and welfare	70,720	85,300	91,960
Housing	8,470	8,990	9,140
Recreation, culture and religious affairs	10,820	12,720	11,840
Fuel and energy	420	460	430
Agriculture, forestry and fishing	114,750	162,060	132,510
Industrial and economic services	4,980	6,410	5,180
Transport and communications	35,030	41,200	45,360
Interest payments	203,510	233,470	277,430
Gross current expenditure	970,140	1,114,290	1,363,820

* Excluding grants, loans and food account transactions.
† Revised figures.
‡ Budget figures.
§ Non-development expenditure, excluding loans and advances, domestic and foreign debt, food account operations and structural adjustment.

Note: Totals may not be equal to the sum of components, owing to rounding.

Source: Ministry of Finance (Finance Division).

PUBLIC SECTOR DEVELOPMENT EXPENDITURE
(departmental allocation, million taka, year ending 30 June)

	2011/12	2012/13*	2013/14†
Agriculture	31,960	36,370	42,170
Local government and rural development	91,130	125,440	125,160
Industrial and economic services	10,810	20,940	26,870
Fuel and energy	79,270	99,440	113,080
Transport and communications	59,500	91,160	160,600
Housing	4,900	4,930	8,650
Education and technology	43,890	64,620	90,710
Health	26,120	36,230	36,020
Social security and welfare	19,150	27,410	31,740
Public order and safety	5,800	7,420	9,700
Defence	2,520	2,140	2,280
Recreation, culture and religious affairs	3,930	4,900	5,600
Public services	7,490	17,580	20,690
Total development expenditure‡	386,470	538,600	673,270

* Revised figures.
† Budget figures.
‡ Including transfers (million taka): 12,840 in 2011/12; 14,930 in 2012/13; 14,570 in 2013/14.

Note: Totals may not be equal to the sum of components, owing to rounding.

Source: Ministry of Finance (Economic Relations Division).

INTERNATIONAL RESERVES
(US $ million at 31 December)

	2010	2011	2012
Gold*	613.2	682.5	719.9
IMF special drawing rights	659.6	733.8	637.2
Reserve position in IMF	0.6	0.6	0.8
Foreign exchange	9,904.1	7,775.1	11,393.3
Total	11,177.5	9,192.0	12,751.2

* Valued at market-related prices.

Source: IMF, *International Financial Statistics*.

MONEY SUPPLY
(million taka at 31 December)

	2010	2011	2012
Currency outside depository corporations	523,528	574,700	641,984
Transferable deposits	466,526	493,958	531,510
Other deposits	3,115,468	3,827,251	4,652,992
Securities other than shares	574,059	575,111	575,771
Broad money	4,679,581	5,471,020	6,402,257

Source: IMF, *International Financial Statistics*.

COST OF LIVING
(Consumer Price Index, year ending 30 June; base: 1995/96 = 100)

	2010/11	2011/12	2012/13
Food, beverages and tobacco	268.0	295.9	317.6
Rent, fuel and lighting	197.9	218.3	238.9
Household requisites	231.8	259.1	280.7
Clothing and footwear	191.9	225.7	252.5
Transport and communications	244.2	276.3	292.5
All items (incl. others)	241.0	266.6	287.1

Source: Bangladesh Bank.

NATIONAL ACCOUNTS
('000 million taka at current prices, year ending 30 June)

Expenditure on the Gross Domestic Product

	2010/11	2011/12	2012/13*
Government final consumption expenditure	460.9	512.9	569.3
Private final consumption expenditure	5,969.4	6,900.0	7,812.2
Gross capital formation	2,003.8	2,436.9	2,786.1
Statistical discrepancy	226.9	153.4	58.0
Total domestic expenditure	8,661.0	10,003.2	11,225.6
Exports of goods and services	1,824.5	2,127.5	2,371.1
Less Imports of goods and services	2,518.4	2,949.2	3,216.7
GDP in purchasers' values	7,967.0	9,181.4	10,379.9
GDP at constant 1995/96 prices	3,850.5	4,090.5	4,337.2

Gross Domestic Product by Economic Activity

	2010/11	2011/12	2012/13*
Agriculture and forestry	1,135.8	1,257.5	1,369.9
Fishing	270.0	310.0	356.7
Mining and quarrying	90.6	104.5	124.1
Manufacturing	1,355.5	1,557.5	1,760.3
Electricity, gas and water	82.1	96.0	111.7
Construction	639.8	766.3	899.8
Wholesale and retail trade	1,159.6	1,306.8	1,434.9
Hotels and restaurants	60.0	71.4	82.5
Transport, storage and communications	854.6	1,018.1	1,187.5
Finance and insurance	144.8	175.8	205.3
Real estate, renting and business services	503.4	589.5	656.5
Public administration and defence	223.8	253.2	284.3
Education	213.1	240.9	279.4
Health and social work	175.8	205.7	235.8
Other community, social and personal services	778.8	914.9	1,041.0
Sub-total	7,687.7	8,868.1	10,029.7
Import duties	279.3	313.3	350.2
GDP in purchasers' values	7,967.0	9,181.4	10,379.9

* Provisional figures.

BALANCE OF PAYMENTS
(US $ million)

	2010	2011	2012
Exports of goods	19,209.4	24,537.2	24,915.9
Imports of goods	–25,081.6	–32,607.4	–32,289.7
Balance on goods	–5,872.2	–8,070.2	–7,373.8
Exports of services	2,445.1	2,452.9	2,676.9
Imports of services	–4,389.2	–5,270.7	–5,370.5
Balance on goods and services	–7,816.3	–10,888.0	–10,067.5
Primary income received	109.6	154.7	171.1
Primary income paid	–1,566.7	–1,674.6	–1,949.3
Balance on goods, services and primary income	–9,273.4	–12,407.9	–11,845.7
Secondary income received	11,740.6	12,727.2	14,772.1
Secondary income paid	–361.3	–484.3	–278.8
Current balance	2,105.9	–164.9	2,647.6
Capital account (net)	603.4	512.4	420.2
Direct investment assets	–1.5	–3.3	–1.1
Direct investment liabilities	918.2	1,137.9	1,178.4
Portfolio investment assets	–824.5	22.5	–318.0
Portfolio investment liabilities	166.0	98.2	214.3
Other investment assets	–2,683.2	–2,299.0	–3,945.8
Other investment liabilities	787.2	64.5	3,759.4
Net errors and omissions	–51.6	–1,182.2	–441.2
Reserves and related items	1,019.7	–1,813.9	3,513.9

Source: IMF, *International Financial Statistics*.

FOREIGN ECONOMIC ASSISTANCE DISBURSEMENTS
(US $ million, year ending 30 June)

	2006/07	2007/08	2008/09
Bilateral donors			
Canada	18	42	19
Denmark	50	33	22
Germany	20	30	64
Japan	32	89	103
Kuwait	—	55	32
Norway	47	—	—
Sweden	57	42	25
United Kingdom	69	128	132
USA	62	15	—
Multilateral donors			
Asian Development Bank	342	448	618
International Development Association	680	796	508
European Union	66	70	33
UN System	85	178	143
UNICEF	30	52	78
Total (incl. others)	1,631	2,063	1,847

Total Foreign Economic Assistance Disbursements (US $ million, year ending 30 June): 2,228 in 2009/10; 1,777 in 2010/11 (Source: Ministry of Finance (Economic Relations Division), Dhaka).

2011/12 (US $ million, year ending 30 June): *Bilateral donors* Canada 5; China, People's Republic 112; Denmark 45; Germany 43; Japan 248; Korea, Republic 60; Kuwait 13; Sweden 34; United Kingdom 137. *Multilateral donors* Asian Development Bank 461; International Development Association 621; UN System 142; UNICEF 59; Total (incl. others) 2,126 (Source: Ministry of Finance (Economic Relations Division), Dhaka).

External Trade

PRINCIPAL COMMODITIES
(US $ million, year ending 30 June)

Imports c.i.f.	2010/11	2011/12	2012/13*
Food grains	1,911	902	722
Edible oil	1,067	1,644	1,402
Petroleum products	3,221	3,922	3,621
Chemicals	1,254	1,210	1,302
Plastics, rubber and articles thereof	1,302	1,366	1,366
Cotton	2,689	2,084	2,006
Yarn	1,391	1,384	1,355
Textiles	2,680	3,021	3,273
Iron and steel	2,004	2,224	2,335
Machinery	2,325	2,005	1,835
Total (incl. others)†	33,658	35,516	33,969

Exports f.o.b.	2010/11	2011/12	2012/13*
Raw jute	357	266	230
Jute goods (excl. carpets)	758	701	801
Leather and leather products	298	330	399
Frozen shrimp and fish	611	578	513
Ready-made garments	8,432	9,603	11,040
Knitwear and hosiery products	9,482	9,486	10,476
Total (incl. others)‡	22,928	24,302	27,018

* Provisional figures.

† Figures include imports from Export Processing Zones (EPZs): 2,140 in 2010/11; 2,114 in 2011/12; 2,505 in 2012/13.

‡ Figures include exports from Export Processing Zones (EPZs): 2,801 in 2010/11; 3,426 in 2011/12; 3,829 in 2012/13.

Source: Bangladesh Bank.

PRINCIPAL TRADING PARTNERS
(US $ million)

Imports c.i.f.	2010	2011	2012
China, People's Republic	4,681	6,575	7,103
Hong Kong	868	744	737
India	3,860	4,870	4,862
Indonesia	753	1,051	1,019
Japan	1,163	1,431	1,344
Korea, Republic	965	1,334	1,488
Kuwait	857	1,332	1,192
Malaysia	1,316	1,766	1,693
Singapore	1,493	1,431	1,771
Thailand	755	1,140	754
Total (incl. others)	27,813	36,193	36,363

Exports f.o.b.	2010	2011	2012
Belgium	353	596	500
Canada	553	783	805
France	998	1,451	1,142
Germany	2,075	3,251	2,870
India	307	n.a.	n.a.
Italy	561	870	750
Netherlands	890	832	587
Spain	507	836	907
United Kingdom	1,244	1,982	1,918
USA	3,247	3,824	3,834
Total (incl. others)	16,497	23,100	22,937

Note: Data reflect the IMF's direction of trade methodology, and, as a result, the totals may not be equal to those presented for trade in commodities.

Source: Asian Development Bank.

Transport

RAILWAYS
(traffic, year ending 30 June)

	2009/10	2010/11	2011/12*
Passengers ('000)	65,627	63,536	66,139
Passenger-km (million)	7,305	8,052	8,787
Freight ('000 metric tons)	2,714	2,554	2,192
Freight ton-km (million)	710	685	582

* Provisional figures.

Source: Bangladesh Railway.

ROAD TRAFFIC
(motor vehicles in use at 31 December)

	2008	2009	2010
Passenger cars	177,638	281,706	310,436
Buses and coaches	71,264	72,768	74,3412
Lorries and vans	138,512	71,505	81,561
Motorcycles and mopeds	768,121	868,165	975,682

Source: IRF, *World Road Statistics*.

SHIPPING

Flag Registered Fleet
(at 31 December)

	2011	2012	2013
Number of vessels	179	180	196
Total displacement ('000 grt)	1,227.8	1,283.5	1,381.8

Source: Lloyd's List Intelligence (www.lloydslistintelligence.com).

International Sea-borne Freight Traffic
('000 metric tons, year ending 30 June)

	2008	2009	2010
Total goods loaded	924	4,056	4,656
Total goods unloaded	18,012	31,944	38,604

Source: UN, *Monthly Bulletin of Statistics*.

CIVIL AVIATION
(traffic on scheduled services)

	2010	2011
Kilometres flown (million)	37	40
Passengers carried ('000)	2,237	2,487
Passenger-km (million)	4,931	5,195
Total ton-km (million)	568	589

Source: UN, *Statistical Yearbook*.

Passengers carried ('000): 2,430.0 in 2012 (Source: World Bank, World Development Indicators database).

Tourism

TOURIST ARRIVALS BY COUNTRY OF NATIONALITY

	2005	2006	2007
Canada	4,519	5,085	10,573
China, People's Republic	6,892	6,955	11,825
India	86,231	60,516	78,568
Japan	6,269	4,370	5,851
Korea, Republic	5,332	4,135	6,020
Malaysia	1,045	2,671	6,408
Nepal	3,378	3,422	4,537
Pakistan	5,671	6,680	12,224
United Kingdom	27,292	37,136	51,314
USA	13,422	16,516	34,638
Total (incl. others)	207,662	200,311	289,110

Tourism receipts (US $ million, excl. passenger transport): 81 in 2010; 87 in 2011; 110 in 2012 (provisional).

Total tourist arrivals ('000): 267 in 2009; 303 in 2010.

Source: World Tourism Organization.

Communications Media

	2010	2011	2012
Telephones ('000 main lines in use)	1,280.8	977.7	961.6
Mobile cellular telephones ('000 subscribers)	67,923.9	84,368.7	97,180.0
Internet users ('000)	940.0	1,150.0	n.a.
Broadband subscribers ('000)	413.0	468.5	516.6

Source: International Telecommunication Union.

Education

(2011/12 unless otherwise indicated)

	Institutions	Teachers	Students
Primary schools*	89,712	403,800	18,432,499
Secondary schools†	21,015	262,213	8,197,004
Universities (government)†‡	25	8,534	71,178

* 2010/11.

† Estimates.

‡ Includes three public and private Islamic universities, but excludes one medical, one veterinary and nine science and technology universities. In addition there were 67 private universities.

Technical and vocational institutes (2004/05): 2,728 institutions, 18,185 teachers, 241,336 students.

Source: Ministry of Education.

Pupil-teacher ratio (primary education, UNESCO estimate): 40.2 in 2010/11 (Source: UNESCO Institute for Statistics).

Adult literacy rate (UNESCO estimates): 57.7% (males 62.0%; females 53.4%) in 2011 (Source: UNESCO Institute for Statistics).

Directory

The Government

HEAD OF STATE

President: Mohammed Abdul Hamid (elected unopposed by members of Parliament 22 April 2013).

Office of the President (Bangabhaban): Motijheel, Dhaka 1222; internet www.bangabhaban.gov.bd.

COUNCIL OF MINISTERS

(April 2014)

The Council of Ministers is formed by the Bangladesh Awami League (AL), the Jatiya Party (JP), the Jatiya Samajtantrik Dal (JSD) and the Workers' Party of Bangladesh (WP).

Prime Minister and Minister of the Armed Forces Division, the Cabinet Division, Defence, and Public Administration: Sheikh Hasina Wajed (AL).

Minister of Foreign Affairs: Abul Hasan Mahmood Ali (AL).

Minister of Finance: A. M. A. Muhith (AL).

Minister of Industries: Amir Hossain Amu (AL).

Minister of Commerce: Tofail Ahmed (AL).

Minister of Agriculture: Matia Chowdhury (AL).

Minister of Post and Telecommunications, and of Information and Communication Technology: Abdul Latif Siddiqui (AL).

Minister of Health and Family Welfare: Mohammad Nasim (AL).

Minister of Local Government, Rural Development and Cooperatives: Syed Ashraful Islam (AL).

Minister of Expatriates' Welfare and Overseas Employment, and of Labour and Employment: Khandker Mosharraf Hossain (AL).

Minister of Civil Aviation and Tourism: Rashed Khan Menon (WP).

Minister of Religious Affairs: Principal Matior Rahman (AL).

Minister of Housing and Public Works: Mosharraf Hossain (AL).

Minister of Liberation War Affairs: A. K. M. Mozammel Huq (AL).

Minister of Fisheries and Livestock: Mohammed Sayedul Haque (AL).

Minister of Textiles and Jute: Md Emaz Uddin Pramanik (AL).

Minister of Communications: Obaidul Quader (AL).

Minister of Information: Hasanul Haq Inu (JSD).

Minister of Water Resources: Anisul Islam Mahmud (JP).

Minister of Environment and Forests: Anwar Hussain (AL).

Minister of Education: Nurul Islam Nahid (AL).

Minister of Shipping: Shahjahan Khan (AL).

Minister of Law, Justice and Parliamentary Affairs: Anisul Haque (AL).

Minister of Disaster Management and Relief: Mofazzal Hossain Chowdhury Maya (AL).

Minister of Railways: Mujibul Hoque (AL).

Minister of Planning: A. H. M. Mustafa Kamal (AL).

Minister of Primary and Mass Education: Dr Mostafizur Rahman (AL).

Minister of Cultural Affairs: Asaduzzaman Noor (AL).

Minister of Social Welfare: Syed Mohsin Ali (AL).

Minister of Land: Shamsur Rahman Sherif (AL).

Minister of Food: Md Kamrul Islam (AL).

Special Envoy to the Prime Minister: Hussain Muhammad Ershad (JP).

In addition, there were 18 Ministers of State, two Deputy Ministers and five cabinet-level Advisers to the Prime Minister.

MINISTRIES

Prime Minister's Office: Old Sangsad Bhaban, Tejgaon, Dhaka 1215; tel. (2) 8151159; fax (2) 8113244; e-mail info@pmo.gov.bd; internet www.pmo.gov.bd.

Ministry of Agriculture: Bangladesh Secretariat, Bhaban 4, Dhaka 1000; tel. (2) 7169277; fax (2) 7171555; e-mail minister@moa.gov.bd; internet www.moa.gov.bd.

Ministry of Chittagong Hill Tracts Affairs: Bangladesh Secretariat, Bhaban 4, Dhaka 1000; tel. (2) 9540044; fax (2) 9565300; e-mail minister@mochta.gov.bd; internet www.mochta.gov.bd.

Ministry of Civil Aviation and Tourism: Bangladesh Secretariat, Bhaban 6, 19th Floor, Dhaka 1000; tel. (2) 9545835; fax (2) 9515499; e-mail info@mocat.gov.bd; internet www.mocat.gov.bd.

Ministry of Commerce: Bangladesh Secretariat, Bhaban 3, Dhaka 1000; tel. (2) 7169687; fax (2) 7167999; e-mail minister@mincom.gov.bd; internet www.mincom.gov.bd.

Ministry of Communications: Bangladesh Secretariat, Bhaban 7, 8th Floor, Dhaka 1000; tel. (2) 9511122; fax (2) 9553900; e-mail info@moc.gov.bd; internet www.moc.gov.bd.

Ministry of Cultural Affairs: Bangladesh Secretariat, Bhaban 6, 10th Floor, Dhaka 1000; tel. (2) 9570667; fax (2) 7169008; e-mail sas-moca@mailcity.com; internet www.moca.gov.bd.

Ministry of Defence: Gonobhaban Complex, Sher-e-Bangla Nagar, Dhaka 1207; tel. (2) 9110111; fax (2) 8117985; e-mail modgob@bttb.net.bd; internet www.mod.gov.bd.

Ministry of Disaster Management and Relief: 92 and 93 Mohakhali C/A, Dhaka 1212; tel. (2) 8858755; fax (2) 8851615; e-mail info@dmb.gov.bd; internet www.dmb.gov.bd.

Ministry of Education: Bangladesh Secretariat, Bhaban 6, 17th–18th Floors, Dhaka 1000; tel. (2) 9576679; fax (2) 9514114; e-mail info@moedu.gov.bd; internet www.moedu.gov.bd.

Ministry of Environment and Forests: Bangladesh Secretariat, Bhaban 6, 13th Floor, Chamber 1307, Dhaka 1000; tel. (2) 9545166; fax (2) 9540210; e-mail secretary@moef.gov.bd; internet www.moef.gov.bd.

Ministry of Expatriates' Welfare and Overseas Employment: 71 and 72 Old Elephant Rd, Eskaton Garden, Dhaka; tel. (2) 7263753; fax (2) 7171622; e-mail secretary@probashi.gov.bd; internet probashi.gov.bd.

Ministry of Finance: Bangladesh Secretariat, Bhaban 7, 3rd Floor, Dhaka 1000; tel. (2) 9512201; fax (2) 9180788; e-mail fkabir@finance.gov.bd; internet www.mof.gov.bd.

Ministry of Fisheries and Livestock: Bangladesh Secretariat, Bhaban 6, 5th and 14th Floors, Dhaka 1000; tel. (2) 7164700; fax (2) 7161117; e-mail secmofl@gmail.com; internet www.mofl.gov.bd.

Ministry of Food: Bangladesh Secretariat, Bhaban 4, Dhaka 1000; tel. (2) 9540121; fax (2) 9514678; e-mail info@mofood.gov.bd; internet www.mofood.gov.bd.

Ministry of Foreign Affairs: Segunbagicha, Dhaka 1000; tel. (2) 9556020; fax (2) 9562188; e-mail ict1@mofa.gov.bd; internet www.mofa.gov.bd.

Ministry of Health and Family Welfare: Bangladesh Secretariat, Bhaban 3, Dhaka 1000; tel. (2) 9574490; fax (2) 9559216; e-mail sasadmin2@mohfw.gov.bd; internet www.mohfw.gov.bd.

Ministry of Home Affairs: Bangladesh Secretariat, Bhaban 8, Dhaka 1000; tel. (2) 7169076; fax (2) 7164788; e-mail info@mha.gov.bd; internet www.mha.gov.bd.

Ministry of Housing and Public Works: Bangladesh Secretariat, Bhaban 5, Dhaka 1000; tel. (2) 9540465; fax (2) 9571984; e-mail secretary@mohpw.gov.bd; internet www.mohpw.gov.bd.

Ministry of Industries: Shilpa Bhaban, 91 Motijheel C/A, Dhaka 1000; tel. (2) 9567024; fax (2) 9563553; e-mail indsecy@moind.gov.bd; internet www.moind.gov.bd.

Ministry of Information: Bangladesh Secretariat, Bhaban 4, 8th Floor, Dhaka 1000; tel. (2) 9576618; fax (2) 9576617; e-mail secretary@moi.gov.bd; internet www.moi.gov.bd.

Ministry of Posts, Telecommunications and Information Technology: BANSDOC Bhaban, E-14/X, Sher-e-Bangla Nagar, Dhaka 1207; tel. (2) 8181547; fax (2) 8181565; e-mail secretary@moict.gov.bd; internet www.ictd.gov.bd.

Ministry of Labour and Employment: Bangladesh Secretariat, Bhaban 7, 5th Floor, Dhaka 1000; tel. (2) 9575587; fax (2) 9575583; e-mail info@mole.gov.bd; internet www.mole.gov.bd.

Ministry of Land: Bangladesh Secretariat, Bhaban 4, 3rd Floor, Dhaka 1000; tel. (2) 7169644; fax (2) 7162989; e-mail min-mol@bdonline.com; internet www.minland.gov.bd.

Ministry of Law, Justice and Parliamentary Affairs: Bangladesh Secretariat, Bhaban 4, 7th Floor, Dhaka 1000; tel. (2) 7164693; e-mail info@minlaw.gov.bd; internet www.minlaw.gov.bd.

Ministry of Liberation War Affairs: Transport Pool Bhaban, Secretariat Link Rd, Dhaka; tel. (2) 9550149; fax (2) 9550127; e-mail info.molwa@yahoo.com; internet www.molwa.gov.bd.

Ministry of Local Government, Rural Development and Co-operatives: Bangladesh Secretariat, Bhaban 7, 6th and 7th Floors, Dhaka 1000; tel. (2) 7169179; fax (2) 7169176; e-mail info@lgd.gov.bd; internet www.lgd.gov.bd.

Ministry of Planning: Block No. 7, Sher-e-Bangla Nagar, Dhaka 1207; fax (2) 8117581; e-mail info@plandiv.gov.bd; internet www.plandiv.gov.bd.

Ministry of Posts, Telecommunications and Information Technology: BANSDOC Bhaban, E-14/X, Sher-e-Bangla Nagar, Dhaka 1207; tel. (2) 8181547; fax (2) 8181565; e-mail secretary@moict.gov.bd; internet www.ictd.gov.bd.

Ministry of Post and Telecommunications: Bangladesh Secretariat, Bhaban 7, Dhaka 1000; tel. (2) 7168689; fax (2) 7166670; e-mail info@mopt.gov.bd; internet www.mopt.gov.bd.

Ministry of Power, Energy and Mineral Resources: Bidyut Bhaban, 10th Floor, 1 Abdul Gani Rd, Dhaka 1000; tel. (2) 9551261; fax (2) 9572097; e-mail info@powerdivision.gov.bd; internet www.powerdivision.gov.bd.

Ministry of Primary and Mass Education: Bangladesh Secretariat, Bhaban 6, Dhaka 1000; tel. (2) 9515548; fax (2) 9576690; e-mail jsadmn@mopme.gov.bd; internet www.mopme.gov.bd.

Ministry of Public Administration: Bangladesh Secretariat, Bhaban 1, Dhaka 1000; tel. (2) 9540485; fax (2) 9540592; e-mail info@mopa.gov.bd; internet www.mopa.gov.bd.

Ministry of Railways: Rail Bhaban, 16 Abdul Gani Rd, Dhaka 1000; tel. (2) 9564139; internet www.railway.gov.bd.

Ministry of Religious Affairs: Bangladesh Secretariat, Bhaban 8, Dhaka 1000; tel. (2) 9514533; fax (2) 9511116; e-mail info@mora.gov.bd; internet www.mora.gov.bd.

Ministry of Science and Technology: Bangladesh Secretariat, Bhaban 6, 9th Floor, Dhaka 1000; tel. (2) 7170840; fax (2) 9576538; e-mail section16@most.gov.bd; internet www.most.gov.bd.

Ministry of Shipping: Bangladesh Secretariat, Bhaban 6, 8th Floor, Dhaka 1000; tel. (2) 9576770; fax (2) 915529; e-mail sec@mos.gov.bd; internet www.mos.gov.bd.

Ministry of Social Welfare: Bangladesh Secretariat, Bhaban 6, 3rd Floor, Dhaka 1000; tel. (2) 7160452; fax (2) 7168969; e-mail sec@msw.gov.bd; internet www.msw.gov.bd.

Ministry of Textiles and Jute: Bangladesh Secretariat, Bhaban 6, 7th and 11th Floors, Dhaka 1000; tel. (2) 7167266; fax (2) 9540766; e-mail sectext@gmail.com; internet www.motj.gov.bd.

Ministry of Water Resources: Bangladesh Secretariat, Bhaban 6, Dhaka 1000; tel. (2) 9512221; fax (2) 9573805; e-mail secretary@mowr.gov.bd; internet www.mowr.gov.bd.

Ministry of Women and Children's Affairs: Bangladesh Secretariat, Bhaban 6, 4th Floor, Dhaka 1000; tel. (2) 7160568; fax (2) 7162892; e-mail mowcanews@gmail.com; internet www.mowca.gov.bd.

Ministry of Youth and Sports: Bangladesh Secretariat, Bhaban 7, Dhaka 1000; tel. (2) 9575506; fax (2) 9585725; e-mail ds.admin@moysports.gov.bd; internet www.moysports.gov.bd.

Legislature

PARLIAMENT
(Jatiya Sangsad)

Bangladesh Parliament: Bangladesh Parliament Secretariat, Dhaka; tel. (2) 9129039; fax (2) 9143504; e-mail pdspo.bdparliament@gmail.com; internet www.parliament.gov.bd.

Speaker: SHIRIN SHARMIN CHAUDHURY.

Deputy Speaker: FAZLE RABBI.

General Election, 5 January 2014, provisional results

	Seats*
Bangladesh Awami League (AL)	231
Jatiya Party	34
Workers' Party of Bangladesh	6
Jatiya Samajtantrik Dal	5
Jatiya Party (Manju)	2
Bangladesh Tarikat Federation	2
Bangladesh Nationalist Front	1
Independents	16
Undecided	3
Total	300

The election was boycotted by an opposition alliance led by the Bangladesh Nationalist Party: 153 seats were uncontested, and members of the AL or its allies were declared elected unopposed in those constituencies

* In addition to the 300 directly elected members, a further 50 seats are reserved for women members.

Election Commission

Bangladesh Election Commission: Block 5/6, Election Commission Secretariat, Sher-e-Bangla Nagar, Dhaka 1207; tel. (2) 9111491; fax (2) 8119819; e-mail becs.info@gmail.com; internet www.ecs.gov.bd; f. 1972; independent; commrs appointed by the President; Chief Election Commr KAZI RAKIBUDDIN AHMAD.

Political Organizations

Bangladesh Awami League (AL): 23 Bangabandhu Ave, Dhaka; tel. (2) 9677881; fax (2) 8621155; e-mail alparty1949@gmail.com; internet www.albd.org; f. 1949; supports parliamentary democracy; advocates socialist economy, but with a private sector, and a secular state; pro-Indian; 28-member central executive committee, 15-member central advisory committee and a 13-member presidium; Pres. Sheikh HASINA WAJED; Gen. Sec. SYED ASHRAFUL ISLAM; c. 1,025,000 mems.

Bangladesh Islami Front: 205/5, Fakirapool, Culvert Rd, Dhaka 1000; fax (2) 9355737; Chair. Allama al-Haj M. A. MANNAN; Gen. Sec. al-Haj M. A. MATIN.

Bangladesh Jamaat-e-Islami (BJI): 505 Elephant Rd, Bara Moghbazar, Dhaka 1217; tel. (2) 933123; fax (2) 831299; e-mail info@jamaat-e-islami.org; internet www.jamaat-e-islami.org; f. 1941; fmrly known as Jamaat-e-Islami Bangladesh; renamed as above in 2008; Islamist party striving to establish an Islamic state through the democratic process; mem. of the BNP-led opposition alliance; Chair. MAQBUL AHMAD (acting); Sec.-Gen. Dr SHAFIQUR RAHMAN (acting).

Bangladesh Jatiya Party (BJP): 50 DIT Extension Rd, Eastern-view, 5th Floor, Naya Paltan, Dhaka 1000; tel. (2) 8317634; fax (2) 8319694; f. 1999 as breakaway faction of Jatiya Party; Chair. ANDALIB RAHMAN PARTHO; Gen. Sec. SHAMIM AL MAMUN.

Bangladesh Kalyan Dal (Bangladesh Welfare Party): House 325, Rd 22, DOHS Mohakhali, Dhaka 1206; tel. (2) 9555864; e-mail info@bkp-bd.org; internet www.bkp-bd.org; f. 2007; Chair. Maj.-Gen. (retd) SYED MUHAMMAD IBRAHIM; Gen. Sec. MOHANNAD ABDUL MALEK CHOUDHURY.

Bangladesh Khelafat Andolon (Bangladesh Caliphate Movement): 314/2 J. N. Saha Rd, Lalbagh Kellar Morr, Dhaka 1211; tel. (2) 8612465; fax (2) 8653249; e-mail khelafat@dhaka.net; internet bangladeshkhelafatandolan.blogspot.com; f. 1981; Supreme Leader Maulana SHAH AHMADULLAH ASHRAF IBN HAFEZZEE HUZUR; Sec.-Gen. Maulana MUHAMMAD ZAFRULLAH KHAN.

Bangladesh Khelafat Majlis: 59/3/3 Purana Paltan, 5th Floor, Dhaka 1000; tel. (2) 9553693; fax (2) 9569002; e-mail info@bangladeshkhelafatmajlis.org; internet www.bangladeshkhelafatmajlis.org; f. 1989; movement for an Islamic state of Bangladesh; Ameer HABIBUR RAHMAN; Gen. Sec. MOHAMMAD HUMAYUN KABIR.

Bangladesh Nationalist Party (BNP): 28/1 Naya Paltan, VIP Rd, Dhaka 1000; tel. (2) 8351929; fax (2) 8318678; e-mail bnpbd@e-fsbd.net; f. 1978 by merger of groups supporting Ziaur Rahman, including Jatiyatabadi Gonotantrik Dal (Jagodal—Nationalist Democratic Party); right of centre; favours multi-party democracy and parliamentary system of govt; Chair. Begum KHALEDA ZIA; Sr Vice-Chair. TARIQUE RAHMAN; Sec.-Gen. MIRZA FAKHRUL ISLAM ALAMGIR (acting).

Bangladesh Samajtantrik Dal (Socialist Party of Bangladesh—SPB): 23/2 Topkhana Rd, 3rd Floor, Shahbagh, Dhaka 1000; tel. (2) 9852206; fax (2) 9554772; e-mail mail@spb.org.bd; internet www.spb.org.bd; f. 1980; Gen. Sec. Comrade KHALEQUZZAMAN.

Bangladesh Tariqat Federation: 1/4, Block A, Section 1, Protishthanik Elaka, Mirpur Housing Estate, Dhaka 1212; tel. (2) 8362622; fax (2) 9349134; e-mail tariqatfederation@yahoo.com; f. 2005; Chair. al-Haj SYED NAJIBUL BASHAR MAIZBHANDARI; Gen. Sec. M. A AWAL.

Bikalpa Dhara Bangladesh (BDB): House 19, Rd 12, Block K, Baridhara, Dhaka 1212; tel. (2) 8855252; fax (2) 9890978; e-mail bchowdhury@dbn-bd.net; f. 2004; Pres. Prof. A. Q .M. BADRUDDOZA CHOWDHURY; Sec.-Gen. Major (retd) ABDUL MANNAN.

Communist Party of Bangladesh (CPB): 'Mukti Bhaban', 2 Comrade Moni Singh Rd, Purana Paltan, Dhaka 1000; tel. (2) 9558612; fax (2) 9552333; e-mail info@cpb.org.bd; internet www.cpb.org.bd; f. 1968 following split from Communist Party of Pakistan; Pres. MUJAHIDUL ISLAM SELIM; Gen. Sec. SYED ABU ZAFAR AHMED; c. 22,000 mems.

Gono Forum (People's Forum): Eden Complex, 2/1A Arambagh, Dhaka 1000; tel. (2) 7194899; fax (2) 7193991; f. 1993; Pres. Dr KAMAL HOSSAIN; Gen. Sec. MUSTAFA MOHSIN.

Gono Front: 24/1/A, Topkhana Rd, Dhaka 1000; tel. (2) 9551332; fax (2) 9567757; f. 1979; Chair. MOHAMMAD ZAKIR HOSSAIN; Gen. Sec. AHMED ALI SHEIKH.

Gonotantrik Party: 79, Kakryle, Mayakanan, 3rd Floor, Dhaka 1000; tel. (2) 9330584; fax (2) 8114820; e-mail gonotantri@gmail.com; Pres. MOHAMMAD AFZAL; Gen. Sec. NURUR RAHMAN SELIM.

Islami Andolan Bangladesh (IAB): 55B Purana Paltan, 3rd Floor, Dhaka 1000; tel. (2) 9567130; internet www.islamiandolanbd.org; Ameer Maulana Mufti SYED MOHAMMAD REZAUL KARIM; Gen. Sec. HAFEZ MAULANA YUNUS AHMAD.

Islami Oikya Jote (Islamic Unity Front—IOJ): 57 Kazi Riyazuddin Rd, Lalbagh, Dhaka 1211; tel. (2) 8631490; mem. of the BNP-led alliance; Chair. Maulana MOHAMMAD ABDUL LATIF NEZAMI; Gen. Sec. MUFTI FAIZULLAH.

Islamic Front Bangladesh: 60A Purana Paltan, 4th Floor, Dhaka 1000; tel. (2) 9565524; fax (2) 9565524; e-mail islamicfront@gmail.com; Chair. SYED BAHADUR SHAH MUJADDEDI; Gen. Sec. ABUL BASHAR MOHAMMAD ZAINUL ABEDIN (ZUBAIR).

Jamiat-e-Ulema-e-Islam Bangladesh: 116/2 Naya Paltan, 4th Floor, Culvert Rd, Dhaka 1000; e-mail jamiateulama1919@gmail.com; Chair. Hazrat Maulana SHEIKH ABDUL MOMIN; Gen. Sec. Maulana Mufti MUHAMMAD WAKKAS.

Jatiya Gonotantrik Party: Rd 1, House 2, Asad Gate Rd, Mohammad, Dhaka 1207; Leader SHAFIUL ALAM PRADHAN; Gen. Sec. KHANDKAR LUTFAR REHMAN.

Jatiya Party (National Party): 75E, Rajni Gandha 17A, Banani, Dhaka 1213; tel. (2) 9571658; fax (2) 8813433; e-mail ershad@dhaka.agni.com; internet www.jatiyo-party.org; f. 1983 as Jana Dal; reorg. 1986, following merger with the four other parties of the pro-Ershad National Front; advocates nationalism, democracy, Islamic ideals and progress; Chair. Lt-Gen. HOSSAIN MOHAMMAD ERSHAD; Sec.-Gen. ZIAUDDIN AHMED BABLU.

Jatiya Samajtantrik Dal (JSD): 35–36 Bangobondhu Ave, Dhaka 1000; tel. (2) 9559972; fax (2) 9559972; e-mail jsd@dhaka.net; f. 1972; Pres. HASANUL HAQ INU; Gen. Sec. SHARIF NURUL AMBIA.

Jatiya Samajtantrik Dal (Rab): 65 Bangobondhu Ave, 4th Floor, Dhaka 1000; tel. (2) 9560300; fax (2) 9562668; e-mail amr.reforms@yahoo.com; f. 2002; Pres. A. S. M. ABDUR RAB; Gen. Sec. ABDUL MALEK RATAN.

Khelafat Majlis: 16 Bijoy Nagar, Dhaka 1000; tel. (2) 9349907; fax (2) 8314747; Ameer Maulana MOHAMMAD IS-HAQUE; Gen. Sec. AHMAD ABDUL KADER.

Krishak Sramik Janata League (KSJL) (Peasants' and Workers' People's Party): 80 Motijheel Banijjyik Elaka, Dhaka; tel. (2) 8114393; fax (2) 8114761; f. 1999; Pres. Bangabir KADER SIDDIQUI; Gen. Sec. HABIBUR RAHMAN TALUKDAR.

Liberal Democratic Party (LDP): 102 Park Rd, New DOHS, Mohakhali, Dhaka 1206; tel. (2) 8752166; fax (2) 8752633; e-mail dr.oliahmad@gmail.com; internet www.ldp-bangladesh.com; f. 2006; comprises several former members of BNP; split into two factions June 2007; Pres. Col (retd) OLI AHMAD; Sec.-Gen. Redwan AHMED.

National Awami Party—Bangladesh (NAP): 85 Naya Paltan, 5th Floor, Masjid Gali, Dhaka 1000; tel. (2) 8836271; fax (2) 8836273; e-mail bd_nap@yahoo.com; f. 1957; Maoist; Pres. JEBEL RAHMAN GANI; Gen. Sec. M. GULAM MOSTAFA BHUIYAN.

National Awami Party—Muzaffar (NAP—M): 20–21 Dhanmandi Hawkers' Market, 2nd Floor, Dhaka 1205; tel. (2) 9669948; f. 1957; reorg. 1967; Pres. MUZAFFAR AHMED; Sec.-Gen. ENAMUL HAQUE; c. 500,000 mems.

National People's Party (NPP): 106 Kakrail Rd, Dhaka 1000; tel. (2) 9361174; f. 2007; Chair. Sheikh SHAWKAT HOSSAIN NILU; Gen. Sec. FARIDDUZAMAN FARHAD.

Workers' Party of Bangladesh: 31F, Topkhana Rd, Dhaka 1000; tel. (2) 9567975; fax (2) 9558545; e-mail wpartybd@bangla.net; f. 1980; Pres. RASHED KHAN MENON; Gen. Sec. ANISUR RAHMAN MALLICK.

Zaker Party: House 19, Rd 3, Block I, Banani, Gulshan, Dhaka 1213; tel. (2) 9895510; fax (2) 9895478; f. 1989; supports sovereignty and the introduction of an Islamic state system; Chair. Peerzada al-Haj MOSTAFA AMIR FAISAL MUJADDEDI; Gen. Sec. MUNSI ABDUL LATIF.

Diplomatic Representation

EMBASSIES AND HIGH COMMISSIONS IN BANGLADESH

Afghanistan: House CWN(C) 2A, 24 Gulshan Ave, Gulshan Model Town, Dhaka 1212; tel. (2) 9895994; fax (2) 9884767; e-mail afghanembdk@dhaka.net; Ambassador ABDUL RAHIM QRAZ.

Australia: 184 Gulshan Ave, Gulshan 2, Dhaka 1212; tel. (2) 8813105; fax (2) 8811125; e-mail ahc.dhaka@dfat.gov.au; internet www.bangladesh.embassy.gov.au; High Commissioner GREG WILCOCK.

Bhutan: House 12, Rd 107, Gulshan 2, Dhaka 1212; tel. (2) 8826863; fax (2) 8823939; e-mail bhtemb@bdmail.net; Ambassador PEMA CHODEN.

Brunei: House 26, Rd 6, Baridhara, Dhaka 1212; tel. (2) 8819552; fax (2) 8819551; e-mail dhaka.bangladesh@mfa.gov.bn; High Commissioner Pengiran Haji ABDUL HARIS Pengiran Haji SHABUDIN.

Canada: United Nations Rd, Baridhara, Dhaka 1212; tel. (2) 8851111; fax (2) 8851139; e-mail dhaka@international.gc.ca; internet www.international.gc.ca/bangladesh; High Commissioner HEATHER CRUDEN.

China, People's Republic: Plots 2 and 4, Embassy Rd, Block 1, Baridhara, Dhaka; tel. (2) 9887923; fax (2) 8823004; e-mail chinaemb_bd@mfa.gov.cn; internet bd.china-embassy.org; Ambassador LI JUN.

Denmark: House 1, Rd 51, Gulshan Model Town, POB 2056, Dhaka 1212; tel. (2) 8821799; fax (2) 8823638; e-mail dacamb@um.dk; internet www.ambdhaka.um.dk; Ambassador HANNE FUGL ESKJÆR.

Egypt: House 9, Rd 90, Gulshan 2, Dhaka 1212; tel. (2) 8858737; fax (2) 8858747; e-mail egypt.emb.dhaka@mfa.gov.eg; internet www.mfa.gov.eg/dhaka_emb; Ambassador MAHMOUD EZZAT.

France: House 18, Rd 108, Gulshan, Dhaka; tel. (2) 8813811; fax (2) 8813612; e-mail admin-etrangers.dacca-amba@diplomatie.gouv.fr; internet www.ambafrance-bd.org; Ambassador MICHEL TRINQUIER.

Germany: 178 Gulshan Ave, Gulshan 2, POB 6126, Dhaka 1212; tel. (2) 9853521; fax (2) 9853260; internet www.dhaka.diplo.de; Ambassador ALBRECHT CONZE.

Holy See: United Nations Rd 2, Diplomatic Enclave, Baridhara Model Town, Gulshan, POB 6003, Dhaka 1212; tel. (2) 8822018; fax (2) 8823574; e-mail nuntius@dhaka.net; Apostolic Nuncio GEORGE KOCHERRY.

India: House 2, Rd 142, Gulshan-I, Dhaka; tel. (2) 9889339; fax (2) 9893050; e-mail hc@hcidhaka.org; internet www.hcidhaka.org; High Commissioner PANKAJ SARAN.

Indonesia: Plot No. 14, Rd 53, Gulshan 2, Dhaka 1212; tel. (2) 8812260; fax (2) 8825391; e-mail contactus@indonesia-dhaka.org; internet www.indonesia-dhaka.org; Ambassador IWAN WIRANTAATMADJA.

Iran: House No. 13A, Rd 75, Gulshan 2, Dhaka 1212; tel. (2) 8825896; fax (2) 8828780; e-mail iranembassydhaka@persiabd.com; internet dhaka.mfa.ir; Ambassador (vacant).

Italy: Plot 2/3, Rd 74/79, Gulshan 2, POB 6062, Dhaka 1212; tel. (2) 8822781; fax (2) 8822578; e-mail amb.dhaka@esteri.it; internet www.ambdhaka.esteri.it; Ambassador GIORGIO GUGLIELMINO.

Japan: 5 and 7, Dutabash Rd, Baridhara, Dhaka 1212; tel. (2) 8810087; fax (2) 8826737; e-mail eojbd@dc.mofa.go.jp; internet www.bd.emb-japan.go.jp; Ambassador SHIRO SADOSHIMA.

Korea, Democratic People's Republic: House 5A, Rd 54, Gulshan 2, Dhaka; tel. (2) 8811893; fax (2) 8810813; Ambassador SIN HONG CHOL.

Korea, Republic: 4 Madani Ave, Diplomatic Enclave, Baridhara, Dhaka 1212; tel. (2) 8812088; fax (2) 8823871; e-mail embdhaka@mofat.go.kr; internet bgd.mofat.go.kr; Ambassador LEE YUN-YOUNG.

Kuwait: Plot 39, Rd 23, Block J, Banani, Dhaka 1213; tel. (2) 8822700; fax (2) 8823753; e-mail dhaka@mofa.gov.kw; Ambassador AHMAD IBRAHIM AL-DHUFAIRI.

Libya: 4 CWN (C), Gulshan Ave (N), Gulshan Model Town, Dhaka 1212; tel. (2) 9895808; fax (2) 8823417; Chargé d'affaires Kamel AL-MAHJOUB.

Malaysia: House 19, Rd 6, Baridhara Diplomatic Enclave, Dhaka 1212; tel. (2) 8827759; fax (2) 8823115; e-mail maldhaka@kln.gov.my; internet www.kln.gov.my/perwakilan/dhaka; High Commissioner NORLIN BINTI OTHMAN.

Maldives: House 45, United Nations Rd, Baridhara, Dhaka 1212; tel. (2) 9882199; fax (2) 9899986; e-mail admin@maldiveshighcommission.org.bd; High Commissioner (vacant).

Morocco: House 44, United Nations Rd, POB 6112, Baridhara, Dhaka 1212; tel. (2) 8823176; fax (2) 8810018; e-mail sifmadac@citech-bd.net; Ambassador MOHAMMED HOURORO.

Myanmar: House 3, Block NE(L), Rd 84, Gulshan 2, Dhaka 1212; tel. (2) 9888903; fax (2) 8823740; e-mail mynembdk@dhaka.net; Ambassador MYO MYINT THAN.

Nepal: United Nations Rd, Rd 2, Diplomatic Enclave, Baridhara, Dhaka; tel. (2) 9892490; fax (2) 8826401; e-mail eondhaka@dhaka.net; internet www.nepembassy-dhaka.org; Ambassador HARI KUMAR SHRESHTHA.

Netherlands: House 49, Rd 90, Gulshan 2, POB 166, Dhaka; tel. (2) 8822715; fax (2) 8823326; e-mail dha@minbuza.nl; internet bangladesh.nlembassy.org; Ambassador GERBEN DE JONG.

Norway: House 9, Rd 111, Gulshan, Dhaka 1212; tel. (2) 8816276; fax (2) 8823661; e-mail emb.dhaka@mfa.no; internet www.norway.org.bd; Ambassador RAGNE BIRTE LUND.

Pakistan: House NE(C) 2, Rd 71, Gulshan 2, Dhaka 1212; tel. (2) 8825388; fax (2) 8850673; e-mail pahicdhaka76@gmail.com; internet www.mofa.gov.pk/bangladesh; High Commissioner AFRASIAB MEHDI HASHMI.

Philippines: House 17, Rd 7, Baridhara, Dhaka 1212; tel. (2) 9881590; fax (2) 8823686; e-mail philemb2@aknetbd.com; internet www.philembassydhaka.org; Ambassador VICENTE VIVENCIO T. BANDILLO.

Qatar: House 1, Rd 79/81, Gulshan 2, Dhaka 1212; tel. (2) 8823346; fax (2) 9896071; e-mail dhaka@mofa.gov.qa; Ambassador ABDULLAH ABDULAZIZ MOHAMED AL MANA.

Russia: NE(J) 9, Rd 79, Gulshan 2, Dhaka 1212; tel. (2) 9884847; fax (2) 9863285; e-mail rusembbd@gmail.com; internet www.bangladesh.mid.ru; Ambassador ALEXANDER NIKOLAEV.

Saudi Arabia: House 5 (NE) L, Rd 83, Gulshan 2, Dhaka 1212; tel. (2) 8829333; fax (2) 8823616; e-mail bdemb@mofa.gov.sa; internet embassies.mofa.gov.sa/sites/bangladesh/AR/Pages/default.aspx; Ambassador ABDULLAH BIN NASSER AL-BUSSAIRI.

Sri Lanka: House 4B, Rd 118, Gulshan Model Town, Dhaka 1212; tel. (2) 9896353; fax (2) 8823971; e-mail slhc@citec-bd.com; internet www.slhcdhaka.org; High Commissioner W. A. SARATH K. WERAGODA.

Sweden: House 1, Rd 51, Gulshan, Dhaka 1212; tel. (2) 8852600; fax (2) 8823948; e-mail ambassaden.dhaka@gov.se; internet www.swedenabroad.com/dhaka; Ambassador ANNELI LINDAHL KENNY.

Switzerland: Bir Bikram Major Hafiz Sarak, House 31B, Rd 18, Banani, Dhaka 1213; tel. (2) 8812874; fax (2) 8823872; e-mail dha.vertretung@eda.admin.ch; internet www.eda.admin.ch/dhaka; Ambassador Dr CHRISTIAN FOTSCH.

Thailand: 18 & 20, Madani Ave, Baridhara, Dhaka 1212; tel. (2) 8812795; fax (2) 8854280; e-mail thaidac@mfa.go.th; internet www.thaidac.com; Ambassador MADURAPOCHANA ITTARONG.

Turkey: House 7, Rd 2, Baridhara, Dhaka 1212; tel. (2) 8822198; fax (2) 8823873; e-mail embassy.dhaka@mfa.gov.tr; internet dhaka.emb.mfa.gov.tr; Ambassador HÜSEYIN MÜFTÜOĞLU.

United Arab Emirates: House 41, Rd 113, Gulshan Model Town, POB 6014, Dhaka 1212; tel. (2) 9882244; fax (2) 8823225; e-mail dhaka@mofa.gov.ae; Ambassador KHALFAN BATTAL AL-MANSOURI.

United Kingdom: United Nations Rd, Baridhara, POB 6079, Dhaka 1212; tel. (2) 8822705; fax (2) 8823437; e-mail Dhaka.Press@fco.gov.uk; internet ukinbangladesh.fco.gov.uk; High Commissioner ROBERT WINNINGTON GIBSON.

USA: Madani Ave, Baridhara, POB 323, Dhaka 1212; tel. (2) 8855500; fax (2) 8823744; e-mail DhakaPA@state.gov; internet dhaka.usembassy.gov; Ambassador DAN W. MOZENA.

Viet Nam: Vintage Bldg, Plot 7, Rd 104, Gulshan 2, Dhaka 1212; tel. (2) 8854052; fax (2) 8854051; e-mail dhaka@mofa.gov.vn; internet www.vietnamembassy-bangladesh.org; Ambassador NGUYEN QUANG THUC.

Judicial System

A judiciary, comprising a Supreme Court with a High Court and an Appellate Division, is in operation. On 1 November 2007 the Government announced the formal separation of the judiciary from the executive.

Supreme Court: Ramna, Dhaka 1000; tel. (2) 433585; fax (2) 9565058; e-mail supremec@bdcom.com; internet www.supremecourt.gov.bd.

Chief Justice: MUZAMMEL HOSSAIN.

Office of the Attorney-General: Bangladesh Supreme Court, Dhaka 1000; tel. (2) 9562868; internet www.minlaw.gov.bd/attornygenarloffice.htm; Attorney-General MAHBUBEY ALAM.

Religion

The results of the 2004 census classified 89.5% of the population as Muslims (the majority of whom were of the Sunni sect), 9.6% as caste Hindus and scheduled castes, and the remainder as Buddhists, Christians, animists and others.

Freedom of religious worship is guaranteed under the Constitution, but, under the 1977 amendment to the Constitution, Islam was declared to be one of the nation's guiding principles and, under the 1988 amendment, Islam was established as the state religion. However, in 2011 a constitutional amendment restored secularism as a fundamental principle of the nation, while Islam was retained as the state religion.

ISLAM

Islamic Foundation Bangladesh: Agargaon, Sher-e-Bangla Nagar, Dhaka 1207; tel. (2) 8181516; fax (2) 9144235; e-mail islamicfoundationbd@yahoo.com; internet www.islamicfoundation.org.bd; f. 1975; supervised by the Ministry of Religious Affairs; Dir-Gen. SHAMIM MOHAMMAD AFZAL.

BUDDHISM

World Fellowship of Buddhists Regional Centre: Dharmarajik Buddhist Monastery, Atish Dipanker Sarak, Basabo, Dhaka 1214; tel. (2) 7205665; fax (2) 7202503; f. 1962; Pres. Ven. SUDDHANANDA MAHATHERO; Sec.-Gen. P. K. BARUYA.

CHRISTIANITY

Jatiyo Church Parishad (National Council of Churches): 395 New Eskaton Rd, Dhaka; tel. (2) 9332869; fax (2) 8312996; e-mail nccb@bangla.net; internet www.ncc-b.org; f. 1949 as East Pakistan Christian Council; 4 mem. churches; Pres. PAUL S. SARKER; Gen. Sec. DAVID A. DAS.

Church of Bangladesh—United Church

After Bangladesh achieved independence, the Diocese of Dacca (Dhaka) of the Church of Pakistan (f. 1970 by the union of Anglicans, Methodists, Presbyterians and Lutherans) became the autonomous Church of Bangladesh. In 2001 the Church had an estimated 14,000 members. In 1990 a second diocese, the Diocese of Kushtia, was established.

Church of Bangladesh: 54/1 Barobag, Mirpur 2, Dhaka 1216; tel. (2) 8020876; e-mail sarkerps@gmail.com; internet www.churchofbangladesh.org; Moderator Rt Rev. PAUL SARKAR.

Bishop of Dhaka: Rt Rev. PAUL S. SARKER.

Bishop of Kushtia: Rt Rev. SAMUEL SUNIL MANKHIN.

The Roman Catholic Church

For ecclesiastical purposes, Bangladesh comprises one archdiocese and five dioceses. At 31 December 2007 there were an estimated 318,603 adherents in the country.

Catholic Bishops' Conference of Bangladesh (CBCB): 24C Asad Avenue, Mohammadpur, Dhaka 1207; tel. (2) 9123108; fax (2) 9127339; e-mail cbcbsec@dhaka.net; internet www.cbcbsec.org; f. 1971; Pres. Most Rev. PATRICK D'ROZARIO (Archbishop of Dhaka).

Secretariat: CBCB Centre, 24C Asad Ave, Mohammadpur, Dhaka 1207; tel. and fax (2) 9127339; e-mail cbcbsg@bdonline.com; Sec.-Gen. Rt Rev. THEOTONIUS GOMES (Titular Bishop of Zucchabar).

Archbishop of Dhaka: Most Rev. PATRICK D'ROZARIO; Archbishop's House, 1 Kakrail Rd, Ramna, POB 3, Dhaka 1000; tel. (2) 9358247; e-mail abpcosta@bangla.net.

Other Christian Churches

Bangladesh Baptist Sangha: 33 Senpara Parbatta, POB 8018, Mirpur 10, Dhaka 1216; tel. (2) 802967; fax (2) 803556; e-mail bbsangha@bdmail.net; f. 1922; 35,150 mems (2004); Pres. Dr JOYANTO ADHIKARI; Gen. Sec. MILTON BISWAS.

Bangladesh Evangelical Lutheran Church: POB 6, Lutheran Mission, Auliapur, Dinajpur 5200; e-mail bnelc_din@yahoo.com.

Bangladesh Lutheran Church: Jogdal Mission, Birganj, District Dinjapur 5220; tel. (531) 89152; e-mail blcmiss@btcl.net.bd; Moderator Rev. AROBINDU BORMON.

In 2002 there were about 51 denominational churches active in the country, including the Bogra Christian Church, the Evangelical Christian Church, the Garo Baptist Union, the Reformed Church of Bangladesh and the Sylhet Presbyterian Synod. The Baptist Sangha was the largest Protestant Church.

HINDUISM

Bangladesh Hindu Kalyan Trust (Hindu Religious Welfare Trust): 1/I, Paribag, Shahbagh, Dhaka; tel. (2) 9677449; fax (2) 9677894; e-mail hindutrustbd@ymail.com; internet www.hindutrust.gov.bd; f. 1983; administered by the Ministry of Religious Affairs; Chair. SHAHJAHAN MIA.

Bangladesh Jatio Hindu Mohajote (Bangladesh National Hindu Grand Alliance): Ram Shita Complex, 1st floor, 19 Jaykali Mondir Rd, Dhaka 1000; e-mail info@hindumohajote.org; internet www.hindumohajote.org; f. 2006; promotes social and political rights of Hindus; Pres. SHAMOL KUMAR ROY; Sec.-Gen. GOBINDO CHANDRA PRAMANIK.

The Press

PRINCIPAL DAILIES

Bengali

Amar Desh: BSEC Bhaban, 102 Kazi Nazrul Islam Ave, Karwan Bazar, Dhaka 1215; tel. (2) 8159575; e-mail info@amardeshonline.com; internet www.amardeshonline.com; f. 2004; Editor MAHMUDUR RAHMAN (acting); circ. 200,000.

Bangladesh Protidin: 371A, Block D, Bashundhara Residential Area, Baridhara, Dhaka; tel. (2) 8402361; fax (2) 8402364; e-mail ibdpratidin@gmail.com; internet www.bd-pratidin.com; Editor NAEEM NIZAM.

Daily Inqilab: 2/1 Ramkrishna Mission Rd, Dhaka 1203; tel. (2) 7122771; fax (2) 9552881; e-mail inqilab08@dhaka.net; internet www.dailyinqilab.com; Editor A. M. M. BAHAUDDIN; circ. 180,025.

Daily Jugantor: 12/7, North Kamalpur, Dhaka 1217; tel. (2) 8419211; fax (2) 8419218; e-mail info@jugantor.com; internet www.jugantor.com; Editor SALMA ISLAM.

Daily Kaler Kantho: Bashundhara R/A, Plot 371/A, Block D, Baridhara, Dhaka 1229; tel. (2) 8402372; fax (2) 8402368; e-mail info@kalerkantho.com; internet www.dailykalerkantho.com; f. 2010; current affairs, sports and entertainment; Editor IMDADUL HAQ MILON (acting).

Daily Naya Diganta: 167/2E, Inner Circular Rd, Motijheel, Dhaka 1000; tel. (2) 7191017; fax (2) 7101877; e-mail info@dailynayadiganta.com; internet www.dailynayadiganta.com; f. 2004; Editor ALAMGIR MOHIUDDIN.

Daily Sangbad: 36 Purana Paltan, Dhaka 1000; tel. (2) 9567557; fax (2) 9558900; e-mail sangbaddesk@gmail.com; internet www.sangbad.com.bd; Editor ALTAMASH KABIR; circ. 77,109.

Dainik Azadi: 9 CDA. C/A, Momin Rd, Chittagong; tel. (31) 612380; e-mail info@dainikazadi.net; internet www.dainikazadi.org; f. 1960; Editor M. A. MALEK; circ. 13,000.

Dainik Bhorer Kagoj: Karnaphuli Media Point, 3rd Floor, 70 Shahid Sangbadik Selina Parveen Sarak (New Circular Rd, Malibagh), Dhaka 1217; tel. (2) 9360285; fax (2) 9362734; e-mail info@bhorerkagoj.net; internet www.bhorerkagoj.net; Editor SHYAMAL DUTTA; circ. 50,000.

Dainik Ittefaq: 40 Kawran Bazar, Dhaka 1215; tel. (2) 7122660; fax (2) 7554974; e-mail dailyittefaq@yahoo.com; internet new.ittefaq.com.bd; f. 1953; Editor ANWAR HOSSAIN; circ. 200,000.

Dainik Jahan: 3/B Shehra Rd, Mymensingh; e-mail dainikjahan@gmail.com; f. 1980; Chief Editor HABIBUR RAHMAN SHEIKH; circ. 4,000.

Dainik Janakantha (Daily People's Voice): Janakantha Bhaban, 24/A New Eskaton Rd, POB 3380, Dhaka 1000; tel. (2) 9347780; fax (2) 9351317; e-mail news@dailyjanakantha.com; internet www.dailyjanakantha.com; f. 1993; Editor MD ATIKULLAH KHAN MASUD; circ. 100,000.

Dainik Janata: Khalil Mansion, 3rd, 5th and 6th Floors, 149/A DIT Extension Ave, Dhaka 1000; tel. (2) 8311068; fax (2) 8314174; e-mail info@dailyjanatabd.com; internet www.dailyjanatabd.com; Editor AHSAN ULLAH.

Dainik Karatoa: Chalkjadu Rd, Bogra 5800; tel. (51) 63660; fax (51) 60422; e-mail dkaratoa@yahoo.com; internet www.karatoa.com.bd; f. 1976; Editor MOZAMMEL HAQUE LALU; circ. 44,000.

Dainik Khabar: 260/C Tejgaon I/A, Dhaka 1208; e-mail khabar@dekko.net.bd; f. 1985; Editor MIZANUR RAHMAN MIZAN; circ. 18,000.

Dainik Purbanchal: Purbanchal House, 38 Iqbal Nagar, Mosque Lane, Khulna 9100; tel. (41) 722251; fax (41) 721013; e-mail liakat@purbanchal.com; internet www.purbanchal.com; f. 1974; Man. Editor FERDOUSI ALI; Editor Al-Haj LIAKAT ALI; circ. 46,000.

Dainik Sangram: 423 Elephant Rd, Magh Bazar, Dhaka 1217; tel. (2) 9346448; fax (2) 9337127; e-mail dsangram@gmail.com; internet www.dailysangram.com; f. 1970; Chair. ALI AHSAN MUHAMMAD MUJAHID; Editor ABUL ASAD; circ. 50,000.

Jaijaidin: Jaijaidin Mediaplex, Love Rd, Tejgaon Industrial Area, Dhaka 1208; tel. (2) 8832222; fax (2) 8832233; e-mail admin@jjdbd.com; internet www.jjdin.com; f. 1984; Chief Editor SAID HUSSAIN CHOWDHURY; circ. 100,000.

Manab Zamin (Human Land): 149 Tejgaon Industrial Area, Dhaka 1208; tel. (2) 8189160; fax (2) 8128313; internet www.mzamin.com; f. 1998; tabloid; Editor MEHBOOBA CHOUDHURY.

Prothom Alo: C. A. Bhaban, 100 Kazi Nazrul Islam Ave, Karwan Bazar, Dhaka 1215; tel. (2) 8110081; fax (2) 9130496; e-mail info@prothom-alo.com; internet www.prothom-alo.com; f. 1998; publ. by MediaStar Ltd; Editor MATIUR RAHMAN.

Shamokal: 136 Tejgaon Industrial Area, Dhaka 1208; tel. (2) 8870179; fax (2) 8870191; e-mail info@samakal.com.bd; internet www.shamokal.com; Editor GOLAM SARWAR.

English

The Bangladesh Today: Concord Royal Court, 4th Floor, Plot No. 275G, Dhanmondi R/A, Dhaka 1209; tel. (2) 9118807; fax (2) 9127103; e-mail editor@thebangladeshtoday.com; internet www.thebangladeshtoday.com; Editor SYED SAJJAD AHMED.

Daily Star: 64–65 Kazi Nazrul Islam Ave, POB 3257, Dhaka 1215; tel. (2) 9102973; fax (2) 8125155; e-mail editor@thedailystar.net; internet www.thedailystar.net; f. 1991; Publr and Editor MAHFUZ ANAM; circ. 40,000 (weekdays), 60,000 (weekends).

Daily Sun: East West Media Group Ltd, 371/A, Block D, Bashundhara R/A, Dhaka 1229; tel. (2) 8402046; fax (2) 8402096; e-mail editor@daily-sun.com; internet www.daily-sun.com; f. 2010; owned by the Bashundhara Group; Editor Dr SYED ANWAR HUSAIN.

Daily Tribune: 38 Iqbal Nagar Mosque Lane, Khulna 9100; tel. (41) 721944; fax (41) 721013; e-mail ferdousi@purbanchal.com; f. 1978; morning; Editor FERDOUSI ALI; circ. 24,000.

Dhaka Tribune: FR Tower, 8/C Panthpath, Shukrabad, Dhaka 1207; tel. (2) 9132093; internet www.dhakatribune.com; f. 2013; Editor ZAFAR SOBHAN.

Financial Express: Tropicana Tower, 4th Floor, 45 Topkhana Road, POB 2526, Dhaka 1000; tel. (2) 9568154; fax (2) 9567049; e-mail editor@thefinancialexpress-bd.com; internet www.thefinancialexpress-bd.com; f. 1993; Editor MOAZZEM HOSSAIN.

The Independent: BEL Tower, 5th and 6th Floors, 19 Dhanmondi, Rd No. 1, Dhaka 1205; tel. (2) 9672091; fax (2) 8629785; e-mail editor@bol-online.com; internet www.theindependent-bd.com; f. 1995; Editor MAHBUBUL ALAM.

New Age: Holiday Bldg, 30 Tejgaon Industrial Area, Dhaka 1208; tel. (2) 8153034; fax (2) 8153033; e-mail newagebd@global-bd.net; internet newagebd.com/newspaper1; f. 2003; Editor NURUL KABIR.

New Nation: 1 Ramkrishna Mission Rd, Dhaka 1203; tel. (2) 7122654; fax (2) 7122650; e-mail n_editor@bangla.net; internet thenewnationbd.com; f. 1981; privately owned; Editor MOSTAFA KAMAL MAJUMDER; circ. 15,000.

The News Today: Shah Ali Tower, 3rd Floor, 33 Karwan Bazar, Dhaka 1215; tel. (2) 9111395; fax (2) 9140721; e-mail newstoday@dhaka.net; internet www.newstoday.com.bd; Editor REAZUDDIN AHMED.

People's View: 253 Nazir Ahmed Chowdhury Rd, Chittagong; tel. (31) 2854333; fax (31) 2854577; e-mail editor@peoples-view.net; internet www.peoples-view.net; f. 1969; Chief Editor NAZIMUDDIN MOSTAN; circ. 3,000.

PERIODICALS

Bengali

Ajker Surjodoy: 212 Shahid Syed Najrul Islam Sarani, 2nd Floor, Bijoy Nagar, Dhaka; tel. (2) 9557360; fax (2) 9567757; f. 1991; weekly; news; Editor KHANDAKER MOZAMMEL HAQUE.

Amod: Chowdhury Para, Comilla 3500; tel. (81) 65193; e-mail bakin_302002@yahoo.com; internet www.weeklyamod.com; f. 1955; weekly; Editor SHAMSUN NAHAR RABBI; circ. 10,000.

Bank Parikrama: Bangladesh Institute of Bank Management, Plot 4, Main Road 1 (South), Mirpur 2, Dhaka 1216; fax (2) 9006756; e-mail office@bibm.org.bd; internet www.bibm-bd.org; banking and finance; quarterly.

Bartaman Sanglap: Jyoti Bhavan, Section 6, Block C, Rd 13, Plot 5, Pallabi, Mirpur, Dhaka 1216; tel. (2) 9002663; e-mail sanglap@bartamansanglap.com; internet www.bartamansanglap.com; weekly; news and culture; Editor SHEIKH ABDUL HANIF.

Begum: 66 Loyal St, Dhaka 1; tel. (2) 7390681; f. 1947; women's illustrated weekly; Editor NURJAHAN BEGUM; circ. 25,000.

Computer Jagat: House 29, Rd 6, Dhanmondi, Dhaka 1205; tel. (2) 8610445; fax (2) 9664723; e-mail jagat@comjagat.com; internet www.comjagat.com; monthly; computers and IT; Editor GOLAP MUNIR.

Kali O Kalam: Bengal Center, Plot No. 2, New Airport Rd, Khilkhet, Dhaka 1229; e-mail mail@kaliokalam.com; internet www.kaliokalam.com; f. 1927; monthly; focus on literature and arts; Editor ABUL HASNAT.

Muktibani: 28 A/3, Toyenbee Circular Rd, Motijheel C/A, Dhaka 1000; tel. (2) 9553522; e-mail muktibani@yahoo.com; f. 1972; Editor NIZAM UDDIN AHMED; circ. 35,000.

Natun Katha: 31E Topkhana Rd, Dhaka; weekly; Editor HAJERA SULTANA; circ. 4,000.

Parjatan Bichitra: M. R. Centre, 7th Floor, House 49, Rd 17, Banani C/A, Dhaka 1213; tel. (2) 8829692; fax (2) 8829809; e-mail info@parjatanbichitra.com; internet www.parjatanbichitra.com; monthly; tourism, wildlife and travel magazine; Editor MOHIUDDIN HELAL.

Protirodh: Ansar and VDP Headquarters, Khilgaon, Dhaka 1219; tel. (2) 7214937; e-mail editor_protirod@ansarvdp.gov.bd; internet www.ansarvdp.gov.bd; f. 1977; fortnightly; publ. of the Bangladesh Ansar and Village Defence Party; circ. 20,000.

Robbar: 1 Ramkrishna Mission Rd, Dhaka; tel. and fax (2) 7122660; f. 1978; weekly; Exec. Editor KAMAL HOSSAIN BABLU; circ. 25,000.

Sachitra Bangladesh: 112 Circuit House Rd, Dhaka 1000; tel. (2) 9333149; internet www.dfp.gov.bd; f. 1979; weekly publ. of the Dept of Films and Publs, Ministry of Information; fortnightly; Editor ROKASANA AKTER.

Sachitra Sandhani: Dhaka; f. 1978; weekly; Editor GAZI SHAHABUDDIN MAHMUD; circ. 13,000.

Shaptahik 2000: 52 Motijheel C/A, Dhaka 1000; tel. (2) 9350951; internet www.shaptahik-2000.com; f. 1998; weekly; entertainment and news; Editor MOINUL AHSAN SABER.

Shaptahik Ekhon: Dhaka; internet www.weeklyekhon.com; weekly; Editor ATAUS SAMAD.

Shishu: Bangladesh Shishu Academy, Old High Court Compound, Dhaka 1000; tel. (2) 9564128; e-mail shishubsa@yahoo.com; internet www.shishuacademy.gov.bd/pub_bok_mn.htm; f. 1977; children's monthly; Exec. Editor SHUJAN BIKASH BARUA; circ. 5,000.

Sonar Bangla: 423 Elephant Rd, Magh Bazar, Dhaka 1217; tel. (2) 8319065; fax (2) 8315571; e-mail weeklysonarbangla@yahoo.com; internet www.weeklysonarbangla.net; f. 1961; Editor MUHAMMED QAMARUZZAMAN; circ. 25,000.

Tarokalok: 622 Boro Moghbazar, Romna, Dhaka; tel. (2) 9668326; fax (2) 8614330; e-mail tarokalok_bd@yahoo.com; fortnightly; Editor IBRAHIM KHALIL KHOKON.

Weekly Ekota: Dhaka; e-mail info@cpb.org.bd; internet www.cpb.org.bd/Ekota.htm; f. 1970; weekly; organ of the Communist Party of Bangladesh; Editor AFROZA NAHAR.

English

Bangladesh Gazette: Bangladesh Government Press, Tejgaon, Dhaka; tel. (2) 9117415; e-mail info@bgpress.gov.bd; internet www.bgpress.gov.bd; f. 1947; name changed 1972; weekly; official notices; Editor MASUM KHAN.

The Bangladesh Monitor: City Heart, 9th Floor, 67 Naya Paltan, Dhaka 1000; tel. (2) 8351148; fax (2) 8314306; e-mail info@bangladeshmonitor.net; internet www.bangladeshmonitor.net; f. 1991; fortnightly; aviation and tourism; Editor KAZI WAHIDUL ALAM.

Bangladesh Quarterly: Department of Films and Publications, 112 Circuit House Rd, Dhaka 1000; internet www.dfp.gov.bd; current affairs and history; Chief Editor KAMRUN NAHAR.

Dhaka Courier: Cosmos Centre, 69/1 New Circular Rd, Malibagh, Dhaka 1217; e-mail info@dhakacourier.com.bd; internet www.dhakacourier.com.bd; f. 1984; weekly; Editor ENAYETULLAH KHAN.

First News: House 52, Road 7/A, Dhanmondi R/A, Dhaka 1207; tel. (2) 8191485; fax (2) 8191484; e-mail firstnews@dhaka.net; internet www.firstnewsmagazine.com; f. 2010; Editor MOHAMMAD BADRUL AHSAN.

Holiday: Holiday Bldg, 30 Tejgaon Industrial Area, Dhaka 1208; tel. (2) 9122950; fax (2) 9127927; e-mail holiday@bangla.net; internet www.weeklyholiday.net; f. 1965; weekly; independent; Editor SAYED KAMALUDDIN; circ. 18,000.

Weekly Blitz: Eastern Commercial Complex, 3rd Floor, Suite 308, 73 Kakrail, Dhaka 1000; tel. 1191350884 (mobile); e-mail ediblitz@yahoo.com; internet www.weeklyblitz.net; f. 2003; weekly (Wednesdays); Publr and Editor SALAH UDDIN SHOAIB CHOUDHURY; circ. 39,000.

NEWS AGENCIES

Bangladesh Sangbad Sangstha (BSS) (Bangladesh News Agency): 68/2 Purana Paltan, Dhaka 1000; tel. (2) 9555036; fax (2) 9568970; e-mail bssadmin@bssnews.org; internet www.bssnews.net; f. 1972; Man. Dir and Chief Editor IHSANUL KARIM HELAL; Man. Editor AZIZUL ISLAM BHUIYAN.

United News of Bangladesh (UNB): Cosmos Centre, 69/1 New Circular Rd, Malibagh, Dhaka 1217; tel. (2) 9345543; fax (2) 9344556; e-mail unb_news@yahoo.com; internet www.unbnews.org; f. 1988; independent; Chair. AMANULLAH KHAN.

PRESS ASSOCIATIONS

Bangladesh Press Council: 40 Topkhana Rd, Dhaka 1000; tel. and fax (2) 7172049; e-mail info@presscouncilbd.com; internet presscouncil.gov.bd; f. 1974; established under an act of Parliament to preserve the freedom of the press and maintain and develop standards of newspapers and news agencies; Chair. Justice B. K. DAS.

Bangladesh Sangbadpatra Press Sramik Federation (Newspaper Press Workers' Federation): 1 Ramkrishna Mission Rd, Dhaka 1203; f. 1960; Pres. M. ABDUL KARIM; Sec.-Gen. BOZLUR RAHMAN MILON.

Dhaka Union of Journalists: National Press Club, Dhaka 1000; f. 1947; Pres. ABDUS SHAHEED.

Newspaper Owners' Association of Bangladesh (NOAB): c/o The Independent, Beximco Media Complex, 149—150 Tejgaon I/A, Dhaka 1208; tel. (2) 9672091; f. 2002; promotes interests of the newspaper industry; Pres. MAHBUBUL ALAM.

Overseas Correspondents' Association of Bangladesh (OCAB): 18 Topkhana Rd, Dhaka 1000; tel. (2) 7215388; e-mail naweed@bdonline.com; f. 1979; Pres. ZAHIDUZZMAN FARUQUE; Gen. Sec. SHAMIM AHMED; 60 mems.

Press Institute of Bangladesh: 3 Circuit House Rd, Dhaka 1000; tel. (2) 9330081; fax (2) 8317458; e-mail dgpib@yahoo.com; internet www.pib.gov.bd; f. 1976; trains journalists, conducts research, operates a newspaper library and data bank; Chair. HABIBUR RAHMAN MILON.

Publishers

Academic Press and Publishing Library (APPL): 70/1 Prantik Apts, Rd 6, Dhanmondi 1209; tel. (2) 8125394; fax (2) 8117277; e-mail appl@dhaka.net; internet www.applbooks.com; f. 1982; social sciences and sociology; Chair. Dr MIZANUR RAHMAN SHELLEY.

Agamee Prakashani: 36 Bangla Bazar, Dhaka 1100; tel. (2) 7111332; fax (2) 7110021; e-mail info@agameeprakashani-bd.com; f. 1986; fiction and academic; CEO and Proprietor OSMAN GANI.

Ahmed Publishing House: 7 Zindabahar 1st Lane, Dhaka; tel. (2) 36492; f. 1942; literature, history, science, religion, children's, maps and charts; Man. Dir KAMALUDDIN AHMED; Man. MESBAHUDDIN AHMED.

Ankur Prakashani: 40/1 Purana Paltan, Dhaka 1000; tel. (2) 9564799; fax (2) 7410986; e-mail info@ankur-prakashani.com; internet www.ankur-prakashani.com; f. 1984; academic and general; Dir MESBAHUDDIN AHMED.

Ashrafia Library: 4 Hakim Habibur Rahman Rd, Chawk Bazar, Dhaka 1000; Islamic religious books, texts, and reference works of Islamic institutions.

Asiatic Society of Bangladesh: 5 Old Secretariat Rd, Nimtali, Ramna, Dhaka 1000; tel. (2) 7168940; fax (2) 7168853; e-mail info@asiaticsociety.org.bd; internet www.asiaticsociety.org.bd; f. 1952; periodicals on science, Bangla and humanities; Pres. Prof. SIRAJUL ISLAM.

Bangla Academy (National Academy of Arts and Letters of Bangladesh): Burdwan House, 3 Kazi Nazrul Islam Ave, Dhaka 1000; tel. (2) 8619577; fax (2) 8612352; e-mail bacademy@citechco.net; internet www.banglaacademy.org.bd; f. 1955; higher education textbooks in Bengali, books on language, literature and culture, language planning, popular science, drama, encyclopedias, translations of world classics, dictionaries; Dir-Gen. Prof. SHAMSUZZAMAN KHAN.

Bangladesh Books International Ltd: Ittefaq Bhaban, 1 Ramkrishna Mission Rd, POB 377, Dhaka; tel. (2) 256071; f. 1975; reference, academic, research, literary and children's books, in Bengali and English; Chair. MOINUL HOSSEIN; Man. Dir ABDUL HAFIZ.

Gatidhara: 38/2-Ka Bangla Bazar, POB 2723, Dhaka 1000; tel. (2) 7117515; fax (2) 7123472; e-mail gatidara@gmail.com; internet www.gatidhara.com; f. 1992; academic, general and fiction; Publr and Chief Exec. SIKDER ABUL BASHAR.

Gono Prakashani: House 14/E, Rd 6, Dhanmondhi R/A, Dhaka 1205; tel. (2) 8617208; fax (2) 8613567; e-mail gk@citechco.net; f. 1978; science and medicine; Man. Dir SHAFIQ KHAN; Editor BAZLUR RAHIM.

Muktadhara: 74 Farashganj, Dhaka 1100; tel. (2) 7111374; e-mail muktadhara1971@yahoo.com; f. 1971; educational and literary; Bengali and English; Dir JAHAR LAL SAHA; Man. Dir BIJALI PRAVA SAHA.

Mullick Brothers: 160–161 Dhaka New Market, Dhaka; tel. (2) 8619125; fax (2) 8610562; educational; Man. Dir KAMRUL HASAN MULLICK.

Prothoma Prokashoni: CA Bhaban, 100 Kazi Nazrul Islam Ave, Karwan Bazar, Dhaka 1215; tel. (2) 8110081; fax (2) 9130496; e-mail info@prothom-alo.info.

Shahitya Prakash: 87 Purana Paltan Line, Paltan Tower, 7th Floor, Dhaka 1000; tel. (2) 9355058; fax (2) 9559091; e-mail shahityap@gmail.com; f. 1970; Prin. Officer MOFIDUL HOQUE.

Somoy Prokashon: 38/2-Ka Bangla Bazar, Dhaka 1100; tel. (2) 7121652; e-mail somoy@somoy.com; internet www.somoy.com; publr of fiction, history and studies on arts and sciences; Dir FARID AHMED.

University Press Ltd: Red Crescent House, 61 Motijheel C/A, POB 2611, Dhaka 1000; tel. (2) 9565444; fax (2) 9565443; e-mail upl@btcl.net.bd; internet www.uplbooks.com.bd; f. 1975; educational, academic and general; Man. Dir MOHIUDDIN AHMED.

GOVERNMENT PUBLISHING HOUSES

Bangladesh Bureau of Statistics: Parishankhan Bhaban, E-27/A, Agargaon, Sher-e-Bangla Nagar, Dhaka 1207; tel. (2) 9112589; fax (2) 9111064; e-mail dg@bbs.gov.bd; internet www.bbs.gov.bd; f. 1971; statistical year book and pocket book, censuses, surveys, agricultural year book, special reports, etc.; Dir-Gen. MOHAMMAD SHAHJAHAN ALI MOLLAH.

Bangladesh Government Press: Tejgaon, Dhaka 1209; tel. (2) 9117415; fax (2) 8891250; e-mail info@bgpress.gov.bd; internet www.bgpress.gov.bd; f. 1972; Dir-Gen. A. L. M. ABDUR RAHMAN.

Department of Films and Publications: 112 Circuit House Rd, Dhaka 1000; tel. (2) 8331034; fax (2) 8331030; e-mail dfp_bd@yahoo.com; internet www.dfp.gov.bd; Dir-Gen. Dr MOHAMMAD JAHANGIR HOSSAIN.

Press Information Department: Bhaban 6, Bangladesh Secretariat, Dhaka 1000; tel. (2) 7161091; fax (2) 7165942; e-mail pid_1@bangla.net; internet www.bdpressinform.org; Prin. Information Officer HARUN UR-RASHID.

PUBLISHERS' ASSOCIATIONS

Bangladesh Publishers' and Booksellers' Association: 3 Liaquat Ave, 3rd Floor, Dhaka 1100; tel. (2) 7111666; f. 1972; Pres. ABU TAHER; 2,500 mems.

National Book Center of Bangladesh: 5C Bangabandhu Ave, Dhaka 1000; tel. (2) 9555745; e-mail info@nbc.org.bd; internet www.nbc.org.bd; f. 1963; est. to promote the cause of 'more, better and cheaper books'; organizes book fairs, publishes monthly journal; Dir RAFIQ AZAD.

Broadcasting and Communications

TELECOMMUNICATIONS

According to the Bangladesh Telecommunication Regulatory Commission, in mid-2013 there were over 104m. active mobile cellular telephone subscriptions and more than 35m. internet subscriptions.

Airtel Bangladesh Ltd: POB 3016, Dhaka; fax (2) 8951786; e-mail customerservice@bd.airtel.com; internet www.bd.airtel.com; fmrly Warid Telecom International; awarded licence to provide mobile cellular telephone services in 2005; service commenced in 2007; renamed as above following acquisition of a 70% stake by Bharti Airtel Ltd, India, in Jan. 2010; 7.1m. subscribers (Dec. 2012); CEO CHRIS TOBIT.

Bangladesh Telecommunications Co Ltd (BTCL): Central Office, Telejogajog Bhaban, 37/E Eskaton Garden, Dhaka 1000; tel. (2) 8311500; fax (2) 832577; e-mail md@btcl.net.bd; internet www.btcl.gov.bd; formed through division of Bangladesh Telegraph and Telephone Board in 2008; govt-owned provider of fixed-line telephone and internet services; Chair. SUNIL KANTI BOSE; Man. Dir ASHRAFUL ALIM.

GrameenPhone Ltd: GP House, Bashundhara, Baridhara, Dhaka 1229; tel. (2) 9882990; fax (2) 9882970; e-mail info@grameenphone.com; internet www.grameenphone.com; f. 1996 by Grameen Bank to expand cellular telephone service in rural areas; 55.8% owned by Telenor (Norway), 34.2% by Grameen Telecom Corpn and 10% by general retail and institutional investors; launched third generation (3G) mobile service in Sept. 2013; the leading telecommunications service provider in Bangladesh with more than 40.0m. subscribers (Dec. 2012); CEO TORE JOHNSEN.

Orascom Telecom Bangladesh Ltd (Banglalink): 4 Gulshan Ave, Gulshan Model Town, Dhaka 1212; tel. (2) 9885770; fax (2) 8827265; e-mail info@banglalinkgsm.com; internet www.banglalinkgsm.com; f. 1998; provides mobile cellular telephone services; 25.9m. subscribers (Dec. 2012); Man. Dir and CEO AHMED ABOU DOMA.

Pacific Bangladesh Telecom Ltd (Citycell): Pacific Centre, 14 Mohakhali C/A, Dhaka 1212; tel. (2) 8822186; fax (2) 8823575; e-mail customerservice@citycell.com; internet www.citycell.com; 1.5m. subscribers (Dec. 2012); CEO MEHBOOB CHOWDHURY.

Robi Axiata Ltd (Robi): 53 Gulshan Ave, Dhaka 1212; tel. (2) 9887146; fax (2) 9885463; e-mail info@axiata.com; internet www.robi.com.bd; f. 1996; jt venture between Axiata Group Berhad, Malaysia (70%) and NTT DoCoMo Inc, Japan (30%); mobile cellular telephone services; 21.0m. subscribers (Dec. 2012); Man. Dir and CEO MICHAEL KUEHNER.

Teletalk Bangladesh Ltd: 41 Rd 27, Blk A, Banani, Dhaka 1213; tel. (2) 8851060; fax (2) 9882828; e-mail info@teletalk.com.bd; internet www.teletalk.com.bd; f. 2004; govt-owned provider of mobile cellular telephone services; affiliated to Bangladesh Telecommunications Co; 1.7m. subscribers (Dec. 2012); Man. Dir MUHAMMAD MUJIBUR RAHMAN.

Regulatory Authority

Bangladesh Telecommunication Regulatory Commission (BTRC): IEB Bhaban, 5th, 6th and 7th Floors, Ramna, Dhaka 1000; tel. (2) 7162277; fax (2) 9556677; e-mail btrc@btrc.gov.bd; internet www.btrc.gov.bd; f. 2002; regulates the telecommunications sector; Chair. Maj.-Gen. (retd) ZIA AHMED; Sec. MUHAMMAD MAHBOOB AHMED.

BROADCASTING

Radio

ABC Radio: Dhaka Trade Centre, 3rd Floor, 99 Kazi Nazrul Islam Ave, Karwan Bazar, Dhaka 1215; tel. (2) 8142038; fax (2) 9128141; e-mail program@abcradiobd.fm; internet abcradiobd.fm; f. 2007; regular news bulletins, documentaries and talk shows; Bangla and English; CEO MOHAMMAD SANAULLAH.

Bangladesh Betar: 121 Kazi Nazrul Islam Ave, Shahabag, Dhaka 1000; tel. (2) 8651083; fax (2) 9662600; e-mail dgbetar@btcl.net.bd; internet www.betar.org.bd; f. 1939; govt-controlled; 12 regional stations broadcast a total of approximately 255 hours daily; external service broadcasts 8 transmissions daily in Arabic, Bengali, English, Hindi, Nepalese and Urdu; Dir-Gen. A. K. M. SHAMEEM CHOWDHURI.

Radio Aamar: Uniwave Broadcasting Co Ltd, Silver Tower, 12th Floor, 52 Gulshan Ave, Dhaka 1212; tel. (2) 9886800; internet www.radioaamar.com; f. 2007; bilingual news and Bangla music.

Radio Foorti: 10 Kazi Nazrul Islam Ave, 5th Floor, Jahangir Tower, Karwan Bazar, Dhaka 1215; tel. (2) 9125792; e-mail info@radiofoorti.fm; internet www.radiofoorti.fm; f. 2006; Bangla music; CEO DANIEL AFZALUR RAHMAN.

Radio Today: 34 Kamal Ataturk Ave, 13th and 19th Floors, Awal Centre, Banani, Dhaka 1213; tel. (2) 9820370; fax (2) 9820369; e-mail info@radiotodaybd.fm; internet www.radiotodaybd.fm; f. 2006; owned by Radio Broadcasting FM (Bangladesh) Co Ltd; contemporary music; Chair. MOHAMMAD MOZAMMEL HAQUE; Man. Dir MOHAMMAD RAFIQUL HAQUE.

Television

Bangladesh Television (BTV): Television House, Rampura, Dhaka 1219; tel. (2) 9330131; fax (2) 8312927; e-mail news@btt.net.bd; internet www.btv.gov.bd; f. 1964; govt-controlled; daily broadcasts on one channel from Dhaka station for 12 hours; transmissions also from nationwide network of 15 relay stations; Dir-Gen. KAZI ABU ZAFAR MOHAMMAD HASSAN SIDDIQUI; Gen. Man. MUHAMMAD MONWARUL ISLAM.

ATN Bangla: WASA Bhaban, 1st Floor, 98 Kazi Nazrul Islam Ave, Karwan Bazar, Dhaka 1215; tel. (2) 8111207; fax (2) 8111876; e-mail atn@dhaka.agni.com; internet www.atnbangla.tv; f. 1997; private satellite channel; broadcasts in Bengali; Chair. and Man. Dir MAHFUZUR RAHMAN.

Banglavision: Bir Uttam C. R. Dutta Rd, Dhaka 1205; tel. (2) 8653175; e-mail info@banglavision.tv; internet www.banglavision.tv; owned by Shamol Bangla Media Ltd; Chair. ABDUL HAQUE; Man. Dir AMINUL HUQ.

Desh Television Ltd: 70 Shaheed Sangbadik Selina Parveen Sarak Malibagh, Dhaka 1217; tel. (2) 8332958; fax (2) 8332981; e-mail web@desh.tv; internet www.desh.tv; f. 2009; private satellite channel; broadcasts in Bengali.

Ekushey Television: Jahangir Tower, 10 Karwan Bazar, Dhaka 1215; tel. (2) 8126535; fax (2) 8121270; e-mail info@ekushey-tv.com; internet www.ekushey-tv.com; private entertainment channel; broadcasts in Bengali; Chair. and CEO ABDUS SALAM.

Islamic TV: 34/1 Paribag, 3rd Floor, Sonargaon Rd, Hatirpul, Dhaka 1000; tel. (2) 8610769; fax (2) 8610866; e-mail info@islamictv.com.bd; internet www.islamictv.com.bd; f. 2007; programmes on Islamic doctrine, culture and news.

NTV Bangladesh: BSEC Bhaban, 6th Floor, 102 Kazi Nazrul Islam Ave, Karwan Bazar, Dhaka 1215; tel. (2) 9143381; fax (2) 9143386; e-mail info@ntvbd.com; internet www.ntvbd.com; f. 2003; private satellite channel; Chair. AL-HAJ MUHAMMAD MOSADDAK ALI.

Sangsad Bangladesh Television: 121 Kazi Nazrul Islam Ave, Dhaka 1000; tel. (2) 9330131; fax (2) 8312927; f. 2011; currently under the supervision of the Development Channel of Bangladesh Television (BTV); broadcasts foreign parliamentary proceedings and documentaries on legislative systems in other countries.

Finance

(cap. = capital; res = reserves; dep. = deposits; m. = million; brs = branches; amounts in taka)

BANKING

Central Bank

Bangladesh Bank: Motijheel C/A, POB 325, Dhaka 1000; tel. (2) 7126101; fax (2) 9566212; e-mail governor@bangla.net; internet www.bangladesh-bank.org; f. 1971; cap. 30m., res 93,546m., dep. 331,680m. (June 2009); Gov. ATIUR RAHMAN; 9 brs.

Nationalized Commercial Banks

Agrani Bank Ltd: 9D Dilkusha C/A, Dhaka 1000; tel. (2) 9566160; fax (2) 9562346; e-mail agrani@agranibank.org; internet www.agranibank.org; f. 1972; 100% state-owned; cap. 9,011.7m., res 11,952.6m., dep. 247,115m. (Dec. 2011); Chair. Dr KHONDOKER BAZLUL HOQUE; Man. Dir and CEO SYED ABDUL HAMID; 867 brs.

Janata Bank Ltd: 110 Motijheel C/A, POB 468, Dhaka 1000; tel. (2) 9552078; fax (2) 9564644; e-mail id-obd@janatabank-bd.com; internet www.janatabank-bd.com; f. 1972; 100% state-owned; cap. 8,125m., res 14,155.2m., dep. 358,632.5m. (Dec. 2011); CEO and Man. Dir S. M. AMINUR RAHMAN; 856 brs in Bangladesh, 4 brs in the UAE.

Rupali Bank Ltd: Rupali Bhaban, 34 Dilkusha C/A, POB 719, Dhaka 1000; tel. (2) 9551525; fax (2) 9564148; e-mail rblhocom@bdcom.com; internet www.rupalibank.org; f. 1972; cap. 1,375m., res 13,115.7m., dep. 105,896.5m. (Dec. 2011); scheduled for privatization; Chair. Dr AHMED AL-KABIR; Man. Dir M. FARID UDDIN; 492 brs.

Sonali Bank Ltd: 35–44 Motijheel C/A, POB 3130, Dhaka 1000; tel. (2) 9550426; fax (2) 9561410; e-mail sbhoid@bdmail.net; internet www.sonalibank.com.bd; f. 1972; 100% state-owned; cap. 11,250m., res 32,047.3m., dep. 523,911.2m. (Dec. 2011); Chair. QUAZI BAHARUL ISLAM; CEO and Man. Dir PRADIP KUMAR DATTAR; 1,189 brs incl. 2 overseas brs.

Private Commercial Banks

AB Bank Ltd: Head Office, BCIC Bhaban, 30–31 Dilkusha C/A, POB 3522, Dhaka 1000; tel. (2) 9560312; fax (2) 9555098; e-mail info@abbank.com.bd; internet www.abbank.com.bd; f. 1981; fmrly known as Arab Bangladesh Bank Ltd; name changed as above in 2007; 99.3% owned by Bangladesh nationals and 0.7% by Bangladesh Govt; cap. 3,686.1m., res 5,955.9m., dep. 125,271.8m. (Dec. 2011); Chair. M. WAHIDUL HAQUE; Pres. and Man. Dir M. FAZLUR RAHMAN; 81 brs in Bangladesh, 1 br. in India.

Al-Arafah Islami Bank Ltd: 6th–9th Floors, 36 Dilkusha C/A, Dhaka 1000; tel. (2) 7123255; fax (2) 9569351; e-mail aibl@al-arafahbank.com; internet www.al-arafahbank.com; f. 1995; 100% owned by 23 sponsors; cap. 5,893.3m., res 2,437.4m., dep. 81,434.3m. (Dec. 2011); Chair. BADIUR RAHMAN; Man. Dir EKRAMUL HOQUE; 91 brs.

The City Bank Ltd: 136 Gulshan Ave, Gulshan-2, Dhaka 1212; tel. (2) 8813483; fax (2) 9884446; e-mail mail@thecitybank.com; internet www.thecitybank.com; f. 1983; 50% owned by sponsors and 50% by public; cap. 5,055m., res 11,199.7m., dep. 82,734.5m. (Dec. 2011); Chair. RUBEL AZIZ; Man. Dir and CEO K. MAHMOOD SATTAR; 88 brs.

Dhaka Bank Ltd: 1st Floor, Biman Bhaban, 100 Motijheel C/A, Dhaka 1000; tel. (2) 9554514; e-mail info@dhakabank.com.bd; internet www.dhakabankltd.com; f. 1995; cap. 3,590m., res 4,191m., dep. 84,177m. (Dec. 2011); Chair. RESHADUR RAHMAN; Man. Dir KHONDKER FAZLE RASHID; 55 brs.

Dutch-Bangla Bank Ltd: 4th Floor, Sena Kalyan Bhaban, 195 Motijheel C/A, Dhaka 1000; tel. (2) 7176390; fax (2) 9561889; internet www.dbbl.com.bd; f. 1996; cap. 2,000m., res 5,201m., dep. 99,601m. (Dec. 2011); Chair. ABEDUR RASHID KHAN; Man. Dir SHAMSHI TABREZ; 120 brs.

Eastern Bank Ltd: Jiban Bima Bhaban, 10 Dilkusha C/A, Dhaka; tel. (2) 9556360; fax (2) 9558392; internet www.ebl.com.bd; f. 1992; appropriated assets and liabilities of fmr Bank of Credit and Commerce International (Overseas) Ltd; 83% owned by public, 17% owned by govt and private commercial banks; cap. 4,527m., res 8,144m., dep. 74,389m. (Dec. 2011); Chair. MOHD. GHAZIUL HAQUE; Man. Dir and CEO ALI REZA IFTEKHAR; 49 brs.

ICB Islamic Bank Ltd: T. K. Bhaban, 15th Floor, 13 Kazi Nazrul Islam Ave, Karwan Bazar, Dhaka 1215; tel. (2) 9143361; fax (2) 9111994; e-mail enquiry@icbislamic-bd.com; internet www.icbislamic-bd.com; f. 1987 on Islamic banking principles; fmrly Al-Baraka Bank Bangladesh Ltd, later Oriental Bank Ltd; cap. 6,647m., res 632.7m., dep. 12,475.5m. (Dec. 2011); Chair. Tan Sri Dr HADENAN BIN ABDUL JALIL; Man. Dir MAMOON MAHMOOD SHAH; 33 brs.

International Finance Investment and Commerce Bank Ltd (IFICB): BSB Bldg, 8th–10th & 16th–19th Floors, 8 Rajuk Ave, POB 2229, Dhaka 1000; tel. (2) 9563020; fax (2) 9562015; e-mail info@

ificbankbd.com; internet www.ificbankbd.com; f. 1983; 58.63% owned by public, 32.75% owned by Govt and 8.62% owned by private industry; cap. 2,768.4m., res 2,726.3m., dep. 71,735.6m. (Dec. 2011); Chair. SALMAN F. RAHMAN; Man. Dir MOHAMMAD ABDULLAH; 87 brs.

Islami Bank Bangladesh Ltd (IBBL): Islami Bank Tower, 40 Dilkusha C/A, POB 233, Dhaka 1000; tel. (2) 9563040; fax (2) 9564532; e-mail info@islamibankbd.com; internet www.islamibankbd.com; f. 1983 on Islamic banking principles; cap. 10,007.7m., res 14,590m., dep. 338,991.8m. (Dec. 2011); Chair. Prof. ABU NASSER MUHAMMED ABDUZ ZAHER; Man. Dir MOHAMMAD ABDUL MANNAN; 251 brs.

Meghna Bank Ltd: Doreen Tower, 7th–8th Floors, 6-A, North Ave C/A Gulshan-2, Dhaka 1212; tel. (2) 9857251; fax (2) 9857124; e-mail hob.prb@meghnabank.com.bd; internet www.meghnabank.com.bd; f. 2013; Man. Dir KAISER A. CHOWDHURY.

Mercantile Bank Ltd: 61 Dilkusha C/A, Dhaka 1000; tel. (2) 9559333; fax (2) 9561213; e-mail mbl@bol-online.com; internet www.mblbd.com; f. 1999; cap. 4,968m., res 3,513m., dep. 92,946m. (Dec. 2011); Chair. MOHAMMED ABDUL JALIL; Man. Dir and CEO M. EHSANUL HAQUE; 86 brs.

Midland Bank Ltd: N. B. Tower, 5th–9th Floors, 40/7 North Ave, Gulshan-2, Dhaka 1212; tel. (2) 8834671; fax (2) 8837735; e-mail ho.mdbl@midlandbankbd.net; internet www.midlandbankbd.net; f. 2013; Chair. MONIRUZZAMAN KHANDAKER; Man. Dir and CEO A. K. M. SHAHIDUL HAQUE.

National Bank Ltd: 18 Dilkusha C/A, Dhaka 1000; tel. (2) 9563081; fax (2) 9563953; e-mail nblho@nblbd.com; internet www.nblbd.com; f. 1983; 50% owned by sponsors and 50% by general public; cap. 8,603m., res 7,802.9m., dep. 125,457m. (Dec. 2011); Chair. ZAINUL HAQUE SIKDER; Man. Dir NEAZ AHMED; 154 brs.

National Credit and Commerce Bank Ltd (NCC Bank): 7–8 Motijheel C/A, Dhaka 1000; tel. (2) 9561902; fax (2) 9566290; e-mail nccbl@bdmail.net; internet www.nccbank.com.bd; f. 1993; 50% owned by sponsors, 50% by general public; cap. 5,941m., res 3,784m., dep. 79,371.9m. (Dec. 2011); Chair. NURUN NEWAZ; Man. Dir and CEO MUHAMMAD NURUL AMIN; 80 brs.

NRB Bank Ltd: Richmond Concord, 7th Floor, 68 Gulshan Ave, Gulshan Circle -1, Dhaka 1212; tel. (2) 9855161; fax (2) 9855001; internet www.nrbbankbd.com; f. 2013; Chair. IQBAL AHMED; Man. Dir MUKLESUR RAHMAN.

NRB Commercial Bank: 114, Motijheel C/A, Dhaka 1000; tel. (2) 9573426; fax (2) 9573421; internet www.nrbcommercialbank.com; f. 2013; Chair. FARASATH ALI; Man. Dir and CEO DEWAN MUJIBUR RAHMAN.

ONE Bank Ltd: HRC Bhaban, 46 Karwan Bazar C/A, Dhaka 1215; tel. (2) 9118161; fax (2) 9134794; e-mail info@onebankbd.com; internet www.onebankbd.com; f. 1999; cap. 3,188.6m., res 1,931m., dep. 56,577m. (Dec. 2011); Chair. SAYEED HOSSAIN CHOWDHURY; Man. Dir FARMAN R. CHOWDHURY.

Prime Bank Ltd: Adamjee Court, Annex Bldg No. 2, 119–120 Motijheel C/A, Dhaka 1000; tel. (2) 9567265; fax (2) 9567230; e-mail info@primebank.com; internet www.primebank.com.bd; f. 1995; cap. 7,798m., res 8,538m., dep. 156,835m. (Dec. 2011); Chair. MOHD SHIRAJUL ISLAM MOLLAH; Man. Dir M. EHSAN KHASRU; 94 brs.

Pubali Bank Ltd: 26 Dilkusha C/A, POB 853, Dhaka 1000; tel. (2) 9551614; fax (2) 9564009; e-mail info@pubalibankbd.com; internet www.pubalibangla.com; f. 1959 as Eastern Mercantile Bank Ltd; name changed as above in 1972; privately owned; cap. 6,707.6m., res 8,164.9m., dep. 120,879.8m. (Dec. 2011); Chair. HAFIZ AHMED MAJUMDER; Man. Dir and CEO HELAL AHMED CHOWDHURY; 410 brs.

Social Islami Bank Ltd: 103 Motijheel C/A, Dhaka 1000; tel. (2) 9559014; fax (2) 9568098; e-mail info@sibl-bd.com; internet www.siblbd.com; f. 1995 as Social Investment Bank; renamed as above in 2009; cap. 6,393.9m., res 2,307m., dep. 65,556m. (Dec. 2010); Chair. AL-HAJ NASIRUDDIN; Man. Dir MUHAMMAD ALI; 64 brs.

South Bangla Agriculture and Commerce Bank Ltd (SBAC): Sun Moon Star Tower, 37 Dilkusha C/A, Dhaka 1000; tel. (2) 9577207; internet www.sbacbank.com; f. 2013; Chair. S. M. AMZAD HOSSAIN; Man. Dir RAFIQUL ISLAM.

Southeast Bank Ltd: Eunoos Trade Center, 2nd, 3rd, 4th and 16th Floors, 52–53 Dilkusha C/A, Dhaka 1000; tel. (2) 9571115; fax (2) 9550093; e-mail info@southeastbank.com.bd; internet www.southeastbank.com.bd; f. 1995; cap. 8,317m., res 8,991m., dep. 125,660m. (Dec. 2011); Chair. ALAMGIR KABIR; Man. Dir MAHBUBUL ALAM; 65 brs.

Trust Bank Ltd: 2nd, 16th and 17th Floors, People's Insurance Bhaban, 36 Dilkusha C/A, Dhaka 1000; tel. (2) 9570261; fax (2) 9572315; e-mail info@trustbanklimited.com; internet www.trustbank.com.bd; f. 1999; cap. 2,661m., res 1,830.7m., dep. 65,374.3m. (Dec. 2011); Chair. Gen. ABDUL MUBEEN; Man. Dir M. SHAH ALAM SARWAR; 45 brs.

United Commercial Bank Ltd: Plot CWS(A) 1, Rd 34, Gulshan Ave, Dhaka 1212; tel. and fax (2) 8852500; e-mail info@ucbl.com; internet www.ucbl.com; f. 1983; 54.17% owned by sponsors and 45.83% by general public; cap. 7,274.9m., res 6,714.2m., dep. 137,011.6m. (Dec. 2011); Chair. AKHTARUZZAMAN CHOWDHURY; Man. Dir M. SHAHIDUL ISLAM; 122 brs.

Union Bank Ltd: Bahela Tower, 72 Gulshan Ave, Dhaka 1212; tel. (2) 9859313; internet www.unionbank.com.bd; f. 2013; Chair. SHAHIDUL ALAM; Man. Dir ABDUL HAMID MIAH.

Uttara Bank Ltd: Uttara Bank Bhaban, 47, Bir Uttom Shahid Ashfaq us-Samad Rd, 90 Motijheel C/A, POB 217 and 818, Dhaka 1000; tel. (2) 9551162; fax (2) 7168376; e-mail uttara@citechco.net; internet www.uttarabank-bd.com; f. 1965 as Eastern Banking Corpn Ltd; name changed to Uttara Bank in 1972 and to Uttara Bank Ltd in 1983; 100% publicly owned; cap. 2,875m., res 5,716.7m., dep. 70,203.3m. (Dec. 2011); Chair. AZHARUL ISLAM; Man. Dir SHAIKH ABDUL AZIZ; 211 brs.

Development Finance Organizations

Bangladesh Development Bank Ltd (BDBL): 8 Rajuk Ave, Dhaka; tel. (2) 9558326; fax (2) 9562061; e-mail md@bdbl.com.bd; internet www.bdbl.com.bd; f. 2010 as result of merger of Bangladesh Shilpa Bank and Bangladesh Shilpa Rin Sangstha; 100% state-owned; auth. cap. 4,100m., res 10,688.5m., dep. 4,657.8m. (Dec. 2011); Chair. NAZEM AHMED CHOWDHURY; Man. Dir Dr MOHAMMAD ZILLUR RAHMAN; 21 brs.

Bangladesh House Building Finance Corpn (BHBFC): 22 Purana Paltan, Dhaka 1000; tel. (2) 9561315; fax (2) 9561324; e-mail bhbfc@bangla.net; internet bhbfc.gov.bd; f. 1952; provides low-interest credit for residential house-building; 100% state-owned; Chair. M. YEASIN ALI; Man. Dir MD NURUL ALAM TALUKDER; 9 zonal offices, 13 regional offices and 2 camp offices.

Bangladesh Krishi Bank (BKB): Krishi Bank Bhaban, 83–85 Motijheel C/A, Dhaka 1000; tel. (2) 9560021; fax (2) 9561211; e-mail info@krishibank.org.bd; internet www.krishibank.org.bd; f. 1961; fmrly the Agricultural Development Bank of Pakistan, name changed as above in 1973; provides credit for agricultural and rural devt; also performs all kinds of banking; 100% state-owned; cap. 9,000m., res 2,059.9m., dep. 128,322.9m. (June 2011); Chair. KHONDKAR IBRAHIM KHALED; Man. Dir MUKTER HUSSAIN; 976 brs.

BASIC Bank Ltd: Bana Sena Kalyan Bhaban, 5th Floor, 195 Motijheel C/A, Dhaka 1000; tel. (2) 9568190; fax (2) 9564829; e-mail basicho@citechco.net; internet www.basicbanklimited.com; f. 1988 as Bangladesh Small Industries and Commerce Bank Ltd; renamed as above in 2001; 100% state-owned; cap. 2,357.5m., res 2,511m., dep. 62,058.8m. (Dec. 2011); Chair. SHEIKH ABDUL HYE BACCHU; Man. Dir KAZI FAQURUL ISLAM; 50 brs.

Export-Import Bank of Bangladesh Ltd: Plot SE(F) 9, Rd 142, Gulshan Ave, Dhaka 1212; tel. (2) 9889363; fax (2) 8828962; e-mail itd@eximbankbd.com; internet www.eximbankbd.com; f. 1999; cap. 9,223.5m., res 3,924.2m., dep. 106,588.7m. (Dec. 2011); Chair. NAZRUL ISLAM MAZUMDER; Man. Dir and CEO MD HAIDER ALI MIAH; 73 brs.

Grameen Bank: Grameen Bank Bhavan, Mirpur 2, Dhaka 1216; tel. (2) 8011138; fax (2) 8013559; e-mail grameen.bank@grameen.net; internet www.grameen.com; f. 1976; provides credit for the landless rural poor; 10% owned by Govt; Chair. (vacant); Man. Dir MOHAMMAD SHAHJAHAN (acting); 2,565 brs.

Infrastructure Development Co Ltd (IDCOL): UTC Bldg, 16th Floor, 8 Panthapath, Karwan Bazar, Dhaka 1215; tel. (2) 9102171; fax (2) 8116663; e-mail contact@idcol.org; internet www.idcol.org; f. 1997; state-owned; Chair. IQBAL MAHMOOD; Exec. Dir and CEO ISLAM SHARIF.

Investment Corpn of Bangladesh (ICB): BDBL Bldg, 12th–15th Floors, 8 Rajuk Ave, Dhaka 1000; tel. (2) 9563455; fax (2) 9563313; e-mail icb@agni.com; internet www.icb.gov.bd; f. 1976; provides investment banking services; 27% owned by Govt; cap. 500.0m., res 1,646.1m. (June 2008); Chair. S. M. MAHFUZUR RAHMAN; Man. Dir MOHAMMAD FAYEKUZZAMAN; 7 brs.

Rajshahi Krishi Unnayan Bank: Kazihata, Rajshahi 6000; tel. (721) 775008; fax (721) 775947; e-mail info@rakub.org.bd; internet www.rakub.org.bd; f. 1987; 100% state-owned; Chair. Dr M. SHAH NOWAZ ALI; Man. Dir MD ABU HANIF KHAN; 365 brs.

Banking Association

Bangladesh Association of Banks: Jabbar Tower, 16th Floor, Rd 135, 42 Gulshan Ave, Gulshan-1, Dhaka 1212; tel. (2) 8859885; fax (2) 8851015; e-mail admin@bab.com.bd; internet www.bab.com.bd; f. 1993; Chair. MD NUZRUL ISLAM MAZUMDER.

STOCK EXCHANGES

Chittagong Stock Exchange: CSE Bldg, 1080 Sheikh Mujib Rd, Agrabad, Chittagong; tel. (31) 714632; fax (31) 714101; e-mail info@

cse.com.bd; internet www.cse.com.bd; f. 1995; Man. Dir SYED SAJID HUSAIN.

Dhaka Stock Exchange Ltd: Stock Exchange Bldg, 9F Motijheel C/A, Dhaka 1000; tel. (2) 9564601; fax (2) 9564727; e-mail dse@bol-online.com; internet www.dsebd.org; f. 1954; 284 listed cos; Pres. MD RAKIBUR RAHMAN; CEO MUSHARRAF M. HUSSAIN.

Regulatory Authority

Bangladesh Securities and Exchange Commission: Jiban Bima Tower, 15th, 16th and 20th Floors, 10 Dilkusha C/A, Dhaka 1000; tel. (2) 9568101; fax (2) 9563721; e-mail secbd@bdmail.net; internet www.secbd.org; f. 1993; Chair. M. KHAIRUL HOSSAIN.

INSURANCE

Bangladesh General Insurance Co Ltd (BGIC): 42 Dilkusha C/A, Dhaka 1000; tel. (2) 9555073; fax (2) 9564212; e-mail bgic@citechco.net; internet www.bgicinsure.com; f. 1985; Chair. TOWHID SAMAD; Man. Dir A. K. AZIZUL HUQ CHAUDHURI.

Bangladesh Insurance Association: Rupali Bima Bhaban, 7th Floor, 7 Rajuk Ave, Dhaka 1000; tel. (2) 9557330; fax (2) 9562345; e-mail bia@bdcom.com; internet bia-bd.org; Chair. SHEIKH KABIR HOSSAIN; 60 mem. cos.

Eastern Insurance Co Ltd: 2nd Floor, 44 Dilkusha C/A, Dhaka 1000; tel. (2) 9563033; fax (2) 9569735; e-mail eicl@dhaka.net; internet www.easterninsurancebd.com; f. 1986; Chair. MUJIBUR RAHMAN; Man. Dir MOHAMMAD HAROON PATWARY.

Jiban Bima Corpn (JBC): 24 Motijheel C/A, Dhaka 1000; tel. (2) 9551414; e-mail mds@jbc.gov.bd; internet www.jbc.gov.bd; state-owned; life insurance; Chair. and Dir MOHAMMED SOHRAB UDDIN; Man. Dir PARIKSHIT DATTA CHOUDHURY.

Pioneer Insurance Co Ltd: Symphony, 5th Floor, SE(F)9, Rd 142, South Ave, Gulshan, Dhaka 1212; tel. (2) 8817512; fax (2) 8817234; e-mail piclho@pioneerinsurance.com.bd; internet www.pioneerinsurance.com.bd; f. 1996; Chair. TAPAN CHOWDHURY; Man. Dir Q. A. F. M. SERAJUL ISLAM.

Pragati Insurance Ltd: Pragati Rhone–Poulence Centre, 6th Floor, 20–21 Kawran Bazar, Dhaka 1215; tel. (2) 8189184; fax (2) 9124024; e-mail info@pragatilife.com; internet www.pragatilife.com; Chair. KHALILUR RAHMAN; Man. Dir QUAMRUL HASAN.

Reliance Insurance Ltd: Shanta Western Tower, Level 5, 186 Tejgaon I/A, Dhaka 1208; tel. (2) 8878836; fax (2) 8878831; e-mail info@reliance-bd.com; internet www.reliance.com.bd; f. 1988; Chair. SHAMSUR RAHMAN; Man. Dir and CEO AKHTAR AHMED.

Sadharan Bima Corpn: Sadharan Bima Bhaban, 33 Dilkusha C/A, Dhaka 1000; e-mail head-office@sbc.org.bd; internet www.sbc.gov.bd; state-owned; general insurance; Chair. M. SHAMSUL ALAM; Man. Dir MD REZAUL KARIM.

Regulatory Authority

Insurance Development and Regulatory Authority (IDRA): Dhaka; e-mail idra.bd@gmail.com; internet www.idra.org.bd; f. 2011, to replace the office of the Chief Controller of Insurance; regulator for 62 insurance cos (2012); Chair. SHEFAQ AHMED.

Trade and Industry

GOVERNMENT AGENCIES

Bangladesh Export Processing Zones Authority (BEPZA): BEPZA Complex, House 19/D, Rd 6, Dhanmondi R/A, Dhaka 1000; tel. (2) 9670530; fax (2) 8650060; e-mail chairman@bepza.org; internet www.epzbangladesh.org.bd; f. 1983 to plan, develop, operate and manage export processing zones (EPZs) in Bangladesh; Exec. Chair. Maj.-Gen. A. T. M. SHAHIDUL ISLAM; Sec. MD SHAWKAT NABI.

Board of Investment: Jiban Bima Tower, 19th Floor, 10 Dilkusha C/A, Dhaka 1000; tel. (2) 7169580; fax (2) 9562312; e-mail service@boi.gov.bd; internet boi.gov.bd; f. 1989; Exec. Chair. Dr S. A. SAMAD.

Export Promotion Bureau: TCB Bhaban, 2nd and 4th Floors, 1 Karwan Bazar, Dhaka 1215; tel. (2) 9144821; fax (2) 9119531; e-mail info@epb.gov.bd; internet www.epb.gov.bd; f. 1972; semi-autonomous govt org., chaired by Minister of Commerce; regional offices in Chittagong, Khulna, Rajshahi; br. offices in Narayanganj, Comilla and Sylhet; Vice-Chair. SHUBHASHISH BOSE.

Planning Commission: Planning Commission Secretariat, Sher-e-Bangla Nagar, Dhaka 1207; e-mail masuddhk@gmail.com; internet www.plancomm.gov.bd; f. 1972; chaired by Prime Minister, with Minister of Planning serving as Vice-Chair.; responsible for all aspects of economic planning and development including the preparation of the five-year plans and annual development programmes (in conjunction with appropriate govt ministries), promotion of savings and investment, compilation of statistics, and evaluation of development schemes and projects; Planning Division Sec. BHUIYAN SHAFIQUL ISLAM.

Privatization Commission: Transport Pool Bldg, Levels 8, 9 & 10, Secretariat Link Rd, Dhaka 1000; tel. (2) 9551986; fax (2) 9556433; e-mail pc@intechworld.net; internet www.pc.gov.bd; f. 1993; Chair. MOLLA WAHEED.

Tariff Commission: Ministry of Commerce, 9th Floor, Govt Office Bldg, Segunbagicha, Dhaka 1000; tel. (2) 9335930; fax (2) 8315685; e-mail btariff@intechworld.net; internet www.bdtariffcom.org; f. 1973; advises the govt on trade and fiscal policies, regional and multilateral trade negotiations and issues facing indigenous industries; Chair. Dr MOHAMMAD MOZIBUR RAHMAN.

Trading Corpn of Bangladesh: 2nd Floor, TCB Bhaban, 1 Kawran Bazar, Dhaka 1215; tel. (2) 8141827; fax (2) 8120853; e-mail tcb@tcb.gov.bd; f. 1972; national trade org. of the Ministry of Commerce; imports, exports and markets goods through appointed dealers and agents; Chair. Brig.-Gen. SARWAR JAHAN TALUKDER; Dir ABU SYED MOHAMMAD HASHIM.

DEVELOPMENT ORGANIZATIONS

Bangladesh Agricultural Development Corpn: 49–51 Krishi Bhaban, Dilkusha Commercial Area, Dhaka 1000; tel. (2) 9556080; fax (2) 9564357; e-mail info@badc.gov.bd; internet www.badc.gov.bd; f. 1961; successor org. to the East Pakistan Agricultural Devt Corpn; responsible for devt of agricultural sector to ensure national food security; production and supply of seed varieties and fertilizers, and provision of irrigation and other technologies; Chair. ZAHIR UDDIN AHMED.

Bangladesh Fisheries Development Corpn (BFDC): 24–25 Dilkusha C/A, Dhaka 1000; tel. (2) 9553975; fax (2) 9563990; e-mail bfdc_64@yahoo.com; internet bfdc-gov.org; f. 1964; under Ministry of Fisheries and Livestock; development and commercial activities; Chair. KHURSHIDA KHATUN.

Bangladesh Forest Industries Development Corpn (BFIDC): Bana Shilpa Bhaban, 73 Motijheel C/A, Dhaka 1000; tel. (2) 9560086; fax (2) 9563035; e-mail cm.bfidc@gmail.com; internet bfidc.info; f. 1959; state-owned; Chair. MOHAMMAD FARHAD UDDIN.

Bangladesh Small and Cottage Industries Corpn (BSCIC): 137–138 Motijheel C/A, Dhaka 1000; tel. (2) 9556191; fax (2) 9550704; e-mail info@bscic.gov.bd; internet www.bscic.gov.bd; f. 1957; Chair. MOHAMMAD FAKRUL ISLAM.

Bangladesh Tea Board: 171–172 Baizid Bostami Rd, Nasirabad, Chittagong; tel. (31) 682903; fax (31) 682863; e-mail secretary@teaboard.gov.bd; internet www.teaboard.gov.bd; f. 1951; regulates, controls and promotes the cultivation and marketing of tea, both in Bangladesh and abroad; Chair. Maj.-Gen. MOHAMMAD MAHBUBUL HASAN.

Chittagong Development Authority (CDA): CDA Bldg, Court Rd, Chittagong; tel. (31) 620988; e-mail secretary@cda.gov.bd; internet portal.cda.gov.bd; f. 1959; oversees devt and expansion of Chittagong metropolitan area; Chair. ABDUS SALAM.

CHAMBERS OF COMMERCE

Federation of Bangladesh Chambers of Commerce and Industry (FBCCI): Federation Bhaban, 60 Motijheel C/A, Dhaka 1000; tel. (2) 9560102; fax (2) 7176030; e-mail fbcci@bol-online.com; internet www.fbcci-bd.org; f. 1973; comprises 259 trade asscns and 81 chambers of commerce and industry; Pres. A. K. AZAD; Sec.-Gen. MIR SHAHABUDDIN MOHAMMAD.

Barisal Chamber of Commerce and Industry: Chamber Bhaban, Nasir Pool, Shaw Rd, POB 30, Barisal; tel. (431) 52020; Pres. Sheikh ABDUR RAHIM.

Chittagong Chamber of Commerce and Industry: World Trade Centre, 102/103 Agrabad C/A, Chittagong; tel. (31) 713366; fax (31) 710183; e-mail info@chittagongchamber.com; internet www.chittagongchamber.com; f. 1959; more than 5,000 mems; Pres. MURSHED MURAD IBRAHIM; Sec. OSMAN GANI CHOWDHURY.

Dhaka Chamber of Commerce and Industry: Dhaka Chamber Bldg, 65–66 Motijheel C/A, POB 2641, Dhaka 1000; tel. (2) 9552562; fax (2) 9560830; e-mail info@dhakachamber.com; internet www.dhakachamber.com; f. 1958; more than 4,500 mems; Pres. ASIF IBRAHIM.

Foreign Investors' Chamber of Commerce and Industry: Shama Home, Apt C3, House 59, Rd 1, Blk 1, Banani, Dhaka 1212; tel. (2) 9893049; fax (2) 9893058; e-mail ficci@bdcom.net; internet www.ficci.org.bd; f. 1963 as Agrabad Chamber of Commerce and Industry, name changed as above in 1987; Pres. SYED ERSHAD AHMED; Exec. Dir M. A. MATIN.

Khulna Chamber of Commerce and Industry: Chamber Mansion, 5 KDA C/A, Khulna 9100; tel. (41) 721695; fax (41) 725365; e-mail khulnachamber@gmail.com; internet www.khulnachamber.com; f. 1934; Pres. KAZI AMINUL HAQUE.

Metropolitan Chamber of Commerce and Industry: Chamber Bldg, 4th Floor, 122–124 Motijheel C/A, Dhaka 1000; tel. (2) 9565208; fax (2) 9565211; e-mail info@mccibd.org; internet www.mccibd.org; f. 1904; Pres. Maj.-Gen. AMJAD KHAN CHOUDHURY; Sec.-Gen. FAROOQ AHMED.

Rajshahi Chamber of Commerce and Industry: Chamber Bhaban, Station Rd, PO Ghoramara, Rajshahi 6100; tel. (721) 812122; fax (721) 812133; e-mail rcci_raj@yahoo.com; internet rajshahichamber.org; f. 1951; Pres. Al-Haj MD ABU BAKKER ALI.

Sylhet Chamber of Commerce and Industry: Chamber Bldg, Jail Rd, POB 97, Sylhet 3100; tel. (821) 714403; fax (821) 715210; e-mail scci@btsnet.net; internet www.sylhetchamber.org; f. 1966; Pres. FARUQUE AHMED MISBAH.

INDUSTRIAL AND TRADE ASSOCIATIONS

Bangladesh Association of Pharmaceutical Industries (BAPI) (Bangladesh Aushad Shilpa Samity): F-41, Rd No. 4, Banani, Dhaka 1213; tel. and fax (2) 8816767; e-mail bdass@bol-online.com; internet www.bapibd.com; f. 1972; Pres. SALMAN F. RAHMAN.

Bangladesh Ceramic Wares Manufacturers' Association: 3rd Floor, 52/1 New Eskaton Rd, Dhaka 1000; tel. (2) 8314531; fax (2) 8314933; Pres. IFTAKHER UDDIN FARHAD.

Bangladesh Finished Leather, Leather Goods and Footwear Exporters' Association: 32/A Rd 2, Dhanmondi, Dhaka 1209; tel. (2) 8622167; internet www.bfllfea.org; f. 2007; more than 100 gen. mems and 40 commercial mems; Chair. M. ABU TAHER.

Bangladesh Frozen Foods Exporters' Association: Skylark Point, 10th Floor, 24/A Bijoynagar, North South Rd, Dhaka 1000; tel. (2) 8316882; fax (2) 8317531; e-mail bffea@dhaka.net; internet www.bffea.net; f. 1984; Pres. KAZI SHANEWAZ.

Bangladesh Garment Manufacturers and Exporters Association (BGMEA): BGMEA Complex, 23/1 Panthapath Link Rd, Karwan Bazar, Dhaka 1215; tel. (2) 9144552; fax (2) 8113951; e-mail info@bgmea.com; internet www.bgmea.com.bd; Pres. MD SHAFIUL ISLAM.

Bangladesh Jute Association: BJA Bldg, 77 Motijheel C/A, Dhaka; tel. (2) 9552916; fax (2) 9561122; e-mail bjute@bangla.net; Chair. MAHFUZUL HAQUE.

Bangladesh Jute Mills Association: Adamjee Court, 4th Floor, 115–120 Motijheel C/A, Dhaka 1000; tel. (2) 9560071; fax (2) 9566472; e-mail info@bjma-bd.org; Chair. NAZMUL HAQUE.

Bangladesh Jute Spinners Association (BJSA): 55A Purana Paltan, 3rd Floor, Dhaka 1000; tel. (2) 9551317; fax (2) 9562772; e-mail bjsa_bd@yahoo.com; internet www.juteyarn-bjsa.org; f. 1979; 92 mems; Chair. SHABBIR YOUSUF; Sec. SHAHIDUL KARIM.

Bangladesh Knitwear Manufacturers and Exporters Association (BKMEA): Press Club Bhaban, 1st Floor, 233/1, B. B. Rd, Banglamotor, Dhaka; tel. (2) 7640535; fax (2) 7630609; e-mail fair@bkmea.com; internet www.bkmea.com; f. 1996; Pres. A. K. M. SALIM OSMAN.

Bangladesh Marine Fisheries Association (BMFA): 13/A Center Point Concord, Dhaka 1215; tel. (2) 9120234; e-mail info@bmfabd.com; internet www.bmfabd.com; f. 1980; asscn of 18 trawler companies; exports frozen shrimp and saltwater fish; Chair. A. K. SHAMSUDDIN KHAN.

Bangladesh Sugar Refiners' Association: Mostafa Centre, House 59, Rd No. 27, Blk K, Banani, Dhaka 1213; tel. (2) 8816763; fax (2) 9891456; Pres. FAZLUR RAHMAN.

Bangladesh Tea Association (Bangladeshiyo Cha Sangsad): 'Progressive Tower', 4th Floor, 1837 Sheikh Mujib Rd (Badamtali), Agrabad, Chittagong 4100; tel. (31) 716407; f. 1952; Chair. MOHAMMAD SAFWAN CHOUDHURY; Sec. G. S. DHAR.

Bangladesh Textile Mills Association (BTMA): Unique Trade Centre, 8th Floor, 8 Panthapath, Karwan Bazar, Dhaka 1215; tel. (2) 9143461; fax (2) 9125338; e-mail btmasg@gmail.com; internet www.btmadhaka.com; Pres. JAHANGIR ALAMIN.

UTILITIES

Regulatory Authority

Bangladesh Energy Regulatory Commission (BERC): TCB Bhaban, 3rd Floor, 1 Karwan Bazar, Dhaka 1215; tel. (2) 9140125; fax (2) 8155743; internet www.berc.org.bd; f. 2004; regulates activities of gas, electricity and petroleum sectors; Chair. SYED YUSUF HOSSAIN.

Electricity

Bangladesh Power Development Board (BPDB): WAPDA Bldg, 1st Floor, Motijheel C/A, Dhaka; tel. (2) 9562154; fax (2) 9564765; e-mail chbpdb@bol-online.com; internet www.bpdb.gov.bd; f. 1972; under Ministry of Power, Energy and Mineral Resources; generation, transmission and distribution of electricity; installed capacity 5,202 MW (2008); Chair. ABDUL WAHAB KHAN.

Dhaka Electric Supply Co Ltd (DESCO): House 3, Rd 24, Block K, Banani Model Town, Dhaka 1213; tel. (2) 8859642; fax (2) 8854648; e-mail info@desco.org.bd; internet www.desco.org.bd; f. 1997; Chair. SHAHJAHAN SIDDIQUI; Man. Dir MD MONZUR RAHMAN.

Dhaka Power Distribution Co Ltd (DPDC): Biddut Bhaban, 1 Abdul Gani Rd, Dhaka 1000; e-mail md@dpdc.org; internet www.dpdc.org.bd; f. 2005 to replace Dhaka Electric Supply Authority; under Ministry of Power, Energy and Mineral Resources; Chair. TAPOS KUMAR ROY; Man. Dir MD ABDUS SOBHAN.

Power Grid Company of Bangladesh Ltd (PGCB): IEB Bldg, 3rd and 4th Floors, Ramna, Dhaka 1000; tel. (2) 9553663; fax (2) 7171833; e-mail info@pgcb.org.bd; internet www.pgcb.org.bd; f. 1996; responsible for power transmission throughout Bangladesh; Chair. MD ABUL KALAM AZAD; Sec. MOHAMMAD ASHRAF HOSSAIN.

Rural Electrification Board: House 3, Rd 12, Nikunja-2, Khilkhet, Dhaka 1229; tel. (2) 8916424; fax (2) 8916400; e-mail seict@reb.gov.bd; internet www.reb.gov.bd; under Ministry of Power, Energy and Mineral Resources; Chair. Brig.-Gen. MOIN UDDIN.

Gas

Gas Transmission Company Ltd (GTCL): Red Crescent Borak Tower, Levels 3–6, 71–72 Old Elephant Rd, Eskaton, Romna, Dhaka 1000; tel. (2) 9362800; fax (2) 9358100; e-mail info@gtcl.org.bd; internet www.gtcl.org.bd; f. 1993; CEO AMINUR RAHMAN.

Water

Bangladesh Water Development Board (BWDB): WAPDA Bldg, Motijheel C/A, Dhaka 1000; tel. (2) 9552194; fax (2) 9564763; e-mail cm-bwdb@bangla.net; internet www.bwdb.gov.bd; f. 1972; fmrly part of East Pakistan Water and Power Development Authority; water resources management and development; Dir-Gen. ABUL KALAM MOHD AZAD.

Chittagong Water Supply and Sewerage Authority: WASA Bhaban, Dampara, Chittagong; tel. (31) 621606; internet cwasa.org; f. 1963; govt corpn; Chair. SULTAN MAHMUD CHOWDHURY.

Dhaka Water Supply and Sewerage Authority: 98 Kazi Nazrul Islam Ave, Karwan Bazar, Dhaka 1215; tel. (2) 8116792; fax (2) 8112109; e-mail secretary@dwasa.org.bd; internet www.dwasa.org.bd; f. 1963; govt corpn; Man. Dir TAQSEM A. KHAN.

Water Resources Planning Organization (WARPO): House 103, Rd 1, Banani, Dhaka 1213; tel. (2) 8814217; fax (2) 9883456; e-mail dg@warpo.gov.bd; internet www.warpo.gov.bd; f. 1992; fmrly Master Plan Organization; macro-level planning org. for integrated water resources management; Dir-Gen. MD SHAHIDUR RAHMAN.

STATE HOLDING COMPANIES

The following holding companies, under the supervision of the Ministry of Industries, are responsible for the management of the public sector companies in the relevant sectors.

Bangladesh Chemical Industries Corpn (BCIC): BCIC Bhaban, 30–31 Dilkusha C/A, Dhaka 1000; tel. (2) 9562140; fax (2) 9564120; e-mail bcic.info@gmail.com; internet www.bcic.gov.bd; f. 1976; state-owned; manages 13 enterprises incl. Chhatak Cement Co, Chittagong Urea Fertilizer Co, Karnaphuli Paper Mills Ltd, Urea Fertilizer Factory Ltd, Natural Gas Fertilizer Factory Ltd; Chair. MD GOLAM RABBANI.

Bangladesh Steel and Engineering Corpn (BSEC): BSEC Bhaban, 102 Kazi Nazrul Islam Ave, Dhaka 1215; tel. (2) 9115144; fax (2) 8189642; e-mail bsecheadoffice@gmail.com; internet www.bsec.gov.bd; f. 1976; 9 industrial units; Chair. MD ATAUR RAHMAN; 2,581 employees.

Bangladesh Sugar and Food Industries Corpn (BSFIC): Chini Shilpa Bhaban, 3 Dilkusha C/A, Dhaka 1000; tel. (2) 9565869; fax (2) 9550481; e-mail chinikal@btcl.net.bd; internet www.bsfic.gov.bd; f. 1976; Chair. MAHMUDUL HAQUE BHUIYAN.

TRADE UNIONS

Bangladesh Free Trade Union Congress (BFTUC): 6A 1/19 Mirpur, Dhaka 1216; tel. (2) 8017001; fax (2) 8015919; e-mail bftuc@agni.com; f. 1983; Gen. Sec. M. R. CHOWDHURY; 95,000 mems.

Bangladesh Jatiyatabadi Sramik Dal: 28/1 Naya Paltan, 4th Floor, VIP Rd, Dhaka 1000; tel. (2) 418214; fax (2) 869723; e-mail bils@agni.com; f. 1979; affiliated with the Bangladesh Nationalist Party; Sec.-Gen. MD ZAFRUL HASAN.

Bangladesh Labour Federation: Sadharan Bima Sadan, 8th Floor, 24–25 Dilkusha C/A, POB 2514, Dhaka 1000; tel. (2) 9560104; fax (2) 7171335; e-mail mdhk_blf@yahoo.com; Pres. SHAH MOHAMMAD ABU ZAFAR.

Bangladesh Mukto Sramik Federation: House 86, Rd No. 11A, Dhanmondhi, Dhaka; tel. 1713007814 (mobile); e-mail mojiburbhuiyan1950@yahoo.com; f. 1973; Gen. Sec. MUHAMMAD MOJIBUR RAHMAN BHUIYAN; 20,050 mems.

Bangladesh Sanjukta Sramik Federation: 2/2 Purana Paltan, 2nd Floor, Dhaka 1000; tel. (2) 7174065; fax (2) 9125078; e-mail bssfhq@intechworld.net; f. 1978.

Jatio Sramik League (JSL): 23 Bangabandhu Ave, POB 2730, Dhaka 1000; tel. (2) 9554499; fax (2) 7162222; e-mail jsl@mail.aitlbd.net; f. 1969; Pres. ABDUL MATIN MASTER; 62,000 mems.

Transport

RAILWAYS

In 2006 the total length of Bangladesh's rail network was estimated at 2,835 km. Plans to modernize and extend the network through an Asian Development Bank-funded Railway Sector Investment Programme were finalized in 2008. Plans to establish direct rail links with Nepal and Bhutan via India were also under consideration. In 2013 plans were finalized for the construction of a 15-km rail link between Akhaura in eastern Bangladesh and Agartala in Tripura, India, which would greatly improve rail connectivity between the Indian mainland and its north-eastern states, via Bangladesh.

Bangladesh Railway: Rail Bhaban, 16 Abdul Ghani Rd, Dhaka 1000; tel. (2) 9561200; fax (2) 9563413; e-mail dg@railway.gov.bd; internet www.railway.gov.bd; f. 1862; supervised by the Ministry of Railways; divided into East and West Zones, with East Zone HQ at Chittagong (tel. (31) 843200; fax (31) 843215) and West Zone HQ at Rajshahi (tel. (721) 761576; fax (721) 761982); total length of 2,835 route km (2009); 440 stations (2009); Dir-Gen. MOHAMMAD ABU TAHER; Gen. Man. (East Zone) (vacant); Gen. Man. (West Zone) FERDOUS ALAM.

ROADS

In 2010 the total length of the main road network (including national and regional highways and district roads under the supervision of the Roads and Highways Dept) was 21,269 km, of which 9.5% were paved. However, when all rural roads are also taken into account, the total road network has been estimated at over 270,000 km. The 4.8-km Bangabandhu Jamuna Multipurpose Bridge, which linked the east and the west of the country with a railway and road network, was opened in 1998. In 2011 funding arrangements were finalized for the 6.1-km, combined road and rail Padma Multipurpose Bridge, the country's largest-ever infrastructure project, which would connect Dhaka with the less-developed south-west of the country; the project was expected to cost an estimated US $2,900m. However, in mid-2012, owing to allegations of corruption in the tendering process, the World Bank withdrew its planned funding of $1,200m. and other major funders followed suit, leading to the postponement of the project. In 2013 the Government formally withdrew its application for World Bank finance and pledged to seek alternative funding arrangements.

Bangladesh Road Transport Corpn: Paribahan Bhaban, 21 Rajuk Ave, Dhaka; tel. (2) 9555786; fax (2) 9555788; e-mail info@brtc.gov.bd; internet www.brtc.gov.bd; f. 1961; state-owned; operates transport services, incl. truck division; transports govt food grain; Chair. Major (retd) M. M. IQBAL.

Roads and Highways Dept: Sarak Bhaban, Tejgaon, Dhaka 1208; tel. (2) 8879299; e-mail info@rhd.gov.bd; internet www.rhd.gov.bd; f. 1962; responsible for devt and maintenance of the road network and for road safety; under the Ministry of Communications; Chief Engineer MOZIFUL ISLAM RAJ KHAN.

INLAND WATERWAYS

In Bangladesh there are some 8,433 km of navigable waterways, which transport 70% of total domestic and foreign cargo traffic and on which are located the main river ports of Dhaka, Narayanganj, Chandpur, Barisal and Khulna.

Bangladesh Inland Water Transport Corpn: 5 Dilkusha C/A, Dhaka 1000; tel. (2) 9555031; fax (2) 9563653; e-mail info@biwtc.gov.bd; internet www.biwtc.gov.bd; f. 1972; Chair. GOLAM MOSTAFA KAMAL; 608 vessels.

SHIPPING

In 2010 the Government launched a major programme to expand and develop the country's ports. Chittagong, comprising two container terminals, is the chief port and handles more than 90% of sea-borne traffic; in 2011 the port handled 1.4m. 20-ft equivalent units (TEUs) and 43.1m. tons of cargo. The port at Mongla, situated some 100 km upstream on the Pasur River, also receives sea-going vessels. Mongla handled some 2.6m. tons of cargo in 2011/12. At December 2013 Bangladesh's flag registered fleet had a total of 196 vessels, with a total displacement of 1,381,809 grt.

Chittagong Port Authority: Bandar Bihar, POB 2013, Chittagong 4100; tel. (31) 2522200; fax (31) 2510889; e-mail info@cpa.gov.bd; internet www.cpa.gov.bd; f. 1887; management and development of Chittagong Port, and provision of bunkering, ship repair, towage and lighterage facilities; Chair. Rear Adm. MOHAMMAD NIZAMUDDIN AHMED.

Mongla Port Authority: Mongla, Bagerhat 9351; tel. (4662) 75200; fax (4662) 75224; e-mail cech@mpa.gov.bd; internet www.mpa.gov.bd; f. 1950; govt-owned; Chair. H. R. BHUYAN.

Principal Shipping Companies

Atlas Shipping Lines Ltd: 142 Sir Iqbal Rd, 3rd Floor, Khulna; tel. and fax (4) 1732669; e-mail atlas@khulna.bangla.net; internet www.atlas-bd.com; Man. Dir S. U. CHOWDHURY; Gen. Man. MUHAMMAD ABU RASEL.

Bangladesh Shipping Corpn: BSC Bhaban, Saltgola Rd, POB 641, Chittagong 4100; tel. (31) 2521162; fax (31) 710506; e-mail md@bsc.gov.bd; internet www.bsc.gov.bd; f. 1972; maritime shipping; 13 vessels; state-owned; Chair. SHAHJAHAN KHAN (Minister of Shipping); Man. Dir Cdre MOQSUMUL QUADER.

Bengal Shipping Line Ltd: Palm View, 100A Agrabad C/A, Chittagong 4100; tel. (31) 500692; fax (31) 710488; e-mail bsl@mkrgroup.com; Chair. MOHAMMED ABDUL AWWAL; Man. Dir MOHAMMED ABDUL MALEK.

Brave Royal Shipping Ltd: Kabir Manzil, Sheikh Mujib Rd, Agrabad C/A, Chittagong 4100; tel. (31) 715222; internet brsml.com; manufactures and operates bulk carrier vessels; Man. Dir MOHAMMAD SHAHJAHAN; Gen. Man. MEHERUL KARIM.

Continental Liner Agencies: Facy Bldg, 3rd Floor, 87 Agrabad C/A, Chittagong; tel. (31) 721572; fax (31) 710965; Chair. SHAH ALAM; Dir (Technical and Operations) Capt. MAHFUZUL ISLAM.

CIVIL AVIATION

There is an international airport at Dhaka (Shahjalal International Airport—as Zia International Airport was renamed in early 2010), situated at Kurmitola, with the capacity to handle 5m. passengers annually. There are two further international airports at Chittagong and Sylhet. The main domestic airports are located at Barisal, Cox's Bazar, Jessore, Rajshahi and Saidpur.

Civil Aviation Authority, Bangladesh (CAAB): Kurmitola, Dhaka 1229; tel. (2) 8901424; e-mail caab@bracnet.net; internet www.caab.gov.bd; Chair. Air Vice-Marshal MAHMUD HUSSAIN.

Best Air: 43 Rd 1/A, Blk J, Baridhara Diplomatic Area, Dhaka 1212; tel. (2) 9888780; fax (2) 8860248; e-mail info@bestairbd.com; internet www.bestairbd.com; f. 1999; est. as helicopter operator, later freight airline; currently operates one domestic passenger service; international services to India, Thailand and China; 80% of shares purchased by Destiny Group in 2010; Man. Dir M. HAIDER UZZAMAN; Chair. MOHAMMAD RAFIQUL AMIN.

Biman Bangladesh Airlines: Head Office, Balaka, Kurmitola, Dhaka 1229; tel. (2) 8917400; fax (2) 8913005; e-mail dgmpr@bdbiman.com; internet www.biman-airlines.com; f. 1972; fmrly state-owned; transferred to private ownership in 2007; domestic services to 4 major towns; international services to 18 destinations in the Middle East, the Far East, Europe and North America; Chair. Air Marshal (retd) JAMAL UDDIN AHMED; CEO and Man. Dir Air Cdre (retd) MUHAMMAD ZAKIUL ISLAM.

GMG Airlines: Plot Nos 1 and 3, Rd 21, Nikunja 2, Dhaka 1229; tel. (2) 8900460; fax (2) 8924390; e-mail info@gmgairlines.com; internet www.gmgairlines.com; f. 1997; private, domestic airline; Man. Dir SHAHAB SATTAR.

Regent Airways: Plot No. 15, Dhaka Mymensingh Rd, Sector 3, Uttara Model Town, Dhaka 1230; tel. (2) 8953003; e-mail info@flyregent.com; internet www.flyregent.com; f. 2010; subsidiary of Habib Group; domestic flights to 5 destinations; CEO IMRAN ASIF.

United Airways (BD) Ltd: 1 Jasimuddin Ave, Uttara Tower, 5th Floor, Uttara, Dhaka 1230; tel. (2) 8931712; fax (2) 8932339; e-mail info@uabdl.com; internet www.uabdl.com; privately owned domestic airline; gained permit for international flights 2008; Chair. and CEO Capt. TASBIRUL AHMED CHOUDHURY.

Tourism

Tourist attractions include the cities of Dhaka and Chittagong, Cox's Bazar—which has the world's longest beach (120 km)—on the Bay of Bengal, and Teknaf, at the southernmost point of Bangladesh. In 2010 an estimated 303,000 tourists visited Bangladesh, and receipts from tourism amounted to about US $110m. (excluding passenger transport) in 2012.

Bangladesh Parjatan Corpn (Govt Tourism Organization): 83–88 Mohakhali Commercial Area, Dhaka 1212; tel. (2) 8833229; fax (2)

8833900; e-mail info@bangladeshtourism.gov.bd; internet www.parjatan.gov.bd; f. 1973; in addition to the one in Dhaka, there are tourist information centres in Bogra, Chittagong, Cox's Bazar, Dinajpur, Khulna, Kuakata, Mongla, Rangamati, Rangpur, Rajshahi, Sylhet, Teknaf and Tungi Para; Chair. MD MAKSUDUL HASAN KHAN.

Bangladesh Tourism Board: Bangladesh House Building Finance Corporation's Building, 7th Floor, 22 Purana Paltan, Dhaka 1000; tel. (2) 9513328; e-mail btbnto@gmail.com; internet www.tourismboard.gov.bd; national tourism org.; responsible for formulating plans and policies for the devt of tourism; CEO AKHTARAUZ ZAMAN KHAN KABIR.

Tour Operators' Association of Bangladesh: 5/8, 1st Floor, Sangsad Ave, Monipuripara, Dhaka 1215; tel. (2) 9114266; fax (2) 9886984; e-mail office@toab.org; f. 1992; Pres. HASAN MANSUR.

Defence

As assessed at November 2013, the total active armed forces numbered 157,050: the army had a total strength of 126,150, the navy 16,900 and the air force 14,000. The paramilitary forces, which totalled 63,900, comprised an armed police reserve of 5,000, a coastguard of 900, a 20,000-strong security guard and the Bangladesh Rifles (or Border Guard Bangladesh), numbering 38,000. Military service is voluntary.

Defence Budget: Estimated at 132,880m. taka for 2012/13 (equivalent to 11.9% of total budgetary expenditure).

Chief of Army Staff: Gen. IQBAL KARIM BHUIYAN.

Chief of Naval Staff: Vice-Adm. M. FARID HABIB.

Chief of Air Staff: Air Marshal MUHAMMAD ENAMUL BARI.

Dir-Gen. of Border Guard Bangladesh: Maj.-Gen. AZIZ AHMED.

Education

The Government provides free schooling for all children for eight years. Primary education, which is compulsory, begins at six years of age and lasts for five years. Secondary education, beginning at the age of 11, lasts for up to seven years, comprising a first cycle of three years, a second cycle of two years and a third cycle of two further years. A Second Primary Education Development Program was initiated in 2004, with substantial funding from international agencies. The initiative, which concluded in mid-2011, aimed to improve the quality of infrastructure, materials and teacher-training in the primary sector, as well as lowering the pupil-teacher ratio. In 2010 an estimated 92% of children (90% of boys; 93% of girls) in the relevant age-group were enrolled at primary schools, while in 2011 the enrolment ratio at secondary schools was 46% (42% of boys; 49% of girls). In 2011/12 there were 89,712 primary schools and 21,015 secondary schools. Secondary schools and colleges in the private sector vastly outnumber government institutions. In 2012, according to the Ministry of Education, there were 34 public and 52 private universities. In the same year there were 3,327 technical colleges, vocational institutes and colleges offering general education. The 2013/14 budget allocated 170,220m. taka to education and technology (equivalent to 12.4% of total projected government expenditure).

BARBADOS

Introductory Survey

LOCATION, CLIMATE, LANGUAGE, RELIGION, FLAG, CAPITAL

Barbados is the most easterly of the Caribbean islands, lying about 320 km (200 miles) north-east of Trinidad. The island has a total area of 430 sq km (166 sq miles). There is a rainy season from July to November and the climate is tropical, tempered by constant sea winds, during the rest of the year. The mean annual temperature is about 26°C (78°F). Average annual rainfall varies from 1,250 mm (49 ins) on the coast, to 1,875 mm (74 ins) in the interior. The official language is English. Almost all of the inhabitants profess Christianity, but there are small groups of Hindus, Muslims and Jews. The largest denomination is the Anglican church, but about 90 other Christian sects are represented. The national flag (proportions 2 by 3) has three equal vertical stripes, of blue, gold and blue; superimposed on the centre of the gold band is the head of a black trident. The capital is Bridgetown.

CONTEMPORARY POLITICAL HISTORY

Historical Context

Barbados was formerly a British colony. The Barbados Labour Party (BLP) won a general election in 1951, when universal adult suffrage was introduced, and held office until 1961. Although the parliamentary system dates from 1639, ministerial government was not established until 1954, when the BLP's leader, Sir Grantley Adams, became the island's first Premier. He was subsequently Prime Minister of the West Indies Federation from January 1958 until its dissolution in May 1962.

Domestic Political Affairs

Barbados achieved full internal self-government in October 1961. The Democratic Labour Party (DLP), formed in 1955 by dissident members of the BLP, won an election in December. The DLP's leader, Errol Barrow, became Premier, succeeding Dr Hugh Cummins of the BLP. When Barbados achieved independence on 30 November 1966, Barrow became the island's first Prime Minister, following another electoral victory by his party earlier in the month.

The DLP retained power in 1971, but in the 1976 general election the BLP, led by J. M. G. M. (Tom) Adams (Sir Grantley's son), ended Barrow's 15-year rule. The BLP was returned to office at a general election in 1981. Adams died in 1985 and was succeeded as Prime Minister by his deputy, Bernard St John. At a general election in 1986 the DLP won a decisive victory, and Barrow returned as Prime Minister. However, Barrow died the year later and was succeeded by L. Erskine Sandiford (hitherto the Deputy Prime Minister).

At a general election in 1991 the DLP won a majority of seats in the enlarged House of Assembly. The creation of a Ministry of Justice and Public Safety by the new Government and the reintroduction of flogging for convicted criminals reflected widespread concern over increased levels of violent crime. Moreover, as a result of serious economic problems, a series of austerity measures was proposed, resulting in public unrest. The increasing unpopularity of Sandiford's premiership provoked demands for his resignation, culminating, in June 1994, in his narrow defeat in a parliamentary motion of confidence. At a general election in September the BLP won a decisive victory and Owen Arthur was subsequently appointed Prime Minister.

The BLP in power

In May 1995 Arthur announced the formation of a commission to advise the Government on possible reforms of the country's Constitution and political institutions. The commission was asked to consider, in particular, the continuing role of the British monarch as Head of State in Barbados. The commission's report, published in December 1998, recommended, as expected, the replacement of the British monarch with a ceremonial President. It also proposed the substitution of a jointly administered regional court for the existing highest judicial body, the Privy Council in the United Kingdom; Caribbean leaders agreed to establish such a court (see below) in 2001.

In November 1998, owing to a recent significant increase in the number of violent crimes, stricter penalties for unlawful possession of firearms were introduced. Amid fears that the escalation in gun crime might affect the country's tourism industry, an anti-firearms unit within the police force was established in 1999. In 2002 the Government established a National Commission on Law and Order to help develop a plan of action to combat the rising crime rate. By 2006 the annual murder rate of 13 people per 100,000 was among the lowest in the Caribbean, but still double the level of the mid-1990s.

The BLP won an overwhelming victory at the general election held in January 1999. The heavy defeat for the DLP was largely attributed to the Government's recent successes in reviving the Barbadian economy, particularly in reducing unemployment.

In August 2000 Arthur announced that there would be a referendum on the replacement of the monarchy with a republic, a move that had the support of all political parties. New constitutional legislation was drafted in 2002; however, the only change made was an amendment to override human rights judgments by the Privy Council, making it easier to make use of the death penalty. In June 2003 the Governor-General announced that the Government intended to transform Barbados into a republic. In February 2005 Arthur stated that a referendum on the issue would be held by the end of the year, but, owing to legislative obstacles, the referendum was suspended.

Owen Arthur's BLP won a third successive victory at the general election of 21 May 2003, attracting 56% of the votes cast, and securing 23 of the 30 seats in the enlarged House of Assembly. The DLP did, however, increase its share of the popular vote to 44% (from 35% in 1999) and its parliamentary strength to seven. Clyde Mascoll, a former Central Bank economist, was appointed DLP leader. Arthur, meanwhile, appointed Mia Mottley, the Attorney-General and Minister of Home Affairs, as Deputy Prime Minister.

In November 2005 the former DLP leader David Thompson was again elected to lead the party, replacing Mascoll. In January 2006 Mascoll defected from the DLP to join the BLP, and was rapidly appointed to the Cabinet as Minister of State in the Ministry of Finance. Among several other ministerial changes effected by Arthur, the most significant was the transfer of Deputy Prime Minister Mottley to the new Ministry of Economic Affairs and Development.

A DLP Government

The opposition DLP won a majority in the general election held on 15 January 2008, securing 52.7% of the votes cast and 20 seats in the House of Assembly. The BLP won the remaining 10 seats. Thompson was appointed Prime Minister, and a new Cabinet was also installed. Following his party's defeat, Arthur announced his retirement from politics; Mottley replaced him as BLP leader.

Thompson effected a major reorganization of his Cabinet in November 2008, which included the removal of Christopher Sinckler as Minister of Foreign Affairs, Foreign Trade and International Business and the appointment of the Attorney-General and Minister of Home Affairs, Freundel Stuart, as Deputy Prime Minister in addition to his existing portfolios. Maxine McClean assumed responsibility for foreign affairs and foreign trade, and George Hutson was appointed to head the new Ministry of International Business and International Transport. Another cabinet reorganization was carried out in March 2010, although the main portfolios were left unaltered.

In March 2009 Thompson survived an opposition-led motion of no confidence in the House of Assembly over his handling of the financial instability that was precipitated by the collapse of CLICO Holdings, an insurance company based in Trinidad and the largest in the region. He was accused by the BLP of failing in his duty to safeguard Barbadian jobs, pensions and policy-holders' interests. The Government announced a new immigration policy in May: to avoid deportation, Caribbean Community and Common Market (CARICOM, see p. 223) nationals living illegally in Barbados would have until the end of the year to prove they had lived in Barbados for at least eight years prior to 2005, pass a security background check and produce evidence of their employment. This policy was expected to impact mostly on nationals from Guyana, who comprised the majority of the estimated 20,000 illegal immigrants in the country, and seemed to be supported by Barbadians as a response to the increasingly grave economic situation and rising levels of unemployment.

Recent developments: Stuart's premiership

Thompson went on medical leave in July 2010, with Stuart serving as acting Prime Minister during his absence. Although Thompson returned to work at the end of August, it was announced that he had pancreatic cancer, but he would remain as Prime Minister. Thompson died on 23 October. Stuart was sworn in as Prime Minister and Minister of National Security later the same day, while Adriel Brathwaite took over the new premier's previous responsibilities, becoming Minister of Home Affairs and Attorney-General. Thompson's vacant legislative seat was won by his widow, Mara, in a by-election held in January 2011. Stuart implemented a cabinet reorganization in June, with most of the changes affecting the economic portfolios, underlining the Government's priorities.

Meanwhile, Mottley, after losing the support of some of her colleagues, was replaced by Arthur as BLP leader in October 2010, creating divisions within the party. Aware of the need for unity prior to the next general election, in April 2011 Arthur made efforts to reconcile with Mottley. However, despite subsequent proclamations of rapprochement, tensions within the BLP remained. Internal party dissent was also evident within the DLP in late 2011, arising from concerns that the ruling party would be defeated in the election under Stuart's stewardship. Opinion polls in 2012 suggested that there was widespread popular dissatisfaction with the Stuart administration, owing to the anaemic state of the island's economy; nevertheless, the DLP won 16 of the 30 seats in the House of Assembly in the general election of 21 February 2013. Stuart was sworn into office for a second term and a new Cabinet was installed, although many ministers were retained from the previous Government. Among the reallocation of portfolios John Boyce was appointed Minister of Health, while Michael Lashley assumed Boyce's previous portfolio, transport and works. The former Minister of Health, Donville Inniss, took charge of the Ministry of Industry, International Business, Commerce and Small Business Development. The disappointing election result for the BLP prompted the party to designate Mottley as its new leader on 25 February.

Crime, particularly against foreign tourists, continued to be a pressing concern to the Government in 2013. In January two British tourists were stabbed in their accommodation in the north-west of the island, while in March two cruise passengers were injured by gunshots walking back to their ship. The incidents attracted negative publicity to the economically vital tourism industry, particularly following the release in December 2012 of a man who had been imprisoned for 18 months after being wrongly convicted of raping two British tourists in 2010. The victims claimed that the police had made no effort to find the real offender, an assertion that the police commissioner, Darwin Dottin, repudiated.

The Caribbean Court of Justice

In April 2005, following many delays, the Caribbean Court of Justice (CCJ), which replaced the United Kingdom-based Privy Council, was inaugurated in Trinidad and Tobago; however, by early 2014 only Barbados, Guyana and Belize had instituted the Court as their supreme appellate body. The CCJ issued its first seminal ruling in November 2006, endorsing a decision of the Appeal Court of Barbados to reduce to life imprisonment the death penalties requested against two convicted murderers, and thus demonstrating the CCJ's disinclination to reinstate capital punishment (the last execution in Barbados was in 1984).

Foreign Affairs

The Governments of Barbados and Trinidad and Tobago agreed in 1999 to draft a boundary delimitation treaty and to establish a negotiating mechanism to resolve trade disputes. The issue of boundary delimitation, however, remained unresolved, and in 2004 the Prime Minister of Trinidad and Tobago indicated that he would refer the matter to CARICOM. Relations between the two countries worsened after several Barbadian fishermen were arrested in Trinidad and Tobago's waters; in response, the Government imposed sanctions against Trinidad and Tobago manufacturers. Later that month Barbados referred the dispute for arbitration under the UN Convention on the Law of the Sea. In 2005 the Barbados Government formed a committee to investigate whether a significant natural gas discovery off east Trinidad fell within Barbadian maritime territory. The Government of Trinidad and Tobago insisted the discovery was within its jurisdiction. Hearings on the boundary dispute commenced in October at the International Dispute Resolution Centre, and in April 2006 a tribunal ruling established a boundary between the two states. This gave Barbados a large area to the south-east of the island, which had been claimed by Trinidad and Tobago, and was thought to have potential for deep-water oil and gas exploration. The tribunal rejected the Barbadian claim to a large area to the north of Tobago, but instructed the two countries to negotiate a fishing agreement for this area 'in good faith'. However, despite initial progress, by 2011 talks to establish an agreement had stalled and no substantive progress was reported during 2012–13. Construction of a 300-km gas pipeline between the two countries was expected to commence in 2014. When completed, the pipeline would allow Barbados to benefit from cheaper Trinidadian gas imports, and plans were in place to extend the link to other islands in the region.

In October 2009 Barbados signed an agreement with France on the delimitation of the maritime boundary between Barbados, Martinique and Guadeloupe. Barbados opened an embassy in the People's Republic of China in 2010. In particular, the Government hoped to strengthen investment, tourism, energy and education ties. Some Bds $16m. was secured from the Chinese Government in September 2011 to finance a number of projects on the island, and the two countries signed an economic co-operation accord in August 2012. During a visit to the Caribbean in June 2013, Chinese President Xi Jinping met with Stuart to discuss bilateral trade relations; Xi also agreed to provide Barbados with another Bds $16m. grant to support domestic programmes.

In 1996 Barbados signed an agreement with the USA to co-operate with a regional initiative to combat the illegal drugs trade. The Government signed a similar agreement with the Organization of American States (OAS) in 2005. In 2000 Barbados officially declared its acceptance of the compulsory jurisdiction of the Inter-American Court of Human Rights (see p. 395), an institution of the OAS. Meanwhile, Barbados joined CARICOM's Caribbean Single Market and Economy (CSME), which was established on 1 January 2006. The CSME was intended to enshrine the free movement of goods, services and labour throughout the CARICOM region, although only six of the organization's 15 members were signatories to the new project from its inauguration. The CSME had originally been expected to be fully operational by 2015, but Stuart, in his role as Lead Head of Government with Responsibility for the CSME, announced in mid-2011 that this target would not be attained. No clear schedule for CSME implementation had been formulated by early 2014, raising doubts about whether the single market would ever be realized. Stuart insisted that the CSME was still viable, although there appeared to be a lack of enthusiasm for the project among other CARICOM heads of government.

CONSTITUTION AND GOVERNMENT

Executive power is vested in the British monarch, represented by a Governor-General, who acts on the advice of the Cabinet. The Governor-General appoints the Prime Minister and, on the latter's recommendation, other members of the Cabinet. Legislative power is vested in the bicameral Parliament, comprising a Senate of 21 members, appointed by the Governor-General, and a House of Assembly with 30 members, elected by universal adult suffrage for five years (subject to dissolution) from single-member constituencies. The Cabinet is responsible to Parliament. The island is divided into 11 parishes, all of which are administered by the central Government.

REGIONAL AND INTERNATIONAL CO-OPERATION

Barbados is a member of the Caribbean Community and Common Market (CARICOM, see p. 223) and of CARICOM's Caribbean Single Market and Economy, launched in 2006 (see Foreign Affairs), the Inter-American Development Bank (see p. 331), the Latin American Economic System (see p. 452), the Association of Caribbean States (see p. 449), and of the Community of Latin American and Caribbean States (see p. 464), which was formally inaugurated in December 2011.

Barbados acceded to the UN in 1966, upon independence. As a contracting party to the General Agreement on Tariffs and

Trade, Barbados joined the World Trade Organization (see p. 434) on its establishment in 1995. The country became a member of the Commonwealth (see p. 236) upon independence.

ECONOMIC AFFAIRS

In 2009, according to estimates by the World Bank, the island's gross national income (GNI), measured at average 2007–09 prices, was US $3,454m., equivalent to US $12,380 per head (or US $18,400 on an international purchasing-power parity basis). Between 2003 and 2012 the population increased at an average rate of 0.5% per year. Barbados' gross domestic product (GDP) per head, increased, in real terms, at an average rate of 0.4% per year during 2003–09. Overall GDP increased, in real terms, at an average annual rate of 1.1% in 2003–12, according to official estimates; real GDP was stagnant in 2012.

Agriculture (including hunting, forestry and fishing) contributed an estimated 1.4% of GDP in 2012, according to official estimates, while the sector engaged an estimated 2.6% of the employed labour force in the first quarter of 2013. Rum was the principal domestic export commodity. In 2013 rum contributed 16.1% of the value of domestic exports, while sugar accounted for 3.0%. The other principal crops, primarily for local consumption, are sweet potatoes, carrots, yams, and other vegetables and fruit. The Government was seeking investors to fund diversification of the failing sugar industry. The GDP of the agricultural sector declined, in real terms, at an average rate of 1.9% per year during 2003–12; sectoral GDP declined by an estimated 3.4% in 2012.

In 2012 industry accounted for an estimated 15.1% of GDP, according to official figures, and 18.6% of the working population were employed in all industrial activities (manufacturing, construction, quarrying and utilities) in the first quarter of 2013. In real terms, industrial GDP decreased at an average rate of 1.7% annually in 2003–12; real industrial GDP increased by 1.8% in 2011, but decreased by an estimated 5.3% in 2012.

According to official estimates, in 2012 mining contributed an estimated 0.3% of GDP. The mining and construction sector employed 9.6% of the working population in the first quarter of 2013. The sector decreased by an average annual rate of 6.5% in 2003–12; mining GDP contracted by an estimated 8.0% in 2012.

In 2012 manufacturing contributed a preliminary 6.7% of GDP and employed 6.5% of the working population in the first quarter of 2013. Excluding sugar factories and refineries, the principal branches of manufacturing were chemical, petroleum, rubber and plastic products, food products and beverages, and tobacco. According to official estimates, manufacturing GDP decreased, in real terms, at an average rate of 3.3% per year during 2003–12; it contracted by an estimated 6.8% in 2012.

The construction sector contributed 5.1% of GDP in 2012 and employed 9.6% (including mining) of the working population in the first quarter of 2013. During 2003–12 the GDP of the sector decreased at an average annual rate of 1.9%, according to official estimates; construction GDP increased by 10.5% in 2011, but decreased by an estimated 7.4% in 2012.

Production of natural gas stood at an estimated 16.0m. cu m in 2011. Barbados traditionally has high fuel import costs; imports of mineral fuels accounted for 31.0% of total imports in 2012. In that year the Government announced plans to modernize the energy sector, to improve efficiency and to reduce import costs. Construction of a natural gas pipeline from Trinidad and Tobago to Barbados was scheduled to begin in 2014. Barbados was expected to start receiving supplies via the US $300m. pipeline in 2016. Production of crude petroleum stood at a provisional 300,000 barrels in 2011.

Service industries are the main sector of the economy, accounting for 83.5% of GDP in 2012, and 78.8% of employment in the first quarter of 2013. The combined GDP of the services sector increased, in real terms, at an average rate of 1.9% per year during 2003–12, according to official figures; the sector expanded by an estimated 1.3% in 2012. Business and financial services contributed 30.5% of GDP in 2012. The Government has encouraged the growth of 'offshore' financial facilities, particularly through the negotiation of double taxation agreements with other countries. In November 2013 there were 46 'offshore' banks registered. Barbados has an active anti-money-laundering regime. Tourism made a direct contribution of an estimated 13.2% to GDP in 2012, and it employed 10.8% of the working population in the first quarter of 2013. Tourism and travel indirectly contributed 39.4% of GDP in 2012, according to the World Travel and Tourism Council. In 2012 the number of stop-over tourist arrivals stood at a provisional 536,303, a fall of 5.5% on the previous year's total. Cruise ship passenger numbers also decreased in 2012, to a provisional 517,436 (from 609,844 in the previous year). Receipts from tourism declined to a provisional $916m. in 2012. Visitors from the United Kingdom comprised a provisional 32.4% of total stop-over visitors in 2012, followed by the USA (24.4%).

In 2010 Barbados recorded a visible merchandise trade deficit of Bds $2,153.3m., while there was a deficit of $517.2m. on the current account of the balance of payments. In 2011 the USA was the principal source of imports, accounting for 42.4% of the total. Other important trading partners were the countries of the Caribbean Community and Common Market (CARICOM, see p. 223). CARICOM partners were the principal source of exports in 2011 (accounting for 40.7% of total exports). The USA was another important purchaser in that year. The principal exports in 2011 were chemicals, miscellaneous manufactured articles, beverages and tobacco, food and live animals, manufactured goods classified chiefly by material, and machinery and transport equipment. The principal imports were machinery and transport equipment, food and live animals, miscellaneous manufactured articles, and manufactured goods classified chiefly by material.

For the financial year ending 31 March 2012 there was an estimated total budgetary deficit of Bds $677.3m., equivalent to 8.0% of GDP. Barbados's general government gross debt was Bds $7,275m. in 2012, equivalent to 85.9% of GDP. In 2006 the total external debt of Barbados was some Bds $2,946m. In that year, the cost of servicing long-term public and publicly guaranteed debt and repayments to the IMF, at Bds $253.2m., was equivalent to 6.3% of the value of exports of goods, services and income (excluding workers' remittances). According to official estimates, the total external debt of Barbados stood at Bds $2,649.0m. in 2012. According to ILO, the average annual rate of inflation was 5.6% in 2003–12. Consumer prices rose by an average of 4.5% in 2012. In the first quarter of 2013 the unemployment rate was 11.5%.

Political stability and consensus have contributed to the economic strengths of Barbados. Tourism dominates the economy but the international financial services sector is also important. Following the economic contraction of 2009, economic activity remained slow in 2010, resulting in negligible real GDP growth and rising rates of unemployment and government debt. Among the unpopular measures announced in the 2010 austerity budget were a temporary 2.5% rise in value-added tax (which was made permanent in 2012) and the withdrawal of a range of tax breaks. The economy expanded by a disappointing 0.8% in 2011. Inflation also increased in that year—the result of rising food and fuel prices on international markets—and levels of public debt were still unsustainably high. The construction industry staged a modest recovery in 2012, but this was offset by a decline in visitor numbers, which placed further pressure on the Government's finances. There was zero growth in 2012, and the country's fragile fiscal position and high unemployment rates continued to provoke deep concern. The economy re-entered recession in 2013, owing to the poor performance of the tourism, construction, financial and export sectors, with the IMF estimating the contraction at 0.8%. The consequent decline in domestic demand and government revenues exacerbated the country's fiscal problems, and credit ratings agencies downgraded the Barbadian economy on multiple occasions during the year. Following an unsuccessful bond issue in September, the Government confirmed in late 2013 that a stringent austerity programme would be effected, entailing civil service retrenchment, tax increases and a reduction in public spending. A five-year plan to increase foreign exchange earnings in the international business sector was also announced in early 2014. The IMF expected real GDP to decline by a further 1.1% in 2014, with a return to growth largely contingent upon economic developments within the United Kingdom and the USA, the countries of origin of most of the island's tourists. The Central Bank predicted that the deficit would decrease to the equivalent of 5% of GDP in 2014 following the implementation of further budget cuts.

PUBLIC HOLIDAYS

2015: 1 January (New Year's Day), 21 January (Errol Barrow Day), 3 April (Good Friday), 6 April (Easter Monday), 28 April (National Heroes' Day), 1 May (Labour Day), 25 May (Whit Monday), 1 August (Emancipation Day), 3 August (Kadooment Day), 30 November (Independence Day), 25–26 December (Christmas).

Statistical Survey

Sources (unless otherwise stated): Barbados Statistical Service, National Insurance Bldg, 3rd Floor, Fairchild St, Bridgetown; tel. 427-7841; fax 435-2198; e-mail barstats@caribsurf.com; internet www.barstats.gov.bb; Central Bank of Barbados, Tom Adams Financial Centre, Spry St, POB 1016, Bridgetown; tel. 436-6870; fax 427-9559; e-mail cbb.libr@caribsurf.com; internet www.centralbank.org.bb.

AREA AND POPULATION

Area: 430 sq km (166 sq miles).

Population: 268,792 at census of 1 May 2000; 277,821 (males 133,018, females 144,803) at census of 2 May 2010. *Mid-2014* (UN estimate): 286,063 (Source: UN, *World Population Prospects: The 2012 Revision*).

Density (at mid-2014): 665.3 per sq km.

Population by Age and Sex (UN estimates at mid-2014): *0–14:* 53,688 (males 27,317, females 26,371); *15–64:* 200,733 (males 102,043, females 98,690); *65 and over:* 31,642 (males 13,371, females 18,271); *Total* 286,063 (males 142,731, females 143,332) (Source: UN, *World Population Prospects: The 2012 Revision*).

Ethnic Groups (2010 census): Black 209,109; White 6,135; Mixed race 7,034; Total (incl. others) 226,193. Note: Data exclude institutional population (2,513) and adjustment for underenumeration (49,115).

Parishes (population at 2010 census): Christ Church 54,336; St Andrew 5,139; St George 19,767; St James 28,498; St John 8,963; St Joseph 6,620; St Lucy 9,758; St Michael 88,529; St Peter 11,300; St Philip 30,662; St Thomas 14,249; *Total* 277,821.

Principal Towns (population at 2000 census, preliminary): Bridgetown (capital) 5,996; Speightstown 2,604; Holetown 1,087; Oistins 1,203. *Mid-2011* (population in '000, incl. suburbs): Bridgetown 122 (Source: UN, *World Urbanization Prospects: The 2011 Revision*).

Births, Marriages and Deaths (2007, unless otherwise indicated): Live births 3,537 (birth rate 12.9 per 1,000); Marriages (2000) 3,518 (marriage rate 13.1 per 1,000); Deaths 2,213 (death rate 8.1 per 1,000). Source: partly UN, *Population and Vital Statistics Report*. *2012:* Crude birth rate 12.2 per 1,000; Crude death rate 8.4 per 1,000 (Source: Pan American Health Organization).

Life Expectancy (years at birth): 75.0 (males 72.6; females 77.4) in 2011 (Source: World Bank, World Development Indicators database).

Economically Active Population (labour force sample surveys, '000 persons aged 15 years and over, excl. armed forces, January–March 2013): Agriculture, forestry and fishing 3.3; Manufacturing 8.2; Electricity, gas and water 3.2; Construction and quarrying 12.1; Wholesale and retail trade 20.2; Tourism 13.7; Transport, storage and communications 6.4; Finance and insurance 6.0; Professional, scientific and technical services 4.9; Administrative and support services 7.0; Public administration and defence 10.2; Education 7.7; Health and social welfare 6.3; Household employees 5.1; Other services 12.0; *Total employed* 126.3 (males 64.2, females 62.0); Unemployed 16.4 (males 8.6, females 7.7); *Total labour force* 142.6 (males 72.9, females 69.8).

HEALTH AND WELFARE

Key Indicators

Total Fertility Rate (children per woman, 2011): 1.6.

Under-5 Mortality Rate (per 1,000 live births, 2011): 20.

HIV/AIDS (% of persons aged 15–49, 2011, estimate): 0.9.

Physicians (per 1,000 head, 2005): 1.8.

Hospital Beds (per 1,000 head, 2009): 6.8.

Health Expenditure (2010): US $ per head (PPP): 1,520.

Health Expenditure (2010): % of GDP: 6.7.

Health Expenditure (2010): public (% of total): 65.0.

Total Carbon Dioxide Emissions ('000 metric tons, 2010): 1,503.5.

Total Carbon Dioxide Emissions Per Head (metric tons, 2010): 5.4.

Human Development Index (2012): ranking: 38.

Human Development Index (2012): value: 0.825.

For sources and definitions, see explanatory note on p. vi.

AGRICULTURE, ETC.

Principal Crops ('000 metric tons, 2012, FAO estimates): Sweet potatoes 0.6; Yams 0.2; Avocados 0.7; Pulses 1.9; Coconuts 2.0; Tomatoes 0.9; Cucumbers 1.2; Chillies and peppers, green 0.4; Onions, dry 0.4; String beans 0.9; Carrots and turnips 0.2; Okra 0.3; Maize 0.3; Bananas 1.0.

Livestock ('000 head, year ending September 2012, FAO estimates): Horses 1.3; Asses 2.3; Mules 2.0; Cattle 11.0; Pigs 22.5; Sheep 13.0; Goats 5.3; Poultry 3,660.

Livestock Products ('000 metric tons, 2012, FAO estimates): Cattle meat 0.2; Pig meat 3.0; Chicken meat 14.7; Cows' milk 6.0; Hen eggs 2.1.

Forestry ('000 cubic metres, 2012, FAO estimates): Roundwood removals 10.9.

Fishing (metric tons, live weight, 2011, FAO estimates): Total catch 1,837 (Yellowfin tuna 131; Flying fishes 908; Common dolphinfish 505).

Source: FAO.

MINING

Production (2011, provisional): Natural gas 16.0m. cu m; Crude petroleum 300,000 barrels; Cement 300,000 metric tons. Source: US Geological Survey.

INDUSTRY

Selected Products (2009 unless otherwise indicated): Raw sugar 33,000 metric tons; Rum 11,000,000 litres (2003); Beer 8,500,000 litres (2007); Cigarettes 65m. (1995); Batteries 17,165 (official estimate, 1998); Electric energy 1,022.9m. kWh. Sources: partly UN Industrial Commodity Statistics Database, and IMF, *Barbados: Statistical Appendix* (May 2004).

FINANCE

Currency and Exchange Rates: 100 cents = 1 Barbados dollar (Bds $). *Sterling, US Dollar and Euro Equivalents* (31 December 2013): £1 sterling = Bds $3.294; US $1 = Bds $2.000; €1 = Bds $2.758; Bds $100 = £30.36 = US $50.00 = €36.26. *Exchange Rate*: Fixed at US $1 = Bds $2.000 since 1986.

Budget (Bds $ million, year ending 31 March 2013, estimates): *Revenue:* Tax revenue 2,193.7 (Direct taxes 847.5, Indirect taxes 1,346.2); Non-tax revenue and grants 147.0; Total 2,340.7. *Expenditure:* Current 2,895.2 (Wages and salaries 870.4, Other goods and services 391.8, Interest payments 559.5, Transfers and subsidies 1,073.5); Capital (incl. net lending) 122.8; Total 3,018.0.

International Reserves (US $ million at 31 December 2012): IMF special drawing rights 86.83; Reserve position in IMF 8.92; Foreign exchange 743.97; Total 839.72. Source: IMF, *International Financial Statistics*.

Money Supply (Bds $ million at 31 December 2009): Currency outside depository corporations 494.0; Transferable deposits 3,098.2; Other deposits 7,355.6; *Broad money* 10,947.8. Source: IMF, *International Financial Statistics*.

Cost of Living (Consumer Price Index; base: 2005 = 100): All items 132.4 in 2010; 149.3 in 2011; 153.1 in 2012. Source: IMF, *International Financial Statistics*.

Gross Domestic Product (Bds $ million at constant 1974 prices): 1,067.9 in 2010, 1,076.0 in 2011; 1,076.1 in 2012.

Expenditure on the Gross Domestic Product (Bds $ million at current prices, 2012): Government final consumption expenditure 1,364.4; Private final consumption expenditure 6,780.0; Gross capital formation 1,204.2; *Total domestic expenditure* 9,348.6; Exports of goods and services 3,589.6; *Less* Imports of goods and services 4,590.8; Statistical discrepancy 102.5; *GDP in purchasers' values* 8,449.7.

Gross Domestic Product by Economic Activity (estimates, Bds $ million at current prices, 2012): Agriculture, hunting, forestry and fishing 103.7; Mining and quarrying 20.8; Manufacturing 489.9; Electricity, gas and water 224.2; Construction 370.9; Wholesale and retail trade 741.9; Hotels and restaurants 965.9; Transport, storage and communications 846.0; Finance, insurance, real estate and business services 2,233.1; Government services 951.7; Other community, social and personal services 379.0; *Sub-total* 7,327.1; *Less* Financial intermediation services indirectly measured (FISIM) 166.2; *GDP at factor cost* 7,160.9; Indirect taxes, less subsidies 1,391.3; Statistical discrepancy –102.5; *GDP in purchasers' values* 8,449.7.

Balance of Payments (Bds $ million, 2010): Exports of goods f.o.b. 861.4; Imports of goods f.o.b. –3,014.7; *Trade balance* –2,153.3; Exports of services 3,247.4; Imports of services –1,465.3; *Balance on goods and services* –371.2; Other income received 472.4; Other income paid –696.2; *Balance on goods, services and income* –595.0; Current transfers received 222.3; Current transfers paid –144.5; *Current balance* –517.2; Capital and financial accounts (net) 512.1; Net errors and omissions 66.1; *Overall balance* 61.0.

EXTERNAL TRADE

Principal Commodities (excl. petroleum, Bds $ million, 2011, provisional): *Imports c.i.f.:* Food and live animals 512.9; Beverages and tobacco 95.9; Crude materials (inedible) except fuels 81.8; Mineral fuels, lubricants, etc. 45.1; Animal and vegetable oils and fats 21.4; Chemicals 351.6; Manufactured goods classified chiefly by material 406.8; Machinery and transport equipment 682.9; Miscellaneous manufactured articles 413.5; Miscellaneous transactions and commodities 15.0; Total 2,627.0. *Exports f.o.b.:* Food and live animals 83.5; Beverages and tobacco 93.4; Crude materials (inedible) except fuels 7.4; Mineral fuels, lubricants, etc. 1.2; Animal and vegetable oils and fats 6.3; Chemicals 191.4; Manufactured goods classified chiefly by material 68.7; Machinery and transport equipment 47.4; Miscellaneous manufactured articles 108.0; Miscellaneous transactions and commodities 7.7; Total 615.0 (incl. re-exports 120.2).

Principal Trading Partners (excluding petroleum, Bds $ million, 2011, provisional): *Imports c.i.f.:* Canada 112.0; CARICOM 277.2; Germany 72.3; Japan 82.5; United Kingdom 143.1; USA 1,114.4; Total (incl. others) 2,627.0. *Exports f.o.b.:* Canada 15.1; CARICOM 250.0; United Kingdom 110.1; USA 137.0; Total (incl. others) 615.0 (incl. re-exports 120.2).

TRANSPORT

Road Traffic (motor vehicles in use, 2007): Passenger cars 103,535; Buses and coaches 631; Lorries and vans 15,151; Motorcycles and mopeds 2,525. Source: IRF, *World Road Statistics*.

Shipping (estimated freight traffic, '000 metric tons, 1990): Goods loaded 206; Goods unloaded 538 (Source: UN, *Monthly Bulletin of Statistics*). *Total Goods Handled* ('000 metric tons, 2010): 1,082 (Source: Barbados Port Authority). *Flag Registered Fleet* (at 31 December 2013): Number of vessels 138; Total displacement 882,619 grt (Source: Lloyd's List Intelligence—www.lloydslistintelligence.com).

Civil Aviation (1994): Aircraft movements 36,100; Freight loaded 5,052.3 metric tons; Freight unloaded 8,548.3 metric tons.

TOURISM

Tourist Arrivals ('000 persons): *Stop-overs:* 532.2 in 2010; 567.7 in 2011; 536.3 in 2012 (provisional). *Cruise-ship passengers:* 664.7 in 2010; 609.8 in 2011; 517.4 in 2012 (provisional).

Tourist Arrivals by Country ('000 visitor stop-overs, 2012, provisional): Canada 72.0; Germany 9.2; Trinidad and Tobago 38.0; Other CARICOM 58.5; United Kingdom 173.5; USA 130.8; Total (incl. others) 536.3.

Tourism Receipts (US $ million, excl. passenger transport): 1,034 in 2010; 963 in 2011; 916 in 2012 (provisional) (Source: World Tourism Organization).

COMMUNICATIONS MEDIA

Telephones (2012): 144,000 main lines in use.

Mobile Cellular Telephones (2012): 347,000 subscribers.

Internet Subscribers (2009): 61,000.

Broadband Subscribers (2012): 65,400.

Source: International Telecommunication Union.

EDUCATION

Pre-primary (2010/11 unless otherwise indicated): 84 schools (1995/96); 348 teachers (males 14, females 334); 5,620 pupils (males 2,836, females 2,784).

Primary (2010/11 unless otherwise indicated): 109 schools (2005/06); 1,720 teachers (males 382, females 1,338); 22,509 pupils (males 11,559, females 10,950).

Secondary (2005/06 unless otherwise indicated): 32 schools; 1,430 teachers (males 589, females 841); 19,696 pupils (males 9,809, females 9,887) (2010/11).

Tertiary (2010/11 unless otherwise indicated): 4 schools (2002); 786 teachers (males 403, females 383) (2006/07); 12,421 students (males 3,833, females 8,588).

Sources: Ministry of Education, Science, Technology and Innovation and UNESCO Institute for Statistics.

Pupil-teacher Ratio (primary education, UNESCO estimate): 13.1 in 2010/11 (Source: UNESCO Institute for Statistics).

Adult Literacy Rate (UN estimates): 99.7% (males 99.7%; females 99.7%) in 2003. Source: UN Development Programme, *Human Development Report*.

Directory

The Government

HEAD OF STATE

Queen: HM Queen ELIZABETH II.

Governor-General: Sir ELLIOT FITZROY BELGRAVE (took office 1 June 2012).

THE CABINET
(April 2014)

The Cabinet is formed by the Democratic Labour Party.

Prime Minister and Minister of National Security, the Public Services and Urban Development: FREUNDEL JEROME STUART.

Attorney-General and Minister of Home Affairs: ADRIEL BRATHWAITE.

Minister of Finance and Economic Affairs: CHRISTOPHER SINCKLER.

Minister of Education, Science, Technology and Innovation: RONALD JONES.

Minister of Housing, Lands and Rural Development: DENIS KELLMAN.

Minister of Tourism and International Transport: RICHARD SEALY.

Minister of Social Care, Constituency Empowerment and Community Development: STEVEN BLACKETT.

Minister of Transport and Works: MICHAEL LASHLEY.

Minister of Culture, Sports and Youth: STEPHEN LASHLEY.

Minister of Drainage and the Environment: DENIS LOWE.

Minister of Agriculture, Food, Fisheries and Water Resource Management: DAVID ESTWICK.

Minister of Health: JOHN BOYCE.

Minister of Foreign Affairs and Foreign Trade: MAXINE MCCLEAN.

Minister of Industry, International Business, Commerce and Small Business Development: DONVILLE INNISS.

Minister of Labour, Social Security and Human Resource Development: Dr ESTHER BYER SUCKOO.

Minister of State in the Prime Minister's Office: PATRICK TODD.

MINISTRIES

Office of the Prime Minister: Government HQ, Bay St, St Michael; tel. 436-6435; fax 436-9280; e-mail info@primeminister.gov.bb; internet www.primeminister.gov.bb.

Ministry of Agriculture, Food, Fisheries and Water Resource Management: Graeme Hall, POB 505, Christ Church; tel. 434-5000; fax 420-8444; e-mail info@agriculture.gov.bb; internet www.agriculture.gov.bb.

Ministry of Culture, Sports and Youth: Constitution Rd, St Michael; tel. 430-2704; fax 436-8909.

Ministry of Drainage and the Environment: S. P. Musson Bldg, Hinks St, St Michael; tel. 467-5700; fax 437-8859; e-mail ps_environment@gob.bb.

Ministry of Education, Science, Technology and Innovation: Elsie Payne Complex, Constitution Rd, St Michael; tel. 430-2709; fax 436-2411; e-mail ps@mes.gov.bb; internet www.mes.gov.bb.

Ministry of Finance and Economic Affairs: East Wing, Warrens Office Complex, St Michael; tel. 426-3179; fax 436-9280; e-mail pspowlett@gob.bb.

Ministry of Foreign Affairs and Foreign Trade: 1 Culloden Rd, St Michael; tel. 429-7108; fax 429-6652; e-mail barbados@foreign.gov.bb; internet www.foreign.gov.bb.

Ministry of Health: Jemmott's Lane, St Michael; tel. 426-5570; fax 426-4669.

Ministry of Home Affairs: General Post Office Bldg, Level 5, Cheapside, St Michael; tel. 228-8950; fax 437-3794; e-mail mha@caribsurf.com; e-mail ps@mha.gov.bb.

Ministry of Housing, Lands and Rural Development: National Housing Corpn Bldg, 'The Garden', Country Rd, St Michael; tel. 426-5041; fax 435-0174; e-mail info@bhta.org.

Ministry of Industry, International Business, Commerce and Small Business Development: British American Insurance Bldg, 2nd Floor, Magazine Lane, Bridgetown, St Michael; tel. 439-7483; fax 271-6155.

Ministry of Labour, Social Security and Human Resource Development: The Warrens Office Complex, 3rd Floor West, Warrens, St Michael; tel. 310-1400; fax 425-0266; e-mail vburnett@labour.gov.bb; internet labour.caribyte.com/index.

Ministry of National Security, the Public Services and Urban Development: E. Humphrey Walcott Bldg, Culloden Rd, St Michael; tel. 426-4617.

Ministry of Social Care, Constituency Empowerment and Community Development: The Warrens Office Complex, 4th Floor, Warrens, St Michael; tel. 310-1604; fax 424-2908; e-mail info@socialtransformation.gov.bb; internet www.socialcare.gov.bb.

Ministry of Tourism and International Transport: Lloyd Erskine Sandiford Centre, Two Mile Hill, St Michael; tel. 430-7500; fax 436-4828; e-mail info@tourism.gov.bb; internet www.tourism.gov.bb.

Ministry of Transport and Works: Pine East West Blvd, St Michael; tel. 429-2191; fax 437-8133; e-mail mpttech@caribsurf.com; internet www.mtw.gov.bb.

Office of the Attorney-General: Cedar Court, Wildey Business Park, Wildey Rd, St Michael; tel. 431-7700; fax 228-5433; e-mail ps@oag.gov.bb.

Legislature

PARLIAMENT

Senate

President: KERRYANN F. IFILL.

There are 21 members.

House of Assembly

Speaker: MICHAEL A. CARRINGTON.

General Election, 21 February 2013

Party	Seats
Democratic Labour Party (DLP)	16
Barbados Labour Party (BLP)	14
Total	30

Election Commission

Electoral and Boundaries Commission: National Insurance Bldg, Ground Floor, Fairchild St, Bridgetown BB11122; tel. 227-5817; fax 437-8229; e-mail electoral@barbados.gov.bb; internet www.electoral.barbados.gov.bb; Chief Electoral Officer ANGELA TAYLOR.

Political Organizations

Barbados Labour Party (BLP): Grantley Adams House, 111 Roebuck St, Bridgetown; tel. 429-1990; fax 427-8792; e-mail will99@caribsurf.com; internet www.blp.org.bb; f. 1938 as Barbados Progressive League, name changed as above 1946; moderate social democrat; Leader MIA MOTTLEY; Gen. Sec. GEORGE PAYNE.

Clement Payne Movement (CPM): Crumpton St, Bridgetown; tel. 435-2334; fax 437-8216; e-mail cpmbarbados2@yahoo.com; f. 1988 in honour of national hero; non-electoral founding assoc. of the PEP; links to the Pan-Caribbean Congress and promotes international Pan-Africanism; Pres. DAVID A. COMISSIONG; Gen. Sec. BOBBY CLARKE.

People's Empowerment Party (PEP): Clement Payne Cultural Centre, Crumpton St, Bridgetown; tel. 423-6089; fax 437-8216; e-mail pepbarbados@gmx.com; internet pepbarbados.blogspot.com; f. 2006 by the Clement Payne Movt; left-of-centre; Leader DAVID COMISSIONG.

Democratic Labour Party (DLP): 'Kennington', George St, Belleville, St Michael; tel. 429-3104; fax 427-0548; internet www.dlpbarbados.org; f. 1955; Pres. and Leader FREUNDEL STUART; Gen. Sec. CHRISTOPHER SINCKLER.

Diplomatic Representation

EMBASSIES AND HIGH COMMISSIONS IN BARBADOS

Brazil: The Courtyard, Hastings, POB BB15156, Christ Church; tel. 427-1735; fax 427-1744; e-mail brasemb.bridgetown@itamaraty.gov.br; internet bridgetown.itamaraty.gov.br; Ambassador APPIO CLAUDIO MUNIZ ACQUARONE.

Canada: Bishops Court Hill, Pine Rd, POB 404, Bridgetown; tel. 429-3550; fax 429-3780; e-mail bdgtn@international.gc.ca; internet www.canadainternational.gc.ca/barbados-barbade; High Commissioner RICHARD HANLEY.

China, People's Republic: 17 Golf View Terrace, Golf Club Rd, POB 428, Rockley, Christ Church; tel. 435-6890; fax 435-8300; e-mail chinaemb_bb@mfa.gov.cn; internet bb.chineseembassy.org; Ambassador WANG KE.

Cuba: No. 13, Edgehill Heights, Phase 2, St Thomas; tel. 271-9209; fax 271-9325; e-mail consulcuba@caribsurf.com; internet www.cubadiplomatica.cu/barbados; Ambassador LISSETTE BÁRBARA PÉREZ PÉREZ.

New Zealand: Lower Collymore Rock, Bridgetown; High Commissioner JAN HENDERSON.

United Kingdom: Lower Collymore Rock, POB 676, Bridgetown; tel. 430-7800; fax 430-7860; e-mail ukinbarbados@fco.gov.uk; internet www.gov.uk/world/barbados; High Commissioner VICTORIA GLYNIS DEAN.

USA: Wildey Business Park, Wildey, POB 302, Bridgetown BB14006; tel. 227-4000; fax 227-4088; e-mail BridgetownPublicAffairs@state.gov; internet bridgetown.usembassy.gov; Ambassador LARRY LEON PALMER.

Venezuela: Hastings, Main Rd, Christ Church; tel. 435-7619; fax 435-7830; e-mail embavenbdos@gmail.com; Ambassador JOSÉ GÓMEZ FEBRES.

Judicial System

Justice is administered by the Supreme Court of Judicature, which consists of a High Court and a Court of Appeal. Final appeal lies with the Caribbean Court of Justice, which was inaugurated in Port of Spain, Trinidad and Tobago, in April 2005; previously, final appeals were administered by the Judicial Committee of the Privy Council in the United Kingdom. There are Magistrates' Courts for lesser offences, with appeal to the Court of Appeal.

Supreme Court: Supreme Court Complex, Whitepark Rd, Bridgetown; tel. 434-9970; fax 426-2405; e-mail registrar@lawcourts.gov.bb; internet www.lawcourts.gov.bb; Chief Justice MARSTON GIBSON; Registrar LAURIE-ANN SMITH-BOVELL.

Office of the Attorney-General: Jones Bldg, Wildey Business Park, Wildey, St Michael; tel. 621-0110; fax 228-5433; e-mail attygen@caribsurf.com; Attorney-Gen. ADRIEL BRATHWAITE.

Religion

More than 100 religious denominations and sects are represented in Barbados, but the vast majority of the population profess Christianity.

CHRISTIANITY

Barbados Christian Council: Caribbean Conference of Churches Bldg, George St and Collymore Rock, St Michael; tel. 426-6014; Chair. Mgr VINCENT BLACKETT.

The Anglican Communion

According to the latest available census figures (2000), some 28% of the population are Anglicans. Anglicans in Barbados are adherents of the Church in the Province of the West Indies, comprising eight dioceses. The Archbishop of the Province currently is the Bishop of Barbados.

Bishop of Barbados: Rt Rev. JOHN WALDER DUNLOP HOLDER, Diocese of Barbados, Mandeville House, Henry's Lane, Collymore Rock, St Michael; tel. 426-2761; fax 426-0871; e-mail mandeville@sunbeach.com; internet www.anglican.bb.

The Roman Catholic Church

According to the 2000 census, some 4% of the population are Roman Catholics. Barbados comprises a single diocese, which is suffragan to the archdiocese of Port of Spain (Trinidad and Tobago). The Bishop participates in the Antilles Episcopal Conference (currently based in Port of Spain, Trinidad and Tobago).

Bishop of Bridgetown: CHARLES JASON GORDON, Bishop's House, Ladymeade Gardens, St Michael, POB 1223, Bridgetown; tel. 426-3510; fax 429-6198; e-mail rcbishopbgl@caribsurf.com.

Other Churches

According to the 2000 census, other significant denominations in terms of number of adherents include Pentecostal (19% of the population), Adventist (5%), Methodist (5%), Church of God (2%), Jehovah's Witnesses (2%) and Baptist (2%).

Church of God: Chapman St, POB 1, St Michael; tel. 426-5327; fax 228-2184; e-mail generalassemblychog@caribsurf.com; internet chogbarbados.org; Chair., Gen. Assembly Rev. M. GOODRIDGE; Pres. Rev. LIONEL L. GIBSON.

Church of Jesus Christ of Latter-Day Saints (Mormons): Black Rock Main Rd, Black Rock, St Michael; tel. 228-0210.

Church of the Nazarene (Barbados District): District Office, POB 3003E, Eagle Hall, St Michael; tel. 435-4444; fax 435-6486; internet nazarenebb.org; f. 1926; Supt Rev. Dr. ORLANDO D. SEALE.

Jerusalem Apostolic Spiritual Baptist Church: Ealing Grove, Christ Church; f. 1957; 10,000 mems; Archbishop GRANVILLE WILLIAMS.

Methodist Church: Bethel Church Office, Bay St, Bridgetown; tel. and fax 426-2223; e-mail methodist@caribsurf.com.

Seventh-day Adventists (East Caribbean Conference): Brydens Ave, Brittons Hill, POB 223, St Michael; tel. 429-7234; fax 429-8055; e-mail thepresident@eastcarib.org; internet www.eastcarib.org; f. 1926; Pres. DAVID BECKLES.

Spiritual Baptist Social and Community Development Ministries: Bridgetown; f. 2010; Chair. Rev. ODAIN BLACKMAN.

Wesleyan Holiness Church: Barbados District, POB 59, Bridgetown; tel. 429-3692; e-mail w.h.bdist@caribsurf.com; f. 1912 in Barbados; 38 churches; Gen. Supt Rev. ANTHONY WORRELL.

Other denominations include the Apostolic Church, the Bethel Evangelical Church, the Moravian Church, the Pentecostal Assemblies of the West Indies, the Salvation Army, Presbyterian congregations, the African Methodist Episcopal Church and the United Holy Church of America.

ISLAM

According to the 2000 census, around 1% of the population are Muslims.

Islamic Teaching Centre: Harts Gap, Hastings, Bridgetown; tel. 427-0120.

JUDAISM

According to the 2000 census, there are 96 Jews on the island (less than 1% of the population).

Jewish Community: Shaare Tzedek Synagogue, Rockley New Rd, Christ Church; Nidhe Israel Synagogue, Synagogue Lane, POB 651, Bridgetown; tel. 437-0970; fax 437-0829; Pres. JACOB HASSID; Sec. SHARON ORAN.

HINDUISM

According to the census of 2000, there are 840 Hindus on the island (less than 1% of the population).

Hindu Community: Hindu Temple, Synagogue Lane, Bridgetown; tel. 434-4638.

The Press

Barbados Advocate: POB 230, St Michael; tel. 467-2000; fax 434-2020; e-mail news@barbadosadvocate.com; internet www.barbadosadvocate.com; f. 1895; daily; Publr ANTHONY T. BRYAN; Man. Editor YAJAIRA ARCHIBALD; circ. 11,413.

The Broad Street Journal: Boarded Hall House, Boarded Hall, St. George; tel. 437-4592; e-mail bsjbarbados@gmail.com; internet www.broadstreetjournalbarbados.com; f. 1993; online; business; Publr and Editor PATRICK R. HOYOS.

The Nation: Nation House, Fontabelle, POB 1203, St Michael BB11000; tel. 430-5400; fax 427-6968; e-mail webmaster@nationnews.com; internet www.nationnews.com; f. 1973; daily; also publishes *The Midweek Nation*, *The Weekend Nation*, *The Sun on Saturday*, *The Sunday Sun* (q.v.) and *The Visitor* (a free publ. for tourists); owned by One Caribbean Media Ltd; Publr VIVIAN-ANNE GITTENS; Editor-in-Chief ROY MORRIS; circ. 31,533 (Daily), 51,440 (Sun.).

Sunday Advocate: POB 230, St Michael; tel. 467-2000; fax 434-1000; e-mail news@sunbeach.net; internet www.barbadosadvocate.com; f. 1895; Exec. Editor GILLIAN MARSHALL; circ. 17,490.

The Sunday Sun: Nation House, Fontabelle, POB 1203, St Michael BB11000; tel. 430-5400; fax 427-6968; e-mail webmaster@nationnews.com; internet www.nationnews.com; f. 1977; owned by One Caribbean Media Ltd; Publr VIVIAN-ANNE GITTENS; Editor-in-Chief KAYMAR JORDAN; circ. 48,824.

NEWS AGENCY

Caribbean Media Corporation (CMC): Harbour Industrial Estate, Unit 1B, Bldg 6A, St Michael BB11145; tel. 467-1000; fax 429-4355; e-mail admin@cmccaribbean.com; internet www.cananews.net; f. 2000; formed by merger of Caribbean News Agency (CANA) and Caribbean Broadcasting Union; Dir PATRICK COZIER.

Publishers

Advocate Publishers (2000) Inc: POB 230, Fontabelle, St Michael; tel. 467-2000; fax 434-2020; e-mail news@barbadosadvocate.com; internet www.barbadosadvocate.com; Dir HENRY MOULTON.

Miller Publishing Co: Edgehill, St Thomas; tel. 421-6700; fax 421-6707; e-mail info@barbadosbooks.com; internet www.barbadosbooks.com; f. 1983; publishes general interest books, tourism and business guides; Jt Man. Dirs KEITH MILLER, SALLY MILLER.

Nation Publishing Co Ltd: Nation House, Fontabelle, POB 1203, Fontabelle, St Michael BB11000; tel. 430-5400; fax 427-6968; internet www.nationpublishing.com; f. 1973; owned by One Caribbean Media Ltd; publishes daily edns of *The Nation* newspaper, as well as *The Midweek Nation*, *The Weekend Nation*, *The Sun on Saturday*, *The Sunday Sun* (q.v.) and *The Visitor* (a free publ. for tourists), *Friends*, *Ignition Plus*, *Barbados Business Authority*, *Better Health* and *Nation Work Book*; Chair. HAROLD HOYTE; Publr and CEO VIVIAN-ANNE GITTENS.

National Cultural Foundation of Barbados: West Terrace, St James; tel. and fax 417-6610; internet www.ncf.bb; Chair. KENNETH D. KNIGHT; CEO DEVERE BROWNE.

Broadcasting and Communications

TELECOMMUNICATIONS

Columbus International Inc: Suite 205-207, Dowell House, cnr Roebuck and Palmetto St, Bridgetown; tel. 602-4668; internet www.columbus.co; f. 2004; internet and private telecommunications network provider; CEO BRENDAN PADDICK.

Digicel Barbados Ltd: The Courtyard, Hastings, Christ Church; tel. 434-3444; fax 426-3444; e-mail BDS_CustomerCare_External@digicelgroup.com; internet www.digicelbarbados.com; f. 2001; awarded licence to operate cellular telephone services in 2003; approval granted in 2006 for the acquisition of Cingular Wireless' operation in Barbados; owned by an Irish consortium; CEO BARRY O'BRIEN.

LIME: Carlisle House, Hincks St, Bridgetown, St Michael; tel. 292-5050; e-mail CallCenterSupport@lime.com; internet www.lime.com; f. 1984; fmrly Cable & Wireless (Barbados) Ltd; Barbados External Telecommunications Ltd became Cable & Wireless BET Ltd; name changed as above in 2008; owned by Cable & Wireless PLC (United Kingdom); provides international telecommunications and internet services; contact centres in Jamaica and Saint Lucia; CEO (Caribbean) MARTIN JOOS (acting); Man. Dir ALEX MCDONALD.

Sunbeach Communications: 'San Remo', Belmont Rd, St Michael; tel. 233-6092; fax 228-6330; e-mail customerservice@sunbeach.net; internet www.sunbeach.net; f. 1995 as an internet service provider; licence to operate cellular telephone services obtained in 2003; launch of cellular operations postponed indefinitely in 2007; Vtel (Saint Lucia) acquired controlling 52.9% share in Dec. 2006; CEO JUDY TROTTER.

BROADCASTING

Radio

Barbados Broadcasting Service Ltd: Astoria, St George, Bridgetown; tel. 437-9550; fax 437-9203; e-mail action@sunbeach.net; f. 1981; operates BBS FM and Faith 102.1 FM (religious broadcasting); Man. Dir GAIL S. PADMORE.

Caribbean Broadcasting Corporation (CBC): The Pine, POB 900, Wildey, St Michael; tel. 467-5400; fax 429-4795; e-mail customerservices@cbc.bb; internet www.cbc.bb; f. 1963; state-owned; operates 3 radio stations; Gen. Man. LARS SÖDERSTRÖM.

CBC Radio 900 AM: Caribbean Broadcasting Corpn, The Pine, St Michael; tel. 434-1900; fax 429-4795; e-mail pbowen@cbc.bb; internet www.947fm.bb; f. 1963; spoken word and news.

Quality 100.7 FM: Caribbean Broadcasting Corpn, The Pine, St Michael; tel. 434-1007; fax 429-4795; e-mail dsthill@cbc.bb; internet www.qfm.bb; international and regional music, incl. folk, classical, etc.

The One 98.1 FM: Caribbean Broadcasting Corpn, The Pine, St Michael; tel. 434-1981; fax 429-4795; e-mail webmaster@theone.bb; internet www.theone.bb; f. 1984; popular music.

One Caribbean Media Ltd (OCM): River Rd, POB 1267, Bridgetown; tel. 430-7300; fax 426-5377; e-mail ocmnetwork@ocmnetwork.net; internet ocmnetwork.net; f. 2007 after Starcom Network Inc (SNI) with CCCL and GBN became the OCM Network; operates 4 radio stations: Gospel 790 AM, Hott 95.3 FM, LOVE FM 104, VOB 92.9 FM; Group CEO DAWN THOMAS.

Television

CBC-TV 8: The Pine, POB 900, Wildey, St Michael; tel. 467-5400; fax 429-4795; e-mail news@cbc.bb; internet www.cbc.bb; f. 1964; part of the Caribbean Broadcasting Corpn (q.v.); Channel Eight is the main national service, broadcasting 24 hours daily; a maximum of 115 digital subscription channels will be available through Multi-Choice Television; Dir of Television CECILY CLARKE-RICHMOND.

DIRECTV: Nation House, Roebuck St, Bridgetown, St Michael; tel. 435-7362; fax 228-5553; e-mail info@directvtt.com; internet www.directvcaribbean.com/bb; digital satellite television service; owned by the OCM Network; Administrator M. OWANA SKEETE.

Finance

In 2013 there were 46 'offshore' banks registered in Barbados

REGULATORY AUTHORITY

Financial Services Commission: 34 Warrens Industrial Park, St Michael; tel. 421-2142; fax 421-2146; e-mail seccom@caribsurf.com; internet www.fsc.gov.bb; f. 2011 to regulate and supervise the operations of the non-banking financial sector.

BANKING

(cap. = capital; res = reserves; dep. = deposits; brs = branches; m. = million; amounts in Barbados dollars unless otherwise indicated)

Central Bank

Central Bank of Barbados: Tom Adams Financial Centre, Spry St, POB 1016, Bridgetown BB11126; tel. 436-6870; fax 436-7836; e-mail info@centralbank.org.bb; internet www.centralbank.org.bb; f. 1972; bank of issue; cap. 2.0m., res 6.5m., dep. 712.3m. (Dec. 2009); Gov. R. DELISLE WORRELL.

Commercial Banks

FirstCaribbean International Bank (Barbados) Ltd: Warrens, POB 503, St Michael; tel. 367-2300; fax 424-8977; e-mail firstcaribbeanbank@firstcaribbeanbank.com; internet www.firstcaribbeanbank.com; f. 2002; previously known as CIBC West Indies Holdings, adopted present name following merger of CIBC West Indies and Caribbean operations of Barclays Bank PLC; Barclays relinquished its stake to CIBC in June 2006; cap. US $1,117.3m., res US $–234.5m., dep. US $7,971.6m. (Oct. 2010); Chair. MICHAEL K. MANSOOR; CEO RIK PARKHILL; Man. Dir (Barbados) DONNA WELLINGTON; 9 brs.

First Citizens Bank (Barbados) Ltd: The Mutual Bldg, 1 Beckwith Pl., Lower Broad St, Bridgetown; tel. 431-4500; fax 429-5734; e-mail contact@firstcitizensbb.com; internet www.firstcitizensbb.com/barbados; f. 2003 as Mutual Bank of the Caribbean, name later changed to Butterfield Bank (Barbados); acquired by First Citizens Bank (Trinidad and Tobago) in 2012; cap. 36.9m., res 11.2m., dep. 481.5m. (Dec. 2010); CEO GLYNE HARRISON.

RBC Royal Bank Barbados: Broad St, POB 68, Bridgetown BB11000; tel. 467-4000; fax 426-4139; internet www.rbcroyalbank.com/caribbean/barbados; f. 1911; subsidiary of RBC Financial Group, Canada; CEO (Caribbean) SURESH SOOKOO.

Republic Bank (Barbados) Ltd: Independence Sq., POB 1002, Bridgetown, St Michael; tel. 431-5700; fax 429-2606; e-mail info@republicbarbados.com; internet www.republicbarbados.com; f. 1978; fmrly Barbados National Bank Inc; present name adopted 2012; cap. 48.0m., res 146.6m., dep. 1,754.2m. (Sept. 2010); Chair. RONALD F. D. HARFORD; Man. Dir and CEO DAVID DULAL-WHITEWAY; 9 brs.

Scotiabank (Canada): CGI Tower, 1st Floor, Warrens, St Michael; tel. 431-3100; fax 421-7110; internet www.scotiabank.com/bb; f. 1956; Man. Dir (Caribbean East) DAVID NOEL; 8 brs.

Regional Development Bank

Caribbean Development Bank: POB 408, Wildey, St Michael BB11000; tel. 431-1600; fax 426-7269; e-mail info@caribank.org; internet www.caribank.org; f. 1970; cap. US $186.3m., res US $14.1m., dep. US $20.0m., total assets US $1,543.1m. (Dec. 2011); Pres. Dr WARREN SMITH.

Trust Companies

Alexandria Trust Corpn: Deighton House, Cnr of Deighton and Dayrell's Rds, St Michael BB14030; tel. 228-8402; fax 228-3847; e-mail barbara.ogorman@atcbarbados.com; internet www.alexandriabancorp.com; wholly owned by Guardian Capital Group Ltd (Canada); Man. Dir ROBERT F. MADDEN; Gen. Man. BARBARA O'GORMAN.

The Blue Financial Group: Braemar Court, Deighton Rd, St Michael BB14017; tel. 467-6677; fax 467-6678; e-mail info@stmichael.bb; internet www.thebluefinancialgroup.com; f. 1987; fmrly St Michael Trust Corpn; Pres. IAN HUTCHISON.

Capita Financial Services Inc: Walrond St, Bridgetown BB11127; tel. 431-4716; fax 426-6168; e-mail info@capitacaribbean.com; internet www.capitacaribbean.com; f. 1984; incorporated as Clico Mortgage & Finance Corpn; name changed as above in 2010; subsidiary of Barbados Public Workers' Cooperative Credit Union Ltd; Chair. CARLOS HOLDER; Pres. and CEO PAUL MAXWELL.

CCG Trust Corpn: 1 Chelston Park, Collymore Rock, St Michael; tel. 427-8174; fax 429-7995; owned by CIT Group, Inc.

Concorde Bank Ltd: The Corporate Centre, Bush Hill, Bay St, POB 1161, Bridgetown BB11000; tel. 430-5320; fax 429-7996; e-mail concorde@concordebb.com; f. 1987; Pres. and Chair. GERARD LUSSAN.

DGM Trust Corpn: Hastings Financial Centre, 2nd Floor, Hastings, Christ Church B15154; tel. 434-4850; fax 431-3439; e-mail info@dgmgroup.com; internet www.dgmbank.com; f. 1996, fmrly Altamira International Bank; Chair. GEOFFREY CAVE.

FirstCaribbean International Trust and Merchant Bank (Barbados) Ltd: Warrens, POB 503, St Michael; tel. 367-2300; fax 424-8977; internet www.cibcfcib.com; known as CIBC Trust and Merchant Bank until 2002; Exec. Chair. MICHAEL MANSOOR; CEO MARK ST HILL.

Globe Finance Inc: Rendezvous Court, Suite 6, Rendezvous Main Rd, Christ Church BB15112; tel. 426-4755; fax 426-4772; e-mail info@globefinanceinc.com; internet www.globefinanceinc.com; f. 1998; Man. Dir RONALD DAVIS.

J&T Bank and Trust: Lauriston House, Lower Collymore Rock, POB 1132, Bridgetown, St Michael BB11000; tel. 430-8650; fax 430-5335; e-mail info@jtbanktrust.com; internet www.jtbanktrust.com; fmrly known as Bayshore Bank and Trust; Chief Financial Officer KWESI MARSHALL.

Republic Finance and Trust Corpn: BNB Bldg, 2nd Floor, Independence Sq., Bridgetown; tel. 431-5700; fax 429-8389; internet www.republicbarbados.com; f. as BNB Finance and Trust Corpn; subsidiary of Republic Bank (Barbados) Ltd; Man. ERIC SCOTT.

Royal Bank of Canada Financial Corporation: Bldg 2, 2nd Floor, Chelston Park, Collymore Rock, POB 986, St Michael; tel. 467-4300; fax 429-3800; internet www.rbcroyalbank.com; Pres. and CEO GORDON M. NIXON; Man. N. L. (ROY) SMITH.

Royal Fidelity Merchant Bank and Trust (Barbados) Ltd: Royal Fidelity House, 27 Pine Rd, POB 1338, St Michael BB11113; tel. 435-1955; fax 435-1964; e-mail info@royalfidelity.com; internet www.royalfidelity.com/barbados; Pres. MICHAEL A. ANDERSON.

Signia Financial Group Inc: Carlisle House, Hinks St, Bridgetown; tel. 434-2360; fax 434-0057; e-mail info@signiafinancial.com; internet www.signiafinancial.com; f. 2003, fmrly General Finance; Chair. GEOFFREY CAVE; CEO PAUL ASHBY.

STOCK EXCHANGE

Barbados Stock Exchange Inc (BSE): Eighth Ave, Belleville, St Michael BB11114; tel. 436-9871; fax 429-8942; e-mail marlon.yarde@bse.com.bb; internet www.bse.com.bb; f. 1987 as the Securities Exchange of Barbados; in 1989 the Govts of Barbados, Trinidad and

Tobago and Jamaica agreed to link exchanges; cross-trading began in April 1991; reincorporated in 2001; CEO and Gen. Man. MARLON YARDE.

INSURANCE

The leading British and a number of US and Canadian companies have agents in Barbados. In 2009 there were 228 exempt and qualified exempt insurance companies registered in the country. Local insurance companies include the following:

Insurance Corporation of Barbados Ltd (ICBL): Roebuck St, POB 11000, Bridgetown; tel. 434-6000; fax 426-3393; e-mail icb@icb.com.bb; internet www.icb.com.bb; f. 1978; 51% owned by BF&M Ltd of Bermuda; cap. Bds $39m.; Chair. R. JOHN WIGHT; Man. Dir and CEO INGRID INNES.

McLarens: Warrens Complex, 106 Warrens Terrace East, Suite 3, POB 5004, St Michael BB28000; tel. 438-9231; e-mail david.hobson@mclarens.com; internet www.mclarens.com; fmrly McLarens Young International; renamed as above in 2012; Regional Dir, Caribbean KEVIN INNES.

Sagicor: Sagicor Financial Centre, Lower Collymore Rock, Wildey, St Michael; tel. 467-7500; fax 436-8829; e-mail info@sagicor.com; internet www.sagicor.com; f. 1840 as Barbados Mutual Life Assurance Society (BMLAS); changed name as above in 2002 after acquiring majority ownership of Life of Barbados (LOB) Ltd; Chair. STEPHEN MCNAMARA; Pres. and CEO DODRIDGE D. MILLER.

United Insurance Co Ltd: United Insurance Centre, Lower Broad St, POB 1215, Bridgetown; tel. 430-1900; fax 436-7573; e-mail mail@unitedinsure.com; internet unitedinsure.com; f. 1976; CEO HOWARD HALL; Regional Man. CECILE COX.

USA Risk Group (Barbados) Ltd: Golden Anchorage Complex, Sunset Crest, St James; tel. 432-6467; fax 483-1850; e-mail mhole@usarisk.bb; internet www.usarisk.com/; Man. MARTIN HOLE.

Association

Insurance Association of the Caribbean Inc (IAC): The Thomas Pierce Bldg, Lower Collymore Rock, St Michael BB11115; tel. 427-5608; fax 427-7277; e-mail info@iac-caribbean.com; internet www.iac-caribbean.com; regional asscn; Pres. DAVID ALLEYNE; Man. JANELLE THOMPSON.

Trade and Industry

GOVERNMENT AGENCY

Barbados Agricultural Management Co Ltd (BAMC): Warrens, POB 719C, St Michael; tel. 425-0010; fax 421-7879; e-mail lparris@bamc.net.bb; f. 1993; Gen. Man. LESLIE PARRIS.

DEVELOPMENT ORGANIZATIONS

Barbados Agriculture Development and Marketing Corpn (BADMC): Fairy Valley Plantation House, Fairy Valley, Christ Church; tel. 428-0250; fax 428-0152; e-mail badmc@agriculture.gov.bb; internet www.agriculture.gov.bb; f. 1993 by merger; programme of diversification and land reforms; CEO FAY BEST.

Barbados Investment and Development Corpn (BIDC): Pelican House, Princess Alice Hwy, POB 1250, Bridgetown BB11000; tel. 427-5350; fax 426-7802; e-mail bidc@bidc.org; internet www.bidc.com; f. 1992 by merger; facilitates the devt of the industrial sector, especially in the areas of manufacturing, information technology and financial services; offers free consultancy to investors; provides factory space for lease or rent; administers the Fiscal Incentives Legislation; Chair. BENSON STRAKER; CEO LEROY MCCLEAN.

Barbados Small Business Association: 1 Pelican Industrial Park, Bridgetown; tel. 228-0162; fax 228-0163; e-mail theoffice@sba.org.bb; internet www.sba.org.bb; f. 1982; non-profit org. representing interests of small businesses; Pres. CELESTE FOSTER.

CHAMBER OF COMMERCE

Barbados Chamber of Commerce and Industry: Braemar Court, Deighton Rd, St Michael; tel. 434-4750; fax 228-2907; e-mail bcci@bdscham.com; internet www.barbadoschamberofcommerce.com; f. 1825; 220 mem. firms; some 345 reps; Exec. Dir LISA GALE.

INDUSTRIAL AND TRADE ASSOCIATIONS

Barbados Agricultural Society: The Grotto, Beckles Rd, St Michael; tel. 436-6683; fax 435-0651; e-mail agrofest@basonevoice.org; internet www.basonevoice.org; CEO JAMES PAUL.

Barbados Association of Professional Engineers: Christie Bldg, Garrison Hill, St Michael BB14038; tel. 429-6105; fax 434-6673; e-mail info@bape.org; internet www.bape.org; f. 1964; Pres. GREG PARRIS; Hon. Sec. JASON MARSHALL; 213 mems.

Barbados International Business Association (BIBA): 19 Pine Rd, Belleville, St Michael; tel. 436-2422; fax 434-2423; e-mail biba@biba.bb; internet www.biba.bb; f. 1993 as Barbados Asscn of International Business Cos and Offshore Banks (BAIBCOB); changed name as above in 1997; org. comprising cos engaged in int. business; Pres. RYLE WEEKES; Exec. Dir HENDERSON HOLMES; 182 mem. cos.

Barbados Manufacturers' Association: Suite 201, Bldg 8, Harbour Industrial Park, St Michael; tel. 426-4474; fax 436-5182; e-mail info@bma.bb; internet www.bma.bb; f. 1964; Pres. KARLENE NICHOLLS; Exec. Dir BOBBI MCKAY; 110 mem. firms.

Barbados Sugar Industry Ltd (BSIL): Bridgetown; f. 1973; operates sugar factories and supervises transport and storage of sugar products; Chair. Dr ATLEE BRATHWAITE.

EMPLOYERS' ORGANIZATION

Barbados Employers' Confederation (BEC): Braemar Court, Deighton Rd, POB 33B, Brittons Hill, St Michael; tel. 435-4753; fax 435-2907; e-mail becon@barbadosemployers.com; internet barbadosemployers.com; f. 1956; Pres. IAN GOODING-EDGHILL; Exec. Dir TONY WALCOTT; 235 mems (incl. assoc. mems).

UTILITIES

Electricity

Barbados Light and Power Co (BL & P): POB 142, Garrison Hill, St Michael; tel. 626-4300; fax 228-1396; internet www.blpc.com.bb; f. 1911; 80% owned by Emera (Canada); electricity generator and distributor; operates 3 stations with a combined capacity of 209,500 kW; Chair. ANDREW GITTENS; Man. Dir MARK KING.

Gas

Barbados National Oil Co Ltd (BNOCL): POB 175, Woodbourne, St Philip; tel. 420-1800; fax 420-1818; e-mail gibbsw@bnocl.com; internet www.bnocl.com; f. 1982; state-owned; exploration and extraction of petroleum and natural gas; Chair. Dr LEONARD NURSE; Gen. Man. WINTON GIBBS; 88 employees.

National Petroleum Corporation (NPC): Wildey, POB 175, St Michael; tel. 430-4020; fax 426-4326; e-mail customerserv@npc.com.bb; internet npc.com.bb; gas production and distribution; Chair. HARCOURT LEWIS; Gen. Man. JAMES BROWNE.

Water

Barbados Water Authority: Pine East-West Blvd, The Pine, St Michael; tel. 424-1650; fax 424-2362; e-mail bwa@caribsurf.com; internet www.bwa.bb; f. 1980; Exec. Chair. ARNI WALTERS; Gen. Man. CHARLES MARVILLE (acting).

TRADE UNIONS

Barbados Workers' Union (BWU): 'Solidarity' House, Harmony Hall, POB 172, St Michael; tel. 426-3492; fax 436-6496; e-mail bwu@caribsurf.com; internet www.bwu-bb.org; f. 1941; Pres.-Gen. LINDA BROOKS; Gen. Sec. Sir ROY TROTMAN; 25,000 mems.

Caribbean Congress of Labour (CCL): St Michael, Barbados; f. 1960; regional trade union fed; Pres. DAVID MESSIAH; Gen.-Sec. LINCOLN LEWIS.

National Union of Public Workers: Dalkeith Rd, POB 174, St Michael; tel. 426-1764; fax 436-1795; e-mail nupwbarbados@sunbeach.net; internet www.nupwbarbados.com; f. 1944 as the Barbados Civil Service Asscn, present name adopted in 1971; Pres. WALTER MALONEY; Gen. Sec. DENNIS L. CLARKE; c. 8,000 mems.

Transport

ROADS

In 2012 there was a network of 1,600 km (994 miles) of paved roads.

Barbados Transport Board: Weymouth, Roebuck St, St Michael BB11083; tel. 310-3500; fax 310-3573; e-mail customerservice@transportboard.com; internet www.transportboard.com; f. 1955; part of the Ministry of Transport and Works; Gen. Man. SANDRA FORDE.

SHIPPING

Bridgetown harbour has berths for eight ships and simultaneous bunkering facilities for five. A new cruise ship pier was built in the mid-2000s. In December 2013 the flag registered fleet comprised 138 vessels, totalling 882,619 grt, of which 21 were bulk carriers and 58 were general cargo ships.

Barbados Port Inc: University Row, Princess Alice Hwy, Bridgetown; tel. 430-6100; fax 429-5348; e-mail administrator@barbadosport.com; internet www.barbadosport.com; f. 1979 as the Barbados Port Authority and was incorporated in 2003; Chair. LARRY TATEM; Man. Dir and CEO EVERTON WALTERS.

The Shipping Association of Barbados: Trident House, 2nd Floor, Broad St, Bridgetown; tel. 427-9860; fax 426-8392; e-mail info@shippingbarbados.com; internet www.shippingbarbados.com; f. 1981; Pres. MARC SAMPSON; Exec. Vice-Pres. ROVEL MORRIS.

Principal Shipping Companies

Barbados Shipping and Trading Co Ltd (B. S. & T.): The Auto Dome, 1st Floor, Warrens, St Michael; tel. 417-5110; fax 417-5116; e-mail info@bsandtco.com; internet www.bsandtco.com; f. 1920; acquired by energy and industrial asscn Neal & Massy (Trinidad and Tobago) in 2008; CEO ANTHONY KING.

Bernuth Agencies: T. Geddes Grant White Park Rd, Bridgetown; tel. 431-3343; e-mail info@bernuth.com; internet www.bernuth.com; Pres. Capt. JORDAN MONOCANDILOS; Port Co-ordinator YAILEEN RODRIGUEZ.

Booth Steamship Co (Barbados) Ltd: Prescod Blvd, St Michael BB11124; tel. 436-6094; fax 426-0484; e-mail info@boothsteamship.com; internet www.boothsteamship.com; f. 1961; represents Crowley Liner Services, Mediterranean Shipping Co (MSC), Inchcape Shipping Services; Chair. RANDALL I. BANFIELD; Gen. Man. NOEL M. NURSE.

DaCosta Mannings Inc (DMI): Brandons, POB 103, St Michael; tel. 430-4800; fax 431-0051; e-mail sales@dmishipping.com; internet www.dmishipping.com; f. 1995 following merger of DaCosta Ltd and Manning, Wilkinson & Challenor Ltd; shipping and retail company; acquired the shipping lines of of T. Geddes Grant Bros in 2002; agent for P & O Nedlloyd, Princess Cruises, Bernuth Agencies, Columbus/Hamburg Sud and K Line; Exec. Dir MARK SEALY; Gen. Man. GLYNE ST HILL.

Eric Hassell and Son Ltd: Carlisle House, Hincks St, Bridgetown; tel. 436-6102; fax 429-3416; e-mail info@erichassell.com.bb; internet www.erichassell.com.bb; f. 1969; shipping agent, stevedoring contractor and cargo forwarder; represents Seaboard Marine; Man. Dir ERICA LUKE; Operations Man. MITCHELL FORDE.

Sea Freight Agencies and Stevedoring Ltd: Atlantis Bldg, Shallow Draught, Bridgetown Port, Bridgetown; tel. 429-9688; fax 429-5107; e-mail operations@seafrt.com; internet www.seafrt.com; f. 2011; ship agent and stevedoring contractor; represents the Geest Line and Clipper Inter-American Line; Man. Dir ROVEL MORRIS; Man. (Operations) GLADSTONE WHARTON.

Seaboard International Shipping Company Ltd, Barbados: St James House, Second St, St James; tel. 432-4000; fax 432-4004; e-mail melb@seaboardintl.com; internet www.seaboardintl.com; f. 1936; parent co in Vancouver, Canada; Rep. MEL BJORNDAL.

Tropical Shipping: Goddards Shipping & Tours Ltd, Goddards Complex, Fontabelle Rd, POB 1283, St Michael; tel. 426-9918; fax 426-7322; e-mail gst_shipagent@goddent.com; internet www.tropical.com; Pres. MIKE PELLICCI; Gen. Man. ROVEL MORRIS.

CIVIL AVIATION

The principal airport is Grantley Adams International Airport, at Seawell, 18 km (11 miles) from Bridgetown and with a runway over 11,000 feet long. Barbados is served by a number of regional and international airlines, including Air Jamaica, LIAT Airlines (see Antigua and Barbuda), Air Canada and British Airways. The first low-fare airline servicing the Caribbean region, Redjet, suspended operations in 2012.

Barbados Civil Aviation Department: Grantley Adams Industrial Park, Bldg 4, Christ Church BB17089; tel. 428-0930; fax 428-2539; e-mail civilav@sunbeach.net; internet www.bcad.gov.bb; Dir MITCHINSON H. BECKLES.

Tourism

The natural attractions of the island consist chiefly of the warm climate and varied scenery. In addition, there are many facilities for outdoor sports of all kinds. In 2012 the number of stop-over tourist arrivals was an estimated 536,300, while the number of visiting cruise ship passengers was an estimated 517,400. Tourism receipts (excluding passenger transport) totalled a provisional US $916m. in 2012. In that year the Inter-American Development Bank confirmed a US $55m. loan for the construction of an eco-friendly Four Seasons hotel.

Barbados Hotel and Tourism Association (BHTA): Fourth Ave, Belleville, St Michael; tel. 426-5041; fax 429-2845; e-mail info@bhta.org; internet www.bhta.org; f. 1952 as the Barbados Hotel Asscn; adopted present name in 1994; non-profit trade asscn; Pres. PATRICIA AFFONSO-DASS.

Barbados Tourism Authority: Harbour Rd, POB 242, Bridgetown; tel. 427-2623; fax 426-4080; e-mail btainfo@visitbarbados.org; internet www.visitbarbados.org; f. 1993 to replace Barbados Board of Tourism; to be restructured in 2014 as the Barbados Tourism Product Authority and Barbados Tourism Marketing Inc; Chair. ADRIAN ELCOCK; Pres. and CEO DAVID RICE.

Defence

The Barbados Defence Force is divided into regular defence units and a coastguard service with armed patrol boats. The total strength of the armed forces, as assessed at November 2013, was an estimated 610, comprising an army of 500 members and a navy (coastguard) of 110. There was also a reserve force of 430 members.

Defence Budget: an estimated Bds $66m. in 2013.

Chief of Staff: Col ALVIN QUINTYNE.

Education

Education is compulsory for 12 years, between five and 16 years of age. Primary education begins at the age of five and lasts for seven years. Secondary education, beginning at 12 years of age, lasts for six years. In 2010/11 22,509 pupils were enrolled at primary schools, while there were 19,696 pupils at secondary schools. Tuition at all government schools is free. There were 12,421 students in higher education in 2010/11. Degree courses in arts, law, education, natural sciences and social sciences are offered at the Cave Hill campus of the University of the West Indies. A two-year clinical-training programme for medical students is conducted by the School of Clinic Medicine and Research of the University, while an in-service training programme for teachers is provided by the School of Education. Non-university post-secondary education is offered by the Samuel Jackman Prescod Polytechnic and the Barbados Community College. Approved government expenditure on education for 2012/13 was Bds $509.0m.

BELARUS

Introductory Survey

LOCATION, CLIMATE, LANGUAGE, RELIGION, FLAG, CAPITAL

The Republic of Belarus is a landlocked state in north-eastern Europe. It is bounded by Lithuania and Latvia to the north-west, by Ukraine to the south, by Russia to the east, and by Poland to the west. The climate is of a continental type, with an average January temperature, in Minsk, of –5°C (23°F) and an average for July of 19°C (67°F). Average annual precipitation is between 560 mm and 660 mm. The official languages of the Republic are Belarusian and Russian. The major religion is Eastern Orthodox Christianity. The national flag (proportions 1 by 2) consists of two unequal horizontal stripes, of red over light green, with a red-outlined white vertical stripe at the hoist, bearing in red a traditional embroidery pattern. The capital is Minsk (Miensk).

CONTEMPORARY POLITICAL HISTORY

Historical Context

Following periods of Lithuanian and Polish rule, Belarus became a part of the Russian Empire in the late 18th century. After Belarus was briefly under German power from early 1918, a Belarusian National Republic (BNR) was declared in March, but the Bolsheviks subsequently occupied Minsk. A Belarusian Soviet Socialist Republic (SSR) was declared on 1 January 1919, but this was merged with Lithuania in February, as 'Litbel'. In April Polish armed forces entered Litbel, which was declared part of Poland. In July 1920 the Bolsheviks recaptured Minsk, and in August the Belarusian SSR was re-established; Lithuania became an independent state. However, the Belarusian SSR comprised only the eastern regions of the lands populated by Belarusians. Western territories were granted to Poland by the Treaty of Rīga, signed on 18 March 1921. Meanwhile, Belarus, with Ukraine and the Transcaucasian Federation (Armenia, Azerbaijan and Georgia), had joined with Russia to establish the Union of Soviet Socialist Republics (USSR) in December 1922.

After the invasion of Poland by German and Soviet forces in September 1939, Belarus was enlarged by the inclusion of the lands that it had lost to Poland in 1921. Between 1941 and 1944 Belarus was occupied by Nazi German forces; an estimated 2.2m. people were killed in the Republic. At the Yalta conference, in February 1945, the Allies agreed to recognize the 'Curzon line' as the basis for the western border of the USSR, thus endorsing the unification of western and eastern Belarus. The requirements of the post-war reconstruction programme and the local labour shortage led to an increase in Russian immigration and an ensuing process of 'russification'.

The relative prosperity of the Republic effectively permitted the ruling Communist Party of Belarus (KPB) to resist implementing the economic and political reforms supported by the Soviet leader, Mikhail Gorbachev, from 1985. A Belarusian Popular Front (BNF), established in October 1988, enjoyed some success at elections to the all-Union Congress of People's Deputies, held in March 1989. In 1990 Belarusian was declared to be the state language of the Republic.

The BNF was not officially permitted to participate in elections to the Belarusian Supreme Soviet (Supreme Council) in March 1990. Instead, its members joined other pro-reform groups in the Belarusian Democratic Bloc, which secured about one-quarter of the 310 seats that were decided by popular election; most of the remainder were won by KPB members. The opposition won most seats in the large cities, notably Gomel and Minsk, where Zyanon Paznyak, the leader of the BNF, was elected. On 27 July the Belarusian Supreme Soviet unanimously adopted a Declaration of State Sovereignty. None the less, the Belarusian Government took part in the negotiation of a new Treaty of Union from late 1990. The all-Union referendum on the preservation of the USSR took place in the Belarusian SSR on 17 March 1991; of the 83% of the electorate who participated, 83% voted in favour of Gorbachev's proposals for a renewed federation.

Following a general strike in April 1991, the Government agreed to economic concessions, but the strikers' political demands were rejected. When the Belarusian Supreme Soviet was convened in May, the authority of the KPB was threatened by internal dissent. In June 33 deputies joined an opposition 'Communists for Democracy' faction, led by Alyaksandr Lukashenka, the director of a state farm.

The Belarusian leadership did not strongly oppose the attempted coup, led by conservative communists, in Moscow, the Russian and Soviet capital, in August 1991. Following the failure of the coup, Mikalay Dzemyantsei, the Chairman of the Belarusian Supreme Soviet (republican head of state), was forced to resign; he was replaced in an interim capacity by Stanislau Shushkevich. The Supreme Soviet agreed to nationalize KPB property and to suspend the party's operations. On 25 August the legislature voted to grant constitutional status to the July 1990 Declaration of State Sovereignty.

Domestic Political Affairs

On 19 September 1991 the Belarusian Supreme Soviet voted to rename the Belarusian SSR the Republic of Belarus, and also elected Shushkevich as its Chairman. On 8 December Shushkevich, with the Russian and Ukrainian Presidents, signed the Minsk Agreement, establishing a Commonwealth of Independent States (CIS, see p. 243), which was to have its headquarters in Minsk, effectively signalling the dissolution of the USSR. On 21 December the leaders of 11 Soviet republics confirmed this decision by the Almaty (Alma-Ata) Declaration.

In March 1993 the KPB and 17 other groups supportive of reunification with Russia formed an alliance, the Popular Movement of Belarus. Despite the opposition of Shushkevich and the BPF to the proposals, a new Constitution, providing for a presidential system of government, was adopted in March 1994. Although Shushkevich and the BNF opposed signing the Collective Security Treaty concluded by six other CIS states in May 1992, on the grounds that this would contravene the Declaration of State Sovereignty, which defined Belarus as a neutral state, in April 1993 the Supreme Council voted to authorize the signing of the Treaty. After Shushkevich delayed doing so, he was removed by a vote in the Supreme Council, held in January 1994 (by which time he had signed the Treaty). He was replaced by Mechislau Gryb. Meanwhile, in February 1993 the suspension on the KPB was lifted, and the party was re-established.

Lukashenka elected as President

Allegations of corruption against the premier, Vyacheslau Kebich, and leading members of the Council of Ministers, together with the worsening economic situation, culminated in a BNF-led general strike in Minsk in February 1994, as a consequence of which Gryb announced an early presidential election. Six candidates, including Kebich, Shushkevich, Paznyak and Lukashenka, head of the Supreme Council's anti-corruption committee, contested the first round of voting in June. In the second round, held on 10 July, Lukashenka received 85% of the votes cast, defeating Kebich. Lukashenka was inaugurated as the first President of Belarus on 20 July. Mikhail Chigir, an economic reformist, became Chairman of a new Council of Ministers (Prime Minister).

In early 1995 there were repeated confrontations between Lukashenka and the Supreme Council. In January the Council voted to adopt legislation that would permit the removal of the President by a two-thirds quorum. In March Lukashenka announced that a referendum would be held on four questions in May, concurrently with scheduled legislative elections. In April, following the Council's rejection of all but one of the proposed questions (on closer integration with Russia), Lukashenka threatened to dissolve the legislature. A number of opposition deputies (including Paznyak), who had declared a hunger strike, were forcibly evicted from the legislative building. Shortly afterwards, deputies voted to incorporate the three remaining questions in the text of the referendum: on granting Russian equal status with Belarusian as an official language; on the abandonment of the state insignia and flag of independent Belarus in favour of a modified version of those of the Belarusian SSR; and on the amendment of the Constitution to empower the President to suspend the Supreme Council in the event of unconstitutional acts. Some 65% of the electorate participated in the referendum, held on 14 May, at which all four questions were approved.

On the same day, at Belarus's first post-Soviet legislative elections, only 18 of the 260 seats in the Supreme Council were filled. A further 101 deputies were elected at 'run-off' elections held on 28 May 1995, but the necessary two-thirds quorum was only achieved after two further rounds of voting, held on 29 November and 10 December, brought the total membership of the Supreme Council to 198. The KPB emerged with the largest number of seats in the new legislature (42), followed by the Belarusian Agrarian Party (BAP, with 33) and the United Civic Party (AHP, with nine); 95 independent candidates were elected. The BNF failed to win representation in the Council; the 62 seats remaining vacant, largely owing to low electoral participation, were mostly those representing the regions in which the BNF commanded its strongest support. In January 1996 Syamyon Sharetski, the leader of the BAP, was appointed Chairman of the new Supreme Council.

Despite substantial opposition, President Lukashenka and the Russian President, Boris Yeltsin, signed the Treaty on the Formation of a Community of Sovereign Republics in Moscow on 2 April 1996, which provided for extensive military, economic and political co-operation between the two countries. Following the Treaty's endorsement, confrontation between Lukashenka and the opposition parties intensified. A warrant was issued in April for the arrest of Paznyak, who was accused of organizing the anti-Union demonstrations; he fled the country and later applied for political asylum in the USA.

Lukashenka scheduled another national referendum for 24 November 1996. The revocation by presidential decree, in November, of a ruling of the Constitutional Court that any constitutional amendments agreed by referendum would not be legally binding, provoked fierce criticism. The referendum ballot papers contained seven questions, four of which were proposed by Lukashenka: that amendments be made to the Constitution to extend the President's term of office from 1999 until 2001, to enable the President to issue decrees that would carry legal force, and to grant him extensive powers of appointment both to the judiciary and to an envisaged bicameral legislature; that Belarusian Independence Day be moved from 27 July (the anniversary of the Declaration of State Sovereignty) to 3 July (the anniversary of the liberation from the Nazis); that there be an unrestricted right to purchase and sell land; and that the death penalty be abolished. The remaining questions were submitted by the Supreme Council, and proposed significant reductions in presidential powers. After the Chairman of the central electoral commission, Viktar Hanchar, stated that he would not approve the results of the voting, owing to electoral violations, Lukashenka dismissed him. In November 1996 Chigir resigned as Chairman of the Council of Ministers, urging that the referendum be cancelled; he was replaced by Syarhey Ling. Some 10,000 people attended an anti-Government rally in Minsk, protesting against the restrictions on freedom of expression. The Council of Europe (see p. 252) declared that the draft of the amended Constitution did not comply with European standards. Meanwhile, 75 deputies in the Supreme Council submitted a motion to the Constitutional Court to begin impeachment proceedings against the President; although the Court had already found 17 decrees issued by Lukashenka to be unconstitutional, it was forced to abandon the motion, as deputies retracted their support. According to the official results of the referendum, in which some 84% of the electorate participated, none of the proposals of the Supreme Council was approved, while two of the President's proposals—on the date on which national independence would be celebrated, and on constitutional amendments—obtained the requisite majority of votes; the other two proposals—on the right to buy and sell land and on the abolition of the death penalty—were overwhelmingly rejected. The amended Constitution was published on 27 November and took effect immediately.

Following the referendum, the Supreme Council divided into two factions. More than 100 deputies declared their support for Lukashenka, establishing a 110-member Palata Predstaviteley (House of Representatives), which was to be the lower chamber of the new bicameral Natsionalnoye Sobraniye (National Assembly), to replace the Supreme Council. Some 50 other deputies declared themselves to be the legitimate legislature, denouncing the referendum as invalid. The House of Representatives convened shortly afterwards and elected Anatol Malafeyeu as its Chairman. Deputies were granted a four-year mandate, while the term of office of those opposed to the new legislature was curtailed to two months. Deputies elected in the by-elections held simultaneously with the referendum were denied registration. Legislation governing the formation of the new upper house of the legislature, the 64-member Soviet Respubliki (Council of the Republic), was approved by Lukashenka in December 1996: eight members were to be appointed by the President and the remaining 56 elected by regional councils. The Council of the Republic convened in January 1997. Meanwhile, in protest at the constitutional amendments, the Chairman of the Constitutional Court and several judges announced their resignations.

In January 1997 a 'shadow' cabinet comprising politicians opposed to the new arrangements, the Public Coalition Government-National Economic Council (PCG-NEC), was formed, chaired by Genadz Karpenka. Meanwhile, international organizations expressed doubts as to the legitimacy of the referendum; the Council of Europe suspended Belarus's 'guest status', while the Permanent Council of the Parliamentary Assembly of the Organization for Security and Co-operation in Europe (OSCE, see p. 387) recognized a delegation from the former Supreme Council, rather than from the House of Representatives, as official Belarusian representatives.

Treaty of Union with Russia

The signing with Russia of the Treaty of Union, and initialling of the Charter of the Union on 2 April 1997, by Presidents Lukashenka and Yeltsin (see Foreign Affairs) prompted a protest demonstration in Minsk, which was suppressed by the police. Nevertheless, support for the treaty appeared to be widespread, and some 15,000 people participated in a pro-Union rally in Minsk in mid-May. The Charter of the Union was signed in Moscow on 23 May. The Treaty and Charter entered into effect in mid-June.

In November 1997 the opposition launched a campaign for the next presidential election to be held in 1999. A number of senior BNF members and other demonstrators were arrested in April 1998 during protest rallies. In June legislation was approved that rendered defamation of the President an offence punishable by up to five years' imprisonment. A new law on local elections was approved by the House of Representatives in December, effectively banning those with a police record or fine from standing in the local elections that were to be held in April 1999. In the event, the opposition organized an electoral boycott, and the majority of the seats in the elections were each contested by a single candidate.

Meanwhile, in January 1999 the Central Electoral Commission of the former Supreme Council scheduled a 'shadow presidential election' for 16 May. Chigir was registered as a candidate for the election in March, but was arrested and detained in April. (In May 2000 he was convicted of abuse of office and received a three-year, suspended sentence.) In the event, it proved impossible to organize fixed polling stations for the poll, which was not recognized by the Government or by the international community. In July 1999 Sharetski fled to Lithuania to avoid arrest after the Supreme Council designated him 'acting President' of Belarus. By September 17 of the 28 existing official parties had been re-registered, in compliance with a January decree by Lukashenka that political parties, trade unions and other organizations seek re-registration by July, or be dissolved. In October Vintsuk Vyachorka was elected Chairman of the BNF, which was renamed Revival—BNF in December. (Supporters of Paznyak had formed a breakaway party in the previous month.) Subsequently, a number of critics of the President disappeared in unexplained circumstances, including Hanchar and a former Minister of the Interior, Yuriy Zakharenka.

In February 2000 Ling resigned as Chairman of the Council of Ministers; he was replaced by Uladzimir Yermoshin. In that month opposition parties agreed to boycott the forthcoming parliamentary elections. The staging, in March, of an anti-Government 'Freedom March' (after a similar rally the previous October) was followed by the prohibition of demonstrations in central Minsk. A further demonstration on 25 March, to commemorate the creation of the BNR in 1918 was suppressed by the security forces and resulted in hundreds of arrests. In April the Minister of Internal Affairs, Yuriy Sivakow, resigned, ostensibly for health reasons.

A large-scale rally by opposition activists preceded the elections to the National Assembly, which were held in two rounds on 15 and 29 October 2000. The OSCE described the elections, in which nominally independent candidates obtained the majority of seats, as neither free nor fair. In March 2001 President Lukashenka signed a decree imposing severe restrictions on the use of foreign financial assistance by both individuals and national organizations.

In June 2001 two former investigators at the Office of the Prosecutor-General, who had been granted asylum in the USA, claimed that senior Belarusian government officials had organized the assassinations of political opponents, and alleged them to be responsible for the deaths of Hanchar and Zakharenka, as well as of Dmitrii Zavadski, a cameraman for a Russian television channel, whose location had been unknown since July 2000. The allegations were supported by the Chairman of the Federation of Trade Unions of Belarus, Uladzimir Hancharyk, who in July 2001 revealed documents that apparently linked the Prosecutor-General, Viktar Sheyman, and former Minister of Internal Affairs Sivakow with the disappearance and presumed murder of Hanchar and Zakharenka. In July the main opposition parties selected Hancharyk as their joint candidate for the presidential election scheduled for September. In August two state security agents released to the media a recorded testimony, in which they supported claims that Hanchar, together with a business associate, had been kidnapped and killed in September 1999 by a special police unit.

An increase in repression

On 9 September 2001 Lukashenka was re-elected to the presidency with 75.7% of votes cast. Hancharyk received 15.7% of the votes, and the only other candidate, the leader of the Liberal Democratic Party of Belarus (LDPB), Syarhey Haydukevich, received just 2.5%. The election was described as flawed by the OSCE, and Hancharyk urged the public to protest against Lukashenka's victory, to little effect. Following Lukashenka's inauguration on 20 September, Yermoshin tendered the resignation of his Government. On 10 October the House of Representatives approved the nomination of former Deputy Prime Minister Genadz Navitsky as premier of a reorganized Council of Ministers. In late 2001 and early 2002 a number of state officials and managers of state enterprises were arrested (several were subsequently imprisoned) as part of an 'anti-corruption' campaign.

In March 2002 two former police officers were sentenced to life imprisonment, having been found guilty of kidnapping Zavadski. However, there were claims that the charges had been fabricated to divert attention from the involvement of more senior government officials in the abduction. In September the Government began to reduce the diffusion in Belarus of Russian broadcast media, which were often critical of Lukashenka, and imposed new registration requirements on radio and television companies.

Local elections were held in March 2003, amid opposition allegations of electoral irregularities. In July the President dismissed premier Navitsky, Deputy Prime Minister Alyaksandr Papkow and the Minister of Agriculture and Food, Mikhail Rusy. The First Deputy Prime Minister, Syarhey Sidorsky, was appointed acting premier. In the same month Navitsky was elected Chairman of the Council of the Republic. In December Sidorsky was confirmed as Prime Minister, and a further reorganization of the Council of Ministers took place.

State repression continued in 2003–04, with the closure of several non-governmental organizations (NGOs), efforts to prevent the publication of several independent newspapers, and the imposition of further restrictions on access to Russian media. In November 2003 the Belarusian Party of Labour, the Belarusian Social Democratic Hramada (Assembly), Revival—BNF, the Party of Communists of Belarus (PKB) and the AHP announced the formation of an opposition alliance, the 'Five Plus' Popular Coalition. Restrictions on political parties increased, and in August 2004 the Supreme Court proscribed the Belarusian Party of Labour. Meanwhile, a prominent opponent of the Government, Mikhail Marinich, was arrested in April, on charges of theft and embezzlement, prompting a widely observed strike in June and other incidents of unrest. (In December Marinich was sentenced to five years' imprisonment, although the term was subsequently reduced.) No opposition candidates secured seats at the legislative elections, which took place on 17 October; 96 nominally independent candidates were elected, while the KPB obtained eight mandates, the BAP three, and the LDPB one. According to official results of a constitutional referendum, held concurrently with the elections, 77.3% of those participating voted to approve an amendment that would permit Lukashenka to contest a third presidential term. The official rate of participation was almost 90%.

In March 2005 police forcibly dispersed a demonstration of up to 1,500 people demanding the resignation of Lukashenka. In April Assembly and the Belarusian Social Democratic Party (National Hramada) merged to form the Assembly (Hramada)—Belarusian Social-Democratic Party (BSDP); Alyaksandr Kazulin was elected as the party's Chairman in July. In June two opposition leaders were sentenced to terms of corrective labour for having organized a series of unauthorized demonstrations. In the same month the organizer of the March demonstration was imprisoned for 18 months. In October a congress of opposition groups nominated civil society activist Alyaksandr Milinkevich as its candidate in the forthcoming presidential election, which was subsequently scheduled for 19 March 2006. In December 2005 the Council of the Republic approved legislative amendments to the criminal code that were widely interpreted as a further effort to curb opposition activity, including measures to penalize citizens for activities deemed to threaten personal or public security, or to discredit Belarus internationally.

Lukashenka elected to a third term

In the period preceding the presidential election many opposition politicians and supporters were detained by the authorities. Preliminary results of the election on 19 March 2006 indicated that Lukashenka had been returned to office by a significant majority, and precipitated immediate protests by opposition supporters at alleged electoral malpractice. Meanwhile, the OSCE declared that the election had failed to meet democratic standards, and Milinkevich demanded that the poll be repeated. According to the final results, Lukashenka received 83.0% of the votes cast, and Milinkevich was placed second, with 6.1%, ahead of Haydukevich and Kazulin. Kazulin was arrested on 25 March, prompting international protests. Both the USA and the European Union (EU, see p. 273) imposed visa bans and financial sanctions on Belarusian officials allegedly involved in electoral malpractice. Lukashenka was inaugurated as President on 8 April; Sidorsky was subsequently reappointed as Prime Minister. The Parliamentary Assembly of the Council of Europe urged the Belarusian authorities to hold a new presidential election in accordance with the demands of the opposition. Later in April Milinkevich was detained and sentenced to 15 days' imprisonment, having been found guilty of participating in an unauthorized demonstration. In July Kazulin was convicted on charges of disorderly conduct, and was sentenced to a prison term of five-and-a-half years.

Meanwhile, in May 2006 Lukashenka effected a government reorganization. In October the House of Representatives voted to amend Belarus's electoral legislation, prior to local elections that were scheduled to take place in January 2007. In the local elections, conducted on 14 January, the opposition secured only two seats on local councils, despite presenting 300 candidates. The USA and the EU declared that the conduct of the elections had failed to meet democratic standards.

In March 2007 an authorized opposition demonstration was staged in Minsk, to mark the anniversary of the creation of the BNR in 1918; opposition leaders declared that up to 10,000 supporters had attended the rally, of whom 100 had been detained. A series of arrests of youth opposition leaders in mid-2007 prompted the EU to suspend its participation in a proposed second round of negotiations with Belarus on energy security. The most prominent of those arrested, Zmitser Dashkevich, received an 18-month term of imprisonment in November, on charges of engaging in activities for an unregistered political organization. Meanwhile, the Ministry of Justice continued to reject applications for official registration by new opposition parties, including Milinkevich's For Freedom Movement. In November a new public association supportive of Lukashenka, White Rus, chaired by Minister of Education Alyaksandr Radzkow, was established. In January 2008 special police violently dispersed an unauthorized demonstration in Minsk, which had been organized in protest at a presidential decree restricting small-business activities. Dashkevich and another youth opposition leader were granted an early release in January, following protests by the EU and USA. In February Andrey Klimau, another opponent of Lukashenka who had been imprisoned for 'inciting revolution', was also released before he had served his full two-year sentence.

In June 2008 the Council of the Republic imposed additional restrictions on media outlets. On 4 July a bomb exploded at a concert held in Minsk to commemorate Independence Day, injuring 54 people. A number of opposition activists were subsequently arrested, including former members of a banned nationalist organization, the Belarusian Union of Military Personnel. Several days later Lukashenka dismissed the State Secretary of the Security Council and the head of the presidential administration, criticizing them for failing to prevent the bomb attack. In August, shortly after Kazulin was temporarily released to attend the funeral of his father-in-law, Lukashenka granted him a pardon. Although he had been replaced as Chairman of the BSDP earlier in August and had subsequently resigned from the party, Kazulin confirmed that he would remain in political life. European Commission and other international officials welcomed Lukashenka's decision and urged the release of the remaining political prisoners.

The 2008 legislative elections

Elections to the House of Representatives, which some 500 OSCE observers were invited to monitor by the Belarusian authorities, were conducted on 28 September 2008. While some 70 opposition candidates were permitted to participate in the poll, none obtained representation; it was reported that all of the 110 elected deputies were pro-Government, although 103 were nominally independent. Opposition supporters staged a protest against the conduct of the election on the same day. A preliminary OSCE report stated that the election process had again failed to meet international democratic standards. Following the election of 56 senators by regional councils on 3–10 October (and appointment of the remaining eight deputies by Lukashenka), a new Council of the Republic was installed. In December, to conform with EU demands, the Ministry of Justice registered Milinkevich's For Freedom Movement as a political party.

Police violently dispersed the annual opposition rally organized in Minsk in February 2009. On 6 April Uladzimir Naumau, Minister of Internal Affairs since 2000, resigned. He was succeeded by Anatol Kulyashou. In June the hitherto Minister of Labour and Social Protection, Uladzimir Patupchyk, was appointed as a Deputy Prime Minister. In September police in Minsk detained the leaders of the AHP and the PKB as they attempted to distribute material critical of the Government's economic policies. In October the House of Representatives voted to amend the electoral code. A more substantial reorganization of the Government was implemented on 4 December, as part of measures that were reportedly intended to address popular dissatisfaction with the economic downturn. Notably, Yuri Zhadobin, the hitherto Secretary of the Security Council, succeeded Leanid Maltsaw as Minister of Defence (who was appointed to Zhadobin's former position), Maryana Shchotkina was appointed as Minister of Labour and Social Protection, Mikalay Snapkou became Minister of the Economy, and Aleh Pralyaskouski, who had advocated the imposition of stricter restrictions on the operations of media organs, was appointed Minister of Information. In March 2010 the offices of a pro-democracy group, Charter 97, in Minsk, were raided by police, apparently in response to the publication of a report on the group's website to the effect that Andrey Sannikau, the leader of an unregistered opposition group, European Belarus, was intending to contest the presidential election due in 2011.

In September 2010 a prominent journalist and opposition activist, Oleh Bebenin, was found hanged. Opposition figures, including Sannikau, expressed doubt at the official attribution of the cause of Bebenin's death to suicide, and the OSCE urged that an independent inquiry be conducted into his death. On 14 September, meanwhile, an extraordinary session of the House of Representatives voted to schedule a presidential election for 19 December, several months earlier than constitutionally required. Lukashenka subsequently confirmed his intention of seeking re-election, and by September some 17 candidates had been registered. Although seven of these subsequently withdrew from the contest, or were unable to gather the requisite 100,000 signatures, several of the opposition candidates were, unprecedentedly, allowed a limited degree of access to state media to campaign, and around 3,000 people attended an opposition protest rally in Minsk in early December. However, the principal opposition leaders, including Kazulin and Milinkevich declined to contest the election.

The 2010 presidential election

The presidential election, held on 19 December 2010, was contested by 10 candidates. According to the official results, Lukashenka was overwhelmingly re-elected to a further term of office, receiving 79.7% of the votes cast, with about 84% of the electorate participating. His nearest rival was Sannikau, with only 2.4%; about 6.5% of the votes cast were 'against all candidates'. The announcement of the preliminary results of the elections, several hours after the polls closed, precipitated demonstrations of some 10,000 people outside the parliamentary buildings in central Minsk, who protested against alleged electoral improprieties. Lukashenka harshly condemned the demonstrators, and riot police forcibly dispersed the crowds. Seven of the nine opposition candidates, including Sannikau, together with his wife, journalist Irina Khalip, were among several hundred people who were arrested, and at least one candidate, Uladzimer Nyaklyaeu, was beaten by police. In total, around 600 demonstrators were detained. Observers from the OSCE criticized the conduct of the election, stating that the counting of votes lacked transparency, although an observer mission from the CIS described the poll as being both 'free and fair'. On the following day police officers beat and arrested members of numerous human rights organizations. By the end of the month four of the opposition candidates had been charged with organizing riots, while three other candidates remained under judicial investigation. During the second half of December the homes and offices of several independent journalists were raided by law enforcement or security officials. Western Governments, the OSCE and the EU criticized the harsh treatment of the opposition, as well as the conduct of the election. At the end of the month the OSCE closed its mission in Minsk, in response to the demands of the Belarusian authorities, which claimed that the organization had fulfilled its mandate in the country. In January 2011 Nyaklyaeu and Khalip were released from detention. At the end of the month, however, the EU sanctions against Belarusian officials, which had been suspended in 2008, were reinstated (see Regional relations).

Meanwhile, on 28 December 2010 Mikhail Myasnikovich, who had served as Head of the Presidential Administration in 1995–2001, was appointed Prime Minister, replacing Sidorsky. Several new ministerial appointments, including those of three new deputy premiers, were made shortly afterwards. On 21 January 2011 Lukashenka was formally inaugurated to a new presidential term.

On 11 April 2011 a bomb exploded at a station on the Minsk Metro, killing 15 people and injuring almost 400. In May Sannikau was sentenced to five years' imprisonment on charges of organizing mass protests after the December 2010 election. (During his trial he claimed that he had been subject to physical torture while in detention.) Khalip subsequently received a suspended prison sentence, having been found guilty of similar charges.

Economic crisis and popular protests

From late May 2011 unauthorized demonstrations, many organized through social networking websites, were staged on a weekly basis in Minsk and other cities, to protest against the deteriorating economic situation in the country; some 400 people were reported to have been detained during June. On 29 June, when a further unauthorized anti-Government demonstration took place in central Minsk, protesters clapped their hands in unison; police subsequently dispersed the demonstration, detaining around 50 people. Similar 'clapping' demonstrations continued to take place in Minsk and across the country during July. By the end of that month it was reported that around 2,000 people had been detained during the protests, and some 500 had received short prison sentences, while the Government had published draft legislation that was intended to prevent the protests by prohibiting groups of people from assembling to take part in any expression of 'action or inaction'. In early August a prominent human rights activist, Ales Byalyatski, was arrested and formally charged with tax evasion (owing to his use of personal bank accounts in Lithuania and Poland to receive funding from international donors); in November he was sentenced to four-and-a-half years' imprisonment.

In November 2011 Lukashenka declared that the Chairmen of the Executive Committees of Minsk and the six oblasts (regions) would be granted the military rank of Major-General, and that they would have additional responsibilities pertaining to territorial defence. In the same month Lukashenka announced the formation of a territorial army numbering 120,000, and established an advisory body, the Council for the Development of an Informational Society, headed by himself, with his eldest son, Viktar, as deputy. At the end of November two Belarusian nationals were convicted and sentenced to death for organizing the metro bomb attack in April, as well as the attack at the 2008 Independence Day concert in Minsk and another bombing in the north-eastern city of Vitebsk in 2005, after they pleaded guilty to the charges against them (although one of them later withdrew his confession). Domestic and international human rights groups cast doubt on the evidence against the two men, petitioning the Government to commute the death sentence against them, while the Council of Europe urged an immediate moratorium on capital punishment in Belarus. None the less, both men were executed in March 2012. Lukashenka dismissed Valery Ivanou as a Deputy Prime Minister in April, appointing Rusy in his place. In the same month Lukashenka announced that he had granted a presidential pardon to Sannikau and to an associate of Sannikau, Zmitser Bandarenka (who had been serving a two-year prison sentence on charges of participating in the unrest after the 2010 election); both detainees were consequently released. In May Lukashenka dismissed Kulyashou as Minister of Internal Affairs, appointing Col Ihar Shunevich to succeed him.

In July 2012 Lukashenka reacted strenuously to an initiative by Swedish human rights activists, who illicitly flew into Belarusian airspace and parachuted to the ground a number of children's toys bearing pro-human rights messages. A Belarusian journalist who photographed the incident was detained shortly afterwards, together with another Belarusian citizen accused of aiding the activists. At the end of the month Lukashenka removed the heads of the border security service and the air force, who were held responsible for failure to prevent the action. Following diplomatic measures taken against Sweden (see Regional relations), in August Lukashenka also dismissed the Minister of Foreign Affairs, Syarhey Martynau, who was replaced by the hitherto head of the presidential administration, Uladzimir Makei. In the same month Leanid Zayets was appointed Minister of Agriculture and Food.

Recent developments: the 2012 legislative elections

Elections were conducted to the House of Representatives on 23 September 2012. Milinkevich had been unable to secure registration to contest the elections, while the AHP and Revival—BNF withdrew from the poll a week beforehand and urged a boycott, arguing that the electoral process was flawed. A total of 104 nominally independent candidates, all of whom were reported to be supporters of Lukashenka, were elected, together with three members of the KPB, one member of the BAP and one member of the Republican Party of Labour and Justice. Although the authorities announced that 71.6% of the electorate had participated in the poll, opposition parties claimed that the rate was as low as 30%. OSCE monitors strongly criticized the conduct of the elections as neither free nor impartial, and also cited continued restrictions on the ability of opposition candidates to campaign beforehand, although the CIS pronounced the poll to have been conducted in accordance with democratic standards. (A second round of voting was to take place in one constituency at an unspecified later date.) Elections for 56 members of the Council of the Republic by regional councils took place on 6–25 September; a new Chairman of the upper chamber assumed office in mid-October. Minor changes to government personnel were implemented in the period following the legislative elections. On 18 January 2013 Piotr Prakapovich, hitherto a presidential aide, was appointed as a Deputy Prime Minister. In April Lukashenka dismissed Alyaksandr Azyarets as Minister of Energy, expressing dissatisfaction with the management of the country's energy sector (the First Deputy Minister of Energy and the Director-General of the state energy company Belenergo/Belenerha were also removed); Azyarets was succeeded by Uladzimir Patupchyk later that month.

In mid-2013 Belarus market traders staged a nationwide strike, in protest at a new requirement for certification, imposed under the regulations of the Russian-led Customs Union (see Regional relations); the authorities subsequently agreed to postpone introduction of the new measure until 2014. In August 2013 the leader of the Young Front opposition group, Dzmitry Dashkevich, who had been declared a prisoner of conscience by human rights organization Amnesty International, was granted early release. However, human rights groups reported that 11 political prisoners remained in detention at late 2013, notably prominent activist Byalyatski. Meanwhile, in October the Central Elections Commission announced that the forthcoming local elections were to be conducted in March 2014. Following an upsurge of popular unrest in Ukraine (in response to its Government's failure to sign an EU Eastern Partnership agreement—see below), in December 2013 large numbers of opposition and youth activists from Belarus joined pro-EU protests in the Ukrainian capital, Kyiv. In January 2014 it was announced that Belarus's main military court had sentenced two Belarusian nationals to eight and 10 years' imprisonment, respectively, on charges of spying for Lithuania. At an OSCE meeting in Vienna, Austria, in February, Sannikau (who had been granted asylum in the United Kingdom) denounced continued human rights violations by the Belarusian Government. In mid-February Lukashenka appointed several new officials in the Ministry of Communications and Information Technologies. Notably, Mikalay Pantsyaley was dismissed as minister; he was succeeded by Syarhey Popkov.

Foreign Affairs

Regional relations

Following the dissolution of the USSR, Belarus's closest relations continued to be with member states of the CIS, particularly Russia. Belarus signed the CIS Collective Security Treaty in December 1993, and accords on closer economic co-operation with CIS states followed. With the dissolution of the USSR, Belarus effectively became a nuclear power, with approximately 80 intercontinental ballistic missiles stationed on its territory. However, in May 1992 Belarus signed the Lisbon Protocol to the Treaty on the Non-Proliferation of Nuclear Weapons (see p. 119), under which it pledged to transfer all nuclear missiles to Russia, and the country's final nuclear warhead was transported to Russia in 1996.

In April 1994 Belarus and Russia concluded an agreement on eventual monetary union, and in April 1996 concluded a Treaty on the Formation of a Community of Sovereign Republics, providing for closer economic, political and military integration. On 2 April 1997 a further Treaty of Union, providing for the 'voluntary unification of the member states', was signed by Presidents Yeltsin and Lukashenka. The Union's Parliamentary Assembly (which had convened in March) was to comprise 36 members from the legislature of each country. A Charter detailing the process of integration was signed in Moscow on 23 May. The respective legislatures ratified the documents in June, before the first official session of the Parliamentary Assembly. In November 1998 the Parliamentary Assembly of the Russia-Belarus Union voted for the creation of a unified, bicameral parliament. (However, establishment of the proposed unified legislature was held in abeyance.) The signature of a treaty formally creating the Union State of Russia and Belarus took place in Moscow on 8 December 1999. The treaty was ratified and took effect in January 2000, when Lukashenka was appointed Chairman of the Supreme State Council of the Union State (comprising the Presidents, Prime Ministers and the heads of each of the parliamentary chambers in both countries). An agreement on the introduction of a single currency was signed on 30 November, and was ratified by the National Assembly in April 2001. (However, the two counties subsequently failed to reach a final agreement on the details of monetary union.)

During 2002 disagreements over the nature of the planned union arose. Although Belarus and Russia reached agreement on the harmonization of customs and tax laws and the removal of trade barriers, in June Vladimir Putin, who had succeeded Yeltsin as President of Russia in 2000, publicly criticized Lukashenka's proposals for union, and in August presented Lukashenka with a new unification plan, providing for the absorption of the seven administrative regions of Belarus (rather than of Belarus as a country) into the Russian Federation; Lukashenka denounced the plan as an insult to Belarus's sovereignty. In October 2005 a draft constitutional act was drawn up; it was envisaged that it would be submitted for approval at referendums to be held in both countries (although no further action on the plan was subsequently taken).

Bilateral relations were strained in 2003–04 by inconclusive negotiations over the settlement of Belarusian fuel arrears, which led to the repeated suspension of gas supplies by the Russian state-controlled energy supplier Gazprom. An agreement was reached in June 2004, whereupon Gazprom resumed supplies to Belarus; a further agreement was signed in December 2005. In January 2007 Belarus imposed a retaliatory levy on Russian oil passing through its territory, after Gazprom more than doubled the price of gas supplied to Belarus, and Russia introduced an oil export duty. Russia subsequently accused Belarus of abstracting Russian crude oil in transit through the country, and again suspended the transit of oil through Belarus. The situation was resolved three days later, when Belarus agreed to lift the transit duty and Russia in turn reduced its duty on oil exports.

In May 2008 Lukashenka (in his capacity as Chairman of the Supreme State Council of the Union State of Russia and Belarus) announced that he had appointed Putin, who had become the Russian Chairman of the Government (premier) following the election of Dmitrii Medvedev to the presidency, Prime Minister of the Union State. Lukashenka expressed support for the military action taken by Russia in Georgia in early August to assist separatists in South Ossetia (see Georgia) (although he subsequently failed to adhere to his pledge that Belarus would extend formal recognition to the Georgian separatist regions of South Ossetia and Abkhazia as independent states.) Russia granted Belarus a loan of some US $2,000m. towards energy supplies in November and later agreed concessionary prices in the payment of natural gas, following the deteriorating financial position in Belarus. In February 2009 it was announced that Belarus and Russia had signed an official treaty providing for the creation of a joint air defence system. The Belarusian Ministry of Defence reported that the two countries had commenced joint training operations, although Belarus subsequently expressed reluctance to participate in a proposed rapid-response unit that the Collective Security Treaty Organization (CSTO, see p. 464) was intending to establish. Relations with Russia deteriorated somewhat during 2009–10, partly in response to the development of warmer relations between Belarus and the EU (see below). In May 2009 Russia announced that it was to delay the release of a tranche worth US $500m. of a loan agreed in late 2008, and in June 2009 it imposed a ban on the import of many items of dairy produce from Belarus, ostensibly because they failed to meet Russian packaging requirements. In protest at this development, Lukashenka boycotted a meeting of the CSTO held in Moscow in mid-June, at which Belarus had been due to assume the rotational chairmanship of the Organization. In March 2010 Putin visited Belarus, where he met Belarusian Prime Minister Sidorsky and chaired a meeting, in Brest, of the Council of Ministers of the Union State. However, at the time of Putin's visit Lukashenka had undertaken a visit to Venezuela, where he met President Hugo Chávez. It was reported that Belarus had offered military assistance to Venezuela, and that Venezuela was to supply petroleum to Belarus. Relations deteriorated further when a state-controlled TV channel in Russia broadcast a series of documentary programmes that were particularly critical of Lukashenka, and which criticized abuses of human rights in Belarus. However, in early December, shortly before a presidential election, terms were agreed on a reduction in the duties paid by Belarus on imports of Russian petroleum, and for Belarus to pay to Russia all the duties that it received from re-exporting Russian petroleum products. Following the election, Belarus's relations with many Western countries deteriorated further, with the effect that its ties with Russia were concomitantly strengthened.

In March 2011 Belarus reached an agreement with Russia on the construction of Belarus's first nuclear power station, for which Russia would provide a US $9,400m. loan over 25 years. In June, amid an increasing economic crisis, Russian electricity exporting company Inter RAO temporarily suspended electricity supplies to Belarus, as a result of unpaid debts. In November Putin announced that the Russian Government had granted a substantial discount in the price of natural gas supplied by Russia from the beginning of 2012, with the aim that Belarus would pay the price charged to neighbouring regions of Russia from 2014. In exchange, the Russian state-owned corporation Gazprom acquired the remaining 50% of Belarus's gas transport network Beltransgaz, thereby obtaining total control of the network. The agreement increased Western concerns about Russia's dominant influence in Belarus (after Putin had, in August 2011, publicly suggested that Belarus become part of Russia). In January 2013 the Russian Government completed ratification of the agreement with Belarus on gas prices and the sale of Beltransgaz.

In August 2013 Vladislav Baumgertner, the Chief Executive of the Russian potash fertilizer company Uralkali, was arrested in Minsk, after the company withdrew from a joint Russian-Belarusian venture the Belarusian Potash Co, in response to what it claimed were violations of the agreement by the Belarusian Government. Baumgertner, who had been invited to Belarus to enter into negotiations with the Government, was charged with abuse of office and placed under house arrest. Following the ensuing strain in bilateral relations, Russia imposed trade restrictions against Belarus, including the introduction of a ban on imports of pork products, and announced that it was to reduce its fuel exports (while denying that these measures were related to Baumgertner's arrest). After one of the joint owners of Uralkali, Russian businessman Suleiman Kerimov (who had also been charged by the Belarusian authorities), agreed to sell his share in the enterprise at the demand of Lukashenka, Baumgertner was extradited to Russia in November on condition that he would remain under investigation there. In December Dmitrii Osipov, hitherto a senior executive at Russian fertilizer producer Uralchem (whose owner originated from Belarus), was appointed to replace Baumgertner. It was reported at the end of January 2014 that Osipov had met the head of the Belarusian Potash Co for co-operation discussions in Moscow.

In March 1996 Belarus, Kazakhstan, Kyrgyzstan and Russia signed the Quadripartite Treaty, which envisaged a common market and a customs union between the four countries, as well as joint transport, energy and communications systems (Tajikistan signed the Treaty in 1998). In April 2003 Armenia, Belarus, Kazakhstan, Kyrgyzstan, Russia and Tajikistan had formally inaugurated a new regional defence structure as the successor to the CIS Collective Security Treaty, the CSTO. Belarus was, together with Kazakhstan, Kyrgyzstan, Russia and Tajikistan, a founding member of the Eurasian Economic Community (EURASEC, see p. 451) in 2001; Armenia, Moldova and Ukraine were subsequently granted observer status, and Uzbekistan acceded to full membership in 2006. In October 2007 EURASEC leaders approved the legal basis for the establishment of a new customs union that was initially to comprise Belarus, Kazakhstan and Russia, with Kyrgyzstan, Tajikistan and Uzbekistan expected to join later. In November 2009 Belarus, Kazakhstan and Russia formalized their agreement on the customs union, which, following the unification of customs tariffs on 1 January 2010, entered into effect from 1 July. Meanwhile, in April Lukashenka announced that Belarus had granted asylum to the recently deposed President of Kyrgyzstan, Kurmanbek Bakiyev, and declined the request of the new Kyrgyzstani authorities for his extradition. In November 2011 Lukashenka, Medvedev and President Nursultan Nazarbaev of Kazakhstan signed an accord in Moscow that provided for the creation of a body to regulate their countries' closer economic integration, with the stated aim of establishing a 'Eurasian economic union' by 2015.

Although the parliamentary elections of October 2008 were judged to have failed to meet democratic standards, EU officials increasingly favoured dialogue with the Belarusian Government, a policy that was supported by principal opposition leaders Kazulin and Milinkevich. At a summit meeting in that month EU ministers of foreign affairs suspended for an initial period of six months the entry visa ban imposed against Lukashenka and a number of other senior officials, in recognition of improvements in the authorities' observance of human rights. (The suspension of the entry visa ban was subsequently extended until January 2011.) However, visa restrictions remained in place against a number of officials. The EU continued to insist that the Belarusian authorities release designated political prisoners, end restrictions on independent newspapers and media, and allow the freedom of assembly of political associations before it would normalize relations. After acknowledging commitments made by the Government towards reform, in March 2009 EU officials confirmed the inclusion of Belarus in the EU's proposed Eastern Partnership programme, which envisaged enhanced free trade and visa arrangements with a number of regional countries. In April President Lukashenka visited Italy and Vatican City, where he met Italian premier Silvio Berlusconi and Pope Benedict XVI. In late November Berlusconi undertook a reciprocal visit to Belarus, becoming the first senior leader of an EU state to visit the country for more than a decade. None the less, in November a meeting of EU foreign affairs ministers voted to maintain the sanctions against various members of the Government (while extending the suspension of certain of these sanctions). Following the December 2010 presidential election, and an escalation in human rights abuses in Belarus, relations with the EU deteriorated sharply, and in January 2011 the EU reinstated the sanctions that it had suspended in 2008, and increased the number of officials subject to restrictions. In January 2012 the EU noted a further worsening in the human rights situation in Belarus, and announced that it intended to expand further its list of banned officials (then numbering 210). In response to the expansion of sanctions, on 28 February the Belarusian authorities announced the immediate expulsion from the country of the Polish ambassador and the EU representatives. On the following day all EU member states withdrew their ambassadors from Belarus, in protest at the expulsions. The ambassadors of the EU member states returned to Minsk, after Lukashenka released a former presidential candidate, Andrey Sannikau, from prison in mid-April (see Domestic Political Affairs). In August the Swedish ambassador was expelled from the country and Sweden was ordered to close its embassy, following an initiative by a Swedish human rights group (see above). (Sweden took reciprocal action towards Belarusian diplomatic staff based in Stockholm, Sweden.) In October EU member states renewed for a further year the sanctions in force against Belarus. As a concession, in June 2013 the EU ended its travel ban against the Belarusian Minister of Foreign Affairs, Uladzimir Makei, in order to facilitate Eastern Partnership negotiations. In October, however, the EU again extended sanctions (henceforth comprising visa bans and asset freezes on 232 officials and 25 companies) for a further year. Makei led the Belarusian delegation at an Eastern Partnership summit meeting, which took place in Vilnius, Lithuania, at the end of November; the participants adopted a declaration that incorporated a roadmap for further development of the regional programme. In February 2014 it was announced that the Belarus authorities had suspended the import of pork products from Poland (following a Russian embargo on pork products from the EU), officially on grounds of safety.

Other external relations

In October 2004 the US Congress approved the Belarus Democracy Act of 2004, which authorized financial assistance to organizations campaigning for democracy within Belarus and also prohibited US government agencies from providing non-humanitarian aid to the Belarusian Government. In January 2005 the US Secretary of State, Condoleezza Rice, described Belarus as an 'outpost of tyranny', and in April she urged that the presidential election due to take place in March 2006 be free and fair. Following the election, relations with the USA deteriorated further, as the USA imposed visa bans and financial sanctions on prominent Belarusian officials (see Domestic Political Affairs). In December the US House of Representatives approved an extension to the Belarus Democracy Act until 2008. The USA subsequently implemented additional financial sanctions, freezing assets belonging to Belarus's largest petrochemical company, Belneftekhim. The US Administration announced that it would impose similar measures against other Belarusian enterprises unless the authorities released political prisoners. In March 2008 the USA extended sanctions to include all Belarusian petrochemical companies in which the State's share was 50% or more. Belarus responded by recalling its ambassador in the USA for consultations; the USA subsequently complied with Belarus's request that the US ambassador leave the country. In May Belarus expelled a further 10 US diplomats from the country. In September, in response to the release of Kazulin and other political prisoners, the US Administration announced the suspension of sanctions against two of the main subsidiaries of Belneftekhim, initially for a period of six months; the suspension was subsequently extended on a further three occasions. In January 2011, in common with the EU, the USA announced additional travel restrictions and the reimposition of sanctions against the two Belneftekhim subsidiaries (with a further four subject to sanctions from August), in response to the mass arrests of opposition supporters after the December 2010 presidential election. The US Administration extended the sanctions in force against Belarus in January 2012, and again, for a period of one year, in June 2013, when it cited the Belarusian Government's failure to meet international standards and the arbitrary detention of citizens during the period of the 2012 elections. In August a court in Ecuador ruled that a Belarusian former financial crimes investigator, Alyaksandr Barankov, should not be extradited to Belarus; Barankov had been granted political asylum in Ecuador in 2010, after claiming that he had discovered corruption involving relatives of Lukashenka. Meanwhile, after establishing strong ties with Venezuela in 2010, Lukashenka attended the funeral of Venezuelan President Hugo Chávez in the capital, Caracas, in March 2013, and a number of commemorative events were staged in Minsk. In November the Belarusian Government announced plans for the expansion of economic co-operation with Venezuela.

CONSTITUTION AND GOVERNMENT

Under the Constitution of March 1994, which was amended in November 1996, legislative power is vested in the bicameral Natsionalnoye Sobraniye (National Assembly). The lower chamber, the 110-member Palata Predstaviteley (House of Representatives), is elected by universal adult suffrage for a term of four years. The upper chamber, the Soviet Respubliki (Council of the Republic), comprises 64 members: 56 members elected by organs of local administration, and eight members appointed by the President. The President is the Head of State, and is elected by popular vote for five years. Executive authority is exercised by the Council of Ministers, which is led by the Chairman (Prime Minister) and is responsible to the National Assembly. Judicial authority is exercised by the Supreme Court, the Supreme Economic Court and regional courts. For administrative purposes, Belarus is divided into six regions (oblasts) and the capital city of Minsk; the regions are divided into districts (rayons).

REGIONAL AND INTERNATIONAL CO-OPERATION

Belarus is a founder member of the Commonwealth of Independent States (CIS, see p. 243), the headquarters of which are located in the Belarusian capital city, Minsk. Belarus is also a member of the Eurasian Economic Community (EURASEC, see p. 451) and the Collective Security Treaty Organization (CSTO, see p. 464). A customs union comprising Belarus, Kazakhstan and Russia was established in 2010.

Belarus was, as the Belarusian Soviet Socialist Republic, a founder member of the UN. Prior to the dissolution of the USSR in 1991, both Belarus and Ukraine had formally separate UN membership from that of the USSR, despite both republics forming integral parts of the Union. Belarus is a permanent member of the Non-aligned Movement (see p. 467).

ECONOMIC AFFAIRS

In 2012, according to estimates by the World Bank, Belarus's gross national income (GNI), measured at average 2010–12 prices, was US $61,781m., equivalent to $6,530 per head. In terms of purchasing power parity, GNI in 2012 was equivalent to $15,220 per head. During 2003–12 the population declined at an average annual rate of 0.4%, while gross domestic product (GDP) per head increased at an average annual rate of 7.5%, in real terms. During 2003–12, overall GDP increased, in real terms, by an average of 7.1% annually. Real GDP increased by 1.5% in 2012.

Agriculture (including forestry) contributed 9.5% of GDP and engaged 10.1% of the employed labour force in 2012. The principal crops are potatoes, grain and sugar beet. Large areas of arable land (some 1.6m. ha) remain unused after being contaminated in 1986, following the accident at the Chornobyl nuclear power station in Ukraine. The Belarusian authorities have largely opposed private farming, and by 1999 collective and state farms still accounted for some 83% of agricultural land. However, private farms produced the majority of Belarus's potatoes, fruit and vegetables, as well as a significant proportion of total livestock-product output. In 1998, according to the IMF, 49.8% of total crop output was produced by the private sector. During 2003–12, according to UN figures, real agricultural GDP increased at an average annual rate of 5.6%. In 2012 agricultural output grew by 6.0%.

Industry (comprising mining, manufacturing, construction and power) provided 43.2% of GDP and engaged 33.3% of the employed labour force in 2012. According to the UN figures, industrial GDP increased, in real terms, at an average annual rate of 10.2% during 2003–12. Real industrial GDP grew by 7.7% in 2011 and by a further 1.8% in 2012.

Belarus has relatively few mineral resources, although there are small deposits of petroleum and natural gas, and important peat reserves. Peat extraction, however, was severely affected by the disaster at Chornobyl, since contaminated peat could not be burned. Some 2.9m. metric tons of peat for fuel were mined in 2011, according to the US Geological Survey. Belarus produced 50% of the former USSR's output of potash, and remained one the world's largest producers; annual production of potash fertilizers (measured in terms of potassium oxide) amounted to 4.8m. metric tons in 2012. Only 0.4% of the labour force were engaged in mining and quarrying in 2012.

The manufacturing sector contributed 31.1% of GDP and engaged 22.7% of the employed labour force in 2012. Machine-building, power generation and chemicals are the principal branches of the sector. During 2003–12 manufacturing GDP increased, in real terms, at an average annual rate of 10.5%, according to UN figures. Overall sectoral GDP grew by 6.3% in 2012.

The construction sector contributed 7.7% of GDP and engaged 7.7% of the employed labour force in 2012. During 2003–12, according to UN figures, the GDP of the sector increased at an average annual rate of 13.5%. Construction GDP increased by 5.8% in 2011, but decreased by 9.8% in 2012.

In 2011 some 98.3% of Belarus's supply of energy was provided by natural gas. Mineral fuels and lubricants comprised 38.5% of the total value of imports in 2012. There are two large petroleum refineries, at Novopolotsk and Mozyr. Construction of a nuclear power plant near the border with Lithuania commenced in

November 2013, in co-operation with Russian state nuclear agency Rosatom.

The services sector provided 47.4% of GDP and accounted for 56.6% of total employment in 2012, with transport and communications, and trade and catering being of particular importance. According to UN figures, during 2003–12 the GDP of the services sector increased, in real terms, at an average annual rate of 6.2%. Sectoral GDP increased by 9.8% in 2011, and by 1.7% in 2012.

In 2012 Belarus recorded a visible merchandise trade surplus of US $565.4m., and there was a deficit of $1,687.8m. on the current account of the balance of payments. In 2012 Russia was Belarus's principal supplier of imports, providing 59.4% of the total. Germany and the People's Republic of China were also major sources of imports. Russia was also Belarus's principal export partner, receiving 35.4% of total exports. The Netherlands, Ukraine and Latvia were also major recipients of exports. In 2012 the principal exports were mineral fuels and lubricants, chemicals and related products, machinery and transport equipment, basic manufactures, food and live animals, and miscellaneous manufactured articles. The principal imports were mineral fuels and lubricants, machinery and transport equipment, basic manufactures, chemicals and related products, and food and live animals.

According to the IMF, in 2013 the general government budget, including the social protection fund, bank-restructuring and outlays related to guaranteed debt, was projected to record a deficit of 18,800m. roubles. Belarus's general government gross debt was 136,382,309m. roubles in 2011, equivalent to 45.9% of GDP. Belarus's total external debt was US $29,120m. at the end of 2011, of which $9,152m. was public and publicly guaranteed debt. In that year, the cost of servicing long-term public and publicly guaranteed debt and repayments to the IMF was equivalent to 4.5% of the value of exports of goods, services and income (excluding workers' remittances). During 2002–10 consumer prices increased at an average rate of 13.3% per year. The annual average rate of inflation was 7.7% in 2010. In 2012 the rate of unemployment was 0.6%. However, the true rate of unemployment was believed to be far higher, as many people were unwilling to register, owing to the low level of official benefits.

Following the dissolution of the USSR, the Belarusian State continued to play a prominent economic role. In 2010 Belarus joined a customs union with Russia and Kazakhstan. Amid a sharp deterioration in the country's financial situation, in early 2011 the Government sought emergency financing from the IMF and Russia. The IMF strongly criticized government policies and demanded the implementation of substantial reforms. In June Belarus was granted a loan of US $3,000m. over a period of three years from the crisis fund of EURASEC (see p. 451). In November the Russian Government agreed to grant Belarus a substantial discount on the price of natural gas, while it was agreed that gas-transport network Beltransgaz would be acquired by Russia. Meanwhile, the USA and the European Union (EU, see p. 273) increased sanctions imposed against Belarus in response to the authorities' human rights record (see Foreign Affairs). By the end of 2012 government measures, supported by EURASEC funding, and several devaluations of the national currency, had succeeded in effecting some recovery from fiscal crisis, with a sharp reduction in inflation. However, the decision, in July 2013, of Russian potash fertilizer company Uralkali to withdraw from a joint state venture, and the subsequent arrest of its head (see Regional relations), caused a diplomatic dispute and the temporary imposition of Russian trade restrictions against Belarus. After the strain in bilateral relations eased later that year, the Belarusian Government continued to seek the removal of tariffs under the Russian-led Customs Union. Meanwhile, negotiations continued with the People's Republic of China on a joint project to construct a large-scale industrial park near Minsk. In December the IMF noted that the country's current account deficit had again amounted to more than 9% of GDP and that currency reserves were becoming depleted, while growth had slowed significantly in 2012–13, attributing the renewed crisis to the Government's continued policy of granting wage increases and issuing of directed lending. Moreover, the release of the final $440m. tranche of EURASEC aid, which was due in late 2013, was postponed. However, in December Russia agreed to extend a further loan of $2,000m. to Belarus, releasing the first funds in January 2014.

PUBLIC HOLIDAYS

2015: 1 January (New Year's Day), 7 January (Orthodox Christmas), 8 March (International Women's Day), 15 March (Constitution Day), 5 April (Catholic Easter), 12 April (Orthodox Easter), 21 April (Radunitsa, Remembrance Day), 1 May (Labour Day), 9 May (Victory Day), 3 July (Independence Day), 7 November (October Revolution Day), 25 December (Catholic Christmas).

Statistical Survey

Source: mainly National Statistical Committee of the Republic of Belarus, 220070 Minsk, pr. Partizanski 12; tel. (17) 249-42-78; fax (17) 249-22-04; e-mail minstat@mail.belpak.by; internet www.belstat.gov.by.

Area and Population

AREA, POPULATION AND DENSITY

Area (sq km)	207,595*
Population (census results)	
16 February 1999†	10,045,237
14–24 October 2009	
Males	4,420,039
Females	5,083,768
Total	9,503,807
Population (official estimates at 1 January)	
2011	9,481,193
2012	9,465,150
2013	9,463,840
Density (per sq km) at 1 January 2013	45.6

* 80,153 sq miles.

† Figure refers to the *de jure* population.

POPULATION BY AGE AND SEX

(official estimates at 1 January 2013)

	Males	Females	Total
0–14	750,878	709,387	1,460,265
15–64	3,232,588	3,465,353	6,697,941
65 and over	414,060	891,574	1,305,634
Total	4,397,526	5,066,314	9,463,840

POPULATION BY ETHNIC GROUP

(2009 census, % of total population)

Belarusian	84
Russian	8
Polish	3
Ukrainian	2
Others	3
Total	100

ADMINISTRATIVE DIVISIONS*
(official population estimates at 1 January 2013)

	Area (sq km)	Population	Density (per sq km)
Oblasts (Regions)			
Brest (Bieraście)	32,785	1,390,364	42.4
Gomel (Homiel)	40,372	1,427,638	35.4
Grodno (Horadnia)	25,127	1,058,415	42.1
Minsk (Miensk)	39,847	1,401,861	35.2
Mogilev (Mahiloŭ)	29,068	1,076,485	37.0
Vitebsk (Viciebsk)	40,048	1,208,018	30.2
Capital City			
Minsk (Miensk)	348	1,901,059	5,462.8
Total	207,595	9,463,840	45.6

* The Belarusian names are given in parentheses after the more widely used Russian names.

PRINCIPAL TOWNS
(estimated population at 1 January 2013)*

Minsk (Miensk, capital)	1,901,059	Borisov (Barysau)	145,659
Gomel (Homiel)	514,968	Pinsk	135,619
Vitebsk (Viciebsk)	369,392	Orsha (Vorsha)	131,791
Mogilev (Mahiloŭ)	366,839	Mozyr (Mazyr)	111,324
Grodno (Horadnia)	352,485	Novopolotsk (Navapolatsk)	107,075
Brest (Bieraście)	326,428	Soligorsk (Salihorsk)	104,745
Bobruysk (Babrujsk)	217,127	Lida	99,430
Baranovichi (Baranavichy)	170,685	Molodechno (Maladzyechna)	93,802

* The Belarusian names are given in parentheses after the more widely used Russian names, where they differ.

BIRTHS, MARRIAGES AND DEATHS

	Registered live births		Registered marriages		Registered deaths	
	Number	Rate (per 1,000)	Number	Rate (per 1,000)	Number	Rate (per 1,000)
2005	90,508	9.3	73,333	7.5	141,857	14.5
2006	96,721	9.9	78,979	8.1	138,426	14.2
2007	103,626	10.7	90,444	9.3	132,993	13.7
2008	107,876	11.1	77,201	8.0	133,879	13.8
2009	109,263	11.5	78,800	8.3	135,097	14.2
2010	108,050	11.4	76,978	8.1	137,132	14.4
2011	109,147	11.5	86,785	9.2	135,090	14.3
2012	115,893	12.2	76,245	8.1	126,531	13.4

Life expectancy (official estimates, years at birth): 72.2 (males 66.6; females 77.6) in 2012.

EMPLOYMENT
(monthly averages, '000 persons)

	2010	2011	2012
Agriculture, hunting and forestry	492.2	480.2	458.5
Fishing	2.3	2.4	2.4
Mining and quarrying	16.3	16.8	16.5
Manufacturing	1,045.5	1,052.9	1,036.5
Electricity, gas and water supply	121.1	118.5	117.2
Construction	407.2	400.8	353.2
Wholesale and retail trade; repair of motor vehicles, motorcycles and personal and household goods	638.4	628.8	637.2
Hotels and restaurants	92.4	93.3	93.9
Transport and communications	350.3	344.1	341.3
Financial intermediation	71.6	73.2	73.3
Real estate, renting and business activities	300.2	315.0	320.1
Public administration	168.5	165.9	163.2

—*continued*	2010	2011	2012
Health and social services	314.6	315.8	321.1
Education, culture and science	458.3	460.6	456.7
Other community, social and personal service activities	186.3	185.5	183.8
Sub-total	4,665.2	4,653.8	4,574.9
Activities not classified*	0.7	0.7	2.2
Total employed	4,665.9	4,654.5	4,577.1
Unemployed	39.2	31.5	28.5
Total labour force	4,705.1	4,686.0	4,605.6
Males	2,252.3	2,294.0	2,239.3
Females	2,452.8	2,392.0	2,366.3

* Figures obtained as residuals.

Health and Welfare

KEY INDICATORS

Total fertility rate (children per woman, 2011)	1.5
Under-5 mortality rate (per 1,000 live births, 2011)	6
HIV/AIDS (% of persons aged 15–49, 2012)	0.4
Physicians (per 1,000 head, 2011)	3.8
Hospital beds (per 1,000 head, 2009)	11.1
Health expenditure (2010): US $ per head (PPP)	762
Health expenditure (2010): % of GDP	5.6
Health expenditure (2010): public (% of total)	77.7
Access to sanitation (% of persons, 2011)	93
Total carbon dioxide emissions ('000 metric tons, 2010)	62,221.7
Carbon dioxide emissions per head (metric tons, 2010)	6.6
Human Development Index (2012): ranking	50
Human Development Index (2012): value	0.793

For sources and definitions, see explanatory note on p. vi.

Agriculture

PRINCIPAL CROPS
('000 metric tons)

	2010	2011	2012
Wheat	1,739.1	2,132.4	2,554.2
Barley	1,965.8	1,978.8	1,917.6
Maize	550.6	1,213.1	954.1
Rye	734.6	800.5	1,082.5
Oats	442.0	448.1	422.2
Buckwheat	18.4	44.5	39.3
Triticale (wheat-rye hybrid)	1,253.9	1,312.4	1,819.1
Potatoes	7,831.1	7,147.9	6,910.9
Sugar beet	3,773.4	4,486.7	4,773.8
Beans, dry	147.9	157.8	227.3
Peas, dry	36.0	47.5	61.6
Walnuts, with shell*	13.5	16.0	16.5
Sunflower seed†	22.0	23.0	40.0
Rapeseed	374.5	379.2	704.5
Linseed	10.4	13.1	8.7
Cabbages and other brassicas	580.9	518.7	380.5
Tomatoes	310.2	118.6	138.3
Cucumbers and gherkins	325.1	250.3	189.4
Onions, dry	183.2	169.3	181.3
Carrots and turnips	358.1	306.6	272.4
Apples	525.6	190.8	511.5
Pears	73.3	61.4	17.5
Plums and sloes	77.7	82.0	8.3
Sour (Morello) cherries	51.1	14.6	10.7
Flax fibre and tow	45.8	46.0	51.6

* FAO estimates.
† Unofficial figures.

Aggregate production ('000 metric tons, may include official, semi-official or estimated data): Total cereals 6,725.5 in 2010, 7,980.6 in 2011, 8,829.1 in 2012; Total roots and tubers 7,831.1 in 2010, 7,147.9 in 2011, 6,910.9 in 2012; Total pulses 262.3 in 2010, 292.3 in 2011, 398.3 in 2012; Total vegetables (incl. melons) 2,341.8 in 2010, 1,822.6 in 2011, 1,587.7 in 2012; Total fruits (excl. melons) 810.2 in 2010, 425.3 in 2011, 611.8 in 2012.

Source: FAO.

LIVESTOCK
('000 head at 1 January)

	2010	2011	2012
Horses	126	113	100
Cattle	4,151	4,151	4,247
Pigs	3,782	3,887	3,989
Sheep	53	52	53
Goats	75	72	73
Chickens*	32,000	35,200	37,300

* Unofficial figures.

Source: FAO.

LIVESTOCK PRODUCTS
('000 metric tons)

	2010	2011	2012
Cattle meat	308.1	297.8	297.9
Sheep meat	1.4	1.3	1.3
Pig meat	398.4	419.3	435.2
Chicken meat*	259.0	297.2	318.0
Cows' milk	6,594.5	6,485.2	6,753.6
Hen eggs*	198.1	204.3	215.0

* Unofficial figures.

Source: FAO.

Forestry

ROUNDWOOD REMOVALS
('000 cubic metres, excl. bark)

	2008*	2009	2010
Sawlogs, veneer logs and logs for sleepers	3,703	3,223	3,486
Pulpwood	1,861	1,353	2,067
Other industrial wood	1,847	2,142	2,521
Fuel wood	1,345	2,094†	2,292†
Total	8,756	8,812	10,364

* FAO estimates.
† Unofficial figure.

2011–12: Annual production assumed to be unchanged from 2010 (FAO estimates).

Source: FAO.

SAWNWOOD PRODUCTION
('000 cubic metres, incl. railway sleepers, FAO estimates)

	2008	2009	2010
Coniferous (softwood)	1,945	2,102	2,300
Broadleaved (hardwood)	514	277	271
Total	2,458	2,379	2,571

2011–12: Annual production assumed to be unchanged from 2010 (FAO estimates).

Source: FAO.

Fishing

(metric tons, live weight)

	2009	2010	2011
Capture	826	897	1,122
Freshwater bream	224	212	258
Common carp	41	42	40
Northern pike	52	59	68
Aquaculture	15,659	16,265	16,293
Common carp	13,609	12,834	12,625
Crucian carp	445	641	765
Total catch	16,485	17,162	17,415

Source: FAO.

Mining

('000 metric tons unless otherwise indicated)

	2009	2010	2011
Crude petroleum	1,720	1,700	1,682
Natural gas (million cu metres)	205	213	222
Peat: for fuel	2,216	2,352	2,914

Source: US Geological Survey.

Industry

SELECTED PRODUCTS
('000 metric tons unless otherwise indicated)

	2010	2011	2012
Refined sugar	816	986	863
Sausages	317	290	299
Wine ('000 hectolitres)	146	155	166
Beer ('000 hectolitres)	3,990	4,720	4,320
Soft drinks ('000 hectolitres)	3,900	4,610	4,710
Cigarettes (million)	25,100	29,600	33,200
Overcoats, semi-coats, raincoats, warm jackets and similar articles, excluding knitted ('000)	2,637	2,345	2,357
Footwear (excluding rubber, '000 pairs)	13,100	17,100	16,500
Plywood ('000 cu metres)	178	160	164
Paper and paperboard	342	357	381
Nitrogenous fertilizers (a)*	761	798	814
Phosphate fertilizers (b)*	192	185	213
Potash fertilizers (c)*	5,223	5,306	4,831
Rubber tyres: for agricultural and other off-road vehicles ('000)	511	679	733
Rubber tyres: for road motor vehicles ('000)	3,181	3,191	3,466
Quicklime	804	794	747
Cement	4,531	4,604	4,906
Refrigerators and freezers ('000)	1,106	1,197	1,263
Bicycles ('000)	134	176	185
Watches ('000)	916	958	1,224
Electric energy (million kWh)	34,900	32,200	30,800

* Production in terms of (a) nitrogen (N); (b) phosphorous pentoxide (P_2O_5); or (c) potassium oxide (K_2O).

2013 (figures are rounded): Footwear ('000 pairs) 14,495; Cement ('000 metric tons) 5,057; Tractors 63,000 units; Refrigerators and freezers 1,200,700 units; Television receivers 245,100 units; Electric energy (million kWh) 31,200.

2009 ('000 metric tons unless otherwise indicated): Wheat flour 675; Ethyl alcohol ('000 hectolitres) 863; Spirits, liqueurs and other spirituous beverages ('000 hectolitres) 1,706; Mineral water ('000 hectolitres) 1,748; Bed linen, articles ('000) 7,152; Shirts, men's and boys' ('000) 2,199; Blankets ('000) 382; Carpets, tufted ('000 sq metres) 5,488 (Source: UN Industrial Commodity Statistics Database).

Finance

CURRENCY AND EXCHANGE RATES

Monetary Units
100 kopeks = 1 Belarusian rouble (rubel).

Sterling, Dollar and Euro Equivalents (31 December 2013)
£1 sterling = 15,661.07 roubles;
US $1 = 9,510.00 roubles;
€1 = 13,115.24 roubles;
10,000 Belarusian roubles = £0.64 = $1.05 = €0.76.

Average Exchange Rate (Belarusian roubles per US $)
2011 4,974.63
2012 8,336.90
2013 8,880.05

GOVERNMENT FINANCE

(general government transactions, '000 million roubles)

Revenue	2010	2011*	2012†
Personal income tax	5,400	9,300	16,400
Profit tax	5,600	8,700	13,700
Value-added tax	16,200	26,500	45,100
Excise taxes	4,400	5,600	10,100
Property tax	1,900	2,500	4,600
Customs duties	5,800	15,100	27,800
Other income	6,700	12,700	20,400
Revenue of budgetary funds	2,900	5,100	6,600
Total	48,800	85,600	144,600

Expenditure (incl. changes in expenditure arrears)	2010	2011*	2012†
Wages and salaries	11,500	18,600	33,100
Social protection fund contributions	3,100	5,000	8,900
Goods and services	10,000	15,400	27,700
Interest	1,100	3,300	10,500
Subsidies and transfers	13,700	21,300	36,900
Capital expenditures	13,600	15,200	28,000
Net lending	–100	400	400
Total (incl. others)	53,000	79,100	145,600

Note: Figures are rounded to nearest 100,000 million roubles.
* Preliminary figures.
† Projections.

2013 (rounded figures, projections): *Revenue:* Personal income tax 22,700, Profit tax 18,900, Value-added tax 62,400, Excise taxes 14,000, Property tax 6,400, Customs duties 39,100, Other income 28,100, Revenue of budgetary funds 8,500, Total 199,900. *Expenditure (incl. changes in expenditure arrears)* Wages and salaries 46,500, Social protection fund contributions 12,600, Goods and services 37,700, Interest 12,600, Subsidies and transfers 50,400, Capital expenditures 41,800, Total 201,500.

Note: Figures exclude the accounts of the Social Security Fund: *Revenue:* 19,700 in 2010; 29,600 in 2011 (preliminary); 49,600 in 2012 (projection); 68,500 in 2013 (projection). *Expenditure:* 18,400 in 2010; 27,500 in 2011 (preliminary); 48,700 in 2012 (projection); 69,800 in 2013 (projection). Also excluded are expenditures on bank restructuring: 2,100 in 2010; 14,500 in 2011 (preliminary); 7,400 in 2012 (projected); 10,300 in 2013 (projected) and outlays related to guaranteed debt: 2,100 in 2010; 2,200 in 2011 (preliminary); 4,000 in 2012 (projected); 5,600 in 2013 (projected).

Source: IMF, *Article IV Consultation and Second Post-Program Monitoring Discussions—Staff Report; Informational Annex*; and *Public Information Notice on the Executive Board Discussion* (May 2012).

INTERNATIONAL RESERVES

(US $ million at 31 December)

	2010	2011	2012
IMF special drawing rights	567.73	572.40	567.55
Reserve position in IMF	0.03	0.03	0.03
Foreign exchange	2,863.27	5,438.80	5,241.41
Total	3,431.03	6,011.24	5,808.99

Source: IMF, *International Financial Statistics*.

MONEY SUPPLY

(million roubles at 31 December)

	2010	2011	2012
Currency outside depository corporations	4,493.9	6,711.8	11,307.3
Transferable deposits	14,220.9	28,453.9	38,754.2
Other deposits	28,822.1	70,145.4	104,125.4
Securities other than shares	2,723.2	5,884.3	6,574.5
Broad money	50,260.1	111,195.3	160,761.4

Source: IMF, *International Financial Statistics*.

COST OF LIVING

(Consumer Price Index; base: 2000 = 100)

	2006	2007	2008
Food (incl. beverages)	380.1	417.4	491.1
Fuel and light	1,810.1	1,999.3	2,825.4
Clothing (incl. footwear)	223.0	227.5	233.6
Rent	4,097.7	4,313.3	4,917.1
All items (incl. others)	411.2	445.9	512.0

2009: Food (incl. beverages) 559.8; All items (incl. others) 578.3.

2010: Food (incl. beverages) 595.7; All items (incl. others) 622.9.

Source: ILO.

NATIONAL ACCOUNTS

('000 million roubles at current prices)

Expenditure on the Gross Domestic Product

	2010	2011	2012
Final consumption expenditure	117,215.0	183,034.1	325,636.8
Households	88,470.2	139,955.1	246,475.1
Non-profit institutions serving households	1,106.7	1,691.7	2,355.6
Government	27,638.1	41,387.3	76,806.1
Gross capital formation	67,816.7	111,791.3	181,779.8
Gross fixed capital formation	64,698.4	113,230.1	173,242.0
Changes in inventories	3,118.3	–1,438.8	8,537.8
Total domestic expenditure	185,031.7	294,825.4	507,416.6
Exports of goods and services	89,270.9	241,080.9	430,540.1
Less Imports of goods and services	111,657.7	244,287.1	406,645.8
Statistical discrepancy	1,831.2	5,538.5	–3,925.8
GDP in market prices	164,476.1	297,157.7	527,385.1

Gross Domestic Product by Economic Activity

	2010	2011	2012
Agriculture, forestry and fishing	15,178.4	24,626.8	44,811.0
Mining and quarrying	561.9	3,372.3	5,790.1
Manufacturing	39,513.1	83,338.7	147,073.1
Electricity, gas and water supply	4,820.0	5,081.1	14,555.7
Construction	15,714.5	19,682.4	36,631.9
Transport and communications	12,577.1	21,693.9	37,607.3
Trade; repair of motor vehicles and household and personal goods	19 956.2	45,526.0	75,484.1
Hotels and restaurants	1,345.5	2,191.4	3,762.8
Financial activities	7,163.2	14,233.1	19,951.5
Real estate, renting, and business services	10,430.7	18,106.2	28,544.0
Public administration	6,330.9	8,897.6	14,918.7
Health and social work	4,762.1	7,218.5	14,989.6
Education	7,040.2	11,265.2	20,263.7
Community, social and personal services	3,337.5	5,087.7	8,460.4
Sub-total	148,731.3	270,320.9	472,843.9
Less Financial intermediation services indirectly measured (FISIM)	5,124.1	9,359.2	12,808.8
GDP at factor cost	143,607.2	260,961.7	460,035.1
Taxes, less subsidies, on products	20,868.9	36,196.0	67,350.0
GDP in market prices	164,476.1	297,157.7	527,385.1

BALANCE OF PAYMENTS
(US $ million)

	2010	2011	2012
Exports of goods	24,506.1	40,927.6	45,574.3
Imports of goods	–33,794.8	–44,394.4	–45,008.9
Balance on goods	–9,288.7	–3,466.8	565.4
Exports of services	4,795.6	5,609.5	6,286.4
Imports of services	–3,007.0	–3,351.6	–3,843.4
Balance on goods and services	–7,500.1	–1,208.9	3,008.4
Primary income received	503.3	705.0	916.7
Primary income paid	–1,599.9	–2,066.4	–2,389.9
Balance on goods, services and primary income	–8,596.7	–2,570.3	1,535.2
Secondary income received	885.0	1,870.9	1,974.0
Secondary income paid	–568.4	–4,353.1	–5,197.0
Current balance	–8,280.1	–5,052.5	–1,687.8
Capital account (net)	—	4.1	3.7
Direct investment assets	–50.6	–125.5	–155.5
Direct investment liabilities	1,393.4	4,002.4	1,463.6
Portfolio investment assets	–59.4	–10.8	27.9
Portfolio investment liabilities	1,245.0	864.9	–218.9
Financial derivatives and employee stock options (net)	—	–594.6	51.2
Other investment assets	–1,178.2	–2,672.9	452.4
Other investment liabilities	4,750.9	4,101.1	–552.6
Net errors and omissions	701.6	1,034.3	722.6
Reserves and related items	–1,477.4	1,550.5	106.6

Source: IMF, *International Financial Statistics*.

External Trade

PRINCIPAL COMMODITIES
(distribution by SITC, US $ million)

Imports c.i.f.	2010	2011	2012
Food and live animals	2,249.2	2,546.8	2,916.5
Crude materials (inedible) except fuels	1,272.0	1,660.9	1,616.9
Mineral fuels, lubricants, etc.	12,058.1	18,723.3	17,869.9
Petroleum, petroleum products and related materials	7,695.5	12,871.0	13,710.3
Gas, natural and manufactured	4,188.0	5,434.4	3,564.4
Chemicals and related products	3,601.3	4,079.2	4,371.6
Basic manufactures	5,281.3	6,106.1	6,450.3
Textile yarn, fabrics, etc.	527.2	645.0	640.2
Iron and steel	2,111.6	2,467.3	2,376.1
Machinery and transport equipment	8,010.0	10,074.1	10,086.1
Machinery specialized for particular industries	1,236.6	1,278.1	1,338.5
General industrial machinery and equipment	1,601.5	1,823.3	1,900.4
Electric machinery, apparatus and appliances, etc.	1,215.8	1,219.1	1,503.3
Road vehicles	1,989.9	3,460.7	2,108.4
Miscellaneous manufactured articles	1,550.7	1,733.0	1,959.9
Total (incl. others)	34,884.4	45,759.1	46,404.4

Exports f.o.b.	2010	2011	2012
Food and live animals	3,131.5	3,751.6	4,382.5
Crude materials (inedible) except fuels	633.4	778.0	724.3
Mineral fuels, lubricants, etc.	7,016.0	14,516.7	16,390.9
Petroleum, petroleum products, etc.	6,765.7	14,215.1	16,010.4
Gas, natural and manufactured	208.9	261.7	329.1
Chemicals and related products	3,731.8	7,106.6	8,283.1
Fertilizers, manufactured	2,445.5	3,782.2	3,007.0
Basic manufactures	3,789.3	4,865.4	5,109.5
Textile yarn, fabrics, etc.	615.0	745.3	729.0
Iron and steel	1,106.1	1,437.8	1,429.3
Other metal manufactures	681.6	857.1	882.3
Machinery and transport equipment	4,561.8	7,859.3	7,897.6
Machinery specialized for particular industries	1,123.5	1,627.5	1,680.1
Electrical machinery, apparatus and appliances, etc.	940.0	1,090.0	1,162.9
Road vehicles	1,662.1	4,022.8	3,675.7
Miscellaneous manufactured articles	1,723.5	2,001.3	2,308.6
Clothing and accessories (excl. footwear)	485.1	548.9	618.6
Total (incl. others)	25,283.5	41,418.7	46,059.9

PRINCIPAL TRADING PARTNERS
(US $ million)

Imports c.i.f.	2010	2011	2012
Azerbaijan	6.0	825.8	12.2
China, People's Republic	1,684.1	2,193.9	2,373.5
Czech Republic	317.1	354.1	440.9
France	384.6	430.1	436.0
Germany	2,385.3	2,558.2	2,732.1
Italy	772.4	968.4	956.3
Netherlands	316.3	400.5	448.4
Poland	1,079.8	1,289.2	1,349.2
Russia	18,080.6	24,930.2	27,550.9
Switzerland	184.4	271.8	378.6
Ukraine	1,879.3	2,035.0	2,309.5
United Kingdom	313.4	356.1	358.2
USA	421.8	556.7	634.1
Total (incl. others)	34,884.4	45,759.1	46,404.4

Exports f.o.b.	2010	2011	2012
Brazil	705.5	1,224.1	801.7
China, People's Republic	475.8	636.6	432.6
Estonia	126.3	578.1	485.9
Germany	460.8	1,826.4	1,737.1
India	330.8	333.0	266.4
Italy	195.4	552.3	676.7
Kazakhstan	464.8	674.0	806.9
Latvia	929.5	3,151.3	3,269.7
Lithuania	450.5	857.2	1,181.2
Netherlands	2,845.6	6,128.5	7,551.3
Poland	885.5	1,124.8	949.7
Russia	9,953.6	14,508.6	16,308.9
Ukraine	2,560.1	4,159.8	5,557.2
United Kingdom	935.2	404.0	556.6
Venezuela	302.4	198.8	254.4
Total (incl. others)	25,283.5	41,418.7	46,059.9

Transport

RAILWAYS
(traffic)

	2011	2012	2013*
Passengers carried ('000)	89,000	100,500	99,300
Passenger-km (million)	7,941	8,977	n.a.
Freight carried ('000 tons)	152,775	153,673	140,039
Freight ton-km (million)	49,414	48,451	n.a.

* Preliminary.

ROAD TRAFFIC
(motor vehicles in use at 31 December)

	2010	2011	2012
Passenger cars	2,601,415	2,750,548	2,748,575
Buses	44,657	43,078	44,883
Freight vehicles	277,204	275,328	279,841

CIVIL AVIATION
(traffic on scheduled services)

	2010	2011	2012
Passengers carried ('000)	1,000	1,000	1,300
Passenger-km (million)	1,571	1,643	2,035
Total ton-km (million)	44	27	34

Tourism

FOREIGN TOURIST ARRIVALS

Country of nationality	2009	2010	2011
Estonia	690	595	464
Germany	2,568	2,245	2,191
Israel	956	925	339
Italy	2,531	2,275	1,816
Latvia	1,550	1,409	1,550
Lithuania	2,979	4,357	3,170
Poland	3,729	4,006	2,983
Russia	56,547	80,881	83,843
Turkey	4,680	4,707	3,596
United Kingdom	4,962	6,220	2,412
USA	864	683	527
Total (incl. others)	94,719	119,370	115,653

Total foreign tourist arrivals ('000): 119 in 2012 (provisional).

Tourism receipts (US $ million, excl. passenger transport): 440 in 2010; 487 in 2011; 664 in 2012 (provisional).

Source: World Tourism Organization.

Communications Media

	2010	2011	2012
Telephones ('000 main lines in use)	4,138.6	4,208.0	4,407.0
Mobile cellular telephones ('000 subscribers)	10,332.9	10,694.9	10,676.5
Internet subscribers ('000)	2,044.1	2,312.6	n.a.
Broadband subscribers ('000)	1,665.9	2,097.3	2,503.9
Book production (incl. pamphlets):			
titles	11,040	11,084	11,344
copies ('000)	43,100	34,300	33,100
Newspapers (daily and non-daily):			
number	713	693	662
average circulation ('000)	8,100	7,300	6,500
Other periodicals:			
number	885	918	897
annual circulation ('000)	59,100	60,500	65,400

Source: International Telecommunication Union.

Education

(2012/13 unless otherwise indicated)

	Institutions	Teachers	Students
Pre-primary	4,064	54,100	398,000
Primary (Grades 1–4) } Secondary (Grades 5–11) }	3,579	128,100	928,200
Vocational and technical	226	14,772*	79,900
Specialized secondary	225	12,748*	152,200
Higher	54	21,684*	428,400
Institutions offering post-graduate studies*	377	9,000	570,000

* 2001/02.

Source: partly Ministry of Education, Minsk.

Pupil-teacher ratio (primary education, UNESCO estimate): 14.9 in 2011/12 (Source: UNESCO Institute for Statistics).

Adult literacy rate (UNESCO estimates): 99.6% (males 99.8%; females 99.5%) in 2009 (Source: UNESCO Institute for Statistics).

Directory

The Government

HEAD OF STATE

President: ALYAKSANDR R. LUKASHENKA (elected 10 July 1994; inaugurated 20 July; re-elected 9 September 2001; re-elected 19 March 2006; re-elected 19 December 2010).

COUNCIL OF MINISTERS
(April 2014)

Prime Minister: MIKHAIL U. MYASNIKOVICH.

First Deputy Prime Minister: ULADZIMIR I. SEMASHKA.

Deputy Prime Minister: ANATOL M. KALININ.

Deputy Prime Minister: PIOTR P. PRAKAPOVICH.

Deputy Prime Minister: MIKHAIL I. RUSY.

Deputy Prime Minister: ANATOLIY A. TOZIK.

Minister of Agriculture and Food: LEANID K. ZAYETS.

Minister of Architecture and Construction: ANATOL B. CHORNY.

Minister of Communications and Information Technologies: SYARHEY P. POPKOV.

Minister of Culture: BARYS U. SVYATLOU.

Minister of Defence: YURIY V. ZHADOBIN.

Minister of the Economy: MIKALAY H. SNAPKOU.

Minister of Education: SYARHEY A. MASKEVICH.

Minister of Emergency Situations: ULADZIMIR A. VASHCHANKA.

Minister of Energy: ULADZIMIR M. PATUPCHYK.

Minister of Finance: ANDREY M. KHARKAVETS.

Minister of Foreign Affairs: ULADZIMIR U. MAKEI.

Minister of Forestry: MIKHAIL M. AMELYANOVICH.

Minister of Health: VASIL I. ZHARKO.

Minister of Housing and Municipal Services: ANDREY V. SHORATS.

Minister of Industry: DZMITRY S. KATSYARYNICH.

Minister of Information: ALEH V. PRALYASKOUSKI.

Minister of Internal Affairs: Col IHAR A. SHUNEVICH.

Minister of Justice: ALEH L. SLIZHEUSKI.

Minister of Labour and Social Protection: MARYANA A. SHCHOTKINA.

Minister of Natural Resources and Environmental Protection: ULADZIMIR H. TSALKO.

Minister of Sports and Tourism: ALYAKSANDR I. SHAMKO.

Minister of Taxes and Duties: ULADZIMIR M. PALUYAN.

Minister of Trade: VALYANTSIN S. CHAKANAU.

Minister of Transport and Communications: ANATOL A. SIVAK.

MINISTRIES

Office of the President: 220016 Minsk, vul. K. Marksa 38, Dom Urada; tel. (17) 222-35-03; fax (17) 222-30-20; e-mail press@president.gov.by; internet president.gov.by.

Office of the Council of Ministers: 220010 Minsk, vul. Savetskaya 11; tel. (17) 222-41-73; fax (17) 222-66-65; e-mail contact@government.by; internet government.by.

Ministry of Agriculture and Food: 220030 Minsk, vul. Kirava 15; tel. (17) 327-37-51; fax (17) 327-42-96; e-mail kanc@mshp.minsk.by; internet mshp.minsk.by.

Ministry of Architecture and Construction: 220048 Minsk, vul. Myasnikova 39; tel. (17) 327-19-34; fax (17) 220-74-24; e-mail mas@mas.by; internet mas.by.

Ministry of Communications and Information Technologies: 220050 Minsk, pr. Nezalezhnastsi 10; tel. (17) 287-87-06; fax (17) 327-21-57; e-mail mpt@mpt.gov.by; internet mpt.gov.by.

Ministry of Culture: 220004 Minsk, pr. Pobeditelei 11; tel. (17) 203-75-74; fax (17) 223-90-45; e-mail ministerstvo@kultura.by; internet kultura.by.

Ministry of Defence: 220034 Minsk, vul. Kamunistychnaya 1; tel. and fax (17) 297-15-81; e-mail modmail@mod.mil.by; internet mod.mil.by.

Ministry of the Economy: 220050 Minsk, vul. Bersona 14; tel. (17) 222-60-48; fax (17) 200-37-77; e-mail minec@economy.gov.by; internet www.economy.gov.by.

Ministry of Education: 220010 Minsk, vul. Savetskaya 9; tel. (17) 222-64-58; fax (17) 200-84-83; e-mail root@minedu.unibel.by; internet edu.gov.by.

Ministry of Emergency Situations: 220050 Minsk, vul. Revolutsionnaya 5; tel. (17) 203-94-28; fax (17) 203-77-81; e-mail mail@mchs.gov.by; internet www.mchs.gov.by.

Ministry of Energy: 220030 Minsk, vul. K. Marksa 14; tel. (17) 218-21-02; fax (17) 218-24-68; e-mail info@min.energo.net.by; internet minenergo.gov.by.

Ministry of Finance: 220010 Minsk, vul. Savetskaya 7; tel. (17) 309-41-59; fax (17) 222-45-93; e-mail minfin@minfin.gov.by; internet minfin.gov.by.

Ministry of Foreign Affairs: 220030 Minsk, vul. Lenina 19; tel. (17) 327-29-22; fax (17) 327-45-21; internet mfa.gov.by.

Ministry of Forestry: 220048 Minsk, vul. Myasnikova 39; tel. (17) 200-46-01; fax (17) 200-44-97; e-mail mail@ministry.mlh.by; internet www.mlh.by.

Ministry of Health: 220048 Minsk, vul. Myasnikova 39; tel. (17) 222-65-47; fax (17) 222-47-09; e-mail mzrb@belcmt.by; internet minzdrav.gov.by.

Ministry of Housing and Municipal Services: 220030 Minsk, vul. Bersona 16; tel. (17) 220-15-45; fax (17) 220-87-08; e-mail info@mjkx.gov.by; internet mjkx.gov.by.

Ministry of Industry: 220033 Minsk, pr. Partizansky 2; tel. (17) 224-95-95; fax (17) 224-87-84; e-mail minprom4@minprom.gov.by; internet minprom.gov.by.

Ministry of Information: 220004 Minsk, pr. Pobeditelei 11; tel. (17) 203-77-65; fax (17) 203-34-35; e-mail info@mininform.gov.by; internet mininform.gov.by.

Ministry of Internal Affairs: 220030 Minsk, vul. Gorodskoy Val 4; tel. (17) 218-79-89; fax (17) 218-70-35; e-mail miapress@mia.by; internet mvd.gov.by.

Ministry of Justice: 220004 Minsk, vul. Kalektarnaya 10; tel. (17) 200-86-87; fax (17) 200-97-55; e-mail kanc@minjust.by; internet minjust.by.

Ministry of Labour and Social Protection: 220004 Minsk, pr. Pobeditelei 23, kor. 2; tel. (17) 306-38-84; fax (17) 306-37-90; e-mail mlsp@mintrud.gov.by; internet mintrud.gov.by.

Ministry of Natural Resources and Environmental Protection: 220004 Minsk, vul. Kalektarnaya 10; tel. (17) 200-66-91; fax (17) 200-52-63; e-mail minproos@mail.belpak.by; internet www.minpriroda.gov.by.

Ministry of Sports and Tourism: 220000 Minsk, vul. Kirava 8, kor. 2; tel. (17) 227-72-37; fax (17) 226-10-33; e-mail info@mst.gov.by; internet mst.by.

Ministry of Taxes and Duties: 220010 Minsk, vul. Savetskaya 9; tel. (17) 229-79-29; fax (17) 226-51-22; e-mail gnk@mail.belpak.by; internet www.nalog.gov.by.

Ministry of Trade: 220030 Minsk, vul. Kirava 8, kor. 1; tel. and fax (17) 227-24-80; e-mail mail@mintorg.gov.by; internet mintorg.gov.by.

Ministry of Transport and Communications: 220029 Minsk, vul. Chicherina 21; tel. (17) 259-79-10; fax (17) 239-42-26; e-mail mail@mintrans.mtk.by; internet www.mintrans.gov.by.

President

Presidential Election, 19 December 2010

Candidates	Votes	%
Alyaksandr Lukashenka	5,130,557	79.65
Andrey Sannikau	156,419	2.43
Others	674,588	10.47
Against all candidates	416,925	6.47
Total*	6,441,031	100.00

* Including 62,542 invalid votes (0.97% of the total).

Legislature

NATIONAL ASSEMBLY
(Natsionalnoye Sobraniye)

Council of the Republic
(Soviet Respubliki)

220016 Minsk, vul. Chervonoarmeiskaya 9; tel. (17) 227-46-74; fax (17) 227-23-18; e-mail cr@sovrep.gov.by; internet www.sovrep.gov.by.

Chairman: ANATOL M. RUBINAU.

The Council of the Republic is the upper chamber of the legislature and comprises 64 deputies. Of the total, 56 deputies are elected by regional councils (eight each from the six oblasts and the city of Minsk) and eight deputies are appointed by the President of the Republic. The most recent elections took place on 6–25 September 2012.

House of Representatives
(Palata Predstaviteley)

220010 Minsk, vul. Savetskaya 11; tel. (17) 222-32-62; fax (17) 327-37-84; e-mail admin@house.gov.by; internet house.gov.by.

Chairman: ULADZIMIR P. ANDREYCHENKO.

General Election, 23 September 2012*

Parties or groups	Seats
Independents	104
Communist Party of Belarus	3
Belarusian Agrarian Party	1
Republican Party of Labour and Justice	1
Vacant	1
Total	110

* An election was to be re-run in one constituency at a future date.

Election Commission

Central Commission of the Republic of Belarus for Elections and Referendums: 220010 Minsk, vul. Savetskaya 11, Dom Pravitelstva; tel. and fax (17) 227-19-03; e-mail centrizb@pmrb.gov.by; internet www.rec.gov.by; f. 1989; Chair. LYDIA M. YERMOSHINA.

Political Organizations

At January 2012 there were 15 officially registered political parties operating in Belarus, of which the most important are listed below.

Belarusian Agrarian Party (BAP) (Belaruskaya Agrarnaya Partya): 220073 Minsk, vul. Zakharava 31; tel. (17) 220-38-29; fax (17) 249-50-18; f. 1992; Leader MIKHAIL V. SHYMANSKI.

Belarusian Party of Greens (Belaruskaya Partya Zyaleny): 220029 Minsk, pr. Masherova, 9/109; tel. 334-0827; e-mail info@belgreens.org; internet belgreens.org; f. 1994; Leader ALEH NOVIKAU.

Belarusian Party of the Left 'Fair World' (Belaruskaya partya levyh 'Spravyadlivy mir'): 220012 Minsk, POB 373, per. Kalinina 12/312; tel. and fax (17) 292-25-73; e-mail ck_smir@tut.by; f. 1991; Chair. SYARHEY KALYAKIN.

Belarusian Social-Democratic Party (Hramada) (Belaruskaya Satsyal-demakratychnaya Partya 'Hramada'—BSDP): 224030 Brest, vul. 17 Verasnya 22–23; tel. and fax (33) 621-78-16; e-mail bsdpps@tut.by; internet www.bsdp.org; f. 1991; the Belarusian Social Democratic Party (National Hramada), f. 1991, and the Belarusian Social-Democratic Hramada (f. 1998) merged in April 2005, although a dissenting faction of the Belarusian Social-Democratic Hramada remained; Chair. IRYNA VESHTARD.

Communist Party of Belarus (CPB) (Kamunistychnaya Partya Belarusi): 220029 Minsk, vul. Chicherina 412; tel. (17) 293-48-88; fax (17) 222-43-79; e-mail karpenko@house.gov.by; internet www.comparty.by; f. 1996 as revival of Soviet-era party; First Sec. IHOR V. KARPENKO.

Conservative Christian Party of the 'Revival' Belarusian Popular Front (Kanservatyuna-Khrystsiyanskaya Partiya Belaruski Narodny Front 'Adradzhennye'): 220005 Minsk, pr. Masherova 8; tel. (17) 285-34-70; internet www.narodnaja-partyja.org; f. 1999; political and legal successor of the political movement, Belarusian Popular Front (f. 1988); Chair. ZYANON S. PAZNYAK; 3,500 mems.

For Freedom Movement (Rukh 'Za Svabodu'): 220005 Minsk, POB 248; tel. and fax (17) 280-88-63; e-mail info@pyx.by; internet www.pyx.by; f. 2006; officially registered Dec. 2008; Chair. ALYAKSANDR U. MILINKEVICH.

Liberal Democratic Party of Belarus (Liberalna-Demakratychnaya Partya Belarusi): 223000 Minsk, vul. Surganova 61; tel. and fax (17) 290-21-38; e-mail ldpb@rambler.ru; internet www.ldpb.net; f. 1994; advocates continued independence of Belarus, increased co-operation with other European countries and eventual membership of the European Union, and expansion of the private sector; Leader SYARHEY V. HAYDUKEVICH; approx. 40,000 mems (2010).

Republican Party of Labour and Justice (Respublikanskaya Partya Pratsy i Spravyadlivasti): 220004 Minsk, pr. Pobeditelei 23/3; tel. (17) 203-43-98; fax (17) 203-63-13; e-mail info@rpts.by; internet www.rpts.by; f. 1993; Chair. VASIL V. ZADNYAPRANY.

Revival—Belarusian Popular Front (Belaruski Narodny Front 'Adradzhennye'): 220012 Minsk, vul. Charnyshevskaga 3/39; tel. and fax (17) 284-50-12; e-mail chairman@narodny.org; internet narodny.org; f. 1988; fmrly the Belarusian Popular Front, name changed as above Dec. 1999; anti-communist movement campaigning for democracy, genuine independence for Belarus, and national and cultural revival; Chair. AYLAKSEY YANUKEVICH.

United Civic Party (Abyadnanaya Hramadzyanskaya Partya): 220123 Minsk, vul. Khoruzhey 22/1701; tel. and fax (17) 289-50-09; e-mail info@ucpb.org; internet www.ucpb.org; f. 1995; liberal-conservative; Chair. ANATOL U. LYABEDZKA.

Diplomatic Representation

EMBASSIES IN BELARUS

Armenia: 220050 Minsk, vul. Kirava 17; tel. (17) 297-92-57; fax (17) 297-93-09; e-mail armbelarusembassy@mfa.am; Ambassador ARMEN KHACHATRYAN.

Azerbaijan: 220113 Minsk, vul. Vostochnaya 133/167; tel. (17) 293-33-99; fax (17) 293-34-99; e-mail minsk@mission.mfa.gov.az; internet www.azembassy.by; Ambassador ISFANDIYAR VAHABZADĂ.

Brazil: 220030 Minsk, vul. Engelsa 34A; tel. (17) 283-19-89; fax (17) 210-47-90; Ambassador RENATO LUIZ RODRIGUES MARQUES.

Bulgaria: 220034 Minsk, pl. Svoboda 11; tel. (17) 328-65-58; fax (17) 328-65-59; e-mail embassy.minsk@mfa.bg; internet www.mfa.bg/embassies/belarus; Ambassador ANGEL GANEV.

China, People's Republic: 220071 Minsk, vul. Brestyanskaya 22; tel. (17) 285-36-82; fax (17) 285-36-81; e-mail chinaemb_by@mfa.gov.cn; internet by.china-embassy.org; Ambassador CUI QIMING.

Cuba: 220005 Minsk, vul. Chervanazornaya 13; tel. (17) 200-03-83; fax (17) 200-23-45; e-mail embacuba@bn.by; internet www.cubadiplomatica.cu/belarus; Ambassador GERARDO SUÁREZ ÁLVAREZ.

Czech Republic: 220030 Minsk, Muzychny zav. 1/2; tel. (17) 226-52-44; fax (17) 211-01-37; e-mail minsk@embassy.mzv.cz; internet www.mzv.cz/minsk; Ambassador MILAN EKERT.

Estonia: 220034 Minsk, Platonova 1B; tel. (17) 217-70-61; fax (17) 217-70-69; e-mail embassy.minsk@mfa.ee; internet www.estemb.by; Ambassador JAAK LENSMENT.

France: 220030 Minsk, pl. Svabody 11; tel. (17) 229-18-00; fax (17) 229-18-30; e-mail webmestreby@diplomatie.fr; internet www.ambafrance-by.org; Ambassador DOMINIQUE GAZUY.

Georgia: 220030 Minsk, pl. Svabody 4; tel. (17) 227-61-93; fax (17) 227-62-19; e-mail minsk.emb@mfa.gov.ge; internet www.belarus.mfa.gov.ge; Ambassador DAVID KOTHARI.

Germany: 220034 Minsk, vul. Zakharava 26; tel. (17) 217-59-00; fax (17) 294-85-52; e-mail info@minsk.diplo.de; internet www.minsk.diplo.de; Ambassador WOLFRAM JOSEF MAAS.

Holy See: 220050 Minsk, vul. Valadarskaga 6; tel. (17) 289-15-84; fax (17) 289-15-17; e-mail nuntius@catholic.by; internet nunciature.catholic.by; Apostolic Nuncio CLAUDIO GUGEROTTI (Titular Archbishop of Rebellum).

Hungary: 222034 Minsk, vul. Platonova 1 B; tel. (17) 233-91-68; fax (17) 233-91-69; e-mail mission.msk@kum.hu; internet www.mfa.gov.hu/emb/minsk; Ambassador VILMOS SZIKLAVÉRI.

India: 220040 Minsk, vul. Sobinova 63; tel. (17) 262-93-99; fax (17) 288-47-99; e-mail amb@indemb.bn.by; internet www.indembminsk.in; Ambassador MANOJ KUMAR BHARTI.

Iran: 220012 Minsk, vul. Kalinina 7B; tel. (17) 385-60-00; fax (17) 237-79-53; e-mail info@iranembassy.by; Ambassador MOHAMMAD REZA SABOURI.

Israel: 220033 Minsk, pr. Partizansky 6A; tel. (17) 330-25-00; fax (17) 330-25-55; e-mail ambass-sec@minsk.mfa.gov.il; Ambassador YOSEF SHAGAL.

Italy: 220004 Minsk, vul. Rakovskaya 16B; tel. (17) 220-29-69; fax (17) 306-20-37; e-mail ambasciata.minsk@esteri.it; internet www.ambminsk.esteri.it; Ambassador STEFANO BIANCHI.

Japan: 220004 Minsk, pr. Pobeditelei 23/1, 8th Floor; tel. (17) 223-62-33; fax (17) 210-21-69; e-mail nippon_emb@telecom.by; Chargé d'affaires a.i. SHIGEHIRO MIRORI.

Kazakhstan: 220029 Minsk, vul. Kuibysheva 12; tel. (17) 288-10-26; fax (17) 334-96-50; e-mail kazemb@nsys.by; internet www.kazembassy.by; Ambassador YERGALI B. BULEGENOV.

Korea, Republic: 220035 Minsk, pr. Pobeditelei 59, 5th Floor; tel. (17) 306-01-47; fax (17) 306-01-60; e-mail belemb@mofat.go.kr; internet blr.mofat.go.kr; Ambassador YANG JOONG-MO.

Kyrgyzstan: 220002 Minsk, vul. Starovilenskaya 57; tel. (17) 334-91-17; fax (17) 334-16-02; e-mail manas@nsys.by; internet www.kgembassy.by; Chargé d'affaires a.i. TALANT SULTANOV.

Latvia: 220013 Minsk, vul. Doroshevicha 6A; tel. (17) 211-30-33; fax (17) 28-26-71; e-mail embassy.belarus@mfa.gov.lv; internet www.am.gov.lv/belarus; Ambassador MIHAILS POPKOVS.

Libya: 220000 Minsk, vul. Belaruskaya 4; tel. (17) 328-39-92; fax (17) 328-39-97; Chargé d'affaires a.i. DELFO ALMABROUK.

Lithuania: 220088 Minsk, vul. Zakharava 68; tel. (17) 217-64-91; fax (17) 285-33-37; e-mail amb.by@urm.lt; internet by.mfa.lt; Ambassador EVALDAS IGNATAVIČIUS.

Moldova: 220030 Minsk, vul. Belaruskaya 2; tel. (17) 289-14-41; fax (17) 289-11-47; e-mail minsk@mfa.md; internet www.belarus.mfa.md; Ambassador GHEORGHE HIOARĂ.

Poland: 220034 Minsk, vul. Rumyantsava 6; tel. (17) 288-21-14; fax (17) 233-97-50; e-mail ambasada@minsk.polemb.net; internet www.minsk.polemb.net; Ambassador LESZEK SZEREPKA.

Romania: 220012 Minsk, Kaliningradskii per. 12; tel. (17) 292-73-99; fax (17) 292-73-83; e-mail romania@mail.belpak.by; Chargé d'affaires a.i. CONSTANTIN EREMIA.

Russia: 220053 Minsk, vul. Novovilenskaya 1A; tel. (17) 334-54-97; fax (17) 233-35-97; e-mail rusemb-minsk@yandex.ru; internet www.belarus.mid.ru; Ambassador ALEKSANDR A. SURIKOV.

Serbia: 220034 Minsk, vul. Rumyantseva 4; tel. (17) 284-29-84; fax (17) 233-92-26; e-mail embassy.minsk@mfa.rs; internet www.minsk.mfa.gov.rs; Ambassador VLASTIMIR ĐURIČANIN.

Slovakia: 220034 Minsk, vul. Volodarskogo 6; tel. (17) 285-29-99; fax (17) 283-68-48; e-mail emb.minsk@mzv.sk; internet www.mzv.sk/minsk; Chargé d'affaires a.i. MIROSLAV MOJŽITA.

Sweden: 222030 Minsk, vul. Revalyutsyynaya 15; tel. (17) 226-55-40; fax (17) 226-55-43; e-mail ambassaden.minsk@gov.se; internet www.swedenabroad.com/minsk; Ambassador MARTIN ÅBERG.

Syria: 220049 Minsk, vul. Suvorova 2; tel. (17) 280-37-08; fax (17) 280-72-00; e-mail syrembmin@yahoo.com; Chargé d'affaires a.i. ADNAN AL-HAMWI.

Tajikistan: 223033 Minsk, vul. Zelenaya 42; tel. and fax (17) 549-01-83; e-mail tajemb-belarus@mail.ru; internet www.tajembassy.by; Ambassador KOZIDAVLAT KOIMDODOV.

Turkey: 220050 Minsk, vul. Valadarskaya 6; tel. (17) 227-13-83; fax (17) 227-27-46; e-mail trembassy@mail.bn.by; internet minsk.emb.mfa.gov.tr; Ambassador CEVAT NEZIHI ÖZKAYA.

Turkmenistan: 220050 Minsk, vul. Kirava 17; tel. and fax (17) 335-24-51; Ambassador MURAT YAZBERDIYEV.

Ukraine: 220002 Minsk, vul. Staravilenskaya 51; tel. (17) 283-19-89; fax (17) 283-19-80; e-mail emb_by@mfa.gov.ua; internet belarus.mfa.gov.ua; Ambassador MIKHAYLO B. YEZHEL.

United Arab Emirates: 220018 Minsk, vul. Privabnaya 6/8; tel. (17) 313-26-01; fax (17) 313-26-04; e-mail mail@uaeembassy.by; internet uaeembassy.by; Ambassador MOHAMED AL-GAHFLI.

United Kingdom: 220030 Minsk, vul. K. Marksa 37; tel. (17) 229-82-00; fax (17) 220-23-06; e-mail ukin.belarus@fconet.fco.gov.uk; internet www.gov.uk/government/world/belarus; Ambassador BRUCE BUCKNELL.

USA: 220002 Minsk, vul. Starovilenskaya 46; tel. (17) 210-12-83; fax (17) 234-78-53; e-mail webmaster@usembassy.minsk.by; internet minsk.usembassy.gov; Chargé d'affaires a.i. ETHAN A. GOLDRICH.

Venezuela: 220029 Minsk, vul. Kuibysheva 14; tel. (17) 284-50-99; fax (17) 284-93-47; e-mail info@embavenez.by; internet www.embavenez.by; Ambassador AMÉRICO DÍAZ NUÑEZ.

Viet Nam: 222040 Minsk, vul. Mozhaiskogo 3; tel. and fax (17) 293-15-38; e-mail dsqvn.belarus@mofa.gov.vn; internet www.vietnamembassy-belarus.org; Ambassador DON VAN MAI.

Judicial System

Supreme Court: 220030 Minsk, vul. Lenina 28; tel. (17) 226-12-06; fax (17) 327-62-38; e-mail scjustrb@pmrb.gov.by; internet www.court.by; f. 1923; Chair. VALENTIN O. SUKALO.

Supreme Economic Court: 220050 Minsk, vul. Valadarskaya 8; tel. and fax (17) 220-23-27; e-mail bxc@court.by; Chair. VIKTAR S. KAMYANKOV.

Office of the Prosecutor-General: 220030 Minsk, vul. Internatsionalnaya 22; tel. and fax (17) 226-43-57; e-mail info@prokuratura.gov.by; internet www.prokuratura.gov.by; Prosecutor-General ALYAKSANDR U. KONYUK.

Constitutional Court: 220016 Minsk, vul. K. Marksa 32; tel. (17) 327-32-73; e-mail interdept@kc.gov.by; internet www.kc.gov.by; f. 1994; 12 mem. judges; Chair. PYOTR MIKLASHEVICH.

Religion

CHRISTIANITY

The major grouping is the Eastern Orthodox Church, but there are also an estimated 1.4m. adherents of the Roman Catholic Church. Of these, some 25% are ethnic Poles, while there are a significant number of Catholics of the Eastern (Byzantine) Rites.

The Eastern Orthodox Church

In 1990 Belarus was designated an exarchate of the Russian Orthodox Church (Moscow Patriarchate), known as the Belarusian Orthodox Church.

Belarusian Orthodox Church (Moscow Patriarchate): 220004 Minsk, vul. Osvobozhdeniya 10; tel. (17) 203-46-01; e-mail press-service@church.by; internet www.church.by; 1,277 parishes (2006); Metropolitan of Minsk and Slutsk, Patriarchal Exarch of All Belarus PAVEL (PONOMARYOV).

The Roman Catholic Church

Belarus comprises one archdiocese and three dioceses. In 1989 an apostolic administration to Belarus was established, and in April 1991 an archbishop was appointed to the recently formed Archdiocese of Minsk-Mogilev (Mahiloŭ). At 31 December 2007 the Catholic Church had an estimated 1,402,605 adherents in Belarus (about 18.8% of the population).

Archdiocese of Minsk and Mogilev: 220030 Minsk, ul. Revolutsionna 1A; tel. (17) 203-68-44; fax (17) 226-90-92; e-mail info@catholic.by; internet catholic.by; Archbishop Mgr TADEUSZ KONDRUSIEWICZ.

Protestant Church

Union of Evangelical Christian Baptists in the Republic of Belarus: 220107 Minsk, POB 25; tel. and fax (17) 295-67-84; e-mail office@baptist.by; internet www.baptist.by; f. 1989; Pres. VIKTAR KRUTSKO.

The Press

PRINCIPAL DAILIES

In Russian, except where otherwise stated. The Russian-based newspapers *Argumenty i Fakty* and *Komosomolskaya Pravda* (in a special edition, *Komsomolskaya Pravda v Belorusii*) also maintain a high rate of circulation in the country.

BDG Delovaya Gazeta (BDG Business Newspaper): 220039 Minsk, vul. Chekalova 12; tel. (17) 216 25 83; fax (17) 216-25-85; e-mail bdgsite2012@gmail.com; internet www.bdg.by; f. 1994; 2 a week; business affairs; suspended for three months in May 2003; subsequently printed in Smolensk, Russia; independent; present name adopted 2005; Editor-in-Chief PETR P. MARTSEV.

Belaruskaya Niva (Belarusian Cornfield): 220013 Minsk, vul. B. Hmyalnitskaga 10A; tel. (17) 287-16-20; fax (17) 232-39-62; e-mail info@belniva.by; internet belniva.by; f. 1921; 5 a week; organ of the Council of Ministers; in Belarusian and Russian; Editor E. SEMASHKO; circ. 34,021 (Aug. 2004).

Narodnaya Hazeta (The People's Newspaper): 220013 Minsk, vul. B. Hmyalnitskaga 10A; tel. and fax (17) 287-18-70; e-mail veche@ng.by; internet www.ng.by; f. 1990; 5 a week; official publication; in Belarusian and Russian; Editor-in-Chief VLADIMIR V. ANDREYVICH.

Narodnaya Volya (People's Will): 220030 Minsk, vul. Engelsa 34A; tel. and fax (17) 328-68-71; e-mail nv@promedia.by; internet www.nv-online.info; f. 1995; daily; independent; 5 a week; in Belarusian and Russian; Editor-in-Chief IOSIF R. SYAREDZICH; circ. 27,000.

Respublika (Republic): 220013 Minsk, vul. B. Hmyalnitskaga 10A; tel. (17) 287-16-15; fax (17) 287-16-12; e-mail info@respublika.info; internet www.respublika.info; 5 a week; publ. of Council of Ministers; in Belarusian and Russian; Editor ANATOLII I. LEMIASHENOK; circ. 101,000 (2005).

Sovetskaya Belorussiya (Soviet Belarus): 220013 Minsk, vul. B. Hmyalnitskaga 10A; tel. and fax (17) 292-51-01; e-mail admin@sb.by; internet www.sb.by; 5 a week; Editor-in-Chief PAVEL I. YAKUBOVICH; circ. 400,000 (2004).

Znamya Yunosti (Banner of Youth): 220013 Minsk, vul. B. Hmyalnitskaga 10A; tel. and fax (17) 292-02-63; e-mail zn@zn.by; internet www.zn.by; f. 1938; 5 a week; organ of the Ministry of Education; Editor-in-Chief EUGENE K. MELESHKO; circ. 32,000 (2007).

Zvyazda (Star): 220013 Minsk, vul. B. Hmyalnitskaga 10A; tel. and fax (17) 287-19-19; e-mail info@zvyazda.minsk.by; internet www.zviazda.by; f. 1917; 5 a week; publ. by the National Assembly and the Council of Ministers; in Belarusian; Editor-in-Chief ALEKSANDR M. KARLYUKEVICH; circ. 30,000 (2012).

PRINCIPAL PERIODICALS

In Belarusian, except where otherwise stated.

7 Dnei (7 Days): 222030 Minsk, vul. Engelsa 30; tel. (17) 227-86-22; internet 7days.belta.by; f. 1990; weekly; in Russian; domestic and international affairs, culture, general; Chief Editor VIKTOR V. CHIKIN; circ. 40,000 (2011).

Agropanorama: 220013 Minsk, vul. B. Hmyalnitskaga 10A; 6 a year; in Belarusian and Russian; agriculture and agricultural technology.

Alesya (Rabotnitsa i Sialianka) (Alesya—Working Woman and Peasant Woman): 220013 Minsk, pr. Nezalezhnastsi 77; tel. and fax (17) 292-43-03; e-mail magalesya@mail.ru; f. 1924; monthly; Editor TAMARA BUNTO; circ. 6,500.

Belaruska Dumka (Belarusian Thought): 222030 Minsk, vul. Engelsa 30; tel. (17) 227-55-33; fax (17) 289-19-55; e-mail beldumka@belta.by; internet www.beldumka.belta.by; f. 1991; monthly; publ. of the Presidential Administration; socio-political and popular science; Chief Editor VADZIM HIHIN.

Detekivnaya Gazeta (Detective Magazine): 220014 Minsk, vul. M. Lynkova 15B/2; tel. (17) 250-36-05; monthly; crime stories; Chief Editor VLADIMIR KHACHIRASHVILI.

Holas Radzimy (Voice of the Motherland): 220005 Minsk, pr. Nezalezhnastsi 44; tel. and fax (17) 288-12-80; e-mail mail@golas.by; internet www.golas.by; f. 1955; weekly; articles of interest to Belarusians in other countries; Editor-in-Chief VIKTAR KHARKOŬ.

Kultura (Culture): 220013 Minsk, pr. Nezalezhnastsi 77; tel. (17) 290-22-50; fax (17) 334-57-41; e-mail kultura@tut.by; internet www.kimpress.by; f. 1991; weekly; colour illustrated; incorporates *Mastatstva* (Arts); Editor-in-Chief LUDMILA KRUSHINSKAYA; circ. 9,000 (2012).

Litaratura i Mastatstva (Literature and Arts): 220034 Minsk, vul. Zakharava 19; tel. (17) 284-79-85; fax (17) 284-66-73; e-mail main_lim@mail.ru; internet www.main.lim.by; f. 1932; weekly; Editor ALES KARLYUKEVICH; circ. 3,428 (2007).

Maladosts (Youth): 220005 Minsk, pr. Nezalezhnastsi 39; tel. (17) 284-85-24; e-mail maladost@bk.ru; f. 1953; monthly; publ. by the state media holding, Litaratura i Mastatstva; novels, short stories, essays, translations, etc., for young people; Editor-in-Chief RAISA A. BARAVIKOVA.

Narodnaya Asveta (People's Education): 220023 Minsk, vul. Makayenka 12; tel. (17) 267-64-69; fax (17) 267-62-68; e-mail info@n-asveta.com; internet www.n-asveta.na.by; f. 1924; publ. by the Ministry of Education; Editor-in-Chief ALLA V. MASLAVA.

Nasha Niva (Our Field): 220050 Minsk, POB 537; tel. and fax (17) 284-73-29; e-mail nn@nn.by; internet www.nn.by; f. 1991 as revival of publication originally founded in 1906; independent; weekly; Editor-in-Chief ANDREY SKURKO; circ. 10,500 (2009).

Tsarkovnae Slova (Words of the Church): 222004 Minsk, vul. Rakovskaya 4; tel. (017) 203-33-44; e-mail tsar.sl@open.by; internet www.sppsobor.by; f. 1992; publ. of the Belarusian Orthodox Church (Moscow Patriarchate); in Russian and Belarusian; Chief Editor ANDREI KHARITONOV; circ. 9,000 (2010).

PRESS ASSOCIATIONS

Belarusian Association of Journalists (Belaruskaya Asatsyyatsyya Zhurnalistau): 220030 Minsk, vul. Kamsamolskaya 7/32; tel. (17) 203-63-66; fax (17) 226-70-98; e-mail baj@baj.by; internet www.baj.by; f. 1995; Chair. ZHANNA LITVINA.

Belarusian Union of Journalists: 220034 Minsk, vul. Rumyantsava 3; tel. and fax (17) 294-51-95; internet www.buj.by; 3,000 mems; Chair. ANATOLY LEMESHENOK.

NEWS AGENCIES

BelaPAN: 222012 Minsk, vul. Akademecheskaya 17/3; tel. (17) 292-55-01; fax (17) 292-56-57; e-mail redactor@belapan.com; internet www.belapan.com; f. 1991; in Belarusian, English and Russian; independent, commercial information company; Dir ALES LIPAY.

Belta—Belarusian Telegraph Agency: 220030 Minsk, vul. Kirava 26; tel. (17) 227-19-92; fax (17) 227-13-46; e-mail oper@belta.by; internet www.belta.by; f. 1918; Gen. Dir DMITRIY A. ZHUK.

Interfaks Zapad (Interfax-West): 222013 Minsk, vul. Brovki 3/2; tel. (17) 284-05-71; fax (17) 284-05-76; e-mail info@interfax.by; internet www.interfax.by; f. 1994; affiliated with Interfaks (Russia); regional bureau in Mogilev; online political and business news; publs *Belarus Business Daily*, *Belarus News Wire*; Dir-Gen. VYACHESLAV ZENKOVICH.

Publishers

Aversev: 220090 Minsk, vul. Oleshva 1; tel. (17) 268-09-79; e-mail info@aversev.by; internet www.aversev.by; f. 1994; teaching and methodical literature.

Belaruskaya Navuka (Belarusian Science): 220141 Minsk, Staroborisovsky trakt 40; tel. and fax (17) 263-76-18; e-mail belnauka@infonet.by; internet www.belnauka.by; f. 1924; scientific, technical, reference books, educational literature and fiction in Belarusian and Russian; Dir ALYAKSANDR STASHKEVICH.

Belarusky Dom Druku (Belarusian Printing House): 220013 Minsk, pr. Nezalezhnastsi 79; tel. (17) 292-81-28; fax (17) 331-91-15; e-mail lan@domdruku.by; internet www.domdruku.by; f. 1917; social, political, children's and fiction in Belarusian, Russian and other European languages, newspapers and magazines; Gen. Dir ROMAN OLEINIK.

Belblankavyd: 220038 Minsk, vul. Botanicheska 6A; tel. (17) 375-29-49; fax (17) 294-91-16; reference books in Belarusian and Russian; Dir VALENTINA MILOVANOVA.

Litaratura i Mastatstva (Literary Fiction and Fine Arts): 220034 Minsk, vul. Zakharava 19; tel. (17) 288-12-94; fax (17) 284-84-61; e-mail main_lim@main.ru; internet www.lim.by; f. 2002; fiction in Belarusian and Russian; Dir ALES M. KARLYUKEVICH.

Mastatskaya Litaratura (Fine Arts Literature): 220004 Minsk, pr. Pobeditelei 11; tel. (17) 203-83-63; fax (17) 203-58-09; e-mail director@mastlit.by; internet www.mastlit.by; f. 1972; state-owned; Dir VLADISLAV A. MACHULSKY.

Narodnaya Asveta (People's Education): 220004 Minsk, pr. Pobeditelei 11; tel. (17) 203-61-84; fax (17) 203-89-25; e-mail director@narasveta.by; internet www.narasveta.by; f. 1951; scientific, educational, reference literature and fiction in Belarusian, Russian and other European languages; Dir LARISA MINKO.

Petrus Brovka Belarusian Encyclopedia Publishing House (Belaruskaya Entsiklopediya): 220072 Minsk, vul. Akademicheska 15A; tel. and fax (17) 284-17-67; e-mail belen@mail.belpak.by; f. 1967; encyclopedias, dictionaries, directories and scientific books; Editor-in-Chief T. V. BELOVA.

Vysheyshaya Shkola (Higher School): 220048 Minsk, pr. Pobeditelei 11; tel. (17) 223-54-15; fax (17) 203-70-08; e-mail info@vshph.by; internet www.vshph.com; f. 1954; textbooks and science books for higher educational institutions; in Belarusian, Russian and other European languages; absorbed the Universitetskaye publishing house in 2002; Dir ANATOL A. ZHADAN; Editor-in-Chief TETYANA K. MAIBORODA.

Broadcasting and Communications

TELECOMMUNICATIONS

Belarus is behind its neighbours in upgrading telecommunications infrastructure. The state-owned company, Beltelecom, dominates the provision of fixed-line telephones, while the mobile communications market consists of four major service providers. In 2011 there were 4.2m. fixed telephone lines and 10.7m. subscriptions to mobile telephone services in Belarus.

BelCel: 22005 Minsk, vul. Zolotaya Gorka 5; tel. (17) 282-02-82; fax (17) 476-11-11; e-mail belcel@belcel.by; internet www.belcel.by; f. 1993; jtly owned by SIV BV (Netherlands) and Beltelecom; mobile telecommunications services; Gen. Dir VIKTOR NOVIKOV.

Beltelecom: 220030 Minsk, vul. Engelsa 6; tel. (17) 217-10-05; fax (17) 227-44-22; e-mail info@main.beltelecom.by; internet www.beltelecom.by; f. 1995; national telecommunications operator; Dir-Gen. SYARHEY POPKOV.

Life:): 220030 Minsk, vul. Chervonoarmeiskaya 24; tel. (17) 295-99-99; fax (17) 328-58-86; e-mail info@life.com.by; internet www.life.com.by; f. 2008; fmrly BeST; mem. of Turkcell Group (Turkey); provides mobile cellular telecommunications services; Dir-Gen. ISMET YAZICI.

MTS Belarus: 222043 Minsk, pr. Nezalezhnastsi 95; tel. (17) 237-98-98; e-mail info@mts.by; internet company.mts.by; f. 2002; mobile cellular communications; 49% owned by Mobile TeleSystems (Russia); Dir-Gen. VLADIMIR S. KARPOVICH.

Velcom: 220030 Minsk, vul. Internatsionalnaya 36; tel. (17) 222-49-01; fax (17) 206-62-52; e-mail pr@velcom.by; internet www.velcom.by; f. 1999; mobile cellular telecommunications; 4.7m. subscribers (2012); Gen. Dir HELMUT DUHS.

BROADCASTING

National State Television and Radio Company of Belarus (Belteleradiocompany): 220807 Minsk, vul. A. Makayenka 9; tel. (17) 389-62-83; fax (17) 267-81-82; e-mail tvr@tvr.by; internet www.tvr.by; f. 1925; parent co of Belarusian Radio (q.v.) and Belarusian Television (q.v.); Chair. HENADZ B. DAVYDZKA.

Radio

Belarusian Radio: 220807 Minsk, vul. Chyrvonaya 4; tel. (17) 284-84-24; fax (17) 290-62-42; e-mail radio1@tvr.by; internet www.tvr.by; f. 1925; stations include Culture Channel, First National Channel (news), Radio Stalitsa (Capital Radio) and Radio Belarus (foreign service in Belarusian, Russian, German and English); Dir ANTON B. VASYUKEVICH.

Television

Belarusian Television: 220807 Minsk, vul. A. Makayenka 9; tel. (17) 269-97-72; fax (17) 263-21-78; e-mail pr@tvr.by; internet www.tvr.by; f. 1956; Dir ULADZIMIR V. ISAT.

Belarus-TV: 220807 Minsk, vul. A. Makayenka 9; tel. (17) 389-61-45; e-mail belarus24@tvr.by; internet www.belarus24.by; f. 2005; international satellite channel; Dir ALENA A. LADUTSKO.

Belarus 2: 220807 Minsk, vul. A. Makayenka 9; tel. (17) 389-63-12; fax (17) 267-81-82; e-mail mail@belarus2.by; internet www.belarus2.by; f. 2003; family channel; Gen. Dir NATALIYA V. MARINOVA.

Belsat TV: 220013 Minsk, POB 383; tel. 22 547-69-07; e-mail office@belsat.eu; internet www.belsat.eu; f. 2007; also broadcasts to Warsaw, Poland; owned by Telewizja Polska (Poland); Dir AGNIESZKA ROMASZEWSKA-GUZY.

ONT—Obshchenatsionalnoye Televideniye (Nationwide TV): 220029 Minsk, ul. Kommunisticheskaya 6; tel. (17) 290-66-72; e-mail reklama@ont.by; internet www.ont.by; f. 2002; 51% state-owned; Chair. GRIGORIY L. KISEL.

TVS—Televizionnaya Veshchatelnaya Set (TBN—Television Broadcasting Network): 220072 Minsk, pr. Nezalezhnastsi 15A; tel. (17) 284-09-13; fax (17) 284-10-86; e-mail tbn@promedia.by; f. 1995; comprises 16 private television cos in Belarus's largest cities and an advertising co.

Finance

(cap. = capital; res = reserves; dep. = deposits; m. = million; brs = branches; amounts in readjusted Belarusian roubles, unless otherwise indicated)

BANKING

In 2011 there were 32 commercial banks registered in Belarus, of which 26 had at least some foreign capital.

Central Bank

National Bank of the Republic of Belarus: 220008 Minsk, pr. Nezalezhnastsi 20; tel. (17) 219-23-03; fax (17) 327-48-79; e-mail email@nbrb.by; internet www.nbrb.by; f. 1990; cap. 250,000.0m., res 198,547.4m., dep. 20,353,567.3m. (Dec. 2009); Chair. NADEZHDA A. ERMAKOVA.

Commercial Banks

Alfa-Bank: 220030 Minsk, vul. Savetskaya 12; tel. (17) 217-64-64; fax (17) 200-17-00; e-mail office@alfa-bank.by; internet www.alfa-bank.by; f. 1999; 93.8% owned by ABH Belarus Ltd (Cyprus); fmrly ITI Bank—International Trade and Investment Bank; present name adopted 2008; cap. 469,882m., res 733m., dep. 2,005,555m. (Dec. 2012); Chair. of Bd DENIS A. KALIMOV; 11 brs.

Bank Moskva-Minsk (Moscow-Minsk Bank): 220002 Minsk, vul. Kamunistychnaya 49; tel. (17) 237-97-97; fax (17) 239-17-84; e-mail mmb@mmbank.by; internet www.mmbank.by; f. 2000; wholly owned by Bank of Moscow (Russia); cap. 253,070m., res 63,586m., dep. 3,099,834m. (Dec. 2012); Gen. Dir Dr ALEKSANDR RAKOVETS; 5 brs.

Bank Torgovyi Kapital (Trade Capital Bank): 220035 Minsk, vul. Timirazeva 65A; tel. (17) 312-10-12; fax (17) 312-10-08; e-mail info@tcbank.by; internet www.tcbank.by; f. 2008; Chair. DMITRIY V. MUSHINSKIY.

Belagroprombank: 220036 Minsk, pr. Zhukov 3; tel. (17) 218-57-77; fax (17) 218-57-14; e-mail info@belapb.by; internet www.belapb.by; f. 1991; 99.8% state-owned; cap. 20,868,682m., res 10,987m., dep. 28,948,509m. (Dec. 2012); Chair. VLADIMIR I. PODKOVIROV; 284 brs.

Belarusbank: 220050 Minsk, vul. Myasnikova 32; tel. (17) 218-84-31; fax (17) 226-47-50; e-mail info@belarus-bank.by; internet www.belarus-bank.by; f. 1995 following merger with Sberbank; cap. 15,266,805m., res –60,726m., dep. 89,818,165m. (Dec. 2012); Chair. SIARHEI PISARYK; 106 brs.

Belgazprombank: 220121 Minsk, vul. Pritytsky 60/2; tel. (17) 229-16-29; fax (17) 259-45-25; e-mail bank@bgpb.by; internet www.belgazprombank.by; f. 1990; present name adopted 1997; 49% owned by Gazprombank (Russia), 49% owned by OAO Gazprom (Russia); cap. 2,310,695m., res 8,564m., dep. 6,390,185m. (Dec. 2012); Chair. of Bd VIKTAR D. BABARIKO; 6 brs.

Belinvestbank—Belarusian Bank for Development and Reconstruction: 220002 Minsk, pr. Masherova 29; tel. (17) 289-28-12; fax (17) 289-35-22; e-mail belbb@belinvestbank.by; internet www.belinvestbank.by; f. 2001 by merger; 85.8% owned by the State Committee for Property; 6.5% owned by National Bank of the Republic of Belarus (q.v.); universal bank; cap. 567,408m., res 1,772,351m., dep. 13,439,984m. (Dec. 2012); Chair. of Bd ANATOLIY A. LYSYUK; 11 brs.

Belvneshekonombank (Belarusian Bank for Foreign Economic Affairs): 220004 Minsk, pr. Pobeditelei 29; tel. (17) 209-29-44; fax (17) 226-48-09; e-mail office@bveb.minsk.by; f. 1991; 97.4% owned by Vneshekonombank (Bank for Foreign Economic Affairs—Russia); cap. 3,494,902m., res 60,169m., dep. 12,716,751m. (Dec. 2012); Chair. of Bd PETR M. FRADKOV; 19 brs.

BPS-Sberbank: 220005 Minsk, Blvd Muliavin 6; tel. (17) 289-41-48; fax (17) 210-03-42; e-mail inbox@bps-sberbank.by; internet www.bps-sberbank.by; f. 1923; fmrly Belpromstroibank; 98.4% owned by Sberbank—Russia; cap. 2,215,132m., res 242,807m., dep. 17,735,529m. (Dec. 2012); Dir-Gen. VASILII S. MATUSHEVSKII; 159 brs.

BTA Bank: 220123 Minsk, vul. V. Khoruzhey 20; tel. (17) 289-58-00; fax (17) 289-58-22; e-mail info@btabank.by; internet www.btabank.by; f. 2002 as Astanaekssimbank; present name adopted 2008; 99.7% owned by BTA Bank, Almatı (Kazakhstan); cap. 197,285m., res 16,866m., dep. 405,432m. (Dec. 2012); Chair. of Bd SULTAN T. MARENOV.

Minski Tranzitnyi Bank (Minsk Transit Bank—MTBank): 220033 Minsk, pr. Partizansky 6A; tel. (17) 213-29-14; fax (17) 213-29-09; e-mail cor@mtbank.by; internet www.mtbank.by; f. 1994; 99% owned by MTB Investments Holdings Ltd; cap. 421,212m., res –1,037m., dep. 2,820,559m. (Dec. 2012); Chair. of Bd ANDREY K. ZHISHKEVICH; 6 brs.

Paritetbank: 220002 Minsk, vul. Kiseleva 61 A; tel. (17) 335-46-41; fax (17) 228-38-37; e-mail info@paritetbank.by; internet www.paritetbank.by; f. 1992; present name adopted 2004; 99.7% owned by the National Bank of the Republic of Belarus (q.v.); cap. 761,394m., res –881m., dep. 617,084m. (Dec. 2012); Chair. of Bd VLADISLAV N. GOROZHANKIN.

Priorbank: 220002 Minsk, vul. V. Khoruzhey 31A; tel. (17) 289-90-90; fax (17) 289-91-91; e-mail info@priorbank.by; internet www.priorbank.by; f. 1989, present name since 1991; 87.7% owned by Raiffeisen International Bank-Holding AG (Austria); cap. 2,189,493m., res 10,990m., dep. 12,480,859m. (Dec. 2012); Chair. of Bd SERGEY A. KOSTYUCHENKO; 21 brs.

Trustbank: 220035 Minsk, vul. Ignatenka 11; tel. (17) 250-43-88; fax (17) 228-52-31; e-mail cbis@trustbank.by; internet www.trustbank.by; f. 1994; jt-stock co; fmrly Infobank, present name adopted Feb. 2005; cap. 336,765m., dep. 396,562m., total assets 740,501m. (Dec. 2012); Chair. VALENTINA M. SAKSON.

VTB Bank (Belarus): 220004 Minsk, vul. Tsetkin 51; tel. (17) 309-15-15; fax (17) 309-15-30; e-mail info@vtb-bank.by; internet www.vtb-bank.by; f. 1996 as Slavneftebank; name changed as above 2007; 97.3% owned by VTB Bank (Russia); cap. 393,187m., res 162,306m., dep. 5,365,836m. (Dec. 2012); Chair. of Bd ULADZIMIR V. IVANOV; 6 brs.

BANKING ASSOCIATION

Association of Belarusian Banks: 220005 Minsk, vul. Smolyachkova 9; tel. (17) 227-78-90; fax (17) 227-58-41; e-mail mail@abbanks.by; Chair. FELIX CHERNYAVSKY.

COMMODITY AND STOCK EXCHANGES

Belarusian Currency and Stock Exchange (Belorusskaya Valyutno-Fondovaya Birzha): 220013 Minsk, vul. Surganova 48 A; tel. (17) 209-41-03; fax (17) 209-41-10; e-mail bcse@bcse.by; internet www.bcse.by; f. 1998; currency and securities exchange trading organization, depository, clearing and information activities; value of trade US $8,934.5m. (2004); Gen. Dir PAVEL TSEKHANOVICH.

Belarusian Universal Commodity Exchange (BUTB): 220099 Minsk, vul. Kazintsa 2/200; tel. (17) 224-48-25; e-mail info@butb.by; internet www.butb.by; f. 2004; jt-stock co; trades in timber, metal and agricultural produce; Pres. ARKADII S. SALIKOV.

INSURANCE

B & B Insurance Co: 220013 Minsk, vul. Kolas 38; tel. (17) 285-76-22; e-mail info@bbinsurance.by; internet www.bbinsurance.by; f. 1995; life and non-life.

Beleksimgarant: 220004 Minsk, vul. Melnikaite 2; tel. (17) 209-40-28; fax (17) 209-40-67; e-mail info@eximgarant.by; internet eximgarant.by; f. 2001; state-owned; Gen. Dir GENADZ MITSKEVICH.

Belgosstrakh Belarusian Republican Unitary Insurance Co: 220036 Minsk, vul. K. Libknekht 70; tel. (17) 269-26-00; fax (17) 213-08-05; e-mail info@bgs.by; internet www.bgs.by; f. 1921; Dir-Gen. SERHEY LEONIDOVICH; 145 brs.

Belingosstrakh: 220050 Minsk, pr. Myasnikov 40; tel. (17) 203-58-78; fax (17) 217-84-19; e-mail office@belingo.by; internet belingo.by; f. 1992; non-life, property, vehicle and cargo insurance; Dir-Gen. ALYAKSANDR K. KHAMYAKOV.

Belkoopstrakh: 220004 Minsk, pr. Pobeditelei 17; tel. (17) 226-80-64; e-mail office@belcoopstrakh.by; internet www.belcoopstrakh.by; f. 1992; non-life.

Belneftestrakh: 220004 Minsk, pr. Pobeditelei 23/1; tel. (17) 336-51-21; fax (17) 226-78-88; e-mail insurance@bns.by; internet www.bns.by; f. 1996; life and non-life; Dir-Gen. YURIY I. NESMASHNY; 10 brs.

Belrosstrahe: 220034 Minsk, vul. Ulyanovsk 31; tel. (17) 222-47-48; fax (17) 210-46-33; e-mail info@brs.by; internet www.belrosstrakh.by; f. 1991; Belarusian-German jt-stock co; renamed as above after merging with Brolly in March 2009; Dir-Gen. SERHEY KOVALEV.

Kupala: 220004 Minsk, vul. Nemiga 40; tel. (17) 200-80-27; fax (17) 200-80-13; e-mail office@kupala.by; internet www.kupala.by; f. 1993; affiliate of Wiener Städtische Allgemeine Versicherung AG (Austria); Dir-Gen. VIKTOR S. NOVIK.

Promtransinvest: 220039 Minsk, vul. Voronyanskogo 7A; tel. (17) 228-12-48; fax (17) 219-77-88; e-mail insurance@promtransinvest.by; internet promtransinvest.by; f. 1993; life and non-life; Dir-Gen. VASILIY I. SENKO.

TASK: 220053 Minsk, vul. Chervyukova 46; tel. (17) 290-10-45; fax (17) 290-10-47; e-mail office@task.by; internet www.task.by; f. 1991; partly state-owned; life and non-life; Gen. Dir IHOR I. VOLKOV.

INSURANCE ASSOCIATION

Belarusian Insurance Union (BIU) (Belaruskii Strakhovoi Soyuz): 220114 Minsk, pr. Nezalezhnastsi 169/905; tel. (17) 206-30-46; fax (17) 206-30-44; e-mail info@biu.by; internet www.biu.by; f. 1992; 28 mems; Pres. VIKTAR HOMYARCHUK.

Trade and Industry

GOVERNMENT AGENCIES

Belarusian Foreign Investment Promotion Agency (BFIPA): 220004 Minsk, pr. Pobeditelei 7; tel. (17) 226-81-02; fax (17) 203-07-78; e-mail ncm@export.by; internet www.export.by; Dir BORIS SMOLKIN.

Belarusian Fund for the Financial Support of Entrepreneurs (BFFSE): 220048 Minsk, vul. Myasnikova 39; e-mail fund@belpak.minsk.by; f. 1996.

CHAMBER OF COMMERCE

Belarusian Chamber of Commerce and Industry (Belorusskaya Torgovo-promyshlennaya Palata): 220029 Minsk, vul. Kammunisticheska 11; tel. (17) 290-72-49; fax (17) 290-72-48; e-mail mbox@cci.by; internet www.cci.by; f. 1952; brs in Brest, Gomel, Grodno, Mogilev and Vitebsk; Pres. MIKHAIL M. MYATLIKOV.

EMPLOYERS' ORGANIZATION

Business Union of Entrepreneurs and Employers (Biznes Soyuz Predprinimatelei i Nanimatelei): 220033 Minsk, vul. Fabrichnaya 22; tel. (17) 298-11-49; fax (17) 298-27-92; e-mail org@bspn.by; internet www.bspn.by; f. 1990; Pres. GEORGY BADEY.

UTILITIES

Electricity

Belenergo/Belenerha (Belarusian Energy Co): 220030 Minsk, vul. K. Marksa 14; tel. (17) 218-23-59; fax (17) 218-26-39; e-mail info@min.energo.by; internet www.energo.by; f. 1995; generation, transmission and distribution of electric power; Dir-Gen. YEVGENIY O. VORONOV.

Gas

Beltopgaz: 220002 Minsk, vul. V. Khoruzhey 3; tel. (17) 288-23-93; fax (17) 284-37-86; e-mail mail@topgas.by; internet www.topgas.by; f. 1992; distributes natural gas to end-users; Dir-Gen. LEONID I. RUDINSKII.

Beltransgaz: 220040 Minsk, vul. Nekrasov 9; tel. (17) 280-01-01; fax (17) 285-63-36; e-mail mail@btg.by; internet www.btg.by; 100% owned by Gazprom (Russia); natural gas transportation and supply; underground gas storage; Dir VLADIMIR MAYAROU.

TRADE UNIONS

Automobile and Agricultural Machinery Workers' Union: 220126 Minsk, pr. Pobeditelei 21/1103; tel. and fax (17) 203-84-27; e-mail acmbel7@mail.belpak.by; internet www.acmprof.by; f. 1990; Pres. VALERY KUZMICH.

Belarusian Congress of Democratic Trade Unions (BKDP): 220095 Minsk, vul. Yakubova 80/80, etazh 15/2; tel. (17) 214-89-05; fax (17) 214-89-06; e-mail bkdp.by@gmail.com; internet www.bkdp.org; f. 1993; alliance of four independent trade unions; Pres. ALYAKSANDR YARASHUK; International Sec. OLEG PODOLINSKI; 10,000 mems (2010).

Belarusian Free Trade Union (BFTU) (Svobodnyi Profsoyuz Belorusskiy—SPB): 220095 Minsk, vul. Yakubova 80/80; tel. (17) 214-89-05; e-mail spby.org@gmail.com; internet www.spby.org; f. 1991; Pres. MIKHAIL KOVALKOV.

Belarusian Independent Trade Union (BITU) (Belorusskiy Nezavisimyy Profsoyuz): 223710 Minsk, vul. Naberezhnaya 8; tel. and fax (17) 422-65-73; e-mail bnpsoligorsk@gmail.com; internet www.belnp.org; f. 1991 as Independent Trade Union of Miners (ITUMB); renamed as above in 1993; for miners, chemists, oil-refiners, transport workers, builders and other workers; Chair. NIKOLAY ZIMIN; 7,000 mem. employees.

Federation of Trade Unions of Belarus (FPB): 220126 Minsk, pr. Pobeditelei 21; tel. (17) 203-90-31; fax (17) 210-43-37; e-mail press@fpb.by; internet www.fpb.by; f. 1990; Chair. LEANID P. KOZIK.

Transport

RAILWAYS

In 2010 the total length of railway lines in use was around 5,502 km, of which 898 km were electrified. There is an underground railway in Minsk.

Belarusian State Railways (Belorusskaya Zheleznaya Doroga): 220030 Minsk, vul. Lenina 17; tel. (17) 225-49-46; fax (17) 227-56-48; e-mail ns@rw.by; internet www.rw.by; f. 1992; Dir ULADZIMIR M. MOROZOV.

Minsk Metro: 220007 Minsk, pr. Kooperativny 12; tel. (17) 219-86-01; fax (17) 222-94-84; e-mail info@minsktrans.by; internet www.minsktrans.by; f. 1984; two lines (30.3 km) with 25 stations (2007); Gen. Dir LEONTIY T. PAPENOK.

ROADS

In 2010 the total length of roads in Belarus was 86,392 km (comprising 15,541 km of main roads and 70,851 km of secondary roads). Some 86.4% of the total network was hard-surfaced.

CIVIL AVIATION

Minsk has two airports.

State Committee for Aviation: 220029 Minsk, vul. Chicherin 21; tel. (17) 334-75-56; fax (17) 222-77-28; e-mail gka@ivcavia.com; internet www.avia.by; Chair. ULADZIMIR B. KOSTIN.

Belavia Belarusian Airlines: 220004 Minsk, vul. Nemiga 14; tel. (17) 220-25-55; fax (17) 220-23-83; e-mail info@belavia.by; internet www.belavia.by; f. 1996; state carrier; operates services in Europe and to the CIS and the Middle East; Dir-Gen. ANATOLIY GUSAROV.

Tourism

Tourism is not developed, although the Government has sought to promote Belarus as a destination for those interested in hunting a variety of animals and birds, and for those who wish to visit sites associated with the Second World War. According to the World Tourism Organization, there were 119,000 tourist arrivals in 2012; according to provisional figures, receipts from tourism (excluding passenger transport) in that year amounted to US $664m.

Belintourist: 220004 Minsk, pr. Pobeditelei 19; tel. (17) 226-91-00; fax (17) 226-93-52; e-mail info@belintourist.by; internet www.belintourist.by; f. 1992; national tour operator; Dir MARIA I. FILIPOVICH.

Defence

As assessed at November 2012, the total strength of Belarus's armed forces was 48,000, comprising ground forces of 22,500 and an air force of 15,000, as well as 10,500 in centrally controlled units and Ministry of Defence staff. Reserves totalled 289,500. There are also paramilitary forces, controlled by the Ministry of Internal Affairs, which number 110,000, including a border guard of 12,000 and a militia of 87,000. Military service is compulsory and lasts for between nine and 12 months. The formation of a new territorial defence force, in which regional governors were to play a leading role, was announced in 2011. Belarus joined the North Atlantic Treaty Organization's 'Partnership for Peace' programme of military co-operation in January 1995.

Defence Expenditure: Budgeted at 4,610,000m. readjusted roubles in 2012.

Chief of the General Staff: Maj.-Gen. OLEH A. BELOKONEV.

Commander of the Army: Maj.-Gen. ALYAKANSDR NIKITIN.

Commander of the Air Force and Air Defence: Maj.-Gen. OLEH DVIGALEV.

Education

In 2011/12 the total enrolment at pre-primary level included 97% of children in the relevant age-group. In that year enrolment at primary level included 94% of pupils in the relevant age-group. Education is compulsory for nine years, but usually lasts for 11 years, between the ages of six and 17 years. Secondary education comprises a first cycle of five years and a second of two years. In 2011/12 secondary enrolment included 96% of pupils in the relevant age-group. At early 2007 there were 43 state-owned and 12 private higher education institutions, including 29 universities. In 2012/13 there were 54 institutions of higher education and 428,400 students in higher education. General government expenditure on education was 7,358,100m. roubles (equivalent to 11.6% of total spending) in 2008.

BELGIUM

Introductory Survey

LOCATION, CLIMATE, LANGUAGE, RELIGION, FLAG, CAPITAL

The Kingdom of Belgium lies in north-western Europe, bounded to the north by the Netherlands, to the east by Luxembourg and Germany, to the south by France, and to the west by the North Sea. The climate is temperate. Temperatures in the capital, Brussels, are generally between 0°C (32°F) and 23°C (73°F). Dutch (also known as Flemish), spoken in the north (Flanders), and French, spoken in the south (Wallonia), are the two main official languages. Brussels (which is situated in Flanders) has bilingual status. Nearly 60% of the population are Dutch-speaking and about 40% are French-speaking. There is a small German-speaking community, comprising less than 1% of the population, in eastern Wallonia. The majority of the inhabitants profess Christianity, and about three-quarters of the population are Roman Catholics. The national flag (proportions 13 by 15) consists of three equal vertical stripes, of black, yellow and red.

CONTEMPORARY POLITICAL HISTORY

Historical Context

In the latter half of the 20th century Belgium's linguistic divisions were exacerbated by the political and economic polarization of Dutch-speaking Flanders in the north and francophone Wallonia in the south. The faster-growing and relatively prosperous population of Flanders traditionally supported the conservative Flemish Christelijke Volkspartij (CVP—Christian People's Party) and the nationalist Volksunie—Vlaamse Vrije Democraten (VU, People's Union—Flemish Free Democrats), while Wallonia was a stronghold of socialist political sympathies. Moderate constitutional reforms, introduced in 1971, were followed by further concessions to regional and cultural sensitivities: in 1972 the German-speaking Community gained representation in the Council of Ministers for the first time, and in 1973 linguistic parity was assured in central government. Provisional legislation, adopted in 1974, established separate Regional Councils and Ministerial Committees. The administrative status of Brussels remained contentious: the majority of the city's inhabitants are francophone, but the Flemish parties were, until the late 1980s, unwilling to grant the capital equal status with the other two regional bodies.

Domestic Political Affairs

In June 1977 the Prime Minister, Leo Tindemans (who had held office since 1974), formed a coalition composed of the CVP and the francophone Parti Social Chrétien (PSC—Christian Social Party), which were collectively known as the Christian Democrats, together with the Flemish and French-speaking Socialist parties, the Front Démocratique des Francophones (FDF—Francophone Democratic Front) and the VU. The Council of Ministers, in what became known as the Egmont Pact, proposed the abolition of the virtually defunct nine-province administration, and devolution of power from the central Government to create a federal Belgium, comprising three political and economic regions (Flanders, Wallonia and Brussels) and two linguistic communities. However, these proposals were not implemented. Tindemans resigned in October 1978 and the Minister of Defence, Paul Vanden Boeynants, was appointed Prime Minister in a transitional Government. Legislative elections in December caused little change to the distribution of seats in the Chamber of Representatives. Four successive prime ministerial nominees failed to form a new government, the main obstacle being the future status of Brussels. The six-month crisis was finally resolved when a new coalition Government was formed in April 1979 under Dr Wilfried Martens, the President of the CVP.

During 1980 the linguistic conflict worsened, sometimes involving violent incidents. Legislation was formulated, under the terms of which Flanders and Wallonia were to be administered by regional assemblies, with control of cultural matters, public health, roads, urban projects and 10% of the national budget, while Brussels was to retain its three-member executive. Belgium suffered severe economic difficulties during the late 1970s and early 1980s, and disagreement over Martens' proposals for their resolution resulted in the formation of four successive coalition Governments between April 1979 and October 1980. Proposed austerity measures provoked demonstrations and lost Martens the support of the Socialist parties. Martens also encountered widespread criticism over plans to install North Atlantic Treaty Organization (NATO, see p. 370) nuclear missiles in Belgium. In April 1981 a new Government was formed, comprising a coalition of the Christian Democrats and the Socialist parties and led by Mark Eyskens (of the CVP), hitherto Minister of Finance. However, lack of parliamentary support for his policies led to Eyskens' resignation in September. In December Martens formed a new centre-right Government, comprising the Christian Democrats and the two Liberal parties. In 1982 Parliament granted special powers for the implementation of economic austerity measures; these were effective until 1984 and similar powers were approved in March 1986. Opposition to reductions in public spending was vigorous, with public sector trade unions undertaking damaging strike action throughout the 1980s.

In July 1985 six Liberal government ministers resigned in connection with a riot at the Heysel football stadium in Brussels in May during which 39 people died. This led to the collapse of the governing coalition. A general election held in October returned the Christian Democrat-Liberal alliance to power, and in November Martens formed his sixth Council of Ministers.

The Government collapsed in October 1987, as a result of continuing division between the French- and Dutch-speaking parties of the coalition. At the ensuing general election in December, no party won a clear mandate for power, and negotiations for a new coalition lasted 146 days, as a series of mediators, appointed by King Baudouin, attempted to reach a compromise. In May 1988 Martens was sworn in at the head of his eighth administration, after agreement was finally reached by the French- and Dutch-speaking wings of both the Christian Democrats and Socialists and by the VU.

Constitutional reform

The five-party coalition agreement committed the new Government to a programme of further austerity measures, together with tax reforms and increased federalization. In August 1988 Parliament approved the first phase of the federalization plan, whereby increased autonomy would be granted to the country's language communities and regions in several areas of jurisdiction, including education and socio-economic policy. It was also agreed that Brussels would have its own regional council, with an executive responsible to it, giving the city equal status with Flanders and Wallonia. In January 1989 Parliament approved the second phase of the federalization programme, allocating the public funds necessary to give effect to the regional autonomy that had been approved in principle in August 1988. The relevant constitutional amendments formally came into effect in July 1989.

A brief constitutional crisis in 1990 provoked widespread demands for a review of the powers of the monarch, as defined by the Constitution. In March proposals for the legalization of abortion (in strictly controlled circumstances) received parliamentary approval. However, King Baudouin had previously stated that his religious convictions would render him unable to give royal assent to any such legislation. A compromise solution was reached in April, whereby Article 82 of the Constitution, which makes provision for the monarch's 'incapacity to rule', was invoked. Baudouin thus abdicated for 36 hours, during which time the new legislation was promulgated. A joint session of Parliament was then convened to declare the resumption of Baudouin's reign. The incident was widely perceived in Belgium as setting a dangerous precedent for the reinterpretation of the Constitution.

The Government was weakened by the resignation of both VU ministers in September 1991 and by the resultant loss of its two-thirds' parliamentary majority. Further linguistic conflict between the remaining coalition partners led to Martens' resignation as Prime Minister in October. The results of a general election in November reflected a significant decline in popular support for all five parties represented in the outgoing Government. In March 1992 the Christian Democrats and the Socialists (which together controlled 120 seats in the 212-member Chamber of Representatives) agreed to form a new four-party administration; Jean-Luc Dehaene of the CVP was appointed Prime Minister.

In February 1993 Parliament voted to amend the Constitution to create a federal state of Belgium, comprising the largely autonomous Flemish, Walloon and Brussels-Capital Regions. The three regions, and the country's three linguistic groups, were to be represented by the following directly elected administrations: a combined administration for the Flemish Region and Community; regional administrations for Wallonia and Brussels; and separate administrations for French- and German-speakers. The regional administrations were to assume sole responsibility for the environment, housing, transport and public works, while the language community administrations were to supervise education policy and culture. Legislation to implement the reforms was enacted in July.

The second coalition under Dehaene

A general election was held in May 1995, concurrently with elections to the regional assemblies. The Christian Democrat-Socialist coalition was re-formed shortly after the election, having secured a total of 82 seats in the Chamber of Representatives (membership of which had been reduced to 150), and in June a new Council of Ministers was appointed, under Dehaene. The Government introduced several strict economic austerity measures in late 1995; public sector trade unions organized strike action in response. In May 1996 Parliament granted the Dehaene administration special emergency powers to implement economic austerity measures by decree.

The latter half of 1996 was dominated by public concern over allegations of endemic official corruption, following the discovery, in August, of an international paedophile network based in Belgium, and subsequent widespread speculation that this had received protection from the police force and from the judicial and political establishment. During September King Albert II (who had succeeded to the throne in 1993) promised a thorough investigation of the network and, in an unprecedented gesture, demanded a review of the judicial system. In April 1997 a parliamentary committee investigating allegations of official corruption and mismanagement claimed that rivalry between the country's various police and judicial divisions often prevented their effective co-operation, but that there was little evidence that paedophile networks had received official protection. In February 1998 the Government announced that, in place of the establishment of an integrated national police force, as recommended by the committee, efforts would be made to facilitate 'voluntary co-operation contracts' between the various law enforcement services. In April Marc Dutroux, a convicted paedophile whose arrest in August 1996 on charges of child kidnapping and murder had prompted the review of judicial institutions, briefly escaped from police custody. The incident precipitated the resignations of several high-ranking figures, including the Ministers of the Interior and Justice. A proposed vote of no confidence in the Government, also ensuing from Dutroux's escape, was defeated in the Chamber of Representatives.

In June 1999 two ministers resigned following the revelation that farms throughout Belgium had been supplied with animal feed contaminated with industrial oil containing dioxin (a carcinogenic chemical). At a general election later in June, the Christian Democrats suffered heavy losses, mainly at the hands of the Liberals and the ecologist parties. The Vlaamse Liberalen en Demokraten—Partij van de Burger (VLD, Flemish Liberals and Democrats—Citizens' Party) emerged as the largest single party in the 150-member Chamber of Representatives, with 23 seats, while the extreme right-wing Vlaams Blok (Flemish Bloc) became the fifth largest party, with 15 seats.

The Verhofstadt Governments

In July 1999 a new six-party coalition Government was sworn in, led by the President of the VLD, Guy Verhofstadt, and comprising the VLD, the francophone Parti Réformateur Libéral (PRL—Reformist Liberal Party), the two Socialist parties and the two ecologist parties, Anders Gaan Leven (Agalev) and Ecolo (the Ecologistes Confédérés pour l'Organisation des Luttes Originales). The new administration was the first Belgian Government in 40 years not to include the Christian Democrats, the first to include the ecologist parties and the first to be headed by a Liberal Prime Minister since 1884.

In 2001 the CVP changed its name to the Christen-Democratisch en Vlaams (CD&V—Christian Democratic and Flemish), emphasizing its commitment to Flemish issues, while the Flemish Socialist party, which had moved towards a more centrist ideological position, adopted the name SP.A (formally, the Socialistische Partij Anders—Socialist Party Otherwise). In late 2001 the VU disbanded and split into two parties: Spirit, which adopted a social-liberal stance and later formed an alliance with the SP.A, and a Flemish nationalist grouping, the Nieuw-Vlaamse Alliantie (N-VA—New Flemish Alliance). The PSC adopted a new statute in 2002, ceased to espouse an explicitly Christian Democratic philosophy and was renamed the Centre Démocrate Humaniste (CDH).

At the general election on 18 May 2003 the outgoing centre-left coalition was returned to power. The VLD won 25 seats in the Chamber of Representatives, as did the francophone Parti Socialiste (PS). The Mouvement Réformateur (MR) coalition, which included the PRL, obtained 24 seats, while the SP.A-Spirit alliance won 23 seats and the CD&V secured 21. The ecologist parties Ecolo and Agalev (later renamed Groen!), which had together won 20 seats in the 1999 election, were reduced to four representatives, while the controversial Vlaams Blok achieved the best result in its 25-year history, gaining 18% of the Flemish vote and winning 18 seats. A new coalition Government, led by Verhofstadt and comprising the VLD, the MR, the PS, the SP.A and Spirit, took office in July. The Government pledged to reduce personal income tax, to increase expenditure on health and justice, and to create 200,000 new jobs by 2007.

In the European and regional elections concurrently held on 10 June 2004, the Vlaams Blok increased its representation in the European Parliament to three of Belgium's 24 seats and became the second largest party in the Flemish Parliament (while the VLD was only the fourth largest). In November the Court of Cassation found the Vlaams Blok guilty of promoting racial discrimination and ruled that freedom of speech should be curtailed in the interests of national security and to protect the rights of other people. The party was fined and lost access both to state funding and to television exposure, thus effectively forcing it to disband; it consequently changed its statutes and renamed itself Vlaams Belang (Flemish Interest).

In October 2005 government proposals to reform the pension and social security systems, most controversially, by raising the minimum retirement age, prompted the first general strike in 12 years. Later that month some 80,000 protesters participated in a demonstration in Brussels against the reforms. Following the Government's introduction of a number of minor amendments, employers' groups agreed to the reforms, but the trade unions remained dissatisfied and organized further industrial action.

In municipal elections held on 8 October 2006 Vlaams Belang, which had campaigned against immigration and in favour of independence for Flanders, expanded its influence beyond its traditional base in Antwerp, winning more than 20% of the vote in the 308 municipal councils in Flanders. In Antwerp Vlaams Belang won 33.5% of the vote, slightly less than the SP.A-Spirit alliance which secured 35.5%. The VLD and other members of the governing coalition performed poorly in the municipal elections, largely reflecting voter dissatisfaction with federal policies, notably attempts at economic reform.

The 2007 general election

At the general election of 10 June 2007 the CD&V made significant gains in Flanders, mainly at the expense of the VLD, which contested the election as Open Vld in alliance with two smaller Flemish liberal parties, Liberaal Appèl Plus and Vivant. The MR replaced the PS as the leading francophone party, securing 23 of the 150 seats in the Chamber of Representatives to the latter's 20, while an alliance of the CD&V and the nationalist N-VA emerged as the largest group, winning 30 seats, while the Open Vld won 18 seats. A collapse in support for the SP.A-Spirit alliance, which won just 14 seats, allowed Vlaams Belang to become the fifth largest party in the Chamber of Representatives, despite a reduction in its own representation to 17 seats. The CDH won 10 seats. In response to the poor electoral performance of the main coalition parties, Verhofstadt announced the resignation of the Council of Ministers, to come into effect following the conclusion of a new coalition agreement.

The Chairman of the CD&V, Yves Leterme, was charged with forming a new government, and initiated formal discussions regarding a coalition agreement between the Christian Democrats and the Liberals. However, divisions quickly emerged between the Flemish and French-speaking parties over proposals to devolve further powers to the regional and community administrations and to divide the electoral constituency of Brussels-Halle-Vilvoorde. (This comprised the Brussels-Capital Region together with 35 districts surrounding the capital but located in the Flemish Region, some of which contained a majority of French-speaking inhabitants. Voters in these districts were thus able to vote for francophone parties at federal and European elections, an anomaly that had been ruled unconstitutional by the Court of Arbitration in May 2003.) In August 2007 the talks were suspended by King Albert, who requested the newly appointed President of the Chamber of Representatives, Herman Van Rompuy of the CD&V, to assess the willingness of the main political parties to recommence talks. Following the completion of Van Rompuy's mission in September, the King again asked Leterme to lead attempts to form a government. On 1 December Leterme resigned as formateur (prime ministerial nominee), having failed to broker an accord. Two days later King Albert asked Verhofstadt to preside over negotiations to form an interim administration, which would have the power to adopt a budget. On 21 December an interim coalition Government, comprising the CD&V, the MR, Open Vld, the PS and the CDH, was sworn in. Verhofstadt remained as Prime Minister, while Leterme was appointed Deputy Prime Minister and Minister for the Budget and Structural Reform.

Verhofstadt resigned as Prime Minister on 20 March 2008, after the five parties of the interim coalition agreed a programme for government. Leterme was sworn in as Prime Minister, while Didier Reynders, the leader of the MR, was appointed as one of five Deputy Prime Ministers and retained the role of Minister of Finance. The agreed government programme focused principally on economic issues, including increasing pension benefits and reducing taxation. The prospects for devolution continued to be considered by a group of senior politicians, with a deadline of mid-July set for agreement on constitutional reform.

Having failed to meet this self-imposed deadline, on 14 July 2008 Leterme submitted his resignation as Prime Minister. However, this was rejected by King Albert. In an attempt to break the impasse, the King announced the appointment of a commission comprising two prominent francophone politicians, François-Xavier de Donnea and Raymond Langendries, and the Minister-President of the German Community, Karl-Heinz Lambertz, to explore possible solutions to the ongoing crisis. The commission published its report in September, defining the basis for negotiations and recommending that a partial agreement be reached prior to the next regional elections in June 2009. However, the report was criticized by some politicians from both linguistic communities for its moderation. The N-VA withdrew its parliamentary support for the federal Government, citing the lack of progress on constitutional reform, while the party's sole member of the Flemish regional Government, Geert Bourgeois, resigned from his post.

Leterme's resignation and return

In early December 2008 the Brussels Court of Appeal ordered the suspension of the proposed sale of a 75% stake in Fortis Bank, which had been nationalized in October, following a successful court case brought by the bank's former shareholders. It was subsequently alleged that government officials had sought to influence the court's decision, although Yves Leterme and his ministers denied any wrongdoing. However, the President of the Court of Cassation wrote in an open letter to the President of the Chamber of Representatives that, while no admissible evidence existed to confirm any impropriety on the part of government officials, there remained 'significant indications' of interference. On 19 December Leterme announced the resignation of the Council of Ministers, after Jo Vandeurzen of the CD&V stood down as Deputy Prime Minister and Minister of Justice and of Institutional Reform, claiming that suspicion of improper conduct impeded him from effectively carrying out his duties. Later that month the President of the Chamber of Representatives, Van Rompuy of the CD&V (who had served as Deputy Prime Minister in 1993–99), was appointed as Prime Minister at the head of a similarly constituted five-party coalition Government.

In July 2009 the Deputy Prime Minister and Minister of Foreign Affairs, Karel De Gucht of Open Vld, was appointed to the European Commission and duly resigned from his cabinet post. In the ensuing cabinet reorganization, Leterme was brought back into the Government to replace De Gucht as Minister of Foreign Affairs, while Guy Vanhengel of Open Vld was appointed Deputy Prime Minister and Minister of the Budget. Van Rompuy was nominated in November to be the first permanent President of the European Council following the entry into force of the Treaty of Lisbon in December. On 25 November the King appointed Leterme (who had reportedly been exonerated from involvement in the Fortis Bank affair) as Prime Minister for a second time. Steven Vanackere, also of the CD&V, succeeded Leterme as Minister of Foreign Affairs and Institutional Reform, while remaining one of the five Deputy Prime Ministers. The King asked former Prime Minister Jean-Luc Dehaene to mediate between the political parties in order to find a solution to the dispute over constitutional reform, including the Brussels-Halle-Vilvoorde question, before mid-April 2010. As no negotiated settlement was reached by the agreed deadline, Open Vld withdrew from the ruling coalition on 22 April. Leterme submitted the resignation of the Government, which was accepted by the King on 26 April. The Government continued in office in an interim capacity, pending the formation of a new administration following a general election.

The 2010 general election and continued political stalemate

At the general election on 13 June 2010 the Flemish separatist N-VA, led by Bart De Wever, won the largest number of seats in the Chamber of Representatives, with 27 of the 150 seats, closely followed by the French-speaking PS of Elio Di Rupo, which increased its representation to 26 seats. The other major parties all suffered a loss of support: the MR secured 18 seats in the lower chamber, while the CD&V obtained 17, the SP.A and Open Vld 13 each, Vlaams Belang 12 and the CDH nine. The strong performance of the N-VA, which advocated a gradual move towards independence for Flanders, inevitably intensified uncertainty about Belgium's future. On 17 June King Albert designated De Wever as informateur, charged with exploring the possibilities for the formation of a new coalition government. De Wever submitted his report to the King on 8 July, suggesting that the differences between the parties were still too substantial to be able to form a government, and was relieved of his mission. King Albert appointed Di Rupo as préformateur to lead negotiations between the parties with the aim of establishing the basis for a stable coalition. However, Di Rupo was unable to broker a coalition agreement. In September the King asked the Presidents of the two legislative chambers to mediate between the parties in order to revive the coalition talks. Negotiations collapsed in early October, after the N-VA withdrew, citing the unwillingness of the francophone parties to devolve greater responsibility for financial affairs to the regions and communities. On 8 October the King set De Wever a 10-day deadline to attempt to resolve the political stalemate, but on 18 October the francophone parties rejected the N-VA leader's proposals on constitutional reform, notably his suggestion that tax-raising powers should be transferred from the federal authorities to the regional administrations. The King then appointed Johan Vande Lanotte, a former leader of the SP.A, to mediate between the seven parties hitherto involved in the negotiations—the Flemish N-VA, CD&V, SP.A and Groen! (which became simply Groen in 2012), and the French-speaking PS, CDH and Ecolo.

Lanotte presented a compromise plan for government to the leaders of the seven parties in early January 2011, but it was rejected by the N-VA and the CD&V. Lanotte resigned as mediator, declaring that it had been impossible to overcome the impasse between the parties. In an indication of public frustration with the continued uncertainty, at least 34,000 people had participated in a march in Brussels demanding national unity and the formation of a permanent government. Meanwhile, amid increasing concern in the financial markets regarding Belgium's mounting government debt, the King asked Leterme's interim Government, which was operating with only limited powers, to prepare an austerity budget for 2011. The budget was finally approved in May.

Didier Reynders of the MR, the Deputy Prime Minister and Minister of Finance and of Institutional Reform, was appointed informateur by the King at the beginning of February 2011. His unsuccessful attempts to resolve the impasse similarly ended a month later. The role of royal mediator was subsequently taken by Wouter Beke of the CD&V, who expanded the negotiations to include the Liberal MR and Open Vld. However, Beke also resigned as mediator in mid-May, following the failure of these talks, and King Albert appointed Di Rupo as formateur. Relations between the linguistic communities deteriorated further later that month, when the parliament of the French Community voted in favour of renaming the Community as the Wallonia-Brussels Federation, noting the strong alliance between francophones in Wallonia and Brussels. The Minister-President of the Flemish Region and Community, Kris Peeters, denounced this move as unconstitutional, refusing to recognize the Federation as an official body. However, it appeared that the new name would be used as an additional name and not in official documents in which the constitutional name of the French Community would be required.

Legislation outlawing the wearing in public of face-covering veils came into force in July 2011, following its approval by an overwhelming majority in the Chamber of Representatives in April 2010. Two Muslim women who wore full veils launched an immediate challenge at the Constitutional Court against the law, which followed the introduction of a similar ban in France in April, on the grounds that it violated fundamental rights, including freedom of expression and religion.

Meanwhile, Di Rupo tendered his resignation as formateur on 9 July 2011, following the rejection of his draft programme for government by De Wever, who claimed that the institutional reforms proposed would provide insufficient autonomy for the regions. However, King Albert refused to accept Di Rupo's resignation, and later that month hopes of a resolution of the protracted political crisis were raised when the CD&V agreed to continue coalition negotiations without the N-VA's participation, on which it had hitherto insisted.

Di Rupo presented a revised programme for government in early September 2011. Later that month it was announced that the eight negotiating parties had reached an agreement on the division of the Brussels-Halle-Vilvoorde electoral constituency, thereby removing one of the principal obstacles to the formation of a new government. In October, moreover, the eight parties concluded an accord on wide-ranging institutional reforms, which, *inter alia*, provided for the devolution of further powers from the federal Government to the regional and community authorities, including some tax-raising powers and responsibility for public expenditure amounting to some €17,000m. (around 4% of national income), notably in the areas of health care and social welfare; and, with effect from May 2014, an increase in the term of office of the Chamber of Representatives to five years and the transformation of the Senate into a non-permanent assembly of 50 representatives of the three linguistic communities plus 10 co-opted members. Shortly afterwards Di Rupo announced that discussions would continue in the absence of the two ecologist parties (other negotiating parties having urged a reduction in the number of coalition partners), and would focus on budgetary and socio-economic issues. Meanwhile, pressure from the financial markets to form a new government with a mandate to introduce much-needed austerity measures and structural reforms was mounting, with the announcement that Dexia Bank Belgium was to be nationalized prompting heightened concerns regarding the country's rising public debt.

Recent developments: new government formed

Di Rupo again submitted his resignation as formateur on 21 November 2011, after the two Liberal parties rejected his proposed budget for 2012, but King Albert asked him to reconsider. Finally, on 26 November, a day after the credit rating agency Standard and Poor's downgraded Belgium's sovereign debt rating, a budget was agreed, followed by a comprehensive programme for government a few days later. A new coalition Government, comprising the Dutch and French-speaking Socialists, Christian Democrats and Liberals (which held a total of 96 of the 150 seats in the Chamber of Representatives), was sworn in on 6 December, 541 days after the general election, with Di Rupo becoming the first francophone Prime Minister in more than 30 years. Five of the six coalition partners had participated in the outgoing administration (the SP.A being the only new addition), and 13 of the 19 individuals appointed to positions in the new Council of Ministers had also served in Leterme's Government. The N-VA questioned the Government's legitimacy on the grounds that it did not represent a majority of Flemish members of Parliament, while trade unions expressed concern regarding the potential impact of the planned austerity measures, organizing a public sector strike in late December and a general strike in January 2012 in protest against pension reforms. Despite further protests by workers in subsequent months, additional austerity measures were announced in March, amid concerns that the budget deficit would exceed the level targeted.

The arrest of a Muslim woman in the Sint-Jans-Molenbeek municipality of Brussels in May 2012 for refusing to remove her niqab prompted violent unrest outside a police station in the capital. Several members of a radical Islamist group, Sharia4-Belgium, were arrested in early June in connection with the disturbances, while Filip Dewinter, a prominent member of Vlaams Belang, declared that the party would pay €250 to anyone who reported a woman wearing a face-covering veil to the police in an effort to ensure the enforcement of the ban that took effect in July 2011. A few days later a French Islamist was arrested after stabbing and injuring two police officers in Molenbeek. He was subsequently found guilty and sentenced to 17 years' imprisonment. Some 230 Muslim demonstrators were detained in September, following a violent protest in Antwerp against an anti-Islam film posted on the video-sharing website YouTube, which had also provoked demonstrations in several other countries. A leading member of Sharia4Belgium was arrested on suspicion of organizing the Antwerp unrest. In mid-2013 the interior minister, Joëlle Milquet, announced that additional government funds were to be made available to combat the radicalization of young Muslims in Belgium.

Meanwhile, some progress was made on the implementation of the agreement on institutional reforms concluded in late 2011. Most notably, in July 2012 Parliament approved constitutional amendments providing for the division of the Brussels-Halle-Vilvoorde electoral constituency, which had been a long-standing source of tension between the Flemish and francophone communities. Still to be completed were changes to the Senate (which were finally approved in December 2013), while discussions regarding the transfer of more powers to the regional and community authorities, as well as the revision of the law regulating the distribution of public finances between the various levels of government, were expected to prove particularly difficult.

At municipal elections in mid-October 2012 the N-VA became the strongest party in Flanders, winning the largest percentage of votes in 20 of the region's 35 provincial districts and securing the mayoralty of Antwerp (which had been held by Socialists for some 90 years hitherto) for De Wever, who immediately demanded greater autonomy for Flanders. The parties in the ruling coalition performed better in Wallonia and Brussels. Two candidates representing a newly established Muslim political organization, the Islam Party, were elected in the Anderlecht and Molenbeek municipalities of Brussels. The results of the municipal elections resulted in minor changes to the federal Government. Vincent Van Quickenborne of Open Vld resigned as Deputy Prime Minister and Minister of Pensions in October, following his election as mayor of Kortrijk, being replaced by Alexander De Croo, the President of Open Vld, while in January 2013 Jean-Pascal Labille of the PS was appointed as Minister of Public Enterprise, Science Policy and Development, in charge of Larger Towns, to succeed Paul Magnette, who had stood down to take office as mayor of Charleroi and as the newly elected President of the PS. (Thierry Giet had acted as interim President of the PS since the appointment of the previous incumbent, Di Rupo, to the premiership in December 2011.) Meanwhile, in December 2012 Gwendolyn Rutten was elected to replace De Croo as President of Open Vld.

The federal Government Deputy Prime Minister and Minister of Finance and of Sustainable Development, Steven Vanackere, resigned in March 2013 after allegations in the media, which he denied, surrounding his involvement in dealings between Belfius (formerly Dexia) Bank and an organization with which he had links. Vanackere was replaced as Deputy Prime Minister by the Minister of Defence, Pieter De Crem, and as Minister of Finance and Sustainable Development by Koen Geens.

On 23 July 2013 King Albert II announced his abdication as monarch, citing his age and failing health as reasons for his decision. However, many commentators speculated that a series of scandals undermining the royal family had contributed to his decision. Following the success of Flemish nationalist parties in the local elections, the King appeared to warn against the dangers of populist nationalist movements in his Christmas address to the nation, in which he spoke of the dangers of seeking scapegoats for current economic difficulties and appeared to draw parallels with the rise of fascism in the 1930s. De Wever, a staunch republican, accused the Prime Minister, Di Rupo, of supporting such views by allowing them to be broadcast in the King's speech. In a separate royal scandal, in January 2013 the elderly dowager Queen Fabiola, widow of King Baudouin (who had died in 1993), was accused of avoiding death duties by using a foundation to channel funds to her Spanish relatives. Her annual allowance was subsequently reduced in value by one-third as part of a wider review of the cost of the royal family, and members of the royal household were required to pay taxes for the first time. In a further incident the King became the focus of controversy when a well-known artist initiated legal action in June to obtain a sample of his DNA to prove that she was his daughter born as the result of an extra-marital affair. Despite these episodes, the royal family appeared to continue to enjoy a significant level of public support and was widely acknowledged as having the ability to unite the country across its linguistic divisions. Moreover, the King's decisive role in guiding the country's political leaders through a prolonged period of instability, in the absence of a permanent government following the 2010 general election, led to increased public respect for the monarch. Crown Prince Philippe, Albert's son, was sworn in as King on 21 July.

Foreign Affairs

Regional relations

Since the Second World War, Belgium has promoted international co-operation in Europe. It was a founder member of many important international organizations, including the North Atlantic Treaty Organization (NATO, see p. 370), the European Community (now the European Union—EU, see p. 273), the Council of Europe (see p. 252) and the Benelux Economic Union (see p. 449). In July 2008 Belgium completed the parliamentary ratification of the EU's Treaty of Lisbon, which was designed to reform the institutions of the EU to improve decision-making following the enlargement of the Union to 27 members. The treaty entered into force in December 2009, following its ratification by all 27 member states. At early 2014 Belgium had yet fully to ratify the Treaty on Stability, Co-ordination and Governance in the Economic and Monetary Union (the so-called fiscal compact), which provided for new, stricter fiscal arrangements and had been signed in March 2012 by all EU member states with the exception of the Czech Republic and the United Kingdom. The approval of the regional and community parliaments was required, in addition to that of the federal legislature.

At a summit meeting held in The Hague, Netherlands, in June 2008 the heads of government of Belgium, the Netherlands and Luxembourg signed a new Benelux Treaty on political and economic co-operation. The document expanded the scope of the previous treaty, signed in 1958, to provide for greater co-operation between the three Governments on justice and home affairs, as well as customs and cross-border trade. In recognition of this, the official title was to change from the Benelux Economic Union to the Benelux Union. The new treaty entered into force on 1 January 2012, following its ratification by the national legislatures of the three countries and by the parliaments of the German-speaking Community, the Flemish Region and Community, the Brussels-Capital Region in Belgium, the Walloon Region and the French Community.

Other external relations

From the late 1980s Belgium's hitherto cordial relations with its former colonies underwent considerable strain. Proposals made by Prime Minister Wilfried Martens in November 1988 regarding the relief of debts owed to Belgium by Zaire (formerly the Belgian Congo, renamed the Democratic Republic of the Congo—DRC—in 1997) provoked allegations in the Belgian press of corruption within the Zairean Government. President Mobutu Sese Seko of Zaire responded by ordering the withdrawal of all Zairean state-owned businesses from Belgium and by demanding that all Zairean nationals resident in Belgium remove their assets from, and leave, their host country. Following the collapse of public order in Zaire in September 1991, the Belgian Government dispatched 1,000 troops to Zaire for the protection of the estimated 11,000 Belgian nationals resident there. By the end of 1991 all the troops had been withdrawn and about 8,000 Belgian nationals had been evacuated. Prospects for the normalization of relations improved following the establishment of a transitional Government in Zaire in July 1992 and the removal of Zairean sanctions against Belgium. Relations deteriorated again, however, in January 1993, when, in response to rioting by forces loyal to President Mobutu, Belgium dispatched 520 troops to evacuate the remaining 3,000 Belgian nationals in Zaire. Following the deposition of Mobutu's regime in May 1997 by the forces of Laurent-Désiré Kabila, it was announced that normal relations between Belgium and the DRC (as Zaire was now renamed) would be gradually restored.

The election of a new Government in Belgium in June 1999 led to improved relations with the DRC. The new Belgian Minister of Foreign Affairs, Louis Michel, was determined to develop a new strategy towards the central African countries with which Belgium had historical ties. Following the assassination of Kabila in January 2001, the Belgian Government intensified its attempts to relaunch the peace initiative in the region. During a visit to Belgium by the new DRC President, Kabila's son, Joseph, the Belgian Prime Minister urged Kabila to commit to peace negotiations under the auspices of the UN. Michel also aimed to add an 'ethical' dimension to Belgian foreign policy, which included an official apology in February 2002 for the Belgian Government's role in the murder of the Belgian Congo's first Prime Minister, Patrice Lumumba, in 1961. Following a peace accord formalized in April 2003 and the installation in June of Joseph Kabila as leader of an interim DRC Government, in October the Belgian Government announced its intention to double its aid to the DRC to €82m. in 2004. In October 2004, however, the Government of the DRC recalled its ambassador from Brussels, in protest at remarks made by the Belgian Minister of Foreign Affairs, Karel De Gucht, criticizing the DRC authorities for their alleged continuing corrupt practices and lack of democracy. In May 2008 the DRC again recalled its ambassador from Brussels, in protest at similar remarks made by De Gucht. By 2010 cordial relations had been restored, and in June King Albert visited the DRC, at Kabila's invitation, to attend the celebration of the 50th anniversary of the country's independence. During an official visit to the DRC in August 2013 the Belgian Minister of Foreign Affairs, Didier Reynders, launched a number of significant projects for which Belgium had provided finance. Reynders also urged the international community to increase its efforts to improve the security of the eastern region of DRC, which continued to suffer from the violent activities of Rwandan-backed rebel groups.

In October 1990 the Martens Government dispatched 600 troops to protect some 1,600 Belgian nationals resident in Rwanda (part of the former Belgian territory of Ruanda-Urundi), when exiled opponents of the incumbent regime invaded that country. In late October a ceasefire agreement came into effect and Belgian forces were withdrawn. Nevertheless, the conflict in Rwanda continued during 1991–94. Following the signing of a peace accord in August 1993, some 420 Belgian troops were redeployed as part of a UN peacekeeping force; this was, however, unable to prevent an outbreak of extreme violence, beginning in April 1994, which resulted in the deaths of many hundreds of thousands of people. Following the execution of 10 Belgian troops in April, the Belgian Government withdrew its peacekeeping contingent. It also dispatched some 800 paratroopers to Rwanda to co-ordinate the evacuation of the estimated 1,500 Belgian expatriates remaining in the country, as well as other foreign nationals. In September 2010 a civil trial commenced in Brussels in a case filed against the Belgian state and three former Belgian army officers by survivors of a massacre of more than 2,000 refugees in Rwanda in April 1994. The defendants, who were accused of failing to act to prevent or put an end to violations of international human rights, maintained that they had been acting on the orders of the UN when they had evacuated 92 Belgian UN troops from a school in which the refugees had sought sanctuary and were subsequently killed. In an interim judgment in December 2010, however, the court ruled that the decision to withdraw the troops from the school had been taken by the Belgian authorities rather than the UN. Relations with Rwanda faltered in January 2013 when the authorities in Kigali expelled a Belgian official working as an aide to the military attaché in the Belgian embassy. Although the Rwandan Government failed to explain the expulsion, it was acknowledged that tensions between the two countries had increased following the decision by Belgium, as well as by a number of other western donor countries, to suspend military aid to Rwanda in November 2012. The decision followed a report by the UN team monitoring the arms embargo in the DRC, in which Rwanda was accused of giving military support to rebel groups fighting in the eastern region of the DRC. During an official visit to Rwanda in June 2013, the Belgian Minister of Public Enterprises and Development Co-operation, Jean-Pascal Labille, urged a strengthening of co-operation between the two countries and announced additional funding and support for healthcare, energy and governance projects in Rwanda.

Legislation introduced in 1993 endowed Belgian courts with universal jurisdiction in human rights cases. In June 2001, in the first case to be successfully conducted under the new law, four Rwandan nationals were convicted of war crimes for their role in the ethnic violence in Rwanda in 1994. In February 2002, however, the International Criminal Court ruled that Belgium did not have the right to try suspects who were protected by diplomatic immunity. Moreover, in June judges ruled that a case against the Israeli Prime Minister, Ariel Sharon, for war crimes allegedly committed against Palestinian refugees in Lebanon in 1982 (when he was Minister of Defence), could not be brought to trial since, according to the Belgian criminal code, alleged crimes committed outside the country required subjects to be on Belgian territory in order to be investigated and tried. Another human rights case, against President Laurent Gbagbo of Côte d'Ivoire, was similarly dismissed. In February 2003 the Court of Cassation reversed the earlier ruling regarding Sharon, but recognized his diplomatic immunity so that proceedings against him were inadmissible while he remained the Israeli premier.

The 1993 law also jeopardized relations with the USA, particularly in the wake of the US-led invasion of Iraq in March 2003 (which was opposed by the Belgian Government). In May Gen. Tommy Franks, the retiring US commander in Iraq, was indicted under the legislation by a Belgian lawyer representing 19 Iraqis. Although the case was swiftly ended under new procedures introduced to prevent the legislation being used for political ends, the US Government demanded the repeal of the legislation. The USA claimed that its officials would be unable to attend meetings of NATO and threatened to withdraw US funding for a new NATO headquarters in Belgium. In July 2003 cases were initiated (and dismissed) against several other prominent US politicians, including President George W. Bush, as well as against the British Prime Minister, Tony Blair, for their roles in the military action in Afghanistan and Iraq. Legislation was adopted in August that substantially amended the 1993 law, establishing a procedure for nullifying pending cases and limiting its jurisdiction to cases involving Belgian citizens and long-term residents. Moreover, it granted automatic legal immunity to all officials attending meetings at NATO and the EU.

In September 2005 a Belgian court issued a warrant for the arrest of Hissène Habré, President of Chad during 1982–90, over alleged human rights abuses committed during his presidency; several of the alleged victims of these abuses had since been granted Belgian citizenship. The Belgian Government subsequently sought to secure Habré's extradition from Senegal, where he had fled after being deposed in 1990, but its requests were denied. In February 2009 the Belgian Government appealed to the International Court of Justice (ICJ) in The Hague, Netherlands, to compel Senegal either to try Habré or to extradite him to Belgium for prosecution under the amended universal jurisdiction law. In July 2012 the ICJ issued its judgment in the case, ruling that Senegal should commence procedures to prosecute Habré 'without further delay' or, failing that, extradite him to Belgium. In the following month the Senegalese Government and the African Union signed an agreement whereby Senegal would establish a special court to try Habré; in December the Senegalese Assemblée nationale adopted legislation providing for the creation of such a court.

Since March 2002 Belgium has contributed troops to the International Security Assistance Force (ISAF) in Afghanistan, which was established following the US-led military campaign against the Taliban and al-Qa'ida militants in 2001 and was placed under the command of NATO in August 2003; the number of Belgian troops participating in ISAF was reduced during the course of 2012 from 520 to 265, with the withdrawal of the contingent responsible for guarding the airport in Kabul, the capital of Afghanistan. By August 2013 a total of 180 Belgian troops were involved in the ISAF mission in Afghanistan. Following the outbreak of civil conflict in Libya in early 2011, and the UN Security Council's adoption in March of Resolution 1973, permitting UN member states to take 'all necessary measures' (short of military occupation) to protect civilians in that country, Belgian military forces participated in the enforcement of an air exclusion zone over Libya and a naval blockade of that country. NATO military action in Libya ended in October, following the death of the Libyan leader, Col Muammar al-Qaddafi. In January 2013 Belgium provided non-combat military support to the French-led operation to assist Malian forces in ousting armed Islamist groups occupying large areas of northern Mali.

CONSTITUTION AND GOVERNMENT

The Belgian Constitution, originally promulgated in 1831, was revised and consolidated in 1993 to provide for a federal structure of government. It has been subsequently amended on a number of occasions. Belgium is a constitutional and hereditary monarchy, consisting of a federation of the largely autonomous regions of Brussels, Flanders and Wallonia and of the Dutch-, French- and German-speaking language communities. The central legislature consists of a bicameral Parliament (the Chamber of Representatives and the Senate). The Chamber has 150 members, all directly elected for a term of four years (which was to rise to five years with effect from May 2014) by universal adult suffrage, on the basis of proportional representation. The Senate at April 2014 comprised 71 normal members, of whom 40 were directly elected at intervals of four years, also by universal suffrage on the basis of proportional representation, 21 were appointed by the legislative bodies of the three language communities, and 10 were co-opted by the elected members. In addition, children of the King were entitled to honorary membership of the Senate from 18 years of age and acquired voting rights at the age of 21. Executive power, nominally vested in the King, is exercised by the Council of Ministers. The King appoints the Prime Minister and, on the latter's advice, other ministers. The Council of Ministers is responsible to the Chamber of Representatives. The three regions and three linguistic communities are represented by the following directly elected legislative administrations: a combined administration for the Flemish Region and Community; administrations for the Walloon and Brussels-Capital Regions; and separate administrations for the French and German communities. The regional administrations have sole responsibility for the environment, housing, transport and public works, while the language community administrations supervise education policy and culture. Under a constitutional amendment approved by the Chamber of Representatives in June 2001, the regions were also granted greater autonomy over taxation and public expenditure, agriculture, and policies regarding foreign aid and trade. The coalition Government that took office in December 2011 proposed the introduction of a number of constitutional reforms, including the devolution of further powers to the regions and communities, an increase in the term of office of the Chamber of Representatives to five years and the transformation of the Senate, with effect from May 2014, into a non-permanent body, comprising 50 indirectly elected members representing the three linguistic communities and 10 co-opted members.

REGIONAL AND INTERNATIONAL CO-OPERATION

Belgium was a founder member of the European Community, now the European Union (EU, see p. 273), the principal institutions of which are based in Brussels. Belgium uses the European single currency, the euro. Belgium was also a founder member of the Benelux Economic Union (see p. 449), the Council of Europe (see p. 252) and the Organization for Security and Co-operation in Europe (OSCE, see p. 387).

Belgium was a founder member of the UN in 1945. As a contracting party to the General Agreement on Tariffs and Trade, Belgium joined the World Trade Organization (WTO, see p. 434) on its establishment in 1995. Belgium was also a founder member of the North Atlantic Treaty Organization (NATO, see p. 370), which has its headquarters in Brussels, and the Organisation for Economic Co-operation and Development (OECD, see p. 379).

ECONOMIC AFFAIRS

In 2012, according to estimates by the World Bank, Belgium's gross national income (GNI), measured at average 2010–12 prices, was US $501,305m., equivalent to $44,990 per head (or $40,170 per head on an international purchasing-power parity basis). During 2003–12, it was estimated, the population increased at an average annual rate of 0.8%, while gross domestic product (GDP) per head increased, in real terms, by an average of 0.6% per year. Overall GDP increased, in real terms, at an average annual rate of 1.4% during 2003–12; GDP decreased by 0.3% in 2012. According to chain-linked methodologies, GDP increased by 1.8% in 2011, but decreased by 0.1% in 2012.

Agriculture (including hunting, forestry and fishing) contributed 0.7% of GDP in 2012 and engaged 1.2% of the employed labour force in 2012. The principal agricultural products are sugar beet, potatoes and cereals. Dairy products and pig meat are also important. Exports of food and live animals accounted for 2.6% of Belgium's total export revenue in 2012. According to estimates by the World Bank, agricultural GDP declined, in real terms, at an average annual rate of 1.2% in 2002–10; it declined by 0.7% in 2010. According to chain-linked methodologies, sectoral GDP decreased by 1.9% in 2011, but increased by 2.3% in 2012.

Industry (including mining and quarrying, manufacturing, power and construction) contributed 21.8% of GDP in 2012 and engaged 21.8% of the employed labour force in 2012. According to estimates by the World Bank, although real industrial GDP remained constant with 0.6% growth in 2002–10, it decreased by 6.7% in 2009 but increased by 3.2% in 2010. According to chain-linked methodologies, sectoral GDP (excluding construction) decreased by 1.1% in 2011 and by 2.4% in 2012.

Belgium has few mineral resources and the country's last coal mine closed in 1992. Extractive activities accounted for only 0.1% of GDP in 2012 and engaged only 0.2% of the employed labour force in 2012. Belgium is, however, an important producer of copper, zinc and aluminium, smelted from imported ores. In 2011, according to chain-linked methodologies, the mining and quarrying sector's GDP increased by 25.8%.

Manufacturing contributed 12.8% of GDP in 2012 and, with mining and other industries, engaged 13.2% of the employed labour force in 2012. In 2012 the main branches of manufacturing, in terms of value added, were food products, beverages and tobacco (accounting for 15.8% of the total), chemical products and man-made fibres (15.6%) and basic metals and fabricated metal products (14.0%). According to estimates by the World Bank, during 2000–07 manufacturing GDP increased at an average annual rate of 1.1%; it rose by 2.6% in 2007.

Construction contributed 5.9% of GDP in 2012 and engaged 7.2% of the employed labour force in 2012. According to chain-linked methodologies, sectoral GDP increased by 8.1% in 2011 and by 1.0% in 2012.

Belgium's seven nuclear reactors accounted for 52.1% of total electricity generation in 2012. In 2012 26.6% was produced by natural gas power stations and 7.1% by coal-fired stations. The country's dependence on imported petroleum and natural gas has increased since 1988, following the announcement by the Government in that year of the indefinite suspension of its nuclear programme and of the construction of a gas-powered generator. In 2003 legislation was enacted to phase out the use of nuclear power by 2025, with the first nuclear power station scheduled to be closed in 2015. In October 2009 the Government agreed to postpone closure until 2025. However, legislation to this effect was not adopted by the legislature, owing to a change of government in April 2010. The coalition Government that took office in December 2011 stated its intention to phase out the use of nuclear power, but did not immediately set a date to do so. Mineral fuels imports comprised an estimated 21.8% of the value of Belgium's total imports in 2012.

The services sector contributed 77.4% of GDP in 2012 and engaged 77.1% of the employed labour force in 2012. Financial services and the insurance sector provide significant contributions to GDP. The presence in Belgium of the offices of many international organizations and businesses is a significant source of revenue. Tourism is an expanding industry in Belgium, and in 2012 an estimated 7.6m. foreign tourists visited the country. According to provisional figures, tourism receipts totalled US $11,381m. in 2012. According to estimates by the World Bank, the GDP of the services sector increased at an average annual rate of 1.7% in 2002–10; it decreased by 1.8% in 2009 but increased by 1.7% in 2010. According to chain-linked methodologies, sectoral GDP increased by 2.4% in 2011 and by 0.1% in 2012.

In 2012 Belgium recorded a visible merchandise trade deficit of US $13,737m., and a deficit of $9,698m. on the current account of the balance of payments. Belgium's principal source of imports in 2012 was the Netherlands (providing 25.5% of the total); other major suppliers were Germany, France and the United Kingdom. The principal markets for exports in that year were Germany (accounting for 16.1% of the total) and France (15.5%); other major purchasers were the Netherlands, the United Kingdom and the USA. The principal exports in 2012 were chemicals and related products, mineral products, machinery and equipment, transport equipment (including road vehicles), base metals and related products, plastics and rubber and related materials, natural or cultured pearls, precious or semi-precious stones, pharmaceutical products, and prepared foodstuffs, tobacco and beverages. The principal imports in that year were mineral products, machinery and equipment, chemicals and related products, transport equipment, base metals and related products, and natural or cultured pearls, precious or semi-precious stones.

In 2012 there was a budget deficit of €15,276m., equivalent to 4.1% of GDP. Belgium's general government gross debt was €375,390m. in 2012, equivalent to 99.8% of GDP. The country's total public debt was equivalent to 89.8% of GDP in 2008. The annual rate of inflation averaged 2.4% in 2004–12. Consumer prices increased by 2.9% in 2012. In 2012 the unemployment rate was 10.9%.

Belgium is a small, open economy, which, as it is reliant on exports, was affected by adverse global economic conditions in 2008–12, recording visible trade deficits throughout that period, following years of modest surpluses. The Belgian authorities acted swiftly in late 2008 to stabilize financial institutions that had been weakened by the international financial crisis, and were forced to nationalize Dexia Bank Belgium in 2011, after it suffered difficulties resulting from the sovereign debt crisis in the eurozone. Having contracted by 2.7% in 2009, real GDP rose by 2.4% in 2010, driven by strong export growth. Growth decelerated to 1.8% in 2011, however, partly owing to weaker external demand, and GDP contracted slightly, by some 0.1%, in 2012, before registering neither growth nor contraction in 2013. Forecasts for 2014 predicted a GDP growth rate of 1.2%. Moreover, the interventions in financial institutions and the costs of the recovery plan had a detrimental effect on the already high debt-to-GDP ratio. Having increased from 84.1% of GDP in 2007 (already significantly above the 60% stipulated by the EU), general government gross debt rose to 97.8% in 2011, to 99.8% in 2012 and further to 100.7% in 2013. The increase was partly attributed to the joint recapitalization with France of Dexia Group (agreed in late 2012), loans to Greece, Ireland and Portugal, and contributions to the European Stability Mechanism. Furthermore, the political deadlock during 2011 prompted concern within the financial markets regarding Belgium's ability to service the mounting public debt. The coalition Government that took office in December 2011 announced spending reductions of €11,300m. for 2012 with the aim of achieving a balanced budget by 2015. A deficit equivalent to 2.5% of GDP was estimated for 2013, compared with 3.3% in the previous year. In early 2014 the continued recovery of the Belgian economy was threatened by weak domestic demand, slow growth in export markets, a relatively high unemployment rate, very high levels of public debt and the financial pressures associated with an ageing population. Despite reforms to the pensions and health-care systems announced in 2012, the European Commission estimated that by 2060 some 8.5% of Belgium's GDP would need to be allocated to meet the needs of this section of the population.

PUBLIC HOLIDAYS

2015: 1 January (New Year's Day), 6 April (Easter Monday), 1 May (Labour Day), 14 May (Ascension Day), 25 May (Whit Monday), 11 July (Flemish Community), 21 July (Independence Day), 15 August (Assumption), 27 September (French Community), 1 November (All Saints' Day), 11 November (Armistice Day), 15 November (German-speaking Community), 25 December (Christmas Day).

Statistical Survey

Sources (unless otherwise stated): Direction générale Statistique et Information économique, 30 blvd Simon Bolivar, 1000 Brussels; tel. (2) 277-70-76; e-mail info.stat@economie.fgov.be; internet www.statbel.fgov.be; National Bank of Belgium, 14 blvd de Berlaimont, 1000 Brussels; tel. (2) 221-21-11; fax (2) 221-31-00; e-mail info@nbb.be; internet www.nbb.be.

Area and Population

AREA, POPULATION AND DENSITY

Area (sq km)	30,528*
Population (census results)‡	
1 March 1991	9,848,647
1 October 2001†	
Males	5,035,446
Females	5,260,904
Total	10,296,350
Population (register-based census at 1 January)‡	
2011	10,951,266
2012	11,035,948
2013	11,099,554
Density (per sq km) at 1 January 2013	363.6

* 11,787 sq miles.

† Refers to the General Socio-Economic Survey, which replaced the methodology of previous censuses.

‡ A register-based system of continuous enumeration replaced the 2001 General Socio-Economic Survey from 1 January 2011; population is *de jure*.

POPULATION BY AGE AND SEX
(population register at 1 January 2013)

	Males	Females	Total
0–14	963,517	921,239	1,884,756
15–64	3,645,556	3,610,117	7,255,673
65 and over	838,415	1,120,710	1,959,125
Total	5,447,488	5,652,066	11,099,554

REGIONS AND PROVINCES
(population register at 1 January 2013)

	Area (sq km)	Population	Density (per sq km)	Capital
Flemish Region	13,521	6,381,859	472.0	
Antwerpen (Antwerp)	2,867	1,793,377	625.5	Antwerpen
Limburg	2,422	853,239	352.3	Hasselt
Oost-Vlaanderen (East Flanders)	2,982	1,460,944	489.9	Gent
Vlaams-Brabant (Flemish Brabant)	2,106	1,101,280	522.9	Leuven
West-Vlaanderen (West Flanders)	3,144	1,173,019	373.1	Brugge
Walloon Region	16,845	3,563,060	211.5	
Brabant Wallon (Walloon Brabant)	1,091	388,526	356.1	Wavre
Hainaut	3,786	1,328,760	351.0	Mons
Liège	3,862	1,087,729	281.6	Liège
Luxembourg	4,440	275,594	62.1	Arlon
Namur	3,666	482,451	131.6	Namur
Brussels-Capital Region	162	1,154,635	7,127.4	Brussels
Total	30,528	11,099,554	363.6	

PRINCIPAL TOWNS
(population register, city proper at 1 January 2013)

Antwerpen (Antwerp)	507,911*	Molenbeek-Saint-Jean	94,653
Gent (Ghent)	248,813	Mons	93,941
Charleroi	203,753	Mechelen	82,602
Liège	195,931	Aalst	82,587
Bruxelles/Brussel (Brussels—capital)	168,576	La Louvière	79,486
Brugge (Bruges)	117,577	Hasselt	75,579
Anderlecht	113,462	Kortrijk	75,120
Namur	110,500	Sint-Niklaas	73,280
Leuven	97,692	Oostende (Ostende)	69,969

* Including Deurne and other suburbs.

BIRTHS, MARRIAGES AND DEATHS

	Registered live births		Registered marriages*		Registered deaths†	
	Number	Rate (per 1,000)	Number	Rate (per 1,000)	Number	Rate (per 1,000)
2002	111,225	10.8	40,434	3.9	105,642	10.2
2003	112,149	10.8	41,777	4.0	107,039	10.3
2004	115,618	11.1	43,296	4.2	101,946	9.8
2005	118,002	11.3	43,141	4.1	103,278	9.9
2006	121,382	11.5	44,813	4.3	101,587	9.7
2007	120,663	11.4	45,561	4.3	100,658	9.5
2008	128,049	12.0	45,613	4.3	n.a.	n.a.
2009	127,297	11.9	43,303	4.0	n.a.	n.a.

* Including marriages among Belgian armed forces stationed outside the country and alien armed forces in Belgium, unless performed by local foreign authority.

† Including Belgian armed forces stationed outside the country, but excluding alien armed forces stationed in Belgium.

Registered marriages: 42,159 (3.9 per 1,000 persons) in 2010; 41,001 in 2011.

Life expectancy (years at birth): 80.5 (males 77.9; females 83.2) in 2011 (Source: World Bank, World Development Indicators database).

ECONOMICALLY ACTIVE POPULATION*
(labour force sample survey, persons aged 15–64 years)

	2011	2012
Agriculture, hunting, forestry and fishing	58,644	53,020
Mining and quarrying	4,890	7,108
Manufacturing	641,405	594,957
Electricity, gas and water supply	63,866	57,305
Construction	337,510	324,858
Wholesale and retail trade	588,392	607,046
Hotels and restaurants	149,478	153,999
Transport, storage and communications	410,204	405,166
Financial intermediation	161,037	156,953
Real estate, renting and business activities	234,319	238,364
Public administration and defence	588,725	640,028
Education	412,932	410,991
Health and social work	614,080	656,966
Other community, social and personal service activities	168,263	161,817
Extra-territorial organizations and bodies	75,530	55,335
Total employed	4,509,274	4,523,913
Unemployed	346,698	88,229
Total labour force	4,855,972	4,612,142
Males	2,650,267	2,516,386
Females	2,205,704	2,095,756

* Includes professional armed forces, but excludes compulsory military service.

Health and Welfare

KEY INDICATORS

Total fertility rate (children per woman, 2011)	1.8
Under-5 mortality rate (per 1,000 live births, 2011)	4
HIV/AIDS (% of persons aged 15–49, 2011)	0.3
Physicians (per 1,000 head, 2010)	3.8
Hospital beds (per 1,000 head, 2010)	6.5
Health expenditure (2010): US $ per head (PPP)	3,975
Health expenditure (2010): % of GDP	10.5
Health expenditure (2010): public (% of total)	75.6
Total carbon dioxide emissions ('000 metric tons, 2010)	108,946.6
Carbon dioxide emissions per head (metric tons, 2010)	10.0
Human Development Index (2012): ranking	17
Human Development Index (2012): value	0.897

For sources and definitions, see explanatory note on p. vi.

Agriculture

PRINCIPAL CROPS
('000 metric tons)

	2010	2011	2012
Wheat	1,850	1,688	1,738
Barley	373	340	340
Maize	746	860	702
Oats	25	18	16
Triticale (wheat-rye hybrid)	44	30	42
Potatoes	3,456	4,129	2,930
Sugar beet	4,465	5,409	5,438
Rapeseed	46	52	52
Cabbages and other brassicas	26	26	26
Lettuce and chicory	67	61	56
Spinach	93	100	79
Tomatoes	228	218	232
Cauliflowers and broccoli	82	100	98
Leeks and other alliaceous vegetables	182	170	162
Beans, green	89	90	86
Peas, green	61	64	67
Carrots and turnips	314	317	317
Mushrooms and truffles*	42	42	42
Chicory roots	393	361	375*
Apples	344	228	220
Pears	307	285	236
Strawberries	35	38	41

* FAO estimate(s).

Aggregate production ('000 metric tons, may include official, semi-official or estimated data): Total cereals 3,042 in 2010, 2,939 in 2011, 2,862 in 2012; Total roots and tubers 3,456 in 2010, 4,129 in 2011, 2,930 in 2012; Total vegetables (incl. melons) 1,924 in 2010, 1,928 in 2011, 1,925 in 2012; Total fruits (excl. melons) 700 in 2010, 564 in 2011, 507 in 2012.

Source: FAO.

LIVESTOCK
('000 head, year ending September)

	2010	2011	2012
Horses	37	34	39
Cattle	2,593	2,535	2,438
Pigs	6,430	6,521	6,448
Sheep	120	114	119
Goats	22	36	36
Chickens	34,375	35,376	35,618
Turkeys	190*	197*	200†

* Unofficial figure.
† FAO estimate.

Source: FAO.

LIVESTOCK PRODUCTS
('000 metric tons)

	2010	2011	2012
Cattle meat	263	272*	262*
Sheep meat	3	2	2†
Pig meat	1,124	1,108	1,150†
Horse meat†	2	2	2
Chicken meat	497	502	512*
Turkey meat	8	9	9†
Cows' milk	3,067	3,101	3,432*
Hen eggs	158*	161*	165†

* Unofficial figure.
† FAO estimate(s).

Source: FAO.

Forestry

ROUNDWOOD REMOVALS
('000 cubic metres, excluding bark)

	2010	2011	2012
Sawlogs, veneer logs and logs for sleepers	2,601	2,677	2,677
Pulpwood	1,345*	1,385*	1,385†
Other industrial wood	168	173	173
Fuel wood	714	893	893
Total	4,827	5,128	5,128

* Unofficial figure.
† FAO estimate.

Source: FAO.

SAWNWOOD PRODUCTION
('000 cubic metres, including railway sleepers, unofficial figures)

	2009	2010	2011
Coniferous (softwood)	1,075	1,142	1,174
Broadleaved (hardwood)	180	241	195
Total	1,255	1,383	1,369

2012: Production assumed to be unchanged from 2011 (FAO estimates).

Source: FAO.

Fishing

('000 metric tons, live weight)

	2009	2010	2011
Capture	21.7	22.4	22.5
European plaice	5.0	5.2	6.3
Lemon sole	0.7	0.7	0.8
Common sole	4.0	3.9	3.5
Atlantic cod	1.1	0.8	0.9
Monkfishes (Angler)	0.9	1.0	1.3
Rays	0.6	0.5	0.3
Aquaculture	0.6*	0.5*	0.0
Total catch	22.3*	23.0*	22.5

* FAO estimate.

Source: FAO.

Mining

('000 metric tons unless otherwise indicated)

	2009	2010	2011
Barite (Barytes)*	28	28	28
Lime and dead-burned dolomite, quicklime*	2,400	2,400	2,400
Clay, kaolin*	460	460	460
Copper (primary and secondary, refined)	374	381	380*
Distillate fuel oil ('000 barrels)	88,289	93,075	93,000*

* Estimated production.

Source: US Geological Survey.

Industry

SELECTED PRODUCTS

('000 metric tons unless otherwise indicated)

	2008	2009	2010
Wheat flour	1,195	1,185	n.a.
Mechanical wood pulp*	150	426	228
Newsprint*	299	250	265
Other paper and paperboard	566	540	517
Jet fuels	1,878	1,838	1,755
Motor spirit (petrol)	4,338	3,355	3,572
Kerosene	31	66	44
Distillate fuel oils	12,959	12,248	n.a.
Residual fuel oil	7,268	5,039	n.a.
Petroleum bitumen (asphalt)	1,300	1,342	1,294
Liquefied petroleum gas (from refineries)	524	463	n.a.
Coke-oven coke	2,309	1,574	1,935
Cement	9,700†	8,500	8,300
Pig iron	7,125	3,087	4,688
Crude steel	10,676	5,635	7,973
Refined copper—unwrought	396	374	381
Refined lead—unwrought	81	109	105
Zinc—unwrought	279†	54	300
Tin—unwrought (metric tons)	9,200	8,700	8,700†
Electric energy (million kWh)	84,930	91,225	95,120

* Unofficial figures.

† Estimate.

2011 ('000 metric tons unless otherwise indicated): Mechanical wood pulp 231 (unofficial figure); Newsprint 259 (unofficial figure); Other paper and paperboard 573; Pig iron 4,725; Crude steel 8,026; Refined copper—unwrought 380 (estimate); Refined lead—unwrought 88; Zinc—unwrought 322 (estimate); Tin—unwrought (metric tons) 8,700 (estimate).

2012 ('000 metric tons unless otherwise indicated): Mechanical wood pulp 227 (unofficial figure); Newsprint 259 (unofficial figure); Other paper and paperboard 573.

Sources: UN Industrial Commodity Statistics Database; FAO; US Geological Survey.

Finance

CURRENCY AND EXCHANGE RATES

Monetary Units

100 cents = 1 euro (€).

Sterling and Dollar Equivalents (31 December 2013)

£1 sterling = 1.194 euros;
US $1 = 0.725 euros;
€10 = £8.37 = $13.79.

Average Exchange Rate (euros per US $)

2011	0.7194
2012	0.7783
2013	0.7532

Note: The national currency was formerly the Belgian franc. From the introduction of the euro, with Belgian participation, on 1 January 1999, a fixed exchange rate of €1 = 40.3399 Belgian francs was in operation. Euro notes and coins were introduced on 1 January 2002. The euro and local currency circulated alongside each other until 28 February, after which the euro became the sole legal tender.

GENERAL GOVERNMENT BUDGET

(€ million)

Revenue	2010	2011	2012
Fiscal and parafiscal receipts	153,569	160,991	168,250
Direct taxes	55,393	59,109	61,899
Individuals	45,334	47,693	49,083
Companies	9,891	11,274	12,678
Indirect taxes	45,494	46,539	48,465
Actual social contributions	50,193	52,676	54,746
Taxes on capital	2,490	2,667	3,139
Non-fiscal and non-parafiscal receipts	19,691	22,142	23,326
Total	173,2611	183,133	191,576

Expenditure	2010	2011	2012
Current expenditure (excluding interest charges)	164,835	173,018	179,897
Compensation of employees	44,667	46,554	48,382
Intermediate consumption and paid taxes	13,246	13,675	13,961
Subsidies to companies	9,201	10,175	10,128
Social benefits	88,407	92,877	97,596
Current transfers to the rest of the world	4,043	4,108	4,239
Other current transfers	5,271	5,630	5,592
Interest charges	12,470	12,743	13,071
Capital expenditure	9,721	11,662	13,884
Gross capital formation	5,829	6,510	6,756
Other capital expenditure	3,892	5,151	7,129
Total	187,026	197,422	206,852

INTERNATIONAL RESERVES

(US $ million at 31 December)

	2010	2011	2012
Gold (Eurosystem valuation)	10,315	11,514	12,169
IMF special drawing rights	6,789	6,500	6,522
Reserve position in IMF	1,831	3,426	3,627
Foreign exchange	7,880	7,992	8,451
Total	26,815	29,432	30,769

Source: IMF, *International Financial Statistics*.

MONEY SUPPLY

(incl. shares, depository corporations, national residency criteria, € million at 31 December)

	2010	2011	2012
Currency issued	28,229	29,809	30,544
Banque Nationale de Belgique	9,769	13,447	16,858
Demand deposits	113,972	110,446	123,186
Other deposits	352,145	363,469	373,385
Securities other than shares	75,260	72,315	66,658
Money market fund shares	1,524	3,533	768
Shares and other equity	66,546	68,756	70,363
Other items (net)	–107,811	–83,850	–89,811
Total	529,865	564,479	575,093

Source: IMF, *International Financial Statistics*.

COST OF LIVING

(Consumer Price Index; base: 2004 = 100)

	2010	2011	2012
Food and beverages	117.2	120.1	123.7
Housing, water, electricity, gas and other fuels	124.1	134.2	139.3
Clothing and footwear	104.3	105.4	106.7
Health	103.2	103.3	103.6
Communication	87.2	87.5	89.4
Transport	114.3	120.9	124.0
Education	116.2	116.6	119.4
All items (incl. others)	113.7	117.7	121.1

NATIONAL ACCOUNTS
(€ million at current prices)

National Income and Product

	2010	2011	2012
Compensation of employees	182,291	190,596	197,096
Gross operating surplus and mixed income	136,139	141,149	139,317
Taxes, less subsidies, on production and imports	37,309	37,514	39,468
GDP in market prices	355,740	369,259	375,881
Primary incomes (net)	6,213	3,439	1,022
Gross national income (GNI)	361,953	372,698	376,903

Expenditure on the Gross Domestic Product

	2010	2011	2012
Private final consumption expenditure	188,455	194,667	198,898
Government final consumption expenditure	86,212	90,278	93,788
Gross fixed capital formation	71,510	76,502	76,535
Increase in stocks	2,058	4,748	2,513
Total domestic expenditure	348,235	366,195	371,734
Exports of goods and services	283,965	313,811	323,734
Less Imports of goods and services	276,461	310,748	319,587
GDP in market prices	355,740	369,259	375,881
GDP in chain linked prices	362,840	369,259	368,756

Gross Domestic Product by Economic Activity

	2010	2011	2012
Agriculture, forestry and fishing	2,458	2,061	2,488
Industry (excl. construction)	53,546	54,094	53,445
Construction	17,957	19,514	19,748
Wholesale and retail trade; transport; accommodation and food service activities	63,564	66,043	66,628
Information and communication	13,221	13,645	13,930
Financial intermediation	21,022	21,712	21,700
Real estate, renting and business activities	69,239	72,804	73,949
Public administration and defence; compulsory social security; education	46,114	48,165	50,135
Health and social work	23,898	25,261	26,472
Arts, entertainment and recreation; other service activities; activities of private households and extra-territorial organizations and bodies	6,455	6,749	6,888
Sub-total	317,474	330,048	335,383
Taxes, less subsidies, on products	38,266	39,211	40,500
GDP at market prices	355,740	369,259	375,881

BALANCE OF PAYMENTS
(US $ million)

	2010	2011	2012
Exports of goods	269,425	322,842	301,753
Imports of goods	–275,028	–337,271	–315,489
Balance on goods	–5,603	–14,429	–13,737
Exports of services	93,960	99,506	103,504
Imports of services	–82,776	–90,176	–93,449
Balance on goods and services	5,581	–5,099	–3,682
Primary income received	69,237	68,243	58,477
Primary income paid	–58,434	–59,364	–54,408
Balance on goods, services and primary income	16,384	3,780	386
Secondary income received	11,732	12,248	11,050
Secondary income paid	–19,647	–21,491	–21,134
Current balance	8,468	–5,463	–9,698

—continued	2010	2011	2012
Capital account (net)	–1,340	–1,001	–567
Direct investment assets	–23,396	–94,950	34,103
Direct investment from liabilities	78,185	117,161	–36,755
Portfolio investment assets	–9,490	4,415	39,288
Portfolio investment liabilities	–25,933	–26,432	21,489
Financial derivatives and employee stock options (net)	1,878	–2,783	2,836
Other investment assets	12,172	–31,559	41,610
Other investment liabilities	–40,889	43,287	–89,140
Net errors and omissions	1,164	–1,175	–2,499
Reserves and related items	819	1,499	666

Source: IMF, *International Financial Statistics*.

External Trade

PRINCIPAL COMMODITIES
(distribution by HS, € million)

Imports c.i.f.	2010	2011	2012
Vegetable products	6,418.1	7,212.0	8,280.7
Prepared foodstuffs, tobacco and beverages, etc.	8,781.5	9,568.2	10,026.3
Mineral products	39,879.1	52,911.0	54,784.6
Mineral fuels, oils and products of their distillation	36,971.4	49,481.6	51,862.3
Chemicals and related products	27,339.8	29,129.0	32,349.4
Organic chemicals	9,716.5	10,785.2	11,616.7
Pharmaceutical products	7,777.9	7,163.6	9,501.8
Plastics and rubber and related materials	11,391.5	12,619.0	12,508.5
Plastics and related materials	8,625.8	9,457.5	9,592.1
Textiles and textile products	6,417.6	6,967.6	6,538.9
Natural or cultured pearls, precious or semi-precious stones	12,841.1	16,916.8	16,683.1
Base metals and related products	18,535.7	21,488.9	19,789.9
Iron and steel	7,572.5	9,081.4	7,615.3
Machinery and mechanical appliances and electrical equipment, etc.	29,241.5	32,789.2	32,361.7
Boilers, general industrial machinery, equipment and parts	17,472.3	20,397.8	20,727.1
Electrical machinery, apparatus, etc.	11,769.1	12,391.4	11,634.6
Transport equipment	24,367.6	26,887.2	26,640.6
Road vehicles (incl. air cushion vehicles) and parts	23,035.7	25,337.7	25,013.9
Total (incl. others)	212,996.2	248,175.1	251,000.3

Exports f.o.b.	2010	2011	2012
Prepared foodstuffs, tobacco and beverages, etc.	11,037.2	12,048.2	12,795.3
Mineral products	24,149.9	31,885.3	33,500.6
Mineral fuels, oils and products of their distillation	22,868.5	30,753.1	32,453.6
Chemicals and related products	35,531.5	38,488.5	40,024.6
Organic chemicals	10,417.4	11,527.7	11,590.7
Pharmaceutical products	10,972.4	11,220.0	13,252.3
Plastics and rubber and related materials	19,464.8	20,982.4	20,936.9
Plastics and related materials	16,689.1	18,020.5	18,146.2
Textiles and textile articles	6,761.3	7,042.5	6,862.1
Natural or cultured pearls, precious or semi-precious stones	14,794.8	18,591.2	18,095.9
Base metals and related products	21,103.7	23,351.2	21,916.3
Iron and steel	11,429.9	13,012.9	11,705.3
Machinery and mechanical appliances and electrical equipment, etc.	22,744.0	25,346.1	25,834.4
Nuclear reactors, boilers, general industrial machinery, equipment and parts	14,356.5	17,247.6	17,933.0
Electrical machinery, apparatus, etc.	8,387.5	8,098.5	7,901.4
Transport equipment	21,736.0	25,036.2	25,650.6
Road vehicles (incl. air cushion vehicles) and parts	20,511.9	24,100.9	24,571.4
Total (incl. others)	208,709.6	236,968.0	239,846.3

PRINCIPAL TRADING PARTNERS
(€ million)*

Imports c.i.f.	2010	2011	2012
China, People's Republic	6,173.1	6,795.3	6,220.5
France†	26,294.2	28,980.1	29,491.4
Germany	34,111.9	37,786.7	38,520.3
India	2,854.9	4,203.3	3,175.4
Ireland	2,471.6	2,515.7	2,518.6
Italy	6,429.2	7,067.6	7,570.2
Japan	5,038.0	5,315.6	5,256.5
Netherlands	50,576.2	60,355.7	64,028.2
Norway	3,068.2	3,829.6	4,413.2
Poland	2,443.0	2,759.3	2,623.6
Russia	5,645.1	8,111.3	7,633.1
Spain	5,131.0	5,519.6	5,434.7
Sweden	4,007.2	4,850.7	4,800.0
Switzerland	1,933.2	2,757.0	2,564.2
United Kingdom	13,241.4	16,436.4	14,336.9
USA	8,529.8	9,900.6	10,649.5
Total (incl. others)	212,996.2	248,175.1	251,000.3

* Imports by country of production; exports by country of last consignment.
† Including trade with Overseas Departments.

Transport

RAILWAYS
(domestic and international traffic)

	2008	2009	2010
Passenger journeys (million)	216.7	219.8	224.0
Passenger-km (million)	10,403	10,427	10,564
Freight carried ('000 metric tons)	57,328	36,521	38,998
Freight ton-km (million)	7,782	5,442	5,729

ROAD TRAFFIC
(motor vehicles in use at 1 August)

	2011	2012	2013
Passenger cars	5,407,015	5,443,807	5,493,472
Buses and coaches	16,100	16,031	15,822
Lorries and vans	714,370	726,237	739,402
Road tractors	46,844	46,774	45,000
Motorcycles and mopeds	433,958	441,324	450,793

SHIPPING

Flag Registered Fleet
(at 31 December)

	2011	2012	2013
Number of vessels	406	403	399
Total displacement ('000 grt)	4,532.9	4,210.8	4,158.7

Source: Lloyd's List Intelligence (www.lloydslistintelligence.com).

International Sea-borne Freight Traffic
('000 metric tons, estimates)

	2001	2002	2003
Goods loaded	422,700	439,900	419,400
Goods unloaded	436,900	447,100	427,000

Source: UN, *Monthly Bulletin of Statistics*.

CIVIL AVIATION
(traffic)

	2010	2011
Kilometres flown (million)	53	53
Passengers carried ('000)	3,372	3,544
Passenger-km (million)	3,994	4,195
Total ton-km (million)	375	392

Source: UN, *Statistical Yearbook*.

Passengers carried ('000): 5,850 in 2012 (Source: World Bank, World Development Indicators database).

Tourism

TOURIST ARRIVALS BY COUNTRY OF ORIGIN
('000 persons)*

Country of residence	2010	2011	2012
China, People's Rep.	80	101	122
France	1,154	1,211	1,205
Germany	815	838	813
Italy	258	279	274
Japan	81	91	112
Netherlands	1,934	1,920	1,922
Spain	342	367	340
United Kingdom	870	876	907
USA	293	325	327
Total (incl. others)	7,186	7,494	7,591

* Non-residents staying in accommodation establishments.

Tourism receipts (US $ million, excl. passenger transport): 10,367 in 2010; 11,651 in 2011; 11,381 in 2012 (provisional) (Source: World Tourism Organization).

Communications Media

	2010	2011	2012
Telephones ('000 main lines in use)	4,639.8	4,633.5	4,630.9
Mobile cellular telephones ('000 subscribers)	12,154.0	12,957.6	12,879.1
Internet subscribers ('000)	3,415.8	3,543.8	n.a.
Broadband subscribers ('000)	3,373.1	3,528.8	3,679.2

Source: International Telecommunication Union.

Education

(2012/13 unless otherwise indicated)

	Institutions		Students	
	French*	Flemish	French†	Flemish
Pre-primary	1,861‡	2,298	179,393	267,976
Primary	1,960‡	2,396	322,178	420,832
Secondary	645	1,067	365,894	438,994
Non-university higher education	329	21	84,875	132,120
University level	9	7	73,249	84,177

* 2004/05.
† 2008/09.
‡ Figure includes 1,640 joint pre-primary and primary institutions.

Teachers: *French (2004/05):* Pre-primary and primary 30,645; Secondary 36,038; Special education (pre-primary, primary and secondary) 6,450; Non-university higher education 10,055; University level 1,822. *Flemish (2012/13 unless otherwise indicated):* Pre-primary 22,853; Primary 49,062; Secondary 76,999; Non-university higher education 12,705; University level 12,016 (2010/11).

Sources: Entreprise des Technologies Nouvelles de l'Information et de la Communication, *Short statistical overview of full-time and social promotion education*; Vlaams Ministerie van Onderwijs en Vorming, *Vlaams onderwijs in beeld*.

German-speaking communities (2011/12 unless otherwise indicated): Students 14,251 (pre-primary 2,311, primary 5,028, secondary 5,357, part-time 46, higher 188, special 291, training 1,030); teachers (at May 2009) 2,047 (Source: Ministerium der Deutschsprachigen Gemeinschaft, Eupen).

Pupil-teacher ratio (primary education, UNESCO estimate): 11.0 in 2009/10 (Source: UNESCO Institute for Statistics).

Directory

The Government

HEAD OF STATE

King of the Belgians: HM King PHILIPPE (succeeded to the throne 21 July 2013).

THE COUNCIL OF MINISTERS

(April 2014)

A coalition of Parti Socialiste (PS), Christen-Democratisch en Vlaams (CD&V), Mouvement Réformateur (MR), Centre Démocrate Humaniste (CDH), Socialistische Partij Anders—Socialist Party (SP.A) and Open Vld.

Prime Minister: ELIO DI RUPO (PS).

Deputy Prime Minister and Minister of Defence: PIETER DE CREM (CD&V).

Deputy Prime Minister and Minister of Foreign Affairs, Foreign Trade and European Affairs: DIDIER REYNDERS (MR).

Deputy Prime Minister and Minister of Economy, Consumer Affairs and the North Sea: JOHAN VANDE LANOTTE (SP.A).

Deputy Prime Minister and Minister of Pensions: ALEXANDER DE CROO (Open Vld).

Deputy Prime Minister and Minister of the Interior and Equal Opportunities: JOËLLE MILQUET (CDH).

Deputy Prime Minister and Minister of Social Affairs and Health, in charge of Beliris and Federal Cultural Institutions: LAURETTE ONKELINX (PS).

Minister of Small and Medium-sized Enterprises, the Self-employed and Agriculture: SABINE LARUELLE (MR).

Minister of Justice: ANNEMIE TURTELBOOM (Open Vld).

Minister of the Budget and Administrative Simplification: OLIVIER CHASTEL (MR).

Minister of Employment: MONICA DE CONINCK (SP.A).

Minister of Public Enterprises and Development Co-operation, in charge of Larger Towns: JEAN-PASCAL LABILLE (PS).

Minister of Finance, in charge of Civil Service: KOEN GEENS (CD&V).

There are six Secretaries of State.

FEDERAL PUBLIC SERVICES AND MINISTRIES

Federal Public Service Chancellery of the Prime Minister: 16 rue de la Loi, 1000 Brussels; tel. (2) 501-02-11; fax (2) 512-69-52; e-mail info@premier.fed.be; internet www.premier.be.

Federal Public Service of the Budget and Management Control: 138/2 rue Royale, 1000 Brussels; tel. (2) 212-37-11; fax (2) 212-39-37; e-mail info.bb@budget.fed.be; internet www.budgetfederal.be.

Ministry of Defence: 1 rue d'Evere, 1140 Evere, Brussels; tel. (2) 550-28-11; fax (2) 550-29-19; e-mail cabinet@mod.mil.be; internet www.mil.be.

Federal Public Service of the Economy, Small and Medium-sized Enterprises, the Self-Employed and Energy: 50 rue du Progrès, 1210 Brussels; tel. (2) 277-51-11; fax (2) 277-51-11; e-mail stefaan.jacobs@economie.fgov.be; internet www.economie.fgov.be.

Federal Public Service of Employment, Labour and Social Dialogue: 12 rue de la Loi, 1000 Brussels; tel. (2) 233-41-11; fax (2) 233-44-88; e-mail info@ckfin.minfin.be; internet www.emploi.belgique.be.

Federal Public Service of Finance: 33 blvd du Roi Albert II, BP 70, 1030 Brussels; tel. (2) 572-57-57; e-mail info.tax@minfin.fed.be; internet www.minfin.fgov.be.

Federal Public Service of Foreign Affairs, Foreign Trade and Development Co-operation: 15 rue des Petits Carmes, 1000 Brussels; tel. (2) 501-81-11; fax (2) 501-81-70; e-mail contact@diplobel.fed.be; internet www.diplomatie.be.

Federal Public Service of Health, Food Chain Safety and Environment: Eurostation II, 40 pl. Victor Horta, BP 10, 1060 Brussels; tel. (2) 524-94-94; fax (2) 524-95-27; e-mail info@health.fgov.be; internet www.health.belgium.be.

Federal Public Service of Information and Communication Technology: WTC III, blvd Simon Bolivar, 1000 Brussels; tel. (2)

212-96-00; fax (2) 212-96-99; e-mail info@fedict.belgique.be; internet www.fedict.belgium.be.

Federal Public Service of the Interior: 1 rue de Louvain, 1000 Brussels; tel. (2) 500-21-11; fax (2) 500-20-39; e-mail info@ibz.fgov.be; internet www.ibz.be.

Federal Public Service of Justice: 115 blvd de Waterloo, 1000 Brussels; tel. (2) 542-65-11; fax (2) 542-70-39; e-mail info@just.fgov.be; internet www.just.fgov.be.

Federal Public Service of Mobility and Transport: 56 rue du Progrès, 1210 Brussels; tel. (2) 277-31-11; e-mail info@mobilit.fgov.be; internet www.mobilit.belgium.be.

Federal Public Service of Personnel and Organization: 51 rue de la Loi, 1040 Brussels; tel. (2) 790-58-00; fax (2) 790-58-99; e-mail info@p-o.belgium.be; internet www.fedweb.belgium.be.

Federal Public Service of Social Security: Centre Administratif Botanique, Finance Tower, 50 Blvd du Jardin Botanique, bte 100, 1000 Brussels; tel. (2) 528-60-11; fax (2) 528-69-53; e-mail social.security@minsoc.fed.be; internet socialsecurity.fgov.be.

Legislature

Chamber of Representatives (Chambre des Représentants/Kamer van Volksvertegenwoordigers)

Palais de la Nation, 1008 Brussels; tel. (2) 549-81-11; e-mail info@lachambre.be; internet www.lachambre.be.

President: ANDRÉ FLAHAUT (PS).

General Election, 13 June 2010

Party	Votes cast	% of votes	Seats
N-VA	1,135,617	17.40	27
PS	894,543	13.70	26
MR	605,617	9.28	18
CD&V	707,986	10.85	17
SP.A	602,867	9.24	13
Open Vld	563,873	8.64	13
Vlaams Belang	506,697	7.76	12
CDH	360,441	5.52	9
Ecolo	313,047	4.80	8
Groen!	285,989	4.38	5
Lijst Dedecker	150,577	2.31	1
Parti Populaire	84,005	1.29	1
Total (incl. others)	6,527,367	100.00	150

Senate (Sénat/Senaat)

Palais de la Nation, 1009 Brussels; tel. (2) 501-70-70; internet www.senate.be.

President: SABINE DE BETHUNE (CD&V).

General Election, 13 June 2010

Party	Votes cast	% of votes	Seats
N-VA	1,268,780	19.61	9
PS	880,828	13.62	7
CD&V	646,375	9.99	4
SP.A	613,079	9.48	4
MR	599,618	9.27	4
Open Vld	533,124	8.24	4
Vlaams Belang	491,547	7.60	3
Ecolo	353,111	5.46	2
CDH	331,870	5.13	2
Groen!	251,546	3.89	1
Total (incl. others)	6,469,103	100.00	40

In addition, the Senate has 21 members appointed by and from within the legislative bodies of the three language communities and 10 members co-opted by the elected and appointed members. Children of the monarch are entitled to honorary membership of the Senate from 18 years of age and acquire voting rights at the age of 21, although they do not exercise their voting rights in practice.

Advisory Councils

Conseil Central de l'Economie/Centrale Raad voor het Bedrijfsleven: 17–21 ave de la Joyeuse entrée, 1040 Brussels; tel. (2) 233-88-11; fax (2) 233-89-12; e-mail mail@ccecrb.fgov.be; internet www.ccecrb.fgov.be; f. 1948; representative and consultative body; advises the authorities on economic issues; 108 mems; Pres. Baron ROBERT TOLLET.

Conseil d'Etat/Raad van State: 33 rue de la Science, 1040 Brussels; tel. (2) 234-96-11; e-mail info@raadvst-consetat.be; internet www.raadvst-consetat.be; f. 1946; advisory body on legislative and regulatory matters; supreme administrative court; hears complaints against the actions of the legislature; 44 mems; First Pres. ROBERT ANDERSEN.

Regional and Community Administrations

Belgium is a federal state, and considerable power has been devolved to the regional administrations for Brussels, Wallonia and Flanders, and to the Flemish, French and German-speaking Communities. The regional authorities have sole responsibility for the environment, housing, transport and public works and for certain aspects of social welfare, while the community administrations are primarily responsible for cultural affairs and education. In June 2001 Parliament granted the regions greater responsibility for taxation and public expenditure, agriculture and matters relating to foreign aid and trade. The Sixth State Reform agreement of December 2011 provided for greater fiscal autonomy for the communities and regions. The Flemish Region and the Flemish Community share a combined administration.

FLEMISH REGION AND COMMUNITY

Minister-President: KRIS PEETERS (CD&V).

Vlaamse Regering (Flemish Government): Boudewijnlaan 30, 1000 Brussels; tel. (2) 553-29-11; fax (2) 553-29-05; e-mail communicatie@vlaanderen.be; internet www.vlaamseregering.be; 10 mems.

Vlaams Parlement (Flemish Parliament): Leuvensweg 86, 1011 Brussels; tel. (2) 552-11-11; fax (2) 552-11-22; e-mail algemeen@vlaamsparlement.be; internet www.vlaamsparlement.be; f. 1972.

President of the Parliament: JAN PEUMANS (N-VA).

Election, 7 June 2009

Party	Seats
CD&V	31
Vlaams Belang	21
Open Vld	21
SP.A	19
N-VA	16
Lijst Dedecker	8
Groen!	7
Union des Francophones	1
Total	124

WALLOON REGION

Minister-President: RUDY DEMOTTE (PS).

Gouvernement Wallon (Walloon Government): 25–27 rue Mazy, 5100 Namur; tel. (81) 33-12-11; fax (81) 33-13-66; e-mail vancau@gov.wallonie.be; internet gouvernement.wallonie.be; 8 mems.

Parlement Wallon (Walloon Parliament): 6 square Arthur Masson, 5012 Namur; tel. (81) 23-10-36; fax (81) 23-12-20; e-mail mail@parlement-wallon.be; internet www.parlement-wallon.be; elects Walloon Govt.

President of the Parliament: PATRICK DUPRIEZ (Ecolo).

Election, 7 June 2009

Party	Seats
PS	29
MR	19
Ecolo	14
CDH	13
Total	75

BRUSSELS-CAPITAL REGION

Minister-President: RUDI VERVOORT (PS).

Gouvernement de la Région de Bruxelles-Capitale/Brussels Hoofdstedelijke Regering (Government of Brussels-Capital): 7–9 rue Ducale, 1000 Brussels; tel. (2) 506-32-11; fax (2) 514-40-22; internet www.bruxelles.irisnet.be; 8 mems.

Parlement de la Région de Bruxelles-Capitale/Brussels Hoofdstedelijk Parlement (Parliament of the Region of Brussels-Capital): 22 rue du Chêne, 1005 Brussels; tel. (2) 549-62-11; fax (2) 549-62-12; e-mail greffe@parlbru.irisnet.be; internet www.parlbru.irisnet.be.

President of the Parliament: FRANÇOISE DUPUIS (PS).

Election, 7 June 2009

Party	Seats
French-speaking group	
MR	24
PS	21
Ecolo	16
CDH	11
N-VA	1
Dutch-speaking group	
SP.A	4
Open Vld	4
Vlaams Belang	3
CD&V	3
Groen!	2
Total (incl. both groups)	89

FRENCH COMMUNITY

Minister-President: RUDY DEMOTTE (PS).

Gouvernement de la Communauté Française Wallonie-Bruxelles (Government of the French Community): 15–17 pl. Surlet de Chokier, 1000 Brussels; tel. (2) 801-72-11; fax (2) 227-33-53; internet gouvernement.cfwb.be; 7 mems.

Parlement de la Communauté Française de Belgique (Parliament of the French Community): 6 rue de la Loi, 1000 Brussels; tel. (2) 506-38-11; fax (2) 506-38-08; e-mail cellule-internet@pcf.be; internet www.pcf.be; 94 mems, comprising the 75 mems of the Walloon Parliament and 19 French-speaking mems of the Council of the Region of Brussels-Capital.

President of the Parliament: JEAN-CHARLES LUPERTO (PS).

GERMAN-SPEAKING COMMUNITY

Minister-President: KARL-HEINZ LAMBERTZ (SP).

Regierung der Deutschsprachigen Gemeinschaft Belgiens (Government of the German-speaking Community): Klötzerbahn 32, 4700 Eupen; tel. (87) 59-64-00; fax (87) 74-02-58; e-mail regierung@dgov.be; internet www.dglive.be; 4 mems.

Parlament der Deutschsprachigen Gemeinschaft in Belgien (Parliament of the German-speaking Community): Kaperberg 8, 4700 Eupen; tel. (87) 59-07-20; fax (87) 59-07-30; e-mail info@dgparlament.be; internet www.dgparlament.be.

President of the Parliament: FERDEL SCHRÖDER (PFF).

Election, 7 June 2009

Party	Seats
CSP	7
SP	5
PFF	4
ProDG	4
Ecolo	3
Vivant	2
Total	25

Election Commission

Direction des Elections/Directie van de Verkiezingen: Parc Atrium, 11 rue des Colonies, 1000 Brussels; tel. (2) 518-21-81; fax (2) 518-21-19; e-mail marina.devos@rrn.ibz.fgov.be; internet www.ibz.rrn.fgov.be; part of the General Directorate of Institutions and Population, a department of the Federal Public Service of the Interior; Dir-Gen. ISABELLE MAZZARA.

Political Organizations

DUTCH-SPEAKING PARTIES

Christen-Democratisch en Vlaams (CD&V) (Christian Democratic and Flemish): Wetstraat 89, 1040 Brussels; tel. (2) 238-38-11; fax (2) 230-43-60; e-mail info@cdenv.be; internet www.cdenv.be; f. 1945 as Parti Social Chrétien/Christelijke Volkspartij (PSC/CVP); CVP separated from PSC by 1972 and adopted current name in 2001; Chair. WOUTER BEKE.

Groen (Green): Sergeant De Bruynestraat 78–82, 1070 Anderlecht; tel. (2) 219-19-19; fax (2) 223-10-90; e-mail info@groen.be; internet www.groen.be; f. 1982 as Anders Gaan Leven (Agalev); adopted current name in 2003; absorbed the Sociaal-Liberaal Partij in 2009; known as Groen! until Jan. 2012; ecologist; Chair. WOUTER VAN BESIEN; Vice-Chair. ELKE VAN DEN BRANDT.

Libertair, Direct, Democratisch: Troonstraat 38, Postbus 53, 8400 Ostend; tel. (9) 210-03-80; fax (9) 210-03-89; e-mail info@lijstdedecker.com; internet www.lijstdedecker.com; f. 2007 as Lijst Dedecker; name changed to present 2011; advocates economic liberalism and greater independence for Flanders; Leader JEAN-MARIE DEDECKER.

Nieuw-Vlaamse Alliantie (N-VA) (New-Flemish Alliance): Koningsstraat 47, Postbus 6, 1000 Brussels; tel. (2) 219-49-30; fax (2) 217-35-10; e-mail info@n-va.be; internet www.n-va.be; f. 2001 following disintegration of the Volksunie (VU, f. 1954); Flemish nationalist party advocating an independent Flemish state within a federal Europe; Chair. BART DE WEVER; 11,000 mems.

Open Vld: Melsensstraat 34, 1000 Brussels; tel. (2) 549-00-20; fax (2) 512-60-25; e-mail info@openvld.be; internet www.openvld.be; f. 1846 as Liberale Partij; name changed to Vlaamse Liberalen en Demokraten (VLD—Flemish Liberals and Democrats) in 1992; adopted the name Open Vld in 2007 to contest the general election in alliance with 2 minor parties, Liberaal Appèl Plus and Vivant; Pres. GWENDOLYN RUTTEN; c. 70,000 mems.

SP.A (Socialistische Partij Anders—Socialist Party): Grasmarkt 105/37, 1000 Brussels; tel. (2) 552-02-00; fax (2) 552-02-55; e-mail info@s-p-a.be; internet www.s-p-a.be; f. 1885; fmrly Socialistische Partij; adopted current name in 2001; Chair. BRUNO TOBBACK.

Vlaams Belang (Flemish Interest): Madouplein 8, Postbus 9, 1210 Brussels; tel. (2) 219-60-09; fax (2) 219-50-47; e-mail info@vlaamsbelang.org; internet www.vlaamsbelang.org; f. 2004 as the successor to the Vlaams Blok (f. 1979), which had been forced to disband; advocates Flemish separatism and is anti-immigration; Chair. GEROLF ANNEMANS.

FRENCH-SPEAKING PARTIES

Centre Démocrate Humaniste (CDH) (Humanist Democrats): 41 rue des Deux-Eglises, 1000 Brussels; tel. (2) 238-01-11; fax (2) 238-01-29; e-mail info@lecdh.be; internet www.lecdh.be; f. 1945 as Parti Social Chrétien/Christelijke Volkspartij (PSC/CVP); PSC separated from CVP by 1972 and adopted current name in 2002; Pres. BENOÎT LUTGEN.

Démocratie Nationale (DN): 6 rue Emile Vandervelde, 1460 Virginal; tel. (487) 38-68-48; e-mail info@dnat.be; internet www.dnat.be; f. 1985; extreme right-wing nationalist party; fmrly Front National (FN); Pres. MARCO SANTI.

Ecolo (Ecologistes Confédérés pour l'Organisation des Luttes Originales): 52 ave de Marlagne, 5000 Namur; tel. (81) 22-78-71; fax (81) 23-06-03; e-mail info@ecolo.be; internet www.ecolo.be; f. 1980; ecologist; Co-Pres EMILY HOYOS, OLIVIER DELEUZE.

Fédéralistes Démocrates Francophones (FDF) (Francophone Federalist Democrats): 127 chaussée de Charleroi, 1060 Brussels; tel. (2) 538-83-20; fax (2) 539-36-50; e-mail fdf@fdf.be; internet www.fdf.be; f. 1964 as Front Démocratique des Francophones; adopted current name in Jan. 2010; aims to preserve the French character of Brussels; Pres. OLIVIER MAINGAIN.

Mouvement des Citoyens pour le Changement (MCC): 50 rue de la Vallée, 1000 Brussels; tel. (2) 642-29-99; fax (2) 642-29-90; e-mail info@lemcc.be; internet www.lemcc.be; part of Mouvement Réformateur; Pres. GÉRARD DEPREZ.

Mouvement Réformateur (MR) (Reformist Movement): 84–86 ave de la Toison d'Or, 1060 Brussels; tel. (2) 500-35-11; fax (2) 500-35-00; e-mail contact@mr.be; internet www.mr.be; f. 2002; asscn of three parties: Mouvement des Citoyens pour le Changement, Parti Réformateur Libéral and Partei für Freiheit und Fortschritt; Pres. CHARLES MICHEL; 5,900 mems.

Parti Réformateur Libéral (PRL) (Reformist Liberal Party): 84–86 ave de la Toison d'Or, 1060 Brussels; tel. (2) 500-35-11; fax (2) 500-35-00; f. 1846; part of Mouvement Réformateur.

Parti Socialiste (PS) (Socialist Party): Maison du PS, 13 blvd de l'Empereur, 1000 Brussels; tel. (2) 548-32-11; fax (2) 548-32-90; e-mail info@ps.be; internet www.ps.be; f. 1885 as the Parti Ouvrier Belge; split from the Socialistische Partij in 1978; Pres. PAUL MAGNETTE; Sec.-Gen. GILLES MAHIEU.

GERMAN-SPEAKING PARTIES

Christlich Soziale Partei (CSP) (Christian Social Party): Kaperberg 6, 4700 Eupen; tel. (87) 55-59-86; fax (87) 55-59-82; e-mail csp-fraktion@dgparlament.be; internet www.csp-dg.be; Pres. LUC FRANK.

Partei für Freiheit und Fortschritt (PFF): Kaperberg 6, 4700 Eupen; tel. (87) 55-59-88; fax (87) 55-59-83; e-mail info@pff.be; internet www.pff.be; German-speaking wing of the Parti Réformateur Libéral (see French-speaking Parties); part of Mouvement Réformateur; Pres. KATTRIN JADIN.

ProDG (Pro Deutsche Gemeinschaft) (Pro-German-speaking Community): Kaperberg 6, 4700 Eupen; tel. and fax (87) 55-59-87; e-mail info@prodg.be; internet www.prodg.be; f. 2008; comprises fmr members of Partei der Deutschsprachigen Belgier (PJU-PDB, f. 1971); promotes equality for the German-speaking minority; Chair. NORBERT SCHOLZEN; Parliamentary Leader ALFONS VELZ.

Sozialistische Partei (SP): Kaperberg 6, 4700 Eupen; tel. (87) 55-44-81; fax (87) 55-59-85; e-mail info@sp-dg.be; internet www.sp-dg.be; German-speaking section of the Parti Socialiste (see French-speaking Parties); Pres. ANTONIOS ANTONIADIS; Sec. BERNI SCHMITZ.

OTHER PARTIES

Partij van de Arbeid van België/Parti du Travail de Belgique (PvdA/PTB) (Workers' Party of Belgium): 171 blvd M. Lemonnier, BP 2, 1000 Brussels; tel. (2) 504-01-12; e-mail international@ptb.be; internet www.ptb.be; f. 1979; Marxist; publ. *Solidaire/Solidair* (weekly); Pres. PETER MERTENS.

Parti Populaire/Personenpartij (People's Party): 42 ave du Houx, 1170 Brussels; tel. (2) 672-62-32; fax (2) 672-53-74; e-mail info@partipopulaire.be; internet www.partipopulaire.be; f. 2009; advocates economic liberalism, administrative simplification and greater emphasis on justice and security; Pres. MISCHAËL MODRIKAMEN.

Vivant (Voor Individuele Vrijheid en Arbeid in een Nieuwe Toekomst): Transportstraat 1, 3980 Hasselt; tel. (11) 60-66-52; e-mail info@vivant.org; internet www.vivant.org; liberal; contested the 2007 legislative elections as part of Open Vld alliance; Chair. ROLAND DUCHÂTELET.

Diplomatic Representation

EMBASSIES IN BELGIUM

Afghanistan: 61 ave de Wolvendael, 1180 Uccle; tel. (2) 761-31-66; fax (2) 761-31-67; e-mail ambassade.afghanistan@skynet.be; Ambassador HUMAYUN TANDAR.

Albania: 11 ave des Scarabées, 1000 Brussels; tel. (2) 640-14-22; fax (2) 640-28-58; e-mail embassy.brussels@mfa.gov.al; Ambassador ILIR TEPELENA.

Algeria: 207 ave Molière, 1050 Brussels; tel. (2) 343-50-78; fax (2) 343-51-68; e-mail info@algerian-embassy.be; internet www.algerian-embassy.be; Ambassador AMAR BENDJAMA.

Andorra: 10 rue de la Montagne, 1000 Brussels; tel. (2) 513-28-06; fax (2) 513-07-41; Ambassador EVA DESCARREGA GARCIA.

Angola: 182 rue Franz Merjay, 1050 Brussels; tel. (2) 346-87-48; fax (2) 346-18-80; e-mail angola.embassy.belgium@skynet.be; Ambassador MARIA ELIZABETH A. SIMBRÃO DE CARVALHO.

Argentina: 225 ave Louise, 3e étage, 1050 Brussels; tel. (2) 647-78-12; fax (2) 647-93-19; e-mail info@embargentina.be; Ambassador JOSÉ MARÍA VÁZQUEZ OCAMPO.

Armenia: 28 rue Montoyer, 1000 Brussels; tel. (2) 348-44-00; fax (2) 348-44-01; e-mail armembel@skynet.be; internet www.armembassy.be; Ambassador AVET ADONTS.

Australia: 56 ave des Arts, 1000 Brussels; tel. (2) 286-05-00; fax (2) 286-05-76; e-mail austemb.brussels@dfat.gov.au; internet www.eu.mission.gov.au; Ambassador DUNCAN LEWIS.

Austria: 5 pl. du Champ de Mars, BP 5, 1050 Brussels; tel. (2) 289-07-00; fax (2) 513-66-41; e-mail bruessel-ob@bmeia.gv.at; internet www.bmeia.gv.at/botschaft/bruessel; Ambassador KARL SCHRAMEK.

Azerbaijan: 464 ave Molière, 1050 Brussels; tel. (2) 345-26-60; fax (2) 345-91-58; e-mail office@azembassy.be; internet www.azembassy.be; Ambassador FUAD ISKANDAROV.

Bahrain: 250 ave Louise, 1050 Brussels; tel. (2) 627-00-30; fax (2) 647-22-74; e-mail brussels.mission@mofa.gov.bh; Ambassador AHMED MUHAMMAD YOUSUF AL-DOSERI.

Bangladesh: 29–31 rue Jacques Jordaens, 1000 Brussels; tel. (2) 640-55-00; fax (2) 646-59-98; e-mail bdootbrussels@skynet.be; internet www.bangladeshembassy.be; Ambassador ISMAT JAHAN.

Barbados: 100 ave F. D. Roosevelt, 1050 Brussels; tel. (2) 732-17-37; fax (2) 732-32-66; e-mail brussels@foreign.gov.bb; Ambassador SAMUEL JEFFERSON CHANDLER.

Belarus: 192 ave Molière, 1050 Brussels; tel. (2) 340-02-70; fax (2) 340-02-87; e-mail belgium@mfa.gov.by; internet belgium.mfa.gov.by; Ambassador ANDREI YEUDACHENKA.

Belize: 136 blvd Brand Witlock, 1200 Brussels; tel. (2) 732-62-04; fax (2) 732-62-46; e-mail embelize@skynet.be; Ambassador DYLAN GREGORY VERNON.

Benin: 5 ave de l'Observatoire, 1180 Brussels; tel. (2) 374-91-92; fax (2) 375-83-26; e-mail ambabenin_benelux@yahoo.fr; Ambassador CHARLES BORROMÉE TODJINOU.

Bhutan: 70 ave Jules César, 1150 Brussels; tel. (2) 761-95-70; fax (2) 761-95-77; e-mail infobhutan@bhutanembassy.be; Ambassador SONAM TSHONG.

Bolivia: 176 ave Louise, 1050 Brussels; tel. (2) 627-00-10; fax (2) 647-47-82; Ambassador RENÉ ERNESTO FERNÁNDEZ REVOLLO.

Bosnia and Herzegovina: 22 rue de l'Industrie, 1040 Brussels; tel. (2) 502-01-88; fax (2) 644-32-54; e-mail info@bhembassy.be; internet www.bhembassy.be; Ambassador BISERA TURKOVIĆ.

Botswana: 169 ave de Tervueren, 1150 Brussels; tel. (2) 735-20-70; fax (2) 735-63-18; e-mail botswana@brutele.be; Ambassador SAMUEL OTSILE OUTLULE.

Brazil: 350 ave Louise, 6e étage, 1050 Brussels; tel. (2) 640-20-15; fax (2) 640-81-34; e-mail brasbruxelas@brasbruxelas.be; internet bruxelas.itamaraty.gov.br; Ambassador ANDRÉ MATTOSO MAIA AMADO.

Brunei: 238 ave F. D. Roosevelt, 1050 Brussels; tel. (2) 675-08-78; fax (2) 672-93-58; e-mail info@bruneiembassy.be; Ambassador Dato' Paduka SERBINI bin Haji ALI.

Bulgaria: 58 ave Hamoir, 1180 Brussels; tel. (2) 374-59-63; fax (2) 375-53-82; e-mail embassy@bulgaria.be; internet www.bulgaria.be; Ambassador VESSELIN PETROV VALKANOV.

Burkina Faso: 16 place Guy d'Arezzo, 1180 Brussels; tel. (2) 345-99-12; fax (2) 345-06-12; e-mail ambassade.burkina@skynet.be; internet www.ambassadeduburkina.be; Ambassador FRÉDÉRIC KORSAGA.

Burundi: 46 square Marie-Louise, 1000 Brussels; tel. (2) 230-45-35; fax (2) 230-78-83; e-mail ambassade.burundi@skynet.be; internet :www.ambaburundi.be; Ambassador FÉLIX NDAYISENGA.

Cambodia: 264A ave de Tervueren, 1150 Brussels; tel. (2) 772-03-72; fax (2) 772-89-99; e-mail amcambel@skynet.be; Ambassador HEM SAEM.

Cameroon: 131 ave Brugmann, 1190 Brussels; tel. (2) 345-18-70; fax (2) 344-57-35; e-mail embassy@cameroon.be; Ambassador DANIEL EVINA ABÉE.

Canada: 2 ave de Tervueren, 1040 Brussels; tel. (2) 741-06-11; fax (2) 741-06-43; e-mail bru@international.gc.ca; internet www.canadainternational.gc.ca/belgium-belgique; Ambassador DENIS ROBERT.

Cape Verde: 29 ave Jeanne, 1050 Brussels; tel. (2) 643-62-70; fax (2) 646-33-85; e-mail emb.caboverde@skynet.be; Ambassador MARIA DE JESUS VEIGA MIRANDA MASCARENHAS.

Central African Republic: 46 rue de la Fusée, 1130 Brussels; tel. (2) 242-28-80; fax (2) 705-56-02; e-mail ambassade.rca.be@hotmail.com; Chargé d'affaires a.i. ABEL SABONO.

Chad: 52 blvd Lambermont, 1030 Brussels; tel. (2) 215-19-75; fax (2) 216-35-26; e-mail contact@ambassadedutchad.be; Ambassador BEADRONE TOMBALBAYE.

Chile: 106 rue des Aduatiques, 1040 Brussels; tel. (2) 743-36-60; fax (2) 736-49-94; e-mail embachile@embachile.be; internet www.embachile.be; Ambassador CARLOS APPELGREN BALBONTÍN.

China, People's Republic: 443–445 ave de Tervueren, 1150 Brussels; tel. (2) 771-14-97; fax (2) 779-28-95; e-mail chinaemb_be@mfa.gov.cn; internet www.chinaembassy-org.be; Ambassador LIAO LIQIANG.

Colombia: 96A ave F. D. Roosevelt, 1050 Brussels; tel. (2) 649-56-79; fax (2) 646-54-91; e-mail embcolombia@emcolbru.org; Ambassador JOSÉ RODRIGO RIVERA SALAZAR.

Comoros: 64 rue de la Fusée, 1130 Brussels; tel. and fax (2) 779-58-38; e-mail ambacom.bxl@skynet.be; Ambassador SAID MDAHOMA ALI.

Congo, Democratic Republic: 30 rue Marie de Bourgogne, 1000 Brussels; tel. (2) 213-49-81; fax (2) 213-49-95; e-mail secretariat@ambardc.be; internet www.ambardc.be; Ambassador HENRI MOVA SAKANYI.

Congo, Republic: 5 rue du Congrès, 1000 Brussels; tel. (2) 648-38-56; fax (2) 646-22-20; e-mail contact@ambacobrazza.eu; internet www.ambacobrazza.eu; Ambassador ROGER JULIEN MENGA.

Costa Rica: 489 ave Louise, 1050 Brussels; tel. (2) 640-55-41; fax (2) 648-31-92; e-mail info@costaricaembassy.be; internet www.costaricaembassy.be; Ambassador FRANCISCO TOMÁS DUEÑAS LEIVA.

Côte d'Ivoire: 234 ave F. D. Roosevelt, 1050 Brussels; tel. (2) 672-23-57; fax (2) 672-04-91; e-mail mailbox@ambcibnl.be; internet www.ambacibnl.be; Ambassador JEAN VINCENT ZINSOU.

Croatia: 425 ave Louise, 1050 Brussels; tel. (2) 639-20-36; fax (2) 512-03-38; e-mail croemb.bruxelles@mvep.hr; internet be.mvp.hr; Ambassador MARIO NOBILO.

Cuba: 80 ave Brugmann, 1190 Brussels; tel. (2) 343-00-20; fax (2) 344-96-91; e-mail mision@embacuba.be; internet www.embacuba .be; Ambassador MIRTHA MARÍA HORMILLA CASTRO.

Cyprus: 61 ave de Cortenbergh, 1000 Brussels; tel. (2) 650-06-10; fax (2) 650-06-20; e-mail cyprusembassybe@mfa.gov.cy; internet www .mfa.gov.cy/embassybrussels; Ambassador ANTONIS GRIVAS.

Czech Republic: 154 ave Adolphe Buyl, 1050 Brussels; tel. (2) 641-89-30; fax (2) 641-89-31; e-mail brussels@embassy.mzv.cz; internet www.mzv.cz/brussels; Ambassador IVO ŠRÁMEK.

Denmark: 73 rue d'Arlon, 1040 Brussels; tel. (2) 233-09-00; fax (2) 233-09-32; e-mail bruamb@um.dk; internet belgien.um.dk; Ambassador POUL SKYTTE CHRISTOFFERSEN.

Djibouti: 204 ave F. D. Roosevelt, 1050 Brussels; tel. (2) 347-69-67; fax (2) 347-69-63; e-mail amb_djib@yahoo.fr; Ambassador BADRI ALI BOGOREH.

Dominican Republic: 130A ave Louise, 3e étage, 1050 Brussels; tel. (2) 346-49-35; fax (2) 346-51-52; e-mail embajadombxl@gmail.com; Ambassador ALEJANDRO GONZÁLEZ PONS.

Eastern Caribbean States (Dominica, Saint Christopher and Nevis, Saint Lucia, Saint Vincent and the Grenadines): 42 rue de Livourne, 1000 Brussels; tel. (2) 534-26-11; fax (2) 539-40-09; e-mail ecs.embassies@oecs.org; Ambassador SHIRLEY SKERRITT-ANDREW.

Ecuador: 363 ave Louise, 9e étage, 1050 Brussels; tel. (2) 644-30-50; fax (2) 644-28-13; e-mail amb.equateur@skynet.be; Ambassador PABLO VILLAGOMEZ REINEL.

Egypt: 19 ave de l'Uruguay, 1000 Brussels; tel. (2) 663-58-00; fax (2) 675-58-88; e-mail eg.sec.be@hotmail.com; Ambassador EHAB MOHAMED MUSTAFA FAWZY.

El Salvador: 171 ave de Tervueren, 1150 Brussels; tel. (2) 733-04-85; fax (2) 735-02-11; e-mail embajadabruselas@rree.gob.sv; Ambassador EDGAR HERNAN VARELA ALAS.

Equatorial Guinea: 6 pl. Guy Arezzo, 1180 Brussels; tel. (2) 346-25-09; fax (2) 346-33-09; Ambassador CARMELO NVONO NCA.

Eritrea: 15–17 ave Wolvendael, 1180 Brussels; tel. (2) 374-44-34; fax (2) 372-07-30; Ambassador (vacant).

Estonia: 11–13, rue Guimard, 1040 Brussels; tel. (2) 779-07-55; fax (2) 779-28-17; e-mail embassy.brussels@mfa.ee; internet www .estemb.be; Ambassador GERT ANTSU.

Ethiopia: 231 ave de Tervueren, 1150 Brussels; tel. (2) 771-32-94; fax (2) 771-49-14; e-mail etebru@brutele.be; Ambassador TESHOME TOGA CHANAKA.

Fiji: 92–94 square Eugène Plasky, 5e étage, 1030 Brussels; tel. (2) 736-90-50; fax (2) 736-14-58; e-mail info@fijiembassy.be; Ambassador PECELI VUNIWAQA VOCEA.

Finland: 80 ave de Cortenbergh, 1000 Brussels; tel. (2) 287-12-12; fax (2) 287-12-00; e-mail sanomat.bry@formin.fi; internet www .finlande.be; Ambassador PER-MIKAEL ENGBERG.

France: 65 rue Ducale, 1000 Brussels; tel. (2) 548-87-11; fax (2) 548-87-32; e-mail ambafr@ambafrance-be.org; internet www .ambafrance-be.org; Ambassador BERNARD VALERO.

Gabon: 112 ave Winston Churchill, 1180 Brussels; tel. (2) 340-62-10; fax (2) 346-46-69; e-mail ambassadedugabon@brutele.be; Ambassador FÉLICITÉ ONGOUORI NGOUBILI.

Gambia: 126 ave F. D. Roosevelt, 1050 Brussels; tel. (2) 640-10-49; fax (2) 646-32-77; e-mail info@gambiaembassy.be; internet www .gambiaembassy.be; Ambassador MAMOUR A. JAGNE.

Georgia: 62 ave de Tervueren, 1040 Brussels; tel. (2) 761-11-91; fax (2) 761-11-99; e-mail info@georgia-embassy.be; internet www .belgium.mfa.gov.ge; Ambassador NATALIE SABANADZE.

Germany: 8–14 rue Jacques de Lalaing, 1040 Brussels; tel. (2) 787-18-00; fax (2) 787-28-00; e-mail info@bruessel.diplo.de; internet www .bruessel.diplo.de; Ambassador Dr ECKART CUNTZ.

Ghana: 7 blvd Général Wahis, 1030 Brussels; tel. (2) 705-82-20; fax (2) 705-66-53; e-mail ghanaemb@chello.be; internet www .ghanaembassy.be; Ambassador MORGAN ADOKWEI BROWN.

Greece: 10 rue des Petits Carmes, 1000 Brussels; tel. (2) 545-55-00; fax (2) 545-55-85; e-mail ambagre@skynet.be; Ambassador CONSTANTIN CHALASTANIS.

Grenada: 183 ave Molière, 1050 Brussels; tel. (2) 223-73-03; fax (2) 223-73-09; e-mail office@embassyofgrenadabxl.net; Ambassador STEPHEN FLETCHER.

Guatemala: 185 ave Winston Churchill, 1180 Brussels; tel. (2) 345-90-58; fax (2) 344-64-99; e-mail guatemala@skynet.be; Ambassador JORGE SKINNER-KLEE ARENALES.

Guinea: 108 blvd Auguste Reyers, 1030 Brussels; tel. (2) 771-01-26; fax (2) 762-60-36; Ambassador OUSMANE SYLLA.

Guinea-Bissau: 70 ave F. D. Roosevelt, 1050 Brussels; tel. (2) 290-51-81; fax (2) 290-51-56; Ambassador ALFREDO LOPES CABRAL.

Guyana: 12 ave du Brésil, 1000 Brussels; tel. (2) 672-62-16; fax (2) 675-55-98; Ambassador PATRICK IGNASIUS GOMES.

Haiti: 139 chaussée de Charleroi, 1060 Brussels; tel. (2) 649-73-81; fax (2) 640-60-80; e-mail ambassade@amb-haiti.be; Ambassador JOSUÉ PIERRE-LOUIS.

Holy See: 9 ave des Franciscains, 1150 Brussels; tel. (2) 762-20-05; fax (2) 762-20-32; Apostolic Nuncio Most Rev. GIACINTO BERLOCO (Titular Archbishop of Fidenae).

Honduras: 3 ave des Gaulois, 5e étage, 1040 Brussels; tel. (2) 734-00-00; fax (2) 735-26-26; e-mail ambassade.honduras@chello.be; Ambassador ROBERTO FLORES BERMÚDEZ.

Hungary: 44 ave du Vert Chasseur, 1180 Brussels; tel. (2) 348-18-00; fax (2) 347-60-28; e-mail mission.bxl@mfa.gov.hu; internet www .mfa.gov.hu/emb/bxl; Ambassador TAMÁS IVÁN KOVÁCS.

Iceland: 11 rond point Robert Schuman, 1040 Brussels; tel. (2) 238-50-00; fax (2) 230-69-38; e-mail emb.brussels@mfa.is; internet www .iceland.org/be; Ambassador THORIR IBSEN.

India: 217 chaussée de Vleurgat, 1050 Brussels; tel. (2) 640-91-40; fax (2) 648-96-38; e-mail info@indembassy.be; internet www .indembassy.be; Ambassador MANJEEV SINGH PURI.

Indonesia: 38 blvd de la Woluwe, 1200 Brussels; tel. (2) 779-09-15; fax (2) 772-82-10; e-mail primebxl@skynet.be; internet www .embassyofindonesia.eu; Ambassador ARIF HAVAS OEGROSENO.

Iran: 15 ave F. D. Roosevelt, 1050 Brussels; tel. (2) 627-03-50; fax (2) 762-39-15; e-mail secretariat@iranembassy.be; internet brussels .mfa.gov.ir; Ambassador MAHMOUD BARIMANI.

Iraq: 115 ave F. D. Roosevelt, 1050 Brussels; tel. (2) 374-59-92; fax (2) 374-76-15; e-mail ambassade.irak@skynet.be; Ambassador MOHAMMED ABDULLAH AL-HUMAIMIDI.

Ireland: 180 chaussée d'Etterbeek, 5e étage, 1040 Brussels; tel. (2) 282-34-00; fax (2) 282-33-95; e-mail embassybrussels@dfa.ie; internet www.embassyofireland.be; Ambassador EAMONN MAC AODHA.

Israel: 40 ave de l'Observatoire, 1180 Brussels; tel. (2) 373-55-00; fax (2) 373-56-17; e-mail info@brussels.mfa.gov.il; internet brussels.mfa .gov.il; Ambassador YAACOV JACQUES REVAH.

Italy: 28 rue Emile Claus, 1050 Brussels; tel. (2) 643-38-50; fax (2) 648-54-85; e-mail ambbruxelles@esteri.it; internet www .ambbruxelles.esteri.it; Ambassador ROBERTO BETTARINI.

Jamaica: 77 ave Hansen-Soulie, 1040 Brussels; tel. (2) 230-11-70; fax (2) 234-69-69; e-mail emb.jam.brussels@skynet.be; internet www .jamaica-brussels.be; Ambassador VILMA MCNISH.

Japan: 5–6 square de Meeûs, 1000 Brussels; tel. (2) 513-23-40; fax (2) 513-15-56; e-mail info.embjapan@skynet.be; internet www.be .emb-japan.go.jp; Ambassador MITSUO SAKABA.

Jordan: 104 ave F. D. Roosevelt, 1050 Brussels; tel. (2) 640-77-55; fax (2) 640-27-96; e-mail jordan.embassy@skynet.be; internet www .jordanembassy.be; Ambassador Dr MONTASER OKLAH AL-ZOU'BI.

Kazakhstan: 30 ave Van Bever, 1180 Brussels; tel. (2) 373-38-90; fax (2) 374-50-91; e-mail kazakhstan.embassy@swing.be; internet www .kazakhstanembassy.be; Ambassador ALMAZ KHAMZAYEV.

Kenya: 208 ave Winston Churchill, 1180 Brussels; tel. (2) 340-10-40; fax (2) 340-10-50; e-mail info@kenyabrussels.com; internet www .kenyabrussels.com; Ambassador JOHNSON MWANGI WERU.

Korea, Republic: 175 chaussée de la Hulpe, 1170 Brussels; tel. (2) 662-57-77; fax (2) 675-52-21; e-mail eukorea@mofat.go.kr; internet bel.mofat.go.kr; Ambassador KIM CHANG-BEOM.

Kosovo: 38 ave Roger Vandendriessche, 1150 Brussels; tel. (2) 773-27-00; fax (2) 773-27-09; e-mail embassy.belgium@ks-gov.net; Ambassador MIMOZA AHMETAJ.

Kuwait: 43 ave F. D. Roosevelt, 1050 Brussels; tel. (2) 647-79-50; fax (2) 646-12-98; e-mail embassy.kwt@skynet.be; Ambassador DHARRAR ABDUL-RAZZAK RAZZOOQI.

Kyrgyzstan: 47 rue de l'Abbaye, 1050 Brussels; tel. (2) 640-18-68; fax (2) 640-01-31; e-mail kyrgyz.embassy@skynet.be; internet www .kyrgyz-embassy.be; Chargé d'affaires a.i. ASEIN ISAEV.

Laos: 19–21 ave de la Brabançonne, 1000 Brussels; tel. (2) 740-09-50; fax (2) 734-16-66; e-mail laoembassy@ambalao.be; internet www .ambalao.be; Ambassador MANOROM PHONSEYA.

Latvia: 23 ave des Arts, 1000 Brussels; tel. (2) 238-32-36; fax (2) 238-32-54; e-mail embassy.belgium@mfa.gov.lv; internet www.mfa.gov .lv/belgium; Ambassador LELDE LĪCE-LĪCĪTE.

Lebanon: 2 rue Guillaume Stocq, 1050 Brussels; tel. (2) 645-77-65; fax (2) 645-77-69; e-mail ambliban@yahoo.fr; internet www .libanbelux.blogspot.com; Ambassador RAMI MORTADA.

Lesotho: 45 blvd Général Wahis, 1030 Brussels; tel. (2) 705-39-76; fax (2) 705-67-79; e-mail lesothobrussels@hotmail.com; Ambassador MPEO MAHASE-MOILOA.

Liberia: 50 ave du Château, 1081 Brussels; tel. (2) 411-01-12; fax (2) 411-09-12; e-mail info@embassyofliberia.be; internet www.embassyofliberia.be; Ambassador JARJAR MASSAQUOR KAMARA.

Libya: 28 ave Victoria, 1000 Brussels; tel. (2) 647-37-37; fax (2) 640-90-76; e-mail libyan_bureau_br@yahoo.com; Sec. of the People's Bureau (vacant).

Liechtenstein: 1 pl. du Congrès, 1000 Brussels; tel. (2) 229-39-00; fax (2) 219-35-45; e-mail ambassade.liechtenstein@bru.llv.li; Ambassador KURT JÄGER.

Lithuania: 41–43 rue Belliard, 1040 Brussels; tel. (2) 401-98-95; fax (2) 401-98-98; e-mail amb.be@urm.lt; internet be.mfa.lt; Ambassador GEDIMINAS VARVUOLIS.

Luxembourg: 75 ave de Cortenbergh, 1000 Brussels; tel. (2) 737-57-00; fax (2) 737-57-10; e-mail bruxelles.amb@mae.etat.lu; internet bruxelles.mae.lu; Ambassador JEAN-JACQUES WELFRING.

Macedonia, former Yugoslav republic: 20 rue Vilain XIV, 1050 Brussels; tel. (2) 734-56-87; fax (2) 732-07-17; e-mail ambassade.mk@skynet.be; Ambassador LAZAR ELENOVSKI.

Madagascar: 276 ave de Tervueren, 1150 Brussels; tel. (2) 770-17-26; fax (2) 772-37-31; e-mail info@madagascar-embassy.eu; internet www.madagascar-embassy.eu; Chargé d'affaires a.i. IBRAHIM NORBERT RICHARD.

Malawi: 46 ave Hermann Debroux, 1160 Brussels; tel. (2) 231-09-80; fax (2) 231-10-66; e-mail embassy.malawi@skynet.be; internet www.embassymalawi.be; Ambassador BRAVE NDISALE.

Malaysia: 414A ave de Tervueren, 1150 Brussels; tel. (2) 776-03-40; fax (2) 762-50-49; e-mail malbrussels@kln.gov.my; Ambassador Dato' ZAINUDDIN YAHYA.

Maldives: 11 rond point Schuman, 1040 Brussels; tel. (2) 256-75-67; fax (2) 256-75-69; Chargé d'affaires a.i. MOHAMED ASIM.

Mali: 487 ave Molière, 1050 Brussels; tel. (2) 345-74-32; fax (2) 344-57-00; e-mail info@amba-mali.be; internet www.amba-mali.be; Ambassador SEKOUBA CISSE.

Malta: 25 rue Archimède, 5e étage, 1000 Brussels; tel. (2) 343-01-95; fax (2) 230-45-83; e-mail maltaembassy.brussels@gov.mt; internet www.mfa.gov.mt/belgium; Ambassador RAY AZZOPARDI.

Mauritania: 6 ave de la Colombie, 1000 Brussels; tel. (2) 672-47-47; fax (2) 672-20-51; e-mail info@amb-mauritania.be; Ambassador MARIEM AOUFFA.

Mauritius: 68 rue des Bollandistes, 1040 Brussels; tel. (2) 733-99-88; fax (2) 734-40-21; e-mail ambmaur@skynet.be; Ambassador JAGDISH DHARAMCHAND KOONJUL.

Mexico: 94 ave F. D. Roosevelt, 1050 Brussels; tel. (2) 629-07-77; fax (2) 644-08-19; e-mail embamex@embamex.eu; internet www.embamex.eu; Ambassador JUAN JOSÉ GÓMEZ CAMACHO.

Moldova: 57 ave F. D. Roosevelt, 1050 Brussels; tel. (2) 626-00-80; fax (2) 732-96-60; e-mail bruxelles@mfa.md; Ambassador MIHAI GRIBINCEA.

Monaco: 17 place Guy d'Arezzo, 1180 Brussels; tel. (2) 347-49-87; fax (2) 343-49-20; e-mail ambassade.monaco@skynet.be; Ambassador GILLES TONELLI.

Mongolia: 18 ave Besme, 1190 Brussels; tel. (2) 344-69-74; fax (2) 344-32-15; e-mail info@embassy-mongolia.be; internet www.embassy-mongolia.be; Ambassador KHISHIGDELGER DAVAADORJ.

Morocco: 29 blvd St-Michel, 1040 Brussels; tel. (2) 736-11-00; fax (2) 734-64-68; e-mail sifamabruxe@skynet.be; Ambassador SAMIR ADDAHRE.

Mozambique: 97 blvd St-Michel, 1040 Brussels; tel. (2) 736-25-64; fax (2) 732-06-64; e-mail maria_manuelalucas@yahoo.com; Ambassador ANA NEMBA UAIENE.

Myanmar: 9 blvd Général Wahis, 1030 Brussels; tel. (2) 701-93-81; fax (2) 705-50-48; Ambassador U PAW LWIN SEIN.

Namibia: 454 ave de Tervueren, 1150 Brussels; tel. (2) 771-14-10; fax (2) 771-96-89; e-mail info@namibiaembassy.be; internet www.namibiaembassy.be; Ambassador HANNO BURKHARD RUMPF.

Nepal: 210 ave Brugmann, 1050 Brussels; tel. (2) 346-26-58; fax (2) 344-13-61; e-mail embn@skynet.be; internet www.nepalembassy.be; Ambassador RAM MANI POKHAREL.

Netherlands: Kortenberglaan 4-10, 1040 Brussels; tel. (2) 679-17-11; fax (2) 679-17-75; e-mail bru@minbuza.nl; internet www.nederlandseambassade.be; Ambassador HENDRIK JAN JURRIAAN (HENNE) SCHUWER.

New Zealand: 9–31 ave des Nerviens, 7e étage, 1000 Brussels; tel. (2) 512-10-40; fax (2) 513-48-56; e-mail nzemb.brussels@skynet.be; internet www.nzembassy.com/belgium; Ambassador VANGELIS VITALIS.

Nicaragua: 55 ave de Wolvendael, 1180 Brussels; tel. (2) 375-65-00; fax (2) 375-71-88; e-mail embanic.bruselas@skynet.be; Ambassador MAURICIO LAUTARO SANDINO MONTES.

Niger: 78 ave F. D. Roosevelt, 1050 Brussels; tel. (2) 648-61-40; fax (2) 648-27-84; e-mail ambanigerbrux@skynet.be; Ambassador ADANI ILLO.

Nigeria: 288 ave de Tervueren, 1150 Brussels; tel. (2) 762-52-00; fax (2) 762-37-63; e-mail ambassador@nigeriabrussels.be; internet www.nigeriabrussels.be; Ambassador FELIX AWANBOR.

Norway: 17 rue Archimède, 1000 Brussels; tel. (2) 238-73-00; fax (2) 238-73-90; e-mail emb.brussels@mfa.no; internet www.norvege.be; Ambassador NIELS ENGELSCHIØN.

Oman: 236 ave F. D. Roosevelt, 1050 Brussels; tel. (2) 679-70-10; fax (2) 534-79-92; e-mail oman@omanembassy.be; Ambassador NUJEEM BIN SULAIMAN BIN NUJEEM AL-ABRI.

Pakistan: 57 ave Delleur, 1170 Brussels; tel. (2) 673-80-07; fax (2) 675-83-94; e-mail parepbrussels@skynet.be; internet www.embassyofpakistan.be; Ambassador MUNAWAR SAEED BHATTI.

Panama: 150 ave de la Foret, 1000 Brussels; tel. (2) 649-07-29; fax (2) 648-92-16; e-mail info@embpanamabxl.be; Ambassador ELENA BARLETTA DE NOTTEBOHM.

Papua New Guinea: 430 ave de Tervueren, 1150 Brussels; tel. (2) 779-06-09; fax (2) 772-70-88; e-mail kundu.brussels@skynet.be; Chargé d'affaires a.i. KAPI TAU MARO.

Paraguay: 475 ave Louise, BP 12, 1050 Brussels; tel. (2) 649-90-55; fax (2) 647-42-48; e-mail embapar@skynet.be; Chargé d'affaires a.i. MARIO FRANCISCO SANDOVAL FERNÁNDEZ.

Peru: 179 ave de Tervueren, 1150 Brussels; tel. (2) 733-33-19; fax (2) 733-48-19; e-mail info@embaperu.be; Ambassador CRISTINA RONQUILLO.

Philippines: 297 ave Moliere, 1050 Brussels; tel. (2) 340-33-77; fax (2) 345-64-25; e-mail brussels@philembassy.be; internet www.philembassy.be; Ambassador VICTORIA SISANTE BATACLAN.

Poland: 139 rue Stévin, 1000 Brussels; tel. (2) 780-45-00; fax (2) 736-18-81; e-mail bebruamb2@msz.gov.pl; internet bruksela.msz.gov.pl; Ambassador ARTUR HARAZIM.

Portugal: 12 ave de Cortenbergh, 1040 Brussels; tel. (2) 286-43-60; fax (2) 286-43-62; e-mail ambassade.portugal@skynet.be; Ambassador (vacant).

Qatar: 51 rue de la Vallée, 1000 Brussels; tel. (2) 643-47-30; fax (2) 223-11-66; e-mail info@qatarembassy.be; internet www.qatarembassy.be; Ambassador Sheikh ALI BIN JASSIM AL THANI.

Romania: 105 rue Gabrielle, 1180 Brussels; tel. (2) 345-26-80; fax (2) 346-23-45; e-mail secretariat@roumanieamb.be; internet bruxelles.mae.ro; Ambassador ŞTEFAN TINCA.

Russia: 66 ave de Fré, 1180 Brussels; tel. (2) 374-34-00; fax (2) 374-26-13; e-mail amrusbel@skynet.be; internet www.belgium.mid.ru; Ambassador ALEKSANDR A. ROMANOV.

Rwanda: 1 ave des Fleurs, 1150 Brussels; tel. (2) 761-94-20; fax (2) 763-07-53; e-mail secretariat@ambarwanda.be; internet www.ambarwanda.be; Ambassador ROBERT MASOZERA MUTANGUHA.

Samoa: 20 ave de l'Orée, BP 4, 1000 Brussels; tel. (2) 660-84-54; fax (2) 675-03-36; e-mail info@samoaembassy.be; internet www.samoaembassy.be; Ambassador FATUMANAVA PA'OLELEI LUTERU.

San Marino: 62 ave F. D. Roosevelt, 1050 Brussels; tel. (2) 644-22-24; fax (2) 644-20-57; e-mail ambrsm.bxl@scarlet.be; Ambassador GIAN NICOLA FILIPPI BALESTRA.

São Tomé and Príncipe: 175 ave de Tervueren, 1150 Brussels; tel. (2) 734-89-66; fax (2) 734-88-15; e-mail ambassade@saotomeeprincipe.be; Chargé d'affaires a.i. HORACIO DA FONSECA PURVIS.

Saudi Arabia: 45 ave F. D. Roosevelt, 1050 Brussels; tel. (2) 649-20-44; fax (2) 647-24-92; e-mail beemb@mofa.gov.sa; Ambassador ABD AL-RAHMAN BIN SULEIMAN AL-AHMAD.

Senegal: 196 ave F. D. Roosevelt, 1050 Brussels; tel. (2) 673-00-97; fax (2) 675-04-60; e-mail ambassadesenegal@skynet.be; internet www.ambassadesenegal.be; Ambassador AMADOU DIOP.

Serbia: 11 ave Emile de Mot, 1000 Brussels; tel. (2) 647-26-52; fax (2) 647-29-41; e-mail ambaserbie@skynet.be; Ambassador VESNA ARSIC.

Seychelles: 28 blvd Saint Michel, BP 23, 1040 Brussels; tel. (2) 733-60-55; fax (2) 732-60-22; e-mail brussels@seychellesgov.com; Ambassador VIVIANNE FOCK TAVE.

Sierra Leone: 410 ave de Tervueren, 1150 Brussels; tel. (2) 771-00-53; fax (2) 771-82-30; e-mail sierraleoneembassy@brutele.be; internet www.sierraleoneembassy.be; Ambassador IBRAHIM SORIE.

Singapore: 85 ave F. D. Roosevelt, 1050 Brussels; tel. (2) 660-29-79; fax (2) 660-86-85; e-mail singemb_bru@sgmfa.gov.sg; internet www.mfa.gov.sg/brussels; Ambassador ENG CHUAN ONG.

Slovakia: 195 ave Molière, 1050 Brussels; tel. (2) 340-14-60; fax (2) 340-14-64; e-mail emb.brussel@mzv.sk; internet www.mzv.sk/brusel; Ambassador JÁN KUDERJAVÝ.

Slovenia: 44 rue du Commerce, 1000 Brussels; tel. (2) 213-63-37; fax (2) 213-64-29; e-mail vbr@gov.si; internet www.bruselj.veleposlanistvo.si; Ambassador MATJAZ SINKOVEC.

Solomon Islands: 17 ave Edouard Lacomble, 1040 Brussels; tel. (2) 732-70-85; fax (2) 732-68-85; e-mail siembassy@skynet.be; Ambassador CORNELIUS WALEGEREA.

Somalia: 66 ave F. D. Roosevelt, 1050 Brussels; tel. (2) 646-64-88; fax (2) 649-28-88; e-mail somalrep@gmail.com; Ambassador ALI SAÏD FAQI.

South Africa: 17–19 rue Montoyer, 1040 Brussels; tel. (2) 285-44-00; fax (2) 285-78-03; e-mail embassy@southafrica.be; internet www.southafrica.be; Ambassador Dr MXOLISI NKOSI.

South Sudan: 30 blvd Brand Whitlock, 1200 Woluwe St Lambert; tel. (2) 280-23-55; fax (2) 280-31-44; e-mail info@goss-brussels.com; internet www.goss-brussels.com; Ambassador LUMUMBA MAKELELE NYAJOK.

Spain: 19 rue de la Science, 1040 Brussels; tel. (2) 230-03-40; fax (2) 230-93-80; e-mail emb.bruselas@maec.es; internet www.exteriores.gob.es/embajadas/bruselas; Ambassador IGNACIO MATELLANES MARTÍNEZ.

Sri Lanka: 27 rue Jules Lejeune, 1050 Brussels; tel. (2) 344-53-94; fax (2) 344-67-37; e-mail secretariat@srilankaembassy.be; internet www.srilankaembassy.be; Ambassador P. M. AMZA.

Sudan: 124 ave F. D. Roosevelt, 1050 Brussels; tel. (2) 647-94-94; fax (2) 648-34-99; e-mail sudanbx@yahoo.com; Ambassador ELTIGANI SALIH FIDAIL.

Suriname: 200 ave F. D. Roosevelt, 1000 Brussels; tel. (2) 640-11-72; fax (2) 646-39-62; e-mail sur.amb.bru@online.be; Ambassador WILFRED EDUARD CHRISTOPHER.

Swaziland: 188 ave Winston Churchill, 1180 Brussels; tel. (2) 347-47-71; fax (2) 347-46-23; e-mail brussels@swaziembassy.be; internet www.swaziembassy.be; Ambassador JOEL MUSA NHLEKO.

Switzerland: 26 rue de la Loi, BP 9, 1040 Brussels; tel. (2) 285-43-50; fax (2) 230-37-81; e-mail bru.vertretung@eda.admin.ch; internet www.eda.admin.ch/bruxelles; Ambassador BÉNÉDICT DE CERJAT.

Syria: 3 ave F. D. Roosevelt, 1050 Brussels; tel. (2) 648-01-35; fax (2) 646-40-18; e-mail ambsyrie@skynet.be; internet www.syrianembassy.be; Ambassador (vacant).

Tajikistan: 16 blvd Général Jacques, 1050 Brussels; tel. (2) 640-69-33; fax (2) 649-01-95; e-mail tajemb-belgium@skynet.be; internet www.taj-emb.be; Ambassador RUSTAMJON A. SOLIEV.

Tanzania: 72 ave F. D. Roosevelt, 1050 Brussels; tel. (2) 640-65-00; fax (2) 640-80-26; e-mail tanzania@skynet.be; internet www.tanzaniaembassy.be; Ambassador Dr DIODORUS KAMALA.

Thailand: 876 Chaussée de Waterloo, 1000 Brussels; tel. (2) 640-68-10; fax (2) 648-30-66; e-mail thaibxl@thaiembassy.be; internet www.thaiembassy.be; Ambassador NOPADOL GUNAVIBOOL.

Timor-Leste: 92–94 sq. Eugène Plasky, 1030 Brussels; tel. (2) 735-96-71; fax (2) 733-90-03; e-mail tlembassy.brussels@skynet.be; Ambassador NELSON SANTOS.

Togo: 264 ave de Tervueren, 1150 Brussels; tel. (2) 770-55-63; fax (2) 771-50-75; e-mail ambassadetogo@ambassadetogo.be; Ambassador FÉLIX KODJO SAGBO.

Trinidad and Tobago: 14 ave de la Faisanderie, 1150 Brussels; tel. (2) 762-94-00; fax (2) 772-27-83; e-mail info@embtrinbago.be; Ambassador MARGARET KING-ROUSSEAU.

Tunisia: 278 ave de Tervueren, 1150 Brussels; tel. (2) 771-73-95; fax (2) 771-94-33; e-mail amb.detunisie@brutele.be; Ambassador TAHAR CHERIF.

Turkey: 4 rue Montoyer, 1000 Brussels; tel. (2) 513-40-95; fax (2) 514-07-48; e-mail embassy.brussels@mfa.gov.tr; internet www.bruksel.be.mfa.gov.tr; Ambassador MEHMET HAKAN OLCAY.

Turkmenistan: 15 blvd Général Jacques, 1030 Brussels; tel. (2) 648-18-74; fax (2) 648-19-06; e-mail turkmenistan@skynet.be; Ambassador KAKADJAN MOMMADOV.

Tuvalu: 17 Ave Edouard Lacomble, 2e étage, 1040 Brussels; tel. (2) 742-10-67; fax (2) 742-28-69; Ambassador TINE LEUELU.

Uganda: 317 ave de Tervueren, 1150 Brussels; tel. (2) 762-58-25; fax (2) 763-04-38; e-mail contactugandaembassy@gmail.com; Ambassador MIRJAM BLAAK.

Ukraine: 30–32 ave Albert Lancaster, 1180 Brussels; tel. (2) 379-21-00; fax (2) 379-21-79; e-mail emb_be@mfa.gov.ua; internet www.ukraine.be; Ambassador Dr IHOR DOLHOV.

United Arab Emirates: 11 rue des Colonies, 1000 Brussels; tel. (2) 640-60-00; fax (2) 646-24-73; e-mail info@uaeembassy.be; internet www.uaeembassybrussels.be; Ambassador SULAIMAN HAMID SALEM AL-MAZROUI.

United Kingdom: 10 ave d'Auderghem, Oudergemselaan, 1040 Brussels; tel. (2) 287-62-11; fax (2) 287-63-55; e-mail info@britain.be; internet www.ukinbelgium.fco.gov.uk; Ambassador JONATHAN BRENTON.

USA: 27 blvd du Régent, 1000 Brussels; tel. (2) 811-40-00; fax (2) 811-45-00; internet belgium.usembassy.gov; Ambassador DENISE BAUER.

Uruguay: 22 ave F. D. Roosevelt, 1050 Brussels; tel. (2) 640-11-69; fax (2) 648-29-09; e-mail uruemb@skynet.be; Ambassador Dr RUBEN WALTER CANCELA VILANOVA.

Uzbekistan: 99 ave F. D. Roosevelt, 1050 Brussels; tel. (2) 672-88-44; fax (2) 672-39-46; e-mail embassy@uzbekistan.be; internet www.uzbekistan.be; Ambassador VLADIMIR NOROV.

Vanuatu: 380 ave de Tervueren, 1150 Brussels; tel. (2) 772-71-41; fax (2) 771-74-94; e-mail info@embassyvanuatu.net; Ambassador ROY MICKEY JOY.

Venezuela: 10 ave F. D. Roosevelt, 1050 Brussels; tel. (2) 639-03-40; fax (2) 647-88-20; e-mail embajada@venezuela-eu.org; internet www.venezuela-eu.gob.ve; Ambassador ANTONIO GUILLERMO GARCÍA DANGLADES.

Viet Nam: 1 blvd Général Jacques, 1050 Brussels; tel. (2) 379-27-37; fax (2) 374-93-76; e-mail vnemb.brussels@skynet.be; Ambassador PHAM SANH CHAU.

Yemen: 114 ave F. D. Roosevelt, 1050 Brussels; tel. (2) 646-52-90; fax (2) 646-29-11; e-mail yemen@skynet.be; Ambassador (vacant).

Zambia: 469 ave Molière, 1050 Brussels; tel. (2) 343-56-49; fax (2) 347-43-33; e-mail zambians_brussels@brutele.be; Ambassador GRACE M. MUTALE KABWE.

Zimbabwe: 11 sq. Joséphine Charlotte, 1200 Brussels; tel. (2) 762-58-08; fax (2) 762-96-05; e-mail zimbrussels@skynet.be; Ambassador MARGARET MUCHADA.

Judicial System

The independence of the judiciary is based on the constitutional division of power between the legislative, executive and judicial bodies, each of which acts independently. Judges are appointed by the Crown for life, and cannot be removed except by judicial sentence. The judiciary is organized on four levels, from the judicial canton to the district, regional and national courts. The lowest courts are those of the Justices of the Peace and the Police Tribunals. Each district has one of each type of district court, including the Tribunals of the First Instance, Tribunals of Commerce and Labour Tribunals, and there is a Court of Assizes in each province. There are civil and criminal Courts of Appeal and Labour Courts in five regional centres (Antwerp, Brussels, Ghent, Liège and Mons). The Constitutional Court (formerly the Court of Arbitration), which must comprise an equal number of Dutch- and French-speaking judges, ensures that legislation conforms to the Constitution and has jurisdiction in cases concerning the division of competencies between the different levels of the federal state. With the Court of Cassation, these are the highest courts in the country. The Military Court of Appeal is in Brussels.

Constitutional Court: 7 pl. Royale, 1000 Brussels; tel. (2) 500-12-11; internet www.const-court.be; Co-Pres ANDRÉ ALEN (Dutch-speaking group), JEAN SPREUTELS (French-speaking group).

Court of Cassation: Palais de Justice, 1 pl. Poelaert, 1000 Brussels; tel. (2) 508-62-74; fax (2) 508-69-53; internet www.cassonline.be; First Pres. JONKHEER ETIENNE GOETHALS; Pres. C. STORCK; Presidents of Chambers F. CLOSE, E. DIRIX, A. FETTWEISS, E. FORRIER, C. JEAN DE CODT; Attorney-General JEAN-FRANÇOIS LECLERCQ; First Advocate-General M. DE SWAEF.

CIVIL AND CRIMINAL COURTS OF APPEAL

Antwerp: Waalse Kaai 35A, 2000 Antwerp; tel. (3) 247-97-11; fax (3) 247-97-82; internet www.juridat.be/beroep/antwerpen; Pres. MICHEL ROZIE; Attorney-Gen. DIRK DE WAELE.

Brussels: Palais de Justice, 1 pl. Poelaert, 1000 Brussels; tel. (2) 508-65-91; fax (2) 508-64-50; internet www.juridat.be/beroep/brussel; First Pres. ANTOON BOYEN; Attorney-Gen. MARC DE LE COURT.

Ghent: Gerechtsgebouw, Koophandelspl. 23, 9000 Ghent; tel. (9) 267-41-11; fax (9) 267-41-03; internet www.juridat.be/beroep/gent; First Pres. HENRI DEBUCQUOY; Attorney-Gen. ANITA HARREWYN.

Liège: Palais de Justice, 16 pl. Saint Lambert, 4000 Liège; tel. (4) 232-56-16; fax (4) 232-56-30; internet www.juridat.be/appel/liege; First Pres. MICHEL JOACHIM; Attorney-Gen. CHRISTIAN DE VALKENEER.

Mons: 1 rue des Droits de l'Homme, 7000 Mons; tel. (65) 37-93-70; fax (65) 37-93-80; internet www.juridat.be/appel/mons; First Pres. JEAN-LOUIS FRANEAU; Attorney-Gen. CLAUDE MICHAUX.

LABOUR COURTS

Antwerp: Cockerillkaai 39, 2000 Antwerp; tel. (3) 247-99-15; fax (3) 247-99-81; internet www.juridat.be/arbeidshof/antwerpen; First Pres. LOLA BOEYKENS.

Brussels: 3 pl. Poelaert, 1000 Brussels; tel. (2) 508-61-27; fax (2) 519-81-48; internet www.juridat.be/arbeidshof/brussel; First Pres. BEATRIX CEULEMANS.

Ghent: Brabantdam 33B, 9000 Ghent; tel. (9) 266-02-11; fax (9) 266-02-32; First Pres. ROGER VAN GREMBERGEN.

Liège: 89 rue St Gilles, 4000 Liège; tel. (4) 232-85-50; fax (4) 223-04-13; First Pres. JOËL HUBIN.

Mons: 1 rue des Droits de l'Homme, 7000 Mons; tel. (65) 37-92-50; fax (65) 37-92-53; First Pres. DANIEL PLAS.

Religion

CHRISTIANITY

The Roman Catholic Church

Belgium comprises one archdiocese and seven dioceses. At 31 December 2006 adherents numbered some 7,389,919 (71.2% of the total population).

Bishops' Conference: Bisschoppenconferentie van België/Conférence Episcopale de Belgique, 1 rue Guimard, 1040 Brussels; tel. (2) 509-96-93; e-mail ce.belgica@interdio.be; f. 1965; Pres. Most Rev. ANDRÉ-JOSEPH LÉONARD (Archbishop of Mechelen-Brussels).

Archbishop of Mechelen-Brussels: Most Rev. ANDRÉ-JOSEPH LÉONARD, Aartsbisdom, Wollemarkt 15, 2800 Mechelen; tel. (15) 29-26-28; fax (15) 20-94-85; e-mail aartsbisdom@kerknet.be.

Protestant Churches

Church of England: Holy Trinity Pro-Cathedral, 29 rue Capitaine Crespel, 1050 Brussels; tel. (2) 511-71-83; fax (2) 511-10-28; e-mail admin@holytrinity.be; internet www.holytrinity.be; Senior Chaplain and Chancellor Canon Dr ROBERT INNES.

Eglise Protestante Unie de Belgique (EPUB): Brogniezstraat 44, 1070 Brussels; tel. (2) 511-44-71; fax (2) 510-61-74; e-mail synodevoorzitter@vpkb.be; internet www.vpkb.be; f. 1979; Pres. Rev. Dr STEVEN H. FUITE; 50,000 mems; publ. *Mosaïque* (monthly).

Evangelical Lutheran Church in Belgium: Tabakvest 59, 2000 Antwerp; tel. (2) 233-62-50; e-mail lutherse.kerk@skynet.be; internet users.skynet.be/lutherse.kerk; f. 1939; 160 mems (2010); Pres. Pastor GIJSBERTUS VAN HATTEM.

Mission Evangélique Belge: 158 blvd Lambermont, 1030 Brussels; tel. (2) 241-30-15; fax (2) 245-79-65; e-mail information@b-e-m.org; internet www.bez-meb.be; f. 1919; Dir WILFRIED GOOSSENS; c. 12,000 mems.

Union of Baptists in Belgium (UBB): Spermaliestraat 147, 8433 Middelkerke; tel. and fax (5) 932-46-10; e-mail samuel.verhaeghe1@telenet.be; f. 1922 as Union of Protestant Baptists in Belgium; mem. of the European Baptist Federation and the Baptist World Alliance; Gen. Sec. Rev. SAMUEL VERHAEGHE; c. 1,100 mems, 23 churches.

The Orthodox Church

There are about 70,000 Greek and Russian Orthodox believers in Belgium.

Archbishop of Belgium (Ecumenical Patriarchate of Constantinople): Metropolitan PANTELEIMON OF BELGIUM, 71 ave Charbolaan, 1030 Brussels; tel. (2) 736-52-78; fax (2) 735-32-64; e-mail eglise.orthodoxe@skynet.be; internet www.eglise-orthodoxe.be.

Archbishop of Brussels and Belgium (Moscow Patriarchate): Archbishop SIMON , 29 rue des Chevaliers, 1050 Brussels; tel. and fax (2) 513-33-74; e-mail info@archiepiskopia.be; internet www.archiepiskopia.be.

ISLAM

In 2007 there were more than 500,000 Muslims in Belgium, constituting about 5% of the total population.

Exécutif des Musulmans de Belgique/Executieve van de Moslims van België (EMB): 166–168 rue de Laaken, 1000 Brussels; tel. (2) 210-02-30; fax (2) 218-07-92; e-mail contact@embnet.be; internet www.embnet.be; f. 1999; promotes dialogue between the Muslim community and the Government; Pres. SEMSETTIN UGURLU; 17 mems.

JUDAISM

The Jewish population in Belgium was estimated at between 40,000 and 50,000 in 2007.

Consistoire Central Israélite de Belgique (Central Council of the Jewish Communities of Belgium): 2 rue Joseph Dupont, 1000 Brussels; tel. (2) 512-21-90; fax (2) 512-35-78; e-mail consis@online.be; internet www.jewishcom.be; f. 1808; central body representing the 17 Jewish communities in Belgium; Chair. Prof. JULIEN KLENER; Sec.-Gen. MICHEL LAUB.

The Press

Article 25 of the Belgian Constitution states: 'The press is free; no form of censorship may ever be instituted; no cautionary deposit may be demanded from writers, publishers or printers. When the author is known and is resident in Belgium, the publisher, printer or distributor may not be prosecuted.'

There is a trend towards concentration of ownership by a number of organizations, which control chains of publications, mostly divided along linguistic lines. The largest of those organizations are as follows:

Corelio NV: Gossetlaan 30, 1702 Groot-Bijgaarden; tel. (2) 467-22-11; internet www.corelio.be; f. 1914 as NV De Standaard; fmrly De Vlaamse Uitgeversmaatschappij (VUM), present name adopted 2006; owns 5 newspapers, incl. *De Standaard*, *Het Nieuwsblad* and *De Gentenaar*; 10 magazines and 3 radio stations; Chair. THOMAS LEYSEN; CEO LUC MISSORTEN.

Groupe Rossel: 100 rue Royale, 1000 Brussels; tel. (2) 225-55-99; fax (2) 225-59-02; e-mail micheline.demeurisse@viarossel.be; internet www.rossel.be; f. 1887; newspapers and magazines; French titles: *L'Echo*, *Le Soir* and Sud Presse newspapers; also publishes *GrenzEcho* and *De Tijd*; Pres. PATRICK HURBAIN; CEO BERNARD MARCHANT.

Roularta Media Group NV: Meiboomlaan 33, 8800 Roeselare; tel. (5) 126-61-11; fax (5) 126-68-66; e-mail info@roularta.be; internet www.roularta.be; f. 1954; magazines and regional newspapers; Chair. Baron HUGO VANDAMME; CEO RIK DE NOLF.

Sanoma: Stationsstraat 55, 2800 Mechelen; tel. (15) 67-80-00; fax (2) 776-23-99; e-mail info@sanoma.com; internet www.sanoma.be; f. 2002; periodicals; CEO HANS COOLS.

PRINCIPAL DAILIES

Antwerpen
(Antwerp)

Gazet van Antwerpen: Katwilgweg 2, 2050 Antwerp; tel. (3) 210-02-10; fax (3) 219-40-41; e-mail servicecenter@gazetvanantwerpen.be; internet www.gva.be; f. 1891; Christian Democrat; Editor JAN MULLEMAN (acting); circ. 119,005 (2011).

De Lloyd NV: Jan van Gentstraat 1, Postbus 102, 2000 Antwerp; tel. (3) 234-05-50; fax (3) 226-08-50; internet www.deltapublishing.be; f. 1858; owned by Delta Publishing NV; weekly; commerce, industry, logistics, transport (shipping, air, rail, road); Dir MICHEL SCHUURING; Editor-in-Chief PHILIPPE VAN DOOREN; circ. 5,600 (2012).

De Nieuwe Gazet: Brusselsesteenweg 347, 1730 Asse; tel. (3) 212-13-48; fax (3) 212-13-46; f. 1897; liberal; Chief Editor LUC VAN DER KELEN.

Arlon

L'Avenir du Luxembourg: 235 ave Général Patton, 6700 Arlon; tel. (63) 23-10-20; fax (63) 23-10-51; e-mail infoal@actu24.be; internet www.actu24.be; f. 1894; 100% owned by Corelio NV; Catholic; Editor-in-Chief DANIEL LAPRAILLE; circ. 103,924 (2011, with *Vers l'Avenir, Le Courrier de l'Escaut, Le Jour, Le Courrier*).

Bruxelles/Brussel
(Brussels)

La Capitale: 120 rue Royale, 1000 Brussels; tel. (2) 225-56-41; fax (2) 225-59-13; e-mail redaction.generale@sudpresse.be; internet www.lacapitale.be; f. 1944 as *La Lanterne*; present name adopted 2002; independent; owned by Sud Presse; Dir THIERRY DELHAYE; Editor-in-Chief KARIM FADOUL.

La Dernière Heure/Les Sports: 179 rue des Francs, 1000 Brussels; tel. (2) 211-28-49; fax (2) 211-28-70; e-mail dh.redaction@dh.be; internet www.dhnet.be; f. 1906; independent liberal; Dir FRANÇOIS LE HODEY; Chief Editor RALPH VANKRINKELVELDT; circ. 80,000 (2011).

L'Echo: 86C ave du Port, BP 309, 1000 Brussels; tel. (2) 423-16-11; e-mail info@lecho.be; internet www.lecho.be; f. 1881; economic and financial; Dir FREDERIK DELAPLACE; circ. 19,457 (2011).

Het Laatste Nieuws: Brusselsesteenweg 347, 1730 Asse-Kobbegem; tel. (2) 454-22-11; fax (2) 454-28-22; e-mail redactie.hln@persgroep.be; internet www.hln.be; f. 1888; Dutch; independent; Editor-in-Chief PAUL DAENEN; circ. 340,235 (2011, incl. *De Nieuwe Gazet*).

La Libre Belgique: 79 rue des Francs, 1040 Brussels; tel. (2) 744-44-44; fax (2) 211-28-32; e-mail llb.redaction@saipm.com; internet www.lalibre.be; f. 1884; independent; Editor-in-Chief VINCENT SLITS; circ. 52,473 (2011, with *La Libre Belgique—Gazette de Liège*).

De Morgen: Arduinkaai 29, 1000 Brussels; tel. (2) 556-68-11; fax (2) 520-35-15; e-mail info@demorgen.be; internet www.demorgen.be; Editor-in-Chief PETER MIJLEMANS; circ. 68,815 (2011).

Het Nieuwsblad: Gossetlaan 28, 1702 Groot-Bijgaarden; tel. (2) 467-22-50; fax (2) 466-30-93; e-mail nieuws@nieuwsblad.be; internet www.nieuwsblad.be; f. 1923; Dir PETER VANDEMEERSCH; Editor-in-Chief GUY FRANSEN; circ. 299,400 (2011, with *De Gentenaar*).

Le Soir: 100 rue Royale, 1000 Brussels; tel. (2) 225-54-32; fax (2) 225-59-10; e-mail journal@lesoir.be; internet www.lesoir.be; f. 1887; independent; Dir-Gen. BERNARD VAN MARCHANT; Editor-in-Chief DIDIER HAMANN; circ. 91,767 (2011).

De Standaard: Gossetlaan 28, 1702 Groot-Bijgaarden; tel. (2) 467-22-11; fax (2) 467-32-99; e-mail hoofdredactie@standaard.be; internet www.standaard.be; f. 1914; Editor-in-Chief BART STURTEWAGEN; circ. 108,828 (2011).

De Tijd: Havenlaan 86C, Postbus 309, 1000 Brussels; tel. (2) 423-16-11; e-mail persberichten@tijd.be; internet www.tijd.be; f. 1968; economic and financial; Editor-in-Chief ISABEL ALBERS; circ. 39,660 (2011).

Charleroi

La Nouvelle Gazette (Charleroi, La Louvière, Philippeville, Namur, Nivelles); La Province (Mons): 2 quai de Flandre, 6000 Charleroi; tel. (71) 27-89-79; fax (71) 66-74-27; e-mail redaction.generale@sudpresse.be; internet www.lanouvellegazette.be; f. 1878; owned by Sud Presse; Dir PHILIPPE MIEST; Editor-in-Chief MICHEL MARTEAU.

Vers L'Avenir Entre-Sambre et Meuse: 1 blvd du Centenaire, 5600 Philippeville; tel. (71) 66-23-40; fax (71) 66-23-49; e-mail philippeville@lavenir.net; internet www.actu24.be; f. 1900; Editor-in-Chief BRUNO MALTER.

Eupen

GrenzEcho: Marktpl. 8, 4700 Eupen; tel. (87) 59-13-22; fax (87) 55-34-57; e-mail redaktion@grenzecho.be; internet www.grenzecho.be; f. 1927; German; independent Catholic; Dir ALFRED KÜCHENBERG; Editor-in-Chief GERARD CREMER; circ. 13,581 (2011).

Gent
(Ghent)

De Gentenaar: Kouter 150, 9000 Ghent; tel. (9) 268-72-75; fax (9) 269-09-87; e-mail de.gentenaar@nieuwsblad.be; internet www.gentenaar.be; f. 1879; Editor-in-Chief GERT DE VOS.

Hasselt

Het Belang van Limburg: Herckenrodesingel 10, 3500 Hasselt; tel. (11) 87-81-11; fax (11) 87-89-06; e-mail hbvlsecretariaat@concentra.be; internet www.hbvl.be; f. 1879; Dir DOMINIC STAS; Editor-in-Chief IVO VANDEKERCKHOVE; circ. 112,861 (2011).

Liège

La Libre Belgique—Gazette de Liège: 26 blvd d'Avroy, 4000 Liège; tel. (4) 290-04-80; fax (4) 290-04-81; e-mail llb.gazettedeliege@saipm.com; internet www.lalibre.be; f. 1840; Editor-in-Chief VINCENT SLITS.

La Meuse: 38 blvd de la Sauvenière, 4000 Liège; tel. (4) 220-08-40; fax (4) 220-08-59; e-mail redliege.lameuse@sudpresse.be; internet www.lameuse.be; f. 1856; owned by Sud Presse; Dir THIERRY DELHAYE; Editor-in-Chief RODOLPHE MAGIS.

Mons

La Province: 29 rue des Capucins, 7000 Mons; tel. (65) 39-49-70; fax (65) 33-84-77; e-mail redaction.generale@sudpresse.be; internet www.laprovince.be; f. 1907; owned by Sud Presse; Dir PHILIPPE MIEST; Editor-in-Chief MICHEL MARTEAU.

Namur

Le Quotidien de Namur: 134 rue de Coquelet, 5010 Namur; tel. (81) 20-82-11; fax (81) 20-83-72; internet www.lequotidiendenamur.be; f. as *La Meuse Namur*; present name adopted 2002; owned by Sud Presse; Dir THIERRY DELHAYE; Editor-in-Chief CHRISTINE BOLINNE.

Vers l'Avenir Namur et Basse Sambre: 38 route de Hannut, 5000 Namur; tel. (81) 24-88-11; fax (81) 22-00-87; e-mail infonam@actu24.be; internet www.actu24.be; f. 1918; 100% owned by Médiabel; Editor-in-Chief JEAN-FRANÇOIS PACCO.

Tournai

Le Courrier de l'Escaut: 101 ave de Maire, 7500 Tournai; tel. (69) 88-96-20; fax (69) 88-96-60; e-mail infoce@actu24.be; internet www.actu24.be; f. 1829; 100% owned by Médiabel; Editor-in-Chief JEAN-PIERRE DE ROUCK.

Verviers

Le Jour: 87 ave de Spa, 4802 Heusy; tel. (87) 32-20-90; fax (87) 32-20-89; e-mail infolj@lavenir.net; internet www.actu24.be; f. 1894; 100% owned by Médiabel; Editor-in-Chief CLAUDE GILLET.

WEEKLIES

Atlas Weekblad: Condédreef 89, 8500 Kortrijk; tel. (56) 26-10-10; fax (56) 21-35-93; e-mail atlas@atlasweekblad.be; internet www.atlasweekblad.be; f. 1946; classified advertising, regional news and sports.

Boer en Tuinder: Diestsevest 40, 3000 Leuven; tel. (16) 28-60-01; fax (16) 28-60-09; internet www.boerenbond.be; f. 1891; agriculture and horticulture; Chair. PIET VANTHEMSCHE; circ. 20,619 (2010).

De Bond: Sylvain Van Der Guchtlaan 24, 9300 Aalst; tel. (53) 82-60-80; fax (53) 82-60-90; e-mail com@publicarto.be; internet www.publicarto.be; f. 1921; general interest; Dir SONIA VERMEIRE; circ. 279,919 (2011).

Brugsch Handelsblad: 20 Sint-Jorisstraat, 8000 Brugge; tel. (50) 44-21-59; fax (50) 44-21-66; e-mail redactie.bhblad@roularta.be; internet www.kw.be; f. 1906; local news; includes *De Krant van West-Vlaanderen* as a supplement; Dir EDDY BROUCKAERT; Editor-in-Chief JAN GHEYSEN; circ. 40,000.

Ciné Télé Revue: 101 ave Reine Marie-Henriette, 1190 Brussels; tel. (2) 345-99-68; fax (2) 343-12-72; e-mail redaction@cineterevue.be; internet www.cinetelerevue.be; f. 1944 as *Theatra Ciné Revue*; present name adopted 1984; TV listings, celebrity news, family issues; circ. 359,727 (2011).

Dag Allemaal: Brandekensweg 2, 2627 Schelle; tel. (3) 880-84-50; internet www.dagallemaal.be; Tue.; general, celebrity gossip; owned by Persgroep Publishing; Editor-in-Chief ILSE BEYERS; 486,462 (2011).

European Voice: International Press Centre, Résidence Palace, rue de la Loi 155, BP 6, 1040 Brussels; tel. (2) 540-90-90; fax (2) 540-90-71; e-mail info@europeanvoice.com; internet www.europeanvoice.com; f. 1995; Thur.; publ. by The Economist Newspaper Ltd (United Kingdom); EU policy-making, politics and business; Editor TIM KING; circ. 18,388 (2008).

Femmes d'Aujourd'hui: Stationsstraat 55, 2800 Mechelen; tel. (15) 67-87-24; e-mail info@femmesdaujourdhui.be; internet www.femmesdaujourdhui.be; f. 1933; French; women's interest; publ. by Sanoma; Editor-in-Chief ANOUK VAN GESTEL; circ. 126,998 (2011).

Flair: Uitbreidingstraat 82, 2600 Berchem; tel. (3) 290-13-92; e-mail flairsec@flair.be; internet www.flair.be; women's interest; publ. by Sanoma; Editor-in-Chief AN BROUCKMANS; circ. (2006) 166,622 (Dutch); 62,056 (French).

Humo: Harensesteenweg 226, 1800 Vilvoorde; tel. (2) 776-24-20; fax (2) 776-23-24; e-mail redactie@humo.be; internet www.humo.be; general weekly and TV and radio guide in Dutch; circ. 259,664 (2011).

Joepie: Brandekensweg 2, 2627 Schelle; tel. (3) 880-84-65; fax (3) 844-61-52; f. 1973; owned by Persgroep Publishing; teenagers' interest; Dir-Gen. KOEN CLEMENT; Chief Editor TINNE MARANT; circ. 82,976 (2011).

Kerk en Leven: Halewijnlaan 92, 2050 Antwerp; tel. (3) 210-08-31; fax (3) 210-08-36; e-mail redactie.kerkenleven@kerknet.be; internet www.kerknet.be; f. 1942; Catholic; 5 regional edns; Editor BERT CLAERHOUT; circ. 346,874 (2011).

Knack: Raketstraat 50, 1130 Brussels; tel. (2) 702-46-51; fax (2) 702-46-52; e-mail knack@knack.be; internet www.knack.be; f. 1971; news magazine; owned by Roularta Media Group; Editor-in-Chief JÖRGEN OOSTERWAAL; circ. 130,128 (2011).

Kortrijks Handelsblad: Doorniksewijk 83B, 8500 Kortrijk; tel. 495-50-71-35; fax (56) 27-00-12; e-mail luc.demiddele@gmail.com; regional news; owned by Roularta Media Group; includes *De Krant van West-Vlaanderen* as a supplement; Chief Editor LUC DEMIDDELE.

De Krant van West-Vlaanderen: Meiboomlaan 33, 8800 Roeselare; tel. (51) 26-66-44; fax (51) 26-65-87; e-mail jan.gheysen@kw.be; internet www.kw.be; regional news and sport; owned by Roularta Media Group; 11 different edns; included as a supplement with titles *De Weekbode*, *Het Wekelijks Nieuws*, *De Zeewacht*, *Brugsch Handelsblad*, *Kortrijks Handelsblad*; Dir EDDY BROUCKAERT; Editor-in-Chief JAN GHEYSEN; circ. 88,776 (2011).

Landbouwleven/Le Sillon Belge: 92 ave Léon Grosjean, 1140 Brussels; tel. (2) 730-34-00; fax (2) 730-33-24; e-mail info@landbouwleven.be; internet www.sillonbelge.be; f. 1952; agriculture; Editorial Man. ANDRÉ DE MOL; circ. 28,343 (2011).

Le Soir Magazine: 100 rue Royale, 1000 Brussels; tel. (2) 225-55-55; fax (2) 225-59-11; e-mail redaction@lesoirmagazine.com; internet soirmag.lesoir.be; f. 1928; independent; illustrated; Dir-Gen. DANIEL VAN WYLICK; Editor-in-Chief JÉRÉMIE DEMEYER; circ. 70,890 (2010).

Libelle: Uitbreidingstraat 82, 2600 Berchem; tel. (3) 290-14-42; fax (3) 290-14-44; e-mail libelle@libelle.be; internet www.libelle.be;

f. 1945; Dutch; women's interest; publ. by Sanoma; Dir CHRISTINE FESTJENS; Editor-in-Chief DITTE VAN DE VELDE; circ. 278,906 (2011).

Médias Catholiques Belges Francophones: Chaussée de Bruxelles 67/2, 1300 Wavre; tel. (10) 23-59-00; fax (10) 23-59-08; e-mail info@mcbf.be; internet www.mcbf.be; Catholic; current affairs; Gen. Man. LUC TIELEMANS.

Moustique: Stationsstraat 55, 2800 Mechelen; e-mail ensie.rojas@moustique.be; internet www.moustique.be; f. 1924; radio and TV; publ. by Sanoma; Dir AIMÉ VAN HECK; Editor JEAN-LUC CAMBIER; circ. 119,130 (2011).

Spirou: 52 rue Jules Destrée, 6001 Marcinelle; tel. (71) 60-05-00; fax (71) 60-05-99; e-mail spirou@dupuis.com; internet www.spirou.com; children's interest; publ. by Editions Dupuis SA; Editor-in-Chief FRÉDÉRIC NIFFLE; circ. 25,289 (2011).

Sport/Foot Magazine and Sport/Voetbal Magazine: 50 rue de la Fusée, BP 5, 1130 Brussels; tel. (2) 702-45-71; fax (2) 702-45-72; e-mail sportmagazine@roularta.be; internet www.sport.be/sportmagazine; f. 1980; Dutch and French; football; owned by Roularta Media Group; Editors-in-Chief JACQUES SYS, JOHN BAETE; circ. 61,000 (2013).

Story: Stationsstraat 55, 2800 Mechelen; tel. (15) 67-80-14; fax (15) 67-97-58; e-mail story@sanomamedia.be; internet www.storymagazine.be; f. 1975; Wed.; Dutch; women's interest; publ. by Sanoma; Dir AIMÉ VAN HECK; Editor-in-Chief THOMAS SIFFER; circ. 212,238 (2011).

De Streekkrant/De Weekkrant: Meiboomlaan 33, 8800 Roeselare; tel. (51) 26-61-11; fax (51) 26-68-66; e-mail streekkrant@roularta.be; internet www.streekkrant.be; f. 1949; local news; distributed free of charge; Propr Roularta Media Group; Editor JEAN-PIERRE VAN GIMST; circ. 2,551,981 (2011).

Télépro/Telepro: 50 rue de la Fusée, 1130 Brussels; tel. (87) 30-87-61; fax (87) 31-35-37; e-mail courrier@telepromagazine.be; internet www.telepro.be; f. 1954; TV listings; co-owned by Bayard Group and Roularta Media Group; Editor-in-Chief NADINE LEJAER; circ. 135,675 (2011).

TeVe-Blad: Stationsstraat 55, 2800 Mechelen; tel. (15) 67-80-14; fax (15) 67-97-58; e-mail story@sanomamedia.be; internet www.teveblad.be; f. 1981; Tue.; TV listings; Editor-in-Chief JAN VAN DE VLOEDT; circ. 155,693 (2011).

Trends/Trends Tendances: Brussels Media Centre, rue de la Fusée, 50, BP 4, 1130 Brussels; tel. (2) 702-48-00; fax (2) 702-48-02; e-mail trends@trends.be; internet www.trends.be; Dutch and French; economic analysis and business news; owned by Roularta Media Group; Editor-in-Chief JOHAN VAN OVERTVELDT; circ. 54,878 (2011).

Le Vif/L'Express: rue de la Fusée 50, BP 6, 1130 Brussels; tel. (2) 702-47-01; fax (2) 702-47-02; e-mail levif@levif.be; internet www.levif.be; f. 1971; current affairs; owned by Roularta Media Group; Dir-Gen. AMID FALJAOUI; Editor-in-Chief CHRISTINE LAURENT; circ. 82,330 (2011).

De Weekbode: Meiboomlaan 33, 8800 Roeselare; tel. (51) 26-61-11; fax (51) 26-65-87; regional news; owned by Roularta Media Group; includes *De Krant van West-Vlaanderen* as a supplement; Editor-in-Chief JAN GHEYSEN.

Het Wekelijks Nieuws Kust: Meiboomlaan 33, 8800 Roeselare; tel. (51) 26-62-60; fax (51) 26-65-87; e-mail sandra.rosseel@roularta.be; internet www.kw.be; Furnes, Dixmude and Belgian West Coast local news; owned by Roularta Media Group; includes *De Krant van West-Vlaanderen* as a supplement; Editor-in-Chief SANDRA ROSSEEL.

Het Wekelijks Nieuws West: Meiboomlaan 33, 8800 Roeselare; tel. (51) 26-65-55; fax (51) 26-55-87; e-mail matthias.vanderaspoilden@roularta.be; internet www.kw.be; local newspaper; Editor MATTHIAS VANDERASPOILDEN; circ. 56,000.

De Zeewacht: Meiboomlaan 33, 8800 Roeselare; tel. (51) 26-62-74; fax (51) 26-65-87; e-mail sandra.rosseel@kw.be; internet www.kw.be; Ostend local news; owned by Roularta Media Group; includes *De Krant van West-Vlaanderen* as a supplement.

Zondag Nieuws: Brandekensweg 2, 2627 Schelle; tel. (2) 220-22-11; fax (2) 217-98-46; f. 1958; general interest; circ. 48,101.

SELECTED OTHER PERIODICALS

axelle: 111 rue de la Poste, 1030 Brussels; tel. (2) 227-13-19; fax (2) 223-04-42; e-mail axelle@viefeminine.be; internet www.axellemag.be; f. 1917; 11 a year; feminist; circ. 9,209 (2013).

Bizzy: Onder den Toren 7, 2800 Mechelen; tel. (15) 21-08-01; fax (15) 21-81-31; e-mail info@bizzy.be; internet www.bizzy.be; monthly; lifestyle magazine; circ. 260,231 (2013).

Elle België: Leuvensesteenweg 431D, 1380 Lasne; tel. (2) 379-29-90; fax (2) 379-29-99; e-mail elle@ventures.be; internet www.elle.be; monthly; fashion; Editor-in-Chief NICA BROUCKE; circ. 36,968 (2013).

Feeling: Uitbreidingstraat 82, 2600 Berchem; tel. (3) 290-13-51; fax (3) 290-13-52; e-mail feeling@feeling.be; internet www.feeling.be; monthly; publ. by Sanoma; women's interest; Editor-in-Chief NATHALIE BALSING; circ. 101,636 (2013).

Femma: Urbain Britsierslaan 5, 1030 Brussels; tel. (2) 246-51-11; e-mail femma@femma.be; internet www.femma.be; f. 1920; fmrly called KAV; name changed to present 2012; women's interest; circ. 75,210 (2013).

Goed Gevoel: Brandekensweg 2, 2627 Schelle; tel. (3) 880-84-50; e-mail redactie@goedgevoel.be; internet www.goedgevoel.be; monthly; health, psychology; owned by Persgroep Publishing; Editor-in-Chief FEMKE ROBBERECHTS; circ. 111,040 (2013).

Goedele: Duboisstraat 50, 2060 Antwerp; tel. (3) 680-24-88; e-mail redactie@goedele.be; internet www.gdlmagazine.be; f. 2008; monthly; lifestyle, society; Editor-in-Chief DANNY ILEGEMS; circ. 84,684 (2010).

International Engineering News (IEN Europe): Hendrik Consciencestraat 1B, 2800 Mechelen; tel. (15) 45-86-00; fax (15) 45-86-10; e-mail p.bondi@tim-europe.com; internet www.ien.eu; f. 1975; 10 a year; English; Man. Dir ORHAN ERENBERK; Editor JÜRGEN WIRTZ; circ. 50,990.

Jet Magazine: Herckenrodesingel 10, 3500 Hasselt; tel. (11) 87-81-11; fax (11) 87-82-04; e-mail jetinfo@concentra.be; internet www.jetmagazine.be; fortnightly; distributed free of charge; general; circ. (2010) 401,595 (Antwerp), 364,025 (Limburg).

Marie Claire Belgique: Telecomlaan 5-7, 1831 Diegem; tel. (2) 776-22-11; fax (2) 776-23-30; e-mail marieclaire@sanoma-magazines.be; f. 1960; monthly; women's interest; Editor-in-Chief FABIENNE WILLAERT; circ. 33,316 (2013).

Le Moniteur de l'Automobile: 56 ave Général Dumonceau, 1190 Brussels; tel. (2) 333-32-11; fax (2) 333-32-61; e-mail info@produpress.be; internet www.moniteurautomobile.be; fortnightly; motoring; Editor-in-Chief XAVIER DAFFE; circ. 24,806 (2006).

Nest: 50 rue de la Fusée, BP 3, 1130 Brussels; tel. (2) 702-45-21; fax (2) 702-45-42; e-mail info@nest.be; internet www.nest.be; 8 a year; Dutch and French; lifestyle; owned by Roularta Media Group; Dir PHILIPPE BELPAIRE; Editor-in-Chief PETER VANDEWEERDT; circ. 171,543 (2013).

Plus Magazine: 50 rue de la Fusée, BP 10, 1130 Brussels; tel. (2) 702-49-01; fax (2) 702-46-02; e-mail redactie@plusmagazine.be; internet www.plusmagazine.be; monthly; Dutch and French; fmrly *Notre Temps / Onze Tijd*; aimed at people over 45 years of age; owned by Senior Publications N.V; Editor-in-Chief ANNE VANDERDONCKT; circ. 139,300 (2013).

Reader's Digest: 20 blvd Paepsem, 1070 Brussels; tel. (2) 526-81-11; fax (2) 526-81-12; e-mail service@readersdigest.be; internet www.readersdigest.be; f. 1947; monthly; general; Editor-in-Chief (vacant); circ. 29,147 (2013).

Vrouwen met Vaart: Remylaan 4B, 3018 Wijgmaal-Leuven; tel. (2) 624-39-99; fax (2) 624-39-09; e-mail kvlv@ons.be; internet www.kvlv.be; f. 1911; 10 a year; women's interest; Editor-in-Chief ANNEMIE MORRIS; circ. 102,152 (2013).

NEWS AGENCIES

Belga News Agency: 8B rue F. Pelletier, 1030 Brussels; tel. (2) 743-23-11; fax (2) 743-34-91; e-mail redaction@belga.be; internet www.belga.be; f. 1920; largely owned by daily newspapers; Man. Dir EGBERT HANS; Editor-in-Chief (vacant).

Agence Europe SA: 36 rue de la Gare, 1040 Brussels; tel. (2) 737-94-94; fax (2) 736-37-00; e-mail info@agenceurope.com; internet www.agenceurope.info; f. 1952; daily bulletin on EU activities; Editor-in-Chief LIONEL CHANGEUR.

PRESS ASSOCIATIONS

Association belge des Editeurs de Journaux/Belgische Vereniging van de Dagbladuitgevers: 22 blvd Paepsem, bte 7, 1070 Brussels; tel. (2) 558-97-60; fax (2) 558-97-68; f. 1964; 17 mems; Pres BRUNO DE CARTIER; Gen. Secs ALEX FORDYN (Dutch), MARGARET BORIBON (French).

Association des Journalistes professionnels/Algemene Vereniging van de Beroepsjournalisten (AGJPB/AVBB): 21 rue de la Senne, 1000 Brussels; tel. (2) 777-08-60; fax (2) 777-08-69; e-mail info@ajp.be; internet www.agjpb.be; f. 1978 by merger of the Association Générale de la Presse Belge and the Union Professionnelle de la Presse Belge; 4,899 mems; affiliated to International Federation of Journalists (IFJ); Nat. Secs MARTINE SIMONIS (AGJPB), POL DELTOUR (AVBB).

Association des Journalistes de la Presse Périodique/Vereniging van Journalisten van de Periodieke Pers: 54 rue Charles Martel, 1000 Brussels; tel. (2) 230-09-99; e-mail info@ajpp-vjpp.be; internet www.ajpp-vjpp.be; f. 1891; Pres. CLAUDE MUYLS.

The Ppress (Fédération de la Presse Périodique): 175 rue Bara, 1070 Brussels; tel. (2) 558-97-50; fax (2) 558-97-58; e-mail info@theppress.be; internet www.theppress.be; f. 1956; operates through 5 orgs:

B2B Press for professional publications; Custo for trade and industry magazines; OPPAb online professional publishers asscn; FEBELMAG (q.v.); and Free Press for free publications; Pres. HANS COOLS; 48 mem. orgs publishing more than 250 titles.

Fédération Belge des Magazines/Federatie van de Belgische Magazines (FEBELMAG): 175 rue Bara, 1070 Brussels; tel. (2) 558-97-50; fax (2) 558-97-58; e-mail info@theppress.be; internet www.theppress.be/febelmag; f. 1956 as Fédération Nationale des Hebdomadaires d'Information; present name adopted 1999; became part of Ppress in 2007; Pres. HANS COOLS; Dir-Gen. ALAIN LAMBRECHTS.

Principal Publishers

Acco CV: Blijde-Inkomststraat 22, 3000 Leuven; tel. (1) 662-80-00; fax (1) 662-80-01; e-mail uitgeverij@acco.be; internet www.acco.be; f. 1960; general reference, scientific books, periodicals; Gen. Man. HERMAN PEETERS.

Uitgeverij Altiora Averbode NV: Abdijstraat 1, Postbus 54, 3271 Averbode; tel. (1) 378-01-11; fax (1) 378-01-83; e-mail info@verbode.be; internet www.averbode.com; f. 1993; educational and children books; publishing dept of Uitgeverij Averbode; Int. Rights Man. JEAN-MARIE DELMOTTE.

Anthemis SA: Pl. Albert I, 9, 1300 Limal; tel. (10) 42-02-90; fax (10) 40-21-84; e-mail info@anthemis.be; internet www.anthemis.be; f. 2005; economics, law; Publrs ANNE ELOY, PATRICIA KEUNINGS.

Brepols Publishers NV: Begijnhof 67, 2300 Turnhout; tel. (1) 444-80-20; fax (1) 442-89-19; e-mail info@brepols.net; internet www.brepols.net; f. 1796; academic; Dir PAUL DE JONGH.

Bruylant SA: 39 rue des Minimes, 1000 Brussels; tel. (2) 548-07-11; fax (2) 513-90-09; e-mail projet@larciergroup.com; internet fr.bruylant.larciergroup.com; f. 1838; law; Pres. and Dir-Gen. JEAN VANDEVELD.

Editions Casterman SA: Cantersteen 47, Postbus 4, 1000 Brussels; tel. (2) 209-83-00; fax (2) 209-83-01; internet www.casterman.com; f. 1780; children's books (fiction, non-fiction, activity books), graphic books; subsidiary of Flammarion (France); Man. Dir (vacant).

Davidsfonds vzw: Blijde-Inkomststraat 79–81, 3000 Leuven; tel. (1) 631-06-00; fax (1) 631-06-08; e-mail info@davidsfonds.be; internet www.davidsfonds.be; f. 1875; general, reference, textbooks; Dir KATRIEN DE VREESE.

Groupe De Boeck SA: Belpairestraat 20, 2600 Berchem; tel. (3) 200-45-00; fax (3) 200-45-99; e-mail informatie@deboeck.com; internet www.deboeck.com; f. 1795; 100% stake acquired by Ergon Capital in 2011; French imprints: De Boeck Education, De Boeck Université, Duculot, Estem, Larcier; Dutch imprints: Uitgeverij De Boeck, Uitgeverij Larcier; educational, scientific, academic, medical, legal; Chair. ALAIN KOUCK; Man. Dir GEORGES HOYOS.

Editions Dupuis SA: 52 rue Jules Destrée, 6001 Marcinelle; tel. (7) 160-50-00; fax (7) 160-05-99; e-mail dupuis@dupuis.be; internet www.dupuis.com; f. 1938; children's fiction, periodicals and comic books for children and adults, multimedia and audiovisual; Dir-Gen. DIMITRI-NOËL KENNES.

Editions Erasme SA: 2 place Baudouin 1er, 5004 Bouge; tel. and fax (8) 120-86-80; e-mail info@editionserasme.be; internet www.editionserasme.be; f. 1945; school books; Dir BENOÎT DUBOIS.

Uitgeverij EPO: Lange Pastoorstraat 25–27, 2600 Berchem; tel. (3) 239-68-74; fax (3) 218-46-04; e-mail uitgeverij@epo.be; internet www.epo.be; history, literature, travel, politics and social sciences; Dir MARTINE UYTTERHOEVEN; Publr JOS HENNES.

Glénat Bénélux: 21 ave Georges Benoidt, 1170 Brussels; tel. (1) 41-46-11-11; fax 41-46-11-00; internet www.glenat.com; f. 1985; owned by Glénat France; comics, magazines, books; CEO JACQUES GLÉNAT.

Editions Hemma SA: 106 rue Chevron, 4987 Chevron; tel. (86) 43-01-01; fax (86) 43-36-40; e-mail info@hemma.be; internet www.hemma.be; f. 1953; juveniles, educational books and materials; Dir GÉRALD DEWIT.

Houtekiet NV: Katwilgweg 2, 2000 Antwerp; tel. (3) 210-30-50; fax (3) 238-80-41; e-mail info@linkeroeveruitgevers.be; internet www.houtekiet.com; f. 1983; subsidiary of Linkeroever Uitgevers nv; Publr LEO DE HAES.

Intersentia NV: Groenstraat 31, 2640 Mortsel; tel. (3) 680-15-50; fax (3) 658-71-21; e-mail mail@intersentia.be; internet www.intersentia.com; Publrs KRIS MOEREMANS, HANS KLUWER, EWOUT LACROIX.

Die Keure NV: Kleine Pathoekeweg 3, 8000 Brugge; tel. (50) 47-12-72; fax (50) 34-37-68; e-mail info@diekeure.be; internet www.diekeure.be; f. 1948; textbooks, law, political and social sciences; Dirs B. VANDENBUSSCHE (secondary schools), NIC PAPPIJN (primary schools).

Uitgeverij De Klaproos: Ezelstraat 79, 8000 Brugge; tel. (5) 034-97-59; e-mail info@klaproos.be; internet www.klaproos.be; f. 1992; historical works; Dir SIEGFRIED DEBAEKE.

Kluwer: Ragheno Business Park, Motstraat 30, 2800 Mechelen; tel. (15) 36-10-00; fax (15) 36-11-91; e-mail info@kluwer.be; internet www.kluwer.be; law, business, scientific; subsidiary of Wolters Kluwer NV (Netherlands); CEO HANS SUIJKERBUIJK.

Lannoo Publishing Group: Kasteelstraat 97, 8700 Tielt; tel. (51) 42-42-11; fax (51) 40-11-52; e-mail lannoo@lannoo.be; internet www.lannoo.com; f. 1909; general, reference; Man. Dir MATTHIAS LANNOO.

Linkeroever Uitgevers: Katwilgweg 2, 2050 Antwerp; tel. (3) 210-30-50; e-mail info@linkeroeveruitgevers.be; internet www.linkeroeveruitgevers.be; f. 2009.

Editions du Lombard SA: 7 ave Paul-Henri Spaak, 1060 Brussels; tel. (2) 526-68-11; fax (2) 520-44-05; e-mail info@lombard.be; internet www.lelombard.be; f. 1946; graphic novels, comics; Gen. Man. FRANÇOIS PERNOT.

Manteau: Mechelsesteenweg 203, 2018 Antwerp; tel. (3) 285-72-00; fax (3) 285-72-99; e-mail info@wpg.be; internet www.wpg.be; f. 1932; literature; imprint of WPG Uitgevers NV; Dir PETER QUAGHEBEUR.

Mercatorfonds: Zuidstraat 2, 1000 Brussel; tel. (2) 548-25-35; fax (2) 502-16-28; e-mail kunstboeken@mercatorfonds.be; internet www.mercatorfonds.be; f. 1965; art, ethnography, literature, music, geography and history; Dir BERNARD STEVAERT.

Peeters: Bondgenotenlaan 153, 3000 Leuven; tel. (1) 623-51-70; fax (1) 622-85-00; e-mail peeters@peeters-leuven.be; internet www.peeters-leuven.be; f. 1857; academic; Dir P. PEETERS.

Uitgeverij Pelckmans NV: Brasschaatsteenweg 308, 2950 Kalmthout; tel. (3) 660-27-20; fax (3) 660-27-01; e-mail uitgeverij@pelckmans.be; internet www.pelckmans.be; f. 1892 as De Nederlandsche Boekhandel; present name adopted 1988; school books, scientific, general; Publr THOM PELCKMANS.

Plantyn NV: Motstraat 32, 2800 Mechelen; tel. (15) 36-36-36; fax (15) 36-36-37; e-mail klantendienst@plantyn.com; internet www.plantyn.com; f. 1959; education; Dir DRIES VANHOVE.

Editions Racine: Tour & Taxis, Entrepôt Royal, 86C ave du Port, 1000 Brussels; tel. (2) 646-44-44; fax (2) 646-55-70; e-mail info@racine.be; internet www.racine.be; f. 1993; literature, art, history; Dir MICHÈLE POSKIN.

Roularta Books: Meiboomlaan 33, 8800 Roeselare; tel. (5) 126-61-11; fax (5) 126-68-66; e-mail info@roularta.be; internet www.roularta.be; f. 1988; owned by Roularta Media Group; Publr JAN INGELBEEN.

Sanoma: Stationsstraat 55, 2800 Mechelen; tel. (15) 67-80-00; fax (2) 776-23-99; e-mail info@sanoma.be; internet www.sanoma.be; f. 2002; periodicals; CEO HANS COOLS.

Editions Versant Sud: 20 blvd Général Jacques, 1050 Brussels; tel. (2) 646-08-90; fax (2) 646-21-68; e-mail info@versant-sud.com; internet www.versant-sud.com; f. 2001; independent; history, music, tourism, comics; Editor ELISABETH JONGEN.

WPG Uitgevers Belgie NV: Mechelsesteenweg 203, 2018 Antwerp; tel. (3) 285-72-00; fax (3) 285-72-99; e-mail info@wpg.be; internet www.wpg.be; f. 1924; general, fiction, non-fiction, comics and professional literature; Dirs PETER QUAGHEBEUR, ERWIN PROVOOST, JOHAN VAN HULLE.

Yoyo Books: Hagelberg 33, 2250 Olen; tel. (1) 428-23-40; fax (1) 428-23-49; e-mail jo.dupre@yoyo-books.com; internet www.yoyo-books.com; imprints: Yoyo, Allegrio; educational, cookery; Man. Dir JO DUPRÉ.

PUBLISHERS' ASSOCIATIONS

Association des Editeurs Belges (ADEB): 34 ave Huart Hamoir, 1030 Brussels; tel. (2) 241-65-80; fax (2) 216-71-31; e-mail adeb@adeb.be; internet www.adeb.be; f. 1922; asscn of French-language book publrs; Dir BERNARD GÉRARD.

Vlaamse Uitgevers Vereniging (VUV): Te Boelaerlei 37, 2140 Borgerhout; tel. (3) 287-66-92; fax (3) 281-22-40; e-mail geert.vandenbossche@boek.be; internet www.boekenvak.be; asscn of Flemish-language book publrs; Dir GEERT VAN DEN BOSSCHE.

Broadcasting and Communications

TELECOMMUNICATIONS

Belgacom: 27B blvd du Roi Albert II, 1030 Brussels; tel. (2) 202-41-11; fax (2) 203-65-93; e-mail about@belgacom.be; internet www.belgacom.be; f. 1992; total service operator; Chair. STEFAAN DE CLERCK; CEO DOMINIQUE LEROY.

Belgacom Mobile SA (Proximus): 27B blvd du Roi Albert II, 1030 Brussels; tel. (2) 205-40-00; fax (2) 205-40-40; internet www.proximus.be; wholly owned subsidiary of Belgacom; mobile cellular telephone operator; Chair. ETIENNE SCHOUPPE.

BT Ltd (Belgium): Telecomlaan 9, 1831 Diegem; tel. (2) 700-22-11; fax (2) 700-32-11; e-mail info.belgium@bt.com; internet www.bt.be; subsidiary of BT Group PLC (UK); Group Chair. Sir MICHAEL RAKE.

KPN Group Belgium SA/NV: 105 rue Neerveld, 1200 Brussels; tel. (486) 19-99-99; fax (484) 00-62-01; e-mail help@base.be; internet www.base.be; fmrly BASE SA/NV; present name adopted in 2009; mobile cellular telephone operator; subsidiary of Koninklijke KPN NV (Netherlands); CEO ERIC HAGEMAN.

Mobistar: 3 ave du Bourgetlaan, 1140 Brussels; tel. (2) 745-71-11; fax (2) 745-70-00; internet www.mobistar.be; f. 1995; mobile cellular telephone and fixed-line operator; owned by Orange SA (France); CEO JEAN MARC HARION; 3.5m. customers (Sept. 2011).

Numericable: 26 rue des Deux Eglises, 1000 Brussels; tel. (2) 226-52-00; fax (2) 226-54-10; e-mail business-solutions@coditel.be; internet www.coditel.be; fmrly Coditel SA; acquired by Apax (France), Deficom Telecom and Altice (France) in 2011; main cable operator in the Brussels Region; Dir-Gen. PASCAL DORMAL.

Scarlet SA: Belgicastraat 5, 1930 Zaventem; tel. (2) 275-27-27; internet www.scarlet.be; f. 1997; offers fixed-line telephone and broadband internet services; acquired by Belgacom in 2008.

Telenet NV: Liersesteenweg 4, 2800 Mechelen; tel. (15) 33-30-00; fax (15) 33-39-99; internet www.telenet.be; f. 1996; total service operator; acquired UPC Belgium 2007; CEO JOHN PORTER.

Verizon Belgium Luxembourg NV: Culliganlaan 2E, 1831 Diegem; tel. (2) 400-80-00; fax (2) 400-84-00; e-mail info@be.verizonbusiness.com; internet www.verizonbusiness.com/be; subsidiary of Verizon Communications (USA); Group CEO LOWELL MCADAM.

Voo: 25 rue Louvrex, 4000 Liège; internet www.voo.be; f. 2006 by merger of ALE-Télédis and Brutélé; owned by TECTEO; digital television, fixed-line telephone and broadband internet service provider; provides services to Brussels-Capital and Walloon Regions.

Regulatory Authority

Institut Belge des Services Postaux et des Télécommunications/Belgisch Instituut voor Postdiensten en Telecommunicatie (Belgian Institute for Postal Services and Telecommunications—IBPT/BIPT): 35 Blvd du Rol Albert II, 1030 Brussels; tel. (2) 226-88-88; fax (2) 226-88-77; e-mail info@ibpt.be; internet www.ibpt.be; ensures regulatory frameworks are observed, consumer rights are protected and certain tasks of public interest are carried out; Chair. LUC HINDRYCKX.

PUBLIC BROADCASTING ORGANIZATIONS

Flemish Community

TV Brussel: Flageygebouw, Belvédèrestraat 27A, Postbus 1, 1050 Elsene; tel. (2) 702-87-30; fax (2) 702-87-41; e-mail nieuws@tvbrussel.be; internet www.tvbrussel.be; f. 1993; broadcasts news and Dutch-language programmes in Brussels-Capital and Flanders Regions; funded by the Flemish Community; Editor-in-Chief ROBERT ESSELINCKX.

Vlaamse Radio- en Televisieomroep NV (VRT): Auguste Reyerslaan 52, 1043 Brussels; tel. (2) 741-31-11; fax (2) 734-93-51; e-mail info@vrt.be; internet www.vrt.be; f. 1998; shares held by Flemish Community; operates 7 radio stations (Radio 1, Radio 2, Klara, Donna, MNM, Radio Brussel and RVi) and 3 television stations (Eén, Canvas and Ketnet); Chair. LUC VAN DEN BRANDE; Man. Dir SANDRA DE PRETER.

French Community

Radio-Télévision Belge de la Communauté Française (RTBF): 52 blvd Auguste Reyers, 1044 Brussels; tel. (2) 737-21-11; fax (2) 737-25-56; internet www.rtbf.be; operates 6 radio stations (La Première, VivaCité, Musiq'3, Classic 21, Pure FM and RTBF International) and 3 television stations (La Une, La Deux and RTBF Sat); Dir-Gen. JEAN-PAUL PHILIPPOT; Dir of Radio FRANCIS GOFFIN; Dir of Television FRANÇOIS TRON.

Télé Bruxelles: 32 rue Gabrielle Petit, 1080 Brussels; tel. (2) 421-21-21; fax (2) 421-21-22; e-mail contact@telebruxelles.be; internet www.telebruxelles.net; f. 1985; broadcasts programmes in French to Brussels-Capital and Walloon Regions; funded mainly by the French Community; Dir-Gen. MARC DE HAAN.

German-speaking Community

Belgisches Rundfunk- und Fernsehzentrum der Deutschsprachigen Gemeinschaft (BRF): Kehrweg 11, 4700 Eupen; tel. (87) 59-11-11; fax (87) 59-11-99; e-mail info@brf.be; internet www.brf.be; operates 3 radio stations (BRF1, BRF2 and BRF-DLF) and 1 television station (BRF TV); Dir TONI WIMMER.

COMMERCIAL, CABLE AND PRIVATE BROADCASTING

PRIME: Liersesteenweg 4, 2800 Mechelen; tel. (2) 716-53-53; fax (2) 716-54-54; e-mail service@prime.be; internet www.prime.be; f. 1989; operated by Telenet NV; broadcasts in Dutch.

Regionale TV Media: Z.1 Research Park 120, 1731 Zellik; tel. (2) 467-58-77; fax (2) 467-56-54; e-mail contact@rtvm.be; internet www.rtvm.be; group of 11 regional news broadcasters within Flanders; commercial; Dir FRÉDÉRIC DEVOS.

RTL TVI: 2 ave Jacques Georgin, 1030 Brussels; tel. (2) 337-68-11; fax (2) 337-68-12; internet www.rtltvi.be; owned by RTL Group, Luxembourg; commercial station; broadcasts in French; Chief Exec. PHILIPPE DELUSINNE.

Medialaan: Medialaan 1, 1800 Vilvoorde; tel. (2) 255-32-11; fax (2) 252-37-87; e-mail info@vtm.be; internet www.vtm.be; f. 1987; commercial; broadcasts in Dutch; CEO PETER BOSSAERT.

Finance

(cap. = capital; res = reserves; dep. = deposits; m. = million; brs = branches; amounts in euros, unless otherwise indicated)

BANKING

L'Autorité des Services et Marchés Financiers (The Financial Services and Markets Authority): 12–14 rue du Congrès, 1000 Brussels; tel. (2) 220-52-11; fax (2) 220-52-75; internet www.fsma.be; f. 2004 by merger; fmrly known as Commission bancaire, financière et des assurances; name changed to present in 2011; supervisory body for the financial sector; Chair., Management Bd JEAN-PAUL SERVAIS; Sec.-Gen. ALBERT NIESTEN.

Central Bank

Banque Nationale de Belgique (National Bank of Belgium): 14 blvd de Berlaimont, 1000 Brussels; tel. (2) 221-21-11; fax (2) 221-31-00; e-mail info@nbb.be; internet www.nbb.be; f. 1850; bank of issue; cap. 10m., res 2,661.8m., dep. 15,376.6m. (Dec. 2009); Gov. LUC COENE; 2 brs.

Major Commercial Banks

ABN AMRO Bank NV: Kanselarijstraat 17A, 1000 Brussels; tel. (2) 229-58-00; fax (2) 229-59-10; e-mail info@abnamro.be; internet www.abnamro.be; f. 1824; acquired by Fortis Bank (Netherlands), Banco Santander Centro Hispano (Spain), Royal Bank of Scotland PLC (UK) in 2007; Netherlands Govt acquired Dutch operations of Fortis Bank, incl. stake in ABN AMRO in 2008; Chair., Management Bd GERRIT ZALM; Chair., Supervisory Bd HESSEL LINDENBERGH; 7 brs.

Antwerpse Diamantbank NV/Banque Diamantaire Anversoise SA/Antwerp Diamond Bank NV: Pelikaanstraat 54, 2018 Antwerp; tel. (3) 204-72-04; fax (3) 233-90-95; e-mail jmampaey@adia.be; internet www.antwerpdiamondbank.com; f. 1934; owned by KBC Bank NV; cap. 34.4m., res 119.8m., total assets 1,817.6m. (Dec. 2012); Chair. DIRK MAMPAEY; CEO PIERRE DE BOSSCHER.

AXA Bank Europe NV: 25 blvd du Souverain, 1170 Brussels; tel. (2) 678-61-11; fax (2) 678-93-40; e-mail contact@axa-bank.be; internet www.axa.be; f. 1881 as ANHYP Bank NV; fmrly AXA Bank Belgium NV; present name adopted 2008; cap. 546.3m., res –27.1m., dep 18,131.3m. (Dec. 2012); Chair., Bd of Dirs ALFRED BOUCKAERT; CEO EUGÈNE THYSEN; 5 brs.

Banca Monte Paschi Belgio SA/NV: 24 rue Joseph II, 1000 Brussels; tel. (2) 220-72-11; fax (2) 218-83-91; e-mail info@montepaschi.be; internet www.montepaschi.be; f. 1947 as Banco di Roma (Belgique); name changed 1992; 99% owned by Banca Monte dei Paschi di Siena SpA; cap. 50.9m., res 31.8m., dep. 1,115.2m. (Dec. 2012); Gen. Dir and Pres. of Exec. Cttee LUIGI MACCHIOLA; 1 br.

Bank J. Van Breda & Co NV: Ledeganckkaai 7, 2000 Antwerp; tel. (3) 217-53-33; fax (3) 271-10-94; e-mail info@bankvanbreda.be; internet www.bankvanbreda.be; f. 1930; present name adopted 1998; cap. 17.5m., res 11.4m., dep. 3,396.6m. (Dec. 2012); Pres., Exec. Cttee and Gen. Man. CARLO HENRIKSEN; 41 brs.

Bank Degroof SA/Banque Degroof SA: 44 rue de l'Industrie, 1040 Brussels; tel. (2) 287-91-11; fax (2) 230-67-00; e-mail info@degroof.be; internet www.degroof.be; f. 1871; present name adopted 1998; cap. 47.5m., res 532.5m., dep. 4,084.1m. (Sept. 2013); Chair. ALAIN PHILIPPSON; CEO REGNIER HAEGELSTEEN.

Bank Delen NV/Banque Delen SA: Jan Van Rijswijcklaan 184, 2020 Antwerp; tel. (3) 244-55-66; fax (3) 216-04-91; e-mail info@delen.be; internet www.delen.be; f. 1928; name changed as above in 1996; cap. 42.3m., res 3.8m., dep. 1,132.3m. (Dec. 2012); Pres. JACQUES DELEN; Chair. JAN SUYKENS; 7 brs.

Belfius Banque: 44 blvd Pachéco, 1000 Brussels; tel. (2) 222-11-11; fax (2) 222-11-22; internet www.belfius.be; f. 1860 as Crédit Communal de Belgique SA; present name changed from Dexia

Bank Belgium 2012; Belgian Govt acquired 100% of the shares of Dexia SA in Dexia Bank Belgium in Oct. 2011; cap. 3,458.1m., res –1,457m., dep. 90,573.1m. (Dec. 2012); Chair., Supervisory Bd JOS CLIJSTERS; Chair., Exec. Cttee MARC RAISIÈRE; 818 brs.

Beobank NV/SA: 263 blvd Général Jacques, 1050 Brussels; tel. (2) 626-64-63; fax (2) 626-64-28; internet www.beobank.be; f. 1919; subsidiary of Crédit Mutuel Nord Europe (France); fmrly Citibank Belgium SA; present name adopted 2013; CEO. BRENDAN CARNEY; 192 brs.

BNP Paribas Fortis: 3 Montagne du Parc, 1000 Brussels; tel. (2) 511-26-311; fax (2) 565-49-29; e-mail info@fortisbank.com; internet www.fortisbanking.be; f. 1990 as Fortis Group; present name adopted May 2009 following acquisition by BNP Paribas (France) of a 75% stake in Fortis Bank SA/NV; 25% owned by Belgian Govt; banking, insurance and investments; cap. 9,605m., res 562m., dep. 173,378m. (Dec. 2012); Chair. HERMAN DAEMS; CEO MAXIME JADOT; 906 brs.

Byblos Bank Europe SA: 10 rue Montoyer, 1000 Brussels; tel. (2) 551-00-20; fax (2) 513-05-26; e-mail byblos.europe@byblosbankeur.com; internet www.byblosbank.com.lb; f. 1976 as Byblos Arab Finance Bank (Belgium) SA; present name adopted 1998; cap. 20m., res 35.9m., dep. 499.7m. (Dec. 2012); Chair. and Gen. Man. Dr FRANÇOIS S. BASSIL; Exec. Dir SAMI HADDAD; 2 brs.

CBC Banque SA: 5 Grand-Place, 1000 Brussels; tel. (2) 547-12-11; fax (2) 547-11-10; e-mail info@cbc.be; internet www.cbc.be; f. 1958; name changed as above in 1998 following merger; cap. 145.7m., res 371.4m., dep. 8,868.3m. (Dec. 2012); Chair., Bd of Dirs JOHAN THIJS; Chair., Exec. Cttee DANIEL FALQUE; 107 brs.

Centrale Kredietverlening (CKV): Mannebeekstraat 33, 8790 Waregem; tel. (56) 62-92-81; fax (56) 61-10-79; e-mail info@ckv.be; internet www.ckv.be; f. 2013; by merger of CKV and Goffin Bank NV.

Crédit Professionnel SA/Beroepskrediet NV: 6–9 ave des Arts, 1210 Brussels; tel. (2) 289-82-00; fax (2) 289-89-90; e-mail info@bkcp.be; internet www.bkcp.be; f. 1946 as Caisse Nationale de Crédit Professionnel SA; name changed as above 1997; cap. 153.9m., res 160.3m., dep. 3,884.9m. (Dec. 2012); Chair., Bd of Dirs ERIC CHARPENTIER; Chair., Exec. Bd JACQUES FAVILLIER.

Crelan SA: 251 blvd Sylvain Dupuis, 1070 Brussels; tel. (2) 558-71-11; fax (2) 558-76-33; internet www.crelan.be; f. 1937; present name adopted after the merger of Crédit Agricole SA/Landbouwkrediet NV and Centea NV; Pres FRANÇOIS MACÉ; CEO LUC VERSELE.

Delta Lloyd Bank NV: 23 ave de l'Astronomie, 1210 Brussels; tel. (2) 229-76-00; fax (2) 229-76-99; e-mail info@dlbank.be; internet www.deltalloydbank.be; f. 1966 as Bankunie NV; above name adopted 2001; subsidiary of Delta Lloyd Group (Netherlands); cap. 288.4m., res 27.8m., dep. 5,574.2m. (Dec. 2012); Pres. JOOST MELIS.

Euroclear Bank SA: 1 blvd du Roi Albert II, 1210 Brussels; tel. (2) 326-12-11; fax (2) 326-12-87; e-mail info@euroclear.com; internet www.euroclear.com; f. 2000; 100% owned by Euroclear SA/NV; cap. 285.5m., res 652.1m., dep. 16,963.6m. (Dec. 2012); CEO and Chair., Management Cttee YVES POULLET.

Europabank NV: Burgstraat 170, 9000 Ghent; tel. (9) 224-73-11; fax (9) 223-34-72; e-mail info@europabank.be; internet www.europabank.be; f. 1964; 99.9% owned by Crédit Agricole SA/Landbouwkrediet NV; cap. 1.6m., res 107.3m., dep. 863.3m. (Dec. 2012); Chair. LUC VERSELE; Pres. LUK OSTE; 47 brs.

ING Belgium SA/NV: 24 ave Marnix, 1000 Brussels; tel. (2) 547-21-11; fax (2) 547-38-44; e-mail info@ing.be; internet www.ing.be; f. 1975 as Bank Brussels Lambert; acquired in 1998 by ING Group (Netherlands); name changed as above in April 2003; cap. 2,350m., res 805.6m., dep. 99,134m. (Dec. 2012); Chair., Bd of Dirs ERIC BOYER DE LA GIRODAY; CEO RALPH HAMERS; 770 brs.

KBC Bank NV: Havenlaan 2, 1080 Brussels 8; tel. (2) 429-11-11; fax (2) 429-81-31; e-mail kbc.telecenter@kbc.be; internet www.kbc.be; f. 1935 as Kredietbank NV; merged with Bank von Roeselare NV and CERA Investment Bank NV in 1998; cap. 8,948m., res 2,613m., dep. 160,975m. (Dec. 2012); Chair. THOMAS LEYSEN; CEO JOHAN THIJS; 956 brs.

Keytrade Bank SA: 100 blvd de Souverain, 1170 Brussels; tel. (2) 679-90-00; fax (2) 679-90-01; e-mail info@keytradebank.com; internet www.keytradebank.com; f. 2002 by merger of RealBank SA and VMS Keytrade.com; owned by Crelan SA; cap. 48.3m., res 82.6m., dep. 2,346.2m. (Dec. 2012); Pres., CEO THIERRY TERNIER; Man. Dir PATRICK BOULIN.

Santander Benelux SA/NV: Guldensporenpark 81, 9820 Merelbeke; tel. (9) 235-50-60; e-mail info@santander.be; internet www.santander.be; f. 1914 as Société Hollandaise de Banque; present name adopted 2004; owned by Banco Santander Centro Hispano SA (Spain); cap. 1,139.6m., res 17.8m., dep. 7,614.4m. (Dec. 2012); Man. Dir GUILLERMO SANZ MURAT.

Development Bank

Gewestelijke Investeringsmaatschappij voor Vlaanderen (GIMV): Karel Oomsstraat 37, 2018 Antwerp; tel. (3) 290-21-00; fax (3) 290-21-05; e-mail info@gimv.be; internet www.gimv.com; f. 1980; promotes creation, restructuring and expansion of private cos; net assets 446m. (2007); Chair. URBAIN VANDEURZEN; CEO KOEN DEJONCKHEERE.

Banking Association

Association Belge des Banques et des Sociétés de Bourse/Belgische Vereniging van Banken en Beursvennootschappen (ABB/BVB): 82 rue d'Arlon, BP 5, 1040 Brussels; tel. (2) 507-68-11; fax (2) 888-68-11; e-mail info@febelfin.be; internet www.febelfin.be; f. 1936; part of Fédération Belge du Secteur Financier (FEBELFIN); Pres. FILIP DIERCKX; CEO MICHEL VERMAERKE.

STOCK EXCHANGE

Euronext Brussels SA/NV: Palais de la Bourse, 1000 Brussels; tel. (2) 509-12-11; fax (2) 509-12-12; e-mail info.be@euronext.com; internet www.euronext.com; formed in 2000 by merger of Amsterdam, Paris and Brussels exchanges, and joined in 2002 by the Lisbon stock exchange and the London futures exchange LIFFE; merged with New York Stock Exchange in 2007 to form NYSE Euronext; Chair. JAN-MICHIEL HESSELS; CEO DUNCAN L. NIEDERAUER.

INSURANCE

Principal Insurance Companies

AG Insurance: 53 blvd Emile Jacqmain, 1000 Brussels; tel. (2) 664-81-11; fax (2) 664-81-50; e-mail info@aginsurance.be; internet www.aginsurance.be; f. 2006 as Fortis Insurance Belgium by merger of Fortis AG and FBAssurances; current name adopted in 2009; 75% owned by Ageas, 25% by BNP Paribas Fortis; both life and non-life insurance; CEO ANTONIO CANO.

Ageas: Rue du Marquis 1, 1000 Brussels; tel. (2) 557-57-11; fax (2) 557-57-50; internet www.ageas.com; fmrly Fortis; name changed in 2010; both life and non-life insurance; Chair. JOZEF DE MEY; CEO BART DE SMET.

Allianz: 35 rue de Laeken, 1000 Brussels; tel. (2) 214-61-11; internet www.allianz.be; f. 1890; insurance and financial services; CEO ROBERT FRANSSEN.

AXA: 25 blvd du Souverain, 1170 Brussels; tel. (2) 678-61-11; fax (2) 678-93-40; internet www.axa.be; f. 1853; member of the AXA group; all branches; CEO EMMANUEL DE TALHOUËT.

Baloise Insurance: Posthofbrug 16, 2600 Antwerp; tel. (3) 247-21-11; fax (3) 247-27-77; e-mail info@baloise.be; internet www.baloise.be; f. 2013; the result of merger between Mercator Verzekeringen and Avéro et Nateus; non-life; owned by Bâloise-Gruppe (Switzerland); CEO GERT DE WINTER.

Delta Lloyd Life SA: 38 ave Fonsny, 1060 Brussels; tel. (2) 238-88-11; fax (2) 238-88-99; e-mail quality@deltalloydlife.be; internet www.deltalloydlife.be; f. 2001; by the merger of three Belgian companies; subsidiary of Delta Lloyd Group; life insurance; Chair. ONNO VERSTEGHEN; CEO JAN VAN AUTREVE.

ERGO: 1–8 blvd Bischoffsheim, 1000 Brussels; tel. (2) 535-57-11; fax (2) 535-57-00; e-mail info@ergo.be; internet www.ergo.be; f. 1960; both life and non-life insurance; Chair. Dr JOHANNES LÖRPER.

Ethias: 24 rue des Croisiers, 4000 Liège; tel. (4) 220-31-11; fax (4) 220-30-05; e-mail info@ethias.be; internet www.ethias.be; f. 1919; fmrly Société Mutuelle des Administrations Publiques (SMAP), name changed as above in 2003; institutions, civil service employees, public administration and enterprises; CEO BERNARD THIRY.

Generali Belgium SA: 149 ave Louise, 1050 Brussels; tel. (2) 403-87-00; fax (2) 403-88-99; e-mail generali_belgium@generali.be; internet www.generali.be; f. 1901; all branches; Chair. FRANS HEUS; Dir Gen. THIERRY DELVAUX.

ING Life & Non-Life Belgium SA/NV: 70 cours Saint-Michel, 1040 Brussels; tel. (2) 547-21-11; fax (2) 547-38-44; e-mail info@ing.be; internet www.ing.be; f. 2007; as two new insurance companies ING Life Belgium SA/NV and ING Non-Life Belgium SA/NV; Chair. ERIC BOYER DE LA GIRODAY.

KBC SA/NV: Overstraetenplein 5, 3000 Leuven; tel. (07) 815-21-54; fax (03) 283-29-50; e-mail kbc24plus@verz.kbc.be; internet www.kbc.be; f. 1998; Chair. JOHAN THIJS.

P & V: Koningsstraat 151, 1210 Brussels; tel. (2) 250-91-11; fax (2) 250-90-46; e-mail infonl@pv.be; internet www.pv.be; f. 1907; both life and non-life; Chair. HILDE VERNAILLEN.

Insurance Associations

Assuralia: 29 square de Meeûs, 1000 Brussels; tel. (2) 547-56-11; fax (2) 547-56-01; e-mail info@assuralia.be; internet www.assuralia.be;

f. 1921; affiliated to Fédération des Entreprises de Belgique; Pres. BART DE SMET; 95 mems.

Fédération des Courtiers d'Assurances et Intermédiaires Financiers de Belgique (FEPRABEL): 40 ave Albert-Elisabeth, 1200 Brussels; tel. (2) 743-25-60; fax (2) 735-44-58; e-mail contact@feprabel.be; internet www.feprabel.be; f. 1934; Pres. VINCENT MAGNUS; 500 mems.

Trade and Industry

GOVERNMENT AGENCIES

Flanders Investment and Trade: Gaucheretstraat 90, 1030 Brussels; tel. (2) 504-88-71; fax (2) 504-88-70; e-mail invest@fitagency.be; internet www.investinflanders.com; f. 2005 by merger of Flanders Foreign Investment Office (FFIO) and Export Vlaanderen; promotes foreign investment in Flanders and Flemish business abroad; CEO CLAIRE TILLEKAERTS.

Société de Développement pour la Région de Bruxelles-Capitale (SDRB): 6 rue Gabrielle Petit, 1080 Brussels; tel. (2) 422-51-11; fax (2) 422-51-12; e-mail info@sdrb.be; internet www.sdrb.irisnet.be; f. 1974; promotes economic development in the capital; Pres. D. GRIMBERGHS; Man. Dir J. MEGANCK.

Société Régionale d'Investissement de Wallonie: 13 ave Destenay, 4000 Liège; tel. (4) 221-98-11; fax (4) 221-99-99; e-mail info@sriw.be; internet www.sriw.be; f. 1979; promotes private enterprise in Wallonia; Chair. JEAN-PASCAL LABILLE (suspended from post while serving as mem. of Govt).

PRINCIPAL CHAMBERS OF COMMERCE

There are chambers of commerce and industry in all major towns and industrial areas.

Chambre de Commerce de Bruxelles (BECI): 500 ave Louise, 1050 Brussels; tel. (2) 648-50-02; fax (2) 640-93-28; e-mail info@beci.be; internet www.beci.be; f. 1875; Pres. EMMANUEL VAN INNIS; 3,000 mems.

Chambre de Commerce et d'Industrie de Liège et de Verviers: 35 rue Renkin, 4800 Verviers; tel. (87) 29-36-36; fax (87) 26-86-35; e-mail info@ccilv.be; internet www.ccilv.be; f. 1866; Man. Dir JEAN-FRANÇOIS COUTELIER; 2,000 mems.

Voka—Kamer van Koophandel Antwerpen-Waasland: Markgravestraat 12, 2000 Antwerp; tel. (3) 232-22-19; fax (3) 233-64-42; e-mail info.antwerpen@voka.be; internet www.voka.be/antwerpen-waasland; f. 1969; Pres. STÉPHANE VERBEECK; 3,000 mems.

INDUSTRIAL AND TRADE ASSOCIATIONS

Fédération des Entreprises de Belgique (VBO-FEB) (Federation of Belgian Companies): 4 rue Ravenstein, 1000 Brussels; tel. (2) 515-08-11; fax (2) 515-09-15; e-mail info@vbo-feb.be; internet www.vbo-feb.be; f. 1895; federates all the main industrial and non-industrial asscns; Chair. PIERRE ALAIN DE SMEDT; CEO RUDI THOMAES; 38 full mems.

Agoria—Fédération Multisectorielle de l'Industrie Technologique (Multisector Federation for the Technology Industry): 80 blvd Auguste Reyers, 1030 Brussels; tel. (2) 706-78-00; fax (2) 706-78-01; e-mail info@agoria.be; internet www.agoria.be; f. 1946; present name adopted 2000; more than 1,200 mem. cos; Chair. CHRIST'L JORIS; CEO PAUL SOETE.

Association des Fabricants de Pâtes, Papiers et Cartons de Belgique (COBELPA) (Paper): 306 ave Louise, BP 11, 1050 Brussels; tel. (2) 646-64-50; fax (2) 646-82-97; e-mail general@cobelpa.be; internet www.cobelpa.be; f. 1940; Gen. Man. FIRMIN FRANÇOIS.

Belgian Petroleum Federation (Petroleum): 39 ave des Arts, BP 2, 1040 Brussels; tel. (2) 508-30-00; fax (2) 511-05-91; e-mail info@petrolfed.be; internet www.petrolfed.be; f. 1926; Pres. DAVE BROWNELL; Sec.-Gen. JEAN-LOUIS NIZET.

Brasseurs Belges (Belgian Brewers): Maison des Brasseurs, 10 Grand'Place, 1000 Brussels; tel. (2) 511-49-87; fax (2) 511-32-59; e-mail belgian.brewers@beerparadise.be; internet www.beerparadise.be; f. 1971; Chair. THEO VERVLOET.

Confédération Nationale de la Construction (CNC) (Civil Engineering, Road and Building Contractors and Auxiliary Trades): 34–42 rue du Lombard, 1000 Brussels; tel. (2) 545-56-00; fax (2) 545-59-00; e-mail info@confederatiebouw.be; internet www.cnc.be; f. 1946; Pres. MARC LEFEBVRE; Man. Dir FRANCIS CARNOY; 15,000 mems.

Creamoda (Clothing): Leliegaarde 22, 1731 Zellik; tel. (2) 238-10-11; fax (2) 238-10-10; e-mail info@creamoda.be; internet www.belgianfashion.be; f. 1946; Dir-Gen. ERIK MAGNUS.

Fédération Belge de la Brique (Bricks): 19 rue des Chartreux, BP 19, 1000 Brussels; tel. (2) 511-25-81; fax (2) 513-26-40; e-mail info@baksteen.be; internet www.brique.be; f. 1947; Pres. BURT NELISSEN; Dir JO VAN DEN BOSSCHE; 25 mems.

Fédération Belge de l'Industrie de l'Automobile et du Cycle (FEBIAC) (Motor Vehicles and Bicycles): 46/6 blvd de la Woluwe, 1200 Brussels; tel. (2) 778-64-00; fax (2) 762-81-71; e-mail info@febiac.be; internet www.febiac.be; f. 1936; Sec.-Gen. FRANÇOIS-XAVIER DUBOIS.

Fédération Belge de l'Industrie Textile, du Bois et de l'Ameublement (FEDUSTRIA) (Textiles, Wood and Furniture): 5/1 allée Hof-ter-Vleest, 1070 Brussels; tel. (2) 528-58-11; fax (2) 528-58-29; e-mail info@fedustria.be; internet www.fedustria.be; f. 2006 by merger of Febelbois and Fébeltex; Pres. PHILIPPE CORTHOUTS; Man. Dir FA QUIX.

Fédération Belge des Industries Chimiques et des Sciences de la Vie (Essenscia) (Chemical Industries and Life Sciences): 80 blvd Auguste Reyers, 1030 Brussels; tel. (2) 238-97-11; fax (2) 231-13-01; e-mail info@essenscia.be; internet www.essenscia.be; incorporates Lubricants Asscn Belgium; Pres. FRANK BECKX; Man. Dir YVES VERSCHUEREN; 800 mem. cos.

Fédération Belge des Industries Graphiques (FEBELGRA) (Graphic Industries): Barastraat 175, 1070 Brussels; tel. (2) 411-22-96; fax (2) 513-56-76; e-mail febelgra.bru@skynet.be; internet www.febelgra.be; f. 1978; Pres. MICHEL PATTYN; 750 mems.

Fédération d'Employeurs pour le Commerce International, le Transport et les Branches d'Activité Connexes (Employers' Federation of International Trade, Transport and Related Activities); incl. Fédération Patronale des Ports Belges: Brouwersvliet 33, Postbus 7, 2000 Antwerp; tel. (3) 221-97-11; fax (3) 232-38-26; e-mail cepa@cepa.be; internet www.cepa.be; f. 1937; Pres. MARINO VERMEERSCH; Dir RENÉ DE BROUWER.

Fédération de l'Industrie Alimentaire/Federatie Voedingsindustrie (FEVIA) (Food): 43 ave des Arts, BP 7, 1040 Brussels; tel. (2) 550-17-40; fax (2) 550-17-59; e-mail info@fevia.be; internet www.fevia.be; f. 1937; Dir-Gen. CHRIS MORIS.

Fédération de l'Industrie du Béton (FEBE) (Precast Concrete): 68 blvd du Souverain, 1170 Brussels; tel. (2) 735-80-15; fax (2) 734-77-95; e-mail mail@febe.be; internet www.febe.be; f. 1936; Pres. LUDO PANIS; Dir EDDY DANO; 80 mem. cos.

Fédération de l'Industrie Cimentière Belge (FEBELCEM) (Cement): 68 blvd du Souverain, 1170 Brussels; tel. (2) 645-52-11; fax (2) 640-06-70; e-mail info@febelcem.be; internet www.febelcem.be; f. 1949; Pres. L. EPPLE; Dir ANDRÉ JASIENSKI.

Fédération des Industries Extractives et Transformatrices de Roches non-Combustibles (FEDIEX) (Extraction and Processing of Non-fuel Rocks): 7 rue Edouard Belin, 1435 Mont-Saint-Guibert; tel. (2) 511-61-73; fax (2) 511-12-84; e-mail info@fediex.org; internet www.fediex.be; f. 1942 as Union des Producteurs Belges de Chaux, Calcaires, Dolomies et Produits Connexes; name changed (as above) 1990; co-operative society; Pres. JEAN MARBEHANT.

Fédération des Industries Transformatrices de Papier et Carton (FETRA) (Paper and Cardboard): 5 blvd de la Plaine, 1050 Brussels; tel. (2) 344-19-62; fax (2) 344-86-61; e-mail info@fetra.be; internet www.fetra.be; f. 1946; Pres. PAUL PISSENS; Sec.-Gen. LIEVE VANLIERDE.

Fédération de l'Industrie du Verre (Glass): 5 blvd de la Plaine, 1050 Brussels; tel. (2) 542-61-20; fax (2) 542-61-21; e-mail info@vgi-fiv.be; internet www.vgi-fiv.be; f. 1947; Pres. J. F. HERIS; Gen. Man. ROLAND DERIDDER.

Fédération Patronale des Ports Belges: Brouwersvliet 33, Postbus 7, 2000 Antwerp 1; tel. (3) 221-99-87; fax (3) 221-99-09; e-mail rene.debrouwer@cepa.be; Pres. PAUL VALKENIERS; Dir RENÉ DE BROUWER.

Groupement des Sablières (Sand and Gravel): Quellinstraat 49, 2018 Antwerp; tel. (3) 223-66-11; fax (3) 223-66-47; e-mail cathy.blervacq@sibelco.be; f. 1937; Pres. ALAIN SPEECKAERT.

Groupement de la Sidérurgie (Iron and Steel): 5 ave Ariane, 1200 Brussels; tel. (2) 509-14-11; fax (2) 509-14-00; e-mail gsv@steelbel.be; internet www.steelbel.be; f. 1953; Pres. GEERT VAN POELVOORDE; Dir-Gen. ROBERT JOOS; 13 mems.

Syndicat de l'industrie diamantaire belge (SBD) (Diamonds): Hoveniersstraat 22, 2018 Antwerp; tel. (3) 233-11-29; fax (3) 227-46-30; e-mail sbd@sbd.be; internet www.sbd.be; f. 1927; Pres. EDUARD DENCKENS.

Synergrid (Gas and Electricity Grid Operators): 4 ave Palmerston, 1000 Brussels; tel. (2) 237-11-11; fax (2) 230-44-80; e-mail info@synergrid.be; internet www.synergrid.be; f. 1946; Pres. DANIEL DOBBENI; Sec.-Gen. BÉRÉNICE CRABS.

Union Professionnelle des Producteurs Belges de Fibres-Ciment (Fibre-Cement): Aarschotstraat 114, 9100 Sint-Niklaas;

tel. (3) 760-49-38; fax (3) 760-49-90; e-mail carry.peeters@svk.be; f. 1941; Pres. KRIS ASSELMAN; Sec. CARRY PEETERS.

Union Royale des Armateurs Belges (Shipowners): 8 Ernest van Dijckkaai, 2000 Antwerp; tel. (3) 232-72-32; fax (3) 231-39-97; e-mail info@brv.be; internet www.brv.be; f. 1909; Chair. PETER VIERSTRAETE; Man. Dir PETER VERSTUYFT.

Fédération Belge des Dragueurs de Gravier et de Sable (BELBAG) (Quarries): Maasstraat 82, Postbus 2, 3640 Kinrooi; tel. (8) 956-08-08; fax (8) 956-08-09; e-mail info@belbag.be; internet www.belbag.be; f. 1967; Pres. LUC SEVERIJNS.

Fédération des Carrières de Petit Granit—Pierre Bleue de Belgique ASBL (Limestone): 1 chemin des Carrières, 7063 Neufvilles; tel. (67) 34-68-05; fax (67) 33-08-49; e-mail info@federationpierrebleue.be; internet www.federationpierrebleue.be; f. 1948; Pres. JEAN-FRANZ ABRAHAM.

UTILITIES

Regulatory Authorities

Commission de Régulation de l'Electricité et du Gaz/Commissie voor de Regulering van de Elektriciteit en het Gas (CREG): 26–38 rue de l'Industrie, 1040 Brussels; tel. (2) 289-76-11; fax (2) 289-76-09; e-mail info@creg.be; internet www.creg.be; regulatory body for both gas and electricity markets; Pres. MARIE-PIERRE FAUCONNIER.

Commission de Régulation pour l'Energie en Région de Bruxelles-Capitale (BRUGEL): 46 ave des Arts, 1000 Brussels; tel. (2) 563-02-00; fax (2) 563-02-13; e-mail info@brugel.be; internet www.brugel.be; regulatory body for electricity and gas markets in Brussels-Capital region; Pres. MARIE-PIERRE FAUCONNIER.

Commission Wallonne pour l'Energie (CWaPE): 4 rue de Louvain-la-Neuve, bte 12, 5001 Namur; tel. (81) 33-08-10; fax (81) 33-08-11; e-mail energie@mrw.wallonie.be; internet www.cwape.be; f. 2002; Pres. FRANCIS GHIGNY.

Vlaams reguleringsinstantie voor de elektriciteits- en gasmarkt (VREG) (Flemish Electricity and Gas Market Regulatory Authority): Graaf de Ferrarisgebouw, Koning Albert II-laan 20–19, 1000 Brussels; tel. (2) 553-13-79; fax (2) 553-13-50; e-mail info@vreg.be; internet www.vreg.be; f. 2001; responsible for regulation of distribution of gas and electricity at low voltage and production of electricity from renewable sources; Chair. KURT DEKETELAER; Dir-Gen. ANDRÉ PICTOEL.

Electricity

EDF Luminus NV/SA: 1 rue du Marquis, 1000 Brussels; tel. (2) 229-19-50; fax (2) 218-61-34; e-mail info@spe.be; internet www.spe.be; fmrly SPE NV; named changed as above in 2011; builds, operates and maintains power plants; supplies electricity and gas under brand name Luminus; CEO GRÉGOIRE DALLEMAGNE.

Electrabel: 34 blvd Simon Bolivar, 1000 Brussels; tel. (2) 510-72-22; internet www.electrabel.com; f. 1905 as Electriciteitsmaatschappij der Schelde; name changed to Ebes following merger in 1956; present name adopted 1990; generates and distributes electricity and natural gas; part of GDF Suez Group; CEO DIRK BEEUWSAERT.

Gas

Distrigas NV/SA: Guimardstraat 1A, 1040 Brussels; tel. (2) 557-30-01; fax (2) 557-31-12; e-mail info@distri.be; internet www.distrigas.eu; supply and sale of natural gas; f. 2001; 100% subsidiary of Eni, Italy; CEO ERWIN VAN BRUYSEL.

EDF Luminus NV/SA: see Electricity.

Fluxys NV/SA: Kunstlaan 31, 1040 Brussels; tel. (2) 282-72-11; fax (2) 230-02-39; e-mail berenice.crabs@fluxys.com; internet www.fluxys.com; owns and operates Belgian gas transmission network; CEO WALTER PEERAER.

Total Belgium: 52 rue de l'Industrie, 1040 Brussels; tel. (2) 288-91-11; fax (2) 288-32-60; e-mail gaznat.ventes@total.com; internet www.be.total.com; CEO MICHEL DEL MARMOL.

Water

Société Wallonne des Eaux: 41 rue de la Concorde, 4800 Verviers; tel. (87) 87-87-87; fax (87) 34-28-00; e-mail info@swde.be; internet www.swde.be; f. 1986; water production and distribution; Pres. RENÉ THISSEN; Dir-Gen. ERIC VAN SEVENANT.

Vlaamse Maatschappij voor Watervoorziening: Vooruitgangstraat 189, 1030 Brussels; tel. (2) 238-94-11; fax (2) 230-97-98; e-mail info@vmw.be; internet www.vmw.be; Chair. LUC ASSELMAN; Dir-Gen. BOUDEWIJN VAN DE STEENE.

TRADE UNIONS

National Federations

Algemeen Belgisch Vakverbond/Fédération Générale du Travail de Belgique (ABVV/FGTB): 42 rue Haute, 1000 Brussels; tel. (2) 506-82-11; fax (2) 506-82-29; e-mail anne.demelenne@abvv.be; internet www.abvv.be; f. 1898; 7 branch unions; affiliated to the International Trade Union Confederation (ITUC); Pres. RUDY DE LEEUW; Gen. Sec. ANNE DEMELENNE; 1,503,000 mems.

Algemeen Christelijk Vakverbond/Confédération des Syndicats Chrétiens (ACV-CSC): Haachtsesteenweg 579, 1031 Brussels; tel. (2) 246-31-11; fax (2) 246-30-10; e-mail international@acv-csc.be; internet www.acv-online.be; 13 affiliated unions; Pres. MARC LEEMANS; Sec.-Gen. CLAUDE ROLIN; 1.7m. mems.

Algemene Centrale der Liberale Vakbonden van België/Centrale Générale des Syndicats Libéraux de Belgique (ACLVB/CGSLB) (General Federation of Liberal Trade Unions of Belgium): 72–74 blvd Poincaré, 1070 Brussels; tel. (2) 558-51-50; fax (2) 558-51-51; e-mail siegesocial@cgslb.be; internet www.cgslb.be; f. 1891; present name adopted 1939; affiliated to the European Trade Union Confederation (ETUC) and the International Trade Union Confederation (ITUC); Nat. Pres. JAN VERCAMST; 274,308 mems (2010).

Transport

RAILWAYS

The Belgian railway network is one of the densest in the world. Train services are operated by the Société Nationale des Chemins de Fer Belges (SNCB), while the infrastructure is owned and managed by Infrabel. In 2011 there were 3,558 km of standard-gauge railways, of which some 3,008 km were electrified. A high-speed railway network for northern Europe, linking Belgium, France, Germany, the Netherlands and the United Kingdom, was fully operational by November 2007.

Société Nationale des Chemins de Fer Belges/Nationale Maatschappij der Belgische Spoorwegen (SNCB/NMBS): 40 ave de la Porte de Hal, 1060 Brussels; tel. (2) 525-21-11; e-mail infocorporate@sncb.be; internet www.b-rail.be; f. 2005; 100% owned by SNCB Holding; 217m. passengers were carried in 2009; CEO MARC DESCHEEMAECKER.

Infrabel: 2 place Marcel Broodthaers, 1060 Brussels; tel. (2) 525-21-11; fax (2) 525-22-03; e-mail anik.cornil@infrabel.be; internet www.infrabel.be; f. 2005; responsible for rail infrastructure management; 93.6% owned by SNCB Holding, 6.4% owned by Federal Govt; CEO LUC LALLEMAND.

Thalys International: 20B place Stéphanie, 1050 Brussels; tel. (2) 548-06-00; fax (2) 504-05-32; internet www.thalys.com; f. 1995 as Westrail International; present name adopted 1999; operates rail passenger services between Brussels and Amsterdam (Netherlands), Cologne (Germany) and Paris (France); 62% owned by Société Nationale des Chemins de fer Français (SNCF—France), 28% by SNCB and 10% by Deutsche Bahn (Germany); CEO FRANCK GERVAIS.

ROADS

In 2010 there were 1,763 km of motorways and some 12,900 km of other main or national roads. There were also 1,349 km of secondary or regional roads and an additional 138,000 km of minor roads.

Société Régionale Wallonne du Transport: 96 ave Gouverneur Bovesse, 5100 Namur; tel. (81) 32-27-11; e-mail info@tec-wl.be; internet www.infotec.be; f. 1991; operates light railways, buses and trams; Dir-Gen. JEAN-MARC VANDENBROUCKE.

Société des Transports Intercommunaux de Bruxelles: 76 rue Royale, 1000 Brussels; tel. (2) 515-20-00; fax (2) 515-32-84; e-mail flauscha@stib.irisnet.be; internet www.stib.be; operates a metro service, buses and trams; operates in 19 communes in Brussels and in 11 outlying communes; Dir-Gen. ALAIN FLAUSCH.

Vlaamse Vervoermaatschappij (De Lijn): Motstraat 20, 2800 Mechelen; tel. (15) 44-07-11; fax (15) 40-89-98; e-mail marketing.cd@delijn.be; internet www.delijn.be; f. 1991; operates bus and tram services under commercial name De Lijn; Dir-Gen. ROGER KESTELOOT.

INLAND WATERWAYS

There are over 1,520 km of inland waterways in Belgium, of which 660 km are navigable rivers and 860 km are canals. Waterways administration is divided between the Flemish Region (1,055 km), the Walloon Region (450 km) and the Brussels-Capital Region (15 km).

Flemish Region:

De Scheepvaart NV: Havenstraat 44, 3500 Hasselt; tel. (11) 29-84-00; fax (11) 22-12-77; e-mail info@descheepvaart.be; internet www

.descheepvaart.be; f. 2004; manages inland waterway system between Antwerp and Netherlands border; Chair. WILLY CLAES.

Waterwegen en Zeekanaal NV (W&Z): Oostdijk 110, 2830 Willebroek; tel. (3) 860-62-11; fax (3) 860-62-00; e-mail info@wenz.be; internet www.wenz.be; f. 2006 to replace Departement Leefmilieu en Infrastructuur Administratie Waterwegen en Zeewezen; Chair. ALBERT ABSILLIS; Gen. Man. ERIC VAN DEN EEDE.

Walloon Region:

Direction Générale de la Mobilité et des Voies Hydrauliques: Centre administratif du MET, 8 blvd du Nord, 5000 Namur; tel. (81) 77-26-80; fax (81) 77-37-60; internet voies-hydrauliques.wallonie.be; Dir-Gen. JACQUES LAURENT.

Brussels-Capital Region:

Port de Bruxelles/Haven van Brussel: 6 place des Armateurs, 1000 Brussels; tel. (2) 420-67-00; fax (2) 420-69-74; e-mail portdebruxelles@port.irisnet.be; internet www.havenvanbrussel.irisnet.be; f. 1993; Pres. M. BENOIT HELLINGS; Dir-Gen. ALFONS MOENS.

SHIPPING

The modernized port of Antwerp is the second largest in Europe and handles about 80% of Belgian foreign trade by sea and inland waterways. It is also the largest railway port and has one of the biggest petroleum refining complexes in Europe. Antwerp has 160 km of quayside and 17 dry docks. Other ports include Zeebrugge, Ostend, Ghent, Liège and Brussels. At 31 December 2013 the flag registered fleet comprised 399 vessels, totalling 4.2m. grt, of which 22 were bulk carrier and 24 general cargo ships.

Antwerp Port Authority: Havenhuis, Entrepotkaai 1, 2000 Antwerp; tel. (3) 205-20-11; fax (3) 205-20-28; e-mail info@portofantwerp.com; internet www.portofantwerp.com; an autonomous, municipally owned company, responsible for planning, development, modernization and maintenance of the port infrastructure; offers a number of ancillary services such as tugging, dredging and renting out dock cranes and floating cranes; also responsible for safe and smooth shipping movements within the dock complex, and operates the bridges and locks; CEO EDDY BRUYNINCKX.

Principal Shipping Companies

Ahlers Logistic and Maritime Services: Noorderlaan 139, 2030 Antwerp; tel. (3) 543-72-11; fax (3) 542-00-23; e-mail info@ahlers.com; internet www.ahlers.com; shipping agency, ship and crew management, forwarding; Exec. Chair. CHRISTIAN LEYSEN.

De Keyser Thornton: Brouwersvliet 25, 2000 Antwerp; tel. (3) 205-31-00; fax (3) 401-74-08; e-mail info@dkt.be; internet www.dkt.be; f. 1853; shipping agency, forwarding and warehousing services; Chair. GUY FOUCHEROT; Man. Dir and CEO PHILIP VAN TILBURG.

Manuport Group: Atlantic House, 3rd Floor, Noorderlaan 147, 2030 Antwerp; tel. (3) 204-95-00; fax (3) 204-95-05; e-mail info@manuport-logistics.be; internet www.manuportgroup.com; forwarding, customs clearance, liner and tramp agencies, chartering, Rhine and inland barging, multi-purpose bulk/bags fertilizer, minerals and agri-bulk terminal; Pres. and CEO WALTER SIJMONS.

Transeuropa Ferries NV: Slijkensesteenweg 2, 8400 Ostend; tel. (5) 934-02-60; fax (5) 934-02-61; e-mail info@transeuropaferries.com; internet www.transeuropaferries.com; f. 2001; 5 ships; shipping, stevedoring and line representation; operates between Ostend and Ramsgate (United Kingdom).

CIVIL AVIATION

The main international airport is at Brussels, with a direct train service between the air terminal and central Brussels. There are also international airports at Antwerp, Charleroi, Kortrijk-Wevelgem, Liège and Ostend.

Brussels Airlines: b.house, Airport Building 26, Ringbaan, 1831 Diegem; tel. (2) 754-19-00; internet www.brusselsairlines.be; f. 2007 by merger of SN Brussels Airlines and Virgin Express; co-owned by SN Airholding and Lufthansa Group; scheduled services within Europe and to Africa, Asia, the Middle East and North America; Man. Dir BERNARD GUSTIN.

Tourism

Belgium has several towns of rich historic and cultural interest, such as Antwerp, Bruges, Brussels, Durbuy, Ghent, Liège, Namur and Tournai. The country's seaside towns attract many visitors. The forest-covered Ardennes region is renowned for hill-walking and gastronomy. In 2012 tourist arrivals totalled some 7.6m., while receipts from tourism totalled an estimated US $11,381m. in 2012.

Office de Promotion du Tourisme Wallonie et Bruxelles: 30 rue Saint-Bernard, 1060 Brussels; tel. (70) 22-10-21; fax (2) 513-69-50; e-mail info@walloniebruxellestourisme.be; internet www.opt.be; f. 1981; promotion of tourism in French-speaking Belgium; Dir-Gen. VIVIANE JACOBS.

Toerisme Vlaanderen: Grasmarkt 61, 1000 Brussels; tel. (2) 504-03-90; fax (2) 513-04-75; e-mail info@toerismevlaanderen.be; internet www.toerismevlaanderen.be; f. 1985; official promotion and policy body for tourism in the Flemish Region; Administrator-Gen. PETER DE WILDE.

Defence

Belgium is a member of the North Atlantic Treaty Organization (NATO), which is headquartered in the country. As assessed at November 2013, the total strength of the Belgian armed forces was 30,700 (including 1,400 in the Medical Service and 10,500 in the Joint Service), comprising an army of 11,300, a navy of 1,500 and an air force of 6,000. Total reserves numbered 6,800. Compulsory military service was abolished in 1995. In 1996 the Belgian and Netherlands navies came under a joint operational command, based at Den Helder, Netherlands. In November 2004 the European Union (EU) defence ministers agreed to create a number of 'battlegroups' (each comprising about 1,500 men), which could be deployed at short notice to carry out peacekeeping activities at crisis points around the world. The EU battlegroups, two of which were to be ready for deployment at any one time, following a rotational schedule, reached full operational capacity from 1 January 2007.

Defence Expenditure: Budget estimated at €3,820m. for 2013.

Chief of Defence: Gen. GERARD VAN CAELENBERGE.

Education

Responsibility for education policy lies with the administrations of the Flemish, French and German-speaking Communities. Education may be provided by the Communities, by other public authorities (provinces and municipalities) or by private interests. All educational establishments, whether official or 'free' (privately organized), receive most of their funding from the Communities. Roman Catholic schools constitute the greatest number of 'free' establishments.

Full-time education in Belgium is compulsory between the ages of six and 16 years. Thereafter, pupils must remain in education for a further two-year period, but may do so on a part-time basis. Children may be enrolled in nursery schools, attached to elementary schools, from between the ages of two-and-a-half and three years. Elementary education begins at six years of age and consists of three courses of two years each. Secondary education, beginning at the age of 12, lasts for six years and is divided into three two-year cycles or, in a few cases, two three-year cycles. According to UNESCO, enrolment at primary schools in 2011/12 included 99% of children in the relevant age-group.

The requirement for university entrance is a pass in the certificate of secondary education, taken after the completion of secondary studies. Reforms to the higher education system entered into effect in 2004 in both the Flemish and the French communities, introducing a three-year bachelor's degree, followed by a master's degree lasting one or two years. (Courses were previously divided into two to three years of general preparation, followed by two to three years of specialization.) There are nine university-level institutions in the French Community and seven such institutions in the Flemish Community. In 2008/09 there were 73,249 students enrolled in French university-level establishments; in 2012/13 there were 84,177 students at Flemish establishments of that level. Non-university institutions of higher education provide arts education, technical training and teacher training; in 2008/09 some 84,875 students were enrolled at French establishments, while in 2012/13 some 132,120 students were enrolled at Flemish non-university institutions. In 2006 enrolment at tertiary level was equivalent to 63% of those in the relevant age-group (males 56%; females 70%). A national study fund provides grants where necessary and about one-fifth of students receive scholarships.

In 2013 the education budget in the Flemish Community was €10,650.0m. and €6,986.5m. in the French Community; education (including training and employment) was budgeted at €106.74m. in the German-speaking Community for 2011.

BELIZE

Introductory Survey

LOCATION, CLIMATE, LANGUAGE, RELIGION, FLAG, CAPITAL

Belize lies on the Caribbean coast of Central America, with Mexico to the north-west and Guatemala to the south-west. The climate is sub-tropical, tempered by trade winds. The temperature averages 24°C (75°F) from November to January, and 27°C (81°F) from May to September. Annual rainfall ranges from 1,290 mm (51 ins) in the north to 4,450 mm (175 ins) in the south. The average annual rainfall in Belize City is 1,650 mm (65 ins). Belize is ethnically diverse, the population (according to the 2000 census) consisting of 49% Mestizos (Maya-Spanish), 25% Creoles (those of predominantly African descent), 11% Amerindian (mainly Maya), 6% Garifuna ('Black Caribs', descendants of those deported from the island of Saint Vincent in 1797) and communities of Asians, Portuguese, German Mennonites and others of European descent. English is the official language and an English Creole is widely understood. Spanish is the mother-tongue of some 15% of the population but is spoken by many others. There are also speakers of Garifuna (Carib), Maya and Ketchi, while the Mennonites speak a German dialect. Most of the population profess Christianity, with about one-half being Roman Catholics. The national flag (proportions usually 3 by 5) is dark blue, with narrow horizontal red stripes at the upper and lower edges; at the centre is a white disc containing the state coat of arms, bordered by an olive wreath. The capital is Belmopan.

CONTEMPORARY POLITICAL HISTORY

Historical Context

Belize, known as British Honduras until June 1973, was first colonized by British settlers (the 'Baymen') in the 17th century, but was not recognized as a British colony until 1862. In 1954 a new Constitution granted universal adult suffrage and provided for the creation of a legislative assembly. The territory's first general election, in 1954, was won by the only party then organized, the People's United Party (PUP), led by George Price. The PUP won all subsequent elections until 1984. In 1961 Price was appointed First Minister under a new ministerial system of government. The colony was granted internal self-government in 1964, with the United Kingdom retaining responsibility for defence, external affairs and internal security. Following an election in 1965, Price became Premier and a bicameral legislature was introduced. In 1970 the capital of the territory was moved from Belize City to the newly built town of Belmopan.

Domestic Political Affairs

Much of the recent history of Belize has been dominated by the territorial dispute with Guatemala, particularly in the years prior to Belize's independence (see Foreign Affairs). This was achieved on 21 September 1981, within the Commonwealth, and with Price becoming Prime Minister. However, party disunity and the failure of the 1981 draft treaty with Guatemala undermined the dominance of the PUP, and the party's 30 years of rule ended at the general election of December 1984 when the United Democratic Party (UDP), led by Manuel Esquivel, took power. However, the PUP returned to office following the general election of September 1989 and Price was again appointed Prime Minister. The PUP performed poorly at the general election of June 1993, and an alliance of the UDP and the National Alliance for Belizean Rights was able to form a Government. Esquivel was appointed Prime Minister.

The PUP Government of Said Musa

At the general election of August 1998 the PUP, led by Said Musa, won an overwhelming victory. The result reflected popular discontent with the outgoing Government's structural adjustment policies, including the introduction of value-added tax (VAT), which the PUP had pledged to repeal. Following the defeat of his party, Esquivel, who had lost his seat in the House of Representatives, resigned as leader of the UDP. He was succeeded by Dean Barrow.

In July 1999 Prime Minister Musa issued a statement rejecting allegations that Michael Ashcroft, a businessman with dual British/Belizean nationality and Belize's ambassador to the UN, had used improper influence in Belizean affairs and was involved in money-laundering. Ashcroft resigned his UN post in March 2000. In late 2000 the remit of an inquiry commissioned by the British Government into Belize's financial system was expanded to investigate public investment companies, including Ashcroft's Carlisle Holdings. In December 2001 it was announced that the Government had refused the United Kingdom's offer of £10m. of debt relief in exchange for a reform of its financial regime and an end to tax relief given to Carlisle Holdings and another company.

On 14 February 2001 the leaders of 11 Caribbean countries, including Belize, signed an agreement to establish a Caribbean Court of Justice (CCJ), based in Trinidad and Tobago. In July 2004 parliament approved legislation sanctioning Belize's membership of the CCJ in its original jurisdiction. In February 2010 the House of Representatives unanimously passed legislation replacing the Privy Council (based in the United Kingdom) with the CCJ as Belize's final court of appeal. The law came into effect on 1 June.

In February 2002 the controversial policy of economic citizenship was formally abolished. However, a report produced in July by the Ministry of Foreign Affairs substantiated claims that the immigration authorities had apparently continued the practice illegally until that month.

Musa became the country's first Prime Minister to be sworn in for a second term in office following the PUP's victory in the March 2003 general election. The PUP won 22 seats in the House of Representatives, while the UDP increased its legislative representation to seven seats (from three). The PUP, which had repealed the unpopular VAT during its 1998–2003 administration, promised that, if re-elected, it would abolish sales tax on basic items and move towards the eradication of personal income tax.

Despite some implementation of pre-election pledges the PUP struggled to maintain popular support during 2004 as protracted financial crises in the Development Finance Corporation (DFC) and the Social Security Board (SSB) forced the Government to reduce spending on social projects. An audit into the SSB's financial operations found that it had made a series of unsecured loans, incurring substantial financial losses. A Senate Select Committee, established to investigate allegations of maladministration by the SSB, found evidence of negligence and recklessness in the purchase and sale of mortgage loans. The Government subsequently dismissed the SSB's General Manager and board of directors, and dissolved the DFC.

BTL ownership

In 2005 controversy arose over the ownership of Belize Telecommunications Ltd (BTL, later renamed Belize Telemedia Ltd). In 2001 the Government had sold the company to Carlisle Holdings. Three years later, in 2004, it bought back those shares and immediately sold them to US company Innovative Communication Corporation (ICC). However, in February 2005 the Government resumed control of BTL after it claimed that ICC had not met a payment deadline. ICC maintained that the default was owing to government failure to meet certain conditions regarding licensing agreements and guaranteed rates of return. In March the Chief Justice launched an inquiry into the various ownerships of BTL between 2001 and 2005. In March 2005 ICC was granted a temporary injunction by a US court that returned control of BTL to it and reinstated four ICC-appointed board members. However, the Supreme Court of Belize ruled that the injunction was not enforceable in Belize. Meanwhile, members of the Belize Communication Workers' Union demanded that majority ownership of BTL be transferred to the company's employees. In mid-April anti-Government feeling led to a strike by BTL employees and several days of violent protests by union members and students, during which shops were looted and more than 100 people arrested. The armed forces were deployed to restore order in the capital. In June the House of Representatives approved the sale of BTL shares: 20% would be sold to employees, 12.5% to a subsidiary of Carlisle Holdings and 5% to other Belizeans. However, the Court of Appeals two months later overturned earlier supreme court rulings upholding government action in BTL, and ruled that control of the telecommunications company be returned to ICC and that all sales of BTL shares since 9 February be annulled.

The UDP in power

The opposition UDP won a convincing victory in the general election held on 7 February 2008, securing 25 of the 31 legislative seats and 57% of the valid votes cast. The PUP's representation was significantly reduced, to six remaining seats, after obtaining 41% of the vote. Some 74.5% of eligible voters participated in the poll. The UDP had campaigned against what it perceived as corruption and mismanagement in the Musa administration. UDP leader Dean Barrow was sworn in as Prime Minister on 8 February. In a concurrent referendum, 61.5% of voters supported proposals for an elected Senate.

In late 2008 former Prime Minister Musa was arrested and charged with diverting US $20m. in Venezuelan grant funds intended for social and construction projects, to the Belize Bank, in order to pay the debt of the privately owned Universal Hospital. In addition, Musa's Government had initially stated that it had received the sum of $10m., a gross discrepancy with the amount Venezuela claimed to have given. Musa's case was referred to the Supreme Court; however, in June 2009 this court overturned a lower court ruling that Musa should stand trial.

Rising levels of violent crime prompted Barrow to create a Ministry of Police and Public Security in June 2010. Douglas Singh was given responsibility for the new portfolio, while Carlos Perdomo, erstwhile Minister of National Security, was appointed Minister of Defence. The annual murder rate in the country rose steeply in 2010, from 97 to 129, while the rate of detection remained low. In an attempt to address this, in September the new security minister announced plans to introduce a witness protection programme. Moreover, in April 2011 the Government announced new bail restrictions, and from August the right to trial by jury was removed from defendants accused of murder, with such cases to be determined solely by a Supreme Court judge. A Caribbean Community and Common Market (CARICOM, see p. 223) initiative to address gang-related criminal activity commenced in Belize during October. Nevertheless, there were 125 murders in 2011.

The CCJ adjudged in July 2011 that two members of the previous PUP administration, Florencio Marin and José Coye, could be brought to trial by the Belizean Government on charges of misfeasance relating to allegedly corrupt land deals. The use of the tort system against former cabinet ministers was without precedent. Following his resignation on grounds of ill health, John Briceño was replaced as PUP leader by Francis Fonseca in October. Some commentators claimed that Briceño had stepped down because his position had become untenable as a result of the chronic infighting and factionalism that had characterized his tenure.

Renationalization of BTL

Following the approval of an amendment to the Telecommunications Law in the House of Representatives in August 2009, the Barrow administration announced the renationalization of BTL. The former owners again protested against the decision, claiming it was unconstitutional, and referred the matter to the Supreme Court. In August 2010 that body ruled that the Government's decision had been lawful. In October some 45% of shares in BTL went on sale to the public. A further 10% of shares were to be reserved for BTL employees. It was intended that majority ownership of the company would remain in Belizean hands. However, in June 2011 the Court of Appeal overturned the Supreme Court's 2010 judgment, declaring that the 2009 renationalization had indeed been in breach of the Constitution. In response, the Government asserted that it would only relinquish control of BTL if an enforcement order were issued—arguing that the Court of Appeal's ruling was merely 'declaratory'—and proposed a constitutional amendment to 'enshrine Belizean public ownership of the utilities'. This change to the Constitution was duly approved by the House of Representatives in October 2011, ostensibly ending any further legal challenges to the control of BTL by the state. (An appeal against this amendment, lodged by the Ashcroft-owned British Caribbean Bank, had been rejected by the CCJ in August.) However, further confusion was caused in June 2012 when the Supreme Court issued an ambiguous ruling on the matter. The Court declared that, while the Government was entitled to retain ownership of BTL, some of the actions that it had taken during the previous year to secure control of the company had been unlawful. Meanwhile, in June 2011 the financially troubled Belize Electricity Ltd (BEL) was also renationalized, although its former owner, Canadian company Fortis, commenced legal action against the Government in October, claiming that this purchase had violated the Constitution. In early 2014 the Court of Appeal was considering multiple petitions regarding the BTL and BEL renationalizations, the legal status of which remained unclear.

The Barrow administration generated further controversy in June 2013 after it seized control of the International Business Companies Registry and the International Merchant Marine Registry. In addition, Belize International Services Ltd (BISL), which had ostensibly been contracted to manage the registries until 2020, was furnished with a BZ $30m. tax bill. BISL vehemently protested against the takeover and the 'arbitrary' tax assessment and threatened the Government with litigation. Barrow claimed that BISL's contract had expired and denied any wrongdoing.

Recent developments: Barrow's second term

General and municipal elections were held on 7 March 2012. The UDP secured re-election, albeit with a much reduced majority, winning 17 of the 31 legislative seats and 49.3% of the valid votes cast. The PUP garnered almost as many votes (49.1%), but this translated into just 14 seats in the House of Representatives. The UDP also performed well in the local elections, retaining control of six of the country's nine municipalities, including Belmopan and Belize City. Prime Minister Barrow indicated that his priority at the beginning of a second term would be renegotiation of Belize's debt-servicing obligations (see Economic Affairs).

A truce between criminal gangs in Belize City, which had been agreed in September 2011, with government mediation, disintegrated in April 2012 following a sharp rise in gang-related violence during that month. In response, the Government deployed a contingent of soldiers to Belize City, increased police patrols, and established vehicle checkpoints. In spite of these measures, a record 145 homicides occurred in 2012, although a decline in the murder rate was reported in 2013.

Foreign Affairs

The frontier with Guatemala was agreed by a convention in 1859, but this was declared invalid by Guatemala in 1940. Guatemalan claims to sovereignty of Belize date back to the middle of the 19th century and were written into Guatemala's Constitution in 1945. In November 1975 and July 1977 British troops and aircraft were sent to protect Belize from the threat of Guatemalan invasion, and a battalion of troops and a detachment of fighter aircraft remained in the territory. In November 1980 the UN General Assembly overwhelmingly approved a resolution urging that Belize be granted independence (similar resolutions having been adopted in 1978 and 1979), and the United Kingdom decided to proceed with a schedule for independence, after having excluded the possibility of any cession of land to Guatemala. A tripartite conference in March 1981 appeared to produce a sound basis for a final settlement, with Guatemala accepting Belizean independence in exchange for access to the Caribbean Sea through Belize and the use of certain offshore cayes and their surrounding waters. Further tripartite talks in the same year collapsed, however, as a result of renewed claims by Guatemala to Belizean land. With Belizean independence imminent, Guatemala made an unsuccessful appeal to the UN Security Council to intervene, severing diplomatic relations with the United Kingdom and sealing its border with Belize on 7 September. Tripartite talks in January 1983 collapsed when Belize rejected Guatemala's proposal that Belize should cede the southern part of the country.

At independence the United Kingdom had agreed to leave troops as protection and for training of the Belize Defence Force. In 1987 renewed discussions were held between Guatemala, the United Kingdom and Belize (although Belize was still regarded by Guatemala as being only an observer at the meetings), and in 1988 the formation of a permanent joint commission (which, in effect, entailed a recognition of the Belizean state by Guatemala) was announced.

In 1991 Belize and Guatemala signed an accord under the terms of which Belize pledged to legislate to reduce its maritime boundaries and to allow Guatemala access to the Caribbean Sea and use of its port facilities. In return, Guatemala officially recognized Belize as an independent state and established diplomatic relations, although it maintained its territorial claim over the country. In January 1992 the Maritime Areas Bill was approved in the Belizean House of Representatives. In April 1993 Belize and Guatemala signed a non-aggression pact, affirming their intent to refrain from the threat or use of force against each other, and preventing either country from being used as a base for aggression against the other.

In 1994 responsibility for the defence of Belize was transferred to the Belize Defence Force; all British troops were withdrawn, with the exception of some 180 troops who remained to organize training for jungle warfare. In March Guatemala formally reaffirmed its territorial claim to Belize, prompting the Belizean Minister of Foreign Affairs to seek talks with the British Government regarding assistance with national defence. In 1996 the Ministers of Foreign Affairs of Belize and Guatemala conducted preliminary talks in New York, USA, concerning a resumption of negotiations on the territorial dispute. Further such discussions were conducted in the following year. In November 1998, at a meeting of ambassadors and officials of both countries, agreement was reached on the establishment of a joint commission to deal with immigration, cross-border traffic and respect for the rights of both countries' citizens.

In June 2002 the Ministers of Foreign Affairs from both countries met under the auspices of the Organization of American States (OAS) to discuss the border dispute issue. Following further, OAS-mediated, negotiations, in September proposals were outlined for a solution to the dispute. These included the provision that Guatemala would recognize Belize's land boundary as laid out in the treaty of 1859. Guatemala would be granted a 200 sq mile Exclusive Economic Zone in the Gulf of Honduras, although Belize and Honduras would retain fishing rights and 50% of any mineral resources discovered in the seabed. A Commission comprising Belize, Guatemala and Honduras would manage fishing in the Gulf of Honduras. However, in 2003 the Guatemalan Government announced it would reject the OAS-proposed agreement. Delegations from the two countries met for further OAS-mediated negotiations in May 2004, and in September 2005 representatives of the two countries signed a new Agreement on a Framework of Negotiation and Confidence-Building Measures. The first meetings under the new accord were held in November in Belize, with future meetings scheduled to take place every 45 days thereafter. Following almost two years of negotiations, in March 2007 representatives of Belize and Guatemala signed a preliminary trade accord, allowing 150 products to be traded duty-free. However, a lack of progress in the talks prompted the Secretary-General of the OAS to suggest that the two countries take the dispute to the International Court of Justice (ICJ). In September 2010 the House of Representatives finally voted to hold a plebiscite to ascertain public support for the ICJ's intervention in the dispute. Under OAS mediation, in November 2011 the foreign ministers of Belize and Guatemala agreed that concurrent referendums on the issue would be conducted by the end of 2013; the date for the plebiscites was later set for 6 October, although this was postponed at Guatemala's request in April. Bilateral discussions were ongoing in 2014, and an agreement was signed by both countries in January, but it remained unclear when the referendums would be held.

The Government signed a reciprocal ship-boarding agreement with the USA in 2005 in an attempt to prevent the transportation of weapons of mass destruction, and in 2009 the USA agreed to provide US $1.1m. in funding for an initiative to combat organized crime and drugs-trafficking. However, in an unprecedented move, reflecting the growing significance of Belize to criminals involved in the transshipment of illegal drugs, the country was added to the USA's black list of significant drugs-producing and -trafficking nations in September 2011.

GOVERNMENT AND CONSTITUTION

The Constitution of Belize came into effect at independence on 21 September 1981. Belize is a constitutional monarchy, with the British sovereign as Head of State. Executive authority is vested in the sovereign and is exercised by the Governor-General, who is appointed on the advice of the Prime Minister, must be of Belizean nationality, and acts, in almost all matters, on the advice of the Cabinet. The Governor-General is also advised by an appointed Belize Advisory Council. Legislative power is vested in the bicameral National Assembly, comprising a Senate (12 members appointed by the Governor-General) and a House of Representatives (31 members elected by universal adult suffrage for five years, subject to dissolution). The Governor-General appoints the Prime Minister and, on the latter's recommendation, other ministers. The Cabinet is responsible to the House of Representatives.

REGIONAL AND INTERNATIONAL CO-OPERATION

Belize is a member of the Caribbean Community and Common Market (CARICOM, see p. 223), the Association of Caribbean States (see p. 449), the Organization of American States (OAS, see p. 394), the Inter-American Development Bank (IDB, see p. 331), and of the Community of Latin American and Caribbean States (see p. 464), which was formally inaugurated in December 2011. Belize is also a member of the Central American Integration System (SICA, see p. 229). Belize joined CARICOM's Caribbean Single Market and Economy (CSME), which was established on 1 January 2006. The CSME was intended to enshrine the free movement of goods, services and labour throughout the CARICOM region, although only six of the organization's 15 members were signatories to the new project from its inauguration.

Belize became a member of the UN upon independence in 1981. The country became a contracting party to GATT (which was superseded by the World Trade Organization, WTO, see p. 434 in 1995) in 1983. As a member of the Commonwealth (see p. 236), Belize enjoys guaranteed access to the EU under the Cotonou Agreement (see p. 324), and tariff-free access to the USA under the Caribbean Basin Initiative.

ECONOMIC AFFAIRS

In 2011, according to estimates by the World Bank, Belize's gross national income (GNI), measured at average 2009–11 prices, was US $1,322m., equivalent to US $4,180 per head (or $6,880 per head on an international purchasing-power parity basis). During 2003–12 Belize's population grew at an average annual rate of 2.6%, while in 2003–11 gross domestic product (GDP) per head increased, in real terms, at an average annual rate of 0.2%. According to official figures, overall GDP increased, in real terms, at an average rate of 3.0% per year in 2003–12; growth was an estimated 4.0% in 2012.

Although 38% of the country is considered suitable for agriculture, only an estimated 6.9% of the total area was used for agricultural purposes in 2011. Nevertheless, agriculture, hunting, forestry and fishing contributed 13.9% of GDP in 2012, according to preliminary figures, and employed 20.7% of the working population in 2006. About 34,000, or 23.0% of the working population, were engaged in the agricultural sector in 2014, according to FAO. The principal cash crops are citrus fruits, sugar cane and bananas. Agricultural policy promotes the cultivation of crops for domestic consumption and the diversification of crops for export. Maize, rice and red kidney beans are the principal domestic food crops, and the development of crops such as soybeans (soya beans), papayas, organic rice and cocoa is being encouraged. The country is largely self-sufficient in fresh meat and eggs. Belize has considerable timber reserves, particularly of tropical hardwoods, and the forestry sector is being developed. The fishing sector increased in the 2000s, largely owing to an expansion in farmed shrimp production. In 2012 marine products provided 10.4% of total export revenue. The fishing catch totalled 268,200 metric tons in 2011, according to FAO estimates. According to preliminary official figures, agricultural GDP increased, in real terms, by an average annual rate of 0.3% in 2003–12; sectoral GDP decreased by 4.3%, in 2011, but increased by an estimated 6.8% in 2012.

Industry (including mining, manufacturing, construction, water and electricity) employed 15.7% of the working population in 2006 and contributed 19.3% of GDP in 2011, according to preliminary figures. According to preliminary official figures, industrial GDP increased at an average annual rate of 4.6% in 2003–12; industrial GDP decreased by a provisional 4.5% in 2012.

Mining accounted for 0.5% of GDP in 2012, according to preliminary figures, and employed 0.4% of the working population in 2006. Mining GDP increased at an average rate of 4.4% per year during 2003–12. The sector expanded significantly from the mid-2000s following the discovery of high-quality crude petroleum in 2005; the sector recorded an estimated increase of 9.2% in 2012.

According to preliminary official figures, manufacturing accounted for 13.1% of GDP in 2012 and employed 7.2% of the working population in 2006. Dominant activities are petroleum-refining, the manufacture of clothing and the processing of agricultural products, particularly sugar cane (for sugar and rum). According to preliminary figures, manufacturing GDP increased at an average rate of 5.9% per year during 2003–12, fuelled mainly by a growth in petroleum refining; however, the sector decreased by 2.6% in 2011 and by a further estimated 7.6% in 2012.

Construction accounted for 3.1% of GDP in 2012, according to preliminary figures, and employed 7.2% of the working population in 2006. Construction GDP decreased at an average rate of 1.9% per year during 2003–12. The sector decreased by 2.6% in 2011, but recovered in 2012, expanding by 15.2% in that year.

Imports of fuels and lubricants accounted for 16.3% of the total cost of imports in 2012. Belize Natural Energy discovered Belize's first commercially viable oilfield in 2005, with proven recoverable reserves of 10m. barrels. In addition to the Mollejón hydroelectric station on the Macal River, a hydroelectric dam at Chalillo on the Macal River provided an estimated 7.3 MW of electricity annually and, according to the Government, would meet Belize's energy needs for 50 years. The dam was operated by its Canadian contractor, Fortis Inc, before transfer to state ownership in 2031. Belize was a signatory of the Petrocaribe agreement with Venezuela, under which it could purchase petroleum at reduced prices. A 30 MW bagasse-fuelled co-generation facility, adjacent to the Tower Hill sugar factory, which began operations in 2010, supplied about 25% of electricity production.

The services sector employed 63.5% of the working population in 2006 and contributed 66.8% of GDP in 2012, according to preliminary figures. Tourism development is concentrated on promoting eco-tourism, based on the attraction of Belize's natural environment, particularly its rainforests and the barrier reef, the second largest in the world. Revenue from tourism totalled US $299m. in 2012, compared with US $248m. in the previous year. The number of tourist arrivals fell by 6.1% in 2012; a decrease was recorded in the number of cruise ship passengers (576,661, compared with 654,790 in the previous year), whereas the number of stop-over visitors, a traditionally higher-spending sector, increased (257,291 in 2012, compared with 233,257 in 2011). According to preliminary official figures, the GDP of the services sector increased, in real terms, at an average annual rate of 3.3% in 2003–12; real sectoral GDP increased by 4.0% in 2012.

According to IMF estimates, in 2012 Belize recorded a merchandise trade deficit of US $208.8m. and a deficit of US $27.5m. on the current account of the balance of payments. In 2012 the principal source of imports was the USA (accounting for 29.2% of the total), followed by the People's Republic of China, Mexico and the United Kingdom. The USA was also the principal export market, accounting for 45.1% of total exports in 2012, followed by the United Kingdom. The principal exports in 2012 were crude petroleum (27.4%), orange concentrate, sugar, bananas and marine products. The principal imports in that year were machinery and transport equipment (18.1%), mineral fuels and lubricants, manufactured goods, food and live animals, chemicals, and miscellaneous manufactured articles. The commercial free zone provided 20.0% of imports in 2012.

For the financial year 2013–14 there was an estimated budgetary deficit of BZ $61.6m. Belize's general government gross debt was BZ $2,477m. in 2012, equivalent to 77.7% of GDP. Belize's total external debt was estimated at $1,278m. in 2011, of which $1,018m. was public and publicly guaranteed debt. In that year the cost of servicing long-term public and publicly guaranteed debt and repayments to the IMF was equivalent to 13.9% of the value of exports of goods, services and income (excluding workers' remittances). The annual rate of inflation averaged 2.1% in 2005–12. Consumer prices fell by 1.9% in 2011, but increased by 4.2% in 2012. In September 2012 some 16.1% of the total labour force were unemployed. Many Belizeans, however, work abroad, and remittances to the country from such workers are an important source of income.

The credibility of Belize's leading financial institutions and its ability to access sources of external finance were severely damaged following a sovereign default in 2006. At the same time, the economy had to contend with restructuring in the agricultural sector (following the cessation of European Union preferential prices for sugar and bananas). However, amendments to the Income and Business Tax Act in 2007 significantly increased revenue, enabling the Government to direct 40% of total revenues from the emerging petroleum sector into budgetary operations. This sector had enjoyed impressive growth following the discovery of a large deposit of high-quality crude petroleum in 2005, although output appeared to have peaked by 2009, precipitating a period of gradual decline. Further uncertainty was generated in the petroleum industry in April 2013 when the Supreme Court, citing alleged environmental violations, annulled six offshore drilling agreements previously approved by the Government. Although this ruling was overturned in June following a successful government appeal, the Prime Minister declared that additional studies would need to be carried out before the authorization of any new offshore contracts. Meanwhile, there were concerns that the renationalization of Belize Telemedia Ltd and Belize Electricity Ltd during 2009–11 would deter investors and exacerbate the country's debt problems. In August 2012 the Government effectively defaulted again on its debt obligations when it confirmed that it was unable to honour an interest payment on a US $547m. 'superbond', which had been created in the aftermath of the 2006 default. Following lengthy negotiations with creditors, a debt-restructuring agreement was reached in February 2013. Growth of 2.1% in 2011 and 4.0% in 2012 was driven by a recovery in the agricultural sector and an increase in stay-over tourist arrivals. Although tourism indicators remained positive in 2013, economic expansion decelerated to around 2.5% in that year, according to IMF estimates, owing to the poor performance of the agricultural and oil sectors.

PUBLIC HOLIDAYS

2015: 1 January (New Year's Day), 9 March (National Heroes' and Benefactors' Day), 3–6 April (Easter), 1 May (Labour Day), 25 May (for Sovereign's Day), 10 September (National Day), 21 September (Independence Day), 12 October (Day of the Americas), 19 November (Garifuna Settlement Day), 25–26 December (Christmas).

Statistical Survey

Sources (unless otherwise stated): Statistical Institute of Belize, 1902 Constitution Drive, Belmopan; tel. 822-2207; internet www.statisticsbelize.org.bz; Central Bank of Belize, Gabourel Lane, POB 852, Belize City; tel. 223-6194; fax 223-6226; e-mail cenbank@btl.net; internet www.centralbank.org.bz.

AREA AND POPULATION

Area: 22,965 sq km (8,867 sq miles).

Population: 240,204 at census of 12 May 2000; 312,698 (males 157,935, females 154,763) at census of 12 May 2010. *Mid-2014:* (UN estimate): 339,758 (Source: UN, *World Population Prospects: The 2012 Revision*).

Density (at mid-2014): 14.8 per sq km.

Population by Age and Sex (UN estimates at mid-2014): *0–14:* 113,316 (males 57,345, females 55,971); *15–64:* 212,789 (males 106,075, females 106,714); *65 and over:* 13,653 (males 6,250, females 7,403); *Total* 339,758 (males 169,670, females 170,088). Source: UN, *World Population Prospects: The 2012 Revision*.

Districts (population at 2010 census): Belize 89,247; Cayo 72,899; Orange Walk 45,419; Corozal 40,354; Stann Creek 32,166; Toledo 30,538. Note: Figures exclude homeless (118) and institutionalized population (1,957).

Principal Towns (population at 2010 census): Belize City (former capital) 65,042; San Ignacio/Santa Elena 16,977; Orange Walk 13,400; Belmopan (capital) 13,351; San Pedro 11,510; Corozal 9,901; Dangriga (fmrly Stann Creek) 9,096; Benque Viejo 5,824; Punta Gorda 5,205. *Mid-2011* (UN estimate, incl. suburbs): Belmopan 14,472 (Source: UN, *World Urbanization Prospects: The 2011 Revision*).

Births, Marriages and Deaths (2009 unless otherwise indicated): Registered live births 7,126 (birth rate 22.1 per 1,000, 2008); Registered marriages 1,895 (marriage rate 5.7 per 1,000); Registered deaths 1,453 (death rate 4.4 per 1,000).

Life Expectancy (years at birth): 73.5 (males 70.6; females 76.6) in 2011. Source: World Bank, World Development Indicators database.

Economically Active Population (April 2006): Agriculture 18,406; Forestry 733; Fishing 2,070; Mining and quarrying 434; Manufacturing 7,363; Electricity, gas and water 879; Construction 7,390; Wholesale and retail trade and repairs 16,722; Tourism (incl. restaurants and hotels) 13,981; Transport, storage and communications 4,352; Financial intermediation 1,800; Real estate, renting and business activities 2,431; General government services 9,345; Community, social and personal services 16,041; Other 285; *Total employed* 102,233. *Total labour force* (persons aged 14 years and over, September 2009): 144,363 (employed 126,188, unemployed 18,176). *2010 Census:* Total employed 100,537; Unemployed 30,180; Total labour force 130,717 (males 79,760, females 50,957). *September 2012:* Total employed 126,624; Unemployed 24,387; Total labour force 151,011 (males 89,763, females 61,248).

HEALTH AND WELFARE

Key Indicators

Total Fertility Rate (children per woman, 2011): 2.7.

Under-5 Mortality Rate (per 1,000 live births, 2011): 17.

HIV/AIDS (% of persons aged 15–49, 2012): 1.4.

Physicians (per 1,000 head, 2009): 0.8.

Hospital Beds (per 1,000 head, 2010): 1.2.

Health Expenditure (2010): US $ per head (PPP): 428.

Health Expenditure (2010): % of GDP: 5.8.

Health Expenditure (2010): public (% of total): 66.0.

Access to Water (% of persons, 2011): 99.

Access to Sanitation (% of persons, 2011): 90.

Total Carbon Dioxide Emissions ('000 metric tons, 2010): 21.7.

Carbon Dioxide Emissions Per Head (metric tons, 2010): 1.4.

Human Development Index (2012): ranking: 96.

Human Development Index (2012): value: 0.702.

For sources and definitions, see explanatory note on p. vi.

AGRICULTURE, ETC.

Principal Crops ('000 metric tons, 2012): Rice, paddy 22.0*; Maize 65.0*; Sorghum 12.0*; Sugar cane 1,070.0; Beans, dry 4.0*; Fresh vegetables 4.5*; Bananas 76.0*; Plantains 12.0*; Oranges 190.0; Grapefruit and pomelos 56.0*; Papayas 24.0*. *Aggregate Production* ('000 metric tons, may include official, semi-official or estimated data): Vegetables (incl. melons) 11.8; Fruits (excl. melons) 362.9.

Livestock ('000 head, year ending September 2012, FAO estimates): Horses 6; Cattle 92; Pigs 17; Sheep 13; Chickens 1,550.

Livestock Products ('000 metric tons, 2012, FAO estimates): Cattle meat 1.6; Chicken meat 14.4; Pig meat 1.4; Cows' milk 5.4; Hen eggs 2.0.

Forestry (2012): *Roundwood Removals* ('000 cubic metres, excl. bark, FAO estimates): Sawlogs, veneer logs and logs for sleepers 41; Fuel wood 126; Total 167. *Sawnwood Production* ('000 cubic metres, incl. railway sleepers, FAO estimates): Coniferous (softwood) 5; Broadleaved (hardwood) 30; Total 35.

Fishing ('000 metric tons, live weight, 2011): Capture 263.4 (Albacore 10.0; Caribbean spiny lobster 0.8; Stromboid conchs 2.9; Yellowfin tuna 3.2); Aquaculture 4.8* (White leg shrimp 4.0*); Total catch 268.2*.

* FAO estimate.

Source: FAO.

INDUSTRY

Production (2005, unless otherwise indicated): Raw sugar 118,339 long tons (2012/13); Molasses 34,508 long tons (2012/13); Cigarettes 78 million; Beer 1,891,000 gallons; Batteries 6,000; Flour 26,959,000 lb; Fertilizers 26,874,000 short tons; Garments 611,900 items; Soft drinks 4,929,000 gallons; Citrus concentrates 2,973,000 gallons (2004); Single strength juices 2,102,000 gallons (2004). Source: mainly IMF, *Belize: Selected Issues and Statistical Appendix* (October 2006).

FINANCE

Currency and Exchange Rates: 100 cents = 1 Belizean dollar (BZ $). *Sterling, US Dollar and Euro Equivalents* (31 December 2013): £1 sterling = BZ $3.294; US $1 = BZ $2.000; €1 = BZ $2.758; BZ $100 = £30.36 = US $50.00 = €36.26. *Exchange rate*: Fixed at US $1 = BZ $2.000 since May 1976.

Budget (BZ $ million, year ending 31 March 2014, provisional): *Revenue:* Taxation 727.0 (Taxes on income and profits 233.8, Taxes on property 7.2, Taxes on goods and services 282.6, International trade and transactions 203.5); Other current revenue 99.3; Capital revenue 5.1; Total 831.4, excl. grants (41.1). *Expenditure:* Current expenditure 777.9 (Personal emoluments 313.2, Pensions 55.2, Goods and services 181.5, Debt service 95.9, Subsidies and current transfers 132.0); Capital expenditure 156.2; Total 934.1.

International Reserves (US $ million at 31 December 2012): IMF special drawing rights 30.80; Reserve position in the IMF 6.51; Foreign exchange 251.61 Total 288.92. Source: IMF, *International Financial Statistics*.

Money Supply (BZ $ million at 31 December 2012): Currency outside depository corporations 193.06; Transferable deposits 909.81; Other deposits 1,340.65; *Broad money* 2,443.51. Source: IMF, *International Financial Statistics*.

Cost of Living (Consumer Price Index; base: 2005 = 100): All items 113.2 in 2010; 111.1 in 2011; 115.8 in 2012. Source: IMF, *International Financial Statistics*.

Expenditure on the Gross Domestic Product (BZ $ million at current prices, 2012 preliminary): Government final consumption expenditure 471.6; Private final consumption expenditure 2,212.8; Gross fixed capital formation 505.7; Change in inventories –1.9; *Gross domestic expenditure* 3,188.1; Exports of goods and services 1,913.5; *Less* Imports of goods and services 1,980.6; Statistical discrepancy 24.2; *GDP at market prices* 3,145.2.

Gross Domestic Product by Economic Activity (BZ $ million at current prices, 2012, preliminary): Agriculture, hunting, forestry and fishing 398.7; Mining and quarrying 15.1; Electricity, gas and water 72.7; Manufacturing 374.9; Construction 87.8; Wholesale and retail trade, repairs 466.0; Hotels and restaurants 137.7; Transport, storage and communications 345.5; Financial intermediation 236.9; Real estate, renting and business activities 195.4; Government services 320.6; Other activities 208.1; *Sub-total* 2,859.5; *Less* Financial intermediation services indirectly measured (FISIM) 121.8; *GDP at factor cost* 2,737.7; Taxes on products, less subsidies 407.5; *GDP at market prices* 3,145.2.

Balance of Payments (US $ million, 2012): Exports of goods 628.2; Imports of goods –837.0; *Balance on goods* –208.8; Exports of services 413.6; Imports of services –187.8; *Balance on goods and services* 17.0; Primary income received 5.1; Primary income paid –125.4; *Balance on goods, services and primary income* –103.3; Secondary income (net) 75.7; *Current balance* –27.5; Capital account (net) 22.5; Financial account (net) 73.1; Net errors and omissions –12.7; *Reserves and related items* 55.5 (Source: IMF, *International Financial Statistics*).

EXTERNAL TRADE

Principal Commodities (BZ $ million, 2012): *Imports c.i.f.:* Food and live animals 193.2; Mineral fuels and lubricants 286.4; Chemicals and related products 159.4; Manufactured goods 203.1; Miscellaneous manufactured articles 106.2; Machinery and transport equipment 319.0; Commercial free zone 351.3; Export processing zone 64.9; Total (incl. others) 1,760.4. *Exports f.o.b.:* Citrus concentrate 123.1; Marine products 70.9; Sugar 107.8; Bananas 92.6; Papaya 15.5; Crude petroleum 186.3; Total (incl. others) 680.9.

Principal Trading Partners (BZ $ million, 2012): *Imports c.i.f.:* China, People's Republic 220.1; Costa Rica 22.0; Jamaica 14.2; Mexico 184.4; Panama 69.3; Trinidad and Tobago 32.8; United Kingdom 17.9; USA 514.8; Total (incl. others) 1,760.4. *Exports f.o.b.:* China, People's Republic 6.0; Jamaica 26.8; Mexico 8.9; Trinidad and Tobago 32.4; United Kingdom 155.0; USA 307.1; Total (incl. others) 680.9.

TRANSPORT

Road Traffic (vehicles in use, 2007): Public vehicles 3,612 (Buses 769, Taxis 2,843); Passenger cars 14,156; Motorcycles 2,389; Pick-up vehicles 15,181; Goods vehicles 4,757; Total vehicles (incl. others) 56,094.

Shipping (sea-borne freight traffic, '000 metric tons, 1996): Goods loaded 255.4; Goods unloaded 277.1. *Flag Registered Fleet* (at 31 December 2013): Number of vessels 1,038; Total displacement 2,372,268 grt (Source: Lloyd's List Intelligence—www.lloydslistintelligence.com).

Civil Aviation (traffic at Philip Goldson International Airport, 2011): Aircraft movement 27,135; Passengers carried 464,732 (Passenger arrivals 244,006, Passenger departures 220,726) Freight carried 1,006 metric tons.

TOURISM

Tourist Arrivals: 914,797 (cruise ship passengers 688,165, stop-over visitors 226,632) in 2010; 888,047 (cruise ship passengers 654,790, stop-over visitors 233,257) in 2011; 833,952 (cruise ship passengers 576,661, stop-over visitors 257,291) in 2012.

Stop-over Visitors by Country of Origin (2012): Guatemala 958; Mexico 5,048; USA 175,957; Total (incl. others) 257,291.

Tourism Receipts (US $ million, excl. passenger transport): 249 in 2010; 248 in 2011; 299 in 2012 (provisional). Source: World Tourism Organization.

COMMUNICATIONS MEDIA

Telephones (2012): 25,400 main lines in use.

Mobile Cellular Telephones (2012): 164,200 subscribers.

Internet Subscribers (2010): 9,400.

Broadband Subscribers (2012): 10,000.

Source: International Telecommunication Union.

EDUCATION

Pre-primary (2011/12): 209 schools, 436 teachers, 7,116 students (males 3,611, females 3,505).

Primary (2011/12): 292 schools, 3,215 teachers, 69,331 students (males 35,478, females 33,853).

Secondary (2011/12): 53 schools, 1,413 teachers, 19,665 students (males 9,465, females 10,200).

Higher (2011/12, unless otherwise indicated): 12 institutions (1997/98), 229 teachers, 4,629 students (males 1,654, females 2,975).

Vocational/Technical (2011/12): 81 teachers, 566 students (males 432, females 134).

Pupil-teacher Ratio (primary education, UNESCO estimate): 21.6 in 2011/12.

Source: Ministry of Education, Youth and Sports; UNESCO Institute for Statistics.

Adult Literacy Rate (UNESCO estimates): 76.9% (males 77.1%; females 76.7%) in 2003. Source: UN Development Programme, *Human Development Report*.

Directory

The Government

HEAD OF STATE

Queen: HM Queen ELIZABETH II.

Governor-General: Sir COLVILLE YOUNG (appointed 17 November 1993).

THE CABINET
(April 2014)

The Government is formed by the United Democratic Party.

Prime Minister and Minister of Finance and Economic Development: DEAN O. BARROW.

Deputy Prime Minister and Minister of Natural Resources and of Agriculture: GASPAR VEGA.

Attorney-General and Minister of Foreign Affairs: WILFRED ELRINGTON.

Minister of Trade, Investment Promotion, Private Sector Development and Consumer Protection: ERWIN CONTRERAS.

Minister of Education, Youth and Sports: PATRICK FABER.

Minister of National Security: JOHN SALDIVAR.

Minister of Housing and Urban Development: MICHAEL FINNEGAN.

Minister of Works and Transport: RENE MONTERO.

Minister of Tourism and Culture: MANUEL HEREDIA, Jr.

Minister of Health: PABLO MARIN.

Minister of Labour, Local Government, Rural Development and National Emergency Management: GODWIN HULSE.

Minister of the Public Service and Elections and Boundaries: CHARLES GIBSON.

Minister of Forestry, Fisheries and Sustainable Development: LISELLE ALAMILLA.

Minister of Human Development, Social Transformation and Poverty Alleviation: ANTHONY MARTINEZ.

Minister of Energy, Science and Technology and Public Utilities: JOY GRANT.

There are, in addition, six Ministers of State.

MINISTRIES

Office of the Prime Minister: Sir Edney Cain Bldg, 3rd Floor, Left Wing, Belmopan; tel. 822-2346; fax 822-0898; e-mail secretarypm@opm.gov.bz; internet www.opm.gov.bz.

Ministry of Agriculture: West Block Bldg, 2nd Floor, Belmopan; tel. 822-2241; fax 822-2409; e-mail info@agriculture.gov.bz; internet www.agriculture.gov.bz.

Ministry of Education, Youth and Sports: West Block Bldg, 3rd Floor, Belmopan; tel. 822-2380; fax 822-3389; e-mail moeducation.moes@gmail.com; internet www.moes.gov.bz.

Ministry of Energy, Science and Technology and Public Utilities: Market Sq., Cayo District, Belmopan; tel. 822-0160; fax 822-0433; e-mail minister.sec@mysc.gov.bz; internet estpu.gov.bz.

Ministry of Finance and Economic Development: New Administration Bldg, Belmopan; tel. 822-2362; fax 822-2886; e-mail econdev@btl.net; internet www.mof.gov.bz.

Ministry of Foreign Affairs: NEMO Bldg, 2nd Floor, POB 174, Belmopan; tel. 822-2167; fax 822-2854; e-mail belizemfa@btl.net; internet www.mfa.gov.bz.

Ministry of Forestry, Fisheries and Sustainable Development: Sir Edney Cain Bldg, Ground Floor, Left Wing, Belmopan; tel. 822-2526; fax 822-3673; internet www.forestdepartment.gov.bz (Forestry), www.agriculture.gov.bz/Fisheries_Dept.html (Fisheries), www.doe.gov.bz (Environment).

Ministry of Health: East Block Bldg, Independence Plaza, Belmopan; tel. 822-2068; fax 822-2942; e-mail seniorsecretary@health.gov.bz; internet health.gov.bz/moh.

Ministry of Housing and Urban Development: Sir Edney Cain Bldg, 2nd Floor, Left Wing, Belmopan; tel. 822-1039; fax 822-3337; e-mail ministry@housing.gov.bz.

Ministry of Human Development, Social Transformation and Poverty Alleviation: West Block Bldg, Independence Plaza, Belmopan; tel. 822-2161; fax 822-3175; e-mail secretary@humandev.gov.bz.

Ministry of Labour, Local Government, Rural Development and National Emergency Management: 6/8 Trinity Blvd, Belmopan; tel. 822-2297; fax 822-0156; e-mail labour.comm@labour.gov.bz.

Ministry of National Security: Curl Thompson Bldg, Belmopan; tel. 822-2817; fax 822-2195; e-mail minofnatsec@mns.gov.bz.

Ministry of Natural Resources: Market Sq., Belmopan; tel. 822-3286; fax 822-2333; e-mail minister@mnrei.gov.bz; internet www.mnrei.gov.bz.

Ministry of the Public Service and Elections and Boundaries: Sir Edney Cain Bldg, Ground Floor, Left Wing, Belmopan; tel. 822-0929; fax 822-2206; e-mail ceo@mps.gov.bz; internet www.gob.gov.bz.

Ministry of Tourism and Culture: 106 South St, Belize City; tel. 227-2801; fax 227-2810; e-mail dcabelize@btl.net; internet www.belizetourism.org (Tourism); www.nichbelize.org (Culture).

Ministry of Trade, Investment Promotion, Private Sector Development and Consumer Protection: Sir Edney Cain Bldg, Ground Floor, Left Wing, Belmopan; tel. 822-2526; fax 822-3673; e-mail foreigntrade@btl.net.

Ministry of Works and Transport: New 2 Power Lane, Belmopan; tel. 822-2136; fax 822-3282; e-mail works@btl.net, departmentoftransport@yahoo.com.

Office of the Attorney-General: General Office, Belmopan; tel. 822-2504; fax 822-3390; e-mail agministrybze@yahoo.com.

Legislature

NATIONAL ASSEMBLY

The Senate

President: MARCO PECH.

There are 12 nominated members in addition to the current ex officio President.

House of Representatives

Speaker: MICHAEL PEYREFITTE.

Clerk: EDDIE WEBSTER.

General Election, 7 March 2012

	Valid votes cast	% of total	Seats
United Democratic Party (UDP)	61,903	49.33	17
People's United Party (PUP)	61,556	49.05	14
Others	2,032	1.62	—
Total valid votes*	125,491	100.00	31

* In addition, there were 4,767 blank, invalid or spoiled votes cast.

Election Commissions

Elections and Boundaries Commission: Belize City; f. 1978; appointed by Governor-Gen; comprises Chair. and 4 mems; separate entity to the Elections and Boundaries Dept; Chair. BERNARD PITTS.

Elections and Boundaries Department: Charles Bartlett Hyde Bldg, Mahogany St Extension, POB 913, Belize City; tel. 222-4042; fax 222-4991; e-mail electbound@btl.net; internet www.elections.gov.bz; f. 1989; dept under the Ministry of the Public Service and Elections and Boundaries; Chief Elections Officer JOSEPHINE TAMAI.

Political Organizations

People's National Party (PNP): 57 Main St, Punta Gorda Town, Toledo Dist; tel. 610-0978; fax 225-2571; e-mail info@pnpbelize.org; internet www.pnpbelize.org; f. 2007; Leader WIL MAHEIA.

People's United Party (PUP): 3 Queen St, Belize City; tel. 677-9169; fax 223-3476; internet www.pup.org.bz; f. 1950; based on organized labour; publs *The Belize Times*; Leader FRANCIS WILLIAM FONSECA; Chair. HENRY USHER; Sec.-Gen. MYRTLE PALACIO.

United Democratic Party (UDP): South End Bel-China Bridge, POB 1898, Belize City; tel. 227-2576; fax 227-6441; e-mail unitedd@btl.net; internet www.udp.org.bz; f. 1974 by merger of People's Development Movement, Liberal Party and National Independence Party; conservative; Leader DEAN BARROW; Chair. ALBERTO AUGUST.

Vision Inspired by the People (VIP): VIP Secretariat, Unit 2, Garden City Hotel, Belmopan, Belize City; e-mail vipbelize@gmail.com; f. 2005; Chair. ROBERT (BOBBY) LOPEZ.

Diplomatic Representation

EMBASSIES AND HIGH COMMISSION IN BELIZE

Brazil: 12 Floral Park Ave, POB 548, Belmopan; tel. 822-0460; fax 822-0461; e-mail brasemb.belmopan@itamaraty.gov.br; internet belmopan.itamaraty.gov.br; Ambassador LUCIO PIRES DE AMORIM.

Costa Rica: 1 Marigold St, Orchid Garden Extension, POB 288, Belmopan; tel. 822-1582; fax 822-1583; e-mail embaticabz@gmail.com; Ambassador INGRID HERMANN ESCRIBANO.

Cuba: 6087 Manatee Dr., Buttonwood Bay, POB 1775, Belize City; tel. 223-5345; fax 223-1105; e-mail embacuba@btl.net; internet www.cubadiplomatica.cu/belice; Ambassador JOSÉ PRIETO CINTADO.

El Salvador: 13 Citron St, Cohune Walk, POB 215, Belmopan; tel. 823-3404; fax 823-3569; e-mail embasalva@btl.net; Ambassador ROLANDO ROBERTO BRIZUELA RAMOS.

Guatemala: 8A St, King's Park, POB 1771, Belize City; tel. 223-3150; fax 223-5140; e-mail embbelice@minex.gob.gt; Ambassador MANUEL ARTURO TÉLLEZ MIRALDA.

Honduras: 2½ Miles, Northern Hwy, POB 285, Belize City; tel. 224-5889; fax 223-0562; e-mail embahonbe@yahoo.com; Ambassador SANDRA ROSALES ABELLA.

Mexico: 3 North Ring Rd, Embassy Sq., Belmopan; tel. 822-2480; fax 822-2487; e-mail embamexbze@btl.net; internet www.sre.gob.mx/belice; Ambassador MARIO VELÁZQUEZ SUAREZ.

Nicaragua: 1 South St, Belize City; tel. and fax 227-0335; e-mail belkysgrl@yahoo.com; Ambassador GILDA MARIA BOLT GONZÁLEZ (resident in El Salvador).

Taiwan (Republic of China): 20 North Park St, POB 1020, Belize City; tel. 227-8744; fax 223-3082; e-mail embroc@btl.net; internet www.taiwanembassy.org/bz; Ambassador DAVID C. K. WU.

United Kingdom: Embassy Sq., POB 91, Belmopan; tel. 822-2146; fax 822-2761; e-mail brithicom@btl.net; internet ukinbelize.fco.gov.uk; High Commissioner PETER HUGHES.

USA: Floral Park Rd, POB 286, Belmopan; tel. 822-4011; fax 822-4012; e-mail embbelize@state.gov; internet belize.usembassy.gov; Ambassador CARLOS MORENO.

Venezuela: 17 Orchid Garden St, POB 49, Belmopan; tel. 822-2384; fax 822-2022; e-mail embaven@btl.net; Ambassador YOEL DE VALLE PÉREZ MARCANO.

Judicial System

Summary Jurisdiction Courts (criminal jurisdiction) and District Courts (civil jurisdiction), presided over by magistrates, are established in each of the six judicial districts. Summary Jurisdiction Courts have a wide jurisdiction in summary offences and a limited jurisdiction in indictable matters. Appeals lie to the Supreme Court, which has jurisdiction corresponding to the English High Court of Justice. From the Supreme Court further appeals lie to a Court of Appeal. Since June 2010 final appeals are made to the Caribbean Court of Justice, based in Trinidad and Tobago, rather than to the Privy Council in the United Kingdom.

Court of Appeal: Belize City; tel. 227-3490; internet www.belizejudiciary.org/web/court-of-appeal-2/; f. 1967; Pres. MANUEL SOSA.

Supreme Court: Supreme Court Bldg, Belize City; tel. 227-7377; fax 227-0181; e-mail info@belizejudiciary.org; internet www.belizejudiciary.org; Chief Justice KENNETH BENJAMIN; Registrar VELDA FLOWERS.

Magistrates' Court: Paslow Bldg, Belize City; tel. 227-7164; fax 227-6268; e-mail magistratecourtbz@gmail.com; internet www.belizejudiciary.org/web/magistracy; Chief Magistrate ANN MARIE SMITH.

Attorney-General: WILFRED ELRINGTON.

Religion

CHRISTIANITY

Most of the population are Christian, the largest denomination being the Roman Catholic Church.

Belize Council of Churches: 149 Allenby St, POB 508, Belize City; tel. 227-7077; f. 1957 as Church World Service Cttee; present name adopted 1984; 9 mem. churches, 4 assoc. bodies; Pres. Rev. ROOSEVELT PAPOULOUTE; Sec. KAREN TAYLOR.

The Roman Catholic Church

According to the 2010 census, 40.4% of the population are Roman Catholics. Belize comprises the single diocese of Belize City-Belmopan, suffragan to the archdiocese of Kingston in Jamaica. The Bishop participates in the Antilles Episcopal Conference (whose secretariat is based in Port of Spain, Trinidad and Tobago).

Bishop of Belize City-Belmopan: DORICK MCGOWAN WRIGHT, Bishop's House, 144 North Front St, POB 616, Belize City; tel. 223-6919; fax 223-1922; e-mail info@catholic.bz; internet catholic.bz.

The Anglican Communion

Anglicans in Belize, accounting for some 4.6% of the population at the 2010 census, belong to the Church in the Province of the West Indies, comprising eight dioceses. The Archbishop of the Province currently is the Bishop of Barbados.

Bishop of Belize: Rt Rev. PHILIP S. WRIGHT, Rectory Lane, POB 535, Belize City; tel. 227-3029; fax 227-6898; e-mail diocese@belizeanglican.org; internet www.belize.anglican.org.

Protestant Churches

According to the 2010 census, some 8.5% of the population are Pentecostalists, 5.5% Seventh-day Adventists, 3.8% Mennonites, 3.6% Baptists and 2.9% Methodists.

Mennonite Congregations in Belize: POB 427, Belize City; tel. 823-0137; fax 823-0101; f. 1958; in 2010 there were an estimated 11,658 mems living in Mennonite settlements, the largest of which was Altkolonier Mennonitengemeinde, followed by Beachy Amish Mennonite Fellowship, Caribbean Light and Truth, Church of God in Christ, Evangelical Mennonite Mission Conference, Iglesia Evangélica Menonita de Belice, among others; Bishop AARON HARDER.

Methodist Church in the Caribbean and the Americas (Belize/Honduras District) (MCCA): 75 Albert St, POB 212, Belize City; tel. 227-7173; fax 227-5870; e-mail roodypap@btl.net; internet www.mccalive.org; f. 1824; c. 1,827 mems; District Pres. Rev. ROOSVELT PAPOULOUTE.

Other denominations active in the country include the Nazarene Church, Jehovah's Witnesses, Mormons and the Salvation Army.

OTHER RELIGIONS

There are also small communities of Hindus (612, according to the census of 2010), Muslims (577 in 2010) and Bahá'ís (202 in 2010), together accounting for less than 1% of the population.

The Press

Amandala: Amandala Press, 3304 Partridge St, POB 15, Belize City; tel. 202-4476; fax 222-4702; e-mail info@amandala.com.bz; internet www.amandala.com.bz; f. 1969; 2 a week; independent; Publr EVAN X. HYDE; Editor RUSSELL VELLOS; circ. 45,000.

Ambergris Today: Pescador Dr., POB 23, San Pedro Town, Ambergris Caye; tel. 226-3462; fax 226-3483; e-mail ambergristoday@yahoo.com; internet www.ambergristoday.com; weekly; independent; Editor DORIAN NUÑEZ.

The Belize Ag Report: POB 150, San Ignacio, Cayo District; tel. 663-6777; e-mail belizeagreport@gmail.com; internet belizeagreport.com; agriculture newsletter; fortnightly; Editor BETH GOULD ROBERSON.

The Belize Times: 3 Queen St, POB 506, Belize City; tel. 671-8385; fax 223-1940; e-mail editortimes@yahoo.com; internet www.belizetimes.bz; f. 1956; weekly; party political paper of PUP; Editor-in-Chief ALBERTO VELLOS; circ. 6,000.

Government Gazette: Print Belize Ltd, 1 Power Lane, Belmopan; tel. 822-0194; fax 822-3367; e-mail admin@printbze.com; f. 1871; official; weekly; CEO LAWRENCE J. NICHOLAS.

The Guardian: Ebony St and Bel-China Bridge, POB 1898, Belize City; tel. 207-5346; fax 227-5343; e-mail guardian@btl.net; internet www.guardian.bz; weekly; party political paper of UDP; Editor ALFONSO NOBLE; circ. 5,000.

The National Perspective: 25 Nanche St, Belmopan; tel. 635-3506; e-mail nationalperspectiveeditor@gmail.com; internet nationalperspectivebz.com; f. 2008; weekly; PUP oriented; Publr and Editor OMAR SILVA.

The Reporter: 147 West St, POB 707, Belize City; tel. 227-2503; fax 227-8278; e-mail editor@belizereporter.bz; internet www.reporter.bz; f. 1967; weekly; Editor DYON ELLIOT; circ. 6,500.

The San Pedro Sun: 63 Barrier Reef Dr., POB 35, San Pedro Town, Ambergris Caye; tel. 226-2070; fax 226-2905; e-mail spsun@sanpedrosun.com; internet www.sanpedrosun.com; f. 1993; weekly; Publr RON SNIFFIN; Editor TAMARA SNIFFIN.

Publishers

Angelus Press Ltd: 10 Queen St, POB 1757, Belize City; tel. 223-5777; fax 227-8825; e-mail angel@btl.net; f. 1885; owned by the Santiago Castillo Group since 1997; Gen. Man. AMPARO MASSON NOBLE.

Cubola Productions: Montserrat Casademunt, 35 Elizabeth St, Benque Viejo del Carmen; tel. 823-2083; fax 823-2240; e-mail cubolabz@btl.net; internet www.cubola.com; Dir MONTSERRAT CASADEMUNT.

Print Belize Ltd: 1 Power Lane, Belmopan; tel. 822-2293; fax 882-3367; e-mail admin@printbelize.com; internet www.printbelize.com; f. 1871; responsible for printing, binding and engraving requirements of all govt depts and ministries; publications include annual govt estimates, govt magazines and the official *Government Gazette*; CEO LAWRENCE J. NICHOLAS.

Broadcasting and Communications

TELECOMMUNICATIONS

Belize Telemedia Ltd: Esquivel Telecom Centre, St Thomas St, POB 603, Belize City; tel. 223-2868; fax 223-1800; e-mail prdept@btl.net; internet www.belizetelemedia.net; f. May 2007; fmrly Belize Telecommunications Ltd (subsidiary of Innovative Communication Corpn (ICC) until taken over by the Govt in 2005); nationalized Aug. 2009; partially privatized in 2010; Exec. Chair. NESTOR VASQUEZ.

SpeedNet Communications Ltd: 2½ miles Northern Hwy, Belize City; tel. 280-1000; fax 223-1919; e-mail sduncan@speednet-wireless.com; internet www.smart-bz.com; f. 2003, commenced services in 2005; mobile cellular telecommunications provider under the brand name Smart; Man. (IT) SEAN DUNCAN.

Regulatory Authority

Public Utilities Commission (PUC): see Utilities—Regulatory Body.

BROADCASTING

Radio

KREM Radio Ltd: 3304 Partridge St, POB 15, Belize City; tel. 202-4409; fax 222-4220; e-mail contact@krembz.com; internet www.krembz.com; f. 1989; commercial; private radio station; Station Man. MICHAEL HYDE.

Love FM: 7145 Slaughterhouse Rd, POB 1865, Belize City; tel. 203-0528; fax 203-0529; e-mail lovefmbelize@yahoo.com; internet www.lovefm.com; f. 1992; purchased Friends FM in 1998; CEO RENE VILLANUEVA, Sr.

Other private radio stations broadcasting in Belize include: Estereo Amor, More FM, My Refuge Christian Radio, Radio 2000 and Voice of America.

Television

Centaur Cable Network (CTV): 31 Clarke St, Orange Walk; tel. 670-2216; fax 322-2216; e-mail jeb@centaurcablenetwork.com; internet www.ctv3belizenews.com; f. 1989; commercial; Man. Dir JAIME BRICEÑO.

Channel 5 Belize: Great Belize Productions Ltd, 2882 Coney Dr., POB 1314, Belize City; tel. 223-7781; fax 223-4936; e-mail gbtv@btl.com; internet www.channel5belize.com; f. 1991; CEO AMALIA MAI.

Tropical Vision (Channel 7): 73 Albert St, Belize City; tel. 223-5589; fax 227-5602; e-mail tvseven@btl.net; internet 7newsbelize.com; commercial; Man. Dir NESTOR VASQUEZ.

Regulatory Authority

Belize Broadcasting Authority (BBA): 7 Gabourel Lane, Belize City; tel. and fax 223-3953; e-mail broadcasting_bze@hotmail.com; regulatory authority; Chair. LOUIS LESLIE.

Finance

(cap. = capital; res = reserves; dep. = deposits; brs = branches; amounts in BZ $, unless otherwise indicated)

BANKING

Central Bank

Central Bank of Belize: Gabourel Lane, POB 852, Belize City; tel. 223-6194; fax 223-6226; e-mail cenbank@btl.net; internet www.centralbank.org.bz; f. 1982; cap. 10m., res 23.9m., dep. 337.9m. (2009); Gov. GLENFORD YSAGUIRRE; Chair. Sir MANUEL ESQUIVEL.

Development Bank

Development Finance Corporation: Bliss Parade, Belmopan; tel. 822-2360; fax 822-3096; e-mail info@dfcbelize.org; internet www.dfcbelize.org; f. 1972; issued cap. 10m.; 5 brs; Chair. DENNIS JONES.

Other Banks

Atlantic Bank Ltd: Cnr Freetown Rd and Cleghorn St, POB 481, Belize City; tel. 223-4123; fax 223-3907; e-mail atlantic@atlabank.com; internet www.atlabank.com; f. 1971; 52% owned by Honduran co Sociedad Nacional de Inversiones, SA (SONISA); dep. 161.0m., total assets 191.9m. (2001); Gen. Man. SANDRA BEDRAN; 8 brs.

Atlantic International Bank Ltd: Cnr Withfield Tower, 2nd Floor, 4792 Coney Dr., POB 1811, Belize City; tel. 223-3152; fax 223-3528; e-mail info@atlanticibl.com; internet www.atlanticibl.com; affiliated to Atlantic Bank Ltd; Gen. Man. RICARDO PELAYO.

Belize Bank International: Matalon Business Center, 2nd Floor, POB 364, Belize City; tel. 227-0697; fax 227-0983; e-mail services@bcbankinternational.com; internet bcbankinternational.com; fmrly British Caribbean Bank International; name changed as above in 2012.

Belize Bank Ltd: 60 Market Sq., POB 364, Belize City; tel. 227-7132; fax 227-2712; e-mail bblbz@belizebank.com; internet www.belizebank.com; subsidiary of BCB Holdings; cap. US $2.2m., res US $2.1m., dep. US $489m. (March 2010); Chair. LYNDON GUISEPPI; 10 brs.

Caye International Bank Ltd (CIBL): Coconut Dr., San Pedro, POB 11, Ambergris Caye; tel. 226-2388; fax 226-2892; e-mail cibl@btl.net; internet www.cayebank.bz; Chair. JOEL NAGEL.

FirstCaribbean International Bank (Barbados) Ltd (Barbados): 21 Albert St, POB 363, Belize City; tel. 227-7211; fax 227-8572; e-mail care@firstcaribbeanbank.com; internet www.firstcaribbeanbank.com; f. 2002 by merger of CIBC West Indies Holdings and Barclays Bank PLC Caribbean operations; Barclays relinquished its stake to CIBC in June 2006; Exec. Chair. MICHAEL MANSOOR; Exec. Dir RIK PARKHILL; 5 brs.

Heritage Bank Ltd: 106 Princess Margaret Dr., POB 1988, Belize City; tel. 223-6783; fax 223-6785; e-mail services@banking.bz; internet www.heritageibt.com/domestic; f. 2001 as Alliance Bank of Belize Ltd; name changed as above in 2010; dep. 6,876m., total assets 113.7m.; Dir CRESENCIA BRADLEY; 3 brs.

Heritage International Bank and Trust Ltd: 35 Barrack Rd, POB 1867, Belize City; tel. 223-5698; fax 223-0368; e-mail services@banking.bz; internet www.heritageibt.com/international; f. 1998 as Provident Bank and Trust of Belize; name changed as above in 2010; cap. US $6.0m., res US $1.5m., dep. US $105.9m. (2004); Man. Dir STEPHEN DUNCAN.

Scotiabank Belize Ltd (Canada): Albert St, POB 708, Belize City; tel. 227-7027; fax 227-7416; e-mail belize.scotia@scotiabank.com; internet www.scotiabank.com/bz/en; f. 1968; Pres. and CEO RICHARD E. WAUGH; Man. Dir PAT ANDREWS; 11 brs.

INSURANCE

The insurance sector is regulated by the Office of the Supervisor of Insurance, part of the Ministry of Finance and Economic Development.

Atlantic Insurance Company Ltd: Atlantic Bank Bldg, 3rd Floor, Cnr Cleghorn St and Freetown Rd, POB 1447, Belize City; tel. 223-2657; fax 223-2658; e-mail info@atlanticinsurancebz.com; internet www.atlanticinsurancebz.com; f. 1991; part of the Atlantic Group of Cos; holding co, Sociedad Nacional de Inversiones, SA, (SONISA); Gen. Man. MARTHA GUERRA.

Belize Insurance Centre: 212 North Front St, Belize City; tel. 227-7310; fax 227-4803; e-mail info@belizeinsurance.com; internet www.belizeinsurance.com; f. 1972; insurance broker; subsidiary of Fraser Fontaine & Kong Ltd (Jamaica); Chair. G. RICHARD FONTAINE; Gen. Man. CYNTHIA AWE.

Insurance Corporation of Belize Ltd: 7 Daly St, Belize City; tel. 224-5328; fax 223-1317; e-mail icb@icbinsurance.com; internet www.icbinsurance.com; f. 1982; general insurance; Exec. Dir ERDULFO NUÑEZ.

RF & G Insurance Co Ltd: Gordon House, 1 Coney Dr., POB 661, Belize City; tel. 223-5734; fax 223-6734; e-mail info@rfginsurancebelize.com; internet www.rfginsurancebelize.com; f. 2005 by merger of F&G Insurance and Regent Insurance; underwriters of all major classes of insurance; mem. of the Roe Group of Cos; Chair. CHRISTOPHER ROE; Man. Dir GUY HOWISON.

RF & G Life Insurance Company Ltd: Gordon House, 4th Floor, 1 Coney Dr., POB 661, Belize City; tel. 223-5734; fax 223-6734; e-mail info@rfglife.com; internet www.rfglife.com; f. 2005 through merger of the Life and Medical portfolios of F&G Insurance Co into Regent Life; mem. of the Roe Group of Cos; Chair. BRIAN D. ROE; Gen. Man. RHONDA LECKY.

Trade and Industry

STATUTORY BODIES

Belize Agricultural Health Authority: Cnr Forest Dr. and Hummingbird Hwy, POB 169, Belmopan; tel. 822-0818; fax 822-0271; e-mail baha@btl.net; internet www.baha.bz; Man. Dir EMIR CRUZ.

Belize Marketing and Development Corporation (BMDC): 117 North Front St, POB 633, Belize City; tel. 227-7402; fax 227-7656; f. 1948 as Belize Marketing Board to encourage the growing of staple food crops; renamed as above in 2003; promotes domestic produce; Man. Dir ROQUE MAI.

Belize Social Investment Fund: 1902 Constitution Dr., Belmopan; tel. 822 0239; fax 822 0508; e-mail daniel.cano@sifbelize.org; internet sifbelize.org; f. 1996; Exec. Dir DANIEL CANO.

Coastal Zone Management Authority and Institute (CZMAI): POB 1884, Belize City; tel. 223-0719; fax 223-5738; e-mail czmbze@btl.net; internet www.coastalzonebelize.org; Man. Dir VINCENT GILLETT.

Pesticides Control Board (PCB): Central Farm, Cayo District; tel. 824-2640; fax 824-3486; e-mail pcbinfo@btl.net; internet www.pcbbelize.com; Chair. EUGENE WAIGHT.

DEVELOPMENT ORGANIZATION

Belize Trade and Investment Development Service (BELTRAIDE): 14 Orchid Garden St, Belmopan; tel. 822-3737; fax 822-0595; e-mail beltraide@belizeinvest.org.bz; internet www.belizeinvest.org.bz; f. 1986 as a joint govt and private sector institution to encourage export and investment; Exec. Chair. MICHAEL SINGH; Exec. Dir NICOLAS RUIZ.

CHAMBERS OF COMMERCE

American Chamber of Commerce of Belize: 5½ Miles Western Hwy, Cucumber Beach, Marina, POB 75, Belize City; tel. 222-4344; fax 222-4265; e-mail office@amchambelize.org; internet www.amchambelize.org; Pres. PHIL HAHN; Sec. CON MURPHY.

Belize Chamber of Commerce and Industry (BCCI): 4792 Coney Dr., Withfield Tower, 1st Floor, POB 291, Belize City; tel. 223-5330; fax 223-5333; e-mail bcci@belize.org; internet www.belize.org; f. 1920; Pres. KAY MENZIES; CEO KIM AIKMAN; 300 mems.

EMPLOYERS' ASSOCIATIONS

Banana Growers' Association: Big Creek, Independence Village, Stann Creek District; tel. 523-2000; fax 523-2112; e-mail banana@btl.net; Chair. ANTONIO (TONY) ZABANEH.

Belize Citrus Growers Association (BCGA): Mile 9, Stann Creek Valley Rd, POB 7, Dangriga, Stann Creek District; tel. 522-3585; fax 522-2686; e-mail cga@belizecitrus.org; internet www.belizecitrus.org; f. 1967; Chair. ECCLESTON IRVING; CEO HENRY N. ANDERSON.

Belize Livestock Producers' Association (BLPA): 47½ miles Western Hwy, POB 183, Belmopan; tel. 822-3883; e-mail blpa@btl.net; internet www.blpabz.org; f. 1972; Chair. JOHN CARR.

Belize Sugar Cane Farmers' Association (BSCFA): 34 San Antonio Rd, Orange Walk; tel. 322-2005; fax 322-3171; f. 1959 to assist cane farmers and negotiate with the Sugar Cane Board and manufacturers on their behalf; Chair. RAMON ABAN; Dir ALFREDO ORTEGA; 16 district brs.

United Cane Farmers' Association (UCFA): Orange Walk; f. 2009; breakaway faction of the BSCFA; Chair. WILFREDO MAGAÑA.

UTILITIES

Regulatory Body

Public Utilities Commission (PUC): 41 Gabourel Lane, POB 300, Belize City; tel. 223-4938; fax 223-6818; e-mail info@puc.bz; internet www.puc.bz; f. 1999; regulatory body, headed by commissioners; replaced the Offices of Electricity Supply and of Telecommunications following enaction of the Public Utilities Commission Act in 1999; Chair. JOHN AVERY.

Electricity

Belize Electricity Co Ltd (BECOL): 115 Barrack Rd, POB 327, Belize City; tel. 227-0954; fax 223-0891; e-mail bel@btl.net; internet www.fortisinc.com; wholly owned subsidiary of Fortis Inc (Canada); operates Mollejón 25.2-MW hydroelectric plant and Chalillo 7.3-MW hydroelectric facility, which supply electricity to Belize Electricity Ltd (BEL—see below); Pres. and CEO H. STANLEY MARSHALL.

Belize Electricity Ltd (BEL): 2½ miles Northern Hwy, POB 327, Belize City; tel. 227-0954; fax 223-0891; e-mail pr@bel.com.bz; internet www.bel.com.bz; fmrly Belize Electricity Board, changed name upon privatization in 1992; nationalized in 2011; 70.2% owned by the Govt of Belize and 26.9% owned by Social Security Board; Pres. and CEO JEFFREY LOCKE; Chair. RODWELL WILLIAMS; 251 employees.

Belize Co-Generation Energy Ltd (BELCOGEN): Tower Hill, Orange Walk Town; operations began 2009; jtly owned by BEL and Belize Sugar Industries Ltd; 31.5 MW biomass plant fuelled by bagasse (sugar cane fibre); Man. Dir JOEY MONTALVO.

Water

Belize Water Services Ltd: 7 Central American Blvd, POB 150, Belize City; tel. 222-4757; fax 222-4759; e-mail bws_ceosec@btl.net; internet www.bws.bz; f. 1971 as Water and Sewerage Authority (WASA); changed name upon privatization in 2001; renationalized in Oct. 2005 prior to partial reprivatization in early 2006; Chair. ALBERTO AUGUST; CEO ALVAN HAYNES.

TRADE UNIONS

National Trade Union Congress of Belize (NTUCB): POB 2359, Belize City; tel. 227-2678; fax 227-2864; e-mail ntucb@btl.net; f. 1966; Pres. DYLAN RENEAU; Gen. Sec. REBECCA SUAZO.

Transport

Department of Transport: NEMO Bldg, Belmopan; tel. 822-2135; fax 822-3317; e-mail departmentoftransport@yahoo.com; Commr GARRET MURILLO.

RAILWAYS

There are no railways in Belize.

ROADS

There are 2,872 km of roads, of which some 2,210 km (1,600 km of gravel roads, 300 km of improved earth roads and 310 km of unimproved earth roads) are unpaved. A double-lane bridge was built over the Sibun River in 2004, and over Silver Creek in 2006. The Middlesex Bridge over Stann Creek was reconstructed at a cost of BZ $2.2m. in 2010. There are four major highways that connect all the major cities and towns and lead to the Mexican and Guatemalan borders. In 2011 work began on the BZ $48m. Southern Highway connecting the south of the country to the Guatemala border. The project was financed by the Kuwaiti Fund for Economic Development and the Development Fund of the Organization of Petroleum Exporting Countries.

SHIPPING

There is a deep-water port at Belize City and a second port at Commerce Bight, near Dangriga (formerly Stann Creek), to the south of Belize City. There is a port for the export of bananas at Big Creek and additional ports at Corozal and Punta Gorda. At 31 December 2013 the flag registered fleet comprised 1,038 vessels, totalling 2,372,268 grt, of which nine were gas tankers, 25 were bulk carriers and 386 were general cargo ships.

Belize Ports Authority: 120 North Front St, POB 633, Belize City; tel. 223-0752; fax 223-0710; e-mail bzportauth@btl.net; internet www.portauthority.bz; f. 1980; Commr of Ports Maj. (retd) J. M. A. FLOWERS.

Marine & Services Ltd: Blake Bldg, Suite 203, Cnr Hudson and Eyre St, POB 611, Belize City; tel. 227-2113; fax 227-5404; e-mail info@marineservices.bz; internet www.marineservices.bz; f. 1975; shipping and cargo services, cruise line agent; Man. JOSE GALLEGO.

Port of Belize Ltd: Caesar Ridge Rd, POB 2674, Belize City; tel. and fax 223-2439; fax 223-3571; e-mail info@portofbelize.com; internet www.portofbelize.com; operates the main port facility; CEO ARTURO VASQUEZ; Deputy CEO FRANZINE WAIGHT.

CIVIL AVIATION

Philip S. W. Goldson International Airport, 16 km (10 miles) from Belize City, can accommodate medium-sized jet-engined aircraft. There are 37 airstrips for light aircraft on internal flights near the major towns and offshore islands.

Belize Airports Authority (BAA): POB 1564, Belize City; tel. 225-2045; fax 225-2439; e-mail bzeaa@btl.net; Chair. JOHN WAIGHT; Gen. Man. (vacant).

Department of Civil Aviation: POB 367, Belize City; tel. 225-2052; fax 225-2533; e-mail dcabelize@btl.net; internet www.civilaviation.gov.bz; f. 1931; Dir JOSE A. CONTRERAS.

Maya Island Air: Municipal Airstrip, Bldg 1, 2nd Floor, POB 458, Belize City; tel. 223-1140; fax 223-0576; e-mail regional@mayaislandair.com; internet www.mayaregional.com; f. 1961 as merger between Maya Airways Ltd and Island Air; operated by Belize Air Group; internal services, centred on Belize City, and charter flights to neighbouring countries; CEO LOUIS ZABANEH; Gen. Man. CARLOS VARGAS.

Tropic Air: San Pedro, POB 20, Ambergris Caye; tel. 226-2012; fax 226-2338; e-mail reservations@tropicair.com; internet www.tropicair.com; f. 1979; operates internal services and services to Guatemala; Chair. CELI MCCORKLE.

Tourism

The main tourist attractions are the beaches and the barrier reef, diving, fishing and the Mayan archaeological sites. There are nine major wildlife reserves, and government policy is to develop eco-tourism, based on the attractions of an unspoiled environment and Belize's natural history. The country's wildlife includes howler monkeys and 500 species of birds, and its barrier reef is the second largest in the world. In 2012 there were 833,952 tourist arrivals, of which some 576,661 were cruise ship passengers and 257,291 were stop-over visitors. Tourism receipts totalled a provisional US $299m. in 2012.

Belize Tourism Board: 64 Regent St, POB 325, Belize City; tel. 227-2420; fax 227-2423; e-mail info@travelbelize.org; internet www.belizetourism.org; f. 1964; fmrly Belize Tourist Bureau; 8 mems; CEO TRACY PANTON; Chair. IAN LIZARRAGA.

Belize Tourism Industry Association (BTIA): 10 North Park St, POB 62, Belize City; tel. 227-1144; fax 227-8710; e-mail info@btia.org; internet www.btia.org; f. 1985; promotes sustainable tourism; Pres. JIM SCOTT; Exec. Dir WENDY LEMUS; 500 mems.

Defence

The Belize Defence Force was formed in 1978 and was based on a combination of the existing Police Special Force and the Belize Volunteer Guard. Military service is voluntary, but provision has been made for the establishment of National Service, if necessary, to supplement normal recruitment. As assessed at November 2013, the regular armed forces totalled approximately 1,050 and there were some 700 militia reserves. The British Army Training Support Unit Belize was withdrawn at the end of 2010. In 2005 the Belize National Coast Guard Service was inaugurated to combat drugs-trafficking, illegal immigration and illegal fishing in Belize's territorial waters. The Coast Guard comprised 58 volunteer officers from the Belize Defence Force, the Belize Police Department, the Customs and Excise Department, the National Fire Service, the Department of Immigration and Nationality Services, the Ports Authority, and the Fisheries Department.

Defence Budget: an estimated BZ $36m. in 2013.

Belize Defence Force Commandant: Col DAVID NEJEMIAH JONES.

Education

Education is compulsory for all children for a period of 10 years between the ages of five and 14 years. Primary education, beginning at five years of age and lasting for eight years, is provided free of charge, principally through subsidized denominational schools under government control. In 2011/12 there were 69,331 pupils enrolled in primary institutions. Secondary education, beginning at the age of 13, lasts for four years. Some 19,665 students were enrolled in secondary education in 2011/12.

In 2011/12 there were 5,195 students enrolled in higher, technical or vocational colleges. The main institution of higher education is the University of Belize, which was formed in 2000 through the amalgamation of five higher education institutions. The private Galen University also offers degree courses. There is an extra-mural branch of the University of the West Indies in Belize. Government expenditure on education in the financial year 2013/14 was projected at BZ $207.2m.

BENIN

Introductory Survey

LOCATION, CLIMATE, LANGUAGE, RELIGION, FLAG, CAPITAL

The Republic of Benin is a narrow stretch of territory in West Africa. The country has an Atlantic coastline of about 100 km (60 miles), flanked by Nigeria to the east and Togo to the west; its northern borders are with Burkina Faso and Niger. Benin's climate is tropical, and is divided into three zones: the north has a rainy season between July and September, with a hot, dry season in October–April; the central region has periods of abundant rain in May–June and in October; and there is year-round precipitation in the south, the heaviest rains being in May–October. Average annual rainfall in Cotonou is 1,300 mm. French is the official language, but each of the indigenous ethnic groups has its own language. Bariba and Fulani are the major languages in the north, while Fon and Yoruba are widely spoken in the south. It is estimated that 38% of the people are Christians, mainly Roman Catholics, 24% are Muslims, while 23% follow traditional beliefs and customs. The national flag (proportions 2 by 3) has a vertical green stripe at the hoist, with equal horizontal stripes of yellow over red in the fly. The administrative capital is Porto-Novo, but most government offices and other state bodies are presently in the economic capital, Cotonou.

CONTEMPORARY POLITICAL HISTORY

Historical Context

Benin, called Dahomey until 1975, was formerly part of French West Africa. It became a self-governing republic within the French Community in December 1958, and an independent state on 1 August 1960. Hubert Maga became the country's first President, but was deposed by the military in October 1963. The early years of independence were characterized by chronic political instability and by periodic regional unrest, fuelled by long-standing rivalries between north and south.

A new Constitution, providing for a return to civilian rule, was approved by referendum in March 1968; however, the presidential election held in May was declared void, and in June the military regime nominated Dr Emile-Derlin Zinsou as President. In December 1969 Zinsou was deposed by Kouandété, then Commander-in-Chief of the Army, and a three-member military Directoire (Directorate) assumed power. In March 1970 a presidential election was abandoned when counting revealed roughly equal support for the three main candidates—Justin Ahomadegbé, Sourou-Migan Apithy, both southerners, and Maga—to whom the Directorate ceded power in May: it was intended that each member of this Presidential Council would act as Head of State, in rotation, for a two-year period. Maga was the first to hold this office, and was succeeded in May 1972 by Ahomadegbé.

In October 1972 the civilian leadership was deposed by Maj. (later Brig.-Gen.) Mathieu Kérékou, Deputy Chief of Staff of the armed forces and a northerner. In September 1973 a Conseil National Révolutionnaire (National Revolutionary Council—CNR) was established. Strategic sectors and financial institutions were acquired by the State, under Kérékou's regime, which pursued Marxist-based policies. In late 1975 the Parti de la Révolution Populaire du Bénin (PRPB) was established as the sole party, and Dahomey was renamed the People's Republic of Benin

In August 1977 the CNR adopted a *Loi fondamentale* decreeing new structures in government. Elections to a new 'supreme authority', the Assemblée Nationale Révolutionnaire (National Revolutionary Assembly—ANR), took place in November 1979, when a single list of 336 People's Commissioners was approved by 97.5% of voters. At the same time a Comité Exécutif National (National Executive Committee—CEN) was established to replace the CNR. The PRPB designated Kérékou as the sole candidate for President of the Republic, and in February 1980 the ANR unanimously elected him to this office. A gradual moderation in Benin's domestic policies followed. At legislative elections in June 1984 the single list of People's Commissioners was approved by 98% of voters, and in July the ANR re-elected Kérékou, again the sole candidate, as President.

In January 1987 Kérékou resigned from the army to become a civilian Head of State. At elections to the ANR in June 1989 89.6% of voters endorsed the single list of PRPB-approved candidates. In August the ANR re-elected Kérékou (once again the sole candidate) as President. At the end of the year Kérékou instituted major political changes, abandoning Marxism-Leninism as the official state ideology.

Domestic Political Affairs

In February 1990 delegates at a conference of the 'active forces of the nation' voted to adopt a national charter that was to form the basis of a new constitution. An interim Haut Conseil de la République (High Council of the Republic—HCR) was appointed to assume the functions of the ANR. Presidential and legislative elections, to be held in the context of a multi-party political system, were scheduled for early 1991. Nicéphore Soglo, a former World Bank official (who had briefly been Minister of Finance and Economic Affairs in the 1960s), was designated interim Prime Minister. The conference also voted to change the country's name to the Republic of Benin. The HCR was inaugurated in March 1990, and Soglo appointed a transitional Government; of the previous administration, only Kérékou remained in office. Legislation permitting the registration of political parties was promulgated in August.

A national referendum on the draft Constitution was conducted on 2 December 1990. Voters were asked to choose between two proposed documents, one of which incorporated a clause stipulating upper and lower age-limits for presidential candidates, and would therefore prevent the candidatures of Ahomadegbé, Maga and Zinsou. It was reported that 95.8% of those who voted approved one or other of the versions, with 79.7% of voters favouring the age-restriction clause.

Following legislative elections on 17 February 1991, the largest grouping in the new, 64-member Assemblée Nationale (National Assembly) was an alliance of three pro-Soglo parties, which secured 12 seats. Kérékou and Soglo were among 13 candidates at the first round of the presidential election on 10 March. Soglo, who won 36.2% of the total votes cast, received his greatest support in the south of the country, while Kérékou, who received 27.3% of the overall vote, was reported to have secured the support of more than 80% of voters in the north. Soglo and Kérékou proceeded to a second round of voting on 24 March, at which Soglo took 67.7% of the total votes cast. Soglo was inaugurated as President on 4 April.

In July 1992 Soglo, who had previously asserted his political neutrality, had made public his membership of a political party, La Renaissance du Bénin (RB), formed by his wife, Rosine Soglo, earlier that year; he was appointed leader of the RB in July 1994.

In November 1994 the National Assembly voted to establish an independent electoral supervisory body, the Commission Electorale Nationale Autonome (CENA), despite resistance from Soglo, who also opposed a planned increase in the number of deputies from 64 to 83. Some 31 political organizations participated in the legislative elections held on 28 March 1995. In April the Constitutional Court annulled the results of voting for 13 seats on the grounds of irregularities. Following by-elections in May, the RB held 20 seats in the National Assembly, and other supporters of Soglo 13. Opposition parties together held 49 seats, the most prominent being the Parti du Renouveau Démocratique (PRD), with 19 seats, and the Front d'Action pour le Renouveau et le Développement—Alafia (FARD—Alafia), with 10; the latter had attracted considerable support from Kérékou supporters in the north, although the former President had not actively campaigned in the election.

The first round of the presidential election, on 3 March 1996, was contested by seven candidates. Soglo secured 35.7% of the valid votes, Kérékou 33.9%, and Adrien Houngbédji, the leader of the PRD, 19.7%. Most of the defeated candidates quickly expressed their support for Kérékou. He and Soglo proceeded to a second round of voting, on 18 March. Several days later the Constitutional Court announced Kérékou's election, with 52.5% of the valid votes. Some 78.1% of those eligible had voted.

Elections to the National Assembly were held on 30 March 1999, and international monitors reported that the elections had been conducted peacefully and democratically. The combined opposition parties won a slender majority in the legislature, with 42 of the 83 seats. The RB won the largest number of seats (27), principally in the south and centre, while FARD—Alafia, the Parti Social-Démocrate (PSD) and other parties loyal to the President performed strongly in the north and west. The incoming legislature elected Houngbédji as its Speaker.

The 2001 presidential election

In the period preceding the 2001 presidential election, Soglo was widely regarded as the sole credible challenger to Kérékou. In the first round of the election, held on 4 March, Kérékou won the largest share of the vote but failed to secure an absolute majority; a second round, to be contested by Kérékou and Soglo, the second-placed candidate, was scheduled for 18 March. As campaigning proceeded, the Constitutional Court conducted a review of the election results declared by the CENA. Revised provisional results of the first round gave Kérékou 45.4% of the votes cast, Soglo 27.1%, Houngbédji 12.6% and Bruno Amoussou 8.6%. Following the declaration of the revised results, which indicated a participation rate of around 80%, there were opposition calls for a boycott of the second round of voting, owing to alleged irregularities in the conduct of the first round. Soglo appealed to the Constitutional Court to annul the disputed results and order a re-run. On 16 March Soglo, having had his appeal rejected, withdrew his candidature. The second round of the election, now to be contested by Kérékou and Houngbédji, was postponed until 22 March. On 19 March, however, Houngbédji also withdrew from the second round, declaring his dissatisfaction with the conduct of the election. Amoussou, who had previously declared his support for Kérékou, became by default his challenger for the presidency. Nine opposition members of the CENA resigned in protest at the election process. Voter participation at the second round of voting, duly held on 22 March, was significantly lower than at the first, at about 55%. Two days after polling the CENA announced that Kérékou had won 84.1% of the valid votes cast. Kérékou was declared President for a further term, despite protests that the depleted CENA was not qualified to organize the election.

The legislative elections held on 30 March 2003 produced a secure pro-presidential majority for the first time since the introduction of multi-party politics in Benin. Pro-Kérékou parties and alliances won 52 of the 83 seats in the National Assembly, and the PRD, which had secured 11 seats, also announced that it would also support the Government. The Union pour le Bénin du Futur (UBF) emerged as the largest single party, with 31 seats. The representation of the RB, the largest party in the outgoing assembly, was reduced from 27 to 15 seats. Nine other parties or alliances also won representation. In the new Government, announced in June, Amoussou was appointed to the most senior ministerial post in the new Government, as Minister of State, responsible for Planning and Development.

President Kérékou effected a major cabinet reorganization in February 2005. Amoussou was removed from the Government and was replaced by Zul Kifl Salami. Towards the end of the year senior members of the Government stated that a lack of funds could prevent the presidential election from being held as scheduled in March 2006, and suggested that presidential polling be held concurrently with the legislative elections scheduled for 2007. Notwithstanding the controversial appointment, in January 2006, of Col (retd) Martin Dohou Azonhiho as Minister of State, responsible for National Defence (Azonhiho, who had held several senior positions in Kérékou's military and Marxist governments from the mid-1970s, and had also served a prison sentence for embezzlement, had of late been a vocal advocate of the postponement of the elections), Kérékou, who was constitutionally prohibited from seeking a further term of office, announced that funding for the elections would be forthcoming.

The first Boni Yayi administration

The first round of the presidential election proceeded on 5 March 2006. Boni Yayi, who had recently resigned as President of the Banque Ouest-Africaine de Développement (BOAD) in order to contest the election, received the largest share of the votes cast (35.6%), followed by Houngbédji, with 24.1%. Amoussou was placed third, with 16.2%; and Léhadi Vinagnon Vitoun Soglo, son of Nicéphore and Rosine Soglo to contest the election, fourth, with 8.4%. Around 75% of the electorate participated, and international monitors described the election as broadly free and fair. A second round of voting, contested by Yayi and Houngbédji on 19 March, resulted in Yayi being decisively elected, with 74.5% of the votes cast. The new President was inaugurated on 6 April. He subsequently appointed a 22-member Council of Ministers. Pascal Irénée Koupaki was appointed was appointed to the most senior position, as Minister of Development, the Economy and Finance.

Legislative elections were held on 31 March 2007, following a one-week delay caused by organizational difficulties. According to provisional results released by the Constitutional Court in mid-April, the Force Cauris pour un Bénin Emergent (FCBE), a pro-Yayi coalition of some 20 parties, took 35 of the 83 seats, while the Alliance pour une Dynamique Démocratique, which included Soglo's RB, secured 20 seats. The PRD won 10 seats, and a further nine parties and alliances also secured parliamentary representation. The rate of voter participation was recorded at 58.7%. In June President Yayi named a new Government; of the 17 new appointments, the most notable included Lawani, who was awarded the finance portfolio, and Moussa Okanla, who became Minister of Foreign Affairs, African Integration, Francophone Affairs and Beninois Abroad. Koupaki was again appointed to the most senior position, namely that of Minister of State, in charge of Planning, Development and the Evaluation of Public Action. An enlarged, 30-member Council of Ministers was named in October 2008, including several opposition party members. Among new appointees was Armand Zinzindohoué, who was assigned the interior and public security portfolio.

In mid-2009, following the emergence of a financial scandal concerning the construction of infrastructure for the 10th summit of the Community of Sahel-Saharan States (CEN-SAD, see p. 450) held in Cotonou in 2008, Yayi, who had during his election campaign pledged to combat corruption, dismissed Lawani and the Minister of Town Planning, Housing, Land Reform and the Fight against Coastal Erosion, François Noudégbéssi, for mismanagement of government funds and alleged irregularities in the tendering process. The economy and finance portfolio was assigned to Idrissou Daouda, hitherto Managing Director of the Banque Centrale des Etats de l'Afrique de l'Ouest.

In June 2010 President Yayi implemented a cabinet reorganization, appointing eight new ministers—among them Modeste Kérékou, the son of former head of state Mathieu Kérékou, as Minister of Youth, Sports and Leisure. Yayi also reappointed Noudégbéssi, who had been cleared of any wrongdoing by a commission of enquiry, to his former position. Daouda retained his post as Minister of the Economy and Finance. In the following month some 100,000 people demonstrated in Cotonou after a further financial scandal was revealed: protesters demanded that the Government act to recover the failed investments of Investment Consultancy and Computing Services. The company, which was perceived as having ties with the Government, had promised returns of up to 50%, but had caused combined losses of more than 100,000m. francs CFA in deposits, allegedly defrauding between 50,000 and 70,000 small investors. Zinzindohoué was subsequently dismissed from the Government, and responsibility for his vacated portfolio was assumed on an acting basis by the Minister of Industry, Candide Azanaï. In August it was reported that more than one-half of the members of the National Assembly had requested that impeachment proceedings be brought against Yayi; however, this demand was refused by the President of the legislature, Mathurin Nago.

In preparation for the presidential election scheduled for March 2011, both France and the European Union (EU) gave financial support for the implementation of a permanent, digital electoral list. By the end of 2010 a number of presidential candidates had been announced: notably, Houngbédji was selected as the candidate of the Union Fait la Nation (UN) alliance. In January 2011 Abdoulaye Bio Tchané, hitherto head of the BOAD and a former Minister of the Economy and Finance under Kérékou, declared his candidacy. A coalition of opposition parties, trade unions and non-governmental organizations, including the UN alliance and Bio Tchané's supporters, joined together to form the anti-Yayi Front de Défense de la Démocratie.

Recent developments: Yayi re-elected; alleged plots against the President

The presidential election was held on 13 March 2011 (having twice been postponed as a result of technical difficulties), contested by 14 candidates. Yayi was re-elected outright, having secured 53.1% of the votes cast. Houngbédji was placed second, with 35.6% of the votes, and Bio Tchané third, with 6.1%. The rate of voter participation was officially recorded at 84.8% of the registered electorate. Following the release of the results, which were confirmed by the Constitutional Court on 21 March, Houngbédji publicly denounced the outcome, and there were protests outside the office of the CENA. The Economic Community of West African States (ECOWAS, see p. 260) voiced deep concern at rising tensions in Benin, and appealed to all candidates to refrain from undermining the electoral process.

Legislative elections followed on 30 April 2011. Results validated by the Constitutional Court on 12 May gave the pro-Yayi FCBE 41 of the 83 seats in the National Assembly. The UN became the second largest party in the legislature, with 31 seats. On 28 May President Yayi announced a new Government, in which the number of ministers was reduced from 35 to 26. In accordance with his campaign promise to establish a post of Prime Minister, Yayi appointed Koupaki to lead the Council of Ministers. The new administration included eight women, among them Adidjatou Mathys, as Benin's first female Minister of the Economy and Finance, and Marie-Elise Gbédo, as Keeper of the Seals, Minister of Justice, Legislation and Human Rights, and Government Spokesperson.

In April 2011 the Government agreed to award a 25% salary increase to civil servants at the Ministry of the Economy and Finance, who had undertaken regular strike action over a period of several months. Staff at other ministries subsequently began industrial action to demand equal treatment. The pay award was overturned by the Constitutional Court in June, prompting renewed stoppages. In July the Government conceded a 25% pay rise for all civil servants, to be implemented at the Ministry of the Economy and Finance in 2011, and incrementally elsewhere in 2011–14. In September 2011 the National Assembly approved legislation removing the right to strike from customs officers, and military and paramilitary personnel (including public officials working in the forestry and water industries); this followed a recent 48-hour strike by customs officers at the Port of Cotonou, which had resulted in losses estimated at 3,000m. francs CFA. The measure, which was signed into law by President Yayi in October, was denounced as intimidatory by the Confédération Générale des Travailleurs du Bénin and by opposition parties.

In April 2012 President Yayi carried out a reorganization of the Government, assuming personal responsibility for the defence portfolio. Notably, Adidjatou Mathys was dismissed as Minister of the Economy and Finance, and Issifou Kogui N'Douro, hitherto Minister of State, in charge of National Defence, was appointed Minister of State, in charge of Presidential Affairs. Mathys was replaced by Jonas Gbian, hitherto Minister of Energy, Mining and Petroleum Research, Water and the Development of Renewable Energy Sources. Three senior officials were dismissed in September, among them the director-general of the Port of Cotonou and the Secretary-General at the Presidency, accused of receiving bribes in relation to a construction project for a dry port at Tori-Bossito.

In October 2012 an alleged plot was revealed to poison the President. The head of the Société de Développement du Coton (SODECO), Moudjaïdou Soumanou (who had held the position of Minister of Trade and Industry under the first Yayi administration), Yayi's personal physician, Dr Ibrahim Mama Cissé, and a niece of the President, Zouberath Kora-Seke, were detained in Benin on charges of conspiracy and attempted murder. Following an extradition request made by Benin, the alleged instigator of the plot, Patrice Talon, a prominent business figure and erstwhile ally of the President, was briefly detained in the French capital in early December, before being released under judicial supervision. Benin had also requested the extradition of an associate of Talon, Olivier Bocco.

In mid-January 2013 the director of Benin's Canal 3 television station, Berthe Cakpossa, was fined 500,000 francs CFA and sentenced to three months' imprisonment, having been convicted on charges of offending President Yayi. The case followed the broadcast by her station, in September 2012, of a press conference by a former adviser to the President, Lionel Agbo, at which he made allegations of corruption within the presidential entourage. Agbo himself was sentenced to six months' imprisonment. At the end of January, however, Yayi pardoned both Cakpossa (who had appealed against sentence) and Agbo, reportedly in the interests of easing tensions.

The Minister of the Environment, Housing and Town Planning, Blaise Ahanhanzo-Glèlè, was briefly detained in January 2013, as part of an investigation into alleged embezzlement in connection with an abandoned project for a new parliament building (on which the Government had spent some 12,500m. francs CFA). In late February the National Assembly authorized the High Court of Justice to try five former ministers, including Lawani and Zinzindohoué, on corruption charges. Yayi implemented a minor government reshuffle in early February 2013.

It was announced in early March 2013 that an attempted military coup, apparently linked to the poisoning plot disclosed in late 2012, had been foiled by security forces in the previous month, while President Yayi was attending a summit meeting in Equatorial Guinea. A prominent business figure and cousin of Talon, Johannes Dagnon, was arrested in connection with the alleged plot, as was Col Pamphile Zomahoun, the former head of the Cotonou gendarmerie. A third alleged conspirator was believed to be at large in Equatorial Guinea. In late May 2013 the investigating judge in the cases of the attempted poisoning and coup plot against Yayi, Angelo Houssou, who had recently dismissed the cases on grounds of lack of evidence, was intercepted at the border with Nigeria and escorted back to his home by Beninois security forces. Although, in early July, the Court of Appeal in Cotonou upheld Houssou's decision, those of the accused who had already been arrested remained in detention pending a higher appeal to the Supreme Court, while the Beninois Government continued to seek Talon's extradition from France. The extradition request was rejected by a court in Paris, France, in late October, on the grounds that Talon could not be guaranteed a fair trial in Benin, and because the death penalty (although no longer applied) remained on Benin's statutes. This ruling was upheld at appeal in Paris in early December. Shortly before that decision, it was reported that Houssou had fled Benin and was seeking asylum in the USA, citing threats to his life.

In early August 2013, meanwhile, President Yayi unexpectedly dismissed Koupaki's Government. The successor administration, named two days later, did not include a Prime Minister among its 26 members. There was some media speculation that Koupaki, a likely contender in the 2016 presidential election, was considered to be too closely linked with Talon. The most senior figure in the new Council of Ministers, after Yayi, was the Minister of State, in charge of Higher Education and Scientific Research, François Adébayo Abiola. One-half of the members of the incoming administration were new appointees, although the Minister of the Economy and Finance, Jonas Gbian, and the Minister of Foreign Affairs, African Integration, Francophone Affairs and Beninois Abroad, Nassirou Arifari Bako, retained their previous positions. François Houéssou was allocated the interior, public security and religious affairs portfolio, and Valentin Djénontin-Agossou that of justice, legislation and human rights.

Maritime Insecurity in the Gulf of Guinea

In July 2011 President Yayi made a request to the UN Secretary-General for international assistance in countering a rapid escalation in sea piracy in the Gulf of Guinea, emphasizing the potentially severe consequences for the economy of Benin of sea piracy and drugs-trafficking. In the following month an influential group of international maritime insurers added the maritime waters off Benin to a list of areas deemed to be of high risk. In October the UN Security Council adopted its first ever resolution (No. 2018) regarding piracy in the Gulf of Guinea, expressing deep concern about the threat posed by piracy and armed robbery to international navigation, security and the economic development of countries of the region, and welcoming the decision of the Secretary-General to dispatch an assessment mission to the region. The report of the UN mission, submitted in early 2012, emphasized the heavy dependence of Benin's economy on port activities, and concluded that a failure to act against sea piracy in the Gulf of Guinea could be 'catastrophic'. The mission also considered that an enduring regional strategy to combat piracy would also need to take into account its causes: high levels of youth unemployment, income disparities, the circulation of illicit weapons and the prevalence of corruption. Joint Beninois-Nigerian patrols, meanwhile, commenced off the coast of Benin in September 2011. Support was also forthcoming from the EU, which had in late 2010 implemented a regional programme to strengthen maritime security and safety in the Gulf of Guinea, as well as from countries including France, the People's Republic of China and the USA.

Foreign Affairs

Benin maintains generally good relations with neighbouring countries, and joined CEN-SAD in March 2002. None the less, in mid-2000 a long-term dispute between Benin and Niger over the ownership of various small islands in the Niger river erupted after Nigerien soldiers reportedly sabotaged the construction of a Beninois administrative building on Lété Island. Meetings between representatives of the two Governments and arbitration by the Organization of African Unity (now the African Union, see p. 186) failed to resolve the dispute, and in April 2002 the two countries officially ratified an agreement (signed in 2001) to refer the dispute to the International Court of Justice (ICJ) in The Hague, Netherlands, for arbitration. In July 2005 the ICJ issued a final ruling to the effect that 16 of the 25 disputed islands, including Lété, belonged to Niger; the Governments of both countries announced their acceptance of the ruling.

Benin and Nigeria began joint police patrols along their common border in August 2001. However, renewed concerns about cross-border crime resulted in the unilateral closure, by the Nigerian authorities, of the frontier in August 2003. The border was reopened later that month, and the Beninois and Nigerian authorities announced a series of measures intended to enhance co-operation to combat cross-border crime, including restrictions of certain types of export trade from Benin to Nigeria. Following his inauguration in April 2006 President Yayi's first official foreign visit was to Nigeria, and in August he signed a treaty with President Gen. Olusegun Obasanjo regarding the maritime boundary between the two countries. In February 2007 the two Presidents, along with President Faure Gnassingbé of Togo, announced the formation of a Co-Prosperity Alliance Zone, aimed at the further integration of their economies and the promotion of peace, stability and development in West Africa. In April 2009 the Nigerian Senate requested that troops be deployed to stop cross-border incursions from Benin; in one such incident, involving 2,000 Beninois villagers, the entire village of Tungar-Kungi in northern Kebbi State was destroyed, leaving 1,500 people (mostly women and children) displaced. In September 2011, further to an agreement made by Yayi and his Nigerian counterpart, President Goodluck Jonathan, at a meeting in Abuja, Nigeria, in the previous month, Benin and Nigeria commenced joint naval patrols in the Gulf of Guinea, as part of a co-ordinated effort to counter an escalation in sea piracy (see Maritime Insecurity in the Gulf of Guinea, above).

An ongoing border dispute between Benin and Burkina Faso came close to armed conflict in 2005, and there was further tension in 2007 following the death of an inhabitant of the contested area while in custody in Benin. In March 2008, at a meeting of high-level officials of the two countries, an undertaking was made that neither side would make any 'visible sovereignty act' in the 68-sq km area of contested territory (such as building paramilitary or police stations), and that joint security patrols would be carried out at the common border. In 2009 both countries agreed to refer the unresolved border issue to the ICJ. Pending a decision, the area was to remain neutral and to be administered and financed jointly. The case had not been formally submitted by late 2013.

From late April 2005 thousands of Togolese sought refuge in Benin, having fled the violence that followed a presidential election in that country. In December the office of the UN High Commissioner for Refugees (UNHCR) estimated that some 26,632 Togolese refugees had fled to Benin. In April 2007 Benin, Togo and UNHCR signed an agreement on the voluntary repatriation of the remaining refugees. At the end of 2012 there were 4,188 Togolese refugees of concern to UNHCR in Benin.

CONSTITUTION AND GOVERNMENT

The Constitution of the Republic of Benin, which was approved in a national referendum on 2 December 1990, provides for a civilian, multi-party political system. Executive power is vested in the President of the Republic, who is elected by direct universal adult suffrage with a five-year mandate, renewable only once. The legislature is the 83-member Assemblée Nationale (National Assembly), elected for a period of four years by universal suffrage. The President of the Republic appoints the Council of Ministers, subject to formal parliamentary approval.

For the purposes of local administration, Benin is divided into 12 departments, each administered by a civilian prefect. These departments are further divided into a total of 77 communes.

REGIONAL AND INTERNATIONAL CO-OPERATION

Benin is a member of the African Union (see p. 186), of the Economic Community of West African States (ECOWAS, see p. 260), of the West African organs of the Franc Zone (see p. 330), of the Community of Sahel-Saharan States (CEN-SAD, see p. 450), of the African Petroleum Producers' Association (APPA, see p. 445), of the Conseil de l'Entente (see p. 450) and of the Niger Basin Authority (see p. 452).

Benin became a member of the UN in 1960, and was admitted to the World Trade Organization (WTO, see p. 434) in 1996.

ECONOMIC AFFAIRS

In 2012, according to estimates by the World Bank, Benin's gross national income (GNI), measured at average 2010–12 prices, was US $7,514m., equivalent to $750 per head (or $1,570 on an international purchasing-power parity basis). During 2003–12, it was estimated, the population increased at an average annual rate of 3.1%, while gross domestic product (GDP) per head increased, in real terms, by an average of 0.6% per year. Overall GDP increased, in real terms, at an average annual rate of 3.7% in 2003–12; growth in 2012 was 5.4%.

According to the African Development Bank (AfDB), agriculture (including forestry and fishing) contributed 36.1% of GDP in 2012. In mid-2013 an estimated 41.4% of the labour force were employed in the sector, according to FAO. The principal cash crops are cotton (exports of which accounted for an estimated 34.2% of total exports in 2012) and rice. Benin is in most years self-sufficient in basic foods; the main subsistence crops are cassava, yams and maize. In September 2011 plans were adopted that aimed to increase rice production from 152,000 metric tons in 2010 to 550,000 from 2015 onwards. According to the World Bank, agricultural GDP increased at an average annual rate of 3.2% in 2003–10; growth in 2012 was estimated at 6.3%, according to the AfDB.

According to the AfDB, industry (including mining, manufacturing, construction and power) contributed 14.4% of GDP in 2012 and engaged 13.0% of the employed labour force at the time of the 2002 census. According to the World Bank, industrial GDP increased at an average annual rate of 2.7% in 2003–10; it grew by 3.4% in 2010.

Mining contributed only 0.3% of GDP in 2012, and engaged 1.4% of the employed labour force in 2002. Marble and limestone are exploited commercially. There were plans to commence production of petroleum on shore in 2014, and to resume output from the Sémé offshore field (exploitation of which had ceased in the late 1990s) in 2015. There are also deposits of gold, phosphates, natural gas, iron ore, silica sand, peat and chromium. The GDP of the mining sector declined at an average annual rate of 28.6% in 1994–2001; growth in mining GDP was 6.0% in 2012, according to the AfDB.

The manufacturing sector, which contributed 8.4% of GDP in 2012, engaged 9.0% of the employed labour force in 2002. The sector is based largely on the processing of primary products (principally cotton-ginning and oil-palm processing). Construction materials and some simple consumer goods are also produced for the domestic market. According to the World Bank, manufacturing GDP increased at an average annual rate of 1.7% in 2003–10; it increased by 6.0% in 2012, according to the AfDB.

Construction contributed 4.7% of GDP in 2012 and engaged 2.5% of the employed labour force at the time of the 2002 census. According to the AfDB, the sector's GDP grew by 6.0% in 2012.

Benin is highly dependent on imports of electricity from Ghana's Akosombo dam. There is also a hydroelectric installation on Benin's border with Togo, at Nangbeto, on the Mono river. In 2009 the Communauté Electrique du Bénin commissioned Sinohydro, of the People's Republic of China, to construct a second dam on the Mono river, at Adjarala, with the aim of achieving eventual self-sufficiency in power for both Benin and Togo. Benin, together with Togo and Ghana, is connected to the West African Gas Pipeline, transporting natural gas from Nigeria, but the project has been subject to delays. According to World Bank estimates, in 2011, 99.4% of Benin's electricity production was derived from petroleum. Imports of mineral fuels accounted for 21.9% of the value of total imports in 2012.

The services sector contributed 49.5% of GDP in 2012, and engaged 39.8% of the employed labour force in 2002. The port of Cotonou, taken over in 2009 by a French group on a 25-year concession, is of considerable importance as a hub for regional trade. The port accounts for some 70% of Benin's GDP, and for 80% of annual fiscal revenue, according to UN data. According to the AfDB, the GDP of the services sector increased at an average annual rate of 4.0% in 2003–10; the output of the sector increased by 3.2% in 2010.

In 2012, according to preliminary data by IMF, Benin recorded a visible merchandise trade deficit of 416,000m. francs CFA, while there was a deficit of 326,000m. francs CFA on the current account of the balance of payments. In 2012 the principal source of imports (13.8%) was France; other major sources were Togo, the People's Republic of China and Belgium. The principal market for exports in that year was People's Republic of China (25.4%); other important purchasers were Chad, India, Nigeria, Malaysia, Côte d'Ivoire and Niger. The principal exports in 2012 were cotton, vegetables and vegetable products, iron and steel, base metals and articles of base metal, mineral products, and prepared foodstuffs and beverages. The main imports in that year were mineral products, vegetables and vegetable products, live animals and animal products, iron and steel, base metals and articles of base metal, textile and textile articles, and vehicles (other than railway and tramway).

In 2012, according to preliminary data by IMF, Benin recorded an estimated overall budgetary deficit of 49,800m. francs CFA. Benin's general government gross debt was 1,097m. francs CFA in 2011, equivalent to 31.9% of GDP. The country's total external debt at the end of 2011 was US $1,423m., of which $1,190m. was public and publicly guaranteed debt. In 2010 the cost of servicing long-term public and publicly guaranteed debt and repayments to the IMF was equivalent to 2.5% of the value of exports of goods, services and income (excluding workers' remittances). The annual rate of inflation increased by an average of 3.4% per year in 2003–12, according to ILO estimates. Consumer prices increased by 6.7% in 2012. According to the 2002 census, 0.7% of the total labour force was unemployed.

The global financial crisis of the late 2000s had a severe impact on the Beninois economy; GDP growth fell from 5.0% in 2008 to 2.7% in 2009. Growth slowed further in 2010, to 2.6%, as a result of devastating floods, which displaced 200,000 people and destroyed some 128,000 ha of crops. Furthermore, there was considerable concern regarding the potential impact for Benin's economy of the escalation of piracy in the Gulf of Guinea from 2010, in view of the country's dependence on revenue from the port of Cotonou, as well as cotton exports via the port. The report of a UN assessment mission (see Contemporary Political History), released in January 2012, drew attention to the fact that increased insurance rates incurred as a result of the listing of Benin as a high-risk country by international maritime insurers in August 2011 had resulted in a 70% decline in the number of vessels entering Cotonou. The economy, none the less, began to recover in 2011, with GDP growth of 3.5%. Official data reported growth of 5.4% in 2012, reflecting in particular improved cotton output (the Government had intervened in order to address operational concerns in the sector), increased production of both basic foods and cash crops, and the positive impact of customs reforms on port and trading activity. However, higher import levels meant that the deficit on the current account of the balance of payments (excluding grants) widened to 9.3% of GDP (from 8.1% in 2011). Annual inflation, which increased sharply from early 2012 with the reduction in fuel price subsidies in neighbouring Nigeria and averaged 6.7% for the year, notably slowed during 2013. In an assessment of the economy published in August 2013, the IMF forecast real GDP growth of 5.0% and average inflation of 2.8% for that year. (The assessment was conducted in the context of the fifth review under the three-year Extended Credit Facility granted in 2010, the review having been previously delayed as a result of earlier difficulties in the implementation of the customs reform, and an extension of the Facility to April 2014 was thus sought.) In his submission to the IMF, Benin's Minister of the Economy and Finance noted progress in infrastructure development and towards raising living standards and in achievement of the country's Millennium Development Goals, including the introduction of a universal health insurance scheme, but recognized that further efforts would be necessary particularly in the areas of health, primary education, water and sanitation. Furthermore, the IMF, while acknowledging advances in the implementation of structural reforms, noted Benin's continued vulnerability to the impact of adverse weather on its dominant agricultural sector and to the impact of fluctuations in international markets, as well as its exposure to policy developments in Nigeria, and cautioned that the conditions for sustained high growth were not yet in place.

PUBLIC HOLIDAYS

2015: 1 January (New Year's Day), 2 January*† (Mouloud, Birth of the Prophet), 10 January (Vodoun national holiday), 1 April (Youth Day), 6 April (Easter Monday), 1 May (Workers' Day), 14 May (Ascension Day), 25 May (Whit Monday), 17 July* (Id al-Fitr, end of Ramadan), 1 August (Independence Day), 15 August (Assumption), 23 September* (Id al-Adha, Feast of the Sacrifice), 1 November (All Saints' Day), 23 December*† (Mouloud, Birth of the Prophet), 25 December (Christmas Day).

* These holidays are dependent on the Islamic lunar calendar and may vary by one or two days from the dates given.

† This festival occurs twice (in the Islamic years AH 1436 and 1437) within the same Gregorian year.

Statistical Survey

Source (unless otherwise stated): Institut National de la Statistique et de l'Analyse Economique, BP 323, Cotonou; tel. 21-30-82-43; fax 21-30-82-46; e-mail insae@insae-bj.org; internet www.insae-bj.org.

Area and Population

AREA, POPULATION AND DENSITY

Area (sq km)	112,622*
Population (census results)	
11 February 2002	6,769,914
11-31 May 2013 (preliminary)	
Males	4,868,180
Females	5,115,704
Total	9,983,884
Population (UN estimates at mid-year)†	
2012	10,050,701
2013	10,323,474
2014	10,599,511
Density (per sq km) at mid-2014	94.1

* 43,484 sq miles.

† Source: UN, *World Population Prospects: The 2012 Revision*; estimates not adjusted to take account of results of 2013 census.

POPULATION BY AGE AND SEX

(UN estimates at mid-2014)

	Males	Females	Total
0–14	2,271,169	2,227,319	4,498,488
15–64	2,885,797	2,909,301	5,795,098
65 and over	127,203	178,722	305,925
Total	5,284,169	5,315,342	10,599,511

Source: UN, *World Population Prospects: The 2012 Revision.*

ETHNIC GROUPS

2002 (percentages): Fon 39.2 (incl. Fon 17.6; Goun 6.3; Aïzo 4.3; Mahi 3.5; Ouémè 2.5; Torri 2.4; Kotafon 1.4; Tofin 1.3); Adja 15.2 (incl. Adja 8.7; Sahouè 2.6; Xwla 1.4; Mina 1.2); Yoruba 12.3 (incl. Nagot 6.8; Yoruba 1.8; Idaasha 1.5; Holli-Djè 1.4); Bariba 9.2 (incl. Bariba 8.3); Peulh 6.9 (incl. Peulh Fulfuldé 5.5); Otamari 6.1 (incl. Berba 1.4; Ditamari 1.3; Waama 1.0); Yoa Lokpa 4.5 (incl. Yoa 1.8; Lokpa 1.2); Dendi 2.5 (incl. Dendi 2.4); Others 2.7.

ADMINISTRATIVE DIVISIONS
(population at 2013 census, preliminary)

Département	Area (sq km)	Population	Population density (per sq km)
Alibori	25,683	868,046	33.8
Atacora	20,459	769,337	37.6
Atlantique	3,233	1,396,548	432.0
Borgou	25,310	1,202,095	47.5
Collines	13,561	716,558	52.8
Couffo	2,404	741,895	308.6
Donga	10,691	542,605	50.8
Littoral	79	678,874	8,593.3
Mono	1,396	495,307	354.8
Ouémé	2,835	1,096,850	386.9
Plateau	1,865	624,146	334.7
Zou	5,106	851,623	166.8
Total	112,622	9,983,884	88.6

PRINCIPAL TOWNS
(population at 2013 census, preliminary)

Cotonou	678,874	Bohicon	170,604
Djougou	266,522	Aplahoue	170,069
Porto-Novo (capital)	263,616	Kalale	168,520
Parakou	254,254	Malanville	168,006
Banikoara	248,621	Ketou	156,497
Seme-Kpodji	224,207	Savalou	144,814
Tchaourou	221,108		

BIRTHS AND DEATHS
(annual averages, UN estimates)

	1995–2000	2000–05	2005–10
Birth rate (per 1,000)	43.6	41.7	39.1
Death rate (per 1,000)	12.9	11.7	10.3

Source: UN, *World Population Prospects: The 2012 Revision*.

2012: Birth rate 33.3 per 1,000; Death rate 8.7 per 1,000 (Source: African Development Bank).

Life expectancy (years at birth): 58.9 (males 57.6; females 60.4) in 2011 (Source: World Bank, World Development Indicators database).

ECONOMICALLY ACTIVE POPULATION
(persons aged 10 years and over, 1992 census)

	Males	Females	Total
Agriculture, hunting, forestry and fishing	780,469	367,277	1,147,746
Mining and quarrying	609	52	661
Manufacturing	93,157	67,249	160,406
Electricity, gas and water	1,152	24	1,176
Construction	50,959	696	51,655
Trade, restaurants and hotels	36,672	395,829	432,501
Transport, storage and communications	52,228	609	52,837
Finance, insurance, real estate and business services	2,705	401	3,106
Community, social and personal services	126,122	38,422	164,544
Sub-total	1,144,073	870,559	2,014,632
Activities not adequately defined	25,579	12,917	38,496
Total employed	1,169,652	883,476	2,053,128
Unemployed	26,475	5,843	32,318
Total labour force	1,196,127	889,319	2,085,446

Source: ILO, *Yearbook of Labour Statistics*.

2002 (census results): Total employed 2,811,753 (males 1,421,474, females 1,390,279); Unemployed 19,123 (males 12,934, females 6,189); Total labour force 2,830,876 (males 1,434,408, females 1,396,468).

Mid-2013 (estimates in '000): Agriculture, etc. 1,643; Total labour force 3,966 (Source: FAO).

Health and Welfare

KEY INDICATORS

Total fertility rate (children per woman, 2011)	5.2
Under-5 mortality rate (per 1,000 live births, 2011)	106
HIV/AIDS (% of persons aged 15–49, 2012)	1.1
Physicians (per 1,000 head, 2008)	0.06
Hospital beds (per 1,000 head, 2010)	0.5
Health expenditure (2010): US $ per head (PPP)	70
Health expenditure (2010): % of GDP	4.3
Health expenditure (2010): public (% of total)	51.2
Access to water (% of persons, 2011)	76
Access to sanitation (% of persons, 2011)	14
Total carbon dioxide emissions ('000 metric tons, 2010)	5,188.8
Carbon dioxide emissions per head (metric tons, 2010)	0.5
Human Development Index (2012): ranking	166
Human Development Index (2012): value	0.436

For sources and definitions, see explanatory note on p. vi.

Agriculture

PRINCIPAL CROPS
('000 metric tons)

	2010	2011	2012
Rice, paddy	125.0	219.6	219.1
Maize	1,012.6	1,166.0	1,174.6
Millet	26.9	24.7	31.0
Sorghum	168.1	133.2	108.0
Sweet potatoes	77.3	49.0	69.8
Cassava (Manioc)	3,445.0	3,645.9	3,295.8
Yams	2,624.0	2,734.9	2,739.1
Sugar cane	48.0*	48.0†	50.0†
Beans, dry	107.4	85.5	93.2
Cashew nuts, with shell	102.1	163.0	170.0†
Groundnuts, with shell	154.4	131.8	121.5
Coconuts	18.6*	18.8*	19.0†
Oil palm fruit†	360	390	400
Seed cotton	137.0	265.2	240.0
Cottonseed	76†	146†	180*
Tomatoes	186.9	163.7	244.7
Chillies and peppers, green	44.6	38.5	67.8
Okra	45.6	48.3	68.2
Pineapples	266.0	246.7	375.6
Cotton (lint)†	48.0	93.0	115.0

* Unofficial figure.
† FAO estimate(s).

Aggregate production ('000 metric tons, may include official, semi-official or estimated data): Total cereals 1,333 in 2010, 1,544 in 2011, 1,534 in 2012; Total roots and tubers 6,148 in 2010, 6,432 in 2011, 6,108 in 2012; Total pulses 150 in 2010, 125 in 2011, 135 in 2012; Total vegetables (incl. melons) 302 in 2010, 280 in 2011, 465 in 2012; Total fruits (excl. melons) 444 in 2010, 426 in 2011, 554 in 2012.

Source: FAO.

LIVESTOCK
('000 head, year ending September)

	2010	2011	2012
Cattle	2,005	2,058	2,111
Sheep	808	825	842
Goats	1,605	1,640	1,678
Pigs	368	383	398
Chickens	16,550	17,087	17,634

Source: FAO.

LIVESTOCK PRODUCTS
('000 metric tons)

	2010	2011	2012
Cattle meat*	28.7	30.1	30.8
Goat meat*	5.2	5.4	5.4
Pig meat*	4.6	4.8	5.0
Chicken meat*	22.4	23.8	24.0
Game meat*	7.8	8.0	8.0
Cows' milk*	32.0	32.5	33.0
Goats' milk*	8.2	8.6	8.9
Hen eggs	9.9	10.7	11.6

* FAO estimates.

Source: FAO.

Forestry

ROUNDWOOD REMOVALS
('000 cubic metres, excl. bark, FAO estimates)

	2010	2011	2012
Sawlogs, veneer logs and logs for sleepers	130	130	130
Other industrial wood	297	297	297
Fuel wood	6,275	6,318	6,363
Total	6,702	6,745	6,790

Source: FAO.

SAWNWOOD PRODUCTION
('000 cubic metres, incl. railway sleepers)

	2005	2006	2007
Total (all broadleaved)	31*	146	84

* FAO estimate.

2008–12: Production assumed to be unchanged from 2007 (FAO estimates).

Source: FAO.

Fishing

('000 metric tons, live weight)

	2009	2010	2011
Capture	38.9*	39.8*	38.8
Tilapias	13.4*	13.7*	13.7
Black catfishes	1.9*	1.9*	2.2
Torpedo-shaped catfishes	1.9*	1.9*	2.0
Mullets	2.7*	2.8*	3.0
Sardinellas	0.8	1.3	0.8
Bonga shad	0.5	0.3	0.3
Freshwater crustaceans	2.3*	2.0*	2.0
Penaeus shrimps	1.2*	1.0*	1.2
Aquaculture	0.3	0.4	0.4*
Total catch (incl. others)*	39.3	40.2	39.2

* FAO estimate(s).

Note: Figures exclude catches by Beninois canoes operating from outside the country.

Source: FAO.

Mining

	2006	2007	2008
Clay ('000 metric tons)	72.2	77.3	77.0
Gold (kg)	24	19	20
Gravel ('000 cu m)	10.6	25.3	25.0

2009–11: Production assumed to be unchanged from 2008 (estimates).

Source: US Geological Survey.

Industry

SELECTED PRODUCTS
('000 metric tons unless otherwise indicated)

	2010	2011	2012
Cement (hydraulic)	1,305	1,300	n.a.
Beer of barley*	47.0	47.0	n.a.
Palm oil†	46	46	53
Palm kernel oil	13.2†	14.1†	14.1*

* Estimate(s).
† Unofficial figure(s).

Beer of sorghum ('000 metric tons): 32.8 in 2000; 35.0 in 2001; 41.8 in 2002 (Source: FAO).

Salted, dried or smoked fish ('000 metric tons): 2.0 in 2001; 2.0 in 2002; 2.4 in 2003 (Source: FAO).

Electric energy (million kWh): 229 in 2008; 128 in 2009; 150 in 2010.

Sources: US Geological Survey; FAO; UN Industrial Commodity Statistics Database.

Finance

CURRENCY AND EXCHANGE RATES

Monetary Units

100 centimes = 1 franc de la Communauté Financière Africaine (CFA).

Sterling, Dollar and Euro Equivalents (31 December 2013)

£1 sterling = 783.286 francs CFA;
US $1 = 475.641 francs CFA;
€1 = 655.957 francs CFA;
10,000 francs CFA = £12.77 = $21.02 = €15.24.

Average Exchange Rate (francs CFA per US $)

2011	471.866
2012	510.527
2013	494.040

Note: An exchange rate of 1 French franc = 50 francs CFA, established in 1948, remained in force until January 1994, when the CFA franc was devalued by 50%, with the exchange rate adjusted to 1 French franc = 100 francs CFA. This relationship to the French currency remained in effect with the introduction of the euro on 1 January 1999. From that date, accordingly, a fixed exchange rate of €1 = 655.957 francs CFA has been in operation.

BUDGET
('000 million francs CFA)

Revenue	2011	2012*	2013†
Tax revenue	534.7	598.2	666.0
Taxes on international trade and transactions‡	261.2	318.1	356.0
Direct and indirect taxes	273.5	280.1	310.0
Non-tax revenue	70.9	124.4	118.4
Grants	76.8	43.4	62.3
Total	682.4	765.9	846.7

Expenditure	2011	2012*	2013†
Salaries	253.2	279.4	298.9
Pensions and scholarships	48.7	55.5	62.5
Other expenditure and current transfers	198.8	234.5	247.7
Investment	226.6	217.3	272.9
Budgetary contribution	107.5	129.6	143.0
Financed from abroad	119.1	87.7	129.9
Interest due	14.9	23.1	23.0
External debt	7.8	10.6	10.9
Net lending	12.5	6.0	8.0
Total	754.7	815.7	913.0

* Preliminary figures.
† Projections.
‡ Including value-added taxes on imports.

2014 ('000 million francs CFA, projections): *Revenue:* Tax revenue 732.0 (International trade 392.8, Direct and indirect taxes 339.2); Non-tax revenue 89.6; Total revenue 821.6 (excl. grants received 73.8). *Expenditure:* Salaries 316.9; Pensions and scholarships 66.9; Other expenditure and current transfers 265.3; Investment 304.2 (Budgetary contribution 160.6, Financed from abroad 143.6); Interest payments 25.7 (External debt 10.2); Net lending 0.0; Total expenditure 979.0.

Source: IMF, *Benin: Fifth Review Under the Extended Credit Facility and Request for Extension of the Arrangement* (September 2013).

INTERNATIONAL RESERVES
(excluding gold, US $ million at 31 December)

	2010	2011	2012
IMF special drawing rights	76.6	76.3	76.4
Reserve position in IMF	3.4	3.4	3.5
Foreign exchange	1,120.1	807.7	632.9
Total	1,200.1	887.4	712.8

Source: IMF, *International Financial Statistics.*

MONEY SUPPLY
('000 million francs CFA at 31 December)

	2010	2011	2012
Currency outside banks	347.6	376.8	398.5
Demand deposits at deposit money banks	449.0	483.4	468.5
Checking deposits at post office	9.1	8.3	4.9
Total money (incl. others)	806.2	869.5	872.4

Source: IMF, *International Financial Statistics.*

COST OF LIVING
(Consumer Price Index in Cotonou; base: 2000 = 100)

	2010	2011	2012
Food, beverages and tobacco	141.6	149.6	156.6
All items (incl. others)	133.7	137.4	146.6

Source: ILO.

NATIONAL ACCOUNTS
('000 million francs CFA at current prices)

Expenditure on the Gross Domestic Product

	2010	2011	2012
Government final consumption expenditure	385.4	400.0	436.5
Private final consumption expenditure	2,489.1	2,638.3	2,837.3
Gross fixed capital formation	666.0	712.9	770.7
Change in inventories	17.5	22.7	22.0
Total domestic expenditure	3,558.0	3,773.9	4,066.5
Exports of goods and services	490.8	494.2	546.2
Less Imports of goods and services	800.7	824.7	890.7
GDP in purchasers' values	3,248.2	3,443.5	3,722.1

Gross Domestic Product by Economic Activity

	2010	2011	2012
Agriculture	1,053.8	1,149.0	1,234.5
Mining and quarrying	7.4	8.0	8.7
Manufacturing	250.6	264.7	285.9
Electricity, gas and water	33.7	35.9	38.8
Construction	137.7	148.8	160.9
Wholesale and retail trade, restaurants and hotels	537.0	554.9	604.7
Finance, insurance and real estate	358.2	379.6	411.7
Transport and communication	263.9	273.7	300.7
Public administration and defence	330.9	352.2	375.1
Sub-total	2,973.2	3,166.8	3,421.0
Indirect taxes	328.8	333.8	363.4
Less Imputed bank service charge	54.0	57.3	62.5
GDP in purchasers' values	3,248.2	3,443.5	3,722.1

Source: African Development Bank.

BALANCE OF PAYMENTS
('000 million francs CFA)

	2010	2011	2012*
Exports of goods f.o.b.	446.7	362.0	385.0
Imports of goods f.o.b.	–755.6	–717.0	–801.0
Trade balance	–308.9	–355.0	–416.0
Exports of services	221.0	216.0	228.0
Imports of services	–255.0	–238.0	–266.0
Balance on goods and services	–342.8	–377.0	–454.0
Income (net)	–26.5	–7.0	–19.0
Balance on goods, services and income	–369.3	–384.0	–473.0
Private unrequited transfers	35.2	52.0	58.0
Public unrequited transfers	97.1	64.0	89.0
Current balance	–237.0	–269.0	–326.0
Capital account (net)	19.2	77.0	43.0
Medium- and long-term public capital	68.3	28.0	23.0
Medium- and long-term private capital	49.6	–6.0	62.0
Foreign direct investment	96.4	48.0	62.0
Portfolio investment	24.4	28.0	34.0
Deposit money banks	–57.5	–141.0	–176.0
Short-term capital	31.6	3.0	81.0
Net errors and omissions	30.0	78.0	89.0
Statistical discrepancy	—	1.0	—
Overall balance	25.0	–153.0	–108.0

* Preliminary figures.

Source: IMF, *Benin: Fifth Review Under the Extended Credit Facility and Request for Extension of the Arrangement* (September 2013).

External Trade

PRINCIPAL COMMODITIES
(distribution by HS, US$ million)

Imports c.i.f.	2010	2011	2012
Live animals and animal products	186.1	275.4	292.0
Meat and meat products	139.4	209.1	221.5
Meat and edible offal of poultry	138.8	208.4	220.2
Vegetables and vegetable products	111.6	233.2	394.6
Cereals	80.4	172.8	327.3
Rice	78.6	160.9	311.9
Animal or vegetable fats and oils, and products thereof	92.4	118.7	78.6
Palm oil	72.6	106.4	57.3
Prepared foodstuffs; beverages, spirits, vinegars; tobacco and articles thereof	87.9	119.4	117.7
Mineral products	361.8	474.2	585.3

Imports c.i.f.—*continued*	2010	2011	2012
Salt, sulphur, earth, stone, plaster, lime and cement	52.9	122.2	91.8
Cements, portland, aluminous, slag, supersulphate and similar hydraulic	45.7	106.2	80.5
Mineral fuels, oils, distillation products, etc.	308.9	352.0	493.4
Petroleum oils	182.1	208.2	362.8
Electrical energy	113.4	127.5	123.9
Chemicals and related products	100.9	166.3	124.8
Pharmaceutical products	65.1	80.3	77.4
Medicament mixtures	56.9	73.5	72.8
Textiles and textile articles	136.1	146.4	135.8
Other made textile articles, sets, worn clothing etc.	54.2	69.9	58.2
Worn clothing and articles	52.0	49.6	55.5
Iron and steel; other base metals and articles of base metal	89.6	148.5	155.3
Iron and steel	64.5	117.5	129.8
Bars and rods,of iron or non-alloy steel	39.7	71.6	84.8
Machinery and mechanical appliances; electrical equipment; parts thereof	93.9	139.0	98.9
Machinery, boilers, etc.	54.6	80.9	62.0
Vehicles, aircraft, vessels and associated transport equipment	120.0	157.6	128.8
Vehicles other than railway, tramway	118.6	157.3	128.6
Cars (incl. station wagon)	48.0	73.5	57.4
Total (incl. others)	1,494.3	2,128.6	2,250.3

Exports f.o.b.	2010	2011	2012
Live animals and animal products	94.7	1.3	1.6
Meat and edible meat offal	93.2	—	—
Meat and edible offal of poultry	93.2	—	—
Vegetables and vegetable products	138.8	68.8	82.7
Edible fruit, nuts, peel of citrus fruit, melons	30.7	54.2	60.1
Brazil nuts, cashew nuts and coconuts	23.7	40.0	51.3
Other nuts	7.0	14.3	8.8
Cereals	100.3	9.4	13.8
Rice	90.6	9.4	4.1
Animal or vegetable fats and oils, and products thereof	16.7	17.0	20.0
Prepared foodstuffs; beverages, spirits, vinegars; tobacco and articles thereof	15.1	15.8	27.4
Mineral products	0.4	46.8	42.7
Mineral fuels, oils, distillation products, etc.	0.1	46.4	38.1
Petroleum oils	—	44.0	37.9
Wood, wood charcoal, cork, and articles thereof	4.6	6.6	16.5
Wood and articles of wood, wood charcoal	4.6	6.6	15.8

Exports f.o.b.—*continued*	2010	2011	2012
Textiles and textile articles	105.5	115.5	146.1
Cotton	105.1	115.1	145.7
Woven cotton fabrics	4.9	14.7	12.9
Iron and steel; other base metals and articles of base metal	29.3	65.2	71.4
Iron and steel	27.8	61.4	68.7
Bars and rods, wound coils, of iron or non-alloy steel	10.2	18.9	32.3
Other bars and rods of iron or non-alloy steel	12.7	25.5	19.6
Machinery and mechanical appliances; electrical equipment; parts thereof	17.9	14.7	7.0
Machinery, boilers, etc.	7.2	14.3	6.4
Total (incl. others)	434.5	363.2	426.0

Source: Trade Map-Trade Competitiveness Map, International Trade Centre, www.intracen.org/marketanalysis.

PRINCIPAL TRADING PARTNERS
(US $ million)

Imports c.i.f.	2010	2011	2012
Belgium	60.9	99.9	116.8
Brazil	21.9	50.5	82.8
China, People's Repub.	188.7	198.0	173.4
Côte d'Ivoire	37.7	66.2	99.5
France	243.1	343.6	311.5
Germany	53.9	93.1	37.5
India	15.0	24.6	97.3
Italy	22.4	31.9	20.9
Japan	14.8	31.6	10.1
Malaysia	69.1	86.7	57.8
Netherlands	106.0	100.4	103.0
Nigeria	56.2	78.9	93.3
Portugal	4.4	22.1	1.3
Singapore	16.1	23.1	39.5
South Africa	16.9	23.7	26.2
Spain	36.0	46.3	43.5
Sweden	7.8	31.0	4.8
Switzerland	22.6	43.2	62.3
Thailand	44.5	98.0	110.6
Togo	162.2	235.4	228.1
Turkey	15.6	19.6	41.1
United Arab Emirates	26.7	33.8	58.1
United Kingdom	52.8	82.0	105.3
USA	36.3	51.5	40.5
Total (incl. others)	1,494.3	2,128.6	2,250.3

Exports f.o.b.	2010	2011	2012
Burkina Faso	1.5	7.2	3.6
Cameroon	4.7	3.1	2.3
Chad	17.7	41.0	60.1
China, People's Repub.	50.6	54.6	108.3
Côte d'Ivoire	2.8	18.6	30.3
Denmark	7.0	11.6	7.1
France	1.2	8.2	3.8
Ghana	2.1	6.5	7.9
India	22.5	39.9	52.1
Indonesia	14.7	23.9	1.5
Italy	5.1	4.3	0.3
Malaysia	7.6	14.1	30.9
Mali	0.1	4.4	0.8
Netherlands	7.0	3.3	2.8
Niger	14.0	10.3	23.5
Nigeria	210.8	47.3	41.4
Portugal	7.8	2.6	7.9
Singapore	4.4	2.1	2.2
South Africa	1.7	10.8	5.5
Spain	0.3	4.7	0.1
Thailand	4.1	6.1	1.8
Togo	8.8	9.1	8.1
Viet Nam	10.0	6.3	5.2
Total (incl. others)	434.5	363.2	426.0

Source: Trade Map-Trade Competitiveness Map, International Trade Centre, www.intracen.org/marketanalysis.

Transport

RAILWAYS
(traffic)

	2004	2005	2006
Passenger-km (million)	45.4	17.0	—
Freight ton-km (million)	33.8	23.0	28.9

Source: mainly IMF, *Benin: Selected Issues and Statistical Appendix* (August 2008).

ROAD TRAFFIC
(motor vehicles in use)

	1994	1995	1996
Passenger cars	26,507	30,346	37,772
Buses and coaches	353	405	504
Lorries and vans	5,301	6,069	7,554
Road tractors	2,192	2,404	2,620
Motorcycles and mopeds	220,800	235,400	250,000

2007: Passenger cars 149,310; Buses and coaches 1,114; Lorries and vans 35,656; Motorcycles and mopeds 15,600.

Source: IRF, *World Road Statistics*.

SHIPPING

Flag Registered Fleet
(at 31 December)

	2010	2011	2012
Number of vessels	5	6	6
Total displacement (grt)	662	991	991

2013: Figures assumed to be unchanged from 2012.

Source: Lloyd's List Intelligence (www.lloydslistintelligence.com).

International Sea-borne Freight Traffic
(at Cotonou, including goods in transit, '000 metric tons)

	2004	2005	2006
Goods loaded	488.2	596.1	514.3
Goods in transit	n.a.	n.a.	2.1
Goods unloaded	3,520.6	4,556.8	4,854.8
Goods in transit	n.a.	n.a.	2,462.1

Source: IMF, *Benin: Selected Issues and Statistical Appendix* (August 2008).

CIVIL AVIATION
(traffic on scheduled services, domestic and international)*

	1999	2000	2001
Kilometres flown (million)	3	3	1
Passengers carried ('000)	84	77	46
Passenger-km (million)	235	216	130
Total ton-km (million)	36	32	19

* Including an apportionment of the traffic of Air Afrique.

Source: UN, *Statistical Yearbook*.

Tourism

FOREIGN VISITORS BY COUNTRY OF ORIGIN*

	2009	2010	2011
Angola	609	11,410	9,872
Belgium	2,162	4,670	3,600
Burkina Faso	9,700	9,122	6,980
Cameroon	5,357	10,620	12,500
Congo, Republic	6,839	25,953	22,897
Côte d'Ivoire	7,550	18,937	15,813
France	2,519	13,206	20,386
Gabon	8,313	6,589	1,807
Ghana	5,126	4,400	5,500
Netherlands	4,120	900	8,900
Niger	5,900	6,000	5,500
Nigeria	13,184	15,975	17,614
Senegal	3,059	4,600	3,100
Switzerland	6,571	1,234	5,500
Togo	11,551	5,400	7,600
Total (incl. others)	190,000	199,491	209,475

* Arrivals of non-resident tourists at national borders, by country of residence.

Receipts from tourism (US $ million, excl. passenger transport): 131 in 2009; 199 in 2010; 209 in 2011.

Source: World Tourism Organization.

Communications Media

	2010	2011	2012
Telephones ('000 main lines in use)	133.4	152.7	156.7
Mobile cellular telephones ('000 subscribers)	7,074.9	7,765.2	8,407.8
Broadband subscribers	3,569	3,897	5,032

2009: Internet subscribers ('000) 19.4.

Source: International Telecommunication Union.

Education

(2011/12 unless otherwise indicated)

			Students ('000)		
	Institutions	Teachers	Males	Females	Total
Pre-primary	283*	4,454	55.3	56.3	111.6
Primary	4,178†	45,010	1,055.3	931.9	1,987.2
Secondary	145‡	14,410§	449.6‖	274.1‖	723.7‖
Tertiary‖	n.a.	6,385	86.8	23.4	110.2

* 1995/96.
† 1999/2000.
‡ 1993/94.
§ 2003/04.
‖ 2010/11.

Source: UNESCO, *Statistical Yearbook* and Institute for Statistics.

Pupil-teacher ratio (primary education, UNESCO estimate): 44.1 in 2011/12 (Source: UNESCO Institute for Statistics).

Adult literacy rate (UNESCO estimates): 42.4% (males 55.2%; females 30.3%) in 2010 (Source: UNESCO Institute for Statistics).

Directory

The Government

HEAD OF STATE

President: Dr BONI YAYI (inaugurated 6 April 2006; re-elected 13 March 2011).

COUNCIL OF MINISTERS
(April 2014)

Minister of State, in charge of Higher Education and Scientific Research: FRANÇOIS ADÉBAYO ABIOLA.

Minister of Development, Economic Analysis and Planning: MARCEL ALAIN DE SOUZA.

Minister of the Economy and Finance: JONAS GBIAN.

Minister of National Defence: ALI YÉRIMA.

Minister of the Interior, Public Security and Religious Affairs: FRANÇOIS HOUÉSSOU.

Keeper of the Seals, Minister of Justice, Legislation and Human Rights: VALENTIN DJÈNONTIN-AGOSSOU.

Minister of Foreign Affairs, African Integration, Francophone Affairs and Beninois Abroad: NASSIROU ARIFARI BAKO.

Minister of Public Works and Transport: AKÉ NATONDÉ.

Minister of Secondary Education, Technical and Professional Training, Career Change and the Integration of Youths: ALASSANE SOUMANOU DJIMBA.

Minister of Nursery and Primary Education: ERIC KOUAGOU N'DAH.

Minister of Health: DOROTHÉE AKOKO KINDÉ GAZARD.

Minister of Agriculture, Stockbreeding and Fisheries: FATOUMA AMADOU DJIBRIL.

Minister of Labour, the Civil Service, Administrative and Institutional Reform, in charge of Social Dialogue: MARTIAL SOUNTON.

Minister in charge of Climate Change Management, Reforestation and the Protection of Natural and Forest Resources: RAPHAËL EDOU.

Minister of the Environment, Sanitation, Housing and Town Planning: CHRISTIAN SOSSOUHOUNTO.

Minister of Energy, Mining and Petroleum Research, Water and the Development of Renewable Energy Sources: BARTHÉLEMY KASSA.

Minister of Culture, Literacy, Crafts and Tourism: JEAN-MICHEL HERVÉ ABIMBOLA.

Minister of the Evaluation of Public Policy and Denationalization: ANTONIN DOSSOU.

Minister of Communications and Information and Communication Technology: KOMI KOUTCHÉ.

Minister in charge of Microfinance and Youth and Women's Employment: FRANÇOISE ASSOGBA.

Minister of Youth, Sports and Leisure: NAHOMI AZARIA.

Minister of Industry, Commerce and Small and Medium-sized Enterprises: AFFO IDRISSOU SAFIOU.

Minister of the Family, Social Affairs, National Solidarity, the Disabled and Senior Citizens: MARIE LAURE SRANON SOSSOU.

Minister of Decentralization, Local Government, Administration and Land Settlement: ISIDORE GNONLONFOUN.

Minister in charge of Relations with the Institutions: BIO TOROU OROU DJIWA.

Minister of the Maritime Economy and Port Infrastructure: ADJOUAVI MARTINE FRANÇOISE DOSSA.

MINISTRIES

Office of the President: BP 1288, Cotonou; tel. 21-30-00-90; fax 21-30-06-36; internet www.gouv.bj.

Ministry of Agriculture, Stockbreeding and Fisheries: 03 BP 2900, Cotonou; tel. 21-30-04-10; fax 21-30-03-26; e-mail sgm@agriculture.gouv.bj; internet www.agriculture.gouv.bj.

Ministry of Climate Change Management, Reforestation and the Protection of Natural and Forest Resources: Cotonou.

Ministry of Communications and Information and Communication Technology: Cotonou.

Ministry of Culture, Literacy, Crafts and Tourism: Cotonou.

Ministry of Decentralization, Local Government, Administration and Land Settlement: Cotonou; tel. 21-30-40-30.

Ministry of Development, Economic Analysis and Planning: Route de l'Aéroport, 08 BP 755, Cotonou; e-mail contact@developpement.bj; internet www.developpement.bj.

Ministry of the Economy and Finance: BP 302, Cotonou; tel. 21-30-02-81; fax 21-31-18-51; e-mail sgm@finance.gouv.bj; internet www.finances.bj.

Ministry of Energy, Mining and Petroleum Research, Water and the Development of Renewable Energy Sources: Cotonou.

Ministry of the Environment, Sanitation, Housing and Town Planning: 01 BP 3621, Cotonou; tel. 21-31-55-96; fax 21-31-50-81; e-mail sg@environnement.gouv.bj.

Ministry of the Evaluation of Public Policy and Denationalization: Cotonou.

Ministry of the Family, Social Affairs, National Solidarity, the Disabled and Senior Citizens: 01 BP 2802, Cotonou; tel. 21-31-67-08; fax 21-31-64-62.

Ministry of Foreign Affairs, African Integration, Francophone Affairs and Beninois Abroad: Zone Résidentielle, route de l'Aéroport, 06 BP 318, Cotonou; tel. 21-30-09-06; fax 21-38-19-70; e-mail infos@maebenin.bj; internet www.diplomatie.gouv.bj.

Ministry of Health: Immeuble ex-MCAT, 01 BP 882, Cotonou; tel. 21-33-21-41; fax 21-33-04-64; e-mail sgm@sante.gouv.bj; internet www.ministeresantebenin.com.

Ministry of Higher Education and Scientific Research: 01 BP 348, Cotonou; tel. 21-30-06-81; fax 21-30-57-95; e-mail sgm@recherche.gouv.bj; internet www.mesrs.bj.

Ministry of Industry, Commerce and Small and Medium-sized Enterprises: BP 363, Cotonou; tel. and fax 21-30-30-24; e-mail mic@mic.bj; internet www.mic.bj.

Ministry of the Interior, Public Security and Religious Affairs: BP 925, Cotonou; tel. 21-30-11-06; fax 21-30-01-59.

Ministry of Justice, Legislation and Human Rights: BP 2493, Cotonou; tel. 21-30-08-90; fax 21-30-18-21; e-mail sgm@justice.gouv.bj; internet www.justice.gouv.bj.

Ministry of Labour, the Civil Service, Administrative and Institutional Reform: BP 907, Cotonou; tel. 21-31-26-18; fax 21-31-06-29; e-mail sgm@travail.gouv.bj; internet www.travail.gouv.bj.

Ministry of the Maritime Economy and Port Infrastructure: Cotonou.

Ministry of Microfinance and Youth and Women's Employment: BP 302, Cotonou; tel. 21-30-02-81; fax 21-30-18-51.

Ministry of National Defence: BP 2493, Cotonou; tel. 21-30-08-90; fax 21-30-18-21.

Ministry of Nursery and Primary Education: 01 BP 10, Porto-Novo; tel. 20-21-33-27; fax 20-21-50-11; e-mail sgm@enseignement.gouv.bj; internet www.enseignement.gouv.bj.

Ministry of Public Works and Transport: 01 BP 372, Cotonou; tel. 21-31-46-64; fax 21-31-06-17; internet www.mtpt-benin.net.

Ministry of Relations with the Institutions: Cotonou.

Ministry of Secondary Education, Technical and Professional Training, Career Change and the Integration of Youths: 10 BP 250, Cotonou; tel. and fax 21-30-56-15.

Ministry of Trade: BP 363, Cotonou; tel. 21-30-76-46; fax 21-30-30-24; e-mail sgm@commerce.gouv.bj; internet www.commerce.gouv.bj.

Ministry of Youth, Sports and Leisure: 03 BP 2103, Cotonou; tel. 21-30-36-14; fax 21-38-21-26; internet www.mjsl.bj.

President

Presidential Election, 13 March 2011

Candidate	Votes	% of votes
Boni Yayi	1,579,550	53.14
Adrien Houngbédji	1,059,396	35.64
Abdoulaye Bio Tchané	182,484	6.14
Issa Salifou	37,219	1.25
Christian Eunock Lagnidé	19,221	0.65
François Janvier Yahouédéhou	16,591	0.56
Others*	77,984	2.62
Total	2,972,445	100.00

* There were eight other candidates.

Legislature

National Assembly: BP 371, Porto-Novo; tel. 20-21-22-19; fax 20-21-36-44; e-mail assemblee.benin@yahoo.fr; internet www.assembleebenin.org.

President: MATHURIN NAGO.

General Election, 30 April 2011

Party	Seats
Force Cauris pour un Bénin Emergent (FCBE)	41
Union Fait la Nation (UN)	30
Alliance G13 Baobab	2
Alliance Amana	2
Alliance Cauris	2
Alliance Forces dans l'Unité (AFU)	2
Union pour la Bénin (UB)	2
Union pour la Relève-Force Espoir (UPR-FE)	2
Total	83

Election Commission

Commission Electorale Nationale Autonome (CENA): 01 BP 443, Cotonou; tel. 21-31-69-90; e-mail info@cena-benin.org; internet www.cena-benin.org; f. 1994; 11 mems, of whom 9 are appointed by the National Assembly, 1 by the President of the Republic, 1 by civil society; there are additionally 4 members of the Commission's permanent administrative secretariat; Chair. JOSEPH GNONLONFOUN.

Advisory Council

Economic and Social Council (Conseil Economique et Social—CES): ave Jean-Paul II, 08 BP 679, Cotonou; tel. 21-30-03-91; fax 21-30-03-13; e-mail noc@ces-benin.org; internet www.ces-benin.org; f. 1994; 30 mems, representing the executive, legislature and 'all sections of the nation'; reviews all legislation relating to economic and social affairs; competent to advise on proposed economic and social legislation, as well as to recommend economic and social reforms; Pres. RAPHIOU TOUKOUROU.

Political Organizations

Some 19 political parties or alliances contested the 2011 legislative elections.

Alliance pour une Dynamique Démocratique (ADD): Leader NICÉPHORE SOGLO.

Mouvement Africain pour la Démocratie et le Progrès (MADEP): BP 1509, Cotonou; tel. 21-31-31-22; f. 1997; Leader El Hadj SÉFOU L. FAGBOHOUN.

Parti Social-Démocrate (PSD): Leader EMMANUEL GOLOU.

La Renaissance du Bénin (RB): BP 2205, Cotonou; tel. 21-31-40-89; f. 1992; Chair. ROSINE VIEYRA SOGLO.

Union des Forces Démocratiques (UFD): Parakou; f. 1994; Leader SACCA GEORGES ZIMÉ.

Alliance Etoile: f. 2002; Leader SACCA LAFIA.

Union pour la Démocratie et la Solidarité Nationale (UDS): BP 1761, Cotonou; tel. 21-31-38-69; Pres. SACCA LAFIA.

Les Verts du Bénin—Parti Écologiste du Bénin: 06 BP 1336, Cotonou; tel. and fax 21-35-19-47; e-mail greensbenin@yahoo.fr; internet www.greensbenin.org; f. 1995; Pres. TOUSSAINT HINVI; Sec. PIERRE AHOUANOZIN.

Alliance des Forces du Progrès (AFP): Assemblée nationale, BP 371, Porto-Novo; Leader VALENTIN ADITI HOUDE.

Alliance du Renouveau (AR): Leader MARTIN DOHOU AZONHIHO.

Force Cauris pour un Bénin Emergent (FCBE): tel. 95861100 (mobile); e-mail fcbe@gmail.com; internet www.fcbe2007.org; Pres. EXPÉDIT HOUESSOU; Sec.-Gen. DAVID NAHOUAN.

Force Clé: Carré 315, ScoaGbéto, 01 BP 1435, Cotonou; tel. 21-35-09-36; f. 2003 on basis of Mouvement pour une Alternative du Peuple; Leader LAZARE SÈHOUÉTO.

Force Espoir (FE): Leader ANTOINE DAYORI.

G13: f. 2008 by fmr supporters of President Yayi; Leader ISSA SALIFOU.

Mouvement pour le Développement et la Solidarité (MDS): BP 73, Porto-Novo; Leader SACCA MOUSSÉDIKOU FIKARA.

Nouvelle Alliance: Cotonou; f. 2006; Leader CORENTIN KOHOUE.

Parti pour la Démocratie et le Progrès Social (PDPS): Leader EDMOND AGOUA.

Parti du Renouveau Démocratique (PRD): Immeuble Babo Oganla, 01 BP 1157, Porto-Novo; tel. 21-30-07-57; f. 1990; Leader ADRIEN HOUNGBÉDJI.

Rassemblement pour la Démocratie et le Panafricanisme (RDP): 03 BP 1050, Cotonou; tel. 21-32-02-83; fax 21-32-35-71; e-mail cotrans@leland.bj; f. 1995; Pres. DOMINIQUE O. HOUNGNINOU; Treas. JANVIER SETANGNI.

Restaurer l'Espoir (RE): Leader CANDIDE AZANNAÏ.

Union pour le Bénin du Futur (UBF): 03 BP 1972, Cotonou; tel. 21-33-12-23; e-mail amoussou@avu.org; f. 2002 by supporters of then Pres. Kérékou; separate faction, UBF 'Aller Plus Loin', formed Oct. 2004 under leadership of JOSEPH GANDAHO, comprising more than 30 pro-presidential parties and asscns; further, smaller faction, the 'Alliance UBF' formed April 2005, led by ALAIN ADIHOU; Co-ordinator BRUNO AMOUSSOU.

Front d'Action pour le Renouveau, la Démocratie et le Développement—Alafia (FARD—Alafia): 01 BP 3238, Cotonou; tel. 21-33-34-10; f. 1994; Sec.-Gen. DANIEL TAWÉMA.

Union pour la Relève (UPR): Gbégamey; internet www.uprbenin.org; Leader ISSA SALIFOU.

Diplomatic Representation

EMBASSIES IN BENIN

China, People's Republic: 2 route de l'Aéroport, 01 BP 196, Cotonou; tel. 21-30-07-65; fax 21-30-08-41; e-mail prcbenin@serv.eit.bj; internet bj.chineseembassy.org; Ambassador TAO WEIGUANG.

Congo, Democratic Republic: Carré 221, Ayélawadjè, Cotonou; tel. 21-30-00-01.

Cuba: ave de la Marina, face Hôtel du Port, 01 BP 948, Cotonou; tel. 21-31-52-97; fax 21-31-65-91; e-mail embacuba@benin.cubaminrex.cu; internet www.cubadiplomatica.cu/benin; Chargé d'affaires a.i. JOSÉ LUIS NORIEGA SÁNCHEZ.

Denmark: Lot P7, Les Cocotiers, 04 BP 1223, Cotonou; tel. 21-30-38-62; fax 21-30-38-60; e-mail cooamb@um.dk; internet www.ambcotonou.um.dk; Ambassador STEPHAN SCHÖNEMANN.

Egypt: Lot G26, route de l'Aéroport, BP 1215, Cotonou; tel. 21-30-08-42; fax 21-30-14-25; Ambassador RAMADAN MOHAMED E. BAKR.

France: ave Jean-Paul II, BP 966, Cotonou; tel. 21-36-55-33; fax 21-36-55-30; e-mail contact@ambafrance-bj.org; internet www.ambafrance-bj.org; Ambassador ALINE KUSTER-MÉNAGER.

Germany: 7 ave Jean-Paul II, 01 BP 504, Cotonou; tel. 21-31-29-67; fax 21-31-29-62; e-mail info@cotonou.diplo.de; internet www.cotonou.diplo.de; Ambassador HANS JÖRG NEUMANN.

Ghana: route de l'Aéroport, Lot F, Les Cocotiers, BP 488, Cotonou; tel. 21-30-07-46; fax 21-30-03-45; e-mail ghaemb02@leland.bj; Ambassador MODESTUS AHIABLE.

Holy See: 08 BP 400, Cotonou; tel. 21-30-03-08; fax 21-30-03-10; e-mail nonciaturebenin@gmail.com; Apostolic Nuncio Archbishop BRIAN UDAIGWE (Titular Archbishop of Suelli).

Japan: Villa A2, Complexe CEN-SAD, Laico-Benin, blvd de la Marina, Cotonou; tel. 21-30-59-86; fax 21-30-59-94; internet www.bj.emb-japan.go.jp; Ambassador DAINI TSUKAHARA.

Korea, Democratic People's Republic: Cotonou; Ambassador KIM PYONG GI.

Kuwait: Cotonou; Ambassador FAEYEZ MISHARI AL-JASSIM.

Libya: Carré 36, Cotonou; tel. 21-30-04-52; fax 21-30-03-01; Ambassador TOUFIK ASHOUR ADAM.

Netherlands: ave Pape Jean Paul II, route de l'Aéroport, derrière le Tri Postal, 08 BP 0783, Cotonou; tel. 21-30-04-39; fax 21-30-41-50; e-mail cot@minbuza.nl; internet larepubliquedubenin.nlambassade.org; Ambassador JOS VAN AGGELEN.

Niger: derrière l'Hôtel de la Plage, BP 352, Cotonou; tel. 21-31-56-65; Ambassador LOMPO SOULEYMANE.

Nigeria: ave de France, Marina, BP 2019, Cotonou; tel. 21-30-11-42; fax 21-30-11-13; Ambassador LAWRENCE OLUFEMI OBISAKIN.

Qatar: Novotel Hotel Area, Cotonou; tel. 21-31-72-00; e-mail cotonou@mofa.gov.qa; Ambassador MOHAMMED JABER AHMAD AL-KUWARI.

South Africa: Marina Hotel, blvd de la Marina, 01 BP 1901, Cotonou; tel. 21-30-72-17; fax 21-30-70-58; e-mail saembassybenin@gmail.com; Ambassador GLADSTONE DUMISANI GWADISO.

Russia: Zone résidentielle, ave de la Marina, face Hôtel du Port, BP 2013, Cotonou; tel. 21-31-28-34; fax 21-31-28-35; e-mail ambrusben@

mail.ru; internet www.benin.mid.ru; Ambassador OLEG V. KOVALCHUK.

USA: rue Caporal Anani Bernard, 01 BP 2012, Cotonou; tel. 21-30-06-50; fax 21-30-03-84; e-mail irccotonou@state.gov; internet cotonou.usembassy.gov; Ambassador MICHAEL RAYNOR.

Judicial System

Constitutional Court: BP 2050, Cotonou; tel. 21-31-16-10; fax 21-31-37-12; e-mail cconstitutsg@yahoo.fr; internet www.cour-constitutionnelle-benin.org; f. 1990; inaug. 1993; 7 mems; 4 appointed by the National Assembly, 3 by the President of the Republic; exercises highest jurisdiction in constitutional affairs; determines the constitutionality of legislation, oversees and proclaims results of national elections and referendums, responsible for protection of individual and public rights and obligations, charged with regulating functions of organs of state and authorities; Pres. ROBERT DOSSOU; Sec.-Gen. MARCELLINE-CLAIRE GBÈHA AFOUDA.

High Court of Justice: 01 BP 2958, Porto-Novo; tel. 20-21-26-81; fax 20-21-27-71; tel. hcjbenin@intnet.bj; internet www.gouv.bj; f. 1990; officially inaugurated in 2001; comprises the 6 members of the Constitutional Court (other than its President), 6 deputies of the National Assembly and the First President of the Supreme Court; competent to try the President of the Republic and members of the Government in cases of high treason, crimes committed in, or at the time of, the exercise of their functions, and of plotting against state security; Pres. Prof. THÉODORE HOLO.

Supreme Court: 01 BP 330, Cotonou; tel. and fax 20-21-26-77; fax 20-21-32-08; e-mail info@coursupreme.gouv.bj; internet www.coursupreme.gouv.bj; f. 1960; highest juridical authority in administrative and judicial affairs and in matters of public accounts; competent in disputes relating to local elections; advises the executive on jurisdiction and administrative affairs; comprises a President (appointed by the President of the Republic, after consultation with the President of the National Assembly, senior magistrates and jurists), presidents of the component chambers, a public prosecutor, 4 assistant procurators-fiscal, counsellors and clerks; Pres. OUSMANE BATOKO; Attorney-Gen. JEAN-BAPTISTE MONSI; Pres. of the Judicial Chamber JACQUES MAYABA; Pres. of the Administrative Chamber GRÉGOIRE Y. ALAYÈ; Pres. of the Chamber of Accounts JUSTIN BIOKOU; Chief Clerk FRANÇOISE TCHIBOZO-QUENUM.

Religion

Religious and spiritual cults, which were discouraged under the military regime, re-emerged as a prominent force in Beninois society during the 1990s. At the time of the 2002 census it was estimated that some 38% of the population were Christians (mainly Roman Catholics), 24% were Muslims, and 17% followed the traditional *vodoun* religion, with a further 6% being adherents of other traditional religions.

CHRISTIANITY

The Roman Catholic Church

Benin comprises two archdioceses and eight dioceses. An estimated 27.6% of the population were Roman Catholics.

Bishops' Conference: Conférence Episcopale du Bénin, Archevêché, 01 BP 491, Cotonou; tel. 21-30-66-48; fax 21-30-07-07; e-mail cepiscob@usa.net; Pres. Most Rev. ANTOINE GANYÉ (Archbishop of Cotonou).

Archbishop of Cotonou: Most Rev. ANTOINE GANYÉ, Archevêché, 01 BP 491, Cotonou; tel. 21-30-01-45; fax 21-30-07-07; e-mail mhlagbot@yahoo.fr.

Archbishop of Parakou: PASCAL N'KOUÉ, Archevêché, BP 75, Parakou; tel. 23-61-02-54; fax 23-61-01-09; e-mail archeveche@borgou.net.

Protestant Church

Eglise Protestante Méthodiste en République du Bénin (EPMB): 54 ave Mgr Steinmetz, 01 BP 34, Cotonou; tel. and fax 21-31-11-42; e-mail epmbenin@intnet.bj; f. 1843; Pres. Rev. Dr NICODÈME ALAGBADA; Sec. Rev. Dr ZABULON ANDRÉ DJARRA; 101,000 mems (1997).

VODOUN

The origins of the traditional *vodoun* religion can be traced to the 14th century. Its influence is particularly strong in Latin America and the Caribbean, owing to the shipment of slaves from the West African region to the Americas in the 18th and 19th centuries.

Communauté Nationale du Culte Vodoun (CNCV): Ouidah; Pres. HOUNGUÈ TOWAKON GUÈDÉHOUNGUÈ II.

ISLAM

Union Islamique du Bénin (UIB): Cotonou; Pres. Imam El Hadj MOHAMED AMED SANNI; Sec.-Gen. FAÏSSOU ADÉGBOLA.

BAHÁ'Í FAITH

National Spiritual Assembly: BP 1252, Cotonou.

The Press

In 2010 there were some 75 dailies and periodicals recognized by the Haute Autorité de l'Audiovisuel et de la Communication in Benin.

DAILIES

Actu-Express: 01 BP 2220, Cotonou; tel. 97981047 (mobile); internet www.actuexpress.com; Dir of Publication MÉDÉRIC FRANÇOIS GOHOUNGO.

L'Adjinakou: Lot AC, Parcelle 1 Avakpa-Tokpa, Immeuble Radio école APM, 03 BP 105, Porto-Novo; tel. 20-22-06-76; e-mail adjinakou2004@yahoo.com; internet www.journal-adjinakou-benin.info; f. 2003; Dir of Publication MAURILLE AGBOKOU.

L'Araignée: siège du cyber DOPHIA, face Cité Houeyiho, 10 BP 1199, Cotonou; tel. 95953458 (mobile); e-mail info@laraignee.org; internet www.laraignee.org; f. 2001; online only; politics, public affairs, culture, society, sport; Dir of Publishing FÉLIX ANIWANOU HOUNSA.

L'Aurore: face Clinique Boni, 05 BP 464, Cotonou; tel. 21-33-70-43; e-mail laurore1998@yahoo.fr; Dir PATRICK ADJAMONSI; circ. 1,500.

L'Autre Quotidien: Lot 115 Z, rue Capitaine Anani, Face PNUD, Zone Résidentielle, 01 BP 6659, Cotonou; tel. 21-31-01-99; fax 21-31-02-05; e-mail lautreredaction@yahoo.fr; internet www.lautrequotidien.com; Dir ROMAIN TOÏ; Editor-in-Chief LÉON BRATHIER.

Bénin-Presse Info: 01 BP 72, Cotonou; tel. 21-31-26-55; fax 21-31-13-26; e-mail abpben@bow.intnet.bj; internet www.gouv.bj/presse/abp/index.php; bulletin of Agence Bénin-Presse; Dir YAOVI R. HOUNKPONOU; Editor-in-Chief JOSEPH VODOUNON.

Le Confrère de la Matinée: Esplanade du Stade de l'Amitié, Cotonou; tel. 21-04-20-14; e-mail info@leconfrere.com; internet www.leconfrere.com; Dir of Publication FAUSTIN BABATOUNDÉ ADJAGBA.

Djakpata: Quartier Todote C/410, Maison Bokononhui, 02 BP 2744, Cotonou; tel. 21-32-43-73; e-mail quotidiendjakpata@yahoo.fr; internet djakpata.info; Editor CYRILLE SAÏZONOU.

Les Echos du Jour: Carré 136, Sodjatimè, 08 BP 718, Cotonou; tel. 21-33-18-33; fax 21-33-17-06; e-mail echos@intnet.bj; independent; Dir MAURICE CHABI; Editor-in-Chief SÉBASTIEN DOSSA; circ. 3,000.

Fraternité: face Station Menontin, 05 BP 915, Cotonou; tel. 21-38-47-70; fax 21-38-47-71; e-mail fraternite@yesouikend.com; internet yesouikend.com/fraternite; Dir of Publication BRICE U. HOUSSOU; Editor-in-Chief GÉRARD GANSOU.

L'Informateur: Etoile Rouge, Bâtiment Radio Star, Carré 1072C, 01 BP 5421, Cotonou; tel. and fax 21-32-66-39; f. 2001; Dir CLÉMENT ADÉCHIAN; Editor-in-Chief BRICE GUÈDÈ.

Le Matin: Carré 54, Tokpa Hoho, 06 BP 2217, Cotonou; tel. 21-31-10-80; fax 21-33-42-62; e-mail lematinonline@moncourrier.com; f. 1994; independent; Dir MOÏSE DATO; Editorial Dir IGNACE FANOU.

Le Matinal: Carré 153–154, Atinkanmey, 06 BP 1989, Cotonou; tel. 90948332 (mobile); e-mail infodumatinal@yahoo.fr; internet www.actubenin.com; f. 1997; daily; Dir-Gen. MAXIMIN TCHIBOZO; Editor-in-Chief NAPOLÉON MAFORIKAN; circ. 5,000.

La Nation: Cadjèhoun, 01 BP 1210, Cotonou; tel. 21-30-02-99; fax 21-30-34-63; e-mail onipben@intnet.bj; internet www.gouv.bj/presse/lanation/index.php; f. 1990; official newspaper; Dir AKUÉTÉ ASSEVI; Editor-in-Chief HUBERT O. AKPONIKPE; circ. 4,000.

La Nouvelle Tribune: Immeuble Zonon, Lot 1498, P Quartier Missogbè à Vêdoko, 09 BP 336, Cotonou; tel. 21-38-34-88; e-mail redaction@lanouvelletribune.info; internet www.lanouvelletribune.info; f. 2001; Dir-Gen. and Dir of Publication VINCENT FOLY; Editorial Dir EMMANUEL S. TACHIN.

L'Oeil du Peuple: Carré 743, rue PTT, Gbégamey, 01 BP 5538, Cotonou; tel. 21-30-22-07; e-mail loeildupeuple@yahoo.fr; Dir CELESTIN ABISSI; Editor-in-Chief PAUL AGBOYIDOU.

Le Point au Quotidien: 332 rue du Renouveau, 05 BP 934, Cotonou; tel. 90916945 (mobile); fax 21-32-25-31; e-mail info@lepointauquotidien.com; independent; Dir and Editor-in-Chief FERNANDO HESSOU; circ. 2,000.

La Presse du Jour: 01 BP 1719, Cotonou; tel. 21-30-51-75; internet www.lapressedujour.net; Dir of Publication PASCAL HOUNKPATIN.

Le Progrès: 05 BP 708, Cotonou; tel. 21-32-52-73; e-mail journalprogres@hotmail.com; internet www.leprogres.info; f. ; Dir of Publication LUDOVIC AGBADJA.

Le Républicain: Les Presses d'Afrique, Carré 630, Tanto, 05 BP 1230, Cotonou; tel. and fax 21-33-83-04; e-mail lerepublicain@lerepublicain.org; independent; Editor-in-Chief ISIDORE ZINSOU.

La Tribune de la Capitale: Lot 03-46, Parcelle E, Houinmè, Maison Onifadé, Catchi, 01 BP 1463, Porto-Novo; tel. 20-22-55-69; e-mail latribunedelacapitale@yahoo.fr; internet www.latribunedelacapitale.com; Dir of Publication SETH EVARISTE HODONOU; Editor-in-Chief KPAKOUN CHARLES.

PERIODICALS

Agri-Culture: 03 BP 0380, Cotonou; tel. and fax 21-36-05-46; e-mail agriculture@uva.org; f. 1999; monthly; Editor-in-Chief JOACHIM SAÏZONOU; circ. 1,000.

L'Autre Gazette: 02 BP 1537, Cotonou; tel. 21-32-59-97; e-mail collegi@beninweb.org; Editor-in-Chief WILFRIED AYIBATIN.

L'Avenir: Carré 911, 02 BP 8134, Cotonou; tel. 21-32-21-23; fortnightly; political analysis; Dir CLAUDE FIRMIN GANGBE.

Le Canard du Golfe: Carré 240, Midombo, Akpakpa, 06 BP 59, Cotonou; tel. 21-32-72-33; e-mail lecanardugolfe@yahoo.fr; satirical; weekly; Dir F. L. TINGBO; Editor-in-Chief EMMANUEL SOTIKON.

Le Continental: BP 4419, Cotonou; tel. 21-30-04-37; fax 21-30-03-21; Editor-in-Chief ARNAULD HOUNDETE.

La Croix du Bénin: Centre Paul VI, 01 BP 105, Cotonou; tel. and fax 21-32-12-07; e-mail andrequenum@yahoo.com; internet www.lacroixdubenin.com; f. 1946; weekly; Roman Catholic; Editor Rev. Dr ANDRÉ S. QUENUM.

Emotion Magazine: 06 BP 1404, Cotonou; tel. 95401707 (mobile); fax 21-32-21-33; e-mail emomagazine@yahoo.fr; f. 1998; every 2 months; cultural and social affairs; Dir of Publication ERIC SESSINOU HUANNOU; Editor-in-Chief BERNARD HERMANN ZANNOU; circ. 3,000 (2006).

La Gazette du Golfe: Immeuble La Gazette du Golfe, Carré 902E, Sikècodji, 03 BP 1624, Cotonou; tel. 21-32-68-44; fax 21-32-52-26; e-mail gazettedugolfe@serv.eit.bj; internet www.golfemediaonline.com; f. 1987; weekly; Dir ISMAËL Y. SOUMANOU; Editor MARCUS BONI TEIGA; circ. 18,000 (nat. edn), 5,000 (int. edn).

Le Gongonneur: 04 BP 1432, Cotonou; tel. 90906095 (mobile); fax 21-35-04-22; e-mail dahoun@yahoo.com; f. 1998; owned by Prix Etoile Internationale à la Qualité; Dir MATHIAS C. SOSSOU; Editor-in-Chief GAFFAROU RADJI.

Le Héraut: 03 BP 3417, Cotonou; tel. 21-36-00-64; e-mail franck.kouyami@auf.org; internet leheraut.org; monthly; current affairs; analysis; produced by students at Université nationale du Bénin; Dir GEOFFREY GOUNOU N'GOYE; Editor-in-Chief GABRIEL DIDEH.

Journal Officiel de la République du Bénin: BP 59, Porto-Novo; tel. 20-21-39-77; f. 1890; present name adopted 1990; official govt bulletin; fortnightly; Dir AFIZE DÉSIRÉ ADAMO.

Madame Afrique: Siège Mefort Inter Diffusion, Carré 1066, quartier Cadjehoun, 05 BP 1914, Cotonou; tel. 97682290 (mobile); e-mail madafric@yahoo.fr; f. 2000; monthly; women's interest; Dir of Publication BERNARD G. ZANKLAN.

Le Magazine de l'Entreprise: BP 850, Cotonou; tel. 21-30-80-79; fax 21-30-47-77; e-mail oliviergat@hotmail.com; f. 1999; monthly; business; Dir A. VICTOR FAKÈYÈ.

Le Perroquet: Carré 478, Quartier Bar-Tito, 03 BP 880, Cotonou; tel. 21-32-18-54; e-mail leperroquet2003@yahoo.fr; internet www.leperroquet.fr.gd; f. 1995; 2 a month; independent; news and analysis; Dir DAMIEN HOUESSOU; Editor-in-Chief CHARLES RICHARD NZI; circ. 4,000 (2004).

Press Association

Union des Journalistes de la Presse Privée du Bénin (UJPB): blvd de la République, près Cadmes Plus, 03 BP 383, Cotonou; tel. 21-32-52-73; e-mail ujpb@h2com.com; internet www.h2com.com/ujpb; f. 1992; asscn of independent journalists; Pres. AGAPIT N. MAFORIKAN.

NEWS AGENCY

Agence Bénin-Presse (ABP): BP 72, Cotonou; tel. and fax 21-31-26-55; e-mail abpben@intnet.bj; internet www.abp.gouv.bj; f. 1961; nat. news agency; Dir YAOVI R. HOUNKPONOU.

Publishers

AFRIDIC: 01 BP 269, 01 Porto-Novo; tel. 20-22-32-28; f. 1996; poetry, essays, fiction; Dir ADJIBI JEAN-BAPTISTE.

Editions de l'ACACIA: 06 BP 1978, Cotonou; tel. 21-33-04-72; e-mail zoundin@yahoo.fr; f. 1989; fmrly Editions du Flamboyant; literary fiction, history, popular science; Dir OSCAR DE SOUZA.

Editions des Diasporas: 04 BP 792, Cotonou; e-mail camouro@yahoo.fr; poetry, essays; Editor CAMILLE AMOURO.

Editions Ruisseaux d'Afrique: 04 BP 1154, Cotonou; tel. and fax 90947925 (mobile); fax 21-30-31-86; e-mail ruisseau@leland.bj; f. 1992; children's literature; Dir BÉATRICE GBADO.

Imprimerie Notre Dame: BP 109, Cotonou; tel. 21-32-12-07; fax 21-32-11-19; f. 1974; Roman Catholic publs; Dir BARTHÉLÉMY ASSOGBA CAKPO.

Société Tunde: 06 BP 1925, Cotonou; tel. 21-30-15-68; fax 21-30-42-86; e-mail tunde.sa@tunde-sa.com; internet www.tunde-sa.com; f. 1986; economics, management; Pres. BABATOUNDÉ RASAKI OLLOFINDJI; Dir-Gen. ALFRED LAMBERT SOMA.

Star Editions: 01 BP 367, Recette principale, Cotonou; tel. 90-94-66-28; fax 21-33-05-29; e-mail star_editions@yahoo.fr; business, economics, science, poetry; Editor JOACHIM ADJOVI.

GOVERNMENT PUBLISHING HOUSE

Office National d'Edition, de Presse et d'Imprimerie (ONEPI): 01 BP 1210, Cotonou; tel. 21-30-02-99; fax 21-30-34-63; f. 1975; Dir-Gen. INNOCENT ADJAHO.

Broadcasting and Communications

TELECOMMUNICATIONS

Benin's fixed-line telephone sector is dominated by the state operator, Bénin Télécoms. In 2011 there were five providers of mobile cellular telephone services, of which four were privately owned and one, Libercom, was state-owned. At December 2007 there were 110,254 subscribers to fixed-line telephone services, while at June 2010 there were 6.3m. subscribers to mobile services.

Bénin Télécoms: Ganhi, 01 BP 5959, Cotonou; tel. 21-31-20-45; fax 21-31-38-43; e-mail sp.dgbttelecoms@intnet.bj; internet www.benintelecoms.bj; f. 2004; Dir-Gen. URBAIN FADÉGNON (acting); 110,254 subscribers (Dec. 2007).

Bell Bénin Communications (BBCOM): 02 BP 1886, Gbégamey; tel. 21-30-52-84; fax 21-30-84-84; internet www.bellbenin.net; f. 2002; mobile cellular telephone operator; Chief Exec. ISSA SALIFOU; 443,550 subscribers (2008).

Glo Mobile Bénin: Aïdjèdo, Lot 817 Parcelle C, ave de la Libération, 01 BP 8050, Cotonou; tel. 21-32-44-56; Dir-Gen. FEMMY OGUNLUSI; 560,090 subscribers (2008).

Libercom: blvd Saint-Michel, face Hall des Arts et de la Culture, 01 BP 5959, Cotonou; tel. 21-31-46-48; fax 21-31-49-42; e-mail renseignements@libercom.bj; internet www.libercom.bj; f. 2000; mobile cellular telephone operator in Cotonou and Porto-Novo; Dir-Gen. ISIDORE DÉGBÈLO; 194,888 subscribers (2008).

MTN Bénin: 01 BP 5293, Cotonou; tel. 21-31-66-41; internet www.mtn.bj; f. 2000 as BéninCell; renamed as Areeba in 2005; mobile cellular telephone operator in Cotonou, Porto-Novo and Parakou under network name Areeba; owned by Mobile Telephone Network International (South Africa); CEO MOHAMAD BADER; 267,583 subscribers (2005).

Moov Bénin: Immeuble Kougblenou, 5è étage, ave Mgr Steinmetz, Cotonou; e-mail moov@moov.bj; internet www.moov.bj; f. 2000 as Telcel Bénin; mobile cellular telephone operator in Cotonou, Porto-Novo, Abomey, Lokossa, other regions of southern Benin and in Parakou; Dir-Gen. TALIBI HAÏDRA; 950,584 subscribers (2008).

Regulatory Authority

Autorité Transitoire de Régulation des Postes et Télécommunications (ATRPT): ave Steinmetz, Von opposé ancien Air Gabon, Immeuble Suzanne Loko, 01 BP 2034, Cotonou; tel. 21-31-72-76; fax 21-31-72-76; e-mail infos@atrpt.bj; internet www.atrpt.bj; f. 2007; Pres. FIRMIN DJIMENOU.

BROADCASTING

Since 1997 the Haute Autorité de l'Audiovisuel et de la Communication has issued licences to private radio and television stations.

Haute Autorité de l'Audiovisuel et de la Communication (HAAC): 01 BP 3567, Cotonou; tel. 21-31-17-45; fax 21-31-17-42; e-mail infohaac@haacbenin.org; internet www.haacbenin.org; f. 1994; Pres. THÉOPHILE NATA.

Radio

Office de Radiodiffusion et de Télévision du Bénin (ORTB): 01 BP 366, Cotonou; tel. 21-30-46-19; fax 21-30-04-48; e-mail drp@ortb.bj; internet www.ortb.bj; state-owned; radio programmes broadcast from Cotonou and Parakou in French, English and 18 local languages; Dir-Gen. JULIEN PIERRE AKPAKI; Dir of Radio CHRISTIAN DE SOUZA.

Atlantic FM: 01 BP 366, Cotonou; tel. 21-30-20-41; Dir JOSEPH OGOUNCHI.

Radiodiffusion Nationale du Bénin: BP 366, Cotonou; tel. 21-30-10-96; f. 1953; Dir MOUFALIOU LIADY.

Radio Régionale de Parakou: BP 128, Parakou; tel. 23-61-07-73; Dir SÉNI SOUROU.

Bénin-Culture: BP 21, Association pour l'Institutionnalisation de la Mémoire et de la Pensée Intellectuelle Africaine, 01 BP 21, Porto-Novo; tel. 20-22-69-34; Head of Station ARMAND COVI.

Golfe FM-Magic Radio: 03 BP 1624, Cotonou; tel. 21-32-42-08; fax 21-32-42-09; e-mail golfefm@serv.eit.bj; internet www.eit.bj/golfefm.htm; Dir ISMAËL SOUMANOU.

Radio Carrefour: 03 BP 432, Cotonou; tel. 21-32-70-50; fax 22-51-16-55; e-mail chrisdavak@yahoo.fr; f. 1999; production and broadcast of radio and television programmes; Dir-Gen. CHRISTOPHE DAVAKAN.

Radio FM-Ahémé: BP 66, Bopa, Mono; tel. 95055818 (mobile); f. 1997; informative, cultural and civic education broadcasts; Dir AMBROISE COKOU MOUSSOU.

Radio Immaculée Conception: BP 88, Allada; tel. 21-36-80-97; e-mail satric@immacolata.com; internet www.immacolata.com; operated by the Roman Catholic Church of Benin; broadcasts to Abomey, Allada, Bembéréke, Cotonou, Dassa-Zoume, Djougou and Parakou; Dir Fr ALFONSO BRUNO.

Radio Maranatha: 03 BP 4113, Cotonou; tel. and fax 21-32-58-82; e-mail maranatha.fm@serv.eit.bj; internet www.eit.to/RadioMaranatha.htm; operated by the Conseil des Eglises Protestantes Evangéliques du Bénin; Dir Rev. CLOVIS ALFRED KPADE.

Radio Planète: 02 BP 1528, Immeuble Master Soft, Cotonou; tel. 21-30-30-30; fax 21-30-24-51; internet www.planetefm.com; Dir JANVIER YAHOUEDEHOU.

Radio Tokpa: Dantokpa, Cotonou; tel. 21-31-45-32; internet www.radiotokpa.net; Dir-Gen. GUY KPAKPO.

La Voix de la Lama: 03 BP 3772, Cotonou; tel. 21-37-12-26; fax 21-37-13-67; e-mail voix_delalama@yahoo.fr; f. 1998; non-commercial FM station, broadcasting on 103.8 Mhz from Allada; Dir SÉRAPHINE DADY.

Radio Wêkê: 05 BP 436, Cotonou; tel. 20-21-38-40; fax 20-21-37-14; e-mail issabadarou@hotmail.com; Promoter ISSA BADAROU-SOULÉ.

Benin also receives broadcasts from Africa No. 1, the British Broadcasting Corporation World Service and Radio France International.

Television

ORTB: (see Radio); Dir of Television STÉPHANE TODOME.

ATVS: BP 7101, Cotonou; tel. 21-31-43-19; owned by African Television System-Sobiex; Dir JACOB AKINOCHO.

Canal 3 Bénin: Cotonou; tel. 21-38-47-70.

Golfe TV: Quartier Sikècodji, 03 BP 1624, Cotonou; tel. 21-32-42-08; internet www.golfemediaonline.com.

LC2 Media (LC2): 05 BP 427, Cotonou; tel. 21-33-47-49; fax 21-33-46-75; e-mail lc2@lc2tv.com; internet www.lc2tv.com; commenced broadcasts 1997; CEO CHRISTIAN LAGNIDE; Man. NADINE LAGNIDE WOROU.

Telco: 44 ave Delorme, 01 BP 1241, Cotonou; tel. 21-31-34-98; e-mail telco@serv.eit.bj; relays 5 int. channels; Dir JOSEPH JÉBARA.

TV+ International/TV5: 01 BP 366, Cotonou; tel. 21-30-10-96; Dir CLAUDE KARAM.

Finance

(cap. = capital; res = reserves; dep. = deposits; m. = million; br(s). = branch(es); amounts in francs CFA)

BANKING

In 2012 there were 12 banks and one financial institution in Benin.

Central Bank

Banque Centrale des Etats de l'Afrique de l'Ouest (BCEAO): ave Jean-Paul II, BP 325, Cotonou; tel. 21-31-24-66; fax 21-31-24-65; e-mail akangni@bceao.int; internet www.bceao.int; HQ in Dakar, Senegal; f. 1962; bank of issue for the mem. states of the Union Economique et Monétaire Ouest-Africaine (UEMOA, comprising Benin, Burkina Faso, Côte d'Ivoire, Guinea-Bissau, Mali, Niger, Senegal and Togo); cap. 134,120m., res 1,474,195m., dep. 2,124,051m. (Dec. 2009); Gov. KONÉ TIÉMOKO MEYLIET; Dir in Benin EVARISTE SÉBASTIEN BONOU; br. at Parakou.

Commercial Banks

Bank of Africa—Bénin (BOAB): ave Jean-Paul II, 08 BP 0879, Cotonou; tel. 21-31-32-28; fax 21-31-31-17; e-mail information@boabenin.com; internet www.boabenin.com; f. 1990; cap. 10,072.6m., res 39,871.0m., dep. 533,552.7m. (Dec. 2012); Chair. PAULIN L. COSSI; Dir-Gen. FAUSTIN AMOUSSOU; 28 brs.

Banque Atlantique du Bénin: rue du Gouverneur Bayol, 08 BP 0682 Cotonou; tel. 21-31-10-18; fax 21-31-31-21; e-mail babn_support@banqueatlantique.net; internet www.banqueatlantique.net; cap. 6,500m., res 898m., dep. 114,474m. (2012); Chair. DOSSONGUI KONÉ; 6 brs.

Banque Internationale du Bénin (BIBE): carrefour des Trois Banques, ave Giran, 03 BP 2098, Jéricho, Cotonou; tel. 95070102 (mobile); fax 21-31-23-65; e-mail bibedi@leland.bj; internet www.bibebank.com; f. 1989; owned by Nigerian commercial interests; cap. 9,000m., dep. 48,577m. (Dec. 2002); Chair. Dr G. A. T. OBOH; Man. Dir JEAN-PAUL K. AIDDO; 4 brs.

Diamond Bank Bénin: 308 rue du Révérend Père Colineau, 01 BP 955, Cotonou; tel. 21-31-79-27; fax 21-31-79-33; e-mail info@benin.diamondbank.com; internet www.benin.diamondbank.com; f. 2001; 80% owned by Diamond Bank (Nigeria); cap. and res 1,939m., total assets 20,645m. (Dec. 2003); Chair. PASCAL GABRIEL DOZIE; Dir-Gen. BENEDICT IHEKIRE; 9 brs.

Ecobank Bénin: rue du Gouverneur Bayol, 01 BP 1280, Cotonou; tel. 21-31-40-23; fax 21-31-33-85; e-mail ecobankbj@ecobank.com; internet www.ecobank.com; f. 1989; 79% owned by Ecobank Transnational Inc (operating under the auspices of the Economic Community of West African States); cap. 5,000.0m., res 13,777.8m., dep. 318,187.7m. (Dec. 2012); Pres., Chair. and Dir RAPHIOU TOUKOUROU; Man. Dir ROGER DAH-ACHINANON; 6 brs.

Orabank Bénin SA (FBB): ave du Gouverneur Général Ponty, 01 BP 2700, Cotonou; tel. 21-31-31-00; fax 21-31-31-02; e-mail secretariat.fbbj@financial-bank.com; internet www.orabank.net; f. 1996; 93.18% owned by Oragroup (Togo), 5.11% owned by Caisse Nationale de Sécurité Sociale; cap. 12,635.7m., res 520.1m., dep. 82,517.4m. (Dec. 2010); Pres. IBRAHIM PEDRO BONI; Dir-Gen. RIZWAN HAÏDER; 8 brs.

Finadev: ave du Commandant Decoeur, 01 BP 6335, Cotonou; tel. 21-31-40-81; fax 21-31-79-22; e-mail info.bj@finadev-groupe.com; f. 1998; 25% owned by Financial Bank Bénin, 25% owned by FMO (Netherlands); cap. and res 1,016.0m., total assets 6,254.6m. (Dec. 2005); Pres. RÉMY BAYSSET; Dir-Gen. CHRISTINE WESTERCAMP; 4 brs.

Société Générale de Banques au Bénin (SGBBE): ave Clozel, Quartier Ganhi, 01 BP 585, Cotonou; tel. 21-31-83-00; fax 21-31-82-95; e-mail hotline.sogebenin@socgen.com; internet www.societegenerale.bj; f. 2002; 67% owned by Genefitec, a wholly owned subsidiary of Groupe Société Générale (France); cap. and res 2,044.0m., total assets 25,503.0m. (Dec. 2003); Pres. GILBERT MEDJE; Dir-Gen. CHRISTIAN METAUX; 4 brs.

UBA Bénin: ave Jean-Paul II, carrefour des Trois Banques, 01 BP 2020, Cotonou; tel. 21-31-24-24; fax 21-31-51-77; e-mail contact@cbankbenin.com; f. 1993 to assume activities of Crédit Lyonnais Bénin; fmrly Continental Bank—Bénin (La Continentale); present name adopted 2012; cap. 3,600m., res 2,720m., dep. 43,407m. (Dec. 2007); Pres. FOGAN SOSSAH; Dir-Gen. GWEN OLOKÉ-ABIOLA; 16 brs.

Savings Bank

Caisse Nationale d'Epargne: Cadjèhoun, route Inter-Etat Cotonou-Lomé, Cotonou; tel. 21-30-18-35; fax 21-31-38-43; e-mail fdossou@opt.bj; internet www.cne.opt.bj; Pres. CHARLES PRODJINOTHO.

Credit Institutions

Crédit du Bénin: 08 BP 0936, Cotonou; tel. 21-31-30-02; fax 21-31-37-01; Man. Dir GILBERT HOUNKPAIN.

Equipbail Bénin: blvd Jean-Paul II, 08 BP 0690, Cotonou; tel. 21-31-11-45; fax 21-31-46-58; e-mail equip.be@bkofafrica.com; internet www.bkofafrica.net/equipbail.htm; f. 1995; 58.7% owned by Bank of Africa—Bénin; cap. and res 1,229.2m., total assets 5,966.3m. (Dec. 2006); Pres. PAUL DERREUMAUX.

Financial Institution

Caisse Autonome d'Amortissement du Bénin: BP 59, Cotonou; tel. 21-31-47-81; fax 21-31-53-56; e-mail caa@firstnet.bj; f. 1966; govt owned; manages state funds; Man. Dir ADAM DENDE AFFO.

STOCK EXCHANGE

Bourse Régionale des Valeurs Mobilières (BRVM): Antenne Nationale des Bourses du Bénin, Immeuble Chambre de Commerce et d'Industrie du Bénin, ave Charles de Gaulle, 01 BP 2985, Cotonou; tel. 21-31-21-26; fax 21-31-20-77; e-mail patioukpe@brvm.org; internet www.brvm.org; f. 1998; nat. branch of BRVM (regional stock exchange based in Abidjan, Côte d'Ivoire, serving the member states of UEMOA); Man. in Benin PAULINE ATIOUKPE.

INSURANCE

Allianz Bénin Assurances: Carré 5, ave Delorme, 01 BP 5455, Cotonou; tel. 21-31-67-35; fax 21-31-67-34; e-mail allianz.benin@allianz-bj.com; internet www.allianz-africa.com/benin; f. 1998; Dir-Gen. XAVIER GUILLAUME SERGE.

A&C Bénin: Carré 21, 01 BP 3758, ave Delorme, Cotonou; tel. 21-31-09-32; fax 21-31-08-70; e-mail info@acbenin.com; internet www.acbenin.com; f. 1996; broker specializing in all branches of insurance; Man. Dir JUSTIN HUBERT AGBOTON.

Africaine des Assurances: Place du Souvenir, 01 BP 3128, Cotonou; tel. 21-30-04-83; fax 21-30-14-06; e-mail assuraf@intnet.bj; internet www.africaine-assur.com; Pres. ANTOINE ZOUNON; Dir-Gen. VINCENT MAFORIKAN.

ASA Bénin: 01 BP 5508, Cotonou; tel. and fax 21-30-00-40; internet asabenin.org; fmrly Société Nationale d'Assurance; Sec.-Gen. ARMAND YEHOUENOU.

Assurances et Réassurance du Golfe de Guinée (ARGG): 04 BP 0851, Cadjehoun, Cotonou; tel. 21-30-56-43; fax 21-30-55-55; e-mail argg@intnet.bj; internet arggbenin.org; non-life insurance and re-insurance; Man. Dir PAULIN HOUECHENOU.

Avie Assurances: Immeuble Notre-Dame, ave Clozel, 01 BP 7061, Cotonou; tel. 21-31-83-55; fax 21-31-83-57; e-mail contact@avieassur.com; f. 2004; Dir-Gen. EVELYNE MARIE S. FASSINOU.

Colina Vie Bénin: Lot 636, Quartier Les Cocotiers, 04 BP 1419, Cotonou; tel. 21-30-85-23; fax 21-30-55-46; e-mail benin@groupecolina.com; Dir-Gen. MARIAM NASSIROU.

Fédérale d'Assurances (FEDAS): 01 BP 4201, Cotonou; tel. 21-31-56-77; fax 21-31-49-79; e-mail fedasbenin@yahoo.fr; f. 1998; Dir-Gen. FAISSOU ADEYEMAN.

Gras Savoye Bénin: Immeuble Aboki Hounkpehedji, 1er étage, ave Mgr Steinmetz, face de l'Immeuble Kougblenou, 01 BP 294 RP Cotonou; tel. 21-31-69-22; fax 21-31-69-79; e-mail gsbenin@leland.bj; affiliated to Gras Savoye (France); Man. GUY BIHANNIC.

Nouvelle Société Interafricaine d'Assurances du Bénin: Immeuble Kougblénou, ave Mgr Steinmetz, 08 BP 0258, Cotonou; tel. 21-31-33-69; fax 21-31-35-17; e-mail nsab@nsiabenin.com; f. 1997; Dir-Gen. ALAIN LATH HOUNGUE.

Union Béninoise d'Assurance-Vie: Place du Souvenir, 08 BP 0322, Cotonou; tel. 21-30-02-12; fax 21-30-07-69; e-mail uba@ubavie.com; f. 1994; cap. 500m.; 53.5% owned by Groupe SUNU (France); Man. Dir VENANCE AMOUSSOUGA.

Association

Association des Sociétés d'Assurance du Bénin: 01 BP 5508, Cotonou; tel. 21-30-00-40; fax 21-30-15-61; e-mail info@asabenin.org; internet www.asabenin.org; f. 1999.

Trade and Industry

GOVERNMENT AGENCIES

Centre Béninois du Commerce Extérieur (CBCE): pl. du Souvenir, BP 1254, Cotonou; tel. 21-30-13-20; fax 21-30-04-36; e-mail cbce@bow.intnet.bj; f. 1988; provides information to export cos.

Centre Béninois de la Recherche Scientifique et Technique (CBRST): 03 BP 1665, Cotonou; tel. 21-32-12-63; fax 21-32-36-71; e-mail cbrst@yahoo.fr; internet www.cbrst-benin.org; f. 1986; promotes scientific and technical research and training; 10 specialized research units; Dir-Gen. BIAOU FIDÈLE DIMON.

Centre de Promotion de l'Artisanat: à côté du Hall des Arts et de la Culture, 01 BP 2651, Cotonou; tel. 21-30-34-32; fax 21-30-34-91; e-mail cpainfos@ifrance.com; internet www.cpabenin.bj; f. 1987; Dir LATIFOU ALASSANE.

Centre de Promotion et d'Encadrement des Petites et Moyennes Entreprises (CEPEPE): face à la Mairie de Xlacondji, 01 BP 2093, Cotonou; tel. 21-31-22-61; fax 21-31-59-50; e-mail cepepe@firstnet.bj; internet www.cepepe.org; f. 1989; promotes business and employment; offers credits and grants to small businesses; undertakes management training and recruitment; publishes bi-monthly journal, *Initiatives*; Dir-Gen. THÉOPHILE CAPO-CHICHI.

Conseil d'Analyse Economique: Palais de la Marina, 01 BP 2028, Cotonou; tel. 21-30-08-07; fax 21-30-18-03; e-mail contact@caebenin.org; internet www.caebenin.org/web; f. 2006; Pres. FULBERT AMOUSSOUGA GERO.

Institut National de Recherches Agricoles du Bénin (INRAB): 01 BP 884, Cotonou; tel. 21-30-02-64; fax 21-30-37-70; e-mail inrabdg4@intnet.bj; internet www.inrab.bj.refer.org; f. 1992; undertakes research into agricultural improvements; publicizes advances in agriculture; Dir DAVID YAO ARODOKOUN.

Office Béninois de Recherches Géologiques et Minières (OBRGM): 04 BP 1412, Cotonou; tel. 21-31-03-09; fax 21-31-41-20; e-mail nestorved@yahoo.fr; internet www.energie.gouv.bj/obrgm/index.htm; f. 1996 as govt agency responsible for mining policy, exploitation and research; Dir-Gen. CYRIAQUE TOSSA.

Office National d'Appui à la Sécurité Alimentaire (ONASA): PK3, route de Porto-Novo, 06 BP 2544, Cotonou; tel. 21-33-15-02; fax 21-33-02-93; e-mail onasa@onasa.org; internet www.onasa-benin.org; f. 1992; distribution of cereals; Pres. IMAROU SALÉ; Dir-Gen. IRENÉE BIO ABOUDOU.

Office National du Bois (ONAB): PK 3,5 route de Porto-Novo, 01 BP 1238, Cotonou; tel. 21-33-16-32; fax 21-33-39-83; e-mail contact@onab-benin.net; f. 1983; reorganized and partially privatized in 2002; forest devt and management, manufacture and marketing of wood products; industrial activities privatized in 2009; Dir-Gen. Dr CLEMENT KOUCHADE.

DEVELOPMENT ORGANIZATIONS

Agence Béninoise pour la Réconciliation et le Développement (ABRD): Haie Vive, Les Cocotiers, 04 BP 1460, Cotonou; tel. 21-00-75-48; internet www.abrd.net; Dir-Gen. AMONKÈ AYICHATOU BEEN FAFOUMI.

Agence Française de Développement (AFD): blvd de France, 01 BP 38, Cotonou; tel. 21-31-35-80; fax 21-31-20-18; e-mail afdcotonou@groupe-afd.org; internet www.afd.fr; fmrly Caisse Française de Développement; Country Dir CATHERINE BONNAUD.

Conseil des Investisseurs Privés au Bénin (CIPB): Carré 85 ave Stenmetz, Tokpa Hoho, 03 BP 4304, Cotonou; tel. 21-31-47-67; fax 21-31-65-29; e-mail info@cipb.bj; internet cipb.bj; f. 2002; Pres. ROLAND RIBOUX; Sec.-Gen. MOUFTAOU SOUHOUIN.

France Volontaires: BP 344, Recette Principale, Cotonou; tel. 21-30-06-21; fax 21-30-07-78; e-mail afvpbn@intnet.bj; internet www.france-volontaires.org; f. 1964; name changed as above in 2009; Nat. Delegate LOVASOA RATSIMBA.

Projet d'Appui au Développement des Micro-entreprises (PADME): C/226 F-Jéricho, 08 BP 712, Cotonou; tel. 21-32-48-02; fax 21-32-48-65; e-mail padme@padmebenin.org; internet www.padmebenin.org; f. 1994; Dir-Gen. DIDIER DJOI.

SNV Bénin (Organisation Néerlandaise de Développement): 01 BP 1048, Carré 107, Zone Résidentielle, Rue du PNUD, Cotonou; tel. 21-31-21-22; fax 21-31-35-59; e-mail benin@snvworld.org; internet www.snvworld.org; Country Dir BRIGITTE GOBERT DIA.

CHAMBER OF COMMERCE

Chambre de Commerce et d'Industrie du Bénin (CCIB): ave du Général de Gaulle, 01 BP 31, Cotonou; tel. 21-31-20-81; fax 21-31-32-99; e-mail ccib@bow.intnet.bj; internet www.ccibenin.org; f. 1908; present name adopted 1962; Pres. ATAOU SOUFIANO; brs at Parakou, Mono-Zou, Natitingou and Porto-Novo.

EMPLOYERS' ORGANIZATIONS

Conseil National des Chargeurs du Bénin (CNCB): 06 BP 2528, Cotonou; tel. 21-31-59-47; fax 21-31-59-60; e-mail cncb@intnet.bj; internet www.cncbenin.com; f. 1983; represents interests of shippers; Dir-Gen. DIANE TOSSA GBOSSOU AGOSSA.

Conseil National du Patronat du Bénin (CNP–Bénin): 01 BP 1260, Cotonou; tel. 21-30-74-06; fax 21-30-83-22; e-mail cnpbenin@yahoo.fr; internet www.cnpbenin.org; f. 1984 as Organisation Nationale des Employeurs du Bénin; Pres. SÉBASTIEN AJAVON; Sec.-Gen. VICTOR FAKEYE.

Fédération des Unions de Producteurs du Bénin (FUPRO): Quartier Zakpo Houdanou, Immeuble Tossou Lazard, SACLO, BP 372, Bohicon; tel. 22-11-18-51; fax 22-51-09-46; e-mail fuproben@yahoo.fr; internet www.fupro.org; f. 1994; Pres. LIONEL GUEZODJE; Sec.-Gen. JUSTIN SEKOU KOUNOU.

Fondation de l'Entrepreneurship du Bénin (FEB): pl. du Québec, 08 BP 1155, Cotonou; tel. 21-31-35-37; fax 21-31-37-26; e-mail fonda@intnet.bj; internet www.placequebec.org; non profit-making org.; encourages the devt of the private sector and of small and medium-sized businesses; Dir PIERRE DOVONOU LOKOSSOU.

UTILITIES

Communauté Electrique du Bénin (CEB): Vedoko, BP 537, Cotonou; tel. 21-30-06-75; fax 21-38-06-75; internet www.cebnet.org; f. 1968; jt venture between Benin and Togo to exploit energy resources in the 2 countries; Dir-Gen. DJIBRIL SALIFOU.

Société Béninoise d'Energie Electrique (SBEE): 01 BP 2047, Cotonou; tel. 21-31-21-45; fax 21-31-50-28; f. 1973; state-owned; production and distribution of electricity; Dir-Gen. MARIUS Z. HOUNKPATIN.

Société Nationale des Eaux du Bénin (SONEB): 92 ave Pope Jean-Paul II, 01 BP 216, RP Cotonou; tel. 21-31-20-60; fax 21-31-11-08; e-mail info@soneb.com; internet www.soneb.com; f. 2003 to assume water activities of Société Béninoise d'Electricité et d'Eau; operates under supervision of ministry responsible for water resources; utilises about 60 systems of drinkable water adductions, feeding 69 municipalities; Pres. EMILE LOUIS PARAÏSO; Dir-Gen. DAVID BABALOLA.

TRADE UNIONS

Centrale Syndicale des Travailleurs du Bénin (CSTB): 03 BP 0989, Cotonou; tel. 21-30-13-15; fax 21-33-26-01; actively opposes privatization and the influence of the international financial community; linked to the Parti Communiste du Bénin; Sec.-Gen. PAUL ESSÈ IKO.

Centrale des Syndicats Autonomes du Bénin (CSA—Bénin): 1 Blvd St Michel, Bourse du Travail, 04 BP 1115, Cotonou; tel. 21-30-31-82; fax 21-30-23-59; e-mail csabenin@intnet.bj; internet csa-benin.org; principally active in private sector enterprises; Sec.-Gen. DIEUDONNÉ LOKOSSOU.

Centrale des Syndicats du Secteur Privé et Informel du Bénin (CSPIB): 03 BP 2961, Cotonou; tel. 21-33-53-53; Sec.-Gen. CHRISTOPHE C. DOVONON.

Centrale des Syndicats Unis du Bénin (CSUB): Cotonou; tel. 21-33-10-27; Sec.-Gen. JEAN SOUROU AGOSSOU.

Confédération Générale des Travailleurs du Bénin (CGTB): 06 BP 2449, Cotonou; tel. 21-31-73-11; fax 21-31-73-10; e-mail cgtbpdd@bow.intnet.bj; principally active in public administration; Sec.-Gen. PASCAL TODJINOU; 33,275 mems (2002).

Confédération des Organisations Syndicales Indépendantes du Bénin (COSI—Benin): Bourse du Travail, 03 BP 1218, Cotonou; tel. 21-30-39-65; fax 21-33-27-82; e-mail cosibenin@intnet.bj; Sec.-Gen. GOERGES KAKAÏ GLELE.

Union Nationale des Syndicats de Travailleurs du Bénin (UNSTB): 1 blvd Saint-Michel, BP 69, Recette Principale, Cotonou; tel. and fax 21-30-36-13; e-mail unstb@unstb.org; internet www.unstb.org; principally active in public administration; sole officially recognized trade union 1974–90; 40,000 members in 2005, of which 25,000 in the informal sector; Sec.-Gen. EMMANUEL ZOUNON.

Transport

RAILWAYS

In 2006 there were 758 km of railway track in operation. There are plans to extend the 438-km Cotonou–Parakou line to Dosso, Niger.

Organisation Commune Bénin-Niger des Chemins de Fer et des Transports (OCBN): BP 16, Cotonou; tel. 21-31-28-57; fax 21-31-41-50; e-mail ocbn@intnet.bj; f. 1959; 50% owned by Govt of Benin, 50% by Govt of Niger; total of 579 track-km; main line runs for 438 km from Cotonou to Parakou in the interior; br. line runs westward via Ouidah to Segboroué (34 km); also line of 107 km from Cotonou via Porto-Novo to Pobé (near the Nigerian border); extension to the Republic of Niger proposed; Dir-Gen. RIGOBERT AZON.

ROADS

In 2011 there were some 30,000 km of roads, including 1,823 km of paved roads.

Agence Générale de Transit et de Consignation (AGETRAC): blvd Maritime, BP 1933, Cotonou; tel. 21-31-32-22; fax 21-31-29-69; e-mail agetrac@leland.bj; f. 1967; goods transportation and warehousing.

Compagnie de Transit et de Consignation du Bénin (CTCB Express): Cotonou; f. 1986; Pres. SOULÉMAN KOURA ZOUMAROU.

Fonds Routier du Bénin: Cotonou; internet www.fondsroutier.bj; Dir-Gen. SYLVESTRE KOCHOFA.

SHIPPING

The main port is at Cotonou. In 2006 the port handled some 5.4m. metric tons of goods. In December 2013 the flag registered fleet of Benin comprised six vessels, with a total displacement of 991 grt.

Port Autonome de Cotonou (PAC): BP 927, Cotonou; tel. 21-31-28-90; fax 21-31-28-91; e-mail pac@leland.bj; internet www.portdecotonou.com; f. 1965; state-owned port authority; Dir-Gen. KASSIM TRAORÉ.

Compagnie Béninoise de Navigation Maritime (COBENAM): pl. Ganhi, 01 BP 2032, Cotonou; tel. 21-31-27-96; fax 21-31-09-78; e-mail cobenam@elodia.intnet.bj; f. 1974 by Govts of Algeria and Dahomey (now Benin); 100% state-owned; Pres. ABDEL KADER ALLAL; Man. Dir ARMAND PRIVAT KANDISSOUNON.

Maersk Bénin: Maersk House, Zone OCBN Lot 531, Parcelle B, 01 BP 2826, Cotonou; tel. 21-31-39-93; fax 21-31-56-60; e-mail coocuscal@maersk.com; internet www.maerskline.com/bj; subsidiary of Maersk Line (Denmark); Dir DAVID SKOV.

Société Béninoise d'Entreprises Maritimes (SBEM): BP 1733, Cotonou; tel. 21-31-23-57; fax 21-31-59-26; warehousing, storage and transportation; Dir RÉGIS TISSER.

Société Béninoise des Manutentions Portuaires (SOBEMAP): blvd de la Marina, BP 35, Cotonou; tel. 21-31-41-45; fax 21-31-53-71; e-mail infos@sobemap.com; internet www.sobemap.com; f. 1969; state-owned; Dir-Gen. SOUMANOU SÉIBOU TOLÉBA.

Société Béninoise Maritime (SOBEMAR): Carré 8, Cruintomé, 08 BP 0956, Cotonou; tel. 21-31-49-65; fax 21-31-52-51; e-mail adm@sobemar-benin.com; internet www.navitrans.fr; f. 1992; Pres. RODOLPHE TORTORA.

CIVIL AVIATION

There is an international airport at Cotonou-Cadjehoun and secondary airports at Parakou, Natitingou, Kandi, Savè, Porga and Djougou.

Aviation Civile du Bénin: 01 BP 305, Cotonou; tel. 21-30-92-17; fax 21-30-45-71; e-mail anacaero@anac.bj; internet www.anac.bj; Dir-Gen. ARISTIDE DE SOUZA.

Trans Air Benin (TAB): ave Jean Paul II, Lot No 14, Les Cocotiers, Cotonou; tel. 21-00-61-65; fax 21-30-92-75; e-mail transairbenin@aol.com; f. 2000; regional flights; Dir BRICE KIKI.

Tourism

Benin's rich cultural diversity and its national parks and game reserves are the principal tourist attractions. About 200,000 tourists visited Benin in 2010. Receipts from tourism were estimated at US $209.0m. in 2011.

Direction de la Promotion et des Professions Touristiques: BP 2037, Cotonou; tel. 21-32-68-24; fax 21-32-68-23; internet www.benintourism.com.

Defence

As assessed at November 2013, the Beninois Armed Forces numbered an estimated 6,950 active personnel (land army 6,500, navy about 200, air force 250). Paramilitary forces comprised a 2,500-strong gendarmerie. Military service is by selective conscription, and lasts for 18 months.

Defence Expenditure: Estimated at 42,500m. francs CFA in 2013.

Chief of Defence Staff: Brig.-Gen. CHABI A. BONI.

Chief of Staff of the Army: Col DOMINIQUE M. AHOUANDJINOU.

Chief of Staff of the Navy: Capt. FERNAND MAXIME AHOYO.

Chief of Staff of the Air Force: Col CAMILLE MICHODJEHOUN.

Education

The Constitution of Benin obliges the state to make a quality compulsory primary education available to all children. Primary education was declared free of charge in 2006. Primary education begins at six years of age and lasts for six years. Secondary education, beginning at 12 years of age, lasts for up to seven years, comprising a first cycle of four years and a second of three years. According to UNESCO estimates, primary enrolment in 2011 included 94% of children (males 100%; females 88%) in the appropriate age-group, while enrolment at secondary schools in that year was equivalent to 48% of children in the appropriate age-group (males 59%; females 36%). The Université Nationale du Bénin, at Cotonou, was founded in 1970 and a second university, in Parakou, opened in 2001. In 2010/11 a total of 110,200 students were enrolled at tertiary education institutes. According to UNESCO estimates, in 2010 spending on education represented 27.8% of total budgeted government expenditure.

BHUTAN

Introductory Survey

LOCATION, CLIMATE, LANGUAGE, RELIGION, FLAG, CAPITAL

The Kingdom of Bhutan lies in the Himalaya range of mountains, with Tibet (the Xizang Autonomous Region), part of the People's Republic of China, to the north and India to the south. The average monthly temperature ranges from 4.4°C (40°F) in January to 17°C (62°F) in July. Rainfall is heavy, ranging from 150 cm (60 in) to 300 cm (120 in) per year. The official language is Dzongkha, spoken mainly in western Bhutan. Written Dzongkha is based on the Tibetan script. The state religion is Mahayana Buddhism, primarily the Drukpa school of the Kagyupa sect, although Nepalese settlers, who comprise about one-quarter of the country's total population, practise Hinduism. The Nepali-speaking Hindus dominate southern Bhutan and are referred to as southern Bhutanese. The national flag (proportions 2 by 3) is divided diagonally from the lower hoist to the upper fly, so forming two triangles, one yellow and the other orange, with a white dragon superimposed in the centre. The capital is Thimphu.

CONTEMPORARY POLITICAL HISTORY

Historical Context

Following decades of domestic strife and warfare, the first hereditary King of Bhutan was installed in December 1907. An Anglo-Bhutanese Treaty, signed in 1910, placed Bhutan's foreign relations under the supervision of the Government of British India. After India became independent, this treaty was replaced in August 1949 by the Indo-Bhutan Treaty of Friendship, whereby Bhutan agreed to seek the advice of the Government of India with regard to its foreign relations but remained free to decide whether or not to accept such advice. King Jigme Dorji Wangchuck, who was installed in 1952, established the National Assembly (tshogdu chenmo) in 1953 and a Royal Advisory Council (lodoi tsokde) in 1965. He formed the country's first Council of Ministers (lhengye zhungtshog) in 1968. Bhutan became a member of the UN in 1971 and of the Non-aligned Movement in 1973.

King Jigme Dorji Wangchuck died in 1972 and was succeeded by the Western-educated, 16-year-old Crown Prince, Jigme Singye Wangchuck. The new King introduced the concept of 'Gross National Happiness' (GNH) to his country, a measure of Bhutan's prosperity that sought to balance material progress with spiritual wellbeing; the four pillars of GNH were defined as the promotion of sustainable development, the preservation and promotion of cultural values, the conservation of the natural environment and the establishment of good governance. He also stated his wish to preserve the Indo-Bhutan Treaty and further to strengthen friendship with India. In 1979, however, during the Non-aligned Conference and later at the UN General Assembly, Bhutan voted in opposition to India, in favour of Chinese policy. In 1983 India and Bhutan signed a new trade agreement concerning overland trade with Bangladesh and Nepal. India raised no objection to Bhutan's decision to negotiate directly with the People's Republic of China over the Bhutan–China border, and discussions between Bhutan and China commenced in 1984 (see Foreign Affairs).

When Chinese authority was established in Tibet (Xizang) in 1959, Bhutan granted asylum to more than 6,000 Tibetan refugees. In response to allegations that many refugees were engaged in spying and subversive activities, the Bhutanese Government decided in 1976 to disperse them in small groups, introducing a number of Bhutanese families into each settlement. In June 1979 the National Assembly approved a directive establishing the end of the year as a time limit for the refugees to decide whether to acquire Bhutanese citizenship or accept repatriation to Tibet. By September 1985 most of the Tibetans had chosen Bhutanese citizenship, and the remainder were to be accepted by India. A revised Citizenship Act, adopted by the National Assembly in 1985, confirmed residence in Bhutan in 1958 as a fundamental basis for automatic citizenship (as provided for by the 1958 Nationality Act), but this was to be interpreted flexibly. Provision was also made for citizenship by registration for Nepalese immigrants who had resided in the country for at least 20 years (15 years if employed by the Government) and who could meet linguistic and other tests of commitment to the Bhutanese community.

Domestic Political Affairs

Important institutional changes were introduced in mid-1998, whereby King Jigme relinquished his role as head of government (while remaining Head of State) in favour of a smaller elected Council of Ministers, which was to consist of six ministers and all nine members of the Royal Advisory Council, and which was to enjoy full executive power under the leadership of a Chairman (elected by ministers, on a rotational basis, for a one-year term) who would be head of government. An act to regulate the Council of Ministers was presented to the National Assembly in mid-1999 and was subjected to extensive discussion and amendment. The rules as finally endorsed explicitly specified that the King had full power to dissolve the Council of Ministers.

At a summit meeting of the South Asian Association for Regional Cooperation (SAARC, see p. 420) held in Kathmandu, Nepal, in January 2002, the incumbent Chairman of the Council of Ministers, Lyonpo Khandu Wangchuk, was referred to as 'Prime Minister' of Bhutan, a title that subsequently became accepted usage. Meanwhile, a committee to draft a written constitution for Bhutan was inaugurated in November 2001. The 39-member committee was chaired by the Chief Justice and included the Chairman and members of the Royal Advisory Council, five government representatives, the Speaker of the National Assembly, representatives from each of the 20 districts (dzongkhags) and two lawyers from the High Court. In December 2002 the preliminary draft of the constitution was presented to King Jigme, who subsequently referred the document to the Prime Minister for further scrutiny. In November 2004 King Jigme presented a fourth draft of the proposed constitution to the Council of Ministers for discussion; the draft was made available for public review in March 2005.

Meanwhile, the creation of four new ministerial positions (as part of a general reorganization of ministries) was announced in June 2003, bringing the total number of ministers to 10. In October 2004 the Crown Prince, Dasho Jigme Khesar Namgyel Wangchuck, was formally installed as the heir to the throne (chhoetse penlop). In December 2005 King Jigme announced that he intended to abdicate in favour of his son in 2008, the year in which Bhutan was scheduled to hold its first national elections. Meanwhile, appointments to the country's first constitutional posts were announced at the end of 2005. Dasho Kuenzang Wangdi became Bhutan's first Chief Election Commissioner, while an Anti-Corruption Commission (ACC) was also created.

In December 2004 a ban on sales of tobacco throughout the kingdom came into effect, making Bhutan the first country in the world to declare such a policy. Imports of tobacco were permitted for private consumption, although these attracted duty of up to 200%. In February 2005 a complete ban on smoking in public places was announced.

The fifth draft of the Constitution, which was published in August 2005, provided for, among other things: the establishment of a democratic constitutional monarchy in accordance with the principle of hereditary succession; the establishment of a parliament consisting of the monarch, a 25-member National Council (upper house) and a 47-member National Assembly (lower house), with members of the latter body to be elected by universal secret ballot from constituencies with approximately equivalent populations; and for two political parties to be represented in the National Assembly, the election campaigns of which would be funded by the state. Within the National Council, 20 members—one representing each district—were to be directly elected by a national vote, with the remaining five 'eminent members' to be selected by royal appointment.

In September 2006 the incumbent Minister of Foreign Affairs, Lyonpo Khandu Wangchuk, succeeded Lyonpo Sangay Ngedup as Prime Minister of Bhutan. Later in the month the Chief Election Commissioner announced that all registered parties would be able to contest the first round of the 2008 general election, following which the two parties with the largest number of votes would compete for parliamentary seats in the second and third rounds. A draft list of about 400,000 potential voters had already been prepared and electoral registration forms were subsequently sent out. In March 2007 details were announced of the 47 constituencies for the National Assembly. 'Mock' elections were held in two rounds, in April and May. Meanwhile, on 9 December 2006 King Jigme issued a royal decree (kasho) in which he formally transferred his responsibilities as Head of State to Crown Prince Jigme Khesar Namgyel, who succeeded to the throne on 21 December. In his first public speech King Jigme Khesar promised to continue on the path towards the establishment of parliamentary democracy.

In June 2007 the King instructed the Chief Election Commissioner to conduct elections for the National Council in December of that year, a primary round for the National Assembly in February 2008, and a general election for the Assembly in March 2008. The Election Commission declared itself open to receive party nominations from 1 July 2007. In that month the Prime Minister and Minister of Foreign Affairs, Lyonchhen Khandu Wangchuk, tendered the resignation of himself and six other ministers prior to joining the political process. Lyonpo Kinzang Dorji, hitherto Minister of Works and Human Settlement, assumed the role of Prime Minister at the head of a much smaller Council of Ministers. The National Assembly was dissolved on 31 July, and, prompted by the depleted status of the Council of Ministers, from August the Royal Advisory Council similarly stood dissolved, in advance of its proposed termination in October, in preparation for the inauguration of the new governmental structure.

Candidates in the National Council elections campaigned without party affiliation, and the Election Commission ruled that only university graduates from approved institutions were eligible to stand. This restriction meant that the requisite minimum of two candidates was not forthcoming in five districts before the date of the poll, 31 December 2007. Consequently, a second stage of voting was held in these districts, on 29 January 2008. Overall, some 53% of registered voters participated in the ballot. The 20 successful candidates, four of whom were women, were to serve five-year terms. An additional five members were to be appointed to the National Council by the King.

By January 2008 only two parties had successfully registered with the Election Commission ahead of elections to the National Assembly—the Druk Phuensum Tshogpa (DPT, Bhutan Peace and Prosperity Party), led by former Prime Minister Lyonpo Jigmi Yozer Thinley, and the People's Democratic Party (PDP), headed by Lyonpo Sangay Ngedup, another former Prime Minister. A third party, the recently formed Bhutan National Party, had its application for registration cancelled, while the application of the Bhutan People's United Party (established by a breakaway faction of the DPT) was rejected by the Election Commission in November 2007. Consequently, the Commission announced that elections to the new National Assembly would be completed in one day (rather than in two rounds as originally envisaged) and the election date was set as 24 March 2008.

A series of bomb blasts occurred in Bhutan in early 2008. On 20 January four bombs were detonated in different locations, including one in the capital Thimphu, and a further explosion occurred behind a government office in Samtse district on 4 February. No one was seriously hurt in the incidents. Leaflets of the Bhutan Communist Party (Marxist-Leninist-Maoist) (BCP—MLM) were recovered from the site of the February explosion, and police subsequently raided two training camps in southern Bhutan and arrested eight members of the party, which officials believed was attempting to disrupt preparations for the general election. A group entitled the United Revolutionary Front of Bhutan (URFB), which was believed to be the military wing of the BCP—MLM, claimed responsibility for the bomb blasts in January. The URFB also claimed responsibility for a bomb explosion in Sarpang district in December, which killed four Bhutanese forest guards.

Democratic elections and a new Constitution

The DPT won an overwhelming majority in the elections to the National Assembly, which were held as scheduled on 24 March 2008, securing 45 of the 47 legislative seats and 67% of valid votes cast, while the PDP won only two seats (despite widespread expectation that representation would be roughly evenly split). Voter turnout was high, at 79.4% of the electorate. Lyonpo Jigmi Yozer Thinley was subsequently nominated as Prime Minister, and his premiership was endorsed by the King on 9 April. The new Council of Ministers was installed two days later and included key appointments for a number of former ministers: Khandu Wangchuk, who had previously served two terms as Prime Minister, was appointed Minister of Economic Affairs, while the finance portfolio was assigned to Wangdi Norbu, who had formerly held the same post. Ugyen Tshering and Yeshey Zimba were given responsibility for the Ministry of Foreign Affairs and Ministry of Works and Human Settlement, respectively. The opening session of the first Parliament of Bhutan was inaugurated as a joint session of the National Assembly and the National Council on 8 May. The draft Constitution was debated throughout May, and was formally signed on 18 July. The bicameral Parliament subsequently discussed six bills, which were eventually adopted as the National Council Act, the National Assembly Act, the Election Act, the Election Fund Act, the Parliamentary Entitlements Act and the National Referendum Act.

The formal coronation of Jigme Khesar Namgyel Wangchuck as the fifth hereditary king of Bhutan took place in Thimphu on 6 November 2008, and was attended by hundreds of foreign dignitaries, including the President of India.

The second session of the National Assembly was held in December 2008–January 2009 (the National Council met concurrently but separately). It was widely agreed that security should be given priority in light of the 2008 bomb blasts in the south of the country. (The establishment of an élite special forces counter-terrorism unit within the Royal Bhutan Police was subsequently announced.) In September 2009, as part of an ongoing programme of decentralization and devolution of power, the Local Government Act of Bhutan was approved by Parliament. The Act established 20 district councils (dzongkhag tshogdus) to function as the highest decision-making body in each of Bhutan's districts. The councils, which were ultimately to be under the authority of the Ministry of Home and Cultural Affairs, were to be assigned a variety of tasks, including the promotion of local business, the preservation of culture and tradition, the protection of public health, the co-ordination of government agency activities, and the review of local government regulations and ordinances. The councils were also to be responsible for the supervision of the district officers (dzongdas), who are appointed by the Royal Civil Service Commission and act as the chief executive of each district.

In June 2010 the Minister of Finance announced the introduction of additional taxes in his budget address to the National Assembly. The parliamentary Opposition Leader, Tshering Tobgay, objecting to the Minister's attempt to implement the measures without first allowing the Assembly to discuss and vote on them, instigated a legal challenge against the Government. The case, which was heard in the Thimphu High Court, represented Bhutan's first constitutional court case. The High Court ruled that the Government was in violation of constitutional procedures by not introducing the revised tax schedule as a fiscal bill subject to discussion and vote. The Government appealed to the Supreme Court, which, in February 2011, upheld the lower court's decision, with some revisions.

Notwithstanding the ongoing evolution of the country's nascent democracy, the King continued to play an active role in helping to develop and strengthen institutions in contemporary Bhutan. In February 2010 the King issued a royal decree establishing the Bhutan Media Foundation (BMF), which aimed to strengthen Bhutanese media through training aided by scholarships. The BMF, which was inaugurated in March 2011, was also expected to promote the readership of printed media through subscription grants, the publication of local editions of newspapers, and the activities of journalists' associations and press clubs. In February 2011 the Kidu Foundation was established under the patronage of the King, with the stated goal of 'complementing' the Government's efforts in the development of education, the rule of law, democracy, the media, environmental protection and cultural heritage. The Foundation was to be funded by voluntary donations. These initiatives were regarded by some observers as potentially undermining the principles of Bhutan's fledgling democracy in that, so they believed, they represented the emergence of a separate administration, centred on the King, in parallel to the elected DPT Government.

In 2011 Bhutan's first democratic local government elections (which were originally scheduled to be held in 2008) took place, on a non-party basis, throughout the country. The polling was to appoint officials to the lower levels of local government—the village block councils (gewog tshogdes) and the municipalities (thromdes). In January elections were completed for the municipalities of four large towns (Thimphu, Phuentsholing,

Samdrup Jongkhar and Gelephu), after issues with residence qualifications and a shortage of qualified candidates were resolved. (All candidates were required to pass functional literacy and administrative skills tests.) Further local elections took place nationwide in June, following the long-delayed confirmation of local government electoral boundaries. The Election Commission reported a turnout of around 56% and, according to official observers, the polling was conducted in a peaceful and proper manner. Although some 1,104 representatives were elected to various lower levels of local government, a total of 373 positions remained vacant after the elections, owing to a general lack of eligible candidates. Comprehensive local government polls—including elections to the 20 recently created district councils—were declared by the Election Commission to be possible only after 2013 (i.e. after the next parliamentary elections).

On 13 October 2011 the highly popular King Jigme Khesar married a Bhutanese commoner, Jetsun Pema, in an elaborate Buddhist ceremony at a monastic fortress in Punakha. Following their marriage, the couple embarked on a nine-day state visit to India.

Recent developments: the 2013 legislative elections

During 2012 it was reported that several new political parties had applied for registration in advance of the forthcoming legislative elections. In January 2013 three new parties were granted formal registration by the Election Commission—the Bhutan Kuen-Nyam Party (BKP, headed by Sonam Tobgay), the Druk Nyamrup Tshogpa (DNT—Solidarity, Justice and Freedom—led by Aum Dorji Choden from March of that year) and the Druk Chirwang Tshogpa (DCT, led by Lily Wangchhuk, the Executive Director of the BMF). Another prospective new party, the Druk Mitsher Tshogpa, had abandoned plans to gain registration and reorganized itself as a youth organization. In November 2012, in a bid to keep state affairs separate from religion, the Election Commission issued a directive forbidding the organization of any religious public event from January 2013 until the scheduled holding later in the year of the country's second general election.

The DPT Government suffered a considerable setback in March 2013 when, following an investigation by the ACC into alleged corruption relating to a controversial land deal some 10 years earlier, the Speaker of the National Assembly, Jigme Tshultim, and the Minister of Home and Cultural Affairs, Lyonpo Minjur Dorji, were convicted on charges of official misconduct and sentenced to terms of imprisonment of two-and-a-half years and one year, respectively (although, with the option of paying a fine to avoid imprisonment). Thirteen other plot allotment committee members received similar sentences.

Elections to the upper house of the parliament, the National Council, were successfully concluded in a single round on 23 April 2013, with 67 non-partisan candidates contesting the 20 elective seats. The majority of those elected were new representatives, with only six incumbent members of the upper house securing reelection. While the outgoing Council included four female representatives, no women were elected in the latest poll. Although the number of voters taking part (over 171,000) increased slightly compared with the previous election in 2008, the participation rate declined to around 45% of registered voters, against 53% in 2008. In accordance with the Constitution, the incumbent Government formally stood down at the end of April 2013 in preparation for the elections to the National Assembly, which took place in two rounds, on 31 May and 13 July; the polls were presided over by an interim Government headed by the Chief Justice of the Supreme Court. Following the elimination of the DNT and the DCT in the primary electoral round, the PDP, hitherto the sole opposition party in government, won a convincing victory in the second round, securing 32 of the 47 seats; the DPT won the remaining 15 seats. The second round of the elections reportedly attracted a turnout of 66.1%. In late July Lyonchhen Tshering Tobgay was sworn in as the country's new Prime Minister at the head of an 11-member PDP Council of Ministers. Of especial note was the appointment of Bhutan's first female cabinet minister, Aum Dorji Choden, who—together with the six other erstwhile DNT parliamentary candidates (including the new Minister of Economic Affairs, Norbu Wangchuk)—had transferred her political allegiance from the DNT to the PDP after the primary elections; she was assigned the works and human settlement portfolio. Although, according to the Constitution, the leader of the winning party in a general election automatically becomes Prime Minister, Tshering Tobgay insisted on being elected by his party, in line with PDP ideology. Also in late July, the DPT elected former Minister of Agriculture and Forests Dr Pema Gyamtsho as Opposition Leader in the National Assembly.

In August 2013 former Prime Minister Lyonpo Jigmi Yozer Thinley submitted his resignation as a member of the lower house. A by-election held in November to fill the seat vacated by Thinley was won by the DPT candidate, thus maintaining the political balance in the National Assembly. In December Thinley completed his exit from political life when he stood down as President of the DPT and was replaced by Pema Gyamtsho. The standing of women in Bhutanese political/diplomatic life was given a further boost, in January 2014, when the country's first female ambassadors were appointed—one to represent Bhutan at the UN permanent mission in New York, the USA, and the other to head the embassy in Dhaka, Bangladesh.

Assamese Militancy

By mid-1998 the most pressing security issue confronting the country was the perceived threat from the presence of Assamese (Asomese) tribal (Bodo) and Maoist (United Liberation Front of Assam—ULFA) militants from India, who had established military training bases in the jungle border regions of south-eastern Bhutan. Concern was expressed regarding a brief Indian military incursion into Bhutanese territory in a raid on suspected militants (for which the Government of India subsequently apologized). In mid-1999 the Bhutanese Minister of Home Affairs reported that recent talks with ULFA leaders had elicited the response that members of the ULFA had been forced to enter Bhutanese territory in 1992, but that they were not ready to leave Bhutan for at least another 18 months. They asserted that they were determined to fight until independence for Assam (Asom), India, was achieved, but offered to reduce their military presence in Bhutan. After detailed discussion, assembly members decided that all supplies of food and other essentials to the ULFA and National Democratic Front of Bodoland (NDFB) must be stopped. In July 2000 the National Assembly adopted a resolution stating that the problem should be solved through peaceful means, but that if negotiations failed military force should be used to evict the insurgents from Bhutanese territory. Some groups of militants began to return to India. However, most ULFA and Bodo militants, who had hitherto refrained from carrying out violent activities in Bhutan, were angered by the Assembly's decision. In December some 13 people were killed when members of the Bodo Liberation Tigers (a group allegedly supported by the Indian security forces) attacked a convoy of Bhutanese vehicles on the Bhutan–India border. The act was perceived as a warning to the Bhutanese Government not to shelter ULFA and NDFB militants.

Following discussions in June 2001, representatives of the ULFA agreed to remove four of their nine military camps in Bhutan by December and reduce the strength of the cadres in the remaining camps. Although the four designated ULFA camps had been abandoned by the end of the year, there were concerns that the militants had repositioned their camps elsewhere in Bhutan. In the mean time, the NDFB maintained three main camps and four mobile camps on Bhutanese territory and the Minister of Home Affairs reported that the Indian militant Kamtapur Liberation Organization (KLO) had also established camps in Bhutan. The KLO armed militants were Rajbansi tribals of north Bengal, India, bordering Chhukha and Samtse districts, who were campaigning for separate statehood for the Kamtapuris.

In mid-2003 the ULFA was reported to have increased its total number of camps inside Bhutan to eight, with an estimated 1,560 militants; the NDFB had eight camps, with about 740 militants; and the KLO had three camps, with an estimated 430 militants. The Council of Ministers approved a contingency budget of up to Nu 2,000m. in the event of military action. Subsequent efforts by the Bhutanese Government in the latter half of the year to seek a peaceful resolution by directly addressing the three armed groups proved fruitless.

A 48-hour notice to leave Bhutan, issued to the militants by the Government on 13 December 2003, went unheeded. Accordingly, on 15 December the Royal Bhutan Army (RBA) launched simultaneous attacks on most of the training camps (which now totalled 30), concentrating on the elimination of the ULFA headquarters. By the end of the month the Government reported that all of the camps had been captured and destroyed (14 of the camps belonged to the ULFA, the NDFB operated 11 camps and the KLO had five camps). Large quantities of armaments and ammunition were seized during the operation. In February 2004 the Chief of Staff of the Indian Army stated that the offensive, which had resulted in the deaths of at least 420 insurgents, had been highly successful. In March it was reported that the RBA had launched another offensive against the remaining militants. In September a bomb explosion in Gelephu killed two people (both of Indian nationality) and injured a further 27; the NDFB was believed to have been responsible for the attack. Meanwhile, more than 100 people in a number of locations in Bhutan were convicted of aiding and abetting the insurgents and were sentenced to prison terms of various lengths. However, in late 2008 the Assam police force expressed its concern that the militants had re-established camps in southern Bhutan, after a bomb that killed 30 people in Assam in October was linked to dissident groups based in Bhutan. The Bhutanese Government, for its part, claimed to have no evidence of any renewal in Assamese insurgent activity within its borders. In late 2012 senior Indian security officials again reported an increase in activities by Indian militants in Bhutan and in mid-2013 there were reports in the Indian media that members of the NDFB were carrying out joint operations (including kidnappings) with Bhupali Maoist militants in southern Bhutan.

Ethnic Unrest, the Southern Bhutanese and the Refugee Camps in Nepal

The violent ethnic Nepalese agitation in India for a 'Gurkha homeland' in the Darjiling-Kalimpong region during the late 1980s and the populist movement in Nepal in 1988–90 (see the respective chapters on India and Nepal) spread into Bhutan in 1990. Ethnic unrest became apparent in that year when a campaign of intimidation and violence, directed by militant Nepalese against the authority of the Government in Thimphu, was initiated. In September–October thousands of southern Bhutanese villagers, and Nepalese who entered Bhutan from across the Indian border, organized demonstrations in border towns in southern Bhutan to protest against domination by the indigenous Buddhist Drukpa. The 'anti-nationals' (ngolops), as they were called by the Bhutanese authorities, demanded a greater role in the country's political and economic life and were bitterly opposed to official attempts to strengthen the Bhutanese sense of national identity through an increased emphasis on Tibetan-derived, rather than Nepalese, culture and religion (including a formal dress code, Dzongkha as the sole official language, etc.).

Most southern villagers were relatively recent arrivals from Nepal, and many of them had made substantial contributions to the development of the southern hills. The provision of free education and health care by the Bhutanese Government for many years attracted Nepalese who had been struggling to survive in their own country and who came to settle illegally in Bhutan. This population movement was largely ignored by local administrative officials, many of whom accepted incentives to disregard the illegal nature of the influx. The Government's policy of encouraging a sense of national identity, together with rigorous new procedures (introduced in 1988) to check citizenship registration, revealed the presence of thousands of illegal residents in southern Bhutan—many of whom had lived there for a decade or more, married local inhabitants and raised families. During the ethnic unrest in 1990 the majority of southern villagers were allegedly coerced into participating in the demonstrations by groups of armed and uniformed young men (including many of Nepalese origin who were born in Bhutan). Many of these dissidents had fled Bhutan in 1989 and early 1990 and had taken up residence in tea gardens and villages in eastern Nepal. Following the demonstrations that took place in Bhutan in 1990, other ethnic Nepalese left Bhutan. In January 1991 more than 200 persons, claiming to be Bhutanese refugees, reportedly arrived in the Jhapa district of eastern Nepal. In September, at the request of the Nepalese Government, the office of the UN High Commissioner for Refugees (UNHCR, see p. 66) inaugurated a relief programme providing food and shelter for more than 300 people in the ad hoc camps. By December the number of people in the camps had risen to about 6,000. This number was substantially augmented by landless and unemployed Nepalese, who had been expelled from Assam (Asom) and other eastern states of India. The small and faction-ridden ethnic Nepalese Bhutan People's Party (BPP) purported to lead the agitation for 'democracy' but presented no clear set of objectives and attracted little support from within Bhutan itself.

Between 1988 and the end of 1999 King Jigme personally authorized the release of more than 1,700 militants captured by the authorities. The King asserted that, while he had an open mind regarding the question of the pace and extent of political reform (including a willingness to hold discussions with any discontented minority group), his Government could not tolerate pressures for change if based on intimidation and violence. Although several of the main leaders of the dissident movement remained in custody, the King stated that they would be released upon a return to normal conditions of law and order. Violence continued in the disturbed areas of Samtse, Chhukha, Tsirang, Sarpang and Gelephu throughout the early 1990s, and companies of trained militia volunteers were posted to these areas to relieve the forces of the regular army.

A number of southern Bhutanese officials (including the Director-General of Power, Bhim Subba, and the Managing Director of the State Trading Corporation, R. B. Basnet) absconded in June 1991 and went directly to Nepal, where they reportedly sought political asylum on the grounds of repression and atrocities against southern Bhutanese. These accusations were refuted by the Government in Thimphu. The former Secretary-General of the BPP, D. K. Rai, was tried by the High Court in Thimphu in May 1992 and was sentenced to life imprisonment for terrorist acts; a further 35 defendants received lesser sentences. Tek Nath Rizal, who had founded the People's Forum for Human Rights–Bhutan (the precursor to the BPP) in exile in Nepal in 1989 and who was alleged to be primarily responsible for the ethnic unrest, came to trial (having been held in prison since November 1989), and was sentenced to life imprisonment in November 1993, having been found guilty of offences against the Tsawa Sum ('the country, the King, and the people'). (Rizal, together with 40 other 'political prisoners', was pardoned by the King and released from prison in December 1999.)

In 1991 'Rongthong' Kinley Dorji, a former Bhutanese businessman accused of unpaid loans and of acts against the state, had absconded to Nepal and joined the anti-Government movement. In 1992 he established and became President of the Druk National Congress, claiming human rights violations in Bhutan. Following the signing of an extradition treaty between India and Bhutan in December, Kinley was arrested by the Indian authorities during a visit to Delhi in April 1997; he was released on bail in June 1998. Despite repeated demands made by the Bhutanese National Assembly that Kinley be extradited from India, in April 2010 the Delhi High Court ruled against the extradition proceedings and Kinley was absolved of all pending charges.

In late 1991 and throughout 1992 several thousand legally settled villagers left southern Bhutan for the newly established refugee camps in eastern Nepal. The Bhutanese Government alleged that the villagers were being enticed or threatened to leave their homes by militants based outside Bhutan, in order to augment the population of the camps and gain international attention; the dissidents, by contrast, claimed that the Bhutanese Government was forcing the villagers to leave. The formation of the Bhutan National Democratic Party (BNDP), including members drawn from supporters of the BPP and with R. B. Basnet as its President, was announced in Kathmandu in February 1992. Incidents of ethnic violence, almost all of which involved infiltration from across the border by ethnic Nepalese who had been trained and dispatched from the camps in Nepal, reportedly diminished substantially in the first half of 1993, as talks continued between Bhutanese and Nepalese officials. The Nepalese Government steadfastly refused to consider any solution that did not include the resettlement in Bhutan of all ethnic Nepalese 'refugees' living in the camps (by November 1993 the number of alleged ethnic Nepalese refugees from Bhutan totalled about 85,000). This proposal was rejected by the Bhutanese Government, which maintained that the majority of the camp population merely claimed to be from Bhutan, had absconded from Bhutan (and thus forfeited their citizenship, according to Bhutan's citizenship laws), or had departed voluntarily after selling their properties and surrendering their citizenship papers and rights. The deadlock was broken, however, when a joint statement was signed by the two countries' Ministers of Home Affairs in July, which committed each side to establishing a 'high-level committee' to work towards a settlement and, in particular, to fulfilling the following mandate prior to undertaking any other related activity: to determine the different categories of people claiming to have come from Bhutan in the refugee camps in eastern Nepal (which now numbered eight); and to specify the positions of the two Governments on each of these categories, which would provide the basis for the resolution of the problem. The first meeting of the ministerial joint committee (MJC) was held in Kathmandu in October, at which it was agreed that four categories would be established among the people in the refugee camps: '(i) bona fide Bhutanese who had been evicted forcefully; (ii) Bhutanese who had emigrated; (iii) non-Bhutanese; and (iv) Bhutanese who had committed criminal acts' (henceforth referred to as Categories I, II, III and IV, respectively). Further MJC meetings were held in 1994 and the first half of 1995, but little progress was made. Nepal's new communist Government demanded that all persons in the camps (regardless of status) be accepted by Bhutan; the Bhutanese authorities, on the other hand, were prepared to accept only the unconditional return of any Category I camp residents.

During 1996–98 further MJC talks proved relatively fruitless. At the eighth round of negotiations, which was held in Kathmandu in September 1999, the Bhutanese Minister of Foreign Affairs agreed that some of those previously classified as voluntary emigrants (under Category II) might be reclassified as Category I (according to the Bhutanese Government, the number of people in this latter category totalled only about 3,000, while the Nepalese Government claimed that all of the camp dwellers—who now numbered about 100,000—had been compelled to leave Bhutan).

At the 10th round of MJC negotiations, held in December 2000, it was agreed that nationality would be verified on the basis of the head of the refugee family for those under 25 years of age, and that refugees over 25 years of age would be verified on an individual basis. This agreement signified a major concession by Bhutan, which had hitherto insisted that verification be conducted on an individual basis. Verification of the nationalities of those claiming refugee status (including some 13,000 minors born in the camps) began in March 2001—commencing with the Khudanabari camp—under a Joint Verification Team (JVT), consisting of five officials each from the Nepalese and Bhutanese Governments. However, following disagreements between the two sides over the categorization of the refugees, the process had come to a standstill by the end of the year.

In January 2003 Bhutan hosted the 12th meeting of the MJC, at which the two Governments finally harmonized their positions on each of the four categories. Details of the results of the verification process at Khudanabari were published in June: only 2.4% of the camp's inhabitants were classified as belonging to Category I (forcefully evicted Bhutanese people); 70.5% to Category II (Bhutanese who had emigrated); 24.2% to Category III (non-Bhutanese people); and 2.8% to Category IV (Bhutanese who had committed criminal acts). Arrangements were made to conduct the repatriation to Bhutan of most of the families in Category I by the end of the year. The MJC also decided that Bhutan would be fully responsible for any Category I persons, while Category II people could apply for either Bhutanese or Nepalese citizenship. However, in December the Bhutanese members of the JVT, while explaining procedures to Category I residents of the Khudanabari camp, were attacked by several thousand other camp members protesting against the terms and conditions of the agreement. The JVT members were subsequently withdrawn to Thimphu, the repatriation process was halted, and talks between Bhutan and Nepal were suspended.

In October 2006 the US Government offered to resettle (after interviews and screening) as many as 60,000 of the refugees over a period of three to four years. This met with a mixed response: some argued that third-country resettlement would amount to an exoneration of Bhutan's actions, while others welcomed the proposal. In the following month Australia, Canada and New Zealand also offered asylum to the refugees. UNHCR, which had urged Bhutan to allow repatriation, and the Nepalese Government began a census of the estimated 106,000 refugees in the Jhapa and Morang districts of Nepal in November.

In January 2007 the Bhutanese Movement Steering Committee, a prominent refugee organization chaired by Tek Nath Rizal, urged the Nepalese Government to terminate discussions with Bhutan and to resolve the matter with the help of India. In May an attempt by a group of 15,000 refugees to cross the Indo–Nepalese border was foiled by Indian troops, who reportedly killed two people and injured a further 60. The march was organized by the National Front for Democracy, a coalition of exiled Bhutanese political groups, to coincide with the second round of 'mock' elections in Bhutan (see Domestic Political Affairs). Following a visit to the refugee camps in November, the US Assistant Secretary of State for Population, Refugees and Migration claimed that the refugees faced 'severe intimidation' from political leaders who were opposed to the offers of resettlement abroad on the grounds that this would undermine their political struggle to settle all the 'camp people' in Bhutan. Nevertheless, in February 2008 Nepal began issuing exit permits to those who had opted for resettlement, and in March the first group of refugees left the camps for the USA and New Zealand. According to the International Organization for Migration, by February 2009 more than 10,000 people claiming to be from Bhutan had been resettled overseas (more than 9,000 in the USA), with many more expected to follow. Despite several pledges by the leaders on both sides to reopen the stalled MJC talks, by early 2014 there had been no resumption of direct negotiations between Bhutan and Nepal on the refugee issue. The third-country resettlement programme increasingly appeared to offer the only practical solution for most of the inhabitants of the refugee camps.

According to UNHCR, at early December 2013 some 31,000 persons remained in the camps (the number of which had now decreased to two), the majority of whom had expressed an interest in third-country resettlement, while the others had requested repatriation to Bhutan. By that date nearly 85,000 persons claiming Bhutanese refugee status had been resettled in third countries: the USA had accepted the largest number (more than 71,000 individuals), followed by Canada, Australia, New Zealand, Denmark, Norway, the United Kingdom and the Netherlands. UNHCR estimated that the number of refugees resettled in third countries would reach 100,000 by the end of 2014, although it stated that it would continue to hold talks with the Bhutanese Government on the option of voluntary repatriation.

Foreign Affairs

In December 2006 Bhutan and India concluded most of a border demarcation process that had been instigated more than four decades earlier. In 2007 Indo-Bhutanese relations entered a new phase: a revised India-Bhutan Friendship Treaty, which was ratified in March, ensured greater autonomy for Bhutan in external and military affairs and increased economic co-operation between the two countries, including free trade. The Treaty also allowed Bhutan to import arms from and through India, and guaranteed equality of justice for citizens of each country when residing in the other. Relations between the two countries were further strengthened in May 2008 when the Indian Prime Minister, Dr Manmohan Singh, paid an official visit to Bhutan, during which he dedicated the Tala Hydroelectric Project, the largest joint venture between India and Bhutan to date, to the two countries. King Jigme Khesar made a state visit to India in December 2009, in the course of which several important agreements were signed between the two countries relating to co-operation in further education, the provision of hydroelectric power, air transport, the prevention of illicit drugs-trafficking and the development of the IT sector. An agreement was also signed to construct a strategically important 20-km railway line linking the two countries across the foothills of the Himalayas. Bhutan's first railway line, which was to be funded and built by India, was to run between Hasimara in West Bengal to Toribari in south Bhutan. (However, the rail project was subsequently delayed owing to opposition to the proposed route from various groups in West Bengal; by early 2014 construction work had yet to commence.) A Bhutanese delegation headed by the King held talks with the Indian Prime Minister in New Delhi in January 2013 focusing on India's support for Bhutan's 11th Five-Year Plan, which was due to be launched in July 2013. During a visit to India in February, Prime Minister Jigmi Yozer Thinley expressed his wish that the Indian Government's ongoing campaign to reduce its fiscal deficit should not affect the strong economic ties between the two countries, particularly the major hydroelectric projects being undertaken by India in Bhutan. However, in July India temporarily halted fuel subsidies to Bhutan—a move that some interpreted as a form of punishment by India prompted by Bhutan's ever closer engagement with China; the vital subsidies were restored in August. A number of observers held that India's withdrawal of subsidies had played a notable part in the defeat of the incumbent DPT Government in the legislative elections in July and accused India of interfering in Bhutanese internal affairs by influencing the outcome of the poll. Notably, the first official foreign visit undertaken by newly appointed Prime Minister Tshering Tobgay, in late August/early September, was to India.

Following the relaxation of many policies in China from 1978, and anticipating improved relations between India and China, Bhutan moved cautiously to assert positions on regional and world affairs that took into account the views of India but were not necessarily identical to them. Discussions with China regarding the formal delineation and demarcation of Bhutan's northern border began in 1984, and substantive negotiations commenced in 1986. At the 12th round of talks, held in Beijing, China, in December 1998, the Ministers of Foreign Affairs of Bhutan and China signed an official interim agreement (the first agreement ever to be signed between the two countries) to maintain peace and tranquillity in the Bhutan–China border area and to observe the status quo of the border as it was prior to May 1959, pending a formal agreement on the border alignment. Following a series of negotiations between Bhutan and China in the first half of the 2000s, the disputed border area, which was 1,128 sq km during the early rounds of talks, was reduced to 764 sq km in the north-west of Bhutan. However, road construction and maintenance work carried out by China in the disputed area caused some tension from 2004, with the Bhutanese Government expressing concern that the work encroached upon its territory. In addition, the Bhutanese authorities alleged that the Chinese army had, on around 40 occasions during 2008–09, intruded into Bhutan's border patrol camps. Despite such alleged aggressive manoeuvres on the part of the Chinese military, boundary negotiations were resumed in January 2010 (following a hiatus of three years). An expert group meeting in Beijing in July concluded that ongoing disagreements regarding a mutually acceptable common claim line would have to be resolved before the Bhutan–China border issue could be finalized. Meeting on the sidelines of a UN conference in Brazil in June 2012, Bhutanese Prime Minister Thinley and the Chinese Premier, Wen Jiabao, both expressed their willingness to establish formal diplomatic ties between their two countries and to conclude the border demarcation process as soon as possible. However, it was subsequently reported in the Indian media, in June 2013, that there had been further intrusions by the Chinese army into the border area of north-eastern Bhutan. The 21st round of Sino-Bhutanese border talks was held in Thimphu in August, with little evidence of any real progress being achieved.

In response to the increasing volume of bilateral trade between Bhutan and Nepal, a draft preferential trade agreement was drawn up by the two countries in March 2010. A second round of talks on the issue was held in Thimphu in May 2011. In 2010 the Nepalese authorities proposed opening a diplomatic mission in the Bhutanese capital; however, by early 2014 Bhutan had given no official response to this proposal.

Bangladesh's Prime Minister, Sheikh Hasina Wajed, made a three-day state visit to Bhutan in November 2009, during which the existing Bhutan-Bangladesh Trade Agreement was renewed for a further five years. The two sides also discussed the possibility of Bhutan exporting electricity to Bangladesh. Amicable relations between the two countries were further strengthened following two state visits made to Bangladesh by King Jigme Khesar in March 2011 and February 2013.

The 16th SAARC summit was held in Thimphu in April 2010. Bhutan had previously declined to host the meeting, on the grounds that its facilities were inadequate, but in the event the Thimphu meeting was rated as highly successful by the leaders in attendance. The establishment of a new SAARC Development Fund (SDF), the permanent secretariat of which was to be located in Thimphu, was announced at the summit. The SDF was created to fund regional projects involving poverty alleviation and economic development; Bhutan's projected contribution was US $15m., payable over five years.

In recent years an increasingly important aspect of Bhutan's foreign policy has been the expansion of diplomatic ties beyond South Asia, in a bid to afford the country a higher profile on the world stage. In the year to August 2012 Bhutan established formal diplomatic relations with 14 additional countries and appointed another six honorary consuls in various locations throughout the world; by mid-March 2013 Bhutan had established diplomatic relations with a total of 52 countries (as well as with the European Union). Furthermore, following months of intense diplomatic lobbying, in October 2012 Bhutan contested the Asian seat for a non-permanent member at the UN Security Council for the 2013–14 term; however, the bid proved unsuccessful, with the Republic of Korea winning the seat.

CONSTITUTION AND GOVERNMENT

In accordance with the provisions of a draft constitution, which had been formally presented to King Jigme Singye Wangchuck in December 2002, Bhutan's first general election took place in March 2008, and was followed by the installation of a new Council of Ministers and a bicameral legislature, composed of a National Council (upper house) and National Assembly (lower house). The National Council comprises 20 members elected by universal suffrage for a five-year term in office, together with five royal nominees; none of the members of the National Council are affiliated to any political party. The National Assembly consists of 47 representatives with party affiliations, who are elected for a term of five years by adult franchise from each district in proportion to its population. The final version of the draft Constitution was adopted by the new Parliament (comprising the King and both legislative houses) in July 2008.

There are 20 districts (dzongkhags), each headed by a district officer (dzongda, in charge of administration and law and order) and a magistrate (drangpon, in charge of judicial matters, formerly known as a thrimpon). District officers are appointed by the Royal Civil Service Commission and are responsible to the Commission and the Ministry of Home and Cultural Affairs. Magistrates answer to the authority of the High Court. In September 2009 the Local Government Act of Bhutan established 20 district councils (dzongkhag tshogdus) to function as the highest decision-making body in each of Bhutan's districts. Seven of the districts are further sub-divided into sub-districts (dungkhags), and the next level down of administrative unit in all districts is the block (gewog) of several villages, of which there are 205. According to the 2009 Local Government Act, each block is administered by a block council (gewog tshogde), which is subordinate to the district council. The block council is composed of a headman (gup), a deputy (mangmi), and between five and eight democratically elected village elders (tshogpas). The blocks, in turn, are divided into chiwogs for elections and thromdes (municipalities) for administration.

REGIONAL AND INTERNATIONAL CO-OPERATION

Bhutan is a member of the Asian Development Bank (ADB, see p. 207), the Colombo Plan (see p. 449), BIMSTEC (Bay of Bengal Initiative for Multi-Sectoral Technical and Economic Cooperation) and the South Asian Association for Regional Cooperation (SAARC, see p. 420), all of which seek to improve regional co-operation, particularly in economic development. Having joined the UN in 1971, Bhutan is also a member of the Economic and Social Commission for Asia and the Pacific (ESCAP, see p. 28). Bhutan applied for membership of the World Trade Organization (WTO) in 1999 and was granted observer status the following year. In 2011 the Bhutan Government began the accession process to join the International Labour Organization (ILO, see p. 137).

ECONOMIC AFFAIRS

In 2012, according to estimates by the World Bank, Bhutan's gross national income (GNI), measured at average 2009–12 prices, was US $1,797m., equivalent to $2,420 per head (or $6,310 per head on an international purchasing-power parity basis). During 2003–12, it was estimated, the population increased at an average annual rate of 2.1%, while gross domestic product (GDP) per head rose, in real terms, by an average of 6.5% per year. Overall GDP increased, in real terms, at an average annual rate of 8.7% in 2003–12. According to the Asian Development Bank (ADB), GDP grew by 5.2% in the fiscal year ending 30 June 2013.

Agriculture (including livestock and forestry) contributed an estimated 18.1% of GDP in 2012. About 62.2% of the employed labour force were engaged in the sector in that year. The principal sources of revenue in the agricultural sector are apples, oranges, potatoes, ginger and cardamom. Timber production is also important; about 60% of the total land area is covered by forest. Agricultural GDP increased, in real terms, at an average annual rate of 1.8% in 2006–12; it grew by 3.4% in 2012. According to the ADB, agricultural GDP grew by 2.6% in 2012/13.

In 2012 industry (including mining, manufacturing, utilities and construction) engaged about 8.6% of the employed labour force and contributed an estimated 41.9% of GDP. Industrial GDP increased at an average annual rate of 10.9% in 2006–12; the sector grew by 2.9% in 2012. According to the ADB, industrial GDP increased by 5.0% in 2012/13.

In 2012 mining and quarrying contributed an estimated 2.1% of GDP and employed just 0.2% of the labour force. Calcium carbide is the most significant mineral export (contributing 3.2% of total export revenue in 2012). Mineral products (including fuels) accounted for 10.0% of total exports in 2011. Gypsum, coal, limestone, slate and dolomite are also mined. Mining GDP increased at an average rate of 10.3% per year in 2006–12; it grew by 24.2% in 2011, but contracted by 2.2% in 2012.

In 2012 manufacturing contributed 9.6% of GDP and employed 5.0% of the employed labour force. The most important sectors are base metals and related products, and cement production. Small-scale manufacturers produce, *inter alia*, textiles, soap, matches, candles and carpets. Manufacturing GDP increased at an average annual rate of 12.6% in 2006–12; the sector grew by 8.9% in 2012.

In 2012 construction contributed 17.0% of GDP, although a mere 1.5% of the employed population were engaged in the sector. Construction GDP increased at an average annual rate of 8.0% in 2006–12; the sector grew by 14.7% in 2011 and by 4.2% in 2012.

Energy is derived principally from hydroelectric power. Bhutan's potential hydroelectric production capacity has been estimated at up to 30,000 MW. A number of hydroelectric power installations, developed in partnership with India, provide electricity for domestic consumption and also for export to India (see below). In 2011 exports of electricity provided 31.2% of total export revenue, while in the same year the value of imports of mineral products (including fuels) was equivalent to 18.4% of total import costs.

In 2012 the services sector contributed 40.0% of GDP and employed about 29.2% of the employed labour force. The tourism sector has become increasingly significant, with tourist arrivals rising from 17,342 in 2006 to 43,943 in 2012 (revenue from tourism grew from US $13m. in 2004 to $63m. in 2012). The GDP of the services sector increased at an average annual rate of 8.7% in 2006–12; sectoral GDP rose by 15.0% in 2011 and by 2.0% in 2012. According to the ADB, the GDP of the services sector increased by 3.8% in 2012/13.

In the financial year ending 30 June 2012, according to provisional official estimates, Bhutan recorded a visible merchandise trade deficit of Nu 23,985.1m. (There has been a series of widening annual deficits in recent years as a result of increased import costs). In 2011/12, according to provisional estimates, there was a deficit of Nu 17,585.2m. on the current account of the balance of payments. In 2012 the principal source of imports (providing an estimated 78.7% of the total) was India, which was also the main market for exports (accounting for an estimated 61.2% of the total). The principal exports in 2011 were base metals and related products, hydroelectric power, mineral products (including fuels) and chemical products (including medicines). The principal imports in 2011, were machinery, mechanical appliances and electrical appliances and equipment; mineral products (including fuels), base metals and related products, and transport vehicles and equipment were also significant imports.

According to revised estimates, the 2012/13 budget recorded a deficit of Nu 7,350.3m., equivalent to 7.4% of GDP for 2012. In 2012/13, according to the ADB, the overall fiscal deficit of the central Government amounted to the equivalent of 0.9% of GDP. Bhutan's total external debt amounted to US $1,705m. at the end of 2013. In that year, the cost of debt-servicing long-term public and publicly guaranteed debt and repayments to the IMF was equivalent to 215.6% of the value of goods, services and income (excluding workers' remittances). According to the ADB, the average annual rate of inflation was 6.6% in 2003–12, and consumer prices increased by 8.6% in 2012/13. The unemployment rate was 2.1% in 2011/12.

Over the last decade or so Bhutan's economic performance has been impressive and notable progress has been made in the areas of poverty reduction and social and infrastructural development. The country's economic development has been guided by a series of five-year plans. The 11th Plan (2013–18) was projected to involve expenditure of around Nu 213,000m. (compared with an estimated Nu 148,000m. under the previous plan) and was to focus on further reducing poverty, lowering unemployment, tackling corruption and addressing the problem of a serious shortage in the supply of Indian rupees. Bhutan is primarily dependent upon the sale of electricity (principally to India) to earn rupees for regional expenditure, and on the continued influx of foreign tourists to earn hard currency for expenses outside the region. The completion of three major Indian-funded hydroelectric power (HEP) projects between 1988 and 2008 helped to stimulate growth in the industrial sector and contributed to strong economic growth throughout the 2000s. Bhutan and India set a target of achieving 10,000 MW of power generation in Bhutan by 2020; however, at early 2014 construction work on five Indian-funded HEP projects (totalling some 4,680 MW), including Bhutan's largest single HEP undertaking, the 2,560 MW Sankosh project, had not yet commenced. In 1999 Bhutan was opened up to foreign investment, although the stock exchange remained closed to external investors. In 2009 the Government announced that it was planning to permit foreign direct investment (FDI) of 100% in certain sectors, and greater liberalization was also to be introduced in Bhutan's financial sector. In an attempt to address unemployment—particularly among young people—in recent years the Government has focused on the promotion of local entrepreneurs and the establishment of training programmes in the industrial sector. By 2011/12 the overall unemployment rate had fallen to 2.1%, compared with 4.0% in 2008/09, while youth unemployment decreased from 12.9% to 7.2% over the same period. Bhutan's first IT park, Thimphu TechPark, was inaugurated in November 2011; however, by early 2013 it was reported that the Park was struggling to attract much interest from either foreign or domestic companies. From late 2011, mainly as a result of excessive imports from India fuelled by the increasing amount of loans provided by Bhutanese financial institutions, Bhutan suffered a severe shortage in the supply of Indian rupees. As a result of persistent pressure on rupee liquidity (which led the Royal Monetary Authority to impose curbs on import expenditure and bank withdrawals), the rate of GDP growth decreased sharply, from 8.6% in 2011 to 4.6% in 2012, according to official estimates. However, with continuing expansion in the hydropower and tourism sectors, a steady resurgence in GDP growth was expected: the ADB estimated growth at 5.2% in the fiscal year ending 30 June 2013, and forecast growth of 6.0% in 2013/14. The rate of inflation reached a record high of 13.6% in the fourth quarter of 2011/12, but moderated thereafter, to average 8.6% in 2012/13, in response to a depreciation of the Indian rupee (to which the Bhutanese currency is pegged), falling food prices, and the Government's imposition of stringent credit measures and foreign exchange restrictions. Nevertheless, sustained growth in the medium term would be dependent on economic diversification and the continued application of strong economic (and particularly financial) management to counter persistent structural imbalances—including rising public debt.

PUBLIC HOLIDAYS

2015: The usual Buddhist holidays are observed, as well as the Winter Solstice (1 January), the Traditional Day of Offering (21 January), Losar (Tibetan New Year, 19 February), the Birthday of the fifth King Jigme Khesar Namgyel Wangchuck (21–23 February), Zhabdrung Kuchoe (Anniversary of the death of Zhabdrung Ngawang Namgyel, 28 April), the Birthday of the late third King Jigme Dorji Wangchuck (2 May), the Anniversary of the death of the late third King (7 August), two days for Thimphu Tsechu (September/October, in Thimphu district only), the movable Hindu feast of Dashain/Dussehra (13 October), the Coronation Day of the fifth King (1 November), the Birthday of the fourth King Jigme Singye Wangchuck and Constitution Day (11 November) and the National Day of Bhutan (17 December).

Statistical Survey

Source (unless otherwise stated): National Statistics Bureau, POB 338, Thimphu; tel. (2) 322753; fax (2) 323069; internet www.nsb.gov.bt.

Area and Population

AREA, POPULATION AND DENSITY

Area (sq km)	38,394*
Population (census results)	
30–31 May 2005†	
Males	364,482
Females	307,943
Total	672,425
Population (official projected estimates at mid-year)	
2012	720,679
2013	733,004
2014	745,153
Density (per sq km) at 2014	19.4

* 14,824 sq miles.

† Including adjustment for estimated 37,443 persons with no permanent residence; the enumerated total was 634,982. The number of Bhutanese nationals was 552,996.

POPULATION BY AGE AND SEX

(official projected estimates at mid-2014)

	Males	Females	Total
0–14	112,003	110,032	222,035
15–64	257,473	230,278	487,751
65 and over	18,044	17,323	35,367
Total	387,520	357,633	745,153

DISTRICTS

(official population projections at mid-2014)

	Area ('000 sq km)*	Population	Density (per sq km)
Bumthang	2.6	18,692	7.2
Chhukha	1.7	86,991	51.2
Dagana	1.3	27,042	20.8
Gasa	4.2	3,637	0.9
Haa	1.7	13,327	7.8
Lhuentse	2.8	17,413	6.2
Mongar	1.9	43,558	22.9
Paro	1.2	24,919	20.8
Pemagatshel	0.5	42,518	85.0
Punakha	0.9	27,415	30.5
Samdrup Jongkhar	2.2	40,093	18.2
Samtse	1.5	69,612	46.4
Sarpang	2.2	44,781	20.4
Thimphu	1.8	113,669	63.1
Trashigang	2.2	55,480	25.2
Trashi Yangtse	1.4	20,574	14.7
Trongsa	1.7	15,760	9.3
Tsirang	0.6	21,517	35.9
Wangdue Phodrang	3.8	36,922	9.7
Zhemgang	2.0	21,233	10.6
Total	38.4	745,153	19.4

* Data approximated from percentage distribution.

PRINCIPAL TOWNS

(official figures at 2005 census)

Thimphu (capital)	79,185	Gelephu	9,199
Phuentsholing	20,537	Wangdue	6,714

Mid-2011 (incl. suburbs, UN estimate): Thimphu 99,337 (Source: UN, *World Urbanization Prospects: The 2011 Revision*).

BIRTHS AND DEATHS

(annual averages, UN estimates)

	1995–2000	2000–05	2005–10
Birth rate (per 1,000)	30.4	25.0	21.5
Death rate (per 1,000)	9.9	8.1	6.9

Source: UN, *World Population Prospects: The 2012 Revision*.

2005 census (year ending 31 May 2005): Live births 12,538 (birth rate 20 per 1,000); Deaths 4,498 (death rate 7 per 1,000).

Life expectancy (years at birth): 67.5 (males 67.2; females 67.8) in 2011 (Source: World Bank, World Development Indicators database).

ECONOMICALLY ACTIVE POPULATION

(labour force survey, '000 persons aged 15 years and over)

	2010	2011	2012
Agriculture and forestry	190.8	194.7	205.0
Mining and quarrying	0.8	1.2	0.5
Manufacturing	12.5	16.9	16.5
Electricity, gas and water supply	5.3	7.2	6.5
Construction	2.9	4.5	5.0
Wholesale and retail trade; repairs of motor vehicles and personal and household goods	30.8	27.8	12.5
Hotels and restaurants	4.1	6.1	6.0
Transport, storage and communications	9.4	8.9	8.4
Financial intermediation	2.5	2.3	2.4
Real estate, renting and business activities	13.4	8.4	2.0
Public administration and defence; compulsory social security	26.2	27.2	27.3
Education	9.7	9.7	11.4
Health and social work	5.3	2.8	4.5
Other community, social and personal service activities	6.8	3.9	15.3
Private households with employed persons	0.4	2.1	6.2
Total employed	320.9	323.7	329.5
Unemployed	11.0	10.5	6.9
Total labour force	331.9	334.2	336.4
Males	170.5	173.4	164.5
Females	161.4	160.8	171.9

Note: Employed persons include those engaged in at least one hour's work during the week prior to the survey.

Source: Ministry of Labour and Human Resources, Thimphu.

Health and Welfare

KEY INDICATORS

Total fertility rate (children per woman, 2011)	2.3
Under-5 mortality rate (per 1,000 live births, 2011)	54
HIV/AIDS (% of persons aged 15–49, 2012)	0.2
Physicians (per 1,000 head, 2012)	0.3
Hospital beds (per 1,000 head, 2012)	1.8
Health expenditure (2010): US $ per head (PPP)	226
Health expenditure (2010): % of GDP	4.3
Health expenditure (2010): public (% of total)	84.6
Access to water (% of persons, 2011)	97
Access to sanitation (% of persons, 2011)	45
Total carbon dioxide emissions ('000 metric tons, 2010)	476.7
Carbon dioxide emissions per head (metric tons, 2010)	0.7
Human Development Index (2012): ranking	140
Human Development Index (2012): value	0.538

For sources and definitions, see explanatory note on p. vi.

Agriculture

PRINCIPAL CROPS
('000 metric tons)

	2010	2011	2012
Rice, paddy	72	79	87*
Maize	58	80	69†
Potatoes	44	52	55*
Sugar cane*	13	13	14
Oranges	53	61	62*
Apples	17	21	22*
Nutmeg, mace and cardamom	1	1	1*

* FAO estimate(s).
† Unofficial figure.

Aggregate production ('000 metric tons, may include official, semi-official or estimated data): Total cereals 145 in 2010, 184 in 2011, 183 in 2012; Total roots and tubers 67 in 2010, 77 in 2011, 80 in 2012; Total vegetables (incl. melons) 21 in 2010, 24 in 2011, 25 in 2012; Total fruits (excl. melons) 97 in 2010, 110 in 2011, 113 in 2012.

Source: FAO.

LIVESTOCK
('000 head, year ending September)

	2010	2011	2012
Horses	18	18	18*
Asses*	18	18	18
Mules	5	6	6*
Cattle	312	297	304
Buffaloes	1	1	1*
Pigs	20	21	23*
Sheep	13	12	13*
Goats	43	44	44*
Chickens	349	435	435*

* FAO estimate(s).

Source: FAO.

LIVESTOCK PRODUCTS
('000 metric tons, FAO estimates)

	2009	2010	2011
Cattle meat	5.1	5.1	5.1
Pig meat	1.0	1.0	1.0
Cows' milk	38.8	38.9	38.6
Hen eggs	0.3	0.3	0.3

2012: Production assumed to be unchanged from 2011 (FAO estimates).

Source: FAO.

Forestry

ROUNDWOOD REMOVALS
('000 cubic metres, excl. bark)

	2010	2011	2012
Sawlogs, veneer logs and logs for sleepers	99	36	36*
Pulpwood	3	4	4*
Other industrial wood*	88	88	88
Fuel wood*	4,845	4,897	4,950
Total*	5,035	5,025	5,078

* FAO estimate(s).

Source: FAO.

SAWNWOOD PRODUCTION
('000 cubic metres, incl. railway sleepers)

	2009	2010	2011
Coniferous (softwood)	2	7	9
Broadleaved (hardwood)*	18	18	18
Total*	20	25	27

* FAO estimates.

2012: Production assumed to be unchanged from 2011 (FAO estimates).

Source: FAO.

Fishing

(metric tons, live weight, capture of freshwater fishes, FAO estimates)

	2009	2010	2011
Total catch	180	160	160

Source: FAO.

Mining

('000 metric tons unless otherwise indicated)

	2010	2011	2012
Dolomite	1,192	1,082	1,500
Limestone	716	649	677
Gypsum	344	352	313
Coal	88	109	99
Marble (sq m)	71	72	60
Quartzite	111	95	89
Talc	40	9	16
Stone	6,650	1,843	1,494

Industry

GROSS SALES AND OUTPUT OF SELECTED INDUSTRIES
(million ngultrum)

	2010	2011	2012
Penden Cement Authority	1,936.6	1,840.6	1,982.9
Bhutan Ferro Alloys	1,920.0	1,815.5	2,084.0
Bhutan Fruit Products	169.8	205.8	1,753.3
Army Welfare Project*	573.8	712.4	805.8
Bhutan Carbide and Chemicals	1,404.1	1,632.5	1,270.4
Bhutan Board Products	287.2	320.4	151.0
Eastern Bhutan Coal Company	243.6	441.8	473.3
Druk Satair Corporation Ltd	473.6	527.5	494.6

* Manufacturer of alcoholic beverages.

Source: Royal Monetary Authority of Bhutan.

Electric energy (million kWh, year ending 30 June): 6,997.6 in 2009/10; 7,066.5 in 2010/11; 6,823.7 in 2011/12 (Source: Department of Power, Royal Government of Bhutan).

Revenue from the Chhukha, Basochhu, Kurichhu and Tala Hydroelectric Projects (million ngultrum): 11,321.0 (internal consumption 909.6, exports 10,411.5) in 2010; 10,584.8 (internal consumption 759.8, exports 9,825.0) in 2011; 10,477.9 (internal consumption 763.3, exports 9,714.6) in 2012 (Source: Department of Power, Royal Government of Bhutan).

Finance

CURRENCY AND EXCHANGE RATES

Monetary Units
100 chetrum (Ch) = 1 ngultrum (Nu).

Sterling, Dollar and Euro Equivalents (31 December 2013)
£1 sterling = 101.932 ngultrum;
US $1 = 61.897 ngultrum;
€1 = 85.362 ngultrum;
1,000 ngultrum = £9.81 = $16.16 = €11.71.

Average Exchange Rate (ngultrum per US $)

2011	46.670
2012	53.437
2013	58.598

Note: The ngultrum is at par with the Indian rupee, which also circulates freely within Bhutan. The foregoing figures relate to the official rate of exchange, which is applicable to government-related transactions alone. Since April 1992 there has also been a market rate of exchange, which values foreign currencies approximately 20% higher than the official rate of exchange.

GOVERNMENT FINANCE

(general government transactions, million ngultrum, year ending 30 June)

Revenue	2010/11	2011/12	2012/13
Tax revenue	11,593.5	14,676.9	15,282.4
Direct taxes	8,025.6	8,987.0	9,387.3
Business income tax	1,109.9	1,576.6	1,489.4
Corporate income tax	5,109.9	5,186.1	5,089.1
Royalties	711.4	1,114.6	—
Indirect taxes	3,567.9	5,689.9	5,895.1
Bhutan sales tax	1,636.4	2,392.4	2,022.7
Excise duties	1,605.3	2,836.9	3,488.1
Non-tax revenue	5,865.3	5,677.5	5,875.1
Fees, dividends and profits	5,772.0	5561.7	5,749.9
Dividends	2,997.2	2,946.9	3,010.0
Capital revenue	93.3	105.8	125.2
Total revenue	17,458.8	20,354.5	21,157.5
Grants	10,497.7	12,501.5	10,691.2
From India	7,882.8	9,003.4	7,504.3
Total revenue and grants	27,956.5	32,856.0	31,848.7

Expenditure by function*	2010/11	2011/12	2012/13
General services	7,180.3	9,122.9	10,787.2
Social services	8,253.6	9,679.7	9,380.4
Education	5,964.7	6,725.0	6,773.6
Health	2,288.9	2,954.7	2,606.8
Economic services	10,223.7	11,416.9	11,632.5
Agriculture	3,849.1	4,734.2	4,551.3
Mining and manufacturing industries	237.4	239.2	886.6
Transport and communication	3,818.9	5,181.1	5,460.6
Energy	1,627.7	600.6	734.0
Other economic services	690.6	661.7	—
Housing and community amenities	1,068.3	1,071.4	1,731.1
Public order and safety	1,626.9	2,115.0	3,283.6
Religion and culture services	1,169.1	1,436.9	1,229.5
Total	29,521.9	34,842.8	38,044.2

* Excluding lending minus repayments (million ngultrum): –65.7 in 2009/10; 320.5 in 2010/11; 1,154.8 in 2011/12.

2012/13 (revised): *Revenue:* Tax revenue 15,561.8; Non-tax revenue 5,621.8; Grants 15,798.6 (From India 10,497.0); Total revenue and grants 36,982.1. *Expenditure:* Current 18,626.1; Capital 20,717.3; Total expenditure 39,343.4 (excl. lending minus repayment –739.0).

2013/14 (budget): *Revenue:* Tax revenue 15,324.8; Non-tax revenue 6,536.1; Grants 8,109.5 (From India 5,332.3); Total revenue and grants 29,970.4. *Expenditure:* Current 19,160.1; Capital 16,953.8; Total expenditure 36,113.9 (excl. lending minus repayment –1,898.0).

Source: partly Ministry of Finance, Thimphu.

FOREIGN EXCHANGE RESERVES

(at 30 June)

	2009/10	2010/11	2011/12
Indian rupee reserves (million Indian rupees)	1,378.6	774.6	1,516.3
Royal Monetary Authority	137.3	91.2	229.9
Bank of Bhutan	923.0	329.4	857.3
Bhutan National Bank	196.3	99.5	171.8
T Bank Ltd	50.0	39.8	53.3
Druk PNB Bank Ltd	72.1	214.7	204.1
Rupee reserves expressed as dollars (US $ million)	29.6	17.2	27.1
Convertible currency reserves (US $ million)	762.0	888.8	742.9
Royal Monetary Authority	730.7	841.7	719.0
Bank of Bhutan	15.4	35.1	9.0
Bhutan National Bank	15.8	10.0	14.2
T Bank Ltd	0.0	0.2	0.1
Druk PNB Bank Ltd	0.2	1.7	0.5
Total reserves (US $ million)	791.6	906.0	770.0

Source: Royal Monetary Authority of Bhutan.

MONEY SUPPLY

(million ngultrum at 31 December)

	2010	2011	2012
Currency outside depository corporations	5,609	6,913	5,257
Transferable deposits	23,465	26,303	28,119
Other deposits	22,912	21,027	24,800
Broad money	51,987	54,243	58,175

Source: IMF, *International Financial Statistics*.

COST OF LIVING

(Consumer Price Index at 31 December, excluding rent; base: 30 September 2003 = 100)

	2010	2011	2012
Food	163.2	179.8	204.9
Non-food items	139.5	150.9	164.8
All items	146.9	160.0	177.5

Source: Royal Monetary Authority of Bhutan.

NATIONAL ACCOUNTS

(million ngultrum at current prices)

Expenditure on the Gross Domestic Product

	2010	2011	2012
Government final consumption expenditure	14,487.8	17,047.8	18,691.2
Private final consumption expenditure	34,221.2	37,564.7	45,524.4
Changes in stocks	372.1	–315.8	–118.1
Gross fixed capital formation	43,437.4	57,135.5	63,661.8
Total domestic expenditure	92,518.5	111,432.3	127,759.3
Exports of goods and services	31,241.6	34,450.4	35,835.4
Less Imports of goods and services	51,263.5	59,969.7	64,139.6
GDP in purchasers' values	72,496.6	85,913.0	99,455.1
GDP at constant 2000 prices	45,432.0	49,318.5	51,597.0

Gross Domestic Product by Economic Activity

	2010	2011	2012
Agriculture, forestry and livestock	12,177.8	13,868.4	16,893.5
Mining and quarrying	1,616.9	1,941.7	1,962.0
Manufacturing	6,324.1	7,044.8	8,934.5
Electricity and water	12,763.6	11,911.6	12,303.1
Construction	10,308.9	13,916.6	15,887.5
Wholesale and retail trade	3,752.6	4,641.8	6,236.4
Restaurants and hotels	608.0	948.7	1,378.5
Transport, storage and communications	6,943.3	9,489.1	10,345.5
Finance, insurance and real estate and business services	5,545.9	7,007.7	7,712.5
Public administration	5,517.3	6,478.0	6,775.7
Education and health	3,745.2	4,404.2	4,473.2
Personal services and recreational activities	298.0	338.0	390.1
Sub-total	69,601.6	81,990.7	93,292.5
Taxes, less subsidies, on products	2,895.1	3,922.4	6,162.5
GDP at current prices	72,496.6	85,913.0	99,455.1

BALANCE OF PAYMENTS
(million ngultrum, year ending 30 June, estimates)

	2009/10	2010/11	2011/12*
Merchandise exports f.o.b.	25,401.8	30,160.1	29,890.4
Merchandise imports c.i.f.	–39,340.0	–53,705.0	–53,875.5
Trade balance	–13,938.2	–23,544.9	–23,985.1
Exports of services	3,213.6	3,707.9	5,142.5
Imports of services	–4,220.6	–5,261.4	–7,097.6
Balance on goods and services	–14,945.2	–25,098.4	–25,940.2
Other income received	762.3	753.9	875.4
Other income paid	–3,599.1	–4,417.2	–4,747.9
Balance on goods, services and income	–17,782.0	–28,761.7	–29,812.7
Current transfers received	12,880.4	12,517.8	14,356.2
Current transfers paid	–1,733.3	–2,355.5	–2,128.6
Current balance	–6,634.9	–18,599.4	–17,585.2
Capital transfers	3,719.5	3,652.0	1,318.6
Direct investment from abroad	885.9	1,181.6	483.7
Other investment	5,015.9	16,585.1	11,332.8
Net errors and omissions	1,987.0	1,516.1	–1,006.0
Overall balance	4,973.4	4,335.4	–5,456.1

* Provisional.

Source: Royal Monetary Authority of Bhutan, *Annual Report*.

External Trade

PRINCIPAL COMMODITIES
(million ngultrum)

Imports	2009	2010	2011
Animal products	992.7	1,188.3	1,311.8
Fruit, vegetables and cereal crops (incl. tea, coffee and spices)	1,295.0	1,559.7	2,056.7
Vegetable fats and oils	414.1	508.9	667.7
Processed foods and beverages (incl. alcohol)	1,161.1	1,425.0	1,742.5
Mineral products (incl. fuels)	5,059.9	7,344.3	8,936.6
Chemical products (incl. medicines and pharmaceuticals)	970.9	1,317.5	1,868.9
Plastics and rubber products	840.1	1,207.3	1,584.3
Wood, woodpulp and products thereof	1,179.8	1,414.4	2,134.8
Textiles, clothing and footwear	384.1	537.0	597.1
Articles of stone, plaster, cement, etc.	371.1	539.6	756.2
Pearls and products of precious and semi-precious metal and stones	138.1	17.7	84.0
Base metals and articles of base metals	4,405.6	8,002.8	8,565.7
Machinery, mechanical appliances and electrical appliances and equipment	5,230.8	9,159.9	10,253.4
Transport vehicles and equipment	2,448.4	3,989.0	7,381.3
Total (incl. others)	25,523.0	39,075.2	48,687.4

Exports	2009	2010	2011
Fruit, vegetables and cereal crops (incl. tea, coffee and spices)	1,135.1	1,010.3	1,325.2
Processed foods and beverages (incl. alcohol)	326.0	334.9	432.4
Mineral products (incl. fuels)	2,872.8	3,191.2	3,149.6
Chemical products (incl. medicines and pharmaceuticals)	1,051.8	1,454.5	1,476.9
Plastics and rubber products	308.4	246.1	309.8
Wood, woodpulp and products thereof	323.8	320.5	318.1
Textiles, clothing and footwear	67.1	41.5	32.4
Base metals and articles of base metals	7,061.9	10,024.3	10,476.0
Electricity*	10,072.5	10,411.5	9,825.0
Total (incl. others)	23,973.9	29,324.0	31,485.9

* Trade with India only.

Source: Royal Monetary Authority of Bhutan, *Annual Report*.

2012 (million ngultrum): Total imports 52,977.5; Total exports 28,600.1.

PRINCIPAL TRADING PARTNERS
(million ngultrum)

Imports c.i.f.	2009	2010	2011
China, People's Republic	487.3	611.0	878.3
Germany	222.7	362.0	639.2
India	19,840.8	29,329.1	35,190.8
Indonesia	68.6	567.7	n.a.
Japan	558.5	845.1	1,536.6
Korea, Republic	383.8	2,004.7	2,916.2
Malaysia	374.5	n.a.	n.a.
Nepal	369.8	585.5	n.a.
Singapore	744.0	903.0	1,844.5
Sweden	462.4	550.3	581.4
Thailand	348.9	988.1	1,223.7
Total (incl. others)	25,522.9	39,075.2	48,687.4

Exports f.o.b.	2009	2010	2011
Bangladesh	758.0	906.1	1,226.7
Hong Kong	677.6	2,188.3	3,404.9
India	22,415.5	26,000.9	26,378.0
Nepal	84.8	39.7	76.1
Singapore	8.6	19.6	12.1
Total (incl. others)	23,973.9	29,324.4	31,485.9

Source: Royal Monetary Authority of Bhutan, *Annual Report*.

2012 (million ngultrum): *Imports c.i.f.:* Austria 939.7; China, People's Republic 1,330.2; India 41,709.5; Japan 1,260.8; Korea, Republic 1,658.9; Singapore 783.5; Sweden 609.2; Thailand 740.7; Total (incl. others) 52,977.5. *Exports f.o.b.:* Bangladesh 1,172.2; India 17,502.2; Italy 125.0; Japan 113.7; Total (incl. others) 28,600.1.

Transport

ROAD TRAFFIC
(registered vehicles, excl. military)

	2010	2011	2012
Heavy vehicles	6,634	7,972	8,443
Medium vehicles	1,013	1,261	1,330
Light vehicles	31,563	36,085	39,189
Two-wheelers	8,954	9,429	9,734
Taxis	3,600	4,856	5,354
Industrial and plant	1,277	1,716	1,918
Others (incl. tractors)	1,010	1,308	1,411
Total	54,051	62,627	67,379

CIVIL AVIATION
(traffic on scheduled services)

	2007	2008	2009
Kilometres flown (million)	3	3	3
Passengers carried ('000)	54	53	49
Passenger-km (million)	80	78	72
Total ton-km (million)	7	7	7

Source: UN, *Statistical Yearbook*.

Passengers carried (Druk Air only): 132,615 in 2010; 166,264 in 2011; 194,283 in 2012.

Tourism

FOREIGN VISITORS BY COUNTRY OF ORIGIN

	2010	2011	2012
Australia	1,318	1,773	1,926
Canada	786	1,061	1,061
China, People's Republic	1,494	2,896	3,766
France	1,454	1,585	1,847
Germany	2,250	2,287	2,880
Italy	1,028	1,014	786
Japan	2,963	3,943	6,967
Malaysia	356	788	1,307
Netherlands	847	933	993
Singapore	785	1,349	1,605
Switzerland	789	781	932
Thailand	875	2,235	3,573
United Kingdom	1,772	2,795	2,466
USA	5,189	6,226	6,007
Total (incl. others)	27,195	37,479	43,943

Tourism receipts (US $ million): 36.0 in 2010; 47.7 in 2011; 62.8 in 2012.

Communications Media

	2010	2011	2012
Telephones ('000 main lines in use)	26.3	27.5	27.0
Mobile cellular telephones ('000 subscribers)	394.3	484.2	560.9
Internet subscribers ('000)	9.8	14.0	n.a.
Broadband subscribers ('000)	8.7	13.2	16.8

Source: International Telecommunication Union.

Education

(2012)

	Institutions	Teachers	Students
Primary schools	353	2,467	50,733
Lower secondary schools	94	1,997	49,998
Middle secondary schools	58	1,774	39,963
Higher secondary schools	48	1,548	32,702
Institutes*	21	1,172	12,727
Non-formal education (NFE) centres	953	949	13,360
Daycare centres	96	229	2,586

* Including tertiary education (excluding students studying abroad), vocational institutes and Sanskrit Pathshala.

Source: Ministry of Education, Thimphu.

Pupil-teacher ratio (primary education, UNESCO estimate): 24.0 in 2011/12 (Source: UNESCO Institute for Statistics).

Adult literacy rate (UNESCO estimates): 55.6% (males 67.1%; females 42.2%) in 2007 (Source: UNESCO Institute for Statistics).

Directory

The Government

HEAD OF STATE

Druk Gyalpo ('Dragon King'): HM Jigme Khesar Namgyel Wangchuck (succeeded to the throne on 21 December 2006).

COUNCIL OF MINISTERS

(April 2014)

The Government is formed by the People's Democratic Party.

Prime Minister: Lyonchhen Tshering Tobgay.

Minister of Economic Affairs: Lyonpo Norbu Wangchuk.

Minister of Finance: Lyonpo Namgay Dorji.

Minister of Foreign Affairs: Lyonpo Rinzin Dorji.

Minister of Health: Lyonpo Tandin Wangchuk.

Minister of Home and Cultural Affairs: Lyonpo Damchoe Dorji.

Minister of Education: Lyonpo Mingbo Dukpa.

Minister of Works and Human Settlement: Lyonpo Dorji Choden.

Minister of Agriculture and Forests: Lyonpo Yeshey Dorji.

Minister of Information and Communications: Lyonpo D. N. Dhungyel.

Minister of Labour and Human Resources: Lyonpo Ngeema Sangay Chenpo.

MINISTRIES AND OTHER MAJOR GOVERNMENT BODIES

Ministry of Agriculture and Forests: POB 252, Thimphu; tel. (2) 323765; fax (2) 324520; e-mail pgyamtsho@moa.gov.bt; internet www.moaf.gov.bt.

Ministry of Economic Affairs: Tashichhodzong, POB 141, Thimphu; tel. (2) 322211; fax (2) 323617; e-mail info@moea.gov.bt; internet www.moea.gov.bt.

Ministry of Education: Peling Lam, POB 112, Thimphu; tel. (2) 325816; fax (2) 325183; e-mail minister@education.gov.bt; internet www.education.gov.bt.

Ministry of Finance: Tashichhodzong, POB 117, Thimphu; tel. (2) 322223; fax (2) 323154; e-mail wnorbu@mof.gov.bt; internet www.mof.gov.bt.

Ministry of Foreign Affairs: Gyalyong Tshokhang, POB 103, Thimphu; tel. (2) 322459; fax (2) 331465; e-mail ugyen@mofa.gov.bt; internet www.mfa.gov.bt.

Ministry of Health: Kawajangsa, POB 726, Thimphu; tel. (2) 322602; fax (2) 324649; e-mail webmaster@health.gov.bt; internet www.health.gov.bt.

Ministry of Home and Cultural Affairs: Tashichhodzong, POB 133, Thimphu; tel. (2) 322301; fax (2) 324320; e-mail lmd@mohca.gov.bt; internet www.mohca.gov.bt.

Ministry of Information and Communications: Thori Lam, Lower Motithang, POB 278, Thimphu; tel. (2) 322144; fax (2) 324860; e-mail secretary@moic.gov.bt; internet www.moic.gov.bt.

Ministry of Labour and Human Resources: Thongsel Lam, Lower Motithang, POB 1036, Thimphu; tel. (2) 333867; fax (2) 326731; e-mail webadmin@molhr.gov.bt; internet www.molhr.gov.bt.

Ministry of Works and Human Settlement: POB 791, Thimphu; tel. (2) 327998; fax (2) 323122; e-mail webmaster@mowhs.gov.bt; internet www.mowhs.gov.bt.

Anti-Corruption Commission: POB 1113, Thimphu; tel. (2) 334863; fax (2) 334865; e-mail netenz@druknet.bt; internet www.anti-corruption.org.bt; f. 2006; Chair. Dasho Aum NETEN ZANGMO; Commrs THINLAY WANGDI, KEZANG JAMTSHO.

Cabinet Secretariat: Tashichhodzong, POB 1011, Thimphu; tel. (2) 321437; fax (2) 321438; e-mail cabinet@druknet.bt; internet www.cabinet.gov.bt.

Gross National Happiness Commission: Convention Centre, POB 127, Thimphu; tel. (2) 325192; fax (2) 322928; e-mail info@gnhc.gov.bt; internet www.gnhc.gov.bt; f. 2008 to replace Planning Commission (f. 1971); Chair. TSHERING TOBGAY; Vice-Chair. Lyonpo WANGDI NORBU; Sec. KARMA TSHITEEM.

His Majesty's Secretariat: Tashichhodzong, Thimphu; tel. (2) 335530; fax (2) 335519; Sec. Dasho AGAY UGEN DORJI TRONGSA DRONGYER.

National Environment Commission: POB 466, Thimphu; tel. (2) 323384; fax (2) 323385; e-mail secretary@nec.gov.bt; internet www.nec.gov.bt; Sec. Dr UGYEN TSHEWANG.

National Land Commission: Thimphu; tel. (2) 336062; fax (2) 336063; e-mail sangaykhandu@hotmail.com; internet www.land.gov.bt; f. 2007; Sec. SANGAY KHANDU.

Royal Audit Authority: POB 191, Kawajangsa, Thimphu; tel. (2) 322111; fax (2) 323491; e-mail info@bhutanaudit.gov.bt; internet www.bhutanaudit.gov.bt; f. 1985; Auditor-Gen. UGEN CHEWANG.

Royal Civil Service Commission: POB 163, Thimphu; tel. (2) 322491; fax (2) 323086; e-mail misd@rcsc.gov.bd; internet www.rcsc.gov.bt; f. 1982 under Royal Charter; successor to Dept of Manpower; Chair. KARMA TSHITEEM; Commrs LHENDUP WANGCHUK, INDRAMAN CHETTRI, KARMA HAMU DORJI, KESANG DEKI.

Royal Privy Council (Gyal Doen Tshokdey): Thimphu; tel. (2) 337336; fax (2) 337258; f. 2009; Chair. Lyonpo CHENKYAB DORJI; Mems Dasho NADO RINCHEN, Dasho SANGAY WANGCHUG, Dr JAGAR DORJI.

Legislature

NATIONAL COUNCIL (UPPER HOUSE)

Within the National Council, 20 members—one representing each of the 20 electoral districts—are directly elected by a national vote, with the remaining five 'eminent persons' selected by royal appointment. The second elections to the National Council were held on 23 April 2013.

National Council: POB 200, Thimphu; tel. (2) 337370; fax (2) 325543; e-mail sonamtobgye@nationalcouncil.bt; internet www.nationalcouncil.bt.

Chairperson: Dasho SONAM KINGA.

Vice-Chairperson: TSHERING DORJI.

NATIONAL ASSEMBLY (LOWER HOUSE)

National Assembly: Gyelyong Tshokhang, POB 139, Thimphu; tel. (2) 322729; fax (2) 324210; e-mail sdhendup@nab.gov.bt; internet www.nab.gov.bt.

Speaker: JIGME ZANGPO.

Deputy Speaker: CHIMI DORJI.

Opposition Leader: PEMA GYAMTSHO.

General Election, second round, 13 July 2013

Party	% of votes	Seats
People's Democratic Party (PDP)	54.9	32
Druk Phuensum Tshogpa (DPT)	45.1	15
Total	100	47

Note: two other parties, the Druk Nyamrup Tshogpa and the Druk Chirwang Tshogpa, were eliminated in a primary round on 31 May 2013

Election Commission

Election Commission of Bhutan: Olakha, POB 2008, Thimphu; tel. (2) 334852; fax (2) 334763; e-mail cec@election-bhutan.org.bt; internet www.election-bhutan.org.bt; f. 2006; appointed by the King; Chief Election Commr Dasho KUNZANG WANGDI; Election Commrs Dasho CHOGYAL DAGO RIGDZIN, Aum DEKI PEMA.

Political Organizations

Having previously been banned in accordance with long-standing legislation, the formal registration of political parties commenced in 2007. By March 2008, when Bhutan's first national elections were held, only two parties—the Druk Phuensum Tshogpa and the People's Democratic Party—had successfully registered with the Election Commission. In January 2013 three new parties were granted formal registration.

Bhutan Kuen-Nyam Party (BKP): Thimphu; tel. (2) 324949; e-mail kuengyam@bkp.bt; internet bkp.bt; f. 2012; Pres. SONAM TOBGAY.

Druk Chirwang Tshogpa: Thimphu; tel. (2) 335336; fax (2) 322007; e-mail drukchirwangtshogpa@gmail.com; internet www.dct.bt; f. 2012; Pres. LILY WANGCHHUK.

Druk Nyamrup Tshogpa (DNT) (Solidarity, Justice and Freedom): Thimphu; tel. 77104849 (mobile); e-mail nyamrup@druknyamrup.info; internet www.druknyamrup.info; f. 2012; Pres. DORJI CHODEN; Vice-Pres. ACHYUT BHANDARI; Gen. Sec. TENZIN LEKPHELL.

Druk Phuensum Tshogpa (DPT) (Bhutan Peace and Prosperity Party): Chang Lam, Thimphu; tel. (2) 336337; fax (2) 335845; e-mail dpt@dpt.bt; internet www.dpt.bt; f. 2007 following merger of short-lived All People's Party and Bhutan United People's Party; Pres. Dr PEMA GYAMTSHO; Sec.-Gen. UGYEN DORJI.

People's Democratic Party (PDP): POB 835, Thimphu; tel. (2) 335557; fax (2) 335757; e-mail info@pdp.bt; internet www.pdp.bt; f. 2007 in asscn with a minister of the outgoing Govt; Pres. Lyonpo TSHERING TOBGAY; Sec.-Gen. SONAM JATSHO.

Outside of Bhutan, there are a number of anti-Government organizations, composed principally of Nepali-speaking former residents of Bhutan, based in Kathmandu, Nepal, and New Delhi, India.

Bhutan Communist Party (Marxist-Leninist-Maoist) (BCP—MLM): Nepal; f. 2003; advocates complete revolution in Bhutan; Gen. Sec. VIKALPA.

Bhutan Gurkha National Liberation Front (BGNLF): Nepal; f. 1994; mem. National Front for Democracy in Bhutan, a coalition also involving the BPP and the DNC; Vice-Pres. D. R. KATEL; Gen. Sec. LALIT PRADHAN.

Bhutan National Democratic Party (BNDP): POB 3334, Kathmandu, Nepal; tel. (1) 525682; f. 1992; also has offices in Delhi and Varanasi, India, and in Jhapa, Nepal; Acting Pres. D. N. S. DHAKAL; Gen. Sec. Dr HARI P. ADHIKARI.

Bhutan People's Party (BPP): POB 13, Anarmani-4, Bhadrapur Rd, Birtamode, Jhapa, Nepal; tel. and fax (23) 542561; e-mail bpparty@ntc.net.np; f. 1990 as a successor to the People's Forum for Human Rights–Bhutan (f. 1989); advocates unconditional release of all political prisoners, judicial reform, freedom of religious practices, linguistic freedom, freedom of press, speech and expression, and equal rights for all ethnic groups; Pres. BALA RAM POUDYAL; Gen. Sec. DURGA GIRI.

Druk National Congress (DNC): Boudha 6, POB 5754, Kathmandu, Nepal; tel. (1) 2298060; e-mail dnc2006@gmail.com; internet www.bhutandnc.com; f. 1994; advocates democracy and human rights in Bhutan; Pres. KESANG LHENDUP; Gen. Sec. KARMA DUPTHO.

Druk National Congress (Democratic) (DNC—D): Kakarvitta, Jhapa, Nepal; tel. (23) 563190 (Nepal); e-mail general@dncbhutan.com; breakaway faction of the Druk National Congress; Pres. RINZIN DORJI; Gen. Sec. KARJAY.

Human Rights Organization of Bhutan (HUROB): Patan Dhoka, POB 172, Lalitpur, Kathmandu, Nepal; tel. (1) 525046 (Nepal); fax (1) 526038 (Nepal); e-mail hurob1991@gmail.com; f. 1991; documents alleged human rights violations in Bhutan and co-ordinates welfare activities in eight refugee camps in Nepal for ethnic Nepalese claiming to be from Bhutan; Chair. S. B. SUBBA; Gen. Sec. OM DHUNGEL.

Diplomatic Representation

EMBASSIES IN BHUTAN

Bangladesh: Plot HIG 3, Upper Chubachu, POB 178, Thimphu; tel. (2) 322539; fax (2) 322629; e-mail bdoot@druknet.bt; Ambassador JISHNU ROY CHOUDHURY.

India: India House Estate, Jungshina, POB 193, Thimphu; tel. (2) 322162; fax (2) 323195; e-mail eoiprothi@gmail.com; internet www.indianembassythimphu.bt; Ambassador V. P. HARAN.

Judicial System

Bhutan has Civil and Criminal Codes, which are based on those laid down by the Shabdrung Ngawang Namgyal in the 17th century. A substantially revised Civil and Criminal Procedure Code was endorsed by the National Assembly in 2001. Following the promulgation of the new Constitution in July 2008, the Supreme Court of Bhutan was established as the highest appellate authority in the country; the Court was first convened in 2010. The Supreme Court is a Court of Record and acts as the guardian of the Constitution; it is the highest appellate authority to entertain appeals against the judgments, orders or decisions of the High Court. The Supreme Court normally consists of a Chief Justice and four judges (or drangpons), appointed by the King on the recommendation of the National Judicial Commission.

The High Court was established in 1967 to review appeals from Lower Courts, although some cases are heard at the first instance. The Full Bench is presided over by the Chief Justice. There are a maximum of eight other judges. Three judges form a quorum.

There is a district court in each of Bhutan's administrative districts (dzongkhags), which tries most cases within its territorial jurisdiction. Appeals are made to the High Court, and less serious civil disputes may be settled by a village headman (gup or mandal) through written undertakings (genja) by the parties concerned. In accordance with the new Constitution adopted in 2008, all 15 subdistricts (dungkhags) had functioning separate courts.

All citizens have the right to make informal appeal for redress of grievances directly to the King, through the office of the gyalpoi zimpon (court chamberlain).

Supreme Court: POB 132, Royal Court of Justice, Thimphu; tel. (2) 322613; fax (2) 322921; e-mail judiciary@druknet.bt; internet www.judiciary.gov.bt; Chief Justice Lyonpo SONAM TOBGYE.

High Court: Thimphu; tel. (2) 322344; fax (2) 322921; internet www.judiciary.gov.bt; f. 1967; Chief Justice of the High Court SANGAY KHANDU (acting).

Office of the Attorney-General: POB 1045, Thori Lam, Lower Motithang, Thimphu; tel. (2) 326889; fax (2) 324606; e-mail oag@oag.gov.bt; internet oag.gov.bt; f. 2006; fmrly Office of Legal Affairs; Chief Prosecutor (vacant); Attorney-Gen. PHUNTSHO WANGDI.

Religion

The state religion is Mahayana Buddhism. An estimated 75% of the population practice Buddhism. The southern Bhutanese, however, are predominantly followers of Hinduism, and the faith accounts for around 22% of the population. The main Buddhist monastic group, the Central Monastic Body, led by an elected Head Abbot (Je Khenpo), is directly supported by the state and spends six months of the year at Tashichhodzong and at Punakha, respectively. The various District Monastic Bodies are sustained by the lay population.

Commission for Religious Organizations (Chhoedey Lhentshog): c/o Department of Culture, Ministry of Home and Cultural Affairs, POB 233, Thimphu; tel. (2) 336500; fax (2) 336500; e-mail crogovbt@gmail.com; internet www.cro.gov.bt; f. 2009.

Council for Ecclesiastical Affairs (Dratshang Lhentshog): POB 254, Thimphu; tel. (2) 322754; fax (2) 323867; e-mail dratshang@druknet.bt; f. 1984, replacing the Central Board for Monastic Studies, to oversee the national memorial chorten (a mound-like structure containing Buddhist relics) and all Buddhist meditational centres and schools of Buddhist studies, as well as the Central and District Monastic Bodies; daily affairs of the Council are run by the Central Monastic Secretariat; Chair. His Holiness the 70th Je Khenpo TRULKU JIGME CHOEDRA; Sec. KARMA PENJOR.

Hindu Dharma Samudaya of Bhutan (HDSB): Motithang, Thimphu; tel. (2) 329245; fax (2) 326267; e-mail hindudharma@druknet.bt; internet www.bhutanhindudharma.com; f. 2007; promotes Hindu religion and values; Chair. Dasho MEGHRAJ GURUNG; Exec. Dir DIPENDRA GIRI.

The Press

Some of the main newspapers and periodicals are listed below.

Bhutan Observer: POB 1112, Norzin Lam, Thimphu; tel. (2) 334891; fax (2) 327981; e-mail editor@bhutanobserver.bt; internet www.bhutanobserver.bt; f. 2006; weekly newspaper; publ. in English and Dzongkha; Man. Dir TENZIN WANGDI; Man. Editor RABI C. DAHAL.

Bhutan Times: POB 1365, Top Floor, Etho Metho Plaza, Norzim Lam, Thimphu; tel. (2) 335006; fax (2) 328451; e-mail bttimes@druknet.bt; internet www.bhutantimes.bt; f. 2006; weekly newspaper; publ. by Bhutan Times Ltd; English and Dzongkha edns; publ. *Bhutan NOW* magazine; Chair. UGEN TSHECHUP; Man. Ed. NAMKHAI NORBU.

Bhutan Today: POB 1532, Thimphu; tel. (2) 336806; fax (2) 336805; internet www.bhutantoday.bt; f. 2008; bi-weekly newspaper; Publr and Chair. NGAWANG DORJI; Man. Dir TENZIN DORJI; Editor M. B. SUBBA.

The Bhutanese: Changangkha, Thegchen Lam, POB 1694, Thimphu; tel. (2) 335605; fax (2) 335593; e-mail editor.thebhutanese@gmail.com; internet www.thebhutanese.bt; f. 2012; bi-weekly; English; CEO TENZING LAMSANG.

Business Bhutan: Norzim Lam, POB 1190, Thimphu; tel. (2) 339904; fax (2) 339882; e-mail editor@businessbhutan.bt; internet www.businessbhutan.bt; f. 2009; weekly newspaper; English and Dzongkha edns; CEO TSHERING WANGCHUK; Editor PHURBA D. DORJI.

Druk Neytshuel: POB 488, Thimphu; tel. (2) 326717; fax (2) 326705; e-mail drukneytshuel@gmail.com; f. 2010; weekly; the country's first exclusively Dzongkha newspaper; CEO SINGYE DORJI; Editor CHIMI DORJI.

Drukpa: POB 885, Thimphu; tel. (2) 324177; fax (2) 324178; e-mail drukpaletters@gmail.com; internet www.drukpa.bt; f. 2009; monthly news magazine; Publr JIGME TSHULTIM, Jr; Editor MITRA RAJ DHITAL.

The Journalist: POB 1336, Norzim Lam, Thimphu; tel. (2) 327540; fax (2) 321680; e-mail iamthejournalist@gmail.com; internet www.thejournalist.bt; f. 2009; weekly Sun. newspaper; CEO SONAM GYELTSHEN; Editor KINLEY TSHERING.

Kuensel: POB 204, Thimphu; tel. (2) 322483; fax (2) 322975; e-mail editor@kuensel.com.bt; internet www.kuenselonline.com; f. 1965 as a weekly govt bulletin; reorg. as a national weekly newspaper in 1986; became autonomous corporation in 1992 (previously under Dept of Information), incorporating former Royal Government Press; 6 issues weekly from 2009; in English and Dzongkha; offered 49% of shares to public in 2006, while Government retained controlling 51%; Man. Dir CHENCHO TSHERING; Editor UGYEN PENJOR.

PRESS ORGANIZATIONS AND ASSOCIATIONS

Bhutan Media Foundation (BMF): POB 1655, Thori Lam, Thimphu; tel. (2) 331705; fax (2) 331702; e-mail bhutanmediafoundation@gmail.com; internet www.bmf.bt; f. 2010; est. through a Royal Charter; fosters responsible media development; promotes use of Dzongkha in national media; Chair. CHENCHO TSHERING; Exec. Dir DAWA PENJOR.

Journalists' Association of Bhutan: Gawa Building, Motithang, Thimphu; tel. (2) 327827; e-mail generalsecretary.jab@gmail.com; internet www.jabbhutan.com; f. 2006; dissolved in 2007, revived in 2012; Pres. PASSANG DORJI; Gen. Sec. KINLEY TSHERING.

Publishers

Absolute Bhutan Books: POB 698, Thimphu; tel. (2) 335336; fax (2) 332007; e-mail abs@druknet.bt; internet www.absolutebhutanbooks.com.bt; publr of books and journals; CEO LILY WANGCHHUK.

KMT Printers and Publishers: Thimphu; tel. (2) 325026; fax (2) 324081; publs incl. books, journals and textbooks; organizer of National Book Fair, Thimphu; Gen. Man. PEMA TASHI; Man. Dir LOPEN KINZANG THINLEY.

Rabsell Media Services: POB 1321, Thimphu; tel. (2) 334641; publr of books on history of Bhutanese royal family; co-publr of Discover Bhutan magazine; Gen. Man. TSHERING WANGCHUCK.

Broadcasting and Communications

REGULATORY AUTHORITY

Bhutan Infocomm and Media Authority (BICMA): POB 1072, Olakha, Thimphu; tel. (2) 321506; fax (2) 326909; e-mail bicma@bicma.gov.bt; internet www.bicma.gov.bt; f. 2000 as Bhutan Telecommunications Authority under Bhutan Telecommunications Act; telecommunications and media regulatory body; regulatory remit extended to include Information and Communication Technology and media services in 2005; began operations as autonomous authority, independent of Ministry of Information and Communications, from 1 January 2007; Dir SONAM PHUNTSHO.

TELECOMMUNICATIONS

In December 2012, according to the Ministry of Information and Communications, there were 560,890 mobile cellular telephone subscribers (77.8% of the total population) and 27,005 fixed-line subscribers. In addition, there were 133,289 internet subscribers.

Bhutan Telecom Ltd: 2/28 Drophen Lam, Thimphu; tel. (2) 322026; fax (2) 324312; e-mail bt@bt.bt; internet www.telecom.net.bt; f. 2000; state-owned public corpn; fmr regulatory authority and monopoly provider of telecommunications services; latterly a provider of fixed-line, mobile and internet services; responsible for the development of national telecommunications infrastructure; CEO NIDUP DORJI.

B-Mobile: Drophen Lam, POB 134, Thimphu; tel. (2) 320194; fax (2) 320193; e-mail mkto@telecom.net.bt; internet www.telecom.net.bt; f. 2002; offered mobile cellular tel. services from Nov. 2003; c. 420,000 subscribers (2012); subsidiary of Bhutan Telecom Ltd; Gen. Man. PUSHPA MANI PRADHAN.

DrukNet: 2/28 Drophen Lam, POB 134, Thimphu; tel. (2) 320118; fax (2) 328160; e-mail info@druknet.bt; internet www.druknet.bt; f. 1999; internet service provider; subsidiary of Bhutan Telecom Ltd; Gen. Man. TSHERING NORBU.

Tashi InfoComm Ltd (TashiCell): POB 1502, Norzim Lam, Thimphu; tel. 77889977 (mobile); fax 77229977; e-mail mail@tashicell.com; internet www.tashicell.com; f. 2008; first privately owned mobile cellular tel. co in Bhutan; c. 139,000 subscribers (2012); Chair. WANGCHUK DORJI; Man. Dir TASHI TSHERING.

BROADCASTING

Radio

The country's first private radio stations were granted FM operating licences in 2006. By December 2012 there were six private stations in operation.

Bhutan Broadcasting Service (BBS): POB 101, Thimphu; tel. (2) 323071; fax (2) 323073; e-mail bbs@bbs.com.bt; internet www.bbs.com.bt; f. 1973 as Radio Nat. Youth Asscn of Bhutan (NYAB); became autonomous corpn in 1992, but remains 100% state-owned; short-wave radio station broadcasting daily in Dzongkha, Sharchopkha, Nepali (Lhotsamkha) and English; FM broadcasts are 24 hours a day in Dzongkha, 7 hours a day in Nepali and Sharchopkha and 12 hours a day in English; a television service was launched in 1999; in early 2012 a second TV channel (BBS 2) was launched; Chair. Aum SANGAY ZAM; Man. Dir THINLEY DORJI; Gen. Man. (TV) TASHI DORJI.

Centennial Radio 101 FM: Kawajangsa, POB 778, Thimphu; tel. (2) 336188; fax (2) 333533; e-mail centennialradio@gmail.com; internet www.centennialradio.com; f. 2008; news, current affairs, music and entertainment programmes; Chair. DORJI WANGCHUK.

Kuzoo FM: POB 419, Thimphu; tel. and fax (2) 335262; e-mail fm@kuzoo.net; internet www.kuzoo.net; f. 2006; broadcasts 24 hours a day on FM in Dzongkha and English; news, information and entertainment programmes; CEO KINCHHO TSERING (acting).

Radio Valley: Rabten Lam, above Pension Board Colony, POB 1373, Thimphu; tel. (2) 322567; fax (2) 331299; e-mail radiovalley@gmail.com; f. 2007; broadcasts 12 hours a day on FM; music, entertainment and information programmes to be broadcast upon commencement of full operations; Founder KINLEY CHOZOM.

Television

Television was officially introduced as recently as 1999, when the state broadcaster BBS launched a limited service in Thimphu. A nation-wide television service via satellite commenced in 2006, allowing BBS to broadcast to almost 40 countries. BBS broadcasts are limited to 10 hours a day and consist principally of national news and documentaries. In 1999 the Government issued the first licences to cable television operators. By mid-2007, according to official figures, there were 52 cable television operators providing more than 40 channels. Limited 'direct-to-home' private satellite services were approved in 2009.

Bhutan Broadcasting Service (BBS): see Radio.

Finance

(cap. = capital; auth. = authorized; p.u. = paid up; res = reserves; dep. = deposits; m. = million; brs = branches; amounts in ngultrum)

BANKING

Central Bank

Royal Monetary Authority (RMA): POB 154, Thimphu; tel. (2) 323111; fax (2) 322847; e-mail rmarsd@rma.org.bt; internet www.rma.org.bt; f. 1982; bank of issue; frames and implements official monetary policy, co-ordinates the activities of financial institutions and holds foreign exchange deposits on behalf of the Govt; cap. 800m., res 15,391.5m., total financial assets 59,336m. (Dec. 2013); Gov. and Chair DAW TENZIN.

Commercial Banks

Bank of Bhutan Ltd: Samdrup Lam, POB 75, Phuentsholing; tel. (5) 252402; fax (5) 252955; e-mail gm_pmb@bob.bt; internet www.bob.bt; f. 1968; 20% owned by the State Bank of India and 80% by the Govt of Bhutan; wholly managed by Govt of Bhutan from 1997; cap. 400m., res 2,424.8m., dep. 22,302.9m. (Dec. 2011); Chair. KARMA W. PENJOR; 41 brs (April 2014).

Bhutan National Bank Ltd (BNB): POB 439, Thimphu; tel. (2) 328577; fax (2) 328839; internet www.bnb.com.bt; f. 1996; Bhutan's second commercial bank; partially privatized in 1998; 13.6% owned by Govt and 20.1% by Asian Development Bank; cap. 675.8m., res 2,232m., dep. 20,230m. (Dec. 2011); Chair. KUNZANG DECHEN; CEO KIPCHU TSHERING; 10 brs.

Druk PNB Bank Ltd: Norzim Lam, POB 502, Thimphu; tel. (2) 324497; fax (2) 333156; e-mail corporate@drukpnbbank.bt; internet www.drukpnbbank.bt; f. 2010; 51% owned by Punjab National Bank (India), 19% by local promoters and 30% by Bhutanese public; share cap. 499.027m. (Dec. 2012), dep. 4,143.4m. (Dec. 2011); CEO MUKESH DAVE; five brs.

T Bank Ltd: TCC Complex Bldg, Norzin Lam, POB 631, Thimphu; tel. (2) 337283; fax (2) 336236; e-mail ho@tbank.bt; internet www.tbankltd.com; f. 2010; 60% owned by Tashi Group, 40% owned by public; cap. 220m., dep. 3,204.3 (Dec. 2011); CEO TSHERING DORJI.

Development Bank

Bhutan Development Bank Ltd (BDBL): POB 256, Thimphu; tel. (2) 322579; fax (2) 323428; e-mail info@bdb.bt; internet www.bdb.bt; f. 1988; provides industrial loans and short- and medium-term agricultural loans; fmrly Bhutan Development Finance Corpn Ltd, name changed as above 2011; 93.50% state-owned; cap. p.u. 100m., receivable loans 2,220.9m. (2008); Chair. NIM DORJI; Man. Dir PEMA TSHERING; 3 regional offices, 29 brs and 2 sub-brs.

STOCK EXCHANGE

Royal Securities Exchange of Bhutan Ltd (RSEB): POB 742, Thimphu; tel. (2) 323994; fax (2) 323849; e-mail rseb@druknet.bt; internet www.rsebl.org.bt; f. 1993; supervised by the Royal Monetary Authority; open to Bhutanese nationals only; 21 listed cos (2014); Chair. DAW TENZIN; CEO DORJI PHUNTSHO.

INSURANCE

Bhutan Insurance Ltd: Chorten Lam, POB 779, Thimphu; tel. (2) 339893; fax (2) 339895; e-mail bhutaninsurancelimited@gmail.com; internet www.bhutaninsurance.com.bt; f. 2009; 40% owned by private investors, 60% to be offered to public shareholders; provides personal, commercial and industrial insurance, and motor vehicle third-party liability insurance; Chair. UGYEN RINZIN; Man. Dir and CEO TSHERING GYALTSHEN.

Royal Insurance Corporation of Bhutan Ltd: POB 315, Thimphu; tel. (2) 322426; fax (2) 323677; e-mail insure@druknet.bt; internet www.ricb.com.bt; f. 1975; provides general and life insurance and credit investment services; Chair. Dasho TOPGYAL DORJI; CEO Dasho NAMGYAL LHENDUP; 10 brs and development centres.

Trade and Industry

GOVERNMENT AGENCIES

Druk Holding and Investments Ltd (DHI): POB 1127, Motithang, Thimphu; tel. (2) 336257; fax (2) 336259; e-mail info@dhi.bt; internet www.dhi.bt; f. 2007 to manage the existing and future investments of the Govt; managed an initial grouping of 14 cos in sectors incl. hydropower, banking, minerals and natural resources; cap. p.u. Nu 44,268.3m. (2009); Chair. Lyonpo OM PRADHAN; Man. Dir KARMA YONTEN.

Food Corporation of Bhutan (FCB): POB 080, Phuentsholing; tel. (5) 252241; fax (5) 252289; e-mail drukfood@druknet.bt; internet www.fcb-bhutan.com; f. 1974; activities include procurement and distribution of food grains and other essential commodities through appointed FCB agents; marketing of surplus agricultural and horticultural produce through FCB-regulated market outlets; maintenance of buffer stocks to offset any emergency food shortages; export of cash crop products; Chair. TENZIN DHENDUP; CEO KARMA NIDUP.

State Trading Corpn of Bhutan Ltd (STCB): POB 76, Phuentsholing; tel. (5) 252745; fax (5) 252619; e-mail stcbl@druknet.bt; internet www.stcb.bt; f. 1969; manages imports and exports of vehicles, IT and construction materials on behalf of the Govt; 51% govt-owned; initial public offering of 49% of shares in 1997; Man. Dir DORJI NAMGAY; brs in Thimphu (POB 272; tel. (2) 324785; fax (2) 323781; e-mail stcbthim@druknet.bt) and Kolkata (Calcutta), India (e-mail stcbkol@vsnl.net).

DEVELOPMENT ORGANIZATIONS

Construction Development Board: POB 1349, Thimphu; tel. (2) 326035; fax (2) 321989; e-mail cdb@druknet.bt; internet www.cdb.gov.bt; Chair Lyonpo DORJI CHODEN (Minister of Works and Human Settlement).

DHI Infra: POB 980, Langjophakha; tel. (2) 331853; fax (2) 332057; e-mail rinchenphuntsho@dhi.bt; internet www.dhiinfra.bt; f. 2011; est. to develop infrastructure projects and to accelerate socio-economic devt; projects incl. Bhutan Education City, Amochhu Land Reclamation and Township Project, and the est. of Special Economic Zones; subsidiary of Druk Holding and Investments Ltd; Chair. CHHEWANG RINZIN.

Natural Resources Development Corporation Ltd (NRDCL): POB 192, Thimphu; tel. (2) 323834; fax (2) 325585; e-mail info@nrdcl.bt; internet www.nrdcl.bt; fmrly Forestry Devt Corpn; renamed as above in 2007; fixes price of sand and timber; oversees quarrying and mining of sand, stone and other natural resources; Chair. PHUNTSHO NORBU; CEO KARMA DUKPA.

CHAMBER OF COMMERCE

Bhutan Chamber of Commerce and Industry (BCCI): Doebum Lam, POB 147, Thimphu; tel. (2) 322742; fax (2) 323936; e-mail bccihrd@gmail.com; internet www.bcci.org.bt; f. 1980; reorg. 1988; promotion of trade and industry and privatization, information dissemination, private sector human resource devt; 14 exec. mems; 20-mem. district exec. cttee; Pres. UGEN TSHECHUP DORJI; Sec.-Gen. PHUB TSHERING.

INDUSTRIAL AND TRADE ASSOCIATIONS

Association of Bhutanese Industries: POB 54, Phuentsholing; tel. (5) 251340; fax (5) 251341; e-mail abi@abibhutan.com; internet www.abibhutan.com; Pres. Dasho RINCHEN DORJI.

Bhutan Exporter Association: POB 256, Phuentsholing; tel. (5) 251917; fax (5) 251918; e-mail beap@druknet.bt; internet www.bhutaniea.org; Pres. GELEG NIMA.

Construction Association of Bhutan: POB 1075, Thimphu; tel. (2) 327830; fax (2) 327831; e-mail cab@druknet.bt; f. 2000; Pres. AUM PHUB ZAM.

Handicraft Association of Bhutan: POB 870, Thimphu; tel. (2) 338089; e-mail officehab@gmail.com; internet www.handicraftsbhutan.org; f. 2005; Pres. TEN DORJI.

Wood Based Industries Association: POB 1601, Phuentsholing; tel. (2) 337364; Pres THUBDRUP GYELTSHEN.

UTILITIES

Electricity

Bhutan Electricity Authority (BEA): c/o Ministry of Economic Affairs, Tashichhodzong, POB 1557, Thimphu; tel. (2) 327317; fax (2) 337076; e-mail bea@druknet.bt; internet www.bea.gov.bt; f. 1991; regulates the electricity supply industry; CEO SAMDRUP K. THINLEY.

Bhutan Power Corporation Ltd: POB 580, Thimphu; tel. (2) 325095; fax (2) 322279; e-mail hrad@bpc.bt; internet www.bpc.bt; f. 2002; responsible for ensuring electricity supply for the whole country at an affordable cost by 2020 and for providing uninterrupted transmission access for export of surplus power; operations in 19 districts; Chair. ZIMPON PENJORE; Man. Dir BHARAT TAMANG YONZEN.

Department of Renewable Energy: c/o Ministry of Economic Affairs, Tashichhodzong, POB 266, Thimphu; tel. (2) 322709; fax (2) 324676; e-mail info@moea.gov.bt; internet www.moea.gov.bt/departments/department.php?id=5; Dir KARMA TSHERING.

Druk Green Power Corpn Ltd: POB 1351, Thimphu; tel. (2) 336413; fax (2) 336417; internet www.drukgreen.bt; f. 2008 on amalgamation of management of Basochhu Hydropower Corpn, Chhukha Hydropower Corpn and Kurichhu Project Authority; assumed control of Tala Hydroelectric Project Authority in April 2009; combined installed capacity 1,480 MW; Dagachhu Project (114 MW) to be commissioned in near future; intended to manage all future power projects in Bhutan; cap. p.u. Nu 6,855m. (2009); Chair. KARMA TSHITEEM; Man. Dir Dasho CHHEWANG RINZIN.

Water

Thimphu City Corporation (Water Supply Unit): POB 215, Thimphu; tel. (2) 324710; fax (2) 324315; e-mail tda@druknet.bt; f. 1982; responsible for water supply of Thimphu municipality; Head BHIMLAL DHUNGEL.

TRADE UNIONS

Under long-standing legislation, trade union activity is illegal in Bhutan. In 2007 a Labour Act was passed, permitting (among other things) the formation of 'workers' associations'.

Transport

ROADS AND TRACKS

Prior to the 1960s, Bhutan had no paved roads. Construction of an east–west highway, connecting Phuentsholing in the south-west with Trashigang in the east and running mainly through central areas of the country, commenced in the early 1960s. By 2010 there were 6,920 km of roads in Bhutan, of which some 2,794 km were black-topped and included 2,259 km of national highways. Surfaced roads link the important border towns of Phuentsholing, Gelephu, Sarpang and Samdrup Jongkhar in southern Bhutan to towns in West Bengal and Assam in India. A Roads Sector Master Plan (2007–27) envisaged the construction of more than 2,500 km of feeder roads throughout Bhutan, a second east–west highway (794 km) in southern Bhutan, and 410 km of highways to improve inter-connectivity between districts.

The number of vehicles on Bhutan's roads increased almost threefold during 2001–11: in December 2011 there were 62,707 registered vehicles, compared with just 22,527 in 2001. By the end of 2013 there were 67,926 motor vehicles, almost 90% of which were registered in the Thimphu and Phuentsholing districts. The provision of public bus services has also expanded rapidly in recent years.

Road Safety and Transport Authority: Thimphu; tel. (2) 321284; fax (2) 321281; e-mail dg@rsta.gov.bt; internet www.rsta.gov.bt; f. 1995; under Ministry of Information and Communications; regulates all motor vehicle activities and surface transport services; Dir LHAM DORJI.

Bhutan Postal Corpn: GPO Bldg, Chang Lam, Thimphu; tel. (2) 325734; fax (2) 323108; e-mail citybus@bhutanpost.com.bt; internet www.bhutanpost.com.bt/index.php?id=71; in addition to postal services, operates a number of bus routes linking Thimphu with surrounding areas, a Thimphu–Phuentsholing service and a Phuentsholing–Kolkata (India) service.

RAILWAYS

In 2009 an agreement was signed by Bhutan and India to construct Bhutan's first rail link: a strategically important 18-km line connecting Hasimara in West Bengal with Toribari in southern Bhutan. However, by late 2011, with opposition to the proposed route from various groups in West Bengal, the India-funded project had stalled and alternative routes were under consideration.

CIVIL AVIATION

There is an international airport at Paro, and a runway strip at Trashigang. Two domestic airports, at Yonphula (34 km south of Trashigang) and Bumthang became operational in late 2011; a third domestic airport, at Gelephu, was inaugurated in October 2012. In December 2011 Bhutan's first private airline, Tashi Air (also known as Bhutan Airlines), launched domestic services from Paro to Bumthang and Yonphula. However, in 2013 domestic services to Gelephu and Yonphula were suspended for repairs and upgrade works. In addition there are some 60 helicopter landing pads.

Department of Civil Aviation: c/o Ministry of Information and Communications, POB 1229, Woochu, Paro; tel. (8) 271347; fax (8) 271909; e-mail aviation@druknet.bt; internet www.dca.gov.bt; state-owned; f. 1986; Dir WANGDI GYALTSHEN.

Druk Air Corpn Ltd (Royal Bhutan Airlines): Head Office, POB 1219, Nemeyzampa, Paro; tel. (8) 271856; fax (8) 271861; e-mail drukair@druknet.bt; internet www.drukair.com.bt; national airline; f. 1981; became fully operational in 1983; domestic routes and services from Paro to destinations in India (Delhi, Kolkata, Bagdogra, Guwahati and Gaya), Bangladesh, Myanmar, Nepal, Singapore and Thailand; Chair. KESANG WANGDI; CEO TANDIN JAMTSHO; 210,453 int. passengers (2012).

Tashi Air (Bhutan Airlines): Phuentsholing; tel. (5) 252109; fax (5) 252110; e-mail tashi@tashigroup.bt; internet www.tashigroup.bt;

f. 2011; owned by the Tashi Group; domestic routes and services to Bangkok (Thailand) via Kolkata (India); CEO Capt. DAVID YOUNG.

Tourism

Bhutan was opened to tourism in 1974. Tourists travel in organized 'package', cultural or trekking tours, or individually, accompanied by trained guides; independent, unaccompanied travel is not permitted within the kingdom. In 1991 the Government began transferring the tourism industry to the private sector and licences were issued to new private tourism operators. In 2008 the Tourism Council of Bhutan was established as an autonomous intergovernmental agency, replacing the Department of Tourism, to optimize the role of the industry. The previously closed north-eastern region of Merak-Sakteng was opened to tour groups from September 2010. In 2012, according to the Royal Monetary Authority, tourist arrivals rose significantly: 43,929 foreign tourists visited the kingdom and receipts from tourism increased to US $62.8m.

Tourism Council of Bhutan (TCB): POB 126, Thimphu; tel. (2) 323251; fax (2) 323695; e-mail info@tourism.gov.bt; internet www.tourism.gov.bt; f. 2008 to replace the Department of Tourism; autonomous intergovernmental agency; manages and develops the tourism industry; Chair. Lyonchhen TSHERING TOBGAY (Prime Minister); Dir-Gen. THUJI DORJI NADIK (acting).

Association of Bhutanese Tour Operators (ABTO): POB 938, Thimphu; tel. (2) 322862; fax (2) 325286; e-mail abto@druknet.bt; internet www.abto.org.bt; f. 2000 to provide forum for mems' views and to unite, supervise and co-ordinate activities of mems; Chair. KARMA LOTEY; Exec. Dir SONAM DORJI; 245 mem. tour operators (March 2011).

Defence

The strength of the Royal Bhutan Army (RBA), which was established in the 1950s and which is under the direct command of the King, was officially said to number 9,021 at June 2007. Membership of the RBA is based on voluntary recruitment augmented by a form of conscription. The RBA includes the Royal Bodyguards, an élite branch of the armed forces responsible for the security of the King, the royal family, and other high-ranking officials. Regular army training facilities are provided, on a functional basis, by an Indian military training team (IMTRAT), whose main personnel are stationed at Haa. The RBA and the Royal Bhutan Police were significantly strengthened from 2000 owing to the growing numbers of armed Indian militants who had established military camps on southern Bhutanese territory. In 2007, however, army officials proposed a reduction in military personnel to 8,000. In addition, the National Assembly resolved that recruitment and training of militia should be renewed.

No reference is made in the Indo-Bhutan Treaty to any aid by India for the defence of Bhutan. In November 1958, however, the Prime Minister of India declared that any act of aggression against Bhutan would be regarded as an act of aggression against India.

Expenditure on Public Order and Safety: 3,283.6m. ngultrum in 2012/13.

Supreme Commander in Chief of the Royal Bhutan Army: HM JIGME KHESAR NAMGYEL WANGCHUCK.

Chief of Operations, Royal Bhutan Army: Goongloen Wogma BATOO TSHERING.

Commandant of the Royal Bodyguards: Goongloen Wogma DHENDUP TSHERING.

Education

Traditionally, education in Bhutan was purely monastic, and the establishment of the contemporary state education system was the result of the reforming zeal of the third King, Jigme Dorji Wangchuck. In 2012/13 government expenditure on education totalled Nu 6,773.6m. (17.8% of total expenditure). In 2012 there were 61 privately operated schools (the majority in Thimphu), including 35 kindergartens; these schools were under the supervision of the Ministry of Education. In that year government operated schools included 44 primary and 183 secondary institutions. English is the medium of instruction, and Dzongkha is a compulsory subject.

The total number of enrolled students in Bhutan was 14,000 in 1974. By 2012, however, the total had risen to more than 176,000. Primary education begins with a pre-primary year (the minimum entry age being six years) and lasts for seven years. Secondary education lasts a further six years, with two years spent at each of three levels (lower, middle and higher). Tertiary education includes various first degree courses offered by 10 colleges under the supervision of the Royal University of Bhutan (RUB), which was established in 2003.

In 2012 enrolment at primary schools included 91% of children in the relevant age-group (boys 89%; girls 92%), while the ratio for secondary enrolment was 57% of pupils in the relevant age-group (boys 53%; girls 61%). Enrolment at primary schools increased from 9,039 (including only 456 girls, and excluding community primary schools) in 1970 to 50,733 (including 25,157 girls) in 2012. Between 1970 and 2012, enrolment at secondary schools increased from 714 (boys 690; girls 24) to 122,663 (boys 60,902; girls 61,761). In 2012 there 6,245 students attending tertiary institutes under the RUB.

BOLIVIA

Introductory Survey

LOCATION, CLIMATE, LANGUAGE, RELIGION, FLAG, CAPITAL

The Plurinational State of Bolivia is a landlocked state in South America, bordered by Chile and Peru to the west, by Brazil to the north and east, and by Paraguay and Argentina to the south. The climate varies, according to altitude, from humid tropical conditions in the northern and eastern lowlands, which are less than 500 m (1,640 ft) above sea level, to the cool and cold zones at altitudes of more than 3,500 m (about 11,500 ft) in the Andes mountains. The official languages are Spanish, Quechua and Aymara. Almost all of the inhabitants profess Christianity, and the great majority are adherents of the Roman Catholic Church. The national civil flag (proportions 2 by 3) has three equal horizontal stripes, of red, yellow and green. The state flag has, in addition, the national coat of arms in the centre of the yellow stripe. The legal capital is Sucre. The administrative capital and seat of government is La Paz.

CONTEMPORARY POLITICAL HISTORY

Historical Context

The Incas of Bolivia were conquered by Spain in 1538 and, although there were many revolts against Spanish rule, independence was not achieved until 1825. Bolivian history has been characterized by recurrent internal strife, resulting in a lengthy succession of presidents, and frequent territorial disputes with its neighbours, including the 1879–83 War of the Pacific between Bolivia, Peru and Chile, which resulted in the loss of Bolivia's coastline, and the Chaco Wars of 1928–30 and 1932–35 against Paraguay.

Domestic Political Affairs

At a presidential election in 1951 the largest share of the vote was won by Dr Víctor Paz Estenssoro, the candidate of the Movimiento Nacionalista Revolucionario (MNR), who had been living in Argentina since 1946. He was denied permission to return to Bolivia and contested the election *in absentia*. However, he failed to gain an absolute majority, and the incumbent President transferred power to a junta of army officers. This regime was overthrown in 1952, when a popular uprising enabled Paz Estenssoro to return from exile and assume the presidency. His Government, a coalition of the MNR and the Labour Party, committed itself to profound social revolution. The coalition nationalized the tin mines and introduced universal suffrage and land reform. Dr Hernán Siles Zuazo, a leading figure in the 1952 revolution, was elected President for the 1956–60 term, and Paz Estenssoro was again elected President in 1960. However, the powerful trade unions came into conflict with the Government, and in 1964, following widespread strikes and disorder, Paz Estenssoro was overthrown by the Vice-President, Gen. René Barrientos Ortuño, who was supported by the army. Barrientos served as Co-President alongside Gen. Alfredo Ovando Candía under a military junta, before his election to the presidency in July 1966.

President Barrientos encountered strong opposition from left-wing groups, including mineworkers' unions. There was also a guerrilla uprising in south-eastern Bolivia, led by Dr Ernesto ('Che') Guevara, the Argentine-born revolutionary who had played a leading role in the Castro regime in Cuba. However, the insurgency was suppressed by government troops, with the help of US advisers, and guerrilla warfare ended in October 1967, when Guevara was captured and killed. In April 1969 Barrientos was killed in an air crash and Vice-President Luis Adolfo Siles Salinas succeeded to the presidency. In September, however, Siles Salinas was deposed by the armed forces, who reinstated Gen. Ovando. He was forced to resign in October 1970, when, after a power struggle between right-wing and left-wing army officers, Gen. Juan José Torres González, supported by leftists, emerged as President, pledging support for agrarian reform and worker participation in management. A 'People's Assembly', formed by Marxist politicians, radical students and leaders of trade unions, was allowed to meet and demanded the introduction of extreme socialist measures, causing disquiet in right-wing circles. President Torres was deposed in August 1971 by Col (later Gen.) Hugo Banzer Suárez, who drew support from the right-wing Falange Socialista Boliviana and a section of the MNR, as well as from the army. In June 1973 Banzer announced an imminent return to constitutional government, but elections were postponed to June 1974. The MNR withdrew its support and entered into active opposition.

Following an attempted military coup in June 1974, all portfolios within the Cabinet were assigned to military personnel. After another failed coup attempt in November Banzer declared that elections had been postponed indefinitely and that his military regime would retain power until at least 1980. All political and union activity was banned. Political and industrial unrest in 1976, however, led Banzer to announce that elections would be held in July 1978. Allegations of fraud rendered the elections void, but Gen. Juan Pereda Asbún, the armed forces candidate in the elections, staged a successful military coup. In November his right-wing Government was overthrown in another coup, led by Gen. David Padilla Aranciba, Commander-in-Chief of the Army, with the support of national left-wing elements.

Presidential and congressional elections were held in July 1979. The presidential poll resulted in almost equal support for two ex-Presidents, Siles Zuazo and Paz Estenssoro, who were now leading rival factions of the MNR. An interim Government was formed under Walter Guevara Arce, but this administration was overthrown on 1 November by a right-wing army officer, Col Alberto Natusch Busch. He withdrew 15 days later after failing to gain the support of the Congreso (Congress), which elected Dra Lidia Gueiler Tejada, President of the Cámara de Diputados (Chamber of Deputies), as interim Head of State pending further elections.

The result of the 1980 presidential election was inconclusive, and in July, before the Congress could meet to decide between the two main contenders (again Siles Zuazo and Paz Estenssoro), a military junta led by an army commander, Gen. Luis García Meza, staged a coup—the 189th in Bolivia's 154 years of independence. In August 1981 a military uprising forced García to resign and transferred power to Gen. Celso Torrelio Villa, who declared his intention to return the country to democracy within three years. Labour unrest, provoked by Bolivia's severe economic crisis, was appeased by restitution of trade union and political rights, and a mainly civilian Cabinet was appointed in April 1982. The political liberalization disturbed the armed forces, who attempted to create a climate of violence, and President Torrelio resigned in July 1982, amid rumours of an impending coup. The junta installed the less moderate Gen. Guido Vildoso Calderón, the Army Chief of Staff, as President. Unable to resolve the worsening economic crisis or to control a general strike, the military regime announced that power would be handed over to the Congress that had originally been elected in 1980. Siles Zuazo was duly elected President by the Congress, and was sworn in for a four-year term in October 1982.

A return to democratic rule

President Siles Zuazo appointed a coalition Cabinet consisting of members of his own party, the Movimiento Nacionalista Revolucionario de Izquierda (MNRI), as well as the Movimiento de la Izquierda Revolucionaria (MIR) and the Partido Comunista de Bolivia (PCB). Economic aid from the USA and Europe was resumed, but the Government found itself unable to fulfil the expectations created by the return to democratic rule. The entire Cabinet resigned in August 1983, and the President appointed a Government that included more members of the right-wing of the MNRI, the Partido Demócrata Cristiano (PDC) and independents. The MIR and the MNR joined business interests in rejecting the Government's policy of complying with IMF conditions for assistance, which involved harsh economic measures. The Government lost its majority in the Congress and was confronted by strikes and mass labour unrest. Following a 48-hour general strike in December, the whole Cabinet again resigned, in anticipation of an opposition motion of censure. In

January 1984 President Siles Zuazo appointed a new coalition Cabinet.

At elections in July 1985, amid reports of electoral malpractice, the right-wing Acción Democrática Nacionalista (ADN), whose presidential candidate was the former dictator Gen. Hugo Banzer Suárez, received 29% of the votes cast, and the MNR obtained 26%, while the MIR was the leading left-wing party. At a further round of voting in the Congress in August, an alliance between the MNR and the leading left-wing groups, including the MIR, enabled Víctor Paz Estenssoro of the MNR to return to the presidency. The armed forces pledged their support for the new Government.

The new Government immediately introduced a very strict economic programme, designed to reduce inflation, which was estimated to have reached 14,173% in the year to August 1985. The trade union confederation, the Central Obrera Boliviana (COB), rejected the programme and called an indefinite general strike in September. The Government responded by declaring the strike illegal and by ordering a 90-day state of siege throughout Bolivia. Leading trade unionists were detained or banished, and thousands of strikers were arrested. The strike ended in October, when union leaders agreed to hold talks with the Government. However protests continued throughout 1986 and 1987, culminating in April 1988 with a national hunger strike, called by the COB.

Presidential and congressional elections took place in May 1989. No candidate had gained the requisite absolute majority, but Gen. Banzer Suárez of the ADN withdrew his candidacy in order to support his former adversary, Jaime Paz Zamora of the MIR, in a congressional vote. Paz Zamora was duly elected to the presidency in August and a coalition Government of 'national unity', the Acuerdo Patriótico, was then formed.

From 1988 the Government increased its efforts to suppress the illegal production of coca. As a result, during 1989 clashes between the drugs-control troops, Unidad Móvil de Patrullaje Rural (UMOPAR), and drugs-traffickers intensified. It soon became clear that the Government had failed to attain the targets of its coca eradication programme, having encountered staunch opposition from the powerful coca growers' organizations. Paz Zamora was critical of the militaristic approach of the USA to coca eradication and emphasized the need for economic and social support. In 1990, however, he accepted US $35m. in military aid from the USA.

In March 1991 the reputation of the Government was seriously undermined when three of its senior officials were forced to resign amid allegations of corruption. The appointment in February of Col Faustino Rico Toro as the new head of Bolivia's anti-drugs-trafficking force had provoked widespread outrage, owing to his alleged connections with drugs-traffickers and involvement in human rights abuses during his tenure as Chief of Army Intelligence in 1980–81, and led to his resignation. Meanwhile, following US accusations linking them with illegal drugs-traffickers, the Minister of the Interior, Migration and Justice and the Chief of Police also resigned. In 1993 the Supreme Court found the former military dictator Gen. Luis García Meza guilty on 49 charges of murder, human rights abuses, corruption and fraud, and sentenced him, *in absentia*, to 30 years' imprisonment. Similar sentences were imposed on 14 of his collaborators. García Meza was extradited from Brazil in 1994 and began his prison sentence in 1995.

A presidential election was held in June 1993. Again, no candidate secured the requisite absolute majority, so a congressional vote was scheduled to take place in August to decide between the two main contenders, Sánchez de Lozada of the MNR and Banzer Suárez, who was supported by both the ADN and the MIR. However, Banzer withdrew from the contest, thereby leaving Sánchez de Lozada's candidacy unopposed. At concurrent legislative elections the MNR secured the most seats in the bicameral Congress, although it had to form a coalition with the Unión Cívica Solidaridad (UCS) and the Movimiento Bolivia Libre (MBL) in order to secure a congressional majority.

In early 1995 government plans to privatize much of the education system and to restrict teachers' rights to union membership provoked industrial action by teachers nationwide. In response to a call by the COB for an indefinite strike the Government declared a state of siege for 90 days. Military units were deployed throughout the country, and 370 union leaders were arrested and banished to remote areas. The state of siege was extended by a further 90 days in July, owing to continued civil unrest, which had become particularly intense in the Chapare valley of Cochabamba, where UMOPAR forces had begun to occupy villages and to destroy coca plantations. Almost 1,000 coca growers were arrested in violent clashes between peasant farmers and UMOPAR personnel between July and September. Human rights organizations expressed alarm at the number of peasants killed and injured.

Continued opposition to the Government's capitalization programme led to further industrial unrest and a general strike in 1996. In April more than 100,000 transport workers took part in protests at the sale of the Eastern Railway to a Chilean company, and riots in La Paz resulted in damage to Chilean-owned railway property. In December a group of miners occupied a pit at Amayapampa in northern Potosí to protest at the actions of the mine's Canadian operators, who, they alleged, had failed to pay local taxes and had caused damage to the environment. When troops arrived at the site to remove the miners 10 protesters were killed and 50 others injured in ensuing clashes.

A presidential election was held in June 1997. The MNR's candidate was Juan Carlos Durán, the MIR presented Paz Zamora, while Banzer Suárez was the nominee of the ADN. In the event, Banzer secured 22% of the total votes, Durán won 18% and Paz Zamora received 17%. At legislative elections held concurrently the ADN failed to secure a majority of seats, but secured a congressional majority by means of a pact with the MIR, the UCS and Condepa. As a result, Banzer was elected President for a newly extended term of five years.

In early 1998 coca producers in the Cochabamba region announced their rejection of the Government's new anti-coca policy, claiming that an agreement, signed in the previous year, to provide alternative development programmes had not been honoured. Many observers believed that similar policies had been ineffective, as, despite the provision of US finance worth US $500m. since 1990 to eradicate the crop, there had been no net reduction in coca production. Violent clashes ensued when army and police personnel converged on the region in April 1998 to implement the eradication programme. More than 1,000 coca growers undertook an 800-km protest march from Chapare to La Paz in August. Demonstrations and roadblocks by coca growers in La Paz and Cochabamba during September were disrupted by security forces, leading to violent confrontations.

President Banzer resigned owing to ill health in August 2001 and was replaced by the Vice-President, Jorge Quiroga Ramírez. At a presidential election in June 2002 the main contenders were Sánchez de Lozada, again representing the MNR, Manfred Reyes Villa of the centre-right Nueva Fuerza Republicana, and Juan Evo Morales Aima, a coca grower leader, representing the left-wing Movimiento al Socialismo—Instrumento Político por la Soberanía de los Pueblos (MAS). In the event, Sánchez de Lozada won the largest share of the ballot (23%). Morales, who opposed the Government's free market economic policy and its coca eradication programme, performed unexpectedly well, coming second with 21% of the votes cast. As no candidate had achieved an absolute majority, however, the Congress voted to appoint Sánchez de Lozada to the presidency once more. Sánchez de Lozada formed a fragile coalition Government dominated by MNR and MIR members.

In February 2003 the Government's proposal to raise income tax rates drew widespread condemnation from representatives of middle- and lower-income groups, and prompted civil unrest. Following the Government's dismissal of their 40% wage-increase demand, approximately 7,000 armed police officers joined civilian protests in central La Paz. During the ensuing confrontation with military personnel some 32 people were killed and the President was forced to withdraw to safety. The riots prompted the resignation, on 19 February, of the entire Cabinet. In the following month the Government withdrew the proposed tax increase.

Civil unrest and the presidency of Carlos Mesa

Increasing civil unrest in El Alto, an industrial suburb of La Paz, prompted by dissatisfaction with the Government's management of Bolivia's natural energy resources, culminated in military intervention, resulting in the deaths of some 36 people on 12 October 2003. The following day protests in La Paz fuelled by the events in El Alto resulted in more violent clashes with the army, and a further 13 deaths. The violent suppression of the protests prompted the resignation of the Vice-President, Carlos Mesa Gisbert, and the Minister of Economic Development, and the COB declared an indefinite general strike. In an attempt to restore order, the Government announced that it would hold a referendum on gas exports and would revise existing energy legislation. Nevertheless, the civil unrest continued unabated and the death toll rose to an estimated 74. On 17 October Sánchez de Lozada resigned as President and fled to the USA. The Congress approved erstwhile Vice-President Mesa to succeed him. Mesa was sworn in as President on 18 October.

President Mesa appointed a Cabinet largely composed of independent technocrats, and notably restored the indigenous affairs portfolio abolished in February 2003. He pledged to re-examine the contentious gas export plan and announced proposals to reduce the coca eradication programme, attracting the cautious approval of peasant and coca growers' leaders. In September 2004 Mesa announced funding of some US $969m. over four years, for a strategy replacing forcible eradication with the cultivation of alternative crops. Accordingly, in November the Government signed an agreement with Evo Morales (in his capacity as leader of the coca growers) to suspend forcible eradication in the Chapare region. In October the Congress voted to prosecute former President Sánchez de Lozada and his Government on charges of genocide relating to the violent suppression of civil unrest in October 2003 in El Alto. By mid-2009 no such trial had been opened and consequently the Congress voted to suspend the President of the Supreme Court, Eddy Fernández. Nevertheless, in August 2011 the Ministers of Labour and Sustainable Development in the Sánchez de Lozada administration each received three-year gaol terms (subsequently suspended) for their involvement in the violence, while five senior military officers were given prison sentences of up to 15 years after being convicted on genocide charges. However, Sánchez de Lozada and most of the members of his former Cabinet continued to reside abroad, beyond the reach of the Bolivian judicial system.

In July 2004 a referendum was held on energy policy. The electorate was asked if it agreed with the abrogation of the hydrocarbons law that had been reintroduced by President Sánchez de Lozada; if state intervention in the oil and gas industry should be increased; if the state oil company, Yacimientos Petrolíferos Fiscales Bolivianos (YPFB), should reclaim shares in privatized energy companies; if Bolivia's gas reserves should be used as a negotiating tool to regain access to the Pacific Ocean; and if reform of the energy sector under broadly left-wing principles should be allowed to proceed. All five of the Government's proposals were accepted, but, despite this clear mandate for change, the resulting draft legislation caused great controversy. Specifically, there was disagreement as to whether extant contracts with energy sector companies should be voided and rewritten to provide for greater state control and revenue. Although various congressional, popular and indigenous groups strongly supported such moves, several foreign companies (notably, BP and Repsol) and foreign government delegations acting in their interests (notably, those of the USA, Brazil, Spain and the United Kingdom) voiced their opposition to any proposals they considered illegal under international law.

Also in late 2004 a broad-based coalition that included politicians, employers and trade unions from Santa Cruz and the oil- and gas-producing department of Tarija made increasingly vociferous demands for a referendum on greater regional autonomy or even full secession. This grouping was also opposed to an increased role for central government in the energy sector. A general strike was held in Santa Cruz and Tarija in November in support of greater autonomy. Civil unrest intensified and spread nationwide in the following month, in protest at significant increases in fuel prices. Throughout early 2005 the country suffered severe disruption from roadblocks and other acts of civil disobedience by protesters demanding, inter alia, a decrease in the price of fuel and greatly increased government revenues from the hydrocarbons sector. In response, Mesa announced that the fuel increases would be reduced from 23% to 15%. However, this was not enough to appease the protesters in Santa Cruz, where at a mass rally the Comité Cívico pro Santa Cruz declared the department to be autonomous and announced that it was to establish a provincial interim government. On the same day Mesa announced that provincial gubernatorial elections would be held on 12 June (departmental prefects were hitherto appointed by the President). However, this measure first required approval by referendum in order to be constitutional, and a constituent assembly was duly appointed. Confronted with continued protests, on 8 March Mesa submitted his resignation to the Congress, although this was rejected. On 16 March the upper house passed legislation that provided for a state royalty of 18% on hydrocarbons at the point of extraction and a further tax of 32%. Final approval of the legislation was given by the lower house on 5 May. Nevertheless, throughout April and May blockades, demonstrations and marches caused great disruption and shortages of goods and services nationwide. On 6 June President Mesa again submitted his resignation to the Congress, which was accepted. Owing to fears of exacerbating the civil conflict, the speakers of the Senado Nacional (Senate) and the Chamber of Deputies both waived their constitutional right to assume the presidency, which was instead assumed in a temporary capacity by a less partisan figure, Eduardo Rodríguez Veltzé, hitherto President of the Supreme Court.

The Government of Evo Morales

Legislative and presidential elections were held on 18 December 2005. Evo Morales, candidate of the MAS, was elected to the presidency with 54% of valid votes cast, while former Vice-President Jorge Quiroga Ramírez of the conservative Poder Democrático y Social (PODEMOS) received 29% of the ballot. The MAS also secured the most votes in the concurrent legislative elections, winning 72 of 130 seats in the Chamber of Deputies and 12 of the 27 seats in the Senate. Despite Morales' close alignment with the left-wing regimes of Venezuela and Cuba and his opposition to US counter-narcotics policy, the US Administration expressed its desire to work closely with the new Government.

Upon taking office, President Morales reiterated his electoral pledge to 'refound' the Bolivian state, by drafting a new constitution. To this end, in March 2006 a Government-sponsored enabling law was approved by the Congress allowing for the election of a constituent assembly and a concurrently held referendum on regional autonomy. The referendums were held on 2 July. The MAS garnered 54.4% of the vote, which translated into 137 seats in the 255-seat Constituent Assembly, considerably short of the two-thirds' majority Morales needed to be sure of gaining approval for his proposed reforms. PODEMOS secured only 15.0% of the ballot, or 60 seats, leaving it reliant on the support of other opposition parties to block government proposals. In the vote on regional autonomy, four of the country's nine departments were in favour of further devolution—Beni, Pando, Santa Cruz and Tarija. The Constituent Assembly was to draft a proposed constitution by August 2007, which would then be put to another referendum for approval. However, in September 2006 opposition members withdrew from the Assembly after MAS representatives endorsed a resolution that decisions would need approval only by a simple majority, rather than the two-thirds' majority originally agreed. The impasse was ended in November, after 10 independent members of the Assembly aligned themselves with the pro-Government bloc: it was agreed that the final proposed text of the constitution would require the approval of two-thirds of the members, but that individual clauses only needed a majority decision. Following further opposition, in January 2007 it was agreed that any individual clauses not accepted by a two-thirds' majority would also be put to a referendum, as well as the constitution as a whole.

In November 2006 the President attempted to weaken the power of the regional prefects (six of whom were from opposition parties) by proposing legislation that would allow the Congress to censure and dismiss departmental heads. The Government claimed the move would allow it better to distribute revenues from oil-producing regions to poorer areas. In response, the Governor of Cochabamba, Manfredo Reyes Villa, demanded that a further referendum on autonomy should be held in the region. Although the electorate in Cochabamba had voted against autonomy in July, if another vote returned a different result, it would put the pro-autonomy departments into a majority. Government supporters in Cochabamba held a massive rally against the proposal in January 2007. The protests and subsequent counter-protests descended into violence, with over 100 people injured and two killed. Reyes Villa was forced to flee the department, taking refuge in Santa Cruz, although he refused to resign.

Meanwhile, on 1 May 2006 President Morales issued a decree establishing the state's ownership of the hydrocarbons sector and increasing taxes for foreign companies operating in the sector from 50% to 82%. Foreign companies had 180 days to sign new contracts with the state hydrocarbons company YPFB or else cease operations in Bolivia. Although the announcement was widely viewed as 'nationalization' of the hydrocarbons sector, foreign concerns would be allowed to remain in the country as minority share-holders. In the following month Morales issued another decree giving the state the power to seize land it deemed unproductive, in order to redistribute it to landless farmers. It was estimated that some 20m.–30m. ha of land could be affected. In the face of much protest from land-owners, particularly in eastern Bolivia, the President pledged that productive farms would be left alone, as would any land gained legally. In late November the Government succeeded in gaining first congressional and then senate approval for the law (and for numerous new contracts with foreign oil companies). The new contracts with the foreign oil concerns were approved in April 2007.

The Constituent Assembly finally came into operation in February 2007. Morales' proposals for the new constitution included new rights of determination for the indigenous majority, with their own political systems and legally recognized leaders, greater state control of the economy, the election of supreme court judges by popular vote (rather than their appointment by the Congress) and the allowance of two consecutive five-year terms for Presidents. By July, however, disagreements over a proposal to transfer the seat of government back from La Paz to Sucre (where it had been located until 1899) led to disruption. A demonstration in La Paz, one of the largest in the country's history, was held in protest against the proposal. In August MAS delegates on the Assembly voted to exclude the issue from the agenda, prompting several weeks of unrest in Sucre. Some observers believed that the issue of relocating the capital from the poor western highlands to the relatively prosperous eastern region was being used by critics of Morales to sabotage his attempts to establish a more inclusive constitution, in which the country's wealth was more evenly distributed. Meanwhile, some 10,000 supporters of Morales marched from El Alto to the opposition-controlled Senate in La Paz, condemning the delegates in Sucre for stalling progress on the new constitution. The constitution was approved on 9 December by the required two-thirds of members present, although not by two-thirds of the membership, owing to a boycott by opposition delegates. Claims of procedural irregularities led the opposition to denounce the vote as illegal.

In February 2008 President Morales approved legislation setting 4 May as the date for an initial national referendum on the draft constitution. However, resistance from the PODEMOS-led opposition—particularly regional prefects of the affluent 'media luna' region (Bolivia's gas-rich eastern lowlands, comprising four of the nine regional departments) who claimed the charter favoured the country's indigenous population, and announced concurrent referendums on proposals for greater regional autonomy—provoked considerable political turmoil. The Corte Nacional Electoral (CNE—National Electoral Court), Bolivia's supreme electoral authority, subsequently ruled that all referendums were to be postponed indefinitely owing, *inter alia*, to the logistical obstacles to public consultations at such short notice. Nevertheless, the authorities in Santa Cruz held a referendum on the autonomy proposal on 4 May. Similar referendums were held in Beni, Pando and Tarija in June. In all of the plebiscites, which were deemed illegal by the Government, roughly four-fifths of votes cast were in favour of autonomy. Only days after the Santa Cruz vote, the opposition-controlled Senate approved legislation that instituted recall referendums for the President, Vice-President and departmental Prefects, in an attempt to force Morales to resign and thus postpone indefinitely a referendum to approve the constitution. In fact, the recall referendums, which were held on 10 August, resulted in a decisive victory for Morales and Vice-President Alvaro García Linera, whose continuance in office was supported by some 67% of valid votes.

The ongoing constitutional crisis descended into violence in September 2008. Opponents of Morales raided government buildings, set up roadblocks, sabotaged gas pipelines and fought with government supporters in the opposition-controlled departments of Beni, Pando, Santa Cruz, Chuquisaca and Tarija. In one incident on 11 September in Pando at least 18 government supporters were ambushed and shot dead and many others were injured or found to be missing. In response the Government imposed martial law and the Prefect of the department, Leopoldo Fernández, was arrested and charged with ordering the massacre. The heads of state of the 12 member countries of UNASUR (the Union of South American Nations, see p. 469) held an emergency summit in Chile on 15 September in response to the crisis, at which they declared their overwhelming support for Morales and stated that their nations would not tolerate any attempts to destabilize the Government.

Following further negotiations in late 2008 between the Government and a moderate faction of PODEMOS, agreement was secured on the final draft constitution and a referendum finally took place on 25 January 2009. Some 61% of the electorate voted in favour of the new Constitution, with support being highest in the western highlands, where the indigenous majority is concentrated, while the eastern lowlands rejected the charter. Legislation on electoral reform and the new Constitution was signed into law on 9 February. Under the new charter three new ministries were created, one of which, the Ministry of Autonomy, was charged with the task of restructuring local government and overseeing land reform. An electoral law was finally approved by the opposition-dominated Senate in April, which allowed for a presidential ballot to be held on 6 December. The legislation also set out the framework for votes on autonomy to be held in five regions.

Morales' second term

Morales was decisively re-elected as President on 6 December 2009, receiving 64.2% of the total votes cast, compared with Manfred Reyes Villa, candidate of the newly formed right-wing Plan Progreso para Bolivia–Convergencia Nacional, who garnered 26.5% of the ballot. The legislative election held concurrently resulted in a majority for the MAS in both chambers, with 88 of the 130 seats in the Chamber of Deputies and 26 of the 36 seats in the newly enlarged Senate. An estimated 95% of the eligible voters participated in the poll. Morales' victory, and particularly his party's new majority in the Senate, was seen as a powerful mandate for his ongoing programme of socialist reforms.

Gubernatorial and municipal elections in 4 April 2010 resulted in further success for the MAS, which won six of the nine gubernatorial posts. The elections carried added significance since they facilitated a key principle enshrined in the new Constitution, namely the decentralization of government. This process was formalized in July, when the legislature approved an autonomy framework law delineating the responsibilities of the new four-tier local governance system (comprising departmental, regional, municipal and indigenous levels). Morales' opponents censured the legislation for disregarding the 2008 autonomy referendums held in the 'media luna' region and for its vagueness in relation to the allocation of fiscal resources. Controversially, the autonomy law also barred those accused of corruption, or other 'formal' charges, from public office. This rule was enforced to suspend the opposition Governors of Tarija and Beni in December 2010 and December 2011, respectively, and also to remove two opposition mayors. Moreover, in late 2011 the sole remaining opposition Governor, Rubén Costas of Santa Cruz, was charged with contempt of court, and an investigation was begun into his financial affairs following allegations of corruption.

The approval of the autonomy law marked the end of a flurry of legislation that established the legal foundations for the new Constitution to come into effect. Laws adopted to this end, the *leyes orgánicas* (organic laws), included a judicial reform bill, to improve efficiency in the courts and permit the establishment of separate indigenous judicial systems, and new electoral rules, which politically empowered social movements (generally perceived as MAS affiliates) and restricted referendums.

Meanwhile, the Government's announcement in May 2010 of a 5% increase in public sector salaries precipitated nationwide protests orchestrated by the COB, hitherto a strong supporter of the Morales administration, demanding pay rises of up to 25%. A deal was subsequently agreed, in what was viewed as a triumph for Morales, whereby the 5% rise was maintained in exchange for a proposed reduction in the retirement age and additional wage increases for the lowest paid workers.

Former President Jorge Quiroga Ramírez was sentenced, *in absentia*, to 32 months' imprisonment in September 2010 for 'defamation and slander' after he accused the government-owned Banco Unión of corruption in 2009. Furthermore, in September 2011 Quiroga and another former President, Sánchez de Lozada, were charged with concluding unfavourable deals with foreign hydrocarbons companies during their tenures in office.

In October 2010 Morales promulgated a contentious anti-racism law, which gave the Government the authority to fine or shut down media outlets that disseminated 'racist and discriminatory ideas'. The legislation was widely viewed as an attempt by Morales to weaken the country's media corporations, predominantly owned by right-wing elements fiercely critical of the Morales administration. In addition to vehement opposition from the local media, the bill also prompted expressions of concern from the UN and national and international press freedom organizations, which feared that the legislation could be misused by the authorities to silence legitimate political debate.

In December 2010 the Government announced that fuel subsidies would be withdrawn, resulting in petrol prices increasing by up to 83%. Nationwide protests were rapidly organized by trade unions and the Government was forced to reinstate the subsidies. During a series of cabinet changes in the first half of 2010 María Cecilia Chacón Rendón became the first female Minister of National Defence and Claudia Peña Claros became the Minister of Autonomy, thereby fulfilling the President's pledge to achieve ministerial gender equality.

Unprecedented elections were conducted in October 2011 to appoint senior judicial personnel to serve in, *inter alia*, the Supreme Court and the Constitutional Court. Morales asserted that the vote would ensure judicial independence, but all of the candidates had been pre-selected by the MAS-controlled legislature. Although the rate of participation by the electorate was high, the majority of ballots were spoiled or left blank in accordance with an opposition-led protest campaign against the Government.

In early 2012 Morales identified the issue of 'citizen security' as a key priority for his Government following a marked increase in the crime rate in recent months. In March the Attorney-General, Mario Uribe, recommended an urgent revision of the criminal code in order to deal with the problem, and demonstrations were held in El Alto demanding the return of the death penalty for serious violent crimes. In the same month 2,300 troops were deployed to assist policing in La Paz, El Alto, Cochabamba and Santa Cruz, the four cities most affected by the increased crime rate. In late July the 'Law of Citizen Security' was promulgated, which provided for the creation of a new system of community policing and an air police service (the first of its kind in the country) for Santa Cruz. Regional governments were required to assign at least 10% of revenue from the hydrocarbons tax to fund the new policies. Corruption, however, continued to be a factor in the effective administration of law and order. In December Col Alberto Aracena Martínez became the country's eighth police chief in six years when he replaced Col Víctor Santos Maldonado, who had been accused of corrupt practices. The appointment of Aracena himself, however, attracted controversy owing to his alleged links to drugs-traffickers. In August 2013 the Government launched the Comités de Defensa Patriótica (CDP—Patriotic Defence Committees) intended to form a strategic alliance between the military and various social organizations, which could provide assistance not only in times of emergency, such as natural disaster, but also in maintaining law and order. Critics of the Government accused Morales of creating the committees as a way of extending the influence of the military in Bolivian society. In December of that year Walter Jonny Villarpando Moya replaced Aracena Martínez, in accordance with Morales' new policy of appointing a new police chief every 12 months. The stated aim of the policy was to strengthen the institution and to address ongoing concerns about corruption, the latter having been highlighted in a report published in mid-2013 by non-governmental organization Transparency International, which rated the Bolivian police force as one of the most corrupt in the region, awarding it a score of 4.5 on a scale of 1–5 (with 5 signifying 'extremely corrupt').

In March 2012 the national summit of the MAS unanimously selected Morales as their presidential candidate for the 2014 election. The selection prompted speculation that, despite recent reverses in the President's popularity (including ongoing disputes with the COB over increases to the minimum wage and pension payments during 2013, and the highly controversial highway project in Cochabamba—see below), Morales had no clear successor and that the success of the MAS was closely bound up in its leader's personal appeal to large sections of the Bolivian population. The opposition claimed that Morales' bid for a third term in office would be unconstitutional, as only two consecutive presidential terms were now permitted. Morales' argument that this would be only a first re-election under the 2009 Constitution was supported by a ruling of the Constitutional Court in April 2013. The rejection in August 2013 of an application by the Movimiento Social Democrático (MSD—Social Democratic Movement) to register itself as a political party with the Tribunal Supremo Electoral (TSE) provoked opposition accusations that the court lacked independence from the Government. The TSE maintained that its ruling upheld the 1999 law governing political parties, which prohibits citizen groups from forming official political entities.

Recent developments: the Cochabamba road project

The hitherto strong relations between the Morales administration and indigenous groups (see below) deteriorated in mid-2011 as a result of a government scheme to build a major road through indigenous territory in Cochabamba. Approximately 1,000 indigenous rights activists, who claimed that the construction of the highway breached multiple constitutional protections guaranteed to their communities and to the environment, began a 500-km protest march from Beni to La Paz in August. The police attempted to stop the march by force in the following month, prompting widespread condemnation of the authorities and the resignations of Minister of National Defence Cecilia Chacón Rendón and Minister of the Interior Sacha Sergio Llorenti Soliz in protest at the repression (they were replaced by Rubén Saavedra Soto and Wilfredo Franz Chávez Serrano, respectively); the march continued, none the less, reaching La Paz in October. Under increasing pressure, Morales terminated the highway project later that month, although the episode had severely damaged his popularity. Nevertheless, in February 2012 the legislature approved a non-binding referendum in Cochabamba on the road project. The plebiscite, due to take place by 10 May, was cancelled, following a recommendation by the UN, and a public consultation exercise was announced, to run from May until December. At the same time the Government announced the cancellation of its contract with the Brazilian company due to begin construction of the road. However, by October a new agreement had been signed with two Bolivian companies to undertake the first section of the project, leading to accusations that the Government's consultation with local communities in the region, which still had two months to run, was not genuine. The Government's declaration that the consultation process had been a success and showed strong support for the road project was questioned by an independent commission formed by representatives of the Catholic church and human rights groups. In its findings the commission alleged that communities had not been given full access to the facts, that only a small minority of residents had been consulted, and that bribes and gifts had distorted the result. Bolivia's human rights ombudsman, Rolando Villena, was similarly critical, describing the process as 'authoritarian, colonialist and unilateral'. In April 2013 Morales announced that the project would not be undertaken until extreme poverty had been eliminated in the communities affected by the scheme, and committed government expenditure of some US $14m. over the following two years for the provision of basic services. Indigenous leaders, however, remained sceptical about the Government's intentions regarding the construction of the highway, which was widely predicted to resume in late 2015.

The Role of Coca in Recent Bolivian Politics

One of Morales' campaign pledges was to legalize the cultivation of coca. On taking office, the new President appointed a former coca grower, Felipe Cáceres García, to lead the country's anti-narcotics effort. In May 2006, however, the Government announced that voluntary eradication was to resume, although growers in the Caranavi region were allowed to cultivate about 1,600 sq m of coca per household, a compromise already extended to the Chapare and Yungas regions. In December Morales announced that the amount of land legally permitted for coca cultivation would be increased from 12,000 ha to 20,000 ha by 2010. The decision was criticized in a 2007 US report, which also berated Morales for advocating the industrialization of coca production. In December the Constituent Assembly approved a measure urging the UN to decriminalize coca and to refrain from 'using the name of the sacred leaf in their products'. The motion resulted from complaints that the US-based multinational drinks company Coca-Cola used the name 'coca' to promote its products while exports of Bolivian products containing coca were banned. In October 2012 Morales appointed US actor Sean Penn as 'ambassador for Bolivia's noble causes', chief among which was to seek the acceptance of coca consumption by the UN. Meanwhile, according to UN figures published in late 2012, coca production decreased in Bolivia for the first time since 2006, with an estimated 27,200 ha under cultivation in 2011, compared with 31,000 ha in 2010. Morales used the announcement to reiterate his position regarding the Bolivian people's right to cultivate coca and, in a statement apparently aimed at the US authorities, urged coca producers to take legal action against anyone accusing them of drugs-trafficking. In January 2013 the UN granted Bolivia a special dispensation recognizing coca consumption as legal in the country. The move allowed

Bolivia to rejoin the 1961 UN Single Convention on Narcotic Drugs, from which the Morales Government had withdrawn in June 2011 in protest at a clause in the agreement banning the chewing of coca leaves. The Government had claimed that the Convention was in breach of the 2007 UN Declaration on the Rights of Indigenous People and Bolivia's new Constitution, both of which enshrined the cultural significance of coca consumption in Bolivian society. The publication in November 2013 of an EU-funded report on the legal uses of coca in Bolivia found that just 58% of the country's coca crop could be justified by estimated legal consumption. At the time of the study's commission in 2004, the Government and coca growers had agreed that the legal ceiling of the crop would be decided by the findings of the independent survey. Its findings, however, appeared to cast serious doubt over the success of Morales' administration's policy of 'coca sí, cocaína no'. Ongoing antagonism towards the coca eradication programme continued during 2013, with 15 coca growers injured in clashes with officials in May, and four members of the security forces killed in the La Paz department while trying to destroy coca crops in October.

Indigenous Peoples' Rights

The issue of the participation of the Aymara, Quechua and Guaraní indigenous peoples in Bolivia's public life reached a critical phase in the early 21st century, following limited progress in the 1990s. Government decrees issued in 1990 acknowledging as Indian territory more than 1.6m. ha of tropical rainforest in northern Bolivia constituted an unprecedented act of recognition of Indian land rights. In 2002 the Sánchez de Lozada administration announced a Land Reform Programme, under which some 1.2m. ha were to be bought by the Government and redistributed to some 11,000 landless families, at a cost of approximately US $2,500m. Despite government claims that some 500,000 ha of land was available for redistribution, landless peasants continued to occupy farms illegally throughout 2004. In August land owned by the multinational hydrocarbons company BP was occupied until the Government agreed to accelerate the process of land redistribution.

The election in December 2005 of Bolivia's first President of indigenous descent, Evo Morales, was seen as a key development in indigenous peoples' political participation. In 2006, following the issuing of a decree on land reform (see above), Morales handed over title deeds to 3.1m. ha of land in the east of the country to indigenous leaders. The gesture was largely symbolic, but it was expected that the land reform would grant indigenous and landless farmers almost 200,000 sq km of land by 2011. The 2009 Constitution granted far-reaching powers to the country's indigenous majority in relation to government, the judiciary and land ownership. In August of that year, in line with the provisions of the new Constitution, Morales enacted the Law of Indigenous Autonomies, which detailed the conditions under which indigenous people could vote for autonomy. In June 2010 the legislature adopted a judicial reform bill, which most notably granted indigenous peoples the right to establish judicial structures in accordance with traditional principles, separate from and equal to the national justice system. This controversial law was denounced by opponents, who highlighted a series of lynchings to draw parallels between indigenous justice and vigilantism. Further legislation was approved in December, limiting the range of crimes under the jurisdiction of indigenous communities and banning lynchings.

Foreign Affairs

Regional relations

Bolivia's relations with Peru and Chile have been dominated by the long-standing issue of possible Bolivian access to the Pacific Ocean. An agreement with Peru, completed in 1993, granted Bolivia free access from its border town of Desaguadero to the Peruvian port of Ilo until 2091. In 2004 the Presidents of Bolivia and Peru signed a declaration of intent to create a special zone in Ilo for the exportation of Bolivian gas (see Economic Affairs). In 2010 Peru broadened the scope of the original 1993 agreement, granting Bolivia permission to construct docks, storage facilities, a free trade area and a naval academy, although by early 2014 the agreement had still not been ratified by the Peruvian Government.

Bolivia's desire to regain sovereign access to the Pacific has continued to impair relations with Chile. The Chilean Government's decision to privatize the port of Arica in 2004 elicited vehement objections from the Mesa administration, which feared this would adversely affect Bolivia's external trade, owing to significant increases in port tariffs (supposedly in contravention of the 1904 treaty that guaranteed duty-free passage of Bolivian goods through Arica). Although bilateral relations improved during Morales' presidency, leading some observers to speculate on the possibility of a permanent access agreement, the new Chilean administration of Sebastián Piñera announced in 2010 that it would not grant Bolivia sovereign rights to any part of its territory, precipitating a sharp deterioration in relations. In April 2013 Bolivia initiated proceedings at the International Court of Justice in an attempt to resolve the matter. Relations had been strained by the arrest of three members of the Bolivian armed forces in January 2013 for entering Chilean territory. Morales maintained that the soldiers had been pursuing smugglers and used a speech in February marking the anniversary of the start of the War of the Pacific to demand their release. Another formal complaint was made against the Chilean authorities in December 2013 to the World Customs Association, following a strike by Chilean customs officials, during which more than 2,000 Bolivian lorries had been stranded at the border, and which, according to the Bolivian Government, had resulted in losses to the Bolivian economy of some US $5m.

Bolivia signed a border agreement with Paraguay in May 2009, resolving a dispute over the Chaco region that had led to war between the two countries during the 1920s and 1930s, in which more than 100,000 people had died. In December 2013 Bolivia and Paraguay formally re-established diplomatic relations, which the Bolivian Government had severed in June of the previous year in protest at the impeachment of former President Fernando Lugo. Bolivia and Brazil concluded an agreement to combat drugs-trafficking along their shared border in March 2011, and a further accord was signed in January 2012. Brazil pledged to provide Bolivia with training and equipment, and Brazilian unmanned aircraft commenced surveillance operations in Bolivian territory. In February 2013 the Bolivian authorities announced plans for a trilateral agreement with Brazil and Peru to combat drugs-trafficking through joint border operations and the sharing of police and financial information. Moreover, in June President Dilma Rousseff of Brazil stated that joint military efforts to police the border with Bolivia would henceforth become a permanent arrangement. Relations between the two countries, however, had been strained by Brazil's decision in June 2012 to grant political asylum to a Bolivian right-wing opposition politician, Roger Pinto, who claimed he was being persecuted by Morales' Government.

Other external relations

Allegations by the Bolivian Government that the US ambassador had given support to opposition activists in the 'media luna' region led to a deterioration in the already strained relationship between the two countries in 2008, and in September President Morales announced the expulsion of the ambassador. Relations continued to deteriorate with Morales' decision to suspend indefinitely all operations by the US Drug Enforcement Administration, which it accused of spying and of fomenting political unrest in the country. In retaliation, the US Government announced the suspension of Bolivia from the Andean Trade Promotion and Drug Eradication Act (ATPDEA) programme and in July 2009 the US Administration of Barack Obama announced the permanent withdrawal of trade privileges for Bolivian goods in the USA under the ATPDEA. This decision was widely criticized in Bolivia, and Morales accused Obama of dishonesty in his stated promise to work towards an equal partnership between the USA and Latin America. Despite a pledge to re-establish diplomatic relations in late 2011 the US Government's refusal in September of the following year to extradite former President Sánchez de Lozada to Bolivia to face charges of genocide for his role in the violence of 2003 (see above) made this seem unlikely. In September 2013 Bolivia's Attorney-General Ramiro Guerrero led a delegation to the USA to file a second request for the extradition of Sánchez de Lozada. Tensions had been heightened in April of that year by US Secretary of State John Kerry's reference to Latin America as the USA's 'backyard', and in the following month Morales expelled the US Agency for International Development from the country, accusing it of seeking to conspire against his Government.

Bolivia and Iran established closer bilateral relations in 2007 following the signing of an industrial co-operation agreement and the investment by Iran of US $1,000m. in technology and trade and industry projects in Bolivia. The presidents of the two countries also signed a framework agreement expressing support for nuclear research for peaceful energy purposes. The US Government expressed concern at Iran's apparently increasing influence in the region. In 2010 Iran agreed to lend the Bolivian Government $254m. to finance a variety of mining projects and further agreements, including an additional $276m. loan, were concluded later that year.

Bolivia's relations with Spain deteriorated in early 2013 following the announcement by President Morales that his Government was to nationalize Servicios de Aeropuertos Bolivianos (SABSA), the Bolivian airport operator owned by private Spanish interests. Morales claimed that the company had failed to invest sufficient funds in the three airports it operated (El Alto, Santa Cruz and Cochabamba), despite making large profits, and described its privatization in 1997 as 'robbery'. The Spanish authorities expressed regret at the action, branding it 'unfriendly'. Furthermore, Bolivia's diplomatic relations with Spain as well as Italy, Portugal and France were severely damaged by an incident in July 2013, when the four European countries refused to allow Morales' presidential jet through their airspace, en route from Russia to Bolivia, thus forcing it to make an unscheduled landing in Vienna, Austria. The decision followed suspicions (proven to be unfounded) that the fugitive US 'whistleblower', Edward Snowden, was on board the aeroplane. Morales described the grounding and extensive searching of his jet as an act of 'state terrorism' and summoned diplomatic representatives from the four countries to La Paz to explain their actions.

CONSTITUTION AND GOVERNMENT

A revised Constitution was signed into law in February 2009, which provided for greater autonomy for indigenous communities, enshrined state control over key economic sectors (most notably natural resources), imposed restrictions on the size of land holdings, removed Roman Catholicism as the state religion and aimed to make the judiciary more transparent and accountable. It also enlarged the Senado Nacional (Senate) and allowed the President, who is elected by direct suffrage for a five-year term, to seek re-election for a second consecutive term. Legislative power is held by the bicameral Congreso Nacional (Congress), comprising a Senate, with 36 members and a Cámara de Diputados (Chamber of Deputies), comprising 130 members. Both houses are elected for a five-year term by universal adult suffrage. Executive power is vested in the President and the Cabinet, which is appointed by the President. If no candidate gains an absolute majority of votes, the President is chosen by the Congress. The country is divided, for administrative purposes, into nine departments, each of which is governed by a prefect.

REGIONAL AND INTERNATIONAL CO-OPERATION

In May 1991 Bolivia was one of five Andean Pact countries to sign the Caracas Declaration providing the foundation for a common market. Bolivia is a member of the Andean Community (see p. 193). In December 2012 Bolivia signed a protocol to become a full member of Mercosur (see p. 429), following 15 years of associate membership. The country is also a member of the Organization of American States (OAS, see p. 394), of the Latin American Integration Association (ALADI, see p. 361), and of the Community of Latin American and Caribbean States (see p. 464), which was formally inaugurated in December 2011. Bolivia was a member of the Bolivarian Alliance for the Peoples of our America-People's Trade Treaty (Alianza Bolivariana para los Pueblos de Nuestra América-Tratado de Comercio de los Pueblos—ALBA-TCP, see p. 463), inaugurated in 2002 and intended as an alternative to the proposed Free Trade Area of the Americas advanced by the USA. In 2004 Bolivia was one of the founder signatories to the agreement signed in Cusco, Peru, creating the South American Community of Nations (Comunidad Sudamericana de Naciones), intended to promote greater regional economic integration and further the unification of Mercosur and the Andean Community. A treaty for the community—referred to as the Union of South American Nations (UNASUR, see p. 469) since its reinvention at the first South American Energy Summit in April 2007—was signed by heads of state meeting in Brasília, Brazil, in May 2008, with full functionality of economic union tentatively scheduled for 2019.

Bolivia became a member of the UN in 1945. The country has been a member of the World Trade Organization (see p. 434) since September 1995.

ECONOMIC AFFAIRS

In 2012, according to World Bank estimates, Bolivia's gross national income (GNI), measured at average 2010–12 prices, totalled US $23,304m., equivalent to about $2,220 per head (or $4,960 per head on an international purchasing-power parity basis). During 2003–12, it was estimated, the population grew at an average annual rate of 1.7% per year, while gross domestic product (GDP) per head increased at an average annual rate of 2.9% per year. Bolivia's overall GDP increased, in real terms, at an average annual rate of 4.7% in 2003–12; GDP increased by a preliminary 5.2% in 2012.

Agriculture (including forestry and fishing) contributed 12.3% of GDP in 2012, according to preliminary figures. According to FAO estimates, 40.0% of the economically active population were engaged in agriculture in mid-2014. The principal cash crop is soya, particularly soya oil. During 2003–12 agricultural GDP increased at an average annual rate of 2.3%; sectoral GDP increased by a preliminary 4.1% in 2012.

Industry (including mining, manufacturing, construction and power) provided 36.8% of GDP in 2012, according to preliminary figures. According to International Labour Organization (ILO) estimates, some 19.7% of the working population was employed in industry in 2007. In 2003–12 industrial GDP increased at an average annual rate of 6.0%; the sector grew by a preliminary 5.2% in 2012.

Mining (including petroleum exploration) contributed 18.4% of GDP in 2012, according to preliminary figures. The sector employed about 1.5% of the working population in 2007. President Evo Morales' policy of bringing the country's hydrocarbons sector under state control led to a significant decrease in foreign investment, although revenue from mineral resources remained relatively high. Natural gas accounted for a preliminary 46.5% of export earnings in 2012. Zinc, silver, tin, gold, wolfram and antimony are the major mineral exports. Exports of zinc and silver earned a preliminary US $738.9m. and $986.4m., respectively, in 2012. In 2003–12 the GDP of the mining sector increased at an estimated average annual rate of 7.6%; mining GDP increased by a preliminary 4.9% in 2012.

In 2012 manufacturing accounted for 12.8% of GDP, according to preliminary figures. In 2007 the sector engaged some 11.0% of the working population. The GDP of this sector increased during 2003–12 at an average annual rate of 4.7%; it increased by 4.7% in 2012.

The construction sector accounted for 3.3% of GDP in 2012, according to preliminary figures, and engaged 6.8% of the economically active population in 2007, according to the ILO. During 2003–12 construction GDP increased at an average annual rate of 8.3%; construction GDP increased by a preliminary 8.0% in 2012.

Energy is derived principally from natural gas and hydroelectricity. In 2010 electricity generation totalled 5,870m. kWh, according to the US Energy Information Administration (EIA). Hydroelectricity accounted for 32.8% of Bolivia's total installed generating capacity in 2010 (2.2 GW), with thermal power stations accounting for most of the remainder (64.8%). According to EIA, in 2012 production of crude petroleum averaged a reported 56,568 barrels per day. Output increased by 14.8% in 2012. In 2012 imports of mineral products comprised a preliminary 15.7% of total merchandise imports. Earnings from exports of mineral products (including gas and petroleum) accounted for a preliminary 50.1% of total export earnings in 2012. At the end of 2012 the country's proven reserves of gas stood at 317,000m. cu m. Bolivia has considerable reserves of lithium (estimated at some 20m. metric tons in 2010), an essential component of electric vehicle batteries, found in the Salar de Uyuni salt flats.

The services sector accounted for 50.8% of GDP in 2012, according to preliminary figures. According to ILO, it engaged some 44.2% of the employed population in 2007. During 2003–12 the GDP of the services sector increased at an average annual rate of 4.2%; the sector expanded by a preliminary 5.4% in 2012.

In 2012 Bolivia recorded a visible merchandise trade surplus of US $3,415.8m., and there was a surplus of $2,127.5m. on the current account of the balance of payments. In 2012 the main sources of imports were Brazil (18.4%), the People's Republic of China, Argentina, the USA, Peru and Venezuela. Brazil was also the main recipient of exports (31.1%) in that year, followed by Argentina, the USA and Peru. The principal imports in that year included machinery and transport equipment, base metals and their manufactures, mineral fuels and lubricants, chemicals and chemical products, miscellaneous manufactured articles, and food and live animals. The principal legal exports were mineral fuels and lubricants, crude materials, food and live animals, and base metals and their manufactures. It was estimated that a large proportion of Bolivia's export earnings came from the illegal trade in coca and its derivatives (mainly cocaine).

In 2012 a consolidated public sector budgetary surplus of 3,288.0m. bolivianos was recorded, according to preliminary figures. Bolivia's general government gross debt was 62,440m. bolivianos in 2012, equivalent to 33.4% of GDP. Bolivia's total external debt at the end of 2011 was US $6,474m., of which $3,414m. was public and publicly guaranteed debt. In that year, the cost of servicing long-term public and publicly guaranteed debt and repayments to the IMF was equivalent to 4.9% of the value of exports of goods, services and income (excluding workers' remittances). According to ILO, in 2003–12 the average annual rate of inflation was 6.3%. Consumer prices increased by 4.6% in 2012. According to official estimates, some 2.7% of the labour force was unemployed in 2011.

The Morales administration's strategic economic objectives of increased financial independence for Bolivia and redistributive social policies were laid out in its 2006–11 development plan, and were largely renewed in its next five-year plan. The global recession from late 2008 had a negligible impact on the Bolivian economy, largely owing to the underdeveloped financial system and comparatively low levels of short-term capital investment, and the country recorded one of the highest levels of economic growth in the region at 3.4% in 2009, which rose to 6.1% in 2010. The hydrocarbons sector provided the majority of this growth, both directly—via export receipts—and indirectly, as the state increased its stake in production, a move that enabled large fiscal surpluses, which the Government used to increase spending on its social programmes. Investment in the gas and mining sectors were buoyant in 2012, gas exports having increased by 37% in 2011, following the inauguration of a new pipeline connecting Bolivia and Argentina. In 2012 the Government announced plans for the state hydrocarbons company to double the area under exploration for gas, and three new exploration agreements were signed with Petrobras, Brazil's state oil company (responsible for more than 50% of Bolivia's gas production in 2011). A further major gas exploration agreement was signed in August 2013 when Russian company Gazprom and French multinational Total agreed to invest US $130m. each in operations in the Bloque Azero in the south of the country. The production of lithium, which officially began in August 2012 with the inauguration of a facility in Uyuni, was expected to provide a significant source of revenue in the coming years. The success of the Government's decision to sell 10-year bonds, which raised $500m. in 2012, the first time that such a sale had occurred since the 1920s, was seen by many observers as an expression of confidence in the Bolivian economy and was repeated in August 2013. The Government's increased state control of the hydrocarbons sector was strengthened by legislation promulgated in September 2013 permitting the state to seize inactive mining concessions from private companies. It was estimated that the law would enable the Government to recover some 70% of the 2,454 concessions thought to be in private ownership. GDP growth of 5.2% was recorded in both 2011 and 2012, rising to an estimated 6.5% in 2013; growth was projected at 5.7% in 2014. The Government's spending on social programmes had a pronounced effect on poverty and human development, with the proportion of Bolivians living in extreme poverty measured at 24% in 2012, compared with 38% in 2008.

PUBLIC HOLIDAYS

2015: 1 January (New Year), 22 January (Plurinational State Foundation Day), 17–18 February (Carnival), 3 April (Good Friday), 1 May (Labour Day), 4 June (Corpus Christi), 21 June (Aymara New Year/Summer Solstice), 16 July (La Paz only), 6 August (Independence), 14 September (Cochabamba only), 24 September (Santa Cruz and Pando only), 2 November (All Souls' Day), 25 December (Christmas).

Statistical Survey

Sources (unless otherwise indicated): Instituto Nacional de Estadística, José Carrasco 1391, Casilla 6129, La Paz; tel. (2) 222-2333; internet www.ine.gob.bo; Banco Central de Bolivia, Avda Ayacucho, esq. Mercado, Casilla 3118, La Paz; tel. (2) 240-9090; fax (2) 240-6614; e-mail bancocentraldebolivia@bcb.gob.bo; internet www.bcb.gob.bo.

Area and Population

AREA, POPULATION AND DENSITY

Area (sq km)	
Land	1,084,391
Inland water	14,190
Total	1,098,581*
Population (census results)†	
5 September 2001	8,274,325
21 November 2012	
Males	5,005,365
Females	5,021,889
Total	10,027,254
Population (UN estimates at mid-year)‡	
2013	10,671,201
2014	10,847,660
Density (per sq km) at mid-2014	9.9

* 424,164 sq miles.

† Figures exclude adjustment for underenumeration.

‡ Source: UN, *World Population Prospects: The 2012 Revision*; estimates not adjusted to take account of the results of the 2012 census.

POPULATION BY AGE AND SEX

(population at 2012 census)

	Males	Females	Total
0–14	1,597,872	1,512,650	3,110,522
15–64	3,119,500	3,184,003	6,303,503
65 and over	287,993	325,236	613,229
Total	5,005,365	5,021,889	10,027,254

DEPARTMENTS

(population at census of November 2012)

	Area (sq km)*	Population	Density (per sq km)	Capital (population)†
Beni	213,564	421,196	2.0	Trinidad (99,443)
Chuquisaca	51,524	576,153	11.2	Sucre (312,024)
Cochabamba	55,631	1,758,143	31.6	Cochabamba (631,304)
La Paz	133,985	2,706,351	20.2	La Paz (852,438)
Oruro	53,588	494,178	9.2	Oruro (218,882)
Pando	63,827	110,436	1.7	Cobija (44,867)
Potosí	118,218	823,517	7.0	Potosí (168,831)
Santa Cruz	370,621	2,655,084	7.2	Santa Cruz de la Sierra (1,697,630)
Tarija	37,623	482,196	12.8	Tarija (216,138)
Total	1,098,581	10,027,254	9.1	

* As at 2001 census.

† Official population projections, 2011.

PRINCIPAL TOWNS
(official projections, 2011)

Santa Cruz de la Sierra	1,697,630	Sacaba	183,386
El Alto	974,754	Potosí	168,831
La Paz (administrative capital)	852,438	Quillacollo	145,594
Cochabamba	631,304	Yacuiba	141,595
Sucre (legal capital)	312,024	Riberalta	102,993
Oruro	218,882	Montero	101,224
Tarija	216,138	Trinidad	99,443

BIRTHS AND DEATHS
(annual averages, UN estimates)

	1995–2000	2000–05	2005–10
Birth rate (per 1,000)	32.7	30.3	27.3
Death rate (per 1,000)	8.9	8.1	7.5

Source: UN, *World Population Prospects: The 2012 Revision*.

Life expectancy (years at birth): 66.6 (males 64.5; females 68.9) in 2011 (Source: World Bank, World Development Indicators database).

ECONOMICALLY ACTIVE POPULATION
(labour force survey, '000 persons aged 10 years and over)

	2005	2006	2007
Agriculture, hunting, forestry and fishing	1,643.6	1,797.4	1,686.7
Mining and quarrying	71.0	55.5	72.4
Manufacturing	465.5	477.8	514.9
Electricity, gas and water supply	13.9	13.0	15.4
Construction	275.3	248.1	316.3
Wholesale and retail trade; repair of motor vehicles, motorcycles and personal and household goods	629.3	647.3	673.8
Hotels and restaurants	171.4	186.7	159.3
Transport, storage and communications	256.3	251.5	272.4
Financial intermediation	13.1	23.3	28.0
Real estate, renting and business activities	104.6	152.0	136.9
Public administration and defence; compulsory social security	91.1	115.2	152.3
Education	192.7	217.9	222.9
Health and social work	64.0	96.9	109.3
Other community, social and personal service activities	153.0	147.5	149.0
Private households with employed persons	108.3	119.6	160.7
Extra-territorial organizations and bodies	4.0	0.6	1.9
Total employed	4,257.2	4,550.3	4,672.4
Unemployed	245.2	243.5	255.0
Total labour force	4,502.4	4,793.8	4,927.4
Males	2,468.2	2,624.6	2,699.4
Females	2,034.2	2,169.2	2,228.0

Source: ILO.

2011 (household survey in November—December, persons aged 10 years and over): Total employed 5,361,425; Unemployed 146,766; Total labour force 5,508,191.

Health and Welfare

KEY INDICATORS

Total fertility rate (children per woman, 2011)	3.3
Under-5 mortality rate (per 1,000 live births, 2011)	51
HIV/AIDS (% of persons aged 15–49, 2012)	0.3
Physicians (per 1,000 head, 2001)	1.2
Hospital beds (per 1,000 head, 2009)	1.1
Health expenditure (2010): US $ per head (PPP)	264
Health expenditure (2010): % of GDP	5.5
Health expenditure (2010): public (% of total)	66.2
Access to water (% of persons, 2011)	88
Access to sanitation (% of persons, 2011)	46
Total carbon dioxide emissions ('000 metric tons, 2010)	15,456.4
Carbon dioxide emissions per head (metric tons, 2010)	1.5
Human Development Index (2012): ranking	108
Human Development Index (2012): value	0.675

For sources and definitions, see explanatory note on p. vi.

Agriculture

PRINCIPAL CROPS
('000 metric tons)

	2010	2011	2012
Wheat	255.4	249.7	200.0*
Rice, paddy	449.5	471.5	440.0*
Barley	47.6	51.1	49.0†
Maize	718.0	1,020.2	1,006.0†
Sorghum	335.5	389.5	478.0†
Potatoes	975.4	966.4	900.0*
Cassava (Manioc)	255.3	242.6	250.0*
Sugar cane	5,826.2	5,869.6	6,500.0*
Brazil nuts*	45.0	45.0	45.0
Chestnuts*	54.0	56.0	57.0
Soybeans (Soya beans)	1,917.2	2,299.9	2,400.0†
Sunflower seeds	310.8	152.7	250.0†
Tomatoes	53.1	49.5	50.0*
Pumpkins, squash and gourds*	20.1	20.2	22.0
Onions, dry	81.0	88.5	92.0*
Peas, green*	25.8	25.9	26.0
Carrots and turnips	26.9	27.0	30.0*
Maize, green	22.2	21.3	23.0*
Watermelons	15.6	15.4	16.5*
Bananas	158.2	203.4	210.0*
Plantains	338.9	336.3	350.0
Oranges	170.8	172.6	175.0
Tangerines, mandarins, clementines and satsumas	130.1	135.2	137.0
Lemons and limes	17.8	17.9	19.0
Grapes	25.0	26.9	28.0*
Papayas	7.6	7.4	7.2*
Coffee, green	28.8*	28.5	35.0*

* FAO estimate(s).
† Unofficial figure.

Aggregate production ('000 metric tons, may include official, semi-official or estimated data): Total cereals 1,849 in 2010, 2,227 in 2011, 2,218 in 2012; Total roots and tubers 1,290 in 2010, 1,267 in 2011, 1,210 in 2012; Total vegetables (incl. melons) 358 in 2010, 359 in 2011, 379 in 2012; Total fruits (excl. melons) 973 in 2010, 1,016 in 2011, 1,046 in 2012.

Source: FAO.

LIVESTOCK
('000 head, year ending September)

	2010	2011	2012
Horses*	478	483	487
Asses*	635	635	635
Mules*	82	82	82
Cattle	8,190	8,400	8,611
Pigs	2,641	2,713	2,800*
Sheep	8,701	8,878	8,900*
Goats	2,199	2,255	2,300*
Chickens	198,380	195,001	195,000*
Ducks*	300	305	307
Turkeys*	155	155	155

* FAO estimate(s).

Source: FAO.

LIVESTOCK PRODUCTS
('000 metric tons)

	2010	2011	2012
Cattle meat	202.3	205.2	215.3
Sheep meat	12.5	13.0	14.0*
Goat meat	5.3	5.3	5.5*
Pig meat	83.9	86.3	88.0*
Chicken meat	383.1	376.1	373.9
Cows' milk	371.7	381.5	392.0*
Sheep's milk*	33.5	33.5	34.0
Goats' milk	26.9	28.3	30.0*
Hen eggs†	69.8	73.1	74.8
Wool, greasy*	6.6	6.6	6.6

* FAO estimate(s).
† Unofficial figures.

Source: FAO.

Forestry

ROUNDWOOD REMOVALS
('000 cubic metres, excl. bark)

	2010	2011	2012
Sawlogs, veneer logs and logs for sleepers	913*	913*	913†
Fuel wood†	2,350	2,368	2,386
Total†	3,263	3,281	3,299

* Unofficial figure.
† FAO estimate(s).

Source: FAO.

SAWNWOOD PRODUCTION
('000 cubic metres, incl. railway sleepers, unofficial figures)

	2008	2009	2010
Coniferous (softwood)	2	3	7
Broadleaved (hardwood)	459	459	459
Total	461	462	466

2011–12: Production assumed to be unchanged from 2010 (FAO estimates).

Source: FAO.

Fishing

(metric tons, live weight)

	2009	2010	2011
Capture	7,568	6,946	6,677
Freshwater fishes	6,568	6,196	6,510
Silversides (sand smelts)	1,000	750	167
Aquaculture	775	856	966
Rainbow trout	325	360	414
Total catch	8,343	7,802	7,643

Note: Figures exclude crocodiles and alligators, recorded by number rather than by weight. The number of spectacled caimans caught was: 27,885 in 2009; 24,192 in 2010; 33,663 in 2011.

Source: FAO.

Mining

(metric tons unless otherwise indicated; figures for metallic minerals refer to the metal content of ores)

	2009	2010	2011
Crude petroleum ('000 barrels)	12,329	12,607	12,600*
Natural gas (million cu m)	13,411	15,227	15,714
Copper	882	2,063	4,176
Tin	19,575	20,190	20,373
Lead	84,538	72,803	100,051
Zinc	430,879	411,409	427,129
Tungsten (Wolfram)	1,023	1,204	1,124
Antimony	2,990	4,980	3,947
Silver (kg)	1,325,729	1,259,388	1,213,586
Gold (kg)	7,217	6,394	6,513

* Estimate.

Source: US Geological Survey.

Industry

SELECTED PRODUCTS
('000 42-gallon barrels unless otherwise indicated)

	2009	2010	2011
Cement ('000 metric tons)	2,292	2,414	2,658
Liquefied petroleum gas	645*	945	950*
Distillate fuel oil	4,100*	4,043	4,000
Kerosene	100*	127	125
Motor spirit (petrol)	5,530*	5,492	5,500

* Estimate.

Electric energy (million kWh): 4,778 in 2005.

Source: partly US Geological Survey.

Finance

CURRENCY AND EXCHANGE RATES

Monetary Units
100 centavos = 1 boliviano (B).

Sterling, Dollar and Euro Equivalents (31 December 2013)
£1 sterling = 11.379 bolivianos;
US $1 = 6.910 bolivianos;
€1 = 9.530 bolivianos;
100 bolivianos = £8.79 = $14.47 = €10.49.

Average Exchange Rate (bolivianos per US $)

2011	6.94
2012	6.91
2013	6.91

GOVERNMENT FINANCE
(consolidated public sector accounts, million bolivianos)

Revenue	2010	2011	2012*
Tax revenue	23,018.5	29,433.5	34,198.1
Internal	20,678.6	26,144.2	30,914.1
Customs	1,544.9	2,095.9	2,317.0
Mining royalties	795.0	1,193.4	967.0
Duties on hydrocarbons	2,252.8	2,432.2	2,447.9
Sale of hydrocarbons	26,392.9	30,830.1	39,560.6
Other public sector sales	3,465.6	5,248.6	5,393.3
Other current revenue	3,552.5	4,780.8	3,366.3
Current transfers	1,312.6	1,514.9	1,770.6
Capital revenue	1,577.5	1,374.5	1,253.2
Total	61,572.4	75,614.6	87,990.0

Expenditure	2010	2011	2012*
Current expenditure	44,519.4	52,119.2	59,446.2
Personal services	14,050.0	16,726.4	18,082.6
Goods and services	19,272.8	22,764.1	25,785.4
Interest on debt	2,221.1	1,991.4	1,887.4
External	482.0	734.2	573.9
Internal	1,739.1	1,257.2	1,313.5
Current transfers	8,011.0	9,519.4	11,497.6
Other current expenditure	964.5	1,117.9	2,193.2
Capital expenditure	14,737.2	22,113.3	25,255.9
Total	59,256.6	74,232.5	84,702.0

* Preliminary figures.

INTERNATIONAL RESERVES
(US $ million at 31 December)

	2010	2011	2012
Gold (national valuation)	1,596.2	2,109.1	2,267.3
IMF special drawing rights	254.0	253.2	254.2
Reserve position in IMF	13.7	13.6	13.6
Foreign exchange	7,866.2	9,643.9	11,391.4
Total	9,730.1	12,019.8	13,926.5

Source: IMF, *International Financial Statistics*.

MONEY SUPPLY
(million bolivianos at 31 December)

	2010	2011	2012
Currency outside depository corporations	22,485	25,814	29,305
Transferable deposits	22,763	30,956	39,073
Other deposits	47,774	56,638	68,322
Securities other than shares	140	758	1,211
Broad money	93,162	114,165	137,911

Source: IMF, *International Financial Statistics*.

COST OF LIVING
(Consumer Price Index for urban areas; base: 2000 = 100)

	2010	2011	2012
Food and beverages	127.8	145.6	151.3
All items (incl. others)	159.7	175.4	183.4

Source: ILO.

NATIONAL ACCOUNTS
(million bolivianos at current prices, preliminary)

Expenditure on the Gross Domestic Product

	2010	2011	2012
Government final consumption expenditure	19,069.9	22,901.9	25,152.8
Private final consumption expenditure	85,894.4	101,250.6	111,089.7
Increase in stocks	599.4	967.3	−1,066.6
Gross fixed capital formation	22,849.1	31,531.1	34,075.0
Total domestic expenditure	128,412.8	156,650.9	169,250.9
Exports of goods and services	56,787.4	73,294.3	88,273.4
Less Imports of goods and services	47,324.6	63,814.1	70,711.5
GDP at market prices	137,875.6	166,131.0	186,812.6
GDP at constant 1990 prices	32,585.7	34,271.6	36,045.7

Gross Domestic Product by Economic Activity

	2010	2011	2012
Agriculture, hunting, forestry and fishing	14,325.1	16,246.6	18,371.2
Mining and quarrying	19,332.4	25,767.1	27,375.0
Manufacturing	15,538.6	17,192.7	19,123.4
Electricity, gas and water	3,010.7	3,301.1	3,546.1
Construction	3,679.4	4,242.3	4,872.0
Trade	10,195.3	11,832.4	12,505.8
Transport, storage and communications	12,375.6	13,959.6	14,941.2
Finance, insurance, real estate and business services	11,997.9	13,378.5	16,095.4
Government services	16,423.2	19,340.7	21,373.3
Other services	9,056.3	9,949.8	10,871.5
Sub-total	115,934.5	135,210.8	149,074.9
Value-added tax Import duties }	26,423.1	36,459.9	44,974.2
Less Imputed bank charge	4,481.9	5,539.7	7,236.5
GDP in purchasers' values	137,875.6	166,131.0	186,812.6

BALANCE OF PAYMENTS
(US $ million)

	2010	2011	2012
Exports of goods	6,129.3	8,174.8	11,109.8
Imports of goods	−5,006.8	−7,126.4	−7,694.0
Balance on goods	1,122.5	1,048.5	3,415.8
Exports of services	707.7	948.0	1,062.2
Imports of services	−1,148.8	−1,650.7	−1,986.9
Balance on goods and services	681.4	345.8	2,491.0
Primary income received	81.7	136.8	141.4
Primary income paid	−970.6	−1,122.5	−1,770.7
Balance on goods, services and primary income	−207.5	−640.0	861.7
Secondary income received	1,187.6	1,299.3	1,416.8
Secondary income paid	−106.3	−122.2	−151.0
Current balance	873.7	537.2	2,127.5
Capital account (net)	−7.2	5.9	5.7
Direct investment assets	28.8	−0.3	—
Direct investment liabilities	622.0	858.9	1,060.0
Portfolio investment assets	90.1	156.0	−360.3
Other investment assets	−32.3	−127.8	−2,342.1
Other investment liabilities	151.4	636.0	2,171.1
Net errors and omissions	−802.3	94.8	−950.1
Reserves and related items	924.3	2,160.8	1,711.7

Source: IMF, *International Financial Statistics*.

External Trade

PRINCIPAL COMMODITIES

(distribution by SITC, US $ million)

Imports c.i.f.	2010	2011	2012*
Food and live animals	375.5	564.0	520.0
Crude materials (inedible) except fuels	62.2	81.8	82.1
Mineral fuels, lubricants, etc.	687.2	1,111.2	1,301.1
Chemicals and related products	949.5	1,117.5	1,250.7
Basic manufactures	1,099.6	1,418.8	1,479.5
Machinery and transport equipment	1,911.0	2,981.7	2,904.9
Miscellaneous manufactured articles	446.0	575.2	598.0
Total (incl. others)	5,603.9	7,935.7	8,281.0

Exports f.o.b.	2010	2011	2012*
Food and live animals	679.4	746.8	965.2
Crude materials (inedible) except fuels	2,028.9	2,589.9	2,382.2
Mineral fuels, lubricants, etc.	3,014.9	4,148.7	5,909.9
Animal and vegetable oils, fats and waxes	286.3	326.8	368.1
Basic manufactures	523.7	799.1	640.3
Machinery and transport equipment	6.2	8.5	2.3
Miscellaneous manufactured articles	160.7	116.4	126.0
Total (incl. others)	6,966.1	9,145.8	11,793.7

* Preliminary figures.

PRINCIPAL TRADING PARTNERS

(US $ million)

Imports c.i.f.	2010	2011	2012*
Argentina	713.5	966.4	1,086.0
Brazil	1,001.2	1,395.5	1,523.1
Canada	63.4	40.0	47.7
Chile	281.2	308.5	382.1
China, People's Republic	652.9	1,112.7	1,088.3
Colombia	118.5	195.0	161.5
France (incl. Monaco)	87.0	47.3	58.7
Germany	112.5	142.9	162.0
India	56.8	76.3	83.7
Italy	69.6	93.8	170.9
Japan	328.3	598.9	369.2
Mexico	128.3	188.9	232.4
Peru	389.1	472.3	557.6
Spain	74.5	101.9	96.0
Sweden	62.1	169.3	85.9
USA	733.2	889.6	910.0
Venezuela	321.9	526.2	446.1
Total (incl. others)	5,603.9	7,935.7	8,281.0

Exports	2010	2011	2012*
Argentina	553.7	1,059.1	2,109.4
Australia	67.5	125.1	113.2
Belgium-Luxembourg	384.5	377.7	334.6
Brazil	2,407.4	3,030.1	3,665.3
Canada	88.4	194.2	152.3
Chile	85.6	149.8	224.0
China, People's Republic	208.6	336.6	314.4
Colombia	229.6	259.3	414.6
Japan	460.3	540.0	441.8
Korea, Republic	367.1	419.1	358.0
Netherlands	60.4	54.4	32.8
Panama	39.4	47.9	39.2
Peru	393.4	461.0	622.6
Spain	59.4	93.6	63.8
Switzerland (incl. Liechtenstein)	167.3	306.0	272.5
United Kingdom	101.3	155.7	106.7
USA	690.7	876.5	1,746.2
Venezuela	341.4	286.4	303.8
Total (incl. others)	6,966.1	9,145.8	11,793.7

* Preliminary.

Transport

RAILWAYS

(traffic)

	2002	2003	2004
Passenger-km (million)	280	283	286
Net ton-km (million)	873	901	1,058

Source: UN, *Statistical Yearbook*.

ROAD TRAFFIC

(motor vehicles in use at 31 December)

	2002	2003	2004
Passenger cars	26,229	127,222	138,729
Buses	27,226	43,588	49,133
Lorries and vans	30,539	225,028	251,801
Motorcycles	1,125	15,467	19,426

2007: Passenger cars 174,912; Buses 6,996; Lorries and vans 468,763; Motorcycles 34,982.

Source: IRF, *World Road Statistics*.

SHIPPING

Flag Registered Fleet

(at 31 December)

	2011	2012	2013
Number of vessels	117	131	118
Total displacement ('000 grt)	170.1	210.2	132.4

Source: Lloyd's List Intelligence (www.lloydslistintelligence.com).

CIVIL AVIATION

(traffic on scheduled services, millions)

	2010	2011
Kilometres flown	22	26
Passengers carried	1.8	2.1
Passenger-km	1,603	2,097
Total ton-km	161	226

Source: UN, *Statistical Yearbook*.

Passengers carried (million): 1.8 in 2012 (Source: World Bank, World Development Indicators database).

Tourism

TOURIST ARRIVALS

(non-resident tourists arriving at hotels and similar establishments)

Country of origin	2008	2009	2010
Argentina	50,205	52,960	55,680
Brazil	38,967	41,670	44,274
Canada	10,933	10,641	10,658
Chile	23,352	23,536	25,769
France	29,888	27,762	30,925
Germany	23,626	30,327	31,396
Italy	9,768	9,407	10,748
Peru	92,993	93,676	100,396
Spain	14,662	17,823	16,469
Switzerland	9,818	10,367	9,669
United Kingdom	25,031	27,982	28,312
USA	47,303	46,821	50,625
Total (incl. others)	490,783	505,704	530,860

Total arrivals ('000): 946 in 2011.

Tourism receipts (US $ million, excl. passenger transport): 379 in 2010; 481 in 2011; 532 in 2012 (provisional).

Source: World Tourism Organization.

Communications Media

	2010	2011	2012
Telephones ('000 main lines in use)	851.5	878.7	880.6
Mobile cellular telephones ('000 subscribers)	7,179.3	8,355.1	9,493.6
Internet subscribers ('000)	114.0	116.8	n.a.
Broadband subscribers ('000)	95.9	65.9	110.6

Source: International Telecommunication Union.

Education

(2010/11 unless otherwise indicated, estimates)

			Students ('000)		
	Institutions	Teachers	Males	Females	Total
Pre-primary	2,294*	6,126†	131.9	126.2	258.1
Primary	12,639‡	62,430†	713.9	675.8	1,389.7
Secondary:					
general	n.a.	57,912†	540.2§	518.1§	1,058.3§
technical/vocational	n.a.	2,148‖	17.3¶	32.3¶	49.6¶
Tertiary†	n.a.	15,685	193.8	158.8	352.6

* 1988.

† 2006/07.

‡ 1987.

§ 2010/11.

‖ 2003/04.

¶ 2002/03.

Pupil-teacher ratio (primary education, UNESCO estimate): 24.2 in 2006/07.

Adult literacy rate (UNESCO estimates): 91.2% (males 95.8%; females 86.8%) in 2009.

Source: UNESCO Institute for Statistics.

Directory

The Government

HEAD OF STATE

President: JUAN EVO MORALES AIMA (took office 22 January 2006, re-elected 6 December 2009).

Vice-President: ALVARO MARCELO GARCÍA LINERA.

THE CABINET

(April 2014)

The Cabinet is composed of members of the Movimiento al Socialismo.

Minister of Foreign Affairs and Worship: DAVID CHOQUEHUANCA CÉSPEDES.

Minister of the Interior: CARLOS GUSTAVO ROMERO BONIFAZ.

Minister of National Defence: RUBÉN SAAVEDRA SOTO.

Minister of Justice: ELIZABETH ZAIDA GUTIÉRREZ SALAZAR.

Minister of Economy and Public Finance: LUIS ALBERTO ARCE CATACORA.

Minister of Development Planning: ELBA VIVIANA CARO HINOJOSA.

Minister of the Presidency: JUAN RAMÓN QUINTANA.

Minister of Autonomy: CLAUDIA PEÑA CLAROS.

Minister of Institutional Transparency and the Fight against Corruption: NARDI SUXO ITURRY.

Minister of Health and Sports: JUAN CARLOS CALVIMONTES CAMARGO.

Minister of Labour, Employment and Social Security: DANIEL SANTALLA TÓRREZ.

Minister of Education: ROBERTO AGUILAR GÓMEZ.

Minister of Rural Development and Lands: NEMESIA ACHACOLLO TOLA.

Minister of Hydrocarbons and Energy: JUAN JOSÉ SOSA SORUCO.

Minister of Mines and Metallurgy: CÉSAR NAVARRO.

Minister of Public Works, Services and Housing: VLADIMIR SÁNCHEZ ESCOBAR.

Minister of Water and the Environment: JOSÉ ZAMORA GUTIÉRREZ.

Minister of Culture and Tourism: PABLO CÉSAR GROUX CANEDO.

Minister of Productive Development and Plural Economy: ANA TERESA MORALES OLIVERA.

Minister of Communications: AMANDA DÁVILA TORRES.

MINISTRIES

Office of the Vice-President: Edif. de la Vicepresidencia del Estado, Calle Ayacucho, esq. Mercado 308, Casilla 7056, La Paz; tel. (2) 214-2000; fax (2) 220-1211; internet www.vicepresidencia.gob.bo.

Ministry of Autonomy: Edif. Ex CONAVI, Avda 20 de Octubre, esq. Fernando Guachalla 2230, Casilla 1397, La Paz; tel. (2) 211-0930; fax (2) 211-3613; e-mail contacto@autonomia.gob.bo; internet www.autonomia.gob.bo.

Ministry of Communications: Edif. La Urbana, 4°, Avda Camacho 1485, La Paz; tel. (2) 220-0402; fax (2) 220-0509; e-mail comunicacion@comunicacion.gob.bo; internet www.comunicacion.gob.bo.

Ministry of Culture and Tourism: Palacio Chico, Calle Ayacucho, esq. Potosí, Casilla 7846, La Paz; tel. (2) 220-0910; fax (2) 220-2628; e-mail despacho@minculturas.gob.bo; internet www.minculturas.gob.bo.

Ministry of Development Planning: Avda Mariscal Santa Cruz, esq. Oruro 1092, Casilla 12814, La Paz; tel. (2) 211-6000; fax (2) 231-7320; e-mail comunicacion@planificacion.gob.bo; internet www.planificacion.gob.bo.

Ministry of Economy and Public Finance: Edif. Palacio de Comunicaciones, 19°, CP 3744, La Paz; tel. (2) 220-3434; fax (2) 235-9955; e-mail ministro_web@economiayfinanzas.gob.bo; internet www.economiayfinanzas.gob.bo.

Ministry of Education: Avda Arce 2147, Casilla 3116, La Paz; tel. and fax (2) 244-2414; e-mail webmaster@minedu.gob.bo; internet www.minedu.gob.bo.

Ministry of Foreign Affairs and Worship: Plaza Murillo, Calle Ingavi, esq. Calle Junín, La Paz; tel. (2) 240-8900; fax (2) 240-8905; e-mail mreuno@rree.gob.bo; internet www.rree.gob.bo.

Ministry of Health and Sports: Plaza del Estudiante, esq. Cañada Strongest s/n, La Paz; tel. (2) 249-0554; fax (2) 248-6654; e-mail info@sns.gob.bo; internet www.sns.gob.bo.

Ministry of Hydrocarbons and Energy: Edif. Centro de Comunicaciones, 12°, Avda Mariscal Santa Cruz, esq. Calle Oruro, La Paz; tel. (2) 237-4050; fax (2) 214-1307; e-mail minehidro@hidrocarburos.gob.bo; internet www.hidrocarburos.gob.bo.

Ministry of Institutional Transparency and the Fight against Corruption: Edif. Capitán Ravelo, 3°–9°, Calle Capitán Ravelo 2101, esq. Montevideo, La Paz; tel. 211-5773; fax 215-3084; internet www.transparencia.gob.bo.

Ministry of the Interior: Avda Arce 2409, esq. Belisario Salinas 2409, Casilla 7110, La Paz; tel. (2) 244-0466; fax (2) 244-0466; e-mail mail@mingobierno.gob.bo; internet www.mingobierno.gob.bo.

Ministry of Justice: Avda 16 de Julio (El Prado) 1769, La Paz; tel. (2) 212-4725; fax (2) 231-5468; e-mail ministerio@justicia.go.bo; internet www.justicia.gob.bo.

Ministry of Labour, Employment and Social Security: Calle Yanacocha, esq. Mercado, Zona Central, La Paz; tel. (2) 240-8606; fax (2) 237-1387; e-mail info@mintrabajo.gob.bo; internet www.mintrabajo.gob.bo.

Ministry of Mines and Metallurgy: Edif. Palacio de Comunicaciones, 14°, Avda Mariscal Santa Cruz, Casilla 8686, La Paz; tel. (2) 237-1165; fax (2) 239-1241; e-mail mineria@mineria.gob.bo; internet www.mineria.gob.bo.

Ministry of National Defence: Calle 20 de Octubre 2502, esq. Pedro Salazar, La Paz; tel. (2) 243-2525; fax (2) 243-3153; e-mail utransparencia@mindef.gob.bo; internet www.mindef.gob.bo.

Ministry of the Presidency: Palacio de Gobierno, Calle Ayacucho, esq. Comercio s/n, Casilla 3278, La Paz; tel. (2) 220-2321; fax (2) 237-1388; e-mail correo@presidencia.gob.bo; internet www.presidencia.gob.bo.

Ministry of Productive Development and Plural Economy: Edif. Centro de Comunicaciones, 20°, Avda Mariscal Santa Cruz, esq. Calle Oruro, La Paz; tel. (2) 212-4235; fax (2) 212-4240; e-mail escribanos@produccion.gob.bo; internet www.produccion.gob.bo.

Ministry of Public Works, Services and Housing: Edif. Centro de Comunicaciones, 5°, Avda Mariscal Santa Cruz, esq. Calle Oruro, La Paz; tel. (2) 211-9999; e-mail obraspublicas@oopp.gob.bo; internet www.oopp.gob.bo.

Ministry of Rural Development and Lands: Avda Camacho 1471, entre Calle Bueno y Loayza, La Paz; tel. (2) 211-1103; fax (2) 211-1067; e-mail contacto@agrobolivia.gob.bo; internet www.agrobolivia.gob.bo.

Ministry of Water and the Environment: Capitán Castrillo 434, entre Calles 20 de Octubre y Héroes del Acre, Zona San Pedro, La Paz; tel. (2) 211-5571; fax (2) 211-8582; e-mail gary.suarez@minagua.gov.bo; internet www.mmaya.gob.bo.

President and Legislature

PRESIDENT

Election, 6 December 2009

Candidate	Valid votes	% of valid votes cast
Juan Evo Morales Aima (MAS)	2,943,209	64.22
Manfred Reyes Villa Leopoldo Fernández (PPB—CN)	1,212,795	26.46
Samuel Doria Medina (UN)	258,971	5.65
René Joaquino Suárez González (AS)	106,027	2.31
Others	61,784	1.35
Total (incl. others)*	4,582,786	100.00

* In addition, there were 156,290 blank votes and 120,364 spoiled votes.

PLURINATIONAL LEGISLATIVE ASSEMBLY
(Asamblea Legislativa Plurinacional)

President of the Senate: EUGENIO ROJAS APAZA (MAS).

President of the Chamber of Deputies: MARCELO WILLIAM ELIO CHÁVEZ (MAS).

General Election, 6 December 2009

Party	Seats: Chamber of Deputies	Seats: Senate
Movimiento al Socialismo (MAS)	88	26
Plan Progreso para Bolivia—Convergencia National (PPB—CN)	37	10
Frente de Unidad Nacional (UN)	3	—
Alianza Social (AS)	2	—
Total	130	36

Governors

DEPARTMENTS
(April 2014)

Beni: CARMELO LENZ FREDERIKSEN.

Chuquisaca: ESTEBAN URQUIZU CUÉLLAR.

Cochabamba: EDMUNDO NOVILLO AGUILAR.

La Paz: CÉSAR HUGO COCARICO YANA.

Oruro: SANTOS JAVIER TITO VÉLIZ.

Pando: LUIS ADOLFO FLORES ROBERTS.

Potosí: FÉLIX GONZÁLEZ BERNAL.

Santa Cruz: RUBÉN DARÍO COSTAS AGUILERA.

Tarija: LINO CONDORI ARAMAYO.

Election Commission

Organo Electoral Plurinacional (OEP): Plaza Abaroa, Avda Sánchez Lima 2440, esq. Pedro Salazar, Sopocachi, CP 8748, La Paz; tel. (2) 242-4221; fax (2) 242-3175; internet www.oep.org.bo; f. 1956 as Corte Nacional Electoral; replaced by OEP in 2010; consists of the Supreme Electoral Tribunal (Tribunal Supremo Electoral—TSE) and nine Departmental Electoral Tribunals, as well as Electoral Judges, the Juries at Election Tables, and Electoral Notaries; the TSE has the highest national jurisdiction; Pres. Dr WILMA VELASCO AGUILAR.

Political Organizations

Alianza Social (AS): Calle Fortunato Gumiel s/n, Potosí; tel. (2) 622-6150; f. 2006; Leader RENÉ JOAQUINO CABRERA.

Bolivia Social Demócrata (BSD): Edif. Arco Iris, planta baja, Of. 01, Calle Yanacocha 441, La Paz; tel. (2) 247-0768; e-mail rimech@hotmail.com; f. 2003; Pres. Dr RIME FRANCISCO CHOQUEHUANCA AGUILAR.

Comité Cívico de Tarija (CCT): Tarija; right-wing autonomist grouping; Pres. PATRICIA GALARZA.

Comité pro Santa Cruz (CSC): Avda Cañada Strongest 70, CP 1801, Santa Cruz; tel. (3) 334-2777; fax (3) 334-1812; e-mail comiteproscz@gmail.com; f. 1950; right-wing autonomist grouping; Pres. Dr HERLAND VACA DÍEZ BUSCH.

Consenso Popular (CP): alle Solíz de Olguín 447, esq. Avda Velarde, Santa Cruz; e-mail oscarortizantelo@gmail.com; internet www.consensopopular.org.bo; f. 2009; fmr dissident grouping of PODEMOS; Leader OSCAR ORTIZ ANTELO.

Frente Revolucionario de Izquierda (FRI): Avda Busch 1191 y Pasaje Jamaica, Miraflores, La Paz; tel. (2) 222-5488; e-mail siemprefri@gmail.com; left-wing; f. 1978; Leader OSCAR ZAMORA MEDINACELI.

Frente de Unidad Nacional (UN): Calle Fernando Guachalla, esq. Jacinto Benavente 2190, La Paz; tel. and fax (2) 211-5110; e-mail info@unidad-nacional.com; f. 2003; left-wing; Leader SAMUEL DORIA MEDINA.

Frente para la Victoria (FPV): Edif. Ugarte de Ingeniería, Penthouse 1, Calle Loayza, La Paz; e-mail fpvbolivia@hotmail.com; f. 2006; Leader PEDRO NUNI.

Movimiento sin Miedo (MSM): Avda 20 de Octubre 1743, La Paz; tel. (2) 248-9935; e-mail somossimiedo@msm.bo; internet www.msm.bo; f. 1999; left-wing; Leader JUAN DEL GRANADO COSÍO.

Movimiento Nacionalista Revolucionario (MNR): Avda Hernando Siles 21, Curva Sur del Estado Hernando Siles, La Paz; tel. (2) 212-8475; fax (2) 212-8479; e-mail mnr@bolivian.com; internet www.bolivian.com/mnr; f. 1942; centre-right; Pres. GUILLERMO BEDREGAL GUTIÉRREZ; 165,000 mems.

Movimiento al Socialismo (MAS): Calle Benedicto Vincenti 960, Sopocachi, La Paz; tel. 72970205 (mobile); e-mail info@masbolivia.com; internet www.masbolivia.com; f. 1987; also known as the Movimiento al Socialismo—Instrumento Político por la Soberanía de los Pueblos (MAS—IPSP); left-wing; promotes equality for indigenous people, peasants and workers; Leader JUAN EVO MORALES AIMA.

Partido Demócrata Cristiano (PDC): Calle Colón 812, 2°, esq. Sucre, Casilla 4345, La Paz; tel. 70655693 (mobile); e-mail josuva2002@hotmail.com; f. 1954; contested the 2009 election in alliance with PODEMOS; Pres. JORGE SUÁREZ VARGAS.

Partido Obrero Revolucionario (POR): Correo Central, La Paz; internet www.por-bolivia.org; f. 1935; Trotskyist; Leader GUILLERMO LORA.

Plan Progreso para Bolivia—Convergencia Nacional (PPB—CN): Plaza del Estudiante 1907, Of. Radio Ciudad, Zona Central, La Paz; tel. 71520200 (mobile); e-mail jlparedesm@hotmail.com; internet www.planprogreso.org; f. 2007; Leader José Luis Paredes Muñoz.

Unión Cívica Solidaridad (UCS): Edif. La Primera Bloque B, 17°, Of. 7 y 8, Avda Mariscal Santa Cruz 1364, La Paz; tel. (2) 236-0297; fax (2) 237-2200; e-mail unidadcivicasolidaridad@hotmail.com; f. 1989; populist; Leader Johnny Fernández Saucedo; 102,000 mems.

OTHER ORGANIZATION

Confederación de Pueblos Indígenas de Bolivia (CIDOB): Blvd San Juan, Calle 2, Santa Cruz; tel. (3) 344-6858; fax (3) 341-5929; e-mail cidob@cidob-bo.org; internet www.cidob-bo.org; f. 1982; represents indigenous peoples and communities; Pres. Adolfo Chávez Beyuma.

Diplomatic Representation

EMBASSIES IN BOLIVIA

Argentina: Calle Aspiazú 497, esq. Sánchez Lima, Casilla 64, La Paz; tel. (2) 241-7737; fax (2) 242-2727; e-mail ebolv@mrecic.gov.ar; internet www.ebolv.mrecic.gov.ar; Ambassador Sergio Ariel Basteiro.

Brazil: Edif. Multicentro, Torre B, Avda Arce s/n, esq. Rosendo Gutiérrez, Sopocachi, Casilla 429, La Paz; tel. (2) 216-6400; fax (2) 244-0043; e-mail embajadabrasil@brasil.org.bo; internet www.brasil.org.bo; Ambassador Raymundo Santos Rocha Magno.

China, People's Republic: Calle 1 8532, Los Pinos, Calacoto, Casilla 10005, La Paz; tel. (2) 279-3851; fax (2) 279-7121; e-mail chinaemb_bo@mfa.gov.cn; internet bo.china-embassy.org/esp; Ambassador Li Dong.

Colombia: Calle Roberto Prudencio 797, entre Calle 15 y 16 de Calacoto, Casilla 1418, Calacoto, La Paz; tel. (2) 279-0386; fax (2) 277-5670; e-mail bolivia@cancilleria.gov.co; internet bolivia.embajada.gov.co; Ambassador Martha Cecilia Pinilla Perdomo.

Cuba: Calle Gobles 6246, entre calles 11 y 12, Bajo Irpavi, Zona Sur, La Paz; tel. (2) 272-1646; fax (2) 272-3419; e-mail embajador@embacubabol.com; internet www.cubadiplomatica.cu/bolivia; Ambassador Rolando Antonio Gómez González.

Denmark: Edif. Fortaleza, 9°, Avda Arce 2799, esq. Cordero, Casilla 9860, La Paz; tel. (2) 243-2070; fax (2) 243-3150; e-mail lpbamb@um.dk; internet www.amblapaz.um.dk; Ambassador Ole Thonke.

Ecuador: Calle 14, No 8136, Calacoto, Casilla 406, La Paz; tel. (2) 211-5869; fax (2) 279-5079; e-mail eecuabolivia@mmrree.gov.ec; Ambassador Ricardo Ulcuango.

Egypt: Avda Ballivián 599, esq. Calle 12, Casilla 2956, La Paz; tel. (2) 278-6511; fax (2) 278-4325; e-mail embassy.lapaz@mfa.gov.eg; internet www.mfa.gov.eg/Lapaz_Emb; Ambassador Hani Muhammad Bassiyoni Mahmoud.

France: Avda Hernando Silés 5390, esq. Calle 8 de Obrajes, Casilla 717, La Paz; tel. (2) 214-9900; fax (2) 214-9901; e-mail information@ambafrance-bo.org; internet www.ambafrance-bo.org; Ambassador Michel Pinard.

Germany: Avda Arce 2395, esq. Belisario Salinas, Casilla 5265, La Paz; tel. (2) 244-0066; fax (2) 244-1441; e-mail info@la-paz.diplo.de; internet www.la-paz.diplo.de; Ambassador Peter Linder.

Holy See: Avda Arce 2990, San Jorge, Casilla 136, La Paz; tel. (2) 243-1007; fax (2) 243-2120; e-mail nunciaturabolivia@gmail.com; Apostolic Nuncio Most Rev. Giambattista Diquattro (Titular Archbishop of Giru Mons).

Iran: Calle 11, No 7805, esq. Avda Infouentes Calacoto, La Paz; tel. (2) 277-5749; fax (2) 277-5747; e-mail iranbolivi@yahoo.com; Ambassador Alireza Ghezili.

Italy: Calle 5 (Jordán Cuellar) 458, Obrajes, Casilla 626, La Paz; tel. (2) 278-8506; fax (2) 278-8178; e-mail segreteria.lapaz@esteri.it; internet www.amblapaz.esteri.it; Ambassador Luigi de Chiara.

Japan: Calle Rosendo Gutiérrez 497, esq. Sánchez Lima, Casiila 2725, La Paz; tel. (2) 241-9110; fax (2) 241-1919; e-mail coopjapon@acelerate.com; internet www.bo.emb-japan.go.jp; Ambassador Hidehiro Tsubaki.

Korea, Republic: Edif. Torre Lucía, 6°, Calle 13, Calacoto, La Paz; tel. (2) 211-0361; fax (2) 211-0365; e-mail coreabolivia@gmail.com; internet bol.mofat.go.kr; Ambassador Chun Young-Wook.

Mexico: Avda Ballivián 1174, entre Calles 17 y 18, Calacoto, Casilla 430, La Paz; tel. (2) 277-1871; fax (2) 277-1855; e-mail embamex@embamexbolivia.org; internet www.sre.gob.mx/bolivia; Ambassador Armando Arriazola Peto-Rueda.

Nicaragua: Calle 6 de Obrajes, entre Avda 14 de Setiembre y Avda Hernando Siles 481, La Paz; tel. (2) 211-5563; e-mail echevez@cancilleria.gob.ni; Ambassador Elías Chévez Obando.

Panama: Calle 10, No 7853, Calacoto, Casilla 678, La Paz; tel. (2) 278-7334; fax (2) 279-7290; e-mail empanbol@ceibo.entelnet.bo; internet www.empanbol.org; Ambassador Afranio Herrera García.

Paraguay: Edif. Illimani II, 1°, Of. 101, Avda 6 de Agosto, esq. Pedro Salazar, Sopocachi, Casilla 882, La Paz; tel. (2) 243-3176; fax (2) 243-2201; e-mail embaparbolivia@mre.gov.py; Chargé d'affaires a.i. Osvaldo Bittar Vicioso.

Peru: Calle Fernando Guachalla 300, Sopocachi, Casilla 668, La Paz; tel. (2) 244-1250; fax (2) 244-1240; e-mail embbol@caoba.entelnet.bo; internet www.embaperubolivia.com; Ambassador Silvia Elena Alfaro Espinosa.

Russia: Avda Walter Guevara Arce 8129, Calacoto, Casilla 5494, La Paz; tel. (2) 278-6419; fax (2) 278-6531; e-mail embrusia@acelerate.com; Ambassador Alexéi Sazonov.

Spain: Avda 6 de Agosto 2827, Casilla 282, La Paz; tel. (2) 243-3518; fax (2) 243-2752; e-mail emb.lapaz@maec.es; internet www.maec.es/embajadas/lapaz; Ambassador Ángel María Vázquez Díaz de Tuesta.

Sweden: Edif. Multicine, 11°, Avda Arce 2631, La Paz; tel. (2) 297-9630; fax (2) 297-9631; e-mail ambassaden.la-paz @foreign.ministry.se; internet www.swedenabroad.com; Ambassador Marie Andersson de Frutos.

Switzerland: Calle 13, esq. Avda 14 de Setiembre, Obrajes, Casilla 9356, La Paz; tel. (2) 275-1225; fax (2) 214-0885; e-mail paz.vertretung@eda.admin.ch; internet www.eda.admin.ch/lapaz; Ambassador Peter Bischof.

United Kingdom: Avda Arce 2732, Casilla 694, La Paz; tel. (2) 243-3424; fax (2) 243-1073; e-mail ukinbolivia@gmail.com; internet www.ukinbolivia.fco.gov.uk; Ambassador Ross Patrick Denny.

USA: Avda Arce 2780, Casilla 425, La Paz; tel. (2) 216-8000; fax (2) 216-8111; e-mail consularlapaz@state.com; internet bolivia.usembassy.gov; Chargé d'affaires a.i. Larry L. Memmott.

Uruguay: Calle 16, No 8247, entre Calle B y Roberto Prudencio, Calacoto, La Paz; tel. (2) 279-1482; fax (2) 279-3976; e-mail urulivia@acelerate.com; internet www.embauruguaybol.com; Ambassador Carlos Mario Flanagan Bentos.

Venezuela: Calle 12, esq. Costanerita 1000, Obrajes, Casilla 441, La Paz; tel. (2) 278-8501; fax (2) 278-8711; e-mail embve.bopaz@mppre.gob.ve; internet bolivia.embajada.gob.ve; Ambassador Crisbeylee Gonzáles Hernández.

Judicial System

In October 2011, following a constitutional amendment, direct elections were held to elect judges to the Constitutional Court, Supreme Court, Council of Magistrates and a newly established Agro-Environmental Court.

CONSTITUTIONAL COURT

Tribunal Constitucional Plurinacional: Avda del Maestro 300, Sucre; tel. (4) 644-0455; fax (4) 642-1871; e-mail tcp@tcpbolivia.bo; internet www.tcpbolivia.bo; f. 1994; seven mems; Pres. (vacant).

SUPREME COURT

Judicial power is vested in the Supreme Tribunal of Justice. There are nine judges and a further nine alternates, directly elected for a term of six years. The court is divided into five chambers. One chamber deals with civil cases, two chambers deal with criminal cases, a further two deal with administrative and social cases. The President of the Supreme Tribunal of Justice presides over joint sessions of the courts and attends the joint sessions for cassation cases.

Tribunal Suprema de Justicia: Parque Bolívar, Casilla 211 y 321, Sucre; tel. (4) 645-3200; fax (4) 646-2696; e-mail cortesuprema@poderjudicial.gob.bo; internet suprema.poderjudicial.gob.bo; Pres. Jorge von Borries.

COUNCIL OF MAGISTRATES

Consejo de la Magistratura: Calle Luis Paz (Ex Pilinco) 290, Sucre; tel. (4) 646-1600; internet www.organojudicial.gob.bo/consejo; f. 2011; five judges, with five alternates; Pres. Cristina Mamani Aguilar.

AGRO-ENVIRONMENTAL COURT

The Agro-Environmental Court was founded in 2011. It comprises seven judges, elected by popular vote for a six-year term.

President: Bernardo Huarachi.

DISTRICT COURTS

There is a District Court sitting in each Department, and additional provincial and local courts to try minor cases.

ATTORNEY-GENERAL

In addition to the Attorney-General at Sucre (appointed by the President on the proposal of the Senate), there is a District Attorney in each Department as well as circuit judges.

Attorney-General: HUGO RAÚL MONTERO LARA.

Religion

CHRISTIANITY

The Roman Catholic Church

Some 83% of the population are Roman Catholics. Bolivia comprises four archdioceses, six dioceses, two Territorial Prelatures and five Apostolic Vicariates.

Bishops' Conference: Conferencia Episcopal Boliviana, Calle Potosí 814, Casilla 2309, La Paz; tel. (2) 240-6855; fax (2) 240-6941; e-mail asc@scbbs-bo.com; internet www.iglesia.org.bo; f. 1972; Pres. Cardinal OSCAR APARICIO (Bishop of Castrense).

Archbishop of Cochabamba: Most Rev. TITO SOLARI CAPELLARI, Avda Heroínas 152, esq. Zenteno Anaya, Casilla 129, Cochabamba; tel. (4) 425-6562; fax (4) 425-0522; e-mail arzobispado@iglesiacbba.org; internet www.iglesiacbba.org.

Archbishop of La Paz: Most Rev. EDMUNDO LUIS FLAVIO ABASTOFLOR MONTERO, Calle Ballivián 1277, Casilla 259, La Paz; tel. (2) 220-3690; fax (2) 220-3672; e-mail arzobispadodelapaz@yahoo.es; internet www.arzobispadolapaz.org.

Archbishop of Santa Cruz de la Sierra: Cardinal SERGIO ALFREDO GUALBERTI CALANDRINA, Calle Ingavi 49, Manzana Uno, Casilla 25, Santa Cruz; tel. (3) 332-4416; fax (3) 333-0181; e-mail cancilleria@cotas.com.bo; internet www.iglesiasantacruz.org.

Archbishop of Sucre: Most Rev. JESÚS JUÁREZ PÁRRAGA, Calle Guillermo Loayza 100B, Casilla 205, Sucre; tel. (4) 645-1587; fax (4) 646-0336; e-mail pascar@arquidiocesisdesucre.org.bo; internet www.arquidiocesisdesucre.org.bo.

The Anglican Communion

The diocese of Bolivia falls within the province of Iglesia Anglicana del Cono Sur de América (Anglican Church of the Southern Cone of America).

Inglesia Anglicana Episcopal de Bolivia: Avda Simón López, esq. Melchor Perez, Casilla 848, Cochabamba; tel. (4) 440-1168; e-mail BpFrank@sams-usa.org; internet iglesiaanglicanadebolivia.org; Bishop Rev. FRANK RAYMOND LYONS.

Other Christian Churches

Church of Jesus Christ of Latter-Day Saints (Mormons): Avda Melchor Urquidi 1500, Alto Queru, Cochabamba; tel. (4) 429-3161; internet www.lds.org; 182,964 mems.

Convención Bautista Boliviana (Baptist Convention of Bolivia): Avda Cesar Cronembold 109, Casilla 3147, Santa Cruz; tel. (3) 343-0717; e-mail convencion@cotas.com.bo; internet conbabol.org; f. 1947; Pres. RUTH NOEMÍ COULTHARD DE MANSILLA.

Iglesia Evangélica Luterana Boliviana: Calle Rio Pirai 958, Casilla 8471, La Paz; tel. (2) 238-3442; fax (2) 238-0073; e-mail eaf2000@hotmail.es; f. 1972; Pres. Rev. EMILIO ASLLA.

Iglesia Evangélica Metodista en Bolivia (Evangelical Methodist Church in Bolivia): Avda 16 de Julio 1636, Casillas 356 y 8347, La Paz; tel. (2) 290-0710; fax (2) 290-0726; internet www.iemb.cc; autonomous since 1969; 10,000 mems; Bishop Rev. JAVIER ROJAS TERÁN.

Unión Bautista Boliviana (Baptist Union of Bolivia): Calle Jordan O-0369, Casilla 2199, La Paz; tel. (2) 458-3538; fax (2) 425-0212; e-mail info@ubb.org.bo; internet ubb.org.bo; Pres. Rev. REYES BALTAZAR QUISPE YAPITA; Exec. Dir YOLANDA OROPEZA DE FLORES.

BAHÁ'Í FAITH

National Spiritual Assembly of the Bahá'ís of Bolivia: Avda Libertador 1, Obrajes, Casilla 1613, La Paz; tel. (2) 278-5058; e-mail secretariat@bahai.org.bo; internet bahai.org.bo; f. 1961; mems resident in 5,161 localities; Sec. JOAN HERNANDEZ.

The Press

DAILY NEWSPAPERS

Cochabamba

Opinión: Calle General Achá 252, Casilla 287, Cochabamba; tel. (4) 425-4400; fax (4) 441-5121; e-mail opinion@opinion.com.bo; internet www.opinion.com.bo; f. 1985; Dir FEDERICO SABAT LARA; Chief Editor MARÍA LUISA MERCADO.

Los Tiempos: Edif. Los Tiempos, Plaza Quintanilla, Casilla 525, Cochabamba; tel. (4) 425-4562; fax (4) 425-7773; e-mail lostiempos@lostiempos-bolivia.com; internet www.lostiempos.com; f. 1943; morning; independent; Pres. EDUARDO CANELAS TÁRDIO; Man. Editor ELIZABETH ARRÁZOLA SANDOVAL; circ. 19,000.

La Paz

El Diario: Calle Loayza 118, Casilla 5, La Paz; tel. (2) 215-0900; fax (2) 215-0902; e-mail redinfo@diario.net; internet www.eldiario.net; f. 1904; morning; conservative; Gen. Man. JORGE CARRASCO GUZMÁN; Man. Editor FERNANDO VALDIVIA DELGADO; circ. 55,000.

Jornada: Edif. Almirante Grau 672, Zona San Pedro, Casilla 1628, La Paz; tel. (2) 248-8163; fax (2) 248-7487; e-mail cartas@jornadanet.com; internet www.jornadanet.com; f. 1964; evening; independent; Dir DAVID RÍOS ARANDA; circ. 11,500.

Página Siete: Calle Rosendo Reyes 16, esq. 27, Cota Cota, La Paz; tel. (2) 261-1700; e-mail paginasiete@paginasiete.bo; internet www.paginasiete.bo; Dir RAÚL PEÑARANDA UNDURRAGA; Editor MARTÍN ZELAYA SÁNCHEZ.

La Prensa: Mayor Lopera 230, Villa Fátima, Casilla 5614, La Paz; tel. (2) 221-8821; fax (2) 220-2509; e-mail laprensa@laprensa.com.bo; internet www.laprensa.com.bo; Dir-Gen. DIEGO CANELAS MONTAÑO; Chief Editor FABIANA CARRAZANA PAZ.

La Razón: Colinas de Santa Rita, Alto Auquisamaña (Zona Sur), Casilla 13100, La Paz; tel. (2) 277-1415; fax (2) 277-0908; e-mail larazon@la-razon.com; internet www.la-razon.com; f. 1990; Dir CLAUDIA BENAVENTE P.; Man. Editor CARLOS ORÍAS B.; circ. 35,000.

Oruro

La Patria: Avda Camacho 1892, entre Murguía y Aldana, Casilla 48, Oruro; tel. (2) 525-0780; fax (2) 525-0782; e-mail info@lapatria.com.bo; internet www.lapatriaenlinea.com; f. 1919; morning; independent; Dir ENRIQUE MIRALLES BONNECARRERE; Chief Editor JORGE LAZZO QUINTEROS; circ. 6,000.

Potosí

El Potosí: Calle Cochabamba 35 (Junto a Unidad Sanitaria), Potosí; tel. (2) 622-2601; fax (2) 622-7835; e-mail elpotosi@entelnet.bo; internet www.elpotosi.net; f. 2001; Dir JUAN JOSÉ TORO MONTOYA; Man. Editor GUILLERMO BULLAÍN IÑIGUEZ.

Santa Cruz

El Deber: Avda El Trompillo 1144, 2°, Casilla 1144, Santa Cruz; tel. (3) 353-8000; fax (3) 353-9053; e-mail web@eldeber.com.bo; internet www.eldeber.com.bo; f. 1953; morning; independent; Exec. Dir Dr PEDRO RIVERO MERCADO; Man. Editor TUFFÍ ARÉ VÁZQUEZ; circ. 35,000.

El Día: Avda Cristo Redentor 3355, Casilla 5344, Santa Cruz; tel. (3) 343-4040; fax (3) 342-4041; e-mail eldia@edadsa.com.bo; internet www.eldia.com.bo; f. 1987; Dir ALDO AGUIERA; Man. Editor RÓGER CUÉLLAR.

La Estrella del Oriente: Calle Republiquetas 353, Santa Cruz; tel. (3) 332-9011; fax (3) 332-9012; e-mail laestrelladeloriente@laestrella.bo; internet www.laestrelladeloriente.com; f. 1864; Dir CARLOS SUBIRANA SUÁREZ; Chief Editor MAURICIO MELGAR.

El Mundo: Parque Industrial, Manzana-7, Casilla 1984, Santa Cruz; tel. (3) 346-4646; fax (3) 346-3322; e-mail redaccion@mail.elmundo.com.bo; internet www.elmundo.com.bo; f. 1979; morning; owned by Santa Cruz Industrialists' Asscn; Pres. JOSÉ LUIS DURÁN SAUCEDO; Chief Editor CARLOS CALIZAYA AYAVIRI; circ. 15,000.

Sucre

Correo del Sur: Calle Kilómetro 7, No 202, Casilla 242, Sucre; tel. (4) 646-3202; fax (4) 646-0152; e-mail correo7@entelnet.bo; internet www.correodelsur.com; f. 1987; Dir MARCO ANTONIO DIPP MUKLED; Man. Editor RAYKHA FLORES COSSIO.

PERIODICALS

Actualidad Boliviana Confidencial (ABC): Edif. Villazón, 10°, Of. 10A, Avda Villazón, La Paz; tel. (2) 231-3781; internet www.abceconomia.com; f. 1966; weekly; Dir HUGO GONZÁLEZ RIOJA; circ. 6,000.

Agricultura Ecológica: Pasaje F, No 2958, Urb. El Profesional, Casilla 1999, Cochabamba; tel. (4) 442-3838; fax (4) 442-3636; e-mail info@agrecolandes.org; internet www.agrecolandes.org; f. 2005; publ. by the Centro de Información e Intercambio para la Agricultura Ecológica (AGRECOL); yearly; Exec. Dir and Editor RUBÉN MALDONADO.

ANF-Notas: Edif. Mariscal de Ayacucho, 5°, Of. 501, Calle Loayza 233, Casilla 5782, La Paz; tel. (2) 233-5577; fax (2) 233-7607; e-mail anf@noticiasfides.com; internet www.noticiasfides.com; f. 1963; publ. by ANF; weekly; political analysis; Dir P. SERGIO MONTES.

Cosas: Calle Inofuentes 1348, entre calles 19 y 20 de Calacoto, La Paz; tel. (2) 215-0191; e-mail cosasbolivia@cosas.com; internet www.cosasbolivia.com; monthly; lifestyle; Dir CARLA TEJERINA DE CABEZAS; Editor MARTHA OIAZO.

Datos: Edif. Quipus, 5°, Pasaje Jauregui No 2248, Sopocachi, Casilla 14390, La Paz; tel. (2) 244-0621; e-mail datos@datos-bo.com; internet www.datos-bo.com; monthly; politics and current affairs; Dir CARLOS RODRÍGUEZ.

Ecos: Calle Kilómetro 7 No 202, Sucre; tel. (4) 646-1531; e-mail contacto@ecos.com.bo; internet www.ecos.com.bo; weekly; entertainment and fashion; Editor OSCAR DÍAZ ARNAU.

Miradas: Edif. Torre Azul, 18°, Avda 20 de Octubre 2665, La Paz; tel. (2) 261-1700; e-mail paginasiete@paginasiete.bo; internet www.paginasiete.bo; weekly; arts; Editor MARCO ZELAYA.

Nueva Economía: Pedro Salazar 2477, La Paz; tel. (2) 291-1600; e-mail dgutierrez@nuevaeconomia.com.bo; internet nuevaeconomia.com.bo; financial; weekly; Gen. Man. JORGE VACA HEREDIA; Editor DANIEL GUTIÉRREZ CARRIÓN.

Oxígeno: Calle Harrison 1957-A, entre Diaz Romero y Villalobos, Miraflores, La Paz; tel. (2) 224-8040; e-mail oxigeno@oxigenobolivia.com; internet www.oxigenobolivia.com; monthly; society, general affairs; Dir GROVER YAPURA ARUQUIPA; Editor LILIANA CARRILLO VALENZUELA.

PRESS ASSOCIATIONS

Asociación Nacional de la Prensa (ANP): Claudio Aliaga 1290, 2°, San Miguel, La Paz; tel. (2) 279-4208; internet www.anpbolivia.com; f. 1976; private; Pres. ANA MARÍA TINEO; Exec. Dir JUAN LEÓN CORNEJO.

Asociación de Periodistas de La Paz (APLP): Edif. Las Dos Torres, Avda 6 de Agosto 2170, Casilla 477, La Paz; tel. (2) 243-0345; fax (2) 243-6006; internet www.aplp.org.bo; f. 1929; Pres. ANTONIO VARGAS RÍOS; Sec.-Gen. GHILKA SULMA SANABRIA PRADEL.

NEWS AGENCIES

Agencia Boliviana de Información: Calle Colón, casi esq. Ballivian, Casilla 6500, La Paz; tel. (2) 211-3782; fax (2) 220-4370; e-mail abi@abi.bo; internet www.abi.bo; govt-owned; Dir JORGE REY CUBA AKIYAMA; Man. Editor RUBÉN DAVID SANDI LORA.

Agencia de Noticias Fides (ANF): Edif. Mariscal de Ayacucho, 5°, Of. 501, Calle Loayza, Casilla 5782, La Paz; tel. (2) 236-5152; fax (2) 236-5153; e-mail anf@noticiasfides.com; internet www.noticiasfides.bo; f. 1963; owned by the Roman Catholic Church; Dir SERGIO RICARDO MONTES RONDÓN; Editor JAIME LOAYZA ZEGARRA.

Publishers

Editorial los Amigos del Libro: Edif. Alba I, 3°, Of. 312, Calle España O-153, Cochabamba; tel. (4) 425-6005; fax (4) 450-4151; e-mail gutten@librosbolivia.com; internet www.librosbolivia.com; f. 1945; general; Gen. Man. INGRID GUTTENTAG.

Editorial Bruño: Loayza 167, Casilla 4809, La Paz; tel. (2) 233-1254; fax (2) 233-5043; f. 1964; Dir IGNACIO LOMA GUTIÉRREZ.

Editorial Comunicarte: Avda Cañoto 360, Santa Cruz; tel. (3) 332-3111; fax (3) 336-9332; e-mail comunicarte@comunicarte.com.bo; internet www.comunicarte.com.bo; Gen. Man. ANA MARÍA ARTIGAS.

Editorial Don Bosco: Villa Tejada Rectangular, Avda La Paz, esq. Avda Cívica, Casilla 4458, La Paz; tel. (2) 281-7325; fax (2) 281-7294; e-mail editorialdonbosco@gmail.com; internet www.editorial-donbosco.com; f. 1896; social sciences and literature.

Editorial Gente Comun: Villa Fátima, Avda de las Américas 764, La Paz; tel. (2) 221-4493; e-mail marcel@editorialgentecomun.com; internet editorialgentecomun.com; Man. Dir ARIEL MUSTAFÁ.

Editorial Icthus: Calle Miguel Angel Valda 121, Sucre; tel. (4) 642-7345; e-mail icthus@entelnet.bo; internet www.innset.com.bo; f. 1967; general and textbooks; Man. Dir FABIOLA GORENA.

Editorial Verbo Divino: Avda Juan de la Rosa O-2216, Casilla 191, Cochabamba; tel. (4) 428-6297; fax (4) 442-0733; e-mail info@verbodivino-bo.com; internet www.verbodivino-bo.com; f. 1997; Christian literature; part of Grupo Editorial Verbo Divino; Gen. Man. PEDRO PITURA.

Gisbert y Cía, SA: Calle Comercio 1270, Casilla 195, La Paz; tel. (2) 220-2626; fax (2) 220-2911; e-mail info@libreriagisbert.com; internet www.libreriagisbert.com; f. 1907; textbooks, history, law and general; Pres. ANTONIO SCHULCZEWSKI GISBERT; Promotions Man. MARÍA DEL CARMEN SCHULCZEWSKI; Admin. Man. SERGIO GARCÍA.

Grupo Editorial La Hoguera: Edif. Gabriela, 2°, Calle Beni 678, Santa Cruz; tel. (3) 335-4426; fax (3) 311-7821; e-mail lahoguera@lahoguera.com; internet www.lahoguera.com; f. 1990; Pres. ALFONSO CORTEZ; Dir-Gen. MAURICIO MÉNDEZ.

Idearia: Calle 8, Este 19, Barrio Hamacas, Santa Cruz; tel. (3) 339-8381; e-mail idearia@idearia.net; internet www.idearia.net; children's literature and magazines; Gen. Man. GABRIELA ICHASO.

Librería Editorial Juventud: Plaza Murillo 519, Casilla 1489, La Paz; tel. (2) 240-6248; f. 1946; textbooks and general; Dir GUSTAVO URQUIZO MENDOZA.

Martínez Acchini, SRL Libros: Edif. Illampu, Avda Arce 2132, La Paz; tel. (2) 244-1112; internet martinezacchini.com; f. 1975; Man. Dir ERNESTO MARTÍNEZ.

Master Bolivia: Calle Velasco 268, Santa Cruz; tel. (3) 333-2413; fax (3) 311-2260; e-mail info@masterbolivia.com; internet masterbolivia.com.

El Pauro Ediciones: Calle Vallegrande 424, Santa Cruz; tel. (3) 339-4916; e-mail elpauroed@cotas.com.bo; internet elpauroediciones.com; Gen. Man. MAGDALENA MÁRQUEZ.

Plural Editores: Calle Rosendo Gutiérrez 595, esq. Avda Ecuador, La Paz; tel. (2) 241-1018; e-mail plural@plural.bo; internet www.plural.bo; f. 1999; Exec. Dir JOSÉ ANTONIO QUIROGA.

Rodel Ediciones: Calle Mandioré 46, Santa Cruz; tel. (3) 337-8689; fax (3) 337-0246; e-mail info@rodelediciones.com; internet rodelediciones.com; Pres. JORGE LUIS RODRÍGUEZ.

Santillana de Ediciones, SA: Calle 13, No 8078, Calacoto, La Paz; tel. (2) 277-4242; fax (2) 277-1056; e-mail info@santillanabo.com; internet www.santillanabo.com; f. 1994; Gen. Man. CAROLA OSSIO.

PUBLISHERS' ASSOCIATION

Cámara Boliviana del Libro: Calle Capitán Ravelo 2116, Casilla 682, La Paz; tel. and fax (2) 211-3264; e-mail cabolib@entelnet.bo; internet www.camaralibrolapaz.org.bo; f. 1947; Pres. ERNESTO MARTÍNEZ ACCHINI; Vice-Pres. CARLA MARÍA BERDEGUÉ; Gen. Man. ANA PATRICIA NAVARRO.

Broadcasting and Communications

TELECOMMUNICATIONS

Bolitel, SRL (Bolivia Telecomunicación, SRL): Calle Mercado, esq. Independencia, Santa Cruz; tel. (3) 364-2424; fax (3) 364-3973; e-mail info@libre.com.bo; internet www.libre.com.bo; f. 2008; part of the UNAGRO corpn; Man. MAURICIO PINTO.

Empresa Nacional de Telecomunicaciones, SA (ENTEL): Calle Federico Suazo 1771, Casilla 4450, La Paz; tel. (2) 214-1010; fax (2) 239-1789; e-mail contacto@entelsa.entelnet.bo; internet www.entel.bo; f. 1965; privatized under the Govt's capitalization programme in 1995; reverted to state ownership in 2008; Pres. CARLOS REYES MONTAÑO; Gen. Man. ROY ROQUE MÉNDEZ.

Tigo (Telefónica Celular de Bolivia): Avda Viedma 648, Santa Cruz; tel. (3) 333-5227; fax (3) 335-8790; e-mail atencionalcliente@tigo.com.bo; internet www.tigo.com.bo; f. 2005; part of Millicom International Cellular, SA (MIC); Chief Officer, Latin America MARIO ZANOTTI; Gen. Man. PABLO GUARDIA.

Viva GSM (NuevaTel PCS de Bolivia, SA): Edif. Multicentro, Calle Capitán Ravelo, esq. R. Gutiérrez 2289, Casilla 11875, Sopocachi, La Paz; tel. (2) 244-2420; fax (2) 244-2353; e-mail infoa@nuevatel.com; internet www.nuevatel.com; f. 1999; Regional Man. VIRGINIA RETAMOSO.

Regulatory Authorities

Autoridad de Fiscalización y Control Social de Transportes y Telecomunicaciones (ATT): Calle 13, Nos 8260 y 8280, entre Sauces y Costanera, Calacoto, Casilla 6692, La Paz; tel. (2) 277-2266; fax (2) 277-2299; e-mail informaciones@att.gob.bo; internet www.att.gob.bo; supervises and regulates the activities and services provided by telecommunications operators; Exec. Dir PEDRO CLIFFORD PARAVICINI HURTADO.

Superintendencia de Telecomunicaciones: Calle 13, No 8260, Calacoto, La Paz; tel. (2) 277-2266; fax (2) 277-2299; e-mail supertel@ceibo.entelnet.bo; internet www.sittel.gov.bo; f. 1995; govt-controlled broadcasting authority; Supt JORGE NAVA AMADOR.

BROADCASTING

Radio

Educación Radiofónica de Bolivia (ERBOL): Edif. Smith, Calle Ballivián 1323, 4°, Casilla 5946, La Paz; tel. (2) 204-0111; fax (2) 220-3888; e-mail erbol@erbol.com.bo; internet www.erbol.com.bo; f. 1967; asscn of 28 educational radio stations in Bolivia; Dir WINDSOR JOSÉ SALAS GUISBERT.

Radio Fides: La Paz; e-mail sistemas@radiofides.com; internet www.radiofides.com; f. 1939; network of 28 radio stations; Roman Catholic; Dir EDUARDO PÉREZ IRIBARNE.

Red Patria Nueva: Avda Camacho 1485, 6°, La Paz; tel. (2) 220-0473; fax (2) 200-390; e-mail illimani@comunica.gov.bo; internet www.patrianueva.bo; f. 1932 as Compañía Radio Boliviana; govt-owned network; broadcasts across the country, often as Radio Illimani; Dir IVÁN MALDONADO CORTÉZ.

Television

ATB Red Nacional (Canal 9): Avda Argentina 2057, Casilla 9285, La Paz; tel. and fax (2) 222-9922; e-mail noticias@atb.com.bo; internet www.atb.com.bo; f. 1984; privately owned television network; part of Grupo Prisa, SA; Man. ROXANA ALCOBA.

Bolivisión (Canal 4): Parque Demetrio Canelas 1543, Casilla 6067, Cochabamba; tel. (4) 428-4318; fax (4) 428-4319; e-mail jimmystrauch@redbolivision.tv; internet www.redbolivision.tv.bo; f. 1997; privately owned television network; Exec. Pres. ERNESTO ASBÚN GAZAUI; Gen. Man. JAVIER CARMONA DEL SOLAR.

Red Uno: Calle Romecín Campos 592, Sopocachi, La Paz; tel. (2) 242-1111; fax (2) 241-0939; e-mail notivision@reduno.com.bo; internet www.reduno.com.bo; f. 1985; commercial television station; offices in La Paz, Santa Cruz and Cochabamba; Dir MARIO ROJAS; Gen. Man. JULIO ROMERO.

Televisión Boliviana (TVB—Canal 7): Edif. La Urbana, 6°, Avda Camacho 1485, Casilla 900, La Paz; tel. (2) 220-3404; fax (2) 220-3973; e-mail info@boliviatv.bo; internet www.boliviatv.bo; f. 1969; govt network operating stations in La Paz, Oruro, Cochabamba, Potosí, Chuquisaca, Pando, Beni, Tarija and Santa Cruz; Gen. Man. MARCO ANTONIO SANTIVAÑEZ SORIA.

Televisión Universitaria (Canal 13): Edif. Hoy, 12°–13°, Avda 6 de Agosto 2170, Casilla 13383, La Paz; tel. and fax (2) 244-1313; e-mail canal13@umsa.bo; internet tvu.umsa.bo; f. 1980; educational programmes; stations in Oruro, Cochabamba, Potosí, Sucre, Tarija, Beni and Santa Cruz; Dir OMAR GÓMEZ LIZARRO.

Unitel (Canal 9): Km 5, Carretera antigua a Cochabamba, Santa Cruz; tel. (3) 352-7686; fax (3) 352-7688; e-mail canal9@unitel.com.bo; internet www.unitel.tv; f. 1997; privately owned television network; Vice-Pres. HUGO PÁRRAGA.

Regulatory Authority

Asociación Boliviana de Radiodifusoras (ASBORA): Edif. Jazmín, 10°, Avda 20 de Octubre 2019, Casilla 5324, La Paz; tel. (2) 236-5154; fax (2) 236-3069; broadcasting authority; Pres. RAÚL NOVILLO ALARCÓN.

Finance

(cap. = capital; res = reserves; dep. = deposits; m. = million; br(s) = branch(es); amounts are in bolivianos, unless otherwise stated)

BANKING

Supervisory Authority

Autoridad de Supervisión del Sistema Financiero: Plaza Isabel la Católica 2507, Casilla 447, La Paz; tel. (2) 243-1919; fax (2) 243-0028; e-mail asfi@asfi.gov.bo; internet www.asfi.gov.bo; f. 1928; fmrly Superintendencia de Bancos y Entidados Financieras; name changed as above in 2009; Exec. Dir Lic. REYNALDO YUJRA SEGALES.

Central Bank

Banco Central de Bolivia: Avda Ayacucho, esq. Mercado, Casilla 3118, La Paz; tel. (2) 240-9090; fax (2) 240-6614; e-mail bancocentraldebolivia@bcb.gob.bo; internet www.bcb.gob.bo; f. 1911 as Banco de la Nación Boliviana; name changed as above in 1928; bank of issue; cap. 515.7m., res 7,807.9m., dep. 47,441.2m. (Dec. 2009); Pres. MARCELO ZABALAGA ESTRADA; Gen. Man. EDUARDO PARDO.

Commercial Banks

Banco Bisa, SA: Avda 16 de Julio 1628, Casilla 1290, La Paz; tel. (2) 231-7272; fax (2) 239-0033; e-mail bancobisa@grupobisa.com; internet www.bisa.com; f. 1963; cap. 731.1m., res 141.5m., dep. 7,850.3m. (Dec. 2010); Pres., CEO and Chair. Ing. JULIO LEÓN PRADO.

Banco de Crédito de Bolivia, SA: Calle Colón, esq. Mercado 1308, Casilla 907, La Paz; tel. (2) 233-0444; fax (2) 231-9163; e-mail cnavarro@bancred.com.bo; internet www.bancodecredito.com.bo; f. 1993 as Banco Popular del Perú, SA; name changed as above 1994; owned by Banco de Crédito del Perú; cap. 315.5m., res 234.1m., dep. 6,813.4m. (Dec. 2010); Chair. DIONISIO ROMERO; Gen. Man. DIEGO A. CAVERO BELAUNDE; 8 brs.

Banco Económico, SA-SCZ: Calle Ayacucho 166, Casilla 5603, Santa Cruz; tel. (3) 315-5500; fax (3) 336-1184; e-mail baneco@baneco.com.bo; internet www.baneco.com.bo; f. 1990; dep. US $244.9m., cap. US $24.4m., total assets US $269.3m. (Dec. 2006); Pres. IVO MATEO KULJIS FÜCHTNER; 25 brs.

Banco Ganadero, SA-Santa Cruz: Calle Bolivar 99, esq. Beni, Santa Cruz; tel. (3) 336-1616; fax (3) 336-1617; internet www.bg.com.bo; f. 1994; cap. 148.5m., res 17.7m., dep. 3,702.9m. (Dec. 2009); Pres. JORGE MARCOS SALVADOR; Gen. Man. RONALD GUTIÉRREZ LÓPEZ.

Banco Mercantil Santa Cruz, SA: Calle Ayacucho, esq. Mercado 295, Casilla 423, La Paz; tel. (2) 240-9040; fax (2) 240-9158; e-mail asalinas@bancomercantil.com.bo; internet www.bmsc.com.bo; f. 1905 as Banco Mercantil, SA; acquired Banco Santa Cruz in 2006 and changed name as above; cap. 413.3m., res 296.9m., dep. 10,827.2m. (Dec. 2010); Exec. Vice-Pres. ALBERTO VALDES ANDREATTA; Pres. EMILIO UNZUETA ZEGARRA; 37 brs.

Banco Nacional de Bolivia: Avda Camacho, esq. Colón 1296, Casilla 360, La Paz; tel. (2) 233-2323; fax (2) 231-0695; e-mail info@bnb.com.bo; internet www.bnb.com.bo; f. 1871; 67.27% owned by Grupo Bedoya; cap. 549.5m., res 57.2m., dep. 8,800.7m. (Dec. 2010); Pres. IGNACIO BEDOYA SÁENZ; Gen. Man. PABLO BEDOYA SÁENZ; 9 brs.

Banco Solidario, SA (BancoSol): Calle Nicolás Acosta 289, Casilla 13176, La Paz; tel. (2) 248-4242; fax (2) 248-6533; e-mail info@bancosol.com.bo; internet www.bancosol.com.bo; f. 1992; cap. 147.7m., res 36.8m., dep. 2,935.1m. (Dec. 2009); Gen. Man. KURT KÖNIGSFEST SANABRIA.

Banco Unión, SA: Calle Loayza 255, Edif. de Ugarte Ingeniería, 10°, Of. 1001, La Paz; e-mail info@bancounion.com.bo; internet www.bancounion.com.bo; f. 1982; cap. 132.9m., res 124.2m., dep. 3,876.4m. (Dec. 2009); Pres. FERNANDO ARTEAGA MONTERO; Gen. Man. MARCIA VILLARROEL GONZÁLES; 9 brs.

Credit Institution

PRODEM: Avda Camacho 1277, esq. Colón, La Paz; tel. (2) 211-3227; fax (2) 214-7632; e-mail info@prodemffp.com.bo; internet www.prodemffp.com; f. 2000; microcredit institution; Gen. Man. JOSÉ NOEL ZAMORA; 250 brs.

Banking Association

Asociación de Bancos Privados de Bolivia (ASOBAN): Edif. Cámara Nacional de Comercio, 15°, Avda Mariscal Santa Cruz, esq. Colombia 1392, Casilla 5822, La Paz; tel. (2) 237-6164; fax (2) 239-1093; e-mail info@asoban.bo; internet www.asoban.bo; f. 1957; Pres. KURT KÖENIGSFEST SANABRIA; Vice-Pres ANTONIO VALDA, MIGUEL NAVARRO; 18 mems.

STOCK EXCHANGE

Bolsa Boliviana de Valores, SA: Calle Montevideo 142, Casilla 12521, La Paz; tel. (2) 244-3232; fax (2) 244-2308; e-mail info@bolsa-valores-bolivia.com; internet www.bbv.com.bo; f. 1989; Pres. JOSÉ TRIGO VALDIVIA; Gen. Man. JAVIER ANEIVA.

INSURANCE

Supervisory Authority

Autoridad de Fiscalización y Control de Pensiones y Seguros (APS): Edif. Torres Gundlach Este, 6°, Calle Reyes Ortiz, esq. Federico Zuazo, Casilla 10794, La Paz; tel. (2) 233-1212; fax (2) 231-2223; e-mail contactenos@aps.gob.bo; internet www.aps.gob.bo; Exec. Dir IVÁN ROJAS YANGUAS.

Major Companies

Alianza, Cía de Seguros y Reaseguros, SA: Avda 20 de Octubre 2680, esq. Campos, Zona San Jorge, Casilla 1043, La Paz; tel. (2) 243-2121; fax (2) 243-2713; e-mail info@alianzaseguros.com; internet www.alianza.com.bo; f. 1991; Exec. Dir ALEJANDRO YBARRA CARRASCO.

Alianza Vida Seguros y Reaseguros, SA: Avda Viedma 21, esq. Melchor Pinto, Casilla 7181, Santa Cruz; tel. (3) 337-5656; fax (3) 337-5666; e-mail vida@alianzaseguros.com; internet www.alianza.com.bo; f. 1999; Gen. Man. ALEJANDRO YBARRA CARRASCO.

Bisa Seguros y Reaseguros, SA: Edif. San Pablo, 13°, Avda 16 de Julio 1479, Casilla 3669, La Paz; tel. (2) 235-2123; fax (2) 214-8724; e-mail JZeballos@grupobisa.com; internet www.bisaseguros.com; f. 1991; part of Grupo Bisa; Pres. JULIO LEÓN PRADO; Exec. Vice-Pres. ALEJANDRO MACLEAN CÉSPEDES.

La Boliviana Ciacruz de Seguros y Reaseguros, SA: Edif. La Boliviana Ciacruz, Calle Colón 288, Casilla 628, La Paz; tel. (2) 220-3131; fax (2) 220-4087; e-mail info@lbc.bo; internet www.lbc.bo; f. 1964; owned by Zurich Bolivia group; all classes; Pres. GONZALO BEDOYA HERRERA; Vice-Pres. RODRIGO BEDOYA DIEZ DE MEDINA.

Bupa Insurance (Bolivia), SA: Calle 9 este, No 9, esq. Pasillo A, Zona Equipetrol, Santa Cruz; tel. (3) 341-2842; fax (3) 341-2832; e-mail bolivia@bupa.com.bo; internet bolivia.ihi.com; health insurance; Pres. ANTHONY CABRELLI; Gen. Man. DIEGO NORIEGA.

Cía de Seguros y Reaseguros Fortaleza, SA: Avda Arce 2799, esq. Cordero, La Paz; tel. and fax (2) 243-4142; e-mail grupo@grupofortaleza.com.bo; internet www.grupofortaleza.com.bo; Pres. GUIDO EDWIN HINOJOSA CARDOSO; Gen. Man. MARTHA O. LUCCA SUÁREZ.

Credinform International, SA de Seguros: Edif. Credinform, Calle Potosí, esq. Ayacucho 1220, Casilla 1724, La Paz; tel. (2) 231-5566; fax (2) 220-3917; e-mail credinform@credinformsa.com; internet www.credinformsa.com; f. 1954; all classes; Pres. Dr ROBÍN BARRAGÁN PELÁEZ; Gen. Man. MIGUEL ANGEL BARRAGÁN IBARGÜEN.

Latina Seguros Patrimoniales, SA: Avda Monseñor Rivero 223, esq. Asunción, Casilla 3087, Santa Cruz; tel. (3) 371-6565; fax (3) 371-6905; e-mail latinaseguros@latinaseguros.com.bo; internet www.latina-seguros.com.bo; f. 2007; part of Grupo Nacional Vida; Exec. Vice-Pres. JOSÉ LUÍS CAMACHO MISERENDINO; Gen. Man. RAMIRO JESÚS QUIROGA SAN MARTÍN.

Nacional Vida Seguros de Personas, SA: Avda Monseñor Rivero 223, esq. Asunción, Santa Cruz; tel. (3) 371-6262; fax (3) 333-7969; e-mail nacionalvida@nacionalvida.com.bo; internet www.nacionalvida.com.bo; f. 1999; Pres. MARIO AVELINO MORENO VIRUEZ; Gen. Man. LUIS ALVARO TOLEDO PEÑARANDA.

Seguros Illimani, SA: Edif. Mariscal de Ayacucho, 10°, Calle Loayza 233, Casilla 133, La Paz; tel. (2) 220-3040; fax (2) 239-1149; e-mail info@segurosillimani.com.bo; internet www.segurosillimani.com.bo; f. 1979; all classes; Exec. Pres. FERNANDO ARCE G.

La Vitalicia Seguros y Reaseguros de Vida, SA: Edif. Hoy, Avda 6 de Agosto 2860, Casilla 8424, La Paz; tel. (2) 215-7800; fax (2) 211-3480; e-mail aibanez@grupobisa.com; internet www.lavitaliciaseguros.com; f. 1988; part of Grupo Bisa; Pres. JULIO LEÓN PRADO; Exec. Vice-Pres. LUIS ALFONSO IBAÑEZ MONTES.

Insurance Association

Asociación Boliviana de Aseguradores: Edif. Castilla, 5°, Of. 510, Calle Loayza, esq. Mercado 250, Casilla 4804, La Paz; tel. (2) 220-1014; fax (2) 220-1088; e-mail aba@ababolivia.org; internet www.ababolivia.org; f. 1950; Pres. ALEJANDRO YBARRA CARRASCO; Gen. Man. Dr JUSTINO AVENDAÑO RENEDO.

Trade and Industry

DEVELOPMENT ORGANIZATIONS

Centro de Estudios para el Desarrollo Laboral y Agrario (CEDLA): Avda Jaimes Freyre 2940, esq. Muñoz Cornejo, Casilla 8630, La Paz; tel. (2) 241-2429; fax (2) 241-4625; e-mail jgomez@cedla.org; internet www.cedla.org; f. 1985; agrarian and labour development; Exec. Dir JAVIER GÓMEZ AGUILAR.

Fondo Nacional de Desarrollo Regional (FNDR): Calle Pedro Salazar, esq. Andrés Muñoz 631, Sopocachi, Casilla 12613, La Paz; tel. (2) 241-7575; fax (2) 242-2267; e-mail transparencia@fndr.gob.bo; internet www.fndr.gob.bo; f. 1987; promotes local and regional devt, offering financing and support; assumed temporary responsibility for water supply in La Paz in Jan. 2007 following annulment of contracts with private water cos; Exec. Dir EDSON VALDA GÓMEZ.

CHAMBERS OF COMMERCE

Cámara de Comercio de Oruro: Edif. Cámara de Comercio, Pasaje Guachalla, La Plata, Casilla 148, Oruro; tel. (2) 525-0606; fax (2) 525-2615; e-mail contacto@camaradecomerciodeoruro.com; internet www.camaradecomerciodeoruro.com; f. 1895; Pres. RAMIRO DULÓN PEREZ; Gen. Man. VÍCTOR HUGO RODRÍGUEZ GARCÍA; 165 mems.

Cámara de Comercio y Servicios de Cochabamba: Calle Sucre E-0336, Casilla 493, Cochabamba; tel. (4) 425-7715; fax (4) 425-7717; e-mail gerencia@cadeco.org; internet www.cadeco.org; f. 1922; Pres. ALDO GASTÓN VACAFLORES CHIARELLA; Gen. Man. JOSÉ RIVERA ETEROVIC.

Cámara Departamental de Industria, Comercio y Servicios de Tarija: Calle Bolívar, entre Mendez y Suipacha, Zona Central, Casilla 74, Tarija; tel. (4) 664-2737; fax (4) 611-3636; e-mail caincotar@entelnet.bo; internet www.cictja.org; f. 2005; Pres. VÍCTOR FERNÁNDEZ.

Cámara de Exportadores de La Paz (CAMEX): Avda Arce 2021 esq. Goitia, Sopocachi, Casilla 789, La Paz; tel. (2) 244-4310; fax (2) 244-2842; e-mail info@camexbolivia.com; internet www.camexbolivia.com; f. 1993; Pres. LARRY SERRATE; Gen. Man. BEATRIZ ESPINOZA CALDERÓN.

Cámara de Exportadores de Santa Cruz (CADEX): Avda Velarde 131, Santa Cruz; tel. (3) 336-2030; fax (3) 332-1509; e-mail cadex@cadex.org; internet www.cadex.org; f. 1986; Pres. RAMIRO MONJE; Gen. Man. OSWALDO BARRIGA KARLBAUM.

Cámara de Industria y Comercio de Chuquisaca: Calle España 64, 2°, Casilla 33, Sucre; tel. (4) 645-1194; fax (4) 645-1850; e-mail empresario@caincochuquisaca.net; internet www.caincochuquisaca.net; f. 1893; Pres. LUIS MARÍA PORCEL IBAÑEZ; Gen. Man. LORENZO CATALÁ SUBIETA.

Cámara de Industria, Comercio, Servicios y Turismo de Santa Cruz (CAINCO): Torre Cainco, Avda Las Américas, 7°, Casilla 180, Santa Cruz; tel. (3) 333-4555; fax (3) 334-2353; e-mail contact.center@cainco.org.bo; internet www.cainco.org.bo; f. 1915; Pres. LUIS FERNANDO BARBERY.

Cámara Nacional de Comercio: Edif. Cámara Nacional de Comercio, Avda Mariscal Santa Cruz 1392, 1° y 2°, Casilla 7, La Paz; tel. (2) 237-8606; fax (2) 239-1004; e-mail cnc@boliviacomercio.org.bo; internet www.boliviacomercio.org.bo; f. 1929; 30 brs and special brs; Pres. OSCAR ALBERTO CALLE ROJAS; Gen. Man. JÓSE LUIS VALENCIA AQUINO.

Cámara Nacional de Comercio Boliviano Brasileña: Edif. San Pablo, 11°, Of. 1105, Avda 16 de Julio 1472, La Paz; tel. (2) 231-4249; fax (2) 231-4247; e-mail cambobra@entelnet.bo; internet www.cambobra.com; f. 1984; Pres. JOÃO GERALDO RAYMUNDO; Gen. Man. CARLOS A. LARRAZÁBAL ANTEZANA.

Cámara Nacional de Exportadores (CANEB): Avda Arce 2017, esq. c. Goitia, Casilla 12145, La Paz; tel. (2) 244-3529; fax (2) 244-1491; e-mail secretaria@caneb.org.bo; internet www.caneb.org.bo; f. 1969; fmrly Asociación Nacional de Exportadores de Bolivia; adopted current name in 1993; Pres. GORAN VRANICIC.

Cámara Nacional de Industrias de Bolivia: Edif. Cámara Nacional de Comercio, 14°, Avda Mariscal Santa Cruz 1392, Casilla 611, La Paz; tel. (2) 237-4477; fax (2) 236-2766; e-mail cni@cnibolivia.com; internet www.cnibolivia.com; f. 1937; 8 depts throughout Bolivia; Pres. ARMANDO GUMUCIO KARSTULOVIC; Gen. Man. FERNANDO HINOJOSA.

INDUSTRIAL AND TRADE ASSOCIATIONS

Asociación Nacional de Exportadores de Café (ANDEC): Calle Nicaragua 1638, Casilla 9770, La Paz; tel. (2) 224-4290; fax (2) 224-4561; e-mail cobalca@ceibo.entelnet.bo; controls the export, quality and marketing of coffee producers; Exec. Pres. CARMEN DONOSO DE ARAMAYO.

Cámara Agropecuaria del Oriente: Avda Roca y Coronado s/n, (Predios de Fexpocruz), Casilla 116, Santa Cruz; tel. (3) 352-2200; fax (3) 352-2621; e-mail comunicacion@cao.org.bo; internet www.cao.org.bo; f. 1964; agriculture and livestock asscn for eastern Bolivia; Gen. Man. EDILBERTO OSINAGA ROSADO.

Cámara Boliviana de Hidrocarburos: Radial 17 1/2 y Sexto Anillo, Casilla 3920, Santa Cruz; tel. (3) 353-8799; fax (3) 357-7868; e-mail cbhe@cbhe.org.bo; internet www.cbhe.org.bo; f. 1986; Pres. CARLOS DELIUS S.; Exec. Dir RAÚL KIEFFER GUZMAN.

Cámara Forestal de Bolivia: Prolongación Manuel Ignacio Salvatierra 1055, Casilla 346, Santa Cruz; tel. (3) 333-2699; fax (3) 333-1456; e-mail camaraforestal@cfb.org.bo; internet www.cfb.org.bo; f. 1969; represents the interests of the Bolivian timber industry; Pres. PABLO ALBERTO ANTELO GIL.

Instituto Boliviano de Comercio Exterior (IBCE): Of. 1010, 10°, Edif. 16 de Julio, Paseo El Prado, Casilla 4738, La Paz; tel. (2) 290-0424; fax (2) 290-0425; internet www.ibce.org.bo; f. 1986; trade promotion institute; Pres. WILFREDO ROJO PARADA; Gen. Man. GARY A. RODRÍGUEZ A.

EMPLOYERS' ASSOCIATIONS

Asociación Nacional de Mineros Medianos: Calle Pedro Salazar 600, esq. Presbítero Medina, Casilla 6190, La Paz; tel. (2) 241-7522; fax (2) 241-4123; e-mail anmm@caoba.entelnet.bo; f. 1939; asscn of 14 private medium-sized mining cos; Pres. HUMBERTO RADA; Sec.-Gen. Dr EDUARDO CAPRILLES.

Confederación de Empresarios Privados de Bolivia (CEPB): Calle Méndez Arcos 117, Plaza España, Zona Sopacachi, Casilla 4239, La Paz; tel. (2) 242-0999; fax (2) 242-1272; e-mail cepb@cepb

.org.bo; internet www.cepb.org.bo; largest national employers' org.; Pres. DANIEL SÁNCHEZ SOLIZ; Exec. Sec. RODRIGO AGREDA GÓMEZ.

Confederación Nacional de la Micro y Pequeña Empresa de Bolivia (Conamype): Edif. de Col, 11°, Of. 1102, Avda Montes 768, La Paz; e-mail conamype_bolivia_2011_2013@hotmail.com; internet conamype.galeon.com; f. 2003; small businesses' org.; Pres. MANUEL RODRÍGUEZ.

STATE HYDROCARBONS COMPANIES

Corporación Minera de Bolivia (COMIBOL): Avda Camacho 1396, esq. Loayza, La Paz; tel. (2) 268-2100; fax (2) 235-7979; e-mail info@comibol.gob.bo; internet www.comibol.gob.bo; f. 1952; state mining corpn; owns both mines and processing plants; Pres. EDGAR ESTEBAN HURTADO MOLLINEDO; 26,000 employees.

Empresa Metalúrgica Karachipampa (EMK): Potosí; f. 1985, but not operational until 2013; part of COMIBOL; lead, zinc, silver and gold smelting.

Empresa Metalúrgica Vinto (EMV): Carretera Potosí Km 7.5, Casilla 612, Oruro; tel. (2) 527-8094; fax (2) 527-8024; e-mail info@vinto.gob.bo; internet www.vinto.gob.bo; f. 1966; smelting of non-ferrous minerals and special alloys; majority of shares previously owned by Glencore (Switzerland); renationalized in 2007; took control of Glencore-owned Vinto-Antimony plant in 2010 following renationalization; Gen. Man. RAMIRO VILLAVICENCIO NIÑO DE GUZMÁN; 950 employees.

Empresa Minera Corocoro (EMC): Corocoro, La Paz; tel. (2) 213-9374; fax (2) 213-4365; e-mail info@mineracorocoro.com; internet www.mineracorocoro.com; f. 2009; copper production; Gen. Man. GUSTAVO CHOQUE VELÁSQUEZ.

Yacimientos Petrolíferos Fiscales Bolivianos (YPFB): Calle Bueno 185, 6°, Casilla 401, La Paz; tel. (2) 217-6300; fax (2) 237-3375; e-mail webmaster@ypfb.gob.bo; internet www.ypfb.gob.bo; f. 1936; exploration, drilling, production, refining, transportation and distribution of petroleum; re-nationalized in 2006; Pres. CARLOS VILLEGAS QUIROGA; 4,900 employees.

YPFB Andina, SA: Avda José Estenssoro 100, Santa Cruz; tel. (3) 371-3529; fax (3) 371-3540; e-mail Jorge.roca@ypfb-andina.com.bo; internet www.ypfb-andina.com.bo; f. 2008; fmrly Repsol YPF Bolivia; exploration and production in the San Antonio and San Alberto regions; produces 60% of the country's natural gas; Pres. JORGE ORTÍZ PAUCARA.

YPFB Chaco, SA: Edif. Centro Empresarial Equipetrol, 6°, Avda San Martín 1700, Equipetrol Norte, Casilla 6428, Santa Cruz; tel. (3) 345-3700; fax (3) 345-3710; e-mail transparencia@ypfbchaco.com.bo; internet www.ypfbchaco.com.bo; f. 1999; wholly owned subsidiary of BP (United Kingdom); oil and gas exploration and production; Exec. Pres. RAFAEL MARTÍNEZ VACA; Gen. Man. CARLOS EDUARDO SÁNCHEZ CHAVARRÍA.

YPFB Petroandina, SAM: Edif. Londres, 4°, Avda Busch 1689, La Paz; tel. (2) 237-0209; internet www.ypfbpetroandina.com.bo; f. 2007; 60% shares owned by YPFB and 40% shares owned by PDVSA, Venezuela; Gen. Man. FERNANDO SALAZAR.

YPFB Refinación, SA: Edif. Nago, Calle Celso Castedo 39, Casilla 804, Santa Cruz; tel. (3) 363-2000; fax (3) 363-2023; internet www.ypfbrefinacion.com.bo; fmrly Petrobras Bolivia Refinación; name changed as above in 2010; Pres. MAURICIO TRIBEÑO CONTRERAS; Gen. Man. GUILLERMO LUIS ACHÁ MORALES.

UTILITIES

Electricity

Autoridad de Fiscalización y Control Social de Electricidad (AE): Avda 16 de Julio 1571, Zona Central, La Paz; tel. (2) 231-2401; fax (2) 231-2393; e-mail autoridaddeelectricidad@ae.gob.bo; internet www.ae.gob.bo; f. 1994; fmrly Superintendencia de Electricidad; regulates the electricity sector; Exec. Dir RICHARD ALCOCER GARNICA.

Alternative Energy Systems Ltd (Talleres AES): Calle Manuel Cespedes 0451, Condominio Mistic, Casilla 1C, Cochabamba; tel. and fax (4) 441-3124; e-mail aesbol@freeyellow.com; internet aesbol.freeyellow.com; f. 1986; specialist manufacturers of alternative energy products including small water turbines, equipment for small hydro plants and pumping stations; Gen. Man. MIGUEL ALANDIA.

Compañía Boliviana de Energía Eléctrica, SA (COBEE): Avda Hernando Siles 5635, Casilla 353, La Paz; tel. (2) 278-2474; fax (2) 278-5920; e-mail cobee@cobee.com; internet www.cobee.com; f. 1925; largest private power producer and distributor, serving the areas of La Paz and Oruro; mainly hydroelectric; Pres. and Gen. Man. RENÉ SERGIO PEREIRA.

Compañía Eléctrica Central Bulo Bulo, SA (CECBB): Avda San Martín 1700, Centro Empresarial Equipetrol Norte, 6°, Casilla 6428, Santa Cruz; tel. (3) 366-3606; fax (3) 366-3601; e-mail ramon.bascope@chaco.com.bo; f. 1999; generator co; owned by Empresa Petrolera Chaco, SA; Gen. Man. RAMÓN BASCOPE PARADA.

Compañía Eléctrica Sucre, SA (CESSA): Calle Ayacucho 254, Sucre; tel. (4) 645-3126; fax (4) 646-0292; e-mail cessa@mara.scr.entelnet.bo; internet www.cessasucre.com; f. 1924; electricity distributor; Pres. MILTON BARÓN; Gen. Man. ALFREDO DEHESA.

Cooperativa Rural de Electrificación Ltda (CRE): Avda Busch, esq. Honduras, Santa Cruz; tel. (3) 336-6666; fax (3) 332-4936; e-mail webmaster@cre.com.bo; internet www.cre.com.bo; f. 1965; electricity distributor; Gen. Man. CARMELO PAZ DURÁN; Sec.-Gen. JOSÉ ERNESTO ZAMBRANA.

Electropaz: Avda Illimani 1973, Miraflores, Casilla 10511, La Paz; tel. (2) 222-2200; fax (2) 222-3756; e-mail cpacheco@electropaz.com.bo; internet www.electropaz.com.bo; f. 1995; distributor serving La Paz area; owned by Iberdrola (Spain), renationalized in Jan. 2013; Gen. Man. Ing. MAURICIO VALDEZ CÁRDENAS.

Empresa Luz y Fuerza Eléctrica de Oruro, SA (ELFEOSA): Calle Catacora y 12 de Octubre, Zona Cementerio, Casilla 53, Oruro; tel. (2) 525-2233; fax (2) 525-2233; e-mail info@elfeosa.info; internet www.elfeosa.info; f. 1921; distributor serving Oruro; owned by Iberdrola (Spain), renationalized in Jan. 2013.

Empresa Nacional de Electricidad, SA (ENDE): Avda Ballivián 503, Edif. Colón, 8°, Casilla 565, Cochabamba; tel. (4) 452-0317; fax (4) 452-0318; e-mail ende@ende.bo; internet www.ende.bo; f. 1962; former state electricity co; privatized under the Govt's capitalization programme in 1995 and divided into three arms concerned with generation, transmission and distribution, respectively; Gen. Man. NELSON CABALLERO; the following companies were renationalized in May 2010 and placed under the control of ENDE:

Empresa Corani, SA: Edif. Las Torres Sofer I, 9°, Avda Oquendo 654, Casilla 5165, Cochabamba; tel. (4) 423-5700; fax (4) 425-9148; e-mail corani@corani.com; internet www.corani.com; f. 1995; generator co; 802.60 GWh generation in 2006 in conjunction with Santa Isabel; Pres. FREDERICK P. RENNER.

Empresa Eléctrica Valle Hermoso, SA (EVH): Calle Tarija 1425, esq. Adela Zamudio, Cala Cala, Cochabamba; tel. (4) 424-0544; fax (4) 428-6838; e-mail central@evh.com.bo; internet www.evh.com.bo; f. 1995; generator co; Pres. ENRIQUE HERRERA SORIA.

Empresa de Generación Guaracachi, SA (EGSA): Avda Brasil y Tercer Anillo Interno, Casilla 336, Santa Cruz; tel. (3) 346-4632; fax (3) 346-5888; e-mail central@egsa.com.bo; internet www.guaracachi.com.bo; f. 1995; generator co; 445 MW capacity in 2008; Pres. PETER EARL.

Empresa de Luz y Fuerza Eléctrica Cochabamba, SA (ELFEC): Avda Heroínas 0-686, Casilla 89, Cochabamba; tel. (4) 420-0125; fax (4) 425-9427; e-mail vustariz@elfec.com; internet www.elfec.com; f. 1908; electricty distributor; Gen. Man. ALVARO HERBAS.

Hidroeléctrica Boliviana, SA: Avda Fuerza Naval 22, Zona Calcoto, La Paz; tel. (2) 277-0765; fax (2) 277-0933; e-mail hb@hidrobol.com; internet www.hidrobol.com; 317 GWh generation in 2008; Gen. Man. Ing. ANGEL ZANNIER CLAROS.

Transportadora de Electricidad, SA (TDE): Calle Colombia O-0655, Casilla 640, Cochabamba; tel. (4) 425-9500; fax (4) 425-9516; e-mail tde@tde.com.bo; internet www.tde.com.bo; f. 1997; fmrly subsidiary of Red Eléctrica Española (REE), Spain; nationalized in May 2012; Pres. LUIS ATIENZA SERNA; Exec. Vice-Pres. JAVIER DE QUINTO ROMERO.

Gas

Numerous distributors of natural gas exist throughout the country, many of which are owned by the petroleum distributor, Yacimientos Petrolíferos Fiscales Bolivianos (YPFB)—see State Hydrocarbons Companies.

Gas TransBoliviano, SA (GTB): Km. 7.5 Carretera a Cochabamba, Casilla 3137, Santa Cruz; tel. (3) 371-4900; fax (3) 371-4009; e-mail rquintana@gtb.com.bo; internet www.gastransboliviano.com; Pres. SANTIAGO SOLOGUREN PAZ; Gen. Man. KATYA DIEDERICH.

Water

Autoridad de Fiscalización y Control Social de Agua Potable y Saneamiento Básico (AAPS): Edif. Cámara de Comercio, Avda Mariscal Santa Cruz 1392, 4° y 16°, Casilla 4245, La Paz; tel. (2) 231-0801; fax (2) 231-0554; e-mail contactos@aaps.gob.bo; internet www.aaps.gob.bo; f. 1999; fmrly Superintendencia de Saneamiento Básico (SISAB); decentralized regulatory authority for urban water supplies and grants service concessions and licences; Exec. Dir JAMES AVILA.

Empresa Pública Social de Agua y Saneamiento (EPSAS): Avda de las Américas 705, Villa Fátima, Casilla 9359, La Paz; tel. (2) 221-0295; fax (2) 221-2454; e-mail info@epsas.com.bo; internet www.epsas.com.bo; f. 2007; state-owned water and sewerage provider in La Paz and El Alto; Gen. Man. VÍCTOR RICO.

TRADE UNIONS

Central Obrera Boliviana (COB): Edif. COB, Calle Pisagua 618, Casilla 6552, La Paz; tel. (2) 352-426; fax (2) 281-201; e-mail postmast@cob-bolivia.org; f. 1952; main union confederation; 800,000 mems; Exec. Sec. JUAN CARLOS TRUJILLO.

Confederación General de Trabajadores Fabriles de Bolivia (CGTFB): Avda Armentia 452, Casilla 21590, La Paz; tel. (2) 228-1524; fax (2) 228-5783; e-mail cgtfb@hotmail.com; f. 1951; manufacturing workers' union; Exec. Sec. VICTOR PEDRO QUISPE TICONA.

Federación Nacional de Cooperativas Mineras de Bolivia (FENCOMIN): Edif. Hansa, 16°, Avda Mariscal Santa Cruz, entre Yanacocha y Socabaya, La Paz; tel. (2) 212-0552; internet www.fencomin.com; Pres. ALEJANDRO SANTOS.

Transport

RAILWAYS

In 2009 there were 2,866 km of railway lines in the country. There are direct rail links with Argentina, Brazil and Chile. A ferry connects the railhead at Guaqui, Bolivia to the railhead at Puno in Peru across Lake Titicaca.

Empresa Nacional de Ferrocarriles (ENFE): Estación Central de Ferrocarriles, Plaza Zalles, Casilla 428, La Paz; tel. (2) 232-7401; fax (2) 239-2677; f. 1964; privatized in 1995; renationalized in 2010; total networks: 3,698 km (2008); Andina network: 2,274 km; Oriental (Eastern) network: 1,424 km; Pres. JOSÉ MANUEL PINTO CLAURE.

Empresa Ferroviaria Andino, SA (Red Occidental): Calle Quintin Barrios 791, entre Avda Ecuador y Calle Cervantes, Plaza España, Casilla 4350, La Paz; tel. and fax (2) 241-4400; e-mail efasa@fca.com.bo; internet www.fca.com.bo; f. 1996; has two lines: *Expreso del Sur* connects Oruro to Uyuni, towards the border of Argentina and *Wara Wara del Sur* connects Uyuni Salt Flats to Chile; other sections of the line connect La Paz with Cochabamba, Sucre and Potosí; Pres. MIGUEL SEPÚLVEDA CAMPOS; Gen. Man. EDUARDO MACLEAN ABAROA.

Empresa Ferroviaria Oriental, SA (FCOSA): Avda Montes Final s/n, Casilla 3569, Santa Cruz; tel. (3) 338-7000; fax (3) 338-7105; e-mail ferroviaria@fo.com.bo; internet www.fo.com.bo; f. 1996; connects Santa Cruz with Sao Paulo, Brazil and Yacuiba on the Argentine border; Chair. RAFAEL ENRIQUE ABREU ANSELMI; Gen. Man. RICARDO FERNANDEZ DURÁN.

ROADS

In 2010 Bolivia had some 80,488 km of roads, of which an estimated 8.5% were paved. Of the total 16,515 km were under the national road network and 23,716 km formed the regional road network. Almost the entire road network is concentrated in the *altiplano* region and the Andes valleys. The Pan-American Highway, linking Argentina and Peru, crosses Bolivia from south to north-west. In 2010 the Administradora Boliviana de Carreteras commenced work on consolidating the Corredor al Norte, which would integrate the departments of La Paz, Beni and Pando. Also known as the Corredor Amazónico, the 1,357-km stretch would also improve Bolivia's connections with neighbouring countries.

Administradora Boliviana de Carreteras (ABC): Edif. Centro de Comunicaciones, 8°, Avda Mariscal Santa Cruz, La Paz; tel. (2) 235-7220; fax (2) 239-1764; e-mail abc@abc.gob.bo; internet www.abc.gob.bo; f. 2006; planning and devt of national highways; Pres. LUIS SÁNCHEZ.

INLAND WATERWAYS AND SHIPPING

By agreement with Paraguay in 1938, Bolivia has an outlet on the River Paraguay. This arrangement, together with navigation rights on the Paraná, gives Bolivia access to the River Plate and the sea. The River Paraguay is navigable for vessels of 12-ft draught for 288 km beyond Asunción, in Paraguay, and for smaller boats another 960 km to Corumbá in Brazil.

Bolivia has duty-free access to the Brazilian coastal ports of Belém and Santos and the inland ports of Corumbá and Port Velho, as well as to free port facilities at Rosario, Argentina, on the River Paraná, and to the Peruvian port of Ilo. Most of Bolivia's foreign trade is handled through the ports of Matarani (Peru), Antofagasta and Arica (Chile), Rosario and Buenos Aires (Argentina) and Santos (Brazil). An agreement between Bolivia and Chile to reform Bolivia's access arrangements to the port of Arica came into effect in 1996. At 31 December 2013 the flag registered fleet comprised 118 vessels, totalling 132,356 grt.

CIVIL AVIATION

Bolivia has 30 airports, including the three international airports at La Paz (El Alto), Santa Cruz (Viru-Viru) and Cochabamba. In 2013 the Government of Evo Morales announced the nationalization of these three airports, hitherto operated by a Spanish company. Later that year plans to open two more international airports, in Cochabamba and Chuquisaca, in 2014, were announced.

Dirección General de Aeronaútica Civil: Edif. Multicine, 9°, Avda Arce 2631, Casilla 9360, La Paz; tel. (2) 244-4450; fax (2) 211-9323; internet www.dgac.gob.bo; f. 1947; Exec. Dir Gen. LUIS COÍMBRA BUSCH.

AeroSur: Avda Irala 616, Casilla 3104, Santa Cruz; tel. (3) 336-4446; fax (3) 363-1384; e-mail ventas@aerosur.com; internet www.aerosur.com; f. 1992; Pres. SERGIO SANZETENEA; Gen. Man. CARLOS MEYER.

Boliviana de Aviación: Calle Jordán 202, esq. Nataniel Aguirre, Cochabamba; tel. (4) 411-4643; fax (4) 411-6477; e-mail ventasweb@boa.bo; internet boa.bo; f. 2007; state-owned; Gen. Man. RONALD SALVADOR CASSO CASSO.

Transportes Aéreos Bolivianos (TAB): El Alto, Internacional Aeropuerto, Casilla 12237, La Paz; tel. (2) 284-0556; e-mail tabair@tabairlines.com; internet www.tabairlines.com; f. 1977; Gen. Man. LUIS GUERECA PADILLA.

Transportes Aéreos Militares: Avda Montes 738, esq. Jose Maria Serrano, La Paz; tel. (2) 268-1101; fax (2) 268-1102; internet www.tam.bo; internal passenger and cargo services; Dir-Gen. REMBERTO DURÁN.

Tourism

Bolivia's tourist attractions include Lake Titicaca, at 3,810 m (12,500 ft) above sea level, pre-Incan ruins at Tiwanaku, Chacaltaya, in the Andes mountains, which has the highest ski-run in the world, and the UNESCO World Cultural Heritage Sites of Potosí and Sucre. In 2012 receipts from tourism totalled a provisional US $532m. Visitor arrivals totalled 946,000 in 2011. Tourists come mainly from South American countries, the USA and Europe.

Asociación Boliviana de Agencias de Viajes y Turismo (ABAVYT): Calle Boliviar 27, 2°, Zonca Central, Santa Cruz; tel. (3) 332-7110; fax (3) 332-1634; e-mail abavyt@acelerate.com; f. 1984; Pres. LOURDES OMOYA BENITEZ.

Dirección General de Turismo: Edif. Cámara Nacional de Comercial, Avda Mariscal Santa Cruz, 11°, Casilla 1868, La Paz; tel. (2) 236-3326; fax (2) 220-2628; Vice-Minister of Tourism MARKO MARCELO MACHICAO BANKOVIC.

Defence

As assessed at November 2013, Bolivia's armed forces numbered 46,100: army 34,800 (including 25,000 conscripts), navy 4,800, air force 6,500. There was also a paramilitary force numbering 37,100. Military service, lasting one year, is selective.

Defence Expenditure: budgeted at 2,560m. bolivianos in 2013.

Commander-in-Chief of the Armed Forces: Adm. VÍCTOR BALDIVIESO HACHÉ.

General Commander of the Army: Maj.-Gen. FERNANDO ZEBALLOS CORTÉS.

General Commander of the Air Force: Maj.-Gen. WALTER MONTECINOS GUERRERO.

General Commander of the Naval Forces: Vice-Adm. VÍCTOR BALDIVIESO HACHE.

Education

Primary education, beginning at six years of age and lasting for eight years, is officially compulsory and is available free of charge. Secondary education, which is not compulsory, begins at 14 years of age and lasts for up to four years. In 2011 enrolment at primary schools included 83% of pupils in the relevant age-group. In 2011 enrolment at secondary schools included 68% of students in the relevant age-group. There are 17 state universities and 68 private universities. The provision for education in the 2012 central government budget was 11,000m. bolivianos.

BOSNIA AND HERZEGOVINA

Introductory Survey

LOCATION, CLIMATE, LANGUAGE, RELIGION, FLAG, CAPITAL

Bosnia and Herzegovina is situated in south-eastern Europe. It is bounded by Croatia to the north, west and south-west, by Serbia to the east and by Montenegro to the south-east. There is a short south-western coastline on the Adriatic Sea, and an exclave of Croatia, around Dubrovnik, lies to the south-east. Bosnia and Herzegovina is a largely mountainous territory with a continental climate and steady rainfall throughout the year; in areas nearer the coast the climate is more Mediterranean. The designated official languages (all of which were, in the 20th century, considered to be variants of Serbo-Croat) are Bosnian, Croatian and Serbian. Bosnian and Croatian are written in the Latin script, while Serbian has traditionally been written in the Cyrillic script, but is sometimes also written in the Latin script. The Muslims (Bosniaks), the majority of whom belong to the Sunni sect, are the largest religious grouping in Bosnia and Herzegovina, comprising 43.7% of the population in 1991. Religious affiliation is roughly equated with ethnicity, the Serbs (31.4% of the population) belonging to the Serbian Orthodox Church and the Croats (17.3%) mostly being members of the Roman Catholic Church. The national flag (proportions 1 by 2) consists of two unequal vertical sections of blue, separated by a yellow triangle, which is bordered on the left by a diagonal line of nine white, five-pointed stars. The capital is Sarajevo.

CONTEMPORARY POLITICAL HISTORY

Historical Context

The provinces of Bosnia and Herzegovina formed part of the Turkish Osmanlı (Ottoman) Empire for almost 400 years, but, following the Congress of Berlin of 1878, were administered by the Habsburg Empire of Austria-Hungary, which formally annexed the territories in 1908. The population of the provinces was composed of a mixture of Orthodox Christian Serbs, Roman Catholic Croats and Muslims (Bosniaks). Serbian expansionist aims caused tension from the late 19th century, and in 1914, following the assassination of the heir to the Habsburg throne by a Bosnian Serb extremist in Sarajevo, Austria-Hungary declared war on Serbia, precipitating the First World War. On 4 December 1918 the Kingdom of Serbs, Croats and Slovenes was proclaimed, under the Serbian monarchy. Bitter disputes ensued between Serbs and Croats, and in 1929 King Aleksandar imposed a dictatorship, formally renaming the country Yugoslavia in October.

Although proscribed in 1921, the Communist Party of Yugoslavia operated clandestinely, and in 1937 Josip Broz (Tito) became its General Secretary. During the Second World War (1939–45) intense fighting took place in Bosnia and Herzegovina, which was incorporated into a fascist Independent State of Croatia in 1941. After the war, Bosnia and Herzegovina became one of the six constituent republics of the Yugoslav federation. In the 1960s Tito sought to maintain a balance of power between the ethnic groups in both Bosnia and Herzegovina and the Socialist Federal Republic of Yugoslavia (SFRY—as the country was renamed in 1963) as a whole. Slav Muslims were granted a recognized official ethnic status, as a nation of Yugoslavia, prior to the 1971 census. In that year a collective state presidency was established for Bosnia and Herzegovina, with a regular rotation of posts.

Domestic Political Affairs

At elections to the republican legislature, the Skupština Republike Bosne i Hercegovine (Republic of Bosnia and Herzegovina Assembly), held in November and December 1990, the three main ethnically based parties secured the greatest representation: the (principally Muslim) Stranka Demokratske Akcije (SDA—Party of Democratic Action), with 86 seats; the Srpska demokratska stranka (SDS—Serbian Democratic Party), with 72 seats; and the Hrvatska Demokratska Zajednica Bosne i Hercegovine (HDZ BiH—Croatian Democratic Union of Bosnia and Herzegovina), with 44 seats. These parties also took all the seats on the directly elected seven-member collective Presidency, forming a coalition administration. On 20 December the leader of the SDA, Alija Izetbegović, was named President of the Presidency.

Following the declarations of independence by Slovenia and Croatia in June 1991, and the ensuing conflict, particularly in Croatia, Serb-dominated territories in Bosnia and Herzegovina declared their intent to remain within the Yugoslav federation. On 16 September a 'Serb Autonomous Region' (SAR) of Bosnian Krajina, based in the north-western city of Banja Luka, was proclaimed; this SAR was formed on the basis of a Serb 'Community of Municipalities of Bosnian Krajina', which had been formed in April, and which had announced its unification with the neighbouring 'SAR of Krajina' in Croatia in June. The formation of further SARs was proclaimed, amid accusations that Serb nationalist elements sought to establish a 'Greater Serbia', with the support of the Yugoslav People's Army (JNA). In October the JNA took control of the southern city of Mostar, north-west of the predominantly Serb 'Old' Herzegovina.

In early October 1991 both the republican Presidency (with the dissenting votes of the Bosnian Serb members) and the SDA proposed that the republic declare its independence. Later that month the Serb deputies rejected a resolution in the Assembly to that end, and withdrew from the chamber. On 15 October the remaining parliamentarians approved a resolution declaring the sovereignty of Bosnia and Herzegovina. In response, the SARs, which rejected the declaration of sovereignty, declared that, henceforth, only the federal laws and Constitution would apply on their territory. On 24 October the Serb deputies of the republican legislature announced that they were to form their own Narodna skupština (People's Assembly). On 9–10 November a referendum, organized by this body, indicated strong support among Bosnian Serbs for remaining in a common state with Serbs elsewhere in Yugoslavia. On 9 January 1992 the formation of a 'Serb Republic (Republika Srpska) of Bosnia and Herzegovina', comprising Serb-held areas of the republic (about 65% of the total area), was proclaimed, headed by Radovan Karadžić, the leader of the SDS. The republican Government immediately declared this secessionist Republic, based in Banja Luka, to be illegal; in August it was renamed 'Republika Srpska'. Meanwhile, in a republic-wide referendum on 29 February–1 March, boycotted by the majority of Bosnian Serbs, 99.4% of the participating 63% of the electorate expressed support for the independence of Bosnia and Herzegovina, which was then duly declared by Izetbegović.

Renewed Serb–Muslim tension led to clashes in Sarajevo and elsewhere. On 18 March 1992, following mediation by the European Community (EC, now European Union—EU), the leaders of the Serb, Croat and Muslim communities signed an agreement providing for the division of Bosnia and Herzegovina into three autonomous units. In April fighting between the JNA on one side, and Muslim and Croat forces on the other, intensified, particularly after the EC and the USA recognized Bosnia and Herzegovina's independence on 7 April; Serb troops besieged Sarajevo and launched mortar attacks on the city, while Serb fighters and irregular troops conducted a campaign of 'ethnic cleansing' in the east and north-west of Bosnia. Izetbegović requested foreign military intervention to support the Government, but the UN, while deploying a UN Protection Force (UNPROFOR) in Croatia, decided against the deployment of a peacekeeping force in Bosnia and Herzegovina. On 20 May the Government of Bosnia and Herzegovina declared the JNA to be an 'occupying force' and announced the formation of a republican army. Two days later, Bosnia and Herzegovina was admitted to the UN. On 30 May the UN imposed economic sanctions against the recently established Federal Republic of Yugoslavia (comprising Serbia and Montenegro), in response to its involvement in the conflict in Bosnia and Herzegovina. In early June, in an apparent effort to placate the UN, Serbian leaders in Belgrade (the Yugoslav and Serbian capital) ordered the Bosnian Serbs to end their siege of Sarajevo.

The proclamation, on 3 July 1992, by Croats in western and central Bosnia and Herzegovina, of an autonomous 'Croat Community of Herzeg-Bosna', covering about 30% of the territory of the country and headed by Mate Boban, was immediately declared to be illegal by Izetbegović. After several months of increasing tensions, hostilities erupted between Croats and Muslims in October, and Croat forces captured the towns of Mostar, Novi Travnik and Vitez. Mostar was subsequently proclaimed the capital of Herzeg-Bosna, with the city effectively being split into Croat- and Muslim-controlled zones, the Serb population of the city (around 20% of the pre-conflict population) having largely fled. In November the Croatian Government admitted that Croatian army units had been deployed in Bosnia and Herzegovina, and accordingly became a signatory to the latest ceasefire agreement in the Republic. In December the UN Human Rights Commission declared that Bosnian Serbs were largely responsible for violations of human rights in Bosnia and Herzegovina. Later that month the UN Security Council unanimously adopted a resolution condemning the atrocities, particularly the widespread rape of Bosniak women, and demanding access to all Serb detention camps.

Geneva peace proposals

In January 1993 the Co-Chairmen of the Geneva Peace Conference (a forum for talks on the conflict), Lord (David) Owen (a former British Secretary of State for Foreign and Commonwealth Affairs) and Cyrus Vance (the UN mediator and a former US Secretary of State), visited Belgrade in order to secure the support of the President of Serbia, Slobodan Milošević, for a plan under which Bosnia and Herzegovina would be divided into 10 provinces (with three provinces allocated to each ethnic group and Sarajevo as a province with special status). Under pressure from Milošević and the President of Yugoslavia, Karadžić agreed to the constitutional proposals included in the peace plan and, subsequently, to the military arrangements. On 22 February the UN Security Council adopted a resolution providing for the establishment of an international court to try alleged war criminals for acts committed since 1991 in the territories formerly included in the SFRY. On 31 March 1993 the UN Security Council adopted a resolution permitting the taking of 'all necessary measures' by UN member states or regional organizations to enforce a 'no-fly zone' imposed on the airspace of Bosnia and Herzegovina in October 1992. In March 1993 Izetbegović agreed to both the military arrangements and the proposed territorial divisions included in the Vance-Owen plan. In May Karadžić signed the Vance-Owen plan in Geneva, Switzerland, but two days later it was rejected by the Bosnian Serb People's Assembly.

In May 1993 the USA, France, Russia, Spain and the United Kingdom signed a communiqué declaring that the arms embargo on the post-SFRY states would continue and that international armed forces would not intervene in the conflict, proposing instead, with effect from 22 July, the creation of six designated 'safe areas' (Sarajevo, Bihać, Tuzla, Goražde, Srebrenica and Žepa), in which disarmed Bosniaks would be settled. In June a UN Security Council resolution permitted UNPROFOR to use force, including air power, in response to attacks against these 'safe areas'. In July intense fighting between Croats and Bosniaks for the control of Mostar commenced.

On 30 July 1993, following new peace proposals by Owen and Thorvald Stoltenberg (who had replaced Vance as the UN mediator), the three factions reached a constitutional agreement in Geneva on the reconstruction of Bosnia and Herzegovina as a confederation of three ethnically determined states, under a central government with limited powers. However, fighting continued. On 28 August a 'Croat Republic of Herzeg-Bosna' was proclaimed in Grude, which proceeded to accept the Owen-Stoltenberg plan on condition that the Serbs and Bosniaks also accepted it. On the same day the Bosnian Serb Assembly also voted in favour, but the plan was rejected by the Republic of Bosnia and Herzegovina Assembly three days later. On 10 September Fikret Abdić, a Bosniak member of the state Presidency, announced the creation of an 'Autonomous Province of Western Bosnia' in the north-western region around Bihać. On 27 September Abdić was elected 'President' of the 'province' by a 'Constituent Assembly'. Abdić (who signed a peace agreement with representatives of the Bosnian Serbs) was subsequently dismissed from the state Presidency of Bosnia and Herzegovina. Izetbegović imposed martial law on the area, and government forces attacked troops under Abdić's command.

In February 1994 the shelling of a Sarajevo market place, killing at least 68 people, prompted the UN to threaten military intervention against Serb forces. Following the issuing of an ultimatum by the North Atlantic Treaty Organization (NATO, see p. 370), the Bosnian Serbs withdrew most of their heavy weaponry from a 20-km 'exclusion zone' around the city, which, however, remained blockaded. In late February NATO forces near Banja Luka shot down four Serb aircraft, which had violated the UN prohibition of non-humanitarian flights over the country—the first aggressive military action ever taken by NATO. Following a ceasefire agreed by the republican Government and Herzeg-Bosna in late February, Haris Silajdžić (Prime Minister of Bosnia and Herzegovina since October 1993) and Kresimir Zubak (who had replaced Boban as the leader of Herzeg-Bosna) signed an agreement on 18 March 1994, in Washington, DC, USA, providing for the creation of a Federation on those territories in Bosnia and Herzegovina controlled by Croats and Bosniaks. A further agreement was signed by Izetbegović and President Franjo Tuđman of Croatia, providing for the eventual creation of a loose confederation of the Federation and Croatia. In late March the accords were approved by the Herzeg-Bosna assembly, and the new Constitution was ratified by the Republic of Bosnia and Herzegovina Assembly. In April, in response to the continued shelling of the 'safe area' of Goražde by Bosnian Serb forces, UN-sanctioned air strikes were launched by NATO aircraft on Serb ground positions. However, Serb forces captured Goražde later that month, prompting strong criticism from the Russian Government. Bosnian Serb forces withdrew from Goražde in late April. In late April a new negotiating forum, the Contact Group, comprising representatives from France, Germany, Russia, the United Kingdom and the USA, was established.

In May 1994 the Ustavotvorna skupština Federacije Bosne i Hercegovine (Federation of Bosnia and Herzegovina Constituent Assembly) elected Zubak to the largely ceremonial post of President of the Federation at its inaugural meeting. Ejup Ganić, a Bosniak, was elected Vice-President of the Federation (he was concurrently a Vice-President of the collective Presidency of the Republic of Bosnia and Herzegovina), and Silajdžić was appointed Prime Minister of the Federation. A joint Government of the Federation and the Republic, led by Silajdžić, was appointed in June.

By the end of June 1994, however, despite a declared ceasefire, government forces had captured Serb-held areas of central Bosnia. The Contact Group presented new peace proposals in July, according to which the Federation would be granted 51% of the country's territory. On 17 July Izetbegović and Tuđman endorsed the Contact Group plan, which was also approved by the Republic of Bosnia and Herzegovina Assembly, but the Bosnian Serb People's Assembly rejected proposals requiring the Bosnian Serbs to cede around one-third of the territory they controlled. On 5 August NATO air strikes (the first since April) were launched against Bosnian Serb targets, in response to attacks against UN forces and the renewed shelling of Sarajevo. In late August 96% of participants of a referendum held in the Bosnian Serb-held areas reportedly voted to reject the Contact Group plan; this rejection was unanimously approved by the Bosnian Serb Assembly on 1 September. Meanwhile, on 21 August Bihać had been captured by the government army of Bosnia and Herzegovina. In December the Contact Group issued proposals based on the July peace plan, which indicated the possibility of confederal links between a Bosnian Serb polity and Yugoslavia or Serbia. On 31 December the Bosnian Serb authorities and the republican Government signed a four-month ceasefire agreement. However, intense fighting continued in the Bihać enclave between government forces and troops loyal to Abdić, who was supported by troops from the adjoining 'Republic of Serb Krajina' in Croatia.

On 20 February 1995 representatives of the Bosnian Serbs and the Croatian Serbs signed a military pact, guaranteeing mutual assistance in the event of attack and providing for the establishment of a joint Supreme Defence Council. In early March, in response, a formal military alliance was announced between the armies of Croatia, the authorities of Herzeg-Bosna and the Government of the Republic of Bosnia and Herzegovina. On 8 April President Zubak of the Federation and Ganić, the Vice-President of both the Federation and of Bosnia and Herzegovina, signed an agreement in Bonn, Germany, on the implementation of principles for the entity. On 25 May, following a UN request in response to the continued bombardment of Sarajevo, NATO aircraft carried out strikes on Bosnian Serb ammunition depots. Serb forces responded by shelling five of the six 'safe areas' and, following further NATO air strikes on 26 May, undertook a massive bombardment of Tuzla, killing at least 70 people. Bosnian Serb troops subsequently disarmed and took hostage 222 UNPROFOR personnel in Goražde. In June NATO and European defence ministers agreed to form a 10,000-strong 'rapid reaction force' for Bosnia and Herzegovina, which would operate under UN command from mid-July, so as to provide 'enhanced protection' to UNPROFOR. Meanwhile, the release of the remaining hostages coincided with the withdrawal of UNPROFOR from Bosnian Serb-controlled territory around Sarajevo.

On 11 July 1995 the eastern 'safe area' of Srebrenica was captured by Bosnian Serb fighters, after Dutch UNPROFOR troops based in the town were taken hostage, despite NATO air strikes on Bosnian Serb tanks approaching the town. Following the capture of Srebrenica, an estimated 7,000–8,000 Muslim male civilians were massacred by Bosnian Serb forces, the largest atrocity to take place in Europe since the end of the Second World War.

Bihać was attacked on 20 July 1995, in a concerted effort by Bosnian Serbs, Croatian Serbs, and rebel Bosniaks led by Abdić, precipitating the signature of a military co-operation agreement between Izetbegović and Tuđman. Croatian government forces invaded the Croatian Serb-held Krajina on 4 August, and rapidly recaptured the entire enclave. On 6–7 August the siege of Bihać was ended by Bosnian government and Croatian troops. On 28 August a mortar attack on a market in central Sarajevo, attributed to Bosnian Serb forces, resulted in at least 38 deaths. Two days later NATO responded by commencing a series of air strikes ('Operation Deliberate Force') on Serb positions throughout Bosnia and Herzegovina, which continued for several weeks.

On 8 September 1995 the Ministers of Foreign Affairs of Bosnia and Herzegovina, Croatia and Yugoslavia (the latter acting on behalf of the Bosnian Serbs), meeting in Geneva under the auspices of the Contact Group, signed an agreement determining the basic principles for a peace accord. These principles included the continuing existence of Bosnia and Herzegovina within its present borders, but comprising two administrative units, known as entities: the Federation of Bosnia and Herzegovina; and Republika Srpska. In mid-September 'Operation Deliberate Force' was suspended, following the withdrawal of Bosnian Serb weaponry from the 'exclusion zone' around Sarajevo. Agreement on further basic principles for a peace accord was reached by the Ministers of Foreign Affairs of Bosnia and Herzegovina, Croatia and Yugoslavia, meeting in New York, USA, on 26 September. A 60-day ceasefire took effect on 12 October.

The Dayton accords

On 1 November 1995 peace negotiations between the three warring parties in the conflict began in Dayton, Ohio, USA. A comprehensive peace agreement was reached on 21 November, when Izetbegović, Tuđman and Milošević (the latter representing both Yugoslavia and the Bosnian Serbs) initialled a General Framework Agreement for Peace in Bosnia and Herzegovina, dividing the country, to be known officially as Bosnia and Herzegovina, between the Federation of Bosnia and Herzegovina, with 51% of the territory, and Republika Srpska, with 49%. Whereas the Government of Republika Srpska was to be highly centralized, with a directly elected presidency and no level of local government other than that of municipality, power in the Federation was devolved to 10 cantonal administrations, as well as to municipalities. The Federation was to have a bicameral legislature, whereas that of Republika Srpska was to be unicameral. A state government (encompassing the whole country) was to have an elected collective Presidency and a parliament. Within the state parliament, Republika Srpska was to be apportioned one-third and the Federation two-thirds of the seats (legislative decisions were only to be implemented, however, with the approval of at least one-third of the deputies of each entity), while the Presidency was also to be organized according to the one-third Serb to two-thirds Bosniak-Croat proportional division. The agreement stipulated the right of all refugees and displaced persons to return to their homes and either to have seized property returned to them or to receive fair compensation. Several suburbs of Sarajevo were to form part of Republika Srpska, although most of the city was to be in the Federation. An international, NATO-commanded, 60,000-strong Implementation Force (IFOR) was to be mandated to oversee the withdrawal of the warring parties from zones of separation and to monitor the agreed exchanges of territory. It was estimated that around 200,000 people had been killed in the conflict in Bosnia and Herzegovina, and some 2.7m. were believed to have been displaced.

Following the initialling of the Dayton peace accords, the UN suspended the remaining economic sanctions against Yugoslavia and voted to remove gradually the arms embargo against the post-SFRY states. At a conference on the implementation of the accords, held in London, United Kingdom, in early December 1995, it was agreed that an Organization for Security and Co-operation in Europe (OSCE, see p. 387) mission would organize and monitor parliamentary elections in Bosnia and Herzegovina and that the Contact Group would be replaced by a Peace Implementation Council (PIC) based in Brussels, Belgium. The Swedish former Prime Minister and EU envoy to the peace talks, Carl Bildt, was appointed High Representative of the International Community in Bosnia and Herzegovina, with responsibility for the implementation of the civilian aspects of the accords. On 14 December the Dayton peace agreement was formally signed by Izetbegović, Tuđman and Milošević, and by President Bill Clinton of the USA and a number of European political leaders in Paris, France. The formal transfer of power from UNPROFOR to IFOR took place on 20 December.

On 30 January 1996 Hasan Muratović was elected by the state assembly as Prime Minister of Bosnia and Herzegovina, following the resignation from the premiership of Silajdžić; a new state Government was appointed on the same day, and a new Federation Government was appointed one day later. In February a joint Croat-Bosniak security patrol, accompanied by officers from the UN International Police Task Force and Western European Union, was deployed in Mostar (where tensions between Croats and Bosniaks remained intense). However, the exchange of territory between the two entities did not proceed as envisaged. From January there had been a mass exodus of Serbs from the suburbs of Sarajevo that were to be transferred to the control of the Federation. The Republika Srpska authorities in Pale were criticized for using intimidation to coerce the Serb inhabitants of these districts to resettle in towns in regions of Republika Srpska from which Muslims had been driven during the war. By late March only about 10% of the pre-war Serb population in Sarajevo remained. In May Bosniak and Croat leaders, meeting in Washington, DC, agreed on the merger of their armed forces and the return of refugees.

Since Karadžić had been indicted by the International Criminal Tribunal for the former Yugoslavia (ICTY, see p. 22), based in The Hague, Netherlands, for war crimes, his continued position as President of Republika Srpska (and that of Gen. Ratko Mladić as head of the armed forces) was in breach of the Dayton agreement, which prohibited those indicted for war crimes from holding public office. Karadžić subsequently delegated some of his powers to his deputy, Dr Biljana Plavšić. In June 1996 Western European countries issued an ultimatum to Karadžić to resign, on penalty of the reimposition of sanctions against Republika Srpska that had been suspended in April. Nevertheless, the SDS re-elected Karadžić as party leader. At the end of June Karadžić announced his temporary resignation and the appointment of Plavšić as the acting President of Republika Srpska. Plavšić was subsequently nominated as the SDS candidate to contest the election to the presidency of Republika Srpska. In mid-July the ICTY issued arrest warrants for Karadžić and Mladić. Following intensive negotiations convened by US Assistant Secretary of State Richard Holbrooke with Milošević and Bosnian Serb leaders, on 19 July Karadžić resigned from the presidency and as head of the SDS.

Post-conflict elections

In August 1996 the OSCE announced that municipal elections were to be postponed, in response to evidence that the Republika Srpska authorities were forcibly registering displaced Serbs in formerly Muslim-dominated localities. Elections were held on 14 September to the state Presidency and Predstavnički dom/Zastupnički dom (House of Representatives, the lower chamber of the bicameral Parlamentarna skupština Bosne i Hercegovine—Bosnia and Herzegovina Parliamentary Assembly). Elections also took place at entity level, to the Republika Srpska presidency and legislature, to cantonal authorities within the Federation and to the Predstavnički dom Federacije/Zastupnički dom Federacije (Federation House of Representatives, the lower chamber of a bicameral Parlament Federacije—Federation Parliament). At the election to the state collective Presidency, Izetbegović won 80% of the Bosniak votes cast; Zubak (contesting the election as the candidate of the HDZ BiH) 88% of the Croat votes; and Momčilo Krajišnik (of the SDS) 67% of the Serb votes; Izetbegović became Chairman of the Presidency. The SDA and the HDZ BiH dominated both the Federation section of the House of Representatives and the Federation lower chamber; none the less, an alliance of social democratic Bosniak and Croat parties, the Joint List of Bosnia and Herzegovina, and the Party for Bosnia and Herzegovina (SBiH—led by Silajdžić) won a significant number of votes in the elections to both the state and

Federation legislatures. The SDS secured a majority of votes in both the Serb section of the House of Representatives and in the Republika Srpska People's Assembly. Plavšić was elected President of Republika Srpska, receiving 59% of the votes cast. Following the OSCE's endorsement of the election results, on 1 October the UN Security Council decided to remove sanctions against Yugoslavia and Republika Srpska. The inauguration of the state Presidency took place on 5 October. In November Plavšić announced that she had dismissed Gen. Mladić as Commander of the Bosnian Serb armed forces.

Following a Peace Implementation Conference, held in London, it was announced that IFOR would be replaced by a Stabilization Force (SFOR) from 20 December 1996. In mid-December the Presidency appointed the two Co-Prime Ministers of the state Council of Ministers: Silajdžić, and Boro Bosić of the SDS. Later in the month the dissolution of Herzeg-Bosna was announced and a Federation Prime Minister elected. The state Council of Ministers was appointed by the Co-Prime Ministers and approved at the inaugural session of the bicameral Parliamentary Assembly (comprising the indirectly elected Dom Naroda—House of Peoples—and the House of Representatives) on 3 January 1997.

In June 1997 Bildt was replaced as High Representative by Carlos Westendorp. In July Plavšić announced the dissolution of the Republika Srpska People's Assembly, following the Assembly's opposition to the suspension of the entity's Minister of Internal Affairs by Plavšić (who was also expelled from the SDS in response). In August the Constitutional Court ruled that Plavšić's dissolution of the legislature had been illegal; the People's Assembly proceeded to vote to disregard future decrees by her. At municipal elections, held on 13–14 September in both entities, three main nationalist parties, the SDA, the HDZ BiH and the SDS, received the majority of the votes cast.

Elections to the Republika Srpska People's Assembly were held on 22–23 November 1997, under the supervision of the OSCE. Although the representation of the SDS was much reduced, to 24 seats, it remained the largest party in the legislature. A newly formed electoral alliance, the Coalition for a Single and Democratic Bosnia and Herzegovina, which included the SDA and the SBiH, secured 16 seats, while the Serb National Alliance (SNS), recently established by Plavšić, and the Serbian Radical Party (SRS) each received 15 seats. In January 1998, following protracted inter-party talks, Milorad Dodik, the leader of the Party of Independent Social Democrats of Republika Srpska (SNSRS), secured sufficient parliamentary support to form a new government. At the end of that month Dodik announced that government bodies were to be transferred from Pale to Banja Luka. In April the OSCE dissolved the municipal assembly of Srebrenica in Republika Srpska, owing to its failure to assist in the resettlement of displaced Muslims there, replacing it with a provisional executive council, headed by a senior OSCE official. In June the UN Security Council officially voted in favour of extending the mandate of SFOR indefinitely, with six-monthly reviews.

Tensions between the state and Republika Srpska authorities

In September 1998 elections took place to the state Presidency and legislature, to the presidency and legislature of Republika Srpska, and to the Federation House of Representatives. Izetbegović was re-elected as the Bosniak member of the collective Presidency. The Chairman of the Socialist Party of Republika Srpska (SPRS, a member of the SNS-led Accord Coalition), Živko Radišić, replaced Krajišnik, and the Chairman of the HDZ BiH, Ante Jelavić, was elected as the Croat member of the Presidency. In the election to the presidency of Republika Srpska, the Chairman of the SRS, Dr Nikola Poplasen, defeated Plavšić. The SDS retained 19 of the 83 seats in the Republika Srpska People's Assembly, while the Coalition for a Single and Democratic Bosnia and Herzegovina won 15 seats; the latter also secured 14 of the 42 seats in the House of Representatives and 68 of the 140 seats in the Federation lower chamber.

On 13 October 1998 the state Presidency was inaugurated. Poplasen took office as President of Republika Srpska. The Accord Coalition, which held 32 seats in the Republika Srpska People's Assembly, rejected Poplasen's nomination of SDS Chairman Dragan Kalinić as Prime Minister of the entity, and supported the reappointment of Dodik to the post. In December the Federation Parliament re-elected Ganić as President (to which post he had been elected in December 1997) and a new Federation Council of Ministers was established. In January 1999 the People's Assembly rejected Poplasen's nomination of Brane Miljus, a member of the SNSRS, as Prime Minister of Republika Srpska.

In February 1999 Westendorp declared that supreme command of the armed forces of the two entities was to be transferred to the members of the collective state Presidency. However, the Republika Srpska Government announced that Poplasen would remain Commander of the entity's armed forces, pending a ruling by the state Constitutional Court. In March, after Poplasen proposed a motion in favour of Dodik's dismissal in the Republika Srpska People's Assembly, Westendorp announced Poplasen's removal from office, on the grounds that he had exceeded his authority. (Mirko Šarović, the incumbent Vice-President, provisionally assumed the presidential office.) In the same month international arbitrators ruled that Serb control of Brčko would end, and that the town would henceforth be governed jointly by Republika Srpska and the Federation, under international supervision. (In March 2000 Brčko was established as a neutral district, and an Interim District Government was established.)

In June 1999 NATO announced that the strength of the SFOR contingent was to be reduced to about 16,500. In August Wolfgang Petritsch, hitherto the Austrian ambassador to Yugoslavia, succeeded Westendorp as High Representative. In February 2000 the SPRS withdrew from the Accord Coalition of Republika Srpska, after Dodik dismissed the SPRS Deputy Prime Minister, Tihomir Gligorić. In March a senior Bosnian Croat commander, Gen. Tihomir Blaškić, was sentenced by the ICTY to 45 years' imprisonment (reduced to nine years' on appeal) for war crimes perpetrated against Muslims in 1992–93. In April 2000 Krajišnik was arrested by SFOR troops and extradited to the ICTY, where his trial commenced in February 2004.

At local elections, held on 8 April 2000, the SDS won control of 49 of the 145 municipal councils, the HDZ BiH secured 25 and the SDA 23; the multi-ethnic Socijaldemokratska Partija BiH (SDP BiH—Social Democratic Party of Bosnia and Herzegovina) made significant electoral gains in the Federation. In the same month the House of Representatives approved the restructuring of the state Council of Ministers, which was to comprise a Chairman (appointed by the collective Presidency for an eight-month term) and five ministers. In June a new state Council of Ministers was appointed, after the House of Representatives confirmed the nomination of a non-party candidate, Spasoje Tusevljak, as Chairman. In October Izetbegović retired from the collective state Presidency. (Halid Genjac of the SDA replaced him as the Bosniak member of the Presidency on an acting basis.) A member of the HDZ BiH, Martin Raguž, subsequently became Chairman of the Council of Ministers, replacing Tusevljak.

Decline in support for the nationalist parties

On 11 November 2000 elections were conducted to the House of Representatives, to the legislatures of both entities and to the presidency of Republika Srpska. In the elections to the 42-member House of Representatives, the SDP BiH secured nine seats, the SDA eight seats, the SDS six seats and the HDZ BiH five seats, while in the 140-member Federation House of Representatives the SDA won 38 seats, the SDP BiH 37 seats, the HDZ BiH 25 seats and the SBiH 21 seats; in both cases, the results were considered to reflect a relative decline in support for the nationalist parties. The SDS secured 31 of the 83 seats in the Republika Srpska People's Assembly, while the SPRS and the Partija Demokratskog Progresa (PDP—Party of Democratic Progress) each received 11 seats. Mirko Šarović, the SDS candidate, was elected to the presidency of Republika Srpska, with some 49.8% of the votes cast, defeating Dodik. The SDS subsequently announced that it was to establish a parliamentary coalition with the PDP, the SPRS and the SDA, thereby securing a majority in the People's Assembly.

In December 2000 Šarović designated Mladen Ivanić, the leader of the PDP, as Prime Minister of Republika Srpska. In the following month Ivanić formed the entity's first multi-ethnic Council of Ministers. Meanwhile, the SDP BiH established parliamentary coalitions with a further nine non-nationalist parties (the Alliance for Change), which held 17 seats in the House of Representatives, in addition to 69 seats in the Federation lower chamber.

In January 2001 Plavšić surrendered to the ICTY, following her indictment in April 2000 on charges of involvement in the organization of genocide and deportation of Bosniaks and Croats in 1991–92. In February 2001 three Bosnian Serbs were sentenced to terms of imprisonment by the ICTY for crimes against humanity perpetrated against Bosniak women in Foča in 1992 (the first case at the Tribunal concerning systematic rape and sexual enslavement). In the same month a former Herzeg-Bosna official received a custodial term of 25 years for authorizing crimes against humanity to be committed against Bosniaks in 1993–94.

On 22 February 2001 the House of Representatives approved a new state Council of Ministers, after endorsing the nomination by the Presidency of SDP BiH candidate Božidar Matić as Chairman. On 28 February the Federation House of Representatives elected Karlo Filipović of the SDP BiH as President of the Federation. Meanwhile, in response to the rejection of Raguž's candidacy to the state premiership, a newly formed grouping of parties led by the HDZ BiH, the self-styled 'Croat People's Assembly', declared self-government in three Croat-majority cantons. Petritsch subsequently dismissed Jelavić from the collective Presidency. On 28 March the House of Representatives voted to appoint Jozo Križanović of the SDP BiH as the Croat member of the collective Presidency (while Beriz Belkić of the SBiH replaced Genjac). Following negotiations with federal and international community officials, the Croat alliance agreed to end its boycott of state institutions in May.

Following the resignation of Matić in June 2001, on 18 July the Parliamentary Assembly approved the nomination of Zlatko Lagumdžija, the leader of the SDP BiH and the hitherto Minister of Foreign Affairs, as Chairman of the Council of Ministers. In August the ICTY obtained its first conviction on charges of genocide, sentencing a former senior Serb army officer, Radislav Krstić, to 46 years' imprisonment (reduced to 35 years' on appeal) for his responsibility for the massacre at Srebrenica in 1995. In October 2001 the Republika Srpska People's Assembly adopted legislation requiring its security forces actively to pursue and to extradite war crime suspects to the ICTY. In November Milošević—who had been extradited to the ICTY in June and charged with crimes against humanity relating to Croatia in 1991–92 and to Kosovo in 1999—was additionally indicted on the basis of responsibility for genocide in Bosnia and Herzegovina in 1992–95. (Milošević died in March 2006, while on trial.)

In March 2002 Dragan Mikerević of the PDP was appointed to the rotating chairmanship of the state Council of Ministers. Later in March the leading political parties, under pressure from Petritsch, agreed on constitutional reforms (implemented the following month), to ensure the representation at all levels of government of Bosniaks, Croats and Serbs throughout the country. A Vijeće naroda (Council of Peoples—comprising eight Bosniaks, eight Croats, eight Serbs and four others) was established within the Republika Srpska People's Assembly (which was to elect the members of the Council).

Lord Ashdown as High Representative

In late May 2002 Lord Ashdown, a British politician and former diplomat, succeeded Petritsch as High Representative, being additionally appointed to a new position, that of EU Special Representative for Bosnia and Herzegovina. In June Ashdown dismissed the Federation Deputy Prime Minister and Minister of Finance, Nikola Grabovac, while the Republika Srpska Minister of Finance, Milenko Vracar, tendered his resignation, following pressure from Ashdown, who had criticized official malpractice in both entities. In September 2002 an organ of the Republika Srpska Government issued a report (which was strongly condemned by the Bosniak community and by Ashdown) disputing the veracity of the Srebrenica massacre and claiming that only some 2,000 members of the republican armed forces had been killed in the region.

On 5 October 2002 elections were conducted to the state Presidency, the presidency of Republika Srpska, the state and entity legislatures, and to the Federation cantonal assemblies. In the three ballots to the state Presidency the Chairman of the SDA, Sulejman Tihić, was elected the Bosniak member, while Dragan Čović of the HDZ BiH became the Croat member and Šarović of the SDS the Serb member. Dragan Čavić of the SDS was elected President of Republika Srpska. The SDP BiH-led alliance lost its majority in the House of Representatives following the polls, and the SDA became the largest single party, with 10 seats. The SDA also secured the highest number of seats (32) in the Federation House of Representatives (which was reduced in size to 98 deputies), while the HDZ BiH, contesting the elections in alliance with the Croatian Christian Democratic Union—Bosnia and Herzegovina, obtained 16 seats. The SDP BiH and the SBiH each won 15 seats. In the elections to the Republika Srpska People's Assembly, the SDS remained the largest party, with 26 seats, while the Savez nezavisnih socijaldemokrata (SNSD, Alliance of Independent Social Democrats—as the SNSRS had become) obtained 19. At the end of October both the Minister of Defence and the army Chief of the General Staff of Republika Srpska resigned, after it emerged that an aviation company owned by the Republika Srpska authorities had exported military equipment to Iraq, in contravention of UN sanctions.

In December 2002 Čavić nominated Mikerević as Prime Minister of Republika Srpska. Also in December Ashdown introduced new legislation to strengthen the powers of the state Government: two new ministries, of security and justice, were to be established and the Prime Minister was to be appointed for a four-year term (replacing the system of rotation between the three ethnic representatives). At the end of 2002 the mandate of the principally civilian security force, the UN Mission in Bosnia and Herzegovina (UNMIBH), officially expired, and the UN transferred responsibility for peacekeeping to an EU Police Mission, which was to supervise the reorganization and training of the country's security forces.

In January 2003 the House of Representatives approved the appointment of Adnan Terzić of the SDA as Chairman of the state Government and a new Council of Ministers was formed. Although this Government was dominated by the three main nationalist parties, representatives of the PDP and the SBiH were also included to ensure a legislative majority. Subsequently, the Republika Srpska People's Assembly approved Mikerević's nomination as entity Prime Minister and the formation of a new Government, which, in accordance with recently approved constitutional amendments, comprised eight Serb, five Bosniak and three Croat representatives. Later that month the Federation House of Representatives elected Niko Lozančić, a Croat, to the presidency, and a Bosniak and a Serb to the office of joint Vice-President. The appointment of a new Federation Government, led by Ahmet Hadžipašić, was approved in February.

On 2 April 2003 Šarović resigned as the Serb member of the state Presidency, after being implicated in illicit exports to Iraq and alleged espionage activities by the Republika Srpska military. Ashdown announced the abolition of the Republika Srpska Supreme Military Council; command of the armed forces was transferred provisionally to the entity's President. Ashdown also removed all references of statehood from the Constitution of Republika Srpska. On 10 April the House of Representatives confirmed the nomination of Borislav Paravać, also of the SDS, to replace Šarović.

Meanwhile, on 27 February 2003 the ICTY sentenced Plavšić to 11 years' imprisonment on the charge of crimes against humanity. In July a former mayor of Prijedor, Dr Milomir Stakić, was sentenced to life imprisonment by the ICTY for his involvement in the campaign of 'ethnic cleansing' of non-Serbs from the region in 1992–95. In December 2003 a Bosnian Serb former army commander, Momir Nikolić, was sentenced at the ICTY to 27 years' imprisonment for his involvement in the Srebrenica massacre.

Bosnian Serb authorities issue apology for Srebrenica massacre

In January 2004 Ashdown issued a decree providing for the reunification of Mostar (divided between six Croat- and Bosniak-controlled municipalities since 1993) into a single administration, thereby fulfilling one of the preconditions for signature of a Stabilization and Association Agreement (SAA) with the EU. In February 2004 Ashdown announced the dismissals of three security officials of Republika Srpska and the removal of Mirko Šarović from the presidium of the SDS, owing to suspicions of their complicity in attempts to prevent Karadžić's capture. The SDS refused to approve Šarović's dismissal, and the party's leader, Kalinić, subsequently resigned in protest at Ashdown's decision. In mid-March the House of Representatives approved the nomination of Nikola Radovanović of the SDS as the first state Minister of Defence. In April Ashdown dismissed the Republika Srpska army Chief of Staff, who had failed to provide information required by a commission investigating the Srebrenica massacre. In June Ashdown dismissed 60 Republika Srpska officials, including the Minister of the Interior, who were reportedly implicated in the continued failure of the authorities to locate and apprehend Karadžić. In September the ICTY sentenced Radislav Brđanin, the self-styled Deputy Prime Minister of Republika Srpska during 1992, to 32 years' imprisonment for involvement in crimes committed against Croats and Muslims in the Krajina region. In municipal elections, held in October 2004, the SDA received the highest proportion of votes in the Federation, while in Republika Srpska the SDS lost support to the SNSD. In mid-October the commission established by the Republika Srpska authorities to investigate the Srebrenica massacre submitted a final report acknowledging that Bosnian Serb forces had, on that occasion, killed an estimated 7,800 Muslim males. In November the Republika Srpska Government issued an official apology for the Srebrenica massacre.

On 22 November 2004 the UN Security Council approved a resolution authorizing the establishment of a new peacekeeping contingent under the command of the EU, and in December SFOR officially transferred authority to the new, 7,000-member EU Force (EUFOR Operation Althea). In December, after NATO rejected for the second time Bosnia and Herzegovina's application to join the 'Partnership for Peace' (PfP) programme, Ashdown announced the acceleration of military reforms: the entity Ministries of Defence were to be abolished by 2005, while a single police force under the state Minister of Security was to replace the three existing police and security agencies. In addition, Ashdown removed nine Republika Srpska security officials accused of complicity in the evasion from arrest of war crime suspects. On 17 December Mikerević resigned as Prime Minister of Republika Srpska in protest at the dismissals. On 8 January 2005 Cavić nominated Pero Bukejlović of the SDP as Prime Minister of Republika Srpska.

In February 2005 the Republika Srpska People's Assembly approved the SDS-dominated entity Government nominated by Bukejlović, while Ivanić announced that the PDP was to remain in the state-level administration. Later that month the Croat member of the state Presidency, Dragan Čović, was charged with corruption during his former tenure as Minister of Finance of the Federation; he was removed from office by Ashdown in March. In May Ivo Miro Jović became the new Croat member of the state Presidency.

The new War Crimes Chamber of the Court of Bosnia and Herzegovina (which had been established in January 2003 as the country's highest judicial organ) commenced operations in March 2005. In July a special defence reform commission endorsed legislation providing for the establishment of a joint multi-ethnic army with a unified command structure by 2007; the entity Ministries of Defence and system of military conscription were to be abolished. In August 2005 the Republika Srpska People's Assembly approved the transfer of entity defence powers to the state Government from January 2006. In October 2005 the People's Assembly finally approved the proposals for police reform, which were subsequently adopted by the Bosnia and Herzegovina Parliamentary Assembly. Also in October the European Commissioner responsible for Enlargement, Olli Rehn, recommended that the Government of Bosnia and Herzegovina be invited to begin discussions on the signature of an SAA with the EU; these officially opened in November. The Federation and Republika Srpska Ministries of Defence and armed forces were officially dissolved on 1 January 2006, when authority over the military was transferred to the central state authorities.

On 26 January 2006, after Ivanić announced the withdrawal of the PDP's support for the Republika Srpska Government in the Republika Srpska People's Assembly, a motion of no confidence, initiated by the SNSD, was approved by 44 deputies in the 83-member chamber. On 31 January a German politician and former government minister, Dr Christian Schwarz-Schilling, succeeded Ashdown as High Representative. On 4 February Cavić nominated Dodik as the new Prime Minister of Republika Srpska; Dodik's administration was approved by the People's Assembly on 28 February. In March, following the convening of US-supported discussions in Sarajevo in January, the principal parties reached agreement on a number of draft constitutional reforms. However, on 26 April the Parliamentary Assembly failed to approve the reforms by the requisite majority of two-thirds of deputies, after four dissenting HDZ BiH representatives formed a breakaway party, the Hrvatska Demokratska Zajednica 1990 (HDZ 1990—Croatian Democratic Union 1990 of Bosnia and Herzegovina).

The 2006 elections

In June 2006 Schwarz-Schilling announced plans for the closure of the Office of the High Representative at the end of June 2007, although the position of EU Special Representative (to which Schwarz-Schilling also had been appointed simultaneously) was to continue. The elections at national, entity and cantonal level, held on 1 October 2006, were pronounced by the OSCE to have been conducted satisfactorily. In the ballot for the Bosniak member of the tripartite presidency, Silajdžić was elected with 62.8% of the votes cast, defeating the incumbent Bosniak representative, Tihić. Nebojša Radmanović, a member of the SNSD, secured the post of Serb member of the Presidency, with 53.3%, while the SDS candidate took only 24.2% of votes. The successful Croat candidate, Željko Komšić, won 39.6% of the votes cast, defeating the incumbent Croat member of the presidency, Jović, who received 26.1%. In the election to the 42-member House of Representatives, the SDA secured nine seats, while the SBiH increased its representation to eight seats, the SNSD obtained seven seats, and the SDP BiH five seats. The SDA also remained the leading party in the Federation House of Representatives, with 28 seats; the SBiH won 24 seats, and the SDP BiH 17 seats. The SNSD achieved the largest representation in the Republika Srpska People's Assembly, with 41 seats, two fewer than required for an absolute majority, while the SDS won only 17 seats. Milan Jelić of the SNSD was elected to the Republika Srpska presidency with 48.8% of the votes cast, defeating Cavić.

In October 2006 Krajišnik was convicted at the ICTY on five charges of crimes against humanity and sentenced to 27 years' imprisonment (later reduced); he was acquitted of genocide and complicity in genocide. The three members of the collective Presidency were inaugurated on 6 November 2006. In mid-November Jelić nominated Dodik as Prime Minister of Republika Srpska. Dodik renewed the ruling coalition of the SNSD with the PDP and SDA, and a new Government was approved by the new People's Assembly Republike Srpske on 30 November.

Following a summit meeting on 14 December 2006, Bosnia and Herzegovina was admitted to the NATO PfP programme. The ICTY Prosecutor, Carla Del Ponte, criticized NATO's decision and declared that the co-operation of the Bosnian authorities with the Tribunal remained unsatisfactory. Also in December, the EU announced a staged reduction in EUFOR troops, to 2,500. (EUFOR was again reconstituted in September 2012, after which it comprised 600 troops.)

On 3 January 2007 agreement was reached on the appointment of Nikola Špirić of the SNSD as Chairman of the state Council of Ministers, and his Government was approved by the House of Representatives on 9 February. At the end of January the Constitutional Court of Bosnia and Herzegovina abolished the coats of arms and flags of both Republika Srpska and the Federation, and the anthem of Republika Srpska, after both entity Governments failed to comply with a previous court ruling that the symbols should represent equally the three constituent ethnic groups. On 28 February 2007 the PIC announced that the operations of the Office of the High Representative, which had been expected to end in June, were to be extended for a further year, although Schwarz-Schilling was to leave the post as scheduled. A new coalition Federation Government, headed by Nedžad Branković of the SDA (hitherto the Minister of Transport and Communications), was approved in the Federation House of Representatives on 30 March.

In May 2007 a former Bosnian Serb army officer, Zdravko Tolimir, who was a former close associate of Mladić, was arrested in Republika Srpska, and extradited to the ICTY. (Tolimir was sentenced to life imprisonment on charges of genocide relating to his involvement in the Srebrenica massacre in December 2012.) On 1 July 2007 a Slovakian diplomat, Miroslav Lajčák, officially succeeded Schwarz-Schilling as High Representative. Later that month the state and entity Governments signed an accord on public administration reform, which was required for the disbursement of EU funds. However, a new police reform plan, agreed between Silajdžić and Dodik, was rejected by Lajčák as failing to meet EU criteria.

In October 2007 Lajčák announced a number of measures for reforming parliamentary and government decision-making procedures, including new regulations to prevent representatives of one ethnic group from obstructing the adoption of legislation. On 1 November Špirić resigned from the state premiership, after the PIC expressed support for the reforms. At the end of November Bosnian Serb leaders ended resistance to the proposed legislation. Following an agreement by the political leaders to proceed with police reforms in accordance with the EU criteria, the SAA was initialled on 4 December, with its signature remaining dependent on the implementation of the reforms.

On 9 December 2007 an election to the Republika Srpska presidency was conducted, following the death of Jelić in September; Rajko Kuzmanović of the SNSD was elected to the post with 41.3% of the votes cast. On 28 December Špirić was reappointed to the state premiership. A police reform plan, proposed by Lajčák, was approved by the House of Representatives on 10 April 2008 and by the House of Peoples on 16 April; the agreement abandoned the stipulation for the creation of a single police force, and provided for the establishment of seven state-level co-ordination bodies, with authority over the entity police forces. EU officials recognized the measure as satisfying the final requirement for signature of the SAA, which duly took place on 16 June; however, the Agreement's entry into force was subsequently suspended, owing to a lack of progress in implementing stipulated reforms. Later in June PIC officials announced that the mandate of the Office of the High Representative would continue until the Government fulfilled a number of stipulated objectives and conditions.

The arrest of Radovan Karadžić

In May 2008 Željko Mejakić, the Bosnian Serb commander of the Omarska detention camp, was sentenced by the ICTY to 21 years' imprisonment, while a further two Serb officials received terms of 31 and 11 years, respectively, for involvement in atrocities perpetrated at the camp. In June a former Bosnian Serb police commander and close aide to Karadžić and Mladić, Stojan Župljanin, was arrested in Serbia; he was subsequently transferred to the ICTY on charges relating to crimes committed against Croats and Muslims in the Bosnian Krajina region. (Župljanin and his associate, Mićo Stanišić, who had surrendered to the authorities in March 2005, were both sentenced to 22 years' imprisonment in March 2013.) On 21 July 2008 the office of Serbian President Boris Tadić announced that Karadžić had been arrested by Serbian security officers; it was subsequently revealed that he had been a long-term resident of Belgrade. Karadžić was transferred to the War Crimes Panel of the Belgrade District Court and was extradited to the ICTY on 30 July. Appearing before the Tribunal on the following day, he refused to recognize its jurisdiction, and alleged that, under a private agreement reached with Richard Holbrooke in 1996, he had been guaranteed immunity from prosecution if he left politics. (Holbrooke strenuously denied such claims.) In February 2009 the ICTY approved an amended indictment of 11 charges against Karadžić, including two counts of genocide, of which one related to war crimes in 1992 and one to the massacre of Srebrenica. In March a plea of not guilty was entered on his behalf.

Elections to municipal councils and mayoralties nationwide, and to the Assemblies of Brčko and Banja Luka, and the City Council of Mostar were conducted on 5 October 2008; the overall rate of voter participation was recorded at 55%. Council of Europe observers concluded that the elections had been organized in accordance with international standards. The SNSD again performed strongly in Republika Srpska, securing 39 mayoralties overall, including that of Banja Luka, while the SDA received 36 mayoralties, gaining support from the HDZ BiH, which obtained 16 mayoralties. (In February 2009 the Brčko Assembly elected Dragan Pajić of the SNSD as the new mayor.)

On 23 January 2009 Lajčák announced his resignation from the Office of the High Representative to assume the post of Slovakian Minister of Foreign Affairs. Later in January Dodik, Tihić and Čović, after resuming constitutional discussions, issued a statement on a draft agreement envisaging the redivision of the country into four regions. In February, however, Dodik withdrew from the discussions, after Tihić and Čović rejected his demand that the right of Bosnian Serbs to secession following a referendum be recognized in a new constitution. In March EU member states approved the appointment of Valentin Inzko, hitherto Austrian ambassador to Slovenia, as EU Special Representative for the period of one year (subsequently extended); Inzko officially assumed the post of High Representative on 26 March. On 27 May Branković resigned from the post of Prime Minister of the Federation, following charges against him and former premier Edhem Bičakčić of misappropriating entity funds to obtain real estate. Mustafa Mujezinović of the SDA was approved as the new Federation Prime Minister on 25 June.

In July 2009 a Serb paramilitary leader, Milan Lukić (who had been extradited from Argentina in February 2006), received a term of life imprisonment at the ICTY for war crimes committed in Višegrad in 1992–94, while his cousin Sredoje was sentenced to 30 years' imprisonment. In September it was announced that Plavšić (who had been transferred to a Swedish prison after her sentence) was to be granted early release under Swedish law; associations representing Bosnian war victims expressed outrage at the decision, which had been approved by the ICTY. She was released on 27 October. Karadžić's trial officially began in late October.

In June 2009, meanwhile, a resolution adopted by the Republika Srpska People's Assembly, obligating the entity's institutions to oppose any future transfer of powers to the central state, was repealed by Inzko on the grounds that it was in violation of the Constitution. In November the PIC concluded that the conditions required for the closure of the Office of the High Representative had not yet been met. On 18 December Mostar City Council, which had proved unable to form a coalition administration following the municipal elections of October 2008, finally elected Ljubo Bešlić of the HDZ BiH as mayor, after Inzko ordered that the voting be conducted by a simple majority rather than a two-thirds' majority. Also in December 2009 Inzko extended the mandate of international judges and prosecutors at the Court of Bosnia and Herzegovina, thereby overruling a vote in the state legislature in October. Dodik condemned his decision, and later in December it was rejected as unconstitutional by the People's Assembly, which demanded that a referendum be conducted on the issue in Republika Srpska. Later that month the European Court of Human Rights (ECHR) ruled that the state Constitution discriminated against members of minority ethnic groups, on the grounds that only Serbs, Croats and Bosniaks were entitled to contest elections to the state Presidency and upper legislative chamber. On 10 February 2010 the House of Representatives voted in favour of amending the Constitution and electoral code in accordance with the Court's ruling. On the same day legislation allowing Republika Srpska wide-ranging powers on the organization of referendums was approved by the People's Assembly. In April the Constitutional Court of Republika Srpska ruled that the legislation on referendums was valid, thereby rejecting a motion against it that had been adopted by the Bosniak members of the Council of Peoples.

In May 2010 the appellate chamber of the Court of Bosnia and Herzegovina acquitted a Bosnian Serb former commander of the special police, Miloš Stupar, of charges relating to the 1995 Srebrenica massacre, thereby reversing his conviction in July 2008 (when he had been sentenced to 40 years' imprisonment). In June 2010 two Bosnian Serb former senior security officers were convicted by the ICTY on charges of genocide and other war crimes at Srebrenica and sentenced to life imprisonment, while a further five military and police officers received lesser terms. In the same month an Islamist extremist was arrested, after staging a bomb attack against a police station in the central town of Bugojno in which one officer was killed and several injured. (He was sentenced to 45 years' imprisonment in December 2013.)

The 2010 elections

Elections to the state Presidency, the presidency of Republika Srpska, the state and entity legislatures, and to the Federation cantonal assemblies were conducted on 3 October 2010. In the election to the state Presidency, Bakir Izetbegović of the SDA was elected as the Bosniak member, with 34.9% of votes cast, defeating Fahrudin Radončić of the newly established Savez za bolju budućnost BiH (SBB BiH—Union for a Better Future of Bosnia and Herzegovina, 30.5% of votes), and the incumbent Silajdžić of the SBiH (25.1%); Komšić of the SDP BiH was re-elected as the Croat member, with 60.6% of votes cast; and Radmanović of the SNSD was re-elected as the Serb member, with 48.9% of votes, narrowly defeating Ivanić of the PDP. Silajdžić's replacement by Bakir Izetbegović (the son of Alija Izetbegović), who was regarded as a moderate, was welcomed by international observers. Dodik was elected as President of Republika Srpska, with 50.5% of votes cast; Emil Vlajki of the (predominately Serb) PDP and Enes Suljkanović of the SDP BiH were elected as the entity's Croat and Bosniak Vice-Presidents, respectively. In the elections to the House of Representatives, the SDP BiH and the SNSD won eight seats each, while the SDA received seven seats. The SDP BiH significantly increased its representation in the Federation House of Representatives, to 28 seats, replacing the SDA (which took 23 seats) as the leading party in the chamber. The SNSD remained the dominant party in the Republika Srpska People's Assembly, with 37 seats, while the SDS received 18 seats. In the elections of the Federations's 10 cantons, the SDP BiH won 61 and the SDA 55 seats of the contested 289 seats in the cantonal assemblies.

The three members of the state Presidency were sworn in on 10 November 2010. On 15 November, after the new Republika Srpska People's Assembly was convened, Dodik was inaugurated as President of Republika Srpska; he declared that the entity would accept no further legislation or resolutions imposed by the High Representative and stated that he sought its eventual independence from Bosnia and Herzegovina. On 24 November

Dodik nominated Aleksandar Džombić, hitherto the Republika Srpska Minister of Finance, to succeed him as the entity's Prime Minister. On 29 December the People's Assembly approved a new Government, headed by Džombić and principally comprising representatives of the SNSD. However, in January 2011 the Bosniak members of the Council of Peoples opposed the appointment of the new Government, claiming that for none of the entity's six main institutions to be headed by a Bosniak breached the constitutional right to equal representation. Local elections took place in eight municipalities on 16 January. At the end of that month the Republika Srpska Constitutional Court ruled against the challenge of the Bosniak members of the Council of Peoples, allowing the installation of Džombić's administration to proceed. Meanwhile, the 12 parties represented in the House of Representatives had failed to reach agreement on the formation of a state-level coalition government, with the SDP BiH and the SNSD (which had formed a parliamentary alliance with the SDS) remaining in conflict over the appointment of a new premier. In the Federation, on 17 March the Dom naroda Federacije (Federation House of Peoples—upper chamber of the Federation legislature) elected Živko Budimir of the extreme nationalist Hrvatska stranka Prava BiH (HSP BiH—Croatian Party of Rights of Bosnia and Herzegovina) as President of the Federation and endorsed a new entity Government, largely comprising members of the SDP BiH and the SDA, and under the premiership of SDP BiH Secretary-General Nermin Nikšić. Following their boycott of the entity's new legislature, the two main Croat parties, the HDZ BiH and HDZ 1990, denounced the election as illegitimate, on the grounds that three Croat-dominated cantons had failed to nominate their delegates to the Federation House of Peoples. On 24 March the Central Election Commission, upholding a complaint by outgoing President of the Federation Borjana Krišto of the HDZ BiH, annulled the election of Budimir; however, Inzko subsequently reversed the decision of the Commission.

On 13 April 2011, following an initiative by Dodik, the Republika Srpska People's Assembly voted in support of a referendum being conducted in the entity on legislation imposed by the High Representative that the SNSD considered to be biased against Serbs, notably concerning the Court of Bosnia and Herzegovina and Prosecutor's Office. Inzko warned that he would prohibit the referendum, which was also strongly opposed by the US Administration and the EU. On 13 May Dodik agreed to postpone the planned referendum in Republika Srpska, following a meeting in Banja Luka with the EU High Representative for Foreign Affairs and Security Policy, Catherine Ashton. Meanwhile, on 26 May Serbian security forces arrested Mladić in a village in northern Serbia; he was extradited to the ICTY five days later, and his trial commenced on 3 June. In July an appeals court in the Netherlands ruled that the Dutch State was responsible for the deaths of three Bosnian Muslims, who had been ceded to Bosnian Serb forces by Dutch members of the UN peacekeeping force prior to the massacre at Srebrenica in 1995; the Dutch Government was ordered to pay compensation to the relatives of the three men. (The verdict was upheld by the Dutch Supreme Court in September 2013.)

At the end of August 2011 Inzko's mandate as EU Special Representative expired, and on 1 September a Danish diplomat, Peter Sørensen, who had been appointed by Ashton in May, assumed the office (while Inzko continued as High Representative). Unsuccessful discussions between the leaders of the six principal parties on the formation of a state-level Council of Ministers took place in Sarajevo and Brčko during September, with continuing disagreement between the main Croat parties and the SDP BiH over the allocation of portfolios. It was reported that President of the Federation Budimir had additionally proposed the creation of a separate Croat entity, thereby threatening to undermine the existing Federation. In October a Serbian national, subsequently named as Mevlid Jašarević and believed to be a member of the Wahhabi Islamic movement, staged an armed assault against the US embassy in Sarajevo, shooting and injuring a police officer, before being arrested. In November a number of suspected associates of Jašarević were arrested and armaments were seized in a police operation against suspected Wahhabi members in the north-eastern village of Gornja Maoča. (In November 2013 Jašarević was sentenced to 15 years' imprisonment for the attack.)

On 28 December 2011, following several further meetings, it was announced that the six main political party leaders had finally agreed on the formation of a new state Council of Ministers, having reached a compromise arrangement whereby the new administration would be chaired by a Croat representative, and comprise a further two Croats, four Bosniaks and three Serbs. On 12 January 2012 the nomination by the collective Presidency of an economist and former Vice-President of the Federation, Vjekoslav Bevanda of the HDZ BiH, as the new Chairman was approved in the House of Representatives. On 1 February the SNSD and SDS proposed a motion in the state legislature for the abolition of the Court of Bosnia and Herzegovina and the Prosecutor's Office, following the Chief Prosecutor's decision to abandon a criminal investigation against 14 former senior officials regarding a May 1992 incident, in which JNA and Serbian soldiers were killed. On 10 February 2012 a new Council of Ministers, headed by Bevanda, was finally approved in the House of Representatives; its members included former premiers Lagumdžija of the SDP BiH as Minister of Foreign Affairs and Spirić of the SNSD as Minister of Finance and the Treasury.

In May 2012 two former Bosnian Serb police chiefs were sentenced to 35 and 30 years' imprisonment, respectively, after being convicted by the Court of Bosnia and Herzegovina on charges of aiding genocide in Srebrenica. In June four Bosnian Serb officers who were convicted by the Court of participation in the Srebrenica massacre received sentences of between 19 and 43 years. Later that month the ICTY acquitted Karadžić of one of the 11 charges brought against him.

New state government coalition

At the end of May 2012 the stability of the newly established state coalition Government was threatened, when the SDA voted against the state budget for that year (which was, nevertheless, adopted by the Parliamentary Assembly). The SDP BiH subsequently formed a new alliance with the SBB BiH, and demanded that the three SDA representatives in the coalition Council of Ministers be replaced. In late October the SDP BiH secured the dismissal of the two ministers (responsible for defence and security, respectively) and one deputy minister belonging to the SDA in a parliamentary vote, after the HDZ BiH failed to oppose the proposal. In November SBB BiH leader Radončić was appointed as the Minister of Security (despite controversy over his alleged connections with an organized crime leader), while Zekerijah Osmić of the SDP BiH became the new Minister of Defence.

Meanwhile, local elections were conducted throughout Bosnia and Herzegovina on 7 October 2012, with a recorded rate of participation by the electorate of some 56%. (The organization of polls was postponed in Mostar until the local authorities complied with a Constitutional Court order for the reform of electoral law to address disproportionate representation in the City Council.) According to official results, the SDA secured the highest number of mayoralties, with 34; the SDS's local representation increased significantly to 27 mayoralties, while the SNSD, winning only 15 mayoralties, registered a loss in support. The HDZ BiH obtained 14 mayoralties and the SDP BiH 11. The mandate of Mostar's City Council officially expired in November, while the local branches of the HDZ BiH and the SDA remained in dispute over the stipulated changes to the electoral system. Subsequent mediation attempts by the Office of the High Representative proved unsuccessful.

After agreement with the EU in June 2012, on a 'roadmap' for Bosnia and Herzegovina's membership application (see Other external relations), the leaders of the ruling coalition parties, meeting in Mostar on 20 November, confirmed their commitment to the principles of constitutional reform. However, negotiations on the constitutional amendments notably required by the ECHR ruling of 2009 subsequently failed to yield progress, principally owing to dissension over a new electoral system for the state Presidency. (The Croat member of the state Presidency, Komšić, had resigned from the SDP BiH in July 2012, after rejecting the party's proposals for the amendments.) In December a crisis developed within the Federation Government, after Prime Minister Nikšić requested the dismissal of eight ministers belonging to the SDA and two other parties, following the changes in the ruling parliamentary coalition. Federation President Budimir refused to remove the ministers concerned, causing Nikšić to accuse him of violating constitutional procedures. On 12 February 2013 a vote of no confidence in the entity's Government was adopted in the Federation House of Representatives by the deputies of the new coalition. However, the SDA deputies in the Federation House of Peoples subsequently prevented endorsement of the motion, claiming that it endangered Bosniak ethnic interests in contravention of a constitutional provision, and the issue was referred to the entity's Constitutional Court.

Meanwhile, on 27 February 2013, amid deteriorating economic conditions in Republika Srpska, Džombić submitted the resignation of his Government, citing differences with Dodik. On the same day Dodik designated Željka Cviljanović of the SNSD, hitherto Deputy Prime Minister, Minister of Economic Affairs and Regional Co-operation, as the new premier. Cviljanović's new Government was approved by the People's Assembly on 12 March.

In late March 2013 two former senior Bosnian Serb officials, Mićo Stanišić and Stojan Župljanin, were both sentenced to 22 years' imprisonment by the ICTY, having been found guilty of crimes against humanity and war crimes committed in 1992. On 26 April 2013 Budimir (who had left the HSP BiH to form a new party, Stranka pravde i povjerenja—the Party of Justice and Trust) and 18 other officials were arrested on charges of corruption and accepting bribes; Budimir was temporarily suspended from the office of President of the Federation. However, Budimir was released from custody on 28 May after the state Constitutional Court ruled that his detention was unconstitutional. Meanwhile, in late May Jadranko Prlić, the 'Prime Minister' of the unrecognized Bosnian Croat state of 'Herceg-Bosna' in 1992–96, was sentenced to 25 years' imprisonment for war crimes by the ICTY; five of his associates also received custodial terms.

In early June 2013 protests were staged outside the parliamentary buildings in Sarajevo, against the Parliamentary Assembly's failure to approve new legislation granting identification numbers and documentation to newborn babies (thereby preventing them from receiving medical treatment abroad). The delay in approval resulted in part from a dispute over whether the identification numbers issued should reflect entity citizenship, as demanded by deputies representing Republika Srpska, and opposed by Bosniak representatives. (The necessary legislation was finally adopted by the House of Peoples on 5 November.)

In mid-August 2013 Komšić (who had acceded to the chairmanship of the state Presidency in July) warned that any secession attempt by the Republika Srpska authorities risked renewed civil conflict. The country's first post-conflict census (which had been postponed from April, owing to organizational difficulties) was conducted during 1–15 October, in compliance with a principal EU requirement. However, despite pressure from Sørensen, the main political parties failed to meet a further deadline of 1 October that had been imposed for adoption of the constitutional amendments required by the ECHR ruling of 2009, thereby incurring financial penalties from the EU. On 27 November 2013 Budimir and several other officials, including the Minister of Justice in the Federation, Zoran Mikulić, were indicted on charges of abuse of power and approving a number of amnesties for severe offences on suspicious grounds.

In early December 2013 the failure of the Parliamentary Assembly to adopt a state budget for 2014 by the IMF-stipulated deadline resulted in a delay in the release of essential IMF funds. Although the entity budgets were adopted by the deadline, in Republika Srpska opposition deputies withdrew from the parliamentary session in protest against perceived shortcomings in the proposals. Following intensive debate, the national budget was finally adopted at the end of December. In the same month the Office of the State Prosecutor initiated an investigation to determine responsibility for the failure to approve the required constitutional amendments, after EU officials announced that some €45m. in EU pre-accession funding was to be withheld, with possible further suspensions of assistance. In early January 2014 Budmir dismissed the Minister of Finance of the Federation, Ante Krajina, reportedly following complaints over the non-payment of Croat war veterans' pensions (amid continued antagonism between Budimir and Prime Minister Nikšić), prompting concerns that governance in the Federation would be further impaired. In mid-January the entity Constitutional Court ruled that Krajina should resume his post temporarily in order to prevent a budget crisis, pending a final decision on the constitutionality of his dismissal. Later that month the Parliamentary Assembly adopted changes to the state electoral law (harmonizing it with that of Republika Srpska), to allow legislative elections to be scheduled for October. Meanwhile, in January Mladić was subpoenaed as a defence witness in the trial of Karadžić at the ICTY, but refused to testify.

Recent developments: anti-Government protests

On 5 February 2014 anti-Government protests that began in the industrial town of Tuzla in response to the closure of privatized businesses and the consequent deterioration in economic conditions erupted into violent rioting. Demonstrations of support in Sarajevo, Mostar and other major towns in the Federation also degenerated into violence, with protesters setting fire to government and municipal buildings, and they were forcibly suppressed by police. Several senior officials, including the heads of the Sarajevo and Tuzla cantonal governments, ceded to pressure to resign, and by 8 February the violence, in which several hundred people had been injured, had subsided. However, further protests were staged in Sarajevo and many other towns to demand the release of protesters from detention and, subsequently, the resignation of the Government of the Federation. In March the House of Representatives voted in favour of the removal of Fahrudin Radončić as state Minister of Security, following his failure to prevent the violence in February.

Foreign Affairs

Regional relations

Bosnia and Herzegovina established diplomatic relations with the Federal Republic of Yugoslavia in December 2000, following the overthrow of the Government of Slobodan Milošević. In February 2006 the International Court of Justice (ICJ, see p. 24) at The Hague, Netherlands, began consideration of an appeal that had been brought in 1993 by Bosnia and Herzegovina against Yugoslavia (represented by Serbia, as its successor state), claiming reparations for acts of genocide perpetrated against the Bosniak population in 1992–95. On 26 February 2007 the ICJ ruled that Serbia was not directly responsible for genocide or complicity in genocide in Bosnia and Herzegovina in 1992–95, but that the state was in violation of its obligation under international law in having failed to prevent the 1995 massacre in Srebrenica and to co-operate fully with the ICTY. In May 2007 the newly appointed Serbian Minister of Foreign Affairs, Vuk Jeremić, met his Bosnian counterpart for discussions in Sarajevo, in an initiative to improve bilateral relations. In February 2010 it was announced that Serbia had accepted the appointment of a new Bosnian ambassador (the post having remained vacant since 2007). In March 2010 Ejup Ganić, the former President of the Federation of Bosnia and Herzegovina, was arrested in London, in response to a request for extradition issued by Serbia on war crimes charges relating to an attack on a Yugoslav army convoy near Sarajevo in May 1992. (In July 2010 a British court rejected the Serbian authorities' attempt to extradite Ganić from the United Kingdom, describing it as politically motivated.) On 31 March the Serbian legislature narrowly adopted a resolution condemning the Srebrenica massacre of July 1995 and formally apologizing for Serbia's failure to prevent it. Following several meetings between the Bosnian and Serbian Ministers of Foreign Affairs, with Turkish mediation, in April 2010 the Chairman of the Bosnian collective Presidency Silajdžić, the Serbian President, Boris Tadić, and Turkish President, Abdullah Gül, met in İstanbul, Turkey; Silajdžić and Tadić pledged commitment to improve bilateral relations and to resolve outstanding disputes. In January 2013 Bosnian and Serbian prosecutors, meeting in Brussels, signed a protocol on co-operation in the prosecution of war crimes suspects. In November the Bosnian and Serbian Governments signed a security agreement in Belgrade.

Meanwhile, a 'special relations' agreement was signed by Republika Srpska and Serbia in September 2006. Following Kosovo's unilateral declaration of independence from Serbia on 17 February 2008, the Bosnian Presidency announced that it would not extend recognition to Kosovo in the near future, owing to the opposition of the Serb population. Large-scale protests against Kosovo's independence were staged in Banja Luka, and secessionist sentiments increased within Republika Srpska; on 21 February the Republika Srpska People's Assembly adopted a resolution denouncing the declaration. After the subsequent recognition of Kosovo's independence by the USA and leading EU member states, Republika Srpska Prime Minister Dodik attended a nationalist protest rally in Belgrade and intensified demands for a referendum on the proposed secession of Republika Srpska. In July 2010 a non-binding ruling issued by the ICJ that Kosovo's declaration of independence had not breached international law was denounced by the Serbian and Republika Srpska authorities.

A Free Trade Agreement was signed between Bosnia and Herzegovina and Croatia in December 2000. Following a meeting in the Croatian town of Motovun in July 2012, the Bosnian Minister of Foreign Affairs, Zlatko Lagumdžija, and his Croatian counterpart reaffirmed their commitment to resolve an outstanding dispute regarding the delineation of a small border area on the Adriatic Sea, including the status of Neum and the Croatian port of Ploče. In February 2013 the two ministers, meeting in Brussels, reached agreement on a number of bilateral issues prior to Croatia's scheduled accession to the EU in July, including Bosnia and Herzegovina's continued use of Ploče. After reported pressure from the European Commission, in June the Governments of Bosnia and Herzegovina and Croatia signed three agreements to ensure the normal movement of people and goods between the two countries after Croatia's EU accession.

Other external relations

Following the beginning of discussions with the European Commission on visa liberalization in May 2008, the Commission announced in November 2009 that Bosnia and Herzegovina had failed to meet the criteria for the abolition of visa requirements for Bosnian citizens, urging further efforts to combat corruption and improve border controls. On 22 April 2010 NATO announced the extension of a Membership Action Plan (MAP) to Bosnia and Herzegovina, although a number of questions concerning the registration of the ownership of military property remained unresolved. In November the EU officially agreed to end visa requirements for citizens of Bosnia and Herzegovina, with effect from mid-December. In June 2012 a dialogue on Bosnia and Herzegovina's EU accession process officially began in Brussels, where agreement was reached on a 'roadmap' for the country's membership application; however, the main political parties subsequently failed to adopt reforms by the deadlines stipulated. An EU progress report, which was released in October, concluded that the Bosnian authorities had advanced little in meeting obligations for EU integration, following continuing political disagreements in the governing coalition. The adoption of two laws providing for the organization of a new national census, and for the control of budget funds, respectively, was cited as the only progress. The Commission expressed particular disappointment at the continued failure of the ruling coalition parties to agree on constitutional amendments required by the ECHR ruling of 2009 (which notably stated that the state Constitution was discriminatory to minority ethnic groups—see Domestic Political Affairs). This constitutional impasse continued during 2013, and the EU report issued in October of that year again concluded that Bosnia and Herzegovina had made limited progress in implementing reforms and meeting political criteria.

CONSTITUTION AND GOVERNMENT

In accordance with the General Framework Agreement for Peace in Bosnia and Herzegovina ('the Dayton accords'), signed in December 1995, Bosnia and Herzegovina is a single state, which consists of two autonomous entities: the Federation of Bosnia and Herzegovina and Republika Srpska. In March 2000, following completion of a demilitarization process, the north-eastern town of Brčko was established as a neutral district and placed under joint Serb, Croat and Bosniak authority. Its status was confirmed under a constitutional amendment adopted in March 2009. A civilian High Representative of the International Community in Bosnia and Herzegovina oversees government institutions and the implementation of the peace accords. Between 2002 and 2011 the High Representative of the International Community concurrently served as a Special Representative of the European Union. The state Government of Bosnia and Herzegovina has a three-member collective Presidency consisting of one Bosniak, one Croat and one Serb. Members of the Presidency are directly elected for a term of four years, and are eligible to serve for only two consecutive terms. Chairmanship of the Presidency is rotated between the members every eight months. The bicameral Parlamentarna skupština Bosne i Hercegovine (Bosnia and Herzegovina Parliamentary Assembly) comprises the Dom naroda (House of Peoples) and the Predstavnički dom/Zastupnički dom (House of Representatives). The House of Representatives has 42 deputies, who serve for a four-year term, of whom 28 are directly elected from the Federation and 14 are directly elected from Republika Srpska. The House of Peoples has 15 deputies, who serve for a four-year term, of whom 10 are selected by the Federation's legislature and five by the Republika Srpska legislature. The Presidency appoints a Chairman of the state Council of Ministers (subject to the approval of the House of Representatives), who subsequently appoints the other ministers.

The Federation of Bosnia and Herzegovina and Republika Srpska each retain an executive presidency, government and legislature. The bicameral Parlament Federacije (Federation Parliament) has a 98-member Predstavnički dom Federacije/ Zastupnički dom Federacije (Federation House of Representatives), which is directly elected for a four-year term, and a 58-member Dom naroda Federacije (Federation House of Peoples), comprising 17 Serb, 17 Bosniak, 17 Croat and seven other deputies, who are elected by the assemblies of each of the 10 cantons within the Federation. The Federation Parliament elects a President and two joint Vice-Presidents, comprising one Bosniak, one Croat and one Serb, for a term of four years. Each canton of the Federation has an elected assembly, President, and Government.

The legislature of Republika Srpska comprises an 83-member Narodna skupština Republike Srpske (Republika Srpska People's Assembly), which is directly elected for a four-year term. This Assembly elects 28 delegates, of whom eight are Bosniaks, eight Croats, eight Serbs, and four representatives of other ethnic groups, to a Vijeće naroda (Council of Peoples), which is responsible, inter alia, for electing the entity's representatives to the House of Peoples. The President and two Vice-Presidents of Republika Srpska are directly elected, for a four-year term.

The judicial system of each entity comprises a Constitutional Court, a Supreme Court and local district courts. The Court of Bosnia and Herzegovina is the country's highest judicial organ, and includes both national and international judges.

Bosnia and Herzegovina comprises a total of 143 municipalities, of which 79 are in the Federation, 63 in Republika Srpska, and one in Brčko district.

REGIONAL AND INTERNATIONAL CO-OPERATION

Bosnia and Herzegovina is a member of the Organization for Security and Co-operation in Europe (OSCE, see p. 387), the Council of Europe (see p. 252) and the Central European Free Trade Agreement (CEFTA, see p. 449). In 2006 the North Atlantic Treaty Organization (NATO, see p. 370) invited Bosnia and Herzegovina to join its 'Partnership for Peace' programme. In 2008 Bosnia and Herzegovina, together with Montenegro, joined the Adriatic Charter, a US-supported initiative that had been established by Albania, Croatia and the former Yugoslav republic of Macedonia in 2003 for accelerated military reform and regional security co-operation in the process of integration into NATO. Bosnia and Herzegovina signed a Stabilization and Association Agreement with the European Union (EU, see p. 273) in June 2008.

Bosnia and Herzegovina was admitted to the UN in 1992. The country became a non-permanent member of the UN Security Council in January 2010.

ECONOMIC AFFAIRS

In 2012, according to World Bank estimates, Bosnia and Herzegovina's gross national income (GNI), measured at average 2010–12 prices, was US $17,839m., equivalent to $4,650 per head (or $9,380 per head on an international purchasing-power parity basis). During 2003–12, it was estimated, the population of Bosnia and Herzegovina decreased at an average annual rate of 0.2%, while gross domestic product (GDP) per head increased, in real terms, by an average annual rate of 3.2%. According to World Bank estimates, overall GDP increased, in real terms, at an average annual rate of 3.1% in 2003–12. In 2011 real GDP increased by 1.3%, but it declined by 0.7% in 2012, measured at constant prices; according to chain-linked methodologies, GDP decreased by 1.7% in that year.

Agriculture (including forestry and fishing) contributed 7.4% of GDP in 2012, according to preliminary figures, and 18.9% of the employed labour force was engaged in the sector in April 2013. The major agricultural products are tobacco and fruit, and the livestock sector is also significant. Foodstuffs and live animals comprised 18.5% of total imports in 2012. According to World Bank estimates, the GDP of the agricultural sector increased, in real terms, at an average annual rate of 4.8% in 2003–12. The sector's GDP grew by 3.0% in 2012, measured at constant prices.

Industry (mining, manufacturing, utilities and construction) contributed 25.5% of GDP in 2012, according to preliminary figures. Some 29.8% of the employed labour force was engaged in the industrial sector in April 2013. According to World Bank estimates, industrial GDP increased, in real terms, at an average annual rate of 4.9% in 2003–12. Industrial GDP increased by 3.0% in 2012.

The mining and quarrying sector contributed 2.7% of GDP in 2012, according to preliminary figures. The sector's GDP increased by 13.4% in 2011, but declined by 4.7% in 2012, according to chain-linked methodologies. Bosnia and Herzegovina possesses extensive mineral resources, including iron ore, lignite, copper, lead, zinc and gold.

According to preliminary figures, manufacturing contributed 12.5% of GDP in 2012. The manufacturing sector is based largely on the processing of iron ore, non-ferrous metals, coal, and wood and paper products. According to World Bank estimates, manufacturing GDP increased, in real terms, at an average annual rate of 4.3% in 2003–12. Manufacturing GDP increased by 3.0% in 2012, measured at constant prices.

Construction contributed 4.7% of GDP in 2012, according to preliminary figures. The sector's GDP decreased by 3.0% in 2012, according to chain-linked methodologies.

The civil conflict in the first half of the 1990s resulted in the destruction of much of the electric power system in Bosnia and Herzegovina. In 2011 some 70.7% of electricity production was derived from coal and 28.7% from hydroelectric power. Mineral fuels accounted for 20.6% of total imports in 2012.

The services sector contributed 67.1% of GDP in 2012, according to preliminary official estimates, and the sector engaged some 51.3% of the employed labour force in April 2013. According to World Bank estimates, the GDP of the services sector increased, in real terms, at an average annual rate of 3.0% in 2003–12. The GDP of the services sector increased by 4.5% in 2012.

In 2012 Bosnia and Herzegovina recorded a visible merchandise trade deficit of US $5,542.7m., and there was a deficit of $1,632.7m. on the current account of the balance of payments. In 2012 the principal source of imports was Croatia (which accounted for 14.5% of total imports); other important suppliers were Germany, Russia, Serbia, Italy, the People's Republic of China and Slovenia. In that year the main market for exports were Germany and Croatia (accounting for 15.4% and 14.8% of the total, respectively); other significant purchasers were Italy, Serbia, Austria and Slovenia. The principal imports in 2012 were basic manufactures, mineral fuels and lubricants, food and live animals, machinery and transport equipment, and chemicals and related products. The principal exports in that year were basic manufactures, machinery and transport equipment, mineral fuels and lubricants, miscellaneous manufactured articles, and food and live animals.

Bosnia and Herzegovina's overall budget surplus for 2012 was KM 815.6m. Bosnia and Herzegovina's general government gross debt was KM 11,669m. in 2012, equivalent to 44.3% of GDP. The country's total external debt was estimated at US $10,729m. in 2011, of which $3,874m. was public and publicly guaranteed debt. In that year, the cost of servicing long-term public and publicly guaranteed debt and repayments to the IMF was equivalent to about 10.9% of the value of exports of goods, services and income (excluding workers' remittances). According to the International Labour Organization (ILO), the average annual rate of inflation was 3.4% in 2005–11. Consumer prices increased by 1.6% in 2011, but declined by 1.5% in 2012, according to official estimates. The rate of unemployment was some 27.4% in April 2013.

A Stabilization and Association Agreement (SAA) was signed with the EU in June 2008; however, its entry into force was subsequently suspended, owing to a lack of progress in implementing required reforms (although an interim trade agreement took effect in July). In September 2012 the IMF approved a new, two-year credit arrangement, totalling €405.3m., to support the Government's economic programme. In December the Federation and Republika Srpska Governments secured approval of their respective entity budgets for 2013, thereby becoming eligible for the first disbursement of IMF credit. In May 2013 the IMF approved a further tranche of funding, of €39m., after both entity Governments agreed to reductions in expenditure, which included cuts to war veterans' pensions in the Federation, as prescribed under the credit arrangement. Later that year, however, the Federation Government indicated that the entity was near bankruptcy; its budget for 2014 projected exceptionally high expenditure as a result of required debt repayments. Furthermore, failure to adopt a state budget for 2014 by the IMF-stipulated deadline resulted in a postponement in the release of the forthcoming tranche of IMF funds; the budget was finally adopted at the end of December 2013. In the same month the EU protested that operations of the state power transmission company were endangered, after draft legislation was adopted to allow the entity authorities to take a proportion of its revenue. Meanwhile, owing to the continued inability of the governing political factions to approve required constitutional amendments, the entry into force of the SAA remained suspended and some €45m. in EU pre-accession funding was additionally withheld; EU officials considered that the lack of a mechanism to facilitate co-ordination between the different levels of government could deprive the country of an additional €80m. each year in funding. Following a small contraction in GDP in 2012, growth (estimated at 0.6%) began to be recorded again in 2013. In early 2014, however, the closure of privatized businesses in Tuzla, which had increased economic hardship, precipitated nationwide protests against government corruption and mismanagement (see Domestic Political Affairs).

PUBLIC HOLIDAYS

2015: 1 January (New Year), 6–7 January (Serbian Orthodox Christmas), 1 March (Independence Day), 3–6 April (Catholic Easter), 10–13 April (Orthodox Easter), 1–2 May (Labour Day), 9 May (Victory Day), 17 July* (Ramadan Bayram, end of Ramadan), 23 September* (Kurban Bayram, Feast of the Sacrifice), 1 November (Catholic All Saints' Day), 21 November (General Framework Agreement Day), 25 November (National Statehood Day), 25 December (Catholic Christmas).

* These holidays are dependent on the Islamic lunar calendar and may vary by one or two days from the dates given.

Statistical Survey

Source (unless otherwise stated): Agencija za statistiku Bosne i Hercegovine, 71000 Sarajevo, trg Bosne i Hercegovine 1; tel. and fax (33) 2206222; e-mail bhas@bih.net.ba; internet www.bhas.ba.

Area and Population

AREA, POPULATION AND DENSITY

Area (sq km)	
Land	51,197
Inland water	12
Total	51,209*
Population (census results)	
31 March 1991	
Males	2,183,795
Females	2,193,238
Total	4,377,033
30 September 2013 (preliminary)†	3,791,622
Density (per sq km) at 2013 census	74.0

* 19,772 sq miles.

† Comprising the Federation of Bosnia and Herzegovina 2,371,603, Republika Srpska 1,326,991 and Brčko District 93,028.

POPULATION BY AGE AND SEX

(household budget survey, 2007)

	Males	Females	Total
0–17	383,839	361,664	745,503
18–64	1,076,349	1,105,045	2,181,394
65 and over	224,061	296,199	520,260
Total	1,684,249	1,762,908	3,447,157
Federation of Bosnia and Herzegovina	1,079,998	1,133,785	2,213,783
0–17	261,306	247,762	509,068
18–64	692,567	718,480	1,411,047
65 and over	126,125	167,543	293,668
Republika Srpska	571,049	595,124	1,166,173
0–17	115,719	106,828	222,547
18–64	362,412	366,017	728,429
65 and over	92,918	122,279	215,197
Brčko District	33,202	33,999	67,201
0–17	6,814	7,074	13,888
18–64	21,370	20,548	41,918
65 and over	5,018	6,377	11,395

POPULATION BY ETHNIC GROUP

(according to official declaration of nationality, 1991 census, provisional)

	Number	% of total population
Muslim	1,905,829	43.7
Serb	1,369,258	31.4
Croat	755,892	17.3
Yugoslav	239,845	5.5
Others	93,750	2.1
Total	4,364,574	100.0

CANTONS WITHIN THE FEDERATION

(population at 2013 census, preliminary)

Canton	Population	Principal city (with population)
Bosna-Podrinje	25,336	Goražde (22,080)
Central Bosnia	273,149	Travnik (57,543)
Herzegovina-Neretva	236,278	Mostar (113,169)
Posavina	48,089	Orašje (21,584)
Sarajevo	438,443	Sarajevo (291,422)
Tuzla	477,278	Tuzla (120,441)
Una-Sana	299,343	Bihać (61,186)
West Herzegovina	97,893	Široki Brijeg (29,809)
Zenica-Doboj	385,067	Zenica (115,134)
'Canton 10'*	90,727	Livno (37,487)
Total	2,371,603	

* Formerly known as Herceg-Bosna Canton.

PRINCIPAL TOWNS

(population at 2013 census, preliminary)

Sarajevo (capital)	291,422*	Ilidža	71,892
Banja Luka	199,191	Cazin	69,411
Tuzla	120,441	Zvornik	63,686
Zenica	115,134	Živinice	61,201
Bijeljina	114,663	Bihać	61,186
Mostar	113,169	Travnik	57,543
Prijedor	97,588	Gradišca	56,727
Doboj	77,223		

* Excluding Istočno Novo Sarajevo municipality (with a population of 11,477 according to preliminary results of the 2013 census) located in Republika Srpska.

BIRTHS, MARRIAGES AND DEATHS

	Registered live births		Registered marriages		Registered deaths	
	Number	Rate (per 1,000)	Number	Rate (per 1,000)	Number	Rate (per 1,000)
2005	34,627	9.0	21,698	5.6	34,402	9.0
2006	34,033	8.9	21,501	5.6	33,221	8.6
2007	33,835	8.8	23,494	6.1	35,044	9.1
2008	34,176	8.9	22,151	5.8	34,026	8.9
2009	34,550	9.0	20,633	5.4	34,904	9.1
2010	33,779	8.8	19,731	5.1	34,633	9.0
2011	31,875	8.3	20,084	5.2	35,522	9.3
2012	32,072	n.a.	18,980	n.a.	35,692	n.a.

Note: Rates are based on official mid-year estimates of de facto population.

Life expectancy (years at birth): 76.0 (males 73.5; females 78.6) in 2011 (Source: World Bank, World Development Indicators database).

EMPLOYMENT

(labour force survey at 31 March 2003)

	Males	Females	Total
Agriculture, hunting and forestry	14,503	3,447	17,950
Fishing	393	98	491
Mining and quarrying	18,203	2,051	20,254
Manufacturing	92,867	55,958	148,825
Electricity, gas and water supply	19,013	4,999	24,012
Construction	29,500	4,857	34,357
Wholesale and retail trade; repair of motor vehicles, motorcycles and personal and household goods	40,062	35,432	75,494
Hotels and restaurants	9,703	9,543	19,246
Transport, storage and communications	30,123	8,973	39,096
Financial intermediation	3,949	6,317	10,266
Real estate, renting and business activities	8,725	4,657	13,382
Public administration and defence; compulsory social security	26,565	20,351	46,916
Education	19,875	28,042	47,917
Health and social work	13,211	27,565	40,776
Other community, social and personal service activities	13,904	7,997	21,901
Sub-total	340,596	220,287	560,883
Activities not adequately defined	42,773	18,164	60,937
Total	383,369	238,451	621,820

Registered unemployed at mid-year: 525,978 in 2011; 538,151 in 2012; 548,300 in 2013.

2013 (labour force survey at April, '000 persons aged 15 years and over, preliminary): Total employed 822; Unemployed 311; *Total labour force* 1,133.

Health and Welfare

KEY INDICATORS

Total fertility rate (children per woman, 2011)	1.1
Under-5 mortality rate (per 1,000 live births, 2011)	8
HIV/AIDS (% of persons aged 15–49, 2007)	<0.1
Physicians (per 1,000 head, 2009)	1.6
Hospital beds (per 1,000 head, 2009)	3.4
Health expenditure (2010): US $ per head (PPP)	893
Health expenditure (2010): % of GDP	10.2
Health expenditure (2010): public (% of total)	68.1
Access to water (% of persons, 2011)	99
Access to sanitation (% of persons, 2011)	96
Total carbon dioxide emissions ('000 metric tons, 2010)	31,125.5
Carbon dioxide emissions per head (metric tons, 2010)	8.1
Human Development Index (2012): ranking	81
Human Development Index (2012): value	0.735

For sources and definitions, see explanatory note on p. vi.

Agriculture

PRINCIPAL CROPS
('000 metric tons)

	2010	2011	2012
Wheat	145.4	210.0	225.1
Barley	50.1	65.7	65.3
Maize	853.4	764.1	539.4
Rye	7.4	9.7	10.7
Oats	19.8	27.0	26.8
Potatoes	378.7	412.7	299.9
Beans, dry	11.4	10.7	8.5
Soybeans (Soya beans)	8.0	6.7	6.7
Cabbages and other brassicas	80.7	72.3	62.1
Tomatoes	36.6	45.9	44.0
Chillies and peppers, green	38.4	37.1	35.4
Onions, dry	37.2	39.9	32.9
Garlic	6.3	5.6	4.8
Carrots and turnips	22.9	20.7	13.7
Watermelons	13.0*	12.3	18.7
Grapes	23.2	21.6	25.9
Apples	71.7	75.3	50.0
Pears	22.9	28.3	18.0
Plums	157.6	157.5	111.0
Tobacco, unmanufactured	1.9	1.8	1.5

* FAO estimate.

Aggregate production ('000 metric tons, may include official, semi-official or estimated data): Total cereals 1,104.1 in 2010, 1,118.3 in 2011, 906.0 in 2012; Total roots and tubers 378.7 in 2010, 412.7 in 2011, 299.9 in 2012; Total vegetables (incl. melons) 732.7 in 2010, 732.0 in 2011, 726.4 in 2012; Total fruits (excl. melons) 321.3 in 2010, 330.9 in 2011, 244.5 in 2012.

Source: FAO.

LIVESTOCK
('000 head, year ending September)

	2010	2011	2012
Horses	19.3	19.1	18.4
Cattle	462.4	455.3	444.6
Pigs	590.4	576.8	539.0
Sheep	1,046.0	1,020.7	1,005.5
Chickens	21,802	18,703	19,401
Ducks	530*	500*	500†
Geese and guinea fowls	630*	600*	600†
Turkeys	330*	300*	300†

* Unofficial figure.
† FAO estimate.

Source: FAO.

LIVESTOCK PRODUCTS
('000 metric tons)

	2010	2011	2012
Cattle meat	23.4	22.4	22.9
Sheep meat	2.0	2.3	2.3
Pig meat	13.3	16.6	15.7
Chicken meat	37.6	45.7	53.4
Cows' milk	715.6	689.0	674.0
Sheep's milk	18.9	18.0	17.0
Hen eggs*	20.8	18.3	23.0

* Unofficial figures.

Source: FAO.

Forestry

ROUNDWOOD REMOVALS
('000 cubic metres, excluding bark)

	2010	2011	2012
Sawlogs, veneer logs and logs for sleepers	1,658	1,783	1,790
Pulpwood	488	514	519
Other industrial wood	209	238	220
Fuel wood	1,260	1,314	1,268
Total	3,615	3,849	3,797

Source: FAO.

SAWNWOOD PRODUCTION
('000 cubic metres, including railway sleepers)

	2010	2011	2012
Coniferous (softwood)	513	560	552
Broadleaved (hardwood)	473	548	541
Total	986	1,108	1,093

Source: FAO.

Fishing

(metric tons, live weight)

	2009*	2010*	2011
Capture	2,005	2,005	2,005*
Aquaculture	7,620	7,620	8,009
Common carp	2,740	2,740	2,920
Rainbow trout	3,880	3,880	3,994
Total catch	9,625	9,625	10,014*

* FAO estimate(s).

Source: FAO.

Mining

('000 metric tons unless otherwise indicated)

	2009	2010	2011
Brown coal and lignite	11,515	10,976	12,732
Iron ore: metal content*	678	588	794
Bauxite	556	844	708
Barite (Barytes) concentrate (metric tons)	30	57	13
Salt	556	663	832
Gypsum (crude)	74	65	72

* Estimates.

Source: US Geological Survey.

Industry

SELECTED PRODUCTS

('000 metric tons unless otherwise indicated)

	2009	2010	2011
Crude steel	519	591	649
Aluminium (metal ingot)	130	150	164
Cement	1,074	949	893
Electric energy (million kWh)	15,668	17,124	n.a.

2003 ('000 metric tons, excluding figures for the Federation): Beer 1,316; Cigarettes 5,062.

Sources: US Geological Survey; UN Industrial Commodity Statistics Database.

Finance

CURRENCY AND EXCHANGE RATES

Monetary Units

100 pfeninga = 1 konvertibilna marka (KM or convertible marka).

Sterling, Dollar and Euro Equivalents (31 December 2013)

£1 sterling = KM 2.335;
US $1 = KM 1.418;
€1 = KM 1.956;
KM 100 = £42.82 = $70.51 = €51.13.

Average Exchange Rate (KM per US $)

2011 1.4069
2012 1.5222
2013 1.4731

Note: The new Bosnia and Herzegovina dinar (BHD) was introduced in August 1994, with an official value fixed at 100 BHD = 1 Deutsche Mark (DM). The DM, the Croatian kuna and the Yugoslav dinar also circulated within Bosnia and Herzegovina. On 22 June 1998 the BHD was replaced by the KM, equivalent to 100 of the former units. The KM was thus at par with the DM. From the introduction of the euro, on 1 January 1999, the German currency had a fixed exchange rate of €1 = DM 1.95583.

CONSOLIDATED BUDGET

(KM million)*

Revenue	2010	2011	2012
Tax revenue	5,640.2	6,032.2	6,037.9
Taxes on income, profits and capital gains	721.7	795.0	818.4
Taxes on payroll and workforce	—	13.9	9.2
Taxes on property	87.2	89.1	84.4
Taxes on goods, services, international trade and transactions	4,824.2	5,101.2	5,103.8
Other taxes	7.2	32.8	22.1
Social security contributions	3,813.0	4,036.3	4,046.6
Grants	48.5	46.7	60.0
Other revenue	1,360.9	1,241.7	1,315.0
Total	10,862.5	11,357.0	11,459.5

Expenditure†	2010	2011	2012
Compensation of employees	3,169.8	3,336.8	3,323.8
Use of goods and services	2,593.1	2,088.2	2,156.4
Interest payments	122.7	161.4	200.6
Subsidies and grants	476.7	409.1	417.1
Social security benefits	3,770.3	4,330.2	4,394.4
Other expenditure	707.7	582.6	678.5
Total	10,840.2	10,908.7	11,170.8

* Figures represent a consolidation of the budgetary accounts of: the central state Government; the federation and cantonal authorities, and social security and road maintenance funds in the Federation; the central republican authorities, local and district administrations, social security and road maintenance funds in Republika Srpska; the central government and health insurance and employment funds in Brčko District.

† Excluding net lending (KM million): –611.9 in 2010; –322.7 in 2011; –526.9 in 2012.

Source: Central Bank of Bosnia and Herzegovina, *Annual Statement of Government Operations*.

INTERNATIONAL RESERVES

(US $ million at 31 December)

	2010	2011	2012
Gold (national valuation)	45.70	100.08	107.25
IMF special drawing rights	0.02	0.74	3.05
Reserve position in IMF	0.07	0.07	0.07
Foreign exchange	4,366.10	4,148.75	4,280.37
Total	4,411.89	4,249.64	4,390.74

Source: IMF, *International Financial Statistics*.

MONEY SUPPLY

(KM million at 31 December)

	2010	2011	2012
Currency outside depository corporations	2,211	2,366	2,414
Transferable deposits	4,900	4,919	4,781
Other deposits	6,517	7,133	7,715
Broad money	13,628	14,418	14,910

Source: IMF, *International Financial Statistics*.

COST OF LIVING

(Consumer Price Index; annual averages; base: previous year = 100)

	2010	2011	2012
Food and non-alcoholic beverages	99.3	106.0	101.8
Clothing and footwear	95.4	92.7	93.9
Housing, utilities and fuels	103.1	103.1	102.9
All items (incl. others)	102.1	103.7	102.1

Source: Central Bank of Bosnia and Herzegovina, *Statistical Bulletin*.

NATIONAL ACCOUNTS

(KM million at current prices)

Expenditure on the Gross Domestic Product

(preliminary figures)

	2010	2011	2012
Government final consumption expenditure	5,779.8	5,975.1	6,015.8
Private final consumption expenditure	21,338.0	21,927.3	22,328.7
Non-profit institutions serving households	249.0	266.7	279.5
Gross capital formation	4,032.7	4,858.8	4,952.6
Total domestic expenditure	31,399.5	33,027.9	33,576.6
Exports of goods and services	7,237.5	8,040.1	7,884.0
Less Imports of goods and services	12,708.3	14,290.8	14,261.9
GDP in purchasers' values	25,928.7	26,777.2	27,198.8

Note: GDP estimates may differ from respective figures for GDP by economic activity owing to differing methods of data compilation.

Gross Domestic Product by Economic Activity

	2011	2012*
Agriculture, hunting, forestry and fishing	1,768.5	1,604.7
Mining and quarrying	569.1	587.2
Manufacturing	2,810.4	2,707.2
Electricity, gas and water	1,211.6	1,192.8
Construction	1,061.4	1,022.0
Wholesale and retail trade; repair of motor vehicles, motorcycles, etc.	3,355.7	3,443.3
Hotels and restaurants	519.9	526.6
Transport, storage and communications	2,031.9	2,059.4
Financial intermediation	994.9	973.0
Real estate, renting and business activities	2,176.1	2,220.1
Public administration and defence	2,382.3	2,371.3
Education	1,253.5	1,267.9
Health and social welfare	1,189.5	1,225.3
Other community, social and personal service activities	390.6	405.2
Sub-total	21,715.3	21,606.1
Less Financial intermediation services indirectly measured	735.4	707.8
Gross value added in basic prices	20,979.9	20,898.4
Taxes, *less* subsidies, on products	4,700.3	4,756.0
GDP in market prices†	25,680.1	25,654.3

* Preliminary figures.

† Comprising (KM million): Federation 16,401.8 in 2011; 16,459.0 in 2012 (preliminary); Republika Srpska 8,682.4 in 2011; 8,585.0 in 2012 (preliminary); Brčko District 595.9 in 2011; 610.3 in 2012 (preliminary).

BALANCE OF PAYMENTS
(US $ million)

	2010	2011	2012
Exports of goods	2,896.4	3,653.3	3,306.2
Imports of goods	–8,056.8	–9,590.6	–8,849.0
Balance on goods	–5,160.4	–5,937.3	–5,542.7
Exports of services	1,998.7	2,068.4	1,905.1
Imports of services	–536.5	–578.7	–511.0
Balance on goods and services	–3,698.2	–4,447.6	–4,148.6
Primary income received	596.7	664.2	572.1
Primary income paid	–317.1	–511.4	–415.4
Balance on goods, services and primary income	–3,418.7	–4,294.8	–3,991.9
Secondary income received	2,563.8	2,689.6	2,541.4
Secondary income paid	–174.4	–198.1	–182.3
Current balance	–1,029.3	–1,803.3	–1,632.7
Capital account (net)	263.7	252.9	196.2
Direct investment assets	–81.2	4.7	0.3
Direct investment liabilities	443.8	468.7	349.6
Portfolio investment assets	–86.0	5.8	29.5
Portfolio investment liabilities	–35.0	–40.8	–41.3
Other investment assets	501.9	410.0	330.7
Other investment liabilities	–144.4	590.6	492.7
Net errors and omissions	106.2	87.3	192.6
Reserves and related items	–60.3	–24.1	–82.3

Source: IMF, *International Financial Statistics*.

External Trade

SELECTED COMMODITIES
(KM million*)

Imports	2010	2011	2012
Food and live animals	2,502.4	2,770.0	2,816.5
Vegetable products	602.2	681.8	705.8
Prepared foodstuffs	1,425.2	1,527.1	1,513.9
Mineral fuels, lubricants, etc.	2,743.9	3,456.7	3,229.0
Chemicals and related products	1,345.7	1,475.5	1,522.5
Basic manufactures	3,989.0	4,451.3	4,367.7
Plastics and rubber	725.1	800.4	846.8
Wood and wood products	526.4	566.7	511.3
Textiles and textile articles	708.1	754.9	734.7
Articles of stone, plaster, cement and asbestos	283.6	297.0	284.3
Base metals and articles thereof	1,209.2	1,384.0	1,330.1
Machinery and transport equipment	2,519.9	2,924.0	2,791.0
Machinery and mechanical appliances	1,764.4	1,870.2	1,881.1
Transport equipment	755.5	1,053.7	909.9
Total (incl. others)	13,616.2	15,525.4	15,252.9

Exports	2010	2011	2012
Food and live animals	553.1	612.2	638.0
Prepared foodstuffs	260.9	323.3	336.7
Mineral fuels, lubricants, etc.	1,215.7	1,316.0	872.0
Basic manufactures	3,263.4	3,894.8	3,900.7
Wood and wood products	630.1	739.3	732.1
Textiles and textile articles	316.0	353.1	332.2
Footwear and headgear	412.4	461.4	476.3
Base metals and articles thereof	1,609.0	1,934.6	1,908.8
Machinery and transport equipment	850.4	1,004.1	994.3
Machinery and mechanical appliances	696.3	815.1	791.3
Transport equipment	154.0	189.0	203.0
Miscellaneous manufactured articles	678.2	760.1	821.2
Total (incl. others)	7,095.5	8,222.1	7,858.0

* Figures from the Customs Administration of the Federation, the Customs Administration of Republika Srpska and the Customs Service of Brčko District, not including adjustments.

Source: Central Bank of Bosnia and Herzegovina.

PRINCIPAL TRADING PARTNERS
(KM million)

Imports	2010	2011	2012
Austria	489.1	491.7	504.1
China, People's Republic	655.5	774.9	816.4
Croatia	2,058.9	2,226.5	2,202.5
France	273.1	n.a.	n.a.
Germany	1,425.0	1,648.4	1,725.8
Hungary	416.8	379.2	413.0
Italy	1,210.4	1,381.7	1,429.4
Russia	1,189.1	1,635.1	1,493.9
Serbia	1,429.5	1,465.6	1,431.5
Slovenia	808.9	828.6	803.4
Switzerland	93.2	n.a.	n.a.
USA	485.5	626.7	388.2
Total (incl. others)	13,616.2	15,525.4	15,252.9

Exports	2010	2011	2012
Austria	470.6	619.0	654.8
Croatia	1,070.6	1,204.4	1,165.0
France	87.0	n.a.	n.a.
Germany	1,085.9	1,216.0	1,210.1
Hungary	126.2	n.a.	n.a.
Italy	862.0	963.5	939.2
Montenegro	310.2	300.4	249.2
Serbia	894.8	1,001.9	710.0
Slovenia	611.7	706.8	653.3
Switzerland	160.4	n.a.	n.a.
Total (incl. others)	7,095.5	8,222.1	7,858.0

Source: Central Bank of Bosnia and Herzegovina.

Transport

RAILWAYS
(traffic)

	2010	2011	2012
Passengers ('000 journeys)	898	821	846
Freight carried ('000 metric tons)	12,882	14,224	13,556
Passenger-km (million)	59	55	54
Freight ton-km (million)	1,232	1,298	1,150

CIVIL AVIATION
(traffic on scheduled services)

	2008	2009
Kilometres flown (million)	2	3
Passengers carried ('000)	56	80
Passenger-km (million)	115	111
Total ton-km (million)	10	9

Source: UN, *Statistical Yearbook*.

Passengers carried ('000): 85 in 2011; 36 in 2012 (Source: World Bank, World Development Indicators database).

Tourism

FOREIGN TOURIST ARRIVALS BY COUNTRY OF ORIGIN*

Country of origin	2010	2011	2012
Austria	14,344	14,786	15,990
Croatia	56,100	64,028	72,587
France	10,734	9,609	10,141
Germany	17,281	18,220	19,581
Italy	23,749	26,379	26,137
Montenegro	8,392	7,679	7,474
Poland	17,888	22,633	27,017
Serbia	56,370	54,169	57,380
Slovenia	40,246	41,267	39,949
Turkey	24,024	25,893	32,502
USA	8,239	8,537	9,743
Total (incl. others)	365,454	391,945	438,585

* Figures refer to arrivals at frontiers by visitors from abroad, and include same-day visitors.

Tourism receipts (US $ million, excl. passenger transport): 594 in 2010; 643 in 2011; 603 in 2012 (provisional) (Source: World Tourism Organization).

Communications Media

	2010	2011	2012
Telephones ('000 main lines in use)	998.6	955.9	878.4
Mobile cellular telephones ('000 subscribers)	3,110.2	3,171.3	3,352.3
Internet subscribers ('000)	522.4	515.3	n.a.
Broadband subscribers ('000)	307.5	364.5	404.1

Source: International Telecommunication Union.

Education

(2012/13)

	Institutions	Teachers*	Students: Males	Students: Females	Students: Total
Pre-primary	243	1,301	9,859	8,958	18,817
Primary/Basic	1,829	24,174	155,773	148,214	303,987
Primary/Basic—special needs	54	310	639	346	985
Secondary (incl. special needs)	313	13,045	84,245	81,877	166,122
Higher	43	9,144	45,937	56,420	102,357

* Full-time and part-time teaching staff.

Adult literacy rate (UNESCO estimates): 98.0% (males 99.5%; females 96.7%) in 2011 (Source: UNESCO Institute for Statistics).

Directory

The Government

(April 2014)

HIGH REPRESENTATIVE OF THE INTERNATIONAL COMMUNITY IN BOSNIA AND HERZEGOVINA

High Representative of the International Community to Bosnia and Herzegovina: Dr Valentin Inzko.

SPECIAL REPRESENTATIVE OF THE EUROPEAN UNION TO BOSNIA AND HERZEGOVINA

Special Representative of the European Union to Bosnia and Herzegovina: Peter Sørensen.

STATE GOVERNMENT

A coalition of the Savez nezavisnih socijaldemokrata (SNSD—Alliance of Independent Social Democrats), Hrvatska Demokratska Zajednica Bosne i Hercegovine (HDZ BiH—Croatian Democratic Union of Bosnia and Herzegovina), Hrvatska Demokratska Zajednica 1990 (Croatian Democratic Union 1990 of Bosnia and Herzegovina—HDZ 1990), Srpska demokratska stranka (SDS—Serbian Democratic Party), Socijaldemokratska Partija BiH (Social Democratic Party of Bosnia and Herzegovina—SDP BiH) and Savez za bolju budućnost BiH (SBB BiH—Union for a Better Future of Bosnia and Herzegovina).

Chairman of the Presidency (March–November 2014): Bakir Izetbegović (Stranka Demokratske Akcije—SDA, Party of Democratic Action).

Member of the Presidency: ŽELJKO KOMŠIĆ (Independent).

Member of the Presidency: NEBOJŠA RADMANOVIĆ (SNSD).

Note: The post of Chairman of the Presidency rotates every eight months between Bosniak, Croat and Serb representatives.

Chairman of the Council of Ministers: VJEKOSLAV BEVANDA (HDZ BiH).

Minister of Foreign Affairs: ZLATKO LAGUMDŽIJA (SDP BiH).

Minister of Security: (vacant).

Minister of Defence: ZEKERIJAH OSMIĆ (SDS).

Minister of Finance and the Treasury: NIKOLA ŠPIRIĆ (SNSD).

Minister of Justice: BARIŠA ČOLAK (HDZ BiH).

Minister of Foreign Trade and Economic Relations: BORIS TUČIĆ.

Minister of Communications and Transport: DAMIR HADŽIĆ (SDP BiH).

Minister of Human Rights and Refugees: DAMIR LJUBIĆ (HDZ 1990).

Minister of Civil Affairs: SREDOJE NOVIĆ (SNSD).

FEDERATION GOVERNMENT

A coalition principally comprising members of Hrvatska stranka Prava BiH (HSP BiH—Croatian Party of Rights of Bosnia and Herzegovina), Hrvatska Demokratska Zajednica Bosne i Hercegovine (HDZ BiH—the Croatian Democratic Union of Bosnia and Herzegovina), Stranka Demokratske Akcije (SDA—Party of Democratic Action), Narodna stranka Radom za boljitak (NSRZB—People's Party Working For Betterment) and Socijaldemokratska Partija BiH (SDP BiH—Social Democratic Party of Bosnia and Herzegovina).

President: ŽIVKO BUDIMIR (Stranka pravde i povjerenja—Party of Justice and Trust).

Vice-President: SVETOZAR PUDARIĆ (SDP BiH).

Vice-President: MIRSAD KEBO (SDA).

Prime Minister: NERMIN NIKŠIĆ (SDP BiH).

Deputy Prime Minister, Minister of Physical Planning: DESNICA RADIVOJEVIĆ (SDA).

Minister of Agriculture, Water Management and Forestry: JERKO IVANKOVIĆ-LIJANOVIĆ (NSRZB).

Minister of Internal Affairs: PREDRAG KURTEŠ (SDP BiH).

Minister of Justice: ZORAN MIKULIĆ (SDP BiH).

Minister of Finance: ANTE KRAJINA (HSP BiH).

Minister of Energy, Mining and Industry: ERDAL TRHULJ (SDA).

Minister of Transport and Communications: ENVER BIJEDIĆ (SDP BiH).

Minister of Labour and Social Policy: VJEKOSLAV ČAMBER (HDZ BiH).

Minister of Displaced Persons and Refugees: ADIL OSMANOVIĆ (SDA).

Minister of Veterans and the Disabled of the War of Defensive Liberation: ZUKAN HELEZ (SDP BiH).

Minister of Health: RUSMIR MESIHOVIĆ (SDP BiH).

Minister of Education and Science: DAMIR MAŠIĆ (SDP BiH).

Minister of Culture and Sport: SALMIR KAPLAN (SDA).

Minister of Trade: MILORAD BAHILJ-BAJA (NSRZB).

Minister of Development, Entrepreneurship and Crafts: SANJIN HALIMOVIĆ (SDA).

Minister of the Environment and Tourism: BRANKA ĐURIĆ (SDP BiH).

Note: substantial powers are devolved further to each of the constituent 10 cantons of the Federation.

REPUBLIKA SRPSKA GOVERNMENT

A coalition of the Savez nezavisnih socijaldemokratska (SNSD—Alliance of Independent Social Democrats), Hrvatska Demokratska Zajednica Bosne i Hercegovine (HDZ BiH—the Croatian Democratic Union of Bosnia and Herzegovina), Stranka Demokratske Akcije (SDA—Party of Democratic Action), Narodna Demokratska Stranka (NDS—the People's Democratic Party), Socijalistička Partija (SP—Socialist Party) and independents.

President: MILORAD DODIK (SNSD).

Vice-President: EMIL VLAJKI (NDS).

Vice-President: ENES SULJKANOVIĆ (Socijal-demokratska Partija BiH—SDP BiH, Social Democratic Party of Bosnia and Herzegovina).

Prime Minister: ŽELJKA CVIJANOVIĆ (SNSD).

Minister of Economic Affairs and Regional Co-operation: IGOR VIDOVIĆ (SNSD).

Minister of Education and Culture: GORAN MUTABDŽIJA (SNSD).

Minister of Finance: ZORAN TEGELTIJA (SNSD).

Minister of Internal Affairs: RADISLAV JOVIČIĆ (SNSD).

Minister of Justice: GORAN ZLATKOVIĆ (SDA).

Minister of Administration and Local Government: LEJLA REŠIĆ (NDS).

Minister of Labour and Veterans: PETAR ĐOKIĆ (SP).

Minister of Trade and Tourism: MAIDA IBRIŠAGIĆ-HRSTIĆ (Independent).

Minister of Industry, Energy and Mining: Dr ŽELJKO KOVAČEVIĆ (SNSD).

Minister of Transport and Communications: NEDELJKO ČUBRILOVIĆ (NDS).

Minister of Agriculture, Forestry and Water Management: Dr STEVO MIRJANIĆ (SNSD).

Minister of Physical Planning, Civil Engineering and the Environment: SREBRENKA GOLIĆ (SNSD).

Minister of Refugees and Displaced Persons: DAVOR ČORDAŠ (HDZ BiH).

Minister of Health and Social Welfare: Dr DRAGAN BOGDANIĆ (Independent).

Minister of Science and Technology: Dr JASMIN KOMIĆ (Independent).

Minister of the Family, Youth and Sport: NADA TEŠANOVIĆ (SNSD).

BRČKO DISTRICT

Principal Deputy High Representative of the International Community and International Supervisor of Brčko District: RODERICK W. MOORE.

Chairman of the Government, Mayor of Brčko District: ANTO DOMIĆ.

OFFICES AND MINISTRIES

Office of the High Representative of the International Community

Office of the High Representative of the International Community: 71000 Sarajevo, Emerika Bluma 1; tel. (33) 283500; fax (33) 283501; e-mail sarajevo.rd@ohr.int; internet www.ohr.int.

Office of the Special Representative of the European Union

Delegation of the European Union to Bosnia and Herzegovina and the European Union Special Representative: 71000 Sarajevo, Skenderija 3A; tel. (33) 560800; fax (33) 668390; e-mail delegation-bih@eeas.europa.eu; internet www.europa.ba.

State Government

Office of the State Presidency: 71000 Sarajevo, Maršala Tita 16; tel. (33) 567510; fax (33) 555620; e-mail press@predsjednistvobih.ba; internet www.predsjednistvobih.ba.

Office of the Chairman of the Council of Ministers: 71000 Sarajevo, trg Bosne i Hercegovine 1; tel. (33) 282611; fax (33) 282613; e-mail predsjedatelj@vm.gov.ba; internet www.vijeceministara.gov.ba.

Ministry of Civil Affairs: 71000 Sarajevo, trg Bosne i Hercegovine 1; tel. (33) 221073; fax (33) 221074; e-mail zorica.rulj@mcp.gov.ba; internet www.mcp.gov.ba.

Ministry of Communications and Transport: 71000 Sarajevo, trg Bosne i Hercegovine 1; tel. (33) 284750; fax (33) 284751; e-mail info@mkt.gov.ba; internet www.mkt.gov.ba.

Ministry of Defence: 71000 Sarajevo, Hamdije Kreševljakovića 98; tel. (33) 285500; fax (33) 206094; e-mail info@mod.gov.ba; internet www.mod.gov.ba.

Ministry of Finance and the Treasury: 71000 Sarajevo, trg Bosne i Hercegovine 1; tel. (33) 205345; fax (33) 202930; e-mail trezorbih@mft.gov.ba.

Ministry of Foreign Affairs: 71000 Sarajevo, Musala 2; tel. (33) 281100; fax (33) 227156; e-mail info_mvpbih@mvp.gov.ba; internet www.mfa.gov.ba.

Ministry of Foreign Trade and Economic Relations: 71000 Sarajevo, Musala 9; tel. (33) 220093; fax (33) 220091; e-mail info@mvteo.gov.ba; internet www.mvteo.gov.ba.

Ministry of Human Rights and Refugees: 71000 Sarajevo, trg Bosne i Hercegovine 1; tel. (33) 202600; fax (33) 206140; e-mail kabmin@mhrr.gov.ba; internet www.mhrr.gov.ba.

Ministry of Justice: 71000 Sarajevo, trg Bosne i Hercegovine 1; tel. (33) 223501; fax (33) 223504; e-mail info@mpr.gov.ba; internet www.mpr.gov.ba.

Ministry of Security: 71000 Sarajevo, trg Bosne i Hercegovine 1; tel. (33) 213623; fax (33) 213628; e-mail glasnogovornik@msb.gov.ba; internet www.msb.gov.ba.

Federation Government

Office of the Federation Presidency (Mostar): 88000 Mostar, Ante Starčevića bb; tel. (36) 318905; fax (36) 313255; e-mail info@predsjednikfbih.gov.ba; internet www.predsjednikfbih.gov.ba.

Office of the Federation Presidency (Sarajevo): 71000 Sarajevo, Musala 9; tel. (33) 212986; fax (33) 220437; e-mail info@fbihvlada.gov.ba; internet www.fbihvlada.gov.ba.

Office of the Prime Minister: 71000 Sarajevo, Alipašina 41; tel. (33) 212986; fax (33) 220437; e-mail info@fbihvlada.gov.ba; internet www.fbihvlada.gov.ba.

Ministry of Agriculture, Water Management and Forestry: 71000 Sarajevo, ul. Marka Marulica 2; tel. (33) 726551; fax (33) 726669; e-mail kabinet@fmpvs.gov.ba; internet www.fmpvs.gov.ba.

Ministry of Culture and Sport: 71000 Sarajevo, ul. Obala Maka Dizdara 2; tel. (33) 254103; fax (33) 254151; e-mail kabinet@fmksa.com; internet www.fmks.gov.ba.

Ministry of Development, Entrepreneurship and Crafts: 88000 Mostar, ul. Ante Starčevića bb; tel. (36) 449120; fax (36) 449122; e-mail fmrpo@fmrpo.gov.ba; internet www.fmrpo.gov.ba.

Ministry of Displaced Persons and Refugees: 71000 Sarajevo, Alipašina 41; tel. (33) 663977; fax (33) 204552; e-mail kabinet@fmroi.gov.ba; internet www.fmroi.gov.ba.

Ministry of Education and Science: 88000 Mostar, Ante Starčevića bb; tel. (36) 355700; fax (33) 355742; e-mail kabinet@fmroi.gov.ba; internet www.fmon.gov.ba.

Ministry of Energy, Mining and Industry: 88000 Mostar, Alekse Šantića bb; tel. (36) 513800; fax (36) 580015; e-mail kabinet.fmeri@bih.net.ba; internet www.fmeri.gov.ba.

Ministry of the Environment and Tourism: 71000 Sarajevo, ul. Mark Marulića 2; tel. (33) 726700; fax (33) 726747; e-mail fmoit@fmoit.gov.ba; internet www.fmoit.gov.ba.

Ministry of Finance: 71000 Sarajevo, Mehmeda Spahe 5; tel. (33) 253400; fax (33) 250534; e-mail info@fmf.gov.ba; internet www.fmf.gov.ba.

Ministry of Health: 71000 Sarajevo, Titova 9; tel. (33) 226635; fax (33) 226637; e-mail kab.moh@bih.net.ba; internet www.fmoh.gov.ba.

Ministry of Internal Affairs: 71000 Sarajevo, Mehmeda Spahe 7; tel. and fax (33) 280020; e-mail info@fmup.gov.ba; internet www.fmup.gov.ba.

Ministry of Justice: 71000 Sarajevo, Valtera Perića 15; tel. (33) 213151; fax (33) 213155; e-mail jedinica.info@fmp.gov.ba; internet www.fmp.gov.ba.

Ministry of Labour and Social Policy: 71000 Sarajevo, Marka Marulića 2; tel. (33) 661782; fax (33) 255461; e-mail info@fmrsp.gov.ba; internet www.fmrsp.gov.ba.

Ministry of Physical Planning: 71000 Sarajevo, Marka Marulića 2; tel. (33) 726500; fax (33) 652743; e-mail info@fmpu.gov.ba; internet www.fmpu.gov.ba.

Ministry of Trade: 88000 Mostar, Ante Starčevića bb; tel. (36) 310148; fax (36) 318684; internet www.fmt.gov.ba.

Ministry of Transport and Communications: 88000 Mostar, Braće Fejića bb; tel. (36) 550025; fax (36) 550024; e-mail fmpiksa@bih.net.ba; internet www.fmpik.gov.ba.

Ministry of Veterans and the Disabled of the War of Defensive Liberation: 71000 Sarajevo, Alipašina 41; tel. (33) 212932; fax (33) 222679; e-mail kabinet@bih.net.ba; internet www.fmbi.gov.ba.

Republika Srpska Government

Office of the President: 78000 Banja Luka, Bana Milosavljevića 4; tel. (51) 248100; fax (51) 248161; e-mail info@predsjednikrs.net; internet www.predsjednikrs.net.

Office of the Prime Minister: 78000 Banja Luka, trg Republike Srpske 1; tel. (51) 339103; fax (51) 339119; e-mail kabinet@vladars.net; internet www.vladars.net.

Ministry of Administration and Local Government: 78000 Banja Luka, trg Republike Srpske 1; tel. (51) 339545; fax (51) 339648; e-mail muls@muls.vladars.net; internet www.vladars.net/sr-SP-Cyrl/Vlada/Ministarstva/muls/OMin/Pages/Splash.aspx.

Ministry of Agriculture, Forestry and Water Management: 78000 Banja Luka, trg Republike Srpske 1; tel. (51) 338415; fax (51) 338865; e-mail mps@mps.vladars.net; internet www.vladars.net/sr-SP-Cyrl/Vlada/Ministarstva/mps.

Ministry of Economic Affairs and Regional Co-operation: 78000 Banja Luka, trg Republike Srpske 1; tel. (51) 339324; fax (51) 339647; e-mail meoi@meoi.vladars.net; internet www.vladars.net/sr-SP-Cyrl/Vlada/Ministarstva/meoi.

Ministry of Education and Culture: 78000 Banja Luka, trg Republike Srpske 1; tel. (51) 338461; fax (51) 338853; e-mail mp@mp.vladars.net; internet www.vladars.net/sr-SP-Cyrl/Vlada/Ministarstva/mpk.

Ministry of the Family, Youth and Sport: 78000 Banja Luka, trg Republike Srpske 1; tel. (51) 338332; fax (51) 338846; e-mail mpos@mpos.vladars.net; internet www.vladars.net/sr-SP-Cyrl/Vlada/Ministarstva/mpos.

Ministry of Finance: 78000 Banja Luka, trg Republike Srpske 1; tel. (51) 339768; fax (51) 339645; e-mail mf@mf.vladars.net; internet www.vladars.net/sr-SP-Cyrl/Vlada/Ministarstva/mf.

Ministry of Health and Social Welfare: 78000 Banja Luka, trg Republike Srpske 1; tel. (51) 339486; fax (51) 339652; e-mail ministarstvo-zdravlja@mzsz.vladars.net; internet www.vladars.net/sr-SP-Cyrl/Vlada/Ministarstva/MZSZ.

Ministry of Industry, Energy and Mining: 78000 Banja Luka, trg Republike Srpske 1; tel. (51) 339581; fax (51) 339651; e-mail mier@mier.vladars.net; internet www.vladars.net/sr-sp-cyrl/vlada/ministarstva/mper.

Ministry of Internal Affairs: 78000 Banja Luka, Desanke Maksimović 4; tel. (51) 338478; fax (51) 338844; e-mail mup@mup.vladars.net; internet www.mup.vladars.net.

Ministry of Justice: 78000 Banja Luka, trg Republike Srpske 1; tel. (51) 339325; fax (51) 339650; e-mail mpr@mpr.vladars.net; internet www.vladars.net/sr-sp-cyrl/vlada/ministarstva/mpr.

Ministry of Labour and Veterans: 78000 Banja Luka, trg Republike Srpske 1; tel. (51) 338602; fax (51) 338845; e-mail mpb@mpb.vladars.net; internet www.vladars.net/sr-sp-cyrl/vlada/ministarstva/mpb.

Ministry of Physical Planning, Civil Engineering and the Environment: 78000 Banja Luka, trg Republike Srpske 1; tel. (51) 339592; fax (51) 339653; e-mail kabinetministra@mgr.vladars.net; internet www.vladars.net/sr-sp-cyrl/vlada/ministarstva/mgr.

Ministry of Refugees and Displaced Persons: 78000 Banja Luka, trg Republike Srpske 1; tel. (51) 338642; fax (51) 338847; e-mail mirl@mirl.vladars.net; internet www.vladars.net/sr-sp-cyrl/vlada/ministarstva/mirl.

Ministry of Science and Technology: 78000 Banja Luka, Administrativni Centar Vlade RS; tel. (51) 338731; fax (51) 338856; e-mail mnk@mnk.vladars.net; internet www.vladars.net/sr-sp-cyrl/vlada/ministarstva/mnk.

Ministry of Trade and Tourism: 78000 Banja Luka, trg Republike Srpske 1; tel. (51) 338769; fax (51) 338864; e-mail mtt@mtt.vladars.net; internet www.vladars.net/sr-sp-cyrl/vlada/ministarstva/mtt.

Ministry of Transport and Communications: 78000 Banja Luka, trg Republike Srpske 1; tel. (51) 339603; fax (51) 339649; e-mail msv@msv.vladars.net; internet www.vladars.net/sr-sp-cyrl/vlada/ministarstva/msv.

Brčko District

Office of the Principal Deputy High Representative of the International Community and International Supervisor of Brčko District: 76100 Brčko, Musala bb; tel. (49) 240300; fax (49) 217560; internet www.ohr.int/ohr-offices/brcko.

Office of the Government of Brčko District: 76100 Brčko, bul. Mira 1; tel. (49) 240600; fax (49) 490008; e-mail gradonacelnik@bdcentral.net; internet www.bdcentral.net.

The Presidency

STATE PRESIDENCY*

Election, 3 October 2010

	Votes	% of votes
Bosniak Candidates		
Bakir Izetbegović (SDA)	162,831	34.86
Fahrudin Radončić (SBB BiH)	142,387	30.49
Haris Silajdžić (SBiH)	117,240	25.10
Others	44,581	9.55
Total	467,039	100.00
Croat Candidates		
Željko Komšić (Independent)	337,065	60.61
Borjana Krišto (HDZ BiH)	109,758	19.74
Martin Raguž (HDZ 1990)	60,266	10.84
Jerko Ivanković-Lijanović (NSRZB)	45,397	8.16
Others	3,625	0.65
Total	556,111	100.00

—continued	Votes	% of votes
Serb Candidates		
Nebojša Radmanović (SNSD)	295,629	48.92
Mladen Ivanić (PDP)	285,951	47.31
Rajko Papović (Alliance for a Democratic Srpska)	22,790	3.77
Total	604,370	100.00

* The Presidency of Bosnia and Herzegovina comprises three members: one Bosniak, one Croat and one Serb. The Serb is elected from within Republika Srpska, and the Bosniak and Croat members from within the Federation of Bosnia and Herzegovina. The position of Chairman of the Presidency is filled on a rotating basis for a term of eight months by each member of the Presidency.

REPUBLIKA SRPSKA PRESIDENCY

Election, 3 October 2010

Candidate	Votes	% of votes
Milorad Dodik (SNSD)	319,618	50.52
Ognjen Tadić (SDS)	227,239	35.92
Others	85,817	13.56
Total	632,674	100.00

Legislature

STATE LEGISLATURE

The **Parliamentary Assembly of Bosnia and Herzegovina** (Parlamentarna Skupština Bosne i Hercegovine) comprises two chambers: a directly elected lower chamber, the **House of Representatives** (Predstavnički dom/Zastupnički dom); and an indirectly elected **House of Peoples** (Dom naroda).

House of Representatives (Predstavnički dom/Zastupnički dom)

71000 Sarajevo, trg Bosne i Hercegovine 1; tel. (33) 284410; fax (33) 284456; e-mail denis.becirovic@parlament.ba; internet www.parlament.ba.

The Predstavnički dom/Zastupnički dom has 42 deputies directly elected for a four-year term, of whom 28 are elected from the Federation and 14 from Republika Srpska.

Speaker: Dr MILORAD ŽIVKOVIĆ.

General Election, 3 October 2010

	% of votes			
Party	FBiH*	RS†	Overall	Seats
SDP BiH	26.07	2.96	17.33	8
SNSD	0.86	43.30	16.92	8
SDA	19.40	2.64	13.05	7
SDS	—	22.19	8.40	4
SBB BiH	12.16	1.02	7.95	4
HDZ BiH	10.99	0.38	6.97	3
SBiH	7.25	2.04	5.28	2
Croatian Coalition‡	4.86	0.08	3.05	2
PDP	—	6.45	2.44	1
NSRZB	4.81	—	2.99	1
DNS	0.11	4.59	1.80	1
DNZ BiH	1.45	0.05	0.92	1
Others	12.04	14.30	12.90	—
Total	100.00	100.00	100.00‖	42

* Federation of Bosnia and Herzegovina.
† Republika Srpska.
‡ A coalition of the HDZ 1990 and the HSP BiH.
‖ A total of 1,641,569 valid votes were cast, of which 1,020,293 were cast in the Federation of Bosnia and Herzegovina and 621,276 were cast in Republika Srpska.

House of Peoples (Dom naroda)

71000 Sarajevo, trg Bosne i Hercegovine 1; tel. (33) 284454; fax (33) 286056; e-mail ognjen.tadic@parlament.ba; internet www.parlament.ba.

There are 15 deputies in the Dom naroda (House of Peoples), of whom 10 are elected by the Dom naroda Federacije (Federation House of Peoples) and five by the Vijeće naroda (Council of Peoples) of the Narodna skupština Republike Srpske (National Assembly of Republika Srpska).

Speaker: Dr DRAGAN ČOVIĆ.

FEDERATION LEGISLATURE

The **Federation Parliament** (Parlamentarna Federacije) comprises two chambers: a directly elected lower chamber, the **Federation House of Representatives** (Predstavnički dom Federacije/Zastupnički dom Federacije) and an indirectly elected **Federation House of Peoples** (Dom Naroda Federacije). Each of the 10 cantons also has an elected assembly.

Federation House of Representatives (Predstavnički dom Federacije/Zastupnički dom Federacije)

71000 Sarajevo, Hamdije Kreševljakovića 3; tel. (33) 263585; fax (33) 223623; e-mail kabinet.predsjedavajuceg@parlamentfbih.gov.ba; internet www.parlamentfbih.gov.ba.

The 98 deputies of the Predstavnički dom Federacije/Zastupnički dom Federacije are directly elected for a four-year term.

Speaker: SAFET SOFTIĆ (PDA).

General Election, 3 October 2010

Party	Votes	% of votes	Seats
SDP BiH	251,053	24.53	28
SDA	206,926	20.22	23
SBB BiH	121,697	11.89	13
HDZ BiH	108,943	10.64	12
SBiH	78,086	7.63	9
NSRZB	48,286	4.72	5
Croatian Coalition*	47,941	4.68	5
A-SDA	19,254	1.88	1
DNZ BiH	15,082	1.47	1
SNSD	9,505	0.93	1
Others	116,819	11.41	—
Total	1,023,529	100.00	98

* A coalition of the HDZ 1990 and the HSP BiH.

Federation House of Peoples (Dom Naroda Federacije)

71000 Sarajevo, Hamdije Kreševljakovića 3; tel. (33) 666681; fax (33) 223622; e-mail parlamentfbih@parlamentfbih.gov.ba; internet www.parlamentfbih.gov.ba.

The 58-member Dom Naroda Federacije comprises 17 Bosniak, 17 Croat, 17 Serb and seven other deputies, who are elected by the cantonal assemblies.

Speaker: TOMISLAV MARTINOVIĆ.

REPUBLIKA SRPSKA LEGISLATURE

The legislature of Republika Srpska comprises the monocameral, directly elected **Republika Srpska People's Assembly** (Narodna Skupština Republike Srpske).

Republika Srpska People's Assembly (Narodna skupština Republike Srpske)

51000 Banja Luka, Vuka Karadžića 2; tel. (51) 338104; fax (51) 301087; internet www.narodnaskupstinars.net.

Speaker: IGOR RADOJIČIĆ.

Election, 3 October 2010

Party	Votes	% of votes	Seats
SNSD	240,727	38.00	37
SDS	120,136	18.97	18
PDP	47,806	7.55	7
DNS	38,547	6.09	6
SP–Party of United Pensioners alliance	26,824	4.23	4
DP	21,604	3.41	3
SDP BiH	19,297	3.05	3
SDA	16,861	2.66	2
NDS	13,440	2.12	2
SRSRS	15,166	2.39	1
Others	73,021	11.53	—
Total	633,429	100.00	83

The Republika Srpska People's Assembly elects 28 delegates to a Council of Peoples (Vijeće naroda), who are responsible for, *inter alia*, nominating the entity's representatives to the state House of Peoples. These 28 members comprise eight Bosniaks, eight Croats, eight Serbs and four others.

Council of Peoples of Republika Srpska (Vijeće naroda Republike Srpske): 51000 Banja Luka, Vuka Karadžića 4; tel. (51) 247446; fax (51) 247653; e-mail predsjedavajuci@vijecenarodars.net; internet www.vijecenarodars.net; Chair. MOMIR MALIĆ.

BRČKO DISTRICT

Note: residents of Brčko District are entitled to vote in elections to state institutions, to those of the entity that they are a citizen of, and in elections to the local district institutions.

Election Commission

Centralna Izborna Komisija Bosne i Hercegovine (Central Election Commission of Bosnia and Herzegovina): 71000 Sarajevo, Danijela Ozme 7; tel. (33) 251300; fax (33) 251329; e-mail kontakt@izbori.ba; internet www.izbori.ba; independent; Pres. STJEPAN MIKIĆ.

Political Organizations

Bosanska Stranka (BOSS) (Bosnian Party): 75000 Tuzla, Kojšino 7; tel. (35) 251035; fax (35) 251431; e-mail predsjednik@boss.ba; internet www.boss.ba; socialist, supports policies of former Yugoslav leader Josip Broz (Tito); Chair. MIRNES AJANOVIĆ.

Bosanskohercegovačka patriotska stranka—Sefer Halilović (BPS) (Bosnian-Herzegovinan Patriotic Party—Sefer Halilović): Sarajevo, ul. Maršala Tita 9A; tel. (33) 208643; fax (33) 201294; e-mail bps@bih.net.ba; internet bps-seferhalilovic.ba; f. 1996; Pres. SEFER HALILOVIĆ; Sec.-Gen. ZAIM BACKOVIĆA.

Demokratska narodna zajednica BiH (DNZ BiH) (Democratic People's Community of Bosnia and Herzegovina): 77230 Velika Kladuša, Sulejmana Topića 7; tel. (37) 775340; fax (37) 770307; e-mail dnzbih@gmail.com; internet www.dnzbih.ba; f. 1993; Chair. RIFAT DOLIĆ.

Demokratska Partija (DP) (Democratic Party): 78000 Banja Luka, Petra Kočića 41; tel. (51) 217000; e-mail demokratska.partija@gmail.com; internet www.dp-rs.org; f. 2009; Pres. DRAGAN CAVIĆ.

Demokratski Narodni Savez (DNS) (Democratic People's Alliance): 78000 Banja Luka, Aleja Svetog Save 20; tel. (51) 219033; fax (51) 219020; internet www.dnsrs.org; f. 2000 by fmr mems of the Serb National Alliance; Chair. Dr MARKO PAVIĆ.

Hrvatska Demokratska Zajednica 1990 (HDZ 1990) (Croatian Democratic Union 1990 of Bosnia and Herzegovina): 88000 Mostar, Nikole Šubića Zrinjskog 11/I; tel. (36) 449730; fax (36) 449737; e-mail hdz1990@tel.net.ba; internet www.hdz1990.org; f. 2006 by fmr mems of the Croatian Democratic Union of Bosnia and Herzegovina; contested 2010 legislative elections as mem. of Croatian Coalition; Pres. MARTIN RAGUŽ.

Hrvatska Demokratska Zajednica Bosne i Hercegovine (HDZ BiH) (Croatian Democratic Union of Bosnia and Herzegovina): 88000 Mostar, Kneza Domagoja bb; tel. (36) 314686; fax (36) 322799; e-mail hdzbih@hdzbih.org; internet www.hdzbih.org; f. 1990; affiliate of the CDU in Croatia; adopted new party statute May 2007; Croat nationalist party; Pres. DRAGAN ČOVIĆ.

Hrvatska seljačka stranka—Nova Hrvatska Inicijativa (HSS—NHI) (Croatian Peasants' Party—New Croatian Initiative): 71000 Sarajevo, Titova 9A; tel. (33) 214602; e-mail hss.nhi@gmail.com; internet www.hss-nhi.ba; f. 2007 by merger of the Croatian Peasants' Party and New Croatian Initiative; Pres. DRAGO DŽAMBAS.

Hrvatska stranka Prava BiH (HSP BiH) (Croatian Party of Rights of Bosnia and Herzegovina): 88000 Mostar, Kneza Mihajla Viševića Humskog 39; tel. (36) 333028; fax (36) 333020; e-mail tajnistvo@hsp-bih.ba; internet www.hsp-bih.ba; Croat nationalist; contested 2010 legislative elections as mem. of Croatian Coalition; Pres. Dr ZVONKO JURIŠIĆ.

Narodna Demokratska Stranka (NDS) (People's Democratic Party): 78000 Banja Luka, Miloša Obilića 9; tel. and fax (51) 465675; e-mail info@ndsrs.org; internet ndsrs.org; fmrly People's Democratic Party of Republika Srpska; Chair. KRSTO JANDRIĆ.

Narodna stranka Radom za boljitak (NSRZB) (People's Party Working for Betterment): 71000 Sarajevo, Zmaja od Bosne 4, Holiday Inn-1011, 1012; tel. (33) 586386; fax (33) 586385; e-mail zaboljitak@zaboljitak.ba; internet www.zaboljitak.ba; f. 2001; multi-ethnic party supporting integration of Bosnia and Herzegovina into European structures; Pres. MLADEN IVANKOVIĆ-LIJANOVIĆ.

Naša Stranka (NS) (Our Party): 71000 Sarajevo, Jezero 8; tel. (33) 551225; fax (33) 551226; e-mail nasastranka@nasastranka.ba; internet www.nasastranka.ba; f. 2008; multi-ethnic; contested 2011 elections in alliance with the New Socialist Party; Chair. DENNIS GRATZ.

Nova Socijalistička Partija (NSP) (New Socialist Party): 78000 Banja Luka, ul. Stepe Stepanović bb; tel. (51) 217032; internet www.novasocijalistickapartija.com; f. 2009; contested 2010 elections in coalition with Our Party; Chair. ZDRAVKO KRSMANOVIĆ.

Partija Demokratskog Progresa (PDP) (Party of Democratic Progress): 78000 Banja Luka, ul. Prvog Krajiškog Korpusa 130; tel. (51) 346210; fax (51) 300956; e-mail pdp@blic.net; internet www.pdpinfo.net; f. 1999; fmrly Party of Democratic Progress of Republika Srpska; moderate, supports equal rights for all ethnic groups, supports closer co-operation of Republika Srpska with the European Union; Chair. MLADEN IVANIĆ.

Savez nezavisnih socijaldemokrata (SNSD) (Alliance of Independent Social Democrats): 78000 Banja Luka, Petra Kočića 5; tel. (51) 318492; fax (51) 318495; e-mail snsd@snsd.org; internet www.snsd.org; f. 1997 as Party of Independent Social Democrats; present name adopted 2001, following merger with Democratic Socialist Party; Chair. MILORAD DODIK; Sec.-Gen. RAJKO VASIĆ.

Savez za bolju budućnost BiH (SBB BiH) (Union for a Better Future of Bosnia and Herzegovina): 71000 Sarajevo, Tešanjska 24A; tel. (33) 942551; fax (33) 261255; e-mail info@sbbbh.ba; internet www.sbbbh.ba; f. 2009; Pres. FAHRUDIN RADONČIĆ.

Socijaldemokratska Partija BiH (SDP BiH) (Social Democratic Party of Bosnia and Herzegovina): 71000 Sarajevo, Alipašina 41; tel. (33) 563910; fax (33) 563913; e-mail predsjednik@sdp.ba; internet www.sdp.ba; Chair. Dr ZLATKO LAGUMDŽIJA; Sec.-Gen. NERMIN NIKŠIĆ.

Socijalistička Partija (SP) (Socialist Party): 78000 Banja Luka, Jovana Dulića 25; tel. (51) 328750; fax (51) 328753; e-mail info@socijalisti.ba; internet www.socijalisti.ba; f. 1993 as br. of Socialist Party of Serbia; fmrly Socialist Party of Republika Srpska; Chair. PETAR ĐOKIĆ.

Srpska demokratska stranka (SDS) (Serbian Democratic Party): 78000 Banja Luka, Nikole Tesle 1B; tel. (51) 225130; fax (51) 212984; e-mail sds@teol.net; internet www.sdsrs.com; f. 1990; allied to SDP of Serbia; Serb nationalist party; Chair. MLADEN BOSIĆ.

Srpska Radikalna Stranka Republike Srpske (SRSRS) (Serbian Radical Party of Republika Srpska): 78000 Banja Luka, Vidovdanska 53; tel. (51) 219428; e-mail kontakt@srs-rs.org; radical Serb nationalist, supports the notion of a 'Greater Serbia'; Chair. MILANKO MIHAJLICA.

Stranka Demokratske Akcije (SDA) (Party of Democratic Action): 71000 Sarajevo, Mehmeda Spahe 14; tel. (33) 216906; fax (33) 225363; e-mail sda@bih.net.ba; internet www.sda.ba; f. 1990; moderate Bosniak nationalist party that supports admission of Bosnia and Herzegovina to the European Union and formation of a Republic of Bosnia and Herzegovina as a decentralized state composed of multi-ethnic regions, with Bosniaks, Croats and Serbs as members of a common Bosnian nation; Chair. SULEJMAN TIHIĆ; Sec.-Gen. AMIR ZUKIĆ.

Stranka Demokratske Aktivnosti (A-SDA) (Party of Democratic Activities): 77220 Cazin, Cazinskih Brigada; tel. and fax (37) 512005; e-mail info@asda.ba; f. 2008 by fmr mems of Party of Democratic Action (q.v.); supports greater integration with Europe, state involvement in the economy; Pres. ISMET KURTAGIĆ.

Stranka pravde i povjerenja (SPP) (Party of Justice and Trust): Sarajevo; f. 2013 by fmr mems of Croatian Party of Rights of Bosnia and Herzegovina; conservative; Pres. ŽIVKO BUDIMIR; 1,071 mems (2013).

Stranka za Bosnu i Hercegovinu (SBiH) (Party for Bosnia and Herzegovina): 71000 Sarajevo, Fra Grge Martića 2/II; tel. (33) 573470; fax (33) 475597; e-mail zabih@zabih.ba; internet www.zabih.ba; f. 1996; integrationist; Pres. AMER JERLAGIĆ.

Diplomatic Representation

EMBASSIES IN BOSNIA AND HERZEGOVINA

Albania: 71000 Sarajevo, ul. Telali 19; tel. (33) 574420; fax (33) 574421; e-mail embassy.sarajevo@mfa.gov.al; Ambassador FLAMUR GASHI.

Austria: 71000 Sarajevo, Džidžikovac 7; tel. (33) 279400; fax (33) 668339; e-mail sarajewo-ob@bmeia.gv.at; internet www.austrijska-ambasada.ba; Ambassador MARTIN PAMMER.

Bulgaria: 71000 Sarajevo, Radnička 30; tel. (33) 668191; fax (33) 668189; e-mail embassy.sarajevo@mfa.bg; Ambassador ANGEL ANGELOV.

China, People's Republic: 71000 Sarajevo, Braće Begića 17; tel. (33) 215102; fax (33) 215108; e-mail emprcbh@bih.net.ba; internet ba.chineseembassy.org; Ambassador DONG CHUNFENG.

Croatia: 71000 Sarajevo, Mehmeda Spahe 16; tel. (33) 251640; fax (33) 472434; e-mail croemb.sarajevo@mvpei.hr; internet ba.mvp.hr; Ambassador IVAN DEL VECCHIO.

Czech Republic: 71000 Sarajevo, Franjevačka 19; tel. (33) 447525; fax (33) 447526; e-mail sarajevo@embassy.mzv.cz; internet www.mzv.cz/sarajevo; Ambassador TOMÁŠ SZUNYOG.

Egypt: 71000 Sarajevo, Nurudina Gackića 58; tel. (33) 666498; fax (33) 666499; e-mail eg.em.sa@bih.net.ba; internet www.mfa.gov.eg/english/embassies/egyptian_embassy_sarajevo/pages/default.aspx; Ambassador YASSER SAYED MAHMOUD EL-ATTAWI.

France: 71000 Sarajevo, Kapetanović Ljubušak 18; tel. (33) 282050; fax (33) 282052; e-mail ambsarajevo.presse@diplomatie.gouv.fr; internet www.ambafrance-ba.org; Ambassador ROLAND GILLES.

Germany: 71000 Sarajevo, Skenderija 3; tel. (33) 565300; fax (33) 206400; e-mail info@sarajewo.diplo.de; internet www.sarajewo.diplo.de; Ambassador ULRIKE MARIA KNOTZ.

Greece: 71000 Sarajevo, Obala Maka Dizdara I; tel. (33) 560550; fax (33) 203512; e-mail greekemb@bih.net.ba; internet www.mfa.gr/sarajevo; Ambassador KAROLOS GADIS.

Holy See: 71000 Sarajevo, Pehlivanuša 9; tel. (33) 551055; fax (33) 551057; e-mail nunbosnia@bih.net.ba; Apostolic Nuncio LUIGI PEZZUTO (Titular Archbishop of Hyccarum).

Hungary: 71000 Sarajevo, Splitska 2; tel. (33) 205302; fax (33) 268930; e-mail mission.sjj@mfa.gov.hu; internet www.mfa.gov.hu/kulkepviselet/bh/hu; Ambassador JÓZSEF PANDUR.

Iran: 71000 Sarajevo, Obala Maka Dizdara 6; tel. (33) 650210; fax (33) 663910; e-mail iries2@bih.net.ba; Ambassador SEYYED HOSSEIN RAJABI.

Italy: 71000 Sarajevo, Čekaluša 39; tel. (33) 218022; fax (33) 659368; e-mail ambsara@bih.net.ba; internet www.ambsarajevo.esteri.it/ambasciata_sarajevo; Ambassador RUGGERO CORRIAS.

Japan: 71000 Sarajevo, Bistrik 9; tel. (33) 209580; fax (33) 209583; e-mail japanbih@sx.mofa.go.jp; internet www.bosnia.emb-japan.go.jp; Ambassador HIDEO YAMAZAKI.

Libya: 71000 Sarajevo, Drinska 8; tel. (33) 200621; fax (33) 226423; e-mail libijskaambasada@hotmail.com; Ambassador AREBI S. A. HALLOUDI.

Macedonia, former Yugoslav republic: 71000 Sarajevo, Splitska 57; tel. and fax (33) 810760; e-mail sarajevo@mfa.gov.mk; internet www.missions.gov.mk/saraevo; Ambassador RAMI REXHEPI.

Malaysia: 71000 Sarajevo, Radnička 4A; tel. (33) 201578; fax (33) 810036; e-mail malsrjevo@kln.gov.my; internet www.kln.gov.my/perwakilan/sarajevo; Ambassador ANUAR KASMAN.

Montenegro: 71000 Sarajevo, Talirovića 4; tel. (33) 239925; fax (33) 239928; e-mail bosniaandherzegovina@mfa.gov.me; Ambassador DRAGAN ĐUROVIĆ.

Netherlands: 71000 Sarajevo, Grbavička 4; tel. (33) 562600; fax (33) 223413; e-mail sar@minbuza.nl; internet bosnieherzegovina.nlambassade.org; Ambassador JURRIAAN KRAAK.

Norway: 71000 Sarajevo, Ferhadija 20; tel. (33) 254000; fax (33) 666505; e-mail emb.sarajevo@mfa.no; internet www.norveska.ba; Ambassador VIBEKE LILLOE.

Pakistan: 71000 Sarajevo, Emerika Bluma 17; tel. (33) 211836; fax (33) 211837; e-mail parepsarajevo@yahoo.com; Ambassador KHALID AMIR JAFFERY.

Poland: 71000 Sarajevo, Dola 13; tel. (33) 201142; fax (33) 226844; e-mail agata.grabska@msz.gov.pl; internet www.sarajewo.polemb.net; Ambassador ANDRZEJ KRAWCZYK.

Portugal: 71000 Sarajevo, Čobanija 12/1; tel. (33) 200835; fax (33) 233796; e-mail embaport@bih.net.ba; Ambassador (vacant).

Qatar: 71000 Sarajevo, Dajanli Ibrahim-bega 23; tel. (33) 565810; fax (33) 205351; e-mail qr.embassy@bih.net.ba; Chargé d'affaires a.i. JASSIM AL-HAMADI.

Romania: 71000 Sarajevo, Čobanja nr. 28; tel. (33) 207447; fax (33) 668940; e-mail rumunska@bih.net.ba; internet sarajevo.mae.ro; Ambassador FILIP TEODORESCU.

Russia: 71000 Sarajevo, Urjan Dedina 93; tel. (33) 668147; fax (33) 668148; e-mail rusembbih@bih.net.ba; internet www.sarajevo.mid.ru; Ambassador ALEKSANDR A. BOTSAN-KHARCHENKO.

San Marino: 71000 Sarajevo, ul. Mjedenica 33; tel. and fax (33) 223447; e-mail amb.bosniaerzegovina@gov.sm; Ambassador MICHELE CHIARUZZI.

Saudi Arabia: 71000 Sarajevo, Koševo 44; tel. (33) 211861; fax (33) 212204; e-mail saudiembassy@epn.ba; Ambassador EID MUHAMMAD A. AL-THAKAFI.

Serbia: 71000 Sarajevo, Obala Maka Dizdara 3A; tel. (33) 260080; fax (33) 221469; e-mail srbamba@bih.net.ba; internet www.sarajevo.mfa.gov.rs; Ambassador STANIMIR VUKIČEVIĆ.

Slovakia: 71000 Sarajevo, Trnovska 6; tel. (33) 716440; fax (33) 716410; e-mail emb.sarajevo@mzv.sk; internet www.mzv.sk/sarajevo; Ambassador JÁN PŠENICA.

Slovenia: 71000 Sarajevo, Bentbaša 7; tel. (33) 271260; fax (33) 271270; e-mail vsa@gov.si; internet sarajevo.veleposlanistvo.si; Ambassador IZTOK GRMEK.

Spain: 71000 Sarajevo, Maguda 18; tel. (33) 584000; fax (33) 239155; e-mail emb.sarajevo@maec.es; Ambassador MARÍA AURORA MEJÍA ERRASQUÍN.

Sweden: 71000 Sarajevo, Ferhadija 20; tel. (33) 276030; fax (33) 276060; e-mail ambassaden.sarajevo@gov.se; internet www.swedenabroad.com/sv-se/ambassader/sarajevo; Ambassador FREDRIK SCHILLER.

Switzerland: 71000 Sarajevo, Josipa Štadlera 15; tel. (33) 275850; fax (33) 570120; e-mail sar.vertretung@eda.admin.ch; internet www.eda.admin.ch/sarajevo; Ambassador ANDRÉ SCHALLER.

Turkey: 71000 Sarajevo, Hamdije Kreševljakovića 5; tel. (33) 568750; fax (33) 267261; e-mail embassy.sarajevo@mfa.gov.tr; internet www.sarajevo.emb.mfa.gov.tr; Ambassador AHMET YILDIZ.

United Kingdom: 71000 Sarajevo, Hamdije Čemerlića 39A; tel. (33) 282200; fax (33) 282203; e-mail britemb@bih.net.ba; internet ukinbih.fco.gov.uk; Ambassador EDWARD FERGUSON.

USA: 71000 Sarajevo, ul. Roberta C. Frasurea 1; tel. (33) 704000; fax (33) 659722; e-mail bhopa@state.gov; internet sarajevo.usembassy.gov; Chargé d'affaires a.i. NICHOLAS M. HILL.

Judicial System

The Court of Bosnia and Herzegovina, which was officially inaugurated on 27 January 2003, represents the country's highest judicial organ. The judicial system of each entity comprises a Constitutional Court, a Supreme Court and local district courts.

Court of Bosnia and Herzegovina: 71000 Sarajevo, Kraljice Jelene 88; tel. (33) 707100; fax (33) 707321; e-mail pios@sudbih.gov.ba; internet www.sudbih.gov.ba; inaugurated 2003; state-level court; comprises 53 judges (51 national and 2 international); 3 divisions (Criminal, Administrative and Appellate); War Crimes Chamber est. 2005; Pres. KRESO MEDDŽIDA.

Constitutional Court of Bosnia and Herzegovina: 71000 Sarajevo, Reisa Džemaludina Causevića 6; tel. (33) 251226; fax (33) 561134; e-mail info@ccbh.ba; internet www.ccbh.ba; f. 1997; nine mems appointed until the age of 70, three of whom are non-nationals selected by the President of the European Court of Human Rights, and six of whom are nationals; four of the latter are elected by the Predstavnički dom Federacije/Zastupnički dom Federacije and two by the Narodna skupština Republike Srpske; Pres. VALERIJA GALIĆ.

Office of the Prosecutor of Bosnia and Herzegovina: 71000 Sarajevo, Kraljice Jelene 88; tel. (33) 707200; fax (33) 707463; e-mail info@tuzilastvobih.gov.ba; internet www.tuzilastvobih.gov.ba; Chief Prosecutor GORAN SALIHOVIĆ.

FEDERATION OF BOSNIA AND HERZEGOVINA

Constitutional Court of the Federation of Bosnia and Herzegovina: 71000 Sarajevo, Valtera Perića 15; tel. (33) 251650; fax (33) 251651.

Supreme Court of the Federation of Bosnia and Herzegovina: 71000 Sarajevo, Valtera Perića 15; tel. (33) 226752; fax (33) 226754; four chambers; Pres. AMIR JAGANJAĆ.

Office of the Federation Prosecutor: 71000 Sarajevo, Valtera Perića 11; tel. (33) 214990; Prosecutor ZDRAVKO KNEŽEVIĆ.

REPUBLIKA SRPSKA

Constitutional Court of Republika Srpska: 78000 Banja Luka, Kralja Alfonsa 11; tel. (51)217390; fax (51) 217970; e-mail ustsudrs@inecco.net; internet www.ustavnisud.org; nine mems; Pres. DŽERARD SELMAN.

Supreme Court of Republika Srpska: 78000 Banja Luka, Aleja Svetog Save bb; tel. (51) 211690; fax (51) 226071; e-mail vrhovnisudrs@vrhovnisudrs.com; Pres. ŽELIMIR BARIĆ.

Office of the Chief Prosecutor of Republika Srpska: 78000 Banja Luka, Kralja Petra I Karađorđevića 12; tel. (51) 218827; fax (51) 218834; e-mail rjt@inecco.net; Prosecutor MAHMUT ŠVRAKA.

Religion

The dominant religion in Bosnia and Herzegovina is Islam, but around one-half of the population are Christian, either adhering to the Serbian Orthodox Church or the Roman Catholic Church. There is a small Jewish community.

ISLAM

Islamic Community of Bosnia and Herzegovina (Islamska Zajednica u Bosni i Hercegovini): 71000 Sarajevo, Reisa Demaludina Cauevića 2; tel. (33) 200355; fax (33) 441573; internet www.rijaset.bà; Reis-ul-ulema Dr MUSTAFA EFENDI CERIĆ.

CHRISTIANITY

The Serbian Orthodox Church

Metropolitan of Dabrobosna: NICOLAJ (MRDA), 71000 Sarajevo, Zelenih Beretki 3; tel. and fax (71) 210518; e-mail info@mitropolijadabrobosanska.org; internet www.mitropolija dabrobosanska.org.

The Roman Catholic Church

Bosnia and Herzegovina comprises one archdiocese and two dioceses. At 31 December 2008 adherents of the Roman Catholic Church numbered 458,861, representing about 15.4% of the total population.

Bishops' Conference: 71000 Sarajevo, Kaptol 32; tel. and fax (33) 666867; e-mail kaptolka@bih.net.ba; f. 1995; Pres. Cardinal VINKO PULJIĆ (Archbishop of Vrhbosna, Sarajevo).

Archbishop of Vrhbosna, Sarajevo: Cardinal VINKO PULJIĆ, 71000 Sarajevo, Kaptol 7; tel. (33) 218823; fax (33) 212937; e-mail kaptolka@bih.net.ba.

The Press

PRINCIPAL DAILIES

Capital: 78000 Banja Luka, Vlašićka 25c; tel. and fax (51) 281407; e-mail info@capital.ba; internet www.capital.ba; Editor-in-Chief SINIŠA VUKELIĆ.

Dnevni Avaz (Daily Herald): 71000 Sarajevo, Tešanjska 24B; tel. (33) 281391; fax (33) 281414; e-mail redakcija@avaz.ba; internet www.dnevniavaz.ba; f. 1995; Editor-in-Chief FADIL MANDAL; circ. 15,700 (2001).

Dnevni List (Daily News): 88000 Mostar, Kralja Petra Krešimira 66/2; tel. (36) 313370; fax (36) 333437; e-mail dnevni@bih.net.ba; internet www.dnevni-list.ba; Editor-in-Chief DARIO LUKIĆ.

Fokus: 78000 Banja Luka, Jovana Raškovića 16; tel. (51) 243900; fax (51) 243945; e-mail redakcija@fokus.ba; internet www.fokus.ba; Editor-in-Chief DALIBOR ĐEKIĆ.

Glas Srpske (Voice of Republika Srpska): 78000 Banja Luka, Skendera Kulenovića 1; tel. (51) 342900; fax (51) 342910; e-mail info@glassrpske.com; internet www.glassrpske.com; fmrly *Glas Srpski* (Serbian Voice); Editor-in-Chief MIRJANA KUSMUK.

Nezavisne novine (The Independent): 78000 Banja Luka, Braće Pišteljića 1; tel. (51) 331800; fax (51) 331810; e-mail desk@nezavisne.com; internet www.nezavisne.com; f. 1995; Editor-in-Chief BORJANA RADMANOVIĆ-PETROVIĆ; circ. 7,500.

Oslobođenje (Liberation): 71000 Sarajevo, Džemala Bijedića 185; tel. (33) 468142; fax (33) 468090; e-mail info@oslobodjenje.de; internet www.oslobodjenje.ba; f. 1943; morning; Editor-in-Chief VILDANA SELIMBEGOVIĆ.

San (Dream): 71000 Sarajevo, Bistrik 9; tel. (33) 254300; fax (33) 254301; e-mail redakcija@san.ba; Editor-in-Chief MENSUR OSMOVIĆ.

WEEKLY NEWSPAPERS

Dani (Days): 71000 Sarajevo, Džemala Bijedića 185; tel. (33) 276900; fax (33) 651789; e-mail dani@oslobodjenje.ba; internet www.bhdani.com; independent; political and cultural; Editor-in-Chief DŽENANA KARUP DRUŠKO; circ. 25,000.

Hercegovačke Novine (Herzegovina News): 88000 Mostar, Krpića 3; tel. and fax (36) 581124; e-mail novine@hercegovacke.ba; Editor-in-Chief ALIJA LIZDE; circ. 15,000 (2010).

Slobodna Bosna (Free Bosnia): 71000 Sarajevo, Čekaluša Čikma 6; tel. (33) 444041; fax (33) 444895; e-mail sl.bos@bih.net.ba; internet www.slobodna-bosna.ba; independent; national and international politics; Editor SENAD AVDIĆ; circ. 28,000.

Start: 71000 Sarajevo, La Benevolencije 6; tel. (33) 260210; fax (33) 215321; e-mail redakcija@startbih.info; internet www.startbih.info; f. 1998; independent; Editor-in-Chief DARIO NOVALIĆ.

PERIODICALS

Auto Magazin: 71000 Sarajevo, Skenderpašina 25; tel. (33) 553850; e-mail info@automagazin.ba; monthly; Editor-in-Chief EDIS JASAREVIĆ.

Buka: 78000 Banja Luka, Aleja Svetog Save 24; tel. and fax (51) 222210; e-mail info@6yka.com; internet www.6yka.com; internet magazine published by the Banja Luka Centre for Informational Decontamination of the Young (Centar za informativnu dekontaminaciju mladih iz Banjaluke); Editor-in-Chief ALEKSANDAR TRIFUNOVIĆ.

Business Magazine: 71000 Sarajevo, Muhameda ef. Pandže 67; tel. (33) 557118; fax (33)223165; e-mail info@business-magazin.ba; internet www.business-magazin.ba; f. 2006; two a month; Editor-in-Chief AIDA DELIĆ.

Gracija: 71000 Sarajevo, Skenderija 31 A; tel. (33) 261710; fax (33) 261711; e-mail redakcija@gracija.ba; internet www.gracija.ba; women's affairs; bi-weekly; Editor-in-Chief ALMA DURAKOVIĆ.

Gusto: 71000 Sarajevo, Zmaja od Bosne 7–7A; tel. (33) 279312; fax (33) 279310; e-mail gusto@oxygen.ba; internet www.gusto.ba; f. 2008; gastronomy; monthly; Editor SARA KRAJINA-JAZVIĆ.

Info: 71000 Sarajevo, Trebevićka 18; tel. and fax (33) 211673; internet www.info.ba; f. 1997; information technology; monthly; Editor-in-Chief GORAN MILIĆ.

In Store: 71000 Sarajevo, Hasana Brkića 2; tel. (33) 710616; fax (33) 710615; e-mail redakcija@instore.ba; internet www.instore.ba; trade; monthly; Editor ZLATA KARKIN.

Magazine: 71000 Sarajevo, Zmaja od Bosne 7–7 A; tel. (33) 279311; fax (33) 279310; e-mail info@magazine.ba; internet www.magazine.ba; lifestyle; monthly; Editor-in-Chief ANDREA TOMAŠEVIĆ; circ. 20,000 (2010).

Naša Ognjišta—Hrvatski katolički mjesečnik (Our Hearth—Croat Catholic Monthly): 80240 Tomislavgrad, trg fra Mije Čuića 1; tel. (34) 352295; fax (34) 352808; e-mail nasa.ognjista@tel.net.ba; internet nasa-ognjista.com; f. 1971; monthly; Editor-in-Chief GABRIJEL MIOČ.

Naša Riječ (Our Word): 72000 Zenica, Kralja Tvrtka I/1; tel. (32) 408003; fax (32) 403055; e-mail redakcija@nasarijec.ba; internet www.nasarijec.ba; f. 1956; weekly; Editor-in-Chief SAJTO ČEHOVIĆ.

Novi Izraz (New Expression): 7100 Sarajevo, Vrazova 1; tel. (33) 200155; fax (33) 217854; e-mail pencentar@bih.net.ba; internet www.penbih.ba; f. 1992 as successor to *Izraz*; literary and art criticism; four a year; published by P. E. N. Centar Bosne i Hercegovine; Editor-in-Chief HANIFA KAPIDŽIĆ-OSMANAGIĆ.

Novi Reporter (New Reporter): 78000 Banja Luka, Duška Koščice 49; tel. (51) 229922; fax (51) 229921; e-mail rep@inecco.net; internet www.novireporter.com; f. 2003 as successor to *Reporter*; independent; Editor-in-Chief SLAVA GOVEDARICA.

Odjek (Echo): 71000 Sarajevo, Obala Maka Dizdara 2; tel. and fax (33) 204463; e-mail redakcija@odjek.ba; internet www.odjek.ba; arts, science and society; quarterly; Editor-in-Chief NERMINA KURSPAHIĆ.

Sarajevske Sveske (Sarajevo Notebook): Mediacentar Sarajevo, 71000 Sarajevo, Kolodvorska 3; tel. and fax (33) 715861; fax (33) 715840; e-mail sarajevske.sveske@media.ba; f. 2002; quarterly; literature and social issues; Editor-in-Chief VELIMIR VISKOVIĆ.

Svjetlo Riječi (Light of the Word): 71000 Sarajevo, Zagrebačka 18; tel. (33) 726200; fax (33) 812247; e-mail redakcija@svjetlorijeci.ba; internet www.svjetlorijeci.ba; f. 1983; Franciscan; monthly; Dir JANKO ĆURO; Editor-in-Chief DRAGO BOJIĆ.

Zehra: 71000 Sarajevo, Zenička 3; tel. (33) 651401; fax (33) 712545; e-mail magazinzehra@gmail.com; internet www.zehra.ba; f. 2001; monthly; family and society; published by women's org., Kewser; Editor MEDIHA DŽAKMIĆ.

Zrno (The Grain): 71000 Sarajevo, Trg sarajevske olimpijade; tel. (61) 485106; e-mail zrno@zrno.ba; internet www.zrno.ba; weapons, technology and security; in Croatian; monthly.

NEWS AGENCIES

FENA—Federalna Novinska Agencija (Federation News Agency): 71000 Sarajevo, Cemalusa 1; tel. (33) 445247; fax (33) 265460; e-mail fena@fena.ba; internet www.fena.ba; f. 2000; Dir FARUK BORIĆ; Editor-in-Chief ZDRAVKO NIKIĆ.

NINA—Nezavisna Informativna Novinska Agencija (Independent Information and News Agency): 88000 Mostar, Kralja Petra Krešimira IV 66/2; tel. (36) 313370; fax (33) 719755; e-mail info@nina.ba; internet www.nina.ba; f. 2003; independent; Dir MIROSLAV RAŠIĆ; Editor-in-Chief ŽELJKO MARJANOVIĆ.

ONASA Independent News Agency: 71000 Sarajevo, Zmaja od Bosna 4; tel. (33) 276580; fax (33) 276599; e-mail onasa@onasa.com.ba; internet www.onasa.com.ba; f. 1994; Gen. Man. ELVIRA BEGOIĆ.

SNRA—Novinska Agentsija Republike Srpske (News Agency of Republika Srpska): 76300 Bijeljina, Sofke Nikolić 51; tel. (55) 211500; fax (55) 201810; e-mail srna@srna.rs; internet www.snra.rs; f. 1992; bureaux in Banja Luka and East Sarajevo; Man. Dir DRAGAN DAVIDOVIĆ.

Publishers

Sarajevo Publishing: 71000 Sarajevo, Obala Kulina Bana 4; tel. (33) 220809; fax (33) 217164; e-mail redakcija@sarajevopublishing.ba; internet www.sarajevopublishing.ba; f. 1950; history, literature, philosophy and culture; Dir MUSTAFA ALAGIĆ.

Službeni List BiH Sarajevo: 71000 Sarajevo, Džemala Bijedića 39/III; tel. and fax (33) 722061; e-mail info@sllist.ba; internet www.sllist

.ba; publishes legislation and other official publications; Dir MEHMEDALIJA HUREMOVIĆ.

Svjetlost (Light): 71000 Sarajevo, Petra Preradovića 3; tel. (33) 212144; fax (33) 272352; internet www.svjetlost.ba; f. 1945; textbooks and literature, religion; Dir SAVO ZIROJEVIĆ.

TKD Šahinpašić: 71020 Sarajevo, Vreoca b.b.; tel. (33) 771180; fax (33) 771188; e-mail info@btcsahinpasic.com; internet www.btcsahinpasic.com; f. 1989; contemporary literature, philosophy and children's books; publishers, importers, exporters and retailers; Dir-Gen. TAJIB ŠAHINPAŠIĆ.

Zoro (Sarajevo): 71000 Sarajevo, Šenoina 14; tel. (33) 214454; fax (33) 213879; e-mail zorosa@bih.net.ba; internet www.zoro.hr; f. 1994 in Zagreb (Croatia); Dir SAMIR FAZLIĆ.

PUBLISHERS' ASSOCIATION

Assen of Publishers and Booksellers of Bosnia and Herzegovina: 71000 Sarajevo, Maršala Tita 9A; tel. (33) 207945; fax (33) 266630; e-mail ibrosa@bih.net.ba; internet www.uik.ba; f. 2005; Pres. IBRAHIM SPAHIĆ.

Broadcasting and Communications

TELECOMMUNICATIONS

Three principal service providers of telecommunications operate in Bosnia and Herzegovina: BH Telecom, which operates chiefly in Sarajevo and in Bosniak-majority cantons of the Federation; HT Mostar in Croat-majority cantons of the Federation; and Telekom Srpske in Republika Srpska.

BH Telecom d.d. Sarajevo: 71000 Sarajevo, Obala Kulina Bana 8; tel. (33) 255150; fax (33) 221111; e-mail nedzad.residbegovic@bhtelecom.ba; internet www.bhtelecom.ba; f. 1993; 90% owned by Govt of Federation of Bosnia and Herzegovina; operates mobile cellular network under the brand name 'BH Mobile'; also provides internet services; Dir-Gen. NEDŽAD REŠIDBEGOVIĆ.

HT Eronet—Hrvatske telekomunikacije Mostar: 88000 Mostar, Kneza Branimira bb; tel. (36) 395000; fax (36) 395425; e-mail press@hteronet.ba; internet www.hteronet.ba; f. 1995; fmrly HT Mostar; name changed as above after merger with Eronet in 2012; 50.1% owned by Govt of Federation of Bosnia and Herzegovina, 39.1% by T-Hrvatski Telekom (Croatia); provider of telephone and internet services; Pres. STIPE PRLIĆ.

M:Tel: 78000 Banja Luka, Mladena Stojanovića 4; e-mail korisnicka.podrska@mtel.ba; internet www.mtel.ba; f. 1999; fmrly Mobi's; subsidiary of Telekom Srpske; present name adopted 2007; mobile cellular communications; provides coverage in a majority of regions of Bosnia and Herzegovina; Gen. Dir PREDRAG ĆULIBRK; 506,500 subscribers (2003).

Telekom Srpske: 78000 Banja Luka, Kralja Petra I Karađorđevića 61A; tel. (51) 240100; fax (51) 211150; e-mail korisnicki.servis@mtel.ba; internet www.mtel.ba; 65% share owned by Telekom Srbija (Serbia); Dir-Gen. PREDRAG ĆULIBRK.

BROADCASTING

Regulatory Authority

Communications Regulatory Agency (Regulatorna agencija za komunikacije—RAK): 71000 Sarajevo, Mehmeda Spahe 1; tel. (33) 250600; fax (33) 713080; e-mail info@rak.ba; internet www.rak.ba; f. 2001; Dir-Gen. KEMAL HUSEINOVIĆ.

Radio and Television

In 2010 there were 144 registered radio stations, of which 63 were publicly owned. At that time there were 44 registered terrestrial television stations, of which 14 were publicly owned.

Alternativna Televizija Informisanje: 78000 Banja Luka, Gunduliceva 33; tel. and fax (51) 348248; e-mail info@atvbl.com; internet www.atvbl.com; f. 1996; Dir NATAŠA TEŠANOVIĆ.

NTV Hayat: 71320 Sarajevo, Vogošća, Jošanička 55; tel. (33) 492900; fax (33) 492911; e-mail elvir@hayat.ba; internet www.hayat.ba; f. 1991; broadcasts 4 channels; Dir-Gen. ELVIR ŠVRAKIĆ.

Public Broadcasting Service of Bosnia and Herzegovina: 71000 Sarajevo, Bulevar Meše Selimovića 12; tel. (33) 464073; e-mail smaila.resic@bhrt.ba; internet www.bhrt.ba; f. 1945; Dir-Gen. MUHAMED BAKAREVIĆ; Dir of Radio MILAN TRIVIĆ; Dir of TV OLIVERA DODIG.

Radio-Televizija Federacije Bosne i Hercegovine (Radio and Television of the Federation of Bosnia and Herzegovina): 71000 Sarajevo, Bulevar Meše Selimovića 12; tel. (33) 464070; fax (33) 455103; e-mail press@rtvfbih.ba; internet www.rtvfbih.ba/loc; Dir-Gen. DŽEMAL ŠABIĆ; Dir of Radio LEJLA TAFRO-SEFIĆ; Dir of Television ZVONIMIR JUKIĆ.

Radio-Televizija Republike Srpske (RTRS) (Radio and Television of Republika Srpska): 78000 Banja Luka, Kralja Petra I Karađorđevića 129; tel. (51) 339800; fax (51) 339924; e-mail rtrs@rtrs.tv; internet www.rtrs.tv; f. 1992; Gen. Man. DRAGAN DAVIDOVIĆ.

Studio 99: 71000 Sarajevo, Skenderija; tel. (33) 221101; fax (33) 262690; e-mail oko22@ntv99.ba; internet www.ntv99.ba; f. 1995; independent radio and TV station; political and current affairs; Editor-in-Chief ADIL KULENOVIĆ.

Finance

(cap. = capital; res = reserves; dep. = deposits; m. = million; amounts in konvertibilna marka—KM, convertible marka; brs = branches)

BANKING

In 2012 some 28 banks were operating in Bosnia and Herzegovina (of which 18 were licensed by the Banking Agency of the Federation and 10 by the Banking Agency of Republika Srpska).

Central Bank

Central Bank of Bosnia and Herzegovina (Centralna banka Bosne i Hercegovine): 71000 Sarajevo, Maršala Tita 25; tel. (33) 278222; fax (33) 215094; e-mail contact@cbbh.ba; internet www.cbbh.ba; f. 1997; cap. 25.0m., res 477.4m., dep. 3,437.7m. (Dec. 2009); Gov. KEMAL KOZARIĆ.

Selected Banks

Hypo Alpe-Adria-Bank a.d. Banja Luka: 78000 Banja Luka, Aleja Svetog Save 13; tel. (51) 336500; fax (51) 336518; e-mail info@hypo-alpe-adria.rs.ba; internet www.hypo-alpe-adria.rs.ba; f. 2002; 99.6% owned by Hypo Alpe-Adria-Bank International AG (Austria); cap. 129.2m., res 86.2m., dep. 935.4m. (Dec. 2012); Dir GORAN BABIĆ.

Hypo Alpe-Adria-Bank d.d.: 88000 Mostar, Kneza Branimira 2B; tel. (36) 444200; fax (36) 444235; e-mail bank.bih@hypo-alpe-adria.com; internet www.hypo-alpe-adria.ba; f. 1999; present name adopted 2001; subsidiary of Hypo Alpe-Adria-Bank International AG (Austria); cap. 213.0m., res 267.5m., dep. 963.0m. (Dec. 2012); Dir ALEKSANDAR PICKER.

NLB Banka d.d. Tuzla: 75000 Tuzla, Maršala Tita 34; tel. (35) 259259; fax (35) 302802; e-mail info@nlb.ba; internet www.nlb.ba; f. 1990 as Tuzlanska Banka d.d. Tuzla; renamed NLB Tuzlanska Banka d.d. Tuzla in 2006; 96.3% owned by NLB d.d. (Slovenia); current name adopted 2012; cap. 39m., res 32m., dep. 617m. (Dec. 2012); Man. ALMIR ŠAHINPAŠIĆ; 16 brs.

NLB Razvojna Banka a.d.: 78000 Banja Luka, Milana Tepića 4; tel. (51) 221610; fax (51) 221623; e-mail helpdesk@nlbrazvojnabanka.com; internet www.nlbrazvojnabanka.com; f. 1998; present name adopted 2006; 99.85% owned by NLB d.d. (Slovenia); cap. 62m., res 34m., dep. 798m. (Dec. 2012); Gen. Dir RADOVAN BAJIĆ; 13 brs.

Nova Banka a.d. Banja Luka: 78000 Banja Luka, Kralja Alfonsa XIII 37A; tel. (55) 230300; fax (55) 201410; e-mail office@novabanka.com; internet www.novabanka.com; f. 1992; fmrly Nova Banka a.d. Bijeljina; present name adopted 2007; cap. 71.0m., res 17.0m., dep. 847.3m. (Dec. 2012); Pres. GORAN RADANOVIĆ; Gen. Man. MILAN RADOVIĆ; 11 brs.

Raiffeisen Bank d.d. Bosna i Hercegovina: 71000 Sarajevo, Danijela Ozme 3; tel. (33) 287100; fax (33) 213851; e-mail info.rbbh@rbb-sarajevo.raiffeisen.at; internet www.raiffeisenbank.ba; f. 1992; present name adopted 2000; cap. 237.4m., res 107.0m., dep. 2,757.0m. (Dec. 2012); Pres. Dr MICHAEL G. MÜLLER; 30 brs.

Sberbank BH d.d.: 71000 Sarajevo, Fra Anđela Zvizdovića 1; tel. (33) 295601; fax (33) 263832; e-mail info@sberbank.ba; internet www.sberbank.ba; f. 2000 as Volksbank BH d.d.; renamed as above in 2013; owned by Sberbank Europe (Austria); cap. 47.0m., res 53.0m., dep. 510.2m. (Dec. 2012); Dir EDIN KARABEG; 15 brs.

UniCredit Bank d.d.: 88000 Mostar, Kardinala Štepinca bb; tel. (36) 312112; fax (36) 312116; e-mail info@unicreditgroup.ba; internet www.unicreditbank.ba; f. 1992; 66% owned by Zagrebačka Banka d.d. Zagreb (Croatia); present name adopted 2008; cap. 119.2m., res 69.2m., dep. 2,806.7m. (Dec. 2012); Chief Exec. BERISLAV KUTLE; 51 brs.

Banking Agencies

Banking Agency of the Federation of Bosnia and Herzegovina (Agencija za Bankarstvo Federacije Bosne i Hercegovine): 71000 Sarajevo, Koševo 3; tel. (33) 721400; fax (33) 668811; e-mail agencija@fba.ba; internet www.fba.ba; f. 1996; Chair. HARIS IHTIJAREVIĆ; Dir ZLATKO BARŠ.

Banking Agency of Republika Srpska (Agencija za Bankarstvo Republike Srpske): 78000 Banja Luka, Vase Pelagića 11A; tel. (51) 218111; fax (51) 216665; e-mail office@abrs.ba; internet www.abrs.ba; f. 1998; Chair. of Bd MIRA BIJELAC; Dir SLAVICA INJAC.

INSURANCE

In 2013 there were 17 insurance companies operating in Bosnia and Herzegovina, including the following:

ASA Osiguranje d.d. Sarajevo: Sarajevo, Bul. M. Selimovića 16; tel. (33) 774730; fax (33) 774733; e-mail info@asa-osiguranje.ba; internet www.asa-osiguranje.ba; Dir FEĐA MORANKIĆ.

Aura Osiguranje d.d. Banja Luka: 78000 Banja Luka, Veljka Mlađenovića 7D; tel. (51) 456680; fax (51) 456681; e-mail auraos@teol.net; internet www.auraosiguranje.com; f. 2007; non-life; Chair. of Bd ZORAN TUNJIĆ.

Bosna Sunce Osiguranje d.d. Sarajevo: 71000 Sarajevo, trg Međunarodnog Prijateljstva 20; tel. (33) 755450; fax (33) 755490; e-mail info@bosna-sunce.ba; internet www.bosna-sunce.ba; life and non-life; Chair. ŽELJKO PERVAN; 6 brs.

Drina Osiguranje d.d.: 75446 Milići, trg rudara 1; tel. and fax (56) 741610; e-mail office@drina-osiguranje.com; internet www.drina-osiguranje.com; f. 1996; non-life; Gen. Dir MILOMIR DURMIĆ; 9 brs.

Euroherc Osiguranje d.d. Sarajevo: 71000 Sarajevo, trg Međunarodnog Prijateljstva 20; tel. (33) 755515; e-mail euroherc@euroherc.ba; internet www.euroherc.ba; f. 1992; Dir DINKO MUSULIN.

Jahorina Osiguranje d.d.: 71420 Pale, ul. Svetosavska; tel. (57) 201320; fax (57) 201321; e-mail direkcija@jahorinaosiguranje.com; internet www.jahorinaosiguranje.com; f. 1992; non-life; Dir-Gen. Dr MIROSLAV MIŠKIĆ.

Kosig Dunav Osiguranje d.d. Banja Luka: 78000 Banja Luka, Veselina Masleše 26; tel. (51) 246100; fax (51) 211686; e-mail info@dunav.ba; internet www.dunav.ba; Man. Dir SAŠA ĆUDIĆ.

Lido Osiguranje d.d. Sarajevo: 71210 Ilidža, Hifzi Bjelevca 82/1; tel. (33) 776388; fax (33) 776399; e-mail info@lido-osiguranje.com; f. 1994; non-life; Dir-Gen. HALID ĐULIĆ; 11 brs in the Federation of Bosnia and Herzegovina.

Sarajevo Osiguranje d.d. Sarajevo: 71000 Sarajevo, Čobanija 14; tel. (33) 203270; fax (33) 443581; e-mail info@sarajevoosiguranje.ba; internet www.sarajevoosiguranje.ba; life and non-life, insurance and reinsurance; Dir-Gen. MIDHAT TERZIĆ; 13 brs.

Triglav Osiguranje d.d.: 71000 Sarajevo, ul. Dolina 8; tel. (33) 252110; fax (33) 252177; e-mail info@triglav.ba; internet www.triglav.ba; f. 2002; subsidiary of Triglav (Slovenia); Chair. of Management EDIB GALIJATOVIĆ; 8 brs.

UNIQA Osiguranje d.d. Sarajevo: Sarajevo, Obala Kulina Bana 19; tel. (33) 289000; fax (33) 289010; e-mail info@uniqa.ba; internet www.uniqa.ba; f. 2005; Exec. Dir AMELA OMERAŠEVIĆ; 26 brs.

STOCK EXCHANGES

Sarajevo Stock Exchange (Sarajevska berza-burza): 71000 Sarajevo, Đoke Mazalića 4; tel. (33) 251462; fax (33) 559460; e-mail contact@sase.ba; internet www.sase.ba; f. 2002; Dir-Gen. TARIK KURBEGOVIĆ.

Banja Luka Stock Exchange (Banjalučka berza): 78000 Banja Luka, Petra Kočića bb; tel. (51) 326040; fax (51) 326056; e-mail office@blberza.com; internet www.blberza.com; f. 2001; Chief Exec. MILAN BOŽIĆ.

Trade and Industry

GOVERNMENT AGENCIES

Foreign Investment Promotion Agency of Bosnia and Herzegovina (FIPA): 71000 Sarajevo, Tešanjska 24A, Avaz Twist Tower; tel. (33) 278080; fax (33) 278081; e-mail fipa@fipa.gov.ba; internet www.fipa.gov.ba; f. 1999; Dir JELICA GRUJIĆ.

Federation of Bosnia and Herzegovina

Privatization Agency of the Federation of Bosnia and Herzegovina (Agencija za privatizaciju u Federaciji BiH—APF): 71000 Sarajevo, Alipašina 41; tel. (33) 212884; fax (33) 212883; e-mail apfbih@bih.net.ba; internet www.apf.com.ba; Dir ENES GANIĆ.

Securities Commission of the Federation of Bosnia and Herzegovina (Komisija za vrijednosne papire Federacije Bosne i Hercegovine): 71000 Sarajevo, Cemalusa 9/2; tel. (33) 203862; fax (33) 211655; e-mail info@komvp.gov.ba; internet www.komvp.gov.ba; f. 1999; Pres. HASAN ĆELAM.

Republika Srpska

Republika Srpska Directorate for Privatization: 78000 Banja Luka, Mladena Stoganovića 4; tel. (51) 308311; fax (51) 311245; e-mail dip@inecco.net; Dir BORISLAV OBRADOVIĆ.

Republika Srpska Securities Commission (Komisija za khartije od vrijednosti Republike Srpske): 78000 Banja Luka, Vuka Karadžića 6; tel. (51) 218362; fax (51) 218361; e-mail kontakt@secrs.gov.ba; internet www.secrs.gov.ba; Pres. MIODRAG JANDRIĆ.

DEVELOPMENT ORGANIZATION

Federation Development Planning Institution (Federacija BiH Federalni zavod za programiranje razvoja): 71000 Sarajevo, Cemalusa 9/3; tel. (33) 667272; fax (33) 212625; e-mail info@fzzpr.gov.ba; internet www.fzzpr.gov.ba; Dir LJUBIŠA ĐAPAN.

CHAMBERS OF COMMERCE

Chamber of Commerce of Bosnia and Herzegovina (Privredna Komora BiH): 71000 Sarajevo, Branislava Đurđeva 10; tel. (33) 566222; fax (33) 214292; internet www.komorabih.ba; Pres. VESELIN POLJAŠEVIĆ.

Chamber of Commerce of the Federation of Bosnia and Herzegovina—Mostar (Privredna Komora FBiH—Mostar): 88000 Mostar, Zagrebačka 10; tel. (36) 332963; fax (36) 332966; e-mail gkfbih@tel.net.ba; internet www.kfbih.com; Sec. ŽELJANA BEVANDA.

Chamber of Commerce of the Federation of Bosnia and Herzegovina—Sarajevo (Privredna Komora FBiH—Sarajevo): 71000 Sarajevo, Branislava Đurđeva 10; tel. (33) 217782; fax (33) 217783; e-mail info@kfbih.com; internet www.kfbih.com; f. 1999; Pres. JAGO LASIĆ.

Chamber of Commerce of Republika Srpska (Privredna komora RS): 78000 Banja Luka, Đure Daničića 1/2; tel. (51) 215744; fax (51) 215565; e-mail info@komorars.ba; internet www.komorars.ba; Pres. BORKO ĐURIĆ.

UTILITIES

Electricity

Elektroprivreda BiH: 71000 Sarajevo, Vilsonovo Šetalište 15; tel. (33) 751000; fax (33) 751008; internet www.elektroprivreda.ba; generation, transmission and distribution of electric energy; Gen. Man. AMER JERLAGIĆ.

Gas

BH-Gas: 71000 Sarajevo, Hamdije Cemerlića 2/1; tel. (33) 279000; fax (33) 661621; e-mail management@bh-gas.ba; internet www.bh-gas.ba; f. 1997; Man. Dir ALMIR BEČAREVIĆ.

Water

Vodno Područje Slivova Rijeke Save: 71000 Sarajevo, ul. Grbavička 4/3; tel. (33) 565400; fax (33) 565423; e-mail info@voda.ba; internet www.voda.ba; Dir SEJAD DELIĆ.

TRADE UNIONS

Confederation of Independent Trade Unions of Bosnia and Herzegovina (Savez samostalnih sindikata Bosne i Hercegovine—SSSBiH): 71000 Sarajevo, Obala Kulina Bana 1; tel. (33) 202029; fax (33) 442321; e-mail sssbih@sindikatbih.ba; internet www.sindikatbih.ba; Chair. ISMET BAJRAMOVIĆ.

Confederation of Trade Unions of Republika Srpska (Savez sindikata Republike Srpske—SSRS): 78000 Banja Luka, Srpska 32; tel. (51) 214543; fax (51) 304241; e-mail ssrs-bl@blic.net; internet www.savezsindikatars.org; f. 1992; Pres. RANKA MISIĆ.

Transport

RAILWAYS

In 2009 there were 1,016 km of railway lines in Bosnia and Herzegovina.

Željeznice Federacije Bosne i Hercegovine (ŽFBH) (Railways of the Federation of Bosnia and Herzegovina): 71000 Sarajevo, Musala 2; tel. (33) 251120; fax (33) 652396; e-mail kabinez@bih.net.ba; internet www.zfbh.ba; CEO Dr NEDŽAD OSMANAGIĆ.

Željeznice Republike Srpske (ŽRS) (Railways of Republika Srpska): 74000 Doboj, Svetog Save 71; tel. (53) 241369; fax (53) 222247; e-mail zrs.kp@doboj.net; internet www.zrs-rs.com; Dir-Gen. PETKO STANOJEVIĆ.

ROADS

Bosnia and Herzegovina's road network covers some 22,703 km, including 3,785 km of main roads and 4,681 km of regional roads.

CIVIL AVIATION

The country has an international airport at Sarajevo, and three smaller civil airports, at Tuzla, Banja Luka and Mostar.

Bosnia and Herzegovina Directorate of Civil Aviation: 78000 Banja Luka, Vojvode Pere Krece bb; tel. (51) 921222; fax (51) 921520; e-mail bhdca@bhdca.gov.ba; internet www.bhdca.gov.ba; f. 1997; Dir-Gen. ĐORĐE RATKOVIĆ.

Federation Civil Aviation Department (FEDCAD) (Federalna Direkcija za Civilnu Avijaciju): 88000 Mostar, Ante Starčevića bb; tel. (36) 449230; fax (36) 327811; e-mail info@fedcad.gov.ba; internet www.fmpik.gov.ba/sektori/civ_avio.html; Dir AMADEO MANDIĆ.

Republika Srpska Civil Aviation Department (RSCAD): 78250 Laktaši, Mahovljani bb, Banja Luka International Airport; tel. (51) 337500; fax (51) 337503; e-mail rscad@rscad.org; internet www.rscad.org; Dir DAMIR ĆOPIĆ.

B&H Airlines: 71000 Sarajevo, Kurta Schorka 36; tel. (33) 460783; fax (33) 466338; e-mail nrecica@bhairlines.ba; internet www.bhairlines.ba; f. 1994 as Air Bosna; ceased operations in 2003, re-launched as B&H Airlines in 2005; 51% state-owned; regular services to Croatia, Germany, Switzerland and Turkey; Dir-Gen. NUDŽEIM REČICA.

Tourism

Bosnia and Herzegovina has many sites of potential interest to tourists, including mountain scenery, rivers and waterfalls, the historic cities of Sarajevo, Mostar, Travnik, Trebinje and Jajce. Provisional figures indicated there were some 438,585 foreign tourist arrivals in 2012. Receipts from tourism (excluding passenger transport) totalled US $603m. in that year, according to provisional figures.

Tourism Asscn of the Federation of Bosnia and Herzegovina: 71000 Sarajevo, Branilaca Sarajeva 21/2; tel. (33) 252900; fax (33) 252901; e-mail media@tourism.ba; internet www.bhtourism.ba.

Tourism Organization of Republika Srpska (Turistička organizacija Republike Srpske): 78000 Banja Luka, Bana Milosavljevića 8; tel. (51) 229720; fax (51) 229721; e-mail tors@teol.net; internet www.turizamrs.org; Exec. Dir NADA JOVANOVIĆ.

Defence

As assessed at November 2013 the active armed forces of Bosnia and Herzegovina numbered 10,500, including air force and air defence brigades of 800. Bosnia and Herzegovina was admitted to the 'Partnership for Peace' (PfP) programme of the North Atlantic Treaty Organization (NATO) on 14 December 2006.

An EU Force (EUFOR), authorized to maintain peace and to support the country's progress towards European integration, established in 2004, comprises around 600 personnel.

Defence Expenditure: Budgeted at KM 352m. in 2012.

Chief of Joint Defence Staff of the Bosnia and Herzegovina Armed Forces: Maj.-Gen. ANTHONY JELEČ.

Commander of the European Union Force (EUFOR—ALTHEA) in Bosnia and Herzegovina: Maj.-Gen. DIETER HEIDECKER.

Education

A nine-year system of elementary education is free and compulsory for children between the ages of six and 15 years. Secondary education is provided in general secondary schools, vocational schools, and technical schools. The entities and the District of Brčko have separate ministries of education, and authority over schooling in the Federation is further divided between the 10 cantons. In 2011/12 enrolment at pre-primary schools included 12% of children in the relevant age-group. In 2012/13 some 304,972 pupils were enrolled in a total of 1,883 primary schools (including those for children with special needs), while 166,122 students were enrolled in 313 institutions of secondary education. Some 102,357 students were enrolled in 43 higher education institutions. In 2010/11 there were eight universities in Bosnia and Herzegovina.

BOTSWANA

Introductory Survey

LOCATION, CLIMATE, LANGUAGE, RELIGION, FLAG, CAPITAL

The Republic of Botswana is a landlocked country in southern Africa, with South Africa to the south and east, Zimbabwe to the north-east and Namibia to the west and north. A short section of the northern frontier adjoins Zambia. The climate is generally sub-tropical, with hot summers. Annual rainfall averages about 457 mm (18 ins), varying from 635 mm (25 ins) in the north to 228 mm (9 ins) or less in the western Kalahari desert. The country is largely near-desert, and most of its inhabitants live along the eastern border, close to the main railway line. English is the official language, and Setswana the national language. Most of the population follow traditional animist beliefs, but several Christian churches are also represented. The national flag (proportions 2 by 3) consists of a central horizontal stripe of black, edged with white, between two blue stripes. The capital is Gaborone.

CONTEMPORARY POLITICAL HISTORY

Historical Context

Botswana was formerly Bechuanaland, which became a British protectorate, at the request of the local rulers, in 1885. It was administered as one of the High Commission Territories in southern Africa, the others being the colony of Basutoland (now Lesotho) and the protectorate of Swaziland. The British Act of Parliament that established the Union of South Africa in 1910 also allowed for the inclusion in South Africa of the three High Commission Territories, on condition that the local inhabitants were consulted. Until 1960 successive South African Governments asked for the transfer of the three territories, but the native chiefs always objected to such a scheme. Bechuanaland became the independent Republic of Botswana, within the Commonwealth, on 30 September 1966, with Sir Seretse Khama, the leader of the Botswana Democratic Party (BDP) taking office as the country's first President. The BDP won elections to the National Assembly, with little opposition, in 1969, 1974 and 1979.

Domestic Political Affairs

Upon Khama's death in July 1980, Dr Quett Masire (later Sir Ketumile Masire), hitherto Vice-President and Minister of Finance, was appointed to the presidency. Following elections to the National Assembly in September 1984, at which the BDP again achieved a decisive victory, Masire was re-elected President by the legislature. In October 1989 the BDP received 65% of the votes cast at a general election to the National Assembly, winning 27 of the 30 elective seats (the remaining three seats were won by the principal opposition party, the Botswana National Front—BNF), and the new legislature re-elected Masire for a third term as President. At the general election held in October 1994 the BDP won 26 of the 40 available seats, while the BNF increased its representation to 13 seats. The National Assembly subsequently re-elected Masire to the presidency.

In August 1997 the National Assembly formally adopted a constitutional amendment restricting the presidential mandate to two terms of office and providing for the automatic succession to the presidency of the Vice-President, in the event of the death or resignation of the President. In September a national referendum endorsed further revisions, lowering the age of eligibility to vote from 21 to 18 years and providing for the establishment of an independent electoral commission. In November Masire announced his intention to retire from politics in March 1998. In accordance with the amended Constitution, Vice-President Festus Mogae was inaugurated as President on 1 April, pending elections to be held in 1999, and subsequently appointed a new Cabinet, in which the only new minister was Lt-Gen. Seretse Khama Ian Khama, son of Sir Seretse Khama and hitherto Commander of the Botswana Defence Force (BDF). Khama was sworn in as Mogae's Vice-President in July 1998.

Meanwhile, hostility between Kenneth Koma, the leader of the BNF, and his deputy, Michael Dingake, had led to a split in the party. In June 1998 the Botswana Congress Party (BCP) was formed, under the leadership of Dingake and the following month the BCP was declared the official opposition, after 11 of the BNF's 13 deputies joined the new party.

At the general election, held in mid-October 1999, the BDP increased its representation in the National Assembly from 26 to 33 seats, while the number of seats held by the BNF fell significantly, to only six seats. The BCP obtained just one seat; 77.3% of the electorate participated in the polls. Mogae was re-elected to the presidency by the National Assembly on 20 October.

In July 2000 the Government established a constitutional commission to investigate allegations of discrimination against minority groups, including the Kalanga, Wayeyi and San. The Kalanga, together with numerous other ethnic groups, were not recognized in the Constitution as one of the eight tribes with the right to be represented in the House of Chiefs, Botswana's second legislative house. On the basis of the recommendations of the commission, in December 2001 the Government presented a number of draft constitutional amendments. Under the proposals, the House of Chiefs would be renamed the Ntlo ya Dikgosi and its membership increased from 15 to 35, comprising 30 members elected by senior tribal authorities and five members appointed by the President. Elections to the Ntlo ya Dikgosi would be held every five years. In April 2002 the draft amendments were revised to allow the eight paramount chiefs to retain their ex officio status in the chamber, and approval of the increase in membership was announced in December 2005.

Meanwhile, in June 2002 the National Assembly approved legislation providing for an expansion in its directly elected membership from 40 to 57, with effect from the next general election, and a gradual increase in the number of ministries, from 12 to 16.

At the election to the newly enlarged legislature, held on 30 October 2004, the BDP secured 44 seats, although it obtained a smaller share of the vote than at the previous general election. The BNF increased its representation to 12 seats, while the BCP retained its solitary parliamentary seat. The rate of voter participation was recorded at 74.6%. President Mogae was sworn in for a second and final term of office on 2 November. Eleven new appointees were included in the reorganized Cabinet.

Recent developments: the Khama presidency

In July 2007 President Mogae announced that, as expected, he would relinquish the presidency in March 2008. In accordance with the Constitution, Vice-President Khama was sworn in as his successor on 1 April. Lt-Gen. Mompati Merafhe, hitherto Minister of Foreign Affairs and International Co-operation, was appointed to the vice-presidency and a new Cabinet was named. Later in April Kwelagobe was appointed Chairman of the BDP.

Despite the dominant status of the BDP in national politics, the party was increasingly affected by internal divisions. In September 2009 factional rivalry within the BDP resulted in the dismissal of the party's Secretary-General, Gomolemo Motswaledi. Motswaledi had challenged Khama's decision to appoint five additional members to the party's central committee in an attempt to reduce the influence of Kwelagobe, whose supporters had secured the majority of executive positions on the committee. Motswaledi was subsequently suspended from the BDP for a period of five years.

Meanwhile, at the elections to the National Assembly, which took place on 16 October 2009, the BDP increased the number of seats it held in the legislature by one, to 45. The BNF's representation was reduced from 12 seats to just six, while the BCP won four seats, compared with the one seat it secured in 2004. Observers from the Southern African Development Community (SADC, see p. 424) declared the elections 'credible, peaceful, free and fair'. On 20 October President Khama was inaugurated for his first full five-year term of office and the following day he appointed a new Cabinet, which featured five new ministers. Merafhe retained the vice-presidency, while Lesego Motsumi replaced Kwelagobe as Minister of Presidential Affairs and Public Administration.

Continuing factionalization within the BDP precipitated the creation of the Botswana Movement for Democracy (BMD), which separated from the ruling party in May 2010. The BMD was formed by four BDP parliamentarians, dissatisfied with

Khama's autocratic leadership style and his treatment of Motswaledi, and portrayed itself as a younger, more progressive political alternative. A further four elected BDP members, along with several councillors, defected to the BMD in mid-2010, making the splinter party the largest opposition grouping in the National Assembly. (Interim deputy leader of the BMD Botsalo Ntuane was officially named Leader of the Opposition in November.) Two of the defectors subsequently rejoined the BDP, however, with the BMD claiming that they had been seduced by financial incentives and offers of ministerial jobs, allegations that the ruling party denied. Meanwhile, the main opposition parties—the BMD, the BCP, the BNF and the Botswana People's Party (BPP)—held discussions in 2010 with the aim of forming an informal coalition to challenge the dominance of the BDP. However, opposition co-operation efforts suffered a reverse in September, when the BDP candidate in the Tonota North by-election comprehensively defeated the BCP's representative, who had been supported by the other coalition parties. Mutual mistrust and ideological differences among the opposition groups continued to undermine the cohesion of the coalition. None the less, in mid-2011 the three main opposition parties decided to ally themselves against the BDP for the forthcoming legislative elections in 2014. Consequently, in late 2012 the BMD, the BNF and the BPP established the Umbrella for Democratic Change (UDC); Motswaledi, the President of the BMD, was installed as the group's Secretary-General. It was agreed in September 2013 that the constituent parties of the UDC would field unified candidates in the general election.

Meanwhile, the Minister of Defence, Justice and Security, and cousin of the President, Brig. Dikgakgamatso Seretse, tendered his resignation in August 2010 after allegedly failing to reveal his role as a director of a company that had been awarded government supply contracts, in contravention of anti-corruption legislation. Seretse was charged by public prosecutors with corruption in October, although he was exonerated in the following year and reappointed to the Cabinet.

Some 100,000 civil servants began industrial action in April 2011 in response to the Government's refusal to increase wages by 16%. The unprecedented civil action—the country's first national strike—was believed to have adversely affected the health and education sectors, although the Government was quick to downplay the crisis. The strike was organized by the Botswana Federation of Public Sector Unions (BFPSU), which maintained that the Government had not increased wages for public sector workers for three consecutive years. The public sector is Botswana's largest employer, and in order to maintain services, the Government redeployed members of the police and military, prompting the trade unions to accuse them of intimidation and the use of illegal substitute workers. Meanwhile, the Industrial Court ordered all workers in essential service sectors to return to work. In May many doctors, nurses, pharmacists and cleaners lost their jobs as a result of the strike action, which finally ended in June with the unions accepting a wage increase of 3%. In September the BFPSU requested that the courts reinstate about 2,600 workers from the public sector who had lost their jobs as a result of the industrial action. Following the end of the strike the Ministry of Labour and Home Affairs classified teachers and diamond workers (among others) as providing essential services in order that they would not be able to take part in future strikes. In mid-2012 Botswana's Court of Appeal suspended a court order requiring the Government to reinstate almost 600 essential service workers who had lost their jobs during the strike action. The suspension was to last until the state's appeal was heard. The Court of Appeal ruled in favour of the Government in March 2013.

Citing ill health, Vice-President Merafhe announced in mid-2012 that he was to retire from the Government. He was replaced by Ponatshego Kedikilwe, who was sworn in on 2 August. In October Botswana's High Court ruled that traditional and preferential rights of males to inherit the family home contravened the country's Constitution, which upholds gender equality. The Court found in favour of four sisters, whose claim to a family property had been challenged by their nephew. The High Court's judgment was upheld by the Court of Appeal in September 2013. In early 2013 the BCP announced that it would present a bill in Parliament requiring all members of the legislature publicly to declare their assets and liabilities (a similar requirement existed in South Africa). Such legislation had been tabled over a decade before, but it had not been passed amid speculation at the time that the then Vice-President, Ian Khama, opposed it. In 2010 the proposed piece of legislation had been presented once more, but a subsequent draft bill required members to disclose their assets to President Khama only.

Indigenous Peoples' Rights

The Government's attempts to relocate San (Bushmen) people from their homeland within the Central Kalahari Game Reserve to a new settlement outside the Reserve provoked international concern from 1996. It was claimed that officials had forced many San to move by disconnecting water supplies and threatening military intervention; 2,160 San had been resettled by mid-2001, according to reports. In January 2002 the Government withdrew services to the remaining San living in the Reserve (estimated to number 500–700), in accordance with a decision announced in August 2001. A legal appeal brought to a halt the process of relocation but the return of hunting rights to the San was rejected on a technicality in April 2002. In August a delegation from the European Union (EU, see p. 273) accused the Government of providing false information about the number of San remaining in the Reserve, and of failing to fulfil their human rights requirements, including the supply of fresh water. In October the Government awarded some P2m. in compensation to more than 3,000 San who had been removed from the Reserve. In late 2002 Survival International, a lobby group for the rights of indigenous peoples, alleged that the Government had relocated the San in order to allow mining companies to explore for diamonds in the Reserve; the Government vehemently rejected these claims, maintaining that it was acting in the socio-economic interests of the San. Some 243 San commenced legal action against the Government in late 2003 in order to be permitted to live in the Reserve. In mid-2005 the Government removed a clause in the Constitution granting protection to San and other minorities. In December 2006 the High Court ruled that the removal of the San from the Reserve had been 'unlawful and unconstitutional' and confirmed their right to live on the Reserve, but also decreed that the Government was not obliged to provide services to them. Following the announcement of the decision some 100 San returned to the Reserve, although it was reported that the Government was attempting to limit the number of returnees. In June 2008 Khama reasserted the Government's firm stance on the issue and maintained that the authorities would not provide the San with any amenities in the Reserve. The Government attracted criticism in July 2010 when it defeated a legal challenge by San demanding the right to reopen a well on the Reserve that had been sealed by the authorities. The ruling also denied the San the right to drill other water-holes, forcing them to rely upon water transported from distant settlements. The San contested the verdict and in January 2011 the Court of Appeal ruled that the San were entitled to use the existing well on the Reserve and also granted them permission to drill for new sources of water. In an effort to reverse an alarming decline in wildlife populations, the Government introduced a ban on commercial hunting in January 2014. The decision could threaten local San communities, but the Ministry of Environment, Wildlife and Tourism promised that the Government would continue to issue game licences for traditional hunting by some local communities.

Foreign Affairs

From independence, it was the Botswana Government's stated policy not to permit any guerrilla groups to operate from its territory. Relations with South Africa deteriorated in May 1984, when President Masire accused the South African Government of exerting pressure on Botswana to sign a non-aggression pact, aimed at preventing the alleged use of Botswana's territory by guerrilla forces of the (then outlawed) African National Congress of South Africa (ANC). In the second half of the 1980s South African forces launched a number of raids on alleged ANC bases in Botswana, resulting in several deaths. Owing to Botswana's vulnerable position, however, the Government did not commit itself to the imposition of economic sanctions against South Africa when this was recommended by the Southern African Development Co-ordination Conference (subsequently SADC) in August 1986. In 1988–89 Botswana took action against the extension onto its territory of hostilities between South African government and anti-apartheid forces. Two South African commandos, who had allegedly opened fire on Botswana security forces while engaged in a raid, were sentenced to 10 years' imprisonment, nine South Africans were expelled for 'security reasons', and five ANC members were convicted on firearms charges. It was reported in August 1989 that the South African army had erected an electrified fence along a 24-km section of the

South Africa–Botswana border, in order to halt the reputed threat of guerrilla infiltration into South Africa via Botswana.

With the dismantling of apartheid in the first half of the 1990s, Botswana's relations with South Africa improved markedly, and full diplomatic relations were established in June 1994. In November 2000 the inaugural meeting of the Botswana-South Africa joint permanent commission on defence and security was held in Gaborone.

In September 2011, the South African High Court criticized Botswana for not aligning itself with the majority of African countries that had abandoned the death penalty. (Capital punishment remains in force in Botswana: between 1966 and 1998 a total of 32 people were hanged in the country, while a further six people were executed in 2001–06.) Moreover, it was ruled unconstitutional for South Africa to extradite a suspect to Botswana unless that country gave assurances that the suspect would not face the death penalty.

Botswana and Zimbabwe established full diplomatic relations in May 1983 and the first meeting of the Botswana-Zimbabwe joint commission for co-operation was held in October 1984. In the mid-1990s the Botswana Government expressed concern at the growing number of illegal immigrants in the country, the majority of whom were from Zimbabwe. Following the controversial re-election of Robert Mugabe to the Zimbabwean presidency in March 2002, the Botswana authorities became more critical of government policy in Zimbabwe, as the economic crisis in that country prompted an influx of immigrants into Botswana, with many entering illegally. In late 2003 the Botswana Government began erecting a 3m-high electrified fence along the border with Zimbabwe, ostensibly to prevent the spread of foot-and-mouth disease, although it was widely regarded as a measure to prevent the entry of further illegal immigrants, with those already in Botswana estimated to number more than 100,000 in early 2004; by the end of that year the number was estimated at more than 200,000. The Government sought to amend the Immigration Act of 2003 to impose higher fines and stricter sentences on those deemed to have entered the country illegally. During April–September 2006 the Botswana Government deported some 30,000 illegal Zimbabwean immigrants.

Following the disputed presidential election in Zimbabwe in March 2008, a campaign of state-sponsored violence was launched against those people who had supported the opposition Movement for Democratic Change (MDC). Many of those displaced as a result of the violence fled to Botswana and other neighbouring countries. The crisis threatened the stability of the region; however, the Botswana Government was one of only a few in Africa openly to condemn Mugabe's regime. President Khama instigated an extraordinary summit of SADC in Lusaka, Zambia, to discuss the crisis, which he attended with MDC leader Morgan Tsvangirai. (Tsvangirai had been granted temporary refuge in Gaborone following the election.) At an African Union (AU, see p. 186) summit in July Vice-President Merafhe urged that Zimbabwe be excluded from the organization's meetings as well as those of SADC, and Botswana became the first African state publicly to declare that it would not recognize Mugabe as President of Zimbabwe. In October a statement was issued by the Ministry of Foreign Affairs and International Co-operation to SADC proposing a re-run of the election. Bilateral relations deteriorated further in January 2010, when three members of Botswana's Department of Wildlife crossed into Zimbabwe while pursuing a pride of lions. The officers were arrested by the Zimbabwean authorities and imprisoned. Frustrated with the Zimbabwean Government's lack of response, Botswana threatened a partial withdrawal of diplomatic personnel from Zimbabwe, precipitating the release of the officers in February after the payment of a fine. Nevertheless, in October Khama announced his support for the removal of sanctions on Zimbabwe. In late 2012 Botswana extended credit worth some US $70m. to help revive Zimbabwe's industry sector.

Botswana questioned the legitimacy of Zimbabwe's July 2013 elections—which resulted in Mugabe securing a further term in office—and unsuccessfully appealed for the establishment of an independent investigation into the conduct of the polls. The number of Zimbabweans deported from Botswana reportedly increased sharply during that year. An estimated 135,000 undocumented Zimbabwean immigrants were repatriated from Botswana during January 2009–July 2013.

Following Namibian independence, in July 1990 it was announced that a commission for bilateral co-operation was to be established by Botswana and Namibia. In 1992, however, a border dispute developed between the two countries regarding their rival territorial claims over a small island (Sedudu-Kasikili) in the Chobe river. In early 1995 the two states agreed to present the issue of the demarcation of their joint border for arbitration at the International Court of Justice (ICJ), in The Hague, Netherlands, and in February 1996 the two countries signed an agreement committing themselves in advance to the Court's eventual judgment. In early 1997 it was reported that Namibia had been angered by Botswana's erection of a fence along Namibia's Caprivi Strip, which separates the two countries to the north; Botswana insisted, however, that the fence was simply a measure to control the spread of livestock diseases. In January 1998 an emergency meeting of the Botswana-Namibia joint commission on defence and security was held to discuss ownership of another island (Situngu) in the Chobe river, following allegations by Namibia that the BDF had occupied the island and was stealing crops planted by Namibian farmers resident there. In December 1999 the ICJ granted Botswana control over Sedudu-Kasikili. A joint technical commission was subsequently established to consider other demarcation disputes between Botswana and Namibia, and in March 2003 its report was accepted by the Presidents of both countries.

Meanwhile, in late 1998 relations between the two countries were further strained by the arrival in Botswana of more than 300 refugees (a number of whom were reportedly leading political dissidents) from the Caprivi Strip (now the Zambezi Region) in Namibia. President Mogae rejected Namibian demands for the extradition of the refugees, whose number had increased to more than 2,000 by early 1999. In May, however, a formal agreement was signed by the two Governments, according to which prominent dissidents among the refugees would be allowed to leave Botswana for another country and an amnesty would be extended to other refugees returning to Namibia. In response to a request from the Namibian Government, in September 2001 the Gaborone Magistrates' Court ruled in favour of the extradition of a group of 13 suspected Caprivi separatists who were wanted to stand trial for alleged high treason; however, this decision was reversed by Botswana's High Court in December 2002. Meanwhile, in April 2002 officials from Botswana and Namibia concluded a tripartite agreement with the office of the UN High Commissioner for Refugees (UNHCR) on the voluntary repatriation of Namibian refugees in Botswana. Between August and October around 800 refugees were repatriated to Namibia (although UNHCR reported that none of them originated from the Caprivi Strip), leaving some 1,200 in Botswana, who remained reluctant to return. In December 2003 UNHCR and human rights groups criticized the deportation from Botswana to Namibia of a further eight Caprivians, seven of whom were subsequently charged with high treason over alleged separatist activities; the authorities in Botswana claimed that the eight had lost their refugee status by visiting Namibia after being granted asylum in Botswana. Tensions between the two countries increased after two Namibians were shot and killed by the BDF in July 2012. The BDF claimed that the two men had been poaching in Chobe National Park, although the Namibian authorities refuted this allegation.

During the civil unrest in Libya, which persisted throughout 2011 and led to the overthrow of Col Muammar al-Qaddafi's regime, many African countries remained neutral. Botswana was, however, one of the first in the region to sever diplomatic ties with Libya as a result of the violent repression of the political opposition by forces loyal to Qaddafi. Botswana also swiftly granted recognition to the National Transitional Council as the legitimate representative of the Libyan people.

CONSTITUTION AND GOVERNMENT

The Constitution of the Republic of Botswana took effect at independence on 30 September 1966; it was amended in August and September 1997. Legislative power is vested in Parliament, consisting of the President and the National Assembly. The National Assembly is elected for a term of five years and comprises 57 members directly elected by universal adult suffrage, together with four members who are elected by the National Assembly from a list of candidates submitted by the President; the President and the Attorney-General are also ex officio members of the Assembly. The President is restricted to two terms of office. He appoints and leads a Cabinet, which is responsible to the Assembly. The President has powers to delay implementation of legislation for six months, and certain matters also have to be referred to the Ntlo ya Dikgosi for approval, although this advisory body has no power of veto. The Ntlo ya Dikgosi has a total of 35 members, comprising 30 members elected by senior tribal authorities and five members appointed by the President; elections to the Ntlo ya Dikgosi are held every five years. Local government is effected through nine district councils and four town councils. The Constitution contains a code of human rights, enforceable by the High Court.

REGIONAL AND INTERNATIONAL CO-OPERATION

Botswana is a member of the Southern African Development Community (SADC, see p. 424) and the organization's headquarters are located in Gaborone. Botswana is also a member of the Southern African Customs Union and of the African Union (see p. 186).

Botswana became a member of the UN in 1966, and was admitted to the World Trade Organization (WTO, see p. 434) in 1995.

ECONOMIC AFFAIRS

In 2012, according to estimates by the World Bank, Botswana's gross national income (GNI), measured at average 2010–12 prices, was US $14,884m., equivalent to $7,430 per head (or $15,880 on an international purchasing-power parity basis). During 2003–12, it was estimated, the population increased by an average of 1.0% per year, while gross domestic product (GDP) per head increased, in real terms, by an average of 2.8% per year. Overall GDP increased, in real terms, at an average annual rate of 3.8% in 2003–12; overall GDP grew by 3.7% in 2012.

Agriculture (including hunting, forestry and fishing) contributed 2.9% of GDP in 2012, and engaged 29.9% of the total labour force in 2006. However, according to FAO, the sector was estimated to engage 41.2% of the total labour force in mid-2014. The principal agricultural activity is cattle-raising (mainly beef production), which supports about one-half of the population and contributes more than 80% of agricultural GDP. As a member of the African, Caribbean and Pacific (ACP) group of states and a signatory to successive Lomé Conventions, Botswana has traditionally enjoyed preferential trade relations with the European Union (EU, see p. 273), including a quota to supply 18,916 metric tons of beef per year. Under the Cotonou Agreement, which was concluded in mid-2000, the quota was to be phased out by 2007, when Botswana and the other ACP states were to establish reciprocal trade arrangements with the EU in order to achieve compatibility with the rules of the WTO (see p. 434). In November 2007 it was announced that an interim agreement had been concluded that allowed Botswana to export beef duty free to the EU market and removed any limitations on export quotas. Negotiations were continuing in 2014 with the aim of finalizing an Economic Partnership Agreement between the EU and SADC (see p. 424) members. Meanwhile, in early 2011 the EU halted Botswana's beef exports following an outbreak of foot-and-mouth disease. The country resumed exports to the EU in July 2012. The Botswana Meat Commission recorded operating losses of P233m. and P283m. in 2011 and 2012, respectively, but forecast a profit in 2013 as a result of lucrative sales to Italy, Hong Kong and Norway. The main subsistence crops are roots and tubers, sorghum, maize, sunflower seeds pulses, although Botswana is not self-sufficient in basic foods. Agricultural GDP increased by 2.9% per year during 2003–12; it grew by 6.4% in 2012.

Industry (including mining, manufacturing, construction and power) engaged 15.2% of the employed labour force in 2006, and provided 35.2% of GDP in 2012. Industrial GDP decreased at an average annual rate of 1.1% in 2003–12; the sector's GDP rose by 4.9% in 2011, but declined by 1.7% in 2012.

Mining contributed 21.9% of GDP in 2012, although the sector engaged only 2.6% of the employed labour force in 2006. In terms of value, Botswana is the world's largest producer of diamonds (which accounted for 79.4% of export earnings in 2012); copper-nickel matte and textiles are also exported. In addition, coal, gold, cobalt, salt and soda ash are mined, and there are known reserves of plutonium, asbestos, chromite, fluorspar, iron, manganese, potash, silver, talc and uranium. The GDP of the mining sector decreased, in real terms, at an average annual rate of 5.8% in 2003–12; mining GDP decreased by 8.1% in 2012.

Manufacturing engaged 6.7% of the employed labour force in 2006, and provided 6.4% of GDP in 2012. The GDP of the manufacturing sector increased at an average annual rate of 6.9% in 2003–12; the GDP of the sector grew by 1.8% in 2012.

Construction engaged 5.1% of the employed labour force in 2006, and provided 7.4% of GDP in 2012. The GDP of the construction sector increased at an average annual rate of 9.7% in 2003–12; the GDP of the sector grew by 14.4% in 2012.

Energy is derived principally from fuel wood and coal; the use of solar power is currently being promoted as an alternative source of energy. According to official figures, imports of fuels accounted for 16.3% of the value of total imports in 2012.

The services sector contributed 61.9% of GDP in 2012, and engaged 54.9% of the employed labour force in 2006. Within the sector, tourism is of considerable importance, traditionally being the third largest source of total foreign exchange. The GDP of the services sector increased at an average annual rate of 7.3% in 2003–12; sectoral growth in 2012 was 6.8%.

In 2012 Botswana recorded a visible merchandise trade deficit of US $1,932.4m., while there was a deficit of $1,077.2m. on the current account of the balance of payments. In 2012 South Africa provided 62.8% of imports; other major suppliers were the United Kingdom and Namibia. The United Kingdom took 60.7% of exports in that year; other important purchasers were South Africa and Israel. The principal exports in 2012 were diamonds and copper-nickel matte. The principal imports were diamonds, fuels, machinery and electrical equipment, food, beverages and tobacco, vehicles and transport equipment, and chemicals and rubber products.

In the financial year to 31 March 2013 the central Government recorded an estimated budgetary surplus of P834.9m. Botswana's general government gross debt was P13.938m. in 2009, equivalent to 16.1% of GDP. Botswana's external debt totalled US $2,396m. in 2011, of which $1,897m. was public and publicly guaranteed debt. In 2010 the cost of servicing long-term public and publicly guaranteed debt and repayments to the IMF was equivalent to 1.4% of the value of exports of goods, services and income (excluding workers' remittances). The average annual rate of inflation was 8.6% in 2003–12; consumer prices increased by 7.5% in 2012. Some 17.6% of the labour force were unemployed in 2006.

Since the 1970s Botswana's development from one of the poorest countries in the world to a stable middle-income country has been based predominantly on the successful exploitation of diamonds and other minerals. However, the need to reduce the country's dependence on the mining industry has been recognized in recent years. The Government's 10th National Development Plan (2008/09–2013/14) aimed to continue the economic diversification effected by previous plans; poverty alleviation and public works programmes were also to be financed. The Government continued its efforts to exploit Botswana's natural resources, with the aim of uncovering deposits of rare metals (particularly platinum), and in July 2009 the Government announced plans to open up the Central Kgalagadi Game Reserve to mineral exploration, granting some 100 mining licences to 14 foreign companies. Other immediate government priorities included the creation of new employment opportunities and the maintenance of macroeconomic stability and financial discipline. Thus, in early 2013 the Government announced it was planning a large-scale agriculture project to channel water from the Chobe-Zambezi system in order to improve food security, contribute to economic growth and create employment. Nevertheless, the HIV/AIDS pandemic represents a significant threat to continued economic growth, diminishing the workforce and depleting government resources through the expenditure required to counter the disease. Approximately one-quarter of the adult population was believed to be infected with HIV in 2012. Significantly, in mid-2012 Botswana announced that, as part of its latest sales agreement with De Beers Diamond Trading Company, that organization would be moving some of its aggregation operations (including processing, sorting, marketing and retail) from London to Gabarone. This transfer, which was completed in November 2013, was expected to generate increased revenue in the diamond sector and create further jobs. The economy returned to growth in 2010, following a contraction in 2009. Growth remained strong in 2011, but slowed in 2012–13 as a result of uncertainty in the global market and significantly lower mineral export demand. According to IMF data, real GDP grew by 4.2% in 2012 and by 3.9% in 2013; growth of 4.1% was forecast for 2014. Following three years of budget deficits, largely resulting from the global economic crisis (which had led to a reduction in diamond sales and foreign direct investment in the country), the IMF estimated that Botswana achieved a budget surplus equivalent to 0.2% of GDP in both 2012/13 and 2013/14.

PUBLIC HOLIDAYS

2015: 1–2 January (New Year), 3–6 April (Easter), 1 May (Labour Day), 14 May (Ascension Day), 1 July (Sir Seretse Khama Day), 20–21 July (President's Day), 30 September (Botswana Day), 25–26 December (Christmas).

Statistical Survey

Source (unless otherwise stated): Central Statistics Office (Statistics Botswana), Plot 8843, Finance House, Khama Crescent, Gaborone; tel. 3671300; e-mail csobots@gov.bw; internet www.cso.gov.bw.

Area and Population

AREA, POPULATION AND DENSITY

Area (sq km)	581,730*
Population (census results)	
17 August 2001	1,680,863†
9-18 August 2011	
Males	989,128
Females	1,035,776
Total	2,024,904
Population (UN estimates at mid-year)‡	
2012	2,003,908
2013	2,021,145
2014	2,038,585
Density (per sq km) at mid-2014	3.5

* 224,607 sq miles.

† Excluding 60,716 non-Botswana enumerated at the time of the census.

‡ Source: UN, *World Population Prospects: The 2012 Revision*; estimates not revised to take account of results of 2011 census.

POPULATION BY AGE AND SEX

(UN estimates at mid-2014)

	Males	Females	Total
0–14	341,964	336,300	678,264
15–64	655,590	629,556	1,285,146
65 and over	29,207	45,968	75,175
Total	1,026,761	1,011,824	2,038,585

Source: UN, *World Population Prospects: The 2012 Revision*.

DISTRICTS AND SUB-DISTRICTS

(population at 2011 census)

Central		Kweneng West	47,797
Bobonong	71,936	*North-East*	
Boteti	57,376	Francistown	98,961
Mahalapye	118,875	North-East	60,264
Orapa	9,531	*North-West*	
Selebi-Phikwe	49,411	Chobe	23,347
Serowe/Palapye	180,500	Ngamiland West	59,421
Sowa Town	3,598	Ngamiland East†	92,863
Tutume	147,377	*South-East*	
Ghanzi		Gaborone	231,592
Ghanzi*	43,355	Lobatse	29,007
Kgalagadi		South-East	85,014
Kgalagadi North	20,476	*Southern*	
Kgalagadi South	30,016	Barolong	54,831
Kgatleng		Jwaneng	18,008
Kgatleng	91,660	Ngwaketse	129,247
Kweneng		Ngwaketse West	13,689
Kweneng East	256,752	**Total**	2,024,904

* Including Central Kalahari Game Reserve (CKGR) sub-district.

† Including Delta sub-district.

PRINCIPAL TOWNS

(population at 2011 census)

Gaborone (capital)	231,592	Serowe	50,820
Francistown	98,961	Selebi-Phikwe	49,411
Molepolole	66,466	Kanye	47,007
Maun	60,263	Mochudi	44,815
Mogoditshane	58,079	Mahalapye	43,289

BIRTHS AND DEATHS

(annual averages, UN estimates)

	1995–2000	2000–05	2005–10
Birth rate (per 1,000)	29.0	26.1	24.9
Death rate (per 1,000)	11.3	15.2	17.2

Source: UN, *World Population Prospects: The 2012 Revision*.

2009 (Health Statistics Report estimates): Live births 46,624; deaths 6,952.

Marriages: 4,416 (marriage rate 4.8) in 2010.

Life expectancy (years at birth): 46.7 (males 47.3; females 46.0) in 2011 (Source: World Bank, World Development Indicators database).

EMPLOYMENT

(number of persons aged 7 years and over, 2006 labour force survey)

	Males	Females	Total
Agriculture, hunting, forestry and fishing	98,805	62,561	161,367
Mining and quarrying	12,457	1,716	14,173
Manufacturing	16,010	19,962	35,973
Electricity, gas and water supply	2,626	1,537	4,163
Construction	23,111	4,476	27,587
Wholesale and retail trade; repair of motor vehicles, motorcycles and personal and household goods	27,924	49,478	77,401
Hotels and restaurants	3,770	10,898	14,667
Transport, storage and communications	10,496	5,555	16,050
Financial intermediation	3,018	5,406	8,424
Real estate, renting and business services	15,554	9,701	25,255
Public administration and defence; compulsory social security	34,539	25,618	60,157
Education	15,182	28,063	43,245
Health and social work	5,393	8,609	14,002
Other community, social and personal service activities	5,213	5,342	10,554
Private households with employed persons	7,208	18,027	25,235
Extra-territorial organizations and bodies	456	439	895
Total employed	281,762	257,388	539,150

2011 (paid employees in formal sector, labour force survey at June): Total employed 387,426 (central and local government 182,466).

Mid-2014 ('000 persons, FAO estimates): Agriculture, etc. 334; Total labour force 809 (Source: FAO).

Health and Welfare

KEY INDICATORS

Total fertility rate (children per woman, 2011)	2.7
Under-5 mortality rate (per 1,000 live births, 2011)	26
HIV/AIDS (% of persons aged 15–49, 2012)	23.0
Physicians (per 1,000 head, 2006)	0.3
Hospital beds (per 1,000 head, 2010)	1.8
Health expenditure (2010): US $ per head (PPP)	711
Health expenditure (2010): % of GDP	5.1
Health expenditure (2010): public (% of total)	64.5
Access to water (% of persons, 2011)	97
Access to sanitation (% of persons, 2011)	64
Total carbon dioxide emissions ('000 metric tons, 2010)	5,232.8
Carbon dioxide emissions per head (metric tons, 2010)	2.7
Human Development Index (2012): ranking	119
Human Development Index (2012): value	0.634

For sources and definitions, see explanatory note on p. vi.

Agriculture

PRINCIPAL CROPS
('000 metric tons)

	2010	2011	2012
Maize	10.6	29.1	10.0*
Sorghum	32.8	44.8	38.0*
Sunflower seed	5.0	5.5†	6.0†
Roots and tubers†	92.9	97.0	99.0
Pulses	3.9	3.8	4.0†

* Unofficial figure.
† FAO estimate(s).

Aggregate production ('000 metric tons, may include official, semi-official or estimated data): Total cereals 50.3 in 2010, 79.1 in 2011, 53.8 in 2012; Total vegetables (incl. melons) 39.8 in 2010, 40.2 in 2011, 40.7 in 2012; Total fruits (excl. melons) 5.9 in 2010, 6.6 in 2011; 7.1 in 2012.

Source: FAO.

LIVESTOCK
('000 head, year ending September)

	2010	2011	2012*
Cattle	2,649	2,554	2,500
Horses	41	42*	42
Asses	339	339*	341
Sheep	279	296	290
Goats	1,938	1,770	1,700
Pigs*	13	13	14
Poultry*	5,100	5,500	5,500

* FAO estimate(s).

LIVESTOCK PRODUCTS
('000 metric tons, FAO estimates)

	2010	2011	2012
Cattle meat	46.0	47.0	47.0
Goat meat	5.6	5.7	5.8
Chicken meat	6.0	6.2	6.5
Other meat	1.0	1.0	1.0
Cows' milk	114.2	114.5	115.5
Goats' milk	4.1	4.1	4.1
Hen eggs	4.5	4.5	4.6

Source: FAO.

Forestry

ROUNDWOOD REMOVALS
('000 cubic metres, excl. bark, FAO estimates)

	2010	2011	2012
Industrial wood	105.0	105.0	105.0
Fuel wood	683.3	686.4	689.5
Total	788.3	791.4	794.5

Source: FAO.

Fishing

(capture in metric tons, live weight)

	2009*	2010	2011
Tilapias	52	43	166
Torpedo-shaped catfishes	19	16	51
Other freshwater fishes	2	1	17
Total catch	73	60	234

* FAO estimates.

Source: FAO.

Mining

(metric tons, unless otherwise indicated)

	2010	2011	2012
Hard coal	988,240	787,729	1,454,404
Copper ore*†	20,833	14,231	17,620
Nickel ore†	23,053	13,842	17,942
Gold (kg)	1,774	1,562	1,377
Cobalt*†	252	129	195
Salt	346,761	446,525	367,749
Diamonds ('000 carats)	22,019	22,903	20,619
Soda ash (natural)	240,898	257,851	248,629
Sand and gravel ('000 cu m)‡	3,000	3,000§	n.a.

* Figures refer to the metal content of matte; product smelted was granulated nickel-copper-cobalt matte.
† Figures refer to the nickel content of matte and include some product not reported as milled.
‡ Source: US Geological Survey.
§ Estimate.

Source (unless otherwise stated): Bank of Botswana, *Annual Report 2012*.

Industry

SELECTED PRODUCTS

	2001	2002	2003
Beer ('000 hl)	1,692	1,396	1,198
Soft drinks ('000 hl)	431	389	405
Electric energy (million kWh)	1,035	1,044	936

Electric energy (million kWh): 697 in 2008; 621 in 2009; 532 in 2010.

Source: UN Industrial Commodity Statistics Database.

Finance

CURRENCY AND EXCHANGE RATES

Monetary Units
100 thebe = 1 pula (P).

Sterling, Dollar and Euro Equivalents (31 December 2013)
£1 sterling = 14.362 pula;
US $1 = 8.721 pula;
€1 = 12.027 pula;
100 pula = £6.96 = $11.47 = €8.31.

Average Exchange Rate (pula per US $)
2011 6.8382
2012 7.6191
2013 8.3989

BUDGET
(million pula, year ending 31 March)

Revenue*	2011/12	2012/13†	2013/14†
Taxation	35,533.1	39,141.5	40,966.1
Mineral revenue	15,823.1	12,038.0	13,254.0
Customs and excise	8,424.3	14,151.0	13,683.1
Non-mineral income taxes	6,112.7	7,877.0	8,967.9
Other taxes	5,173.2	5,075.5	5,061.1
General sales tax/VAT	4,851.0	4,769.8	4,747.1
Other current revenue	2,420.1	2,418.9	2,619.8
Interest	58.6	29.4	30.5
Other property income	122.6	47.5	135.2
Bank of Botswana revenues	863.8	780.0	500.0
Fees, charges, etc.	1,269.0	1,487.9	1,884.6
Sales of fixed assets and land	106.1	74.0	69.6
Total	37,953.2	41,560.3	43,585.9

Expenditure‡	2011/12	2012/13†	2013/14†
General services (incl. defence)	9,826.3	10,659.5	11,046.7
Social services	17,205.7	17,795.9	20,015.3
Education	8,379.9	8,439.7	9,212.5
Health	4,381.1	4,448.5	4,816.2
Housing, urban and regional development	2,861.6	2,738.4	3,025.6
Food and social welfare programme	719.1	1,157.2	1,689.4
Other community and social services	864.0	1,012.1	1,271.7
Economic services	8,498.3	8,091.9	8,429.6
Agriculture, forestry and fishing	1,289.4	1,283.6	1,596.9
Mining	729.8	280.3	293.4
Electricity and water supply	2,522.4	2,839.1	2,718.6
Transport	3,074.5	3,005.2	2,745.0
Others	882.1	683.7	1,075.7
Transfers	3,137.2	4,528.3	3,750.9
Deficit grants to local authorities	2,550.6	2,936.4	2,973.2
Interest on public debt	586.6	1,591.9	777.7
Total	38,667.5	41,075.6	43,242.4

* Excluding grants received (million pula): ; 532.8 in 2011/12; 350.2 in 2012/13 (estimate); 435.8 in 2013/14 (estimate).

† Estimates.

‡ Including net lending (million pula): ; –124.4 in 2011/12; –54.4 in 2012/13 (estimate); –55.1 in 2013/14 (estimate).

Source: Bank of Botswana, *Annual Report 2012*.

INTERNATIONAL RESERVES

(US $ million at 31 December)

	2010	2011	2012
IMF special drawing rights	143.19	133.57	131.52
Reserve position in IMF	20.86	41.88	43.15
Foreign exchange	7,721.16	7,906.44	7,453.30
Total	7,885.21	8,081.89	7,627.97

Source: IMF, *International Financial Statistics*.

MONEY SUPPLY

(million pula at 31 December)

	2010	2011	2012
Currency outside depository corporations	1,241	1,431	1,558
Transferable deposits	8,023	7,244	8,997
Other deposits	33,596	36,088	38,247
Broad money	42,860	44,763	48,802

Source: IMF, *International Financial Statistics*.

COST OF LIVING

(Consumer Price Index; annual averages; base: September 2006 = 100)

	2010	2011	2012
Food	155.2	165.9	179.1
Alcohol and tobacco	175.3	190.0	204.6
Clothing (incl. footwear)	122.3	133.2	143.1
Housing	125.3	135.9	146.3
Health	127.4	133.0	140.8
Transport	127.3	144.1	159.6
Communication	95.8	92.9	91.6
Education	120.5	133.2	141.7
All items (incl. others)	136.9	148.4	159.6

NATIONAL ACCOUNTS

(million pula at current prices, provisional figures)

Expenditure on the Gross Domestic Product

	2010	2011	2012
Government final consumption expenditure	17,162	19,407	21,196
Private final consumption expenditure	42,692	48,629	59,151
Increase in stocks	3,815	6,856	–481
Gross fixed capital formation	29,202	33,641	38,488
Total domestic expenditure	92,871	108,533	118,353
Exports of goods and services	33,402	46,380	49,173
Less Imports of goods and services	40,314	52,423	55,263
Statistical discrepancy	7,431	2,083	–1,752
GDP in purchasers' values	93,390	104,573	110,511
GDP at constant 2006 prices	66,549	70,610	73,560

Gross Domestic Product by Economic Activity

	2010	2011	2012
Agriculture, hunting, forestry and fishing	2,717	2,636	2,963
Mining and quarrying	22,868	25,841	22,049
Manufacturing	5,548	6,074	6,441
Water and electricity	394	187	–493
Construction	5,056	6,247	7,471
Trade, restaurants and hotels	13,084	15,366	16,792
Transport, post and telecommunications	4,471	5,109	6,230
Finance, insurance and business services	11,610	13,481	16,017
Government services	13,380	14,464	16,566
Social and personal services	5,243	5,881	6,842
GDP at basic prices	84,371	95,286	100,878
Import duties	4,570	4,722	5,055
Taxes on products	4,932	5,114	5,173
Less Subsidies on products	483	548	595
GDP in purchasers' values	93,390	104,573	110,511

Source: Bank of Botswana, Gaborone.

BALANCE OF PAYMENTS

(US $ million)

	2010	2011	2012
Exports of goods	4,629.7	6,446.9	6,016.6
Imports of goods	–5,634.4	–7,194.1	–7,949.0
Balance on goods	–1,004.7	–747.1	–1,932.4
Exports of services	283.4	517.0	268.2
Imports of services	–723.3	–858.1	–670.4
Balance on goods and services	–1,444.6	–1,088.3	–2,334.6
Primary income received	255.7	248.6	214.1
Primary income paid	–278.4	–575.3	–714.7
Balance on goods, services and primary income	–1,467.3	–1,415.0	–2,835.2
Secondary income received	1,295.5	1,317.7	1,941.6
Secondary income paid	–126.5	–226.3	–183.6
Current balance	–298.3	–323.6	–1,077.2
Capital account (net)	3.4	0.4	—
Direct investment assets	–1.3	10.9	–7.7
Direct investment liabilities	–6.1	413.6	333.7
Portfolio investment assets	–413.1	–193.1	–166.6
Portfolio investment liabilities	11.0	–20.2	–8.6
Other investment assets	–222.4	–434.5	–209.3
Other investment liabilities	211.4	–31.2	153.7
Net errors and omissions	–330.7	1,389.5	845.4
Reserves and related items	–1,046.2	811.8	–136.6

Source: IMF, *International Financial Statistics*.

External Trade

PRINCIPAL COMMODITIES
(million pula)

Imports c.i.f.	2010	2011	2012
Food, beverages and tobacco	4,812.7	5,240.3	5,679.9
Fuels	5,521.5	8,290.4	9,981.6
Chemicals and rubber products	4,206.7	4,555.3	5,393.1
Textiles and footwear	1,562.8	1,787.5	1,881.1
Metals and metal products	2,857.0	3,704.2	2,902.8
Machinery and electrical equipment	6,768.0	11,461.6	9,065.2
Vehicles and transport equipment	3,707.0	4,568.1	5,489.5
Diamonds	4,471.3	5,882.1	16,512.4
Total (incl. others)	38,474.7	49,737.7	61,348.6

Exports f.o.b.	2010	2011	2012
Meat and meat products	1,084.0	356.7	498.9
Diamonds	21,779.9	30,247.7	36,143.0
Copper-nickel matte	4,240.2	2,940.3	3,294.3
Textiles	1,118.5	1,817.7	609.6
Total (incl. others)	31,817.5	40,007.0	45,495.0

PRINCIPAL TRADING PARTNERS
(million pula)

Imports c.i.f.	2010	2011	2012
Belgium	349.0	578.5	800.2
China, People's Republic	2,075.1	5,430.0	1,709.0
India	286.0	677.5	831.8
Israel	713.6	687.1	922.0
SACU*	28,323.8	33,181.6	42,121.3
Namibia	282.0	421.8	3,466.8
South Africa	28,001.9	32,687.32	38,521.9
United Kingdom	3,563.3	4,915.2	10,289.0
USA	507.0	1,068.9	1,201.3
Total (incl. others)	38,474.7	49,737.7	61,348.6

Exports f.o.b.	2010	2011	2012
Belgium	1,042.2	1,086.8	1,978.9
India	277.7	512.9	520.3
Israel	1,680.0	2,069.3	2,458.2
Norway	2,971.1	1,906.5	2,269.7
SACU*	4,328.0	5,709.2	6,828.0
Namibia	113.5	212.1	849.4
South Africa	4,201.9	5,460.6	5,957.8
Switzerland	493.2	609.4	776.4
United Kingdom	17,710.1	24,961.1	27,623.0
USA	385.1	426.5	553.3
Zambia	262.4	518.2	367.1
Zimbabwe	1,191.7	1,187.4	865.0
Total (incl. others)	31,817.5	40,007.0	45,495.0

* Southern African Customs Union, of which Botswana is a member; also including Lesotho, Namibia, South Africa and Swaziland.

Transport

RAILWAYS
(traffic)

	2007	2008	2009
Number of passengers ('000)	382.8	415.9	97.6*
Freight ('000 metric tons)	1,750.7	1,759.5	1,927.5

* Preliminary figure.

Freight carried ('000 metric tons): 2,010.8 in 2010; 2,034.8 in 2011; 1,984.9 in 2012.

ROAD TRAFFIC
(registered vehicles)

	2010	2011	2012
Cars	177,131	121,344	189,661
Light duty vehicles	100,978	67,083	93,551
Trucks	22,220	14,785	21,701
Buses	14,155	8,856	12,753
Tractors	5,180	2,634	4,959
Others (incl. trailers, motorcycles and tankers)	25,055	15,741	24,376
Total	344,719	230,443	347,001

CIVIL AVIATION
(traffic on scheduled services, million)

	2007	2008	2009
Kilometres flown	4	4	4
Passenger-km	116	118	113
Total ton-km	10	11	10

Source: UN, *Statistical Yearbook*.

Passengers carried: 774,771 in 2010; 788,461 in 2011; 764,972 in 2012.

Freight carried (metric tons): 1,098.2 in 2007; 1,067.8 in 2008; 936.9 in 2009.

Tourism

FOREIGN TOURIST ARRIVALS

Country of origin	2007	2008	2009
Namibia	99,417	115,219	122,518
South Africa	627,437	666,690	686,431
United Kingdom and Ireland	27,481	30,591	30,104
Zambia	153,487	278,335	158,389
Zimbabwe	801,998	1,027,177	839,347
Total (incl. others)	1,983,427	2,338,383	2,065,195

2010: Total tourist arrivals ('000) 2,145; Receipts from tourism (US $ million, excl. passenger transport) 218 (Source: World Tourism Organization).

Communications Media

	2010	2011	2012
Telephones ('000 main lines in use)	137.4	149.6	160.5
Mobile cellular telephones ('000 subscribers)	2,363.4	2,900.3	3,081.7
Broadband subscribers ('000)	12.0	15.7	16.1

Internet subscribers: 12,000 in 2009.

Source: International Telecommunication Union.

Education

(2012 unless otherwise indicated)

	Institutions	Teachers	Students
Primary	812	14,220	337,206
Secondary	274	11,553	171,478
General programmes	n.a.	11,910*	171,986†
Technical and vocational programmes	43†	992‡	10,094‡
Tertiary	2§	529‖	17,218

* 2006/7.

† 2008.

‡ 2007.

§ 2001; number of colleges of education.

‖ 2004/05.

Sources: Ministry of Education, Gaborone; UNESCO Institute for Statistics.

Agricultural college (2006): Teachers 106; students 960.

University (2011/12): Teachers 877; students 17,678 (Source: University of Botswana).

Pupil-teacher ratio (primary education): 23.8 in 2012.

Adult literacy rate (UNESCO estimates): 85.1% (males 84.6%; females 85.6%) in 2011 (Source: UNESCO Institute for Statistics).

Directory

The Government

HEAD OF STATE

President: Lt-Gen. SERETSE KHAMA IAN KHAMA (took office 1 April 2008).

Vice-President: Dr PONATSHEGO H. KEDIKILWE.

CABINET
(April 2014)

The Government is formed by the Botswana Democratic Party.

President: Lt-Gen. SERETSE KHAMA IAN KHAMA.

Vice-President: Dr PONATSHEGO H. KEDIKILWE.

Minister of Defence, Justice and Security: RAMADELUKA SERETSE.

Minister of Presidential Affairs and Public Administration: MOKGWEETSI ERIC MASISI.

Minister of Foreign Affairs and International Co-operation: PHANDU T. C. SKELEMANI.

Minister of Finance and Development Planning: KENNETH O. MATAMBO.

Minister of Infrastructure, Science and Technology: JOHNNIE K. SWARTZ.

Minister of Lands and Housing: LEBONAMANG MOKALAKE.

Minister of Labour and Home Affairs: EDWIN BATSU.

Minister of Youth, Sports and Culture: SHAW KGATHI.

Minister of Trade and Industry: DORCAS MAKGATO-MALESU.

Minister of Local Government: PETER SIELE.

Minister of Agriculture: CHRISTIAN DE GRAAF.

Minister of Transport and Communications: NONOFO MOLEFHI.

Minister of Minerals, Energy and Water Resources: ONKOKAME KITSO MOKAILA.

Minister of Education and Skills Development: PELONOMI VENSON-MOITOI.

Minister of Environment, Wildlife and Tourism: TSHEKEDI KHAMA.

Minister of Health: JOHN SEAKGOSING.

Attorney-General: Dr ATHALIAH MOLOKOMME.

Secretary to the Cabinet: ERIC MOLALE.

In addition, there were eight Assistant Ministers.

MINISTRIES

Office of the President: PMB 001, Gaborone; tel. 3950825; fax 3950858; e-mail op.registry@gov.bw; internet www.gov.bw/government/ministry_of_state_president.html#office_of_the_president.

Ministry of Agriculture: PMB 003, Gaborone; tel. 33689000; fax 3975805; e-mail mkojane@gov.bw; internet www.moa.gov.bw.

Ministry of Education and Skills Development: Chief Education Officer, Block 6 Bldg, 2nd Floor, Government Enclave, Gaborone; PMB 005, Gaborone; tel. 3655400; fax 3655458; e-mail cde.registry@gov.bw; internet www.moe.gov.bw.

Ministry of Environment, Wildlife and Tourism: PMB BO199, Standard House, 2nd Floor, Main Mall, Bontleng, Gaborone; tel. 3914955; fax 3191346; internet www.mewt.gov.bw.

Ministry of Finance and Development Planning: Government Enclave, Khama Cres., Blk 25, State Dr., PMB 008, Gaborone; tel. 3950100; fax 3905742; e-mail kmutasa@gov.bw; internet www.finance.gov.bw.

Ministry of Foreign Affairs and International Co-operation: Government Enclave, PMB 00368, Gaborone; tel. 3600700; fax 3913366; e-mail mofaic-admin@lists.gov.bw; internet www.mofaic.gov.bw.

Ministry of Health: PMB 0038, Gaborone; tel. 3170585; e-mail moh-webmaster@gov.bw; internet www.moh.gov.bw.

Ministry of Infrastructure, Science and Technology: PMB 007, Gaborone; tel. 3958500; fax 3913303; internet www.mist.gov.bw.

Ministry of Labour and Home Affairs: PMB 002, Gaborone; tel. 3611100; fax 3913584; e-mail msetimela@gov.bw; internet www.gov.bw/government/ministry_of_labour_and_home_affairs.html.

Ministry of Lands and Housing: PMB 00434, Gaborone; tel. 3682000; fax 3911591; e-mail lrtlhaloso@gov.bw; internet www.mlh.gov.bw.

Ministry of Local Government: PMB 006, Gaborone; tel. 3658400; fax 3952382; internet www.mlg.gov.bw.

Ministry of Minerals, Energy and Water Resources: Khama Cres., PMB 0018, Gaborone; tel. 3656600; fax 3972738; internet www.mmewr.gov.bw.

Ministry of Trade and Industry: PMB 004, Gaborone; tel. 3601200; fax 3971539; internet www.mti.gov.bw.

Ministry of Transport and Communications: PMB 00414, Gaborone; tel. 3907230; fax 3907236.

Ministry of Youth, Sports and Culture: Plot 50626, Samora Machel Dr., next to Cresta Lodge, PMB 00514, Gaborone; tel. 3682600; fax 3913473; e-mail mysc_pro@gov.bw; internet www.mysc.gov.bw.

Legislature

NTLO YA DIKGOSI

Following a review, in December 2005 the membership of the Ntlo ya Dikgosi was increased from 15 to 35 members.

Chairperson: Chief MOSADI SEBOKO.

NATIONAL ASSEMBLY

Speaker: Dr MARGARET NASHA.

General Election, 16 October 2009

Party	Votes	% of votes	Seats
Botswana Democratic Party	290,099	53.26	45
Botswana National Front	119,509	21.94	6
Botswana Congress Party	104,302	19.15	4
Botswana Alliance Movement	12,387	2.27	1
Independents	10,464	1.92	1
Botswana People's Party	7,554	1.39	–
MELS Movement of Botswana	292	0.05	–
Botswana Tlhoko Tiro Organisation	40	0.01	–
Total	544,647	100.00	57†

† The President and the Attorney-General are also ex officio members of the National Assembly.

Election Commission

Independent Electoral Commission (IEC): Fair Ground Holdings, Plot 63726, PMB 00284, Gaborone; tel. 3612400; fax 3900581; e-mail iec_info@gov.bw; internet www.iec.gov.bw; f. 1997; Chair. A. B. TAFA.

Political Organizations

Botswana Congress Party (BCP): Plot 364, Extension 4, Independence Ave, Gaborone; POB 2918, Gaborone; tel. and fax 3181805; e-mail thatoosupile@hotmail.com; internet www.bcp.org.bw; f. 1998 following split from the BNF; Pres. DUMELANG SALESHANDO; Nat. Chair. BATISANI MASWIBILI; Sec.-Gen. TAOLO LUCAS.

Botswana Democratic Party (BDP) (Domkrag): Plot 695, behind Tsholetsa House, POB 28, Gaborone; tel. 3952564; fax 3913911; e-mail bserema@bdp.org.bw; internet www.bdp.org.bw; f. 1962 as the Bechuanaland Democratic Party; Pres. SERETSE KHAMA IAN KHAMA; Chair. DANIEL K. KWELAGOBE; Sec.-Gen. MPHO BALOPI.

Botswana National Front (BNF): POB 40065, Gaborone; tel. and fax 3182921; e-mail botswananationalfront@yahoo.com; f. 1966; incl. fmr mems of the United Socialist Party (PUSO), which split from the BNF in 1994 later to re-affiliate in 2005; Pres. OTSWELETSE MOUPO; Chair. NEHEMIAH MODUBULE; Sec.-Gen. MOHAMMED KHAN.

Botswana Movement for Democracy (BMD): Gaborone; f. 2010 by fmr mems of the Botswana Democratic Party; Chair. GOMOLEMO MOTSWALEDI.

Botswana People's Party (BPP): POB 685, Francistown; tel. 72610603 (mobile); f. 1960; Pres. WHYTE MAROBELA.

Botswana Workers' Front (BWF): PMB 00704, Jwaneng; tel. 3552877; fax 3956866; f. 1993 following split from the BNF; mems may retain dual membership of the BNF; Leader SHAWN NTHAILE.

MELS Movement of Botswana: POB 501818, Gaborone; tel. 3933140; fax 3933241; e-mail joinaandass@botsnet.bw; f. 1984; Marxist-Leninist; Leader THEMBA JOINA; Vice-Pres. EPHRAIM MAKGETHO.

New Democratic Front (NDF): Gaborone; f. 2003 following split from the BNF; affiliated to the BCP since mid-2006; Leader DICK BAYFORD.

Diplomatic Representation

EMBASSIES AND HIGH COMMISSIONS IN BOTSWANA

Angola: Plot 13232, Khama Cres., Nelson Mandela Rd, PMB BR 111, Gaborone; tel. 3900204; fax 3975089; Ambassador JOSÉ AGOSTINHO NETO.

Brazil: Plot 11245, Main Mall, Standard House, 3rd Floor, PMB 475, Gaborone; tel. 3951061; fax 3972581; e-mail brasemb.gaborone@itamaraty.gov.br; internet gaborone.itamaraty.gov.br; Ambassador MARCIO ARAUJO LAGE.

China, People's Republic: Plot 3096 North Ring Rd, POB 1031, Gaborone; tel. 3952209; fax 3900156; e-mail chinaemb_bw@mfa.gov.cn; internet bw.china-embassy.org; Ambassador LIU HUANXING.

Cuba: Plot 5504, Kolobe, Partial, Extension 17, POB 40261, Gaborone; tel. 3911485; fax 3951750; e-mail secretario@botsnet.bw; internet www.cubadiplomatica.cu/botswana; Ambassador JUAN CARLOS ARENCIBIA CORRALES.

France: 761 Robinson Rd, POB 1424, Gaborone; tel. 3680800; fax 3680801; e-mail frambbots@orangemail.co.bw; internet www.ambafrance-bw.org; Ambassador ANNE DE LA BLACHE.

Germany: Professional House, 3rd Floor, Segoditshane Way, Broadhurst, POB 315, Gaborone; tel. 3953143; fax 3953038; e-mail info@gaborone.diplo.de; internet www.gaborone.diplo.de; Ambassador ROLF ULRICH.

India: Plot 5375, President's Dr., PMB 00249, Gaborone; tel. 3972676; fax 3974636; e-mail counsellor@hci.org.bw; internet www.hcigaborone.org.bw; High Commissioner MADHAVA CHANDRA.

Kenya: Plot 2615, Zebra Way, off Chuma Dr., PMB 297, Gaborone; tel. 3951408; fax 3951409; e-mail info@khcbotswana.org.bw; internet www.khcbotswana.com; High Commissioner JEAN W. KIMANI.

Libya: Plot 8851, Government Enclave, POB 180, Gaborone; tel. 3952481; fax 356928; Chargé d'affaires ASSED MOHAMED ALMUTAA.

Mozambique: Phuti Cres. 2638, POB 00215, Gaborone; tel. 3191251; fax 3191262; e-mail anuvunga@info.bw; High Commissioner BELMIRO JOSÉ MALATE.

Namibia: Plot 186, Morara Close, POB 987, Gaborone; tel. 3902181; fax 3902248; e-mail namibhc@botsnet.bw; High Commissioner H. T. HISHONGWA.

Nigeria: Plot 1086–92, Queens Rd, The Mall, POB 274, Gaborone; tel. 3913561; fax 3913738; e-mail nigeriabotswana@it.bw; internet nhcbotswana.org; High Commissioner OKUBOTIN CHARLES COCODIA.

Russia: Plot 4711, Tawana Close, POB 81, Gaborone; tel. 3953389; fax 3952930; e-mail embrus@info.bw; internet www.botswana.mid.ru; Ambassador ANATOLY NIKOLAEVICH KORSUN.

South Africa: Plot 29, Queens Rd, PMB 00402, Gaborone; tel. 3904800; fax 3905501; e-mail sahcgabs@botsnet.bw; High Commissioner L. SHOPE.

United Kingdom: Plot 1079–1084, Main Mall, off Queens Rd, PMB 0023, Gaborone; tel. 3952841; fax 3956105; e-mail bhc@botsnet.bw; internet ukinbotswana.fco.gov.uk; High Commissioner NICHOLAS JOHN PYLE.

USA: Embassy Enclave, off Khama Cres., POB 90, Gaborone; tel. 3953982; fax 3956947; internet botswana.usembassy.gov; Chargé d'affaires a.i. MICHAEL J. MURPHY.

Zambia: Plot 1120, Queens Rd, The Mall, POB 362, Gaborone; tel. 3951951; fax 3953952; High Commissioner MARINA MALOKOTA NSINGO.

Zimbabwe: Plot 8850, POB 1232, Gaborone; tel. 3914495; fax 3905863; e-mail zimembassy@zimgaborone.gov.zw; internet www.zimgaborone.gov.zw; Ambassador THOMAS MANDIGORA.

Judicial System

There is a High Court at Lobatse and a branch at Francistown, and Magistrates' Courts in each district. Appeals lie to the Court of Appeal of Botswana. The Chief Justice and the President of the Court of Appeal are appointed by the President.

Chief Justice: MARUPING DIBOTELO.

Court of Appeal: Lobatse; Pres. IAN KIRBY.

High Court: PMB 1, Lobatse; tel. 5330396; fax 5332317; Judges ISAAC K. B. LESETEDI, MARUPING DIBOTELO, UNITY DOW, MOATLHODI MARUMO, STANLEY SAPIRE, LEATILE DAMBE, LOT MOROKA; Registrar and Master GODFREY NTHOMIWA.

Office of the Attorney-General: PMB 009, Gaborone; tel. 3954700; fax 3957089; Attorney-General Dr ATHALIAH MOLOKOMME.

Religion

In 2006, according to official figures, the majority of the population aged 10 years and above were Christians (approximately 62%); an estimated 2% held animist beliefs. There are Islamic mosques in Gaborone and Lobatse. Hinduism and the Bahá'í Faith are also represented.

CHRISTIANITY

Botswana Council of Churches (Lekgotla la Dikereke mo Botswana): POB 355, Gaborone; tel. and fax 3951981; e-mail bots.christ.c@info.bw; f. 1966; Pres. Rev. MPHO MORUAKGOMO; Gen. Sec. DAVID J. MODIEGA; 24 mem. churches and orgs.

The Anglican Communion

Anglicans are adherents of the Church of the Province of Central Africa, covering Botswana, Malawi, Zambia and Zimbabwe. The Church comprises 15 dioceses, including one in Botswana. The current Archbishop of the Province is the Bishop of Northern Zambia. The Province was established in 1955, and the diocese of Botswana was formed in 1972. There were some 10,500 adherents at mid-2000.

Bishop of Botswana: Rt Rev. METLHAYOTLHE BELEME, POB 769, Gaborone; tel. 3953779; fax 3952075; e-mail info@anglicanbotswana.org.bw; internet www.diobot.org.

Protestant Churches

There were an estimated 178,000 adherents in the country at mid-2000.

African Methodist Episcopal Church: POB 141, Lobatse; tel. 5407520; e-mail tmobea@gmail.com; Presiding Elder Rev. TIROYAONE MOBEA.

Evangelical Lutheran Church in Botswana (Kereke ya Luthere ya Efangele mo Botswana): POB 1976, Serotologane St, Plot 28570, Gaborone; tel. 3164612; fax 3164615; e-mail elcb@info.bw; f. 1979; Bishop Dr COSMOS MOENGA; 43 congregations; 18,650 mems (2010).

Evangelical Lutheran Church in Southern Africa (Botswana Diocese): Bontleng, POB 201012, Gaborone; tel. and fax 302144; f. 1982; Bishop Rev. G. EKSTEEN.

Methodist Church of Southern Africa (Gaborone Circuit): POB 260, Gaborone; tel. 3167627; Circuit Supt Rev. ODIRILE E. MERE.

United Congregational Church of Southern Africa (Synod of Botswana): POB 1263, Gaborone; tel. 3952491; synod status since 1980; Chair. Rev. D. T. MAPITSE; Sec. Rev. M. P. P. DIBEELA; c. 24,000 mems.

Other denominations active in Botswana include the Church of God in Christ, the Dutch Reformed Church, the Mennonite Church, the United Methodist Church and the Seventh-day Adventists.

The Roman Catholic Church

Botswana comprises one diocese and one apostolic vicariate. The metropolitan see is Bloemfontein, South Africa. The church was established in Botswana in 1928, and adherents comprised some 5% of the total population. The Bishop participates in the Southern African Catholic Bishops' Conference, currently based in Pretoria, South Africa.

Bishop of Gaborone: Rt Rev. VALENTINE TSAMMA SEANE, POB 218, Bishop's House, Plot 162, Queens Rd, Gaborone; tel. 3912958; fax 3956970; e-mail gabs.diocese@botsnet.bw.

Vicar Apostolic of Francistown: Rt Rev. FRANKLYN NUBUASAH, POB 702, Tsane Rd, 14061 Area W, Francistown; tel. 2413601; fax 2417183; e-mail catholicoffice@botsnet.bw.

The Press

DAILY NEWSPAPERS

Dikgang tsa Gompieno (Daily News): 37795 Wellie Seboni Dr., PMB BR 139, Gaborone; tel. 3653500; fax 3901675; e-mail dailynews@gov.bw; internet www.dailynews.gov.bw; f. 1964; Mon.–Fri.; publ. by Dept of Information and Broadcasting; Setswana and English; Editor THEBEYAME RAMOROKA; circ. 60,000.

Mmegi/The Reporter: Segogwane Way, Plot 8901, Broadhurst, PMB BR 50, Gaborone; tel. 3974784; fax 3905508; e-mail dikgang@mmegi.bw; internet www.mmegi.bw; f. 1984 as *Mmegi wa Dikgang*; daily; publ. by Dikgang Publishing Co; Setswana and English; Man. Editor TITUS MBUYA; circ. 20,000; also publishes the weekly *Mmegi Monitor* (f. 2000, Monday, circ. 16,000).

PERIODICALS

Botswana Advertiser/Northern Advertiser: 5647 Nakedi Rd, Broadhurst Industrial, POB 130, Gaborone; tel. 3914788; fax 3182957; e-mail sales@northernadvertiser.co.bw; internet www.theadvertiser.co.bw; f. 1971; owned by Screen Print (Pty) Ltd; weekly; English; circ. 90,000 (*Botswana Advertiser*), 35,000 (*Northern Advertiser*); Gen. Man. MARTIN CHIBANDA.

The Botswana Gazette: 125 Sedimosa House, Millennium Park, Kgale View, POB 1605, Gaborone; tel. 3912833; fax 3972283; e-mail editor@gazette.com; internet www.gazette.bw; f. 1985; publ. by News Co Botswana; weekly; Man. Dir CLARA OLSEN; Editor OARABILE MOTSETA; circ. 23,500.

Botswana Guardian: Plot 14442, Kamushungo Rd, G-West Industrial Site, POB 1641, Gaborone; tel. 3908432; fax 3908457; internet www.botswanaguardian.co.bw; f. 1983; weekly; publ. by Pula Printing & Publishing (Pty) Ltd; English; Editor OUTSA MOKONE; circ. 21,505.

Business and Financial Times: Unit 9, Plot 64, Gaborone International Commerce Park, POB 402396, Gaborone; tel. 3939911; fax 3939910; e-mail businesstimes@botsnet.bw; internet www.businesstimes.co.bw; Publr JAFFAR KATERYA MBUI; Editor JIMMY SWIRA.

Francistown News and Reviews: POB 632, Francistown; tel. and fax 2412040; weekly; English.

Kutlwano: Willie Sebonie Rd, PMB BR 139, Gaborone; tel. 3653500; fax 3653630; e-mail kutlwano@gov.bw; internet www.kutlwano.gov.bw; monthly; publ. by Dept of Information Services; Setswana and English; Editor THOMAS NKHOMA; circ. 15,000.

The Midweek Sun: Plot 14442, Kamushungo Rd, G-West Industrial Site, POB 00153, Gaborone; tel. 3908408; fax 3908457; internet www.midweeksun.co.bw; f. 1989; weekly; English; Editor MIKE MOTHIBI; circ. 17,971.

Mokgosi Newspaper: Plot 134, Madirelo, Tlokweng, POB 46530, Gaborone; tel. 3936868; fax 3936869; e-mail mokgosi@mmegi.bw.

The Ngami Times: Mabudutsa Ward, PMB BO 30, Maun; tel. 6864807; fax 6860257; e-mail tnt@info.bw; internet www.ngamitimes.com; f. 1999; owned by The Ngami Times Printing and Publishing Co Botswana (Pty) Ltd; weekly; English; Editor NORMAN CHANDLER.

The Oriental Post: Gaborone; f. 2009; weekly; Chinese; Dir MILES NAN.

Sunday Standard: Postnet Kgale View, PMB 351, Suite 287, Gaborone; tel. 3188784; fax 3188795; internet www.sundaystandard.info; Editor OUTSA MOKONE.

Sunday Tribune: POB 41458, Gaborone; tel. and fax 3926431; weekly.

Tautona Times: Office of the President, PMB 001, Gaborone; tel. 71318598 (mobile); e-mail jramsay@gov.bw; f. 2003; weekly; electronic press circular publ. by the Office of the Pres.; Communications Co-ordinator Dr JEFF RAMSAY.

The Voice: Plot 170, Unit 7, Commerce Park, POB 40415, Gaborone; tel. 3161585; fax 3932822; e-mail voicebw@yahoo.com; internet www.thevoicebw.com; f. 1992 as *The Francistowner*; weekly; Publr BEATA KASALE; Man. Editor DONALD MOORE; Editor EMANG BOKHUTLO; circ. 30,000.

Wena Magazine: POB 201533, Gaborone; tel. and fax 3907678; e-mail environews@it.bw; f. 1998; 6 a year; English and Setswana; environmental issues; Editor and Publr FLORA SEBONI-MMEREKI; circ. c. 8,000.

The Zebra's Voice: National Museum, 331 Independence Ave, PMB 00114, Gaborone; tel. 3974616; fax 3934351; e-mail bemotswakhumo@gov.bw; internet www.botswana-museum.gov.bw; f. 1980; twice a year; cultural affairs; Editor BERLINAH MOTSWAKHUMO; circ. 5,000.

NEWS AGENCY

Department of Information Services, Botswana Press Agency (BOPA): PMB BR 139, Gaborone; tel. 3653525; fax 3653626; e-mail bopa@gov.bw; f. 1981; News Editor NDIYANE MASOLE.

PRESS ORGANIZATIONS

Botswana Journalists' Association (BOJA): POB 60518, Gaborone; tel. 3974435; e-mail penlite@info.bw; internet www.botswanamedia.bw/boja.htm; f. 1977; represents professional journalists; Chair. SECHELE SECHELE; Sec.-Gen. RAMPHOLO MOLEFHE; 55 mems (1999).

Botswana Media Consultative Council (BMCC): POB 2679, Gaborone; tel. 71624382 (mobile); e-mail botswanamedia@info.bw; internet www.botswanamedia.bw; f. 1998; promotes the devt of a democratic media; Chair. Dr JEFF RAMSAY; Exec. Sec. ANTOINETTE O. CHIGODORA; 40 mem. orgs (1999).

Publishers

A. C. Braby (Botswana) (Pty) Ltd: Unit 3/A/2, Western Industrial Estate, 22100 Phase 4 Industrial, POB 1549, Gaborone; tel. 3971444; fax 3973462; e-mail customercare@brabys.co.za; internet www.brabys.com/bw/; business directories.

Bay Publishing: POB 832, Gaborone; tel. and fax 3937882; e-mail baybooks@orangemail.co.bw; f. 1994; Dir LENE BAY.

Botsalo Books: Gaborone International Commerce Park, Kgale, Plot 59/60, Unit 5, POB 1532, Gaborone; tel. 3912576; fax 3972608; e-mail botsalo@botsnet.bw; internet www.abcdafrica.com/botsalobooks.

The Botswana Society (BotSoc): Kgale Siding Office 1A, Kgale, POB 71, Gaborone; tel. and fax 3919745; fax 3919673; e-mail botsoc@

info.bw; internet www.botsoc.org.bw; f. 1968; archaeology, arts, history, law, sciences; Chair. JOSEPH TSONOPE.

Heinemann Educational Botswana (Pty) Ltd: Plot 20695, Unit 4, Magochanyana Rd, POB 10103, Village Post Office, Gaborone; tel. 3972305; fax 3971832; e-mail hein@info.bw; internet www.heinemann.co.za; Man. Dir LESEDI SEITEI.

Lentswe la Lesedi (Pty): POB 2365, Gaborone; tel. 3903994; fax 3914017; e-mail publisher@lightbooks.net; f. 1992; Publr CHARLES BEWLAY.

Lightbooks Publishers: Digitec House, 685 Botswana Rd, The Mall, POB 2365, Gaborone; tel. 3903994; fax 3914017; e-mail publisher@lightbooks.net; internet www.lightbooks.net; f. 1992; commercial publishing division of Lentswe la Lesedi (Pty); scholarly, research, women's issues, journals, reports; Publr CHARLES BEWLAY.

Longman Botswana (Pty) Ltd: Plot 14386, West Industrial Site, New Lobatse Rd, POB 1083, Gaborone; tel. 3922969; fax 3922682; e-mail connie.burford@pearsoned.com; f. 1981; subsidiary of Pearson Education, UK; educational; Man. Dir J. K. CHALASHIKA.

Macmillan Botswana Publishing Co (Pty) Ltd: Plot 50635, Block 10, Airport Rd, POB 1155, Gaborone; tel. 3911770; fax 3911987; e-mail leburu.siangaf@macmillan.bw; Man. Dir WIM UITERWIJK.

Medi Publishing: Phakalane Phase 1, Medie Close, Plot No. 21633, POB 47680, Gaborone; tel. 3121110; e-mail medi@it.bw; f. 1995; scholarly; Publishing Dir PORTIA TSHOAGONG.

Mmegi Publishing House (MPH): Plot 8901, Segogwane Way, Broadhurst, PMB BR 50, Gaborone; tel. 3952464; fax 3184977; e-mail editor@mmegi.bw; internet www.mmegi.bw; owned by Dikgang Publishing Co; academic and general.

Printing and Publishing Co (Botswana) (Pty) Ltd (PPCB): Plot 5634 Nakedi Rd, Broadhurst Industrial, POB 130, Gaborone; tel. 3912844; fax 3913054; e-mail ppcb@info.bw; internet www.ppcb.co.bw; educational; Man. Dir Y. MUSSA; Gen. Man. GAVIN BLAMIRE.

GOVERNMENT PUBLISHING HOUSE

Department of Government Printing and Publishing Service: PMB 0081, Gaborone; tel. 353202; fax 312001; Dir O. ANDREW SESINYI.

Broadcasting and Communications

TELECOMMUNICATIONS

Botswana Telecommunications Corpn (BTC): POB 700, Gaborone; tel. 3958000; fax 3913355; internet www.btc.bw; f. 1980; state-owned; privatization pending; fixed-line telecommunications provider; Chair. LEONARD MUSA MAKWINJA; CEO PAUL TAYLOR.

Mascom: Tsholetsa House, Plot 4705/6, Botswana Rd, Main Mall, PMB BO298, Bontleng, Gaborone; tel. 3903396; fax 3903445; e-mail backoffice@mascom.bw; internet www.mascom.bw/home; f. 1998; 60% owned by DECI; 40% owned by Econet Wireless; mobile cellular telecommunications provider; CEO JOSE VIEIRA COUCEIRO.

Orange Botswana: Camphill Bldg, Plot 43002/1, PMB BO64, Bontleng, Gaborone; tel. 3163370; fax 3163372; internet www.orange.co.bw; f. 1998 as Vista Cellular; present name adopted in 2003; 49% owned by Orange SA, France; 46% owned by Mosokelatsebeng Cellular; mobile cellular telecommunications provider; CEO PHILLIPE BAUDIN.

Regulatory Authority

Botswana Telecommunications Authority (BTA): 206–207 Independence Ave, PMB 00495, Gaborone; tel. 3957755; fax 3957976; e-mail pro@bta.org.bw; internet www.bta.org.bw; f. 1996; Chair. Dr MASEGO AYO MPOTOKWANE; CEO THARI G. PHEKO.

BROADCASTING

The Department of Information and Broadcasting operates 21 radio stations across the country from bureaux in Gaborone, Kanye, Serowe and Francistown. The National Broadcasting Board was preparing to issue three further licences for private commercial radio stations in addition to those already held by Yarona FM and GABZ FM.

Department of Information and Broadcasting: PMB 0060, Gaborone; tel. 3658000; fax 564416; e-mail otsiang@btv.gov.bw; internet www.dib.gov.bw; f. 1978 following merger between Information Services and Radio Botswana; Dir O. ANDREW SESINYI.

Radio

Radio Botswana (RB1): PMB 0060, Gaborone; tel. 3952541; fax 3957138; e-mail rbeng@info.bw; state-owned; f. 1965; fmrly Radio Bechuanaland; culture, entertainment, news and current affairs programmes; broadcasts 18 hours daily in Setswana and English; Dir ANDREW SESINYI; Head of Programmes M. GABAKGORE.

Radio Botswana (RB2) (FM 103): PMB 0060, Gaborone; tel. 3653000; fax 3653346; e-mail mmphusu@gov.bw; f. 1992; contemporary entertainment; Head of Programmes MONICA MPHUSU.

GABZ FM 96.2: PMB 319, Gaborone; tel. 3956962; fax 3181443; e-mail feedback@gabzfm.co.bw; internet www.gabzfm.com; f. 1999; owned by Thari Investment; entertainment, news and politics; broadcasts in Setswana and English; Man. Dir KENNEDY OTSHELENG.

Yarona FM 106.6: POB 1607, Gaborone; tel. 3912305; fax 3901063; e-mail info@yaronafm.co.bw; internet www.yaronafm.co.bw; f. 1999; owned by Copacabana Investment; Station Man. DUMI LOPANG.

Television

Botswana Television (BTV): PMB 0060, Gaborone; tel. 3658000; fax 3900051; e-mail marketing@btv.gov.bw; internet www.btv.gov.bw; f. 2000; broadcasts local and international programmes 8 hours daily (Mon.–Fri.) and 10 hours (Sat.–Sun.); 60% local content; Gen. Man. MOLEFHE SEJOE.

E-Botswana: Plot 53996, Mogochama St, opposite Coca Cola, POB 921, Gaborone; tel. 3957654; fax 3901875; e-mail info@ebotswana.co.bw; internet www.ebotswana.co.bw; f. 1988; present name adopted 2010; operated by Gaborone Broadcasting Co (Pty) Ltd; 49% owned by Sabido (South Africa); Setswana and English; rebroadcasts foreign TV programmes; Man. Dir MIKE KLINCK.

Finance

(cap. = capital; res = reserves; dep. = deposits; m. = million; brs = branches; amounts in pula, unless otherwise stated)

At the end of 2012 there were 10 commercial banks, one investment bank and four development financial institutions in Botswana.

BANKING

Central Bank

Bank of Botswana: POB 712, PMB 154,17938 Khama Cres., Gaborone; tel. 3606301; fax 3974859; e-mail selwej@bob.bw; internet www.bankofbotswana.bw; f. 1975; bank of issue; cap. 25m., res 34,609.1m., dep. 20,898.3m. (Dec. 2009); Gov. LINAH MOHOHLO.

Commercial Banks

BancABC: 86/384 BancABC House, Plot 62433, Fairground Office Park, POB 00303, Gaborone; tel. 3674300; fax 3901583; e-mail info@bancabc.com; internet www.bancabc.co.bw; f. 1989 as ulc (Pty) Ltd; name changed to African Banking Corpn (Pty) Ltd in 2001; present name adopted in 2009; subsidiary of ABC Holdings Ltd; financial services and investment banking; operates in Botswana, Mozambique, Tanzania, Zambia and Zimbabwe; cap. 34.1m., res 6.1m., dep. 1,405.0m. (Dec. 2009); Chair. HOWARD BUTTERY; CEO DOUGLAS MUNATSI.

Bank Gaborone Ltd: Plot 5129, Pilane/Queens Rd, The Mall, PMB 00325, Gaborone; tel. 3671500; fax 3904007; e-mail info@bankgaborone.co.bw; internet www.bankgaborone.co.bw; f. 2006; cap. 175m., res 0.7m., dep. 2,259.0m. (Dec. 2012); Chair. JACOBUS CHRISTIAAN BRANDT; Man. Dir ANDRÉ BARNARD.

Bank of Baroda (Botswana) Ltd: AKD House, Plot 1108, Queens Rd, The Main Mall, Bontleng, POB 21559, Gaborone; tel. 3188878; fax 3188879; e-mail botswana@barodabank.co.bw; internet www.bankofbaroda.co.bw; f. 2001; subsidiary of the Bank of Baroda, India; Chair. S. K. JAIN; Man. Dir B. NANDHA GOPAL.

Barclays Bank of Botswana Ltd: Barclays House, 6th Floor, Plot 8842, Khama Cres., POB 478, Gaborone; tel. 3952041; fax 3913672; e-mail botswana.customerservice@barclays.com; internet www.barclays.com/africa/botswana; f. 1975 as local successor to Barclays Bank Int. Ltd; 74.9% owned by Barclays Bank PLC, UK; cap. 17.1m., res 67.5m., dep. 9,542.9m. (Dec. 2012); Chair. RIZWAN DESAI; Man. Dir AUPA MONYATSI (acting); 52 brs.

Capital Bank Ltd: Plot 17954, Old Lobatse Rd, POB 5548, Gaborone; tel. 3907801; fax 3922818; internet www.capitalbank.co.bw; f. 2007; cap. 58.5m., res 3.0m., dep. 844.4m. (Dec. 2011); CEO SRIRAM GADE.

First National Bank of Botswana Ltd: Finance House, 5th Floor, Plot 8843, Khama Cres., POB 1552, Gaborone; tel. 3642600; fax 3906130; e-mail ddesilva@fnbbotswana.co.bw; internet www.fnbbotswana.co.bw; f. 1991; 69.5% owned by First Nat. Bank Holdings Botswana Ltd; cap. 51.0m., res 256.9m., dep. 11,840.7m. (June 2012); Chair. PREMCHAND DEPAL SHAH; CEO LORATO BOAKGOMO-NTAKHWANA; 18 brs.

Stanbic Bank Botswana Ltd: Stanbic House, 1st Floor, Plot 50672, Fairground (off Machel Dr.), PMB 00168, Gaborone; tel. 3901600; fax 3900171; e-mail stanbic@mega.bw; internet www.stanbicbank.co.bw; f. 1992; subsidiary of Standard Bank Investment Corpn Africa Holdings Ltd; cap. 390.1m., res 36.8m., dep. 9,095.0m. (Dec. 2012); CEO LEINA GABARAANE; 6 brs.

Standard Chartered Bank Botswana Ltd: Standard House, 5th Floor, Plots 1124–1127, The Mall, POB 496, Gaborone; tel. 3601500; fax 3918299; internet www.standardchartered.com/bw; f. 1975; 75% owned by Standard Chartered Holdings (Africa) BV, Amsterdam; cap. 44.5m., res 60.0m., dep. 7,512.6m. (Dec. 2009); Man. Dir MOATLHODI LEKAUKAU; 11 brs; 5 agencies.

Investment Bank

Kingdom Bank Africa Limited: Plot 115, Unit 23, Kgale Mews International Financial Park, POB 45078, Riverwalk, Gaborone; tel. 3906926; fax 3906874; e-mail kbal@kingdombotswana.co.bw; internet www.kingdombotswana.com; f. 2003; 52.57% owned by Brotherhood Holdings Ltd; cap. US $5.1m., res. –1.9m., dep. $6.6m. (Dec. 2009); Chair. MICHAEL MCNAUGHT; Man. Dir SIBONGINKOSI MOYO.

Other Banks

Botswana Savings Bank: Tshomarelo House, Plot 53796, cnr Lekgarapa and Letswai Rds, Broadhurst Mall, POB 1150, Gaborone; tel. 3912555; fax 3952608; e-mail marketing@bsb.bw; internet www.bsb.bw; f. 1992; cap. and res 48.4m., dep. 101.5m. (March 2000); Chair. F. MODISE; Man. Dir LANDRICK OTENG SIANGA.

Letshego: POB 318, Gaborone; tel. 3180635; fax 3957949; e-mail letshego@info.bw; internet www.letshego.co.bw; f. 1998; micro-finance; 43.8% owned by Micro Provident Ltd; 34.9% owned by the Int. Finance Corpn, Netherlands Devt Finance Co, Pan-African Investment Partners and Pan-Commonwealth African Partners; total assets 328.0m. (Oct. 2005); Chair. LEGODILE E. SEREMA; Man. Dir FREDRICK MMELESI.

National Development Bank: Development House, Plot 1123, The Mall, POB 225, Gaborone; tel. 3952801; fax 3974446; e-mail bmojalemotho@ndb.bw; internet www.ndb.bw; f. 1963; cap. 77.7m., res 49.8m. (March 2009); Chair. LESEDI VINCENT SEITEI; CEO LORATO C. MORAPEDI; 3 brs.

STOCK EXCHANGE

Botswana Stock Exchange: Exchange House, Office Block 6, Plot 64511, Fairgrounds, PMB 00417, Gaborone; tel. 3180201; fax 3180175; e-mail enquiries@bse.co.bw; internet www.bse.co.bw; f. 1989; commenced formal functions of a stock exchange in 1995; Chair. LIPALESA SIWAWA; CEO Dr HIRAN MENDIS; 27 cos and 32 securities firms listed in 2004.

INSURANCE

At the end of 2012 there were 20 insurance companies in Botswana, of which seven were life insurers.

Botswana Eagle Insurance Co Ltd: Eagle House, Plot 54479, Fairgrounds, POB 1221, Gaborone; tel. 3188888; fax 3188911; e-mail john.main@botswanaeagle.co.za; f. 1976; subsidiary of Zurich Insurance Co South Africa Ltd, fmrly South African Eagle Insurance Co Ltd; Man. JOHN MAIN.

Botswana Insurance Co. Ltd: BIC House, Gaborone Business Park, Plot 50372, Gaborone Show Grounds, POB 715, Gaborone; tel. 3600500; fax 3972867; internet www.bic.co.bw; f. 1975; Man. Dir DZIKAMANI NGANUNU.

Botswana Insurance Holdings Ltd (BIHL): Block A, Fairground Office Park, POB 336, Gaborone; tel. 3645100; fax 3905884; f. 1975; 54% owned by African Life Assurance Co Ltd (Aflife), South Africa; total assets 80.8m. (Dec. 2006); Chair. BATSHO DAMBE-GROTH; CEO REGINA SIKALESELE-VAKA.

Botswana Life Insurance Ltd: Block A, Fairground Office Park, Plot 50676, Gaborone; tel. 3645100; fax 3905884; e-mail Webmaster@blil.co.bw; internet www.botswanalifeinsurance.com; subsidiary of BIHL; life insurance; CEO CATHERINE LESETEDI-LETEGELE.

General Insurance Botswana (GIB): 767 Tati Rd, PMB 00315, Gaborone; tel. 3184310; fax 3950008; internet www.gib.co.bw; Man. Dir SOPHIE K. TSHEOLE.

Hollard Insurance Botswana: Plot 50676, 2nd Floor, Block A, BIFM Bldg, Fairgrounds Business Park, POB 45029, Gaborone; tel. 3958023; fax 3958024; internet www.hollard.co.bw; Man. THEMBA MPOFU.

Metropolitan Life of Botswana Ltd: Standard House, 1st Floor, Queens Rd, Main Mall, PMB 231, Gaborone; tel. 3624300; fax 3624423; e-mail omothibatsela@metropolitan.co.bw; internet www.metropolitan.co.bw; f. 1996; 75% owned by Metropolitan South Africa, 25% owned by the Botswana Devt Corpn; Man. Dir OUPA MOTHIBATSELA.

Mutual and Federal Insurance Co of Botswana Ltd: Bldg B, Fairground Office Park, PMB 00347, Gaborone; tel. 3903333; fax 3903400; e-mail jbekker@mf.co.za; f. 1994; subsidiary of Mutual and Federal, South Africa; Man. Dir JACK BEKKER.

Regent Insurance Botswana: Plot 50370, Twin Towers, East Wing Fairgrounds Office Park, PMB BR 203, Gaborone; tel. 3188153; fax 3188063; Man. Dir A. A. BOTES; also **Regent Life Botswana**, life insurance.

Regulatory Authority

Non-Bank Financial Institutions Regulatory Authority (NBFIRA): MVA House, 1st Floor, Showgrounds, Private Bag 00314, Gaborone; tel. and fax 3102595; internet www.nbfira.org.bw; Chair. M. DUBE; CEO O. M. RAMASEDI.

Trade and Industry

GOVERNMENT AGENCIES

Botswana Housing Corpn (BHC): Plot 4773, cnr Mmaraka and Station Rds, POB 412, Gaborone; tel. 3605100; fax 3952070; e-mail info@bhc.bw; internet www.bhc.bw; f. 1971; provides housing for central govt and local authority needs and assists with private sector housing schemes; Chair. BOJOSI K. OTHOGILE; CEO MOOTIEMANG REGINALD MOTSWAISO.

Citizen Entrepreneurial Development Agency (CEDA): Leseding House, 1st Floor, Plot 204, Independence Ave, PMB 00504, Gaborone; tel. 3170895; fax 3170896; e-mail info@ceda.co.bw; internet www.ceda.co.bw; f. 2001; develops and promotes citizen-owned enterprises; provides business training and financial assistance; Chair. LUCAS PHIRIE GAKALE; CEO THABO PRINCE THAMANE.

Competition Authority: Paledi Morrison House, Ground Floor, Fairgrounds, Plot 50664, PMB 00101, Gaborone; tel. 3934278; e-mail competitionauthority@gmail.com; internet www.competitionauthority.co.bw; f. 2011; monitors, controls and prohibits anti-competitive trade or business practices; Chair. Dr ZEIN KEBONANG; CEO THULA GILBERT KAIRA.

Department of Town and Regional Planning: PMB 0042, Gaborone; tel. 3658596; fax 3913280; e-mail rchephethe@gov.bw; f. 1972; responsible for physical planning policy and implementation; Dir R. CHEPHETHE.

Public Enterprises Evaluation and Privatisation Agency (PEEPA): Twin Towers, East Wing, 2nd Floor, Fairground Office Park, PMB 00510, Gaborone; tel. 3188807; fax 3188662; e-mail peepa@peepa.co.bw; internet www.peepa.co.bw; f. 2001; responsible for commercializing and privatizing public parastatals; Chair. B. MAROLE; CEO KGOTLA RAMAPHANE.

DEVELOPMENT ORGANIZATIONS

Botswana Council of Non-Governmental Organisations (BOCONGO): Bonokopila House, Plot 53957, Machel Dr., PMB 00418, Gaborone; tel. 3911319; fax 3912935; e-mail bocongo@bocongo.org.bw; internet www.bocongo.org.bw; Chair. OSCAR MOTSUMI; 84 mem. orgs.

Botswana Development Corpn Ltd: Moedi, Plot 50380, Gaborone International Showgrounds (off Machel Dr.), PMB 160, Gaborone; tel. 3651300; fax 3904193; e-mail enquiries@bdc.bw; internet www.bdc.bw; f. 1970; Chair. BLACKIE MAROLE; Man. Dir MARIA M. NTHEBOLAN.

Botswana Investment and Trade Centre (BITC): Plot 54351, Exponential Building, next to Masa Centre, Private Bag 00445, Gaborone; tel. 3633300; fax 3170452; e-mail enquiries@bitc.co.bw; internet www.bitc.co.bw; f. 2012; following merger of the Botswana Export Development and Investment Authority (BEDIA) and the Botswana International Financial Services Centre; promotes and facilitates local and foreign investment, and the devt of cross-border financial services based in Botswana; Chair. VICTOR SENNYE; CEO LETSEBE SEJOE (acting).

RETENG: the Multicultural Coalition of Botswana: POB 402786, Gaborone; tel. 71654345 (mobile); fax 3937779; f. 2003; umbrella org. composed of human rights advocacy and conservation groups, and public service and private sector unions; Sec.-Gen. Prof. LYDIA NYATHI-RAMAHOBO.

INDUSTRIAL AND TRADE ASSOCIATIONS

Botswana Agricultural Marketing Board (BAMB): Plot 130, Unit 3–4, Gaborone International Finance Park, Nkwe Sq., PMB 0053, Gaborone; tel. 3951341; fax 3952926; e-mail info@bamb.co.bw; internet www.bamb.co.bw; Chair. D. TIBE; CEO E. NCAAGAE (acting).

Botswana Meat Commission (BMC): Plot 621, 1 Khama Ave, PMB 4, Lobatse; tel. 5330321; fax 5332228; e-mail marketing@bmc.bw; internet www.bmc.bw; f. 1966; slaughter of livestock, export of hides and skins, carcasses, frozen and chilled boneless beef; operates tannery and beef products cannery; CEO Dr AKOLANG RUSSIA TOMBALE (acting); Gen. Man. JOHNSON BOJOSI.

EMPLOYERS' ORGANIZATIONS

Botswana Chamber of Mines (BCM): Plot 22, Khama Cres., POB AD 80 ABE Postnet, Kgaleview, Gaborone; tel. 3914685; fax 3914684; e-mail bcm@info.bw; internet www.bcm.org.bw; Pres. MONTY MPHATHI; CEO CHARLES SIWAWA.

Botswana Confederation of Commerce, Industry and Manpower (BOCCIM): BOCCIM House, Old Lobatse Rd, Plot 5196, POB 432, Gaborone; tel. 3953459; fax 3973142; e-mail publicrelations@boccim.co.bw; internet www.boccim.co.bw; f. 1971; Pres. LEKWALO LETA MOSIENYANE; CEO MARIA MACHAILO-ELLIS; 2,000 mems.

Botswana Teachers' Union (BTU): Unit 21, Kgale Court, Gaborone; PMB 0019, Mogoditshane; tel. 3906774; fax 3909838; e-mail btu@it.bw; internet www.botswanateachersunion.org; f. 1937 as the Bechuanaland Protectorate African Teachers' Asscn; present name adopted 1966; Pres. SIMON MAPULELO; Sec.-Gen. IBO NANA KENOSI; 13,000 mems.

UTILITIES

Electricity

Botswana Power Corpn (BPC): Motlakase House, Macheng Way, POB 48, Gaborone; tel. 3603000; fax 3973563; e-mail contact@bpc.bw; internet www.bpc.bw; f. 1971; parastatal; operates power station at Morupule (132 MW); Chair. EWETSE RAKHUDU; CEO JACOB N. RALERU.

Water

Department of Water Affairs: Plot No 25019, Old Lobatse Rd, Private Bag 0029, Gaborone; tel. 3607100; fax 3903508; e-mail folesitse@gov.bw; internet www.water.gov.bw; provides public water supplies for rural areas; Dir O. T. OBAKENG.

Water Utilities Corpn: PMB 00276, Gaborone; tel. 3604400; fax 3973852; e-mail contactcentre@wuc.bw; internet www.wuc.bw; f. 1970; 100% state-owned; supplies water to main urban centres; Chair. NOZIPHO MABE; CEO GODFREY WISISO MUDANGA.

CO-OPERATIVES

Department for Co-operative Development: POB 86, Gaborone; tel. 3950500; fax 3951657; e-mail vmosele@gov.bw; f. 1964; promotes marketing and supply, consumer, dairy, horticultural and fisheries co-operatives, thrift and loan societies, credit societies, a co-operative union and a co-operative bank; Commissioner VIOLET MOSELE.

TRADE UNION

Botswana Federation of Trade Unions (BFTU): POB 440, Gaborone; tel. and fax 3952534; f. 1977; Pres. ALLEN KEITSENG; Sec.-Gen. GAZHANI MHOTSHA; 25,000 mems (2001).

Transport

RAILWAYS

The 960-km railway line from Mafikeng, South Africa, to Bulawayo, Zimbabwe, passes through Botswana and has been operated by Botswana Railways (BR) since 1987. In 2010 there were 888 km of 1,067-mm-gauge track within Botswana, including three branches serving the Selebi-Phikwe mining complex (56 km), the Morupule colliery (16 km) and the Sua Pan soda-ash deposits (175 km). Through its links with Transnet, which operates the South African railways system, and the National Railways of Zimbabwe, BR provides connections with Namibia and Swaziland to the south, and an uninterrupted rail link to Zambia, the Democratic Republic of the Congo, Angola, Mozambique, Tanzania and Malawi to the north. However, freight traffic on BR was severely reduced following Zimbabwe's construction, in 1999, of a rail link from Bulawayo to Beitbridge, on its border with South Africa. In April 2009 BR suspended all passenger services owing to continuing losses. In 2010 plans were under way for the construction of a trans-Kalahari railway linking the Mmamabula coal deposits in Botswana with the port of Walvis Bay, Namibia. A 1,100-km railway project linking Botswana with a new port in southern Mozambique was also under consideration.

Botswana Railways (BR): A1 Mahalapye Main Rd, Mowana Ward, PMB 52, Mahalapye; tel. 4711375; fax 4711385; e-mail info@botrail.bw; internet www.botswanarailways.co.bw; f. 1986; Chair. RAYMOND WATSON; CEO DOMINIC NTWAAGAE.

ROADS

In 2011 there were 25,798 km of roads, including 8,916 km of secondary roads. Some 33% of the road network was paved, including a main road from Gaborone, via Francistown, to Kazungula, where the borders of Botswana, Namibia, Zambia and Zimbabwe meet. The construction of a 340-km road between Nata and Maun was completed in the late 1990s. Construction of the 600-km Trans-Kalahari Highway, from Jwaneng to the port of Walvis Bay on the Namibian coast, commenced in 1990 and was completed in 1998. A car-ferry service operates from Kazungula across the Zambezi river into Zambia.

Department of Road Transport and Safety: PMB 0054, Gaborone; tel. 3905442; e-mail amotshegwe@gov.bw; internet www.roadtransport.gov.bw; responsible for national road network; Dir ORAPELENG M. B. MOSIGI.

CIVIL AVIATION

The main international airport is at Gaborone. The four other major airports are located at Kasane, Maun, Francistown and Ghanzi. In addition, in 2000 there were 108 airfields throughout the country. Scheduled services of Air Botswana are supplemented by an active charter and business sector. In 2011 there were 14 non-scheduled air operators in Botswana.

Civil Aviation Authority of Botswana (CAAB): Plot 61920, Letsema Office Park, POB 250, Fairgrounds, Gaborone; tel. 3688200; fax 3931883; e-mail caab@caab.co.bw; internet www.caab.co.bw; f. 2009; Chair. MARK SAMPSON; CEO MAJ. GEN. (RETD) JEFFERSON G. TLHOKWANE.

Air Botswana: POB 92, Sir Seretse Khama Airport, Gaborone; tel. 3952812; fax 3974802; internet www.airbotswana.co.bw; f. 1972; 45% state-owned; domestic services and regional services to countries in eastern and southern Africa; Chair. NIGEL DIXON-WARRE; Gen. Man. SAKHILE NYONI-REILING; 150,000 passengers per year.

Moremi Air: 1st Floor, Maun Airport Bldg, PMB 187, Maun; tel. 6863632; fax 6862078; e-mail info@moremiair.com; internet www.moremiair.com; air charter operator; Gen. Man. KELLY SEROLE.

Tourism

There are three game reserves and three national parks, including Chobe, near Victoria Falls, on the Zambia–Zimbabwe border. Efforts to expand the tourism industry include plans for the construction of new hotels and the rehabilitation of existing hotel facilities. The Okavango Delta is famed for its wildlife and attracts many foreign visitors. In 2010 foreign tourist arrivals were estimated at 2.1m. Receipts from tourism totalled $218m. (excluding passenger transport) in that year.

Botswana Tourism Board: Plot 50676, Fairground Office Park, Block B, Ground Floor, Gaborone; tel. 3913111; fax 3959220; e-mail board@botswanatourism.co.bw; internet www.botswanatourism.co.bw; f. 2003; CEO BRAIN DITHEBE (acting).

Department of Wildlife and National Parks: POB 131, Gaborone; tel. 3971405; fax 3912354; e-mail dwnp@gov.bw; Dir J. MATLHARE.

Hospitality and Tourism Association of Botswana (HATAB): PMB 00423, Gaborone; tel. 3957144; fax 3903201; internet www.hatab.bw; f. 1982; fmrly Hotel and Tourism Asscn of Botswana; CEO MORONGOE NTLOEDIBE-DISELE.

Defence

Military service is voluntary. Botswana established a permanent defence force in 1977. As assessed at November 2013, the total strength of the Botswana Defence Force (BDF) was some 9,000, comprising an army of 8,500 and an air force of 500. In addition, there was a paramilitary police force of 1,500. There are plans to enlarge the strength of the army to 10,000 men. In 2007 Botswana began recruiting women into the BDF for the first time.

Defence Expenditure: Budgeted at P3,730m. in 2013.

Defence Force Commander: Maj.-Gen. TEBOGO H. C. MASIRE.

Education

Although education is not compulsory, enrolment ratios are high. Primary education begins at six years of age and lasts for up to seven years. Secondary education, beginning at the age of 13, lasts for a further five years, comprising a first cycle of three years and a second of two years. In 2012 a total of 337,206 pupils were enrolled in primary education, while a total of 171,478 pupils were enrolled in secondary education in that year. According to UNESCO estimates, enrolment at primary schools in 2009 included 84% of children in the relevant age-group (boys 83%; girls 84%), while the ratio for secondary enrolment in 2008 was 61% (boys 56%; girls 65%). Tertiary education is provided by the University of Botswana and the affiliated College of Technical and Vocational Education. A total of 17,218 students were enrolled in tertiary education in 2012. There are also more than 40 other technical and vocational training centres, including the Institutes of Health Sciences, the Botswana College of Agriculture, the Roads Training College, the Colleges of Education (Primary and Secondary), and the Botswana Institute of Administration and Commerce. Expenditure on education by the central Government in 2012/13 was budgeted at P8,444.7m. (representing 20.2% of total spending by the central Government).

BRAZIL

Introductory Survey

LOCATION, CLIMATE, LANGUAGE, RELIGION, FLAG, CAPITAL

The Federative Republic of Brazil, the fifth largest country in the world, lies in central and north-eastern South America. To the north are Venezuela, Colombia, Guyana, Suriname and French Guiana, to the west Peru and Bolivia, and to the south Paraguay, Argentina and Uruguay. Brazil has a very long coastline on the Atlantic Ocean. Climatic conditions vary from hot and wet in the tropical rainforest of the Amazon basin to temperate in the savannah grasslands of the central and southern uplands, which have warm summers and mild winters. In Rio de Janeiro temperatures are generally between 17°C (63°F) and 29°C (85°F). The official language is Portuguese. Almost all of the inhabitants profess Christianity, and about 84% are adherents of the Roman Catholic Church. The national flag (proportions 7 by 10) is green, bearing, at the centre, a yellow diamond containing a blue celestial globe with 26 white five-pointed stars (one for each of Brazil's states), arranged in the pattern of the southern firmament, below an equatorial scroll with the motto 'Ordem e Progresso' ('Order and Progress'), and a single star above the scroll. The capital is Brasília.

CONTEMPORARY POLITICAL HISTORY

Historical Context

Formerly a Portuguese possession, Brazil became an independent monarchy in 1822, and a republic in 1889. A federal constitution for the United States of Brazil was adopted in 1891. Following social unrest in the 1920s, the economic crisis of 1930 resulted in a major revolt, led by Dr Getúlio Vargas, who was installed as President. He governed the country as a benevolent dictator until forced to resign by the armed forces in December 1945. During Vargas's populist rule, Brazil enjoyed internal stability and steady economic progress. He established a strongly authoritarian corporate state, similar to fascist regimes in Europe, but in 1942 Brazil entered the Second World War on the side of the Allies.

A succession of ineffectual presidential terms (including another by Vargas, who was re-elected in 1950) failed to establish stable government in the late 1940s and early 1950s. President Jânio Quadros, elected in 1960, resigned after only seven months in office, and in September 1961 the Vice-President, João Goulart, was sworn in as President. Military leaders suspected Goulart, the leader of the Partido Trabalhista Brasileiro (PTB), of communist sympathies, and they were reluctant to let him succeed to the presidency. As a compromise, the Constitution was amended to restrict the powers of the President and to provide for a Prime Minister. However, following the appointment of three successive premiers during a 16-month period of mounting political crisis, the system was rejected when a referendum, conducted in January 1963, approved a return to the presidential system of government.

Following a period of economic crisis, exacerbated by allegations of official corruption, the left-wing regime of President Goulart was overthrown in April 1964 by a bloodless right-wing military coup led by Gen. (later Marshal) Humberto Castelo Branco, the Army Chief of Staff, who was promptly elected President by the National Congress (Congresso Nacional). In October 1965 President Castelo Branco assumed dictatorial powers, and all political parties were banned. In December, however, two artificially created parties, the pro-Government Aliança Renovadora Nacional (ARENA) and the opposition Movimento Democrático Brasileiro (MDB), were granted official recognition. Castelo Branco nominated as his successor Marshal Artur da Costa e Silva, who was elected in October 1966 and took office in March 1967 as President of the redesignated Federative Republic of Brazil (a new Constitution was introduced simultaneously). The ailing President da Costa e Silva was forced to resign in September 1969 and was replaced by a triumvirate of military leaders.

Domestic Political Affairs

The military regime granted the President wide-ranging powers to rule by decree. In October 1969 the ruling junta introduced a revised Constitution, vesting executive authority in an indirectly elected President. The National Congress, suspended since December 1968, was recalled and elected Gen. Emílio Garrastazu Médici as President. Médici was succeeded as President by Gen. Ernesto Geisel and then Gen. João Baptista de Figueiredo. Despite the attempts of both Presidents to pursue a policy of *abertura*, or opening to democratization, opposition to military rule intensified throughout the 1970s and early 1980s. In November 1982 the government-sponsored Partido Democrático Social (PDS) suffered significant losses at elections to the Câmara dos Deputados (Chamber of Deputies), state governorships and municipal councils, but secured a majority of seats in the Senado Federal (Federal Senate).

In 1984 Vice-President Antônio Chaves de Mendonça and the influential Marco de Oliveira Maciel, a former Governor of Pernambuco, formed an alliance of liberal PDS members with members of the Partido do Movimento Democrático Brasileiro (PMDB), which became an official political party, the Partido Frente Liberal (PFL). In January 1985 the PFL candidate, Tancredo Neves, was elected by electoral college as Brazil's first civilian President for 21 years. However, Neves died before being inaugurated, and the PFL vice-presidential candidate, José Sarney, took office as President in April. In May the National Congress approved a constitutional amendment restoring direct elections by universal suffrage.

Support for Sarney's Government was demonstrated in November 1986 at elections to the National Congress, which was to operate as a Constitutional Assembly (Assembleia Constitucional). The first round of voting for the presidential election was provisionally set for 15 November 1989, thereby enabling Sarney to remain in office until March 1990. This de facto victory for the President led to the resignations of some leading members of the PMDB, who formed a new centre-left party, the Partido da Social Democracia Brasileira (PSDB). The Constitution was approved by the Congresso Nacional on 22 September 1988 and promulgated in October. Among its 245 articles were provisions transferring many hitherto presidential powers to the legislature. The Constitution offered no guarantees of land reform, and was thought by many to be nationalistic and protectionist.

Brazil's first presidential election by direct voting since 1960 took place in two rounds in November and December 1989. The conservative Fernando Collor de Mello of the newly formed Partido de Reconstrução Nacional (PRN) defeated Luiz Inácio Lula da Silva of the left-wing Partido dos Trabalhadores (PT), with 53% of the votes cast. Following his inauguration in March 1990, the new President announced an ambitious programme of economic reform, the 'Collor Plan', with the principal aim of reducing inflation, which had reached a monthly rate of more than 80%. A second economic plan was implemented in February 1991. In March Collor de Mello announced further deregulation and rationalization of many state-controlled areas.

Collor de Mello's position became increasingly precarious towards the end of 1991, after accusations of mismanagement of federal funds were made against his wife and several associates. In May 1992 the President became the focus of further revelations, which appeared to implicate him in a number of corrupt practices. The National Congress established a special commission of inquiry to investigate the affair and on 29 September, after the commission had delivered its report, the Chamber of Deputies voted to proceed with the impeachment of the President for abuses of authority and position, prompting the immediate resignation of the Cabinet. In December the Senate voted overwhelmingly to proceed with Collor de Mello's impeachment and to indict the President for 'crimes of responsibility'. At the opening of the impeachment trial on 29 December, however, Collor de Mello resigned the presidency; Vice-President Itamar Franco was sworn in to serve the remainder of his term. On the following day the Senate announced the removal of the former President's political rights (including immunity from prosecution). In December 1994, however, the Supreme Federal Court voted to acquit Collor de Mello of charges of passive corruption and criminal association, owing to insufficient evidence. In January 1998 the former President was cleared of charges of illegal enrichment.

Allegations of corruption and misconduct preceding the elections in October 1994 forced the replacement of the vice-presidential running mates of both Minister of the Economy Fernando Henrique Cardoso and of Lula da Silva and the withdrawal from the contest of the presidential candidate of the Partido Liberal (PL). Cardoso, whose candidacy was supported by the PFL, the PTB, the PL and the business community, won the presidential contest in the first round, following a campaign that had focused largely on the success of his economic initiatives, which included the introduction of a new currency, the real.

Cardoso's presidency

Cardoso was inaugurated as President on 1 January 1995. Opposition to the ongoing programme of economic stabilization and to renewed efforts by the Government to introduce constitutional amendments, including those that would end state monopolies in the telecommunications and petroleum sectors, resulted in a general strike in May. A number of amendments, including to the petroleum and telecommunication sectors, were none the less subsequently approved by the Senate.

By December 1995, however, Cardoso's integrity had been seriously compromised by the alleged involvement of a number of his political associates in irregular financial transactions organized by the Banco Econômico, and by an influence-peddling scandal arising from the award to a US company of the contract for development of an Amazon Regional Surveillance System (Sivam). Investigation of the so-called 'pink folder' of politicians, recovered from the ailing Banco Econômico, continued during 1996, as the banking sector was plunged into further crisis.

In 1996 the Government announced details of the next phase of its massive divestment programme. Several companies in the power sector and 31 ports were among those state concerns to be offered for sale. In March 1997 legislation was approved ending the long-standing monopoly of Petróleo Brasileiro, SA (Petrobras).

In October 1998 Cardoso, again the PSDB's candidate, became the first President to be re-elected for a second consecutive term, following a constitutional amendment in the previous year. At the concurrent legislative elections, the PSDB also performed well, as did its electoral allies—the PFL, PMDB, Partido Progressista (PP) and PTB.

In January 1999 Itamar Franco, the newly elected Governor of Minas Gerais, declared that the state was defaulting on its debt to the federal Government, indirectly precipitating the devaluation of the Brazilian currency. In the same month the National Congress endorsed long-proposed reforms to the country's munificent pension system, considerably enhancing the prospects of President Cardoso's programme of fiscal austerity. However, the Government suffered a setback in March following the withdrawal of the PTB from the ruling coalition.

In October 1999 a congressional commission of inquiry into allegations of organized crime exposed a nationwide criminal network that allegedly encompassed politicians, government and banking officials, judges, police officers and business executives. Embarrassed by the scale of the revelations, Cardoso announced the establishment of a new anti-corruption force. In an effort to improve accountability and to strengthen congressional powers of investigation, the Senate approved a constitutional amendment to restrict presidential use of provisional measures, to which successive Governments had frequently resorted as a means to circumvent the cumbersome legislative process.

At the presidential election of 6 October 2002, Lula, once again the PT's candidate, secured 46% of the votes cast in the first round. José Serra, the government-backed PMDB candidate, was second placed, followed by Partido Socialista Brasileiro (PSB) nominee Anthony Garotinho. Lula defeated Serra in a second round of voting on 27 October, securing a record 61% of the votes cast. At the congressional elections, also held on 6 October, Lula's party took 91 of the 513 seats in the Chamber of Deputies and increased its representation in the Senate to 14 seats.

Lula's first term

President Lula took office on 2 January 2003. The new President needed support from the centrist parties in order to form a Government, and duly entered a coalition agreement with the PFL and the PMDB. Lula's new Cabinet was dominated by members of the PT, although it also included representatives from the Partido Popular Socialista (PPS), the Partido Democrático Trabalhista (PDT), the PSB and the PL. Lula affirmed his intention to proceed with a promised 'zero hunger' poverty alleviation programme funded by spending cuts, to effect public sector pension reform, and to modernize Brazil's tax system. By the end of the year the Government had enacted legislation taxing public sector pensions and raising the retirement age, despite discontent among government workers and the PT's traditional allies in the trade union movement. Changes to the tax system, which included standardizing the rate of value-added tax (which varied between states) and replacing the federal property tax with a state levy had also been approved by the Congress.

In 2004 evidence emerged that the former deputy of Cabinet Chief José Dirceu, Waldomiro Diniz, had offered government contracts in exchange for contributions towards the 2002 presidential campaign from the head of an illegal gambling operation in the state of Rio de Janeiro. In 2006 a parliamentary investigation committee recommended that Diniz, as well as former Minister of Finance Antônio Palocci (see below) and a close associate of the President, Paulo Okamoto, be indicted on corruption charges.

Divisions within the Government emerged in December 2004 when the PPS left the coalition. One day later members of the PMDB also departed the coalition Government, citing Lula's failure to pursue an active social policy. However, the party's two cabinet members and several of its senators and deputies refused to abide by the decision (the vote was ruled invalid by the high court).

In June 2005 footage was shown on national television that appeared to show proof that bribes had been offered to employees of the state-run postal service and a reinsurance company in return for contracts. A recipient of the bribes accused Roberto Jefferson, the President of the PTB, of organizing the cash incentive scheme; Jefferson denied the allegation and, in turn, accused the PT leadership of running a system of institutional bribery in 2003 and 2004. Under this scheme, deputies from other parties allegedly received a monthly allowance (*mensalão*) for supporting government-sponsored legislation. Jefferson cited Dirceu as the organizer of the scheme. Dirceu resigned, followed in July by Sílvio Pereira, Delúbio Soares and José Genoíno, respectively Secretary-General, Treasurer and President of the PT. Dirceu was replaced as Cabinet Chief by Dilma Vana Rousseff.

In August 2005 Valdemar Costa Neto, the President of the PL, a party allied to the Government, resigned owing to his alleged involvement in the *mensalão* scheme. Lula's problems worsened when his Minister of Finance, Antônio Palocci, was also accused of having accepted illegal payments. At the end of August Jefferson further alleged that the PT also received payments from a state-owned electricity company. A congressional report into the *mensalão* and post office corruption scandals published in September recommended that 18 deputies, including Dirceu, be impeached for their role in the affairs. All but one of the deputies belonged to the PT or allied parties. In mid-September the legislature voted to dismiss Jefferson from the Chamber of Deputies. One week later Severino Cavalcanti, the President of the Chamber of Deputies (and a member of the PP), resigned following allegations that he too had accepted bribes, although this was unconnected to the *mensalão* scandal.

In November 2005 the congressional committee investigating the corruption scandals concluded that the PT had given money to deputies from pro-Government parties in return for legislative support. It also reported that public funds had been illegally transferred to the PT. It recommended that former PT Treasurer Soares be charged in relation to the bribes and related money-laundering. In December Dirceu was finally dismissed from the Chamber of Deputies after deputies voted to impeach him. In August 2007 the Supreme Federal Court indicted 40 people on charges related to the *mensalão* affair, including Jefferson, Dirceu, Soares and Genoíno. (Their trial took place in the second half of 2012—see Mensalão trial.)

Palocci resigned as Minister of Finance in March 2006. He was replaced by Guido Mantega, President of the Banco Nacional do Desenvolvimento Econômico e Social and a former minister.

In the first round of voting in the 2006 presidential election, held on 1 October, Lula failed to secure the necessary amount of votes to avoid a run-off ballot, garnering 49% of the valid votes cast, while Geraldo Alckmin, the former Governor of the state of São Paulo and the PSDB's candidate, won 42% of the ballot. Nevertheless, in a second round ballot on 29 October Lula comfortably secured a second term in office, attracting some 61% of the valid votes. In the congressional elections, also held on 1 October, the PMDB won the most seats, 89, in the 513-seat lower chamber, while the PT returned 83 deputies. The PSDB and the PFL both secured 65 seats, followed by the PP with 42 and the PFL (an ally of the PSDB) with 27. Some 27 seats were contested in the 81-seat Senate: following voting the PMDB held 20 upper house seats, the PFL and the PSDB 16 each, the PT 12, and the PTB and the PDT four each. Lacking an absolute majority in the Congress, the President immediately announced that he intended to govern 'by consensus' in his second term. To this end, in November he secured the congressional support of the PT and of most of the factions of the internally divided PMDB.

Lula's second term

President Lula was inaugurated on 1 January 2007. The President declared that his main priority in his second term in office would be economic growth and the poverty alleviation programmes initiated in his first term, in particular the successful Bolsa Família (Family Allowance) cash transfer programme.

Cases of corruption continued to affect the Lula administration. In May 2007 a police investigation into embezzlement of federal funds implicated the Minister of Mines and Energy, Silas Rondeau, as well as two state governors. Rondeau resigned, although he maintained his innocence. Later in May the magazine *Veja* alleged that the President of the Senate, Renan Calheiros, a close ally of Lula, had accepted bribes from the construction company Mendes Júnior. The Senate's ethics committee recommended the impeachment of Calheiros, but a substantial majority of senators voted not to indict him. None the less, he resigned as President in December, following the emergence of evidence of his involvement in further illegal practices. The controversy surrounding Calheiros contributed to the Senate's rejection, later in December, of legislation to extend a temporary tax on financial transactions for a further four-year period, representing the Government's first major defeat in the Congress. Meanwhile, Walfrido dos Mares Guia, the Minister of Institutional Relations, also resigned in November after being accused by the public prosecution service of fraud in a 1998 gubernatorial election.

In February 2009 the PMDB's candidates, Michel Temer, the party leader, and José Sarney, a former President (1985–90), secured the presidencies of both the Chamber of Deputies and the Senate, respectively. The PMDB strengthened its position further by gaining control of an additional two states in February and April, bringing its total to nine, following the impeachment of the Governors of Paraíba (of the PSDB) and Maranhão (of the PDT), after they were found guilty by the Higher Electoral Court of bribing voters in gubernatorial elections in 2006.

Tension between senators of the PMDB and the PT delayed the passage of legislation in the first half of 2009, amid mutual allegations of corruption, including the misuse of arrangements to compensate legislators for expenses. It also emerged that appointed employees of the Senate had been paid R $6.2m. in overtime in January 2009, when the upper house was in recess. In March Sarney initiated a review of the Senate's administrative structure, which revealed that 'secret directives' had been issued to appoint political associates of senators to administrative positions in the upper house and to reinstate officials who had been dismissed following accusations of corruption. Although senators from all the major parties were alleged to have benefited from these directives, attention was focused particularly on Sarney, who had also presided over the Senate in 1995–97, when the practice was believed to have been introduced, and several of whose relatives were alleged to have been on the upper chamber's payroll, despite not having worked there. The PSDB and Demócratas (DEM—as the PFL had been renamed in 2007) withdrew their support for Sarney in June, but Lula, who hoped to secure the support of Sarney's PMDB for his preferred successor, Cabinet Chief Rousseff, in the 2010 presidential election, staunchly defended the senate President, and in August the chamber's ethics committee decided not to investigate the accusations any further.

In August 2009 Lula submitted to the National Congress a proposed new regulatory framework for the exploitation of major offshore petroleum and natural gas reserves discovered in 2007, envisaging overall state control and the extensive involvement of Petrobras. The framework was approved and signed into law in December 2010. Petrobras was to be the sole operator for all new projects in the offshore fields and was to hold a minimum 30% stake in all new joint venture agreements. However, Lula vetoed a plan to divide the income from royalties and tax revenue related to the oil sector equally between all states and municipalities.

Another corruption scandal emerged in November 2009, involving the Governor of the Federal District of Brasília, José Roberto Arruda of the DEM, and a number of other politicians from various parties. Arruda was accused of receiving illegal payments from lobbyists and companies seeking to win contracts for public works projects. He was arrested in February 2010 and his gubernatorial mandate was revoked in March.

2010 general election

Lula strongly supported Rousseff's candidacy for the PT presidential nomination: his regular attendance, with Rousseff, in 2009 and 2010 at the inauguration of infrastructure projects funded under the Government's Growth Acceleration Programme (Programa de Aceleração do Crescimento—PAC), which was principally co-ordinated by the Cabinet Chief, prompted opposition parties to accuse the President of using the events to campaign prematurely on Rousseff's behalf. (The Higher Electoral Court upheld a complaint by the PSDB to that effect in March 2010, fining Lula R $5,000.) In October the PMDB agreed to support Rousseff's presidential bid in return for the vice-presidential candidacy.

Rousseff was confirmed as the PT's presidential candidate in February 2010. Serra declared his presidential candidacy for the PSDB in April. Rousseff and eight other ministers also resigned from the Government in order to run for office in October. Former Minister of the Environment Marina Silva, who had resigned from the PT in 2009, confirmed her presidential candidacy for the Partido Verde in May. A number of controversies subsequently threatened to damage Rousseff's electoral prospects, including claims that government officials had illegally accessed the tax and bank account details of several senior PSDB politicians and of members of Serra's family and passed them to Rousseff's campaign team. Moreover, Rousseff's successor, Erenice Guerra, was forced to resign as Cabinet Chief in September following corruption allegations.

In the first round of voting in the presidential election, held on 3 October 2010, Rousseff failed to secure sufficient votes to avoid a run-off ballot, winning 46.9% of the valid votes cast, while Serra obtained 32.6%. In third place, securing a far greater share of the ballot than forecast, was Marina Silva, with 19.3% of the valid votes cast. The six other candidates all took less than 1% of the ballot. Some 81.9% of the electorate participated in the poll. Rousseff defeated Serra in a second round of voting on 31 October, receiving 56.0% of the valid votes cast. A turnout of 78.5% was recorded. The PT and its allies also performed well at the congressional elections, held concurrently with the first round of the presidential vote, securing a majority of seats in both chambers. The PT became the largest party in the 513-member Chamber of Deputies, with 88 seats, while the PMDB won 79, the Partido da República (PR) and the PP 41 each, the PSB 34 and the PDT 28. The opposition PSDB and DEM secured 53 and 43 seats, respectively, in the lower house. The PT also increased its representation in the Senate (where 54 of the 81 seats were contested), to 15 seats, while the PMDB retained the most upper house seats, with 20; following the election, other allied parties held an additional 19 seats, including the PR, the PP and the PDT, with four each, and the PSB, with three. The PSDB was represented by 11 senators, and the DEM and the PTB by six each. In gubernatorial elections, 16 of the 27 governors elected were deemed to be supportive of Rousseff.

Rousseff in office

Rousseff took office as Brazil's first female President on 1 January 2011. Her 37-member coalition Government included 17 ministers from the PT and six from the PMDB, as well as representatives of the PP, the PSB, the PDT, the PR and the Partido Comunista do Brasil (PC do B) and a number of independents. The new administration was expected broadly to continue the social and economic policies of its predecessor, with the reform of the education sector and the eradication of extreme poverty identified as particular priorities. This continuity was signalled by the retention of several ministers from the outgoing Cabinet, while Antônio Palocci, Rousseff's election campaign manager, notably returned to the Government as Cabinet Chief.

Rousseff's first year in office was marked by the resignations of seven ministers from her Cabinet, in six cases following their alleged implication in corruption scandals (although they all refuted the accusations). First to stand down, in June 2011, was Palocci, after a newspaper reported that his personal wealth had increased 20-fold during 2006–10, when he had worked as a political consultant while also serving as a deputy. Palocci denied any wrongdoing. He was replaced as Cabinet Chief by Gleisi Hoffmann. Palocci's departure was followed in July 2011 by that of the Minister of Transport, Alfredo Nascimento, amid allegations of irregularities in the granting of public works contracts. Paulo Sérgio Passos succeeded Nascimento. Two PMDB ministers resigned in August: the Minister of Defence, Nelson Jobim, after reportedly criticizing government colleagues; and the Minister of Agriculture, Livestock and Food Supply, Wagner Rossi, following accusations that he had accepted bribes from agricultural companies. Celso Amorim was appointed to head the Ministry of Defence, while Mendes Ribeiro replaced Rossi. In a further setback for Rousseff, the PR announced its withdrawal from the ruling coalition that month. The Government retained its congressional majorities, however, and the PR allowed Passos, its only representative in the Cabinet, to remain in his post. In September the Minister of Tourism, Pedro Novais of the PMDB, resigned from the Cabinet over accusations that he had used public funds to employ domestic staff; in the previous month, moreover, Novais's deputy minister and more than 30 other officials at the Ministry of Tourism had been arrested in connection with a separate investigation into alleged embezzlement of public funds. The Minister of Sport, Orlando Silva of the PC do B, stood down from office in October after allegations of his involvement in a ministry scheme in which illicit payments were received from non-governmental organizations (NGOs). José Aldo Rebelo, also of the PC do B, succeeded him. Finally, in December Carlos Lupi, the PDT Minister of Labour and Employment, resigned when he and other officials at his ministry were also accused, *inter alia*, of demanding payments from NGOs in return for funding or contracts. The Government suffered yet another casualty in February of that year when the Minister of Cities, Mário Negromonte, resigned after allegations of corruption.

Nevertheless, President Rousseff's popularity remained high, indicating public admiration for her professed 'zero tolerance' approach to corruption. Several further government changes, this time not related to corruption, took place in early 2012. Fernando Haddad resigned as Minister of Education in January in order to contest the mayoralty of São Paulo for the PT in municipal elections scheduled to be held in October; he was replaced by Aloízio Mercadante. Marcelo Bezerra Crivella succeeded the PT's Luiz Sérgio Nobrega de Oliveira as Minister of Fisheries and Aquaculture in February, and in the following month Gilberto José Vargas of the PT was appointed as Minister of Agrarian Development, replacing party colleague Alfonso Florence.

Meanwhile, notwithstanding the instability caused by the tensions and frequent changes within her Cabinet, Rousseff attempted to proceed with implementing her election pledges. In June 2011 she launched the Brasil Sem Miséria social welfare plan, which aimed to lift 16.2m. Brazilians out of extreme poverty by 2014, partly through the expansion of existing initiatives, such as the Bolsa Família programme, and by increasing access to essential services, including utilities, education, health care and housing. A new centrist party, the Partido Social Democrático (PSD), led by the incumbent mayor of São Paulo, Gilberto Kassab (formerly of the DEM), pledged its legislative support for Rousseff's coalition following its registration in September 2011. Comprising dissidents from the opposition DEM and PSDB, among other parties, the PSD became the third largest party in the Chamber of Deputies, displacing the PSDB. Legislation providing for the creation of a National Truth Commission, which had provoked controversy when first proposed in 2009, was finally approved by the Congress in October and enacted by Rousseff in November. The seven-member Commission was inaugurated in May 2012, with a two-year mandate to investigate human rights violations committed in Brazil between 1946 and 1988.

A strike in Bahia by military police officers demanding a pay rise led to a significant increase in violent crime in the north-eastern state in February 2012, with the murder rate approximately doubling. In response, the Government dispatched some 3,000 troops to Bahia to restore order and to end the occupation of the state legislature by 245 police officers, while the Governor of the state agreed to a salary increase. Meanwhile, military and civil police officers in the state of Rio de Janeiro also undertook industrial action in February.

Tensions between the President and the ruling coalition parties were evident in March 2012, when the National Congress refused to endorse Rousseff's decision to reappoint a technocrat to serve a second term as Director-General of the national land transport agency, the Agência Nacional de Transportes Terrestres, with the PMDB, in particular, aggrieved at perceived sidelining by the President. Rousseff promptly sought to reassert her authority, replacing the coalition leaders in both congressional chambers. Meanwhile, a new political scandal emerged when several legislators and state governors were implicated in an illegal gambling and money-laundering operation allegedly run by businessman Carlos Augusto Ramos, who had been arrested in February. A parliamentary committee of inquiry was established in April to investigate Ramos's political links. One of those under investigation, Demóstenes Torres, a senator representing the DEM, resigned from his party that month and was expelled from the Senate in July.

Municipal elections were conducted on 7 and 28 October 2012. In São Paulo the PT mayoral candidate, Fernando Haddad, secured a notable victory in a second round of voting, narrowly defeating Serra of the PSDB. However, the PT failed to win its other main target, the mayoralty of Salvador, capital of Bahia, where the DEM candidate, Antônio Carlos Magalhães Neto was successful, while Eduardo Paes of the PMDB was overwhelmingly re-elected as mayor of Rio de Janeiro. Overall, the PT increased the number of municipalities it controlled, but lost five state capitals to its coalition ally, the PSB. The recently formed PSD also performed well, largely at the expense of the DEM.

Mensalão trial

The trial of those accused of involvement in the *mensalão* scandal, which first emerged in June 2005 (see Lula's first term), commenced in August 2012 and was concluded in December. Of the 37 defendants, 25 were convicted by the Supreme Federal Court for their role in the incentive scheme, under which the PT paid deputies from other parties a monthly allowance from public funds in return for their support for government-sponsored legislation. Businessman Marcos Valério de Souza, who was found guilty of operating the scheme, was sentenced to more than 40 years' imprisonment, with several of his associates also receiving long prison sentences. Among the most prominent politicians charged, Dirceu was convicted of bribery and conspiracy and was sentenced to 10 years and 10 months in prison, while Soares, Jefferson and Genoíno received prison terms of between six and eight years. Fines were also imposed on those convicted. The court ruled that three serving deputies convicted in the case should lose their congressional seats: João Paulo Cunha of the PT (who was President of the Câmara dos Deputados in 2003–05), Pedro Henry Neto of the PP and Valdemar Costa Neto of the PR (formerly of the PL). Several of those convicted announced plans to appeal against their sentences, including Genoíno, who was controversially sworn in as a member of the Chamber of Deputies in January 2013 (replacing a deputy who had been elected as a mayor in the municipal elections). Meanwhile, a further corruption scandal emerged in November 2012, when six people were arrested at government offices in Brasília and São Paulo on suspicion of awarding government contracts to private companies in return for bribes. President Rousseff dismissed all those accused of involvement, who included the cabinet chief of the regional office of the presidency in São Paulo, the Deputy Attorney-General and the directors of two federal agencies.

A protracted dispute over the division of income from royalties related to the oil sector was renewed in early November 2012, when a new regulatory framework was endorsed by the Chamber of Deputies, having already been approved by the Senate. The issue had first provoked controversy in late 2010, when President Lula had vetoed a plan to divide the royalties income equally between all states and municipalities, whether oil-producing (Rio de Janeiro, Espírito Santo and São Paulo) or not, and in November 2011 a new proposal to increase the share of royalties received by non-producing states had prompted a protest in Rio de Janeiro by more than 100,000 people, led by Governor Sérgio Cabral. The need to finalize the framework had become increasingly urgent as auctions for new oil concessions could not take place until a new system had been agreed. In late November 2012 some 200,000 people participated in a demonstration in Rio de Janeiro against the newly approved framework, which would lower the share of royalties apportioned to oil-producing states from 26% to 20%. Cabral claimed that his state could lose some R $77,000m. in revenue from royalties by 2020 under the arrangements approved by the National Congress, which would hinder its ability to host the 2016 Olympic Games. At the end of the month President Rousseff vetoed provisions of the framework that would have affected existing concessions and added a measure mandating that 100% of the royalties derived from future concessions be allocated to education. An initial attempt by non-oil-producing states to overturn Rousseff's veto failed in December, when the Supreme Federal Court granted an injunction (sought by oil-producing states) blocking a fast-track congressional vote on the matter. Consequently, in March 2013 both houses of the Congress approved the law; however, later in the month the state of Rio de Janeiro successfully appealed to the Supreme Federal Court to suspend implementation of the law, on the grounds that it affected state income. The law was finally passed by the Chamber of Deputies on 14 August (having already been approved by the Senate) and decreed that 75% of the federal Government's royalties from future concessions be allocated to education and the remaining 25% to health programmes. None the less, the allocation of the royalties between oil-producing and non-oil-producing states remained unresolved.

On 4 February 2013 Henrique Eduardo Alves of the PMDB was elected President of the Chamber of Deputies, three days after Renan Calheiros was voted in as chairman of the Senate for the third time, giving the PMDB a commanding position within parliament. A few days later over 100 national guard officers were deployed in the city of Florianópolis, in Santa Catarina state, to help combat the wave of violence against local security forces that had started at the end of January, organized by crime gangs within state prisons, apparently in an effort to improve conditions for inmates. The unrest continued into the following week, when further reinforcements were sent to the region.

On 18 February 2013 port workers in Santos seized a Chinese ship in protest at the Government's proposed privatization of a number of Brazilian ports, which was intended to attract US $27,600m. in investment to the sector. However, a national strike, scheduled for the end of March, was called off after successful negotiations between the Government and the workers, grouped under the Força Sindical union. On 16 May legislation to allow the ports sector to open up to private investment was passed by the National Congress.

On 18 May 2013 the PSDB elected Aécio Neves, senator for Minas Gerais, to the party leadership with an overwhelming majority. Neves had the backing of former President Cardoso, as well as party figures hitherto associated with defeated presidential candidate José Serra. Following his election Serra offered Neves his full support, as did Governor of São Paulo Geraldo Alckmin which, with the landslide nature of his victory, suggested that he would contest the presidency on behalf of the PSDB in 2014.

Recent developments: civil unrest

A rise in public transport fares in early June 2013 gave rise to several weeks of public protests across the country, the worst civil unrest in Brazil for two decades, which, at its peak, on 20 June, involved over 1m. demonstrators. The protests began in São Paulo the day after the fare increase, on 11 June, with some 10,000 people gathering in the city centre. Violence broke out when the police attempted to disperse the crowds. By 17 June, as the FIFA Confederations Cup got under way, some 200,000 had taken to the streets of the major cities. Apart from the rise in transport costs demonstrators cited as their grievances the rate of inflation, widespread corruption, the massive public expenditure on preparations for the FIFA World Cup in 2014 and poor public services. On 24 June Rousseff, following a meeting with the organizers of the demonstration, the Movimento Passe Libre, along with state governors and city mayors, made a televised address in which she proposed that the National Congress approve a referendum on widespread political reform. The President, who was experiencing the first fall in popularity since taking office, also called for increased spending on public transport, health care and education. The following day, responding to one of the demands of the protesters, parliament rejected a controversial law that would have removed the role of federal prosecutors in conducting investigations into criminal activities within the Government, giving exclusive power to the police. Despite these measures, the protests continued, with a crowd of some 50,000 demonstrating outside a football stadium in Belo Horizonte at the time of the Confederation Cup semi-final match on 26 June. On 2 July Rousseff presented five proposed political reforms to be put to a national plebiscite by the start of October; this was declared unfeasible, however, by both Alves and Vice-President Michel Miguel Elias Temer Lulia, also of the PMDB. On 11 July the country's major trade unions staged a general strike (the first in 22 years) to demand improvements in public services and a reduction in the working week to 40 hours. Although the organizers of the strike claimed that some 100,000 had participated, figures were thought to be considerably lower.

Two high-profile corruption scandals emerged in mid-2013. The first concerned alleged anti-competitive practices in relation to the construction and maintenance of the train and metro networks in São Paulo and Brasília, which involved several foreign engineering companies including Siemens (of Germany), Mitsui (of Japan) and Alstom (of France). An investigation into the possible price-rigging cartel by the Brazilian authorities was announced in mid-July. Siemens, which had admitted to belonging to the cartel in return for immunity from prosecution, also reported that it had paid bribes in order to secure the contracts to construct the São Paulo metro system. Major figures in the PSDB, namely Alckmin and Serra, were linked to the affair, but denied any involvement. In mid-August it was announced that the state of São Paulo planned to file a lawsuit against Siemens to recover funds lost to as a result of the actions of the cartel. Meanwhile, a news magazine, *Epoca*, claimed that state energy company Petrobras had been involved with paying bribes from companies involved with its foreign contracts to political parties, in particular the PMDB. On 26 August foreign minister Antonio Patriota resigned following a diplomatic incident with Bolivia (see Foreign Affairs). He was replaced by Luiz Alberto Figueiredo.

In late August 2013 the Supreme Federal Court rejected an appeal by José Dirceu against the sentence he received for his role in the *mensalão* scandal. The court's sentencing in the trial, judged by some to be unusually harsh, was in keeping with the national sentiment in the wake of the street protests in June. However, in September the Supreme Federal Court made a controversial decision to allow the retrial in early 2014 of 12 of those who had appealed part of their convictions, including Dirceu and Genoíno. Two months later, on 13 November, the court voted that the gaol terms for 16 of those convicted be executed immediately. (Those like Dirceu who were among their number, but awaiting an appeal, were ordered to start serving their sentences for those crimes for which the verdict was final.) On 6 December Valdemar Costa Neto of the PR (formerly of the PL) resigned his parliamentary seat in order to avoid impeachment proceedings. In late February 2014 the Supreme Federal Court ruled that eight of those imprisoned over the scandal, including Dirceu, be absolved of the charge of conspiracy.

Meanwhile, in mid-September 2013 the PSB withdrew its two ministers from the Government in order that Eduardo Henrique Accioly Campos, Governor of the north-eastern state of Pernambuco, could run for President in the 2014 election. On 7 October, two days after she had failed to register her environmental movement, Rede Sustentabilidade, as a political party, Marina Silva joined the PSB and announced that she would support Campos in his campaign. On 28 November Silva officially announced Campos as the presidential candidate for the alliance between her ecological movement and the PSB.

On 25 January 2014 a demonstration in São Paulo of some 2,500 people in protest against the FIFA World Cup became violent; 135 people were reportedly arrested but all were subsequently released. Two weeks later in Rio de Janeiro a television cameraman was fatally wounded during violent clashes between police and demonstrators who had gathered to protest a 9% increase in bus fares.

President Rousseff carried out a minor cabinet reshuffle in late January 2014 in anticipation of the October elections. The appointments included that of José Henrique Paim Fernandes, of the PT, who became Minister of Education, while Arturo Chioro, also of the PT, was promoted to Minister of Health. In early February Campos launched his campaign for the presidency, accusing Rousseff of being 'desperate' at the thought of losing power and stressing the need for political change. By March there were signs that relations between the PT and the PMDB were becoming increasingly strained, with PMDB congressional leader João Paulo Cunha threatening to withdraw from the coalition unless the party's number of ministries be increased from five to six. In an attempt to placate the PMDB Rousseff pledged the PT's support in six states in the regional elections; none the less a number of PMDB deputies boycotted the swearing-in ceremony of new cabinet ministers the following week. Pressure on Rousseff increased when it was reported at this time that the opposition was to seek approval for a congressional inquiry into her handling of the purchase of an oil refinery in 2006, when as Lula's chief of staff she presided over the advisory board of Petrobras. However, public support for the President reportedly remained high.

On 25 March 2014, after almost three years of debate and despite the efforts of congressional rebels to block it, a law was approved in the Chamber of Deputies that aimed to guarantee civil rights for the use of the internet. The inclusion of a controversial clause on 'net neutrality', whereby internet service providers would be unable to discriminate between websites, was the result of US spying allegations of mid-2013 (see Foreign Affairs).

Land Occupations

From the mid-1990s the Landless Peasant Movement, the Movimento dos Trabalhadores Rurais Sem Terra (MST), came to increasing prominence. During 1995 the MST organized a number of illegal occupations of disputed land in support of demands for an acceleration of the Government's programme of expropriation of uncultivated land for distribution to landless rural families. Rapidly deteriorating relations between the authorities and the MST were exacerbated in April 1996 by the violent intervention of the local military police in a demonstration in the state of Pará, which resulted in the deaths of 19 demonstrators. Widespread public outrage prompted the Government to announce new measures to accelerate the process of land reform in 1997. In March 1998 thousands of activists occupied government premises in a campaign that led to the suspension of São Paulo's land expropriation proceedings. In May 2000 more than 30,000 members of the MST occupied a number of public buildings prompting the Government to introduce legislation preventing further land invasions.

Following the election of Lula to the presidency, the MST in 2002 agreed to a temporary suspension of illegal land occupations. However, in March 2003 the MST resumed its policy of land invasions. In January 2007 the Government announced that it had reached 95% of its resettlement targets in 2003–06; however, this figure was disputed by landless organizations. Following a truce with the PT during Lula's re-election campaign in 2006, in April 2007 the MST again resumed its policy of land invasions. In February 2009 four security guards were killed during land occupations by MST members in Pernambuco state and some 2,000 activists from a dissident group within the MST invaded 20 plantations across eastern areas of São Paulo state. Following the killings the President of the Supreme Federal Court, Gilmar Ferreira Mendes, controversially alleged that militant groups linked to the MST were illicitly receiving public funding. Further land invasions in the state of Pará in April ended in violent clashes with the security forces. In October, following the destruction of a productive farm in São Paulo state by MST members, the opposition succeeded in initiating a congressional investigation into the disbursement of government funds to the movement and the alleged use of such funds to finance criminal activities.

The MST marked its 30th anniversary in 2014 by initiating a new campaign for agrarian reform. Some 20,000 landless farmers protested in Brasília on 12 February in advance of a meeting between MST leaders and President Rousseff, in which she pledged to advance the reform programme and to improve the quality of the land given to farmers through irrigation and drainage systems.

Environmental Issues

Widespread concern was expressed from the late 1980s that large-scale development projects, together with the 'slash-and-burn' farming techniques of cattle ranchers, peasant smallholders and loggers, and the release of large amounts of mercury into the environment by gold prospectors (*garimpeiros*) in the Amazon region, presented a serious threat to the survival of both the indigenous Indians and the rainforest. Of particular concern to many international observers was the plight of the Yanomami Indian tribe in Roraima. It was estimated that, since the arrival of the *garimpeiros* in the region, some 10%–15% of the Yanomami's total population had been exterminated as a result of pollution and disease. Legislation to provide greater protection for Brazil's natural resources, through the establishment of criminal penalties for illegal activities, was introduced in 1998. In 2002 Cardoso's Government created the world's biggest national park in the Tumucumaque Mountains. In 2005 the Government approved the creation of an Indian reservation of 1.75m. ha, Raposa Serra do Sol, in northern Roraima. The constitutionality of the reservation was contested in the Supreme Federal Court by a group of farmers; however, in March 2009 the Court ruled in favour of maintaining the reservation as a single unbroken territory. The judgment meant that the farmers and all other non-indigenous inhabitants of the designated area would have to leave. At least 26 people involved in illegal gold-mining in Roraima were arrested in July 2012, after police identified five criminal groups that had caused severe environmental damage through mining activities.

A contract for the construction of the Belo Monte hydroelectric dam on the Xingu river, in the state of Pará (which, on completion, would be the third largest dam in the world), was signed in August 2010, despite concerns regarding the project's potential social and environmental impact, as well as its economic viability. A court in Pará suspended the contract in February 2011, on the grounds that the developers, Norte Energia, had failed to meet environmental standards. This ruling was overturned in March, however, allowing preparatory work on the 11,000-MW dam to commence, and in June permission for construction work was granted by the state environmental agency. In September a judge barred Norte Energia from undertaking any infrastructure work that would interfere with the natural flow of the Xingu river, ruling in favour of an appeal by a fisheries group that the dam would affect fish stocks, but he reversed his decision in December. However, legal challenges and protests against the project continued. In August 2012 a regional federal judge ordered that work on the project be halted on the grounds that indigenous communities had not been properly consulted, but the Supreme Federal Court overturned this decision two weeks later. Indigenous protesters occupied the construction site for several days in October, leaving only after Norte Energia agreed to their demands for the provision of new schools, hospitals and housing for indigenous communities. In October 2013 a judge of the Regional Federal Court of the First Region suspended construction of the dam on the grounds that Norte Energia had failed to meet its environmental commitments. However, again, this ruling was reversed several days later.

In May 2011 the Chamber of Deputies approved controversial amendments to the forestry code, essentially easing restrictions designed to protect the rainforest. The proposals notably provided for a reduction in the amount of forest that farmers were required to conserve on their land and for partial amnesty from fines imposed on those who deforested illegally prior to 2008. A revised version of the bill was approved by the Senate in December 2011 and by the Chamber of Deputies in April 2012. In May Rousseff vetoed or amended several of the changes, including the proposed amnesty for illegal deforestation, and returned the code to the National Congress. The new forestry code was finally enacted in October, after the President vetoed further congressional amendments. Although the requirement to maintain forest cover on 80% of private land in the Amazon region was retained in the new code, environmentalists remained dissatisfied with the level of protection afforded, noting particularly the decision to allow landowners to include in their calculations of the total area of forest cover river margins and steep hillsides, where preservation of forest was already mandatory and previously additional. There was concern, moreover, that the complexity of the code would hinder its enforcement. In January 2013 the Government announced plans to undertake an inventory of the trees in the Amazon rainforest; the census was expected to take four years. Despite a 27% decrease in deforestation in the region between August 2011 and July 2012, the following year official figures indicated a 28% increase, with a total of 5,843 ha having been illegally cleared during that period.

Foreign Affairs

Regional relations

A Southern Common Market (Mercado Comum do Sul—Mercosul, see p. 429), comprising Brazil, Argentina, Paraguay and Uruguay, came into effect on 1 January 1995 (Venezuela became a full member in 2012). Customs barriers on 80%–85% of mutually exchanged goods were removed immediately.

Relations between Brazil and Bolivia threatened to become strained in 2006, after President Evo Morales of Bolivia announced the effective nationalization of his country's hydrocarbons industry. The state-owned Petrobras was a significant investor in Bolivia's petroleum and gas sectors: although the Brazilian Government accepted the 82% tax increase on profits, it refused to accept any increases in the cost of gas imports, or any expropriation of Petrobras assets in Bolivia. Relations had improved by August 2009, when Morales and Lula signed various bilateral agreements (notably allowing Brazil to reduce the amount of gas purchased from Bolivia). In January 2012, moreover, a tripartite accord, additionally involving the USA, was signed with the aim of further improving the monitoring of illegal coca cultivation in Bolivia. In late August 2013 relations between the two countries worsened when it emerged that a Brazilian diplomat had assisted Roger Pinto Molina, a Bolivian senator accused of corruption, in fleeing across the Brazilian border. Despite Bolivian demands for his immediate return, in October the Brazilian Government announced that Pinto would be allowed to remain in Brazil.

In July 2009 President Lula and his Paraguayan counterpart, Fernando Lugo, signed an agreement aimed at ending a dispute over the Itaipú hydroelectric plant on their joint border. Under the accord, Brazil was to triple the amount it paid Paraguay for surplus electricity from Itaipú and to allow Paraguay to sell energy direct to Brazilian utility companies. However, the Brazilian Government refused Paraguayan demands for a renegotiation of the terms of the 1973 bilateral Treaty of Itaipú (not due to expire until 2023), which provided for an equal division of the electricity generated at Itaipú, but obliged each country to sell any of its allocation that remained unused to the other at below the market rate. The agreement was finally ratified by the Brazilian legislature in May 2011. Following the controversial impeachment of Lugo in June 2012, Rousseff supported the suspension of Paraguay's membership of Mercosul and of the Union of South American Nations (UNASUR, or União das Nações Sul-Americanas, see p. 469). (Paraguay resumed active membership of the grouping at the Mercosul summit in early 2014.)

Other external relations

At the fifth Ministerial Conference of the World Trade Organization (WTO) in 2003 Brazil led a group of countries opposed to the policy of subsidizing agricultural products as practised by the USA and the European Union (EU). The group of developing nations, which came to be known as the Group of 20 (G20), demanded an end to subsidies in industrialized countries, in return for opening up their markets. The failure of the Doha round of WTO negotiations in 2007 was partly attributed to Brazilian–US failure to reach consensus on agricultural subsidies. The Lula administration greatly expanded trade links with the People's Republic of China, particularly in the energy sector, and in March 2009 that country became Brazil's principal trading partner. Further bilateral agreements on trade and energy co-operation were signed by Brazilian and Chinese officials at the second summit of the BRIC group of nations (Brazil, Russia, India and China), in April 2010. In December of that year the IMF Board of Governors approved reforms that, subject to the approval of member states, would increase the voting powers of the BRIC countries within the Fund. Brazil constituted the largest recipient of Chinese foreign direct investment in 2010. Concerns regarding weak global economic conditions, particularly in the eurozone, dominated the fourth BRICS summit, which was held in the Indian capital, New Delhi, in March 2012. BRICS leaders discussed the proposed establishment of a new development bank and urged the implementation of the IMF reforms agreed in December 2010. In January 2013 Brazil's representative at the IMF, Paulo Nogueira Batista, criticized the failure of the Fund to meet a self-imposed deadline to agree on a comprehensive revision of the formula used to apportion voting rights. Meanwhile, in June 2012 President Rousseff and Chinese Premier Wen Jiabao sought to elevate bilateral relations to the level of a 'global strategic partnership', signing a series of agreements aimed at increasing investment and trade flows between their countries; a 10-year plan of co-operation, covering a wide range of areas, was also announced.

Brazil's opposition to imposing further UN sanctions on Iran over the latter's nuclear programme frustrated the US Administration in 2010 (although, as a non-permanent member of the Security Council, Brazil did not have the power of veto), as did its involvement in brokering an agreement, signed in May, to allow Iran to send low-enriched uranium to Turkey in return for reactor fuel. None the less, Brazilian-US relations remained cordial, and a bilateral defence co-operation agreement was signed in April of that year. President Rousseff sought to strengthen relations with the USA after taking office in January 2011. This was achieved to some extent during a visit to Brazil by US President Barack Obama in March and by a reciprocal visit by Rousseff to Washington, DC, in April 2012, when talks covered a wide range of issues, including the importance of further expanding bilateral trade and investment. On both occasions Obama acknowledged Brazil's rising global significance, but failed fully to endorse the country's aspiration to secure a permanent seat on the UN Security Council (Brazil served as a non-permanent member of the Council in 2010–11). While in Washington, Rousseff expressed concern that the expansionist monetary policies being pursued by developed countries were adversely affecting the competitiveness and growth prospects of emerging countries. Brazil's relationship with the USA came under pressure in early July 2013, when allegations emerged in a report in *O Globo* newspaper that the US National Security Agency (NSA) had gathered data on electronic and telephone communications in Brazil. In August the Brazilian Government protested the arrest of a Brazilian citizen, David Miranda, at Heathrow airport in the United Kingdom. Miranda was the partner of British journalist Glenn Greenwald, who had reported on US and British intelligence-gathering activities. While the British Government denied that it was aware that the arrest take place, it was alleged that the US Administration had prior knowledge that Miranda would be detained. On 20 August the British ambassador to Brazil was summoned to the foreign ministry to explain the incident. Further claims of espionage emerged in early September when it was reported that the NSA had intercepted the personal communications of both Rousseff and Mexican President Enrique Peña Nieto during his electoral campaign. The allegations caused Rousseff to postpone her trip to Washington, DC, scheduled for October. It was hoped that the passage of internet legislation in March 2014 (see Domestic Political Affairs) would improve relations between the two countries.

CONSTITUTION AND GOVERNMENT

Under the Constitution, which was promulgated on 5 October 1988, the country is a federal republic comprising 26 states and a Federal District (Brasília). Legislative power is exercised by the bicameral Congresso Nacional (National Congress), comprising the Senado Federal (Federal Senate—members elected by the majority principle in rotation for eight years) and the Câmara dos Deputados (Chamber of Deputies—members elected by a system of proportional representation for four years). The number of deputies is based on the size of the population. Election is by universal adult suffrage. Executive power is exercised by the President, elected by direct ballot for four years. The President appoints and leads the Cabinet. Each state has a directly elected Governor and an elected legislature. Judicial power is exercised by the Supreme Federal Court; the Higher Court of Justice; the regional federal courts; labour courts; electoral courts; military courts; and the courts of the states. For the purposes of local government, the states are divided into municipalities.

REGIONAL AND INTERNATIONAL CO-OPERATION

Brazil is a member of the Latin American Integration Association (see p. 361), of the Southern Common Market (Mercado Comum do Sul—Mercosul, see p. 429), of the Union of South American Nations (see p. 469) (União das Nações Sul-Americanas, UNASUR) and the associated South American Defence Council, and of the Community of Latin American and Caribbean States (see p. 464), which was formally inaugurated in December 2011.

Brazil was a founder member of the UN in 1945. As a contracting party to the General Agreement on Tariffs and Trade, Brazil joined the World Trade Organization (see p. 434) on its establishment in 1995. Brazil participates in the Group of 20 (G20, see p. 456) leading industrialized and developing nations, and is also a member of the Association of Tin Producing Countries, of the Cairns Group (see p. 505), and of the Comunidade dos Países de Língua Portuguesa (see p. 464). Brazil is a member of the Inter-American Development Bank (see p. 331) and the Organization of American States (see p. 394).

ECONOMIC AFFAIRS

In 2012, according to estimates by the World Bank, Brazil's gross national income (GNI), measured at average 2010–12 prices, was US $2,311,146m., equivalent to US $11,630 per head (or $11,720 per head on an international purchasing-power parity basis). During 2003–12, it was estimated, the population increased at an average annual rate of 1.0%, while gross domestic product (GDP) per head increased, in real terms, by an average of 2.8% per year. Overall GDP increased, in real terms, at an average annual rate of 3.9% in 2003–12; real GDP grew by 0.9% in 2012.

Agriculture (including hunting, forestry and fishing) contributed 5.3% of GDP and engaged 14.2% of the economically active population, according to official figures, in 2012. The principal cash crops are sugar cane, soya beans, coffee, tobacco and cocoa beans. Subsistence crops include maize, cassava, rice, wheat, potatoes and beans. Beef and poultry production are also important, as is fishing (particularly tuna, crab and shrimp). In 2005 the National Congress approved a law permitting the use of genetically modified crops. During 2003–12, according to the World Bank, agricultural GDP increased at an average annual rate of 2.5%; the sector's GDP increased by 3.9% in 2011, but decreased by 2.3% in 2012.

Industry (including mining, manufacturing, construction and power) provided 26.0% of GDP and employed 22.8% of the working population in 2012. During 2003–12, according to the World Bank, industrial GDP increased at an average annual rate of 2.9%; the sector's GDP increased by 1.5% in 2011, but decreased by 0.8% in 2012.

Mining contributed 4.3% of GDP in 2012. The GDP of the mining sector increased by an impressive 45.5% in 2009. The major mineral exports are iron ore (haematite—in terms of iron content, Brazil is the largest producer in the world), manganese, tin and aluminium. Gold, phosphates, platinum, uranium, copper and coal are also mined. In 2012 Brazil supplied an estimated 91.3% of the world's total output of columbium and was among the largest producers of bauxite, graphite, iron ore, manganese, niobium, tantalum and tin. In 2011 gold production totalled 60,250 kg, compared with 62,047 kg in the previous year. Copper output stood at 232,900 metric tons in 2011, a 3.8% increase on 2010. The state-run oil company Petróleo Brasileiro, SA (Petrobras) estimated Brazil's reserves of petroleum to be 13,123m. 42-gallon barrels in 2013 following discoveries of oil in the pre-salt layer off the coast of Rio de Janeiro.

Manufacturing contributed 13.0% of GDP and engaged 13.3% of the economically active population in 2012. While traditionally dominant areas, including textiles and clothing, footwear and food- and beverage-processing, continue to contribute a large share to the sector, more recent developments in the sector have resulted in the emergence of machinery and transport equipment (including road vehicles and components, passenger jet aircraft and specialist machinery for the petroleum industry), construction materials (especially iron and steel), wood and sugar cane derivatives, and chemicals and petrochemicals as significant new manufacturing activities. According to the World Bank, manufacturing GDP increased at an average rate of 1.9% per year in 2003–12; the sector's GDP increased by just 0.1% in 2011, and decreased by 2.5% in 2012.

Construction provided 5.7% of GDP and employed 8.8% of the working population in 2012.

In 2011, according to the World Bank, 80.6% of total electricity production was provided by hydroelectric power. Other energy sources, including petroleum, coal and nuclear power, accounted for the remaining 12.7%. The country's vast hydroelectric needs were met, in part, by the 14-GW dam at Itaipú, on the border with Paraguay, and at Tucuruí, on the Tocantins river. According to official figures, imports of mineral fuels and lubricants comprised 19.1% of the value of total merchandise imports in 2013.

The services sector contributed 68.7% of GDP and engaged 63.0% of the employed labour force in 2012. Tourism was an important contributor to the economy. Tourism receipts (excluding passenger transport) totalled a provisional US $6,645m. in 2012. In that year foreign tourists reached 5,676,843, a 4.5% increase on the total in 2011. According to the World Bank, the GDP of the services sector increased at an average rate of 3.7% per year in 2003–12; the sector's GDP increased by 1.6% in 2012.

Brazil recorded a visible merchandise trade surplus of US $19,431m. in 2012, while there was a deficit of $54,246m. on the current account of the balance of payments. In 2013 the principal sources of imports were the People's Republic of China and the USA (contributing 15.6% and 15.1%, respectively, of the total). Other import trading partners were Argentina and Germany. China was the principal market for exports (19.0%). Other major export trading partners were the USA, Argentina and the Netherlands. The principal exports in 2013 were mineral products, vegetable products, prepared foodstuffs, beverages, spirits and tobacco, vehicles, aircraft, vessels and transport equipment, machinery and mechanical appliances, electrical equipment, live animals and animal products, and base metals and articles thereof. The principal imports in that year were machinery and mechanical appliances, electrical equipment, mineral products, chemicals and related products, vehicles, aircraft, vessels and transport equipment, base metals and articles thereof, and plastics, rubber and their articles.

The 2012 federal budget recorded expenditure of R $986,344m. and revenue of R $1,062,206m., creating a surplus equivalent to 1.7% of GDP. Brazil's general government gross debt was R $2,994,571m. in 2012, equivalent to 68.0% of GDP. Brazil's external debt was US $404,317m. at the end of 2011, of which US $94,977m. was public and publicly guaranteed debt. In that year, the cost of servicing long-term public and publicly guaranteed debt and repayments to the IMF was equivalent to 19.4% of the value of exports of goods, services and income (excluding workers' remittances). According to the International Labour Organization, the annual rate of inflation averaged 5.4% in 2003–12. Consumer prices increased by 5.4% in 2012. Official figures indicated an average unemployment rate of 6.1% of the labour force in 2012.

On taking office in 2011, Rousseff inherited a rapidly expanding economy, which had recovered strongly from the recession of 2008–09, driven by increasing domestic demand and investment, as well as rising prices for Brazil's commodity exports. However, GDP growth slowed sharply, from 7.5% in 2010 to 2.7% in 2011, and further, to 0.9% in 2012, amid weak global economic conditions. The projected growth figure for 2013 was, however, 2.5%, led by a dramatic increase in agricultural output (in particular soy production). Having set the interest rate to a new record low of 7.25% in October 2012, by November 2013 the central bank had raised it to 10%, representing the sixth successive rise and the highest rate since March 2012. This move signified the Government's commitment to combating inflation, which in October 2013 had risen by 5.8% year-on-year, a figure significantly higher than the target of 4.5%. The rise in consumer prices was, in part, brought about by the fall in value of the real. By the end of 2013 Rousseff was coming under increasing pressure to change direction on economic policy. At the start of her presidency she had initiated the second phase of the Growth Acceleration Programme (Programa de Aceleração do Crescimento) begun by her predecessor, Lula da Silva, in 2007, which set out investment plans aimed at improving Brazil's failing infrastructure, as well as preparing for the upcoming FIFA World Cup in 2014 and the 2016 Olympics. In January 2014 it was reported that Brazil had awarded private sector infrastructure concessions worth some R $80,300m. in 2013. In addition, Rousseff's economic policy included tax relief, subsidies and protection for industry and increased social welfare benefits. In accordance with the five pacts proposed by the Government in response to the large-scale public unrest of 2013, in late October funding of R $13,500m. and R $5,400m. was announced for sanitation and paving and urban transport projects, respectively. By late 2013 there were signs that Rousseff might be forced to adjust economic policy; in October the President was criticized by leading Brazilian economists for the degree of state intervention in the economy and for her preference for so-called 'big government', which, they argued, was deterring investment, hindering competitiveness and isolating the country from international markets. Furthermore, in December Brazil was forced to answer charges of protectionism brought by the EU at the World Trade Organization over its import taxes.

PUBLIC HOLIDAYS

2015: 1 January (New Year's Day—Universal Confraternization Day), 16–18 February (Carnival), 3 April (Good Friday), 21 April (Tiradentes Day—Discovery of Brazil), 1 May (Labour Day), 4 June (Corpus Christi), 7 September (Independence Day), 12 October (Our Lady Aparecida, Patron Saint of Brazil), 2 November (All Souls' Day), 15 November (Proclamation of the Republic), 20 November (Death of Zumbi dos Palmares—Black Awareness Day), 25 December (Christmas Day).

Other local holidays include 20 January (Foundation of Rio de Janeiro) and 25 January (Foundation of São Paulo).

Statistical Survey

Sources (unless otherwise stated): Economic Research Department, Banco Central do Brasil, SBS, Quadra 03, Bloco B, 70074-900 Brasília, DF; tel. (61) 3414-1074; fax (61) 3414-2036; e-mail coace.depec.@bcb.gov.br; internet www.bcb.gov.br; Instituto Brasileiro de Geografia e Estatística (IBGE), Centro de Documentação e Disseminação de Informações (CDDI), Rua Gen. Canabarro 706, 2° andar, Maracanã, 20271-201 Rio de Janeiro, RJ; tel. (21) 2142-4781; fax (21) 2142-4933; e-mail ibge@ibge.bov.br; internet www.ibge.gov.br.

Area and Population

AREA, POPULATION AND DENSITY

Area (sq km)	8,514,877*
Population (census results)†	
1 August 2000	169,590,693
1 August 2010	
Males	93,406,990
Females	97,348,809
Total	190,755,799
Population (official estimates at mid-year)	
2011	192,379,287
2012	193,946,886
2013	201,032,714
Density (per sq km) at mid-2013	23.6

* 3,287,611 sq miles.

† Excluding Indian jungle population (numbering 45,429 in 1950).

POPULATION BY AGE AND SEX

(official estimates at mid-2013)

	Males	Females	Total
0–14	24,776,943	23,754,709	48,531,652
15–64	68,179,905	69,451,071	137,630,976
65 and over	6,380,010	8,490,076	14,870,086
Total	99,336,858	101,695,856	201,032,714

ADMINISTRATIVE DIVISIONS

(official population estimates at mid-2013)

State	Area (sq km)	Population	Density (per sq km)	Capital
Acre (AC)	152,581	776,463	5.1	Rio Branco
Alagoas (AL)	27,768	3,300,935	118.9	Maceió
Amapá (AP)	142,815	734,996	5.1	Macapá
Amazonas (AM)	1,570,746	3,807,921	2.4	Manaus
Bahia (BA)	564,693	15,044,137	26.6	Salvador
Ceará (CE)	148,826	8,778,576	59.0	Fortaleza
Distrito Federal (DF)	5,802	2,789,761	480.8	Brasília
Espírito Santo (ES)	46,078	3,839,366	83.3	Vitória
Goiás (GO)	340,087	6,434,048	18.9	Goiânia
Maranhão (MA)	331,983	6,794,301	20.5	São Luís
Mato Grosso (MT)	903,358	3,182,113	3.5	Cuiabá
Mato Grosso do Sul (MS)	357,125	2,587,269	7.2	Campo Grande
Minas Gerais (MG)	586,528	20,593,356	35.1	Belo Horizonte
Pará (PA)	1,247,690	7,969,654	6.4	Belém
Paraíba (PB)	56,440	3,914,421	69.4	João Pessoa
Paraná (PR)	199,315	10,997,465	55.2	Curitiba
Pernambuco (PE)	98,312	9,208,550	93.7	Recife
Piauí (PI)	251,529	3,184,166	12.7	Teresina
Rio de Janeiro (RJ)	43,696	16,369,179	374.6	Rio de Janeiro
Rio Grande do Norte (RN)	52,797	3,373,959	63.9	Natal
Rio Grande do Sul (RS)	281,749	11,164,043	39.6	Porto Alegre
Rondônia (RO)	237,576	1,728,214	7.3	Porto Velho
Roraima (RR)	224,299	488,072	2.2	Boa Vista
Santa Catarina (SC)	95,346	6,634,254	69.6	Florianópolis
São Paulo (SP)	248,209	43,663,669	175.9	São Paulo
Sergipe (SE)	21,910	2,195,662	100.2	Aracaju
Tocantins (TO)	277,621	1,478,164	5.3	Palmas
Total	8,514,877	201,032,714	23.6	—

PRINCIPAL TOWNS

(official estimates at mid-2013)*

São Paulo	11,821,873	Uberlândia	646,673
Rio de Janeiro	6,429,923	Contagem	637,961
Salvador	2,883,682	Sorocaba	629,231
Brasília (capital)	2,789,761	Aracaju	614,577
Fortaleza	2,551,806	Feira de Santana	606,139
Belo Horizonte	2,479,165	Cuiabá	569,830
Manaus	1,982,177	Joinville	546,981
Curitiba	1,848,946	Juíz de Fora	545,942
Recife	1,599,513	Londrina	537,566
Porto Alegre	1,467,816	Aparecida de Goiânia	500,619
Belém	1,425,922	Niterói	494,200
Goiânia	1,393,575	Ananindeua	493,976
Guarulhos	1,299,249	Porto Velho	484,992
Campinas	1,144,862	Belford Roxo	477,583
São Luís	1,053,922	Campos dos Goytacazes	477,208
São Gonçalo	1,025,507	Serra	467,318
Maceió	996,733	Caxias do Sul	465,304
Duque de Caxias	873,921	São João de Meriti	460,799
Natal	853,928	Vila Velha	458,489
Teresina	836,475	Florianópolis	453,285
Campo Grande	832,352	Mauá	444,136
São Bernardo do Campo	805,895	Macapá	437,256
Nova Iguaçu	804,815	São José do Rio Preto	434,039
João Pessoa	769,607	Santos	433,153
Santo André	704,942	Mogi das Cruzes	414,907
Osasco	691,652	Diadema	406,718
Jaboatão dos Guararapes	675,599	Betim	406,474
São José dos Campos	673,255	Campina Grande	400,002
Ribeirão Preto	649,556		

* Figures refer to *municípios*, which may contain rural districts.

BIRTHS, MARRIAGES AND DEATHS

(official estimates based on annual registrations)

	Live births		Marriages	Deaths	
	Number*	Rate (per 1,000)	Number	Number	Rate (per 1,000)
2005	3,329,431	18.2	835,846	996,931	5.4
2006	3,172,000	17.1	889,828	1,023,814	5.5
2007	3,080,266	16.4	916,006	1,036,405	5.5
2008	3,107,927	16.4	959,901	1,060,365	5.6
2009	3,045,696	15.9	935,116	1,083,399	5.7
2010	2,985,406	15.7	977,620	1,132,701	5.1
2011	3,044,594	15.8	1,026,736	1,163,740	6.0
2012	2,998,281	15.5	1,041,440	1,165,751	6.0

* Including births registered but not occurring during that year: 448,243 in 2005; 368,062 in 2006; 324,895 in 2007; 309,885 in 2008; 281,054 in 2009; 224,445 in 2010; 219,818 in 2011; 185,764 in 2012.

Life expectancy (years at birth): 73.3 (males 69.8; females 77.0) in 2011 (Source: World Bank, World Development Indicators database).

ECONOMICALLY ACTIVE POPULATION

('000 persons aged 10 years and over, labour force sample survey at September)*

	2009	2011†	2012
Agriculture, hunting, forestry and fishing	15,715	14,682	13,368
Industry (excl. construction)	13,598	12,509	13,161
Manufacturing industries	12,815	11,787	12,441
Construction	6,895	7,814	8,218
Commerce and repair of motor vehicles and household goods	16,484	16,660	16,688
Hotels and restaurants	3,623	4,570	4,471
Transport, storage and communication	4,436	5,109	5,252
Public administration	4,754	5,081	5,178
Education, health and social services	8,681	8,627	9,100
Domestic services	7,223	6,653	6,355
Other community, social and personal services	3,928	3,538	3,748
Other activities	7,150	8,120	8,307
Sub-total	92,487	93,363	93,846
Activities not adequately defined	202	130	69
Total employed	92,689	93,493	93,915
Unemployed	8,421	6,730	6,149
Total labour force	101,110	100,223	100,064

* Data coverage excludes rural areas of Acre, Amapá, Amazonas, Pará, Rondônia and Roraima.

† No survey was conducted in 2010, owing to the population census in that year.

Health and Welfare

KEY INDICATORS

Total fertility rate (children per woman, 2011)	1.8
Under-5 mortality rate (per 1,000 live births, 2011)	16
HIV/AIDS (% of persons aged 15–49, 2011)	0.3
Physicians (per 1,000 head, 2008)	1.8
Hospital beds (per 1,000 head, 2010)	2.4
Health expenditure (2010): US $ per head (PPP)	1,009
Health expenditure (2010): % of GDP	9.0
Health expenditure (2010): public (% of total)	47.0
Access to water (% of persons, 2011)	97
Access to sanitation (% of persons, 2011)	81
Total carbon dioxide emissions ('000 metric tons, 2010)	419,754.2
Carbon dioxide emissions per head (metric tons, 2010)	2.2
Human Development Index (2012): ranking	85
Human Development Index (2012): value	0.730

For sources and definitions, see explanatory note on p. vi.

Agriculture

PRINCIPAL CROPS

('000 metric tons)

	2010	2011	2012
Wheat	6,171	5,690	4,418
Rice, paddy	11,236	13,477	11,550
Barley	279	304	265
Maize	55,364	55,660	71,073
Oats	395	373	431
Sorghum	1,532	1,931	2,017
Buckwheat*	57	57	60
Potatoes	3,548	3,917	3,732
Sweet potatoes	495	545	479
Cassava (Manioc)	24,967	25,349	23,045
Yams*	233	244	246
Sugar cane	717,464	734,006	721,077
Beans, dry	3,159	3,435	2,795
Brazil nuts, with shell	40	42	44*
Cashew nuts, with shell	104	231	81
Soybeans (Soya beans)	68,756	74,815	65,849
Groundnuts, with shell	261	311	334
Coconuts	2,843	2,944	2,888

—continued	2010	2011	2012
Oil palm fruit	1,293	1,301	1,241
Castor oil seed	95	120	26
Sunflower seed	87	78	124
Tomatoes	4,107	4,417	3,874
Onions, dry	1,753	1,523	1,519
Garlic	104	143	107
Watermelons	2,053	2,199	2,080
Cantaloupes and other melons	478	499	575
Bananas	6,969	7,329	6,902
Oranges	18,503	19,811	18,013
Tangerines, mandarins, clementines and satsumas	1,122	1,005	960
Lemons and limes	1,021	1,127	1,208
Grapefruit and pomelos*	71	75	78
Apples	1,279	1,339	1,335
Peaches and nectarines	222	222	233
Grapes	1,355	1,542	1,515
Guavas, mangoes, mangosteens	1,190	1,250	1,176
Avocados	153	160	160
Pineapples	2,206	2,365	2,478
Persimmons	167	155	158
Cashew-apple*	1,694	1,788	1,805
Papayas	1,872	1,854	1,518
Coffee, green	2,907	2,700	3,038
Cocoa beans	235	249	253
Mate	430	444	513
Sisal	247	284	89
Tobacco, unmanufactured	788	952	811
Natural rubber	134	164	177

* FAO estimate(s).

Aggregate production ('000 metric tons, may include official, semi-official or estimated data): Total cereals 75,161 in 2010, 77,586 in 2011, 89,908 in 2012; Total roots and tubers 29,243 in 2010, 30,055 in 2011, 27,502 in 2012; Total vegetables (incl. melons) 11,233 in 2010, 11,611 in 2011, 11,055 in 2012; Total fruits (excl. melons) 38,793 in 2010, 40,997 in 2011, 38,369 in 2012.

Source: FAO.

LIVESTOCK

('000 head, year ending September)

	2010	2011	2012
Cattle	209,541	212,815	211,279
Buffaloes	1,185	1,278	1,262
Horses	5,514	5,511	5,363
Asses	1,002	975	903
Mules	1,277	1,269	1,222
Pigs	38,957	39,307	38,796
Sheep	17,381	17,668	16,789
Goats	9,313	9,386	8,646
Chickens	1,238,912	1,268,209	1,245,269
Ducks*	3,700	3,750	3,800
Turkeys*	26,900	27,100	28,300

* FAO estimates.

Source: FAO.

LIVESTOCK PRODUCTS

('000 metric tons)

	2010	2011	2012
Cattle meat*	9,115	9,030	9,307
Sheep meat†	82	84	85
Goat meat†	29	29	30
Pig meat	3,195*	3,370	3,465
Horse meat†	22	22	23
Chicken meat	10,693	11,422	11,533
Cows' milk	30,715	32,096	32,304
Goats' milk†	148	149	150
Hen eggs*	1,948	2,037	2,084
Other poultry eggs	139	156	160†
Natural honey	38	42	34
Wool, greasy	12	12	12

* Unofficial figures.

† FAO estimate(s).

Source: FAO.

Forestry

ROUNDWOOD REMOVALS
('000 cubic metres, excl. bark, FAO estimates)

	2010	2011	2012
Sawlogs, veneer logs and logs for sleepers	50,574	55,289	62,950
Pulpwood	69,779	75,882	73,837
Other industrial wood	8,047	8,798	10,017
Fuel wood	143,101	144,050	145,016
Total	271,501	284,019	291,820

Source: FAO.

SAWNWOOD PRODUCTION
('000 cubic metres, incl. railway sleepers)

	2010	2011	2012
Coniferous (softwood)*	8,970	9,100	9,200
Broadleaved (hardwood)	16,110†	16,110*	16,110†
Total	25,080	25,210	25,310

* Unofficial figure(s).
† FAO estimate.

Source: FAO.

Fishing

('000 metric tons, live weight)

	2009	2010	2011
Capture	825.4	785.4	803.3
Characins	84.3	90.4	91.0
Freshwater siluroids	35.6	30.0	30.3
Weakfishes	51.5	48.6	45.4
Whitemouth croaker	45.8	43.2	43.2
Brazilian sardinella	83.3	62.1	76.0
Aquaculture*	415.6	479.4	629.3
Common carp	80.9	94.6	14.0
Tilapias	133.0	155.5	253.8
Whiteleg shrimp	65.2	69.4	65.7
Total catch*	1,241.0	1,264.8	1,432.6

* FAO estimates.

Note: Figures exclude aquatic mammals, recorded by number rather than by weight. The number of whales and dolphins caught was: 25 in 2009; 70 in 2010; 42 in 2011. Also excluded are crocodiles: the number of broad-nosed, black and spectacled caimans caught was: 9,116 in 2009; 1,101 in 2010; 9,036 in 2011.

Source: FAO.

Mining

('000 metric tons unless otherwise indicated)

	2009	2010	2011[1]
Hard coal[2]	5,818	6,310	6,330
Crude petroleum ('000 barrels)	714,041	752,253	770,179
Natural gas (million cu m)	21,142	22,922	24,090
Iron ore:[3]			
gross weight	298,528	372,120	391,098
metal content	198,771	247,772	260,408
Copper (metric tons)	231,399	224,292	232,900
Nickel ore (metric tons)[4]	41,059	108,983	110,960
Bauxite	26,074	32,028	34,494
Lead concentrates (metric tons)[4]	15,890	19,650	19,700
Zinc (metric tons)	242,136	288,107	281,190
Tin concentrates (metric tons)[4]	9,500	10,400	9,550
Chromium ore (metric tons)[5]	246,900	258,308	258,300
Tungsten concentrates (metric tons)[4]	192	166	170
Ilmenite (metric tons)	52,800	166,000	166,000
Rutile (metric tons)	2,737	2,519	2,520
Zirconium concentrates (metric tons)[6]	34,248	23,235	23,200
Silver (kg)[7]	35,500	37,000	36,500
Gold (kg)	60,330	62,047	60,250
Bentonite (beneficiated)	264	532	532
Kaolin (beneficiated)	1,987	2,200	1,712
Magnesite (beneficiated)	410	484	484
Phosphate rock[8]	6,084	6,192	6,200
Potash salts[9]	452	418	418
Fluorspar (Fluorite) (metric tons)[10]	43,964	25,814	25,850
Barite (Barytes) (beneficiated) (metric tons)	49,847	41,385	41,400
Quartz (natural crystals) (metric tons)	11,588	13,024	13,000
Salt (unrefined):			
marine	4,462	5,615	5,600
rock	1,443	1,415	1,400
Gypsum and anhydrite (crude)	2,348	2,750	2,750
Graphite (natural) (metric tons)[2]	59,425	72,623	76,330
Asbestos (fibre) (metric tons)	288,452	302,257	302,300
Mica (metric tons)[11]	4,000	4,000	4,000
Vermiculite concentrates (metric tons)	50,438	49,976	55,000
Talc and pyrophyllite (crude)	578	655	655
Diamonds, gem and industrial ('000 carats)[11,12]	21	25	25

[1] Preliminary figures.
[2] Figures refer to marketable products.
[3] Includes sponge iron (metric tons) 270,000 in 2009–11 (estimates).
[4] Figures refer to the metal content of ores and concentrates.
[5] Figures refer to the chromic oxide (Cr_2O_3) content.
[6] Including production of baddeleyite-caldasite.
[7] Figures refer to primary production only. The production of secondary silver (in kg, estimates): was: 31,000 in 2009; 32,000 in 2010; 32,000 in 2011 (preliminary figure).
[8] Figures refer to the gross weight of concentrates. The phosphoric acid (P_2O_5) content (in '000 metric tons) was: 2,163 in 2009; 2,179 in 2010; 2,200 in 2011 (preliminary figure).
[9] Figures refer to the potassium oxide (K_2O) content.
[10] Acid-grade and metallurgical-grade concentrates.
[11] Estimated production.
[12] Figures refer to officially reported diamond output plus official Brazilian estimates of diamond output by independent miners (*garimpeiros*).

Source: US Geological Survey.

Industry

SELECTED PRODUCTS
('000 metric tons unless otherwise indicated)

	2009	2010	2011
Beef—fresh or chilled	3,476	3,492	4,675
Frozen poultry meats and giblets	5,687	6,842	7,869
Sugar (granulated)	17,583	19,794	17,536
Beer ('000 hl)	n.a.	130,432	137,435
Soft drinks ('000 hl)	142,041	166,323	167,252
Gas-diesel oil (distillate fuel oil, '000 cu m)	45,949	44,173	50,725
Residual fuel oils ('000 cu m)	30,720	29,948	26,974
Naphthas for petrochemicals ('000 cu m)	9,187	9,022	8,233
Liquefied petroleum gas	12,159	13,379	13,274
Ethylene—unsaturated	2,772	n.a.	1,035
Fertilizers with nitrogen, phosphorus and potassium	15,057	17,207	18,944
Chemical wood pulp, cellulose	9,856	10,467	10,467
Iron	5,028	6,670	7,009
Iron ore*	315,744	299,304	316,878

—continued	2009	2010	2011
Hot rolled coils of carbon steel—uncoated	4,961	2,917	2,504
Trucks (units)†	100,832	144,412	164,243
Motorcycles (units)	1,391,865	1,590,697	1,928,754
Mobile cellular telephones ('000 units)	55,854	57,618	60,842

* Prepared forms, including concentrates, ball bearings, etc.

† Vehicles with diesel engines and maximum load capacity in excess of five metric tons.

Motor vehicles (excl. trucks): 2,473,586 in 2007.

Electric energy (million kWh): 463,120 in 2008; 466,158 in 2009; 515,798 in 2010 (Source: UN Industrial Commodity Statistics Database).

Finance

CURRENCY AND EXCHANGE RATES

Monetary Units

100 centavos = 1 real (plural: reais).

Sterling, Dollar and Euro Equivalents (31 December 2013)

£1 sterling = 3.876 reais;
US $1 = 2.354 reais;
€1 = 3.246 reais;
100 reais = £25.80 = $42.48 = €30.81.

Average Exchange Rates (reais per US $)

2011	1.6728
2012	1.9531
2013	2.156

Note: In March 1986 the cruzeiro (CR $) was replaced by a new currency unit, the cruzado (CZ $), equivalent to 1,000 cruzeiros. In January 1989 the cruzado was, in turn, replaced by the new cruzado (NCZ $), equivalent to CZ $1,000 and initially at par with the US dollar (US $). In March 1990 the new cruzado was replaced by the cruzeiro (CR $), at an exchange rate of one new cruzado for one cruzeiro. In August 1993 the cruzeiro was replaced by the cruzeiro real, equivalent to CR $1,000. On 1 March 1994, in preparation for the introduction of a new currency, a transitional accounting unit, the Unidade Real de Valor (at par with the US $), came into operation, alongside the cruzeiro real. On 1 July 1994 the cruzeiro real was replaced by the real (R $), also at par with the US $ and thus equivalent to 2,750 cruzeiros reais.

BUDGET
(R $ million)

Revenue	2011	2012	2013
National treasury revenues	741,297	783,439	871,158
Gross revenues*	757,429	802,831	894,678
Restitutions	−15,858	−19,249	−23,468
Fiscal incentives	−274	−142	−52
Social security revenues	245,892	275,765	307,147
Urban	240,536	270,002	300,991
Rural	5,356	5,763	6,156
Central bank revenues	3,217	3,002	2,795
Total	990,406	1,062,206	1,181,100

Expenditure	2011	2012	2013
Transfers to state and local governments	172,483	181,377	189,987
Treasury expenditures	439,191	484,623	552,925
Payroll*	179,277	186,097	202,744
Worker support fund (FAT)	34,660	39,330	44,688
Economic subsidies and grants†	10,517	11,272	44,688
Assistance benefits (LOAS/RMV)	24,905	29,207	33,523
Other current and capital expenditures	187,696	216,399	251,853
Transfer to central bank	2,136	2,317	2,112
Social security benefits	281,438	316,590	357,003
Central bank expenditures	3,769	3,755	4,113
Total	896,881	986,344	1,104,028

* Excludes the employer share of federal civil service payments from revenues originating in contributions to the Social Security Plan (CPSS) and personnel outlays.

† Includes judicially determined repayments related to the Rural Unified and Industrial Unified initiatives.

Source: Ministério da Fazenda, Brasília, DF.

INTERNATIONAL RESERVES
(US $ million at 31 December)

	2010	2011	2012
Gold (national valuation)	1,519	1,654	3,581
IMF special drawing rights	4,450	3,979	3,986
Reserve position in the IMF	2,037	2,993	3,483
Foreign exchange	280,570	343,384	362,097
Total	288,576	352,010	373,147

Source: IMF, *International Financial Statistics*.

MONEY SUPPLY
(R $ million at 31 December)

	2010	2011	2012
Currency outside depository corporations	121,969	131,727	149,627
Transferable deposits	159,005	152,579	182,279
Other deposits	2,239,882	2,603,033	2,413,439
Securities other than shares	74,434	193,472	810,387
Broad money	2,595,291	3,080,811	3,555,732

Source: IMF, *International Financial Statistics*.

COST OF LIVING
(Consumer Price Index; base: 2000 = 100)

	2010	2011	2012
Food	204.6	222.7	240.8
All items (incl. others)	190.4	203.0	214.0

Source: ILO.

NATIONAL ACCOUNTS
(R $ million at current prices)

National Income and Product

	2010	2011	2012
Gross domestic product (GDP) in market prices	3,770,085	4,143,013	4,392,094
Wages and salaries	879	948	1,001
Primary incomes received from abroad (net)	−68,907	−79,076	−69,818
Gross national income (GNI)	3,702,057	4,064,885	4,323,277
Current transfers received from abroad (net)	5,112	4,998	5,581
Net national disposable income	3,707,169	4,069,883	4,328,858

Expenditure on the Gross Domestic Product

	2010	2011	2012
Final consumption expenditure	3,045,956	3,356,136	3,686,020
Households	2,248,624	2,499,489	2,750,191
General government	797,332	856,647	935,829
Gross capital formation	763,012	817,260	769,606
Gross fixed capital formation	733,712	798,720	798,142
Changes in inventories	29,300	18,540	−28,537
Total domestic expenditure	3,808,968	4,173,396	4,455,626
Exports of goods and services	409,868	492,570	552,843
Less Imports of goods and services	448,752	522,953	616,374
GDP in market prices	3,770,085	4,143,013	4,392,094

Gross Domestic Product by Economic Activity

	2010	2011	2012
Agriculture, hunting, forestry and fishing	171,177	192,653	198,137
Mining and quarrying	95,886	143,924	159,002
Manufacturing	523,616	515,441	482,494
Electricity, gas and water	103,873	108,724	114,637
Construction	182,477	204,067	213,100
Trade, restaurants and hotels	404,007	446,606	474,743
Transport, storage and communications	161,936	180,997	201,226
Information services	103,977	107,589	107,519
Financial intermediation, insurance, and related services	242,410	262,482	266,793
Real estate and renting	252,824	278,402	305,726
Government, health and education services	522,777	576,541	618,464
Other services	462,221	513,445	583,228
Gross value added in basic prices	3,227,181	3,530,871	3,725,069
Taxes, less subsidies, on products	542,904	612,142	667,025
GDP in market prices	3,770,085	4,143,013	4,392,094

BALANCE OF PAYMENTS
(US $ million)

	2010	2011	2012
Exports of goods	201,915	256,040	242,580
Imports of goods	–181,768	–226,233	–223,149
Balance on goods	20,147	29,807	19,431
Exports of services	31,821	38,209	39,864
Imports of services	–62,592	–76,161	–80,939
Balance on goods and services	–10,624	–8,145	–21,645
Primary income received	7,405	10,753	10,888
Primary income paid	–46,892	–58,072	–46,335
Balance on goods, services and primary income	–50,111	–55,464	–57,092
Secondary income received	4,661	4,915	4,626
Secondary income paid	–1,873	–1,931	–1,780
Current balance	–47,323	–52,480	–54,246
Capital account (net)	1,119	1,573	–1,877
Direct investment assets	–16,426	–3,850	–8,017
Direct investment liabilities	53,345	71,539	76,111
Portfolio investment assets	–4,784	16,858	–8,260
Portfolio investment liabilities	67,795	18,453	16,534
Financial derivatives assets	133	252	150
Financial derivatives liabilities	–245	–249	–125
Other investment assets	–42,636	–38,984	–24,278
Other investment liabilities	41,415	46,796	22,525
Net errors and omissions	–3,313	–1,274	384
Reserves and related items	49,080	58,635	18,899

Source: IMF, *International Financial Statistics*.

External Trade

PRINCIPAL COMMODITIES
(distribution by HS, US $ million)

Imports f.o.b.	2011	2012	2013
Mineral products	44,559.2	42,218.5	48,027.4
Mineral fuels, oils, distillation products, etc.	41,968.2	40,187.2	45,693.8
Crude petroleum oils	14,080.6	13,405.8	16,320.0
Petroleum oils, not crude	16,905.1	16,365.1	17,757.0
Petroleum gases	4,592.4	5,959.6	7,997.9
Chemicals and related products	34,600.7	35,628.4	38,233.1
Organic chemicals	9,396.6	9,914.7	10,735.8
Pharmaceutical products	6,499.2	6,840.9	7,420.1
Fertilizers	9,138.4	8,583.8	8,885.5
Plastics, rubber and articles of plastics and rubber	13,206.9	12,507.4	13,599.4
Plastics and articles thereof	8,104.3	7,967.7	8,848.6

Imports f.o.b.—*continued*	2011	2012	2013
Base metals and articles thereof	14,246.8	13,788.4	13,704.7
Machinery and mechanical appliances, electrical equipment	60,098.2	60,163.1	64,032.0
Machinery, boilers, etc.	33,703.1	34,674.0	35,757.5
Electrical and electronic equipment	26,395.1	25,489.1	28,274.4
Vehicles, aircraft, vessels and transport equipment	26,374.3	25,208.0	26,497.8
Vehicles other than railway, tramway	22,620.9	21,309.4	22,418.6
Cars (incl. station wagons)	11,891.4	9,566.7	9,081.2
Parts and accessories of motor vehicles	6,317.6	6,771.5	8,296.7
Optical, medical apparatus, etc.; clocks and watches; musical instruments; parts thereof	6,762.4	6,913.2	7,533.2
Total (incl. others)	226,243.4	223,149.1	239,620.9

Exports f.o.b.	2011	2012	2013
Live animals and animal products	15,214.5	15,364.6	16,630.8
Meat and edible meat offal	13,722.9	13,703.0	14,786.2
Vegetable products	30,040.9	31,357.0	36,112.9
Coffee, tea, mate and spices	8,324.9	6,022.8	4,954.3
Coffee	8,026.4	5,740.3	4,598.1
Oil seed, oleagic fruits, grain, seed, fruit, etc.	16,531.3	17,682.0	23,027.2
Soya beans	16,327.3	17,248.3	22,812.3
Prepared foodstuffs, beverages, spirits, tobacco, etc.	31,786.7	31,419.9	30,277.3
Sugars and sugar confectionery	15,154.1	13,030.3	12,013.9
Cane or beet sugar and chemically pure sucrose in solid form	14,941.7	12,650.8	11,842.5
Mineral products	76,613.6	65,433.8	53,705.6
Ores, slag and ash	44,216.6	33,244.4	35,082.7
Iron ores and concentrates (incl. roasted iron pyrites)	41,817.3	30,989.3	32,491.5
Mineral fuels, oils, distillation products, etc.	31,619.4	31,420.0	17,822.2
Crude petroleum oils	21,603.3	20,305.9	12,956.6
Chemicals and related products	12,258.4	11,570.0	11,156.6
Base metals and articles thereof	18,940.9	17,240.1	14,805.3
Iron and steel	12,013.9	10,711.0	8,372.3
Machinery and mechanical appliances, electrical equipment	19,225.4	18,805.5	17,638.1
Machinery, boilers, etc.	14,084.4	13,880.6	12,890.2
Vehicles, aircraft, vessels and transport equipment	19,575.4	19,436.7	26,573.9
Vehicles other than railway, tramway	13,760.9	12,569.5	14,089.3
Ships, boats and other floating structures	1,152.8	1,548.8	7,933.7
Light vessels, dredgers; floating docks; floating/submersible drill platforms	1,042.9	1,457.8	7,735.5
Total (incl. others)	256,038.7	242,579.8	242,178.6

Source: Trade Map-Trade Competitiveness Map, International Trade Centre, www.intracen.org/marketanalysis.

PRINCIPAL TRADING PARTNERS
(US $ million)

Imports f.o.b.	2011	2012	2013
Algeria	3,136.8	3,197.9	3,074.8
Argentina	16,906.1	16,444.1	16,462.9
Bolivia	2,863.4	3,431.0	3,937.7
Canada	3,553.3	3,072.1	3,001.5
Chile	4,569.5	4,164.6	4,328.3
China, People's Republic	32,788.4	34,248.5	37,302.2
France (incl. Monaco)	5,471.3	5,918.6	6,509.4
Germany	15,212.9	14,208.9	15,182.0
India	6,081.0	5,042.8	6,357.3
Italy	6,228.3	6,206.9	6,724.1
Japan	7,871.8	7,734.7	7,081.7
Korea, Republic	10,097.0	9,097.7	9,491.3
Malaysia	2,287.4	2,083.6	2,211.7
Mexico	5,130.2	6,075.1	5,794.8
Netherlands	2,265.4	3,106.4	2,344.6
Nigeria	8,386.4	8,012.2	9,647.5
Russia	2,944.2	2,790.7	2,676.1
Saudi Arabia	3,093.0	3,192.9	3,194.2
Spain	3,298.2	3,540.1	4,486.4
Switzerland (incl. Liechtenstein)	2,845.9	2,782.8	2,951.9
Taiwan	3,509.4	3,168.8	2,937.8
Thailand	2,399.3	2,503.9	2,383.9
United Kingdom	3,375.6	3,505.2	3,614.9
USA	34,233.5	32,607.9	36,279.6
Total (incl. others)	226,243.4	223,149.1	239,620.9

Exports f.o.b.	2011	2012	2013
Argentina	22,709.3	17,997.7	19,615.4
Belgium-Luxembourg	3,959.7	3,741.6	3,593.8
Canada	3,129.5	3,079.9	2,701.7
Chile	5,418.1	4,602.2	4,483.8
China, People's Republic	44,314.6	41,227.5	46,026.2
Colombia	2,577.4	2,834.5	2,703.1
Egypt	2,624.0	2,711.9	2,201.6
France (incl. Monaco)	4,359.3	4,139.4	3,423.4
Germany	9,039.1	7,277.1	6,551.7
Hong Kong	2,176.3	2,458.1	3,339.2
India	3,200.7	5,576.9	3,130.1
Italy	5,440.9	4,580.7	4,098.1
Japan	9,473.1	7,955.7	7,964.0
Korea, Republic	4,693.9	4,501.1	4,720.0
Mexico	3,959.7	4,003.0	4,230.3
Netherlands	13,639.7	15,040.7	17,325.9
Panama	418.7	397.4	4,423.1
Paraguay	2,968.6	2,617.5	2,996.6
Peru	2,262.9	2,415.2	2,147.2
Russia	4,216.3	3,140.8	2,974.1
Saint Lucia	2,943.3	1,253.5	100.7
Saudi Arabia	3,476.4	3,000.1	2,838.8
Singapore	2,786.5	2,942.6	1,905.4
Spain	4,705.5	3,688.7	3,576.0
United Arab Emirates	2,169.2	2,456.8	2,588.8
United Kingdom	5,229.8	4,519.4	4,101.9
USA	25,943.0	26,849.9	24,861.8
Venezuela	4,591.8	5,056.0	4,849.8
Total (incl. others)	256,038.7	242,579.8	242,178.6

Source: Trade Map-Trade Competitiveness Map, International Trade Centre, www.intracen.org/marketanalysis.

Transport

RAILWAYS
(figures are rounded)

	2005	2006	2007
Passengers ('000)			
Long distance	1,451	1,481	1,414
Metropolitan	144,300	n.a.	n.a.
Passenger-km ('000, long distance only)	451,943	463,517	444,094
Freight ('000 metric tons)	388,592	389,109	414,926
Freight ton-km (million)	221,633	238,054	257,118

2008: Freight ('000 metric tons) 426,514; Freight ton-km (million) 266,967.

Source: Agência Nacional de Transportes Terrestres (ANTT), Ministério dos Transportes, Brasília.

ROAD TRAFFIC
(motor vehicles in use at 31 December)

	2007	2008	2009
Passenger cars	30,282,855	32,054,684	34,536,667
Vans and lorries	5,709,063	7,528,326	n.a.
Buses and coaches	1,985,761	633,122	673,084
Motorcycles and mopeds	10,921,686	13,088,074	14,688,678
Total (incl. others)	48,899,365	53,304,206	n.a.

Source: IRF, *World Road Statistics*.

SHIPPING

Flag Registered Fleet
(at 31 December)

	2011	2012	2013
Number of vessels	744	781	823
Total displacement ('000 grt)	2,914.8	2,920.4	3,156.5

Source: Lloyd's List Intelligence (www.lloydslistintelligence.com).

International Sea-borne Freight Traffic
('000 metric tons)

	2003	2004	2005
Goods loaded	376,188	417,723	452,742
Goods unloaded	194,602	202,997	196,677

CIVIL AVIATION

	2008	2009	2010
Passengers carried ('000)*	58,763	67,946	77,255
Passenger-km (million)	n.a.	78,282	95,845
Freight ton-km ('000)†	8,403,749	6,615,013.	8,024,365

* Source: partly UN Economic Commission for Latin America and the Caribbean, *Statistical Yearbook*.

† Including mail and cargo.

Source: mostly Departamento de Aviação Civil (DAC), Comando da Aeronáutica, Ministério da Defesa, Brasília.

Tourism

FOREIGN TOURIST ARRIVALS

Country of origin	2010	2011	2012
Argentina	1,399,592	1,593,775	1,671,604
Bolivia	99,359	85,429	112,639
Chile	200,724	217,200	250,586
Colombia	85,567	91,345	100,324
France	199,719	207,890	218,626
Germany	226,630	241,739	258,437
Italy	245,491	229,484	230,114
Paraguay	194,340	192,730	246,401
Portugal	189,065	183,728	168,649
Spain	179,340	190,392	180,406
United Kingdom	167,355	149,564	155,548
USA	641,377	594,947	586,463
Uruguay	228,545	261,204	253,864
Total (incl. others)	5,161,379	5,433,354	5,676,843

Source: Instituto Brasileiro de Turismo—EMBRATUR, Brasília.

Receipts from tourism (US $ million, excl. passenger transport): 5,702 in 2010; 6,555 in 2011; 6,645 in 2012 (provisional) (Source: World Tourism Organization).

Communications Media

	2010	2011	2012
Telephones in use ('000 main lines)	42,141.4	43,025.8	44,305.3
Mobile cellular telephones ('000 subscribers)	202,944.0	234,357.5	248,323.7
Internet subscribers ('000)	20,992.4	22,898.3	n.a.
Broadband subscribers ('000)	13,266.3	16,855.1	18,187.0

Source: International Telecommunication Union.

Education

(2012 unless otherwise indicated)

	Institutions	Teachers	Students
Pre-primary	107,791	443,405	7,295,512
Literacy classes (Classe de Alfabetização)*	27,670	37,508	598,589
Primary	144,705	1,405,552	29,702,498
Secondary	27,164	497,797	8,376,852
Special	4,161	29,492	199,656
Technical and vocational	4,285	71,896	1,063,655
Higher	2,416	378,939	5,923,838

* 2003 figures.

Source: Ministério da Educação, Brasília.

Pupil-teacher ratio (primary education, UN estimate): 21.3 in 2010/11 (Source: UNESCO Institute for Statistics).

Adult literacy rate (UNESCO estimates): 90.4% (males 90.1%; females 90.7%) in 2010 (Source: UNESCO Institute for Statistics).

Directory

The Government

HEAD OF STATE

President: DILMA VANA ROUSSEFF (PT) (took office 1 January 2011).

Vice-President: MICHEL MIGUEL ELIAS TEMER LULIA (PMDB).

THE CABINET
(April 2014)

The Cabinet is composed of members of the Partido dos Trabalhadores (PT), the Partido do Movimento Democrático Brasileiro (PMDB), the Partido da República (PR), the Partido Republicano Brasiliero (PRB), the Partido Comunista do Brasil (PC do B), the Partido Democrático Trabalhista (PDT), the Partido Republicano da Ordem Social (PROS), and Independents (Ind.).

Cabinet Chief: ALOÍZIO MERCADANTE (PT).

Minister of Foreign Affairs: LUIZ ALBERTO FIGUEIREDO MACHADO (Ind.).

Minister of Justice: JOSÉ EDUARDO CARDOZO (PT).

Minister of Finance: GUIDO MANTEGA (PT).

Minister of Defence: CELSO AMORIM (PT).

Minister of Agriculture, Livestock and Food Supply: NERI GELLER (PMDB).

Minister of Agrarian Development: MIGUEL ROSSETTO (PT).

Minister of Labour and Employment: MANOEL DIAS (PDT).

Minister of Transport: CÉSAR BORGES (PR).

Minister of Cities: GILBERTO MAGALHÃES OCCHI (Ind.).

Minister of Planning, Budget and Administration: MIRIAM BELCHIOR (PT).

Minister of Mines and Energy: EDISON LOBÃO (PMDB).

Minister of Culture: MARTA SUPLICY (PT).

Minister of the Environment: IZABELLA MÔNICA VIEIRA TEIXEIRA (Ind.).

Minister of Development, Industry and Foreign Trade: FERNANDO PIMENTEL (PT).

Minister of Education: JOSÉ HENRIQUE PAIM FERNANDES (PT).

Minister of Health: ARTHUR CHIORO (PT).

Minister of National Integration: FRANCISCO JOSÉ COELHO TEIXEIRA (PROS).

Minister of Social Security: GARIBALDI ALVES FILHO (PMDB).

Minister of Social Development and the Fight against Hunger: TEREZA CAMPELO (PT).

Minister of Communications: PAULO BERNARDO SILVA (PT).

Minister of Science, Technology and Innovation: CLÉLIO CAMPOLINA DINIZ (PMDB).

Minister of Sport: JOSÉ ALDO REBELO FIGUEIREDO (PC do B).

Minister of Tourism: VINICIUS NOBRE LAGES (PMDB).

Minister of Fisheries and Aquaculture: EDUARDO LOPES (PRB).

Attorney-General: ROBERTO MONTEIRO GURGEL SANTOS.

Comptroller-General: JORGE HAGE SOBRINHO.

Chief Minister of the Office of Institutional Security: Gen. JOSÉ ELITO CARVALHO SIQUEIRA.

SECRETARIES

Secretary of Strategic Affairs: MARCELO CÔRTES NERI.

Secretary of Civil Aviation: MOREIRA FRANCO.

Secretary of Social Communication: THOMAS TRAUMANN.

Secretary of Human Rights: MARIA DO ROSÁRIO.

Secretary of Policies for the Promotion of Racial Equality: LUIZA HELENA DE BAIRROS.

Secretary of Women's Policies: ELEONORA MENICUCCI DE OLIVEIRA.

Secretary of Ports: ANTONIO HENRIQUE PINHEIRO SILVEIRA (acting).

Secretary of Institutional Relations: IDELI SALVATTI.

Secretary for Small- and Micro-Businesses: GUILHERME AFIF DOMINGOS.

Secretary-General: GILBERTO CARVALHO.

MINISTRIES AND SECRETARIATS

Office of the President: Palácio do Planalto, 3° andar, Praça dos Três Poderes, 70150-900 Brasília, DF; tel. (61) 3411-1221; fax 3411-2222; e-mail protocolo@planalto.gov.br; internet www2.planalto.gov.br.

Office of the Civilian Cabinet: Palácio do Planalto, 4° andar, Praça dos Três Poderes, 70150-900 Brasília, DF; tel. (61) 3411-1221; fax (61) 3411-2222; e-mail sicplanalto@planalto.gov.br; internet www.casacivil.planalto.gov.br.

Ministry of Agrarian Development: Esplanada dos Ministérios, Bloco A, 8º andar, Ala Norte, 70050-902 Brasília, DF; tel. (61) 2020-0002; fax (61) 2020-0061; e-mail miguel.rossetto@mda.gov.br; internet www.mda.gov.br.

Ministry of Agriculture, Livestock and Food Supply: Esplanada dos Ministérios, Bloco D, Anexo B, 70043-900 Brasília, DF; tel. (61) 3218-2828; fax (61) 3218-2401; e-mail gm@agricultura.gov.br; internet www.agricultura.gov.br.

Ministry of Cities: Edif. Telemundi II, 14º andar, Setor de Autarquias Sul, Quadra 01, Lote 01/06, Bloco H, 700700-10 Brasília, DF; tel. (61) 2108-1000; fax (61) 2108-1415; e-mail cidades@cidades.gov.br; internet www.cidades.gov.br.

Ministry of Communications: Esplanada dos Ministérios, Bloco R, 8° andar, 70044-900 Brasília, DF; tel. (61) 2027-6200; fax (61) 3311-6731; e-mail falecomoministerio@comunicacoes.gov.br; internet www.mc.gov.br.

Ministry of Culture: Esplanada dos Ministérios, Bloco B, 4° andar, 70068-900 Brasília, DF; tel. (61) 2024-2000; fax (61) 3225-9162; e-mail gm@cultura.gov.br; internet www.cultura.gov.br.

Ministry of Defence: Esplanada dos Ministérios, Bloco Q, 70049-900 Brasília, DF; tel. (61) 3312-4000; fax (61) 3225-4151; e-mail faleconosco@defesa.gov.br; internet www.defesa.gov.br.

Ministry of Development, Industry and Foreign Trade: Esplanada dos Ministérios, Bloco J, 70053-900 Brasília, DF; tel. (61) 2027-7000; fax (61) 2027-7230; e-mail asint@desenvolvimento.gov.br; internet www.desenvolvimento.gov.br.

Ministry of Education: Esplanada dos Ministérios, Bloco L, 8º andar, Sala 805, 70047-900 Brasília, DF; tel. (61) 2022-7828; fax (61) 2022-7858; e-mail gabinetedoministro@mec.gov.br; internet www.mec.gov.br.

Ministry of the Environment: Esplanada dos Ministérios, Bloco B, 5°–9° andares, 70068-900 Brasília, DF; tel. (61) 2028-1057; fax (61) 2028-1756; e-mail webmaster@mma.gov.br; internet www.mma.gov.br.

Ministry of Finance: Esplanada dos Ministérios, Bloco P, 5° andar, 70048-900 Brasília, DF; tel. (61) 3412-2000; fax (61) 3412-1721; e-mail gabinete.df.gmf@fazenda.gov.br; internet www.fazenda.gov.br.

Ministry of Fisheries and Aquaculture: Edif. Carlton Tower, SBS Quadra 2, Lote 10, Bloco J, 70043-900 Brasília DF; tel. (61) 2023-3000; fax (61) 2023-3916; e-mail comunicacao@mpa.gov.br; internet www.mpa.gov.br.

Ministry of Foreign Affairs: Palácio do Itamaraty, Térreo, Esplanada dos Ministérios, Bloco H, 70170-900 Brasília, DF; tel. (61) 3411-8006; fax (61) 3225-8002; e-mail imprensa@itamaraty.gov.br; internet www.itamaraty.gov.br.

Ministry of Health: Esplanada dos Ministérios, Bloco G, 70058-900 Brasília, DF; tel. (61) 3315-3283; e-mail leandro.viegas@saude.gov.br; internet www.saude.gov.br.

Ministry of Justice: Esplanada dos Ministérios, Bloco T, 70064-900 Brasília, DF; tel. (61) 3429-3000; fax (61) 3224-0954; e-mail acs@mj.gov.br; internet www.mj.gov.br.

Ministry of Labour and Employment: Esplanada dos Ministérios, Bloco F, 5° andar, 70059-900 Brasília, DF; tel. (61) 3317-6000; fax (61) 3317-8245; e-mail ouvidoria@mte.gov.br; internet www.mte.gov.br.

Ministry of Mines and Energy: Esplanada dos Ministérios, Bloco U, 70065-900 Brasília, DF; tel. (61) 3319-5555; fax (61) 3319-5074; e-mail gabinete@mme.gov.br; internet www.mme.gov.br.

Ministry of National Integration: Esplanada dos Ministérios, Bloco E, 8º andar, 70067-901 Brasília, DF; tel. (61) 3414-5814; fax (61) 3321-5914; e-mail impresa@integracao.gov.br; internet www.integracao.gov.br.

Ministry of Planning, Budget and Administration: Esplanada dos Ministérios, Bloco K, 7º andar, 70040-906 Brasília, DF; tel. (61) 2020-4102; fax (61) 2020-5009; e-mail ministro@planejamento.gov.br; internet www.planejamento.gov.br.

Ministry of Science, Technology and Innovation: Esplanada dos Ministérios, Bloco E, 4° andar, 70067-900 Brasília, DF; tel. (61) 3317-7500; fax (61) 3317-7764; e-mail webgab@mct.gov.br; internet www.mct.gov.br.

Ministry of Social Development and the Fight against Hunger: Esplanada dos Ministérios, Bloco C, 5° andar, 70046-900 Brasília, DF; tel. (61) 3433-1029; e-mail ministro.mds@mds.gov.br; internet www.mds.gov.br.

Ministry of Social Security: Esplanada dos Ministérios, Bloco F, 8º andar, 70059-900 Brasília, DF; tel. (61) 2021-5000; fax (61) 2021-5407; e-mail gm.mps@previdencia.gov.br; internet www.mps.gov.br.

Ministry of Sport: Esplanada dos Ministérios, Bloco A, 70054-906 Brasília, DF; tel. (61) 3217-1800; fax (61) 3217-1707; e-mail gabmin@esporte.gov.br; internet www.esporte.gov.br.

Ministry of Tourism: Esplanada dos Ministérios, Bloco U, 2º e 3º andar, 70065-900 Brasília, DF; tel. (61) 2023-7024; fax (61) 2023-7096; e-mail ouvidoria@turismo.gov.br; internet www.turismo.gov.br.

Ministry of Transport: Esplanada dos Ministérios, Bloco R, 6º andar, 70044-900 Brasília, DF; tel. (61) 2029-7000; fax (61) 2029-7876; e-mail paulo.passos@transportes.gov.br; internet www.transportes.gov.br.

Office of Institutional Security: Brasília, DF.

Secretariat-General of the Presidency: Praça dos Três Poderes, Palácio do Planalto, 4º andar, 70150-900 Brasília, DF; tel. (61) 3411-1225; e-mail sg@planalto.gov.br; internet www.secretariageral.gov.br.

Secretariat of Civil Aviation: Brasília, DF.

Secretariat of Human Rights: Edif. Parque Cidade Corporate, Torre A, 10º andar, Setor Comercial Sul B, Quadra 9, Lote C, 70308-200 Brasília, DF; tel. (61) 2025-3536; fax (61) 2025-3106; e-mail direitoshumanos@sedh.gov.br; internet www.direitoshumanos.gov.br.

Secretariat of Institutional Relations: Palácio do Planalto, 4º andar, Sala 404, Praça dos Três Poderes, 70150-900 Brasília, DF; tel. (61) 3411-1585; fax (61) 3411-1503; e-mail sri.gabinete@planalto.gov.br; internet www.relacoesinstitucionais.gov.br.

Secretariat of Policies for the Promotion of Racial Equality: Esplanada dos Ministérios, Bloco A, 9º andar, 70054-906 Brasília, DF; tel. (61) 2025-7043; fax (61) 3226-5625; e-mail seppir.imprensa@planalto.gov.br; internet www.seppir.gov.br.

Secretariat of Ports: Centro Empresarial Varig, Pétala C Mezanino, Sala 1403, SCN Quadra 04, Bloco B, 70714-900 Brasília, DF; tel. (61) 3411-3704; fax (61) 3326-3025; e-mail faleconosco@portosdobrasil.gov.br; internet www.portosdobrasil.gov.br.

Secretariat of Small- and Micro-Businesses: Brasília, DF.

Secretariat of Social Communication: Esplanada dos Ministérios, Bloco A, 70054-900 Brasília, DF; tel. (61) 3411-1279; fax (61) 3226-8316; internet www.secom.gov.br.

Secretariat of Strategic Affairs: Esplanada dos Ministérios, Bloco O, 7° andar, 8° e 9° andares, 70052-900 Brasília, DF; tel. (61) 3411-4674; e-mail falecomministro.sae@presidencia.gov.br; internet www.sae.gov.br.

Secretariat of Women's Policies: Via N1 Leste, Pavilhão das Metas, Praça dos Três Poderes, Zona Cívico-Administrativa, 70150-908 Brasília, DF; tel. (61) 3411-4246; fax (61) 3327-7464; e-mail spmulheres@spmulheres.gov.br; internet www.sepm.gov.br.

President and Legislature

PRESIDENT

Election, First Round, 3 October 2010

Candidate	Votes	% of valid votes
Dilma Vana Rousseff (PT)	47,651,434	46.91
José Serra (PSDB)	33,132,283	32.61
Marina Silva (PV)	19,636,359	19.33
Plínio de Arruda Sampaio (PSOL)	886,816	0.87
José Maria Eymael (PSDC)	89,350	0.09
José Maria de Almeida (PSTU)	84,609	0.08
Levy Fidelix (PRTB)	57,960	0.06
Ivan Pinheiro (PCB)	39,136	0.04
Rui Costa Pimenta (PCO)	12,206	0.01
Total*	101,590,153	100.00

* In addition, there were 3,479,340 blank and 6,124,254 spoiled votes.

Election, Second Round, 31 October 2010

Candidate	Votes	% of valid votes
Dilma Vana Rousseff (PT)	55,725,529	56.04
José Serra (PSDB)	43,711,388	43.96
Total*	99,436,917	100.00

* In addition, there were 2,452,597 blank ballots and 4,689,428 spoiled ballots.

NATIONAL CONGRESS

Chamber of Deputies
(Câmara dos Deputados)

Chamber of Deputies: Palácio do Congresso Nacional, Edif. Principal, Praça dos Três Poderes, 70160-900 Brasília, DF; tel. (61) 3216-0000; e-mail presidencia@camara.gov.br; internet www.camara.gov.br.

President: HENRIQUE EDUARDO ALVES (PMDB).

The Chamber has 513 members who hold office for a four-year term.

General Election, 3 October 2010

Party	Votes	% of valid votes	Seats
Partido dos Trabalhadores (PT)	16,289,199	16.9	88
Partido do Movimento Democrático Brasileiro (PMDB)	12,537,252	13.0	79
Partido da Social Democracia Brasileira (PSDB)	11,477,380	11.9	53
Democratas (DEM)	7,301,171	7.6	43
Partido da República (PR)	7,311,655	7.6	41
Partido Progressista (PP)	6,330,062	6.6	41
Partido Socialista Brasileiro (PSB)	6,851,053	7.1	34
Partido Democrático Trabalhista (PDT)	4,854,602	5.0	28
Partido Trabalhista Brasileiro (PTB)	4,038,239	4.2	21
Partido Social Cristão (PSC)	3,072,546	3.2	17
Partido Verde (PV)	3,710,366	3.8	15
Partido Comunista do Brasil (PC do B)	2,748,290	2.8	15
Partido Popular Socialista (PPS)	2,536,809	2.6	12
Partido Republicano Brasileiro (PRB)	1,633,500	1.7	8
Partido da Mobilização Nacional (PMN)	1,086,705	1.1	4
Partido Socialismo e Liberdade (PSOL)	1,142,737	1.2	3
Partido Trabalhista do Brasil (PT do B)	642,422	0.7	3
Partido Humanista da Solidariedade (PHS)	764,412	0.8	2
Partido Renovador Trabalhista Brasileira (PRTB)	307,925	0.3	2
Partido Republicano Progressista (PRP)	307,188	0.3	2
Partido Trabalhista Cristão (PTC)	595,431	0.6	1
Partido Social Liberal (PSL)	499,963	0.5	1
Total (incl. others)	96,580,011	100.0	513

Federal Senate
(Senado Federal)

Federal Senate: Palácio do Congresso Nacional, Praça dos Três Poderes, 70165-900 Brasília, DF; tel. (61) 3311-4141; fax (61) 3311-3190; e-mail asimpre@senado.gov.br; internet www.senado.gov.br.

President: RENAN CALHEIROS (PMDB).

The 81 members of the Senate are elected by the 26 states and the Federal District (three senators for each) according to the principle of majority. The Senate's term of office is eight years, with elections after four years for one-third of the members and after another four years for the remaining two-thirds.

In the elections of 3 October 2010 54 seats were contested. In that month the PMDB was represented by 20 senators, the PT by 15, the PSDB by 11, the PTB and the DEM by six each, the PR, the PP and the PDT by four each, the PSB by three, the PSOL and the PC do B by two each and the PRB, the PPS, the PSC and the PMN by one each.

Governors

STATES
(April 2014)

Acre: SEBASTIÃO AFONSO VIANA MACEDO NEVES (PT).
Alagoas: TEOTÔNIO BRANDÃO VILELA FILHO (PSDB).
Amapá: CARLOS CAMILO GÓES CAPIBERIBE (PSB).
Amazonas: JOSÉ MELO DE OLIVEIRA (PROS).
Bahia: JACQUES WAGNER (PT).
Ceará: CID GOMES (PSB).
Espírito Santo: RENATO CASAGRANDE (PSB).
Goiás: MARCONI FERREIRA PERILLO JÚNIOR (PSDB).
Maranhão: ROSEANA SARNEY (PMDB).
Mato Grosso: SILVAL CUNHA BARBOSA (PMDB).
Mato Grosso do Sul: ANDRÉ PUCCINELLI (PMDB).
Minas Gerais: ALBERTO PINTO COELHO JÚNIOR (PP).
Pará: SIMÃO ROBSON OLIVEIRA JATENE (PSDB).
Paraíba: RICARDO VIEIRA COUTINHO (PSB).
Paraná: CARLOS ALBERTO RICHA (PSDB).
Pernambuco: JOÃO SOARES LYRA NETO (PMDB).
Piauí: ANTÔNIO JOSÉ DE MORAES SOUZA FILHO (PMDB).
Rio de Janeiro: LUIZ FERNANDO PEZÃO (PMDB, acting).
Rio Grande do Norte: ROSALBA CIARLINI ROSADO (DEM).
Rio Grande do Sul: TARSO FERNANDO HERZ GENRO (PT).
Rondônia: CONFÚCIO AIRES DE MOURA (PMDB).
Roraima: FRANCISCO (CHICO) DE ASSIS RODRIGUES (PSB).
Santa Catarina: JOÃO RAIMUNDO COLOMBO (DEM).
São Paulo: GERALDO ALCKMIN FILHO (PSDB).
Sergipe: JACKSON BARRETO DE LIMA (acting, PT).
Tocantins: SANDOVAL LOBO CARDOSO (PMDB).

FEDERAL DISTRICT

Brasília: AGNELO SANTOS QUEIROZ FILHO (PT).

Election Commission

Tribunal Superior Eleitoral (TSE): Setor de Administração Federal Sul (SAFS), Quadra 7, Lotes 1/2, 70070-600 Brasília, DF; tel. (61) 3030-7000; fax (61) 3030-9850; e-mail webmaster@tse.gov.br; internet www.tse.gov.br; f. 1945; Pres. CÁRMEN LÚCIA ANTUNES ROCHA; Inspector-Gen., Elections LAURITA HILÁRIO VAZ.

Political Organizations

Democratas (DEM): Senado Federal, Anexo 1, 26° andar, 70165-900 Brasília, DF; tel. (61) 3311-4305; fax (61) 3224-1912; e-mail democratas25@democratas.org.br; internet www.dem.org.br; f. 1985 as the Partido da Frente Liberal; refounded in 2007 under present name; Pres. JOSÉ AGRIPINO MAIA; Sec.-Gen. ONYX LORENZONI.

Partido da Causa Operaria (PCO): SCS, Quadra 2, Edif. São Paulo, Sala 310, 70314-900 Brasília, DF; tel. (11) 5584-9322; fax (11) 5584-9322; e-mail pco@pco.org.br; internet www.pco.org.br; f. 1997; Pres. RUI COSTA PIMENTA.

Partido Comunista do Brasil (PC do B): Rua Rego Freitas 192, 01220-907 São Paulo, SP; tel. and fax (11) 3054-1800; e-mail comitecentral@pcdob.org.br; internet www.pcdob.org.br; f. 1922; Pres. JOSÉ RENATO RABELO; Sec.-Gen. WALTER SORRENTINO; 185,000 mems.

Partido Democrático Trabalhista (PDT): Rua do Teatro 39, Praça Tiradentes, 20010-190 Rio de Janeiro, RJ; tel. (21) 2232-1016; fax (21) 2232-0121; e-mail fio@pdt.org.br; internet www.pdt.org.br; f. 1980; fmrly the Partido Trabalhista Brasileiro, renamed 1980 when that name was awarded to a dissident group following controversial judicial proceedings; mem. of Socialist International; Pres. CARLOS LUPI; Sec.-Gen. MANOEL DIAS.

Partido Ecológico Nacional (PEN): SHN, Quadra 2, Bloco F, Conj. 1510, Sala B, Asa Norte, 70702-000 Brasília, DF; tel. and fax (61) 3326-4555; e-mail pen@pen51.org.br; internet www.pen51.org.br; f. 2012; Pres. ADILSON BARROSO OLIVEIRA.

Partido Humanista da Solidariedade (PHS): SHI/SUL, QL 2, Conj. 3, Casa 13, Lago Sul, 71610-035 Brasília, DF; tel. (61) 3321-3131; fax (61) 3224-0726; e-mail contato@phs.org.br; internet www.phs.org.br; f. 2013; Pres. EDUARDO MACHADO E SILVA RODRIGUES.

Partido da Mobilização Nacional (PMN): Rua Martins Fontes 197, 3º andar, Conj. 32, 01050-906 São Paulo, SP; tel. (11) 3214-4261; fax (11) 3120-2669; e-mail pmn33@pmn.org.br; internet www.pmn.org.br; f. 1984; Pres. OSCAR NORONHA FILHO; Sec.-Gen. TELMA RIBEIRO DOS SANTOS.

Partido do Movimento Democrático Brasileiro (PMDB): Câmara dos Deputados, Edif. Principal, Ala B, Sala 6, Praça dos Três Poderes, 70160-900 Brasília, DF; tel. (61) 3215-9206; fax (61) 3215-9220; e-mail pmdb@pmdb.org.br; internet www.pmdb.org.br; f. 1980 by moderate elements of fmr Movimento Democrático Brasileiro; merged with Partido Popular in 1982; Pres. MICHEL TEMER; Sec.-Gen. MAURO LOPES; factions include the Históricos and the Movimento da Unidade Progressiva (MUP).

Partido Pátria Livre (PPL): SCS, Quadra 1, Bloco L, 17°, Sala 1114, 70301-000 Brasília, DF; tel. (61) 3225-1396; fax (61) 3225-1396; e-mail df.patrialivre@hotmail.com; f. 2011; Pres. SÉRGIO RUBENS DE ARAÚJO TORRES.

Partido Popular Socialista (PPS): SCS, Quadra 7, Bloco A, Edif. Executive Tower, Sala 826/828, Pátio Brasil Shopping, Setor Comercial Sul, 70307-901 Brasília, DF; tel. (61) 3218-4123; fax (61) 3218-4112; e-mail pps23@pps.org.br; internet www.pps.org.br; f. 1922; Pres. ROBERTO JOÃO PEREIRA FREIRE; Sec.-Gen. RUBENS BUENO.

Partido Progressista (PP): Senado Federal, Anexo 1, 17° andar, Sala 1704, 70165-900 Brasília, DF; tel. (61) 3311-3041; fax (61) 3322-6938; e-mail pp@pp.org.br; internet www.pp.org.br; f. 1995 as Partido Progressista Brasileiro by merger of Partido Progressista Reformador, Partido Progressista and Partido Republicano Progressista; adopted present name 2003; right-wing; Pres. CIRO NOGUEIRA; Sec.-Gen. ALDO DA ROSA.

Partido Renovador Trabalhista Brasileiro (PRTB): SHN, Quadra 2, Bloco F, Edif. Executive Tower, 70702-906 Brasília, DF; tel. (61) 3328-6128; fax (11) 5097-9993; e-mail prtb@prtb.org.br; internet www.prtb.org.br; f. 2004; Pres. JOSÉ LEVY FIDELIX DA CRUZ.

Partido da República (PR): SCN, Edif. Liberty Mall, Quadra 02, Bloco D, Torre A, Salas 601/606, Asa Norte, 70712-903 Brasília, DF; tel. and fax (61) 3202-9922; e-mail pr22@partidodarepublica.org.br; internet www.partidodarepublica.org.br; f. 2006 by merger of Partido Liberal and Partido de Reedificação da Ordem Nacional; Pres. ALFREDO PEREIRA DO NASCIMENTO.

Partido Republicano Brasileiro (PRB): SDS, Bloco L 30, Edif. Miguel Badya, 3° andar, Sala 320, 70394-901 Brasília, DF; tel. and fax (61) 3223-9069; e-mail faleconosco@prb10.org.br; internet www.prb10.org.br; f. 2005 as Partido Municipalista Renovador; name changed as above in 2006; political wing of Igreja Universal do Reino de Deus; Pres. MARCOS ANTÔNIO PEREIRA; Sec.-Gen. EVANDRO GARLA.

Partido Republicano da Ordem Social (PROS): SAS, Quadra 05, Bloco K, Salas 1007–08, Asa Sul, 70070-937 Brasília, DF; tel. (61) 3322-4030; fax (61) 3223-8053; e-mail contato@pros.org.br; internet www.pros.org.br; f. 2013; Pres. EURÍPEDES GOMES DE MACEDO JÚNIOR.

Partido Republicano Progressista (PRP): SRTVS, Quadra 701, Bloco E, Edif. Palácio do Rádio II, 70340-902 Brasília, DF; tel. (61) 3037-4044; fax (61) 3039-4044; e-mail prpnacionalsrp@terra.com.br; internet www.prp.org.br; f. 2013; Pres OVASCO ROMA ALTIMARI RESENDE.

Partido Social Cristão (PSC): Rua Pouso Alegre 1388, Santa Teresa, 31015-030 Belo Horizonte, MG; tel. (31) 3467-1390; fax (31) 3467-6522; e-mail psc@psc.org.br; internet www.psc.org.br; f. 1970 as Partido Democrático Republicano; Pres. VITOR JORGE ADBALA NÓSSEIS; Sec.-Gen. ANTONIO OLIBONI.

Partido da Social Democracia Brasileira (PSDB): SGAS, Quadra 607, Edif. Metrópolis, Asa Sul, Cobertura 2, 70200-670 Brasília, DF; tel. (61) 3424-0500; fax (61) 3424-0515; e-mail tucano@psdb.org.br; internet www.psdb.org.br; f. 1988; centre-left; formed by dissident mems of parties incl. the PMDB, PFL, PDT, PSB and PTB; Pres. AÉCIO NEVES; Sec.-Gen. ANTÔNIO CARLOS MENDES THAME.

Partido Social Democrata Cristão (PSDC): SCS, Quadra 1, Bloco I, Edif. Central, Sala 402, 70304-900 Brasília, DF; tel. (61) 3225-1427; fax (61) 3225-1427; e-mail secretaria@psdc.org.br; internet www.psdc.org.br; f. 2011; Pres. JOSÉ MARIA EYMAEL.

Partido Social Democrático (PSD): e-mail contato@psd.org.br; internet www.psd.org.br; f. 2011; Pres. GILBERTO KASSAB; Sec.-Gen. SAULO QUEIROZ.

Partido Social Liberal (PSL): SCS, Quadra 01, Bloco E, Edif. Ceará, Sala 1004, 70303-900 Brasília, DF; tel. (61) 3322-1721; fax (61) 3032-6832; e-mail contato@pslnacional.org.br; internet www.pslnacional.org.br; f. 1994; Pres. LUCIANO CALDAS BIVAR; Sec.-Gen. ROBERTO SIQUEIRA GOMES.

Partido Socialismo e Liberdade (PSOL): SCS, Quadra 01, Bloco E, Edif. Ceará, Salas 1203–04, 70303-900 Brasília, DF; tel. (61) 3963-1750; fax (61) 3039-6356; e-mail secretariageral@psol50.org.br; internet psol50.org.br; f. 2004 by fmr PT mems; Pres. IVAN VALENTE; Secs-Gen. EDILSON FRANCISCO DA SILVA, MARIO AGRA JUNIOR.

Partido Socialista Brasileiro (PSB): SCLN 304, Bloco A, Sobreloja 1, Entrada 63, 70736-510 Brasília, DF; tel. and fax (61) 3327-6405; e-mail psb@psbnacional.org.br; internet www.psbnacional.org.br; f. 1945 as the Esquerda Democrática, renamed 1947; Pres. EDUARDO HENRIQUE ACCIOLY CAMPOS; Sec.-Gen. JOSÉ RENATO CASAGRANDE.

Partido Socialista dos Trabalhadores Unificado (PSTU): SCS, SL 215, Quadra 6, Bloco A, Edif. Carioca 240, Asa Sul, 70306-000 Brasília, DF; tel. (61) 3226-1016; fax (61) 3226-1016; e-mail pstu@pstu.org.br; internet www.pstu.org.br; f. 2010; Pres. JOSÉ MARIA ALMEIDA.

Partido Social Liberal (PSL): SCS, SL 1203, Quadra 1, Bloco E, Edif. Ceará, Setor Comercial Sul, 70303-900 Brasília, DF; tel. (61) 3322-1721; fax (61) 3225-1805; e-mail contato@pslnacional.org.br; internet www.psl.org.br; f. 1998; Pres. LUCIANO CALDAS BIVAR.

Partido dos Trabalhadores (PT): SCS, Quadra 2, Bloco C, Edif. Toufic, Sala 256, 70302-000 São Paulo, SP; tel. (11) 3213-1313; fax (11) 3213-1360; e-mail presidencia@pt.org.br; internet www.pt.org.br; f. 1980; first independent labour party; associated with the *autêntico* br. of the trade union movt; 500,000 mems; Pres. RUI FALCÃO; Sec.-Gen. PAULO TEIXEIRA.

Partido Trabalhista Nacional (PTN): SRTVS 701, Torre 1, SL 422, Edif. Assis Chateaubriand, Asa Sul, 70340-000 Brasília, DF; tel. (61) 3368-1323; fax (61) 3368-1323; e-mail ptnbrasil@ptn.org.br; internet www.ptn.org.br; f. 1997; Pres. JOSÉ MASCI DE ABREU.

Partido Trabalhista Brasileiro (PTB): SEPN, Quadra 504, Bloco A, Edif. Ana Carolina, Sala 100, Cobertura, 70730-521 Brasília DF; tel. (61) 2101-1414; fax (61) 2101-1400; e-mail ptb@ptb.org.br; internet www.ptb.org.br; f. 1980; Pres. ROBERTO JEFFERSON MONTEIRO FRANCISCO; Sec.-Gen. ANTÔNIO CARLOS DE CAMPOS MACHADO.

Partido Trabalhista do Brasil (PT do B): SHIS, QI 5, BlocoF, 130°, Centro Comercial Gilberto Salomão, Sobreloja 224, Lago Sul, 71615-907 Brasília, DF; tel. (61) 3248-1929; fax (61) 3248-5909; e-mail ptdobnac@yahoo.com.br; internet www.ptdob.org.br; f. 1994; Pres. LUIS HENRIQUE DE OLIVEIRA RESENDE.

Partido Trabalhista Cristão (PTC): Edif. Rodolpho De Paoli, Sala 506, Av. Nilo Peçanha 50, Centro, 20020-906 Rio de Janeiro, RJ; tel. (21) 2220-1832; e-mail ptcnacional@uol.com.br; internet www.ptc36nacional.com.br; f. 1989 as the Partido da Reconstrução Nacional, renamed 1997; Christian party; Pres. DANIEL S. TOURINHO.

Partido Verde (PV): Edif. Miguel Badya, Bloco L, Sala 218, Asa Sul, 70394-901 Brasília, DF; tel. (61) 3366-1569; e-mail nacional@pv.org.br; internet www.pv.org.br; f. 1990; Pres. JOSÉ LUIS DE FRANÇA PENNA; Organizing Sec. CARLA PIRANDA.

Solidariedade: Rua Colônia da Glória 390, Salas 3 e 6, Vila Mariana, 04113-000 São Paulo, SP; tel. (11) 3053-4700; e-mail falecom@solidariedade.org.br; internet www.solidariedade.org.br; f. 2012; Pres. PAULO PEREIRA DA SILVA.

OTHER ORGANIZATIONS

Movimento dos Trabalhadores Rurais Sem Terra (MST): Alameda Barão de Limeira, 1232 Campos Elíseos, 01202-002 São Paulo, SP; tel. (11) 3361-3866; e-mail semterra@mst.org.br; internet www.mst.org.br; f. 1984; landless peasant movt; Pres. JOÃO PEDRO STÉDILE; Nat. Co-ordinator MARINA DOS SANTOS.

Other rural movements include the Organização da Luto no Campo (OLC) and the Movimento de Liberação dos Sem Terra (MLST), a dissident faction of the MST.

Diplomatic Representation

EMBASSIES IN BRAZIL

Albania: SMDB, Conj. 4, Lote 3, Casa D, Lago Sul, 71680-040 Brasília, DF; tel. (61) 3364-0519; fax (61) 3364-0619; e-mail embassy.brasilia@mfa.gov.al; Ambassador TATIANA GJONAJ.

Algeria: SHIS, QI 09, Conj. 13, Casa 01, Lago Sul, 70472-900 Brasília, DF; tel. (61) 3248-4039; fax (61) 3248-4691; e-mail sanag277@terra.com.br; internet www.embaixadadaargelia.com.br; Ambassador DJAMEL-EDDINE OMAR BENNAOUM.

Angola: SHIS, QL 06, Conj. 5, Casa 01, 71620-055 Brasília, DF; tel. (61) 3248-0761; fax (61) 3248-1567; e-mail embangola@embaixadadeangola.com.br; internet www.embaixadadeangola.com.br; Ambassador NELSON MANUEL COSME.

Argentina: SES Quadra 803, Lote 12, 70200-030 Brasília, DF; tel. (61) 3212-7600; fax (61) 3364-7666; e-mail ebras@mrecic.gov.br; internet www.brasil.embajada-argentina.gov.ar; Ambassador LUIS MARÍA KRECKLER.

Armenia: SHIS, QL 28, Conj. 3, Casa 04, South Lake, 71665-235 Brasília, DF; e-mail armgenconsulatesan-paulo@mfa.am; Ambassador ASHOT GALOYAN.

Australia: SES, Av. das Nações, Quadra 801, Conj. K, Lote 7, 70200-010 Brasília, DF; tel. (61) 3226-3111; fax (61) 3226-1112; e-mail embaustr@dfat.gov.au; internet www.brazil.embassy.gov.au; Ambassador PATRICK LAWLESS.

Austria: SES, Av. das Nações, Quadra 811, Lote 40, 70426-900 Brasília, DF; tel. (61) 3443-3111; fax (61) 3443-5233; e-mail brasilia-ob@bmeia.gv.at; internet www.embaixadadaaustria.com.br; Ambassador MARIANNE FELDMANN.

Azerbaijan: SHIS, QI 9, Conj. 15, Casa 15, Lago Sul, 71625-150 Brasília, DF; tel. (61) 3253-9803; fax (61) 3253-9812; e-mail embaixada@azembassy.org.br; internet www.azembassy.org.br; Ambassador ELNUR SULTANOV.

Bangladesh: SHIS, QL 24, Conj. 8, Casa 3, Lago Sul, 71665-085 Brasília, DF; tel. (61) 3367-3699; fax (61) 3522-8634; e-mail bdoot.brasilia@gmail.com; Ambassador SHAMEEM AHSAN.

Barbados: SHIS, QI 13, Conj. 10, Casa 03, Lago Sul, 71635-100 Brasília, DF; tel. (61) 3526-8310; fax (61) 3546-8310; e-mail brasilia@foreign.gov.bb; Ambassador YVETTE GODDARD.

Belarus: SHIS, Lago Sul, Quadra 12, Conj. 06, Casa 09, 71630-265 Brasília, DF; tel. (61) 3543-0481; fax (61) 3543-0469; e-mail belarus.emb@terra.com.br; internet brazil.mfa.gov.by; Ambassador LEONID KRUPETS.

Belgium: SES, Av. das Nações, Quadra 809, Lote 32, 70422-900 Brasília, DF; tel. (61) 3443-1133; fax (61) 3443-1219; e-mail brasilia@diplobel.org; internet www.diplomatie.be/brasilia; Ambassador JOZEF SMETS.

Benin: SHIS, QI 9, Conj. 11, Casa 24, Lago Sul, 71625-110 Brasília, DF; tel. (61) 3248-2192; fax (61) 3263-0739; e-mail ambabeninbrasilia@yahoo.fr; Ambassador ISIDORE BENJAMIN AMÉDÉE MONSI.

Bolivia: SHIS, QI 19, Conj. 13, Casa 19, Lago Sul, 71655-130 Brasília, DF; tel. (61) 3366-3432; fax (61) 3366-3136; e-mail embolivia@embolivia.org.br; internet www.embolivia.org.br; Ambassador JERJES JUSTINIANO TALAVERA.

Botswana: SHIS, QI 09, Conj. 17, Casa 16, Lago Sul, 70316-000 Brasília, DF; tel. (61) 3366-5563; fax (61) 3120-1271; e-mail info@botbraz.org.br; Ambassador BERNADETTE SEBAGE RATHEDI.

Bulgaria: Asa Norte, SEN 8, 70800-911 Brasília, DF; tel. (61) 3223-6193; fax (61) 3323-3285; e-mail Embassy.Brasilia@mfa.bg; internet www.mfa.bg/embassies/brazil; Ambassador VALERIY IVANOV YOTOV.

Burkina Faso: SHIS QI 09, Conj. 13, Casa 12, Lago Sul, 71605-001 Brasília, DF; tel. (61) 3366-4636; fax (61) 3366-3210; e-mail amburkinabras@gmail.com; internet www.burkina.org.br; Ambassador ALAIN FRANCIS GUSTAVE ILBOUDO.

Burundi: SHIS, QI 21, Conj. 1, Casa 10, Lago Sul, 71655-210, Brasília, DF; tel. (61) 3248-1814; fax (61) 3248-1569; e-mail ambaburundibrasilia@gmail.com; Ambassador GAUDENCE SINDAYIGAYA.

Cameroon: SHIS, QI 15, Conj. 14, Casa 17, 71635-340 Brasília, DF; tel. (61) 3248-5403; fax (61) 3248-0443; e-mail embcameroun@embcameroun.org.br; internet www.embcameroun.org.br; Ambassador MARTIN AGBOR MBENG.

Canada: SES, Av. das Nações, Quadra 803, Lote 16, 70410-900 Brasília, DF; tel. (61) 3424-5400; fax (61) 3424-5490; e-mail brsla@international.gc.ca; internet www.canadainternational.gc.ca/brazil; Ambassador JAMAL KHOKHAR.

Cape Verde: SHIS, QL 14, Conj. 03, Casa 08, Lago Sul, 71640-035 Brasília, DF; tel. (61) 3248-0543; fax (61) 3364-4059; e-mail embcvbrasil@embcv.org.br; internet www.embcv.org.br; Ambassador DOMINGOS DIAS PEREIRA MASCARENHAS.

Chile: SES, Av. das Nações, Quadra 803, Lote 11, Asa Sul, 70407-900 Brasília, DF; tel. (61) 2103-5151; fax (61) 3322-2966; e-mail embchile@embchile.org.br; internet chileabroad.gov.cl/brasil; Ambassador JAIME GAZMURI MUJICA.

China, People's Republic: SES, Av. das Nações, Quadra 813, Lote 51, Asa Sul, 70443-900 Brasília, DF; tel. (61) 2198-8200; fax (61) 3346-3299; e-mail chinaemb_br@mfa.gov.cn; internet br.china-embassy.org/por; Ambassador LI JINZHANG.

Colombia: SES, Av. das Nações, Quadra 803, Lote 10, 70444-900 Brasília, DF; tel. (61) 3214-8900; fax (61) 3224-4732; e-mail ebrasili@cancilleria.gov.co; internet www.embajadaenbrasil.gov.co; Chargé d'affaires a.i. RICARDO ALFREDO MONTENEGRO CORAL.

Congo, Democratic Republic: SHIS, QL 13, Conj. 08, Casa 21, Lago Sul, 71635-080 Brasília, DF; tel. (61) 3214-8900; fax (61) 3536-1285; e-mail ambaredeco@ig.com.br; Chargé d'affaires a.i. NADINE OSÓRIO TCHAMLESSO.

Congo, Republic: SHIS, QL 8, Conj. 05, Casa 06, Lago Sul, 71620-255 Brasília, DF; tel. and fax (61) 3532-0440; e-mail ambacobrazza@gmail.com; Ambassador LOUIS-SYLVAIN GOMA.

Costa Rica: SRTV/N 701, Conj. C, Ala A, Salas 308/310, Edif. Centro Empresarial Norte, 70719-903 Brasília, DF; tel. (61) 3032-8450; fax (61) 3032-8452; e-mail embcr.brasil@gmail.com; Ambassador VÍCTOR MONGE CHACÓN.

Côte d'Ivoire: SEN, Av. das Nações, Lote 09, 70473-900 Brasília, DF; tel. (61) 3321-7320; fax (61) 3321-1306; e-mail cotedivoire@cotedivoire.org.br; internet www.cotedivoire.org.br; Ambassador SYLVESTRE AKA AMON KASSI.

Croatia: SHIS, QI 09, Conj. 11, Casa 03, 71625-110 Brasília, DF; tel. (61) 3248-0610; fax (61) 3248-1708; e-mail croemb.brasilia@mvpei.hr; Ambassador DRAGO STAMBUK.

Cuba: SHIS, QI 05, Conj. 18, Casa 01, Lago Sul, 71615-180 Brasília, DF; tel. (61) 3248-4710; fax (61) 3248-6778; e-mail embacuba@uol.com.br; internet embacu.cubaminrex.cu/brasil; Ambassador MARÍA ELENA RUÍZ CAPOTE.

Cyprus: SHIS, QI 09, Conj. 20, Casa 2, Lago Sul, 71625-200 Brasília, DF; tel. (61) 3541-6892; e-mail mmavrommatis@mfa.gov.cy; Ambassador MARTHA A. MAVROMMATIS.

Czech Republic: SES 805, Lote 21A, Via L3 Sul, Asa Sul, 70200-901 Brasília, DF; tel. (61) 3242-7785; fax (61) 3242-7833; e-mail brasilia@embassy.mzv.cz; internet www.mzv.cz/brasilia; Ambassador JIRÍ HAVLÍK.

Denmark: SES, Av. das Nações, Quadra 807, Lote 26, 70200-900 Brasília, DF; tel. (61) 3878-4500; fax (61) 3878-4509; e-mail bsbamb@um.dk; internet www.ambbrasilia.um.dk; Ambassador SVEND ROED NIELSEN.

Dominican Republic: SHIS, QL 06, Conj. 07, Casa 02, 71626-075 Brasília, DF; tel. (61) 3248-1405; fax (61) 3364-3214; e-mail embaixada@republicadominicana.org.br; internet www.republicadominicana.org.br; Ambassador HÉCTOR DIONISIO PÉREZ FERNÁNDEZ.

Ecuador: SHIS, QL 10, Conj. 08, Casa 01, 71630-085 Brasília, DF; tel. (61) 3248-5560; fax (61) 3248-1290; e-mail embeq@solar.com.br; internet www.embequador.org.br; Ambassador HORACIO SEVILLA BORJA.

Egypt: SEN, Av. das Nações, Lote 12, 70435-900 Brasília, DF; tel. (61) 3323-8800; fax (61) 3323-1039; e-mail embegito@opendf.com.br; internet www.opengate.com.br/embegito; Ambassador HOSSAM ELDIN MOHAMED IBRAHIM ZAKI.

El Salvador: SHIS, QL 22, Conj. 7, Casa 8, Lago Sul, 71650-275 Brasília, DF; tel. (61) 3364-4141; fax (61) 3541-4101; e-mail elsalvador@embelsalvador.brte.com.br; Ambassador RINA DEL SOCORRO ANGULO.

Equatorial Guinea: SHIS, QL 10, Conj. 09, Casa 01, Lago Sul, 70630-095 Brasília, DF; tel. (61) 3364-4185; fax (61) 3364-1641; e-mail embaixada@embrge.brtdata.com.br; Ambassador BENIGNO PEDRO MATUTE TANG.

Ethiopia: SHIS QI 7, Conj. 2, Casa 6, Lago Sul, Brasília, DF; tel. (61) 3248-0361; fax (61) 3248-0367; e-mail ethiobrazil@ethiopianembassy.org.br; internet www.ethiopianembassy.org.br; Ambassador SINKNESH EJIGU.

Fiji: QI 22, Conj. 10, Casa 13, Lago Sul, 71650-035 Brasília, DF; tel. (61) 3548-8100; Ambassador CAMA TUIQILAQILA TUILOMA.

Finland: SES, Av. das Nações, Quadra 807, Lote 27, 70417-900 Brasília, DF; tel. (61) 3443-7151; fax (61) 3443-3315; e-mail sanomat.bra@formin.fi; internet www.finlandia.org.br; Ambassador JARÍ LUOTO.

France: SES, Av. das Nações, Quadra 801, Lote 04, 70404-900 Brasília, DF; tel. (61) 3222-3999; fax (61) 3222-3917; e-mail france@ambafrance.org.br; internet ambafrance-br.org; Ambassador DENIS PIETTON.

Gabon: SHIS, QL 09, Conj. 09, Casa 19, Lago Sul, 71625-160 Brasília, DF; tel. (61) 3248-3536; fax (61) 3248-2241; e-mail embgabao@yahoo.com.br; Ambassador JÉRÔME ANGOUO.

Georgia: SHIS, QI 7, Conj. 11, Casa 01, Lago Sul, 71615-310 Brasília, DF; tel. (61) 3366-1101; fax (61) 3366-1161; e-mail brazil.emb@mfa.gov.ge; Ambassador OTAR BERDZENISHVILI.

Germany: SES, Av. das Nações, Quadra 807, Lote 25, 70415-900 Brasília, DF; tel. (61) 3442-7000; fax (61) 3443-7508; e-mail info@alemanja.org; internet www.brasilia.diplo.de; Ambassador WILFRIED GROLIG.

Ghana: SHIS, QL 10, Conj. 08, Casa 02, 71630-085 Brasília, DF; tel. (61) 3248-6047; fax (61) 3248-7913; e-mail ghaembra@zaz.com.br; Ambassador Brig.-Gen. WALLACE GBEDEMAH.

Greece: SES, Av. das Nações, Quadra 805, Lote 22, 70480-900 Brasília, DF; tel. (61) 3443-6573; fax (61) 3443-6902; e-mail gremb.bra@mfa.gr; internet www.emb-grecia.org.br; Ambassador DIMITRI ALEXANDRAKIS.

Guatemala: SHIS, QI 03, Conj. 09, Casa 07, Lago Sul, 71615-330 Brasília, DF; tel. (61) 3248-4175; fax (61) 3248-6678; e-mail embaguate.brasil@gmail.com; Ambassador JULIO ARMANDO MARTINI-HERRERA.

Guinea: SHIS, QL 02, Conj. 07, Casa 09, Lago Sul, 71610-075 Brasília, DF; tel. (61) 3365-1301; fax (61) 3365-4921; e-mail ambaguibrasil@terra.com.br; Ambassador MOHAMED YOULA.

Guinea-Bissau: SHIS, QL 02, Conj. 3, Casa 18, Lago Sul, 71610-035 Brasília, DF; tel. (61) 3366-1098; fax (61) 3366-1554; Ambassador EUGÉNIA PEREIRA SALDANHA ARAÚJO.

Guyana: SHIS, QI 05, Conj. 19, Casa 24, 71615-190 Brasília, DF; tel. (61) 3248-0874; fax (61) 3248-0886; e-mail embguyana@embguyana.org.br; internet www.embguyana.org.br; Ambassador MERLIN UDHO.

Haiti: SHIS, QI 13, Conj. 08, Casa 18, Lago Sul, 71635-080 Brasília, DF; tel. (61) 3248-6860; fax (61) 3248-7472; e-mail embhaiti@terra.com.br; Ambassador MADSEN CHÉRUBIN.

Holy See: SES, Av. das Nações, Quadra 801, Lote 01, 70401-900 Brasília, DF; tel. (61) 3223-0794; fax (61) 3224-9365; e-mail nunapost@solar.com.br; Apostolic Nuncio Most Rev. GIOVANNI D'ANIELLO (Titular Archbishop of Pesto).

Honduras: SHIS, QI 19, Conj. 07, Casa 34, Lago Sul, 71655-070 Brasília, DF; tel. (61) 3366-4082; fax (61) 3366-4618; e-mail embajada@embajadahondurasbrasil.com; internet www.embajadahondurasbrasil.com; Ambassador JAIME GÜELL BOGRÁN.

Hungary: SES, Av. das Nações, Quadra 805, Lote 19, 70413-900 Brasília, DF; tel. (61) 3443-0836; fax (61) 3443-3434; e-mail mission.brz@kum.hu; internet www.mfa.gov.hu/emb/brasilia; Ambassador Dr CSABA SZIJJARTO.

India: SES 805, Lote 24, 70452-901 Brasília, DF; tel. (61) 3248-4006; fax (61) 3248-7849; e-mail indemb@indianembassy.org.br; internet www.indianembassy.org.br; Ambassador ASHOK TOMAR.

Indonesia: SES, Av. das Nações, Quadra 805, Lote 20, 70479-900 Brasília, DF; tel. (61) 3443-8800; fax (61) 3443-6732; e-mail contato@embaixadadaindonesia.org; internet www.embaixadadaindonesia.org; Ambassador SUDARYOMO HARTOSUDARMO.

Iran: SES, Av. das Nações, Quadra 809, Lote 31, 70421-900 Brasília, DF; tel. (61) 3242-5733; fax (61) 3224-9640; e-mail secretaria@irembassy.com; internet brasilia.mfa.gov.ir; Ambassador MOHAMMAD ALI GHANEZADEH EZABADI.

Iraq: SES, Av. das Nações, Quadra 815, Lote 64, 70430-900 Brasília, DF; tel. (61) 3346-2822; fax (61) 3346-7442; e-mail brzemb@mofaml.gov.iq; Ambassador ADEL MUSTAFA KAMIL AL-KURDI.

Ireland: SHIS, QL 12, Conj. 05, Casa 09, Lago Sul, 71630-255 Brasília, DF; tel. (61) 3248-8800; fax (61) 3248-8816; e-mail brasiliaembassy@dfa.ie; internet www.embaixada-irlanda.org.br; Ambassador FRANK SHERIDAN.

Israel: SES, Av. das Nações, Quadra 809, Lote 38, 70424-900 Brasília, DF; tel. (61) 2105-0500; fax (61) 3443-8107; e-mail info@brasilia.mfa.gov.il; internet brasilia.mfa.gov.il; Ambassador RAFAEL ELDAD.

Italy: SES, Av. das Nações, Quadra 807, Lote 30, 70420-900 Brasília, DF; tel. (61) 3442-9900; fax (61) 3443-1231; e-mail ambasciata.brasilia@esteri.it; internet www.ambbrasilia.esteri.it; Ambassador RAFFAELE TROMBETTA.

Jamaica: SHIS, QL 02, Conj. 04, Casa 02, Lago Sul, 71610-045 Brasília, DF; tel. (61) 2192-9774; fax (61) 2192-9772; e-mail jamaicanembassy.brazil@gmail.com; Ambassador ALISON STONE ROOFE.

Japan: SES, Av. das Nações, Quadra 811, Lote 39, 70425-900 Brasília, DF; tel. (61) 3442-4200; fax (61) 3442-2499; e-mail consularjapao@yawl.com.br; internet www.br.emb-japan.go.jp; Ambassador KUNIO UMEDA.

Jordan: SHIS, QI 09, Conj. 18, Casa 14, Lago Sul, 71625-180 Brasília, DF; tel. (61) 3248-5414; fax (61) 3248-1698; e-mail emb.jordania@apis.com.br; Ambassador MALEK EID OTALLA TWAL.

Kazakhstan: SHIS, QI 9, Conj. 03, Casa 8, Lago Sul, 71625-030 Brasília, DF; tel. (61) 3879-4602; fax (61) 3879-4604; e-mail embassykz@gmail.com; Ambassador BAKYTZHAN ORDABAYEV.

Kenya: SHIS, QL 10, Conj. 08, Casa 08, Lago Sul, 71630-085 Brasília, DF; tel. (61) 3364-0691; fax (61) 3364-0978; e-mail info@kenyaembassybrazil.com.br; internet www.kenyaembassy.com.br; Ambassador PETER KIRIMI KABERIA.

Korea, Democratic People's Republic: SHIS, QI 25, Conj. 10, Casa 11, Lago Sul, 71660-300 Brasília, DF; tel. (61) 3367-1940; fax (61) 3367-3177; e-mail embrpdcoreia@hotmail.com; Ambassador KIM THAE JONG.

Korea, Republic: SEN, Av. das Nações, Lote 14, 70436-900 Brasília, DF; tel. (61) 3321-2500; fax (61) 3321-2508; e-mail emb-br@mofat.go.kr; internet bra-brasilia.mofat.go.kr; Ambassador BON-WOO KOO.

Kuwait: SHIS, QI 05, Chácara 30, Lago Sul, 71600-550 Brasília, DF; tel. (61) 3213-2333; fax (61) 3248-0969; e-mail kuwait@opendf.com.br; Ambassador AYADA MEBRED AL-SAIDI.

Lebanon: SES, Av. das Nações, Quadra 805, Lote 17, 70411-900 Brasília, DF; tel. (61) 3443-5552; fax (61) 3443-8574; e-mail embaixada@libano.org.br; internet www.libano.org.br; Ambassador JOSEPH SAYAH.

Libya: SHIS, QI 15, Chácara 26, Lago Sul, 71600-750 Brasília, DF; tel. (61) 3248-6710; fax (61) 3248-0598; e-mail emblibia@terra.com.br; Ambassador JOSEPH SAYAH.

Malawi: SHIS, QI 15, Conj. 01, Casa 03, Lago Sul, 71635-230 Brasília, DF; tel. (61) 3366-1337; fax (61) 3365-2149; e-mail malawiembassybrasil@bol.com.br; Ambassador FRANCIS MOTO.

Malaysia: SHIS, QI 05, Chácara 62, Lago Sul, 70477-900 Brasília, DF; tel. (61) 3248-5008; fax (61) 3248-6307; e-mail mwbrasilia@terra.com.br; internet www.kln.gov.my/perwakilan/brasilia; Ambassador SUDHA DEVI.

Mauritania: SHIS, QI 9, Conj. 3, Casa 09, Lago Sul, 71625-030 Brasília, DF; tel. (61) 3797-3995; fax (61) 3365-3079; e-mail ambarimbrasilia@mauritania.org.br; internet www.mauritania.org.br; Ambassador KABA MOUHAMED ALIOU.

Mexico: SES, Av. das Nações, Quadra 805, Lote 18, 70412-900 Brasília, DF; tel. (61) 3204-5200; fax (61) 3204-5201; e-mail embamexbra@cabonet.com.br; internet portal.sre.gob.mx/brasil; Ambassador BEATRIZ ELENA PAREDES RANGEL.

Mongolia: Brasilia, DF; Ambassador CHULUUNBAATARYN SOSORMAA.

Morocco: SEN, Av. das Nacões, Quadra 801, Lote 02, Asa Norte, 70432-900 Brasília, DF; tel. (61) 3321-3994; fax (61) 3321-0745; e-mail sifamabr@onix.com.br; Ambassador LARBI MOUKHARIQ.

Mozambique: SHIS, QL 12, Conj. 07, Casa 09, Lago Sul, 71630-275 Brasília, DF; tel. (61) 3248-4222; fax (61) 3248-3917; e-mail embamoc-bsb@uol.com; internet www.mozambique.org.br; Ambassador MANUEL TOMÁS LUBISSE.

Myanmar: SHIS, QI 25, Conj. 05, Casa 14, Lago Sul, 71660-250 Brasília, DF; tel. (61) 3248-3747; fax (61) 3364-2747; e-mail mebrsl@brnet.com.br; internet www.myanmarbsb.org; Ambassador THIRI PIYANCHI U TUN NAY LINN.

Namibia: SHIS, QI 09, Conj. 08, Casa 11, Lago Sul, 71625-080 Brasília, DF; tel. (61) 3248-6274; fax (61) 3248-7135; e-mail info@embassyofnamibia.org.br; internet www.embassyofnamibia.org.br; Ambassador LINEEKELA JOSEPHAT MBOTI.

Nepal: SHIS, QI 11, Conj.03, Casa 20, Lago Sul, 71625-230 Brasília, DF; tel. (61) 3541-1232; fax (61) 3541-1229; e-mail embaixadanepal@gmail.com; Ambassador PRADHUMNA BIKRAM SHAH.

Netherlands: SES, Av. das Nações, Quadra 801, Lote 05, 70405-900 Brasília, DF; tel. (61) 3961-3200; fax (61) 3961-3234; e-mail bra@minbuza.nl; internet www.mfa.nl/brasil; Ambassador KEES PIETER RADE.

New Zealand: SHIS, QI 09, Conj. 16, Casa 01, 71625-160 Brasília, DF; tel. (61) 3248-9900; fax (61) 3248-9916; e-mail zelandia@nwi.com.br; internet www.nzembassy.com/brazil; Ambassador JEFFREY McALISTER.

Nicaragua: SHIS, QL 21, Conj. 10, Casa 14, Lago Sul, 71655-340 Brasília, DF; tel. (61) 3366-3297; e-mail embanicbrasil@cancilleria.gob.ni; Ambassador LORENA DEL CARMEN MARTÍNEZ.

Nigeria: SEN, Av. das Nações, Lote 05, 70800-400 Brasília, DF; tel. (61) 3208-1700; fax (61) 3226-5192; e-mail admin@nigerianembassy-brazil.org; internet www.nigerianembassy-brazil.org; Ambassador VINCENT ADAMU EMOZOZO.

Norway: SES, Av. das Nações, Quadra 807, Lote 28, 70418-900 Brasília, DF; tel. (61) 3443-8720; fax (61) 3443-2942; e-mail emb.brasilia@mfa.no; internet www.noruega.org.br; Ambassador AUD MARIT WIIG.

Pakistan: SHIS, QL 12, Conj. 02, Casa 19, Lago Sul, 71630-225 Brasília, DF; tel. (61) 3364-1632; fax (61) 3248-0246; e-mail parepbrasilia@yahoo.com; internet www.pakistan.org.br; Ambassador NASRULLAH KHAN.

Panama: SES, Av. das Nações, Quadra 803, Lote 09, 70200-030 Brasília, DF; tel. (61) 3323-6177; fax (61) 3323-2885; e-mail contacto@panaembabrasil.com.br; Ambassador GABRIELA GARCÍA CARRANZA.

Paraguay: SES, Av. das Nações, Quadra 811, Lote 42, 70427-900 Brasília, DF; tel. (61) 3242-3732; fax (61) 3242-4605; e-mail secretaria@embaparaguai.org.br; internet www.embaparaguai.org.br; Ambassador MANUEL MARÍA CÁCERES CARDOZO.

Peru: SES, Av. das Nações, Quadra 811, Lote 43, 70428-900 Brasília, DF; tel. (61) 3242-9933; fax (61) 3225-9136; e-mail embperu@embperu.org.br; internet www.embperu.org.br; Ambassador JORGE PORFIRIO BAYONA MEDINA.

Philippines: SEN, Av. das Nações, Lote 01, 70431-900 Brasília, DF; tel. (61) 3223-5143; fax (61) 3226-7411; e-mail brasiliape@turbo.com.br; Ambassador EVA G. BETITA.

Poland: SES, Av. das Nações, Quadra 809, Lote 33, 70423-900 Brasília, DF; tel. (61) 3212-8000; fax (61) 3242-8543; e-mail brasilia

.embaixada@msz.gov.pl; internet www.brasilia.msz.gov.pl; Ambassador ANDRZEJ MARIA BRAITER.

Portugal: SES Sul, Av. das Nações, Quadra 801, Lote 02, 70402-900 Brasília, DF; tel. (61) 3032-9600; fax (61) 3032-9642; e-mail embaixadadeportugal@embaixadadeportugal.org.br; internet www.embaixadadeportugal.org.br; Ambassador FRANCISCO MARIA DE SOUSA RIBEIRO TELLES.

Qatar: SHIS, QL 20, Conj. 01, Casa 19, Lago Sul, 71650-115 Brasília, DF; tel. (61) 3366-1005; fax (61) 3366-1115; e-mail qatarbsb@embcatar.org.br; Ambassador MOHAMED AHMAD AL-HAYKI.

Romania: SEN, Av. das Nações, Lote 06, 70456-900 Brasília, DF; tel. (61) 3226-0746; fax (61) 3226-6629; e-mail romenia@solar.com.br; Ambassador DIANA ANCA RADU.

Russia: SES, Av. das Nações, Quadra 801, Lote A, 70476-900 Brasília, DF; tel. (61) 3223-3094; fax (61) 3226-7319; e-mail emb@embrus.brte.com.br; internet www.brazil.mid.ru; Ambassador SERGUEY POGÓSSOVITCH AKOPOV.

Saudi Arabia: SHIS, QL 9, Conj. 09, Casa 18, 71625-090 Brasília, DF; tel. (61) 3248-3523; fax (61) 3284-1142; e-mail bremb@mofa.gov.sa; internet www.saudiembassy.org.br; Ambassador HISHAM SULTAN BIN ZAFIR ALQAHTANI.

Senegal: SEN, Av. das Nações, Lote 18, 70800-400 Brasília, DF; tel. (61) 3223-6110; fax (61) 3322-7822; e-mail senebrasilia@senebrasilia.com.br; internet www.senebrasilia.org.br; Ambassador El Hadj AMADOU NIANG.

Serbia: SES, Av. das Nações, Quadra 803, Lote 15, 70409-900 Brasília, DF; tel. (61) 3223-7272; fax (61) 3223-8462; e-mail embaixadaservia@terra.com.br; Ambassador LJUBOMIR MILIC.

Singapore: SHIS QL 24, Conj. 3, Casa 11, Lago Sul, 71665-035 Brasília, DF; tel. (61) 2191-6565; fax (61) 2191-6580; e-mail singemb_bsb@sgmfa.gov.sg; internet www.mfa.gov.sg/brasilia; Ambassador CHIAU BENG CHOO.

Slovakia: SES, Av. das Nações, Quadra 805, Lote 21B, 70200-902 Brasília, DF; tel. (61) 3443-1263; fax (61) 3443-1267; e-mail emb.brasilia@mzv.sk; internet www.mzv.sk/brazilia; Ambassador MILAN CIGÁŇ.

Slovenia: SHIS, QL 08, Conj. 08, Casa 07, Lago Sul, 71620-285 Brasília, DF; tel. (61) 3365-1445; fax (61) 3365-1440; e-mail vbi@gov.si; internet www.brasilia.embassy.si; Ambassador MILENA ŠMIT.

South Africa: SES, Av. das Nações, Quadra 801, Lote 06, 70406-900 Brasília, DF; tel. (61) 3312-9500; fax (61) 3322-8491; e-mail brasilia.general@foreign.gov.za; internet www.africadosul.org.br; Ambassador MOHAKAMA NYANGWENI MBETE.

Spain: SES, Av. das Nações, Quadra 811, Lote 44, 70429-900 Brasília, DF; tel. (61) 3701-1600; fax (61) 3242-1781; e-mail emb.brasilia@maec.es; Ambassador MANUEL DE LA CÁMARA HERMOSO.

Sri Lanka: SHIS, QI 13, Conj. 13, Casa 01, Lago Sul, 71635-130 Brasília, DF; tel. (61) 3248-2701; fax (61) 3364-5430; e-mail lankaemb@yawl.com.br; Ambassador RAJA A. EDIRISURIYA.

Sudan: SHIS, QI 11, Conj. 05, Casa 13, Lago Sul, 71625-250 Brasília, DF; tel. (61) 3248-4835; fax (61) 3248-4833; e-mail sudanbrasilia@yahoo.com; Ambassador ABD ELGHANI ELNAIM AWAD ELKARIM.

Suriname: SHIS, QI 09, Conj. 08, Casa 24, 71625-080 Brasília, DF; tel. (61) 3248-6706; fax (61) 3248-3791; e-mail surinameemb@terra.com.br; Ambassador MARLON FAISAL MOHAMED HOESEIN.

Sweden: SES, Av. das Nações, Quadra 807, Lote 29, 70419-900 Brasília, DF; tel. (61) 3442-5200; fax (61) 3443-1187; e-mail ambassaden.brasilia@gov.se; internet www.suecia.org.br; Ambassador MAGNUS ROBACH.

Switzerland: SES, Av. das Nações, Quadra 811, Lote 41, 70448-900 Brasília, DF; tel. (61) 3443-5500; fax (61) 3443-5711; e-mail bra.vertretung@eda.admin.ch; internet www.dfae.admin.ch/brasilia; Ambassador ANDRÉ REGLI.

Syria: SEN, Av. das Nações, Lote 11, 70434-900 Brasília, DF; tel. (61) 3226-0970; fax (61) 3223-2595; e-mail embsiria@uol.com.br; Chargé d'affaires a.i. GHASSAN NSEIR.

Tanzania: SHIS, QI 09, Conj. 16, Casa 20, Lago Sul, 71615-190 Brasília, DF; tel. (61) 3364-2629; fax (61) 3248-3361; e-mail tanrepbrasilia@yahoo.com.br; Ambassador FRANCIS AMBAKISYE MALAMBUGI.

Thailand: SEN, Av. das Nações, Lote 10, 70800-912 Brasília, DF; tel. (61) 3224-6943; fax (61) 3223-7502; e-mail thaiembbrazil@gmail.com; internet www.thaiembassybrazil.com; Ambassador PITCHAYAPHANT CHARNBHUMIDOL.

Timor-Leste: SHIS, QI 11, Conj. 10, Casa 19, Lago Sul, 71625-300 Brasília, DF; tel. and fax (61) 3366-2755; e-mail embaixada@embaixadatimorleste.com.br; Ambassador DOMINGOS FRANCISCO DE JESUS DE SOUSA.

Trinidad and Tobago: SHIS, QL 02, Conj. 02, Casa 01, 71665-028 Brasília, DF; tel. (61) 3365-1132; fax (61) 3365-1733; e-mail trinbagoemb@gmail.com; Ambassador Dr HAMZA RAFEEQ.

Tunisia: SHIS, QI 11, Conj. 06, Casa 06, Lago Sul, 71625-260 Brasília, DF; tel. (61) 3248-7366; fax (61) 3248-7355; e-mail at.brasilia@terra.com.br; Ambassador SABRI BACHTOBJI.

Turkey: SES, Av. das Nações, Quadra 805, Lote 23, 70452-900 Brasília, DF; tel. (61) 3242-1850; fax (61) 3242-1448; e-mail embassy.brasil@mfa.gov.tr; internet brasilia.emb.mfa.gov.tr; Ambassador HÜSEYIN LAZIP DIRIÖZ.

Ukraine: SHIS, QI 05, Conj. 04, Casa 02, Lago Sul, 71615-040 Brasília, DF; tel. (61) 3365-1457; fax (61) 3365-2127; e-mail emb_br@mfa.gov.ua; internet www.mfa.gov.ua/brazil; Ambassador ROSTYSLAV TRONENKO.

United Arab Emirates: SHIS, QI 05, Chácara 54, 70800-400 Brasília, DF; tel. (61) 3248-0717; fax (61) 3248-7543; e-mail uae@uae.org.br; internet www.uae.org.br; Ambassador SULTAN RASHED AL-KAITOOB.

United Kingdom: SES, Av. das Nações, Quadra 801, Conj. K, Lote 08, 70408-900 Brasília, DF; tel. (61) 3329-2300; fax (61) 3329-2369; e-mail press.brasilia@fco.gov.uk; internet ukinbrazil.fco.gov.uk; Ambassador ALEXANDER WYKEHAM ELLIS.

USA: SES, Av. das Nações, Quadra 801, Lote 03, 70403-900 Brasília, DF; tel. (61) 3312-7000; fax (61) 3225-9136; e-mail ircbsb@state.gov; internet brasilia.usembassy.gov; Ambassador LILIANA AYALDE.

Uruguay: SES, Av. das Nações, Quadra 803, Lote 14, 70450-900 Brasília, DF; tel. (61) 3322-1200; fax (61) 3322-6534; e-mail urubras@emburuguai.org.br; internet www.emburuguai.org.br; Ambassador CARLOS DANIEL AMORÍN TENCONI.

Venezuela: SES, Av. das Nações, Quadra 803, Lote 13, 70451-900 Brasília, DF; tel. (61) 2101-1011; fax (61) 3321-0871; e-mail emb@embvenezuela.org.br; internet www.embvenezuela.org.br; Ambassador DIEGO ALFREDO MOLERO BELLAVIA.

Viet Nam: SHIS, QI 09, Conj. 10, Casa 01, Lago Sul, 71625-100 Brasília, DF; tel. (61) 3364-5876; fax (61) 3364-5836; e-mail embavina@yahoo.com; internet www.vietnamembassy-brazil.org/vi; Ambassador NGUYÊN VAN KIEN.

Zambia: SHIS, QL 10, Conj. 10, Casa 17, Lago Sul, 71630-065 Brasília, DF; tel. and fax (61) 3248-3277; fax (61) 3248-3494; e-mail zambiansbrasil@embaixadazambia.org.br; Ambassador CYNTHIA JANGULO.

Zimbabwe: SHIS, QI 03, Conj. 10, Casa 13, Lago Sul, 71605-300 Brasília, DF; tel. (61) 3365-4801; fax (61) 3365-4803; e-mail zimbrasilia@uol.com.br; Ambassador THOMAS SUKUTAI BVUMA.

Judicial System

The judicial powers of the State are held by the following: the Supreme Federal Court (Supremo Tribunal Federal), the Higher Court of Justice, the five Regional Federal Courts and Federal Judges, the Higher Labour Court, the 24 Regional Labour Courts, the Conciliation and Judgment Councils and Labour Judges, the Higher Electoral Court, the 27 Regional Electoral Courts, the Electoral Judges and Electoral Councils, the Higher Military Court, the Military Courts and Military Judges, the Courts of the States and Judges of the States, the Court of the Federal District and of the Territories and Judges of the Federal District and of the Territories.

The Supreme Federal Court comprises 11 ministers, nominated by the President and approved by the Senado. Its most important role is to rule on the final interpretation of the Constitution. The Supreme Federal Court has the power to declare an act of Congress void if it is unconstitutional. It judges offences committed by persons such as the President, the Vice-President, members of the Congresso Nacional, Ministers of State, its own members, the Attorney-General, judges of other higher courts, and heads of permanent diplomatic missions. It also judges cases of litigation between the Union and the States, between the States, or between foreign nations and the Union or the States, disputes as to jurisdiction between higher Courts, or between the latter and any other court, in cases involving the extradition of criminals, and others related to the writs of habeas corpus and habeas data, and in other cases.

The Higher Court of Justice comprises 33 members, appointed by the President and approved by the Senado. Its jurisdiction includes the judgment of offences committed by State Governors. The Regional Federal Courts comprise at least seven judges, recruited when possible in the respective region and appointed by the President of the Republic. The Higher Labour Court comprises 17 members, appointed by the President and approved by the Senado. The judges of the Regional Labour Courts are also appointed by the President. The Regional Electoral Courts are composed of seven members. The Higher Military Court comprises 15 life members, appointed by the President and approved by the Senado: three from the navy, four from the army, three from the air force and five civilian members. The States are responsible for the administration of their own justice, according to the principles established by the Constitution.

SUPREME FEDERAL COURT

Supremo Tribunal Federal: Praça dos Três Poderes, 70175-900 Brasília, DF; tel. (61) 3217-3000; fax (61) 3217-4412; internet www.stf.jus.br; Pres. JOAQUIM BENEDITO BARBOSA GOMES; Vice-Pres. ENRIQUE RICARDO LEWANDOWSKI.

Attorney-General: ROBERTO MONTEIRO GURGEL SANTOS.

Religion

CHRISTIANITY

Conselho Nacional de Igrejas Cristãs do Brasil (CONIC) (National Council of Christian Churches in Brazil): Edif. Ceará, Sala 713, SCS, Quadra 01, Bloco E, 70303-900 Brasília, DF; tel. and fax (61) 3321-4034; e-mail conic@conic.org.br; internet www.conic.org.br; f. 1982; eight mem. churches; Pres. Bishop MANOEL JOÃO FRANCISCO; Exec. Sec. Pastor ROMI MÁRCIA BENCKE.

The Roman Catholic Church

Brazil comprises 44 archdioceses, 213 dioceses (including one each for Catholics of the Maronite, Melkite and Ukrainian Rites), 11 territorial prelatures and one personal apostolic administration. The Archbishop of São Sebastião do Rio de Janeiro is also the Ordinary for Catholics of other Oriental Rites in Brazil. In December 2011 some 84% of the population were Roman Catholics.

Bishops' Conference: Conferência Nacional dos Bispos do Brasil, SES, Quadra 801, Conj. B, 70401-900 Brasília, DF; tel. (61) 2103-8300; fax (61) 2103-8303; e-mail cnbb@cnbb.org.br; internet www.cnbb.org.br; f. 1952; statutes approved 2002; Pres. RAYMUNDO DAMASCENO ASSIS (Archbishop of Aparecida, SP); Sec.-Gen. ANTÔNIO SILVA DA PAIXÃO.

Latin Rite

Archbishop of São Salvador da Bahia, BA, and Primate of Brazil: MURILO SEBASTIÃO RAMOS KRIEGER, Cúria Metropolitana, Av. Leovigildo Filgueiras, García 270, 40100-000 Salvador, BA; tel. (71) 4009-6666; e-mail contato@arquidiocesesalvador.org.br; internet www.arquidiocesesalvador.org.br.

Archbishop of Aparecida, SP: Cardinal RAYMUNDO DAMASCENO ASSIS.

Archbishop of Aracaju, SE: JOSÉ PALMEIRA LESSA.

Archbishop of Belém do Pará, PA: ALBERTO TAVEIRO CORRÊA.

Archbishop of Belo Horizonte, MG: WALMOR OLIVEIRA DE AZEVEDO.

Archbishop of Botucatu, SP: MAURÍCIO GROTTO DE CAMARGO.

Archbishop of Brasília, DF: SÉRGIO DA ROCHA.

Archbishop of Campinas, SP: AIRTON JOSÉ DOS SANTOS.

Archbishop of Campo Grande, MS: DIMAS LARA BARBOSA.

Archbishop of Cascavel, PR: MAURO APARECIDO DOS SANTOS.

Archbishop of Cuiabá, MT: MILTON ANTÔNIO DOS SANTOS.

Archbishop of Curitiba, PR: MOACYR JOSÉ VITTI.

Archbishop of Diamantina, MG: JOÃO BOSCO OLIVER DE FARIA.

Archbishop of Feira de Santana, BA: ITAMAR NAVILDO VIAN.

Archbishop of Florianópolis, SC: WILSON TADEU JÖNCK.

Archbishop of Fortaleza, CE: JOSÉ ANTÔNIO APARECIDO TOSI MARQUES.

Archbishop of Goiânia, GO: WASHINGTON CRUZ.

Archbishop of Juíz de Fora, MG: GIL ANTÔNIO MOREIRA.

Archbishop of Londrina, PR: ORLANDO BRANDES.

Archbishop of Maceió, AL: ANTÔNIO MUNIZ FERNANDES.

Archbishop of Manaus, AM: SÉRGIO EDUARDO CASTRANI.

Archbishop of Mariana, MG: GERALDO LYRIO ROCHA.

Archbishop of Maringá, PR: ANUAR BATTISTI.

Archbishop of Montes Claros, MG: JOSÉ ALBERTO MOURA.

Archbishop of Natal, RN: JAIME VIEIRA ROCHA.

Archbishop of Niterói, RJ: JOSÉ FRANCISCO REZENDE DIAS.

Archbishop of Olinda e Recife, PE: ANTONIO FERNANDO SABURIDO.

Archbishop of Palmas, PR: PEDRO BRITO GUIMARÃES.

Archbishop of Paraíba, PB: ALDO DE CILLO PAGOTTO.

Archbishop of Passo Fundo, RS: ANTÔNIO CARLOS ALTIERI.

Archbishop of Pelotas, RS: JACINTO BERGMANN.

Archbishop of Porto Alegre, RS: JAIME SPENGLER.

Archbishop of Porto Velho, RO: ESMERALDO BARRETO DE FARIAS.

Archbishop of Pouso Alegre, MG: RICARDO PEDRO CHAVES PINTO FILHO.

Archbishop of Ribeirão Preto, SP: MOACIR SILVA.

Archbishop of Santa Maria, RS: HÉLIO ADELAR RUBERT.

Archbishop of São Luís do Maranhão, MA: JOSÉ BELISÁRIO DA SILVA.

Archbishop of São Paulo, SP: Cardinal ODILO PEDRO SCHERER.

Archbishop of São Sebastião do Rio de Janeiro, RJ: Cardinal ORANI JOÃO TEMPESTA.

Archbishop of Sorocaba, SP: EDUARDO BENES DE SALES RODRIGUES.

Archbishop of Teresina, PI: JACINTO FURTADO DE BRITO SOBRINHO.

Archbishop of Uberaba, MG: PAULO MENDES PEIXOTO.

Archbishop of Vitória, ES: LUIZ MANCILHA VILELA.

Archbishop of Vitória da Conquista, BA: LUIS GONZAGA SILVA PEPEU.

Maronite Rite

Bishop of Nossa Senhora do Líbano em São Paulo, SP: EDGAR MADI.

Melkite Rite

Bishop of Nossa Senhora do Paraíso em São Paulo, SP: FARES MAAKAROUN.

Ukrainian Rite

Bishop of São João Batista em Curitiba, PR: VOLODÊMER KOUBETCH.

The Anglican Communion

Anglicans form the Episcopal Anglican Church of Brazil (Igreja Episcopal Anglicana do Brasil), comprising eight dioceses.

Igreja Episcopal Anglicana do Brasil: Praça Olavo Bilac 63, Campos Elíseos, 01201-050 São Paulo, SP; tel. and fax (11) 3667-8161; e-mail sec.geral@ieab.org.br; internet www.ieab.org.br; f. 1890; 103,021 mems (1997); Primate Rt Rev. MAURÍCIO JOSÉ ARAÚJO DE ANDRADE; Sec.-Gen. Rev. ARTHUR CAVALCANTE.

Other Christian Churches

According to the 2000 census, 15% of the population are Evangelical Christians.

Church of Jesus Christ of Latter-Day Saints (Mormons): Av. Prof. Francisco Morato 2390, Caxingui 05512-900 São Paulo, SP; tel. (11) 3723-7600; internet www.lds.org; 1.2m. mems.

Igreja Cristã Reformada do Campo Belo (Christian Reformed Church of Campo Belo): Rua Gabrielle D'annuzio 952, Campo Belo, Zona Sul, São Paulo, SP; tel. (11) 5561-6399; internet www.icrcampobelo.com.br; f. 1958; Pastor Rev. VALDECI SANTOS.

Igreja Evangélica de Confissão Luterana no Brasil (IECLB): Rua Senhor dos Passos 202, 4° andar, 90020-180 Porto Alegre, RS; tel. (51) 3284-5400; fax (51) 3284-5419; e-mail presidencia@ieclb.org.br; internet www.luteranos.org.br; f. 1949; 717,000 mems; Pres. Pastor Dr NESTOR PAULO FRIEDRICH; Sec.-Gen. INGRIT VOGT.

Igreja Evangélica Congregacional do Brasil: Rua Mauá 33, Centro, 98900-000 Santa Rosa, RS; tel. (55) 3512-6449; e-mail pastorivo@iecb.org.br; internet www.iecb.org.br; f. 1942; 148,836 mems (2000); Pres. Rev. IVO KÖHN.

Igreja Evangélica Luterana do Brasil: Av. Cel. Lucas de Oliveira 894, Bairro Mont'Serrat, 90440-010 Porto Alegre, RS; tel. (51) 3332-2111; fax (51) 3332-8145; e-mail ielb@ielb.org.br; internet www.ielb.org.br; f. 1904; 233,416 mems; Pres. Rev. EGON KOPERECK; Sec. Rev. Dr REUBENS JOSÉ OGG.

Igreja Maná do Brasil: Rua Arthur Guilardi 153, Jardin Recreio, 12910-150 Bragança Paulista, SP; tel. (11) 4032-8104; e-mail faleconosco@igrejamana.com.br; internet www.igrejamana.com.br; Pastor JORGE TADEU.

Igreja Metodista do Brasil: Av. Piassanguaba 3031, Planalto Paulista, 04060-004 São Paulo, SP; tel. (11) 2813-8600; fax (11) 2813-8632; e-mail sede.nacional@metodista.org.br; internet www.metodista.org.br; 136,470 mems (2002); Exec. Sec. Bishop JOÃO CARLOS LOPES.

Igreja Presbiteriana Unida do Brasil (IPU): Edif. Vitória Center, Av. Princesa Isabel 629, 29010-360 Vitória, ES; tel. and fax (27) 3222-8024; e-mail ipu@ipu.org.br; internet www.ipu.org.br; f. 1978; Moderator Rev. ANITA SUE WRIGHT TORRES.

BAHÁ'Í FAITH

Assembleia Espiritual Nacional dos Bahá'ís do Brasil (National Spiritual Assembly of Bahá'ís of Brazil): SHIS, QL 08, Conj. 02, CP 7035, 71620-970 Brasília, DF; tel. (61) 3255-2200; fax (61) 3364-3470; e-mail info@bahai.org.br; internet www.bahai.org.br; f. 1965; Nat.-Sec. CARLOS ALBERTO SILVA.

BUDDHISM

Sociedade Budista do Brasil (Buddhist Society—Rio Buddhist Vihara): Dom Joaquim Mamede 45, Lagoinha, Santa Tereza, 20241-390 Rio de Janeiro, RJ; tel. (21) 2245-4331; e-mail sbb@sociedadebudistadobrasil.org; internet www.sociedadebudistadobrasil.org; f. 1972; Pres. JOÃO NERY RAFAEL.

OTHER RELIGIONS

Sociedade Taoísta do Brasil (Taoist Society): Rua Cosme Velho 355, Cosme Velho, 22241-090 Rio de Janeiro, RJ; tel. (21) 2285-1937; e-mail secretaria@taoismo.org.br; internet www.taoismo.org.br; f. 1991; Pres. WU JYH CHERNG.

The Press

The most striking feature of the Brazilian press is the relatively small circulation of newspapers in comparison with the size of the population. This is mainly owing to high costs resulting from distribution difficulties. In consequence, there are no national newspapers.

DAILY NEWSPAPERS

Belém, PA

O Liberal: Av. 25 de Setembro 2473, Marco, 66093-000 Belém, PA; tel. (91) 3216-1138; e-mail redacao@orm.com.br; internet www.orm.com.br/oliberal; f. 1946; Gen. Man. MICHEL PSAROS; Editor ELISÂNGELA SOARES; circ. 43,000.

Belo Horizonte, MG

Diário do Comércio: Av. Américo Vespúcio 1660, Nova Esperança, 31230-250 Belo Horizonte, MG; tel. (31) 3469-2000; fax (31) 3469-2043; e-mail redacaodc@diariodocomercio.com.br; internet www.diariodocomercio.com.br; f. 1932; Editor-in-Chief AMAURY PIMENTA DE PINHO; Exec. Dir YVAN MULLS.

Estado de Minas: Av. Getúlio Vargas 291, 8º andar, 30112-020 Belo Horizonte, MG; tel. (31) 3263-5800; fax (31) 3263-5424; e-mail fale.conosco@em.com.br; internet www.em.com.br; f. 1928; morning; independent; Chief Editor CARLOS MARCELO CARVALHO; circ. 80,136.

Hoje em Dia: Rua Padre Rolim 652, Santa Efigênia, 30130-916 Belo Horizonte, MG; tel. (31) 3236-8000; fax (31) 3236-8010; e-mail jornalismo@hojeemdia.com.br; internet www.hojeemdia.com.br; Pres. FLÁVIO JACQUES CARNEIRO; Editor-in-Chief CHICO MENDONÇA; circ. 48,800.

Blumenau, SC

Jornal de Santa Catarina: Rua Bahia 2291, 89031-002 Blumenau, SC; tel. (47) 3221-1400; fax (48) 3221-1405; e-mail redacao@santa.com.br; internet jornaldesantacatarina.clicrbs.com.br/sc; f. 1971; Chief Editor EVANDRO ASSIS; circ. 19,402.

Brasília, DF

Correio Braziliense: Edif. Edilson Varela, SIG, Quadra 02, Lote 340, 70610-901 Brasília, DF; tel. (61) 3342-1000; fax (61) 3342-1306; e-mail anadubeux.df@dabr.com.br; internet www.correiobraziliense.com.br; f. 1960; Pres. and Dir ALVARO TEIXEIRA DA COSTA; Editor-in-Chief ANA DUBEUX; circ. 56,321.

Jornal de Brasília: SIG, Trecho 1, Lote 765, 70610-410 Brasília, DF; tel. (61) 3343-8000; fax (61) 3226-6735; e-mail redacao@jornaldebrasilia.com.br; internet www.jornaldebrasilia.com.br; f. 1972; Editor-in-Chief PAULO GUSMÃO; circ. 25,000.

Campinas, SP

Correio Popular: Rua 7 de Setembro 189, Vila Industrial, 13035-350 Campinas, SP; tel. (19) 3736-3050; fax (19) 3234-8984; e-mail correiopontocom@rac.com.br; internet www.cpopular.com.br; f. 1927; Editorial Dir NELSON HOMEM DE MELLO; circ. 32,044.

Contagem, MG

Super Notícia: Av. Babita Camargos 1645, 32210-180 Contagem, MG; tel. (31) 2101-3901; e-mail luciacastro@otempo.com.br; internet www.supernoticia.com.br; f. 2002; Editor LÚCIA CASTRO; circ. 293,572.

Curitiba, PR

O Estado do Paraná: Rua José Loureiro 282, Centro, 80010-020 Curitiba, PR; tel. (41) 3321-5000; fax (41) 3331-5167; e-mail fale@pron.com.br; internet www.parana-online.com.br; f. 1951; Pres. ANA AMÉLIA CUNHA PEREIRA FILIZOLA; Editorial Dir RAFAEL TAVARES DE MELLO; circ. 15,000.

Gazeta do Povo: Rua Pedro Ivo 459, Centro, 80010-020 Curitiba, PR; tel. (41) 3321-5470; fax (41) 3321-5300; e-mail guia@gazetadopovo.com.br; internet www.gazetadopovo.com.br; f. 1919; Editorial Dir MARIA SANDRA GONÇALVES; circ. 43,513.

Jornal Bem Paraná: Rua Dr Roberto Barrozo 22, Centro Cívico, 80530-120 Curitiba, PR; tel. (41) 3350-6600; fax (41) 3350-6650; e-mail contato@bemparana.com.br; internet www.bemparana.com.br; f. 1983 as Jornal do Estado; adopted present name in 2013; Editor-in-Chief JOSIANNE RITZ.

Fortaleza, CE

Diário do Nordeste: Editora Verdes Mares Ltda, Praça da Impresa, C.G.C. 07209-299 Fortaleza, CE; tel. (85) 3266-9773; fax (85) 3266-9797; e-mail aloredacao@diariodonordeste.com.br; internet diariodonordeste.globo.com; Editorial Dir ILDEFONSO RODRIGUES; circ. 33,114.

Jornal O Povo: Av. Aguanambi 282, 60055 Fortaleza, CE; tel. (85) 3255-6250; fax (85) 3231-5792; e-mail centraldeatendimento@opovo.com.br; internet www.opovo.com.br; f. 1928; evening; Exec. Editor FÁTIMA SUDÁRIO; circ. 23,216.

Goiânia, GO

Diário da Manhã: Av. Anhanguera 2833, Setor Leste Universitário, 74610-010 Goiânia, GO; tel. (62) 3267-1000; e-mail opiniao@dm.com.br; internet www.dm.com.br; f. 1980; Editor BATISTA CUSTÓDIO; circ. 16,000.

O Popular: Rua Thómas Edson, Quadra 07, No 400, Setor Serrinha, 74835-130 Goiânia, GO; tel. (62) 3250-1028; fax (62) 3250-1260; e-mail dca@opopular.com.br; internet www.opopular.com.br; f. 1938; Editor-in-Chief CILEIDE ALVES; circ. 31,971.

João Pessoa, PB

Correio da Paraíba: Av. Pedro II, Centro, João Pessoa, PB; tel. (83) 3216-5000; fax (83) 3216-5009; e-mail assinante@portalcorreio.com.br; internet www.correiodaparaiba.com.br; Exec. Dir BEATRIZ RIBEIRO; Editor-in-Chief WALTER GALVÃO.

Londrina, PR

Folha de Londrina: Rua Piauí 241, 86010-420 Londrina, PR; tel. (43) 3374-2020; fax (43) 3339-1412; e-mail contato@folhadelondrina.com.br; internet www.folhaweb.com.br; f. 1948; Editor-in-Chief FERNANDA MAZZINI; circ. 33,113.

Manaus, AM

A Crítica: Av. André Araújo 1924A, Aleixo-Cidade das Comunicações, 69060-001 Manaus, AM; tel. (92) 3643-1200; fax (92) 3643-1234; e-mail aruana@acritica.com.br; internet www.acritica.com.br; f. 1949; Chair. RITTA ARAÚJO CALDERARO; Editorial Dir ARUANA BRIANEZI; circ. 19,000.

Natal, RN

Diario de Natal: Av. Deodoro da Fonseca 245, Petrópolis, 59012-600 Natal, RN; tel. (84) 4009-0166; e-mail redacao.rn@diariosassociados.com.br; internet www.diariodenatal.com.br; Exec. Editor JULISKA AZEVEDO.

Niterói, RJ

O Fluminense: Rua Visconde de Itaboraí 184, Centro, 24035-900 Niterói, RJ; tel. (21) 2125-3000; fax (21) 2620-8636; e-mail reportagem@ofluminense.com.br; internet www.ofluminense.com.br; f. 1878; Man. Editor SANDRA DUARTE; circ. 80,000.

A Tribuna: Rua Barão do Amazonas 31, Ponta D'areia, 2403-0111 Niterói, RJ; tel. (21) 2719-1886; e-mail icarai@urbi.com.br; internet www.atribunarj.com.br; f. 1936; daily; Dir-Supt GUSTAVO SANTANO AMÓRO; circ. 10,000.

Palmas, TO

O Girassol: Edif. Office Center, Salas 408–410, Av. Teotônio Segurado, 101 Sul, Conj. 01, Lote 06, 77015-002 Palmas, TO; tel. and fax (63) 3225-5456; e-mail ogirassol@uol.com.br; internet www.ogirassol.com.br; f. 2000; Editor-in-Chief WILBERGSON ESTRELA GOMES; Exec. Editor SONIELSON LUCIANO DE SOUSA.

Porto Alegre, RS

Zero Hora: Av. Ipiranga 1075, Azenha, 90169-900 Porto Alegre, RS; tel. (51) 3218-4300; fax (51) 3218-4700; e-mail leitor@zerohora.com.br; internet zerohora.clicrbs.com.br/rs; f. 1964; Editor-in-Chief NILSON VARGAS; circ. 188,561.

Recife, PE

Diário de Pernambuco: Rua do Veiga 600, Santo Amaro, 50040-110 Recife, PE; tel. (81) 2122-7555; fax (81) 2122-7544; e-mail faleconosco@diariodepernambuco.com.br; internet www.diariodepernambuco.com.br; f. 1825; morning; independent; Editorial Dir VERA OGANDO; circ. 24,762.

Ribeirão Preto, SP

Jornal Tribuna da Ribeirão Preto: Rua São Sebastião 1380, Centro, 14015-040 Ribeirão Preto, SP; tel. and fax (16) 3632-2200; e-mail tribuna@tribunaribeirao.com.br; internet www.tribunaribeirao.com.br; Editor HILTON HARTMANN; circ. 16,000.

Rio de Janeiro, RJ

O Dia: Rua Riachuelo 359, Centro, 20235-900 Rio de Janeiro, RJ; fax (21) 2507-1228; e-mail aziz.filho@odia.com.br; internet odia.ig.com.br; f. 1951; morning; centrist labour; Publr RAMIRO ALVES; Editor-in-Chief AZIZ FILHO; circ. 50,288.

O Globo: Rua Irineu Marinho 35, CP 1090, 20233-900 Rio de Janeiro, RJ; tel. (21) 2534-5000; fax (21) 2534-5510; internet oglobo.globo.com; f. 1925; morning; Editor-in-Chief ASCÂNIO SELEME; circ. 256,259.

Jornal do Brasil: Av. Paulo de Frontin 568, Fundos, Rio Comprido, 20261-243 Rio de Janeiro, RJ; tel. (21) 2323-1000; e-mail cartas@jb.com.br; internet www.jb.com.br; f. 1891; print edn suspended July 2010, online only; Catholic, liberal; Editor TALES FARIA.

Lance: Rua Santa Maria 47, Cidade Nova, 20211-210 Rio de Janeiro, RJ; tel. (21) 4063-6350; internet www.lancenet.com.br; sports, daily; Editor LUIZ FERNANDO GOMES; circ.84,983.

Salvador, BA

Correio da Bahia: Rua Aristides Novis 123, Federação, 40310-630 Salvador, BA; tel. (71) 3533-3030; fax (71) 3203-1045; e-mail redacao@correio24horas.com.br; internet www.correio24horas.com.br; f. 1978; Editor-in-Chief SERGIO COSTA; circ. 34,681.

A Tarde: Rua Prof. Milton Cayres de Brito 204, Caminho das Árvores, 41820-570 Salvador, BA; tel. (71) 3340-8500; fax (71) 3231-8800; e-mail suporte@atarde.com.br; internet www.atarde.com.br; f. 1912; evening; Editor-in-Chief VAGUINALDO MARINHEIRO; circ. 45,377.

Santarém, PA

O Impacto—O Jornal da Amazônia: Av. Presidente Vargas 3721, Caranazal, 68040-060 Santarém, PA; tel. (93) 3523-3330; fax (93) 3523-9131; e-mail oimpacto@oimpacto.com.br; internet www.oimpacto.com.br; Editor-in-Chief JERFFESON ROCHA.

Santo André, SP

Diário do Grande ABC: Rua Catequese 562, Bairro Jardim, 09090-900 Santo André, SP; tel. (11) 4435-8100; fax (11) 4434-8250; e-mail online@dgabc.com.br; internet www.dgabc.com.br; f. 1958; Editor-in-Chief EVALDO NOVELINI; circ. 78,500.

Santos, SP

A Tribuna: Rua João Pessoa 129, 2º e 3º andares, Centro, 11013-900 Santos, SP; tel. (13) 2102-7000; fax (13) 3219-7329; e-mail redacao@atribuna.com.br; internet www.atribuna.com.br; f. 1984; Exec. Editor ARMINDA AUGUSTO; Editor-in-Chief CARLOS CONDE; circ. 20,751.

São Luís, MA

O Imparcial: Empresa Pacotilha Ltda, Rua Assis Chateaubriand s/n, Renascença 2, 65075-670 São Luís, MA; tel. (98) 3212-2000; e-mail redacao@oimparcial.com.br; internet www.oimparcial.com.br; f. 1926; Editor-in-Chief PEDRO HENRIQUE FREIRE; circ. 8,000.

São Paulo, SP

DCI (Diário Comércio, Indústria e Serviços): Rua Major Quedinho 90, 7° andar, centro, 01050-030 São Paulo, SP; tel. (11) 5095-5200; fax (11) 5095-5308; e-mail redacao@dci.com.br; internet www.dci.com.br; f. 1933; morning; Editor-in-Chief LILIANA LAVORATTI; circ. 50,000.

Diário do Comércio: Associação Comercial de São Paulo, Rua Boa Vista 51, 6° andar, Centro, 01014-911 São Paulo, SP; tel. (11) 3244-3322; fax (11) 3244-3046; e-mail faleconosco@dcomercio.com.br; internet www.dcomercio.com.br; Editorial Dir. MOISÉS RABINOVICI.

Diário de São Paulo: Rua Américo Vespúcio 1001, Menck, 06273-070 Osasco, SP; tel. (11) 3235-7800; e-mail contato@diariosp.com.br; internet www.diariosp.com.br; f. 1884; fmrly *Diário Popular*; evening; owned by O Globo; Editor-in-Chief CARLOS FREY DE ALENCAR; circ. 38,840.

O Estado de São Paulo: Av. Engenheiro Caetano Alvares 55, Bairro do Limão, 02598-900 São Paulo, SP; tel. (11) 3856-5400; fax (11) 3856-2940; e-mail falecom.estado@grupoestado.com.br; internet www.estado.com.br; f. 1875; morning; independent; Editor-in-Chief ROBERTO GAZZI; circ. 263,046.

Folha de São Paulo: Alameda Barão de Limeira 425, 6° andar, Campos Elíseos, 01202-900 São Paulo, SP; tel. (11) 3224-4759; fax (11) 3224-7550; e-mail falecomagente@folha.com.br; internet www.folha.uol.com.br; f. 1921; morning; Editorial Dir OTAVIO FRIAS FILHO; circ. 286,398.

Vitória, ES

A Gazeta: Rua Charic Murad 902, 29050 Vitória, ES; tel. (27) 3321-8333; fax (27) 3321-8720; e-mail ahees@redegazeta.com.br; internet gazetaonline.globo.com; f. 1928; Exec. Editor ANDRÉ HEES; circ. 26,785.

PERIODICALS

Rio de Janeiro, RJ

Antenna-Eletrônica Popular: Av. Marechal Floriano 151, Centro, 20080-005 Rio de Janeiro, RJ; tel. (21) 2223-2442; fax (21) 2263-8840; e-mail antenna@anep.com.br; internet www.anep.com.br; f. 1926; monthly; telecommunications and electronics, radio, TV, hi-fi, amateur and CB radio; Dir MARIA BEATRIZ AFFONSO PENNA; circ. 15,000.

Conjuntura Econômica: Rua Barão de Itambi 60, 7º andar, Botafogo, 22231-000 Rio de Janeiro, RJ; tel. (21) 2559-6040; fax (21) 2559-6039; e-mail eleonora@conjunturainstitucional.com.br; internet www.fgv.br/ibre/cecon; f. 1947; monthly; economics and finance; published by Fundação Getúlio Vargas; Editor-in-Chief CLAUDIO CONCEIÇÃO; circ. 15,000.

ECO21: Av. Copacabana 2, Gr. 301, 22010-122 Rio de Janeiro, RJ; tel. (21) 2275-1490; e-mail eco21@eco21.com.br; internet www.eco21.com.br; f. 1990; monthly; ecological issues; Editor RENÉ CAPRILES.

São Paulo, SP

Ana Maria: Editora Abril, Av. das Nações Unidas 7221, 05425-902 São Paulo, SP; tel. (11) 3037-2000; fax (11) 3037-4734; e-mail anamaria.abril@atleitor.com.br; internet mdemulher.abril.com.br/revistas/anamaria; weekly; women's interest; Dir HELENA BAGNOLI; Editor-in-Chief LIDICE BÁ; circ. 222,171.

Caras: Av. Juscelino Kubitschek 1400, 13º andar, 04543-000 São Paulo, SP; tel. (11) 2197-2000; fax (11) 3086-4738; e-mail atendimento@caras.com.br; internet novoportal.caras.uol.com.br; f. 1993; weekly; celebrities; Editor VALENÇA SOTERO; circ. 308,465.

Caros Amigos: Rua Paris 856, Sumaré, 01257-040 São Paulo, SP; tel. (11) 3123-6600; fax (11) 3123-6609; e-mail atendimento@carosamigos.com.br; internet www.carosamigos.com.br; f. 1997; monthly; political; Editor ARAY NABUCO (acting); circ. 37,000.

CartaCapital: Alameda Santos 1800, 7º andar, Cerqueira César, 01418-200 São Paulo, SP; tel. (11) 3474-0161; e-mail redacao@cartacapital.com.br; internet www.cartacapital.com.br; f. 1994; weekly; politics and economics; Editor-in-Chief SERGIO LIRIO; circ. 32,570.

Casa e Jardim: Av. Jaguaré 1485, 05346-902 São Paulo, SP; tel. (11) 3767-7000; fax (11) 3767-7936; e-mail casaejardim@edglobo.com.br; internet revistacasaejardim.globo.com; f. 1953; monthly; homes and gardens, illustrated; Editor-in-Chief THAÍS LAUTON; circ. 100,811.

Claudia: Editora Abril, Av. das Nações Unidas 7221, Pinheiros, 05425-902 São Paulo, SP; tel. (11) 3037-2000; fax (11) 5087-2100; e-mail claudia.abril@atleitor.com.br; internet claudia.abril.com.br; f. 1962; monthly; women's interest; Dir PAULA MAGESTE; Editor-in-Chief DAGMAR SERPA; circ. 402,940.

Contigo!: Editora Abril, Av. das Nações Unidas 7221, 5° andar, 05425-902 São Paulo, SP; tel. (11) 3037-2000; fax (11) 3037-4734; e-mail contigo.abril@atleitor.com.br; internet contigo.abril.com.br; f. 1963; weekly; entertainment and celebrity news; Editor-in-Chief DENISE GIANOGLIO; circ. 148,569.

Cult: Praça Santo Agostinho 70, 10º andar, Paraíso, 01533-070 São Paulo, SP; tel. (11) 3385-3385; fax (11) 3385-3386; e-mail redacao@revistacult.com.br; internet revistacult.uol.com.br; f. 1997; monthly; art and culture; Editorial Dir DAYSI BREGANTINI.

Digesto Econômico: Associação Comercial de São Paulo, Rua Boa Vista 51, 6° andar, Centro, 01014-911 São Paulo, SP; tel. (11) 3244-3055; fax (11) 3244-3046; e-mail admdiario@acsp.com.br; internet www.dcomercio.com.br; fortnightly; Chief Editor JOSÉ GUILHERME RODRIGUEZ FERREIRA.

Elle: Editora Abril, Av. das Nações Unidas 7221, 16° andar, Pinheiros, 05425-902 São Paulo, SP; tel. (11) 3037-3545; fax (11) 3037-5451; e-mail elle.abril@atleitor.com.br; internet elle.abril.com.br; f. 1988; monthly; women's interest; Editor-in-Chief RENATA PIZA; circ. 100,000.

Época: Av. Jaguaré 1485, 05346-902 São Paulo, SP; tel. (11) 3767-7000; e-mail epoca@edglobo.com.br; internet revistaepoca.globo.com; f. 1998; news weekly; Editor-in-Chief João Gabriel de Lima; circ. 416,744.

Exame: Editora Abril, Av. das Nações Unidas 7221, Pinheiros, 05425-902 São Paulo, SP; tel. (11) 3037-2000; fax (11) 3037-2027; e-mail redacao.exame@abril.com.br; internet www.exame.com.br; f. 1967; 2 a week; business; Editor-in-Chief Tiago Lethbridge; circ. 168,300.

Glamour: Rua de Rocio 350, 04552-000 São Paulo, SP; tel. (11) 2322-4617; fax (11) 2322-4699; e-mail glamour@edglobo.com.br; internet revistaglamour.globo.com; f. 2012; monthly; women's interest; Editor-in-Chief Mônica Salgado.

ISTOÉ: Rua William Speers 1088, 05067-900 São Paulo, SP; tel. (11) 3618-4200; fax (11) 3618-4324; e-mail leitor@istoe.com.br; internet www.istoe.com.br; politics and current affairs; Editorial Dir Carlos José Marques; circ. 340,764.

Máquinas e Metais: Alameda Olga 315, 01155-900 São Paulo, SP; tel. (11) 3824-5300; fax (11) 3666-9585; e-mail infomm@arandanet.com.br; internet www.arandanet.com.br; f. 1964; monthly; machine and metal industries; Editorial Dir José Roberto Gonçalves; circ. 15,000.

Marie Claire: Av. Jaguaré 1485, 05346-902 São Paulo, SP; tel. (11) 3767-7000; fax (11) 3767-7833; e-mail mclaire@edglobo.com.br; internet revistamarieclaire.globo.com; monthly; women's interest; Editorial Dir Mônica de Albuquerque Lins Serino; circ. 199,831.

Micromundo-Computerworld do Brasil: Rua Caçapava 79, 01408 São Paulo, SP; tel. (11) 3289-1767; e-mail cw@nowdigital.com.br; internet www.computerworld.com.br; f. 1976; bimonthly; computers; Exec. Editor Edileuza Soares; circ. 38,000.

Nova Escola: Editora Abril, Av. das Nações Unidas 7221, 6° andar, 05425-902 São Paulo, SP; tel. (11) 3037-2000; fax (11) 3037-4322; e-mail novaescola@atleitor.com.br; internet revistaescola.abril.com.br; f. 1986; monthly; education; Editor-in-Chief Denise Pellegrini; circ. 451,125.

Pais & Filhos: Av. Rebouças 3181, Pinheiros, 05401-400 São Paulo, SP; tel. (11) 3511-2200; fax (11) 3512-9458; e-mail revista@revistapaisefilhos.com.br; internet revistapaisefilhos.com.br; monthly; child health; Editor Mariana Setubal.

Placar: Editora Abril, Av. das Nações Unidas 7221, 14° andar, Pinheiros, 05425-902 São Paulo, SP; tel. (11) 3037-2000; fax (11) 5087-2100; e-mail placar.abril@atleitor.com.br; internet placar.abril.com.br; f. 1970; monthly; soccer; Editor-in-Chief Marcos Sergio Silva; circ. 127,000.

Quatro Rodas: Av. das Nações Unidas 7221, 14° andar, 05425-902 São Paulo, SP; fax (11) 3037-5039; internet quatrorodas.abril.com.br; f. 1960; monthly; motoring; Editor-in-Chief Zeca Chaves; circ. 190,139.

Revista O Carreteiro: Rua Palacete das Aguias 395, Vila Alexandria, 04635-021 São Paulo, SP; tel. (11) 5035-0000; fax (11) 5031-8647; e-mail revista@ocarreteiro.com.br; internet www.revistaocarreteiro.com.br; f. 1970; monthly; transport; Editor João Geraldo; circ. 100,000.

Saúde: Editora Abril, Av. das Nações Unidas 7221, 16° andar, Pinheiros, 05425-902 São Paulo, SP; tel. (11) 3037-4885; fax (11) 3037-4867; e-mail saude.abril@atleitor.com.br; internet saude.abril.com.br; monthly; health; Editor-in-Chief Fábio de Oliveira; circ. 183,250.

Superinteressante: Editora Abril, Av. das Nações Unidas 7221, 8º andar, 05425-902 São Paulo, SP; tel. (11) 3037-2000; fax (11) 3037-5891; e-mail superleitor.abril@atleitor.com.br; internet super.abril.com.br; f. 1987; monthly; popular science; Editor-in-Chief Rafael Kenski; circ. 354,947.

Veja: Editora Abril, Av. das Nações Unidas 7221, Pinheiros, 05425-902 São Paulo, SP; tel. (11) 3347-2121; fax (11) 3037-5638; e-mail veja@abril.com.br; internet veja.abril.com.br; f. 1968; news weekly; Editor-in-Chief Fábio Altman; circ. 1,099,078.

NEWS AGENCIES

Agência o Estado de São Paulo: Av. Eng. Caetano Alvares 55, Bairro do Limão, 02588-900 São Paulo, SP; tel. (11) 3856-3500; fax (11) 3856-2940; e-mail falecom.estado@grupoestado.com.br; internet www.estadao.com.br; Rep. Samuel Dirceu F. Bueno.

Agência O Globo: Rua Irineu Marinho 70, 4° andar, Cidade Nova, 20230-901 Rio de Janeiro, RJ; tel. (21) 2534-5656; e-mail agenciaoglobo@oglobo.com.br; internet www.agenciaoglobo.com.br; f. 1974; Man. Ricardo Mello.

PRESS ASSOCIATIONS

Associação Brasileira de Imprensa (ABI): Rua Araújo Porto Alegre 71, Centro, 20030-012 Rio de Janeiro, RJ; tel. (21) 2282-1292; e-mail abi@abi.org.br; internet www.abi.org.br; f. 1908; asscn for journalistic rights and assistance; 4,000 mems; Pres. Maurício Azêdo.

Associação Nacional de Editores de Revistas (ANER): Rua Deputado Lacerda Franco 300, 15°, Conj. 155, 05418-000 São Paulo, SP; tel. (11) 3030-9390; fax (11) 3030-9393; e-mail info@aner.org.br; internet www.aner.org.br; f. 1986; Pres. Frederic Kachar; Exec. Dir Maria Célia Furtado.

Federação Nacional dos Jornalistas (FENAJ): SCLRN 704, Bloco F, Loja 20, 70730-536 Brasília, DF; tel. (61) 3244-0650; fax (61) 3242-6616; e-mail fenaj@fenaj.org.br; internet www.fenaj.org.br; f. 1946; represents 31 regional unions; Pres. Celso Schröder; Sec.-Gen. Guto Camargo.

Publishers

Aymará Edições e Tecnologia, Ltda: Rua Lamenha Lins 1709, Rebouças, 80220-080 Curitiba, PR; tel. (41) 3213-3500; fax (41) 3213-3501; e-mail debora.nunes@aymara.com.br; internet www.aymara.com.br; academic; Pres. André Caldeira.

Barsa Planeta Internacional: Edif. New York, 4º andar, Centro Empresarial Agua Branca, Av. Francisco Matarazzo 1500, 05001-100 São Paulo, SP; tel. (11) 3225-1990; fax (11) 3225-1960; e-mail atendimento@barsaplaneta.com.br; internet brasil.planetasaber.com; f. 1949; reference books.

Cengage Learning: Prédio 11, Torre A, Conj. 12, Condomínio E-Business Park, Rua Werner Siemens 111, Lapa de Baixo, 05069-900 São Paulo, SP; tel. (11) 3665-9900; fax (11) 3665-9901; e-mail milagros.valderrama@cengage.com; internet www.cengage.com.br; f. 1960 as Editora Pioneira; architecture, computers, political and social sciences, business studies, languages, children's books; Dir Milagros Valderrama.

Cortez Editora: Rua Monte Alegre 1074, 05014-001 São Paulo, SP; tel. (11) 3611-9696; fax (11) 3864-0111; e-mail erivan@cortezeditora.com.br; internet www.cortezeditora.com.br; f. 1980; children's literature, linguistics and social sciences; Dir Erivan Gomes.

Ediouro Publicações, SA: Rua Nova Jerusalém 345, CP 1880, Bonsucesso, 21042-235 Rio de Janeiro, RJ; tel. (21) 3882-8416; fax (21) 3882-8200; e-mail livros@ediouro.com.br; internet www.ediouro.com.br; f. 1939; part of Empresas Ediouro; general interest, leisure magazines, textbooks; Pres. Jorge Carneiro.

Editora Abril, SA: Av. das Nações Unidas 7221, Pinheiros, 05425-902 São Paulo, SP; tel. (11) 3037-2000; fax (11) 5087-2100; e-mail abril@abril.com.br; internet www.abril.com.br; f. 1950; magazines; Pres. and Editorial Dir Roberto Civita.

Editora Atica, SA: Rua Barão de Iguape 110, 01507-900 São Paulo, SP; tel. (11) 3346-3000; fax (11) 3277-4146; e-mail editora@atica.com.br; internet www.atica.com.br; f. 1965; acquired by Grupo Abril in 2004; textbooks, Brazilian and African literature; Pres. Vicente Paz Fernandez.

Editora Atlas, SA: Rua Conselheiro Nébias 1384, 01203-904 São Paulo, SP; tel. (11) 3357-9144; fax (11) 3331-7830; e-mail atendimento@editora-atlas.com.br; internet www.editoraatlas.com.br; f. 1944; business administration, economics, accounting, law, education, social sciences; Pres. Luiz Herrmann, Jr.

Editora Blucher: Rua Pedroso Alvarenga 1245, 4º andar, 04531-012 São Paulo, SP; tel. (11) 3078-5366; fax (11) 3079-2707; e-mail eduardo@blucher.com.br; internet www.blucher.com.br; f. 1957; science and engineering; Dir Eduardo Blücher.

Editora do Brasil, SA: Rua Conselheiro Nébias 887, Campos Elíseos, CP 4986, 01203-001 São Paulo, SP; tel. (11) 3226-0211; fax (11) 3222-5583; e-mail editora@editoradobrasil.com.br; internet www.editoradobrasil.com.br; f. 1943; education; Pres. Maria Apparecida Cavalcante Costa.

Editora Brasiliense, SA: Rua Mourato Coelho 111, Pinheiros, 05417-010 São Paulo, SP; tel. and fax (11) 3087-0000; e-mail brasilienseedit@uol.com.br; internet www.editorabrasiliense.com.br; f. 1943; education, racism, gender studies, human rights, ecology, history, literature, social sciences; Pres. Yolanda C. da Silva Prado.

Editora Campus-Elsevier: Rua Sete de Setembro 111, 16° andar, 20050-002 Rio de Janeiro, RJ; tel. (21) 3970-9300; fax (21) 2507-1991; e-mail info@elsevier.com.br; internet www.campus.com.br; f. 1976; business, computing, non-fiction; imprint of Elsevier since 2002; Pres. Claudio Rothmuller; Dir Igdal Parnes.

Editora Canção Nova: Rua São Bento 43, Centro, 01011-000 São Paulo, SP; tel. (11) 3106-9080; e-mail editora@cancaonova.com; internet editora.cancaonova.com; f. 1996; spiritual literature and children's books; Dir Cristiana Maria Negrão.

Editora Delta, SA (Mundo da Criança): Av. Nilo Peçanha 50, Centro 2817, 20020-100 Rio de Janeiro, RJ; tel. (21) (21) 2533-6673; e-mail faleconosco@mundodacrianca.com; internet www.mundodacrianca.com; f. 1930; reference books; Pres. ANDRÉ KOOGAN BREITMAN.

Editora FTD, SA: Rua Rui Barbosa 156, Bairro Bela Vista, 01326-010 São Paulo, SP; tel. (11) 3253-5011; fax (11) 3288-0132; e-mail ftd@ftd.com.br; internet www.ftd.com.br; f. 1902; textbooks; Pres. DÉLCIO AFONSO BALESTRIN; Dir CECILIANY ALVES.

Editora Globo, SA: Av. Jaguaré 1485, 3º andar, 05346-902 São Paulo, SP; tel. (11) 3767-7400; fax (11) 3767-7870; e-mail globolivros@edglobo.com.br; internet globolivros.globo.com; f. 1957; fiction, engineering, agriculture, cookery, environmental studies; Dir-Gen. FREDERIC ZOGHAIB KACHAR.

Editora Lê, SA: Rua Januária 437, Floresta, 31110-060 Belo Horizonte, MG; tel. (31) 3423-3200; fax (31) 2517-3003; e-mail editora@le.com.br; internet www.le.com.br; f. 1967; textbooks; Dir JOSÉ ALENCAR MAYRINK.

Editora Manole: Av. Ceci 672, Tamboré, 06460-120 Barueri, SP; tel. (11) 4196-6000; e-mail info@manole.com.br; internet www.manole.com.br; includes the imprints Minha Editora and Amarilys Editora; Dir AMARYLIS MANOLE.

Editora Melhoramentos, Ltda: Rua Tito 479, Vila Romana, 05051-000 São Paulo, SP; tel. (11) 3874-0800; fax (11) 3874-0855; e-mail sac@melhoramentos.com.br; internet www.livrariamelhoramentos.com.br; f. 1890; general non-fiction, children's books, dictionaries; Dir BRENO LERNER.

Editora Moderna, Ltda: Rua Padre Adelino 758, Belenzinho, 03303-904 São Paulo, SP; tel. (11) 2790-1300; fax (11) 2602-5510; e-mail faleconosco@moderna.com.br; internet www.moderna.com.br; f. 1968; Pres. RICARDO ARISSA FELTRE.

Editora Nova Fronteira, SA: Rua Nova Jerusalém 345, Bonsucesso, 21042-230 Rio de Janeiro, RJ; tel. (21) 2131-1111; fax (21) 2537-2009; e-mail sac@novafronteira.com.br; internet www.novafronteira.com.br; f. 1965; acquired by Empresas Ediouro in 2006; fiction, psychology, history, politics, science fiction, poetry, leisure, reference; Exec. Dir MAURO PALERMO.

Editora Positivo: Rua Major Heitor Guimarães 174, Seminário, 80400-120 Curitiba, PR; tel. (41) 3212-3500; fax (41) 3336-5135; e-mail vendas@editorapositivo.com.br; internet www.editorapositivo.com.br; f. 1980; Dir-Gen. EMERSON SANTOS.

Editora Record, SA: Rua Argentina 171, São Cristóvão, CP 884, 20921-380 Rio de Janeiro, RJ; tel. (21) 2585-2000; fax (21) 2585-2085; e-mail record@record.com.br; internet www.record.com.br; f. 1942; part of Grupo Editorial Record; general fiction and non-fiction, education, textbooks, fine arts; Pres. SÉRGIO MACHADO.

Editora Revista dos Tribunais, Ltda: Rua do Bosque 820, 01136-000 São Paulo, SP; tel. (11) 3613-8400; fax (11) 3613-8450; e-mail sac@rt.com.br; internet www.rt.com.br; f. 1912; acquired by Thomson Reuters in 2010; law and jurisprudence books and periodicals; Pres. GONZALO LISSARRAGUE; CEO BELINELO ANTONIO.

Editora Rideel, Ltda: Av. Casa Verde 455, Casa Verde, 02519-000 São Paulo, SP; tel. and fax (11) 2238-5100; e-mail sac@rideel.com.br; internet www.rideel.com.br; f. 1971; general; Dir ITALO AMADIO.

Editora Saraiva: Rua Henrique Schaumann 270, Cerqueira César, 05413-909 São Paulo, SP; tel. (11) 3613-3000; fax (11) 3611-3308; e-mail saceditorasaraiva@editorasaraiva.com.br; internet www.editorasaraiva.com.br; f. 1914; education, textbooks, law, economics, general fiction and non-fiction; Pres. JORGE EDUARDO SARAIVA.

Editora Sçipione, Ltda: Av. Otaviano Alves de Lima 4400, Freguesia do Ó, 02909-900 São Paulo, SP; tel. (11) 3990-1788; e-mail scipione@scipione.com.br; internet www.scipione.com.br; f. 1983; owned by Editora Abril, SA; school books, literature, reference; Chair. DOUGLAS DURAN; Dir LUIZ ESTEVES SALLUM.

Editora Vozes, Ltda: Rua Frei Luís 100, CP 90023, Centro, 25689-900 Petrópolis, RJ; tel. (24) 2233-9000; fax (24) 2231-4676; e-mail editorial@vozes.com.br; internet www.universovozes.com.br; f. 1901; Catholic publrs; theology, philosophy, history, linguistics, science, psychology, fiction, education, etc.; Dir ANTÔNIO MOSER.

Global Editora: Rua Pirapitingüi 111, Liberdade, 01508-020 São Paolo, SP; tel. (11) 3277-7999; fax (11) 3277-8141; e-mail global@globaleditora.com.br; internet www.globaleditora.com.br; f. 1973; Dir LUIZ ALVES JÚNIOR.

Instituto Brasileiro de Edições Pedagógicas, Ltda (Editora IBEP): Av. Alexandre Mackenzie 619, Jaguaré, 05322-000 São Paulo, SP; tel. (11) 2799-7799; fax (11) 6694-5338; e-mail editoras@ibep-nacional.com.br; internet www.editoraibep.com.br; f. 1965; part of Grupo IBEP; textbooks; Dirs JORGE YUNES, PAULO CORNADO MARTI.

Lex Editora, SA: Rua da Consolação 77, Centro, 01301-000 São Paulo, SP; tel. (11) 2126-6000; fax (11) 2126-6020; e-mail editorial@lex.com.br; internet www.lex.com.br; f. 1937; legislation and jurisprudence; Pres. CARLOS SERGIO SERRA; Exec. Dir FÁBIO PAIXÃO.

Pallas Editora: Rua Frederico de Albuquerque 56, Higienópolis, 21050-840 Rio de Janeiro, RJ; tel. and fax (21) 2270-0186; e-mail pallas@pallaseditora.com.br; internet www.pallaseditora.com.br; f. 1980; Afro-Brazilian culture; Pres. CRISTINA FERNANDES WARTH.

Yendis Editora: Rua Major Carlos del Prete 510, 09530-000 São Caetano do Sul, SP; tel. (11) 4224-9400; fax (11) 4224-9403; e-mail max@yendis.com.br; internet www.yendis.com.br; Dir MAXWELL MEDEIROS FERNANDES.

PUBLISHERS' ASSOCIATIONS

Associação Brasileira de Difusão do Livro (ABDL) (Brazilian Association of Door-to-Door Booksellers): Rua Marquês de Itu 408-71, CP 01223-000, São Paulo, SP; internet www.abdl.com.br; f. 1987; non-profit org.; Pres. LUÍS ANTONIO TORELLI.

Associação Brasileira de Editores de Livros Escolares (Abrelivros): Rua Funchal 263, Conj. 61/62, Vila Olímpia, 04551-060 São Paulo, SP; tel. and fax (11) 3826-9071; e-mail contato@abrelivros.org.br; internet www.abrelivros.org.br; f. 1991; 28 mems; Pres. JORGE YUNES; Gen. Man. BEATRIZ GRELLET.

Associação Brasileira do Livro (ABL): Av. 13 de Maio 23, 16° andar, Sala 1619/1620, 20031-000 Rio de Janeiro, RJ; tel. and fax (21) 2240-9115; e-mail abralivro@uol.com.br; internet www.abralivro.com.br; f. 1955; Pres. ADENILSON JARBAS CABRAL.

Câmara Brasileira do Livro: Rua Cristiano Viana 91, Pinheiros, 05411-000 São Paulo, SP; tel. and fax (11) 3069-1300; e-mail cbl@cbl.org.br; internet www.cbl.org.br; f. 1946; Pres. ROSELY BOSCHINI.

Sindicato Nacional dos Editores de Livros (SNEL): Rua da Ajuda 35, 18° andar, Centro, 20040-000 Rio de Janeiro, RJ; tel. (21) 2533-0399; fax (21) 2533-0422; e-mail snel@snel.org.br; internet www.snel.org.br; 200 mems; Pres. SONIA MACHADO JARDIM.

Broadcasting and Communications

TELECOMMUNICATIONS

AT&T Brazil: Torre Sul, 7°, Rua James Joule 65, São Paulo, SP; tel. (11) 3885-0080; internet www.att.com.br; Vice-Pres. (Caribbean and Latin America) MARY LIVINGSTON.

Claro: Rua Florida 1970, Bairro Cidade Monções, 40432-544 São Paulo, SP; internet www.claro.com.br; f. 2003 by mergers; owned by América Móvil, SA de CV (Mexico); mobile cellular provider; 67m. subscribers (2013); CEO CARLOS ZENTENO DE LOS SANTOS.

CTBC (Companhia de Telecomunicações do Brasil Central): Rua Machado de Assis 333, Centro, 38400-112 Uberlândia, MG; tel. (34) 3256-2033; fax (34) 3236-7723; e-mail tatianes@ctbc.com.br; internet www.ctbc.com.br; f. 1954; owned by Grupo Algar; mobile and fixed line provider in central Brazil; Pres. DIVINO SEBASTIÃO DE SOUZA.

Empresa Brasileira de Telecomunicações, SA (Embratel): Av. Presidente Vargas 1012, CP 2586, 20179-900 Rio de Janeiro, RJ; tel. (21) 2519-8182; e-mail cmsocial@embratel.net.br; internet www.embratel.com.br; f. 1965; operates national and international telecommunications system; owned by Telmex (Teléfonos de Mexico, SA); Pres. JOSÉ FORMOSO MARTÍNEZ.

Nextel Telecomunicações Ltda: Av. das Nações Unidas 14171, Morumbi, 04795-100 São Paulo, SP; tel. (11) 4004-6611; e-mail assessoria.imprensa@nextel.com.br; internet www.nextel.com.br; f. 1997; part of NII Holdings, Inc. (USA); digital radio, mobile cellular and wireless services provider; Pres. SERGIO CHAIA.

Oi (Tele Norte Leste Participações, SA): Rua Lauro Müller 116, 22° andar, Botafogo, Rio de Janeiro, RJ; tel. (21) 2815-2921; fax (21) 2571-3050; internet www.novaoi.com.br; f. 1998 as Telemar; 22% owned by Portugal Telecom, full merger planned in early 2014; fixed line and mobile operator; 50m. subscribers (2013); CEO ZEINAL BAVA.

Sercomtel Celular, SA: Rua João Cândido 555, 86010-000 Londrina, PR; e-mail casc@sercomtel.com.br; internet www.sercomtelcelular.com.br; f. 1998; mobile cellular network provider; Pres. OSWALDO PITOL.

Telefônica SP: Rua Martiniano de Carvalho 851, Bela Vista, 01321-000 São Paulo, SP; tel. (11) 3549-7200; fax (11) 3549-7202; e-mail telefonicabr@telefonica.com.br; internet www.telefonica.com.br; fmrly Telecomunicações de São Paulo (Telesp), privatized in 1998; subsidiary of Telefónica, SA (Spain); 41m. customers; Pres. ANTONIO CARLOS VALENTE DA SILVA.

Telemig Celular: internet www.telemigcelular.com.br; mobile cellular provider in Minas Gerais; 2.6m. customers.

Vivo: Av. Chucri Zaidan 2460, 5º, 04583-110 São Paulo, SP; tel. (11) 5105-1001; internet www.vivo.com.br; owned by Telefónica Móviles, SA of Spain; Telefónica bought Portugal Telecom's share in 2010; 77m. customers (2013); CEO PAULO CESAR TEIXEIRA.

TIM (Telecom Italia Mobile): Av. das Américas 3434, 5° andar, Barra da Tijuca, 22640-102 Rio de Janeiro, RJ; internet www.tim.com.br; f. 1998 in Brazil; subsidiary of Telecom Italia (Italy); mobile cellular provider; 73m. customers (2013); Pres. MANOEL HORÁCIO FRANCISCO DA SILVA; Dir ANDREA MANGONI.

Regulatory Authority

Agência Nacional de Telecomunicações (ANATEL): SAUS Quadra 06, Blocos C, E, F e H, 70070-940 Brasília, DF; tel. (61) 2312-2000; fax (61) 2312-2264; e-mail biblioteca@anatel.gov.br; internet www.anatel.gov.br; f. 1998; regional office in each state; Pres. JOÃO BATISTA DE REZENDE; Exec. Supt MARILDA MOREIRA.

BROADCASTING

Empresa Brasil de Comunicação (EBC): Edif. Venâncio 2000, 1° andar Inferior, SCS, Quadra 08, Bloco B–60, Asa Sul, 70333-900 Brasília, DF; tel. (61) 3799-5700; e-mail comunicacao@ebc.com.br; internet www.ebc.com.br; f. 1975, as Empresa Brasileira de Radiodifusão (RADIOBRÁS); re-established as above in 2007; state-run radio and television network; manages public broadcasters; Pres. NELSON BREVE; Dir-Gen. EDUARDO CASTRO.

Radio

The main broadcasting stations in Rio de Janeiro are: Rádio Nacional, Rádio Globo, Rádio Eldorado, Rádio Jornal do Brasil, Rádio Tupi and Rádio Mundial. In São Paulo the main stations are Rádio Bandeirantes, Rádio Mulher, Rádio Eldorado, Rádio Gazeta and Rádio Excelsior; and in Brasília: Rádio Nacional, Rádio Alvorada, Rádio Planalto and Rádio Capital.

The state-run corporation Empresa Brasil de Comunicação (q.v.) owns the following radio stations:

Rádio MEC AM/FM do Rio de Janeiro: Praça da República 141-A, Centro, 20211-350 Rio de Janeiro, RJ; tel. (21) 2117-7853; e-mail ouvinte@radiomec.com.br; internet radiomec.com.br; f. 2004; Supt ORLANDO GUILHON.

Rádio Nacional AM de Brasília: CP 259, 70710-750 Brasília, DF; tel. (61) 3799-5167; fax (61) 3799-5169; e-mail centraldoouvinte@ebc.com.br; f. 1958; Man. CRISTINA GUIMARÃES.

Rádio Nacional da Amazônia-OC: CP 258, 70359-970 Brasília, DF; f. 1977; Regional Man. SOFÍA HAMMOE; Co-ordinator LUCIANA COUTO.

Rádio Nacional FM de Brasília: CP 070747, 70720-502 Brasília, DF; e-mail ouvinte@radiomec.com.br; f. 1976; broadcasts to the Federal District and surrounding areas; Man. CARLOS SENNA.

Television

The main television networks are:

RBS TV: Rua do Acampamento 2550, Passo do Príncipe, 96425-250 Bagé, RS; tel. (53) 3240-5300; fax (53) 3240-5305; internet www.rbs.com.br; f. 1957; major regional network; operates Canal Rural and TVCOM; Group Pres. NELSON PACHECO SIROTSKY; Exec. Dir EDUARDO SIROTSKY MELZER.

TV Bandeirantes: Rádio e Televisão Bandeirantes Ltda, Rua Radiantes 13, Morumbi, 05699-900 São Paulo, SP; tel. (11) 3742-3011; fax (11) 3745-7622; e-mail cat@band.com.br; internet www.band.com.br; 65 TV stations and repeaters throughout Brazil; Pres. JOÃO CARLOS SAAD.

TV Brasil Internacional (TVBI): CP 8640, 70312-970 Brasília, DF; tel. (61) 3799-5889; fax (61) 3799-5888; e-mail tvbrasilinternacional@ebc.com.br; internet www.tvbrasil.ebc.com.br/internacional; f. 2010; owned by Empresa Brasil de Comunicação (EBC); broadcasts internationally via satellite in Portuguese; Programme Dir RICARDO SOARES; Programme Man. MAX GONÇALVES.

TV Nacional/TV Brasil (Canal 2): Rua da Relação 18, Lapa, 20231-110 Rio de Janeiro, RJ; tel. (21) 2117-6208; e-mail sap@tvbrasil.org.br; internet www.tvbrasil.org.br; public tv station; broadcasts to the Federal District and surrounding areas; operated by Empresa Brasil de Comunicação (EBC); Dir-Gen. NELSON BREVE.

TV Record—Rádio e Televisão Record, SA: Rua de Bosque 1393, Barra Funda, 01136-001 São Paulo, SP; tel. (11) 3660-4761; fax (11) 3660-4756; e-mail tvrecord@rederecord.com.br; internet rederecord.r7.com; f. 1953; Dir ALEXANDRE RAPOSO.

TV Rede Globo: Rua Lopes Quintas 303, Jardim Botânico, 22460-010 Rio de Janeiro, RJ; tel. (21) 2444-4725; fax (21) 2294-2092; e-mail cgcom-br@tvglobo.com.br; internet redeglobo.globo.com; f. 1965; 8 stations; national network; Exec. Pres. ROBERTO IRINEU MARINHO.

TV SBT—Sistema Brasileira de Televisão—Canal 4 de São Paulo, SA: Av. das Comunicações 4, Vila Jaraguá, Osasco, 06278-905 São Paulo, SP; tel. (11) 7087-3000; fax (11) 7087-3509; internet www.sbt.com.br; 107 local TV channels; Dir-Gen. DANIEL SLAVIERO.

Broadcasting Associations

Associação Brasileira de Emissoras de Rádio e Televisão (ABERT): Edif.Via Esplanada, SAF/SUL Quadra 02, Lote 04, Bloco D, Sala 101, 70770-600 Brasília, DF; tel. (61) 2104-4600; fax (61) 2104-4611; e-mail abert@abert.org.br; internet www.abert.org.br; f. 1962; Pres. DANIEL PIMENTEL SLAVIERO; Exec. Dir VICENTE JORGE RODRIGUES.

There are regional associations for Bahia, Ceará, Goiás, Minas Gerais, Rio Grande do Sul, Santa Catarina, São Paulo, Amazonas, Distrito Federal, Mato Grosso and Mato Grosso do Sul (combined), and Sergipe.

Finance

(cap. = capital; res = reserves; dep. = deposits; m. = million; brs = branches; amounts in reais, unless otherwise stated)

BANKING

Conselho Monetário Nacional (CMN): Setor Bancário Sul, Quadra 03, Bloco B, Edif. Sede do Banco do Brasil, 21° andar, 70074-900 Brasília, DF; tel. (61) 3414-1945; fax (61) 3414-2528; e-mail cmn@bcb.gov.br; internet www.bcb.gov.br/?CMN; f. 1964 to formulate monetary policy and to supervise the banking system; Pres. GUIDO MANTEGA (Minister of Finance).

Central Bank

Banco Central do Brasil: SBS, Quadra 03, Mezanino 01, Bloco B, 70074-900 Brasília, DF; tel. (61) 3414-1414; fax (61) 3414-2553; e-mail secre.surel@bcb.gov.br; internet www.bcb.gov.br; f. 1965; est. to execute the decisions of the Conselho Monetário Nacional; bank of issue; total assets 1,157,596.2m. (Dec. 2009); Gov. ALEXANDRE ANTONIO TOMBINI; 10 brs.

State Commercial Banks

Banco da Amazônia, SA: Av. Presidente Vargas 800, 3° andar, 66017-000 Belém, PA; tel. (91) 4008-3888; fax (91) 4008-3243; e-mail cambio@bancoamazionia.com.br; internet www.bancoamazonia.com.br; f. 1942; state-owned; cap. 1,219.7m., res 36.4m., dep. 2,339.6m. (Dec. 2011); Pres. ABIDIAS JOSÉ DE SOUZA JÚNIOR; 104 brs.

Banco do Brasil, SA: SBS, Quadra 01, Bloco C, Lote 32, Edif. Sede III, 70073-901 Brasília, DF; tel. (61) 3102-1124; fax (61) 3102-1435; e-mail ri@bb.com.br; internet www.bb.com.br; f. 1808; cap. 33,122.6m., res 24,999.1m., dep. 443,627.6m. (Dec. 2011); Pres. ALDEMIR BENDINE.

Banco do Estado do Pará: Edif. Banpará, 4° andar, Av. Presidente Vargas 251, Campina, 66010-000 Belém, PA; tel. (91) 3210-3233; fax (91) 3241-7163; internet www.banparanet.com.br; f. 1961; cap. 264.1m., res 109m., dep. 2,239.8m. (Dec. 2011); Pres. AUGUSTO SÉRGIO AMORIM COSTA; 24 brs.

Banco do Estado do Rio Grande do Sul, SA (Banrisul): Rua Capitão Montanha 177, Centro, 90010-040 Porto Alegre, RS; tel. (51) 3215-2501; fax (51) 3215-1715; e-mail cambio_dg@banrisul.com.br; internet www.banrisul.com.br; f. 1928; cap. 3,200m., res 1,199.5m., dep. 23,921.4m. (Dec. 2011); Pres. TÚLIO LUIZ ZAMIN; 352 brs.

Banco do Nordeste do Brasil, SA: Av. Pedro Ramalho 5700, Passaré, CP 628, 60743-902 Fortaleza, CE; tel. (85) 3299-3000; fax (85) 3299-3674; e-mail info@banconordeste.gov.br; internet www.banconordeste.gov.br; f. 1952; cap. 2,010m., res 319.5m., dep. 9,676m. (Dec. 2011); Pres. ARY JOEL DE ABREU LANZARIN; 186 brs.

BANESTES, SA—Banco do Estado do Espírito Santo: Edif. Palas Center, Bloco B, 9° andar, Av. Princesa Isabel 574, Centro, 29010-931 Espírito Santo, ES; tel. (27) 3383-1545; fax (27) 3383-1398; e-mail ri@banestes.com.br; internet www.banestes.com.br; f. 1937; cap. 694m., res 136.8m., dep. 5,986.4m. (Dec. 2011); CEO BRUNO PESSANHA NEGRIS.

Private Banks

Banco ABC Brasil, SA: Av. Juscelino Kubitschek 1400, 3°–5° andares, Itaim Bibi, 04543-000 São Paulo, SP; tel. (11) 3170-2000; fax (11) 3170-2001; e-mail sac.abcbrasil@abcbrasil.com.br; internet www.abcbrasil.com.br; f. 1989 as Banco ABC—Roma SA; 84% owned by Arab Banking Corpn BSC (Bahrain); cap. 1,004.4m., res 495.2m., dep. 4,202m. (Dec. 2011); Pres. and Gen. Man. ANIS CHACUR NETO; 4 brs.

Banco Alfa de Investimento, SA: Alameda Santos 466, Cerqueira César, 01418-000 Paraíso, SP; tel. (11) 4004-3344; fax (11) 3171-2438; e-mail alfanet@alfanet.com.br; internet www.alfanet.com.br; f. 1998; cap. 476m., res 620m., dep. 4,011m. (Dec. 2011); Chair. PAULO GUIHERME MONTEIRO LOBATO RIBEIRO; Pres. FABIO ALBERTO AMOROSINO; 12 brs.

Banco BBM, SA: Rua Miguel Calmon 398, 2º andar, Parte Comércio, 40015-010 Salvador, BA; tel. (71) 3326-4721; fax (71) 3254-2703; e-mail bancobbm@bancobbm.com.br; internet www.bancobbm.com.br; f. 1858; est. as Banco de Bahia; present name adopted 1998; cap. 413.1m., res 123.1m., dep. 805.2m. (Dec. 2011); Pres. PEDRO HENRIQUE MARIANI BITTENCOURT; 6 brs.

Banco BMG, SA: Av. Alvares Cabral 1707, Santo Agostinho, 30170-001 Belo Horizonte, MG; tel. (31) 3290-3000; fax (31) 3290-3100; e-mail faleconosco@bancobmg.com.br; internet www.bancobmg.com.br; f. 1930; cap. 2,500m., res 1,117.5m., dep. 8,918.1m. (Dec. 2011); Pres. RICARDO ANNES GUIMARÃES; 14 brs.

Banco Bradesco, SA: Cidade de Deus, Vila Yara, 06029-900 Osasco, SP; tel. (11) 3684-4011; fax (11) 3684-4630; internet www.bradesco.com.br; f. 1943; est. as Banco Brasileiro de Descontos; present name adopted 1989; cap. 30,000m., res 18,042.8m., dep. 334,619.5m. (Dec. 2010); Pres. and CEO LUIZ CARLOS TRABUCO CAPPI; 3,628 brs.

Banco Brascan, SA: Av. Almirante Barroso 52, 30° andar, Centro, 20031-000 Rio de Janeiro, RJ; tel. (21) 3231-3000; fax (21) 3231-3231; internet www.bancobrascan.com.br; f. 1968; cap. 155.6m., res 6.4m., dep. 224.1m. (Dec. 2011); Pres. VALDECYR MACIEL GOMES.

Banco BTG Pactual, SA: Torre Corcovado, 6°, Praia de Botafago 501, 22250-040 Rio de Janeiro, RJ; tel. (21) 3262-9600; fax (21) 2514-8600; internet www.btgpactual.com; f. 1983; fmrly Banco UBS Pactual; present name adopted 2008 following acquisition by BTG Pactual; cap. 3,242.5m., res 3,090.8m., dep. 44,106.2m. (Dec. 2011); Pres. ANDRÉ ESTEVES; 5 brs.

Banco Fibra: Av. Presidente Juscelino Kubitschek 360, 4°–9° andares, 04543-000 São Paulo, SP; tel. (11) 3847-6700; fax (11) 3847-6962; e-mail bancofibra@bancofibra.com.br; internet www.bancofibra.com.br; f. 1989; cap. 966.4m., res 153.2m., dep. 6,315.4m. (Dec. 2011); CEO ANTONIO DE LIMA NETO.

Banco Industrial do Brasil: Av. Juscelino Kubitschek 1703, 2°–4° andares, Itaim Bibi, 04543-000 São Paulo, SP; tel. (11) 3049-9671; fax (11) 3049-9810; internet www.bancoindustrial.com.br; f. 1994; cap. 367.2m., res 52.7m., dep. 1,171.3m. (Dec. 2011); Pres. CARLOS ALBERTO MANSUR.

Banco Industrial e Comercial, SA (Bicbanco): Av. Brigadeiro Faria Lima 4440, 2º andar, 04538-132 São Paulo, SP; tel. (11) 2173-9000; fax (11) 2173-9101; internet www.bicbanco.com.br; f. 1938; 72% bought by China Construction Bank in Oct. 2013; cap. 1,257.5m., res 738.5m., dep. 9,386.8m. (Dec. 2008); Pres. JOSÉ BEZERRA DE MENEZES; 30 brs.

Banco Indusval & Partners, SA (Banco Indusval Multistock): Rua Iguatemi 151, 6° andar, Centro, 01451-011 São Paulo, SP; tel. (11) 3315-6777; fax (11) 3315-0130; e-mail banco@indusval.com.br; internet www.bip.b.br; f. 1980; fmrly Banco Indusval; adopted present name in 2011; cap. 572.4m., res 7.9m., dep. 1,657.9m. (Dec. 2011); Chair. MANOEL FELIX CINTRA NETO; Pres. JAIR RIBEIRO DA SILVA NETO.

Banco Itaú BBA, SA: Av. Brig. Faria Lima 3400, 3° ao 8° andar, 04538-132 São Paulo, SP; tel. (11) 3708-8000; fax (11) 3708-8172; e-mail bancoitaubba@itaubba.com.br; internet www.itaubba.com.br; f. 1967; est. as Banco do Estado de Minas Gerais, SA; acquired by Banco Itaú in 2002; present name adopted 2004; cap. 4,224.1m., res 2,607.7m., dep. 137,531.7m. (Dec. 2011); Pres. and CEO CANDIDO BOTELHO BRACHER; 6 brs.

Banco Mercantil do Brasil, SA: Rua Rio de Janeiro 680, Centro, 30160-912 Belo Horizonte, MG; tel. (31) 3057-4450; fax (31) 3079-8422; e-mail sac@mercantil.com.br; internet www.mercantil.com.br; f. 1943; est. as Banco Mercantil de Minas Gerais, SA; cap. 332.7m., res 370.9m., dep. 8,165.2m. (Dec. 2011); Pres. MILTON DE ARAÚJO; 171 brs.

Banco Paulista, SA: Av. Brigadeiro Faria Lima, 1355 Jardim Paulistano, 2° andar, 01452-002 São Paulo, SP; tel. (11) 3299-2000; fax (11) 3299-2362; e-mail cambiobp@bancopaulista.com.br; internet www.bancopaulista.com.br; f. 1989; cap. 127m., res 0.09m., dep. 726.7m. (Dec. 2011); Pres. ALVARO AUGUSTO VIDIGAL.

Banco Pine, SA: Eldorado Business Tower, Av. das Nações Unidas 8501, 30° andar, 05425-070 São Paulo, SP; tel. (11) 3372-5200; fax (11) 3372-5404; e-mail bancopine@uol.com.br; internet www.bancopine.com.br; f. 1997; cap. 796m., res 229.9m., dep. 7,172.5m. (Dec. 2011); Chair. NORBERTO NOGUEIRA PINHEIRO.

Banco Rural, SA: Rua Rio de Janeiro 927, 13º andar, Centro, 30160-041 Belo Horizonte, MG; tel. (31) 2126-5000; fax (31) 2126-5802; e-mail seger@rural.com.br; internet www.bancorural.com.br; f. 1964; est. as Banco Rural de Minas Gerais; present name adopted 1980; cap. 440.7m., res 26.3m., dep. 3,166.8m. (Dec. 2011); Pres. JOÃO HERALDO LIMA; 22 brs.

Banco Safra, SA: Av. Paulista 2100, 9° andar, Cerqueira Cesar, 01310-930 São Paulo, SP; tel. (11) 3175-7575; fax (11) 3175-7211; internet www.safra.com.br; f. 1940; cap. 3,980.3m., res 2,035.3m., dep. 40,118.1m. (Dec. 2011); Pres. ROSSANO MARANHÃO; 98 brs.

Banco Santander Brasil, SA: Av. Presidente Juscelino Kubitschek 2041, E 2235, Bloco A, Vila Olimpia, 04543-011 São Paulo, SP; tel. (11) 3553-5447; fax (11) 3553-7778; internet www.santander.com.br; f. 2006; est. as Banco Santander Banespa, SA by merger; present name adopted 2007; owned by Banco Santander, SA (Spain); cap. 62,634.6m., res 7,630.5m., dep. 245,521.3m. (Dec. 2011); Pres. MARCIAL ANGEL PORTELA ALVAREZ.

Banco Société Générale Brasil, SA: Av. Paulista 2300, 9° andar, Cerqueira Cesar, 01310-300 São Paulo, SP; tel. (11) 3217-8000; fax (11) 3217-8090; e-mail faleconosco@sgcib.com; internet www.sgbrasil.com.br; f. 1981; est. as Banco Sogeral; present name adopted 2001; cap. 1,757.9m., res –48.6m., dep. 843.4m. (Dec. 2011); Pres. SÉRGIO LEIFERT.

Banco Votorantim, SA: Av. das Nações Unidas 14171, Torre A, 18° andar, Vila Gertrudes, 04794-000 São Paulo, SP; tel. (11) 5171-1000; fax (11) 5171-1900; e-mail sac@bancovotorantim.com.br; internet www.bancovotorantim.com.br; f. 1991; cap. 5,026.8m., res 2,204m., dep. 30,766.2m. (Dec. 2011); Pres. JOÃO TEIXEIRA.

Banif—Banco Internacional do Funchal (Brasil), SA: Rua Minas de Prata 30, 16°–17° andares, Vila Olímpia, 04552-080 São Paulo, SP; tel. (11) 3165-2000; fax (11) 3167-3960; e-mail bc_matriz@bancobanif.com.br; internet www.bancobanif.com.br; f. 1999 as Banco Banif Primus, SA; present name adopted 2005; owned by Banif Comercial SGPS, SA (Portugal); cap. 194.3m., res 8.9m., dep. 1,195.3m. (Dec. 2011); Pres. ANTONIO JÚLIO MACHADO RODRIGUES.

Itaú Unibanco, SA: Praça Alfredo Egydio de Souza Aranha 100, Torre Olavo Setubal, Parque Jabaquara, 04344-902 São Paulo, SP; tel. (11) 5019-8101; fax (11) 5019-8103; e-mail investor.relations@itau-unibanco.com.br; internet www.itau-unibanco.com.br; f. 1944; est. as Banco Central de Crédito; renamed Banco Itaú, SA in 1973; named changed as above in 2008 following merger with Unibanco; cap. 39,676.3m., res 450.2m., dep. 404,881.3m. (Dec. 2011); Pres. and CEO ROBERTO SETUBAL; 3,044 brs.

Development Banks

Banco de Desenvolvimento de Minas Gerais, SA (BDMG): Rua da Bahia 1600, Lourdes, 30160-907 Belo Horizonte, MG; tel. (31) 3219-8000; fax (31) 3226-3292; internet www.bdmg.mg.gov.br; f. 1962; owned by the state of Minas Gerais; long-term credit operations; cap. 1,087.7m., res 63m., dep. 100.2m. (Dec. 2011); Pres. PAULO DE TARSO ALMEIDA PAIVA.

Banco Nacional do Desenvolvimento Econômico e Social (BNDES): Av. República do Chile 100, Centro, 20031-917 Rio de Janeiro, RJ; tel. (21) 2172-7447; fax (21) 2172-6266; e-mail gerai@bndes.gov.br; internet www.bndes.gov.br; f. 1952 to act as main instrument for financing of govt devt schemes and to support programmes for the devt of the national economy; socio-environmental devt and the modernization of public administration; cap. 36,340.5m., res 24,672.5m., dep. 22,605.2m. (Dec. 2011); Pres. LUCIANO COUTINHO.

Investment Bank

BES Investimento do Brasil, SA- Banco de Investimento: Av. Brigadeiro Faria Lima 3729, 6º andar, 04538-905 São Paulo, SP; tel. (11) 3074–7444; fax (11) 3074-7469; e-mail besinvestimento@besinvestimento.com.br; internet www.besinvestimento.com.br; f. 2000; part of Banco Espírito Santo de Investimento, SA (Portugal); cap. 320m., res 202.2m., dep. 4,269.1m. (2011); Gen. Man. JANKIEL SANTOS.

State-owned Savings Bank

Caixa Econômica Federal: SBS, Quadra 04, Lotes 3–4, 16° andar, 70092-900 Brasília, DF; tel. (61) 3206-9840; fax (61) 3206-0175; e-mail genit04@caixa.gov.br; internet www.caixa.gov.br; f. 1861; cap. 15,154.8m., res 5,579.1m., dep. 270,790.4m. (Dec. 2011); Pres. JORGE FONTES HEREDA; 2,500 brs.

Foreign Banks

Banco Sumitomo Mitsui Brasileiro, SA: Av. Paulista 37, 11° andar, Conj. 112, Bela Vista, 01311-902 São Paulo, SP; tel. (11) 3178-8000; fax (11) 3178-8189; internet www.smbcgroup.com.br; f. 1958; present name adopted 2001; cap. 667.8m., res 2m., dep. 608.4m. (Dec. 2011); Pres. TERUHISA KONISHI; 1 br.

Banco de Tokyo-Mitsubishi UFJ Brasil, SA: Av. Paulista 1274, Bela Vista, 01310-925 São Paulo, SP; tel. (11) 3268-0211; fax (11) 3268-0453; internet www.br.bk.mufg.jp; f. 1972 as Banco de Tokyo; cap. 853m., res 216.9m., dep. 644.3m. (Dec. 2011); Pres. TOSHIFUMI MURATA; 2 brs.

Deutsche Bank, SA—Banco Alemão: Av. Brigadeiro Faria Lima 3900, 13–15° andares, Itaim Bibi, 04598-132 São Paulo, SP; tel. (11) 2113-5000; fax (11) 2113-5100; internet www.deutsche-bank.com.br; f. 1911; cap. 415.2m., res 575.3m., dep. 4,613.8m. (Dec. 2010); Pres. BERNARDO PARNES.

HSBC Bank Brasil, SA—Banco Multiplo: Edif. Palácio Avenida, 4° andar, Travessa Oliveira Belo 34, Centro, 80020-030 Curitiba, PR; tel. (41) 3321-6161; fax (41) 3321-6075; internet www.hsbc.com.br; f. 1997; cap. 5,568.9m., res 108.1m., dep. 88,084.7m. (Dec. 2011); Pres. and CEO ANDRE BRANDÃO; 399 brs.

Scotiabank Brasil, SA Banco Múltiplo (Canada): Av. Brig. Faria Lima 2277, 7° andar, 01452-000 São Paulo, SP; tel. (11) 2202-8100; fax (11) 2202-8200; e-mail scotiabank.saopaulo@br.scotiabank.com; internet www.br.scotiabank.com.

Banking Associations

Associação Brasileira das Entidades dos Mercados Financeiro e de Capitais (ANBIMA): Edif. Eldorado Business Tower, Av. das Nações Unidas 8501, 21° andar, Conj. A, Pinheiros, 05425-070 São Paulo, SP; tel. (11) 3471-4200; fax (11) 3471-4230; e-mail anbid@anbid.com.br; internet www.anbima.com.br; fmrly Associação Nacional dos Bancos de Investimentos; changed name as above in 2009 following re-integration; investment banks; Pres. DENISE PAULI PAVARINA; Supt JOSÉ CARLOS DOHERTY.

Federação Brasileira dos Bancos: Av. Brigadeiro Faria Lima 1485, 14° andar, Torre Norte, Pinheiros, 01452-921 São Paulo, SP; tel. (11) 3244-9800; fax (11) 3031-4106; e-mail imprensa@febraban.org.br; internet www.febraban.org.br; f. 1966; Pres. MURILO PORTUGAL FILHO; Dir-Gen. WILSON ROBERTO LEVORATO; 120 mems.

Federação dos Empregados em Estabelecimentos Bancários de São Paulo e Mato Grosso do Sul (Feeb-SP/MS): Rua Boa Vista 76, 10º andar, Centro, 01014-000 São Paulo, SP; tel. (11) 3116-7070; fax (11) 3104-2422; internet www.feeb-spms.org.br; f. 1956; Pres. DAVID ZAIA.

Sindicato dos Bancos dos Estados do Rio de Janeiro e Espírito Santo: Rua do Ouvidor 50, 20° andar, 20040-004 Rio de Janeiro, RJ; tel. (21) 2253-1538; fax (21) 2253-6032; e-mail aberj@aberj.com.br; internet www.aberj.com.br; f. 1935; Pres. CARLOS ALBERTO VIEIRA.

There are other banking associations in Maceió, Salvador, Fortaleza, Belo Horizonte, João Pessoa, Recife and Porto Alegre.

STOCK EXCHANGES

Comissão de Valores Mobiliários (CVM): Rua 7 de Setembro 111, Centro, 20050-901 Rio de Janeiro, RJ; tel. (21) 3554-8531; fax (21) 3554-8211; e-mail ouvidor@cvm.gov.br; internet www.cvm.gov.br; f. 1977 to supervise the operations of the stock exchanges and develop the Brazilian securities market; regional offices in Brasília and São Paulo; Chair. LEONARDO GOMES PEREIRA.

BM&F BOVESPA, SA (Bolsa de Valores, Mercadorias e Futuros): Praça Antônio Prado 48 Centro, 01010-901 São Paulo, SP; tel. (11) 2565-4000; fax (11) 2565-5314; e-mail ri@bmfbovespa.com.br; internet www.bmfbovespa.com.br; f. 2008 by merger of Bolsa de Mercadorias e Futuros (BM&F—Mercantile and Futures Exchange) and Bolsa de Valores de São Paulo (BOVESPA—São Paulo Stock Exchange); offices in São Paulo, Rio de Janeiro, New York (USA), Shanghai (People's Republic of China) and London (UK); Pres. PEDRO PARENTE; CEO EDEMIR PINTO.

There are commodity exchanges at Paraná, Porto Alegre, Vitória, Recife, Santos and São Paulo.

INSURANCE

Supervisory Authorities

Conselho de Recursos do Sistema Nacional de Seguros Privados, de Previdência Abierta e de Capitalização (CRSNSP): Av. Presidente Vargas 730, 20071-900 Rio de Janeiro, RJ; tel. (21) 3233-4115; internet www.fazenda.gov.br/portugues/orgaos/crsnsp/crsnsp.html; f. 1966 as Conselho Nacional de Seguros Privados (CNSP); changed name in 1998; part of the Ministry of Finance; Pres. FRANCISCO TEIXEIRA DE ALMEIDA; Sec. THERESA CHRISTINA CUNHA MARTINS.

Superintendência de Seguros Privados (SUSEP): Av. Presidente Vargas, 730 Centro, 20071-900 Rio de Janeiro, RJ; tel. (21) 3233-4000; e-mail gabinete.rj@susep.gov.br; internet www.susep.gov.br; f. 1966; part of the Ministry of Finance; offices in Brasília, São Paulo and Porto Alegre; Supt LUCIANO SANTANNA.

Principal Companies

The following is a list of the principal national insurance companies, selected on the basis of assets. The total assets of insurance companies operating in Brazil were R $283,040m. in 2011.

Bradesco Seguros e Previdência, SA: Rua Barão de Itapagipe 225, 20261-901 Rio de Janeiro, RJ; tel. (21) 2503-1101; fax (21) 2293-9489; internet www.bradescoseguros.com.br; f. 1934; general; Pres. MARCO ANTONIO ROSSI.

Bradesco Vida e Previdência, SA: Cidade de Deus s/n, Vila Yara, São Paulo, SP; tel. (11) 3684-2122; fax (11) 3684-5068; internet www.bradescoprevidencia.com.br; f. 2001; life insurance; Pres. LÚCIO FLÁVIO DE OLIVEIRA.

Brasilprev Seguros e Prevedência, SA: Rua Alexandre Dumas 1671, 04717-004 São Paulo, SP; tel. (11) 5185-4240; e-mail atendimento@brasilprev.com.br; internet www.brasilprev.com.br; f. 1993; all classes; 50% owned by Banco do Brasil; Pres. SÉRGIO ROSA.

Caixa Seguros: Edif. No 1, 15° andar, SCN Quadra 01, Bloco A, Asa Norte, 70711-900 Brasília, DF; tel. (61) 2192-2400; fax (61) 3328-0600; internet www.caixaseguros.com.br; f. 1967; fmrly Sasse, Cia Nacional de Seguros; adopted current name 2000; general; Pres. THIERRY MARC CLAUDE CLAUDON.

Caixa Vida e Previdência, SA: Edif. No 1, 13° andar, SCN Quadra 1, Bloco A, 70711-900 Brasília, DF; tel. (61) 2192-2400; fax (61) 3328-0600; internet www.caixavidaeprevidencia.com.br; part of Caixa Seguros group; Dir JUVÊNCIO CAVALCANTE BRAGA.

Cia de Seguros Aliança do Brasil, SA (BB Seguros): Rua Manuel da Nóbrega 1280, 9° andar, 04001-004 São Paulo, SP; tel. (11) 4689-5638; e-mail imprensa@aliancadobrasil.com.br; internet www.aliancadobrasil.com.br; f. 1996; Pres. ROBERTO BARROSO.

Crédito y Caución Seguradora de Crédito à Exportação, SA: Av. Angélica 2530, 10° andar, Consolaçao, 01228-200 São Paulo, SP; tel. (11) 3100-1100; fax (11) 3100-1109; e-mail saopaulo@creditoycaucion.com.br; internet www.creditoycaucion.com.br; f. 1997 (in Brazil); Dir-Gen. JACINTO IGLESIAS RUBIO.

HSBC Vida e Previdência (Brasil), SA: Rua Teniente Francisco Ferreira de Souza 805, Bloco 1, Ala 4, Vila Hauer, 81630-010 Curitaba, PR; tel. (41) 3777-4400; fax (41) 3523-2320; e-mail spariz@hsbc.com.vr; internet www.hsbc.com.br; f. 1938; all classes; Supt Dir FERNANDO ALVES MOREIRA.

Icatu Hartford Seguros, SA: Praça 22 de Abril 36, 20021-370 Rio de Janeiro, RJ; tel. (21) 3824-3900; fax 3824-6678; e-mail atendimento_internet@icatuseguros.com.br; internet www.icatuseguros.com.br; Pres. MARIA SILVIA BASTOS MARQUES.

IRB-Brasil Resseguros: Av. Marechal Câmara 171, Castelo, 20020-901 Rio de Janeiro, RJ; tel. (21) 2272-0200; fax (21) 2272-2800; e-mail info@irb-brasilre.com.br; internet www.irb-brasilre.com.br; f. 1939; state-owned reinsurance co; fmrly Instituto de Resseguros do Brasil; Pres. LEONARDO ANDRÉ PAIXÃO.

Itaú Seguros, SA: Praça Alfredo Egydio de Souza Aranha 100, Bloco A, 04344-920 São Paulo, SP; tel. (11) 5019-3322; fax (11) 5019-3530; e-mail itauseguros@itauseguros.com.br; internet www.itauseguros.com.br; f. 1921; all classes; Pres. ROBERTO EGYDIO SETUBAL; Supt MARCOS DE BARROS LISBOA.

Liberty Seguros, SA: Rua Dr Geraldo Campos Moreira 110, 04571-020 São Paulo, SP; tel. (11) 5503-4000; fax (11) 5505-2122; internet www.libertyseguros.com.br; f. 1906; general; Pres. LUIS EMILIO MAURETTE.

Marítima Seguros, SA: Rua Col Xavier de Toledo 114 e 140, 10° andar, São Paulo, SP; tel. (11) 3156-1000; fax (11) 3156-1712; internet www.maritima.com.br; f. 1943; Pres. FRANCISCO CAIUBY VIDIGAL; Exec. Dir MARIO JORGE PEREIRA.

Porto Seguro Cia de Seguros Gerais: Rua Guaianazes 1238, 12° andar, Campos Elíseos, 01204-001 São Paulo, SP; tel. (11) 3366-5963; fax (11) 3366-5175; internet www.portoseguro.com.br; f. 1945; life, automotive and risk; Pres. JAYME BRASIL GARFINKEL.

Santander Seguros, SA: internet www.santander.com.br; part of Banco Santander.

Sul América Cia Nacional de Seguros, SA: Rua da Beatriz Larragoiti Lucas 121, Cidade Nova, 20211-903 Rio de Janeiro, RJ; tel. (21) 2506-8585; fax (21) 2506-8807; internet www.sulamerica.com.br; f. 1895; life and risk; Chair. PATRICK ANTONIO DE LARRAGOITI LUCAS; CEO THOMAZ LUIZ CABRAL DE MENEZES.

Tokio Marine Seguradora, SA: Rua Samapiao Viana 44, 04004-902 Paraíso, SP; tel. (11) 3054-7000; internet www.tokiomarine.com.br; f. 1969 as Real Seguros, SA; adopted current name 2008; owned by Tokio Marine Holdings (Japan); general; Pres. AKIRA HARASHIMA.

Insurance Associations

Confederação Nacional das Empresas de Seguros Gerais, Previdência Privada e Vida, Saúde Suplementar e Capitalização (CNseg): Rua Senador Dantas 74, 12° andar, Centro, 20031-205 Rio de Janeiro, RJ; tel. (21) 2510-7777; e-mail suporte@cnseg.org.br; internet www.cnseg.org.br; f. 1951 as Federação Nacional das Empresas de Seguros Privados e de Capitalização; reformulated as above 2008; four subordinate feds; Pres. JORGE HILÁRIO GOUVÊA VIEIRA.

Federação Nacional de Capitalização (FenaCap): Pres. PAULO ROGÉRIO CAFFARELLI.

Federação Nacional de Previdência Privada e Vida (FenaPrevi): Pres. MARCO ANTONIO ROSSI.

Federação Nacional de Saúde Suplementar (FenaSaúde): Pres. MARCIO SERÔA DE ARAUJO CORIOLANO.

Federação Nacional de Seguros Gerais (FenSeg): Pres. JAYME BRASIL GARFINKEL.

Federação Nacional dos Corretores de Seguros Privados e de Resseguros, de Capitalização, de Previdência Privada e das Empresas Corretoras de Seguros e de Resseguros (FENACOR): Rua Senador Dantas 74, 10° andar, 20031-205 Rio de Janeiro, RJ; tel. (21) 3077-4777; fax (21) 3077-4799; e-mail presidencia@fenacor.com.br; internet www.fenacor.com.br; f. 1975; Pres. ARMANDO VERGÍLIO DOS SANTOS, Jr.

Trade and Industry

GOVERNMENT AGENCIES

Agência Nacional de Petróleo, Gás Natural e Biocombustíveis (ANP): Av. Rio Branco 65, 12°–22° andar, 20090-004 Rio de Janeiro, RJ; tel. (21) 2112-8100; fax (21) 2112-8129; e-mail imprensa@anp.gov.br; internet www.anp.gov.br; f. 1998; regulatory body of the petroleum, natural gas and biofuels industries; Dir-Gen. MAGDA MARIA DE REGINA CHAMBRIARD.

Agência de Promoção de Exportações do Brasil (APEX Brasil): Edif. Apex-Brasil, SBN, Quadra 02, Lote 11, 70040-020 Brasília, DF; tel. (61) 3426-0202; fax (61) 3426-0263; e-mail apex@apexbrasil.com.br; internet www.apexbrasil.com.br; f. 2003; promotes Brazilian exports; CEO MAURICIO BORGES.

Câmara de Comércio Exterior (CAMEX): Ministério do Desenvolvimento, Indústria e Comércio Exterior, Bloco J, 70053-900 Brasília, DF; tel. (61) 2109-7483; e-mail camex@desenvolvimento.gov.br; internet www.desenvolvimento.gov.br; f. 2003; part of Ministry of Development, Industry and Foreign Trade; formulates and co-ordinates export policies; Exec. Sec. EMILIO GAROFALO.

Companhia de Pesquisa de Recursos Minerais (CPRM): Av. SGAN, Quadra 603, Conj. J, Parte A, 1° andar, 70830-030 Brasília, DF; tel. (61) 2192-8252; fax (61) 3224-1616; e-mail cprmsede@df.cprm.gov.br; internet www.cprm.gov.br; mining research, attached to the Ministry of Mines and Energy; 8 regional offices; Exec. Dir MANOEL BARRETTO DA ROCHA NETO.

Confederação Nacional da Agricultura e Pecuária do Brasil (CNA): SGAN, Quadra 601, Módulo K, 70830-903 Brasília, DF; tel. (61) 2109-1400; fax (61) 2109-1490; internet ww.canaldoprodutor.com.br; represents and defends the interests of farmers; 27 agricultural fed. mems; Pres. KÁTIA ABREU.

Conselho Nacional de Desenvolvimento Científico e Tecnológico (CNPq): Edif. Santos Dumont, SHIS, Quadra 01, Conj. B, Blocos A, B, C e D, Lago Sul, 71605-001 Brasília, DF; tel. (61) 2108-9000; fax (61) 2108-9394; e-mail presidencia@cnpq.br; internet www.cnpq.br; f. 1951; scientific and technological development council; Pres. GLAUCIUS OLIVA.

Conselho Nacional de Desenvolvimento Rural Sustentável (CONDRAF): Edif. Sarkis, SBN, Quadra 01, Bloco D, 70057-900 Brasília, DF; tel. (61) 2020-0285; e-mail condraf@mda.gov.br; internet sistemas.mda.gov.br/condraf; f. 2000 to promote sustainable rural development; Sec. JERÔNIMO RODRIGUES.

Empresa Brasileira de Pesquisa Agropecuária (EMBRAPA): Edif. Sede, Parque Estação Biológica (PqEB) s/n, Av. W3 Norte (final), CP 40315, 70770-901 Brasília, DF; tel. (61) 3448-4433; fax (61) 3448-4890; e-mail presid@sede.embrapa.br; internet www.embrapa.br; f. 1973; attached to the Ministry of Agriculture, Livestock and Food Supply; agricultural research; Pres. PEDRO ANTONIO ARRAES PEREIRA.

Instituto Brasileiro do Meio Ambiente e Recursos Naturais Renováveis (IBAMA): Edif. Sede IBAMA, SCEN Trecho 2, 70818-900 Brasília, DF; tel. (61) 3316-1001; fax (61) 3226-1025; e-mail presid.sede@ibama.gov.br; internet www.ibama.gov.br; f. 1989; authorizes environmentally sensitive devt projects; Pres. Dr VOLNEY ZANARDI.

Instituto Nacional de Colonização e Reforma Agraria (INCRA): Edif. Palácio do Desenvolvimento, SBN, Quadra 01, Bloco D, 70057-900 Brasília, DF; tel. (61) 3411-7474; fax (61) 3411-7404; e-mail publico@incra.gov.br; internet www.incra.gov.br; f. 1970; land reform agency; Pres. CELSO LISBOA DE LACERDA.

Instituto Nacional da Propriedade Industrial (INPI): Praça Mauá 7, 18° andar, Centro, 20081-240 Rio de Janeiro, RJ; tel. (21) 2139-3000; fax (21) 2263-2539; e-mail sic@inpi.gov.br; internet www.inpi.gov.br; f. 1970; part of Ministry of Development, Industry and Foreign Trade; intellectual property, etc.; Pres. JORGE DE PAULA COSTA ÁVILA.

Instituto de Pesquisa Econômica Aplicada (IPEA): Av. Presidente Antônio Carlos 51, 15° andar, 20020-010 Rio de Janeiro, RJ; tel. (21) 3804-8000; fax (21) 2240-1920; e-mail faleconosco@ipea.gov.br; internet www.ipea.gov.br; f. 1970; economics and planning institute; Pres. VANESSA PETRELLI CORRÊA.

REGIONAL DEVELOPMENT ORGANIZATIONS

Companhia de Desenvolvimento dos Vales do São Francisco e do Parnaíba (CODEVASF): Edif. Manoel Novaes, SGAN, Quadra 601, Conj. 1, 70830-901 Brasília, DF; tel. (61) 3312-4611; fax (61) 3312-4680; e-mail tenio.pereira@codevasf.gov.br; internet www.codevasf.gov.br; f. 1974; promotes integrated development of resources of São Francisco and Parnaíba Valley; part of Ministry of National Integration; Pres. ELMO VAZ BASTOS DE MATOS.

Superintendência do Desenvolvimento da Amazônia (SUDAM): Av. Almirante Barroso 426, Marco, 66090-900 Belém, PA; tel. (91) 4008-5443; fax (91) 4008-5456; e-mail ouvidoria@sudam.gov.br; internet www.sudam.gov.br; f. 2001 to co-ordinate the devt of resources in Amazon region; Supt DJALMA BEZERRA MELLO.

Superintendência de Desenvolvimento do Nordeste (SUDENE): Praça Ministro João Gonçalves de Souza s/n, Engenho do Meio, 50670-900 Recife, PE; tel. (81) 2102-2114; fax (81) 2102-2575; e-mail gabinete@sudene.gov.br; internet www.sudene.gov.br; f. 2007 to replace Agência de Desenvolvimento do Nordeste (f. 2001); Supt LUIZ GONZAGA PAES LANDIM.

Superintendência da Zona Franca de Manaus (SUFRAMA): Av. Ministro João Gonçalves de Souza 1424, Distrito Industrial, 69075-830 Manaus, AM; tel. (92) 3321-7000; fax (92) 3237-6549; e-mail super@suframa.gov.br; internet www.suframa.gov.br; assists in the devt of the Manaus Free Zone; Supt THOMAZ AFONSO QUEIROZ NOGUEIRA.

AGRICULTURAL, INDUSTRIAL AND TRADE ORGANIZATIONS

Associação Brasileira do Alumínio (ABAL): Rua Humberto I 220, 4° andar, Vila Mariana, 04018-030 São Paulo, SP; tel. (11) 5904-6450; fax (11) 5904-6459; e-mail aluminio@abal.org.br; internet www.abal.org.br; f. 1970; represents aluminium producing and processing cos; 66 mem. cos; Pres. ADJARMA AZEVEDO.

Associação Brasileira de Celulose e Papel—Bracelpa: Rua Olimpíadas, 66, 9° and Bairro Vl. Olímpia São Paulo, São Paulo, SP; tel. (11) 3018-7800; fax (11) 3018-7813; e-mail faleconosco@bracelpa.org.br; internet www.bracelpa.org.br; f. 1932; pulp and paper asscn; Exec. Dir ELIZABETH CARVALHAES.

Associação Brasileira das Empresas Importadoras de Veículos Automotores (ABEIVA): Rua Dr Renato Paes de Barros 717, Conjunto 113, 11º andar, Itaim Bibi, 04530–001 São Paulo, SP; tel. (11) 3078-3989; e-mail abeiva@abeiva.com.br; internet www.abeiva.com.br; f. 1991; car importers' asscn; Pres. FLÁVIO PADOVAN; Exec. Man. JOSÉ NELSON CORREA.

Associação Brasileira das Indústrias de Óleos Vegetais (Abiove) (Brazilian Association of Vegetable Oil Industries): Av. Vereador José Diniz 3707, 7° andar, Conj. 73, 04603-004 São Paulo, SP; tel. (11) 5536-0733; fax (11) 5536-9816; e-mail abiove@abiove.com.br; internet www.abiove.com.br; f. 1981; 11 mem. cos; Pres. MANOEL TEIXEIRA PEREIRA.

Associação Brasileira da Infraestrutura e Indústrias de Base (ABDIB): Praça Monteiro Lobato, 36 Butantã, 05506-030 São Paulo, SP; tel. (11) 3094-1950; fax (11) 3094-1949; e-mail abdib@abdib.org.br; internet www.abdib.org.br; f. 1955; Pres. PAULO GODOY; 144 mems.

Associação Brasileira dos Produtores de Algodão (ABRAPA): Edif. Barão do Rio Branco, Terraço 02, 4º andar, SIG, Quadra 01, Lotes 495, 505 e 515, 70610-410 Brasília, DF; tel. (61) 3028-9700; fax (61) 3028-9707; e-mail faleconosco@abrapa.com.br; internet www.abrapa.com.br; f. 1999; cotton producers' asscn; Pres. SÉRGIO DE MARCO; Exec. Dir MARCIO PORTOCARRERO.

Associação Comercial do Rio de Janeiro (ACRJ): Rua da Calendária 9, 11°–12° andares, Centro, 20091-020 Rio de Janeiro, RJ; tel. and fax (21) 2514-1229; e-mail acrj@acrj.org.br; internet www.acrj.org.br; f. 1820; Pres. DANIEL CORRÊA HOMEM DE CARVALHO.

Associação Comercial de São Paulo (ACSP): Rua Boa Vista 51, Centro, 01014-911 São Paulo, SP; tel. (11) 3244-3322; fax (11) 3244-3355; e-mail infocem@acsp.com.br; internet www.acsp.com.br; f. 1894; Pres. ROGÉRIO PINTO COELHO AMATO.

Associação de Comércio Exterior do Brasil (AEB) (Brazilian Foreign Trade Association): Av. General Justo 335, 4° andar, 20021-130 Rio de Janeiro, RJ; tel. (21) 2544-0048; fax (21) 2544-0577; e-mail aebbras@aeb.org.br; internet www.aeb.org.br; exporters' asscn; Pres. JOSÉ AUGUSTO DE CASTRO.

Associação Nacional dos Exportadores de Cereais (ANEC): Av. Brigadeiro Faria Lima 1656, 8º andar, Conj. 81, Jardim Paulistano, 01451-001 São Paulo, SP; tel. (11) 3039-5599; fax (11) 3039-5598; e-mail anec@anec.com.br; internet www.anec.com.br; f. 1965; grain exporters' asscn; Pres. FELÍCIO PASCHOAL DA C. AGUIAR; Dir-Gen. SÉRGIO CASTANHO TEIXEIRA MENDES.

Associação Nacional dos Fabricantes de Veículos Automotores (ANFAVEA): Av. Indianópolis 496, 04062-900 São Paulo, SP;

tel. (11) 2193-7800; fax (11) 2193-7825; internet www.anfavea.com.br; f. 1956; motor vehicle manufacturers' asscn; 27 mems; Pres. CLEDORVINO BELINI.

Centro das Indústrias do Estado de São Paulo (CIESP): Av. Paulista 1313, 01311-923 São Paulo, SP; tel. (11) 3549-3232; e-mail atendimento@ciesp.com.br; internet www.ciesp.org.br; f. 1928; asscn of small and medium-sized businesses; Pres. PAULO ANTONIO SKEF.

Confederação da Agricultura e Pecuária do Brasil (CNA): SGAN, Quadra 601, Modulo K, 70830-903 Brasília, DF; tel. (61) 2109-1400; fax (61) 2109-1490; e-mail cna@cna.org.br; internet www.canaldoprodutor.com.br; f. 1964; national agricultural confederation; Pres. KÁTIA REGINA DE ABREU.

Confederação Nacional do Comércio (CNC): Av. General Justo 307, 20021-130 Rio de Janeiro, RJ; tel. (21) 3804-9200; e-mail cncrj@cnc.com.br; internet www.portaldocomercio.org.br; 35 affiliated feds of commerce; Pres. ANTÔNIO JOSÉ DOMINGUES DE OLIVEIRA SANTOS.

Confederação Nacional da Indústria (CNI) (National Confederation of Industry): Edif. Roberto Simonsen, SBN, Quadra 01, Bloco C, 70040-903 Brasília, DF; tel. (61) 3317-9993; fax (61) 3317-9994; e-mail sac@cni.org.br; internet www.cni.org.br; f. 1938; comprises 27 state industrial feds; Pres. ROBSON BRAGA DE ANDRADE.

Conselho dos Exportadores de Café Verde do Brasil (CECAFE): Av. Nove de Julho 4865, Torre A, Conj. 61, Chácara Itaim, 01407-200 São Paulo, SP; tel. (11) 3079-3755; fax (11) 3167-4060; e-mail cecafe@cecafe.com.br; internet www.cecafe.com.br; f. 1999 through merger of Federação Brasileira dos Exportadores de Café and Associação Brasileira dos Exportadores de Café; council of green coffee exporters; Pres. JOÃO ANTÔNIO LIAN; Dir-Gen. GUILHERME BRAGA ABREU PIRES FILHO.

Federação das Indústrias do Estado do Rio de Janeiro (FIRJAN): Centro Empresarial FIRJAN, Av. Graça Aranha 1, Rio de Janeiro, RJ; tel. (21) 2563-4389; e-mail centrodeatendimento@firjan.org.br; internet www.firjan.org.br; Pres. EDUARDO EUGENIO GOUVÊA VIEIRA; regional manufacturers' asscn; 103 affiliated syndicates representing almost 16,000 cos.

Federação das Indústrias do Estado de São Paulo (FIESP): Av. Paulista 1313, 01311-923 São Paulo, SP; tel. (11) 3549-4499; e-mail relacionamento@fiesp.org.br; internet www.fiesp.org.br; regional manufacturers' asscn; Pres. PAULO ANTONIO SKAF.

Instituto Aço Brasil: Av. Rio Branco 181, 28° andar, 20040-007 Rio de Janeiro, RJ; tel. (21) 3445-6300; fax (21) 2262-2234; e-mail acobrasil@acobrasil.org.br; internet www.acobrasil.org.br; f. 1963; fmrly Instituto Brasileiro de Siderurgia (IBS); steel cos' org.; Pres. ANDRÉ BIER GERDAU JOHANNPETER; Exec. Chair MARCO POLO DE MELLO LOPES.

Instituto Brasileiro do Mineração (IBRAM) (Brazilian Mining Association): SHIS, Quadra 12, Conj. 0, Casa 4, 71630-205 Brasília, DF; tel. (61) 3364-7200; fax (61) 3364-7272; e-mail ibram@ibram.org.br; internet www.ibram.org.br; f. 1976 to foster the devt of the mining industry; Pres. and Dir JOSÉ FERNANDO COURA.

Instituto Nacional de Tecnologia (INT): Av. Venezuela 82, 8° andar, 20081-312 Rio de Janeiro, RJ; tel. (21) 2123-1100; fax (21) 2123-1284; e-mail dcom@int.gov.br; internet www.int.gov.br; f. 1921; co-operates in national industrial devt; Dir DOMINGOS MANFREDI NAVEIRO.

Serviço de Apoio às Micro e Pequenas Empresas (Sebrae): SEPN, Quadra 515, Lote 03, Bloco C, Asa Norte, 70770-530 Brasília, DF; tel. (61) 3348-7100; fax (61) 3347-3581; internet www.sebrae.com.br; f. 1972; supports small and medium-sized enterprises; Exec. Dir LUIZ EDUARDO PEREIRA BARRETTO FILHO.

União Democrática Ruralista (UDR): Av. Col Marcondes 983, 6° andar, Sala 62, Centro, 19010-080 Presidente Prudente, SP; tel. (11) 3221-1082; fax (11) 3232-4622; e-mail udr.org@uol.com.br; internet www.udr.org.br; landowners' org.; Pres. LUIZ ANTÔNIO NABHAN GARCIA.

União da Industria de Cana-de-Açúcar (UNICA): Av. Brigadeiro Faria Lima 2179, 9° andar, Jardim Paulistano, 01452-000 São Paulo, SP; tel. (11) 3093-4949; fax (11) 3812-1416; e-mail unica@unica.com.br; internet www.unica.com.br; f. 1997; sugar and bioethanol asscn; offices in USA and Belgium; Pres. ANTONIO DE PADUA RODRIGUES (acting); Exec. Dir EDUARDO LEÃO DE SOUSA.

STATE HYDROCARBONS COMPANIES

Petróleo Brasileiro, SA (Petrobras): Av. República do Chile 65, Centro, 20031-912 Rio de Janeiro, RJ; tel. (21) 3224-1510; fax (21) 3224-6055; e-mail sac@petrobras.com.br; internet www.petrobras.com.br; f. 1953; production of petroleum and petroleum products; owns 16 oil refineries; CEO MARIA DAS GRAÇAS SILVA FOSTER; Sec.-Gen. HÉLIO SHIGUENOBU FUJIKAWA; 53,933 employees; subsidiary cos are Petrobras Transporte, SA (Transpetro), Petrobras Comercializadora de Energia, Ltda, Petrobras Negócios Eletrônicos, SA, Petrobras International Finance Co (PIFCO) and Downstream Participações, SA, and cos listed below:

Petrobras Biocombustível, SA (Petrobras Biofuel): Av. República do Chile 500, 27°, Centro, 20031-912 Rio de Janeiro, RJ; tel. (21) 3224-6283; fax (21) 3224-6055; e-mail biocombustivel@petrobras.com.br; internet www.petrobrasbiocombustivel.com.br; f. 2008; 5 biodiesel plants; 10 ethanol plants, 9 in Brazil and 1 in Mozambique; Pres. MIGUEL SOLDATELLI ROSSETTO.

Petrobras Distribuidora, SA: Rua General Canabarro 500, Maracanã, 20271-900 Rio de Janeiro, RJ; tel. (21) 3876-4477; fax (21) 3876-4977; internet www.br.com.br; f. 1971; distribution of all petroleum by-products; Pres. JOSÉ LIMA DE ANDRADE NETO; 3,758 employees.

Petrobras Gás, SA (Gaspetro): Av. República do Chile 65, Centro, 20031-912 Rio de Janeiro, RJ; tel. (21) 3534-0439; fax (21) 3534-1080; e-mail sac@petrobras.com.br; internet www.gaspetro.com.br; f. 1998; Pres. JOSÉ MARIA CARVALHO RESENDE.

Petrobras Química, SA (Petroquisa): Av. República do Chile 65, 9° andar, Centro, 20031-912 Rio de Janeiro, RJ; tel. (21) 3224-1455; fax (21) 2262-1521; e-mail contato.petroquisa@petrobras.com.br; internet www.petroquisa.com.br; f. 1968; petrochemicals industry; controls 27 affiliated cos and 4 subsidiaries; Dir PATRICK FAIRON.

Pré-Sal Petróleo, SA: f. 2010; state-owned; manages exploration of petroleum and natural gas beneath the salt layer along the Brazilian coast; Pres. EDISON LOBÃO (Minister of Mines and Energy).

Refinaria de Petróleos de Manguinhos: Av. Brasil 3141, Manguinhos, 20930-041 Rio de Janeiro, RJ; tel. (21) 3891-2000; e-mail webmaster@rpdm.com.br; internet www.manguinhosrefinaria.com.br; f. 1954; acquired by Grupo Andrade Magro in 2008; nationalization announced in Nov. 2012; Chair. CARLOS FILIPE RIZZO; Pres. and CEO PAULO HENRIQUE OLIVEIRA DE MENEZES.

UTILITIES

Regulatory Agencies

Agência Nacional de Energia Elétrica (ANEEL): SGAN 603, Módulo J, 70830-030 Brasília, DF; tel. (61) 2192-8600; e-mail aneel@aneel.gov.br; internet www.aneel.gov.br; f. 1939 as Conselho Nacional de Águas e Energia Elétrica, present name adopted 1996; Dir-Gen. NELSON JOSÉ HÜBNER MOREIRA.

Comissão Nacional de Energia Nuclear (CNEN): Rua General Severiano 90, Botafogo, 22290-901 Rio de Janeiro, RJ; tel. (21) 2173-2000; fax (21) 2173-2003; e-mail corin@cnen.gov.br; internet www.cnen.gov.br; f. 1956; management of nuclear power programme; Pres. ODAIR DIAS GONÇALVES.

Operador Nacional do Sistema Elétrico (ONS): Rua Júlio do Carmo 251, Cidade Nova 20211-160, Rio de Janeiro, RJ; tel. (21) 3444-9400; internet www.ons.org.br; operates national electricity grid; regulated by ANEEL; Dir-Gen. HERMES CHIPP.

Electricity

Ampla Energia e Serviços, SA (Ampla): Praça Leoni Ramos 1, Bloco 1, 7° andar, São Domingos, 24210-205 Niterói, RJ; tel. (21) 2613-7000; fax (21) 2613-7153; e-mail ampla@ampla.com; internet www.ampla.com; f. 1907, privatized in 2004; fmrly Companhia de Eletricidade do Estado do Rio de Janeiro-CERJ; Pres. MARCELO LLÉVENES.

CPFL Energia, SA (Companhia Paulista de Força e Luz): Rua Gomes de Carvalho 1510, 14° andar, Conj. 1402, 04547-005 Vila Olímpia, SP; tel. (19) 3756-8018; fax (19) 3252-7644; internet www.cpfl.com.br; provides electricity through govt concessions; operates 21 subsidiaries; Pres. MURILO CESAR LEMOS DOS SANTOS PASSOS; Exec. Dir WILSON PINTO FERREIRA JÚNIOR.

Centrais Elétricas Brasileiras, SA (Eletrobras): Av. Presidente Vargas 409, 13° andar, Centro, 20071-003 Rio de Janeiro, RJ; tel. (21) 2514-5151; fax (21) 2514-6479; e-mail pr@eletrobras.gov.br; internet www.eletrobras.com; f. 1962; 54% govt-owned; Pres. JOSÉ ANTONIO MUNIZ LOPES; controls 6 electricity generation and transmission subsidiaries and 6 distribution subsidiaries:

Eletrobras Amazonas Energia: Av. Sete de Setembro 2414, Cachoeirinha, 69005-141 Manaus, AM; tel. (92) 3621-1201; fax (92) 3633-2406; internet www.amazonasenergia.gov.br; f. 1895; name changed as above in 2010; distribution; Exec. Dir PEDRO CARLOS HOSKEN VIEIRA.

Eletrobras CGTEE (Companhia de Geração Térmica de Energia Elétrica): Rua Sete de Setembro 539, 90010-190 Porto Alegre, RS; tel. (51) 3287-1500; fax (51) 3287-1566; internet www.cgtee.gov.br; f. 1997; became part of Eletrobras in 2000; generation and transmission; Pres. VALTER LUIZ CARDEAL DE SOUZA; Exec. Dir SERENO CHAISE.

Eletrobras Chesf (Companhia Hidro Eléctrica do São Francisco): 333 Bongi, Rua Delmiro Golveia, 50761-901 Recife, PE; tel. (81) 3229-2000; fax (81) 3229-2390; e-mail chesf@chesf.com.br; internet www.chesf.gov.br; f. 1948; generation and transmission;

Pres. UBIRAJARA ROCHA MEIRA; Exec. Dir DILTON DA CONTI OLIVEIRA.

Eletrobras Distribuição Acre (ELETROACRE): Rua Valério Magalhães 226, Bairro do Bosque, 69909-710 Rio Branco, AC; tel. (68) 3212-5700; fax (68) 3223-1142; e-mail ouvidoria@eletroacre.com.br; internet www.eletroacre.com.br; f. 1965; distribution; Exec. Dir PEDRO CARLOS HOSKEN VIEIRA.

Eletrobras Distribuição Alagoas (CEAL): Av. Fernandes Lima 3349, Gruta de Lourdes, 57057-900 Maceió, AL; tel. (82) 2126-9247; fax (82) 2126-9326; e-mail ape@ceal.com.br; internet www.ceal.com.br; f. 1961; electricity distribution; Exec. Dir PEDRO CARLOS HOSKEN VIEIRA.

Eletrobras Distribuição Piauí (CEPISA): Av. Maranhão 759, Sul, 64001-010 Teresina, PI; tel. (86) 3228-8000; internet www.cepisa.com.br; f. 1962, bought by Eletrobras in 1997; distribution; Exec. Dir PEDRO CARLOS HOSKEN VIEIRA.

Eletrobras Distribuição Rondônia, SA (CERON): Av. Imigrantes 4137, Industrial, 76821-063 Porto Velho, RO; tel. (69) 3216-4000; internet www.ceron.com.br; f. 1968; distribution; Exec. Dir PEDRO CARLOS HOSKEN VIEIRA.

Eletrobras Distribuição Roraima (Boa Vista Energia): Av. Capitão Ene Garcêz 691, Centro, 69310-160 Boa Vista, RR; tel. (95) 2621-1400; e-mail frvcarvalho@boavistaenergia.gov.br; internet www.boavistaenergia.gov.br; f. 1997; distribution; Exec. Dir PEDRO CARLOS HOSKEN VIEIRA.

Eletrobras Eletronorte: SCN, Quadra 6, Conj. A, Blocos B e C, Entrada Norte 2, Asa Norte, 70716-901 Brasília, DF; tel. (61) 3429-5151; fax (61) 3328-1463; e-mail ouvidoria@eln.gov.br; internet www.eln.gov.br; f. 1973; generation and transmission; serves Amapá, Acre, Amazonas, Maranhão, Mato Grosso, Pará, Rondônia, Roraima and Tocantins; Pres. ASTROGILDO FRAGUGLIA QUENTAL; Exec. Dir JOSIAS MATOS DE ARAUJO.

Eletrobras Eletronuclear: Rua da Candelária 65, Centro, 20091-906 Rio de Janeiro, RJ; tel. (21) 2588-7000; fax (21) 2588-7200; internet www.eletronuclear.gov.br; f. 1997 by merger of the nuclear br. of Furnas with Nuclebrás Engenharia (NUCLEN); operates 2 nuclear facilities, Angra I and II; Pres. MIGUEL COLASUONNO; Exec. Dir OTHON LUIZ PINHEIRO DA SILVA.

Eletrobras Eletrosul: Rua Deputado Antônio Edu Vieira 999, Pantanal, 88040-901 Florianópolis, SC; tel. (48) 3231-7000; fax (48) 3234-4040; internet www.eletrosul.gov.br; f. 1968; generation and transmission; Pres. VALTER LUIZ CARDEAL DE SOUZA; Exec. Dir EURIDES LUIZ MESCOLOTTO.

Eletrobras Furnas: Rua Real Grandeza 219, Bloco A, 16° andar, Botafogo, 22281-900 Rio de Janeiro, RJ; tel. (21) 2528-3112; fax (21) 2528-5858; e-mail webfurnas@furnas.com.br; internet www.furnas.com.br; f. 1957; generation and transmission; Pres. FLÁVIO DECAT; Exec. Dir CARLOS NADALUTTI FILHO.

Companhia de Eletricidade do Estado da Bahia (COELBA): Av. Edgard Santos 300, 300 Narandiba, 41186-900 Salvador, BA; tel. (71) 3370-5130; fax (71) 3370-5135; internet www.coelba.com.br; f. 1960; Pres. JOILSON RODRIGUES FERREIRA CHAVES; Exec. Dir MOISÉS AFONSO SALES FILHO.

Companhia Energética de Brasília (CEB): SIA/SAPS, Trecho 01, Lotes C, Asa Sul, 71215-000 Brasília, DF; tel. (61) 3363-4011; fax (61) 3363-2657; e-mail info@ceb.com.br; internet www.ceb.com.br; generation and distribution of electricity in Distrito Federal; also operates gas distribution co CEBGAS; Pres. and CEO PAULO VICTOR RADA DE REZENDE.

Companhia Energética do Ceará (COELCE): Rua Padre Valdevino 150, 1° andar, Joaquim Távora, 60135-040 Fortaleza, CE; tel. (85) 3247-1444; fax (85) 3216-4088; e-mail gercom@coelce.com.br; internet www.coelce.com.br; f. 1971; part of Endesa (Spain); Pres. ABEL ROCHINHA.

Companhia Energética do Maranhão (CEMAR): Av. Coronel Colares Moreira 477, Renascença II, 65075-441 São Luís, MA; tel. (98) 3217-2211; fax (98) 3321-7161; e-mail corporativo@cemar-ma.com.br; internet www.cemar-ma.com.br; f. 1958 as Centrais Elétricas do Maranhão; changed name as above in 1984; owned by PPL Global, Inc (USA); Exec. Dir AUGUSTO MIRANDA DA PAZ JÚNIOR.

Companhia Energética de Minas Gerais (CEMIG): Av. Barbacena 1200, 5° andar, Ala B1, Bairro Santo Agostinho, 30161-970 Belo Horizonte, MG; tel. (31) 3299-4900; fax (31) 3299-3700; e-mail atendimento@cemig.com.br; internet www.cemig.com.br; f. 1952; 51% state-owned, 33% owned by Southern Electric Brasil Partipações, Ltda; Exec. Dir DJALMA BASTOS DE MORAIS.

Companhia Energética de Pernambuco (CELPE): Av. João de Barros 111, Sala 301, Boa Vista, 50050-902 Recife, PE; tel. (81) 3217-5168; e-mail rodrigo.carvalho@celpe.com.br; internet www.celpe.com.br; Pres. JOILSON RODRIGUES FERREIRA; Exec. Dir LUIZ ANTÔNIO CIARLINI.

Companhia Energética de São Paulo (CESP): Av. Nossa Senhora do Sabará 5312, Bairro Pedreira, 04447-011 São Paulo, SP; tel. (11) 5613-2100; fax (11) 3262-5545; e-mail inform@cesp.com.br; internet www.cesp.com.br; f. 1966; Pres. DILMA SELI PENA; Exec. Dir VILSON DANIEL CHRISTOFARI.

Companhia Paranaense de Energia (COPEL): Rua Coronel Dulcídio 800, 80420-170 Curitiba, PR; tel. (41) 3331-5050; fax (41) 3331-4376; e-mail copel@copel.com; internet www.copel.com; f. 1954; Pres. LÉO DE ALMEIDA NEVES; Exec. Dir LINDOLFO ZIMMER.

Eletropaulo Metropolitana Eletricidade de São Paulo, SA (AES Eletropaulo): Av. Lourenço Marques 158, 3° andar, Vila Olímpia, 04547-100 São Paulo, SP; tel. (11) 2195-2000; fax (11) 2195-2511; e-mail administracao@eletropaulo.com.br; internet www.aeseletropaulo.com.br; f. 1899; acquired by AES in 2001; Pres. and Exec. Dir BRITALDO PEDROSA SOARES.

Energisa Minas Gerais: Praça Rui Barbosa 80, Centro, 36770-901 Cataguases, MG; tel. (32) 3429-6000; fax (32) 3429-6317; e-mail secretaria@energisa.com.br; internet www.minasgerais.energisa.com.br; f. 1905 as Companhia Força e Luz Cataguazes-Leopoldina, adopted present name in 2008; subsidiary of Grupo Energisa, SA; Pres. IVAN MÜLLER BOTELHO; Exec. Dir GABRIEL ALVES PEREIRA JÚNIOR.

Espírito Santo Centrais Elétricas, SA (EDP Escelsa): Rua José Alexandre Buaiz 160, 8° andar, Enseada do Suá, 29050-955 Vitória, ES; tel. (27) 3321-9000; fax (27) 3322-9109; e-mail escelsa@enbr.com.br; internet www.escelsa.com.br; f. 1968; subsidiary of EDB; Pres. ANTÓNIO MANUEL BARRETO PITA DE ABREU; Exec. Dir MIGUEL NUNO FERREIRA SETAS.

Indústrias Nucleares do Brasil, SA (INB): Av. João Cabral de Mello Netto 400, 101 a 304 Barra da Tijuca, 22775-057 Rio de Janeiro, RJ; tel. (21) 3797-1600; fax (21) 3793-1757; e-mail inbrio@inb.gov.br; internet www.inb.gov.br; f. 1988; Pres. AQUILINO SENRA MARTINEZ.

Itaipu Binacional: Av. Tancredo Neves 6731, 85866-900 Foz de Iguaçu, PR; tel. (45) 3520-5252; fax (45) 3520-3015; e-mail itaipu@itaipu.gov.br; internet www.itaipu.gov.br; f. 1974; hydroelectric power station on Brazilian–Paraguayan border; jtly owned by Brazil and Paraguay; 98,630 GWh produced in 2013; Dir-Gen. (Brazil) JORGE MIGUEL SAMEK; Dir-Gen. (Paraguay) JAMES EDWARD CLIFTON SPALDING HELLMERS.

LIGHT—Serviços de Eletricidade, SA: Av. Marechal Floriano 168, CP 0571, 20080-002 Rio de Janeiro, RJ; tel. (21) 2211-7171; fax (21) 2233-1249; e-mail light@lightrio.com.br; internet www.lightrio.com.br; f. 1905; electricity generation and distribution in Rio de Janeiro; fmrly state-owned, sold in 1996; 79.4% owned by Rio Minas Energia Participaçoes, SA (RME), 10% by EdF (France); generating capacity of 850 MW; Pres. SÉRGIO ALAIR BARROSO; Exec. Dir JERSON KELMAN.

Gas

Companhia Distribuidora de Gás do Rio de Janeiro (CEG): Av. Pedro II 68, São Cristóvão, 20941-070 Rio de Janeiro, RJ; tel. (21) 2585-7575; fax (21) 2585-7070; internet www.ceg.com.br; f. 1969, privatized in 1997; Pres. SERGIO ARANDA MORENO; Exec. Dir BRUNO ARMBRUST.

Companhia de Gás de Alagoas, SA (ALGÁS): Rua Artur Vital da Silva, 04, Gruta de Lourdes, 57052-790 Maceió, AL; tel. (82) 3218-7767; fax (82) 3218-7742; e-mail algas@algas.com.br; internet www.algas.com.br; 51% state-owned; Exec. Dir GERSON FONSECA.

Companhia de Gás de Bahia (BAHIAGÁS): Av. Tancredo Neves 450, Edif. Suarez Trade, 20° andar, Caminho das Arvores, 41820-901 Salvador, BA; tel. (71) 3206-6000; fax (71) 3206-6001; e-mail atendimento@bahiagas.com.br; internet www.bahiagas.com.br; f. 1991; 51% state-owned; Pres. WILSON ALVES DE BRITO FILHO; Exec. Dir DAVIDSON DE MAGALHÃES SANTOS.

Companhia de Gás do Ceará (CEGÁS): Av. Santos Dumont 7700, 5°–8° e 11° andares, Manoel Dias Branco, 60190-800 Fortaleza, CE; tel. (85) 3266-6900; fax (85) 3265-2026; e-mail ouvidoria@cegas.com.br; internet www.cegas.com.br; 51% owned by the state of Amazonas; Pres. Dr JOSÉ REGO FILHO.

Companhia de Gás de Minas Gerais (GASMIG): Av. do Contorno 6594, 10° andar, Funcionários, 30110-044 Belo Horizonte, MG; tel. (31) 3265-1000; fax (31) 3265-1103; e-mail gasmig@gasmig.com.br; internet www.gasmig.com.br; Exec. Dir MÁRCIO AUGUSTO VASCONCELOS NUNES.

Companhia de Gás de Pernambuco (COPERGÁS): Av. Mal. Mascarenhas de Morais 533, Imbiribeira, 51150-904 Recife, PE; tel. (81) 3184-2000; e-mail copergas@copergas.com.br; internet www.copergas.com.br; 51% state-owned; Exec. Dir ALDO GUEDES.

Companhia de Gás do Rio Grande do Sul (SULGÁS): Rua 7 de Setembro 1069, Edif. Santa Cruz, 5° andar, Centro, 90010-190 Porto Alegre, RS; tel. (51) 3287-2200; fax (51) 3287-2205; internet www.sulgas.rs.gov.br; f. 1993; 51% state-owned; 49% owned by Petrobras; Pres. DANIEL ANDRADE; Exec. Dir ANTÔNIO GREGÓRIO GOIDANICH.

Companhia de Gás de Santa Catarina (SCGÁS): Rua Antônia Luz 255, Centro Empresarial Hoepcke, 88010-410 Florianópolis, SC;

tel. (48) 3229-1200; fax (48) 3229-1230; internet www.scgas.com.br; f. 1994; 51% state-owned; Exec. Dir Ivan César Ranzolin.

Companhia de Gás de São Paulo (COMGÁS): Av. Pres. Juscelino Kubitschek 1327, 14° andar, Vila Nova Conceição, 04543-011 São Paulo, SP; tel. (11) 4504-5000; fax (11) 4504-5027; e-mail investidores@comgas.com.br; internet www.comgas.com.br; f. 1872; owned by Cosan Group and Royal Dutch Shell Group; Chair. Rubens Ometto Silveira Mello; Exec. Dir Luis Henrique Guimarães.

Companhia Paraibana de Gás (PBGÁS): Av. Presidente Epitácio Pessoa 4756, Cabo Branco, 58045-001 João Pessoa, PB; tel. (83) 3247-7609; fax (83) 3247-2244; e-mail cicero@pbgas.com.br; internet www.pbgas.pb.gov.br; f. 1995; 51% state-owned; Exec. Dir Antônio Carlos Fernandes Regis.

Companhia Paranaense de Gás (COMPAGÁS): Rua Pasteur 463, Edif. Jatobá, 7° andar, Batel, 80250-080 Curitaba, PR; tel. (41) 3312-1900; fax (41) 3312-1922; e-mail compagas@compagas.com.br; internet www.compagas.com.br; f. 1998; 51.0% owned by Copel Participaçoes, SA, 24.5% by Gaspetro and 24.5% by Mitsui Gás e Energia do Brasil; Pres. Dr Antônio Fernando Krempel; Exec. Dir Stênio Jacob.

Companhia Potiguar de Gás (POTIGÁS): Av. Brancas Dunas 485, Lojas 1 e 2, Salas de 101 a 106, Candelária, 59064-720 Natal, RN; tel. (84) 3204-8500; fax (84) 3206-8504; e-mail mauricio@potigas.com.br; internet www.potigas.com.br; 17% state-owned; Pres. Francisco Cipriano de Paula Segundo; Exec. Dir Nelson Hermógenes de Medeiros Freire.

Companhia Rondoniense de Gás, SA (RONGÁS): Av. Carlos Gomes 1223, Sala 403, 4° andar, Centro, 78900-030 Porto Velho, RO; tel. and fax (69) 3229-0333; e-mail rongas@rongas.com.br; internet www.rongas.com.br; f. 1997; 17% state-owned; Exec. Dir José Sanguanini.

Empresa Sergipana de Gás, SA (EMSERGÁS): Av. Heráclito Rollemberg 1712, Conj. Augusto Franco, 49030-640 Farolândia, SE; tel. (79) 3243-8500; fax (79) 3243-8508; e-mail emsergas@infonet.com.br; internet www.sergipegas.com.br; f. 1993; 51% state-owned; Exec. Dir Fernando Akira Ota.

Water

Águas e Esgotos do Piauí (AGESPISA): Av. Marechal Castelo Branco 101, Norte, Cabral, 64000-810 Teresina, PI; tel. (86) 3216-6300; fax (86) 3216-8182; e-mail marcosvenicius@agespisa.com.br; internet www.agespisa.com.br; f. 1962; state-owned; Exec. Dir Marcos Venícius Medeiros Costa.

Companhia de Agua e Esgosto de Ceará (CAGECE): Av. Dr Lauro Vieira Chaves 1030, Vila União, 60420-280 Fortaleza, CE; tel. (85) 3101-1805; fax (85) 3101-1834; e-mail asimp-cagece@cagece.com.br; internet www.cagece.com.br; f. 1971; state-owned; Pres. Joaquim Cartaxo Filho; Exec. Dir Henrique Vieira Costa Lima.

Companhia Algoas Industrial (CINAL): Rodovia Divaldo Suruagy, BR 424, Km 12, 57160-000 Marechal Deodoro, AL; tel. (82) 3218-2500; fax (82) 3269-1199; e-mail airton@cinal.com.br; internet www.cinal.com.br; f. 1982; Pres. Roberto Prisco Paraíso Ramos; Exec. Dir Francisco Carlos Ruga.

Companhia Espírito Santense de Saneamento (CESAN): Av. Governador Bley 186, Edif. BEMGE, 3º andar, Centro, 29010-150 Vitória, ES; tel. (27) 2127-5353; fax (27) 2127-5000; e-mail comunica@cesan.com.br; internet www.cesan.com.br; f. 1968; state-owned; Exec. Dir Paulo Ruy Valim Carnelli.

Companhia Estadual de Aguas e Esgotos (CEDAE): Rua Sacadura Cabral 103, 9° andar, 20081-260 Rio de Janeiro, RJ; tel. (21) 2332-3600; fax (21) 2296-0416; internet www.cedae.rj.gov.br; f. 1975; state-owned; Pres. Alberto José Mendes Gomes; Exec. Dir Wagner Granja Victer.

Companhia Pernambucana de Saneamento (COMPESA): Rua da Aurora 777, Boa Vista, 50040-905 Recife, PE; tel. (81) 3412-9693; fax (81) 3412-9181; internet www.compesa.com.br; state-owned; Pres. João Bosco de Almeida.

Companhia Riograndense de Saneamento (CORSAN): Rua Caldas Júnior 120, 18° andar, 90010-260 Porto Alegre, RS; tel. (51) 3215-5600; e-mail ascom@corsan.com.br; internet www.corsan.com.br; f. 1965; state-owned; Exec. Dir Luis Zaffalon.

Companhia de Saneamento Básico do Estado de São Paulo (SABESP): Rua Costa Carvalho 300, Pinheiros, 05429-000 São Paulo, SP; tel. (11) 3388-8200; fax (11) 3813-0254; internet www.sabesp.com.br; f. 1973; state-owned; Pres. Dilma Seli Pena; Exec. Dir Gesner José de Oliveira Filho.

TRADE UNIONS

Central Unica dos Trabalhadores (CUT): Rua Caetano Pinto 575, Brás, 03041-000 São Paulo, SP; tel. (11) 2108-9200; fax (11) 2108-9310; e-mail duvaier@cut.org.br; internet www.cut.org.br; f. 1983; central union confederation; left-wing; 3.5m. mems; Pres. Vagner Freitas de Moraes; Gen. Sec. Sérgio Nobre.

Confederação Nacional dos Metalúrgicos (Metal Workers): Av. Antártico, 480-Jardim do Mar, São Bernardo do Campo, 09726-150 São Paulo, SP; tel. (11) 4122-7700; e-mail cnmcut@cnmcut.org.br; internet www.cnmcut.org.br; f. 1992; Pres. Paulo Cayres; Gen. Sec. João Cayres.

Confederação Nacional das Profissões Liberais (CNPL) (Liberal Professions): SCS, Quadra 02, Bloco D, Edif. Oscar Niemeyer, 9º andar, 70316-900 Brasília, DF; tel. (61) 2103-1683; fax (61) 2103-1684; e-mail secretaria@cnpl.org.br; internet www.cnpl.org.br; f. 1953; 260,000 mems (2007); Pres. Carlos Alberto Schmitt de Azevedo; Sec.-Gen. José Alberto Rossi.

Confederação Nacional dos Trabalhadores na Indústria (CNTI) (Industrial Workers): SEP/NORTE, Quadra 505, Conj. A, 70730-540 Brasília, DF; tel. (61) 3448-9900; fax (61) 3448-9956; e-mail cnti@cnti.org.br; internet www.cnti.org.br; f. 1946; Pres. José Calixto Ramos; Sec.-Gen. Aprígio Guimarães.

Confederação Nacional dos Trabalhadores no Comércio (CNTC) (Commercial Workers): Av. W/5 Sul, SGAS Quadra 902, Bloco C, 70390-020 Brasília, DF; tel. (61) 3217-7100; fax (61) 3217-7122; e-mail cntc@cntc.org.br; internet www.cntc.com.br; f. 1946; Pres. Levi Fernandes Pinto.

Confederação Nacional dos Trabalhadores em Transportes Aquaviários e Aéreos, na Pesca e nos Portos (CONTTMAF) (Maritime, River and Air Transport Workers): SDS, Edif. Venâncio V, Grupos 501/503, 70393-900 Brasília, DF; tel. (61) 3226-5263; fax (61) 3322-6383; e-mail conttmaf@conttmaf.org.br; internet www.conttmaf.org.br; f. 1957; Pres. Severino Almeida Filho; Sec.-Gen. Odilon dos Santos Braga.

Confederação Nacional dos Trabalhadores em Comunicações e Publicidade (CONTCOP) (Communications and Advertising Workers): SCS, Quadra 02, Edif. Serra Dourada, Sala 705–709, 70300-902 Brasília, DF; tel. (61) 3224-7926; fax (61) 3224-5686; e-mail faleconosco@contcop.org.br; internet www.contcop.org.br; f. 1964; 350,000 mems; Pres. Antônio Maria Thaumaturgo Cortizo; Sec.-Gen. Benedito Antonio Marcello.

Confederação Nacional dos Trabalhadores nas Empresas de Crédito (CONTEC) (Workers in Credit Institutions): SEP-SUL, Av. W/4, EQ 707/907, Conj. A/B, 70390-078 Brasília, DF; tel. (61) 3244-5833; fax (61) 3224-2743; e-mail contec@contec.org.br; internet www.contec.org.br; f. 1958; Pres. Lourenço Ferreira do Prado; Sec.-Gen. Gilberto Antonio Vieira.

Confederação Nacional dos Trabalhadores em Estabelecimentos de Educação e Cultura (CNTEEC) (Workers in Education and Culture): SAS, Quadra 04, Bloco B, 70070-908 Brasília, DF; tel. (61) 3321-4140; fax (61) 3321-2704; internet www.cnteec.org.br; f. 1966; Pres. Miguel Abrão Neto.

Confederação Nacional dos Trabalhadores na Agricultura (CONTAG) (Agricultural Workers): SMPW, Quadra 01, Conj. 02, Lote 02, Núcleo Bandeirante, 71735-102 Brasília, DF; tel. (61) 2102-2288; fax (61) 2102-2299; e-mail contag@contag.org.br; internet www.contag.org.br; f. 1964; represents 25 state feds and 3,630 syndicates, 15m. mems; Pres. Alberto Ercílio Broch; Sec.-Gen. David Wylkerson Rodrigues de Souza.

Força Sindical (FS): Rua Rocha Pombo, 94 Liberdade, 01525-010 São Paulo, SP; tel. and fax (11) 3348-9000; e-mail secgeral@fsindical.org.br; internet www.fsindical.org.br; f. 1991; 2.1m. mems (2007); Pres. Paulo Pereira da Silva; Sec.-Gen. João Carlos Gonçalves.

União Geral dos Trabalhadores (UGT): Rua Aguiar de Barrios, 144 Bela Vista, 01316-020 São Paulo, SP; tel. (11) 2111-7300; fax (11) 2111-7501; e-mail ugt@ugt.org.br; internet www.ugt.org.br; f. 2007 by merger of Confederação Geral dos Trabalhadores with two other unions; Pres. Ricardo Patah; Sec.-Gen. Francisco Canindé Pegado do Nascimento.

Transport

Ministry of Transport: see section on the Government (Ministries).

Agência Nacional de Transportes Terrestres (ANTT): Edif. Phenícia, SBN, Quadra 02, Bloco C, Lote 17, 70040-020 Brasília, DF; tel. (61) 3410-8100; fax (61) 3410-1189; e-mail ouvidoria@antt.gov.br; internet www.antt.gov.br; f. 2002; govt agency; oversees road and rail infrastructure; Dir-Gen. Bernardo Figueiredo.

RAILWAYS

In 2013 there were 30,051 km of railway lines. There were also railways owned by state governments and several privately owned railways. Construction of a new high-speed rail link connecting Rio de Janeiro, São Paulo and Campinas was originally scheduled to begin in 2010, but this was postponed until 2013. The estimated cost of the project was R $38,000m. In addition, the first part of a 24 km urban transit system was scheduled to begin operations in São Paulo in early 2014, with completion of the monorail system by the end of 2016. Construction of a metro system in Salvador, originally begun in 2000, was finally under way in 2014. In 2012 the federal Government announced an additional US $63,600m. in expenditure on transport infrastructure.

América Latina Logística do Brasil, SA (ALL): Rua Emilio Bertolini 100, Vila Oficinas, Cajuru, Curitiba, PR; tel. (41) 2141-7555; e-mail caall@all-logistica.com; internet www.all-logistica.com; f. 1997; 6,586 km in 2003; acquired Ferrovia Novoeste, SA in 2006; Pres. WILSON FERRO DE LARA; Dir-Gen. PAULO LUIZ ARAÚJO BASÍLIO.

Ferrovia Bandeirante, SA (Ferroban): Av. Paulista 1.499, 17° andar, Sala 5, São Paulo, SP; tel. (11) 3138-2048; fax (11) 3138-2054; f. 1971 by merger of five railways operated by São Paulo State; transferred to private ownership in 1998; fmrly Ferrovia Paulista; 4,236 km open in 2003; Dir JOÃO GOUVEIA FERRÃO NETO.

Associação Brasileira da Indústria Ferroviáia (ABIFER): Av. Paulista 1313, 8° andar conjunto 801, 01311-923 São Paulo, SP; tel. (11) 3289-1667; fax (11) 3171-2286; e-mail abifer@abifer.org.br; internet www.abifer.org.br; f. 1977; rail industry asscn; Pres. VICENTE ABATE.

Associação Nacional dos Transportadores Ferroviários (ANTF): Edif. CNT, Torre A, 6° andar, Sala 605, Quadra 01, Bloco J, 70070-010 Brasília, DF; tel. (61) 3226-5434; fax (61) 3221-0135; e-mail imprensa@antf.org.br; internet www.antf.org.br; promotes railway devt; 11 mem. cos; Pres. EDUARDO PARENTE; Exec. Dir RODRIGO VILAÇA.

Cia Brasileira de Trens Urbanos (CBTU): Estrada Velha da Tijuca 77, Usina, 20531-080 Rio de Janeiro, RJ; tel. (21) 2575-3399; fax (21) 2571-6149; e-mail imprensa@cbtu.gov.br; internet www.cbtu.gov.br; f. 1984; fmrly responsible for suburban networks and metro systems throughout Brazil; operates 5 metro systems; Pres. FRANCISCO COLOMBO.

Metrô BH (Superintendência de Trens Urbanos de Belo Horizonte): Rua Janúaria 181m, 31110-060 Belo Horizonte, MG; tel. (31) 3250-3900; fax (31) 3250-4053; e-mail stu-bh@cbtu.gov.br; f. 1981 as DEMETRÔ; present name adopted 2003; operates 3 lines; Supt JOSÉ DÓRIA.

METROREC (Superintendência de Trens Urbanos de Recife): Rua José Natário 478, Areias, 50900-000 Recife, PE; tel. (81) 2102-8500; fax (81) 3455-4422; e-mail ouvidoria@metrorec.com.br; internet www2.cbtumetrorec.gov.br; f. 1985; 71 km open in 2010; Supt RICARDO BELTRÃO.

Superintendência de Trens Urbanos de João Pessoa (GTU/JOP): Praça Napoleão Laureano 1, Varadouro, 58010-040 João Pessoa, PB; tel. (83) 3241-4240; fax (83) 3241-6388; e-mail gecomjp@cbtu.gov.br; internet joaopessoa.cbtu.gov.br; 30 km; Supt LUCÉLIO CARTAXO.

Superintendência de Trens Urbanos de Maceió (STU/MAC): Rua Barão de Anadia 121, Centro, 57020-630 Maceió, AL; tel. (82) 2123-1700; fax (82) 2123-1445; e-mail orleanes@cbtu.gov.br; internet www.cbtu.gov.br; f. 1996; 32 km; Supt MARCELO DE AGUIAR GOMES.

Superintendência de Trens Urbanos de Natal (STU/NAT): Praça Augusto Severo, 302 Ribeira, 59012-380 Natal, RN; tel. (84) 3221-3355; fax (84) 3211-4122; e-mail stunat@cbtu.gov.br; internet natal.cbtu.gov.br; f. 1984; 56 km; Supt ERLY BASTOS.

Cia Cearense de Transportes Metropolitanos, SA (Metrofor): Rua 24 de Maio 60, 60020-001 Fortaleza, CE; tel. (85) 3101-7100; fax (85) 3101-4744; e-mail metrofor@metrofor.ce.gov.br; internet www.metrofor.ce.gov.br; f. 1997; 46 km; Pres. RÔMULO DOS SANTOS FORTES.

Cia do Metropolitano de São Paulo: Rua Boa Vista 175, 01014-001, São Paulo, SP; tel. (11) 3291-7800; fax (11) 3371-7329; e-mail ouvidoria@metrosp.com.br; internet www.metro.sp.gov.br; f. 1968; 4-line metro system, 61.3 km open in 2007; Dir-Gen. SÉRGIO HENRIQUE PASSOS AVELLEDA.

Cia Paulista de Trens Metropolitanos (CPTM): Av. Paulista 402, 5° andar, 01310-000 São Paulo, SP; tel. (11) 3371-1530; fax (11) 3285-0323; e-mail usuario@cptm.sp.gov.br; internet www.cptm.sp.gov.br; f. 1992 to incorporate suburban lines fmrly operated by the CBTU and FEPASA; 286 km; Pres. Dr JURANDIR FERNANDES; Dir-Gen. MARIO MANUEL SEABRA RODRIGUES BANDEIRA.

Empresa de Trens Urbanos de Porto Alegre, SA: Av. Ernesto Neugebauer 1985, 6° andar, Humaitá, 90250-140 Porto Alegre, RS; tel. (51) 3363-8000; fax (51) 3363-8166; e-mail atendimento@trensurb.com.br; internet www.trensurb.gov.br; f. 1985; Pres. ROBERTO DE OLIVEIRA MUNIZ; Dir-Gen. HUMBERTO KASPER.

Estrada de Ferro do Amapá (EFA): Av. Santana 429, Porto de Santana, 68925-000 Macapá, AP; tel. (96) 281-1845; fax (96) 281-1175; f. 1957; operated by Indústria e Comércio de Minérios, SA; 194 km open in 2007; Dir Supt JOSÉ LUIZ ORTIZ VERGULINO.

Estrada de Ferro Campos do Jordão: Rua Martin Cabral 87, CP 11, 12400-020 Pindamonhangaba, SP; tel. (12) 3642-3233; fax (12) 242-2499; internet www.efcj.sp.gov.br; f. 1914; operated by the Tourism Secretariat of the State of São Paulo; Dir SILVIO CAMARGO.

Estrada de Ferro Carajás: Av. Graça Aranha 26, 20030-000 RJ; tel. (21) 3814-4477; fax (21) 3814-4040; f. 1985 for movement of minerals from the Serra do Carajás to the port at Ponta da Madeira; operated by Vale, SA (CVRD); Supt JUARES SALIBRA.

Estrada de Ferro do Jari: Vila Munguba s/n, Monte Dourado, 68230-000 Pará, PA; tel. (91) 3736-6526; fax (91) 3736-6490; e-mail ascarvalho@jari.com.br; f. 1979; transportation of timber; 70 km open; Operations Man. PABLO ASSIS GUZZO.

Estrada de Ferro Paraná-Oeste, SA (FERROESTE): Av. Iguaçú 420, 7° andar, Rebouças, 80230-902 Curitiba, PR; tel. (41) 3281-9800; fax (41) 3233-2147; e-mail ferroest@pr.gov.br; internet www.ferroeste.pr.gov.br; f. 1988; serves the grain-producing regions in Paraná and Mato Grosso do Sul; Pres. MAURICIO QUERINO THEODORO.

Estrada de Ferro Vitória-Minas: Av. Aarão Reis 423, Centro, Belo Horizonte, MG; tel. (31) 273-5976; fax (31) 3279-4676; f. 1942; operated by Vale, SA (CVRD); transport of iron ore, general cargo and passengers; Dir ALVARO ALBERGARIA.

Ferrovia Centro Atlântica, SA: Rua Sapucaí 383, Floresta 30150-904, Belo Horizonte, MG; tel. (31) 3279-5323; fax (31) 3279-5709; e-mail thiers@centro-atlantica.com.br; internet www.fcasa.com.br; f. 1996 following the privatization of Rede Ferroviária Federal, SA; owned by Vale, SA (CVRD) since 2003; industrial freight; 8,000 km; Dir-Gen. MARCELLO SPINELLI.

Ferrovia de Integração Oeste-Leste (FIOL): Av. Soares Lopes, 956 Casa, Centro, 45653-005 Ilhéus, BA; tel. (73) 3231-5769; internet www.valec.gov.br; 1,527 km from Bahia to Tocantins; Supt NEVILLE BARBOSA.

Ferrovia Norte-Sul: Av. Marechal Floriano 45, Centro, 20080-003 Rio de Janeiro, RJ; tel. (21) 2291-2185; fax (21) 2263-9119; e-mail valecascom@ferrovianortesul.com.br; 2,066 km from Belém to Goiânia; Dir JOSÉ FRANCISCO DAS NEVES.

Ferrovia Tereza Cristina, SA (FTC): Rua dos Ferroviários 100, Bairro Oficinas, 88702-230 Tubarão, SC; tel. (48) 3621-7724; fax (48) 3621-7747; e-mail comunicacao@ftc.com.br; internet www.ftc.com.br; 164 km in 2007; Man. Dir BENONY SCHMITZ FILHO.

Metrô-DF (Cia do Metropolitano do Distrito Federal): Av. Jequitibá, lote 155, Águas Claras, 71929-540 Brasília, DF; tel. (61) 3353-7373; fax (61) 3352-1472; e-mail atendimentoaousuario@metro.df.gov.br; internet www.metro.df.gov.br; f. 1991; Pres. IVELISE MARIA LONGHI PEREIRA DA SILVA.

Metrô Rio: Av. Presidente Vargas 2000, Col. Centro, 20210-031 Rio de Janeiro, RJ; tel. (21) 3211-6300; e-mail sac@metrorio.com.br; internet www.metrorio.com.br; 2-line metro system; operated by Opportans Concessão Metroviária, SA.

MRS Logística, SA: Praia de Botafogo 228, Sala 1201E, Ala B, Botafogo, 22359-900 Rio de Janeiro, RJ; tel. (21) 2559-4610; e-mail daf@mrs.com.br; internet www.mrs.com.br; f. 1996; CEO EDUARDO PARENTE.

SuperVia, SA: Rua da América 210, Santo Cristo, 20220-590 Rio de Janeiro, RJ; tel. (21) 2111-9646; internet www.supervia.com.br; f. 1998; operates commuter trains in Rio de Janeiro; Pres. CARLOS JOSÉ CUNHA.

Transnordestina Logística, SA: Av. Francisco de Sá 4829, Bairro Carlito Pamplona, 60310-002 Fortaleza, CE; tel. (85) 4008-2500; fax (85) 4008-2525; e-mail kerley@cfn.com.br; internet www.cfn.com.br; fmrly Cia Ferroviária do Nordeste; changed name as above in 2008; subsidiary of Grupo CSN (Cia Siderúrgica Nacional); 4,534 km in 2003; Dir-Gen. TUFI DAHER FILHO.

Transporte Urbano do Distrito Federal (DFTRANS): SAIN, Estação Rodoferroviária, Ala Sul, Sobreloja, 70631-900 Brasília, DF; tel. (61) 3043-0401; e-mail ouvidoriadftrans@yahoo.com.br; internet www.dftrans.df.gov.br; the first section of the Brasília metro, linking the capital with the western suburb of Samambaia, was inaugurated in 1994; Dir MARCO ANTONIO CAMPANELLA.

ROADS

In 2010 there were 1,580,964 km of roads in Brazil, of which 13.5% were paved. Of the total, 99,220 km were part of the national road network and 219,999 km formed the regional road network. Brasília has been a focal point for inter-regional development, and paved roads link the capital with every region of Brazil. Major projects include the Interportos Highway, linking the ports of Paraná, Paranaguá, Antonina and the future port terminals of Pontal and Emboguaçu. A 3.5-km bridge linking Manaus with Iranduba over the Rio Negro, a tributary of the Amazon, was inaugurated in 2011. In the same year a 2,600-km road, linking Rio Branco, the capital of Acre, with Nazca on the coast of Peru, was opened.

Departamento Nacional de Infra-Estrutura de Transportes (DNIT) (National Roads Development): Edif. Núcleo dos Transportes, SAN, Quadra 3, Bloco A, Lote A, 70040-902 Brasília, DF; tel. (61) 3315-4000; fax (61) 3315-4050; e-mail diretoria.geral@dnit.gov.br; internet www.dnit.gov.br; f. 1945 to plan and execute federal road policy and to supervise state and municipal roads in order to integrate them into the national network; Dir-Gen. JORGE ERNESTO PINTO FRAXE; Exec. Dir TARCÍSIO GOMES DE FREITAS.

INLAND WATERWAYS

River transport plays only a minor part in the movement of goods. There are three major river systems, the Amazon, the Paraná and the São Francisco, with a total of 28,000 km of waterways. The Amazon is navigable for 3,680 km, as far as Iquitos in Peru, and ocean-going ships can reach Manaus, 1,600 km upstream.

Agência Nacional de Transportes Aquaviários (ANTAQ): Edif. ANTAQ, SEPN, Quadra 514, Conj. E, 70760-545 Brasília, DF; tel. (61) 2029-6500; fax (61) 3447-1040; e-mail asc@antaq.gov.br; internet www.antaq.gov.br; Dir-Gen. FERNANDO ANTÔNIO BRITO FIALHO.

Administração das Hidrovias da Amazônia Ocidental (AHIMOC): Rua Marquês de Santa Cruz 264, Centro, 69005-050 Manaus, AM; tel. (92) 3633-3061; fax (92) 3232-5156; e-mail ahimoc@ahimoc.com.br; internet www.ahimoc.com.br; Supt SEBASTIÃO DA SILVA REIS.

Administração das Hidrovias da Amazônia Oriental (AHIMOR): Rua Joaquim Nabuco 8, Nazaré, 66055-300 Belém, PA; tel. (91) 3039-7700; fax (91) 3039-7721; e-mail ahimor@ahimor.gov.br; internet www.ahimor.gov.br; Supt ALBERTINO DE OLIVEIRA E SILVA.

Administração das Hidrovias do Nordeste (AHINOR): Rua da Paz 561, Centro, 65020-450 São Luiz, MA; tel. and fax (98) 3231-5122; fax (98) 3232-6707; e-mail ahinor@elo.com.br; internet www.ahinor.gov.br; Pres. JOSÉ OSCAR FRAZÃO FROTA.

Administração da Hidrovia do Paraguai (AHIPAR): Rua Treze de Junho 960, 79300-040 Corumbá, MS; tel. (67) 3234-3200; fax (67) 3231-2661; internet www.ahipar.gov.br; Supt ANTÔNIO PAULO DE BARROS LEITE.

Administração da Hidrovia do Paraná (AHRANA): Av. Brig. Faria Lima 1912, 16° andar, Jardim Paulistano, 01451-000 São Paulo, SP; tel. (11) 2106-1600; fax (11) 3815-5435; e-mail ahrana@ahrana.gov.br; internet www.ahrana.gov.br; Supt ANTONIO BADIH CHENIN.

Administração da Hidrovia do São Francisco (AHSFRA): Praça do Porto 70, Distrito Industrial, 39270-000 Pirapora, MG; tel. (38) 3741-2555; fax (38) 3741-3046; e-mail superint@ahsfra.gov.br; internet www.ahsfra.gov.br; Supt SEBASTIÃO JOSÉ MARQUES DE OLIVEIRA.

Administração das Hidrovias do Sul (AHSUL): Praça Oswaldo Cruz 15, 3° andar, Sala 311–314, 90030-160 Porto Alegre, RS; tel. (51) 3225-0700; fax (51) 3226-9068; e-mail ahsul@uol.com.br; internet www.ahsul.com.br; Supt JOSÉ LUIZ FAY DE AZAMBUJA.

Administração das Hidrovias do Tocantins e Araguaia (AHITAR): ACSE Conj. 02, Lote 33, 1° andar, Sala 02, 77020-024 Palmas, TO; tel. (62) 3215-3171; fax (62) 3213-1904; e-mail ahitar@terra.com.br; internet www.ahitar.gov.br; Supt TARLES JUNQUEIRA CALEMAN.

SHIPPING

There are more than 40 deep-water ports in Brazil, all but one of which (Imbituba) are directly or indirectly administered by the Government. The majority of ports are operated by state-owned concerns (Cia Docas do Pará, Estado de Ceará, Estado do Rio Grande do Norte, Bahia, Paraíba, Espírito Santo, Rio de Janeiro and Estado de São Paulo), while a smaller number (including Suape, Cabedelo, São Sebastião, Paranaguá, Antonina, São Francisco do Sul, Porto Alegre, Itajaí, Pelotas and Rio Grande) are administered by state governments. The Government was seeking some US $26,000m. investment in the ports in 2013 in order to improve efficiency and upgrade facilities.

The ports of Santos, Rio de Janeiro and Rio Grande have specialized container terminals handling more than 1,200,000 TEUs (20-ft equivalent units of containerized cargo) per year. Santos is the major container port in Brazil, accounting for 800,000 TEUs annually. The ports of Paranaguá, Itajaí, São Francisco do Sul, Salvador, Vitória and Imbituba cater for containerized cargo to a lesser extent.

Brazil's flag registered fleet comprised 823 vessels in 2013, with a combined aggregate displacement of some 3,156,535 grt.

Departamento de Marinha Mercante: Coordenação Geral de Transporte Maritimo, Av. Rio Branco 103, 6° e 8° andar, 20040-004 Rio de Janeiro, RJ; tel. (21) 2221-4014; fax (21) 2221-5929; Dir DÉBORA TEIXEIRA.

Secretariat of Ports: see The Government—Ministries.

Port Authorities

Administração do Porto de Manaus (SNPH): Rua Marquês de Santa Cruz 25, Centro, 69005-050 Manaus, AM; tel. (92) 2123-4350; fax (92) 2123-4358; e-mail falecom@portodemanaus.com.br; internet www.portodemanaus.com.br; private; operates the port of Manaus; Dir ALESSANDRO BRONZE.

Administração dos Portos de Paranaguá e Antonina (APPA): Av. Conde Matarazzo 2500, 83370-000 Antonina, PR; Av. Ayrton Senna da Silva 161D, Pedro II, 83203-800 Paranaguá, PR; tel. (41) 3420-1100; fax (41) 3423-4252; e-mail superintendencia@appa.pr.gov.br; internet www.portosdoparana.pr.gov.br; Supt AIRTON VIDAL MARON.

Administração do Porto de São Francisco do Sul (APSFS): Av. Eng. Leite Ribeiro 782, CP 71, 89240-000 São Francisco do Sul, SC; tel. (47) 3471-1200; fax (47) 3471-1211; e-mail porto@apsfs.sc.gov.br; internet www.apsfs.sc.gov.br; Pres. PAULO CÉSAR CORTES CORSI.

Cia Docas do Espírito Santo (CODESA): Av. Getúlio Vargas 556, Centro, 29010-945 Vitória, ES; tel. (27) 3132-7360; fax (27) 3132-7311; e-mail dirpre@codesa.gov.br; internet www.portodevitoria.com.br; f. 1983; Dir-Gen. CLOVIS LASCOSQUE.

Cia das Docas do Estado de Bahia (CODEBA): Av. da França 1551, Comércio, 40010-000 Salvador, BA; tel. (71) 3320-1100; fax (71) 3320-1375; e-mail business@codeba.com.br; internet www.codeba.com.br; f. 1977; port authority of state of Bahia and administers the ports of Salvador, Aratu and Ilhéus; CEO JOSÉ MUNIZ REBOUÇAS.

Cia Docas do Estado de Ceará (CDC): Praça Amigos da Marinha s/n, Mucuripe, 60182-640 Fortaleza, CE; tel. (85) 3266-8800; internet www.docasdoceara.com.br; administers the port of Fortaleza; Dir-Gen. PAULO ANDRÉ DE CASTRO HOLANDA.

Cia Docas do Estado de São Paulo (CODESP): Av. Conselheiro Rodrigues Alves s/n, Macuco, 11015-900 Santos, SP; tel. (13) 3202-6565; fax (13) 3202-6411; internet www.portodesantos.com; administers the ports of Santos, Charqueadas, Estrela, Cáceres and Corumbá/Ladário, and the waterways of Paraná (AHRANA), Paraguai (AHIPAR) and the South (AHSUL); Dir-Gen. JOSÉ ROBERTO CORREIA SERRA.

Cia Docas de Imbituba (CDI): Av. Presidente Vargas 100, CP 01, 88780-000 Imbituba, SC; tel. (48) 3355-8900; fax (48) 3255-0701; e-mail docas@cdiport.com.br; internet www.cdiport.com.br; private sector concession; Pres. NILTON GARCIA DE ARAUJO; Port Administrator JEZIEL PAMATO DE SOUZA.

Cia Docas do Pará (CDP): Av. Presidente Vargas 41, 2° andar, Centro, 66010-000 Belém, PA; tel. (91) 3182-9029; fax (91) 3182-9139; e-mail asscom@cdp.com.br; internet www.cdp.com.br; f. 1967; administers the ports of Belém, Miramar, Santarém Obidos, Altamira, São Francisco, Marabá and Vila do Conde; Dir-Gen. CARLOS J. PONCIANO DA SILVA.

Cia Docas da Paraíba (DOCAS-PB): Porto de Cabedelo, Rua Presidente João Pessoa s/n, Centro, 58310-000 Cabedelo, PB; tel. (83) 3250-3000; fax (83) 3250-3001; e-mail gvp@docaspb.com.br; internet www.docaspb.com.br; administers the port of Cabedelo; Dir-Gen. WILBUR JÁCOME.

Cia Docas do Rio de Janeiro (CDRJ): Rua do Acre 21, Centro, 20081-000 Rio de Janeiro, RJ; tel. (21) 2219-8617; fax (21) 2253-0528; e-mail aleconosco@portosrio.gov.br; internet www.portosrio.gov.br; administers the ports of Rio de Janeiro, Niterói, Itaguaí and Angra dos Reis; Dir-Gen. JORGE LUZ DE MELLO.

Cia Docas do Rio Grande do Norte (CODERN): Av. Hildebrando de Góis 220, Ribeira, 59010-700 Natal, RN; tel. (84) 4005-5311; e-mail administrativo@codern.com.br; internet www.codern.com.br; administers the ports of Areia Branca, Natal and Maceió; Dir-Gen. PEDRO TERCEIRO DE MELO.

Empresa Maranhense de Administração Portuária (EMAP): Av. dos Portugueses s/n, Itaquí, 65085-370 São Luís, MA; tel. (98) 3216-6000; fax (98) 3216-6060; e-mail csl@emap.ma.gov.br; internet www.emap.ma.gov.br; f. 2001 to administer port of Itaquí as concession from the state of Maranhão; Pres. LUIZ CARLOS FOSSATI.

Sociedade de Portos e Hidrovias do Estado de Rondônia (SOPH): Rua Terminal dos Milagres 400, Bairro da Balsa, 78900-750 Porto Velho, RO; tel. (69) 3229-2134; fax (69) 3229-3904; e-mail soph@soph.ro.gov.br; internet www.soph.ro.gov.br; operates the port of Porto Velho; Dir-Gen. MATEUS SANTOS COSTA.

SUAPE—Complexo Industrial Portuário Governador Eraldo Gueiros: Rodovia PE-060, Km 10, Engenho Massangana, 55590-972 Ipojuca, PE; tel. (81) 3527-5000; fax (81) 3527-5066; e-mail presidencia@suape.pe.gov.br; internet www.suape.pe.gov.br; administers the port of Suape; Pres. MÁRCIO STEFANNI MONTEIRO.

Superintendência do Porto de Itajaí: Rua Blumenau 5, Centro, 88305-101 Itajaí, SC; tel. (47) 3341-8000; fax (47) 3341-8075; e-mail atendimento@portoitajai.com.br; internet www.portoitajai.com.br; Supt ANTÔNIO AYRES DOS SANTOS, Jr.

Superintendência do Porto de Rio Grande (SUPRG): Av. Honório Bicalho s/n, CP 198, 96201-020 Rio Grande do Sul, RS; tel. (53) 3231-1366; fax (53) 3231-1857; e-mail dirceu.lopes@portoriogrande.com.br; internet www.portoriogrande.com.br; f. 1996; Supt DIRCEU DA SILVA LOPES.

Superintendência do Porto de Tubarão: Ponta de Tubarão, CP 1078, 29072-970 Vitória, ES; tel. (27) 3335-4666; fax (27) 3335-3535; operated by Vale, SA (CVRD); handles iron ore cargoes; Exec. Dir TITO MARTINS.

Superintendência de Portos e Hidrovias do Estado do Rio Grande do Sul (SPH): Av. Mauá 1050, 4° andar, 90010-110 Porto Alegre, RS; tel. and fax (51) 3288-9200; e-mail executiva@sph.rs.gov.br; internet www.sph.rs.gov.br; f. 1921; administers the ports of Porto Alegre, Porto Pelotas, Porto Cachoeira, the São Gonçalo canal and other waterways; Dir-Supt PEDRO HOMERO FLORES OBELAR.

Private Companies

Aliança Navegação e Logística, Ltda: Rua Verbo Divino 1547, Bairro Chácara Santo Antônio, 04719-002 São Paulo, SP; tel. (11) 5185-3100; fax (11) 5185-5624; e-mail alianca@sao.alianca.com.br; internet www.alianca.com.br; f. 1951; cargo services to Argentina, Uruguay, Europe, Baltic, Atlantic and North Sea ports; Pres. ARSÊNIO CARLOS NÓBREGA.

Cia Libra de Navegação: Av. Rio Branco, 4, 6° e 7° andares, 20090-000 Rio de Janeiro; tel. and fax (21) 2213-9700; e-mail atendimento.brasil@csavgroup.com; internet www.libra.com.br.

Cia de Navegação da Amazônia (CNA): Edif. Vieiralves Business Center, Rua Salvador 120, 11º andar, Adrianópolis, Manaus, AM; tel. (92) 2125-1200; fax (92) 2125-1212; internet www.cnamazon.com.br; f. 1942; Exec. Pres. RENÉ LEVY AGUIAR.

Cia de Navegação Norsul: Av. Augusto Severo 8, 8º andar, 20021-040 Rio de Janeiro, RJ; tel. (21) 2139-0505; fax (21) 2507-1547; e-mail norsul@norsul.com; internet www.norsul.com; f. 1963; largest private fleet, more than 28 vessels; Pres. CARLOS TEMKE.

Petrobras Transporte, SA (TRANSPETRO): Edif. Visconde de Itaboraí, Av. Presidente Vargas 328, 20091-060 Rio de Janeiro, RJ; tel. (21) 3211-7848; e-mail ouvidoria@transpetro.com.br; internet www.transpetro.com.br; f. 1998; absorbed the Frota Nacional de Petroleiros (FRONAPE) in 1999; transport of petroleum and related products; 53 vessels; Pres. JOSÉ SERGIO DE OLIVEIRA MACHADO.

Wilson Sons Agência Marítima: Rua Jardim Botânico 518, 3° andar, 22461-000 Rio de Janeiro, RJ; tel. (21) 2126-4222; fax (21) 2126-4190; e-mail box@wilsonsons.com.br; internet www.wilsonsons.com.br; f. 1837; shipping agency, port operations, towage, small shipyard; CEO AUGUSTO CEZAR TAVARES BAIÃO.

CIVIL AVIATION

Of the 67 principal airports, 22 are international, although most international traffic is handled by the two airports at Rio de Janeiro and two at São Paulo. In 2012 the Government reached agreement with foreign consortia to expand or upgrade the two São Paulo airports and the airport at Brasília.

Agência Nacional de Aviação Civil: Edif. Parque Cidade Corporate Torre A, SCS, Quadra 09, Lote C, 70308-200 Brasília, DF; tel. (61) 3314-4105; internet www.anac.gov.br; f. 2006; Dir-Pres. MARCELO PACHECO DOS GUARANYS.

Empresa Brasileira de Infra-Estrutura Aeroportuária (Infraero): Estrada do Aeroporto, Setor de Concessionárias, Lote 5, Edif. Sede, 71608-900 Brasília, DF; tel. (61) 3312-3222; fax (61) 3321-0512; e-mail webmaster@infraero.gov.br; internet www.infraero.gov.br; Pres. GUSTAVO DO VALE.

Secretariat of Civil Aviation: see The Government—Ministries.

Principal Airlines

Avianca: Av. Marechal Câmara 160, Sala 1532, Centro, 20020-080 Rio de Janeiro, RJ; tel. (21) 2544-2181; fax (21) 2215-7181; e-mail reservas@avianca.com.br; internet www.avianca.com.br; f. 1998 as Oceanair Linhas Aéreas, Ltda; changed name as above 2010; domestic services; Pres. JOSÉ EFROMOVICH.

Azul Linhas Aéreas Brasileiras: São Paulo, SP; tel. (11) 4831-1245; e-mail imprensa@voeazul.com.br; internet www.voeazul.com.br; f. 2009; plan to merge with TRIP (q.v.) announced in 2012; Pres. DAVID NEELEMAN.

GOL Transportes Aéreos, SA: Rua Tamios 246, Jardim Aeropuerto, 04630-000 São Paulo, SP; tel. (11) 5033-4200; e-mail faleconosco@golnaweb.com.br; internet www.voegol.com.br; f. 2001; low-cost airline, acquired VARIG, SA in 2007; Man. Dir CONSTANTINO OLIVEIRA JÚNIOR.

Líder Aviação, SA: Av. Santa Rosa 123, São Luiz, 31270-750 Belo Horizonte, MG; tel. (31) 3490-4500; fax (31) 3490-4600; internet www.lideraviacao.com.br; f. 1958 as Líder Táxi Aéreo; changed name 2005; helicopters and small jets; Pres. JOSÉ AFONSO ASSUMPÇÃO.

TAM Linhas Aéreas, SA (TAM Airlines—TAM): Av. Jurandir 856, Jardim Aeroporto, 04072-000 São Paulo, SP; tel. (11) 5582-8811; e-mail relacoesinstitucionais@tam.com.br; internet www.tam.com.br; f. 1976; part of LATAM Airlines Group, SA following a merger with LAN Airlines, SA (Chile) in 2012, although still operates under TAM brand; scheduled passenger and cargo services from São Paulo to destinations throughout Brazil and in Argentina, Paraguay, Europe and the USA; CEO, LATAM Airlines ENRIQUE CUETO PLAZA; CEO, TAM Airlines MARCO ANTONIO BOLOGNA.

TRIP Linhas Aéreas: Av. Brigadeiro Faria Lima 2601, 9º andar, Paulistano, 01451-001 São Paulo, SP; tel. (11) 3643-2700; internet www.voetrip.com.br; f. 1998; part of Grupos Caprioli; plan to merge with Azul (q.v.) announced in May 2012; Pres. JOSÉ MARIO CAPRIOLI.

Tourism

In 2012 some 5.7m. tourists visited Brazil and receipts from tourism totalled US $6,645m., according to provisional figures. Rio de Janeiro, with its famous beaches, is the centre of the tourist trade. Like Salvador, Recife and other towns, it has excellent examples of Portuguese colonial and modern architecture. The modern capital, Brasília, incorporates a new concept of city planning and is the nation's showpiece. Other attractions are the Iguaçu Falls, the seventh largest (by volume) in the world, the tropical forests of the Amazon basin and the wildlife of the Pantanal.

Associação Brasileira da Indústria de Hotéis (ABIH): Edif. América Office Tower, 17º andar, Salas 1712 e 1713, SCN, Quadra 01, Bloco F, 70711-905 Brasília, DF; tel. and fax (61) 3326-1177; e-mail secretariaabih@abih.com.br; internet www.abih.com.br; f. 1936; hoteliers' asscn; Pres. ENRICO FERMI TORQUATO.

Federação Nacional de Turismo (FENACTUR): Largo do Arouche 290, 6° andar, São Paulo, SP; tel. (11) 3331-4590; fax (11) 3221-6947; e-mail fenactur@uol.com.br; internet www.fenactur.com.br; f. 1990; Pres. MICHEL TUMA NESS.

Instituto Brasileiro de Turismo (EMBRATUR): Edif. Embratur, 3° andar, SCN, Quadra 02, Bloco G, 70712-907 Brasília, DF; tel. (61) 3429-7777; fax (61) 3429-7710; e-mail presidencia@embratur.gov.br; internet www.braziltour.com; f. 1966; Pres. FLÁVIO DINO DE CASTRO E COSTA.

Defence

As assessed at November 2013, Brazil's armed forces numbered 318,500: army 190,000 (including 70,000 conscripts); navy 59,000 (including at least 3,200 conscripts; also including 2,500 in the naval air force and 15,000 marines); and air force 69,500. Reserves numbered 1,340,000 and there were some 395,000 in the paramilitary Public Security Forces, state militias under army control. Military service lasts for 12 months and is compulsory for men between 18 and 45 years of age.

Defence Budget: R $67,800m. in 2013.

Chief of Staff of the Air Forces: Gen. JUNITI SAITO.

Chief of Staff of the Army: Gen. ENZO MARTINS PERI.

Chief of Staff of the Navy: Adm. JÚLIO SOARES DE MOURA NETO.

Education

Education is free in official schools at primary and secondary level. Primary education is compulsory between the ages of six and 14 years and lasts for nine years. Secondary education begins at 15 years of age and lasts for three years. In 2008 enrolment in primary schools included 94% of children in the relevant age-group, while enrolment in secondary schools included 82% of those in the relevant age-group. The federal Government is responsible for higher education, and in 2011 there were 190 universities, of which 102 were state-administered. Numerous private institutions exist at all levels of education. Federal government expenditure on education was R $7,746.2m. in 2010.

BRUNEI

Introductory Survey

LOCATION, CLIMATE, LANGUAGE, RELIGION, FLAG, CAPITAL

The Sultanate of Brunei (Negara Brunei Darussalam) lies in South-East Asia, on the north-west coast of the island of Borneo (most of which comprises the Indonesian territory of Kalimantan). It is surrounded and bisected on the landward side by Sarawak, one of the two eastern states of Malaysia. The country has a tropical climate, characterized by consistent temperature and humidity. Annual rainfall averages about 2,540 mm (100 in) in coastal areas and about 3,300 mm (130 in) in the interior. Temperatures are high: average daily temperatures range from 24°C (75°F) to 32°C (90°F). The principal language is Malay, although Chinese is also spoken and English is widely used. The Malay population (accounting for 65.7% of the total, according to the 2011 census) are mainly Sunni Muslims. Most of the Chinese in Brunei (10.3% of the population in 2011) are Buddhists, and some are adherents of Confucianism and Daoism. Europeans and Eurasians are predominantly Christians, and the majority of indigenous tribespeople (Iban, Dayak and Kelabit—3.6% of the population in 2006) adhere to various animist beliefs. The flag (proportions 1 by 2) is yellow, with two diagonal stripes, of white and black, running from the upper hoist to the lower fly; superimposed in the centre is the state emblem (in red, with yellow Arabic inscriptions). The capital is Bandar Seri Begawan (formerly Brunei Town).

CONTEMPORARY POLITICAL HISTORY

Historical Context

Brunei, a traditional Islamic monarchy, formerly included most of the coastal regions of North Borneo (now Sabah) and Sarawak, which later became states of Malaysia. During the 19th century the rulers of Brunei ceded large parts of their territory to the United Kingdom, reducing the sultanate to its present size. In 1888, when North Borneo became a British Protectorate, Brunei became a British Protected State. In accordance with an agreement made in 1906, a British Resident was appointed to the court of the ruling Sultan as an adviser on administration. Under this arrangement, a form of government that included an advisory body, the State Council, emerged.

Brunei was invaded by Japanese forces in December 1941, but reverted to its former status in 1945, when the Second World War ended. The British-appointed Governor of Sarawak was High Commissioner for Brunei from 1948 until the territory's first written Constitution was promulgated in September 1959, when a further agreement was made between the Sultan and the British Government. The United Kingdom continued to be responsible for Brunei's defence and external affairs until the Sultanate's declaration of independence in 1984.

In December 1962 a large-scale revolt broke out in Brunei and in parts of Sarawak and North Borneo. The rebellion was undertaken by the 'North Borneo Liberation Army', an organization linked with the Parti Rakyat Brunei (PRB—Brunei People's Party), led by Sheikh Ahmad Azahari, which was strongly opposed to the planned entry of Brunei into the Federation of Malaysia. The rebels proclaimed the 'revolutionary State of North Kalimantan', but the revolt was suppressed, after 10 days' fighting, with the aid of British forces from Singapore. A state of emergency was declared, the PRB was banned, and Azahari was given asylum in Malaya. In the event, the Sultan of Brunei, Sir Omar Ali Saifuddin III, decided in 1963 against joining the Federation. From 1962 he ruled by decree, and the state of emergency remained in force. In October 1967 Saifuddin, who had been Sultan since 1950, abdicated in favour of his son, Hassanal Bolkiah. In November 1971 an amended version of the 1959 agreement between the Sultan and the British Government was signed, granting Brunei full internal self-government.

In December 1975 the UN General Assembly adopted a resolution advocating British withdrawal from Brunei, the return of political exiles and the holding of a general election. Negotiations in 1978, following assurances by Malaysia and Indonesia that they would respect Brunei's sovereignty, resulted in an agreement (signed in January 1979) that Brunei would become fully independent within five years. Independence was duly proclaimed on 1 January 1984, and the Sultan took office as Prime Minister and Minister of Finance and of Home Affairs, presiding over a cabinet of six other ministers (including two of the Sultan's brothers and his father, Saifuddin, the former Sultan).

The Chinese population, which controlled much of Brunei's private commercial sector but which had become stateless since independence, appeared threatened in 1985, when the Sultan indicated that Brunei would become an Islamic state in which the indigenous, mainly Malay, inhabitants, known as *bumiputras* ('sons of the soil'), would receive preferential treatment.

Domestic Political Affairs

In May 1985 a new political party, the Parti Kebangsaan Demokratik Brunei (PKDB—Brunei National Democratic Party), was formed, comprising business executives loyal to the Sultan. However, the Sultan forbade employees of the Government (about 40% of the country's working population) to join the party, which based its policies on Islam and a form of liberal nationalism; persons belonging to the Chinese community were also excluded from membership. Divisions within the new party led to the formation of a second group, the Parti Perpaduan Kebangsaan Brunei (PPKB—Brunei National Solidarity Party), in February 1986. This party, which also received the Sultan's official approval, placed greater emphasis on co-operation with the Government, and was open to both Muslim and non-Muslim ethnic groups.

During 1985–86 a more progressive style of government was adopted. The death of Sir Omar Ali Saifuddin, the Sultan's father, in September 1986 was expected to accelerate modernization. In October the cabinet was enlarged to 11 members, and commoners and aristocrats were assigned portfolios that had previously been held by members of the royal family. In February 1988, however, the PKDB was dissolved by the authorities after it had demanded the resignation of the Sultan as head of government (although not as head of state), an end to the 26-year state of emergency and the holding of democratic elections. The official reason for the dissolution of the party was its connections with a foreign organization, the Pacific Democratic Union. The leaders of the PKDB, Abdul Latif Hamid and Abdul Latif Chuchu, were arrested, under the provisions of the Internal Security Act, and detained until March 1990.

In 1990 the Government encouraged the population to embrace *Melayu Islam Beraja* (MIB—Malay Islamic Monarchy) as the state ideology. This affirmation of traditional Bruneian values for Malay Muslims was widely believed to be a response to an increase in social problems, including alcohol and narcotics abuse. Muslims were urged to adhere more closely to the tenets of Islam, greater emphasis was laid on Islamic holiday celebrations, and the distribution of alcohol was discouraged.

In 1994 a constitutional committee, appointed by the Government and chaired by the Minister of Foreign Affairs, Prince Mohamed Bolkiah, submitted a recommendation that the Constitution be amended to provide for an elected legislature. In February 1997, in the first major cabinet change for 10 years, the Sultan replaced his brother, Prince Jefri Bolkiah, as Minister of Finance. It was reported that the Sultan's assumption of the finance portfolio was due to alleged financial disagreements rather than Prince Jefri's frequently criticized profligate lifestyle (including allegations of misconduct with a number of foreign women and of large-scale financial malpractice).

On 10 August 1998 the Sultan's son, Prince Haji Al-Muhtadee Billah Bolkiah, was installed as the heir to the throne. Meanwhile, Prince Jefri, who had left Brunei in April, was removed as Chairman of the Brunei Investment Agency (BIA) in July, following the collapse of his business conglomerate, the Amedeo Development Corporation. (Amedeo was formally liquidated in 1999, with reported debts of at least US $3,500m.) Prince Jefri, who was also removed from the boards of seven telecommunications companies, claimed that he was the victim of a conspiracy of conservative Islamists, led by his estranged brother, Prince Mohamed Bolkiah (the Minister of Foreign Affairs), and the Minister of Education, Pehin Dato' Haji Abdul Aziz bin Pehin

Haji Umar. Prince Jefri's removal from positions of authority took place amid a more rigorous enforcement of the ban on alcohol and the confiscation from retailers of non-Islamic religious artefacts. In September 1998 Abdul Aziz, who had replaced Prince Jefri as Chairman of the BIA, announced that large amounts of government funds had been misappropriated during Prince Jefri's tenure. Prince Jefri returned to Brunei from his self-imposed exile in January 2000. In the following month the Government and the BIA began civil proceedings against him, alleging his improper withdrawal and use of substantial BIA funds while Minister of Finance and Chairman of the BIA (it was estimated that more than US $28,000m. had been misappropriated); 71 other people were named in the action, including Prince Jefri's eldest son, Prince Muda Abdul Hakeem. In May an out-of-court settlement was reached whereby the assets that had been acquired by Prince Jefri with funds derived from the BIA were to be returned to the state. Some of these assets were sold, for £5.5m., at a public auction in August 2001.

In 2000 a new political party, Parti Kesedaran Rakyat (PAKAR—People's Consciousness Party), was established. PAKAR outwardly pledged its support to the Sultan and the system of governance, but was critical of administrative deficiencies. In October of that year Haji Awang Kassim, Prince Jefri's former confidential secretary, who was also former deputy managing director of the BIA and a prominent figure in Amedeo management, was arrested, following his extradition from the Philippines. Civil proceedings were also instigated against another six of Prince Jefri's former colleagues. In October 2001 the Sultan requested his newly created local company, Global Evergreen, to resolve the long-standing dispute over responsibility for Amedeo's huge losses, with more than 300 creditors owed an estimated combined total of B $1,000m. Negotiations proceeded swiftly, and creditors were strongly recommended to accept a new, highly favourable offer whereby they would be repaid on a 'sliding scale' according to the magnitude of their claim against Amedeo. The settlement brought to an end much of the legal contention arising from the closure of the company.

Reconvening of the Legislative Council

In September 2004 the 21-member Legislative Council, suspended in 1983 prior to Brunei's declaration of independence and formally disbanded in 1984 (the relevant constitutional provision having been in abeyance since the revolt of 1962), was reconvened and approved a series of constitutional amendments. These envisaged, *inter alia*, the direct election—by a governmental committee—of 15 members of an expanded Legislative Council of up to 45 members; the remaining members would be appointed by the Sultan. However, no schedule was established for the holding of elections, nor was there any reference to the lifting of the national state of emergency that had been in place since 1962.

In May 2005 the Sultan effected a major cabinet reorganization, in which four prominent ministers were dismissed, including the Minister of Home Affairs and Special Adviser to the Prime Minister, Pehin Dato' Haji Isa Ibrahim, and the Minister of Education, Pehin Dato' Haji Abdul Aziz. Crown Prince Haji Al-Muhtadee Billah Bolkiah was appointed to the newly formed position of Senior Minister at the Prime Minister's Office. The changes also included the creation of a new Ministry of Energy and the appointment of the first ethnic Chinese official within the Bruneian cabinet, Pehin Dato' Lim Jock Seng, who was installed as the Minister of Foreign Affairs II. Furthermore, the Sultan appointed 10 new Deputy Ministers, including two from the corporate sector. The Ministry of Foreign Affairs was renamed the Ministry of Foreign Affairs and Trade in August.

In September 2005 the Sultan dissolved the incumbent Legislative Council and appointed 29 new members. The enlargement of the Council received widespread approval, but by early 2014 there was still no indication of a date for the holding of elections. In March 2006 the Legislative Council held a six-day session principally for the purpose of approving the National Budget. The Council convened in March each year thereafter. In May the Government announced that state laws governing the granting of citizenship to foreign nationals resident in Brunei were to be relaxed. Henceforth, any foreign male national married to a Bruneian woman for 15 years, if he had been born in Brunei (or for 20 years if born outside Brunei), could apply for permanent citizenship. Furthermore, foreign nationals possessing professional skills of direct benefit to the country and those contributing to Brunei's economic growth and commanding assets and/or investments worth in excess of B $500,000 would also be eligible. However, all applicants would still be required to demonstrate both written and oral proficiency in Malay and be expected to possess a comprehensive understanding of Bruneian culture.

Recent developments

In August 2006 the number of legal political organizations in Brunei was increased to three upon the official recognition of the Parti Pembangunan Bangsa (PPB, National Development Party). Founded by the former Secretary-General of the PRB, Muhammad Yasin Affendy bin Abdul Rahman, the deeply conservative PPB—the stated goal of which was to support the Government by promoting adherence to the values of MIB—held its first congress in April 2006. However, in 2007 both the PPKB and PAKAR were deregistered—PAKAR in March, as a result of the internal leadership disputes that had resulted in the party splitting into two opposing factions, and the PPKB in November, following its failure to supply annual reports to the relevant authority. The PPKB's subsequent appeal against its deregistration was rejected in February 2008 by the Minister of Home Affairs, thereby confirming the dissolution and consolidating the PPB's status as the only active party within the country. The PPB's fifth party congress was held in June 2010, but the party remained largely ineffectual. Owing to ill health, Yasin Affendy resigned as the PPB's President in February 2011, and was subsequently replaced by the party's deputy leader, Mahmud Morshidi Othman.

Meanwhile, in 2004 the BIA had initiated further legal proceedings against Prince Jefri, alleging that he had failed to relinquish ownership of properties in Europe and the USA as prescribed by the out-of-court settlement of 2000. Prince Jefri disputed the legitimacy of the BIA's actions, and the case was referred to the Privy Council in London, United Kingdom, where the Prince now resided. In November 2007 the Privy Council, which remained Brunei's highest court of appeal, dismissed Prince Jefri's defence as 'hopeless' and ruled that he return assets valued at more than US $1,000m. Citing Prince Jefri's continued failure to honour the court ruling, the Sultanate referred the case to the High Court of England and obtained an order compelling Prince Jefri to attend a hearing for contempt of court in June 2008. When Prince Jefri failed to appear at the proceedings, the presiding judge issued a warrant for his arrest. Prince Jefri returned to Brunei in October 2009, whereupon he visited the Sultan, prompting speculation that relations between the two brothers might have improved and that the ongoing legal dispute might soon be resolved. Photographs published in local media during 2010–11 of the Prince in the company of the Sultan and other senior members of the royal family suggested that a reconciliation between the brothers had been achieved; over the following two years the Prince's rehabilitation within royal circles appeared to be complete.

In various *titah* (royal addresses) in the second half of the 2000s, the Sultan repeatedly stressed the need to revive the religious education system, insisting that emphasis be given to the teaching of Islamic religious knowledge in schools. In August 2007 the Sultanate's first Islamic university, Universiti Islam Sultan Sharif Ali (UNISSA), welcomed its first intake of students. In August 2009 Datin Hayati Salleh was appointed to the position of Attorney-General, a role that had been conferred with ministerial status in 2005, thus becoming the first woman to attain full cabinet rank in Brunei (although Princess Hajah Masna, Brunei's ambassador-at-large, had frequently served as Minister of Foreign Affairs in an acting capacity).

A major cabinet reorganization was implemented in May 2010. Significant ministerial promotions included that of Pehin Dato' Paduka Haji Badaruddin bin Haji Othman as the new Minister of Home Affairs and of Pehin Dato' Haji Col (retd) Mohammad Yasmin bin Haji Umar as Minister of Energy at the Prime Minister's Office. Pengiran Dato' Dr Haji Mohammad bin Haji Abdul Rahman was appointed Minister of Religious Affairs, in place of Pehin Zain Serudin, who left the Council of Cabinet Ministers after 24 years' service. Another notable departure was that of Minister of Education Pehin Abdul Rahman Taib, a cabinet minister since independence in 1984. Datin Adina Othman, a high-ranking civil servant, was appointed Deputy Minister of Culture, Youth and Sports, thereby becoming the second woman to attain full ministerial status in Brunei (after Attorney-General Salleh).

In July 2010 the Sultan announced the establishment of the Autoriti Monetari Brunei Darussalam (AMBD), which was to be responsible for overseeing monetary policy, supervising financial institutions and currency management (in effect, performing the role of a central bank). Crown Prince Al-Muhtadee Bolkiah was appointed Chairman of the AMBD, which was formally inaugurated on 1 January 2011; the Prince retained the post of Senior Minister at the Prime Minister's Office.

Pengiran Anak Kemaludin, the elderly uncle of the Sultan, resigned as Speaker of the Legislative Council in February 2011 and was replaced by Pehin Dato' Haji Isa Ibrahim, the former Minister of Home Affairs and Special Adviser to the Prime Minister. In mid-March the Legislative Council was dissolved and a new membership (again, totally nominated) was announced in June; among the Council's new members were two women. The country's sole political party, the PPB, was not represented in the Legislative Council. Meanwhile, in March the Sultan decreed that, following the undermining of Islamic jurisprudence by British intervention during the colonial era, Bruneian law must henceforth be more closely aligned with Syariah (*Shari'a*—Islamic) law, which had constituted the main body of law in Brunei prior to the implementation of British civil law. A working committee was subsequently established to ensure that criminal justice was restructured according to the requirements of Islamic teachings, and any discrepancies between existing civil legislation and Syariah law were to be eliminated. In April the Sultan appointed Princes Abdul Azim, Abdul Malik and Abdul Mateen to the Privy Council, appearing to indicate the potential emergence of a new generation of Bruneian leaders.

During 2012–13 the profile of Islam in Brunei was considerably strengthened by a series of official measures. In October 2012 the Sultan ordered that all businesses be closed during Friday prayers and from January 2013 the undertaking of religious education for a period of seven years was made compulsory for all Muslim children. In addition, in October the Sultan announced that the long-considered Syariah Criminal Penal Code Order was finally to be implemented (in stages) in Brunei in 2014; however, civil law would continue to be used when appropriate. Human rights activists feared that the implementation of the stringent new code, which was to be applied only to Muslim nationals, would involve draconian punishments such as flogging, stoning and limb amputation. To date, the country's Syariah courts had handled civil cases regarding primarily family-related matters, including marriage and inheritance.

Foreign Affairs

Regional relations

Brunei has developed close relations with its fellow members of the Association of Southeast Asian Nations (ASEAN, see p. 211), in particular Singapore, with which it has concluded numerous bilateral agreements covering a wide range of areas. Some members of the Singapore Armed Forces, including national servicemen, continue to undergo their training in the jungles of Temburong in eastern Brunei.

Conflicting claims (from Brunei, the People's Republic of China, Malaysia, the Philippines, Taiwan and Viet Nam) to all, or some, of the uninhabited Spratly Islands, situated in the South China Sea, have proved a source of tension in the region. Brunei is the only claimant not to have stationed troops on the islands, which are not only strategically important but also possess potentially large reserves of petroleum and natural gas. During the 1990s attempts to resolve the dispute through a negotiated settlement resulted in little progress, and military activity in the area increased. However, during the annual ASEAN summit meeting held in Cambodia in November 2002, the members of the grouping signed an agreement with China approving a 'code of conduct' for the islands. Following the ASEAN summit meeting held in Viet Nam in October 2010, it was announced that China and the ASEAN member states had agreed to adopt a more legally binding code of conduct for the islands, which it was hoped would reduce political and security instability in the area and strengthen regional co-operation. An agreement on guidelines for the establishment of such a code of conduct was signed in July 2011, following talks, held in Bali, Indonesia, between ASEAN ministers responsible for foreign affairs and Chinese foreign officials; at January 2014, however, despite heightened tensions in the South China Sea, no legally binding code of conduct had been drawn up.

Protracted land and maritime border disputes between Brunei and Malaysia were deemed by the Governments of both countries to have been concluded by the signing of an Exchange of Letters in March 2009 by the Sultan and Malaysian Prime Minister Abdullah Badawi. As well as the final settlement of the maritime border between Brunei and Malaysia, the agreement also provided for, *inter alia*, the establishment of a joint petroleum/gas revenue area and the eventual joint demarcation of the common land border. Relations with Malaysia were further boosted by the signing, in October 2010, of a Memorandum of Understanding (MOU) intended to bolster co-operation in higher education and, in December of that year, of a bilateral agreement providing for the joint development of two petroleum blocks off the coast of Borneo. The completion in December 2013 of a 'friendship bridge' across the Pandaruan River, providing a road link between Temburong (Brunei) and Limbang (Sarawak), was expected to facilitate greater trade and tourism between the two countries.

At the end of the seventh summit meeting of ASEAN leaders, hosted by Brunei in November 2001, the Sultanate pledged its support for a programme proposed by Philippine President Gloria Macapagal Arroyo, which sought to encourage close regional cooperation in countering international terrorism in the aftermath of the September suicide attacks on the USA; the ASEAN leaders thereupon signed a Declaration on Counter-Terrorism with the USA. In January 2010 the Sultanate hosted an ASEAN Tourism Forum summit meeting. In November 2011 the seventh ASEAN Ministerial Meeting on Rural Development and Poverty Eradication was hosted by Brunei, and in April 2012 the Sultanate played host to the 19th ASEAN-European Union (EU) Ministerial Meeting (since 2009 Brunei had been responsible for co-ordinating ASEAN's relations with the EU); during the meeting it was announced that the EU and Brunei were to launch negotiations on a bilateral Partnership and Cooperation Agreement. Brunei resumed the annually rotating chair of ASEAN in 2013. In this capacity, Brunei hosted the East Asia Summit (EAS) in October of that year; EAS members include the 10 ASEAN countries, as well as Australia, China, India, Japan, New Zealand, Russia, the Republic of Korea (South Korea) and the USA, which joined the leadership forum in 2011 as part of its new focus on the Asia-Pacific region.

Relations with China, with which full diplomatic relations were established in 1991, have strengthened in recent years. In September 2004, during an official visit to the People's Republic, the Sultan and Chinese President Hu Jintao signed a number of MOUs intended to increase co-operation in areas such as trade and investment, education and judicial affairs. During a reciprocal visit to Brunei by President Hu in April 2005, several more bilateral agreements were signed, under the terms of which the need for diplomatic and official visas for travel between the two countries was waived; other areas of focus included energy, public health, tourism and military training. During a visit to Bandar Seri Begawan by Chinese Premier Wen Jiabao in November 2011, Wen asserted that continuing Chinese-Bruneian co-operation had engendered tangible benefits to both countries and had helped to promote regional stability and prosperity—a view reiterated by the new Chinese Premier, Li Keqiang, when he visited Brunei in October 2013. In April of that year Sultan Hassanal was the first foreign leader to be received by the newly elected Chinese President, Xi Jinping. During the Sultan's state visit to China, Brunei National Petroleum Co and the China National Offshore Oil Corpn signed an agreement relating to joint exploration of maritime oil and gas resources.

Japan remains a major market for Bruneian exports, and in July 2007 the Sultan and Japanese Prime Minister Shinzo Abe signed a free trade agreement—the Brunei-Japan Economic Partnership Agreement—in the Japanese capital, Tokyo. Bilateral relations were further consolidated during a meeting between the Sultan and Japanese Emperor Akihito in Tokyo in November 2010. In June 2013 the Japanese Chief of the Joint Staff, Gen. Shigeru Iwasaki, visited Brunei with the aim of promoting military co-operation between the two countries. Meanwhile, in April 2009 Brunei and the Philippines signed an MOU that was intended to increase bilateral co-operation in a number of areas, including agriculture and farming-related trade and investment; a further MOU, pertaining to the field of information and communications technology, was signed between the two countries in July 2010.

Other external relations

Relations with the United Kingdom became strained during 1983, following the Brunei Government's decision, in August, to transfer the management of its investment portfolio from the British Crown Agents to the newly created BIA. However, normal relations were restored in September, when the British Government agreed that a battalion of Gurkha troops, stationed in Brunei since 1971, should remain in the country after independence, at the Sultanate's expense, specifically to guard the oil- and gasfields. In June 2009 it was agreed that the battalion would continue to be stationed in the Sultanate for a further five years from September.

In July 1990, in response to the uncertainty over the future of US bases in the Philippines, Brunei offered the USA the option of operating its forces from Brunei. A bilateral MOU was subsequently signed, providing for up to three visits a year to Brunei by US warships. Under the terms of the memorandum, Bruneian and US armed forces engage in regular joint military exercises and training programmes. Senior-level state visits to the USA in recent years have included those of the Sultan to Washington, DC, in December 2002 and to New York in November 2008 and that of the Crown Prince to Washington, DC, and New York in September 2011, during which he addressed the UN General Assembly. Meanwhile, bilateral tension was provoked in June 2010 by the inclusion of Brunei on the USA's Trafficking in Persons Report, an annual document containing a list of countries perceived by the US Administration to be a significant destination for forced labour and prostitution. None the less, the meeting between the Sultan and US President Barack Obama in Washington DC, USA, in March 2013—following a two-day visit by US Secretary of State Hillary Clinton to Bandar Seri Begawan in September 2012—was considered a notable diplomatic success.

Since 2010 Brunei has participated in negotiations regarding the proposed establishment of a new free trade agreement—the Trans-Pacific Partnership. At early 2014 the 11 other countries involved in the negotiating process (which notably did not include China) were the USA, Australia, Chile, Canada, Japan, Malaysia, Mexico, New Zealand, Peru, Singapore and Viet Nam.

Diplomatic relations were established with numerous countries in 2005–12, the most recent being Djibouti in November 2012. Meanwhile, Brunei's relations with other Islamic nations continued to develop; in April 2006 the Sultan made his first state visits to Qatar and the United Arab Emirates, and in April 2009 he made official visits to Kuwait and Oman. In October 2011 the Sultan revisited Kuwait in order to attend the 10th Ministerial Meeting of the Asia Cooperation Dialogue—established in 2002 to promote Asian co-operation at a continental level and to help to integrate separate regional organizations such as ASEAN, the Gulf Cooperation Council and the South Asian Association for Regional Cooperation.

During a visit to Russia in October 2009, the Sultan met with Prime Minister Vladimir Putin and President Dmitrii Medvedev, signing several bilateral agreements intended to improve co-operation in the areas of defence, the economy, education and tourism. The Russian embassy in Brunei was formally opened in April 2010. In September 2012, prior to attending the annual Leaders' Meeting of the Asia-Pacific Economic Co-operation (APEC) forum in Vladivostok, Russia, the Sultan and President Putin (who had succeeded Medvedev as Russian head of state in May) expressed their commitment to furthering co-operation between the two countries, particularly in the fields of energy and defence.

CONSTITUTION AND GOVERNMENT

The 1959 Constitution confers supreme executive authority on the Sultan. He is assisted and advised by four Constitutional Councils: the Religious Council, the Privy Council, the Council of Cabinet Ministers and the Council of Succession. Following the rebellion of 1962, certain provisions of the Constitution (including those pertaining to elections and to a fifth Council, the Legislative Council) were suspended, and the Sultan has since ruled by decree. However, in September 2004 the 21-member Legislative Council was convened for the first time since the country became independent in 1984 and approved several constitutional amendments, including one providing for the direct election of 15 members of an expanded 45-member Legislative Council. The remaining members were to be appointed by the Sultan. In June 2011 the Sultan appointed a new, enlarged Legislative Council comprising 33 full members and three ex officio members. At early 2014 no schedule had been established for the holding of the elections.

REGIONAL AND INTERNATIONAL CO-OPERATION

Brunei is a member of the Association of Southeast Asian Nations (ASEAN, see p. 211), of the Asia-Pacific Economic Co-operation (APEC, see p. 201) forum, of the Asian Development Bank (ADB, see p. 207), and of the UN's Economic and Social Commission for Asia and the Pacific (ESCAP, see p. 28).

Brunei became a member of the UN in 1984, and was admitted to the World Trade Organization (WTO) in 1995. In 2007 Brunei was admitted to the International Labour Organization (ILO, see p. 137). Brunei is also a member of the Organization of the Islamic Conference (OIC, see p. 403) and of the Non-aligned Movement (see p. 467).

ECONOMIC AFFAIRS

In 2009, according to estimates by the World Bank, Brunei's gross national income (GNI), measured at average 2007–09 prices, was US $12,460m., equivalent to US $31,800 per head (or US $49,790 on an international purchasing-power parity basis). In 2003–12, it was estimated, the population increased by an average of 1.7% per year. Gross domestic product (GDP) per head, in real terms, decreased at an average annual rate of 0.8% over the same period. According to the World Bank, Brunei's overall GDP increased at an estimated average annual rate of 0.9% during 2003–12. According to the Asian Development Bank (ADB), real GDP expanded by 0.9% in 2012, but declined by 1.4% in 2013.

Agriculture (including forestry and fishing) employed just over 0.5% of the working population in 2011, according to FAO estimates, and provided 0.7% of GDP in 2012. The principal crops include rice, cassava, bananas and pineapples. According to the World Bank, in 2003–12 the GDP of the agricultural sector increased, in real terms, at an estimated average annual rate of 1.9%. According to the ADB, agricultural GDP grew by 4.6% in 2011 and by 11.8% in 2012.

Industry (comprising mining, manufacturing, construction and utilities) employed 21.4% of the working population, according to the results of the 2001 census, and contributed 71.1% of GDP in 2012. According to figures from the World Bank, total industrial GDP decreased at an average annual rate of 1.4% in 2003–12. According to the ADB, industrial GDP increased by 3.2% in 2011, but decreased by 1.8% in 2012.

Brunei's economy has continued to rely almost entirely on its petroleum and natural gas resources. However, according to the 2001 census, mining and quarrying employed only 2.7% of the working population. The contribution to GDP of the sector increased from 50.8% in 2010 to 55.7% in 2012. Proven reserves of petroleum at the end of 2012 amounted to 1,100m. barrels, sufficient to sustain production at that year's levels (averaging 166,000 barrels per day) for almost 19 years. Output of natural gas in 2012 totalled an estimated 12,600m. cu m. According to industry sources, proven reserves at the end of that year totalled 288,000m. cu m (a level sustainable for nearly 23 years). In 2012, according to official figures, exports of petroleum and gas accounted for 95.7% of total exports. According to figures from the ADB, the GDP of the mining sector decreased by an average of 2.2% per year in 2003–12, expanding by 3.1% in 2011, before declining by 3.6% in 2012. Commercial operations at Brunei's inaugural petrochemical plant, a methanol production facility at the Sungai Liang Industrial Park in Belait district, commenced in 2010.

The manufacturing sector employed 8.5% of the working population, according to the 2001 census, and contributed 11.8% of GDP in 2012. The textile and garment industry provides modest revenue; other industries include cement, mineral water, canned food, dairy products, silica sands products, footwear and leather products, the design and manufacture of printed circuits, publishing and printing. According to ADB figures, during 2003–12 manufacturing GDP declined at an average annual rate of 0.8%; sectoral GDP increased by 3.4% in 2011 and by 0.7% in 2012.

Construction employed 8.4% of the working population, according to the 2001 census, and contributed 2.9% of GDP in 2012. According to figures from the ADB, the GDP of the sector increased at an average annual rate of 2.9% during 2003–12; sectoral GDP grew by 4.0% in 2012.

Services employed 77.2% of the working population, according to the 2001 census, and provided 28.2% of GDP in 2012. In addition to efforts to develop Brunei as a financial centre, the tourism sector has also been actively promoted, and in 2009 receipts from tourism totalled US $254m. In 2012, according to official figures, a total of 209,108 tourists visited Brunei. During 2003–12, according to the World Bank, the combined GDP of the service sectors increased, in real terms, at an average annual rate of 4.3%. The GDP of the services sector expanded by 3.7% in 2011 and 3.8% in 2012.

In 2013, according to the ADB, Brunei recorded a visible merchandise trade surplus of US $7,823m. ($9,410m. in 2012), predominantly attributable to receipts from petroleum exports. In the same year there was a surplus equivalent to 43.0% of GDP

(47.0% in 2012)on the current account of the balance of payments. In 2012 the principal source of imports (providing 23.5% of the total) was Singapore; other major suppliers were Malaysia (15.4%), the People's Republic of China, the USA, Japan and Thailand. In that year the principal market for exports was Japan, which accounted for 45.2% of total exports (mainly natural gas on a long-term contract); other significant purchasers were the Republic of Korea (also a purchaser of natural gas), India, and Australia. In 2012 the principal imports comprised machinery and transport equipment, basic manufactures, food and live animals, miscellaneous manufactured articles and chemicals; the principal exports were crude petroleum and liquefied natural gas.

For the fiscal year ending March 2013, according to the ADB, there was an overall budgetary surplus of B $388m., equivalent to 1.8% of GDP. Brunei has no external public debt. Annual inflation averaged 1.0% in 2003–12. According to the ADB, consumer prices increased by 0.1% in 2012 and by 0.4% in 2013. Foreign workers, principally from Malaysia and the Philippines, have helped to ease the labour shortage arising from the small size of the population, and comprised about 41% of the labour force in 2000. However, the rate of unemployment was 1.1% in 2012, according to the ADB., reflecting a shortage of non-manual jobs for well-educated Bruneians.

Largely as a result of the global economic slowdown and a weakening of international petroleum prices, GDP contracted by 1.9% in 2008 and by 1.8% in 2009. The economy recovered in 2010, when GDP increased by 2.6%. The rate of GDP growth rose to 3.4% in 2011, but declined to 0.9% in 2012, and GDP contracted by 1.4% in 2013, owing to lower production and exports of crude petroleum, partly as a result of scheduled infrastructure maintenance activities and the depletion of oil wells. The Government's 10th National Development Plan, encompassing the period 2012–17, focused on improving workforce capability and the quality of education, and on promoting research and development and the expansion of small and medium enterprises. Expenditure of B $6,500m. was allocated to the plan, which formed part of the Wawasan (National Vision) Brunei 2035, a long-term development strategy intended to improve per caput incomes and to diversify economic activities. In addition to expanding Islamic financial services, the Government planned to diversify into the petrochemicals sector. The Brunei Methanol Company (a joint venture between Bruneian and Japanese interests) commenced operations at the Sungai Liang Industrial Park (SPARK) in May 2010. Further downstream petrochemical plants were to be constructed at the SPARK as part of an integrated gas-based petrochemical complex. In December 2011 the Chinese firm Zhejiang Hengyi Group was awarded the development rights for an integrated oil refinery and aromatics cracker complex to be located at Pulau Muara Besar. Following completion of the first phase of the project, which was to include petroleum products, paraxylene and benzene, and which was expected to create more than 800 jobs (the majority of which were to be offered to local workers), the Chinese firm planned to expand the refinery to produce olefins, creating an additional 1,200 employment opportunities. Other infrastructural developments envisaged under the Plan, which were expected to boost future growth, included a port at Pulau Muara Besar, a high-speed broadband network and the construction of three new bridges. In addition, upgrade work on Brunei International Airport continued in 2014 with the aim of increasing the terminal's annual capacity to 3m. passengers by the end of the year. Meanwhile, following the establishment in January 2011 of the Autoriti Monetari Brunei Darussalam, which was to perform the functions of a central bank in helping to maintain fiscal stability, it was confirmed that the currency interchangeability agreement with Singapore (in force since 1967) was to remain in place. The arrangement helped mitigate inflationary pressures, as did the Government's continued subsidies on various consumer items; consumer prices increased by only 0.1% in 2012 and 0.4% in 2013, according to the ADB, although it forecast a moderate increase to 0.5% in 2014 and 0.6% in 2015.

PUBLIC HOLIDAYS

2015: 1 January (New Year's Day), 2 January*† (Hari Mouloud, Birth of the Prophet), 18 February‡ (Chinese New Year), 23 February (National Day), 15 May* (Israk Mikraj, Ascension of the Prophet Muhammad), 31 May (Royal Brunei Armed Forces Day), 17 June* (Beginning of Ramadan), 15 July (Sultan's Birthday), 16 July* (Memperingati Nuzul Al-Quran, Anniversary of the Revelation of the Koran), 17 July* (Hari Raya Aidilfitri, end of Ramadan), 23 September* (Hari Raya Aidiladha, Feast of the Sacrifice), 13 October* (Hijrah, Islamic New Year), 23 December*† (Hari Mouloud, Birth of the Prophet), 25 December (Christmas Day),

* These holidays are dependent on the Islamic lunar calendar and may vary by one or two days from the dates given.

† This holiday occurs twice in 2015.

‡ The first day of the first moon of the lunar calendar.

Statistical Survey

Sources (unless otherwise stated): Department of Economic Planning and Development, Prime Minister's Office, Block 2A, Jalan Ong Sum Ping, Bandar Seri Begawan BA 1311; tel. 2244433; fax 2230236; e-mail info@jpke.gov.bn; internet www.depd.gov.bn; Brunei Economic Development Board, Block 2K, Bangunan Kerajaan, Jalan Ong Sum Ping, Bandar Seri Begawan BA 1311; tel. 2230111; fax 2230063; e-mail info@bedb.com.bn; internet www.bedb.com.bn.

AREA AND POPULATION

Area: 5,765 sq km (2,226 sq miles); *By District:* Brunei/Muara 571 sq km (220 sq miles), Seria/Belait 2,724 sq km (1,051 sq miles), Tutong 1,166 sq km (450 sq miles), Temburong 1,304 sq km (503 sq miles).

Population (excluding transients afloat): 332,844 at census of 21 August 2001; 393,372 (males 203,149, females 190,223) at census of 20 June 2011. *2012* (official estimates at mid-year): 399,800 (males 206,700, females 193,100). *By District* (official estimates at mid-2012): Brunei/Muara 285,300; Seria/Belait 61,500; Tutong 44,100; Temburong 8,900; Total 399,800.

Density (at mid-2012): 69.3 per sq km.

Population by Age and Sex (UN estimates at mid-2014): *0–14:* 105,427 (males 54,094, females 51,333); *15–64:* 298,442 (males 150,844, females 147,598); *65 and over:* 19,338 (males 9,391, females 9,947); *Total* 423,207 (males 214,329, females 208,878) (Source: UN, *World Population Prospects: The 2012 Revision*). *Population by Age* ('000 persons at mid-2012, official estimates): *0–19:* 134.6; *20–64:* 250.5; *65 and over:* 14.7; *Total* 399.8. Note: UN estimates not adjusted to take account of results of 2011 census; totals may not be equal to the sum of components, owing to rounding.

Ethnic Groups (official estimates at mid-2012): Malay 262,800, Chinese 41,000, Others 96,000, Total 399,800.

Principal Towns: Bandar Seri Begawan (capital): population 27,285 at 2001 census; Kuala Belait: population 21,200 at 1991 census; Seria: population 21,100 at 1991 census; Tutong: population 13,000 at 1991 census. *Mid-2011* (incl. suburbs, UN estimate): Bandar Seri Begawan 16,381 (Source: UN, *World Urbanization Prospects: The 2011 Revision*).

Births, Marriages and Deaths (2012): Live births 6,909 (birth rate 17.3 per 1,000); Marriages 2,671 (marriage rate 6.7 per 1,000); Deaths 1,216 (death rate 3.0 per 1,000).

Life Expectancy (years at birth): 78.2 (males 76.3; females 80.1) in 2011. Source: World Bank, World Development Indicators database.

Economically Active Population (persons aged 15 years and over, 2001 census, provisional): Agriculture, hunting, forestry and fishing 1,994; Mining and quarrying 3,954; Manufacturing 12,455; Electricity, gas and water 2,639; Construction 12,301; Trade, restaurants and hotels 20,038; Transport, storage and communications 4,803; Financing, insurance, real estate and business services 8,190; Community, social and personal services 79,880; *Total employed* 146,254 (males 85,820, females 60,434); Unemployed 11,340 (males 6,734, females 4,606); *Total labour force* 157,594 (males 92,554, females 65,040). *2012:* Total employed 187,000; Unemployed 2,000; Total labour force 189,000. (Sources: Asian Development Bank).

HEALTH AND WELFARE

Key Indicators

Total Fertility Rate (children per woman, 2011): 2.0.

Under-5 Mortality Rate (per 1,000 live births, 2011): 7.

HIV/AIDS (% of persons aged 15–49, 2005): <0.1.

Physicians (per 1,000 head, 2010): 1.4.

Hospital Beds (per 1,000 head, 2009): 2.6.

Health Expenditure (2010): US $ per head (PPP): 1,503.

Health Expenditure (2010): % of GDP: 2.9.

Health Expenditure (2010): public (% of total): 85.4.

Total Carbon Dioxide Emissions ('000 metric tons, 2010): 9,160.2.

Carbon Dioxide Emissions Per Head (metric tons, 2010): 22.9.

Human Development Index (2012): ranking: 30.

Human Development Index (2012): value: 0.855.

For sources and definitions, see explanatory note on p. vi.

AGRICULTURE, ETC.

Principal Crops ('000 metric tons, 2012): Rice, paddy 1.2 (FAO estimate). *Aggregate Production* ('000 metric tons, may include official, semi-official or estimated data): Total vegetables (incl. melons) 12.4; Total fruits (excl. melons) 6.5.

Livestock ('000 head, 2012, FAO estimates): Cattle 0.9; Buffaloes 4.2; Sheep 4.0; Goats 7.2; Pigs 1.3; Chickens 15,500.

Livestock Products ('000 metric tons, 2012, FAO estimates): Cattle meat 0.6; Chicken meat 19.4; Hen eggs 7.1.

Forestry ('000 cubic metres, 2012, FAO estimates): *Roundwood Removals:* Sawlogs, veneer logs and logs for sleepers 96.3; Other industrial roundwood 11.0; Fuel wood 11.7; Total 119.0. *Sawnwood Production:* Total (all broad-leaved) 50.9.

Fishing (metric tons, live weight, 2011, FAO estimates): Capture 2,100; Aquaculture 530 (Blue Shrimp 320); *Total catch* 2,630.

Source: FAO.

MINING

Production (2011): Crude petroleum ('000 barrels, incl. condensate) 59,400; Natural gas (million cu m, gross) 12,300. Source: US Geological Survey.

INDUSTRY

Production ('000 metric tons, 2010, unless otherwise indicated): Motor spirit (petrol) 197; Distillate fuel oils 173 (2009); Residual fuel oil 91; Cement 275 (estimate) (2011); Electric energy (million kWh) 3,929 (2012). Sources: mainly UN Industrial Commodity Statistics Database; and US Geological Survey.

FINANCE

Currency and Exchange Rates: 100 sen (cents) = 1 Brunei dollar (B $). *Sterling, US Dollar and Euro Equivalents* (31 December 2013): £1 sterling = B $2.090; US $1 = B $1.269; €1 = B $1.750; B $100 = £47.84 = US $78.78 = €57.13. *Average Exchange Rate* (Brunei dollars per US $): 1.2579 in 2011; 1.2496 in 2012; 1.2512 in 2013. Note: The Brunei dollar is at par with the Singapore dollar.

Budget (B $ million, year ending 31 March 2013): *Revenue:* Oil and gas revenue 5,521; Revenues from government operations 757 (Taxes 398, Fees, charges and rent 323, Others 36); Returns from investment and savings 10; Total 6,288. *Expenditure:* Current expenditure 4,327 (Wages and salaries 1,940, Other annual recurrent charges 1,718, Charged expenditure 669); Capital expenditure 1,573 (Special expenditure charges 523, Development expenditure 1,050); Total 5,900. Source: IMF, *Brunei Darussalam: Statistical Appendix* (June 2013).

International Reserves (excl. gold, US $ million at 31 December 2012): IMF special drawing rights 332.71; Reserve position in IMF 21.01; Foreign exchange 2,931.59; Total 3,285.31. Source: IMF, *International Financial Statistics*.

Money Supply (B $ million at 31 December 2012): Currency outside depository corporations 926.0; Transferable deposits 3,367.4; Other deposits 9,668.2; Securities other than shares 0.0; *Broad money* 13,961.6. Source: IMF, *International Financial Statistics*.

Cost of Living (Consumer Price Index; base: 2005 = 100): All items 104.8 in 2010; 106.9 in 2011; 107.4 in 2012.

Gross Domestic Product (B $ million at constant 2000 prices): 11,846.5 in 2010; 12,252.8 in 2011; 12,369.0 in 2012.

Expenditure on the Gross Domestic Product (B $ million in current prices, 2012, preliminary): Government final consumption expenditure 3,659.4; Private consumption expenditure 4,333.2; Gross capital formation 2,880.6; *Total domestic expenditure* 10,873.2; Exports of goods and services 17,237.3; *Less* Imports of goods and services 6,605.4; Statistical discrepancy –319.9; *GDP in purchasers' values* 21,185.1.

Gross Domestic Product by Economic Activity (B $ million in current prices, 2012, preliminary): Agriculture, hunting, forestry and fishing 151.5; Mining and quarrying 11,803.6; Manufacturing 2,498.4; Electricity, gas and water 141.7; Construction 614.6; Wholesale and retail trade 704.2; Transport and communications 682.3; Finance 585.1; Public administration 2,479.6; Others 1,524.1; *GDP in purchasers' values* 21,185.1.

Balance of Payments (US $ million, 2011): Exports of goods 9,042; Imports of goods –2,079; *Trade balance* 6,963; Exports of services 1,091; Imports of services –1,892; *Balance on goods and services* 6,162; Other income received 1,185; Other income paid –1,506; *Balance on goods, services and income* 5,842; Current transfers (net) –548; *Current balance* 5,294; Capital account (net) –11; Direct investment (net) 393; Portfolio investment (net) 165; Other investment assets 113; Net errors and omissions –5,031; *Overall balance* 924. Source: IMF, *Brunei Darussalam: Statistical Appendix* (June 2013).

EXTERNAL TRADE

Principal Commodities (B $ million, 2012): *Imports c.i.f.:* Food and live animals 549.2; Chemicals 301.9; Basic manufactures 1,001.2; Machinery and transport equipment 1,292.5; Miscellaneous manufactured articles 664.1; Total (incl. others) 4,461.9. *Exports f.o.b.:* Crude petroleum 7,824.4; Liquefied natural gas 7,706.1; Methanol 303.4; Total (incl. others) 16,220.7 (incl. re-exports 374.2).

Principal Trading Partners (B $ million, 2012): *Imports:* China, People's Republic 508.0; Germany 123.5; Japan 334.8; Korea, Republic 169.2; Malaysia 686.4; Singapore 1,048.5; Thailand 260.4; United Kingdom 115.9; USA 348.2; Total (incl. others) 4,461.9. *Exports:* Australia 1205.4; China, People's Republic 432.8; India 1,444.0; Indonesia 571.9; Japan 7,158.5; Korea, Republic 2,550.5; Malaysia 17.4; New Zealand 823.1; Singapore 588.0; Thailand 588.0; Viet Nam 738.1; Total (incl. others) 15,840.5 (incl. re-exports 374.2).

TRANSPORT

Road Traffic (registered vehicles at 31 December 2008): Passenger cars 190,393; Lorries and vans 8,071; Buses 1,476; Motorcycles and mopeds 3,470. Source: IRF, *World Road Statistics*.

Flag Registered Fleet (at 31 December 2013): Number of vessels 80; Total displacement (grt) 542,238. Source: Lloyd's List Intelligence (www.lloydslistintelligence.com).

International Sea-borne Shipping (freight traffic, '000 freight tons, 2012): Goods loaded 21.8; Goods unloaded 1,189.7. Note: One freight ton equals 40 cu ft (1.133 cu m) of cargo.

Civil Aviation (2011): Kilometres flown (million) 30; Passengers carried ('000) 1,313; Passenger-km (million) 4,988; Total ton-km (million) 600. *Passengers Carried* ('000): 1,063.6 in 2012. Sources: mainly UN, *Statistical Yearbook* and World Bank, World Development Indicators database.

TOURISM

Foreign Visitor Arrivals by Nationality (tourist arrivals at national borders, 2011): Australia 18,845; China, People's Republic 32,853; Indonesia 20,350; Japan 4,140; Malaysia 61,470; New Zealand 10,381; Philippines 17,446; Singapore 16,221; Thailand 4,809; United Kingdom 18,222; USA 4,200; Total (incl. others) 242,061.

Tourism Receipts (US $ million, excl. passenger transport): 233 in 2007; 241 in 2008; 254 in 2009.

Source: World Tourism Organization.

COMMUNICATIONS MEDIA

Telephones (2012): 70,933 main lines in use.

Mobile Cellular Telephones ('000 subscribers, 2012): 469.7.

Internet Subscribers ('000, 2011): 27.4.

Broadband Subscribers ('000, 2012): 19.8.

Source: International Telecommunication Union.

EDUCATION

Pre-primary and Primary (2012): 200 schools (incl. some schools also offering secondary education), 4,946 teachers and 55,848 pupils.

General Secondary (2012): 40 schools (excl. schools offering primary education also), 4,655 teachers and 40,025 pupils.

Nursing/Technical/Vocational (2012): 12 colleges, 606 teachers and 6,267 students.

Teacher Training (2008): 1 college, 37 teachers and 437 students.

Higher Education (2012): 7 institutes; 709 teachers and 9,092 students.

Pupil-teacher Ratio (primary education, UNESCO estimate): 10.6 in 2011/12. Source: UNESCO Institute for Statistics.

Adult Literacy Rate (UNESCO estimates): 95.4% (males 97.0%; females 93.9%) in 2011. Source: UNESCO Institute for Statistics.

Directory

The Government

HEAD OF STATE

Sultan and Yang Di-Pertuan: HM Sultan Haji HASSANAL BOLKIAH (succeeded 5 October 1967; crowned 1 August 1968).

COUNCIL OF CABINET MINISTERS

(April 2014)

Prime Minister, Minister of Defence and of Finance: HM Sultan Haji HASSANAL BOLKIAH.

Senior Minister at the Prime Minister's Office: HRH Prince Haji AL-MUHTADEE BILLAH BOLKIAH.

Minister of Energy at the Prime Minister's Office: Pehin Dato' Haji Col (retd) MOHAMMAD YASMIN BIN Haji UMAR.

Minister of Foreign Affairs and Trade: HRH Prince Haji MOHAMED BOLKIAH.

Minister of Home Affairs: Pehin Dato' Paduka Haji BADARUDDIN BIN Haji OTHMAN.

Minister of Education: Pehin Dato' Seri Haji ABU BAKAR BIN Haji APONG.

Minister of Industry and Primary Resources: Pehin Dato' Paduka Haji YAHYA BIN Haji BAKAR.

Minister of Religious Affairs: Pengiran Dato' Dr Haji MOHAMMAD BIN Haji ABDUL RAHMAN.

Minister of Development: Pehin Dato' Seri Haji SUYOI BIN Haji OSMAN.

Minister of Health: Pehin Dato' Seri Haji ADANAN BIN Pehin Dato' Haji MOHAMMAD YUSOF.

Minister of Culture, Youth and Sports: Pehin Dato' Haji HAZAIR BIN Haji ABDULLAH.

Minister of Communications: Pehin Dato' Paduka Haji ABDULLAH BIN Haji BAKAR.

Minister of Finance II: Pehin Dato' Seri Haji ABDUL RAHMAN BIN Haji IBRAHIM.

Minister of Foreign Affairs and Trade II: Pehin Dato' Seri Paduka LIM JOCK SENG.

MINISTRIES

Prime Minister's Office (Jabatan Perdana Menteri): Jalan Kumbang Pasang, Bandar Seri Begawan BA 1311; tel. 2224645; fax 2233743; e-mail info@jpm.gov.bn; internet www.jpm.gov.bn.

Ministry of Communications (Kementerian Perhubungan): Jalan Menteri Besar, Bandar Seri Begawan BB 3910; tel. 2383838; fax 2380884; e-mail info.mincom@mincom.gov.bn; internet www.mincom.gov.bn.

Ministry of Culture, Youth and Sports (Kementerian Kebudayaan, Belia dan Sukan): Simpang 336-17, Jalan Kebangsaan, Bandar Seri Begawan BA 1210; tel. 2382911; fax 2380652; e-mail info@kkbs.gov.bn; internet www.kkbs.gov.bn.

Ministry of Defence (Kementerian Pertahanan): Bolkiah Garrison, Bandar Seri Begawan BB 3510; tel. 2386371; fax 2381934; e-mail pru@mindef.gov.bn; internet www.mindef.gov.bn.

Ministry of Development (Kementerian Pembangunan): Old Airport, Jalan Berakas, Bandar Seri Begawan BB 3510; tel. 2383222; fax 2380298; e-mail info@mod.gov.bn; internet www.mod.gov.bn.

Ministry of Education (Kementerian Pendidikan): Old Airport, Berakas, Bandar Seri Begawan BB 3510; tel. 2381133; fax 2380050; e-mail feedback@moe.gov.bn; internet www.moe.gov.bn.

Ministry of Energy: Office of the Prime Minister, Tingkat 5, Bahirah Bldg, Jalan Menteri Besar, Bandar Seri Begawan BB 3910; tel. 2384488; fax 2384444; e-mail energy@jpm.gov.bn; internet www.energy.gov.bn.

Ministry of Finance (Kementerian Kewangan): Tingkat 15, Bangunan Kementerian Kewangan, Commonwealth Dr., Jalan Kebangsaan, Bandar Seri Begawan BB 3910; tel. 2383950; fax 2226132; e-mail administration@mof.gov.bn; internet www.mof.gov.bn.

Ministry of Foreign Affairs and Trade (Kementerian Hal Ehwal Luar Negeri dan Perdagangan): Jalan Subok, Bandar Seri Begawan BD 2710; tel. 2261293; fax 2262904; e-mail info@mfa.gov.bn; internet www.mofat.gov.bn.

Ministry of Health (Kementerian Kesihatan): Jalan Menteri Besar, Commonwealth Dr., Bandar Seri Begawan BB 3910; tel. 2381640; fax 2381440; e-mail prohealth@moh.gov.bn; internet www.moh.gov.bn.

Ministry of Home Affairs (Kementerian Hal Ehwal Dalam Negeri): Jalan James Pearce, Bandar Seri Begawan BS 8610; tel. 2223225; fax 2241367; e-mail info.moha@home-affairs.gov.bn; internet www.home-affairs.gov.bn.

Ministry of Industry and Primary Resources (Kementerian Perindustrian dan Sumber-sumber Utama): Jalan Menteri Besar, Bandar Seri Begawan BB 3910; tel. 2382822; fax 2382474; e-mail helpdesk@industry.gov.bn; internet www.bruneimipr.gov.bn.

Ministry of Religious Affairs (Kementerian Hal Ehwal Ugama): Jalan Menteri Besar, Bandar Seri Begawan BB 3910; tel. 2382525; fax 2382330; e-mail info@religious-affairs.gov.bn; internet www.religious-affairs.gov.bn.

Legislature

THE LEGISLATIVE COUNCIL

In March 2011 the Sultan dissolved the existing Legislative Council, and a new Council, comprising 33 full members and three ex officio members, was appointed in June. The Council usually convenes annually, in March.

Speaker: Pehin Dato' Haji ISA IBRAHIM.

Political Organizations

At early 2014 there was only one legally registered political organization in Brunei.

Parti Pembangunan Bangsa (PPB) (National Development Party): Limbaruh Hijau, Simpang 323, Jalan Jerudong, Kampong Jerudong, Brunei Muara, BG 3122; tel. 2610703; fax 2610701; e-mail aspirasi@aspirasi-ndp.com; internet www.aspirasi-ndp.com; f. 2005; 2,000 mems; Pres. Haji MAHMUD MORSHIDI OTHMAN; Sec.-Gen. Haji JEFRI MOHD DAUD.

Political organizations that have officially ceased activities include: Parti Rakyat Brunei (PRB—Brunei People's Party), banned in 1962 and leaders all exiled; Barisan Kemerdeka'an Rakyat (BAKER—People's Independence Front), f. 1966 but no longer active; Parti Perpaduan Kebangsaan Rakyat Brunei (PERKARA—Brunei People's National United Party), f. 1968 but no longer active; Parti Kebangsaan Demokratik Brunei (PKDB—Brunei National Democratic Party—BNDP), f. 1985 and dissolved by government order in 1988; Parti Kesedaran Rakyat (PAKAR—People's Consciousness Party), f. 2000 and subsequently split into two opposing factions, prior to being deregistered in 2007; and Parti Perpaduan Kebangsaan Brunei (PPKB—Brunei National Solidarity Party—BNSP), f. 1986 but deregistered in 2008.

Diplomatic Representation

EMBASSIES AND HIGH COMMISSIONS IN BRUNEI

Australia: Level 6, DAR Takaful IBB Utama, Jalan Pemancha, Bandar Seri Begawan BS 8711; tel. 2229435; fax 2221652; e-mail austhicom.brunei@dfat.gov.au; internet www.bruneidarussalam.embassy.gov.au; High Commissioner TODD MERCER.

Bangladesh: 10 Simpang 83-20, Jalan Sungai Akar, Kampong Sungai Akar, Bandar Seri Begawan BC 3915; tel. 2342420; fax 2342421; e-mail bdoot@brunet.bn; internet www.hcbangladesh.org.bn; High Commissioner MOHAMMED ABDUL HYE.

Cambodia: Jalan Kebangsaan 336-71, Bandar Seri Begawan; tel. 2426450; fax 2426452; e-mail camemb.brn@mfa.gov.kh; Ambassador CHHAY SOKHAN.

Canada: 5th Floor, Jalan McArthur Bldg, 1 Jalan McArthur, Bandar Seri Begawan BS 8711; tel. 2220043; fax 2220040; e-mail bsbgn@international.gc.ca; internet www.canadainternational.gc.ca/brunei_darussalam; High Commissioner MARCEL GAUMOND.

China, People's Republic: 1, 3 & 5 Simpang 462, Jalan Muara, Kampong Sungai Hanching, Bandar Seri Begawan BC 2115; tel. 2339609; fax 2335710; e-mail chinaemb_bn@mfa.gov.cn; internet bn.chineseembassy.org/eng; Ambassador ZHENG XIANGLIN.

France: Kompleks Jalan Sultan, Units 301–306, 3rd Floor, 51–55 Jalan Sultan, Bandar Seri Begawan BS 8811; tel. 2220960; fax 2243373; e-mail france@brunet.bn; internet www.ambafrance-bn.org; Ambassador JEAN-YVES BERTHAULT.

Germany: Kompleks Yayasan Sultan Haji Hassanal Bolkiah, Blk A, 2nd Floor, Unit 2.01, Jalan Pretty, Bandar Seri Begawan BS 8711; tel. 2225547; fax 2225583; e-mail prgerman@brunet.bn; internet www.bandar-seri-begawan.diplo.de; Ambassador ROLAND CHRISTIAN GRAFE.

India: Baitussyifaa, Simpang 40-22, Jalan Sungai Akar, Bandar Seri Begawan BC 3915; tel. 2339947; fax 2339783; e-mail hicomind@brunet.bn; internet www.hcindiabrunei.org.bn; High Commissioner Dr ASHOK KUMAR AMROHI (designate).

Indonesia: Simpang 528, Lot 4498, Jalan Muara, Kampong Sungai Hanching Baru, Bandar Seri Begawan BC 2115; tel. 2330180; fax 2330646; e-mail kbribsb@brunet.bn; internet www.kemlu.go.id/bandarseribegawan; Ambassador NURUL QOMAR.

Iran: 2 Jalan Dato Ratna, Kampong Kiarong, Bandar Seri Begawan BE 1318; tel. 2424873; fax 2424875; e-mail iranemb2@brunet.bn; Ambassador MUHAMMAD REZA HAVASELI ASHTIANI.

Japan: 1 & 3 Jalan Jawatan Dalam, Lot 37355, 33 Simpang 122, Kampong Kiulap, Bandar Seri Begawan BE 1518; tel. 2229265; fax 2229481; e-mail embassy@japan.com.bn; internet www.bn.emb-japan.go.jp; Ambassador KENICHI SUGANUMA (outgoing).

Korea, Republic: 17 Simpang 462, Jalan Muara, Kampong Hancing Baru, Bandar Seri Begawan BC 2115; tel. 2330248; fax 2330254; e-mail brunei@mofat.go.kr; internet brn.mofat.go.kr; Ambassador CHOI BYUNG-KOO.

Kuwait: POB 729, Bandar Seri Begawan BS 8675; tel. 2457176; fax 2457179; e-mail kuwait@brunet.bn; Ambassador (vacant).

Laos: 159 Simpang 336, Jalan Kebangsaan, Kampong Sungai Akar, Bandar Seri Begawan BB 4313; tel. 2384382; fax 2384381; e-mail laosemba@brunet.bn; Ambassador SOUVANNA PHOUYAVONG (outgoing).

Malaysia: 61 Simpang 336, Jalan Kebangsaan, Kampong Sungai Akar, Bandar Seri Begawan BA 1211; tel. 2381095; fax 2381278; e-mail malbrnei@kln.gov.my; internet www.kln.gov.my/perwakilan/seribegawan; High Commissioner Datuk AWANG SAHAK AWANG SALLEH.

Myanmar: 14 Lot 2185/46292, Simpang 212, Jalan Kampong Rimba, Gadong, Bandar Seri Begawan BE 3119; tel. 2451960; fax 2451963; e-mail myanmar@brunet.bn; Ambassador YIN YIN MYINT.

Oman: 35 Simpang 100, Jalan Tungku Link, Kampong Pengkalan, Gadong, Bandar Seri Begawan BE 3719; tel. 2446953; fax 2446956; e-mail omnembsb@brunet.bn; Ambassador Sheikh AHMED BIN HASHIL AL MASKARI.

Pakistan: 8 Simpang 31, Jalan Bunga Jasmine, Kampong Beribi, Gadong, Bandar Seri Begawan BE 1118; tel. 2424600; fax 2424606; e-mail hcpak@brunet.bn; High Commissioner MUHAMMAD IJAZ HUSSAIN AWAN (outgoing).

Philippines: 17 Simpang 336, Jalan Kebangsaan, Bandar Seri Begawan BA 1210; tel. 2241465; fax 2237707; e-mail bruneipe@brunet.bn; internet www.philippine-embassybrunei.com; Ambassador NESTOR Z. OCHOA.

Qatar: Lot 188897, Simpang 898, Kampong Jangsak, Gadong, Bandar Seri Begawan; tel. 2447777; fax 2443333; e-mail qatarembassybru@gmail.com; Ambassador AHMED IBRAHIM AL-ABDULLA.

Russia: The Holiday Lodge Hotel, 97192, Jalan Palau Kubu, Kampong Jerudong, Bandar Seri Begawan; tel. 2611413; fax 2411424; e-mail ruembr@yandex.ru; internet www.brunei.mid.ru; Ambassador VIKTOR A. SELEZNEV.

Saudi Arabia: 1 Simpang 570, Jalan Muara, Kampong Salar, Bandar Seri Begawan BU 1429; tel. 2792821; fax 2792826; e-mail bnemb@mofa.gov.sa; Ambassador MUHAMMAD JAMIL ABD AL-JALEEL HASHIM (outgoing).

Singapore: 8 Simpang 74, Jalan Subok, Bandar Seri Begawan; tel. 2262741; fax 2262752; e-mail singhc_bwn@sgmfa.gov.sg; internet www.mfa.gov.sg/brunei; High Commissioner JAYA RATNAM.

Thailand: 2 Simpang 682, Jalan Tutong, Kampong Bunut, Bandar Seri Begawan BF 1320; tel. 2653108; fax 2653032; e-mail thaiemb@brunet.bn; internet www.thaiembassybrunei.org; Ambassador APICHART PHETCHARATANA.

United Kingdom: Kompleks Yayasan Sultan Haji Hassanal Bolkiah, Blk D, 2nd Floor, Unit 2.01, Bandar Seri Begawan BS 8711; tel. 2222231; fax 2234315; e-mail bsbconsularenquiries@fco.gov.uk; internet ukinbrunei.fco.gov.uk; High Commissioner DAVID CAMPBELL.

USA: Simpang 336-52-16-9, Jalan Kebangsaan, Bandar Seri Begawan BC 4115; tel. 2384616; fax 2384604; e-mail amembassy_bsb@state.gov; internet brunei.usembassy.gov; Ambassador DANIEL L. SHIELDS, III.

Viet Nam: 9 Simpang 148-3, Jalan Telanai, Bandar Seri Begawan BA 2312; tel. 2651580; fax 2651574; e-mail vnembassy@yahoo.com; internet www.vietnamembassy-brunei.org; Ambassador NGUYEN TRUONG GIANG.

Judicial System

Syariah (*Shari'a*) courts co-exist with the Supreme Court and deal with Islamic laws.

Supreme Court: Km 11/2, Jalan Tutong, Bandar Seri Begawan BA 1910; tel. 2243939; fax 2241984; internet www.judicial.gov.bn; the Supreme Court consists of the Court of Appeal and the High Court; the Court of Appeal considers criminal and civil appeals against the decisions of the High Court and the Intermediate Court and is the highest appellate court for criminal cases; in civil cases an appeal may be referred to the Judicial Committee of Her Majesty's Privy Council in London if all parties agree to do so before the hearing of the appeal in the Brunei Court of Appeal; the High Court considers appeals in criminal and civil matters against the decisions of the Subordinate Courts and has unlimited original jurisdiction in criminal and civil matters; President (Court of Appeal) JOHN BARRY MORTIMER; Chief Justice (High Court) Dato' Seri Paduka Haji KIFRAWI KIFLI.

Intermediate Courts: have jurisdiction to try all offences other than those punishable by the death sentence and civil jurisdiction to try all actions and suits of a civil nature where the amount in dispute or value of the subject/matter does not exceed B $100,000.

Magistrates' Courts: Law and Courts' Bldg, Bandar Seri Begawan BA 1910; internet www.judicial.gov.bn; function as subordinate courts; have limited original jurisdiction in civil and criminal matters and civil jurisdiction to try all actions and suits of a civil nature where the amount in dispute does not exceed B $50,000 (for Chief Magistrate) and B $30,000 (for magistrates); Chief Magistrate ABDULLAH SOEFRI BIN Pengiran Haji ABIDIN.

Courts of Kathis: deal with questions concerning Islamic religion, marriage and divorce; appeals lie from these courts to the Sultan in the Religious Council; Chief Kathi Dato' Seri Setia Haji ABDULLAH SALIM BIN Haji BESAR.

Attorney-General's Chambers: The Law Bldg, Km 1, Jalan Tutong, Bandar Seri Begawan BA 1910; tel. 2244872; fax 2227954; e-mail info.agc@agc.gov.bn; internet www.agc.gov.bn; Attorney-General Datin Paduka Hajah HAYATI Dato' Seri Paduka Haji MOHD SALLEH.

Religion

The official religion of Brunei is Islam, and the Sultan is head of the Islamic community. The majority of the Malay population are Muslims of the Shafi'is school of the Sunni sect; at the 2011 census Muslims accounted for 78.8% of the total population. The Chinese population is either Buddhist (accounting for 7.8% of the total population at the 2011 census), Confucianist, Daoist or Christian. Large numbers of the indigenous ethnic groups practise traditional animist forms of religion. The remainder of the population are mostly Christians, generally Roman Catholics, Anglicans or members of the American Methodist Church of Southern Asia. At the 2011 census Christians accounted for 8.7% of the total population.

ISLAM

Supreme Head of Islam: HM Sultan Haji HASSANAL BOLKIAH (Sultan and Yang Di-Pertuan).

CHRISTIANITY

The Anglican Communion

Within the Church of the Province of South East Asia, Brunei forms part of the diocese of Kuching (Malaysia).

The Roman Catholic Church

Brunei comprises a single apostolic vicariate. At 31 December 2007 there were an estimated 18,427 adherents in the country, equivalent to 5.0% of the population.

Prefect Apostolic: Rev. CORNELIUS SIM, Church of Our Lady of the Assumption, Jalan Kumbang Pasang, Bandar Seri Begawan BS 8670; tel. 2222261; fax 2238938; e-mail frcsim@brunet.bn.

The Press

NEWSPAPERS

Borneo Bulletin: Lot 8 and 11, Perindustrian Beribi II, Gadong BE 1118; tel. 2451468; fax 2451461; e-mail borneobulletin@brunet.bn; internet borneobulletin.brunei-online.com; f. 1953; daily; English; independent; owned by QAF Group; Editor PRABHAKAR NATARAJAN; circ. 20,000 (weekdays), 25,000 (Sat.), 25,000 (Sun.).

Brunei Darussalam Newsletter: Dept of Information, Prime Minister's Office, Istana Nurul Iman, Berakas, Bandar Seri Begawan BB 3510; tel. 2383400; fax 2382012; e-mail bd.newsletter@information.gov.bn; monthly; English; govt newspaper; distributed free; Editor SASTRA SARINI BINTI Haji JULAINI; circ. 3,000.

The Brunei Times: Wisma Haji Mohd Taha, 3rd Floor, Jalan Gadong, Bandar Seri Begawan BE 4119; tel. 2428333; fax 2428555; e-mail bruneitimes@bt.com.bn; internet www.bt.com.bn; f. 2006; daily; English; Editor-in-Chief Haji BUJANG BIN MASU'UT; circ. 15,500.

Media Permata: Locked Bag No. 2, MPC (Old Airport, Berakas), Bandar Seri Begawan BB 3510; tel. 2451468; fax 2451461; e-mail mediapermata@brunet.bn; internet www.brunei-online.com/mp; f. 1995; daily (not Sun.); Malay; owned by QAF Group; Editor MUHAMMAD NOOR; circ. 10,000.

Pelita Brunei: Dept of Information, Prime Minister's Office, Old Airport, Berakas, Bandar Seri Begawan BB 3510; tel. 2383941; fax 2381004; e-mail e.pelita@yahoo.com; internet www.pelitabrunei.gov.bn; f. 1956; 3 a week (Mon., Wed. and Sat.); Malay; govt newspaper; distributed free; Editor Haji JAAFAR BIN Haji IBRAHIM; circ. 19,000.

Salam: c/o Brunei Shell Petroleum Co Sdn Bhd, Jalan Utara, Panaga, Seria KB 3534; tel. 3373018; fax 3374189; e-mail editorial@shell.com; internet www.bsp.com.bn/main/mediacentre/publications.asp; f. 1953; monthly; Malay and English; distributed free to employees and shareholders of the Brunei Shell Petroleum Co Sdn Bhd; Exec. Editor Malai AYLA SURYA Malai Haji ABDULLAH; circ. 46,000.

Publishers

Borneo Printers & Trading Sdn Bhd: POB 2211, Bandar Seri Begawan BS 8674; tel. 2651387; fax 2654342; e-mail bptl@brunet.bn.

Brunei Press Sdn Bhd: Lots 8 & 11, Perindustrian Beribi II, Jalan Gadong, Bandar Seri Begawan BE 1118; tel. 2451468; fax 2451462; e-mail brupress@brunet.bn; internet www.bruneipress.com.bn; f. 1953; Gen. Man. REGGIE SEE.

Capital Trading & Printing Pte Ltd: POB 1089, Bandar Seri Begawan; tel. 2244541.

Leong Bros: 52 Jalan Bunga Kuning, POB 164, Seria; tel. 322381.

Offset Printing House: Lot Q37, 4 Simpang 5, Lambak Kanan Industrial Area, Berakas, Bandar Seri Begawan BB 1714; tel. 2390797; fax 2390798; e-mail offset@brunei.bn; f. 1980; Gen. Man. KENNY TEO.

GOVERNMENT PUBLISHING HOUSES

Dewan Bahasa dan Pustaka (Language and Literature Bureau): c/o Ministry of Culture, Youth and Sports, Berakas BB 3510; tel. 2382511; fax 2381817; e-mail pengarahdbp@brunet.bn; internet www.dbp.gov.bn; f. 1961; publs incl. children's books, textbooks, novels, poetry and translations of foreign works; promotion and preservation of Malayan literature and folklore; library services; Dir-Gen. Datuk TERMUZI ABDUL AZIZ.

Jabatan Percetakan Kerajaan (Government Printing Dept): Prime Minister's Office, Bandar Seri Begawan BB 3510; tel. 2382541; fax 2381141; e-mail info@printing.gov.bn; internet www.printing.gov.bn; f. 1975; Dir Haji DAUD BIN Haji AHMAD.

Broadcasting and Communications

TELECOMMUNICATIONS

B-Mobile Communications Sdn Bhd (b-mobile): Old Airport, Berakas, Bandar Seri Begawan BB 3510; tel. 2221010; fax 2384040; e-mail contact@bmobile.com.bn; internet www.bmobile.com.bn; f. 2005; 3G mobile service provider; jt venture between Telekom Brunei Bhd (TelBru) and QAF Comserve.

DST Communications Sdn Bhd: Jalan Tungku Link, Bandar Seri Begawan BE 3619; tel. 2410888; fax 2410142; e-mail dstmarketing@simpur.net.bn; internet www.dst-group.com/dstcom; mobile and internet broadband services provider; mem. of DST Group; signed agreement with Alcatel in 2003 to improve provision of mobile services in Brunei; Chief Operating Officer (DST Group) Haji MARSAD BIN Haji ISMAIL.

Telekom Brunei Bhd (TelBru): Jalan Lapangan Terbang Lama, Berakas, Bandar Seri Begawan BB 3510; tel. 2321321; fax 2382444; e-mail info@telbru.com.bn; internet www.telbru.com.bn; fmrly Jabatan Telekom Brunei (Dept of Telecommunications of Brunei); name changed as above upon corporatization in April 2006; telecommunications services provider; Chair. Dato' Paduka Haji HISHAM BIN Haji MOHAMMAD HANIFAH; CEO DAVID KAY.

Regulatory Authority

Authority for Info-Communications Technology Industry (AITI): Blk B14, Simpang 32–35, Kampong Anggrek Desa, Jalan Berakas, Bandar Seri Begawan BB 3713; tel. 2323232; fax 2382447; e-mail info@aiti.gov.bn; internet www.aiti.gov.bn; f. 2003; assumed responsibility for regulating and representing telecommunications industry following corporatization of Dept of Telecommunications of Brunei in April 2006; also entrusted with devt of ICT industry; Chair. ALAIHUDDIN BIN Haji MOHAMMED TAHA.

BROADCASTING

Radio

KRISTALfm: Jalan Tungku Link, Bandar Seri Begawan BE 3619; tel. 2410888; fax 2411788; e-mail kristalfm@dst-group.com; internet www.kristal.fm; f. 1999; subsidiary of Kristal Media Sdn Bhd; mem. of DST Group; two networks; Malay and English.

Radio Televisyen Brunei (RTB): Prime Minister's Office, Jalan Elizabeth II, Bandar Seri Begawan BS 8610; tel. 2243111; fax 2241882; e-mail gts@rtb.gov.bn; internet www.rtb.gov.bn; f. 1975; five radio networks; Malay, Chinese (Mandarin), English and Arabic; also broadcasts on the internet; Dir Haji MOHAMAD YUNOS BIN Haji BOLHASSAN.

Television

Kristal Astro Sdn Bhd: Unit 1-345, 1st Floor, Gadong Properties Centre, Gadong, Bandar Seri Begawan BE 4119; e-mail mdnoh.koya@dst-group.com; tel. 2456855; fax 2456848; f. 2000; jt venture between DST Communications Sdn Bhd and Astro Malaysia; provides over 100 digital satellite subscription channels; Sen. Man. H. K. NOH.

Radio Televisyen Brunei (RTB): Prime Minister's Office, Jalan Elizabeth II, Bandar Seri Begawan BS 8610; tel. 2243111; fax 2241882; e-mail director@rtb.gov.bn; internet www.rtb.gov.bn; f. 1975; five TV channels; five radio channels; Dir Haji MOHAMAD YUNOS BIN Haji BOLHASSAN.

Finance

(cap. = capital; res = reserves; dep. = deposits; brs = branches; amounts in Brunei dollars unless otherwise stated)

BANKING

In 2013 there were 13 banks in operation, including three offshore banks. In January 2011 the Monetary Authority of Brunei Darussalam formally assumed responsibility for the functions of the Brunei Currency and Monetary Board. In April 2013, it entered into a Memorandum of Understanding (MOU) with Bank Negara Malaysia to establish a collaborative framework towards enhancing mutual co-operation in the development of the financial services sector.

Autoriti Monetari Brunei Darussalam (AMBD) (Monetary Authority of Brunei Darussalam): Ministry of Finance Bldg, Tingkat 14, Commonwealth Dr., Bandar Seri Begawan BB 3910; tel. 2384626; fax 2383787; internet www.ambd.gov.bn; f. 2011; performs functions of central bank; responsible for monetary policy, supervision of financial institutions and currency management; Chair. HRH Prince Haji AL-MUHTADEE BILLAH BOLKIAH; Man. Dir Haji MOHD ROSLI BIN Haji SABTU.

Commercial Banks

Baiduri Bank Bhd: Blk A, Units 1–4, Kiarong Complex, Lebuhraya Sultan Hassanal Bolkiah, Bandar Seri Begawan BE 1318; tel. 2268300; fax 2455599; e-mail bank@baiduri.com; internet www.baiduri.com; f. 1994; cap. 100m., res 96.8m., dep. 3,196.1m. (Dec. 2011); Chair. Pengiran Anak ISTERI Pengiran Anak Hajjah ZARIAH; Gen. Man. PIERRE IMHOF; 11 brs.

Bank Islam Brunei Darussalam: Lot 159, Bangunan IBB, Jalan Pemancha, Bandar Seri Begawan BS 8711; tel. 2238181; fax 2235722; internet www.bibd.com.bn; f. 1981; est. as Island Devt Bank; fmrly Islamic Bank of Brunei; merged with Islamic Devt Bank of Brunei Bhd in 2006; practises Islamic banking principles; cap. 724.7m., res 237.1m., dep. 4,895.5m. (Dec. 2012); Chair. Dato' Seri Setia Haji ABDULLAH BIN BEGAWAN MUDIM Dato' Paduka Haji BAKAR; Man. Dir JAVED AHMED; 14 brs.

Citibank NA (USA): Darussalam Complex, 12–15 Jalan Sultan, Bandar Seri Begawan BS 8811; tel. 2243983; fax 2237344; Country Head TERRENCE CUDDYRE; 2 brs.

The Hongkong and Shanghai Banking Corpn Ltd (HSBC) (Hong Kong): Jalan Sultan, cnr Jalan Pemancha, Bandar Seri Begawan BS 8670; tel. 2252252; fax 2241316; e-mail hsbc@hsbc.com.bn; internet www.hsbc.com.bn; f. 1947; acquired assets of Nat. Bank of Brunei in 1986; CEO TODD WILCOX; 11 brs.

Maybank (Malaysia): 1 Jalan McArthur, Bandar Seri Begawan BS 8711; tel. 2242494; fax 2226101; e-mail maybank@brunet.bn; f. 1960; Country Man. MOHAMAD HASSANEL BIN JARAI; 3 brs.

RHB Bank Bhd (Malaysia): Kompleks Yayasan Sultan Haji Hassanal Bolkiah, Blk D, Unit G.02, Jalan Pretty, Bandar Seri Begawan BS 8711; tel. 2222515; fax 2237487; e-mail iskandar_yusoff@rhbislamicbank.com.my; fmrly Sime Bank Bhd; Country Man. ISKANDAR BIN MOHD YUSSOF; 1 br.

Standard Chartered Bank (United Kingdom): Kompleks Jalan Sultan, Tingkat 1, 51–55 Jalan Sultan, Bandar Seri Begawan BS 8811; tel. 2220345; fax 2234811; e-mail scb.brunei@sc.com; internet www.standardchartered.com/bn; f. 1958; CEO LAI PEI-SI; 7 brs.

Perbadanan Tabung Amanah Islam Brunei Berhad (TAIB): Bangunan Ibu Pejabat Perbadanan TAIB, Jalan Sultan, Bandar Seri Begawan BS 8811; tel. 2232222; fax 2240316; internet www.taib.com.bn; f. 1991; Man. Dir Puan Hajah FA'AIZAH Haji ABIDIN; 8 brs.

United Overseas Bank Ltd (Singapore): Units 10–11, Bangunan D'Amin Jaya, Lot 54989, Kampong Kiarong, Mukim Gadong, Bandar Seri Begawan BE 1318; tel. 2225477; fax 2240792; f. 1973; Gen. Man. ABDUL RAZAK BIN ABDUL MALEK; 2 brs.

Offshore Banks

The Brunei International Financial Centre (BIFC—see Government Agencies), under the Ministry of Finance, supervises the activities of the offshore banking sector in Brunei.

Oversea-Chinese Banking Corpn Ltd: Unit 2, 5th Floor, Dar Takaful IBB Utama, Jalan Pemancha, Bandar Seri Begawan BS 8711; tel. 2230826; fax 2230283; Country Head KHALID AFFENDY BIN MOHAMMAD KASIM.

Royal Bank of Canada: 1 Jalan McArthur, 4th Floor, Unit 4A, Bandar Seri Begawan BS 8711; tel. 2224366; fax 2224368; Gen. Man. SUHAILA KANI.

Sun Hung Kai International Bank (Brunei) Ltd (Hong Kong): Britannia House, Unit 41, 4th Floor, Jalan Cator, Bandar Seri Begawan BS 8811; tel. 2223919; fax 2223920; e-mail cs@shkf.com; f. 2004; Dir PAK HUNG MAK.

STOCK EXCHANGE

International Brunei Exchange Ltd (IBX): The Empire, Muara-Tutong Highway, Jerudong BG 3122; tel. 2611222; fax 2611020; e-mail info@ibx.com.bn; f. 2001; CEO B. C. YONG.

INSURANCE

General Companies

Audley Insurance Co Sdn Bhd: Ministry of Finance Bldg, 9th Floor, Commonwealth Dr., Jalan Kebangsaan, Bandar Seri Begawan BB 3910; tel. 2383535; fax 2383548; e-mail audley@bia.com.bn; Man. Dir Datuk HAJAH UMI SALAMAH Haji ISMAIL.

Etiqa Insurance Bhd: B7, Ground Floor, Shakirin Kompleks, Kampong Kiulap, Bandar Seri Begawan BE 1518; tel. 2443393; fax 2427451; e-mail tsangpy@brunet.bn; fmrly known as Malaysia National Insurance Bhd; Man. TSANG POH YEE.

MBA Insurance Sdn Bhd: First Floor, Units 15–17, Lot 9784, Bangunan Haji Hassan Abdullah, Jalan Gadong, Kampong Menglait, Bandar Seri Begawan BE 3978; tel. 2441535; fax 2441534; e-mail mbabrunei@brunet.bn; Gen. Man. SHIM WEI HSUING.

Mitsui Sumitomo Insurance (Malaysia) Bhd: Unit 311, 3rd Floor, Kompleks Mohamad Yussof, Km 4, Jalan Tutong, Bandar Seri Begawan; tel. 2223632; fax 2220965; Sr Exec. DAVID ENG.

National Insurance Co Bhd: Units 12 and 13, Blk A, Regent Sq., Simpang 150, Kampong Kiarong BE1318; tel. 2226222; fax 2429888; e-mail insurance@national.com.bn; internet www.national.com.bn; f. 1969; Gen. Man. KOLJA KLAWUNN.

South East Asia Insurance (B) Sdn Bhd: Unit 2, Blk A, Abdul Razak Complex, 1st Floor, Jalan Gadong, Bandar Seri Begawan BE 3919; tel. 2443842; fax 2420860; Gen. Man. SHIM WEI HSIUNG.

Standard Insurance (B) Sdn Bhd: 2 Bangunan Hasbullah I, Ground Floor, Bandar Seri Begawan BE 3719; tel. 2450077; fax 2450076; e-mail feedback@standard-ins.com; internet www.standard-ins.com; Man. PAUL KONG.

Tokio Marine Insurance Singapore Ltd: Units A1 & A2, 1st Floor, Blk A, Bangunan Hau Man Yong, Simpang 88, Kampong Kiulap, Bandar Seri Begawan BE 1518; tel. 2236100; fax 2236102; e-mail davidwong@tmasiainsurance.com; f. 1929; Br. Man. DAVID WONG KOK MIN.

Life Companies

American International Assurance Co Ltd: Unit 509, Wisma Jaya, 5th Floor, 85–94 Jalan Pemancha, Bandar Seri Begawan BS 8811; tel. 2239113; fax 2221667; e-mail Kenneth-WC.Ling@aia.com; Gen. Man. PETER LIM.

The Great Eastern Life Assurance Co Ltd: Unit 17 & 18, Blk B, Bangunan Habza, Simpang 150, Kampong Kiarong, Bandar Seri Begawan BA 1318; tel. 2233118; fax 2238118; e-mail carolinesim@greateasternlife.com; internet www.greateasternlife.com/bn; Head CAROLINE SIM (acting).

TM Asia Life Singapore Ltd: Unit 2, 1st Floor, Blk D, Abdul Razak Complex, Jalan Gadong, Bandar Seri Begawan BE 4119; tel. 2423755; fax 2423754; e-mail tmasialife@brunet.bn; fmrly Asia Life Assurance Society Ltd; Br. Man. JOSEPH WONG SIONG LION.

Takaful (Composite Insurance) Companies

Insurans Islam TAIB Sdn Bhd: Perbadanan TAIB, Jalan Sultan, Bandar Seri Begawan BS 8811; tel. 2232222; fax 2237729; e-mail ict@insuranstaib.com.bn; internet www.insuranstaib.com.bn; f. 1993; provides Islamic insurance products and services; Gen. Man. OSMAN MOHAMAD JAIR.

Takaful Bank Pembangunan Islam Sdn Bhd (TBPISB): Unit 10, Komplex Seri Kiulap, Kampong Kiulap, Gadong, Bandar Seri Begawan BE 1518; tel. 2237220; fax 2237045; internet www.takafulbpisb.com; f. 2001; fmrly Takaful IDBB Sdn Bhd; name changed as above in 2003; Islamic life and non-life insurance products; Chair. Pehin Dato' Haji AHMAD WALLY SKINNER; Man. Dir Haji AISHATUL AKMAR SIDEK.

Takaful IBB Bhd: Levels 2 & 7–8, Dar Takaful IBB Utama, Jalan Pemancha, Bandar Seri Begawan BS 8711; tel. 2239338; fax 2451808; e-mail takaful@brunet.bn; f. 1993; Chair. Pehin Dato' Haji ABU BAKAR BIN Haji APONG DAUD.

Insurance Association

General Insurance Association of Negara Brunei Darussalam (GIAB): Unit C2-2, Blk C, Shakirin Complex, Kampong Kiulap, Bandar Seri Begawan BE 1518; tel. 2237898; fax 2237858; e-mail giab@brunet.bn; internet www.giab.com.bn; f. 1986; 15 mems; Chair. HELEN YEO.

Trade and Industry

GOVERNMENT AGENCIES

Brunei International Financial Centre (BIFC): Tingkat 14, Ministry of Finance, Commonwealth Dr., Jalan Kebangsaan, Bandar Seri Begawan BB 3910; tel. 2383747; fax 2383787; e-mail bifc@mof.gov.bn; internet www.mof.gov.bn/english/bifc; f. 2000; regulates international financial sector and encourages devt of Brunei as investment destination; Dir MOHAMED ROSLI SABTU.

Brunei Investment Agency (BIA): Tingkat 11, Bangunan Kementerian Kewangan, Commonwealth Dr., Jalan Kebangsaan, Bandar Seri Begawan BB 3910; tel. 2383535; fax 2383539; e-mail dramin.abdullah@bia.com.bn; f. 1983; Chair. Pehin Dato' Haji ABU BAKAR BIN Haji APONG; Man. Dir Haji MOHAMMAD AMIN LIEW ABDULLAH.

DEVELOPMENT ORGANIZATIONS

Brunei Economic Development Board (BEDB): Blk 2K, Jalan Kumbang Pasang, Bandar Seri Begawan BA 1311; tel. 2230111; fax 2230063; e-mail info@bedb.com.bn; internet www.bedb.com.bn; f. 2001; promotes Brunei as an investment destination; facilitates and assists industrial devt; under control of Prime Minister's Office since late 2010; Chair. Dato' Paduka Awang Haji ALI Haji APONG; CEO Dr HAJI ABDUL MANAF Haji METUSSIN.

Brunei Industrial Development Authority (BINA): Ministry of Industry and Primary Resources, Km 8, Jalan Gadong, Bandar Seri Begawan BE 1118; tel. 2444100; fax 2423300; e-mail bruneibina@brunet.bn; internet www.bina.gov.bn; f. 1996; Dir Pengiran SHARIFUDDIN BIN Pengiran Haji METALI.

Brunei Islamic Trust Fund (Tabung Amanah Islam Brunei): Bangunan Kewangaan Utama, Jalan Sultan, Bandar Seri Begawan BS 8811; tel. 2232222; fax 2240316; e-mail administration@taib.com.bn; internet www.taib.com.bn; f. 1991; promotes trade and industry; Chair. Dato' Paduka Dr Haji MAT SUNY Haji MUHAMMAD HUSSEIN.

Semaun Holdings Sdn Bhd: Unit 10, Blk B, Warisan Mata-Mata Complex, Kampong Mata-Mata, Gadong, Bandar Seri Begawan BE 1718; tel. 2456064; fax 2456070; e-mail semaun@brunet.bn; internet www.semaunholdings.com; f. 1994; promotes industrial and commercial devt through direct investment in key industrial sectors; 100% govt-owned; bd of dirs is composed of ministers and senior govt officials; chaired by Minister of Industry and Primary Resources; Man. Dir Hajah ASMAH Binti Haji SAMAN.

CHAMBERS OF COMMERCE

Brunei Darussalam International Chamber of Commerce and Industry: Units 401–403A, 4th Floor, Wisma Jaya, Jalan Pemancha, Bandar Seri Begawan BS 8811; tel. 2236601; fax 2228389; Chair. Haji AHMAD BIN Haji ISA; Sec. Haji SHAZALI BIN Dato' Haji SULAIMAN; 30 mems.

Brunei Malay Chamber of Commerce and Industry: Suite 301, 2nd Floor, Bangunan Guru-Guru Melayu Brunei, Jalan Kianggehi, Bandar Seri Begawan 1910; tel. 2227297; fax 2227278; f. 1964; Pres. Haji RAZALI BIN Haji JOHARI; 160 mems.

Chinese Chamber of Commerce: Chinese Chamber of Commerce Bldg, 4th Floor, 72 Jalan Roberts, Bandar Seri Begawan BS 8711; tel. 2235494; fax 2235493; e-mail ccc@brunet.bn; Pres. Dr CHAN SUI KIAT.

Indian Chamber of Commerce: Unit 13–15, Blk B, Delima Jaya Complex, Jalan Muara, Kampong Serusop, Bandar Seri Begawan BB 2313; tel. and fax 2340972; Pres. NAZEER AHMAD.

National Chamber of Commerce and Industry of Brunei Darussalam (NCCIBD): Unit 1, Blk D, Beribi Industrial Complex 1, Jalan Gadong, Bandar Seri Begawan BE 1118; tel. 2421840; fax 2421839; e-mail nccibd@brunet.bn; internet www.nccibd.com; Pres. Haji RAZALI BIN Haji JOHARI; Sec.-Gen. Haji ABDUL SAMAN AHMAD.

STATE HYDROCARBON COMPANIES

Brunei LNG Sdn Bhd (BLNG): Lumut, Seria KC 2935; tel. 3236901; fax 3236892; e-mail enquiry@bruneilng.com; internet www.blng.com.bn; f. 1969; natural gas liquefaction; owned jtly by the Brunei Govt (50%), Shell and Mitsubishi Corpn; operates LNG plant at Lumut, which has a capacity of 7.2m. metric tons per year; Man. Dir and CEO Haji SALLEH BOSTAMAN Haji ZAINAL ABIDIN.

Brunei National Petroleum Co Sdn Bhd (PetroleumBrunei): 2nd Floor, Blk A, B, C, Kompleks Yayasan Sultan Haji Hassanal Bolkiah, Jalan Pretty, Bandar Seri Begawan BS 8711; tel. 2230720; fax 2230654; e-mail pb@pb.com.bn; internet www.pb.com.bn; f. 2002; wholly govt-owned; CEO MATSATEJO Dató Paduka SOKIAW.

Brunei Shell Marketing Co Bhd: Ground & 12th Floor, PGGMB Bldg, Jalan Kianggeh, Bandar Seri Begawan BS 8811; tel. 2229304; fax 2240470; e-mail edyzurina.awang@shell.com; internet www.bsm.com.bn; f. 1978; est. from Shell Marketing Co of Brunei Ltd as jt venture between Shell and the Bruneian Govt; markets petroleum and chemical products throughout Brunei; Man. Dir MAT SUNY Haji MOHD HUSSEIN.

Brunei Shell Petroleum Co Sdn Bhd (BSP): Jalan Utara, Panagia, Seria KB 3534; tel. 3373999; fax 3372040; internet www.bsp.com.bn; f. 1957; the largest industrial concern in the country; 50% state holding; Man. Dir GRAHAEME HENDERSON.

Jasra International Petroleum Sdn Bhd: RBA Plaza, 2nd Floor, Jalan Sultan, Bandar Seri Begawan 2085; tel. 2228968; fax 2228929; petroleum exploration and production; Man. Dir ROBERT A. HARRISON.

TRADE UNIONS

All trade unions must be registered with the Government. Authorization for affiliation with international trade union organizations is required. In 2008 the three officially registered trade unions were all in the petroleum sector, which collectively represented about 1,500 workers (less than 1% of the total workforce). Two of the unions, representing the sector's office workers, were reported to be inactive.

Brunei Oilfield Workers' Union: XDR/11, BSP Co Sdn Bhd, Seria KB 3534; f. 1964; 470 mems; Pres. SUHAINI Haji OTHMAN; Sec.-Gen. ABU TALIB BIN Haji MOHAMAD.

Transport

RAILWAYS

There are no public railways. The Brunei Shell Petroleum Co Sdn Bhd maintains a 19.3-km section of light railway between Seria and Badas.

ROADS

In 2010 there were 3,029 km of roads in Brunei (excluding roads maintained by the Brunei Shell Petroleum Co Sdn Bhd), of which 80.1% were permanent. The main highway connects Bandar Seri Begawan, Tutong and Kuala Belait.

Land Transport Department: Jalan Beribi Gadong, Bandar Seri Begawan BE 1110; tel. 2451979; fax 2424775; e-mail latis@brunet.bn; internet www.land-transport.gov.bn; f. 1962; Dir MOHAMMAD RIZA BIN Haji MOHAMMAD YUNOS.

SHIPPING

Most sea traffic is handled by a deep-water port at Muara, 28 km from the capital. It has a container terminal, warehousing, freezer facilities and cement silos. In September 2007 a cruise ship centre was opened at Muara. The port at Kuala Belait takes shallow-draught vessels and serves mainly the Shell petroleum field and Seria. The jetty at Lumut handles liquefied natural gas (LNG) carriers.

Four main rivers, with numerous tributaries, are an important means of communication in the interior. Water taxis operate daily to the Temburong district.

Shipping Association of Brunei Darussalam (SABD): POB 476, Bandar Seri Begawan BS 8670; tel. 2421572; fax 2421453; e-mail seatradefang@brunet.bn; Pres. Haji RAZALI BIN Haji JOHARI; Sec.-Gen. FANG TECK SIONG.

Bee Seng Shipping Co: 30 Blk D, Madang Complex, Mukim Berakas, POB 1777, Bandar Seri Begawan BC 3715; tel. 2220033; fax 2221815; e-mail enquiry@beeseng.com; internet www.beeseng.com.

Brunei Gas Carriers Sdn Bhd (BGC): Units 1–3, Lot 8632, Lim Kah Sik Bldg, Jalan Jerudong, Bandar Seri Begawan BG 3122; tel. 2613000; fax 2238790; e-mail bgc@brunet.bn; internet www.syarikatbgc.com; f. 1998; LNG shipping co; owned jtly by the Prime Minister's Corpn (80%), Shell Gas BV (10%) and Mitsubishi subsidiary Diamond Gas Carriers BV (10%); one vessel operated by Shell Int. Trading and Shipping Co Ltd; Man. Dir Haji SHAHBUDIN BIN MUSA.

Brunei Shell Tankers Sdn Bhd: Seria KB 3534; tel. 3372722; f. 1986; owned jtly by the Minister for Finance Corpn (50%), Shell Petroleum Ltd (25%) and Diamond Gas BV (25%); four vessels operated by Shell Int. Trading and Shipping Co Ltd; delivers LNG to regional customers; Man. Dir KEN MARNOCH.

Harper Wira Sdn Bhd: B2, 1st Floor, Bangunan Pehin, Simpang 27, Lot 12284, Km 3, Jalan Gadong, Bandar Seri Begawan 3180; tel. and fax 2448529.

IDS Borneo Sdn Bhd: Km 4, Jalan Gadong, Bandar Seri Begawan BE 4119; tel. 2422396; fax 2232537; f. 1856; Gen. Man. CHONG SOO HENG.

Pansar Co Sdn Bhd: Unit A6, 2nd Floor, Bangunan Urairah, Jalan Gadong, Kampong Kiulap Mukim, Bandar Seri Begawan BE 1518; tel. 2233641; fax 2233643; e-mail pscbwn-admin@pansar.com.my; internet pansar.com.my; Man. Dir JASON TAI HEE.

Seatrade Shipping Co: POB 476, Bandar Seri Begawan BS 8670; tel. 2421457; fax 2425824; e-mail info@seatradeshpg.com; internet www.seatradeshpg.com; Gen. Man. FANG TECK SIONG.

Silver Line (B) Sdn Bhd: 2nd Floor, 6 Abdul Razak Complex, Simpang 137, Jalan Gadong, Bandar Seri Begawan BE 4119; tel. 2445069; fax 2430276; e-mail silvline@brunet.bn.

Tri-Star Shipping and Trading Co Sdn Bhd: Unit 16, Simpang 584, Jalan Tutong, Bandar Seri Begawan; tel. 2653013; fax 2652685; e-mail enquiry@tristarbrunei.com; internet www.tristarbrunei.com.

CIVIL AVIATION

There is an international airport at Berakas, near Bandar Seri Begawan. The Brunei Shell Petroleum Co Sdn Bhd operates a private airfield at Anduki for helicopter services.

Department of Civil Aviation: Brunei International Airport, Bandar Seri Begawan BB 2513; tel. 2330142; fax 2340971; e-mail info@civil-aviation.gov.bn; internet www.civil-aviation.gov.bn; Dir Pengiran ADNAN BIN Pengiran BADARUDIN (acting).

Royal Brunei Airlines (RBA) Ltd: RBA Plaza, Jalan Sultan, POB 737, Bandar Seri Begawan BS 8671; tel. 2240500; fax 2244737; e-mail feedback@rba.com.bn; internet www.bruneiair.com; f. 1974; operates services within the Far East and to the Middle East, Australia and Europe; Chair. Dato' Paduka Haji BAHRIN BIN ABDULLAH; Dep. Chair. and CEO DERMOT MANNION.

Syabas Aviation Services Sdn Bhd: Unit 47, 1st Floor, Haji Uthman Kompleks, Simpang 13, Jalan Lapangan Terbang Antarabangsa, Bandar Seri Begawan BB 2513; tel. 2342657; fax 2342658; e-mail info@syabasaviation.com; internet syabasaviation.com; f. 2009; Chair. ABAS MOHAMMED.

Tourism

Tourist attractions in Brunei include the flora and fauna of the rain forest and the national parks, as well as mosques and water villages. In 2011 the number of tourist arrivals was estimated at 242,000. International tourism receipts totalled US $254m. in 2009.

Brunei Tourism: c/o Ministry of Industry and Primary Resources, Jalan Menteri Besar, Bandar Seri Begawan BB 3910; tel. 2382822; fax 2382824; e-mail info@bruneitourism.travel; internet www.bruneitourism.travel.

Defence

As assessed at November 2013, the total strength of the Royal Brunei Malay Regiment was 7,000: army 4,900; navy 1,000; air force 1,100. Military service (for which only ethnic Malays are eligible) is voluntary. Paramilitary forces comprise an estimated 2,250, of whom an estimated 400–500 belong to the Gurkha Reserve Unit and 1,750 are members of the Royal Brunei Police. A Gurkha battalion of the British army guards the petroleum and gas fields. Singaporean troops operate a training school in Brunei.

Defence Budget: B $516m. in 2013.

Commander of the Royal Brunei Armed Forces: Pehin Datu Pekerma Jaya Maj.-Gen. Dato Seri Pahlawan MOHD TAWIH ABDULLAH.

Commander of the Royal Brunei Land Force: Col YUSSOF BIN Haji ABD RAHMAN.

Commander of the Royal Brunei Navy: Dato Seri Pahlawan ABD AZIZ Haji MOHAMED TAMIT.

Commander of the Royal Brunei Air Force: Brig.-Gen. Haji WARDI BIN Haji ABD LATIP.

Education

Education is free and is compulsory for 12 years from the age of five years, and in 2010 the adult literacy rate was 95.2%. Islamic studies form an integral part of the school curriculum. There are three official languages of instruction, Malay, English and Chinese (Mandarin), with schools being divided accordingly. In 2011/12 enrolment at primary level included 92% of pupils in the relevant age group, while enrolment at secondary level included 95% of pupils in the relevant age-group. In 2012 there were 200 pre-primary and primary schools, 40 secondary schools, 12 vocational colleges and five higher education institutions. In the budget for 2011/12 the Government allocated B $693m. to the Ministry of Education.

BULGARIA

Introductory Survey

LOCATION, CLIMATE, LANGUAGE, RELIGION, FLAG, CAPITAL

The Republic of Bulgaria lies in the eastern Balkans, in south-eastern Europe. It is bounded by Romania to the north, by Turkey and Greece to the south, by Serbia to the west and by the former Yugoslav republic of Macedonia to the south-west. The country has an eastern coastline on the Black Sea. The climate is one of fairly sharp contrasts between winter and summer. Temperatures in the capital, Sofia, are generally between −5°C (23°F) and 28°C (82°F). The official language is Bulgarian, a Southern Slavonic language, written in the Cyrillic alphabet. Minority languages include Turkish and Macedonian. The majority of the population is Christian; most are members of the Bulgarian Orthodox Church, although there is a substantial minority of Muslims. The national flag (proportions 2 by 3) has three equal horizontal stripes, of white, green and red.

CONTEMPORARY POLITICAL HISTORY

Historical Context

After almost 500 years of Ottoman rule, Bulgaria declared itself an independent kingdom in 1908. In both the First and Second World Wars, Bulgaria allied itself with Germany, and in 1941 joined in the occupation of Yugoslavia. In September 1942 the Fatherland Front, a newly formed left-wing alliance, seized power, with help from the USSR, and installed a Government, led by Kimon Georgiev. Soviet troops occupied Bulgaria in 1944. In September 1946 the monarchy was abolished following a popular referendum, and a republic was proclaimed. The first post-war elections were held in October, when the Fatherland Front won 364 seats—277 of which were held by the Bulgarian Communist Party (BCP)—in the 465-member National Assembly. In November Georgi Dimitrov, the First Secretary of the BCP, became Chairman of the Council of Ministers (Prime Minister) in a Government formed by the Fatherland Front. All opposition parties were abolished and a new Constitution was adopted in December 1947, when Bulgaria was designated a People's Republic. Dimitrov was replaced as Prime Minister by Vasil Kolarov in March 1949, but remained leader of the BCP until his death in July. His successor as party leader, Vulko Chervenkov, became Prime Minister in February 1950.

Todor Zhivkov succeeded Chervenkov as leader of the BCP in 1954, although Chervenkov remained Prime Minister until 1956, when he was replaced by Anton Yugov. Following an ideological struggle within the BCP, Zhivkov was Prime Minister from 1962 until 1971, when, after the adoption of a new Constitution, he became the first President of the newly formed State Council. At a BCP Congress in 1981 the party's leader was restyled General Secretary. In June, following elections to the National Assembly, a new Government was formed: Grisha Filipov, a member of the BCP's Political Bureau, succeeded Stanko Todorov, who had been Prime Minister since 1971. In March 1986 Filipov was replaced by Georgi Atanasov, a former Vice-President of the State Council.

In local elections in March 1988 the nomination of candidates other than those endorsed by the BCP was permitted. Candidates presented by independent public organizations and workers' collectives obtained about one-quarter of the total votes cast. On 10 November 1989 Zhivkov was removed from his post of General Secretary of the BCP and from the Political Bureau. He was replaced as General Secretary by Petar Mladenov, Minister of Foreign Affairs since 1971, who also became President of the State Council. In mid-November 1989 the National Assembly voted to abolish part of the penal code prohibiting 'anti-State propaganda' and to grant an amnesty to those convicted under its provisions. Zhivkov was subsequently denounced by the BCP, and an investigation into corruption during his tenure was initiated. (In January 1994 Zhivkov was sentenced to seven years' imprisonment on charges of embezzlement of state funds, but in February 1996 his appeal against the sentence was upheld.)

Domestic Political Affairs

In early December 1989 Angel Dimitrov became leader of the Bulgarian Agrarian People's Union (BAPU, the sole legal political party apart from the BCP, with which it was originally allied); the BAPU was subsequently reconstituted as an independent opposition party. In mid-December the BCP proposed amendments to the Constitution and the adoption of a new electoral law to permit free elections to be held. In January 1990 the National Assembly voted to remove from the Constitution the article guaranteeing the BCP's dominant role in society and approved legislation permitting citizens to form independent groups and to stage demonstrations. Discussions regarding political and economic reforms commenced between the BCP, the BAPU and the Sayuz na Demokratichnite Sili (SDS—Union of Democratic Forces), which comprised several dissident and independent groups. In February the BCP adopted a new manifesto, pledging its commitment to the separation of party and state, and the introduction of a multi-party system, while retaining its Marxist orientation. Nevertheless, the new Council of Ministers, appointed on 8 February, was composed solely of BCP members, chaired by Andrei Lukanov.

In February 1990 some 200,000 supporters of the SDS protested in Sofia to demand the end of BCP rule. Following discussions in March, it was finally agreed that Mladenov was to be re-elected as President, pending elections to a Grand National Assembly, which would be empowered to approve a new constitution. It was also decided to dissolve the State Council. In April the National Assembly adopted an electoral law, together with legislation that guaranteed the right to form political parties. Meanwhile, the BCP was reconstituted as the Balgarska Sotsialisticheska Partiya (BSP—Bulgarian Socialist Party).

Elections to a 400-member Grand National Assembly were held in two rounds in June 1990. The BSP won 211 seats, while the SDS obtained 144. The Dvizhenie za Prava i Svobodi (DPS—Movement for Rights and Freedoms), which had been established in 1990 to represent the country's Muslim minority (principally ethnic Turks), secured 23 seats. The BAPU won 16 seats. In July Mladenov resigned as President, following a campaign of protests led by students. Zhelyu Zhelev, the Chairman of the SDS, was elected to replace him in August. Zhelev was succeeded as Chairman of the SDS by Petar Beron, and, from December, by Filip Dimitrov.

In November 1990 16 BSP delegates to the Grand National Assembly formed a separate group, as a result of which the party no longer held an absolute majority. Following a general strike prompted by increased economic hardship, Lukanov's Government resigned at the end of the month. A new 'Government of national consensus' was formed in December, comprising members of the BSP, the SDS, the BAPU and four independents, and chaired by Dimitar Popov, a lawyer with no party affiliation.

Meanwhile, in November 1990 the Grand National Assembly voted to rename the country the Republic of Bulgaria and to remove from the national flag the state emblem, which included communist symbols. The Grand National Assembly adopted a new Constitution in July 1991; it subsequently voted to dissolve itself. The new Constitution provided for elections to be held, on an ad hoc basis, to a Grand National Assembly, the sole body empowered to adopt a new constitution and sanction territorial changes or certain constitutional amendments, although the permanent legislative body was to be the National Assembly. The Constitution stipulated a five-year residency qualification for presidential candidates, effectively disqualifying the candidacy of Simeon Sakskoburggotski (Saxe-Coburg Gotha—'Simeon II'), the pretender to the Bulgarian throne, who had lived in exile since 1946. At the elections to the new, 240-seat National Assembly, held on 13 October 1991, the SDS obtained 110 seats, narrowly defeating an alliance led by the BSP, which won 106 seats. The DPS secured 24 seats. The new Council of Ministers, composed principally of SDS members, was announced in November. Dimitrov, the leader of the SDS, was elected Chairman of the new Government. A direct presidential election was held in January 1992, in two rounds; Zhelev was re-elected for a five-year term, receiving 53% of the votes cast in the 'run-off' poll.

In April 1992 the Government adopted legislation restoring ownership of land and property that had been transferred to the state during 1947–62 (the deadline for property restitution was extended by three years in 1995); legislation approving the privatization of state-owned companies followed. In May Dimitrov implemented an extensive reorganization of the Council of Ministers. Meanwhile, relations between President Zhelev and the SDS became increasingly strained. In October 1992 DPS and BSP deputies in the National Assembly defeated the Government in a motion of confidence proposed by Dimitrov. In December the DPS nominated an academic, Prof. Lyuben Berov, hitherto an economic adviser to Zhelev, as Prime Minister. The SDS accused Berov of collaborating with the former communist regime and organized a large rally to protest against his candidacy. Although the majority of SDS deputies abstained, Berov was approved as Prime Minister on 30 December, heading a Council of Ministers principally composed of 'technocrats'.

In March 1993 a breakaway faction of the SDS formed a new, pro-Berov organization, the New Union for Democracy (NUD). Demonstrations were staged by the SDS in June, accusing Zhelev of attempting to restore communism, and demanding immediate elections. In June the Vice-President, Blaga Dimitrova, resigned. The crisis subsided when three votes expressing no confidence in Berov's Government, proposed by the SDS in the National Assembly, proved unsuccessful.

In September 1994 Berov's Government submitted its resignation, owing to criticism of the organization of the privatization programme, and in October Zhelev dissolved the National Assembly. At the general election, which was held on 18 December, the BSP (in alliance with two small parties) obtained an outright majority in the National Assembly, with 125 seats; the SDS won 69 seats. A new Government, headed by the Chairman of the BSP, Zhan Videnov, was appointed in January 1995.

In March 1995 the Government drafted a programme for mass privatization. At municipal elections in October–November, the ruling coalition won 195 of a total of 255 mayoralties, although the SDS secured the mayoralties in the country's three main cities. In January 1996 an unsuccessful motion of no confidence in the Videnov administration led to the resignations of the Deputy Prime Minister and two ministers. In October former Prime Minister Andrei Lukanov was assassinated.

In the first round of the presidential election of 27 October 1996, Petar Stoyanov, a lawyer and senior member of the SDS, secured 44.1% of the votes cast; Ivan Marazov of the BSP, the candidate of a newly formed electoral alliance, Together for Bulgaria, received 27.0% of the votes. In the second round of voting, which took place on 3 November, Stoyanov was elected to the presidency, with 59.7% of the votes cast.

Decline in BSP support

In December 1996 the SDS staged a series of demonstrations to demand early legislative elections and the resignation of the Government. On 21 December Videnov tendered his resignation as Prime Minister and BSP leader. Georgi Parvanov, a supporter of Videnov, subsequently replaced him as Chairman of the BSP. At the end of December the National Assembly voted to accept the resignation of Videnov's Government. The SDS, however, intensified its campaign of demonstrations.

On 19 January 1997 Stoyanov was inaugurated as President. After Nikolai Dobrev relinquished the BSP mandate to form a government, the legislature approved recommendations by the consultative National Security Council that the President should appoint an interim council of ministers, dissolve the National Assembly and schedule legislative elections. In March the interim Government, led by the Mayor of Sofia, Stefan Sofiyanski, announced that Videnov was to be charged with criminal negligence over government policies that had caused severe grain shortages in 1995–96; the Minister of Agriculture under Videnov was also prosecuted.

At the elections to the National Assembly, conducted on 19 April 1997, the SDS secured 137 seats, while the BSP (again contesting the elections in alliance with other parties, as the Democratic Left) obtained only 58 seats. Later in April the SDS nominated the party Chairman, Ivan Kostov, as Prime Minister, and in May he was confirmed in that position by the National Assembly.

In January 2001, in advance of presidential and legislative elections, the BSP attempted to consolidate support by forming an alliance, the Coalition for Bulgaria, with smaller leftist and nationalist groups. In April the former monarch, Simeon Sakskoburggotski, who had returned to Bulgaria at the beginning of the month, was prevented from registering his new National Movement as a party. In May, however, the Movement was permitted to form an alliance with two smaller, registered parties, the Party of Bulgarian Women and the Oborishte Party for National Revival, as the National Movement Simeon II (NMSII), in order to participate in the legislative elections. Sakskoburggotski (who was not permitted officially to lead the Movement) emphasized that he had no desire to restore the monarchy, and pledged to combat official corruption and reform the economy, in order to fulfil the criteria for membership of the European Union (EU, see p. 273).

In the general election, held on 17 June 2001, the NMSII obtained 120 seats, while the SDS secured 51 seats. The NMSII held just one seat fewer than the 121 required to secure an absolute majority in the National Assembly, and it approached the DPS (which held 21 legislative seats) and the SDS as potential partners. The SDS refused to participate in an administration that included members of the DPS, and the BSP consequently became an informal coalition partner. Sakskoburggotski was sworn in as Prime Minister on 24 July. The Council of Ministers, in which two ministerial portfolios were allocated to both the DPS and the BSP, was approved by the National Assembly on the same day. Kostov subsequently resigned his leadership of the SDS. In March 2002 five members of the National Assembly left the NMSII, in protest against Sakskoburggotski's perceived failure to fulfil electoral pledges. In April the NMSII was finally legally registered as a political party, and Sakskoburggotski was elected as its Chairman.

Meanwhile, in the first round of voting in the presidential election held on 11 November 2001 Parvanov, contesting the election for the Coalition for Bulgaria, won 36.4% of the votes cast, and the incumbent, Stoyanov, who stood as an independent candidate, secured 34.9% of the votes. However, the rate of participation by the electorate was just 39.2% (less than the 50% demanded by the Constitution). Parvanov confirmed his victory in a second round of voting on 18 November, in which he obtained 54.1% of the votes cast; the rate of voter participation was some 54.6%. Parvanov took office on 22 January 2002. In February 2003 five legislative deputies had left the NMSII, alleging widespread corruption within the Government, thereby reducing the governing coalition's legislative majority to just 10 seats. Nadezhda Mihailova was re-elected as leader of the SDS in February 2004, prompting 26 SDS members, including the former Chairman, Kostov, to leave the party. Kostov founded a new party, Demokrati za silna Balgariya (DSB—Democrats for a Strong Bulgaria).

The return of the BSP

In February 2005 the National Assembly voted by a narrow majority to dismiss its Chairman, Ognyan Gerdzhikov. He was replaced by Borislav Velikov. In the same month, in an attempt to strengthen the ruling coalition before the legislative elections due to take place later that year, the Prime Minister reorganized the Council of Ministers.

At the elections to the National Assembly, held on 25 June 2005, the BSP-led Coalition for Bulgaria secured 82 of the 240 seats in the legislature and 34.2% of the votes cast; the NMSII received 53 seats and 22.1% of the votes, and the DPS secured 34 seats and 14.2% of the votes. A newly formed coalition of extreme right-wing and nationalist parties, the Attack National Union (Attack, subsequently the Attack Party—Partiya Ataka), secured 21 seats (8.8% of the votes). The rate of participation by the electorate was 55.7%. On 16 August the National Assembly approved a three-party coalition Government led by BSP leader Sergei Stanishev. The new Council of Ministers comprised nine members of the BSP, five members of the NMSII, three members of the DPS and one independent minister. Meanwhile, in July Georgi Pirinski, a former Minister of Foreign Affairs and Deputy Chairman of the BSP, was elected as the new Chairman of the National Assembly.

In October 2005 former President Stoyanov was appointed as leader of the SDS, replacing Mihailova. The first round of presidential voting, held on 22 October 2006 and contested by seven candidates, proved inconclusive because the rate of electoral participation was below the requisite 50%. The first-placed candidate, the incumbent, Parvanov, who secured some 64.1% of the votes cast, progressed to a 'run-off' vote against Volen Siderov of Ataka (who secured 21.5% of the votes cast) on 29 October. Parvanov won 76.0% of the votes in the second round of voting (which had no minimum required rate of participation), thereby becoming the first post-communist President of Bulgaria to be elected to a second term of office. Parvanov was inaugurated on 22 January 2007.

Following Bulgaria's accession to the EU on 1 January 2007 (see Foreign Affairs), elections to the European Parliament were held in May. Both the SDS and the DSB failed to secure representation, prompting the resignations of Stoyanov and Kostov from the leadership of their respective parties. The BSP and Grazhdani za evropeysko razvitie na Balgariya (GERB—Citizens for European Development of Bulgaria), a newly established centre-right opposition party unofficially headed by the Mayor of Sofia, Boyko Borisov, each secured five of the 18 available seats. The NMSII obtained one seat, and in the following month reconstituted itself as the Natsionalno dvizhenie za stabilnost i vazhod (NDSV—National Movement for Stability and Progress). At municipal elections, conducted on 28 October and 4 November, GERB won the mayoral polls in the country's principal towns, with Borisov re-elected as Mayor of Sofia.

A new State Agency for National Security was established in December 2007 to investigate cases of corruption and organized crime. In April 2008 the Minister of the Interior, Rumen Petkov, resigned from the Government, after allegations of corruption emerged. The BSP, the DPS and the NDSV reached agreement on a government reorganization, in which four ministers (including Petkov) were replaced. Hitherto ambassador to Germany, Meglena Plugchieva was appointed to the new post of Deputy Prime Minister, with responsibility for EU funds, while Mihail Mikov became Minister of the Interior. In May a new political organization, Balgarska Nova Demokratsia (BND—Bulgarian New Democracy), was created by former members of the NDSV, including 16 deputies who had left the party owing to their opposition to the NDSV leadership. None the less, the ruling three-party coalition retained a large majority in the National Assembly. In January 2009 more than 2,000 people attended an anti-Government demonstration outside the parliament building in Sofia to protest against corruption and poverty; the police detained around 160 people. On the following day 15 opposition deputies participated in a second demonstration.

In April 2009 the National Assembly approved the introduction of a mixed system of voting in legislative elections: 31 of the 240 deputies were to be directly elected by majority vote, while the remaining seats continued to be distributed by proportional representation. At elections to the European Parliament held on 7 June, GERB secured five of the 17 seats allocated to Bulgaria, with 24.4% of the votes cast, while the BSP-led Coalition for Bulgaria took four (18.5% of the votes) and the DPS three (14.1%). Ataka and the NDSV each obtained two seats, with the remaining seat won by the recently formed Blue Coalition, led by the SDS and the DSB. A rate of participation of 37.5% was recorded.

The 2009 legislative elections

In the general election held on 5 July 2009, GERB won 39.7% of the votes cast and 116 of the 240 seats; the Coalition for Bulgaria received 17.7% of the votes and 40 seats, the DPS secured 14.4% of the votes and 38 seats, while the NDSV failed to obtain representation. Ataka, the Blue Coalition and the centre-right Red, zakonnost i spravedlivost (Order, Law and Justice party, founded in late 2005) secured 21, 15 and 10 seats, respectively. At 60.9%, the rate of voter participation was notably higher than at the 2005 elections. Tsetska Tsacheva, of GERB, was elected to chair the new National Assembly at its first session on 14 July. A minority GERB Government, led by Borisov and supported by Ataka, the Blue Coalition and Order, Law and Justice, was approved by the legislature on 27 July. In February 2010 a recount of votes at 23 Turkish polling stations (after the Constitutional Court invalidated some 18,350 votes cast in Turkey) led to a ruling that increased the number of parliamentary seats held by GERB to 117, and reduced the representation of the DPS by one seat, to 37.

Borisov swiftly introduced measures intended to address corruption. In August 2009 a six-member ministerial council, chaired by Deputy Prime Minister and Minister of Finance Simeon Dyankov, was established to manage EU resources, while the Ministry of the Interior and the police force initiated a project aimed at detecting and preventing the misuse of EU funds. The Government also instigated investigations into alleged corruption by the previous Government. Borisov had been barred from assuming the official leadership of the party while holding the position of Mayor of Sofia. In November Yordanka Fandakova was elected Mayor, and Borisov was elected as Chairman of GERB in January 2010, with Deputy Prime Minister and Minister of the Interior Tsvetan Tsvetanov as his deputy. In mid-March Tomislav Donchev, hitherto Mayor of the central city of Gabrovo, was appointed as Minister for the Management of EU Funds. In November 2010 a new, independent commission was established to investigate high-level corruption.

The GERB Government and the election of a new President

In November 2010 it was reported that Parvanov had launched a new movement, the Alternative for Bulgarian Revival, which included former members of the BSP. In December it emerged that almost one-half of the members of Bulgaria's diplomatic service had co-operated with the communist-era security services. The National Assembly subsequently voted in favour of the recall of 33 ambassadors. Bozhidar Dimitrov, who was also known to have collaborated with the security services, resigned from his post as Minister without Portfolio in late December. In January 2011 illicitly obtained recordings released in the media appeared to implicate members of the Government, including Borisov, in corrupt practices, and to reveal severe internal divisions. The Government, which denied the authenticity of the recordings, subsequently won two votes of confidence in the National Assembly. In February a bomb exploded outside the offices of opposition newspaper *Galeria*, which had notably published transcripts of the recordings. The Director of the State Agency for National Security subsequently tendered his resignation. In March a large-scale anti-Government demonstration was organized by the BSP in Sofia, in protest at economic hardship. In June the Government survived a further parliamentary motion of no confidence.

The first round of the presidential election held on 23 October 2011 was contested by 18 candidates. Rosen Plevneliev of GERB (who had previously held the position of Minister of Regional Development and Public Works) secured 40.1% of the votes cast, while the BSP candidate, Ivaylo Kalfin, received 29.0%. (Parvanov, having served two terms in office, was prohibited from seeking re-election.) At the subsequent second round of voting, contested by the two leading candidates on 30 October, Plevneliev was elected to the presidency with 52.6% of the votes cast. The rate of participation by the electorate was estimated at 48.3%. Municipal elections were conducted in two rounds concurrently with the presidential voting: GERB retained control of the principal towns, including the mayoralties of Sofia and Burgas. In mid-December the Constitutional Court officially ruled the results of the presidential election to be legitimate, and Plevneliev was inaugurated on 22 January 2012.

In early December 2011 the National Assembly voted to adopt pension reforms, which included proposals for a gradual increase in the retirement age from 2012. Opposition parties strongly opposed the measures, while the two main trade union federations, which had previously negotiated an agreement with the Government allowing the retirement age to remain unchanged until 2021, began a campaign of national protests. In January 2012 a 'special court' that was designed to expedite trials relating to organized crime opened in Sofia.

In July 2012 a suicide bomb attack killed five Israeli tourists and a Bulgarian bus driver at Burgas Airport, and more than 30 other people were wounded; the attack was alleged by the Ministry of the Interior to be linked to the Lebanese militant Shi'ite grouping Hezbollah (which denied involvement). In mid-January 2013 there was an apparent attempt to assassinate the Chairman of the DPS, Ahmed Dogan, who was speaking at a party conference in Sofia; Dogan, who was unharmed, resigned his party post on the same day, and a man was arrested and later charged with attempted murder. Dogan was succeeded by Lyutvi Mestan.

In January 2013 Stefan Vodenicharov was appointed as Minister of Education, Youth and Science, replacing Sergey Ignatov. The latter had resigned as a result of a scandal involving the Scientific Research Fund, which included irregularities in the assessment of research funding; in the previous month hundreds of scientists and researchers had protested against alleged attempts to cover up the scandal.

Recent developments: the 2013 legislative elections

In mid-February 2013 large-scale popular protests against economic hardship and rising electricity prices prompted Borisov to dismiss Deputy Prime Minister and Minister of Finance Dyankov. On the following day an unemployed man set himself on fire outside the local branch of a major bank, and later died, in the first in a series of cases of self-immolation throughout Bulgaria. On 20 February Borisov announced the resignation of his Government, after the protests in the capital became violent. The Government's resignation was approved by the National Assembly the next day. An interim cabinet, led by Marin Raykov, was officially appointed by President Plevneliev on 13 March, pending early legislative elections, scheduled for 12 May. At the elections, which took place as scheduled, GERB was the highest-placed party, with 30.6% of the votes and 97 seats; the BSP-led Coalition for Bulgaria obtained 26.6% of the votes and 84 seats, the DPS secured 11.3% and 36 seats, and Ataka 7.3% and 23 seats. On 29 May a new Government, comprising members of the BSP, the DPS and unaffiliated ministers, took office, under the leadership of Plamen Oresharski, who had been Minister of Finance in 2005–09. Notable appointments included that of Tsvetlin Yovchev of the BSP as Minister of the Interior and, from June, Deputy Prime Minister.

In May–July 2013 Tsvetan Tsvetanov, the former Minister of the Interior, was charged in connection with allegations of the illicit monitoring of members of the previous Government and of the National Assembly, and with obstructing justice; a tax evasion case originally launched in 2011 was also re-opened, and in November 2013 Tsvetanov was charged with embezzlement.

Meanwhile, popular protests resumed on 14 June 2013, in response to the approval by the National Assembly of Delyan Peevski, a businessman with substantial media interests who had previously been investigated over corruption allegations, as the new Chairman of the State Agency for National Security (DANS); President Plevneliev questioned Peevski's suitability for the post, and Peevski resigned the next day. On 19 June Oresharski apologized for the controversial appointment of Peevski, but stated that he would not resign as premier, as that risked deepening the political crisis. Vladimir Pisanchev was appointed as Chairman of DANS in the following month. Meanwhile, Oresharski swiftly implemented measures to regulate the energy sector in an attempt to prevent further demonstrations. The Government also enacted a series of legislative amendments to overturn actions taken by its predecessor, particularly with the aim of improving the accountability of state agencies. The GERB-appointed heads of the National Security Service (NSO), the National Investigative Service and the National Audit Office were all to be replaced. None the less, large-scale demonstrations continued to take place. On 23–24 July protesters blockaded the National Assembly following the approval of the draft budget, trapping around 100 deputies and parliamentary staff inside; some 20 people were injured in clashes between protesters and the police. In late October students at Sofia University joined the anti-Government protests, occupying a university building. The protests persisted into the early months of 2014. In February 2014 the Government survived a third vote of no confidence in the National Assembly.

Foreign Affairs

Regional relations

Bulgaria's establishment of formal relations with the former Yugoslav republic of Macedonia (FYRM) in January 1992 prompted criticism from the Greek Government. In December 1993 Bulgaria announced that it was to open an embassy in the FYRM and relax border procedures between the two states. In February 1999 Prime Minister Kostov and the Prime Minister of the FYRM, Ljubčo Georgievski, signed a declaration pledging that neither country had a territorial claim on the other. In March the Ministers of Defence of Bulgaria and the FYRM signed a joint declaration providing for increased military co-operation, in connection with the aim of both countries to join the North Atlantic Treaty Organization (NATO, see p. 370).

Bulgaria's relations with Serbia were strained in March 2008, following the Bulgarian Government's decision to recognize Kosovo's independence, which had been unilaterally declared by the former Serbian province in the previous month. None the less, in September the Governments of Bulgaria, Serbia and Romania signed an agreement on co-operation in combating cross-border crime. Moreover, in December 2012 it was reported that Prime Minister Borisov and Serbian premier Ivica Dačić had signed a deal to build a 150-km natural gas pipeline connecting the two countries' transmission grids. The deal, worth some €120m., was to be financed by the European Union (EU) and construction was expected to be completed by 2017.

Relations between Bulgaria and Russia improved in 1992, following the signature of co-operation agreements, and the visit of the Russian President, Boris Yeltsin, to Sofia in August. In April 1998 the Bulgarian Government signed an agreement with the Russian national gas company, Gazprom, providing for the supply and transit of Russian gas. In December 2000 Russia expressed its disappointment at Bulgaria's decision to terminate, in accordance with conditions for accession to the EU, a 1978 bilateral agreement on visa-free travel, with effect from June 2001. However, in March 2003 Russian President Vladimir Putin visited Bulgaria, resulting in strongly enhanced economic relations, despite failing to persuade Bulgaria to withdraw its support for US-led military action in Iraq (see below). In March 2007 the Russian, Bulgarian and Greek Governments signed an agreement on the construction of a pipeline to transport Russian petroleum from the Bulgarian Black Sea port of Burgas to Alexandroupolis, on the Greek Aegean coast. In early 2008 the two countries also signed an accord on Bulgaria's participation in Russia's so-called South Stream project, which was being pursued jointly with Italian energy company Eni and involved the establishment of a pipeline to deliver Russian natural gas to Italy and Austria, via Bulgaria. In mid-2010 French energy company EDF joined the project. Meanwhile, in July 2009 the Governments of Bulgaria, Austria, Hungary, Romania and Turkey signed an agreement on the construction of the 3,300-km Nabucco pipeline, which was intended to transport natural gas from Central Asia through Turkey to Europe, thus reducing dependence on Russian supplies. In November 2010 Putin, by this time the Russian premier, visited Sofia, where he and Prime Minister Boyko Borisov signed an agreement on the establishment of a joint company for the construction of the South Stream pipeline route. In November 2012 Bulgaria signed a six-year arrangement with the Russian gas monopoly Gazprom, which provided for a 20% reduction in the cost of Bulgaria's gas imports. Bulgaria also signed a final investment agreement with Gazprom on the South Stream pipeline; construction of the pipeline commenced in the following month. Meanwhile, in December 2011 the Bulgarian Government had announced its withdrawal from the Burgas–Alexandroupolis pipeline, citing financial concerns.

Relations with Turkey were intermittently strained from the mid-1980s, when the Zhivkov regime began a campaign of forced assimilation of Bulgaria's ethnic Turkish minority (8% of the total population, according to 2011 census data). In May 1989 Bulgarian militia units violently suppressed demonstrations by an estimated 30,000 ethnic Turks in eastern Bulgaria, and in June more than 80,000 ethnic Turks were expelled from Bulgaria, although the Bulgarian authorities claimed that the Turks had chosen to settle in Turkey. By mid-August an estimated 310,000 Bulgarian Turks had crossed into Turkey, and in late August the Turkish Government closed the border. In the following month a substantial number of the Bulgarian Turks, disillusioned with conditions in Turkey, began to return to Bulgaria. The Turkish Government repeatedly proposed that discussions with the Bulgarian Government be held, under the auspices of the UN High Commissioner for Refugees (UNHCR), to establish the rights of the Bulgarian Turks and to formulate a clear immigration policy. Finally, Bulgaria agreed to negotiations, and friendly relations between Bulgaria and Turkey were restored by late 1991.

Meanwhile, in December 1989 some 6,000 Pomaks (ethnic Bulgarian Muslims) held demonstrations to demand religious and cultural freedoms, as well as an official inquiry into alleged atrocities against Pomaks during Zhivkov's tenure of office. In March 1990 the National Assembly approved legislation that permitted ethnic Turks and Pomaks to use their original, non-Slavic names. In May 1992 Prime Minister Dimitrov visited Turkey, and the two countries signed a treaty of friendship and co-operation. In June 1998 the National Assembly ratified an agreement demarcating the border between Bulgaria and Turkey.

Negotiations on Bulgaria's accession to the EU began in March 2000. In June 2004 Bulgaria (along with Romania) officially concluded the negotiation process. Bulgaria and Romania signed formal accession agreements with the EU on 25 April 2005. In October the European Commission emphasized that Bulgaria's accession remained dependent on its ability, *inter alia*, to combat organized crime and reform the judicial system. Bulgaria (and Romania) formally acceded to the EU on 1 January 2007. However, many existing EU members imposed extensive labour market restrictions; only nine countries guaranteed unlimited access to migrant workers from Bulgaria and Romania following their accession. The Czech Republic and Italy removed their labour market restrictions in January 2012, and France eased restrictions in October; transitional migration restrictions were lifted altogether on 1 January 2014. Additional constraints on membership rights, together with domestic power deficits following the closure of two nuclear reactors at the end of 2006, in compliance with EU accession preconditions, provoked some animosity between Bulgaria and the original bloc members and led to reciprocal restrictions against economic migrants from those countries refusing or limiting access to Bulgarians. In early 2008 the Government initiated an official campaign to gain support for the reopening of the nuclear reactors, despite the opposition of the EU. The European Commission suspended nearly €500m. in development aid to Bulgaria in July 2008, after releasing a report that strongly criticized the country's continued failure to reduce levels of organized crime and corruption, including the alleged misuse of EU funds by public officials. In November €220m. of this funding was forfeited. After taking office in July 2009, the administration of Boyko Borisov introduced measures aimed at improving the management of EU funds (see Contemporary Political History). In September it was announced that the European Commission was to resume farm subsidy payments and other agricultural aid to Bulgaria. Further suspended funds, amounting to some €340m., were released in November. In January 2014 the European Commission published a report on Bulgaria's progress in implementing judicial reform, and combating corruption and organized crime, which noted that although some important measures had been implemented in the judicial reform process, corruption continued to be perceived to be endemic within Bulgaria, while combating organized crime remained a major challenge.

Other external relations

Bulgaria's relations with the USA strengthened during 2002, and in February 2003 the National Assembly voted to allow US forces to make use of Bulgarian airspace, as well as the airbase at Sarafovo, on the Black Sea, for military operations during the impending US-led campaign to remove the regime of Saddam Hussain in Iraq; Bulgaria had previously offered its support to the USA during its military campaign in Afghanistan from late 2001. Bulgaria dispatched some 470 troops to support the US-led military campaign in Iraq, which commenced in March 2003. The troops were withdrawn after the Iraqi parliamentary elections in December 2005. Bulgarian troops continued to participate in the NATO-led International Security Assistance Force (ISAF) in Afghanistan, their contingent numbering 581 in early 2013. Meanwhile, a defence co-operation agreement on the sharing of Bulgarian military bases with US troops was signed by Kalfin and the US Secretary of State, Condoleezza Rice, in Sofia in April 2006, and entered into force in June; further agreements on the joint use of military facilities were signed in early 2008. Several bilateral accords were signed during an official visit to the USA by Bulgarian Prime Minister Stanishev in June 2008.

As a result of the civil conflict in Syria, the number of Syrian refugees arriving in Bulgaria, via Turkey, increased significantly in 2013, totalling more than 6,000 people. The Government struggled to accommodate the number of asylum-seekers; according to the UN High Commissioner for Refugees (UNHCR), some 1,400 police officers had been deployed along the Turkish border and a 30-km fence was constructed in an effort to reduce the number of displaced people entering the country.

CONSTITUTION AND GOVERNMENT

The Constitution of the Republic of Bulgaria took effect upon its promulgation, on 13 July 1991. Legislative power is held by the unicameral National Assembly (National Assembly), comprising 240 members, who are elected for four years by universal adult suffrage. The President of the Republic (Head of State) is directly elected for a period of five years, and is also Supreme Commander-in-Chief of the Armed Forces. The Council of Ministers, the highest organ of state administration, is elected by the National Assembly. The judicial branch of government is independent. The Supreme Court of Cassation exercises supreme judicial responsibility for the application of the law by all courts, while the Supreme Administrative Court rules on all challenges to the legality of acts of any organ of government. For local administration purposes, Bulgaria comprises 28 regions (divided into a total of 259 municipalities).

REGIONAL AND INTERNATIONAL CO-OPERATION

Bulgaria is a member of the European Bank for Reconstruction and Development (EBRD, see p. 267), of the Council of Europe (see p. 252) and of the Organization of the Black Sea Economic Co-operation (BSEC, see p. 401). In January 2007 Bulgaria acceded to the European Union (EU, see p. 273).

Bulgaria became a member of the UN in 1955, and was admitted to the World Trade Organization (WTO, see p. 434) in 1996. In 2004 Bulgaria joined the North Atlantic Treaty Organization (NATO, see p. 370).

ECONOMIC AFFAIRS

In 2012, according to estimates by the World Bank, Bulgaria's gross national income (GNI), measured at average 2010–12 prices, was US $50,163m., equivalent to $6,870 per head (or $15,390 per head on an international purchasing-power parity basis). During 2003–12, it was estimated, the population decreased at an average rate of 0.8% per year, while gross domestic product (GDP) per head increased, in real terms, at an average annual rate of 4.0%. Bulgaria's overall GDP increased, in real terms, by an average of 3.2% annually during 2003–12; real GDP increased by 0.8% in 2012, according to official preliminary figures.

According to official preliminary figures, agriculture (including hunting, forestry and fishing) contributed 6.4% of GDP in 2012. The sector engaged 6.4% of the employed labour force in 2012. In 1990 private farming was legalized, and by the end of 1999 some 96% of farmland had been restituted, in its former physical boundaries, to former owners and their heirs. The principal crops are wheat, maize, sunflower seeds, barley, potatoes, grapes, tomatoes and watermelons. Bulgaria is a major exporter of wine, and there is a large exportable surplus of processed agricultural products. During 2003–12 the average annual GDP of the agricultural sector declined, in real terms, by 2.6%; the GDP of the sector declined by 1.1% in 2011, but increased by 3.5% in 2012.

According to official preliminary figures, industry (including mining, manufacturing, construction and utilities) provided some 30.4% of GDP in 2012. The sector engaged 31.3% of the employed labour force in 2012. Industrial GDP increased, in real terms, at an average annual rate of 3.2% in 2003–12; industrial GDP increased by 5.9% in 2011 and by 0.7% in 2012.

In 2005 mining accounted for some 1.6% of GDP, and in 2012 mining and quarrying engaged 0.9% of the employed labour force. Coal, iron ore, copper, manganese, lead and zinc are mined, and petroleum is extracted on the Black Sea coast.

According to World Bank estimates, the manufacturing sector contributed 16.6% of GDP in 2011. The sector engaged 20.6% of the employed labour force in 2012. The GDP of the manufacturing sector increased at an average annual rate of 5.4%, in real terms, in 2003–11; the GDP of the sector increased by 9.0% in 2011.

According to official preliminary figures, the construction sector contributed 5.9% of GDP in 2012, when it engaged 7.0% of the employed labour force. The GDP of the sector increased at an average annual rate of 3.5% in 2003–12, in real terms. Sectoral GDP declined by 3.5% in 2012.

Bulgaria's production of primary energy in 2011 was equivalent to 62.4% of gross consumption. Coal and nuclear power, the latter produced by the country's sole nuclear power station, at Kozloduy, are the main domestic sources of energy. Four of the plant's six reactors were closed by 2006, in compliance with conditions for membership of the European Union (EU, see p. 273). There were plans for the construction of a new reactor at Kozloduy, although this would not be completed before 2016. Bulgaria's proven coal reserves stood at 2,366m. metric tons at the end of 2012. In 2011 nuclear power provided 32.6% of electric energy, while coal accounted for 55.0% of electricity production. Crude petroleum and natural gas comprised 18.8% of the value of merchandise imports in 2012.

According to official preliminary figures, in 2012 the services sector contributed some 63.2% of GDP. In 2012 the sector engaged 62.2% of the employed labour force. Tourism revenue increased significantly from 2002. Revenue totalled US $3,967m. in 2011, but decreased to $3,748m. in 2012. The real GDP of the services sector increased at an average annual rate of 4.1% during 2003–12; the GDP of the sector increased by 0.7% in 2011, but declined by 0.2% in 2012.

In 2012 Bulgaria recorded a visible merchandise trade deficit of US $4,455.7m., and there was a deficit of $735.3m. on the current account of the balance of payments. In that year the principal sources of imports were Russia (which provided 20.3% of the total), Germany, Italy, the People's Republic of China, Romania and Greece. The main market for exports in 2012 was Germany (taking 10.2% of the total). Turkey, Italy, Romania and

Greece were also significant purchasers. The principal exports in 2012 were petroleum products, metals (including iron and steel), raw materials for the food industry, and clothing and footwear. The principal imports in that year were mineral fuels, crude petroleum and natural gas, machines and equipment, food, beverages and tobacco, spare parts and equipment, and ores.

In 2012 Bulgaria recorded a budgetary deficit of 359m. new leva (equivalent to 0.5% of GDP). Bulgaria's general government gross debt was 13,674m. new leva in 2012, equivalent to 17.6% of GDP. Bulgaria's total external debt in 2011 was US $39,930m., of which $4,138m. was public and publicly guaranteed debt. In that year the cost of servicing long-term public and publicly guaranteed debt and repayments to the IMF was equivalent to 12.2% of the value of exports of goods, services and income (excluding workers' remittances). The annual rate of inflation averaged 5.7% in 2003–12. Consumer prices increased by 3.0% in 2012. According to Bulgaria's National Statistical Institute, 12.3% of the labour force were registered as unemployed in 2012.

Large inflows of foreign investment followed the conclusion, in 2004, of negotiations on Bulgaria's membership of the EU and continued after accession at the beginning of 2007, allowing infrastructure projects to proceed rapidly. In July 2010 Bulgaria's budget deficit triggered the EU's Excessive Deficit Procedure (EDP), which compels countries to correct errors relating to fiscal policy, and Bulgaria swiftly introduced measures to curb public expenditure. Bulgaria exited the EDP in 2012, and met its target of reducing the fiscal deficit to 1.3% of GDP by the end of that year; the country's level of public debt was the second lowest in the EU. However, Bulgaria remains the poorest EU member in terms of income per head. According to EU statistics, the rate of unemployment was 13.1% in January 2014, while the rate of youth unemployment had reached 30.0%; poverty was also widespread. Although GDP growth resumed in 2010, and continued in 2011–12, continuing uncertainties in the external environment were hampering the country's recovery, despite the maintenance of strong macroeconomic policies. The IMF projected real GDP growth of 0.5% for 2013, based on the export market remaining relatively sound amid hampered demand domestically, and 1.6% for 2014, as both domestic demand and European trade and foreign direct investment recovered. The European Commission projected that Bulgaria's recovery would be slower than those of comparable economies because of the continued decline in the population level. The Government that took office in May 2013 pledged to prioritize macroeconomic stability and, notably, established a Ministry of Investment Projects. However, government wariness over the public unrest that ultimately led to the collapse of the Borisov Government in February of that year meant that the energy sector remained uncompetitive and in need of reform; prices were reduced three times in 2013 and were to remain frozen in 2014. The IMF observed that structural reforms remained necessary to stimulate both growth and incomes, and criticized the Borisov Government's reversal of reforms aimed at strengthening the sustainability of the pension system.

PUBLIC HOLIDAYS

2015: 1 January (New Year), 3 March (National Day), 12–13 April (Eastern Orthodox Easter), 1 May (Labour Day), 6 May (St George's Day), 24 May (Education Day), 6 September (Unification Day), 22 September (Independence Day), 24–26 December (Christmas).

Statistical Survey

Sources (unless otherwise indicated): National Statistical Institute, 1038 Sofia, ul. P. Volov 2; tel. (2) 985-77-00; fax (2) 985-76-40; e-mail info@nsi.bg; internet www.nsi.bg; Bulgarian National Bank, 1000 Sofia, pl. Knyaz Aleksandar I 1; tel. (2) 914-59; fax (2) 980-24-25; e-mail press_office@bnbank.org; internet www.bnb.bg; Center for Economic Development, 1408 Sofia, ul. J. K. Ivan Vazov 1/9; tel. (2) 953-42-04; e-mail stat@ced.bg; internet www.stat.bg.

Area and Population

AREA, POPULATION AND DENSITY

Area (sq km)*	110,994†
Population (census results)	
1 March 2001	7,928,901
1 February 2011	
Males	3,586,571
Females	3,777,999
Total	7,364,570
Population (official estimate at 31 December)	
2012	7,284,552
Density (per sq km) at 31 December 2012	65.6

* Including territorial waters of frontier rivers (261.4 sq km).

† 42,855 sq miles.

POPULATION BY AGE AND SEX

(official estimates at 31 December 2012)

	Males	Females	Total
0–14	508,975	481,014	989,989
15–64	2,469,854	2,429,238	4,899,092
65 and over	566,244	829,227	1,395,471
Total	3,545,073	3,739,479	7,284,552

ETHNIC GROUPS

(2011 census)

	Number	%
Bulgarian	5,664,624	76.9
Turkish	588,318	8.0
Roma	325,343	4.4
Others*	786,285	10.7
Total	7,364,570	100.0

* Including 53,391 (0.7% of the total) who chose not to be defined by ethnic group.

ADMINISTRATIVE REGIONS

(population at 31 December 2012, official estimates)

	Area (sq km)	Population	Density (per sq km)
City Oblast			
Sofia City	1,038.8	1,302,316	1,253.7
Oblasts			
Blagoevgrad	6,468.8	320,160	49.5
Burgas	7,610.6	414,154	54.4
Dobrich	4,692.5	186,445	39.7
Gabrovo	2,069.5	119,971	58.0
Haskovo	4,032.0	241,676	59.9
Kardzhali	4,023.0	151,340	37.6
Kyustendil	3,004.2	132,813	44.2
Lovech	4,131.0	137,718	33.3
Montana	3,587.6	143,662	40.0
Pazardzhik	4,382.2	271,721	62.0
Pernik	2,356.7	130,240	55.3
Pleven	4,187.1	262,969	62.8
Plovdiv	5,595.1	678,860	121.3
Razgrad	2,647.9	122,166	46.1
Ruse	2,625.9	231,580	88.2
Shumen	3,376.5	178,814	53.0
Silistra	2,878.1	117,214	40.7
Sliven	3,731.7	195,345	52.3

—*continued*	Area (sq km)	Population	Density (per sq km)
Smolyan	3,520.6	118,751	33.7
Sofia	7,389.4	243,254	32.9
Stara Zagora	4,905.6	329,832	67.2
Targovishche	2,756.0	118,786	43.1
Varna	3,822.8	473,415	123.8
Veliko Tarnovo	4,693.5	253,580	54.0
Vidin	3,112.3	97,546	31.3
Vratsa	4,189.1	181,574	43.3
Yambol	4,165.1	128,650	30.9
Total	110,993.6	7,284,552	65.6

Note: Each oblast is named after its capital city.

PRINCIPAL TOWNS
(population at 31 December 2012, official estimates)

Sofia (capital)	1,302,316	Sliven	123,891
Varna	343,602	Pazardzhik	113,365
Plovdiv	339,129	Pernik	95,043
Burgas (Bourgas)	211,535	Haskovo	92,788
Ruse (Roussé)	165,884	Shumen	92,693
Stara Zagora	159,516	Dobrich	89,627
Pleven	128,328	Veliko Tarnovo	88,286

BIRTHS, MARRIAGES AND DEATHS

	Registered live births		Registered marriages		Registered deaths	
	Number	Rate (per 1,000)	Number	Rate (per 1,000)	Number	Rate (per 1,000)
2006	73,978	9.6	26,159	4.3	113,438	14.8
2007	75,349	9.8	29,640	3.9	113,004	14.8
2008	77,712	10.2	27,722	3.6	110,523	14.5
2009	80,956	10.7	25,923	3.4	108,068	14.3
2010	75,513	10.0	24,286	3.2	110,165	14.6
2011	70,846	9.7	21,448	2.9	108,258	14.8
2012	69,121	9.5	21,167	2.9	109,281	15.0

Life expectancy (years at birth): 74.2 (males 70.7; females 77.8) in 2011 (Source: World Bank, World Development Indicators database).

ECONOMICALLY ACTIVE POPULATION
(labour force survey, '000 persons aged 15 years and over)

	2010	2011	2012
Agriculture, hunting, forestry and fishing	208.1	201.0	189.0
Mining and quarrying	33.0	26.3	26.0
Manufacturing	637.4	593.0	603.5
Electricity, gas and water supply	76.3	84.6	83.4
Construction	268.5	228.7	206.0
Wholesale and retail trade; repair of motor vehicles, motorcycles and personal and household goods	531.1	544.4	526.9
Hotels and restaurants	159.7	159.2	152.7
Transport and communications	247.6	241.2	245.2
Financial intermediation	52.7	55.0	52.7
Real estate, renting and business activities	170.9	173.8	192.8
Public administration and defence; compulsory social security	226.2	224.1	230.4
Education	184.4	187.5	188.2
Health and social work	159.4	153.2	145.0
Other community, social and personal service activities	97.4	93.2	92.3
Total employed	3,052.8	2,965.2	2,934.0
Unemployed	348.0	376.2	410.3
Total labour force	3,400.9	3,341.4	3,344.3
Males	1,804.7	1,786.1	1,782.8
Females	1,596.2	1,555.3	1,561.5

Health and Welfare

KEY INDICATORS

Total fertility rate (children per woman, 2011)	1.5
Under-5 mortality rate (per 1,000 live births, 2011)	12
HIV/AIDS (% of persons aged 15–49, 2011)	0.1
Physicians (per 1,000 head, 2009)	3.7
Hospital beds (per 1,000 head, 2009)	6.6
Health expenditure (2010): US $ per head (PPP)	1,057
Health expenditure (2010): % of GDP	7.6
Health expenditure (2010): public (% of total)	55.7
Total carbon dioxide emissions ('000 metric tons, 2010)	44,678.7
Carbon dioxide emissions per head (metric tons, 2010)	5.9
Human Development Index (2012): ranking	57
Human Development Index (2012): value	0.782

For sources and definitions, see explanatory note on p. vi.

Agriculture

PRINCIPAL CROPS
('000 metric tons)

	2010	2011	2012
Wheat	4,094.6	4,458.5	4,455.1
Rice, paddy	56.0	59.6	54.9
Barley	833.3	707.0	661.9
Maize	2,047.4	2,209.2	1,717.8
Rye	17.5	19.8	22.0
Oats	40.0	29.2	30.8
Triticale (wheat-rye hybrid)	26.3	26.5	26.5
Potatoes	251.1	232.3	194.2
Beans, dry	2.1	1.0	1.6
Sunflower seed	1,536.3	1,439.7	1,387.8
Cabbages and other brassicas	78.9	44.6	47.3
Asparagus*	6.5	5.9	6.0
Tomatoes	114.6	103.1	94.0
Pumpkins, squash and gourds	14.8	0.8	5.1
Cucumbers and gherkins	65.7	58.9	38.0
Aubergines (eggplants)	10.7	6.8	7.8
Chillies and peppers, green	69.1	66.3	47.1
Onions, dry	19.1	16.8	10.3
Beans, green	4.3	1.6	2.0
Carrots and turnips	10.6	12.0	9.6
Mushrooms and truffles	1.6	2.2	2.1
Watermelons	70.8	83.2	73.4
Apples	43.2	40.4	30.9
Apricots	11.6	11.9	10.2
Sweet cherries	25.0	30.1	19.5
Peaches and nectarines	24.5	28.4	25.2
Plums and sloes	33.7	32.4	22.9
Strawberries	5.7	7.0	4.8
Grapes	230.2	243.8	260.7
Tobacco, unmanufactured	41.1	40.6	28.1

* FAO estimates.

Aggregate production ('000 metric tons, may include official, semi-official or estimated data): Total cereals 7,130.0 in 2010, 7,520.6 in 2011, 6,986.8 in 2012; Total roots and tubers 251.1 in 2010, 232.3 in 2011, 194.2 in 2012; Total vegetables (incl. melons) 509.8 in 2010, 472.5 in 2011, 390.5 in 2012; Total fruits (excl. melons) 396.5 in 2010, 420.0 in 2011, 397.3 in 2012.

Source: FAO.

LIVESTOCK
('000 head at 1 January each year)

	2010	2011	2012
Horses	112.8	69.5	60.0*
Asses*	45.0	40.3	35.0
Cattle	539.6	544.5	557.6
Pigs	729.8	664.0	608.3
Sheep	1,400.3	1,368.0	1,454.6
Goats	360.8	356.3	341.1
Chickens	16,002	14,063	13,150

* FAO estimate(s).

Source: FAO.

LIVESTOCK PRODUCTS
('000 metric tons)

	2010	2011	2012
Cattle meat	19.6	20.9	20.4
Sheep meat	13.3	11.8	13.8
Goat meat	3.7	4.1	3.2
Pig meat	70.5	72.5	73.2
Poultry meat*	111.0	107.0	111.9
Cows' milk	1,124.4	1,125.8	1,093.0
Buffaloes' milk	7.9	8.9	8.1
Sheep's milk	85.0	89.3	87.4
Goats' milk	60.4	61.5	53.3
Hen eggs	89.3	73.5	71.9
Other poultry eggs	0.4	0.4	0.4
Honey	10.6	9.6	9.2
Wool: greasy*	7.0	7.0	7.0

* FAO estimates.

Source: FAO.

Forestry

ROUNDWOOD REMOVALS
('000 cubic metres, excl. bark)

	2009	2010	2011
Sawlogs, veneer logs and logs for sleepers	952	1,320	1,520
Pulpwood	1,225	1,613	1,754
Other industrial wood	47	78	90
Fuel wood	2,375	2,657	2,841
Total	4,599	5,668	6,205

2012: Production assumed to be unchanged from 2011 (FAO estimates).

Source: FAO.

SAWNWOOD PRODUCTION
('000 cubic metres, incl. sleepers)

	2009	2010	2011
Coniferous (softwood)	338	437	570
Broadleaved (hardwood)	113	117	158
Total	451	554	728

2012: Production assumed to be unchanged from 2011 (FAO estimates).

Source: FAO.

Fishing

('000 metric tons, live weight)

	2009	2010	2011
Capture	9.0	10.8	9.6
Common carp	0.8	0.5	0.6
European sprat	4.6	4.0	4.0
Sea snails	2.2	4.8	3.1
Aquaculture	6.7	7.9	5.5
Common carp	1.9	1.9	1.4
Rainbow trout	2.4	2.9	1.5
Total catch	15.7	18.7	15.2

Source: FAO.

Mining

('000 metric tons unless otherwise indicated)

	2009	2010	2011
Other hard coal	23	26*	20*
Lignite	25,015	27,000*	34,900*
Other brown coal	2,244	2,200*	2,200*
Crude petroleum	24	23	23*
Natural gas (million cu metres)	17	74	434
Copper ore*†	110	107	110
Copper concentrate†	105	105	105
Lead—mine output†	12	12	12
Lead concentrate†	12	12*	12*
Zinc—mine output†	9	13	10
Zinc concentrate*†	7.6	7.6	7.6
Silver—mine output (kilograms)*†	55	55	55
Gold (kilograms)‡	4,482	4,400*	4,400*
Bentonite	108	100*	100*
Kaolin (raw)	939	900*	900*
Salt (unrefined)	1,300	1,300*	1,300*
Gypsum and anhydrite (crude)	128	130*	130*

* Estimated production.

† Figures relate to the metal content of ores and concentrates.

‡ Figures relate to metal production.

Iron ore: gross weight ('000 metric tons): 83 in 2004.

Iron ore: metal content ('000 metric tons): 27 in 2004.

Barite (Barytes) ('000 metric tons): 237 in 2004.

Source: US Geological Survey.

Industry

SELECTED PRODUCTS
('000 metric tons unless otherwise indicated)

	2010	2011	2012
Wheat flour	444	446	447
Refined sugar	120	97	45
Wine ('000 hectolitres)	1,279	1,103	1,114
Beer ('000 hectolitres)	4,893	4,913	5,156
Cotton yarn (metric tons)*	2.3	1.5	1.2
Woven cotton fabrics†‡	11,195	8,490	7,505
Woven woollen fabrics‡	3,187	2,831	2,797
Footwear (excl. rubber, '000 pairs)	4,391	4,604	4,553
Cement (kilograms)	1,988	1,896	1,771
Crude steel (ingots)§	740	834	n.a.
Lathes (number)	646	854	907
Fork-lift trucks (number)‖	654	770	797
Electric energy (million kWh)	46,011	50,330	47,406

* Other than sewing thread. Figures for wool include yarn of man-made staple.

† Pure and mixed fabrics, after undergoing finishing processes.

‡ Million square metres.

§ Source: US Geological Survey.

‖ Electrical and motorized.

Cigarettes (million): 17,353 in 2006; 20,763 in 2007; 17,766 in 2008.

Clay building bricks (million): 354 in 2006; 425 in 2007.

Pig iron, steel-making (incl. foundry) ('000 metric tons): 1,147 in 2006; 1,069 in 2007; 441 in 2008.

Finance

CURRENCY AND EXCHANGE RATES

Monetary Units
100 stotinki (singular: stotinka) = 1 new lev (plural: leva).

Sterling, Dollar and Euro Equivalents (31 December 2013)
£1 sterling = 2.337 new leva;
US $1 = 1.419 new leva;
€1 = 1.957 new leva;
100 new leva = £42.79 = $70.47 = €51.10.

Average Exchange Rate (new leva per US $)
2011 1.4065
2012 1.5221
2013 1.4736

Note: On 5 July 1999 a new lev, equivalent to 1,000 old leva, was introduced. In January 1999 the value of the old lev had been linked to the German currency, the Deutsche Mark (DM), when an official exchange rate of 1 DM = 1,000 old leva was established. The new lev was thus at par with the DM. From the establishment of the euro, on 1 January 1999, the German currency had a fixed exchange rate of €1 = 1.95583 DM.

GENERAL GOVERNMENT BUDGET
(million new leva)

Revenue

	2010	2011	2012
Taxes	14,045	15,085	15,933
Taxes on income, profits and capital gains	3,385	3,676	3,776
Taxes on goods and services	6,267	6,612	7,152
Custom duties	119	131	118
Excises	3,568	3,860	4,048
Other taxes	706	806	840
Social contributions	4,970	5,510	5,596
Non-tax revenue	3,315	3,321	3,573
Grants	1,603	1,463	2,368
Total	23,933	25,378	27,469

Expenditure

Expenditure by economic type	2010	2011	2012
Compensation of employees	5,047	5,121	5,208
Use of goods and services	4,442	4,454	4,482
Interest	486	547	573
External	336	350	374
Internal	150	197	199
Subsidies	1,485	1,595	1,233
Social benefits	10,959	11,296	11,843
Other expenses	4,337	3,855	4,490
Total	26,755	26,867	27,828

Expenditure by functions of government	2010	2011	2012
General public services	1,669	1,708	1,675
Defence	3,223	2,832	2,802
Social support and security	9,593	9,702	10,061
Economic affairs	3,403	3,454	3,859
Housing, community services and environmental protection	1,534	1,428	1,359
Health	3,001	3,248	3,303
Recreation, culture and religion	499	513	587
Education	2,678	2,655	2,799
Other expenditure	1,156	1,326	1,382
Total	26,755	26,867	27,828

Source: Ministry of Finance, Sofia.

INTERNATIONAL RESERVES
(US $ million at 31 December)

	2010	2011	2012
Gold*	1,812.5	2,020.0	2,131.8
IMF special drawing rights	940.8	937.9	939.2
Reserve position in IMF	52.2	52.4	52.4
Foreign exchange	14,427.5	14,261.6	17,379.4
Total	17,233.0	17,271.9	20,502.8

* Valued at market-related prices.

Source: IMF, *International Financial Statistics*.

MONEY SUPPLY
(million new leva at 31 December)

	2010	2011	2012
Currency outside depositary corporations	7,356	7,794	8,499
Transferable deposits	11,032	13,234	14,515
Other deposits	32,283	35,860	38,598
Securities other than shares	75	71	109
Broad money	50,746	56,959	61,722

Source: IMF, *International Financial Statistics*.

COST OF LIVING
(Consumer Price Index; base: 2000 = 100)

	2010	2011	2012
Food	161.7	172.9	178.1
All items (incl. others)	178.2	185.8	191.3

Source: ILO.

NATIONAL ACCOUNTS
(million new leva at current prices)

Expenditure on the Gross Domestic Product

	2010	2011	2012*
Government final consumption expenditure	11,719	12,089	12,368
Private final consumption expenditure	43,990	46,725	49,595
Gross fixed capital formation	16,077	16,225	16,600
Changes in inventories	61	284	1,887
Total domestic expenditure	71,847	75,324	80,450
Exports of goods and services	40,481	50,077	51,691
Less Imports of goods and services	41,817	50,094	54,559
GDP in market prices	70,511	75,308	77,582

* Preliminary figures.

Gross Domestic Product by Economic Activity

	2010	2011	2012*
Agriculture, hunting, forestry and fishing	2,976	3,519	4,264
Mining and quarrying; manufacturing; electricity, gas and water supply	13,540	15,690	16,313
Construction	4,341	4,218	3,936
Wholesale and retail trade; repair of motor vehicles and household goods; hotels and restaurants; transport and communications	16,202	17,066	16,950
Financial intermediation	4,889	5,441	5,452
Real estate, renting and business activities	9,231	9,551	9,515
Other services	9,538	9,688	10,213
Gross value added in basic prices	60,716	65,174	66,642
Taxes, less subsidies, on products	9,795	10,134	10,940
GDP in market prices	70,511	75,308	77,582

* Preliminary figures.

Note: Financial intermediation services indirectly measured assumed to be distributed by activity.

BALANCE OF PAYMENTS
(US $ million)

	2010	2011	2012
Exports of goods	20,583.8	28,248.2	26,677.6
Imports of goods	–24,255.2	–31,221.5	–31,133.3
Balance on goods	–3,671.4	–2,973.3	–4,455.7
Exports of services	6,543.5	7,497.2	7,295.9
Imports of services	–4,159.1	–4,230.0	–4,381.4
Balance on goods and services	–1,287.1	293.9	–1,541.2
Primary income received	816.4	860.6	931.5
Primary income paid	–2,296.2	–3,384.6	–2,796.1
Balance on goods, services and primary income	–2,766.9	–2,230.2	–3,405.9
Secondary income received	2,700.0	3,127.1	3,504.9
Secondary income paid	–729.5	–764.3	–834.3
Current balance	–796.3	132.7	–735.3
Capital account (net)	391.4	683.8	691.6
Direct investment assets	–580.9	–485.5	–547.0
Direct investment liabilities	1,866.6	2,124.2	2,094.8
Portfolio investment assets	–701.8	–52.4	–1,887.7
Portfolio investment liabilities	–106.5	–424.0	684.7
Financial derivatives and employee stock options assets	–29.6	–81.9	–38.3
Financial derivatives and employee stock options liabilities	–3.3	–8.9	–4.6
Other investment assets	–53.5	–1,030.2	1,249.5
Other investment liabilities	–1,378.4	–1,368.6	1,134.0
Net errors and omissions	788.8	771.1	88.2
Reserves and related items	–603.5	260.2	2,729.9

Source: IMF, *International Financial Statistics*.

External Trade

PRINCIPAL COMMODITIES
(€ million)

Imports c.i.f.	2010	2011	2012
Food, beverages and tobacco	1,176.0	1,381.7	1,508.8
Furniture and household appliances	672.9	640.2	640.7
Medicines and cosmetics	801.5	911.9	940.7
Ores	998.3	1,489.1	1,381.4
Iron and steel	636.0	960.4	823.1
Textiles	927.5	1,090.1	1,061.8
Plastics and rubber	971.0	1,120.1	1,203.1
Machines and equipment	1,349.2	1,569.7	1,709.8
Electrical machines	772.4	778.6	819.4
Vehicles	574.4	861.1	1,023.5
Spare parts and equipment	746.6	1,075.1	1,406.8
Mineral fuels	3,410.2	4,179.0	5,181.1
Crude petroleum and natural gas	3,116.8	3,830.8	4792.0
Total (incl. others)	19,244.8	23,406.2	25,459.1

Exports f.o.b.	2010	2011	2012
Food, beverages and tobacco	839.1	902.7	989.6
Clothing and footwear	1,359.0	1,525.3	1,456.2
Medicines and cosmetics	534.3	635.6	701.0
Furniture and household appliances	573.2	655.0	748.1
Iron and steel	658.7	900.3	720.4
Other metals	1,784.5	2,485.6	2,291.9
Raw materials for the food industry	1,309.0	1,835.3	1,732.6
Machines and equipment	700.9	951.9	1,001.9
Spare parts and equipment	580.5	765.5	859.9
Petroleum products	1,661.1	2,225.6	2,928.3
Other mineral fuels and electricity	452.5	589.3	553.0
Total (incl. others)	15,561.2	20,264.3	20,770.2

PRINCIPAL TRADING PARTNERS
(€ million)

Imports c.i.f.	2010	2011	2012
Austria	394.9	461.6	491.4
Belgium	269.0	320.3	319.7
Brazil	109.3	207.9	399.3
China, People's Republic	1,045.1	1,397.5	1,656.4
Czech Republic	342.3	366.3	446.0
France	650.5	783.6	753.4
Germany	2,004.9	2,275.8	2,473.6
Greece	1,032.5	1,170.8	1,355.0
Hungary	386.4	434.3	459.7
Italy	1,458.0	1,695.9	1,675.2
Macedonia, former Yugoslav republic	253.8	249.3	254.1
Netherlands	341.3	367.5	441.7
Poland	437.8	476.9	586.8
Romania	1,134.9	1,361.6	1,405.2
Russia	3,292.2	3,875.1	5,157.7
Serbia	216.3	262.1	258.2
Spain	361.8	358.7	380.6
Switzerland	202.7	234.6	311.2
Turkey	1,067.0	1,076.1	1,194.1
Ukraine	456.6	699.0	571.8
United Kingdom	290.2	373.4	395.5
USA	292.6	371.2	393.9
Total (incl. others)	19,244.8	23,406.2	25,459.1

Exports f.o.b.	2010	2011	2012
Austria	293.8	388.2	380.4
Belgium	587.3	999.3	765.9
China, People's Republic	187.4	293.7	595.0
Czech Republic	146.4	217.7	254.2
France	628.4	855.2	830.0
Georgia	144.1	230.1	285.1
Germany	1,658.7	2,355.2	2,126.5
Greece	1,236.8	1,423.6	1,494.6
Hungary	198.1	255.4	241.3
Italy	1,511.2	1,760.8	1,763.8
Macedonia, former Yugoslav republic	332.4	461.3	392.6
Netherlands	234.5	359.6	379.3
Poland	267.5	360.3	363.2
Romania	1,417.4	1,933.3	1,674.1
Russia	441.3	542.1	562.5
Serbia	549.9	478.4	442.4
Spain	415.9	543.8	540.2
Turkey	1,317.2	1,733.1	1,957.7
Ukraine	198.0	288.9	244.9
United Kingdom	303.0	370.4	398.3
USA	212.0	265.0	370.8
Total (incl. others)	15,561.2	20,264.3	20,770.2

Transport

RAILWAYS
(traffic)

	2010	2011	2012
Passengers carried ('000)	30,101.9	29,308.2	26,523.2
Passenger-kilometres (million)	2,099.7	2,067.5	1,876.0
Freight carried ('000 metric tons)	12,939.5	14,152.0	12,469.8
Freight net ton-kilometres (million)	3,063.5	3,291.2	2,907.6

ROAD TRAFFIC
(motor vehicles in use at 31 December)

	2002	2003	2004
Passenger cars	2,254,222	2,309,343	2,438,383
Buses and coaches	44,255	43,687	36,000
Lorries and vans	262,641	293,487	317,681
Motorcycles and mopeds	220,296	n.a.	137,955

2008: Passenger cars 2,366,196; Buses and coaches 24,622; Lorries and vans 291,161; Motorcycles 106,911.

2009: Passenger cars 2,502,020; Buses and coaches 24,448; Lorries and vans 317,808; Motorcycles 117,595.

Source: IRF, *World Road Statistics*.

INLAND WATERWAYS
(traffic)

	2000	2001	2002
Passengers carried ('000)	76	67	60
Passenger-kilometres (million)	1	—	—
Freight carried ('000 metric tons)	1,846	1,300	1,621
Freight ton-kilometres (million)	397	365	571

SHIPPING

Flag Registered Fleet
(at 31 December)

	2011	2012	2013
Number of vessels	94	91	87
Total displacement ('000 grt)	327.4	236.3	135.4

Source: Lloyd's List Intelligence (www.lloydslistintelligence.com).

Sea-borne Traffic
(international and coastal)

	2000	2001	2002
Freight ('000 metric tons)	18,619	16,737	15,557
Freight ton-kilometres (million)	74,391	67,551	60,814

CIVIL AVIATION
(traffic)

	2010	2011
Passengers carried ('000)	708	933
Kilometres flown (million)	13	15
Passenger-kilometres (million)	1,109	1,239
Total ton-kilometres (million)	103	115

Source: UN, *Statistical Yearbook*.

2012 ('000): Passengers carried 946.7 (Source: World Bank, World Development Indicators database).

Tourism

ARRIVALS OF FOREIGN VISITORS
(including same day visitors)

Country of origin	2010	2011	2012
Austria	181,577	186,438	185,242
Czech Republic	184,440	176,135	173,739
France	181,317	182,407	180,060
Germany	853,430	836,845	784,678
Greece	1,017,914	1,120,640	1,087,260
Macedonia, former Yugoslav republic*	409,970	439,679	424,182
Poland	294,131	289,742	286,267
Romania*	1,445,342	1,499,415	1,468,179
Russia	389,864	469,772	609,630
Serbia and Montenegro*	307,838	365,644	396,448
Turkey	943,137	860,654	984,212
Ukraine	199,080	251,803	325,944
United Kingdom	309,482	306,939	282,076
Total (incl. others)	8,374,034	8,712,821	8,866,552

* Includes 'shuttle traders'.

Tourism receipts (US $ million, excl. passenger transport): 3,637 in 2010; 3,967 in 2011; 3,748 in 2012 (provisional) (Source: World Tourism Organization).

Communications Media

	2010	2011	2012
Telephones ('000 main lines in use)	2,222.5	2,355.7	2,252.5
Mobile cellular telephones ('000 subscribers)	10,199.9	10,475.1	10,780.7
Internet subscribers ('000)	1,091.1	1,227.9	n.a.
Broadband subscribers ('000)	1,088.3	1,224.7	1,305.4
Book production*:			
titles	4,614	4,524	7,213
copies ('000)	3,220	2,717	4,100
Newspapers:			
titles	359	369	354
total circulation ('000 copies)	340,812	373,111	374,660
Magazines:†			
titles	695	668	635
total circulation ('000 copies)	32,099	27,831	24,109

* Including pamphlets.
† Including bulletins.

Source: partly International Telecommunication Union.

Education

(2012/13)

	Institutions	Teachers	Students
Kindergartens	2,070*	20,015	235,015
General and special schools:			
primary	153	14,565	253,675
basic	1,402	n.a.	n.a.
lower secondary	11	19,315	221,839
upper secondary	140	24,684†	273,498
combined schools	406	n.a.	n.a.
Vocational	494	13,063	142, 733
Colleges	8	1,091	14,688‡
Universities and equivalent	45	22,365	269,271§

* Excluding dependent half-day kindergartens.
† Including teaching staff in interschools centres.
‡ Qualification degree 'specialist'.
§ Including 4,703 post-graduate students studying for 'specialist' degrees.

Pupil-teacher ratio (primary education, UNESCO estimate): 17.5 in 2010/11 (Source: UNESCO Institute for Statistics).

Adult literacy rate (UNESCO estimates): 98.4% (males 98.7%; females 98.0%) in 2011 (Source: UNESCO Institute for Statistics).

Directory

The Government

HEAD OF STATE AND VICE-PRESIDENT

President: Rosen Plevneliev (took office 22 January 2012).

Vice-President: Margarita Popova.

COUNCIL OF MINISTERS

(April 2014)

The Government comprises members of the Balgarska Sotsialisticheska Partiya (BSP—Bulgarian Socialist Party), the Dvizhenie za Prava i Svobodi (DPS—Movement for Rights and Freedoms) and Independents.

Prime Minister: Plamen Oresharski (Independent).

Deputy Prime Minister and Minister of Justice: Zinaida Zlatanova (BSP).

Deputy Prime Minister and Minister of the Interior: Tsvetlin Yovchev (BSP).

Deputy Prime Minister: Daniela Bobeva (Independent).

Minister of Foreign Affairs: Kristian Vigenin (BSP).

Minister of Finance: Petar Chobanov (BSP).

Minister of Defence: Angel Naydenov (BSP).

Minister of the Economy and Energy: Dragomir Stoynev (BSP).

Minister of Labour and Social Policy: Hasan Ademov (DPS).

Minister of Investment Projects: Ivan Danov (Independent).

Minister of Agriculture and Food: Dimitar Grekov (BSP).

Minister of Regional Development: Desislava Terzieva (Independent).

Minister of Transport, Communications and Information Technology: Danail Papazov (BSP).

Minister of the Environment and Water: Iskra Mihaylova-Koparova (DPS).

Minister of Health: Tanya Andreeva-Raynova (BSP).

Minister of Education and Science: Aneliya Klisarova (BSP).

Minister of Culture: Petar Stoyanovich (Independent).

Minister of Youth and Sports: Mariana Georgieva (DPS).

MINISTRIES

Office of the President: 1123 Sofia, bul. Dondukov 2; tel. (2) 923-93-33; e-mail priemna@president.bg; internet www.president.bg.

Council of Ministers: 1594 Sofia, bul. Dondukov 1; tel. (2) 940-29-99; fax (2) 980-21-01; e-mail gis@government.bg; internet www.government.bg.

Ministry of Agriculture and Food: 1040 Sofia, bul. Hristo Botev 55; tel. (2) 985-11-238; fax (2) 980-91-19; e-mail press@mzh.government.bg; internet www.mzh.government.bg.

Ministry of Culture: 1040 Sofia, bul. A. Stamboliyski 17; tel. (2) 940-09-00; fax (2) 981-81-45; e-mail press@mc.government.bg; internet www.mc.government.bg.

Ministry of Defence: 1092 Sofia, ul. Dyakon Ignatiy 3; tel. (2) 922-09-22; fax (2) 987-96-93; e-mail presscntr@mod.bg; internet www.mod.bg.

Ministry of the Economy and Energy: 1000 Sofia, ul. Slavyanska 8; tel. (2) 940-70-01; fax (2) 987-21-90; e-mail e-docs@mee.government.bg; internet www.mee.government.bg.

Ministry of Education and Science: 1540 Sofia, bul. Knyaz Dondukov 2a; tel. (2) 921-77-99; fax (2) 988-24-85; e-mail contact@mon.bg; internet www.mon.bg.

Ministry of the Environment and Water: 1000 Sofia, bul. Maria Luiza 22; tel. (2) 940-61-94; fax (2) 986-25-33; e-mail minister@moew.government.bg; internet www.moew.government.bg.

Ministry of Finance: 1040 Sofia, ul. G. S. Rakovski 102; tel. (2) 639-26-34; fax (2) 987-05-81; e-mail feedback@minfin.bg; internet www.minfin.bg.

Ministry of Foreign Affairs: 1113 Sofia, ul. Al. Zhendov 2; tel. (2) 948-29-99; fax (2) 297-136-20; e-mail info@mfa.bg; internet www.mfa.bg.

Ministry of Health: 1000 Sofia, pl. Sv. Nedelya 5; tel. (2) 930-11-07; fax (2) 981-26-39; e-mail press@mh.government.bg; internet www.mh.government.bg.

Ministry of the Interior: 1000 Sofia, ul. 6-ti Septemvri 29; tel. (2) 982-25-74; fax (2) 982-20-47; e-mail press@mvr.bg; internet www.mvr.bg.

Ministry of Investment Projects: Sofia.

Ministry of Justice: 1040 Sofia, ul. Slavyanska 1; tel. (2) 923-75-55; fax (2) 981-91-57; e-mail pr@justice.government.bg; internet www.justice.government.bg.

Ministry of Labour and Social Policy: 1051 Sofia, ul. Triaditsa 2; tel. (2) 811-94-43; fax (2) 988-44-05; e-mail mlsp@mlsp.government.bg; internet www.mlsp.government.bg.

Ministry of Regional Development: 1000 Sofia, ul. Kiril i Metodiy 17–19; tel. (2) 940-54-30; fax (2) 987-25-17; e-mail press@mrrb.government.bg; internet www.mrrb.government.bg.

Ministry of Transport, Communications and Information Technology: 1000 Sofia, ul. Dyakon Ignatiy 9; tel. and fax (2) 988-50-94; e-mail mail@mtitc.government.bg; internet www.mtitc.government.bg.

Ministry of Youth and Sports: 1000 Sofia, ul. V. Levski 75; tel. (2) 930-05-55; e-mail info@mms.government.bg.

President

Presidential Election, First Round, 23 October 2011

Candidate	Votes	% of votes
Rosen Plevneliev (Grazhdani za evropeysko razvitie na Balgariya)	1,349,380	40.11
Ivaylo Kalfin (Balgarska Sotsialisticheska Partiya)	974,300	28.96
Meglena Kuneva (Independent)	470,808	14.00
Others	569,590	16.93
Total	3,364,078	100.00

Second Round, 30 October 2011

Candidate	Votes	% of votes
Rosen Plevneliev (Grazhdani za evropeysko razvitie na Balgariya)	1,698,136	52.58
Ivaylo Kalfin (Balgarska Sotsialisticheska Partiya)	1,531,193	47.42
Total	3,229,329	100.00

Legislature

National Assembly (Narodno Sobranie)

1169 Sofia, pl. Narodno Sobranie 2; fax (2) 981-31-31; e-mail infocenter@parliament.bg; internet www.parliament.bg.

Chairman: Mihail Mikov.

General Election, 12 May 2013

Party	Votes	% of votes	Seats
Grazhdani za evropeysko razvitie na Balgariya	1,081,605	30.55	97
Coalition for Bulgaria*	942,541	26.62	84
Dvizhenie za Prava i Svobodi	400,466	11.31	36
Partiya Ataka	258,481	7.30	23
Total	3,541,745†	100.00	240

* A coalition of eight parties, led by the Balgarska Sotsialisticheska Partiya.

† Including others.

Election Commission

Central Election Committee: 1169 Sofia, pl. A. Battenberg 1; tel. (2) 987-92-42; fax (2) 986-64-56; e-mail cik@cik.bg; internet www.cik.bg; Chair. Ivilina V. Aleksieva.

Political Organizations

Balgarska Nova Demokratsia (BND) (Bulgarian New Democracy): 1614 Sofia, ul. Nikola Pekov 143 a; tel. (0895) 567–801; e-mail bnd2008@abv.bg; internet www.bnd.bg; f. 2008 by fmr mems of the

Nat. Movement for Stability and Progress; centre-right; Chair. VASIMIR RADULOV.

Balgarski Sotsialdemokrati (Bulgarian Social Democrats): 1000 Sofia, ul. Aksakov 31; tel. and fax (2) 988-15-69; e-mail sdms@pbs-d.bg; internet www.pbs-d.bg; fmrly Bulgarian Social Democratic Party (United); contested 2013 legislative elections as part of the Coalition for Bulgaria; Pres. GEORGI ANASTASOV.

Balgarska Sotsialisticheska Partiya (BSP) (Bulgarian Socialist Party): 1000 Sofia, ul. Positano 20; tel. (2) 810-72-00; fax (2) 981-21-85; e-mail bsp@bsp.bg; internet www.bsp.bg; f. 1891 as the Bulgarian Social Democratic Party (BSDP); renamed as above in 1990; contested 2013 legislative elections as part of the Coalition for Bulgaria; Chair. SERGEY STANISHEV.

Demokraticheskata Partiya (Democratic Party): 1303 Sofia, bul. Botev 61; tel. (2) 930-80-30; fax (2) 930-80-31; internet www.demparty.eu; re-formed 1990; Chair. ALEKSANDAR PRAMATARSKI.

Demokrati za silna Balgariya (DSB) (Democrats for a Strong Bulgaria): 1000 Sofia, bul. Vitosha 18; tel. (2) 400-99-21; fax (2) 400-99-48; e-mail dsb@dsb.bg; internet www.dsb.bg; f. 2004; right-wing; Chair. RADAN KANEV.

Dvizhenie za Prava i Svobodi (DPS) (Movement for Rights and Freedoms): 1301 Sofia, bul. Al. Stamboliyski 45A; tel. (2) 811-44-52; fax (2) 811-44-53; e-mail mestan@dps.bg; internet www.dps.bg; f. 1990 to represent interests of Muslim minority in Bulgaria; supported integration of Bulgaria into the European Union (EU) and North Atlantic Treaty Organization (NATO); Chair. LYUTVI MESTAN.

Grazhdani za evropeysko razvitie na Balgariya (GERB) (Citizens for European Development of Bulgaria): 1463 Sofia, pl. Balgariya 1, NDK Administration Bldg 17; tel. (2) 490-13-13; fax (2) 490-09-51; e-mail pr@gerb.bg; internet www.gerb.bg; f. 2006; centre-right; Chair. BOYKO BORISOV.

Komunisticheska Partiya na Balgariya (Communist Party of Bulgaria): 1000 Sofia, ul. Tsar Kaloyan 10; tel. and fax (2) 981-60-93; e-mail comparty@abv.bg; internet www.comparty-bg.com; f. 1996; breakaway party of fmr Bulgarian Social Democratic Party; contested 2013 legislative elections as part of the Coalition for Bulgaria; Chair. ALEKSANDAR PAUNOV.

Natsionalno dvizhenie za stabilnost i vazhod (NDSV) (National Movement for Stability and Progress): 1000 Sofia, ul. Vrabcha 23; tel. (2) 921-81-83; fax (2) 921-81-81; e-mail presscenter@ndsv.bg; internet www.ndsv.bg; f. 2001 by supporters of the former monarch; registered as a political party, Nat. Movement Simeon II, in 2002; name changed June 2007; Pres. Dr ANTONIYA S. PURVANOVA.

Novoto vreme (The New Time): Sofia, bul. 6 Septembri 7A; tel. (89) 999-76-26; e-mail party@novotovreme.bg; internet www.novotovreme.bg; f. 2003 by fmr mems of Nat. Movement Simeon II; Chair. ROSICHA Y. KABZEVA-DIKINA.

Partiya Ataka (Attack Party): 1000 Sofia, ul. Vrabcha 1; tel. and fax (2) 980-55-70; e-mail atakacentrala@abv.bg; internet www.ataka.bg; f. 2005 as Attack Nat. Union by coalition of the Nat. Movement for the Salvation of the Fatherland, the Bulgarian Nat. Patriotic Party and the Union of Patriotic Forces and Militaries of the Defence Reserve; subsequently constituted as a political party; nationalist, populist, anti-Western; Leader VOLEN SIDEROV.

Politicheska Partia LIDER (LIDER Political Party—Liberal Initiative for Democratic European Development): Sofia, bul. Cherni Vrykh 39; tel. (2) 421-11-55; e-mail lider@lider-bg.org; internet www.lider-bg.org; f. 2007; Chair. KANCHO FILIPOV.

Red, zakonnost i spravedlivost (RZS) (Order, Law and Justice): 1000 Sofia, bul. Knyaz Dondukov 15; tel. (2) 981-03-07; fax (2) 981-10-89; e-mail centrala@rzs.bg; internet www.rzs.bg; f. 2005; Leader YANE YANEV.

Sayuz na Demokratichnite Sili (SDS) (SUnion of Democratic Forces): 1000 Sofia, bul. Rakovski 134; tel. (2) 930-61-33; fax (2) 981-01-19; e-mail presscenter@sds.bg; internet www.sds.bg; f. 1989; supported the integration of Bulgaria into the EU; pro-market; contested 2013 legislative elections as part of the Blue Coalition; Chair. BOZHIDAR LUKARSKI.

Sayuz na svobodnite demokrati (SSD) (Union of Free Democrats): 1000 Sofia, bul. Levski 91; tel. (2) 989-59-99; fax (2) 989-69-99; e-mail ssd_centrala@abv.bg; internet www.ssd.bg; f. 2001 as a breakaway faction of the Union of Democratic Forces; supports greater integration of Bulgaria into the EU and NATO; Chair. RADOSLAV KATSAROV.

VMRO—Balgarsko natsionalno dvizhenie (VMRO—BND) (IMRO—Bulgarian National Movement): 1301 Sofia, ul. Pirotska 5; tel. (2) 980-25-82; fax (2) 980-25-83; e-mail vmro@vmro.bg; internet www.vmro.bg; f. 2000; fmrly Inner Macedonian Revolutionary Org.—Bulgarian Nat. Movement; in March 2010 it was reported that a splinter group had been formed, under the leadership of Petko Atansov; Chair. KRASSIMIR KARAKACHANOV.

Zelenite (The Greens): 1412 Sofia, ul. Biser 7; e-mail info@zelenite.bg; internet www.zelenite.bg; f. 2008; Co-Chair. BORISLAV SANDOV, SOIYAN YOTOV, GEORG TUPAREV.

Zemedelski Naroden Sayuz (ZNS) (Agrarian People's Union): 1000 Sofia, bul. N. I. Vapstarov 23; tel. and fax (2) 987-05-77; e-mail office@zns.bg; internet www.zns.bg; fmrly Bulgarian Agrarian Nat. Union—People's Union; present name adopted 2006; Pres. ROUMEN IONTCHEV.

Diplomatic Representation

EMBASSIES IN BULGARIA

Afghanistan: 1700 Sofia, Simeonovsko shose 57/3; tel. (2) 962-51-93; fax (2) 962-74-86; e-mail embassy_in_sofia@yahoo.com; Ambassador SIAULLAH MAHMUD.

Albania: 1504 Sofia, ul. Krakra 10; tel. (2) 943-38-57; fax (2) 943-30-69; e-mail aembassy.sofia@mfa.gov.al; Ambassador PETRIT KARABINA.

Algeria: 1000 Sofia, ul. Slavyanska 16; tel. (2) 980-22-50; fax (2) 981-03-28; e-mail ambalgsf@abv.bg; internet www.ambalg-sofia.org; Ambassador AHMED BOUTACHE.

Argentina: 1040 Sofia, ul. D. Tsankov 36, Interpred B, 8th Floor, POB 635; tel. (2) 971-25-39; fax (2) 969-30-28; e-mail ebulg@mrecic.gov.ar; Ambassador GUILLERMO AZRAK.

Armenia: 1111 Sofia, ul. Zagorichane 3; tel. and fax (2) 946-12-72; fax (2) 946-12-74; e-mail armembsof@omega.bg; Ambassador ARSEN SKHOIAN.

Austria: 1000 Sofia, ul. Shipka 4; tel. (2) 932-90-32; fax (2) 981-05-67; e-mail sofia-ob@bmeia.gv.at; internet www.bmeia.gv.at/botschaft/sofia; Ambassador GERHARD REIWEGER.

Azerbaijan: 1113 Sofia, zh. k. Iztok, ul. Charlz Darvin 6; tel. (2) 817-00-70; fax (2) 817-00-77; e-mail sofia@mission.mfa.gov.az; internet www.azembassy.bg; Ambassador EMIL KARIMOV.

Belarus: 1505 Sofia, kv. Reduta, ul. N. Karadzhov 3; tel. (2) 971-95-28; fax (2) 973-31-00; e-mail bulgaria@mfa.gov.by; internet www.bulgaria.mfa.gov.by; Ambassador VLADIMIR A. VORONKOVICH.

Belgium: 1407 Sofia, ul. Dzheimz Baucher 103; tel. (2) 988-72-90; fax (2) 963-36-38; e-mail sofia@diplobel.fed.be; internet www.diplomatie.be/sofia; Ambassador ANICK VAN CALSTER.

Bosnia and Herzegovina: 1000 Sofia, ul. Al. Zhendov 1; tel. (2) 973-37-75; fax (2) 973-37-29; e-mail ambihsofia@dir.bg; Chargé d'affaires a.i. MITAR PAVIĆ.

Brazil: 1000 Sofia, bul. Knyaz Dondukov 54B; tel. (2) 971-98-19; fax (2) 971-28-18; e-mail brasemb.sofia@itamaraty.gov.br; internet sofia.itamaraty.gov.br; Chargé d'affaires a.i. RICARDO GUERRA DE ARAÚJO.

China, People's Republic: 1113 Sofia, ul. A. fon Khumbolt 7; tel. (2) 973-38-73; fax (2) 971-10-81; e-mail chnemb_bg@live.cn; internet www.chinaembassy.bg; Ambassador WEI JINGHUA.

Croatia: 1504 Sofia, ul. Veliko Tarnovo 32; tel. (2) 861-12-11; fax (2) 946-13-55; e-mail sofia@mvep.hr; internet bg.mvp.hr; Ambassador LJERKA ALAJBEG.

Cuba: 1113 Sofia, ul. K. Sharkelov 1; tel. (2) 872-09-96; fax (2) 872-04-60; e-mail protocolo@embacuba-bg.com; internet www.cubadiplomatica.cu/bulgaria; Ambassador TERESITA CAPOTE CAMACHO.

Cyprus: 1164 Sofia, ul. Dzheimz Baucher i Plachkovitsa 1A/1; tel. (2) 961-77-30; fax (2) 862-94-70; e-mail cyprus@mbox.contact.bg; Ambassador STAVROS AMVROSIOU.

Czech Republic: 1504 Sofia, bul. Ya. Sakazov 9; tel. (2) 948-68-00; fax (2) 948-68-18; e-mail sofia@embassy.mzv.cz; internet www.mzv.cz/sofia; Ambassador PAVEL VACEK.

Denmark: 1504 Sofia, bul. Dondukov 54, POB 37; tel. (2) 917-01-00; fax (2) 980-99-01; e-mail sofamb@um.dk; internet www.bulgarien.um.dk; Ambassador KAARE ERHARD JANSON.

Egypt: 1000 Sofia, ul. 6-ti Septemvri 5; tel. (2) 988-15-09; fax (2) 980-12-63; e-mail egembsof@spnet.net; internet www.mfa.gov.eg/english/embassies/egyptian_embassy_bulgaria/Pages/default.aspx; Ambassador MANAL EL-SHINNAWI.

Finland: 1000 Sofia, ul. Bacho Kiro 26–28, 5th Floor; tel. (2) 810-21-10; fax (2) 810-21-20; e-mail sanomat.sof@formin.fi; internet www.finland.bg; Ambassador HARRI SALMI.

France: 1504 Sofia, ul. Oborishte 27–29; tel. (2) 965-11-00; fax (2) 965-11-20; e-mail presse@ambafrance-bg.org; internet www.ambafrance-bg.org; Ambassador XAVIER LAPEYRE DE CABANES.

Georgia: 1164 Sofia, kv. Lozenets, ul. Krichim 65; tel. (2) 868-54-04; fax (2) 868-34-27; e-mail bulgaria.emb@mfa.gov.ge; internet www.bulgaria.mfa.gov.ge; Ambassador ZURAB BERIDZE.

Germany: 1113 Sofia, ul. F. Zholio-Kyuri 25; tel. (2) 918-38-00; fax (2) 963-16-58; e-mail info@sofia.diplo.de; internet www.sofia.diplo.de; Ambassador MATTHIAS HÖPFNER.

Greece: 1504 Sofia, ul. San Stefano 33; tel. (2) 946-10-30; fax (2) 946-12-49; e-mail gremb.sof@mfa.gr; internet www.mfa.gr/sofia; Ambassador DIMOSTHENIS STOIDIS.

Holy See: 1000 Sofia, ul. 11-ti Avgust 6, POB 9; tel. (2) 981-21-97; fax (2) 981-61-95; e-mail nunziatura.bulgaria@gmail.com; Chargé d'affaires a.i. JÁN MALEČEK.

Hungary: 1000 Sofia, ul. 6-ti Septemvri 57; tel. (2) 963-11-35; fax (2) 963-21-10; e-mail embassy.sof@mfa.gov.hu; internet www.mfa.gov.hu/emb/sofia; Ambassador ANDRÁS KLEIN.

India: 1421 Sofia, kv. Lozenets, ul. Sv. Sedmochislenitsi 23; tel. (2) 963-56-75; fax (2) 963-56-86; e-mail ambassador@indembsofia.org; internet www.indembsofia.org; Ambassador DIVYABH MANCHANDA.

Indonesia: 1700 Sofia, Iosef Valdkhart 5; tel. (2) 962-52-40; fax (2) 962-44-18; e-mail kbrisofia@indonesia.bg; internet www.indonesia.bg; Ambassador BUNYAN SAPTOMO.

Iran: 1087 Sofia, ul. V. Levski 77; tel. (2) 987-85-46; fax (2) 981-41-72; e-mail iranembassy@abv.bg; Ambassador ABDOLLAH NOROUZI.

Iraq: 1113 Sofia, ul. A. Chekhov 21; tel. (2) 973-33-48; fax (2) 971-11-97; e-mail sofemb@mofaml.gov.iq; Ambassador ASAD AL-SAMMARRAIE.

Ireland: 1000 Sofia, ul. Bacho Kiro 26–30; tel. (2) 985-34-25; fax (2) 983-33-02; e-mail sofiaembassy@dfa.ie; internet www.embassyofireland.bg; Ambassador JOHN BIGGAR.

Israel: 1113 Sofia, bul. Shipchenski prohod 18; tel. (2) 951-50-44; fax (2) 952-11-01; e-mail info@sofia.mfa.gov.il; internet sofia.mfa.gov.il; Ambassador SHAUL KAMISA-RAZ.

Italy: 1000 Sofia, ul. Shipka 2; tel. (2) 921-73-00; fax (2) 980-37-17; e-mail ambasciata.sofia@esteri.it; internet www.ambsofia.esteri.it; Ambassador MARCO CONTICELLI.

Japan: 1113 Sofia, ul. Lyulyakova gradina 14; tel. (2) 971-27-08; fax (2) 971-10-95; e-mail emb-jp-bg@sf.mofa.go.jp; internet www.bg.emb-japan.go.jp; Ambassador TAKASHI KOIZUMI.

Kazakhstan: 1000 Sofia, ul. Galichitsa 38; tel. (2) 862-41-52; fax (2) 862-41-70; e-mail kazembassy@bulpost.net; internet www.kazembassy.bulpost.net; Chargé d'affaires TEMIRTAY IZBASTIN.

Korea, Democratic People's Republic: 1756 Sofia, kv. Darvenitsa, ul. Sofiysko pole 3; tel. (2) 974-61-11; fax (2) 974-55-67; e-mail koembg12@yahoo.com; Ambassador ZU UANG HUAN.

Korea, Republic: 1040 Sofia, bul. D. Tsankov 36, et. 7A; tel. (2) 971-21-81; fax (2) 971-33-88; e-mail korean-embassy@mofat.go.kr; internet bgr.mofa.go.kr/worldlanguage/europe/bgr/main/index.jsp; Ambassador SHIN MAENG-HO.

Kosovo: 1000 Sofia, ul. Batcho Kiro 23; tel. (2) 983-39-99; fax (2) 983-52-22; e-mail embassy.bulgaria@rks-gov.net; Ambassador SHPEND KALLABA.

Kuwait: 1700 Sofia, Simeonovsko shose 15; tel. (2) 962-56-89; fax (2) 962-45-84; e-mail kuwaitembassy-bulgaria@hotmail.com; Ambassador FAISAL AL-ADWANI.

Lebanon: 1113 Sofia, ul. F. Zholio-Kyuri 155/13; tel. (2) 971-27-23; fax (2) 973-34-97; e-mail amblibansofia@gmail.com; Ambassador FARES EID.

Libya: 1784 Sofia, Mladost 1, bul. A. Sakharov 1; tel. (2) 974-35-56; fax (2) 974-32-73; e-mail libya_embbg@yahoo.com; Chargé d'affaires a.i. YOUSEF ZURGANI.

Lithuania: 1504 Sofia, ul. Oborishte 15; tel. (2) 980-61-04; fax (2) 980-61-05; e-mail amb.bg@urm.lt; internet bg.mfa.lt; Chargé d'affaires a.i. DARIUS GAIDYS.

Macedonia, former Yugoslav republic: 1113 Sofia, ul. F. Zholio-Kyuri 17/2/1; tel. (2) 870-15-60; fax (2) 971-28-32; e-mail sofia@mfa.gov.mk; Ambassador BLAGOJ HANDZISKI.

Moldova: 1142 Sofia, bul. G. S. Rakovski 152; tel. (2) 935-60-11; fax (2) 980-64-75; e-mail secretary@ambasadamd.org; Ambassador ALEXANDRU PRIGORSCHI.

Mongolia: 1113 Sofia, ul. F. Zholio-Kyuri 52; tel. (2) 865-90-12; fax (2) 963-07-45; e-mail mongemb@gmail.com; Ambassador LKHAMSÜRENGIIN DÜGERJAV.

Morocco: 1421 Sofia, ul. Chervena stena 1/1; tel. (2) 865-11-26; fax (2) 865-48-11; e-mail ambmarsofia@mbox.contact.bg; Ambassador LATIFA AKHARBACH.

Netherlands: 1504 Sofia, ul. Oborishte 15; tel. (2) 816-03-00; fax (2) 816-03-01; e-mail sof@minbuza.nl; internet www.netherlandsembassy.bg; Ambassador THOMAS VAN OORSCHOT.

Norway: 1000 Sofia, ul. Bacho Kiro 26–30; tel. (2) 803-61-00; fax (2) 803-61-99; e-mail emb.sofia@mfa.no; internet www.norvegia.bg; Ambassador GURO KATHARINA VIKØR.

Pakistan: 1040 Sofia, bul. D. Tsankov 36; tel. (2) 971-96-19; fax (2) 971-01-94; e-mail parepsofia@gmail.com; Ambassador MUHAMMAD JAMSHAID IFTIKHAR.

Poland: 1000 Sofia, ul. Khan Krum 46; tel. (2) 987-26-10; fax (2) 987-29-39; e-mail sofia.amb.sekretariat@msz.gov.pl; internet www.sofia.msz.gov.pl; Ambassador LESZEK HENSEL.

Portugal: 1000 Sofia, ul. Pozitano 7/3, et. 5; tel. (2) 448-41-10; fax (2) 448-41-02; e-mail embpor@sofia.dgaccp.pt; Chargé d'affaires LUIS FERRAZ.

Qatar: 1504 Sofia, ul. Vasil Aprilov 4; tel. (2) 865-01-94; fax (2) 865-02-39; Ambassador MUHAMMAD ALI SAID AL-NUAYMI.

Romania: Sofia, bul. Mihai Eminesku 4; tel. (2) 971-28-58; fax (2) 973-34-12; e-mail ambrosofia@mfaro.bg; internet sofia.mae.ro; Ambassador ANTON PĂCUREȚU.

Russia: 1113 Sofia, bul. D. Tsankov 28; tel. (2) 963-09-14; fax (2) 963-41-03; e-mail info@russia.bg; internet www.russia.bg; Ambassador YURII N. ISAKOV.

Serbia: 1504 Sofia, ul. Veliko Tarnovo 3; tel. (2) 946-16-33; fax (2) 946-10-59; e-mail sofia@emb-serbia.com; internet www.emb-serbia.com; Ambassador VLADIMIR CURGUS.

Slovakia: 1504 Sofia, bul. Ya. Sakazov 9; tel. (2) 942-92-10; fax (2) 942-92-35; e-mail emb.sofia@mzv.sk; internet www.mzv.sk/sofia; Ambassador MARIÁN JAKUBÓCY.

South Africa: 1000 Sofia, ul. Bacho Kiro 26; tel. (2) 939-50-15; fax (2) 939-50-17; e-mail sofia.admin@foreign.gov.za; internet www.dfa.gov.za/sofia; Chargé d'affaires a.i. BOIKI P. MOTLOUNG.

Spain: 1504 Sofia, ul. Sheynovo 27, POB 381; tel. (2) 943-36-20; fax (2) 946-12-01; e-mail emb.sofia@maec.es; internet www.embespbg.com; Ambassador JOSÉ LUIS TAPIA VICENTE.

Sudan: 1113 Sofia, ul. F. Zholio-Kyuri 19/156/1, ap. 2; tel. (2) 971-29-91; fax (2) 971-70-38; e-mail scgs@online.bg; Ambassador ELTAYEB ABUELGASIM FADUL ABUELGASIM.

Switzerland: 1504 Sofia, ul. Shipka 33, POB 132; tel. (2) 942-01-00; fax (2) 946-16-22; e-mail sof.vertretung@eda.admin.ch; internet www.eda.admin.ch/sofia; Ambassador REGINA ESCHER.

Syria: 1700 Sofia, Simeonovsko shose 13A; tel. (2) 962-57-42; fax (2) 962-43-14; e-mail syrembabg@gmail.com; Chargé d'affaires a.i. BASHAR SAFIEY.

Turkey: 1000 Sofia, bul. V. Levski 80; tel. (2) 935-55-00; fax (2) 981-93-58; e-mail embassy.sofia@mfa.gov.tr; internet www.sofya.be.mfa.gov.tr; Ambassador SÜLEYMAN GÖKÇE.

Ukraine: 1618 Sofia, Ovcha Kupel, ul. Boryana 29; tel. (2) 818-68-28; fax (2) 955-52-47; e-mail emb_bg@mfa.gov.ua; internet www.mfa.gov.ua/bulgaria; Ambassador MYKOLA BALTAZHI.

United Kingdom: 1000 Sofia, ul. Moskovska 9; tel. (2) 933-92-22; fax (2) 933-92-50; e-mail britishembassysofia@fco.gov.uk; internet www.gov.uk/government/world/bulgaria; Ambassador JONATHAN ALLEN.

USA: 1407 Sofia, ul. Kozyak 16; tel. (2) 937-51-00; fax (2) 937-53-20; e-mail sofia@usembassy.bg; internet bulgaria.usembassy.gov; Ambassador MARCIE RIES.

Venezuela: 1421 Sofia, ul. Arsenalski 11, 4th Floor; tel. (2) 963-16-37; fax (2) 963-16-42; e-mail embavenezuela@abv.bg; Ambassador RAFAEL ANGEL BARRETO CASTILLO.

Viet Nam: 1113 Sofia, ul. Zhetvarka 1; tel. and fax (2) 963-36-58; e-mail vnemb.bg@mofa.gov.vn; internet www.mofa.gov.vn/vnemb.bg; Ambassador LE DUC LUU.

Yemen: 1784 Sofia, Mladost 1, bul. A. Sakharov 50; tel. (2) 870-41-19; fax (2) 974-34-63; e-mail yemb-sofia@mofa.gov.ye; Chargé d'affaires AHMED AL-KADASI.

Judicial System

The 1991 Constitution provides for justice to be administered by the Supreme Court of Cassation, the Supreme Administrative Court, courts of appeal, courts of assizes, military courts and district courts. The main legal officials are the justices, or judges, of the higher courts, the prosecutors and investigating magistrates. The judicial system is independent, most appointments being made or recommended by the Supreme Judicial Council, a permanent, supervisory body. The military courts handle cases involving military personnel. Administrative courts review appeals of government acts. The Supreme Judicial Council comprises 25 members, who serve a 5-year term; 11 members are elected by the National Assembly and 11 are elected by the judiciary. The Chairmen of the two Supreme Courts and the Prosecutor-General are senior *ex officio* members. The Supreme Judicial Council is responsible for all judicial appointments and administers the judiciary. The Constitutional Court is the final arbiter of constitutional issues. It comprises 12 judges, who serve 9-year terms, four of whom are appointed by the President, four by the National Assembly and four by the Supreme Courts. A new 'special court' opened in Sofia in January 2012, designed to expedite organized crime trials.

Supreme Court of Cassation (Varkhoven kasatsionen sad): 1000 Sofia, bul. Vitosha 2; tel. (2) 987-17-34; fax (2) 987-60-24; internet www.vks.bg; Chair. LAZAR GRUEV.

Supreme Administrative Court (Varkhoven Administrariven Sad): 1301 Sofia, bul. A. Stamboliyski 18; tel. (2) 988-49-02; fax (2) 981-87-51; e-mail chairman@sac.government.bg; internet www.sac.government.bg; Chair. GEORGI KOLEV.

Constitutional Court (Konstitutsionen Sad): 1594 Sofia, bul. Dondukov 1; tel. (2) 987-50-08; fax (2) 987-19-86; e-mail secretariat@constcourt.bg; internet www.constcourt.bg; Chair. DIMITAR TOKUSHEV.

Supreme Judicial Council (Vissh Sadeben Savet): 1000 Sofia, ul. Ekzarh Yosif 12; tel. (2) 930-49-17; fax (2) 980-76-32; e-mail representative@vss.justice.bg; internet www.vss.justice.bg; Sec.-Gen. SLAVKA KAMENOVA.

Office of the Prosecutor-General: 1061 Sofia, bul. Vitosha 2; tel. (2) 921-92-09; fax (2) 981-58-32; e-mail press@prb.bg; internet www.prb.bg; Prosecutor-Gen. SOTIR TSATSAROV.

Religion

Most of the population professes Christianity, the main denomination being the Bulgarian Orthodox Church. The 1991 Constitution guarantees freedom of religion, although Eastern Orthodox Christianity is declared to be the 'traditional religion in Bulgaria'. There is a significant Islamic minority, most of whom are ethnic Turks, although there are also some ethnic Bulgarian Muslims, known as Pomaks. There is a small Jewish community.

CHRISTIANITY

Bulgarian Orthodox Church: 1090 Sofia, ul. Oborishte 4, Synod Palace; tel. (2) 987-56-11; fax (2) 989-76-00; f. AD 865; autocephalous Exarchate 1870 (recognized 1945); administered by the Bulgarian Patriarchy; 11 dioceses in Bulgaria and two dioceses abroad (Diocese of North and South America and Australia, and Diocese of West Europe), each under a Metropolitan; Chair. of the Bulgarian Patriarchy NEOFIT DMITROV.

Armenian Apostolic Orthodox Church: Sofia 1080, ul. Nishka 31; tel. (2) 988-02-08; 20,000 adherents (1996); administered by Bishop DIRAYR MARDIKIYAN, resident in Bucharest, Romania; Chair. of the Diocesan Council in Bulgaria OWANES KIRAZIAN.

The Roman Catholic Church

The Latin (Roman) Rite, which is organized in two dioceses, both directly responsible to the Holy See, has some 63,000 adherents. The Byzantine-Slav (Eastern) Rite is organized in one apostolic exarchate, which has some 10,000 adherents.

Bishops' Conference: 1606 Sofia, ul. Lulin Planina 5; tel. (2) 953-04-06; fax (2) 952-61-86; e-mail proykov@gmail.com; internet www.catholic-bg.org; f. 1991; Pres. Most Rev. CHRISTO NIKOLOV PROYKOV (Titular Bishop of Briula).

Latin Rite

Bishop of Nicopolis: Most Rev. PETKO CHRISTOV, 7000 Ruse, ul. Bratya Simeonovi 26A; tel. (82) 83-52-45; fax (82) 82-28-81; e-mail dio_nicop@elits.rousse.bg.

Bishop of Sofia and Plovdiv: Most Rev. GEORGI ZHOVCHEV, 4000 Plovdiv, bul. Maria Luisa 3; tel. (32) 62-20-42; fax (32) 62-15-22; e-mail manolov@seznam.cz.

Byzantine Rite

Apostolic Exarch of Sofia: CHRISTO PROYKOV (Titular Bishop of Briula), 1606 Sofia, ul. Lulin Planina 5; tel. (2) 953-04-06; fax (2) 952-61-86; e-mail cproykov@technolink.bg.

ISLAM

National Muslim Conference: 1000 Sofia, ul. Bratya Miladinovi 27; tel. (2) 981-60-01; fax (2) 980-30-58; e-mail gl.mufti@genmuftibg.net; internet www.genmuftibg.net; f. 1909; an estimated 1,200 imams; Chair. SHABANALI AHMED; Grand Mufti MUSTAFA HADZHI.

JUDAISM

Central Jewish Theological Council: 1000 Sofia, ul. Ekzarkh Yosif 16; tel. (2) 983-12-73; fax (2) 983-50-85; e-mail sofia_synagogue@mail.orbitel.bg; internet www.sofiasynagogue.com; Head ROBERT DJERASSI.

The Press

There were 354 newspapers and 635 periodicals, including bulletins, published in 2012.

PRINCIPAL DAILIES

24 Chasa (24 Hours): 1504 Sofia, bul. Tsarigradsko 47; tel. (2) 942-25-14; fax (2) 942-28-19; e-mail mnenia@24chasa.bg; internet www.24chasa.bg; f. 1991; wholly owned by Westdeutsche Allgemeine Zeitung (Germany); Editor-in-Chief DANKA VASILEVA; circ. 330,000.

Capital Daily: 1000 Sofia, ul. I. Vazov 16; tel. (2) 461-54-14; fax (2) 461-52-35; e-mail pisma@capital.bg; internet www.capital.bg; f. 2011 through merger of the print editions of *Dnevnik* and *Pari*; Editor-in-Chief STANKA TOSHEVA.

Chernomorsky Far (The Black Sea Lighthouse): 8000 Burgas Oblast, Burgas, ul. Hristo Botev 101/2; tel. (56) 80-17-33; fax (56) 83-10-00; e-mail far@chfar.com; internet www.chernomorskifar.com; f. 1920; regional independent; Chief Editor RUMYANA EMANUILIDU.

Dneven Trud (Daily Labour): 1000 Sofia, bul. Dondukov 52; tel. (2) 921-42-40; fax (2) 980-26-26; e-mail trud@trud.bg; internet www.trud.bg; f. 1936; owned by Westdeutsche Allgemeine Zeitung (Germany); Editor TOSHO TOSHEV.

Dnevnik (The Daily): 1000 Sofia, ul. I. Vazov 20; tel. (2) 461-53-00; fax (2) 461-52-35; e-mail dnevnik@dnevnik.bg; internet www.dnevnik.bg; f. 2001; online only from 2011; Editor-in-Chief VELISLAVA POPOVA.

Duma (Word): 1301 Sofia, bul. Pozitano 20A; tel. (2) 970-52-00; fax (2) 975-26-04; e-mail duma@duma.bg; internet www.duma.bg; f. 1990; leftist; Chief Editor IVELIN NIKOLOV.

Monitor: 1784 Sofia, bul. Tsarigradsko shose 113A; tel. (2) 960-22-09; fax (2) 975-24-44; e-mail monitor@monitor.bg; internet www.monitor.bg; f. 1998; Editorial Dir IRENA KRASTEVA.

Narodno Delo (People's Cause): 9000 Varna, bul. Miladinovi 68; tel. (52) 66-36-03; fax (52) 61-50-80; e-mail office@narodnodelo.bg; internet www.narodnodelo.bg; f. 1944; 6 a week; regional independent; business, politics and sport; Chief Editor MARTIN MARKOV; circ. 20,000 (Oct. 2010).

Novinar: 1000 Sofia, ul. Iskar 31; tel. and fax (2) 943-45-32; e-mail novinar@novinar.bg; internet www.novinar.net; f. 1992; Editor-in-Chief STOYAN SIRAKOV.

Sega: 1463 Sofia, pl. Balgaria 1; tel. (2) 428-23-00; e-mail prepress@segabg.com; internet www.segabg.com; f. 1998; Chief Editor TEODORA PEEVA.

Standart News: 1404 Sofia, bul. Balgaria 49, Biznis tsentar 'Vitosha'; tel. (2) 818-23-11; fax (2) 818-23-55; e-mail office@standartnews.com; internet www.standartnews.com; f. 1992; Editor-in-Chief SLAVKA BOZUKOVA.

Trud (Labour): 1000 Sofia, bul. Dondukov 52; tel. (2) 921-42-12; fax (2) 980-11-40; internet www.trud.bg; f. 1936; organ of the Confederation of Independent Trade Unions in Bulgaria; Editor-in-Chief SVETLANA DZHAMDZHIEV; circ. 200,000.

PRINCIPAL PERIODICALS

168 Chasa (168 Hours): 1504 Sofia, bul. Tsarigradsko 47; tel. (2) 433-92-88; fax (2) 433-93-15; internet www.168chasa.bg; f. 1990; weekly; business, politics, entertainment; owned by Westdeutsche Allgemeine Zeitung (Germany); Editor-in-Chief BORISLAV ZYUMBYULEV; circ. 93,000.

AMICA: 1504 Sofia, bul. Shipka 21; tel. (2) 470-07-00; fax (2) 946-12-87; e-mail amica@amica.bg; internet www.amica.bg; monthly; fashion; in Bulgarian; owned by Bulgarian Textile; Editor-in-Chief BOGDANA ZLATEVA; circ. 20,000 (2007).

Az Buki (Alphabet): 1113 Sofia, bul. Tsarigradsko 125; tel. (2) 425-04-70; e-mail azbuki@mon.bg; internet www.azbuki.bg; f. 1991; weekly; for schools; sponsored by the Ministry of Education and Science; Editor-in-Chief NADYA KANTAREVA-BARUH; circ. 4,000 (2009).

Bankera: 1421 Sofia, ul. Tsvetna gradina 5; tel. (2) 440-94-40; fax (2) 440-94-35; e-mail info@banker.bg; internet www.banker.bg; weekly; banking and finance; Editor-in-Chief BISTRA GEORGIEVA.

Bulka (Bride): 1784 Sofia, POB 138; tel. (89) 787-77-63; e-mail bulka@gbg.bg; internet www.spisaniebulka.com; quarterly; fashion and weddings; owned by 75 GROUP Ltd; Chief Editor VIOLETA TSACHEVA.

Durzhaven Vestnik (State Gazette): 1169 Sofia, bul. K. Aleksandar 1; tel. (2) 939-35-03; fax (2) 981-17-11; e-mail dv@parliament.bg; internet dv.parliament.bg; f. 1879; 2 a week; official publication of the Republic of Bulgaria; 2 bulletins of parliamentary proceedings and the publ. in which all legislation is promulgated; Editor-in-Chief ISKRA KOEVA; circ. 4,000.

EVA: 1000 Sofia, Hristo Belchev 1/5; tel. (2) 987-34-39; fax (2) 980-94-54; e-mail eva@eva.bg; internet www.eva.bg; monthly; fashion and lifestyle; in Bulgarian; Editor-in-Chief MILENA POPOVA.

Galeria (Gallery): Sofia, Tsarigradsko Shosse 17; f. 2009; weekly; politics; Editor-in-Chief KRISTINA PATRASHKOVA.

Kultura (Culture): 1164 Sofia, kv. Lozenets, ul. Milin Kamak 14; tel. (2) 963-21-06; fax (2) 963-21-05; e-mail kultura@online.bg; internet www.kultura.bg; f. 1957; weekly; arts, publicity and cultural affairs; Chief Editor KOPRINKA CHERVENKOVA; circ. 5,000.

Napravi Sam (Do It Yourself): 1527 Sofia, ul. Panayot Volov 11; tel. (2) 857-65-65; e-mail nsam@newteck.bg; internet www.napravisam.net; f. 1980; monthly; Editor-in-Chief GEORGI BALANSKI; circ. 115,000 (2012).

Novo Vreme (New Time): 1000 Sofia, ul. Pozitano 20; tel. (2) 810-72-70; fax (2) 810-72-69; e-mail novovreme@novovreme.com; internet www.novovreme.com; f. 1897; 6 a year; organ of the Bulgarian Socialist Party; Editor-in-Chief I. BORISOV.

Pro i Anti: 1000 Sofia, pl. Slaveykov 11; tel. (2) 980-44-45; fax (2) 963-42-36; e-mail v.proanti@gmail.com; f. 1991; weekly; politics, culture; Editor VASIL STANILOV; circ. 7,000.

Sofia Ekho (Sofia Echo): 1000 Sofia, ul. Ivan Vazov 16; tel. (2) 937-63-49; e-mail editor@sofiaecho.com; internet www.sofiaecho.com; f. 1997; weekly; business, law, property, travel and tourism, lifestyle and sports; in Bulgarian and English; owned by the media company Economedia; Editor-in-Chief CLIVE LEVIEV-SAWYER; circ. 3,000 (2008).

Starshel (The Hornet): 1000 Sofia, pl. Slaveykov 4; tel. and fax (2) 988-08-16; e-mail info@starshel.bg; internet www.starshel.bg; f. 1946; weekly; satirical; Chief Editor MIKHAIL VESHIM; circ. 45,200.

Tema: 1000 Sofia, bul. Vitosha 19; tel. (2) 933-09-10; fax (2) 933-09-39; e-mail tema@temanews.com; internet www.temanews.com; weekly; society, economics, politics; Chief Editor VALERI ZAPRYANOV; circ. 10,000.

Zhenata Dnes (Women Today): 1164 Sofia, bul. Dzheimz Baucher 23; tel. and fax (2) 969-41-97; e-mail jenatadnes@rispress.com; internet www.jenatadnes.com; f. 1946; monthly; Chief Editor MIRA BADZHEVA; circ. 50,000.

NEWS AGENCIES

Balgarska Telegrafna Agentsia (BTA) (Bulgarian Telegraph Agency): Sofia, bul. Tsarigradsko 49; tel. (2) 988-17-19; fax (2) 988-54-63; e-mail bta@bta.bg; internet www.bta.bg; f. 1898; official news agency; domestic, Balkan and international news in Bulgarian and English; also economic and sports news; publishes weekly surveys of science and technology, international affairs, literature and art; Gen. Dir MAKSIM MINCHEV.

Sofia News Agency: 1000 Sofia, ul. Khan Asparuh 54; tel. and fax (2) 421-11-51; internet www.novinite.com; f. 2001; English-language news provider; part of One Click Media Group; Man. Dir NEDA PELITEVA.

Sofia-Press Agency: 1000 Sofia, ul. Slavyanska 29/7; tel. (2) 988-28-78; e-mail office@sofia-press.com; internet www.sofia-press.com; f. 1967; publishes socio-political and scientific literature, fiction, children's and tourist literature, publs on the arts, a newspaper, magazines and bulletins in foreign languages.

PRESS ASSOCIATIONS

Bulgarian Journalists' Union: 1000 Sofia, Graf Ignatiev 4; tel. (2) 987-28-08; fax (2) 988-30-47; e-mail sbj_bg@mail.bg; internet www.sbj-bg.eu; f. 1944; Chair. SNEZHANA TODOROVA (acting).

Union des Journalistes Bulgares Podkrepa: 1000 Sofia, Angel Kantchev 2; tel. (2) 987-68-82; fax (2) 987-05-57; e-mail press_center@podkrepa.org; internet www.podkrepa.org; Pres. KONSTANTIN TRANCHEFF.

Publishers

Balgarski Hudozhnik (Bulgarian Artist) Publishing House: 1504 Sofia, ul. Shipka 6; tel. (2) 944-61-15; fax (2) 946-02-12; e-mail info@sbhart.com; internet www.sbhart.com; f. 1952; owned by Union of Bulgarian Artists; art books, children's books; Chair. LYUBEN GENOV.

Balgarski Pisatel (Bulgarian Writer) Publishing House: 1000 Sofia, ul. 6-ti Septemvri 35; tel. (2) 87-58-73; fax (2) 87-24-95; publishing house of the Union of Bulgarian Writers; Bulgarian fiction and poetry, literary criticism; Dir GERTCHO ATANASOV.

Khristo G. Danov State Publishing House (Darzhavno Izdatelstvo 'Khristo G. Danov'): 4005 Plovdiv, ul. S. Chalakov 1; tel. (32) 63-25-52; fax (32) 26-05-60; f. 1855; fiction, poetry, literary criticism; Dir NACHO KHRISTOSKOV.

Prof. Marin Drinov Academic Publishing House (Bulgarian Academy of Sciences) (Izdatelstvo na Bulgarskata Akademiya na Naukite 'Prof. Marin Drinov'): 1113 Sofia, ul. G. Bonchev 6; tel. (2) 872-09-22; fax (2) 870-40-54; e-mail aph@aph.bas.bg; internet www.baspress.com; f. 1869; scientific works and periodicals of the Bulgarian Academy of Sciences; Dir MARTIN KRASTEV.

Medizina i Fizkultura (Medicine and Physical Culture) Publishing House (Izdatelstvo 'Medizina i Fizkultura'): 1000 Sofia, pl. Slaveykov 11; tel. (2) 987-99-75; e-mail medpubl@abv.bg; internet www.medpubl.com; f. 1956; privately owned; medicine; Dir EMILIA NIKOLOVA.

Military Publishing House (Voenno Izdatelstvo): 1080 Sofia, ul. I. Vazov 12; tel. (2) 987-39-34; fax (2) 980-27-79; e-mail plamstoyanov@abv.bg; internet www.vi-books.com; f. 1888; Dir PLAMEN STOYANOV.

Narodna Kultura (National Culture) Publishing House: 1000 Sofia, ul. A. Kanchev 1, POB 421; tel. (2) 987-80-63; e-mail nauk-izk@sigma-bg.com; f. 1944; general; Dir PETAR MANOLOV.

Nauka i Izkustvo (Sciences and Arts) Publishing House: 1000 Sofia, pl. Slaveykov 11; tel. (2) 987-47-90; fax (2) 987-24-96; e-mail nauk_izk@sigma-bg.com; f. 1948; language and psychology; Man. LORETA PUSHKAROVA.

Prosveta (Enlightenment) Publishing House: 1618 Sofia, ul. Zemedelska 2; tel. (2) 818-20-20; fax (2) 818-20-19; e-mail prosveta@prosveta.bg; internet www.prosveta.bg; f. 1945; educational publishing house; Chair. JOANA TOMOVA.

Reporter Publishing House: 1784 Sofia, bul. Tsarigradsko 113; tel. and fax (2) 832-80-50; e-mail reporter7@abv.bg; f. 1990; private publishers of fiction and documentary literature; Man. KRUM BLAGOV.

RIVA Publishers: 1000 Sofia, ul. Graf Ignatiyev 53B; tel. and fax (2) 986-56-86; e-mail riva@rivapublishers.com; internet www.rivapublishers.com; f. 1990; history, philosophy, social sciences, literature and musicology; Man. YONKO YONTCHEV.

Sinodalno (Synodal) Publishing House: 1000 Sofia, ul. Oborishte 4; tel. (2) 87-56-11; religious publishing house; Dir ANGEL VELITEHKOV.

Tangra TanNakRa: 1124 Sofia, POB 1832; tel. (2) 986-44-19; fax (2) 986-69-45; e-mail mail@tangra-bg.org; internet www.tangra-bg.org; history.

Technica Publishing House: 1000 Sofia, pl. Slaveykov 1; tel. (2) 987-12-83; fax (2) 987-49-06; e-mail office@technica-bg.com; internet www.technica-bg.com; f. 1958; textbooks for professional, higher and university education, technical literature, dictionaries and handbooks; Exec. Man. MARIA TSANKOVA.

Zemizdat Publishing House: 1504 Sofia, bul. Tsarigradsko 47; tel. (2) 44-18-29; f. 1949; specializes in works on agriculture, shooting, fishing, forestry, livestock-breeding, environmental studies, and popular scientific literature and textbooks; Dir PETAR ANGELOV.

PUBLISHERS' ASSOCIATIONS

Bulgarian Book Association: 1463 Sofia, bul. Vitosha; tel. (2) 958-15-25; fax (2) (2) 958-92-11; e-mail office@abk.bg; internet www.abk.bg; f. 1994; Chair. VESSELIN TODOROV; Sec. SILVA PAPAZIAN.

Union of Publishers in Bulgaria (UPB): 1000 Sofia, ul. Alabin 58; tel. (2) 988-47-84; fax (2) 987-33-75; e-mail office@sib.bg; internet www.sib.bg; f. 2000; independent union of publrs of newspapers, magazines and books; Chair. LYUBOMIR PAVLOV; 18 mem. orgs.

Broadcasting and Communications

TELECOMMUNICATIONS

Blizoo Media and Broadband: 1700 Sofia, bul. Nikola Gabrovski 83; tel. (2) 480-07-83; fax (4) 480-07-48; e-mail info@blizoo.bg; internet www.blizoo.bg; f. 2009; provides fixed-line, mobile telephone and internet services; CEO HARALD RÖSCH.

Bulsatcom: Sofia, ul. Voynishko Vastanie 61/3; tel. (2) 411-94-41; e-mail info@bulsat.com; internet www.bulsat.com; f. 2004; provides fixed-line and mobile telephone, internet and internet TV services; CEO PLAMEN GENCHEV.

Globul: 1766 Sofia, bul. Mladost 4, POB 10; fax (2) 415-41-23; e-mail career@globul.bg; internet www.globul.bg; f. 2001; wholly owned by Telenor ASA (Norway); mobile telecommunications services; CEO STEIN-ERIK VELLAN.

Mobiltel EAD: 1309 Sofia, Ilinden, ul. Kukush 1/8; tel. (88) 808-80-88; fax (88) 850-08-85; e-mail pr@mobiltel.bg; internet www.mtel.bg; f. 1994; owned by Telekom Austria AG from 2006; provides mobile and fixed telecommunications services, digital TV and high-speed internet; 5.3m. subscribers (Nov. 2011); CEO THANASIS KATSIROUBAS.

Vivacom: 1784 Sofia, Tsarigradsko shosse 115; tel. (2) 949-46-24; fax (2) 952-10-98; internet www.vivacom.bg; 90% owned by AIG

Investments (USA); formerly known as Bulgarian Telecommunications Co (BTC); merged with BTC Mobile (Vivatel) in Jan. 2009; name changed as above in Sept. 2009; provides fixed-line and mobile telecommunications, and internet services; Chair. ZLATOZAR K. SURLEKOV; CEO ATANAS I. DOBREV; 23,000 employees.

Regulatory Authority

Communications Regulation Commission (CRC): 1000 Sofia, ul. Gurko 6; tel. (2) 949-27-75; fax (2) 971-27-29; e-mail info@crc.bg; internet www.crc.bg; f. 2002; Chair. VESELIN BOZHKOV.

BROADCASTING

National Radio and Television Council: 1504 Sofia, ul. San Stefano 29; Dir IVAN BORISLAVOV.

Association of Bulgarian Broadcasters (ABBRO): 1463 Sofia, pl. Bulgaria 1; tel. (2) 946-16-20; fax (2) 916-63-51; e-mail office@abbro-bg.org; internet www.abbro-bg.org; f. 1997; independent non-profit org.; represents 60 private media companies, incl. 160 radio and TV stations; Exec. Dir GRISHA KAMBUROV.

Radio

In 2009 there were 86 licensed local radio stations, and two principal nation-wide stations: Bulgaria National Radio (BNR) and Darik Radio. At the end of 2008 BNR and Darik Radio reached 96% and 95% of the population, respectively.

Bulgarian National Radio (Balgarsko Natsionalno Radio): 1040 Sofia, bul. D. Tsankov 4; tel. (2) 933-66-38; fax (2) 933-67-15; internet www.bnr.bg; f. 1929; two Home Service programmes; local stations at Blagoevgrad, Plovdiv, Shumen, Stara Zagora and Varna; Foreign Service broadcasts in Bulgarian, Albanian, Arabic, English, French, German, Greek, Russian, Serbian, Spanish and Turkish; Dir VALERI TODOROV.

BG Radio: 1000 Sofia, POB 48; tel. (2) 952-38-07; fax (2) 952-38-45; e-mail office@bgradio.net; internet www.bgradio.net; f. 2001; commercial music station; wholly owned by Metromedia Int. Telecommunications Inc (USA); Chief Exec. NIKOLAY YANCHOVICHIN.

Television

At the end of 2009 there were 20 terrestrial television broadcasters. Of these, the three most significant were the state-owned Bulgarian National Television, and two private stations, bTV and Nova Television. There were also 532 cable television operators, offering a total of 2,811 channels.

bTV: 1463 Sofia, pl. Bulgaria 1, NDK Administration Bldg; tel. (2) 917-68-00; fax (2) 917-68-86; internet www.btv.bg; f. 2000; daily transmission of commercial news, family entertainment and locally produced programmes, on bTV channel; owned by Central European Media Enterprises; Gen. Dir PAVEL STANCHEV.

Bulgarian National Television (Bulgarska Natsionalna Televiziya): 1504 Sofia, ul. San Stefano 29; tel. (2) 944-49-99; fax (2) 946-12-10; internet www.bnt.bg; f. 1959; daily transmission of programmes on Channel 1 and Efir 2 and on the satellite channel TV Bulgaria; Dir VYARA ANKOVA; 3,000 employees.

Nova Television: 1592 Sofia, bul. Khristopfer Kolumb 41, Porsche Business Centre; tel. (2) 805-00-00; fax (2) 805-05-06; e-mail office@ntv.bg; internet www.ntv.bg; f. 1994; privately owned; news and entertainment; CEO DIDIER STOESSEL.

Finance

(cap. = capital; res = reserves; dep. = deposits; m. = million; brs = branches; amounts in new leva)

BANKING

At mid-2012 31 commercial banks were licensed to operate in Bulgaria (of which six were branches of foreign banks).

Central Bank

Bulgarian National Bank (Bulgarska Narodna Banka): 1000 Sofia, pl. Knyaz Aleksandar I 1; tel. (2) 914-59; fax (2) 980-24-25; e-mail press_office@bnbank.org; internet www.bnb.bg; f. 1879; bank of issue; cap. 20.0m., res 4,326.7m., dep. 12,315.1m. (Dec. 2010); Gov. IVAN ISKROV; 3 brs.

Commercial Banks

Allianz Bank Bulgaria: 1202 Sofia, bul. Mariya Luiza 79; tel. (2) 981-93-07; fax (2) 921-55-06; e-mail admin@bank.allianz.bg; internet www.bank.allianz.bg; f. 1997; 79.26% owned by Allianz Bulgaria Holding AD; cap. 85.3m., res 10.1m., dep. 1,462.0m. (Dec. 2011); CEO SVETOSLAV GAVRIISKI; 54 brs.

Bulgarian Development Bank: 1000 Sofia, ul. Stefan Karadzha 10; tel. (2) 930-63-33; fax (2) 930-63-21; e-mail office@bdbank.bg; internet www.bdbank.bg; f. 1999 as Encouragement Bank; name changed as above 2008; 99.99% owned by the Ministry of Finance; cap. 602.0m., res 59.0m., dep. 241.3m. (Dec. 2011); Chair. and CEO DIMO SPASSOV.

Central Co-operative Bank (Tsentralna Kooperativna Banka): 1086 Sofia, bul. G. S. Rakovski 103; tel. (2) 926-65-23; fax (2) 980-43-86; e-mail office@ccbank.bg; internet www.ccbank.bg; f. 1991; cap. 113.2m., res 81.0m., dep. 3,108.4m. (Dec. 2012); Chair. of Managing Bd IVO KAMENOV; 36 brs.

CIBank: 1612 Sofia, bul. Tsar Boris III/1; tel. (2) 939-92-40; fax (2) 981-25-26; e-mail info@cibank.bg; internet www.cibank.bg; f. 1994 as Bulgarian Russian Investment Bank; name changed to BRIBank in 1999, and to Economic and Investment Bank in 2000; current name adopted 2011; wholly owned by KBC Bank NV (Belgium); cap. 79.4m., res 58.3m., dep. 1,541.0m. (Dec. 2012); Chair. and Exec. Dir PETAR ANDRONOV; 41 brs.

Corporate Commercial Bank (Korporativna Targovska Banka): 1000 Sofia, ul. Graf Ignatiev 10, POB 632; tel. (2) 937-56-06; fax (2) 937-56-07; e-mail corpbank@corpbank.bg; internet www.corpbank.bg; f. 1989; 50.66% owned by Bromak Ltd and 30.35% by Bulgarian Acquisition Co; cap. 60.0m., res 334.0m., dep. 4,739.3m. (Dec. 2012); Chair. of Supervisory Bd TZVETAN VASILEV; 30 brs.

DSK Bank (Banka DSK): 1036 Sofia, ul. Moskovska 19; tel. 0700-10-375; fax (2) 980-64-77; e-mail call_center@dskbank.bg; internet www.dskbank.bg; f. 1951 as State Savings Bank; present name adopted 1998; provides general retail banking services throughout the country; owned by Nat. Savings and Commercial Bank—OTP Bank (Hungary); cap. 154m., res 1,085m., dep. 6,819m. (Dec. 2012); Chair. and Chief Exec. VIOLINA MARINOVA; 231 brs.

Eurobank Bulgaria (Postbank): 1048 Sofia, bul. Tsar Osvoboditel 14; tel. (2) 816-60-00; fax (2) 988-81-10; e-mail main@postbank.bg; internet www.postbank.bg; f. 2007 as Eurobank EFG Bulgaria (Postbank) by merger of Postbank and DZI Bank; name changed as above in 2013; 63.6% owned by EFG Eurobank Ergasias SA (Greece); cap. 453m., res –7m., dep. 4,456.1m. (Dec. 2012); Chief Exec. PETYA DIMITROVA; 28 brs.

First Investment Bank (Parva Investitsionna Banka): 1797 Sofia, bul. Dragan Tzankov 37; tel. (2) 817-11-00; fax (2) 970-95-97; e-mail fib@fibank.bg; internet www.fibank.bg; f. 1993; 15% owned by Bulgarian Stock Exchange; cap. 110m., res 140m., dep. 6,192.3m. (Dec. 2012); Chair. of Supervisory Bd DIMITAR KOSTOV; 34 brs.

Investbank: 1404 Sofia, bul. Bulgaria 85; tel. (2) 818-61-44; fax (2) 854-81-99; e-mail office@ibank.bg; internet www.ibank.bg; f. 1994; present name adopted 2002; cap. 119.4m., res 48.0m., dep. 1,162.0m. (Dec. 2012); Chair. of Supervisory Bd PETYA SLAVOVA; 29 brs.

Municipal Bank (Obshchinska Banka): 1000 Sofia, ul. Vrabcha 6; tel. (2) 930-01-11; fax (2) 930-02-70; e-mail contacts@municipalbank.bg; internet www.municipalbank.bg; f. 1996; 67.65% owned by the Municipality of Sofia; cap. 43.5m., res 25.3m., dep. 891.1m. (Dec. 2012); Chair. of Supervisory Bd STEFAN NENOV; 11 brs.

Piraeus Bank Bulgaria AD: 1000 Sofia, bul. Vitosha 3; tel. (2) 700-12-002; fax (2) 800-43-62; e-mail customerservice@piraeusbank.bg; internet www.piraeusbank.bg; f. 1994; 99.8% owned by Piraeus Bank (Greece); cap. 316.7m., res 33.0m., dep. 2,305.0m. (Dec. 2012); Chair. ILIAS MILIS; 46 brs.

Raiffeisenbank (Bulgaria) EAD: 1504 Sofia, ul. Gogol 18–20; tel. (2) 919-85-101; fax (2) 943-45-28; internet www.rbb.bg; f. 1994; 100% owned by Raiffeisen Int. Bank Holding AG (Austria); cap. 603.4m., res 86.0m., dep. 4,424.3m. (Dec. 2012); Chair. and Exec. Dir MOMCHIL ANDREEV; 86 brs.

Société Générale Expressbank AD Varna: 9000 Varna, bul. Vl. Varnenchik 92; tel. (52) 68-61-00; fax (52) 60-16-81; e-mail sgeb.contact@socgen.com; internet www.sgeb.bg; f. 1993; present name adopted 2005; 97.95% owned by Société Générale (France); cap. 33.7m., res 100.4m., dep. 2,790.0m. (Dec. 2012); CEO PHILIPPE LHOTTE; 19 brs.

UniCredit Bulbank AD: 1000 Sofia, pl. Sveta Nedelia 7; tel. (2) 923-21-11; fax (2) 988-46-36; e-mail pr@unicreditgroup.bg; internet www.unicreditbulbank.bg; f. 1964; present name adopted 2007; 96.47% owned by UniCredit Bank Austria AG (Austria); cap. 286.0m., res 491.3m., dep. 10,117.0m. (Dec. 2012); Chair. and Chief Exec. LEVON HAMPARTZOUMIAN; 34 brs.

United Bulgarian Bank (Obedinena Balgarska Banka): 1040 Sofia, ul. Sv. Sofia 5; tel. (2) 811-28-30; fax (2) 988-08-22; e-mail info@ubb.bg; internet www.ubb.bg; f. 1992; universal commercial bank; 99.9% owned by National Bank of Greece SA; cap. 76m., res 1,038m., dep. 4,781m. (Dec. 2012); Chair. STILIYAN VATEV; 75 brs.

STOCK EXCHANGE

Bulgarian Stock Exchange: 1303 Sofia, ul. Triushi 10; tel. (2) 937-09-34; fax (2) 937-09-46; e-mail bse@bse-sofia.bg; internet www.bse-sofia.bg; f. 1997; Chair. ASEN YAGODIN; CEO IVAN TAKEV.

INSURANCE

In 2013 there were 47 insurance companies operating in Bulgaria, of which 17 were life and 27 non-life.

Allianz Bulgaria: 1504 Sofia, bul. Knyaz Al. Dondukov 59; tel. (2) 930-22-00; fax (2) 930-22-30; e-mail life@allianz.bg; internet www.allianz.bg; f. 1991; Chair. and CEO PLAMEN YALAMOV.

Bulstrad: 1000 Sofia, pl. Pozitano 5; tel. (2) 985-66-10; fax (2) 985-61-03; e-mail public@bulstrad.bg; internet www.bulstrad.bg; f. 1961; 31% owned by TBIH Group (Netherlands); all classes of insurance and reinsurance; Chair. of Bd and Chief Exec. RUMEN YANCHEV; 14 brs.

DZI Insurance: 1000 Sofia, Georgi Benkovski St 3; tel. (2) 981-57-99; fax (2) 987-45-33; e-mail general.ins@dzi.bg; internet www.dzi.bg; f. 1946; privatization approved in 2002; all areas of insurance; Chair. and CEO KOSTA CHULAKOV; 27 agencies, 101 brs.

Evroins: 1592 Sofia, bul. Christopher Columbus 43; tel. (2) 965-15-25; fax (2) 489-55-26; e-mail office@euroins.bg; internet www.euroins.bg; f. 1996; business and general insurance; Chair. of Supervisory Bd VIOLETA DARAKOVA; 88 agencies and offices.

Generali Life Insurance: 1504 Sofia, bul. Knyaz Al. Dondukov 68; tel. (2) 926-71-11; fax (2) 926-71-12; e-mail information@generali.bg; internet www.generali.bg; Chair. IVAYLO YOSIFOV.

Municipal Insurance Co (Obshchinska Zastrakhovatelna Kompaniya): 1301 Sofia, bul. Sveta Sofia 7, 5th Floor; tel. (2) 981-31-22; fax (2) 981-43-51; e-mail headoffice@ozk.bg; internet www.ozk.bg; f. 1996; 65.7% owned by L.M. Impex; Exec. Dir ALEKSANDER LICHEV.

Uniqa Insurance Plc Bulgaria: 1612 Sofia, ul. Yunak 11–13; tel. (2) 915-63-33; fax (2) 915-63-00; e-mail info@uniqa.bg; internet www.uniqa.bg; f. 1992; subsidiary of Uniqa (Austria); fmrly Vitosha-Zhivot (Vitosha Life) Insurance Co; CEO and Chair. NIKOLAI GENCHEV; 10 agencies, 28 brs.

Trade and Industry

GOVERNMENT AGENCY

Privatization and Post-privatization Control Agency: 1113 Sofia, bul. Dr G. M. Dimitrov 52A; tel. (2) 970-16-15; fax (2) 970-16-80; f. 2010 by merger of the Privatization Agency and the Agency for Post-privatization Control; Exec. Dir EMIL KARANIKOLOV.

INTERNATIONAL FREE TRADE ZONES

Burgas Free Trade Zone: 8000 Burgas, ul. Trapezitsa 5, POB 154; tel. (56) 84-20-47; fax (56) 84-15-62; e-mail info@freezoneburgas.com; internet www.freezonebourgas.com; f. 1989; Exec. Dir VASSILIY SKRIPKA.

Dragoman Free Trade Zone: 2210 Dragoman, ul. Z. Stoianov 16; tel. and fax (2) 954-93-39.

Plovdiv Free Trade Zone: 4003 Plovdiv, ul. Vasil Levski 242A, POB 75; tel. (32) 90-62-33; fax (32) 96-08-33; e-mail frzone@mbox.contact.bg; internet www.freezone-plovdiv.com; f. 1990; Exec. Dir VASIL CHUCHULEV.

Ruse (Rousse) Free Trade Zone: 7000 Ruse, Tutrakan bul. 71, POB 107; tel. (82) 88-08-00; fax (82) 83-11-12; e-mail manager@freezone-rousse.bg; internet www.freezone-rousse.bg; f. 1988; Exec. Dir DIMITAR NEDYALKOV.

Svilengrad Free Trade Zone: 6500 Svilengrad, bul. Bulgaria 60; tel. (359) 379-74-45; fax (359) 379-75-41; e-mail sbz@svilengrad.com; f. 1990; Exec. Dir DIMO HARAKCHIEV.

Vidin Free Trade Zone: 3700 Vidin; tel. (94) 60-20-60; fax (94) 60-20-46; e-mail ftzvd@vidin.net; f. 1988; Gen. Man. K. MARINOV.

CHAMBER OF COMMERCE

Bulgarian Chamber of Commerce and Industry (BCCI): 1058 Sofia, ul. Iskar 9; tel. (2) 987-26-31; fax (2) 987-32-09; e-mail bcci@bcci.bg; internet www.bcci.bg; f. 1895; promotes economic relations and business contacts between Bulgarian and foreign cos and orgs; organizes participation in international fairs and exhibitions; publishes economic publs in Bulgarian and foreign languages; organizes foreign trade advertising and publicity; provides legal and economic consultations, etc.; registers all Bulgarian cos trading internationally (more than 53,000 at the end of 2013); Pres. TSVETAN SIMEONOV; 28 regional chambers.

EMPLOYERS' ASSOCIATIONS

Bulgarian Industrial Association—Union of Bulgarian Business (Balgarska Stopanska Kamara—Sayuz na balgarskiya biznes): 1000 Sofia, ul. Alabin 16–20; tel. (2) 932-09-11; fax (2) 987-26-04; e-mail office@bia-bg.com; internet www.bia-bg.com; f. 1980; assists Bulgarian economic enterprises with promotion and foreign contacts; economic analysis; legal and arbitration services; intellectual property protection; training and qualifications; Chair. and Exec. Pres. BOZHIDAR DANEV.

Employers' Association of Bulgaria (EABG) (Sayuz na Rabotodatelite v Balgariya): 1202 Sofia, ul. Industrialna 11; tel. (2) 917-88-68; fax (2) 917-88-61; f. 2000; Chair. VASIL VASILEV.

Union for Private Economic Enterprise in Bulgaria (UPEE) (Sayuz za Stopansko Initsiativa—SSI): 1407 Sofia, ul. T. Notchev 30; tel. (2) 962-47-84; fax (2) 962-13-76; e-mail bborisov@unwe.acad.bg; internet www.ssi-bg.org; f. 1989; voluntary asscn of private enterprises; Pres. Dr BORISLAV BORISOV; 140 brs.

Vazrazhdane (Renaissance) Union of Bulgarian Private Entrepreneurs (UPBE) (Vazrazhdane sayuz na chastnite predpremachi): 1504 Sofia, bul. Dondukov 68; tel. (2) 926-24-17; fax (2) 926-74-12; e-mail vuzrazdane@union-vuzrazdane.com; internet www.union-vuzrazdane.eu; f. 1989; Chair. VANIYA TODOROVA.

UTILITIES

Electricity

National Electricity Company (Natsionalna Elektricheska Kompania—NEK): 1040 Sofia, ul. Veslets 5; tel. (2) 926-36-36; fax (2) 980-12-43; e-mail nek@nek.bg; internet www.nek.bg; f. 1991; wholly state-owned subsidiary of Bulgarian Energy Holding EAD; responsible for hydroelectric power generation; national transmission of electricity; centralized purchase and sale of electrical energy; supervision of national power system; Chair. of Bd EVGENY NAGELOV; Exec. Dir KRASSIMIR PARVANOV.

Gas

Bulgargaz: 1336 Sofia, bul. P. Vladigerov 66, POB 3; tel. (2) 939-64-00; fax (2) 925-03-94; e-mail hq@bulgargaz.bg; internet www.bulgargaz.bg; f. 1973; renamed 1990; state-owned subsidiary of Bulgarian Energy Holding EAD; import, transmission, distribution, storage and transit of natural gas; Chair. VORIS TODOROV; Exec. Dir DIMITAR GOGOV.

Overgaz: 1407 Sofia, ul. F. Kutev 5; tel. (2) 428-33-54; fax (2) 962-17-24; e-mail press@overgas.bg; internet www.overgas.bg; f. 1992; 50% owned by Gazprom (Russia), 50% by Overgas Holding AD (Bulgaria); controlling interest in five local gas distribution cos; Exec. Dir SASHO DONTCHEV.

TRADE UNION CONFEDERATIONS

Confederation of Independent Trade Unions in Bulgaria (CITUB) (Konfederatsia na Nezavisitimite Sindikati v Bulgaria—KNSB): 1040 Sofia, bul. Makedonia 1; tel. (2) 401-05-01; fax (2) 988-59-69; e-mail pldimitrov@citub.net; internet knsb-bg.org; f. 1904; name changed from Bulgarian Professional Union and independence declared from all parties and state structures in 1990; Pres. PLAMEN DIMITROV; Sec. MILADIN STOYNOV; 250,000 mems (2013).

Podkrepa (Support) Trade Union Confederation of Labour: 1000 Sofia, ul. A. Kanchev 2; tel. (2) 987-98-87; fax (2) 981-29-28; e-mail intdept@podkrepa.org; internet www.podkrepa.org; f. 1989; 36 regional and 24 branch union orgs; Pres. Dr KONSTANTIN TRENCHEV; 154,350 mems (2013).

Transport

RAILWAYS

In 2010 there were 4,097 km of railway lines.

Bulgarian State Railways EAD (Balgarski Darzhavni Zheleznitsi—BDZh/BDZ): 1080 Sofia, ul. I. Vazov 3; tel. (2) 981-11-10; fax (2) 981-71-51; e-mail bdz@bdz.bg; internet www.bdz.bg; f. 1888; operates passenger and freight railway services; wholly state-owned; Chair. of Bd of Dirs VELIK ZANCHEV; CEO CHAVDAR TRENDAFILOV; 17,832 employees (2006).

National Railway Infrastructure Company (Natsionalna Kompania 'Zhelezoputna Infrastruktura'): 1233 Sofia, bul. Maria Luiza 110; tel. (2) 932-34-13; e-mail office@rail-infra.bg; internet www.rail-infra.bg; f. 2002 to assume infrastructure responsibilities of Bulgarian State Railways; Chair. ATANAS TONEV; Dir-Gen. ANTON GINEV.

Railway Administration Executive Agency (Zhelezoputna Administratsiya): 1080 Sofia, ul. Gurko 5; tel. (2) 940-94-28; fax (2) 987-67-69; e-mail iaja@mtitc.government.bg; internet www.iaja

.government.bg; f. 2001; regulatory and control functions; Exec. Dir VESELIN VASILEV.

ROADS

There were 19,456 km of roads in Bulgaria in 2010, of which 2,970 km were main roads and 4,030 km were secondary roads; 98.6% of the road network was paved. Two international motorways traverse the country, and a motorway links Sofia to the coast.

SHIPPING AND INLAND WATERWAYS

At December 2013 Bulgaria's flag registered fleet had 87 vessels, with a total displacement of 135,363 grt. The largest Black Sea ports in Bulgaria are at Varna and Burgas. The Danube (Dunav) River is the main waterway, with Ruse (Rousse) and Lom the two main ports.

Bulgarian Ports National Co (BPA) (Natsionalna Kompania 'Pristanishta'): 1000 Sofia, ul. Gen. Gurko 5; tel. (2) 940-97-73; fax (2) 987-94-80; e-mail bpa@port.bg; internet www.port.bg; f. 2000; Gen. Dir Capt. PEYCHO MANOLOV.

Bulgarian River Shipping Co (Parakhodstvo Balgarsko Rechno Plavane): 7000 Ruse, pl. Otets Paisiy 2; tel. (82) 833-37-77; fax (82) 822-21-30; e-mail main@brp.bg; internet www.brp.bg; f. 1935; shipment of cargo and passengers on the Danube; storage, handling and forwarding of cargo; 100% privately owned; Exec. Dir DRAGOMIR KOCHANOV.

Bulgarski Morski Flot Co: 9000 Varna, ul. Panaguirishte 17; tel. (52) 22-63-16; fax (52) 22-53-94; carriage of goods and passengers on waterways; Dir-Gen. ATANAS YONKOV.

Burgas (Bourgas) Port Authority: 8000 Burgas, ul. A. Battenberg 1; tel. (56) 82-22-22; fax (56) 82-21-56; e-mail headoffice@port-burgas.com; internet www.port-burgas.com; Chair. NELY BENEVA; Exec. Dir ARGIR BOIADJIEV.

Navigation Maritime Bulgare: 9000 Varna, Primorski bul. 1; tel. (52) 68-33-72; fax (52) 68-39-32; e-mail office@navbul.com; internet www.navbul.com; f. 1892; 70% of shares sold to KG Maritime Shipping (Bulgaria/Germany) in 2008; sea transport and ship repair; owns 78 tankers, bulk carriers, and container, ferry, cargo and passenger vessels with a capacity of 1.35m. dwt; owns Varna shipyard; Dir-Gen. Capt. HRISTO DONEV; 5,000 employees.

Varna Port Authority: 9000 Varna, pl. Slaveykov 1; tel. (52) 69-22-32; fax (52) 63-29-53; e-mail headoffice@port-varna.bg; internet port-varna.bg; Exec. Dir DANAIL PAPAZOV.

CIVIL AVIATION

There are three international airports in Bulgaria, at Sofia, Varna and Burgas, and seven other airports for domestic services.

Civil Aviation Administration (Grazhdanska Vazdukhoplavatelna Administratsiya): 1000 Sofia, ul. Dyakon Ignatiy 9; tel. (2) 937-10-47; fax (2) 980-53-37; e-mail caa@caa.bg; internet www.caa.bg; Dir-Gen. MINTCHO TZVETKOV.

Bulgaria Air: 1540 Sofia, bul. Brussels 1, Sofia Airport; tel. (2) 402-03-06; fax (2) 937-32-54; e-mail office@air.bg; internet www.air.bg; f. 2002 as successor to Balkan Bulgarian Airlines (Balkanair); 99.99% owned by Balkan Hemus Group; international passenger and cargo services; Chief Exec. YANKO GEORGIEV.

Tourism

Bulgaria's tourist attractions include the resorts on the Black Sea coast, mountain scenery, ski resorts and historic centres. There were 8.9m. foreign tourist arrivals in Bulgaria in 2012, when receipts from tourism (excluding passenger transport) totalled US $3,748m., according to provisional data.

Bulgarian Tourist Chamber: 1000 Sofia, ul. Sv. Sofia 8; tel. (2) 987-40-59; fax (2) 986-51-33; e-mail btch@btch.org; internet www.btch.org; f. 1990; assists tourism enterprises, provides training, and co-ordinates non-governmental orgs; Chair. TSVETAN TONCHEV.

State Agency for Tourism: 1052 Sofia, ul. Slavianska 8; tel. (2) 933-58-14; e-mail secretary@bulgariatravel.org; Chair. ANELIYA KRUSHKOVA.

Defence

The total strength of the armed forces, as assessed at November 2013, was 31,300, comprising an army of 16,300, an air force of 6,700, a navy of 3,450, and 4,850 centrally controlled staff. There were also 16,000 paramilitary forces and a total of 303,000 reserves. Bulgaria joined the North Atlantic Treaty Organization's (NATO) 'Partnership for Peace' programme of military co-operation in 1994 and became a full member of the Alliance on 29 March 2004. The modernization of the national defence force and its operation on a professional basis, which were stipulated as preconditions of Bulgaria's accession to the EU, were agreed in November 2006. Compulsory military service was officially ended on 1 December 2007.

Defence Expenditure: Budgeted at 1,100m. new leva in 2014.

Chief of the General Staff: Gen. SIMEON HRISTOV SIMEONOV.

Education

Education is free and compulsory between the ages of seven and 16 years. Children between the ages of three and six years may attend kindergartens (in 2010/11 some 82% of pre-school age children attended). A 12-year system of schooling was introduced in 1998. Primary education (grades one to four), beginning at seven years of age, lasts for four years. Secondary education (grades five to 12), from 11 years of age, lasts for up to eight years, comprising two cycles of four years each. Secondary education is undertaken at general schools, which provide a general academic course, or vocational and technical schools, and art schools, which offer specialized training. In addition, basic schools cover both primary and lower secondary grades, while combined schools can cater for pupils from grades one to 12. In 2010/11, according to official figures, primary enrolment included 97% of children in the relevant age-group, while enrolment at secondary schools included 85% of those in the relevant age-group. In 2012/13 there were a total of 45 universities and equivalent higher educational institutions, with a total enrolment of 269,271 students (including 4,703 post-graduate students studying for 'specialist' degrees), and an additional eight colleges. Tuition fees for university students were introduced in mid-1999. General government expenditure on education in 2012 amounted to 2,799m. new leva (representing 10.1% of total spending).

BURKINA FASO

Introductory Survey

LOCATION, CLIMATE, LANGUAGE, RELIGION, FLAG, CAPITAL

Burkina Faso is a landlocked state in West Africa, bordered by Mali to the west and north, by Niger to the east, and by Benin, Togo, Ghana and Côte d'Ivoire to the south. The climate is hot and mainly dry, with an average temperature of 27°C (81°F) in the dry season (December–May). A rainy season occurs between June and October. Levels of rainfall are generally higher in the south than in the north; average annual rainfall in Ouagadougou is 718 mm (28 ins). The official language is French, and there are numerous indigenous languages (principally Mossi), with many dialects. The majority of the population are Muslims (61%), while some 23% are Christians, mainly Roman Catholics, and 15% follow animist beliefs. The national flag (proportions 2 by 3) has two equal horizontal stripes, of red and green, with a five-pointed gold star in the centre. The capital is Ouagadougou.

CONTEMPORARY POLITICAL HISTORY

Historical Context

Burkina Faso became a self-governing republic (as Upper Volta) within the French Community in December 1958 and achieved independence on 5 August 1960, with Maurice Yaméogo as President. In January 1966 Yaméogo was deposed in a coup, led by Lt-Col (later Gen.) Sangoulé Lamizana, the army Chief of Staff, who took office as President and Prime Minister. The new regime dissolved the legislature, suspended the Constitution and established a Conseil Suprême des Forces Armées (Supreme Council of the Armed Forces). A new Constitution, approved by referendum in June 1970, provided for a return to civilian rule after a four-year transitional period. The Union Démocratique Voltaïque (UDV) won 37 of the 57 seats in elections for an Assemblée Nationale (National Assembly), held in December.

In February 1974 Lamizana announced that the army had again assumed power. Political activity resumed in October 1977, and in the following month a referendum approved a draft Constitution providing for a return to civilian rule. The UDV won 28 of the 57 seats at elections to a new National Assembly, held in April 1978, while the Union Nationale pour la Défense de la Démocratie (UNDD), led by Hermann Yaméogo (the son of the former President), secured 13 seats. In May Lamizana was elected President, and in July the National Assembly elected Lamizana's nominee, Dr Joseph Conombo, as Prime Minister.

In November 1980 Lamizana was overthrown in a bloodless coup, led by Col Saye Zerbo, and a new Government, comprising both army officers and civilians, was formed. Opposition to the Zerbo regime soon emerged, and in November 1982 Zerbo was deposed by a group of non-commissioned army officers. Maj. Jean-Baptiste Ouédraogo emerged as leader of the new regime, and a predominantly civilian Government was installed. A power struggle within the Government became apparent with the arrest, in May 1983, of radical left-wing elements, including Capt. Thomas Sankara, the recently appointed Prime Minister. Sankara and his supporters were released following a rebellion by commandos under the leadership of Capt. Blaise Compaoré.

In August 1983 Sankara seized power in a violent coup. A Conseil National Révolutionnaire (National Revolutionary Council—CNR) was established, and Jean-Baptiste Ouédraogo and other opponents of the new administration were placed under house arrest. Compaoré, as Minister of State at the Presidency, became the regime's second-in-command. Administrative, judicial and military reforms were announced, and citizens were urged to join Comités pour la Défense de la Révolution (Committees for the Defence of the Revolution), which played an important role in consolidating Sankara's position. In August 1984 the country was renamed Burkina Faso ('Land of the Incorruptible Men').

In December 1985 a long-standing border dispute with Mali erupted into a six-day armed conflict, centred on the reputedly mineral-rich Agacher strip, which left some 50 people dead. Following a ceasefire and as a result of an interim decision on the dispute delivered by the International Court of Justice (ICJ) in January 1986, troops were withdrawn from the contested area; both countries accepted the ICJ's ruling, issued in December, that the territory be divided equally between the two.

Domestic Political Affairs

In October 1987 a self-styled Front Populaire (Popular Front—FP), led by Compaoré, overthrew the CNR in a coup, in which Sankara was killed. A predominantly civilian Council of Ministers included seven members of the previous administration. Compaoré became Head of State. In April 1989 a new political grouping, the Organisation pour la Démocratie Populaire/Mouvement du Travail (ODP/MT), was established, under the leadership of Clément Oumarou Ouédraogo. The dismissal of government members who had declined to join the new party signalled that the ODP/MT was to assume a prominent role in Compaoré's regime.

The final draft of a new constitution, which was completed in late 1990, referred to Burkina Faso as a 'revolutionary, democratic, unitary and secular state'. Multi-party legislative and presidential elections, by universal suffrage, were to take place, while provision was made for the establishment of a second, appointed and consultative chamber of the legislature, the Chambre des Représentants (Chamber of Representatives). In March 1991 the ODP/MT adopted Compaoré as the party's presidential candidate; the party also renounced its Marxist-Leninist ideology. In May a congress was convened to restructure the FP and to provide for the separation, upon the adoption of the draft constitution, of the functions of the FP and the organs of state. Delegates also approved the rehabilitation of Maurice Yaméogo, and an appeal was made to all political exiles to return to Burkina.

About 49% of the registered electorate voted in the constitutional referendum, which took place on 2 June 1991: of these, 93% were reported to have endorsed the new Constitution, which thereby took effect on 11 June. A transitional Government, in which the ODP/MT retained a dominant role, was subsequently appointed, its most senior member being Roch Marc-Christian Kaboré (as Minister of State, responsible for the Co-ordination of Government Action).

A presidential election proceeded on 1 December 1991, when Compaoré (who had resigned from the army to contest the presidency as a civilian) was elected, unopposed, with the support of 90.4% of those who voted. Compaoré was inaugurated as President on 24 December. Four opposition members were appointed to the Government in February 1992, including Hermann Yaméogo (now leader of the Alliance pour la Démocratie et la Fédération—ADF) as Minister of State.

Some 27 political parties contested the legislative elections, which were held on 24 May 1992. The ODP/MT won 78 of the 107 seats in the Assemblée des Députés du Peuple (Assembly of People's Deputies—ADP), and nine other parties secured representation. In June Compaoré appointed Youssouf Ouédraogo, hitherto President of the Economic and Social Council, as Prime Minister. Although his Council of Ministers included representatives of seven political parties, the ODP/MT held most strategic posts.

In March 1994 Youssouf Ouédraogo resigned, apparently prompted by the failure of the Government to negotiate a settlement for salary increases acceptable to workers' representatives, following the 50% devaluation of the CFA franc in January. Kaboré was appointed as the new premier. In February 1996 Kadré Désiré Ouédraogo, hitherto Deputy Governor of the Banque Centrale des Etats de l'Afrique de l'Ouest, replaced Kaboré as Prime Minister. At this time the ODP/MT and 10 other parties merged to form the Congrès pour la Démocratie et le Progrès (CDP), which was dominated by close allies of Compaoré, and the new premier subsequently joined the party.

Constitutional amendments and a new electoral code were approved by the ADP in January 1997. Notably, restrictions were removed on the renewal of the presidential mandate (hitherto renewable only once); the number of parliamentary seats was to be increased to 111 with effect from the forthcoming elections; and the ADP was renamed the National Assembly. At legislative elections in May the CDP won a resounding victory, securing 101 seats.

Several prominent opposition figures, among them Hermann Yaméogo, whose party had become the Alliance pour la Démocratie et la Fédération—Rassemblement Démocratique Africain (ADF—RDA), and Joseph Ki-Zerbo, the leader of the principal opposition party in the legislature, the Parti pour la Démocratie et le Progrès (PDP), declined to participate in the presidential election held on 15 November 1998. Compaoré was challenged by two minor candidates, and provisional results confirmed his decisive victory with 87.5% of the valid votes cast. A new Government, again headed by Ouédraogo, was appointed in January 1999.

The political climate deteriorated rapidly after Norbert Zongo, the managing editor of *L'Indépendant* newspaper, was found dead, together with three colleagues, in December 1998. Zongo, a frequent critic of the Compaoré regime, had been investigating allegations that David Ouédraogo, a driver employed by François Compaoré, younger brother and special adviser of the President, had been tortured and killed by members of the presidential guard. However, the commission of inquiry set up to investigate the deaths stated that it was unable to prove the identity of the perpetrators.

Political reform

In June 1999 President Compaoré established a 16-member Collège des Sages (College of the Wise), composed of Burkinabè state elders, and religious and ethnic leaders, the function of which was to promote national reconciliation and to investigate unpunished political crimes since independence. The College's report, published in August, recommended the formation of both a government of national unity and a commission of truth and justice to oversee the transition to a truly plural political system and to investigate unresolved political murders, including that of Thomas Sankara. The College further recommended the creation of a commission to consider possible political reforms. The two commissions were established in November. Opposition groups had, however, condemned the proposed amnesty for those implicated during the investigations of the commission of truth and justice, and criticized the recommendation for the President to assent to any proposed reforms. Meanwhile, proposals to form a government of national unity were impeded by the demands of most opposition parties that legal action be expedited in the cases of David Ouédraogo and Norbert Zongo. Thus, a reorganized Council of Ministers, announced in October, included just two representatives of the opposition.

In January 2000 the governing CDP organized a public rally in favour of the proposals made by the commission on political reform, including a restriction of the presidential mandate to no more than two successive terms. The National Assembly subsequently voted to revise the electoral code and to accord greater powers to a restructured independent electoral commission (the Commission Electorale Nationale Indépendante—CENI). However, the opposition criticized what they perceived to be the limited nature of the reforms, and expressed their determination to boycott any elections until the Ouédraogo and Zongo cases had been fully resolved. The commission on national reconciliation published its report in February, urging the prosecution of persons suspected of involvement in the embezzlement of public funds and in political killings. The commission also appealed for greater freedom of speech, of the press and of assembly; the resolution of legal proceedings in the Ouédraogo and Zongo cases; the enactment of an amnesty law; and the construction of a monument to Sankara.

The National Assembly approved revisions to the electoral code in April 2000. Under the new regulations, which introduced a system of proportional representation, 90 deputies would be elected from regional lists, with 21 to be elected from a national list. The new legislation also reduced the presidential mandate from seven years to five, renewable only once. However, as the new limits would not take effect until the next election, Compaoré would be permitted to contest the presidential elections due in 2005 and 2010. The Assembly also approved significant judicial reforms, providing for the abolition of the Supreme Court and the replacement of its four permanent chambers with four new state institutions: a Constitutional Council, a Council of State, a Court of Appeal and a National Audit Court.

Kadré Désiré Ouédraogo resigned in November 2000; he was succeeded as Prime Minister by Paramanga Ernest Yonli, hitherto the Minister of the Civil Service and Institutional Development. Compaoré subsequently appointed a 36-member Council of Ministers, including 12 members of the opposition.

Meanwhile, the trial of the soldiers accused of murdering David Ouédraogo began in August 2000. The military tribunal sentenced two members of Compaoré's presidential guard, including Marcel Kafando, head of the guard at the time of Ouédraogo's death, to 20 years' imprisonment; a third member received a 10-year prison sentence. In February 2001 Kafando was further charged with arson and with the murder of Norbert Zongo and three others. In March, at a rally attended by some 30,000 people, President Compaoré formally apologized for 176 unpunished crimes allegedly committed by state representatives since independence. This act constituted the most significant element of a 'day of forgiveness' that had been proposed by the College of the Wise, but which was boycotted by, among others, relatives of Sankara and Zongo. Dissatisfaction at the Government's failure to resolve the Zongo case persisted, and in June several thousand people participated in a demonstration in Ouagadougou to demand that those whom they believed to have ordered the killing of Zongo, including François Compaoré, be brought to justice. In November it was announced that the judicial investigation into Kafando's alleged involvement in Zongo's death had been hampered by the poor health of the defendant. (Eventually, in August 2006 an appeals court confirmed the dismissal of all charges against Kafando.)

Some 30 parties contested elections to the National Assembly, held on 5 May 2002. The CDP remained the largest party, securing 57 of the 111 seats, with 49.5% of the votes cast, although its representation was much reduced. The ADF—RDA won 17 seats, with 12.6% of the votes cast, becoming the largest opposition party, followed by the PDP—PS (as the PDP had become, following its merger with the Parti Socialiste Burkinabè in mid-2001), with 10 seats. Kaboré was elected as President of the National Assembly in June, prior to the reappointment of Yonli as Prime Minister. Despite the slim overall majority held by the CDP in the National Assembly, and the precedent set by the inclusion of ministers from opposition parties in the outgoing administration, the new, 31-member Government did not contain any representatives of the opposition.

The 2005 presidential election

In March 2005 it was announced that the first round of the presidential election would take place on 13 November. Numerous candidates subsequently emerged, among them three candidates representing a 12-party opposition alliance, Alternance 2005, namely: Hermann Yaméogo, now of the Union Nationale pour la Démocratie et le Développement (UNDD); Philippe Ouédraogo, of the Parti Africain de l'Indépendance; and Bénéwendé Stanislas Sankara, of the Union pour la Renaissance—Mouvement Sankariste. In June Compaoré announced his intention to contest a further term as the candidate of the CDP. This widely anticipated announcement prompted several opposition groups to seek a ruling by the Constitutional Court as to whether the amendments approved in 2000 (which, notably, restricted the President to two terms of office) applied retroactively. The Constitutional Court duly confirmed in October 2005 that Compaoré was entitled to contest both the forthcoming election and that scheduled to be held in 2010. Hermann Yaméogo subsequently announced that he was to withdraw from the contest (although his name remained on the ballot paper), and the UNDD called for a campaign of civil disobedience against what it termed a 'forceful step towards the installation of an absolute republican monarch'.

The presidential election was held, as scheduled, on 13 November 2005. According to official results, Compaoré took an overwhelming 80.4% of the votes cast; the second-placed candidate was Sankara, with just 4.9%. Around 57% of the registered electorate participated in the election, and international election observers declared themselves largely satisfied with the conduct of the poll. In January 2006 Compaoré reappointed Yonli as Prime Minister, heading a new Government that included several members of opposition parties, although many of the principal positions remained unchanged from the outgoing administration.

The premiership of Tertius Zongo

A total of 47 parties contested legislative elections held on 6 May 2007. The CDP increased its majority in the National Assembly, winning 73 of the 111 available seats; the ADF—RDA retained 14 seats; and 11 other parties also won representation. Voter turnout was reported to be 56.4%. The following month Prime Minister Yonli tendered his resignation and that of his Government. President Compaoré subsequently named Tertius Zongo, hitherto the Burkinabè ambassador to the USA, as Yonli's successor, and a new Council of Ministers was sworn in.

Following civil unrest in 2006 involving demonstrations against escalating fuel prices, in February 2008 there were protests over the rising cost of living, in particular the sharp increase in food prices (in the year to March the price of maize had reportedly doubled). In Banfora, Ouahigouya and Bobo-Dioulasso rioters attacked government offices, shops and petrol stations; the violence lasted for two days, leading to hundreds of arrests. The Government responded by suspending import taxes on certain staple goods. Violent protests took place in Ouagadougou later in February, after opposition groups called for a day of strikes and civil action in the capital. In early March it was reported that 29 people had been sentenced to between three and 36 months' imprisonment for their part in the protests,. A new coalition of civil society organizations, including human rights groups and trade unions, was formed, and in mid-March the coalition led a demonstration in the capital to demand an increase in salaries and a reduction in the price of basic goods, threatening a two-day general strike if the Government did not comply. Similar demonstrations took place in other towns, but there was no repeat of the violence that had occurred in February. The Government continued to refuse to meet the demands of the protesters, and the two-day strike proceeded peacefully in April.

In April and May 2009 the National Assembly adopted several amendments to the electoral system, including a stipulation that women should make up at least 30% of political organizations' candidate lists for legislative and municipal elections, and a reduction in the percentage of votes that parties were required to secure at election to be eligible for state funding from 5% to 3%. Also approved was a specification that the official leader of the parliamentary opposition should not come from a pro-Government party: the ADF—RDA had hitherto provided the holder of this position, being the second largest party in the legislature, despite its support for Compaoré's administration.

Recent developments: Compaoré's fourth elected term

In February 2010 the Government announced that the first round of voting for the presidential election would take place on 21 November. In August the CDP approved Compaoré's candidature for the presidency, and requested that the constitutional restriction be removed on the number of presidential terms that could be served. In October legislation was adopted postponing municipal elections, previously scheduled to take place in April 2011, to be run concurrently with legislative elections due in May 2012.

The presidential election proceeded as scheduled on 21 November 2010. According to provisional results, released by the CENI four days later, Compaoré won an overwhelming 80.2% of the votes cast. His closest rivals among six other candidates, Hama Arba Diallo, the deputy mayor of Dori, and Bénéwendé Stanislas Sankara, took just 8.2% and 6.3% of the votes, respectively. The rate of voter participation was recorded at some 55% of the registered electorate. The Constitutional Council confirmed Compaoré's re-election on 8 December, having made only minor adjustments to the number of votes allocated to each candidate.

Compaoré was thus sworn in for what was due to be his final five-year presidential term on 21 December 2010. Tertius Zongo was reappointed as Prime Minister in January 2011. A new, 38-member Council of Ministers, again formed by members of the CDP, was subsequently named. Among eight incoming members was the former President of the National Assembly, Bognessan Arsène Ye, as Minister of State, Minister at the Presidency, in charge of Political Reform; he was to oversee constitutional changes and the creation of an upper legislative chamber. In April an advisory council was created to consider political reforms; however, the Conseil Consultatif sur les Réformes Politiques (Consultative Council on Political Reforms—CCRP) was boycotted by several opposition parties and civil society organizations.

The death of a student in police custody in Koudougou, the main town of the Centre-ouest region, provoked violent protests in February 2011, in which six people were reportedly killed. The regional governor was subsequently dismissed. There followed a period of considerable instability, during which Compaoré's position for a time appeared in doubt. In late March troops from two army camps protested in Ouagadougou, and tensions escalated in mid-April, when a mutiny by members of the presidential guard, over unpaid housing and food allowances, apparently caused Compaoré to leave the capital for several hours. The following day, on his return to Ouagadougou, Compaoré dismissed Zongo and his Government, and imposed an overnight curfew in the capital. The Chief of the General Staff of the Armed Forces and the head of the presidential guard were also replaced. Luc Adolphe Tiao, hitherto ambassador to France, was appointed as the new Prime Minister, and a new Government (reduced in size from 38 to 29 ministers) was announced. Yipènè Djibril Bassolet, who had been Minister of Foreign Affairs and Regional Co-operation in Zongo's first administration, returned to that post, while Compaoré assumed personal responsibility for the defence portfolio. Later in April there were protests involving students and members of the police force, and a reported 10,000 civilians joined nationwide protests against high food and fuel prices. In early May the Government introduced a series of emergency measures aimed at addressing public discontent over the high cost of living, including a reduction in the prices of certain staple foodstuffs and a 10% cut in taxes on salaries. Nevertheless, in mid-May thousands of women participated in an anti-government protest in Ouagadougou. The curfew was ended two days later. Further protests by soldiers and gendarmes to demand the payment of allowances took place in several towns in that month, and in early June forces loyal to Compaoré intervened to quell a mutiny by soldiers in Bobo-Dioulasso. Order was restored there, but six soldiers and a teenage girl were killed in an exchange of gunfire.

In June 2011 Compaoré replaced the country's 13 regional governors. In July 566 soldiers were discharged from the armed forces, and 217 were detained on charges of rebellion. Three police officers were gaoled in August for their involvement in the death of the student in Koudougou, and in September the military chiefs in Kaya and Bobo-Dioulasso were replaced. In late 2011 a 5% increase in salary and pension benefits was announced for public sector workers (trade unions had demanded a 30% rise), and the Government pledged to create some 50,000 new jobs, along with 45,000 apprenticeships for young people, by the end of 2014.

Also in June 2011 opposition members resigned from the CENI, citing a lack of confidence in the ability of its President to organize transparent legislative elections (due in May 2012). In August 2011 Barthélemy Kéré was elected as President of the CENI and in October it was announced that legislative and municipal elections would be deferred until November 2012, to allow for the introduction of a system of biometric voter cards. The CCRP's reform proposals were discussed at a series of regional and national conferences held in late 2011. Its proposals included the establishment of an upper legislative body, an increase in the number of National Assembly deputies, and the adoption of minimum and maximum ages for presidential candidates of 35 and 75 years, respectively.

In February 2012 Compaoré dismissed the Minister of Justice and the Promotion of Human Rights, Keeper of the Seals, Jérôme Traoré, in response to allegations that he ordered the beating and arrest of a mechanic following a traffic-related incident. A government reorganization followed, in which Salamata Sawadogo Tapsoba became Minister of Justice, Keeper of the Seals. A new Ministry of Human Rights and Civic Promotion was established under Albert Ouédraogo, hitherto Minister of Secondary and Higher Education. At a CDP congress in March Assimi Kouanda replaced Roch Marc Christian Kaboré at the head of a revised party structure. Kouanda, the head of the presidential administration, had led Compaoré's election campaign in 2010, and it was noted that many of the members of the party's new executive secretariat were close associates of the President.

In April 2012 the National Assembly approved an increase in the number of deputies from 111 to 127 with effect from the forthcoming elections, which were subsequently scheduled for 2 December. In June, in a vote boycotted by opposition parties, the Assembly approved legislation granting amnesty, through immunity from prosecution, to Compaoré and to all the country's heads of state since independence. The same session also approved the establishment of an upper house, the Sénat (Senate), as well as the introduction of upper and lower age limits for presidential candidates, as proposed by the CCRP.

In November 2012 seven gendarmes received custodial sentences of between 18 months' and five years' duration, having been convicted on charges including disobedience, illegal detention, revolt and illicit possession of weaponry. The trial, which related to events in May 2011, was the first arising from the mutinies in March–June of that year. Proceedings were ongoing in late 2013, at which time it was reported that the series of trials that had begun in late 2012 involved some 222 serving and former armed forces personnel.

Legislative elections took place, according to the revised schedule, on 2 December 2012, together with local elections. Official results of the parliamentary elections, released by the CENI on 7 December and validated by the Constitutional Council two weeks later, confirmed that pro-Compaoré parties retained an overall majority in the enlarged, 127-member National Assembly, with the CDP returning the largest number of deputies (70, including eight of the 16 national list seats); allies of Compaoré and the CDP secured a further 27 seats. The opposition Union pour le Progrès et le Changement (UPC), formed in early 2010 by Zéphirin Diabré, who had held several ministerial posts under Compaoré, won 19 seats, including two national list seats, matching the number now held by the ADF—RDA. The UPC had expressed scepticism regarding an earlier delay in the announcement of results for Kadiogo province (in which Ouagadougou is situated), where, in the event, both Diabré and the President's brother, François Compaoré, were elected. None the less, election observers assessed that the conduct of voting had been largely free and transparent. The rate of participation by voters in the national legislative elections was 76.0% of a registered electorate of some 4.37m. Turnout also exceeded 75% for the local elections, in which the CDP won some 66% of all seats. In late December Soungalo Apollinaire Ouattara, hitherto Minister of the Civil Service, Labour and Social Security, was elected to succeed Kaboré as President of the incoming National Assembly.

Luc Adolphe Tiao formally resigned and was then reappointed as Prime Minister at the end of December 2012. A new Government was formed in early January 2013, in which most of the key portfolios remained unaltered. Among notable new appointments, Dramané Yaméogo replaced Salamata Sawadogo Tapsoba as Minister of Justice, Keeper of the Seals, and the CDP leader, Assimi Kouanda, became Minister of State, Minister in Charge of Presidential Affairs.

A focus of political debate following the legislative elections was the proposed Senate, the establishment of which was planned for September 2013. The National Assembly approved provisions in May concerning the new chamber, although parties opposed to the legislation, including the UPC and the ADF—RDA, expressed concern that the Compaoré administration would seek, through its likely dominance of the Senate, a revision of Article 37 of the Constitution to remove the limit on the renewal of the presidential mandate and thus allow Compaoré to stand for election once again in 2015. Of the 89 members of the Senate, 39 were to be indirectly elected at regional level, 29 were to be appointed by the Head of State, and 21 were to be selected by traditional and religious leaders, trade unions, employers' groups and representatives of Burkinabè abroad. There was also opposition to the second chamber on grounds of cost. At the end of June 2013 police in Ouagadougou used tear gas to disperse demonstrators who were protesting against the establishment of the new chamber, and there were further mass protests at the end of July as the regional selection process took place for the indirectly elected Senate seats. It was subsequently reported that the CDP had won 36 of these 39 seats. Meanwhile, in a televised address, Prime Minister Tiao undertook to meet with trade union representatives following widespread demonstrations against the rising costs of staple goods, but he did not refer to the protesters' parallel concerns regarding the establishment of the Senate. In mid-August Compaoré announced that the installation of the upper house would be deferred, and requested that Tiao set up a review committee to make recommendations regarding the new chamber. The report of this committee of elders, released in early September, concluded that the establishment of the Senate should proceed, although it suggested that membership of the upper house should be reduced to 71 members, to include 20 presidential nominees. Political opposition to the Senate continued, however, and church leaders notably issued a statement in that month to the effect that they would not take up their seats. Traditional leaders, for their part, stated that they wished to see the Senate established, and would be prepared to participate, but that the Government must first consult with the opposition and take account of its concerns. At a meeting between Compaoré and opposition leaders in mid-November, the UPC's Zéphirin Diabré reiterated that the opposition's stance with regard to the Senate, and to the possible revision of Article 37, remained unchanged. In December, none the less, in both his address on the anniversary of the country's independence and in his new year statement, the President emphasized his continued commitment to the establishment of the Senate. His remarks concerning Article 37 of the Constitution were interpreted as an indication that he would refer the matter to a national referendum in the event that he were to seek a revision of the limit on the presidential mandate.

In early January 2014, following several weeks of rumours regarding divisions within the presidential party, several senior figures with long associations with the Compaoré regime, among them Kaboré, announced their withdrawal from the CDP, prompting speculation that they would establish a new political organization. In an open letter to the CDP's executive secretariat, the defectors notably cited what they termed repeated violations of fundamental texts, as well as attempts by the governing party to impose the Senate in order to achieve a revision of Article 37.

Foreign Affairs

Compaoré has, in recent years, gained wide recognition for his efforts as a regional mediator and as a proponent of inter-African conflict-resolution initiatives. In the early 1990s, however, relations with some members of the Economic Community of West African States (ECOWAS, see p. 260) were difficult, owing to the Compaoré Government's support for Charles Taylor's rebel National Patriotic Front of Liberia (NPFL) and Burkina's initial refusal to participate in the military intervention by the ECOWAS ceasefire monitoring group (ECOMOG) in Liberia. In early 1999 President Ahmed Tejan Kabbah of Sierra Leone and the Nigerian Government alleged that Burkina Faso and Liberia were co-operating to provide support and supply arms to the rebel fighters of the Revolutionary United Front (RUF) in Sierra Leone. In early 2000 a report to the UN Security Council accused Burkina of having supplied weapons to the RUF in exchange for diamonds on several occasions. It was also alleged that Burkina had supplied weapons to Liberia and to Angolan rebel groups, despite international embargoes on the supply of weapons to those countries. The report was strenuously denied by the Burkinabè Government. Two missions from the UN Security Council visited Burkina Faso in mid-2000, at the invitation of the Burkinabè authorities, to investigate the claims regarding the breaching of arms embargoes against Angola and Sierra Leone. In July 2002 the Burkinabè Government hosted a conference intended to promote a peaceful resolution of the political crisis in Liberia, at which Taylor's Government was not represented. Moreover, Compaoré stated that he regarded Taylor's resignation as President of Liberia in August 2003 as a positive development, which would encourage the stabilization of the region.

In November 1999 a dispute over land rights between Burkinabè settlers in the south-west of Côte d'Ivoire and the indigenous minority Krou population led to the violent and systematic expulsion from the region of several hundred Burkinabè plantation workers. Several deaths were reported, and some 20,000 expatriates subsequently returned to Burkina. Following the coup in Côte d'Ivoire in December of that year, the military authorities assured the Government of Burkina that the expulsions would cease and that measures would be taken in order to allow workers to return. None the less, tensions between the two countries intensified as the former Prime Minister of Côte d'Ivoire, Alassane Ouattara, was excluded from participation in the Ivorian presidential election of October 2000 on grounds of nationality (the authorities in Côte d'Ivoire maintained that Ouattara was of Burkinabè origin and thus ineligible to stand for office). Following a coup attempt in Abidjan, Côte d'Ivoire, in January 2001, which the Ivorian Government attributed to the influence of unnamed, neighbouring states, attacks on Burkinabè expatriates in Côte d'Ivoire reportedly increased; it was subsequently reported that up to 10,000 Burkinabè were returning to Burkina each week.

Following the outbreak of unrest in northern Côte d'Ivoire in September 2002, Gbagbo again claimed that an unnamed neighbouring country was implicated in the rebellion; these allegations were widely believed to refer to Burkina, although the Burkinabè Government denied any involvement in the uprising. A statement by Compaoré in an interview with the French newspaper *Le Parisien*, in late January 2003, to the effect that the restoration of peace in Côte d'Ivoire would necessitate the resignation of Gbagbo as President of that country, led to a further deterioration in relations between the two countries. As a result of the upsurge in violence in Côte d'Ivoire, at least 350,000 Burkinabè citizens were reported to have fled Côte d'Ivoire for Burkina by mid-2003. The Burkinabè authorities closed the border between the two countries in September 2002, reopening it one year later. Relations between the two countries subsequently eased, and in March 2007 Compaoré brokered a peace agreement between Gbagbo and former rebel leader Guillaume

Soro, providing for the reunification of the country, the disarmament of rebels and the dismantling of militia groups, and the establishment of an electoral timetable. In December 2008 Compaoré was again instrumental in the signing of a further accord between Gbagbo and Soro (who had been appointed Prime Minister in April 2007) to integrate rebel troops into the Ivorian police force. Following the presidential election run-off in Côte d'Ivoire of November 2010, and Gbagbo's refusal to relinquish the presidency to the internationally recognized victor, Alassane Ouattara, Compaoré was among a number of African heads of state who endorsed efforts by ECOWAS and the African Union to secure Gbagbo's eventual removal from power.

In March 2008 Burkina Faso and Benin reached an agreement in respect of a long-running border dispute between the two countries, with a commitment from both sides that neither would make any further 'visible sovereignty acts' (including building police stations or displaying national flags) in the 68-sq km contested zone. In 2009 the two countries agreed to refer the case to for arbitration by the ICJ; pending a resolution, the contested area would be regarded as neutral, and would be administered and financed jointly. The case had not been formally submitted by late 2013.

In July 2010, in accordance with an agreement reached in early 2009, Burkina and Niger made a joint submission to the ICJ for arbitration in the demarcation of part of their joint border. Hearings took place in October 2012, and in April 2013 the ICJ delivered its ruling, determining the border based on a map published by the French Institut Géographique National in 1960. Both countries declared themselves satisfied with the outcome.

In early December 2012, in his capacity as chief ECOWAS mediator for the crisis in northern Mali, President Compaoré hosted the first direct talks between the Malian transitional Government and Tuareg and Islamist groups. Burkina was expected at this time to be a principal contributor, together with Niger and Nigeria, to an ECOWAS military intervention force of some 3,300 personnel for northern Mali, the deployment of which was agreed by ECOWAS heads of state and government in November. The situation escalated with the arrest of the Malian Prime Minister, Cheikh Modibo Diarra, who had supported ECOWAS intervention, and the installation in mid-December of a new Government headed by Diango Cissoko. Following French military intervention in Mali in January 2013, Burkina Faso committed some 500 troops to the African-led International Support Mission to Mali (AFISMA), established by ECOWAS to assist Mali's armed forces in combating the Islamist insurgency. In April 2013 the UN Security Council approved the establishment of the UN Multidimensional Integrated Stabilization Mission in Mali, which took over authority from AFISMA with effect from July. In June, meanwhile, Compaoré mediated in talks between rebel Tuaregs and the Malian authorities that allowed Malian government forces to retake control of the northern town of Kidal, thus allowing voting in the following month's presidential election to proceed there. By December, according to statistics of the UN High Commissioner for Refugees (UNHCR), there remained some 43,000 Malian refugees in Burkina. UNHCR anticipated that some 5,000 of this refugee population would return voluntarily to Mali in 2014.

CONSTITUTION AND GOVERNMENT

Under the terms of the Constitution of June 1991, as subsequently revised, executive power is vested in the President and in the Government, and is counterbalanced by a legislative Assemblée Nationale (National Assembly), and by an independent judiciary. The President is empowered to appoint a Prime Minister; however, the National Assembly has the right to veto any such appointment. Presidential and legislative elections are conducted by universal adult suffrage, in the context of a multi-party political system. The membership of the National Assembly, the term of which is five years, was increased from 111 to 127 members at the 2012 elections, including 16 national list seats. Legislation adopted in April of that year provided for the establishment of an upper chamber, the Sénat (Senate). Provisions for an 89-member Senate were approved by the National Assembly in May 2013, but the installation of the new chamber, planned for September 2013, was subsequently deferred (see Contemporary Political History).

An amendment to the electoral code in April 2004 changed the electoral unit from the region to the province. Each province is administered by a civilian governor.

REGIONAL AND INTERNATIONAL CO-OPERATION

Burkina Faso is a member of numerous regional organizations, including the Economic Community of West African States (ECOWAS, see p. 260), the West African organs of the Franc Zone (see p. 330), the Community of Sahel-Saharan States (see p. 450), the Conseil de l'Entente (see p. 450), the Liptako–Gourma Integrated Development Authority (see p. 452), and the Permanent Inter-State Committee on Drought Control in the Sahel (CILSS, see p. 453). Burkina Faso is also a member of the African Union (see p. 186)

Burkina Faso became a member of the UN in 1960 and was admitted to the World Trade Organization (WTO, see p. 434) in 1995. In May 2008 the country was elected to sit on the 47-member UN Human Rights Council for a term of three years, and in 2012 Burkina began a three-year term on the UN Economic and Social Council (UNESCO).

ECONOMIC AFFAIRS

In 2012, according to estimates by the World Bank, Burkina Faso's gross national income (GNI), measured at average 2010–12 prices, was US $10,948m., equivalent to $670 per head (or $1,510 on an international purchasing-power parity basis). During 2003–12, it was estimated, the population increased at an average annual rate of 3.0%, while gross domestic product (GDP) per head also increased, in real terms, by an average of 3.0% per year. Overall GDP increased, in real terms, at an average annual rate of 6.0% in 2003–12; growth in 2012 was 10.0%.

Agriculture (including forestry and fishing) contributed an estimated 33.3% of GDP in 2011, according to the African Development Bank (AfDB). According to FAO estimates, 92.0% of the employed labour force were engaged in agriculture in mid-2013. The principal cash crop is cotton (exports of which accounted for an estimated 14.2% of the value of total exports in 2012). Smaller amounts of other crops, including karité nuts (sheanuts) and sesame seed, are also exported. The main subsistence crops are sorghum, maize and millet. Burkina is almost self-sufficient in basic foodstuffs in non-drought years. Livestock-rearing is of considerable significance. According to the World Bank, during 2003–11 agricultural GDP increased at an average annual rate of 2.5%. Agricultural GDP increased by 4.3% in 2012, according to the AfDB.

Industry (including mining, manufacturing, construction and power) contributed an estimated 25.1% of GDP in 2011, according to the AfDB, but engaged only 10.1% of the employed labour force in 2007, according to official figures. According to the World Bank, during 2003–11 industrial GDP increased at an average annual rate of 5.8%; industrial GDP increased by 11.1% in 2011.

Although Burkina has considerable mineral resources, extractive activities accounted for just 12.8% of GDP in 2011, according to the AfDB, and engaged only 4.8% of the employed labour force in 2007. However, the commercial development of reserves of gold (exports of which contributed an estimated 74.8% of the value of total exports in 2012) has brought about a rapid increase in the sector's economic importance, while there is considerable potential, subject to the development of an adequate infrastructure, for the exploitation of manganese, zinc and limestone. Gold production amounted to some 22,939 kg in 2010, according to the US Geological Survey, and output reached 31,774 kg in 2011, with the entry into production of the Essakane reserve. The country's other known mineral reserves include phosphates, silver, lead and nickel.

The manufacturing sector engaged only 3.2% of the employed labour force in 2007, and, according to the AfDB, contributed 7.5% of GDP in 2011. The sector is dominated by the processing of primary products: major activities are cotton-ginning, the production of textiles, food-processing (including milling and sugar-refining), brewing and the processing of tobacco and of hides and skins. According to the World Bank, manufacturing GDP increased at an average annual rate of 1.3% in 2003–11; the GDP of the sector increased by 3.1% in 2012, according to the AfDB.

The construction sector engaged only 1.9% of the employed labour force in 2007. The sector contributed 4.0% of GDP in 2011, according to the AfDB. The sector declined by 0.2% in 2011, but grew by 9.0% in 2012.

In 2008 some 78.1% of Burkina's total electricity production came from hydroelectric sources; the remainder (21.9%) was derived from thermal power stations (using imported fuel). The country's hydropower capacity is being expanded, and in 2000 the interconnection of the south of Burkina Faso with the electricity network of Côte d'Ivoire was finalized. A link with Ghana's electricity grid is also planned, and in late 2013 members of the Niger Basin Authority approved plans including the joint exploitation of resources as part of which Burkina would eventually receive electricity from the Taoussa dam in Mali. Imports of petroleum accounted for an estimated 24.5% of the value of total merchandise imports in 2012.

The services sector contributed an estimated 41.6% of GDP in 2011, according to the AfDB, and engaged 22.3% of the employed labour force in 2007. According to the World Bank, the GDP of the services sector increased at an average annual rate of 7.0% in 2003–11; growth was 5.8% in 2011.

According to preliminary figures by the IMF, in 2011 Burkina recorded a visible merchandise trade surplus of 2,400m. francs CFA, while there was a deficit of 54,300m. francs CFA on the current account of the balance of payments. In 2012 the principal sources of imports were Côte d'Ivoire and the People's Republic of China (which provided 9.7% and 9.3% of the total, respectively) and other major trading partners were France, the United Kingdom and the USA. The principal market for exports in that year was Switzerland (taking 66.6% of exports). The other major trading partner was South Africa. The principal exports in 2012 were pearls, precious stones, metals and coins, cotton and oil seeds. In the same year the principal imports were mineral fuels, boilers and machinery, vehicles, and electrical and electronic equipment.

In 2013 Burkina was projected to have an estimated overall budget deficit of 151,700m. francs CFA. Burkina's general government gross debt was 1,185,166m. francs CFA in 2010, equivalent to 27.1% of GDP. Burkina's total external debt was US $2,420m. at the end of 2011, of which $2,056m. was public and publicly guaranteed debt. In 2010 the cost of servicing long-term public and publicly guaranteed debt and repayments to the IMF was equivalent to 2.5% of the value of exports of goods, services and income (excluding workers' remittances). In 2003–12 the average annual rate of inflation was 2.8%. Consumer prices increased by 3.9% in 2012. Some 123,739 people were unemployed in 2006, according to the national census, equivalent to only 2.4% of the total labour force. According to official figures the unemployed population represented 2.6% in 2007 and the inactive population represented 21.2%, giving a combined rate of 23.8%.

Burkina Faso has a narrow productive base, and remains one of the poorest nations in the world: largely owing to its very poor health and education indicators, it was ranked 183rd of 187 countries on the UN Development Programme's human development index for 2012. Economic activity in the late 2000s was negatively affected by the global economic crisis, with the country being particularly adversely affected by high prices for basic foods and fuel, although there was considerable benefit from high global prices for gold at the time of the rapid development of Burkina's reserves. By 2009 gold outranked cotton as the country's principal export. Burkina was declared to be compliant under the international Extractive Industries Transparency Initiative in early 2013, and adoption of a new mining code was pending in that year. A five-year (2011–15) strategy for sustainable development (Stratégie de Croissance Accélérée et de Développement Durable—SCADD) aimed to strengthen the capacity of the Burkinabè economy to withstand various shocks, while promoting inclusive growth and poverty reduction through, *inter alia*: agricultural and rural development; investment in energy, transport and other infrastructure; employment creation and training, particularly for young people; and efforts to promote social protection. An IMF assessment in mid-2013, in the context of the three-year Extended Credit Facility agreed in 2010, noted that government spending on poverty reduction had now reached almost 30% of total public spending, and commended progress towards achievement of the country's Millennium Development Goals in certain areas of health and education. Upon completion of the final review under the ECF, in December 2013, the IMF noted that, despite external shocks (including, in 2012–13, the impact of a large refugee flow from neighbouring Mali), Burkina had maintained one of the highest average growth rates in sub-Saharan Africa. Growth of 6.8% was anticipated for 2013. (This represented a slight downward revision from the 7% projected at mid-year, in part reflecting the subsequent contraction in international gold prices.) Disbursements under the investment budget were slower than anticipated in 2013, and the IMF reiterated the need to ensure more inclusive growth arising from the country's strong overall economic performance. A new three-year ECF, worth SDR 27.09m. was approved by the IMF at the end of December.

PUBLIC HOLIDAYS

2015: 1 January (New Year's Day), 2 January*† (Mouloud, Birth of the Prophet), 3 January (Revolution Day), 8 March (International Women's Day), 6 April (Easter Monday), 1 May (Labour Day), 14 May (Ascension Day), 17 July* (Aid es Segheir, end of Ramadan), 5 August (Independence Day), 15 August (Assumption), 23 September* (Aid el Kebir—Tabaski, Feast of the Sacrifice), 1 November (All Saints' Day), 11 December (Proclamation of the Republic), 23 December*† (Mouloud, Birth of the Prophet), 25 December (Christmas).

* These holidays are dependent on the Islamic lunar calendar and may vary by one or two days from the dates given.

† This festival occurs twice (in the Islamic years AH 1436 and 1437) within the same Gregorian year.

Statistical Survey

Source (except where otherwise stated): Institut National de la Statistique et de la Démographie, 555 blvd de la Révolution, 01 BP 374, Ouagadougou 01; tel. 50-32-49-76; fax 50-32-61-59; e-mail insd@cenatrin.bf; internet www.insd.bf.

Area and Population

AREA, POPULATION AND DENSITY

Area (sq km)	274,222*
Population (census results)	
10 December 1996	10,312,609
9–23 December 2006	
Males	6,768,739
Females	7,248,523
Total	14,017,262
Population (official estimates at mid-year)	
2012	16,779,206
2013	17,322,796
2014	17,880,386
Density (per sq km) at mid-2014	65.2

* 105,878 sq miles.

POPULATION BY AGE AND SEX

(official estimates at mid-2014)

	Males	Females	Total
0–14	4,378,270	4,160,397	8,538,667
15–64	4,000,984	4,805,256	8,806,240
65 and over	248,576	286,903	535,479
Total	8,627,830	9,252,556	17,880,386

PROVINCES
(official population estimates at mid-2014)

	Population	Capital	Population of capital*
Balé	264,980	Boromo	14,594
Bam	344,628	Kongoussi	25,172
Banwa	332,828	Solenzo	16,850
Bazèga	283,035	Kombissiri	23,460
Bougouriba	127,857	Diébougou	17,937
Boulgou	681,954	Tenkodogo	44,491
Boulkiemdé	614,531	Koudougou	88,184
Comoé	556,354	Banfora	75,917
Ganzourgou	393,778	Zorgho	20,462
Gnagna	514,821	Bogandé	14,929
Gourma	391,282	Fada N'Gourma	41,785
Houet	1,233,224	Bobo-Dioulasso	489,967
Ioba	233,599	Dano	17,068
Kadiogo	2,429,718	Ouagadougou	1,475,839
Kénédougou	370,272	Orodara	23,356
Komandjari	106,089	Gayéri	6,060
Kompienga	107,100	Pama	8,541
Kossi	340,024	Nouna	22,166
Koulpélogo	330,503	Ouargaye	10,103
Kouritenga	414,863	Koupéla	28,151
Kourwéogo	166,999	Boussé	15,868
Léraba	156,705	Sindou	4,185
Loroum	178,017	Titao	19,131
Mouhoun	368,606	Dédougou	38,862
Nahouri	197,053	Pô	24,320
Namentenga	411,815	Boulsa	17,925
Nayala	198,987	Toma	12,401
Noumbiel	89,036	Batié	10,105
Oubritenga	291,759	Ziniaré	18,619
Oudalan	253,325	Gorom-Gorom	8,882
Passoré	392,489	Yako	22,685
Poni	322,481	Gaoua	25,104
Sanguié	360,386	Réo	28,694
Sanmatenga	746,551	Kaya	54,365
Séno	332,886	Dori	21,078
Sissili	264,473	Léo	26,779
Soum	442,973	Djibo	28,990
Sourou	266,471	Tougan	17,050
Tapoa	444,852	Diapaga	8,400
Tuy	294,865	Houndé	39,458
Yagha	204,375	Sebba	5,906
Yatenga	682,184	Ouahigouya	73,153
Ziro	229,576	Sapouy	12,438
Zondoma	208,740	Gourcy	24,616
Zoundwéogo	303,342	Manga	19,860
Total	17,880,386		

* Data as at 2006 census.

PRINCIPAL TOWNS
(population at 2006 census)

Ouagadougou (capital)	1,475,839	Kaya	54,365
Bobo-Dioulasso	489,967	Tenkodogo	44,491
Koudougou	88,184	Fada N'gourma	41,785
Banfora	75,917	Houndé	39,458
Ouahigouya	73,153	Dédougou	38,862
Pouytenga	60,618	Garango	35,015

Mid-2011 (incl. suburbs, UN estimate): Ouagadougou 2,052,530 (Source: UN, *World Urbanization Prospects: The 2011 Revision*).

BIRTHS AND DEATHS
(annual averages, UN estimates)

	1995–2000	2000–05	2005–10
Birth rate (per 1,000)	46.7	45.6	43.8
Death rate (per 1,000)	16.2	14.6	12.8

Source: UN, *World Population Prospects: The 2012 Revision.*

Life expectancy (years at birth): 55.4 (males 54.9; females 56.0) in 2011 (Source: World Bank, World Development Indicators database).

ECONOMICALLY ACTIVE POPULATION
(2006 census, persons aged 15–64 years)

	Males	Females	Total
Agriculture, hunting, forestry and fishing	2,057,719	1,891,402	3,949,121
Mining and quarrying	17,674	4,550	22,224
Manufacturing	97,751	86,923	184,674
Electricity, gas and water	4,974	540	5,514
Construction	55,632	1,012	56,644
Trade, restaurants and hotels	218,220	205,707	423,927
Transport, storage and communications	12,866	1,832	14,698
Financial intermediation	3,192	1,966	5,158
Real estate and business services	6,489	2,100	8,589
Public administration	37,202	7,619	44,821
Education	40,526	17,165	57,691
Health and social work	16,581	11,138	27,719
Community, social and personal services	45,251	31,965	77,216
Private households with employed persons	5,057	14,443	19,500
Extra-territorial organizations and bodies	1,234	545	1,779
Sub-total	2,620,368	2,278,907	4,899,275
Activities not adequately defined	96,070	40,546	136,616
Total employed	2,716,438	2,319,453	5,035,891
Unemployed	84,180	39,559	123,739
Total labour force	2,800,618	2,359,012	5,159,630

Note: In addition, the 2006 census recorded 1,417,821 children aged between 5 and 14 years engaged in mostly agricultural work within the family, and a further 261,986 employed persons aged 65 years and above.

Mid-2013 ('000, estimates): Agriculture, etc. 7,652; Total labour force 8,317 (Source: FAO).

Health and Welfare

KEY INDICATORS

Total fertility rate (children per woman, 2011)	5.8
Under-5 mortality rate (per 1,000 live births, 2011)	146
HIV/AIDS (% of persons aged 15–49, 2012)	1.0
Physicians (per 1,000 head, 2008)	0.06
Hospital beds (per 1,000 head, 2010)	0.4
Health expenditure (2010): US $ per head (PPP)	92
Health expenditure (2010): % of GDP	7.4
Health expenditure (2010): public (% of total)	55.4
Access to water (% of persons, 2011)	80
Access to sanitation (% of persons, 2011)	18
Total carbon dioxide emissions ('000 metric tons, 2010)	1,683.2
Carbon dioxide emissions per head (metric tons, 2010)	0.1
Human Development Index (2012): ranking	183
Human Development Index (2012): value	0.343

For sources and definitions, see explanatory note on p. vi.

Agriculture

PRINCIPAL CROPS
('000 metric tons)

	2010	2011	2012
Rice, paddy	270.7	240.9	319.4
Maize	1,133.5	1,076.8	1,556.3
Millet	1,147.9	828.7	1,078.4
Sorghum	1,990.2	1,505.5	1,923.8
Sweet potatoes	92.5	140.1	92.8
Yams	97.6	99.7	113.3
Sugar cane*	455	460	485
Cow peas, dry	626.1	441.0	598.5
Bambara beans	59.5	48.8	50.0*
Groundnuts, with shell	340.2	265.3	310.8
Okra*	23	23	24
Cotton lint*	190	150.0	206.0
Cottonseed†	328	274	440
Seed cotton	529.6	441.1	607.0

* FAO estimate(s).
† Unofficial figures.

Aggregate production ('000 metric tons, may include official, semi-official or estimated data): Total cereals 4,560.5 in 2010, 3,666.4 in 2011, 4,898.5 in 2012; Total pulses 704.1 in 2010, 507.3 in 2011, 666.5 in 2012; Total roots and tubers 196.1 in 2010, 246.0 in 2011, 212.7 in 2012; Total vegetables (incl. melons) 300.6 in 2010, 283.0 in 2011, 287.5 in 2012; Total fruits (excl. melons) 93.8 in 2010, 97.7 in 2011, n.a. in 2012.

LIVESTOCK
('000 head, year ending September)

	2010	2011	2012
Cattle	8,398	8,566	8,738
Sheep	8,243	8,491	8,745
Goats	12,342	12,713	13,094
Pigs	2,167	2,211	2,255
Chickens*	39,000	40,000	42,000
Horses	39	39	39
Asses	1,050	1,071	1,093
Camels	17	17	18

* FAO estimates.

Source: FAO.

LIVESTOCK PRODUCTS
('000 metric tons,)

	2010	2011	2012
Cattle meat	123.4	125.8	128.4
Sheep meat	19.9	20.5	21.1
Goat meat	31.8	32.7	33.7
Pig meat*	31.2	31.8	31.9
Chicken meat*	37.3	38.2	38.8
Cows' milk	129.9	132.5	135.1
Goats' milk	103.3	106.4	109.6
Hen eggs*	57.8	58.8	59.5

* FAO estimates.

Source: FAO.

Forestry

ROUNDWOOD REMOVALS
('000 cubic metres, excluding bark, FAO estimates)

	2010	2011	2012
Sawlogs, veneer logs and logs for sleepers	73	73	73
Other industrial wood	1,098	1,098	1,098
Fuel wood	12,785	12,963	13,145
Total	13,956	14,134	14,316

Source: FAO.

SAWNWOOD PRODUCTION
('000 cubic metres)

	2005	2006	2007
Total (all broadleaved)	1.1	0.7	5.2

2008–12: Production assumed to be unchanged from 2007 (FAO estimates).
Source: FAO.

Fishing

(metric tons, live weight)

	2009	2010*	2011
Capture	11,800*	14,520	15,000
Freshwater fishes	11,800*	14,520	15,000
Aquaculture	205	300	205
Total catch	12,005*	14,820	15,205

* FAO estimate(s).

Source: FAO.

Mining

('000 metric tons unless otherwise indicated)

	2009	2010	2011
Cement	450	450	450
Gold (kg)*	11,581	22,939	31,774

* Does not include artisanal mining, which was estimated to fluctuate between 1,600 and 5,000 kg annually.

Source: US Geological Survey.

Industry

SELECTED PRODUCTS
(metric tons unless otherwise indicated)

	2000	2001	2002
Edible oils	17,888	19,452	19,626
Shea (karité) butter	186	101	21
Flour	12,289	13,686	10,005
Pasta	211	n.a.	n.a.
Sugar	43,412	46,662	47,743
Beer ('000 hl)	494	500	546
Soft drinks ('000 hl)	221	222	250
Cigarettes (million packets)	85	78	78
Printed fabric ('000 sq m)	275	n.a.	n.a.
Soap	12,079	9,240	9,923
Matches (cartons)	9,358	4,956	3,009
Bicycles (units)	22,215	17,718	20,849
Mopeds (units)	16,531	19,333	19,702
Tyres ('000)	397	599	670
Inner tubes ('000)	2,655	3,217	2,751
Electric energy ('000 kWh)	390,322	364,902	361,000

Electric energy ('000 kWh): 619,400 in 2008; 699,790 in 2009; 565,370 in 2010.

Source: mainly IMF, *Burkina Faso: Selected Issues and Statistical Appendix* (September 2005).

Raw sugar ('000 metric tons): 40 in 2006–09 (Source: UN Industrial Commodity Statistics Database).

Finance

CURRENCY AND EXCHANGE RATES

Monetary Units

100 centimes = 1 franc de la Communauté Financière Africaine (CFA).

Sterling, Dollar and Euro Equivalents (31 December 2013)

£1 sterling = 783.286 francs CFA;
US $1 = 475.641 francs CFA;
€1 = 655.957 francs CFA;
10,000 francs CFA = £12.77 = $21.02 = €15.24.

Average Exchange Rate (francs CFA per US $)

2011	471.866
2012	510.527
2013	494.040

Note: An exchange rate of 1 French franc = 50 francs CFA, established in 1948, remained in force until January 1994, when the CFA franc was devalued by 50%, with the exchange rate adjusted to 1 French franc = 100 francs CFA. This relationship to French currency remained in effect with the introduction of the euro on 1 January 1999. From that date, accordingly, a fixed exchange rate of €1 = 655.957 francs CFA has been in operation.

BUDGET

('000 million francs CFA)

Revenue*	2010	2011†	2012‡
Tax revenue	565.7	695.6	812.1
Income and profits	133.6	201.0	229.4
Domestic goods and services	318.4	366.8	416.8
International trade	96.8	112.0	149.8
Non-tax revenue	115.5	98.0	90.4
Total	681.3	793.6	902.5

Expenditure§	2010	2011†	2012‡
Current expenditure	530.9	628.3	785.3
Wages and salaries	245.8	281.4	334.4
Goods and services	90.8	97.1	124.2
Interest payments	21.4	28.3	28.5
Current transfers	172.9	221.4	298.2
Capital expenditure	484.7	488.6	678.8
Expenditure carried forward from previous year	67.7	46.6	0.0
Total	1,083.3	1,163.5	1,464.1

* Excluding grants received ('000 million francs CFA): 198.9 in 2010; 253.7 in 2011 (preliminary); 397.7 in 2012 (projection).

† Preliminary figures.

‡ Projections.

§ Excluding net lending ('000 million francs CFA): –6.2 in 2010; 2.7 in 2011 (preliminary); 8.1 in 2012 (projection).

2013 ('000 million francs CFA, projections): *Revenue:* Tax revenue 886.8 (Income and profits 257.8; Domestic goods and services 456.9; International trade 152.9); Non-tax revenue 112.0; Total revenue 998.7 (excl. grants received 386.4). *Expenditure:* Current expenditure 740.2 (Wages and salaries 349.6, Goods and services 113.8, Interest payments 29.4, Current transfers 247.5); Capital expenditure 791.7; Total expenditure 1,531.9 (excl. net lending 4.9).

2014 ('000 million francs CFA, projections): *Revenue:* Tax revenue 979.8 (Income and profits 287.0; Domestic goods and services 505.9; International trade 165.0); Non-tax revenue 115.9; Total revenue 1,095.7 (excl. grants received 415.1). *Expenditure:* Current expenditure 818.5 (Wages and salaries 381.4, Goods and services 130.6, Interest payments 33.3, Current transfers 273.2); Capital expenditure 862.5; Total expenditure 1,681.0 (excl. net lending 10.0).

Source: IMF, *Burkina Faso: Fifth Review Under the Three-Year Arrangement Under the Extended Credit Facility and Request for Modification of Performance Criteria—Staff Report; Press Release on the Executive Board Discussion* (January 2013).

INTERNATIONAL RESERVES

(excluding gold, US $ million at 31 December)

	2010	2011	2012
IMF special drawing rights	74.2	73.9	74.0
Reserve position in IMF	11.5	11.6	11.6
Foreign exchange	982.5	871.5	938.9
Total	1,068.2	957.0	1,024.5

Source: IMF, *International Financial Statistics*.

MONEY SUPPLY

('000 million francs CFA at 31 December)

	2010	2011	2012
Currency outside banks	215.1	189.6	230.3
Demand deposits at deposit money banks*	437.9	593.5	678.4
Checking deposits at post office	3.9	5.5	5.5
Total money (incl. others)	659.2	790.7	917.2

* Excluding the deposits of public establishments of an administrative or social nature.

Source: IMF, *International Financial Statistics*.

COST OF LIVING

(Consumer Price Index; base: 2000 = 100)

	2010	2011	2012
Food, beverages and tobacco	152.7	162.0	170.7
All items (incl. others)	131.4	135.0	140.2

Source: ILO.

NATIONAL ACCOUNTS

('000 million francs CFA in current prices)

Expenditure on the Gross Domestic Product

	2009	2010	2011
Government final consumption expenditure	855	918	920
Private final consumption expenditure	2,711	2,799	3,545
Gross fixed capital formation	887	1,014	863
Change in stocks	87	108	145
Total domestic expenditure	4,540	4,839	5,473
Exports of goods and services	497	931	1,015
Less Imports of goods and services	1,096	1,316	1,402
GDP in purchasers' values	3,942	4,454	5,085

Gross Domestic Product by Economic Activity

	2009	2010	2011
Agriculture, livestock, forestry and fishing	1,279	1,444	1,537
Mining	109	288	589
Manufacturing	317	304	344
Electricity, gas and water	45	33	42
Construction and public works	178	209	183
Wholesale and retail trade, restaurants and hotels	509	606	572
Finance, insurance and real estate	226	243	309
Transport and communications	176	175	167
Public administration and defence	713	726	776
Other services	86	89	95
Sub-total	3,639	4,116	4,614
Indirect taxes	353	384	530
Less Imputed bank service charge	51	46	59
GDP in purchasers' values	3,942	4,454	5,085

Source: African Development Bank.

BALANCE OF PAYMENTS
('000 million francs CFA)

	2010	2011*	2012†
Exports of goods f.o.b.	785.2	1,066.2	1,290.6
Imports of goods f.o.b.	–854.2	–1,063.8	–1,398.7
Trade balance	–68.9	2.4	–108.1
Services (net)	–261.6	–325.0	–417.1
Balance on goods and services	–330.5	–322.6	–525.2
Income (net)	–3.2	0.2	6.4
Balance on goods, services and income	–333.7	–322.4	–518.8
Private unrequited transfers (net)	61.9	64.7	64.1
Official unrequited transfers (net)	170.2	203.4	198.9
Current balance	–101.7	–54.3	–255.8
Capital account (net)	98.8	121.2	270.6
Financial account‡	75.6	–19.2	–48.1
Net errors and omissions	6.5	–13.8	0.0
Overall balance	79.3	34.0	–33.4

* Preliminary.
† Projections.
‡ Including portfolio investment and direct foreign investment.

Source: IMF, *Burkina Faso: Fifth Review Under the Three-Year Arrangement Under the Extended Credit Facility and Request for Modification of Performance Criteria—Staff Report; Press Release on the Executive Board Discussion* (January 2013).

External Trade

PRINCIPAL COMMODITIES
(distribution by HS, US $ million)

Imports f.o.b.	2010	2011	2012
Vegetable and vegetable products	129.1	171.4	205.3
Cereals	83.8	121.7	146.2
Rice	63.7	92.8	116.6
Prepared foodstuffs; beverages, spirits, vinegar, tobacco and articles thereof	143.3	177.9	207.8
Mineral products	542.7	665.5	972.1
Mineral fuels, lubricants and related materials	453.6	575.7	856.3
Petroleum oils	424.8	534.3	800.0
Salt, sulphur, earth, stone, plaster, lime and cement	89.1	89.8	115.6
Cement, etc.	73.7	72.9	94.4
Chemicals and related products	261.9	339.4	418.5
Fertilizers	82.4	80.2	130.3
Pharmaceutical products	96.0	141.6	123.3
Plastics, rubber and articles thereof	87.2	93.8	133.6
Textile and textile articles	61.6	51.8	60.8
Iron and steel, other base metals and articles of base metal	177.1	191.3	263.5
Iron and steel	85.9	89.4	117.6
Iron and steel articles	71.0	74.5	114.2
Machinery and mechanical appliances; electrical equipment; parts thereof	296.5	336.6	557.3
Boilers, machinery, etc.	182.4	192.7	368.1
Electrical, electronic equipment	114.1	144.0	189.2
Vehicles, aircraft, vessels and associated transport equipment	174.7	184.6	227.7
Vehicles other than railway, tramway	171.7	173.0	219.9
Total (incl. others)	2,048.2	2,406.4	3,271.5

Exports f.o.b.	2010	2011	2012
Vegetables and vegetable products	105.1	173.2	165.4
Oil seed, oleagic fruits, grain, seed, fruit, etc.	71.6	89.8	112.4
Oil seeds	71.1	89.1	111.7
Textile and textile articles	230.3	275.9	309.2
Cotton	228.1	272.9	304.9
Pearls, precious stones, metals, coins, etc.	883.7	1,790.4	1,603.2
Total (incl. others)	1,288.1	2,312.4	2,143.1

Source: Trade Map-Trade Competitiveness Map, International Trade Centre, www.intracen.org/marketanalysis.

PRINCIPAL TRADING PARTNERS
(US $ million)

Imports c.i.f.	2010	2011	2012
Belgium	43.6	40.8	57.9
Benin	2.5	27.1	8.6
Brazil	20.2	35.7	26.4
Canada	50.1	29.5	37.3
China, People's Repub.	198.2	235.8	302.9
Côte d'Ivoire	328.0	257.0	316.1
France	211.5	291.7	295.1
Germany	81.3	94.1	111.9
Ghana	56.0	65.9	98.0
India	57.4	89.3	115.6
Italy	23.7	32.7	47.6
Japan	53.9	58.1	77.5
Mali	20.5	51.1	74.1
Netherlands	90.4	95.6	99.6
Nigeria	26.4	84.1	62.8
Russia	31.2	41.3	37.2
Senegal	21.9	40.9	50.5
South Africa	54.8	37.0	80.6
Spain	31.4	32.9	52.6
Sweden	11.0	29.9	36.7
Thailand	21.0	37.9	39.3
Togo	91.9	93.4	156.0
Turkey	22.8	25.0	33.5
Ukraine	25.4	24.7	68.6
United Kingdom	75.9	106.0	263.4
USA	82.9	104.1	170.3
Total (incl. others)	2,048.2	2,406.4	3,271.5

Exports f.o.b.	2010	2011	2012
Belgium	18.0	51.1	3.0
Benin	8.5	7.6	5.8
Côte d'Ivoire	18.9	23.7	19.6
Denmark	3.5	14.4	11.0
France	29.9	55.9	48.8
Ghana	35.1	48.1	38.2
Mali	12.0	9.5	13.0
Netherlands	20.4	41.6	42.9
Niger	23.4	14.8	10.9
Singapore	62.8	107.7	105.8
South Africa	144.3	237.4	222.8
Switzerland	817.3	1,599.8	1,426.9
Togo	14.3	13.1	12.7
United Kingdom	38.1	19.3	27.1
Total (incl. others)	1,288.1	2,312.4	2,143.1

Source: Trade Map-Trade Competitiveness Map, International Trade Centre, www.intracen.org/marketanalysis.

Transport

RAILWAYS

	2007	2008	2009
Freight carried ('000 metric tons)	907.4	832.7	871.6
Freight ton-km ('000)	840,374	779,620	820,784
Passengers ('000 journeys)	500*	n.a.	n.a.

* Estimate.

ROAD TRAFFIC
('000 motor vehicles in use)

	2009	2010	2011
Passenger cars	110.9	120.2	131.5
Vans	26.1	27.9	30.1
Trucks	15.8	17.2	18.9
Tractors, trailers and semi-trailers	18.6	20.2	22.7
Motorbikes and mopeds	551.3	689.8	868.1

CIVIL AVIATION
(traffic on scheduled services)*

	2003	2004	2005
Kilometres flown (million)	1	1	1
Passengers carried ('000)	54	61	66
Passenger-km (million)	29	33	37
Total ton-km (million)	3	3	3

* Including an apportionment of the traffic of Air Afrique.

Source: UN, *Statistical Yearbook*.

Passengers carried ('000): 160.0 in 2010; 133.7 in 2011; 125.7 in 2012 (Source: World Bank, World Development Indicators database).

Tourism

FOREIGN VISITORS BY COUNTRY OF ORIGIN*

	2009	2010	2011
Belgium	7,806	7,344	6,491
Benin	11,138	11,754	10,032
Canada	6,434	8,833	7,442
Côte d'Ivoire	18,090	19,251	18,276
France	67,866	63,715	42,296
Germany	7,193	6,855	6,420
Ghana	8,412	8,402	10,152
Italy	6,726	5,892	4,875
Mali	14,474	15,643	14,846
Niger	14,888	14,342	12,486
Nigeria	5,561	4,297	4,045
Senegal	9,875	10,638	9,570
Togo	9,110	11,125	9,837
USA	8,592	9,094	7,255
Total (incl. others)	269,227	274,330	237,725

* Arrivals at hotels and similar establishments.

Receipts from tourism (US $ million, excl. passenger transport): 64 in 2009; 72 in 2010; 133 in 2011.

Source: World Tourism Organization.

Communications Media

	2010	2011	2012
Telephones ('000 main lines in use)	144.0	141.5	141.4
Mobile cellular telephones ('000 subscribers)	5,707.8	7,682.1	9,976.1
Internet subscribers ('000)	28.7	31.2	n.a.
Broadband subscribers ('000)	13.7	14.1	14.3

Source: International Telecommunication Union.

Education

(2011/12 unless otherwise indicated)

			Students ('000)		
	Institutions	Teachers	Males	Females	Total
Pre-primary	147*	2,527	30.1	29.4	59.5
Primary	9,726†	48,592	1,225.0	1,119.0	2,344.0
Secondary (general)	922†	22,381	364.5	284.5	649.0
Secondary (technical and vocational)	119†	3,303	14.7	12.7	27.4
Tertiary	52†	3,671	46.5	22.4	68.9

* 1997/98.
† 2008/09.

Source: mostly UNESCO Institute for Statistics.

Pupil-teacher ratio (primary education, UNESCO estimate): 48.2 in 2011/12 (Source: UNESCO Institute for Statistics).

Adult literacy rate (UNESCO estimates): 28.7% (males 36.7%; females 21.6%) in 2007 (Source: UNESCO Institute for Statistics).

Directory

The Government

HEAD OF STATE

President: BLAISE COMPAORÉ (assumed power as Chairman of the Front Populaire 15 October 1987; elected President 1 December 1991; re-elected 15 November 1998, 13 November 2005 and 21 November 2010).

COUNCIL OF MINISTERS

(April 2014)

President and Minister of Defence and War Veterans: BLAISE COMPAORÉ.

Prime Minister: LUC ADOLPHE TIAO.

Minister of State, Minister in charge of Parliamentary Affairs and Political Reform: BONGNESSAN ARSÈNE YÉ.

Minister of State, Minister in charge of Presidential Affairs: ASSIMI KOUANDA.

Minister of State, Minister of Foreign Affairs and Regional Co-operation: YIPÈNÈ DJIBRIL BASSOLÉ.

Minister of the Economy and Finance: LUCIEN MARIE NOËL BEMBAMBA.

Minister of Territorial Administration and Security: JÉRÔME BOUGOUMA.

Minister of Justice, Keeper of the Seals: DRAMANE YAMÉOGO.

Minister of Agriculture and Food Security: MAHAMA ZOUNGRANA.

Minister of Mines and Energy: ABDOULAYE LAMOUSSA SALIF KABORÉ.

Minister of Industry, Trade and Crafts: PATIENDÉ ARTHUR KAFANDO.

Minister of Communication and Government Spokesperson: ALAIN EDOUARD TRAORÉ.

Minister for the Promotion of Women and Gender Equality: NESTORINE SANGARÉ COMPAORÉ.

Minister of Culture and Tourism: BABA HAMA.

Minister of Infrastructure, Improving Access to Isolated Regions and Transport: JEAN BERTIN OUÉDRAOGO.

Minister of Health: LENÉ SEBGO.

Minister of Housing: YACOUBA BARRY.

Minister of Secondary and Higher Education: Prof. MOUSSA OUATTARA.

Minister of National Education and Literacy: KOUMBA BOLY BARRY.

Minister of the Civil Service, Labour and Social Security: VINCENT ZAKANÉ.

Minister of Scientific Research and Innovation: GNISSA ISAÏE KONATÉ.

Minister of the Environment and Sustainable Development: SALIF OUÉDRAOGO.

Minister of Youth, Professional Training and Employment: BASGA EMILE DIALLA.

Minister of Animal Resources and Fisheries: JÉRÉMIE TINGA OUÉDRAOGO.

Minister of Water, Management of Water Resources and Sanitation: MAMOUNATA BÉEM OUÉDRAOGO.

Minister of Development of the Digital Economy and Posts: JEAN KOULIDIATI.

Minister of Sport and Leisure: YACOUBA OUÉDRAOGO.

Minister of Social Action and National Solidarity: ALAIN ZOUBGA.

Minister of Human Rights and Civic Promotion: PRUDENCE JULIE M. N. K. NIGNA SOMDA.

Minister of Town and Country Planning and Decentralization: TOUSSAIN ABEL COULIBALY.

Minister-delegate to the Minister of the Economy and Finance, responsible for the Budget: CLOTILDE KI NIKIÉMA.

Minister-delegate to the Minister of Foreign Affairs and Regional Co-operation, responsible for Regional Co-operation: THOMAS PALÉ.

Minister-delegate to the Minister of National Education and Literacy, responsible for Literacy: AMADOU DIEMDIODA DICKO.

Minister-delegate to the Minister of Infrastructure, Improving Access to Isolated Regions and Transport, responsible for Transport: BABA DIÉMÉ.

MINISTRIES

Office of the President: 03 BP 7030, Ouagadougou 03; tel. 50-50-66-30; fax 50-31-49-26; e-mail info@presidence.bf; internet www.presidence.bf.

Office of the Prime Minister: 03 BP 7027, Ouagadougou 03; tel. 50-32-48-89; fax 50-33-05-51; e-mail webmaster@primature.gov.bf; internet www.gouvernement.gov.bf.

Ministry of Agriculture and Food Security: 03 BP 7005, Ouagadougou 03; tel. 50-32-41-14; fax 50-31-08-70; internet www.agriculture.gov.bf.

Ministry of Animal Resources and Fisheries: 03 BP 7026, Ouagadougou 03; tel. 50-39-96-15; fax 50-31-84-75; e-mail pinidie.banaon@mra.gov.bf; internet www.mra.gov.bf.

Ministry of the Civil Service, Labour and Social Security: Immeuble de la Modernisation, 922 ave Kwamé N'Krumah, 03 BP 7006, Ouagadougou 03; tel. 50-50-19-52; fax 50-50-19-55; internet www.fonction-publique.gov.bf.

Ministry of Communication and Government Spokesperson: 387 ave Georges Conseiga, 01 BP 5175, Ouagadougou 01; tel. 50-49-00-00; fax 50-33-73-87; internet www.mptic.gov.bf.

Ministry of Culture and Tourism: 11 BP 852, CMS, Ouagadougou 11; tel. 50-33-09-63; fax 50-33-09-64; e-mail mctc@cenatrin.bf; internet www.culture.gov.bf.

Ministry of Defence and War Veterans: 01 BP 496, Ouagadougou 01; tel. 50-50-72-14; fax 50-31-36-10; internet www.defense.gov.bf.

Ministry of Development of the Digital Economy and Posts: Ouagadougou.

Ministry of the Economy and Finance: 395 ave Ho Chi Minh, 01 BP 7008, Ouagadougou 01; tel. 50-32-42-11; fax 50-31-27-15; e-mail webmaster@finances.gov.bf; internet www.finances.gov.bf.

Ministry of the Environment and Sustainable Development: 565 rue Agostino Neto, Koulouba, 03 BP 7044, Ouagadougou 03; tel. 50-32-40-74; fax 50-50-70-39; internet www.environnement.gov.bf.

Ministry of Foreign Affairs and Regional Co-operation: rue 988, blvd du Faso, 03 BP 7038, Ouagadougou 03; tel. 50-32-47-34; fax 50-50-87-92; e-mail webmaster.mae@mae.gov.bf; internet www.mae.gov.bf.

Ministry of Health: 03 BP 7009, Ouagadougou 03; tel. 50-32-63-40; internet www.sante.gov.bf.

Ministry of Housing: Ouagadougou; tel. and fax 50-50-57-86.

Ministry of Human Rights and Civic Promotion: Ouagadougou.

Ministry of Industry, Trade and Crafts: 01 BP 514, Ouagadougou 01; tel. 50-32-48-28; fax 50-31-70-53; internet www.commerce.gov.bf.

Ministry of Infrastructure, Improving Access to Isolated Regions and Transport: 03 BP 7011, Ouagadougou 03; tel. 50-50-73-33; fax 50-31-84-08; internet www.mith.gov.bf.

Ministry of Justice: 01 BP 526, Ouagadougou 01; tel. 50-32-48-33; fax 50-31-71-37; e-mail webmestre@justice.bf; internet www.justice.gov.bf.

Ministry of Labour and Social Security: 01 BP 7016, Ouagadougou 01; tel. 50-50-09-60; fax 50-31-88-01; e-mail emploi@metss.gov.bf; internet www.emploi.gov.bf.

Ministry of Mines and Energy: 01 BP 644, Ouagadougou 01; tel. 50-31-84-29; fax 50-31-84-30; internet www.mines.gov.bf.

Ministry of National Education and Literacy: 03 BP 7032, Ouagadougou 03; tel. 50-50-66-00; fax 50-31-42-76; internet www.meba.gov.bf.

Ministry of Parliamentary Affairs and Political Reform: 01 BP 2079, Ouagadougou 01; tel. 50-32-40-70; fax 50-50-78-94; e-mail cab_mrp@yahoo.fr; internet www.mrp.gov.bf.

Ministry for the Promotion of Women and Gender Equality: 01 BP 303, Ouagadougou 01; tel. 50-50-01-04; fax 50-50-01-02; e-mail secretariat@mpf.gov.bf; internet www.mpf.gov.bf.

Ministry of Scientific Research and Innovation: Ouagadougou.

Ministry of Secondary and Higher Education: 03 BP 7047, Ouagadougou 03; tel. 50-33-73-34; fax 50-50-02-32; e-mail messrsxxsg@yahoo.ca; internet www.messrs.gov.bf.

Ministry of Social Action and National Solidarity: 01 BP 515, Ouagadougou 01; tel. 50-50-68-75; fax 50-31-67-37; internet www.action-sociale.gov.bf.

Ministry of Sport and Leisure: 03 BP 7035, Ouagadougou 03; tel. 50-32-47-86; fax 50-33-08-18; internet www.sports.gov.bf.

Ministry of Territorial Administration and Security: 01 BP 526, Ouagadougou 01; tel. 50-32-48-33; fax 50-31-72-00; internet www.matd.gov.bf.

Ministry of Town and Country Planning and Decentralization: Ouagadougou.

Ministry of Water, Management of Water Resources and Sanitation: Ouagadougou.

Ministry of Youth, Professional Training and Employment: 01 BP 7016, Ouagadougou 01; tel. 50-50-09-60; fax 30-31-84-80; internet www.emploi.gov.bf.

President

Presidential Election, 21 November 2010

Candidate	Votes	% of votes
Blaise Compaoré	1,357,315	80.15
Hama Arba Diallo	138,975	8.21
Bénéwendé Stanislas Sankara	107,310	6.34
Boukary Kaboré	39,186	2.31
Maxime Kaboré	25,077	1.48
Pargui Emile Paré	14,560	0.86
Ouampoussoga François Kaboré	10,962	0.65
Total	1,693,385	100.00

Legislature

National Assembly: 01 BP 6482, Ouagadougou 01; tel. 50-31-46-84; fax 50-31-45-90.

President: SOUNGALO APOLLINAIRE OUATTARA.

General Election, 2 December 2012

Parties	Provincial list seats	National list seats	Total seats
CDP	62	8	70
UPC	17	2	19
ADF—RDA	16	2	18
UPR	4	1	5
UNIR/PS	3	1	4
CFD/B	2	1	3
PDS/Metba	1	1	2
CNPB	1	—	1
FA	1	—	1
ODT	1	—	1
RDB	1	—	1
RDS	1	—	1
UNDD	1	—	1
Total	111	16	127

Election Commission

Commission Electorale Nationale Indépendante (CENI): 01 BP 5152, Ouagadougou 01; tel. 50-50-00-52; fax 50-50-80-44; e-mail ceni@fasonet.bf; internet www.ceni.bf; f. 2001; 15 mems; Pres. BARTHÉLEMY KÉRÉ.

Advisory Council

Economic and Social Council (Conseil Economique et Social): 01 BP 6162, Ouagadougou 01; tel. 50-32-40-91; fax 50-31-06-54; e-mail ces@ces.gov.bf; internet www.ces.gov.bf; f. 1985; present name adopted in 1992; 90 mems; Pres. THOMAS SANON.

Political Organizations

A total of 74 political parties contested the legislative elections held in December 2012.

Alliance pour la Démocratie et la Fédération—Rassemblement Démocratique Africain (ADF—RDA): 01 BP 1991, Ouagadougou 01; tel. 50-43-03-69; e-mail contact@adf-rda.com; internet www.adf-rda.com; f. 1990 as Alliance pour la Démocratie et la Fédération; absorbed faction of Rassemblement Démocratique Africain in 1998; Pres. GILBERT NOËL OUÉDRAOGO; Sec.-Gen. AÏSSATA SIDIBÉ.

Congrès pour la Démocratie et le Progrès (CDP): 1146 ave Kwamé N'Krumah, 01 BP 1605, Ouagadougou 01; tel. 50-31-50-18; fax 50-31-43-93; e-mail contact@cdp-burkina.org; internet www.cdp.bf; f. 1996; Nat. Exec. Sec. ASSIMI KOUANDA.

Convention des Forces Démocratiques du Burkina (CFD/B): Ouagadougou; Leader AMADOU DIEMDIODA DICKO.

Convention Nationale du Progrès du Burkina (CNPB): f. 2009; Pres. MOUSSA BOLY.

Le Faso Autrement (FA): Ouagadougou; Pres. ABLASSÉ OUÉDRAOGO.

Mouvement du Peuple pour le Progrès (MPP): Ouagadougou; f. 2014; Pres. ROCH MARC CHRISTIAN KABORÉ.

Organisation pour la Démocratie et le Travail (ODT): 02 BP 5274, Ouagadougou 02; tel. 50-35-64-61; Pres. MOÏSE SAWADOGO.

Parti pour la Démocratie et le Progrès—Parti Socialiste (PDP—PS): 11 BP 26, Ouagadougou 11; tel. and fax 78-04-12-53 (mobile); e-mail pdp-ps@fasonet.bf; f. 2001 by merger of the Parti pour la Démocratie et le Progrès and the Parti Socialiste Burkinabè; Nat. Pres. THÉOPHILE DENTIOGUÉ.

Parti pour la Démocratie et le Socialisme/Parti des Bâtisseurs (PDS/METBA): Ouagadougou; tel. 50-34-34-04; Pres. SAMBO YOUSSOUF BA.

Parti de l'Indépendance, du Travail et de la Justice (PITJ): Ouagadougou; f. 2012; Sec.-Gen. SOUMANE TOURÉ.

Parti de la Renaissance Nationale (PAREN): Ouagadougou; tel. 50-43-12-26; f. 2000; social-democratic; Pres. KILACHIA LAURENT BADO.

Rassemblement pour la Démocratie et le Socialisme (RDS): Ouagadougou.

Rassemblement pour le Développement du Burkina (RDB): Pres. CÉLESTIN SEYDOU COMPAORÉ.

Union Nationale pour la Démocratie et le Développement (UNDD): 03 BP 7114, Ouagadougou 03; tel. 50-31-15-15; internet www.undd.org; f. 2003 by fmr mems of the ADF—RDA; liberal; Pres. Me HERMANN YAMÉOGO.

Union pour le Progrès et le Changement (UPC): Ouagadougou; f. 2010; Pres. ZÉPHIRIN DIABRÉ.

Union pour la Renaissance—Parti Sankariste (UNIR—PS): Ouagadougou; tel. 50-36-30-45; f. 2000 as Union pour la Renaissance—Mouvement Sankariste; renamed as above in 2009; Pres. BÉNÉWENDÉ STANISLAS SANKARA.

Union pour la République (UPR): 01 BP 5111, Ouagadougou 01; tel. 50-35-23-92; Leader TOUSSAINT ABEL COULIBALY.

Diplomatic Representation

EMBASSIES IN BURKINA FASO

Algeria: Secteur 13, Zone du Bois, 295 ave Babanguida, 01 BP 3893, Ouagadougou 01; tel. 50-36-81-81; fax 50-36-81-79; Ambassador ABDELKRIM BENCHIAH.

Belgium: Immeuble Me Benoit Sawadogo, 994 rue Agostino Neto, Koulouba, 01 BP 1624, Ouagadougou 01; tel. 50-31-21-64; fax 50-31-06-60; e-mail ouagadougou@diplobel.fed.be; internet diplomatie.belgium.be/burkina_faso; Ambassador PHILIP EMMANUEL HEUTS.

Brazil: Parcele 20, Lot 38, Section F, Zone A Bogodogo Ouaga 2000, 10 BP 13571, Ouagadougou 10; tel. 50-37-60-30; fax 50-37-69-35; e-mail brasembuagadugu@mre.gov.br; Ambassador SANTIAGO LUIS BENTO FERNANDEZ ALCAZAR.

Canada: 316 ave du Prof. Joseph Ki Zerbo, 01 BP 548, Ouagadougou 01; tel. 50-31-18-94; fax 50-31-19-00; e-mail ouaga@dfait-maeci.gc.ca; internet www.canadainternational.gc.ca/burkinafaso; Ambassador IVAN ROBERTS.

Chad: Ouagadougou; tel. 50-50-09-79; Ambassador MBATNA BANDJANG.

Côte d'Ivoire: pl. des Nations Unies, 01 BP 20, Ouagadougou 01; tel. 50-31-82-28; fax 50-31-82-30; Ambassador ABDOU TOURÉ.

Cuba: rue 4/64, La Rotonde, Secteur 4, Ouagadougou; tel. 50-50-64-91; fax 50-31-73-24; e-mail embacuba.bf@fasonet.bf; internet www.cubadiplomatica.cu/burkinafaso; Ambassador ANA MARIA ROVIRA INGIDUA.

Denmark: 316 ave Pr. Joseph Ki-Zerbo, 01 BP 1760, Ouagadougou 01; tel. 50-32-85-40; fax 50-32-85-77; e-mail ouaamb@um.dk; internet burkinafaso.um.dk; Ambassador BO JENSEN.

Egypt: Zone du Conseil de L'Entente, blvd du Faso, 04 BP 7042, Ouagadougou 04; tel. 50-50-66-39; fax 50-31-38-36; Ambassador HISHAM MOHAMED NAGI ABD EL HAMID.

France: ave du Trésor, 01 BP 504, Ouagadougou 01; tel. 50-49-66-66; fax 50-49-66-09; e-mail ambassade@ambafrance-bf.org; internet www.ambafrance-bf.org; Ambassador GILLES THIBAULT.

Germany: 399 ave Joseph Badoua, 01 BP 600, Ouagadougou 01; tel. 50-50-67-31; fax 50-31-39-91; e-mail amb.allemagne@fasonet.bf; internet www.ouagadougou.diplo.de; Ambassador CHRISTIAN GERMANN.

Ghana: 22 ave d'Oubritenga, 01 BP 212, Ouagadougou 01; tel. 50-50-76-35; e-mail embagna@fasonet.bf; Ambassador Chief MANDEAYA BAWUMIA.

Holy See: Tange Saabé, BP 1902, Ouagadougou 01; tel. 50-31-63-56; fax 50-31-63-55; e-mail nuntiusapbn@yahoo.it; Ambassador VITO RALLO (Titular Archbishop of Alba).

Japan: 01 BP 5560, Ouagadougou 01; tel. 50-37-65-06; fax 50-37-65-81; internet www.bf.emb-japan.go.jp; Ambassador MASATO FUTAISHI.

Korea, Democratic People's Republic: Ouagadougou; Ambassador KIL MUN YONG.

Libya: 01 BP 1601, Ouagadougou 01; tel. 50-50-67-53; fax 50-31-34-70; Ambassador (vacant).

Mali: 2569 ave Bassawarga, 01 BP 1911, Ouagadougou 01; tel. 50-38-19-22; Ambassador DRISSA COULIBALY.

Morocco: Ouaga 2000 Villa B04, pl. de la Cotière, 01 BP 3438, Ouagadougou 01; tel. 50-37-40-16; fax 50-37-41-72; e-mail maroc1@fasonet.bf; Ambassador FARHAT BOUAAZA.

Nigeria: rue de l'Hôpital Yalgado, 01 BP 132, Ouagadougou 01; tel. 50-36-30-15; Ambassador DAVID GAMBAR BALA.

Saudi Arabia: Ouaga 2000, rue de la Francophonie, Villa M05, 01 BP 2069, Ouagadougou 01; tel. 50-37-42-06; fax 50-37-42-10; e-mail bfemb@mofa.gov.sa; internet embassies.mofa.gov.sa/sites/burkinafaso; Ambassador DAHIR MOOTISH ALANZI.

Senegal: Immeuble Espace Fadima, ave de la Résistance du 17 Mai, 01 BP 3226, Ouagadougou 01; tel. 50-31-14-18; fax 50-31-14-01; Ambassador MAMADOU MAKHTAR GUEYE.

South Africa: Villa 1110, Hotel Sofitel, Ouagadougou; tel. 50-37-60-98; fax 50-37-60-97; e-mail saemb.ouaga@dirco.gov.za; Ambassador GANGUMZI M. TSENGIWE.

Sweden: 11 BP 755, CMS, Ouagadougou; tel. 50-49-61-70; e-mail ambassaden.ouagadougou@sida.se; internet www.swedenabroad.com/ouagadougou; Ambassador CARIN WALL.

Taiwan (Republic of China): Immeuble Henri Vimal, ave du Prof. Joseph Ki Zerbo, 01 BP 5563, Ouagadougou 01; tel. 50-31-61-95; fax 50-31-61-97; e-mail ambachine@fasonet.bf; internet www.taiwanembassy.org/BF; Ambassador SHEN CHENG-HONG.

Turkey: Ouagadougou; Ambassador HÜSNÜ MURAT ÜLKÜ.

USA: ave Sembene Ousmane, Ouaga 2000, Secteur 15, Ouagadougou; tel. 50-49-53-00; fax 50-49-56-28; e-mail amembouaga@state.gov; internet ouagadougou.usembassy.gov; Ambassador Dr TULINABO S. MUSHINGI.

Judicial System

In accordance with constitutional amendments approved by the National Assembly in April 2000, the Supreme Court was abolished; its four permanent chambers were replaced by a Constitutional Council, a Council of State, a Court of Cassation and a National Audit Court, all of which commenced operations in December 2002. Judges are accountable to a Higher Council, under the chairmanship of the President of the Republic, in which capacity he is officially responsible for ensuring the independence of the judiciary. A High Court of Justice is competent to try the President and members of the Government in cases of treason, embezzlement of public funds, and other crimes and offences.

Constitutional Council: 40 ave de la Nation, 11 BP 1114, Ouagadougou 11; tel. 50-50-05-53; fax 50-50-08-66; e-mail conseil@conseil-constitutionnel.gov.bf; internet www.conseil-constitutionnel.gov.bf; f. 2002 to replace Constitutional Chamber of fmr Supreme Court; Pres. DÉ ALBERT MILLOGO; Sec.-Gen. HONIBIPÈ MARIAM MARGUERITE OUÉDRAOGO.

Council of State: 01 BP 586, Ouagadougou 01; tel. 50-50-64-18; e-mail webmaster@conseil-etat.gov.bf; internet www.conseil-etat.gov.bf; f. 2002 to replace Administrative Chamber of fmr Supreme Court; comprises 2 chambers: a Consultative Chamber and a Chamber of Litigation; First Pres. HARIDIATA SERE DAKOURÉ; Pres. of Consultative Chamber THÉRÈSE SANOU TRAORÉ; Pres. of Chamber of Litigation VENANT OUÉDRAOGO.

Court of Cassation: 05 BP 6204, Ouagadougou 05; tel. 50-31-20-47; fax 50-31-02-71; e-mail webmaster@courcassation.bf; internet www.cour-cassation.gov.bf; f. 2002 to replace Judicial Chamber of fmr Supreme Court; First Pres. CHEICK DIMKINSEDO OUÉDRAOGO.

High Court of Justice: Ouagadougou; f. 1998; comprises 6 deputies of the Assemblée nationale and 3 magistrates appointed by the President of the Court of Cassation; Pres. DIM-SONGDO BONAVENTURE OUÉDRAOGO; Vice-Pres. SIBILA FRANCK COMPAORÉ.

National Audit Court: 01 BP 2534, Ouagadougou 01; tel. 50-50-36-00; fax 50-50-35-01; e-mail infos@cour-comptes.gov.bf; internet www.cour-comptes.gov.bf; f. 2002 to replace Audit Chamber of fmr Supreme Court; comprises 3 chambers, concerned with: local government organs; public enterprises; and the operations of the State; First Pres. NOUMOUTIÉ HERBERT TRAORÉ; Procurator-Gen. THÉRÈSE TRAORÉ SANOU; Pres of Chambers PASCAL SANOU, SÉNÉBOU RAYMONDD MANUELLA OUILMA TRAORÉ, SABINE OUÉDRAOGO YETA.

Religion

The Constitution provides for freedom of religion, and the Government respects this right in practice. The country is a secular state. Islam, Christianity and traditional religions operate freely without government interference. According to the 2006 census, some 60.5% of the population are Muslims, 23.2% are Christians and 15.3% follow animist beliefs, with the remaining population being adherents of other religions or practising no religion.

ISLAM

Communauté Musulmane du Burkina Faso: 01 BP 368, Ouagadougou 01; tel. 50-31-44-05; fax 50-50-70-30; Pres. El Hadj ADAMA SAKANDÉ (acting).

CHRISTIANITY

The Roman Catholic Church

Burkina Faso comprises three archdioceses and 12 dioceses. Some 19% of the total population are Roman Catholics.

Bishops' Conference: Conférence des Evêques de Burkina Faso et du Niger, 01 BP 1195, Ouagadougou 01; tel. 50-50-60-26; fax 50-31-64-81; e-mail ccbn@fasonet.bf; internet www.egliseduburkina.org; f. 1966; legally recognized 1978; Pres. Most Rev. PAUL YEMBOARO OUÉDRAOGO (Archbishop of Bobo-Dioulasso).

Archbishop of Bobo-Dioulasso: Most Rev. PAUL YEMBOARO OUÉDRAOGO, Archevêché, Lafiaso, 01 BP 312, Bobo-Dioulasso; tel. 20-97-00-35; fax 20-97-19-50; e-mail lafiaso@fasonet.bf.

Archbishop of Koupéla: Most Rev. SÉRAPHIN FRANÇOIS ROUAMBA, Archevêché, BP 51, Koupéla; tel. 40-71-00-30; fax 40-71-02-65; e-mail ardiokou@fasonet.bf.

Archbishop of Ouagadougou: Cardinal PHILIPPE OUÉDRAOGO, Archevêché, 01 BP 1472, Ouagadougou 01; tel. 50-50-67-04; fax 50-50-72-75; e-mail untaani@fasonet.bf.

Protestant Churches

Some 4.2% of the population are Protestants.

Assemblées de Dieu du Burkina Faso: 01 BP 458, Ouagadougou 01; tel. 50-34-35-45; fax 50-34-28-71; e-mail adlagengo@fasonet.bf; f. 1921; Pres. Pastor MICHEL OUÉDRAOGO.

Fédération des Eglises et Missions Evangéliques (FEME): BP 108, Ouagadougou; tel. 50-36-14-26; e-mail feme@fasonet.bf; f. 1961; 10 churches and missions, 82,309 adherents; Pres. Pastor SAMUEL YAMÉOGO.

BAHÁ'Í FAITH

Assemblée Spirituelle Nationale: 01 BP 977, Ouagadougou 01; tel. 50-34-29-95; e-mail gnampa@fasonet.bf; Nat. Sec. JEAN-PIERRE SWEDY.

The Press

Direction de la Presse Ecrite: Ouagadougou; govt body responsible for press direction.

DAILIES

24 Heures: 01 BP 3654, Ouagadougou 01; tel. 50-31-41-08; fax 50-30-57-39; f. 2000; privately owned; Dir BOUBAKAR DIALLO.

Bulletin de l'Agence d'Information du Burkina: 01 BP 2507, Ouagadougou 01; tel. 50-32-46-40; fax 50-33-73-16; e-mail infos@aib.bf; internet www.aib.bf; f. 1964 as L'Agence Voltaïque de Presse; current name adopted in 1984; Dir JAMES DABIRÉ.

L'Express du Faso: 01 BP 1, Bobo-Dioulasso 01; tel. 50-33-50-27; e-mail lexpress.faso@yahoo.fr; internet www.lexpressdufaso.com; f. 1998; privately owned; Dir of Publication JACQUES; Editor-in-Chief KANI MOUNTAMOU; circ. 2,000 (2010).

L'Observateur Paalga (New Observer): 01 BP 584, Ouagadougou 01; tel. 50-33-27-05; fax 50-31-45-79; e-mail lobs@fasonet.bf; internet www.lobservateur.bf; f. 1973; privately owned; also a Friday edn *L'Observateur Dimanche*; Dir EDOUARD OUÉDRAOGO; circ. in 2012 10,000 (daily), 5,000 (weekly).

Le Pays: Cité 1200 logements, 01 BP 4577, Ouagadougou 01; tel. 50-36-20-46; fax 50-36-03-78; e-mail lepays91@yahoo.fr; internet www.lepays.bf; f. 1991; independent; Dir-Gen. BOUREIMA JÉRÉMIE SIGUE; Editor-in-Chief MAHOROU KANAZOE; circ. 12,000 (2010).

Sidwaya Quotidien (Daily Truth): 5 rue du Marché, 01 BP 507, Ouagadougou 01; tel. 50-31-22-89; fax 50-31-03-62; e-mail daouda.ouedraogo@sidwaya.bf; internet www.sidwaya.bf; f. 1984; state-owned; Dir-Gen. RABANKHI ABOU-BÂKR ZIDA; Editor-in-Chief VICTORIEN AIMAR SAWADOGO; circ. 5,000 (2010).

PERIODICALS

Bendré (Drum): 16.38 ave du Yatenga, 01 BP 6020, Ouagadougou 01; tel. 50-33-27-11; fax 50-31-28-53; e-mail bendrekan@hotmail.com; internet www.journalbendre.net; f. 1990; weekly; current affairs; Dir SY MOUMINA CHERIFF; circ. 2,000 (2010).

Evasion: Cité 1200 logements, 01 BP 4577, Ouagadougou 01; tel. 50-36-17-30; fax 50-36-03-78; e-mail lepays91@yahoo.fr; internet www.lepays.fr; f. 1996; publ. by Editions le Pays; weekly; current affairs; Dir-Gen. BOUREIMA JÉRÉMIE SIGUE; Editor-in-Chief CHRISTINE SAWADOGO.

L'Evènement: 01 BP 1860, Ouagadougou 01; tel. and fax 50-36-33-03; e-mail bangreib@yahoo.fr; internet www.evenement-bf.net; f. 2001; bi-monthly; Dir of Publication GERMAIN BITTIOU NAMA; Editor-in-Chief NEWTON AHMED BARRY; circ. 6,000 (2010).

Fasozine: Ouagadougou; tel. 50-50-76-01; fax 50-31-69-73; e-mail ecrire@fasozine.com; internet www.fasozine.com; f. 2005; Dir of Publication MORIN YAMONGBE.

L'Hebdomadaire: Ouagadougou; tel. 50-31-47-62; e-mail hebdcom@fasonet.bf; internet www.hebdo.bf; f. 1999; Fridays; Dir ZÉPHIRIN KPODA; Editor-in-Chief DJIBRIL TOURÉ.

L'Indépendant: 01 BP 5663, Ouagadougou 01; tel. 50-33-37-75; e-mail sebgo@fasonet.bf; internet www.independant.bf; f. 1993 by Norbert Zongo; weekly, Tuesdays; Dir LIERMÉ DIEUDONNÉ SOMÉ; Editor-in-Chief TALATO SIID SAYA; circ. 5,000 (2010).

Le Journal du Jeudi (JJ): 01 BP 3654, Ouagadougou 01; tel. 50-31-41-08; fax 50-50-01-62; e-mail info@journaldujeudi.com; internet www.journaldujeudi.com; f. 1991; weekly; satirical; Dir BOUBAKAR DIALLO; Editor-in-Chief DAMIEN GLEZ; circ. 10,000.

Laabaali: Association Tin Tua, BP 167, Fada N'Gourma; tel. 40-77-01-26; fax 40-77-02-08; e-mail info@tintua.org; internet www.tintua.org/Liens/Laabali.htm; f. 1988; monthly; promotes literacy, agricultural information, cultural affairs; Gourmanche; Dir of Publishing BENOÎT B. OUOBA; Editor-in-Chief SUZANNE OUOBA; circ. 4,000.

Le Marabout: 01 BP 3564, Ouagadougou 01; tel. 50-31-41-08; e-mail info@marabout.net; f. 2001; monthly; publ. by the Réseau Africain pour la Liberté d'Informer; pan-African politics; satirical; Dir BOUBAKAR DIALLO; Editor-in-Chief DAMIEN GLEZ.

L'Opinion: 01 BP 6459, Ouagadougou 01; tel. and fax 50-50-89-49; e-mail zedcom@fasonet.bf; internet www.zedcom.bf; weekly; Dir of Publishing ISSAKA LINGANI.

San Finna: Immeuble Photo Luxe, 12 BP 105, Ouagadougou 12; tel. and fax 50-35-82-64; e-mail sanfinna@yahoo.fr; internet www.sanfinna.com; f. 1999; Mondays; independent; current affairs, international politics; Editor-in-Chief MATHIEU N'DO.

Sidwaya Hebdo (Weekly Truth): 5 rue du Marché, 01 BP 507, Ouagadougou 01; tel. 50-31-22-89; fax 50-31-03-62; e-mail daouda.ouedraogo@sidwaya.bf; internet www.sidwaya.bf; f. 1997; state-owned; weekly; Editor-in-Chief DAOUDA E. OUÉDRAOGO.

Sidwaya Magazine (Truth): 5 rue du Marché, 01 BP 507, Ouagadougou 01; tel. 50-31-22-89; fax 50-31-03-62; e-mail daouda.ouedraogo@sidwaya.bf; internet www.sidwaya.bf; f. 1989; state-owned; monthly; Editor-in-Chief DAOUDA E. OUÉDRAOGO; circ. 2,500.

La Voix du Sahel: 01 BP 5505, Ouagadougou 01; tel. 50-33-20-75; e-mail voixdusahel@yahoo.fr; privately owned; Dir of Publication PROMOTHÉE KASSOUM BAKO.

Votre Santé: Cité 1200 logements, 01 BP 4577, Ouagadougou 01; tel. 50-36-20-46; fax 50-36-03-78; e-mail lepays91@yahoo.fr; internet www.lepays.fr; f. 1996; publ. by Editions le Pays; monthly; Dir-Gen. BOUREIMA JÉRÉMIE SIGUE; Editor-in-Chief ALEXANDRE LE GRAND ROUAMBA.

NEWS AGENCY

Agence d'Information du Burkina (AIB): 01 BP 2507, Ouagadougou 01; tel. 50-32-46-39; fax 50-33-73-16; e-mail aib.redaction@mcc.gov.bf; internet www.aib.bf; f. 1964; fmrly Agence Voltaïque de Presse; state-controlled; Dir JOLIVET EMMAÜS.

PRESS ASSOCIATIONS

Association Rayimkudemdé—Association Nationale des Animateurs et Journalistes en Langues Nationales du Burkina Faso (ARK): Sigh-Noghin, Ouagadougou; f. 2001; Pres. RIGOBERT ILBOUDO; Sec.-Gen. PIERRE OUÉDRAOGO.

Centre National de Presse—Norbert Zongo (CNP—NZ): 04 BP 8524, Ouagadougou 04; tel. and fax 50-34-37-45; internet www.cnpress-zongo.net; f. 1998 as Centre National de Presse; centre of information and documentation; provides journalistic training; incorporates Association des Journalistes du Burkina (f. 1988); Dir ABDOULAYE DIALLO.

Publishers

Editions Contact: 04 BP 8462, Ouagadougou 04; tel. 76-61-28-72 (mobile); e-mail contact.evang@cenatrin.bf; f. 1992; evangelical Christian and other books in French.

Editions Découvertes du Burkina (ADDB): 06 BP 9237, Ouagadougou 06; tel. 50-36-22-38; e-mail jacques@liptinfor.bf; human and social sciences, poetry; Dir JACQUES GUÉGANÉ.

Editions Firmament: 01 BP 3392, Ouagadougou 01; tel. 50-38-44-25; e-mail brkabore@uemoa.int; f. 1994; literary fiction; Dir ROGER KABORÉ.

Editions Flamme: 04 BP 8921, Ouagadougou 04; tel. 50-34-15-31; fax 70-12-52-30; e-mail flamme@fasonet.bf; f. 1994; owned by the Assembleés de Dieu du Burkina Faso; literature of Christian interest in French, in Mooré and in Dioula; Editor-in-Chief DANIEL KABORÉ.

Editions Gambidi: 01 BP 5743, Ouagadougou 01; tel. 50-36-59-42; politics, philosophy; Dir JEAN-PIERRE GUINGANÉ.

Graphic Technic International & Biomedical (GTI): 01 BP 3230, Ouagadougou 01; tel. and fax 50-31-67-69; medicine, literary, popular and children's fiction, poetry; Dir-Gen. SAWADOGO N. TASSERE.

Presses Africaines SA: 01 BP 1471, Ouagadougou 01; tel. 50-50-71-75; general fiction, religion, primary and secondary textbooks; Man. Dir A. WININGA.

Editions Sankofa et Gurli: 01 BP 3811, Ouagadougou 01; tel. 70-24-30-81 (mobile); e-mail sankogur@hotmail.com; f. 1995; literary fiction, social sciences, African languages, youth and childhood literature; in French and in national languages; Dir JEAN-CLAUDE NABA.

Editions Sidwaya: BP 507, Ouagadougou 01; tel. 50-31-22-89; fax 50-31-03-62; internet www.sidwaya.bf; f. 1998 to replace Société Nationale d'Editions et de Presse; state-owned; transfer to private ownership proposed; general, periodicals; Dir IBRAHIMAN SAKANDÉ.

Broadcasting and Communications

TELECOMMUNICATIONS

Airtel Burkina Faso: ave du Président Aboubacar Sangoulé Lamizana, 01 BP 6622, Ouagadougou 01; tel. 50-33-14-00; fax 50-33-14-06; e-mail info@bf.airtel.com; internet africa.airtel.com/burkina; f. 2001; fmrly Zain Burkina Faso, present name adopted 2010; mobile cellular telephone operator in Ouagadougou, Bobo-Dioulasso and 235 other towns; acquired by Bharti Airtel (India) in 2010; Dir-Gen. JOHN NDEGO; 3,014,640 subscribers (Dec. 2011).

Office National des Télécommunications (ONATEL): ave de la Nation, 01 BP 10000, Ouagadougou 01; tel. 50-49-44-02; fax 50-31-03-31; e-mail dcrp@onatel.bf; internet www.onatel.bf; fixed-line telephone and internet services; 51% owned by Maroc Telecom (Morocco, Vivendi); 23% state-owned; Pres. PAUL BALMA; Dir-Gen. MOHAMMED MORCHID; 141,529 subscribers (Dec. 2011).

TELMOB: tel. 49-42-41; fax 50-49-42-78; e-mail wema.d@onatel.bf; f. 2002; mobile cellular telephone operator in 19 cities; Dir DIEUDONNÉ WEMA; 2,970,805 subscribers (Dec. 2011).

Telecel-Faso: 396 ave de la Nation, 08 BP 11059, Ouagadougou 086; tel. 50-33-35-56; fax 50-33-35-58; e-mail infos@telecelfaso.bf; internet www.telecelfaso.bf; f. 2000; mobile cellular telephone operator in Ouagadougou, Bobo-Dioulasso and 19 other towns; 80% owned by Orascom Telecom (Egypt); Dir-Gen. DIMITRI W. OUÉDRAOGO; 1,696,655 subscribers (Dec. 2003).

Regulatory Authority

Autorité de Régulation des Communications Electroniques et des Postes (ARCEP): ave Dimdolobsom, porte 43, rue 3 angle rue 48, 01 BP 6437, Ouagadougou 01; tel. 50-37-53-60; fax 50-37-53-64; e-mail secretariat@arcep.bf; internet www.arce.bf; f. 2009 to replace Autorité Nationale de Régulation des Télécommunications (ARTEL);

Pres. of the Council of Administration BÉLI MATHURIN BAKO; Dir-Gen. SIBIRI OUATTARA.

BROADCASTING

In 2010 there were some 112 radio stations and 14 television stations operating in Burkina Faso.

Regulatory Authority

Conseil Supérieur de la Communication (Higher Council of Communication): 290 ave Ho Chi Minh, 01 BP 6618, Ouagadougou 01; tel. 50-50-11-24; fax 50-50-11-33; e-mail info@csi.bf; internet www.csi.bf; f. 1995 as Higher Council of Information, present name adopted 2005; Pres. MARIE NOËLLIE BÉATRICE DAMIBA; Sec.-Gen. JEAN-PAUL KONSEIBO.

Radio

Radiodiffusion-Télévision du Burkina (RTB): 01 BP 2530, Ouagadougou 01; tel. 50-31-83-53; fax 50-32-48-09; internet www.rtb.bf; f. 2001; Dir-Gen. YACOUBA TRAORÉ.

Horizon FM: 01 BP 2714, Ouagadougou 01; tel. 50-33-23-23; fax 50-50-21-41; e-mail hfm@grouphorizonfm.com; internet www.grouphorizonfm.com; f. 1990; private commercial station; broadcasts in French, English and 8 vernacular languages; operates 10 stations nationally; Dir JUDITH IDA SAWADOGO.

Ouaga FM: blvd France-Afrique, Ouagadougou; tel. 50-37-51-21; fax 50-37-61-77; internet www.ouagafm.bf; Pres. JOACHIM BAKY; Dir-Gen. ZAKARIDJA GNIENHOUN.

Radio Nationale du Burkina (La RNB): 03 BP 7029, Ouagadougou 03; tel. 50-32-43-02; fax 50-31-04-41; e-mail radio@rtb.bf; internet www.radio.bf; f. 1959; state radio service; comprises national broadcaster of informative and discussion programmes, music stations *Canal Arc-En-Ciel* and *Canal Arc-en-Ciel Plus*, and 2 regional stations, broadcasting in local languages, in Bobo-Dioulasso and Gaoua; Dir OUÉZIN LOUIS OULON.

Radio Evangile Développement (RED): 04 BP 8050, Ouagadougou 04; tel. 50-43-51-56; e-mail redbf@laposte.net; internet www.red-burkina.org; f. 1993; broadcasts from Ouagadougou, Bobo-Dioulasso, Ouahigouya, Léo, Houndé, Koudougou, Yako and Fada N'Gourma; evangelical Christian; Dir-Gen. ETIENNE KIEMDE.

Radio Locale-Radio Rurale: 03 BP 7029, Ouagadougou 03; tel. 50-31-27-81; fax 40-79-10-22; f. 1969; community broadcaster; local stations at Diapaga, Djibasso Gasson, Kongoussi, Orodara and Poura; Dir-Gen. BÉLIBIÉ SOUMAÏLA BASSOLE.

Radio Maria: BP 51, Koupela; tel. and fax 40-71-00-10; e-mail administration.bur@radiomaria.org; internet www.radiomaria.org; f. 1993; Roman Catholic; Dir BELEMSIGRI PIERRE CLAVER.

Radio Pulsar: Ave Léo Frobenius, 01 BP 5976, Ouagadougou 01; tel. 50-31-41-99; fax 50-50-75-45; e-mail info@monpulsar.com; internet www.monpulsar.com; f. 1996; Dir FRANÇOIS YESSO.

Radio Salankoloto-Association Galian: 01 BP 1095, Ouagadougou 01; tel. 50-31-64-93; fax 50-31-64-71; e-mail radiosalankoloto@cenatrin.bf; f. 1996; community broadcaster; Dir ROGER NIKIÉMA.

Radio Vive le Paysan: BP 75, Saponé; tel. 50-40-56-21; fax 50-50-52-80; e-mail a2oyigde@yahoo.fr; f. 1995; Dir ADRIEN VITAUX.

Savane FM: 10 BP 500, Ouagadougou 10; tel. 50-43-37-43; internet www.savanefm.bf; Dir-Gen. CHARLEMAGNE ABISSI.

Television

BF1: Ouagadougou; f. 2010; Dir-Gen. LÉOPOLD KOHOUN.

La Télévision Nationale du Burkina: 955 blvd de la Révolution, 01 BP 2530, Ouagadougou 01; tel. 50-31-83-53; fax 50-32-48-09; e-mail television@rtb.bf; internet www.tnb.bf; branch of Radiodiffusion-Télévision du Burkina (q.v.); broadcasts 75 hours per week; Dir PASCAL YEMBOINI THIOMBIANO.

Télévision Canal Viim Koéga—Fréquence Lumière: BP 108, Ouagadougou; tel. 50-50-76-40; e-mail cvktv@cvktv.org; internet www.cvktv.org; f. 1996; operated by the Fédération des Eglises et Missions Evangéliques; broadcasts 6 hours daily (Mon.–Fri.).

TV Canal 3: ave Kwamé N'Krumah, 11 BP 340, Ouagadougou 11; tel. 50-50-06-55; e-mail info@tvcanal3.com; internet www.tvcanal3.com; f. 2002.

TV Maria: Ouagadougou; f. 2009; Roman Catholic; Dir RACHEL ZONGO.

TVZ Africa: 145 ave de Kossodo, 01 BP 70170, Ouagadougou 01; tel. 70-26-28-20 (mobile); internet www.tvzafrica.com; commercial broadcaster; Pres. and Dir-Gen. MOUSTAPHA LAABLI THIOMBIANO.

Finance

(cap. = capital; res = reserves; dep. = deposits; m. = million; br(s). = branch(es); amounts in francs CFA)

BANKING

In 2012 there were 11 banks and five financial institutions in Burkina Faso.

Central Bank

Banque Centrale des Etats de l'Afrique de l'Ouest (BCEAO): ave Bassawarga, BP 356, Ouagadougou; tel. 50-50-60-15; fax 50-31-01-22; e-mail webmaster@bceao.int; internet www.bceao.int; HQ in Dakar, Senegal; f. 1962; bank of issue for the mem. states of the Union Economique et Monétaire Ouest-Africaine (UEMOA, comprising Benin, Burkina Faso, Côte d'Ivoire, Guinea-Bissau, Mali, Niger, Senegal and Togo); cap. 134,120m., res 1,474,195m., dep. 2,124,051m. (Dec. 2009); Gov. KONÉ TIÉMOKO MEYLIET; Dir in Burkina Faso CHARLES LUANGA KI-ZERBO; br. in Bobo-Dioulasso.

Other Banks

Bank of Africa—Burkina Faso (BOA—B): 770 ave du Président Sangoule Lamizana, 01 BP 1319, Ouagadougou 01; tel. 50-50-88-70; fax 50-50-88-74; e-mail information@boaburkinafaso.com; internet www.boaburkinafaso.com; f. 1998; cap. 8,000.0m., res 9,071.4m., dep. 302,886.2m. (Dec. 2012); Chair. MICHEL F. KAHN; 20 brs.

Banque Agricole et Commerciale du Burkina (BAC-B): 2 ave Gamal Abdel Nasser, Secteur 3, 01 BP 1644, Ouagadougou 01; tel. 50-33-33-33; fax 50-31-43-52; e-mail bacb@bacb.bf; internet www.bacb.bf; f. 1980; fmrly Caisse Nationale de Crédit Agricole du Burkina (CNCA-B); present name adopted 2002; 25% state-owned; cap. 3,500m., res 898m., dep. 70,108m. (Dec. 2006); Pres. TIBILA KABORE; Chair. and Gen. Man. LÉONCE KONÉ; 4 brs.

Banque Commerciale du Burkina (BCB): 653 ave Kwamé N'Krumah, 01 BP 1336, Ouagadougou 01; tel. 50-50-78-78; fax 50-31-06-28; e-mail bcb@bcb.bf; internet www.bcb.bf; f. 1988; 50% owned by Libyan Arab Foreign Bank, 25% state-owned, 25% owned by Caisse Nationale de Sécurité Sociale; cap. 26,125m., res –20,259m., dep. 68,756m. (Dec. 2011); Pres. JACQUES ZIDA; Gen. Man. ABDULLA EL MOGADAMI; 4 brs.

Banque Internationale pour le Commerce, l'Industrie et l'Agriculture du Burkina (BICIA—B): 479 ave Kwamé N'Krumah, 01 BP 08, Ouagadougou 01; tel. 50-31-31-31; fax 50-31-19-55; e-mail biciabq@fasonet.bf; internet www.biciab.bf; f. 1973; affiliated to BNP Paribas (France); 25% state-owned; cap. 5,000m., res 7,338m., dep. 127,687m. (Dec. 2008); Pres. MICHEL KOMPAORÉ; Dir-Gen. LUC VIDAL; 11 brs.

Ecobank Burkina: 49 rue de l'Hôtel de Ville, 01 BP 145, Ouagadougou 01; tel. 50-49-64-00; fax 50-31-89-81; e-mail ecobankbf@ecobank.com; internet www.ecobank.com; f. 1996; 82% owned by Ecobank Transnational Inc; cap. 7,495.0m., res 14,122.2m., dep. 339,507.9m. (Dec. 2012); Chair. BARTHÉLEMY DJIBANA DRABO; Dir-Gen. CHEIKH TRAVALY.

Société Générale de Banques au Burkina (SGBB): 248 rue de l'Hôtel de Ville, 01 BP 585, Ouagadougou 01; tel. 50-32-32-32; fax 50-31-05-61; e-mail sgbb.burkina@socgen.com; internet www.societegenerale.bf; f. 1998; 50% owned by Partie Burkinabè, 44% owned by Société Générale (France), 6% owned by FINADEI; cap. and res 5,510m., total assets 95,927m. (Dec. 2004); Dir-Gen. SIONLÉ YEO.

United Bank for Africa Burkina: 1340 ave Dimdolobsom, 01 BP 362, Ouagadougou 01; tel. 75-35-20-95 (mobile); fax 75-35-20-94 (mobile); e-mail info@bibburkinafaso.net; internet www.bibburkinafaso.net; f. 1974; 25% owned by Fonds Burkina de Développement Economique et Social, 24.2% owned by Holding COFIPA (Mali), 22.8% state-owned; fmrly Banque Internationale du Burkina; cap. 18,566.2m., res 11,210.0m., dep. 206,104.3m. (Dec. 2011); Pres. and Dir-Gen. ALPHONSE KADJO; 26 brs.

Credit Institutions

Burkina Bail, SA: 1035 ave du Dr Kwamé N'Krumah, Immeuble SODIFA, 01 BP 1913, Ouagadougou 01; tel. 50-33-26-33; fax 50-50-70-02; e-mail courrierdg@burkinabail.bf; internet www.burkinabail.bf; f. 1998; 28% owned by FBDES, 22% owned by Africapitalpartners, 15% owned by BOAD, 15% owned by BIDC, 15% by FSA, 5% owned by others; total assets 6,478m. (Dec. 2012); CEO KOUAFILANN ABDOULAYE SORY.

Réseau des Caisses Populaires du Burkina (RCPB): Ouagadougou; tel. 50-50-48-41; internet www.rcpb.bf; f. 1972; Dir-Gen. DAOUDA SAWADOGA; 450,000 mems (2006), 104 co-operatives.

Société Burkinabè de Financement (SOBFI): Immeuble Nassa, 1242 ave Dr Kwamé N'Krumah, 10 BP 13876, Ouagadougou 10; tel. 50-31-80-04; fax 50-33-71-62; e-mail sobfi@fasonet.bf; f. 1997; cap. 500.0m., total assets 2,850.9m. (Dec. 2002); Pres. DIAWAR DIACK.

Bankers' Association

Association Professionnelle des Banques et Etablissements Financiers du Burkina (APBEF-B): 1021 ave de la Cathédrale, 01 BP 6215, Ouagadougou 01; tel. 50-31-20-65; fax 50-31-20-66; e-mail apbef@fasonet.bf; f. 1967; Vice-Pres. MAMADI NAPON.

STOCK EXCHANGE

Bourse Régionale des Valeurs Mobilières (BRVM): s/c Chambre de Commerce et d'Industrie du Burkina, 01 BP 502, Ouagadougou 01; tel. 50-50-87-73; fax 50-50-87-19; e-mail louedraogo@brvm.org; internet www.brvm.org; f. 1998; national branch of BRVM (regional stock exchange based in Abidjan, Côte d'Ivoire, serving the member states of UEMOA); Man. LÉOPOLD OUÉDRAOGO.

INSURANCE

In 2008 there were 10 insurance companies in Burkina Faso.

Allianz Burkina Assurances: 99 ave Léo Frobénius, 01 BP 398, Ouagadougou 01; tel. 50-50-62-04; fax 50-31-01-53; e-mail allianz.burkina@allianz-bf.com; internet www.allianz-burkina.com; f. 1978; name changed as above in 2009; subsidiary of Allianz (France); non-life insurance and reinsurance; cap. 400m.; Dir-Gen. THIERRY BROUSSOU; also **Allianz Burkina Assurances Vie**, life insurance; Dir-Gen. THIERRY BROUSSOU.

Générale des Assurances: ave du Président Aboubacar Sangoulé Lamizana, 01 BP 6275, Ouagadougou 01; tel. 50-31-77-75; fax 50-50-87-17; e-mail g.assur@fasonet.bf; internet www.generaledesassurances.com; Dir-Gen. (life insurance) SIMON PIERRE GOUEM; Dir-Gen. (non-life insurance) AUGUSTIN LOADA.

Gras Savoye Burkina Faso: ave de la Résistance du 17 mai, 01 BP 1304, Ouagadougou 01; tel. 50-50-51-69; fax 50-50-51-73; internet www.ga.grassavoye.com; affiliated to Gras Savoye (France); Dir-Gen. LAURENT SAWADOGO.

Raynal SA: ave du Kwamé N'Krumah, 01 BP 6131, Ouagadougou 01; tel. 50-50-25-12; fax 50-50-25-14; e-mail raynal-sa@raynal-sa.com; Dir-Gen. REYNATOU ELÉONOR BADO YAMEOGO.

Société Nationale d'Assurances et de Réassurances (SONAR): 284 ave de Loudun, 01 BP 406, Ouagadougou 01; tel. 50-33-46-66; fax 50-50-89-75; e-mail sonarinfo@sonar.bf; internet www.sonar.bf; f. 1974; 42% owned by Burkinabè interests, 33% by French, Ivorian and US cos, 22% state-owned; life and non-life; cap. 720m. (SONAR-IARD, non-life), 500m. (SONAR-Vie, life); Dir-Gen. ANDRÉ B. BAYALA; 9 brs and sub-brs.

Union des Assurances du Burkina (UAB): 08 BP 11041, Ouagadougou 08; tel. 50-31-26-15; fax 50-31-26-20; e-mail uab@fasonet.bf; f. 1991; 11% owned by AXA Assurances Côte d'Ivoire; cap. 1,000m.; Pres. APPOLINAIRE COMPAORÉ; Dir-Gen. (non-life insurance) JEAN DASMASCÈNE NIGNAN; Dir-Gen. (life insurance) SOUMAÏLA SORGHO.

Trade and Industry

GOVERNMENT AGENCIES

Bureau des Mines et de la Géologie du Burkina (BUMIGEB): 4186 route de Fada N'Gourma, 01 BP 601, Ouagadougou 01; tel. 50-36-48-02; fax 50-36-48-88; e-mail bumigeb@cenatrin.bf; internet www.bumigeb.bf; f. 1978; restructured 1997; research into geological and mineral resources; Pres. BOURI ROGER ZOMBRE; Dir-Gen. PASCALE DIENDÉRÉ.

Comptoir Burkinabè des Métaux Précieux (CBMP): Ouagadougou; tel. 50-50-75-48; fax 50-31-56-34; promotes gold sector, liaises with artisanal producers; transfer to private management pending; Dir-Gen. YACOUBA BARRY.

Office National du Commerce Extérieur (ONAC): 30 ave de l'UEMOA, 01 BP 389, Ouagadougou 01; tel. 50-31-13-00; fax 50-31-14-69; e-mail info@onac.bf; internet www.tradepoint.bf; f. 1974; promotes and supervises external trade; Man. Dir BAYA JUSTIN BAYILI; br. at Bobo-Dioulasso.

DEVELOPMENT ORGANIZATIONS

Agence Française de Développement (AFD): 52 ave de la Nation, 01 BP 529, Ouagadougou 01; tel. 50-50-60-92; fax 50-31-19-66; e-mail afdouagadougou@bf.groupe-afd.org; internet www.afd.fr; Country Dir PASCAL COLLANGE.

Autorité de Régulation des Marchés Publics: 01 BP 2080, Ouagadougou 01; tel. 50-50-69-01; fax 50-50-53-01; e-mail armp@armp.bf; internet www.armp.bf; f. 2007; Perm. Sec. MAMADOU GUIRA.

Bureau d'Appui aux Micro-entreprises (BAME): BP 610, Bobo-Dioulasso; tel. 20-97-16-28; fax 20-97-21-76; f. 1991; supports small business; Dir FÉLIX SANON.

Cellule d'Appui à la Petite et Moyenne Entreprise d'Ouagadougou (CAPEO): 01 BP 6443, Ouagadougou 01; tel. 50-31-37-62; fax 50-31-37-64; internet www.spid.com/capeo; f. 1991; supports small and medium-sized enterprises.

France Volontaires: 01 BP 947, Ouagadougou 01; tel. 50-50-70-43; fax 50-50-10-72; internet www.france-volontaires.org; f. 1973 as Association Française des Volontaires du Progrès; name changed as above in 2009; supports small business; Nat. Delegate EUGÈNE SOME.

Promotion du Développement Industriel, Artisanal et Agricole (PRODIA): Secteur 8, Gounghin, 01 BP 2344, Ouagadougou 01; tel. 50-34-31-11; fax 50-34-71-47; f. 1981; supports small business; Dir (vacant).

CHAMBERS OF COMMERCE

Chambre de Commerce et d'Industrie du Burkina Faso (CCI-BF): 118/220 ave de Lyon, 01 BP 502, Ouagadougou 01; tel. 50-50-61-14; fax 50-50-61-16; e-mail info@cci.bf; internet www.cci.bf; f. 1948; Pres. ALIZÈTA OUÉDRAOGO; Dir-Gen. FRANCK TAPSOBA; brs in Bobo-Dioulasso, Koupéla and Ouahigouya.

Chambre des Mines du Burkina (CMB): 01 BP 126, Ouagadougou; tel. 50-50-60-91; e-mail cmb@chambredesmines.bf; internet www.chambredesmines.bf; f. 2011; Pres. ELIE JUSTIN OUÉDRAOGO; Sec.-Gen. ABOUBAKAR SIDIKOU.

EMPLOYERS' ORGANIZATIONS

Club des Hommes d'Affaires Franco-Burkinabè (CHAFB): 01 BP 6890, Ouagadougou 01; tel. 70-21-20-20 (mobile); fax 50-31-32-81; internet chafb.bf; f. 1990; represents 65 major enterprises and seeks to develop trading relations between Burkina Faso and France; Pres. CHANTAL COMPTE NIKIÈMA.

Conseil National du Patronat Burkinabè (CNPB): 1221 ave du Dr Kwame N'Krumah, 01 BP 1482, Ouagadougou 01; tel. 50-33-03-09; fax 50-50-03-08; e-mail cnpb@liptinfor.bf; internet www.patronat.bf; f. 1974; comprises 70 professional groupings; Pres. BIRAHIMA NACOULMA; Sec.-Gen. PHILOMÈNE YAMEOGO.

Groupement Professionnel des Industriels (GPI): Immeuble CBC, 641 ave Koubemba, 01 BP 5381, Ouagadougou 01; tel. and fax 50-50-11-59; e-mail gpi@fasonet.bf; internet www.gpi.bf; f. 1974; Pres. SANOH MAMADY.

Fédération Nationale des Exportateurs du Burkina (FENEB): 01 BP 389, Ouagadougou 01; tel. 50-31-13-00; fax 50-31-14-69; e-mail fofseydou@hotmail.com; Permanent Sec. SEYDOU FOFANA.

Jeune Chambre Internationale du Burkina Faso: Immeuble Kanazoe, ave du Travail, 11 BP 136, Ouagadougou; tel. 78-85-40-41 (mobile); e-mail kroser73@yahoo.fr; internet www.jci.cc/local/burkina; f. 1976; org. of entrepreneurs aged 18–40; affiliated to Junior Chambers International, Inc; Exec. Pres. K. RODOLPHE S. DJIGUIMDE.

Maison de l'Entreprise du Burkina Faso (MEBF): rue 3-1119, porte 132, 11 BP 379, Ouagadougou 11; tel. 50-39-80-60; fax 50-39-80-62; e-mail info@me.bf; internet www.me.bf; f. 2002; promotes devt of the private sector; Pres. ALAIN ROGER COEFE; Dir-Gen. ISSAKA KARGOUGOU.

Syndicat des Commerçants Importateurs et Exportateurs du Burkina (SCIMPEX): ave Kadiogo, Secteur 2, Immeuble CBC, 1er étage, 01 BP 552, Ouagadougou 01; tel. 50-31-18-70; fax 50-31-30-36; e-mail scimpex@fasonet.bf; internet www.scimpex-bf.com; f. 1959; Pres. LASSINÉ DIAWARA.

Union Nationale des Producteurs de Coton du Burkina Faso (UNPCB): 02 BP 1677, Bobo-Dioulasso 02; tel. 20-97-33-10; fax 20-97-20-59; e-mail unpcb@fasonet.bf; internet www.abcburkina.net/unpcb/unpcb_index.htm; f. 1998; Pres. KARIM TRAORÉ.

UTILITIES

Electricity

Société Générale de Travaux et de Constructions Electriques (SOGETEL): Zone Industrielle, Gounghin, 01 BP 429, Ouagadougou 01; tel. 50-50-23-45; fax 50-34-25-70; e-mail sogetel@cenatrin.bf; internet www.cenatrin.bf/sogetel; transport and distribution of electricity.

Société Nationale Burkinabè d'Electricité (SONABEL): 55 ave de la Nation, 01 BP 54, Ouagadougou 01; tel. 50-50-61-00; fax 50-31-03-40; e-mail courrier@sonabel.bf; internet www.sonabel.bf; f. 1984; state-owned; production and distribution of electricity; Dir-Gen. SIENGUI APOLLINAIRE KI.

Water

Office National de l'Eau et de l'Assainissement (ONEA): 01 BP 170, Ouagadougou 01; tel. 50-43-19-00; fax 50-43-19-11; e-mail onea@fasonet.bf; internet www.oneabf.com; f. 1977; storage, purification and distribution of water; transferred to private management (by Veolia Water Burkina Faso) in 2001; Dir-Gen. HAROUNA YAMBA OUIBIGA.

Veolia Water Burkina Faso: 06 BP 9525, Ouagadougou 06; tel. and fax 50-34-03-00; manages operation of water distribution and sewerage services; subsidiary of Veolia Environnement (France).

CO-OPERATIVE

Union des Coopératives Agricoles et Maraîchères du Burkina (UCOBAM): 01 BP 277, Ouagadougou 01; tel. 50-50-65-27; fax 50-50-65-28; e-mail ucobam@zcp.bf; internet www.ucobam.bf; f. 1968; comprises 8 regional co-operative unions (6,500 mems, representing 35,000 producers); production and marketing of fruit, vegetables, jams and conserves; Dir-Gen. YASSIA OUÉDRAOGO.

TRADE UNIONS

Confédération Générale du Travail Burkina (CGTB): 01 BP 547, Ouagadougou 01; tel. and fax 50-31-36-71; e-mail info@cgtb.bf; internet www.cgtb.bf; f. 1988; confed. of several autonomous trade unions; Sec.-Gen. TOLÉ SAGNON.

Confédération Nationale des Travailleurs Burkinabè (CNTB): 584 ave du Dr Kwamé N'Krumah, 01 BP 445, Ouagadougou 01; tel. 50-31-23-95; e-mail cntb@fasonet.bf; internet www.cntb-bf.org; f. 1972; Sec.-Gen. AUGUSTIN BLAISE HIEN; 10,000 mems.

Confédération Syndicale Burkinabè (CSB): 01 BP 1921, Ouagadougou 01; tel. and fax 50-31-83-98; e-mail cosybu2000@yahoo.fr; f. 1974; mainly public service unions; Sec.-Gen. JEAN MATHIAS LILIOU.

Organisation Nationale des Syndicats Libres (ONSL): 01 BP 99, Ouagadougou 01; tel. and fax 50-34-34-69; e-mail onslbf@yahoo.fr; f. 1960; Sec.-Gen. PAUL NOBILA KABORÉ; 6,000 mems.

Union Syndicale des Travailleurs Burkinabè (USTB): BP 381, Ouagadougou; tel. and fax 50-33-73-09; f. 1958; Sec.-Gen. MAMADOU NAMA; 35,000 mems in 45 affiliated orgs.

Transport

RAILWAY

In 2010 the total length of track in operation was 622 km.

SITARAIL—Transport Ferroviaire de Personnes et de Marchandises: rue Dioncolo, 01 BP 5699, Ouagadougou 01; tel. 50-31-07-35; fax 50-50-85-21; 67% owned by Groupe Bolloré, 15% state-owned, 15% owned by Govt of Côte d'Ivoire; national branch of SITARAIL (based in Abidjan, Côte d'Ivoire); responsible for operations on the railway line between Kaya, Ouagadougou and Abidjan; Regional Dir MOURAMANE FOFANA.

Société de Gestion du Patrimoine Ferroviaire du Burkina (SOPAFER—B): 93 rue de la Culture, 01 BP 192, Ouagadougou 01; tel. 50-31-35-99; fax 50-31-35-94; e-mail dgsopafer@liptinfor.bf; f. 1995; railway network services; Dir-Gen. AHAMADO OUÉDRAGO.

ROADS

In 2004 there were an estimated 92,495 km of roads, including 15,271 km of highways.

Fonds d'Entretien Routier du Burkina (FER): 01 BP 2517, Ouagadougou 01; Dir-Gen. MAMADOU OUATTARA.

Société Africaine de Transports Routiers (SATR): 01 BP 5298, Ouagadougou 01; tel. 50-34-08-62.

Société Nationale du Transit du Burkina (SNTB): 474 rue Ilboudo Waogyandé, 01 BP 1192, Ouagadougou 01; tel. 50-49-30-00; fax 50-50-85-21; f. 1977; 82% owned by Groupe SAGA (France), 12% state-owned; road haulage and warehousing; Dir-Gen. RÉGIS TISSIER.

Société de Transport en Commun de Ouagadougou (SOTRACO): 2257 ave du Sanematenga, 01 BP 5665 Ouagadougou 01; tel. 50-35-67-87; fax 50-35-66-80; e-mail sotraco@fasonet.bf; internet sotraco-bf.net; f. 2003; Dir-Gen. BOUREIMA TARNAGDA.

CIVIL AVIATION

There are international airports at Ouagadougou and Bobo-Dioulasso, 49 small airfields and 13 private airstrips. Plans were announced in 2006 for the construction of a new international airport at Donsin, 35 km north-east of the capital; the first phase of the project from 2007–11 was to cost some 115,000m. francs CFA. Two subsequent phases were projected to extend until 2023.

Air Burkina: 29 ave de la Nation, 01 BP 1459, Ouagadougou 01; tel. 50-49-23-70; fax 50-31-31-65; e-mail resa@airburkina.bf; internet www.air-burkina.com; f. 1967 as Air Volta; 56% owned by Aga Khan Group, 14% state-owned; operates domestic and regional services; Dir MOHAMED GHELALA.

Tourism

Burkina Faso, which possesses some 2.8m. ha of nature reserves, is considered to provide some of the best opportunities to observe wild animals in West Africa. Some big game hunting is permitted. Several important cultural events are also held in Burkina Faso: the biennial pan-African film festival, FESPACO, is held in Ouagadougou, as is the biennial international exhibition of handicrafts, while Bobo-Dioulasso hosts the biennial week of national culture. In 2011 there were 238,000 foreign visitors and receipts from tourism were estimated at US $133m.

Office National du Tourisme Burkinabè (ONTB): ave Frobénius, BP 1318, Ouagadougou; tel. 50-31-19-59; fax 50-31-44-34; e-mail ontb@ontb.bf; internet www.ontb.bf; Dir-Gen. SOULÉMANE OUÉDRAOGO.

Defence

National service is voluntary, and lasts for two years on a part-time basis. As assessed at November 2013, the armed forces numbered 11,200 (army 6,400, air force 600, paramilitary gendarmerie 4,200). There was also a 'security company' of 250 and a part-time people's militia of 45,000.

Defence Expenditure: Estimated at 78,400m. francs CFA in 2014.

Chief of the General Staff of the Armed Forces and Chief of Staff of the Army: Col-Maj. HONORÉ NABÉRÉ TRAORÉ.

Education

Education is provided free of charge, and is officially compulsory for 10 years between the ages of six and 16. Primary education begins at six years of age and lasts for six years, comprising three cycles of two years each. Secondary education, beginning at the age of 13, lasts for a further seven years, comprising a first cycle of four years and a second of three years. Enrolment levels are among the lowest in the region. According to UNESCO estimates, in 2012 primary enrolment included 66% (boys 68%; girls 65%) of children in the relevant age-group, while secondary enrolment included only 20% of children in the appropriate age-group (boys 22%; girls 18%). There are three state-owned higher education institutions: a university in Ouagadougou, a polytechnic university at Bobo-Dioulasso and an institute of teacher training at Koudougou. There are also 11 private higher education institutions. The number of students enrolled at tertiary-level institutions in 2012 was 68,900. In 2011 spending on education was budgeted at 23.3% of total budgeted government expenditure.

BURUNDI

Introductory Survey

LOCATION, CLIMATE, LANGUAGE, RELIGION, FLAG, CAPITAL

The Republic of Burundi is a landlocked country lying on the eastern shore of Lake Tanganyika, in central Africa, a little south of the Equator. It is bordered by Rwanda to the north, by Tanzania to the south and east, and by the Democratic Republic of the Congo (formerly Zaire) to the west. The climate is tropical (hot and humid) in the lowlands, and cool in the highlands, with an irregular rainfall. The population is composed of three ethnic groups: the Hutu (85%), the Tutsi (14%) and the Twa (1%). The official languages are French and Kirundi, while Swahili is used, in addition to French, in commercial circles. Some 70% of the inhabitants profess Christianity, with the great majority of the Christians being Roman Catholics. A large minority still adhere to traditional animist beliefs. The national flag (proportions 3 by 5) consists of a white diagonal cross on a background of red (above and below) and green (hoist and fly), with a white circle, containing three green-edged red stars, in the centre. The capital is Bujumbura.

CONTEMPORARY POLITICAL HISTORY

Historical Context

Burundi (formerly Urundi) became part of German East Africa in 1899. In 1916 the territory was occupied by Belgian forces from the Congo (now the Democratic Republic of the Congo, DRC). Subsequently, as part of Ruanda-Urundi, it was administered by Belgium under a League of Nations mandate and later as a UN Trust Territory. Elections in September 1961, conducted under UN supervision, were won by the Union pour le Progrès National (UPRONA). Internal self-government was granted in January 1962 and full independence on 1 July, when the two parts of the Trust Territory became separate states, as Burundi and Rwanda. Tensions between Burundi's two main ethnic groups, the Tutsi (traditionally the dominant tribe, despite representing a minority of the overall population) and the Hutu, escalated during 1965. Following an unsuccessful attempt by the Hutu to overthrow the Tutsi-dominated Government in October, nearly all the Hutu political élite were executed, eliminating any significant participation by the Hutu in Burundi's political life until the late 1980s.

Burundi was declared a republic in June 1966, and UPRONA became the sole legal party in July 1974. However, in 1976 members of the armed forces, led by Lt-Col (later Col) Jean-Baptiste Bagaza, effected a coup. Bagaza was appointed President by the Supreme Revolutionary Council (composed of army officers), and a new Council of Ministers was formed. The first national congress of UPRONA was held in December 1979, and a party Central Committee, headed by Bagaza, assumed the functions of the Supreme Revolutionary Council in January 1980. A new Constitution, adopted by national referendum in November 1981, provided for the establishment of a unicameral legislature, the Assemblée Nationale (National Assembly). The first legislative elections were held in October 1982. Having been re-elected President of UPRONA in July 1984, Bagaza, the sole candidate, was elected President of Burundi in August, winning 99.6% of the votes cast.

In September 1987 Bagaza was deposed in a military coup, led by Maj. Pierre Buyoya, who accused Bagaza of corruption. Buyoya immediately formed a Comité Militaire pour le Salut National (Military Committee for National Salvation—CMSN) to administer the country. The Constitution was suspended, and the National Assembly was dissolved. On 2 October Buyoya was inaugurated as President of the Third Republic.

In August 1988 tribal tensions erupted into violence in the north of the country when groups of Hutus, claiming Tutsi provocation, slaughtered hundreds of Tutsis in the towns of Ntega and Marangara. The Tutsi-dominated army was immediately dispatched to the region to restore order, and large-scale tribal massacres occurred. In October Buyoya announced government changes, including the appointment of a Hutu, Adrien Sibomana, as Prime Minister, and established a committee to investigate the massacres; nevertheless, political tension persisted.

Domestic Political Affairs

In May 1990, in response to a new draft charter on national unity, Buyoya announced plans to replace military rule with a 'democratic constitution under a one-party government'. In December the CMSN was abolished and its functions transferred to an 80-member Central Committee, with Buyoya as Chairman and with a Hutu, Nicolas Mayugi, as Secretary-General. At a referendum in February 1991 the draft charter on national unity was overwhelmingly approved. Later that month a ministerial reorganization, in which Hutus received 12 of the 23 government portfolios, was viewed with scepticism by political opponents. Proposals to establish a multi-party parliamentary system received the support of more than 90% of the voters in a referendum held on 9 March 1992, and the new Constitution was promulgated on 13 March.

In an extensive government reorganization in April 1992, Hutus were appointed to 15 of the 25 ministries, while Buyoya relinquished the defence portfolio. In the same month Buyoya approved legislation relating to the creation of new political parties in accordance with the new Constitution. New political parties were to be obliged to demonstrate impartiality with regard to ethnic or regional origin, gender and religion, and were to refrain from militarization. In October Buyoya announced the creation of an electoral commission, which included representatives of the eight recognized political parties.

A presidential election on 1 June 1993 was won, with 64.8% of the votes cast, by Melchior Ndadaye, the candidate of the Front pour la Démocratie au Burundi (FRODEBU), who was also supported by the Rassemblement du Peuple Burundien (RPB), the Parti du Peuple and the Parti Libéral. Buyoya received 32.4% of the votes as the UPRONA candidate, with support from the Rassemblement pour la Démocratie et le Développement Economique et Social (RADDES) and the Parti Social Démocrate. At elections to the National Assembly, which were conducted on 29 June, FRODEBU secured 71% of the votes and 65 of the 81 contested seats; UPRONA, with 21.4% of the votes, obtained the remaining 16 seats. Ndadaye, Burundi's first Hutu Head of State, assumed the presidency on 10 July. A Tutsi, Sylvie Kinigi, became Prime Minister, while the new Council of Ministers included a further six Tutsi representatives.

On 21 October 1993 more than 100 army paratroopers occupied the presidential palace and the headquarters of the national broadcasting company. Ndadaye and several other prominent Hutu politicians and officials were detained and subsequently killed by the insurgents, who later proclaimed François Ngeze, one of the few Hutu members of UPRONA and a minister in the Government of former President Buyoya, as head of a Comité National du Salut Public (National Committee of Public Salvation—CNSP). While members of the Government sought refuge abroad and in the offices of foreign diplomatic missions in Bujumbura, the armed forces declared a state of emergency, closing national borders and the capital's airport. However, international condemnation of the coup, together with the scale of renewed tribal violence, undermined support for the insurgents from within the armed forces, and precipitated the collapse of the CNSP, which was dissolved on 25 October. Kinigi ended the curfew, but remained in hiding and urged the deployment of an international force in Burundi to protect the civilian Government. On 28 October the UN confirmed that the Government had resumed control of the country. Ngeze and 10 coup leaders were arrested, while some 40 other insurgents were believed to have fled to Zaire (now the DRC). Meanwhile, following division within FRODEBU, a 'hardline' leader, Léonard Nyangoma, established a new party, Conseil National pour la Défense de la Démocratie (CNDD), with an armed wing, the Forces pour la Défense de la Démocratie (FDD).

In early November 1993 several members of the Government, including Kinigi, left the French embassy with a small escort of French troops. On 8 November the Constitutional Court officially recognized the presidential vacancy resulting from the murder of both Ndadaye and his constitutional successor, Giles Bimazubute, the Speaker of the National Assembly, and stated that presidential power should be exercised by the Council of Ministers, pending a presidential election, which was to be conducted within three months. In December the Minister of External Relations and Co-operation, Sylvestre Ntibantunganya (who had succeeded Ndadaye as leader of FRODEBU), was elected Speaker of the National Assembly.

Meanwhile, in November 1993, following repeated requests by the Government for an international contribution to the protection of government ministers in Burundi, the Organization of African Unity (OAU—now the African Union—AU, see p. 186) agreed to the deployment of an 180-member protection force. In December opposition parties, including UPRONA and the RADDES, organized demonstrations in protest at the deployment of the contingent, scheduled for January 1994, claiming that it infringed Burundi's sovereignty. As a compromise, in March the Government secured a significant reduction in the size of the mission, to comprise a military contingent of 47 and 20 civilian observers; it was finally deployed in February 1995.

In early January 1994 FRODEBU deputies in the National Assembly approved a draft amendment to the Constitution, allowing a President of the Republic to be elected by the National Assembly, in the event of the Constitutional Court's recognition of a presidential vacancy. However, UPRONA deputies, who had boycotted the vote, protested that such a procedure represented election by indirect suffrage, in contravention of the Constitution. On 13 January, following the successful negotiation of a political truce with opposition parties, the FRODEBU candidate, Cyprien Ntaryamira (hitherto the Minister of Agriculture and Livestock), was elected President by the National Assembly. A Tutsi Prime Minister, Anatole Kanyenkiko, was appointed in early February, and the composition of a new multi-party Council of Ministers was subsequently agreed.

Ethnic violence

On 6 April 1994, returning from a regional summit meeting in Dar es Salaam, Tanzania, Ntaryamira and three government ministers were killed when the aircraft of the Rwandan President, Juvénal Habyarimana, in which they were travelling, exploded following a rocket attack above Kigali airport, Rwanda. Habyarimana, who was also killed, was widely acknowledged to have been the intended victim of the attack. On 8 April Ntibantunganya, the Speaker of the National Assembly, was confirmed (in accordance with the Constitution) as interim President for a three-month period.

Having discounted the possibility of organizing a general election, owing to security considerations, in June 1994 all major political parties joined lengthy negotiations to establish a procedure for the restoration of the presidency. The mandate of the interim President was extended for three months by the Constitutional Court in July, and by the end of August it had been decided that a new President would be elected by a broadly representative commission. A new power-sharing agreement, the Convention of Government, was announced on 10 September. Detailing the terms of government for a four-year transitional period (including the allocation of 45% of cabinet posts to opposition parties), it was incorporated into the Constitution on 22 September. The Convention also provided for the creation of a Conseil de Sécurité Nationale (National Security Council—CSN), which was formally inaugurated on 10 October. On 30 September the Convention elected Ntibantunganya to the presidency from a list of six candidates, and he was formally inaugurated on 1 October. In February 1995 Antoine Nduwayo, a UPRONA candidate selected in consultation with other opposition parties, was appointed Prime Minister by presidential decree. A new coalition Council of Ministers was announced on 1 March, but political stability was undermined immediately by the murder of the Hutu Minister of Energy and Mines, Ernest Kabushemeye.

An escalation in the scale and frequency of incidents of politically and ethnically motivated violence during 1995 prompted renewed concern that the security crisis would precipitate a large-scale campaign of ethnic massacres. Government-sponsored military initiatives were concentrated in Hutu-dominated suburbs of Bujumbura and in the north-east, where a campaign was waged against the alleged insurgent activities of the Parti de Libération du Peuple Hutu (PALIPEHUTU—a small, proscribed, Hutu opposition group), resulting in the deaths of hundreds of Hutu civilians. In December, following increasing reports of atrocities perpetrated against civilians by dissident elements of the Tutsi-led armed forces (including militia known as the *Sans Echecs*) and by extremist Hutu rebel groups, the UN Secretary-General urged the Security Council to sanction international military intervention in Burundi to address the crisis.

Representatives of some 13 political parties (including FRODEBU and UPRONA) participated in discussions that began in Mwanza, Tanzania, in April 1996, with mediation by the former President of Tanzania, Julius Nyerere. At a conference of regional powers in Arusha, Tanzania, in June, it was reported that Ntibantunganya and Nduwayo had requested foreign intervention to protect government installations. By July a regional technical commission to examine the request for 'security assistance' (comprising regional defence ministers) had convened in Arusha and had reached preliminary agreement, with UN support, for an intervention force. Meanwhile, significant differences with regard to the mandate of such a force had emerged between Ntibantunganya and Nduwayo (who suggested that the President was attempting to neutralize the country's military capability). At a mass rally in Bujumbura of Tutsi-dominated opposition parties, the Prime Minister joined other leaders in rejecting foreign military intervention. However, full endorsement of the Arusha proposal for intervention was subsequently recorded by member nations of the OAU at a summit meeting convened in Yaoundé, Cameroon.

Military coup: Buyoya declared transitional President

On 25 July 1996 the armed forces seized power in the capital. A statement issued by the Minister of National Defence, Lt-Col Firmin Sinzoyiheba, criticized the failure of the administration to safeguard national security, and announced the suspension of the National Assembly and all political activity, the imposition of a nationwide curfew and the closure of national borders and the airport at Bujumbura. Former President Buyoya was declared interim President of a transitional republic. Ntibantunganya conveyed his refusal to relinquish office, but Nduwayo resigned, attributing his failure to effect national reconciliation principally to Ntibantunganya's ineffective leadership. In response to widespread external condemnation of the coup, Buyoya announced that a largely civilian government of national unity would be promptly installed, and that future negotiations with all Hutu groups would be considered. The forced repatriation of Rwandan Hutu refugees was halted with immediate effect.

Despite the appointment at the end of July 1996 of Pascal-Firmin Ndimira, a Hutu member of UPRONA, as Prime Minister, and an urgent attempt by Buyoya to obtain regional support, the leaders of Ethiopia, Kenya, Rwanda, Tanzania, Uganda and Zaire, meeting in Arusha, under OAU auspices, declared their intention to impose stringent economic sanctions against the new regime unless constitutional government was restored immediately. In early August sanctions were imposed, and in the same month the establishment of a new multi-ethnic Cabinet was announced. In mid-August Buyoya declared that an expanded transitional National Assembly, incorporating existing elected deputies, would be inaugurated during September for a three-year period, but sanctions were maintained due to the continued suspension of the Constitution. Buyoya was formally sworn in as President on 27 September.

By late 1996 the military action in eastern Zaire had led to the repatriation of 30,000 Burundians and had severely weakened FDD fighting capacity. In January 1997 the office of the UN High Commissioner for Refugees (UNHCR) reported that the army had massed more than 100,000 (mainly Hutu) civilians in camps, as part of a 'regroupment' scheme, which the authorities claimed to be an initiative to protect villagers in areas of rebel activity.-Buyoya attended the fourth Arusha summit meeting on the Burundi conflict in April, where the leaders of the Great Lakes countries agreed to ease economic sanctions in the interest of alleviating conditions for the civilian population. The full revocation of sanctions was made dependent on the opening of direct, unconditional peace talks between the Burundian Government and opposition.

On 1 January 1998 an attack on Bujumbura airport by more than 1,000 Hutu rebels resulted in at least 250 deaths. Similar attacks, although on a smaller scale, continued during early 1998. Following negotiations between the Government and the National Assembly concerning the expiry of FRODEBU's electoral mandate, in early June Buyoya and the parliamentary Speaker, Léonce Ngendakumana, signed a political accord, and a new transitional Constitution was promulgated. The new charter provided for institutional reforms, including the creation of two vice-presidencies to replace the office of Prime Minister, the enlargement of the National Assembly from 81 to

121 seats, and the creation of a seven-member Constitutional Court. In accordance with the transitional Constitution, Buyoya was inaugurated as President on 11 June. On the following day the two Vice-Presidents were appointed: Frédérique Bavuginyumvira, a senior member of FRODEBU, who was allocated responsibility for political and administrative affairs, and Mathias Sinamenye (a Tutsi and hitherto the Governor of the central bank), with responsibility for economic and social issues. A new Council of Ministers included 13 Hutus and eight Tutsis. The newly enlarged National Assembly, which was inaugurated in mid-July, incorporated nine representatives from smaller political parties, together with 27 civilian representatives and 21 new representatives of FRODEBU to replace those who had been killed or had fled into exile. Meanwhile, in May dissension between the political and military wings of the CNDD resulted in a division of the organization, into a faction headed by Nyangoma (which retained the name CNDD) and a larger faction comprising most of its armed forces, led by the FDD Chief of Staff, Jean-Bosco Ndayikengurukiye (which became known as the CNDD—FDD).

At a regional summit meeting, which took place in Arusha in January 1999, following an appeal from the UN Security Council earlier in the month, regional heads of state voted to suspend the economic sanctions, although they emphasized that the eventual lifting of the sanctions would be dependent on progress made at inter-party peace talks. However, the continuing discussions failed to result in agreement on a peace plan, with the absence from the negotiations of the two most significant rebel movements, the CNDD—FDD and an armed wing of PALIPEHUTU, known as Forces Nationales de Libération (FNL), regarded as a major impediment. Following the death of Nyerere in October, the former President of South Africa, Nelson Mandela, was nominated as the new mediator of the peace negotiations in December.

Peace negotiations (the first to be attended by Mandela) resumed in Arusha in February 2000. At a further round of discussions in Arusha in March, agreement was reached on draft proposals to fulfil a main requirement for equal representation of Hutu and Tutsi in the armed forces. In July Ndayikengurukiye, as leader of the CNDD—FDD, for the first time accepted an invitation by Mandela to participate in the peace negotiations. In the same month the drafting of a peace accord was finalized; the agreement stipulated the terms for the establishment of a transitional government for a period of three years, the integration of former Hutu rebels into the armed forces, and the creation of an electoral system that would ensure power-sharing between the Tutsi and the Hutu. At a summit meeting, which was attended by several regional heads of state in Arusha, negotiating groups were presented with the draft peace agreement. However, the CNDD—FDD demanded the release by the authorities of political prisoners and bilateral negotiations with the armed forces, as a precondition to the cessation of hostilities. (The FNL had again failed to attend the discussions.) On 28 August the peace agreement was formally endorsed by representatives of the Government, the National Assembly, seven Hutu political associations and seven Tutsi parties. The remaining three Tutsi groups that had attended the previous negotiations subsequently signed the accord at ceasefire discussions, which took place in Nairobi, Kenya, in late September, following assurances by Mandela that measures would be taken to ensure that the Hutu rebels cease hostilities. At the same time an Implementation and Monitoring Committee, comprising representatives of the negotiating parties, and international and civil society representatives, was established.

In January 2001 14 of the 19 signatories of the peace accord agreed on the composition of a new National Assembly, which would allocate Hutu parties 60% and Tutsi 40% representation in the legislature. Nevertheless, hostilities between government troops and Hutu rebels continued, and at the end of February the FNL launched an offensive on the northern outskirts of Bujumbura, which resulted in some 50,000 civilians fleeing to the centre of the capital. Government forces regained control of Bujumbura by early March, but heavy fighting continued in regions outlying the capital. Later that month CNDD—FDD forces launched a major attack against the principal town of Gitega, 100 km east of Bujumbura, which was repelled by government troops. On 18 April, while Buyoya was attending peace negotiations with the CNDD—FDD leadership in Gabon, Tutsi army officers seized control of the state radio station in Bujumbura and announced that the Government had been overthrown. Troops loyal to Buyoya rapidly suppressed the coup attempt, and about 40 members of the armed forces were subsequently arrested in connection with the uprising.

Peace agreement and power-sharing Government

In late July 2001 Mandela chaired a peace summit of regional heads of state in Arusha at which the signatory groups to the Arusha accord finally reached agreement on the nature of the transitional leadership. A new multi-party transitional government, according the Hutu and Tutsi ethnic groups balanced representation, was to be installed on 1 November. The Secretary-General of FRODEBU, Domitien Ndayizeye, was nominated to the vice-presidency of the transitional administration. Buyoya was to continue in the office of President for 18 months (from 1 November), after which time he was to transfer the office to Ndayizeye. However, the CNDD—FDD and the FNL persisted in rejecting the peace accord, while one of the principal Tutsi opposition parties, the Parti pour le Redressement National (PARENA), refused to join the proposed new government.

Following further negotiations in Arusha and in Pretoria, South Africa, in early October 2001, agreement was reached on the composition of the new 26-member transitional Government. FRODEBU and UPRONA were the most dominant parties in the new power-sharing administration, while portfolios were allocated to a further 13 parties that had signed the Arusha agreement. (In total, Hutus received 14 of the 26 ministerial posts.) On 29 October a transitional Constitution, which was drafted by a technical law commission and included principles incorporated in the previous Constitution of 1992 and the Arusha peace accord, was formally adopted by the National Assembly. The new transitional Constitution provided for the establishment of an upper legislative chamber, the Sénat (Senate), and four new commissions to assist in the peace and reconciliation process. Former combatants belonging to political movements were to be integrated into the armed and security forces during the transitional period. Also at the end of October the South African Government dispatched troops to Burundi as part of a proposed 700-member contingent, in an effort, initiated by Mandela, to enforce national security and support the transitional authorities. In a reversal to the peace efforts, however, the CNDD—FDD had divided, with the emergence of a new faction, led by Maj. Jean-Pierre Nkurunziza, which commanded the support of most of the movement's combatants.

On 1 November 2001 the newly established transitional Government was officially installed, as scheduled. However, the FNL continued to launch attacks on the outskirts of Bujumbura, despite the deployment of the South African troops. In January 2002 the Constitutional Court endorsed the nomination to the transitional National Assembly of a number of deputies, representing civil society and 14 of the political parties that had signed the peace agreement. (FRODEBU and UPRONA retained their seats in the chamber.) Jean Minani, the Chairman of FRODEBU, was subsequently elected Speaker of the National Assembly. At the end of that month the Constitutional Court approved the establishment of a 51-member Senate.

Efforts to bring about a ceasefire in the civil conflict continued, with a series of meetings in Pretoria in February 2002. The South African Deputy President, Jacob Zuma (who had replaced Mandela as the principal mediator), hosted further consultations between the militia groups and the Burundi Government in Pretoria in April; however, both the FNL and Nkurunziza's CNDD—FDD faction again refused to participate. Additional discussions between government and rebel delegations regarding the implementation of a ceasefire were scheduled to take place in Dar es Salaam in August. Early that month, following an attempt to remove the FNL 'hardline' leader, Agathon Rwasa, from his post, the movement divided: a new faction, led by Alain Mugabarabona, emerged, while Rwasa remained in control of most of the combatants. The peace negotiations, which commenced on 12 August, were attended for the first time by Mugabarabona's FNL faction and both CNDD—FDD factions.

A summit meeting on Burundi (attended by regional Presidents), which was convened in Dar es Salaam on 7 October 2002, resulted in a ceasefire agreement between the Government, and Ndayikengurukiye's CNDD—FDD and Mugabarabona's FNL faction. Negotiations with the main CNDD—FDD continued, however, amid hostilities between government and rebel forces in central and northern Burundi.

On 3 December 2002, following mediation from Uganda and South Africa, the Government finally reached a ceasefire agreement with Nkurunziza's main CNDD—FDD faction, which was scheduled to enter into effect at the end of that month. Under the Arusha agreement, the rebel factions were to be reconstituted as political parties, while Buyoya was to relinquish the presidency to Ndayizeye at the end of April 2003. However, the ceasefire agreement was not implemented, owing to delays in the arrival of observers from the AU. Hostilities between government and CNDD—FDD forces continued, particularly in Gitega, and Nkurunziza, attributing responsibility for the failure to implement the accord to the Government, suspended further discussions. In February the AU Ceasefire Observer Mission, comprising 35 monitors, arrived in Bujumbura, with a mandate to monitor the peace agreement. In late April the first 100 members of an AU Mission in Burundi (AMIB) arrived in the country; the contingent (which was to comprise troops from South Africa, Ethiopia and Mozambique) was to assist in the enforcement of the ceasefire between the Government and the rebel factions. Despite the reported reluctance of Buyoya to relinquish the presidency, Ndayizeye was officially inaugurated as President for the scheduled period of 18 months on 30 April. On the same day Alphonse-Marie Kadege was appointed Vice-President. On 5 May Ndayizeye appointed a representative of Mugabarabona's FNL faction and Ndayikengurukiye's CNDD—FDD faction to the transitional Council of Ministers, as part of a government reorganization.

In October 2003, under the mediation of Zuma and the South African President, Thabo Mbeki, Ndayizeye signed an agreement with Nkurunziza on political, military and security power-sharing. The CNDD—FDD faction was to be allocated four ministerial portfolios, 40% of army officers' posts, the vice-presidency of the National Assembly, three provincial governorships and two ambassadorial posts, while former CNDD—FDD combatants were to be demobilized. Mugabarabona and Ndayikengurukiye issued a statement condemning the accord, which was finally approved by the legislature on 22 October. On 16 November the Government and Nkurunziza's CNDD—FDD signed a final comprehensive peace agreement, endorsing the accords of December 2002, and of October and November 2003. On the same day regional heads of state issued an ultimatum to Rwasa (as leader of the only rebel faction to remain in conflict with the Government) to join the peace process. Later that month Ndayizeye reorganized the Government of national unity to include four representatives of Nkurunziza's CNDD—FDD faction, including Nkurunziza himself, who was appointed to the third most senior post, Minister of State with responsibility for Good Governance and State Inspection.

In January 2004 Ndayizeye established a Joint Military High Command, comprising 20 members of the existing armed forces and 13 of the former CNDD—FDD. Later that month negotiations between Ndayizeye and an FNL delegation, convened in Oisterwijk, Netherlands, ended without agreement on a ceasefire being reached. The FNL continued to refuse to recognize the transitional authorities, and clashes between government and rebel forces continued in early February. In March the AU renewed the mandate of AMIB (which was due to expire at the beginning of April) for a further month, and urged the UN Security Council to authorize the deployment of UN peacekeeping troops in Burundi. In April Nkurunziza announced the suspension of CNDD—FDD participation in the transitional institutions, on the grounds that the Government had failed to implement the November 2003 power-sharing accord. In May the UN Security Council approved the replacement of the AMIB mission with a UN contingent, the Opération des Nations Unies au Burundi (ONUB). With a maximum strength of 5,650 military personnel, ONUB officially commenced deployment on 1 June.

In July 2004 the International Monitoring Committee charged with overseeing the implementation of the power-sharing arrangements urged political parties to reach consensus in efforts to adopt a new constitution (necessary to allow elections to proceed). A draft power-sharing accord (which provided for a Government and National Assembly of 60% Hutu and 40% Tutsi composition) was reached in Pretoria later that month, but was rejected by predominantly Tutsi parties. (Also in July the CNDD—FDD announced the resumption of its participation in the Government of national unity.) On 6 August the accord, which would allow elections to proceed on 31 October, was signed in Pretoria by 20 of the 30 delegations, with Tutsi parties, notably UPRONA, refusing to accept the proposed power-sharing arrangements. A five-member Commission Electorale Nationale Indépendante (CENI) was established at the end of August. Following the massacre of refugees at the Gatumba camp in August (see below), however, government forces launched further attacks against FNL troop positions.

Nkurunziza becomes President

In September 2004 the International Criminal Court (ICC, see p. 340) announced that Burundi had ratified the signatory treaty, allowing prosecutions for civilian massacres to proceed. Meanwhile, the main political groupings continued to fail to reach agreement on a proposed new constitution, with 11 Tutsi parties, including UPRONA, objecting to the parliamentary ethnic representation vested in the draft. In mid-October the CENI announced that legislative elections, scheduled to take place at the end of that month, were to be postponed until 22 April 2005. On 20 October 2004 a new interim 'post-transitional' Constitution was officially adopted by Ndayizeye, after its approval by both chambers of the legislature. The new Constitution, which was to extend the mandate of the transitional organs of government from 1 November until the elections in April 2005, and which enshrined the power-sharing principles of a Government and National Assembly of 60% Hutu and 40% Tutsi composition, was endorsed at a referendum on 28 February 2005 by some 92% of votes cast (with an estimated 88% of the electorate participating in the ballot). Legislative elections were to proceed on 22 April, to be followed by the election of a President by the new National Assembly and Senate. (Under the terms of the Constitution, subsequent Presidents were to be directly elected.) However, the legislature failed to approve the new electoral code until late April, and the Government subsequently announced that Ndayizeye's mandate was to be extended to allow a further postponement of the elections. According to the new schedule, after local government elections in June, elections were to be conducted to the National Assembly on 4 July, and to the Senate on 19 July, followed by the election of a President by the new legislature on 19 August. Meanwhile, in December 2004 the Government announced the creation of a new Forces de Défense Nationales and of a new police force, comprising equal numbers of the existing Tutsi-dominated armed forces and Hutu former rebel combatants (mainly CNDD—FDD); a Tutsi was appointed head of the new army, while the post of deputy commander was allocated to a Hutu.

On 3 June 2005 communal government elections were conducted under the transitional schedule; of the 3,225 contested seats, the CNDD—FDD secured 1,781, FRODEBU 822, and UPRONA 260 seats. Elections to a reduced number of 100 seats in the National Assembly took place, as scheduled, on 4 July 2005, and received the approval of international observers. According to official results, the CNDD—FDD won 59 seats, FRODEBU 25 and UPRONA 10 seats. A further 18 deputies were subsequently nominated in accordance with the constitutional requirements of balance of ethnic representation (60% Hutu and 40% Tutsi) and a minimum 30% representation of women; in effect, the Twa ethnic group was allocated three seats, while the CNDD—FDD, FRODEBU and UPRONA each received five additional seats. The CNDD—FDD won 30 of the 34 contested seats in elections to the Senate, which followed on 29 July, while FRODEBU won only four seats; four former Presidents were subsequently allocated seats, and the Twa ethnic group was designated three seats. In early August the authorities and political parties agreed to expand the chamber to 49 deputies, in order to guarantee the stipulated minimum representation of women; the four political parties with the highest votes each nominated two women to the additional seats. On 19 August a joint session of the National Assembly and the Senate elected Nkurunziza as President; the sole candidate, he secured about 81.5% of votes cast. Nkurunziza was officially inaugurated on 26 August and subsequently formed a 20-member Government in accordance with the terms of the Constitution, comprising a 60% Hutu and 40% Tutsi balance of representation, with a minimum 30% of women.

In September 2005 the FNL leadership refused an offer by the new Government to enter into reconciliation negotiations. In following months the Government consequently increased military efforts to suppress rebel activity, particularly in the provinces of Bujumbura Rural and Bubanza where the movement was based, causing large displacement of civilians from these regions. As a result of increasing support within the FNL for reconciliation with the Government, Rwasa was ousted from the leadership in December, and was replaced by Jean-Bosco Sindayigaya, who announced that he was prepared to enter into unconditional negotiations with the authorities. However, Rwasa continued to head a smaller faction of the FNL opposed to negotiations and sporadic hostilities continued in early 2006. In December 2005 the UN Security Council extended the mandate of ONUB for a further six months.

In January 2006 Nkurunziza ordered the provisional release of 'political prisoners' imprisoned in connection with the coup attempt of 1993, with the stated aim of promoting national reconciliation. In March 2006 the President of FRODEBU, Léonce Ngendakumana, ordered its representatives to withdraw from the Government and legislature, in protest at the failure of the CNDD—FDD to consult with other coalition parties, and at decisions which he considered to be contrary to democratic principles; however, the three FRODEBU ministers refused to resign from their posts, and were subsequently expelled from the party. Also in March Rwasa agreed to enter into peace negotiations, providing that they constituted direct dialogue with Nkurunziza. Following a request from Nkurunziza that South Africa assist in the negotiations, in May Mbeki appointed the South African Minister of Safety and Security, Charles Nqakula, as mediator. Negotiations commenced in Dar es Salaam later that month. In June government and FNL delegations signed a framework accord for a cessation of hostilities; however, discussions continued throughout July without agreement being reached on a ceasefire. On 30 June the UN Security Council adopted a resolution authorizing the extension of ONUB's mandate to the end of 2006, when the mission was to withdraw and be replaced by a UN office, the Bureau Intégré des Nations Unies au Burundi (BINUB).

In August 2006 several prominent politicians, including former President Ndayizeye, former Vice-President Kadege and FNL faction leader Mugabarabona were arrested on suspicion of involvement in a coup attempt, and subsequently charged. In September, after Rwasa agreed to abandon demands for the restructured armed forces to comprise a higher proportion of Hutus, he and Nkurunziza signed a comprehensive ceasefire agreement, under the aegis of Mbeki, in Dar es Salaam. A Joint Verification and Monitoring Committee, composed of UN officials, together with representatives of the FNL and the Governments of Burundi, South Africa, Tanzania and Uganda, was established at the beginning of October to supervise the implementation of the ceasefire. (Owing to a boycott by the FNL members, however, the Committee subsequently failed to commence operations.)

Also in September 2006 the Second Vice-President, Alice Nzomukunda, a member of the CNDD—FDD, tendered her resignation, citing her opposition to the arrests in connection with the alleged conspiracy to overthrow the Government; she was replaced by Marina Barampama. At the end of 2006 ONUB duly withdrew and BINUB was installed for an initial period of one year (which was subsequently extended), with authorization to continue the process of peace consolidation, including support for the demobilization and reintegration of former combatants and reform of the security sector. Some 850 South African peacekeeping troops previously belonging to ONUB were transferred to the authority of the AU, which announced plans to increase the size of the contingent deployed in the country to 1,700.

In January 2007 Ndayizeye, Kadege and three other suspects were acquitted of the charges of conspiring to overthrow Nkurunziza's Government; however, Mugabarabona was convicted and sentenced to 20 years' imprisonment, while a further defendant received a term of 15 years. The outcome of Ndayizeye's trial precipitated political unrest, with ruling party leaders, particularly the Chairman of the CNDD—FDD, Hussein Radjabu, suspected of fabricating the conspiracy involving opposition figures in order to suppress dissent. The Minister of Development Planning and National Reconstruction (a member of the CNDD—FDD) was removed following an investigation into the sale of a presidential airplane, and subsequently fled abroad, causing further controversy. At the end of January, after discussions in Dar es Salaam, the FNL leadership agreed, in principle, to accept the terms for the implementation of the ceasefire agreement.

In February 2007 Barampama was dismissed from the post of Second Vice-President, after pledging her support to Radjabu, who had been removed from the chairmanship of the CNDD—FDD at a special congress of the party earlier that month. Gabriel Ntiszerana, hitherto the Governor of the central bank, was appointed to replace her as Second Vice-President. In April Radjabu was arrested and detained on charges of recruiting and arming demobilized troops and planning to launch an attack on state forces. (In April 2008 he was convicted by the Supreme Court and sentenced to 13 years in prison.)

The peace process

In June 2007 Rwasa became the last of the rebel leaders to sign the ceasefire agreement drawn up in 2006. However, the following month FNL leaders deserted their roles in a joint monitoring group that had been established to oversee the implementation of the ceasefire, further delaying the peace process, and in September fighting resumed between rebel insurgents. In light of the continued impasse between the Government and opposition parties over the terms of a power-sharing agreement, and the increasing unrest among rebel groups, international observers appealed for renewed peace talks. In October Nkurunziza issued a statement announcing that a power-sharing compromise had been reached; the agreement pledged to guarantee the rights of political parties to meet freely and reinstate members of the opposition who had previously been dismissed from the Government.

President Nkurunziza installed a new, 21-member Council of Ministers (which included eight new ministers) in July 2007, in an effort to address concerns over allegations of corruption and human rights abuses. In August First Vice-President Martin Nduwimana was expelled from UPRONA amid allegations that he had been attempting to sabotage the party, and in the same month the Governor of the central bank, Isaac Bizimana, was arrested for allegedly embezzling state funds. In November Nduwimana resigned from the Government, and was replaced by Yves Sahinguvu. Later that month Nkurunziza announced further changes to the composition of the Government, which included the appointment of Vénant Kamana, hitherto Minister at the Presidency, as Minister of the Interior.

There was a resumption of hostilities between the rebels and government forces in April 2008 when FNL units launched attacks on a number of military positions and towns, and shelled Bujumbura; the Burundian armed forces responded by bombing rebel positions in the north of the country. In late May, however, a ceasefire was signed between the Government and the FNL, and four days later Rwasa returned to Burundi from Tanzania, where he had been living in exile. The following month, at a ceremony in Rugazi Commune to mark the start of the cantonment of FNL fighters, he declared that the armed struggle against the Government had officially ended. Furthermore, at a summit in Bujumbura in December, the FNL agreed to remove the word 'Hutu' from the name of its political wing, the PALIPEHUTU, in accordance with the constitutional ban on such ethnic terminology. This signified a breakthrough in the peace process, and at the same summit Nkurunziza confirmed that he would award government positions to members of the FNL and would release political prisoners and prisoners of war.

Meanwhile, the political situation had deteriorated following FRODEBU's withdrawal, in February 2008, from the National Assembly, in protest at the CNDD—FDD's removal of the parliamentary First Vice-President, Alice Nzomukunda (who had been expelled from the party). Later that month 46 members of the National Assembly sent a letter to the UN Secretary-General, Ban Ki-Moon, expressing their concerns about the security situation in Burundi and requesting international protection from persecution by the Government. In March there were a series of grenade attacks on the homes of four opposition party members (all of whom were signatories to the letter). In June the Constitutional Court expelled 22 parliamentary deputies, who had defected from the ruling CNDD—FDD party in early 2007 in response to Radjabu's dismissal as Chairman and the Government's purge of his supporters. There was further concern regarding government intimidation of the opposition in November 2008, when Alexis Sinduhije, a journalist and leader of the opposition Mouvement pour la Sécurité et la Démocratie, was arrested, along with 30 other members of the party. In December the National Assembly approved a new penal code, which was praised by human rights groups for abolishing capital punishment, as well as defining and prohibiting torture, but also criticized for criminalizing homosexual activity and permitting arbitrary detention.

In January 2009 Nkurunziza reorganized the Council of Ministers; notably, Minister of the Interior Kamana was replaced by Edouard Nduwimana, formerly the governor of Kayanza province. A new CENI, comprising two civil society activists and one representative each from the CNDD—FDD, FRODEBU and UPRONA, was officially appointed in early April. Rwasa symbolically surrendered his weapons at a special ceremony in Bubanza on 18 April, marking the start of the demobilization of FNL combatants, under an agreement between the FNL and the Government whereby 3,500 FNL combatants would be integrated into the national army and police force and a further 5,000 would be demobilized. (However, an estimated 10,000 FNL supporters who were not recognized by the authorities as former combatants remained at large.) The FNL was formally registered as a political party on 21 April. In June Nkurunziza appointed several senior FNL officials to government posts, including Rwasa, who became head of the National Social Security Institute.

The 2010 elections

In December 2009 the Chairman of CENI announced that the first round of a presidential election was to take place on 28 June 2010, on the expiry of Nkurunziza's term of office, and was to be followed by elections to the National Assembly on 23 July and to the Senate on 28 July. A voter registration process was undertaken in January. Meanwhile, reports emerged of division within the FNL, following Rwasa's government appointment, between his supporters and a faction led by the party's spokesman, Pasteur Habimana, which declared that it no longer recognized Rwasa as Chairman. The FNL selected Rwasa as its presidential candidate in that month, while FRODEBU chose Ndayizeye. Nkurunziza was elected as the presidential candidate by the CNDD—FDD at a special congress in late April. Also in April, despite strong opposition from the main FNL, Habimana's faction of the FNL, led by his associate, Jacques Kenese, officially registered as a party, known as FNL Iragi rya Gahutu.

A number of grenade attacks, which prompted the arrest of some 130 suspects, were reported during the campaign period prior to communal government elections. Following the elections on 24 May 2010, it was announced that the CNDD—FDD had secured 64% of votes cast, with the FNL receiving only 14%, UPRONA 6%, and FRODEBU 5% of the votes. While a European Union (EU, see p. 273) observer mission reported that the communal elections had generally proceeded in accordance with international standards, the opposition denounced the results as fraudulent and demanded that the elections be repeated. All principal opposition parties subsequently withdrew from the electoral process in protest at the alleged malpractice, and the five opposition candidates who had registered to contest the presidential election, including Rwasa and Ndayizeye, announced that they would boycott the poll.

Prior to the presidential election in June 2010, at least two prominent members of the CNDD—FDD and an opposition activist were killed in further numerous grenade attacks, mainly directed against CNDD—FDD local offices. The Government ordered the arrest of large numbers of opposition members, particularly of the FNL (which denied any involvement in the attacks), and banned all opposition party gatherings. The presidential election took place, as scheduled, on 28 June. The Constitutional Court confirmed the official results of the election on 8 July, according to which Nkurunziza (who had contested the election as the sole candidate) was re-elected with 91.6% of votes cast. The rate of voter participation was estimated at 77.0% of the registered electorate. At the elections to the National Assembly, which took place on 23 July, the CNDD—FDD increased its number of seats to 81, while UPRONA took 17 and FRODEBU-Nyakuri (a small, pro-Government, breakaway faction of FRODEBU) five. A further three deputies from the Twa ethnic group were subsequently nominated in accordance with the constitutional requirements of balance of ethnic representation. At the elections to the Senate on 28 July, the CNDD—FDD secured 32 of the 34 available seats; the remaining two seats were won by UPRONA. A further four seats were allocated to former Presidents and three to the Twa ethnic group, increasing the total number of senators to 41. At the beginning of August government supporters within the FNL announced that Rwasa had been deposed as party leader and replaced by a presidential adviser, Emmanuel Miburo. On 30 August Nkurunziza appointed a new Government, which included 10 new ministers, notably Thérence Sinunguruza of UPRONA as First Vice-President.

In late 2010 sporadic unrest continued in rural areas and in November the Prosecutor-General announced the establishment of a commission to investigate reports of a number of extra-judicial killings by members of the armed forces. Upon the expiry of BINUB's mandate in mid-December, the UN Security Council adopted a resolution authorizing the establishment of a reduced, 15-member body, the new UN Office in Burundi (BNUB), for an initial 12-month period, beginning on 1 January 2011. (In December 2011 the UN Security Council adopted a resolution extending the mandate of BNUB until mid-February 2013.)

Continued human rights violations

In June 2011 EU ambassadors addressed an official protest to the Burundian Government at 20 incidences of politically motivated extrajudicial killings and a number of torture cases allegedly committed by security officials between June 2010 and March 2011. In October the authorities stated, following a preliminary inquiry, that Rwasa (who was believed to be in hiding in the DRC) had organized an attack in Gatumba, near the border with the DRC, in September; a total of 39 people had been killed in the incident, which followed a series of attacks previously attributed by the Government to armed bandits. The trial of 21 defendants suspected of perpetrating the killings began in Bujumbura High Court in October. In the same month principal international human rights organizations demanded that the Government provide financial support to a newly established independent human rights commission and end the restrictions on media reporting, also citing arrests and legal measures undertaken by the authorities against a number of independent journalists and civil activists in previous months.

In November 2011 Nkurunziza effected an extensive government reorganization, in which six new ministers were appointed. Notably, head of police Gabriel Nizigama was awarded the post of Minister of Public Security, while Laurent Kavakure, hitherto a senior presidential adviser, became Minister of External Relations and International Co-operation. Following the abolition of the Ministry of Planning for Economic Development, Minister of Finance Clotilde Nizigama assumed the additional portfolio. In December one of the defendants accused of participating in the bar attack in Gatumba claimed that he had been recruited by senior police officials, who had planned to eliminate an FNL rebel commander. In January 2012 seven people were sentenced to life imprisonment for involvement in the Gatumba attack; a further nine defendants received terms of between two and five years, and the remaining five, including one army and two police officials, were acquitted. As part of a government reorganization, announced in early February, Tabu Abdallah Manirakiza became Minister of Finance and Planning for Economic Development, replacing Nizigama, while Issa Ngendakumana was appointed Minister at the Presidency, in charge of Good Governance and Privatization.

In February 2012 the EU delegation based in Burundi, after meeting government ministers, expressed concern over violations of human rights and justice on the part of the authorities, with regard to further reported extrajudicial killings. Concerns were also expressed by human rights groups over the case of a journalist, Hassan Ruvakuki, who, with 22 others, had been placed on trial on charges of terrorism; Ruvakuki was accused of involvement in the activities of a new rebel group, Forces pour la Restauration de la Démocratie (FRD—Abanyagihugu), in the east of the country, after travelling to Tanzania to investigate the movement. Also in February, Faustin Ndikumana, the head of an anti-corruption agency, was detained after criticizing senior members of the judiciary, including the Minister of Justice, for alleged corruption, but was released following pressure from the EU. In June it was reported that the leader of FRD—Abanyagihugu, Jean-Petit Nduwimana (a former head of the intelligence services), had been arrested in the DRC, transferred to the custody of the Burundian army and subsequently executed. In July Ruvakuki and 13 others were convicted and sentenced to life imprisonment on terrorism charges (with a further nine defendants receiving terms of 15 years' imprisonment), prompting renewed protests from journalist associations and human rights organizations. In November Nkurunziza appointed new heads of the police and army. Meanwhile, a pledge made by Nkurunziza at the beginning of 2012 that a long-envisaged Truth and Reconciliation Commission would be established by the end of that year remained unfulfilled. Non-governmental organizations cited the continued lack of opposition participation in government institutions (following the opposition boycott of the 2010 elections); in December a coalition of principal opposition parties, the Alliance Démocratique pour le Changement au Burundi, rejected the approval of a new CENI, prior to elections in 2015. In January 2013 an appeals court in Gitega dismissed the terrorism charges against Ruvakuki, but ruled that he was guilty of participating in a criminal group, reducing his sentence of life imprisonment to a term of three years.

In early February 2013 President Nkurunziza carried out a reorganization of the Government, in which seven ministers (including those responsible for communal development, and telecommunications) were replaced. On 13 February the UN Security Council, citing concerns at reports of continuing extrajudicial killings in the country, extended the mandate of BNUB for a further year. In response to the political impasse, a dialogue between government and opposition leaders was organized under the aegis of the UN on 11–13 March in Bujumbura; a general agreement of principles was drafted, and the representatives also pledged to review the electoral law and the Constitution by the end of the year. In March Ruvakuki, was unexpectedly released from detention. In June, however, Nkurunziza enacted media legislation (following its approval by both parliamentary chambers), under which journalists were obliged to reveal their sources and the publication of information considered to undermine national security was prohibited; journalist and human rights organizations strongly protested against the new regulations. Three journalists were detained on suspicion of undermining state security shortly after the promulgation of the legislation. Meanwhile, civil society organizations denounced the involvement of members of the CNDD—FDD youth wing, the Imbonerakure, in criminal activities and the harassment of opponents.

In October 2013 divisions within UPRONA resulted in the resignation of First Vice-President Sinunguruza, after elements of his party accused him of not representing its interests. On 17 October the National Assembly approved Nkurunziza's appointment to the post of another UPRONA member, Bernard Busokoza. In the same month Jacques Bigirimana was elected as the new leader of the FNL (despite objections from Rwasa, who had returned to Burundi in August).

Recent developments: proposed constitutional amendments

In late 2013 plans by the Government radically to amend the Constitution prompted consternation from opposition parties and the country's bishops: the proposed changes, which were submitted to the National Assembly in November, included replacement of the two ethnically balanced vice-presidencies stipulated in the Arusha agreement with the posts of a largely ceremonial Vice-President and an executive Prime Minister, and the reduction of the parliamentary requirement for adoption of legislation from a two-thirds' to a simple majority. In early December former Vice-President Frédéric Bamvuginyumvira, a FRODEBU parliamentary deputy and potential opposition presidential candidate, was arrested and subsequently charged with corruption shortly before a planned protest against the constitutional amendments (which was later cancelled). Following an appeal by the Union Burundaise des Journalistes, in January 2014 the Constitutional Court abrogated part of the new media legislation that had provided for dramatically increased penalties for journalists.

Foreign Affairs

The cross-border movement of vast numbers of refugees, provoked by regional ethnic and political violence, has dominated relations with Rwanda, Tanzania and the DRC (formerly Zaire), and has long been a matter of considerable concern to the international aid community. The uprising by Laurent-Désiré Kabila's Alliance des Forces Démocratiques pour la Libération du Congo-Zaïre in eastern Zaire in January 1997 resulted in the return of large numbers of refugees to Burundi, reportedly undermining the operations from Zaire of FDD combatants. Burundi initially denied any involvement in the civil war that commenced in the DRC in August, but Burundian troops were subsequently reported to be stationed in the east of the country, with the aim of destroying CNDD—FDD camps. (The CNDD—FDD supported the DRC Government in the civil war and used the conflict as an opportunity to regroup and rearm.) In June the DRC instituted proceedings against Burundi, together with Rwanda and Uganda, at the International Court of Justice in The Hague, Netherlands, accusing them of acts of armed aggression in contravention of the terms of both the UN Charter and the Charter of the OAU. In February 2001, however, the DRC abandoned proceedings against Burundi and Rwanda. In January 2002 the Burundian Government made a formal commitment to withdraw all troops (reported to number about 1,000) from the DRC, while the DRC authorities pledged to end their alliance with the CNDD—FDD. In August 2004 some 160 Banyamulenge (Congolese Tutsi) were massacred at a refugee camp at Gatumba, near the border between the two countries. Although the FNL admitted responsibility for the atrocity, the Governments of Burundi and Rwanda maintained that Hutu militia operating within the DRC were involved. (In September 2013 it was announced that the Burundian authorities had launched an investigation into allegations that FNL leader Rwasa had ordered the massacre of the Banyamulenge refugees.) In 2009 Burundi, the DRC and UNHCR signed a tripartite agreement providing for the voluntary repatriation of Burundian and Congolese refugees. With new inflows following continued hostilities in eastern DRC, however, UNHCR estimated that some 35,400 refugees originating from the DRC remained in Burundi at the end of 2013.

With improvement in the security situation in Burundi, the Tanzanian authorities began a UNHCR-supervised programme in 2003 to repatriate Burundian refugees. In early 2008 the Tanzanian Government announced an initiative (commended by UNHCR), under which the remaining Burundian refugees would be permitted to remain in the country and apply for Tanzanian citizenship, or be repatriated; it was reported that some 55,000 had decided to return to Burundi. By October 2009 some 53,500 long-term Burundian refugees had been repatriated under the UNHCR programme since March 2008, while some 162,000 Burundian refugees had applied for Tanzanian citizenship. Prior to the official closure of a large refugee camp in Tanzania in December 2012, the forced repatriation of some 35,000 Burundians to the south of the country commenced in October.

In December 2006 the Presidents of Burundi, Kenya, Uganda, the DRC and Rwanda signed a Pact of Security, Stability and Development in the Great Lakes Region, which was welcomed by the UN Security Council as a significant measure towards regional stabilization. In the same month the East African Community (EAC, see p. 450) officially accepted the membership applications of Burundi and Rwanda. In November 2009 the Heads of State of Tanzania, Kenya, Uganda, Rwanda and Burundi signed a common market protocol in Arusha, allowing the free movement of goods, services, people and capital within the EAC. The common market protocol officially entered into force in July 2010. Burundi for the first time hosted an EAC summit meeting in November 2011, when plans to adopt a single currency (originally envisaged for 2012) were under discussion. On 30 November 2013 the EAC Heads of State, meeting in Kampala, Uganda, signed a protocol on the adoption of full monetary union within 10 years. The Burundian Government contributed troops to AU peacekeeping contingents deployed in Somalia, Mali and, from December 2013, the Central African Republic.

CONSTITUTION AND GOVERNMENT

Following the coup of 25 July 1996, the Constitution of March 1992 was suspended. A peace agreement, which was signed by representatives of the incumbent Government, the Assemblée Nationale (National Assembly) and 17 political groupings on 28 August 2000, provided for the installation of a transitional administration, in which power-sharing between the Hutu and Tutsi ethnic groups was guaranteed (see Contemporary Political History). Under an interim 'post-transitional' Constitution, which was officially adopted by the President on 20 October 2004, legislative elections were conducted in July 2005, and a President, elected by the new National Assembly and the Sénat (Senate), was inaugurated on 26 August. The National Assembly comprised 118 deputies, of whom 100 were elected for a term of five years, and the remainder nominated according to constitutional requirements for a proportion of 60% Hutu and 40% Tutsi representatives, and a minimum 30% of women, while three seats were allocated to the Twa ethnic group. The Senate comprised 49 deputies, of whom 34 were elected (two deputies by ethnically balanced colleges from each of the country's provinces) for a term of five years, and the remainder nominated according to constitutional requirements for balance of ethnic representation and minimum representation of women. The President, who is Head of State and is henceforth directly elected, appoints two Vice-Presidents, and, in consultation with them, the Government.

For the purposes of local government, Burundi comprises 17 provinces (administered by civilian Governors), each of which is divided into districts and further subdivided into communes. Each district has a council, which is directly elected for a term of five years.

REGIONAL AND INTERNATIONAL CO-OPERATION

Burundi is a member of the African Union (see p. 186) and, with neighbouring states Rwanda and the DRC, is a member of the Economic Community of the Great Lakes Countries (see p. 450). Burundi is also a member of the Common Market for Eastern and Southern Africa (see p. 233), and of the International Coffee

Organization (see p. 446). In December 2006 Burundi, together with Rwanda, was admitted to the East African Community (see p. 450).

Burundi was admitted to the UN in 1962, and joined the World Trade Organization (WTO, see p. 434) in 1995.

ECONOMIC AFFAIRS

In 2012, according to estimates by the World Bank, Burundi's gross national income (GNI), measured at average 2010–12 prices, was US $2,382m., equivalent to $240 per head (or $560 per head on an international purchasing-power parity basis). During 2003–12, it was estimated, the population increased at an average annual rate of 3.4%, while gross domestic product (GDP) per head increased, in real terms, by an average of 0.6% per year. Overall GDP increased, in real terms, at an average annual rate of 4.0% in 2003–12; growth was 4.0% in 2012.

Agriculture (including forestry and fishing) contributed a provisional 39.7% of GDP in 2012, according to the African Development Bank (AfDB). According to FAO, some 88.5% of the labour force were estimated to be employed in the sector in mid-2014. The principal cash crops are coffee (which accounted for 27.2% of export earnings in 2012) and cane sugar. The main subsistence crops are cassava, sweet potatoes, dry beans and millet. Although Burundi is traditionally self-sufficient in food crops, population displacement (a consequence of the political crisis) resulted in considerable disruption in the sector. The livestock-rearing sector was also severely affected by the civil war. According to estimates by the World Bank, agricultural GDP declined, in real terms, at an average annual rate of 0.5% in 2003–11; however, it grew by 4.4% in 2011. According to the AfDB, growth in agriculture of 5.7% was recorded in 2012.

Industry (comprising mining, manufacturing, construction and utilities) engaged 21.8% of the employed labour force in 1991. According to the AfDB, the sector contributed a provisional 20.8% of GDP in 2012. According to estimates by the World Bank, during 2003–11, industrial GDP increased at an average annual rate of 1.8%; it increased by 5.9% in 2011.

Mining and power engaged 0.1% of the employed labour force in 1990 and, according to the AfDB, the contribution of mining and quarrying towards GDP was a provisional 0.7% in 2012. Gold (alluvial), tin, tungsten and columbo-tantalite are mined in small quantities, although much activity has hitherto been outside the formal sector. Burundi has important deposits of nickel (estimated at 5% of world reserves), vanadium and uranium. In addition, petroleum deposits have been discovered. The GDP of the mining sector increased at an average annual rate of 3.4% in 1997–2001, according to IMF estimates; growth in 2001 was an estimated 14.3%. According to the AfDB, growth in the mining sector of 5.0% was recorded in 2012.

Manufacturing engaged 1.2% of the employed labour force in 1990 and, according to the AfDB, contributed a provisional 14.6% of GDP in 2012. The sector consists largely of the processing of foodstuffs and agricultural products (coffee, cotton, tea and the extraction of vegetable oils), and of textiles and leather products. Manufacturing GDP increased at an average annual rate of 0.1% in 2005–11, according to World Bank. Manufacturing GDP decreased by 1.0% in 2011. According to the AfDB, growth in manufacturing of 10.7% was recorded in 2012.

According to the AfDB, the construction sector contributed a provisional 4.2% of GDP in 2012. The sector engaged only 0.7% of the employed labour force in 1990. The sector grew by 11.6% in 2012.

Energy is derived principally from hydroelectric power (an estimated 38.6% of electricity consumed in 2001 was imported). Peat is also exploited as an additional source of energy. Imports of mineral fuels and lubricants comprised 17.0% of the value of imports in 2012.

The services sector contributed a provisional 39.5% of GDP in 2012, according to the AfDB. The sector engaged only 4.4% of the employed labour force in 1990. According to estimates by the World Bank, the GDP of the services sector increased at an average annual rate of 9.4% in 2003–11; the sector grew by 3.6% in 2011.

In 2012 Burundi recorded a merchandise trade deficit of US $576.3m., and there was a deficit of $578.3m. on the current account of the balance of payments. In 2012 the principal source of imports was Italy (providing 17.6% of the total); other important suppliers in that year were Saudi Arabia, Belgium, the People's Republic of China, India and Tanzania. The principal market for exports in 2012 was the United Arab Emirates (16.3%). The main imports in 2012 were vegetables and vegetable products and prepared foodstuffs, machinery and mechanical and electrical appliances, chemicals and related products, pearls, precious or semi-precious stones, precious metals, and articles, and vehicles and other transport equipment. The principal exports in that year were pearls, precious stones, metals, coins, etc., vegetables and vegetable products (especially coffee) and mineral products (mainly ores, slag and ash).

In 2012 the budget deficit was estimated at 132,900m. Burundian francs. Burundi's general government gross debt was 1,273,877m. Burundian francs in 2012, equivalent to 35.7% of GDP. Burundi's external debt in 2011 was US $628m., of which $387m. was public and publicly guaranteed debt. In 2011, the cost of debt-servicing long-term public and publicly guaranteed debt and repayments to the IMF in that year was equivalent to 3.4% of the value of exports of goods, services and income (excluding workers' remittances). According to the IMF, the annual rate of inflation averaged 8.7% in 2005–12; consumer prices increased by 18.0% in 2012.

Following a period of extended conflict in Burundi from the mid-1990s, the transitional power-sharing Government installed in 2001 oversaw the beginning of an economic recovery. In August 2005 the IMF and the World Bank's International Development Association (IDA) agreed that, in view of progress demonstrated in economic stabilization and structural reforms, Burundi had qualified for interim debt relief under the enhanced initiative for heavily indebted poor countries (HIPC), thereby enabling it to reduce an unsustainable external debt-servicing burden. Large-scale hostilities in the country finally ended in May 2008, with the signing of a ceasefire agreement (although rebel activity subsequently continued in parts of the country—see Recent History). In January 2009 the IMF and World Bank announced that Burundi had made sufficient progress to reach completion point under the HIPC initiative and had become eligible for further debt relief from the IMF, IDA and the African Development Fund. Following the completion of an IMF-financed economic programme in January 2012, a further three-year arrangement, totalling US $46.5m., was approved for Burundi under the Extended Credit Facility (ECF). Meanwhile, the authorities announced that an extensive revision of the tax collection system during 2009–11 had resulted in a substantial rise in tax revenue, allowing increased funding to the agriculture and health sectors, and the implementation of major infrastructure projects. In August 2013 the World Bank approved a grant of $340m. to finance a project by the Governments of Burundi, Rwanda and Tanzania for the development of a joint hydroelectric dam, which was scheduled for completion in 2020. In November 2013 the East African Community (EAC, see p. 450), which had officially established a common market in July 2010, reached agreement on the adoption of full monetary union within 10 years; the monetary and fiscal policies of the constituent states were to be harmonized and a common central bank established, prior to the introduction of a common currency, which would promote a further expansion of regional trade. The fourth IMF review under the ECF arrangement was conducted in December 2013 (total funds extended under the Facility amounted to $22.6m. at that time, following a disbursement in September). Although regional unrest with concomitant refugee arrivals was cited as a continuing strain on the economy, the Government had succeeded in lowering the inflation rate from high levels in 2012, while GDP growth was projected to rise slightly (to 4.5% in 2013 and to 4.7% in 2014).

PUBLIC HOLIDAYS

2015: 1 January (New Year's Day), 5 February (Unity Day), 6 April (Easter Monday), 1 May (Labour Day), 14 May (Ascension Day), 1 July (Independence Day), 17 July* (Id al-Fitr, end of Ramadan), 15 August (Assumption), 18 September (Victory of UPRONA Party), 13 October (Rwagasore Day), 21 October (Ndadaye Day), 1 November (All Saints' Day), 25 December (Christmas).

* These holidays are dependent on the Islamic lunar calendar and may vary by one or two days from the dates given.

Statistical Survey

Area and Population

AREA, POPULATION AND DENSITY

Area (sq km)	27,834*
Population (census results)†	
16–30 August 1990	5,139,073
16–31 August 2008	
Males	3,964,906
Females	4,088,668
Total	8,053,574
Population (UN estimates at mid-year)‡	
2012	9,849,569
2013	10,162,534
2014	10,482,752
Density (per sq km) at mid-2014	376.6

* 10,747 sq miles.
† Excluding adjustment for underenumeration.
‡ Source: UN, *World Population Prospects: The 2012 Revision*.

POPULATION BY AGE AND SEX
(UN estimates at mid-2014)

	Males	Females	Total
0–14	2,339,036	2,346,494	4,685,530
15–64	2,724,574	2,823,317	5,547,891
65 and over	115,240	134,091	249,331
Total	5,178,850	5,303,902	10,482,752

Source: UN, *World Population Prospects: The 2012 Revision*.

Principal Towns: Bujumbura (capital), population 235,440 (census result, August 1990). *Mid-2011* (urban population, incl. suburbs, UN estimate): Bujumbura 604,732 (Source: UN, *World Urbanization Prospects: The 2011 Revision*).

BIRTHS AND DEATHS
(UN estimates, annual averages)

	1995–2000	2000–05	2005–10
Birth rate (per 1,000)	43.4	42.5	44.8
Death rate (per 1,000)	16.5	15.3	14.2

Source: UN, *World Population Prospects: The 2012 Revision*.

Life expectancy (years at birth): 53.1 (males 53.1; females 55.0) in 2011 (Source: World Bank, World Development Indicators database).

ECONOMICALLY ACTIVE POPULATION*
(persons aged 10 years and over, 1990 census)

	Males	Females	Total
Agriculture, hunting, forestry and fishing	1,153,890	1,420,553	2,574,443
Mining and quarrying	1,146	39	1,185
Manufacturing	24,120	9,747	33,867
Electricity, gas and water	1,847	74	1,921
Construction	19,447	290	19,737
Trade, restaurants and hotels	19,667	6,155	25,822
Transport, storage and communications	8,193	311	8,504
Financing, insurance, real estate and business services	1,387	618	2,005
Community, social and personal services	68,905	16,286	85,191
Sub-total	1,298,602	1,454,073	2,752,675
Activities not adequately defined	8,653	4,617	13,270
Total labour force	1,307,255	1,458,690	2,765,945

* Figures exclude persons seeking work for the first time, totalling 13,832 (males 9,608, females 4,224), but include other unemployed persons.

Source: UN, *Demographic Yearbook*.

Mid-2014 (estimates in '000): Agriculture, etc. 3,926; Total labour force 4,432 (Source: FAO).

Health and Welfare

KEY INDICATORS

Total fertility rate (children per woman, 2011)	4.2
Under-5 mortality rate (per 1,000 live births, 2011)	139
HIV/AIDS (% of persons aged 15–49, 2012)	1.3
Physicians (per 1,000 head, 2004)	0.03
Hospital beds (per 1,000 head, 2011)	1.9
Health expenditure (2010): US $ per head (PPP)	54
Health expenditure (2010): % of GDP	9.1
Health expenditure (2010): public (% of total)	35.0
Access to water (% of persons, 2011)	74
Access to sanitation (% of persons, 2011)	50
Total carbon dioxide emissions ('000 metric tons, 2010)	308.0
Carbon dioxide emissions per head (metric tons, 2010)	0.0
Human Development Index (2012): ranking	178
Human Development Index (2012): value	0.355

For sources and definitions, see explanatory note on p. vi.

Agriculture

PRINCIPAL CROPS
('000 metric tons)

	2010	2011	2012
Wheat	9.0	9.8	4.2
Rice, paddy	83.0	91.4	64.6
Maize	126.4	128.5	140.5
Millet*	11.7	12.0	11.0
Sorghum	83.0	86.9	31.5
Potatoes	29.7	28.2	47.8
Sweet potatoes	966.3	955.1	659.6
Cassava (Manioc)	598.4	508.7	1,244.6
Taro (Coco yam)	58.9	58.3	93.0
Yams	9.9	9.9	6.3
Sugar cane	131.7	203.9	220.3
Beans, dry	201.6	200.7	205.9
Peas, dry	31.5	31.4	16.7
Groundnuts, with shell	7.5*	9.0*	10.0
Oil palm fruit*	84.0	70.0	72.0
Bananas	1,912.7	1,848.7	1,184.1
Coffee, green	6.8	23.9	26.3
Tea	8.0	8.8	9.1

* FAO estimate(s).

Aggregate production ('000 metric tons, may include official, semi-official or estimated data): Total cereals 313.2 in 2010, 328.5 in 2011, 251.9 in 2012. Total roots and tubers 1,663.2 in 2010, 1,560.2 in 2011, 2,051.3 in 2012. Total vegetables (incl. melons) 430.0 in 2010, 435.0 in 2011, 445.0 in 2012. Total fruits (excl. melons) 2,027.7 in 2010, 1,964.7 in 2011, 1,302.1 in 2012.

Source: FAO.

LIVESTOCK
('000 head, year ending September)

	2010	2011	2012
Cattle	596	654	696
Pigs	244	297	377
Sheep	315	332	332
Goats	2,145	2,286	2,489
Chickens	5,050*	5,100*	2,835

* FAO estimate.

Source: FAO.

LIVESTOCK PRODUCTS
('000 metric tons)

	2010	2011	2012
Cattle meat*	7.8	9.9	12.0
Sheep meat*	0.7	0.5	1.2
Goat meat	3.9	2.6*	4.8
Pig meat	3.7	2.1*	5.1
Chicken meat*	6.8	6.9	3.8
Cows' milk	30.4	43.8	31.8
Sheep's milk*	0.8	0.9	0.9
Goats' milk*	17.6	17.6	17.8
Hen eggs*	3.0	3.1	3.1

* FAO estimate(s).

Source: FAO.

Forestry

ROUNDWOOD REMOVALS
('000 cubic metres, excl. bark, FAO estimates)

	2010	2011	2012
Sawlogs, veneer logs and logs for sleepers	307	307	307
Other industrial wood	576	576	576
Fuel wood	9,259	9,397	9,536
Total	10,142	10,280	10,419

Source: FAO.

SAWNWOOD PRODUCTION
('000 cubic metres, incl. railway sleepers)

	2005	2006	2007
Coniferous (softwood)	18.0*	17.8	18.3
Broadleaved (hardwood)*	65.0	65.0	65.0
Total*	83.0	82.8	83.3

* FAO estimate(s).

2008–12: Production assumed to be unchanged from 2007 (FAO estimates).

Source: FAO.

Fishing

(metric tons, live weight)

	2009	2010	2011
Capture	12,615	17,305	10,654
Lake Tanganyika sprat	8,346	11,650	7,264
Sleek lates	2,515	2,499	1,849
Dagaas	1,043	2,208	866
Aquaculture*	50	50	50
Total catch (incl. others)*	12,665	17,355	10,704

* FAO estimates.

Source: FAO.

Mining

(metric tons unless otherwise indicated)

	2009	2010	2011*
Gold (kg)*†	750	750	750
Tin ore†	8	12	12
Tantalum and niobium (columbium) concentrates‡	24.4	67.4	68.0
Peat	11,352	13,111	15,000

* Estimates.

† Figures refer to the metal content of ores.

‡ The estimated tantalum content (in metric tons) was 4.8 in 2009, 13.1 in 2010 and 13.2 in 2011.

Source: US Geological Survey.

Industry

SELECTED PRODUCTS
('000 metric tons unless otherwise indicated)

	2010	2011	2012
Beer ('000 hl)	1,665.2	1,748.8	1,749.9
Soft drinks ('000 hl)	319.9	331.9	291.5
Cottonseed oil ('000 litres)	26.5	43.6	47.8
Sugar	18.9	20.7	23.2
Cigarettes (million)	457.8	510.4	650.5
Paint	0.5	0.6	0.7
Polyethylene film (metric tons)	1.6	—	—
Soap (metric tons)	5,418.9	8,767.9	9,662.1
Plastic racks ('000)	393.2	322.4	592.8
Moulds (metric tons)	39.1	27.7	22.0
PVC tubing (metric tons)	143.2	174.2	65.1
Electric energy (million kWh)	142.0	141.2	141.7

Source: Banque de la République du Burundi.

Finance

CURRENCY AND EXCHANGE RATES

Monetary Units

100 centimes = 1 Burundian franc.

Sterling, Dollar and Euro Equivalents (31 December 2013)

£1 sterling = 2,539.3 francs;
US $1 = 1,542.0 francs;
€1 = 2,126.6 francs;
10,000 Burundian francs = £3.94 = $6.49 = €4.70.

Average Exchange Rate (Burundian francs per US dollar)

2011	1,261.073
2012	1,442.506
2013	1,555.091

GOVERNMENT FINANCE
(central government operations, '000 million Burundian francs)

Revenue*	2011	2012†	2013‡
Tax revenue	424.1	491.8	494.4
Taxes on income, profits and capital gains	131.0	155.9	151.3
Taxes on goods and services	248.6	286.2	299.9
Taxes on international trade	44.5	49.7	43.2
Non-tax revenue	32.9	34.9	49.0
Total	457.0	526.7	543.4

Expenditure	2011	2012†	2013‡
Current expenditure	726.3	792.2	818.5
Compensation of employees	280.2	288.2	303.3
Goods and services	97.9	103.8	106.9
Transfers and subsidies	140.0	163.2	188.1
Interest payments	25.5	26.7	36.0
Other expense	182.6	210.4	184.0
Capital expenditure	463.2	477.6	438.2
Total	1,189.5	1,269.8	1,256.7

* Excluding grants received ('000 million Burundian francs): 615.0 in 2011; 610.2 in 2012 (preliminary figure); 641.8 in 2013 (projected figure).

† Preliminary figures.

‡ Projected figures.

Source: IMF, *Burundi: Third Review Under the Extended Credit Facility Arrangement and Request for Modification of Performance Criteria—Staff Report; Press Release on the Executive Board Discussion; and Statement by the Executive Director for Burundi* (September 2013).

INTERNATIONAL RESERVES

(US $ million at 31 December)

	2010	2011	2012
Gold*	1.36	1.50	1.61
IMF special drawing rights	112.77	121.31	129.17
Reserve position in IMF	0.55	0.55	0.55
Foreign exchange	217.41	172.12	177.44
Total	332.09	295.48	308.77

* Valued at market-related prices.

Source: IMF, *International Financial Statistics*.

MONEY SUPPLY

(million Burundian francs at 31 December)

	2010	2011	2012
Currency outside depository corporations	139,103	153,214	173,872
Transferable deposits	435,553	373,235	449,204
Other deposits	155,472	183,918	196,551
Broad money	730,128	710,367	819,626

Source: IMF, *International Financial Statistics*.

COST OF LIVING

(Consumer Price Index for Bujumbura; base: January 2000 = 100)

	2005	2006	2007
Food	139.4	139.5	151.6
Clothing	126.7	125.9	119.1
Rent	163.2	176.6	195.5
All items (incl. others)	144.8	148.6	161.0

Source: ILO.

All items (Consumer Price Index; base: 2005 = 100): 163.2 in 2010; 179.1 in 2011; 222.6 in 2012 (Source: IMF, *International Financial Statistics*).

NATIONAL ACCOUNTS

(million Burundian francs at current prices)

Expenditure on the Gross Domestic Product

	2009	2010*	2011*
Government final consumption expenditure	362,138	401,938	407,992
Private final consumption expenditure	2,062,873	2,350,181	2,650,980
Gross fixed capital formation	276,693	483,632	627,989
Change in inventories	–17,476	–169,842	–169,580
Total domestic expenditure	2,684,228	3,065,909	3,517,381
Exports of goods and services	193,172	269,453	246,120
Less Imports of goods and services	671,961	769,897	868,304
GDP in purchasers' values	2,205,440	2,565,465	2,895,197

2012 (provisional figures): Government final consumption expenditure 456,105; Private final consumption expenditure 3,490,512; Gross fixed capital formation 658,894; Change in inventories –357,710; *Total domestic expenditure* 4,247,801; Exports of goods and services 294,869; *Less* Imports of goods and services 1,286,245; *GDP in purchasers' values* 3,256,425.

Gross Domestic Product by Economic Activity

	2009	2010*	2011*
Agriculture, hunting, forestry and fishing	827,237	1,022,812	1,104,378
Mining and quarrying	13,007	14,585	18,259
Manufacturing	264,981	328,144	388,469
Electricity, gas and water	17,305	18,343	31,934
Construction	68,865	81,611	106,362
Trade, restaurants and hotels	455,387	450,902	531,171
Finance, insurance and real estate	73,942	81,941	92,817
Transport and communications	63,001	66,873	83,988
Public administration and defence	141,930	164,414	170,120
Other services	165,050	206,095	226,085
Sub-total	2,090,705	2,435,718	2,753,582
Less Imputed bank service charge	67,403	82,123	97,486
GDP at factor cost	2,023,303	2,353,595	2,656,096
Indirect taxes	182,137	211,870	239,101
GDP in purchasers' values	2,205,440	2,565,465	2,895,197

* Estimates.

2012 (provisional figures): Agriculture, hunting, forestry and fishing 1,230,645; Mining and quarrying 22,430; Manufacturing 453,522; Electricity, gas and water 39,164; Construction 130,529; Trade, restaurants and hotels 585,174; Finance, insurance and real estate 106,520; Transport and communications 97,332; Public administration and defence 193,029; Other services 241,263; *Sub-total* 3,099,608; *Less* Imputed bank service charge 112,116; *GDP at factor cost* 2,987,492; Indirect taxes, less subsidies 268,933; *GDP in purchasers' values* 3,256,425.

Source: African Development Bank.

BALANCE OF PAYMENTS

(US $ million)

	2010	2011	2012
Exports of goods	101.2	124.0	134.7
Imports of goods	–438.4	–552.5	–711.0
Balance on goods	–337.2	–428.5	–576.3
Export of services	79.5	111.7	92.8
Import of services	–168.3	–212.9	–211.6
Balance on goods and services	–426.0	–529.7	–695.1
Primary income received	1.1	7.5	11.4
Primary income paid	–12.0	–25.0	–17.9
Balance on goods, services and primary income	–436.9	–547.1	–701.6
Secondary income received	127.2	176.0	133.2
Secondary income paid	–13.6	–13.5	–9.9
Current balance	–323.2	–384.6	–578.3
Capital account (net)	75.7	59.7	123.3
Direct investment liabilities	0.8	3.4	0.6
Other investment assets	–43.6	–46.8	–50.0
Other investment liabilities	108.2	93.6	127.9
Net errors and omissions	6.2	7.7	4.2
Reserves and related items	–175.9	–267.1	–372.3

Source: IMF, *International Financial Statistics*.

External Trade

PRINCIPAL COMMODITIES

(distribution by HS, US $ million)

Imports c.i.f.	2010	2011	2012
Vegetables and vegetable products	30.2	170.0	252.5
Cereals	12.7	27.2	50.5
Milling products, malt, starches, inulin, wheat gluten	13.8	20.0	49.0
Wheat and meslin	2.0	7.5	15.4
Oil seed, oleagic fruits, grain, seed, fruit, etc.	0.8	116.4	148.4
Soya beans	—	113.8	109.5
Flour and meals of oil seeds	—	1.3	37.4
Prepared foodstuffs; beverages, spirits, vinegar; tobacco and articles thereof	22.0	89.3	32.0
Sugars and sugar confectionery	13.0	10.9	13.8
Cane or beet sugar and chemically pure sucrose, in solid form	12.4	9.7	12.5
Miscellaneous edible preparations	1.6	67.9	2.6
Food preparations	0.6	67.1	1.4
Mineral products	45.6	381.9	203.7
Salt, sulphur, earth, stone, plaster, lime and cement	37.0	38.8	33.3
Cements	34.9	34.7	29.7
Mineral fuels, oils, distillation products, etc.	8.6	343.1	170.2
Petroleum oils, not crude	6.5	321.1	161.5
Chemicals and related products	59.5	81.0	93.7
Pharmaceutical products	40.2	50.0	56.5
Medicament mixtures put in dosage	36.4	37.5	41.2
Plastics, rubber, and articles thereof	13.8	20.6	29.9
Pulp of wood, paper and paperboard, and articles thereof	12.2	15.8	24.8
Textiles and textile articles	19.0	26.8	31.0
Iron and steel, other base metals and articles of base metal	39.9	69.6	72.4
Iron and steel	21.9	36.5	36.8
Machinery and mechanical appliances; electrical equipment; parts thereof	71.1	130.3	126.2
Machinery, boilers, etc.	30.5	67.0	62.4
Electrical and electronic equipment	40.6	63.3	63.7
Vehicles, aircraft, vessels and associated transport equipment	50.5	50.5	56.6
Vehicles other than railway, tramway	50.4	57.2	54.5
Total (incl. others)	404.1	1,127.7	1,003.1

Exports f.o.b.	2010	2011	2012
Vegetables and vegetable products	81.7	88.7	80.8
Coffee, tea, mate and spices	80.5	87.9	80.5
Coffee	70.4	75.2	66.1
Tea	10.1	12.7	14.4
Prepared foodstuffs; beverages, spirits, vinegar; tobacco and articles thereof	3.9	3.7	5.9
Sugars, molasses and honey	1.4	1.8	1.2
Mineral products	5.9	11.2	17.8
Ores, slag and ash	3.4	10.5	17.3
Ores and concentrates	0.2	5.9	16.8
Chemicals and related products	1.5	4.5	6.2
Soaps, lubricants, waxes, candles and modelling pastes	1.3	4.3	5.9
Raw hides and skins, leather, furskins, etc., and articles thereof	3.6	6.4	7.0
Raw hides and skins (other than furskins) and leather	3.6	6.4	7.0
Articles of stone, plaster, cement, asbestos; ceramic and glass products	—	3.7	3.0
Glass and glassware	—	3.7	2.9
Pearls, precious or semi-precious stones, precious metals, and articles thereof	13.0	59.3	105.2
Gold (unwrought or semi-manufactured)	13.0	59.0	105.2
Machinery and mechanical appliances; electrical equipment; parts thereof	1.1	11.0	3.4
Electrical and electronic equipment	0.6	8.1	0.7
Vehicles, aircraft, vessels and associated transport equipment	1.6	4.1	6.2
Vehicles other than railway, tramway	1.6	4.1	6.2
Total (incl. others)	118.2	197.8	242.7

Source: Trade Map-Trade Competitiveness Map, International Trade Centre, www.intracen.org/marketanalysis.

PRINCIPAL TRADING PARTNERS

(US $ million)

Imports c.i.f.	2010	2011	2012
Belgium	48.6	69.0	79.6
China, People's Repub.	48.6	60.3	78.4
Denmark	6.5	84.0	9.8
Egypt	11.2	14.8	13.3
France (incl. Monaco)	28.9	42.9	29.8
Germany	6.4	24.7	15.5
India	24.3	38.6	77.9
Italy	5.4	9.8	176.7
Japan	37.9	28.6	22.2
Kenya	29.5	45.7	46.5
Rwanda	2.5	6.8	29.7
Saudi Arabia	2.3	270.0	82.3
South Africa	6.6	19.8	32.4
Tanzania	24.1	161.2	53.1
Turkey	2.0	9.6	12.4
Uganda	27.6	53.5	45.1
United Arab Emirates	18.7	33.8	30.3
United Kingdom	5.1	16.2	9.7
USA	6.0	32.7	35.3
Zambia	34.0	35.0	35.4
Total (incl. others)	404.1	1,127.7	1,003.1

Exports f.o.b.	2010	2011	2012
Belgium	15.4	18.3	0.2
Congo, Democratic Repub.	7.3	10.4	0.1
France (incl. Monaco)	0.8	1.8	2.7
Germany	2.5	3.2	0.2
Hong Kong	2.2	2.8	—
Kenya	10.3	15.2	0.7
Netherlands	0.7	9.1	—
Oman	1.8	2.2	—
Rwanda	3.0	6.1	1.2
Singapore	7.2	1.2	—
Swaziland	1.3	—	—
Switzerland and Liechtenstein	31.8	33.9	0.6
Tanzania	1.8	1.4	2.1
Uganda	2.9	5.7	0.7
United Arab Emirates	10.5	58.2	39.6
United Kingdom	15.8	17.6	0.9
Total (incl. others)	118.2	197.8	242.7

Source: Trade Map-Trade Competitiveness Map, International Trade Centre, www.intracen.org/marketanalysis.

Transport

ROAD TRAFFIC
('000 motor vehicles in use, estimates)

	1998	1999	2000
Passenger cars	6.6	6.9	7.0
Commercial vehicles	9.3	9.3	9.3

2001–03 ('000 motor vehicles in use): Figures assumed to be unchanged from 2000.

Source: UN, *Statistical Yearbook*.

2007 (motor vehicles in use at 31 December): Passenger cars 15,466; Vans and lorries 32,717; Motorcycles and mopeds 11,302 (Source: IRF, *World Road Statistics*).

LAKE TRAFFIC
(Bujumbura, '000 metric tons)

	2010	2011	2012
Goods:			
arrivals	222.8	224.2	183.1
departures	22.8	9.5	16.0

Source: Banque de la République du Burundi.

CIVIL AVIATION
(traffic on scheduled services)

	1996	1997	1998
Passengers carried ('000)	9	12	12
Passenger-km (million)	2	8	8

Source: UN, *Statistical Yearbook*.

Tourism

TOURIST ARRIVALS BY REGION*

	2008	2009	2010
Africa	177,579	186,457	122,045
Americas	5,044	5,297	3,883
Asia	4,237	4,449	2,912
Europe	12,107	12,713	9,985
Unspecified	2,828	2,968	3,486
Total	201,795	211,884	142,311

* Including Burundian nationals residing abroad.

Tourism receipts (US $ million, incl. passenger transport): 2.1 in 2010; 2.0 in 2010; 3.0 in 2011.

Source: World Tourism Organization.

Communications Media

	2010	2011	2012
Telephones ('000 main lines in use)	35.0	30.0	17.4
Mobile cellular telephones ('000 subscribers)	1,678.0	1,914.6	2,247.1
Broadband subscribers	352	352	352

Internet subscribers: 17,700 in 2009.

Source: International Telecommunication Union.

Education

(2011/12 unless otherwise indicated)

	Teachers	Students		
		Males	Females	Total
Pre-primary	1,418	23,235	23,507	46,742
Primary	42,052	984,434	996,412	1,980,846
Secondary:				
General	13,061	226,223	176,510	402,733
Technical and vocational	1,080	11,635	5,749	17,384
Higher*	1,784	18,917	10,352	29,269

* 2009/10 figures.

Institutions (1988/89): Primary 1,512; Secondary 400.

Source: UNESCO Institute for Statistics.

Pupil-teacher ratio (primary education, UNESCO estimate): 47.1 in 2011/12 (Source: UNESCO Institute for Statistics).

Adult literacy rate (UNESCO estimates): 67.2% (males 72.9%; females 61.8%) in 2010 (Source: UNESCO Institute for Statistics).

Directory

The Government

HEAD OF STATE

President: Maj. JEAN-PIERRE NKURUNZIZA (inaugurated 26 August 2005; re-elected 28 June 2010).

First Vice-President: PROSPER BAZOMBANZA.

Second Vice-President: GERVAIS RUFYIKIRI.

COUNCIL OF MINISTERS

(April 2014)

The Government comprises members of the Conseil National pour la Défense de la Démocratie—Forces pour la Défense de la Démocratie (CNDD—FDD), the Front pour la Démocratie au Burundi (FRODEBU-Nyakuri), the Union pour le Progrès National (UPRONA) and independents.

Minister of the Interior: EDOUARD NDUWIMANA (CNDD—FDD).

Minister of Public Security: GABRIEL NIZIGAMA (CNDD—FDD).

Minister of External Relations and International Co-operation: LAURENT KAVAKURE (CNDD—FDD).

Minister at the Presidency, in charge of Good Governance and Privatization: ERNEST MBERAMIHETO (FRODEBU-Nyakuri).

Minister at the Presidency, in charge of East African Community Affairs: HAFSA MOSSI (CNDD—FDD).

Minister of Justice, Keeper of the Seals: PASCAL BARANDAGIYE (CNDD—FDD).

Minister of Finance and Planning for Economic Development: TABU ABDALLAH MANIRAKIZA (CNDD—FDD).

Minister of Communal Development: DIEUDONNÉ GITERUZI (UPRONA).

Minister of National Defence and War Veterans: Maj.-Gen. PONTIEN GACIYUBWENGE (Ind.).

Minister of Public Health and the Fight against AIDS: Dr SABINE NTAKARUTIMANA (CNDD—FDD).

Minister of Higher Education and Scientific Research: JOSEPH BUTORE (CNDD—FDD).

Minister of Primary and Secondary Education, Professional and Vocational Training and Literacy: ROSE GAHIRU (CNDD—FDD).

Minister of Agriculture and Livestock: ODETTE KAYITESI (CNDD—FDD).

Minister of Telecommunications, Information, Communications and Relations with Parliament: THARCISSE NKEZABAHIZI (UPRONA).

Minister of Water, the Environment, Territorial Development and Town Planning: JEAN CLAUDE NDUWAYO (CNDD—FDD).

Minister of Commerce, Industry, Posts and Tourism: MARIE ROSE NIZIGIYIMANA (UPRONA).

Minister of Energy and Mines: CÔME MANIRAKIZA (CNDD—FDD).

Minister of Civil Service, Labour and Social Security: ANNONCIATE SENDAZIRASA (CNDD—FDD).

Minister of Transport, Public Works and Equipment: VIRGINIE CIZA (CNDD—FDD).

Minister of Youth, Sports and Culture: ADOLPHE RUKENKANYA (CNDD—FDD).

Minister of National Solidarity, Human Rights and Gender: CLOTILDE NIRAGIRA (CNDD—FDD).

MINISTRIES

Office of the President: Bujumbura; tel. 22226063; internet www.presidence.bi.

Ministry of Agriculture and Livestock: Bujumbura; tel. 22222087.

Ministry of Civil Service, Labour and Social Security: BP 1480, Bujumbura; tel. 22225645; fax 22228715.

Ministry of Commerce, Industry, Posts and Tourism: BP 492, Bujumbura; tel. 22225330; fax 22225595.

Ministry of Communal Development: Bujumbura; internet www.miniplan.bi.

Ministry of Energy and Mines: BP 745, Bujumbura; tel. 22225909; fax 22223337.

Ministry of External Relations and International Co-operation: Bujumbura; tel. 22222150.

Ministry of Finance and Planning for Economic Development: ave des Non-Aligens, BP 1830, Bujumbura; tel. 22225142; fax 22223128; internet www.finances.gov.bi.

Ministry of Higher Education and Scientific Research: Bujumbura.

Ministry of the Interior: Bujumbura.

Ministry of Justice: Grand Bureau, pl. de la Révolution, ave de la Liberté, Bujumbura; tel. 22253379; e-mail info@justice.gov.bi; internet justice.gov.bi.

Ministry of National Defence and War Veterans: Bujumbura.

Ministry of National Solidarity, Human Rights and Gender: BP 224, Bujumbura; tel. 22225394; fax 22224193; e-mail ministre@miniplan.bi; internet www.cslpminiplan.bi.

Ministry of Primary and Secondary Education, Professional and Vocational Training and Literacy: Bujumbura.

Ministry of Public Health and the Fight against AIDS: rue Pierre Ngendandumwe, Bujumbura.

Ministry of Public Security: Bujumbura.

Ministry of Telecommunications, Information, Communications and Relations with Parliament: BP 2870, Bujumbura.

Ministry of Transport, Public Works and Equipment: BP 2000, Bujumbura; tel. 22222923; fax 22226900; internet www.mttpe-burundi.org.

Minister of Water, the Environment, Territorial Development and Town Planning: BP 631, Bujumbura; tel. 22224976; fax 22228902; e-mail nduwi_deo@yahoo.fr; internet www.meeatu.gov.bi.

Ministry of Youth, Sports and Culture: Bujumbura; tel. 22226822.

President

A presidential election was held on 28 June 2010 at which Jean-Pierre Nkurunziza, representing the Conseil National pour la Défense de la Démocratie—Forces pour la Défense de la Démocratie, was the sole candidate. According to results confirmed by the Constitutional Court on 8 July, Nkurunziza secured 2,482,219 of the 2,709,941 votes cast, equating to 91.60%. (There were 29,195 invalid votes cast.)

Legislature

SENATE

President: GABRIEL NTISEZERANA (CNDD—FDD).

First Vice-President: PERSILLE MWIDOGO (CNDD—FDD).

Second Vice-President: PONTIEN NIYONGABO (UPRONA).

Elections, 28 July 2010

Party	Seats*
CNDD—FDD	32
UPRONA	2
Total	34

* In accordance with constitutional requirements for balance of ethnic representation and a minimum 30% representation of women, a further four seats were allocated to former Presidents and three to the Twa ethnic group, increasing the total number of senators to 41.

NATIONAL ASSEMBLY

President: PIE NTAVYOHANYUMA (CNDD—FDD).

First Vice-President: MO-MAMO KARERWA (CNDD—FDD).

Second Vice-President: FRANÇOIS KABURA (UPRONA).

Elections, 23 July 2010

Party	Seats*
CNDD—FDD	81
UPRONA	17
FRODEBU-Nyakuri	5
Total	103

* In accordance with constitutional requirements for balance of ethnic representation and a minimum 30% representation of women, a further three seats were allocated to the Twa ethnic group, increasing the total number of deputies to 106. The CNDD—FDD, FRODEBU-Nyakuri and UPRONA each received an additional seat.

Election Commission

Commission Electorale Nationale Indépendante (CENI): Commune Ngagara, Quartier Industriel, blvd de l'OUA, rue Nyankoni, Parcelle N° 690/C, BP 1128, Bujumbura; tel. 22274464; tel. info@ceniburundi.bi; internet www.ceniburundi.bi; f. 2004; independent; 5 mems; Chair. PIERRE CLAVER NDAYICARIYE; Vice-Chair. SPÈS CARITAS NDIRONKEYE.

Political Organizations

Political parties are required to demonstrate firm commitment to national unity, and impartiality with regard to ethnic or regional origin, gender and religion, in order to receive legal recognition. By 2010 the number of registered political parties had increased to 44; these included former rebel organizations.

Alliance Burundaise-Africaine pour le Salut (ABASA): Bujumbura; f. 1993; Tutsi; Leader TÉRENCE NSANZE.

Alliance Démocratique pour le Changement au Burundi (ADC—Ikibiri): Bujumbura; f. 2010; coalition of 12 opposition parties, including Front pour la Démocratie au Burundi (FRODEBU); Pres. LÉONCE NGENDAKUMANA.

Conseil National pour la Défense de la Démocratie (CNDD): Bujumbura; e-mail cndd_bur@usa.net; internet www.club.euronet.be/pascal.karolero.cndd.burundi; f. 1994; Hutu; Pres. LÉONARD NYANGOMA.

Conseil National pour la Défense de la Démocratie—Forces pour la Défense de la Démocratie (CNDD—FDD): fmr armed wing of the Hutu CNDD; split into 2 factions in Oct. 2001, one led by JEAN-BOSCO NDAYIKENGURUKIYE and the other by JEAN-PIERRE NKURUNZIZA; Nkurunziza's faction incl. in Govt Nov. 2003, following peace agreement; registered as political org. Jan. 2005; Chair. PASCAL NYABENDA; Sec.-Gen. GÉLASE NDABIRABE.

Forces Nationales de Libération (FNL): fmr armed wing of Hutu Parti de Libération du Peuple Hutu (PALIPEHUTU, f. 1980); split in Aug. 2002 and in Dec. 2005; ceasefire with Govt announced Sept. 2006; formally registered as a political organization in 2009; Chair. JACQUES BIGIRIMANA.

Forces Nationales de Libération—Iragi rya Gahutu: f. 2009; Leader JACQUES KENESE.

Front National de Libération Icanzo (FNL Icanzo): reconstituted Dec. 2002 from fmr faction of Forces Nationales de Libération; Leader Dr ALAIN MUGABARABONA.

Front pour la Démocratie au Burundi (FRODEBU): Bujumbura; internet www.frodebu.bi; f. 1992; Hutu; Chair. LÉONCE NGENDAKUMANA.

FRODEBU-Nyakuri: Bujumbura; f. 2008; Leader JEAN MINANI.

Mouvement pour la Réhabilitation du Citoyen—Rurenzangemero (MRC—Rurenzangemero): Bujumbura; f. June 2001; regd Nov. 2002; Leader Lt-Col EPITACE BAYAGANAKANDI.

Mouvement pour la Sécurité et la Démocratie: tel. 29550803; e-mail msdburundi@yahoo.fr; Pres. ALEXIS SINDUHIJE; Sec.-Gen. FRANÇOIS NYAMOYA.

Mouvement Socialiste Panafricaniste—Inkinzo y'Ijambo Ry'abarundi (MSP—Inkinzo) (Guarantor of Freedom of Speech in Burundi): Bujumbura; f. 1993; Tutsi; Chair. TITE BUCUMI.

Parti Libéral (PL): BP 2167, Bujumbura; tel. 22214848; fax 22225981; e-mail liberalburundi@yahoo.fr; f. 1992; Hutu; Leader GAËTAN NIKOBAMYE.

Parti pour le Développement et la Solidarité des Travailleurs (PML-Abanyamwete): Bujumbura; f. Oct. 2004; Leader PATRICIA NDAYIZEYE.

Parti pour la Réconciliation du Peuple (PRP): Bujumbura; f. 1992; Tutsi; Leader DÉOGRATIAS RUSENGWAMIHIGO.

Parti pour le Redressement Intégral du Burundi (PARIBU): Bujumbura; f. Sept. 2004; Leader BENOÎT NDORIMANA.

Parti pour le Redressement National (PARENA): Bujumbura; f. 1994; Leader JEAN-BAPTISTE BAGAZA.

Parti Social Démocrate (PSD): Bujumbura; f. 1993; Tutsi; Leader GODEFROID HAKIZIMANA.

Rassemblement pour la Démocratie et le Développement Economique et Social (RADDES): Bujumbura; f. 1992; Tutsi; Chair. DISMAS NDITABIRIYE.

Union pour la Paix et le Développement (Zigamibanga): f. Aug. 2002; Leader ZEDI FERUZI.

Union pour le Progrès National (UPRONA): BP 1810, Bujumbura; tel. 22225028; internet www.uprona.org; f. 1958; Chair. BONAVENTURE NIYOYANKANA.

Diplomatic Representation

EMBASSIES IN BURUNDI

Belgium: 18 blvd de la Liberté, BP 1920, Bujumbura; tel. 22226176; fax 22223171; e-mail bujumbura@diplobel.fed.be; internet diplomatie.belgium.be/burundi; Ambassador MARC GEDOPT.

China, People's Republic: 675 sur la Parcelle, BP 2550, Bujumbura; tel. 22224307; fax 22213735; e-mail chinaemb_bi@mfa.gov.cn; internet bi.chineseembassy.org/chn; Ambassador YU XUZHONG.

Congo, Democratic Republic: BP 872, Bujumbura; tel. 22229330; e-mail ambardcbujumbura@yahoo.fr; Ambassador SALOMON BANAMUHERE BALIÈNE.

Egypt: 31 ave de la Liberté, BP 1520, Bujumbura; tel. 22223161; fax 22222918; Ambassador ABDEL MONE'M OMAR ABDEL MONE'M.

France: 60 ave de l'UPRONA, BP 1740, Bujumbura; tel. 22203000; fax 22203010; e-mail cad.bujumbura-amba@diplomatie.gouv.fr; internet www.ambafrance-bi.org; Ambassador GERRIT VAN ROSSUM.

Germany: 22 rue 18 septembre, BP 480, Bujumbura; tel. 22257777; fax 22221004; e-mail info@buju.diplo.de; Ambassador BRUNO BROMMER.

Holy See: 28 ave des Travailleurs, BP 1068, Bujumbura; tel. 22225415; fax 22223176; e-mail na.burundi@diplomat.va; Apostolic Nuncio (vacant).

Kenya: PTA Bank Bldg, 2nd Floor, West Wing Chaussée du Prince Louis Rwagasore, BP 5138, Mutanga, Bujumbura; tel. 22258160; fax 22258161; e-mail information@kenyaembassy.bu; Ambassador BENJAMIN A. W. MWERI.

Nigeria: Bujumbura; tel. 22257076; Ambassador OKWUDILI OBIDIGBO NWOSU.

Russia: 78 blvd de l'UPRONA, BP 1034, Bujumbura; tel. 22226098; fax 22222984; e-mail ustas@cbinf.com; Ambassador VLADIMIR MALYSHEV.

Rwanda: 40 ave de la RDC, BP 400, Bujumbura; tel. 22228755; fax 22215426; e-mail ambabuja@minaffet.gov.rw; internet www.burundi.embassy.gov.rw; Ambassador AUGUSTIN HABIMANA.

South Africa: ave de la Plage, Quartier Asiatique, BP 185, Bujumbura; tel. 22248220; fax 22248219; e-mail bujumbura@foreign.gov.za; Ambassador O. E. MONARENG.

Tanzania: Kabondo, Mpotsa Ave, BP 855, Bujumbura; tel. 22248636; fax 22248637; e-mail tanzanrep@usan-bu.net; Ambassador Dr JAMES MWASI NZAGI.

USA: ave des Etats-Unis, BP 1720, Bujumbura; tel. 22223454; fax 22222926; e-mail jyellin@bujumbura.us-state.gov; internet burundi.usembassy.gov; Ambassador DAWN M. LIBERI.

Judicial System

Constitutional Court: BP 151, Bujumbura; comprises a minimum of 7 judges, who are nominated by the President for a 6-year term; Pres. CHRISTINE NZEYIMANA.

Supreme Court: BP 1460, Bujumbura; tel. and fax 22213544; court of final instance; 3 divisions: ordinary, cassation and administrative; Pres. (vacant).

Courts of Appeal: Bujumbura, Gitega and Ngozi.

Attorney-General: VALENTIN BAGORIKUNDA.

There are also 17 provincial tribunals (one in each commune) and 134 smaller resident tribunals.

Religion

Some 70% of the population are Christians, the majority of whom are Roman Catholics. Anglicans number about 60,000. There are about 200,000 other Protestant adherents, of whom about 160,000 are Pentecostalists. About 23% of the population adhere to traditional beliefs, which include the worship of the god Imana. About 10% of the population are Muslims. The Bahá'í Faith is also active in Burundi.

Conseil Interconfessionnel du Burundi (CICB): 42 ave de France, BP 1390, Bujumbura; tel. 22259153; e-mail info@religionsforpeaceburundi.org; internet religionsforpeaceburundi@gmail.com; f. 2008.

CHRISTIANITY

Conseil National des Eglises Protestantes du Burundi (CNEB): BP 17, Bujumbura; tel. 22224216; fax 22227941; e-mail cneb@cbninf.com; f. 1935; 10 mem. churches; Pres. Rev. JUVÉNAL NZOSABA; Gen. Sec. Rev. NOAH NZEYIMANA.

The Anglican Communion

The Church of the Province of Burundi, established in 1992, comprises seven dioceses.

Archbishop of Burundi and Bishop of Matana: Most Rev. BERNARD NTAHOTURI, BP 447, Bujumbura; tel. 22924595; fax 22229129; e-mail ntahober@cbinf.com.

Provincial Secretary: (vacant), BP 447, Bujumbura; tel. 22270361; fax 22229129; e-mail peab@cbinf.com.

The Roman Catholic Church

Burundi comprises two archdioceses and six dioceses. Some 69% of the total population are Roman Catholics.

Bishops' Conference: Conférence des Evêques Catholiques du Burundi, 5 blvd de l'UPRONA, BP 1390, Bujumbura; tel. 22223263; fax 22223270; e-mail cecab@cbinf.com; f. 1980; Pres. Rev. GERVAIS BANSHIMIYUBUSA (Bishop of Ngozi).

Archbishop of Bujumbura: Rt Rev. EVARISTE NGOYAGOYE, BP 690, Bujumbura; tel. 22231476; fax 22231165; e-mail dicabu@cni.cbinf.com.

Archbishop of Gitega: Most Rev. SIMON NTAMWANA, Archevêché, BP 118, Gitega; tel. 22402160; fax 22402620; e-mail archigi@bujumbura.ocicnet.net.

Other Christian Churches

Union of Baptist Churches of Burundi: Rubura, DS 117, Bujumbura 1; 87 mem. churches; Pres. PAUL BARUHENAMWO; mems 25,505 (2005).

Other denominations active in the country include the Evangelical Christian Brotherhood of Burundi, the Free Methodist Church of Burundi and the United Methodist Church of Burundi.

ISLAM

Communauté Islamique du Burundi: BP 2741, Bujumbura; tel. 22215749; fax 22219371; e-mail comibu2006@yahoo.fr.

BAHÁ'Í FAITH

National Spiritual Assembly: BP 1578, Bujumbura; tel. 79320312; e-mail bahaiburundi@yahoo.fr; f. 1973; Sec. DENIS NDAYIZEYE.

The Press

Conseil National de la Communication (CNC): Immeuble Marcoil, blvd de l'UPRONA, Bujumbura; tel. 22259064; fax 22259066; e-mail info@cnc-burundi.org; internet cnc-burundi.org; f. 2001; responsible for ensuring press freedom; Pres. PIERRE BAMBASI; Sec. ESPÉRANCE NDAYIZEYE.

NEWSPAPER

Le Renouveau du Burundi: BP 2573, Bujumbura; tel. 22225411; e-mail lerenouveaubdi@yahoo.fr; f. 1978; daily; French; govt-owned; Dir of Publication CHANNEL SABIMBONA; Editor-in-Chief PASCALINE BIDUDA; circ. 1,200 (2011).

PERIODICALS

Arc-en-Ciel: Bujumbura; weekly; French; Editor-in-Chief THIERRY NDAYISHIMIYE.

Au Coeur de l'Afrique: Association des conférences des ordinaires du Rwanda et Burundi, BP 1390, Bujumbura; fax 22223027; e-mail cnid@cbinf.com; bimonthly; education; circ. 1,000.

Bulletin Economique et Financier: BP 482, Bujumbura; bimonthly.

Bulletin Mensuel: Banque de la République du Burundi, Service des études, BP 705, Bujumbura; tel. 22225142; monthly.

In-Burundi: c/o Cyber Média, BP 5270, ave du 18 septembre, Bujumbura; tel. 2244464; current affairs internet publication; Editor-in-Chief EDGAR C. MBANZA.

Iwacu: ave de France 6, BP 1842, Bujumbura; tel. 22258957; fax 79991474; internet www.iwacu-burundi.org; f. 2008; weekly; publ. by the Union Burundaise des Journalistes; Editor-in-Chief ANTOINE KABURAHE.

Ndongozi Y'uburundi: Catholic Mission, BP 690, Bujumbura; tel. 22222762; fax 22228907; fortnightly; Kirundi.

Revue Administration et Juridique: Association d'Etudes Administratives et Juridiques du Burundi, BP 1613, Bujumbura; quarterly; French.

Ubumwe: Bujumbura; tel. 22225654; fax 22225894; e-mail ubumwebdi@yahoo.fr; internet www.ppbdi.com; weekly; Editor-in-Chief PACIFIQUE NKESHIMANA; circ. 2,500 (2011).

PRESS ASSOCIATIONS

Association Burundaise des Femmes Journalistes (AFJO): ave Kunkiko, BP 2414, Bujumbura; tel. 79949460; fax 22254920; e-mail nijembazi@yahoo.fr; Pres. ANNICK NSABIMANA.

Union Burundaise des Journalistes (UBJ): Bujumbura; internet www.ubj-burundi.org; fmrly Association Burundaise des Journalistes (ABJ), present name adopted 2009; Pres. ALEXANDRE NIYUNGEKO; Sec.-Gen. BERTRAND BIHIZI.

NEWS AGENCY

Agence Burundaise de Presse (ABP): Quartier Asiatique, ave du Lac, BP 2870, Bujumbura; tel. 22213083; fax 22222282; e-mail abp@cbinf.com; internet www.abpinfo.org; f. 1975; publ. daily bulletin; Dir JEAN PAUL CIZA.

Publishers

Editions Intore: 19 ave Matana, BP 2524, Bujumbura; tel. 22223499; e-mail anbirabuza@yahoo.fr; f. 1992; philosophy, history, journalism, literature, social sciences; Dir Dr ANDRÉ BIRABUZA.

IMPARUDI: ave du 18 septembre 3, BP 3010, Bujumbura; tel. 22223125; fax 22222572; e-mail imparudi.1982@yahoo.fr; f. 1950; Dir-Gen. THÉONESTE MUTAMBUKA.

Imprimerie la Licorne: 29 ave de la Mission, BP 2942, Bujumbura; tel. 22223503; fax 22227225; f. 1991.

Les Presses Lavigerie: 5 ave de l'UPRONA, BP 1640, Bujumbura; tel. 22222368; fax 22220318.

Régie de Productions Pédagogiques: BP 3118, Bujumbura II; tel. 22226111; fax 22222631; e-mail rpp@cbinf.com; f. 1984; school textbooks; Dir ABRAHAM MBONERANE.

GOVERNMENT PUBLISHING HOUSE

Imprimerie Nationale du Burundi (INABU): BP 991, Bujumbura; tel. 22224046; fax 22225399; f. 1978; Dir NICOLAS NIJIMBERE.

Broadcasting and Communications

TELECOMMUNICATIONS

In 2011 there were five providers of cellular mobile telephone communications services. The state-owned ONATEL provided fixed-line services. In 2010 there were some 1.7m. mobile telephone subscribers.

Econet Wireless Burundi: 21 blvd du 28 Novembre, BP 431, Bujumbura; tel. 22243131; fax 22243535; internet www.econet.bi; formerly Spacetel; mobile and fixed telecommunications services and products, satellite services and internet solutions; Dir-Gen. DARLINGTON MANDIVENGA.

Leo Burundi: 1 pl. de l'Indépendance, BP 5186, Bujumbura; tel. 79910910 (mobile); e-mail feliciten@leo.bi; internet www.leo.bi; f. 1993; fmrly Telecel Burundi, Leo Burundi is the trade name of U-Com Burundi; mobile telephone service provider; a subsidiary of Orascom Telecom Holding; Dir-Gen. ABDALLAH EL KABDANI.

Office National des Télécommunications (ONATEL): 1 ave du Commerce, BP 60, Bujumbura; tel. 22266601; fax 22266606; e-mail info@onatelburundi.bi; internet onatel.net; f. 1979; Dir-Gen. DONATIEN NDAYISHIMIYE.

ONAMOB: Bujumbura; mobile cellular telephone operator owned by ONATEL.

Smart Mobile: Immeuble White Stone, blvd de l'Uprona Centre, BP 3150, Bujumbura; internet lacellsu.com; f. 2010; trade name of Lacell SU; Dir-Gen. BHUPENDRA BHANDARI.

Tempo Africell: ave de la RDC, Bujumbura; tel. 78872872; e-mail africell@cbinf.com; internet www.tempo.bi; f. 1999 as Africell; name changed as above in 2008 following acquisition by VTEL Holdings (United Arab Emirates); mobile cellular telephone service provider; CEO YANAL ABZACK.

Regulatory Authority

Agence de Régulation et de Contrôle des Télécommunications (ARCT): 360 ave Patrice Lumumba, BP 6702, Bujumbura; tel. 22210276; fax 22242832; Dir-Gen. SALVATOR NIZIGIYIMANA.

BROADCASTING

In 2010 there were some 15 private radio stations and one private television channel operating in Burundi, in addition to the state-run Radiodiffusion et Télévision Nationale du Burundi.

Radio

Radio Bonesha FM: BP 5314, Bujumbura; tel. 22217068; e-mail umwizero@cbinf.com; f. 1996 as Radio Umwizero; EU-funded, private station promoting national reconciliation, peace and devt projects; broadcasts 9 hours daily in Kirundi, Swahili and French; Dir HUBERT VIEILLE.

Radio Isanganiro: 27 ave de l'Amitié, BP 810, Bujumbura; tel. 22246595; fax 22246600; e-mail isanganiro@isanganiro.org; internet www.isanganiro.org; f. Nov. 2002; controlled by Association Ijambo, f. by Studio Ijambo (see below); broadcasts on 89.7 FM frequency, in Kirundi, French and Swahili; services cover Bujumbura area, and were to be extended to all Great Lakes region; Dir VINCENT NKESHIMANA.

Radio Publique Africaine (RPA): Bujumbura; tel. 79920704; e-mail nfo@rpa-radioyacu.org; internet www.rpa-radiyoyacu.org; f. 2001 with the aim of promoting peace; independent; Dir ALEXIS SINDUHIJE.

Radio Renaissance FM: Bujumbura; f. 2003; Dir-Gen. INNOCENT MUHOZI.

Radio Sans Frontières Bonesha FM: Association Radio Sans Frontières 47, Chemin P. L. Rwagasore, BP 5314, Bujumbura; internet www.bonesha.bi; Dir CORNEILLE NIBARUTA.

Rema FM: Bujumbura; f. 2008.

Studio Ijambo (Wise Words): 27 ave de l'Amitié, BP 6180, Bujumbura; tel. 22219699; e-mail burundi@sfcg.org.bi; internet www.studioijambo.org; f. 1995 by Search for Common Ground; promotes peace and reconciliation.

Voix de la Révolution/La Radiodiffusion et Télévision Nationale du Burundi (RTNB): BP 1900, Bujumbura; tel. 22223742; fax

22226547; internet www.rtnb.bi; f. 1960; govt-controlled; daily radio broadcasts in Kirundi, Swahili, French and English; Pres. SALVATOR NIZIGIYIMANA; Dir FRÉDÉRIC NZEYIMANA.

Television

Télé Renaissance: Bujumbura; f. 2008; Dir-Gen. INNOCENT MUHOZI.

Voix de la Révolution/La Radiodiffusion et Télévision Nationale du Burundi (RTNB): BP 1900, Bujumbura; tel. 22223742; fax 22226547; internet www.rtnb.bi; f. 1960; govt-controlled; television service in Kirundi, Swahili, French and English; Pres. SALVATOR NIZIGIYIMANA; Dir NESTOR BANKUMUKUNZI.

Finance

(cap. = capital; res = reserves; dep. = deposits; m. = million; brs = branches; amounts in Burundian francs)

BANKING

In early 2013 there were 10 commercial banks and 22 microfinancial institutions in Burundi.

Central Bank

Banque de la République du Burundi (BRB): ave du Gouvernement, BP 705, Bujumbura; tel. 22225142; fax 22223128; e-mail brb@brb.bi; internet www.brb.bi; f. 1964 as Banque du Royaume du Burundi; state-owned; bank of issue; cap. 11,000m., res 21,780m., dep. 169,043m. (Dec. 2009); Gov. JEAN CIZA; First Vice-Gov. MELCHIOR WAGARA; 2 brs.

Commercial Banks

Banque Burundaise pour le Commerce et l'Investissement SARL (BBCI): blvd du Peuple Murundi, BP 2320, Bujumbura; tel. 22223328; fax 22223339; e-mail bbci@cbinf.com; f. 1988; cap. and res 2,645.8m., total assets 14,016.2m. (Dec. 2003); Pres. CELESLIN MIZERO; Dir-Gen. CHARLES NIHANGAZA.

Banque Commerciale du Burundi SM (BANCOBU): 84 chaussée Prince Louis Rwagasore, BP 990, Bujumbura; tel. 22222317; fax 22221018; e-mail info@bancobu.com; internet www.bancobu.com; f. 1960; cap. 10,010.0m., res 11,500.7m., dep. 105,607.4m. (Dec. 2012); Pres. LÉA NGABIRE; Dir-Gen. JEAN CIZA; 8 brs.

Banque de Crédit de Bujumbura SM: ave Patrice Emery Lumumba, BP 300, Bujumbura; tel. 22201111; fax 22201115; e-mail info@bcb.bi; internet www.bcb.bi; f. 1964; cap. 13,000.0m., res 14,521.2m., dep. 237,254.5m. (Dec. 2012); Pres. and Dir-Gen THARCISSE RUTUMO; 8 brs.

Banque de Financement et de Leasing S.A.: blvd de la Liberté, BP 2998, Bujumbura; tel. 22243206; fax 22225437; e-mail finalease@cbinf.com; cap. and res 1,400.5m., total assets 8,578.4m. (Dec. 2003); Pres. AUDACE BIREHA; Dir-Gen. ERIC BONANE RUBEGA.

Banque de Gestion et de Financement SA: 1 blvd de la Liberté, BP 1035, Bujumbura; tel. 22221349; fax 22221351; e-mail bgf@onatel.bi; f. 1996; cap. 1,029.0m., res 986.1m., dep. 19,791.7m. (Dec. 2006); Pres. BÉDE BEDETSE; Gen. Man. MATHIAS NDIKUMANA.

Ecobank Burundi: 6 rue de la Science, BP 270, Bujumbura; tel. 22226351; fax 22225437; e-mail ecobankbi@ecobank.com; internet www.ecobank.com; cap. 10,500.1m., res 938.7m., dep. 48,368.0m. (Dec. 2011); Chair. ISAAC BUDABUDA; Man. Dir STEPHANE DOUKOURE.

Interbank Burundi SARL: 15 rue de l'Industrie, BP 2970, Bujumbura; tel. 22220629; fax 22220461; e-mail info@interbankbdi.com; internet www.interbankbdi.com; f. 1993; cap. 18,166.5m., res 4,758.2m., dep. 199,905.0m. (Dec. 2011); Pres. GEORGES COUCOULIS; Dir-Gen. CALLIXTE MUTABAZI.

Development Bank

Banque Nationale pour le Développement Economique SARL (BNDE): 3 ave du Marché, BP 1620, Bujumbura; tel. 22222888; fax 22223775; e-mail bnde@cbinf.com; internet www.bndesm.com; f. 1966; 40% state-owned; cap. 6,190.1m., res 811.3m., dep. 6,526.1m. (Dec. 2009); Chair. and Man. Dir DONATIEN NIJIMBERE.

Co-operative Bank

Banque Coopérative d'Epargne et de Crédit Mutuel (BCM): BP 1340, Bujumbura; operating licence granted in April 1995; Vice-Pres. JULIEN MUSARAGANY.

Financial Institutions

Fonds de Promotion de L'Habitat Urbain (FPHU): ave de la Liberté, BP 1996, Bujumbura; tel. 22224986; fax 22223225; e-mail info@fphu.bi; internet www.fphu.bi; cap. 818m. (2005); Dir-Gen. AUDACE BUKURU.

Société Burundaise de Financement: 6 rue de la Science, BP 270, Bujumbura; tel. 22222126; fax 22225437; e-mail sbf@cbinf.com; cap. and res 2,558.9m., total assets 11,680.4m. (Dec. 2003); Pres. ASTÈRE GIRUKWIGOMBA; Dir-Gen. DARIUS NAHAYO.

INSURANCE

In 2010 there were six insurance companies in Burundi.

Société d'Assurances du Burundi (SOCABU): 14–18 rue de l'Amitié, BP 2440, Bujumbura; tel. 22226520; fax 22226803; e-mail socabu@socabu.bi; internet www.socabu-assurances.com; f. 1977; cap. 180m.; Man. Dir ONÉSIME NDUWIMANA.

Société Générale d'Assurances et de Réassurance (SOGEAR): BP 2432, Bujumbura; tel. 22222345; fax 22229338; f. 1991; Pres. BENOÎT NDORIMANA; Dir-Gen. L. SAUSSEZ.

Union Commerciale d'Assurances et de Réassurance (UCAR): BP 3012, Bujumbura; tel. 22223638; fax 22223695; e-mail ucar@cbinf.com; f. 1986; cap. 150m.; Chair. Lt-Col EDOUARD NZAMBIMANA; Dir-Gen. PASCAL NTAMASHIMIKIRO.

Trade and Industry

GOVERNMENT AGENCIES

Agence Burundaise de Promotion des Investissements: Quartier Kigobe, BP 7057, Bujumbura; tel. 22275996; e-mail info@burundi-investment.com; internet www.burundi-investment.com; f. 2009; Dir-Gen. ANTOINE KABURA.

Agence de Promotion des Echanges Extérieurs (APEE): 27 rue de la Victoire, BP 3535, Bujumbura; tel. 22225497; fax 22222767; e-mail apee@cbinf.com; promotes and supervises foreign exchanges.

Autorité de Régulation de la Filière Café (ARFIC): 279 blvd de Tanzanie, BP 450, Bujumbura; tel. 22223193; fax 22225532; internet arfic.gov.bi; f. 2009 to replace the Office du Café du Burundi, f. 1964; contributes to policy formulation for the coffee sector and supervises coffee plantations and coffee exports; Dir EVARISTE NGAYEMPORE.

Office du Thé du Burundi (OTB): 52 blvd de l'UPRONA, Bujumbura; tel. 22224228; fax 22224657; e-mail otb@cbinf.com; f. 1979; supervises production and marketing of tea; Man. Dir ANICET TUYAGA.

DEVELOPMENT ORGANIZATIONS

Agence Française de Développement (AFD): Immeuble Old East, pl. de l'Indépendance, BP 2740, Bujumbura; tel. 222255931; fax 22255932; internet www.afd.fr; Gen. Man. CAMILLE TIOLLIER.

Fonds de National d'Investissement Communal (FONIC): blvd du 28 Novembre, BP 2799, Bujumbura; tel. 22221963; fax 22243268; e-mail fdc@cbinf.com; internet www.fonic.bi; f. 2007 to replace Fonds de Développement Communal; Pres. DOMITIEN NDIHOKUBWAYO.

Fonds de Promotion de l'Habitat Urbain: 6 ave de la Liberté, BP 1996, Bujumbura; tel. 22227676; fax 22223225; e-mail info@fphu.bi; internet www.fphu.bi; cap. 818m. Burundian francs; Pres. IDI KARIM BUHANGA; Dir-Gen. ALOYS NTAKIRUTIMANA.

Institut des Sciences Agronomiques du Burundi (ISABU): ave de la Cathédrale, BP 795, Bujumbura; tel. 22223390; fax 22225798; e-mail dgisabu@cbinf.com; f. 1962 for the scientific development of agriculture and livestock; Dir-Gen. DIEUDONNÉ NAHIMANA.

Observatoire des Filières Agricoles du Burundi (OFB): 7 ave Imbo, Quartier Asiatique, BP 5, Bujumbura; tel. 22251865; fax 22250567; e-mail info@ofburundi.org; internet www.ofburundi.org; f. 2004; provides information on Burundi's agricultural sector and facilitates dialogue between key figures and orgs; Co-ordinator PATRICE NTAHOMPAGAZE.

Office National de la Tourbe (ONATOUR): route de l'aéroport, BP 2360, Bujumbura; tel. 22226480; fax 22226709; e-mail kariyo@yahoo.fr; f. 1977 to promote the exploitation of peat deposits; Dir-Gen. EMMANUEL MIBURO.

Société d'Economie pour l'Exploitation du Quinquina au Burundi (SOKINABU): 16 blvd Mwezi Gisabo, BP 1783, Bujumbura; tel. 22223469; fax 22218160; e-mail chiastos@yahoo.fr; f. 1975 to develop and exploit cinchona trees, the source of quinine; Dir CHRISTIAN REMEZO.

INDUSTRIAL AND TRADE ASSOCIATIONS

Association des Commerçants du Burundi (ACOBU): 254 ave du Commerce, Rohero, BP 6373, Bujumbura; tel. 22248663; Pres. CONSTANTIN NDIKUMANA.

Association des Employeurs du Burundi (AEB): 187 rue de la Mission, BP 141, Bujumbura; tel. 22221119; fax 22248190; e-mail assoaeb64@yahoo.fr; Pres. THÉODORE KAMWENUBUSA; Exec. Sec. GASPARD NZISABIRA.

Association des Femmes Entrepreneurs du Burundi (AFAB): 127 ave Kunkiko, Rohero II, BP 1628, Bujumbura; tel. 22242784; Pres. CONSOLATA NDAYISHIMIYE.

Association des Industriels du Burundi (AIB): 187 rue de la mission, Rohero, BP 141, Bujumbura; tel. 22221119; fax 22220643; e-mail aib.burundi@yahoo.fr; Pres. ECONIE NIJEMBERE; Exec. Sec. PARFAIT NKERABAGENZI.

CHAMBER OF COMMERCE

Chambre Fédérale de Commerce et d'Industrie du Burundi (CFCIB): ave du 18 Septembre, BP 313, Bujumbura; tel. 22222280; fax 22227895; e-mail ccib@ccib.bi; internet www.cfcib.org; f. 2010 to replace Chambre de Commerce, d'Industrie, d'Agriculture et d'Artisanat du Burundi (CCIB; f. 1923); Pres. ECONIE NIJIMBERE; 130 mems.

UTILITIES

Agence Burundaise pour l'Electrification Rurale (ABER): Bujumbura; f. 2011; Chair. NOLASQUE NDAYIHAYE; Dir-Gen. LÉONARD NTIRWONZA.

Régie de Distribution d'Eau et d'Electricité (REGIDESO): 11 ave de la Science, BP 660, Bujumbura; tel. 222536363; fax 22226563; internet www.regideso.bi; state-owned distributor of water and electricity services; Dir LIBÉRAT MFUMUKEKO.

TRADE UNIONS

Confédération des Syndicats du Burundi (COSYBU): ave du 18 Septembre, Ex Hôtel Central 8, BP 220, Bujumbura; tel. and fax 22248190; e-mail cosybu@yahoo.fr; Pres. THARCISSE GAHUNGU; 32 mem. asscns.

Confédération des Syndicats Libres du Burundi (CSB): BP 1570, Bujumbura; tel. 222229; e-mail csb sq2001@vahoo.fr; Pres. THARCISSE NIBOGORA; Sec.-Gen. MATHIAS RUVARI.

Transport

RAILWAYS

There are no railways in Burundi. Plans have been under consideration since 1987 for the construction of a line passing through Uganda, Rwanda and Burundi, to connect with the Kigoma–Dar es Salaam line in Tanzania. This rail link would relieve Burundi's isolated trade position.

ROADS

In 2004 Burundi had a total of 12,322 km of roads, of which 5,012 km were national highways and 282 km secondary roads. In 2008 some 31.7% of all roads were paved.

Office des Transports en Commun (OTRACO): BP 1486, Bujumbura; tel. 22231313; fax 22232051; 100% govt-owned; operates public transport; Dir-Gen. NICODÈME NIZIGIYIMANA.

INLAND WATERWAYS

Bujumbura is the principal port for both passenger and freight traffic on Lake Tanganyika, and the greater part of Burundi's external trade is dependent on the shipping services between Bujumbura and lake ports in Tanzania, Zambia and the Democratic Republic of the Congo.

Société Concessionnaire de l'Exploitation du Port de Bujumbura (EPB): BP 59, Bujumbura; tel. 22226036; e-mail bujaport@cbinf.com; f. 1967; 43% state-owned; controls Bujumbura port; Dir-Gen. MÉTHODE SHIRAMBERE.

CIVIL AVIATION

The international airport at Bujumbura is equipped to take large jet-engined aircraft.

Air Burundi: 13 ave du Commerce, BP 2460, Bujumbura; tel. 22269417; fax 22223452; e-mail info@flyairburundi.com; internet flyairburundi.com; f. 1971 as Société de Transports Aériens du Burundi; state-owned; operates charter and scheduled passenger services to destinations throughout central Africa; Group Man. Dir EMMANUEL HABIMANA.

Autorité de l'Aviation Civile du Burundi (AACB): Bujumbura; f. 2012; Dir-Gen. ALBERT MANIRATUNGA.

Tourism

Tourism is relatively undeveloped. In 2010, according to the World Tourism Organization, 142,311 tourists visited Burundi. Tourism receipts amounted to an estimated US $3.0m. in 2011.

Office National du Tourisme (ONT): 2 ave des Euphorbes, BP 902, Bujumbura; tel. and fax 22224208; e-mail info@burunditourisme.net; internet www.burunditourisme.net; f. 1972; responsible for the promotion and supervision of tourism; Dir DÉO NGENDAHAYO.

Defence

Burundi's armed forces, as assessed at November 2013, comprised an army of 20,000 and a paramilitary force of 31,050 gendarmes (including a 50-strong marine police force). At the end of 2004 the Government had officially established a reconstituted armed forces (Forces de Défense Nationales—FDN—comprising equal proportions of Hutus and Tutsis), which incorporated some 23,000 former rebel combatants, and a new police force. In April 2003 the deployment of the first members of an African Union Mission in Burundi (AMIB) commenced; the contingent (which comprised mainly South African troops, with reinforcements from Ethiopia and Mozambique) was mandated to assist in the enforcement of the ceasefire between the Government and rebel factions. In May 2004 the UN Security Council approved the deployment of a Opération des Nations Unies au Burundi (ONUB—with a maximum authorized strength of 5,650 military personnel), to replace AMIB. Under a resolution of 30 June 2006, the UN Security Council ended the mandate of ONUB at the end of December, when it was replaced by a UN office, the Bureau Intégré des Nations Unies au Burundi (BINUB). BINUB was established for an initial period of one year, with authorization to continue peace consolidation, including support for the demobilization and reintegration of former combatants and reform of the security sector. BINUB's mandate was subsequently extended until 31 December 2010. In mid-December the Security Council replaced BINUB with the United Nations Office in Burundi, with effect from 1 January 2011 and with an initial mandate of 12 months (subsequently extended until 31 December 2014). Meanwhile, some 100 Burundian troops were sent to Somalia in December 2007 as part of the African Union Mission to Somalia (AMISOM), a peacekeeping force established at the beginning of that year in an attempt to stabilize the war-torn country. By mid-2012 the AU force comprised 15,541 soldiers, including 4,800 from Burundi. In 2012 a total of 4,411 troops were stationed abroad, of whom five were observers.

Defence Expenditure: Budgeted at 102,600m. Burundian francs in 2013.

Chief of Staff of the Forces de Défense Nationales: Maj.-Gen. GODEFROID NIYOMBARE.

Chief of Staff of the Gendarmerie: Col SALVATOR NDAYIYUNVIYE.

Education

Education is provided free of charge. Kirundi is the language of instruction in primary schools, while French is used in secondary schools. Primary education, which is officially compulsory, begins at seven years of age and lasts for six years. Secondary education begins at the age of 13 and lasts for up to seven years, comprising a first cycle of four years and a second of three years. In 2010, according to UNESCO estimates, primary enrolment included 94% of children in the relevant age-group (males 94%; females 94%). Enrolment at secondary schools in 2012 included an estimated 18% of the population (males 20%; females 17%). In 2013 an estimated 15,000 students were enrolled at the Université du Burundi. There are also private universities at Ngozi and Bujumbura, the Université de Ngozi, the Université Lumière de Bujumbura, the Université du Lac Tanganyika and Hope Africa University. The total number of students enrolled in higher education in 2009/10 was 29,269. Public expenditure on education in 2008 was equivalent to 25.1% of total government expenditure.

CAMBODIA

Introductory Survey

LOCATION, CLIMATE, LANGUAGE, RELIGION, FLAG, CAPITAL

The Kingdom of Cambodia occupies part of the Indo-Chinese peninsula in South-East Asia. It is bordered by Thailand and Laos to the north, by Viet Nam to the east and by the Gulf of Thailand to the south. The climate is tropical and humid. There is a rainy season from June to November, with the heaviest rainfall in September. The temperature is generally between 20°C and 36°C (68°F to 97°F), with March and April usually the hottest months; the annual average temperature in Phnom Penh is 27°C (81°F). The official language is Khmer, which is spoken by almost everybody except the Vietnamese and Chinese minorities. The state religion is Theravada Buddhism. The national flag (proportions 2 by 3) consists of three horizontal stripes, of dark blue, red (half the depth) and dark blue, with a stylized representation (in white) of the temple of Angkor Wat, showing three of its five towers, in the centre. The capital is Phnom Penh.

CONTEMPORARY POLITICAL HISTORY

Historical Context

The Kingdom of Cambodia became a French protectorate in the 19th century and was incorporated into French Indo-China. In April 1941 Norodom Sihanouk, then aged 18 years, succeeded his grandfather as King. In May 1947 he promulgated a Constitution which provided for a bicameral Parliament, including an elected National Assembly. Cambodia became an Associate State of the French Union in November 1949 and attained independence on 9 November 1953. In order to become a political leader, King Sihanouk abdicated in March 1955 in favour of his father, Norodom Suramarit, and became known as Prince Sihanouk. He founded a mass movement, the Sangkum Reastr Niyum (Popular Socialist Community), which won all the seats in elections to the National Assembly in 1955, 1958, 1962 and 1966. King Suramarit died in April 1960, and in June Parliament elected Prince Sihanouk as head of state. Prince Sihanouk's Government developed good relations with the People's Republic of China and with North Viet Nam, but it was highly critical of the USA's role in Asia. From 1964, however, the Government was confronted by an underground Marxist insurgency movement, the Khmers Rouges, while it also became increasingly difficult to isolate Cambodia from the war in Viet Nam.

Domestic Political Affairs

In March 1970 Prince Sihanouk was deposed by a right-wing coup, led by the Prime Minister, Lt-Gen. (later Marshal) Lon Nol. The new Government pledged itself to the removal of foreign communist forces and appealed to the USA for military aid. Sihanouk went into exile and formed the Royal Government of National Union of Cambodia (Gouvernement Royal d'Union Nationale du Cambodge—GRUNC), supported by the Khmers Rouges. Sihanoukists and the Khmers Rouges formed the National United Front of Cambodia (Front Uni National du Cambodge—FUNC). Their combined forces, aided by South Viet Nam's National Liberation Front and North Vietnamese troops, posed a serious threat to the new regime, but in October 1970 Marshal Lon Nol proclaimed the Khmer Republic. In June 1972 he was elected the first President. During 1973 several foreign states recognized GRUNC as the rightful government of Cambodia. In 1974 the republican regime's control was limited to a few urban enclaves, besieged by GRUNC forces, mainly Khmers Rouges, who gained control of Phnom Penh on 17 April 1975. Prince Sihanouk was reappointed head of state but did not return from exile until September. The country was subjected to a prearranged programme of radical social deconstruction immediately after the Khmers Rouges' assumption of power; towns were largely evacuated, and their inhabitants forced to work in rural areas. During the following three years an estimated 1.7m. people died as a result of ill-treatment, hunger, disease and executions.

A new Constitution, promulgated in January 1976, renamed the country Democratic Kampuchea, and established a republican form of government; elections for a 250-member People's Representative Assembly were held in March. In April Prince Sihanouk resigned as head of state, and GRUNC was dissolved. The Assembly elected former Deputy Prime Minister Khieu Samphan to be President of the State Presidium (head of state). The little-known Pol Pot (formerly Saloth Sar) was appointed Prime Minister. The Communist Party of Kampuchea (CPK), with Pol Pot as the Secretary of its Central Committee, became the ruling organization.

After 1975 close links with China were developed, while relations with Viet Nam deteriorated. In 1978, following a two-year campaign of raids across the Vietnamese border by the Khmers Rouges, the Vietnamese army launched a series of offensives into Kampuchean territory. In December Viet Nam invaded Kampuchea, supported by the Kampuchean National United Front for National Salvation (KNUFNS—a communist-led movement opposed to Pol Pot, the establishment of which had been announced earlier that month).

On 7 January 1979 Phnom Penh was captured by Vietnamese forces, and three days later the People's Republic of Kampuchea was proclaimed. A People's Revolutionary Council was established, with Heng Samrin, leader of the KNUFNS, as President. The CPK was replaced as the governing party by the Kampuchean People's Revolutionary Party (KPRP). However, the Khmer Rouge forces remained active in the western provinces, near the border with Thailand, and conducted sporadic guerrilla activities elsewhere in the country. Several groups opposing both the Khmers Rouges and the Heng Samrin regime were established, including the Khmer People's National Liberation Front (KPNLF), headed by a former Prime Minister, Son Sann. In July, claiming that Pol Pot's regime had been responsible for 3m. deaths, the KPRP administration sentenced Pol Pot and his former Minister of Foreign Affairs, Ieng Sary, to death *in absentia*. In January 1980 Khieu Samphan assumed the premiership of the deposed Khmer Rouge regime, while Pol Pot became Commander-in-Chief of the armed forces. In 1981 the CPK was reportedly dissolved and was replaced by the Party of Democratic Kampuchea (PDK).

During the early years of the KPRP regime Viet Nam launched regular offensives on the Thai–Kampuchean border against the united armed forces of Democratic Kampuchea, the coalition Government-in-exile of anti-Vietnamese resistance groups formed in June 1982. Thousands of Kampuchean refugees crossed the border into Thailand; in turn, a large number of Vietnamese citizens subsequently settled on Kampuchean territory. The coalition Government-in-exile, of which Prince Sihanouk became President, Khieu Samphan (PDK) Vice-President and Son Sann (KPNLF) Prime Minister, received the support of China and of member states of the Association of Southeast Asian Nations (ASEAN, see p. 211), while retaining the Kampuchean seat in the UN General Assembly.

In the mid-1980s an increasingly conciliatory relationship between the USSR and China led to a number of diplomatic exchanges, aimed at reconciling the coalition Government-in-exile with the Government in Phnom Penh, led by the General Secretary of the KPRP, Heng Samrin; however, the latter rejected peace proposals from ASEAN and the coalition Government-in-exile. In September 1987 the Chinese Government stated that it would accept a Kampuchean 'government of national reconciliation' under Prince Sihanouk, but that the presence of Vietnamese troops in Kampuchea remained a major obstacle. In October, having announced its readiness to conduct negotiations with some PDK leaders (but not Pol Pot), the Heng Samrin Government offered Prince Sihanouk a government post and issued a set of peace proposals, which included the complete withdrawal of Vietnamese troops, internationally observed elections and the formation of a coalition government. In December a meeting held in France between Prince Sihanouk and Hun Sen, the Chairman of the Council of Ministers in the Heng Samrin Government, resulted in a joint communiqué, stating that the conflict was to be settled politically by negotiations involving all the Kampuchean parties.

Under increasing pressure from the USSR and China, the four Kampuchean factions participated in a series of 'informal meetings', held in Indonesia, which were also attended by representatives of Viet Nam, Laos and the six ASEAN members. At the first of these meetings, in July 1988, Viet Nam advanced its deadline for a complete withdrawal of its troops from Kampuchea to late 1989. In April 1989 the National Assembly in Phnom Penh ratified several constitutional amendments, whereby the name of the country was changed to the State of Cambodia, a new national flag, emblem and anthem were introduced, Buddhism was reinstated as the state religion, and the death penalty was abolished. In July the Paris International Conference on Cambodia (PICC) convened, in the French capital, for the first time. The PICC agreed to send a UN reconnaissance party to Cambodia to study the prospects for a ceasefire and the installation of a peacekeeping force.

The Paris Peace Agreement and election of 1993

The withdrawal of Vietnamese forces, completed on schedule in September 1989, was followed by renewed offensives into Cambodia by the resistance forces, particularly the PDK. In November, following substantial military gains by the PDK, the UN General Assembly adopted a resolution supporting the formation of an interim government in Cambodia, which would include members of the PDK; however, the resolution retained a clause, introduced in 1988, relating to past atrocities committed by the organization. The resolution also cast doubt on the Vietnamese withdrawal (since it had not been monitored by the UN) and, in reference to the alleged presence of 1m. Vietnamese settlers in Cambodia, condemned 'demographic changes' imposed in the country. An Australian peace initiative was unanimously approved by the five permanent members of the UN Security Council in January 1990. In February Prince Sihanouk declared that the coalition Government-in-exile would henceforth be known as the National Government of Cambodia.

In July 1990 the USA withdrew its support for the National Government of Cambodia's occupation of Cambodia's seat at the UN. In August the UN Security Council endorsed the framework for a comprehensive settlement in Cambodia. The agreement provided for UN supervision of an interim government, military arrangements for the transitional period, free elections and guarantees for the future neutrality of Cambodia. A special representative of the Secretary-General of the UN was to control the proposed UN Transitional Authority in Cambodia (UNTAC). The UN would also assume control of the Ministries of Foreign Affairs, National Defence, Finance, the Interior and Information, Press and Culture.

At a fourth 'informal meeting', held in Indonesia in September 1990, the four Cambodian factions accepted the UN proposals. They also agreed to the formation of the Supreme National Council (SNC), with six representatives from the Phnom Penh Government and six from the National Government of Cambodia. SNC decisions were to be taken by consensus, effectively allowing each faction the power of veto, and the SNC was to occupy the Cambodian seat at the UN General Assembly. Prince Sihanouk was subsequently elected to the chairmanship of the SNC, and resigned as leader of the resistance coalition and as President of the National Government of Cambodia (in which positions he was replaced by Son Sann). Agreement was also reached on the four factions reducing their armed forces by 70% and the remaining 30% being placed in cantonments under UN supervision; the introduction of a system of multi-party democracy; the Phnom Penh Government abandoning its demand for references to genocide to be included in a draft plan; and the holding of elections to a constituent assembly, which would subsequently become a 120-seat legislative assembly.

Following the release of political prisoners by the Phnom Penh Government in October 1991, including former 'reformist' associates of Hun Sen who had been arrested in 1990 and replaced by supporters of the more conservative Chairman of the National Assembly, Chea Sim, a congress of the KPRP was convened at which the party changed its name to the Cambodian People's Party (CPP). The communist insignia was removed from its emblem, Heng Samrin was replaced as Chairman of the Central Committee (formerly the Politburo) by Chea Sim and Hun Sen was elected as Vice-Chairman.

On 23 October 1991 the four factions signed the UN peace agreement in Paris—commonly known as the Paris Peace Agreement—under the auspices of the PICC. The 300-strong UN Advance Mission in Cambodia (UNAMIC) was in position by the end of the year. The agreement also provided for the repatriation, under the supervision of the UN High Commissioner for Refugees, of the estimated 340,000 Cambodian refugees living in camps in Thailand. (The majority of these refugees had returned to Cambodia by the end of April 2003.) In November 1991 Prince Sihanouk returned to Phnom Penh, accompanied by Hun Sen. The CPP and the National United Front for an Independent, Neutral, Peaceful and Co-operative Cambodia (Front Uni National pour un Cambodge Indépendent Neutre Pacifique et Coopératif—FUNCINPEC), led by Prince Sihanouk, subsequently formed an alliance and announced their intention to establish a coalition government. (The alliance was abandoned in December, in response to objections from the KPNLF and the PDK.) The four factions endorsed the reinstatement of Prince Sihanouk as head of state of Cambodia. In late November, however, an attack by demonstrators on Khieu Samphan on his return to Phnom Penh led senior PDK officials to flee to the Thai capital of Bangkok where the SNC met and agreed that, henceforth, officials of the party would occupy the SNC headquarters in Phnom Penh with members of UNAMIC. Further demonstrations followed. Having reached an agreement with representatives of the UN Security Council, by March 1992 the Phnom Penh Government had released all remaining political prisoners. The UN Security Council expanded UNAMIC's mandate to include mine-clearing operations, and in February authorized the dispatch of a 22,000-member peacekeeping force to Cambodia to establish UNTAC. In March UNAMIC transferred responsibility for the implementation of the peace agreement to UNTAC.

The refugee repatriation programme, which began in March 1992, was threatened by repeated ceasefire violations, which were concentrated in the central province of Kampong Thom. In response to the PDK's continued lack of co-operation regarding the peacekeeping operation, in August Yasushi Akashi (who had been appointed UN Special Representative to Cambodia in charge of UNTAC in January) affirmed that the legislative elections would proceed without the participation of the PDK if it continued to refuse to co-operate. The UN set a deadline for compliance of 15 November. By the end of November, however, no consensus had been reached, and the Security Council adopted a resolution condemning PDK obduracy. The Security Council approved an embargo on the supplies of petroleum products to the PDK and endorsed a ban on the export of timber (a principal source of income for the party). However, the PDK announced the formation of a subsidiary party to contest the forthcoming elections, the Cambodian National Unity Party, led by Khieu Samphan and Son Sen. The Phnom Penh Government subsequently launched an offensive against the PDK in northern and western Cambodia, recovering much of the territory gained by the PDK since the signing of the peace agreement in October 1991. There were also continuing attacks by the PDK on ethnic Vietnamese, and, following several rural massacres, thousands of Vietnamese took refuge in Viet Nam.

Meanwhile, by the final deadline at the end of January 1993 20 parties, excluding the PDK, had registered to contest the elections. On 23–28 May about 90% of the electorate participated in the elections to the Constituent Assembly. The PDK offered support to FUNCINPEC (officially the FUNCINPEC Party from 1992), but, in response to the high electoral turnout, Prince Sihanouk abandoned his proposals for the inclusion of the PDK in a future government. Despite CPP allegations of irregularities, UNTAC rejected requests for fresh elections in at least four provinces. In early June, without prior consultation with the UN and disregarding the incomplete election results, Prince Sihanouk announced the formation of a new Government, with himself as Prime Minister and Prince Norodom Ranariddh and Hun Sen as joint Deputy Prime Ministers. The coalition was created and renounced within hours, owing to objections from Prince Ranariddh, who had not been consulted, and to suggestions by UN officials that it was tantamount to a coup. Two days later the official results of the elections were released: FUNCINPEC had secured 58 of the 120 seats, the CPP 51 seats, the Buddhist Liberal Democratic Party (BLDP, founded by the KPNLF) 10 seats and a breakaway faction from FUNCINPEC, the Movement for the National Liberation of Cambodia (Mouvement pour la Libération Nationale du Kampuchea—MOLINAKA), one seat. Despite the UN's endorsement of the elections as fair, the CPP refused to dissolve the State of Cambodia Government in Phnom Penh. Prince Norodom Chakrapong (a son of Prince Sihanouk who had been appointed to the Council of Ministers of the Phnom Penh Government in December 1991) subsequently led a secessionist movement in the east and north-east of the country, which was reportedly sanctioned by the CPP leadership in an attempt to secure a power-sharing agreement with FUNCINPEC.

On 14 June 1993, at the inaugural session of the Constituent Assembly, Prince Sihanouk was proclaimed head of state, and 'full and special' powers were conferred on him. The Assembly adopted a resolution declaring null and void the overthrow of Prince Sihanouk 23 years previously and recognizing him retroactively as head of state of Cambodia during that period. The secessionist movement collapsed, and Hun Sen and Prince Ranariddh were appointed as Co-Chairmen of the Provisional National Government of Cambodia. Prince Chakrapong returned to Phnom Penh, where he was reconciled with Prince Sihanouk, and the CPP officially recognized the election results.

The PDK had immediately accepted the results of the elections and supported the formation of a coalition government, but continued to engage in military action in pursuit of its demands for inclusion in a future government. In August 1993 the newly formed Cambodian National Armed Forces (later restyled the Royal Cambodian Armed Forces), which had been created through the merger of the forces of the other three factions in June, initiated a successful offensive against PDK positions in north-western Cambodia. The Government rejected an appeal by the PDK for urgent discussions, insisting that the party surrender unconditionally the estimated 20% of Cambodian territory remaining under its control.

The new Constitution and National Assembly

In September 1993 the Constituent Assembly adopted a new Constitution, which provided for an hereditary monarchy. Prince Sihanouk duly promulgated the Constitution, thus terminating the mandate of UNTAC (whose personnel had left the country by mid-November). The Constituent Assembly became the National Assembly (chaired by Chea Sim), and Prince Sihanouk acceded to the throne of the new Kingdom of Cambodia. Government ministers were to be chosen from parties represented in the National Assembly, thus precluding the involvement of the PDK. At the end of October the National Assembly approved the new Royal Government of Cambodia (previously endorsed by King Sihanouk), in which Prince Ranariddh was named First Prime Minister and Hun Sen Second Prime Minister. Subsequent initiatives to incorporate the PDK into the new Government failed, owing to objections from various parties. In the first half of 1994 the fighting between the PDK and the government troops in the north-west of the country reached a severity not witnessed since 1989. Following the failure of peace talks held in Pyongyang, the Democratic People's Republic of Korea (North Korea), in May and June 1994, the Government ordered the PDK to leave Phnom Penh and closed the party's mission in the capital.

In July 1994 the Government claimed to have suppressed a coup attempt led by Prince Chakrapong and Gen. Sin Song, a former Minister of National Security under the State of Cambodia. Following a personal appeal from King Sihanouk, Prince Chakrapong, who protested his innocence, was exiled from Cambodia, while Gen. Sin Song was placed under arrest. (Gen. Sin Song escaped from prison in September and was captured by the Thai authorities in November.) Hun Sen also suspected Deputy Prime Minister and Minister of the Interior Sar Kheng of involvement in the alleged revolt; however, Sar Kheng was protected by his powerful brother-in-law, Chea Sim. The coup attempt was used by the increasingly divided Government as a pretext to suppress criticism of the regime.

Despite King Sihanouk's continued advocacy of national reconciliation, in July 1994 the National Assembly adopted legislation outlawing the PDK. In response, the PDK formed a Provisional Government of National Unity and National Salvation of Cambodia (PGNUNSC), under the premiership of Khieu Samphan, which was to co-ordinate opposition to the Government in Phnom Penh from its headquarters in the northern province of Preah Vihear. In October Sam Rainsy was dismissed as Minister of Finance, apparently owing to his efforts to combat corruption at senior levels. Prince Sirivudh subsequently resigned as Minister of Foreign Affairs in protest at Rainsy's removal, and criticized FUNCINPEC, of which he was Secretary-General, for submitting too readily to CPP demands, as it became increasingly apparent that real power lay with the former communists.

Following his expulsion from FUNCINPEC in May 1995 and from the National Assembly in June, Rainsy formed a new party, the Khmer Nation Party (KNP). Meanwhile, the National Assembly adopted the revised draft of a stringent press law, which imposed substantial fines and prison sentences for reporting issues affecting 'national security' or 'political stability'. In October Prince Sirivudh was also expelled from the National Assembly and charged with conspiring to assassinate Hun Sen. He was allowed to go into exile in France in December on condition that he refrain from political activity, and in January 1996 he was convicted and sentenced to 10 years' imprisonment *in absentia* on charges of criminal conspiracy and possession of unlicensed firearms. Also in January the Government began to adopt repressive measures against the KNP. In March Rainsy nominally merged the KNP with a defunct but still legally registered party, in an attempt to gain legal status. However, in April the Government ordered all parties without parliamentary representation to close their offices. Several KNP officials were assassinated during the year.

In August 1996 the prominent PDK leader Ieng Sary, together with two military divisions that controlled the PDK strongholds of Pailin and Malai, defected from the movement and negotiated a peace agreement with the Government. Ieng Sary denied responsibility for the atrocities committed during Pol Pot's regime, and was granted a royal amnesty in September. He then formed a new political organization, the Democratic National United Movement (DNUM), while his supporters retained control of Pailin and Malai, despite efforts by troops loyal to the PDK leadership to recapture the region (where lucrative mineral and timber resources were situated). An estimated 2,500 PDK troops transferred allegiance to the Government in October. Some 4,000 former PDK troops were integrated into the national army in November.

In September 1996 the partial dissolution of the PDK increased tensions within the ruling coalition: as FUNCINPEC appeared more successful than the CPP at recruiting former PDK troops, Hun Sen became concerned that the alliance between the royalists and the PDK as former resistance forces would be re-established. In February 1997 Prince Ranariddh sent a helicopter mission to Anlong Veng to negotiate with the central PDK faction; however, PDK members opposed to peace talks ambushed the helicopter, killing the majority of the Prince's emissaries. Meanwhile, the two Prime Ministers were stockpiling weapons, violations of human and civil rights were becoming increasingly prevalent, corruption was rampant and labour unrest was widespread. In March Rainsy led a demonstration outside the National Assembly. The rally was attacked by assailants who threw four grenades, killing 19 and injuring more than 100 protesters. Rainsy, who was himself among the injured, accused Hun Sen of organizing the attack.

In April 1997 Ung Phan, a former CPP member who had joined FUNCINPEC in the early 1990s, led a rebellion against the party leadership of Prince Ranariddh, with the support of Hun Sen. The National Assembly, which was due to adopt legislation regarding elections scheduled for 1998, was unable to convene, as FUNCINPEC refused to attend until its dissident members were expelled from the Assembly, whereas the CPP insisted on their retention. In June the dissident FUNCINPEC members formed a rival FUNCINPEC party.

In May 1997 Khieu Samphan announced the creation of a new political party, the National Solidarity Party, which would support the National United Front (an alliance founded in February by Prince Ranariddh) at the next elections. Prince Ranariddh declared that, if the notorious former leadership of the PDK were excluded, he would welcome such an alliance. However, Hun Sen deemed the potential alliance to be a threat to the CPP and, following the seizure of a shipment of weapons destined for Prince Ranariddh, accused the Prince of illegally importing weapons to arm PDK soldiers. The PDK was divided over the issue of peace negotiations. Pol Pot ordered the death of the former Commander-in-Chief of Democratic Kampuchea, Son Sen, and also that of Ta Mok, the south-western regional army commander. Following the execution of Son Sen and his family, many PDK commanders rallied behind Ta Mok, and fighting erupted between the two factions. Pol Pot and his supporters fled into the jungle, with Khieu Samphan as a hostage, but were captured by Ta Mok's forces and returned to the PDK base at Anlong Veng, near the Thai border. In June Prince Ranariddh claimed that Pol Pot was under arrest and that Khieu Samphan would surrender. In July Pol Pot was condemned by a 'people's court' for 'destroying national unity' and for the killing of Son Sen and his family.

In early July 1997, following several attempts by CPP troops to detect the presence of PDK soldiers in FUNCINPEC units, CPP forces disarmed a unit of bodyguards of Prince Ranariddh, who subsequently left the country. On 5 July serious fighting erupted in Phnom Penh, and on 6 July, the day on which Khieu Samphan had been scheduled to broadcast the PDK's agreement with

FUNCINPEC to end its resistance and rejoin the political system, Hun Sen appeared on television to demand Prince Ranariddh's arrest (on charges of negotiating with the PDK, introducing proscribed PDK troops into Phnom Penh and secretly importing weapons to arm those forces) and to urge FUNCINPEC officials to select another leader. More than 24 hours of violence then ensued. The UN subsequently claimed that it had documentary evidence showing that at least 43 people, principally from the royalist army structure, had been murdered by forces loyal to Hun Sen after the events of 5–6 July. Many more FUNCINPEC and KNP officials, as well as many FUNCINPEC members of the legislature, fled the country.

King Sihanouk's appeals for a settlement were rejected by Hun Sen. Prince Ranariddh announced from Paris that a resistance movement was being organized in western Cambodia. Meanwhile, Hun Sen began negotiations with certain prominent members of FUNCINPEC who remained in Phnom Penh in an effort to attain the two-thirds' majority of the National Assembly necessary for the investiture of a new government. By the end of July 1997 the National Assembly had reconvened, with 98 of the 120 deputies present, including 40 of the 58 FUNCINPEC deputies. Hun Sen protested to the international community that his actions did not constitute a *coup d'état*, as he had not abolished the Constitution or the monarchy and had not dissolved the Government or the National Assembly. King Sihanouk, who had been in China since February, insisted on remaining neutral and accepted that Chea Sim should continue to sign royal decrees in his absence. In August the National Assembly voted to remove Ranariddh's legal immunity (a warrant subsequently being issued for his arrest) and elected Ung Huot, the FUNCINPEC Minister of Foreign Affairs, to the post of First Prime Minister.

Troops loyal to Prince Ranariddh, led by Gen. Nhiek Bun Chhay (the former military Deputy Chief of Staff and a principal negotiator with the PDK), were swiftly forced into the north-west of the country by CPP troops. They regrouped near the Thai border in an effective alliance with PDK troops under Ta Mok. Prolonged fighting took place for control of the town of O'Smach, about 70 km west of Anlong Veng, which was the last base for the resistance coalition led by Prince Ranariddh, the Union of Cambodian Democrats. At the end of August 1997 King Sihanouk arrived in Siem Reap. Hun Sen rejected another proposal from the King to act as a mediator in peace talks, insisting that Ranariddh be tried for his alleged crimes.

In September 1997 Hun Sen announced a cabinet reorganization that effectively removed remaining supporters of Prince Ranariddh from the Government. However, in a secret ballot the National Assembly failed by 13 votes to approve the changes by the required two-thirds' majority. Hun Sen continued to encourage the return of all opposition representatives who had fled the country in July, except Ranariddh and Gen. Nhiek Bun Chhay. In late 1997 Rainsy returned to Cambodia and agreed to co-operate with Hun Sen. In December the National Assembly voted to postpone local and legislative elections from May until July 1998 and to increase the number of legislative seats from 120 to 122. In February 1998 Rainsy withdrew the KNP from the electoral process in protest at the unlawful methods allegedly employed by Hun Sen, including the registration of a breakaway faction of the KNP bearing an identical title and logo, and the fatal shooting in January of a KNP official and his daughter. The KNP was subsequently restyled the Sam Rainsy Party (SRP).

Hun Sen and Ranariddh agreed to the terms of a Japanese-brokered peace proposal in February 1998, which provided for the severance of Ranariddh's links with the PDK, the implementation of a ceasefire in the north-west (which came into effect on 27 February), a royal pardon for Ranariddh if he were convicted *in absentia* of the charges against him, and his guaranteed safe return to participate in the general election. Ranariddh was convicted in March of illegally importing weapons and of conspiring with the proscribed PDK, and sentenced to 30 years' imprisonment and a fine of US $54m. for damage caused on 5–6 July 1997. At the formal request of Hun Sen, King Sihanouk granted Ranariddh a royal pardon, but no amnesty was accorded to Gen. Nhiek Bun Chhay or Serei Kosal, the commanders of Ranariddh's troops in the north-west, who were also found guilty. Ranariddh returned to Phnom Penh at the end of March 1998, but FUNCINPEC had been severely weakened by the killing of many of its senior personnel, the closure of its offices and the defection of some of its principal officials.

In March 1998 several divisions of PDK troops mutinied against their leader, Ta Mok, surrendering control of the PDK headquarters, Anlong Veng, to government troops; during the ensuing clashes thousands of civilians were evacuated to Thailand. Pol Pot died on 15 April, shortly after his comrades had offered to surrender him for trial by an international tribunal. It was later reported that he had committed suicide. Ta Mok announced that he was prepared to reach agreement with the Government but demanded autonomy for Anlong Veng. Despite sporadic clashes between government forces and the remnants of the PDK, the grouping was practically defunct by the end of the year, following further significant defections in October and December. In late December Nuon Chea (Pol Pot's former deputy) and Khieu Samphan defected to the Government, seeking sanctuary in Pailin, an area still effectively controlled by Ieng Sary. In February 1999 a final 4,332 PDK troops surrendered to the Co-Ministers of National Defence in Anlong Veng, although Ta Mok remained in the border area.

The coalition Government of 1998–2003

The campaign period for the July 1998 general election was characterized by intimidation and violence. All demonstrations were banned, as was the dissemination of political information by private news media. However, the election, which took place relatively peacefully on 26 July, was deemed free and fair by the UN-co-ordinated Joint International Observer Group; 90% of the electorate participated in the poll, which was contested by 39 parties. Under a newly introduced modified system of proportional representation that favoured larger parties, the CPP secured 64 of the 122 seats, FUNCINPEC 43 seats and the SRP 15 seats. Hun Sen proposed a three-party coalition, but this was rejected by Ranariddh and Rainsy.

In August 1998 Rainsy was detained for questioning, following a grenade explosion at the Ministry of the Interior. Several thousand Cambodians took part in a peaceful demonstration in Phnom Penh, organized by Rainsy, to denounce alleged electoral fraud and to demand the removal of Hun Sen. Following a grenade attack on a disused residence of Hun Sen in September, the protesters were violently dispersed by security forces. Hun Sen ordered the arrest of Rainsy on charges of murder, prompting the latter to take refuge under the protection of the UN. Both Rainsy and Ranariddh abandoned demands for a recount. Sporadic violence continued, and Hun Sen announced that FUNCINPEC and the SRP would be expelled from the National Assembly if they failed to attend its inauguration on 24 September. Following a rocket-propelled grenade attack on a convoy of vehicles en route to the convening ceremony of the National Assembly, Ranariddh and Rainsy fled to Thailand. The situation further deteriorated in October with the arrest, torture and execution of many opposition supporters. Ranariddh subsequently agreed to return to Cambodia to attend a meeting with Hun Sen, under the auspices of King Sihanouk, from which Rainsy was excluded.

In November 1998 agreement was reached on the formation of a CPP-FUNCINPEC coalition Government, with Hun Sen as Prime Minister and Ranariddh as the Chairman of the National Assembly. The accord also provided for the creation of a Senate (to be presided over by Chea Sim), the reintegration of resistance soldiers into the armed forces, and royal pardons for Gen. Nhiek Bun Chhay and Serei Kosal, as well as Prince Sirivudh and Prince Chakrapong. Ranariddh was duly elected Chairman of the National Assembly, with two CPP deputies. The new Royal Government included Co-Ministers for the influential Ministries of Defence and of the Interior, while the CPP controlled the foreign affairs and finance portfolios and FUNCINPEC assumed responsibility for information and health. Rainsy became the official leader of the opposition. The Senate held its inaugural session in March 1999. Representation in the 61-member upper chamber was proportionate to elected strength in the National Assembly; the CPP was allocated 31 seats, FUNCINPEC 21 and the SRP seven, with a further two members being appointed by the King. Chea Sim was duly elected as Chairman, and Gen. Nhiek Bun Chhay became one of the three Deputy Chairmen.

Reform of the Royal Cambodian Armed Forces began in January 1999 with Hun Sen's resignation as Commander-in-Chief. He was replaced by former Chief of the General Staff Gen. Ke Kimyan. Plans announced in November provided for the demobilization of 11,500 troops in 2000, followed by a further 10,000 in both 2001 and 2002.

In March 1999 Ta Mok was captured near the Thai border and placed in detention. In May Kang Khek Ieu (also known as Duch or Kaing Guek Eav), the director of the Tuol Sleng detention centre where more than 15,000 detainees had been tortured and executed during the Democratic Kampuchean regime, was arrested and charged with belonging to a proscribed organization. In September both Ta Mok and Duch were formally charged with genocide, and in 2002 both were also charged with crimes against humanity. (In July 2006, however, Ta Mok died.)

In November 2000 dozens of armed men launched an attack on official buildings in Phnom Penh. At least seven of the gunmen were killed in the raid, responsibility for which was subsequently claimed by the US-based Cambodian Freedom Fighters organization, led by Chhun Yasith (a naturalized citizen of the USA who had fled Cambodia in 1982, having reportedly witnessed the execution of his father by the Khmers Rouges in the late 1970s); the organization was vehemently opposed to Prime Minister Hun Sen, who it argued was obstructing democratic reform in Cambodia. Between June 2001 and February 2002 the trials of more than 70 people (including four US citizens) accused of participating in the apparent coup attempt took place, amid accusations, notably by Rainsy, that the Government had played a part in fomenting the violence so as to facilitate the intimidation of political opponents by local leaders. The majority of defendants were convicted and imprisoned. In June 2005 Chhun Yasith was arrested in the USA; he was convicted on four charges (including conspiracy to kill) by a Californian court in April 2008 and sentenced to life imprisonment in June 2010.

In February 2002 the CPP claimed an overwhelming victory in Cambodia's first multi-party local elections, winning control of more than 98% of the country's communes (*khum*). Despite numerous allegations of intimidation and electoral irregularities, the opposition parties accepted the results; however, according to monitors, the elections could be deemed neither free nor fair. At least 20 of the candidates who planned to mount a challenge to Hun Sen and the ruling CPP had been fatally shot in the course of the election campaign, during which the opposition had been denied access to the state-controlled media.

The 2003 elections, the King's abdication and the new Senate

Following its disappointing performance in the local elections of 2002, a rift developed within FUNCINPEC. As an indirect result, in May Prince Chakrapong founded a new political party, the Prince Norodom Chakrapong Khmer Soul party. Moreover, in June FUNCINPEC was weakened further by the defection of one of its founding members, Hang Dara, who announced the formation of the Hang Dara Movement Democratic Party to contest the next general election.

On 27 July 2003 23 political parties contested elections to the slightly enlarged (by one seat, to 123) National Assembly. The CPP secured 73 seats (failing to obtain the two-thirds' majority necessary to form a single-party government), while FUNCINPEC won 26 seats and the SRP 24. The latter two parties both refused to enter into a multi-party government and, instead, formed the Alliance of Democrats to oppose the CPP. Initially, the Alliance insisted that it would agree to form a tripartite government only if Hun Sen resigned as Prime Minister. Following a series of talks convened by King Sihanouk, in December the CPP and the two opposition parties finally began negotiations on the formation of a new government. However, the CPP continued to reject opposition demands concerning the composition of a new administration, insisting that Hun Sen would continue as Prime Minister. With elections to the upper house of the legislature scheduled for March, in early 2004 King Sihanouk announced that he had approved a request by the Chairman of the Senate, Chea Sim, to extend the Senate's mandate by one year in order to avert a constitutional crisis. The impasse was finally ended when the CPP and FUNCINPEC signed a power-sharing agreement in June. The formation of a new, 207-member coalition Government (in which the CPP held 136 posts and FUNCINPEC 71) was ratified by the National Assembly in July, and Hun Sen was confirmed as Prime Minister by royal decree. Prince Ranariddh of FUNCINPEC was appointed President of the National Assembly, which was boycotted by the SRP in protest at its exclusion from the new Government. Meanwhile, a series of shootings of prominent opposition supporters in the aftermath of the 2003 legislative elections was believed to have been co-ordinated by the CPP.

In October 2004 King Sihanouk unexpectedly announced his intention to abdicate, owing to ill health. The Royal Council of the Throne was convened and subsequently appointed one of Sihanouk's sons, Prince Norodom Sihamoni, to the throne. Sihamoni's coronation took place later in that month.

In February 2005 the National Assembly voted to divest Rainsy and two other SRP members—Cheam Channy and Chea Poch—of their parliamentary immunity, leaving them open to several defamation lawsuits. In August Channy was sentenced to seven years' imprisonment for attempting to form a military group with the aim of overthrowing the Government. In December Rainsy was sentenced *in absentia* to 18 months' imprisonment for defaming leaders of the ruling coalition. In February 2006 King Sihamoni granted royal pardons to both Rainsy and Channy; the former returned to Cambodia later that month.

Meanwhile, in January 2006 the country's first elections to the Senate were held. The ballot was open only to parliamentarians and members of local administrative bodies, with the general public being ineligible to vote. The CPP secured 45 of the 57 elective seats, while FUNCINPEC took 10 seats and the SRP just two. A further four senators were appointed by the National Assembly and King Sihamoni. In September the National Assembly approved a law whereby legislators would no longer be granted immunity from prosecution if they expressed opinions that threatened 'the good customs of society, law and order, and national security'.

In October 2006 Prince Ranariddh was ousted as President of FUNCINPEC, amid allegations of corruption and bribery made by the party's Secretary-General, Gen. Nhiek Bun Chhay; Ranariddh adamantly denied any wrongdoing. Keo Puth Rasmey, the son-in-law of Norodom Sihanouk, was elected as the new party President, and was subsequently also appointed as Deputy Prime Minister of the Kingdom. In November FUNCINPEC filed a lawsuit against Prince Ranariddh, accusing him of embezzling approximately US $3.6m. of party funds. In December Ranariddh lost his seat in the National Assembly, following his decision to assume control of the Khmer Front Party, now renamed the Norodom Ranariddh Party (NRP); according to laws governing the National Assembly, any member who left his or her political party was obliged to relinquish his or her seat in the legislature. In March 2007 Ranariddh, who was by then living in self-imposed exile in Malaysia, was found guilty *in absentia* of defrauding FUNCINPEC in a property transaction.

At the country's second multi-party *khum* elections, held in April 2007, the CPP retained control of the majority of the commune posts. Although conditions were more stable than in 2002, the level of voter participation declined from 87% to less than 68%.

In December 2007 the Special Representative of the UN Secretary-General for Human Rights in Cambodia, Yash Ghai, concluded that the human rights situation was deteriorating; he expressed particular concern with regard to the numerous land expropriations and illegal forced evictions that had left thousands of families homeless. The weakness of the country's judicial system, the prevalence of corruption and the dearth of official land records (most of which had been destroyed by the Khmers Rouges) remained major issues.

The 2008 elections, Rainsy on trial and the death of the King

The CPP secured a resounding victory at the legislative elections held on 27 July 2008, winning 90 seats in the 123-member National Assembly. The SRP secured only 26 seats, while the new Human Rights Party (HRP), formed by Kem Sokha in 2007, was placed third, taking three seats; the NRP and FUNCINPEC won two seats each. Some 75% of the electorate was reported to have participated in the polling, which was described as relatively peaceful. According to Human Rights Watch (a US-based non-governmental organization—NGO), the CPP had used both intimidation and employment incentives to promote the defection of SRP members to its own ranks, and had also targeted journalists who had been critical of the CPP.

Hun Sen was re-elected Prime Minister by the National Assembly in September 2008; his cabinet was largely unchanged, and the CPP's coalition with FUNCINPEC remained intact. A few days later, at the request of Hun Sen, King Sihamoni granted a royal pardon to Prince Ranariddh, overruling his 2007 fraud conviction (see above). Ranariddh returned to Cambodia at the end of September, whereupon he announced his withdrawal from active politics. The NRP was subsequently renamed the Nationalist Party (NP). In December King Sihamoni appointed Prince Ranariddh as President of the Supreme Privy Advisory Council, a position that effectively precluded him from resuming his political career.

In March 2009 Surya Subedi was appointed as the UN Special Rapporteur for Human Rights in Cambodia, following Yash Ghai's resignation in 2008 after months of insults from the Cambodian Government. Subedi made his first visit to Cambodia in July, following which he concluded that improvements to the human rights situation were urgently needed, particularly with regard to the judiciary and 'core political rights', including freedom of speech and peaceful assembly.

Three SRP members were stripped of their parliamentary immunity from prosecution in 2009, prompting widespread accusations that the Government was using the courts as a political instrument for dealing with dissenters. One of the SRP deputies was convicted in August of the defamation of Hun Sen, while another was charged (but acquitted in September) with defaming a number of senior military officers. In October the third SRP deputy, Sam Rainsy, was charged with racial incitement and destruction of public property after leading a group of protesters at the Cambodian–Vietnamese border decrying alleged Vietnamese encroachment on Cambodian territory. The opposition leader, who refused to attend any court proceedings, was convicted *in absentia* in January 2010 and sentenced to two years' imprisonment.

The Government filed a new lawsuit against Rainsy, who was reported to be living in self-imposed exile in France, in February 2010, alleging that he had forged official documents and disseminated false information about the ongoing border dispute with Viet Nam. In September Rainsy was convicted of the fresh charges *in absentia* and sentenced to 10 years' imprisonment. The SRP denounced the verdict as an attempt to discredit the opposition in advance of legislative elections due to be held in 2013.

A new penal code was implemented in December 2010. Controversial new articles that appeared to outlaw criticism of court decisions and public officials elicited severe criticism from human rights organizations. Further consternation was provoked by draft legislation pertaining to NGO activity, the details of which were publicized later that month. The Government stated that the bill was intended to increase transparency among the country's hundreds of NGOs; however, some rights groups claimed that the more stringent registration and reporting regulations proposed by the draft legislation would restrict the activities of NGOs, particularly smaller, more community-based groups.

Following months of public speculation, in December 2010 Prince Ranariddh announced the resumption of his political career at the head of the NP, which later that month readopted its former name, the Norodom Ranariddh Party (NRP). Given Prince Ranariddh's very public ousting from FUNCINPEC in 2006, the development appeared to jeopardize existing plans for a merger between the NRP and FUNCINPEC. The Prince claimed that the FUNCINPEC leadership, including party President Keo Puth Rasmey and Secretary-General Gen. Nhiek Bun Chhay, had lost popular support, implying that it would be in FUNCINPEC's best interests if they were to step down. Meanwhile, Hun Sen issued a warning that any FUNCINPEC government officials who attempted to defect to the NRP would be relieved of their government positions. In an address to NRP members in November 2011, Prince Ranariddh stated that his aim in returning to the political fray was to reunite monarchists across the country and to force the creation of a coalition government with the ruling CPP following the 2013 legislative elections. The Prince also criticized Gen. Nhiek Bun Chhay, reiterating claims that the latter had been responsible for his ousting from FUNCINPEC in 2006.

Meanwhile, in February 2011 three FUNCINPEC officials distributed documents at a party committee meeting purporting to reveal Gen. Nhiek Bun Chhay's involvement in the mismanagement and embezzlement of party property and funds since 2008. Nhiek Bun Chhay adamantly refuted the allegations and filed a defamation suit against the three officials, who, he asserted, were planning to defect to the NRP and had consequently forged the documents and fabricated the case against him to win favour with Prince Ranariddh. Amid the ensuing claims of an internal fissure within FUNCINPEC, the party denied reports that 127 party activists in Kampong Cham province had defected to the NRP in March 2011, contending that such claims were a gross exaggeration fabricated by the NRP as a means of fomenting division within Prince Ranariddh's former party.

At the second indirect elections to the Senate, which were held on 29 January 2012 and contested solely by the CPP and the SRP, the CPP gained one additional seat compared with the 2006 polls, securing 46 of the 57 elective seats, while the SRP increased its representation from two seats to 11. Chea Sim was re-elected as President of the Senate in March. In late October 2011 the Committee for Free and Fair Elections in Cambodia (Comfrel—established in 1995 as a permanent election-monitoring organization) had noted a significant number of irregularities in the voter registration process, which took place during September and October, and an imbalance in political broadcasting, with the ruling CPP dominating television and radio broadcasts. Not surprisingly, therefore, the outcome of the third multi-party local elections, which were held on 3 June 2012, was that the CPP retained control over the majority of the communes, while the opposition parties failed to win control of any of them. In July the SRP and the HRP announced plans to contest the legislative elections scheduled to be held in July 2013 as an electoral alliance, the Cambodia National Rescue Party (CNRP), to be headed by Rainsy. The erstwhile SRP and HRP deputies were subsequently expelled from Parliament for having contravened parliamentary regulations by forming a new party. The CNRP received official approval from the Ministry of the Interior in October 2012. In March 2013 the CNRP announced that it would nominate Rainsy as its candidate for the premiership following the elections, despite his continuing exile abroad and his ineligibility to contest the July poll owing to his criminal convictions. In June, in an apparent attempt by the CPP both to intimidate the opposition and to strengthen its own position in the immediate run-up to the general election, new legislation was adopted by Parliament making the denial (or minimization) of atrocities having been carried out by the Khmer Rouge regime a criminal offence.

Meanwhile, in April 2012 a prominent environmental campaigner, Chut Wutty, who had been an outspoken critic of illegal logging and land expropriation, was killed in an altercation with military police in a remote forest region of south-western Cambodia. The following month the Government temporarily suspended the granting of land for development to private companies in order to carry out a reassessment of the policy. This directive was ordered shortly before a visit to the country that month by Surya Subedi, the UN Special Rapporteur for Human Rights in Cambodia, to investigate the impact of the Government's so-called land concessions on local communities. During his visit, Subedi expressed concern at the increasing use of firearms by the police and military against environmental and human rights campaigners. However, only a few days later, security forces shot dead a 14-year-old girl who was taking part in a protest against land seizures and evictions in the north-eastern province of Kratie.

On 15 October 2012, following several years of ill health, the former King, Norodom Sihanouk, died at the age of 89 years in a hospital in the Chinese capital of Beijing. His state funeral in Phnom Penh on 4 February 2013 was attended by tens of thousands of mourners and by a number of foreign dignitaries, including the French Prime Minister, Jean-Marc Ayrault.

Recent developments: the 2013 elections

Having been granted a royal pardon at the request of Prime Minister Hun Sen (who had come under pressure from the US Government to do so), Rainsy returned to Cambodia from exile in mid-July 2013 and was greeted by thousands of his supporters; however, the CNRP leader remained disqualified from contesting the legislative elections on 28 July. According to the official preliminary results published by the National Election Committee on 12 August, following the general election—which was contested by eight parties—the ruling CPP retained its position as the largest party in the 123-seat National Assembly, albeit with a greatly reduced majority, winning 68 seats (22 fewer than in the 2008 elections), while the opposition CNRP secured the remaining 55 seats. Rainsy refused to recognize the results, alleging that serious irregularities had occurred and lodging 17 complaints with the National Election Committee. The opposition leader, who claimed that his party had won 63 seats and the CPP 60, demanded that an official investigation be undertaken by an independent committee into the allegations of widespread electoral fraud. Following a review of the contested results, on 6 September the Constitutional Council rejected all opposition complaints regarding alleged infringements of due electoral procedure and confirmed the CPP as the rightful winner. None the less, the CNRP continued to dispute the outcome and the opposition deputies refused to assume their seats in the legislature. Against the backdrop of the staging of large (and at times violent) demonstrations by the opposition in the capital earlier that month and despite the parliamentary boycott by the CNRP deputies, on 23 September Hun Sen was reappointed as Prime Minister at the head of a Government composed solely of CPP ministers.

The CNRP, which upheld its boycott of legislative proceedings, continued to stage anti-Government protests in the latter months of 2013 and into January 2014, when it was joined by striking garment workers who were demanding better pay and working conditions. At least four garment workers were killed in clashes with security forces on the outskirts of Phnom Penh on 3 January when the police reportedly opened fire on a group of demonstrators. More than 20 other protesters were arrested and detained and a ban on demonstrations was introduced, although some unauthorized protests continued to take place. Sam Rainsy and his deputy Kem Sokha were asked to appear in court in mid-January to be questioned over accusations of inciting social unrest, although they were not charged. Later in January representatives from human rights and development organizations submitted a petition to foreign embassies in Phnom Penh, calling for assistance in freeing the protesters who remained in detention. The detainees, who were charged with violence and destruction of property, were, however, denied bail by an appeals court in February.

Mass opposition demonstrations resumed in February 2014, following the lifting of the ban on public protests. In March negotiations between officials from the ruling CPP and the opposition CNRP to resolve the crisis resulted in an agreement to discuss a 14-point reform agenda, including voter registration, election financing and institutional reform, notably the reform of the National Election Committee.

The Khmer Rouge Tribunal

The detention of Ta Mok in March and of Duch in May 1999 (see Domestic Political Affairs) resulted in increased domestic and international pressure for the establishment of a tribunal to try former Khmer Rouge leaders for atrocities committed during 1975–79. However, the Cambodian Government was reluctant to indict former Khmer Rouge leaders who had surrendered, for fear that former PDK members might revert to armed insurrection. Furthermore, the Prime Minister, Hun Sen, initially insisted that any trials take place within the existing Cambodian court structure, while the UN favoured an international tribunal. In April 1999, however, Hun Sen conceded that UN-appointed foreign judges could take part in a trial in Cambodia, although he still favoured the nomination of a Cambodian prosecutor.

Legislation providing a formula for the establishment of a tribunal was finally endorsed by the National Assembly in July 2001 and signed into law by King Sihanouk in August, after receiving the approval of the Constitutional Council. Meanwhile, in June Hun Sen accused the UN of interfering with Cambodian sovereignty, a view that was reiterated by Prince Ranariddh. In February 2002 the UN unexpectedly announced that it had decided to abandon negotiations with the Cambodian Government over a UN role in the establishment of a joint tribunal, claiming that the legal framework created by the Government did not conform to international standards of justice and would ensure neither the independence nor impartiality of proceedings. In July Hun Sen announced that Cambodia was prepared to compromise with the UN by amending the laws that would govern the establishment of any tribunal. Following talks in the first half of 2003, the two sides concluded a formal agreement in June providing for the establishment of a bicameral tribunal, composed of a Trial Chamber and a Supreme Court Chamber. Under the legislation approved in 2001, only those individuals deemed 'most responsible' for the atrocities of 1975–79 were to be put on trial, thereby implicitly exempting significant numbers of middle- and lower-ranking former Khmer Rouge officials from prosecution. After a significant delay, owing to the prolonged political dispute that followed the 2003 elections, the legislation establishing the tribunal was finally ratified by the Cambodian legislature and promulgated by the King in October 2004. In December UN officials arrived in Cambodia to begin preparatory work.

In March 2006 the UN Secretary-General submitted to the Cambodian Government a list of international candidates for judicial positions within the tribunal (officially known as the Extraordinary Chambers in the Courts of Cambodia—ECCC). In July the 17 local and 13 international judges and prosecutors selected by the Cambodian Supreme Council of Magistracy—the country's highest judicial body, responsible for all judicial and prosecutorial appointments—were formally sworn in by King Sihamoni; later that month the two newly appointed co-prosecutors began their formal investigations, with former King Sihanouk stating that he would be willing to testify against the Khmers Rouges. At a meeting held in November, however, Cambodian and international judges failed to agree on internal rules governing the operations of the ECCC, further delaying the proceedings. In December Human Rights Watch alleged that Cambodian government interference was responsible for halting the process. In June 2007 agreement was finally reached on the tribunal's rules of procedure, and in July Duch became the first former Khmer Rouge leader to be formally charged with crimes against humanity, in what became known as Case 001.

In August 2007 the removal by royal decree of the President of the Court of Appeal, Ly Louch Leng, following allegations of bribery, and her replacement by You Bunleng, a judge previously appointed to serve with the ECCC, was widely regarded as seriously jeopardizing the independence and efficiency of the judiciary; UN officials questioned the Cambodian authorities' decision to make the appointment without due regard for the country's Constitution. Concerns were reiterated regarding the composition of the Supreme Council of Magistracy, which included a government minister and an official of the ruling party, and the appointment in August of four new members, through executive rather than constitutional channels, further diminished confidence in the system.

In the latter part of 2007 former Khmer Rouge leaders Nuon Chea, Ieng Sary and Khieu Samphan were charged with war crimes and crimes against humanity. Ieng Thirith, former Minister of Social Affairs and wife of Ieng Sary, was also charged with crimes against humanity. In a report released in October, the UN criticized Cambodia's management of the proceedings, in particular the engagement of excessive numbers of apparently unqualified staff, warning that it would withdraw from the trials process if changes were not implemented. In November, in its first public session, the tribunal began its consideration of Duch's request for bail, his lawyers arguing that his detention without trial for eight years constituted a breach of international standards of justice; the request was rejected in December.

Duch was formally indicted in August 2008 and his trial began in March 2009. Duch admitted responsibility, and apologized, for the part that he had played in the torture and execution of inmates as governor of the Tuol Sleng detention centre (see The coalition Government of 1998–2003). The trial was concluded in November and, following protracted delays, Duch was convicted of war crimes and crimes against humanity in July 2010 and sentenced to 30 years' imprisonment. However, this was to be reduced by 11 years owing to time already spent incarcerated, effectively shortening the term of imprisonment to 19 years. The tribunal's President explained that the decision not to award a life sentence (the maximum punishment to which the tribunal had recourse) was due to several mitigating factors, among them Duch's 'co-operation with the chamber, admission of responsibility, limited expressions of remorse, the coercive environment in Democratic Kampuchea and the potential for rehabilitation'.

In August 2010 it was announced that prosecutors were appealing against the 30-year prison sentence. Later that month Duch's lawyers also appealed against the conviction, arguing that the tribunal lacked jurisdiction since it was mandated to prosecute only the most senior leaders and those 'most responsible' for the atrocities committed during 1975–79, while Duch, they insisted, was just one of more than 100 prison guards serving during the Khmer Rouge regime and had merely been following orders. However, the prosecution team maintained that, as governor of the infamous Tuol Sleng detention camp, to which those deemed most dangerous to the Khmer Rouge regime had been sent and where no more than 15 detainees were thought to have survived, Duch had been one of the main protagonists of the regime's atrocities. Following an appeal hearing in March–April 2011, in February 2012 the ECCC's Supreme Court Chamber ruled that the original sentence had been too lenient given the gravity of Duch's crimes and increased his sentence to one of life imprisonment.

In September 2010 the four other, aforementioned defendants awaiting trial by the ECCC were formally indicted for genocide, crimes against humanity and war crimes. The four defendants (collectively known as Case 002), who were to be tried together, denied the charges against them; however, their final appeal was rejected in January 2011. It was announced in September that the trial was to be held in a number of stages, the first of which was to consider charges involving the forced movement of people and crimes against humanity, while subsequent trials would focus on the remaining charges, including genocide. In November, two days prior to the opening of the trial, medical experts deemed Ieng Thirith unfit to stand trial owing to poor mental health and ordered that she be released. (However, in December the ECCC ruled that she remain in detention and be transferred to a medical facility for treatment in the hope that she might subsequently become fit to stand trial.) The trial of Nuon Chea, Khieu Samphan and Ieng Sary opened two days later as planned. Almost 4,000 civil parties, primarily the relatives of victims of the Khmer Rouge regime, were to give evidence during the court proceedings.

Meanwhile, during a meeting with UN Secretary-General Ban Ki-Moon in October 2010, Prime Minister Hun Sen, himself a former junior Khmer Rouge cadre, was reported to have stated that he would not allow further prosecutions to be pursued by the ECCC beyond the long-anticipated second trial, arguing that such action would pose a threat to stability in Cambodia; several prominent Cambodian government officials publicly claimed that pursuing all but the most senior former Khmer Rouge leaders would constitute a breach of the tribunal's stipulated remit. The comments came amid ongoing investigations into two other complaints filed against five other former Khmer Rouge officials still at large. However, as of early 2012 no new cases had been brought before the ECCC. This inaction prompted some observers to accuse certain Cambodian members of the tribunal of wilfully obstructing the ECCC's activity in order to serve the Hun Sen Government's agenda, while one international judge blamed Cambodian government interference for his reticence in pursuing new cases. Indeed, two international judges resigned from the tribunal (one in October 2011 and the other in March 2012), claiming that their work was persistently hindered by co-investigating Cambodian judges. Meanwhile, Hun Sen continued to resist the idea of bringing any further charges against former Khmer Rouge leaders and insisted that no member of his Government was under any obligation to provide testimony to the ECCC. Having provisionally accepted a number of conditions demanded by the prosecution to limit the 80-year-old's freedom, the ECCC released Ieng Thirith, who remained unfit to stand trial (allegedly as a result of suffering from Alzheimer's disease), in September 2012.

In late 2012 it was reported that the ECCC, which relied on voluntary donations, was nearly bankrupt and urgently required funding if any further hearings were to be conducted. International contributions had considerably decreased over the preceding years mainly as a result of the global economic recession, the financial crisis in the eurozone and the 2011 tsunami disaster in Japan (which had provided around one-half of all international funds for the tribunal since 2006). In January 2013 Japan announced that it was to provide US $2.5m. in additional funding for the tribunal. In February the judges were asked to revisit their 2011 decision to hold the trial in a number of stages as it appeared that, owing to slow progress, many significant crimes would never reach the court. With proceedings still unfinished, the former Minister of Foreign Affairs of Democratic Kampuchea, Ieng Sary died in March 2013, prompting further criticism of the many delays. In the closing statements of the trial in October the prosecutors demanded the maximum sentence of life imprisonment for the two remaining defendants, who, in turn, continued to deny the charges against them; a final verdict was expected to be delivered by the ECCC in the first half of 2014.

Foreign Affairs

Regional relations

Regional relations were severely affected by the events of July 1997. ASEAN decided to postpone indefinitely Cambodia's admission to the grouping, which had been scheduled for that month, while Japan, like others in the international donor community, suspended all but humanitarian assistance. At the end of July Hun Sen invited ASEAN to mediate in the Cambodian crisis and held discussions with the grouping in August. Prior to the ASEAN summit meeting in Viet Nam in December 1998, Singapore, Thailand and the Philippines remained opposed to Cambodia's immediate accession to the organization. However, the host country then announced that Cambodia had been accepted as the 10th member of ASEAN. Cambodia duly acceded to ASEAN in April 1999.

In August 2002, following a meeting of ASEAN in Brunei, Cambodia became a signatory to a regional anti-terrorism pact drawn up by Malaysia, Indonesia and the Philippines earlier that year. In November Cambodia hosted the annual ASEAN summit meeting, which was also attended by the Republic of Korea (South Korea), Japan and the People's Republic of China, as well as India (which was present for the first time). During the meeting a framework agreement was signed to establish an ASEAN-China free trade area by 2010; the accord was duly implemented in January 2010. In 2012 Cambodia once again played host to the annual ASEAN summit meeting, which took place in two sessions (in April and November).

Relations between Cambodia and the People's Republic of China (which had formerly supported the PDK) improved from the mid-1990s. In November 2000 President Jiang Zemin paid a two-day official visit to Cambodia, the first by a Chinese head of state in more than 35 years. In August 2005 King Sihamoni undertook an official visit to China, and Chinese Premier Wen Jiabao made a reciprocal visit to Phnom Penh in April 2006. Cambodia prompted international censure in December 2009 when, before their claims for asylum had been heard, it deported 20 Uygur refugees to China, following coercion from the Chinese Government and despite objections from human rights groups and the UN. The members of the Turkic-speaking Muslim minority group had fled to Cambodia in the previous month, claiming that they were being persecuted by the Chinese Government following violent clashes in July between Uygur and Han Chinese in Urumqi, in the Xinjiang region of China. Several of the refugees had declared in written statements that they feared execution if forced to return to China. Two days after the deportations China and Cambodia signed 14 agreements for grants and loans, totalling an estimated US $1,000m., prompting suggestions that the former had abused its position as Cambodia's largest foreign investor to persuade the Cambodian Government to deport the refugees. Following the US Government's suspension of the delivery of military vehicles and uniforms in protest at the repatriation of the Uygur from Cambodia to China, China supplied Cambodia with military trucks in June 2010 and with military uniforms in May 2011. Also in June 2010, a memorandum of understanding (MOU) to increase road and bridge infrastructure co-operation was signed between Cambodia and China. As a result of the rapid development in bilateral relations over the last decade, China is now one of Cambodia's leading trading partners as well as its top investor. Bilateral trade volume between the two countries increased to around $2,900m. in 2012 and was expected to reach $5,000m. by 2017. Between 1994 and 2012 China was reported to have provided Cambodia with some $9,170m. in foreign direct investment.

Thailand remained neutral following the events in Cambodia of mid-1997, but extended humanitarian assistance to the estimated 35,000 Cambodian refugees who crossed into Thailand to avoid the fighting. In January 2003 demonstrators attacked the Thai embassy and several Thai-owned businesses in Phnom Penh, having been provoked by comments, wrongly attributed to a Thai actress, that implied that the temples at Angkor Wat had been stolen from Thailand. The violence escalated, prompting the Thai Government to withdraw its ambassador and to downgrade diplomatic relations. Following a formal apology to the Thai Government by Prime Minister Hun Sen, the Thai ambassador returned to Phnom Penh in April, and at the end of the following month the Cambodian and Thai Cabinets held an unprecedented joint meeting. In October 2004 the Thai embassy in Phnom Penh was finally reopened. Hun Sen visited Bangkok in May 2005 to commemorate the 55th anniversary of bilateral relations. An MOU pertaining to information and broadcasting was signed by the two countries in October of that year and another MOU, which provided for a single tourist visa valid for both countries, was signed in the following month. After the removal of the Government of Thaksin Shinawatra in a military coup in September 2006, Hun Sen stated that relations between the two countries remained unchanged and that Cambodia respected the right of Thailand to resolve its domestic affairs without international interference.

Cambodian-Thai relations were severely tested when the Preah Vihear temple, located on the countries' joint border, was declared a World Heritage Site by UNESCO in July 2008. An International Court of Justice (ICJ) ruling in 1962 had awarded Cambodia ownership of the temple, but sovereignty of the surrounding area remained a point of contention, and the Thai Government's initial approval, without parliamentary consent, of Cambodia's application to UNESCO had prompted considerable consternation in Thailand. As the situation escalated, soldiers from both countries were deployed to the area; following discussions between the two sides, most of the troops were withdrawn in August 2008, but in October the confrontation resulted in the deaths of two Cambodian soldiers. Later that month the Cambodian and Thai Governments agreed to seek a peaceful resolution to the matter, and in November plans for a border demarcation process and the full withdrawal of all remaining troops were drawn up. Following the reported death of four Thai soldiers during an exchange of fire across the border, the Joint Border Committee (JBC) of Cambodia and Thailand convened in April 2009 to discuss plans to accelerate the process of border demarcation. Despite an agreement on the planting of border posts, minor skirmishes in the disputed area continued to be reported during the latter half of 2009 and into 2010.

Meanwhile, in October 2009 Hun Sen had incensed Thai officials at the ASEAN summit meeting, held in Hua Hin, by declaring that Thaksin (who had been convicted *in absentia* of corruption and sentenced to two years' imprisonment by the Thai Supreme Court in October 2008) was welcome to seek refuge in Cambodia. Following the Cambodian Government's appointment of Thaksin as an economic adviser in late October 2009, Thailand recalled its ambassador from Phnom Penh in early November, accusing the Cambodian Government of interfering in Thailand's internal affairs; Cambodia recalled its own ambassador in Bangkok on the following day. In mid-November the Cambodian Government summarily rejected a request by Thai diplomats for the extradition of Thaksin, on the grounds that the latter's conviction had been 'politically motivated'.

Diplomatic relations between Cambodia and Thailand were fully restored following the announcement in August 2010 that Thaksin had resigned from his economic advisory position in Cambodia. From September a series of meetings between Hun Sen and the Thai Prime Minister, Abhisit Vejjajiva, on the sidelines of regional and international conferences, at which the two leaders were reported to have discussed the Preah Vihear issue and measures to prevent future border disputes, led to a further amelioration in relations. However, tensions once again escalated in mid-October, when a senior Thai investigator alleged that 11 members of the anti-Government Red Shirt movement who had been arrested earlier that month on suspicion of involvement in alleged assassination plots—the intended targets of which had included Abhisit—had received training at a Cambodian military base. The Cambodian Government adamantly denied the claims. Fighting broke out again in contested border areas in mid-April 2011, and by the beginning of May at least 18 Cambodian and Thai soldiers were reported to have been killed in the latest bout of violence. Following an appeal by ASEAN for the immediate holding of a formal dialogue, a tentative truce was declared in early May, and the Cambodian–Thai border crossing near the Preah Vihear site was reopened. In the same month Cambodian and Thai representatives appeared before the ICJ in connection with the border dispute, with both sides stating that they would respect the ultimate decision of the Court in its clarification of the 1962 ruling (as requested by Cambodia in April 2011); however, in June the Thai Government formally denounced the 1972 UNESCO World Heritage Convention. In July 2011 the ICJ ordered the withdrawal of all Cambodian and Thai military personnel from the disputed area around the Preah Vihear site and the establishment of a provisional demilitarized zone (PDZ) therein, which would be monitored by ASEAN-appointed observers.

The instalment of Thaksin's sister, Yingluck Shinawatra, as Thailand's Prime Minister in August 2011, engendered hopes of a new era in Cambodian-Thai relations. An official visit to Cambodia by Yingluck in September did appear to indicate a significant improvement in relations. During her stay, the new premier and the Cambodian Minister of Information agreed that both countries must adhere to the ICJ's decisions on the bilateral border dispute, including the redeployment of all military personnel away from the Preah Vihear site; the two also agreed to bolster co-operation in the fields of trade and investment and cross-border crime. Following a meeting in Phnom Penh between the Cambodian Minister of National Defence and his Thai counterpart in December, the two sides agreed to establish a joint working group (JWG) on the simultaneous withdrawal of troops under the observance of Indonesian monitors. In April 2012 the JWG agreed to commence mine-clearing operations around the Preah Vihear site, and, following a meeting between Hun Sen and Yingluck in Siem Reap in July, the two sides began withdrawing their military personnel from the disputed area to the PDZ, in accordance with the ICJ stipulation. The hearings at the ICJ on the border dispute commenced in April 2013 and in its final ruling, which was delivered in November, the court awarded sovereignty of most of the area surrounding the temple to Cambodia and consequently demanded the withdrawal of the Thai personnel stationed there. The ruling, which could not be appealed, was welcomed by the governments of both countries.

In April 1995 Cambodia, Thailand, Viet Nam and Laos signed an agreement providing for the establishment of the Mekong River Commission (see p. 452), which was to co-ordinate the sustainable development of the resources of the Lower Mekong River Basin. In October 1999 the leaders of Cambodia, Laos and Viet Nam convened in the Laotian capital for the first 'unofficial' summit meeting of the Indo-Chinese nations. During a visit to Viet Nam by Prime Minister Hun Sen in November 2005 the two countries signed a supplementary border treaty to complement an existing bilateral treaty signed in 1985; the new agreement envisaged that the demarcation of the border between the two countries would be finalized by December 2008. (However, by mid-2012 the project had still not been completed, with some 27 of the 314 planned border markers not yet having been installed.) King Sihamoni made his first official visit to Viet Nam in March 2006. In December 2009 the two countries signed more than 60 bilateral co-operation agreements and contracts intended to promote Vietnamese investment in Cambodia and estimated to be worth US $6,000m. Bilateral trade between Cambodia and Viet Nam increased from $1,600m. in 2008 to $2,800m. in 2011. At mid-2012 Viet Nam was operating more than 100 investment projects in Cambodia—focusing on telecommunications, banking, energy and agriculture—with a total capital of more than $2,200m. At a regional summit meeting held in Cambodia in November 2010, Cambodia, Laos, Myanmar, Thailand and Viet Nam signed the Phnom Penh Declaration, which was intended to improve economic co-operation across a wide range of activities among the regional neighbours. The signatories also expressed their support for the elimination of visa requirements for 30-day visits by citizens within the five countries, while Cambodia and Thailand signed an agreement exempting Cambodian and Thai citizens holding ordinary passports from visa requirements, in order to facilitate the flow of business people and tourists. At a ministerial meeting on anti-narcotics co-operation held in December, Cambodia, Laos and Viet Nam agreed to intensify co-operation in order to combat illegal drugs activities within the three countries. In June 2011 the Cambodian Government signed an agreement with the Laotian and Vietnamese Governments providing for the establishment of a trilateral economic development zone; however, critics argued that the agreement, which called for an acceleration of the border demarcation process, could result in the ceding of sovereign Cambodian territory to its regional neighbours. Cambodia's relations with Viet Nam were further strengthened in May 2013 following the signing of a defence co-operation plan in Ho Chi Minh City, Viet Nam, by the Cambodian Minister of National Defence, Gen. Tea Banh, and his Vietnamese counterpart.

Cambodia's relations with Japan continued to improve, following talks between the two in 1998–99, which culminated in 1999 in the Japanese Government's resumption of direct funding to Cambodia, which had been suspended after the events of 1997; during the 2000s and early 2010s Japan was a leading donor of development aid to the country (contributing US $130.9m. in 2011), and also made sizeable contributions to the financing of the Khmer Rouge trials. Strengthening bilateral relations were reflected by the first-ever official visit to Japan of King Sihamoni, in May 2010.

Other external relations

As with its regional relations, Cambodia's relations with countries further afield were greatly impeded by the events of July 1997. Like Japan, the USA and many European donors (including Germany) suspended all but humanitarian assistance, and in October 1998 the US House of Representatives adopted a resolution accusing Hun Sen of genocide. A further significant consequence was the decision of the UN Accreditation Committee to leave Cambodia's seat at the UN vacant; however, following the formation of a coalition Government in November 1998, Cambodia regained its seat in December.

Following bilateral negotiations in early 1999, Germany resumed financial aid to Cambodia, as did many within the international donor community. During the 2000s and early 2010s Germany was one of Cambodia's principal bilateral donors (contributing US $41.3m. in 2010), providing significant financial assistance for a wide range of developmental and humanitarian projects (including de-mining operations), as well as support for the Khmer Rouge trials.

US direct funding to Cambodia remained suspended until February 2007. In the same month, for the first time in more than 30 years, a US navy frigate docked in Cambodia, visiting the port of Sihanoukville. Although bilateral relations were hampered by Cambodia's decision to deport 20 Uygur refugees to China in December 2009 (see Regional relations), the damage appeared to be limited and short-lived. In May 2010 a US $1.8m.

peacekeeping training centre, funded by the US Department of Defense, was opened in the Cambodian capital. Furthermore, in July the USA and Cambodia co-organized the 'Angkor Sentinel 10' military exercises, involving 1,200 soldiers from 23 countries. Speaking at the event's inauguration, the US ambassador to Cambodia emphasized the commitment of the US Government to deepening its defence relations and other links with Cambodia. Human Rights Watch and other rights organizations urged the Administration of US President Barack Obama to suspend military aid to Cambodia until the latter country had achieved significant progress on its human rights record. However, given the deepening nature of Sino-Cambodian relations, it was feared by some observers that the US Administration's commitment to the promotion of human rights in Cambodia might be overshadowed by its desire to foster closer strategic relations with Phnom Penh and thereby to contain China's influence in Cambodia and the wider Asian-Pacific region. The USA continued to provide aid to Cambodia, pledging more than $65m. for 2012. While attending the ASEAN summit meeting in Phnom Penh in November 2012, President Obama met Hun Sen for the first time—talks between the two leaders reportedly focused almost exclusively on the issues of human rights and democracy.

In June 2007 the inaugural session of the Cambodia Development Cooperation Forum (CDCF) was held in Phnom Penh. Chaired solely by the Cambodian Government, the new forum replaced the Consultative Group of international donors and was to complement the implementation of the National Strategic Development Plan. Attended by about 25 delegations from the international community, the first meeting resulted in a total of US $689m. being pledged by foreign donors, for the first time including China. A total of $951.5m. was pledged at the second CDCF meeting, held in December 2008, and a further $1,100m. at the third meeting, held in June 2010. In August 2011 the fourth meeting, which had been scheduled to be convened in December of that year, was indefinitely postponed at the request of the Cambodian Government. This development was widely believed to have been linked to the announcement by the World Bank earlier in August that it was suspending the provision of new loans to Cambodia, in response to the forced eviction of thousands of residents living around Boeung Kak lake in Phnom Penh to make way for a luxury property development. One of the companies involved in the development was a Chinese firm alleged to have close links with Hun Sen. The World Bank further stated that it would resume funding only when the Cambodian Government halted such evictions and agreed to compensate all those who had already been evicted. Although, the Government subsequently gave land titles to some of the evicted families, the freeze on funding remained in place at March 2014.

CONSTITUTION AND GOVERNMENT

The Kingdom of Cambodia is a constitutional monarchy. The monarch is the head of state and is selected by the Throne Council from among descendants of three royal lines. Legislative power is vested in the 123-member National Assembly, the lower chamber, which is elected for a term of five years by universal adult suffrage, and the 61-member Senate, the upper chamber, 57 members of which are elected by parliamentarians and members of local administrative bodies, while the remaining four members are appointed by the National Assembly and the King. Executive power is held by the Cabinet (the Royal Government of Cambodia), headed by the Prime Minister, who is appointed by the King at the recommendation of the Chairman of the National Assembly from among the representatives of the majority party.

For local administration the Kingdom of Cambodia is divided into provinces (*khaet*), districts (*srok* or *khan*), municipalities (*krong*) and communes (*sangkat* or *khum*).

REGIONAL AND INTERNATIONAL CO-OPERATION

Cambodia is a member of the Association of Southeast Asian Nations (ASEAN, see p. 211), of the Asian Development Bank (ADB, see p. 207), of the Mekong River Commission (see p. 452), and of the Colombo Plan (see p. 449). Cambodia is also a member of the UN's Economic and Social Commission for Asia and the Pacific (ESCAP, see p. 28).

Cambodia became a member of the UN in 1955, and was admitted to the World Trade Organization (WTO, see p. 434) in 2004. Cambodia is a member of the International Labour Organization (ILO, see p. 137) and of the Non-aligned Movement (see p. 467).

ECONOMIC AFFAIRS

In 2012, according to the World Bank, Cambodia's gross national income (GNI), measured at average 2010–12 prices, was US $13,023m., equivalent to $880 per head (or $2,360 per head on an international purchasing-power parity basis). During 2003–12, it was estimated, the population increased at an average annual rate of 1.6%, while gross domestic product (GDP) per head increased, in real terms, by an average of 6.2% per year during the same period. According to the Asian Development Bank (ADB), Cambodia's overall GDP grew, in real terms, at an average annual rate of 7.9% during 2003–12; GDP increased by 7.2% in 2013.

According to the ADB, in 2012 agriculture (including forestry and fishing) contributed 35.6% of GDP and engaged 71.1% of the employed labour force. Production of paddy rice, a significant source of export revenue, was 9.3m. metric tons in 2012. Other important crops include cassava, maize, sugar cane and bananas. Floods in September and October 2013 adversely affected crop production and reduced the rate of growth of agricultural GDP in that year. Rubber and timber are also major export commodities. However, forestry reserves continued to be depleted and reafforestation remained inadequate. The fishing sector was also adversely affected by deforestation, which caused the silting up of lakes and rivers. According to ADB data, agricultural GDP increased, in real terms, at an average annual rate of 5.2% during 2003–12; sectoral growth was 4.3% in 2012, but declined to 1.8% in 2013.

According to the ADB, industry (including mining, manufacturing, construction and utilities) contributed 24.3% of GDP in 2012. In 2007 15.4% of the employed labour force were engaged in this sector, according to the IMF. In real terms, according to figures from the ADB, industrial GDP increased at an average annual rate of 9.4% during 2003–12. Sectoral GDP rose by 10.5% in 2013.

In 2012, according to the ADB, mining and quarrying contributed 0.8% of GDP and employed 0.7% of the employed labour force. Cambodia's mineral resources include phosphates, gemstones, iron ore, bauxite, silicon, manganese ore and gold. Commercial reserves of offshore petroleum were confirmed by the US energy company Chevron in 2010; by the end of 2012 Cambodia had granted six prospecting licences to a number of international companies. The country also has substantial reserves of natural gas. According to figures from the ADB, the GDP of the mining sector increased, in real terms, at an average annual rate of 20.3% during 2003–12; sectoral growth was 19.8% in 2011 and 26.5% in 2012.

Manufacturing contributed 16.0% of GDP and engaged 9.0% of the employed labour force in 2012, according to the ADB. The sector is dominated by rice milling and the production of garments, household goods, textiles, tyres and pharmaceutical products. The total value of garment exports reached US $4,327.6m. in 2012. According to ADB figures, the GDP of the manufacturing sector increased, in real terms, at an average annual rate of 9.8% during 2003–12. Manufacturing GDP grew by 16.2% in 2011 and by 7.1% in 2012.

According to the ADB, construction contributed 6.9% of GDP in 2012. The sector engaged 3.6% of the employed labour force in 2007, according to the IMF. During 2003–12, according to the ADB, the GDP of the sector increased at an average annual rate of 7.0%; sectoral GDP increased by 7.9% in 2011 and by 16.3% in 2012.

Household energy is derived principally from wood charcoal, which accounted for about 80% of total energy consumption in 2010. Most commercial energy used in Cambodia is imported. In 2010 only 22% of Cambodian households had access to electricity, mostly in Phnom Penh. Cambodia has significant hydropower potential and several dam projects are currently under way. In 2011 petroleum accounted for 90.3% of electricity output. Imports of petroleum products accounted for 13.9% of the cost of total merchandise imports in 2012.

The services sector contributed 40.1% of GDP in 2012, according to the ADB, and engaged 28.7% of the employed labour force in 2007, according to the IMF. The tourism sector has become increasingly significant. Foreign tourist arrivals rose by 24.4% compared with 2011, to reach 3.6m. in 2012, when tourism receipts amounted to US $2,210m. In real terms, the GDP of the services sector increased at an average annual rate of 7.9% during 2002–11, according to data from the ADB. The sector's rate of growth reached 8.1% in 2012 and 8.4% in 2013.

In 2012 Cambodia recorded a visible merchandise trade deficit of US $1,949.2m., and there was a deficit of $1,207.5m. on the current account of the balance of payments. In 2012 the principal source of imports was the People's Republic of China (providing 30.6% of the total). Other major sources were Viet Nam, Thailand, Hong Kong and the Republic of Korea. In the same year the principal market for exports was the USA (taking 25.9% of the total); other important purchasers were Hong Kong, Singapore, the United Kingdom, Germany and Canada. The principal exports in 2012 were textiles and textile products (accounting for 55.2% of the total), and pulp of wood, paper and paperboard, and articles thereof. The country's main imports included textiles and textile products, mineral products, machinery and mechanical appliances, electrical equipment, vehicles, and prepared foodstuffs, beverages, spirits, vinegar and tobacco products.

According to ADB data, Cambodia's overall budgetary deficit in 2012 was 1,325,900m. riels, equivalent to 2.3% of GDP. The fiscal deficit was equivalent to 6.5% of GDP in 2012 and 5.0% in 2013. Cambodia's general government gross debt was 16,307,183m. riels in 2012, equivalent to 28.8% of GDP. The Cambodia Development Cooperation Forum (CDCF), which superseded the Consultative Group of international donors in 2007, has continued to provide support (see Contemporary Political History). According to the ADB, Cambodia's external public debt was estimated at US $4,822m. at the end of 2013. In that year the cost of servicing external public debt was equivalent to 1.6% of the value of exports of goods and services. The annual rate of inflation in Phnom Penh averaged 6.3% during 2003–12, according to the International Labour Organization (ILO); consumer prices increased by 2.9% in 2013, according to the ADB. According to government estimates, the unemployment rate was 0.2% in 2012.

Despite years of mainly vigorous growth, the Cambodian economy has remained narrowly based on the tourism and garment industries, both of which were adversely affected by the global recession of 2008–09; in 2009 the country's GDP growth rate plummeted to only 0.1%. The Government's attempts to counter the economic downturn and to reduce levels of poverty were impeded by an unexpectedly sharp rise (of 25%) in consumer prices in 2008. Inflationary pressures subsided in 2009 but re-emerged in 2010–11, as the costs of food and fuel again increased. Inflation rose to 5.5% in 2011, but fell to 2.9% in 2012 and 2013, mainly as a result of a moderation in food prices; according to the ADB, inflation was projected to reach 3.5% in 2014 and 2015. Cambodia remained the sixth largest exporter of garments internationally; in 2013 exports of garments and footwear to the European Union grew by 26%, according to the ADB, to reach US $2,000m., although the US market, which expanded by 6%, remained marginally larger at $2,100m. The sector is a leading recipient of investment finance; according to the World Bank, total foreign direct investment in Cambodia (much of which was from China) almost doubled from US $785.0m. in 2011 to $1,410.2m. in 2012. However, it declined to $1,300m. in 2013, largely as a result of the political uncertainty following the legislative elections in July 2013. In December 2013 a new ministry, dedicated solely to mines and energy, was established with a view to oil and natural gas production being instigated within the next few years, although the number and size of the deposits discovered were smaller than originally forecast. Light industry (notably the manufacture of automotive parts and processing of agricultural products) was encouraged by the establishment of special economic zones (SEZs) across the country—by 2014 22 SEZs had been approved and 11 had received investment from foreign and local companies. The financial sector was expanding, and trading on the newly launched Cambodia Securities Exchange, which was 55% owned by the Cambodian Government and 45% owned by the South Korean stock exchange, commenced in April 2012. Following the resumption of robust growth (of 6.0%) in 2010, GDP expanded by 7.1% in 2011 and 7.3% in 2012, underpinned by strong exports, consumption and investment and a rise in tourist arrivals. Growth was sustained at 7.2% in 2013, as exports continued to demonstrate robust growth and the services sector expanded strongly. Concerns about growing labour unrest, particularly in the garment sector where workers organized strikes to demand increased wages and better working conditions, raised concerns that the rate of economic growth could slow, but the ADB forecast growth of 7.0% for 2014 and 7.3% for 2015. The Government's 2014–18 National Strategic Development Plan—which emphasizes the promotion of good governance, the development of the private sector, the commercialization of agriculture, infrastuctural development, and the raising of the skills levels of the workforce through vocational training—targets growth of more than 7% a year over the period of the plan and a reduction in the rate of poverty to below 20%, through a decline of 1% annually.

PUBLIC HOLIDAYS

2015: 1 January (International New Year's Day), 7 January (Victory Day over the Genocide Regime), 7 February (Meak Bochea Day), 8 March (for International Women's Day), 14–16 April (Cambodian New Year), 1 May (Labour Day), 9 May (Royal Ploughing Ceremony), 25 May (Visaka Buchea Day), 13 May (King Sihamoni's Birthday), 3 June (for International Children's Day), 18 June (Former Queen's Birthday), 28 September (Bonn Pchum Ben), 24 September (Constitution Day), 29 October (Anniversary of Coronation of King Sihamoni), 31 October (Former King Sihanouk's Birthday), 9 November (for Independence Day), 25 November (Water Festival), 10 December (Human Rights Day).

Statistical Survey

Source (unless otherwise stated): National Institute of Statistics, Ministry of Planning, Sangkat Boeung Keng Kang 1, blvd Monivong, Phnom Penh; tel. (23) 216538; fax (23) 213650; e-mail census@camnet.com.kh; internet www.nis.gov.kh.

Area and Population

AREA, POPULATION AND DENSITY

Area (sq km)	181,035*
Population (census results)†	
3 March 1998	11,437,656
3 March 2008	
Males	6,516,054
Females	6,879,628
Total	13,395,682
Population (UN estimates at mid-year)‡	
2012	14,864,647
2013	15,135,167
2014	15,408,269
Density (per sq km) at mid-2014	85.1

* 69,898 sq miles; figure includes Tonlé Sap lake (approx. 3,000 sq km).
† Excluding adjustments for underenumeration.
‡ Source: UN, *World Population Prospects: The 2012 Revision*.

POPULATION BY AGE AND SEX
(UN estimates at mid-2014)

	Males	Females	Total
0–14	2,454,214	2,336,298	4,790,512
15–64	4,717,982	5,053,724	9,771,706
65 and over	349,775	496,276	846,051
Total	7,521,971	7,886,298	15,408,269

Source: UN, *World Population Prospects: The 2012 Revision*.

PROVINCES
(population at 2008 census)

	Area (sq km)*	Population	Density (per sq km)
Banteay Meanchey	6,679	677,872	101.5
Battambang	11,702	1,025,174	87.6
Kampong Cham	9,799	1,679,992	171.4
Kampong Chhnang	5,521	472,341	85.6
Kampong Spueu	7,017	716,944	102.2
Kampong Thom	13,814	631,409	45.7
Kampot	4,873	585,850	120.2
Kandal	3,568	1,265,280	354.6
Kep	336	35,753	106.4
Koh Kong	11,160	117,481	10.5
Kratie	11,094	319,217	28.8
Mondul Kiri	14,288	61,107	4.3
Oddar Meanchey	6,158	185,819	30.2
Pailin	803	70,486	87.8
Phnom Penh	290	1,327,615	4,578.0
Preah Vihear	13,788	171,139	12.4
Prey Veng	4,883	947,372	194.0
Pursat	12,692	397,161	31.3
Ratanak Kiri	10,782	150,466	14.0
Siem Reap	10,299	896,443	87.0
Sihanoukville (Preah Sihanouk)	868	221,396	255.1
Stung Treng	11,092	111,671	10.1
Svay Rieng	2,966	482,788	162.8
Takeo	3,563	844,906	237.1
Total	178,035	13,395,682	75.2

* Excluding Tonlé Sap lake (approx. 3,000 sq km).

PRINCIPAL TOWNS
(population at 1998 census)

Phnom Penh (capital)	999,804	Bat Dambang (Battambang)	139,964
Preah Sihanouk (Sihanoukville)*	155,690	Siem Reab (Siem Reap)	119,528

* Also known as Kampong Saom (Kompong Som).

Mid-2011 ('000, incl. suburbs, UN estimate): Phnom Penh 1,549,760 (Source: UN, *World Urbanization Prospects: The 2011 Revision*).

BIRTHS AND DEATHS
(annual averages, UN estimates)

	1995–2000	2000–05	2005–10
Birth rate (per 1,000)	29.8	26.5	26.3
Death rate (per 1,000)	9.5	7.6	6.4

Source: UN, *World Population Prospects: The 2012 Revision*.

2004: Live births 384,267; Deaths 124,391 (Source: UN, *Population and Vital Statistics Report*).

Life expectancy (years at birth, WHO estimates): 71.1 (males 68.4; females 73.8) in 2011 (Source: World Bank, World Development Indicators database).

EMPLOYMENT
('000 persons)

	2005	2006	2007
Agriculture, forestry and fishing	4,655	4,619	4,670
Mining and quarrying	19	20	22
Manufacturing	789	870	944
Electricity, gas and water	17	19	21
Construction	234	260	299
Wholesale and retail trade	1,104	1,140	1,196
Restaurants and hotels	43	61	86
Transport and communications	206	217	228
Financial intermediation	23	32	32
Real estate and renting	16	18	20
Public administration	185	184	185
Education	113	120	128
Health and social work	43	49	57
Other social services	89	108	123
Other services	341	336	343
Total employed	7,878	8,053	8,354

Source: IMF, *Cambodia: Statistical Appendix* (February 2009).

2011 ('000 persons): Agriculture 5,168.9; Manufacturing 635.2; Mining 50.7; Others 1,391.7; *Total employed* 7,246.5 (Source: Asian Development Bank).

2012 ('000 persons): Agriculture 5,178.0; Manufacturing 653.8; Mining 50.2; Others 1,405.3; *Total employed* 7,287.4 (Source: Asian Development Bank).

Health and Welfare

KEY INDICATORS

Total fertility rate (children per woman, 2011)	2.5
Under-5 mortality rate (per 1,000 live births, 2011)	43
HIV/AIDS (% of persons aged 15–49, 2012)	0.8
Physicians (per 1,000 head, 2008)	0.2
Hospital beds (per 1,000 head, 2004)	0.1
Health expenditure (2010): US $ per head (PPP)	132
Health expenditure (2010): % of GDP	6.0
Health expenditure (2010): public (% of total)	21.5
Access to water (% of persons, 2011)	67
Access to sanitation (% of persons, 2011)	33
Total carbon dioxide emissions ('000 metric tons, 2010)	4,180.4
Carbon dioxide emissions per head (metric tons, 2010)	0.3
Human Development Index (2012): ranking	138
Human Development Index (2012): value	0.543

For sources and definitions, see explanatory note on p. vi.

Agriculture

PRINCIPAL CROPS
('000 metric tons)

	2010	2011	2012
Rice, paddy	8,245.3	8,779.0	9,290.9
Maize	773.3	717.0	950.9
Sweet potatoes	79.3	46.6	48.8
Cassava (Manioc)	4,247.4	8,033.8	7,613.7
Beans, dry	71.2	76.2	74.7
Soybeans (Soya beans)	156.6	114.6	120.2
Groundnuts, with shell	22.0	22.8	30.3
Sesame seed	29.9	33.5	26.8
Coconuts	65.5*	53.7*	55.0†
Sugar cane	365.6	468.7	573.7*
Tobacco, unmanufactured	14.6	15.1†	16.0†
Natural rubber†	39.2	43.5	43.5
Oranges†	63.5	56.9	58.0
Guavas, mangoes and mangosteens†	48.0	62.0	64.0
Pineapples†	21.3	24.6	26.0
Bananas†	151.2	155.6	160.0

* Unofficial figure.
† FAO estimate(s).

Aggregate production ('000 metric tons, may include official, semi-official or estimated data): Total cereals 9,018.6 in 2010, 9,496.0 in 2011, 10,241.8 in 2012; Total roots and tubers 4,360.8 in 2010, 8,116.3 in 2011, 7,699.0 in 2012; Total vegetables (incl. melons) 527.8 in 2010, 621.5 in 2011; 628.0 in 2012; Total fruits (excl. melons) 385.6 in 2010, 373.3 in 2011; 385.5 in 2012.

Source: FAO.

LIVESTOCK
('000 head, year ending September)

	2010	2011	2012
Horses*	28	29	29
Cattle	3,485	3,407	2,915
Buffaloes	702	690	680*
Pigs	2,057	2,099	2,120*
Chickens	17,448	16,341	14,447
Ducks*	7,000	8,000	8,200

* FAO estimate(s).

Source: FAO.

LIVESTOCK PRODUCTS
('000 metric tons, FAO estimates)

	2010	2011	2012
Cattle meat	62.9	63.1	63.6
Buffalo meat	9.8	9.8	9.8
Pig meat	100.0	97.5	98.5
Chicken meat	19.5	19.0	19.0
Cows' milk	26.8	23.3	23.5
Hen eggs	17.6	18.0	18.5
Other poultry eggs	4.8	4.8	4.8

Source: FAO.

Forestry

ROUNDWOOD REMOVALS
('000 cubic metres, excl. bark)

	2010	2011	2012
Sawlogs, veneer logs and logs for sleepers	69*	161*	161†
Other industrial wood	13†	9	9†
Fuel wood†	8,442	8,299	8,162
Total	8,524	8,469	8,332

* Unofficial figure.
† FAO estimate(s).

Source: FAO.

SAWNWOOD PRODUCTION
('000 cubic metres, incl. railway sleepers)

	2007	2008	2009
Total (all broadleaved)*	162	112	102

* Unofficial figures.

2010–12: Production assumed to be unchanged since 2009 (unofficial figures).

Source: FAO.

Fishing

('000 metric tons, live weight)

	2009	2010	2011
Capture	465.0	490.1*	490.0*
Freshwater fishes	389.7	404.5	404.5*
Marine fishes	55.4	62.7*	61.6*
Natantian decapods	7.0	8.0*	8.0*
Aquaculture	50.0*	60.0*	72.0
Total catch*	515.0	550.1	562.0

* FAO estimate(s).

Note: Figures exclude crocodiles, recorded by number rather than by weight. The total number of estuarine crocodiles caught was: 185,000 in 2009; n.a. in 2010–11. Also excluded are aquatic plants.

Source: FAO.

Mining

('000 metric tons)

	2009	2010	2011*
Gravel	41.9	82.5	82.5
Limestone*	1,000.0	1,000.0	1,000.0
Sand (construction material)	14,035.8	38,367.5	40,000.0

* Estimates.

Source: US Geological Survey.

Industry

SELECTED PRODUCTS

	2010	2011	2012
Plywood ('000 cu m)*†	12	12	12
Electric energy (million kWh)‡	968.4	1,018.5	1,423.1

* Source: FAO.
† Unofficial figures.
‡ Source: Electricity Authority of Cambodia.

Finance

CURRENCY AND EXCHANGE RATES

Monetary Units
100 sen = 1 riel.

Sterling, Dollar and Euro Equivalents (31 December 2013)
£1 sterling = 6,579.0 riels;
US $1 = 3,995.0 riels;
€1 = 5,509.5 riels;
10,000 riels = £1.52 = $2.50 = €1.82.

Average Exchange Rate (riels per US $)
2011 4,058.50
2012 4,033.00
2013 4027.25

BUDGET

('000 million riels)

Revenue	2009	2010*	2011†
Tax revenue	4,332.2	5,070.0	5,750.8
Direct taxes	742.9	967.8	1,097.8
Trade tax	1,064.3	1,112.3	1,261.7
Value-added tax	1,460.6	1,773.0	1,984.3
Excise duties	849.4	919.7	1,029.3
Non-tax revenue	716.2	872.2	989.3
Fishery	6.4	9.1	10.3
Forestry	14.7	18.7	21.2
Factory leases	21.5	22.8	25.9
Civil aviation	56.2	52.9	60.0
Posts and telecommunications	71.5	67.9	77.0
Other non-tax revenues	497.8	653.8	741.6
Capital revenue	29.3	48.0	100.0
Total	5,077.7	5,992.2	6,840.1

Expenditure	2009	2010*	2011†
Current expenditure	4,597.1	5,172.9	5,662.5
Defence and security	1,254.0	1,150.5	1,229.3
General administration	1,332.6	753.1	807.0
Social administration	1,505.8	1,770.6	1,987.6
Economic administration	246.1	299.1	332.6
Interest	86.6	120.0	128.2
Provincial expenditure	157.4	144.1	178.4
Other current expenditure	14.5	935.4	999.5
Capital expenditure	2,951.6	3,326.9	3,534.3
Locally financed	1,019.2	971.0	1,113.6
Externally financed	1,877.3	2,300.0	2,364.1
Provincial expenditure	55.1	55.9	56.6
Total	7,548.6	8,499.8	9,196.8

* Estimates.
† Budget projections.

2012 (budget projections): *Revenue:* Tax revenue 6,529.0 (Direct taxes 1,246.3; Indirect taxes 3,462.9; Trade taxes 1,432.4; Provincial taxes 253.6); Non-tax revenue 1,123.2; Capital revenue 100.0; Total 7,752.1. *Expenditure:* Current expenditure 6,163.0 (Defence and security 1,297.5, Civil administration 4,511.8, Interest 135.3, Provincial expenditure 218.3); Capital expenditure 3,876.3; Total 10,039.3.

Source: Ministry of Economy and Finance, Phnom Penh.

2013 ('000 million riels, general government operations, projections): *Revenue* Tax revenue 7,426 (Income, profits, and capital gains 1,488, Goods and services 4,294, International trade and transactions 1,645); Non-tax revenue 1,268; Total (excl. grants 1,860) 8,694. *Expenditure* Current expenditure 7,325 (Compensation of employees 3,126, Purchase of goods and services 2,252, Interest 180; Other expenditure 1,767); Capital expenditure 4,972 (Externally financed 3,705); Total 12,297 (excl. net lending –1,743) (Source: IMF, *Cambodia: Staff Report for the 2012 Article IV Consultation*—January 2013).

INTERNATIONAL RESERVES

(US $ million at 31 December)

	2010	2011	2012
Gold (national valuation)	547.01	619.32	670.66
IMF special drawing rights	105.43	105.00	105.09
Foreign exchange	3,149.68	3,344.69	4,162.24
Total	3,802.12	4,069.01	4,937.99

Source: IMF, *International Financial Statistics*.

MONEY SUPPLY

('000 million riels at 31 December)

	2010	2011	2012
Currency outside depository corporations	3,103.56	3,782.27	3,777.63
Transferable deposits	3,030.17	2,963.72	5,119.95
Other deposits	13,440.93	13,599.53	19,466.16
Broad money	19,574.66	20,345.51	28,363.73

Source: IMF, *International Financial Statistics*.

COST OF LIVING

(Consumer Price Index for Phnom Penh at January; base: October-December 2006 = 100)

	2011	2012	2013
Food and non-alcoholic beverages	153.8	165.6	167.9
Clothing and footwear	115.0	118.7	124.1
Housing and utilities	122.1	124.4	127.7
Household furnishings, etc.	122.6	125.4	129.3
Medical care and health expenses	116.7	116.1	116.6
Transport	121.4	129.7	131.0
Communication	73.8	72.2	71.3
Recreation and culture	103.4	102.3	105.1
Education	140.2	142.7	n.a.
All items	138.5	146.5	149.2

NATIONAL ACCOUNTS

('000 million riels at current prices)

Expenditure on the Gross Domestic Product

	2010	2011	2012
Government final consumption expenditure	2,985.0	3,134.2	3,280.5
Private final consumption expenditure	38,246.2	43,144.0	46,361.6
Change in stocks	552.1	586.4	644.0
Gross fixed capital formation	7,619.0	8,316.3	8,538.6
Total domestic expenditure	49,402.4	55,180.9	58,824.7
Exports of goods and services	25,444.9	28,159.1	30,926.5
Less Imports of goods and services	28,003.4	30,981.4	33,184.2
Statistical discrepancy	204.2	–289.9	49.8
GDP in purchasers' values	47,048.0	52,068.7	56,616.8
GDP at constant 2000 prices	30,403.3	32,552.7	34,916.5

Gross Domestic Product by Economic Activity

	2009	2010	2011
Agriculture, hunting, forestry and fishing	14,420.0	15,938.3	17,993.5
Mining and quarrying	195.9	279.5	329.7
Manufacturing	6,207.6	6,913.2	7,900.2
Electricity, gas and water	229.7	251.6	269.8
Construction	2,693.7	2,844.5	3,029.2
Trade, hotels and restaurants	5,811.6	6,480.1	7,014.0
Transport, storage and communications	3,223.6	3,565.3	3,961.0
Finance, real estate and other business activities	594.1	670.1	796.9
Public administration	768.5	806.9	844.0
Other services	6,303.9	6,499.6	6,911.9
Sub-total	40,448.6	44,249.0	49,050.3
Less Imputed bank service charge	471.9	529.1	568.5
GDP at factor cost	39,976.7	43,719.8	48,481.8
Indirect taxes, *less* subsidies	3,089.3	3,381.8	3,672.3
Statistical discrepancy	—	–53.6	–85.4
GDP in purchasers' values	43,065.8	47,048.0	52,068.7

2012: Agriculture, hunting, forestry and fishing 18,999.4; Mining and quarrying 438.9; Manufacturing 8,563.0; Electricity, gas and water 294.3; Construction 3,662.5; Trade, hotels and restaurants 7,722.2; Transport, storage and communications 4,263.9; Finance, real estate and other business activities 4,098.7; Public administration 858.3; Other services 4,465.5; *Sub-total* 53,366.7; *Less* Imputed bank service charge 661.3; *GDP at factor cost* 52,705.4; Indirect taxes, less subsidies 4,005.8; Statistical discrepancy –94.4; *GDP in purchaser's values* 56,616.8.

Source: Asian Development Bank.

BALANCE OF PAYMENTS
(US $ million)

	2010	2011	2012
Exports of goods	3,884.3	5,219.5	6,015.7
Imports of goods	–5,466.0	–6,709.5	–7,964.9
Balance on goods	–1,581.6	–1,490.1	–1,949.2
Exports of services	1,669.0	2,212.6	2,545.4
Imports of services	–971.8	–1,323.4	–1,545.6
Balance on goods and services	–884.4	–600.9	–949.4
Primary income received	58.7	61.3	67.6
Primary income paid	–588.5	–756.2	–809.4
Balance on goods, services and primary income	–1,414.2	–1,295.8	–1,691.2
Secondary income received	663.9	605.9	583.0
Secondary income paid	–21.4	–21.9	–99.3
Current balance	–771.7	–711.8	–1,207.5
Capital account (net)	331.0	222.1	276.5
Direct investment assets	–20.6	–29.2	–30.6
Direct investment liabilities	782.6	901.7	1,557.1
Portfolio investment assets	–36.7	–6.1	–32.8
Other investment assets	–685.6	–772.9	–1,783.7
Other investment liabilities	580.6	731.3	1,638.8
Net errors and omissions	–29.4	–26.4	–42.5
Reserves and related items	150.3	308.7	375.4

Source: IMF, *International Financial Statistics*.

External Trade

PRINCIPAL COMMODITIES
(distribution by HS, US $ million)

Imports c.i.f.	2010	2011	2012
Prepared foodstuffs; beverages, spirits, vinegar; tobacco and articles thereof	294.5	331.3	405.3
Tobacco and tobacco manufactures	159.7	144.7	171.8
Mineral products	413.6	917.4	1,068.2
Mineral fuels, oils, distillation products, etc.	356.6	848.6	984.5
Non-crude petroleum	316.8	803.1	910.1
Chemicals and related products	258.5	290.7	340.1
Plastics, rubber, and articles thereof	161.5	173.8	215.6
Textiles and textile articles	1,914.9	2,268.1	2,619.8
Manmade staple fibres	524.6	633.5	713.4
Woven fabrics of synthetic staple fibres	377.8	463.5	554.6
Knitted or crocheted fabric	1,001.4	1,162.9	1,394.9
Knitted or crocheted fabrics of a greater width	334.6	499.5	593.0
Fabrics, knitted or crocheted, excluding warp knit fabrics	623.3	639.0	768.1
Pearls, precious or semi-precious stones, precious metals, and articles thereof	168.4	108.9	118.8
Gold unwrought or in semi-manufactured forms	164.5	88.3	104.9
Iron and steel, other base metals and articles of base metal	201.0	288.5	314.1
Machinery and mechanical appliances; electrical equipment; parts thereof	640.6	682.4	699.4
Machinery, boilers, etc.	420.0	411.8	464.2
Electrical, electronic equipment	220.6	270.6	235.1
Vehicles, aircraft, vessels and associated transport equipment	377.6	452.1	657.5
Road vehicles	353.4	444.4	643.8
Total (incl. others)	4,902.5	6,143.3	7,062.6

Exports f.o.b.	2010	2011	2012
Plastics, rubber, and articles thereof	95.2	202.9	186.0
Pulp of wood, paper and paperboard, and articles thereof	1,778.6	1,579.9	2,289.1
Printed books, newspapers, and pictures	1,777.0	1,576.1	2,283.0
Unused stamps, cheque forms, banknotes, bond certificates	1,777.0	1,574.9	2,282.1
Textiles and textile articles	3,056.6	4,014.4	4,327.6
Articles of apparel, accessories, knit or crochet	2,945.0	3,843.3	4,059.0
Men's suits, jackets, trousers	485.0	685.4	741.1
Women's suits, and dresses	819.9	1,038.9	1,064.8
Women's wear, knitted/crocheted	186.2	201.1	250.1
T-shirts, knitted or crocheted	307.9	485.2	586.8
Jerseys, pullovers, cardigans, etc., knitted or crocheted	641.6	781.8	754.2

Exports f.o.b.—*continued*	2010	2011	2012
Footwear, headgear, umbrellas, walking sticks, etc.	184.1	277.3	311.0
Footwear, gaiters and parts thereof	177.1	267.1	299.5
Vehicles, aircraft, vessels and associated transport equipment	119.8	306.3	297.5
Road vehicles	103.9	298.1	293.5
Total (incl. others)	5,590.1	6,704.1	7,838.1

Source: Trade Map-Trade Competitiveness Map, International Trade Centre, www.intracen.org/marketanalysis.

PRINCIPAL TRADING PARTNERS
(US $ million)

Imports c.i.f.	2010	2011	2012
China, People's Republic	1,186.3	1,738.9	2,162.2
France (incl. Monaco)	50.6	43.6	46.1
Hong Kong	553.3	479.4	495.4
India	52.5	74.0	103.2
Indonesia	175.3	169.3	215.7
Japan	156.7	248.4	223.0
Korea, Republic	248.1	301.1	404.4
Malaysia	165.5	209.7	175.4
Singapore	155.7	238.1	258.4
Switzerland-Liechtenstein	171.4	93.2	111.8
Thailand	690.7	726.5	902.3
USA	129.9	144.9	151.9
Viet Nam	487.3	882.9	937.0
Total (incl. others)	4,902.5	6,143.3	7,062.6

Exports f.o.b.	2010	2011	2012
Belgium	63.8	134.9	163.3
Canada	274.4	382.6	417.0
China, People's Republic	65.0	154.6	182.9
France (incl. Monaco)	57.6	94.9	124.2
Germany	112.4	324.0	469.7
Hong Kong	1,386.4	1,199.0	1,682.7
Japan	89.6	153.4	199.2
Netherlands	235.8	171.4	122.6
Singapore	430.0	441.9	684.7
Spain	101.3	141.2	149.9
Thailand	150.1	190.5	102.3
United Kingdom	235.5	391.1	528.0
USA	1,905.6	2,107.2	2,032.8
Viet Nam	96.1	148.8	116.3
Total (incl. others)	5,590.1	6,704.1	7,838.1

Source: Trade Map-Trade Competitiveness Map, International Trade Centre, www.intracen.org/marketanalysis.

Transport

RAILWAYS
(traffic)

	1997	1998	1999
Freight carried ('000 metric tons)	16	294	259
Freight ton-km ('000)	36,514	75,721	76,171
Passengers ('000)	553	438	431
Passenger-km ('000)	50,992	43,847	49,894

Source: Ministry of Economy and Finance, Phnom Penh.

2000: Passenger-km (million) 15; Freight ton-km (million) 91 (Source: UN, *Statistical Yearbook*).

2005: Passenger-km (million) 45 (Source: World Bank, World Development Indicators database).

ROAD TRAFFIC
(estimated number of motor vehicles in use)

	2002	2003	2004
Passenger cars	209,128	219,602	235,298
Buses and coaches	3,196	3,269	3,502
Trucks	29,968	30,448	31,946
Other vehicles	421	428	440
Motorcycles and mopeds	586,278	619,748	646,944

Sources: Ministry of Public Works and Transport, Phnom Penh, and Phnom Penh Municipal Traffic Police.

2005 (motor vehicles in use at 31 December): Passenger cars 247,322; Buses and coaches 3,681; Vans and Lorries 33,578; Motorcycles and mopeds 680,002 (Source: IRF, *World Road Statistics*).

SHIPPING

Flag Registered Fleet
(at 31 December)

	2011	2012	2013
Number of vessels	1,000	970	859
Displacement ('000 grt)	2,037.5	2,096.5	2,066.9

Source: Lloyd's List Intelligence (www.lloydslistintelligence.com).

International Sea-borne Freight Traffic
(estimates, '000 metric tons)

	1988	1989	1990
Goods loaded	10	10	11
Goods unloaded	100	100	95

Source: UN, *Monthly Bulletin of Statistics*.

Tourism

FOREIGN TOURIST ARRIVALS BY COUNTRY OF RESIDENCE

Country of residence	2010	2011	2012
Australia	93,598	105,010	117,729
China, People's Repub.	177,636	247,197	333,894
France	113,285	117,408	121,175
Germany	62,864	63,398	72,537
Japan	151,795	161,804	179,327
Korea, Republic	289,702	342,810	411,491
Laos	n.a.	128,525	254,022
Malaysia	89,952	102,929	116,764
Philippines	56,156	70,718	97,487
Russia	n.a.	67,747	99,750
Taiwan	91,229	98,363	92,811
Thailand	149,108	116,758	201,422
United Kingdom	103,067	104,052	110,182
USA	146,005	153,953	173,076
Viet Nam	514,289	614,090	763,136
Total (incl. others)	2,508,289	2,881,862	3,584,307

Tourism receipts (US $ million, incl. passenger transport): 1,786 in 2010; 1,912 in 2011; 2,210 in 2012.

Source: Ministry of Tourism, Phnom Penh.

Communications Media

	2010	2011	2012
Telephones ('000 main lines in use)	358.8	530.0	584.5
Mobile cellular telephones ('000 subscribers)	8,150.8	13,757.0	19,105.1
Internet subscribers ('000)	n.a.	47.0	n.a.
Broadband subscribers ('000)	35.7	22.0	29.7

Source: International Telecommunication Union.

Education

(2012/13)

	Institutions	Teachers	Students		
			Males	Females	Total
Pre-primary	2,813	4,152	64,192	64,065	128,257
Primary	6,910	44,840	1,150,401	1,022,983	2,173,384
Secondary	2,055	38,211	425,522	397,977	823,499
Lower secondary	1,622	27,054	271,341	263,369	534,710
Upper secondary	433	11,157	154,181	134,608	288,789

Source: Ministry of Education, Youth and Sport, Phnom Penh.

Tertiary education (2010/11): Teachers 10,758; Students 223,222 (males 139,199, females 84,023) (Source: UNESCO Institute for Statistics).

Pupil-teacher ratio (primary education, UNESCO estimate): 45.7 in 2011/12 (Source: UNESCO Institute for Statistics).

Adult literacy rate (UNESCO estimates): 73.9% (males 82.8%, females 65.9%) in 2009 (Source: UNESCO Institute for Statistics).

Directory

The Government

HEAD OF STATE

King: HM King NORODOM SIHAMONI (appointed by the Royal Council of the Throne on 14 October 2004).

ROYAL GOVERNMENT OF CAMBODIA
(April 2014)

The Government is formed by the Cambodian People's Party.

Prime Minister: HUN SEN.

Permanent Deputy Prime Minister: KEAT CHHON.

Deputy Prime Minister and Minister of the Interior: SAR KHENG.

Deputy Prime Minister and Minister of National Defence: Gen. TEA BANH.

Deputy Prime Minister and Minister of Foreign Affairs and International Co-operation: HOR NAM HONG.

Deputy Prime Minister and Minister in Charge of the Council of Ministers: Dr SOK AN.

Deputy Prime Ministers without Portfolio: YIM CHHAY LY, BIN CHHIN, KE KIM YAN.

Senior Ministers: CHAM PRASIDH, CHAN SARUN, CHIN BUN SEAN, CHHAY THAN, HIM CHHEM, IENG MOLY, IM CHHUN LIM, KHUN HAING, LY THUCH, NHIM VANDA, OM YINTIENG, SEREI KOSAL, SUN CHANTHOL, VAR KIMHONG, YIM NOLA.

Minister of Agriculture, Forestry and Fisheries: OUK RABUN.

Minister of Commerce: SUN CHANTHOL.

Minister of Culture and Fine Arts: PHOEUNG SAKONA.

Minister of Economy and Finance: AUN PORN MONIROTH.

Minister of Education, Youth and Sport: HANG CHUON NARON.

Minister of Environment: SAY SAMAL.

Minister of Health: MAM BUN HENG.

Minister of Industry and Handicrafts: CHAM PRASIDH.

Minister of Mines and Energy: SUY SEM.

Minister of Information: KHIEU KANHARITH.

Minister of Justice: ANG VONG VATHANA.

Minister of Labour and Vocational Training: ITH SAM HENG.

Minister of Land Management, Urban Planning and Construction: IM CHHUN LIM.

Minister of Planning: CHHAY THAN.

Minister of Posts and Telecommunications: PRAK SOKHONN.

Minister of Public Function: PICH BUNTHIN.

Minister of Public Works and Transport: TRAM EAV TOEK.

Minister of Religions and Cults: MIN KHIN.

Minister of Royal Palace Affairs: KONG SAM OL (CPP).

Minister of Rural Development: CHEA SOPHARA.

Minister of Social Affairs, Veterans and Youth Rehabilitation: VORNG SAUT.

Minister of Tourism: THONG KHON.

Minister of Water Resources and Meteorology: LIM KEAN HOR.

Minister of Women's Affairs: ING KANTHA PHAVI.

Secretary of State for Civil Aviation: MAO VANNAL.

MINISTRIES

Office of the Council of Ministers: 41 blvd Confédération de la Russie, Sangkat Toeuk Thla, Khan Sen Sok, Phnom Penh; tel. (12) 804442; fax (23) 880624; e-mail ocm@cambodia.gov.kh; internet www.cambodia.gov.kh.

Ministry of Agriculture, Forestry and Fisheries: 200 blvd Norodom, Sangkat Tonle Bassac, Khan Chamkarmon, Phnom Penh 12301; tel. (23) 211351; fax (23) 217320; e-mail info@maff.gov.kh; internet www.maff.gov.kh.

Ministry of Commerce: 19–61 rue MOC, Sangkat Toeuk Thla, Khan Sen Sok, Phnom Penh; tel. (23) 866088; fax (23) 866188; e-mail moccab@moc.gov.kh; internet www.moc.gov.kh.

Ministry of Culture and Fine Arts: 227 blvd Norodom, Phnom Penh; tel. and fax (23) 218148; e-mail info@mcfa.gov.kh; internet www.mcfa.gov.kh.

Ministry of Economy and Finance: 60 rue 92, Sangkat Wat Phnom, Khan Duan Penh, Phnom Penh; tel. (23) 724664; fax (23) 427798; e-mail admin@mef.gov.kh; internet www.mef.gov.kh.

Ministry of Education, Youth and Sport: 80 blvd Norodom, Phnom Penh; tel. and fax (23) 210134; e-mail info@moeys.gov.kh; internet www.moeys.gov.kh.

Ministry of Environment: 48 blvd Sihanouk, Sangkat Tonle Bassac, Khan Chamkarmon, Phnom Penh; tel. (23) 427894; fax (23) 427844; e-mail moe-cabinet@camnet.com.kh; internet www.camnet.com.kh/moe.

Ministry of Foreign Affairs and International Co-operation: 3 rue Samdech Hun Sen, Sangkat Tonle Bassac, Khan Chamkarmon, Phnom Penh; tel. (23) 214441; fax (23) 216144; e-mail mfaic@mfa.gov.kh; internet www.mfaic.gov.kh.

Ministry of Health: 151–153 blvd Kampuchea Krom, Phnom Penh; tel. (23) 722873; fax (23) 426841; e-mail webmaster@moh.gov.kh; internet www.moh.gov.kh.

Ministry of Industry and Handicrafts: 45 blvd Preah Norodom, Khan Duan Penh, Phnom Penh; tel. (23) 222504; fax (23) 991438.

Ministry of Information: 62 blvd Monivong, Phnom Penh; tel. (23) 724159; fax (23) 724275; e-mail info@information.gov.kh; internet www.information.gov.kh.

Ministry of the Interior: 275 blvd Norodom, Khan Chamkarmon, Phnom Penh; tel. and fax (23) 721905; e-mail moi@interior.gov.kh; internet www.interior.gov.kh.

Ministry of Justice: 240 blvd Sothearos, Phnom Penh; tel. (23) 360327; fax (23) 364119; e-mail moj@cambodia.gov.kh; internet www.moj.gov.kh.

Ministry of Labour and Vocational Training: 3 blvd Confédération de la Russie, Sangkat Toeuk Thla, Khan Sen Sok, Phnom Penh; tel. (23) 884375; e-mail mlvt@camintel.com.

Ministry of Land Management, Urban Planning and Construction: 771–773 blvd Monivong, Boeung Trabek, Khan Chamkarmon, Phnom Penh; tel. (23) 880780; e-mail mlmupc@camnet.com.kh; internet www.mlmupc.gov.kh.

Ministry of Mines and Energy: Phnom Penh.

Ministry of National Assembly-Senate Relations and Inspection: 215 blvd Jawaharlal Nehru, Phnom Penh; tel. (23) 884261; fax (23) 884264; e-mail mnasrl@cambodia.gov.kh; internet www.monasri.gov.kh.

Ministry of National Defence: blvd Confédération de la Russie, cnr rue 175, Sangkat Toeuk Thla, Khan Sen Sok, Phnom Penh; tel. and fax (23) 883274; e-mail info@mond.gov.kh; internet www.mod.gov.kh.

Ministry of Planning: 386 blvd Monivong, Sangkat Boeung Keng Kang 1, Phnom Penh; tel. (23) 212049; fax (23) 210698; e-mail mop@cambodia.gov.kh; internet www.mop.gov.kh.

Ministry of Posts and Telecommunications: Sangkat Wat Phnom, cnr rues 13 & 102, Phnom Penh; tel. (23) 426510; fax (23) 426011; e-mail mptc@cambodia.gov.kh; internet www.mptc.gov.kh.

Ministry of Public Function: Phnom Penh.

Ministry of Public Works and Transport: cnr blvd Norodom, rue 106, Phnom Penh; tel. (23) 427845; e-mail info@mpwt.gov.kh; internet www.mpwt.gov.kh.

Ministry of Religions and Cults: Preah Sisowath Quay, cnr rue 240, Phnom Penh; tel. (23) 725099; fax (23) 725699; e-mail morac@cambodia.gov.kh; internet www.morac.gov.kh.

Ministry of Rural Development: blvd Confédération de la Russie, cnr rue 169, Sangkat Toeuk Thla, Khan Sen Sok, Phnom Penh; tel. and fax (23) 884539; e-mail mrd@cambodia.gov.kh; internet www.mrd.gov.kh.

Ministry of Social Affairs, Veterans and Youth Rehabilitation: 788 blvd Monivong, Phnom Penh; tel. (23) 726103; fax (23) 726086; internet www.mosvy.gov.kh.

Ministry of Tourism: A3 rue 169, Sangkat Veal Vong, Khan 7 Makara, Phnom Penh; tel. (23) 213741; fax (23) 220704; e-mail info@tourismcambodia.org; internet www.tourismcambodia.org.

Ministry of Water Resources and Meteorology: 47 blvd Norodom, Phnom Penh; tel. (23) 724289; fax (23) 426345; e-mail mowram@cambodia.gov.kh; internet www.mowram.gov.kh.

Ministry of Women's Affairs: Bldg 3, Sangkat Wat Phnom, Khan Daun Penh, Phnom Penh; tel. (23) 216704; internet mwa.gov.kh.

Legislature

PARLIAMENT

National Assembly

blvd Samdech Sothearos, cnr rue 240, Phnom Penh; tel. (23) 214136; fax (23) 217769; e-mail kimhenglong@cambodian-parliament.org; internet www.national-assembly.org.kh.

Chairman: HENG SAMRIN.

Distribution of seats following election, 28 July 2013

	% of votes	Seats
Cambodian People's Party	48.79	68
Cambodia National Rescue Party	44.45	55
Total	100.00*	123

* Including others.

Senate

Chamkarmon State Bldg, blvd Norodom, Phnom Penh; tel. (23) 211441; fax (23) 211446; e-mail info@senate.gov.kh; internet www.senate.gov.kh.

President: CHEA SIM (CPP).

First Vice-President: SAY CHHUM (CPP).

Second Vice-President: TEP NGORN (CPP).

Elections, 29 January 2012

	Seats
Cambodian People's Party	46
Sam Rainsy Party*	11
King's appointees	2
National Assembly's appointees	2
Total	61

* Merged with the Human Rights Party in 2012 to form the Cambodia National Rescue Party.

Note: 57 of the 61 Senators were chosen by means of an electoral college system.

Election Commission

National Election Committee (NEC): blvd Preah Norodom, Khan Chamkarmon, Phnom Penh; tel. (12) 855018; fax (23) 214374; e-mail necinfo@forum.org.kh; internet www.necelect.org.kh; independent body, appointed by royal decree; Chair. IM SUOSDEY; Sec.-Gen. TEP NYTHA.

Political Organizations

Eight parties contested the elections to the National Assembly held in July 2013.

Cambodia National Rescue Party (CNRP): Phnom Penh; e-mail rphqpp@gmail.com; internet www.nationalrescueparty.org; f. 2012; est. by merger of the Sam Rainsy Party (f. 1995 as Khmer Nation Party) and the Human Rights Party (f.2007); Pres. SAM RAINSY; Vice-Pres. KEM SOKHA.

Cambodian Nationality Party: Phnom Penh; f. 2012; Leader SENG SOKHENG.

Cambodian People's Party (CPP) (Kanakpak Pracheachon Kampuchea): 203 blvd Norodom, Sangkat Tonle Bassac, Khan Chamkarmon, Phnom Penh; tel. and fax (23) 215801; e-mail cpp@camnet.com.kh; internet www.thecpp.org.kh; f. 1951; known as the Kampuchean People's Revolutionary Party (KPRP) 1979–91; name changed as above in 1991; 30-mem. Standing Cttee of the Cen. Cttee; Cen. Cttee of 268 full mems; Hon. Chair. of Cen. Cttee HENG SAMRIN; Chair. of Cen. Cttee CHEA SIM; Vice-Chair. HUN SEN; Chair. of Permanent Cttee SAY CHHUM.

Solidarity Front for Development of the Cambodian Motherland (SFDCM): Phnom Penh; f. 1978; est. as Kampuchean National United Front for National Salvation (KNUFNS); name changed to Kampuchean United Front for National Construction and Defence (KUFNCD) in 1981, and to United Front for the Construction and Defence of the Kampuchean Fatherland (UFCDKF) in 1989; present name adopted in 2006; mass org. supporting policies of the CPP; an 89-mem. Nat. Council and a seven-mem. hon. Presidium; Chair. of Nat. Council HENG SAMRIN; Gen. Sec. of Nat. Council MIN KHIN.

Democratic Republican Party: Phnom Penh; f. 2012; Leader SOKROTH SOVAN PANHCHAKSEILA.

FUNCINPEC Party (National United Front for an Independent, Neutral, Peaceful and Co-operative Cambodia Party): 11 blvd Monivong (93), Sangkat Sras Chak, Khan Daun Penh, BP 1444, Phnom Penh; tel. (23) 428864; fax (23) 218547; e-mail info@funcinpecparty.org; internet www.funcinpecparty.org; FUNCINPEC altered its title to the FUNCINPEC Party when it adopted political status in 1992; the party's military wing was the National Army of Independent Cambodia (fmrly the Armée Nationale Sihanoukiste—ANS); merged with the Son Sann Party in Jan. 1999 and with the Norodom Ranariddh Party in 2012; Pres. Princess NORODOM ARUN RASMEY; Sec.-Gen. Gen. NHIEK BUN CHHAY.

Khmer Anti-Poverty Party: Phnom Penh; f. 2007; Leader DARAN KRAVANH.

Khmer Economic Development Party: Phnom Penh; f. 2012; Leader HUON REACH CHAMROEUN.

Khmer M'chas Srok (Khmer Sovereign): 14A rue Keo Chea, Phnom Penh; tel. (23) 62365; fax (23) 27340; e-mail khmer.mchas.srok@gmail.com; internet www.khmer-mchas-srok.org; fmrly Khmer Neutral Party; Pres. SAKHONN CHAK.

Khmer Republican Party (KRP): 282 rue 371, Phoum Obekaam, Sangkat Taek Thla, Khan Russey Keo, Phnom Penh; tel. (23) 350842; e-mail krp2005@gmail.com; f. 2006; Pres. LON RITH.

League for Democracy Party: 61A rue 608, Sangkat Boeung Kak II, Khan Tuol Kok, Phnom Penh; tel. (12) 897600; e-mail info@leadparty.org; internet www.camldp.org; f. 2006; Pres. KHEM VEASNA; Sec.-Gen. OK VETH.

Diplomatic Representation

EMBASSIES IN CAMBODIA

Australia: 16B rue Nat. Assembly, Sangkat Tonle Bassac, Khan Chamkarmon, Phnom Penh; tel. (23) 213470; fax (23) 213413; e-mail australian.embassy.cambodia@dfat.gov.au; internet www.cambodia.embassy.gov.au; Ambassador ALISON BURROWS.

Brunei: 237 rue Pasteur 51, Sangkat Boeung Keng Kang 1, Khan Chamkarmon, Phnom Penh; tel. (23) 211457; fax (23) 211456; e-mail brunei@online.com.kh; Ambassador Sheikh Haji FADILAH Sheikh Haji AHMAD.

Bulgaria: 227–229 blvd Norodom, Phnom Penh; tel. (23) 217504; fax (23) 212792; e-mail bulgembpnp@online.com.kh; Chargé d'affaires a.i. SVILEN POPOV.

China, People's Republic: 156 blvd Mao Tse Toung, Phnom Penh; tel. (23) 720920; fax (23) 720922; e-mail chinaemb_kh@mfa.gov.cn; internet kh.china-embassy.org/chn; Ambassador BU JIANGUO.

Cuba: 96–98 rue 214, Sangkat Veal Vong, Khan 7 Makara, Phnom Penh; tel. (23) 213965; fax (23) 217428; e-mail embacambodia1@online.com.kh; Ambassador JOSÉ RAMÓN RODRÍGUEZ VARONA.

France: 1 blvd Monivong, BP 18, Phnom Penh; tel. (23) 430020; fax (23) 430037; e-mail ambafrance.phnom-penh-amba@diplomatie.gouv.fr; internet www.ambafrance-kh.org; Ambassador SERGE MOSTURA.

Germany: 76–78 rue Yougoslavie (rue 214), BP 60, Phnom Penh; tel. (23) 216381; fax (23) 427746; internet www.phnom-penh.diplo.de; Ambassador JOACHIM BARON VON MARSCHALL.

India: 5 rue 466, Phnom Penh; tel. (23) 210912; fax (23) 210914; e-mail embindia@online.com.kh; internet www.indembassyphnompenh.org; Ambassador DINESH K. PATNAIK.

Indonesia: 1 rue 466, cnr blvd Norodom, BP 894, Phnom Penh; tel. (23) 217934; fax (23) 217566; e-mail indoembassy-phnompenh@emaxxtelecom.com; internet www.kemlu.go.id/phnompenh; Ambassador PITONO PURNOMO.

Japan: 194 blvd Preah Norodom, Sangkat Tonle Bassac, Khan Chamkarmon, BP 21, Phnom Penh; tel. (23) 217161; fax (23) 216162; e-mail eojc@online.com.kh; internet www.kh.emb-japan.go.jp; Ambassador KUMAMARU YUJI.

Korea, Democratic People's Republic: 39 blvd Samdech Suramarith, Phnom Penh; tel. and fax (15) 217013; Ambassador HONG KI CHOL.

Korea, Republic: 50–52 rue 214, Sangkat Boeung Raing, Khan Daun Penh, BP 2433, Phnom Penh; tel. (23) 211900; fax (23) 219200; e-mail cambodia@mofa.go.kr; internet khm.mofat.go.kr; Ambassador KIM HAN-SOO.

Kuwait: Raffles Hotel Le Royal, Suite 256, 92 Rukhak Vithei Daum Penh, Sangkat Wat Phnom, Phnom Penh; tel. (23) 981172; fax (23) 981188; e-mail kuwaitembassy.cambodia@gmail.com; Ambassador DHERAR NASER AL-TUWAIJRI.

Laos: 15–17 blvd Mao Tse Toung, Khan Chamkarmon, BP 19, Phnom Penh; tel. (23) 997931; fax (23) 720907; e-mail laoembpp@hotmail.com; Ambassador (vacant).

Malaysia: 220–222 blvd Norodom, Sangkat Tonle Bassac, Khan Chamkarmon, Phnom Penh; tel. (23) 216176; fax (23) 426101; e-mail malppenh@kln.gov.my; internet www.kln.gov.my/web/khm_phnom-penh; Ambassador RASZLAN BIN ABDUL RASHID.

Myanmar: 181 blvd Preah Norodom, Sangkat Boeung Keng Kang 1, Khan Chamkarmon, Phnom Penh; tel. (23) 223761; fax (23) 223763; e-mail mephnompenh@yahoo.com; Ambassador U CHO TUN AUNG.

Pakistan: 45 rue 310, Sangkat Boeung Keng Kang 1, Phnom Penh; tel. (23) 996890; fax (23) 992113; e-mail parepcambodia@mofa.gov.pk; internet www.mofa.gov.pk/cambodia; Ambassador H. E. AMJAD ALI SHER.

Philippines: 15 rue 422, Khan Chamkarmon, Sangkat Tonle Bassac, Phnom Penh; tel. (23) 222203; fax (23) 215143; e-mail phnompenh.pe@dfa.gov.ph; Ambassador NOE A. WONG.

Russia: 213 blvd Samdech Sothearos, Phnom Penh; tel. (23) 210931; fax (23) 216776; e-mail russemba@gmail.com; internet www.embrusscambodia.mid.ru; Ambassador ALEKSANDR IGNATOV (outgoing).

Singapore: 129 blvd Norodom, Phnom Penh; tel. (23) 221875; fax (23) 210862; e-mail singemb_pnh@sgmfa.gov.sg; internet www.mfa.gov.sg/phnompenh; Ambassador KEVIN CHEOK.

Sweden: POB 68, Phnom Penh; tel. (23) 861700; fax (23) 861701; e-mail ambassaden.phnom-penh@gov.se; internet www.swedenabroad.com/sv-SE/Ambassader/Phnom-Penh; Ambassador ANNA MAJ HULTGÅRD.

Thailand: 196 blvd Preah Norodom, Sangkat Tonle Bassac, Khan Chamkarmon, Phnom Penh; tel. (23) 994316; fax (23) 994312; e-mail thaipnp@mfa.go.th; internet www.thaiembassy.org/phnompenh; Ambassador TOUCHAYOOT PAKDI.

Turkey: 18/F, Canadia Tower, 315 blvd Monivong, Phnom Penh; tel. (23) 962459; Ambassador ILHAN KEMAL TUG.

United Kingdom: 27–29 rue 75, Sangkat Srah Chak, Khan Daun Penh, Phnom Penh; tel. (23) 427124; fax (23) 427125; e-mail britemb@online.com.kh; internet www.gov.uk/world/cambodia; Ambassador WILLIAM JESSE LONGHURST.

USA: 1 rue 96, Sangkat Wat Phnom, Khan Daun Penh, Phnom Penh; tel. (23) 728000; fax (23) 728600; e-mail ACSPhnomPenh@state.gov; internet cambodia.usembassy.gov; Ambassador WILLIAM E. TODD.

Viet Nam: 436 blvd Monivong, Khan Chamkarmon, Phnom Penh; tel. (23) 726274; fax (23) 726495; e-mail ttcpc@mofa.gov.vn; internet www.vietnamembassy-cambodia.org; Ambassador NGO ANH DUNG.

Judicial System

An independent judiciary was established under the 1993 Constitution. A council for legal and judicial reform was created in 2003 to co-ordinate the implementation of reforms. A new criminal law code took effect in December 2010, replacing the penal code implemented by the UN Transitional Authority in Cambodia in 1992. The highest judicial body is the Supreme Council of Magistracy.

Supreme Court: 222 blvd Trasak Phaem, Sangkat Boeung Keng Kang I, Khan Chamkarmon, Phnom Penh; e-mail info@supremecourt.gov.kh; tel. and fax (23) 212828; Pres. DITH MUNTY.

Religion

The Government of Democratic Kampuchea banned all religious activity in 1975. Under a constitutional amendment of 1989, Buddhism was reinstated as the national religion and was retained as such under the 1993 Constitution.

BUDDHISM

The principal religion of Cambodia is Theravada Buddhism (Buddhism of the 'Tradition of the Elders'), the sacred language of which is Pali. In 2010 about 93% of the population were Buddhists.

Great Supreme Patriarch: Ven. Patriarch TEP VONG.

Supreme Patriarchs: Ven. Patriarch BOU KRY (Thammayut Nikaya sect), Ven. Patriarch NON NGET (Maha Nikaya sect).

CHRISTIANITY

The Roman Catholic Church

Cambodia comprises the Apostolic Vicariate of Phnom Penh and the Apostolic Prefectures of Battambang and Kampong Cham. At December 2010 the Christian community constituted 2% of the population.

Vicar Apostolic of Phnom Penh: Rev. OLIVIER SCHMITTHAEUSLER (Titular Bishop of Catabum Castra), 787 blvd Monivong (rue 93), BP 123, Phnom Penh; tel. and fax (23) 212462; e-mail evecam@forum.org.kh.

ISLAM

Islam is practised by a minority in Cambodia; in 2010 there were an estimated 464,000 Muslims.

The Press

According to Cambodia's Press Law, newspapers, magazines and foreign press agencies are required to register with the Department of Media at the Ministry of Information.

NEWSPAPERS

Areyathor (Civilization): 609B Author House, Sony Borey, Chey, Phnom Penh; tel. (23) 913662; e-mail areyathor@yahoo.com; internet www.arey-news.com; f. 1994; 2 a week; Editor LEANG HI.

Cambodge Nouveau: 58 rue 302, Sangkat Boeung Keng Kang 1, Khan Chamkarmon, Phnom Penh 12302; tel. (23) 214610; e-mail cn@forum.org.kh; internet www.cambodgenouveau.com; f. 1994; monthly; French; politics, economics and business; Editor-in-Chief ALAIN GASCUEL.

Cambodia Daily: 129 rue 228, Phnom Penh; tel. (23) 426602; fax (23) 426573; e-mail aafc@camnet.com.kh; internet www.cambodiadaily.com; f. 1993; Mon.–Sat.; English and Khmer; distributed free of charge within Cambodia; Editor-in-Chief KEVIN DOYLE; Publr BERNARD KRISHER; circ. 5,000.

Cambodia New Vision: BP 158, Phnom Penh; tel. (23) 219898; fax (23) 360666; e-mail cabinet1b@camnet.com.kh; internet www.cnv.org.kh; f. 1998; official newsletter of the Cambodian Govt.

Cambodia Sin Chew Daily: 107 blvd Josep Broz Tito, rue 214, Sangkat Boeung Prolit, Khan 7 Makara, Phnom Penh 12258; tel. (23) 212628; fax (23) 211728; e-mail sinchew_daily@online.com.kh; internet www.sinchew-i.com/cambodia; f. 2000; daily; Chinese; Editor CHARLES SHAW.

Jian Hua Daily: 116–118 blvd Kampuchea Krom, Sangkat Monorom, Khan 7 Makara, Phnom Penh 12251; tel. (23) 883801; fax (23) 883797; e-mail jianhuadaily@hotmail.com; internet www.jianhuadaily.com; daily; Chinese; Editor-in-Chief YANG WEN.

Kampuchea Thmey (New Cambodia): 805 blvd Kampuchea Krom, rue 128, Sangkat Tuk Laak 1, Khan Tuol Kok, Phnom Penh 12156; tel. (23) 726614; fax (23) 726629; e-mail kampucheathmey@mail2world.com; internet www.kampucheathmey.com; daily; Editor-in-Chief KEV NAVY.

Kampuchea Thnai Nes (Cambodia Today Newspaper): 21 rue 163, Sangkat Veal Vong, Khan 7 Makara, Phnom Penh 12253; tel. and fax (23) 364882; e-mail cambodiatoday@online.com.kh; daily; Editor-in-Chief HONG NARA.

Koh Santepheap (Island of Peace): 41E rue 338, Sangkat Boeung Tumpun, Khan Meanchey, Phnom Penh 12351; tel. (23) 987118; fax (23) 220155; e-mail info@kspg.co; internet www.kohsantepheapdaily.com.kh; daily; Khmer; Dir THONG UY PANG.

Mekong News: POB 623, 576 National Rd 2, Sangkat Chak Angre Krom, Khan Menachey, Phnom Penh; tel. (23) 425353; fax (23) 425363; e-mail mrcs@mrcmekong.org; f. 2005; quarterly; English and Khmer; publ. by Mekong River Commission Secretariat, distributed free of charge; Editor and Publr M. NOOR ULLAH.

Neak Chea: 1 rue 158, Oukghna Toeung Kang, Beng Raing Daun Penh, Phnom Penh; tel. (23) 218653; fax (23) 217229; e-mail adhoc@forum.org.kh; 2 a month; Khmer; bulletin of Cambodia Human Rights and Devt Assen.

Phnom Penh Post: 888 Bldg F, 8th Floor, Phnom Penh Center, cnr Sothearos & Sihanouk Blvd, Sangkat Tonle Bassac, Khan Chamkarmon, Phnom Penh; tel. (23) 214311; fax (23) 214318; e-mail bernie.leo@phnompenhpost.com; internet www.phnompenhpost.com; f. 1992; fortnightly; English; Editor-in-Chief ALAN PARKHOUSE.

Pracheachon (The People): 101 blvd Norodom, Phnom Penh; tel. (23) 723665; f. 1985; 2 a week; organ of the CPP; Editor-in-Chief SOM KIMSUOR; circ. 50,000.

Raja Bori News: 76 rue 57, Sangkat Boeung Kak II, Khan Tuol Kok, Phnom Penh 12152; tel. (12) 840993; weekly; Editor-in-Chief KIM SOMLOT.

Rasmei Angkor (Light of Angkor): 25/25z rue 372, Sangkat Boeung Salang, Khan Tuol Kok, Phnom Penh 12160; tel. (12) 259832; e-mail raksmeiangkor@yahoo.com; f. 1992; 3 a week; Editor-in-Chief EN CHAN SIVUTHA.

Rasmei Kampuchea (Light of Cambodia): T. B. R. Printing Co Ltd, 474 blvd Preah Monivong, Sangkat Tonle Bassac, Khan Chamkarmon, Phnom Penh 12301; tel. and fax (23) 7266555; e-mail rasmei_kampuchea@yahoo.com; internet www.rasmeinews.com; daily; f. 1993; local newspaper in northern Cambodia; Editor PEN SAMITHY; circ. 18,000.

Sahasa Wat Thmey (New Millennium): 48AE blvd Oknha Chun, Sangkat Chaktomuk, Khan Daun Penh, Phnom Penh 12207; tel. (16) 719551; e-mail sahasawatthmey@mail2world.com; f. 2004; 3 a week; Editor-in-Chief MANN BUNTHOEUN.

Samleng Thmei (New Voice): 91 rue 139, Sangkat Veal Vong, Khan 7, Phnom Penh; tel. (15) 920589; Khmer; weekly; Publr and Editor KHUN NGO; circ. 2,000.

Udomkate Khmer (Khmer Ideal): 17 blvd Samdech Sothearos, Sangkat Tuk Laak 3, Khan Tuol Kok, Phnom Penh 12158; tel. (12) 851478; daily; Editor-in-Chief HOR SOK LEN.

PERIODICALS

Angkor Thom: 105 rue 324, Sangkat Boeung Salang, Khan Tuol Kok, Phnom Penh 12253; tel. (23) 996421; fax (23) 996441; e-mail vuthyrith@angkorthommagazine.com; internet ekhmermagazines.com; f. 1998; 3 a month; Khmer; news, current affairs, arts and sport; Editor-in-Chief SING VUTHYRITH; circ. 30,000.

Bayon Pearnik: 3 rue 174, Sangkat Phsar Thmei 3, Khan Daun Penh, Phnom Penh 312210; tel. (12) 803968; e-mail bp@forum.org.kh; internet www.bayonpearnik.com; f. 1996; monthly; English; news for expatriates and tourists; Publr and Editor-in-Chief ADAM PARKER.

Cambodian Scene: 41 blvd Sang Kreach Tieng, rue 222, Sangkat Boeung Raing, Khan Daun Penh, Phnom Penh 12211; tel. (23) 224488; fax (23) 222266; e-mail publisher@cambodianscene.com; internet www.cambodianscene-magazine.com; every 2 months; English; tourism, culture and entertainment guide; Publr and Editor-in-Chief JANE NYE.

L'Echo du Cambodge: 42 blvd Preah Norodom, Sangkat Phsar Thmei 2, Khan Daun Penh, Phnom Penh 12206; e-mail echoducambodge@yahoo.fr; monthly; English and French; Editor-in-Chief MARCEL ZARCA.

Indradevi: 167 blvd Mao Tse Toung, Sangkat Tuol Svay Prey 2, Khan Chamkarmon, Phnom Penh 12309; tel. and fax (23) 215808; e-mail indradevi@camnet.com.kh; f. 2000; Editor-in-Chief CHHEM SARITH.

Kambuja: Kambuja Dept, Agence Kampuchea Presse, Ministry of Information, 62 blvd Preah Monivong, Sangkat Wat Phnom, Khan Daun Penh, Phnom Penh 12202; tel. and fax (23) 427945; e-mail akp@camnet.com.kh; monthly; Khmer; publ. by the AKP; devt, education and int. affairs.

Khmer Apsara: 143A Khum Pring Kang Cheung, Sangkat Chom Chao, Khan Dangkor, Phnom Penh 12405; tel. (17) 391087; e-mail khmer_apsara01@yahoo.com; internet www.khmerapsaramagazine.com; f. 2005; monthly; Khmer; entertainment, fashion, technology, health and culture; Editor-in-Chief EN SOPHANNA.

Pracheaprey (Popular): 71–73 rue 70, Sangkat Sras Chak, Phnom Penh; tel. (12) 890613; fax (12) 890614; e-mail popularmagazine@online.com.kh; f. 2000; 3 a month; Khmer; news, current affairs, politics, arts, science and sport; Editor-in-Chief PRACH SIM.

Samay Thmei (Modern): 127 rue 357, Sangkat Chbar Ampheou 2, Khan Meanchey, Phnom Penh 12355; tel. (23) 359969; fortnightly; Khmer; fashion, contemporary living, sports and entertainment; Editor-in-Chief EK SAMAT.

Suorsadey Magazine: 13A rue 222, Sang Kreach Tieng, Phnom Penh; tel. (23) 224488; fax (23) 222266; e-mail soursadey_info@yahoo.com; internet www.suorsadey.com; f. 2009; quarterly; tourism, culture and entertainment guide; Editor MOEN NHEAN.

NEWS AGENCY

Agence Kampuchea Presse (AKP): 62 blvd Monivong, Phnom Penh; tel. (23) 430564; fax (23) 427945; e-mail ask@akp.gov.kh; internet www.akp.gov.kh; f. 1978; Dir-Gen. SOK MOM NIMUL.

ASSOCIATIONS

Cambodian Association for the Protection of Journalists (CAPJ): BP 816, 58 rue 336, Sangkat Phsar Doeum Kor, Khan Tuol Kok, Phnom Penh; tel. (15) 997004; fax (23) 215834; e-mail umsarin@hotmail.com; Pres. UM SARIN.

Club of Cambodian Journalists: 226 rue 155, Sangkat Tuol Tumpong 1, Khan Chamkarmon, Phnom Penh; tel. and fax (23) 224094; e-mail ccj@online.com.kh; internet www.ccj.com.kh; f. 2000; Pres. PEN SAMITTHY; Sec.-Gen. PRACH SIM.

Press Council of Cambodia: 127 blvd Norodom, Sangkat Tonle Bassac, Khan Chamkarmon, Phnom Penh; tel. (12) 910425; f. 2008; est. as an umbrella body for more than 15 journalists' asscns; Pres. SOK SOVANN.

Broadcasting and Communications

TELECOMMUNICATIONS

Cambodia Advance Communications Co Ltd (CADCOMMS): 825ABC blvd Preah Monivong, Sangkat Phsar Damthkov, Khan Chamkarmon, Phnom Penh; tel. (13) 300313; fax (13) 300317; e-mail info@qbmore.com; internet www.qbmore.com; f. 2006; operates mobile services; Chief Information Officer SANDOS NONG.

Camintel: 1 cnr Terak Vithei Sisowath & Vithei Phsar Dek, Phnom Penh; tel. (23) 986986; fax (23) 986277; e-mail support@camintel.com; internet www.camintel.com; f. 1995; est. as a jt venture between the Ministry of Posts and Telecommunications and Indonesian co Indosat; acquired by KTC Cable Co in 2012; operates domestic telephone network and internet; CEO KIM MYUNG-IL.

Mfone Co Ltd: 721 blvd Preah Monivong, Sangkat Boeung Keng Kang 3, Khan Chamkarmon, Phnom Penh; tel. (23) 303333; fax (23) 361111; e-mail sales@mfone.biz; internet www.mfone.com.kh; f. 1993; fmrly Cambodia Shinawatra Co Ltd; subsidiary of Shenington Investments Pte Ltd and Asia Mobile Holdings Pte Ltd; provides fixed line, mobile (incl. third generation—3G) and internet services; CEO SUTTISAK KHNDHIKAJANA.

MobiTel: 33 blvd Preah Sihanouk, BP 2468, Phnom Penh; tel. (12) 800800; fax (12) 801801; e-mail helpline@mobitel.com.kh; internet www.mobitel.com.kh; f. 1998; wholly owned by The Royal Group since Nov. 2009; operates national GSM 900 mobile network under trade name Cellcard; CEO DAVID SPRIGGS.

Smart Mobile: 464A blvd Monivong, Sangkat Tonle Bassac, Khan Chamkarmon, Phnom Penh; tel. (10) 201000; fax (23) 868882; e-mail info@smart.com.kh; internet www.smart.com.kh; operates GSM mobile services; CEO THOMAS HUNDT.

Telekom Malaysia International (Cambodia) Co Ltd: cnr Sihanouk & Sothearos, Sangkat Tonle Bassac, Khan Chamkarmon,

Phnom Penh; tel. (16) 880002; internet www.hello.com.kh; f. 1992; est. as Cambodia Samart Communication; name changed as above following acquisition by Telekom Malaysia Bhd in 2006; operates a national mobile network under trade name Hello; CEO MUHAMMED YUSOFF ZAMRI.

Regulatory Authority

Telecommunication Regulator of Cambodia (TRC): c/o Ministry of Posts and Telecommunications, Sangkat Wat Phnom, cnr rues 13 & 102, Phnom Penh; f. 2012; sole regulator and licence provider; Chair. MOA CHAKRYA.

BROADCASTING

Radio

There is a single government radio station, the National Radio of Cambodia, and many local private radio stations, which emerged following the deregulation of broadcasting services in 1979.

Apsara Radio (FM 97 MHz): 69 rue 57, Sangkat Boeung Keng Kang 1, Khan Chamkarmon, Phnom Penh; tel. (12) 303002; fax (23) 214302; internet www.apsaratv.com.kh; f. 1996; linked to Cambodian People's Party; Khmer; Dir-Gen. SOK EYSAN.

Bayon Radio (FM 95 MHz): 3 rue 466, Sangkat Tonle Bassac, Khan Chamkarmon, Phnom Penh; tel. (12) 682222; fax (23) 363795; internet www.bayontv.com.kh; f. 1998; linked to Prime Minister Hun Sen; Dir-Gen. HUN MANA; Deputy Dir-Gen. HUOT KHEANGVENG.

Beehive Radio (Sambok Khmoum): 44G rue 360, Sangkat Boeung Keng Kang 1, Khan Chamkarmon, Phnom Penh; tel. (16) 458599; fax (23) 210439; e-mail sbk105kh@gmail.com; internet www.sbk.com.kh; f. 1996; broadcasts incl. news programmes from Voice of America and Radio Free Asia; Dir-Gen. MAM SONANDO.

Family FM 99.5 MHz (Krusa FM): Phnom Penh; e-mail febcam@bigpond.com.kh; internet www.febc.org; f. 2002; controlled by Far East Broadcasting Co; religious and educational programmes from a Christian perspective; Dir SAMOEUN INTAL.

FM 90 MHz: 65 rue 178, Phnom Penh; tel. (16) 709090; fax (23) 368623; news, music and educational programmes; affiliated to the FUNCINPEC Party; Dir-Gen. NHIM BUN THON; Dep. Dir-Gen. TUM VANN DET.

FM 107 MHz: 18 rue 562, Boeung Kak 1, Khan Toul Kork, Phnom Penh; tel. (23) 880874; fax (23) 881935; e-mail info@tv9.com.kh; internet www.tv9.com.kh; news and music; Dir-Gen. KHUN HAING.

National Radio of Cambodia (RNK) (Radio National Kampuchea): Bldg 6, Sangkat Wat Phnom, cnr rues 19 & 102, Phnom Penh; tel. (23) 722869; fax (23) 427319; internet www.rnk.gov.kh; f. 1978; fmrly Vithyu Samleng Pracheachon Kampuchea (Voice of the Cambodian People); controlled by the Ministry of Information; domestic service in Khmer; broadcasts on both AM and FM frequencies; daily external services in English, French, Lao, Vietnamese and Thai; Dir-Gen. TAN YAN.

New Life Radio FM 89.5 MHz: 4 rue 95, Sangkat Boueng Keng Kong II, Khan Chamkarmon, Phnom Penh; tel. (23) 212593; e-mail newliferadio@camnet.com.kh.

Phnom Penh Municipality Radio (103 MHz): 2 blvd Confédération de la Russie, Phnom Penh; tel. (23) 725205; fax (23) 360800; Gen. Man. KHAMPUN KEOMONY.

Royal Cambodian Armed Forces Radio (RCAF Radio) (FM 98.0 MHz): c/o Borei Keila, rue 169, Sangkat Vealvong, Phnom Penh; tel. (23) 306064; fax (23) 884245; f. 1994; Dir THA TANA; News Editor SENG KATEKA.

Ta Prohm Radio (FM 90.5 MHz): 27B rue 472, Phnom Penh; tel. (23) 993206; e-mail taprohm@yahoo.com; f. 2003; launched by FUNCINPEC Party as opposition radio station; broadcasts news programmes in Khmer to Phnom Penh and surrounding area; Propr EAR LIMSUOR.

Women's Radio FM 102 MHz: 30 rue 488, Sangkat Phsar Demthkov, Khan Chamkarmon, Phnom Penh; POB 497, Phnom Penh; tel. (23) 212264; fax (23) 223597; e-mail fm102@wmc.org.kh; internet www.wmc.org.kh; f. 1999; independent; radio station of Women's Media Centre of Cambodia; Exec. Dir CHEA SUNDANETH.

Television

Apsara Television (TV11): 69 rue 57, Sangkat Boeung Keng Kang 1, Khan Chamkarmon, Phnom Penh; tel. (23) 303002; fax (23) 214302; e-mail tv11@camnet.com.kh; internet www.apsaratv.com.kh; broadcasts for 14 hours per day on weekdays, and for 16 hours per day at weekends, in Khmer; linked to Cambodian People's Party; Dir-Gen. SOK EYSAN.

Bayon Television (TV27): 3 rue 466, Sangkat Tonle Bassac, Khan Chamkarmon, Phnom Penh; tel. (12) 682222; fax (23) 363795; e-mail bayontv@camnet.com.kh; internet www.bayontv.com.kh; linked to Prime Minister Hun Sen; Dir-Gen. HUN MANA.

Cambodian Television Network (CTN): POB 2468, Phnom Penh 12104; tel. (12) 999434; e-mail tv@ctn.com.kh; internet www.ctn.com.kh; f. 2003; wholly owned by The Royal Group; operates two free-to-air stations, CTN and MYTV; CTN International available internationally via satellite; Propr KITH MENG; Gen. Man. GLEN FELGATE.

Cambodian Television Station Channel 9 (TV9): 18 rue 562, Phnom Penh; tel. (23) 880874; fax (23) 368212; e-mail info@tv9.com.kh; internet www.tv9.com.kh; f. 1992; Dir-Gen. KHOUN ELYNA; News Editor SOM RATHA.

National Television of Cambodia (TVK): 62 blvd Preah Monivong, Phnom Penh; tel. and fax (12) 554535; e-mail tvk@camnet.gov.kh; internet www.tvk.gov.kh; f. 1983; broadcasts in Khmer, 24 hours per day (TVK) and 12 hours per day (TVK2); Dir-Gen. (Head of Television) KEM GUNAWADH.

Phnom Penh Municipality Television (TV3): 2 blvd Confédération de la Russie, Phnom Penh; tel. (12) 814323; fax (23) 360800; e-mail tv3@kcsradio.com; internet www.tv3.com.kh; jt venture between Phnom Penh Municipality and KCS Cambodia Co Ltd (Thailand); Dir-Gen. KHAMPHUN KEOMONY.

Royal Cambodian Armed Forces Television (TV5 Cambodia): Prek Tloeng Village, Prek Kampoes, Kandal Stoeng, Kandal; tel. (23) 303925; fax (23) 994385; e-mail info@ch5cambodia.com; internet www.ch5cambodia.com; f. 1995; jt venture between Royal Cambodian Armed Forces and MICA Media Co; also operates an FM radio service.

Finance

(cap. = capital; res = reserves; dep. = deposits; brs = branches; amounts in US dollars unless otherwise stated)

BANKING

In 2013 there were 43 banks (excluding the central bank) operating in Cambodia, comprising: seven specialized banks; 32 locally incorporated private banks; and four branches of foreign banks.

Central Bank

National Bank of Cambodia (NBC): 22–24 blvd Preah Norodom, BP 25, Phnom Penh; tel. (23) 722563; fax (23) 426117; e-mail info@nbc.org.kh; internet www.nbc.org.kh; f. 1954; est. as National Bank of Cambodia; name changed to People's National Bank of Cambodia in 1979; name reverted to above in 1992; cap. 100,000m. riels, res 6,537,600m. riels, dep. 3,875,862m. riels (June 2007); Gov. CHEA CHANTO; Dep. Gov. NEAV CHANTHANA.

Specialized Banks

First Investment Specialized Bank (FISB): 72 blvd Preah Sihanouk, Sangkat Tonle Bassac, Khan Daun Penh, Phnom Penh; tel. (23) 222281; fax (23) 221112; e-mail service@fibank.com.kh; internet www.fibank.com.kh; f. 2005; cap. 12m., res 2.6m. (Dec. 2011); Chair. and CEO NEAK OKNHA; Gen. Man. YIP SOREIYOS.

Peng Heng SME Bank: 72 blvd Norodom, Sangkat Chey Chumneas, Khan Daun Penh, Phnom Penh; tel. (23) 219245; fax (23) 219185; e-mail pengheng@camnet.com.kh; f. 2001.

Rural Development Bank: 9–13 rue 7, Sangkat Chaktomouk, Khan Daun Penh, BP 1410, Phnom Penh; tel. (23) 220810; fax (23) 224628; e-mail admin@rdb.com.kh; internet www.rdb.com.kh; f. 1998; state-owned; provides credit to rural enterprises; Chair. and CEO SON KOUN THOR.

Private Banks

ACLEDA Bank PLC: 61 blvd Monivong, Sangkat Srah Chork, Khan Duan Penh, BP 1149, Phnom Penh; tel. (23) 430999; fax (23) 430555; e-mail acledabank@acledabank.com.kh; internet www.acledabank.com.kh; f. 1993; became specialized bank Oct. 2000; awarded commercial banking licence Dec. 2003; provides financial services to all sectors; cap. 113.1m., res 74.3m., dep. 1,507.2m. (Dec. 2012); Chair. CHEA SOK; Pres. and CEO IN CHANNY; 238 brs.

Advanced Bank of Asia Ltd: 148 blvd Preah Sihanouk, Sangkat Boeung Keng Kang 1, Khan Chamkarmon, Phnom Penh; tel. (23) 225333; fax (23) 216333; e-mail info@ababank.com; internet www.ababank.net; f. 1996; Chair. DAMIR KARASSAYEV; CEO ASKHAT AZHIKHANOV; 10 brs.

Cambodia Asia Bank Ltd: 439 blvd Monivong, Ground Floor, Phnom Penh; tel. (23) 220000; fax (23) 426628; e-mail cab@cab.com.kh; internet www.cab.com.kh; incorporated in 1992; cap. 36.5m., dep. 19.0m. (Dec. 2010); Man. WONG TOW FOCK.

Cambodia Mekong Bank: 6 blvd Monivong, Khan Daun Penh, Phnom Penh; tel. and fax (23) 217122; e-mail info@mekongbank.com; f. 1994; cap. 37.0m., dep. 18.4m. (Dec. 2011); Chair. MICHAEL C. STEPHEN; Pres. and CEO KHOV BOUN CHHAY.

Cambodian Commercial Bank Ltd: 26 blvd Preah Monivong, Sangkat Phsar Thmei 2, Khan Daun Penh, Phnom Penh; tel. (23) 426145; fax (23) 426116; e-mail ccbpp@ccb.com.kh; f. 1991; cap. 25m., dep. 83.3m. (Dec. 2011); Chair. NABHENGBHASANG KRISHNAMRA; Dir and Sec. NATTHAWUT CHAKANAN; 4 brs.

Cambodian Public Bank PLC (Campu Bank): Campu Bank Bldg 23, rue Kramoun Sar 114, Sangkat Phsar Thmei 2, Khan Daun Penh, Phnom Penh; tel. (23) 222880; fax (23) 222887; e-mail customerservice@campubank.com.kh; internet www.campubank.com.kh; f. 1992; cap. 90m., res 40m.,dep. 753.9m. (Dec. 2011); wholly owned subsidiary of Public Bank Bhd, Malaysia; Chair. Tan Sri Dato' Sri Dr HONG PIOW TEH; Country Head PHAN YING TONG; 23 brs.

Canadia Bank PLC: 315 rue Preah Ang Duong, cnr blvd Monivong, Khan Daun Penh, Phnom Penh; tel. (23) 868222; fax (23) 23427064; e-mail info@canadiabank.com.kh; internet www.canadiabank.com; f. 1991; est. as Canadia Gold and Trust Corpn Ltd; present name adopted 2004; cap. 130m., res 15m., dep. 1,282.8m. (Dec. 2012); Chair. LOR CHEE LENG; 42 brs.

Foreign Trade Bank: 3 rue Kramoun Sar, Sangkat Phsar Thmei 1, Khan Daun Penh, Phnom Penh; tel. (23) 724466; fax (23) 426108; e-mail info@ftbbank.com; internet www.ftbbank.com; f. 1979; removed from direct management of Nat. Bank of Cambodia in 2000; privatized in 2011; cap. 38.5m., res.2m., dep. 343.3m. (Dec. 2011); Chair. LIM BUN SOUR (acting); Gen. Man. GUI ANVANITH.

Singapore Banking Corporation Ltd: 68 rue Samdech Pan 214, Sangkat Boeung Raing, Khan Daun Penh, BP 688, Phnom Penh; tel. (23) 211211; fax (23) 212121; e-mail info@sbc-bank.com; internet www.sbc-bank.com; f. 1992; cap. 17m., dep. 47.7m. (Dec. 2011); Pres. ANDY KUN SWEE TIONG; Chair. KUN KAY HONG.

Union Commercial Bank PLC: UCB Bldg, 61 rue 130, Sangkat Phsar Chas, Khan Daun Penh, Phnom Penh; tel. (23) 427995; fax (23) 427997; e-mail info@ucb.com.kh; internet www.ucb.com.kh; f. 1994; cap. 37.5m., res 1.2m., dep. 202.0m. (Dec. 2011); Chair. and Pres. YUM SUI SANG; 4 brs.

Vattanac Bank: 89 blvd Preah Norodom, Sangkat Boeung Raing, Khan Daun Penh, Phnom Penh; tel. (23) 212727; fax (23) 216687; e-mail service@vattanacbank.com; internet www.vattanacbank.com; f. 2002; cap. 37.5m., dep. 142.8m. (Dec. 2011); Chair. SAM ANG; Pres. CHHUN LEANG.

Bankers' Association

The Association of Banks in Cambodia: 10 rue Oknha Pich (rue 242), Sangkat Chaktomuk, Khan Daun Penh, Phnom Penh; tel. (23) 218610; fax (23) 224310; e-mail secretariat@abc.org.kh; internet www.abc.org.kh; f. 1994; represents 35 banks and 28 micro-finance institutions; Chair. PHAN YING TONG.

STOCK EXCHANGE

The Cambodia Securities Exchange, a joint venture between the Government and the Korea Exchange (KRX—Republic of Korea), was launched in July 2011.

Stock Exchange

Cambodia Securities Exchange (CSX): Canadia Tower, 25th Floor, 315 rue Preah Ang Duong, Khan Daun Penh, Phnom Penh; tel. (23) 958888; fax (23) 955558; e-mail info@csx.com.kh; internet www.csx.com.kh; f. 2011; 55% govt-owned and 45% owned by Korea Exchange; trading began in April 2012; CEO HONG SOK HOUR.

Supervisory Body

Securities and Exchange Commission of Cambodia (SECC): 99 rue 598, Sangkat Phnom-Penh Thmei, Khan Sen Sok, Phnom Penh; tel. (23) 885611; fax (23) 885622; e-mail sovy_va@secc.gov.kh; internet www.secc.gov.kh; f. 2007; govt-owned; Dir-Gen. MING BANKOSAL; Dir SOVY VA.

INSURANCE

Asia Insurance (Cambodia) Ltd: 5 rue 13, Sangkat Wat Phnom, Khan Daun Penh, Phnom Penh 12201; tel. (23) 427981; fax (23) 216969; e-mail email@asiainsurance.com.kh; internet www.asiainsurance.com.kh; f. 1996; Gen. Man. PASCAL BRANDT-GAGNON.

Cambodia National Insurance Company (CAMINCO): cnr rues 106 & 13, Sangkat Wat Phnom, Khan Daun Penh, Phnom Penh; tel. (23) 722043; fax (23) 427810; e-mail info@caminco.com.kh; internet www.caminco.com.kh; f. 1990; fmrly 100% state-owned; since 2008 75% owned by Viriyah BVB Insurance PLC (Cambodian co est. by local businessman Duong Vibol), 25% state-owned; Chair. LOK CHUM TEAV OKNHA SAT NAVY; Man. Dir DUONG VIBOL.

Forte Insurance (Cambodia) PLC: 325 blvd Mao Tse Toung, BP 565, Phnom Penh; tel. (23) 885077; fax (23) 986922; e-mail info@forteinsurance.com; internet www.forteinsurance.com; f. 1996; Man. Dir CARLO CHEO; Gen. Man. YOUK CHAMROEUNRITH.

Infinity General Insurance PLC: 126 blvd Preah Norodom, Phnom Penh; tel. (23) 999888; fax (23) 999123; e-mail cs@infinity.com.kh; internet www.infinityinsurance.com.kh.

Trade and Industry

DEVELOPMENT ORGANIZATIONS

Council for the Development of Cambodia (CDC): Government Palace, quai Sisowath, Sangkat Wat Phnom, BP 1225, Phnom Penh; tel. (23) 981241; fax (23) 981161; e-mail cdc-cmb@camnet.com.kh; internet www.cdc-crdb.gov.kh; f. 1994; Chair. HUN SEN; Sec.-Gen. SOK CHENDA.

Cambodian Investment Board (CIB): Government Palace, quai Sisowath, Sangkat Wat Phnom, Phnom Penh; tel. (23) 981156; fax (23) 428426; e-mail cdc.cib@bigpond.com.kh; internet www.cambodiainvestment.gov.kh; f. 1993; part of CDC; sole body responsible for approving foreign investment in Cambodia; Chair. HUN SEN; Sec.-Gen. SUON SITTHY.

Cambodian National Petroleum Authority (CNPA): 13–14 blvd Confédération de la Russie, Sangkat Toeuk Thla, Khan Sen Sok, Phnom Penh; tel. (23) 890569; fax (23) 890569; internet cnpa-cambodia.com; f. 1999; Chair. SOK AN; Dir-Gen. TE DUONG TARA.

National Information Communications Technology Development Authority (NiDA): 113 rue 214, Sangkat Bong Prolet, Khan 7 Makara, Phnom Penh; tel. (12) 812282; fax (23) 216793; e-mail info@nida.gov.kh; internet www.nida.gov.kh; f. 2000; promotes IT and formulates policy devt; Chair. HUN SEN; Sec.-Gen. Dr PHU LEEWOOD.

CHAMBERS OF COMMERCE

Cambodia Chamber of Commerce: 7D blvd Confédération de la Russie, Khan Tuol Kok, Phnom Penh; tel. (23) 880795; fax (23) 881757; e-mail info@ppcc.org.kh; internet www.ppcc.org.kh; f. 1995; Pres. KITH MENG; Dir-Gen. NGUON MENG TECH.

Indian Chamber of Commerce (ICC): 34 rue 208, Sangkat Boeung Raing, Khan Duan Penh, Phnom Penh; tel. (12) 895895; e-mail president@icc-cambodia.org; internet www.icc-cambodia.org; f. 2012; Pres. DEBASISH PATTNAIK.

INDUSTRIAL AND TRADE ASSOCIATIONS

Garment Manufacturers' Association in Cambodia (GMAC): 175 blvd Jawaharlal Nehru (rue 215), Sangkat Phsar Doeum Kor, Khan Tuol Kok 12159, Phnom Penh; tel. (23) 882860; fax (23) 331183; e-mail info@gmac-cambodia.org; internet www.gmac-cambodia.org; Chair. VAN SOU IENG; Sec.-Gen. KEN LOO.

Trade Promotion Department: Ministry of Commerce, 65–69 rue 136, Sangkat Phsar Kandal 2, Khan Daun Penh, Phnom Penh; tel. (23) 216948; fax (23) 211745; e-mail info@tpd.gov.kh; internet www.tpd.gov.kh; Dir SEUN SOTHA.

UTILITIES

Electricity

Electricité du Cambodge (EDC): EDC Bldg, rue 19, Sangkat Wat Phnom, Khan Daun Penh, Phnom Penh; tel. (23) 723971; fax (23) 426018; e-mail info@edc.com.kh; internet www.edc.com.kh; f. 1996; state-owned; Chair. TUN LEAN; Man. Dir KEO ROTTANAK.

Electricity Authority of Cambodia (EAC): 2 rue 282, Sangkat Boeung Keng Kang 1, Khan Chamkarmon, Phnom Penh; tel. (23) 217654; fax (23) 214144; e-mail admin@eac.gov.kh; internet www.eac.gov.kh; f. 2001; regulatory authority; Chair. Dr TY NORIN.

Water

Phnom Penh Water Supply Authority (PPWSA): rue 106, Sangkat Srach Chak, Khan Daun Penh, Phnom Penh 12201; tel. (23) 724046; fax (23) 427657; e-mail admin@ppwsa.com.kh; internet www.ppwsa.com.kh; f. 1996; autonomous public enterprise; Dir-Gen. SIM SITHA.

TRADE UNIONS

Cambodia Federation of Independent Trade Unions (CFITU): 45 rue 63, Sangkat Boeung Keng Kang 1, Khan Chamkarmon, Phnom Penh; tel. (23) 213356; e-mail cfitu@online.com.kh; f. 1979 as Cambodia Fed. of Trade Unions; changed name as above in 1999; Chair. ROS SOK.

Cambodian Labour Confederation: No. 2, 3G rue 26BT, Tnotchrum Village, Sangkat Boeung, Tompun, Khan Meanchey, Phnom Penh; tel. (12) 998906; e-mail c.l.ccambodia@online.com.kh; internet clccambodia.org; f. 2006; Pres. ATH THORN.

Cambodian Union Federation (CUF): 16 rue 11 (New World City), Phoum Tropaintling, Sangkat Chomchao, Khan Dongkor, Phnom Penh; tel. (12) 837789; fax (23) 884329; e-mail CUF@online.com.kh; internet cuf-cctu.org; f. 1997; est. with CPP support in response to formation of the Free Trade Union of Workers of the Kingdom of Cambodia (FTUWKC); Pres. CHUON MOMTHOL.

Transport

RAILWAYS

Toll Royal Railways: Central Railway Station, Railway Sq., Sangkat Srach Chak, Khan Daun Penh, Phnom Penh; tel. (23) 992379; fax (23) 992353; e-mail chanvoleak.hong@tollgroup.com; internet www.tollroyalrailway.com; two single-track lines: the original 385-km Phnom Penh to Poipet line (incl. 48-km Sisophon–Poipet link); and a redeveloped 254-km line between Phnom Penh and Sihanoukville, a 117-km section of which, linking Phnom Penh and Kampot, reopened in late 2010; jt venture between Toll (55%) and Royal Group (45%) under 30-year concession agreement with Cambodian govt; Pres. and Dir-Gen. SOKHOM PHEAKAVANMONY; CEO DAVID KERR.

ROADS

In 2010 the total road network was 38,257 km in length, of which 4,757 km were highways and 5,700 km were secondary roads; about 6.3% of the road network was paved. A road bridge across the Mekong River opened in 2001.

INLAND WATERWAYS

The major routes are along the Mekong River, and up the Tonlé Sap River into the Tonlé Sap (Great Lake), covering, in all, about 2,400 km. The inland ports of Neak Luong, Kampong Cham and Prek Kdam have been supplied with motor ferries.

SHIPPING

The main port is Sihanoukville, on the Gulf of Thailand, which has 11 berths and can accommodate vessels of 10,000–15,000 tons. Phnom Penh port lies some distance inland. Koh Kong port, near the border with Thailand, serves as a docking bay for vessels entering Cambodia from Singapore, Malaysia and Thailand.

Phnom Penh Autonomous Port: Preah Sisowath, Sangkat Sras Chak, Khan Daun Penh; tel. and fax (23) 427802; e-mail ppapmpwt@online.com.kh; internet www.ppap.com.kh; state-owned; Chair. and CEO HEI BAVY.

Sihanoukville Autonomous Port (PAS): Terak Vithei Samdech Akka Moha Sena Padei Techo HUN SEN Sangkat No 3, Sihanoukville, Preah Sihanouk; tel. (34) 933416; fax (34) 933693; e-mail pasplan@pas.gov.kh; internet www.pas.gov.kh; Chair. and CEO LOU KIM CHHUN.

CIVIL AVIATION

There are international airports at Pochentong, serving nearby Phnom Penh, at Siem Reap and at Preah Sihanouk.

State Secretariat of Civil Aviation (SSCA): 62 blvd Norodom, Phnom Penh; tel. and fax (23) 211019; e-mail sengvany@camnet.com.kh; internet www.civilaviation.gov.kh; Dir-Gen. MAO HAS VANNAL.

Cambodia Angkor Air: 206A, blvd Norodom, Sangkat Tonle Bassac, Khan Chamkarmon, Phnom Penh; tel. (23) 6666786; fax (23) 224164; e-mail helpdesk_online@cambodiaangkorair.com; internet www.cambodiaangkorair.com; f. 2009; national carrier; jt venture with Viet Nam Airlines; Chair. and CEO TRINH NGOC THANH.

PMT Air: 118 rue 2013, Sangkat Kakab, Khan Dong Kar, Phnom Penh; tel. and fax (23) 23890322; e-mail ticket@pmtair.com; internet www.pmtair.com; f. 2003; domestic and international services.

Royal Khmer Airlines: 36B, 245 blvd Mao Tse Toung, Sangkat Boeung Trabek, Khan Chamkarmon, Phnom Penh; tel. (23) 994888; fax (23) 994508; e-mail rudy@royalkhmerairlines.com; internet www.royalkhmerairlines.com; f. 2000; jt venture with Indonesia; domestic and international services; CEO RUDYANTO WIDJAJA.

Royal Phnom Penh Airways: 209 rue 19, Sangkat Chey Chumneah, Khan Daun Penh, Phnom Penh; tel. (23) 215565; fax (23) 217420; e-mail ppenhairw@bigpond.com.kh; f. 1999; scheduled and charter passenger flights to domestic and regional destinations; Chair. Prince NORODOM CHAKRAPONG.

Siem Reap Airways International: 65 rue 214, Sangkat Boeung Raing, Khan Daun Penh, Phnom Penh; tel. (23) 723962; fax (23) 720522; internet www.siemreapair.com; f. 2000; scheduled domestic and international passenger services; CEO PRASERT PRASARTTONG-OSOTH.

Sky Wings Asia Airlines: IOC, 4th Floor, 254 blvd Monivong, Sangkat Boeung Raing, Khan Daun Penh, Phnom Penh; tel. (23) 217130; fax (23) 217150; e-mail phh@skywingsair.com; internet www.skywingsair.com; f. 2011; domestic and international carrier operating scheduled and charter services; CEO YOON JONG-MAN.

Tonlesap Airlines: 6R rue 208, Sangkat Boeung Raing, Khan Daun Penh, Phnom Penh; tel. (23) 216747; e-mail service@tonlesapairlines.com; internet www.tonlesapairlines.com; f. 2011; scheduled passenger services to domestic and regional destinations; commenced operations to Hong Kong in 2012; CEO YONG HWEE TEO.

Tourism

Cambodia's attractions include the ancient temples of Angkor and the beaches of Sihanoukville. Receipts from tourism totalled US $2,210m. in 2012. In that year visitor arrivals reached 3.6m. Major sources of visitors included Viet Nam, South Korea, the People's Republic of China, Laos, Thailand and Japan.

Directorate-General of Tourism: 3 blvd Monivong, Phnom Penh; tel. (23) 427130; fax (23) 426107; f. 1988; Dir-Gen. THITH CHANTHA.

Defence

As assessed at November 2013, the total strength of the Royal Cambodian Armed Forces was estimated to be 124,300 (including provincial forces): army 75,000, navy 2,800, air force 1,500 and provincial forces about 45,000. Paramilitary forces are organized at village level and numbered some 67,000 men and women in 2013. In that year 219 Cambodian troops were participating in the UN peacekeeping mission in Lebanon and a further 147 in that organization's mission in South Sudan. The defence budget for 2013 was 1,590,000m. riels.

Supreme Commander of the Royal Cambodian Armed Forces: King NORODOM SIHAMONI.

Commander-in-Chief: Gen. POL SAROEUN.

Education

In 2009 the adult literacy rate was 73.9%. In 2011/12 there were 2,575 pre-primary institutions, 6,849 primary schools and 2,023 secondary schools. In that year a total of 121,306 children were attending pre-primary schools, primary pupils totalled 2,142,464, and secondary students totalled 859,312. In 2009/10 enrolment at pre-primary level included 13% of children in the relevant age-group (males 13%; females 13%). Primary education is compulsory for nine years between the ages of six and 15. Enrolment at primary level included 98% of children in the relevant age-group (males 100%; females 97%) in 2011/12. Secondary education comprises two cycles, each lasting three years. Enrolment at secondary level included 38% of children in the relevant age-group (males 40%; females 36%) in 2007/08.

Institutions of higher education include Phnom Penh University, an arts college, a technical college, a teacher-training college, a number of secondary vocational schools and an agricultural college.

The budget for 2012 allocated 1,007,626m. riels to the Ministry of Education, Youth and Sport.

CAMEROON

Introductory Survey

LOCATION, CLIMATE, LANGUAGE, RELIGION, FLAG, CAPITAL

The Republic of Cameroon lies on the west coast of Africa, with Nigeria to the west, Chad and the Central African Republic to the east, and the Republic of the Congo, Equatorial Guinea and Gabon to the south. The climate is hot and humid in the south and west, with average temperatures of 26°C (80°F). Annual rainfall in Yaoundé averages 4,030 mm (159 ins). The north is drier, with more extreme temperatures. The official languages are French and English; many local languages are also spoken, including Fang, Bamileke and Duala. Approximately 53% of Cameroonians profess Christianity, 25% adhere to traditional religious beliefs, and about 22%, mostly in the north, are Muslims. The national flag (proportions 2 by 3) has three equal vertical stripes, of green, red and yellow, with a five-pointed gold star in the centre of the red stripe. The capital is Yaoundé.

CONTEMPORARY POLITICAL HISTORY

Historical Context

In 1919 the former German protectorate of Cameroon (Kamerun) was divided into two zones: a French-ruled area in the east and south, and a smaller British-administered area in the west. In 1946 the zones were transformed into UN Trust Territories, with British and French rule continuing in their respective areas. French Cameroons became an autonomous state within the French Community in 1957. Under the leadership of Ahmadou Ahidjo, a northerner who became Prime Minister in 1958, the territory became independent, as the Republic of Cameroon, on 1 January 1960. The first election for the country's National Assembly, held in April of that year, was won by Ahidjo's party, the Union Camerounaise. In May the new National Assembly elected Ahidjo to be the country's first President.

British Cameroons, comprising a northern and a southern region, was attached to neighbouring Nigeria, for administrative purposes, prior to Nigeria's independence in October 1960. Plebiscites were held, under UN auspices, in the two regions of British Cameroons in February 1961. The northern area voted to merge with Nigeria (becoming the province of Sardauna), while the south voted for union with the Republic of Cameroon, which was effected on 1 October 1961.

The enlarged country was named the Federal Republic of Cameroon, with French and English as joint official languages. It comprised two states: the former French zone became East Cameroon, while the former British portion became West Cameroon. John Ngu Foncha, the Prime Minister of West Cameroon and leader of the Kamerun National Democratic Party, became Vice-President of the Federal Republic. Under the continuing leadership of Ahidjo, who (as the sole candidate) was re-elected President in 1965, the two states became increasingly integrated. In 1966 the two governing parties and several opposition groups combined to form a single party, the Union Nationale Camerounaise (UNC). Ahidjo was re-elected as President in 1970, and Solomon Muna (who had replaced Foncha as Prime Minister of West Cameroon in 1968) became Vice-President.

In 1972, following the approval by referendum of a new Constitution, the federal system was ended, and the country was officially renamed the United Republic of Cameroon. A centralized political and administrative system was rapidly introduced, and in 1973 a new National Assembly was elected for a five-year term. After the re-election of Ahidjo as President in 1975, the Constitution was revised, and a Prime Minister, Paul Biya (a bilingual Christian southerner), was appointed in June. In 1980 Ahidjo was unanimously re-elected to the presidency for a fifth five-year term of office.

Ahidjo resigned as President in November 1982, and nominated Biya as his successor. Biya was elected President in January 1984. The post of Prime Minister was subsequently abolished, and it was announced that the country's name was to revert to the Republic of Cameroon.

Domestic Political Affairs

In April 1984 rebel elements in the presidential guard attempted to overthrow the Biya Government. After three days of intense fighting, in which hundreds of people were reported to have been killed, the rebellion was suppressed by forces loyal to the President; a total of 51 defendants subsequently received death sentences. Following the coup attempt, Biya implemented extensive changes within the military hierarchy, reorganized the Government, and introduced more stringent press censorship. In March 1985 the UNC was renamed the Rassemblement Démocratique du Peuple Camerounais (RDPC).

Biya was re-elected unopposed to the presidency in April 1988. In concurrent elections to the National Assembly, voters were presented with a choice of RDPC-approved candidates; 153 of the 180 deputies elected were new members.

In February 1990 11 people were arrested in connection with their alleged involvement in an unofficial opposition organization, the Social Democratic Front (SDF). In June, in response to mounting civil unrest, Biya stated that he envisaged the future adoption of a multi-party system and announced a series of reforms, including the abolition of laws governing subversion, the revision of the law on political associations, and the reinforcement of press freedom. In December the National Assembly adopted legislation whereby Cameroon officially became a multi-party state. Legislation granting a general amnesty for political prisoners was approved in April 1991. The post of Prime Minister was reintroduced by legislation enacted in the same month, and Biya subsequently appointed Sadou Hayatou, hitherto Secretary-General at the Presidency, to lead a transitional Government. However, the Government's refusal to comply with demands for an unconditional amnesty for all political prisoners, and for the convening of a national conference, prompted a general strike in June. The Government placed seven of Cameroon's 10 provinces under military authority, prohibited opposition gatherings, and, following continued civil disturbances, banned several opposition parties, alleging that they were responsible for terrorist activities. The observance of the general strike declined in subsequent months.

Towards constitutional reform

Following negotiations, the Government and about 40 of the 47 registered opposition parties signed an agreement in November 1991 providing for the establishment of a committee to draft constitutional reforms. The opposition undertook to suspend the campaign of civil disobedience, while the Government agreed to end the ban on opposition meetings and to release all prisoners who had been arrested during anti-Government demonstrations. The ban on opposition gatherings was revoked later in November, and military rule was ended in December. In February 1992 those opposition parties that had not accepted the November 1991 agreement formed the Alliance pour le Redressement du Cameroun (ARC), and announced that they were to boycott the forthcoming elections.

At legislative elections in March 1992 the RDPC won 88 of the National Assembly's 180 seats. The Union Nationale pour la Démocratie et le Progrès (UNDP) obtained 68 seats, the extreme left-wing Union des Populations du Cameroun (UPC) 18, and the Mouvement pour la Défense de la République (MDR) six. The RDPC subsequently formed an alliance with the MDR, thereby securing an absolute majority in the National Assembly. In April Biya formed a 25-member Cabinet, principally comprising members of the previous Government and including five MDR members; Simon Achidi Achu, an anglophone member of the RDPC, was appointed Prime Minister.

The presidential election that had been scheduled for May 1993 was brought forward to 11 October 1992. It was announced that Biya had been re-elected by 39.9% of the votes cast, while the Chairman of the SDF, John Fru Ndi (who had the support of the ARC), had secured 35.9%. The opposition alleged malpractice, and there were violent demonstrations by opposition supporters in many areas. Biya was inaugurated as President on 3 November, and pledged to implement further constitutional reforms. He subsequently appointed a new Cabinet, including representatives of the MDR, the UPC, the UNDP and the Parti National du Progrès.

In May 1993 the Government made public draft constitutional amendments that provided for the installation of a democratic political system, with the establishment of new organs of government, including a Senate as an upper legislative chamber, and restricted the power vested in the President (who was to serve a maximum of two five-year terms of office). The draft retained a unitary state, but, in recognition of pro-federalist demands, envisaged a more decentralized system of local government.

In August 1995 representatives of anglophone movements, most prominently the Southern Cameroons National Council (SCNC), officially presented to the UN demands for the establishment of an independent, English-speaking republic of Southern Cameroons. The organizations claimed that the plebiscite of 1961 whereby the former southern portion of British Cameroons had voted to merge with the Republic of Cameroon on terms of equal status had been rendered invalid by subsequent francophone domination.

In December 1995 the National Assembly adopted revised constitutional amendments that increased the presidential mandate from five years to seven (while restricting the maximum tenure of office to two terms) and provided for the establishment of a Senate and a Constitutional Council. In September 1996 Achu was replaced as Prime Minister by Peter Mafany Musonge, the General Manager of the Cameroon Development Corporation, and a new Cabinet was appointed.

Organizational difficulties meant that National Assembly elections scheduled to take place in March 1997 were postponed until May. The eventual elections were contested by 46 parties. The announcement of provisional results attributing a large majority of seats to the RDPC prompted opposition claims of widespread electoral malpractice, although these were rejected by the Supreme Court. The official results, announced in June, showed that the RDPC had secured 109 of the 180 seats, the SDF 43, the UNDP 13, and the Union Démocratique du Cameroun (UDC) five. A new Cabinet remained virtually unchanged from the previous administration. In August polls were re-run in seven constituencies where the results had been annulled owing to alleged irregularities: the RDPC won all of these seats, thus increasing its representation in the National Assembly to 116 seats.

Prior to the October 1997 presidential election, the SDF, the UNDP and the UDC declared a boycott of all elections, in view of the absence of an independent electoral commission. Biya was overwhelmingly re-elected, with 92.6% of the votes cast, against six other candidates. The level of voter participation in the election was much disputed, with official sources asserting that 81.4% of the electorate took part, while opposition leaders claimed that the abstention rate was higher than 80%. In December, having reappointed Musonge as Prime Minister, Biya made major changes to the composition of the Cabinet. The new administration included representatives of four political groups, although the RDPC retained 45 of the 50 ministerial posts.

There was a sit-down protest by deputies outside the National Assembly building in November 2000, after the security forces prevented a march, organized by the SDF, in support of demands for the creation of an independent electoral commission. In the following month the National Assembly adopted legislation on the establishment of a National Elections Observatory (NEO) and on the regulation of state funding for political parties and electoral campaigns. Five opposition parties boycotted the vote on the NEO, considering that it would be unconstitutional and criticizing the President's role in appointing its 11 members. The new electoral body was inaugurated in October 2001.

Legislative elections were held in June 2002. The RDPC increased its representation to 133 seats. The SDF retained 21 seats, and the UDC five, while the UPC won three seats and the UNDP held just one. Turnout was reported to be less than 50%, and the elections were boycotted by the SCNC. Voting for the remaining 17 National Assembly seats was cancelled by the Supreme Court following complaints of various irregularities in the nine constituencies concerned. Opposition parties alleged widespread electoral fraud, however, and demanded that the entire elections be declared void. The SDF initially refused to participate in the incoming legislature, although by mid-July Fru Ndi announced the end of the boycott. In protest against his decision, several senior SDF officials subsequently resigned from the party and formed the Alliance des Forces Progressistes. In August there was an extensive cabinet reorganization, in which 18 new members were appointed. Voting took place in September for the outstanding 17 National Assembly seats: the RDPC took a further 16 seats, increasing its standing to 149 of the 180 seats, and the SDF won the remaining seat.

Biya's third term

Biya was re-elected to the presidency for a further seven-year term in October 2004, with 70.9% of the vote. His closest rival among 15 other registered candidates, John Fru Ndi of the SDF, received 17.4%. Turnout was officially put at 82.2%. Although opposition groups strongly contested the validity of the result, accusing Biya and his allies of large-scale fraud, international observers declared that the conduct of the election, despite some shortcomings, had been broadly fair.

In December 2004 President Biya appointed a new, anglophone Prime Minister, Ephraïm Inoni, hitherto Assistant Secretary-General of the Presidency. Nevertheless, representatives of Cameroon's English-speaking community continued to assert that there remained a disproportionately large number of francophone ministers. The new Cabinet was again principally made up of members of the RDPC.

In July 2005 the National Assembly approved legislation to harmonize the penal code. Hitherto, the country's English- and French-speaking regions had been subject to distinct penal codes. Although the measure was broadly welcomed as promoting national unity, unrest and secessionist sympathies grew throughout 2005 among anglophones of southern Cameroon. In October public celebrations in Bui County commemorating the anniversary of southern British Cameroons' union with the Republic of Cameroon in 1961 led to violent confrontations. Subsequently, more than 100 SCNC activists, including the movement's National Chairman, Ette Otun Ayamba, were arrested.

The RDPC further increased its majority at elections held in July 2007, winning an initial 152 of the 180 seats in the National Assembly. Voter participation was officially put at some 62%, although the SDF, which alleged malpractice in the conduct of the polls, estimated turnout of just 30%. The Supreme Court subsequently annulled the results in five constituencies, and elections were re-run in the 17 affected seats at the end of September. At the final outcome, the RDPC held 153 seats in the National Assembly, the SDF 16, the UNDP six, the UDC four and the opposition Mouvement Progressiste (MP) one.

In January 2008 it was reported that public meetings and demonstrations had been banned in Littoral province, including in its capital, Douala (the country's largest city and main port), where opposition parties and civil society groups had been intending to organize protests against government plans to seek the abolition of the constitutional limit on the presidential mandate in order to allow Biya to stand for re-election at the end of his current term. Rioting erupted in Douala in February 2008, as a nationwide strike by transport workers to protest against substantial rises in the prices of fuel and basic products coincided with political opposition to constitutional changes, and there were clashes between protesters and heavily armed troops as unrest spread to Yaoundé and other cities. According to official figures, 40 people were killed, and more than 1,500 arrested, during the violence, although one human rights group put the number of deaths at more than 100. In March the Government announced a series of measures intended to offset the impact of rising living costs, including a 15% increase in the salaries of civil servants and military employees, the suspension of duties on imports of certain basic foodstuffs and a reduction in electricity tariffs. Further reductions in the cost of staple goods were announced in July 2009, in an effort to avoid renewed unrest.

In April 2008 the National Assembly approved a number of constitutional amendments, including the removal of the restriction on the renewal of the presidential mandate. The vote was boycotted by SDF deputies, who denounced the revisions as a 'constitutional coup', and there were protests in a number of cities.

In August 2008 Fru Ndi was brought to trial for alleged complicity in the murder of a member of a rival SDF faction in May 2006. (More than 20 members of the SDF had been detained on charges of involvement in the murder, but most were provisionally released in November 2008.) Fru Ndi, who had not been detained, claimed that the charges against him were politically motivated and aimed at preventing him from contesting the 2011 presidential election. Proceedings against him and other SDF members were adjourned indefinitely in July 2009.

Philémon Yang, an English-speaker and long-standing member of the presidential circle, was appointed to replace Inoni as Prime Minister in June 2009. Several ministers were redeployed, and nine were replaced, in an accompanying reorganization of the Cabinet.

A World Bank report published in September 2009 stated that fraud and institutional corruption remained the principal obstacles to development and investment in Cameroon, despite a wide-ranging anti-corruption campaign that had been launched in 2004 by Inoni. A number of high-profile scandals involving ministers and state officials were made public in late 2009 and early 2010, including the arrest of the recently replaced Minister of Basic Education, Haman Adama. Meanwhile, President Biya was severely criticized in the French press for the extravagant cost of a visit to France in September 2009, having two months earlier accepted €537m. in French aid.

In May 2010 security forces acted to prevent a rally by hundreds of members of the Union des Journalists du Cameroun demanding the immediate release of all detained reporters and the conduct of media trials in civil rather than criminal courts. Of particular concern was a series of arrests of journalists investigating corruption at state level, one of whom, Germain Cyrille Ngota (managing editor of *Cameroon Express*), had recently died while in custody. In September a judicial inquiry (established following considerable external pressure, notably from France and the USA) concluded that Ngota had died from complications arising from an existing medical condition; however, his family and press freedom organizations rejected this finding. Subsequently, reports continued to emerge of further arrests, notably of journalists investigating high-level corruption. A report submitted to the UN Human Rights Council by several international media freedom groups in October 2012 criticized the Cameroonian authorities for their ongoing suppression of journalists in the country. In December three of Ngota's colleagues received prison sentences of between two and 15 years, after having been convicted of forging an official document during an investigation into government corruption.

Recent developments: the 2011 and 2013 elections

A new authority to replace the NEO, Elections Cameroon (ELECAM), provision for which had been signed into law in 2006, became fully operational in January 2010. ELECAM was to assume the functions previously undertaken by the Ministry of Territorial Administration and Decentralization in organizing elections, and those of the NEO in supervising and controlling polls. While nominally independent, the impartiality of ELECAM had already been called into question: 11 of its 12 members, appointed at the end of 2008, had been selected from the RDPC. In April 2010 a coalition of 10 opposition parties and 10 civil society groups demanded that ELECAM be dissolved.

The registration process for the 2011 presidential election began in August 2010. SDF leader John Fru Ndi announced his intention to seek a postponement of the election if certain demands were not met. Among these were: the introduction of biometric data on voters' cards and registers; the participation of all political parties at all levels of decision-making regarding the poll; financial autonomy for ELECAM; non-participation of government officials in the election campaign; and the introduction of the right to vote for Cameroon nationals living abroad. This last was met in July 2011, when the National Assembly approved legislation permitting members of the diaspora to vote. In February, meanwhile, the Government established a new agency with authorization to impose price controls on staple foodstuffs during inflationary periods, apparently to offset a potential source of social disorder prior to the election. Fuel subsidies were also maintained during the pre-election period.

At the beginning of October 2011, shortly before the scheduled presidential election, more than 200 SCNC supporters were arrested for attending what was stated to be an unauthorized protest in Buéa. At least 14 members of the SCNC had been detained in April after participating in a meeting that was deemed by the authorities to be illegal.

As the presidential election proceeded on 9 October 2011, the opposition continued to raise concerns regarding the constitutionality of Biya's standing for a further term, the impartiality of ELECAM and the credibility of the rules governing the election. As expected, Biya once again secured a resounding victory, with 78.0% of the votes cast. Of the 22 other candidates, Fru Ndi, for the SDF, won 10.7%, and Garga Haman Adji, of the Alliance pour la Démocratie et le Développement, 3.2%. According to official figures, the rate of participation was 65.8% of the registered electorate. The SDF and other opposition parties demanded that the results be annulled, complaining of widespread procedural irregularities, but the Supreme Court upheld the outcome. While noting numerous deficiencies, international observers were generally satisfied with the conduct of the polls. Biya appointed a new Government in December, retaining Yang as Prime Minister and reorganizing portfolios with a particular focus on the economy.

Meanwhile, in November 2011 the National Anti-Corruption Commission published a report accusing numerous senior public officials, including government ministers, of corrupt practices. Most notably, Minister of Public Works Bernard Messengue Avom was accused of embezzling US $30m. after having issued fraudulent construction contracts. President Biya established a judicial inquiry to examine the allegations, and pledged that legal action would be brought against those responsible.

Marafa Hamidou Yaya, a former minister of state, received a 25-year prison sentence in September 2012, after having been convicted of involvement in a scheme to misappropriate some US $48m. of public funds designated for the purchase of a presidential aircraft in 2004. Former Prime Minister Inoni, who was also implicated in the scandal, was arrested along with Yaya in April, and in January 2013 the newly established Special Criminal Court indicted him on two counts of embezzling state funds while in public office (see below). In the mean time, in October 2012 former Minister of Public Health Titus Edzoa, who had been imprisoned since 1997 on embezzlement charges, was convicted of further corruption offences and given an additional 20-year gaol term.

In October 2012 more than 100 SCNC activists were arrested while attending a meeting in Buéa. Meanwhile, violent clashes between SDF protesters and the security forces broke out in Douala in November, on the 30th anniversary of Biya's assumption of the presidency.

Although legislative elections had been scheduled for July 2012, the mandated term of the National Assembly was extended, at intervals, until May 2013, in order to give ELECAM additional time to implement the new biometric voter registration programme. In preparation for the elections, the legislature approved amendments to the electoral code in April 2012; and in December of that year the code was further amended to reduce the deposit required of candidates for the National Assembly from 3m. francs CFA to 1m. francs CFA. Registration of voters took place between October 2012 and March 2013, but, with only 5m. of a targeted 7m. electorate registered, was reopened in late May. In early May, meanwhile, the legislative elections were once again rescheduled, to take place in late July in tandem with municipal elections which had themselves been deferred from mid-2012. At the beginning of July 2013, however, Biya decreed that both the legislative and municipal elections would take place on 30 September. Registration of voters thus closed with immediate effect: by this time, the electoral register included some 5.4m. eligible voters.

Voting took place among municipal councillors for the 70 elective members of the new Senate on 14 April 2013; seven senators were elected to represent each of the country's 10 provinces. The official results, released by the Supreme Court on 29 April, allocated 56 seats to the RDPC and 14 to the SDF. It appeared that the latter had profited from the disqualification, prior to the election, of the RDPC candidate lists in Adamaoua and West provinces, although John Fru Ndi notably failed to win a seat in North-West province. President Biya proceeded to appoint the 30 other members of the Senate on 8 May. Almost all of the nominees were considered to be closely associated with the RDPC. In mid-June the new Senate, provision for which had been established in the 1995 constitutional amendments, elected Marcel Niat Njifenji (one of the nominated senators, representing West province) as its president; the 14 SDF senators cast blank votes. Under the terms of the Constitution, the president of the Senate would assume the office of Head of State in the event of a vacancy.

The former Minister of Basic Education, Haman Adama, was released from detention in mid-September 2013, after the Special Criminal Court halted proceedings against her and 14 co-accused in respect of charges of misappropriation of public funds and the improper awarding of public contracts. Adama, who had been in custody since her arrest at the beginning of 2010, was reported to have repaid to the state some 212.5m. CFA francs in February 2013. In early October Inoni and former senior minister Jean-Marie Atangana Mebara (who was already in detention following an earlier conviction) were each sentenced to 20 years' imprisonment and ordered to pay 85m. francs CFA, having been found guilty by the Special Criminal Court of conspiracy in the embezzlement of state funds with regard to the 2004 case concerning the purchase of a presidential aircraft.

The deferred legislative and municipal elections proceeded, according to the revised schedule, on 30 September 2013. In the legislative elections, 29 political parties presented candidates for the National Assembly. Official results, published on 17 October by the Supreme Court (which had rejected more than 40 petitions for the outcome of voting for certain seats to be annulled), confirmed a slightly reduced but still decisive majority for the RDPC, which held 148 of the 180 seats in the National Assembly. The SDF returned 18 deputies. Five other parties won representation: the UNDP (five seats), the UDC (four), the UPC (three), the MDR (one) and the Mouvement pour la Renaissance du Cameroun (one). The rate of participation by voters was put at 76.8%. International observer missions confirmed that both the election campaign and voting had proceeded generally peacefully and transparently, although the opposition complained that public funds intended to support political parties had been released too late to have been of benefit to the governing party's challengers. The RDPC also won a clear majority of seats on the 360 municipal councils. As the elections proceeded, Biya announced that the establishment of the Constitutional Council—which, like the Senate, was provided for under the 1995 amendments—would proceed following the proclamation of the election results. (In the absence of this body, the electoral code assigned responsibility for the proclamation of election results to the Supreme Court.)

The announcement of the new Government remained pending in April 2014. Remarks made by Biya at the end of December 2013, in his new year address to the nation, had been widely interpreted as being critical of the Government of Philémon Yang in its management of the economy.

Foreign Affairs

Regional relations

In October 2002 the International Court of Justice (ICJ, see p. 24) issued its final verdict on the demarcation of the land and maritime boundary between Cameroon and Nigeria. Its judgment notably ruled in favour of Cameroon's sovereignty over the strategically and economically important Bakassi peninsula in the Gulf of Guinea, citing a 1913 Anglo-German partition agreement, while upholding Nigeria's offshore boundary claims. Sovereignty over the peninsula had been a source of long-standing tension between Cameroon and Nigeria, and, following a series of armed clashes, Cameroon had in 1994 referred the case for adjudication by the ICJ. Nigeria refused to accept the Court's decision, and troop deployments increased on both sides of the border. In November 2002, however, at a UN-mediated meeting in Geneva, Switzerland, the Presidents of Cameroon and Nigeria signed a joint communiqué announcing the creation of a bilateral commission, to be headed by a UN Special Representative, with a mandate to achieve a peaceful resolution to the Bakassi dispute. At its inaugural meeting in Yaoundé in December, the Cameroon-Nigeria Mixed Commission agreed a 15-point peace agenda and decided to establish a sub-committee to undertake the demarcation of the boundary. In August 2003 Nigeria and Cameroon adopted a framework for the demilitarization of the Bakassi region, and in December Nigeria ceded control of 32 villages on its north-eastern border to Cameroon. Sovereignty over petroleum resources remained under discussion.

In January 2004 the two countries agreed to establish joint security patrols in the disputed region. Following a meeting in Yaoundé in July, it was confirmed that Nigerian troops would withdraw from Bakassi by mid-September. However, the Nigerian Government subsequently reneged on this agreement, in response to legal challenges by Bakassi residents regarding the constitutionality of ceding land held by Nigerians. The Nigerian Federal High Court rejected this appeal in October, but Nigeria maintained its troops in Bakassi, citing difficulties over demarcating maritime boundaries. In June 2006 an agreement was reached, under the auspices of the UN Secretary-General (the so-called Greentree Agreement), whereby Nigeria would withdraw its troops from the Bakassi peninsula within 60 days. Accordingly, Nigeria completed its troop withdrawal in August. Under the terms of the agreement, Nigerian police were to remain in control of the southern and eastern parts of the region until August 2008, in which month Nigeria officially ceded control of the Bakassi peninsula to Cameroon. Joint observation missions would monitor the rights of Nigerian nationals in Bakassi during a five-year transitional period, and implementation of the Greentree Agreement would be overseen by a joint Follow-up Committee. Although there had been speculation that Nigeria would appeal against the ICJ's 2002 ruling, the final deadline for appeal expired in October 2012. There was a brief escalation of tensions at this time, after a secessionist group, the Bakassi Self-Determination Front, unilaterally proclaimed the peninsula's independence in August. None the less, the transitional period ended on 14 August 2013, whereupon Cameroon assumed full sovereignty of the Bakassi peninsula: a declaration to this effect was adopted in October, at the final meeting of the Follow-up Committee on the Greentree Agreement. By the end of 2013, according to the UN, 1,893 km of the estimated 2,100-km land boundary had been demarcated.

Meanwhile, a series of high-profile attacks in Nigeria perpetrated by the militant Islamist Boko Haram organization during 2011 impelled Cameroon to review its border security arrangements. In January 2012 Cameroonian troops were stationed near the border with Nigeria to discourage Boko Haram jihadists from crossing into Cameroon, and in February the two countries agreed to form a border security council. The issue of border security in northern Cameroon remained of concern during 2013. Notably, seven members of a French family, including four children, were held hostage for two months, having been abducted in northern Cameroon by Boko Haram activists in February; and Boko Haram also claimed responsibility for the kidnap there of a French Roman Catholic priest who was held hostage for more than six weeks in late 2013. In June, meanwhile, the office of the UN High Commissioner for Refugees (UNHCR) reported that some 3,000 Nigerians, mainly women and children, had crossed the border into Cameroon to escape violent confrontations between the Nigerian military and Boko Haram insurgents in north-eastern states of Adamawa, Borno and Yobe, where a state of emergency had been declared in May. By the end of October, according to UNHCR, about 8,100 Nigerians had sought refuge in Cameroon.

Relations between Cameroon and Equatorial Guinea have become strained in recent years. The construction of the Cameroon–Chad petroleum pipeline has led to diminished fishing areas inshore, resulting in Cameroonian fishing vessels travelling further out to sea and thus closer to Equatorial Guinean waters. An armed assault against the presidential palace in Equatorial Guinea in February 2009 led to a further deterioration in relations, and the common maritime border was temporarily sealed. Equatorial Guinea closed its land frontier with Cameroon in March 2012 following a violent dispute between Equato-Guinean border troops and Cameroonian traders attempting to enter the country. The border was reopened four months later, following a meeting between the Presidents of the two countries. Immediately prior to the scheduled entry into effect, on 1 January 2014, of an agreement to permit the free movement of nationals among the six member countries of the Communauté Economique et Monétaire de l'Afrique Centrale (CEMAC), it was reported that Equatorial Guinea had closed its border with Cameroon (and also with Gabon). The agreement, reached by CEMAC heads of state in June 2013, allowed nationals to move freely between countries of the bloc for a maximum of three months, but had been opposed by Equatorial Guinea on the grounds that it would undermine efforts to provide employment for its own nationals. The border was reopened three weeks later, following a visit to Equatorial Guinea by Cameroon's Minister of External Affairs to meet with his counterpart there.

Cameroon has for several years hosted a large refugee population from the Central African Republic (CAR): at the end of 2012, according to UNHCR, the CAR refugee and asylum seeker population in Cameroon numbered some 93,000. A renewed escalation of insecurity in the CAR after December 2012—and particularly from March 2013, when the administration of President François Bozizé was deposed by the rebel Seleka alliance—prompted further refugee flows into Cameroon and put additional pressure on facilities for the refugee population. Cameroon temporarily closed its border with the CAR in August, following an exchange of gunfire between Cameroonian security forces and Seleka fighters; and in November Cameroon stated that it had repelled a cross-border raid by some 400 armed men who were, it was alleged, attempting to free the leader of a breakaway faction from Seleka who had been arrested in Cameroon in September. As at January 2014, following the escalation of inter-religious fighting in the CAR at the end of 2013, UNHCR put the total refugee population from the CAR in Cameroon at more than 98,500. Meanwhile, Cameroon contributed military personnel to the African-led International Support

Mission in the Central African Republic (MISCA), deployment of which was authorized by the UN Security Council in December 2013.

CONSTITUTION AND GOVERNMENT

Under the amended 1972 Constitution, the Republic of Cameroon is a multi-party state. Executive power is vested in the President, as Head of State, who is elected by universal adult suffrage for a term of seven years; there is no limit on the number of terms that may be served. Legislative power is held by the National Assembly, which comprises 180 members and is elected for a term of five years. Constitutional amendments adopted in 1995 provided for the establishment of an upper legislative chamber. Elections for 70 members of this Senate took place at municipal council level in April 2013 (with seven senators being elected to represent each province), and a further 30 members (three for each province) were appointed by presidential decree in May. The Cabinet is appointed by the President.

Local administration is based on 10 provinces, each with a governor who is appointed by the President.

REGIONAL AND INTERNATIONAL CO-OPERATION

Cameroon is a member of the African Union (see p. 186), of the Central African organs of the Franc Zone (see p. 329) and of the Communauté Economique des Etats de l'Afrique Centrale (CEEAC, see p. 450). The regional Banque des Etats de l'Afrique Centrale has its headquarters in Yaoundé.

Cameroon became a member of the UN in 1960, and was admitted to the World Trade Organization (WTO, see p. 434) in 1995. Cameroon is also a member of the International Cocoa Organization (see p. 446) and of the International Coffee Organization (see p. 446).

ECONOMIC AFFAIRS

In 2012, according to estimates by the World Bank, Cameroon's gross national income (GNI), measured at average 2010–12 prices, was US $25,395m., equivalent to $1,170 per head (or $2,320 per head on an international purchasing-power parity basis). During 2003–12, it was estimated, the population increased at an average annual rate of 2.6%, while gross domestic product (GDP) per head grew, in real terms, by an average of 0.6% per year. Overall GDP increased, in real terms, at an average annual rate of 3.2% in 2003–12; growth in 2012 was 4.7%.

Agriculture (including hunting, forestry and fishing) contributed 23.0% of GDP in 2012. An estimated 42.6% of the labour force were employed in agriculture in mid-2014, according to FAO. The principal cash crops are cocoa beans (which accounted for 9.2% of export earnings in 2012) and cotton (3.4%). Oil palm and rubber are also increasing in significance. The main subsistence crops are cassava, plaintains, maize and sorghum; Cameroon is not, however, self-sufficient in cereals. In 2011 an estimated 42% of the country's land area was covered by forest, but an inadequate transport infrastructure has impeded the development of the forestry sector. In 2010 Cameroon signed a Voluntary Partnership Agreement (VPA) on Forest Law Enhancement, Governance and Trade with the European Union (EU, see p. 273), to which Cameroon exports 80% of its sawnwood; the VPA, which entered effect in 2011, commits each party to trade only in verified legal timber and timber products. During 2007–12, the real GDP of the agricultural sector increased at an average annual rate of 4.0%; sectoral growth in 2012 was 2.7%.

Industry (including mining, manufacturing, construction and power) employed 8.9% of the labour force in 1990, and contributed 30.1% of GDP in 2012. During 2007–12, industrial GDP increased at an average annual rate of 1.1%; the sector grew by 4.9% in 2012.

Mining contributed 8.8% of GDP in 2012. The sector employed only 0.1% of Cameroon's working population in 1985, although this share is believed to have grown considerably in recent years. Receipts from the exploitation of the country's petroleum reserves constitute a principal source of government revenue. Output decreased from a peak of 185,000 barrels per day (b/d) in the mid-1980s to 63,500 b/d in 2012, according to the US Energy Information Administration, although there was a marginal increase in output in the latter year, and volumes were forecast to rise over the medium term as new oilfields entered production. Significant petroleum reserves have been discovered off shore from the Bakassi peninsula, of which Cameroon assumed full sovereignty in 2013 (see Contemporary Political History—Foreign Affairs). Extraction of natural gas is under way; deposits of limestone are quarried; and there are plans to begin extraction of iron ore at Mbalam, bauxite at Ngaoundéré and diamonds (industrial and gem-quality) at Mobilong. In addition, Cameroon has largely undeveloped reserves of uranium and tin. The GDP of the mining sector declined by an average of 6.2% per year during 2007–12; the real GDP of the mining sector declined by 6.7% in 2011, but increased by 3.7% in 2012.

Manufacturing contributed an estimated 14.7% of GDP in 2012. The sector employed an estimated 7% of the working population in 1995. The sector is based on the processing both of indigenous primary products (petroleum-refining, agro-industrial activities) and of imported raw materials (an aluminium smelter uses alumina imported from Guinea). Manufacturing GDP increased at an average annual rate of 2.5% in 2007–12; the sector grew by 2.3% in 2011 and by 5.1% in 2012.

Construction contributed 5.7% of GDP in 2012. The sector employed 1.8% of the employed labour force in 1985. The GDP of the construction sector increased by an average of 5.7% per year during 2007–12; the sector grew by 6.7% in 2012.

In 2011 hydroelectric power installations supplied 73.3% of Cameroon's energy. A further 18.3% was produced by petroleum sources and 7.3% by gas. In 2012 imports of mineral fuels accounted for 30.4% of the value of total imports.

Services contributed 46.9% of GDP in 2012. The sector engaged 14.7% of the employed labour force in 1985. Cameroon receives royalties from the pipeline linking petroleum reserves at Doba, Chad, to the port of Kribi, which transports some 100,000 b/d. During 2007–12 the GDP of the services sector increased at an average annual rate of 4.1%; growth in 2012 was 5.5%.

In 2012 Cameroon recorded a visible merchandise trade deficit of US $278.5m., and there was a deficit of $956.0m. on the current account of the balance of payments. In 2012 the principal source of imports was Nigeria (providing 17.8% of the total); other major suppliers were France and the People's Republic of China. China was the principal market for exports in that year, taking 15.3% of the total; other significant purchasers were the Portugal, Netherlands, Spain, France and Italy. The principal exports in 2012 were mineral fuels, lubricants and related materials, machinery and mechanical appliances and electrical equipment and their parts, vegetables and vegetable products, chemicals and related products, and vehicles, aircraft, vessels and associated transport equipment. The principal imports in that year were mineral fuels, lubricants and related materials, prepared foodstuffs, beverages, spirits, vinegar, tobacco and their articles, and wood, wood charcoal, cork, and their articles. In January 2009 Cameroon became the first Central African country to sign an interim Economic Partnership Agreement with the EU: this provided for duty-free quota access for Cameroon's exports to EU markets, in parallel with the phased liberalization of 80% of imports from the EU over a 15-year period.

In 2012 there was an estimated budget deficit of 145,000m. francs CFA and it was projected to reach at 496,000m. in 2013. Cameroon's general government gross debt was 2,095,140m. francs CFA in 2012, equivalent to 16.2% of GDP. Cameroon's total external debt in 2011 was US $3,074m., of which $2,101m. was public and publicly guaranteed debt. In 2010, the cost of servicing long-term public and publicly guaranteed debt and repayments to the IMF was equivalent to 3.5% of the value of exports of goods, services and income (excluding workers' remittances). According to ILO, the annual rate of inflation averaged 2.6% in 2003–11. According to official figures, consumer prices increased by 2.4% in 2012. An estimated 7.5% of the labour force were unemployed in 2001.

Despite its rich natural resources, Cameroon's potential for sustained economic development has been notably hindered by its poor physical infrastructure, and its record of endemic fraud and corruption. In an effort to address the inadequacy of infrastructure, the Government embarked on an ambitious programme of public works in the 2000s: notably, the first phase of a new deep-water seaport at Kribi was expected to be operational in mid-2014; and what was termed a 'second generation' of infrastructural expansion, to include projects in the power, transport, water supply, roads, manufacturing and mining sectors, was planned from 2015. Under the budget for 2014, more than 30% of total projected expenditure of 3,312,000m. francs CFA was allocated to public investment. Priority projects for the Bakassi region, focusing especially on the livestock and fisheries sectors, were to be allocated some 1.4m. francs CFA in 2014. Assessing the economy in mid-2013, the IMF noted a modest increase in the rate of GDP growth in 2012, reflecting higher oil revenues (from marginally improved output) and strong growth in the agriculture and forestry sectors. However, it cautioned that apparently robust growth in GDP, projected to reach 5.5% by 2018, remained insufficient to enable Cameroon to achieve its aim of achieving emerging market status by 2035, and furthermore, had not been translated into adequate growth in GDP per head or improved social indicators. Vulnerabilities identified by the IMF included an accumulation of government arrears and payment obligations arising from fuel subsidies (retail fuel prices had remained frozen since 2008, and the cost of subsidies was expected to represent 3.2% of GDP in 2013), an increase in the level of external borrowing at non-concessionary rates, and an unfavourable environment for private investment. At the end of 2013 President Biya emphasized the need for the Government to address issues of purchasing power, employment and living conditions, and reiterated that levels of private investment in the economy remained inadequate. GDP growth for 2013 was estimated at 4.8%, below the Government's target of 6.1%.

PUBLIC HOLIDAYS

2015: 1 January (New Year's Day), 11 February (Youth Day), 3 April (Good Friday), 6 April (Easter Monday), 1 May (Labour Day), 14 May (Ascension Day), 20 May (National Day), 17 July* (Djoulde Soumae, end of Ramadan), 15 August (Assumption), 23 September* (Festival of Sheep), 25 December (Christmas).

* These holidays are dependent on the Islamic lunar calendar and may vary by one or two days from the dates given.

Statistical Survey

Source (unless otherwise stated): Institut National de la Statistique du Cameroun, BP 134, Yaoundé; tel. 2222-0445; fax 2223-2437; internet www.statistics-cameroon.org.

Area and Population

AREA, POPULATION AND DENSITY

Area (sq km)	
Continental	466,050
Maritime	9,600
Total	475,650*
Population (census results)	
9 April 1987	10,493,655
11 November 2005	
Males	8,408,495
Females	8,643,639
Total	17,052,134
Population (UN estimates at mid-year)†	
2012	21,699,633
2013	22,253,959
2014	22,818,632
Density (per sq km) at mid-2014	48.0‡

* 183,649 sq miles.

† Source: UN, *World Population Prospects: The 2012 Revision*.

‡ Continental area only.

POPULATION BY AGE AND SEX

(UN estimates at mid-2014)

	Males	Females	Total
0–14	4,908,647	4,840,365	9,749,012
15–64	6,164,862	6,171,934	12,336,796
65 and over	334,693	398,131	732,824
Total	11,408,202	11,410,430	22,818,632

Source: UN, *World Population Prospects: The 2012 Revision*.

PROVINCES

(official population projections, 2012)

	Area (sq km)*	Population	Density (per sq km)
Centre	68,953	3,730,784	54.1
Littoral	20,248	3,037,633	150.0
West	13,892	1,834,812	132.1
South-West	25,410	1,427,076	56.2
North-West	17,300	1,855,199	107.2
North	66,090	2,222,161	33.6
East	109,002	815,472	7.5
South	47,191	713,538	15.1
Adamaoua	63,701	1,080,500	16.9
Far North	34,263	3,669,624	107.1
Total	466,050	20,386,799	43.7

* Continental area only.

PRINCIPAL TOWNS

(population at 2005 census)

Douala	1,907,479	Maroua	201,371
Yaoundé (capital)	1,817,524	Kumba	144,268
Bamenda	269,530	Nkongsamba	104,050
Bafoussam	239,287	Limbé	84,223
Garoua	235,996		

Mid-2011 ('000, incl. suburbs, UN estimate): Yaoundé 2,432 (Source: UN, *World Urbanization Prospects: The 2011 Revision*).

BIRTHS AND DEATHS

(annual averages, UN estimates)

	1995–2000	2000–05	2005–10
Birth rate (per 1,000)	41.6	40.9	39.6
Death rate (per 1,000)	13.7	14.0	13.2

Source: UN, *World Population Prospects: The 2012 Revision*.

Life expectancy (years at birth): 54.1 (males 53.1; females 55.2) in 2011 (Source: World Bank, World Development Indicators database).

ECONOMICALLY ACTIVE POPULATION

(persons aged six years and over, mid-1985, official estimates)

	Males	Females	Total
Agriculture, hunting, forestry and fishing	1,574,946	1,325,925	2,900,871
Mining and quarrying	1,693	100	1,793
Manufacturing	137,671	36,827	174,498
Electricity, gas and water	3,373	149	3,522
Construction	65,666	1,018	66,684
Trade, restaurants and hotels	115,269	38,745	154,014
Transport, storage and communications	50,664	1,024	51,688
Financing, insurance, real estate and business services	7,447	562	8,009
Community, social and personal services	255,076	37,846	292,922
Sub-total	2,211,805	1,442,196	3,654,001
Activities not adequately defined	18,515	17,444	35,959
Total in employment	2,230,320	1,459,640	3,689,960
Unemployed	180,016	47,659	227,675
Total labour force	2,410,336	1,507,299	3,917,635

Source: ILO, *Yearbook of Labour Statistics*.

Mid-2013 ('000, estimates): Agriculture, etc. 3,571; Total labour force 8,377 (Source: FAO).

Health and Welfare

KEY INDICATORS

Total fertility rate (children per woman, 2011)	4.4
Under-5 mortality rate (per 1,000 live births, 2011)	127
HIV/AIDS (% of persons aged 15–49, 2012)	4.5
Physicians (per 1,000 head, 2009)	0.1
Hospital beds (per 1,000 head, 2010)	1.3
Health expenditure (2010): US $ per head (PPP)	122
Health expenditure (2010): % of GDP	5.1
Health expenditure (2010): public (% of total)	29.6
Access to water (% of persons, 2011)	74
Access to sanitation (% of persons, 2011)	48
Total carbon dioxide emissions ('000 metric tons, 2010)	7,235.0
Carbon dioxide emissions per head (metric tons, 2010)	0.4
Human Development Index (2012): ranking	150
Human Development Index (2012): value	0.495

For sources and definitions, see explanatory note on p. vi.

Agriculture

PRINCIPAL CROPS
('000 metric tons)

	2010	2011	2012
Rice, paddy	153	174	139*
Maize	1,670	1,572	1,622*
Millet	89*	95*	98†
Sorghum*	1,099	1,146	1,102
Potatoes	188	197	200†
Sweet potatoes	289	308	320†
Cassava (Manioc)	3,808	4,083	4,200†
Yams	500	517	520†
Taro (Coco yams)	1,470	1,569	1,600†
Sugar cane†	1,450	1,450	1,200
Beans, dry	354	366	375†
Groundnuts, with shell	536	564	570†
Oil palm fruit†	2,200	2,400	2,500
Melonseed†	62	42	43
Tomatoes	795	853	880†
Pumpkins, squash and gourds†	146	151	155
Onions, dry	65	184	185†
Bananas	1,334	1,395	1,400†
Plantains	3,182	3,426	3,450†
Avocados†	56	70	72
Pineapples	160	165	168
Coffee, green	67	65†	65†
Cocoa beans	264	272*	256*
Natural rubber	55	56†	56†

* Unofficial figure(s).
† FAO estimate(s).

Aggregate production ('000 metric tons, may include official, semi-official or estimated data): Total cereals 3,012 in 2010, 2,988 in 2011, 2,962 in 2012; Total roots and tubers 6,295 in 2010, 6,714 in 2011, 6,882 in 2012; Total vegetables (incl. melons) 2,115 in 2010, 2,335 in 2011, 2,379. in 2012; Total fruits (excl. melons) 4,864 in 2010, 5,219 in 2011, 5,256 in 2012.

Source: FAO.

LIVESTOCK
('000 head, year ending September)

	2010	2011	2012
Horses*	17	18	18
Asses*	40	40	40
Cattle	4,069	4,920	5,001
Pigs	2,150	2,290	1,690
Sheep*	3,850	3,900	4,000
Goats*	4,450	4,500	4,600
Chickens*	45,000	46,000	47,000

* FAO estimates.

Source: FAO.

LIVESTOCK PRODUCTS
('000 metric tons)

	2010	2011*	2012*
Cattle meat	102.0*	114.0	120.0
Sheep meat	16.5	16.8	17.4
Goat meat	20.1	20.3	20.5
Pig meat	37.8*	39.0	40.5
Chicken meat	68.0*	70.0	70.4
Game meat	66.5*	66.5	66.5
Cows' milk	175.0*	177.0	180.0
Sheep's milk	18.6*	18.6	18.7
Goats' milk	48.0*	48.5	50.0
Hen eggs	15.0*	15.0	15.5
Honey	4.2*	4.2	4.3

* FAO estimate(s).

Source: FAO.

Forestry

ROUNDWOOD REMOVALS
('000 cubic metres, excl. bark, FAO estimates, unless otherwise indicated)

	2010	2011	2012
Sawlogs, veneer logs and logs for sleepers	1,825*	1,825*	1,825
Other industrial wood	350	350	350
Fuel wood	9,906	9,993	10,081
Total	12,081	12,168	12,256

* Unofficial figure.

Source: FAO.

SAWNWOOD PRODUCTION
('000 cubic metres, incl. railway sleepers)

	2010	2011	2012
Total (all broadleaved)*	912	993	993

* Unofficial figures.

Source: FAO.

Fishing

('000 metric tons, live weight)

	2008*	2009	2010*
Capture*	139.2	140.0	140.0
Freshwater fishes	74.7	75.0	75.0
Cassava croaker	0.5	0.9	0.9
Sardinellas*	2.1	2.1	2.1
Bonga shad*	41.4	41.4	41.4
Aquaculture*	0.6	0.7	0.8
Total catch*	139.8	140.7	140.8

* FAO estimates.

2011: Figures assumed to be unchanged from 2010 (FAO estimates).

Source: FAO.

Mining

	2010	2011	2012
Crude petroleum (million barrels)	23.3	22.0	23.0
Gold (kg)*†	1,800	1,600	1,500
Pozzolan ('000 metric tons)*	600	600	600
Limestone ('000 metric tons)*	100	100	n.a.

* Estimated figures.

† From artisanal mining.

Source: US Geological Survey.

Industry

SELECTED PRODUCTS

('000 metric tons unless otherwise indicated)

	2008	2009	2010
Palm oil	226	238	327
Raw sugar	100	110	n.a.
Veneer sheets ('000 cu m)*	79	41	53
Plywood ('000 cu m)*	24	21	27
Jet fuels	85	292	332
Motor spirit (petrol)	399	350	383
Kerosene	261	n.a.	n.a.
Gas-diesel (distillate fuel) oil	658	610	n.a.
Residual fuel oils	380	259	329
Liquefied petroleum gas	17	15	n.a.
Cement	982	1,221	n.a.
Electric energy (million kWh)	5,681	5,783	5,899

* Unofficial figures.

2011 ('000 cu metres, unofficial figures): Veneer sheets 55; Plywood 23; Palm oil ('000 metric tons) 354.

2012 ('000 cu metres, unofficial figures): Veneer sheets 55; Plywood 23; Palm oil ('000 metric tons) 322.

Sources: UN Industrial Commodity Statistics Database; FAO.

Finance

CURRENCY AND EXCHANGE RATES

Monetary Units

100 centimes = 1 franc de la Coopération Financière en Afrique Centrale (CFA).

Sterling, Dollar and Euro Equivalents (31 December 2013)

£1 sterling = 783.286 francs CFA;
US $1 = 475.641 francs CFA;
€1 = 655.957 francs CFA;
10,000 francs CFA = £12.77 = $21.02 = €15.24.

Average Exchange Rate (francs CFA per US $)

2011	471.866
2012	510.527
2013	494.040

Note: An exchange rate of 1 French franc = 50 francs CFA, established in 1948, remained in force until January 1994, when the CFA franc was devalued by 50%, with the exchange rate adjusted to 1 French franc = 100 francs CFA. This relationship to French currency remained in effect with the introduction of the euro on 1 January 1999. From that date, accordingly, a fixed exchange rate of €1 = 655.957 francs CFA has been in operation.

BUDGET

('000 million francs CFA)

Revenue*	2011	2012†	2013‡
Petroleum revenue	638	693	711
Non-petroleum revenue	1,552	1,677	1,960
Direct taxes	405	471	520
Special tax on petroleum products	85	97	108
Taxes on international trade	274	294	361
Other taxes on goods and services	701	720	878
Non-tax revenue (excluding privatization proceeds)	88	94	93
Total	2,190	2,370	2,671

Expenditure	2011	2012†	2013‡
Current expenditure	1,842	1,807	2,352
Wages and salaries	685	706	803
Other goods and services	550	575	636
Interest on public debt	45	51	46
Subsidies and transfers	563	474	867
Capital expenditure	761	764	871
Externally financed investment	163	189	252
Domestically financed investment	563	513	554
Restructuring	35	61	65
Total	2,603	2,570	3,223

* Excluding grants received ('000 million francs CFA): 60 in 2011; 55 in 2012 (estimate); 56 in 2013 (projected figure).

† Estimates.

‡ Projected figures.

Source: IMF, *Cameroon: 2013 Article IV Consultation* (September 2013).

INTERNATIONAL RESERVES

(US $ million at 31 December)

	2010	2011	2012
Gold (national valuation)	22.69	45.78	50.43
IMF special drawing rights	27.13	24.92	23.45
Reserve position in IMF	1.34	1.38	1.42
Foreign exchange	3,614.17	3,172.42	3,355.83
Total	3,665.33	3,244.50	3,431.13

Source: IMF, *International Financial Statistics*.

MONEY SUPPLY

('000 million francs CFA at 31 December)

	2009	2010	2011
Currency outside depository corporations	477.87	541.75	577.89
Transferable deposits	834.44	907.34	1,017.98
Other deposits	881.33	1,026.38	1,147.74
Broad money	2,193.63	2,475.46	2,743.60

Source: IMF, *International Financial Statistics*.

COST OF LIVING

(Consumer Price Index; base: 2000 = 100)

	2006	2007	2008
Food	117.9	119.1	130.0
Clothing	100.4	100.3	100.8
Electricity, gas and other fuels	119.3	120.4	124.6
All items (incl. others)	116.2	117.2	123.5

All items: 127.2 in 2009; 128.9 in 2010; 132.7 in 2011.

Source: ILO.

2012 (Consumer Price Index; base: 2011 = 100): Food and non-alcoholic beverages 103.4; Alcoholic beverages and tobacco 102.6; Clothing and footwear 102.2; Housing, water, electricity, gas and other fuels 103.3; Health 100.3; Transportation 102.3; Communications 99.3; Education 103.3; All items 102.4.

NATIONAL ACCOUNTS

('000 million francs CFA at current prices)

Expenditure on the Gross Domestic Product

	2010	2011	2012
Government final consumption expenditure	1,358.4	1,457.2	1,548.2
Private final consumption expenditure	8,776.3	9,519.1	10,403.6
Gross capital formation	2,219.9	2,582.6	2,600.1
Change in inventories	8.0	1.0	18.7
Total domestic expenditure	12,362.6	13,559.9	14,570.6
Exports of goods and services	2,029.6	2,306.8	2,540.1
Less Imports of goods and services	2,692.5	3,321.1	3,595.9
GDP in purchasers' values	11,699.7	12,545.7	13,514.7
GDP at constant 2000 prices	9,156.7	9,535.8	9,973.4

Gross Domestic Product by Economic Activity

	2010	2011	2012
Agriculture	2,534.9	2,727.8	2,894.1
Mining and quarrying	777.5	960.8	1,099.5
Manufacturing	1,756.5	1,679.0	1,845.3
Electricity, gas and water	110.1	120.2	120.6
Construction	597.5	662.8	709.7
Wholesale and retail trade, restaurants and hotels	2,107.2	2,254.8	2,438.7
Finance, insurance and real estate	1,244.8	1,332.8	1,408.0
Transport and communication	757.7	818.7	862.6
Public administration and defence	878.6	943.6	1,033.0
Other services	134.7	140.2	147.1
Sub-total	10,899.5	11,640.7	12,558.6
Indirect taxes	864.1	973.2	1,030.2
Less Imputed bank service charge	64.0	68.2	74.1
GDP in purchasers' values	11,699.6	12,545.7	13,514.7

BALANCE OF PAYMENTS

(US $ million)

	2010	2011	2012
Exports of goods	4,311.7	5,632.8	5,752.7
Imports of goods	–4,625.9	–6,232.5	–6,031.2
Balance on goods	–314.2	–599.6	–278.5
Exports of services	1,286.8	1,851.9	1,623.5
Imports of services	–1,736.3	–1,955.3	–2119.6
Balance on goods and services	–763.7	–703.1	–774.5
Primary income received	93.1	163.2	205.7
Primary income paid	–331.7	–465.9	–650.5
Balance on goods, services and primary income	–1,002.3	–1,005.9	–1,219.3
Secondary income received	334.3	542.4	506.2
Secondary income paid	–188.3	–284.7	–242.9
Current balance	–856.3	–748.2	–956.0
Capital account (net)	147.0	130.4	117.1
Direct investment assets	–502.5	–186.8	284.0
Direct investment liabilities	537.8	652.4	525.8
Portfolio investment assets	–10.8	–55.7	19.2
Portfolio investment liabilities	85.2	–1.2	–20.7
Other investment assets	550.6	–34.6	105.3
Other investment liabilities	–132.8	11.3	206.5
Net errors and omissions	188.8	–93.3	–162.4
Reserves and related items	6.8	–325.7	118.7

Source: IMF, *International Financial Statistics*.

External Trade

PRINCIPAL COMMODITIES

(US $ million)

Imports c.i.f.	2010	2011	2012
Live animals and animal products	239.9	379.9	307.6
Fish, crustaceans, molluscs and other aquatic invertebrates	189.5	316.2	240.3
Frozen and whole fish	188.7	315.0	239.4
Vegetables and vegetable products	423.9	572.8	617.6
Cereals	327.2	471.6	517.8
Wheat and meslin	123.7	178.9	196.6
Rice	196.0	285.2	306.9
Prepared foodstuffs; beverages, spirits, vinegar; tobacco and articles thereof	225.3	312.7	303.6
Mineral products	1,570.6	313.7	2,150.3
Mineral fuels, oils, distillation products, etc.	1,421.1	152.2	1,977.8
Crude petroleum oils	1,231.8	—	1,300.9
Chemicals and related products	487.5	623.5	600.2
Pharmaceutical products	141.0	160.3	180.7
Plastics, rubber, and articles thereof	202.4	227.3	229.6
Pulp of wood, paper and paperboard, and articles thereof	118.9	154.1	137.6
Textiles and textile articles	136.4	207.3	157.0
Iron and steel, other base metals and articles of base metal	298.2	385.6	364.8
Articles of iron or steel	133.5	190.6	163.9
Machinery and mechanical appliances; electrical equipment; parts thereof	693.7	956.3	889.5
Machinery and boilers	431.0	556.5	534.5
Electrical and electronic equipment	262.7	399.9	355.0
Vehicles, aircraft, vessels and associated transport equipment	468.6	657.1	427.9
Vehicles other than railway, tramway	387.5	456.5	381.6
Cars (incl. station wagon)	129.8	155.9	147.1
Ships, boats and other floating structures	67.4	188.0	15.5
Total (incl. others)	5,133.3	5,074.4	6,515.1

Exports f.o.b.	2010	2011	2012
Vegetable and vegetable products	158.3	169.1	169.7
Edible fruit, nuts, peel of citrus fruit and melons	85.1	91.7	77.3
Bananas and plantains (fresh, dried)	82.1	88.7	74.9
Coffee, tea, mate and spices	67.0	72.9	87.3
Coffee	66.8	72.8	87.3
Prepared foodstuffs; beverages, spirits, vinegar; tobacco and articles thereof	777.8	678.3	547.3
Cocoa and cocoa products	717.8	616.6	491.4
Cocoa beans (whole, broken, raw, roasted)	611.0	512.3	394.8
Mineral products	1,924.7	14.8	2,386.5
Mineral fuels, oils, distillation products, etc.	1,921.7	11.8	2,374.3
Crude petroleum oils	1,415.7	—	1,834.1
Non-crude petroleum oils	496.8	1.4	527.5
Chemicals and related products	79.9	96.5	148.8
Plastics, rubber, and articles thereof	107.9	147.1	133.8
Rubber and articles thereof	96.6	132.5	123.4

Exports f.o.b.—*continued*	2010	2011	2012
Natural rubber, balata, gutta-percha etc.	95.6	131.3	121.5
Wood, wood charcoal, cork, and articles thereof	446.4	482.3	452.5
Wood and articles of wood and wood charcoal	446.4	482.3	452.4
Wood in the rough	144.4	141.7	121.8
Wood sawn (chipped lengthwise, sliced or peeled)	249.4	288.2	279.8
Textiles and textile articles	86.0	119.8	150.8
Cotton	82.8	118.0	146.3
Cotton (non-carded or combed)	81.3	114.0	143.7
Iron and steel, other base metals and articles of base metal	151.2	168.6	136.8
Aluminium and articles thereof	120.9	116.8	77.6
Aluminium (unwrought)	98.2	94.4	52.6
Machinery and mechanical appliances; electrical equipment; parts thereof	67.0	166.3	57.6
Machinery and boilers	60.2	122.0	52.3
Total (incl. others)	3,878.4	2,147.4	4,275.0

Source: Trade Map-Trade Competitiveness Map, International Trade Centre, www.intracen.org/marketanalysis.

PRINCIPAL TRADING PARTNERS
(US $ million)

Imports c.i.f.	2010	2011	2012
Argentina	29.9	63.2	51.7
Belgium	152.7	161.5	199.0
Brazil	89.3	155.3	103.4
China, People's Repub.	543.0	722.1	678.3
Côte d'Ivoire	47.9	19.1	133.8
Egypt	22.4	77.8	44.6
Equatorial Guinea	124.0	7.0	103.2
France (incl. Monaco)	748.1	879.3	778.3
Germany	190.6	228.4	191.5
Greece	21.0	135.2	46.2
India	121.0	157.2	257.8
Italy	124.4	197.9	207.8
Japan	155.0	170.3	157.7
Korea, Republic	55.1	37.8	36.0
Malaysia	32.0	54.3	74.6
Mauritania	80.4	111.3	56.5
Netherlands	83.9	103.8	266.2
Nigeria	933.7	19.9	1,157.7
South Africa	109.9	132.2	103.8
Spain	74.9	119.4	126.7
Thailand	155.2	194.5	193.3
Turkey	54.4	115.4	122.7
United Kingdom	73.0	0.0	152.7
USA	169.4	215.3	228.7
Viet Nam	44.2	116.5	62.9
Total (incl. others)	5,133.3	5,074.4	6,515.1

Exports f.o.b.	2010	2011	2012
Belgium	73.4	118.1	116.3
Central African Republic	53.8	24.8	33.2
Chad	337.8	53.5	78.3
China, People's Repub.	329.6	181.9	653.0
Colombia	0.0	26.8	0.0
Congo, Democratic Repub.	173.0	3.8	96.9
Congo, Repub.	0.0	114.7	88.5
Equatorial Guinea	36.2	51.1	99.1
France (incl. Monaco)	242.7	249.2	369.8
Gabon	57.6	66.6	81.5
Germany	63.1	76.4	34.0
Greece	3.7	54.8	2.2
India	138.4	12.3	106.6
Italy	376.6	139.5	223.1
Malaysia	63.5	63.5	49.9
Netherlands	508.6	415.3	481.3
Nigeria	28.3	46.5	149.7
Portugal	73.1	15.3	504.1
Spain	716.6	77.8	480.3
Togo	22.1	3.4	45.7
Turkey	23.5	27.5	19.3
United Kingdom	51.1	0.0	81.9
Uruguay	78.7	0.0	0.0
USA	219.7	79.1	178.7
Viet Nam	34.9	48.0	39.2
Total (incl. others)	3,878.4	2,147.4	4,275.0

Source: Trade Map-Trade Competitiveness Map, International Trade Centre, www.intracen.org/marketanalysis.

Transport

RAILWAYS
(traffic, year ending 30 June)

	2008	2009	2010
Passengers carried ('000)	1,201.6	1,363.8	1,405.0
Passenger-km (million)	379.1	434.7	485.0
Freight carried ('000 tonnes)	1,582.8	1,576.6	1,654.0
Freight ton-km (million)	978.3	1,014.8	1,078.0

ROAD TRAFFIC
(motor vehicles in use)

	2007	2008	2009
Passenger cars	190,341	197,383	204,292
Buses and coaches	17,287	17,926	18,554
Vans and lorries	51,842	53,790	55,642
Motorcycles and mopeds	72,351	75,029	77,655

SHIPPING

Flag Registered Fleet
(at 31 December)

	2011	2012	2013
Number of vessels	52	53	53
Total displacement ('000 grt)	413.7	414.0	296.3

Source: Lloyd's List Intelligence (www.lloydslistintelligence.com).

International Sea-borne Freight Traffic
(freight traffic at Douala, '000 metric tons)

	2008	2009	2011
Goods loaded	2,160	1,824	2,184
Goods unloaded	4,848	5,352	6,348

Note: Data for 2010 were not available.

Source: UN, *Monthly Bulletin of Statistics*.

CIVIL AVIATION
(traffic on scheduled services)

	2006	2007	2008
Kilometres flown (million)	12	13	13
Passengers carried ('000)	425	453	471
Passenger-km (million)	861	910	930
Total ton-km (million)	108	111	113

Source: UN, *Statistical Yearbook*.

Passengers carried ('000): 171.0 in 2011; 248.0 in 2012 (Source: World Bank, World Development Indicators database).

Tourism

FOREIGN VISITORS BY COUNTRY OF ORIGIN*

	2006	2007	2008
Belgium	3,960	4,616	5,673
Canada	2,723	3,536	3,420
France	38,782	43,814	44,619
Italy	4,341	4,358	4,565
Netherlands	3,607	3,889	3,568
Switzerland	2,964	3,195	3,682
United Kingdom	6,847	7,682	18,825
USA	9,862	9,494	10,223
Total (incl. others)	214,360	262,340	297,983

* Arrivals at hotels and similar establishments.

Total tourist arrivals ('000): 573 in 2010; 604 in 2011; 817 in 2012 (provisional).

Receipts from tourism (US $ million, excl. passenger transport): 270 in 2009; 159 in 2010.

Source: World Tourism Organization.

Communications Media

	2010	2011	2012
Telephones ('000 main lines in use)	539.5	669.0	737.4
Mobile cellular telephones ('000 subscribers)	8,636.7	10,486.6	13,108.1
Broadband subscribers	1,000	1,100	1,100

Internet users ('000): 749.6 in 2009.

Source: International Telecommunication Union.

Education

(2011/12 unless otherwise indicated)

	Institutions	Teachers	Students ('000) Males	Females	Total
Pre-primary	1,371*	17,546	193.2	195.4	388.6
Primary	9,459*	84,467	2,064.4	1,784.2	3,848.6
Secondary: general	700*	47,088†	704.3	649.6	1,353.9
Secondary: technical/vocational	324*	18,173†	224.0	135.5	359.5
Universities	6‡	4,235§	141.1†	103.1†	244.2†

* 1997/98.
† 2010/11.
‡ 1996/97.
§ 2009/10.

Source: UNESCO Institute for Statistics.

Pupil-teacher ratio (primary education, UNESCO estimate): 45.6 in 2011/12 (Source: UNESCO Institute for Statistics).

Adult literacy rate (UNESCO estimates): 71.3% (males 78.3%; females 64.8%) in 2010 (Source: UNESCO Institute for Statistics).

Directory

The Government

HEAD OF STATE

President: PAUL BIYA (took office 6 November 1982; elected 14 January 1984; re-elected 24 April 1988, 11 October 1992, 12 October 1997, 11 October 2004 and 9 October 2011).

CABINET
(April 2014)

The Government is a coalition of the Rassemblement Démocratique du Peuple Camerounais (RDPC), the Front pour le Salut National du Cameroun (FSNC), the Union Nationale pour la Démocratie et le Progrès (UNDP) and the Alliance Nationale pour la Démocratie et le Progrès (ANDP).

Prime Minister: PHILÉMON YANG (RDPC).

Deputy Prime Minister, Minister-delegate at the Presidency in charge of Relations with the Assemblies: AMADOU ALI (RDPC).

Ministers of State

Minister of State, Minister of Tourism and Leisure: MAIGARI BELLO BOUBA (UNDP).

Minister of State, Minister of Justice and Keeper of the Seals: LAURENT ESSO (RDPC).

Ministers

Minister of Territorial Administration and Decentralization: RENÉ EMMANUEL SADI (RDPC).

Minister of Social Affairs: CATHERINE LOUISE MARINETTE BAKANG MBOCK (RDPC).

Minister of Agriculture and Rural Development: LAZARE ESSIMI MENYE.

Minister of Art and Culture: AMA TUTU MUNA (RDPC).

Minister of Trade: LUC MAGLOIRE MBARGA ATANGANA.

Minister of Communication: BAKARY ISSA TCHIROMA (FSNC).

Minister of Estates and Land Affairs: JACQUELINE KOUNG À BISSIKE.

Minister of Water and Energy: BASILE ATANGANA KOUNA.

Minister of the Economy, Planning and Land Settlement: EMMANUEL NGANOU DJOUMESSI (RDPC).

Minister of Basic Education: YOUSSOUF ADIDJA ALIM.

Minister of Livestock, Fisheries and Animal Industries: Dr TAIGA.

Minister of Employment and Professional Training: ZACHARIE PÉRÉVET (RDPC).

Minister of Secondary Education: LOUIS BAPES BAPES (RDPC).

Minister of Higher Education: JACQUES FAME NDONGO (RDPC).

Minister of the Environment, the Protection of Nature and Sustainable Development: PIERRE HÉLÉ (RDPC).

Minister of Finance: ALAMINE OUSMANE MEY.

Minister of Public Service and Administrative Reform: MICHEL ANGE ANGOUIN (RDPC).

Minister of Forests and Wildlife: PHILIP NGWESE NGOLE (RDPC).

Minister of Housing and Urban Development: JEAN CLAUDE MBWETCHOU (RDPC).

Minister of Youth and Civic Education: ISMAËL BIDOUNG KPWATT.

Minister of Mines, Industry and Technological Development: EMMANUEL BONDE.

Minister of Small and Medium-sized Enterprises, Social Economy and Crafts: LAURENT SERGE ETOUNDI NGOA (RDPC).

Minister of Posts and Telecommunications: JEAN-PIERRE BYITI BI ESSAM.

Minister of Women's Affairs and the Family: MARIE THÉRÈSE ABENA ONDUA.

Minister of Scientific Research and Innovation: MADELEINE TCHUENTÉ (RDPC).

Minister of External Relations: PIERRE MOUKOKO MBONJO.

Minister of Public Health: ANDRÉ MAMA FOUDA (RDPC).

Minister of Sports and Physical Education: ADOUM GAROUA.

Minister of Transport: ROBERT NKILI.

Minister of Labour and Social Security: GRÉGOIRE OWONA (RDPC).

Minister of Public Works: PATRICE AMBA SALLA.

Ministers-delegate

Minister-delegate at the Presidency, in charge of Defence: EDGARD ALAIN MEBE NGO'O.

Minister-delegate at the Presidency, in charge of the Contrôle Superieur de l'État: HENRI EYEBE AYISSI.

Minister-delegate at the Presidency, in charge of Public Markets: ABBA SADOU.

Minister-delegate at the Ministry of Territorial Administration and Decentralization, in charge of Decentralized Territorial Collectivities: JULES DORET NDONGO (RDPC).

Minister-delegate at the Ministry of Agriculture and Rural Development, in charge of Rural Development: CLÉMENTINE ANTOINETTE ANANGA MESSINA.

Minister-delegate at the Ministry of the Environment, the Protection of Nature and Sustainable Development: NANA ABOUBAKAR DJALLOH (UNDP).

Minister-delegate at the Ministry of the Economy, Planning and Land Settlement, in charge of Planning: ABDOULAYE YAOUBA.

Minister-delegate at the Ministry of Finance: PIERRE TITTI.

Minister-delegate at the Ministry of Justice, Keeper of the Seals: JEAN PIERRE FOGUI.

Minister-delegate at the Ministry of External Relations, in charge of Relations with the Commonwealth: JOSEPH DION NGUTÉ (RDPC).

Minister-delegate at the Ministry of External Relations, in charge of Relations with the Islamic World: ADOUM GARGOUM (RDPC).

Minister-delegate at the Ministry of Transport: MEFIRO OUMAROU.

Secretaries of State

Secretary of State for Defence, in charge of the National Gendarmerie: JEAN BAPTISTE BOKAM.

Secretary of State for Defence, in charge of Former Combatants and War Victims: ISSA KOUMPA.

Secretary of State for Basic Education: BENOÎT NDONG SOUMHET.

Secretary of State for Secondary Education, in charge of Normal Education: MOULOUNA FOUTSOU.

Secretary of State for Forests and Wildlife: ALHADJI KOULSOUMI BOUKAR.

Secretary of State for Housing and Urban Development, in charge of Urban Development: MARIE ROSE DIBONG.

Secretary of State for Justice, in charge of Prisons: JÉRÔME PENBAGA DOOH.

Secretary of State for Industry, Mines and Technological Development: CALISTUS GENTRY FUH.

Secretary of State for Public Health, in charge of the Fight Against Epidemics and Pandemics: ALIM HAYATOU (RDPC).

Secretary of State for Public Works, in charge of Roads: HANS NYETAM NYETAM.

Other Officials with the Rank of Minister

Ministers, Chargés de Mission at the Presidency: HAMADOU MOUSTAPHA, PAUL ATANGA NJI, VICTOR MENGOT ARREY NKONGHO, PHILIPPE MBARGA MBOA.

MINISTRIES

Office of the President: Palais de l'Unité, Yaoundé; tel. 2223-4025; internet www.camnet.cm/celcom/homepr.htm.

Office of the Prime Minister: Yaoundé; tel. 2223-8005; fax 2223-5735; e-mail spm@spm.gov.cm; internet www.spm.gov.cm.

Ministry of Agriculture and Rural Development: Quartier Administratif, Yaoundé; tel. 2223-1190; fax 2222-5091; internet www.minader.cm.

Ministry of Art and Culture: Quartier Hippodrome, Yaoundé; tel. 2222-6579; fax 2223-6579.

Ministry of Basic Education: Quartier Administratif, Yaoundé; tel. 2223-4050; fax 2223-1262.

Ministry of Communication: Quartier Hippodrome, Yaoundé; tel. 2223-3974; fax 2223-3022; e-mail mincom@mincom.gov.cm; internet www.mincom.gov.cm.

Ministry of Defence: Quartier Général, Yaoundé; tel. 2223-4055.

Ministry of the Economy, Planning and Land Settlement: Yaoundé; e-mail lecinfosminepat@gmail.com; internet www.minepat.info.

Ministry of Employment and Professional Training: Yaoundé; tel. 2222-0186; fax 2223-1820.

Ministry of the Environment, the Protection of Nature and Sustainable Development: Yaoundé.

Ministry of Estates and Land Affairs: Yaoundé.

Ministry of External Relations: Yaoundé; tel. 2220-3850; fax 2220-1133; internet www.diplocam.gov.cm.

Ministry of Finance: BP 13750, Quartier Administratif, Yaoundé; tel. and fax 7723-2099; internet www.camnet.cm/investir/minfi/.

Ministry of Forests and Wildlife: BP 1341, Yaoundé; tel. 2220-4258; fax 2222-9487; e-mail onadef@camnet.cm; internet www.camnet.cm/investir/envforet/index.htm.

Ministry of Higher Education: BP 1739, Yaoundé; tel. 2222-1370; fax 2222-9724; e-mail cab@minesup.gov.cm; internet www.minesup.gov.cm.

Ministry of Housing and Urban Development: Yaoundé; tel. 2223-2282.

Ministry of Justice: Quartier Administratif, Yaoundé; tel. 2223-4292; fax 2223-0005; e-mail jpouloumou@yahoo.fr.

Ministry of Labour and Social Security: Yaoundé.

Ministry of Livestock, Fisheries and Animal Industries: Yaoundé; tel. 2222-3311.

Ministry of Mines, Industry and Technological Development: Quartier Administratif, BP 955, Yaoundé; tel. 2223-3404; fax 2223-3400; e-mail minmee@camnet.cm; internet www.camnet.cm/investir/minmee.

Ministry of Posts and Telecommunications: Quartier Administratif, Yaoundé; tel. 2223-0615; fax 2223-3159; internet www.minpostel.gov.cm.

Ministry of Public Health: Quartier Administratif, Yaoundé; tel. and fax 2222-0233; internet www.minsante.gov.cm.

Ministry of Public Service and Administrative Reform: Yaoundé; tel. 2222-0356; fax 2223-0800.

Ministry of Public Works: Quartier Administratif, Yaoundé; tel. 2222-1916; fax 2222-0156.

Ministry of Scientific Research and Innovation: Yaoundé; tel. 2222-1334; fax 2222-1336; internet www.minresi.net.

Ministry of Secondary Education: BP 16185, Yaoundé; tel. 2222-3843; internet www.minesec.cm.

Ministry of Small and Medium-sized Enterprises, Social Economy and Crafts: BP 6096, Yaoundé; tel. 2223-2388; fax 2223-2180; e-mail enngoal1@yahoo.fr.

Ministry of Social Affairs: Quartier Administratif, Yaoundé; tel. 2222-2958; fax 2223-1162; e-mail infos@minas.cm; internet www.minas.cm.

Ministry of Sports and Physical Education: POB 1016, Yaoundé; tel. 2223-1201; fax 2223-2610; e-mail minsepinfos@yahoo.fr; internet www.minsep.cm.

Ministry of Territorial Administration and Decentralization: Quartier Administratif, Yaoundé; tel. 2223-4546; fax 2222-3735; e-mail minatdcm@minatd.cm; internet minatd.cm.

Ministry of Tourism and Leisure: BP 266, Yaoundé; tel. 2222-4411; fax 2222-1295; e-mail mintour@camnet.cm; internet www.mintour.gov.cm.

Ministry of Trade: Yaoundé; tel. 2223-0216.

Ministry of Transport: Quartier Administratif, Yaoundé; tel. 2222-8709; fax 2223-2238; e-mail minetatcam@gmail.com; internet www.mint.gov.cm.

Ministry of Water and Energy: Quartier Administratif, BP 70, Yaoundé; tel. 2222-3400; fax 2223-3400; e-mail courrierminee@yahoo.fr; internet www.minee.cm.

Ministry of Women's Affairs and the Family: Quartier Administratif, Yaoundé; tel. 2223-2550; fax 2223-3965; e-mail cab_minproff@yahoo.fr; internet www.minproff.gov.cm.

Ministry of Youth and Civic Education: Quartier Administratif, Yaoundé; tel. 2223-3257; e-mail minjes@minjes.gov.cm; internet www.minjes.gov.cm.

President

Election, 9 October 2011

Candidate	Votes	% of votes
Paul Biya (RDPC)	3,772,527	77.99
Ni John Fru Ndi (SDF)	518,175	10.71
Garga Haman Adji (ADD)	155,348	3.21
Adamou Ndam Njoya (UDC)	83,860	1.73
Ayah Paul Abine (PAPE)	61,158	1.26
Others*	246,181	5.09
Total	4,837,249	100.00

* There were 18 other candidates.

Legislature

SENATE

Senate: Yaoundé.

President: MARCEL NIAT NJIFENJI.

Election, 14 April 2013

Party	Seats
RDPC	56
SDF	14
Total	70*

* In addition to the 70 elected seats, a further 30 senators are appointed by the President of the Republic of Cameroon.

NATIONAL ASSEMBLY

National Assembly: Yaoundé; tel. 2222-8071; fax 2222-0979; internet www.assemblenationale.cm.

President: CAVAYE YÉGUIÉ DJIBRIL.

General Election, 30 September 2013

Party	Seats
RDPC	148
SDF	18
UNDP	5
UDC	4
UPC	3
MDR	1
MRC	1
Total	180

Election Commission

Elections Cameroon (ELECAM): BP 13506, Yaoundé; tel. 2221-2540; fax 2221-2539; e-mail elecam@elecam.cm; internet www.elecam.cm; f. 2006 to replace Observatoire National des Elections/National Elections Observatory; 12 mems appointed by the Head of State in consultation with political parties represented in the National Assembly and civil society; Pres. SAMUEL FONKAM AZU'U; Dir-Gen. MOHAMAN SANI TANIMOU.

Political Organizations

At December 2012 a total of 282 political parties were registered with the Ministry of Territorial Administration and Decentralization, of which the most important are listed below:

Action for Meritocracy and Equal Opportunity Party (AMEC): BP 20354, Yaoundé; tel. 9991-9154 (mobile); fax 2223-4642; e-mail Tabijoachim@yahoo.fr; Leader JOACHIM TABI OWONO.

Alliance pour la Démocratie et le Développement (ADD): BP 231, Garoua; Sec.-Gen. GARGA HAMAN ADJI.

Alliance des Forces Progressistes (AFP): BP 4724, Douala; f. 2002; Leader BERNARD MUNA.

Alliance Nationale pour la Démocratie et le Progrès: BP 5019, Yaoundé; tel. and fax 2220-9898; Pres. HAMADOU MOUSTAPHA.

Cameroon Anglophone Movement (CAM): advocates a federal system of govt.

Front pour le Salut National du Cameroun (FSNC): Yaoundé; f. 2007; Pres. BAKARY ISSA TCHIROMA.

Mouvement Africain pour la Nouvelle Indépendance et la Démocratie (MANIDEM): BP 10298, Douala; tel. 3342-0076; f. 1995; fmrly a faction of the UPC; Leader PIERRE ABANDA KPAMA.

Mouvement pour la Défense de la République (MDR): BP 6438, Yaoundé; tel. 2220-8982; f. 1991; Leader DAKOLE DAÏSSALA.

Mouvement des Démocrates Camerounais pour la Paix (MDCP): BP 3274, Yaoundé; tel. 2220-8173; f. 2000; Leader GAMEL ADAMOU ISSA.

Mouvement pour la Démocratie et le Progrès (MDP): BP 8379, Douala; tel. 2239-1174; f. 1992; Pres. ARON MUKURI MAKA; Sec.-Gen. RENÉ MBANDA MANDENGUE.

Mouvement pour la Jeunesse du Cameroun (MLJC): BP 26, Eséka; tel. 7714-8750 (mobile); fax 2228-6019; Pres. DIEUDONNÉ TINA; Sec.-Gen. JEAN LÉONARD POM.

Mouvement pour la Libération et le Développement du Cameroun (MLDC): BP 886, Edéa; tel. 3346-4431; fax 3346-4847; f. 1998 by a breakaway faction of the MLJC; Leader MARCEL YONDO.

Mouvement Progressiste (MP): BP 2500, Douala; tel. 9987-2513 (mobile); e-mail djombyves@yahoo.fr; f. 1991; Pres. JEAN JACQUES EKINDI.

Mouvement pour la Renaissance du Cameroun (MRC): Yaoundé; Pres. Prof. MAURICE KAMTO.

Nouvelle Force Populaire (NFP): BP 1139, Douala; f. 2002; Leader LÉANDRE DJINO.

Parti des Démocrates Camerounais (PDC): Nlongkak, BP 4070, Yaoundé; tel. 9961-5297 (mobile); e-mail contact@pdc-cpd.org; internet www.pdc-cpd.org/fr; f. 1991; Leader LOUIS-TOBIE MBIDA; Sec.-Gen. ARNOLD ALBERT MBITI.

Parti Libéral-Démocrate (PLD): BP 4764, Douala; tel. 3337-3792; f. 1991; Pres. JEAN ROBERT LIAPOE; Sec.-Gen. JEAN TCHUENTE.

Parti Républicain du Peuple Camerounais (PRPC): BP 6654, Yaoundé; tel. 2222-2120; f. 1991; Leader ANDRÉ ATEBA NGOUA.

Rassemblement Camerounais pour la République (RCR): BP 452, Bandjoun; tel. 3344-1349; f. 1992; Leader SAMUEL WAMBO.

Rassemblement Démocratique du Peuple Camerounais (RDPC): Palais des Congrès, 2e étage, BP 867, Yaoundé; tel. 2221-2417; fax 2221-2508; e-mail rdpcpdm@rdpcpdm.cm; internet www.rdpcpdm.cm; f. 1966 as Union Nationale Camerounaise by merger of the Union Camerounaise, the Kamerun National Democratic Party and four opposition parties; adopted present name in 1985; sole legal party 1972–90; Pres. PAUL BIYA; Sec.-Gen. RENÉ EMMANUEL SADI.

Social Democratic Front (SDF): BP 490, Mankon, Bamenda; tel. 3336-3949; fax 3336-2991; e-mail webmaster@sdfparty.org; internet www.sdfparty.org; f. 1990; Chair. NI JOHN FRU NDI; Sec.-Gen. Dr ELIZABETH TAMAJONG.

Southern Cameroons National Council (SCNC): BP 131, Eyumojock; tel. 7796-4888 (mobile); e-mail scnc@scncforsoutherncameroons.net; internet www.scncforsoutherncameroons.net; f. 1995; supports the establishment of an independent republic in anglophone Cameroon; Chair. Chief ETTE OTUN AYAMBA.

Union Démocratique du Cameroun (UDC): BP 1638, Yaoundé; tel. 2222-9545; fax 2222-4620; f. 1991; Leader ADAMOU NDAM NJOYA.

Union des Forces Démocratiques du Cameroun (UFDC): BP 7190, Yaoundé; tel. 2223-1644; f. 1991; Leader VICTORIN HAMENI BIELEU.

Union des Mouvements Socialistes (UMS): f. 2011; Leader PIERRE KWEMO.

Union Nationale pour la Démocratie et le Progrès (UNDP): BP 656, Douala; tel. 2220-9898; f. 1991; split in 1995; Chair. MAIGARI BELLO BOUBA; Sec.-Gen. PIERRE FLAMBEAU NGAYAP.

Union Nationale pour l'Indépendance Totale du Cameroun (UNITOC): BP 1301, Yaoundé; tel. 2222-8002; f. 2002; Pres. DANIEL TATSINFANG; Sec.-Gen. JEAN CLAUDE TIENTCHEU FANSI.

Union des Populations du Cameroun (UPC): BP 2860, Yaoundé; tel. 9569-5634 (mobile); fax 3342-8629; e-mail upcbcd@yahoo.fr; internet www.upc-cameroun.org; f. 1948; Pres. ALEXIS NDEMA SAMÉ; Sec.-Gen. ALBERT MOUTOUDOU.

Diplomatic Representation

EMBASSIES AND HIGH COMMISSIONS IN CAMEROON

Algeria: 433 rue 1828, Quartier Bastos, BP 1619, Yaoundé; tel. 2221-5351; fax 2231-5354; Ambassador TOUFIK MILAT.

Belgium: rue 1792, Quartier Nouveau Bastos, Yaoundé; tel. 2204-7040; fax 2220-0521; e-mail yaounde@diplobel.fed.be; internet www.diplomatie.be/yaounde; Ambassador JAN DE BRUYNE.

Brazil: rue 1828, Quartier Bastos, BP 16227, Yaoundé; tel. 2220-1085; fax 2220-2048; e-mail embiaunde@cameroun-online.com; Ambassador NEI FUTURO BITENCOURT.

Canada: Immeuble Stamatiades, pl. de l'Hôtel de Ville, BP 572, Yaoundé; tel. 2223-2311; fax 2222-1090; e-mail yunde@international.gc.ca; internet www.canadainternational.gc.ca/cameroon-cameroun; High Commissioner BENOÎT-PIERRE LARAMÉE.

Central African Republic: 41 rue 1863, Quartier Bastos, Montée du Carrefour de la Vallée Nlongkak, BP 396, Yaoundé; tel. and fax 2220-5155; Ambassador LOUIS OGUÉRÉ NGAÏKOUMON.

Chad: Quartier Bastos, BP 506, Yaoundé; tel. 2221-0624; fax 2220-3940; e-mail ambatchad_yaounde@yahoo.fr; Ambassador YOOSSEM-KONTOU NOUDJIAMLAO.

China, People's Republic: Nouveau Bastos, BP 1307, Yaoundé; tel. 2221-0083; fax 2221-4395; e-mail chinaemb_cm@mfa.gov.cn; Ambassador WO RUIDI.

Congo, Democratic Republic: BP 632, Yaoundé; tel. 2220-5103; Chargé d'affaires a.i. FRANÇOIS LUAMBO.

Congo, Republic: Rheinallée 45, BP 1422, Yaoundé; tel. 2221-2458; fax 2221-1733; Ambassador ERIC EPENI OBONDZO.

Côte d'Ivoire: rue 1983, Résidence 140, Quartier Bastos, BP 1715, Yaoundé; tel. 2221-3291; fax 2221-3592; e-mail contact@ambaci-cam.org; internet www.ambacicam.org; Ambassador DOSSO ADAMA.

Egypt: 718 rue 1828, Quartier Bastos, BP 809, Yaoundé; tel. 2220-3922; fax 2220-2647; Ambassador SHERIF SALAH ELDIN EL-LEITHY.

Equatorial Guinea: 82 rue 1851, Quartier Bastos, BP 277, Yaoundé; tel. and fax 2221-0804; Ambassador ANASTASIO ASUMU MUM MUNOZ.

France: Plateau Atémengué, BP 1631, Yaoundé; tel. 2222-7900; fax 2222-7909; e-mail chancellerie.yaounde-amba@diplomatie.gouv.fr; internet www.ambafrance-cm.org; Ambassador CHRISTINE ROBICHON.

Gabon: Quartier Bastos, Ekoudou, BP 4130, Yaoundé; tel. 2220-2966; fax 2221-0224; Ambassador PAUL PATRICK BIFFOT.

Germany: Nouvelle Route Bastos, Bastos-Usine, BP 1160, Yaoundé; tel. 2221-0056; fax 2221-6211; e-mail info@jaun.diplo.de; internet www.jaunde.diplo.de; Ambassador Dr KLAUS-LUDWIG KEFERSTEIN.

Holy See: rue du Vatican, BP 210, Yaoundé (Apostolic Nunciature); tel. 2220-0475; fax 2220-7513; e-mail nonce.cam@sat.signis.net; Apostolic Pro-Nuncio Most Rev. PIERO PIOPPO (Titular Archbishop of Torcello).

Israel: rue du Club Olympique à Bastos 154, Longkak, BP 5934, Yaoundé; tel. 2221-1291; fax 2221-0823; e-mail info@yaounde.mfa.gov.il; internet yaounde.mfa.gov.il; Ambassador NADAV COHEN.

Italy: Plateau Bastos, BP 827, Yaoundé; tel. 2220-3376; fax 2221-5250; e-mail ambasciata.yaounde@esteri.it; internet www.ambyaounde.esteri.it; Ambassador STEFANO PONTESILLI.

Japan: 1513 rue 1828, Quartier Bastos, Ekoudou, BP 6868, Yaoundé; tel. 2220-6202; fax 2220-6203; internet www.cmr.emb-japan.go.jp; Ambassador TSUTOMU ARAI.

Korea, Democratic People's Republic: Yaoundé; Ambassador KIM RYONG YONG.

Korea, Republic: BP 13286, Yaoundé; tel. 2220-3756; fax 2220-3757; e-mail korean.embassy.yaounde@gmail.com; Ambassador CHO JUNE-HYUCK.

Liberia: Quartier Bastos, Ekoudou, BP 1185, Yaoundé; tel. 2221-1296; fax 2220-9781; Ambassador MASSA JAMES.

Libya: Quartier Nylon Nlongkak, Quartier Bastos, BP 1980, Yaoundé; tel. 2220-4138; fax 2221-4298; Chargé d'affaires a.i. IBRAHIM O. AMAMI.

Morocco: 32 rue 1793, Quartier Bastos, BP 1629, Yaoundé; tel. 2220-5092; fax 2220-3793; e-mail ambmaroccam@yahoo.fr; Ambassador LAHCEN SAIL.

Nigeria: Quartier Bastos, BP 448, Yaoundé; tel. 2222-3455; fax 2223-5551; e-mail nhc_yde@yahoo.com; High Commissioner HADIZA MUSTAPHA.

Russia: Quartier Bastos, BP 488, Yaoundé; tel. 2220-1714; fax 2220-7891; e-mail russie.ambassade@orangemail.cm; internet fr.rusembcam.org; Ambassador NIKOLAY RATSIBORINSKIY.

Saudi Arabia: rue 1951, Quartier Bastos, BP 1602, Yaoundé; tel. 2221-2675; fax 2220-6689; internet cmemb@mofa.gov.sa; Ambassador MUHAMMAD BIN SOULEMAN AL-MASHAR.

South Africa: rue 1801, Quartier Bastos, BP 1636, Yaoundé; tel. 2220-0438; fax 2220-0995; e-mail yaounde@foreign.gov.za; High Commissioner N. M. TSHEOLE.

Spain: blvd de l'URSS, Quartier Bastos, BP 877, Yaoundé; tel. 2220-3543; fax 2220-6491; e-mail embespcm@mail.mae.es; Ambassador MARCELINO CABANAS ANSORENA.

Switzerland: angle rues 1811 et 1814, Quartier Bastos, BP 1169, Yaoundé; tel. 2220-5067; fax 2220-9386; internet www.eda.admin.ch/yaounde; Ambassador CLAUDE ALTERMATT.

Tunisia: rue de Rotary, Quartier Bastos, BP 6074, Yaoundé; tel. 2220-3368; fax 2221-0507; e-mail at.yaounde@camnet.cm; Ambassador ABDERRAZAK LANDOULSI.

Turkey: blvd de l'URSS 1782, Quartier Bastos, BP 35155, Yaoundé; tel. 2220-6775; fax 2220-6778; Ambassador OMER FARUK DOGAN.

United Kingdom: ave Winston Churchill, BP 547, Yaoundé; tel. 2222-0545; fax 2222-0148; e-mail BHC.yaounde@fco.gov.uk; internet ukincameroon.fco.gov.uk; High Commissioner JOHN BRIAN OLLEY.

USA: ave Rosa Parks, BP 817, Yaoundé; tel. and fax 2220-1500; internet yaounde.usembassy.gov; Chargé d'affaires a.i. GREGORY THOME.

Judicial System

The independence of the judiciary is enshrined in the Constitution and judicial power is exercised by the Supreme Court, courts of appeal and tribunals. The President of the Republic guarantees the independence of the judicial power and appoints members of the bench and of the legal department. He is assisted in this task by the Higher Judicial Council (HJC), which gives him its opinion on all nominations for the bench and on disciplinary action against judicial and legal officers. The HJC is composed of six members who serve five-year terms. Justice is rendered in Cameroon by: courts of first instance; high courts; military courts; courts of appeal and the Supreme Court. In 2012 a Special Criminal Court was established in Yaoundé; the new court was to conduct trials relating to the embezzlement of public funds.

Supreme Court: Yaoundé; tel. 2222-0164; fax 2222-0576; internet www.coursupreme.cm; consists of a president, 9 titular and substitute judges, a procureur général, an avocat général, deputies to the procureur général, a registrar and clerks; Pres. ALEXIS DIPANDA MOUELLE.

Attorney-General: MARTIN RISSOUCK MOULONG.

Religion

According to the 2005 census, 69% of the population were Christians (38% Roman Catholics, 26% Protestants), 10% adhered to traditional religious beliefs, and 21% were Muslims.

CHRISTIANITY

Protestant Churches

Conseil des Eglises Protestantes du Cameroun (CEPCA): BP 491, Yaoundé; tel. and fax 2223-8117; e-mail femec_org@yahoo.fr; f. 1968; name changed as above in 2005; 11 mem. churches; Pres. Rev. Dr ROBERT NGOYECK; Admin. Sec. Rev. Dr PHILIPPE NGUETE.

Church of the Lutheran Brethren of Cameroon: POB 16, Garoua; tel. and fax 2227-2573; e-mail eflcsynode@yahoo.fr; Pres. Rev. ROBERT GOYEK DAGA; 105,994 mems (2010).

Eglise Evangélique du Cameroun (Evangelical Church of Cameroon—EEC): 13 rue Alfred Saker, Akwa, Centenaire, BP 89, Douala; tel. 3342-3611; fax 3342-4011; e-mail eec@eeccameroun.org; internet www.eeccameroun.org; f. 1957; 2m. mems; Pres. Rev. ISAAC BATOMEN HENGA; Sec. Rev. JEAN SAMUEL HENDJE TOYA.

Eglise Presbytérienne Camerounaise (Presbyterian Church of Cameroon): BP 519, Yaoundé; tel. 3332-4236; independent since 1957; comprises 4 synods and 16 presbyteries; Gen. Sec. Rev. Dr MASSI GAM'S.

Eglise Protestante Africaine (African Protestant Church): BP 26, Lolodorf; e-mail epacameroun@yahoo.fr; f. 1934; Pres. Rev. FRANÇOIS PUASSE.

Evangelical Lutheran Church of Cameroon: POB 6, Ngaoundéré-Adamaoua; tel. 2225-2066; fax 2225-2299; e-mail evequenational_eelc@yahoo.fr; Pres. Rev. Dr THOMAS NYIWE; 253,000 mems (2010).

Presbyterian Church in Cameroon: BP 19, Buéa; tel. 3332-2487; fax 332-2754; e-mail pcc_modoffice19@yahoo.com; 1.8m. mems; 302 ministers; Moderator Rt Rev. Dr NYANSAKO-NI-NKU.

Union des Eglises Baptistes du Cameroun (Union of Baptist Churches of Cameroon): New Bell, BP 6007, Douala; tel. 3342-4106; e-mail mbangueeboa@yahoo.fr; autonomous since 1957; Gen. Sec. Rev. EMMANUEL MBANGUE EBOA.

Other Protestant churches active in Cameroon include the Cameroon Baptist Church, the Cameroon Baptist Convention, the Presbyterian Church in West Cameroon and the Union of Evangelical

Churches of North Cameroon. The Eglise Evangélique du Cameroun (EEC) et Union des Eglises Baptistes du Cameroun (UEBC) have also formed a Conseil des Eglises Baptistes et Evangéliques du Cameroun (CEBEC).

The Roman Catholic Church

Cameroon comprises five archdioceses and 20 dioceses.

Bishops' Conference: Conférence Episcopale Nationale du Cameroun, BP 1963, Yaoundé; tel. 2231-1592; fax 2231-2977; e-mail cenc20042003@yahoo.ca; f. 1989; Pres. Most Rev. Joseph Atanga (Archbishop of Bertoua); Sec.-Gen. Sébastien Mongo Behong.

Archbishop of Bamenda: Most Rev. Cornelius Fontem Esua, Archbishop's House, BP 82, Bamenda; tel. 3336-1241; fax 3336-3487; e-mail archbishopshouse@yahoo.com.

Archbishop of Bertoua: Most Rev. Joseph Atanga, Archevêché, BP 40, Bertoua; tel. 2224-1748; fax 2224-2585.

Archbishop of Douala: Samuel Kleda, Archevêché, BP 179, Douala; tel. 3342-3714; fax 3343-1837; e-mail mikjp2004@yahoo.fr.

Archbishop of Garoua: Most Rev. Antoine Ntalou, Archevêché, BP 272, Garoua; tel. 2227-1353; fax 2227-2942; e-mail archigaroua@yahoo.fr.

Archbishop of Yaoundé: (vacant), Archevêché, BP 207, Yaoundé; tel. 2201-1048; fax 2221-9735; e-mail simonvita2000@yahoo.fr.

ISLAM

Conseil Supérieur Islamique du Cameroun: BP 4171, Yaoundé; tel. 7400-1072 (mobile); internet www.csicameroun.org; f. 1984; Sec.-Gen. Zounedou Mfonyoumdi.

BAHÁ'Í FAITH

National Spiritual Assembly: 4230 Yaoundé; tel. 2223-0575; e-mail nsacameroon@yahoo.com; f. 1968; Nat. Sec. Silas Banolok; mems in 1,744 localities.

The Press

DAILIES

Cameroon Tribune: route de l'Aéroport, BP 1218, Yaoundé; tel. 2230-4147; fax 2230-4362; e-mail cameroon-tribune@cameroon-tribune.cm; internet www.cameroon-tribune.cm; f. 1974; publ. by the Société de Presse et d'Editions du Cameroun (SOPECAM), which also publishes a weekly *Weekend*, a monthly *Nyanga* and a fortnightly *Alter Ego*; govt-controlled; French and English; Publr Marie Claire Nnana; Man. Editor Raoul Dieudonné Lebogo Ndongo; circ. 25,000.

Mutations: South Media Corporation, 183 rue 1,055, Pl. Repiquet, BP 12348, Yaoundé; tel. 2230-6680; fax 2222-9635; e-mail journalmutations@yahoo.fr; internet quotidienmutations.info; daily; French; independent; Publr Alain Blaise Batongué; Editor Xavier Messe.

The Post: POB 91, Buéa; tel. 3332-3287; fax 7773-8904; e-mail thepostnp@yahoo.com; internet www.thepostwebedition.com; bi-weekly; independent; English; Publr Francis Wache; Editor Charly Ndi Chia.

Le Quotidien de l'Économie: Douala; f. 2012; Dir of Publication Thierry Ekouti; circ. 2000.

PERIODICALS

Accord Magazine: BP 3696, Messa, Yaoundé; tel. 9969-0600 (mobile); e-mail accordmag@hotmail.com; popular culture.

L'Anecdote: face collège Vogt, BP 25070, Yaoundé; tel. 2231-3395; e-mail journalanecdote@yahoo.com; weekly; conservative; Editor-in-Chief François Bikoro.

Aurore Plus: BP 7042, Douala; tel. 3342-9261; fax 3342-4917; e-mail jouraurplus@yahoo.fr; 2 a week; Dir Michel Michaut Moussala.

Les Cahiers de Mutations: South Media Corporation, 183 rue 1,055, Pl. Repiquet, BP 12348, Yaoundé; tel. 2222-5104; fax 2222-9635; monthly; Dir Roger Alain Taakam.

Cameroon Outlook: BP 124, Limbé; f. 1969; 3 a week; independent; English; Editor Jérôme F. Gwellem; circ. 20,000.

Cameroon Panorama: BP 46, Buéa; tel. 3332-2178; e-mail cainsbuea@yahoo.com; f. 1962; monthly; English; Roman Catholic; Editor Rev. Fr Wilson Ngema; circ. 8,000.

Dikalo: BP 4320, Douala; tel. 3337-2122; fax 3337-1906; f. 1991; independent; 2 a week; French; Publications Dir Tetteh M. Armah; Editor Henri Epee Ndoumbe.

Ecovox: BP 1256, Bafoussam; tel. 3344-6668; fax 3344-6669; e-mail ecovox@cipcre.org; internet www.cipcre.org/ecovox; 2 a year; French; ecological news.

L'Effort Camerounais: BP 15231, Douala; tel. 3343-2726; fax 3343-1837; e-mail leffortcamerounais@yahoo.com; internet www.leffortcamerounais.com; bi-monthly; Catholic; f. 1955; Editor-in-Chief Ireneaus Chia Chongwain.

The Herald: BP 1218, Yaoundé; tel. 2231-5522; fax 2231-8497; 3 a week; English; Dir Dr Boniface Forbin; circ. 1,568.

Al Houda: BP 1638, Yaoundé; quarterly; Islamic cultural review.

Le Jeune Observateur: Yaoundé; f. 1991; Editor Jules Koum Koum.

J'informe: Yaoundé; tel. 9993-6605; fax 2220-5336; f. 2002; weekly; French; Editor Delor Magellan Kamgaing.

Journal Officiel de la République du Cameroun: BP 1603, Yaoundé; tel. 2220-1719; fax 2220-2959; weekly; official govt notices; Man. Editor Joseph Marcel; circ. 4,000.

Le Messager: rue des Écoles, BP 5925, Douala; tel. 3342-0214; fax 3342-0439; internet www.lemessager.net; f. 1979; 3 a week; independent; Man. Editor (vacant); circ. 20,000.

The Messenger: BP 15043, Douala; English-language edn of *Le Messager*; Editor Hilary Fokum.

La Nouvelle Expression: 12 rue Prince de Galles, BP 15333, Douala; tel. 3343-2227; fax 3343-2669; internet www.lanouvelleexpression.net; 3 a week; independent; French; Man. Editor Séverin Tchounkeu.

La Nouvelle Presse: face mairie de Yaoundé VIème/Biyem-Assi, BP 2625, Messa, Yaoundé; tel. 9996-6768; e-mail lanvellepresse@iccnet.cm; f. 2001; weekly; Publications Dir Jacques Blaise Mvie.

Nyanga: route de l'Aéroport, BP 1218, Yaoundé; tel. 2230-4147; fax 2230-4362; publ. by the Société de Presse et d'Editions du Cameroun (SOPECAM); Dir Emmanuel Tataw.

Ouest Echos: BP 767, Bafoussam; tel. and fax 3344-1091; e-mail ouechos@wagne.net; internet www.wagne.net/ouestechos; weekly; regional; Dir Michel Eclador Pékoua.

La Sentinelle: BP 24079, Douala; tel. and fax 3339-1627; weekly; lifestyle; circ. 3,200.

Situations: Yaoundé; weekly.

Le Travailleur/The Worker: BP 1610, Yaoundé; tel. 2222-3315; f. 1972; monthly; French and English; journal of Organisation Syndicale des Travailleurs du Cameroun/Cameroon Trade Union Congress; Sec.-Gen. Louis Sombes; circ. 10,000.

Le Triomphe: BP 1862, Douala; tel. 3342-8774; f. 2002; weekly; Publications Dir Sipowa Conscience Parfait.

Weekly Post: BP 30420, Yaoundé; tel. 9990-4866 (mobile); e-mail weeklyp@yahoo.com; internet weeklypost1.tripod.com; English; f. 1992; independent; Editor-in-Chief Bisong Etahoben.

NEWS AGENCY

CamNews: c/o SOPECAM, BP 1218, Yaoundé; tel. 2230-3830; fax 2230-4362; Dir Jean Ngandjeu.

PRESS ASSOCIATIONS

Conseil Camerounais des Médias (CCM): Yaoundé; internet www.ccm-info.org; f. 2005; created by the UJC to strengthen the quality and independence of journalism in Cameroon; 9 mems; Pres. Pierre Essama Essomba; Sec.-Gen. Pierre-Paul Tchindji.

Union des Journalistes du Cameroun (UJC): Yaoundé; Pres. Célestin Lingo.

Publishers

AES Presses Universitaires d'Afrique: 1077 rue Mballa Eloumden, BP 8106, Yaoundé; tel. 2220-2695; fax 2220-2698; e-mail aes@iccnet.cm; internet www.aes-pua.com; f. 1986; literature, social sciences and law; Dir-Gen. Serge Dontchueng Kouam.

Editions Akoma Mba: ave Germaine Ahidjo 20189, Yaoundé; tel. 9992-2955; fax 2222-4343; e-mail akomamba@hotmail.com; educational; Dir Edmond VII Mballa Elanga.

Editions Clé (Centre de Littérature Evangélique): BP 1501, ave Maréchal Foch, Yaoundé; tel. 2222-3554; fax 2223-2709; e-mail editionscle@yahoo.fr; internet www.wagne.net/cle; f. 1963; African and Christian literature and studies; school textbooks; medicine and science; general non-fiction; Dir Dr Marcelin Vounda Etoa.

Editions Ndzé: BP 647, Bertoua; tel. 9950-9295; fax 2224-2585; e-mail editions@ndze.com; internet www.ndze.com; fiction; Commercial Dir Alexis Limbona.

Editions Semences Africaines: BP 5329, Yaoundé-Nlongkak; tel. 9917-1439; e-mail renephilombe@yahoo.fr; f. 1974; fiction, history, religion, textbooks; Man. Dir Réné Léa Philombe.

Presses de l'Université Catholique d'Afrique Centrale (PUCAC): BP 11628, Yaoundé; tel. 2230-5508; fax 2230-5501; e-mail p_ucac@yahoo.fr; internet www.pucac.com; Man. GABRIEL TSALA ONANA.

GOVERNMENT PUBLISHING HOUSES

Centre d'Edition et de Production pour l'Enseignement et la Recherche (CEPER): BP 808, Yaoundé; tel. 7723-1293; f. 1967; transfer pending to private ownership; general non-fiction, science and technology, tertiary, secondary and primary educational textbooks; Man. Dir JEAN CLAUDE FOUTH.

Imprimerie Nationale: BP 1603, Yaoundé; tel. 2223-1277; Dir AMADOU VAMOULKE.

Société de Presse et d'Editions du Cameroun (SOPECAM): route de l'Aéroport, BP 1218, Yaoundé; tel. 2230-4147; fax 2230-4362; e-mail mclairennana@yahoo.fr; internet cameroon-tribune.cm; f. 1977; under the supervision of the Ministry of Communication; Pres. JOSEPH LE; Dir-Gen. MARIE CLAIRE NNANA.

Broadcasting and Communications

TELECOMMUNICATIONS

In 2013 there were three operators of telecommunication services in Cameroon: one fixed-line and two mobile cellular. A third mobile operator (Viettel) was expected to launch its service in 2014.

Cameroon Telecommunications (CAMTEL): BP 1571, Yaoundé; tel. 2223-4065; fax 2223-0303; e-mail camtel@camnet.cm; internet www.camtel.cm; f. 1999 by merger of INTELCAM and the Dept of Telecommunications; 51% privatization pending; Pres. NFON VICTOR MUKETE; Dir-Gen. DAVID NKOTO EMANE.

CREOLINK Telecoms: Bastos, BP 12725, Yaoundé; tel. 2250-2000; internet www.creolink.cm; internet service provider.

Mobile Telephone Networks (MTN) Cameroon Ltd: 360 rue Drouot, Bonamouti, Akwa, BP 15574, Douala; tel. 7900-9000; fax 7900-9040; internet www.mtncameroon.net; f. 1999 as CAMTEL Mobile; acquired by MTN in 2000; mobile cellular telephone operator; 70% owned by MTN Ltd, 30% owned by Broadband Telecom Ltd; CEO KARL OLUTOKUN TORIOLA.

Orange: Immeuble CBC, ave Kennedy, Yaoundé; tel. 2222-4956; e-mail contact@orange.cm; internet www.orange.cm; mobile cellular telephone and internet operator; Dir-Gen. ELISABETH MEDOU BADANG.

Ringo SA: Immeuble La Lekie, ave Winston Churchill, BP 15283, Yaoundé; tel. 2250-5000; internet www.ringo.cm; f. 2008; internet service provider.

Saconets PLC: BP 6064, Yaoundé; tel. 2223-1018; e-mail info@saconets.com; internet saconets.com; f. 2008; internet service provider.

Regulatory Authority

Agence de Régulation des Télécommunications (ART): Immeuble Balanos, rue Valéry Giscard d'Estaing, BP 6132, Yaoundé; tel. 2223-0380; fax 2223-3748; e-mail art@art.cm; internet www.art.cm; f. 1998; Pres. HESSANA MAHAMAT; Dir-Gen. JEAN LOUIS BEH MENGUE.

BROADCASTING

Radio

Office de Radiodiffusion-Télévision Camerounaise (CRTV): BP 1634, Yaoundé; tel. 2221-4077; fax 2220-4340; e-mail infos@crtv.cm; internet www.crtv.cm; f. 1987; broadcasts in French and English; satellite broadcasts commenced in Jan. 2001, reaching some 80% of the national territory; Pres. of Council of Administration BAKARY ISSA TCHIROMA (Minister of Communication); Dir-Gen. AMADOU VAMOULKE.

Radio Yaoundé FM 94: BP 1634, Yaoundé; tel. 2220-2089; fax 2220-4340; e-mail fm94@crtv.cm; Head of Station LOUISE POM.

Television

Television programmes from France were broadcast by the Office de Radiodiffusion-Télévision Camerounaise from early 1990.

Office de Radiodiffusion-Télévision Camerounaise (CRTV): see Radio.

Finance

(cap. = capital; res = reserves; dep. = deposits; m. = million; brs = branches; amounts in francs CFA)

BANKING

In 2013 there were 12 licensed banks in Cameroon.

Central Bank

Banque des Etats de l'Afrique Centrale (BEAC): 736 ave Monseigneur Vogt, BP 1917, Yaoundé; tel. 2223-4060; fax 2223-3329; e-mail beac@beac.int; internet www.beac.int; f. 1973; bank of issue for mem. states of the Communauté Economique et monétaire de l'Afrique Centrale (CEMAC, fmrly Union Douanière et Economique de l'Afrique Centrale): Cameroon, the Central African Repub., Chad, the Repub. of the Congo, Equatorial Guinea and Gabon; cap. 88,000m., res 227,843m., dep. 4,110,966m. (Dec. 2007); Gov. LUCAS ABAGA NCHAMA; Dir in Cameroon JEAN-MARIE BENOÎT MANI; 5 brs in Cameroon.

Commercial Banks

Afriland First Bank: 1063 pl. de l'Indépendance, BP 11834, Yaoundé; tel. 2223-3068; fax 2222-1785; e-mail firstbank@afrilandfirstbank.com; internet www.afrilandfirstbank.com; formerly Caisse Commune d'Epargne et d'Investissement (CCEI); SBF & Co (36.62%), FMO (19.80%), private shareholders (43.58%); cap. 15,800m., res 19,987.8m., dep 477,108.9m. (Dec. 2011); Pres. Dr JEAN PAULIN FONKOUA; Gen. Man. ALPHONSE NAFACK.

Banque Internationale du Cameroun pour l'Epargne et le Crédit (BICEC): ave du Général de Gaulle, BP 1925, Douala; tel. 3343-6000; fax 3343-1226; e-mail bicec@bicec.banquepopulaire.com; internet www.bicec.com; f. 1962 as Banque Internationale pour le Commerce et l'Industrie du Cameroun; name changed as above in 1997, following restructuring; 52.5% owned by Groupe Banques Populaires (France); cap. 6,000m., res 12,157m., dep. 486,058m. (Dec. 2010); Pres. JEAN-BAPTISTE BOKAM; Gen. Man. PIERRE MAHÉ; 32 brs.

Citibank N.A. Cameroon: 96 rue Flatters, Bonanjo, BP 4571, Douala; tel. 3342-2777; fax 3342-4074; internet www.citigroup.com; f. 1997; Dir-Gen. ASIF ZAIDI; COO WILSON CHOLA.

Commercial Bank Cameroon SA (CBC): ave du Général de Gaulle, BP 59, Douala; tel. 3342-0202; fax 3343-3800; e-mail cbcbank@cbc-bank.com; internet www.cbc-bank.com; f. 1997; cap. 7,000.0m., res 4,596.2m., dep. 156,758.3m. (Dec. 2005); Pres. YVES MICHEL FOTSO.

Ecobank Cameroun SA (Togo): blvd de la Liberté, BP 582, Douala; tel. 3343-8251; fax 3343-8609; e-mail ecobankcm@ecobank.com; internet www.ecobank.com; f. 2001; cap. 9,515.0m., res 1,616.8m., dep. 238,292.4m. (Dec. 2011); Chair. MARTIN N. FONCHA; Man. Dir MOUSTAPHA FALL; 24 brs.

National Financial Credit Bank SA (NFC): ave Charles de Gaulle, BP 6578, Yaoundé; tel. 2220-2823; fax 2220-2832; e-mail info@nfcbanksa.com; internet www.nfcbanksa.com; Gen. Man. AWANGA ZACHARIA.

Société Commerciale de Banque Cameroun SA: 530 rue du Roi George, BP 300, Douala; tel. and fax 3343-5300; e-mail ca_scb@scbcameroun.com; internet www.scbcameroun.net; f. 1989 as Société Commerciale de Banque—Crédit Lyonnais Cameroun; renamed Crédit Lyonnais Cameroun SA in 2002, and as above in 2007; 35% state-owned; cap. 6,000.0m., res 13,131.1m., dep. 294,167.7m. (Dec. 2009); Pres. MARTIN ARISTIDE OKOUDA; Gen. Man. FRANCIS DUBUS.

Société Générale de Banques au Cameroun (SGBC): 78 rue Joss, BP 4042, Douala; tel. 3342-7010; fax 3343-0353; e-mail sgbcdla@camnet.cm; internet www.sgbc.cm; f. 1963; 25.6% state-owned; cap. 12,500m., res 24,488m., dep. 387,997m. (Dec. 2010); Chair. MATHURIN NDOUMBÉ EPÉE; Dir-Gen. JEAN PHILIPPE GUILLAUME; 22 brs.

Standard Chartered Bank Cameroon SA: blvd de la Liberté, BP 1784, Douala; tel. 3343-5200; fax 3342-2789; e-mail Paul.Sagnia@cm.standardchartered.com; internet www.standardchartered.com/cm; f. 1980 as Boston Bank Cameroon; name changed 1986; 100% owned by Standard Chartered Bank (United Kingdom); cap. 7,000m., res 5,797m., dep. 127,823m. (June 2005); CEO MATHIEU MANDENG; 2 brs.

Union Bank of Cameroon, Ltd (UBC): NWCA Ltd Bldg, 2nd Floor, Commercial Ave, BP 110, Bamenda, Douala; tel. 3336-2316; fax 3336-2314; e-mail ubc@unionbankcameroon.com; internet www.unionbankcameroon.com; f. 2000; share cap. 5,000m. (2005); Pres. NJONG ERIC NJONG; Gen. Man. VICTOR NOUMOUE.

United Bank for Africa Cameroon: blvd de la Liberté-Akwa, BP 2088, Douala; tel. 3343-3683; fax 3343-3707; e-mail ubacameroon@ubagroup.com; internet www.ubagroup.com/ubacameroon; Dir-Gen. EMEKE E. IWERIEBOR.

Development Banks

Banque de Développement des Etats de l'Afrique Centrale: see Franc Zone.

Crédit Foncier du Cameroun (CFC): 484 blvd du 20 mai 1972, BP 1531, Yaoundé; tel. 2223-5216; fax 2223-5221; internet www.creditfoncier.cm; f. 1977; 75% state-owned; cap. 6,000m. (Dec. 2007); provides assistance for low-cost housing; Chair. JULES DORET NDONGO; Gen. Man. JEAN PAUL MISSI; 10 brs.

Société Nationale d'Investissement du Cameroun (SNI): pl. Ahmadou Ahidjo, BP 423, Yaoundé; tel. 2222-4422; fax 2223-1332; e-mail sni@sni.cm; internet www.sni.cm; f. 1964; state-owned investment and credit agency; cap. 22,000m., total assets 33,341m. (June 2003); Chair. SIMON ACHIDI ACHU; Dir-Gen. YAOU AISSATOU.

Financial Institutions

Alios Finance Cameroun: rue du Roi Albert, BP 554, Douala; tel. 3305-2300; fax 3342-1219; e-mail cameroun@alios-finance.com; internet www.alios-finance.com; fmrly Société Camerounaise de Crédit-Bail; name changed as above in 2006; Dir-Gen. ERIC LECLERE.

Caisse Autonome d'Amortissement du Cameroun: BP 7167, Yaoundé; tel. 2222-2226; fax 2222-0129; e-mail caa@caa.cm; internet www.caa.cm; f. 1985; cap. 5,000m. (1998); Dir-Gen. DIEUDONNÉ EVOU MEKOU.

Société Camerounaise de Crédit Automobile (SOCCA): rue du Roi Albert, BP 554, Douala; tel. 3342-7478; fax 3342-1219; e-mail socca@socca-cm.cm; internet www.giefca.com/english/cameroun.htm; f. 1959; cap. and res 4,770m., total assets 23,748m. (Dec. 2003); Dir-Gen. JOHANN BAUDOT.

STOCK EXCHANGE

Bourse des Valeurs de Douala (Douala Stock Exchange): 1450 blvd de la Liberté, BP 442, Douala; tel. 3343-8583; fax 3353-8584; e-mail dsx@douala-stock-exchange.com; internet www.douala-stock-exchange.com; f. 2003; 23% state-owned; Chair. BÉNÉDICT BELIBI; Dir-Gen. PIERRE EKOULÉ MOUANGUÉ.

INSURANCE

In 2010 there were 24 insurance companies in Cameroon.

Activa Assurances: rue du Prince du Galles 1385, BP 12970, Douala; tel. 3343-4503; fax 3343-4572; e-mail activa.assur@camnet.cm; f. 1999; all branches except life insurance; cap. 400m.; 66% owned by Cameroonian investors, 33% by Ivorian investors; Chair. JEAN KACOU DIAGOU; Gen. Man. RICHARD NZONLIÉ LOWE; also **Activa Vie**, life insurance.

Allianz Cameroun: rue Manga Bell, BP 105, Douala; tel. 3350-2000; fax 3350-2001; e-mail allianz.cameroun@allianz-cm.com; internet www.allianz-africa.com/cameroun; formerly AGF Cameroun Assurances; all classes of insurance; Dir-Gen. BERNARD GIRARDIN (life insurance).

Association des Sociétés d'Assurances du Cameroun (ASAC): BP 1136, Douala; tel. and fax 3342-0668; e-mail contact@asac-cameroun.org; internet asac-cameroun.org; Pres. MARTIN N. FONCHA; Sec.-Gen. GEORGES MANDENG LIKENG.

AXA Assurances Cameroun: 309 rue Bebey-Eyidi, BP 4068, Douala; e-mail axa.cameroun@axacameroun.com; internet www.axacameroun.com; tel. 3342-6772; fax 3342-6453; f. 1974 as Compagnie Camerounaise d'Assurances et de Réassurances; renamed as above in June 2000; Pres. SANDA OUMAROU; Dir-Gen. THIERRY KEPEDEN.

Beneficial Life Insurance SA: BP 2328, Douala; tel. 3342-8408; fax 3342-7754; e-mail beneficial@iccnet.cm; f. 1974; Dir-Gen. ALLEN ROOSEVELT BROWN.

Chanas Assurances: BP 109, Douala; tel. 3342-1474; fax 3342-9960; e-mail chanas@iccnet2000.com; internet www.chanas-assurances.com; f. 1999; Pres. and Dir-Gen. JACQUELINE CASALEGNO.

Colina All Life: blvd de la Liberté, BP 267, Douala; tel. 3343-0904; fax 3343-1237; e-mail colinaalllife@groupecolina.com; internet www.groupecolina.com; f. 1996; life insurance; Dir-Gen. MARTIN FONCHA.

Colina La Citoyenne Cameroun: 34 rue Dinde, BP 12125, Douala; tel. 3342-4446; fax 3342-4727; e-mail citoyenne@groupecolina.com; internet colina.cawad.com; f. 1986; non-life insurance; Dir-Gen. PROTAIS AYANGMA AMANG.

Société Africaine d'Assurances et Réassurances (SAAR): BP 1011, Douala; tel. 3343-1765; fax 3343-1759; internet www.saar-assurances.com; f. 1990; Pres. Dr PAUL K. FOKAM; Dir-Gen. GEORGES LÉOPOLD KAGOU; also **SAAR-Vie**, life insurance; Dir-Gen. FERDINAND MENG.

Trade and Industry

GOVERNMENT AGENCY

Economic and Social Council: BP 1058, Yaoundé; tel. 2223-2474; advises the Govt on economic and social problems; comprises 150 mems, who serve a 5-year term, and a perm. sec.; Pres. LUC AYANG; Sec.-Gen. ESSOME BIKOU RENÉ.

DEVELOPMENT ORGANIZATIONS

Agence Française de Développement (AFD): Plateau Atémengué, BP 46, Yaoundé; tel. 2222-0015; fax 2223-5707; e-mail afdyaounde@afd.fr; internet www.afd.fr; fmrly Caisse Française de Développement; Man. HERVÉ CONAN.

Cameroon Development Corporation (CAMDEV): Bota Area, Limbé; tel. 3333-2251; fax 3333-2680; e-mail info@cdc-cameroon.com; f. 1947; reorg. 1982; cap. 15,626m. francs CFA; statutory corpn established to acquire and develop plantations of tropical crops for local and export markets; operates 3 palm oil mills and 5 rubber factories; Chair. Chief OKIAH NAMATA ELANGWE; Gen. Man. FRANKLIN NGONI IKOME NJIE.

Hévéa-Cameroun (HEVECAM): BP 1298, Douala and BP 174, Kribi; tel. 3346-1919; f. 1975; state-owned; devt of 15,000-ha rubber plantation; 4,500 employees; transferred to private ownership in 1997; Pres. ELIE C. NYOKWEDI MALONGA; Man. Dir ALAIN YOUNG.

Institut de Recherche Agricole pour le Développement (IRAD): BP 2067, Yaoundé; tel. and fax 2222-3538; e-mail contact@irad-cameroun.org; internet www.irad-cameroon.org; Dir-Gen. NOÉ WOIN.

Institut de Recherche pour le Développement (IRD): 1095 rue Joseph Essono Mballa, Quartier Elig Essono, BP 1857, Yaoundé; tel. 2220-1508; fax 2220-1854; e-mail cameroun@ird.fr; internet www.cameroun.ird.fr; f. 1944; Rep. in Cameroon BRUNO BORDAGE.

Mission d'Aménagement et d'Equipement des Terrains Urbains et Ruraux (MAETUR): 716 ave Winston Churchill, Quartier Hippodrome, BP 1248, Yaoundé; tel. 2222-3113; fax 2223-3190; e-mail maetur@maetur.cm; internet www.maetur.cm; f. 1977; Pres. ABDOULAYE ABOUBAKARY; Dir-Gen. LOUIS ROGER MANGA.

Mission d'Aménagement et de Gestion des Zones Industrielles: BP 1431, Yaoundé; tel. and fax 2231–8440; e-mail magzicameroun@yahoo.fr; internet www.magzicameroun.com; f. 1971; state-owned industrial land authority; Dir CHRISTOL GEORGES MANON.

Mission de Développement de la Province du Nord-Ouest (MIDENO): BP 442, Bamenda; Gen. Man. JOHN BEGHENI NDEH.

Office Céréalier dans la Province du Nord: BP 298, Garoua; tel. 2227-1438; f. 1975 to combat effects of drought in northern Cameroon and stabilize cereal prices; Pres. Alhadji MAHAMAT; Dir-Gen. GILBERT GOURLEMOND.

Office National du Cacao et du Café (ONCC): BP 3018, Douala; tel. 3342-9482; fax 3342-0002; Dir-Gen. MICHAËL NDOPING.

Service de Coopération et d'Action Culturelle: BP 1616, Yaoundé; tel. 2223-0412; fax 2222-5065; e-mail mission.coop@camnet.cm; administers bilateral aid from France; Dir LIONEL VIGNACQ.

Société de Développement du Cacao (SODECAO): BP 1651, Yaoundé; tel. 2230-4544; fax 2230-3395; e-mail contact@sodecao.cm; internet www.sodecao.cm; f. 1974; reorg. 1980; cap. 425m. francs CFA; devt of cocoa, coffee and food crop production in the Littoral, Centre, East and South provinces; Pres. JOSEPH-CHARLES DOUMBA; Dir-Gen. JÉRÔME MVONDO.

Société de Développement du Coton (SODECOTON): BP 302, Garoua; tel. 2227-1556; fax 2227-2026; f. 1974; Chair. OTTO WILSON JOSEPH; Man. ABDOU NAMBA.

Société de Développement et d'Exploitation des Productions Animales (SODEPA): BP 1410, Yaoundé; tel. 2220-0810; fax 2220-0809; e-mail courrier@sodepa.org; internet www.sodepa.org; f. 1974; cap. 375m. francs CFA; devt of livestock and livestock products; Man. Dir DIEUDONNÉ BOUBA NDENGUE.

Société d'Expansion et de Modernisation de la Riziculture de Yagoua (SEMRY): BP 46, Yagoua; tel. 2229-6213; internet semry.com; f. 1971; cap. 4,580m. francs CFA; commercialization of rice products and expansion of rice-growing in areas where irrigation is possible; Pres. AUGUSTINE AWA FONKA; Dir-Gen. MARC SAMATANA.

Société Immobilière du Cameroun (SIC): ave de l'Indépendance, BP 387, Yaoundé; BP 924, Douala; BP 94, Garoua; tel. 2223-3411; fax 2222-5119; e-mail sic@sicameroun.com; internet sic.cm; f. 1952; cap. 1,000m. francs CFA; housing construction and devt; Pres. ABDOULAYE HAMAN ADJI; Dir-Gen. GABRIEL BENGONO.

CHAMBERS OF COMMERCE

Chambre d'Agriculture, des Pêches, de l'Elevage et des Forêts du Cameroun (CAPEF): BP 6620, Yaoundé; tel. 2222-0441; fax 2222-2025; e-mail cfe_cameroun@yahoo.fr; f. 1955; 120 mems; Pres. JANVIER MONGUI SOSSOMBA; Sec.-Gen. BERNARD NWANA SAMA; other chambers at Ebolowa, Bertoua, Douala, Ngaoundéré, Garoua, Maroua, Buéa, Bamenda and Bafoussam.

Chambre de Commerce, d'Industrie, des Mines et de l'Artisanat du Cameroun (CCIMA): rue de Chambre de Commerce, BP 4011, Douala; also at BP 36, Yaoundé; BP 211, Limbé; BP 59, Garoua; BP 944, Bafoussam; BP 551, Bamenda; BP 824, Ngaoundéré; BP 86, Bertoua; tel. 3342-6855; fax 3342-5596; e-mail siege@ccima.net; internet www.ccima.net; f. 1921; 160 mems; Pres. CHRISTOPHE EKEN; Sec.-Gen. SAÏDOU ABDOULAYE BOBBOY.

EMPLOYERS' ORGANIZATIONS

Association Professionnelle des Etablissements de Crédit du Cameroun (APECCAM): BP 133, Yaoundé; tel. 2223-5401; fax 2223-5402; Pres. MATHIEU MANDENG; Sec.-Gen. BÉNÉDICT BELIBI.

Groupement des Femmes d'Affaires du Cameroun (GFAC): BP 1940, Douala; tel. 2223-4059; fax 2221-1041; e-mail gfacnational@yahoo.fr; f. 1985; Pres. FRANÇOISE FONING.

Groupement Inter-Patronal du Cameroun (GICAM): Vallée des Ministres, Bonanjo, BP 829, Douala; tel. 3342-3141; fax 3343-3880; e-mail gicam@legicam.org; internet www.legicam.org; Pres. ANDRÉ FOTSO.

Mouvement des Entrepreneurs du Cameroun (MECAM): BP 12443, Douala; tel. 3339-5000; fax 3339-5001; Pres. DANIEL CLAUDE ABATE.

Syndicat des Commerçants Importateurs-Exportateurs du Cameroun (SCIEC): 16 rue Quillien, BP 562, Douala; tel. 3342-0304; Pres. EMMANUEL UGOLINI; Treas. MICHEL CHUPIN.

Syndicat des Industriels du Cameroun (SYNDUSTRICAM): BP 673, Douala; tel. 3342-3058; fax 3342-5616; e-mail syndustricam@camnet.cm; f. 1953; Pres. CHARLES METOUCK; Sec.-Gen. MOÏSE FERDINAND BEKE.

Syndicat des Producteurs et Exportateurs de Bois du Cameroun: BP 570, Yaoundé; tel. 2220-2722; fax 2220-9694; f. 1939; Pres. CARLO ORIANI.

Syndicat Professionnel des Entreprises du Bâtiment, des Travaux Publics et des Activités Annexes: BP 1134, Yaoundé; BP 660, Douala; tel. and fax 2220-2722; Sec.-Gen. FRANCIS SANZOUANGOU.

UTILITIES

Electricity

Electricity Development Corpn: Immeuble Hibiscus, BP 15111, Yaoundé; tel. 2223-1930; fax 2223-1113; e-mail info@edc-cameroon.org; internet edc-cameroon.org; f. 2006; state-owned; Pres. VICTOR MENGOT; Dir-Gen. Dr THÉODORE NSANGOU.

Société Nationale d'Electricité du Cameroun (AES-SONEL): BP 4077, 63 ave de Gaulle, Douala; tel. 3342-1553; fax 3342-2235; e-mail sonel@camnet.cm; internet www.aesoneltoday.com; f. 1974; 56% owned by AES Sirocco, 44% state-owned; Pres. SERAPHIN MAGLOIRE FOUDA; Gen. Man. JEAN-DAVID BILÉ.

Water

Cameroon Water Utilities Corpn (Camwater): BP 4077, Douala; tel. 3342-5444; fax 3342-2247; f. 1967; 73% state-owned; Pres. JÉRÔME OBI ETA; Dir-Gen. JEAN WILLIAMS SOLLO.

PRINCIPAL CO-OPERATIVE ORGANIZATIONS

Centre National de Développement des Entreprises Coopératives (CENADEC): Yaoundé; f. 1970; promotes and organizes the co-operative movement; bureaux at BP 43, Kumba and BP 26, Bamenda; Dir JACQUES SANGUE.

Union Centrale des Coopératives Agricoles de l'Ouest (UCCAO): ave Samuel Wanko, BP 1002, Bafoussam; tel. 3344-4296; fax 3344-1845; e-mail uccao@uccao-cameroun.com; internet www.uccao-cameroon.com; f. 1958; marketing of cocoa and coffee; 120,000 mems; Pres. JACQUES FOTSO KANKEU; Gen. Man. FRANÇOIS MEFINJA FOKA.

West Cameroon Co-operative Association Ltd: BP 135, Kumba; founded as central financing body of the co-operative movement; provides short-term credits and agricultural services to mem. socs; policy-making body for the co-operative movement in West Cameroon; 142 mem. unions and socs representing c. 45,000 mems; Pres. Chief T. E. NJEA.

TRADE UNION FEDERATIONS

Confederation of Cameroon Trade Unions (CCTU): BP 1610, Yaoundé; tel. 2222-3315; f. 1985; fmrly the Union Nationale des Travailleurs du Cameroun (UNTC); Pres. JEAN-MARIE ZAMBO AMOUGOU.

Confédération des Syndicats Autonomes du Cameroun (CSAC): Yaoundé; Pres. (vacant); Sec.-Gen. PIERRE LOUIS MOUANGUE.

Union des Syndicats Libres du Cameroun (USLC): BP 13306, Yaoundé; tel. 2223-4196; Pres. FLAUBERT MOUSSOLÉ.

Other trade union federations include the Union Générale des Travailleurs du Cameroun (UGTC), the Confédération Camerounaise du Travail (CCT), the Confédération Générale du Travail-Liberté du Cameroun (CGT-L), the Confédération des Syndicats Indépendants du Cameroun (CSIC) and the Confédération des Travailleurs Unis du Cameroun (CTUC).

Transport

RAILWAYS

In 2010 there were some 1,103 km of track—the West Line running from Douala to Nkongsamba (166 km), with a branch line leading south-west from Mbanga to Kumba (29 km), and the Transcameroon railway, which runs from Douala to Ngaoundéré (885 km), with a branch line from Ngoumou to Mbalmayo (30 km). There were also plans for the construction of a 450-km railway linking Mbalam with Kribi.

CAMRAIL: Gare Centrale de Bessengué, blvd de la Réunification, BP 766, Douala; tel. 3340-6045; fax 3340-8252; e-mail didier.vandenbon@camrail.net; internet www.camrail.net; f. 1999; passenger and freight transport; Pres. HAMADOU SALI; Dir-Gen. QUENTIN GÉRARD.

Office du Chemin de Fer Transcamerounais: BP 625, Yaoundé; tel. 2222-4433; supervises the laying of new railway lines and improvements to existing lines, and undertakes relevant research; Dir-Gen. LUC TOWA FOTSO.

ROADS

In 2011 there were an estimated 52,743 km of roads, of which 8.4% were paved. In August of that year the Government stated its intention to pave 3,500 km of new roads by 2020.

Fonds Routier du Cameroun: BP 6221, Yaoundé; tel. 2222-4752; fax 2222-4789; e-mail contact@fonds-routier.cm; internet www.fondsroutiercameroun.org; f. 1996; Dir-Gen. PIERRE TITTI; Administrator JEAN CLAUDE ATANGA BIKOE.

Société Camerounaise de Transport Urbain (SOCATUR): BP 1347, Douala; tel. 3340-1297; fax 3340-1297; f. 2000; bus operator in Douala; Dir-Gen. JEAN ERNEST NGALLÉ BIBEHE.

SHIPPING

There are seaports at Kribi and Limbé-Tiko, a river port at Garoua, and an estuary port at Douala-Bonabéri, the principal port and main outlet, which has 2,510 m of quays and a minimum depth of 5.8 m in the channels and 8.5 m at the quays. Total handling capacity is 7m. metric tons annually. The first phase of the Kribi Deep-water Seaport commenced in December 2010 after a concessionary loan of 207,000m. francs CFA was granted by the Export and Import Bank of China; construction work was expected to be completed in 2014. Plans for a similar deep-water seaport project at Limbé-Tiko were under way in 2012. In December 2013 Cameroon's flag registered fleet comprised 53 vessels, totalling 296,327 grt.

Autorité Portuaire Nationale (APN): BP 11538 Yaoundé; tel. 2223-7316; fax 2223-7314; Dir-Gen. JOSUÉ YOUMBA.

Port Autonome de Douala (PAD): 81 rue de la Chambre de Commerce, BP 4020, Douala; tel. 3342-0133; fax 3342-6797; e-mail portdouala@iccnet2000.com; Chair. SHEY JONES YEMBE; Dir-Gen. EMMANUEL ETOUNDI OYONO.

Camtainer: Para-maritime Area, Douala Port, BP 4993, Douala; tel. 3342-7704; fax 3342-7173; e-mail camtainer@douala1.com; internet www.camnet.cm/investir/transpor/camtenair/sommaire.htm; f. 1984; Chair. JOSEPH TSANGA ABANDA; Man. ZACHARIE KUATE.

Conseil National des Chargeurs du Cameroun (CNCC): BP 1588, Douala; tel. 3343-6767; fax 3343-7017; e-mail info@cncc.cm; internet www.cncc.cm; f. 1975; promotion of the maritime sector; Gen. Man. AUGUSTE MBAPPE PENDA.

Consignation et Logistique du Golfe de Guinée (CLGG): Centre des Affaires Maritimes, BP 4054, Douala; tel. 3342-0064; fax 3342-2181; e-mail agencies@clgg-cm.com; internet www.clgg-cm.com; f. 1975; privatized Feb. 1997; 6 vessels trading with Western Europe, the USA, Far East and Africa; Chair. RENÉ MBAYEN; Man. Dir BERNARD ANDRÉ NDENGUE.

MAERSK CAMEROUN SA—Douala: BP 12414, Douala; tel. 3342-1185; fax 3342-1186; Dir-Gen. DAVID WARE.

Société Camerounaise de Manutention et d'Acconage (SOCAMAC): BP 284, Douala; tel. 3342-4051; e-mail socamac@camnet.cm; internet www.camnet.cm/investir/transpor/socamac/socamac.htm; f. 1976; freight handling; Pres. MOHAMADOU TALBA; Dir-Gen. HARRY J. GHOOS.

Société Camerounaise de Transport et d'Affrètement (SCTA): BP 974, Douala; tel. 3342-1724; f. 1951; Pres. JACQUES VIAULT; Dir-Gen. GONTRAN FRAUCIEL.

Société Camerounaise de Transport Maritime: BP 12351, Douala; tel. 3342-4550; fax 3342-4946.

SOCOPAO Cameroun: BP 215, Douala; tel. 3342-6464; f. 1951; shipping agents; Pres. VINCENT BOLLORE; Man. Dir E. DUPUY.

CIVIL AVIATION

There are international airports at Douala, Garoua and Yaoundé; there are, in addition, 11 domestic airports, as well as a number of secondary airfields.

Cameroon Civil Aviation Authority (CCAA): BP 6998 Yaoundé; tel. 2230-3090; fax 2230-3362; e-mail contact@ccaa.aero; internet www.ccaa.aero; Pres. MAXIMIN PAUL NKOUE NKONGO; Dir-Gen. PIERRE TANKAM.

Aéroports du Cameroun (ADC): Nsimalen, BP 13615, Yaoundé; tel. 2223-4521; fax 2223-4520; e-mail adc@iccnet.cm; internet aeroportsducameroun.com; f. 1999; manages major airports; 63% state-owned; Dir-Gen. ROGER NTONGO ONGUENE.

Cameroon Airlines Corpn (CAMAIRCO): f. 2008 to replace Cameroon Airlines; commenced operations in March 2011; Chair. PHILÉMON YANG; Dir-Gen. ALEX VAN ELK.

Tourism

Tourists are attracted by Cameroon's cultural diversity and by its national parks, game reserves and sandy beaches. In 2012, according to the World Tourism Organization, some 817,000 tourists visited Cameroon. Receipts from tourism totalled US $159m. in 2010.

Ministry of Tourism and Leisure: see Ministries.

Defence

As assessed at November 2012, Cameroon's armed forces were estimated to total 14,200 men (army 12,500, navy 1,300, air force 400). There was also a 9,000-strong paramilitary force.

Defence Expenditure: Estimated at 164,000m. francs CFA in 2011.

Commander-in-Chief of the Armed Forces: PAUL BIYA.

Education

Since independence, Cameroon has achieved one of the highest rates of school attendance in Africa, but provision of educational facilities varies according to region. Education, which is bilingual, is provided by the Government, missionary societies and private concerns. Primary education in state schools is available free of charge, and the Government provides financial assistance for other schools. It begins at six years of age, and lasts for six years. Secondary education, beginning at the age of 12, lasts for a further seven years, comprising two cycles of four years and three years in the francophone sub-system and of five years and two years in the anglophone sub-system. In 2009/10, according to UNESCO estimates, 92% of children in the relevant age-group (99% boys; 86% girls) were enrolled at primary schools. In 2011/12 the number of pupils enrolled at secondary schools totalled some 1.71m. There are seven universities, six of which are state-owned. There were 220,300 students enrolled at the state-owned universities in 2009/10; these institutions employed a total of 4,235 teachers in that year. In 2010 expenditure on education was budgeted at 17.9% of total government spending.

CANADA

Introductory Survey

LOCATION, CLIMATE, LANGUAGE, RELIGION, FLAG, CAPITAL

Canada occupies the northern part of North America (excluding Alaska and Greenland) and is the second largest country in the world, after Russia. It extends from the Atlantic Ocean to the Pacific. Except for the boundary with Alaska in the north-west, Canada's frontier with the USA follows the upper St Lawrence Seaway and the Great Lakes, continuing west along latitude 49°N. The climate is an extreme one, particularly inland. Winter temperatures drop well below freezing but summers are generally hot. Rainfall varies from moderate to light and there are heavy falls of snow. The two official languages are English and French, the mother tongues of 57.2% and 21.8%, respectively, at the general census in 2006. About 45% of the population are Roman Catholics. The main Protestant churches are the United Church of Canada and the Anglican Church of Canada. Numerous other religious denominations are represented. The national flag (proportions 1 by 2) consists of a red maple leaf on a white field, flanked by red panels. The capital is Ottawa.

CONTEMPORARY POLITICAL HISTORY

Historical Context

The Dominion of Canada, consisting of the provinces of New Brunswick, Nova Scotia, Ontario and Québec, was established through the British North America Act (or Constitution Act) of 1867; the Act also formed the basis of Canada's legal system and the federal and provincial systems of government. However, the United Kingdom retained control over Canadian foreign policy, and constitutional amendments could only be enacted by the British Parliament. By 1905 the Canadian confederation had been expanded to incorporate the provinces of Manitoba, British Columbia, Prince Edward Island, Saskatchewan and Alberta, and the federal territories of the Yukon and the Northwest Territories. The second British North America Act (Constitution Act) of 1949 enabled the Canadian Parliament to enact constitutional amendments in matters affecting the federal Government. In the same year Newfoundland joined the Canadian confederation as the 10th province.

In September 1939 Canada declared war on Germany, thus entering the Second World War. Following the War the Liberal Party of Canada, which had governed at the federal level since 1935, remained the dominant political party. After a period of Conservative government in 1957–63, the Liberals, under the leadership of Pierre Trudeau, were returned to office at general elections in 1968, 1972 and 1974. A minority Progressive Conservative Party (PC) administration in 1979–80 was followed by a further Liberal victory in 1980. However, after an economic recession during 1981–83, the PC, led by Brian Mulroney, obtained a substantial legislative majority at the 1984 general election.

In 1982 the British Parliament transferred to Canada authority over all matters contained in British statutes relating to Canada, opening the way for institutional reform and the redistribution of legislative powers between Parliament and the provincial legislatures. All the provinces except Québec eventually accepted constitutional provisions that included a charter of rights and a formula whereby constitutional amendments would require the support of at least seven provinces representing more than 50% of the population. Québec, however, maintained that its legislature could exercise the right to veto constitutional provisions.

In the province of Québec, where four-fifths of the population speak French as a first language and which maintains its own cultural identity, the question of political self-determination has long been a sensitive issue. At provincial elections in 1976 the separatist Parti Québécois (PQ) came to power, and in 1977 made French the official language of education, business and government in Québec.

Domestic Political Affairs

The popularity of Mulroney's PC Government was undermined by persistently high unemployment and by criticism of the administration's negotiation of a new US-Canadian trade treaty, which the main opposition parties, the Liberals and the New Democratic Party (NDP), viewed as overly advantageous to US business interests and potentially damaging to Canada's national identity; the treaty was approved by the House of Commons in August 1988. Nevertheless, at a general election in November the PC was re-elected, although with a reduced majority, and full legislative ratification of the free trade agreement followed in December. In February 1990 the federal Government opened negotiations with Mexico to achieve a lowering of trade barriers. The US Government joined these discussions, and in December 1992 Canada, the USA and Mexico finalized terms for a tripartite North American Free Trade Agreement (NAFTA, see p. 369).

Meanwhile, in 1985 the Liberals replaced the PQ as the governing party in Québec, following which the federal Government adopted new initiatives to include Québec in the constitutional arrangements. In April 1987 Mulroney and the provincial premiers met at Meech Lake, Québec, to negotiate a constitutional accommodation for Québec. The resultant agreement, the Meech Lake Accord, recognized Québec as a 'distinct society' within the Canadian federation, and granted each of the provinces substantial new powers. The Accord was subject to ratification, not later than June 1990, by the federal Parliament and all provincial legislatures.

Opposition to the Meech Lake arrangements, on the grounds that they afforded too much influence to Québec and failed to provide Inuit and Indian minorities with the same measure of protection as francophone groups, began to emerge in early 1990. Despite the adoption of a number of compromise amendments, the provinces of Manitoba and Newfoundland upheld their opposition and the Meech Lake Accord duly lapsed in June. The Québec Government responded by refusing to participate in future provincial conferences, and by appointing a commission to examine the province's political choices. In September 1991 the federal Government announced a new series of constitutional reform proposals whereby Québec was to be recognized as a distinct society in terms of its language, culture and legal system, while each province would have full control of its cultural affairs. Native peoples were to receive full self-government within 10 years, inter-provincial trade barriers were to be abolished, and the federal Senate was to become an elected body with limited powers of legislative veto.

Meanwhile, political support for separatist aspirations was extended to the federal Parliament in May 1990, when seven PC members representing Québec constituencies, led by Lucien Bouchard, broke away from the party and formed the independent Bloc Québécois (BQ), with the object of acting in the interests of a 'sovereign Québec'. The BQ later expanded, with disaffected Liberal support, to nine members.

In March 1992 an all-party committee of the federal Parliament recommended new proposals providing for a system of 'co-operative federalism', which would grant Québec powers of veto over future constitutional changes, together with exclusive jurisdiction over the main areas of its provincial affairs. This plan was rejected by the Québec Government, while the western provinces, which sought increased representation in a reformed Senate, were unwilling to concede a constitutional veto to Québec until these changes had been carried out. In August a new programme of constitutional reforms, the Charlottetown Agreement, was finalized for submission to a national referendum. The proposals, which were endorsed by all of the provincial premiers as well as the three main political parties, provided for an equal and elected Senate, and a guarantee in perpetuity to Québec of one-quarter of the seats in the federal House of Commons. There was also to be recognition of provincial jurisdiction in cultural affairs, and increased provincial powers over certain economic affairs and immigration. The inherent right to self-government of the Indian and Inuit population was also to be recognized.

Despite the apparent political consensus, disagreements emerged on a regional basis, as well as among NDP and Liberal supporters, and aspects of the proposed constitution were opposed by the PQ and the BQ, and by the Reform Party (RP), a conservative-populist movement that led opposition in the western provinces. At the referendum, which took place in October 1992, the Charlottetown Agreement was defeated by a margin of 54% to 45%. This defeat, together with the persistence of adverse economic conditions, led to a rapid erosion in the prestige of the Government, and in the Prime Minister's personal popularity. In June 1993 Mulroney stepped down and was succeeded by the former Minister of Defence and Veterans' Affairs, Kim Campbell, who became Canada's first female Prime Minister.

The Campbell Government proved unable to restore the PC's political standing, and at the October 1993 general election the Liberals, led by Jean Chrétien, won a decisive victory. PC representation in the new Parliament was reduced to only two seats. The BQ, with 54 seats, became the official opposition party, and declared that it would pursue the achievement of full sovereignty for Québec. Campbell, who lost her seat in the federal Parliament, resigned as PC leader and was succeeded by Jean Charest.

In December 1993, following the renegotiation of certain treaty protocols with the US Government, NAFTA, which had received Canadian legislative ratification in June, was formally promulgated, to take effect from January 1994.

Separatism in Québec

The issue of separatism in Québec was reopened by provincial elections held in September 1994, in which the PQ, led by Jacques Parizeau, defeated the incumbent Liberal administration. Parizeau, who had pledged to hold a new referendum on independence during 1995, was supported at federal level by the BQ. In June 1995 the PQ and the BQ, together with a smaller provincial nationalist group, the Action Démocratique du Québec (ADQ), agreed a framework for the province's proposed independence, and in September the referendum received provincial legislative approval.

In the referendum, held on 30 October 1995, the sovereignty proposals were defeated by a margin of only 50,000 votes; 49% of eligible voters were in favour of the sovereignty plan, and 51% opposed. In February 1996 Lucien Bouchard, having resigned from the federal House of Commons and relinquished the BQ leadership, succeeded Parizeau as Premier of Québec and leader of the PQ. In September 1997 Bouchard refused to attend a conference of provincial premiers and territorial commissioners, at which a seven-point framework on Canadian unity was agreed. The conference, held in Calgary, recognized the 'unique character' of Québec, but asserted that any future change in the constitutional powers of one province should be applicable to all provinces. By June 1998 the resultant 'Calgary Declaration' had been endorsed by the legislatures of all provinces except Québec.

The Supreme Court, which had been requested in February 1998 to rule on the legality of a unilateral secession by Québec, declared in August that no province had the right, in constitutional or international law, to leave the federation without prior negotiations with the federal and provincial governments, and that secession would require the approval of the federal legislature, together with that of seven of the 10 provinces. It was further stated that an obligation would exist for negotiation with Québec if a clear majority of its voters expressed a wish to leave the federation.

In March 1998 Jean Charest resigned as leader of the PC, to accept the leadership of the Liberal Party of Québec. Although the Liberals narrowly won the popular vote in the provincial legislative election in November, the PQ secured the most seats in the provincial Assembly.

In January 2001 Bouchard announced his intention to resign as Premier of Québec; he also resigned as a member of the provincial legislature and as leader of the PQ, stating that he had failed to achieve independence for the province. Opinion polls continued to show a decline in support for independence. In March Bernard Landry of the PQ was elected Premier of Québec. Landry was succeeded by Charest in April 2003 following an election in which the Liberals secured a majority in the provincial legislature.

Continuing Liberal rule 1997–2006

The Liberals were re-elected at a general election held in June 1997, although with a reduced majority in the House of Commons. The conservative RP replaced the BQ as the main opposition party. In March 2000 members of the RP voted to form the Canadian Alliance (CA), with the aim of uniting the major right-wing parties. The PC declined to join the CA, although a number of the party's prominent members chose to do so. In July Stockwell Day, a former PC member, was elected leader of the CA.

In October 2000 Prime Minister Chrétien announced that a general election would be held on 27 November, despite his Government's mandate being valid until June 2002. At the election, Chrétien's Liberals won 172 of the 301 seats in the House of Commons. The CA secured 66 seats, while the BQ obtained 38, the NDP 13 and the PC 12. The results demonstrated an increasing political polarization between the west of the country, where the CA dominated, and eastern and central areas, where the Liberals retained strong support.

In July 2001, following several months of internal dissent in the CA owing to its poor performance in the legislative elections, 13 members resigned from the party in protest at Day's refusal to resign the leadership. Day eventually resigned in December, and was succeeded by Stephen Harper.

In December 2003 former Minister of Finance Paul Martin succeeded Chrétien as Prime Minister and as leader of the Liberal Party following the latter's retirement. In the same month the PC and the CA announced that they had merged at federal level to form a new party, the Conservative Party of Canada; Stephen Harper was elected leader of the new party in March 2005.

Legislation defining marriage as 'a heterosexual or homosexual union' was approved by the House of Commons in June 2005; the bill received senate approval in the following month. Thus, Canada became only the third country in the world to legalize same-sex marriages (after the Netherlands and Belgium).

From 2002 the Liberal Government was subject to persistent accusations of corruption. In February 2004 a report by the office of the Auditor-General concluded that the Government had misappropriated funds during a state campaign intended to promote national unity in Québec in 1997–2001. It was alleged that contracts worth some C $100m. had been awarded to advertising companies in Québec with links to the Liberal Party, and that some of these contracts were false. Prime Minister Martin denied any involvement in the affair, which coincided with his time as Minister of Finance in the Chrétien Government, and ordered a public inquiry. Nevertheless, the so-called 'sponsorship scandal' was widely believed to have affected support for the Liberal Party in the general election held on 28 June 2004. The incumbent party failed to obtain a parliamentary majority, so Martin formed the first minority Government in Canada since 1979.

The Commission of Inquiry into the alleged misappropriation of campaign funds in Québec held public hearings from September 2004. As details emerged of alleged fraud and systemic mismanagement of sponsorship deals, the Government came under increasing pressure from opposition parties to hold a fresh election. In April 2005 Prime Minister Martin announced that a general election would be held within 30 days of the publication of the Commission's report. In May, with the support of the NDP, the Government narrowly avoided a parliamentary defeat in a vote on the 2006 budget that was treated as a motion of confidence.

The first part of the Commission of Inquiry's report into the sponsorship scandal was published on 1 November 2005. The report concluded, *inter alia*, that the Liberal Party had obtained election funds illegally. Although there was no evidence to link former Prime Minister Chrétien to any wrongdoing, he was held politically accountable for the failures in management; Prime Minister Martin and the current Liberal Government were exonerated. However, in late November the Conservatives tabled a motion of no confidence in the Government. Having lost the support of the NDP earlier in the month—according to NDP officials, because of differences over health policy—the Government was defeated by 171 votes to 133, thus precipitating the dissolution of Parliament.

The 2006 general election

At the general election, held on 23 January 2006, the Conservative Party won 124 of the 308 seats, an increase of 25. As expected, the Liberals' parliamentary representation fell, by 32 seats to 103 seats. In contrast, the NDP increased its share of seats by 10, to 29 seats. The BQ, which was only represented in Québec, won 51 seats, a slight decrease from the 54 seats it held previously. There was one independent seat. Conservative leader Stephen Harper was declared Prime Minister-elect, but was forced to form a minority Government.

Harper was sworn into office on 6 February 2006. The new Prime Minister pledged that his first piece of legislation would be the introduction of a Federal Accountability Act. The proposal reflected the conclusions of the Commission of Inquiry, the final part of which was released on 1 February. The report made 19 recommendations towards improving executive answerability, including: reform of the Government's decision-making process; a curtailment of the powers of the Prime Minister; and an increase in the authority of the federal Parliament. In the same month Martin stood down as Liberal Party leader; he was succeeded by Stéphane Dion.

In November 2006 the House of Commons voted by an overwhelming margin to approve legislation introduced by Prime Minister Harper recognizing Québec as a 'nation within a united Canada'. Although the resolution was largely seen as symbolic, the Minister for Intergovernmental Affairs, Michael D. Chong, resigned from the Cabinet in protest at the legislation's recognition of what he described as 'ethnic nationalism'. In Québec, Charest was re-elected Premier in March 2007; however, the Liberals failed to secure a parliamentary majority, precipitating the formation of a minority Government, the first in 129 years in that province.

Former Prime Minister Brian Mulroney was the subject of corruption allegations in November 2007, regarding payments he reportedly received from businessman Karlheinz Schreiber in 1993–94. Mulroney denied receiving any money while still in office. A federal Commission of Inquiry began public hearings concerning the allegations in March 2009. Testifying in May, Mulroney admitted receiving C $225,000 from Schreiber, but claimed that this was payment for the international promotion of military vehicles to be manufactured in Canada by a German company represented by Schreiber, rather than for illegal domestic lobbying. In a report issued in May 2010 the head of the Commission, Associate Chief Justice Jeffrey Oliphant, concluded that Mulroney was guilty of infringing federal ethics guidelines; Oliphant highlighted Mulroney's acceptance of three large cash payments. However, the report found that the transactions had occurred after the former premier's resignation in June 1993.

The 2008 general election and subsequent events

Parliament was dissolved in September 2008 at the request of Prime Minister Harper, who was seeking a functional mandate for his party after two-and-a-half years of minority government. At a general election held on 14 October, the Conservative Party won 143 of the 308 seats, an increase of 16 but still short of a majority. The Liberal Party garnered 77 seats, the BQ 49 and the NDP 37, while two seats were secured by independent candidates. Turnout was 59.1%, the lowest participation rate ever recorded.

Harper suspended Parliament again in December 2008, thus avoiding a scheduled no-confidence vote in which his minority Government had been expected to be defeated. The Liberal Party and the NDP had intended to form a coalition administration with support from the BQ, having proposed the vote on the grounds that the Conservative Government had failed adequately to address adverse economic conditions. A few days later the leader of the Liberal Party, Stéphane Dion, announced that he was to resign. He was replaced, initially in an acting capacity, by Michael Ignatieff, whose leadership of the party was ratified in May 2009. Meanwhile, following the criticism of its response to the economic downturn, the Government announced a programme of stimulus measures costing some C $40,000m. over two years, which received the approval of Parliament in February.

In Québec, following early legislative elections called by the minority Liberal administration in December 2008, Charest was elected to a third term as Premier and the Liberals secured a majority in the provincial legislature. In May 2009 the House of Assembly of Nova Scotia approved a vote of no confidence in Rodney MacDonald's minority PC Government over its proposed budget. The NDP, led by Darrell Dexter, was victorious in elections held in the province in June, and Dexter duly replaced MacDonald as Premier.

In October 2009 the House of Commons rejected a motion of no confidence in the Government, tabled by the Liberal Party, which again accused Harper's administration of economic mismanagement. Although the BQ had supported the Liberal motion, the NDP abstained from voting, allowing the Conservative Government to survive. The Conservatives performed well in by-elections to fill four vacant seats in the House of Commons in November, increasing their representation to 145 seats.

Parliament was suspended again at Harper's request in December 2009, until March 2010. The Prime Minister claimed that more time was required to review economic policy prior to the presentation of the 2010 budget, but opposition parties accused the Government of attempting to evade questions regarding the alleged torture of prisoners in Afghanistan transferred into local custody by Canadian soldiers (see Foreign Affairs). Demonstrations were held throughout Canada in late January 2010 in protest against the legislative suspension.

In June 2010 Canada hosted two major international forums on economic co-operation: the annual summit of the Group of Eight (G8) was held in Huntsville, Ontario on 25–26 June, and was immediately followed by a summit meeting of the Group of 20 (G20) in Toronto. Despite the Canadian authorities mounting what was described as the country's largest and most expensive security operation, a series of anti-summit protests commenced in Toronto from mid-June. Large demonstrations on 26–27 June escalated into extensive civil disorder, as some protesters became embroiled in violent clashes with the security forces; there were also widespread acts of vandalism aimed at business interests in the city centre. The unrest prompted the largest mass arrests in Canada's history, as more than 1,000 people were detained. Most were released within 48 hours; however, the severity of the security response was strongly criticized by civil rights organizations.

At a provincial election in New Brunswick in September 2010, the PC overturned the Liberal Party's majority, winning 42 of the Legislative Assembly's 55 seats. David Alward was sworn in as provincial Premier in October. In November the Premier of British Columbia, Gordon Campbell of the Liberal Party, announced his intention to resign after almost 10 years in office. In February 2011 Christy Clark won the Liberal Party's provincial leadership contest; she was sworn in as Premier of British Columbia in March. In November 2010 the PC Premier of Newfoundland and Labrador, Danny Williams, announced his resignation; Kathy Dunderdale was sworn in as Premier in December.

In October 2010 David Johnston, an author and former academic, was sworn in as Governor-General. He succeeded Michaëlle Jean, who had held the post since September 2005.

An opposition-sponsored Climate Change Accountability Act, which had been passed in the House of Commons in May 2010, was defeated by Conservatives in the Senate in November. The act required a reduction in emissions of greenhouse gases to 25% below 1990 levels by 2020. The intervention of the upper house in the passage of the legislation, which was described as 'undemocratic' by opposition politicians, was defended by Prime Minister Harper, who insisted that the legislation was 'irresponsible'. Peter Kent was appointed Minister of the Environment in January 2011, replacing Jim Prentice, who had resigned in November 2010. In his inaugural speech, Kent insisted that Canadian environmental regulations would, by necessity, be aligned with those of the USA. (For further background information on climate change policy, see Regional Relations.)

The 2011 general election and majority Conservative rule

In early 2011 the tenure of the minority Government appeared increasingly insecure as a series of misconduct allegations were levelled against the Conservatives. In February four officials were charged with financial irregularities relating to the Conservatives' 2006 general election campaign. In early March 2011 the Speaker of the House approved two opposition motions that accused the Government of being in contempt of Parliament: the administration had allegedly failed to disclose full details of federal spending on crime prevention, and Minister of International Co-operation Beverley Oda was accused of misleading the House over investigations into her role in the falsification of a document on foreign-aid funding. In mid-March the parliamentary Standing Committee on Procedure and House Affairs confirmed that the Government's conduct constituted contempt of Parliament. The three main opposition parties subsequently indicated their intention to vote against the 2011 federal budget, which was presented to the House on 22 March. On 25 March the Liberals presented a parliamentary motion charging Harper's administration with contempt of Parliament and expressing no confidence in the Government; the motion was carried by 156 votes to 145, and thus an early general election was called.

Despite the fact that Harper's Government was the first in Canada's history to be declared in contempt of Parliament, opinion polls showed no reduction in support for the Conservatives. In the event, the general election on 2 May 2011 produced a dramatic transformation in the political status quo. The Conservative Party won an overall majority for the first time, with

166 out of 308 available seats (an increase of 23 seats on the previous election in October 2008). Both the Liberals and the BQ suffered heavy losses: the Liberals retained just 34 seats, compared with 77 at the 2008 election; the BQ held only four seats, compared with 49 in 2008. Michael Ignatieff, leader of the Liberal Party, and his BQ counterpart, Gilles Duceppe, both failed to secure re-election, and each subsequently resigned his party leadership. The NDP became for the first time the largest opposition party, increasing its representation in the House from 37 seats to 103 (with particularly large gains in Québec). In British Columbia a candidate of the Green Party of Canada secured the party's first seat in the federal Parliament. Voter turnout was recorded at 61.1%.

Prime Minister Harper announced a new Federal Ministry in mid-May 2011. Most notably, John Baird replaced the unseated Lawrence Cannon as Minister of Foreign Affairs. Robert Rae was elected as the Liberal Party's interim leader in late May, pending a forthcoming leadership contest (see below). NDP leader Jack Layton died of cancer in August 2011; Nycole Turmel assumed Layton's duties on an interim basis. In March 2012 Thomas Mulcair was elected as the new leader of the NDP and, therefore, became the official opposition leader in the House of Commons. Meanwhile, in December 2011 Daniel Paillé won the BQ's leadership election, and in the following month the ADQ was absorbed by the recently founded Coalition Avenir Québec.

In June 2011 the Government proposed new measures to reform the Senate. Voluntary elections would be held in the provinces and territories to nominate potential senators, who, if selected by the Prime Minister, would serve non-renewable, nine-year terms. Opposition parties criticized the proposals for introducing additional costly elections, for lacking a framework to resolve conflicts between the upper and lower houses, and for failing to address provincial inequalities in relation to the distribution of Senate seats. In mid-November 2013 the Supreme Court began hearings regarding the constitutionality of the Government's Senate reform proposals. The Government's contention was that the proposed reforms were merely technical adjustments that could be introduced without provincial approval. However, a majority of provincial leaders held that such changes to the legislative system represented constitutional amendments and, as such, would require the approval of at least seven provinces, representing 50% of the national population; while abolition of the Senate (which was supported by some members of the federal and provincial legislatures) would require the unanimous consent of all provinces. Meanwhile, in a controversial move to re-emphasize Canada's traditional connections with the British monarchy, in August 2011 Minister of National Defence Peter MacKay proclaimed that the Maritime Command and the Air Command would be redesignated, respectively, as the Royal Canadian Navy and the Royal Canadian Air Force—titles not used since 1968.

Seven provincial and territorial legislative elections were conducted during October–November 2011. Dalton McGuinty won a third term as Premier of Ontario, although the Liberals fell one seat short of a majority in the provincial legislature, while the NDP, under Greg Selinger, secured a fourth consecutive tenure in office in Manitoba. In Saskatchewan, Premier Brad Wall and his Saskatchewan Party were re-elected for a second term, as were Premier Robert Ghiz and the Liberals in Prince Edward Island. The Conservative administration in Newfoundland and Labrador, led by Kathy Dunderdale, was elected to serve a third successive term. The Yukon territorial election was won by the Yukon Party, and incumbent Premier Darrell Pasloski—who had assumed the premiership in June—was sworn in for a full term in October. Robert McLeod was elected as the new Premier of the Northwest Territories. Meanwhile, in October Alison Redford was selected as the new Progressive Conservative leader in Alberta and hence became Premier of the province shortly thereafter, replacing Ed Stelmach. In April 2012 Redford's Conservatives were re-elected to serve a 12th consecutive term in Alberta, winning 61 out of 87 seats in the provincial legislature. The right-wing Wildrose Alliance Party, which had failed to secure representation in the 2008 ballot, garnered 17 seats and replaced the Liberals as the largest opposition party in the province.

In the Québec provincial election, held in September 2012, the PQ secured a narrow victory over the incumbent Liberals. PQ leader Pauline Marois was subsequently inaugurated as Premier, and she formed a minority administration. Marois' victory speech had been disrupted by a deadly shooting incident, which appeared to have been politically motivated. After 10 years in office, Dalton McGuinty announced his resignation as Premier of Ontario in October; he was succeeded by Kathleen Wynne in February 2013.

Meanwhile, legislation increasing the number of seats in the House of Commons, from 308 to 338, was promulgated in December 2011. The change was to come into effect at the next general election (expected to take place in 2015). The Fair Representation Act partially redressed the imbalances in the allocation of seats among the provinces, with Alberta, British Columbia, Ontario and Québec all receiving additional seats to reflect their growing populations.

The Government's policy proposals during 2012 were frequently introduced in the form of expansive 'omnibus bills', which grouped together numerous, sometimes unrelated, initiatives into a single piece of legislation. This strategy provoked controversy since the size and heterogeneity of some of these bills allegedly hindered efforts to analyse and debate the individual proposals in a comprehensive manner. An omnibus anti-crime bill (C-10) received legislative approval in March; an omnibus refugee bill (C-31) was endorsed in June; and two omnibus budgetary implementation bills (C-38 and C-45) were adopted in June and December, respectively. The budget legislation proved to be particularly contentious as the fiscal measures were bundled together with other proposals on, *inter alia*, immigration, the intelligence services and the environment. Bill C-45 also reportedly diluted the laws concerning aboriginal land management rights and the protection of waterways, prompting demonstrations by indigenous communities and the formation of a native protest movement, Idle No More. Harper met with indigenous representatives in January 2013, although his administration appeared reluctant to amend the disputed legislation.

Recent developments

In early 2013 two members of the Conservative Government who were facing misconduct allegations were forced to resign from the Federal Ministry in separate incidents. Minister of Aboriginal Affairs and Northern Development John Duncan, already under pressure over his response to indigenous opposition to recent government legislation, resigned in February, following reports of an inappropriate intervention with the tax authorities on behalf of a constituent in 2011. Duncan was replaced by Bernard Valcourt. In March Minister of Intergovernmental Affairs Peter Penashue stood down, following allegations of funding irregularities related to his 2011 election campaign; Penashue also resigned from his parliamentary seat but vowed to contest the resulting by-election. Penashue's responsibilities were transferred to Denis Lebel, the Minister of Transport, Infrastructure and Communities.

In May 2013 Harper effected a significant government reorganization: most notably, Minister of National Defence Peter MacKay was appointed Attorney-General and Minister of Justice, succeeding Rob Nicholson, who assumed the defence portfolio. In the same month, Nigel Wright, Harper's Chief of Staff, resigned over his role in an intensifying Senate expenses scandal. Three Senators who had either resigned or been expelled from the Conservative caucus to sit as independent members during 2013 were suspended for two years in November over irregularities relating to parliamentary expenses. Wright had reportedly provided one of the disgraced Senators with a loan to repay his illegitimate expenses. It was further alleged that the Office of the Prime Minister had been involved in attempts to suppress reports of the incident, although Prime Minister Harper was not held to be personally involved. None the less, the high-profile scandal undermined the Government's stated objectives of accountability and transparency. Also in November, with growing public dissatisfaction over the expenses scandal and the slow progress of the Government's proposed Senate reforms (see above), the legislative assembly of Saskatchewan approved a motion in support of the abolition of the Senate. A similar motion had earlier been approved by the Manitoba legislature, while an abolition motion was also proposed by NDP members of the Nova Scotia assembly in December. Prior to the Senate suspensions, in September Harper had provoked controversy by proroguing Parliament for the fourth time since he had taken office (with some opponents claiming that the Prime Minister was attempting to avoid interrogation on the expenses scandal). By-elections were held in four federal constituencies in November: the Conservative Party retained the two seats vacated by its outgoing members, as did the Liberals in the other two constituencies.

Meanwhile, in April 2013 Justin Trudeau, son of former Prime Minister Pierre Trudeau, was elected as leader of the Liberal Party. His appointment raised hopes among Liberal supporters for a political resurgence of the beleaguered party. At a provincial election in British Columbia in May, the Liberals won a fourth consecutive term in office, despite widespread predictions that the NDP would claim a victory. (Party leader Christy Clark, however, lost her own seat. Clark, who continued as Premier, was re-elected to the provincial legislature at a by-election in July.) In a further sign that the party was recovering from its recent political setbacks, in October the Liberal Party secured a majority at the Nova Scotia provincial election, returning to office there for the first time since 1998; Stephen McNeil was duly sworn in as Premier. The erstwhile ruling NDP was demoted to third position in the province, behind the PC. Later that month in an election in Nunavut, Premier Eva Aariak lost her seat and was replaced by Peter Taptuna. In January 2014 Newfoundland and Labrador Premier Kathy Dunderdale resigned, and was succeeded by fellow Conservative Tom Marshall.

In March 2014 Alison Redford announced her resignation from the premiership of Alberta. The decision reportedly resulted from disquiet within her own party over her leadership style. Dave Hancock was sworn in as Redford's replacement on an interim basis. In the same month the Premier of Québec, Pauline Marois, called an early election in a bid to secure a majority for the PQ in the provincie after 18 months of minority government. However, it proved a disastrous strategy, as the election, which was held in early April, resulted in a heavy defeat for the PQ and signalled another resurgence for the Liberal Party. The Liberals secured a majority, with 70 out of 125 seats in the provincial legislature; the PQ's representation dropped to 30 seats, while Coalition Avenir Québec and Québec Solidaire gained 22 seats and three seats, respectively. Marois lost her own seat and subsequently announced her resignation from the party leadership. Philippe Couillard, who had replaced Charest as leader of the Québec Liberal Party in March 2013, was sworn in as the new Premier in late April 2014. The result appeared to represent a serious setback for the cause of Québec sovereignty, and especially for the uncompromising brand of separatism that had been espoused by the PQ in advance of the election.

Meanwhile, in March 2014 Jim Flaherty announced his resignation as Minister of Finance, after more than eight years in the post. Joe Oliver, hitherto Minister of Natural Resources, was appointed as his replacement; Minister of State Greg Rickford was given responsibility for the natural resources portfolio. Flaherty died in April.

Land Treaty Claims

The question of land treaty claims by Canada's indigenous peoples came to prominence in the late 20th century, when disputes over land rights arose in Ontario, Manitoba and Québec. In 1988, following 13 years of negotiations, the federal Government formally transferred to indigenous ownership an area covering 673,000 sq km in the Northwest Territories. In the Yukon Territory, an area of 41,000 sq km (representing 8.6% of the Territory's land) was transferred to indigenous control. At the same time, debate had begun to intensify on the formulation of a new constitutional status for the Northwest Territories, in which a population of only 58,000 (of which Inuit and other indigenous peoples comprised about one-half) occupied an area comprising one-third of Canada's land mass. In 1991 specific terms for the creation of a semi-autonomous Nunavut Territory, covering an area of 2.2m. sq km, to the east of a boundary running northwards from the Saskatchewan–Manitoba border, were agreed by Inuit representatives and the federal Government, and in May 1992 a plebiscite on a proposal to divide the Northwest Territories into two self-governing units was approved by the territories' residents.

A formal agreement to settle all outstanding land treaty claims was finalized by the federal Government in May 1993, providing for Nunavut to come into official existence on 1 April 1999. Elections to a new, 17-seat legislature for Nunavut, to be located at Iqaluit, were held in February 1999, and the new territorial Government took office in April. In December 1997 the Supreme Court awarded legal title to 57,000 sq km of ancestral land to two native groups in British Columbia, and in the following month the federal Government offered a formal apology to all native groups for past mistreatment and injustices. The principle of 'aboriginal title', established by the Supreme Court ruling, was again exercised in April 1999 in British Columbia under the Nisga'a Agreement. The Agreement transferred some 2,000 sq km of land, together with substantial powers of self-government and C $196m., to 5,500 Nisga'a people; in return, they ceded their wider aboriginal title. In August 2003 Prime Minister Chrétien signed an agreement that would transfer powers of self-government and 39,000 sq km of land to some 3,000 Tlicho people in the Northwest Territories; the agreement was ratified by the federal Parliament in February 2005. At a summit in British Columbia in November, Prime Minister Martin pledged to spend C $4,300m. over the next 10 years on measures to reduce poverty and improve health, education and housing among the Indian and Inuit communities. An agreement worth C $350m., transferring powers of self-government to 5,300 Inuit people in north-west Labrador, came into effect in December.

In July 2012 the Québec Government signed an accord with the Cree Indian communities of Québec, which provided for the abolition of the municipality of Baie-James and its replacement with a new power-sharing regional administration for the 330,000 sq km Eeyou Istchee/Baie-James (James Bay) territory. The accord, which built on earlier treaties with indigenous peoples in Québec (notably, the James Bay and Northern Québec Agreement of 1975, the first major aboriginal land settlement of the modern era), was expected to grant the Cree increased powers of self-government and greater influence over decisions concerning land and natural resources. The first meeting of the new administration, comprising an equal number of representatives from the Cree and non-aboriginal communities, convened in January 2014. Meanwhile, protests by indigenous peoples, including those led by the Idle No More movement, took place in many urban centres from early 2013, focusing on poor living conditions, high rates of unemployment and imprisonment, and the threat to native lands from proposed logging and energy projects.

Foreign Affairs

Regional relations

Recent administrations have sought to emphasize Canada's independence from the USA in matters of foreign policy, while continuing the increased co-operation in areas such as trade and environmental protection. In the last two decades of the 20th century a number of bilateral environmental agreements were signed, including accords on gaseous emissions, both domestically and in the USA (these move northwards into Canada to produce 'acid rain'), and the elimination of industrial pollution from the Great Lakes. Canada assumed a leading role in the establishment, with seven other circumpolar countries, of the Arctic Council (see p. 448), which commenced operation in September 1996. The aims of the Council include the protection of the environment of the polar region, the formation of co-ordinated policies governing its future, and the safeguarding of the interests of its indigenous population groups. In 1997, at the third Conference of the Parties to the Framework Convention on Climate Change (World Meteorological Organization, see p. 176), held in Kyoto, Japan, Canada undertook to implement reductions of its emissions of greenhouse gases to 6% below 1990 levels by 2012. In December 2002 the Government ratified the Protocol, despite opposition from the gas and petroleum industries and the province of Alberta. However, by April 2007 the country's greenhouse gas emissions were reportedly 30% greater than those recorded in 1990, and the Martin administration conceded that Canada would be unable to satisfy its obligations prescribed under the Kyoto Protocol by 2012. In April 2007 a government initiative targeting a 20% reduction in current emissions from 2006 levels by 2020 was undertaken. In January 2010 the Minister of the Environment, Jim Prentice, announced that Canada's target for lowering emissions would be amended to match that of the USA, which was considering a 17% reduction from 2005 levels by 2020. To avoid financial penalties for failing to attain emissions reduction targets, in December 2012 Canada became the first signatory to the Kyoto Protocol to withdraw from the agreement. The Harper administration claimed that the Kyoto targets were unrealistic and damaging to Canada's economy and argued that the Protocol was ineffective since significant polluters such as the USA and China were not obliged to reduce their greenhouse gas emissions.

Canada, which maintains significant economic and commercial links with Cuba and operates a policy of 'constructive engagement' in its relations with that country, adopted a prominent role in international opposition to efforts, initiated by the US Government in March 1996, to penalize investors whose business involves property in Cuba that was confiscated from US citizens following the 1959 revolution. The imposition of these measures, known as the Helms-Burton Act, led in July 1996 to the exclusion from the USA of nine Canadian businessmen involved in nickel-mining operations in Cuba. The Canadian Government responded by introducing legislation prohibiting Canadian companies from compliance with the Helms-Burton Act, and refused to recognize foreign court rulings arising from the Act. With Mexico, which also conducts significant trade with Cuba, Canada co-ordinated a joint challenge to the US Government through NAFTA dispute procedures. In November 1996 Canada actively promoted a resolution by the UN General Assembly condemning the US trade sanctions against Cuba and joined the European Union (EU) in a complaint against the embargo to the World Trade Organization (WTO, see p. 434). In April 1998 the Canadian Government signed a series of co-operation agreements with Cuba. However, bilateral relations subsequently experienced a marked decline, owing to increasing concern in Canada at the Cuban Government's human rights record. In July 1999 the Canadian Government stated that it would implement no further assistance programmes to Cuba that did not clearly further the protection of human rights.

Meanwhile, relations with the USA (Canada's largest trading partner) improved in June 1999 following the resolution of a long-standing disagreement over the demarcation of salmon-fishing rights off the Pacific coast. However, in September 2000 a dispute arose over the USA's threat to impose export tariffs on Canadian timber, which, the USA claimed, was subsidized by the Canadian Government, and which undercut the price of US timber. Canada requested a WTO investigation into US anti-subsidy policies, after the USA imposed duties of 32% on softwood lumber imports from Canada in response. In August 2001 Canada won a preliminary victory at the WTO, which adopted a report agreeing that the Government was not subsidizing exports. Canada hoped to remove US duties and replace an earlier quota agreement, which expired in March 2001, with a system based on free trade; however, the USA imposed tariffs of 27% on softwood lumber imports from Canada in May 2002. Negotiations to resolve the issue failed, and in August 2004 the WTO ruled that Canada could retaliate with trade sanctions. In August 2005 a NAFTA panel ordered the USA to remove the duties on Canadian softwood and to refund some US $4,000m. already collected. However, the USA refused to comply and in this case received support from the WTO. The trade dispute was resolved in April 2006 when the USA agreed to remove its tariffs and refund the US $4,000m. in duties collected; in return, Canada agreed to restrict its share of the US timber market to 34%. The USA's prohibition of the use of foreign-produced iron, steel and other manufactured goods in projects funded by a US $787,000m. fiscal stimulus programme approved by the US Congress in February 2009 prompted considerable concern in Canada. Prime Minister Harper sought to secure the exemption of Canadian producers and suppliers from the so-called 'buy American' provision, and in February 2010 a bilateral agreement was signed that allowed Canadian companies to participate in some US state and local infrastructure projects for the remainder of the stimulus programme in exchange for access for US companies to construction contracts in Canada.

Following the terrorist attacks on the USA on 11 September 2001 Canada and the USA increased co-operation on intelligence and security matters: under the 'Smart Border Declaration' signed by the two countries in December, 400 US National Guards were to be deployed at 43 crossings along both sides of the 6,400-km (4,000-mile) Canada–USA border. In the same month extensive anti-terrorist legislation was also introduced.

In February 2005 Prime Minister Martin announced that Canada would not participate in a controversial US missile defence programme. However, in 2004 Martin's Government had acceded to a US request to allow installations of the North American Aerospace Defense Command (NORAD—a binational military organization established by the two countries in 1958) to be integrated into the anti-missile warning system, which was regarded as tantamount to Canadian participation. In May 2006 the House of Commons voted to renew the NORAD agreement and to make it a permanent arrangement, subject to review every four years.

In February 2011 Prime Minister Harper and US President Barack Obama announced details of a framework agreement on border co-operation, which envisioned a fully integrated and jointly operated North American security perimeter. An action plan to implement the accord was announced in December. However, political opponents claimed that the border agreement represented a serious threat to Canada's national sovereignty, since it would force Canada to adopt US policy on immigration and security, and would enable US border guards to operate within Canadian territory. Legislation authorizing the latter was approved by Canada in June 2012.

In mid-2007 Russian explorers participating in a research expedition descended to the floor of the Arctic Ocean and planted their nation's flag directly under the North Pole. The incident was widely interpreted, not least in Canada, as an attempt to stake a territorial claim to the Arctic seabed and the vast mineral and energy resources believed to exist therein. Such interpretations were refuted by the Russian authorities. Nevertheless, the Conservative Government of Stephen Harper has pursued an increasingly assertive approach in its defence of Canadian maritime sovereignty in the Arctic. In July 2007 the Government announced its intention to commission up to eight Arctic patrol ships, with ice-breaking capabilities, which would enable the Navy to maintain year-round patrols of Canada's northern waters. In 2011 construction contracts for the vessels were awarded, although the first ships were not expected to be launched until 2018. Further plans aimed at consolidating Canada's presence in the far north included the construction of a naval training facility and the development of a deep-water port in locations adjacent to the Northwest Passage. Under the terms of the UN Convention on the Law of the Sea (UNCLOS), Canada was required to submit its sovereignty claims to the Arctic seabed by 2013 (10 years after ratification of the convention). In December of that year the Government submitted a preliminary claim to the UN Commission on the Limits of the Continental Shelf (CLCS), arguing that the outer limits of Canada's eastern, offshore territory be extended by some 1.2m sq km. While the task of mapping the Arctic sea floor had yet to be completed, the Canadian authorities announced that they had instructed their scientists to complete this project with a view to claiming the 'biggest geographic area possible for Canada'. The final Canadian Arctic submission was expected, controversially, to include a territorial claim on the North Pole.

In early 2014 several other territorial disputes involving Canada remained open: a long-running dispute with Denmark concerning ownership of Hans Island, a small uninhabited island located in the strategic strait between Greenland and Ellesmere Island, Nunavut; a disagreement with the USA concerning delineation of their joint maritime border in the Beaufort Sea; and an ongoing debate with several nations regarding Canada's claimed sovereignty over the Northwest Passage. In 2011 Canadian-Danish plans for a joint-mapping project on the seabed adjacent to Hans Island were under discussion, and in 2012 the solution of splitting the island equally between the two nations was one of several under consideration. In November 2012 Canada and Denmark also concluded a 'tentative' accord delineating their shared maritime boundary in the Lincoln Sea (north of Ellesmere Island and Greenland).

Other external relations

There have been recurrent disagreements between Canada and France concerning the boundary of disputed waters near the French-controlled islands of Saint Pierre and Miquelon, off the southern coast of Newfoundland and Labrador. In June 1992 an international arbitration tribunal presented its report, generally regarded as favourable to Canada, and in December 1994 the two countries agreed a 10-year accord on the allocation of fishing rights around the islands. In September 2001 France and Canada held talks on energy exploration in the waters off Saint Pierre and Miquelon; geologists believed there were large petroleum and natural gas deposits between the islands and Newfoundland and Labrador and Nova Scotia. In May 2009 the French Government lodged a claim at the CLCS to areas of seabed beyond its existing Exclusive Economic Zone (EEZ) around Saint Pierre and Miquelon. The Canadian Government insisted that the matter had been definitively resolved by the arbitration tribunal in 1992. However, Canada's preliminary submission to the CLCS, in December 2013, claiming an expansion of its continental shelf in the Atlantic Ocean (see above), was expected to revive the dispute with France, with the French authorities indicating that they would launch a counter claim during 2014.

In 1994 the Canadian Government vigorously contested a decision by the EU unilaterally to award itself almost 70% of the internationally agreed quota of Greenland halibut caught in the north-west Atlantic fishing grounds. It declared that it would act to prevent EU fishing trawlers (principally from Spain and Portugal) from overfishing the already seriously depleted stocks of Greenland halibut and announced that Canada was extending its maritime jurisdiction beyond its EEZ, already extending 200 nautical miles (370 km) from the coastline. This action was rejected by the EU as contrary to international law. (In November 2003 Canada ratified UNCLOS, which establishes the limit of the EEZ as being 200 nautical miles from the coastline. In July 2006 the Government announced that it would undertake an underwater survey to identify the outer edge of the continental shelf; under the terms of UNCLOS, countries have the right to exploit natural resources on and under the seabed up to an identifiable shelf edge where it extends beyond the EEZ.)

In February 1995 the Canadian Government warned the EU that force would be used if necessary to ensure that total catches by EU vessels did not exceed the Northwest Atlantic Fishing Organization (NAFO)-agreed quota and, in March, its enforcement vessels impounded a Spanish trawler fishing in international waters. The EU responded by suspending all official political contacts with Canada. The impasse was eased by the release of the trawler in the following week, when it was agreed to initiate quota allocation negotiations. A resolution was reached in April, under which Canada and EU countries each consented to accept 41% of the 1996 Greenland halibut quota. It was agreed that independent observers would monitor the activities of trawlers in the north-west Atlantic fishing zone. In early 2002 the Canadian Government imposed a ban on all vessels from Estonia and the Faroe Islands from entering Canadian ports, accusing those fleets of violating NAFO-agreed shrimp quotas off the eastern coast of the country. In September the Government extended the ban to any foreign vessel that violated NAFO-agreed quotas. The ban on the Estonian fleet was lifted in December. In July 2006 the EU and Canada announced that they would begin joint inspection patrols to combat illegal fishing and to enforce the NAFO Regulatory Area.

The EU is Canada's second largest trading partner, after the USA. Negotiations with the EU concerning a Comprehensive Economic and Trade Agreement (CETA) commenced in 2009 and were provisionally concluded in October 2013. The CETA, which was expected to come into force in 2015, would remove almost all tariffs between the two economies, and was predicted to produce an increase of around 23% in the value of bilateral trade within seven years. A potential obstacle to the CETA was a proposed EU directive that would classify oil derived from bituminous sands (or 'oil sands') as a 'carbon intensive' fuel, thus impeding future European imports of Canadian oil. However, as of early 2014 it remained unclear whether a compromise had been reached by European and Canadian negotiators on this influential issue. An EU ban on trade in seal products, which had entered into force in 2010, prompted Canada (a major supplier of such items) to refer the matter to the WTO in 2011. A similar ban came into effect in Russia, Belarus and Kazakhstan in 2011, placing the future of the Canadian sealing industry in serious jeopardy.

Some 750 Canadian troops were deployed in Afghanistan in February 2002 as part of the US-led international forces present in that country, although all Canadian forces had returned home by November. However, in August 2003 around 1,900 Canadian troops were sent to Afghanistan as part of a NATO-led mission to protect the interim Government there and suppress militant resistance. By late 2006 Canada had committed C $1,000m. to fund reconstruction and poverty reduction and to strengthen governance in Afghanistan, over a 10-year period. In July 2011 Canadian combat operations in Afghanistan were officially terminated and approximately 3,000 Canadian armed forces personnel in the country were withdrawn. The Government pledged that Canadian forces would continue to participate in humanitarian and development projects. Furthermore, up to 950 military personnel were to be deployed in training programmes for the Afghan security forces. In March 2014 the final contingent of Canadian troops were withdrawn from Afghanistan. According to reports, some 40,000 Canadian troops had served in Afghanistan since 2001, and 158 Canadian soldiers and four civilians had been killed in the conflict. By 2011 the cost of the mission was estimated at more than US $11,000m.

In February 2007 the Department of National Defence released documents apparently providing evidence of the violent mistreatment by Canadian military personnel of three Afghan prisoners held in Canadian custody near Qandahar. A government inquiry into the scandal was endorsed by NATO in April. In the same month the human rights organization Amnesty International alleged that Canadian military forces had been aware that prisoners transferred from Canadian into Afghan custody had been subject to abuse. Meanwhile, appeals launched in the Supreme Court by three suspected al-Qa'ida operatives, who had been detained in Canada during 2001–03, returned a unanimous ruling in February 2007 that the Government had contravened Canada's Charter of Rights and Freedoms by ratifying legislation in 2002 that permitted the use of undisclosed evidence by the authorities to justify the indefinite detention, or deportation, of non-Canadian terrorist suspects without recourse to trial. The judgment had been suspended by one year to enable Parliament to amend the Immigration and Refugee Protection Act. Controversy regarding the treatment of detainees transferred from Canadian to Afghan custody re-emerged in November 2009, when Richard Colvin, a senior Canadian diplomat who had been based in Afghanistan in 2006–07, alleged that the Canadian authorities had been complicit in the torture of prisoners. Colvin's testimony, before a parliamentary committee, prompted opposition demands for a public inquiry, but was dismissed by the Government. In December 2009 the House of Commons adopted a motion requiring the release of uncensored documents concerning the Afghan detainees to the committee considering the issue. In June 2011 the Government finally released some 4,000 pages of partially redacted documents, proclaiming that they exonerated the military of any malpractice and that the matter was now closed. However, opposition parties expressed concern that a reported 36,000 pages of documents relating to the abuse allegations still remained classified and appealed for a further investigation. The Military Police Complaints Commission (MPCC) issued a report in June 2012 acknowledging the likelihood that the detainees transferred to the Afghan security forces had subsequently been subjected to torture, but exonerating eight Canadian military police officers of any wrongdoing. The report strongly criticized the Harper administration for obstructing the MPCC's investigation.

In February 2011 Canada placed economic sanctions on the Libyan regime of Col Muammar al-Qaddafi and recalled its ambassador from the North African country following attempts by the Libyan authorities to suppress violently a popular uprising. To protect the civilian population from attacks by Qaddafi's forces, in the following month the Canadian military intervened in Libya as part of an international coalition established to enforce a 'no-fly zone' over the country (authorized under UN Security Council Resolution 1973). In June the Canadian Government recognized the rebel 'National Transitional Council of Libya' and pledged aid of C $2m., while in August Qaddafi-appointed diplomats were expelled from Canada. John Baird, the Canadian Minister of Foreign Affairs, announced further funding of $10m. during a visit to Libya in October. The coalition military action, which included Canadian air strikes, contributed significantly to the final defeat of the Qaddafi regime later that month, prompting critics to claim that the alliance had breached the terms of the UN mandate. The Government estimated the cost of Canada's military intervention at $347m.

The Canadian authorities ordered the expulsion of all Syrian diplomats in May 2012 in protest against the massacre of suspected opposition sympathizers in Houla, Syria; the atrocity had allegedly been perpetrated by pro-Government militia. Canada also severed diplomatic ties with Iran in September owing to ongoing concerns about the latter's nuclear programme and its alliance with Syria. In November the Canadian Government withdrew, temporarily, its diplomatic representatives to the UN and the Palestinian (National) Authority following the overwhelming approval by the UN General Assembly of an upgrade in the Palestinians' UN status. The Harper administration had consistently maintained a staunchly pro-Israel stance and regarded the status upgrade as damaging to the Middle East peace process. In January 2014 Harper completed his first official visit to the Middle East, the main focus of which was to reaffirm his Government's unwavering support for Israel; Harper and his Israeli counterpart, Binyamin Netanyahu, signed a memorandum of understanding on a Canada-Israel Strategic Partnership. The one-week trip also included brief visits by the Canadian premier to the Palestinian West Bank territory and Jordan.

At a conference held in Ottawa in December 1997, Canada became the first signatory of the Ottawa Convention, a treaty agreed by 121 countries, undertaking to discontinue the use of landmines and providing for the destruction of existing stockpiles. Humanitarian concerns remained at the forefront of Canadian foreign policy—in early 2014 Canadian humanitarian or peacekeeping forces were deployed in the following locations: Afghanistan, Cyprus, the Democratic Republic of the Congo, the

Golan Heights, Haiti, Kosovo, Mali, Sierra Leone, Sinai and East Jerusalem, South Sudan and Sudan.

CONSTITUTION AND GOVERNMENT

Canada is a federal parliamentary state. Under the Constitution Act 1982, which was enacted as Schedule B to the Canada Act (UK) 1982, and which entered into force on 17 April 1982, executive power is vested in the British monarch, as Head of State, and may be exercised by her representative, the Governor-General, whom she appoints on the advice of the Canadian Prime Minister. The federal Parliament comprises the Head of State, a nominated Senate (a maximum of 112 members, appointed on a regional basis) and a House of Commons (308 members, elected by universal adult suffrage for single-member constituencies). According to the terms of the Fair Representation Act, which was promulgated in December 2011, the number of members in the House of Commons was to be increased to 338 from the next general election, expected to be held in 2015. A Parliament may last no longer than five years. The Governor-General appoints the Prime Minister and, on the latter's recommendation, other ministers to form the Federal Ministry. The Prime Minister should have the confidence of the House of Commons, to which the Cabinet is responsible. Canada comprises 10 provinces (each with a Lieutenant-Governor and a legislature, which may last no longer than five years, from which a Premier is chosen), and three territories constituted by Act of Parliament.

REGIONAL AND INTERNATIONAL CO-OPERATION

Canada is a member of the Organization of American States (see p. 394) and of the Inter-American Development Bank (see p. 331). Together with Mexico and the USA, Canada is a signatory to the North American Free Trade Agreement (NAFTA, see p. 369), which entered into force in 1994 and had been fully implemented by 2008. Canada has also sought to expand trade in Latin America, concluding free trade agreements with Chile, Colombia, Costa Rica, Panama and Peru. Free trade negotiations have also been conducted with the Dominican Republic, El Salvador, Guatemala, Honduras and Nicaragua, and with members of the Caribbean Community and Common Market (see p. 223).

Canada was a founder member of the UN in 1945. As a contracting party to the General Agreement on Tariffs and Trade, Canada joined the World Trade Organization (see p. 434) on its establishment in 1995. Canada is a member of The Commonwealth (see p. 236), of the North Atlantic Treaty Organization (NATO, see p. 370) and of the Organisation for Economic Co-operation and Development (OECD, see p. 379). The country also participates in the Group of Eight (G8, see p. 465) leading industrialized nations and in the Group of 20 (G20, see p. 456). Canada has concluded a free trade accord with the members of the European Free Trade Association (see p. 451) and, in 2013, reached agreement in principle on a Comprehensive Economic and Trade Agreement with the European Union (EU, see p. 273), due to come into force in 2015. In 2012 Canada joined negotiations for the Trans-Pacific Partnership, a proposed Asian-Pacific free trade agreement.

ECONOMIC AFFAIRS

In 2012, according to estimates by the World Bank, Canada's gross national income (GNI), measured at average 2010–12 prices, was US $1,777,860m., equivalent to US $50,970 per head (or US $42,530 on an international purchasing-power parity basis). The country's population increased at an average annual rate of 1.1% in 2003–12, while gross domestic product (GDP) per head increased, in real terms, by an average of 0.7% per year. Overall GDP increased, in real terms, at an average rate of 1.8% per year in 2003–12. According to chain-linked methodologies, the economy grew by 1.7% in 2012.

Agriculture (including forestry and fishing) contributed 1.7% of GDP in 2011, according to the UN, and the sector (excluding forestry and fishing) engaged 1.8% of the economically active population in 2012. In terms of farm receipts, the principal crops are wheat and canola (rapeseed), which, together with livestock production (chiefly cattle and pigs) and timber, provide an important source of export earnings. Canada is a leading world exporter of forest products and of fish and seafood. The production of furs is also important. In real terms, the GDP of the agricultural sector increased at an average annual rate of 0.8% in 2003–11. In 2012, according to chain-linked methodologies, the sector's GDP increased by 0.7%.

Industry (including mining, manufacturing, construction and power) provided 30.9% of GDP in 2011, according to the UN, and the sector (including forestry and fishing) employed 20.3% of the economically active population in 2012. Industrial GDP remained constant, in real terms, in 2003–11. Industrial GDP increased by 3.3% in 2011.

According to the UN, mining (including power) provided 12.7% of GDP in 2011. The mining sector (together with forestry, fishing, petroleum and gas) employed only 2.1% of the economically active population in 2012. Canada is a major world producer of zinc, asbestos, nickel, potash and uranium. Gold, silver, iron, copper, cobalt and lead are also exploited. There are considerable reserves of petroleum and natural gas in Alberta's oil sands, off the Atlantic coast and in the Canadian Arctic islands. At the end of 2012 the country's proven natural gas reserves were estimated at 1,982,503m. cu m. Proven oil reserves were put at 173,888m. barrels in 2012 and crude oil production totalled 3.74m. barrels per day in the same year. These figures included estimated reserves of some 25,851m. barrels 'under active development' in Alberta's oil sands in 2012. However, additional 'established reserves' from Canada's oil sands measured an estimated 167,850m. barrels in 2012. When total oil sands reserves are included, Canada holds the world's third largest reported oil reserves (after Venezuela and Saudi Arabia). The GDP of the mining sector (including power) increased, in real terms, at an average annual rate of 0.2% in 2003–11. Mining GDP increased by 5.2% in 2011 but by only 0.4% in 2012, according to chain-linked methodologies.

Manufacturing contributed 10.9% of GDP in 2011, according to the UN, and employed 10.2% of the economically active population in 2012. The principal branches of manufacturing in 2012, measured by the value of shipments, were transport equipment (accounting for 17.5% of the total), food products, refined petroleum and coal industries, primary metal industries, chemical products, machinery industries (excluding electrical machinery), and fabricated metal products. The GDP of the sector declined, in real terms, at an average rate of 1.5% per year in 2003–11. In 2012, according to chain-linked methodologies, manufacturing GDP increased by 1.4%.

Construction contributed 7.3% of GDP in 2011, according to UN figures, and employed 7.2% of the economically active population in 2012. During 2003–11 the GDP of the sector increased at an average annual rate of 3.3%. Construction GDP increased by 5.2% in 2012, according to chain-linked methodologies.

Energy is derived principally from hydroelectric power (which provided 58.9% of the electricity supply in 2012) and from geothermal and nuclear power stations. In 2010 Canada's total energy production (including nuclear energy) totalled an estimated 607,952m. kWh. In 2012 energy products accounted for 9.6% of imports. In August 2009 Suncor Energy and Petro-Canada merged under the name Suncor, creating Canada's first major oil conglomerate.

Services provided 67.4% of GDP in 2011, according to the UN, and engaged 77.9% of the economically active population in 2012. The combined GDP of the service sectors increased, in real terms, at an average rate of 2.7% per year in 2003–11. Services GDP increased by 1.8% in 2012, according to chain-linked methodologies.

In 2012 Canada recorded a visible merchandise trade deficit of US $12,028m. The current account of the balance of payments showed a deficit of US $62,256m. in that year. In 2012 the USA accounted for 73.2% of Canada's total exports and 62.5% of total imports; the countries of the European Union (notably, the United Kingdom) and Japan were also important trading partners. The principal exports in that year were energy products, motor vehicles and parts, consumer goods, metal and non-metallic mineral products, basic and industrial chemical, plastic and rubber products, forestry products, and farm, fishing and intermediate products. The principal imports were consumer goods, motor vehicles and parts, electronic and electrical equipment, energy products, industrial machinery and equipment, and metal and non-metallic mineral products.

For the financial year 2012/13 there was a consolidated budget deficit of C $45,026m. Canada's general government gross debt was C $1,552,189m. in 2012, equivalent to 85.3% of GDP. The annual rate of inflation averaged 2.0% in 2002–12. Consumer prices increased by an average of 1.5% in 2012. The rate of unemployment averaged 7.2% in 2012.

A sustained period of buoyancy enjoyed by the Canadian economy from the mid-1990s was underpinned by stringent financial policy, low rates of inflation, high international commodity prices and by the beneficial effects of the North American

Free Trade Agreement (NAFTA) on Canadian exports to the USA. Real GDP declined by 2.8% in 2009, amid a global economic downturn; however, a robust recovery in 2010, with real GDP increasing by 3.2%, was attributed to effective macroeconomic intervention and the resilience of the financial sector; although the commencement of a two-year economic stimulus programme in 2009 led to a sharp increase in the budget deficit. GDP expansion slowed in 2011, to 2.6%, as growth was hindered by the volatile global economic climate, the rising value of the local currency and the gradual reduction of stimulus spending. According to the IMF, growth in real GDP slowed further, to 2.0% in 2012 and to 1.6% in 2013, as domestic consumption moderated owing, in part, to the Government's ongoing fiscal austerity programme. A reduction in US demand for Canada's exports and declining commodity prices were further concerns. In January 2012 the US Department of State rejected a Canadian plan to build a 2,700-km oil pipeline, 'Keystone XL', connecting the Alberta oil sands with markets in the USA, pending an assessment of the environmental effects. Nevertheless, in February the Obama Administration approved the first branch of the pipeline, to be constructed in the southern USA. The US Department of State concluded in January 2014 that the pipeline would not significantly increase carbon pollution, although final approval for the project had yet to be granted, with a decision expected in late 2014. Two other proposed pipeline projects were under consideration in 2014: one between Alberta and the Pacific coast of British Colombia, which would facilitate the export of Canadian oil to Asia; and the other between Alberta and New Brunswick, to replace oil imported into eastern Canada, and allow for exports across the Atlantic. The projects have been criticized by environmentalists, since oil sands production is more polluting than conventional petroleum operations. In 2013 a sizeable discovery of oil was found off the coast of Newfoundland and Labrador, estimated at up to 600m. recoverable barrels. In the 2013/14 federal budget, the Government announced plans for a Building Canada Fund, to involve some C $47,000m. in new funding for infrastructural projects over 10 years from 2014/15. The Government forecast in its 2014/15 federal budget that the budget would return to surplus in 2015/16. Meanwhile, from 2012 exports of Canadian goods benefited from the steady fall in the value of the Canadian currency against the US dollar. The IMF forecast a modest revival in economic growth to 2.2% in 2014.

PUBLIC HOLIDAYS

2015: 1 January (New Year's Day), 3 April (Good Friday), 6 April (Easter Monday), 18 May (Victoria Day), 1 July (Canada Day), 7 September (Labour Day), 12 October (Thanksgiving Day), 11 November (Remembrance Day), 25 December (Christmas Day), 26 December (Boxing Day).

Note: standard public holidays comprise the listed days, together with any other day so proclaimed by individual provinces or territories.

Statistical Survey

Source (unless otherwise stated): Statistics Canada, Ottawa, ON K1A 0T6; tel. (613) 951-8116; fax (613) 951-0581; internet www.statcan.gc.ca.

The following Statistics Canada resources have been adapted for use in this survey (with permission). [SC1]: *Population and Dwelling Counts, for Canada, Provinces and Territories, 2011 and 2006 Censuses – 100% Data*; internet www12.statcan.gc.ca/census-recensement/2011/dp-pd/hlt-fst/pd-pl/Table-Tableau.cfm?LANG=Eng&T=101&S=50&O=A. [SC2a]: *Population by sex and age group*; internet www.statcan.gc.ca/pub/91-215-x/2013002/t512-eng.htm. [SC2b]: *Population by year, by province and territory*; internet www.statcan.gc.ca/pub/91-215-x/2013002/t002-eng.htm. [SC3]: *Population of census metropolitan areas (2011 Census boundaries)*; internet www12.statcan.gc.ca/census-recensement/2011/dp-pd/hlt-fst/pd-pl/Table-Tableau.cfm?LANG=Eng&T=205&S=3&RPP=50. [SC4]: *Births and birth rate, by province and territory*; internet www.statcan.gc.ca/tables-tableaux/sum-som/l01/cst01/demo04a-eng.htm. [SC5]: *Marriages by province and territory*; internet www40.statcan.ca/l01/cst01/famil04.htm. [SC6]: *Deaths and death rate, by province and territory*; internet www.statcan.gc.ca/tables-tableaux/sum-som/l01/cst01/demo07a-eng.htm. [SC7]: *Employment by industry*; internet www.statcan.gc.ca/tables-tableaux/sum-som/l01/cst01/econ40-eng.htm. [SC8]: *Labour force characteristics*; internet www.statcan.gc.ca/tables-tableaux/sum-som/l01/cst01/econ10-eng.htm. [SC9]: *Field and speciality crops*; internet www.statcan.gc.ca/tables-tableaux/sum-som/l01/cst01/prim11b-eng.htm. [SC10]: *Fur production, by province and territory*; internet www.statcan.gc.ca/tables-tableaux/sum-som/l01/cst01/prim46a-eng.htm. [SC11]: *Manufacturing shipments, by subsector*; internet www.statcan.gc.ca/tables-tableaux/sum-som/l01/cst01/manuf11-eng.htm. [SC12]: *Consolidated government revenue and expenditures*; internet www5.statcan.gc.ca/cansim/a05?lang=eng&id=3850032&pattern=3850032&searchTypeByValue=1&p2=35. [SC13]: *Consumer price index, by province*; internet www.statcan.gc.ca/tables-tableaux/sum-som/l01/cst01/econ09a-eng.htm. [SC14]: *Gross domestic product, income-based*; internet www.statcan.gc.ca/tables-tableaux/sum-som/l01/cst01/econ03-eng.htm. [SC15]: *Gross domestic product, expenditure-based*; internet www.statcan.gc.ca/tables-tableaux/sum-som/l01/cst01/econ04-eng.htm. [SC16]: *Real gross domestic product, expenditure-based*; internet www.statcan.gc.ca/tables-tableaux/sum-som/l01/cst01/econ05-eng.htm. [SC17]: *Gross domestic product at basic prices by industry*; internet www.statcan.gc.ca/tables-tableaux/sum-som/l01/cst01/econ41-eng.htm. [SC18]: *Imports of goods on a balance-of-payments basis, by product*; internet www.statcan.gc.ca/tables-tableaux/sum-som/l01/cst01/gblec05-eng.htm. [SC19]: *Exports of goods on a balance-of-payments basis, by product*; internet www.statcan.gc.ca/tables-tableaux/sum-som/l01/cst01/gblec04-eng.htm. [SC20]: *Imports, exports and trade balance of goods on a balance-of-payments basis, by country or country grouping*; internet www.statcan.gc.ca/tables-tableaux/sum-som/l01/cst01/gblec02a-eng.htm. [SC21]: *Motor vehicle registrations, by province and territory*; internet www5.statcan.gc.ca/cansim/a05?lang=eng&id=4050004. All data were retrieved December 2013.

Area and Population

AREA, POPULATION AND DENSITY

Area (sq km)	
Land	8,965,121*
Inland water	n.a.
Total	n.a.
Population (census results)†	
16 May 2006	31,612,897
10 May 2011	
Males‡	16,414,230
Females‡	17,062,460
Total	33,476,688
Population (official estimates at 1 July)	
2012	34,754,312
2013 (preliminary)	35,158,304
Density (per sq km) at 1 July 2013	3.9§

* 3,461,451 sq miles (at 2011 census); area of inland water was recorded at 891,163 sq km in 2005, but a full breakdown was not available at 2011 census.

† Excluding census data for one or more incompletely enumerated Indian reserves or Indian settlements and excluding adjustment for under-enumeration.

‡ Figures are rounded to nearest 5.

§ Land area only.

Sources: Statistics Canada, [SC1], [SC2a].

POPULATION BY AGE AND SEX

(official estimates at 1 July 2013, preliminary)

	Males	Females	Total
0–14	2,910,611	2,763,512	5,674,123
15–64	12,103,312	12,001,247	24,104,559
65 and over	2,418,326	2,961,296	5,379,622
Total	17,432,249	17,726,055	35,158,304

Source: Statistics Canada, [SC2a].

PROVINCES AND TERRITORIES
(official estimates of population at 1 July 2013, preliminary)

	Land area (sq km)	Population	Density (per sq km)	Capital
Provinces:				
Alberta	640,082	4,025,074	6.3	Edmonton
British Columbia	922,509	4,581,978	5.0	Victoria
Manitoba	552,330	1,265,015	2.3	Winnipeg
New Brunswick	71,377	756,050	10.6	Fredericton
Newfoundland and Labrador	370,511	526,702	1.4	St John's
Nova Scotia	52,939	940,789	17.8	Halifax
Ontario	908,608	13,537,994	14.9	Toronto
Prince Edward Island	5,686	145,237	25.5	Charlottetown
Québec	1,356,547	8,155,334	6.0	Québec
Saskatchewan	588,239	1,108,303	1.9	Regina
Territories:				
Northwest Territories	1,143,793	43,537	0.0	Yellowknife
Nunavut Territory	1,877,788	35,591	0.0	Iqaluit
Yukon Territory	474,713	36,700	0.1	Whitehorse
Total	8,965,121	35,158,304	3.9	—

Source: Statistics Canada, [SC2b].

PRINCIPAL METROPOLITAN AREAS
(population at 2011 census)

Toronto	5,583,064	London	474,786
Montréal	3,824,221	St Catharines–Niagara	392,184
Vancouver	2,313,328	Halifax	390,328
Ottawa–Gatineau (capital)	1,236,324	Oshawa	356,177
Calgary	1,214,839	Victoria	344,615
Edmonton	1,159,869	Windsor	319,246
Québec	765,706	Saskatoon	260,600
Winnipeg	730,018	Regina	210,556
Hamilton	721,053	Sherbrooke	201,890
Kitchener	477,160		

Source: Statistics Canada, [SC3].

BIRTHS, MARRIAGES AND DEATHS
(year ending 30 June, unless otherwise indicated)

	Registered live births*		Registered marriages†		Registered deaths*	
	Number	Rate (per 1,000)	Number	Rate (per 1,000)	Number	Rate (per 1,000)
2005/06	346,082	10.7	145,842	4.5	225,489	7.0
2006/07	360,916	11.0	147,084	4.5	233,825	7.1
2007/08	373,695	11.2	148,296‡	4.4	236,525	7.1
2008/09	379,290	11.3	148,831‡	4.4	237,708	7.1
2009/10	379,373	11.2	n.a.	n.a.	237,138	7.0
2010/11	376,951	11.0	n.a.	n.a.	244,968	7.1
2011/12	378,762	10.9	n.a.	n.a.	244,645	7.0
2012/13‡	383,822	10.9	n.a.	n.a.	253,241	7.2

* Including Canadian residents temporarily in the USA but excluding US residents temporarily in Canada.
† Figures refer to the first of the two years, from January to December.
‡ Preliminary figure(s).

Sources: Statistics Canada, [SC2b], [SC4], [SC5], [SC6].

Life expectancy (years at birth): 81.1 (males 78.9; females 83.3) in 2011 (Source: World Bank, World Development Indicators database).

ECONOMICALLY ACTIVE POPULATION*
(annual averages, '000 persons aged 15 years and over)

	2010	2011	2012
Agriculture	300.7	305.6	309.2
Forestry, fishing, mining, petroleum and gas	329.4	337.2	369.1
Utilities	148.3	139.8	140.7
Construction	1,217.2	1,262.2	1,267.5
Manufacturing	1,744.3	1,760.2	1,785.5
Trade	2,677.8	2,669.9	2,643.8
Transportation and warehousing	805.7	843.4	849.4
Finance, insurance, real estate and leasing	1,095.7	1,083.4	1,093.2
Professional, scientific and technical services	1,266.7	1,309.2	1,299.3
Business, building and other support services	672.2	677.0	690.5
Educational services	1,217.8	1,219.4	1,287.7
Health care and social assistance	2,030.7	2,091.5	2,128.0
Information, culture and recreation	766.0	784.2	790.4
Accommodation and food services	1,058.4	1,093.4	1,102.4
Other services	753.5	758.7	795.3
Public administration	956.4	971.2	955.9
Total employed	17,041.0	17,306.2	17,507.7
Unemployed	1,484.1	1,393.1	1,368.4
Total labour force	18,525.1	18,699.4	18,876.1
Males	9,763.3	9,858.9	9,950.1
Females	8,761.8	8,840.5	8,926.0

* Figures exclude military personnel, inmates of institutions, residents of the Yukon, Northwest and Nunavut Territories, and Indian Reserves.

Sources: Statistics Canada, [SC7], [SC8].

Health and Welfare

KEY INDICATORS

Total fertility rate (children per woman, 2010)	1.7
Under-5 mortality rate (per 1,000 live births, 2010)	6
HIV/AIDS (% of persons aged 15–49, 2009)	0.2
Physicians (per 1,000 head, 2008)	2.0
Hospital beds (per 1,000 head, 2009)	3.2
Health expenditure (2009): US $ per head (PPP)	4,314
Health expenditure (2009): % of GDP	11.4
Health expenditure (2009): public (% of total)	70.6
Total carbon dioxide emissions ('000 metric tons, 2010)	499,137.4
Carbon dioxide emissions per head (metric tons, 2010)	14.6
Human Development Index (2012): ranking	11
Human Development Index (2012): value	0.911

For sources and definitions, see explanatory note on p. vi.

Agriculture

PRINCIPAL CROPS
('000 metric tons, estimates)

	2011	2012	2013
Wheat	25,288.0	27,205.2	33,026.2
Barley	7,891.5	8,012.3	9,246.5
Corn for grain	11,358.7	13,060.1	12,942.5
Rye	241.4	336.6	196.8
Oats	3,157.6	2,811.9	3,163.3
Peas, dry	2,502.0	3,340.8	3,781.0
Soybeans	4,297.7	5,086.4	4,817.4
Sunflower seed	19.8	86.9	53.6
Rapeseed (Canola)	14,608.1	13,868.5	15,963.1
Canary seed	128.6	149.7	97.5
Lentils	1,573.5	1,537.9	1,708.8
Mustard seed	130.0	118.6	153.7
Tame hay	27,735.3	25,258.8	n.a.

Source: Statistics Canada, [SC9].

LIVESTOCK
('000 head at 1 July)

	2010	2011	2012
Horses*	400	405	407
Cattle	13,013	12,155	12,215
Pigs	12,690	12,785	12,668
Sheep	855	879	887
Chickens*	165,000	164,600	166,000
Ducks*	1,300	1,350	1,400
Turkeys*	5,400	5,500	5,500

* FAO estimates.

Source: FAO.

LIVESTOCK PRODUCTS
('000 metric tons)

	2010	2011	2012
Cattle meat	1,272.3	1,154.2	1,204.6
Sheep meat	16.2	15.9	16.7
Pig meat	1,925.9	1,968.9	1,998.4
Horse meat*	25.6	27.0	28.5
Chicken meat	1,048.5	1,053.2	1,063.7
Turkey meat	159.0	159.6	160.8
Cows' milk†	8,243	8,400	8,450
Hen eggs	433.0	436.8	443.4

* FAO estimates.
† Unofficial figures.

Source: FAO.

Forestry

ROUNDWOOD REMOVALS
('000 cubic metres)

	2010	2011	2012
Sawlogs, veneer logs and logs for sleepers	112,540	118,036	122,097*
Pulpwood	23,409	25,921	26,272*
Other industrial wood	2,853	2,779	2,781*
Fuel wood	3,211	1,443	1,443†
Total	142,013	148,178	152,594†

* Unofficial figures.
† FAO estimate.

Source: FAO.

SAWNWOOD PRODUCTION
('000 cubic metres, incl. railway sleepers)

	2010	2011	2012
Coniferous (softwood)*	37,712	37,409	39,417
Broadleaved (hardwood)	955	1,471	1,298
Total	38,667	38,880	40,715

* Unofficial figures.

Source: FAO.

Fur Industry

NUMBER OF PELTS PRODUCED
('000)

	2007	2008	2009
Alberta	100.7	n.a.	n.a.
British Columbia	n.a.	170.1	162.7
Manitoba	139.9	129.9	124.4
New Brunswick	74.4	84.1	85.6
Newfoundland and Labrador	156.6	130.4	191.7
Northwest Territories	20.4	31.4	27.5
Nova Scotia	1,226.0	1,262.8	1,404.3
Nunavut Territory	8.4	7.3	4.5
Ontario	497.3	517.1	558.5
Prince Edward Island	46.9	51.9	63.9
Québec	248.0	261.7	277.3
Yukon Territory	4.2	4.5	2.3
Total (incl. others)	2,839.1	2,786.0	3,031.1

Source: Statistics Canada, [SC10].

Fishing

('000 metric tons, live weight)

	2010	2011	2012
Cod	19	15	12
Herring	159	142	123
Mackerel	39	12	6
Clams	29	29	28
Scallop*	60	60	53
Lobster	67	67	72
Shrimp	165	151	149
Queen Crab	85	84	93
Hake	59	57	59
Salmon	24	21	9
Total (incl. others)	905	836	783

* Includes meat with roe.

Note: Figures exclude landings of aquatic plants and animals ('000 metric tons): 46 in 2010; 22 in 2011; 17 in 2012.

Source: Department of Fisheries and Oceans, Ottawa.

Mining

('000 metric tons unless otherwise indicated)

	2009	2010	2011*
Metallic:			
Bismuth (metric tons)	87	91	92
Cadmium (metric tons)	322	2,403	1,767
Cobalt (metric tons)	2,275	2,643	2,966
Copper	470	508	551
Gold (kilograms)	96,573	102,147	98,166
Iron ore	31,728	36,178	33,573
Lead	71	62	60
Molybdenum (metric tons)	9,116	8,524	8,404
Nickel	132	156	212
Platinum group (kilograms)	10,925	9,864	21,567
Selenium (metric tons)	131	97	35
Silver (metric tons)	609	570	533
Uranium (metric tons)	10,133	9,927	8,690
Zinc	670	610	576
Non-metallic:			
Gypsum	3,568	3,046	2,555
Lime	1,613	1,863	1,959

—continued	2009	2010	2011*
Nepheline syenite	527	603	610
Potash (K_2O)	4,297	9,700	11,005
Salt	14,676	10,278	12,315
Sulphur, in smelter gas	543	610	609
Sulphur, elemental	6,435	6,247	5,914
Fuels:			
Coal	62,935	68,152	66,736
Structural materials:			
Cement	10,831	11,523	11,972
Stone	153,038	170,664	167,716

* Provisional figures.

Source: Natural Resources Canada.

2012: Natural gas (million cubic metres) 156,546; Crude petroleum ('000 metric tons) 182,571 (Source: BP, *Statistical Review of World Energy 2013*).

Industry

VALUE OF SHIPMENTS
(C $ million)

	2010	2011	2012
Food industries	82,330.0	85,523.0	87,318.2
Beverage and tobacco products industries	10,724.7	11,158.1	11,569.5
Textile mills	1,552.8	1,628.1	1,596.5
Textile product mills	1,664.0	1,734.2	1,750.0
Leather and allied products industries	415.9	399.6	409.2
Paper industries	26,206.8	25,885.0	24,162.2
Printing, publishing and allied industries	9,007.7	8,906.3	9,074.1
Refined petroleum and coal products industries	68,053.3	79,334.4	85,251.0
Chemical and chemical products industries	44,414.9	46,849.9	45,924.0
Plastics and rubber products industries	21,885.3	24,059.2	24,547.4
Clothing industries	2,497.3	2,672.7	2,529.4
Wood product industries	18,487.8	18,480.0	20,350.0
Non-metallic mineral products industries	12,828.1	13,148.2	13,150.9
Primary metal industries	42,188.3	48,638.0	46,318.8
Fabricated metal products industries	30,365.1	33,017.2	35,046.6
Machinery industries (excl. electrical machinery)	28,083.6	33,379.2	35,256.0
Computer and electronic products industries	15,342.2	15,336.0	13,663.6
Electrical equipment, appliance and component industries	9,565.3	10,130.5	10,350.9
Transportation equipment industries	84,682.6	91,719.8	104,013.2
Furniture and fixture industries	10,614.2	10,188.3	10,261.6
Other manufacturing industries	10,482.6	11,730.1	11,306.8
Total	531,392.6	573,917.6	593,849.9

Source: Statistics Canada, [SC11].

Electric energy (gross production, million kWh): 641,051 in 2008; 603,234 in 2009; 607,952 in 2010 (Source: UN Industrial Commodity Statistics Database).

Finance

CURRENCY AND EXCHANGE RATES

Monetary Units:
100 cents = 1 Canadian dollar (C $).

Sterling, US Dollar and Euro Equivalents (31 December 2013):
£1 sterling = C $1.7448;
US $1 = C $1.0595;
€1 = C $1.4612;
C $100 = £57.31 = US $94.38 = €68.44.

Average Exchange Rate (C $ per US $):
2011 0.9895
2012 0.9992
2013 1.0298

BUDGET
(C $ million, year ending 31 March)*

Revenue	2010/11	2011/12	2012/13
Tax revenue	436,725	466,936	480,500
Taxes on income, profits and capital gains	238,668	261,394	268,861
Taxes on payroll and work force	10,967	11,781	11,988
Taxes on property	58,780	59,234	60,181
Taxes on goods and services	118,665	124,337	128,758
Taxes on international trade and transactions	3,510	3,682	3,923
Social contributions	76,178	80,935	85,397
Other revenue	127,217	133,790	131,003
Total revenue	640,120	681,661	696,900

Expenditure	2010/11	2011/12	2012/13
Compensation of employees	216,994	224,446	231,354
Use of goods and services	157,565	161,637	165,915
Consumption of fixed capital	54,419	58,083	61,703
Interest	60,709	62,273	61,314
Subsidies	23,907	23,688	22,687
Grants	44,708	44,785	43,705
Social benefits	134,756	139,055	144,760
Other expense	9,639	10,779	10,488
Total expenditure†	702,697	724,746	741,926

* Figures refer to the consolidated accounts of federal, provincial and territorial governments with state pension plans.

† Including net acquisition of non-financial assets.

Source: Statistics Canada, [SC12].

INTERNATIONAL RESERVES
(US $ million at 31 December)

	2010	2011	2012
Gold*	153	167	181
IMF special drawing rights	9,054	8,966	8,754
Reserve position in IMF	3,056	3,875	4,368
Foreign exchange	44,888	52,811	55,243
Total	57,151	65,819	68,546

* National valuation.

Source: IMF, *International Financial Statistics*.

MONEY SUPPLY
(C $ million at 31 December*)

	2006	2007	2008
Currency outside depository corporations	43,870	44,740	48,610
Transferable deposits	515,470	452,820	566,410
Other deposits	1,791,510	1,257,500	1,404,760
Broad money	2,350,840	1,755,050	2,019,770

* Figures rounded to the nearest $10m.

Source: IMF, *International Financial Statistics*.

COST OF LIVING
(Consumer Price Index; base: 2002 = 100)

	2010	2011	2012
Food	123.1	127.7	130.8
Housing	123.3	125.6	127.1
Household expenses and furnishings	108.8	110.9	113.0
Clothing	91.6	91.9	92.0
Transport	118.0	125.6	128.1
Health and personal care	112.1	117.1	118.7
Recreation, education and reading	104.0	105.3	105.9
Tobacco and alcohol	133.1	135.6	137.6
All items	116.5	119.9	121.7

Source: Statistics Canada, [SC13].

NATIONAL ACCOUNTS

National Income and Product
(C $ million at current prices)

	2010	2011	2012
Compensation of employees	839,376	883,753	923,424
Net operating surplus and mixed income	377,938	411,428	406,047
Domestic factor incomes	1,217,314	1,295,181	1,329,471
Consumption of fixed capital	276,161	288,645	306,583
Gross domestic product (GDP) at factor cost	1,493,475	1,583,826	1,636,054
Indirect taxes, less subsidies	170,428	176,472	184,447
Statistical discrepancy	–1,146	–287	–534
GDP at market prices	1,662,757	1,760,011	1,819,967

Gross national income (C $ '000 million): 1,593.97 in 2010; 1,688.49 in 2011; 1,784.85 in 2012 (Source: IMF, *International Financial Statistics*).

Gross national disposable income (C $ '000 million): 1,505.81 in 2009; 1,591.53 in 2010; 1,684.47 in 2011 (Source: IMF, *International Financial Statistics*).

Expenditure on the Gross Domestic Product
(C $ million at current prices)

	2010	2011	2012
Government final consumption expenditure	366,346	381,774	394,499
Private final consumption expenditure	938,773	980,123	1,012,386
Changes in inventories	125	7,659	9,491
Gross fixed capital formation	387,976	412,037	439,269
Total domestic expenditure	1,693,220	1,781,593	1,855,645
Exports of goods and services	483,212	540,657	546,617
Less Imports of goods and services	514,821	562,525	582,829
Statistical discrepancy	1,146	286	534
GDP at market prices	1,662,757	1,760,011	1,819,967

Gross Domestic Product by Economic Activity
(C $ million at chained 2007 prices)

	2010	2011	2012
Agriculture, hunting, forestry and fishing	23,998	24,794	24,962
Mining, petroleum and gas extraction	117,356	123,469	123,906
Manufacturing	160,917	166,340	168,606
Electricity, gas and water	36,938	37,837	37,974
Construction	103,703	106,980	112,537
Wholesale trade	79,536	83,775	85,161
Retail trade	81,007	82,529	83,940
Transportation and warehousing	61,847	63,717	64,896
Finance, insurance, real estate and leasing	281,699	289,983	297,431
Professional, scientific and technical services	78,230	80,515	82,316

—continued	2010	2011	2012
Administration and support, waste management and remediation services	50,236	50,979	51,592
Education	81,332	81,955	83,185
Health care and social assistance	102,867	104,808	106,739
Information and cultural industries	50,485	51,404	52,224
Arts, entertainment and recreation	11,388	11,250	11,047
Accommodation and food services	30,577	30,716	31,826
Public administration	107,422	109,079	109,176
Other services	29,955	30,490	30,905
Statistical discrepancy	–267	–615	–346
GDP at basic prices	1,489,226	1,530,005	1,558,077

Sources: Statistics Canada, [SC14], [SC15], [SC16], [SC17].

BALANCE OF PAYMENTS
(US $ million)

	2010	2011	2012
Exports of goods	392,338	461,507	462,883
Imports of goods	–401,705	–460,923	–474,911
Balance on goods	–9,367	585	–12,028
Exports of services	76,925	84,808	84,159
Imports of services	–98,183	–107,694	–108,367
Balance on goods and services	–30,624	–22,302	–36,236
Primary income received	61,098	70,108	72,731
Primary income paid	–83,904	–93,352	–95,204
Balance on goods, services and primary income	–53,431	–45,545	–58,709
Secondary income received	9,217	9,555	9,759
Secondary income paid	–12,413	–13,093	–13,307
Current balance	–56,626	–49,083	–62,256
Capital account (net)	–121	–10	–140
Direct investment assets	–35,220	–51,906	–55,611
Direct investment liabilities	28,596	40,132	43,085
Portfolio investment assets	–13,936	–18,375	–35,309
Portfolio investment liabilities	110,233	101,047	83,233
Other investment assets	–42,415	–29,857	–28,803
Other investment liabilities	11,545	23,005	59,080
Net errors and omissions	1,759	–7,035	–1,549
Statistical discrepancy	—	–2	–1
Reserves and related items	3,815	7,916	1,729

Source: IMF, *International Financial Statistics*.

External Trade

PRINCIPAL COMMODITIES
(C $ million)

Imports f.o.b.	2010	2011	2012
Energy products	37,603.7	46,597.2	45,769.9
Crude petroleum	23,297.3	28,118.3	30,857.9
Forestry products	17,439.4	18,574.8	20,468.5
Building and packaging material	14,556.3	15,793.2	17,627.6
Metal and non-metallic mineral products	37,588.4	44,059.8	43,488.7
Intermediate metal products	22,900.6	28,055.6	27,172.2
Basic and industrial chemical, plastic and rubber products	30,758.9	35,823.2	38,084.9
Basic and industrial chemical products	16,570.1	20,339.1	22,224.5
Plastic and rubber products	14,188.7	15,483.9	15,860.4
Industrial machinery and equipment (excl. automotive products)	36,037.6	42,283.4	45,203.6
Electronic and electrical equipment and parts	51,058.5	55,085.6	55,497.5
Communications, audio and video equipment	16,252.6	17,686.2	17,934.4

Imports f.o.b.—*continued*	2010	2011	2012
Motor vehicles and parts	71,675.9	74,152.7	82,813.8
Passenger cars and light trucks	31,081.9	31,022.2	34,049.7
Tyres, motor vehicle engines and parts	33,497.0	34,665.6	38,733.5
Aircraft and other transportation equipment	11,941.7	12,794.0	12,725.2
Consumer goods	86,043.6	89,410.6	93,016.0
Food, beverages and tobacco products	19,138.1	20,897.3	22,592.7
Clothing, footwear and textile products	15,501.4	16,771.4	17,192.2
Pharmaceutical and medicinal products	13,490.9	13,759.4	13,424.3
Cleaning products, appliances, and miscellaneous goods and supplies	23,932.5	24,106.0	25,495.1
Total (incl. others)	413,670.0	456,054.7	474,544.5

Exports f.o.b.	2010	2011	2012
Farm, fishing and intermediate products	20,144.9	24,136.2	27,233.4
Farm and fishing products	16,120.1	18,729.9	21,136.5
Energy products	83,569.2	103,491.9	105,064.7
Crude petroleum	49,906.8	68,326.3	73,016.1
Natural gas	17,591.4	15,562.5	10,597.0
Forestry products	29,393.6	30,461.5	30,621.3
Pulp and paper stock	13,078.1	13,308.1	11,816.3
Building and packaging material	15,860.1	16,484.4	18,149.8
Metal ores and non-metallic minerals	16,826.9	20,231.1	18,512.5
Metal and non-metallic mineral products	48,686.2	59,008.3	54,399.9
Intermediate metal products	39,215.6	47,799.1	43,317.6
Basic and industrial chemical, plastic and rubber products	30,582.3	35,755.6	32,986.0
Basic and industrial chemical products	19,400.9	23,283.1	20,494.3
Industrial machinery and equipment (excl. automotive products)	22,461.8	25,400.1	26,829.5
Electrical and electronic equipment and parts	22,484.2	23,212.0	22,915.4
Motor vehicles and parts	57,357.0	59,583.3	68,486.0
Passenger cars and light trucks	37,967.8	39,303.1	46,921.0
Tyres, motor vehicle engines and parts	17,667.9	18,040.5	19,221.2
Aircraft and other transportation equipment	15,815.7	16,247.9	17,331.5
Aircraft, engines and parts	13,510.8	13,325.5	14,307.0
Consumer goods	47,593.2	49,836.2	48,534.6
Food, beverages and tobacco products	19,514.8	20,835.7	20,912.8
Total (incl. others)	403,966.7	456,807.5	462,528.2

Sources: Statistics Canada, [SC18], [SC19].

PRINCIPAL TRADING PARTNERS
(C $ million, balance of payments basis)

Imports	2010	2011	2012
Japan	10,062.0	9,367.0	10,791.4
United Kingdom	9,556.3	10,559.1	8,310.9
USA	259,934.8	281,460.3	296,458.1
Other European Union countries	30,867.2	35,237.2	36,302.7
Other OECD countries	28,824.7	32,701.4	35,988.1
Other countries	74,424.9	86,730.1	86,693.5
Total	413,670.0	456,054.7	474,544.5

Exports	2010	2011	2012
Japan	9,751.6	11,336.4	10,823.8
United Kingdom	16,971.6	19,371.4	19,829.3
USA	295,113.1	329,928.3	338,440.5
Other European Union countries	20,238.4	23,041.2	21,143.0
Other OECD countries	17,864.7	20,486.3	18,510.4
Other countries	44,027.5	52,643.7	53,781.0
Total	403,966.7	456,807.5	462,528.2

Source: Statistics Canada, [SC20].

Transport

RAILWAYS
(revenue traffic)

	2009	2010	2011
Passengers carried ('000)*	4,538	4,477	4,461
Passenger-km (million)*	1,439	1,412	1,428
Freight carried ('000 metric tons)	244,062	303,258	305,793
Net freight ton-km ('000)	307,880	360,809	372,264

* Intercity trains only.

Source: Railway Association of Canada, *Railway Trends*.

ROAD TRAFFIC
('000 vehicles registered at 31 December)

	2008	2009	2010
On-road motor vehicle registrations	21,087.0	21,387.1	21,847.6
Passenger cars and light trucks	19,612.9	19,877.0	20,268.0
Heavy trucks	823.0	829.7	877.0
Buses	84.2	85.6	86.3
Motorcycles and mopeds	566.9	594.9	616.3
Trailers	5,527.8	5,747.3	5,953.8
Other (off-road, construction, farm vehicles, etc.)	1,851.5	1,920.9	1,896.4
Total vehicle registrations	28,466.3	29,055.3	29,697.8

Note: Light trucks are defined as vehicles weighing less than 4,500 kilograms; heavy trucks are those weighing 4,500 kilograms and over.

Source: Statistics Canada, [SC21].

INLAND WATER TRAFFIC
(St Lawrence Seaway, '000 gross registered metric tons)

	2010	2011	2012
Montréal-Lake Ontario	29,999	33,348	35,812
Welland Canal	36,808	38,379	40,079

Source: St Lawrence Seaway Management Corpn.

SHIPPING

Flag Registered Fleet
(at 31 December)

	2011	2012	2013
Number of vessels	1,379	1,378	1,391
Total displacement ('000 grt)	3,890.9	3,839.9	3,781.2

Source: Lloyd's List Intelligence (www.lloydslistintelligence.com).

CIVIL AVIATION
(scheduled services)

	2010	2011
Kilometres flown (million)	1,162	1,208
Passengers carried ('000)	67,277	70,254
Passenger-km (million)	115,793	123,664
Total ton-km (million)	13,417	14,201

Source: UN, *Statistical Yearbook*.

2012: Passengers carried ('000) 73,573.8 (Source: World Bank, World Development Indicators database).

Tourism

FOREIGN TOURIST ARRIVALS BY COUNTRY OF RESIDENCE

	2009	2010	2011
Australia	204,383	232,855	242,430
China, People's Republic	160,833	194,979	243,692
France	407,653	435,465	459,140
Germany	309,684	332,086	315,901
Hong Kong	107,410	114,973	123,060
India	107,959	127,619	139,213
Japan	197,752	235,510	211,062
Korea, Republic	138,150	164,282	151,101
Mexico	168,724	120,499	132,217
Netherlands	109,133	109,208	105,842
Switzerland	99,457	105,425	110,723
United Kingdom	710,513	711,689	679,828
USA	11,667,233	11,748,814	11,595,363
Total (incl. others)	15,737,150	16,097,369	16,014,405

Total tourist arrivals ('000): 15,972 in 2012.

Tourism receipts (US $ million, excl. passenger transport): 15,842 in 2010; 16,800 in 2011; 17,401 in 2012 (provisional).

Source: World Tourism Organization.

Communications Media

	2010	2011	2012
Telephones ('000 main lines in use)	18,394	18,201	18,010
Mobile cellular telephones ('000 subscribers)	25,825.4	27,387.2	26,263.0
Internet subscribers ('000)	10,953.3	n.a.	n.a.
Broadband subscribers ('000)	10,477.9	10,931.9	11,405.5

Source: International Telecommunication Union.

Education

(2009/10 unless otherwise indicated, UNESCO estimates)

		Students		
	Teachers	Males	Females	Total
Pre-primary	28,624*	261,416	246,506	507,922
Primary	141,045*	1,110,993	1,057,029	2,168,022
Secondary	376,830†	1,352,109	1,259,510	2,611,619
Tertiary	132,230‡	577,784§	748,927§	1,326,711§

* 1999/2000 figure.

† 2007/08 figure.

‡ 2001/02 figure.

§ 2003/04 figure.

Source: UNESCO Institute for Statistics.

Directory

The Government

HEAD OF STATE

Queen: HM Queen ELIZABETH II.

Governor-General: DAVID LLOYD JOHNSTON (took office on 1 October 2010).

FEDERAL MINISTRY
(April 2014)

The Government is formed by the Conservative Party of Canada.

Prime Minister: STEPHEN JOSEPH HARPER.

Minister of Aboriginal Affairs and Northern Development: BERNARD VALCOURT.

Minister of National Defence: ROBERT DOUGLAS NICHOLSON.

Minister of Justice and Attorney-General of Canada: PETER GORDON MACKAY.

Minister of Health: RONA AMBROSE.

Minister of Public Works and Government Services: DIANE FINLEY.

Minister of Foreign Affairs: JOHN BAIRD.

President of the Treasury Board: TONY CLEMENT.

Minister of Finance: JOE OLIVER.

Leader of the Government in the House of Commons: PETER VAN LOAN.

Minister of Employment and Social Development, and of Multiculturalism: JASON KENNEY.

Minister of Agriculture and Agri-Food: GERRY RITZ.

Minister of International Development and Minister for La Francophonie: CHRISTIAN PARADIS.

Minister of Industry: JAMES MOORE.

Minister of Infrastructure, Communities and Intergovernmental Affairs, and Minister of the Economic Development Agency of Canada for the Regions of Quebec: DENIS LEBEL.

Minister of Environment, Minister for the Arctic Council and Minister of the Canadian Northern Economic Development Agency: LEONA AGLUKKAQ.

Minister of Transport: LISA RAITT.

Minister of Fisheries and Oceans: GAIL SHEA.

Minister of Veterans' Affairs: JULIAN FANTINO.

Minister of Public Safety and Emergency Preparedness: STEVEN BLANEY.

Minister of International Trade: EDWARD FAST.

Minister of Natural Resources and for the Federal Economic Development Initiative for Northern Ontario: GREG RICKFORD.

Minister of National Revenue: KERRY-LYNNE D. FINDLAY.

Minister of Canadian Heritage and Official Languages: SHELLY GLOVER.

Minister of Citizenship and Immigration: CHRIS ALEXANDER.

Minister of Labour and Minister for Status of Women: KELLIE LEITCH.

Minister of State (Small Business and Tourism, and Agriculture): MAXIME BERNIER.

Minister of State (Foreign Affairs and Consular Services): LYNNE YELICH.

Minister of State (Federal Economic Development Agency for Southern Ontario): GARY GOODYEAR.

Minister of State (Atlantic Canada Opportunities Agency): ROB MOORE.

Minister of State and Chief Government Whip: JOHN DUNCAN.

Minister of State (Multiculturalism): TIM UPPAL.

Minister of State (Seniors): ALICE WONG.

Minister of State (Sport): BAL GOSAL.

Minister of State (Finance): KEVIN SORENSON.

Minister of State (Democratic Reform): PIERRE POILIEVRE.

Minister of State (Social Development): CANDICE BERGEN.

Minister of State (Science and Technology): ED HOLDER.

Minister of State (Western Economic Diversification): MICHELLE REMPEL.

MINISTRIES

Office of the Prime Minister: Langevin Block, 80 Wellington St, Ottawa, ON K1A 0A2; tel. (613) 941-6888; fax (613) 941-6900; e-mail pm@pm.gc.ca; internet www.pm.gc.ca.

Aboriginal Affairs and Northern Development Canada: Terrasses de la Chaudière, 10 rue Wellington, Tour Nord, Gatineau, QC; Ottawa, ON K1A 0H4; tel. (819) 997-0811; fax (866) 817-3977; e-mail InfoPubs@aadnc-aandc.gc.ca; internet www.aadnc-aandc.gc.ca.

Agriculture and Agri-Food Canada: 1341 Baseline Rd, Ottawa, ON K1A 0C5; tel. (613) 773-1000; fax (613) 773-1081; e-mail info@agr.gc.ca; internet www.agr.gc.ca.

Atlantic Canada Opportunities Agency (ACOA): Blue Cross Centre, 3rd Floor, 644 Main St, POB 6051, Moncton, NB E1C 9J8; tel. (506) 851-2271; fax (506) 851-7403; e-mail information@acoa-apeca.gc.ca; internet www.acoa-apeca.gc.ca.

Canada Economic Development for the Regions of Québec: Edifice Dominion Sq., 1255 rue Peel, Suite 900, Montréal, QC H3B 2T9; tel. (514) 283-6412; fax (514) 283-3302; internet www.dec-ced.gc.ca.

Canada Revenue Agency: Office of the Minister of National Revenue, 7th Floor, 555 McKenzie Ave, Ottawa, ON K1A 0L5; tel. (613) 952-9184; internet www.cra-arc.gc.ca.

Canadian Heritage: 15 rue Eddy, Gatineau, QC K1A 0M5; tel. (819) 997-8409; fax (819) 934-3201; e-mail indemcanada@pch.gc.ca; internet www.pch.gc.ca.

Canadian Northern Economic Development Agency (CanNor): Allavvik Bldg, 2nd Floor, 1106 Iqaluit, NU X0A 0H0; tel. (867) 975-3746; fax (867) 975-3740; e-mail infonorth@cannor.gc.ca; internet www.cannor.gc.ca; devt of the northern territories; brs in Yellowknife and Whitehorse; Pres. PATRICK BORBEY.

Citizenship and Immigration Canada: Jean Edmonds Towers, 21st Floor, 365 Laurier Ave West, Ottawa, ON K1A 1L1; tel. (613) 954-1064; e-mail minister@cic.gc.ca; internet www.cic.gc.ca.

Department of Finance Canada: East Tower, 19th Floor, 140 O'Connor St, Ottawa, ON K1A 0G5; tel. (613) 992-1573; fax (613) 943-0938; e-mail finpub@fin.gc.ca; internet www.fin.gc.ca.

Department of Justice Canada: East Memorial Bldg, 284 Wellington St, Ottawa, ON K1A 0H8; tel. (613) 957-4222; fax (613) 954-0811; e-mail webadmin@justice.gc.ca; internet www.canada.justice.gc.ca.

Department of National Defence: National Defence HQ, Maj.-Gen. George R. Pearkes Bldg, 101 Colonel By Dr., Ottawa, ON K1A 0K2; tel. (613) 995-2534; fax (613) 992-4739; e-mail information@forces.gc.ca; internet www.forces.gc.ca.

Employment and Social Development Canada: Phase IV, 140 promenade du Portage, Gatineau, QC K1A 0J9; tel. (819) 994-5559; fax (819) 953-7260; e-mail media@hrsdc-rhdcc.gc.ca; internet www.hrsdc.gc.ca; manages the Labour Program.

Environment Canada: Les Terrasses de la Chaudière, 28th Floor, 10 Wellington St, Gatineau, QC K1A 0H3; tel. (819) 997-1441; fax (819) 953-0279; e-mail minister@ec.gc.ca; internet www.ec.gc.ca.

Fisheries and Oceans Canada: Centennial Towers, 13th Floor, 200 Kent St, Station 13E228, Ottawa, ON K1A 0E6; tel. (613) 993-0999; fax (613) 990-1866; e-mail info@dfo-mpo.gc.ca; internet www.dfo-mpo.gc.ca.

Foreign Affairs, Trade and Development Canada: Lester B. Pearson Bldg, 125 Sussex Dr., Ottawa, ON K1A 0G2; tel. (613) 944-4000; fax (613) 996-9709; e-mail enqserv@international.gc.ca; internet www.international.gc.ca.

Health Canada: 0900C2, Ottawa, ON K1A 0K9; tel. (866) 225-0709; fax (613) 941-5366; e-mail info@hc-sc.gc.ca; internet www.hc-sc.gc.ca.

Industry Canada: C. D. Howe Bldg, 11th Floor, East Tower, 235 Queen St, Ottawa, ON K1P 5G8; tel. (613) 954-5031; fax (613) 954-2340; e-mail info@ic.gc.ca; internet www.ic.gc.ca.

Infrastructure Canada: 180 Kent St, Suite 1100, Ottawa, ON K1P 0B6; tel. (613) 948-1148; fax (613) 948-9393; e-mail info@infc.gc.ca; internet www.infrastructure.gc.ca.

Intergovernmental Affairs: Privy Council Office, Rm 1000, 85 Sparks St, Ottawa, ON K1A 0A3; tel. (613) 957-5153; fax (613) 957-5043; e-mail info@pco-bcp.gc.ca; internet www.pco-bcp.gc.ca/aia.

Natural Resources Canada: 580 Booth St, Ottawa, ON K1A 0E4; tel. (613) 995-0947; fax (613) 996-9094; e-mail questions@nrcan.gc.ca; internet www.nrcan.gc.ca.

Public Safety Canada: 269 Laurier Ave West, Ottawa, ON K1A 0P8; tel. (613) 944-4875; fax (613) 954-5186; e-mail communications@ps-sp.gc.ca; internet www.ps-sp.gc.ca.

Public Works and Government Services Canada: 11 rue Laurier, PDP III, Gatineau, QC K1A 0S5; tel. (819) 956-3115; fax (819) 956-9062; e-mail questions@tpsgc-pwgsc.gc.ca; internet www.tpsgc-pwgsc.gc.ca.

Status of Women Canada: McDonald Bldg, 10th Floor, 123 Slater St, Ottawa, ON K1P 1H9; tel. (613) 995-3783; fax (613) 947-0761; e-mail infonational@swc-cfc.gc.ca; internet www.swc-cfc.gc.ca.

Transport Canada: 330 Sparks St, Ottawa, ON K1A 0N5; tel. (613) 990-2309; fax (613) 954-4731; e-mail questions@tc.gc.ca; internet www.tc.gc.ca.

Treasury Board of Canada Secretariat: Strategic Communications and Ministerial Affairs, L'Esplanade Laurier, 9th Floor, East Tower, 140 O'Connor St, Ottawa, ON K1A 0R5; tel. (613) 957-2400; fax (613) 941-4000; e-mail info@tbs-sct.gc.ca; internet www.tbs-sct.gc.ca.

Veterans Affairs Canada: 161 Grafton St, POB 7700, Charlottetown, PE C1A 8M9; tel. (866) 522-2122; fax (902) 566-8508; e-mail information@vac-acc.gc.ca; internet www.vac-acc.gc.ca.

Western Economic Diversification Canada: Canada Pl., 9700 Jasper Ave, Suite 1500, Edmonton, AB T5J 4H7; tel. (780) 495-4164; fax (403) 495-4557; e-mail info@wd-deo.gc.ca; internet www.wd-deo.gc.ca.

Federal Legislature

THE SENATE

Senators are appointed by the Governor-General on the recommendation of the Prime Minister of Canada. Senators hold their positions until they attain the age of 75 years.

The Senate of Canada: Ottawa, ON K1A 0A4; tel. (613) 992-4416; e-mail sencom@sen.parl.gc.ca; internet sen.parl.gc.ca.

Speaker: NOËL A. KINSELLA.

Seats at Dec. 2013

Conservative Party	57
Liberal Party	32
Independent	7
Vacant	9
Total	105

HOUSE OF COMMONS

House of Commons: Parliament of Canada, Ottawa, ON K1A 0A9; tel. (613) 992-4793; e-mail info@parl.gc.ca; internet www.parl.gc.ca.

Speaker: ANDREW SCHEER.

General Election, 2 May 2011, official results

	% of votes	Seats at election	Seats at April 2014
Conservative Party	39.6	166	160
New Democratic Party	30.6	103	99
Liberal Party	18.9	34	35
Bloc Québécois	6.1	4	4
Green Party	3.9	1	2
Independent	0.4	—	3
Vacant	—	—	5
Total (incl. others)	100.0	308	308

Provincial Legislatures

ALBERTA

Lieutenant-Governor: DONALD S. ETHELL.

Interim Premier: DAVE HANCOCK.

Election, 23 April 2012

	Seats at election	Seats at Jan. 2014
Progressive Conservative	61	60
Wildrose Alliance Party	17	17
Liberal	5	5
New Democratic Party	4	4
Independent	—	1
Total	87	87

BRITISH COLUMBIA

Lieutenant-Governor: JUDITH GUICHON.

Premier: CHRISTY CLARK.

Election, 14 May 2013

	Seats
Liberal	49
New Democratic Party	34
Green Party	1
Independent	1
Total	85

MANITOBA

Lieutenant-Governor: PHILLIP S. LEE.

Premier: GREGORY SELINGER.

Election, 4 October 2011

	Seats at election	Seats at Jan. 2014
New Democratic Party	37	37
Progressive Conservative	19	17
Liberal	1	1
Vacant	—	2
Total	57	57

NEW BRUNSWICK

Lieutenant-Governor: GRAYDON NICHOLAS.

Premier: DAVID ALWARD.

Election, 27 September 2010

	Seats at election	Seats at Jan. 2014
Progressive Conservative	42	41
Liberal	13	13
Independent	—	1
Total	55	55

NEWFOUNDLAND AND LABRADOR

Lieutenant-Governor: FRANK FAGAN.

Premier: THOMAS W MARSHALL.

Election, 11 October 2011

	Seats at election	Seats at Jan. 2014
Progressive Conservative	37	34
Liberal	6	9
New Democratic Party	5	3
Independent	—	2
Total	48	48

NOVA SCOTIA

Lieutenant-Governor: JOHN JAMES GRANT.

Premier: STEPHEN MCNEIL.

Election, 8 October 2013

	Seats
Liberal	33
Progressive Conservative	11
New Democratic Party	7
Total	51

ONTARIO

Lieutenant-Governor: DAVID C. ONLEY.

Premier: KATHLEEN WYNNE.

Election, 6 October 2011

	Seats at election	Seats at Jan. 2014
Liberal	53	49
Progressive Conservative	37	36
New Democratic Party	17	20
Vacant	—	2
Total	107	107

PRINCE EDWARD ISLAND

Lieutenant-Governor: H. FRANK LEWIS.

Premier: ROBERT GHIZ.

Election, 3 October 2011

	Seats at election	Seats at Jan. 2014
Liberal	22	23
Progressive Conservative	5	3
Independent	—	1
Total	27	27

QUÉBEC

Lieutenant-Governor: PIERRE DUCHESNE.

Premier: PHILIPPE COUILLARD.

Election, 7 April 2014

	Seats
Liberal	70
Parti Québécois	30
Coalition Avenir Québec	22
Québec Solidaire	3
Total	125

SASKATCHEWAN

Lieutenant-Governor: VAUGHN SOLOMON SCHOFIELD.

Premier: BRAD WALL.

Election, 7 November 2011

	Seats
Saskatchewan Party	49
New Democratic Party	9
Vacant	—
Total	58

Territorial Legislatures

NORTHWEST TERRITORIES

Commissioner: GEORGE L. TUCCARO.

Premier: BOB MCLEOD.

The Legislative Assembly consists of 19 independent members without formal party affiliation.

NUNAVUT

Commissioner: EDNA EKHIVALAK ELIAS.

Premier: PETER TAPTUNA.

The Legislative Assembly consists of 22 independent members without formal party affiliation.

YUKON

Commissioner: DOUGLAS GEORGE PHILLIPS.

Premier: DARRELL PASLOSKI.

Election, 11 October 2011

	Seats	Seats at Jan. 2014
Yukon Party	11	12
New Democratic Party	6	6
Liberal	2	1
Vacant	—	—
Total	19	19

Election Commission

Elections Canada: Jackson Bldg, 257 Slater St, Ottawa, ON K1A 0M6; tel. (613) 993-2975; fax (613) 954-8584; e-mail info@elections.ca; internet www.elections.ca; f. 1920; independent; Chief Electoral Officer MARC MAYRAND; Commr YVES CÔTÉ.

Political Organizations

Bloc Québécois: 3730 blvd Crémazie Est, 4e étage, Montréal, QC H2A 1B4; tel. (514) 526-3000; fax (514) 526-2868; e-mail capitale@bloc.org; internet www.blocquebecois.org; f. 1990 by group of seven Progressive Conservative MPs representing Québec constituencies in federal Parliament; seeks negotiated sovereignty for Québec; Leader ANNIE LESSARD (acting).

Canadian Action Party/Parti Action Canadienne: 333 Sockeye Creek, St Terrace, BC V8G 0G5; tel. (705) 727-9827; e-mail communications@actionparty.ca; internet actionparty-ne.ca; f. 1997; Leader JASON CHASE; Sec. SALLY BRAUN.

Christian Heritage Party of Canada: POB 4958, Station E, Ottawa, ON K1S 5J1; tel. (819) 281-6686; fax (819) 281-7174; e-mail nationaloffice@chp.ca; internet www.chp.ca; f. 1986; Leader JIM HNATIUK; Pres. LOUIS (LUKE) KWANTES.

Coalition Avenir Québec: 4020, rue Saint-Ambroise Bureau 499, Montréal, QC H4C 2C7; tel. (514) 800-6000; fax (514) 800-0081; e-mail info@coalitionavenirquebec.org; internet www.coalitionavenirquebec.org; f. 2011; absorbed the Action Démocratique du Québec (f. 1994) after its dissolution in 2012; Leader FRANÇOIS LEGAULT; Pres. DOMINIQUE ANGLADE.

Communist Party of Canada: 290A Danforth Ave, Toronto, ON M4K 1N6; tel. (416) 469-2446; fax (416) 469-4063; e-mail info@cpc-pcc.ca; internet www.parti-communiste.ca; f. 1921; Leader MIGUEL FIGUEROA.

Conservative Party of Canada: 130 Albert St, Suite 1204, Ottawa, ON K1P 5G4; tel. (613) 755-2000; fax (613) 755-2001; internet www.conservative.ca; f. 2003 by merger of federal brs of Canadian Alliance and Progressive Conservative Party of Canada (although most provincial brs of the Progressive Conservative Party retained that name); Leader STEPHEN J. HARPER; Pres. JOHN WALSH.

Green Party of Canada: 85 Albert St, Suite 1507, Ottawa, ON K1P 6A4; POB 997, Station B, Ottawa, ON K1P 5R1; tel. (613) 562-4916; fax (613) 482-4632; e-mail info@greenparty.ca; internet www.greenparty.ca; f. 1983; environmentalist; Leader ELIZABETH MAY.

Liberal Party of Canada: 81 Metcalfe St, Suite 600, Ottawa, ON K1P 6M8; tel. (613) 237-0740; fax (613) 235-7208; e-mail info@liberal.ca; internet www.liberal.ca; Leader JUSTIN TRUDEAU; Pres. MIKE CRAWLEY.

Libertarian Party of Canada: 372 Rideau St, Suite 205, Ottawa, ON K1N 1G7; tel. (613) 288-9089; e-mail info@libertarian.ca; internet www.libertarian.ca; f. 1974; supports the extension of individual freedoms; Leader KATRINA CHOWNE; Pres. ROB BROOKS (acting).

Marxist-Leninist Party of Canada: 1867 Amherst St, Montréal, QC H2L 3L7; tel. and fax (514) 522-1373; e-mail office@mlpc.ca; internet www.mlpc.ca; f. 1970; publishes *The Marxist-Leninist Daily* (English and French); Nat. Leader ANNA DI CARLO.

New Democratic Party of Canada (NDP): 279 Laurier Ave West, Suite 300, Ottawa, ON K1P 5J9; tel. (613) 236-3613; fax (613) 230-9950; internet www.ndp.ca; f. 1961; social democratic; Leader THOMAS MULCAIR; Pres. REBECCA BLAIKIE.

Parti Québécois: 1200 ave Papineau, bureau 150, Montréal, QC H2K 4R5; tel. (514) 526-0020; fax (514) 526-0272; e-mail info@pq.org; internet www.pq.org; f. 1968; social democratic; seeks political sovereignty for Québec; Leader PAULINE MAROIS; Pres. RAYMOND ARCHAMBAULT.

Progressive Canadian Party: Suite 200, 730 Davis Dr., Toronto, ON L3Y 2R4; tel. (905) 853-8949; fax (905) 853-7214; e-mail info@pcparty.org; internet progressivecanadian.ca; f. 2004; Leader SINCLAIR M. STEVENS.

Québec Solidaire: 7105 rue St-Hubert, Suite 304, Montréal H2S 2N1; tel. (514) 278-9014; fax (514) 270-4379; e-mail akhadir-merc@assnat.qc.ca; internet www.quebecsolidaire.net; f. 2006; Pres ANDRÉS FONTECILLA.

Saskatchewan Party: 6135 Rochdale Blvd, Regina, SK S4X 2R1; tel. (306) 359-1638; fax (306) 359-9832; e-mail info@saskparty.com; internet www.saskparty.com; f. 1997; provincial; Leader BRAD WALL; Pres. GARY MESCHISHNICK.

Wildrose Alliance Party: 10th Ave SW, Suite 601, Calgary, AB T2R 0B2; tel. (888) 262-1888; fax (866) 620-4791; e-mail info@wildrose.ca; internet www.wildrose.ca; f. 2008 by merger of Alberta Alliance and Wildrose Alliance Party of Alberta; provincial; Leader DANIELLE SMITH; Pres. DAVID YAGER.

Yukon Party: 211 Elliott St, POB 31113, Whitehorse, YT Y1A 5P7; tel. (867) 668-6505; e-mail info@yukonparty.ca; internet www.yukonparty.ca; provincial; Leader DARRELL PASLOSKI; Pres. PAT MCINROY.

Diplomatic Representation

EMBASSIES AND HIGH COMMISSIONS IN CANADA

Afghanistan: 240 Argyle Ave, Ottawa, ON K2P 1B9; tel. (613) 563-4223; fax (613) 563-4962; e-mail contact@afghanemb-canada.net; internet www.afghanemb-canada.net; Chargé d'affaires a.i. MOHAMMAD DAWOOD QAYOMI.

Albania: 130 Albert St, Suite 302, Ottawa, ON K1P 5G4; tel. (613) 236-3053; fax (613) 236-0804; e-mail embassy.ottawa@mfa.gov.al; Ambassador ELIDA PETOSHATI.

Algeria: 500 Wilbrod St, Ottawa, ON K1N 6N2; tel. (613) 789-8505; fax (613) 789-1406; e-mail info@embassyalgeria.ca; internet www.embassyalgeria.ca; Ambassador SMAIL BENAMARA.

Angola: 189 Laurier Ave East, Ottawa, ON K1N 6P1; tel. (613) 234-1152; fax (613) 234-1179; e-mail info@embangola-can.org; internet www.embangola-can.org; Ambassador AGOSTINHO TAVARES DA SILVA NETO.

Argentina: 81 Metcalfe St, 7th Floor, Ottawa ON K1P 6K7; tel. (613) 236-2351; fax (613) 235-2659; e-mail ecana@mrecic.gov.ar; internet www.ecana.mrecic.gob.ar; Ambassador NORMA ESTER NASCIMBENE.

Armenia: 7 Delaware Ave, Ottawa, ON K2P 0Z2; tel. (613) 234-3710; fax (613) 234-2144; e-mail armcanadaembassy@mfa.am; internet www.canada.mfa.am; Ambassador ARMEN YEGANIAN.

Australia: 50 O'Connor St, Suite 710, Ottawa, ON K1P 6L2; tel. (613) 236-0841; fax (613) 216-1321; internet www.canada.embassy.gov.au; High Commissioner LOUISE HAND.

Austria: 445 Wilbrod St, Ottawa, ON K1N 6M7; tel. (613) 789-1444; fax (613) 789-3431; e-mail ottawa-ob@bmeia.gv.at; internet www.austro.org; Ambassador ARNO RIEDEL.

Azerbaijan: 275 Slater St, Suite 1203, Ottawa, ON K1P 5H9; tel. (613) 288-0497; fax (613) 230-8089; e-mail azerbaijan@azembassy.ca; internet www.azembassy.ca; Ambassador FARID SHAFIYEV.

Bahamas: 50 O'Connor St, Suite 1313, Ottawa, ON K1P 6L2; tel. (613) 232-1724; fax (613) 232-0097; e-mail ottawa-mission@bahighco.com; internet www.bahighco.ca; High Commissioner CALSEY W. JOHNSON.

Bangladesh: 340 Albert St, Suite 1250, Ottawa, ON K1R 7Y6; tel. (613) 236-0138; fax (613) 567-3213; e-mail bangla@rogers.com; internet www.bdhcottawa.ca; High Commissioner KAMRUL AHSAN.

Barbados: 55 Metcalfe St, Suite 470, Ottawa, ON K1P 6L5; tel. (613) 236-9517; fax (613) 230-4362; e-mail ottawa@foreign.gov.bb; High Commissioner EDWARD EVELYN GREAVES.

Belarus: 130 Albert St, Suite 600, Ottawa, K1P 5G4; tel. (613) 233-9994; fax (613) 233-8500; e-mail canada@mfa.gov.by; internet www.canada.belembassy.org; Chargé d'affaires a.i. ROMAN SOBOLEV.

Belgium: 360 Albert St, 8th Floor, Suite 820, Ottawa, ON K1R 7X7; tel. (613) 236-7267; fax (613) 236-7882; e-mail ottawa@diplobel.fed.be; internet www.diplomatie.be/ottawa; Ambassador BRUNO VAN DER PLUIJM.

Benin: 58 Glebe Ave, Ottawa, ON K1S 2C3; tel. (613) 233-4429; fax (613) 233-8952; e-mail amba.benin@yahoo.ca; internet www.benin.ca; Ambassador PAMPHILE C. GOUTONDJI.

Bolivia: 130 Albert St, Suite 416, Ottawa, ON K1P 5G4; tel. (613) 236-5730; fax (613) 236-1312; e-mail mbolivia-ottawa@rree.gov.be; internet www.emboliviacanada.com; Ambassador EDGAR JOSÉ TORREZ-MOSQUEIRA.

Bosnia and Herzegovina: 17 Blackburn Ave, Ottawa, ON K1N 8A2; tel. (613) 236-0028; fax (613) 236-1139; e-mail info@bhembassy.ca; internet www.bhembassy.ca; Chargé d'affaires a.i. MITHAT PASIC.

Brazil: 450 Wilbrod St, Ottawa, ON K1N 6M8; tel. (613) 237-1090; fax (613) 237-6144; e-mail mailbox@brasembottawa.org; internet www.brasembottawa.org; Ambassador PEDRO FERNANDO BRÊTAS BASTOS.

Brunei: 395 Laurier Ave East, Suite 400, Ottawa, ON K1N 6R4; tel. (603) 234-5656; fax (603) 234-4397; e-mail bhco@bellnet.ca; High Commissioner NADIAH AHMAD RAFIE (acting).

Bulgaria: 325 Stewart St, Ottawa, ON K1N 6K5; tel. (613) 789-3215; fax (613) 789-3524; e-mail mailmn@storm.ca; Ambassador NIKOLAY MIKLOV.

Burkina Faso: 48 Chemin Range Rd, Ottawa, ON K1N 8J4; tel. (613) 238-4796; fax (613) 238-3812; e-mail contact@ambabf-ca.org; internet www.burkinafaso.ca; Ambassador AMADOU ADRIEN KONÉ.

Burundi: 340 Albert St, Suite 1301, Ottawa, ON K1R 7Y6; tel. (613) 789-0414; fax (613) 789-9537; e-mail ambabottawa@yahoo.ca; internet www.ambabucanada.com; Ambassador SPECIOSE NZEYIMANA.

Cameroon: 170 Clemow Ave, Ottawa, ON K1S 2B4; tel. (613) 236-1522; fax (613) 238-3885; e-mail cameroun@rogers.com; internet www.hc-cameroon-ottawa.org; High Commissioner ANU'A-GHEYLE SOLOMON AZOH-MBI.

Chile: 50 O'Connor St, Suite 1413, Ottawa, ON K1N 6L2; tel. (613) 235-4402; fax (613) 235-1176; e-mail echileca@chile.ca; internet chileabroad.gov.cl/canada/; Ambassador ROBERTO CHRISTIAN IBARRA.

China, People's Republic: 515 St Patrick St, Ottawa, ON K1N 5H3; tel. (613) 789-3434; fax (613) 789-1911; e-mail chinaemb_ca@mfa.gov.cn; internet www.ca.china-embassy.org; Ambassador ZHANG JUNSAI.

Colombia: 360 Albert St, Suite 1002, Ottawa, ON K1R 7X7; tel. (613) 230-3760; fax (613) 230-4416; e-mail embajada@embajadacolombia.ca; Ambassador NICOLAS LLOREDA RICAURTE.

Congo, Democratic Republic: 18 Range Rd, Ottawa, ON K1N 8J3; tel. (613) 230-6391; fax (613) 230-1945; e-mail info@ambardcongocanada.ca; internet www.ambardcongocanada.ca; Ambassador DOMINIQUE KILUFYA KAMFWA.

Costa Rica: 350 Sparks St, Suite 701, Ottawa, ON K1R 7S8; tel. (613) 562-2855; fax (613) 562-2582; e-mail embcr@costaricaembassy.com; internet www.costaricaembassy.com; Ambassador LUIS CARLOS DELGADO.

Côte d'Ivoire: 9 Marlborough Ave, Ottawa, ON K1N 8E6; tel. (613) 236-9919; fax (613) 563-8287; e-mail info@canada.diplomatie.gouv.ci; internet www.canada.diplomatie.gouv.ci; Ambassador N'GORAN KOUAME.

Croatia: 229 Chapel St, Ottawa, ON K1N 7Y6; tel. (613) 562-7820; fax (613) 562-7821; e-mail croemb.ottawa@mvpei.hr; internet ca.mfa.hr; Ambassador VESELKO GRUBIŠIĆ.

Cuba: 388 Main St, Ottawa, ON K1S 1E3; tel. (613) 563-0141; fax (613) 563-0068; e-mail cuba@embacubacanada.net; internet www.cubadiplomatica.cu/canada; Ambassador JULIO GARMENDÍA PEÑA.

Czech Republic: 251 Cooper St, Ottawa, ON K2P 0G2; tel. (613) 562-3875; fax (613) 562-3878; e-mail ottawa@embassy.mzv.cz; internet www.mzv.cz/ottawa; Chargé d'affaires a.i. ROBERT TRIPES.

Denmark: 47 Clarence St, Suite 450, Ottawa, ON K1N 9K1; tel. (613) 562-1811; fax (613) 562-1812; e-mail ottamb@um.dk; internet www.canada.um.dk; Ambassador NIELS BOEL ABRAHAMSEN.

Dominica: (see entry for Barbados).

Dominican Republic: 130 Albert St, Suite 418, Ottawa, ON K1P 5G4; tel. (613) 569-9893; fax (613) 569-8673; e-mail info@drembassy.org; internet www.drembassy.org; Ambassador HECTOR VIRGILIO ALCANTARA MEJIA.

Ecuador: 99 Bank St, Suite 230, Ottawa, ON K1P 6B9; tel. (613) 563-8206; fax (613) 235-5776; e-mail embassy@embassyecuador.ca; internet www.embassyecuador.ca; Ambassador ANDRES TERAN-PARRAL.

Egypt: 454 Laurier Ave East, Ottawa, ON K1N 6R3; tel. (613) 234-4931; fax (613) 234-9347; e-mail egyptemb@sympatico.ca; internet www.mfa.gov.eg/english/embassies/egyptian_embassy_ottawa; Ambassador WAEL AHMED KAMAL ABOUL MAGD.

El Salvador: 209 Kent St, Ottawa, ON K2P 1Z8; tel. (613) 238-2939; fax (613) 238-6940; e-mail elsalvadorottawa@rree.gob.sv; internet embajadacanada.rree.gob.sv; Ambassador OSCAR MAURICIO DUARTE GRANADOS.

Eritrea: 75 Albert St, Suite 610, Ottawa, ON K1P 5E7; tel. (613) 234-3989; fax (613) 234-6213; Ambassador AHFEROM BERHANE GHEBREMEDHIN.

Estonia: 260 Dalhousie St, Suite 210, Ottawa, ON K1N 7E4; tel. (613) 789-4222; fax (613) 789-9555; e-mail embassy.ottawa@mfa.ee; internet www.estemb.ca; Ambassador GITA KALMET.

Ethiopia: 1501, 275 Slater St, Ottawa, ON K1P 5H9; tel. (613) 565-6637; fax (613) 565-9175; e-mail info@embassyofethiopia.net; internet www.embassyofethiopia.net; Ambassador BIRTUKAN AYANO.

Finland: 55 Metcalfe St, Suite 850, Ottawa, ON K1P 6L5; tel. (613) 288-2233; fax (613) 288-2244; e-mail embassy@finland.ca; internet www.finland.ca; Ambassador RISTO KARLO (CHARLES) MURTO.

France: 42 Sussex Dr., Ottawa, ON K1M 2C9; tel. (613) 789-1795; fax (613) 562-3735; e-mail politique@ambafrance-ca.org; internet www.ambafrance-ca.org; Ambassador PHILIPPE ANDRÉ FRANÇOIS E. ZELLER.

Gabon: 4 Range Rd, POB 368, Ottawa, ON K1N 8J5; tel. (613) 232-5301; fax (613) 232-6916; e-mail ambgabon@sprint.ca; internet gabonembassycanada.org; Chargé d'affaires a.i. FRANÇOIS EBIBI MBA.

Georgia: 150 Metcalfe St, Suite 2101, Ottawa ON K2P 1P1; tel. (613) 421-0460; fax (613) 680-0394; Ambassador ALEXANDER LATSABIDZE.

Germany: 1 Waverley St, Ottawa, ON K2P 0T8; tel. (613) 232-1101; fax (613) 594-9330; e-mail info@ottawa.diplo.de; internet www.ottawa.diplo.de; Ambassador WERNER FRANZ WNENDT.

Ghana: 1 Clemow Ave, Ottawa, ON K1S 2A9; tel. (613) 236-0871; fax (613) 236-0874; e-mail ghanacom@ghc-ca.com; internet www.ghc-ca.com; High Commissioner KWAASI OBENG-KORANTENG (acting).

Greece: 76–80 MacLaren St, Ottawa, ON K2P 0K6; tel. (613) 238-6271; fax (613) 238-5676; e-mail embassy@greekembassy.ca; internet www.mfa.gr/canada; Ambassador ELEFTHERIOS ANGHELOPOULOS.

Grenada: (see entry for Barbados).

Guatemala: 130 Albert St, Suite 1010, Ottawa, ON K1P 5G4; tel. (613) 233-7188; fax (613) 233-0135; e-mail embassy1@embaguate-canada.com; internet www.embaguate-canada.com; Ambassador BLANCA RITA JOSEFINA CLAVERIE DIAZ DE SCIOLLO.

Guinea: 483 Wilbrod St, Ottawa, ON K1N 6N1; tel. (613) 789-8444; fax (613) 789-7560; e-mail infos@ambaguinee-canada.org; internet ambaguinee-canada.org; Chargé d'affaires a.i. LOUNCENY CONDE.

Guyana: Burnside Bldg, 151 Slater St, Suite 309, Ottawa, ON K1P 5H3; tel. (613) 235-7249; fax (613) 235-1447; e-mail guyanahcott@rogers.com; internet www.guyanamissionottawa.org; High Commissioner HARRY NARINE NAWBATT.

Haiti: 85 Albert St, Suite 1110, Ottawa, ON K1P 6A4; tel. (613) 238-1628; fax (613) 238-2986; e-mail bohio@bellnet.ca; Ambassador FRANTZ LIAUTAUD.

Holy See: Apostolic Nunciature, 724 Manor Ave, Rockcliffe Park, Ottawa, ON K1M 0E3; tel. (613) 746-4914; fax (613) 746-4786; e-mail apostolic.nunciature@rogers.com; Nuncio Most Rev. LUIGI BONAZZI (Titular Archbishop of Atella).

Honduras: 151 Slater St, Suite 805, Ottawa, ON K1P 5H3; tel. (613) 233-8900; fax (613) 232-0193; e-mail embhonca@embassyhonduras.ca; internet www.embassyhonduras.ca; Ambassador SOFIA LASTENIA CERRATO RODRIGUEZ.

Hungary: 299 Waverley St, Ottawa, ON K2P 0V9; tel. (613) 230-2717; fax (613) 230-7560; e-mail mission.ott@mfa.gov.hu; internet www.mfa.gov.hu/kulkepviselet/CA/en/mainpage.htm; Ambassador LÁSZLÓ CSABA PORDÁNY.

Iceland: Constitution Sq., 360 Albert St, Suite 710, Ottawa, ON K1R 7X7; tel. (613) 482-1944; fax (613) 482-1945; e-mail icemb.ottawa@utn.stjr.is; internet www.iceland.org/ca; Ambassador THORDUR AEGIR OSKARSSON.

India: 10 Springfield Rd, Ottawa, ON K1M 1C9; tel. (613) 744-3751; fax (613) 744-0913; e-mail hicomind@hciottawa.ca; internet www.hciottawa.ca; High Commissioner NIRMAL K. VERMA.

Indonesia: 55 Parkdale Ave, Ottawa, ON K1Y 1E5; tel. (613) 724-1100; fax (613) 724-1105; e-mail info@indonesia-ottawa.org; internet www.indonesia-ottawa.org; Ambassador DIENNE HARDIANTI MOEHARIO.

Iraq: 215 McLeod St, Ottawa, ON K2P 0Z8; tel. (613) 236-9177; fax (613) 236-9641; e-mail media@iraqembassy.ca; internet www.iraqembassy.ca; Ambassador ABDULRAHMAN HAMID AL-HUSSAINI.

Ireland: 130 Albert St, 11th Floor, Suite 1105, Ottawa, ON K1P 5G4; tel. (613) 233-6281; fax (613) 233-5835; e-mail embassyofireland@rogers.com; Ambassador JOHN RAYMOND BASSETT.

Israel: 50 O'Connor St, Suite 1005, Ottawa, ON K1P 6L2; tel. (613) 567-6450; fax (613) 567-9878; e-mail info@ottawa.mfa.gov.il; internet ottawa.mfa.gov.il; Ambassador RAFAEL BARAK.

Italy: 275 Slater St, 21st Floor, Ottawa, ON K1P 5H9; tel. (613) 232-2401; fax (613) 233-1484; e-mail ambasciata.ottawa@esteri.it; internet www.ambottawa.esteri.it; Ambassador GIAN LORENZO CORNADO.

Jamaica: 151 Slater St, 10th Floor, Suite 1000, Ottawa, ON K1P 5H3; tel. (613) 233-9311; fax (613) 233-0611; e-mail hc@jhcottawa.ca; internet www.jhcottawa.ca; High Commissioner SHEILA IVOLINE SEALY MONTEITH.

Japan: 255 Sussex Dr., Ottawa, ON K1N 9E6; tel. (613) 241-8541; fax (613) 241-9831; e-mail infocul@ot.mofa.go.jp; internet www.ca.emb-japan.go.jp; Ambassador NORIHIRO OKUDA.

Jordan: 100 Bronson Ave, Suite 701, Ottawa, ON K1R 6G8; tel. (613) 238-8090; fax (613) 232-3341; e-mail jordan@on.aibn.com; internet www.embassyofjordan.ca; Ambassador BASHEER FAWWAZ ZOUBI.

Kazakhstan: 150 Metcalfe St, Suite 1603-1604, Ottawa, ON K2P 1P1; tel. (613) 695-8055; e-mail kazakhembassy@gmail.com; internet kazembassy.ca; Ambassador KONSTANTIN ZHIGALOV.

Kenya: 415 Laurier Ave East, Ottawa, ON K1N 6R4; tel. (613) 563-1773; fax (613) 233-6599; e-mail kenyahighcommission@rogers.com; internet www.kenyahighcommission.ca; Chargé d'affaires a.i. LILY C. SAMBU.

Korea, Republic: 150 Boteler St, Ottawa, ON K1N 5A6; tel. (613) 244-5010; fax (613) 244-5034; e-mail canada@mofat.go.kr; internet can-ottawa.mofat.go.kr; Ambassador CHO HEE-YONG.

Kuwait: 333 Sussex Dr., Ottawa, ON K1N 1J9; tel. (613) 780-9999; fax (613) 780-9905; e-mail info@embassyofkuwait.ca; internet www.embassyofkuwait.ca; Ambassador ALI HUSSAIN SALEH AL-SAMMAK.

Latvia: 350 Sparks St, Suite 1200, Ottawa, ON K1R 7S8; tel. (613) 238-6014; fax (613) 238-7044; e-mail embassy.canada@mfa.gov.lv; internet www.ottawa.am.gov.lv; Ambassador JURIS AUDARIŅŠ.

Lebanon: 640 Lyon St, Ottawa, ON K1S 3Z5; tel. (613) 236-5825; fax (613) 232-1609; e-mail info@lebanonembassy.ca; internet www.lebanonembassy.ca; Ambassador MICHELINE ABI-SAMRA.

Lesotho: 130 Albert St, Suite 1820, Ottawa, ON K1P 5G4; tel. (613) 234-0770; fax (613) 234-5665; e-mail lesotho.ottawa@bellnet.ca; internet www.lesothocanada.gov.ls; High Commissioner MATHABO THERESIA TSEPA.

Libya: 81 Metcalfe St, Suite 1000, Ottawa, ON K1P 6K7; tel. (613) 842-7519; fax (613) 842-8627; e-mail info@libyanembassy.ca; internet www.libyanembassy.ca; Ambassador FATHI MOHAMED BAJA.

Lithuania: 150 Metcalfe St, Suite 1600, Ottawa, ON K2P 1P1; tel. (613) 567-5458; fax (613) 567-5315; e-mail litemb@storm.ca; internet www.ca.mfa.lt; Ambassador VYTAUTAS ZALYS.

Macedonia, former Yugoslav republic: 130 Albert St, Suite 1006, Ottawa, ON K1P 5G4; tel. (613) 234-3882; fax (613) 233-1852; e-mail emb.macedonia.ottawa@sympatico.ca; internet www3.sympatico.ca/emb.macedonia.ottawa; Ambassador LJUBEN TEVDOVSKI.

Madagascar: 3 Raymond St, Ottawa, ON K1R 1A3; tel. (613) 567-0505; fax (613) 567-2882; e-mail ambamadcanada@bellnet.ca; internet www.madagascar-embassy.ca; Ambassador SIMON CONSTANT HORACE.

Malaysia: 60 Boteler St, Ottawa, ON K1N 8Y7; tel. (613) 241-5182; fax (613) 241-5214; e-mail malottawa@kln.gov.my; internet www.kln.gov.my/perwakilan/ottawa; High Commissioner HAYATI BINTI ISMAIL.

Mali: 50 Goulburn Ave, Ottawa, ON K1N 8C8; tel. (613) 232-1501; fax (613) 232-7429; e-mail ambassadedumali@rogers.com; internet www.ambamalicanada.org; Ambassador AMI TRAORE.

Mexico: 45 O'Connor St, Suite 1000, Ottawa, ON K1P 1A4; tel. (613) 233-8988; fax (613) 235-9123; e-mail info@embamexcan.com; internet www.sre.gob.mx/canada; Ambassador FRANCISCO SUÁREZ DÁVILA.

Mongolia: 151 Slater St, Suite 503, Ottawa, ON K1P 5H3; tel. (613) 569-3830; fax (613) 569-3916; e-mail mail@mongolembassy.org; internet www.ottawa.mfat.gov.mn; Ambassador TUNDEVDORJIIN ZALAA-UUL.

Montserrat: (see entry for Barbados).

Morocco: 38 Range Rd, Ottawa, ON K1N 8J4; tel. (613) 236-7391; fax (613) 236-6164; e-mail info@ambamaroc.ca; internet www.ambamaroc.ca; Ambassador NOUZHA CHEKROUNI.

Myanmar: 336 Island Park Dr., Ottawa, ON K1Y 0A7; tel. (613) 232-9990; fax (613) 232-6999; e-mail meottawa@rogers.com; internet www.meottawa.org; Ambassador HAU DO SUAN.

Nepal: 408 Queen St, Ottawa, ON K1R 5A7; tel. (613) 680-5513; fax (613) 422-5149; e-mail nepalembassy@rogers.com; internet www.nepalembassy.ca; Ambassador (vacant).

Netherlands: 350 Albert St, Suite 2020, Ottawa, ON K1R 1A4; tel. (613) 237-5031; fax (613) 237-6471; e-mail nid@the-netherlands.org; internet ottawa.the-netherlands.org; Ambassador CORNELIS JOHANNES KOLE.

New Zealand: Clarica Centre, 99 Bank St, Suite 727, Ottawa, ON K1P 6G3; tel. (613) 238-5991; fax (613) 238-5707; e-mail info@nzhcottawa.org; internet www.nzembassy.com/canada; High Commissioner SIMON TUCKER.

Niger: 38 Blackburn Ave, Ottawa, ON K1N 8A3; tel. (613) 232-4291; fax (613) 230-9808; e-mail ambanigeracanada@rogers.com; internet www.ambanigeracanada.ca; Ambassador FADJIMATA MAMAN SIDIBE.

Nigeria: 295 Metcalfe St, Ottawa, ON K2P 1R9; tel. (613) 236-0522; fax (613) 236-0529; e-mail chancery@nigeriahcottawa.com; internet www.nigeriahcottawa.com; High Commissioner OJO MADUEKWE.

Norway: 150 Metcalfe St, Suite 1300, Ottawa, ON K2P 1P1; tel. (613) 238-6571; fax (613) 238-2765; e-mail emb.ottawa@mfa.no; internet www.emb-norway.ca; Ambassador MONA ELISABETH BROETHER.

Pakistan: 10 Range Rd, Ottawa, ON K1N 8J3; tel. (613) 238-7881; fax (613) 238-7296; e-mail parepottawa@rogers.com; internet www.pakmission.ca; High Commissioner MIAN GUL AKBAR ZEB.

Panama: 130 Albert St, Suite 300, Ottawa, ON K1P 5G4; tel. (613) 236-7177; fax (613) 236-5775; e-mail info@embassyofpanama.ca; internet www.embassyofpanama.ca; Ambassador JORGE HERNAN MIRANDA CORONA.

Paraguay: 151 Slater St, Suite 501, Ottawa, ON K1P 5H3; tel. (613) 567-1283; fax (613) 567-1679; e-mail consularsection@embassyofparaguay.ca; internet www.embassyofparaguay.ca; Ambassador MANUEL SCHAERER KANONNIKOFF.

Peru: 130 Albert St, Suite 1901, Ottawa, ON K1P 5G4; tel. (613) 238-1777; fax (613) 232-3062; e-mail emperuca@bellnet.ca; internet www.embassyofperu.ca; Ambassador JOSÉ ANTONIO BELLINA ACEVEDO.

Philippines: 130 Albert St, Suite 606, Ottawa, ON K1P 5G4; tel. (613) 233-1121; fax (613) 233-4165; e-mail embassyofphilippines@rogers.com; internet www.philembassy.ca; Ambassador LESLIE B. GATAN.

Poland: 443 Daly Ave, Ottawa, ON K1N 6H3; tel. (613) 789-0468; fax (613) 789-1218; e-mail ottawa@polishembassy.ca; internet www.ottawa.msz.gov.pl; Ambassador MARCIN BOSACKI.

Portugal: 645 Island Park Dr., Ottawa, ON K1Y 0B8; tel. (613) 729-0883; fax (613) 729-4236; e-mail embportugal@dgaccp.org; Ambassador JOSÉ FERNANDO MOREIRA DA CUNHA.

Qatar: 150 Metcalfe St, 8th Floor, Suite 800, Ottawa ON K2P 1P1; tel. (613) 241-4917; fax (613) 241-3304; e-mail ottawa@mofa.gov.qa; Ambassador FAHAD MOHAMED Y. KAFOUD.

Romania: 655 Rideau St, Ottawa, ON K1N 6A3; tel. (613) 789-3709; fax (613) 789-4365; e-mail romania@romanian-embassy.com; internet ottawa.mae.ro; Ambassador MARIA LIGOR.

Russia: 285 Charlotte St, Ottawa, ON K1N 8L5; tel. (613) 235-4341; fax (613) 236-6342; e-mail info@rusembassy.ca; internet www.rusembassy.ca; Ambassador GEORGIY MAMEDOV.

Rwanda: 294 Albert St, Suite 404, Ottawa, ON K1P 6E6; tel. (613) 569-5420; fax (613) 569-5421; e-mail generalinfo@ambarwaottawa.ca; internet www.rwandahighcommission.ca; High Commissioner EDDA MUKABAGWIZA.

Saudi Arabia: 201 Sussex Dr., Ottawa, ON K1N 1K6; tel. (613) 237-4100; fax (613) 237-0567; e-mail caemb@mofa.gov.sa; internet www.saudiembassy.ca; Ambassador NAIF BIN BANDAR AL-SUDAIRI.

Senegal: 57 Marlborough Ave, Ottawa, ON K1N 8E8; tel. (613) 238-6392; fax (613) 238-2695; e-mail ambassn@sympatico.ca; internet www.ambsencanada.org; Ambassador NANCY NDIAYE NGOM.

Serbia: 17 Blackburn Ave, Ottawa, ON K1N 8A2; tel. (613) 233-6289; fax (613) 233-7850; e-mail diplomat@yuemb.ca; internet www.serbianembassy.ca; Chargé d'affaires a.i. MIRJANA ŠEŠUM-ĆURČIĆ.

Slovakia: 50 Rideau Terrace, Ottawa, ON K1M 2A1; tel. (613) 749-4442; fax (613) 749-4989; e-mail ottawa@slovakembassy.ca; internet www.ottawa.mfa.sk; Ambassador MILAN KOLLÁR.

Slovenia: 150 Metcalfe St, Suite 2200, Ottawa, ON K2P 1P1; tel. (613) 565-5781; fax (613) 565-5783; e-mail vot@gov.si; internet ottawa.embassy.si; Chargé d'affaires a.i. IRENA GRIL.

South Africa: 15 Sussex Dr., Ottawa, ON K1M 1M8; tel. (613) 744-0330; fax (613) 741-1639; e-mail rsafrica@southafrica-canada.ca; internet www.southafrica-canada.ca; Ambassador MEMBATHISI MPHUMZI MDLADLANA.

Spain: 74 Stanley Ave, Ottawa, ON K1M 1P4; tel. (613) 747-2252; fax (613) 744-1224; e-mail emb.ottawa@mae.es; internet www.maec.es/embajadas/ottawa; Ambassador CARLOS GÓMEZ-MÚGICA SANZ.

Sri Lanka: 333 Laurier Ave West, Suite 1204, Ottawa, ON K1P 1C1; tel. (613) 233-8449; fax (613) 238-8448; e-mail slhcit@rogers.com; internet www.srilankahcottawa.org; High Commissioner CHITRANGANEE WAGISWARA.

Sudan: 354 Stewart St, Ottawa, ON K1N 6K8; tel. (613) 235-4000; fax (613) 235-6880; e-mail sudanembassy-canada@rogers.com; internet www.sudanembassy.ca; Chargé d'affaires a.i. MUSA ABDELRAHIM MOHAMED ADAM.

Sweden: 377 Dalhousie St, Ottawa, ON K1N 9N8; tel. (613) 244-8200; fax (613) 241-2277; e-mail sweden.ottawa@foreign.ministry.se; internet www.swedishembassy.ca; Ambassador TEPPO MARKUS TAURIAINEN.

Switzerland: 5 Marlborough Ave, Ottawa, ON K1N 8E6; tel. (613) 235-1837; fax (613) 563-1394; e-mail ott.vertretung@eda.admin.ch; internet www.eda.admin.ch/canada; Ambassador ULRICH LEHNER.

Syria: 46 Cartier St, Ottawa, ON K2P1J3; tel. (613) 569-5556; fax (613) 569-3800; e-mail info@syrianembassy.ca; internet www.syrianembassy.ca; Chargé d'affaires a.i. BASHAR AKBIK (expelled in May 2012).

Tanzania: 50 Range Rd, Ottawa, ON K1N 8J4; tel. (613) 232-1509; fax (613) 232-5184; e-mail tzottawa@synapse.net; internet www.tzrepottawa.ca; High Commissioner ALEX CRESCENT MASSINDA.

Thailand: 180 Island Park Dr., Ottawa, ON K1Y 0A2; tel. (613) 722-4444; fax (613) 722-6624; e-mail contact@thaiembassy.ca; internet www.thaiembassy.ca; Ambassador PISAN MANAWAPAT.

Togo: 12 Range Rd, Ottawa, ON K1N 8J3; tel. (613) 238-5916; fax (613) 235-6425; e-mail ambatogoca@hotmail.com; Chargé d'affaires a.i. PALAKIYEM BOYODE.

Trinidad and Tobago: 200 First Ave, Ottawa, ON K1S 2G6; tel. (613) 232-2418; fax (613) 232-4349; e-mail ottawa@ttmissions.com; internet www.ttmissions.com; High Commissioner PHILIP ANTHONY BUXO.

Tunisia: 515 O'Connor St, Ottawa, ON K1S 3P8; tel. (613) 237-0330; fax (613) 237-7939; e-mail atottawa@comnet.ca; Ambassador RIADH ESSID.

Turkey: 197 Wurtemburg St, Ottawa, ON K1N 8L9; tel. (613) 244-2470; fax (613) 789-3442; e-mail embassy.ottawa@mfa.gov.tr; internet www.ottava.be.mfa.gov.tr; Ambassador TUNCAY BABALI.

Uganda: 231 Cobourg St, Ottawa, ON K1N 8J2; tel. (613) 789-7797; fax (613) 789-8909; e-mail uhc@ugandahighcommission.com; internet ugandahighcommission.com; High Commissioner JOHN CHRYSOSTOM ALINTUMA NSAMBU.

Ukraine: 310 Somerset St West, Ottawa, ON K2P 0J9; tel. (613) 230-2961; fax (613) 230-2400; e-mail emb_ca@ukremb.ca; internet www.canada.mfa.gov.ua; Ambassador VADYM PRYSTAIKO.

United Arab Emirates: 125 Boteler St, Ottawa, ON K1N 0A4; tel. (613) 565-7272; fax (613) 5658007; e-mail safara@uae-embassy.com; Ambassador MOHAMMAD SAIF HILAL AL-SHEHI.

United Kingdom: 80 Elgin St, Ottawa, ON K1P 5K7; tel. (613) 237-1530; fax (613) 237-7980; e-mail generalenquiries@britainincanada.org; internet www.gov.uk/government/world/organisations/british-high-commission-ottawa; High Commissioner HOWARD RONALD DRAKE.

USA: 490 Sussex Dr., POB 866, Station B, Ottawa, ON K1P 5T1; tel. (613) 238-5335; fax (613) 688-3082; internet ottawa.usembassy.gov; Ambassador BRUCE HEYMAN.

Uruguay: 350 Sparks St, Suite 901, Ottawa, ON K1R 7S8; tel. (613) 234-2727; fax (613) 233-4670; e-mail embassy@embassyofuruguay.ca; internet embassyofuruguay.ca; Ambassador ELBIO OSCAR ROSSELLI FRIERI.

Venezuela: 32 Range Rd, Ottawa, ON K1N 8J4; tel. (613) 235-5151; fax (613) 235-3205; e-mail info.canada@misionvenezuela.org; internet www.misionvenezuela.org; Chargé d'affaires a.i. ANA CAROLINA RODRÍGUEZ.

Viet Nam: 55 MacKay St, Ottawa, ON K1M 2B2; tel. (613) 236-0772; fax (613) 236-2704; e-mail vietnamembassy@rogers.com; internet www.vietnamembassy-canada.ca; Ambassador TO ANH DZUNG.

Yemen: 54 Chamberlain Ave, Ottawa, ON K1S 1V9; tel. (613) 729-6627; fax (613) 729-8915; e-mail info@yemenincanada.ca; internet www.yemenembassy.ca; Ambassador KHALED MAHFOODH ABDULLAH BAHAH.

Zambia: 151 Slater St, Suite 205, Ottawa, ON K1B 5H3; tel. (613) 232-4400; fax (613) 232-4410; e-mail embzamb@aol.com; internet www.zambiahighcommission.ca; High Commissioner BOBBY MBUNJI SAMAKAI.

Zimbabwe: 332 Somerset St West, Ottawa, ON K2P 0J9; tel. (613) 421-2824; fax (613) 422-7403; e-mail zimembassy@bellnet.ca; internet www.zimbabweembassy.ca; Ambassador FLORENCE ZANO CHIDEYA.

Judicial System

Responsibility for the administration of justice in Canada is shared between the federal government and the provinces and territories. The administration of justice in the provinces, including the Constitution, maintenance and organization of provincial courts, in both civil and criminal departments, rests with the provincial government. Provincial attorney-generals have responsibility for criminal prosecutions within their province that fall under the terms of the Criminal Code of Canada (1893). The Attorney-General of Canada has responsibility for proceedings under federal statutes other than the Criminal Code. All criminal proceedings in the Northwest Territories and Yukon come under the jurisdiction of the Attorney-General of Canada.

The right to pass legislation on the various aspects of civil law is shared between the federal Parliament and the provincial and territorial legislatures. Provinces and territories have jurisdiction over contract, property and tort laws, while the federal Parliament has jurisdiction over banking, bankruptcy and insolvency, and patents and copyrights. Jurisdiction is shared on corporation and tax laws.

FEDERAL COURTS

The Supreme Court is the ultimate court of appeal in both civil and criminal cases throughout Canada. The Court is also required to advise on questions referred to it by the Governor-General in Council. Questions concerning the interpretation of the Constitution Act, the constitutionality or interpretation of any federal or provincial law, the powers of Parliament or of the provincial legislatures, among other matters, may be referred by the Government to the Supreme Court for consideration.

The Federal Court has jurisdiction in cases arising in the federal domain, including claims by or against the Government of Canada, claims concerning crown officers and servants, challenges to the decisions of Federal Boards, Commissions, and other tribunals, interprovincial and federal-provincial disputes, and civil suits in federally regulated areas. The Federal Court of Appeal has jurisdiction on appeals from the Trial Division, appeals from Federal Tribunals, review of decisions of Federal Boards and Commissions, appeals from Tribunals and Reviews under Section 28 of the Federal Court Act, and references by Federal Boards and Commissions.

The Supreme Court of Canada: Supreme Court Bldg, 301 Wellington St, Ottawa, ON K1A 0J1; tel. (613) 995-4330; fax (613) 996-3063; e-mail reception@scc-csc.gc.ca; internet www.scc-csc.gc.ca; Chief Justice of Canada BEVERLEY MCLACHLIN.

Puisne Judges: LOUIS LEBEL, ROSALIE SIBERMAN ABELLA, MARSHALL ROTHSTEIN, THOMAS ALBERT CROMWELL, MICHAEL J. MOLDAVER, ANDROMACHE KARAKATSANIS, RICHARD WAGNER, MARC NADON.

The Federal Court: Supreme Court Bldg, Kent and Wellington Sts, Ottawa, ON K1A 0H9; tel. (613) 996-6795; fax (613) 952-7226; e-mail reception@cas-satj.gc.ca; internet www.fct-cf.gc.ca; Chief Justice PAUL S. CRAMPTON.

The Federal Court of Appeal: Supreme Court Bldg, Kent and Wellington Sts, Ottawa, ON K1A 0H9; tel. (613) 996-6795; fax (613) 952-7226; e-mail reception@cas-satj.gc.ca; internet www.fca-caf.gc.ca; the Court has one central registry and consists of the principal office in Ottawa and local offices in major centres throughout Canada; Chief Justice PIERRE BLAIS.

PROVINCIAL AND TERRITORIAL COURTS

Provincial courts are constituted under provincial legislation; while their names may vary from province to province, their structures are generally similar. There are three levels of provincial courts. The highest level of court in a province is the Superior or Supreme Court, which hears serious criminal and civil cases and has the authority to grant divorces. All provinces, with the exception of Québec, have an intermediate level of courts, called County or District Courts. These possess immediate jurisdiction, dealing with criminal cases (apart from the most serious) and cases beyond the jurisdiction of the Small Claims Court. Finally, each province has inferior courts which, with some variations, consist of the Juvenile Court, the Family Court, the Provincial Court (Criminal Division) and the Small Claims Court. With the exception of those serving the inferior courts, judges are appointed by the federal Government.

The superior courts of Nunavut and the Northwest Territories are presided over by the Chief Justice of Alberta, while the superior court of Yukon is presided over by the Chief Justice of British Columbia. The Nunavut Court of Justice is a single level court, which hears any type of case, including civil, family and criminal disputes, in both adult and youth courts.

Chief Justice of Alberta: CATHERINE A. FRASER (Edmonton).

Chief Justice of British Columbia: CHRISTOPHER E. HINKSON.

Chief Justice of Manitoba: RICHARD J. CHARTIER.

Chief Justice of New Brunswick: J. ERNEST DRAPEAU.

Chief Justice of Newfoundland and Labrador: J. DEREK GREEN.

Chief Justice of Nova Scotia: MICHAEL MACDONALD.

Chief Justice of Ontario: WARREN K. WINKLER.

Chief Justice of Prince Edward Island: DAVID H. JENKINS.

Chief Justice of Québec: NICOLE DUVAL HESLER.

Chief Justice of Saskatchewan: ROBERT RICHARDS.

Religion

CHRISTIANITY

According to the 2011 census, some 67% of the total population (22.1m. people) were affiliated with a Christian religion (although this figure included non-practising Christians). Of this total, Roman Catholics were the largest group, accounting for about 57% of Canada's Christians. The other main denominations were the United, Anglican and Baptist churches.

Canadian Council of Churches/Conseil canadien des églises: 47 Queen's Park Cres. East, Toronto, ON M5S 2C3; tel. (416) 972-9494; fax (416) 927-0405; e-mail delph@ccc-cce.ca; internet www.councilofchurches.ca; f. 1944; 25 mem. churches, 5 affiliate mems; Pres. Maj. JIM CHAMP (Christian Reformed Church in North America); Gen. Sec. Rev. Dr KAREN HAMILTON.

The Anglican Communion

The Anglican Church of Canada (L'Eglise anglicane du Canada) comprises 30 dioceses in four ecclesiastical provinces (each with a Metropolitan archbishop). According to census figures, there were 1.6m. Anglicans in 2011.

General Synod of the Anglican Church of Canada: 80 Hayden St, Toronto, ON M4Y 3G2; tel. (416) 924-9192; fax (416) 968-7983; e-mail information@national.anglican.ca; internet www.anglican.ca; f. 1893; Gen. Sec. The Venerable MICHAEL THOMPSON.

Primate of the Anglican Church of Canada: Most Rev. FRED HILTZ.

Province of British Columbia and Yukon: Metropolitan Most Rev. JOHN E. PRIVETT (Archbishop of Kootenay).

Province of Canada: Metropolitan Most Rev. CLAUDE E. W. MILLER (Bishop of Fredericton).

Province of Ontario: Metropolitan Most Rev. COLIN JOHNSON (Archbishop of Toronto).

Province of Rupert's Land: Metropolitan Most Rev. DAVID ASHDOWN (Archbishop of Keewatin).

The Orthodox Churches

According to census figures, there were some 550,700 members of Eastern Orthodox churches in Canada in 2011.

Greek Orthodox Metropolis of Toronto (Canada): 86 Overlea Blvd, Toronto, ON M4H 1C6; tel. (416) 429-5757; fax (416) 429-4588; e-mail metropolis@gometropolis.org; internet www.gometropolis.org; 215,175 mems (2001); Metropolitan Archbishop SOTIRIOS ATHANASSOULAS.

The Russian, Ukrainian, Belarusian, Polish, Romanian, Serbian, Coptic, Antiochian and Armenian Churches are also represented in Canada.

The Roman Catholic Church

For Catholics of the Latin rite, Canada comprises 18 archdioceses (including one directly responsible to the Holy See), 46 dioceses and one territorial abbacy. There are also one archdiocese and four dioceses of the Ukrainian rite. In addition, the Maronite, Melkite and Slovak rites are each represented by one diocese (all directly responsible to the Holy See). According to census figures, in 2011 some 12.7m. Canadians identified themselves as Roman Catholic.

Canadian Conference of Catholic Bishops/Conférence des évêques catholiques du Canada: 2500 Don Reid Dr., Ottawa, ON K1H 2J2; tel. (613) 241-9461; fax (613) 241-8117; e-mail cecc@cccb.ca; internet www.cccb.ca; f. 1943 as Canadian Catholic Conference; officially recognized 1948; restyled as above 1977; Pres. Most Rev. PAUL-ANDRÉ DUROCHER (Archbishop of Gatineau); Gen. Sec. Mgr PATRICK POWERS.

Latin Rite

Archbishop of Edmonton: Most Rev. RICHARD SMITH.

Archbishop of Gatineau: Most Rev. PAUL-ANDRÉ DUROCHER.

Archbishop of Grouard-McLennan: Most Rev. GÉRARD PETTIPAS.

Archbishop of Halifax: Most Rev. ANTHONY MANCINI.

Archbishop of Keewatin-Le Pas: Most Rev. MURRAY CHATLAIN.

Archbishop of Kingston: Most Rev. BRENDAN M. O'BRIEN.

Archbishop of Moncton: Most Rev. VALÉRY VIENNEAU.

Archbishop of Montréal: Cardinal CHRISTIAN LÉPINE.

Archbishop of Ottawa: Most Rev. TERRENCE PRENDERGAST.

Archbishop of Québec: Cardinal GÉRALD CYPRIEN LACROIX.

Archbishop of Regina: Most Rev. DANIEL J. BOHAN.

Archbishop of Rimouski: Most Rev. PIERRE-ANDRÉ FOURNIER.

Archbishop of St Boniface: Most Rev. ALBERT LEGATT.

Archbishop of St John's, NL: Most Rev. MARTIN WILLIAM CURRIE.

Archbishop of Sherbrooke: Most Rev. LUC CYR.

Archbishop of Toronto: Cardinal THOMAS COLLINS.

Archbishop of Vancouver: Most Rev. MICHAEL MILLER.

Archbishop of Winnipeg: Most Rev. V. JAMES WEISGERBER.

Ukrainian Rite

Ukrainian Catholic Archeparchy of Winnipeg (Metropolitan See of Canada): 233 Scotia St, Winnipeg, MB R2V 1V7; tel. (204) 338-7801; fax (204) 339-4006; e-mail chancery@archeparchy.ca; internet www.archeparchy.ca; 126,200 mems (2001); Archeparch-Metropolitan of Winnipeg Most Rev. LAWRENCE HUCULAK.

The United Church of Canada

The United Church of Canada (l'Eglise Unie du Canada) was founded in 1925 with the union of Methodist, Congregational and 70% of Presbyterian churches in Canada. The Evangelical United Brethren of Canada joined in 1968. It is the largest Protestant denomination in Canada. In 2012 there were 3,075 congregations. According to 2011 census figures, 2.0m. people identified themselves as adherents of the United Church.

United Church of Canada: 3250 Bloor St West, Suite 300, Toronto, ON M8X 2Y4; tel. (416) 231-5931; fax (416) 231-3103; e-mail info@united-church.ca; internet www.united-church.ca; Moderator Rev. GARY PATERSON; Gen. Sec. NORA SANDERS.

Other Christian Churches

Canadian Baptist Ministries: 7185 Millcreek Dr., Mississauga, ON L5N 5R4; tel. (905) 821-3533; fax (905) 826-3441; e-mail communications@cbmin.org; internet www.cbmin.org; more than 1,000 churches; 250,000 mems (2008); Pres. Dr KEN BELLOUS.

Christian Reformed Church in North America (Canadian Council): 3475 Mainway, POB 5070, Burlington, ON L7R 3Y8; tel. (905) 336-2920; fax (905) 336-8344; e-mail crcna@crcna.ca; internet www.crcna.org; f. 1857; 256 congregations; 75,600 mems (2010); Dir in Canada BEN VANDEZANDE.

Church of Jesus Christ of Latter-day Saints (Mormon): 28 St South, Suite 2410, Lethbridge, AB T1K 2V9; tel. (403) 328-8552; f. 1832; 481 congregations; 166,505 mems in Canada (2004); Dir GORDON GEDLAMAN.

Evangelical Lutheran Church in Canada (ELCIC): 177 Lombard Ave, Suite 600, Winnipeg, MB R3B 0W5; tel. (204) 984-9173; fax (204) 984-9185; e-mail bwiebe@elcic.ca; internet www.elcic.ca; f. 1986 by merger of the fmr Evangelical Lutheran Church of Canada and Lutheran Church in America—Canada Section; 594 congregations; 145,376 mems; Nat. Bishop Rev. SUSAN JOHNSON, Vice-Pres. SHEILA HAMILTON.

Lutheran Church—Canada: 3074 Portage Ave, Winnipeg, MB R3K 0Y2; tel. (204) 895-3433; fax (204) 897-4319; e-mail pres_sec@lutheranchurch.ca; internet www.lutheranchurch.ca; f. 1988 by 3 Canadian congregations of the Lutheran Church—Missouri Synod; more than 325 congregations; 51,650 mems (2010); Pres. Rev. ROBERT BUGBEE.

Pentecostal Assemblies of Canada: 2450 Milltower Court, Mississauga, ON L5N 5Z6; tel. (905) 542-7400; fax (905) 542-7313; e-mail info@paoc.org; internet www.paoc.org; f. 1919; 1,103 congregations; 236,000 mems; Gen. Supt Rev. DAVID WELLS.

Presbyterian Church in Canada: 50 Wynford Dr., Toronto, ON M3C 1J7; tel. (416) 441-1111; fax (416) 441-2825; e-mail communications@presbyterian.ca; internet www.presbyterian.ca; f. 1875; 910 congregations (2010); 105,886 mems (2010); Gen. Sec. Rev. Dr RICHARD W. FEE.

Religious Society of Friends: 91A Fourth Ave, Ottawa, ON K1S 2L1; tel. (613) 235-8553; fax (613) 235-1753; e-mail cym-office@quaker.ca; internet www.quaker.ca; Clerk of Canadian Yearly Meeting CAROL DIXON.

Seventh-day Adventist Church in Canada: 1148 King St East, Oshawa, ON L1H 1H8; tel. (905) 433-0011; fax (905) 433-0982; e-mail communications@sdacc.org; internet www.adventist.ca; 372 congregations, 66,140 mems (2011); f. 1901; Pres. MARK JOHNSON; Sec. CATHY ANDERSON.

BAHÁ'Í FAITH

Bahá'í Community of Canada: 7200 Leslie St, Thornhill, ON L3T 6L8; tel. (905) 889-8168; fax (905) 889-8184; e-mail secretariat@cdnbnc.org; internet www.ca.bahai.org; f. 1902; 34,000 mems (2012); Sec.-Gen. KAREN MCKYE.

BUDDHISM

According to census figures, 366,830 people identified themselves as Buddhist in 2011.

Jodo Shinshu Buddhist Temples of Canada: 11786 Fentiman Pl., Richmond, BC V7E 6M6; tel. (604) 272-3330; fax (604) 272-6865; e-mail jsbtcheadquarters@shaw.ca; internet www.bcc.ca; f. 1905; fmrly Buddhist Churches of Canada; Bishop TATSUYA AOKI.

HINDUISM

According to census figures, there were 497,960 Hindus in Canada in 2011.

Hindu Federation: 270 Export Blvd, Mississauga, ON L5S 1Y9; tel. (905) 670-8439; fax (905) 696-0384; e-mail info@hindufederation.ca; internet www.hindufederation.ca; f. 1999; umbrella body for various Hindu denominations and orgs; Pres. Pandit ROOPNAUTH SHARMA; Sec. JAYANT PATEL.

ISLAM

According to census figures, there were 1,053,945 Muslims in Canada in 2011.

Ahmadiyya Muslim Jama'at (Canada): 10610 Jane St, Maple, ON L6A 3A2; tel. (905) 303-4000; fax (905) 832-3220; e-mail info@ahmadiyya.ca; internet www.ahmadiyya.ca; f. 1965; Pres. LAL KHAN MALIK; Gen. Sec. Dr ASLAM DAUD.

Canadian Islamic Congress (CIC): 115B, 115-2nd Ave North, Saskatoon, SK S7K 2B1; tel. (306) 652-5929; fax (306) 652-5919; e-mail cicnp@canadianislamiccongress.com; internet www.canadianislamiccongress.com; f. 1998; Chair. and Nat. Pres. AMIN ELSHORBAGY.

Canadian Muslim Union (CMU): Toronto, ON; tel. (416) 558-4777; e-mail secretary@muslimunion.ca; internet www.muslimunion.ca; f. 2006 following split from the Muslim Canadian Congress; Sec.-Gen. EL-FAROUK KHAKI.

Council of Muslim Communities of Canada (CMCC): 1521 Trinity Dr., Unit 16, Mississauga, ON L5T 1P6; tel. and fax (416) 564-1566; fax (416) 564-1544; f. 1971; umbrella org. representing c. 30 communities nationwide; Pres. HANNY HASSAN.

Organization of North American Shi'a Itha-Asheri Muslim Communities (NASIMCO): 9200 Dufferin St, POB 20078, Concord, ON L4K 0C0; tel. (905) 763-7512; fax (905) 763-7509; e-mail director@nasimco.org; internet www.nasimco.org; Pres. GULAM-ABBAS NAJAFI; Sec. HABIB M. HABIB.

JUDAISM

According to census figures, there were some 329,500 Jews in Canada in 2011.

Canadian Council for Reform Judaism (CCRJ): 3845 Bathurst St, Suite 301, Toronto, ON M3H 3N2; tel. (416) 630-0375; fax (416) 630-5089; e-mail ccrj@urj.org; internet urj.org/ccrj; f. 1988; Pres. CAROLE STERLING; Exec. Dir Rabbi SHARON L. SOBEL.

United Synagogue of Conservative Judaism: 1000 Finch Ave West, Suite 508, Toronto, ON M3J 2V5; tel. (416) 667-1717; fax (416) 667-1881; e-mail canadian@uscj.org; internet www.uscj.org; Exec. Dir Rabbi STEVEN WERNICK.

SIKHISM

There were 454,965 Sikhs in Canada, according to 2011 census figures.

Canadian Sikh Council (CSC): 4103 Sherbrooke St West, Montréal, QC H3Z 1A7; tel. (416) 630-0375; fax (416) 630-5089; e-mail info@sikhcouncil.ca; internet www.sikhcouncil.ca; f. 2001; Dir Dr MANJIT SINGH.

World Sikh Organization of Canada (WSO Canada): 1183 Cecil Ave, Ottawa, ON K1H 7Z6; tel. (613) 521-1984; fax (613) 521-7454; e-mail info@worldsikh.org; internet worldsikh.org; f. 1984; Pres. PREM SINGH VINNING.

The Press

Traditionally the daily press in Canada was essentially local in coverage, influence and distribution. In October 1998 publication began of Canada's first national newspaper, the *National Post*. A national edition of the Toronto *Globe and Mail*, established in 1981, was also available coast to coast, as was (from 1988) a national edition of the *Financial Post*.

Chain ownership has traditionally been predominant: in 2011 just over one-half (52%) of daily newspaper circulation was represented by two major groups, Postmedia Network Inc and Quebecor Media Inc. Quebecor had become Canada's largest newspaper publishing enterprise in terms of the number of titles produced after it acquired Osprey Media Group Inc in 2007. In 2012 Quebecor, through its subsidiary Sun Media Corpn, owned 42 daily newspapers (and controlled 23% of total paid daily newspaper circulation), Postmedia Network Inc (which had bought CanWest's entire newspaper division in 2010) owned 10 (with the greatest share of total circulation, at 29%), Transcontinental Media owned 12 and Power Corpn of Canada seven.

In 2012 there were 95 paid-for daily newspapers, with a combined daily circulation of some 4.2m.; of these only two were independent. In the same year there were 29 free daily newspapers, with a combined daily circulation of almost 1.8m. In mid-2013 there were 1,019 community newspapers serving mainly the more remote areas of the country, with a combined circulation of more than 19.6m. per week. The vast majority of community newspapers (some 95%) are distributed free.

There were numerous periodicals for business, trade, professional, recreational and special interest readership. In 2011 1,286 consumer titles and 784 business titles were published in Canada.

The following are among the principal newspaper publishing groups:

Gesca Limitée: 7 rue St-Jacques, Montréal, QC H2Y 1K9; tel. (514) 285-7048; fax (514) 285-7331; e-mail recherchemarketing@lapresse.ca; internet publicite.gesca.ca; wholly owned subsidiary of the Power Corpn of Canada; owns 7 daily newspapers (average daily circ. 452,085); Chair. and Co-CEO PAUL DESMARAIS, Jr; Pres. and Co-CEO ANDRÉ DESMARAIS.

Postmedia Network Inc: 1450 Don Mills Rd, Don Mills, ON M3B 3R5; tel. (416) 383-2300; internet www.postmedia.com; f. 2010 to acquire the newspaper division of CanWest Global Communications Corpn; owns 10 English-language daily newspapers (average daily circ. 1,141,616) and 7 community newspapers in Canada; Pres. and CEO PAUL V. GODFREY.

Quebecor Media Inc: 612 rue St-Jacques, Montréal, QC H3C 4M8; tel. (514) 380-1999; e-mail webmaster@quebecor.com; internet www.quebecor.com; f. 1965; acquired Osprey Media Group Inc in 2007; television, cable, telecommunications and publishing interests in 17 countries; Pres. and CEO ROBERT DÉPATIE.

Sun Media Corpn: 333 King St East, Toronto, ON M5A 3X5; tel. (416) 947-2222; e-mail qi_info@quebecor.com; internet www.sunmedia.ca/SunMedia/; f. 1965; publishes 43 English- and French-language dailies and over 250 community papers; Pres. and CEO PIERRE KARL PÉLADEAU.

Torstar Corpn: 1 Yonge St, Toronto, ON M5E 1P9; tel. (416) 869-4010; fax (416) 869-4183; e-mail torstar@torstar.ca; internet www.torstar.com; f. 1958; incorporates the Star Media Group and Metroland Media Group; owns 3 daily newspapers, 10 weekly publs, and 112 community newspapers; Chair. JOHN A. HONDERICH; Pres. and CEO DAVID P. HOLLAND.

Transcontinental Media: 1 Pl. Ville Marie, bureau 3315, Montréal QC H3B 3N2; tel. (514) 954-4000; fax (514) 954-4016; e-mail contact-media@transcontinental.ca; internet www.transcontinentalmedia.com; f. 1978; publs 10 dailies (daily circ. 92,545) and more than 125 weekly, fortnightly and monthly newspapers (circ. 2.4m.); Chair. ISABELLE MARCOUX; Pres. and CEO FRANÇOIS OLIVIER.

PRINCIPAL DAILY NEWSPAPERS

Alberta

Calgary Herald: 215 16th St, SE, POB 2400, Station M, Calgary, AB T2P 0W8; tel. (403) 235-7100; fax (403) 235-7379; e-mail calgaryherald@reachcanada.com; internet www.canada.com/calgaryherald; f. 1883; owned by Postmedia Network Inc; Publr MALCOLM KIRK; Editor-in-Chief LORNE MOTLEY; circ. 127,147.

Calgary Sun: 2615 12th St, NE, Calgary, AB T2E 7W9; tel. (403) 410-1010; fax (403) 250-4176; e-mail callet@calgarysun.com; internet www.calgarysun.com; f. 1980; owned by Sun Media Corpn; Editor-in-Chief JOSÉ RODRIGUEZ; Man. Editor MARTIN HUDSON; circ. 64,654.

Edmonton Journal: 10006 101 St, POB 2421, Edmonton, AB T5J 0S1; tel. (780) 429-5100; fax (780) 429-5536; internet www.edmontonjournal.com; f. 1903; owned by Postmedia Network Inc; Publr JOHN CONNOLLY; Editor-in-Chief MARGO GOODHAND; circ. 101,950.

Edmonton Sun: 4990 92nd Ave, Suite 250, Edmonton, AB T6B 3A1; tel. (780) 468-0100; fax (780) 468-0128; e-mail edm-mailbag@sunmedia.ca; internet www.edmontonsun.com; f. 1978; owned by Sun Media Corpn; Editor-in-Chief STEVE SERVISS; Man. Editor DONNA HARKER; circ. 43,573.

Lethbridge Herald: 504 Seventh St South, POB 670, Lethbridge, AB T1J 2H1; tel. (403) 328-4411; fax (403) 328-4536; e-mail ccampbell@abnewsgroup.com; internet www.lethbridgeherald.com; f. 1907; evening and Sun.; Gen. Man. COLEEN CAMPBELL; Man. Editor DOYLE MACKINNON; circ. 15,492.

Medicine Hat News: 3257 Dunmore Rd, SE, POB 10, Medicine Hat, AB T1A 7E6; tel. (403) 527-1101; fax (403) 527-1244; e-mail apoirier@medicinehatnews.com; internet www.medicinehatnews.com; f. 1887; evening; Publr MICHAEL J. HERTZ; Man. Editor KERRI SANDFORD; circ. 11,002.

Red Deer Advocate: 2950 Bremner Ave, Bag 5200, Red Deer, AB T4R 1M9; tel. (403) 343-2400; fax (403) 341-6560; e-mail editorial@reddeeradvocate.com; internet www.reddeeradvocate.com; f. 1894; Publr FRED GORMAN; Man. Editor JOHN STEWART; circ. 13,318.

British Columbia

Daily Courier: 550 Doyle Ave, Kelowna, BC V1Y 7V1; tel. (250) 470-0741; fax (250) 762-0258; e-mail jon.manchester@ok.bc.ca; internet www.kelownadailycourier.ca; f. 1904; morning; Publr TERRY ARMSTRONG; Man. Editor JON MANCHESTER; circ. 12,382.

Kamloops Daily News: 393 Seymour St, Kamloops, BC V2C 6P6; tel. (250) 372-2331; fax (250) 374-3884; e-mail kamloopsnews@telus.net; internet www.kamloopsnews.ca; f. 1930; evening; Publr TIM SHOULTS; Editor TRACY GILCHRIST; circ. 12,812.

Penticton Herald: 186 Nanaimo Ave West, Suite 101, Penticton, BC V2A 1N4; tel. (250) 492-4002; fax (250) 492-2403; e-mail editor@pentictonherald.ca; internet www.pentictonherald.ca; f. 1906 as Penticton Press; morning; Man. Editor JAMES MILLER; Gen. Man. ED KENNEDY; circ. 6,401.

Prince George Citizen: 150 Brunswick St, POB 5700, Prince George, BC V2L 2B3; tel. (250) 562-2441; fax (250) 562-7453; e-mail info@pgcitizen.ca; internet www.princegeorgecitizen.com; f. 1916; morning; Publr COLLEEN SPARROW; Editor NEIL GODBOUT; circ. 12,743.

The Province: 200 Granville St, Suite 1, Vancouver, BC V6C 3N3; tel. (604) 605-2000; fax (604) 605-2914; e-mail info@png.canwest

.com; internet www.theprovince.com; f. 1898; owned by Postmedia Network Inc; Publr KEVIN D. BENT; Editor-in-Chief WAYNE MORIARTY; circ. 142,300.

Sing Tao Daily News (Eastern Canada Edition): 8508 Ash St, Vancouver, BC V6P 3M2; tel. (416) 596-8140; fax (416) 599-6688; e-mail editor_toronto@singtao.ca; internet news.singtao.ca; f. 1978; Chinese; Editor VICTOR HO; circ. Mon. to Sun. 45,000.

Times Colonist: 2621 Douglas St, Victoria, BC V8T 4M2; tel. (250) 380-5211; fax (250) 380-5353; e-mail customerservice@timescolonist.com; internet www.timescolonist.com; f. 1980 by merger of British Colonist (f. 1858) and Victoria Daily Times (f. 1884); owned by Postmedia Network Inc; Publr BOB MCKENZIE; Editor-in-Chief DAVE OBEE; circ. 56,170.

The Vancouver Sun: 200 Granville St, Suite 1, Vancouver, BC V6C 3N3; tel. (604) 605-2000; fax (604) 605-2308; e-mail pgraham@vancouversun.com; internet www.vancouversun.com; f. 1886; owned by Postmedia Network Inc; Pres. and Publr KEVIN D. BENT; Editor-in-Chief HAROLD MUNRO; circ. 164,507.

World Journal (Vancouver): 2288 Clark Dr., Vancouver, BC V5N 3G8; tel. (604) 876-1338; fax (604) 876-9191; e-mail bcwebmaster@worldjournal.com; internet www.worldjournal.com; f. 1976; Chinese; Publr JACK CHEN; circ. 10,000.

Manitoba

Brandon Sun: 501 Rosser Ave, Brandon, MB R7A 0K4; tel. (204) 727-2451; fax (204) 725-0976; e-mail joconnor@brandonsun.com; internet www.brandonsun.com; f. 1882; evening and Sun.; Publr ERIC LAWSON; Man. Editor JAMES O'CONNOR; circ. 10,749.

Winnipeg Free Press: 1355 Mountain Ave, Winnipeg, MB R2X 3B6; tel. (204) 697-7000; fax (204) 697-7412; e-mail bob.cox@freepress.mb.ca; internet www.winnipegfreepress.com; f. 1872; morning; Publr BOB COX; Editor PAUL SAMYN; circ. 113,251.

Winnipeg Sun: 1700 Church Ave, Winnipeg, MB R2X 3A2; tel. (204) 694-2022; fax (204) 697-0759; e-mail kevin.klein@sunmedia.ca; internet www.winnipegsun.com; f. 1980; owned by Sun Media Corpn; Publr and CEO KEVIN KLEIN; Editor-in-Chief MARK HAMM; circ. 51,145.

New Brunswick

L'Acadie Nouvelle: 476 blvd St-Pierre ouest, CP 5536, Caraquet, NB E1W 1B7; tel. (506) 727-4444; fax (506) 727-7620; e-mail info@acadiemedia.com; internet www.acadienouvelle.com; f. 1984; French; Publr and CEO FRANCIS SONIER; Editor-in-Chief JEAN SAINT-CYR; circ. 18,102.

The Daily Gleaner: 984 Prospect St, POB 3370, Fredericton, NB E3B 2T8; tel. (506) 452-6671; fax (506) 452-7405; e-mail news@dailygleaner.com; internet www.dailygleaner.com; f. 1881; morning; Gen. Man. JEN MACFARLANE; Man. Editor ANNE MOOERS; circ. 17,184.

Telegraph-Journal: 210 Crown St, POB 2350, Saint John, NB E2L 3V8; tel. (506) 633-5599; fax (506) 648-2654; e-mail newsroom@nbpub.com; internet www.telegraphjournal.com; Man. Editor RON BARRY; circ. 28,000.

The Times and Transcript: 939 Main St, POB 1001, Moncton, NB E1C 8P3; tel. (506) 859-4905; fax (506) 859-4904; e-mail news@timestranscript.com; internet timestranscript.canadaeast.com; f. 1983; Mon. to Sat. evening, Sat. morning; Publr ERIC LAWSON; Man. Editor AL HOGAN; circ. 30,747.

Newfoundland and Labrador

The Telegram: 430 Topsail Rd, POB 86, St John's, NL A1E 4N1; tel. (709) 364-6300; fax (709) 364-3939; e-mail telegram@thetelegram.com; internet www.thetelegram.com; f. 1879; evening; Publr and Gen. Man. CHARLES STACEY; Man. Editor KERRY HANN; circ. 25,646.

The Western Star: 106 West St, POB 460, Corner Brook, NL A2H 6E7; tel. (709) 634-4348; fax (709) 634-9824; e-mail newsroom@thewesternstar.com; internet www.thewesternstar.com; f. 1900; Publr and Gen. Man. TRINA BURDEN; Man. Editor TROY TURNER; circ. 5,782.

Nova Scotia

Cape Breton Post: 255 George St, POB 1500, Sydney, NS B1P 6K6; tel. (902) 564-5451; fax (902) 562-7077; e-mail edit@cbpost.com; internet www.capebretonpost.com; f. 1901; Publr ANITA DELAZZER; Editorial Dir TOM AYERS; circ. 20,675.

ChronicleHerald: 2717 Joseph Howe Dr., POB 610, Halifax, NS B3J 2T2; tel. (902) 426-3031; fax (902) 426-1170; e-mail reception@herald.ca; internet thechronicleherald.ca; f. 1875; Publr SARAH DENNIS; Editor-in-Chief BOB HOWSE; circ. 109,210.

The News: 352 East River Rd, POB 159, New Glasgow, NS B2H 5E2; tel. (902) 752-3000; fax (902) 752-1945; e-mail news@ngnews.ca; internet www.ngnews.ca; f. 1910; fmrly known as *The Evening News*; evening; Publr RICHARD RUSSELL; Man. Editor DAVE GLENEN; circ. 5,779.

Truro Daily News: 6 Louise St, POB 220, Truro, NS B2N 5C3; tel. (902) 893-9405; fax (902) 895-6106; e-mail news@trurodaily.com; internet www.trurodaily.com; f. 1891; evening; Publr RICHARD RUSSELL; Man. Editor CARL FLEMING; circ. 5,507.

Ontario

Barrie Examiner: 571 Bayfield St North, Barrie, ON L4M 4Z9; tel. (705) 726-6537; fax (705) 726-5148; internet www.thebarrieexaminer.com; f. 1864; owned by Sun Media Corpn; evening; Publr SANDY DAVIES; Editor BRIAN RODNICK; circ. 7,444.

Beacon Herald: 789 Erie St, Stratford, Ontario N4Z 1A1; tel. (519) 271-2222; fax (519) 271-1026; e-mail jkastner@bowesnet.com; internet www.stratfordbeaconherald.com; f. 1854; owned by Sun Media Corpn; evening; Publr DAVE CARTER; Man. Editor JOHN KASTNER; circ. 7,243.

Chatham Daily News: 138 King St West, POB 2007, Chatham, ON N7M 1E3; tel. (519) 354-2000; fax (519) 354-3448; e-mail news@chathamdailynews.ca; internet www.chathamdailynews.ca; f. 1862; owned by Sun Media Corpn; evening; Publr and Gen. Man. DEAN MUHARREM; Man. Editor ROD HILTS; circ. 6,971.

Chronicle Journal: 75 Cumberland St South, Thunder Bay, ON P7B 1A3; tel. (807) 343-6200; fax (807) 229-0823; e-mail julio.gomes@chroniclejournal.com; internet www.chroniclejournal.com; Publr and Gen. Man. COLIN J. BRUCE; Man. Editor JULIO HELENO GOMES; circ. 23,462 .

Le Droit: 47 rue Clarence, bureau 222, CP 8860, succursale Terminus, Ottawa, ON K1G 3J9; tel. (613) 285-7000; fax (613) 562-7539; e-mail nouvelles@lapresse.ca; internet www.lapresse.ca/le-droit; f. 1913; Publr JACQUES PRONOVOST; Man. Editor ANDRÉ LAROCQUE; circ. 35,535.

The Expositor: 195 Henry St, Brantford, ON N3S 5C9; tel. (519) 756-2020; fax (519) 756-3285; e-mail publisher@theexpositor.com; internet www.brantfordexpositor.ca; f. 1852; owned by Sun Media Corpn; Publr KEN KOYAMA; Man. Editor JEFF DERTINGER; circ. 15,555.

The Globe and Mail: 444 Front St West, Toronto, ON M5V 2S9; tel. (416) 585-5000; fax (416) 585-5698; e-mail newsroom@globeandmail.ca; internet www.globeandmail.com; f. 1844; Publr and CEO PHILLIP CRAWLEY; Editor-in-Chief JOHN STACKHOUSE; circ. 302,190.

Guelph Mercury: 8–14 Macdonnell St, Guelph, ON N1H 6P7; tel. (519) 823-6060; fax (519) 767-1681; e-mail editor@guelphmercury.com; internet www.guelphmercury.com; f. 1867; evening; Publr PAUL MCCUAIG; Man. Editor PHIL ANDREWS; circ. 12,192.

Hamilton Spectator: 44 Frid St, Hamilton, ON L8N 3G3; tel. (905) 526-3333; fax (905) 526-0147; internet www.thespec.com; f. 1846; Publr NEIL OLIVER; Editor-in-Chief PAUL BERTON; circ. 102,088.

Intelligencer: 199 Front St, Suite 535, Century Pl., Belleville, ON K8N 5H5; tel. (613) 962-9171; fax (613) 962-9652; e-mail bglisky@intelligencer.ca; internet www.intelligencer.ca; f. 1870; owned by Sun Media Corpn; evening; Publr MAUREEN KEELER; Man. Editor BILL GLISKY; circ. 8,851.

The Kingston Whig-Standard: 6 Cataraqui St, POB 2300, Kingston, ON K7L 4Z7; tel. (613) 544-5000; fax (613) 530-4122; e-mail whiglocal@thewhig.com; internet www.thewhig.com; f. 1834; owned by Sun Media Corpn; Publr RON LAURIN; Man. Editor DEREK SHELLY; circ. 20,776.

London Free Press: 369 York St, POB 2280, London, ON N6A 4G1; tel. (519) 679-1111; fax (519) 667-4523; e-mail letters@lfpress.com; internet www.lfpress.com; f. 1849; owned by Sun Media Corpn; Publr and CEO SUSAN MUSZAK; Editor-in-Chief JOE RUSCITTI; circ. 70,407.

Ming Pao Daily News: 1355 Huntingwood Dr., Scarborough, ON M1S 3J1; tel. (416) 321-0088; fax (416) 321-9663; e-mail newsdesk@mingpaotor.com; internet www.mingpaotor.com; f. 1993; Chinese; Editor-in-Chief RICHARD KWOK-KAI NG; circ. Mon. to Fri. 68,600, Sat. 97,000, Sun. 102,000.

National Post: 1450 Don Mills Rd, Suite 300, Don Mills, ON M3B 3R5; tel. (416) 383-2300; fax (416) 383-2305; e-mail queries@nationalpost.com; internet www.nationalpost.com; f. 1998; incorporates the *Financial Post* (f. 1907); national newspaper with printing centres in 9 cities; owned by Postmedia Network Inc; Publr DOUGLAS KELLY; Editor-in-Chief STEPHEN MEURICE; circ. 169,566.

Niagara Falls Review: 4801 Valley Way, POB 270, Niagara Falls, ON L2E 1W4; tel. (905) 358-5711; fax (905) 356-0785; e-mail pconradi@nfreview.com; internet www.niagarafallsreview.ca; f. 1879; owned by Sun Media Corpn; morning; Publr MARK CRESSMAN; Man. Editor STEVEN GALLAGHER; circ. 19,003.

North Bay Nugget: 259 Worthington St, North Bay, ON P1B 3B5; tel. (705) 472-3200; fax (705) 472-1438; e-mail news@nugget.ca; internet www.nugget.ca; f. 1909; owned by Sun Media Corpn; evening; Publr DAN JOHNSON; Man. Editor BRUCE COWAN; circ. 10,884.

Orillia Packet and Times: 425 West St North, Suite 15, Orillia, ON L3V 7R2; tel. (705) 325-1355; fax (705) 325-4033; internet www.orilliapacket.com; f. 1926 by merger; owned by Sun Media Corpn; evening; Publr and Gen. Man. JOHN HAMMILL; Editor RANDY LUCENTI; circ. 8,654.

Ottawa Citizen: 1101 Baxter Rd, POB 5020, Ottawa, ON K2C 3M4; tel. (613) 596-1950; fax (613) 726-5852; e-mail apotter@ottawacitizen.com; internet www.ottawacitizen.com; f. 1845 as *The Packet*; owned by Postmedia Network Inc; Publr and Editor-in-Chief GERRY NOTT; Man. Editor ANDREW POTTER; circ. 110,019.

Ottawa Sun: POB 9729, Station T, Ottawa, ON K1G 5H7; tel. (613) 739-7000; fax (613) 739-9383; e-mail ottsun.city@sunmedia.ca; internet www.ottawasun.com; owned by Sun Media Corpn; Publr BRUCE HOLMES; Man. Editor DONALD ERMEN; circ. 41,443.

Peterborough Examiner: 60 Hunter St East, POB 3890, Peterborough, ON K9J 3L4; tel. (705) 745-4641; fax (705) 745-3361; e-mail darren.murphy@sunmedia.ca; internet www.thepeterboroughexaminer.com; f. 1847; owned by Sun Media Corpn; evening; Publr DARREN MURPHY; Man. Editor JIM HENDRY; circ. 16,979.

The Record: 160 King St East, Kitchener, ON N2G 4E5; tel. (519) 894-2231; fax (519) 894-3912; e-mail pmccuaig@therecord.com; internet www.therecord.com; f. 1878; evening; Publr PAUL MCCUAIG; Editor-in-Chief LYNN HADDRALL; circ. Mon. to Fri. 53,839, Sat. 57,455 (2011).

The Recorder and Times: 2479 Parkedale Ave, POB 10, Brockville, ON K6V 3H2; tel. (613) 342-4441; fax (613) 342-4456; e-mail editor@recorder.ca; internet www.recorder.ca; f. 1821; owned by Sun Media Corpn; evening; Publr LIZA NELSON; Man. Editor DEREK GORDANIER; circ. 9,615.

St Catharines Standard: 17 Queen St, St Catharines, ON L2R 5G5; tel. (905) 684-7251; fax (905) 684-6032; e-mail mark.cressman@sunmedia.ca; internet www.stcatharinesstandard.ca; f. 1891; owned by Sun Media Corpn; evening; Publr MARK CRESSMAN; Editor-in-Chief PETER CONRADI; circ. 34,102.

Sarnia Observer: 140 Front St South, POB 3009, Sarnia, ON N7T 7M8; tel. (519) 344-3641; fax (519) 332-2951; e-mail rhilts@theobserver.ca; internet www.theobserver.ca; f. 1853; owned by Sun Media Corpn; evening; Publr LINDA LEBLANC; Man. Editor ROD HILTS; circ. 11,497.

Sault Star: 145 Old Garden River Rd, POB 460, Sault Ste Marie, ON P6A 5M5; tel. (705) 759-3030; fax (705) 759-5947; e-mail frank.rupnik@sunmedia.ca; internet www.saultstar.com; f. 1912; owned by Sun Media Corpn; evening; Publr LOU A. MAULUCCI; Editor FRANK RUPNIK; circ. 12,589.

Sentinel-Review: 16 Brock St, POB 1000, Woodstock, ON N4S 3B4; tel. (519) 537-2341; fax (519) 537-3049; e-mail sentinelreview@bowesnet.com; internet www.woodstocksentinelreview.com; f. 1886; owned by Sun Media Corpn; evening; Publr ANDREA DEMEER; Man. Editor BRUCE URQUHART; circ. 7,700.

Simcoe Reformer: 50 Gilbertson Dr., POB 370, Simcoe, ON N3Y 4L2; tel. (519) 426-5710; fax (519) 426-9255; e-mail refedit@bowesnet.com; internet www.simcoereformer.ca; f. 1858; owned by Sun Media Corpn; evening; Publr KEN KOYOMA; Man. Editor KIMBERLEY NOVAK; circ. 10,933.

Sing Tao Daily News: 417 Dundas St West, Toronto, ON M5T 1G6; tel. (416) 596-8140; fax (416) 599-6688; e-mail editor_toronto@singtao.ca; internet www.singtao.ca; Chinese; Editor-in-Chief ROBERT LEUNG; circ. Mon. to Sun. 160,693.

Standard-Freeholder: 1150 Montreal Rd, Cornwall, ON K6J 1E2; tel. (613) 933-3160; fax (613) 933-7521; e-mail peter.padbury@sunmedia.ca; internet www.standard-freeholder.com; owned by Sun Media Corpn; Publr PETER PADBURY; Man. Editor BRIAN DRYDEN; circ. 13,158.

Sudbury Star: 128 Pine St, Suite 201, Sudbury, ON P3C 1X3; tel. (705) 674-5271; fax (705) 674-6834; e-mail david.kilgour@sunmedia.ca; internet www.thesudburystar.com; f. 1909; owned by Sun Media Corpn; evening; Publr DAVID KILGOUR; Man. Editor BRIAN MACLEOD; circ. 12,752.

Sun Times: 290 Ninth St East, POB 200, Owen Sound, ON N4K 1N7; tel. (519) 376-2250; fax (519) 372-1861; e-mail doug.edgar@sunmedia.ca; internet www.owensoundsuntimes.com; f. 1853 as *The Times*; owned by Sun Media Corpn; evening; Publr CHERYL A. MCMENEMY; Man. Editor DOUG EDGAR; circ. 13,223.

Toronto Star: 1 Yonge St, Toronto, ON M5E 1E6; tel. (416) 367-2000; fax (416) 869-4328; e-mail city@thestar.ca; internet www.thestar.com; f. 1892; Publr JOHN D. CRUICKSHANK; Editor-in-Chief MICHAEL COOKE; circ. 357,612.

Toronto Sun: 333 King St East, Toronto, ON M5A 3X5; tel. (416) 947-2222; fax (416) 947-1664; e-mail wendy.metcalfe@sunmedia.ca; internet www.torontosun.com; f. 1971; owned by Sun Media Corpn; Publr MIKE POWER; Editor-in-Chief WENDY METCALFE; circ. 169,219.

Welland Tribune: 228 East Main St, POB 278, Welland, ON L3B 5P5; tel. (905) 732-2411; fax (905) 732-3660; e-mail dan.dakin@sunmedia.ca; internet www.wellandtribune.ca; f. 1863; owned by Sun Media Corpn; Publr KEN KOYAMA; Man. Editor DAN DAKIN; circ. 13,879.

Windsor Star: 300 Ouellette Ave, Windsor, ON N9A 7B4; tel. (519) 255-5714; fax (519) 255-5515; e-mail mbeneteau@windsorstar.com; internet www.windsorstar.com; f. 1918; owned by Postmedia Network Inc; Publr and Editor MARTY BENETEAU; circ. 52,169.

World Journal (Toronto): 7755 Warden Ave, Unit 9, Markham, ON L3R 0N3; tel. (416) 778-0888; fax (416) 778-1037; e-mail webmaster@worldjournal.com; internet www.worldjournal.com; f. 1976; Chinese; Editor-in-Chief PAUL CHANG; circ. 38,000.

Prince Edward Island

Guardian: 165 Prince St, POB 760, Charlottetown, PE C1A 4R7; tel. (902) 629-6000; fax (902) 566-3808; e-mail newsroom@theguardian.pe.ca; internet www.theguardian.pe.ca; f. 1887; Publr DON BRANDER; Man. Editor GARY MACDOUGALL; circ. 17,724.

The Journal Pioneer: 316 Water St, POB 2480, Summerside, PE C1N 4K5; tel. (902) 436-2121; fax (902) 436-0784; e-mail newsroom@journalpioneer.com; internet www.journalpioneer.com; f. 1865; evening; Publr SANDY RUNDLE; Man. Editor BRAD WORKS; circ. 7,230.

Québec

Le Devoir: 2050 rue de Bleury, 9e étage, Montréal, QC H3A 3M9; tel. (514) 985-3333; fax (514) 985-3360; e-mail clbeliveau@ledevoir.com; internet www.ledevoir.com; Publr BERNARD DESCÔTEAUX; Editor-in-Chief JOSÉE BOILEAU; circ. 34,697.

The Gazette: 1010 rue Ste-Catherine ouest, Suite 200, Montréal, QC H3B 5L1; tel. (514) 987-2222; fax (514) 987-2270; e-mail readtheg@montrealgazette.com; internet www.montrealgazette.com; f. 1778; owned by Postmedia Network Inc; English; Publr ALAN ALLNUTT; Editor-in-Chief LUCINDA CHODAN; circ. 113,888.

Le Journal de Montréal: 4545 rue Frontenac, Montréal, QC H2H 2R7; tel. (514) 521-4545; fax (514) 525-4542; e-mail transmission@journalmtl.com; internet www.canoe.com/journaldemontreal; f. 1964; owned by Sun Media Corpn; Publr and Editor LYNE ROBITAILLE; Editor-in-Chief DANY DOUCET; circ. 287,799.

Le Journal de Québec: 450 ave Béchard, Vanier, QC G1M 2E9; tel. (418) 683-1573; fax (418) 683-8886; e-mail commentaires@journaldequebec.com; internet lejournaldequebec.canoe.ca; f. 1967; owned by Sun Media Corpn; Publr and CEO LOUISE CORDEAU; circ. 145,089.

Le Nouvelliste: 1920 rue Bellefeuille, CP 668, Trois Rivières, QC G9A 3Y2; tel. (819) 376-2501; fax (819) 376-0946; e-mail information@lenouvelliste.qc.ca; internet www.cyberpresse.ca/le-nouvelliste; f. 1920; Pres. and Publr ALAIN TURCOTTE; Editor-in-Chief STÉPHAN FRAPPIER; circ. 44,514.

La Presse: 7 rue St-Jacques, Montréal, QC H2Y 1K9; tel. (514) 285-7000; fax (514) 285-6930; e-mail commentaires@lapresse.ca; internet www.cyberpresse.ca/actualites/regional/montreal; f. 1884; Pres. and Editor GUY CREVIER; circ. 227,206.

Le Quotidien du Saguenay-Lac-St-Jean: 1051 blvd Talbot, Chicoutimi, QC G7H 5C1; tel. (418) 545-4474; fax (418) 690-8824; e-mail redaction@lequotidien.com; internet www.cyberpresse.ca/le-quotidien; f. 1973; Publr and Editor-in-Chief MICHEL SIMARD; circ. 27,940.

Le Soleil: 410 blvd Charest est, CP 1547, succursale Terminus, Québec, QC G1K 7J6; tel. (418) 686-3233; fax (418) 686-3374; e-mail redaction@lesoleil.com; internet www.cyberpresse.ca/le-soleil; f. 1896; Publr CLAUDE GAGNON; Editor-in-Chief PIERRE-PAUL NOREAU; circ. 80,432.

La Voix de L'Est: 76 rue Dufferin, Granby, QC J2G 9L4; tel. (450) 375-4555; fax (450) 777-4865; e-mail redaction@lavoixdelest.qc.ca; internet www.cyberpresse.ca/la-voix-de-lest; f. 1945; Pres. and Publr YVES LALONDE; circ. 15,053.

Saskatchewan

Daily Herald: 30 10th St East, Prince Albert, SK S6V 0Y5; tel. (306) 764-4276; fax (306) 763-3331; e-mail editorial@paherald.sk.ca; internet www.paherald.sk.ca; f. 1894; Publr JOHN MORASH; Editor PERRY BERGSON; circ. 5,237.

Leader-Post: 1964 Park St, POB 2020, Regina, SK S4P 3G4; tel. (306) 781-5211; fax (306) 565-2588; e-mail readerservice@leaderpost.com; internet www.leaderpost.com; f. 1883; owned by Postmedia Network Inc; Publr MARTY KLYNE; circ. 41,598.

StarPhoenix: 204 Fifth Ave North, Saskatoon, SK S7K 2P1; tel. (306) 657-6231; fax (306) 657-6437; e-mail citydesk@thestarphoenix.com; internet www.thestarphoenix.com; f. 1902; owned by Postmedia Network Inc; Editor ROB MCLAUGHLIN; circ. 48,107.

Times Herald: 44 Fairford St West, POB 3000, Moose Jaw, SK S6H 1V1; tel. (306) 692-6441; fax (306) 692-2101; e-mail editorial@mjtimes.sk.ca; internet www.mjtimes.sk.ca; f. 1889; evening; Publr and Gen. Man. ROB CLARK; Man. Editor LESLEY SHEPPARD; circ. Mon. to Sat. 5,023 (2011).

Yukon Territory

Whitehorse Star: 2149 Second Ave, Whitehorse, Yukon, YT Y1A 1C5; tel. (867) 667-4481; fax (867) 668-7130; e-mail star@whitehorsestar.com; internet www.whitehorsestar.com; f. 1900; evening; Publr JACKIE PIERCE; Editor JIM BUTLER; circ. 2,094.

SELECTED PERIODICALS

Alberta

Oilweek: 2nd Floor, 55 Ave, Suite 816, NE, Calgary, AB T2E 6Y4; tel. (403) 209-3500; fax (403) 245-8666; e-mail webmaster@junewarren.com; internet www.oilweek.com; monthly magazine; f. 1948; Publr AGNES ZALEWSKI; Man. Editor DALE LUNAN; circ. 7,500.

British Columbia

BC Outdoors—Sport Fishing and Hunting: OP Publishing Ltd, 200 West Esplanade, Suite 500, North Vancouver, BC V7M 1A4; tel. (604) 998-3310; fax (604) 998-3320; e-mail subscriptions@oppublishing.com; internet www.bcosportfishing.com; f. 1945; 6 a year; Publr MARK YELIC; Editor MIKE MITCHELL; circ. 13,615.

Pacific Yachting: OP Publishing Ltd, 200 West Esplanade, Suite 500, North Vancouver, BC V7M 1A4; tel. (604) 998-3310; fax (604) 998-3320; e-mail editor@pacificyachting.com; internet www.pacificyachting.com; f. 1968; monthly; Editor DALE MILLER; circ. 14,291.

Vancouver Magazine: 2608 Granville St, Suite 560, Vancouver, BC V6H 3V3; tel. (604) 877-7732; fax (604) 877-4848; e-mail mail@vancouvermagazine.com; internet www.vanmag.com; f. 1967; 11 a year; Publr LORI CHALMERS; Editor-in-Chief JOHN BURNS; circ. 60,000.

Western Living: 2608 Granville St, Suite 560, Vancouver, BC V6H 3V3; tel. (604) 877-7732; fax (604) 877-4838; e-mail wlmail@westernlivingmagazine.com; internet www.westernlivingmagazine.com; f. 1971; 10 a year; Editor-in-Chief ANICKA QUIN; circ. 165,000.

WestWorld BC: 4180 Lougheed Hwy, 4th Floor, Burnaby, BC V5C 6A7; tel. (604) 299-7311; fax (604) 299-9188; e-mail cwm@canadawide.com; internet www.canadawide.com/brands/westworld-bc; f. 1974; quarterly; travel and sport; Publr and Pres. PETER LEGGE; Editor-in-Chief TOM GIERASIMCZUK; circ. 540,000.

Manitoba

Canada's History: Bryce Hall, University of Winnipeg, 515 Portage Ave, Winnipeg, MB R3B 2E9; tel. (204) 988-9300; fax (204) 988-9309; e-mail editors@canadashistory.ca; internet www.canadashistory.ca; f. 1920 as *The Beaver—Canada's History Magazine*, present name adopted 2010; 6 a year; Canadian history; Publr, Pres. and CEO DEBORAH MORRISON; Editor-in-Chief MARK REID; circ. 37,956.

Cattlemen: 1666 Dublin Ave, Winnipeg, MB R3H 0H1; tel. (204) 944-5753; fax (204) 954-1422; e-mail gren@fbcpublishing.com; internet www.canadiancattlemen.ca; f. 1938; 13 a year; animal husbandry; Editor GREN WINSLOW; circ. 14,636.

Country Guide: 1666 Dublin Ave, Winnipeg, MB R3H 0H1; tel. (204) 944-5754; fax (204) 954-1422; e-mail tom.button@fbcpublishing.com; internet www.country-guide.ca; f. 1882; 10 a year; agriculture; 2 edns: *Western Edition* and *Eastern Edition*; Publr LYNDA TITYK; Editor TOM BUTTON; circ. 21,751.

Grainews: 1666 Dublin Ave, Winnipeg, MB R3H 0H1; tel. (204) 954-1400; fax (204) 944-1422; e-mail leeann.minogue@fbcpublishing.com; internet www.grainews.ca; f. 1975; 17 a year; grain- and cattle-farming; Publr BOB WILLCOX; Editor LEEANN MINOGUE; circ. 20,974.

Kanada Kurier: 955 Alexander Ave, POB 1054, Winnipeg, MB R3C 2X8; tel. (204) 774-1883; fax (204) 783-5740; f. 1889; weekly; German language and culture; Publr E. ROTZETTER; Editor MARION SCHIRRMANN; circ. 7,442.

The Manitoba Co-operator: 1666 Dublin Ave, Winnipeg, MB R3H 0H1; tel. (204) 954-1400; fax (204) 954-1422; e-mail laura@fbcpublishing.com; internet www.manitobacooperator.ca; f. 1925; owned by Farm Business Communications, a subsidiary of Glacier Ventures International Corpn; weekly; for the farming community; Publr BOB WILLCOX; Editor LAURA RANCE; circ. 11,877 (March 2010).

New Brunswick

Brunswick Business Journal: 175 General Manson Way, Miramichi, NB E1N 6K7; tel. (506) 622-2600; internet nbbusinessjournal.canadaeast.com; f. 1984; monthly; Man. Editor NANCY COOK.

Newfoundland and Labrador

Atlantic Business Magazine: 95 Le Marchant Rd, Suite 302, St John's, NL A1C 2H1; tel. (709) 726-9300; fax (709) 726-3013; e-mail dchafe@atlanticbusinessmagazine.com; internet www.atlanticbusinessmagazine.com; f. 1987; 6 a year; business; Publr HUBERT HUTTON; Exec. Editor DAWN CHAFE; circ. 37,000.

Northwest Territories

L'Aquilon: POB 456, Yellowknife, NT X1A 2N4; tel. (867) 873-6603; fax (867) 873-6663; e-mail direction_aquilon@mac.com; internet www.aquilon.nt.ca; f. 1986; weekly; Editor ALAIN BESSETTE; circ. 1,000.

Hay River Hub: 8–4 Courtoreille St, Hay River, NT X0E 1G2; tel. (867) 874-6577; fax (867) 874-2679; e-mail editor@hayriverhub.com; internet www.hayriverhub.com; f. 1973; weekly; Publr CHRIS BRODEUR; Editor PATRICK TESKEY; circ. 3,000.

Northern News Services: 5108 50th St, POB 2820, Yellowknife, NT X1A 2R1; tel. (867) 873-4031; fax (867) 873-8507; e-mail nnsl@nnsl.com; internet www.nnsl.com; f. 1945 as *News/North*; weekly; Publr JACK SIGVALDASON; Man. Editor BRUCE VALPY; circ. 11,000.

Northern Journal: 207 McDougal Rd, POB 990, Fort Smith, NT X0E 0P0; tel. (867) 872-3000; fax (867) 872-2754; e-mail news@norj.ca; internet www.srj.ca; f. 1978; weekly; fmrly the *Slave River Journal*, renamed as above in 2011; Publr and Man. Editor DON JAQUE; circ. 2,750.

Yellowknifer: POB 2820, Yellowknife, NT X1A 2R1; tel. (867) 873-4031; fax (867) 873-8507; e-mail nnsl@nnsl.com; internet www.nnsl.com; weekly; Publr JACK SIGVALDASON; Man. Editor BRUCE VALPY; circ. 6,200.

Nova Scotia

Canadian Forum: 5502 Atlantic St, Halifax, NS B3H 1G4; tel. (902) 421-7022; fax (902) 425-0166; f. 1920; 10 a year; political, literary and economic; Editor ROBERT CLUDOS; circ. 9,000.

Progress: 1660 Hollis St, Penthouse, Suite 1202, Halifax, NS B3J 1V7; tel. (902) 494-0999; fax (902) 494-0997; e-mail news@progressmedia.ca; internet progressmedia.ca; f. 1993; 8 a year; regional business; Editor PAMELA SCOTT-CRACE; circ. 22,477 (June 2010).

Nunavut

Kivalliq News: Rankin Inlet, NU; tel. (867) 645-3223; fax (867) 645-3225; e-mail kivalliqnews@nnsl.com; internet www.nnsl.com; f. 1994; weekly; owned by Northern News Services; English and Inuktitut; Publr JACK SIGVALDASON; Man. Editor BRUCE VALPY; circ. 1,400.

Nunatsiaq News: POB 8, Iqaluit, NU X0A 0H0; tel. (867) 979-5357; fax (867) 979-4763; e-mail editor@nunatsiaqonline.ca; internet www.nunatsiaq.com; f. 1973; weekly; English and Inuktitut; Publr MICHAEL ROBERTS; Editor JIM BELL; circ. 8,000.

Ontario

Anglican Journal: 80 Hayden St, Toronto, ON M4Y 3G2; tel. (416) 924-9199; fax (416) 925-8811; e-mail editor@anglicanjournal.com; internet www.anglicanjournal.com; f. 1875; 10 a year; official publ. of the Anglican Church of Canada; Man. Editor PAUL FEHELEY (acting); circ. 160,000.

Better Farming: 21400 Service Rd, Vankleek Hill, ON K0B 1R0; tel. (613) 678-2232; fax (613) 678-5993; e-mail admin@betterfarming.com; internet www.betterfarming.com; f. 1999; 10 a year; Publr PAUL NOLAN; Man. Editor ROBERT C. IRWIN; circ. 39,000.

CAmagazine: The Canadian Institute of Chartered Accountants, 277 Wellington St West, Toronto, ON M5V 3H2; tel. (416) 204-3235; fax (416) 204-3409; e-mail camagazineinfo@cica.ca; internet www.camagazine.com; f. 1911; 10 a year; English and French; Publr CAIRINE M. WILSON; Editor-in-Chief OKEY CHIGBO; circ. 90,413 (June 2010).

Campus Canada: 5397 Eglington Ave West, Suite 101, Toronto, ON M9C 5K6; tel. (416) 928-2909; fax (416) 928-1357; internet www.campus.ca; f. 1983; quarterly; 30 campus edns; Man. Editor CHRISTIAN PEARCE; circ. 145,000.

Canada Gazette: Canada Gazette Directorate, Public Works and Govt Services Canada, 5th Floor, 350 Albert St, Ottawa, ON K1A 0S5; tel. (613) 996-1268; fax (613) 991-3540; e-mail info.gazette@pwgsc-tpsgc.gc.ca; internet canadagazette.gc.ca; f. 1841; weekly; official newspaper of the Govt of Canada; English and French; Editor-in-Chief JOSÉE BOISVERT.

Canadian Architect: 12 Concorde Pl., Suite 800, Toronto, ON M3C 4J2; tel. (416) 510-6807; fax (416) 510-5140; e-mail editors@canadianarchitect.com; internet www.canadianarchitect.com;

f. 1955; monthly; Publr TOM ARKELL; Editor IAN CHODIKOFF; circ. 14,000.

Canadian Art: 215 Spadina Ave, Suite 320, Toronto, ON M5T 2C7; tel. (416) 368-8854; fax (416) 368-6135; e-mail info@canadianart.ca; internet www.canadianart.ca; quarterly; Publr ANN WEBB; Editor RICHARD RHODES; circ. 17,385.

Canadian Bar Review/Revue du Barreau canadien: Canadian Bar Foundation, 500–865 Carling Ave, Ottawa, ON K1S 5S8; tel. (613) 237-2925; fax (613) 237-0185; e-mail info@cba.org; internet www.cba.org; f. 1923; quarterly, comprising 3 online issues and 1 yearly consolidated vol.; Editor Prof. BETH BILSON; circ. 36,000.

Canadian Business: 1 Mount Pleasant Rd, 11th Floor, Toronto, ON M4Y 2Y5; tel. (416) 764-1200; fax (416) 764-1255; e-mail help@canadianbusiness.com; internet www.canadianbusiness.com; f. 1928; 18 a year; owned by Rogers Media; Publr KENNETH WHYTE; Editor and Assoc. Publr STEVE MAICH; circ. 80,536.

Canadian Electronics: Annex Business Media, 222 Edward St, Aurora, ON L4G 1W6; tel. (905) 727-0077; fax (905) 727-0017; e-mail kpirker@annexweb.com; internet www.canadianelectronics.ca; f. 1986; 4 a year; Publr KLAUS PIRKER; Editorial Dir MIKE EDWARDS; circ. 17,152 (Nov. 2012).

Canadian Geographic: 1155 Lola St, Suite 200, Ottawa, ON K1K 4C1; tel. (613) 745-4629; fax (613) 744-0947; e-mail editorial@canadiangeographic.ca; internet www.canadiangeographic.ca; f. 1930; 6 a year; publ. of the Royal Canadian Geographical Soc; Publr ANDRÉ PRÉFONTAINE; Editor-in-Chief ERIC HARRIS; circ. 186,805.

Canadian Home Workshop: 54 St Patrick St, Toronto, ON M5T 1V1; tel. (416) 599-2000; fax (416) 599-0800; e-mail editorial@canadianhomeworkshop.com; internet www.canadianhomeworkshop.com; f. 1977; owned by Cottage Life Media Inc; 6 a year; home improvement; Editor-in-Chief and Brand Man. DOUGLAS THOMSON; Man. Editor MATTHEW PIORO; circ. 125,015.

Canadian House & Home: 511 King St West, Suite 120, Toronto, ON M5V 2Z4; tel. (416) 591-0204; fax (416) 591-1630; e-mail chheditorial@hhmedia.com; internet www.houseandhome.com; f. 1982; monthly; Pres. and Publr LYNDA REEVES; Editor-in-Chief SUZANNE DIMMA; circ. 244,436.

Canadian Jewish News (CJN): 1750 Steeles Ave, Suite 218, Vaughan, ON L4K 2L7; tel. (416) 391-1836; fax (416) 391-0829; e-mail cjninfo@gmail.com; internet www.cjnews.com; f. 1971; weekly; Gen. Man. JOE SERGE; Editor MORDECHAI BEN-DAT; circ. 39,000.

Canadian Living: 25 Sheppard Ave West, Suite 100, North York, ON M2N 6S7; tel. (416) 733-7600; fax (416) 733-3398; e-mail letters@canadianliving.com; internet www.canadianliving.com; f. 1975; monthly; Editor-in-Chief SUSAN ANTONACCI; circ. 505,665.

Canadian Medical Association Journal (CMAJ): 1867 Alta Vista Dr., Ottawa, ON K1G 5W8; tel. (613) 731-8610; fax (613) 565-5471; e-mail pubs@cma.ca; internet www.cmaj.ca; f. 1911; 25 a year; Editor-in-Chief Dr JOHN FLETCHER; Man. Editor LEESA D. SULLIVAN; circ. 73,711 (March 2010).

Canadian Musician (CM): 4056 Dorchester Rd 202, Niagara Falls, ON L2E 6M9; tel. (905) 374-8878; fax (888) 665-1307; e-mail mail@nor.com; internet www.canadianmusician.com; f. 1979; 6 a year; Editor ANDREW KING; circ. 27,000.

Canadian Nurse/L'infirmière canadienne: 50 Driveway, Ottawa, ON K2P 1E2; tel. (613) 237-2133; fax (613) 237-3520; e-mail info@canadian-nurse.com; internet www.canadian-nurse.com; f. 1905 as journal of the Canadian Nurses' Asscn; publ. in separate French and English edns since 2000; 9 a year; Editor-in-Chief LISA BRAZEAU; circ. 134,000 (January 2011).

Canadian Travel Press Weekly: 310 Dupont St, Toronto, ON M5R 1V9; tel. (416) 968-7252; fax (416) 968-2377; e-mail ctp@baxter.net; internet www.travelpress.com; 46 a year; Editor-in-Chief EDITH BAXTER; Exec. Editor ROBERT MOWAT; circ. 25,500.

Chatelaine: 1 Mount Pleasant Rd, 8th Floor, Toronto, ON M4Y 2Y5; tel. (416) 764-1888; fax (416) 764-2891; internet www.chatelaine.com; f. 1928; publ. by Rogers Publishing Inc; monthly; women's journal; Publr TARA TUCKER; Editor-in-Chief JANE FRANCISCO; circ. 544,413.

ComputerWorld Canada: 55 Town Centre Ct, Suite 302, Scarborough, ON M1P 4X4; tel. (416) 290-0240; fax (416) 290-0238; e-mail editorial@itwc.ca; internet www.itworldcanada.com; f. 1984; 25 a year; Pres. and Publr FAWN ANNAN; Editor DAVE WEBB; circ. 42,000.

Embassy: 69 Sparks St, Ottawa, ON K1P 5A5; tel. (613) 232-5952; fax (613) 232-9055; e-mail acreskey@embassynews.ca; internet www.embassynews.ca; f. 2004; weekly; Publr ANNE MARIE CRESKEY.

Fashion: 111 Queen St East, Suite 320, Toronto, ON M5C 1S2; tel. (416) 364-3333; fax (416) 594-3374; internet www.fashionmagazine.com; f. 1996 as Elm Street; ceased publication in 2004 but continued to publish quarterly fashion supplement *Elm Street The Look* until 2006 when magazine relaunched under above name; publ. by St Jospeh Media; monthly; women's interest; Editor-in-Chief CERI MARSH.

Flare: 1 Mount Pleasant Rd, 8th Floor, Toronto, ON M4Y 2Y5; tel. (416) 764-2863; fax (416) 764-2866; e-mail laura.lanktree@flare.rogers.com; internet www.teenflare.com; f. 1980; monthly; fashion, beauty and health; Publr MELISSA AHLSTRAND; Editor MIRANDA PURVES; circ. 135,489.

The Hockey News: Transcontinental Publishing, 25 Sheppard Ave West, Suite 100, North York, ON M2N 6S7; tel. (416) 340-8000; fax (416) 340-2786; e-mail editorial@thehockeynews.com; internet www.thehockeynews.com; f. 1947; 34 a year; Man. Editor JASON KAY; circ. 100,027.

Journal of the Canadian Dental Association: 1815 Alta Vista Dr., Ottawa, ON K1G 3Y6; tel. (613) 523-1770; fax (613) 523-7736; e-mail president@cda-adc.ca; internet www.jcda.ca; f. 1935; 11 a year; Editor Dr MICHAEL J. CASAS; circ. 20,000.

Legion Magazine: 86 Aird Pl., Kanata, ON K2L 0A1; tel. (613) 591-0116; fax (613) 591-0146; e-mail info@legionmagazine.com; internet www.legionmagazine.com; f. 1926; 6 a year; publ. for Canadian veterans and Legionnaires; Gen. Man. JENNIFER MORSE; circ. 2,323,308.

Maclean's: 1 Mount Pleasant Rd, 11th Floor, Toronto, ON M4Y 2Y5; tel. (416) 764-1300; fax (416) 764-1332; e-mail letters@macleans.ca; internet www2.macleans.ca; f. 1905 as *The Business Magazine*; present name adopted in 1911; weekly; Publr PENNY HICKS; Editor MARK STEVENSON; circ. 340,610.

The Northern Miner: 80 Valleybrook Dr., Toronto, ON M3B 2S9; tel. (416) 442-2122; fax (416) 442-2191; e-mail northernminer2@northernminer.com; internet www.northernminer.com; f. 1915; owned by the Business Information Group; weekly; Publr DOUGLAS DONNELLY; Editor JOHN CUMMING; circ. 11,000.

Now: 189 Church St, Toronto, ON M5B 1Y7; tel. (416) 364-1300; fax (416) 364-1166; e-mail web@nowtoronto.com; internet www.nowtoronto.com; f. 1981; weekly; young adult; Publr and Editor MICHAEL HOLLETT; CEO and Editor ALICE KLEIN; circ. 115,911.

Ontario Medical Review (OMA): 150 Bloor St West, Suite 900, Toronto, ON M5S 3C1; tel. (416) 599-2580; fax (416) 340-2944; e-mail info@oma.org; internet www.oma.org; f. 1922; monthly; publ. of the Ontario Medical Asscn; Editor JEFF HENRY; Man. Editor ELIZABETH PETRUCELLI; circ. 29,000.

Oral Health: 80 Valleybrook Dr., Toronto, ON M3B 2S9; tel. (416) 510-6785; fax (416) 510-5140; e-mail cwilson@oralhealthjournal.com; internet www.oralhealthjournal.com; f. 1911; monthly; dentistry; Sr Publr MELISSA SUMMERFIELD; Editorial Dir CATHERINE WILSON; circ. 21,000 (2010).

Quill & Quire: POB 819, Markham, ON L3P 8A2; tel. (416) 364-3333; fax (416) 595-5415; e-mail swoods@quillandquire.com; internet www.quillandquire.com; f. 1935; 10 a year; book publishing industry; Publr ALISON JONES; Editor STUART WOODS; circ. 5,000.

Style: 1106–60 Bloor St West, Toronto, ON M4W 3B8; tel. (416) 203-7900; fax (416) 703-6392; e-mail bryan@rivegauchemedia.com; internet www.style.ca; f. 1888; monthly; fashion and clothing trade; owned by Rive Gauche Media; Pres. OLIVIER FELICIO; Editor BRYAN SOROKA; circ. 12,000.

Style at Home: Transcontinental Media Inc, 25 Sheppard Ave West, Suite 100, Toronto, ON M2N 6S7; tel. (416) 733-7600; fax (416) 218-3632; e-mail letters@styleathome.com; internet www.styleathome.com; f. 1997; monthly; owned by Transcontinental Media Inc; Editor ERIN MCLAUGHLIN; circ. 230,002.

Toronto Life Magazine: 111 Queen St East, Suite 320, Toronto, ON M5C 1S2; tel. (416) 364-3333; fax (416) 861-1169; e-mail editorial@torontolife.com; internet www.torontolife.com; f. 1966; monthly; Publr DAVID HAMILTON; Editor SARAH FULFORD; circ. 95,000.

Tribute Magazine: 71 Barber Greene Rd, Don Mills, Toronto, ON M3C 2A2; tel. (416) 445-0544; fax (416) 445-2894; e-mail generalinfo@tribute.ca; internet www.tribute.ca; f. 1981; 6 a year; entertainment; CEO and Editor-in-Chief SANDRA I. STEWART; circ. 1.8m.

TV Guide: POB 815, Markham Station, Markham ON L3P 7Z7; tel. (416) 733-7600; fax (416) 733-3632; e-mail tvguide@indas.on.ca; internet www.tvguide.ca; f. 1976; weekly; Publr CAROLINE ANDREWS; Editor AMBER DOWLING; circ. 243,695.

Québec

L'Actualité: 1200 ave McGill College, bureau 800, Montréal, QC H3B 4G7; tel. (514) 843-2564; fax (514) 843-2186; e-mail redaction@lactualite.rogers.com; internet www.lactualite.com; f. 1976; monthly; current affairs; Publr and Editor-in-Chief CAROLE BEAULIEU; circ. 163,572.

Les Affaires: 1100 blvd René-Lévesque ouest, 24e étage, Montréal, QC H3B 4X9; tel. (514) 392-9000; fax (514) 392-4726; e-mail redaction

.lesaffaires.com@tc.tc; internet www.lesaffaires.com; f. 1978; monthly; Editor-in-Chief DANIEL GERMAIN; circ. 76,274 (June 2010).

Le Bulletin des Agriculteurs: 1 Place du Commerce, Suite 320, Nuns' Island, QC H3E 1A2; tel. (514) 766-9554; fax (514) 766-2665; e-mail info@lebulletin.rogers.com; internet www.lebulletin.com; f. 1918; monthly; Editor-in-Chief YVON THÉRIEN; circ. 12,270 (June 2010).

Châtelaine: 1200 ave McGill College, bureau 800, Montréal, QC H3B 4G7; tel. (514) 845-5141; fax (514) 843-2185; e-mail redaction@chatelaine.rogers.com; internet fr.chatelaine.com; f. 1960; monthly; Publr TARA TUCKER; Editor-in-Chief JANE FRANCISCO; circ. 544,413.

Il Cittadino Canadese: 6020 Jean-Talon est, bureau 209, Montréal, QC H1S 3B1; tel. (514) 253-2332; fax (514) 253-6574; e-mail journal@cittadinocanadese.com; internet www.cittadinocanadese.com; f. 1941; weekly; Italian; Publr NINA GIORDANO; Editor ANTONINA MORMINA; circ. 38,500.

Commerce: 1100 blvd René-Lévesque ouest, 24e étage, Montréal, QC H3B 4X9; tel. (514) 392-9000; fax (514) 392-1489; e-mail commerce@transcontinental.ca; f. 1898; monthly; Editor-in-Chief DIANE BÉRARD; circ. 40,135.

Harrowsmith Country Life: 3100 blvd Concorde est, Suite 213, Laval, QC H7E 2B8; tel. (450) 665-0271; fax (450) 665-2974; e-mail info@harrowsmithcountrylife.ca; internet www.harrowsmithcountrylife.ca; f. 1976; 6 a year; Editor TOM CRUICKSHANK; circ. 126,862.

Le Lundi: 7 chemin Bates, Outremont, QC H2V 1A6; tel. (514) 270-1100; fax (514) 270-5395; f. 1976; weekly; Editor MICHAEL CHOINIÈRE; circ. 25,037.

Photo Life: 185 St Paul St, Québec City, QC G1K 3W2; tel. (800) 905-7468; fax (800) 664-2739; e-mail editor@photolife.com; internet www.photolife.com; f. 1976; 6 a year; Editorial Dir VALÉRIE RACINE; circ. 55,000.

Québec Science: 1251 rue Rachel est, Montréal, QC H2J 2J9; tel. (514) 843-8356; fax (514) 843-4897; e-mail courrier@quebecscience.qc.ca; internet www.quebecscience.qc.ca; f. 1969; 10 a year; Editor-in-Chief RAYMOND LEMIEUX; circ. 32,000.

Le Quotidien: Saguenay, QC G7H 5C1; tel. (418) 545-4474; fax (418) 690-8805; e-mail msimard@lequotidien.com; internet www.cyberpresse.ca/le-quotidien; f. 1964; weekly; also publishes *Le Progrès Dimanche*; Pres. and Editor MICHEL SIMARD; circ. 132,800 (2009).

Reader's Digest: 1100 blvd René-Lévesque ouest, Montréal, QC H3B 5H5; tel. (514) 934-0751; fax (514) 940-3637; internet www.readersdigest.ca; f. 1947; monthly; English edn; Pres. and CEO TONY CIOFFI; Editor-in-Chief ROBERT GOYETTE; circ. 597,229.

Rénovation Bricolage: 1010, rue de Serigny, Longueuil, QC J4K 5G7; fax (514) 848-0309; e-mail renobrico@tvapublications.com; internet www.magazinerenovationbricolage.com; f. 1976; 9 a year; Publr and Editor CLAUDE LECLERC; Editor-in-Chief VINCENT ROY; circ. 31,489.

Sélection du Reader's Digest: 1100 blvd René-Lévesque ouest, Montréal, QC H3B 5H5; tel. (514) 940-0751; fax (514) 940-7340; e-mail manon.sylvain@readersdigest.com; internet www.selection.ca; f. 1947; monthly; Pres. and CEO TONY CIOFFI; Editor-in-Chief ROBERT GOYETTE; circ. 249,843.

La Terre de Chez Nous: 555 blvd Roland-Therrien, Longueuil, QC J4H 3Y9; tel. (450) 679-8483; fax (450) 670-4788; e-mail laterre@laterre.ca; internet www.laterre.ca; f. 1929; weekly; agriculture and forestry; Publr ANDRÉ SAVARD; Editor MICHEL BEAUNOYER; circ. 35,576.

TV Hebdo: 1010 rue de Sérigny, 4th Floor, Longueuil, QC J4K 5G7; tel. (514) 848-7000; fax (514) 848-7070; e-mail tvhebdo@tvapublications.com.com; internet www.tvhebdo.com; f. 1960; weekly; Editor-in-Chief JEAN-LOUIS PODLESAK; circ. 81,007.

Saskatchewan

Farm Light & Power: 2230 15th Ave, Regina, SK S4P 1A2; tel. (306) 525-3305; fax (306) 757-1810; f. 1959; monthly; Editor TOM BRADLEY; circ. 71,000.

Western Producer: 2310 Millar Ave, POB 2500, Saskatoon, SK S7K 2C4; tel. (306) 665-3544; fax (306) 934-2401; e-mail newsroom@producer.com; internet www.producer.com; f. 1923; weekly; agriculture; Editor JOANNE PAULSON; circ. 74,000.

Yukon

Yukon News: 211 Wood St, Whitehorse, YT Y1A 2E4; tel. (867) 667-6285; fax (867) 668-3755; e-mail rmostyn@yukon-news.com; internet www.yukon-news.com; f. 1960; 3 a week; Editor JOHN THOMPSON; circ. 8,000.

NEWS AGENCY

The Canadian Press: 36 King St East, Toronto, ON M5C 2L9; tel. (416) 364-0321; fax (416) 364-0207; internet www.cp.org; f. 1917; national news co-operative; 99 newspaper mems; Editor-in-Chief SCOTT WHITE.

PRESS ASSOCIATIONS

Canadian Business Press (CBP): 2100 Banbury Cres., Oakville, ON L6H 5P6; tel. (416) 239-1022; fax (416) 239-1076; e-mail torrance@cbp.ca; internet www.cbp.ca; f. 1920; Chair. JOHN KERR; Exec. Dir TRISH TORRANCE; over 170 mems.

Canadian Community Newspapers Association (CCNA): 890 Yonge St, Suite 200, Toronto, ON M4W 3P4; tel. (416) 923-3567; fax (416) 923-7206; e-mail info@newspaperscanada.ca; internet www.newspaperscanada.ca; f. 1919; in Jan. 2011 est. Newspapers Canada, a jt initiative with the Canadian Newspaper Asscn, to represent interests of all newspaper mems; Chair. PAUL MACNEILL; Pres. GREG NESBITT; CEO JOHN HINDS; 8 regional asscns; more than 700 mems.

Canadian Newspaper Association (CNA): 890 Yonge St, Suite 200, Toronto, ON M4W 3P4; tel. (416) 923-3567; fax (416) 923-7206; e-mail info@newspaperscanada.ca; internet www.newspaperscanada.ca; f. 1996; in Jan. 2011 est. Newspapers Canada, a jt initiative with the Canadian Community Newspapers Asscn, to represent interests of all newspaper mems; Chair. PETER KVARNSTROM; Pres. and CEO JOHN HINDS.

Magazines Canada (The Magazine Asscn of Canada): 425 Adelaide St West, Suite 700, Toronto, ON M5V 3C1; tel. (416) 504-0274; fax (416) 504-0437; e-mail info@magazinescanada.ca; internet www.magazinescanada.ca; f. 1973 as the Canadian Magazine Publrs Asscn; present name adopted 2005; represents over 370 of the country's consumer titles; Chair. MICHAEL FOX; CEO MARK JAMISON; Gen. Man. and Publr BARBARA ZATYKO.

Publishers

Thomas Allen and Son Ltd: 390 Steelcase Rd East, Markham, ON L3R 1G2; tel. (905) 475-9126; fax (905) 475-4255; e-mail info@t-allen.com; internet www.thomasallen.ca; f. 1916; Pres. and CEO KIRK HOWARD.

Annick Press Ltd: 15 Patricia Ave, Toronto, ON M2M 1H9; tel. (416) 221-4802; fax (416) 221-8400; e-mail annickpress@annickpress.com; internet www.annickpress.com; f. 1975; children's; Dir RICK WILKS.

Arsenal Pulp Press Book Publishers Ltd: 211 East Georgia St, Suite 101, Vancouver, BC V6A 1Z6; tel. (604) 687-4233; fax (604) 687-4283; e-mail info@arsenalpulp.com; internet www.arsenalpulp.com; f. 1982; literary fiction and non-fiction, cultural studies, gay and lesbian; Publr BRIAN LAM.

Editions Bellarmin: 7333, pl. des Roseraies, Suite 100, Anjou, QC H1M 2X6; tel. (514) 745-4290; fax (514) 745-4299; e-mail editions@fides.qc.ca; internet www.fides.qc.ca; f. 1891; religious, educational, politics, sociology, ethnography, history, sport, leisure; Dir-Gen. STÉPHANE LAVOIE.

Black Rose Books: CP 35788, succ. Leo Pariseau, Montréal, QC H2X 0A4; tel. (514) 844-4076; e-mail info@blackrosebooks.net; internet www.blackrosebooks.net; f. 1969; politics, social studies, humanities; Pres. LAWRENCE BARBUB.

Borealis Press Ltd: 8 Mohawk Cres., Nepean, ON K2H 7G6; tel. (613) 829-0150; fax (613) 829-7783; e-mail drt@borealispress.com; internet www.borealispress.com; f. 1972; Canadian fiction and non-fiction, drama, juvenile, poetry; Pres. FRANK TIERNEY.

Breakwater Books: 100 Water St, POB 2188, St John's, NL A1C 6E6; tel. (709) 722-6680; fax (709) 753-0708; e-mail info@breakwaterbooks.com; internet www.breakwaterbooks.com; f. 1973; fiction, non-fiction, children's, educational, folklore; Pres. REBECCA ROSE.

Broadview Press: 280 Perry St, Unit 5, POB 1243, Peterborough, ON K9J 7H5; tel. (705) 743-8990; fax (705) 743-8353; e-mail customerservice@broadviewpress.com; internet www.broadviewpress.com; f. 1985; English studies and philosophy; Pres. and CEO DON LEPAN.

Canada Law Book: 1 Corporate Plaza, 2075 Kennedy Rd, Toronto, ON M1T 3V4; tel. (416) 609-3800; fax (416) 298-5085; e-mail najat@canadalawbook.ca; internet www.canadalawbook.ca; f. 1855; acquired by Thomson Reuters in 2010; law reports, law journals, legal textbooks, online legal research services, etc.; Vice-Pres. RUTH EPSTEIN.

Les Editions CEC, Inc: 9001 blvd Louis-H. La Fontaine, Anjou, Montréal, QC H1J 2C5; tel. (514) 351-6010; fax (514) 351-3534;

e-mail infoped@ceceditions.com; internet www.editionscec.com; f. 1956; textbooks; Pres. and Dir-Gen. CHRISTIAN JETTÉ.

Chenelière Education: 5800 rue Saint-Denis, bureau 900, Montréal, QC H2S 3L5; tel. (514) 273-1066; fax (514) 276-0324; e-mail jrochefort@cheneliere.ca; internet www.cheneliere.ca; f. 1984; owned by TC Transcontinental Inc; French-language educational publr; imprints incl. Beauchemin, Chenelière/McGraw-Hill, Gaëtan Morin Editeur, Graficor; Pres. JACQUES ROCHEFORT.

Coach House Books: 80 bpNichol Lane, behind 401 Huron St, Toronto, ON M5S 3J4; tel. (416) 979-2217; fax (416) 977-1158; e-mail mail@chbooks.com; internet www.chbooks.com; f. 1965; fiction, poetry, drama; Publr STAN BEVINGTON; Editor-in-Chief ALANA WILCOX.

Crabtree Publishing Co, Ltd: 616 Welland Ave, St Catharines, ON L2M 5V6; tel. (905) 682-5221; fax (905) 682-7166; e-mail custserv@crabtreebooks.com; internet www.crabtreebooks.com; f. 1978; children's non-fiction; Pres. PETER A. CRABTREE; CEO JOHN SIEMENS.

D&M Publishers Inc: 4437 Rondeview Rd, P.O.Box 219, Madeira Park, BC V0N 2H0; tel. (604) 883-2730; fax (604) 883-9451; e-mail dm@dmpibooks.com; internet www.dmpibooks.com; f. 1964 as Douglas & McIntyre Publrs; imprints incl. Greystone Books, New Society Publrs; general non-fiction, literary fiction; Chair. and CEO SCOTT MCINTYRE; Exec. Dir MARK SCOTT.

The Dundurn Group: 3 Church St, Suite 500, Toronto, ON M5E 1M2; tel. (416) 214-5544; fax (416) 214-5556; e-mail info@dundurn.com; internet www.dundurn.com; f. 1972; drama and performing arts, history, reference, fiction and non-fiction; Pres. KIRK HOWARD.

Emond Montgomery Publications: 60 Shaftesbury Ave, Toronto, ON M4T 1A3; tel. (416) 975-3925; fax (416) 975-3924; e-mail agrinstead@emp.ca; internet www.emp.ca; f. 1978; educational and professional; Pres. PAUL EMOND.

Fenn Publishing Co Ltd: 34 Nixon Rd, Bolton, ON L7E 1W2; internet www.hbfenn.com; fiction and non-fiction; Pres. HAROLD FENN; Publr C. JORDAN FENN.

Editions Fides: 7333 pl. des Roseraies, Suite 100, Anjou, QC H1M 2X6; tel. (514) 745-4290; fax (514) 745-4299; e-mail editions@groupefides.com; internet www.editionsfides.com; f. 1937; juvenile, history, theology, textbooks and literature; Dir-Gen. STÉPHANE LAVOIE.

Fifth House Publishers Ltd: 195 Allstate Pkwy, Markham, ON L3R 4T8; e-mail tdettman@fitzhenry.ca; internet www.fifthhousepublishers.ca; f. 1982; imprint of Fitzhenry & Whiteside Ltd; native, literary and non-fiction; Publr TRACEY DETTMAN.

Fitzhenry & Whiteside Ltd: 195 Allstate Pkwy, Markham, ON L3R 4T8; tel. (905) 477-9700; fax (905) 477-2834; e-mail godwit@fitzhenry.ca; internet www.fitzhenry.ca; f. 1966; children's fiction and non-fiction, textbooks, trade, educational, poetry; Pres. SHARON FITZHENRY.

Formac Publishing Ltd: 5502 Atlantic St, Halifax, NS B3H 1G4; tel. (902) 421-7022; fax (902) 425-0166; e-mail customerservice@formac.ca; internet www.formac.ca; f. 1971; urban and labour studies, maritime studies, children's, general non-fiction; Publr JAMES LORIMER.

Harlequin Enterprises Ltd: 225 Duncan Mill Rd, Don Mills, ON M3B 3K9; tel. (416) 445-5860; fax (416) 445-8655; e-mail CustomerService@Harlequin.com; internet www.eharlequin.com; f. 1949; fiction, paperbacks; imprints: Silhouette, MIRA Books, Red Dress Ink, LUNA Books, HQN Books, Steeple Hill Books, Steeple Hill Café, Kimani Press, Spice and Harlequin Ginger Blossom; Chair. and CEO DONNA M. HAYES.

HarperCollins Canada Ltd: 1995 Markham Rd, Scarborough, ON M1B 5M8; tel. (416) 321-2241; fax (416) 321-3033; internet www.harpercollins.ca; f. 1989; trade, bibles, dictionaries, juvenile, paperbacks; Pres. and CEO DAVID KENT.

Editions de l'Hexagone: 1010 rue de la Gauchetière est, Montréal, QC H2L 2N5; tel. (514) 523-7993; fax (514) 282-7530; e-mail adpcommandes@messageries-adp.com; internet www.edhexagone.com; f. 1953; part of Quebecor Media Inc; literature; Vice-Pres. MARTIN BALTHAZAR; Editor STÉPHANE BERTHOMET.

Institut de Recherches Psychologiques, Inc/Institute of Psychological Research, Inc: 76 rue Mozart Ouest, Montréal, QC H2S 1C4; tel. (514) 382-3000; fax (514) 382-3007; e-mail pierre@irpcanada.com; internet www.irpcanada.com; f. 1964; educational and psychological; Dir PAUL-JULIEN GROLEAU.

Key Porter Books: 6 Adelaide St East, 10th Floor, Toronto, ON M5C 1H6; tel. (416) 862-7777; fax (416) 862-2304; e-mail rob.howard@keyporter.com; internet www.keyporter.com; f. 1979; majority owned by H. B. Fenn and Co Ltd; general trade; Publr and Vice-Pres. JORDAN FENN.

Leméac Editeur: 4609 rue d'Iberville, 1e étage, Montréal, QC H2H 2L9; tel. (514) 525-5558; fax (514) 524-3145; e-mail lemeac@lemeac.com; internet www.lemeac.com; f. 1957; literary, academic, theatre, general; Gen. Dir LISE P. BERGEVIN.

Lidec Inc: 4350 ave de l'Hôtel-de-Ville, Montréal, QC H2W 2H5; tel. (514) 843-5991; fax (514) 843-5252; e-mail lidec@lidec.qc.ca; internet www.lidec.qc.ca; f. 1965; educational, textbooks; Pres. MARC-AIMÉ GUÉRIN.

McClelland and Stewart Ltd: 75 Sherbourne St, 5th Floor, Toronto, ON M5A 2P9; tel. (416) 364-4449; fax (416) 598-7764; e-mail editorial@mcclelland.com; internet www.mcclelland.com; f. 1906; trade; Publr ELLEN SELIGMAN.

McGill-Queen's University Press: 1010 Sherbrooke St West, Suite 1720, Montréal, QC H3A 2R7; tel. (514) 398-3750; fax (514) 398-4333; e-mail mqup@mcgill.ca; internet mqup.mcgill.ca; f. 1960; scholarly and general interest; Exec. Dir PHILIP J. CERCONE.

McGraw-Hill Ryerson Ltd: 300 Water St, Whitby, ON L1N 9B6; tel. (905) 430-5000; fax (905) 430-5191; e-mail cs_queries@mcgrawhill.ca; internet www.mcgrawhill.ca; f. 1944; general; 3 divisions: educational publishing, higher education and professional publishing; Pres. and CEO DAVID SWAIL.

Nelson Education: 1120 Birchmount Rd, Scarborough, ON M1K 5G4; tel. (416) 752-9448; fax (416) 752-8101; e-mail communications@nelson.com; internet www.nelson.com; f. 1914; owned by OMERS Capital Partners; retailing, consumer affairs, textbooks; Pres. and CEO GREG NORDAL.

Editions du Noroît: 4609 rue d'Iberville, Suite 202, Montréal, QC H2H 2L9; tel. (514) 727-0005; fax (514) 723-6660; e-mail lenoroit@lenoroit.com; internet www.lenoroit.com; f. 1971; poetry; Dir PAUL BÉLANGER.

Oberon Press: 145 Spruce St, Suite 205, Ottawa, ON K1R 6P1; tel. and fax (613) 238-3275; e-mail oberon@sympatico.ca; internet www.oberonpress.ca; f. 1966; poetry, fiction and general non-fiction; Pres. MICHAEL MACKLEM.

Oxford University Press Canada: 8 Sampson Mews, Suite 204, Don Mills, ON M3C 0H5; tel. (416) 441-2941; fax (416) 444-0427; e-mail customer.service.ca@oup.com; internet www.oupcanada.com; f. 1904; general, education, scholarly, Canadiana; Pres. DAVID STOVER.

Pearson Canada Assessment: 55 Horner Ave, Toronto, ON M8Z 4X6; tel. (866) 335-8418; fax (416) 644-2166; e-mail cs.canada@pearson.com; internet pearsonassess.ca; f. 1922; medical, educational, scholarly; Pres. and Publr AURELIO PRIFITERA; Gen. Man. SCOTT PAWSON.

Pearson Education Canada, Inc: 26 Prince Andrew Pl., Don Mills, Toronto, ON M3C 2T8; tel. (416) 447-5101; fax (416) 443-0948; e-mail webinfo.pubcanada@pearsoned.com; internet www.pearsoned.ca; educational; includes Pearson Technology Group Canada; Pres. DAN LEE.

Penguin Group (Canada): 90 Eglinton Ave East, Suite 700, Toronto, ON M4P 2Y3; tel. (416) 925-2249; fax (416) 925-0068; e-mail info@penguin.ca; internet www.penguin.ca; f. 1974; division of Pearson; merged with Random House in 2013; Pres. NICOLE WINSTANLEY; Chair. J. ROBERT PRICHARD.

Pippin Publishing Corpn: POB 242, Don Mills, ON M3C 2S2; tel. (416) 510-2918; fax (416) 510-3359; e-mail jld@pippinpub.com; internet www.pippinpub.com; f. 1995; educational and trade; Pres. JONATHAN LOVAT DICKSON.

Pontifical Institute of Mediaeval Studies: 59 Queen's Park Cres. East, Toronto, ON M5S 2C4; tel. (416) 926-7142; fax (416) 926-7292; e-mail barbara.north@utoronto.ca; internet www.pims.ca; f. 1939; scholarly publs concerning the Middle Ages; Pres. RICHARD ALWAY.

Prentice Hall Canada Inc: 1870 Birchmount Rd, Scarborough, ON M1P 2J7; tel. (416) 293-3621; fax (416) 299-2529; internet www.pearsonhighered.com; f. 1960; imprint of Pearson; trade, textbooks; Pres. BRIAN HEER.

Les Presses de l'Université Laval: Pavillon East, 2180, chemin Saint-Foy, 1st Floor, Québec, QC G1V 0A6; tel. (418) 656-2803; fax (418) 656-3305; e-mail presses@pul.ulaval.ca; internet www.pulaval.com; f. 1950; scholarly; Pres. LOUIS BABINEAU; Dir-Gen. DENIS DION.

Les Presses de l'Université de Montréal: 3744 rue Jean-Brillant, bureau 6310, Montréal, QC H3T 1P1; tel. (514) 343-6933; fax (514) 343-2232; e-mail pum@umontreal.ca; internet www.pum.umontreal.ca; f. 1962; scholarly and general; Dir-Gen. ANTOINE DEL BUSSO.

Les Presses de l'Université du Québec: Edif. le Delta I, 2875 blvd Laurier, Suite 450, Québec, QC G1V 2M2; tel. (418) 657-4399; fax (418) 657-2096; e-mail puq@puq.ca; internet www.puq.ca; f. 1969; scholarly and general; Dir-Gen. CÉLINE FOURNIER.

Random House of Canada Ltd: 1 Toronto St, Unit 300, Toronto, ON M5C 2V6; tel. (416) 364-4449; fax (416) 364-6863; internet www.randomhouse.ca; f. 1944; merger with Penguin announced in Oct. 2012; Chair. MARKUS DOHLE; Pres. and CEO BRAD MARTIN.

Editions du Renouveau Pédagogique, Inc: 5757 rue Cypihot, St-Laurent, QC H4S 1R3; tel. (514) 334-2690; fax (514) 334-4720; e-mail normand.cleroux@erpi.com; internet www.erpi.com; f. 1965; textbooks; Pres. NORMAND CLÉROUX.

Scholastic Canada Ltd: 175 Hillmont Rd, Markham, ON L6C 1Z7; tel. (905) 887-7323; fax (905) 472-7319; e-mail custserv@scholastic.ca; internet www.scholastic.ca; f. 1957; wholly owned subsidiary of Scholastic, Inc; imprints include North Winds Press, Editions Scholastic; Co-Pres LINDA GOSNELL, IOLE LUCCHESE.

Sélection du Reader's Digest (Canada) Ltée/The Reader's Digest Association (Canada) Ltd: 1125 Stanley St, Montréal, QC H3B 5H5; tel. (514) 940-0751; fax (514) 940-3637; e-mail customer.service@readersdigest.com; internet www.rd.ca; Pres. and CEO TONI CIOFFI.

Editions du Septentrion: 1300 ave Maguire, Sillery, QC G1T 1Z3; tel. (418) 688-3556; fax (418) 527-4978; e-mail sept@septentrion.qc.ca; internet www.septentrion.qc.ca; f. 1988; history, essays, general; Pres. DENIS VAUGEOIS; Dir-Gen. and Editor GILLES HERMAN.

Simon & Schuster Canada: 166 King St East, Suite 300, Toronto, ON M5A 1J3; tel. (905) 427-8882; fax (905) 430-9446; e-mail info@simonandschuster.ca; internet www.simonandschuster.com; Pres. KEVIN HANSON.

Thistledown Press Ltd: 20th St West, Suite 118, Saskatoon, SK S7M 0W6; tel. (306) 244-1722; fax (306) 244-1762; e-mail tdpress@thistledownpress.com; internet www.thistledownpress.com; f. 1975; Canadian fiction, non-fiction and poetry; Publr ALLAN FORRIE.

Thompson Educational Publishing Inc: 20 Ripley Ave, Toronto, ON M6S 3N9; tel. (416) 766-2763; fax (416) 766-0398; e-mail info@thompsonbooks.com; internet thompsonbooks.com; f. 1989; textbooks; Pres. KEITH THOMPSON.

Thomson Carswell: 1 Corporate Plaza, 2075 Kennedy Rd, Toronto, ON M1T 3V4; tel. (416) 609-3800; fax (416) 298-5082; e-mail jayne.jackson@thomsonreuters.com; internet www.carswell.com; f. 1864; fmrly Carswell-Thomson Professional Publishing Canada; legal, financial, business; Pres. and CEO DON VAN MEER.

Turnstone Press Ltd: 100 Arthur St, Suite 206, Winnipeg, MB R3B 1H3; tel. (204) 947-1555; fax (204) 942-1555; internet www.turnstonepress.com; f. 1976; literary and regional; Assoc. Publr JAMIS PAULSON.

University of Alberta Press (UAP): Ring House 2, Edmonton, AB T6G 2E1; tel. (780) 492-3662; fax (780) 492-0719; e-mail linda.cameron@ualberta.ca; internet www.uap.ualberta.ca; f. 1969; scholarly, general non-fiction; Dir LINDA D. CAMERON.

University of British Columbia Press (UBC Press): 2029 West Mall, Vancouver, BC V6T 1Z2; tel. (604) 822-5959; fax (604) 822-6083; e-mail frontdesk@ubcpress.ca; internet www.ubcpress.ca; f. 1971; law, politics, history, environmental studies, anthropology, Canadian studies, sociology, military history; Dir MELISSA PITTS.

University of Calgary Press: 2500 University Dr., NW, Calgary, AB T2N 1N4; tel. (403) 220-7578; fax (403) 282-0085; e-mail ucpress@ucalgary.ca; internet www.uofcpress.com; f. 1981; Dir JOHN WRIGHT (interim).

University of Manitoba Press: 301 St John's College, University of Manitoba, Winnipeg, MB R3T 2M5; tel. (204) 474-9495; fax (204) 474-7566; e-mail carr@cc.umanitoba.ca; internet uofmpress.ca; f. 1967; native, Arctic and Canadian history; Icelandic and Canadian literature; Dir DAVID CARR; Man. Editor GLENN BERGEN.

University of Ottawa Press/Les Presses de l'Université d'Ottawa: 542 King Edward Ave, Ottawa, ON K1N 6N5; tel. (613) 562-5246; fax (613) 562-5247; e-mail puo-uop@uottawa.ca; internet www.press.uottawa.ca; f. 1936; university texts, scholarly and literary works in English and French; Dir LARA MAINVILLE.

University of Toronto Press: 10 St Mary St, Suite 700, Toronto, ON M4Y 2W8; tel. (416) 978-2239; fax (416) 978-4738; e-mail publishing@utpress.utoronto.ca; internet www.utpress.utoronto.ca; f. 1901; scholarly books and journals; Pres., Publr and CEO JOHN YATES.

John Wiley and Sons Canada Ltd: 6045 blvd Freemont, Mississauga, ON L5R 4J3; tel. (416) 236-4433; fax (416) 236-8743; e-mail canada@wiley.com; internet ca.wiley.com; f. 1968; general and trade; CEO STEPHEN SMITH.

Wilfrid Laurier University Press: Wilfrid Laurier University, 75 University Ave West, Waterloo, ON N2L 3C5; tel. (519) 884-0710; fax (519) 725-1399; e-mail press@wlu.ca; internet www.wlupress.wlu.ca; f. 1974; academic and scholarly; Dir BRIAN HENDERSON.

GOVERNMENT PUBLISHING HOUSE

Government of Canada Publications: 350 Albert St, 5th Floor, Ottawa, ON K1A 0S5; tel. (613) 941-5995; fax (613) 954-5779; e-mail publications@tpsgc-pwgsc.gc.ca; internet publications.gc.ca; f. 1876; books and periodicals on numerous subjects, incl. agriculture, economics, environment, geology, history and sociology; Dir CHRISTINE LEDUC.

ORGANIZATIONS AND ASSOCIATIONS

Association of Canadian Publishers (ACP): 174 Spadina Ave, Suite 306, Toronto, ON M5T 2C2; tel. (416) 487-6116; fax (416) 487-8815; e-mail admin@canbook.org; internet www.publishers.ca; f. 1976; trade asscn of Canadian-owned English-language book publrs; represents Canadian publishing internationally; 125 mems; Exec. Dir CAROLYN WOOD.

Association of Canadian University Presses/Association des Presses Universitaires Canadiennes: 10 St Mary St, Suite 700, Toronto, ON M4Y 2W8; tel. (416) 978-2239; fax (416) 978-4738; e-mail clarose@utpress.utoronto.ca; internet www.acup.ca; f. 1965; Pres. JOHN YATES.

Canadian Copyright Institute: 192 Spadina Ave, Suite 107, Toronto, ON M5T 2C2; tel. (416) 975-1756; fax (416) 975-1839; e-mail info@thecci.ca; internet www.canadiancopyrightinstitute.ca; 83 mems; Admin. ANNE MCCLELLAND.

Canadian Publishers' Council: 250 Merton St, Suite 203, Toronto, ON M4S 1B1; tel. (416) 322-7011; fax (416) 322-6999; e-mail jhushion@pubcouncil.ca; internet www.pubcouncil.ca; f. 1910; trade asscn of Canadian-owned publrs and Canadian-incorp. subsidiaries of British and US publrs; 24 mems; Pres. KEVIN HANSON; Exec. Dir JACQUELINE HUSHION.

Broadcasting and Communications

The 1968 Broadcasting Act established the Canadian Broadcasting Corporation (CBC) as the national, publicly owned, broadcasting service and created the Canadian Radio-Television and Telecommunications Commission (CRTC) as the agency regulating radio, television and cable television. The CRTC was constituted as an independent public body under the 1985 Canadian Radio-Television and Telecommunications Act. The CRTC derives its regulatory authority over broadcasting from the 1991 Broadcasting Act, and over telecommunications from the 1987 Bell Canada Act and the 1993 Telecommunications Act, and their subsequent amendments.

REGULATORY AUTHORITY

Canadian Radio-Television and Telecommunications Commission (CRTC): Ottawa, ON K1A 0N2; tel. (819) 997-0313; fax (819) 994-0218; internet www.crtc.gc.ca; f. 1968; offices in Dartmouth, Edmonton, Montréal, Toronto, Regina, Vancouver and Winnipeg; regulates c. 2,000 radio, television and cable broadcasters, telecommunications carriers and telephone companies; Chair. and CEO JEAN-PIERRE BLAIS; Vice-Chair. (Broadcasting) TOM PENTEFOUNTAS; Vice-Chair. (Telecommunications) PETER MENZIES; Sec.-Gen. JOHN TRAVERSY.

TELECOMMUNICATIONS

Bell Aliant: 6 South, Maritime Centre, 1505 Barrington St, Halifax, NS B3J 2W3; tel. (902) 487-4609; fax (902) 425-0708; e-mail aliant.business@bellaliant.ca; internet www.bellaliant.ca; f. 2006 by merger of Aliant and Bell operations; part owned by Bell Canada and BCE; operates as Aliant in Atlantic Canada and as Bell in central Canada; worldwide communications and information technology solutions; 5.3m. customers; Chair. GEORGE COPE; Pres. and CEO KAREN H. SHERIFF.

Bell Canada Enterprises Inc (BCE): 1 carrefour Alexander Graham Bell, Edif. A, 4e étage, Verdun, QC H3E 3B3; tel. (888) 932-6666; fax (514) 766-5735; e-mail bcecomms@bce.ca; internet www.bce.ca; f. 1880; provides fixed-line and mobile telecommunications, satellite and internet services; Chair. THOMAS C. O'NEILL; Pres. and CEO GEORGE COPE.

Bell Canada: POB 8716, Station A, Montréal, QC H3C 3P3; e-mail bell.direct@bell.ca; internet www.bell.ca; 80% owned by BCE; holds a monopoly in most of Québec and Ontario; CEO GEORGE COPE.

Bell Mobility: 4 Eglinton Sq., Scarborough, ON M1L 2K1; tel. (416) 755-7157; e-mail mobility@bell.ca; internet www.bellmobility.ca; mobile telecommunications; Pres. WADE OOSTERMAN.

Manitoba Telecom Services Inc (MTS): 333 Main St, POB 6666, Winnipeg, MB R3C 3V6; tel. (204) 225-4249; fax (204) 949-1244; e-mail media.relations@mtsallstream.com; internet www.mts.ca; full-service (wireline voice, data, wireless and television services) telecommunications co for Manitoba; national broadband fibre optic network of 24,300 km; Allstream (National) Division serves business customers nationwide; Chair. DAVID LEITH; CEO PIERRE BLOUIN.

Northwestel Inc: 301 Lambert St, POB 2727, Whitehorse, YT Y1A 4Y4; tel. (867) 668-5300; fax (867) 668-7079; e-mail customerservice@nwtel.ca; internet www.nwtel.ca; f. 1979, bought by BCE Inc in 1988; provides fixed-line and mobile telecommunications services to 110,000 customers in Yukon Territory, Northwest Territories, Nunavut Territory and British Columbia; Chair. CHARLES BROWN; Pres. and CEO PAUL FLAHERTY.

Télébec: 555 ave Centrale, Val-d'Or, QC J9P 1P6; tel. (819) 233-6711; e-mail telebec@telebec.com; internet www.telebec.com; f. 1969; owned by Bell Nordiq Group Inc, subsidiary of BCE; mobile telecommunications (Télébec Mobilité) and internet services (Télébec Internet) for the region of Québec; 150,000 customers; Pres. ROCH L. DUBÉ.

Glentel: 8501 Commerce Ct, Burnaby, BC V5A 4N3; tel. (604) 415-6500; fax (604) 415-6565; e-mail investors@glentel.com; internet www.glentel.com; f. 1963; wireless communications; Chair., Pres. and CEO THOMAS E. SKIDMORE.

Globalstar Canada Co: 115 Matheson Blvd West, Suite 100, Mississauga, ON L5R 3L1; tel. (905) 890-1377; fax (905) 890-2175; e-mail info@globalstar.ca; internet www.globalstar.ca; satellite voice and data communications; Chair. and CEO JAMES (JAY) MONROE, III.

Primus Telecommunications Canada Inc: 5343 Dundas St West, Suite 400, Etobicoke, ON M9B 6K5; tel. (416) 236-3636; e-mail info@primustel.ca; internet www.primustel.ca; f. 1997; long-distance, local fixed-line, international and internet services; CEO ANDREW DAY.

Rogers Communications Inc: 333 Bloor St East, 10th Floor, Toronto, ON M4W 1G9; tel. (416) 935-8080; fax (877) 331-1573; e-mail customer.service@rci.rogers.com; internet www.rogers.com; f. 1986; subsidiaries: Rogers Cable and Telecom provides fixed-line telephony, cable and internet services; Rogers Wireless Inc provides wireless and mobile cellular services; Chair. ALAN D. HORN; Pres. and CEO NADIR MOHAMED; 9.3m. wireless subscribers (2011).

Fido: 333 Bloor St East, 10th Floor, Toronto, ON M4W 1G9; tel. (416) 935-8710; internet www.fido.ca; f. 1996; by Microcell Solutions Inc; subsidiary of Rogers Communications Inc; Gen. Man. FADEL CHBIHNA.

Saskatchewan Telecommunications International (SaskTel): POB 2121, Regina, SK S4P 4C5; tel. (411) 555-1212; fax (306) 359-5651; internet www.sasktel.com; f. 1986; provides mobile, satellite and internet services for Saskatchewan; Chair. GRANT J. KOOK; Pres. and CEO RON STYLES; 568,904 subscribers (2011).

Sierra Wireless, Inc: 13811 Wireless Way, Richmond, BC V6V 3A4; tel. (604) 231-1100; fax (604) 231-1109; e-mail pr@sierrawireless.com; internet www.sierrawireless.com; f. 1993; Chair. CHARLES E. LEVINE; CEO JASON W. COHENOUR; 905 employees.

Telesat: 1601 Telesat Court, Ottawa, ON K1B 5P4; tel. (613) 748-0123; fax (613) 748-8712; e-mail info@telesat.com; internet telesat.com; f. 1969 by Act of Parliament; owns 14 satellites and operates a further 13 on behalf of customers; carrier and distributor of more than 200 TV signals in North America; provides voice and data transmission services to telecommunication carriers in North and South America and wireless data business networks in Canada and the USA; Pres. and CEO DANIEL S. GOLDBERG.

TELUS: TELUS Corpn, 555 Robson St, Vancouver, BC V6B 3K9; tel. (604) 697-8044; fax (604) 432-9681; e-mail ir@telus.com; internet www.telus.com; f. 2001 following merger of TELUS Communications and BC Telecom; Chair. BRIAN A. CANFIELD; Pres. and CEO DARREN ENTWISTLE; 7.7m. wireless subscribers, 3.3m. fixed-line connections, 1.4m. internet subscribers, 743,000 TV customers (2013).

TELUS Mobility: 200 Consilium Pl., Suite 1600, Scarborough, ON M1H 3J3; internet www.telusmobility.com; mobile telecommunications; incorporates Clearnet, QuébecTel and TELUS Mobility West; Vice-Pres. BRENT JOHNSTON.

TELUS Québec: 9 rue Jules-A.-Brillant, CP 2070, Rimouski, QC G5L 7E4; tel. (418) 318-6102; e-mail jacinthe.beaulieu@telus.com; internet www.telusquebec.com; fmrly QuébecTel; adopted current name following acquisition by TELUS corpn in 2001; telecommunications for Québec; Pres. FRANÇOIS CÔTÉ.

TerreStar Canada: 1035 Laurier Ave West, Outremont, QC H2V 2L1; tel. (514) 843-0679; fax (514) 843-0360; e-mail media@terrestar.ca; internet www.terrestar.ca; f. 2010; integrated satellite-terrestrial mobile communications services; Pres. and CEO ANDRE TREMBLAY.

Videotron Ltd: 612 Saint-Jacques St, Montréal, QC H3C 4M8; tel. (514) 281-1711; fax (514) 281-1232; e-mail youann.blouin@videotron.com; internet www.videotron.com; f. 1964; wholly owned subsidiary of Quebecor Media Inc; cable telephone, wireless telephone, internet services; Chair. PIERRE KARL PÉLADEAU; Pres. and CEO ROBERT DÉPATIE.

Wind Mobile: 207 Queens Quay West, Suite 710, POB 114, Toronto, ON M5J 1A7; e-mail info@windmobile.ca; internet www.windmobile.ca; Chair. and CEO ANTHONY LACAVERA.

BROADCASTING

Radio

CBC operates four national networks broadcasting on AM and FM, two each in English and French. CBC's Northern Service (CBC North), created in 1958, provides both national network programming in English and French, and special local and short-wave programmes, some of which are broadcast in the languages of the native Indian and Inuit peoples. CBC also operates a number of satellite and internet radio networks. CBC radio service, which is virtually free of commercial advertising, is within reach of 99.5% of the population. Radio Canada International, CBC's overseas short-wave service, broadcasts daily in nine languages and distributes recorded programmes free for use worldwide.

CBC/Radio-Canada (Canadian Broadcasting Corpn): POB 3220, Station C, Ottawa, ON K1Y 1E4; tel. (613) 288-6033; fax (613) 288-6245; e-mail liaison@cbc.ca; internet www.cbc.radio-canada.ca; f. 1936; Canada's nat. public broadcaster; financed mainly by public funds, with supplementary revenue from commercial advertising on CBC Television and other commercial sources; broadcasts via 29 services (television, radio, internet and satellite-based services); services in French, English and 8 aboriginal languages; production facilities and broadcast transmitters in many locations throughout Canada; Chair. RÉMI RACINE; Pres. and CEO HUBERT T. LACROIX.

French Networks: 1400 blvd René-Lévesque est, CP 6000, Montréal, QC H3C 3A8; tel. (514) 597-6000; fax (514) 597-6013; e-mail auditoire@fr.radio-canada.ca; internet www.cbc.radio-canada.ca; Exec. Vice-Pres. LOUIS LALANDE.

Radio Canada International: 1400 blvd René-Lévesque est, Montréal, QC H2L 2M2; tel. (514) 024-6737; fax 597-7760; e-mail info@rcinet.ca; internet www.rcinet.ca; f. 1945; operates short-wave, satellite and audio internet services; broadcasts in French, English, Spanish, Arabic, Russian, Mandarin and Portuguese; Dir HÉLÈNE PARENT.

Television

CBC operates two national, free-to-air television networks, one in English and one in French. CBC North provides both radio and television services to inhabitants of northern Québec, the Northwest Territories, Nunavut and Yukon; programming is provided in Dene and Inuktitut languages as well as English and French. CBC also provides speciality services, including the CBC Newsworld network and a digital channel (bold). CBC television is available to approximately 99% of the English- and French-speaking population. Many privately owned television and radio stations have affiliation agreements with the CBC and help to distribute the national services.

Canadian Satellite Communication Inc (Cancom, now Shaw Broadcast Services) was licensed in 1981 to operate a multi-channel television and radio broadcasting service via satellite to serve remote and under-served communities. Satellite television services are also provided by Shaw Direct (a subsidiary of Shaw Communications) and Bell TV (a subsidiary of Bell Canada). Global Television Network, acquired by Shaw Communications in 2010, operates 11 stations, broadcasting to some 98.9% of the English-speaking population.

Aboriginal Peoples Television Network (APTN): 339 Portage Ave, 2nd Floor, Winnipeg, MB R3B 2C3; tel. (204) 947-9331; fax (204) 947-9307; e-mail info@aptn.ca; internet www.aptn.ca; f. 1999; fmrly Television Northern Canada—TVNC; broadcasts in English, French and a number of aboriginal languages; Chair. DANIEL VANDAL; CEO JEAN LAROSE.

Corus Entertainment Inc: Corus Quay, 25 Dockside Dr., Toronto, ON M5A 0B5; tel. (416) 479-7000; fax (416) 479-7006; e-mail investor.relations@corusent.com; internet www.corusent.com; f. 1999; operates 37 radio stations and 17 television channels, including 11 special interest television channels; Chair. HEATHER SHAW; Pres. and CEO JOHN M. CASSADAY.

W Network: Corus Quay, 25 Dockside Dr., Toronto, ON M5A 0B5; tel. (416) 479-6786; e-mail comments@wnetwork.com; internet www.wnetwork.com; f. 1995 as Women's Television Network; women's network; owned by Corus Entertainment Inc; Pres. DOUG MURPHY.

CTV Television Network: 9 Channel Nine Court, POB 9, Station O, Scarborough, Toronto, ON M4A 2M9; tel. (416) 384-5000; fax (416) 299-2643; e-mail programming@ctv.ca; internet www.ctv.ca; 25 privately owned affiliated stations from coast to coast (including one satellite-to-cable service), with 247 rebroadcasters; covers 99% of English-speaking Canadian TV households; owned by Bell Media; Pres. and CEO KEVIN CRULL.

CTV British Columbia (CTV): Suite 500, 969 Robson St, Vancouver, BC V6Z 1X5; tel. (604) 608-2868; fax (604) 608-2698; e-mail bccomments@ctv.ca; internet bc.ctvnews.ca; f. 1997, as VTV; rebranded in 2001; Vice-Pres. and Gen. Man. JAMES STUART.

Global Television Network: 81 Barber Greene Rd, Don Mills, ON M3C 2A2; tel. (416) 446-5311; fax (416) 446-5447; e-mail globalnews.bc@globaltv.com; internet www.canada.com/globaltv; 11 stations in 8 provinces; acquired by Shaw Communications in 2010; Sr Vice-Pres. BARBARA WILLIAMS.

Knowledge Network: 4355 Mathissi Pl., Burnaby, BC V5G 4S8; tel. (604) 431-3222; fax (604) 431-3387; e-mail info@knowledge.ca; internet www.knowledge.ca; f. 1981; Chair. NINI BAIRD; Pres. and CEO RUDY BUTTIGNOL.

Réseau TVA: 1600 de Maisonneuve Blvd East, Montréal, QC H2L 4P2; tel. (514) 526-9251; fax (514) 599-5502; e-mail andre.limoges@tva.ca; internet tva.canoe.com; f. 1960 as Corporation Télé-Métropole; runs the Canoë network; French-language network, with 9 stations in Québec and 19 rebroadcasters serving 98% of the province and Francophone communities in Ontario and New Brunswick; Pres. and CEO PIERRE DION.

RNC Media Inc: 1 pl. Ville Marie, bureau 1523, Montréal, QC H3B 2B5; tel. (514) 866-8686; fax (514) 866-8056; e-mail info@rncmedia.ca; internet www.rncmedia.ca; f. 1948 as radio Nord Communications Inc; 16 radio stations and 5 television stations; Pres. and CEO PIERRE R. BROSSEAU; Man. RAYNALD BRIÈRE.

Rogers Broadcasting Ltd (Rogers Media): 333 Bloor St East, 10th Floor, Toronto, ON M4W 1G9; tel. and fax (416) 935-8200; e-mail susan.wheeler@rci.rogers.com; internet www.rogers.com; subsidiary of Rogers Communications Inc; 51 radio stations and 8 television channels; Pres. SCOTT MOORE.

Shaw Communications Inc: 630 Third Ave, SW, Suite 900, Calgary, AB T2P 4L4; tel. (403) 750-4500; fax (403) 750-4501; internet www.shaw.ca; f. 1966 as Capital Cable Television Co Ltd, present name adopted in 1993; Exec. Chair. J. R. SHAW; CEO BRADLEY SHAW.

Shaw Broadcast Services: 2055 Flavelle Blvd, Mississauga, ON L5K 1Z8; tel. (905) 403-2020; fax (905) 403-2022; e-mail shawbroadcastsupport@sjrb.ca; internet www.shawbroadcast.com; fmrly Canadian Satellite Communications Inc (Cancom); present name adopted 2006; a division of Shaw Communications Inc; responsible for providing and managing the distribution of television channels to cable companies via satellite; also operates Shaw Direct, a Canadian direct broadcast satellite service; Vice-Pres. DON FLETCHER.

Taqramiut Nipingat Inc: 185 Dorval Ave, Suite 501, Dorval, QC H9S 5J9; tel. (514) 683-2330; fax (514) 683-1078; e-mail tnigeneral@taqramiut.qc.ca; internet www.taqramiut.qc.ca; f. 1975; broadcasts programming in Inuktitut, French and English to Arctic regions of Québec (Nunavik); Pres. GEORGE KAKAYUK; Dir-Gen. CLAUDE GRENIER.

TVOntario: 2180 Yonge St, POB 200, Station Q, Toronto, ON M4T 2T1; tel. (416) 484-2600; fax (416) 484-6285; internet www.tvo.org; f. 1970; Chair. PETER O'BRIAN; CEO LISA DE WILDE.

ASSOCIATIONS

Canadian Association of Broadcasters/L'Association canadienne des radiodiffuseurs: 45 O'Connor St, Suite 700, POB 627, Station B, Ottawa, ON K1P 5S2; tel. (613) 233-4035; fax (613) 233-6961; e-mail sbissonnette@cab-acr.ca; internet www.cab-acr.ca; f. 1926; over 600 mem. broadcasting stations; Chair. (Board of Dirs) ELMER HILDEBRAND.

Radio Advisory Board of Canada/Conseil Consultatif Canadien de la Radio: 116 Albert St, Suite 811, Ottawa, ON K1P 5G3; tel. (613) 230-3261; fax (613) 728-3278; e-mail rabc.gm@on.aibn.com; internet www.rabc-cccr.ca; 20 mem. asscns; Gen. Man. ROGER POIRIER.

Television Bureau of Canada: 160 Bloor St East, Suite 1005, Toronto, ON M4W 1B9; tel. (416) 923-8813; fax (416) 413-3879; e-mail tvb@tvb.ca; internet www.tvb.ca; f. 1962; 150 mems; Chair. ERROL DA-RÉ; Pres. and CEO THERESA TREUTLER.

Finance

(cap. = capital; auth. = authorized; res = reserves; dep. = deposits; m. = million; brs = branches; amounts in Canadian dollars, unless otherwise indicated)

BANKING

The Bank Act of 1980 created two categories of banking institution: Schedule I banks, in which no one interest was allowed to own more than 10% of the shares; and Schedule II banks, which are either subsidiaries of foreign financial institutions, or are banks controlled by Canadian non-bank financial institutions. In 1999 the Government adopted legislation permitting foreign banks to establish operations in Canada without their being obliged to establish Canadian-incorporated subsidiaries. Foreign bank branches (known as Schedule III banks) are prohibited from accepting deposits of less than C $150,000. The Bank Act Reform, a series of extensive changes to federal financial institutions, entered into effect in 2001. This provided for much greater flexibility of the financial services system and also included an increase in the maximum level of single ownership in large banks from 10% to 20%, while any one interest was henceforth permitted to control as much as 65% of a medium-sized bank.

In February 2014, according to the Office of the Superintendent of Financial Institutions, the banking industry included 29 domestic banks, 26 full-service foreign bank branches, 24 foreign bank subsidiaries and three foreign banks with lending branches. At December 2013 the combined assets of all banks (excluding foreign subsidiaries) totalled C $4,027,357.1m.

Trust and loan companies, which were originally formed to provide mortgage finance and private customer loans, now occupy an important place in the financial system, offering current account facilities and providing access to money transfer services. In February 2014, according to the Office of the Superintendent of Financial Institutions, 44 trust companies and 19 loan companies, which were regulated under the federal Trust and Loan Companies Act, were operating in Canada.

Central Bank

Bank of Canada: 234 Wellington St, Ottawa, ON K1A 0G9; tel. (613) 782-7902; fax (613) 782-7713; e-mail info@bankofcanada.ca; internet www.bankofcanada.ca; f. 1934; bank of issue; cap. and res 212.9m., dep. 24,413.2m. (Dec. 2008); Gov. STEPHEN POLOZ.

Commercial Banks

Schedule I Banks

Bank of Montréal: 1 First Canada Pl., 18th Floor, 100 King St West, Toronto, ON M5X 1A1; tel. (416) 867-6656; fax (416) 867-3367; e-mail feedback@bmo.com; internet www.bmo.com; f. 1817; cap. 14,422m., res 693m., dep. 323,702m. (Oct. 2012); Chair. J. ROBERT S. PRICHARD; Pres. and CEO WILLIAM DOWNE; 1,280 brs; 47,000 employees.

Bank of Nova Scotia (Scotiabank): Scotia Plaza, 44 King St West, Toronto, ON M5H 1H1; tel. (416) 866-6430; fax (416) 866-3750; e-mail email@scotiabank.com; internet www.scotiabank.com; f. 1832; acquired NBG Bank Canada (Greece) in Nov. 2005; cap. 17,523m., res –135m., dep. 463,609m. (Oct. 2012); Chair. JOHN T. MAYBERRY; CEO RICHARD E. WAUGH; 1,037 brs in Canada, 1,907 foreign brs.

Canadian Imperial Bank of Commerce: Commerce Court, Toronto, ON M5L 1A2; tel. (416) 980-2211; fax (416) 363-5347; internet www.cibc.com; f. 1961 by merger of Canadian Bank of Commerce (f. 1867) and Imperial Bank of Canada (f. 1875); cap. 9,475m., res 349m., dep. 247,931m. (Oct. 2012); Chair. CHARLES SIROIS; Pres. and CEO GERALD T. MCCAUGHEY; 1,076 brs in Canada.

Canadian Western Bank: 10303 Jasper Ave, Suite 3000, Edmonton, AB T5J 3X6; tel. (780) 423-8888; fax (780) 423-8897; internet www.cwbankgroup.com; f. 1988 by merger of the Bank of Alberta and the Western and Pacific Bank of Canada; cap. 700m., res 31.7m., dep. 14,144.8m. (Oct. 2012); Chair. ALLAN W. JACKSON; Pres. and CEO CHRIS H. FOWLER; 40 brs.

Laurentian Bank of Canada/Banque Laurentienne du Canada: Laurentian Bank Tower, 1981 ave Collège McGill, Suite 1660, Montréal, QC H3A 3K3; tel. (514) 252-1846; fax (514) 284-3988; e-mail customer_inquiries@laurentianbank.ca; internet www.laurentianbank.ca; f. 1846 as Montreal City and District Savings Bank; name changed as above 1987; cap. 731.8m., res 34.5m., dep. 25,904m. (Oct. 2012); Chair. ISABELLE COURVILLE; Pres. and CEO RÉJEAN ROBITAILLE; 158 brs.

National Bank of Canada/Banque Nationale du Canada: 600 rue de la Gauchetière ouest, Montréal, QC H3B 4L2; tel. (866) 517-5455; fax (514) 394-6196; e-mail investorrelations@nbc.ca; internet www.nbc.ca; f. 1859; cap. 2,837m., res 272m., dep. 101,886m. (Oct. 2012); Chair. JEAN DOUVILLE; Pres. and CEO LOUIS VACHON; 453 brs in Canada.

Pacific and Western Bank of Canada: 140 Fullarton St, Suite 2002, London, ON N6A 5P2; tel. (519) 645-1919; fax (519) 645-2060; e-mail tellus@pwbank.com; internet www.pwbank.com; f. 1980 as Pacific and Western Trust Corpn; granted approval to become a Schedule I Bank in 2002 and name changed as above; subsidiary of Pacific and Western Credit Corpn; assets 1,534m. (Oct. 2012); Chair. SCOTT RITCHIE; Pres. and CEO DAVID R. TAYLOR.

Royal Bank of Canada: 200 Bay St, 9th Floor, South Tower, Toronto, ON M5J 2J5; tel. (514) 974-5151; fax (514) 974-7800; e-mail banks@rbc.com; internet www.rbc.com; f. 1869; bought RBTT Ltd in 2007; cap. 19,136m., res 861m., dep. 508,219m. (Oct. 2012); Chair. DAVID P. O'BRIEN; Pres. and CEO GORDON M. NIXON; 1,443 brs.

Toronto-Dominion Bank: Toronto-Dominion Centre, 55 King St West and Bay St, POB 1, Toronto, ON M5K 1A2; tel. (416) 982-8222;

fax (416) 982-5671; e-mail customer.service@td.com; internet www.td.com; f. 1955 by merger of the Bank of Toronto (f. 1855) and the Dominion Bank (f. 1869); acquired Commerce Bancorp Inc in 2007; subsidiaries incl. TD Canada Trust and TD Commercial Banking; cap. 22,086m., res 3,674m., dep. 526,528m. (Oct. 2012); Chair. BRIAN M. LEVITT; Pres. and CEO W. EDMUND CLARKE; 953 brs.

Principal Schedule II Banks

Amex Bank of Canada (USA): 101 McNabb St, Markham, ON L3R 4H8; tel. (905) 474-0870; fax (905) 940-7702; internet www.americanexpress.com/canada; f. 1990; cap. 206m., res 9m., dep. 334.5m. (Dec. 2012); Chair., Pres. and CEO DENISE PICKETT.

Bank of China (Canada) (People's Republic of China): Exchange Tower, Suite 2730, 130 King St West, POB 356, Toronto, ON M5X 1E1; tel. (416) 362-2991; fax (416) 362-3047; e-mail service_ca@bank-of-china.com; internet www.boc.cn/cn/html/canada; f. 1992; cap. 65m., res 2m, dep. 961m. (Dec. 2012); Pres. and CEO LIJUN WANG.

Bank of Tokyo-Mitsubishi UFJ (Canada) (Japan): Suite 1700, South Tower, Royal Bank Plaza, POB 42, Toronto, ON M5J 2J1; tel. (416) 865-0220; fax (416) 865-9511; f. Jan. 2006 through merger of Bank of Tokyo-Mitsubishi (Canada) (f. 1996) and UFJ Bank Canada (f. 2001); cap. 485m., dep. 3,481m. (Oct. 2012); Pres. and CEO HIROAKI ODAJIMA.

BNP Paribas (Canada) (France): BNP Tower, 1981 ave McGill College, Montréal, QC H3A 2W8; tel. (514) 285-6000; fax (514) 285-6278; e-mail bnpp.canada@americas.bnpparibas.com; internet www.bnpparibas.ca; f. 2000 by merger of Banque Nationale de Paris Canada (f. 1961) into Paribas Bank of Canada (f. 1981); cap. 532.7m., res 3.8m., dep. 1,924.4m. (Dec. 2012); Chair. JACQUES H. WAHL; Pres. and CEO ANNE MARIE VERSTRAETEN.

Citibank Canada (USA): Suite 1900, Citibank Pl., 123 Front St West, Toronto, ON M5J 2M3; tel. (416) 947-5500; fax (416) 947-5628; internet www.citibank.com/canada; f. 1981; subsidiary of Citibank NA (USA); cap. 601m., res –3.9m., dep. 3,410.9m. (Dec. 2011); Chair. and CEO JOHN HASTINGS; 220 brs in Canada.

HSBC Bank Canada: 300–885 West Georgia St, Vancouver, BC V6C 3E9; tel. (604) 685-1000; fax (604) 641-1849; e-mail info@hsbc.ca; internet www.hsbc.ca; f. 1981 as Hongkong Bank of Canada; merged with Barclays Bank of Canada in 1996; subsidiary of HSBC Holdings plc (United Kingdom); cap. 2,171m., res 281m., dep. 54,796m. (Dec. 2012); Pres. and CEO PAULO MAIA; c. 140 brs.

Mizuho Bank Ltd (Canada Branch) (Japan): Suite 1102, 100 Yonge St, POB 29, Toronto, ON M5C 2W1; tel. (416) 874-0222; fax (416) 367-3452; e-mail inquiries@mizuhocbus.com; f. 1982 following merger of Dai-Ichi Kangyo Bank and Industrial Bank of Japan; name changed as above in 2013; Gen. Man. MASAKI SHIMODA.

Société Générale (Canada): 1501 ave Collège McGill, bureau 1800, Montréal, QC H3A 3M8; tel. (514) 841-6000; fax (514) 841-6250; e-mail info.canada@sgcib.com; internet www.sgcib.com/canada; f. 1974; subsidiary of Société Générale SA (France); cap. 5.8m., res 43.0m., dep. 226.3m. (Dec. 2012); CEO PIERRE MATUSZEWSKI; 3 brs.

Sumitomo Mitsui Banking Corpn of Canada (Japan): Toronto-Dominion Centre, Suite 1400, 222 Bay St, Toronto, ON M5K 1H6; tel. (416) 368-4766; fax (416) 367-3565; f. 2001 following merger of Sakura Bank and Sumitomo Bank of Canada; cap. 244m., dep. 1,832.2m. (Oct. 2012); Chair. MASAYUKI OKU; Pres. TAKESHI KUNIBE.

Development Bank

Business Development Bank of Canada: 5 pl. Ville Marie, Suite 300, Montréal, QC H3B 5E7; tel. (514) 283-5904; fax (514) 283-2872; internet www.bdc.ca; f. 1944; fed. govt corpn; total shareholders' equity 4,008m. (March 2011); Chair. THOMAS R. SPENCER (acting); Pres. and CEO JEAN-RENÉ HALDE.

Principal Trust and Loan Companies

Bank of Nova Scotia Trust Co: Scotia Plaza, 44 King St West, Toronto, ON M5H 1H1; tel. (416) 866-6161; fax (416) 866-3750; internet www.scotiabank.com; CEO RICHARD E. WAUGH; Pres. BRIAN J. PORTER.

Canadian Western Trust Corporation: 600–750 Cambie St, Vancouver, BC V6B 0A2; tel. (604) 685-2081; fax (604) 669-6069; e-mail informationservices@cwt.ca; internet www.cwt.ca; Pres. and COO CHRIS FOWLER.

CIBC Mellon: 320 Bay St, 4th Floor, POB 1, Toronto, ON M5H 4A6; tel. (416) 643-5000; e-mail generalinquiries@cibcmellon.com; internet www.cibcmellon.com; f. 1997; privately owned jt venture between CIBC and The Bank of New York Mellon; provides asset sevicing (CIBC Mellon Global Securities Services Co) and issuer services (CIBC Mellon Trust Co); Chair. VINCENT V. SANDS; Pres. and CEO THOMAS S. MONAHAN.

Home Trust Co: 145 King St West, Suite 2300, Toronto, ON M5H 1J8; tel. (416) 360-4663; fax (416) 360-3727; e-mail inquiry.htc@hometrust.ca; internet www.hometrust.ca; f. 1977 as Home Savings and Loan Corpn; above name adopted in 2000; Pres. MARTIN REID; CEO GERALD M. SOLOWAY.

ResMor Trust Co: 3250 Bloor St West, Suite 1400, East Tower, Toronto, ON M8X 2X9; tel. (416) 640-3415; e-mail mortgagesupport@resmor.com; internet www.resmor.com; f. 1964 as Equisure Trust Co; renamed as above following acquisition in 2003 by ResMor Capital Corpn; Pres. and CEO JOHANNE BROSSARD.

Savings Institutions with Provincial Charters

ATB Financial: ATB Pl., 2nd Floor, 9888 Jasper Ave, Edmonton, AB T5J 1P1; tel. (780) 408-7000; fax (780) 408-7523; e-mail apm@atb.com; internet www.atb.com; f. 1938 as Alberta Treasury Branches; name changed as above in 2002; assets 33,700m. (June 2013); Pres. and CEO DAVID MOWAT; 171 brs.

Desjardins Credit Union: 1615 Dundas St East, Whitby, ON L1N 2L1; tel. (905) 743-5790; fax (905) 743-6156; e-mail info@dcu.desjardins.com; internet www.desjardins.com/en/dcu; f. 1921, as Province of Ontario Savings Office; acquired by Desjardins Credit Union in 2003; merged with Meridian Credit Union in June 2011; Chair., Pres. and CEO MONIQUE F. LEROUX; 21 brs.

Bankers' Organization

Canadian Bankers Association: Commerce Court West, Suite 3000, 199 Bay St, Box 348, Toronto, ON M5L 1G2; tel. (416) 362-6092; fax (416) 362-7705; e-mail inform@cba.ca; internet www.cba.ca; f. 1891; Chair. DAVID WILLIAMSON; Pres. TERRY CAMPBELL; 56 mems.

STOCK EXCHANGES

Bourse de Montréal/Montreal Exchange: Tour de la Bourse, CP 61, 800 sq. Victoria, Montréal, QC H4Z 1A9; tel. (514) 871-2424; fax (514) 871-3514; e-mail info@tmx.ca; internet www.m-x.ca; f. 1874; Chair. JEAN TURMEL; Pres. and CEO ALAIN MIQUELON; 91 approved participants.

Toronto Stock Exchange (TSX): The Exchange Tower, 130 King St West, Toronto, ON M5X 1J2; tel. (416) 947-4670; fax (416) 947-4662; e-mail info@tsx.com; internet www.tsx.com; f. 1861; owned by TMX Group; Chair. CHARLES M. WINOGRAD; CEO THOMAS KLOET; 121 mems.

TSX Venture Exchange: Fifth Ave SW, Suite 300, 10th Floor, Calgary, AB T2P 3C4; tel. (403) 218-2800; fax (403) 237-0450; e-mail information@tsxventure.com; internet www.tmx.com; f. 1999 by merger of Alberta and Vancouver Stock Exchanges; incorporated Winnipeg Stock Exchange in 2000; acquired by Toronto Stock Exchange (TSX) in 2001; fmrly Canadian Venture Exchange; Pres. JOHN MCCOACH; 92 mems (2013).

INSURANCE

In February 2014, according to the Office of the Superintendent of Financial Institutions, 260 insurance companies were operating in Canada, including 76 life insurance companies, 14 fraternal benefit societies and 170 property and casualty companies.

Principal Companies

Assumption Life: 770 Main St, POB 160, Moncton, NB E1C 8L1; tel. (506) 853-6040; e-mail comments@assumption.ca; internet www.assumption.ca; f. 1903; Chair. YVON FONTAINE; Pres. and CEO ANDRÉ VINCENT.

Aviva Canada Inc: 2206 Eglinton Ave East, Scarborough, ON M1L 4S8; tel. (416) 701-4409; fax (416) 615–4239; e-mail kimberly_flood@avivacanada.com; internet www.avivacanada.com; f. 1906; fmrly known as CGU Group Canada Ltd following merger of General Accident, Commerical Union and Canadian General Insurance Group in 1999; present name adopted 2003; commercial and personal insurance; Pres. and CEO GREG SOMERVILLE (acting).

Blue Cross Life Insurance Co of Canada: 644 Main St, POB 220, Moncton, NB E1C 8L3; tel. (506) 853-1811; fax (506) 853-4646; e-mail inquiry@medavie.bluecross.ca; internet www.bluecross.ca; life, accident and illness; Pres. and CEO JAMES K. GILLIGAN.

Co-operators General Insurance Co: 130 Macdonell St, Guelph, ON N1H 6P8; tel. (519) 824-4400; fax (519) 824-0599; e-mail service@cooperators.ca; internet www.cooperators.ca; f. 1945; Chair. RICHARD LEMOLNG; Pres. and CEO KATHERINE A. BARDSWICK.

The CUMIS Group Ltd: 151 North Service Rd, POB 5065, Burlington, ON L7R 4C2; tel. (905) 632-1221; e-mail customer.service@cumis.com; internet www.cumis.com; owns CUMIS General Insurance Co (f. 1980) and CUMIS Life Insurance Co (f. 1977); Chair. and CEO KATHY BARDSWICK.

Desjardins sécurité financière/Desjardins Financial Security: 200 rue des Commandeurs, Lévis, QC G6V 6R2; tel. (418) 828-

7800; fax (418) 833-5985; e-mail info@desjardinssecuritefinanciere.com; internet www.desjardinslifeinsurance.com; fmrly Assurance-vie Desjardins-Laurentienne, merged with Imperial Life Assurance in 2001; CEO MONIQUE F. LEROUX.

Dominion of Canada General Insurance Co: 165 University Ave, Toronto, ON M5H 3B9; tel. (416) 362-7231; fax (416) 362-9918; internet www.thedominion.ca; f. 1887; Chair. DUNCAN N. R. JACKMAN; Pres. and CEO GEORGE L. COOKE.

Empire Life Insurance Co: 259 King St East, Kingston, ON K7L 3A8; tel. (613) 548-1881; fax (613) 920-5868; e-mail info@empire.ca; internet www.empire.ca; f. 1923; Chair. DUNCAN N. R. JACKMAN; Pres. and CEO LESLIE (LES) C. HERR.

Equitable Life of Canada: 1 Westmount Rd North, POB 1603, Waterloo, ON N2J 4C7; tel. (519) 886-5110; fax (519) 886-5210; e-mail headoffice@equitable.ca; internet www.equitable.ca; f. 1920; Chair. DOUGLAS W. DODDS; Pres. and CEO RONALD E. BEETTAM.

Foresters Life Insurance Co: 1660 Tech Ave, Suite 3, Mississauga, ON L4W 5S8; tel. (905) 219-8000; fax (905) 219-8121; e-mail info@unitylife.ca; internet www.unitylife.ca; f. 1898; originally the Insurance Dept of Subsidiary High Court of the Ancient Order of Foresters, subsequently Toronto Mutual Life Insurance Co until amalgamation with its subsidiary Western Life Assurance Co in 2002; fmrly Unity Life of Canada; name changed as above in 2012; Chair. RICHARD M. FREEBOROUGH; Pres. and CEO SHARON GIFFEN.

The Great-West Life Assurance Co: 100 Osborne St North, POB 6000, Winnipeg, MB R3C 3A5; tel. (204) 946-1190; fax (204) 946-7838; e-mail contactus@gwl.ca; internet www.greatwestlife.com; f. 1891; subsidiaries incl. London Life Insurance Co (; internet www.londonlife.com) and The Canada Life Assurance Co (; internet www.canadalife.com); Pres. and CEO PAUL A. MAHON; COO (Canada) J. DAVE JOHNSTON.

Industrial Alliance Insurance and Financial Inc: 1080 Grande Allée West, POB 1907 Station Terminus, Québec, QC G1K 7M3; tel. (418) 684-5000; internet www.inalco.com; f. 2000; Pres. and CEO YVON CHAREST.

Intact Financial Corpn: 700 University Ave, Toronto, ON M5G 0A1; tel. (416) 341-1464; fax (416) 941-5320; e-mail info@intact.net; internet www.intactfc.com; f. 1809; Chair. CLAUDE DUSSAULT; Pres. and CEO CHARLES BRINDAMOUR.

La Capitale Civil Service Mutual: 625 Saint-Amable St, Québec, QC G1R 2G5; tel. (418) 644-4276; internet www.lacapitale.com; f. 1940; Chair. and CEO RENÉ ROULEAU.

Manulife Financial: 500 King St North, Waterloo, ON N2J 4C6; tel. (519) 747-7000; e-mail corporate_communications@manulife.com; internet www.manulife.ca; f. 1887; acquired Commercial Union Life Assurance Co of Canada in 2001; merged in 2004 with Maritime Life Assurance's holding co, John Hancock Financial Services, creating the Manulife Financial Group; Pres. and CEO DONALD A. GULOIEN.

Metropolitan Life Insurance Co (MetLife Canada): Constitution Sq., 360 Albert St, Suite 1750, Ottawa, ON K1R 7X7; tel. (613) 237-7171; fax (613) 237-7585; internet www.metlife.com; Chair, Pres. and CEO STEVEN A. KANDARIAN.

RBC Insurance Co of Canada: West Tower, 9th Floor, 6880 Financial Dr., Mississauga, ON L5N 7Y5; internet www.rbcinsurance.com; fmrly Westbury Life; bought Unum Provident Canada and the Canadian operation of Provident Life and Accident Insurance Co in 2004; Pres. and CEO NEIL SKELDING.

Royal & Sun Alliance Insurance Co of Canada: 18 York St, Suite 800, Toronto, ON M5J 2T8; tel. (416) 366-7511; fax (416) 367-9869; internet www.rsagroup.ca; f. 1833 as British America Assurance Co; name changed as above in 1976; Pres. and CEO ROWAN SAUNDERS.

Sun Life Financial Canada: 150 King St West, 6th Floor, Toronto, ON M5H 1J9; tel. (416) 979-9966; fax (416) 598-3121; e-mail service@sunlife.ca; internet www.sunlife.ca; f. 1871; merged with Clarica in 2007; Pres. KEVIN DOUGHERTY.

TD Insurance: 50 Cremazie Pl., 12th Floor, Montréal, QC H2P 1B6; tel. (514) 384-1112; internet www.tdinsurance.com; f. 1949; Pres. and CEO KENNETH W. LALONDE.

Transamerica Life Canada: 5000 Yonge St, Toronto, ON M2N 7J8; tel. (416) 883-5003; fax (416) 883-5520; e-mail lifeservices@transamerica.ca; internet www.transamerica.ca; f. 1927; wholly owned by Aegon NV (Netherlands); Pres. and CEO DOUGLAS W. BROOKS.

Wawanesa Mutual Insurance Co: 400–200 Main St, Winnipeg, R3C 1A8; tel. (204) 985-3923; fax (204) 942-7724; internet www.wawanesa.com; f. 1896; Pres. and CEO KENNETH E. MCCREA.

Western Life Assurance Co: 1010-24th St East, High River, AB T1V 2A7; tel. (403) 652-4356; fax (403) 652-2673; e-mail info@westernlife.com; internet www.westernlifeassurance.net; fmrly Federated Life Insurance Co of Canada, present name adopted 2004; Pres. and CEO DOMINIQUE GREGOIRE.

Insurance Organizations

Advocis (Financial Advisors Association of Canada): 390 Queens Quay West, Suite 209, Toronto, ON M5V 3A2; tel. (416) 444-5251; fax (416) 444-8031; e-mail info@advocis.ca; internet www.advocis.ca; f. 2002 by merger of the Canadian Asscn of Insurance and Financial Advisors and Canadian Asscn of Financial Planners; fmrly Life Underwriters Asscn of Canada (f. 1906); Chair. HARLEY LOCKHART; Pres. and CEO GREG POLLOCK; c. 12,000 mems.

Assuris: 250 Yonge St, Suite 3110, POB 23, Toronto, ON M5B 2L7; tel. (416) 359-2001; fax (416) 777-9802; e-mail info@assuris.ca; internet www.assuris.ca; fmrly Canadian Life and Health Insurance Compensation Corpn (CompCorp), name changed as above in Dec. 2005; Pres. and CEO GORDON M. DUNNING; 86 mems.

Canadian Association of Mutual Insurance Companies: 311 McArthur Ave, Suite 205, Ottawa, ON K1L 6P1; tel. (613) 789-6851; fax (613) 789-7665; e-mail nlafreniere@camic.ca; internet www.camic.ca; Chair. RANDY CLARK; Pres. NORMAN LAFRENIÈRE; 93 mems.

Canadian Life and Health Insurance Association Inc: 1 Queen St East, Suite 1700, Toronto, ON M5C 2X9; tel. (416) 777-2221; fax (416) 777-1895; internet www.clhia.ca; f. 1894; Chair. DOUGLAS W. BROOKS; 75 mems.

Insurance Brokers Association of Canada: 18 King St East, Suite 1210, Toronto, ON M5C 1C4; tel. (416) 367-1831; fax (416) 367-3687; e-mail ibac@ibac.ca; internet www.ibac.ca; f. 1922; Chair. STEPHEN HALSALL; Pres. KEN MYERS; 11 mem. asscns.

Insurance Bureau of Canada: 777 Bay St, Suite 2400, POB 121, Toronto, ON M5G 2C8; tel. (416) 362-2031; fax (416) 361-5952; e-mail consumercentre@ibc.ca; internet www.ibc.ca; f. 1964; Pres. and CEO DON FORGERON.

Insurance Institute of Canada: 18 King St East, 16th Floor, Toronto, ON M5C 1C4; tel. (416) 362-8586; fax (416) 362-1126; e-mail iicmail@insuranceinstitute.ca; internet www.insuranceinstitute.ca; f. 1952; Chair. MAURICE TULLOCH; Pres. PETER G. HOHMAN; 36,565 mems.

Chartered Insurance Professionals' Society (CIP Society): 18 King St East, 6th Floor, Toronto, ON M5C 1C4; tel. (416) 362-8586; fax (416) 362-2692; e-mail cips@insuranceinstitute.ca; a division of the Insurance Institute of Canada; represents c. 15,000 insurance professionals; Dir MARGARET PARENT.

LOMA Canada: 675 Cochrane Dr., East Tower, 6th Floor, Toronto, ON L3R 0B8; tel. (905) 530-2309; fax (905) 530-2001; e-mail lomacanada@loma.org; internet www.loma.org/canada; f. 1924 as Life Insurance Institute of Canada; renamed LOMA Canada in June 2006, following 2002 merger with LOMA; Pres. and CEO ROBERT A. KERZNER; Dir BRENT LEMANSKI; over 1,200 mem. cos in 84 countries.

Trade and Industry

GOVERNMENT AGENCIES

Canada Development Investment Corpn (CDEV): 1240 Bay St, Suite 302, Toronto, ON M5R 2A7; tel. (416) 966-2221; fax (416) 966-5485; e-mail info@cdev.gc.ca; internet www.cdiccei.ca; f. 1982; oversees the management and privatization of relevant state investments; subsidiaries incl. Canada Hibernia Holding Corpn, Canada GEN Investment Corpn and Canada Eldor Inc; Chair. WILLIAM C. ROSS.

Canadian Commercial Corporation (CCC): 50 O'Connor St, 11th Floor, Ottawa, ON K1A 0S6; tel. (613) 996-0034; fax (613) 995-2121; e-mail communications@ccc.ca; internet www.ccc.ca; f. 1946; international contracting and procurement agency; facilitates access for Canadian producers to foreign government contracts; Chair. RAY CASTELLI; Pres. and CEO MARC WHITTINGHAM.

Export Development Canada: 151 O'Connor St, Ottawa, ON K1A 1K3; tel. (613) 598-2500; fax (613) 237-2690; e-mail contactatlantic@edc.ca; internet www.edc.ca; f. 1944; provides trade finance and risk management services to Canadian exporters and investors; Pres. and CEO BENOIT DAIGNAULT.

Federal Economic Development Agency for Southern Ontario (FedDev Ontario): 101 Frederick St, 4th Floor, ON N2H 6R2; tel. (519) 571-5710; fax (519) 571-5750; e-mail info@feddevontario.gc.ca; internet www.feddevontario.gc.ca; f. 2009; federally-funded agency supporting businesses, communities and economic growth in Southern Ontario; Pres. KAREN ELLIS.

Federal Economic Development Initiative in Northern Ontario (FedNor): 19 Lisgar St, Suite 307, Sudbury, ON P3E 3L4; tel. (705) 670-6251; fax (705) 671-0717; e-mail fednor@ic.gc.ca; internet www.fednor.ic.gc.ca; f. 1987; promotes economic growth, diversification, job creation, and sustainable, self-reliant communities in Northern Ontario; Dir-Gen. AIME DIMATTEO.

NAFTA Secretariat—Canadian Section: 111 Sussex Dr., 5th Floor, Ottawa, ON K1N 1J1; tel. (343) 203-4274; fax (613) 992-9392;

e-mail webmaster@nafta-alena.gc.ca; internet www.nafta-alena.gc.ca; f. 1994; responsible for the admin. of the dispute settlement provisions of the North American Free Trade Agreement; Sec. PATRICIA LANGAN-TORELL.

CHAMBER OF COMMERCE

The Canadian Chamber of Commerce: 360 Albert St, Suite 420, Ottawa, ON K1R 7X7; tel. (613) 238-4000; fax (613) 238-7643; e-mail info@chamber.ca; internet www.chamber.ca; f. 1925; part of the Int. Chamber of Commerce, and of the Business and Industry Advisory Cttee to the Organisation for Economic Co-operation and Development (OECD); Chair. RICHARD PAYETTE; Pres. and CEO PERRIN BEATTY; 254 corp. mems.

INDUSTRIAL AND TRADE ASSOCIATIONS

Canadian Association of Importers and Exporters Inc (I. E. Canada): POB 189, Station Don Mills, ON M3C 2S2; tel. (416) 595-5333; fax (416) 595-8226; e-mail info@iecanada.com; internet www.iecanada.com; f. 1932 as the Canadian Importers and Traders Asscn; name changed as above in 2000; Chair. JOHN O'RIELLY; Pres. JOY NOTT; 750 mem. cos.

Canadian Manufacturers and Exporters: 1 Nicholas St, Suite 1500, Ottawa, ON K1N 7B7; tel. (613) 238-8888; fax (613) 563-9218; e-mail jayson.myers@cme-mec.ca; internet www.cme-mec.ca; f. 1871 as the Ontario Manufacturers' Asscn, later renamed the Canadian Manufacturers' Asscn; merged with the Canadian Exporters' Asscn in 1943 to form the Alliance of Manufacturers and Exporters Canada; present name adopted in 2000; Pres. and CEO JAYSON MYERS; Exec. Dir DIANE DEJONG; 10,000 mems.

Agriculture and Horticulture

Canada Beef Inc: 6715 Eighth St, NE, Suite 146, Calgary, AB T2E 7H7; tel. (403) 275-5890; fax (403) 275-9288; e-mail rserapiglia@canadabeef.ca; internet www.canadabeef.ca; f. 2011 following merger of the Canada Beef Export Fed., the Beef Information Centre and the Canadian Beef Cattle Research, Market Development and Promotion Agency; Chair. CHUCK MACLEAN; Pres. ROBERT MEIJER.

Canada Grains Council: Suite 1215, 220 Portage Ave, Winnipeg, MB R3C 0A5; tel. (204) 925-2130; fax (204) 925-2132; e-mail office@canadagrainscouncil.ca; internet www.canadagrainscouncil.ca; f. 1969; Chair. CHANTELLE DONAHUE; 28 mems.

Canadian Federation of Agriculture/Fédération Canadienne de l'agriculture (CFA/FCA): 21 Florence St, Ottawa, ON K2P 0W6; tel. (613) 236-3633; fax (613) 236-5749; e-mail info@cfafca.ca; internet www.cfa-fca.ca; f. 1935; Pres. RON BONNETT; Exec. Dir BRIGID RIVOIRE; 22 mems.

Canadian Horticultural Council (CHC): 9 Corvus Court, Ottawa, ON K2E 7Z4; tel. (613) 226-4880; fax (613) 226-4497; e-mail webmaster@hortcouncil.ca; internet www.hortcouncil.ca; f. 1922; Pres. KEITH KUHL; Exec. Vice-Pres. ANNE FOWLIE.

Canadian Seed Growers' Association: 240 Catherine St, Suite 202, POB 8455, Ottawa, ON K1G 3T1; tel. (613) 236-0497; fax (613) 563-7855; e-mail seeds@seedgrowers.ca; internet www.seedgrowers.ca; f. 1904; Pres. JIM BAILLIE; Exec. Dir DALE ADOLPHE; 3,700 mems (2012).

Canadian Wheat Board: 423 Main St, Station Main, POB 816, Winnipeg, MB R3C 2P5; tel. (204) 983-0239; fax (204) 983-3841; e-mail questions@cwb.ca; internet www.cwb.ca; sole marketing agency for western Canadian wheat and barley exports and for domestic sales of grains for human consumption; Chair. BRUCE JOHNSON; Pres. and CEO IAN WHITE.

National Farmers Union (NFU): 2717 Wentz Ave, Saskatoon, SK S7K 4B6; tel. (306) 652-9465; fax (306) 664-6226; e-mail nfu@nfu.ca; internet www.nfu.ca; f. 1969; Pres. TERRY BOEHM; 10,000 mems.

Union des producteurs agricoles: 555 blvd Roland-Therrien, bureau 100, Longueuil, QC J4H 3Y9; tel. (450) 679-0530; fax (450) 679-4943; e-mail upa@upa.qc.ca; internet www.upa.qc.ca; f. 1924; Pres. MARCEL GROLEAU; 155 base unions, 15 regional feds and 44,000 mems.

Building and Construction

Canadian Construction Association (CCA): 275 Slater St, 19 Floor, Ottawa, ON K1P 5H9; tel. (613) 236-9455; fax (613) 236-9526; e-mail cca@cca-acc.com; internet www.cca-acc.com; f. 1918; Pres. MICHAEL ATKINSON; over 20,000 mems.

Canadian Institute of Steel Construction (CISC-ICCA): 3760 14th Ave, Suite 200, Markham, ON L3R 3T7; tel. (905) 946-0864; fax (905) 946-8574; e-mail info@cisc-icca.ca; internet www.cisc-icca.ca; f. 1930; Chair. JIM MCLAGGAN; Pres. ED WHALEN; 862 mems.

Canadian Paint and Coatings Association (CPCA): 170 Laurier Ave West, Suite 608, Ottawa, ON K1P 5V5; tel. (613) 231-3604; fax (613) 231-4908; e-mail cpca@canpaint.com; internet www.canpaint.com; f. 1913; Chair. DALE CONSTANTINOFF; Pres. and CEO GARY LEROUX; 100 mems.

Canadian Precast/Prestressed Concrete Institute (CPCI): 196 Bronson Ave, Suite 100, Ottawa, ON K1R 6H4; tel. (613) 232-2619; fax (613) 232-5139; e-mail info@cpci.ca; internet www.cpci.ca; Pres. ROBERT BURAK; Man. Dir BRIAN HALL; 55 active, 36 assoc., 3 supporting and 100 professional and student mems.

Clothing and Textiles

Apparel Quebec/Vêtement Québec (Institut des manufacturiers du vêtement du Québec—IMVQ): 1435 rue St Alexandre, Suite 1270, Montréal, QC H3A 2G4; tel. (514) 382-3846; fax (514) 940-5336; e-mail cs@apparelquebec.com; internet www.vetementquebec.com; f. 1974; Pres. EVE GRENIER; Exec. Dir PATRICK THOMAS.

Canadian Apparel Federation: 151 Slater St, Suite 708, Ottawa, ON K1P 5H3; tel. (613) 231-3220; fax (613) 231-2305; e-mail info@apparel.ca; internet www.apparel.ca; f. 1977; Exec. Dir BOB KIRKE.

Canadian Textile Association: 13 Interlacken Dr., Brampton, ON L6X 0Y1; tel. (647) 821-4649; e-mail srglaramee@rogers.com; internet www.cdntexassoc.com; f. 2003 following merger of Canadian Asscn of Textile Chemists and Colourists (Ontario) and the Textile Society of Canada; Pres. JOHN SECONDI.

Electrical and Electronics

Canadian Electrical Contractors' Association (CECA): 170 Attwell Dr., Suite 460, Toronto, ON M9W 5Z5; tel. (416) 675-3226; fax (416) 675-7736; e-mail ceca@ceca.org; internet www.ceca.org; f. 1955; Pres. COLIN CAMPBELL.

Canadian Electricity Association, Inc: see Utilities—Electricity.

Fisheries

Fisheries Council of Canada: 170 Laurier Ave West, Suite 900, Ottawa, ON K1P 5V5; tel. (613) 727-7450; fax (613) 727-7453; e-mail info@fisheriescouncil.org; internet www.fisheriescouncil.ca; f. 1915 as Canadian Fisheries Asscn; present name adopted in 1945; Chair BILL MUIRHEAD; Pres. PATRICK MCGUINNESS; six mem. asscns, over 110 mem. cos.

Food and Beverages

Baking Association of Canada (BAC): 7895 Tranmere Dr., Suite 202, Mississauga, ON L5S 1V9; tel. (905) 405-0288; fax (905) 405-0993; e-mail info@baking.ca; internet www.baking.ca; f. 1947; Chair. GLENN WILDE; Pres. and CEO PAUL HETHERINGTON; 1,400 institutional mems, 200 assoc. mems.

Brewers Association of Canada/L'Association des brasseurs du Canada (BAC): 45 O'Connor St, Suite 650, Ottawa, ON K1P 1A4; tel. (613) 232-9601; fax (613) 232-2283; e-mail info@brewers.ca; internet www.brewers.ca; f. 1943; Chair. JOHN SLEEMAN; Pres. and CEO LUKE HARFORD; 25 mems.

Canadian Meat Council/Conseil des viandes du Canada: 1545 Carling Ave, Suite 407, Ottawa, ON K1Z 8P9; tel. (613) 729-3911; fax (613) 729-4997; e-mail info@cmc-cvc.com; internet www.cmc-cvc.com; f. 1919; Pres. RAY PRICE; Exec. Dir JAMES M. LAWS; 55 regular and 92 assoc. mems (2012).

Canadian National Millers' Association (CNMA): 265 Carling Ave, Suite 200, Ottawa, ON K1S 2E1; tel. (613) 238-2293; fax (613) 235-5866; e-mail gharrison@canadianmillers.ca; internet www.canadianmillers.ca; f. 1920; Pres. GORDON HARRISON; 14 mems.

Canadian Pork Council/Conseil canadien du porc (CPC/CCP): 220 Laurier Ave West, Suite 900, Ottawa, ON K1P 5Z9; tel. (613) 236-9239; fax (613) 236-6658; e-mail info@cpc-ccp.com; internet www.cpc-ccp.com; f. 1966 as the Canadian Swine Council; Chair. JEAN-GUY VINCENT; nine mems.

Confectionery Manufacturers Association of Canada/L'Association canadienne des fabricants confiseries (CMAC): 885 Don Mills Rd, Suite 301, Don Mills, ON M3C 1V9; tel. (416) 510-8034; fax (416) 510-8043; e-mail info@cmaconline.ca; internet www.confectioncanada.com; f. 1919; Exec. Dir LESLIE EWING; 8 regular and 24 assoc. mems.

Food and Consumer Products of Canada (FCPC): 100 Sheppard Ave East, Suite 600, Toronto, ON M2N 6N5; tel. (416) 510-8024; fax (416) 510-8043; e-mail info@fcpc.ca; internet www.fcpc.ca; Chair. DARRYL ROWE; Pres. and CEO NANCY CROITORU; 123 corporate mems.

Food Processors of Canada (FPC): 350 Sparks St, Suite 900, Ottawa, ON K1R 7S8; tel. (613) 722-1000; e-mail fpc@foodprocessors.ca; internet www.foodprocessors.ca; f. 1989; fmrly Food Institute of Canada; Pres. CHRISTOPHER KYTE; 200 mems.

Forestry, Lumber and Allied Industries

Canadian Forestry Association/Association forestière canadienne (CFA/AFC): 1027 Pembroke St East, Suite 200, Pembroke,

ON K8A 3M4; tel. (613) 732-2917; fax (613) 732-3386; e-mail manager@canadianforestry.com; internet www.canadianforestry.com; f. 1900; Chair. BARRY WAITO; Gen. Man. DAVE LEMKAY.

Canadian Wood Council (CWC/CCB): 99 Bank St, Suite 400, Ottawa, ON K1P 6B9; tel. (613) 747-5544; fax (613) 747-6264; e-mail info@cwc.ca; internet www.cwc.ca; f. 1959; Pres. and CEO BRADY WHITTAKER; Chair. CHRIS MCIVER; 11 mem. asscns.

Council of Forest Industries (COFI): I Business Bldg, Suite 1501, 700 West Pender St, Pender Pl., Vancouver, BC V6C 1G8; tel. (604) 684-0211; fax (604) 687-4930; e-mail info@cofi.org; internet www.cofi.org; f. 1960; Pres. and CEO JAMES GORMAN; 17 corp. mems.

Forest Products Association of Canada/Association des produits forestiers du Canada (FPAC/APFC): 99 Bank St, Suite 410, Ottawa, ON KIP 6B9; tel. (613) 563-1441; fax (613) 563-4720; e-mail ottawa@fpac.ca; internet www.fpac.ca; f. 1913; fmrly the Canadian Pulp and Paper Asscn; Pres. and CEO DAVID LINDSAY; Exec. Dir SUSAN MURRAY; 18 mem. cos.

Ontario Forest Industries Association (OFIA): 8 King St East, Suite 300, Toronto, ON M5C 1C3; tel. (416) 368-6188; fax (416) 368-5445; e-mail info@ofia.com; internet www.ofia.com; f. 1943; merged with Canadian Lumbermen's Asscn (f. 1907) in 2009; Pres. and CEO JAMIE LIM; 10 mem. cos, 15 affiliate mems and 4 assoc. mems (2012).

Hotels and Catering

Canadian Restaurant and Foodservices Association (CRFA): 316 Bloor St West, Toronto, ON M5S 1W5; tel. (416) 923-8416; fax (416) 923-1450; e-mail info@crfa.ca; internet www.crfa.ca; f. 1944; Chair SUSAN SENECAL; Pres. and CEO GARTH WHYTE; more than 30,000 mems.

Hotel Association of Canada: 130 Albert St, Suite 1206, Ottawa, ON K1P 5G4; tel. (613) 237-7149; fax (613) 237-8928; e-mail info@hotelassociation.ca; internet www.hotelassociation.ca; f. 1913; Pres. ANTHONY P. POLLARD; 10 provincial asscns; 28 corp. mems.

Mining

Canadian Association of Petroleum Producers (CAPP): 350 Seventh Ave, SW, Suite 2100, Calgary, AB T2P 3N9; tel. (403) 267-1100; fax (403) 261-4622; e-mail communication@capp.ca; internet www.capp.ca; f. 1952; represents the upstream petroleum and natural gas industry; Chair. BRIAN SCHMIDT; Pres. DAVID COLLYER; 150 mems, 125 assoc. mems.

Canadian Gas Association: see Utilities—Gas.

Coal Association of Canada: 205 Ninth Ave, SE, Suite 150, Calgary, AB T2G 0R3; tel. (403) 262-1544; fax (403) 265-7604; e-mail info@coal.ca; internet www.coal.ca; f. 1973; Chair. SEAN MCCAUGHAN; Pres. ANN MARIE HANN; 89 mem. cos.

Mining Association of Canada (MAC): 350 Sparks St, Suite 1105, Ottawa, ON K1R 7S8; tel. (613) 233-9392; fax (613) 233-8897; e-mail communications@mining.ca; internet www.mining.ca; f. 1935; Chair. ZOE YUJINOVICH; Pres. and CEO PIERRE GRATTON; 39 mems, 48 assoc. mems.

Petroleum Services Association of Canada: 800 Sixth Ave, SW, Suite 1150, Calgary, AB T2P 3G3; tel. (403) 264-4195; fax (403) 263-7174; e-mail info@psac.ca; internet www.psac.ca; f. 1981; Chair. MIKE EDMONDS; Pres. MARK SALKELD; over 250 mems.

Pharmaceutical

Canada's Research-Based Pharmaceutical Companies/Les compagnies de recherche pharmaceutique du Canada (Rx&D): 55 Metcalfe St, Suite 1220, Ottawa, ON K1P 6L5; tel. (613) 236-0455; fax (613) 236-6756; e-mail info@canadapharma.org; internet www.canadapharma.org; f. 1914 as Canadian Asscn of Mfrs of Medicinal and Toilet Products, present name adopted 1999; Chair. MARK LIEVONEN; Pres. RUSSELL WILLIAMS.

Canadian Generic Pharmaceutical Association (CGPA): 4120 Yonge St, Suite 409, Toronto, ON M2P 2B8; tel. (416) 223-2333; fax (416) 223-2425; e-mail info@canadiangenerics.ca; internet www.canadiangenerics.ca; fmrly Canadian Drug Mfrs' Asscn; Pres. JIM KEON; Chair. DICK GUEST; 11 mems.

Retailing

Retail Council of Canada (RCC): 1881 Yonge St, Suite 800, Toronto, ON M5R 2A9; tel. (416) 922-6678; fax (416) 922-8011; e-mail info@retailcouncil.org; internet www.retailcouncil.org; f. 1963; Chair. KEVIN MACNAB; Pres. and CEO DIANE J. BRISEBOIS.

Transport

Air Transport Association of Canada: see Transport—Civil Aviation.

Canadian Trucking Alliance: 555 Dixon Rd, Toronto, ON M9W 1H8; tel. (613) 236-9426; fax (613) 563-2701; e-mail info@cantruck.ca; internet www.cantruck.com; f. 1937; Pres. and CEO DAVID BRADLEY; 4,500 mems.

Canadian Vehicle Manufacturers' Association: 170 Attwell Dr., Suite 400, Toronto, ON M9W 5Z5; tel. (416) 364-9333; fax (416) 367-3221; e-mail info@cvma.ca; internet www.cvma.ca; f. 1926; Pres. MARK A. NANTAIS; 4 mems.

Railway Association of Canada: see Transport—Railways.

Shipping Federation of Canada: see Transport—Shipping.

Miscellaneous

Canadian Printing Industries Association (CPIA): 151 Slater St, Suite 1110, Ottawa, ON K1P 5H3; tel. (613) 236-7208; fax (613) 232-1334; e-mail info@cpia-aci.ca; internet www.cpia-aci.ca; f. 1939; Chair. SANDY STEPHENS; Pres. EVAN CAMBRAY; 23 mems.

Shipbuilding Association of Canada: 222 Queen St, Ottawa, ON K1P 5V9; tel. (613) 232-7127; fax (613) 238-5519; e-mail pcairns@cfncon.com; tel. www.canadianshipbuilding.ca; f. 1995; Chair. ANDREW MCARTHUR; Pres. PETER CAIRNS; 5 mems, 23 assoc. mems.

UTILITIES

Regulatory Authorities

Alberta Utilities Commission: Fifth Ave Pl., 4th Floor, 425 First St, SW, Calgary, AB T2P 3L8; tel. (403) 592-8845; fax (403) 592-4406; e-mail info@auc.ab.ca; internet www.auc.ab.ca; f. 2008 after realignment of Alberta Energy and Utilities Bd into two separate bodies; regulates Alberta's electric, natural gas, and water utilities; Chair. WILLIE GRIEVE; CEO BOB HEGGIE.

British Columbia Utilities Commission: 900 Howe St, 6th Floor, POB 250, Vancouver, BC V6Z 2N3; tel. (604) 660-4700; fax (604) 660-1102; e-mail commission.secretary@bcuc.com; internet www.bcuc.com; operates under and administers the Utilities Commission Act; Chair. and CEO LEONARD F. KELSEY.

Energy Resources Conservation Board: Fifth St, SW, Suite 1000, Calgary, AB T2P 0R4; tel. (403) 297-8311; fax (403) 297-7336; e-mail inquiries@ercb.ca; internet www.ercb.ca; f. 2008 after realignment of Alberta Energy and Utilities Bd into two separate bodies; regulates Alberta's oil and gas industries; Chair. GERRY PROTTI.

Manitoba Public Utilities Board: 330 Portage Ave, Suite 400, Winnipeg, MB R3C 0C4; tel. (204) 945-2638; fax (204) 945-2643; e-mail publicutilities@gov.mb.ca; internet www.pub.gov.mb.ca; Chair. RÉGIS GOSSELIN.

National Energy Board: 444 Seventh Ave, SW, Calgary, AB T2P 0X8; tel. (403) 292-4800; fax (403) 292-5503; e-mail info@neb-one.gc.ca; internet www.neb-one.gc.ca; f. 1959; federal regulatory agency; Chair. and CEO GAÉTAN CARON.

New Brunswick Energy and Utilities Board: 15 Market Sq., Suite 1400, POB 5001, Saint John, NB E2L 4Y9; tel. (506) 658-2504; fax (506) 643-7300; e-mail rgorman@pub.nb.ca; internet www.nbeub.ca; Chair. RAYMOND GORMAN; Sec. LORRAINE R. LÉGÈRE.

Newfoundland and Labrador Board of Commissioners of Public Utilities: 120 Torbay Rd, Prince Charles Bldg, Suite E 210, POB 21040, St John's, NL A1A 5B2; tel. (709) 726-8600; fax (709) 726-9604; e-mail ito@pub.nl.ca; internet www.pub.nf.ca; Chair. and CEO ANDY WELLS.

Nova Scotia Utility and Review Board: Summit Pl., 3rd Floor, 1601 Lower Water St, Halifax, NS B3J 3P6; tel. (902) 424-4448; fax (902) 424-3919; e-mail board@gov.ns.ca; internet www.nsuarb.ca; f. 1992; Chair. PETER W. GURNHAM.

Ontario Energy Board: 2300 Yonge St, 27th Floor, POB 2319, Toronto, ON M4P 1E4; tel. (416) 481-1967; fax (416) 440-7656; e-mail boardsec@oeb.gov.on.ca; internet www.oeb.gov.on.ca; Chair. ROSEMARIE T. LECLAIR.

Prince Edward Island Regulatory and Appeals Commission: 134 Kent St, Suite 501, POB 577, Charlottetown, PE C1A 7L1; tel. (902) 892-3501; fax (902) 566-4076; e-mail info@irac.pe.ca; internet www.irac.pe.ca; f. 1991 as Public Utilities Commission; regulatory and appeal body for energy, utilities, etc.; Dir ALLISON MCEWEN.

Québec Energy Board (Régie de l'Énergie du Québec): Tour de la Bourse, bureau 2.55, 2e étage, 800 pl. Victoria, CP 001, Montréal, QC H4Z 1A2; tel. (514) 873-2452; fax (514) 873-2070; internet www.regie-energie.qc.ca.

Electricity

ATCO Ltd: 909 11th Ave, SW, Suite 1400, Calgary, AB T2R 1N6; tel. (403) 292-7500; fax (403) 292-7532; e-mail info@atco.com; internet www.atco.com; f. 1947; conventional thermal and hydro power, and gas; operates ATCO Electric and ATCO Gas cos; Chair., Pres. and CEO NANCY C. SOUTHERN.

BC Hydro: 6911 Southpoint Dr., Burnaby, BC V3N 4X8; tel. (604) 224-9376; e-mail bob@bchydro.bc.ca; internet www.bchydro.com;

f. 1961; c. 1.9m. customers in British Columbia (2012); Chair. (vacant); Pres. and CEO CHARLES REID.

Canadian Electricity Association: 275 Slater St, Suite 1500, Ottawa, ON K1P 5H9; tel. (613) 230-9263; fax (613) 230-9326; e-mail info@electricity.ca; internet www.electricity.ca; f. 1891; Chair. ANTHONY HAINES; Pres. and CEO JIM BURPEE.

Hydro-Québec: 75 blvd René-Lévesque ouest, 19e étage, Montréal, QC H2Z 1A4; tel. (514) 289-2211; fax (514) 289-3691; e-mail morin.josee@hydro.qc.ca; internet www.hydro.qc.ca; f. 1944; generates, transmits and distributes electricity; govt-owned supplier to 4.1m. customer accounts in Québec (2012); Chair. MICHAEL L. TURCOTTE; Pres. and CEO THIERRY VANDAL.

Manitoba Hydro: 360 Portage Ave, POB 815, Winnipeg, MB R3C 2P4; tel. (204) 480-5900; fax (204) 360-6155; e-mail publicaffairs@hydro.mb.ca; internet www.hydro.mb.ca; operates 14 hydroelectric facilities, 2 thermal and 4 diesel generating stations; Chair. BILL FRASER; Pres. and CEO SCOTT THOMSON.

Newfoundland and Labrador Hydro: Hydro Pl., 500 Columbus Dr., POB 12400, St John's, NL A1B 4K7; tel. (709) 737-1400; fax (709) 737-1800; e-mail hydro@nlh.nl.ca; internet www.nlh.nl.ca; publicly owned electricity wholesaler; Pres. and CEO ED MARTIN.

Northwest Territories Power Corpn: 4 Capital Dr., Hay River, NT X0E 1G2; tel. (867) 874-5200; fax (867) 874-5229; e-mail info@ntpc.com; internet www.ntpc.com; f. 1989; Chair. BRENDAN BELL; Pres. and CEO EMANUEL DAROSA.

Nova Scotia Power, Inc: POB 910, Halifax, NS B3J 2W5; tel. (902) 428-6230; fax (902) 428-6108; e-mail jennifer.parker@nspower.ca; internet www.nspower.ca; fmrly Crown Corpn of Nova Scotia; privatized in 1992; distributes power to 490,000 customers; utility subsidiary of Emera; Pres. and CEO BOB HANF.

Ontario Power Generation, Inc (OPG): 700 University Ave, Toronto, ON M5G 1X6; tel. (416) 592-2555; fax (416) 971-3621; e-mail webmaster@opg.com; internet www.opg.com; f. 1907 as Ontario Hydro, renamed as above in 1999; Canada's largest utility and main nuclear power producer; generating capacity in excess of 19,000 MW (2012); crown corpn; Chair. JAKE EPP; Pres. and CEO TOM MITCHELL.

Prince Edward Island Energy Corpn: Jones Bldg, 11 Kent St, 4th Floor, POB 2000, Charlottetown, PE C1A 7N8; tel. (902) 894-0288; fax (902) 894-0290; e-mail dwmacquarrie@gov.pe.ca; internet www.gov.pe.ca/enveng/eam-info/dg.inc.php3; Dir WAYNE MACQUARRIE.

SaskPower: 2025 Victoria Ave, Regina, SK S4P 0S1; tel. (306) 566-2121; fax (306) 566-3306; internet www.saskpower.com; f. 1929; conventional thermal and alternative power; distributes power to over 439,000 customers; Chair. JOEL TEAL; Pres. and CEO ROBERT WATSON.

Gas

Canadian Gas Association (CGA): 350 Sparks St, Suite 809, Ottawa, ON K1R 7S8; tel. (613) 748-0057; fax (613) 748-9078; e-mail info@cga.ca; internet www.cga.ca; f. 1907; represents the natural gas delivery industry; Chair. GUY JARVIS; Pres. and CEO TIMOTHY M. EGAN; 200 corporate mems.

Suncor: 150 Sixth Ave, SW, POB 2844, Calgary, AB T2P 3E3; tel. (403) 296-8000; fax (403) 296-3030; e-mail info@suncormail.com; internet www.suncor.com; f. 2009 following merger of Suncor Energy (f. 1919 as Sun Co Inc, became Suncor in 1979) and Petro-Canada (f. 1975 as a Crown Corpn, privatized from 1991); natural gas and oil producer; also develops oil sands; Chair. JOHN FERGUSON; Pres. and CEO STEVE WILLIAMS.

TransCanada Corpn: 450 1st Street SW, Calgary, AB T2P 5H1; tel. (403) 920-2000; fax (403) 920-2200; e-mail webmaster-e@transcanada.com; internet www.transcanada.com; production, storage, transmission and sale of natural gas; operates more than 68,000 km of gas pipelines in the USA and Canada; several major crude oil pipeline projects under development; diversified power portfolio includes natural gas, nuclear, coal, hydro and wind generation facilities; Chair. S. BARRY JACKSON; Pres. and CEO RUSSELL K. GIRLING.

Water

Centre d'expertise hydrique du Québec/Québec Water Assessment Centre: Edif. Marie-Guyart, 4e étage, 675 blvd René-Lévesque est, Aile Louis-Alexandre-Taschereau, Québec, QC G1R 5V7; tel. (418) 521-3866; fax (418) 643-6900; e-mail cehq@mddep.gouv.qc.ca; internet www.cehq.gouv.qc.ca; administered by Québec's Ministry of Sustainable Development, Environment and Parks; Dir-Gen. PIERRE AUBÉ.

Drinking Water and Wastewater Management, Prince Edward Island Department of Environment, Labour and Justice: Jones Bldg, Fourth Floor, 11 Kent St, POB 2000, Charlottetown, PE C1A 7N8; tel. (902) 368-5028; fax (902) 368-5830; e-mail ghsomers@gov.pe.ca; Man. GEORGE SOMERS.

Manitoba Water Services Board: 2010 Currie Blvd, POB 22080, Brandon, MB R7A 6Y9; tel. (204) 726-6076; fax (204) 726-7196; e-mail mwsb@gov.mb.ca; internet www.gov.mb.ca/ia/mwsb/mwsb.html; Chair. LINDA MCFADYEN.

Manitoba Water Stewardship: 200 Saulteaux Cres., POB 11, Winnipeg, MB R3J 3W3; tel. (204) 945-6398; e-mail msw@gov.mb.ca; internet www.gov.mb.ca/waterstewardship; Minister of Water Stewardship GORD MACKINTOSH.

Northwest Territories Water Board: 5101–50th Ave, Suite 300, Greenstone Bldg, Yellowknife, NT X1A 2N9; tel. (867) 765-0106; fax (867) 765-0114; e-mail info@nwtwb.com; internet www.nwtwb.com; Chair. EDDIE T. DILLON; Exec. Dir RON WALLACE (interim).

Nunavut Water Board: POB 119, Gjoa Haven, NU X0B 1J0; tel. (867) 360-6338; fax (867) 360-6369; e-mail exec@nunavutwaterboard.org; internet www.nunavutwaterboard.org; Chair. THOMAS KABLOONA; Exec. Dir DAMIEN A. CÔTÉ.

Ontario Clean Water Agency/Agence ontarienne des eaux (OCWA): 1 Yonge St, Toronto, ON M5E 1E5; tel. (416) 775-0500; fax (416) 314-8300; e-mail ocwa@ocwa.com; internet www.ocwa.com; f. 1993; Chair. MICHAEL R. GARRETT; Pres. and CEO JANE PAGEL.

Saskwater: 111 Fairford St East, 2nd Floor, Suite 200, Moose Jaw, SK S6H 1C8; tel. (306) 694-3098; fax (306) 694-3207; e-mail customerservice@saskwater.com; internet www.saskwater.com; Chair. GLEN RITTINGER; Pres. DOUG MATTHIES.

Water and Wastewater Branch, Nova Scotia Environment: 5151 Terminal Rd, 5th Floor, POB 442, Halifax, NS B3J 2P8; tel. (902) 424-3600; fax (902) 424-0501; e-mail askus@gov.ns.ca; internet www.gov.ns.ca/nse/water/.

Water and Wastewater Management Section, New Brunswick Department of Environment: Marysville Pl., 20 McGloin St, POB 6000, Fredericton, NB E3B 5H1; tel. (506) 453-7945; fax (506) 453-2390; e-mail kyle.baglole@gnb.ca; internet www.gnb.ca/0009/index-e.asp; Co-ordinator KYLE BAGLOLE.

Water Management Operations, Alberta Environment (WMO): Provincial Bldg, 2nd Floor, 200 Fifth Ave South, Lethbridge, AB T1J 4L1; tel. (403) 381-5300; fax (403) 381-5969; e-mail dave.ardell@gov.ab.ca; internet environment.alberta.ca/01157.html; Dir DAVID ARDELL.

Water Resources Management Division, Newfoundland and Labrador Department of Environment and Conservation: Confederation Bldg, West Block, 4th Floor, POB 8700, St John's, NL A1B 4J6; tel. (709) 729-2563; fax (709) 729-0320; e-mail water@gov.nl.ca; internet www.env.gov.nl.ca/env/department/contact/wrmd.html; f. 1949; Dir HASEEN KHAN.

Water Resources Section, Yukon Department of Environment: POB 2703, Whitehorse, YT Y1A 2C6; tel. (867) 667-3171; fax (867) 667-3195; e-mail water.resources@gov.yk.ca; internet yukonwater.ca; Dir KEVIN MCDONNELL.

Water Stewardship Division, British Columbia Ministry of Environment: 10428 153rd St, Surrey, BC V3R 1E1; tel. (604) 586-4400; fax (604) 586-4434; e-mail water.stewardship@gov.bc.ca; internet www.env.gov.bc.ca/wsd; Exec. Asst SARAH ANDREWS.

Yukon Water Board: 419 Range Rd, Suite 106, Whitehorse, YT Y1A 3V1; tel. (867) 456-3980; fax (867) 456-3890; e-mail ywb@yukonwaterboard.ca; internet www.yukonwaterboard.ca; Chair. RON JOHNSON; Dir CAROLA SCHEU.

TRADE UNIONS

In January 2011 there were 4,625,777 union members in Canada, representing 25.0% of the civilian labour force. Of these, 26.4% belonged to international unions (with headquarters outside of Canada) and 68% belonged to national unions.

In 2007 unions affiliated to the Canadian Labour Congress represented 70.8% of total union membership.

Canadian Labour Congress (CLC): 2841 Riverside Dr., Ottawa, ON K1V 8X7; tel. (613) 521-3400; fax (613) 521-4655; e-mail hyussuff@clc-ctc.ca; internet www.canadianlabour.ca; f. 1956; Pres. KENNETH V. GEORGETTI; Sec.-Treas. HASSAN YUSSUFF; c. 3.3m. mems (2012). Major affiliated unions include:

Canadian Union of Public Employees (CUPE): 1375 St Laurent, Ottawa, ON K1G 0Z7; tel. (613) 237-1590; fax (613) 237-5508; e-mail cupemail@cupe.ca; internet www.cupe.ca; Nat. Pres. PAUL MOIST; 627,000 mems (2013).

National Automobile, Aerospace Transportation and General Workers Union of Canada (CAW–Canada): 205 Placer Court, North York, Willowdale, ON M2H 3H9; tel. (416) 497-4110; fax (416) 495-6552; e-mail cawpres@caw.ca; internet www.caw.ca; f. 1985; Nat. Pres. KEN LEWENZA; 193,000 mems (2013).

National Union of Public and General Employees (NUPGE): 15 Auriga Dr., Nepean, ON K2E 1B7; tel. (613) 228-

9800; fax (613) 228-9801; e-mail national@nupge.ca; internet www.nupge.ca; Nat. Pres. JAMES CLANCY; Nat. Sec.-Treas. LARRY BROWN; 340,000 mems (2013).

Public Service Alliance of Canada (PSAC): 233 Gilmour St, Ottawa, ON K2P 0P1; tel. (613) 560-4200; fax (613) 567-0385; e-mail nat-pres@psac-afpc.com; internet www.psac-afpc.com; f. 1966; Nat. Pres. ROBYN BENSON; 180,000 mems (2012).

Unifor Canada: Ottawa; tel. (613) 565-9449; fax (613) 230-5200; e-mail cepcaw@gmail.com; internet www.newunionconvention.ca; f. 2013, following the merger of the Canadian Auto Workers Union and the Communications, Energy and Paperworkers Union; largest private sector union representing 20 economic sectors; Nat. Pres. JERRY DIAS; c. 300,000 mems.

United Food and Commercial Workers Canada (UFCW): 61 International Blvd, Suite 300, Toronto, ON M9W 6K4; tel. (416) 675-1104; fax (416) 675-6919; e-mail ufcw@ufcw.ca; internet www.ufcw.ca; f. 1979; Nat. Pres. WAYNE HANLEY; over 250,000 mems in 47 local Canadian unions (2012).

United Steel, Paper and Forestry, Rubber, Manufacturing, Energy, Allied Industrial and Service Workers International Union (United Steelworkers): 234 Eglinton Ave East, 8th Floor, Toronto, ON M4P 1K7; tel. (416) 487-1571; fax (416) 482-5548; e-mail info@usw.ca; internet www.usw.ca; f. 1943; Nat. Dir for Canada KEN NEUMANN; over 225,000 mems (2012).

Other Central Congresses

Centrale des syndicats démocratiques: 9405 rue Sherbrooke Est, bureau 2000, Montréal, QC H1L 6P3; tel. (514) 899-1070; fax (514) 899-5113; e-mail caronam@csd.qc.ca; internet www.csd.qc.ca; f. 1972; Pres. FRANÇOIS VAUDREUIL; Sec. ANNE-MARIE CARON; 73,500 mems.

Centrale des syndicats du Québec: 9405 rue Sherbrooke est, Montréal, QC H1L 6P3; tel. (514) 356-8888; fax (514) 356-9999; internet www.csq.qc.net; f. 1974; name changed as above in 2000; Pres. LOUISE CHABOT; 13 affiliated federations, 240 affiliated unions, more than 200,000 mems (2012).

Confédération des syndicats nationaux: 1601 ave de Lorimier, Montréal, QC H2K 4M5; tel. (514) 598-2271; fax (514) 598-2052; e-mail contactus@csn.qc.ca; internet www.csn.qc.ca; f. 1921 as Confédération des travailleurs catholiques du Canada (CTCC); present name adopted 1960; Pres. JACQUES LÉTOURNEAU; 8 federated unions, c. 300,000 mems (2012).

Transport

Owing to the size of the country, Canada's economy is particularly dependent upon its transport infrastructure. The St Lawrence Seaway allows ocean-going ships to reach the Great Lakes. In addition to an extensive railway network, the country's transport facilities are being increasingly augmented by new roads, air services and petroleum pipelines. The Trans-Canada Highway forms a main feature of a network of more than 1m. km of roads and highways.

Canadian Transportation Agency (CTA): Ottawa, ON K1A 0N9; tel. (819) 994-0775; fax (819) 997-6727; e-mail info@otc-cta.gc.ca; internet www.cta.gc.ca; f. 1996 to replace the Nat. Transportation Agency; independent administrative tribunal responsible for dealing with and resolving transportation disputes; improving access to transportation services; and economic regulation of air, rail and marine transportation; Chair. and CEO GEOFFREY C. HARE.

RAILWAYS

Canada's railway system is the fifth largest in the world. In 2011 the total length of the railways was 45,888 route-km. In that year the network carried an estimated 4.5m. passengers and 305.8m. metric tons of freight.

Canadian Pacific (CP): Gulf Canada Sq., 401 Ninth Ave, SW, Suite 500, Calgary, AB T2P 4Z4; tel. (403) 319-7000; e-mail ed_greenberg@cpr.ca; internet www.cpr.ca; f. 1881; 26,208 km (16,300 miles) of mainline track in Canada and the north-east and mid-west of the USA; Chair. PAUL HAGGIS; Pres. and CEO HUNTER HARRISON.

Ontario Northland: 555 Oak St East, North Bay, ON P1B 8L3; tel. (705) 472-4500; fax (705) 476-5598; e-mail info@ontarionorthland.ca; internet www.ontarionorthland.ca; f. 1902; agency of the Govt of Ontario; operates freight and passenger rail services over 1,100 km (684 miles) of track; Commr and Chair. TED HARGREAVES; Pres. and CEO PAUL GOULET.

VIA Rail Canada Inc: Station A, POB 8116, Montréal, QC H3C 3N3; tel. (514) 871-6000; fax (514) 871-6104; e-mail customer_relations@viarail.ca; internet www.viarail.ca; f. 1978; federal govt corpn; proposed transfer to private sector postponed Oct. 2007; operates passenger services over rail routes covering 13,822 km of track throughout Canada; Chair. PAUL G. SMITH; Pres. and CEO MARC LALIBERTÉ.

Association

Railway Association of Canada: 99 Bank St, Suite 901, Ottawa, ON K1P 6B9; tel. (613) 567-8591; fax (613) 567-6726; e-mail rac@railcan.ca; internet www.railcan.ca; f. 1917; Pres. and CEO MICHAEL BOURQUE; 60 mems.

ROADS

Provincial governments are responsible for roads within their boundaries. The federal Government is responsible for major roads in the Yukon, the Northwest Territories and Nunavut, and in National Parks. In 2010 there were 1,042,300 km of roads (including, in 2004, 16,900 km of freeways and 200,400 km of highways). The Trans-Canada Highway extends from St John's, NL, to Victoria, BC.

INLAND WATERWAYS

The St Lawrence River and the Great Lakes provide Canada and the USA with a system of inland waterways extending from the Atlantic Ocean to the western end of Lake Superior, a distance of 3,769 km (2,342 miles). There is a 10.7-m (35-foot) navigation channel from Montréal to the sea and an 8.25-m (27-foot) channel from Montréal to Lake Erie. The St Lawrence Seaway (see below), which was opened in 1959, was initiated partly to provide a deep waterway and partly to satisfy the increasing demand for electric power. Power development has been undertaken by the provinces of Québec and Ontario, and by New York State. The navigation facilities and conditions are within the jurisdiction of the federal governments of the USA and Canada.

Other inland waterways that play a vital role in domestic cargo transportation include the Fraser River system and Burrard Inlet in British Columbia, and the Mackenzie River and Great Slave Lake in the Northwest Territories.

St Lawrence River and Great Lakes Shipping

St Lawrence Seaway Management Corpn: 202 Pitt St, Cornwall, ON K6J 3P7; tel. (613) 932-5170; fax (613) 932-7286; e-mail marketing@seaway.ca; internet www.greatlakes-seaway.com; f. 1998; responsible for management of the St Lawrence Seaway (f. 1959), allowing ocean-going vessels to enter the Great Lakes of North America; operated jtly with the USA; 39.1m. metric tons of freight in 2012; Chair. JONATHAN BAMBERGER; Pres. and CEO TERENCE F. BOWLES.

Algoma Central Corpn: 63 Church St, Suite 600, St. Catharines, ON L2R 3C4; tel. (905) 687-7888; internet www.algonet.com; f. 1899; transportation co moving bulk cargo by water; also has interests in commercial property devt; Chair. DUNCAN N. R. JACKMAN; Pres. and CEO GREG D. WIGHT.

Canada Steamship Lines (CSL): 759 square Victoria, 6th Floor, Montréal, QC H2Y 2K3; tel. (514) 982-3800; fax (514) 982-3910; e-mail info@cslmtl.com; internet www.cslships.com; f. 1913; Pres. LOUIS MARTEL; 23 vessels.

SHIPPING

The most important ports handling international container traffic include Vancouver and Prince Rupert (on the Pacific coast), Montréal (on the St Lawrence River) and Halifax (on the Atlantic coast). Other major commercial ports are located at Toronto, St John's, Québec City, Sept-Iles, Kitimat and Saint John.

At 31 December 2013 the Canadian flag registered fleet comprised 1,391 vessels, with a total displacement of 3,781,171 grt.

British Columbia Ferry Services Inc (BC Ferries): 1321 Blanshard St, Victoria, BC V8W 0B7; tel. (250) 381-1401; fax (250) 381-5452; e-mail customerservice@bcferries.com; internet www.bcferries.com; 7 passenger and car ferries; Chair. DONALD P. HAYES; Pres. and CEO MIKE CORRIGAN.

Canship Ugland Ltd: 1315 Topsail Rd, POB 8040, St John's, NL A1B 3N4; tel. (709) 782-3333; fax (709) 782-0225; e-mail info@canship.com; internet www.canship.com; f. 1995; Pres. and CEO SIDNEY J. HYNES.

Fednav Ltd: 1000 rue de la Gauchetière ouest, Montréal, QC H3B 4W5; tel. (514) 878-6500; fax (514) 878-6642; e-mail info@fednav.com; internet www.fednav.com; f. 1944; shipowners, operators, contractors, terminal operators; owned and chartered fleet of 85 vessels; Chair. LAURENCE G. PATHY; Co-CEO MARK PATHY, PAUL PATHY.

Groupe Desgagnés Inc: 21 rue du Marché-Champlain, bureau 100, Québec, QC G1K 8Z8; tel. (418) 692-1000; fax (418) 692-6044; e-mail info@desgagnes.com; internet www.groupedesgagnes.com; f. 1866; private co; 18 vessels; Chair. and CEO LOUIS-MARIE BEAULIEU.

Marine Atlantic Inc: 10 Fort William Pl., Suite 802, Baine Johnston Centre, St John's, NL A1C 1K4; tel. (709) 772-8957; fax (709) 772-8956; e-mail info@marine-atlantic.ca; internet www

.marine-atlantic.ca; serves Atlantic coast of Canada; 4 vessels, incl. passenger, roll-on/roll-off and freight ferries; 382,522 passengers in 2010/11; Chair. ROBERT CROSBIE; Pres. and CEO PAUL GRIFFIN.

Northumberland Ferries Ltd: 94 Water St, POB 634, Charlottetown, PE C1A 7L3; tel. (902) 566-3838; fax (902) 566-1550; e-mail infodesk@nfl-bay.com; internet www.ferries.ca; f. 1939; Pres. and CEO MARK MACDONALD.

Northern Transportation Co Ltd: Suite 1209, 10104 103rd Ave, Edmonton, AB T5J 0H8; tel. (780) 441-3932; fax (780) 441-3934; e-mail customerservicedesk@ntcl.com; internet www.ntcl.com; f. 1934; Pres. SHIVA DEAN.

Seaspan Marine Corpn: 10 Pemberton Ave, North Vancouver, BC V7P 2R1; tel. (604) 988–3111; fax (604) 984–1613; internet www.seaspan.com; f. 1970; Chair. KYLE WASHINGTON; CEO JONATHAN WHITWORTH.

Associations

Association of Canadian Port Authorities (ACPA): 75 Albert St, Suite 1006, Ottawa, ON K1P 5E7; tel. (613) 232-2036; fax (613) 232-9554; e-mail wzatylny@acpa-ports.net; internet www.acpa-ports.net; f. 1958; Chair. SYLVIE VACHON; Pres. WENDY ZATYLNY.

Canadian Shipowners Association (CSA): 350 Sparks St, Suite 705, Ottawa, ON K1R 7S8; tel. (613) 232-3539; fax (613) 232-6211; e-mail lewis-manning@shipowners.ca; internet www.shipowners.ca; f. 1953; Pres. ROBERT LEWIS-MANNING; 6 mem. cos.

Shipping Federation of Canada: 300 rue du St-Sacrement, bureau 326, Montréal, QC H27 1X4; tel. (514) 849-2325; fax (514) 849-8774; e-mail info@shipfed.ca; internet www.shipfed.ca; f. 1903; Chair. BRIAN MCDONALD; Pres. MICHAEL H. BROAD; 70 mems.

CIVIL AVIATION

In 2012 Canada's national Airport System comprised 26 airports, which, between them, handled over 90% of all scheduled passenger and cargo volumes. In addition there were more than 1,800 other airports, heliports, and land and water aerodromes serving the country's vast expanses.

Principal Companies

Air Canada: Air Canada Centre, 7373 blvd de la Côte-Vertu ouest, Saint-Laurent, Québec, QC H4S 1Z3; tel. (514) 422-5000; e-mail media@aircanada.ca; internet www.aircanada.com; f. 1937; fmrly Trans-Canada Air Lines; subsidiary of ACE Aviation Holdings Inc; acquired Canadian Airlines in Jan. 2001; operates services to 175 cities worldwide; Chair. DAVID I. RICHARDSON; Pres. and CEO CALIN ROVINESCU.

Air Transat: 5959 Côte-Vertu blvd, Montréal, QC H4S 2E6; tel. (514) 636-3630; fax (514) 987-6381; e-mail information@airtransat.com; internet www.airtransat.ca; f. 1986; operates services throughout Canada and USA, also to Europe, the Caribbean, Mexico and South America; flies to 60 destinations in 25 countries; Pres. and CEO JEAN-MARC EUSTACHE.

Jazz Aviation LP (Jazz): 3 Spectacle Lake Dr., Dartmouth, NS B3B 1W8; tel. (902) 873-5000; fax (902) 873-2098; internet www.flyjazz.ca; f. 2001 as Air Canada Regional Inc, following merger of AirBC, Air Nova, Air Ontario, and Canadian Regional; operates regional air services on behalf of Air Canada under the brand name Air Canada Express (fmrly Air Georgian); services 78 destinations in Canada and the USA; owned by Chorus Aviation Inc; Pres. and CEO JOSEPH D. RANDELL.

WestJet: 22 Aerial Pl., NE, Calgary, AB T2E 3J1; tel. (403) 444-2600; fax (866) 477-6535; internet www.westjet.com; f. 1996; services destinations in Canada, the USA, Mexico and the Caribbean; Chair. CLIVE BEDDOE; Pres. and CEO GREGG SARETSKY.

Association

Air Transport Association of Canada (ATAC): 255 Albert St, Suite 700, Ottawa, ON K1P 6A9; tel. (613) 233-7727; fax (613) 230-8648; e-mail atac@atac.ca; internet www.atac.ca; f. 1934 as the Commercial Air Transport and Mfrs' Asscn of Canada; present name adopted in 1962 following withdrawal of industrial mems; mems collectively account for more than 97% of national commercial air transport revenues; Chair. HARVEY J. FRIESEN; Pres. and CEO JOHN MCKENNA.

Tourism

Most tourist visitors are from the USA, accounting for an estimated 11.9m. (74.4%) of a total 16.0m. visitors in 2012, according to the Canadian Tourism Commission. In the same year receipts from tourism were estimated at some US $17,400m.

Canadian Tourism Commission: Four Bentall Centre, 1055 Dunsmuir St, Suite 1400, Box 49230, Vancouver, BC V7X 1L2; tel. (604) 638-8300; e-mail ctx_feedback@ctc-cct.ca; internet corporate.canada.travel/ctc-cct; Chair. STEVE ALLAN; Pres. and CEO MICHELE MCKENZIE.

Tourism Industry Association of Canada: 600-116 Lisgar St, Ottawa, ON K2P 0C2; tel. (613) 238-3883; fax (613) 238-3878; e-mail info@tiac.travel; internet www.tiac.travel; f. 1930; private sector asscn, encourages travel to and within Canada; promotes devt of travel services and facilities; Chair. MICHAEL CROCKATT; Pres. and CEO DAVID F. GOLDSTEIN.

Defence

Canada co-operates with the USA in the defence of North America and is a member of the North Atlantic Treaty Organization. Military service is voluntary. As assessed at November 2013, the armed forces numbered 66,000: army 34,800, navy 11,300, air force 19,900. The Canadian Coast Guard totalled 4,500 personnel. There were 30,950 reserve troops.

Federal Defence Budget: C $16,600m. in 2013.

Chief of the Defence Staff: Gen. THOMAS J. LAWSON.

Commander of the Army: Lt-Gen. J. M. M. HAINSE.

Commander of the Navy and Chief of the Naval Staff: Vice-Adm. MARK A. G. NORMAN.

Commander of the Air Force and Chief of the Air Staff: Lt-Gen. YVAN BLONDIN.

Education

Education policy is a provincial responsibility, and the period of compulsory school attendance varies. French-speaking students are entitled by law, in some provinces, to instruction in French. Primary, or elementary, education is for children between the ages of six and 11 or 13, while secondary, or high, schools cater for those aged 12–14 to 18. In 2010/11 some 5,315,686 pupils were enrolled in primary and secondary schools. In 2010/11 there were 95 university institutions in the country. In 2008/09 total federal, provincial and territorial government expenditure on education totalled C $95,732m., equivalent to 15.3% of total expenditure.

CAPE VERDE

Introductory Survey

LOCATION, CLIMATE, LANGUAGE, RELIGION, FLAG, CAPITAL

The Republic of Cape Verde is an archipelago of 10 islands and five islets in the North Atlantic Ocean, about 500 km (300 miles) west of Dakar, Senegal. The country lies in a semi-arid belt, with little rain and an annual average temperature of 24°C (76°F). The official language is Portuguese, of which the locally spoken form is Crioulo. Virtually all the inhabitants profess Christianity, and some 95% are Roman Catholics. The national flag, adopted in 1992 (proportions 3 by 5), comprises five horizontal stripes: blue (half the depth) at the top, white, red, white (each one-twelfth) and blue. Superimposed, to the left of centre, is a circle of 10 five-pointed gold stars (four on the white stripes and three each on the blue stripes above and below). The capital is Cidade da Praia.

CONTEMPORARY POLITICAL HISTORY

Historical Context

The Cape Verde Islands were colonized by the Portuguese in the 15th century. From the 1950s liberation movements in Portugal's African colonies campaigned for independence, and, in this context, the archipelago was linked with the mainland territory of Portuguese Guinea (now Guinea-Bissau) under one nationalist movement, the Partido Africano da Independência da Guiné e Cabo Verde (PAIGC). Portugal recognized the independence of Guinea-Bissau in September 1974, but the PAIGC leadership in the Cape Verde Islands decided to pursue its independence claims separately, rather than enter into a federation with Guinea-Bissau. In December 1974 representatives of the Portuguese Government and the PAIGC formed a transitional Government; members of other political parties were excluded. On 30 June 1975 elections for a legislative body, the Assembleia Nacional Popular (National People's Assembly—ANP) were held, in which only PAIGC candidates were allowed to participate. Independence was granted to the Republic of Cape Verde on 5 July 1975, with Aristides Pereira, Secretary-General of the PAIGC, becoming the country's first President. Cape Verde's first Constitution was approved in September 1980.

Although Cape Verde and Guinea-Bissau remained constitutionally separate, the PAIGC supervised the activities of both states. Progress towards the ultimate goal of unification was halted by the November 1980 coup in Guinea-Bissau. The Government of Cape Verde condemned the coup, and in January 1981 the Cape Verdean wing of the PAIGC was renamed the Partido Africano da Independência de Cabo Verde (PAICV). In February the ANP re-elected Pereira as President, and all articles concerning an eventual union with Guinea-Bissau were removed from the Constitution. Discussions concerning reconciliation were held in June 1982, however, and diplomatic relations between the two countries were subsequently normalized.

Domestic Political Affairs

Elections to the ANP took place in December 1985. The candidates on the PAICV-approved list obtained 94.5% of the votes cast. In January 1986 Pereira was re-elected for a further five-year term as President by the ANP. In April 1990 a newly formed political organization, the Movimento para a Democracia (MpD), issued a manifesto in Paris, France, which advocated the immediate introduction of a multi-party system. Pereira subsequently announced that the next presidential election would be held, for the first time, on the basis of universal suffrage.

In July 1990 a special congress of the PAICV reviewed proposals for new party statutes and the abolition of Article 4 of the Constitution, which guaranteed the supremacy of the PAICV. Pereira also resigned as Secretary-General of the PAICV, and was later replaced by the Prime Minister, Gen. Pedro Verona Rodrigues Pires. In September the ANP approved a constitutional amendment abolishing the PAICV's monopoly of power and permitting a multi-party system. The MpD subsequently received official recognition as a political party. On 13 January 1991 the first multi-party elections to take place in lusophone Africa resulted in a decisive victory for the MpD, which secured 56 of the 79 seats in the ANP. Later that month Dr Carlos Alberto Wahnon de Carvalho Veiga, the leader of the MpD, was sworn in as Prime Minister at the head of an interim Government, comprising mostly members of the MpD. The presidential election, held in mid-February, resulted in victory for António Mascarenhas Monteiro, supported by the MpD, who secured 73.5% of the votes cast. On 25 September 1992 a new Constitution of the Republic of Cape Verde (also referred to as the 'Second Republic') came into force, enshrining the principles of multi-party democracy.

At legislative elections conducted in December 1995 the MpD secured an outright majority, taking 50 of the 72 seats in the Assembleia Nacional (National Assembly—AN—as the ANP had become in 1992). The PAICV won 21 seats, while the Partido da Convergência Democrática (PCD), which had been formed in 1994, obtained the remaining seat. At a presidential election conducted in February 1996 Mascarenhas, the sole candidate, was re-elected. Veiga, meanwhile, expressed his intention to continue the policies of liberal economic and social reform that had been pursued in his previous term in office.

In municipal elections held in February 2000 the MpD sustained substantial losses, retaining only eight of 17 local councils and losing the capital to the PAICV, which re-emerged as a credible political force. Following the resignation of Pires, who announced his candidacy for the presidential election, the PAICV elected José Maria Neves as its new President in June. In the following month António Gualberto do Rosário was elected Chairman of the MpD.

In July 2000 Veiga announced his resignation as Prime Minister and confirmed his candidacy for the presidential election scheduled to take place in early 2001; he was replaced by do Rosário. In October 2000 it was announced that the PCD, the União Caboverdiana Independente e Democrática (UCID) and the Partido do Trabalho e da Solidariedade (PTS) were to form a coalition (the Aliança Democrática para a Mudança—ADM) to participate in the forthcoming legislative elections. At the legislative elections, held on 14 January 2001, the opposition PAICV secured 40 seats in the AN, compared with 30 seats for the MpD and two seats for the ADM. A new Government, headed by Neves, was announced at the end of January. At the presidential election, conducted in February, Pires narrowly defeated Veiga in a second round of voting, receiving 50.01% of the valid votes cast. The Supreme Court later rejected appeals against the result by Veiga, on the grounds of voting irregularities, and confirmed Pires as the new President. In December Agostinho Lopes was elected unopposed as the new Chairman of the MpD.

Legislative elections were held on 22 January 2006, the PAICV won 41 seats in the AN, while the MpD took 29 seats and the UCID won two seats. The rate of voter participation was recorded at 54.5%.

Pires' second term

In the presidential election held on 12 February 2006 Pires secured 51.0% of the valid votes cast, while Veiga received 49.0%. The new Council of Ministers, again headed by Neves, was appointed on 8 March. At the end of that month Agostinho Lopes resigned as leader of the MpD; he was subsequently replaced by Jorge Santos.

In November 2006 unrest broke out in response to a ruling by the Supreme Court that the approval of decrees on value-added tax by the Council of Ministers in the preceding year had been unconstitutional, as they should have been approved by the legislature. Consequently, the prices of fuel, electricity, water, telecommunications and transport escalated, owing to the suspension of protection from external price fluctuations. In the same month the Minister of the Economy, Growth and Competitiveness, João Pereira Silva, resigned following queries over the legality of certain tourism development contracts.

In February 2007 the PAICV and the MpD each nominated seven deputies to a new commission charged with reaching consensus on issues that required a two-thirds' majority in the AN; these included constitutional reform and changes to the electoral code, in particular the membership and structure of the Comissão Nacional de Eleições (National Election Commission—CNE). After protracted negotiations a new electoral code was approved in June, which included the creation of single electoral regions for each island, with the exception of Santiago (which was split into two regions). However, disagreements regarding the membership of the CNE delayed the restructuring of that body and the compilation of a new electoral census. The delay prompted the resignation in protest of the Minister of Internal Administration, Júlio Lopes Correia. The Minister of State and of Health, Basílio Ramos, was appointed Secretary-General of the PAICV in January 2008.

In February 2010 the AN approved a number of draft changes to the Constitution. The main focus of the reform regarded the composition of the judiciary, and the creation of a Conselho Superior da Magistratura Judicial (Supreme Council of Judiciary) to approve judicial appointments. (Hitherto, judges had been appointed by the Government.) Changes to the electoral code were also approved in that month.

The MpD criticized the Government in July 2010 for delays in the voter registration process for Cape Verdean citizens resident overseas; Veiga claimed that the delays would result in fewer residents abroad being able to participate in the 2011 legislative and presidential elections. Other MpD members also accused the Government of registration irregularities and a lack of transparency. The MpD's election campaign focused on tackling unemployment and poverty by improving education levels and lowering taxes to encourage foreign investment, while the PAICV emphasized its successful infrastructure development projects and burgeoning relations with the European Union (EU).

At the elections to the AN, held on 6 February 2011, the PAICV retained its legislative majority, although it won three fewer seats than in the previous legislature, attaining 38. The MpD took 32 seats, while the UCID again secured two seats. The rate of voter participation was recorded at 76.0%. In mid-March Neves announced the composition of his new Government, which increased in size from 15 to 21 members and included six independents.

Recent developments: the 2011 presidential election

The first round of the presidential election was contested between four candidates on 7 August 2011. Jorge Carlos Fonseca, a former Minister of Foreign Affairs endorsed by the MpD, secured 37.8% of the votes cast, followed by former Minister of Infrastructure, Transport and Telecommunications Manuel Inocêncio Sousa (of the PAICV) with 32.5% and two independent candidates, Aristides Lima and Joaquim Monteiro, who won 27.8% and 2.0%, respectively. Fonseca defeated Sousa in a second round of voting two weeks later, obtaining 54.2% of the ballot. International monitors, while noting some irregularities, declared that the election had been free and fair.

The participation in the election by Lima—a member of the PAICV who had chosen to stand as an independent, thereby placing himself in direct competition with Sousa, the candidate officially supported by the ruling party—created divisions within the PAICV. One consequence of this schism was the resignation in late August 2011 of the Minister of Social Development and Families, Felisberto Vieira, who, to the embarrassment of the PAICV, had publicly endorsed Lima during the election campaign. A party conference was convened in September in an attempt to promote internal unity, but, despite declarations of rapprochement, tensions remained.

Fonseca was inaugurated as President on 9 September 2011, replacing Pires (who had been constitutionally prohibited from standing in the election). This peaceful transfer of power, still a rare event in sub-Saharan Africa, was internationally recognized in October when Pires received the Mo Ibrahim Prize for Achievement in African Leadership, a high-profile annual award honouring African leaders who uphold democratic values. The outcome of the election also resulted in the first instance in the country of the Prime Minister and the President representing different parties.

Local elections were held on 1 July 2012. According to the final results, the MpD gained control of 13 municipalities (including the capital city, Praia), the PAICV won eight and the Grupo Independente para Modernizar Sal secured the remaining mandate. In December Veiga confirmed that he would not stand for re-election as leader of the MpD in 2013, In June 2013 former Minister of Finance and Mayor of Praia, Ulisses Correia e Silva, was elected unopposed as Veiga's successor. He pledged to reform the party and strengthen its electoral infrastructure ahead of the next set of polls due to take place in 2016.

In July 2012 the National Assembly approved a new environmental taxation law that targeted imports of non-biodegradable packaging products in an attempt to reduce pollution. President Fonseca had vetoed the first version of the legislation because of objections that most of the revenue generated by the tax would go to the central Government's environmental fund rather than to the local authorities. However, he was obliged to promulgate the law after the National Assembly adopted it in a second vote.

In March 2013 Neves was re-elected unopposed as President of the PAICV for a third term, although he stated that he would resign in 2015, one year before presidential, legislative and local elections were due to take place.

Foreign Affairs

Cape Verde has traditionally professed a non-aligned stance in foreign affairs and maintains relations with virtually all the power blocs. On taking office in 1991, the MpD Government successfully sought to extend Cape Verde's range of international contacts, with special emphasis on potential new sources of development aid. In 1996 Cape Verde became a full member of the Sommet Francophone, a commonwealth comprising all the French-speaking nations of the world, and benefits in turn from membership of this body's Agence de Coopération Culturelle et Technique. In 2001 the new PAICV administration established diplomatic relations at ambassadorial level with the People's Republic of China; as with numerous other African countries, these relations intensified considerably from the mid-2000s. With Portuguese support, Cape Verde attained special partnership status with the EU in November 2007, paving the way for greater integration and co-operation in relation to trade, development, migration and security. In July 2010 the Government agreed to a US request to resettle a Syrian detainee from the USA's detention centre in Guantánamo Bay, Cuba. Critics alleged that the deal had been arranged in exchange for additional US aid, a claim denied by the Government. Prime Minister Neves held discussions with US Secretary of State Hillary Clinton in January 2012 when she visited the archipelago, and in the following month the US Millennium Challenge Corporation approved aid totalling US $66m. In March 2013 Neves made an official visit to the USA and was one of four African leaders to attend a meeting with US President Barack Obama. Cape Verde also secured more than $100m. in aid and concessionary financing from China in 2012 and $50m. in military funding in 2013. Japan also provided a €60m. loan in 2012 and in 2013 agreed to fund $224m. worth of projects in Cape Verde, including a water desalination, storage and transport initiative and improvements to the power transmission network.

The country has continued to maintain particularly close relations with Portugal and Brazil, and with other lusophone African former colonies—Angola, Guinea-Bissau, Mozambique and São Tomé and Príncipe, known collectively, with Cape Verde, as the Países Africanos da Língua Oficial Portuguesa (PALOP). In July 1996 a 'lusophone commonwealth', the Comunidade dos Países de Língua Portuguesa (CPLP), comprising the five PALOP countries together with Portugal and Brazil, was formed with the intention of benefiting each member state through joint co-operation on technical, cultural and social matters. (Timor-Leste acceded to membership of the CPLP in 2002.) In April 2010 Neves visited São Tomé and Príncipe, where he signed a number of trade agreements, and he paid an official visit to Portugal in June, signing a new friendship and co-operation accord. The construction of three dams on the archipelago was announced by the Government in March 2011, to be funded by a US $72m. Portuguese credit facility, while in June it was confirmed that Brazil would finance the establishment of a $220m. 'administrative city' in Praia. In an attempt to strengthen bilateral ties, Neves hosted discussions with José Ramos Horta, the President of Timor-Leste, and Patrice Emery Trovoada, the Prime Minister of São Tomé and Príncipe, in July and November, respectively. Neves also met Prime Minister Carlos Gomes Júnior of Guinea-Bissau for talks during a visit to that country in November, and several economic and transportation agreements were concluded. In the same month Cape Verde was a signatory to the 'Luanda Declaration', which pledged greater co-operation between the CPLP member states in the fields of, *inter alia*, security, crime prevention and immigration. President Fonseca made an official visit to Timor-Leste in November 2012 to bolster bilateral relations. Nine co-operation agreements, spanning areas such as education, health and economic affairs, were signed by Cape Verde and Portugal in December; earlier that year Portugal had pledged financial support of €71 m. between 2012 and 2015, in addition to four Portuguese credit lines amounting to some €600m. that had been in place since 2009.

CONSTITUTION AND GOVERNMENT

Under the 1992 Constitution, Cape Verde is a multi-party state, although the formation of parties on a religious or geographical basis is prohibited. Legislative power is vested in the Assembleia Nacional (National Assembly), which comprises 72 deputies, elected by universal adult suffrage for a five-year term. The Head of State is the President of the Republic, who is elected by universal suffrage for a five-year term. Executive power is vested in the Prime Minister, who is nominated by the deputies of the National Assembly, appointed by the President and governs with the assistance of a Council of Ministers. A constitutional revision, adopted in July 1999, granted the President the right to dissolve the National Assembly, created a new advisory chamber (Conselho Económico e Social—Economic and Social Council), and granted the state the right to adopt Crioulo as the country's second official language.

REGIONAL AND INTERNATIONAL CO-OPERATION

Cape Verde is a member of the African Union (see p. 186), the Economic Community of West African States (see p. 260), which promotes trade and co-operation in West Africa, and is a signatory to the Lomé Convention and subsequent Cotonou Agreement (see p. 324).

Cape Verde became a member of the UN in 1975, and was admitted to the World Trade Organization (WTO, see p. 434) in 2008.

ECONOMIC AFFAIRS

In 2012, according to estimates from the World Bank, Cape Verde's gross national income (GNI), measured at average 2010–12 prices, was US $1,882m., equivalent to $3,810 per head (or $4,340 per head on an international purchasing-power parity basis). During 2003–12, it was estimated, the population increased at an average annual rate of 0.6%, while gross domestic product (GDP) per head increased, in real terms, by an average of 5.3% per year. Overall GDP increased, in real terms, at an average annual rate of 6.0% in 2003–12; growth in 2012 was 4.3%.

Agriculture (including forestry and fishing) contributed 9.1% of GDP in 2011. According to FAO, the sector employed an estimated 14.6% of the total labour force in mid-2014. The staple crop is sugar cane; tomatoes, bananas, guavas, mangoes and mangosteens, maize, coconuts and sweet potatoes are also cultivated. Limited water resources on the islands restrict the prospects for agricultural activity, however. Export earnings from fish and crustaceans amounted to 3,837.0m. escudos (84.1% of the total value of exports, excluding re-exports) in 2012. Lobster and tuna are among the most important exports. In 2011 the total fish catch was estimated to be 22,500 metric tons. In 2005 an agreement was reached allowing European Union (EU) vessels to fish in Cape Verdean waters; in return the EU would assist with the development of the local fishing industry. According to the World Bank, during 2003–2010 the GDP of the agricultural sector increased, in real terms, at an average annual rate of 6.9%; it increased by 45.9% in 2009 and by 18.8% in 2010.

Industry (including construction and power) contributed 20.6% of GDP in 2011, and employed 24.5% of the labour force in 1990. During 2003–10, according to the World Bank, industrial GDP increased, in real terms, at an average annual rate of 7.4%; growth in 2010 was 4.0%.

Mining employed 0.3% of the labour force in 1990, and contributed 0.5% of GDP in 2011. During 2000–07 the sector's GDP increased, in real terms, at an average annual rate of 9.8%, according to official figures. According to the African Development Bank (AfDB), the mining sector declined by 8.0% in 2010. Salt and pozzolana, a volcanic ash used in cement manufacture, are the main non-fuel minerals produced.

Manufacturing contributed 6.3% of GDP in 2011, according to the World Bank, and employed about 6% of the labour force in 1995. The most important branches, other than fish-processing, are clothing, footwear, rum-distilling and -bottling. Legislation enacted in 1999 provided for the transformation of industrial parks at Mindelo and Praia into free-trade zones, and for the establishment of a further free-trade zone on Sal island. During 2000–07 the GDP of the manufacturing sector decreased, in real terms, at an average annual rate of 1.7%. According to the AfDB, the manufacturing sector grew by 10.3% in 2010.

Construction contributed an estimated 12.1% of GDP in 2011, and employed 18.8% of the labour force in 1990. During 2000–07 construction GDP increased, in real terms, at an average annual rate of 8.5%, according to official figures. According to the AfDB, sectoral GDP declined by 11.0% in 2010.

Energy is derived principally from hydroelectric power and gas. Imports of fuel products comprised 14.2% of the value of total imports in 2012.

Services accounted for 70.3% of GDP in 2011, and employed an estimated 50.7% of total labour in 1990. Tourism has been identified as the area with the most potential for economic development. Two new international airports, one on Santiago and the other on Boavista, which were opened in 2005 and 2007, respectively, were expected to give considerable impetus to the development of the tourism sector. Furthermore, following an upgrade, the airport on São Vicente island commenced handling international flights in 2009. Tourist arrivals increased from 52,000 in 1998 to 533,877 in 2012. During 2003–10 the combined GDP of the services sector increased, in real terms, at an average annual rate of 6.1%, according to the World Bank; growth of 4.3% was recorded in 2010.

In 2012 Cape Verde recorded a visible merchandise trade deficit of US $705.6m. and there was a deficit of $209.3m. on the current account of the balance of payments. In 2012 the principal source of imports was Portugal (providing 48.2% of the total); other major suppliers were the Netherlands, Spain and the USA. In 2012 Spain was the principal recipient of exports (taking 76.3% of the total), while Portugal was the other major purchaser. The principal exports in 2012 were fish and crustaceans, and clothing and footwear. The principal imports in that year were manufactured food products, fuel products, transport equipment, construction materials, and machines.

According to IMF estimates, budget figures for 2012 indicated a preliminary deficit of 16,300m. escudos, equivalent to 11.7% of the GDP in that year. The country's general government gross debt was 134,270m. escudos in 2012, equivalent to 85.9% of GDP. Cape Verde's total external debt at the end of 2011 was US $1,025m., of which $1,004m. was public and publicly guaranteed debt. In that year the cost of servicing long-term public and publicly guaranteed debt and repayments to the IMF was equivalent to 5.0% of the value of exports of goods, services and income (excluding workers' remittances). According to ILO, the annual rate of inflation averaged 2.8% in 2003–12. Consumer prices increased by an annual average of 2.5% in 2012. In 2011 unemployment was estimated to affect 12.2% of the labour force, but was almost double this rate among the youth; the IMF has assessed a shortage of skilled labour and some of the most rigid labour market regulations in the world to be key structural weaknesses.

Having only graduated to the status of middle-income country in 2008, Cape Verde weathered well the initial years following the international economic and financial crisis that emerged in that year, and achieved real GDP growth of 5.2% in 2010. Economic growth then slowed in 2011 and further in 2012, however, reaching just 2.5% in the latter year. Despite the Government's record of 'prudent macroeconomic management', the IMF anticipated that real GDP growth would reach its slowest point in 2013, at 1.5%, in connection with the country's exposure to the challenging economic environment in the eurozone. Not only is the escudo pegged to the euro, but the economy is strongly dependent on remittances, tourism, trade and foreign direct investment (FDI) from Europe. (The tourism sector did, however, benefit from trade displaced by political disruption in North Africa in 2011–12.) The Government's policy of counter-cyclical spending on a large-scale public infrastructure programme, such as upgrading its ports to strengthen its prospects as a transport hub, contributed to growing levels of public debt; this became particularly pertinent because the country was nearing the expiry of a transitional period regarding concessional lending by donors. Despite this and slow levels of domestic demand, the Government maintained its agenda for reforms such as strengthened regulation of the banking sector. The IMF continued to urge improved tax-collection practices and management of state-owned enterprises to aid fiscal consolidation and economic competitiveness, as well as reforms to the business environment and the consolidation of foreign exchange reserves to cushion against external shocks. More broadly, the World Bank assessed that Cape Verde was on course to meet all its Millennium Development Goals by 2015.

PUBLIC HOLIDAYS

2015: 1 January (New Year), 20 January (National Heroes' Day), 1 May (Labour Day), 5 July (Independence Day), 15 August (Assumption), 1 November (All Saints' Day), 25 December (Christmas Day).

Statistical Survey

Sources (unless otherwise stated): Instituto Nacional de Estatística, Av. Amílcar Cabral, CP 116, Praia, Santiago; tel. 613960; e-mail inecv@mail.cvtelecom.cv; internet www.ine.cv; Statistical Service, Banco de Cabo Verde, Av. Amílcar Cabral 117, CP 101, Praia, Santiago; tel. 2607060; fax 2614447; e-mail apericles@bcv.cv; internet www.bcv.cv.

AREA AND POPULATION

Area: 4,033 sq km (1,557 sq miles).

Population: 436,863 (males 211,479, females 225,384) at census of 16 June 2000; 491,875 (males 243,593, females 248,282) at census of 16–30 June 2010. *By Island* (2010 census): Boavista 9,162; Brava 5,995; Fogo 37,051; Maio 6,952; Sal 25,765; Santo Antão 43,915; São Nicolau 12,817; Santiago 273,919; São Vicente 76,107; Total 491,683 (excl. 192 persons of unknown residence). *Mid-2014* (official estimates): 518,467 (males 258,744, females 259,723).

Density (at mid-2014): 128.6 per sq km.

Population by Age and Sex ('000, official estimates at mid-2014): *0–14:* 154.4 (males 77.6, females 76.8); *15–64:* 335.6 (males 170.1, females 165.5); *65 and over:* 28.4 (males 11.0, females 17.4); *Total* 518.5 (males 258.7, females 259.7). Note: Totals may not be equal to the sum of components, owing to rounding.

Municipalities (official population estimates at mid-2014): Boavista 13,376; Brava 5,760; Maio 6,947; Mosteiros 9,394; Paúl 6,261; Porto Novo 17,556; Praia 147,607; Ribeira Brava 7,262; Ribeira Grande 17,375; Ribeira Grande Santiago 8,399; Sal 32,208; Santa Catarina 44,745; Santa Catarina Fogo 5,290; Santa Cruz 26,436; São Domingos 14,004; São Filipe 21,384; São Lourenço Orgaos 7,179; São Miguel 14,867; São Salvador Mundo 8,661; São Vicente 80,140; Tarrafal 18,367; Tarrafal São Nicolau 5,249; *Total* 518,467.

Births, Marriages and Deaths (official estimates): Live births 10,556 (birth rate 2.1 per 1,000, 2013); Deaths 2,942 (death rate 5.6 per 1,000, 2012); Marriages 10,695 (marriage rate 2.1 per 1,000, 2011).

Life Expectancy (years at birth, official estimates): 73.2 (males 69.3; females 76.9) in 2012.

Economically Active Population (persons aged 10 years and over, 1990 census): Agriculture, hunting, forestry and fishing 29,876; Mining and quarrying 410; Manufacturing 5,520; Electricity, gas and water 883; Construction 22,722; Trade, restaurants and hotels 12,747; Transport, storage and communications 6,138; Financial, insurance, real estate and business services 821; Community, social and personal services 17,358; *Sub-total* 96,475; Activities not adequately defined 24,090; *Total labour force* 120,565 (males 75,786, females 44,779), including 31,049 unemployed persons (males 19,712, females 11,337) (Source: ILO). *2000 Census* (persons aged 10 years and over): Total employed 144,310; Unemployed 30,334; Total labour force 174,644. *2010 Census* (persons aged 15 years and over): Total employed 156,129; Unemployed 21,168; Total labour force 177,297. *Mid-2014* (FAO estimates): Agriculture, etc. 30,000; Total (incl. others) 205,000 (Source: FAO).

HEALTH AND WELFARE

Key Indicators

Total Fertility Rate (children per woman, 2011): 2.3.

Under-5 Mortality Rate (per 1,000 live births, 2011): 21.

Physicians (per 1,000 head, 2010): 0.3.

Hospital Beds (per 1,000 head, 2010): 2.1.

Health Expenditure (2010): US $ per head (PPP): 80.

Health Expenditure (2010): % of GDP: 2.3.

Health Expenditure (2010): public (% of total): 49.1.

Access to Water (% of persons, 2011): 89.

Access to Sanitation (% of persons, 2011): 63.

Total Carbon Dioxide Emissions ('000 metric tons, 2010): 335.7.

Carbon Dioxide Emissions Per Head (metric tons, 2010): 0.7.

Human Development Index (2012): ranking: 132.

Human Development Index (2012): 0.586.

For sources and definitions, see explanatory note on p. vi.

AGRICULTURE, ETC.

Principal Crops ('000 metric tons, 2012, FAO estimates): Maize 6.0; Potatoes 5.0; Sweet potatoes 5.5; Cassava 4.0; Sugar cane 27.0; Pulses 3.0; Coconuts 5.6; Cabbages 2.6; Tomatoes 13.5; Onions, dry 3.6; Beans, green 2.8; Cucumbers and gherkins 1.4; Bananas 7.4; Guavas, mangoes and mangosteens 7.0. *Aggregate Production* ('000 metric tons, may include official, semi-official or estimated data): Vegetables (incl. melons) 28.3; Fruits (excl. melons) 20.2; Roots and tubers 14.5.

Livestock ('000 head, 2012, FAO estimates): Cattle 47.0; Pigs 240.0; Sheep 20.6; Goats 240.0; Horses 0.5; Asses 15.3; Mules 1.9; Chickens 750.

Livestock Products ('000 metric tons, 2012, FAO estimates): Pig meat 8.8; Cattle meat 1.0; Cows' milk 12.5; Goats' milk 12.5; Hen eggs 2.2.

Fishing (metric tons, live weight, 2011): Total catch (FAO estimate) 22,500 (Skipjack tuna 7,758; Yellowfin tuna 5,987).

Source: FAO.

MINING

Production (metric tons, 2012): Salt (unrefined) 1,600. Clay, gypsum, limestone and volcanic rock were also produced, at unreported levels. Source: US Geological Survey.

INDUSTRY

Production (metric tons, 2003, unless otherwise indicated): Canned fish 200; Frozen fish 900; Flour 15,901 (1999); Beer 4,104,546 litres (1999); Soft drinks 922,714 litres (1996); Cigarettes and tobacco 77 kg (1999); Paint 628,243 kg (1997); Cement 1,100,000 (2012); Footwear 670,676 pairs (1996); Soap 1,371,045 kg (1999); Electric energy 319m. kWh (2010). Sources: mainly UN Industrial Commodity Statistics Database, US Geological Survey and IMF, *Cape Verde: Statistical Appendix* (October 2001).

FINANCE

Currency and Exchange Rates: 100 centavos = 1 Cape Verde escudo; 1,000 escudos are known as a conto. *Sterling, Dollar and Euro Equivalents* (31 December 2013): £1 sterling = 133.563 escudos; US $1 = 81.105 escudos; €1 = 111.852 escudos; 1,000 Cape Verde escudos = £7.49 = $12.33 = €8.94. *Average Exchange Rate* (escudos per US dollar): 79.323 in 2011; 85.822 in 2012; 83.051 in 2013.

Central Government Budget (million escudos, 2012, budget figures): *Revenue:* Taxation 32,092 (Taxes on income and profits 9,698, Taxes on international trade 5,927, Consumption taxes 15,421, Other tax revenue 1,046); Non-tax revenue 4,617; Grants 4,028; Total 40,737. *Expenditure:* Recurrent 32,209 (Wages and salaries 18,898, Acquisition of goods and services 3,354, Transfers and other subsidies 5,481, Interest payments 2,410, Other recurrent expenditure 2,066); Capital 24,828; Total 57,037. *2013* (projections): Total revenue and grants 46,861; Total expenditure 62,668. Source: IMF, *Cape Verde: Second Review Under the Policy Support Instrument and Requests for Waivers of Nonobservance of Assessment Criteria—Staff Report; Staff Supplements; Press Release on the Executive Board Discussion; and Statement by the Executive Director for Cape Verde* (February 2012).

International Reserves (excluding gold, US $ million at 31 December 2012): IMF special drawing rights 5.20; Reserve position in the IMF 0.02; Foreign exchange 370.62; Total 375.84. Source: IMF, *International Financial Statistics*.

Money Supply (million escudos at 31 December 2012): Currency outside depository corporations 7,894.5; Transferable deposits 39,850.3; Other deposits 75,662.0; *Broad money* 123,406.8. Source: IMF, *International Financial Statistics*.

Cost of Living (Consumer Price Index; base: 2005 = 100): All items 121.1 in 2010; 126.5 in 2011; 129.7 in 2012. Source: IMF, *International Financial Statistics*.

Expenditure on the Gross Domestic Product (million escudos at current prices, 2012 estimates): Government final consumption expenditure 27,002; Private final consumption expenditure 89,871; Gross fixed capital formation 56,219; Increase in stocks 3,612; *Total domestic expenditure* 176,704; Exports of goods and services 50,760; *Less* Imports of goods and services 88,628; *GDP in purchasers' values* 138,837.

Gross Domestic Product by Economic Activity (million escudos at current prices, 2011): Agriculture, hunting and forestry 10,597; Fishing 1,005; Mining and quarrying 612; Manufacturing 8,054; Electricity, gas and water supply 2,157; Construction 15,455; Wholesale and retail trade 19,003; Hotels and restaurants 5,896; Transport, storage and communications 20,283; Financial intermediation

5,077; Other services 39,386; *Gross value added in basic prices* 127,525; Indirect taxes (net) 20,399; *GDP at market prices* 147,924.

Balance of Payments (US $ million, 2012): Exports of goods 173.12; Imports of goods −878.68; *Balance on goods* −705.56; Exports of services 604.24; Imports of services −314.66; *Balance on goods and services* −415.98; Primary income received 12.33; Primary income paid −71.89; *Balance on goods, services and primary income* −475.54; Secondary income received 310.41; Secondary income paid −44.18; *Current balance* −209.31; Capital account (net) 12.92; Direct investment assets −3.97; Direct investment liabilities 74.06; Portfolio investment liabilities 0.19; Other investment assets −86.84; Other investment liabilities 271.60; Net errors and omissions −8.94; *Reserves and related items* 49.71. Source: IMF, *International Finance Statistics*.

EXTERNAL TRADE

Principal Commodities (million escudos, 2012): *Imports c.i.f.:* Consumer goods 23,257.9 (Manufactured food products 13,208.5); Intermediate goods 13,475.8 (Construction materials 6,221.6); Capital goods 13,618.0 (Machines 5,727.5; Transportation 7,548.5); Fuel imports 9,340.1 (Fuel oil 2,432.3; Diesel oil 4,950.3); Other imports 6,019.0; Total 65,710.7. *Exports f.o.b.:* Fish and crustaceans 3,837.0 (Frozen 1,752.8); Clothing 221.3; Footwear 377.8; Total (incl. others) 4,563.9.

Principal Trading Partners (million escudos, 2012): *Imports c.i.f.:* Brazil 2,646.7; ECOWAS 854.5; Germany 679.4; Italy 1,041.1; Netherlands 9,859.4; Portugal 31,672.5; Spain 4,701.2; USA 3,483.7; Total (incl. others) 65,710.7. *Exports f.o.b.:* ECOWAS 6.2; France 2.2; Netherlands 7.5; Portugal 728.9; Spain 3,483.8; USA 58.5; Total (incl. others) 4,563.9.

TRANSPORT

Road Traffic (motor vehicles in use at 31 December 2007): Passenger cars 35,738; Buses and coaches 542; Vans and lorries 13,540; Motorcycles and mopeds 4,333 (Source: IRF, *World Road Statistics*).

Shipping: *Flag Registered Fleet* (at 31 December 2013): Number of vessels 50; Total displacement ('000 grt) 45.4 (Source: Lloyd's List Intelligence—www.lloydslistintelligence.com). *International Seaborne Freight Traffic* ('000 metric tons, 2011): Goods loaded 330.3; Goods unloaded 1,417.5).

Civil Aviation (traffic on scheduled services, 2009): Kilometres flown (million) 12; Passengers carried ('000) 777; Passenger-km (million) 1,216; Total ton-km (million) 115 (Source: UN, *Statistical Yearbook*). *2012:* Passengers carried ('000) 598 (Source: World Bank, World Development Indicators database).

TOURISM

Tourist Arrivals by Country of Residence (2012): Belgium and Netherlands 34,608; France 69,593; Germany 67,306; Italy 30,345; Portugal 67,790; Spain 12,714; Switzerland 3,767; United Kingdom 115,238; USA 4,906; Total (incl. others) 533,877.

Tourism Receipts (US $ million, excl. passenger transport): 278 in 2010; 369 in 2011; 414 in 2012 (provisional).

Source: World Tourism Organization.

COMMUNICATIONS MEDIA

Telephones (2012): 70,220 main lines in use.

Mobile Cellular Telephones (2012): 425,310 subscribers.

Internet Subscribers (2011): 21,700.

Broadband Subscribers (2012): 19,103.

Source: International Telecommunication Union.

EDUCATION

Pre-primary (2011/12 unless otherwise stated): 465 schools (2003/04); 1,113 teachers; 21,933 pupils.

Primary (2011/12 unless otherwise stated): 425 schools (2002/03); 2,956 teachers; 67,903 pupils.

Total Secondary (2011/12 unless otherwise stated): 33 schools (2003/04); 3,689 teachers; 61,956 pupils.

Higher (2011/12): 1,316 teachers; 11,800 pupils.

Teacher Training (2003/04): 3 colleges; 52 teachers; 948 pupils.

Pupil-teacher Ratio (primary education, UNESCO estimate): 23.0 in 2011/12.

Adult Literacy Rate (UNESCO estimates): 84.9% (males 89.7%; females 80.3%) in 2011.

Sources (unless otherwise indicated): Comunidade dos Países de Língua Portuguesa; UNESCO Institute for Statistics.

Directory

The Government

HEAD OF STATE

President: JORGE CARLOS FONSECA (elected 21 August 2011; took office 9 September).

COUNCIL OF MINISTERS

(April 2014)

The Government is composed of members of the Partido Africano da Independência de Cabo Verde and independents.

Prime Minister and Minister of State Reform: JOSÉ MARIA PEREIRA NEVES.

Minister of State and of Health: MARIA CRISTINA LOPES DE ALMEIDA FONTES LIMA.

Minister of Finance and Planning: CRISTINA ISABEL LOPES DA SILVA MONTEIRO DUARTE.

Minister of the Presidency of the Council of Ministers and of National Defence: JORGE HOMERO TOLENTINO ARAÚJO.

Minister of Foreign Affairs: JORGE ALBERTO DA SILVA BORGES.

Minister of Parliamentary Affairs: RUI MENDES SEMEDO.

Minister of Internal Administration: MARISA HELENA DO NASCIMENTO MORAIS.

Minister of Justice: JOSÉ CARLOS LOPES CORREIA.

Minister of Infrastructure and the Maritime Economy: SARA MARIA DUARTE LOPES.

Minister of the Environment, Housing and Spatial Planning: EMANUEL ANTERO GARCIA DA VEIGA.

Minister of Youth, Employment and Human Resources Development: JANIRA ISABEL FONSECA HOPFFER ALMADA.

Minister of Tourism, Industry and Energy: HUMBERTO SANTOS DE BRITO.

Minister of Education and Sport: FERNANDA MARIA DE BRITO MARQUES.

Minister of Rural Development: EVA VERONA TEIXEIRA ORTET.

Minister of Higher Education, Science and Innovation: ANTÓNIO LEÃO DE AGUIAR CORREIA E SILVA.

Minister of Communities: MARIA FERNANDA TAVARES FERNANDES.

Minister of Culture: MÁRIO LÚCIO MATIAS DE SOUSA MENDES.

Secretary of State for Foreign Affairs: JOSÉ LUÍS ROCHA.

Secretary of State for Public Administration: ROMEU FONSECA MODESTO.

Secretary of State for Marine Resources: ADALBERTO FILOMENO CARVALHO SANTOS VIEIRA.

MINISTRIES

Office of the President: Presidência da República, Palácio do Plateau, CP 100, Plateau, Praia, Santiago; tel. 2616555; fax 2614356; internet www.presidenciarepublica.cv.

Office of the Prime Minister: Gabinete do Primeiro Ministro, Palácio do Governo, Várzea, CP 16, Praia, Santiago; tel. 2610411; fax 2613099; e-mail gab.imprensa@gpm.gov.cv; internet www.primeirominstro.cv.

Ministry of Communities: Rua Governador Roçadas 4, Praia, CP 149A, Santiago; tel. 2615778; fax 2616744; e-mail comunidades@mdc.gov.cv; internet www.mdc.gov.cv.

Ministry of Culture: Praia, Santiago; internet www.cultura.gov.cv.

Ministry of Education and Sport: Palácio do Governo, Várzea, CP 111, Praia, Santiago; tel. 2610510; fax 2615873; internet www.minedu.gov.cv.

Ministry of the Environment, Housing and Spatial Planning: Ponta Belém, CP 115, Praia, Santiago; tel. 2615716; fax 2614054; internet www.maap.cv.

Ministry of Finance and Planning: 107 Av. Amílcar Cabral, CP 30, Praia, Santiago; tel. 2607400; e-mail aliciab@gov1.gov.cv; internet www.minfin.cv.

Ministry of Foreign Affairs: Palácio das Comunidades, Achada de Santo António, CP 60, Praia, Santiago; tel. 2607853; fax 2619270; internet www.mirex.gov.cv.

Ministry of Health: Largo Desastre da Assistência, Chã d'Areia, CP 719, Praia, Santiago; tel. 2612167; fax 2613112; e-mail cndsanitario@cvtelecom.cv; internet www.minsaude.gov.cv.

Ministry of Higher Education, Science and Innovation: Praia, Santiago; tel. 2610232; fax 2610166; internet www.mesci.gov.cv.

Ministry of Infrastructure and the Maritime Economy: Ponta Belém, Praia, Santiago; tel. 2615709; fax 2611595; e-mail gsoares@mih.gov.cv.

Ministry of Internal Administration: Praia, Santiago; e-mail samory.araujo@govcv.gov.cv; internet www.mai.gov.cv.

Ministry of Justice: Rua Cidade do Funchal, CP 205, Praia, Santiago; tel. 2609900; fax 2623262; e-mail minjus@govcv.gov.cv; internet www.mj.gov.cv.

Ministry of Parliamentary Affairs: Praia, Santiago.

Ministry of the Presidency of the Council of Ministers and of National Defence: Palácio do Governo, Várzea da Companhia, Praia, Santiago; tel. 2610344; fax 2610337; internet www.defesa.gov.cv.

Ministry of Rural Development: Praia, CP 115, Santiago; tel. 2615713; fax 2614054; e-mail mdr@mdr.gov.cv; internet www.mdr.gov.cv.

Ministry of Tourism, Industry and Energy: Rua do Funchal 2, Achada St Antonio, Praia, CP 15, Santiago; tel. 2604800; fax 2623154; e-mail mtie@mtie.gov.cv; internet www.mtie.gov.cv.

Ministry of Youth, Employment and Human Resources Development: Rua Governador Rossada 4, CP 684,Praia, Santiago; tel. 2615778; fax 2616744; internet www.juventude.cv.

President

Presidential Election, First Round, 7 August 2011

Candidate	Votes	% of votes
Jorge Carlos Fonseca (MpD)	60,438	37.76
Manuel Inocêncio Sousa (PAICV)	51,970	32.47
Aristides Lima (Ind.)	44,500	27.80
Joaquim Monteiro (Ind.)	3,169	1.98
Total	160,077*	100.00

* The total number of votes cast declared by the CNE was 162,229, which included 964 blank votes and 885 spoiled ballots.

Presidential Election, Second Round, 21 August 2011

Candidate	Votes	% of votes
Jorge Carlos Fonseca (MpD)	97,643	54.18
Manuel Inocêncio Sousa (PAICV)	82,634	45.85
Total	180,227*	100.00

* Excluding 1,489 blank votes and 831 spoiled ballots.

Legislature

National Assembly: Achada de Santo António, CP 20A, Praia, Santiago; tel. 2608000; fax 2622660; e-mail an-cv@cvtelecom.cv; internet www.parlamento.cv.

Speaker: Basílio Mosso Ramos.

Legislative Elections, 6 February 2011

Party	Votes	% of votes	Seats
PAICV	117,967	52.68	38
MpD	94,674	42.27	32
UCID	9,842	4.39	2
PSD	1,040	0.46	—
PTS	429	0.19	—
Total	223,952*	100.00	72

* Excluding 1,248 blank votes and 1,742 invalid votes.

Election Commission

Comissão Nacional de Eleições (CNE): Achada de Santo António, Praia, Santiago; tel. 2624323; e-mail cne@cne.cv; internet www.cne.cv; Pres. Rosa Carlota Martins Branco Vicente.

Political Organizations

Grupo Independente para Modernizar Sal (GIMS): Leader Jorge Figueiredo.

Movimento para a Democracia (MpD): Av. Cidade Lisboa, 4° andar, CP 90A, Praia, Santiago; tel. 2614122; e-mail mpd@mpd.cv; internet www.mpd.cv; f. 1990; Chair. Carlos Veiga; Sec.-Gen. Agostinho Lopes.

Partido Africano da Independência de Cabo Verde (PAICV): Av. Amílcar Cabral, CP 22, Praia, Santiago; tel. 2612720; fax 2611410; internet www.paicv.cv; f. 1956 as the Partido Africano da Independência do Guiné e Cabo Verde (PAIGC); name changed in 1981, following the 1980 coup in Guinea-Bissau; sole authorized political party 1975–90; Pres. José Maria Pereira Neves; Sec.-Gen. Armindo Mauricio.

Partido da Renovação Democrática (PRD): Praia, Santiago; f. 2000 by fmr mems of the MpD; Pres. José Luís Barbosa.

Partido Socialista Democrático (PSD): Praia, Santiago; f. 1992; Sec.-Gen. João Além.

Partido do Trabalho e da Solidariedade (PTS): Praia, Santiago; f. 1998; Leader José Augusto Fernandes.

União Cristã, Independente e Democrática (UCID): Achada Santo António-Frente, Restaurante 'O Poeta', Praia, Santiago; tel. 2608134; fax 2624403; Pres. António Monteiro.

Diplomatic Representation

EMBASSIES IN CAPE VERDE

Angola: Av. OUA, Achada de Santo António, CP 78A, Praia, Santiago; tel. 2623235; fax 2623234; e-mail emb.angola@cv.telecom.cv; Ambassador Josefina Guilhermina Coelho da Cruz.

Brazil: Chã de Areia 2, CP 93, Praia, Santiago; tel. 2615607; fax 2615609; e-mail contato@embrasilpraia.org; internet praia.itamaraty.gov.br/pt-br; Ambassador João Inácio Oswald Padilha.

China, People's Republic: Achada de Santo António, CP 8, Praia, Santiago; tel. 2623029; fax 2623047; e-mail chinaemb_cv@mfa.gov.cn; Ambassador Li Chunhua.

Cuba: Achada de Santo António, Praia, Santiago; tel. 2619408; fax 2617527; e-mail ecubacpv@cvtelecom.cv; internet emba.cubaminrex.cu/caboverdepor; Ambassador Narciso Amador Socorro.

France: Achada de Santo António, CP 192, Praia, Santiago; tel. 2615591; fax 2615590; internet www.ambafrance-cv.org; Ambassador Philippe Barbry.

Portugal: Av. OUA, Achada de Santo António, CP 160, Praia, Santiago; tel. 2623037; fax 2623222; e-mail embportpraia@gmail.com; internet www.secomunidades.pt/web/praia; Ambassador Bernardo Fernandes Homem de Lucena.

Russia: Achada de Santo António, CP 31, Praia, Santiago; tel. 2622739; fax 2622738; e-mail embrus@cvtelecom.cv; internet www.capeverde.mid.ru; Ambassador Boris G. Kurdyumov.

Senegal: Rua Abílio Macedo, Plateau, CP 269, Praia, Santiago; tel. 2615621; fax 2612838; e-mail silcarneyni@hotmail.com; Ambassador Mamadou Fall.

Spain: Rua de Espanha 1, Achada de Santo Antonio, Praia; tel. 2601800; fax 2621322; e-mail emb.praia@maec.es; Ambassador José Miguel Corvinos Lafuente.

USA: Rua Abílio Macedo 6, Praia, Santiago; tel. 2608900; fax 2611355; internet praia.usembassy.gov; Ambassador ADRIENNE O'NEAL.

Judicial System

Supreme Court of Justice (Supremo Tribunal de Justiça—STJ): Gabinete do Juiz Presidente, Edif. dos Correios, Rua Cesário de Lacerda, CP 117, Praia, Santiago; tel. 2615810; fax 2611751; e-mail stj@supremo.gov.cv; internet www.stj.cv; f. 1975; Pres. ARLINDO ALMEIDA MEDINA.

Attorney-General: JÚLIO CÉSAR MARTINS TAVARES.

Religion

CHRISTIANITY

An estimated 95% of the population are believed to be adherents of the Roman Catholic Church. Protestant churches, among which the Church of the Nazarene is the most prominent, represent about 1% of the population.

The Roman Catholic Church

Cape Verde comprises two dioceses, directly responsible to the Holy See. The Bishops participate in the Episcopal Conference of Senegal, Mauritania, Cape Verde and Guinea-Bissau, currently based in Senegal.

Bishop of Mindelo: Rt Rev. ILDO AUGUSTO DOS SANTOS LOPES FORTES, CP 447, 2110 Mindelo, São Vicente; tel. 2318870; fax 2318872; e-mail diocesemindelo@cvtelecom.cv.

Bishop of Santiago de Cabo Verde: Rt Rev. ARLINDO GOMES FURTADO, Av. Amílcar Cabral, Largo 5 de Outubro, CP 46, Praia, Santiago; tel. 2611119; fax 2614599; e-mail diocesecv@cvtelecom.cv.

The Anglican Communion

Cape Verde forms part of the diocese of The Gambia, within the Church of the Province of West Africa. The Bishop is resident in Banjul, The Gambia.

Other Christian Churches

Church of the Nazarene: District Office, Av. Amílcar Cabral, Plateau, CP 96, Praia, Santiago; tel. 2613611.

Other churches represented in Cape Verde include the Church of the Assembly of God, the Church of Jesus Christ of Latter-day Saints, the Evangelical Baptist Church, the Maná Church, the New Apostolic Church, the Seventh-day Adventist Church and the Universal Church of the Kingdom of God.

BAHÁ'Í FAITH

National Spiritual Assembly: Rua Madragoa, Plateau, Praia, Santiago; tel. 2617739; f. 1984.

The Press

Boletim Oficial da República de Cabo Verde: Imprensa Nacional, Av. Amílcar Cabral, Calçada Diogo Gomes, CP 113, Praia, Santiago; tel. 2614150; fax 2614209; e-mail incv@gov1.gov.cv; weekly; official announcements.

Expresso das Ilhas: Achada de Santo António, OUA Nº 21, R/C, CP 666, Praia, Santiago; tel. 2619807; fax 2619805; e-mail jornal@expressodasilhas.cv; internet www.expressodasilhas.sapo.cv; f. 2001 by the MpD; daily; Dir JOÃO DO ROSÁRIO; Editor-in-Chief JORGE MONTEZINHO.

Jornal de Cabo Verde: Prédio Gonçalves, 6º piso, Av. Cidade de Lisboa, CP 889, Praia; tel. 2601414; e-mail jornal@liberal-caboverde.com; print version of online news website O Liberal; Dir DANIEL MEDINA; circ. 7,000.

A Nação: CP 690, Cidadela, Praia; tel. 2628677; fax 2628505; e-mail geral@anacao.cv; internet www.anacao.cv; f. 2007; weekly; independent; Dir-Gen. FERNANDO RUI ORTET; circ. 5,000.

A Semana: Rotunda do Palmarejo, Av. Santiago 59, CP 36C, Praia, Santiago; tel. 2629860; fax 2628661; e-mail asemana@cvtelecom.cv; internet www.asemana.publ.cv; f. 1991; weekly; independent; Editor FILOMENA SILVA; circ. 5,000.

Terra Nova: Rua Guiné-Bissau 1, CP 166, Mindelo, São Vicente; tel. 2322442; fax 2321475; e-mail terranova@cabonet.cv; f. 1975; quarterly; Roman Catholic; Editor P. ANTÓNIO FIDALGO BARROS; circ. 3,000.

There is also an online newspaper, **Visão News** (www.visaonews.com), based in the USA. Further news websites include **O Liberal** (liberal.sapo.cv), **AllCaboVerde.com** (www.noscaboverde.com), **Cabonet** (www.cabonet.org), **Sport Kriolu** (www.sportkriolu.com), dedicated to sport, and **Voz di Povo Online** (arquivo.vozdipovo-online.com).

NEWS AGENCY

Inforpress: Achada de Santo António, CP 40A, Praia, Santiago; tel. 2624313; fax 2622554; e-mail inforpress@mail.cvtelecom.cv; internet www.inforpress.publ.cv; f. 1988 as Cabopress; Pres. JOSÉ AUGUSTO SANCHES.

PRESS ASSOCIATION

Associação de Jornalistas de Cabo Verde (AJOC): Rua João Chapuzet (Travessa do mercado), CP 350A, Praia, Santiago; tel. and fax 2622121; e-mail ajoc@ajoc.org.cv; internet www.ajoc.org.cv; f. 1993; Pres. HULDA MOREIRA; 11 media cos and 159 individual mems.

Publishers

Instituto Caboverdeano do Livro e do Disco (ICL): Centro Cultural, CP 158, Praia, Santiago; tel. 2612346; books, journals, music.

GOVERNMENT PUBLISHING HOUSE

Imprensa Nacional: Av. Amílcar Cabral, Calçada Diogo Gomes, CP 113, Praia, Santiago; tel. 2612145; fax 2614209; e-mail incv@gov1.gov.cv; internet www.incv.cv; Admin. JOÃO DE PINA.

Broadcasting and Communications

TELECOMMUNICATIONS

Cabo Verde Telecom (CVTelecom): Rua Cabo Verde Telecom, Várzea, CP 220, Praia, Santiago; tel. 2609200; fax 2613725; e-mail cvtelecom@cvtelecom.cv; internet www.cvtelecom.cv; f. 1995; 40% owned by Portugal Telecom; Chief Exec. ANTÓNIO PIRES CORREIA.

CVMóvel: Chã de Areia, Praia, Santiago 126-A; fax 2622509; e-mail marketing@cvt.cv; internet www.cvmovel.cv; wholly owned subsidiary of Cabo Verde Telecom providing cellular mobile services.

Unitel T+ Telecomunicações: Rua Cidade de Funchal 8, ASA, CP 346-A, Praia, Santiago; tel. 3303030; fax 2619606; e-mail 555@tmais.cv; internet www.uniteltmais.cv; f. 2007; est. as T+ Telecomunicações; acquired by Unitel Internacional of Angola in 2012 and renamed as above; Pres. MARCO BENTO; Dir-Gen. TONY DOLTON.

Regulatory Authority

Agência Nacional das Comunicações (ANAC): Rampa Terra Branca, Chã d'Areia, Piso 5, CP 892, Praia, Santiago; tel. 2604400; fax 2613069; e-mail info.anac@anac.cv; internet www.anac.cv; f. 2006; Pres. DAVID GOMES.

BROADCASTING

Rádiotelevisão Caboverdiana (RTC): Rua 13 de Janeiro, Achada de Santo António, CP 1A, Praia, Santiago; tel. 2605200; fax 2605256; e-mail rtc.infos@rtc.cv; internet www.rtc.cv; govt-controlled; 40 transmitters and relay transmitters; FM transmission only; radio broadcasts in Portuguese and Crioulo for 24 hours daily; 1 television transmitter and 7 relay television transmitters; television broadcasts in Portuguese and Crioulo for 8 hours daily with co-operation of RTP Africa (Portugal) and TV5 Honde; Pres. JOSÉ EMANUEL TAVARES MOREIRA; Dir of Radio ANATÓLIO FONSECA LIMA; Dir of Television JÚLIO RODRIGUES.

Televisão de Cabo Verde: Praia, Santiago; sole television broadcaster; part of RTC; Dir ÁLVARO ANDRADE.

Praia FM: Rua Visconde de S. Januario 19, 4° andar, CP 276C, Praia, Santiago; tel. 2616356; fax 2613515; e-mail atendimento@praiafm.biz; internet praiafm.sapo.cv; f. 1999; Dir GIORDANO CUSTÓDIO.

Rádio Comercial: Av. Liberdade e Democradia 6, Prédio Gomes Irmãos, 3° esq., CP 507, Praia, Santiago; tel. 2623156; fax 2622413; e-mail multimedia.rc@cvtelecom.cv; f. 1997; Admin. HENRIQUE PIRES; Dir CARLOS FILIPE GONÇALVES.

Rádio Educativa de Cabo Verde: Achada de Santo António, Praia, Santiago; tel. 2611161; Dir LUÍS LIMA.

Rádio Morabeza: Rua São João 16, 2º andar, CP 456, Mindelo, São Vicente; tel. 2324429; fax 2324431; e-mail radiomorabeza@cvtelecom.cv; f. 1999; Editor-in-Chief NUNO FERREIRA.

Rádio Nacional de Cabo Verde (RNCV): CP 26, Praia, Santiago; tel. 2613729; Dir CARLOS SANTOS.

Rádio Nova—Emissora Cristã de Cabo Verde: CP 166, Mindelo, São Vicente; tel. 2322082; fax 2321475; internet www.radionovaonline.com; f. 2002; Roman Catholic station; Dir ANTÓNIO FIDALGO BARROS.

Voz de São Vicente: CP 29, Mindelo, São Vicente; fax 2311006; f. 1974; govt-controlled; Dir JOSÉ FONSECA SOARES.

Finance

(cap. = capital; res = reserves; dep. = deposits; m. = million; brs = branches; amounts in Cape Verde escudos)

BANKING

In early 2011 there were nine commercial banks and 14 international 'offshore' financial institutions in Cape Verde.

Central Bank

Banco de Cabo Verde (BCV): Av. Amílcar Cabral 117, CP 101, Praia, Santiago; tel. 2607000; fax 2607095; e-mail avarela@bcv.cv; internet www.bcv.cv; f. 1976; bank of issue; cap. 200.0m., res –288m., dep. 28,470m. (Dec. 2009); Gov. CARLOS AUGUSTO DUARTE DE BURGO.

Other Banks

Banco Africano de Investimentos Cabo Verde SA: Edifício Santa Maria, R/C-Chã DAreia, CP 459, Praia; tel. 2602300; fax 2601726; e-mail bai@bancobai.cv; internet www.bancobai.cv; f. 2008; Pres. Dr LUÍS FILIPE RODRIGUES LÉLIS; Dir-Gen. Dr CARLOS AUGUSTO BESSA VICTOR CHAVES.

Banco Caboverdiano de Negócios (BCN): Av. Amílcar Cabral 97, CP 593, Praia, Santiago; tel. 2604920; fax 2614006; e-mail bcn@bcdenegocios.cv; internet www.bcncv.com; f. 1996 as Banco Totta e Açores (Cabo Verde); renamed as above in 2004; 46% owned by Banif (Portugal); cap. 900,000(Dec. 2008); Pres. Dr MANUEL CASIMIRO DE JESUS CHANTRE; 3 brs.

Banco Comercial do Atlântico (BCA): Praça Alexandre Albuquerque, Av. Amílcar Cabral, CP 474, Praia, Santiago; tel. 2600941; fax 2613668; e-mail bca@bca.cv; internet www.bca.cv; f. 1993; privatized in 2000; main commercial bank; cap. 1,318.6m., res 995.2m., dep. 53,688.1m. (Dec. 2009); Pres. and Gen. Man. ANTÓNIO JOAQUIM DE SOUSA; 25 brs.

Banco Espírito Santo Cabo Verde SA: Av. Cidade de Lisboa-Fazenda, CP 35, Praia, Santiago; tel. 2602626; fax 2602630; e-mail bescv@bescv.cv; internet www.bescv.cv; f. 2010; Pres. PEDRO ROBERTO MENÉRES CUDELL.

Banco Interatlântico: Av. Cidade de Lisboa, CP 131A, Praia, Santiago; tel. 2614008; fax 2614752; e-mail bi@bi.cv; internet www.bi.cv; f. 1999; cap. 600m., res 261m., dep. 14,198m. (Dec. 2009); Pres. of Exec. Comm. Dr JORGE FERNANDO GONÇALVES ALVES.

Caixa Económica de Cabo Verde, SA (CECV): Av. Cidade de Lisboa, CP 199, Praia, Santiago; tel. 2603603; fax 2612055; e-mail antonio.moreira@caixa.cv; internet www.caixa.cv; f. 1928; privatized in 1999; commercial bank; cap. 1,392.0m., res 1,522.8m., dep. 29,229.9m. (Dec. 2009); Pres. and CEO EMANUEL JESUS DA VEIGA MIRANDA; 11 brs.

Ecobank Cabo Verde: Praça Infante Dom Henrique 18, Palmarejo, CP 374C, Praia; tel. 2603660; fax 2611090; e-mail ecobankcv@ecobank.com; internet www.ecobank.com; f. 2010; Pres. EVELINE TALL; Man. Dir MAMADOU MOCTAR SALL.

STOCK EXCHANGE

Bolsa de Valores de Cabo Verde, Sarl (BVC): 16 Achada de Santo António, CP 115 A, Praia, Santiago; tel. 2603030; fax 2603038; e-mail bcv@bvc.cv; internet www.bvc.cv; f. 1998; reopened December 2005; Pres. VERÍSSIMO PINTO.

INSURANCE

Companhia Caboverdiana de Seguros (IMPAR): Rua Amilcar Cabral, CP 469, Praia, S.Vicente; tel. and fax 2603127; fax 2616025; e-mail comercial@impar.cv; internet www.impar.cv; f. 1991; Pres. CORSINO ANTÓNIO FORTES.

Garantia Companhia de Seguros: Chã d'Areia, CP 138, Praia, Santiago; tel. 2608622; fax 2616117; e-mail garantia@cvtelecom.cv; internet www.garantia.cv; f. 1991; privatized in 2000; Pres. Dr ANTÓNIO JOAQUIM DE SOUSA.

Trade and Industry

GOVERNMENT AGENCIES

Agência Caboverdiana de Promoção de Investimentos e das Exportações (CI—Cabo Verde Investimentos): Rotunda da Cruz do Papa 5, CP 89C, Praia, Santiago; tel. 2604110; fax 2622657; e-mail Presidente@cvinvest.cv; internet www.cvinvest.cv; f. 2004; promotes public-private investment partnerships in infrastructure, exports and tourism; Pres. and CEO JOSÉ ARMANDO DUARTE.

Agência Nacional de Segurança Alimentar (ANSA): Início Rampa Chã d'Areia à Terra Branca, 3º andar Prédio Laranja, CP 262, Praia, Santiago; tel. 2626290; fax 2626297; e-mail ansa@cvtelecom.cv; food security agency; Pres. MIGUEL MONTEIRO.

Agência de Regulação e Supervisão dos Produtos Farmacêuticos e Alimentares (ARFA): Achada de Santo António, CP 296A, Praia, Santiago; tel. 2626410; fax 2624970; e-mail arfa@govcv.gov.cv; internet www.arfa.cv; Pres. Dr CARLA DJAMILA MONTEIRO REIS.

Comissão de Investimento Externo e Empresa Franca (CIEF): Praia, Santiago; foreign investment commission.

Gabinete de Apoio à Reestruturação do Sector Empresarial do Estado (GARSEE) (Cabo Verde Privatization): Largo do Tunis, Cruzeiro, CP 323, Praia, Santiago; tel. 2614748; fax 2612334; bureau in charge of planning and supervising restructuring and divestment of public enterprises; Project Dir Dr SÉRGIO CENTEIO.

DEVELOPMENT ORGANIZATION

Instituto Nacional de Investigação e Desenvolvimento Agrário (INIDA): CP 84, Praia, Santiago; tel. 2711147; fax 2711133; f. 1979; research and training on agricultural issues.

TRADE ASSOCIATION

Associação para a Promoção dos MicroEmpresários (APME): Fazenda, Praia, Santiago; tel. 2606056; f. 1988.

CHAMBERS OF COMMERCE

Câmara de Comércio, Indústria e Serviços de Barlavento (CCISB): Rua da Luz 31, CP 728, Mindelo, São Vicente; tel. 2328495; fax 2328496; e-mail camara.com@cvtelecom.cv; internet www.cciasb.org; f. 1996; Pres. MANUEL J. MONTEIRO.

Câmara de Comércio, Indústria e Serviços de Sotavento (CCISS): Rua Serpa Pinto 160, CP 105, Praia, Santiago; tel. 2617234; fax 2617235; e-mail cciss@cvtelecom.cv; internet www.faroldacciss.org; Pres. JORGE SPENCER LIMA; Sec.-Gen. ROSÁRIO LUZ.

STATE INDUSTRIAL ENTERPRISES

Empresa Nacional de Avicultura, SARL (ENAVI): Tira Chapéu Zona Industrial, CP 135, Praia, Santiago; tel. 2627268; fax 2628441; e-mail enavi@cvtelecom.cv; poultry-farming.

Empresa Nacional de Combustíveis, SARL (ENACOL): Largo John Miller's, CP 1, Mindelo, São Vicente; tel. 2306060; fax 2323425; e-mail enacolsv@enacol.cv; internet www.enacol.cv; f. 1979; supervises import and distribution of petroleum; Pres. Dr CARLOS ADOLFO DE MAGALHÃES FERREIRA; Dir CARLITOS FORTES.

Empresa Nacional de Produtos Farmacêuticos, SARL (EMPROFAC): Tira Chapéu Zona Industrial, CP 59, Praia, Santiago; tel. 2627895; fax 2627899; e-mail emprofac@cvtelecom.cv; f. 1979; state monopoly of pharmaceuticals and medical imports; Dir-Gen. ÓSCAR BAPTISTA.

UTILITIES

Electricity and Water

Empresa de Electricidade e Água, SARL (Electra): Av. Baltasar Lopes Silva 10, CP 137, Mindelo, São Vicente; tel. 2303030; fax 2324446; e-mail comercial@electra.cv; internet www.electra.cv; divided into three separate cos: Electra, ELECTRA Norte and ELECTRA-Sul; f. 1982; 51% govt-owned; Pres. ALEXANDRE GUILHERME VIEIRA FONTES.

CO-OPERATIVE

Instituto Nacional das Cooperativas: Achada de Santo António, Praia, Santiago; tel. 2616376; central co-operative org.

TRADE UNIONS

Confederação Caboverdiana dos Sindicatos Livres (CCSL): Rua Dr Júlio Abreu, CP 155, Praia, Santiago; tel. 2613928; fax 2616319; e-mail ccsl@cvtelecom.cv; f. 1992; Pres. JOSÉ MANUEL VAZ.

Federação Nacional dos Sindicatos dos Trabalhadores da Administração Pública (FNSTAP): CP 123, Praia; tel. 2614305; fax 2613629; Pres. MIGUEL HORTA DA SILVA.

Sindicato dos Transportes, Comunicações e Turismo (STCT): Praia, Santiago; tel. 2616338.

União Nacional dos Trabalhadores de Cabo Verde—Central Sindical (UNTC—CS): Av. Cidade de Lisboa, CP 123, Praia, Santiago; tel. 2614305; fax 2613629; e-mail untc@cvtelecom.cv; internet www.untc-cs.cv; f. 1978; Chair. JÚLIO ASCENÇÃO SILVA.

Transport

ROADS

In 2004 there were an estimated 2,250 km of roads, of which 1,750 km were paved.

Associação Apoio aos Reclusos e Crianças de Rua (AAPR): Achada de Santo António, CP 205A, Praia, Santiago; tel. 2618441; fax 2619017; e-mail aapr@cvtelecom.cv; road devt agency.

SHIPPING

Cargo-passenger ships call regularly at Porto Grande, Mindelo, on São Vicente, and at Praia, on Santiago. The ports at Praia, Sal, São Vicente and Porto Novo (Santo Antão) have all been upgraded in recent years. There are small ports on the other inhabited islands. Cape Verde's flag registered merchant fleet at 31 December 2013 consisted of 50 vessels, totalling 45,442 grt.

Cabo Verde Fast Ferry (CVFF): Av. Andrade Corvo 35, 2º andar, CP 796, Chã d'Areia, Praia; tel. 2617552; fax 2617553; e-mail sueila .silva@cvfastferry.com; internet www.cvfastferry.com; f. 2009; Pres. ANDY DE ANDRADE.

Companhia de Navegação Estrela Negra: Av. 5 de Julho 17, CP 91, Mindelo, São Vicente; tel. 2325423; fax 2315382.

Empresa Nacional de Administração dos Portos, SA (ENAPOR, SA): Av. Marginal, CP 82, Mindelo, São Vicente; tel. 2307500; fax 2324337; e-mail info@enapor.cv; internet www.enapor.cv; f. 1982; Chair. and Man. Dir FRANKLIN DO ROSÁRIO SPENCER.

Linhas Marítimas Caboverdianas (LINMAC): CP 357, Praia, Santiago; tel. 2614352; fax 2613715; Dir ESTHER SPENCER.

Seage Agência de Navegação de Cabo Verde: Av. Cidade de Lisboa, CP 232, Praia, Santiago; tel. 2615758; fax 2612524; f. 1986; Chair. CÉSAR MANUEL SEMEDO LOPES.

Since the liquidation of the state ferry company, Arca Verde, in 2003 Transnacional, a maritime transport company, has operated a passenger ferry service between the islands of Santiago, Maio, Boavista, Fogo and Brava.

CIVIL AVIATION

The Amílcar Cabral international airport, at Espargos, on Sal island, can accommodate aircraft of up to 50 metric tons and 1m. passengers per year. The airport's facilities were expanded during the 1990s. A second international airport, Aeroporto da Praia (renamed Aeroporto Nelson Mandela in 2012) on Santiago, was opened in late 2005, and a third, Rabil International Airport on Boavista, commenced operating in 2007. In addition, following upgrade work, São Pedro Airport, on the island of São Vicente, received its first international arrival in December 2009. There is also a small airport on each of the other inhabited islands.

Agência de Aviação Civil (AAC): 34 Av. Cidade de Lisboa, CP 371, Praia, Santiago; tel. 2603430; fax 2611075; e-mail dgeral@acivil.gov .cv; internet www.aac.cv; f. 2005; regulatory agency; Pres. JOÃO DOS REIS MONTEIRO.

Empresa Nacional de Aeroportos e Segurança AEREA, SA (ASA): Aeroporto Amílcar Cabral, CP 58, Ilha do Sal; tel. 2412626; fax 2411570; e-mail pca@asa.cv; internet www.asa.cv; f. 1984; state-owned; airports and air navigation; Pres. MÁRIO PAIXÃO LOPES.

Halcyon Air: CP 142, Ilha do Sal; tel. 2412948; fax 2412362; e-mail comercial@halcyonair.com; f. 2005; inter-island carrier; Dir-Gen. FERNANDO GIL EVORA.

Transportes Aéreos de Cabo Verde (TACV): Av. Amílcar Cabral, CP 1, Praia, Santiago; tel. 2608200; fax 2617275; e-mail pferreira@ tacv.aero; internet www.tacv.cv; f. 1958; internal services connecting the 9 inhabited islands; also operates regional services to Senegal, The Gambia and Guinea-Bissau, and long-distance services to Europe and the USA; scheduled for privatization; Pres. and CEO JOÃO PEREIRA DA SILVA; Gen. Man. PAULO FERREIRA.

A private company, Inter Island Airlines, also offers flights between the islands of Cape Verde.

Tourism

The islands of Santiago, Santo Antão, Fogo and Brava offer attractive mountain scenery. There are extensive beaches on the islands of Santiago, Sal, Boavista and Maio. A total of 533,877 tourists visited Cape Verde in 2012, and in that year tourism receipts totalled some US $414m. (excluding passenger transport). The sector is undergoing rapid expansion, with development in a number of Zonas de Desenvolvimento Turístico Integral. In 2003 the Government began steps to have Fogo, which contains the only live volcano on Cape Verde, designated a UNESCO World Heritage Site. Plans were unveiled in 2004 to promote the island of Santa Luzia as an ecotourism destination.

Defence

The armed forces numbered about 1,200 (army 1,000, air force less than 100, coastguard 100), as assessed at November 2012. There is also a police force, the Police for Public Order, which is organized by the local municipal councils. National service of two years is by selective conscription.

Defence Expenditure: Budgeted at 722m. escudos in 2011.

Chief of Staff of the Armed Forces: Col ANTERO DE MATOS.

Education

Compulsory primary education begins at six or seven years of age and lasts for six years. Secondary education, beginning at 13 years of age, is divided into two cycles, the first comprising a three-year general course, the second a two-year pre-university course. There are three teacher-training units and two industrial and commercial schools of further education. According to UNESCO estimates, primary enrolment in 2012 included 96% of children in the relevant age-group (males 99%; females 96%), while secondary enrolment included 69% of children in the relevant age-group (males 64%; females 74%). In 2011/12 a total of 11,800 Cape Verdean students were enrolled in higher education. In 2002 a private university, the Universidade Jean Piaget de Cabo Verde, opened in Praia. According to UNESCO estimates, in 2010 spending on education represented 14.4% of total budgetary expenditure.

THE CENTRAL AFRICAN REPUBLIC

Introductory Survey

LOCATION, CLIMATE, LANGUAGE, RELIGION, FLAG, CAPITAL

The Central African Republic is a landlocked country in the heart of equatorial Africa. It is bordered by Chad to the north, by South Sudan and Sudan to the east, by the Democratic Republic of the Congo (formerly Zaire) and the Republic of the Congo to the south and by Cameroon to the west. The climate is tropical, with an average annual temperature of 25°C (77°F) and heavy rainfall in the south-western forest areas. The national language is Sango, but French is the official language and another 68 languages and dialects have been identified. It is estimated that about one-half of the population are Christian; another 15% are Muslims, while animist beliefs are held by an estimated 24%. The national flag (proportions 3 by 5) has four equal horizontal stripes, of blue, white, green and yellow, divided vertically by a central red stripe, with a five-pointed yellow star in the hoist corner of the blue stripe. The capital is Bangui.

CONTEMPORARY POLITICAL HISTORY

Historical Context

The former territory of Ubangi-Shari (Oubangui-Chari), within French Equatorial Africa, became the Central African Republic (CAR) on achieving self-government in December 1958. David Dacko led the country to full independence and became its first President, on 13 August 1960. In 1962 a one-party state was established, with the ruling Mouvement d'Evolution Sociale de l'Afrique Noire (MESAN) as the sole authorized party. Dacko was overthrown on 31 December 1965 by a military coup, which brought to power his cousin, Col (later Marshal) Jean-Bédel Bokassa, Commander-in-Chief of the armed forces.

In January 1966 Bokassa formed a new Government, rescinded the Constitution and dissolved the legislature. Bokassa became Life President in March 1972 and Marshal of the Republic in May 1974. In September 1976 the Council of Ministers was replaced by the Council for the Central African Revolution, and former President Dacko was appointed personal adviser to the President. In December the Republic was renamed the Central African Empire (CAE), and a new Constitution was instituted. Bokassa was proclaimed the first Emperor, and Dacko became his Personal Counsellor. However, in September 1979, while Bokassa was in Libya, Dacko deposed him in a bloodless coup, which received considerable support from France. The country was again designated a republic, with Dacko as its President and Henri Maidou as Vice-President.

In February 1981 a new Constitution, providing for a multi-party system, was approved by referendum and promulgated by Dacko. He won a presidential election in March, amid allegations of electoral malpractice, and was sworn in for a six-year term in April. Political tension intensified in subsequent months, and on 1 September the Chief of Staff of the Armed Forces, Gen. André Kolingba, deposed Dacko. Kolingba was declared President, and an all-military Government was formed. All political activity was suspended.

Domestic Political Affairs

In March 1982 the exiled leader of the banned Mouvement pour la Libération du Peuple Centrafricain (MLPC), Ange-Félix Patassé, returned to Bangui and was implicated in an unsuccessful coup attempt. Patassé, who had been Prime Minister under Bokassa in 1976–78 and who had contested the 1981 presidential election, sought asylum in the French embassy in Bangui, from where he was transported to exile in Togo.

In September 1985, for the first time since Kolingba's assumption of power, civilians were appointed to the Council of Ministers. In early 1986 a specially convened commission drafted a new Constitution, which provided for the creation of a sole legal political party, the Rassemblement Démocratique Centrafricain (RDC), and conferred extensive executive powers on the President, while defining a predominantly advisory role for the legislature. At a referendum in November some 91% of voters approved the draft Constitution and granted Kolingba a mandate to serve a further six-year term as President. The RDC was officially established in February 1987, with Kolingba as founding President, and elections to the new Assemblée Nationale (National Assembly) took place in July, at which 142 candidates, all nominated by the RDC, contested the 52 seats.

The appointment during 1988 of former associates of Bokassa, Dacko and Patassé to prominent public offices appeared to represent an attempt by Kolingba to consolidate national unity. In August 1989, however, 12 opponents of his regime, including the leader of the Rassemblement Populaire pour la Reconstruction de la Centrafrique, Brig.-Gen. (later Gen.) François Bozizé Yangouvonda, were arrested in Benin, where they had been living in exile, and extradited to the CAR. Bozizé was subsequently found guilty of complicity in the 1982 coup attempt.

In 1990 opposition movements exerted pressure on the Government to introduce a plural political system. In December the Executive Council of the RDC recommended a review of the Constitution and the re-establishment of the premiership. Accordingly, in March 1991 Edouard Franck, a former Minister of State at the Presidency, was appointed Prime Minister, and in July the National Assembly approved a constitutional amendment providing for the re-establishment of a multi-party political system. Kolingba resigned from the presidency of the RDC in the following month. In December Kolingba pardoned Bozizé.

Kolingba convened a Grand National Debate in August 1992, but it was boycotted by the influential Concertation des Forces Démocratiques, an alliance of opposition groupings. At the end of August the National Assembly approved legislation in accordance with decisions taken by the Grand National Debate: constitutional amendments provided for the strict separation of executive, legislative and judicial powers, and Kolingba was granted temporary powers to rule by decree until the election of a new multi-party legislature. Concurrent legislative and presidential elections commenced in October, but were suspended by presidential decree and subsequently annulled by the Supreme Court, owing to alleged sabotage of the electoral process.

Patassé's presidency

Two rounds of concurrent legislative and presidential elections were held in August and September 1993 in which the MLPC won 34 of the 85 seats in the National Assembly, while the RDC, in second place, secured 13 seats. Patassé, the MLPC leader and former Prime Minister, was elected President, winning 52.5% of the votes cast at a second round of voting. In October Patassé was inaugurated as President. Soon afterwards he appointed Jean-Luc Mandaba, the Vice-President of the MLPC, as Prime Minister; Mandaba formed a coalition Government, which had a working majority of 53 seats in the National Assembly.

A new Constitution, which was adopted in January 1995, included provisions empowering the President to nominate senior military, civil service and judicial officials, and requiring the Prime Minister to implement policies decided by the President. In addition, provision was made for the creation of directly elected regional assemblies and for the establishment of an advisory State Council. Several groups in the governing coalition (notably the Mouvement pour la Démocratie et le Développement—MDD, led by Dacko) expressed concern at the powers afforded to the President.

In April 1995 Mandaba resigned as Prime Minister, pre-empting a threatened vote of no confidence in his administration (initiated by his own party), following accusations of corruption and incompetence. Patassé appointed Gabriel Koyambounou as the new Prime Minister, who subsequently nominated a new Council of Ministers. In December several opposition movements (including the MDD, but not the RDC) united to form the Conseil Démocratique des Partis Politiques de l'Opposition (CODEPO), which aimed to campaign against alleged corruption and mismanagement by the Patassé regime.

In the mid-1990s the Government repeatedly failed to pay the salaries of public sector employees and members of the security forces, prompting frequent strikes and mounting political unrest. In April 1996 CODEPO staged an anti-Government rally in Bangui. Shortly afterwards part of the national army mutinied in the capital and demanded the immediate settlement of all salary arrears. Patassé promised that part of the overdue salaries would be paid and that the mutineers would not be subject to prosecution. The presence of French troops (the Eléments Français d'Assistance Opérationelle—EFAO) in Bangui contributed to the swift collapse of the rebellion. In late April Patassé appointed a new Chief of Staff of the Armed Forces, Col Maurice Regonessa, and banned all public demonstrations. In May, however, a second, more determined insurrection developed. Once again EFAO troops were deployed to protect the Patassé administration; some 500 reinforcements were brought in from Chad and Gabon to consolidate the resident French military presence (numbering 1,400). After five days of fierce fighting between dissident and loyalist troops, the French forces intervened to suppress the rebellion. France's military action prompted intense scrutiny of the role of the former colonial power, and precipitated large pro- and anti-French demonstrations in Bangui. Following extended negotiations, the mutineers and government representatives eventually signed an accord, providing for an amnesty for the rebels, the immediate release of hostages, and the installation of a new government of national unity. This was duly installed in June and Jean-Paul Ngoupandé, hitherto ambassador to France, was appointed as the new Prime Minister. However, CODEPO, dissatisfied with the level of its ministerial representation, immediately withdrew from the Government.

After renewed violence in January 1997, the former transitional President of Mali, Gen. Amadou Toumani Touré was appointed as mediator and helped to create a cross-party Committee of Consultation and Dialogue. The 'Bangui Accords', drawn up by this committee, were signed towards the end of that month; these, as well as offering an amnesty to the mutineers, provided for the formation of a new government of national unity and for the replacement of the EFAO troops by peacekeeping forces from African nations. The opposition at first threatened to boycott the new Government, largely owing to the appointment of Michel Gbezera-Bria (a close associate of Patassé and hitherto the Minister of Foreign Affairs) as Prime Minister. However, with the creation of new ministerial posts for opposition politicians, a 'Government of Action' was formed on 18 February; soon afterwards Gen. Bozizé replaced Gen. Regonessa as Chief of Staff of the Armed Forces. Also in February responsibility for peacekeeping operations was transferred from the EFAO to forces of the newly formed Mission Interafricaine de Surveillance des Accords de Bangui (MISAB), comprising some 700 soldiers from Burkina Faso, Chad, Gabon, Mali, Senegal and Togo (with logistical support from 50 French military personnel).

In June 1997 violent clashes erupted between MISAB forces and former mutineers. Several hundred EFAO troops were redeployed on the streets of Bangui and MISAB forces launched a major offensive in the capital, capturing most of the rebel-controlled districts. This assault led to the arrest of more than 80 former mutineers, but also to some 100 deaths, both of soldiers and of civilians. Subsequently, Touré returned to Bangui in his capacity as Chairman of MISAB, and negotiated a ceasefire agreement, signed at the beginning of July; all of the former mutineers were to be reintegrated into the regular armed forces; the rebels, for their part, were to relinquish their weaponry. In September the nine representatives of opposition parties in the Council of Ministers resumed their vacant posts.

In July 1997 France announced its intention to withdraw its troops from the CAR by April 1998; the first troops left the country in October 1997. A National Reconciliation Conference, held in Bangui in February 1998, led to the signing on 5 March of a National Reconciliation Pact by President Patassé and 40 representatives of all the country's political and social groups. The Pact restated the main provisions of the Bangui Accords and of the political protocol of June 1996. It provided for military and political restructuring, to be implemented by a civilian Prime Minister, supported by all of the country's social and political groups. However, Patassé was to remain President, pending a presidential election, which was scheduled for late 1999.

The signature of the Pact facilitated the authorization, later in March 1998, by the UN Security Council of the establishment of a peacekeeping mission, the UN Mission in the Central African Republic (MINURCA), to replace MISAB. MINURCA, comprising 1,345 troops, was granted an initial three-month mandate, which was subsequently extended until February 1999.

The 1998 elections

Elections to the newly reorganized National Assembly took place on 22 November and 13 December 1998. The MLPC won 47 of the 109 seats in the legislature, but secured the co-operation of seven independent members. The opposition won 55 seats; however, the defection, amid allegations of bribery, of a newly elected deputy belonging to the Parti Social-Démocrate (PSD) gave the ruling MLPC a majority in the Assembly. Patassé's decision to call on erstwhile Minister of Finance, Anicet Georges Dologuélé, to form a new Government provoked public demonstrations and caused the opposition formally to withdraw from the Assembly (the boycott lasted until March 1999). Dologuélé announced the composition of a new coalition Council of Ministers in early January, but 10 opposition ministers immediately resigned in protest at the MLPC's alleged disregard for the results of the election. In mid-January Dologuélé announced the formation of another Council of Ministers, which included four members of the MDD, despite an earlier agreement made by the opposition not to accept posts in the new Government. The MDD leadership subsequently ordered its members to resign from their government positions; three of its four ministers did so.

In February 1999 the UN Security Council extended MINURCA's mandate until mid-November in order that it might assist in the organization of the presidential election, which was scheduled for 29 August. The UN Secretary-General, Kofi Annan, was particularly critical of delays in the appointment of the independent electoral commission, the Commission Electorale Mixte Indépendante (CEMI), the 27 members of which were finally approved in May. In August, at the request of bilateral creditors and the UN, a 45-member body was established to supervise the activities of the CEMI, which comprised members of both opposition and pro-Patassé parties. In the event, the election was not held until 19 September, owing to organizational problems. On 2 October the Constitutional Court announced that Patassé had been re-elected President, with 51.6% of the total votes cast. On 22 October Patassé was sworn in as President for a further six-year term. In early November recently reappointed Prime Minister Dologuélé announced the formation of a new Council of Ministers, which included three opposition representatives.

In October 1999 Kofi Annan requested that the UN Security Council authorize the gradual withdrawal of MINURCA from the CAR over a three-month period following the end of its mandate on 15 November. In December the UN announced the establishment of a Bureau de Soutien à la Consolidation de la Paix en Centrafrique (BONUCA) in Bangui, which would monitor developments in the CAR in the areas of politics, socio-economics, human rights and security, as well as facilitate political dialogue. BONUCA began operations on 15 February 2000, when MINURCA's withdrawal was officially completed. (BONUCA was replaced by the Bureau Intégré de l'Organisation des Nations Unies en Centrafrique—BINUCA in January 2010.)

In April 2001 Patassé dismissed the Dologuélé administration. Martin Ziguélé was appointed as Prime Minister, and a new Government was formed. In late May rebellious soldiers, thought to be supporters of Kolingba, attacked Patassé's official residence in an attempted coup. However, the insurgency was suppressed by troops loyal to Patassé, and at least 59 people were killed. Libya sent troops and helicopters, while a contingent of rebels from the Democratic Republic of the Congo (DRC, formerly Zaire) arrived to support the Patassé regime. Violence ensued throughout the country, with heavy fighting in Bangui resulting in some 300 deaths. In August 2002 Kolingba and 21 associates were sentenced to death *in absentia* for their alleged involvement in the coup; a further 500 defendants were reported to have received prison terms of 10–20 years.

In August 2001 the Council of Ministers was reshuffled; most notably, the Minister of National Defence, Jean-Jacques Démafouth, was replaced, following allegations regarding his involvement in the attempted coup (he was, however, acquitted of all charges in October 2002). In October 2001 Gen. Bozizé was dismissed from the post of Chief of Staff of the Armed Forces because of similar allegations. However, in early November violence erupted in Bangui between supporters of Bozizé and the presidential guard (supported by forces from Libya) after attempts were made to arrest Bozizé, at the request of a judicial commission of inquiry into the failed coup attempt. Efforts to mediate between Bozizé and the CAR administration were unsuccessful, and later that month Bozizé fled to the town of Sarh in southern Chad, where he was granted refuge, with about 300 of his armed supporters. In late December the CAR judiciary abandoned legal proceedings against Bozizé, and in January 2002, during a meeting held in Chad, a government delegation invited Bozizé and his supporters to return to the CAR.

On 25 October 2002 the northern outskirts of Bangui were invaded by forces loyal to Bozizé, who had been granted asylum in France earlier in the month, in accordance with an agreement reached at a summit meeting of the Communauté Economique et Monétaire de l'Afrique Centrale (CEMAC) aimed at improving relations between the CAR and Chad (see Foreign Affairs). After five days of heavy fighting, pro-Government forces, supported by Libyan troops and some 1,000 fighters from a DRC rebel grouping, the Mouvement pour la Libération du Congo (MLC), succeeded in repelling Bozizé's insurgents. None the less, by December the Patassé Government had failed fully to suppress the forces allied to Bozizé, and the CAR was effectively divided between loyalist areas in the south and east and rebel-held northern regions between the Chadian border and Bangui. In December the first contingent of a CEMAC peacekeeping force (eventually to number 350) arrived in Bangui, and in January 2003 Libyan forces were withdrawn. In February MLC fighters also began to withdraw from the CAR, in response to international pressure on the Patassé Government.

Bozizé takes power

On 15 March 2003 armed supporters of Bozizé entered Bangui. President Patassé, who had been attending a regional summit in Niger, was forced to withdraw to the Cameroonian capital, Yaoundé, after shots were fired at his aeroplane as it attempted to land at Bangui. Reports suggested that casualties during the coup had numbered no more than 15 people. Following the surrender of the largely demoralized security forces in Bangui, Bozizé declared himself Head of State, dissolved the National Assembly and suspended the Constitution. Although the coup was condemned by the African Union (AU, see p. 186), the UN, CEMAC, France and the USA, Bozizé insisted that his actions constituted only a 'temporary suspension of democracy' and that a new consensus government would be formed. Following this announcement, Bozizé secured the approval of the Governments of Gabon and the Republic of the Congo at a meeting with the foreign ministers of those countries. France deployed some 300 troops in Bangui to assist foreign nationals intending to leave the CAR. Bozizé also gained the support of opposition parties, which pledged to oppose any attempt by Patassé to return to power. In late March Abel Goumba, the leader of the Front Patriotique pour le Progrès, was appointed as Prime Minister, and a new, broad-based transitional Government was subsequently formed. In May Bozizé inaugurated an advisory Conseil National de Transition (National Transitional Council—CNT) to assist him in exercising legislative power during the transitional period. Bozizé confirmed his intention to return the country to civilian rule in January 2005, and an electoral timetable was announced.

In June 2003 the Government announced plans for the demobilization or integration into the army of 5,700 former fighters. Meanwhile, the Government continued its investigations into widely acknowledged corruption within the country's economic institutions and civil service. Mineral and timber interests controlled by Patassé were suspended, and in August the state prosecutor issued an international arrest warrant for the former President, now in exile in Togo, on charges including murder and embezzlement.

In December 2003 Prime Minister Goumba was appointed Vice-President, and his previous post was allocated to Célestin-Leroy Gaombalet, a former financier. An eight-member inter-ministerial committee, headed by Gaombalet, was established in January 2004 to oversee the forthcoming electoral process. According to a revised schedule, a referendum on a new constitution, which was to be drafted by the CNT, would be held in November, with municipal, presidential and legislative elections to follow between December and January 2005. The new Constitution, which provided for a presidential term of five years, renewable only once, and increased powers for the Prime Minister, was approved by 87.2% of those who voted at a referendum held in December 2004.

Following administrative delays, presidential and legislative elections were held concurrently on 13 March 2005. In the presidential election Bozizé secured 43.0% of the votes cast, while former Prime Minister Ziguélé obtained 23.5%; both proceeded to a second round of voting, held on 8 May, at which Bozizé took 64.7% of the vote. At the legislative elections the pro-Bozizé Convergence 'Kwa na Kwa' ('Work and Only Work') secured 42 of the 105 seats in the new National Assembly, while the MLPC (the principal party supporting Ziguélé) won 11 seats; 34 independent candidates were also elected. In June Bozizé appointed a new Council of Ministers headed by Elie Doté. Also in that month the AU's Peace and Security Council lifted sanctions that had been imposed on the CAR in the wake of Bozizé's seizure of power in March 2003.

In April 2006 the Supreme Court confirmed that the CAR justice system was inadequate to try Patassé and his associates for the atrocities allegedly committed in the country following Bozizé's failed coup attempt of October 2002. The case was therefore referred to the International Criminal Court (ICC). In August 2006 Patassé and one of his advisers were found guilty of financial misconduct by the ICC. They were sentenced to 20 years hard labour *in absentia* and fined 7,000m. francs CFA. In October the rebel coalition, the Union des Forces Démocratiques pour le Rassemblement (UFDR), took control of the north-eastern town of Birao. Following a meeting between Bozizé and his Chadian counterpart, President Idriss Deby Itno, Chadian forces were deployed to assist the CAR military in overcoming the rebels; the French Government also agreed to provide support in the form of logistics and aerial intelligence. In November a major government counter-offensive, in which CEMAC forces were also involved, resulted in the recapture of Birao. In December Ouanda Djalle, the last town to remain under rebel control, was reclaimed, following a series of French air attacks in the region.

In February 2007 Abdoulaye Miskine, leader of the Front Démocratique de Libération du Peuple Centrafricain (FDPC—a faction of the UFDR), and André Ringui Le Gaillard, leader of the Armée Populaire pour la Restauration de la République et la Démocratie (APRD), signed a peace agreement with Bozizé, brokered by the Libyan leader, Col Muammar al-Qaddafi, in Sirte, Libya. In April a further accord was signed by the CAR Government and the leader of the UFDR, Zakaria Damane, on behalf of the northern rebels, granting them an amnesty and providing for the immediate cessation of hostilities. However, the ceasefire was subsequently abandoned and violence continued. The UN encouraged the CAR Government to continue discussions with rebel leaders, and in July Damane was appointed as an adviser to the presidency.

Prime Minister Elie Doté announced his resignation, and that of his Council of Ministers, in mid-January 2008 ahead of a planned vote of no confidence in his leadership. The country had been experiencing civil unrest for several months and a number of trade unions had earlier in January commenced a general strike in protest against unpaid salaries. Prof. Faustin-Archange Touadéra, the Rector of the University of Bangui, who possessed no significant previous political experience, was named as Doté's successor and later in January a new Government was announced.

A national peace process

In mid-May 2008 a peace deal was finally brokered in Libreville, Gabon, between the Government and the APRD, the last remaining rebel group outside the reconciliation process. The agreement provided for an immediate ceasefire and the eventual reintegration of rebel forces into the national army. This was followed in June by the signing of a 'global peace accord' in Libreville between the Government, the APRD and the UFDR. However, in August the APRD withdrew from the peace process, along with several other rebel factions, and violence resumed. Rebel leaders cited dissatisfaction at proposed legislation to grant an amnesty to those implicated in crimes during the conflict as the reason behind the failure of the peace talks. In September the National Assembly approved the new amnesty legislation, with the intent of encouraging the resumption of reconciliation talks. APRD leaders agreed to consider the terms of the new law and political dialogue resumed in December in the presence of Patassé who had recently returned from exile.

Following 12 days of talks between some 200 representatives from the Government, the opposition, civil society groups and rebel movements, Bozizé pledged to appoint a government of national unity. In mid-January 2009 he dismissed the incumbent administration and reappointed Touadéra to the premiership. The new, 32-member Government announced on 20 January contained 13 new ministers. However, in February the FDPC, one of the first groups to have signed the peace accord, announced its rejection of the agreement, citing government non-compliance with its terms, and Miskine declared the formation of a new rebel alliance, the Résistance Nationale. Also in February the northern town of Ndélé was briefly occupied by forces of the newly formed Convention des Patriotes pour la Justice et la Paix (CPJP), led by Charles Massi, a former defence minister. In December 2009 government forces attacked the CPJP base, pre-empting a further assault on Ndélé. Massi had been captured in Chad in June and in December was transferred to the CAR. In January 2010 the CPJP demanded that the Government prove Massi was still alive and in a later communiqué the French-based Secretary of the Forum Démocratique pour la Modernité, of which Massi was a member, stated that he had died from injuries inflicted while in custody.

The 2011 elections

Despite the ongoing violence, the Government proceeded with a three-year project to disarm, demobilize and reintegrate former rebels, which was to be supervised by a UN steering committee. A Commission Electorale Indépendante (CEI) was set up to organize legislative and presidential elections planned for 2010. Although initially a coalition of opposition parties boycotted the commission, President Bozizé acceded to their demands to annul local CEI committees that were considered to have been constituted illegally. In early March a presidential decree scheduled the first round of the elections for 25 April. Also in March an alleged coup plot implicated Patassé, who denounced the accusations as an attempt to eliminate him from the presidential contest. At the end of the month the elections, which, according to the UN, were required to be held before April in order to comply with the Constitution, were postponed until 16 May.

At the end of April 2010 the CEI announced that it required additional funds of €5.3m. to finance the elections, and it became apparent that the polls would be subject to a further delay. An extraordinary session of the National Assembly was called to agree the extension of the presidential mandate (which had been due to expire in June) until the date upon which elections could be held. Legislation was swiftly adopted and the CEI decided that the polls would be held on 24 October. Bozizé, however, subsequently decreed 23 January 2011 as the election date.

The presidential and legislative elections finally took place on 23 January 2011. In the presidential poll Bozizé took 64.4% of the total votes cast (thus obviating the need for a second round of voting), while his nearest challengers Patassé and Ziguélé secured 21.4% and 6.8%, respectively. A total of 35 parliamentary candidates were elected in the first round of the legislative election; however, after a number of challenges by opposition parties regarding the validity of the elections were dismissed, the coalition of opposition forces boycotted the second round on 27 March. Following the conclusion of the second round, of the 105 seats available, 61 were allocated to members of Kwa na Kwa, while 26 were won by independent candidates, 11 were taken by members of the 'Majorité Presidentielle' and two seats were secured by members of the opposition. The results in 14 constituencies were subsequently annulled by the Constitutional Court. On 5 April the death of Patassé (in a hospital in Douala, Cameroon) was announced. Later in April Bozizé reappointed Touadéra to the premiership following the resignation of his Government the previous month. A new Council of Ministers was announced on 22 April. In September by-elections were held in those constituencies where the results had been annulled; Kwa na Kwa secured eight seats, independents three seats, and the MLPC, the PSD and the Parti pour la Démocratie en Centrafrique each won one seat. A number of opposition parties did not participate in the by-elections in continuing protest against the allegedly fraudulent polls conducted earlier in the year.

Meanwhile, clashes between CPJP rebels and the armed forces (supported by pro-Government UFDR fighters) erupted in the north-eastern prefecture of Vakaga in April 2011. Nevertheless, later that month the CPJP declared a truce, which was formalized in June when a ceasefire accord was concluded with the Government; a similar agreement was signed by a dissident CPJP faction in July. Almost 1,500 rebels, from various groupings, had been disarmed by the end of that month under the Government's demobilization programme. In spite of this progress, the seizure by the CPJP of a UFDR-controlled diamond mine in Vakaga provoked renewed fighting between the two groups in September, which resulted in the deaths of at least 50 people. The Government and the UN condemned the resumption of violence and appealed for a ceasefire, an agreement for which was duly signed by both sides in October. The Government announced that the disarmament of the CPJP and the UFDR would be completed by the end of the month.

In July 2011 two journalists were convicted of defamation and fined after accusing Jean-Francis Bozizé—the President's son and Minister-delegate at the Presidency, in charge of National Defence, War Veterans, War Victims and the Restructuring of the Armed Forces—of embezzling €5.2m. in European Union (EU) funds. Press rights organizations condemned the treatment of the journalists and declared that the legal action was in contravention of constitutional provisions guaranteeing press freedom. In January 2012 two journalists were found guilty of defamation and sentenced to short gaol terms after criticizing Lt-Col Sylvain N'Doutingaï, the minister responsible for finance, and nephew of President Bozizé.

In April 2012 Bozizé dismissed Michel Koyt, the Minister in charge of the Secretariat-General of the Government and Relations with the Institutions, and Abdallah Kadre, the Minister-delegate to the Prime Minister, for allegedly embezzling approximately US $5m. of public funds. In June N'Doutingaï was also removed from the Council of Ministers after being accused of planning to stage a coup against Bozizé; N'Doutingaï's duties were assumed by Albert Bessé. Another alleged coup plot was uncovered in October, resulting in the detention of three suspects, including a Chadian.

Renewed conflict and the ouster of Bozizé

The APRD temporarily suspended its participation in the demobilization programme in January 2012 following the arrest of APRD leader Jean-Jacques Démafouth on suspicion of colluding with anti-Government militants. Démafouth, who denied the accusations, was granted bail in April, and in the following month, as part of the disarmament process, he oversaw the dissolution of the APRD. The Government and the CPJP concluded a formal peace agreement in August, although a purported CPJP splinter group registered its opposition to the accord by launching attacks against the towns of Sibut, Damara and Dekoa in September.

There was a sharp escalation of rebel violence during December 2012 as numerous strategically important towns in central and northern regions were overrun by fighters belonging to the recently created Seleka coalition, a loose alliance of various factions of the CPJP, the UFDR, the FDPC and the Convention Patriotique pour le Salut Wa Kodro. Seleka demanded negotiations with the Government, claiming that it had reneged on earlier promises regarding the peace and reintegration process. Bozizé appealed to Chad for military support, and on 18 December a contingent of Chadian soldiers was deployed to the CAR. France rejected a similar appeal but transferred 180 military personnel to Bangui on 30 December to defend its interests in the capital. The Mission for the Consolidation of Peace in the CAR (MICOPAX), a peacekeeping operation that had been established in the CAR by the Communauté Economique des Etats de l'Afrique Centrale (CEEAC) in 2008, was strengthened from late December 2012, with the arrival of CEEAC reinforcements in the country. On 2 January 2013 Jean-Francis Bozizé was stripped of the national defence portfolio and Guillaume Lapo was removed from his post as Chief of Staff of the Armed Forces following the capitulation of the CAR's army during the Seleka offensive; President Bozizé assumed responsibility for defence. However, with international pressure growing on the authorities to reach a peaceful resolution to the crisis, on 8 January the Government was obliged to enter into talks with Seleka and opposition parties, which were held in Libreville. The CEEAC-sponsored discussions yielded a ceasefire agreement on 11 January, as well as the signing of a political transition accord. Consequently, on 12 January Prime Minister Touadéra and the Council of Ministers were dismissed, and on 17 January Nicolas Tiangaye, a prominent opposition figure, was installed as the new premier. A Government of national unity, which included Seleka leader Michel Am Nondroko Djotodia as the First Deputy Prime Minister and Minister of National Defence, was created on 3 February; Prime Minister Tiangaye additionally received the finance portfolio. Bozizé was to remain as President, though he agreed not to contest the next presidential election. Fresh legislative polls were to be conducted within one year. MICOPAX, supported by troops of the Central African Multinational Force (FOMAC—a regional peacekeeping force established by the CEEAC), was tasked with monitoring implementation of the agreement and enforcing the ceasefire. However, a demobilization initiative had made little progress by March, with Seleka continuing to occupy multiple towns. The rebels maintained that Bozizé had failed to abide by a number of pledges made under the accord and withdrew from the power-sharing Government.

On 23 March 2013 some 5,000 Seleka troops entered Bangui and the following day Bozizé fled the country, initially taking refuge in the DRC and then in Cameroon, before seeking asylum in Benin. Djotodia declared himself President on 25 March, and stated his intention to legislate by decree for a period of three years after which time 'free, credible and transparent' elections would be held. In response, the AU announced the suspension of the CAR from the organization, pending the restoration of democratic order. Djotodia installed a new Government on 31 March in which he assumed responsibility for the defence portfolio; Tiangaye was retained as premier.

Regional heads of state, meeting at a CEEAC summit in Chad on 3 April 2013, refused to recognize Djotodia as the President of the CAR. Djotodia subsequently agreed to their recommendations that a new, 105-member CNT be established to serve as an interim legislative body. Djotodia was nevertheless, on 13 April, elected Interim President by the members of the CNT and declared that elections, in which he would not stand as a candidate, would take place within 18 months. Meanwhile, South Africa announced the withdrawal of some 400 troops deployed in the CAR under a military co-operation agreement, following the death of 13 South African soldiers during Seleka's seizure of Bangui. In mid-April an extraordinary CEEAC summit, held in N'Djamena, Chad, recommended that the CNT be enlarged, and on 14 May the transitional body was expanded to 135 members. A new electoral law was adopted by the CNT later in May, providing for the establishment of a seven-member Autorité Nationale des Elections as an independent body responsible for supervising elections. Under international pressure, on 13 June Djotodia reorganized the Government, appointing several new representatives of the opposition and civil society. On 31 May, meanwhile, the Attorney-General issued an international arrest warrant for Bozizé on charges relating to numerous alleged crimes, including murder and arbitrary detentions.

A transitional constitutional charter, which officially designated Djotodia as transitional Head of State, was signed into effect by him on 18 July 2013 (following its adoption on 5 July by the CNT). Amid continued clashes in the capital, later that month Djotodia announced the formation of a new 'Republican Army of Central Africa', comprising former members of the armed forces and Seleka combatants. Meanwhile, on 19 July the AU Peace and Security Council authorized the deployment of the International Support Mission in the Central African Republic (MISCA), which was to succeed the CEEAC-led MICOPAX. On 18 August Djotodia was formally inaugurated as the transitional Head of State.

By October 2013 the security situation in the country had severely deteriorated, with clashes between former Muslim Seleka rebels and Christian militia (known as anti-Balaka—'anti-machete') in the west. At a CEEAC summit meeting on the security crisis in the CAR, held in N'Djamena on 23 October, it was agreed to increase the strength of MISCA to more than 3,600 and to provide air support for the contingent. On 29 October the UN Security Council also approved a proposal by UN Secretary-General Ban Ki-Moon to station a 250-strong military force in Bangui to protect UN personnel there; a further 560 soldiers were later to be deployed in areas of unrest. In late November the French Government announced that its troops in the country (then numbering some 420) would be increased to 1,000 to support the new MISCA force.

On 5 December 2013 the UN Security Council adopted Resolution 2127, which authorized the deployment of MISCA and of the French forces already stationed in the country to support the mission in exercising its mandate. A further reinforcement in the French contingent, to 1,600, was announced and, after more than 185 people were killed in a series of massacres in Bangui, French troops took action to regain control of the capital. In early December two French soldiers were killed in a clash between their patrol and Seleka militia near the airport. The planned maximum strength of MISCA was increased to about 6,000, and on 19 December the AU mission formally succeeded the MICOPAX and FOMAC contingents. Meanwhile, on 15 December Djotodia dismissed three ministers, including Minister of Finance and the Budget Christophe Bremaïdou, together with the head of the treasury, who were held responsible for the collapse of the country's finances.

Recent developments: new transitional authorities

Following the failure of the transitional authorities to bring about stability and organize democratic elections, on 9 January 2014 it was announced that Djotodia and premier Tiangaye had agreed to resign, prompting celebrations in Bangui. On 11 January Djotodia left the country for Benin. On 20 January the CNT elected Catherine Samba-Panza, hitherto Mayor of Bangui, as the new Interim President from a list of eight nominated candidates. Samba-Panza, who was inaugurated on 23 January, appointed a former Banque de Développement des Etats de l'Afrique Centrale official, André Nzapayéké, as Prime Minister two days later. On 27 January Nzapayéké appointed a new Government comprising representatives of both Christian groups and the former Seleka rebels, and including several members of Djotodia's previous administration. In response to the worsening conflict in the west of the country, the new Government appealed to the UN Security Council to approve a recommendation by the UN Secretary-General for the deployment of a 12,000-member UN peacekeeping force in the CAR, while the EU also planned to contribute reinforcements. In February France increased the strength of its military contingent to 2,000; at the request of Samba-Panza, the French troops were expected to remain in the country until after elections due to be held in February 2015. In early March 2014 the head of a UN commission of inquiry announced that it would submit a list of those suspected of having responsibility for the massacres, with the ultimate aim of securing their prosecution.

Foreign Affairs

In May 1997 the CAR recognized the administration of President Laurent-Désiré Kabila in the DRC, and the two countries signed a mutual assistance pact, which provided for permanent consultation on internal security and defence. In June 2003 Bozizé and President Joseph Kabila of the DRC agreed to re-establish existing bilateral security arrangements. Following large refugee movements between the countries from the late 1990s, in August 2004 officials from both countries met to discuss reopening the common border and, subsequently, an agreement was signed under the auspices of the office of the UN High Commissioner for Refugees (UNHCR), allowing some 10,000 Congolese refugees in the CAR to be repatriated. In May 2008 former Congolese Vice-President Jean-Pierre Bemba was arrested in Belgium, and in June the ICC confirmed that it had brought charges against him of war crimes and crimes against humanity for acts committed in the CAR as leader of the MLC in 2002–03. His trial opened at the ICC on 22 November 2010.

In July 2009, according to UN estimates, 1,200 Congolese fleeing attacks by the Ugandan Lord's Resistance Army (LRA), which had bases in the DRC, sought refuge in south-eastern CAR. Cross-border raids had resulted in the deaths of 10 people that month and the internal displacement of some 3,000 CAR civilians. In August 2010, after a campaign of attacks in the north-east of the country and the abduction of villagers, largely comprising children who were coerced into fighting, the CAR pledged to capture the LRA leader, Joseph Kony, with the co-operation of Uganda, France and the USA. A number of US special forces were transferred from Uganda to Obo, in south-eastern CAR, in December 2011 to provide assistance to the CAR military in suppressing LRA activity in the area. Counter-insurgency operations in the CAR had also been bolstered since late 2010 by the provision of French equipment and technical advice. In May 2012 a senior LRA commander, Caesar Acellam Otto, was captured in the CAR by the Ugandan armed forces, although LRA attacks in the country continued throughout that year. An AU mission (comprising troops from Uganda, the CAR, the DRC and South Sudan), which had been formed to combat the LRA, commenced operations in September, replacing the existing Ugandan-led force. Following the rebel Seleka coup of March 2013, however, the Ugandan army suspended participation in the operation to arrest Kony in April. In November the Kenyan transitional authorities announced that they were in negotiations with Kony, who was reported to be demanding guarantees for his security in exchange for his surrender. Kony remained at large at early 2014, but his forces were believed to have declined to only about 170 combatants.

In 1994 the CAR became the fifth member of the Lake Chad Basin Commission (see p. 452). Relations between the CAR and Chad deteriorated, following raids by rebels into southern Chad at the end of 2001, and further border clashes in August 2002 resulted in the death of 20 CAR soldiers. An emergency CEMAC summit took place later that month, chaired by the Gabonese President, Omar Bongo, and an observer mission was dispatched to examine the security situation along the common border. However, Chad's reputed sponsorship of forces loyal to insurgent leader Bozizé further strained relations. In October a CEMAC summit in Libreville sought to resolve tensions between the two countries; under an accord reached at the summit, Bozizé was subsequently granted asylum in France. In December the first contingent of a CEMAC force was deployed in Bangui, initially to protect Patassé and later to monitor joint patrols of the border by Chadian and CAR troops. Relations between the two countries subsequently began to improve, and in January 2003 the Governments of the CAR, Chad and Sudan announced their intention to establish a tripartite committee to oversee the security and stability of their joint borders. Following Bozizé's assumption of power in the CAR in March 2003, the Chadian Government dispatched some 400 troops to Bangui; 120 Chadian troops were subsequently integrated into CEMAC's operations in the CAR.

In September 2007, following the adoption of UN Resolution 1778, the UN Security Council approved the deployment for a period of one year of the UN Mission in the Central African Republic and Chad (MINURCAT), with the mandate to protect refugees, displaced persons and civilians adversely affected by the uprising in the Darfur region of Sudan. MINURCAT was also to facilitate the provision of humanitarian assistance in eastern Chad and the north-east of the CAR, and to create favourable conditions for the reconstruction and economic and social development of those areas. The multidimensional presence was to be supported by the EU bridging military operation in Eastern Chad and North Eastern Central African Republic (EUFOR TCHAD/RCA) comprising some 4,300 troops. In March 2009 UN peacekeepers replaced the EU forces and MINURCAT's mandate was extended until March 2010. However, at the request of the Chadian Government, MINURCAT's mandate was ended in December and all troops withdrew from the region, to be replaced by Chadian military units, causing the UN Secretary-General to express concerns for the security of citizens of both countries.

Attacks by Christians against Chadian Muslims took place in Bangui during late May 2011. Mosques were set ablaze, Muslim homes and shops were looted, and at least 11 people (including eight Chadians) were killed in the violence, which had been prompted by the alleged ritualistic killing of two children by a Muslim. Following discussions with the Chadian Government on measures to alleviate tensions between the two communities, it was agreed that a bilateral security committee would be formed. The CAR and Chad commenced a joint military operation in January 2012, targeting the Front Populaire pour le Redressement (FPR), a Chadian rebel group that had been sheltering in the north of the CAR since 2008. Following UN-mediated discussions, FPR leader Abdel Kader Baba Ladde surrendered to the CAR military in September 2012. A peace agreement between the Chadian Government and the FPR was subsequently signed, and in October–November measures were undertaken to repatriate the FPR fighters remaining in the CAR. Chadian peacekeeping troops were again deployed in the CAR as part of FOMAC from December, and were subsequently incorporated into an AU-led successor mission, MISCA. Following the ousting of President Bozizé by the rebel Seleka group in March 2013, however, he accused Chadian forces of assisting the rebels. Although the Chadian authorities denied the allegations, many former Seleka combatants were reported to be Chadian nationals. In early 2014 non-governmental organization Human Rights Watch corroborated suspicions that Chadian peacekeeping troops were assisting former Seleka rebels.

Relations with Sudan have been strained in recent years, ostensibly owing to the instability in the west of that country, particularly in the Darfur region. In April 2006 the CAR closed the common border, after a number of incursions into its territory from Sudanese-based rebels. Furthermore, the CAR alleged Sudanese involvement in the UFDR's capture of Birao in October and President Bozizé accused his Sudanese counterpart, Omar Hassan Ahmad al-Bashir, of attempting to destabilize the CAR. These claims were refuted by the Sudanese authorities and in August 2007, following a visit by Bozizé to Khartoum, the Sudanese capital, the two countries agreed to normalize bilateral relations and to improve border security through joint patrols. In May 2011 the Presidents of the CAR, Sudan and Chad met in Khartoum for discussions on border security; it was announced that a tripartite border force would be created to prevent smuggling and other illegal cross-border activities.

Following the worsening hostilities between Muslim former Seleka combatants and Christian anti-Balaka militia during 2013, UNHCR reported in March 2014 that most of the Muslim population had fled from the west of the CAR owing to the reprisal violence of anti-Balaka groups. It was estimated at that time that 650,000 people were internally displaced, more than 232,000 of them in the capital, while more than 300,000 had taken refuge in neighbouring countries.

CONSTITUTION AND GOVERNMENT

The Constitution, which was approved by referendum on 5 December 2004 provides for a presidential term of five years, renewable only once. Executive authority is held by the President, who is elected by direct popular vote and who, in turn, appoints a Council of Ministers (headed by a Prime Minister). The legislature comprises a directly-elected 105-member Assemblée Nationale (National Assembly), which remains in office for a five-year term. Following the following the overthrow of President Gen. François Bozizé Yangouvonda in March 2013, a 135-member CNT was installed to act as the legislative body, pending elections.

For administrative purposes, the country is divided into 14 prefectures, two economic prefectures (Gribingui and Sangha), and one commune (Bangui). It is further divided into 67 sub-prefectures and two postes de contrôle administratif. At community level there are 65 communes urbaines, 102 communes rurales and seven communes d'élevage.

REGIONAL AND INTERNATIONAL CO-OPERATION

The CAR is a member of the African Union (see p. 186), the Central African organs of the Franc Zone (see p. 329), the Community of Sahel-Saharan States (see p. 450) and of the Communauté Economique des Etats de l'Afrique Centrale (CEEAC, see p. 450).

The CAR became a member of the UN in 1960, and was admitted to the World Trade Organization (WTO, see p. 434) in 1995. The country is also a member of the International Coffee Organization (see p. 446).

ECONOMIC AFFAIRS

In 2012, according to estimates by the World Bank, the CAR's gross national income (GNI), measured at average 2010–12 prices, was US $2,199m., equivalent to $490 per head (or $860 per head on an international purchasing-power parity basis). During 2003–12, it was estimated, the population increased at an average annual rate of 1.9%, while gross domestic product (GDP) per head, in real terms, increased at an average annual rate of 0.9%. Overall GDP increased, in real terms, at an average annual rate of 2.8% in 2003–12. It increased by 4.1% in 2012.

Agriculture (including hunting, forestry and fishing) contributed 54.3% of GDP in 2012, according to UN estimates. An estimated 59.1% of the economically active population was employed in the sector in mid-2014, according to FAO estimates. The principal cash crops have traditionally been cotton (which accounted for 9.6% of export earnings in 2012) and coffee (only an estimated 0.3% of total exports in 2012, compared with 9.4% in 1999). Livestock and tobacco are also exported. The major subsistence crops are cassava (manioc) and yams. The Government is encouraging the cultivation of horticultural produce for export. The exploitation of the country's large forest resources represents a significant source of export revenue. Rare butterflies are also exported. According to UN estimates, agricultural GDP increased at an average annual rate of 2.4% during 2003–12; the sector's GDP increased by 2.9% in 2012.

Industry (including mining, manufacturing, construction and power) engaged 3.5% of the employed labour force in 1990 and, according to UN estimates, provided 13.7% of GDP in 2012. Industrial GDP increased at an average annual rate of 3.6% in 2003–12; growth in 2012 was 4.1%.

Mining and quarrying engaged a labour force estimated at between 40,000 and 80,000 in the late 1990s, and along with utilities contributed an estimated 2.8% of GDP in 2012, according to UN estimates. The principal activity is the extraction of predominantly gem diamonds (exports of diamonds totalled an estimated 415,000 carats in 2002 and provided some 56.9% of total export revenue in 2012). The introduction of gem-cutting facilities and the eradication of widespread 'black' market smuggling operations would substantially increase revenue from diamond mining. However, in the CAR diamonds are predominantly found in widely scattered 'alluvial' deposits (mainly in the south-west and west of the country), rather than Kimberlite deposits, which are concentrated and, thus, more easily exploited and policed. It was estimated that 50% of the potential revenue from taxes on diamond exports was lost to smuggling and corruption under the Patassé administration. In July 2003 the CAR became a participant in the Kimberley Process, an international certification scheme aimed at excluding diamonds from the world market that have been traded for arms by rebel movements in conflict zones. Deposits of gold are also exploited. The development of uranium resources may proceed, and reserves of iron ore, copper, tin and zinc have also been located, although the country's insecurity and poor infrastructure have generally deterred mining companies from attempting commercial exploitation of these reserves. The GDP of the mining and utilities sector increased by an average of 2.0% per year during

2003–12; sector's GDP increased by 7.2% in 2012, according to UN estimates.

The manufacturing sector engaged 1.6% of the employed labour force in 1988. Manufacturing, which, according to UN estimates, contributed 6.5% of GDP in 2012, is based on the processing of primary products. In real terms, the GDP of the manufacturing sector increased at an average annual rate of 4.0% during 2003–12, and it increased by 3.0% in 2012.

The construction sector engaged 0.5% of the employed labour force in 1988. According to UN estimates, the sector contributed 4.5% of GDP in 2012. Construction GDP increased at an average annual rate of 4.2% during 2003–12; the sector grew by 3.5% in 2012.

In 1999, according to preliminary figures, 97.7% of electrical energy generated within the CAR was derived from the country's two hydroelectric power installations. Imports of petroleum products comprised only 0.8% of the cost of merchandise imports in 2011 compared with 16.9% in 2005.

Services engaged 15.5% of the employed labour force in 1988 and, according to UN estimates, provided 32.0% of GDP in 2012. In real terms the GDP of the services sector decreased at an average rate of 3.3% per year during 2003–12; it increased by 4.7% in 2012.

In 2010 the CAR recorded a preliminary visible merchandise trade deficit of 79,400m. francs CFA and there was a deficit of 97,700m. francs CFA on the current account of the balance of payments. In 2012 the principal source of imports was France (providing 25.2% of the total), while the principal market for exports was Belgium (accounting for 45.0% of the total). Other major trading partners in that year were the People's Republic of China, Japan, Cameroon, India and the United Arab Emirates. The principal exports in 2012 were diamonds and wood products. The principal imports in that year were machinery and transport equipment, prepared foodstuffs, beverages and tobacco, chemical products, vegetable products, food and live animals, and base metals and their articles.

In 2010, according to IMF estimates, there was a preliminary budget deficit of 20,100m. francs CFA which was projected to reach at 30.100m. francs CFA in 2012. The CAR's general government gross debt in 2012 was 338,325m. francs CFA, equivalent to 30.5% of GDP. At the end of 2011 the CAR's total external debt was US $573m., of which $297m. was public and publicly guaranteed debt. In 2009 the cost of servicing long-term public and publicly guaranteed debt and repayments to the IMF was equivalent to 4.9% of the value of exports of goods, services and income (excluding workers' remittances). The annual rate of inflation averaged 3.2% in 2003–10; consumer prices increased by an average of 3.5% in 2009 and by 1.5% in 2010, according to ILO. In 1995 7.6% of the labour force were unemployed.

The CAR's landlocked position, the inadequacy of the transport infrastructure and the country's vulnerability to adverse climatic conditions and to fluctuations in international prices for its main agricultural exports have impeded sustained economic growth. Although economic expansion slowed in 2009 in response to the global financial crisis and problems with the domestic electricity network, a revival in the agricultural sector in 2010 supported increased real GDP growth in 2010–12. However, frequent outbreaks of violence from 2011 placed a strain on public resources and discouraged foreign investment. A three-year Extended Credit Facility, valued at US $63m., was approved by the IMF in June 2012. The rebel offensive, which began in December 2012, caused widespread economic disruption. The African Union (see p. 186) suspended the CAR's membership following the seizure of power by a rebel group in March 2013 (see Domestic Political Affairs). The transitional authorities failed to restore stability, and sectarian violence involving former rebel combatants in the west of the country had severely intensified by the end of the year. Estimated GDP growth fell to 2.2% in that year (nearly one-half of the level projected). The election of a new transitional President by the interim legislature in January 2014 was welcomed by the international community; however, the humanitarian crisis, with mass displacement of civilians, continued. International donors in that month pledged assistance of US $500m. for the CAR in 2014, while the World Bank announced that it would provide $100m. to support damaged government services, as well as in humanitarian aid. The UN World Food Programme began to distribute emergency supplies in February. At the end of that month the UN Development Programme initiated a two-year, $26m. programme to promote peacebuilding and social reparation in the country.

PUBLIC HOLIDAYS

2015: 1 January (New Year), 29 March (Anniversary of the death of Barthélemy Boganda), 6 April (Easter Monday), 1 May (May Day), 14 May (Ascension Day), 25 May (Whit Monday), 30 June (National Day of Prayer), 13 August (Independence Day), 15 August (Assumption), 1 November (All Saints' Day), 1 December (National Day), 25 December (Christmas).

Statistical Survey

Source (unless otherwise stated): Division des Statistiques et des Etudes Economiques, Ministère de l'Economie, du Plan et de la Coopération Internationale, Bangui.

Area and Population

AREA, POPULATION AND DENSITY

Area (sq km)	622,984*
Population (census results)	
8 December 1988	2,463,616
8 December 2003†	
Males	1,569,446
Females	1,581,626
Total	3,151,072
Population (UN estimates at mid-year)‡	
2012	4,525,207
2013	4,616,418
2014	4,709,205
Density (per sq km) at mid-2014	7.6

* 240,535 sq miles.

† Source: UN, *Population and Vital Statistics Report*.

‡ Source: UN, *World Population Prospects: The 2012 Revision*.

POPULATION BY AGE AND SEX
(UN estimates at mid-2014)

	Males	Females	Total
0–14	925,697	933,116	1,858,813
15–64	1,314,578	1,356,463	2,671,041
65 and over	77,485	101,866	179,351
Total	2,317,760	2,391,445	4,709,205

Source: UN, *World Population Prospects: The 2012 Revision*.

PRINCIPAL TOWNS
(estimated population at mid-1994)

Bangui (capital)	524,000	Carnot	41,000
Berbérati	47,000	Bambari	41,000
Bouar	43,000	Bossangoa	33,000

Mid-2011 (incl. suburbs, UN estimate): Bangui 740,062 (Source: UN, *World Urbanization Prospects: The 2011 Revision*).

BIRTHS AND DEATHS
(annual averages, UN estimates)

	1995–2000	2000–05	2005–10
Birth rate (per 1,000)	39.9	38.5	35.8
Death rate (per 1,000)	19.6	19.2	17.3

Source: UN, *World Population Prospects: The 2012 Revision*.

Life expectancy (years at birth): 48.8 (males 47.0; females 50.7) in 2011 (Source: World Bank, World Development Indicators database).

ECONOMICALLY ACTIVE POPULATION
(persons aged 6 years and over, 1988 census)

	Males	Females	Total
Agriculture, hunting, forestry and fishing	417,630	463,007	880,637
Mining and quarrying	11,823	586	12,409
Manufacturing	16,096	1,250	17,346
Electricity, gas and water	751	58	809
Construction	5,583	49	5,632
Trade, restaurants and hotels	37,435	54,563	91,998
Transport, storage and communications	6,601	150	6,751
Financing, insurance, real estate and business services	505	147	652
Community, social and personal services	61,764	8,537	70,301
Sub-total	558,188	528,347	1,086,535
Activities not adequately defined	7,042	4,627	11,669
Total employed	565,230	532,974	1,098,204
Unemployed	66,624	22,144	88,768
Total labour force	631,854	555,118	1,186,972

Source: ILO.

Mid-2014 (estimates in '000): Agriculture, etc. 1,282; Total labour force 2,168 (Source: FAO).

Health and Welfare

KEY INDICATORS

Total fertility rate (children per woman, 2011)	4.5
Under-5 mortality rate (per 1,000 live births, 2011)	164
HIV/AIDS (% of persons aged 15–49, 2011)	4.6
Physicians (per 1,000 head, 2009)	0.05
Hospital beds (per 1,000 head, 2011)	1.0
Health expenditure (2010): US $ per head (PPP)	30
Health expenditure (2010): % of GDP	3.8
Health expenditure (2010): public (% of total)	51.0
Access to water (% of persons, 2011)	67
Access to sanitation (% of persons, 2011)	34
Total carbon dioxide emissions ('000 metric tons, 2010)	264.0
Carbon dioxide emissions per head (metric tons, 2010)	0.1
Human Development Index (2012): ranking	180
Human Development Index (2012): value	0.352

For sources and definitions, see explanatory note on p. vi.

Agriculture

PRINCIPAL CROPS
('000 metric tons)

	2010	2011	2012
Maize	150.0	160.0	161.5
Millet	10.0*	11.0†	11.5
Sorghum	50.0	48.0	45.6
Cassava (Manioc)	679.0	706.1	684.2
Taro (Coco yam)†	118.0	122.7	125.0
Rice, paddy	39.0	40.0	42.0
Yams†	435.0	452.4	460.0
Sugar cane†	96.0	97.0	100.0
Groundnuts, with shell	140.0	160.0	149.3
Oil palm fruit	4.7	5.0†	5.5
Sesame seed	29.0	29.6	28.1
Melonseed†	37.0	35.0	35.0
Pumpkins, squash and gourds	20.7	21.1	20.0
Bananas†	126.0	124.0	128.0
Plantains†	88.0	84.0	85.0
Oranges†	24.0	29.8	30.5
Pineapples†	14.5	15.1	15.6
Coffee, green	5.3	6.0†	6.5
Seed cotton	10.5	10.1	20.8

* Unofficial figure.
† FAO estimate(s).

Aggregate production ('000 metric tons, may include official, semi-official or estimated data): Total cereals 249.0 in 2010, 259.0 in 2011, 260.6 in 2012; Total roots and tubers 1,233.2 in 2010, 1,282.5 in 2011, 1,270.5 in 2012; Total pulses 31.3 in 2010, 34.0 in 2011, 36.5 in 2012; Total vegetables (incl. melons) 85.7 in 2010, 88.3 in 2011, 90.0 in 2012; Total fruits (excl. melons) 274.6 in 2010, 279.2 in 2011, 286.2 in 2012.

Source: FAO.

LIVESTOCK
('000 head, year ending September)

	2010	2011	2012*
Cattle	3,893	4,182	4,250
Goats	4,862	5,744	5,800
Sheep	388	386	400
Pigs	1,087	1,032	1,000
Chickens	6,376	6,604	6,700

* FAO estimates.

Source: FAO.

LIVESTOCK PRODUCTS
('000 metric tons, FAO estimates)

	2010	2011	2012
Cattle meat	85.0	88.0	90.0
Sheep meat	2.2	2.3	2.3
Goat meat	18.0	21.3	21.3
Pig meat	18.5	17.7	16.4
Chicken meat	5.7	5.9	6.0
Game meat	19.7	20.0	21.0
Cows' milk	75.0	77.0	80.0
Hen eggs	3.1	3.2	2.5
Honey	15.0	15.5	16.0

Source: FAO.

Forestry

ROUNDWOOD REMOVALS
('000 cubic metres, excluding bark)

	2009	2010	2011
Sawlogs, veneer logs and logs for sleepers	349	324	424
Other industrial wood	308	308	308
Fuel wood*	2,000	2,000	2,000
Total	2,657	2,632	2,732

* FAO estimates.

2012: Production assumed to be unchanged from 2011 (FAO estimates).

Source: FAO.

SAWNWOOD PRODUCTION
('000 cubic metres, including railway sleepers)

	2009	2010	2011
Total (all broadleaved)	62	45	54

2012: Production assumed to be unchanged from 2011 (FAO estimates).

Source: FAO.

Fishing

('000 metric tons, live weight of capture, FAO estimates)

	2009	2010	2011
Total catch (freshwater fishes)	33.0	35.0	35.0

Source: FAO.

Mining

	2010	2011	2012
Gold (kg)	59	53	55*
Diamonds ('000 carats)†	301.6	323.6	365.9

* Estimate.
† Production is approximately 70% to 80% gem quality.

Source: US Geological Survey.

Industry

SELECTED PRODUCTS
('000 metric tons, unless otherwise indicated)

	2004	2005	2006
Beer ('000 hectolitres)	118.7	118.9	123.1
Sugar (raw, centrifugal)*	12	12	n.a.
Soft drinks ('000 hectolitres)	41.4	46.7	51.8
Cigarettes (million packets)	16.0	n.a.	n.a.
Palm oil*	1.7	1.7	1.7
Groundnut oil*	33.2	33.2	33.2
Plywood ('000 cubic metres)*	2.0	2.0	2.0

* FAO estimates.

Sources: IMF, *Central African Republic: Selected Issues and Statistical Appendix* (January 2008); FAO.

Groundnut oil ('000 metric tons, FAO estimates): 39.4 in 2009; 33.7 in 2010; 38.7 in 2011; 36.0 in 2012 (Source: FAO).

Electric energy (million kWh, estimates): 137 in 2007–08; 136 in 2009; 160 in 2010 (Source: UN, Industrial Commodity Statistics database).

Palm oil ('000 metric tons, FAO estimates): 0.7 in 2009; 0.4 in 2010–12 (Source: FAO).

Plywood ('000 cubic metres, unofficial figures): 1.0 in 2009–12 (Source: FAO).

Finance

CURRENCY AND EXCHANGE RATES

Monetary Units

100 centimes = 1 franc de la Coopération Financière en Afrique Centrale (CFA).

Sterling, Dollar and Euro Equivalents (31 December 2013)

£1 sterling = 783.286 francs CFA;
US $1 = 475.641 francs CFA;
€1 = 655.957 francs CFA;
10,000 francs CFA = £12.77 = $21.02 = €15.24.

Average Exchange Rate (francs CFA per US $)

2011	471.866
2012	510.527
2013	494.040

Note: An exchange rate of 1 French franc = 50 francs CFA, established in 1948, remained in force until January 1994, when the CFA franc was devalued by 50%, with the exchange rate adjusted to 1 French franc = 100 francs CFA. This relationship to French currency remained in effect with the introduction of the euro on 1 January 1999. From that date, accordingly, a fixed exchange rate of €1 = 655.957 francs CFA has been in operation.

BUDGET
('000 million francs CFA)

Revenue*	2010†	2011‡	2012‡
Tax revenue	92.0	97.3	108.5
Taxes on profits and property	17.8	19.2	21.1
Taxes on goods and services	74.2	78.1	87.4
Taxes on international trade	26.9	27.3	30.3
Non-tax revenue	22.3	16.9	17.8
Total	114.3	114.2	126.4

Expenditure§	2010†	2011‡	2012‡
Current primary expenditure	113.3	113.9	117.8
Wages and salaries	43.3	46.2	50.8
Other goods and services	37.6	33.2	31.2
Transfers and subsidies	32.3	34.6	35.8
Interest payments	9.9	8.3	7.9
Capital expenditure	67.2	58.4	62.9
Domestically financed	11.1	19.5	11.2
Externally financed	56.1	38.8	51.7
Total	190.4	180.6	188.6

* Excluding grants received ('000 million francs CFA): 62.2 in 2010 (preliminary figure); 36.2 in 2011 (projected figure); 50.1 in 2012 (projected figure).
† Preliminary figures.
‡ Projections.
§ Excluding adjustment for payment arrears ('000 million francs CFA): 6.2 in 2010 (preliminary figure); 6.8 in 2011 (projected figure); 18.0 in 2012 (projected figure).

Source: IMF, *Central African Republic: 2011 Article IV Consultation—Staff Report; Public Information Notice on the Executive Board Discussion; and Statement by the Executive Director for Central African Republic* (August 2012).

INTERNATIONAL RESERVES
(US $ million at 31 December)

	2010	2011	2012
Gold (national valuation)	4.78	17.01	18.73
IMF special drawing rights	4.28	4.23	4.24
Reserve position in IMF	0.36	0.40	0.40
Foreign exchange	176.54	149.88	153.27
Total	185.96	171.52	176.64

Source: IMF, *International Financial Statistics*.

MONEY SUPPLY
('000 million francs CFA at 31 December)

	2011	2012
Currency outside depository corporations	105.55	105.13
Transferable deposits	53.52	57.65
Other deposits	40.13	39.51
Broad money	199.19	202.29

Source: IMF, *International Financial Statistics*.

COST OF LIVING
(Consumer Price Index for Bangui; base: 2000 = 100)

	2006	2007	2008
Food	118.9	121.1	134.9
Fuel and light	104.9	104.9	111.5
Clothing	131.0	128.1	130.6
All items (incl. others)	119.1	120.3	131.5

2009: All items 136.1.

2010: All items 138.1.

Source: ILO.

NATIONAL ACCOUNTS
(million francs CFA at current prices)

Expenditure on the Gross Domestic Product

	2010	2011	2012
Government final consumption expenditure	81,103	64,658	84,898
Private final consumption expenditure	883,440	933,194	978,932
Gross capital formation	138,771	155,160	163,495
Total domestic expenditure	1,103,314	1,153,012	1,227,324
Exports of goods and services	102,333	119,297	129,037
Less Imports of goods and services	222,020	228,212	241,276
GDP in purchasers' values	983,627	1,044,097	1,115,084

Gross Domestic Product by Economic Activity

	2010	2011	2012
Agriculture, hunting, forestry and fishing	494,655	542,519	571,357
Mining, quarrying and utilities	24,451	27,245	29,175
Manufacturing	61,549	64,735	68,122
Construction	40,002	44,107	47,112
Wholesale and retail trade, restaurants and hotels	120,694	135,503	141,649
Transport, storage and communication	52,180	59,658	62,363
Other services	119,096	114,929	132,107
GDP at factor cost	912,627	988,697	1,051,885
Indirect taxes (net)*	71,000	55,400	63,199
GDP in purchasers' values	983,627	1,044,097	1,115,084

* Figures obtained as residuals.

Source: UN National Accounts Main Aggregates Database.

BALANCE OF PAYMENTS
('000 million francs CFA, preliminary)

	2008	2009	2010
Exports of goods	66.1	61.0	71.7
Imports of goods	−134.4	−128.0	−151.1
Trade balance	−68.4	−66.9	−79.4
Services (net)	−43.5	−43.0	−56.3
Balance on goods and services	−111.9	−109.9	−135.7
Income (net)	−9.9	−2.6	−1.6
Balance on goods, services and income	−121.8	−112.5	−137.3
Current transfers (net)	34.1	36.9	39.6
Current balance	−87.6	−75.7	−97.7
Capital account (net)	29.7	43.0	48.4
Project grants	29.7	32.8	48.4
Capital grants and transfers	0.0	10.2	0.0
Financial account	61.2	26.8	47.1
Direct investment	55.2	19.9	30.4
Other investment	6.0	6.9	16.7
Overall balance	3.3	−5.9	−2.1

Source: IMF, *Central African Republic: 2011 Article IV Consultation—Staff Report; Public Information Notice on the Executive Board Discussion; and Statement by the Executive Director for Central African Republic* (August 2012).

External Trade

PRINCIPAL COMMODITIES
(distribution by HS, US $ million)

Imports c.i.f.	2010	2011	2012
Live animals and animal products	5.7	6.3	6.1
Vegetable products	23.5	28.9	26.2
Malt, starches, milling products, etc.	21.1	26.3	22.7
Wheat or meslin flour	12.3	16.3	17.8
Animal, vegetable fats and oils, etc.	7.3	5.0	4.8
Prepared foodstuffs, beverages and tobacco	22.9	27.7	28.5
Sugars and sugar confectionery	8.0	11.8	11.4
Cane or beet sugar and chemically pure sucrose (solid form)	7.4	11.7	10.7
Mineral products	10.6	9.9	10.1
Salt, sulphur, lime, cement, etc.	8.5	8.1	6.7
Cements	7.1	6.7	5.6
Chemical and related products	33.2	25.1	26.3
Pharmaceutical products	24.0	16.0	18.6
Medicament mixtures in dosage	18.7	12.1	14.0
Plastics and rubber articles	7.5	5.2	6.5
Textiles and textile articles	8.0	7.1	6.9
Other made textile articles, worn clothing, etc.	6.4	5.8	5.4
Base metals and articles	13.5	12.2	11.1
Machinery and electrical equipment	38.0	46.3	44.2
Machinery, boilers, etc.	15.8	28.0	22.2
Electrical, electronic equipment	22.2	18.3	22.0
Electric application for line telephony	5.9	5.8	7.2
Vehicles, aircraft, vessels and transport equipment	19.4	21.5	33.1
Vehicles other than railway, tramway	19.1	21.3	32.9
Cars (incl. station wagons)	5.1	5.9	12.2
Trucks and goods motor vehicles	4.7	3.3	7.6
Total (incl. others)	209.9	214.7	221.2

* Excluding tyres, engines and electrical parts.

Exports f.o.b.	2010	2011	2012
Wood and articles of wood	24.7	26.2	26.2
Wood in the rough	17.2	17.9	18.9
Sawnwood (chipped lengthwise, sliced or peeled)	7.5	8.3	7.3
Textiles and textile articles	7.5	5.7	11.1
Cotton	7.5	5.7	11.1
Pearls, precious stones, metals, coins, etc.	53.3	65.6	67.5
Diamonds, not mounted or set	52.0	63.1	66.1
Machinery and electrical equipment	1.4	2.3	4.2
Machinery and boilers etc.	1.0	2.3	4.0
Vehicles, aircraft, vessels and transport equipment	0.4	1.8	3.8
Vehicles other than railway, tramway	0.4	1.8	3.8
Total (incl. others)	89.8	103.9	116.1

Source: Trade Map-Trade Competitiveness Map, International Trade Centre, www.intracen.org/marketanalysis.

PRINCIPAL TRADING PARTNERS
(US $ million)

Imports c.i.f.	2010	2011	2012
Belgium	6.5	5.7	8.4
Brazil	7.1	0.2	10.9
Cameroon	14.9	16.5	15.6
China, People's Repub.	25.4	14.2	25.3
France (incl. Monaco)	50.7	68.1	55.7
Gabon	5.8	1.0	4.9
Germany	4.5	14.1	6.9
India	11.4	3.0	12.8
Italy	6.1	2.4	6.2
Japan	7.6	29.3	16.3
Malaysia	2.3	2.2	3.4
Namibia	4.3	2.8	3.0
Netherlands	12.9	4.6	3.9
South Africa	4.3	2.8	4.6
Spain	3.2	1.9	3.1
Turks and Caicos	2.3	3.5	4.3
United Arab Emirates	3.1	4.9	3.9
USA	9.7	3.7	8.2
Total (incl. others)	209.9	214.7	221.2

Exports f.o.b.	2010	2011	2012
Belgium	36.7	1.5	52.3
Cameroon	1.0	10.1	2.4
Chad	1.2	0.6	2.8
China, People's Repub.	7.2	8.7	16.0
France (incl. Monaco)	14.4	27.3	11.3
Germany	8.4	6.7	8.5
Israel	6.7	0.2	—
Italy	0.4	1.1	0.1
Japan	—	15.6	0.1
Netherlands	—	3.3	0.1
South Africa	0.1	4.3	—
Spain	0.8	2.8	0.1
Switzerland (incl. Liechtenstein)	1.1	0.3	1.1
United Arab Emirates	6.0	2.8	11.7
United Kingdom	0.1	3.0	—
Total (incl. others)	89.8	103.9	116.1

Source: Trade Map-Trade Competitiveness Map, International Trade Centre, www.intracen.org/marketanalysis.

Transport

ROAD TRAFFIC
(motor vehicles in use)

	1999	2000	2001
Passenger cars	4,900	5,300	5,300
Commercial vehicles	5,800	6,300	6,300

Source: UN, *Statistical Yearbook*.

2007 (motor vehicles in use at 31 December): Passenger cars 1,225; Vans and lorries 58; Motorcycles and mopeds 4,492; Total 5,775 (Source: IRF, *World Road Statistics*).

2008 (motor vehicles in use at 31 December): Passenger cars 2,682; Buses and coaches 22 (Source: IRF, *World Road Statistics*).

SHIPPING
(international traffic on inland waterways, metric tons)

	1996	1997	1998
Freight unloaded at Bangui	60,311	56,206	57,513
Freight loaded at Bangui	5,348	5,907	12,524
Total	65,659	62,113	70,037

Source: Banque des Etats de l'Afrique Centrale, *Etudes et Statistiques*.

CIVIL AVIATION
(traffic on scheduled services)*

	1999	2000	2001
Kilometres flown (million)	3	3	1
Passengers carried ('000)	84	77	46
Passenger-km (million)	235	216	130
Total ton-km (million)	36	32	19

* Including an apportionment of the traffic of Air Afrique.

Source: UN, *Statistical Yearbook*.

Tourism

FOREIGN VISITORS BY COUNTRY OF ORIGIN*

	2008	2009	2010
Cameroon	2,895	4,125	2,861
Chad	1,275	3,221	2,732
Congo, Democratic Rep.	795	588	1,124
Congo, Republic	1,107	734	1,845
Côte d'Ivoire	1,024	1,116	1,236
France	6,975	4,431	7,661
Gabon	912	695	762
Italy	788	2,017	1,229
Senegal	1,127	1,662	1,577
Total (incl. others)	30,611	52,429	53,821

* Arrivals at hotels and similar establishments.

Receipts from tourism (US $ million, incl. passenger transport): 11.8 in 2008; 6.0 in 2009; 7.2 in 2010.

Source: World Tourism Organization.

Communications Media

	2010	2011	2012
Telephones ('000 main lines in use)	5.3	5.4	5.6
Mobile cellular telephones ('000 subscribers)	979.2	1,823.9	1,979.3
Internet subscribers ('000)	0.1	n.a.	n.a.

Source: International Telecommunication Union.

Education

(2011/12 unless otherwise indicated)

			Students		
	Institutions*	Teachers	Males	Females	Total
Pre-primary	162	478†	10,455†	10,708†	21,163†
Primary	930	8,267	377,781	284,536	662,317
Secondary:					
general	46	1,699	80,345	41,712	122,057
vocational	n.a.	149	2,415	1,435	3,850
Tertiary	n.a.	384†	9,153	3,369	12,522

* 1990/91 figures.

† 2010/11 figures.

Source: UNESCO Institute for Statistics.

Pupil-teacher ratio (primary education, UNESCO estimate): 80.1 in 2011/12 (Source: UNESCO Institute for Statistics).

Adult literacy rate (UNESCO estimates): 56.6% (males 69.6%; females 44.2%) in 2011 (Source: UNESCO Institute for Statistics).

Directory

The Government

HEAD OF STATE

Interim President: CATHERINE SAMBA-PANZA (elected by vote of the National Transitional Council on 20 January 2014).

COUNCIL OF MINISTERS

(April 2014)

Interim President: CATHERINE SAMBA-PANZA.

Prime Minister: ANDRÉ NZAPAYÉKÉ.

Minister of State, in charge of Public Works, Town Planning, Housing and Public Buildings: HERBERT GONTRAN DJONO AHABA.

Minister of State, in charge of Rural Development: MARIE NOËLLE ANDET-KOYARA.

Minister of Justice, Keeper of the Seals, in charge of Judicial Reform and Human Rights: ISABELLE GAUDEUILLE.

Minister of Foreign Affairs, African Integration and the Francophonie: TOUSSAINT KONGO DOUDOU.

Minister of National Defence, in charge of the Reorganization of the Armed Forces, Former Combatants, War Victims, Disarmament, Demobilization and Reintegration: Gen. THOMAS THÉOPHILE TCHIMANGOA.

Minister of Territorial Administration, Decentralization and Regionalization: ARISTIDE SOKAMBI.

Minister of the Economy, Planning and International Co-operation, in charge of Poles of Development: FLORENCE LIMBIO.

Minister of Public Security, Emigration and Immigration: Col. DENIS WANGAO KIZIMALE.

Minister of Finance and the Budget: RÉMI YAKORO.

Minister of Mines, Energy and Water Resources: OLIVIER MALIBANGAR.

Minister of the Forest Economy, the Environment and Tourism: HYACINTHE TOUHOUYÉ.

Minister of Public Health, Social Affairs and Humanitarian Action: Dr MARGUERITE SAMBA.

Minister of National and Higher Education and Scientific Research: GISÈLE BEDAN.

Minister of Communication and National Reconciliation: ANTOINETTE MONTAIGNE MOUSSA.

Minister of Posts and Telecommunications, in charge of New Technology: ABDALLAH KADRE HASSAN.

Minister of the Civil Service, Labour, Social Security and Employment: ELOI ANGUIMATÉ.

Minister of Transport and Civil Aviation: ARNAUD DJOUBAYE ABAZENE.

Minister of Trade, Industry, Handicrafts and Small and Medium-sized Enterprises: GERTRUDE ZOUTA.

Minister of Youth, Sport, the Arts and Culture: LÉOPOLD NARCISSE BARA.

Minister, in charge of the Secretariat-General of the Government and of Relations with the Institutions: GASTON MACKOUZANGBA.

MINISTRIES

Office of the President: Palais de la Renaissance, Bangui; tel. 21-61-46-63.

Office of the Prime Minister: BP 932, Bangui; tel. 21-61-59-23; e-mail contact@primature-rca.org; internet www.primature-rca.org.

Ministry of the Civil Service and Administrative Reform: Bangui.

Ministry of Communication, the Promotion of Civic Culture and National Reconciliation: Bangui.

Ministry of the Development of Tourism and Handicrafts: Bangui; tel. 21-61-04-16.

Ministry of the Environment, Ecology and Sustainable Development: Bangui; tel. 21-61-79-21.

Ministry of Equipment, Public Works and Promotion of the Regions: Bangui.

Ministry of Finance and the Budget: BP 696, Bangui; tel. 21-61-38-05.

Ministry of Foreign Affairs, African Integration, the Francophonie and Central Africans Abroad: Bangui.

Ministry of Fundamental, Secondary and Technical Education: Bangui.

Ministry of Higher Education and Scientific Research: BP 791, Bangui; tel. 21-61-08-38.

Ministry of Housing: Bangui.

Ministry of Human Rights: Bangui.

Ministry of Justice: Bangui; tel. 21-61-52-11.

Ministry of Labour, Employment, Professional Training and Social Security: Bangui; tel. 21-61-21-88; fax 21-61-04-14.

Ministry of Mining, Petroleum, Energy and Water Resources: Bangui; tel. 21-61-20-54; fax 21-61-60-76.

Ministry of National Defence and the Restructuring of the Armed Forces: Bangui; tel. 21-61-00-25.

Ministry of Planning, the Economy and International Co-operation: BP 912, Bangui; tel. 21-61-70-55; fax 21-61-63-98.

Ministry of Posts, Telecommunications and New Technology: Bangui; tel. 21-61-29-66.

Ministry of Poles of Development: Bangui.

Ministry of the Promotion of Arts and Culture: Bangui.

Ministry of Public Health, Population and the Fight against AIDS: Bangui; tel. 21-61-16-35.

Ministry of Public Security, Emigration, Immigration and Public Order: Bangui; tel. 21-61-14-77.

Ministry of Rural Development: Bangui; tel. 21-61-28-00.

Ministry of Small and Medium-sized Enterprises: Bangui.

Ministry of Social Affairs, National Solidarity and the Promotion of Gender Equality: Bangui; tel. 21-61-55-65.

Ministry of the Social Economy and Microfinance: Bangui.

Ministry of Stockbreeding and Animal Industries: Bangui.

Ministry of Territorial Administration, Decentralization and Regionalization: Bangui; e-mail aristide@sokambi.com.

Ministry of Town Planning, Land Registry and Land Reform: Bangui; tel. 21-61-69-54.

Ministry of the Programme of Disarmament, Demobilization and Reintegration: Bangui.

Ministry of Trade and Industry: Bangui; tel. 21-61-10-69.

Ministry of Transport and Civil Aviation: BP 941, Bangui; tel. 21-61-70-49; fax 21-61-46-28.

Ministry of Water, Forests, Hunting and Fishing: Bangui.

Ministry of Youth and Sport: Bangui; tel. 21-61-39-69.

President

Presidential Election, 23 January 2011

Candidate	Votes	% of votes
Gen. François Bozizé Yangouvonda	718,801	64.37
Ange-Félix Patassé	239,279	21.43
Martin Ziguélé	75,939	6.80
Emile Gros-Raymond Nakombo	51,469	4.61
Jean-Jacques Démafouth	31,184	2.79
Total	1,116,672	100.00

Legislature

General Election, 23 January and 27 March 2011

Party	Seats
Kwa na Kwa	61
Majorité Présidentielle	11
L'Opposition	2
Independents	26
Total	100*

* Following the second round of elections, five seats remained undeclared. The results in these five constituencies, along with nine others, were subsequently annulled by the Constitutional Court. By-elections were held in these 14 constituencies in September.

Election Commission

Autorité Nationale des Elections (ANE): Bangui; f. 2012; 7 mems.

Political Organizations

Alliance pour la Démocratie et le Progrès (ADP): Bangui; internet alliance-democratie-progres.over-blog.com; f. 1991; progressive; Nat. Pres. EMMANUEL OLIVIER GABIRAULT.

Armée Populaire pour la Restauration de la République et la Démocratie (APRD): Bangui; armed insurrectionary group; Leader JEAN-JACQUES DÉMAFOUTH.

Forum Démocratique pour la Modernité (FODEM): ave Dejean, Sicai, Bangui; tel. 21-61-29-54; e-mail eric.neris@fodem.org; internet www.fodem.org; f. 1997; Pres. (vacant).

Front Démocratique de Libération du Peuple Centrafricain (FDPC): e-mail miskinedardar@yahoo.fr; internet www.centrafriquefdpc.com; Leader ABDOULAYE MISKINE.

Front Patriotique pour le Progrès (FPP): BP 259, Bangui; tel. 21-61-52-23; fax 21-61-10-93; f. 1972; aims to promote political education and debate; Leader ALEXANDRE GOUMBA.

Kwa na Kwa (KNK): Bangui; f. 2004; formally constituted as a political party in 2009; Acting Pres. CÉLESTIN-LEROY GAOMBALET.

Mouvement National pour le Renouveau: Bangui; Leader PAUL BELLET.

Mouvement pour la Démocratie et le Développement (MDD): Bangui; f. 1993; aims to safeguard national unity and the equitable distribution of national wealth; Leader LOUIS PAPENIAH.

Mouvement pour la Démocratie, l'Indépendance et le Progrès Social (MDI-PS): BP 1404, Bangui; tel. 21-61-18-21; e-mail mdicentrafrique@chez.com; internet www.chez.com/mdicentrafrique; Sec.-Gen. DANIEL NDITIFEI BOYSEMBE.

Mouvement pour la Libération du Peuple Centrafricain (MLPC): Bangui; internet www.lemlpc.net; f. 1979; leading party in govt Oct. 1993–March 2003; Pres. MARTIN ZIGUÉLÉ; Sec.-Gen. JEAN-MICHEL MANDABA.

Nouvelle Alliance pour le Progrès (NAP): Bangui; internet www.centrafrique-nap.com; Leader JEAN-JACQUES DÉMAFOUTH.

Parti Social-Démocrate (PSD): BP 543, Bangui; tel. 21-61-59-02; fax 21-61-58-44; Leader ENOCH DERANT LAKOUÉ.

Rassemblement Démocratique Centrafricain (RDC): BP 503, Bangui; tel. 21-61-53-75; f. 1987; sole legal political party 1987–91; Leader (vacant).

Union des Forces Démocratiques pour le Rassemblement (UFDR): Bangui; f. 2006; Chief of Staff ZAKARIA DAMANE.

Front Démocratique Centrafricain (FDC): Bangui; Leader Commdt JUSTIN HASSAN.

Groupe d'Action Patriotique de la Libération de Centrafrique (GAPLC): Bangui; Leader MICHEL AM NONDROKO DJOTODIA.

Mouvement des Libérateurs Centrafricains pour la Justice (MLCJ): Bangui; Leader Capt. ABAKAR SABONE.

Union des Forces Républicaines de Centrafrique: Bangui; f. 2006; armed insurrectionary group; Leader Lt FRANÇOIS-FLORIAN N'DJADDER-BEDAYA.

Union pour un Mouvement Populaire de Centrafrique (UMPCA): Pres. YVONNE M'BOÏSSONA.

Diplomatic Representation

EMBASSIES IN THE CENTRAL AFRICAN REPUBLIC

Cameroon: rue du Languedoc, BP 935, Bangui; tel. 77-59-31-80 (mobile); e-mail ambacambangui@yahoo.fr; Chargé d'affaires a.i. NICOLAS NZOYOUM.

Chad: ave Valéry Giscard d'Estaing, BP 461, Bangui; tel. 21-61-46-77; fax 21-61-62-44; Ambassador MAHAMAT BÉCHIR CHÉRIF.

China, People's Republic: ave des Martyrs, BP 1430, Bangui; tel. 21-61-27-60; fax 21-61-31-83; e-mail chinaemb_cf@mfa.gov.cn; Ambassador SUN HAICHAO.

Congo, Democratic Republic: Ambassador EMBE ISEA MBAMBE.

Congo, Republic: ave Boganda, BP 1414, Bangui; tel. 21-61-03-09; e-mail diplobrazzabangui@yahoo.fr; Ambassador GABRIEL ENTCHA-EBIA.

Egypt: angle ave Léopold Sédar Senghor et rue Emile Gentil, BP 1422, Bangui; tel. 21-61-46-88; fax 21-61-35-45; e-mail ambassadedEgypt_Centreafrique@excite.com; Ambassador AZZA EL-GUIBALI.

France: blvd du Général de Gaulle, BP 884, Bangui; tel. 21-61-30-05; fax 21-61-74-04; e-mail contact@ambafrance-cf.org; internet www.ambafrance-cf.org; Ambassador CHARLES MALINAS.

Holy See: ave Boganda, BP 1447, Bangui; tel. 75041492 (mobile); e-mail na.rca@diplomat.va; Apostolic Nuncio FRANCO COPPOLA.

Japan: Temporarily closed; affairs handled through the embassy of Japan, Yaoundé, Cameroon, since October 2003.

Libya: Bangui; tel. 21-61-46-62; fax 21-61-55-25; Ambassador OMAR ISSA BARUNI.

Morocco: ave de l'Indépendence, BP 1609, Bangui; tel. 21-61-39-51; fax 21-61-35-22; e-mail sifama-bg@intnet.cf; Ambassador MUSTAPHA EL-HALFAOUI.

Nigeria: ave des Martyrs, BP 1010, Bangui; tel. 21-61-07-44; fax 21-61-12-79; e-mail jimgom7@yahoo.com; Ambassador ROLAND OZAWUMI OMOWA.

Qatar: Ledger Plaza, Bangui; tel. 21-61-72-67; fax 21-61-72-66; e-mail bangui@mofa.gov.qa; AHMAD ABDUL RAHMAN MOHAMMED AL-SUNAIDI.

Russia: ave du Président Gamal Abdel Nasser, BP 1405, Bangui; tel. 21-61-03-11; fax 21-61-56-45; e-mail rusconsrca@yandex.ru; internet www.rca.mid.ru; Ambassador ALEKSANDR V. KASPAROV.

Sudan: ave de France, BP 1351, Bangui; tel. 21-61-38-21; Ambassador OMAR SALIH ABU BAKR.

USA: ave David Dacko, BP 924, Bangui; tel. 21-61-02-00; fax 21-61-44-94; internet bangui.usembassy.gov; Ambassador LAURENCE D. WOHLERS; operations temporarily suspended in Dec. 2013.

Judicial System

Supreme Court: BP 926, Bangui; tel. 21-61-41-33; highest judicial organ; acts as a Court of Cassation in civil and penal cases and as Court of Appeal in administrative cases; comprises four chambers: constitutional, judicial, administrative and financial; Pres. TAGBIA SANZIA.

Transitional Constitutional Court: BP 2104, Bangui; tel. 21-61-99-58; fax 21-61-99-52; f. 1995; 9 mems; Pres. ZACHARIE NDOUBA.

Religion

It is estimated that 24% of the population hold animist beliefs, 50% are Christians (25% Roman Catholic, 25% Protestant) and 15% are Muslims. There is no official state religion.

CHRISTIANITY

The Roman Catholic Church

The Central African Republic comprises one archdiocese and eight dioceses. An estimated 25% of the population are Roman Catholics.

Bishops' Conference: Conférence Episcopale Centrafricaine, BP 1518, Bangui; tel. 75-11-41-02; fax 21-61-46-92; e-mail ceca_rca@yahoo.fr; f. 1982; Pres. Most Rev. DIEUDONNÉ NZAPALAINGA.

Archbishop of Bangui: Most Rev. DIEUDONNÉ NZAPALAINGA, Archevêché, BP 1518, Bangui; tel. 21-61-08-98; fax 21-61-46-92; e-mail archbangui@yahoo.fr.

Protestant Church

Eglise Evangélique Luthérienne de la République Centrafricaine: BP 100, Bouar; tel. 70-80-73-36; fax 21-31-41-70; e-mail eelrca@skyfile.com; Pres. Rev. ANDRÉ GOLIKE; 55,000 mems (2010).

Eglise Protestante du Christ Roi: rue des Missions, BP 608, Bangui; tel. 21-61-14-35; fax 21-61-35-61; e-mail sgudeac@intnet.cf; f. 1968.

ISLAM

Conférence Islamique de RCA: Bangui; Pres. Imam OMAR KOBINE LAYAMA.

The Press

The independent press is highly regulated. Independent publications must hold a trading licence and prove their status as a commercial enterprise. They must also have proof that they fulfil taxation requirements. There is little press activity outside Bangui.

DAILIES

Le Citoyen: BP 974, Bangui; tel. 21-61-89-16; e-mail ltdc@yahoo.fr; independent; Dir MAKA GBOSSOKOTTO; circ. 1,000.

Le Confident: BP 427, Bangui; tel. 75-04-64-14; e-mail leconfident2000@yahoo.fr; internet www.leconfident.net; f. 2001; Mon.–Sat; Dir MATHURIN C. N. MOMET; circ. 500.

Le Démocrate: BP 427, Bangui; Dir of Publication FERDINAND SAMBA; circ. 500.

L'Hirondelle: Bangui; independent; Editor-in-Chief JULES YANGANDA; circ. 500.

PERIODICALS

Bangui Match: Bangui; monthly.

Centrafrique-Presse: BP 1058, Bangui; tel. and fax 21-61-39-57; e-mail redaction.centrafrique.presse@gmail.com; internet www.centrafrique-presse.info; weekly; Publr PROSPER N'DOUBA.

Demain le Monde: BP 650, Bangui; tel. 21-61-23-15; f. 1985; fortnightly; independent; Editor-in-Chief NGANAM NÖEL.

Journal Officiel de la République Centrafricaine: BP 739, Bangui; f. 1974; fortnightly; economic data; Dir-Gen. GABRIEL AGBA.

Nations Nouvelles: BP 965, Bangui; publ. by Organisation Commune Africaine et Mauricienne; politics and current affairs.

Le Patriote: Bangui; Dir of Publication AMBROISE YALIMA.

Le Peuple: BP 569, Bangui; tel. 21-61-76-34; f. 1995; weekly; Editor-in-Chief VERMOND TCHENDO.

Le Progrès: BP 154, Bangui; tel. 21-61-70-26; f. 1991; monthly; Editor-in-Chief BELIBANGA CLÉMENT; circ. 2,000.

La Tortue Déchainée: Bangui; independent; satirical; Publr MAKA GBOSSOKOTTO.

PRESS ASSOCIATION

Groupement des Editeurs de la Presse Privée Indépendante de Centrafrique (GEPPIC): Bangui; Pres. PATRICK AGOUNDOU.

Observatoire des Médias Centrafricains (OMCA): Bangui; Pres. PIERRE DÉBATO, II.

Union des Journalistes de Centrafrique (UJCA): Bangui; Pres. MAKA GBOSSOKOTO.

NEWS AGENCY

Agence Centrafrique Presse (ACAP): BP 40, Bangui; tel. 21-61-22-79; e-mail infoacap@yahoo.fr; internet www.acap-cf.info; f. 1960; Gen. Man. ALAIN BERTRAND KOGALAMA.

Publisher

GOVERNMENT PUBLISHING HOUSE

Imprimerie Centrafricaine: ave David Dacko, BP 329, Bangui; tel. 21-61-72-24; f. 1974; Dir-Gen. SERGE BOZANGA.

Broadcasting and Communications

TELECOMMUNICATIONS

In 2013 there were four mobile cellular telephone operators and one fixed-line telephone operator in the country. In 2010, according to the International Telecommunication Union, there were 979,200 subscribers to mobile telephone services and 5,300 subscribers to fixed-line services.

Atlantique Telecom Centrafrique SA: Immeuble Moov, ave du Président Mobutu, BP 2439 Bangui; tel. and fax 21-61-23-85; internet www.moov-rca.com; operates mobile cellular telephone services under Moov network; Dir-Gen. SOULEYMANE DIALLO (Moov Centrafrique); 248,063 subscribers.

Azur RCA: ave de l'Indépendance, Ex FNUAP, BP 1418, Bangui; tel. 21-61-33-97; fax 21-61-33-07; e-mail contact@azur-rca.com; internet www.azur-rca.com; f. 2004; fmrly Nation Link Telecom; mobile cellular telephone operator; Dir-Gen. YANNICK BOURDEU; 96,499 subscribers (2009).

Orange Centrafrique: Imeuble SODIAM, ave Bathélemy Boganda, BP 863, Bangui; tel. 72-27-08-00; e-mail serviceclient@orange.cf; internet www.orange.cf; f. 2007; mobile cellular telephone operator; Pres. MICHEL BARRÉ; Dir-Gen. BRUNO ALLASSONNIÈRE; 211,657 subscribers (2009).

Société Centrafricaine de Télécommunications (SOCATEL): BP 939, Bangui; tel. 21-61-42-68; fax 21-61-44-72; e-mail dg-socatel@socatel.cf; internet www.socatel.cf; f. 1990; 100% state-owned; Dir-Gen. PAUL MARTIAL GUIPI-BOPALA; 1,000 subscribers (2012).

Telecel: BP 939, Bangui; tel. 21-61-19-30; fax 21-61-16-99; f. 1996; mobile cellular telephone operator; Dir-Gen. LIONEL GOUSSI; 238,868 subscribers (2009).

Regulatory Authority

Agence de Régulation des Télécommunications (ART): Immeuble de la Poste, BP 1046, Bangui; tel. 21-61-56-51; fax 21-61-05-82; e-mail art-rca@art-rca.org; internet www.art-rca.org; Dir-Gen. JOSEPH NGANAZOUI.

BROADCASTING

Radiodiffusion-Télévision Centrafricaine: BP 940, Bangui; tel. 21-61-25-88; f. 1958 as Radiodiffusion Nationale Centrafricaine; govt-controlled; broadcasts in French and Sango.

Radio Centrafrique: Bangui; tel. 75-50-36-32; e-mail yakanet.rca@gmail.com; internet www.radiocentrafrique.org; Dir-Gen DAVID GBANGA.

Radio Ndeke Luka: Concession du PNUD, BP 558, ave de l'Indépendance, Bangui; tel. 72-29-52-52; e-mail m.faye@radiondekeluka.org; internet www.radiondekeluka.org; f. 2000; Dir MARTIN FAYE.

TELEVISION

Télévision Centrafricaine (TVCA): Bangui; tel. 21-61-61-02; Dir-Gen. MICHEL OUAMBÉTI.

Finance

(cap. = capital; res = reserves; dep. = deposits; m. = million; br. = branch; amounts in francs CFA)

BANKING

In 2010 there were four commercial banks in the country.

Central Bank

Banque des Etats de l'Afrique Centrale (BEAC): BP 851, Bangui; tel. 21-61-24-00; fax 21-61-19-95; e-mail beacbgf@beac.int; internet www.beac.int; headquarters in Yaoundé, Cameroon; f. 1973; bank of issue for mem. states of the Communauté Economique et Monétaire de l'Afrique Centrale (CEMAC, fmrly Union Douanière et Economique de l'Afrique Centrale), comprising Cameroon, the CAR, Chad, the Repub. of the Congo, Equatorial Guinea and Gabon; cap. 88,000m., res 227,843m., dep. 4,110,966m. (Dec. 2007); Gov. LUCAS ABAGA NCHAMA; Dir in CAR CAMILLE KELEFIO.

Commercial Banks

Banque Populaire Maroco-Centrafricaine (BPMC): rue Guérillot, BP 844, Bangui; tel. 21-61-31-90; fax 21-61-62-30; e-mail bpmc@intnet.cf; f. 1991; 57.5% owned by Groupe Banque Populaire (Morocco); cap. and res 4,183m., total assets 13,331m. (Dec. 2003); Gen. Man. MOHAMMED BENZIANI.

Commercial Bank Centrafrique (CBCA): rue de Brazza, BP 59, Bangui; tel. 21-61-29-90; fax 21-61-34-54; e-mail cbcabank@cbc-bank.com; internet www.cbc-bank.com/cb_centrafrique/page.php?langue=fr; f. 1999; 54.5% owned by Groupe Fotso, 40.5% owned by CAR private shareholders, 5% owned by Commercial Bank Cameroon SA; cap. 1,500.m., res 1,856.3m., dep 22,941.2m. (Dec. 2005); Pres. SERGE PSIMHIS; Dir-Gen. THÉODORE DABANGA; 1 br.

Ecobank Centrafrique: pl. de la République, BP 910, Bangui; tel. 21-61-00-42; fax 21-61-34-38; e-mail ecobankcf@ecobank.com; internet www.ecobank.com; f. 1946 as BAO; cap. 5,000m., res 845m., dep. 53,621m. (Dec. 2009); Pres. KASSIMOU ABOU KABASSI; Man. Dir CHRISTIAN ASSOSSOU.

Development Bank

Banque de Développement des Etats de l'Afrique Centrale: see Franc Zone.

Financial Institutions

Caisse Autonome d'Amortissement de la République Centrafricaine: Bangui; tel. 21-61-53-60; fax 21-61-21-82; management of state funds; Dir-Gen. JOSEPH PINGAMA.

Caisse Nationale d'Epargne (CNE): Office National des Postes et de l'Epargne, Bangui; tel. 21-61-22-96; fax 21-61-78-80; Pres. SIMONE BODEMO-MODOYANGBA; Dir-Gen. AMBROISE DAOUDA; Man. ANTOINE BEKOUANEBANDI.

Bankers' Association

Association Professionnelle des Banques: Bangui.

Development Agencies

Agence Française de Développement: route de la Moyenne Corniche, BP 817, Bangui; tel. 21-61-45-78; fax 21-61-03-06; e-mail afdbangui@groupe-afd.org; internet www.afd.fr; administers economic aid and finances specific development projects; Man. JOCELYN LEVENEUR.

Mission Française de Coopération et d'Action Culturelle: BP 934, Bangui; tel. 21-61-63-34; fax 21-61-28-24; administers bilateral aid from France; Dir HERVÉ CRONEL.

INSURANCE

Agence Centrafricaine d'Assurances (ACA): BP 512, Bangui; tel. 21-61-06-23; f. 1956; Dir R. CERBELLAUD.

Allianz Centrafrique Assurances: blvd Général de Gaulle, BP 343, Bangui; tel. 21-61-36-66; fax 21-61-33-40; e-mail allianz.centrafrique@allianz-cf.com; internet www.allianz-africa.com; f. 1988; Dir of Operations BRUNO RIBEYRON.

Assureurs Conseils Centrafricains (ACCAF): ave Barthélemy Boganda, BP 743, Bangui; tel. 21-61-19-33; fax 21-61-44-70; e-mail centrafrique@ascoma.com; internet www.ascoma.com; f. 1968; owned by Ascoma (Monaco); Man. VENANT EBELA; Dir-Gen. SYLVAIN COUSIN.

Entreprise d'Etat d'Assurances et de Réassurances (SIRIRI): Bangui; tel. 21-61-36-55; f. 1972; Pres. EMMANUEL DOKOUNA; Dir-Gen. MARTIN ZIGUÉLÉ.

Union des Assurances Centrafricaine (UAC): rue de la Victoire, BP 896, Bangui; tel. 21-61-31-02; fax 21-61-18-48; e-mail uac02@yahoo.fr; f. 1999; non-life insurance; Dir-Gen. PATHÉ DIONE.

Trade and Industry

DEVELOPMENT ORGANIZATION

Agence Centrafricaine de Développement Agricole (ACDA): ave David Dacko, BP 997, Bangui; tel. 21-61-54-85; e-mail acda_2010@yahoo.fr; internet www.acda-rca.org; f. 1993; purchasing, transport and marketing of cotton, cotton-ginning, production of cottonseed oil and groundnut oil; Pres. HONORÉ FEIZOURE.

INDUSTRIAL AND TRADE ASSOCIATIONS

Agence Nationale pour le Développement de l'Elevage (ANDE): BP 1509, Bangui; tel. 21-61-69-60; fax 21-61-50-83; assists with development of livestock; Dir-Gen. EMMANUEL NAMKOISSÉ.

Bourse Internationale de Diamant de Bangui: BP 26, Bangui; tel. 21-61-58-63; fax 21-61-60-76; diamond exchange.

Caisse de Stabilisation et de Péréquation des Produits Agricoles (CAISTAB): BP 76, Bangui; tel. 21-61-08-00; supervises marketing and pricing of agricultural produce; Dir-Gen. M. BOUNANDELE-KOUMBA.

Fédération Nationale des Eleveurs Centrafricains (FNEC): ave des Martyrs, BP 588, Bangui; tel. 21-61-23-97; fax 21-61-47-24; Pres. BI AMADOU SOUAIBOU; Sec.-Gen. YOUSSOUFA MANDJO.

Groupement des Industries Centrafricaines (GICA): BP 804, Bangui; umbrella group representing 12 principal companies of various industries; Pres. PATRICK DEJEAN.

Office National de la Forêts (ONF): BP 915, Bangui; tel. 21-61-38-27; f. 1969; afforestation, development of forest resources; Dir-Gen. C. D. SONGUET.

CHAMBERS OF COMMERCE

Chambre d'Agriculture, d'Elevage, des Eaux, Forêts, Chasses, Pêches et du Tourisme: BP 850, Bangui; tel. 21-61-06-38; e-mail chagri_rca@hotmail.com; f. 1964; Sec.-Gen. HENRI OUIKON.

Chambre de Commerce, d'Industrie, des Mines et de l'Artisanat (CCIMA): blvd Charles de Gaulle, BP 823, Bangui; tel. 21-61-16-68; fax 21-61-35-61; e-mail ccima@intnet.cf; internet ccima-rca.com; f. 1935; Pres. ROBERT NGOKI; Treas. THÉODORE LAWSON.

EMPLOYERS' ORGANIZATION

Union Nationale du Patronat Centrafricain (UNPC): Immeuble Tropicana, 1°, BP 2180, Bangui; tel. and fax 21-61-16-79; e-mail unpc-rca@intnet.cf; Pres. GILLES GILBERT GRESENGUET.

UTILITIES

Electricity

Société Energie de Centrafrique (ENERCA): ave de l'Indépendance, BP 880, Bangui; tel. 21-61-20-22; fax 21-61-54-43; e-mail enerca@intnet.cf; f. 1967; state-owned; production and distribution of electric energy; 119.1 GWh produced for the Bangui grid in 2003; Dir-Gen. SAMUEL TOZOUI.

Water

Société de Distribution d'Eau en Centrafrique (SODECA): BP 1838, Bangui; tel. 21-61-59-66; fax 21-61-25-49; e-mail sodeca@intnet.cf; f. 1975 as the Société Nationale des Eaux; state-owned co responsible for supply, treatment and distribution of water; Dir-Gen. PAUL BELLET.

TRADE UNIONS

Confédération Chrétienne des Travailleurs de Centrafrique (CCTC): BP 939, Bangui; tel. 21-61-05-71; fax 21-61-55-81; Pres. LOUIS SALVADOR.

Confédération Nationale de Travailleurs de Centrafrique: BP 2141, Bangui; tel. 75-50-94-36; fax 21-61-35-61; e-mail cnt@intnet.cf; Sec.-Gen. JEAN-RICHARD SANDOS-OULANGA.

Confédération Syndicale des Travailleurs de Centrafrique (CSTC): BP 386, km 5, Bangui; tel. 21-61-38-69; Sec.-Gen. SABIN KPOKOLO.

Union Générale des Travailleurs de Centrafrique (UGTC): BP 346, Bangui; tel. 21-61-05-86; fax 21-61-17-96; Pres. CÉCILE GUÉRÉ.

Union Syndicale des Travailleurs de Centrafrique (USTC): BP 1390, Bangui; tel. 21-61-60-15; e-mail vvesfon@yahoo.fr; Sec.-Gen. NOËL RAMADAN.

Transport

RAILWAYS

There are no railways at present. There are long-term plans to connect Bangui to the Transcameroon railway. A line linking Sudan's Darfur region with the CAR's Vakaga province has also been proposed.

ROADS

In 2010 there were an estimated 20,278 km of roads. Only about 6.8% of the total network is paved. Eight main routes serve Bangui, and those that are surfaced are toll roads. Both the total road length and the condition of the roads are inadequate for current requirements. In 1997 the European Union provided 32,500m. francs CFA to improve infrastructure in the CAR. In September a vast road improvement scheme was launched, concentrating initially on roads to the south and north-west of Bangui. The CAR is linked with Cameroon by the TransAfrican Lagos–Mombasa highway. Roads are frequently impassable in the rainy season (July–October).

Bureau d'Affrètement Routier Centrafricain (BARC): Gare routière, BP 523, Bangui; tel. 21-61-20-55; fax 21-61-37-44; Dir-Gen. J. M. LAGUEREMA-YADINGUIN.

Fonds d'Entretien Routier (FER): BP 962, Bangui; tel. 21-61-62-95; fax 21-61-68-63; e-mail fondsroutier@admn.cf; f. 1981; Dir-Gen. MARIE-CLAIR BITOUANGA.

TBC Cameroun SARL: BP 637, Bangui; tel. 21-61-20-16; fax 21-61-13-19; e-mail rca@tbclogistics.com; internet www.tbclogistics.com; f. 1963.

INLAND WATERWAYS

There are some 2,800 km of navigable waterways along two main water courses. The first, formed by the Congo river and its tributary the Oubangui, can accommodate convoys of barges (of up to 800 metric tons load) between Bangui and Brazzaville and Pointe-Noire in the Republic of the Congo, except during the dry season, when the route is impassable. The second is the river Sangha, also a tributary of the Congo, on which traffic is again seasonal. There are two ports, at Bangui and Salo, on the rivers Oubangui and Sangha, respectively. Bangui port has a handling capacity of 350,000 tons, with 350 m of wharfs and 24,000 sq m of warehousing. Efforts are being made to develop the Sangha upstream from Salo, to increase the transportation of timber from this area and to develop Nola as a timber port.

Agence Centrafricaine des Communications Fluviales (ACCF): BP 822, Bangui; tel. 21-61-09-67; fax 21-61-02-11; f. 1969; state-owned; supervises development of inland waterways transport system; Chair. GUY MAMADOU MARABENA.

Société Centrafricaine de Transports Fluviaux (SOCATRAF): rue Parent, BP 1445, Bangui; tel. and fax 21-61-43-15; e-mail socatraf@intnet.cf; f. 1980; 51% owned by ACCF; Man. Dir FRANÇOIS TOUSSAINT.

CIVIL AVIATION

The international airport is at Bangui-M'Poko. There are also 37 small airports for internal services.

Tourism

Although tourism remains relatively undeveloped, the CAR possesses considerable scenic attractions in its waterfalls, forests and wildlife. In 2010 some 54,000 tourists arrived. In that year receipts from tourism were estimated at US $7.2m.

Office National Centrafricain du Tourisme (OCATOUR): rue Roger Guérillot, BP 645, Bangui; tel. 21-61-45-66.

Defence

As assessed at November 2013, the armed forces numbered about 7,150 men (army 7,000 and air force 150). Military service is selective and lasts for two years. There was also a paramilitary gendarmerie with 1,000 members.

Defence Expenditure: Estimated at 25,500m. francs CFA in 2012.

Chief of Staff of the Armed Forces: Gen. FERDINAND BOMBAYAKÉ.

Education

Education is officially compulsory for eight years between six and 14 years of age. Primary education begins at the age of six and lasts for six years. Secondary education begins at the age of 12 and lasts for up to seven years, comprising a first cycle of four years and a second of three years. In 2009/10, according to UNESCO estimates, enrolment at primary schools included 69% of children in the relevant age-group (78% of boys; 59% of girls), while secondary enrolment included only 14% (18% of boys; 10% of girls). In 2011/12 there were some 12,522 students enrolled in tertiary education. The provision of state-funded education was severely disrupted during the 1990s and early 2000s, owing to the inadequacy of financial resources. In 2010 public spending on education was equivalent to 12% of total government expenditure.

CHAD

Introductory Survey

LOCATION, CLIMATE, LANGUAGE, RELIGION, FLAG, CAPITAL

The Republic of Chad is a landlocked country in north central Africa, bordered to the north by Libya, to the south by the Central African Republic, to the west by Niger, Nigeria and Cameroon, and to the east by Sudan. The climate is hot and arid in the northern desert regions of the Sahara but very wet, with annual rainfall of 5,000 mm (197 ins) in the south. The official languages are French and Arabic, and various African languages are also widely spoken. Almost one-half of the population are Muslims, mainly living in the north. About 30% of the population are Christians. Most of the remainder follow animist beliefs. The national flag (proportions 2 by 3) has three equal vertical stripes, of dark blue, yellow and red. The capital is N'Djamena.

CONTEMPORARY POLITICAL HISTORY

Historical Context

Formerly a province of French Equatorial Africa, Chad achieved independence on 11 August 1960, although the sparsely populated northern territory of Borkou-Ennedi-Tibesti, accounting for some 47% of the area of Chad, remained under French military control until 1965. The first President of the independent republic was François (later Ngarta) Tombalbaye, a southerner and leader of the Parti Progressiste Tchadien. The Muslims of northern Chad have historically been in conflict with their southern compatriots, who are mainly Christians or animists. In 1965 a full-scale insurgency began. The banned Front de Libération Nationale du Tchad (FROLINAT, founded in 1966) assumed leadership of the rebellion, which was partially quelled in 1968, following French military intervention.

Several prominent figures in the regime, including Gen. Félix Malloum, the Army Chief of Staff, were imprisoned in 1973 on charges of conspiracy. Following the death of Tombalbaye in a military coup in 1975, Malloum was released and appointed President of a military regime.

In 1973 Libyan troops occupied the so-called 'Aozou strip', a mineral-rich region in northern Chad, over which Libya claimed sovereignty.

Domestic Political Affairs

In early 1978 FROLINAT, with clandestine military assistance from Libya, seized control of a large area of the north before its advance was halted by French military intervention. In August, after negotiations with President Malloum, Hissène Habré, a former FROLINAT leader, was appointed Prime Minister. However, disagreements developed between Habré (a Muslim from the north) and Malloum over the status of Muslims in Chad.

In February 1979 armed conflict broke out between Habré's Forces Armées du Nord (FAN) and the government Forces Armées Tchadiennes (FAT). The FAN took control of the capital, N'Djamena, and in March Malloum resigned and fled the country. A provisional Government was initially formed, comprising representatives of groups including FROLINAT, the FAN and the FAT, and in August 11 factions formed a Gouvernement d'Union Nationale de Transition (Transitional Government of National Unity—GUNT), with Goukouni Oueddei, the FROLINAT leader, as President and Lt-Col (later Gen.) Wadal Abdelkader Kamougué as Vice-President.

Goukouni's authority was undermined by continual disagreements with Habré, and fighting resumed in 1980. Habré was defeated by the end of the year, after Libyan forces intervened direct in support of Goukouni, and a 15,000-strong Libyan force was established in Chad. Libyan troops were withdrawn in late 1981, and a peacekeeping force was installed under the auspices of the Organization of African Unity (OAU—now the African Union—AU, see p. 186). The conflict intensified, however, and in June 1982 Habré's forces captured N'Djamena. Habré was formally inaugurated as President in October.

In August 1983 some 3,000 French troops imposed an 'interdiction line' to separate the warring factions. Although Libya and France agreed to withdraw their troops and by November all French troops had left the country, it was reported that some 3,000 Libyan troops remained. In February 1986 GUNT forces, with Libyan support, attacked government positions south of the interdiction line. Following an appeal by Habré for military assistance, France established a defensive air strike force (Opération Epervier) in N'Djamena, and the GUNT began to disintegrate. Kamougué, who resigned as Vice-President in June, declared his support for Habré in February 1987. Chad and Libya agreed to an OAU-sponsored ceasefire in September, and in October Goukouni declared himself willing to seek a reconciliation with Habré.

Diplomatic relations were resumed between Chad and Libya in October 1988, and the previous year's ceasefire was reaffirmed, although Chad continued to accuse Libya of violating the conditions of the agreement. Negotiations in August 1989 in the Algerian capital resulted in the signing of an outline peace accord, including provision for the withdrawal of all armed forces from the Aozou region and the release of all prisoners of war. The territorial dispute was referred for adjudication by the International Court of Justice (ICJ) in The Hague, Netherlands.

In December 1989 a new Constitution was approved by 99.94% of voters in a national referendum, according to official reports. In endorsing the document, the electorate also approved Habré in the office of President for a further seven-year term. The new Constitution confirmed the Union Nationale pour l'Indépendance et la Révolution as the sole legal party, and provided for the establishment of an elected legislature. Elections to the new Assemblée Nationale (National Assembly) followed in July 1990.

Idriss Deby takes power

In November 1990 the Mouvement Patriotique du Salut (MPS), led by Idriss Deby (later Idriss Deby Itno), a former Commander-in-Chief of the Armed Forces who had left the country following a failed coup attempt the previous year, invaded Chad from Sudan. Habré fled Chad as the MPS advanced rapidly towards N'Djamena. Deby arrived in N'Djamena in early December. The National Assembly was dissolved, the Constitution was suspended, and Deby became interim Head of State. A new Government was appointed, including several members of the former Habré regime. In March 1991 the Government promulgated a National Charter, to operate for a 30-month transitional period, confirming Deby's appointment as President, Head of State and Chairman of the MPS, and establishing a Council of Ministers and a 31-member legislative Conseil de la République (Council of the Republic). France, meanwhile, which had emphasized its policy of non-interference in Chad's internal affairs at the time of the MPS invasion, responded favourably to the new administration, and the Libyan and Sudanese Governments declared their support for the MPS.

The Deby administration established a commission of inquiry to investigate state crimes committed under Habré in 1982–90, including illegal detentions, assassinations, disappearances and torture, as well as drugs-trafficking and embezzlement of state funds. The commission's report, published in 1992, held the Habré regime responsible for, *inter alia*, the political murder of some 40,000 people. The political police of the Documentation and Security Directorate was cited as being particularly responsible for acts of cruelty, contempt and terror; many of the perpetrators identified by the report continued to serve in state institutions and the armed forces under Deby. Habré remained in Senegal, where he had been granted asylum following his overthrow. (For subsequent developments, see Proceedings against Hissène Habré.)

In September 1991 forces loyal to Habré apparently entered Chad from Niger and attacked military garrisons in the north of the country. In the following month disaffected members of the Armée Nationale Tchadienne (ANT—the national army as reconstituted under Deby) attempted to seize power, attacking an arsenal at N'Djamena airport. Several officials, including the Minister of the Interior, were arrested in connection with the coup attempt. France reaffirmed its support for the MPS, and announced that an additional 300 troops would be dispatched to Chad, while Chad abrogated a recent co-operation agreement with Libya. In December some 3,000 pro-Habré rebels of the

Libyan-based Mouvement pour la Démocratie et le Développement (MDD) attacked towns in the Lake Chad region.

In April 1993 a sovereign national conference, convened in January, adopted a Transitional Charter; elected Dr Fidel Moungar, hitherto Minister of National and Higher Education, as Prime Minister; and established a 57-member interim legislature, the Conseil Supérieur de la Transition (Higher Transitional Council—CST). Under the terms of the Transitional Charter, Deby was to remain Head of State and Commander-in-Chief of the Armed Forces for a one-year period (with provision for one extension). Moungar resigned in October 1993, after the CST approved a motion expressing no confidence in his administration. In November the CST elected Nouradine Kassiré Delwa Coumakoye, hitherto Minister of Justice, Keeper of the Seals, as Prime Minister.

In March 1994 an institutional committee submitted constitutional recommendations, including provisions for the introduction of a five-year presidential term, the installation of a bicameral legislature and of a Constitutional Court, and the establishment of a decentralized administrative structure. In April the CST extended the transitional period by one year. A new electoral schedule was adopted, obliging the Government, by June, to adopt an electoral code, establish a national reconciliation council, and appoint electoral and human rights commissions.

In February 1994 the ICJ ruled in favour of Chad in the issue of the sovereignty of the Aozou region. The withdrawal of Libyan troops from the region was completed by May; and in the following month the two countries signed a co-operation agreement.

In September 1994 it was reported that the Minister of Mines and Energy, Lt-Col Mahamat Garfa (who had recently been dismissed as Chief of Army Staff), had fled N'Djamena and joined rebel forces in the east of the country; Garfa, from exile, subsequently established the Alliance Nationale de la Résistance (ANR), incorporating eight rebel groups operative in eastern Chad.

Deby formally announced in November 1994 that the process of democratic transition would conclude on 9 April 1995, following presidential and legislative elections. A general amnesty for political prisoners and opposition members in exile, announced in December 1994, notably excluded Habré. In early 1995 the CST adopted a new electoral code and approved the draft Constitution, which had been amended in accordance with recommendations made by a national conference in August 1994. In March 1995 the CST extended the transitional period for a further year, and amended the National Charter to debar the incumbent Prime Minister from contesting the forthcoming presidential election or from belonging to a political party. In April the CST, which had criticized the Government's lack of progress in organizing democratic elections, voted to remove Coumakoye and elected Djimasta Koibla, a prominent member of the Union pour la Démocratie et la République (UDR), to replace him as Prime Minister.

In November 1995 the Government and the MDD reached agreement on a ceasefire, an exchange of prisoners and the integration of a number of MDD troops into the ANT. In March 1996, following reconciliation talks in Franceville, Gabon, the Chadian Government and 13 opposition groups signed a ceasefire agreement. Although it appeared that the majority of the armed movements rejected its terms, the conclusion of the Franceville accord allowed the electoral programme to proceed. The new Constitution was endorsed by 63.5% of votes cast at a national referendum on 31 March.

Elections under the new Constitution

At the first round of voting in the presidential election, held on 2 June 1996, Deby won 43.9% of the votes cast. He and his closest rival among 14 other candidates, Wadal Abdelkader Kamougué of the Union pour le Renouveau et la Démocratie (URD), who took 12.4% of votes cast, proceeded to a second round of voting on 3 July. Although most of the other first-round candidates urged a boycott of the second round, the third-placed candidate, Saleh Kebzabo of the Union Nationale pour la Démocratie et le Renouveau (UNDR), announced his support for Deby, who won a decisive victory with 69.1% of votes cast. Following Deby's inauguration as President on 8 August, he reappointed Koibla as Prime Minister. The new, interim Council of Ministers included Kebzabo as Minister of Foreign Affairs. In September representatives of the Government and the MDD signed a peace agreement in Niger.

At legislative elections held on 5 January and 23 February 1997, the MPS secured an absolute majority in the 125-member National Assembly, winning 65 seats; Kamougué's URD won 29 seats, and Kebzabo's UNDR 15. In May Kamougué was elected as the President of the new legislature. Nassour Guélendouksia Ouaïdou, hitherto Secretary-General at the Presidency, was appointed as Prime Minister.

Reports emerged from late 1998 of a rebellion in the Tibesti region of northern Chad, led by the Mouvement pour la Démocratie et la Justice au Tchad (MDJT) of Youssouf Togoimi, who had been dismissed as Minister of the Armed Forces in 1997. In June 1999 FROLINAT announced that it was giving political and logistical support to the Tibesti rebellion. In July 2000 the MDJT attacked a garrison in Bardaï and proclaimed its control of four towns in Tibesti. The Prime Minister visited the region and invited the MDJT to take part in peace talks. At a meeting between Togoimi and Deby, in Sirte, Libya, in September, Togoimi proposed multilateral peace discussions, incorporating all opposition groups and Deby's administration. A conference followed later that month at which Deby met with representatives of some 30 organizations (including trade unions, civil society groups and political parties). Despite these contacts, renewed fighting broke out from October between members of the MDJT and government forces in the far north.

Meanwhile, Ouaïdou resigned as Prime Minister in December 1999. He was replaced by Negoum Yamassoum, whose new Government included five UNDR members, among them Kebzabo as Minister of State, Minister of Agriculture. In July 2000 the National Assembly approved proposals for a Commission Electorale Nationale Indépendante (National Independent Election Commission—CENI), which was to plan a reorganization of constituencies in advance of elections due to be held in 2001. An extensive reorganization of the Government in August 2000 followed the dismissal of ministers belonging to the URD, which was opposed to a new electoral code.

In February 2001 it was announced that the presidential election would take place in May, and that legislative elections, initially scheduled for April, would be postponed until 2002 for financial reasons. Local elections were postponed indefinitely, meaning that the establishment of a proposed upper legislative chamber was also deferred, since members of this Sénat (Senate) were to have been selected at local council level.

The 2001 presidential election

The presidential election took place, as scheduled, on 20 May 2001. Although international and national observers pronounced themselves largely satisfied with the conduct of the polls, the six opposition candidates alleged widespread fraud and malpractice. According to the final results, issued by the Constitutional Council in June, Idriss Deby won 63.2% of the valid votes cast, followed by Ngarledjy Yorongar, with 16.4%. A turnout of 61.4% was declared. Negoum Yamassoum was reappointed as Prime Minister following Deby's inauguration in August.

Following Libyan mediation, a peace agreement was signed by the Chadian Government and the MDJT deputy leader, Adoum Togoi Abbo (a former Chadian ambassador to Libya), in January 2002. According to the agreement, both sides would observe an immediate ceasefire and a general amnesty for prisoners. The MDJT was to participate in the Chadian Government and other state institutions, and rebel fighters were to be incorporated within the regular armed forces. However, Youssouf Togoimi did not support the agreement, and, as a split in the rebel group became evident, the MDJT issued a statement in April accusing the Government of inhibiting the peace process by its refusal to postpone the legislative elections in order to allow the appointment of MDJT representatives to the Government.

At the legislative elections, which took place on 21 April 2002, the MPS significantly increased its parliamentary representation, obtaining 110 of 155 seats in the enlarged National Assembly. The Rassemblement pour la Démocratie et le Progrès (RDP) became the second largest party, with 12 seats; and the Fédération Action pour la République (FAR), with nine seats, became the largest opposition party. Coumakoye's VIVA—Rassemblement National pour la Démocratie et le Progrès (VIVA—RNDP) and the UNDR each won five seats, and the URD's representation was significantly reduced, to just three seats. In June Nassour Guélendouksia Ouaïdou was elected as President of the National Assembly, and Deby appointed Haroun Kabadi, a senior MPS official, as Prime Minister.

Meanwhile, in May 2002 it was reported that Togoi was being held in detention by MDJT forces loyal to Togoimi, who had confirmed his rejection of the peace agreement signed in

January. Following the death of Togoimi, in Libya in September, as a result of injuries sustained in a landmine explosion in Chad in the previous month, Deby visited the north in order to encourage a resumption of negotiations between the Government and the MDJT. The leadership of the MDJT was assumed, in an acting capacity, by Adoum Maurice Hel-Bongo, although a split in the organization between pro-Togoi elements and those loyal to Hel-Bongo subsequently became evident.

Towards a peace process

In January 2003, following negotiations in Libreville, Gabon, the Government and the ANR signed a peace memorandum. During the first half of that year reports emerged of the formation of a new grouping of 'politico-military' organizations opposed to the Deby regime, the Front Uni pour la Démocratie et la Paix (FUDP). By July, when Togoi was elected as head of the FUDP, several organizations had announced their affiliation to the grouping, among them the MDD and the pro-Togoi faction of the MDJT. In August, following the resignation of Hel-Bongo, the faction of the MDJT that had remained outside the FUDP elected Col Hassan Abdallah Mardigué as its leader. In September more than 200 MDJT fighters were reported to have surrendered to government forces near Fada, following the signing of a peace accord between the Minister of National Defence, Veterans and Victims of War, Gen. Mahamat Nouri, and a local MDJT commander, although armed clashes continued elsewhere.

In December 2003 the Government signed a peace agreement with Togoi in Ouagadougou, Burkina Faso (where Togoi had been resident since 2000), providing for an immediate ceasefire, an amnesty for MDJT fighters and supporters, and for the eventual inclusion of an undisclosed number of MDJT ministers in the Chadian Government. The terms of the agreement were, however, rejected by hard-line factions of the MDJT.

Meanwhile, in June 2003 a new Council of Ministers was formed, with a close ally of the President, Moussa Faki Mahamat, as Prime Minister. Deby reorganized the Council of Ministers once again in February 2004.

Despite strong protests by the opposition parties, in May 2004 the National Assembly adopted eight constitutional amendments, the most notable of which removed the two-term limit on the presidential mandate. The Constitutional Council rejected a subsequent opposition appeal to annul the revisions. A national referendum proceeded in June 2005, at which, according to official results, 77.8% of voters approved the amendments to the Constitution, with a turnout of some 71% of the registered electorate. The opposition Coordination des Partis Politiques pour la Défense de la Constitution (CPDC), which included the URD, the UNDR and the RDP, denounced the result as fraudulent.

Faki resigned in February 2005; although no official reason for his departure was given, there was speculation that his resignation—which followed a series of strikes by civil servants, teachers and health workers, in protest at unpaid wages—reflected increasing tension between the Government and the President. Deby nominated Pascal Yoadimnadji, hitherto the Minister of Agriculture, as the new Prime Minister, and new ministers responsible for the economy and for education were also appointed. A further reorganization followed in August, with, notably, responsibility for defence affairs being transferred to the Office of the Presidency. In the same month 15 senior army officers were arrested on charges of plotting a coup.

Also in August 2005 Yoadimnadji announced that former members of Hissène Habré's security forces who remained within state organizations would be removed from office and be subject to legal proceedings in connection with alleged human rights abuses under the former regime. The new Prime Minister also stated that the Government intended to introduce legislation that would provide compensation for the victims of torture and their families.

In October 2005 the Chadian authorities stated that at least 40 soldiers had deserted their posts in N'Djamena and had fled to the east of the country. (Opposition sources claimed the number to be as high as 500.) Some of the deserters formed a new 'politico-military' organization, the Socle pour le Changement, l'Unité Nationale et la Démocratie, which at the end of the year was reported to have formed the Front Uni pour le Changement Démocratique (FUCD) in alliance with another recently formed rebel group, the Sudanese-based Rassemblement pour la Démocratie et les Libertés.

In January 2006 the National Assembly voted to approve legislation, introduced by Deby, that extended its mandate by 18 months, apparently because the Government lacked the funding required to hold the legislative elections due in April. In February a presidential election was, none the less, scheduled for 3 May.

In March 2006 it was announced that an attempt to assassinate Deby had been foiled; two senior army officers were arrested, and it was alleged that the attempt had been plotted by several other former senior officers (including several relatives of Deby) who had recently defected to join the FUCD. At the end of the month the Chief of the Land Forces, Gen. Abakar Youssouf Mahamat Itno, was killed in clashes with rebels near the Sudanese border. The FUCD, under the command of Capt. Mahamat Nour Abdelkerim, advanced on N'Djamena, and there was heavy fighting between the rebels and government forces in the capital in mid-April.

Deby re-elected

The presidential election proceeded as scheduled on 3 May 2006, although opposition parties urged a boycott. According to results released by the Constitutional Council some three weeks later, Idriss Deby won a decisive 64.7% of the votes cast, while his nearest rival among the four other candidates, Kassiré Delwa Coumakoye, took 15.1%. The rate of voter participation was recorded at 53.1%.

In July 2006 some 54 political organizations and civil society groups participated in a 'national dialogue', chaired by Prime Minister Pascal Yoadimnadji; however, the meeting was boycotted by the CPDC and the FAR. Deby was sworn in for a third elected term as President in August, and subsequently announced the composition of an enlarged Council of Ministers, retaining Yoadimnadji as Prime Minister. Three candidates who had stood in the presidential election in May—Coumakoye, Pahimi Padacke Albert and Ibrahim Koullamallah—were appointed to ministerial posts.

In December 2006 the Chadian Government and the FUCD, under the de facto leadership of Mahamat Nour Abdelkerim, signed a peace agreement in Tripoli, Libya, providing, *inter alia*, for an immediate cessation of hostilities, the release of all prisoners of war and the integration of FUCD combatants into the Chadian security forces, and the allocation of government posts to representatives of the FUCD within three months. Meanwhile, several hundred people were reported to have been killed in late 2006 after heavy fighting broke out between government troops and two rebel groups: the Union des Forces pour la Démocratie et le Développement (UFDD), led by Mahamat Nouri (the former defence minister), which had been formed following a split in the FUCD; and the Rassemblement des Forces Démocratiques—Convention Nationale Tchadienne (RAFD—CNT).

In February 2007 Yoadimnadji died following a brain haemorrhage while receiving medical treatment in Paris, France. Coumakoye was subsequently appointed to succeed him as Prime Minister. Nour was notably appointed Minister of National Defence within the new Government. In August Deby and representatives of the civilian opposition signed an agreement on a new electoral code. Provision was made for a review of the electoral system, the holding of a new census, updating of the electoral register and the reorganization of the CENI. It was anticipated that legislative elections would take place before the end of 2009.

In October 2007 the Government and four rebel movements, including the UFDD, the Rassemblement des Forces pour le Changement (RFC, as the RAFD—CNT had become) and the Concorde Nationale Tchadienne, concluded a peace agreement in Sirte. The accord established a ceasefire, granted an amnesty to all members of the signatory organizations, and permitted the rebel movements to reconstitute themselves as political parties. The disarmament of rebel movements was scheduled for November, and provision was made for their integration into the Chadian defence forces. However, the ceasefire broke down in that month, following heavy fighting near Abéché between government forces and rebels of the UFDD and the RFC. Nour was subsequently dismissed as Minister of National Defence.

In February 2008 a coalition of anti-Government forces including the UFDD and the RFC, advanced towards N'Djamena from bases in western Sudan, with the intention of overthrowing Deby. Heavy fighting broke out between government and rebel forces, in the course of which both sides claimed control of the capital, but troops loyal to Deby, with the assistance of intelligence and logistical support provided by the French military, succeeded in repelling the rebels.

Deby dismissed Coumakoye in April 2008, appointing Youssouf Saleh Abbas, a former Chadian special representative to the UN and latterly responsible for liaison between the Government and the EUFOR Tchad/RCA mission (see Foreign Affairs—Regional relations), as Prime Minister. Four ministerial posts in the new Government were assigned to members of the CPDC, among them Jean Bawoyeu Alingué and Wadal Abdelkader Kamougué, who assumed the justice and national defence portfolios, respectively. As part of a government reorganization in September, Gata Ngoulou, formerly Secretary-General of the Banque des Etats de l'Afrique Centrale, became Minister of Finance and the Budget.

In December 2008 the eight main rebel movements, meeting in Khartoum, Sudan, agreed a joint political manifesto to overthrow Deby's regime and establish a transitional government. The leader of the RFC, Timane Erdimi (a nephew of Deby), was in January 2009 chosen as the head of the new rebel coalition, the Union des Forces de la Résistance (UFR). There were violent clashes between UFR fighters and government forces in May, after the UFR launched an attack on the south-eastern city of Am-Timan: according to official reports, the fighting resulted in 247 deaths, including 22 within the military, and the UFR deputy chief of staff was among 212 rebels captured. In July three rebel groups of the Mouvement National coalition signed a peace treaty with Deby's Government in Tripoli.

The reconstituted CENI, with 15 representatives of the Government and 15 from the political opposition, was sworn in during mid-2009. Among its tasks in preparing for the planned elections was the compilation of a new voters' register, to be based on that year's census. The CENI announced in January 2010 that legislative elections would take place in November, to be followed by local elections in December. The presidential election was scheduled for April 2011.

Prime Minister Abbas tendered his resignation in March 2010, following allegations of embezzlement involving several government ministers, four of whom had been suspended earlier in the year. Deby appointed Emmanuel Nadingar, hitherto Minister-delegate to the Prime Minister, responsible for Decentralization, to replace Abbas. Nadingar's 40-member Government included 18 new ministers.

The 2011 elections

Following protracted delays in the process of organizing the elections, agreement was reached between the Government and opposition in October 2010 that legislative elections would take place on 6 February 2011, the presidential election on 3 April, and local elections on 26 June. Initiatives proceeded, meanwhile, to reintegrate former rebels into Chadian society. A ceasefire was signed with the MDJT in April 2010 in Tripoli, with an amnesty declared for the group's fighters and the release of prisoners of war; and in commemoration of the 50th anniversary of independence, in January 2011, President Deby announced an amnesty for all prisoners of war.

Following a one-week delay resulting from the removal of the head of the CENI, who was alleged to have tampered with the list of candidates, the legislative elections finally took place on 13 February 2011. According to official results, the parties of the presidential majority (the MPS, the RDP and VIVA—RNDP), grouped in the Alliance pour la Renaissance du Tchad, secured 132 of the 188 seats in the enlarged National Assembly. The UNDR won 11 seats; the Rassemblement National pour la Démocratie au Tchad—le Réveil (RNDT—le Réveil) eight; and an alliance of the URD and the Parti pour les Libertés et le Développement (PLD) eight. A further 19 parties also secured representation. The rate of participation was put at 56.6% of the registered electorate. The Constitutional Court subsequently upheld a number of opposition complaints of irregularities; none the less, international election monitors considered the overall conduct of the elections to have been generally fair and transparent.

The presidential election was postponed by three weeks, after opposition candidates, in March, threatened a boycott, as they considered that certain procedural requirements had not been met. Voting thus took place on 24–25 April 2011, albeit still boycotted by the main opposition figures, including Saleh Kebzabo of the UNDR, Ngarledjy Yorongar of FAR-Parti Fédération, and Kamougué of the URD (who died in the following month). On 10 May 2011 the CENI declared Deby to have won re-election with some 88.7% of votes cast. The other two candidates, RNDT—le Réveil leader Pahimi Padacke Albert and Nadji Madou of Alliance Socialiste pour un Renouveau Intégral, who received 6.0% and 5.3% of the votes respectively, rejected the result. According to official figures, voter turnout was 64.2%. The Constitutional Council subsequently amended the voting figures; however, the margin of Deby's victory, with a revised 83.6% of the votes cast, remained overwhelming.

Recent developments: Deby's fourth elected term

Idriss Deby was sworn in for a fourth term as elected president on 8 August 2011. He subsequently reappointed Emmanuel Nadingar as Prime Minister; and a new Government, which included five members of the RDP and four of VIVA—RNDP, was formed on 17 August. Among the incoming ministers, former presidential chief of staff Bénando Tatola was appointed as Minister-delegate at the Presidency of the Republic, responsible for National Defence and War Veterans, and Christian Georges Diguimbaye, hitherto the head of the Banque Agricole et Commerciale, became Minister of Finance and the Budget. In January 2012 Deby replaced the Minister of Energy and Petroleum, and the Minister of Planning, the Economy and International Co-operation, following the temporary closure of an oil refinery that had been constructed in a joint venture with China National Petroleum Corporation (see Other external relations).

The country's first local elections, which had been repeatedly postponed, were finally conducted on 22 January 2012. According to the official results, announced by the CENI in early February, the MPS won a majority in 12 of the 43 contested municipalities, and, with its allied parties, secured control of most others, including six of N'Djamena's 10 districts. The opposition CPDC alliance succeeded in gaining control of Chad's second largest city, Moundou, in the south of the country. The Supreme Court subsequently upheld most of the election results, following complaints by the CPDC of irregularities, but required that ballots be repeated in two districts of N'Djamena.

In July 2012 the main trade union association, the Union des Syndicats du Tchad (UST), organized strike action to demand wage increases for public sector workers (in accordance with an undertaking made by the Government the previous year). In September, following the intervention of religious leaders, the UST agreed to suspend industrial action to allow negotiations to take place. In that month, however, the President, Vice-President and General Secretary of the UST were charged with inciting racial hatred, after they circulated a petition denouncing President Deby and the Government for mismanagement of the country's resources; all three officials received suspended custodial sentences of 18 months and fines of 1m. francs CFA. A 12-month suspended sentence and fine of 1m. francs CFA was also imposed on Jean-Claude Nekim, the director of *N'Djamena Bi-Hebdo* newspaper, which had published the petition. In October the Government ordered the expulsion of the Roman Catholic bishop of the petroleum-rich southern region of Doba, after a private radio station broadcast a sermon in which he criticized the Government's management of oil revenues. In January 2013 the authorities announced that the bishop was to be permitted to return to the country.

Deby named Joseph Djimrangar Dadnadji as Prime Minister in late January 2013, following the resignation of Emmanuel Nadingar. A government reorganization followed: although most key portfolios remained unchanged, Djerassem Le Bemadjiel was notably appointed Minister of Energy and Petroleum, and Adrien Beyom Mallo, who had been appointed Secretary-General of the MPS in October 2012, became Minister Counsellor at the Presidency of the Republic. Further government changes were made in mid-February 2013, following the dismissal of the ministers responsible for the interior and public security, and for territorial administration and decentralization; in April, when the interior portfolio again changed hands; and in July. Prior to the ministerial changes in February, the head of the national police had been dismissed, and the entire police force suspended, in response to allegations of corruption, favouritism and abuse of office.

In late March 2013 Timan Erdimi, now based in Qatar, announced that the UFR, which had demobilized with the normalization of relations between Chad and Sudan after 2009, intended to relaunch its armed struggle against the Deby regime. Erdimi stated that the Chadian Government had failed to enter into a dialogue with the UFR, as envisaged under the peace agreement with Sudan.

At the beginning of May 2013 it was announced that an attempted coup had been foiled, and there were reports of several deaths after security forces intervened at a gathering of the alleged conspirators in a suburb of N'Djamena. Among figures arrested in late April and early May were: two army generals (one of whom, Weiding Assi Assoué, was a former defence minister and armed forces chief of staff); the governor of Salamat, in south-eastern Chad; four National Assembly deputies; the head of the Chadian journalists' union; and a prominent UFDD figure, Moussa Tao Mahamat, who had rallied to the Deby regime in 2010. The political opposition denounced the arrests as being without foundation: Saleh Kebzabo stated that the Government was acting to weaken the opposition before the legislative and presidential elections due in 2015 and 2016. For its part, the UFR stated that the action to put down an alleged coup was a pretext for a purge of the armed forces.

Meanwhile, a former chief of the Documentation and Security Directorate—or political police—under Habré, Mahamat Djibrine, was reported to have been arrested in mid-May 2013, on suspicion of involvement in torture and politically motivated killings during the 1980s.

An extensive reorganization of the Government took place in mid-October 2013. Notable among 13 incoming ministers in the 41-member administration were Bedoumra Kordjo, latterly a Vice-President at the African Development Bank, as Minister of Finance and the Budget; Abderahim Birene Hamid, formerly President of the Supreme Court, as Minister of the Interior and Public Security; Mariam Mahamat Nour, as Minister of the Economy, Planning and International Co-operation; and Daoussa Deby Itno, the President's older brother, as Minister of Posts and New Information Technologies.

This fifth set of changes to the Government since the appointment of Dadnadji at the beginning of 2013 was among the factors that prompted National Assembly deputies of the presidential majority to table a motion of no confidence in the Prime Minister in mid-November: *inter alia*, Dadnadji was accused of ordering arbitrary arrests of deputies following the revelation of the alleged destabilization plot in May; of responsibility for chronic instability within the Government; of a failure to address high living costs; and of mishandling education reforms. Before the motion could be debated, Dadnadji announced his resignation. Deby immediately named Kalzeubet Pahimi Deubet, an economist who had latterly been head of the state-controlled CotonTchad, as Prime Minister. Another new Government was thus formed in late November, in which Abderahim Bireme Hamid became Minister of Trade and Industry, and was replaced as Minister of the Interior and Public Security by Gen. Mahamat Yaya Oky Dagache (who had been assigned the territorial administration portfolio in October). New appointees included Ahmat Mahamat Acyl, half-brother of the President's wife, as Minister of Secondary Education and Professional Training. Further minor changes to the Council of Ministers were announced in February 2014, and in April a further reorganization was effected, in which Hamid was again allocated responsibility for the public security portfolio (along with that for territorial administration).

Some controversy surrounded the CENI in late 2013. In early November Jean-Pierre Madjirangue Madjibaye was appointed by presidential decree as head of the incoming CENI (now comprising 17 members for the presidential majority, 17 representatives of the political opposition, and six members of civil society). Subsequently, however, the then Prime Minister, Dadnadji, requested that the Cadre National de Dialogue Politique (National Framework for Political Dialogue—CNDR), the cross-party consultative framework responsible for, *inter alia*, designating the head of the CENI, make another nomination since the 'morality' of Madjirangue was considered in doubt. Although the CNDR concluded that there was no impropriety that would invalidate his appointment, members of the presidential majority insisted that Madjirangue be replaced, and in mid-December the previous month's decree nominating all members of the CENI was annulled. A new presidential decree subsequently named Jean-Pierre Royoumbaye Nadoumngar as the new head of the CENI, but his appointment was in turn challenged by the CPDC on the grounds that, as a member of the PLD executive, he was not politically neutral as required by law.

Proceedings against Hissène Habré

In 2000, in response to a criminal complaint made by representatives of victims of crime and political repression under Habré, and following a judicial ruling in Senegal that he could be tried there, Habré was charged with complicity in acts of torture and crimes against humanity committed in Chad under his regime, and was placed under house arrest. However, the charges were subsequently dismissed on appeal, on the grounds that Senegal lacked the appropriate penal procedure to process the case since the crimes were not committed in the country. Senegal's Court of Cassation upheld this ruling in 2001. In response, the plaintiffs announced their intention to seek Habré's extradition to Belgium, where at this time courts were endowed with universal jurisdiction in human rights cases. In September 2005 a Belgian court issued a warrant for Habré's arrest, under legislation that (as amended in 2003) gave that country's courts universal jurisdiction in cases of human rights abuses and war crimes if Belgian citizens or long-term residents were among the plaintiffs: several of the alleged victims of abuses committed under Habré's regime had been granted Belgian citizenship meanwhile. Habré was remanded in custody in Senegal in November by the appeal court investigating the request for extradition, but, on the recommendation of the Senegalese public prosecutor, the court subsequently found that it had no jurisdiction to rule on Habré's extradition; he was released but then rearrested later in November, and it was announced that a decision on which judicial body was competent to rule on Habré's extradition would be taken at a forthcoming summit of AU leaders. At the summit, held in Khartoum in January 2006, it was agreed that Habré should not be extradited to Belgium, and a resolution was approved to establish a Committee of Eminent African Jurists that would consider all aspects of the Habré case, including where his trial might appropriately be held. Accordingly, at the AU summit held in Banjul, The Gambia, in July, Senegal was formally requested to prosecute Habré.

In August 2008 Habré was, *in absentia*, sentenced to death by a Chadian court, along with 11 rebel leaders (among them Gen. Nour Abdelkerim) held responsible for the attack on N'Djamena earlier in the year, having been convicted of plotting to overthrow the Government. The Chadian authorities emphasized that this case was distinct from the process pending before the Senegalese courts.

The envisaged funding requirement that would allow the case against Habré to proceed in Senegal was eventually met at an international donors' conference held in November 2010. In the same month the Community Court of Justice of the Economic Community of West African States (ECOWAS)—at which Habré had challenged Senegal's jurisdiction in his case—ruled that Senegal could not try Habré in its own courts, but could fulfil the AU mandate for his prosecution by hosting an ad hoc international tribunal. In July 2011 the Senegalese Government announced that it intended to extradite Habré to Chad, but the decision was reversed following intervention by the UN High Commissioner for Human Rights, who expressed concern that Habré might be subjected to torture or the death penalty if returned to Chad. In July 2012 the ICJ issued a legally binding ruling, in response to a case first brought by Belgium in February 2009, that Senegal must try Habré without delay or extradite him for trial in Belgium. In August the AU and Senegal signed an agreement whereby a special tribunal mechanism, with African judges to be appointed by the AU, would be established in the Senegalese capital, Dakar, to try Habré. The Senegalese National Assembly approved legislation providing for the creation of this Extraordinary African Chambers in December, and the tribunal began work in February 2013. In May it was announced that the justice ministers of Chad and Senegal had reached an agreement enabling members of the Senegalese judiciary to conduct investigations in the Habré case within Chad. It was anticipated at this time that pre-trial investigations would take about 15 months, and that Habré's trial would commence in late 2014 or early 2015.

Habré was arrested and taken into custody in Dakar at the end of June 2013, and in early July he was formally charged by the Extraordinary African Chambers tribunal with war crimes, crimes against humanity and acts of torture. In November the ECOWAS Court of Justice rejected a petition by Habré's lawyers that the Extraordinary African Chambers was not legitimate, deciding that the tribunal had been established in conformity with the ECOWAS judgment of 2010.

Foreign Affairs

Regional relations

Although Idriss Deby played a major role in promoting diplomatic efforts to restore peace following the outbreak of violence in the Darfur region of western Sudan in 2003 (see Sudan), relations between Chad and Sudan were at times strained in 2004–05. There was, notably, a series of clashes in mid-2004 between Chadian armed forces and Sudan's *Janjaweed* militias, who were pursuing Sudanese rebels across the border into Chad. In late 2005 Deby accused Sudan of complicity in providing arms and logistical support to Chadian rebels; and, following an attack by Chadian rebels on a barracks in eastern Chad, for which Chad held Sudan responsible, Deby stated that he regarded a 'state of belligerence' as existing between the two countries.

In February 2006, with Libyan mediation, Deby and Sudan's President Lt-Gen. Omar Hassan Ahmad al-Bashir signed an agreement whereby, *inter alia*, Chad and Sudan agreed to cease supporting groups hostile to the other. However, following a rebel attack on the Chadian capital in April, Chad announced that it was to sever diplomatic relations with Sudan with immediate effect. The two countries signed a further agreement in July not to host each other's rebel groups on their territory. In August al-Bashir attended Deby's presidential inauguration, and it was announced that Chad and Sudan had restored diplomatic relations and that the border between the two countries would be reopened. There were, however, numerous reports of violent incidents in the border region during late 2006 and early 2007, and in November 2006 both Chad and the Central African Republic (CAR) appealed for UN peacekeeping troops to be deployed in the area. In February 2007, in view of the extreme instability in eastern Chad arising from the presence of large numbers of refugees from Darfur, compounded by the displacement of Chadians by the protracted civil conflict and by the refugee population from the CAR, the UN Secretary-General proposed the deployment of an 11,000-strong UN peacekeeping mission to protect civilians and deter cross-border attacks. However, the Chadian authorities stipulated that they would not accept a military force, and requested that a civil force comprised solely of police officers be deployed to the area. In May, following mediation by King Abdullah of Saudi Arabia, Presidents Deby and al-Bashir agreed to co-operate with the AU and the UN in attempts to stabilize the Chad–Sudan border. Both countries approved the formation of a joint border force, and pledged to cease training and funding rebel groups and to stop all cross-border attacks. In June, furthermore, Deby announced that Chad had agreed in principle to the deployment of a European Union (EU, see p. 273) force along the border with Sudan. In September, following the adoption of UN Resolution 1778, the UN Security Council approved the deployment of the United Nations Mission in the Central African Republic and Chad (MINURCAT), with an initial one-year mandate to protect refugees, displaced persons and civilians adversely affected by the uprising in Darfur. MINURCAT was also to facilitate the provision of humanitarian assistance in eastern Chad and the north-east of the CAR and create favourable conditions for the reconstruction of those areas. The mission was to be supported by a EU bridging military operation (EUFOR Tchad/RCA), which began deployment in February 2008. EUFOR Tchad/RCA completed its mandate in March 2009, whereupon a military component of MINURCAT was deployed to follow up EUFOR operations.

In May 2008 Sudan accused Chad of supporting rebel activity in the Sudanese capital, Khartoum, subsequently recalling its ambassador from N'Djamena. With AU mediation, the two countries agreed in July to resume diplomatic relations, and in November both countries' ambassadors took up their posts again. In May 2009 Sudan and Chad signed a bilateral agreement in Doha, Qatar, to normalize relations and end support within their borders of rebel groups hostile to the other country. Shortly after the accord was finalized, however, the Chadian Government accused Sudan of involvement in the UFR attack on Am-Timan (see Domestic Political Affairs—Deby re-elected). In retaliation, Chad carried out air raids along the common border and some 40 km into Sudanese territory. In February 2010, following a visit by Deby to Khartoum, Sudan and Chad agreed to end proxy wars and work together to rebuild border regions. In January, meanwhile, the Chadian Government requested that MINURCAT withdraw from Chad by mid-March. Following negotiations between Chad and the UN Secretariat, the terms of a revised mandate were adopted by the UN Security Council (Resolution 1923) in May, extending the MINURCAT mandate to the end of the year; meanwhile, the Chadian Government was to assume full responsibility for the security and the protection of the civilian population in eastern Chad. At August 2013, with the arrival of more than new 30,000 refugees from West Darfur since the beginning of the year, the office of the UN High Commissioner for Refugees put the number of Sudanese refugees in Chad at 348,528.

In December 2011 the International Criminal Court (ICC) announced that Chad, as a party to the Court's founding statute, had not met its obligation to co-operate with the ICC by failing to arrest and surrender al-Bashir when he visited the country (to attend Deby's inauguration) in August. (The Sudanese President, against whom the ICC had issued arrest warrants in 2009 and 2010, had also travelled to Chad in July 2010.)

Following the assumption of power in the CAR by François Bozizé Yangouvonda in March 2003, Chadian troops were reportedly dispatched to the CAR in his support. (Chad had granted Bozizé refuge following a coup attempt in 2001.) Chadian personnel were subsequently integrated into a force deployed by the Communauté Economique et Monétaire de l'Afrique Centrale (CEMAC) from late 2002 to monitor joint patrols of the Chad–CAR border. However, sporadic unrest in the north-east of the CAR continued. In December 2010, following the withdrawal of MINURCAT (see above), it was announced that Chadian troops had assisted the CAR army in repelling rebel attacks on the border between the two countries. At a summit meeting held in Khartoum in May 2011 between Presidents Deby, Bozizé and al-Bashir, it was agreed to establish a tripartite force to address border security issues, and to encourage the voluntary return of refugees. In September 2012 Abdel Kader Baba Laddé, the leader of a Chadian rebel movement active in the CAR border region, the Front Populaire pour le Redressement (FPR), surrendered to the CAR authorities and was subsequently returned to Chad. In December Chadian troops were again dispatched to the CAR, as part of the Central African Multinational Force (FOMAC), to provide support to the Bozizé regime against rebel forces. However, following the seizure of power in the CAR by the rebel Seleka alliance, the deposed Bozizé accused Chadian special forces of assisting the rebels. Although Chad denied Bozizé's assertion, the country was generally considered to have played a decisive role in the change of regime in the CAR. The renewed escalation of insecurity in the CAR prompted further refugee flows into Chad: by August, according to UNHCR, the number of refugees from the CAR exceeded 74,000; and at January 2014, following the escalation of inter-religious fighting in the CAR at the end of 2013, UNHCR put the refugee population at 80,364. In December 2013, meanwhile, six Chadian members of FOMAC were killed in violence in the CAR capital, Bangui. As part of FOMAC, Chadian forces were incorporated within the African-led International Support Mission in the Central African Republic (MISCA), deployment of which was authorized by the UN Security Council in that month. In January 2014 the UN High Commissioner for Human Rights, reporting on abuses of human rights documented in the CAR in late 2013, stated that, *inter alia*, multiple testimonies had been received identifying some ex-Seleka perpetrators as being Chadian nationals, and that credible testimonies had also been received of collusion between some Chadian elements of FOMAC and ex-Seleka forces. Meanwhile, there was speculation that Deby's action to replace the commander of the Chadian FOMAC contingent, Col Djibril Oumar, with Gen. Ousman Bahr Itno (a nephew of the President) at the time of FOMAC's incorporation within MISCA reflected an effort to address the complexities caused by close ties between Chadian and Seleka elements. Chad, which had hosted extraordinary summit meetings of the Communauté Economique des Etats de l'Afrique Centrale (CEEAC) in April 2013 to facilitate the transition in the CAR, again hosted a CEEAC summit, in January 2014, at which the Seleka leader, Michel Am Nondroko Djotodia, resigned as interim President of the CAR.

Following French military intervention against the Islamist insurgency in Mali in January 2013, Chad committed some 2,000 troops to northern Mali to assist French and Malian government forces there. Chadian forces were considered to be particularly well adapted to conduct counter-insurgency operations in the remote desert and mountain terrain of the far north of Mali. At the beginning of March Chad announced that its soldiers in Mali had killed two senior figures of al-Qa'ida in the Islamic Maghreb (AQIM). Although Chad is not a member of ECOWAS, which had deployed the African-led International Support Mission to Mali (AFISMA) in January, the Chadian contingent was incorporated within AFISMA in March. In April, by which time at least 30 members of the Chadian force were understood to have been killed in the Malian intervention, Chad announced that, having accomplished its mission there, it was to withdraw its troops from northern Mali. Chad did, however, contribute military personnel and police to the UN Multidimensional Integrated Stabilization Mission in Mali (MINUSMA), which took over authority from AFISMA with effect from July.

Other external relations

France, which maintained a 950-strong deployment in the country at mid-2013, is considered to have a particular interest in a politically stable Chad, as exemplified by French support in repelling the rebel attempt on N'Djamena in early 2008 (see Domestic Political Affairs—Deby re-elected). Deby has, for his part, in recent years sought to position himself as a key ally, and as a potential power-broker and guarantor of regional stability, as France has realigned its external policy. Chad's contribution to counter-insurgency operations in Mali in early 2013 (see above) apparently underlined its significance as a partner to France, although there was some speculation that the French Government's ability to influence matters such as guarantees of human rights in Chad had been restricted by the importance of Chad's role in the intervention.

In 2006 the People's Republic of China announced that it had resumed diplomatic relations with Chad, after bilateral ties between Chad and Taiwan were severed. China thereafter made further substantial investments in Chadian infrastructure projects. In 2009, notably, China National Petroleum Corporation (CNPC) began work on a pipeline to transport crude petroleum from the southern Koudalwa field to the Djarmaya oil refinery under construction north of N'Djamena. The Djarmaya refinery, operated by CNPC, was inaugurated in mid-2011. However, the Chadian Government temporarily closed the refinery for three weeks in early 2012, in response to a dispute with CNPC over fuel pricing. Furthermore, the Government suspended all operations in Chad by CNPC in August–October 2013, having found violations of environmental standards at Koudalwa.

Chad began a two-year term as one of the five non-permanent members of the UN Security Council in January 2014.

CONSTITUTION AND GOVERNMENT

Under the terms of the 1996 Constitution, as subsequently amended, the Republic of Chad is a unitary state with a multiparty political system. Executive power is vested in the President, elected by direct universal suffrage, who is the Head of State and Commander-in-Chief of the Armed Forces. The President appoints the Prime Minister, who nominates the Council of Ministers. Legislative power is vested in a unicameral legislature, the 188-member Assemblée Nationale (National Assembly), which is elected by direct universal suffrage for a four-year term. Constitutional amendments approved by referendum in 2005 removed the restriction limiting the President to serving two five-year terms of office and abolished the Sénat (Senate) as the upper legislative house.

REGIONAL AND INTERNATIONAL CO-OPERATION

Chad is a member of the African Union (see p. 186), the Central African organs of the Franc Zone (see p. 329) and of the Communauté Economique des Etats de l'Afrique Centrale (CEEAC, see p. 450); the Lake Chad Basin Commission (see p. 452) is based in N'Djamena.

Chad became a member of the UN in 1960, and was admitted to the World Trade Organization (WTO, see p. 434) in 1996.

ECONOMIC AFFAIRS

In 2012, according to estimates by the World Bank, Chad's gross national income (GNI), measured at average 2010–12 prices, was US $9,268m., equivalent to $740 per head (or $1,320 on an international purchasing-power parity basis). During 2003–12, it was estimated, the population increased at an average annual rate of 3.3%, while gross domestic product (GDP) per head increased, in real terms, by an average of 3.8% per year. Overall GDP expanded, in real terms, at an average annual rate of 7.2% in 2003–12, according to the World Bank. GDP increased by 5.0% in 2012.

Agriculture contributed 16.3% of GDP in 2012, according to the African Development Bank (AfDB); some 61.0% of the labour force were employed in the sector in mid-2014, according to estimates by FAO. The principal cash crop is cotton (exports of which contributed 0.1% of total export revenue in 2012, a decline from 41.1% in 2001). The principal subsistence crops are sorghum, millet, cassava, maize and rice. Livestock-rearing also makes an important contribution to the domestic food supply. According to the World Bank, during 2000–08 agricultural GDP increased at an average annual rate of 3.1%. According to AfDB estimates, agricultural GDP declined by 6.6% in 2011, but increased by 3.7 in 2012.

Industry (including mining) contributed 41.5% of GDP in 2012, according to the AfDB. About 4.2% of the population were employed in the sector in 1990. According to the World Bank, during 2000–08 industrial GDP increased at an average annual rate of 23.7%; it increased by 144.5% in 2004, largely owing to the revenues from petroleum extraction (see below), but grew by just 5.0% in 2005, before declining by 3.7% in 2006 and by 13.6% in 2007. The sector underwent a strong recovery in 2008, registering growth of 13.9% in that year.

The mining sector contributed 27.8% of GDP in 2012, according to the AfDB. Petroleum contributed an estimated 74.2% of total revenue (excluding grants) in 2012. For many years the only minerals exploited were natron (sodium carbonate), salt, alluvial gold and materials for the construction industry. However, long-delayed plans to develop sizeable petroleum reserves in the Doba Basin and at Sedigi, in the south of the country, were pursued in the early 2000s, and the production of petroleum at Doba commenced in mid-2003. Some 100,000 barrels per day (b/d) of oil are transported by pipeline from Doba to the port of Kribi in Cameroon. There is believed to be considerable potential for the further exploitation of gold, bauxite and uranium. During 1998–2005 the GDP of the mining sector (including fishing) increased at an average annual rate of 4.3%, according to the IMF; growth of 6.8% was recorded in 2005. According to AfDB estimates, mining GDP increased by 2.7% in 2012.

According to the AfDB, the manufacturing sector (including handicrafts) contributed 6.1% of GDP in 2012. The sector operates mainly in the south of the country, and is dominated by agro-industrial activities, notably the processing of the cotton crop by the state-controlled Société Cotonnière du Tchad (CotonTchad). Chad's first oil refinery, operated by China National Petroleum Corporation (CNPC), began production in 2011. During 1998–2005 manufacturing GDP increased at an average annual rate of 0.9%, according to the IMF. The GDP of the sector increased by 6.9% in 2012, according to AfDB estimates.

Construction contributed 7.0% of GDP in 2012, according to AfDB estimates. The sector grew by 5.0% in 2012.

Chad has historically been heavily dependent on imports of mineral fuels (principally from Cameroon and Nigeria) for the generation of electricity. The use of wood-based fuel products by most households has contributed to the severe depletion of Chad's forest resources. By 2011 only 9.1% of Chad's total land area was forested. In 2002 only 2% of households in Chad had access to electricity.

Services contributed 42.2% of GDP in 2012, according to the AfDB. The GDP of the sector increased at an average annual rate of 8.3% in 2000–08; growth in 2008 was 6.5%.

According to the IMF, in 2012 Chad's preliminary merchandise trade surplus was 671,000m. francs CFA, but there was a preliminary deficit of 93,000m. francs CFA on the current account of the balance of payments. In 2011 Chad's principal source of imports (providing 14.5% of the total) was France; other major suppliers were Cameroon and the USA. In 2011 the principal market for exports was the USA (75.2%), followed by the People's Republic of China and France. The principal exports in 2012 were petroleum and livestock. The principal imports in 2011 were metal working machinery, and natural and manufactured gas.

In 2012, according to the IMF, Chad's projected budgetary deficit was 137,000m. francs CFA. Chad's general government gross debt was 1,830,070m. francs CFA in 2012, equivalent to 27.8% of GDP. Chad's external debt at the end of 2011 totalled US $1,821m., of which $1,710m. was public and publicly guaranteed debt. In 2009, the cost of servicing long-term public and publicly guaranteed debt and repayments to the IMF was equivalent to 4.1% of the value of exports of goods, services and income (excluding workers' remittances). According to the IMF, consumer prices increased at an average annual rate of 3.7% in 2005–12; they declined by 4.9% in 2011, but rose by 15.8% in 2012.

Despite the overall economic expansion arising from the commercial exploitation of Chad's petroleum resources after 2003, development has been impeded by factors including: the country's landlocked position; a relative lack of economic diversification and infrastructural development hitherto; its vulnerability to adverse climatic conditions and to external factors such as fluctuations in international commodity prices; the impact of long-term political instability; and the presence of large numbers of refugees from conflicts, particularly in Sudan and the Central African Republic (CAR). Chad was ranked 184th of 187 countries assessed in 2012 for the UN Development Programme's (UNDP) 2013 Human Development Index. A National Development Plan (NDP), adopted in May 2013, was intended to build on efforts made under two previous poverty reduction strategies implemented in 2003–06 and 2008–11, and aimed to achieve more inclusive economic growth and poverty reduction: a joint assessment of the NDP by the IMF and the International Development Association in mid-2013 noted that the rate of poverty reduction in 2003–11 had been exceeded by the rate of population growth. Priorities under the NDP were to include job creation and human capital development, environmental protection and efforts to counter the negative impact of climate change, and measures to promote good governance. Consistent with the NDP, in September 2013 the Chadian Government and UNDP inaugurated a three-year, US $1,000m. programme to counter food insecurity and enhance progress towards achievement of the country's Millennium Development Goals. The IMF approved a Staff-Monitored Programme (SMP) for Chad in July of that year, covering the period April–December, with a view to facilitating subsequent discussion of a new programme of support under its Extended Credit Facility. In a review under the SMP, conducted in December, the IMF estimated real GDP growth of 3.6% for that year, as agricultural production reverted to normal levels (after an exceptionally strong harvest in 2012) and oil output slowed as a result of technical difficulties at established fields and delays in the entry into production of new projects. Oil revenues were expected to be significantly lower than originally budgeted for 2013, while the overall fiscal deficit was projected to increase to 6.1% of non-oil GDP. Average inflation for the year was projected to decline to 0.4%, reflecting lower food prices. Real GDP growth of 10.8% was forecast for 2014, as new oilfields entered production in the Lake Chad region: Chad's finance minister stated in September 2013 that oil output could increase to 200,000 b/d in 2014 (from 110,000 b/d in 2012) and to 300,000 b/d by 2015. None the less, the IMF emphasized the need for Chad to diversify its economy in order to broaden its revenue base, not least in view of a projected eventual slowing of oil income, with priority to be given to promoting productivity and job creation in the agricultural sector in order to reduce rural poverty. Meanwhile, the Government suspended all operations in Chad by China National Petroleum Corporation in August–October 2013, having found violations of environmental standards at its operation at Koudalwa, in southern Chad; an environmental audit of all oil projects was subsequently commissioned. In March 2013 the UN announced that some $4.9m. was to be allocated from its Central Emergency Response Fund (CERF) in support of operations in Chad to assist refugees from the conflicts in Sudan and the CAR, as well as Chadian returnees from Sudan and Libya. In January 2014 it was announced that a further $10m. was to be allocated from the CERF to support relief operations in Chad.

PUBLIC HOLIDAYS

2015: 1 January (New Year), 2 January*† (Maloud, Birth of the Prophet), 6 April (Easter Monday), 1 May (Labour Day), 24 May (Whit Monday), 25 May ('Liberation of Africa', anniversary of the OAU's foundation), 17 July* (Id al-Fitr, end of Ramadan), 11 August (Independence Day), 15 August (Assumption), 23 September* (Id al-Adha, Feast of the Sacrifice), 1 November (All Saints' Day), 28 November (Proclamation of the Republic), 1 December (Liberation and Democracy Day, anniversary of the 1990 coup), 23 December*† (Maloud, Birth of the Prophet), 25 December (Christmas).

* These holidays are dependent on the Islamic lunar calendar and may vary by one or two days from the dates given.

† This festival occurs twice (in the Islamic years AH 1436 and 1437) within the same Gregorian year.

Statistical Survey

Source (unless otherwise stated): Institut national de la statistique, des études economiques et démographiques, BP 453, N'Djamena; tel. 22-52-31-64; fax 22-52-66-13; e-mail inseed@intnet.td; internet www.inseed-tchad.org.

Area and Population

AREA, POPULATION AND DENSITY

Area (sq km)	
Land	1,259,200
Inland waters	24,800
Total	1,284,000*
Population (census result)	
8 April 1993	6,279,931
20 May–30 June 2009†	
Males	5,509,522
Females	5,666,393
Total	11,175,915
Population (UN estimates at mid-year)‡	
2012	12,448,174
2013	12,825,315
2014	13,211,147
Density (per sq km) at mid-2014	10.3

* 495,800 sq miles.

† Figures are provisional.

‡ Source: UN, *World Population Prospects: The 2012 Revision*.

POPULATION BY AGE AND SEX

(UN estimates at mid-2014)

	Males	Females	Total
0–14	3,206,415	3,151,245	6,357,660
15–64	3,265,868	3,273,187	6,539,055
65 and over	144,892	169,540	314,432
Total	6,617,175	6,593,972	13,211,147

Source: UN, *World Population Prospects: The 2012 Revision*.

ETHNIC GROUPS

1995 (percentages): Sara, Bongo and Baguirmi 20.1; Chadic 17.7; Arab 14.3; M'Bourn 6.3; Masalit, Maba and Mimi 6.1; Tama 6.1; Adamawa 6.0; Sudanese 6.0; Mubi 4.1; Hausa 2.1; Kanori 2.1; Massa 2.1; Kotoko 2.0; Peul 0.5; Others 4.5 (Source: La Francophonie).

REGIONS

(2009 census, preliminary figures)

Barh El Gazel	260,865	Mayo-Kebbi Est	769,178
Batha	527,031	Mayo-Kebbi Ouest	565,087
Borkou	97,251	Moyen-Chari	598,284
Chari-Baguirmi	621,785	N'Djamena	993,492
Ennedi	173,606	Ouaddaï	731,679
Guéra	553,795	Salamat	308,605
Hadjer-Lamis	562,957	Sila	289,776
Kanem	354,603	Tandjilé	682,817
Lac	451,369	Tibesti	21,970
Logone Occidental	683,293	Wadi Fira	494,933
Logone Oriental	796,453		
Mandoul	637,086	**Total**	11,175,915

PRINCIPAL TOWNS

(population at 1993 census)

N'Djamena (capital)	530,965	Koumra	26,702
Moundou	99,530	Pala	26,115
Sarh	75,496	Am-Timan	21,269
Abéché	54,628	Bongor	20,448
Kelo	31,319	Mongo	20,443

Mid-2011 (incl. suburbs, UN estimate): N'Djamena 1,078,640 (Source: UN, *World Urbanization Prospects: The 2011 Revision*).

BIRTHS AND DEATHS
(annual averages, UN estimates)

	1995–2000	2000–05	2005–10
Birth rate (per 1,000)	51.3	50.4	48.7
Death rate (per 1,000)	18.5	17.8	16.4

2001 (preliminary): Live births 397,896; Deaths 138,025.

Sources: UN, *World Population Prospects: The 2012 Revision* and *Population and Vital Statistics Report*.

Life expectancy (years at birth): 50.2 (males 49.4; females 51.1) in 2011 (Source: World Bank, World Development Indicators database).

ECONOMICALLY ACTIVE POPULATION
('000 persons at mid-1990, ILO estimates)

	Males	Females	Total
Agriculture, hunting, forestry and fishing	1,179	1,102	2,281
Industry	105	9	115
Manufacturing	50	6	56
Services	245	100	344
Total labour force	1,529	1,211	2,740

Source: ILO.

1993 census (persons aged six years and over): Total employed 2,305,961; Unemployed 16,268; Total labour force 2,322,229.

Mid-2014 ('000, estimates): Agriculture, etc. 3,097; Total labour force 5,074 (Source: FAO).

Health and Welfare

KEY INDICATORS

Total fertility rate (children per woman, 2011)	5.9
Under-5 mortality rate (per 1,000 live births, 2011)	169
HIV/AIDS (% of persons aged 15–49, 2010)	3.1
Physicians (per 1,000 head, 2006)	0.04
Hospital beds (per 1,000 head, 2005)	0.40
Health expenditure (2010): US $ per head (PPP)	60
Health expenditure (2010): % of GDP	4.0
Health expenditure (2010): public (% of total)	25.0
Access to water (% of persons, 2011)	50
Access to sanitation (% of persons, 2011)	12
Total carbon dioxide emissions ('000 metric tons, 2010)	469.4
Carbon dioxide emissions per head (metric tons, 2010)	<0.1
Human Development Index (2012): ranking	184
Human Development Index (2012): value	0.340

For sources and definitions, see explanatory note on p. vi.

Agriculture

PRINCIPAL CROPS
('000 metric tons)

	2010	2011	2012
Rice, paddy	170.0*	172.6†	180.0*
Maize*	200.0	195.0	200.0
Millet	600.0*	319.0†	924.0†
Sorghum	680.0*	648.0†	1,200.0†
Potatoes*	50	50	52
Sweet potatoes*	88	85	90
Cassava (Manioc)*	231	230	240
Taro (Coco yam)*	26	26	27
Yams*	415	400	420
Sugar cane*	380	390	380
Beans, dry*	73	70	71
Groundnuts, with shell†	400	414	371
Sesame seed†	37	37	39
Melonseed*	21	21	21
Onions, dry*	18	19	20
Dates*	19	20	20
Guavas, mangoes and mangosteens*	33	33	35

* FAO estimate(s).
† Unofficial figure(s).

Aggregate production ('000 metric tons, may include official, semi-official or estimated data): Total cereals 2,150 in 2010, 1,553 in 2011, 3,467 in 2012; Total pulses 122 in 2010, 122 in 2011, 126 in 2012; Total roots and tubers 810 in 2010, 791 in 2011, 829 in 2012; Total vegetables (incl. melons) 99 in 2010, 104 in 2011, 107 in 2012; Total fruits (excl. melons) 118 in 2010, 120 in 2011, 123 in 2012.

Source: FAO.

LIVESTOCK
('000 head, year ending September, FAO estimates)

	2010	2011	2012
Cattle	7,419	7,650	7,800
Goats	6,700	6,750	6,780
Sheep	3,027	3,100	3,150
Pigs	30	32	33
Horses	420	426	432
Asses	460	468	476
Camels	1,400	1,435	1,450
Chickens	5,550	5,600	5,680

Source: FAO.

LIVESTOCK PRODUCTS
('000 metric tons, FAO estimates)

	2010	2011	2012
Cattle meat	94.8	97.2	98.0
Sheep meat	15.4	15.7	15.8
Goat meat	25.2	25.8	26.4
Cows' milk	195.6	198.5	199.0
Sheep's milk	13.1	13.5	13.6
Goats' milk	39.8	39.8	40.0
Hen eggs	4.0	4.0	4.0

Source: FAO.

Forestry

ROUNDWOOD REMOVALS

('000 cubic metres, excl. bark, FAO estimates)

	2010	2011	2012
Sawlogs, veneer logs and logs for sleepers*	14	14	14
Other industrial wood†	747	747	747
Fuel wood	7,070	7,184	7,300
Total	7,831	7,945	8,061

* Output assumed to be unchanged since 1993.
† Output assumed to be unchanged since 1999.

Source: FAO.

SAWNWOOD PRODUCTION

('000 cubic metres, incl. railway sleepers)

	1994	1995	1996
Total (all broadleaved)	2.4*	2.4	2.4

* FAO estimate.

1997–2012: Annual production as in 1996 (FAO estimates).

Source: FAO.

Fishing

('000 metric tons, live weight, FAO estimates)

	2009	2010	2011
Total catch (freshwater fishes)	40.0	50.0	60.0

Source: FAO.

Mining

	2010	2011	2012
Crude petroleum ('000 metric tons)	6,403	5,971	5,309

Source: BP, *Statistical Review of World Energy*.

Industry

SELECTED PRODUCTS

	2002	2003	2004
Sugar (centrifugal, raw, '000 metric tons)	23.1	38.0	40.0
Beer ('000 metric tons)	12.4	11.0	8.4
Cigarettes (million packs)	36.0	37.0	40.0
Electric energy (million kWh)	106.6	86.0	84.0

Source: IMF, *Chad: Selected Issues and Statistical Appendix* (January 2007).

Oil of groundnuts ('000 metric tons): 36.0 in 2010; 38.3 in 2011; 33.2 in 2012 (unofficial figure). Source: FAO.

Raw sugar ('000 metric tons): 35.0 in 2007; 36.0 in 2008; 40.0 in 2009. Source: UN Industrial Commodities Statistics Database.

Electric energy (million kWh): 150.0 in 2008; 183.0 in 2009; 200.0 in 2010. Source: UN Industrial Commodities Statistics Database.

Finance

CURRENCY AND EXCHANGE RATES

Monetary Units

100 centimes = 1 franc de la Coopération Financière en Afrique Centrale (CFA).

Sterling, Dollar and Euro Equivalents (31 December 2013)

£1 sterling = 783.286 francs CFA;
US $1 = 475.641 francs CFA;
€1 = 655.957 francs CFA;
10,000 francs CFA = £12.77 = $21.02 = €15.24.

Average Exchange Rate (francs CFA per US $)

2011 471.866
2012 510.527
2013 494.040

Note: An exchange rate of 1 French franc = 50 francs CFA, established in 1948, remained in force until January 1994, when the CFA franc was devalued by 50%, with the exchange rate adjusted to 1 French franc = 100 francs CFA. This relationship to French currency remained in effect with the introduction of the euro on 1 January 1999. From that date, accordingly, a fixed exchange rate of €1 = 655.957 francs CFA has been in operation.

BUDGET

('000 million francs CFA)

Revenue	2011	2012*	2013†
Petroleum revenue	1,017	1,020	821
Non-petroleum revenue	314	335	403
Tax revenue	296	309	378
Non-tax revenue	18	27	25
Total	1,331	1,375	1,224

Expenditure	2011	2012*	2013†
Current expenditure	736	726	822
Wages and salaries	250	283	343
Goods and services	87	123	128
Transfers	364	123	315
Interest	35	28	36
External	10	12	18
Investment expenditure	548	787	679
Domestically financed	416	543	492
Foreign financed	132	243	187
Total	1,284	1,512	1,501

* Preliminary.
† Programmed.

Source: IMF, *Chad: Staff-Monitored Program* (September 2013).

INTERNATIONAL RESERVES

(US $ million at 31 December)

	2010	2011	2012
Gold*	6.19	17.01	18.73
IMF special drawing rights	4.20	0.09	0.08
Reserve position in IMF	0.43	4.50	4.51
Foreign exchange	627.77	946.51	1,151.07
Total	638.59	968.11	1,174.39

* Valued at market-related prices.

Source: IMF, *International Financial Statistics*.

MONEY SUPPLY

('000 million francs CFA at 31 December)

	2011	2012
Currency outside depository corporations	373.54	400.74
Transferable deposits	258.89	326.00
Other deposits	58.90	57.55
Broad money	691.33	784.28

Source: IMF, *International Financial Statistics*.

COST OF LIVING
(Consumer Price Index for African households in N'Djamena; base: 2005 = 100)

	2010	2011	2012
All items	116.8	111.1	128.6

Source: IMF, *International Financial Statistics*.

NATIONAL ACCOUNTS
('000 million francs CFA)

Expenditure on the Gross Domestic Product

	2010	2011	2012
Government final consumption expenditure	1,193	1,128	1,231
Private final consumption expenditure	3,089	3,402	3,654
Gross fixed capital formation	1,373	1,527	1,577
Change in inventories	179	–141	–67
Total domestic expenditure	5,834	5,916	6,395
Exports of goods and services	1,875	2,382	2,148
Less Imports of goods and services	2,447	2,424	2,349
GDP in purchasers' values	5,263	5,875	6,194

Gross Domestic Product by Economic Activity

	2010	2011	2012
Agriculture	999	929	988
Mining and quarrying	1,335	1,746	1,686
Electricity, gas and water	21	24	35
Manufacturing	304	320	367
Construction	361	398	425
Wholesale and retail trade, restaurants and hotels	982	1,053	1,123
Finance, insurance, real estate, etc.	677	725	824
Transport and communications	73	84	97
Public administration and defence	421	475	510
Less Imputed bank service charge.	25	28	32
GDP at factor cost	5,148	5,726	6,023
Indirect taxes	115	149	171
GDP in purchasers' values	5,263	5,875	6,194

Source: African Development Bank.

BALANCE OF PAYMENTS
('000 million francs CFA)

	2010	2011*	2012†
Exports of goods f.o.b.	1,752	2,032	2,145
Imports of goods f.o.b.	–1,183	–1,272	–1,474
Trade balance	569	760	671
Services (net)	–923	–928	–894
Balance on goods and services	–354	–168	–223
Factor income (net)	–176	–148	–346
Balance on goods, services and income	–530	–316	–569
Private unrequited transfers (net)	294	251	456
Official unrequited transfers (net)	22	17	20
Current balance	–213	–48	–93
Capital transfers	59	85	164
Foreign direct investment	155	133	103
Other medium- and long-term investments	65	99	33
Short-term capital (incl. errors and omissions)	–60	–100	–159
Overall balance	5	169	48

* Estimates.
† Preliminary.

Source: IMF, *Chad: Staff-Monitored Program* (September 2013).

External Trade

PRINCIPAL COMMODITIES
(US $ million)

Imports	2009	2010	2011
Metal working machinery	214	230	210
Natural and manufactured gas	134	171	194
Office machines and automatic data processing machines	124	169	110
Non-ferrous metals	162	134	110
Transport equipment	118	108	99
Total (incl. others)	2,835	3,347	3,251

2012: Total imports 2,992.

Exports	2010	2011	2012
Livestock (mostly cattle)	253	272	258
Crude petroleum	3,222	3,947	3,721
Gum arabic	18	24	23
Cotton	32	70	52
Total (incl. others)	3,713	4,540	4,294

Source: African Development Bank.

PRINCIPAL TRADING PARTNERS
(US $ million)

Imports	2009	2010	2011
Cameroon	216	244	269
France	449	458	471
Germany	98	99	97
Portugal	112	114	121
USA	248	268	241
Total (incl. others)	2,835	3,347	3,251

Exports	2009	2010	2011
China	89	588	290
France	130	57	228
United Kingdom	12	15	16
USA	2,442	2,498	3,415
Total (incl. others)	2,891	3,713	4,540

2012: Total imports 2,992; Total exports 4,294.

Source: African Development Bank.

Transport

ROAD TRAFFIC
(motor vehicles in use at 31 December)

	1994	1995*	1996*
Passenger cars	8,720	9,700	10,560
Buses and coaches	708	760	820
Lorries and vans	12,650	13,720	14,550
Tractors	1,413	1,500	1,580
Motorcycles and mopeds	1,855	2,730	3,640

* Estimates.

Source: IRF, *World Road Statistics*.

2006: Passenger cars 18,867; Vans 24,874; Buses 3,278; Tractors 3,132; Motorcycles 63,036 (Source: Ministère de Travaux Publics et de Transport).

CIVIL AVIATION
(traffic on scheduled services*)

	1999	2000	2001
Kilometres flown (million)	3	3	1
Passengers carried ('000)	84	77	46
Passenger-km (million)	235	216	130
Total ton-km (million)	36	32	19

* Including an apportionment of the traffic of Air Afrique.

Source: UN, *Statistical Yearbook*.

Tourism

FOREIGN VISITORS BY NATIONALITY*

	2008	2009	2010
Belgium	491	335	198
Canada	42	512	230
Egypt	23	190	30
France	6,142	6,564	5,843
Germany	298	285	243
Italy	421	484	224
Libya	12	827	7
Saudi Arabia	1	—	22
Switzerland	216	36	99
United Kingdom	607	518	281
USA	1,699	2,579	1,081
Total (incl. others)	21,871	31,169	14,298

* Arrivals at hotels and similar establishments.

Receipts from tourism (US $ million, incl. passenger transport): 14 in 2000; 23 in 2001; 25 in 2002.

Source: World Tourism Organization.

Communications Media

	2010	2011	2012
Telephones ('000 main lines in use)	51.2	31.2	29.9
Mobile cellular telephones ('000 subscribers)	2,875.3	3,665.7	4,198.6
Broadband subscribers	331	15,799	19,454

Internet subscribers: 4,600 in 2009.

Source: International Telecommunication Union.

Education

(2011/12 unless otherwise indicated)

	Institutions	Teachers	Students		
			Males	Females	Total
Pre-primary	24*	543	9,935	9,164	19,099
Primary	2,660†	34,125	1,194,940	895,818	2,090,758
Secondary	n.a.	15,384	315,454	142,580	458,034
Tertiary‡	n.a.	2,239	19,690	4,659	24,349

* 1994/95 figure; public institutions only.
† 1995/96.
‡ 2010/11.

Source: mainly UNESCO Institute for Statistics.

Pupil-teacher ratio (primary education, UNESCO estimate): 61.3 in 2011/12 (Source: UNESCO Institute for Statistics).

Adult literacy rate (UNESCO estimates): 35.4% (males 45.6%; females 25.4%) in 2011 (Source: UNESCO Institute for Statistics).

Directory

The Government

HEAD OF STATE

President: Gen. IDRISS DEBY ITNO (assumed office 4 December 1990; elected President 3 July 1996; re-elected 20 May 2001, 3 May 2006 and 25 April 2011).

COUNCIL OF MINISTERS
(April 2014)

Prime Minister: KALZEUBÉ PAHIMI DEUBET.

Minister of Foreign Affairs and African Integration: MOUSSA FAKI MAHAMAT.

Minister of Territorial Administration and Public Security: ABDERAHIM BIREME HAMID.

Minister of Finance and the Budget: BEDOUMRA KORDJE.

Minister-delegate at the Presidency of the Republic, responsible for National Defence and War Veterans: BÉNAINDO TATOLA.

Minister of Infrastructure, Transport and Civil Aviation: ADOUM YOUNOUSMI.

Minister of Justice and Human Rights: BÉCHIR MADET.

Minister of Planning and International Co-operation: MARIAM MAHAMAT NOUR.

Minister of Posts and New Information and Communication Technology: DAOUSSA DEBY ITNO.

Minister of Public Health, Social Action and National Solidarity: Dr NGARIERA RIMADJITA.

Minister of Agriculture and the Environment: BAÎWONG DJIBERGUI AMANE ROSINE.

Minister of Stockbreeding and Water Supply: ISSA ALI TAHER.

Minister of Communication, Government Spokesperson: HASSAN SILLA BAKARI.

Minister of Petroleum, Mines and Energy: DJERASSEM LE BEMADJIEL.

Minister of Land Management, Town Planning and Housing: GATA NGOULOU.

Minister of Public Sanitation and the Promotion of Good Governance: ABDERAMAN SALLAH.

Minister of Higher Education and Scientific Research: Prof. MACKAYE HASSANE TAÎSSO.

Minister of the Economy, Trade and Tourism Development: AZIZ MAHAMAT SALEH.

Minister of National Education: AHMAT MAHAMAT ACYL.

Minister of Culture, Youth and Sport: ABDOULAYE NGARDIGUINA.

Minister of the Civil Service, Labour and Employment: ABDERAMANE MOUCTAR MAHAMAT.

Minister, Secretary-General of the Government, in charge of Relations with the National Assembly: ABDOULAYE SABRE FADOUL.

Secretary of State for External Relations, responsible for Chadians Abroad: KASSIRE ISABELLE HOUSNA.

Secretary of State for Finance and the Budget, responsible for Microfinance: BANATA TCHALET SOW.

Secretary of State for Public Health, Social Action and National Solidarity: ASSANE NGUEADOUM.

Secretary of State, responsible for Civil Aviation and Meteorology: HAOUA ACYL.

Secretary of State for National Education: ALBATOUL ZAKARIA.

Deputy Secretary-General of the Government: AMINA KODJIYANA.

MINISTRIES

Office of the President: Palais rose, BP 74, N'Djamena; tel. 22-51-44-37; fax 22-52-45-01; internet www.presidencetchad.org.

Office of the Prime Minister: BP 463, N'Djamena; tel. 22-52-63-39; fax 22-52-69-77; e-mail cpcprimt@intnet.td; internet www.gouvernementdutchad.org.

Ministry of Agriculture and Irrigation: BP 441, N'Djamena; tel. 22-52-65-66; fax 22-52-51-19; e-mail conacils@intnet.td; internet www.minagri-tchad.org.

Ministry of the Civil Service, Labour and Employment: BP 637, N'Djamena; tel. and fax 22-52-21-98; internet minfpt-tchad.org.

Ministry of Communication: BP 892, N'Djamena; tel. 22-52-40-97; fax 22-52-65-60.

Ministry of Culture, the Arts and the Preservation of National Heritage: BP 519, N'Djamena; tel. 22-52-26-58.

Ministry of the Economy, Planning and International Co-operation: N'Djamena; tel. 22-51-45-87; fax 22-51-51-85; e-mail spee@intnet.td; internet www.mepci.org.

Ministry of Energy and Petroleum: BP 816, N'Djamena; tel. 22-52-56-03; fax 22-52-36-66; e-mail mme@intnet.td; internet www.ministere-petrole.td.

Ministry of the Environment and Fisheries: BP 905, N'Djamena; tel. 22-52-60-12; fax 22-52-38-39; e-mail facdrem@intnet.td.

Ministry of External Relations and African Integration: BP 746, N'Djamena; tel. 22-51-80-50; fax 22-51-45-85; e-mail tchaddiplomatie@gmail.com; internet www.tchad-diplomatie.org.

Ministry of Finance and the Budget: BP 816, N'Djamena; tel. 22-52-68-61; fax 22-52-49-08; e-mail d.dette@intnet.td.

Ministry of Higher Education, and Scientific Research: BP 743, N'Djamena; tel. 22-51-61-58; fax 22-51-92-31.

Ministry of Human Rights and the Promotion of Fundamental Liberties: N'Djamena.

Ministry of Infrastructure and Transport: Route de Farcha, Chari Baguirmi, N'Djamena; tel. 22-52-20-96; fax 22-52-21-05; e-mail secretariat@mcie-tchad.com; internet mcie-tchad.com.

Ministry of the Interior and Public Security: BP 916, N'Djamena; tel. 22-52-05-76.

Ministry of Justice: BP 426, N'Djamena; tel. 22-52-21-72; fax 22-52-21-39; e-mail justice@intnet.td.

Ministry of Microfinance for the Promotion of Women and Youth: N'Djamena.

Ministry of Mines and Geology: BP 816, N'Djamena; tel. 22-51-83-06; fax 22-52-75-60; e-mail cons.mines@intnet.td.

Ministry of National Defence and War Veterans: BP 916, N'Djamena; tel. 22-52-35-13; fax 22-52-65-44.

Ministry of Pastoral Development and Animal Production: BP 750, N'Djamena; tel. 22-52-89-43.

Ministry of Posts and New Information Technology: BP 154, N'Djamena; tel. 22-52-15-79; fax 22-52-15-30; e-mail ahmatgamar1@yahoo.fr.

Ministry of Primary Education and Literacy: BP 743, N'Djamena; tel. 22-51-92-65; fax 22-51-45-12.

Ministry of Public Health: BP 440, N'Djamena; tel. 22-51-51-14; fax 22-51-58-00; internet www.sante-tchad.org.

Ministry of Public Sanitation and the Promotion of Good Governance: N'Djamena.

Ministry of Secondary Education and Professional Training: N'Djamena.

Ministry of Social Action, Families and National Solidarity: BP 80, N'Djamena; tel. 22-52-25-32; fax 22-52-48-88.

Ministry of Territorial Administration, Decentralization and Local Freedom: Niamey.

Ministry of Tourism and the Promotion of Handicrafts: BP 86, N'Djamena; tel. 22-52-44-21; fax 22-52-51-19.

Ministry of Town Planning, Housing, Land Affairs and State Property: N'Djamena.

Ministry of Trade and Industry: Palais du Gouvernement, BP 424, N'Djamena; tel. 22-52-21-99; fax 22-52-27-33; e-mail mdjca-dg@intnet.td.

Ministry of Urban and Rural Water Supply: N'Djamena.

Ministry of Youth and Sports: BP 519, N'Djamena; tel. 22-52-52-90; fax 22-52-55-38.

President

Election, 24–25 April 2011

Candidate	Votes	% of vote
Idriss Deby Itno (MPS)	2,072,481	83.59
Pahimi Padacke Albert (RNDT—le Réveil)	213,257	8.60
Nadji Madou (ASRI)	193,617	7.81
Total	2,479,355	100.00

Legislature

National Assembly: Palais du 15 janvier, BP 01, N'Djamena; tel. 22-53-08-25; fax 22-31-45-90; internet www.primature-tchad.org/ass.php.

President: HAROUN KABADI.

General Election, 13 February 2011

Party	Seats
Alliance pour la Renaissance du Tchad (ART)*	132
Union Nationale pour le Développement et le Renouveau (UNDR)	11
Rassemblement National pour la Démocratie au Tchad—le Réveil	8
Union pour le Renouveau et la Démocratie-Parti pour la Liberté et le Développement (URD-PLD)	8
Fédération Action pour la République-Parti Fédération (FAR-PF)	4
Convention Tchadienne pour la Paix et le Développement (CTPD)	2
Parti Démocratique et Socialiste pour l'Alternance (PDSA)	2
Union pour la Démocratie et la République (UDR)	2
Others†	15
Total	184‡

* Comprising the Mouvement Patriotique du Salut, the Rassemblement pour la Démocratie et le Progrès and VIVA—Rassemblement National pour la Démocratie et le Progrès.

† A total of 15 other parties all secured one seat each.

‡ Results in the Mayo-Boneye constituency, which was to return four deputies, were not declared by the Commission Electorale Nationale Indépendante.

Election Commission

Commission Electorale Nationale Indépendante (CENI): N'Djamena; f. 2000; 41 mems; Pres. JEAN-PIERRE ROYOUMBAYE NADOUMNGAR.

Political Organizations

Legislation permitting the operation of political associations, subject to official registration, took effect in October 1991. A total of 101 political organizations contested the 2011 legislative elections, of which the following were among the most important:

Action Tchadienne pour l'Unité et le Socialisme (ACTUS): N'Djamena; e-mail actus@club-internet.fr; f. 1981; Marxist-Leninist; Sec.-Gen. Dr DJIMADOUM LEY-NGARDIGAL.

Alliance Nationale pour la Démocratie et le Développement (ANDD): BP 4066, N'Djamena; tel. 22-51-46-72; f. 1992; Leader SALIBOU GARBA.

Alliance Socialiste pour un Renouveau Intégral (ASRI): tel. 66-28-74-10; e-mail info@asritchad.org; internet www.asritchad.org; Pres. NADJI MADOU.

Alliance Tchadienne pour la Démocratie et le Développement (ATD): N'Djamena; e-mail info@atd-tchad.com; Leader ABDERAMAN DJASNABAILLE.

Concorde Nationale Tchadienne (CNT): Leader Col HASSANE SALEH AL GADAM AL JINEDI.

Convention pour la Démocratie et le Fédéralisme: N'Djamena; f. 2002; socialist; supports the establishment of a federal state; Leader ALI GOLHOR.

Convention Tchadienne pour la Paix et le Développement (CTPD).

Coordination des Partis Politiques pour la Défense de la Constitution (CPDC): f. 2004 to oppose President Deby's proposed constitutional modifications; mems include the URD and the UNDR.

Fédération Action pour la République-Parti Fédération (FAR-PF): BP 4197, N'Djamena; tel. 66-26-89-67 (mobile); fax 22-51-78-60; e-mail yorongar@gmail.com; internet www.yorongar.com; supports the establishment of a federal republic; Leader NGARLEDJY YORONGAR.

Front pour le Salut de la République (FSR): f. 2007 to unite opposition groups in attempt to oust Pres. Deby Itno; member of the Mouvement National Coalition; Pres. Col AHMAT HASSABALLAH SOUBIANE.

Mouvement Patriotique du Salut (MPS): Assemblée nationale, Palais du 15 janvier, BP 01, N'Djamena; e-mail administrateur@

tchad-gpmps.org; internet www.tchad-gpmps.org; f. 1990 as a coalition of several opposition movements; other opposition groups joined during the Nov. 1990 offensive against the regime of Hissène Habré, and following the movement's accession to power in Dec. 1990; Pres. D'IDRISS NDELE MOUSSA; Sec.-Gen. ADRIEN BEYOM MALLO.

Parti Africain pour la Paix et la Justice Sociale (PAP/JS): quartier Abena, N'Djamena; tel. 66-27-09-74; Pres. VALENTIN NÉATOBEI BIDI.

Parti Démocratique et Socialiste pour l'Alternance (PDSA): Pres. MALLOUM YOBOÏDE DJEKARI.

Parti pour les Libertés et le Développement (PLD): N'Djamena; internet www.pldtchad.org; f. 1993; Sec.-Gen. JEAN BAPTISTE LAOKOLÉ.

Rassemblement pour la Démocratie et le Progrès (RDP): N'Djamena; f. 1992; seeks to create a secure political environment by the establishment of a reformed national army; supported the reelection of Pres. Deby in 2001, but withdrew support from the Govt in Nov. 2003; Leader LOL MAHAMAT CHOUA.

Rassemblement National pour la Démocratie au Tchad—le Réveil: Leader ALBERT PAHIMI PADACKE.

Union Nationale pour la Démocratie et le Renouveau (UNDR): N'Djamena; supports greater decentralization and increased limitations on the power of the state; Pres. SALEH KEBZABO; Sec.-Gen. CÉLESTIN TOPONA.

Union pour le Renouveau et la Démocratie (URD): BP 92, N'Djamena; tel. 22-51-44-23; fax 22-51-41-87; f. 1992; Leader (vacant).

VIVA—Rassemblement National pour la Démocratie et le Progrès (VIVA—RNDP): N'Djamena; f. 1992; supports a unitary, democratic republic; Pres. KASSIRÉ DELWA COUMAKOYE.

A number of unregistered dissident groups (some based abroad) are also active. In 2010 these organizations, largely 'politico-military', included the following:

Alliance Nationale de la Résistance (ANR): f. 1996 as alliance of five movements; in early 2003 comprised eight rebel groups based in eastern Chad; signed peace agreement with Govt in Jan. 2003, although FONALT rejected this accord; Leader MAHAMAT ABBO SILECK.

Armée Nationale Tchadienne en Dissidence (ANTD): f. 1994; Leader Col MAHAMAT GARFA.

Forces des Organisations Nationales pour l'Alternance et les Libertés au Tchad (FONALT): rejected ceasefire signed by ANR with Govt in Jan. 2003; Leader Col ABDOULAYE ISSAKA SARWA.

Coordination des Mouvements Armés et Partis Politiques de l'Opposition (CMAP): f. 1999 by 13 'politico-military' orgs; a number of groups subsequently left, several of which later joined the FUDP; Leader ANTOINE BANGUI.

Front Extérieur pour la Rénovation: Leader ANTOINE BANGUI.

Front de Libération Nationale du Tchad—Conseil Provisoire de la Révolution (FROLINAT—CPR): f. 1968 in Sudan; based in Algeria; Leader GOUKOUNI OUEDDEI.

Front Uni pour le Changement Démocratique (FUCD): f. 2005; signed a peace agreement with the Govt in Dec. 2006; Leader Capt. MAHAMAT NOUR ABDELKERIM.

Rassemblement pour la Démocratie et les Libertés (RDL): f. 2005 in eastern Chad; Leader Capt. MAHAMAT NOUR ABDELKERIM.

Socle pour le Changement, l'Unité Nationale et la Démocratie (SCUD): f. 2005 in eastern Chad; Leaders TOM ERDIMI, YAYA DILLO DJÉROU.

Front Uni pour la Démocratie et la Paix (FUDP): f. 2003 in Benin; seeks by all possible means to establish a new constitution and a transitional govt in advance of free and transparent elections; faction of MDJT led by Adoum Togoi Abbo claims membership, but this is rejected by principal faction of MDJT; Pres. Brig.-Gen. ADOUM TOGOI ABBO.

Conseil National de Redressement du Tchad (CNR): e-mail admin@cnrdutchad.com; internet www.cnrdutchad.com; leadership of group forced to leave Benin for Togo in mid-2003; Pres. Col ABBAS KOTY YACOUB.

Convention Populaire de Résistance (CPR): e-mail cpr60@voila.fr; f. 2001 by fmr mems of CNR; Leader ABDEL-AZIZ ABDALLAH KODOK.

Front National du Tchad Renové (FNTR): Dabo, France; e-mail yasaid2001@yahoo.fr; f. 1996; publishes monthly bulletin, *Al-Widha*, in French and Arabic; Hon. Pres. MAHAMAT CHARFADINE; Sec.-Gen. SALAHADINE MAHADI.

Mouvement Nationale des Rénovateurs Tchadiens (MNRT): e-mail fpls@romandie.com; democratic opposition in exile; Sec.-Gen. ALI MUHAMMAD DIALLO.

Rassemblement des Forces pour le Changement (RFC): internet www.rfctchad.com; f. 2006 as Rassemblement des Forces Démocratiques; Pres. TIMANE ERDIMI.

Union des Forces pour le Changement (UFC): f. 2004; advocates suspension of the 1996 Constitution and the composition of a new Charter of the Republic to develop national unity, free elections and the rule of law; National Co-ordinator ACHEIKH IBN OUMAR.

Conseil Démocratique Révolutionnaire (CDR): Leader ACHEIKH IBN OUMAR.

Front Démocratique Populaire (FDP): Leader Dr MAHAMOUT NAHOR.

Front Populaire pour la Renaissance Nationale: Leader ADOUM YACOUB KOUKOU.

Mouvement pour la Démocratie et le Développement (MDD): e-mail mdd@mdd-tchad.com; internet membres.lycos.fr/mddtchad; comprises two factions, led by ISSA FAKI MAHAMAT and BRAHIM MALLAH.

Mouvement pour la Démocratie et la Justice au Tchad (MDJT): based in Tibesti, northern Chad; e-mail admin@mdjt.net; internet www.mdjt.net; fmr deputy leader, Brig.-Gen. ADOUM TOGOI ABBO, signed a peace agreement with Govt in Jan. 2002, although this was subsequently rejected by elements close to fmr leader, YOUSSOUF TOGOIMI (who died in Sept. 2002); split into two factions in 2003; the faction led by Togoi claimed membership of the FUDP and signed a peace agreement with the Govt in Dec. 2003, which was rejected by the faction led by Chair. Col HASSAN ABDALLAH MARDIGUÉ; announced a proposed merger with FROLINAT—CPR in December 2006.

Mouvement pour l'Unité et la République (MUR): f. 2000 by faction of the MDD; Pres. HASSAN DADJOULA.

Union des Forces pour la Démocratie et le Développement (UFDD): f. 2006; Leader Gen. MAHAMAT NOURI.

Union des Forces pour la Démocratie et le Développement—Fondamentale (UFDD—F): Leader ABDELWAHID ABOUD MAKAYE.

Diplomatic Representation

EMBASSIES IN CHAD

Algeria: BP 178, rue de Paris, N'Djamena; tel. 22-52-38-15; fax 22-52-37-92; e-mail amb.algerie@intnet.td; Ambassador NADJIB MAHDI.

Cameroon: rue des Poids Lourds, BP 58, N'Djamena; tel. 22-52-28-94; Ambassador BAH OUMAROU SANDA.

Central African Republic: rue 1036, près du Rond-Point de la Garde, BP 115, N'Djamena; tel. 22-52-32-06; Ambassador LAZARE YAGAO NGAMA.

China, People's Republic: rue 1021, 1er arrondissement, BP 735, N'Djamena; tel. 22-52-29-49; fax 22-53-00-45; internet td.china-embassy.org; Ambassador HU ZHIQIANG.

Congo, Democratic Republic: ave du 20 août, BP 910, N'Djamena; tel. 22-52-21-83.

Egypt: Quartier Clemat, ave Georges Pompidou, auprès rond-point de la SONASUT, BP 1094, N'Djamena; tel. 22-51-09-73; fax 22-51-09-72; e-mail am.egypte@intnet.td; Ambassador NABIH ABDELMADJID AL DAÏROUTI.

France: rue du Lt Franjoux, BP 431, N'Djamena; tel. 22-52-25-75; fax 22-52-28-55; e-mail amba.france@intnet.td; internet www.ambafrance-td.org; Ambassador EVELYNE DECORPS.

Holy See: rue de Béguinage, BP 490, N'Djamena; tel. 22-52-31-15; fax 22-52-38-27; e-mail nonceapo@intnet.td; Apostolic Nuncio Archbishop FRANCO COPPOLA (Titular Archbishop of Vinda).

Korea, Democratic People's Republic: N'Djamena; Ambassador KIM PYONG GI.

Libya: BP 1096, N'Djamena; tel. 22-51-92-89; e-mail alibya1@intnet.td; Ambassador GRÈNE SALEH GRÈNE.

Nigeria: 35 ave Charles de Gaulle, BP 752, N'Djamena; tel. 22-52-24-98; fax 22-52-30-92; e-mail nigndjam@intnet.td; Ambassador GARBA ABDU ZAKARI.

Qatar: N'Djamena; tel. 22-52-41-41; fax 22-52-50-50; e-mail ndjamena@mofa.gov.qa; Ambassador HAMAD ABDULHADI SAEED AL-HAJRI.

Russia: 2 rue Adjutant Collin, BP 891, N'Djamena; tel. 22-51-57-19; fax 22-51-31-72; e-mail amrus@intnet.td; Ambassador VLADIMIR N. MARTYNOV.

Saudi Arabia: BP 974, N'Djamena; tel. 22-52-36-96; fax 22-52-33-28; e-mail tdemb@mofa.gov.sa; internet embassies.mofa.gov.sa/sites/chad; Ambassador FAISAL AL-MANDEEL.

South Africa: Quartier Mardjan Daffac, 1124 rue 3035, ave Gaourang, BP 1243, N'Djamena; tel. 22-52-22-09; fax 22-52-22-59; e-mail ndjamena@foreign.gov.za; Ambassador DAYANAND NAIDOO.

Sudan: rue de la Gendarmerie, BP 45, N'Djamena; tel. 22-52-43-59; e-mail amb.soudan@intnet.td; Ambassador ABDALLAH AL-SHEIKH.

USA: ave Félix Eboué, BP 413, N'Djamena; tel. 22-51-70-09; fax 22-51-56-54; e-mail YingraD@state.gov; internet chad.usembassy.gov; Ambassador JAMES KNIGHT.

Judicial System

The highest judicial authority is the Supreme Court, which comprises a Judicial Chamber, an Administrative Chamber and an Audit Chamber. There is also a Constitutional Council, with final jurisdiction in matters of state. The legal structure also comprises the Courts of Appeal, and magistrate and criminal courts. A High Court of Justice, which is competent to try the President or members of the Government in cases of treason, embezzlement of public funds, and certain other crimes and offences, was inaugurated in June 2003.

Supreme Court: rue 0221, Quartier Résidentiel, 1er arrondissement, BP 5495, N'Djamena; tel. 22-52-01-99; fax 22-52-51-81; e-mail ccsrp@intnet.td; internet www.coursupreme-tchad.org; Pres. SAMIR ADAM ANNOUR; Pres. of the Judicial Chamber BELKOULAYE BEN COUMAREAUX; Pres. of the Administrative Chamber OUSMAME SALAH IDJEMI; Pres. of the Audit Chamber DOLOTAN NOUDJALBAYE; Prosecutor-Gen. AHMAT AGREY.

Constitutional Council: BP 5500, N'Djamena; tel. 22-52-03-41; e-mail conseil.sg@intnet.td; Pres. HOUDEÏNGAR DAVID NGARIMADEN; Sec.-Gen. DARKEM JOSEPH.

Courts of Appeal: N'Djamena: Pres. MADJITANGUE TRAHOGRA; Moundou: Pres. HASSANE MAHAMAT HASSANE KHAYAR; Abéché: Pres. AHMAT NGABO.

High Court of Justice: BP 1407, N'Djamena; tel. 22-52-33-54; fax 22-52-35-35; e-mail dchcj@intnet.td; f. 2003; comprises 15 deputies of the Assemblée nationale, of whom 10 are titular judges and five supplementaries, who serve in the absence of a titular judge. All 15 are elected for the term of four years by their peers; Pres. LOUM ELISE NDOADOUMNGUÉ.

Religion

It is estimated that some 54% of the population are Muslims and about 34% Christians. Most of the remainder follow animist beliefs.

ISLAM

Conseil Suprême des Affaires Islamiques: POB 1101, N'Djamena; tel. 22-51-81-80; fax 22-52-58-84; Pres. CHEIKH HISSEIN HASSAN ABAKAR.

CHRISTIANITY

The Roman Catholic Church

Chad comprises one archdiocese, six dioceses and one apostolic vicariate. Approximately 20% of the total population are Roman Catholics, most of whom reside in the south of the country and in N'Djamena.

Bishops' Conference: Conférence Episcopale du Tchad, BP 456, N'Djamena; tel. 22-51-74-44; fax 22-52-50-51; e-mail cetchad@yahoo.fr; f. 1991; Pres. Most Rev. JEAN-CLAUDE BOUCHARD (Bishop of Pala).

Archbishop of N'Djamena: (vacant), Archevêché, BP 456, N'Djamena; tel. 22-51-74-44; fax 22-52-50-51; e-mail archnja@intnet.td.

Protestant Churches

Approximately 14% of the total population are Protestants.

Entente des Eglises et Missions Evangéliques au Tchad (EEMET): BP 2006, N'Djamena; tel. 22-51-53-93; fax 22-51-87-20; e-mail eemet@intnet.td; f. 1964; asscn of churches and missions working in Chad; includes Assemblées Chrétiennes au Tchad (ACT), Assemblées de Dieu au Tchad (ADT), Eglise Evangélique des Frères au Tchad (EEFT), Eglise Evangélique au Tchad (EET), Eglise Fraternelle Luthérienne au Tchad (EFLT), Eglise Evangélique en Afrique Centrale au Tchad (EEACT), Eglise Evangélique Missionnaire au Tchad (EEMT); also five assoc. mems: Union des Jeunes Chrétiens (UJC), Groupe Biblique des Hôpitaux au Tchad (GBHT), Mission Evangélique contre la Lèpre (MECL), Croix Bleue du Tchad (CBT); Sec.-Gen. SOUINA POTIFAR.

BAHÁ'Í FAITH

National Spiritual Assembly: BP 181, N'Djamena; tel. 22-51-47-05; e-mail ntirandaz@aol.com.

The Press

Audy Magazine: BP 780, N'Djamena; tel. 22-51-49-59; f. 2000; 2 a month; women's interest; Dir TONGRONGOU AGOUNA GRÂCE.

Bulletin Mensuel de Statistiques du Tchad: BP 453, N'Djamena; monthly.

Carrefour: Centre al-Mouna, BP 456, N'Djamena; tel. 22-51-42-54; e-mail almouna@intnet.td; f. 2000; every 2 months; Dir Sister NADIA KARAKI; circ. 1,000 (2001).

Da'kouna: N'Djamena; tel. 66-66-66-71; fax 22-51-46-71; e-mail dakounajournal@yahoo.fr; internet www.dakounajournal.org; monthly.

Grenier: BP 1128, N'Djamena; tel. 22-53-30-14; e-mail cedesep@intnet.td; monthly; economics; finance; Dir KOHOM NGAR-ONE DAVID.

Info-Tchad: BP 670, N'Djamena; tel. 22-51-58-67; news bulletin issued by Agence-Info Tchad; daily; French.

La Lettre: BP 2037, N'Djamena; tel. and fax 22-51-91-09; e-mail ltdh@intnet.td; f. 1993; monthly; publ. by the Ligue Tchadienne des Droits de l'Homme; Dir DOBIAN ASSINGAR.

N'Djamena Bi-Hebdo: BP 4498, N'Djamena; tel. 22-51-53-14; fax 22-52-14-98; e-mail ndjh@intnet.td; internet www.ndjh.org; f. 1989; 2 a week; Arabic and French; Dir YALDET BÉGOTO OULATAR; Editor-in-Chief DIEUDONNÉ DJONABAYE; circ. 3,000 (2010).

Notre Temps: BP 4352, N'Djamena; tel. and fax 22-51-46-50; e-mail ntemps.presse@yahoo.fr; f. 2000; weekly; opposed to the Govt of Pres. Deby Itno; Editorial Dir NADJIKIMO BENOUDJITA; circ. 3,000 (2010).

L'Observateur: BP 2031, N'Djamena; tel. and fax 22-51-80-05; e-mail observer.presse@intnet.td; f. 1997; weekly; Dir NGARADOUMBE SAMBORY; circ. 4,000 (2010).

Le Progrès: 1976 ave Charles de Gaulle, BP 3055, N'Djamena; tel. 22-51-55-86; fax 22-51-02-56; e-mail progres@intnet.td; f. 1993; daily; Dir MAHAMAT HISSÈNE; circ. 3,000 (2010).

Revue Juridique Tchadienne: BP 907, N'Djamena; internet www.cefod.org/Droit_au_Tchad/Revuejuridique/Sommaire_rjt.htm; f. 1999; Dir MAHAMAT SALEH BEN BIANG.

Tchad et Culture: BP 907, N'Djamena; tel. 22-51-54-32; fax 22-51-91-50; e-mail cefod@intnet.td; internet www.cefod.org; f. 1961; monthly; Dir RONELNGUÉ TORIAÏRA; Editor-in-Chief NAYGOTIMTI BAMBÉ; circ. 4,500 (2002).

Le Temps: face Ecole Belle-vue, Moursal, BP 1333, N'Djamena; tel. 22-51-70-28; fax 22-51-99-24; e-mail temps.presse@intnet.td; f. 1995; weekly; Publishing Dir MICHAËL N. DIDAMA; circ. 4,000 (2010).

La Voix: N'Djamena; weekly; circ. 5,000 (2010).

La Voix du Paysan: BP 1671, N'Djamena; tel. 22-51-82-66; monthly; Dir DJALDI TABDI GASSISSOU NASSER.

NEWS AGENCY

Agence Tchadienne de Presse: BP 670, N'Djamena; tel. 22-52-58-67; fax 22-52-37-74; e-mail atp@infotchad.com; internet www.infotchad.com; f. 1966; Dir HASSAN ABDELKERIM BOUYEBRI.

Publishers

Grande Imprimerie du Tchad: route de Farcha, BP 691, N'Djamena; tel. 22-52-51-59.

Imprimerie AGB: ave Ornano, BP 2052, N'Djamena; tel. 22-51-21-67; e-mail agb@intnet.td.

Imprimerie du Tchad (IDT): BP 456, N'Djamena; tel. 22-52-44-40; fax 22-52-28-60; e-mail idt.tchad@intnet.td; Gen. Dir D. E. MAURIN.

Broadcasting and Communications

TELECOMMUNICATIONS

In 2011 there was one fixed-line telephone and three mobile cellular telephone operators in Chad.

Société des Télécommunications du Tchad (SOTEL TCHAD): BP 1132, N'Djamena; tel. 22-52-14-36; fax 22-52-14-42; e-mail sotel@intnet.td; internet www.sotel.td; f. 2000 by merger of telecommunications services of fmr Office National des Postes et des Télécommunications and the Société des Télécommunications Internationales du Tchad; state-owned; 80% to be privatized; Dir-Gen. ADAM ABDERAMANE ANOU.

Salam: N'Djamena; wholly owned subsidiary of SOTEL TCHAD providing mobile cellular telephone services.

Airtel au Tchad: ave Charles de Gaulle, BP 5665, N'Djamena; tel. 22-52-04-18; fax 22-52-04-19; e-mail info.africa@airtel.com; internet africa.airtel.com/chad; f. 2000; acquired by Bharti Airtel (India) in

2010; fmrly Celtel-Tchad, subsequently Zain au Tchad, present name adopted in 2010; Dir-Gen. MBAYE SYLLA KHOUMA.

Millicom Tchad: N'Djamena; internet www.millicom.com; f. 2005; 87% owned by Millicom International Cellular (Luxembourg/Sweden); operates mobile cellular telecommunications network in N'Djamena (with expansion to other cities proposed) under the brand name 'Tigo'.

Regulatory Authority

Office Tchadien de Regulation des Telecommunications: BP 5808, N'Djamena; tel. 22-52-15-13; fax 22-52-15-15; e-mail otrt@intnet.td; internet www.otrt.td; Dir-Gen. IDRISS SALEH BACHAR.

BROADCASTING

Regulatory Authorities

High Council of Communication (HCC): BP 1316, N'Djamena; tel. 22-52-36-00; fax 22-52-31-51; e-mail hcc@intnet.td; f. 1994; responsible for registration and regulation of radio and television stations, in addition to the printed press; funds independent radio stations; Sec.-Gen. ADOUM GUEMESSOU.

Office National de Radiodiffusion et de Télévision du Tchad (ONRTV): ave Mobotu, N'Djamena; tel. 22-52-15-13; fax 22-52-15-17; internet www.onrtv.org; f. 2006; Dir-Gen. DOUBAÏ KLEPTOUIN.

Radio

Private radio stations have been permitted to operate in Chad since 1994, although private broadcasts did not begin until 1997. By mid-2002 15 private and community stations had received licences, of which nine had commenced broadcasts. There was, additionally, a state-owned broadcaster, with four regional stations.

Radio Nationale Tchadienne (RNT): BP 4589, N'Djamena; tel. and fax 22-51-60-71; f. 1955; state-controlled; programmes in French, Arabic and 11 vernacular languages; four regional stations; Dir HASSAN SILLA BAKARI.

Radio Abéché: BP 36, Abéché, Ouaddaï; tel. 22-69-81-49.

Radio Faya-Largeau: Faya-Largeau, Borkou.

Radio Moundou: BP 122, Moundou, Logone Occidental; tel. 22-69-13-22; programmes in French, Sara and Arabic; Dir DIMANANGAR DJAÏNTA.

Radio Sarh: BP 270, Sarh, Bahr Kôh; tel. 22-68-13-61; programmes in French, Sara and Arabic; Dir BIANA FOUDA NACTOUANDI.

Union des Radios Privées du Tchad (URPT): N'Djamena; f. 2002 as a federation of nine private and community radio stations; Pres. ZARA YACOUB; Sec.-Gen. DJEKOURNINGA KAOUTAR LAZAR; includes the following:

DJA FM: BP 1312, N'Djamena; tel. 22-51-64-90; fax 22-52-14-52; e-mail myzara@intnet.td; f. 1999; music, cultural and informative programmes in French, Arabic and Sara; Dir ZARA YACOUB.

Radio Brakoss (Radio de l'Agriculture): Moïssala, Mandoul; f. 1996; community radio station.

Radio Duji Lohar: BP 155, Moundou, Logone Occidental; tel. 22-69-17-14; fax 22-69-12-11; e-mail cdave@intnet.td; f. 2001.

Radio FM Liberté: BP 892, N'Djamena; tel. 22-51-42-53; f. 2000; financed by nine civil society orgs; broadcasts in French, Arabic and Sara; Dir DJEKOURNINGA KAOUTAR LAZAR.

Radio Lotiko: Diocese de Sarh, BP 87, Sarh; tel. 22-68-12-46; fax 22-68-14-79; e-mail lotiko@intnet.td; internet www.lotiko.org; f. 2001; community radio station; Dir ABBÉ FIDÈLE ALLAHADOUMBAYE.

La Voix du Paysan: BP 22, Doba, Logone Oriental; f. 1996; Roman Catholic; Dir DJALDI TABDI GASSISSOU NASSER.

Television

Télévision Nationale Tchadienne (Télé Tchad): BP 274, N'Djamena; tel. 22-52-26-79; fax 22-52-29-23; state-controlled; broadcasts c. 38 hours per week in French and Arabic; Dir HALIMÉ ASSADYA ALI.

Broadcasts from Africa 24, Canal France International, France 24, TV5, CNN and seven Arabic television stations are also received in Chad.

Finance

(cap. = capital; res = reserves; dep. = deposits; m. = million; br(s). = branch(es); amounts in francs CFA)

BANKING

In early 2013 there were nine commercial banks in Chad.

Central Bank

Banque des Etats de l'Afrique Centrale (BEAC): ave Charles de Gaulle, BP 50, N'Djamena; tel. 22-52-21-65; fax 22-52-44-87; e-mail beacndj@beac.int; internet www.beac.int; HQ in Yaoundé, Cameroon; f. 1973; bank of issue for mem. states of the Communauté Economique et Monétaire de l'Afrique Centrale (CEMAC, fmrly Union Douanière et Economique de l'Afrique Centrale), comprising Cameroon, the Central African Repub., Chad, the Repub. of the Congo, Equatorial Guinea and Gabon; cap. 88,000m., res 227,843m., dep. 4,110,966m. (Dec. 2007); Gov. LUCAS ABAGA NCHAMA; Dir in Chad CHRISTIAN NGARDOUM MORNONDE; brs at Moundou and Sarh.

Other Banks

Banque Agricole et Commerciale (BAC): ave el-Niméry, BP 1727, N'Djamena; tel. 22-51-90-41; fax 22-51-90-40; e-mail bast@intnet.td; f. 1997; cap. 1,200m. (2002), total assets 1,845m. (Dec. 1999); Pres. MOUHAMED OUSMAN AWAD; Dir-Gen. ABDELKADER OUSMAN HASSAN; 1 br.

Banque Commerciale du Chari (BCC): ave Charles de Gaulle, BP 757, N'Djamena; tel. 22-51-89-58; fax 22-51-62-49; e-mail bcc@intnet.td; f. 1981 as Banque Tchad-Arabe Libyenne; present name adopted 1995; 50% state-owned, 50% owned by Libya Arab Foreign Bank (Libya); cap. and res 3,567m., total assets 20,931m. (Dec. 2001); Pres. BIDJERE BINDJAKI; Dir-Gen. HAMED EL MISTIRI.

Banque Sahélo-Saharienne pour l'Investissement et le Commerce (BSIC): ave Charles de Gaulle, BP 81, N'Djamena; tel. 22-52-26-92; fax 22-62-26-93; e-mail bsic@bsic-tchad.com; internet www.bsicnet.com; f. 2004; Pres. and Dir-Gen. ALHADJI MOHAMED ALWARFALLI; Dir HABIBA SAHOULIBA.

Commercial Bank Tchad (CBT): rue du Capitaine Ohrel, BP 19, N'Djamena; tel. 22-52-28-29; fax 22-52-33-18; e-mail cbtbank@cbc-bank.com; internet www.cbc-bank.com; f. 1962; 50.7% owned by Groupe FOTSO (Cameroon), 17.5% state-owned; fmrly Banque de Développement du Tchad; cap. 4,020m., res 2,465m., dep. 38,624m. (Dec. 2005); Pres. YOUSSOUF ABBASALAH; Dir-Gen. GEORGES DJADJO; 1 br.

Ecobank Tchad: ave Charles de Gaulle, BP 87, N'Djamena; tel. 22-52-43-14; fax 22-52-23-45; e-mail ecobanktd@ecobank.com; internet www.ecobank.com; f. 2006; following acquisition of the former Banque Internationale pour l'Afrique au Tchad (BIAT); 6,250.0m., res 2,537.1m., dep. 120,375.2m. (Dec. 2011); Pres. MAMBY KOULIBALY; Dir-Gen. MAHAMAT ALI KÉRIM; 11 brs (2008).

Orabank Tchad: ave Charles de Gaulle, BP 804, N'Djamena; tel. 22-52-26-60; fax 22-52-29-05; e-mail info-td@orabank.net; internet www.orabank.net; f. 1992; fmrly Financial Bank Tchad, name changed as above in 2012; 100% owned by Oragroup SA (Togo); cap. 4,350.0m., res 111.6m., dep. 40,191.0m. (Dec. 2009); Pres. PATRICK MESTRALLET; Dir-Gen. LOUKOUMANOU WAIDI.

Société Générale Tchadienne de Banque (SGTB): 2–6 rue Robert Lévy, BP 461, N'Djamena; tel. 22-52-28-01; fax 22-52-37-13; e-mail sgtb@intnet.td; internet www.sgtb.td; f. 1963; 30% owned by Société Générale (France), 15% by Société Générale de Banque au Cameroun; cap. and res 3,603m., total assets 36,579m. (Dec. 2003); Dir-Gen. HAKIM OUZZANI; 3 brs.

United Bank for Africa—Tchad: ave Charles de Gaulle, BP 1148, N'Djamena; tel. 22-52-19-60; fax 22-52-19-61; internet www.ubagroup.com; f. 2009; Dir-Gen. SALAMI ALIYU INDA.

Bankers' Organizations

Association Professionnelle des Banques au Tchad: 2–6 rue Robert Lévy, BP 461, N'Djamena; tel. 22-52-41-90; fax 22-52-17-13; Pres. CHEMI KOGRIMI.

Conseil National de Crédit: N'Djamena; f. 1965 to formulate a national credit policy and to organize the banking profession.

INSURANCE

Assureurs Conseils Tchadiens Cecar et Jutheau: rue du Havre, BP 139, N'Djamena; tel. 22-52-21-15; fax 22-52-35-39; e-mail biliou.alikeke@intnet.td; f. 1966; Dir BILIOU ALIKEKE.

Gras Savoye Tchad: rue du Général Thillo, BP 5620, N'Djamena; tel. 22-52-00-72; fax 22-52-00-71; e-mail gras.savoye@intnet.td; affiliated to Gras Savoye (France); Man. DOMKRÉO DJAMON.

Société Mutuelle d'Assurances des Cadres des Professions Libérales et des Indépendants (SMAC): BP 644, N'Djamena; tel. 22-51-70-19; fax 22-51-70-61.

Société Tchadienne d'Assurances et de Réassurances (La STAR Nationale): ave Charles de Gaulle, BP 914, N'Djamena; tel. 22-52-56-77; fax 22-52-51-89; e-mail star@intnet.td; internet www.lastarnationale.com; f. 1977; privatized in 1996; brs in N'Djamena, Moundou and Abéché; cap. 500m.; Dir-Gen. RAKHIS MANNANY.

Trade and Industry

DEVELOPMENT ORGANIZATIONS

Agence Française de Développement (AFD): route de Farcha, BP 478, N'Djamena; tel. 22-52-70-71; fax 22-52-78-31; e-mail afdndjamena@groupe-afd.org; internet www.afd.fr; Country Dir JEAN-MARC PRADELLE.

Association Tchadienne pour le Développement: BP 470, Quartier Sabangali, N'Djamena; tel. 22-51-43-69; fax 22-51-89-23; e-mail darna.dnla@intnet.td; Dir DIGALI ZEUHINBA.

France Volontaires: BP 448, N'Djamena; tel. 22-52-20-53; fax 22-52-26-56; e-mail afvptchd@intnet.td; internet www.france-volontaires.org; f. 1965; name changed as above in 2009; Nat. Rep. TELNGAR RASSEMBEYE.

Office National de Développement Rural (ONDR): BP 896, N'Djamena; tel. 22-52-23-20; fax 22-52-29-60; e-mail psapdn@intnet.td; f. 1968; Dir HASSAN GUIHINI DADI.

Service de Coopération et d'Action Culturelle: BP 898, N'Djamena; tel. 22-52-42-87; fax 22-52-44-38; administers bilateral aid from France; Advisor FRANÇOISE GIANVITI.

Société de Développement du Lac (SODELAC): BP 782, N'Djamena; tel. 22-52-35-03; f. 1967 to develop the area of Lake Chad; cap. 179m. francs CFA; Pres. HASSANTY OUMAR CHAIB; Dir-Gen. ABBO YOUSSOUF.

CHAMBER OF COMMERCE

Chambre de Commerce, d'Industrie, d'Agriculture, des Mines et d'Artisanat: 13 rue du Col Moll, BP 458, N'Djamena; tel. 22-52-52-64; fax 22-52-52-63; e-mail cciama_tchad@yahoo.fr; internet cciama-tchad.org; f. 1935; brs at Sarh, Moundou, Bol and Abéché; Pres. Dr SOURADJ KOULAMALLAH; Dir-Gen. BEKOUTOU TAIGAM.

TRADE ASSOCIATIONS

Office National des Céréales (ONC): BP 21, N'Djamena; tel. 22-52-37-31; fax 22-52-20-18; e-mail onc1@intnet.td; f. 1978; production and marketing of cereals; Dir-Gen. MAHAMAT ALI HASSABALLAH; 11 regional offices.

Société Nationale de Commercialisation du Tchad (SONACOT): BP 630, N'Djamena; tel. 22-51-30-47; f. 1965; cap. 150m. francs CFA; 76% state-owned; nat. marketing, distribution and import-export co; Man. Dir MARBROUCK NATROUD.

EMPLOYERS' ORGANIZATION

Conseil National du Patronat Tchadien (CNPT): rue Bazelaire, angle ave Charles de Gaulle, BP 134, N'Djamena; tel. and fax 22-52-25-71; e-mail dgastat.tchad@intnet.td; internet cnpttchad.org; Pres. MAHAMAT ADOUM ISMAEL; Sec.-Gen. MARC MADENGAR BEREMADJI; 67 mem. enterprises with total workforce of 8,000 (2002).

UTILITIES

Société Nationale d'Électricité (SNE): 11 rue du Col Largeau, BP 44, N'Djamena; tel. 22-51-28-81; fax 22-51-21-34; internet www.snetchad.com; f. 2010; state-owned; created following the dissolution of the Société Tchadienne d'Eau et d'Electricité (STEE, f.1968); production and distribution of electricity; Dir-Gen. MAHAMAT SÉNOUSSI CHÉRIF.

Société Tchadienne des Eaux (STE): N'Djamena; f. 2010; state-owned; created following the dissolution of the Société Tchadienne d'Eau et d'Electricité (STEE, f.1968); Dir-Gen. FÉLICIEN NGASNA MAÏNGAR.

TRADE UNIONS

Confédération Libre des Travailleurs du Tchad (CLTT): ave Charles de Gaulle, BP 553, N'Djamena; tel. 22-51-76-11; fax 22-52-44-56; e-mail confederationlibre@yahoo.fr; Pres. BRAHIM BEN SAID; 22,500 mems (2001).

Union des Syndicats du Tchad (UST): BP 1143, N'Djamena; tel. 22-51-42-75; fax 22-52-14-52; e-mail ustchad@yahoo.fr; f. 1988; federation of trade unions; Pres. MICHEL BARKA; Sec.-Gen. FRANÇOIS DJONDANG.

Transport

RAILWAYS

Prior to 2012 there were no railways in Chad. In 1962 the Governments of Chad and Cameroon signed an agreement to extend the Transcameroon railway from Ngaoundéré to Sarh, a distance of 500 km. Although the Transcameroon reached Ngaoundéré in 1974, its proposed extension into Chad remains indefinitely postponed. In December 2011 the Government signed an agreement with the China Civil Engineering Construction Corporation to build over 1,300 km of standard gauge railway line (primarily for freight but also for passengers) in Chad. It was planned that two lines would be constructed—one from N'Djamena to Moundou and Koutéré on the border with Cameroon and the other from the capital to the Sudanese border via Abéché and Adré. This latter line would then be extended to Nyala in western Sudan, from where the existing line runs via Sudan's capital Khartoum to Port Sudan on the Red Sea. Building work commenced in 2012. The project was to cost US $5,600m. and was to be partially funded by the Export-Import Bank of China.

ROADS

The total length of the road network in 2006 was an estimated 40,000 km. There are also some 20,000 km of tracks suitable for motor traffic during the October–July dry season. In recent years the European Union has contributed funds towards the construction of a highway connecting N'Djamena with Sarh and Léré, on the Cameroon border, and of a 400-km highway linking Moundou and Ngaoundéré.

Coopérative des Transportateurs Tchadiens (CTT): BP 336, N'Djamena; tel. 22-51-43-55; road haulage; Pres. SALEH KHALIFA; brs at Sarh, Moundou, Bangui (CAR), Douala and Ngaoundere (Cameroon).

Fonds d'Entretien Routier: N'Djamena; internet fer-tchad.org; f. 2000; Dir AHMED DJAMALLADINE.

Société Tchadienne d'Affrètement et de Transit (STAT): 21 ave Félix Eboué, BP 100, N'Djamena; tel. 22-51-88-72; fax 22-51-74-24; e-mail stat.tchad@intnet.td; affiliated to Groupe Saga (France); road haulage.

INLAND WATERWAYS

The Chari and Logone rivers, which converge to the south of N'Djamena, are navigable. These waterways connect Sarh with N'Djamena on the Chari, and Bongor and Moundou with N'Djamena on the Logone.

CIVIL AVIATION

The international airport is at N'Djamena. There are also more than 40 smaller airfields. In late 2011 China CAMC Engineering Co secured a contract of about US $1,060m. to construct a new international airport in Chad.

Autorité de l'Aviation Civile (ADAC): 1 route de Farcha, BP 234, N'Djamena; tel. 22-52-54-14; fax 22-52-26-79; e-mail contact@adac-tchad.com; internet adac-tchad.com; Dir-Gen. YAYA MAHAMAT.

Air Affaires Tchad: BP 256, N'Djamena; tel. 22-51-60-37; fax 22-51-06-20; e-mail airaffaires@yahoo.st; passenger and freight, internal and charter flights.

Minair Tchad: ave Charles de Gaulle, BP 1239, N'Djamena; tel. 22-52-52-45; fax 22-51-07-80; e-mail abdel.ousman@intnet.td; passenger and freight air transport.

Toumaï Air Tchad (TAT): 66 ave Charles de Gaulle, 0036 rue 1020, Beck Ceccaldi, face à la Financial Bank, N'Djamena; tel. 22-52-41-07; fax 22-52-41-06; e-mail tatndj@toumaiair.com; internet www.toumaiair.com; f. 2004; scheduled passenger and cargo flights on domestic routes, and between N'Djamena and destinations in central and West Africa; Pres. and Dir-Gen. ZACHARIA DEBY ITNO.

Tourism

Chad's potential attractions for tourists include a variety of scenery from the dense forests of the south to the deserts of the north. Receipts from tourism in 2002 were estimated at US $25m. According to the World Tourism Organization, a total of only 14,298 tourists visited Chad in 2010, compared with 31,169 in 2009.

Office National Tchadien de Tourisme: BP 1649, N'Djamena; tel. and fax 22-52-02-85; internet www.ott.td; Dir Gen. MAHMOUD YOUNOUS.

Defence

As assessed at November 2012, the Armée Nationale Tchadienne was estimated to number 25,350 (army approximately 20,000, air force 350, Republican Guard 5,000). In addition, there was a 9,500-strong gendarmerie. The army has been undergoing restructuring since 1996. Military service is by conscription. Under defence agreements with France, the army receives technical and other aid: at mid-2013 there were nearly 950 French troops deployed in Chad.

Defence Expenditure: Budgeted at 63,700m. francs CFA for 2011.

Chief of Staff of the Armed Forces: Gen. ZAKARIA NGOBONGUE.

Chief of the Land Forces: Brig.-Gen. MASSOUD DRESSA.
Chief of Naval Staff: Lt MORNADJI MBAISSANEBE.
Chief of Air Force: Brig.-Gen. NADJITA BÉASSOUMAL.

Education

Education is officially compulsory for 10 years between six and 16 years of age and is provided free of charge in public institutions. Primary education begins at the age of six and lasts for six years. Secondary education, from the age of 12, lasts for seven years, comprising a first cycle of four years and a second of three years. In 2011 enrolment in primary education included 63% of students in the relevant age-group (males 71%; females 55%), while in 2012 secondary enrolment was equivalent to only 23% of children in the appropriate age-group (males 31%; females 14%). The Université de N'Djamena was opened in 1971. In addition, there are several technical colleges. Some 24,349 students (19,690 males, 4,659 females) were enrolled at higher education institutions in 2010/11. In 2005 spending on education represented 10.1% of total budgetary expenditure.

CHILE

Introductory Survey

LOCATION, CLIMATE, LANGUAGE, RELIGION, FLAG, CAPITAL

The Republic of Chile is a long, narrow country lying along the Pacific coast of South America, extending from Peru and Bolivia in the north to Cape Horn in the far south. Isla de Pascua (Rapa Nui or Easter Island), about 3,780 km (2,350 miles) off shore, and several other small islands form part of Chile. To the east, Chile is separated from Argentina by the high Andes mountains. Both the mountains and the cold Humboldt Current influence the climate; between Arica in the north and Punta Arenas in the extreme south, a distance of about 4,000 km (2,500 miles), the average maximum temperature varies by no more than 13°C. Rainfall varies widely between the arid desert in the north and the rainy south. The language is Spanish. There is no state religion but the great majority of the inhabitants profess Christianity, and some 70% are adherents of the Roman Catholic Church. The national flag (proportions 2 by 3) is divided horizontally: the lower half is red, while the upper half has a five-pointed white star on a blue square, at the hoist, with the remainder white. The capital is Santiago.

CONTEMPORARY POLITICAL HISTORY

Historical Context

Chile was ruled by Spain from the 16th century until its independence in 1818. For most of the 19th century it was governed by a small oligarchy of landowners. Chile won the War of the Pacific (1879–83) against Peru and Bolivia. The greater part of the 20th century was characterized by the struggle for power between right- and left-wing forces.

Domestic Political Affairs

In September 1970 Dr Salvador Allende Gossens, the Marxist candidate of the left-wing Unidad Popular coalition, was elected to succeed Eduardo Frei Montalva. Allende promised to transform Chilean society by constitutional means, and imposed an extensive programme of nationalization. The Government failed to obtain a congressional majority in the elections of March 1973 and encountered a deteriorating economic situation as well as an intensification of violent opposition to its policies. Accelerated inflation led to food shortages and there were repeated clashes between pro- and anti-Government activists. The armed forces finally intervened in September 1973. President Allende died during the coup. The Congreso (Congress) was subsequently dissolved, all political activity banned and strict censorship introduced. The military junta dedicated itself to the eradication of Marxism and the 'reconstruction' of Chile, and its leader, Gen. Augusto Pinochet Ugarte, became Supreme Chief of State in June 1974 and President in December. The junta was widely criticized abroad for its repressive policies and violations of human rights. Critics of the regime were tortured and imprisoned, and several thousand were abducted or 'disappeared'. Some of those who had been imprisoned were released, as a result of international pressure, and sent into exile.

The Pinochet regime

In September 1976 three constitutional acts were promulgated with the aim of creating an 'authoritarian democracy'. All political parties were banned in March 1977, when the state of siege was extended. Following a UN General Assembly resolution, adopted in December, which condemned the Government for violating human rights, a referendum was held in January 1978 to seek endorsement of the regime's policies. Since more than 75% of the voters supported the President in his defence of Chile 'in the face of international aggression', the state of siege (in force since 1973) was ended and was replaced by a state of emergency.

At a plebiscite held in September 1980 some 67% of voters endorsed a new Constitution, drafted by the Government, although dubious electoral practices were allegedly employed. Although the new Constitution was described as providing a 'transition to democracy' and President Pinochet ceased to be head of the armed forces, additional clauses allowed him to maintain his firm hold on power until 1989. The new Constitution became effective from March 1981.

In February 1984 the Council of State, a government-appointed consultative body, began drafting a law to legalize political parties and to prepare for elections in 1989. Despite the Government's strenuous attempts to eradicate internal opposition through the introduction of anti-terrorist legislation and extensive security measures, a campaign of explosions and public protests continued throughout 1984 and 1985. A number of protesters were killed in violent clashes with security forces, and many opposition leaders and trade unionists were detained and sent into internal exile.

Throughout 1986 President Pinochet's regime came under increasing attack from the Roman Catholic Church, guerrilla organizations (principally the Frente Patriótico Manuel Rodríguez—FPMR) and international critics, including the US Administration, which had previously refrained from condemning the regime's human rights record. In September the FPMR made an unsuccessful attempt to assassinate Pinochet, precipitating the imposition of a state of siege throughout Chile, under which leading members of the opposition were detained and strict censorship was introduced. Right-wing 'death squads' reappeared, which were implicated in a series of murders following the assassination attempt.

President Pinochet clearly indicated his intention to remain in office beyond 1989 by securing, in 1987, the sole presidential candidacy, should it be approved by the same plebiscite that would decide the future electoral timetable. The referendum, to be held on 5 October 1988, asked if the candidate nominated by the Pinochet regime should be confirmed as President. If the Government lost the referendum, it would be obliged to hold open elections within one year. Opposition groups established the 'Comando por el No' campaign to co-ordinate the anti-Government vote. The official result recorded 55% of the votes cast for the anti-Pinochet campaign, and 43% for the President. Following the plebiscite, the opposition made repeated demands for changes to the Constitution, in order to accelerate the democratic process. However, Pinochet rejected the opposition's proposals, and affirmed his intention to remain in office until March 1990.

The restoration of democracy

In mid-1989 Patricio Aylwin Azócar emerged as the sole presidential candidate for the centre-left Concertación de Partidos por la Democracia (CPD, as the Comando por el No had become). The election campaign was dominated by demands from both the CPD and right-wing parties for constitutional reform. Some 54 amendments ratified by the junta were finally accepted by the opposition, with some reservations, and the reforms were approved by voters in a national referendum in July. President Pinochet dismissed the possibility of his candidacy as unconstitutional, but reiterated his intention to continue as Commander-in-Chief of the Army for at least four years.

The presidential and congressional elections were conducted on 14 December 1989. In the presidential ballot, Aylwin won a clear victory over the government-supported candidate, Hernán Büchi Buc. The transfer of power took place on 11 March 1990, but Aylwin's new CPD administration lacked the two-thirds' majority in the Congress necessary to amend the 1981 Constitution significantly. Two members of the outgoing junta remained as commanders of the air force and police.

In April 1990 the Government created a national truth and reconciliation commission, the Comisión Nacional de Verdad y Reconciliación (CNVR), to document and investigate alleged violations of human rights. Although Pinochet had provided for the impunity of the former military junta, it was suggested by human rights organizations that such safeguards might be circumvented by indicting known perpetrators of atrocities on charges of 'crimes against humanity', a provision that gained considerable public support following the discovery, during 1990, of a number of mass graves. The army High Command condemned the Commission for undermining the prestige of the armed forces and attempting to contravene the terms of a comprehensive amnesty declared in 1978. Although a new accord between military leaders and the Government-elect had been negotiated in January 1990, relations between the new Government and the army High Command remained tense. Pinochet became the focus for widespread disaffection with the military élite, but resisted demands for his resignation.

Escalating public and political antagonism towards the former military leadership was fuelled throughout 1990 and 1991 by further revelations of abuses of human rights and financial corruption, and erupted into widespread popular outrage following the publication, in March 1991, of the findings of the CNVR. The report documented the deaths of 2,279 alleged political opponents of the former regime who were executed, died as a result of torture or disappeared in 1973–90. (By 2012 the official death toll had been increased to 3,197.) Those responsible were identified only by the institutions to which they belonged. However, Aylwin pledged full government co-operation for families wishing to pursue private prosecutions. The report concluded that the military Government had embarked upon a 'systematic policy of extermination' of its opponents through the illegal activities of the covert military intelligence agency, Dirección de Inteligencia Nacional. It was also highly critical of the judiciary for failing to protect the rights of individuals by refusing thousands of petitions for habeas corpus. Pinochet denounced the document and declared his opposition to government plans to make material reparation to the families of the disappeared.

The presidential election of December 1993 was won by the CPD candidate Eduardo Frei Ruiz-Tagle, ahead of Arturo Alessandri Besa, the candidate of the right-wing coalition, the Unión por el Progreso de Chile (UPC). However, the ruling coalition failed to make significant gains at concurrently conducted congressional elections, and Frei encountered continuing opposition to constitutional reform (particularly from the right and the upper house).

In November 1995 the Government secured the support of the opposition Renovación Nacional (RN) for revised proposals for new legislation relating to human rights and constitutional reform. However, the compromised nature of the agreement provoked considerable disaffection within the RN, and within the opposition UPC alliance in general, which was effectively dissolved following internal disagreements. During 1997 government efforts to abolish the designated seats in the Senado (Senate) intensified in response to Pinochet's stated intention to assume one of the seats assigned to former Presidents on his retirement as Commander-in-Chief in March 1998. In July 1997 the Senate rejected the Government's latest petition for reform to the system of appointments. In October it was announced that Maj.-Gen. Ricardo Izurieta, previously chief of defence staff, was to succeed Pinochet as Commander-in-Chief. The announcement was made amid a number of changes in the military High Command, which appeared to confirm earlier predictions that military influence was henceforth to be concentrated in the Senate, where it would bolster the political right wing.

Legislative elections to renew all 120 seats in the Cámara de Diputados (Chamber of Deputies) and 20 of the elective seats in the Senate were conducted in December 1997. The governing CPD retained a comfortable majority in the lower house. The elections revealed a shifting balance of power within the two major political groupings, and prompted renewed criticism of the country's binomial system of voting.

Legal proceedings against Pinochet

In January 1998, in response to attempts to begin judicial proceedings against him on charges related to gross abuses of human rights, Pinochet announced that he would continue as Commander-in-Chief until 10 March, the day before he was scheduled to assume his ex officio seat in the Senate, thereby preserving the immunity from prosecution provided by the position for as long as possible. On 6 March the military High Command announced that Pinochet had been named an honorary commander-in-chief—a position with no historical precedent.

In October 1998 Pinochet was arrested during a visit to London, United Kingdom, in response to a preliminary request that he should be extradited to Spain to answer charges of 'genocide and terrorism'. The British House of Lords' hearing of the extradition appeal in November overturned an earlier ruling that Pinochet was entitled to 'sovereign immunity' as a former head of state, and in December formal extradition proceedings commenced. Further legal inquiry, however, found that only charges relating to events subsequent to December 1988 (at which time the 1984 UN Convention against Torture and Other Cruel, Inhuman or Degrading Treatment or Punishment had entered into British law) should be considered relevant, thus reducing the number of draft charges brought by Spain from 33 to three. Formal extradition proceedings were initiated in September 1999, and in October a court found that Pinochet, who remained under effective house arrest, could be lawfully extradited to Spain. However, in March 2000, after an independent doctors' report had concluded that he was physically unfit to undergo further legal proceedings, Pinochet was released, and returned to Chile.

Meanwhile, domestic attention in 1999 was once again focused on the actions of the security forces during Pinochet's regime. In June the arrest of five retired army officers (former commanders of a notorious élite army unit popularly referred to as the 'caravan of death') was ordered by an appeal court judge following renewed investigation into the disappearance of 72 political prisoners in the immediate aftermath of the 1973 coup. The decision to prosecute the five men on charges of aggravated kidnapping was considered a breakthrough in Chilean judicial practice, as the absence of physical or documented evidence of the deaths of the prisoners meant that the crimes were technically in continuance, and thus the accused men were not protected by the 1978 amnesty that guaranteed the impunity of military personnel. In July 1999 the legality of the arrests was confirmed by the Supreme Court.

In June 2000 the Santiago Appeal Court ruled to lift Pinochet's political immunity, and in August, in an historic judgment, the Supreme Court confirmed the decision. The judgment was made possible by changes to Chile's judiciary, several members of which had retired and had been replaced by more independent-minded judges. Foremost among these was Juan Guzmán Tapia, who vigorously took up the legal case against Pinochet and others accused of human rights' infringements. Over 200 lawsuits were filed against the former dictator. In October an Argentine judge requested the extradition of Pinochet to stand trial for the 1974 killing in Buenos Aires of former Chilean army chief Carlos Prats and his wife. In November the Supreme Court ruled that Pinochet must not leave the country, and in December Judge Guzmán indicted the former dictator on charges of aggravated kidnapping and murder in the 'caravan of death' case. In January 2001 Pinochet finally consented to a medical examination to determine whether he was mentally fit to stand trial, and was subsequently questioned by Guzmán, who subsequently issued an order for the former General's arrest on charges of kidnap and murder. However, following an appeal, in March the Santiago Appeals Court ruled that the charges should be reduced to conspiracy to cover up the events, as opposed to responsibility for the 'caravan of death', and in July the Court ruled that the former dictator was mentally unfit to stand trial. In July 2002 the Supreme Court voted to close the case against Pinochet permanently, as he was suffering from dementia. Within days Pinochet relinquished his position as senator-for-life. However, in August 2004 the Supreme Court upheld a decision by the appeals court in May to strip Pinochet of his immunity from prosecution for the crimes allegedly committed as part of Plan Condor, an intelligence operation to eliminate opponents of the Latin American military dictatorships in the 1970s. Guzmán declared Pinochet to be of sufficiently sound mind to stand trial over his role in 'Plan Condor' in December, but in September 2005 the Penal Chamber of the Supreme Court ruled that the charges against Pinochet relating to Plan Condor were inadmissible. In the same month US financial investigators accused Pinochet of accepting bribes totalling more than US $3.5m. from European defence contractors and in October the Supreme Court removed Pinochet's immunity from prosecution on charges of embezzlement and the use of false passports to open foreign bank accounts.

Gen. Pinochet died on 10 December 2006, thus ending the efforts to bring him to trial. In January Pinochet had been charged in relation to Operation Colombo, an operation allegedly undertaken during his dictatorship to abduct and murder 119 opponents of the regime, after the Supreme Court had removed his immunity from prosecution on the charges in the previous month. In October he had been indicted on human rights abuses after a court ruled that he was mentally fit to face trial: some 4,500 political opponents were alleged to have been detained at the notorious Villa Grimaldi detention centre during his regime, and more than 200 people murdered there. Pinochet was charged on one count of murder, 35 kidnappings and 24 cases of torture. In November he was once again put under house arrest. Earlier in the same month the Appeals Court of Santiago also lifted his immunity from prosecution in the case of the 'disappearance' of a Spanish priest in 1974, and charges in the 'caravan of death' case were also once again brought. In addition, he was due to face trial on fraud charges relating to large sums of money that he had allegedly deposited in secret accounts.

The Government of President Lagos

At the presidential poll held in December 1999 the candidate of the CPD, Ricardo Lagos Escobar of the Partido Socialista de Chile, and the nominee of the Alianza por Chile (formed by the RN and the Unión Demócrata Independiente—UDI), Joaquín Lavín, both obtained 48% of the total votes cast. At a second round of voting in January 2000 Lagos emerged victorious with 51% of the total votes. Lagos was sworn in as President in March.

In August 2003 President Lagos announced a series of measures intended to resolve issues relating to human rights violations during the military dictatorship. These included increases in compensation paid to victims of political violence and their relatives, as well as measures to facilitate criminal prosecutions of former military personnel. In November 2004 the Supreme Court—in reference to the prosecution, on charges of involvement in Plan Condor, of four former secret policemen—again ruled against the invocation of the amnesty law in cases of 'disappearance', on the grounds that, until the body of the kidnapped person was found, such unresolved cases of abduction should be considered as ongoing. The Supreme Court's ruling opened the way for many other cases of human rights abuses to be brought. Also in November 2004, the testimonies of some 35,000 victims of abuses under the Pinochet regime were published in a report by the National Commission on Political Imprisonment and Torture. Although victims' and human rights groups welcomed the report, many criticized it for omitting the names of those accused of the abuses. Prior to the report's publication, the Commander-in-Chief of the Chilean Army, Gen. Juan Emilio Cheyre Espinosa, issued on behalf of the armed forces a public apology, in which for the first time institutional responsibility was accepted for the systematic abuse of opponents of the Pinochet regime.

In October and November 2004 the Senate finally approved a number of constitutional reforms. These included: the abolition of non-elected senators and of senators-for-life; the restoration of the President's power to dismiss the head of the armed forces and the police; and a reduction of the presidential term from six years to four. The constitutional reforms received final congressional approval in August 2005. Significantly, the reforms did not include changes to the binomial electoral system.

The Government of President Bachelet

At the presidential election in December 2005 the CPD's candidate, Michelle Bachelet Jeria, obtained 46% of the valid votes cast, while Sebastián Piñera Echeñique of the RN received 25% of the ballot. As no candidate obtained the requisite 50% of the ballot, a run-off election between Bachelet and Piñera was held in January 2006. Bachelet was elected President with 54% of the valid votes cast and took office in March.

In May 2006, in spite of the Government's pledge to increase public spending on education, some 700,000 students attended nationwide demonstrations in protest against the education system. Although the demonstrations were largely peaceful, the police attempted to break up the protests using water cannons and tear gas, and some 700 arrests were made. In response to the students' demands, in June the Government agreed to provide free transport for those attending school or college and to introduce grants to cover entrance examination fees for the poorest students. The unrest led to the dismissal in July of the Minister of the Interior, after the police handling of the demonstrations was criticized. The ministers responsible for education and the economy were also removed from their cabinet posts. The Government was further challenged by frequent outbreaks of industrial unrest during 2006–07, particularly in the copper-mining sector.

A government request for an additional US $92m. in funding for a new public transport system, Transantiago, was rejected by the Senate in November 2007. A Partido Demócrata Cristiano (PDC) senator Adolfo Zaldívar voted with the opposition, precipitating his expulsion from the party. In January 2008 five deputies also announced their departure from the PDC, leaving the ruling coalition in a minority in both legislative chambers. In an attempt to restore confidence in her Government, in the same month President Bachelet carried out another extensive cabinet reorganization. Congressional support for the Government was further eroded in March when Zaldívar was elected President of the Senate. At municipal elections held in October the Alianza por Chile won the greatest share of the votes cast for mayors for the first time since the restoration of democracy. Continuing divisions within the ruling coalition meant that it did not present unified lists of candidates for municipal council seats.

Legislation to reform the education system was approved by the Chamber of Deputies in June 2008. Earlier in June teachers had gone on strike and students and teachers had participated in demonstrations against the reforms, claiming that they would not sufficiently reduce the inequalities inherent in the existing system, which favoured private education. The draft legislation was approved by the Senate in December.

The Government of President Piñera

Presidential and legislative elections took place on 13 December 2009. The right-of-centre grouping, Coalición por el Cambio, secured 58 seats in the Chamber of Deputies (three short of a majority), while the CPD's representation was reduced to 57 seats. As neither grouping achieved a majority in the lower chamber, a period of intense political manoeuvring ensued. In the first round of the presidential poll Sebastián Piñera Echeñique, candidate for Coalición por el Cambio, secured 44.1% of total votes, compared with the CPD's candidate, former President Eduardo Frei Ruiz-Tagle, who won 29.6%. The popular independent candidate Marco Enríquez-Ominami Gumucio secured 20.1% of the total vote. At the second round on 17 January 2010 Piñera was victorious with 51.6% of the vote. The result was significant in marking the end of the CPD's 20-year rule and in giving Chile its first right-wing President since Pinochet.

In February 2010 a huge earthquake, measuring 8.8 on the Richter scale, struck Chile affecting a wide area centred near Concepción. According to official figures, the quake caused the deaths of more than 500 people and damaged or destroyed 370,000 homes. The outgoing Bachelet administration deployed some 14,000 members of the armed forces to the disaster area to re-establish order and prevent looting. The first priority for the incoming Government, which took office in mid-March, was to gain congressional approval for its reconstruction plan, estimated to cost US $20,000m. Although a dispute over funding arrangements delayed its passage, reconstruction legislation was finally adopted in October.

There were numerous reports throughout 2010 of government property on Isla de Pascua (Rapa Nui or Easter Island) being occupied by indigenous protesters demanding land reform and immigration controls. The protesters claimed that the mainland authorities had illegally seized their historical lands. The idea of secession from Chile was also mooted by the island's indigenous leaders, a concept dismissed by the Government. Mainland police units were dispatched to the island to end the occupations, precipitating violent clashes in December between the police and the demonstrators.

To boost revenues, in January 2011 the heavily indebted state-owned petroleum company Empresa Nacional de Petróleo proposed a 17% increase in gas prices in southern Chile, prompting strikes and violent protests in Punta Arenas, which resulted in the deaths of two people and the disruption of transport links with Argentina. The Minister of the National Energy Commission, Ricardo Raineri Bernain, resigned from the Cabinet as a result of the unrest, and his duties were assumed by the Minister of Mining and Energy, Laurence Golborne Riveros. Golborne secured an end to the protests shortly afterwards, agreeing to reduce the price increase to 3% and reinstate gas subsidies. In the same cabinet reorganization, Piñera also appointed Andrés Allamand as Minister of National Defence and Evelyn Matthei Fornet as Minister of Labour and Social Security.

Jacqueline van Rysselberghe, the Governor of Biobío and a prominent member of the UDI (part of the governing Coalición por el Cambio), was forced to resign in April 2011 following relentless pressure from the opposition CPD, which accused her of exaggerating the extent of earthquake damage in Biobío to obtain additional government funds for her region. Another UDI member, Minister of Housing and Urban Development Magdalena Matte Lecaros, resigned later that month after being implicated in the van Rysselberghe scandal; Matte had also been criticized for allegedly mishandling a construction contract for work on Transantiago. The resignations of these high-profile UDI officials signified the growing assertiveness of the left-wing opposition and also exposed tensions between the two main parties within the ruling coalition, the RN and the UDI, which had expected greater RN support for its members. Meanwhile, to improve the transparency of military expenditure, in May the National Congress abrogated a law that allocated 10% of the Corporación Nacional del Cobre de Chile's (CODELCO-Chile—the state-owned copper company) export earnings to the military, a practice that had been enforced, in various forms, since 1942.

In May 2011, amid widespread power shortages, local regulators approved the construction of five hydroelectric plants in the Aisén region of southern Chile, which would boost generating capacity by some 2,750 MW at a cost of US $3,200m. However, throughout May activists concerned about the environmental consequences of the HidroAysén scheme staged large-scale demonstrations against this decision, some of which deteriorated into violence. An opposition-supported legal challenge prompted a local court to suspend the hydroelectric project in June, although this appeal was rejected in October and work was allowed to resume; in April 2012 the Supreme Court also ruled in favour of the development. Nevertheless, fresh doubts about the viability of the scheme were raised in May when one of HidroAysén's major investors partially suspended its participation, citing the lack of popular support for the project. Environmental and technical studies were ongoing in early 2014.

In February–March 2012 the Movimiento Social por la Región de Aysén, a broad-based civic protest movement that had emerged in the wake of the HidroAysén controversy, blockaded roads, ports and airports in the area to draw attention to a range of regional grievances, leading to violent confrontations between the demonstrators and the security forces. Besides a resolution to the HidroAysén dispute, the protesters demanded the relaxation of fishing regulations, greater government investment in the region and measures to offset the high cost of living. The Government reached a preliminary settlement with the movement's leaders in late March, agreeing to a number of concessions, including the introduction of new subsidies and the establishment of a duty-free zone.

In January 2012 the President promulgated a constitutional amendment that granted eligible citizens the automatic, and voluntary, right to vote in elections. (Hitherto, voters had been required to complete a registration process, following which electoral participation was mandatory.) This measure expanded the size of the electorate by almost 5m., with the number of young voters forecast to rise significantly. The CPD performed strongly in municipal elections held on 28 October, winning 168 mayoralties (compared with 121 for the Coalición por el Cambio) and a plurality of council seats. Turnout declined sharply, from 78% in 2008 to just 41%, as a result of the new voluntary voting law. In the following month Allamand and Golborne left the Cabinet to commence their respective campaigns to become the Coalición por el Cambio's nominee in the upcoming presidential election, due to take place in November 2013. In the ensuing government reorganization, Rodrigo Hinzpeter Kirberg was appointed as Minister of National Defence, Loreto Silva Rojas became Minister of Public Works and Andrés Chadwick Piñera was awarded the interior portfolio. Further ministerial withdrawals forced Piñera to reorganize the Cabinet again in mid-2013; new ministers responsible for the economy, labour, social development and culture were duly appointed.

Student protests

Student groups organized several demonstrations in Santiago in June 2011, attended by up to 80,000 people, to demand free higher education and greater government involvement and investment in the country's education system, and also to protest against private, profit-generating universities and the disparities in the standard of education received by rich and poor students. Although the President, in July, announced new measures to reduce the financial burden on students and pledged US $4,000m. in new educational funding, these proposals failed to mollify the demonstrators and the protests continued. (A strike by CODELCO-Chile workers later that month, in response to alleged government plans to privatize the company, placed further pressure on the Government, which denied the rumours.) A cabinet reorganization was implemented by Piñera in mid-July, in which the Minister of Education and the Minister of Mining were replaced. Amid continuing, and often violent, large-scale student protests, a two-day strike was organized by the Central Unitaria de Trabajadores de Chile (CUT) in late August. The CUT claimed that 600,000 people took part in demonstrations throughout the country to demand health care, education, labour and pension reforms. However, these rallies precipitated violent clashes between the police and protesters, one of whom was killed by the security forces, and Chile's head of police was forced to resign as a result. Discussions between the Government and student representatives in September–October foundered. Riot police were deployed during a further student demonstration in mid-October, with reports that firearms and petrol bombs had been used by some demonstrators. Later that month protesters attacked the UDI's headquarters, stormed a senate meeting, forcing Minister of Education Felipe Bulnes Serrano to flee, and launched a failed attempt to occupy the Ministry of Education. Results from an unofficial plebiscite indicated strong public support for the students' demands, whereas Piñera's approval ratings had declined dramatically. The protests, while continuing, appeared to lose momentum following the approval in November of the 2012 budget, which allocated additional funds to education; the Government also expanded the scholarship system and established a new body to regulate the quality and transparency of universities, but rejected most of the protesters' other demands. Student leaders, dissatisfied with these concessions, pledged to resume protests in the new year. Bulnes resigned as Minister of Education in December 2011 and was replaced by Harald Beyer.

In April 2012 further higher education reforms were proposed by the Government, including a restructuring of the scholarship system to provide greater assistance to low-income students and the creation of a state-operated student loans agency to obviate the need for high-interest, private sector loans; additional educational spending was also pledged, to be funded by tax increases. Nevertheless, student demonstrations, which had recommenced in March, continued, with as many as 150,000 protesters taking part in a march through the capital in June, according to figures released by student organizations (police estimates were lower). Outbreaks of violence at these rallies were common. Piñera's tax proposals received congressional approval in September, and the 2013 budget consequently included a large increase in expenditure for the education sector. However, student groups organized fresh demonstrations, arguing that the Government's tax reforms would fail to generate the revenues necessary to address the deficiencies within the educational system.

An investigation by the Ministry of Education in mid-2012 into management of the national accreditation institute (Comisión Nacional de Acreditación—CNA) discovered that payments had been made by private universities in exchange for endorsement by the government-run body. In November the head of the CNA, Luis Eugenio Díaz, was arrested, along with two university rectors, on corruption charges. Minister of Justice Teodoro Ribera resigned in December after being accused of a conflict of interest in relation to the scandal; he was replaced by Patricia Pérez. In January 2013 Piñera presented legislation to the Congress aimed at improving transparency in the education sector.

Beyer was dismissed from his post in April 2013 after the Congress voted to impeach him for failing to investigate allegations of excessive profits being made by the privately run Universidad del Mar. He was replaced by Carolina Schmidt, hitherto head of the National Women's Service. In the previous week another nationwide student demonstration against university fees had been organized, with turnout in Santiago alone put at 150,000 (again, police estimates were lower). Further well-attended marches took place throughout 2013, with the protesters occasionally joined by trade union activists. Recurrent outbreaks of industrial unrest were reported across many sectors during that year; in mid-December workers at the port of Puerto Angamos in Mejillones withdrew their labour to protest in support of the rights of temporary workers. The strike spread to other parts of the country and by mid-January 2014 15 ports were affected by the unrest.

Recent developments: the 2013 elections

A presidential poll was held on 17 November 2013. Former President Bachelet, contesting the election as the representative of the left-wing Nueva Mayoría bloc (comprising the Concertación coalition and the Partido Comunista), garnered 46.7% of the valid votes cast, compared with 25.0% for Evelyn Matthei Fornet of the governing UDI/RN coalition (redesignated as the Alianza). Marco Enríquez-Ominami Gumucio of the Partido Progresista was third-placed, with 11.0% of the ballot. In the second round of voting, which took place on 15 December, Bachelet was re-elected to the presidency with 62.2% of the ballot. Turnout in the two respective rounds was relatively low, at 49% and 42%. Legislative elections were conducted concurrently with the first round of the presidential contest. Nueva Mayoría attracted 47.7% of the vote and gained control of 67 of the 120 seats in the Chamber of Deputies, while the number of Alianza deputies declined to 49. Nueva Mayoría also secured a majority in the Senate. Bachelet took office on 11 March 2014. Included in her new Cabinet was Rodrigo Peñailillo of the Partido por la Democracia, who was appointed to the interior ministry, while his party colleagues Heraldo Muñoz and Nicolás Eyzaguirre were given the foreign affairs and education portfolios, respectively. Alberto Arenas of the Partido Socialista de Chile was named Minister of Finance and Luis Felipe Céspedes of the PDC Minister of the Economy. Bachelet's campaign pledges had most notably included the provision of free higher education (to be financed by an increase in corporation tax) and constitutional reform. Although Nueva Mayoría's legislative position was robust, opposition support would be required to modify the Constitution.

Unrest among the Indigenous Mapuche Communities

A series of mining, dam and forestry projects in the 2000s prompted violent protests by the Mapuche indigenous peoples who were campaigning for the restitution of land they claimed under ancestral right. In 2000 a Historical Truth and New Deal Commission was created to consider the demands and needs of indigenous communities. In November 2003 the Commission produced its final report, which recommended the extension of constitutional and property rights to indigenous peoples and confirmation of their entitlement to participate in national politics. In early 2004 it was alleged that damage to timber industry property and forest fires in the Biobío region were the acts of Mapuche activists opposed to the activities of the timber industry, and in August five Mapuche activists were convicted under anti-terrorism legislation. President Bachelet put forward to the Congress a constitutional amendment in October 2007 that would recognize indigenous ancestral lands as well as promote the rights of the country's indigenous peoples. In January 2008 the Government established a panel to address the issue of Mapuche rights. In a further attempt to improve relations between the Government and the Mapuche community, a member of the Cabinet was designated as Co-ordinator of Indigenous Policy in August 2009. Ongoing unrest led the Government in October to announce its intention to invoke anti-terrorism laws enacted by Gen. Pinochet (which imposed penalties far stricter than those in the penal code). In August 2010 the Government declared that it had received evidence from the Colombian authorities confirming that radical Mapuches had trained with the Fuerzas Armadas Revolucionarias de Colombia—Ejército del Pueblo, a militant Colombian guerrilla group, although Mapuche representatives and high-ranking members of the Chilean police force rejected this claim. Meanwhile, in July a group of Mapuche prisoners had begun a hunger strike in protest against the controversial anti-terrorism laws that were being used to detain them without trial. Under increasing pressure, after four left-wing deputies joined the hunger strike and demonstrations were held in solidarity with the Mapuches, in September President Piñera consented to direct talks with Mapuche leaders and proposed modifications to the anti-terrorism legislation. Dissatisfied with the Government's response, Mapuche protesters in Santiago temporarily took control of UN and International Labour Organization buildings. However, following further negotiations, on 1 October agreement was reached to end the hunger strike in exchange for government pledges to reform the anti-terrorism laws and to re-examine the terrorism charges against the prisoners. In spite of this breakthrough, in November public prosecutors invoked the Pinochet-era anti-terrorism legislation in a trial involving a Mapuche attack on several police officers. Mapuche protests resumed in March 2011, prompted by the sentencing of four high-profile Mapuches to prison terms of between 20 and 25 years after they were convicted of robbery and attempting to murder a district attorney. The four men commenced a hunger strike and lodged an appeal against their convictions with the Supreme Court, which was rejected in June (although their sentences were reduced). The prisoners ended their hunger strike shortly thereafter, following a pledge by the Government to establish a Mapuche rights commission. Broad anti-discrimination legislation, providing new protections for Mapuches and other minorities, was promulgated in July 2012. Nevertheless, tensions between Mapuche communities and the authorities remained high, and Mapuche protest action, sometimes involving violence and arson, occurred frequently throughout the year. The Government suspected that radical Mapuches may have been responsible for a series of forest fires within Mapuche regions during 2011–12, which resulted in significant losses for the logging industry and at least seven deaths. Piñera established an anti-terrorism unit in January 2013 to combat another escalation in Mapuche-related violence. Later that month, in a further effort to quell the unrest, the President proposed a constitutional amendment that would enshrine the rights of indigenous populations, although the momentum behind this initiative dissipated rapidly. A senior UN official at the Office of the High Commissioner for Human Rights censured the Piñera administration in July for its continued application of counter-terrorism legislation against Mapuches.

Foreign Affairs

In 1991 Argentina and Chile reached a settlement regarding disputed territory in the Antarctic region. In 1994 Argentina's claim to the contentious Laguna del Desierto region was upheld by a five-member international arbitration panel. In 1998 agreement on border demarcation of the still disputed 'continental glaciers' territory in the Antarctic region was reached by the Presidents of the two countries and in 2000 both countries ratified the Mining and Co-operation Integration Treaty, allowing joint exploitation of mineral deposits along their shared border. In 2006 a bilateral group was established to resolve disagreements over energy matters. Relations between the two countries deteriorated in 2010 when Argentina granted asylum to Sergio Galvarino Apablaza, who was wanted by the Chilean authorities in relation to the 1991 assassination of Jaime Guzmán, a prominent figure in the Pinochet regime.

The decision in 2003 by the administration of Ricardo Lagos to privatize the port of Arica elicited vehement objections from the Bolivian Government, which feared this would lead to significant increases in port tariffs. (Bolivia had severed ties with Chile in 1978 over the issue of Bolivian access to the Pacific Ocean.) However, bilateral discussions in 2006 included Bolivian claims to Pacific access for the first time in more than a century. In 2008 the two countries signed a memorandum of understanding on defence co-operation, which both Governments described as an important step in the development of bilateral relations. However, President Piñera announced in December 2010 that he would not grant Bolivia sovereign rights to any part of Chile, an option that had been contemplated by President Bachelet. Frustrated by this impasse, Bolivian President Evo Morales referred the matter to the International Court of Justice (ICJ) in April 2013; hearings were expected to commence in 2015.

Relations with Peru suffered in 2007 after a Peruvian government periodical published a map appearing to lay claim to Chilean water, prompting Chile to recall its ambassador from that country. In 2008 Chile again recalled its ambassador after the Peruvian legislature approved legislation revising the maritime border. Public hearings on the delimitation of the maritime boundary were held at the ICJ in December 2012, and in January 2014 the Court promulgated its final judgment on the matter. The redefined border resulted in the transfer of some 21,000 sq km of ocean territory from Chile to Peru. Although disappointed with this decision, Piñera agreed to respect the ICJ's ruling.

Chile has negotiated free trade agreements throughout the South American continent (with the exception of Bolivia) and has also concluded free trade pacts with the USA, Canada, the European Union, the People's Republic of China, Japan, Australia, Malaysia, Thailand, Turkey and Viet Nam.

CONSTITUTION AND GOVERNMENT

Chile is a republic, divided into 14 regions and a metropolitan area. Easter Island enjoys 'special territory' status within Chile. The 1981 Constitution, described as a 'transition to democracy', separated the presidency from the junta and provided for presidential elections and for the re-establishment of the bicameral legislature. Under the terms of the Constitution, executive power is vested in the President, who is directly elected for a four-year term. The President is assisted by a Cabinet. Legislative power is vested in the bicameral Congreso Nacional (National Congress), comprising the 38-member Senado (Senate) and the 120-member Cámara de Diputados (Chamber of Deputies).

REGIONAL AND INTERNATIONAL CO-OPERATION

The country is a member of the Latin American Integration Association (ALADI, see p. 361) and was admitted to the Asia-Pacific Economic Co-operation group (APEC, see p. 201) in 1994. In 2004 Chile was one of 12 countries that were signatories to the agreement, signed in Cusco, Peru, creating the South American Community of Nations (Comunidad Sudamericana de Naciones, which was renamed Union of South American Nations—Unión de Naciones Suramericanas, UNASUR, in 2007, see p. 469). The

Senate ratified UNASUR membership in 2010. In 2006 Chile rejoined the Andean Community of Nations (CAN, see p. 193) as an associate member; it had withdrawn from the organization in 1976 following a dispute. Chile has participated in negotiations towards a Trans-Pacific Partnership. The country was a member of the Community of Latin American and Caribbean States (see p. 464), which was formally inaugurated in December 2011. In June 2012 the Presidents of Chile, Colombia, Mexico and Peru signed a framework agreement in Antofagasta, creating a new regional economic bloc, the Pacific Alliance (Alianza del Pacífico, see p. 453). In early 2014 the countries of the Pacific Alliance reached an agreement, subject to ratification, that would eliminate 92% of import tariffs on goods and services traded between the four countries.

Chile became a member of the UN in 1945. As a contracting party to the General Agreement on Tariffs and Trade Chile joined the World Trade Organization, WTO (see p. 434) on its establishment in 1995. In 2010 Chile became a member of the Organization for Economic Co-operation and Development (see p. 379).

ECONOMIC AFFAIRS

In 2012, according to estimates by the World Bank, Chile's gross national income (GNI), measured at average 2010–12 prices, was US $249,406m., equivalent to $14,280 per head (or $21,310 per head on an international purchasing-power parity basis). During 2003–12, it was estimated, the population increased by an average of 1.0% per year, while gross domestic product (GDP) per head increased, in real terms, at an average annual rate of 3.5%. Overall GDP increased, in real terms, at an average annual rate of 4.5% in 2003–12; real GDP increased by 5.6% in 2012.

Agriculture (including forestry and fishing) contributed 3.6% of GDP in 2012, and employed 8.7% of the employed labour force at the end of September 2013. Important subsistence crops include wheat, maize, oats, rice, barley, beans, lentils and chickpeas. Industrial crops include sugar beet and rapeseed. Fruit and vegetables are also important export commodities (together contributing 7.4% of total export revenues in 2012), particularly grapes, apples, citrus fruits, peaches, avocados, pears, plums and nuts. The production and export of wine was significant: output increased by 14.3% in 2011. Forestry and fishing, and derivatives from both activities, also make important contributions to the sector. During 2003–11 agricultural GDP increased, in real terms, by an average of 3.8% per year, according to the World Bank; agricultural GDP decreased by 0.3% in 2012, according to chain-linked methodologies.

Industry (including mining, manufacturing, construction and power) contributed an estimated 36.0% of GDP in 2012, and accounted for 24.2% of the employed labour force at the end of September 2013. During 2003–11, according to the World Bank, industrial GDP increased by an average of 1.7% per year; growth in the sector was 4.8% in 2012, according to chain-linked methodologies.

Mining contributed 14.2% of GDP in 2012, and engaged 3.2% of the employed labour force at the end of September 2013. Chile, with some 20% of the world's known reserves, is the world's largest producer and exporter of copper. Copper accounted for an estimated 53.9% of Chile's total export earnings (some US $42,184m.) in 2012, compared with 87.5% for copper alone in 1970. Gold, silver, iron ore, nitrates, molybdenum, manganese, lead and coal are also mined. Petroleum and natural gas deposits have been located in the south and offshore. Chile was a major producer of lithium carbonate, producing over one-third of global output. According to the Banco Central de Chile, the sector remained constant during 2003–10. According to chain-linked methodologies, the sector's GDP decreased by 4.4% in 2011, but increased by 4.3% in 2012.

Manufacturing contributed 11.2% of GDP in 2012, and engaged 11.7% of the employed labour force at the end of September 2013. The most important branches of manufacturing are food and non-ferrous metals. According to the World Bank, manufacturing GDP increased by an average of 3.3% per year in 2003–11. Manufacturing GDP increased by 2.6% in 2012, according to chain-linked methodologies.

Construction contributed 8.3% of GDP in 2012, and engaged 8.7% of the employed labour force at the end of September 2013. According to the Banco Central de Chile, construction GDP increased by an average of 3.8% per year in 2003–10; sectoral GDP increased by 8.1% in 2012, according to chain-linked methodologies.

Electric energy was derived mainly from coal (35.1% in 2012), hydroelectric power (28.1%), natural gas (18.3%) and petroleum (9.1%). Chile produces some 40% of its national energy requirements. The controversial project to build five hydroelectric plants in southern Chile (see Domestic Political Affairs) would increase generating capacity by some 2,750 MW at a cost of US $3,200m. In 2012 Chile imported mineral fuels and lubricants equivalent to some 22.7% of the value of total merchandise imports.

The services sector contributed 60.4% of GDP in 2012, and engaged 67.1% of the employed labour force at the end of September 2013. During 2003–11 overall services GDP increased by an average of 6.0% per year. In 2012, according to chain-linked methodologies, services GDP increased, in real terms, by 6.5%.

In 2012 Chile recorded a visible merchandise trade surplus of US $3,422m., and there was a deficit of $9,496m. on the current account of the balance of payments. In 2012 the USA was the principal source of imports (22.9%), while the People's Republic of China was the principal market for exports (23.3%). Other major trading partners were Japan, Argentina, Brazil and the Republic of Korea. In 2012 the principal exports were non-ferrous metals, metalliferous ores and metal scrap, vegetables and fruit and fish. The principal imports in that year were machinery and transport equipment, mineral fuels and lubricants, basic manufactures, chemicals and related products, and miscellaneous manufactured articles.

In 2012 there was a budgetary surplus of some 6,187,986m. pesos, equivalent to 4.7% of GDP. Chile's general government gross debt was 15,517,619m. pesos in 2012, equivalent to 11.9% of GDP. Chile's external debt totalled some US $96,245m. at the end of 2011, of which $16,354m. was long-term public and publicly guaranteed debt. In that year, the cost of servicing long-term public and publicly guaranteed debt and repayments to the IMF was equivalent to 15.2% of the value of exports of goods, services and income (excluding workers' remittances). The annual rate of inflation averaged 3.4% in 2000–09, and stood at 3.1% in 2012. Some 5.7% of the labour force were unemployed in September 2013.

In spite of a recent expansion in agricultural and industrial exports, in early 2014 Chile remained heavily dependent on exports of copper. High international copper prices resulted in Chile recording its 14th successive trade surplus in 2013. Growth in trade was buoyed by foreign direct investment and free trade agreements, although the strong copper prices led to an appreciation in the Chilean peso, which, in turn, adversely affected other merchandise exports. Inflationary pressures and energy supply problems led to a contraction in GDP in 2009. An improvement in the global economic climate and extensive reconstruction activity following the massive earthquake that struck Concepción in February 2010 contributed to real GDP growth of 5.7% in 2010 and 5.8% in 2011. Copper exports increased during this period, benefiting from a recovery in the copper price on international markets. Low levels of unemployment resulted in rising domestic demand, which reinforced the economic revival. The economy expanded by 5.6% in 2012, supported by a further upsurge in internal demand. A modest decrease in copper exports was recorded during that year, although the state-owned copper company, the Corporación Nacional del Cobre de Chile, planned to invest in new mines to boost declining production rates. In spite of an increase in copper output and robust levels of domestic consumption, growth slowed to 4.4% in 2013 following a decline in copper prices and investment inflows. The IMF projected real GDP growth of 4.5% in 2014.

PUBLIC HOLIDAYS

2015: 1 January (New Year's Day), 3 April (Good Friday), 4 April (Holy Saturday), 1 May (Labour Day), 21 May (Navy Day—Battle of Iquique), 29 June (Saints Peter and Paul), 16 July (Our Lady of Carmen), 15 August (Assumption), 11 September (Reconciliation Day), 18 September (Independence Day), 19 September (Army Day), 12 October (Discovery of America), 31 October (Reformation Day), 1 November (All Saints' Day), 8 December (Immaculate Conception), 25 December (Christmas Day).

Statistical Survey

Sources (unless otherwise stated): Instituto Nacional de Estadísticas (INE), Avda Bulnes 418, Casilla 498-3, Correo 3, Santiago; tel. (2) 2366-7777; fax (2) 2671-2169; e-mail inesdadm@reuna.cl; internet www.ine.cl; Banco Central de Chile, Agustinas 1180, Santiago; tel. (2) 2696-2281; fax (2) 2698-4847; e-mail bcch@bcentral.cl; internet www.bcentral.cl.

Area and Population

AREA, POPULATION AND DENSITY*

Area (sq km)	756,096†
Population (census results)‡	
24 April 2002	15,116,435
9 April 2012§	
Males	8,101,890
Females	8,532,713
Total	16,634,603
Population (official estimates at mid-year)‖	
2013	17,556,815
2014	17,711,004
Density (per sq km) at mid-2014	23.4

* Excluding Chilean Antarctic Territory (approximately 1,250,000 sq km).
† 291,930 sq miles.
‡ Excluding adjustment for underenumeration.
§ In November 2013 a government commission investigating claims that the 2012 census results contained compromising irregularities rejected earlier demands that the census should be annulled, but recommended that the published results should be revised with expanded documentation of the irregularities.
‖ Estimates not adjusted to take account of the 2012 census.

POPULATION BY AGE AND SEX
(at 2012 census)

	Males	Females	Total
0–14	1,829,199	1,759,524	3,588,723
15–64	5,534,705	5,791,414	11,326,119
65 and over	737,986	981,775	1,719,761
Total	8,101,890	8,532,713	16,634,603

REGIONS
(population at 2012 census)*

	Area (sq km)	Population	Density (per sq km)	Capital
Tarapacá	42,225.8	300,021	7.1	Iquique
Antofagasta	126,049.1	547,463	4.3	Antofagasta
Atacama	75,176.2	292,054	3.9	Copiapó
Coquimbo	40,579.9	707,654	17.4	La Serena
Valparaíso	16,396.1	1,734,917	105.8	Valparaíso
El Libertador Gen. Bernardo O'Higgins	16,387.0	877,784	53.6	Rancagua
Maule	30,296.1	968,336	32.0	Talca
Biobío	37,068.7	1,971,998	53.2	Concepción
La Araucanía	31,842.3	913,065	28.7	Temuco
Los Lagos	48,583.6	798,141	16.4	Puerto Montt
Aisén del Gen. Carlos Ibáñez del Campo	108,494.4	99,609	0.9	Coyhaique
Magallanes y Antártica Chilena*	1,382,291.1	159,468	0.1	Punta Arenas
Metropolitan Region (Santiago)	15,403.2	6,685,685	434.0	—
Los Ríos	18,429.5	364,592	19.8	Valdivia
Arica y Parinacota	16,873.3	213,816	12.7	Arica
Total	2,006,096.3	16,634,603	8.3	—

* Including Chilean Antarctic Territory (approximately 1,250,000 sq km).

PRINCIPAL TOWNS
(2012 census)

Gran Santiago (capital)	6,685,685	Arica	210,936
Puente Alto	583,471	Coquimbo	202,441
Antofagasta	348,669	Talca	201,142
Viña del Mar	331,399	Los Angeles	187,494
Valparaíso	294,848	Iquique	184,953
San Bernardo	277,802	Chillán	175,869
Temuco	269,992	Valdivia	154,445
Puerto Montt	238,455	Osorno	154,137
Rancagua	232,524	Talcahuano	151,524
Concepción	214,926	Calama	138,722
La Serena	211,275		

BIRTHS, MARRIAGES AND DEATHS

	Registered live births*		Registered marriages		Registered deaths	
	Number	Rate (per 1,000)	Number	Rate (per 1,000)	Number	Rate (per 1,000)
2004	230,352	14.5	53,403	3.3	86,138	5.4
2005	230,831	14.3	53,842	3.3	86,102	5.3
2006	231,383	14.2	58,155	3.5	85,639	5.2
2007	240,569	14.6	57,792	3.5	93,000	5.6
2008	246,581	14.8	56,112	3.3	90,168	5.4
2009	252,240	15.0	56,127	3.3	91,965	5.4
2010	250,643	14.7	60,362	3.5	97,930	5.7
2011	247,358	14.4	64,768	3.8	94,985	5.5

* Adjusted for underenumeration.

Life expectancy (years at birth): 79.3 (males 76.5; females 82.3) in 2011 (Source: World Bank, World Development Indicators database).

ECONOMICALLY ACTIVE POPULATION*
(labour force survey July–September,'000 persons aged 15 years and over, preliminary)

	2011	2012	2013
Agriculture, hunting, forestry and fishing	711.2	717.7	675.7
Mining and quarrying	226.2	254.8	244.9
Manufacturing	881.6	907.4	905.0
Electricity, gas and water	57.8	51.8	52.7
Construction	610.5	630.2	676.1
Trade, restaurants and hotels	1,816.7	1,765.9	1,868.1
Transport, storage and communications	553.8	577.9	574.7
Financing, insurance, real estate and business services	589.5	582.8	652.6
Community, social and personal services	2,041.5	2,119.2	2,109.2
Total employed	7,488.7	7,607.8	7,758.9
Unemployed	600.3	529.2	468.1
Total labour force	8,089.1	8,137.0	8,227.1

* Figures are based on sample surveys, covering 36,000 households, and exclude members of the armed forces. Estimates are made independently, therefore totals are not always the sum of the component parts.

Health and Welfare

KEY INDICATORS

Total fertility rate (children per woman, 2011)	1.8
Under-5 mortality rate (per 1,000 live births, 2011)	9
HIV/AIDS (% of persons aged 15–49, 2012)	0.4
Physicians (per 1,000 head, 2009)	1.0
Hospital beds (per 1,000 head, 2010)	2.1
Health expenditure (2010): US $ per head (PPP)	1,191
Health expenditure (2010): % of GDP	7.4
Health expenditure (2010): public (% of total)	47.2
Access to water (% of persons, 2011)	99
Access to sanitation (% of persons, 2011)	99
Total carbon dioxide emissions ('000 metric tons, 2010)	72,258.2
Carbon dioxide emissions per head (metric tons, 2010)	4.2
Human Development Index (2012): ranking	40
Human Development Index (2012): value	0.819

For sources and definitions, see explanatory note on p. vi.

Agriculture

PRINCIPAL CROPS
('000 metric tons)

	2010	2011	2012
Wheat	1,524	1,576	1,213
Rice, paddy	95	130	150
Barley	97	123	76
Maize	1,358	1,438	1,493
Oats	381	564	451
Potatoes	1,081	1,676	1,093
Sugar beet	1,420	1,951	1,824
Beans, dry	23	24	11
Rapeseed	44	71	114
Cabbages and other brassicas*	44	38	45
Lettuce and chicory*	94	102	99
Tomatoes*	738	726	400
Pumpkins, squash and gourds*	137	141	142
Chillies and peppers, green*	50	46	51
Onions, dry*	297	295	300
Carrots and turnips*	150	161	165
Maize, green*	176	177	180
Watermelons*	52	53	55
Cantaloupes and other melons*	49	49	50
Oranges*	134	141	145
Lemons and limes*	155	153	160
Apples	1,624	1,588	1,625*
Pears*	180	190	191
Peaches and nectarines*	357	320	325
Plums and sloes*	298	293	300
Grapes*	2,904	3,149	3,200
Avocados	166	156	160*
Kiwi fruit*	229	237	240

* FAO estimate(s).

Aggregate production ('000 metric tons, may include official, semi-official or estimated data): Total cereals 3,588 in 2010, 3,950 in 2011, 3,465 in 2012; Total roots and tubers 1,094 in 2010, 1,690 in 2011, 1,107 in 2012; Total vegetables (incl. melons) 2,107 in 2010, 2,123 in 2011, 1,827 in 2012; Total fruits (excl. melons) 6,184 in 2010, 6,391 in 2011, 6,514 in 2012.

Source: FAO.

LIVESTOCK
('000 head, year ending September)

	2010	2011	2012*
Horses	308†	310†	311
Cattle	3,830*	3,759	3,750
Pigs	2,706	2,824	2,940
Sheep	3,644†	3,600*	3,650
Goats*	750	745	747
Chickens	47,479	47,479	48,000
Turkeys*	30,000	32,000	32,000

* FAO estimate(s).
† Unofficial figure.

Source: FAO.

LIVESTOCK PRODUCTS
('000 metric tons)

	2010	2011	2012*
Cattle meat	210.7	191.0	195.0
Sheep meat	10.5	11.2	11.6
Pig meat	498.5	527.9	540.0
Horse meat	7.4	8.3	9.2
Chicken meat	503.8	562.1	572.0
Cows' milk	2,530	2,620	2,650
Goats' milk*	10.3	9.7	10.0
Hen eggs	190.8	198.3	200.0
Wool, greasy	7.8	7.8*	8.0

* FAO estimate(s).

Source: FAO.

Forestry

ROUNDWOOD REMOVALS
('000 cubic metres, excluding bark)

	2009	2010	2011
Sawlogs, veneer logs and logs for sleepers	13,962	14,905	16,147
Pulpwood	22,279	19,424	22,722
Other industrial wood	161	231	281
Fuel wood	14,621	12,655	15,998
Total	51,023	47,215	55,148

2012: Figures are assumed to be unchanged from 2011 (FAO estimates).

Source: FAO.

SAWNWOOD PRODUCTION
('000 cubic metres, including railway sleepers)

	2009	2010	2011
Coniferous (softwood)	5,566	6,050	6,507
Broadleaved (hardwood)	271	304	278
Total	5,837	6,354	6,785

2012: Figures are assumed to be unchanged from 2011 (FAO estimates).

Source: FAO.

Fishing

('000 metric tons, live weight)

	2009	2010	2011
Capture	3,453.8	2,679.7	3,063.4
Patagonian grenadier	78.4	74.3	70.1
Araucanian herring	855.3	750.8	887.3
Anchoveta (Peruvian anchovy)	955.2	755.4	1,191.4
Chilean jack mackerel	834.9	464.8	247.3
Chub mackerel	158.5	95.7	26.1
Jumbo flying squid	56.3	200.4	163.5
Aquaculture	792.9	701.1	954.8
Atlantic salmon	233.3	123.2	264.3
Coho (silver) salmon	157.0	122.7*	159.6
Rainbow trout	214.7	220.2*	224.4
Total catch	4,246.7	3,380.8*	4,018.3

* FAO estimate.

Note: Figures exclude aquatic plants ('000 metric tons): 456.2 (capture 368.0, aquaculture 88.2) in 2009; 380.8 (capture 368.6, aquaculture 12.2) in 2010; 418.2 (capture 403.5, aquaculture 14.5) in 2011.

Source: FAO.

Mining

('000 metric tons unless otherwise indicated)

	2009	2010	2011
Copper (metal content)	5,394	5,419	5,263
Coal	636	619	654
Iron ore*	8,242	9,130	12,625
Calcium carbonate	6,012	6,518	6,270
Zinc—metal content (metric tons)	27,801	27,662	36,602
Molybdenum—metal content (metric tons)	34,925	37,186	40,889
Manganese (metric tons)†	5,722	—	—
Gold (kg)	40,834	39,494	45,137
Silver (kg)	1,301	1,287	1,291
Crude petroleum	1,355	1,536	1,741

* Gross weight. The estimated iron content is 61%.

† Gross weight. The estimated metal content is 32%.

Source: US Geological Survey.

Industry

SELECTED PRODUCTS

('000 metric tons unless otherwise indicated)

	2007	2008	2009
Beer ('000 hl)	5,501	7,091	6,678
Wine*	792	868.3	1,000.1
Soft drinks ('000 hl)	16,870	19,760	n.a.
Cigarettes (million)	18,654	19,498	17,359
Non-rubber footwear ('000 pairs)	3,628	2,821	2,503
Particle board ('000 cu m)	515	n.a.	n.a.
Mattresses ('000)	1,535	2,031	1,896
Jet fuel	537	511	610
Motor spirit (petrol)	2,349	2,230	2,445
Kerosene	93	77	60
Distillate fuel oils	3,623	3,811	3,442
Residual fuel oils	2,445	1,906	1,802
Cement	4,368.5	4,620.7	2,579
Tyres ('000)	5,254	5,036	n.a.
Blister copper	1,936	2,134	2,131
Refined copper, unwrought	124	98	2,407
Electric energy (million kWh)	58,509	59,704	60,722

2010 ('000 metric tons unless otherwise indicated): Wine 915.2*; Electric energy 60,159m. kWh.

2011 ('000 metric tons unless otherwise indicated): Wine 1,046.0*; Electric energy 63,723m. kWh.

* Source: FAO.

Source (unless otherwise indicated): UN Industrial Commodity Statistics Database.

Finance

CURRENCY AND EXCHANGE RATES

Monetary Units

100 centavos = 1 Chilean peso.

Sterling, Dollar and Euro Equivalents (31 December 2013)

£1 sterling = 862.528 pesos;
US $1 = 523.760 pesos;
€1 = 722.317 pesos;
10,000 Chilean pesos = £11.59 = $19.09 = €13.84.

Average Exchange Rate (pesos per US $)

2011	483.668
2012	486.471
2013	495.288

GOVERNMENT FINANCE

(general government transactions, non-cash basis, million pesos)

Summary of Balances

	2010	2011	2012
Revenue	25,577,517	29,508,700	30,890,972
Less Expense	21,523,119	22,729,390	24,702,986
Net operating balance	4,054,398	6,779,310	6,187,986
Less Net acquisition of non-financial assets	4,460,201	5,075,938	5,302,470
Net lending/borrowing	–405,803	1,703,372	885,516

Revenue

	2010	2011	2012
Net tax revenue	19,042,371	22,770,751	24,614,798
Gross copper revenue	3,042,010	2,765,411	1,963,870
Social security contributions	1,493,987	1,623,817	1,802,468
Grants	81,691	156,050	126,288
Property income	481,798	558,816	622,777
Operating revenue	587,285	611,146	702,913
Other revenue	848,376	1,022,709	1,057,859
Total	25,577,517	29,508,700	30,890,972

Expense

Expense by economic type	2010	2011	2012
Compensation of employees	6,339,591	6,745,129	7,405,419
Use of goods and services	3,202,605	3,602,327	3,718,668
Interest	537,523	676,690	765,405
Subsidies and grants	6,364,756	6,435,691	7,284,077
Social benefits	5,027,790	5,207,538	5,448,996
Other expense	50,853	62,016	80,421
Total	21,523,119	22,729,390	24,702,986

Source: Dirección de Presupuestos, Santiago.

INTERNATIONAL RESERVES

(US $ million at 31 December)

	2010	2011	2012
Gold (national valuation)	11.2	12.2	13.1
IMF special drawing rights	1,216.6	1,214.1	1,211.4
Reserve position in IMF	282.0	601.1	691.7
Foreign exchange	26,317.8	40,116.6	39,733.0
Total	27,827.5	41,944.0	41,649.1

Source: IMF, *International Financial Statistics*.

MONEY SUPPLY

('000 million pesos at 31 December)

	2010	2011	2012
Currency outside depository corporations	3,423.2	3,892.3	4,480.0
Transferable deposits	11,243.8	17,536.5	19,954.8
Other deposits	44,212.9	34,704.2	39,738.9
Securities other than shares	30,883.9	35,337.8	36,719.4
Broad money	89,763.8	91,470.8	100,893.0

Source: IMF, *International Financial Statistics*.

COST OF LIVING
(Consumer Price Index; base: 2009 = 100)

	2010	2011	2012
Food (incl. non-alcoholic beverages)	102.2	109.0	117.4
Alcoholic beverages and tobacco	106.6	120.3	129.1
Rent, fuel and light	101.2	108.1	108.5
Clothing (incl. footwear)	82.5	73.1	68.0
Furniture, etc.	99.2	99.8	100.7
Health	101.5	104.1	108.4
Transport	105.4	111.1	114.3
Communications	95.4	92.6	91.9
Recreation and culture	94.5	88.7	88.6
Education	104.0	109.5	114.6
All items (incl. others)	101.4	104.8	108.0

NATIONAL ACCOUNTS
('000 million pesos at current prices)

Expenditure on the Gross Domestic Product

	2010	2011	2012
Government final consumption expenditure	13,645.2	14,576.0	15,833.9
Private final consumption expenditure	65,522.8	74,405.2	81,632.1
Increase in stocks	1,441.2	1,280.7	1,075.3
Gross fixed capital formation	23,406.7	27,248.2	31,513.9
Total domestic expenditure	104,016.0	117,510.2	130,055.3
Exports of goods and services	42,245.9	46,160.8	44,655.8
Less Imports of goods and services	35,254.1	42,178.4	44,184.3
GDP in purchasers' values	111,007.9	121,492.7	130,526.8

Gross Domestic Product by Economic Activity

	2010	2011	2012
Agriculture and forestry	3,029.8	3,590.7	3,752.8
Fishing	509.4	573.5	588.1
Mining and quarrying	17,743.1	18,086.5	16,947.6
Copper	16,360.2	16,131.8	15,143.8
Manufacturing	12,005.1	13,004.4	13,324.6
Electricity, gas and water	3,109.5	3,337.1	2,816.0
Construction	7,555.6	8,420.6	9,883.1
Trade, restaurants and hotels	10,402.6	12,062.8	14,010.1
Transport	4,825.4	4,771.4	5,331.3
Communications	2,205.6	2,410.0	2,599.5
Financial services*	18,742.4	21,309.3	24,043.8
Sale of real estate	5,302.3	5,699.9	5,910.4
Personal services†	11,874.3	13,043.9	14,345.4
Public administration	4,863.9	5,184.1	5,947.4
Sub-total	102,169.1	111,494.2	119,500.1
Value-added tax	8,194.4	9,347.6	10,334.0
Import duties	644.5	650.8	693.0
GDP in purchasers' values	111,007.9	121,492.7	130,526.8

* Including insurance, renting of property and business loans.
† Including education.

BALANCE OF PAYMENTS
(US $ million)

	2010	2011	2012
Exports of goods	71,108	81,455	78,277
Imports of goods	–55,474	–70,911	–74,855
Balance on goods	15,634	10,544	3,422
Exports of services	10,836	13,133	12,626
Imports of services	–12,972	–15,711	–15,061
Balance on goods and services	13,499	7,966	987
Primary income received	9,074	7,918	7,350
Primary income paid	–23,759.5	–22,059	–20,025
Balance on goods, services and primary income	–1,187	–6,175	–11,688
Secondary income received	5,657	4,322	3,891
Secondary income paid	–1,246	–1,430	–1,699
Current balance	3,224	–3,283	–9,496
Capital account (net)	6,241	14	13

—continued	2010	2011	2012
Direct investment assets	–9,461	–20,373	–21,090
Direct investment liabilities	15,373	22,931	30,323
Portfolio investment assets	–15,710	806	–13,891
Portfolio investment liabilities	9,289	10,729	10,481
Financial derivatives and employee stock options assets	8,668	12,270	9,674
Financial derivatives and employee stock options liabilities	–9,602	–14,688	–9,664
Other investment assets	–6,384	648	921
Other investment liabilities	1,883	5,490	3,193
Net errors and omissions	–498	–350	–829
Reserves and related items	3,023	14,192	–366

Source: IMF, *International Financial Statistics*.

External Trade

PRINCIPAL COMMODITIES
(distribution by SITC, US $ million, preliminary)

Imports c.i.f.	2010	2011	2012
Food and live animals	3,713	4,796	5,175
Mineral fuels, lubricants, etc.	11,445	15,933	17,990
Petroleum, petroleum products, etc.	9,017	12,386	14,589
Gas, natural and manufactured	1,724	2,388	2,250
Chemicals and related products	5,857	7,315	8,055
Basic manufactures	6,470	7,170	8,894
Machinery and transport equipment	18,727	22,542	29,110
Power generating machinery and equipment	1,044	1,140	1,099
Machinery specialized for particular industries	2,424	3,385	3,972
General industrial machinery equipment and parts	2,590	3,188	3,666
Telecommunications and sound equipment	2,358	2,697	3,441
Other electrical machinery apparatus, etc.	1,766	2,080	2,687
Road vehicles and parts*	6,319	7,717	9,251
Miscellaneous manufactured articles	4,860	6,042	7,939
Total (incl. others)	58,956	74,199	79,468

* Data on parts exclude tyres, engines and electrical parts.

Exports f.o.b.	2010	2011	2012
Food and live animals	9,981	12,088	12,300
Fish, crustaceans and molluscs and preparations thereof	2,817	3,932	3,788
Vegetables and fruit	4,890	5,612	5,803
Crude materials (inedible) except fuels	21,649	23,002	24,454
Pulp and waste paper	2,429	2,899	2,534
Metalliferous ores and metal scrap	17,395	17,930	19,684
Chemicals and related products	2,795	3,516	3,852
Basic manufactures	30,033	33,666	29,735
Non-ferrous metals	27,495	30,461	26,580
Total (incl. others)	71,028	80,586	78,277

PRINCIPAL TRADING PARTNERS
(US $ million, revised)

Imports c.i.f.	2010	2011	2012
Argentina	4,672	4,385	5,283
Brazil	4,632	6,196	5,186
Canada	708	876	1,032
China, People's Republic	8,296	10,686	14,432
Colombia	1,533	2,186	2,185
Ecuador	798	1,297	2,155
France	810	1,045	1,555
Germany	1,968	2,682	2,862
Italy	924	1,138	1,264
Japan	2,909	2,408	2,596
Korea, Republic	3,372	2,564	2,604
Mexico	2,037	2,438	2,608
Paraguay	613	603	211
Peru	1,331	2,018	2,072
Spain	937	1,050	1,394
United Kingdom	966	1,352	892
USA	9,335	13,948	18,188
Total (incl. others)	58,956	74,199	79,468

Exports f.o.b.	2010	2011	2012
Argentina	987	1,175	1,070
Australia	786	878	1,250
Belgium	1,658	1,364	1,249
Brazil	4,292	4,382	4,294
Canada	1,391	1,468	1,283
China, People's Republic	17,355	17,923	18,218
Colombia	735	939	914
France	1,204	1,418	1,222
Germany	893	1,132	941
India	1,754	1,873	2,586
Italy	2,460	2,731	2,013
Japan	7,593	8,826	8,384
Korea, Republic	4,086	4,330	4,551
Mexico	1,844	1,922	1,346
Netherlands	2,560	3,788	2,739
Peru	1,187	1,492	1,813
Spain	1,293	1,579	1,616
Switzerland	503	767	1,077
Taiwan	2,090	2,110	1,818
United Kingdom	643	727	715
USA	7,002	9,012	9,580
Venezuela	542	685	692
Total (incl. others)	71,028	80,586	78,277

Transport

PRINCIPAL RAILWAYS

	2010	2011	2012
Passenger journeys ('000)	22,020	26,859	29,463
Passenger-km ('000)	696,050	851,582	933,999
Freight ('000 metric tons)	25,215	27,374	27,537
Freight ton-km (million)	3,834	4,123	4,090

ROAD TRAFFIC
(motor vehicles in use)

	2010	2011	2012
Passenger cars and jeeps (excl. taxis)	2,070,060	2,262,436	2,479,813
Minibuses and vans	164,195	174,203	188,941
Light trucks	608,507	653,691	703,616
Motorcycles and mopeds	102,314	112,806	133,640

SHIPPING

Flag Registered Fleet
(at 31 December)

	2011	2012	2013
Number of vessels	596	601	614
Total displacement ('000 grt)	881	800	908

Source: Lloyd's List Intelligence (www.lloydslistintelligence.com).

International Sea-borne Shipping
(freight traffic, '000 metric tons)

	2008	2009	2010
Goods loaded	46,386	48,002	48,770
Goods unloaded	40,904	35,101	41,610

CIVIL AVIATION
(traffic on scheduled services)

	2010	2011	2012
Kilometres flown (million)	153.6	173.2	188.2
Passengers carried ('000)	11,064.5	12,989.3	15,234.0
Passenger-km (million)	25,096.5	28,320.5	31,412.0
Freight carried ('000 metric tons)	295.8	298.5	318.2
Freight ton-km (million)	5,306.2	6,367.0	6,647.7

Tourism

ARRIVALS BY NATIONALITY

	2010	2011	2012
Argentina	1,001,125	1,118,767	1,377,645
Bolivia	307,475	321,488	355,758
Brazil	229,337	324,594	373,840
France	60,091	60,993	60,220
Germany	57,899	58,202	62,891
Peru	308,759	338,916	338,026
Spain	51,874	55,643	62,646
USA	2,222,002	2,532,750	2,899,056
Total (incl. others)	2,800,637	3,137,285	3,554,279

Source: Servicio Nacional de Turismo.

Tourism receipts (US $ million, excl. passenger transport): 1,645 in 2010; 1,889 in 2011; 2,201 in 2012 (provisional) (Source: World Tourism Organization).

Communications Media

	2010	2011	2012
Telephones ('000 main lines in use)	3,457.5	3,366.3	3,275.7
Mobile cellular telephones ('000 subscribers)	19,852.2	22,400.0	24,130.8
Internet subscribers ('000)	1,818.8	2,025.1	n.a.
Broadband subscribers ('000)	1,779.1	2,002.6	2,166.8

Source: International Telecommunication Union.

Education

(2012 unless otherwise indicated)

	Institutions	Teachers	Students
Pre-primary	n.a.*	16,528†	348,495
Special primary		7,673†	159,078
Primary		75,854†	1,976,176
Secondary		49,144†	1,044,233
Adult		1,897‡	131,237†
Higher (incl. universities)	226‡	n.a.	1,127,181

* Many schools offer more than one level of education; a detailed breakdown is given below.

† 2004 figure.

‡ 2003 figure.

Schools (2004): Pre-primary: 640; Special 766; Primary 3,679; Secondary 517; Adult 292; Pre-primary and special 10; Pre-primary and primary 3,172; Pre-primary and secondary 1; Special and primary 22; Special and adult 3; Primary and secondary 380; Primary and adult 82; Secondary and adult 156; Pre-primary, special and primary 52; Pre-primary, primary and secondary 1,070; Pre-primary, primary and adult 261; Special, primary and secondary 2; Primary, secondary and adult 49; Pre-primary, special, primary and secondary 13; Pre-primary, special, primary and adult 7; Pre-primary, primary, secondary and adult 106; Pre-primary, special, primary, secondary and adult 5.

2010/11: *Teachers:* Pre-primary 57,404; Primary 69,191; Secondary 70,903; Tertiary 70,248. *Students:* Pre-primary 544,104; Primary 1,520,405; Secondary 1,493,033; Tertiary 1,061,527 (Source: UNESCO Institute for Statistics).

Pupil-teacher ratio (primary education, UNESCO estimate): 22.0 in 2010/11 (Source: UNESCO Institute for Statistics).

Adult literacy rate (UNESCO estimates): 98.6% (males 98.6%; females 98.5%) in 2009 (Source: UNESCO Institute for Statistics).

Directory

The Government

HEAD OF STATE

President: MICHELLE BACHELET JERIA (took office 11 March 2014).

THE CABINET
(April 2014)

The Government was comprised of members of the Nueva Mayoría coalition and independents.

Minister of the Interior and Public Security: RODRIGO PEÑAILILLO (PPD).

Minister of Foreign Affairs: HERALDO MUÑOZ (PPD).

Minister of National Defence: JORGE BURGOS (PDC).

Minister of Finance: ALBERTO ARENAS (PS).

Minister, Secretary-General of the Presidency: XIMENA RINCÓN (PDC).

Minister, Secretary-General of the Government: ALVARO ELIZALDE (PS).

Minister of the Economy, Development and Tourism: LUIS FELIPE CÉSPEDES (PDC).

Minister of Social Development: FERNANDA VILLEGAS (PS).

Minister of Education: NICOLÁS EYZAGUIRRE (PPD).

Minister of Justice: JOSÉ ANTONIO GÓMEZ (PRSD).

Minister of Labour and Social Security: JAVIERA BLANCO (Ind.).

Minister of Public Works: ALBERTO UNDURRAGA (PDC).

Minister of Health: HELIA MOLINA (PPD).

Minister of Housing and Urban Development: PAULINA SABALL (PS).

Minister of Agriculture: CARLOS FURCHE (PS).

Minister of Mining: AURORA WILLIAMS (PRSD).

Minister of Transport and Telecommunications: ANDRÉS GÓMEZ-LOBO (PPD).

Minister of National Property: VÍCTOR OSORIO (IC).

Minister of Energy: MÁXIMO PACHECO MATTE (PS).

Minister of the Environment: PABLO BADENIER (PDC).

Minister of Sport: NATALIA RIFFO (MAS).

Minister of the National Women's Service (Sernam): CLAUDIA PASCUAL (PC).

Minister of the National Commission for Culture and the Arts: CLAUDIA BARATTINI (Ind.).

MINISTRIES

Ministry of Agriculture: Teatinos 40, 1°, Santiago; tel. (2) 2393-5000; fax (2) 2393-5135; internet www.minagri.gob.cl.

Ministry of the Economy, Development and Tourism: Avda Libertador Bernardo O'Higgins 1449, Santiago Downtown Torre II, CP 8340487, Santiago; tel. (2) 2473-3400; fax (2) 2473-3403; e-mail economia@economia.cl; internet www.economia.cl.

Ministry of Education: Alameda 1371, 7°, Santiago; tel. (2) 2406-6000; fax (2) 2380-0317; e-mail consultas@mineduc.cl; internet www.mineduc.cl.

Ministry of Energy: Edif. Santiago Downtown II, 13° y 14°, Alameda 1449, Santiago; tel. (2) 2365-6800; internet www.minenergia.cl.

Ministry of the Environment: Teatinos 254/258, Santiago; tel. (2) 2240-5600; fax (2) 2240-5758; internet www.mma.gob.cl.

Ministry of Finance: Teatinos 120, 12°, Santiago; tel. (2) 2828-2000; internet www.minhda.cl.

Ministry of Foreign Affairs: Teatinos 180, Santiago; tel. (2) 2827-4200; internet www.minrel.gov.cl.

Ministry of Health: Enrique MacIver 541, 3°, Santiago; tel. (2) 2574-0100; e-mail consulta@minsal.cl; internet www.minsal.cl.

Ministry of Housing and Urban Development: Alameda 924, CP 6513482, Santiago; tel. (2) 2351-3000; fax (2) 2633-7830; e-mail contactenos@minvu.cl; internet www.minvu.cl.

Ministry of the Interior and Public Security: Palacio de la Moneda, Santiago; tel. (2) 2690-4000; fax (2) 2699-2165; internet www.interior.cl.

Ministry of Justice: Morandé 107, Santiago; tel. (2) 2674-3100; fax (2) 2698-7098; internet www.minjusticia.cl.

Ministry of Labour and Social Security: Huérfanos 1273, 6°, Santiago; tel. (2) 2753-0400; fax (2) 2753-0401; e-mail mintrab@mintrab.gob.cl; internet www.mintrab.gob.cl.

Ministry of Mining: Teatinos 120, 9°, Santiago; tel. (2) 2473-3000; fax (2) 2687-9339; internet www.minmineria.cl.

Ministry of National Defence: Edif. Diego Portales, 22°, Villavicencio 364, Santiago; tel. (2) 2222-1202; fax (2) 2633-0568; e-mail correo@defensa.cl; internet www.defensa.cl.

Ministry of National Property: Avda Libertador Bernardo O'Higgins 720, Santiago; tel. (2) 2937-5100; fax (2) 2351-2160; e-mail consultas@mbienes.cl; internet www.bienes.cl.

Ministry of Public Works: Morandé 59, Of. 545, 2°, Santiago; tel. (2) 2449-4000; fax (2) 2441-0914; e-mail dv.secretariatecnica@mop.gov.cl; internet www.vialidad.cl.

Ministry of Social Development: Ahumada 48, 7°, Santiago; tel. (2) 2675-1400; fax (2) 2672-1879; internet www.ministeriodesarrollosocial.gob.cl.

Ministry of Sport: Fidel Oteíza 1956, 3°, Providencia, Santiago; tel. (2) 754-0200; fax (2) 368-9685; internet www.ind.cl.

Ministry of Transport and Telecommunications: Amunátegui 139, 3°, Santiago; tel. (2) 2421-3000; fax (2) 2421-3552; internet www.mtt.cl.

National Commission for Culture and the Arts: Paseo Ahumada 11, 9°-11°, Santiago; tel. (2) 2618-9000; e-mail oirs@cultura.gob.cl; internet www.consejodelacultura.cl.

National Women's Service (Sernam): Huérfanos 1219, Santiago Centro, Santiago; tel. (2) 2549-6100; fax (2) 2549-6247; e-mail sernam@sernam.gov.cl; internet www.sernam.gov.cl.

Office of the Minister, Secretary-General of the Government: Palacio de la Moneda, Santiago; tel. (2) 2690-4000; fax (2) 2697-1756; e-mail cmladini@segegob.cl; internet www.segegob.cl.

Office of the Minister, Secretary-General of the Presidency: Moneda 1160, Entrepiso, Santiago; tel. (2) 2690-4000; fax (2) 2694-5888; e-mail contactenos@minsegpres.gob.cl; internet www.minsegpres.gob.cl.

President and Legislature

PRESIDENT

Election, First Round, 17 November 2013

Candidate	Valid votes	% of valid votes
Michelle Bachelet Jeria (Nueva Mayoría)*	3,073,570	46.69
Evelyn Matthei Fornet (Alianza)†	1,647,490	25.02
Marco Enríquez-Ominami Gumucio (PRO)	723,066	10.98
Franco Aldo Parisi Fernández (Ind.)	665,959	10.11
Marcel Claude Reyes (Partido Humanista)	184,966	2.81
Alfredo Sfeir Younis (PEV)	154,701	2.35
Others	132,722	2.02
Total valid votes‡	6,582,474	100.00

* Comprising the Concertación de Partidos por la Democracia coalition, the Partido Comunista de Chile, the Izquierda Ciudadana and the Movimiento Amplio Social.

† Comprising the Renovación Nacional and the Unión Demócrata Independiente.

‡ In addition, there were 46,394 blank and 67,361 spoiled votes.

Election, Second Round, 15 December 2013

Candidate	Valid votes	% of valid votes
Michelle Bachelet Jeria (Nueva Mayoría)*	3,468,389	62.16
Evelyn Matthei Fornet (Alianza)†	2,111,306	37.83
Total valid votes‡	5,579,695	100.00

* Comprising the Concertación de Partidos por la Democracia coalition, the Partido Comunista de Chile, the Izquierda Ciudadana and the Movimiento Amplio Social.

† Comprising the Renovación Nacional and the Unión Demócrata Independiente.

‡ In addition, there were 32,838 blank and 83,231 spoiled votes.

NATIONAL CONGRESS
(Congreso Nacional)

Senate

President: ISABEL ALLENDE BUSSI.

The Senate has 38 members, who hold office for an eight-year term, with approximately one-half of the seats renewable every four years. The last election, to renew 20 of the 38 seats, was held on 17 November 2013. The table below shows the composition of the Senate following that election.

Distribution of Seats by Legislative Bloc, November 2013

	Seats
Nueva Mayoría	21
Partido Socialista	7
Partido por la Democracia	6
Partido Demócrata Cristiano	6
Independents	2
Alianza	16
Unión Demócrata Independiente	8
Renovación Nacional	8
Independent	1
Total	38

Chamber of Deputies

President: ALDO CORNEJO GONZÁLEZ (PDC).

General Election, 17 November 2013, provisional results

Legislative bloc	% of valid votes	Seats
Nueva Mayoría	47.73	67
Partido Demócrata Cristiano	—	21
Partido Socialista de Chile	—	16
Partido por la Democracia	—	15
Partido Radical Socialdemócrata	—	6
Partido Comunista de Chile	—	6
Izquierda Ciudadana	—	1
Independents	—	2
Alianza	36.17	49
Unión Demócrata Independiente	—	29
Renovación Nacional	—	19
Independent	—	1
Partido Liberal de Chile	5.45	1
Independents	3.31	3
Partido Humanista	3.36	—
Nueva Constitución para Chile*	2.78	—
Partido Regionalista de los Independientes	1.16	—
Total valid votes†	100.00	120

* Electoral alliance led by the Partido Igualdad and the Partido Ecologista Verde.

† In addition there were 257,299 blank votes and 221,100 spoiled votes.

Election Commissions

Servicio Electoral: Esmeralda 611/615, Santiago; tel. (2) 2731-5500; fax (2) 2639-7296; e-mail consultas.servel@servel.cl; internet www.servel.cl; f. 1986; Dir PATRICIO SANTAMARÍA.

Tribunal Calificador de Elecciones (TCE): Calle Compañía de Jesús 1288, Santiago; tel. (2) 2733-9300; fax (2) 2699-4464; e-mail tce@tribunalcalificador.cl; internet www.tribunalcalificador.cl; f. 1980; Pres. PATRICIO VALDÉS ALDUNATE.

Political Organizations

Alianza: f. 1999 as the Alianza por Chile, known as the Coalición por el Cambio in 2009–12, adopted present name to contest the 2013 elections; right-wing alliance.

Renovación Nacional (RN): Antonio Varas 454, Providencia, Santiago; tel. (2) 2799-4200; fax (2) 2799-4212; e-mail clarrain@rn.cl; internet www.rn.cl; f. 1988; right-wing; Pres. CARLOS LARRAÍN PEÑA; Sec.-Gen. MARIO DESBORDES.

Unión Demócrata Independiente (UDI): Avda Suecia 286, Providencia, Santiago; tel. (2) 2241-4200; fax (2) 2233-6189; e-mail contacto@udi.cl; internet www.udi.cl; f. 1989; right-wing; Pres. PATRICIO MELERO; Sec.-Gen. JOSÉ ANTONIO KAST.

Concertación de Partidos por la Democracia (CPD): Londres 57, Santiago; tel. and fax (2) 2639-7170; f. 1988 as the Comando por el No, an opposition front to campaign against the military regime in the plebiscite of 5 Oct. 1988; adopted present name following plebiscite; contested the 2013 elections as the Nueva Mayoría coalition with the Partido Comunista de Chile (q.v.); Nat. Co-ordinator DOMINGO NAMUNCURA.

Partido Demócrata Cristiano (PDC): Alameda 1460, 2°, Santiago; tel. and fax (2) 2376-0136; e-mail info@pdc.cl; internet www.pdc.cl; f. 1957; Pres. IGNACIO WALKER PRIETO; Sec. VÍCTOR MALDONADO ROLDÁN.

Partido por la Democracia (PPD): Santo Domingo 1828, Santiago; tel. and fax (2) 2671-2320; e-mail presidencia@ppd.cl; internet www.ppd.cl; f. 1987; Pres. JAIME DANIEL QUINTANA LEAL; Sec.-Gen. LUIS GONZALO NAVARRETE MUÑOZ.

Partido Radical Socialdemócrata (PRSD): Londres 57, Santiago; tel. and fax (2) 2633-6928; fax (2) 2638-3353; e-mail ernestov@123mail.cl; internet www.partidoradical.cl; centre-left; Pres. JOSÉ ANTONIO GÓMEZ URRUTIA; Sec.-Gen. ERNESTO VELASCO RODRÍGUEZ.

Partido Socialista de Chile (PS): París 873, Santiago; tel. (2) 2549-9900; e-mail pschile@pschile.cl; internet www.pschile.cl; f. 1933; left-wing; mem. of Socialist International; Pres. OSVALDO ANDRADE LARA; Sec.-Gen. ALVARO ELIZALDE SOTO.

Izquierda Ciudadana (IC): Santiago; internet www.izquierdaciudadanadechile.cl; f. 1971 as Izquierda Cristiana de Chile, present name adopted 2013; mem. of the Nueva Mayoría coalition; Pres. CRISTIAN MÉNDEZ; Sec.-Gen. BERNARDA PÉREZ.

Movimiento Amplio Social (MAS): Calle Padre Alonso de Ovalle 726, Santiago; f. 2008; mem. of the Nueva Mayoría coalition; Pres. ALEJANDRO NAVARRO BRAIN; Sec.-Gen. FERNANDO ZAMORANO FERNÁNDEZ.

Partido Comunista de Chile (PC): Avda Vicuña Mackenna 31, Santiago; tel. and fax (2) 2222-2750; e-mail www@pcchile.cl; internet www.pcchile.cl; f. 1912; achieved legal status in 1990; contested the 2013 elections as mem. of the Nueva Mayoría coalition with the Concertación de Partidos por la Democracia (q.v.); Pres. GUILLERMO TEILLIER; Sec.-Gen. LAUTARO CARMONA.

Partido Ecologista Verde (PEV): O'Higgins 1104, Concepción; e-mail admin@partidoecologista.cl; internet partidoecologista.cl; f. 2002 as Partido Ecologista; Pres. ALEJANDRO IVÁN SAN MARTÍN BRAVO; Sec.-Gen. PABLO ANDRÉS PEÑALOZA TORRES.

Partido Humanista (PH): Condell 860, Providencia, Santiago; tel. (2) 2634-7562; e-mail danilo.monteverde.reyes@gmail.com; internet www.partidohumanista.cl; f. 1984; Pres. DANILO MONTEVERDE; Sec.-Gen. MICHELY BRAVO.

Partido Igualdad: Pasaje Huérfanos 1460, Of. 3B4, Santiago; tel. (2) 5792-3426; e-mail contacto@roxanamiranda.cl; internet partidoigualdad.cl; f. 2009; left-wing; Leader ROXANA MIRANDA MENESES.

Partido Liberal de Chile: Of. 613, Paseo Huérfanos 886, Santiago; tel. (2) 2638-0551; e-mail contacto@losliberales.cl; internet www.losliberales.cl; f. 2007 as Chile Primero by fmr mems of the Partido por la Democracia (q.v.), reconstituted in 2012; contested the 2013 legislative elections in alliance with the Partido Progresista; Pres. VLADO MIROSEVIC; Sec.-Gen. IVÁN MORÁN.

Partido Progresista (PRO): Salvador 1029, Providencia; tel. (2) 2204-5274; e-mail cwarner@losprogresistas.cl; internet losprogresistas.cl; f. 2010; Pres. PATRICIA MORALES ERRÁZURIZ; Sec.-Gen. CAMILO LAGOS.

Partido Regionalista de los Independientes (PRI): Avda Miraflores 133, Of. 33, Santiago; tel. (2) 2664-8772; fax (2) 2664-8773; e-mail pri@pricentro.cl; internet www.pricentro.cl; f. 2006 following merger of Alianza National de Independientes and Partido de Acción Regionalista de Chile; Pres. HUMBERTO DE LA MAZA MAILLET; Sec.-Gen. EDUARDO SALAS CERDA.

Wallmapuwen (Partido Nacionalista Mapuche): e-mail wallmapuwen@gmail.com; internet www.wallmapuwen.cl; f. 2005; campaigns for Mapuche rights; not officially registered; Pres. GUSTAVO QUILAQUEO BUSTOS; Sec.-Gen. CLAUDIO CARIHUENTRU MILLALEO.

Diplomatic Representation

EMBASSIES IN CHILE

Algeria: Monseñor Nuncio Sotero Sanz 221, Providencia, Santiago; tel. (2) 2820-2100; fax (2) 2820-2121; e-mail embajadargelia.cl@gmail.com; Ambassador NOURREDINE YAZID.

Argentina: Miraflores 285, Santiago; tel. (2) 2582-2500; fax (2) 2639-3321; e-mail ehile@cancilleria.gov.ar; internet ehile.cancilleria.gov.ar; Ambassador GINÉS GONZÁLEZ GARCÍA.

Australia: Isidora Goyenechea 3621, El Golf Torre B, 12° y 13°, Casilla 33, Correo 10 Las Condes, Santiago; tel. (2) 2550-3500; fax (2) 2331-5960; e-mail dima-santiago@dfat.gov.au; internet www.chile.embassy.gov.au; Ambassador TIMOTHY KANE.

Austria: Barros Errazuriz 1968, 3°, Santiago; tel. (2) 2223-4774; fax (2) 2204-9382; e-mail santiago-de-chile-ob@bmaa.gv.at; internet www.chile-embajadadeaustria.at; Ambassador DOROTHEA AUER.

Belgium: Edif. Forum, Avda Providencia 2653, 11°, Of. 1103, Santiago; tel. (2) 2232-1070; fax (2) 2232-1073; e-mail santiago@diplobel.org; internet www.diplomatie.be/santiago; Chargé d'affaires a.i. TOM VANDER ELST.

Brazil: Padre Alonso Ovalle 1665, Casilla 1497, Santiago; tel. (2) 2698-2486; fax (2) 2671-5961; e-mail embrasil@brasembsantiago.cl; internet www.brasembsantiago.cl; Ambassador GEORGES LAMAZIERE.

Canada: Edif. World Trade Center, Torre Norte, 12°, Nueva Tajamar 481, Santiago; tel. (2) 2652-3800; fax (2) 2652-3912; e-mail stago@international.gc.ca; internet www.canadainternational.gc.ca/chile-chili; Ambassador PATRICIA FULLER.

China, People's Republic: Pedro de Valdivia 550, Santiago; tel. (2) 2233-9880; fax (2) 2335-2755; e-mail embajadachina@entelchile.net; internet cl.china-embassy.org; Ambassador YANG WANMING.

Colombia: Los Militares 5885, 3°, Las Condes, Santiago; tel. (2) 2220-6273; fax (2) 2224-3585; e-mail echile@cancilleria.gov.co; internet chile.embajada.gov.co; Ambassador MAURICIO ECHEVERRY GUTIÉRREZ.

Costa Rica: Zurich 255, Of. 85, Las Condes, Santiago; tel. (2) 2334-9486; fax (2) 2334-9490; e-mail embacostarica@adsl.tie.cl; Ambassador JAN RUGE MOYA.

Croatia: Ezequias Alliende 2370, Providencia, Santiago; tel. (2) 2269-6141; fax (2) 2269-6092; e-mail croemb.santiago@mvep.hr; Chargé d'affaires a.i. IVIN RENEE.

Cuba: Avda Los Leones 1346, Providencia, Santiago; tel. (2) 2596-8553; fax (2) 2596-8584; e-mail emcuchil@embacuba.cl; internet www.embacuba.cl; Ambassador ADOLFO CURBELO CASTELLANOS.

Czech Republic: Avda El Golf 254, Santiago; tel. (2) 2232-1066; fax (2) 2232-0707; e-mail santiago@embassy.mzv.cz; internet www.mfa.cz/santiago; Ambassador ZDENĚK KUBÁNEK.

Denmark: Jacques Cazotte 5531, Casilla 18, Centro Cívico, Vitacura, Santiago; tel. (2) 2941-5100; fax (2) 2218-1736; e-mail sclamb@um.dk; internet chile.um.dk; Ambassador LARS STEEN NIELSEN.

Dominican Republic: Candelaria Goyenechea 4153, Vitacura, Santiago; tel. (2) 2953-5750; fax (2) 2953-5758; e-mail embrepdom@erd.co.cl; Ambassador PABLO ARTURO MARIÑEZ ALVAREZ.

Ecuador: Avda Providencia 1979 y Pedro Valdivia, 5°, Casilla 16007, Correo 9, Santiago; tel. (2) 2231-5073; fax (2) 2232-5833; e-mail embajadaecuador@adsl.tie.cl; internet www.embajadaecuador.cl; Ambassador FRANCISCO BORJA CEVALLOS.

Egypt: Roberto del Río 1871, Providencia, Santiago; tel. (2) 2274-8881; fax (2) 2274-6334; e-mail embassy.santiago@mfa.gov.eg; Ambassador HAZEM AHDY KHAIRAT.

El Salvador: Coronel 2330, 5°, Of. 51, Casilla 16863, Correo 9, Santiago; tel. (2) 2233-8324; fax (2) 2231-0960; e-mail embasalva@adsl.tie.cl; internet www.rree.gob.sv/embajadas/chile.nsf; Ambassador AIDA ELENA MINERO REYES.

Finland: Alcántara 200, Of. 201, Las Condes, Casilla 16657, Correo 9, Santiago; tel. (2) 2263-4917; fax (2) 2263-4701; e-mail sanomat.snt@formin.fi; internet www.finland.cl; Ambassador ILKKA HEISKANEN.

France: Avda Condell 65, Casilla 38D, Providencia, Santiago; tel. (2) 2470-8000; fax (2) 2470-8050; e-mail ambassade@ambafrance-cl.org; internet www.france.cl; Ambassador MARC GIACOMINI.

Germany: Las Hualtatas 5677, Vitacura, Santiago; tel. (2) 2463-2500; fax (2) 2463-2525; e-mail info@santigo-de-chile.diplo.de; internet www.santiago.diplo.de; Ambassador HANS-HENNING BLOMEYER-BARTENSTEIN.

Greece: Jorge Sexto 306, Las Condes, Santiago; tel. (2) 2212-7900; fax (2) 2212-8048; e-mail secretaria@mfa.gr; internet www.mfa.gr/santiago; Ambassador AGLAIA BALTA.

Guatemala: Zurich 255, Of. 55, Las Condes, Santiago; tel. (2) 2326-8133; fax (2) 2326-8142; e-mail embajada@guatemala.cl; internet www.guatemala.cl; Ambassador GUISELA ATALIDA GODINEZ SAZO.

Haiti: Zurich 255, Of. 21, Las Condes, Santiago; tel. (2) 2231-3364; fax (2) 2231-0967; e-mail embajada@embajadahaiti.cl; Ambassador JEAN-VICTOR HARVEL JEAN-BAPTISTE.

Holy See: Nuncio Sótero Sanz 200, Casilla 16836, Correo 9, Santiago (Apostolic Nunciature); tel. (2) 2231-2020; fax (2) 2231-0868; e-mail nunciatura@iglesia.cl; Apostolic Nuncio Most Rev. IVO SCAPOLO (Titular Archbishop of Thagaste).

Honduras: Zurich 255, Of. 51, Las Condes, Santiago; tel. (2) 2234-4069; fax (2) 2334-7946; e-mail secretaria@embajadadehonduras.cl; Ambassador MARÍA DEL CARMEN NASSER DE RAMOS.

Hungary: Avda Los Leones 2279, Providencia, Santiago; tel. (2) 2274-2210; fax (2) 2234-1227; e-mail huembstg@entelchile.net; Ambassador (vacant).

India: Alcantara 971, Casilla 10433, Las Condes, Santiago; tel. (2) 2228-4141; fax (2) 2321-7217; e-mail info@embajadaindia.cl; internet www.embajadaindia.cl; Ambassador DEBRAJ PRADHAN.

Indonesia: Avda Nueva Costanera 3318, Vitacura, Santiago; tel. (2) 2207-6266; fax (2) 2207-9901; e-mail kbristgo@mi.cl; Ambassador ALOYSIUS LELE MADHAAS.

Iran: Estoril 755, Las Condes, Santiago; tel. (2) 2723-3623; fax (2) 2723-3632; e-mail embiranchile@mail.com; internet www.embiranchile.com; Ambassador HOUSHANG KARIMI ABHARI.

Iraq: Enrique Fosters Sur 369, Santiago; tel. (2) 2984-5147; fax (2) 2982-5189; e-mail sanemb@iraqmfamail.com; internet www.mofamission.gov.iq/chl/ab/articles.aspx; Chargé d'affaires a.i. AMER ABDUL HUSSEIN ABBAS AL-FATLAWI.

Israel: San Sebastián 2812, 5°, Las Condes, Santiago; tel. (2) 2750-0500; fax (2) 2750-0555; e-mail amb.sec@santiago.mfa.gov.il; internet santiago.mfa.gov.il; Ambassador DAVID DADONN.

Italy: Clemente Fabres 1050, Providencia, Santiago; tel. (2) 2470-8400; fax (2) 2223-2467; e-mail info.santiago@esteri.it; internet www.ambsantiago.esteri.it; Ambassador MARCO RICCI.

Japan: Avda Ricardo Lyon 520, Santiago; tel. (2) 2232-1807; fax (2) 2232-1812; e-mail contactoembajadajapon@sg.mofa.go.jp; internet www.cl.emb-japan.go.jp; Ambassador HIDENORI MURAKAMI.

Jordan: Of. 1307, Calle Pio X 2460, Providencia, Santiago; tel. (2) 2975-6187; fax (2) 2975-6178; e-mail embajadadejordania@manquehue.net; Ambassador SUHEIL HADDAD.

Korea, Republic: Alcántara 74, Casilla 1301, Santiago; tel. (2) 2228-4214; fax (2) 2206-2355; e-mail coremb@tie.cl; internet chl.mofat.go.kr; Ambassador HWANG EUI-SEUNG.

Kuwait: San José de la Sierra 479, Las Condes, Santiago; tel. (2) 2883-9800; e-mail embajadadekuwaitchile@gmail.com; Ambassador REEM M. AL-KHALED.

Lebanon: Fray Montalva 292, Las Condes, Santiago; tel. (2) 2218-2835; fax (2) 2219-3502; e-mail info@embajadadellibano.cl; internet www.embajadadellibano.cl; Chargé d'affaires a.i. BRIGITTA AL-OJEIL.

Malaysia: Tajamar 183, 10°, Of. 1002, Correo 35, Las Condes, Santiago; tel. (2) 2233-6698; fax (2) 2234-3853; e-mail mwstg@embdemalasia.cl; internet www.kln.gov.my/perwakilan/santiago; Ambassador GANESON SIVAGURUNATHAN.

Mexico: Félix de Amesti 128, Las Condes, Santiago; tel. (2) 2583-8400; fax (2) 2583-8484; e-mail info@emexico.cl; internet www.emexico.cl; Ambassador OTTO RENÉ GRANADOS ROLDÁN.

Morocco: Avda Jorge VI 375, Las Condes, Santiago; tel. (2) 2212-1766; fax (2) 2212-1747; e-mail embamarruecos@yahoo.es; Ambassador ABDELKADER CHAUI LUDIE.

Netherlands: Apoquinado 3500, 13°, Las Condes, Santiago; tel. (2) 2756-9200; fax (2) 2756-9226; e-mail stg@minbuza.nl; internet chile.nlembajada.org; Ambassador MARION S. KAPPEYNE VAN DE COPPELLO.

New Zealand: Avda Isidora Goyenechea 3000, 12°, Las Condes, Santiago; tel. (2) 2616-3000; fax (2) 2951-6138; e-mail embajada@nzembassy.cl; internet www.nzembassy.cl; Ambassador JOHN CAPPER.

Nicaragua: Zurich 255, Of. 111, Las Condes, Santiago; tel. (2) 2234-1808; fax (2) 2234-5170; e-mail embanic@embajadadenicaragua.tie.cl; Ambassador MARÍA LUISA ROBLETO AGUILAR.

Norway: Los Militares 5001, 7°, Las Condes, Santiago; tel. (2) 2234-2888; fax (2) 2234-2201; e-mail emb.santiago@mfa.no; internet www.noruega.cl; Ambassador HEGE ARALDSEN.

Panama: Latadía 5930, Las Condes, Santiago; tel. (2) 2228-1687; e-mail embajadapanamachile@vtr.net; internet www.panamaenelexterior.gob.pa/chile; Ambassador MERCEDES ALFARO DE LÓPEZ.

Paraguay: Carmen Sylva 2437, Providencia, Santiago; tel. (2) 2963-6380; fax (2) 2963-6381; e-mail epychemb@entelchile.net; Ambassador TERUMI MATSUO DE CLAVEROL.

Peru: Avda Andrés Bello 1751, Casilla 16277, Providencia, Santiago; tel. (2) 2339-2600; fax (2) 2235-2053; e-mail embstgo@entelchile.net; Ambassador CARLOS PAREJA RÍOS.

Philippines: Félix de Amesti 367, Las Condes, Santiago; tel. (2) 2208-1313; fax (2) 2208-1400; e-mail embassyphil@vtr.net; Ambassador MARÍA CONSUELO PUYAT-REYES.

Poland: Mar del Plata 2055, Providencia, Santiago; tel. (2) 2204-1213; fax (2) 2204-9332; e-mail santiagodechile.embajada@msz.gov.pl; internet santiagodechile.msz.gov.pl; Ambassador ALEKSANDRA PIATKOWSKA.

Portugal: Nueva Tajamar 555, Torre Costanera 16°, Las Condes, Santiago; tel. (2) 2203-0542; fax (2) 2203-4004; e-mail embajada@embportugal.tie.cl; Ambassador LUIS JOÃO DE SOUSA LORVÃO.

Romania: Benjamín 2955, Las Condes, Santiago; tel. (2) 2231-1893; fax (2) 2232-2325; e-mail embajada@rumania.tie.cl; internet www.rumania.cl; Ambassador FLORIN ANGELO FLORIAN.

Russia: Avda Américo Vespucio 2127, Vitacura, Santiago; tel. (2) 2208-6254; fax (2) 2206-8892; e-mail embajada@rusia.tie.cl; internet www.chile.mid.ru; Ambassador MIKHAIL ORLOVETS.

South Africa: Avda 11 de Septiembre 2353, 17°, Torre San Ramón, Santiago; tel. (2) 2820-0300; fax (2) 2231-3185; e-mail info.chile@dirco.gov.za; internet www.embajada-sudafrica.cl; Ambassador HILTON FISHER.

Spain: Avda Andrés Bello 1895, Casilla 16456, Providencia, Santiago; tel. (2) 2235-2755; fax (2) 2235-1049; e-mail emb.santiagodechile@mae.es; internet www.mae.es/embajadas/santiagodechile; Ambassador IÑIGO DE PALACIO ESPAÑA.

Sweden: Avda 11 de Septiembre 2353, 4°, Providencia, Santiago; tel. (2) 2940-1700; fax (2) 2940-1730; e-mail ambassaden.santiago-de-chile@foreign.ministry.se; internet www.embajadasuecia.cl; Ambassador EVA ZETTERBERG.

Switzerland: Avda Américo Vespucio Sur 100, 14°, Las Condes, Santiago; tel. (2) 2928-0100; fax (2) 2928-0135; e-mail san.vertretung@eda.admin.ch; internet www.eda.admin.ch/santiago; Ambassador YVONNEE BAUMANN.

Syria: Carmencita 111, Casilla 12, Correo 10, Santiago; tel. (2) 2232-7471; fax (2) 2231-1825; e-mail embajadasiria@tie.cl; Chargé d'affaires a.i. KALIL BITAR.

Thailand: Avda Américo Vespucio 100, 15°, Las Condes, Santiago; tel. (2) 2717-3959; fax (2) 2717-3758; e-mail rte.santiago@vtr.net; internet www.thaiembassychile.org; Ambassador SURAPON PETCH-VRA.

Turkey: Edif. Montolin, Of. 71, Monseñor Sotero Sanz 55, Providencia, Santiago; tel. (2) 2231-8952; fax (2) 2231-7762; e-mail embturquia@123.cl; Ambassador NACIYE GÖKÇEN KAYA.

United Arab Emirates: Avda Apoquindo 3039, 7°, Las Condes, Santiago; tel. (2) 2790-0000; fax (2) 2790-0033; e-mail archive.santiago@mofa.gov.ae; Ambassador ABDULLAH MOHAMMED AL MU'INA.

United Kingdom: Avda el Bosque Norte 0125, Santiago; tel. (2) 2370-4100; fax (2) 2370-4160; e-mail embsan@britemb.cl; internet ukinchile.fco.gov.uk; Ambassador FIONA CLOUDER.

USA: Avda Andrés Bello 2800, Las Condes, Santiago; tel. (2) 2232-2600; fax (2) 2330-3710; internet chile.usembassy.gov; Ambassador MICHAEL A. HAMMER.

Uruguay: Avda Pedro de Valdivia 711, Santiago; tel. (2) 2204-7988; fax (2) 2204-7772; e-mail urusgo@uruguay.cl; internet www.uruguay.cl; Ambassador RODOLFO CAMAROSANO BERSANI.

Venezuela: Bustos 2021, Providencia, Santiago; tel. (2) 2365-8700; fax (2) 2981-9087; e-mail embve.chile@mppre.gob.ve; internet chile.embajada.gob.ve; Ambassador ENRIQUE AREVALO MÉNDEZ ROMERO.

Viet Nam: Eliodoro Yañez 2897, Providencia, Santiago; tel. (2) 2244-3633; fax (2) 2244-3799; e-mail sqvnchile@yahoo.com; Ambassador HA THI NGOC HA.

Judicial System

There are Courts of Appeal throughout the country whose members are appointed from a list submitted to the President of the Republic by the Supreme Court. The number of members of each court varies. Judges and ministers of the Supreme Court do not continue in office beyond the age of 75 years.

Corte Suprema: Compañía 1140, 2°, Santiago; tel. (2) 2873-5000; fax (2) 2873-5276; e-mail mgonzalezp@poderjudicial.cl; internet www.poderjudicial.cl; 21 mems; Pres. SERGIO MUÑOZ GAJARDO.

Attorney-General: SABAS CHAHUÁN.

Religion

CHRISTIANITY

The Roman Catholic Church

According to the latest available census figures (2002), some 70% of the population aged 15 years and above are Roman Catholics. Chile comprises five archdioceses, 19 dioceses, two territorial prelatures and one apostolic vicariate.

Bishops' Conference: Conferencia Episcopal de Chile, Echaurren 4, 6°, Casilla 517-V, Correo 21, Santiago; tel. (2) 2671-7733; fax (2) 2698-1416; e-mail prensa@episcopado.cl; internet www.iglesia.cl; f. 1955 (statutes approved 2000); Pres. Cardinal RICARDO EZZATI ANDRELLO (Archbishop of Santiago).

Archbishop of Antofagasta: PABLO LIZAMA RIQUELME, San Martín 2628, Casilla E, Antofagasta; tel. and fax (55) 226-8856; e-mail antofagasta@episcopado.cl; internet www.iglesiadeantofagasta.cl.

Archbishop of Concepción: FERNANDO CHOMALI GARIB, Calle Barros Arana 544, Casilla 65-C, Concepción; tel. (41) 262-6100; fax (41) 223-2844; e-mail amoreno@episcopado.cl; internet www.arzobispadodeconcepcion.cl.

Archbishop of La Serena: RENE OSVALDO REBOLLEDO SALINAS, Los Carrera 450, Casilla 613, La Serena; tel. (51) 222-5658; fax (51) 222-5291; e-mail laserena@episcopado.cl; internet www.arzobispadodelaserena.cl.

Archbishop of Puerto Montt: CRISTIÁN CARO CORDERO, Calle Benavente 385, Casilla 17, Puerto Montt; tel. (65) 225-2215; fax (65) 227-1861; e-mail puertomontt@episcopado.cl; internet www.arzobispadodepuertomontt.cl.

Archbishop of Santiago de Chile: Cardinal RICARDO EZZATI ANDRELLO, Erasmo Escala 1872, Casilla 30-D, Santiago; tel. (2) 2787-5600; fax (2) 2787-5664; e-mail curiasantiago@arzobispado.tie.cl; internet www.iglesiadesantiago.cl.

The Anglican Communion

Anglicans in Chile come within the Diocese of Chile, which forms part of the Anglican Church of the Southern Cone of America, covering Argentina, Bolivia, Chile, Paraguay, Peru and Uruguay.

Bishop of Chile: Rt Rev. HECTOR F. ZAVALA, Corporación Anglicana de Chile, Victoria Subercaseaux 41, Of. 301, Casilla 50675, Correo Central, Santiago; tel. (2) 2638-3009; fax (2) 2639-4581; e-mail diocesis@iach.cl; internet www.iach.cl.

Other Christian Churches

According to the 2002 census, 15% of the population are Evangelical Christians, 1% are Jehovah's Witnesses and 1% are Mormons.

Church of Jesus Christ of Latter-Day Saints (Mormons): Pocuro 1940, Providencia 664-1404, Santiago; tel. (2) 340-5070; internet www.lds.org; 577,716 mems.

Iglesia Católica Apostólica Ortodoxa de la Santísima Virgen María (Orthodox Church of the Patriarch of Antioch): Avda Pedro de Valdivia 92, Providencia, Santiago; tel. (2) 2231-7284; fax (2) 2232-0860; e-mail iglesia@iglesiaortodoxa.cl; internet www.iglesiaortodoxa.cl; Archbishop Mgr SERGIO ABAD.

Iglesia Evangélica Luterana en Chile: Juan Enrique Concha 121, Nuñoa, Casilla 167–11, Santiago; tel. (2) 2223-3195; fax (2) 2205-2193; e-mail secretaria@ielch.cl; internet www.ielch.cl; f. 1937; Pres. Dr LUIS ALVAREZ FIGUEROA; 3,000 mems.

Iglesia Luterana en Chile: Avda Lota 2330, POB 16067, Correo 9, Santiago; tel. (2) 2231-7222; fax (2) 2231-3913; e-mail obispo@iglesialuterana.cl; internet www.iglesialuterana.cl; Bishop SIEGFRIED SANDER; 10,280 mems.

Iglesia Metodista de Chile: Sargento Aldea 1041, Casilla 67, Santiago; tel. (2) 2556-6074; fax (2) 2554-1763; e-mail imech.chile@metodista.cl; internet www.metodistachile.cl; autonomous since 1969; Bishop MARIO MARTÍNEZ TAPIA; 9,882 mems.

Iglesia Pentecostal de Chile: Manuel Rodríguez 1155, Curicó; tel. (75) 231-8640; e-mail iglesia@pentecostaldechile.cl; internet www.pentecostaldechile.cl; f. 1947; Pres. Rev. SERGIO VELOSO TOLOSA; Bishop Rev. LUIS ULISES MUÑOZ MORAGA; 125,000 mems.

Jehovah's Witnesses: Avda Concha y Toro 3456, Casilla 267, Puente Alto; tel. (2) 2428-2600; fax (2) 2428-2609; Dir PEDRO J. LOVATO GROSSO.

Unión de Iglesias Evangélicas Bautistas de Chile: Miguel Claro 755, Providencia, Santiago; tel. (2) 2264-1208; fax (2) 2431-8012; e-mail centrobautista@ubach.cl; internet www.ubach.cl; f. 1908; Pres. Pastor MAURICIO REYES.

JUDAISM

There is a small Jewish community in Chile, numbering 14,976 at the 2002 census (less than 1% of the population).

Círculo Israelita de Santiago: Comandante Malbec 13210, Lo Barnechea, Santiago; tel. (2) 2240-5000; fax (2) 2243-6244; e-mail socios@cis.cl; internet www.cis.cl; f. 1982; Rabbi EDUARDO WAINGORTIN.

Comunidad Israelita Sefardi de Chile: Avda Las Condes 8361, Providencia, Santiago; tel. (2) 2202-0330; fax (2) 2204-7382; e-mail contacto@sefaradies.cl; internet www.sefaradies.cl; Rabbi ANGEL KREIMAN.

ISLAM

There is a small Muslim community in Chile, numbering 2,894 at the 2002 census (less than 1% of the population).

Centro Islámico de Chile: Mezquita As-Salam, Campoamor 2975, esq. Chile-España, Nuñoa, Santiago; tel. (2) 2343-1376; fax (2) 2343-1378; e-mail contacto@islamenchile.cl; internet www.islamenchile.cl; f. 1925 as the Sociedad Unión Musulmana; Sec. MOHAMED RUMIE.

BAHÁ'Í FAITH

National Spiritual Assembly: Manuel de Salas 356, Casilla 3731, Nuñoa, Santiago; tel. (2) 2752-3999; fax (2) 2752-3999; e-mail secretaria@bahai.cl; internet www.bahai.cl.

The Press

DAILIES

Santiago

La Cuarta: Diagonal Vicuña Mackenna 1870, Casilla 2795, Santiago; tel. (2) 2551-7067; fax (2) 2555-7071; e-mail contacto@lacuarta.cl; internet www.lacuarta.cl; f. 1984; morning; popular; Dir SERGIO MARABOLÍ TRIVIÑO; circ. 146,000.

Diario Financiero: Avda Apoquindo 3885, 1°, Las Condes, Santiago; tel. (2) 2339-1000; fax (2) 2231-3340; e-mail ventas@df.cl; internet www.df.cl; f. 1988; morning; Gen. Man. PAULA URENDA WARREN; circ. 20,000.

Diario Oficial de la República de Chile: Dr Torres Boonen 511, Providencia, Santiago; tel. (2) 2486-3600; fax (2) 2698-1059; e-mail consultasdof@interior.gob.cl; internet www.diariooficial.interior.gob.cl; f. 1877; Dir CARMEN CECILIA POWER HELFMANN; circ. 2,000.

Estrategia: Luis Carrera 1289, Vitacura, Santiago; tel. (2) 2655-6100; fax (2) 2655-6439; e-mail estrategia@estrategia.cl; internet www.estrategia.cl; f. 1978; morning; business news; Dir VÍCTOR MANUEL OJEDA MÉNDEZ; circ. 33,000.

La Hora: Avda Vicuña Mackenna 1870, Santiago; tel. (2) 2550-7000; fax (2) 2550-7770; e-mail contacto@lahora.cl; internet www.lahora.cl; f. 1997; Mon.–Fri; distributed free of charge; Editor SALVADOR CARMONA SCHÖNFFELDT; circ. 106,000.

El Mercurio: Avda Santa María 5542, Casilla 13-D, Santiago; tel. (2) 2330-1111; fax (2) 2242-6965; e-mail elmercurio@mercurio.cl; internet www.elmercurio.cl; f. 1900; morning; conservative; Dir CRISTIÁN ZEGERS ARIZTÍA; circ. 154,000 (Mon.–Fri.), 232,000 (weekends).

La Nación: Serrano 14, Casilla 81-D, Santiago; tel. (2) 2787-0100; fax (2) 2698-1059; e-mail contactoln@lanacion.cl; internet www.lanacion.cl; f. 1917 to replace govt-subsidized El Cronista; online only from Dec. 2010; owned by Soc. Periodística La Nación; Dir SAMUEL ROMO; circ. 11,000.

Santiago Times: Avda Santa María 227, Of. 12, Santiago; tel. (2) 2735-9044; fax (2) 2777-5376; e-mail editor@santiagotimes.cl; internet www.santiagotimes.cl; f. 1991; daily; national news in English; Publr STEVE ANDERSON; Editor-in-Chief DAVID PEDIGO; 10,000 subscribers.

La Segunda: Avda Santa María 5542, Casilla 13-D, Santiago; tel. (2) 2330-1111; fax (2) 2242-6965; e-mail cartas@lasegunda.cl; internet www.lasegunda.com; f. 1931; owned by proprs of *El Mercurio*; evening; Dir VÍCTOR CARVAJAL; circ. 40,000.

La Tercera: Avda Vicuña Mackenna 1870, Nuñoa, Santiago; tel. (2) 2550-7000; fax (2) 2555-7071; e-mail contactoweb@grupocopesa.cl; internet www.latercera.cl; f. 1950; morning; Dir ANDRÉS AZÓCAR ZAMUDIO; circ. 91,000 (Mon.–Fri.), 201,000 (weekends).

Las Ultimas Noticias: Bellavista 0112, Providencia, Santiago; tel. (2) 2730-3000; fax (2) 2730-3331; e-mail ultimas.noticias@lun.cl; internet www.lun.cl; f. 1902; owned by the proprs of *El Mercurio*; morning; Dir AGUSTÍN EDWARDS DEL RÍO; circ. 133,000 (Mon.–Fri.), 176,000 (weekends).

Antofagasta

La Estrella del Norte: Manuel Antonio Matta 2112, Antofagasta; tel. (55) 245-3672; fax (55) 245-3671; e-mail cronicanorte@estrellanorte.cl; internet www.estrellanorte.cl; f. 1966; evening; Dir SERGIO MERCADO RICHARDS; circ. 5,000.

El Mercurio de Antofagasta: Manuel Antonio Matta 2112, Antofagasta; tel. (55) 2425-3600; fax (55) 2425-3612; e-mail cartas@mercurioantofagasta.cl; internet www.mercurioantofagasta.cl; f. 1906; morning; conservative ind; owned by Soc. Chilena de Publicaciones; Dir VÍCTOR TOLOZA JIMÉNEZ; circ. 9,000.

Arica

La Estrella de Arica: San Marcos 580, Arica; tel. (58) 235-2828; fax (58) 235-2841; e-mail cronica@estrellaarica.cl; internet www.estrellaarica.cl; f. 1976; Dir EDUARDO CAMPOS CORREA; circ. 10,000.

Atacama

Chañarcillo: Maipú 849, Casilla 198, Copiapó, Atacama; tel. and fax (52) 224-0948; fax (52) 221-9044; internet www.chanarcillo.cl; f. 1992; morning; Dir ALBERTO BICHARA NICOLÁS.

Calama

El Mercurio de Calama: Abaroa 2051, Calama; tel. (55) 245-8571; fax (55) 245-8172; e-mail cronicacalama@mercurio.cl; internet www.mercuriocalama.cl; f. 1968; owned by Soc. Chilena de Publicaciones; Dir JAVIER ORELLANA VERA; circ. 4,500 (weekdays), 7,000 (Sun.).

Chillán

La Discusión: 18 de Septiembre 721, Casilla 479, Chillán; tel. (42) 220-1200; fax (42) 221-3578; e-mail diario@ladiscusion.cl; internet www.diarioladiscusion.cl; f. 1870; morning; ind; Dir FRANCISCO MARTINIC FIGUEROA; circ. 5,000.

Concepción

El Sur: Caupolicán 518, 8°, Casilla 8-C, Concepción; tel. (41) 279-4760; fax (41) 279-4761; e-mail buzon@diarioelsur.cl; internet www.elsur.cl; f. 1882; morning; ind; Dir MAURICIO RIVAS ALVEAR; circ. 28,000 (weekdays), 45,000 (Sun.).

Copiapó

El Diario de Atacama: Atacama 725A, Copiapó; tel. (52) 221-8509; fax (52) 223-2212; e-mail ddoll@diarioatacama.cl; internet www.diarioatacama.cl; f. 1970; morning; ind.; Dir DAVID DOLL PINTO; circ. 6,500.

Coyhaique

El Diario de Aysén: 21 de Mayo 410, Coyhaique; tel. (67) 2234-850; fax (67) 2232-318; e-mail contacto@diarioaysen.cl; internet www.diarioaysen.cl; f. 1981; Dir GABRIELA VICENTINI ROGEL.

Curicó

La Prensa: Sargento Aldea 632, Curicó; tel. (75) 231-0132; fax (75) 231-1924; e-mail correo@diariolaprensa.cl; internet diariolaprensa.cl; f. 1898; morning; right-wing; Dir MANUEL MASSA MAUTINO; circ. 6,000.

Iquique

La Estrella de Iquique: Luis Uribe 452, Iquique; tel. (57) 239-9311; fax (57) 242-7975; e-mail cronica@estrellaiquique.cl; internet www.estrellaiquique.cl; f. 1966; evening; Dir CAUPOLICÁN MÁRQUEZ VERGARA; circ. 10,000.

La Serena

El Día: Brasil 431, La Serena; tel. (51) 220-0400; fax (51) 221-9599; e-mail azenteno@eldia.la; internet diarioeldia.cl; f. 1944; morning; Editor ELEAZAR GARVISO GÁLVEZ; Dir FRANCISCO PUGA VERGARA; circ. 10,800.

Los Angeles

La Tribuna: Colo Colo 464, Casilla 15-D, Los Angeles; tel. (43) 231-3315; fax (43) 231-4987; e-mail gerencia@diariolatribuna.cl; internet www.diariolatribuna.cl; f. 1958; ind; Dir DANIA PINCHEIRA PASCAL; circ. 4,200.

Osorno

El Austral–El Diario de Osorno: O'Higgins 870, Osorno; tel. (64) 222-2300; fax (64) 222-2316; e-mail cronica@australosorno.cl; internet www.australosorno.cl; f. 1982; Dir GUIDO RODRÍGUEZ AVÍLES; circ. 6,500 (weekdays), 7,300 (Sun.).

Ovalle

El Ovallino: Vicuña Mackenna 473, Ovalle; tel. (53) 243-3430; fax (53) 243-3429; e-mail contacto@elovallino.cl; internet www.elovallino.cl; f. 1989; Editor DAVID FLORES BARRIOS.

Puerto Montt

El Llanquíhue: Antonio Varas 167, Puerto Montt; tel. (65) 243-2400; fax (65) 243-2401; e-mail cartasdirector@diariollanquihue.cl; internet www.diariollanquihue.cl; f. 1885; Dir ROBERTO GAETE PARRAGUEZ; circ. 4,800 (weekdays), 5,700 (Sun.).

Punta Arenas

La Prensa Austral: Waldo Seguel 636, Casilla 9-D, Punta Arenas; tel. (61) 220-4000; fax (61) 224-7406; e-mail redaccion@laprensaaustral.cl; internet www.laprensaaustral.cl; f. 1941; morning; ind.; Gen. Editor POLY RAÍN HARO; Dir FRANCISCO KARELOVIC CAR; circ. 8,000 (Mon.–Sat.); *El Magallanes*; f. 1894, circ. 9,500.

Quillota

El Observador: La Concepción 277, Casilla 1-D, Quillota; tel. (33) 234-2209; fax (33) 231-1417; e-mail elobser@entelchile.net; internet www.diarioelobservador.cl; f. 1970; Man. Dir ROBERTO SILVA BIJIT.

Rancagua

El Rancagüino: O'Carroll 518, Casilla 50, Rancagua; tel. (72) 232-7400; e-mail web@elrancaguino.cl; internet www.elrancaguino.cl; f. 1915; ind; Dir ALEJANDRO GONZÁLEZ PINO; circ. 10,000.

Talca

El Centro: Casa Matriz, Avda Lircay 3030, Talca; tel. (71) 251-5300; fax (71) 251-0310; e-mail diario@diarioelcentro.cl; internet www.diarioelcentro.cl; f. 1989; Dir JOSÉ ALVAREZ ESPINOZA.

Temuco

El Austral–El Diario de la Araucanía: Antonio Varas 945, Casilla 1-D, Temuco; tel. (45) 229-2727; fax (45) 223-7765; e-mail cronica@australtemuco.cl; internet www.australtemuco.cl; f. 1916; owned by Soc. Periodística Araucanía; morning; commercial, industrial and agricultural interests; Dir MARCO SALAZAR PARDO; circ. 15,100 (weekdays), 23,500 (Sun.).

Tocopilla

La Estrella de Tocopilla: Bolívar 1244, Tocopilla; tel. (83) 281-3036; e-mail prensa@prensatocopilla.cl; internet www.prensatocopilla.cl; f. 1924; morning; ind; Dir SERGIO MERCADO RICHARDS; circ. 3,000.

Valdivia

El Diario Austral de Valdivia: Yungay 499, Valdivia; tel. (63) 224-2200; fax (63) 224-2209; e-mail cartasdirector@australvaldivia.cl; internet www.australvaldivia.cl; f. 1982; Dir VERÓNICA MORENO AGUILERA; circ. 5,600.

Valparaíso

La Estrella: Esmeralda 1002, Casilla 57-V, Valparaíso; tel. (32) 226-4264; fax (32) 226-4108; e-mail cartasdirector@estrellavalpo.cl; internet www.estrellavalpo.cl; f. 1921; evening; owned by the proprs of *El Mercurio*; Dir CARLOS VERGARA EHRENBERG; circ. 28,000 (weekdays), 35,000 (Sat.).

El Mercurio de Valparaíso: Esmeralda 1002, Casilla 57-V, Valparaíso; tel. (32) 226-4264; fax (32) 226-4248; e-mail sclientevalpo@mercuriovalpo.cl; internet www.mercuriovalpo.cl; f. 1827; owned by the proprs of *El Mercurio*; morning; Dir PEDRO URZÚA BAZIN; circ. 65,000.

PERIODICALS

América Economía: tel. (2) 2290-9400; fax (2) 2206-6005; e-mail rferro@aeconomia.cl; internet www.americaeconomia.com; f. 1986; monthly; business; Publr and Editor ELÍAS SELMAN; Gen. Man. EDUARDO ALBORNOZ.

CA (Ciudad/Arquitectura) Revista Oficial del Colegio de Arquitectos de Chile AG: Avda Libertador Bernardo O'Higgins 115, Santiago; tel. (2) 2353-2321; fax (2) 2353-2355; e-mail revistaca@colegioarquitectos.com; internet www.revistaca.cl; f. 1968; 4 a year; architecture; Dir HUGO MONDRAGÓN L.; circ. 4,000.

Caras: Rosario Norte 555, 18°, Santiago; tel. (2) 2595-5000; e-mail revista@caras.cl; internet www.caras.cl; f. 1988; women's interest; Dir CAROLINA GARCÍA-HUIDOBRO; Editor LORRAINE THOMSON.

Chile Forestal: Paseo Bulnes 265, Of. 601, Santiago; tel. (2) 2663-0208; fax (2) 2696-6724; e-mail mariela.espejo@conaf.cl; internet www.conaf.cl/conaf/seccion-revista-chile-forestal.html; f. 1974; 6 a year; state-owned; technical information and features on forestry sector; Dir RICARDO SAN MARTÍN; Editor MARIELA ESPEJO SUAZO; circ. 4,000.

Cinegrama: Avda Holanda 279, Providencia, Santiago; tel. (2) 2422-8500; fax (2) 2422-8570; e-mail cinegrama@cinegrama.cl; internet www.cinegrama.cl; f. 1987; monthly; cinema; Dir JUAN IGNACIO OTO; Editor LEYLA LÓPEZ.

The Clinic: Santo Domingo 550, Of. 601, Santiago; tel. (2) 2633-9584; fax (2) 2639-6584; e-mail theclinic@theclinic.cl; internet www.theclinic.cl; fortnightly; political and social satire; Editor PABLO BASADRE; Dir PATRICIO FERNÁNDEZ CHADWICK.

Conozca Más: Rosario Norte 555, 18°, Las Condes, Santiago; tel. (2) 2366-7100; fax (2) 2246-2810; e-mail viamail@conozcamas.cl; internet www.conozcamas.cl; monthly; science; Dir PAULA AVILÉS VILLAGRA; circ. 90,000.

Cosas: Almirante Pastene 259, Providencia, Santiago; tel. (2) 2364-5100; fax (2) 2235-8331; e-mail info@cosas.com; internet www.cosas.com; f. 1976; fortnightly; entertainment and lifestyle; Editor Oscar Sepúlveda Pacheco; Dir Mónica Comandari Kaiser; circ. 40,000.

Ercilla: Avda Holanda 279, Providencia, Santiago; tel. (2) 2422-8500; fax (2) 2422-8570; e-mail ercilla@holanda.cl; internet www.ercilla.cl; f. 1936; weekly; general interest; conservative; Dir Juan Ignacio Oto; circ. 28,000.

El Gráfico: Avda Kennedy 5735, Of. 701, Torre Poniente Hotel Marriott, Las Condes, Santiago; tel. (2) 2434-4900; fax (2) 2421-5900; e-mail deportes@publimetro.cl; internet www.elgraficochile.cl; monthly; sport, illustrated; Editor Matías Carvajal.

Paula: Vicuña Mackenna 1962, Nuñoa, Santiago; tel. (2) 2550-7000; fax (2) 2550-7195; e-mail cartas@paula.cl; internet www.paula.cl; f. 1967; monthly; women's interest; Dir Milena Vodanovic; Editor Carolina Díaz; circ. 85,000.

Punto Final: San Diego 31, Of. 606, Casilla 13954, Correo 21, Santiago; tel. and fax (2) 2697-0615; e-mail revistapuntofinal@movistar.cl; internet www.puntofinal.cl; f. 1965; fortnightly; politics; left-wing; Dir Manuel Cabieses Donoso; circ. 15,000.

¿Qué Pasa?: Vicuña Mackenna 1870, Nuñoa, Santiago; tel. (2) 2550-7523; fax (2) 2550-7529; e-mail quepasa@copesa.cl; internet www.quepasa.cl; f. 1971; weekly; general interest; Editor Francisco Aravena; Dir José Luis Santa María; circ. 30,000.

Revista Agrícola: O'Higgin 870, Osorno; tel. (63) 222-2300; e-mail contacto@revistaagricola.cl; internet www.revistaagricola.cl; agricultural research; Dir Guido Rodríguez Avíles.

Revista Mensaje: Cienfuegos 21, Santiago; tel. (2) 2698-0617; fax (2) 2671-7030; e-mail rrpp@mensaje.cl; internet www.mensaje.cl; f. 1951; monthly; national, church and international affairs; Dir Antonio Delfau; circ. 6,000.

Vea: Avda Holanda 279, Providencia, Santiago; tel. (2) 2422-8500; fax (2) 2422-8572; e-mail vea@holanda.cl; internet www.vea.cl; f. 1939; weekly; general interest, illustrated; Dir Martha Beltrán; circ. 150,000.

PRESS ASSOCIATION

Asociación Nacional de la Prensa: Carlos Antúnez 2048, Providencia, Santiago; tel. (2) 2232-1004; fax (2) 2232-1006; e-mail info@anp.cl; internet www.anp.cl; f. 1951; Pres. Alvaro Caviedes Barahona; Sec.-Gen. Sebastián Zárate Rojas.

NEWS AGENCIES

Agencia Chile Noticias (ACN): Carlos Antúnez 1884, Of. 104, Providencia, Santiago; tel. and fax (2) 2717-9121; e-mail prensa@chilenoticias.cl; internet www.chilenoticias.cl; f. 1993; Editor Norberto Parra Hidalgo.

Agencia Orbe: Avda Phillips 56, Of. 66, Santiago; tel. (2) 2251-7800; fax (2) 2251-7801; e-mail prensa@orbe.cl; internet www.orbe.cl; f. 1955; Bureau Chief Patricia Escalona Cáceres.

Business News Americas: San Patricio 2944, Las Condes, Santiago; tel. (2) 2941-0300; fax (2) 2232-9376; e-mail info@bnamericas.com; internet www.bnamericas.com; internet-based business information; CEO Gregory Barton.

UPI Chile Ltd: Avda Nataniel Cox 47, 9°, Santiago; tel. (2) 2657-0874; fax (2) 2698-6605; e-mail prensa@upi.com; internet www.upi.cl; Gen. Man. Jorgeq Iribarren Espejo.

Publishers

Carlos Quiroga Editorial: La Concepción 56, Of. 202, Providencia, Santiago; tel. and fax (2) 2202-9825; e-mail cquiroga@carlosquiroga.cl; internet www.carlosquiroga.cl; children's and educational; Gen. Man. Marianella Medina.

Edebé—Editorial Don Bosco: Avda Gen. Bulnes 35, Santiago; tel. (2) 2437-8050; e-mail contacto@edebe.cl; internet www.edebe.cl; f. 1904 as Editorial Salesiana; adopted present name in 1996; general, political, biography, religious, children's; Chair. Aldo Moltedo; Gen. Man. Pablo Marinkovic.

Ediciones B Chile: Avda Las Torres 1375a, Huechuraba, Santiago; tel. (2) 2729-5400; fax (2) 2231-6300; e-mail mansieta@edicionesbchile.cl; internet www.edicionesbchile.cl; f. 1986; part of Grupo Zeta; children's and fiction; Gen. Man. Marilén Wood.

Ediciones Mil Hojas: Avda Antonio Varas 1480, Providencia, Santiago; tel. (2) 2274-3172; fax (2) 2223-7544; e-mail milhojas@terra.cl; internet www.milhojas.cl; educational and reference; Dir Julieta Melo Cabello.

Ediciones Universitarias de Valparaíso: Universidad Católica de Valparaíso, Calle 12 de Febrero 187, Casilla 1415, Valparaíso; tel. (32) 227-3087; fax (32) 227-3429; e-mail euvsa@ucv.cl; internet www.euv.cl; f. 1970; literature, social and general sciences, engineering, education, music, arts, textbooks; Chair. Patricio Arana Espina; Gen. Man. María Teresa Vega Segovia.

Ediciones Urano: Avda Francisco Bilbao 2790, CP 7510745, Providencia, Santiago; tel. (2) 2341-7493; fax (2) 2225-3896; e-mail info@edicionesurano.cl; internet www.edicionesurano.cl; f. 1983 in Spain, f. 1996 in Chile; self-help, mystical and scholarly; Gen. Man. Ricardo Vlastelica Vega.

Editec (Ediciones Técnicas Ltda): El Condor 844, Of. 205, Ciudad Empresarial, Huechuraba, Santiago; tel. (2) 2757-4200; fax (2) 2757-4201; e-mail editec@editec.cl; internet www.editec.cl; Pres. Ricardo Cortes Donoso; Gen. Man. Roly Solis Sepúlveda.

Editorial Antártica, SA: San Francisco 116, Santiago; tel. (2) 2639-3476; fax (2) 2633-3402; e-mail consulta@antartica.cl; internet www.antartica.cl; f. 1978; Gen. Man. Paul Laborde U.

Editorial Borlando: Avda Victoria 155, Santiago; tel. (2) 2555-9566; fax (2) 2556-7100; e-mail ventas@editorialborlando.cl; internet www.editorialborlando.cl; f. 1984; scholarly, juvenile, educational and reference; Dir-Gen. Sergio Borlando Portales.

Editorial Cuatro Vientos Ltda: Maturana 19, Metro República, entre Brasil y Cumming, Santiago; tel. (2) 2672-9226; fax (2) 2673-2153; e-mail editorial@cuatrovientos.cl; internet cuatrovientos.cl; f. 1980; Man. Editor Juan Francisco Huneeus Cox.

Editorial y Distribuidora Lenguaje y Pensamiento Ltda: Avda 11 de Septiembre 1881, Of. 324, Metro Pedro de Valdivia, Santiago; tel. (2) 2335-2347; e-mail contacto@lenguajeypensamiento.cl; internet www.editoriallenguajeypensamiento.cl; children's, educational; Gen. Man. María Lorena Terán.

Editorial Evolución, SA: Ministro Carvajal 6, Providencia, Santiago; tel. (2) 2681-8072; fax (2) 2236-2071; e-mail info@evolucion.cl; internet www.evolucion.cl; business and management; Dir Juan Bravo Carrasco.

Editorial Fondo de Cultura Económica Chile, SA: Paseo Bulnes 152, Metro Moneda, Santiago; tel. (2) 2594-4100; fax (2) 2594-4101; e-mail info@fcechile.cl; internet fcechile.cl; f. 1954; Gen. Man. Óscar Bravo.

Editorial Jurídica de Chile: Ahumada 131, 4°, Santiago; tel. (2) 2461-9500; fax (2) 2461-9501; e-mail covalle@editorialjuridica.cl; internet www.editorialjuridica.cl; f. 1945; law; Gen. Man. Patricio Rojas.

Editorial Patris: José Manuel Infante 132, Providencia, Santiago; tel. (2) 2235-1343; fax (2) 2235-8674; e-mail gerencia@entelchile.net; internet www.patris.cl; f. 1982; Catholic; Dir José Luis Correa Lira.

Editorial Renacimiento: Amunátegui 458, Santiago; tel. (2) 2345-8300; fax (2) 2345-8320; e-mail pedidos@editorialrenacimiento.com; internet www.editorialrenacimiento.com; f. 1977; Gen. Man. Alberto Aldea.

Editorial San Pablo: Avda Libertador Bernardo O'Higgins 1626, Casilla 3746, Santiago; tel. (2) 2720-0300; fax (2) 2672-8469; e-mail alameda@san-pablo.cl; internet www.sanpablochile.cl; f. 1914; Catholic texts; Dir-Gen. Bruno Bressan.

Editorial Tiempo Presente Ltda: Almirante Pastene 345, Providencia, Santiago; tel. (2) 2364-5100; fax (2) 2235-8331; e-mail info@cosas.com; internet www.cosas.com; Gen. Man. Matías Pfingsthorn Olivares.

Editorial Universitaria, SA: Avda Libertador Bernardo O'Higgins 1050, Santiago; tel. (2) 2487-0700; fax (2) 2487-0702; e-mail comunicaciones@universitaria.cl; internet www.universitaria.cl; f. 1947; general literature, social science, technical, textbooks; Man. Dir Rodrigo Fuentes.

Empresa Editora Zig-Zag SA: Los Conquistadores 1700, 10°, Providencia, Santiago; tel. (2) 2810-7400; fax (2) 2810-7452; e-mail zigzag@zigzag.cl; internet www.zigzag.cl; f. 1905; general publrs of literary works, reference books and magazines; Pres. Alfredo Vercelli; Gen. Man. Ramón Olaciregui.

Grupo Planeta: Avda 11 de Septiembre 2353, 16°, CP 7510058, Providencia, Santiago; tel. (2) 2652-2927; fax (2) 2652-2912; e-mail info@planeta.cl; internet www.editorialplaneta.cl; f. 1968; non-fiction, philosophy, psychology; Gen. Man. Elsy Salazar Campo.

Liberalia Ediciones: Avda Italia 2016, Nuñoa, Santiago; tel. (2) 2432-8003; fax (2) 2326-8805; e-mail liberalia@liberalia.cl; internet www.liberalia.cl; f. 1997; Dir Jaime Oxley Muñoz.

McGraw-Hill/Interamericana de Chile Ltda: Evaristo Lillo 112, 7°, Las Condes, Santiago; tel. (2) 2661-3000; fax (2) 2661-3020; e-mail info_chile@mcgraw-hill.com; internet www.mcgraw-hill.cl; educational and technical; Gen. Man. José Aberg Cobo.

Norma de Chile, SA: Monjitas 527, 17°, Centro, Santiago; tel. (2) 2731-7500; fax (2) 2632-2079; e-mail david.malhue@norma.com; internet www.librerianorma.com; f. 1960; part of Editorial Norma of Colombia; Gen. Man. David Malhue.

Pearson Educación de Chile: José Ananias 505, Macul, Santiago; tel. (2) 2237-2387; fax (2) 2237-3297; e-mail infopear@pearsoned.cl; Gen. Man. EDUARDO GUZMÁN BARROS.

Pehuen Editores, SA: Brown Norte 417, Nuñoa, Santiago; tel. (2) 2795-7130; fax (2) 2795-7133; e-mail editorial@pehuen.cl; internet www.pehuen.cl; f. 1983; literature, sociology and photography; Pres. SEBASTIÁN BARROS CERDA; Gen. Man. JUAN MANUEL GALÁN.

RIL Editores (Red Internacional del Libro Ltda): Los Leones 2258, Providencia, CP 751-1055, Santiago; tel. (2) 2223-8100; fax (2) 2225-4269; e-mail ril@rileditores.com; internet www.rileditores.com; literature, poetry, scholarly and political; f. 1991 as Red Internacional del Libro Ltda; Dir ELEONORA FINKELSTEIN; Dir of Publications DANIEL CALABRESE.

Tajamar Editores: Avda Mariano Sánchez Fontecilla 352, Las Condes, Santiago; tel. (2) 2245-7026; e-mail info@tajamar-editores.cl; internet www.tajamar-editores.cl; f. 2002; literature; Gen. Man. MARÍA PAZ GAETE SILVA.

PUBLISHERS' ASSOCIATIONS

Asociación de Editores de Chile (Asociación de Editores Independientes, Universitarios y Autónomos): Maturana 19, Santiago; tel. (2) 2632-9210; e-mail contacto@editoresdechile.cl; internet www.editoresdechile.cl; Pres. PAULO SLACHEVSKY CHONCHOL; Exec. Dir CARMEN GLORIA ARCE.

Cámara Chilena del Libro, AG: Avda Libertador Bernardo O'Higgins 1370, Of. 502, Casilla 13526, Santiago; tel. (2) 2672-0348; fax (2) 2687-4271; e-mail prolibro@tie.cl; internet www.camaradellibro.cl; f. 1950; Pres. EDUARDO CASTILLO GARCÍA.

Broadcasting and Communications

REGULATORY AUTHORITY

Subsecretaría de Telecomunicaciones (Subtel): Amunátegui 139, 5°, Casilla 120, Correo 21, Santiago; tel. (2) 2421-3500; fax (2) 2421-3553; e-mail subtel@subtel.cl; internet www.subtel.cl; f. 1977; part of the Ministry of Transport and Telecommunications; Under-Sec. JORGE ATTON PALMA.

TELECOMMUNICATIONS

Claro Chile, SA: Avda del Cóndor 820, Ciudad Empresarial, Comuna de Huechuraba, Santiago; tel. (2) 2444-5000; fax (2) 2444-5170; internet www.clarochile.cl; fmrly Smartcom; acquired in 2005 by América Móvil, SA de CV (Mexico); merged with Telmex Chile in 2010; Gen. Man. GERARDO MUÑOZ.

CMET Telecomunicaciones: Avda Los Leones 1412, Providencia, Santiago; tel. (2) 2250-0105; fax (2) 2274-9573; internet www.cmet.cl; f. 1978.

Empresa Nacional de Telecomunicaciones, SA—ENTEL Chile, SA: Andrés Bello 2687, 14°, Casilla 4254, Las Condes, Santiago; tel. (2) 2360-0123; fax (2) 2360-3424; internet www.entel.cl; f. 1964; operates the Chilean land satellite stations of Longovilo, Punta Arenas and Coyhaique, linked to INTELSAT system; 52% owned by Telecom Italia; Pres. JUAN JOSÉ HURTADO VICUÑA; Gen. Man. ANTONIO BÜCHI BUC.

Grupo GTD: Moneda 920, 11°, CP 2099, Santiago; tel. (2) 2413-9400; fax (2) 2413-9100; e-mail soporte@gtdinternet.com; internet www.grupogtd.com; f. 1979; internet and telephone service provider; Pres. JUAN MANUEL CASANUEVA PRÉNDEZ; Gen. Man. MARIO RAÚL DOMÍNGUEZ ROJAS.

Movistar: Providencia 111, CP 16-D, Santiago; tel. (2) 2691-2020; fax (2) 2691-7881; internet www.movistar.cl; f. 1996 as Telefónica Móvil de Chile, present name adopted in 2005 following merger of Telefónica Móviles de Chile with BellSouth Communications (USA); mobile cellular telephone services; Pres. CLAUDIO MUÑOZ ZÚÑIGA; Gen. Man. FERNANDO SAIZ MAREGATTI.

VTR GlobalCom: Reyes Lavalle 3340, 9°, Las Condes, Santiago; tel. (2) 2310-1000; fax (2) 2310-1560; internet www.vtr.cl; f. 1928 as Vía Transradio Chilena; present name adopted in 1999; 80% owned by Liberty Global Inc (USA), 20% owned by Cristalerías Chile of the Claro group; Exec. Pres. MAURICIO RAMOS BORRERO.

BROADCASTING

Radio

Agricultura (AM y FM): Avda Manuel Rodríguez 15, Santiago; tel. (2) 2392-3000; fax (2) 2392-3072; internet www.radioagricultura.cl; owned by Sociedad Nacional de Agricultura; Pres. DOMINGO ROMERO CORTÉS; Gen. Man. LUIS LANGLOIS DIAZ.

Beethoven FM: Avda. Santa María 2670, 2°, Providencia, Santiago; tel. (2) 2571-7056; fax (2) 2274-3323; e-mail director@redfm.cl; internet www.beethovenfm.cl; f. 1981; mainly classical music; affiliate stations in Viña del Mar and Temuco; Dir ADOLFO FLORES.

Bío Bío La Radio: Avda Libertador Bernardo O'Higgins 680, Concepción; tel. (41) 262-0620; fax (41) 222-6742; e-mail internet@laradio.cl; internet www.radiobiobio.cl; affiliate stations in Concepción, Los Angeles, Temuco, Ancud, Castro, Osorno, Puerto Montt, Santiago and Valdivia; Man. PATRICIO ANDRADE.

Duna FM: Avda Santa María 2670, 2°, Providencia, Santiago; tel. (2) 2225-5494; fax (2) 2225-6013; e-mail aholuigue@duna.cl; internet www.duna.cl; affiliate stations in Viña del Mar and Concepción; Pres. FELIPE LAMARCA CLARO; Dir A. HOLUIGUE.

Estrella del Mar AM: Eleuterio Ramírez 207, Ancud, Isla de Chiloé; tel. and fax (65) 262-2722; e-mail secretariaestrelladelmar@gmail.com; internet www.radioestrelladelmar.cl; f. 1982; station of the Roman Catholic diocese of San Carlos de Ancud; affiliate stations in Castro, Quellón, Melinka, Achao, Futaleufú, Palena and Chaitén; Exec. Dir PABLO DURÁN LEIVA.

Festival AM: Quinta 124A, 2°, Casilla 337, Viña del Mar; tel. (32) 268-4251; fax (32) 268-0266; e-mail servicios@festival.cl; internet www.festival.cl; f. 1976; Dir-Gen. ROSSANA CHIESA VENEGAS.

Horizonte: Avda Pocuro 2151, Providencia, Santiago; tel. (2) 2410-5400; fax (2) 2410-5460; internet www.horizonte.cl; f. 1985; affiliate stations in Arica, Antofagasta, Iquique, La Serena, Viña del Mar, Concepción, San Antonio, Temuco, Villarrica, Puerto Montt, Punta Arenas and Osorno; Dir RODRIGO HURTADO.

IberoAmericana Radio Chile: Eliodoro Yáñez 1783, Providencia, Santiago; tel. (2) 2390-2000; fax (2) 2390-2047; e-mail aaguirre@iarc.cl; internet www.iarc.cl; part of Prisa Radio; Exec. Dir MARCELO ZÚÑIGA VETTIGER; Communications Man. JAVIERA BALLACEY T.; the media group operates 11 radio stations.

40 Principales 101.7 FM: e-mail radio@los40.cl; internet www.los40.cl.

ADN Radio Chile 91.7 FM: e-mail radio@adnradio.cl; internet www.adnradio.cl; general and sports news.

Concierto 88.5 FM: e-mail radio@concierto.cl; internet www.concierto.cl; f. 1999; 1980s music; Gen. Man. JAIME VEGA DE KUYPER.

Corazón 101.3 FM: e-mail radio@corazon.cl; internet www.corazon.cl; f. 1997.

FMDos 98.5 FM: e-mail radio@fmdos.cl; internet www.fm2.cl; popular music.

Futuro 88.9 FM: e-mail radio@futuro.cl; internet www.futuro.cl; rock music.

Imagina 88.1 FM: e-mail radio@radioimagina.cl; internet www.radioimagina.cl; women's radio.

Pudahuel 90.5 FM: e-mail radio@pudahuel.cl; internet www.pudahuel.cl; f. 1966; Pres. SUSANA MUTINELLI ANCHUBIDART; Gen. Man. JOAQUÍN BLAYA BARRIOS.

Radioactiva 92.5 FM: e-mail info@radioactiva.cl; internet www.radioactiva.cl; dance music.

Rock & Pop 94.1 FM: e-mail contacto@rockandpop.cl; internet www.rockandpop.cl; retro classics and 1990s music.

Uno 97.1 FM: e-mail contacto@radiounochile.cl; internet www.radiounochile.cl; Chilean national music.

Infinita FM: Avda Los Leones 1285, Providencia, Santiago; tel. (2) 2754-4400; fax (2) 2341-6727; internet www.infinita.cl; f. 1977; affiliate stations in Santiago, Viña del Mar, Concepción and Valdivia; Gen. Man. CARLOS ALBERTO PEÑAFIEL GUARACHI.

Para Ti FM: Vial 775, Puerto Montt, Santiago; tel. (65) 2317-003; internet www.radioparati.cl; 16 affiliate stations throughout Chile; Gen. Man. PATRICIO COROMINAS.

Play FM: Alcalde Dávalos 164, Providencia, Santiago; tel. (2) 2630-2600; fax (2) 2630-2264; e-mail asanchez@13.cl; internet www.playfm.cl; f. 2006; Dir GABRIEL POLGATI; Gen. Man. XIMENA CALLEJÓN.

Radio Carolina: Avda Santa Maria 2670, 2°, Providence, Santiago; tel. (2) 2571-7000; fax (2) 2571-7002; internet www.carolina.cl; f. 1975; owned by COPESA, SA; Contact HÉCTOR CABRERA.

Radio El Conquistador FM: El Conquistador del Monte 4644, Huechuraba, Santiago; tel. (2) 2580-2000; e-mail radio@elconquistadorfm.cl; internet www.elconquistadorfm.cl; f. 1962; affiliate stations in Santiago, Iquique, Antofagasta, La Serena, Viña del Mar, Rancagua, Talca, Chillán, Concepción, Talcahuano, Pucón, Temuco, Villarrica, Lago Llanquihue, Osorno, Puerto Montt, Puerto Varas, Valdivia and Punta Arenas; Pres. JOAQUÍN MOLFINO.

Radio Cooperativa (AM y FM): Antonio Bellet 353, Casilla 16367, Correo 9, Santiago; tel. (2) 2364-8000; fax (2) 2236-0535; e-mail info@cooperativa.cl; internet www.cooperativa.cl; f. 1936; affiliate stations in Copiapó, Arica, Coquimbo, La Serena, Valparaíso, Concepción, Calama, Temuco and Castro; Gen. Man. LUIS AJENJO ISASI.

Radio Nacional de Chile: Roca 931, 2°, Santiago; tel. (61) 222-2957; fax (61) 222-2304; e-mail radionacional@123.cl; internet www.radio-nacional.cl; f. 1974; Gen. Man. SOFIA MANSILLA ALVARADO.

Radio Nueva Belén FM: Benavente 385, 3°, Puerto Montt; tel. (65) 225-8042; fax (65) 225-8084; e-mail nuevabelen@gmail.com; internet www.radionuevabelen.cl; f. 2005; owned by Archbishopric of Puerto Montt; Dir HÉCTOR ASENJO REYES; Gen. Man. CARLOS WAGNER CATALÁN.

Radio Polar: Bories 871, 2° y 3°, Punta Arenas; tel. (61) 224-1417; fax (61) 224-9001; e-mail secretaria@radiopolar.com; internet www.radiopolar.com; f. 1940; Pres. RENÉ VENEGAS OLMEDO.

Superandina FM: Avda Chacabuco 281, Los Andes; tel. (34) 242-2515; fax (34) 290-4091; e-mail radio@superandina.cl; internet www.superandina.cl; f. 1987; Dir JOSÉ ANDRÉS GÁLVEZ VALENZUELA.

Universo FM: Antonio Bellet 223, Providencia, Santiago; tel. (2) 2364-8000; e-mail alfredo@universo.cl; internet www.universo.cl; affiliate stations in 18 cities; Commercial Man. RODRIGO LIU L.

Television

Corporación de Televisión de la Universidad Católica de Chile—Canal 13: Inés Matte Urrejola 0848, Providencia, Santiago; tel. (2) 2251-4000; fax (2) 2630-2683; internet www.canal13.cl; f. 1959; non-commercial; Pres. NICOLÁS EYZAGUIRRE; Exec. Dir DAVID BELMAR.

Corporación de Televisión de la Pontificia Universidad Católica de Valparaíso (UCV TV): Edif. Panorámico, Torre A, Of. 1402, Avda 11 Septiembre 2155, Santiago; tel. (2) 2586-4350; fax (2) 2586-4351; e-mail direccion@ucvtv.cl; internet www.ucvtv.cl; f. 1957; Pres. BERNARDO DONOSO RIVEROS; Exec. Dir ENRIQUE AIMONE GARCÍA.

Red de Televisión SA/Chilevisión—Canal 11: Inés Matte Urrejola 0825, Casilla 16547, Correo 9, Providencia, Santiago; tel. (2) 2461-5100; fax (2) 2461-5371; e-mail contactoweb@chilevision.cl; internet www.chilevision.cl; Exec. Dir JAIME DE AGUIRRE HOFFA; Gen. Man. ALICIA ZALDÍVAR PERALTA.

La Red Televisión TV: Manquehue Sur 1201, Las Condes, Santiago; tel. (2) 2385-4000; fax (2) 2385-4020; e-mail administracion@lared.cl; internet www.redtv.cl; f. 1991; Dir-Gen. JOSÉ MANUEL LARRAÍN; Exec. Dir JAVIER URRUTIA.

Red Televisiva Megavisión, SA—Canal 9: Avda Vicuña Mackenna 1348, Nuñoa, Santiago; tel. (2) 2810-8000; fax (2) 2551-8369; e-mail mega@mcl.cl; internet www.mega.cl; f. 1990; Pres. RICARDO CLARO VALDÉS; Gen. Man. CRISTÓBAL BULNES SERRANO.

Televisión Nacional de Chile—Canal 7: Bellavista 0990, Casilla 16104, Providencia, Santiago; tel. (2) 2707-7777; fax (2) 2707-7766; e-mail relaciones.publicas@tvn.cl; internet www.tvn.cl; f. 1969; govt network of 140 stations and an international satellite signal; Chair. MAURO VALDÉS; Exec. Dir DANIEL FERNÁNDEZ KOPRICH.

Regulatory Authority

Consejo Nacional de Televisión (CNTV): Mar del Plata 2147, Providencia, Santiago; tel. (2) 2592-2700; internet www.cntv.cl; f. 1989; Pres. HERMAN CHADWICK PIÑERA.

Broadcasting Associations

Asociación Nacional de Televisión (ANATEL): Lota 2257, Of. 501, Providencia, Santiago; tel. (2) 2231-3755; fax (2) 2331-9803; e-mail contacto@anatel.cl; internet www.anatel.cl; 7 mem. networks; Pres. ERNESTO CORONA BOZZO; Sec.-Gen. HERNÁN TRIVIÑO OYARZUN.

Asociación de Radiodifusores de Chile (ARCHI): Pasaje Matte 956, 8°, Of. 801, Casilla 10476, Santiago; tel. (2) 2639-8755; fax (2) 2639-4205; e-mail archi@archiradios.cl; internet www.archi.cl; f. 1933; more than 1,000 affiliated stations; Nat. Pres. CARLOS ALBERTO PEÑAFIEL; Sec.-Gen. FERNANDO OCARANZA YÑESTA.

Finance

(cap. = capital; res = reserves; dep. = deposits; m. = million; brs = branches; amounts in pesos, unless otherwise specified)

BANKING

Supervisory Authority

Superintendencia de Bancos e Instituciones Financieras: Moneda 1123, 6°, Casilla 15-D, Santiago; tel. (2) 2887-9200; fax (2) 2381-0410; e-mail superintendente@sbif.cl; internet www.sbif.cl; f. 1925; affiliated to Ministry of Finance; Supt RAPHAEL BERGOEING VELA.

Central Bank

Banco Central de Chile: Agustinas 1180, Santiago; tel. (2) 2670-2000; fax (2) 2670-2099; e-mail bcch@bcentral.cl; internet www.bcentral.cl; f. 1926; autonomous from 1989; bank of issue; cap. and res 806,560.9m., dep. 15,274,011.2m. (Dec. 2009); Pres. RODRIGO VERGARA MONTES; Gen. Man ALEJANDRO ZURBUCHEN SILVA.

State Bank

Banco del Estado de Chile (BancoEstado): Avda Libertador Bernardo O'Higgins 1111, Casilla 240V, Santiago; tel. (2) 2970-7000; fax (2) 2970-5711; internet www.bancoestado.cl; f. 1953; state bank; cap. 278,497m., res 719,674m., dep. 14,160,876m. (Dec. 2011); Pres. SEGISMUNDO SCHULIN-ZEUTHEN SERRANO; CEO PABLO PIÑERA ECHENIQUE; 214 brs.

Commercial Banks

Banco BICE: Teatinos 220, Santiago; tel. (2) 2692-2000; fax (2) 2696-5324; e-mail webmaster@bice.cl; internet www.bice.cl; f. 1979 as Banco Industrial y de Comercio Exterior; adopted present name 1988; cap. 32,142m., res –15,312m., dep. 2,235,310m. (Dec. 2011); Pres. and Chair. BERNARDO MATTE LARRAÍN; Gen. Man. ANDRÉS SCHILING REDLICH; 18 brs.

Banco Bilbao Vizcaya Argentaria Chile: Pedro de Valdivia 100, 17°, Providencia, Santiago; tel. (2) 2679-1000; fax (2) 2698-5640; e-mail ascarito@bbva.cl; internet www.bbva.cl; f. 1883 as Banco Hipotecario de Fomento Nacional; controlling interest acquired by Banco Bilbao Vizcaya (Spain) in 1998; adopted current name 2003; cap. 224,795m., res 243,163m., dep. 4,991,411m. (Dec. 2011); Chair. JOSÉ SAID SAFFIE; Gen. Man. and CEO MANUEL OLIVARES; 108 brs.

Banco de Chile: Ahumada 251, Casilla 151-D, Santiago; tel. (2) 2653-1111; fax (2) 2637-3434; internet www.bancochile.cl; f. 1894; 35.6% owned by SAOS, SA; cap. 1,436,083m., res –142,094m., dep. 14,344,330m. (Dec. 2011); Pres. and Chair. PABLO GRANIFO LAVÍN; CEO ARTURO TAGLE QUIROZ; 422 brs.

Banco de Crédito e Inversiones (Bci): Avda El Golf 125, Las Condes, Santiago; tel. (2) 2692-7000; fax (2) 2695-3775; e-mail webmaster@bci.cl; internet www.bci.cl; f. 1937; cap. 1,026,985m., res 12,172m., dep. 10,216,690m. (Dec. 2011); Pres. and Chair. LUIS ENRIQUE YARUR REY; Gen. Man. LIONEL OLAVARRÍA; 258 brs.

Banco Internacional: Moneda 818, Casilla 135-D, Santiago; tel. (2) 2369-7000; fax (2) 2369-7367; e-mail banco@binter.cl; internet www.bancointernacional.cl; f. 1944; cap. 44,010m., res 4,323m., dep. 770,831m. (Dec. 2011); Pres. JULIO JARAQUEMADA LEDOUX; Gen. Man. JUAN ENRIQUE VILAJUANA R.

Banco Itaú Chile: Enrique Foster Sur 20, 6°, Las Condes, Santiago; tel. (2) 2686-0000; internet www.itau.cl; cap. 219,492m., res 138,113m., dep. 3,104,992m. (Dec. 2011); Pres. RICARDO VILLELA MARINO; Gen. Man. BORIS BUVINIC GUEROVICH.

Banco Penta: Avda El Bosque Norte 440, Las Condes, Santiago; tel. (2) 2873-3062; internet www.bancopenta.cl; cap. 60,754m., res –2,106m., dep. 385,711m. (Dec. 2011); Pres. CARLOS ALBERTO DÉLANO ABBOTT; Gen. Man. ANDRÉS CHECHILNITZKY RODRÍGUEZ.

Banco Santander Chile: Bandera 150, 2°, Casilla 57-D, Santiago; tel. (2) 2320-2000; fax (2) 2320-8877; e-mail webmaster@santander.cl; internet www.santander.cl; f. 1926; cap. 891,303m., res –76,154m., dep. 14,173,755m. (Dec. 2011); subsidiary of Banco Santander (Spain); Chair. MAURICIO LARRAÍN GARCES; CEO CLAUDIO MELANDRI; 72 brs.

Banco Security: Apoquindo 3100, Las Condes, Santiago; tel. (2) 2584-4000; fax (2) 2584-4058; internet www.bancosecurity.cl; f. 1981; fmrly Banco Urquijo de Chile; cap. 185,207m., res 10,226m., dep. 2,552,913m. (Dec. 2011); Pres. and Chair. FRANCISCO SILVA S.; Gen. Man. RAMÓN ELUCHANS O.; 20 brs.

Corpbanca: Rosario Norte 660, Las Condes, Casilla 80-D, Santiago; tel. (2) 2687-8000; fax (2) 2672-6729; e-mail corpbanca@corpbanca.cl; internet www.corpbanca.cl; f. 1871 as Banco de Concepción, current name adopted in 1997; bought by Itaú Unibanco (Brazil) in 2014; cap. 507,108m., res 96,646m., dep. 5,643,328m. (Dec. 2011); Chair. ALVARO SAIEH BENDECK; CEO FERNANDO MASSÚ; 70 brs.

HSBC Bank (Chile): Avda Isidora Goyenechea 2800, 23°, Santiago; tel. (2) 2299-7200; fax (2) 2299-7391; e-mail camilo.jimenez@cl.hsbc.com; internet www.hsbc.cl; f. 2003 as HSBC Bank Chile; present name adopted in 2004; cap. 92,032m., res 1,156m., dep. 857,067m. (Dec. 2011); Chair. FRANK LAWSON; CEO and Gen. Man. GUSTAVO COSTA.

Scotiabank Chile (Canada): Morandé 226, Casilla 90-D, Santiago; tel. (2) 2692-6000; fax (2) 2671-5547; e-mail scotiabank@scotiabank.cl; internet www.scotiabank.cl; f. 1983; fmrly Banco del Desarrollo; renamed as above in 2009; cap. 390,158m., res 37,361m., dep. 3,928,425m. (Dec. 2011); CEO (Chile) FRANCISCO SARDÓN DE TABOADA; 83 brs.

Banking Association

Asociación de Bancos e Instituciones Financieras de Chile AG: Avda Nueva Costanera 4091, 4°, Vitacura; tel. (8) 292-2800; fax

(8) 292-2826; e-mail general@abif.cl; internet www.abif.cl; f. 1945; Pres. JORGE AWAD M.; Gen. Man. RICARDO MATTE E.

Other Financial Supervisory Bodies

Superintendencia de Administradoras de Fondos de Pensiones (SAFP) (Superintendency of Pension Funds): Avda Libertador Bernardo O'Higgins 1449, 1°, Local 8, Santiago; tel. (2) 2753-0100; fax (2) 2753-0122; internet www.safp.cl; f. 1981; Supt MICHEL CANTA.

Superintendencia de Seguridad Social (Superintendency of Social Security): Huérfanos 1376, 5°, Santiago; tel. (2) 2620-4500; fax (2) 2696-4672; e-mail contacto@suseso.cl; internet www.suseso.gov.cl; f. 1927; Supt MARÍA JOSÉ ZALDÍVAR LARRAÍN.

STOCK EXCHANGES

Bolsa de Comercio de Santiago: La Bolsa 64, Casilla 123-D, Santiago; tel. (2) 2399-3000; fax (2) 2318-1961; e-mail chathaway@bolsadesantiago.com; internet www.bolsadesantiago.com; f. 1893; 32 mems; Pres. PABLO YRARRÁZAVAL VALDÉS; Gen. Man. JOSÉ ANTONIO MARTÍNEZ ZUGARRAMURDI.

Bolsa de Corredores—Valores de Valparaíso: Prat 798, Casilla 218-V, Valparaíso; tel. (32) 225-0677; fax (32) 221-2764; e-mail bolsadec.orred001@chilnet.cl; internet www.bovalpo.com; f. 1905; Pres. CARLOS F. MARÍN ORREGO; Man. ARIE JOEL GELFENSTEIN FREUNDLICH.

Bolsa Electrónica de Chile: Huérfanos 770, 14°, Santiago; tel. (2) 2484-0100; fax (2) 2484-0101; e-mail contactoweb@bolchile.cl; internet www.bolchile.cl; f. 1989; Gen. Man. JUAN CARLOS SPENCER OSSA.

INSURANCE

Supervisory Authority

Superintendencia de Valores y Seguros: Avda Libertador Bernardo O'Higgins 1449, Casilla 834-0518, Santiago; tel. (2) 2617-4000; fax (2) 2617-4101; internet www.svs.cl; f. 1931; under Ministry of Finance; Supt FERNANDO COLOMA CORREA.

Principal Companies

ACE Seguros, SA: Miraflores 222, 17°, Centro, Santiago; tel. (2) 2549-8300; fax (2) 2632-8289; e-mail contact.la@acegroup.com; internet www.aceseguros.cl; f. 1999; Finance Man. VERÓNICA CAMPOS.

Aseguradora Magallanes, SA: Avda Alonso de Córdova 5151, 17° y 18°, Of. 1801, Las Condes, Santiago; tel. (2) 2715-4605; fax (2) 2715-4860; e-mail fvarela@magallanes.cl; internet www.magallanes.cl; f. 1957; general; Pres. EDUARDO DOMINGUEZ COVARRUBIAS; Gen. Man. FERNANDO VARELA VILLAROEL.

Axa Asistencia Chile: Josué Smith Solar 390, 6650378 Providencia, Santiago; tel. (2) 2941-8900; fax (2) 2941-8951; e-mail asistencia@axa-assistance.cl; internet www.axa-assistance.cl; f. 1994; general; Gen. Man. MARYLÚ FORTTES VALDIVIA.

Cardif Chile: Vitacura 2670, 13°, Las Condes, Santiago; tel. (2) 2370-4800; fax (2) 2370-4877; e-mail cardif@cardif.cl; internet www.cardif.cl; f. 1997; owned by BNP Paribas (France); Pres. OLIVIER MARTIN; Gen. Man. FRANCISCO VALENZUELA CORNEJO.

Chilena Consolidada Seguros, SA: Avda Pedro de Valdivia 195, Casilla 16587, Correo 9, Providencia, Santiago; tel. (2) 2200-7000; fax (2) 2274-9933; internet www.chilena.cl; f. 1853; owned by Zurich group; general and life; Pres. HERNÁN FELIPE ERRÁZURIZ CORREA; Gen. Man. JOSÉ MANUEL CAMPOSANO LARRAECHEA.

Chubb de Chile Compañía de Seguros Generales, SA: Gertrudis Echeñique 30, 4°, Ofs 41 y 42, Santiago; tel. (2) 2398-7000; fax (2) 2398-7090; e-mail chileinfo@chubb.com; internet www.chubb.com/chile; f. 1992; general; Gen. Man. CLAUDIO MARCELO ROSSI.

Cía de Seguros de Crédito Continental, SA: Avda Isidora Goyenechea 3162, 6°, Edif. Parque 1 Golf, Santiago; tel. (2) 2636-4000; fax (2) 2636-4001; e-mail seguros@continental.cl; internet www.continental.cl; f. 1990; general; Pres. MIGUEL ANGEL PODUJE SAPIAIN; Gen. Man. ANDRÉS MENDIETA VALENZUELA.

Cía de Seguros de Vida Cruz del Sur, SA: Avda El Golf 150, Las Condes, Santiago; tel. (2) 2461-8000; fax (2) 2461-8334; internet www.cruzdelsur.cl; f. 1992; life; Pres. JOSÉ TOMÁS GUZMÁN DUMAS; Gen. Man. JOSÉ ANTONIO LLANEZA TORREALBA.

Consorcio, SA: Edif. Consorcio, Avda El Bosque Sur 180, Las Condes, Santiago; tel. (2) 2230-4000; fax (2) 2230-4050; internet www.consorcio.cl; f. 1916; life and general insurance; Pres. JUAN BILBAO HORMAECHE; Gen. Man. NICOLÁS GELLONA AMUNATEGUI.

Euroamérica Seguros de Vida, SA: Apoquindo 3885, 20°, Las Condes, Santiago; tel. (2) 2581-7000; fax (2) 2581-7722; internet www.euroamerica.cl; f. 1962; life; Pres. NICHOLAS DAVIS LECAROS; Gen. Man. CLAUDIO ASECIO FULGERI.

HDI Seguros, SA: Encomenderos 113, Casilla 185-D, Centro 192, Las Condes, Santiago; tel. (2) 2422-9000; fax (2) 2246-7567; e-mail contacto@hdi.cl; internet www.hdi.cl; f. 1989 in Chile; general; CEO PATRICIO ALDUNATE.

ING Seguros de Vida, SA: Avda Suecia 211, Providencia, Santiago; tel. (2) 2252-1464; fax (2) 2364-2060; e-mail centro.solucionwm@ing.cl; internet www.ingvida.cl; f. 1989; life; CEO ANDRÉS CASTRO.

Mapfre Seguros: Isidora Goyenechea 3520, 14°, Casilla 7550071, Las Condes, Santiago; tel. (2) 2700-4000; fax (2) 2694-7565; internet www.mapfreseguros.cl; f. 1991; general; Gen. Man. JULIO DOMINGO SOUTO.

MetLife Chile Seguros de Vida, SA: Agustinas 640, 9°, Casilla 111, Correo Central, Santiago; tel. (2) 2640-1000; fax (2) 2640-1100; internet www.metlife.cl; f. 1980 as Seguros Interamericana; subsidiary of Metlife Inc. since 2002; Country Man. VÍCTOR HASSI SABAL.

Renta Nacional Compañías de Seguros, SA: Amunátegui 178, 2°, Centro, Santiago; tel. (2) 2670-0200; fax (2) 2670-0039; e-mail renta@rentanac.cl; internet www.rentanac.cl; f. 1982; life; Pres. FRANCISCO JAVIER ERRÁZURIZ TALAVERA; Gen. Man. JORGE SIMS SAN ROMÁN.

RSA Chile (United Kingdom): Providencia 1760, 4°, Santiago; tel. (2) 2396-1000; fax (2) 2396-1291; e-mail servicioaclientes@cl.rsagroup.com; internet www.rsagroup.cl; f. 2000; fmrly known as Royal & Sun Alliance Seguros; Pres. VÍCTOR MANUEL JARPA RIVEROS; Gen. Man. GONZALO SANTOS.

Vida Security, SA: Apoquindo 3150, 8°, Las Condes, Santiago; tel. (2) 2584-2400; internet www.vidasecurity.cl; f. 2002 through merger of Seguros Security and Seguros Previsión Vida; Pres. FRANCISCO SILVA SILVA; Gen. Man. ALEJANDRO ALZÉRRECA LUNA.

Insurance Association

Asociación de Aseguradores de Chile, AG: La Concepción 322, Of. 501, Casilla 2630, Providencia, Santiago; tel. (2) 2834-4900; fax (2) 2834-4920; e-mail seguros@aach.cl; internet www.aach.cl; f. 1931; Pres. FERNANDO CÁMBARA LODIGIANI.

Trade and Industry

GOVERNMENT AGENCIES

Comisión Nacional de Energía (CNE): Miraflores 222, 10°, Santiago; tel. (2) 2797-2600; fax (2) 2797-2627; internet www.cne.cl; Exec. Sec. JUAN MANUEL CONTRERAS SEPÚLVEDA.

Corporación de Fomento de la Producción (CORFO): Moneda 921, Casilla 3886, Santiago; tel. (2) 2631-8200; e-mail info@corfo.cl; internet www.corfo.cl; f. 1939; holding group of principal state enterprises; grants loans and guarantees to private sector; responsible for sale of non-strategic state enterprises; promotes entrepreneurship; Pres. LUIS FELIPE CÉSPEDES (Minister of the Economy, Development and Tourism); Exec. Vice-Pres. HERNÁN CHEYRE VALENZUELA; 13 brs.

PROCHILE (Dirección General de Relaciones Económicas Internacionales): Teatinos 180, Santiago; tel. (2) 2827-5100; fax (2) 2696-0639; e-mail info@prochile.cl; internet www.prochile.cl; f. 1974; bureau of international economic affairs; Dir (vacant).

Servicio Nacional de Capacitación y Empleo (SENCE) (National Training and Employment Service): Teatinos 333, 8°, Santiago; tel. (2) 2870-6222; fax (2) 2696-7103; internet www.sence.cl; attached to Ministry of Labour and Social Security; Nat. Dir JOSÉ JUAN BENNETT URRUTIA.

STATE CORPORATIONS

Corporación Nacional del Cobre de Chile (CODELCO-Chile): Huérfanos 1270, Casilla 150-D, Santiago; tel. (2) 2690-3000; fax (2) 2690-3059; e-mail comunica@codelco.cl; internet www.codelco.com; f. 1976 as a state-owned enterprise with copper-producing operational divisions at Chuquicamata, Radomiro Tomić, Salvador, Andina, Talleres Rancagua and El Teniente; attached to Ministry of Mining; Chair. GERARDO JOFRÉ DE MIRANDA; CEO THOMAS KELLER LIPPOLD; 18,496 employees.

Empresa Nacional de Petróleo (ENAP): Vitacura 2736, 10°, Las Condes, Santiago; tel. (2) 2280-3000; fax (2) 2280-3199; e-mail webenap@enap.cl; internet www.enap.cl; f. 1950; state-owned petroleum and gas exploration and production corpn; subsidiaries include Enap Sipetrol and Enap Refinerías; Pres. MÁXIMO PACHECO MATTE (Minister of Energy); Gen. Man. RICARDO CRUZAT OCHAGAVÍA; 3,286 employees.

DEVELOPMENT ORGANIZATIONS

Comisión Chilena de Energía Nuclear: Amunátegui 95, Santiago; tel. (2) 2470-2500; fax (2) 2470-2570; e-mail oirs@cchen.cl;

internet www.cchen.cl; f. 1965; govt body to develop peaceful uses of atomic energy; concentrates, regulates and controls all matters related to nuclear energy; Pres. RENATO AGURTO COLIMA; Exec. Dir JAIME SALAS KURTE.

Corporación Nacional de Desarrollo Indígena (Conadi): Aldunate 285, Temuco, Chile; tel. (45) 2641-500; fax (45) 2641-520; e-mail ctranamil@conadi.gov.cl; internet www.conadi.cl; promotes the economic and social development of indigenous communities; Nat. Dir JORGE RUBIO RETAMAL.

Corporación Nacional Forestal (CONAF): Paseo Bulnes 285, Santiago; tel. (2) 2663-0000; fax (2) 2225-0641; e-mail consulta@conaf.cl; internet www.conaf.cl; f. 1970 to promote forestry activities, enforce forestry law, promote afforestation, administer subsidies for afforestation projects and to increase and preserve forest resources; manages 13.97m. ha designated as National Parks, Natural Monuments and National Reserves; under Ministry of Agriculture; Exec. Dir EDUARDO VIAL RUIZ-TAGLE.

Empresa Nacional de Minería (ENAMI): MacIver 459, 2°, Casilla 100-D, Santiago; tel. (2) 2637-5278; fax (2) 2637-5452; e-mail eiturra@enami.cl; internet www.enami.cl; promotes the devt of small and medium-sized mines; attached to Ministry of Mining; partially privatized; Exec. Vice-Pres. FELIPE BARROS.

CHAMBERS OF COMMERCE

Cámara Chileno China de Comercio, Industria y Turismo: Morandé 322, Of. 502, Santiago; tel. (2) 2673-0304; fax (2) 2697-1510; e-mail camara@chicit.cl; internet www.chicit.cl; f. 1997; Pres. JUAN ESTEBAN MUSALEM AIACH.

Cámara de Comercio de Santiago: Edif. Del Comercio, Monjitas 392, Santiago; tel. (2) 2360-7000; fax (2) 2633-3595; e-mail cpn@ccs.cl; internet www.ccs.cl; f. 1919; 1,300 mems; Pres. PETER HILL D.; Sec.-Gen. CRISTIAN GARCÍA-HUIDOBRO.

Cámara de Comercio, Servicios y Turismo de Antofagasta: Latorre 2580, 3º, Of. 21, Antofagasta; tel. (55) 2225-175; fax (55) 2222-053; e-mail info@ccantof.cl; internet www.ccantof.cl; f. 1924; Pres. GIANCARLO CORONATO MACKENZIE; Co-ordinator Gen. MARCELA REY LEVA.

Cámara de Comercio, Servicios y Turismo de Temuco, AG: Vicuña Mackenna 396, Temuco; tel. (45) 221-0556; fax (45) 223-7047; e-mail secretaria@camaratemuco.cl; internet www.camaratemuco.cl; Pres. JORGE ARGANDOÑA RAMOS; Gen. Man. RUBÉN RIOS ROJAS.

Cámara Nacional de Comercio, Servicios y Turismo de Chile: Merced 230, Santiago; tel. (2) 2365-4000; fax (2) 2365-4001; internet www.cnc.cl; f. 1858; Pres. RICARDO MEWES; Sec.-Gen. JAIME ALÉ YARAD; 120 mems.

Cámara de la Producción y del Comercio de Concepción: Cauplicán 567, 2°, Concepción; tel. (41) 224-1121; fax (41) 224-1440; e-mail lmandiola@cpcc.cl; internet www.cpcc.cl; f. 1927; Pres. ALBERTO MIRANDA GUERRA; Gen. Man. LEONCIO TORO ARAYA.

INDUSTRIAL AND TRADE ASSOCIATIONS

Asociación de Exportadores de Frutas de Chile, AG (ASOEX): Cruz del Sur 133, Of. 904, Las Condes, Santiago; tel. (2) 2472-4778; internet www.asoex.cl; f. 1935; Pres. RONALD BOWN.

Servicio Agrícola y Ganadero (SAG): Avda Bulnes 140, 8º, Santiago; tel. (2) 2345-1100; fax (2) 2345-1102; e-mail dirnac@sag.gob.cl; internet www.sag.cl; under Ministry of Agriculture; responsible for the protection and devt of safe practice in the sector; Nat. Dir ANÍBAL ARIZTÍA REYES.

Servicio Nacional de Pesca y Acuicultura (SERNAPESCA): Victoria 2832, Valparaíso; tel. (32) 281-9100; fax (32) 225-6311; e-mail informaciones@sernapesca.cl; internet www.sernapesca.cl; f. 1978; govt regulator of the fishing industry; Nat. Dir JUAN LUIS ANSOLEAGA BENGOECHEA.

Sociedad Agrícola y Servicios Isla de Pascua (SASIPA): Hotu Matu'a s/n, Hanga Roa, Isla de Pascua; tel. (32) 210-0212; e-mail atencion@sasipa.cl; internet www.sasipa.cl; f. 1966; administers agriculture and public services on Easter Island; Pres. DANIEL TOMÁS PLATOVSKY TUREK; Gen. Man. PEDRO HEY ICKA.

EMPLOYERS' ORGANIZATIONS

Confederación del Comercio Detallista y Turismo de Chile, AG (CONFEDECH): Merced 380, 8°, Of. 74, Santiago; tel. (2) 2639-1264; fax (2) 2638-0338; e-mail comerciodetallista@confedech.cl; internet www.confedech.cl; f. 1938; retail trade; Nat. Pres. RAFAEL CUMSILLE ZAPAPA; Sec.-Gen. PEDRO ZAMORANO PIÑATS.

Confederación Nacional de Dueños de Camiones de Chile (CNDC): Santiago; internet www.cndc.cl; represents 39,000 truck cos; Pres. JUAN ARAYA JOFRÉ.

Confederación de la Producción y del Comercio: Monseñor Sótero Sanz 182, Providencia, Santiago; tel. (2) 2231-9764; fax (2) 2231-9808; e-mail procomer@entelchile.net; internet www.cpc.cl; f. 1936; Pres. ANDRÉS SANTA CRUZ LÓPEZ; Gen. Man. FERNANDO ALVEAR ARTAZA.

Affiliated organizations:

Asociación de Bancos e Instituciones Financieras de Chile AG: see Finance (Banking Association).

Cámara Nacional de Comercio, Servicios y Turismo de Chile: see Chambers of Commerce.

Cámara Chilena de la Construcción (CChC): Marchant Pereira 10, 3°, Providencia, CP 6640721, Santiago; tel. (2) 2376-3300; fax (2) 2371-3430; internet www.cchc.cl; f. 1951; Pres. DANIEL HURTADO PAROT; 17,442 mems.

Sociedad de Fomento Fabril, FG (SOFOFA): Avda Andrés Bello 2777, 3°, Las Condes, Santiago; tel. (2) 2391-3100; fax (2) 2391-3200; e-mail sofofa@sofofa.cl; internet www.sofofa.cl; f. 1883; largest employers' org.; Pres. HERMAN VON MÜHLENBROCK SOTO; Sec.-Gen. CRISTÓBAL PHILIPPI IRARRAZÁVAL; 2,500 mems.

Sociedad Nacional de Agricultura—Federación Gremial (SNA): Tenderini 187, 2°, CP 6500978, Santiago; tel. (2) 2639-6710; fax (2) 2633-7771; e-mail comunicaciones@sna.cl; internet www.sna.cl; f. 1838; landowners' asscn; controls Radio Stations CB 57 and XQB8 (FM) in Santiago, CB-97 in Valparaíso, CD-120 in Los Angeles, CA-144 in La Serena, CD-127 in Temuco; Pres. PATRICIO CRESPO URETA; Sec.-Gen. JUAN PABLO MATTE FUENTES.

Sociedad Nacional de Minería (SONAMI): Avda Apoquindo 3000, 5°, Santiago; tel. (2) 2335-9300; fax (2) 2334-9700; e-mail monica.cavallini@sonami.cl; internet www.sonami.cl; f. 1883; Pres. ALBERTO SALAS MUÑOZ; Gen. Man. FELIPE CELEDÓN MARDONES; 48 mem. cos.

CONUPIA (Confederación Gremial Nacional Unida de la Mediana y Pequeña Industria, Servicios y Artesanado): Phillips 40, 6°, Of. 63, Providencia, Santiago; tel. (2) 2633-1492; e-mail secgeneral@conupia.cl; internet www.conupia.cl; f. 1966; small and medium-sized industries and crafts; Pres. PEDRO DAVIS URZÚA; Sec.-Gen. JOSÉ LUIS RAMÍREZ ZAMORANO.

UTILITIES

Comisión Nacional de Energía: see Government Agencies.

Superintendencia de Electricidad y Combustibles (SEC): Avda Libertador Bernardo O'Higgins 1449, 13°, Torre 1, Santiago; tel. (2) 2756-5149; fax (2) 2756-5155; e-mail pchotzen@sec.cl; internet www.sec.cl; Supt LUIS AVILA BRAVO.

Electricity

AES Gener, SA: Mariano Sánchez Fontecilla 310, 3°, Las Condes, Santiago; tel. (2) 2686-8900; fax (2) 2686-8991; e-mail gener@gener.cl; internet www.gener.cl; f. 1981 as Chilectra Generación, SA; privatized in 1988; current name adopted in 1998; owned by AES Corpn (USA); responsible for operation of power plants at Renca, Ventanas, Laguna Verde, El Indio, Altalfal, Maitenes, Queltehues and Volcán; Pres. ANDRÉS GLUSKI WEILERT; Gen. Man. LUIS FELIPE CERÓN CERÓN; 1,121 employees (group).

Eléctrica Santiago: Jorge Hirmas 2964, Renca, Santiago; tel. (2) 2680-4760; fax (2) 2680-4743; e-mail electricasantiago@aes.com; internet www.electricasantiago.cl; f. 1994; operates the Renca and the Nueva Renca thermoelectric plants in Santiago; installed capacity of 379 MW; Pres. VICENTE JAVIER GIORGIO; Gen. Man. RODRIGO OSORIO BÓRQUEZ.

Empresa Eléctrica Guacolda, SA: Avda Apoquindo 3885, 10°, Las Condes, Santiago; tel. (2) 2362-4000; fax (2) 2464-3560; internet www.guacolda.cl; operates a thermoelectric power station in Huasco; installed capacity of 304 MW; Pres. JOSÉ FLORENCIO GUZMÁN CORREA; Gen. Man. MARCO ARRÓSPIDE RIVERA.

Energía Verde: Mariano Sánchez Fontecilla 310, 3°, Las Condes, Santiago; tel. (43) 2402-700; fax (43) 2402-709; internet www.energiaverde.cl; operates 2 co-generation power stations at Constitución and Laja and a steam plant at Nacimiento; supplies the Cabrero industrial plant; CEO JAIME ZUAZAGOITÍA VIANCOS.

Norgener, SA: Jorge Hirmas 2960, Renca, Santiago; tel. (2) 2680-4710; fax (2) 2680-4868; northern subsidiary supplying the mining industry; Exec. Dir JUAN CARLOS OLMEDO HIDALGO.

Arauco Generación: El Golf 150, 14°, Las Condes, Santiago; tel. (2) 2461-7200; fax (2) 2698-5987; e-mail gic@arauco.cl; internet www.arauco.cl; f. 1994 to commercialize surplus power from pulp processing facility; Pres. JOSÉ TOMÁS GUZMÁN; Gen. Man. CRISTIÁN INFANTE.

Chilquinta Energía, SA: General Cruz 222, Valparaíso; tel. (32) 250-2000; fax (32) 223-1171; e-mail contactoweb@chilquinta.cl; internet www.chilquinta.cl; f. 1997 as Energas, SA; present name adopted in 2001; owned by Inversiones Sempra and PSEG of the USA; Pres. ARTURO INFANZÓN FAVELA; Gen. Man. CRISTIÁN ARNOLDS REYES.

Compañía Eléctrica del Litoral, SA: Avda Peñablanca 540, Algarrobo, Casilla 14454, Santiago; tel. (2) 2481-195; fax (2) 2483-313; e-mail fmartine@litoral.cl; internet www.litoral.cl; f. 1949; Gen. Man. LUIS CONTRERAS IGLESIAS.

Compañía General de Electricidad, SA (CGE): Teatinos 280, Santiago; tel. (2) 2680-7000; fax (2) 2680-7104; e-mail contacto@cge.cl; internet www.cge.cl; installed capacity of 662 MW; Pres. JORGE EDUARDO MARÍN CORREA; Gen. Man. PABLO GUARDA BARROS.

Compañía Nacional de Fuerza Eléctrica, SA (CONAFE): Norte 13, Of. 810, Viña del Mar; tel. (32) 220-6100; fax (32) 227-1593; e-mail serviciocliente@conafe.cl; internet www.conafe.cl; f. 1945; Pres. JOSÉ LUIS HORNAUER HERRMANN; Gen. Man. RODRIGO VIDAL SÁNCHEZ.

E-CL, SA (Energía Esencial): El Bosque Norte 500, 9°, Vitacura, Santiago; tel. (2) 2353-3200; fax (2) 2353-3210; e-mail contacto@edelnor.cl; internet www.e-cl.cl; f. 1981; acquired by CODELCO and Tractebel, SA (Belgium) in 2002; fmrly Edelnor, changed name as above in 2010 following merger with Electroandina; Pres. JAN FLACHET; Gen. Man. LODEWIJK VERDEYEN.

Empresa Eléctrica de Magallanes, SA (Edelmag, SA): Croacia 444, Punta Arenas; tel. (71) 271-4000; fax (71) 271-4077; e-mail edelmag@edelmag.cl; internet www.edelmag.cl; f. 1981; 55% owned by CGE; Pres. JORGE JORDAN FRANULIC; Gen. Man. CARLOS YÁÑEZ ANTONUCCI.

Empresas Emel, SA: Avda Libertador Bernardo O'Higgins 886, 10°, Santiago; tel. (2) 2344-8000; fax (2) 2344-8001; internet www.emel.cl; holding co for the Emel group of electricity cos, bought by CGE in 2007; Gen. Man. CRISTIÁN SAPHORES MARTÍNEZ; Emel group includes:

ELECDA (Empresa Eléctrica de Antofagasta, SA): José Miguel Carrera 1587, Antofagasta 1250; tel. (55) 268-1401; internet www.elecda.cl; Regional Man. ORLANDO ASSAD MANRÍQUEZ.

ELIQSA (Empresa Eléctrica de Iquique, SA): Zegeres 469, Iquique; tel. (57) 240-5400; fax (57) 242-7181; e-mail eliqsa@eliqsa.cl; internet www.eliqsa.cl; Pres. PABLO GUARDA BARROS; Regional Man. JUAN CARLOS GÓMEZ GAMBOA.

EMELARI (Empresa Eléctrica de Arica, SA): Baquedano 731, Arica; tel. (58) 2201-100; fax (58) 223-1105; internet www.emelari.cl; Regional Man. RICARDO MIRANDA PUEBLA.

EMELAT (Empresa Eléctrica Atacama, SA): Circunvalación Ignacio Carrera Pinto 51, Copiapó; tel. (52) 220-5111; fax (52) 220-5103; internet www.emelat.cl; f. 1981; distribution co; Pres. JOSÉ LUIS HORNAUER HERRMANN; Regional Man. CLAUDIO JACQUES VERGARA.

EMELECTRIC (Empresa Eléctrica de Melipilla, Colchagua y Maule): Ortúzar N° 376, Melipilla; internet www.emelectric.cl; Pres. FRANCISCO JAVIER MARÍN ESTÉVEZ; Regional Mans NOLBERTO PÉREZ PEÑA (Melipilla), JUAN CARLOS OLIVER PÉREZ (Colchagua), JUAN MANUEL ORTEGA MUÑOZ (Maule).

ENERSIS, SA: Santa Rosa 76, Casilla 1557, Vitacura, Santiago; tel. (2) 2353-4400; fax (2) 2378-4788; e-mail comunicacion@e.enersis.cl; internet www.enersis.cl; f. 1981; holding co for Spanish group generating and distributing electricity through its subsidiaries throughout South America; 60.62% owned by Endesa Chile; Pres. PABLO YRARRÁZAVAL VALDÉS; Gen. Man. IGNACIO ANTOÑANZAS ALVEAR; 10,957 employees.

Chilectra, SA: Santo Domingo 789, Casilla 1557, Santiago; tel. (2) 2632-2000; fax (2) 2639-3280; e-mail rrpp@chilectra.cl; internet www.chilectra.cl; f. 1921; transmission and distribution arm of ENERSIS; supplies distribution cos, including the Empresa Eléctrica Municipal de Lo Barnechea, Empresa Municipal de Til-Til, and the Empresa Eléctrica de Colina, SA; holds overseas distribution concessions in Argentina, Peru and Brazil; acquired by ENERSIS of Spain in 1999; Pres. JUAN MARÍA MORENO MELLADO; Gen. Man. CRISTIÁN FIERRO MONTES.

Endesa Chile: Santa Rosa 76, Casilla 1392, Santiago; tel. (2) 2630-9000; fax (2) 2635-4720; e-mail comunicacion@endesa.cl; internet www.endesa.cl; f. 1943; installed capacity 4,035 MW (2002); ENERSIS obtained majority control of Endesa Chile in 1999; operates subsidiaries in Pehuenche, Pangue, San Isidro y Celta; Pres. JORGE ROSENBLUT; Gen. Man. JOAQUÍN GALINDO VÉLEZ.

SAESA (Sociedad Austral de Electricidad, SA): Manuel Bulnes 441, Casilla 21-0, Osorno; tel. (64) 220-6200; fax (64) 220-6309; e-mail saesa@saesa.cl; internet www.saesa.cl; owned by PSEG Corpn of the USA; Pres. JORGE LESSER GARCÍA-HUIDOBRO; Gen. Man. FRANCISCO MUALIM TIETZ.

Gas

Abastible, SA (Abastecedora de Combustible): Avda Vicuña Mackenna 55, Providencia, Santiago; tel. (2) 2693-9000; fax (2) 2693-9304; internet www.abastible.cl; f. 1956; owned by COPEC; Pres. FELIPE LAMARCA CLARO; Gen. Man. JOSÉ ODONE.

Compañía de Consumidores de Gas de Santiago (GASCO, SA): 1061 Santo Domingo, Casilla 8-D, Santiago; tel. (2) 2694-4444; fax (2) 2694-4370; e-mail info@gasco.cl; internet www.gasco.cl; natural gas utility; supplies Santiago and Punta Arenas regions; owned by CGE; Pres. CLAUDIO HORNAUER HERRMANN; Gen. Man. GERARDO COOD SCHOEPKE.

Electrogas: Alonso de Cordova 5900, Of. 401, Las Condes, Santiago; tel. (2) 2299-3400; fax (2) 2299-3490; e-mail carlos.andreani@electrogas.cl; internet www.electrogas.cl/default.asp; f. 1998; subsidiary of Endesa Chile; CEO CARLOS ANDREANI LUCO.

Empresas Lipigas: Las Urbinas 53, 13°, Of. 131, Providencia, Santiago; tel. (2) 2650-3582; e-mail info@empresaslipigas.cl; internet www.lipigas.cl; f. 1950; liquid gas supplier; also operates Agrogas, Enagas and Industrias Codigas; Pres. ERNESTO NOGUERA G.; Gen. Man. ANGEL MAFUCCI.

GasAndes: Avda Chena 11650, Parque Industrial Puerta Sur, San Bernardo, Santiago; tel. (2) 2366-5960; fax (2) 2366-5942; internet www.gasandes.com; distributes natural gas transported from the Argentine province of Mendoza via a 463-km pipeline.

GasAtacama Generación: Isidora Goyenechea 3365, 8°, Las Condes, Santiago; tel. (2) 2366-3800; fax (2) 2366-3802; natural gas producer and transporter; subsidiary of Endesa Chile; Man. RUDOLFO ARANEDA.

GasValpo, SA: Camino Internacional 1420, Viña del Mar; tel. (32) 227-7000; fax (32) 221-3092; e-mail info@gasvalpo.cl; internet www.gasvalpo.cl; f. 1853; owned by AGL of Australia; Pres. GREG MARTIN; Gen. Man. LUIS KIPREOS.

Linde Chile: Paseo Presidente, Errázuriz Echaurren 2631, Casilla 16953, Providencia, Santiago; tel. (2) 2330-8000; fax (2) 2231-8009; e-mail callcentre@cl.aga.com; internet www.linde.cl; f. 1920 as AGA Chile, SA; owned by Linde Gas Corpn of Germany; natural and industrial gases utility.

Water

Aguas Andinas, SA: Avda Presidente Balmaceda 1398, Santiago; tel. (2) 2688-1000; fax (2) 2698-5871; e-mail info@aguasandinas.cl; internet www.aguasandinas.cl; water supply and sanitation services to Santiago and the surrounding area; sold to a French-Spanish consortium in June 1999; Pres. FELIPE LARRAIN ASPILLAGA; Gen. Man. VÍCTOR DE LA BARRA FUENZALIDA.

Empresa de Obras Sanitarias de Valparaíso, SA (Esval): Cochrane 751, Valparaíso; tel. (32) 220-9000; fax (32) 220-9502; e-mail infoesval@entelchile.net; internet www.esval.cl; f. 1989; sanitation and irrigation co serving Valparaíso; Pres. JUAN HURTADO VICUÑA; Gen. Man. FRANCISCO OTTONE VIGORENA; 377 employees.

Sigsig Ltda (Tecnagent) (Servicios de Ingeniería Sigren y Sigren Ltda): Presidente Errázuriz 3262, Casilla 7550295, Las Condes, Santiago; tel. (2) 2335-2001; fax (2) 2334-8466; e-mail tecnagent@tecnagent.cl; internet www.tecnagent.cl; f. 1986; Pres. RAÚL B. SIGREN BINDHOFF; Gen. Man. RAÚL A. SIGREN ORFILA.

TRADE UNIONS

Central Unions

Central Autónoma de Trabajadores (CAT): Sazié 1761, Santiago; tel. and fax (2) 2657-8533; e-mail catchile@catchile.cl; internet www.catchile.cl; 107,000 mems (2007); Pres. OSCAR OLIVOS MADARIAGA; Sec.-Gen. ALFONSO PASTENE URIBE.

Central Unitaria de Trabajadores de Chile (CUT): Alameda 1346, Centro, Santiago; tel. (2) 2352-7600; fax (2) 2672-0112; e-mail cutorganizacion@gmail.com; internet www.cutchile.cl; f. 1988; affiliated orgs: 20 asscns, 28 confederations, 64 federations, 35 unions; 670,000 mems (2009); Pres. BÁRBARA FIGUEROA; Gen. Sec. ARTURO MARTÍNEZ.

Unión Nacional de Trabajadores: Moneda 1447, Santiago; tel. (2) 2688-6344; e-mail info@untchile.cl; internet untchile.cl; Pres. DIEGO OLIVARES ARAVENA; Gen. Sec. LUIS PALOMINOS LIZAM.

Transport

RAILWAYS

In 2010 there were 6,188 km of railway lines in the country.

State Railways

Empresa de los Ferrocarriles del Estado (EFE): Morandé 115, 6°, Santiago; tel. (2) 2376-8500; fax (2) 2776-2609; e-mail principios@efe.cl; internet www.efe.cl; f. 1851; 2,072 km of track in use (2006); Pres. VÍCTOR TOLEDO SANDOVAL; Gen. Man. FRANCO FACCILONGO FORNO.

Ferrocarriles Suburbanos de Concepción (FESUB): Avda Padre Hurtado 570, 4°, Concepción; tel. (41) 286-8015; e-mail contacto@biotren.cl; internet www.fesub.cl; f. 2008; serves Corto

Laja and Regional Victoria Temuco; Pres. JOAQUÍN BRAHM BARRIL; Gen. Man. NELSON HERNÁNDEZ ROLDÁN.

Servicio de Trenes Regionales Terra, SA (TerraSur): Avda Libertador Bernardo O'Higgins 3170, andén 6, 2°, Santiago; tel. (2) 2585-5000; fax (2) 2585-5914; e-mail comunicaciones@terrasur.cl; internet www.terrasur.cl; Pres. GONZALO EDWARDS GUZMÁN; Gen. Man. ANTONIO DOURTHÉ CASTRILLÓN.

Transporte Ferroviario Andrés Pirazolli, SA (Transap): Exterminal Ferroviario Los Lirios, Rancagua; tel. (67) 2222-2242; fax (67) 2222-2039; e-mail contacto@transap.cl; internet www.transap.cl; f. 2000; freight services; Pres. MARCELO PIRAZZOLI; Gen. Man. NABIL KUNCAR.

Private Railways

Empresa de Transporte Ferroviario, SA (Ferronor): Huérfanos 587, Ofs 301 y 302, Santiago; tel. (2) 2938-3170; fax (2) 2638-0464; e-mail ferronor@ferronor.cl; internet www.ferronor.cl; 2,412 km of track (2009); operates cargo services only; interconnected with Argentina, Bolivia, Brazil and Paraguay; Pres. ROBERTO PIRAZZOLI; Gen. Man. JUAN CARLOS GARCÍA-HUIDOBRO.

Ferrocarril de Antofagasta (FCAB): Bolívar 255, Casillas ST, Antofagasta; tel. (55) 220-6100; fax (55) 220-6220; e-mail info@fcab.cl; internet www.fcab.cl; f. 1888; subsidiary of Grupo Antofagasta PLC (United Kingdom); operates an international railway to Bolivia and Argentina; cargo-forwarding services; track length in use 1,000 km (2011); Gen. Man. MIGUEL V. SEPÚLVEDA.

Ferrocarril del Pacífico, SA (FEPASA): Málaga 120, 5°, Las Condes, Santiago; tel. (2) 2837-8000; fax (2) 2837-8005; e-mail oguevara@fepasa.cl; internet www.fepasa.cl; f. 1993; privatized freight services on EFE track; 19.83% owned by EFE; Pres. OSCAR GUILLERMO GARRETÓN PURCELL; Gen. Man. GAMALIEL VILLALOBOS ARANDA.

Association

Asociación Chilena de Conservación de Patrimonio Ferroviario (ACCPF): Casilla 51996, Correo Central, Santiago; tel. (2) 2699-4607; fax (2) 2280-0252; e-mail info@accpf.cl; internet www.accpf.cl; f. 1986; railway preservation asscn; Pres. JOSÉ TOMÁS BRETÓN JARA; Sec.-Gen. EUGENIO TUEVE RIVERA.

METROPOLITAN TRANSPORT

Metro de Santiago: Avda Libertador Bernardo O'Higgins 1414, Santiago; tel. (2) 2250-3000; fax (2) 2937-2000; e-mail comunicaciones@metro.cl; internet www.metrosantiago.cl; f. 1975; 5 lines, 103 km (2012); extension to 140 km scheduled for completion in 2017; Pres. RAPHAEL BERGOEING VELA; Gen. Man. ROBERTO BIANCHI POBLETA.

Metro Valparaíso, SA (MERVAL): Viana 1685, Viña del Mar, V Región, Valparaíso; tel. (32) 252-7511; fax (32) 252-7509; e-mail jmobando@metro-valparaiso.cl; internet www.metro-valparaiso.cl; f. 1995; Pres. JOSÉ LUIS DOMÍNGUEZ; Gen. Man. MARISA KAUSEL CONTADOR.

Transantiago: Nueva York 9, 10°, Santiago; tel. (2) 2428-7900; fax (2) 2428-7926; internet www.transantiago.cl; f. 2005; govt scheme to co-ordinate public transport in Santiago; comprises 10 bus networks and the Metro de Santiago.

Trenes Metropolitanos, SA: Avda Libertador Bernardo O'Higgins 3170, Andén 6 de Estación Central, Santiago; tel. (2) 2585-5000; fax (2) 2776-3304; e-mail contacto@tmsa.cl; internet www.tmsa.cl; f. 1990; subsidiary of Empresa de los Ferrocarriles del Estado (EFE); connects Santiago with several communities near San Fernando; Pres. JUAN ESTEBAN DOÑA NOVOA; Gen. Man. CRISTIÁN MOYA SILVA.

ROADS

In 2010 the road network comprised 77,764 km of roads, of which 23% were paved. Of the total, 9,041 km were part of the national road network and some 14,139 km formed the provincial road network. The road system includes the entirely paved Pan-American Highway, extending 3,455 km from north to south.

Dirección de Vialidad: Morandé 59, 2°, Santiago; tel. (2) 2449-4000; fax (2) 2441-0914; internet www.vialidad.cl; f. 1953; supervising authority; Dir MARIO FERNÁNDEZ RODRÍGUEZ.

SHIPPING

As a consequence of Chile's difficult topography, maritime transport is of particular importance. The principal state and privately owned ports are San Antonio, Quintero, Valparaíso, Lirquén, San Vicente, Patillos, Mejillones, Ventanas, Huasco, Iquique, Tocopilla and Antofagasta. Chile's flag registered fleet comprised 614 vessels, totalling to 907,989 grt at December 2013.

Supervisory Authorities

Asociación Nacional de Armadores: Blanco 869, 3°, Valparaíso; tel. (32) 221-2057; fax (32) 221-2017; e-mail info@armadores-chile.cl; internet www.armadores-chile.cl; f. 1931; shipowners' asscn; Pres. ROBERTO HETZ VORPAHL; Gen. Man. ARTURO SIERRA MERINO.

Cámara Marítima y Portuaria de Chile, AG: Blanco 869, 2°, Valparaíso; tel. (32) 225-0313; fax (32) 225-0231; e-mail info@camport.cl; internet www.camport.cl; Pres. VICTOR PINO TORCHE; Exec. Vice-Pres. RODOLFO GARCÍA SÁNCHEZ.

Dirección General de Territorio Marítimo y Marina Mercante (DIRECTEMAR): Errázuriz 537, 4°, Valparaíso; tel. (32) 220-8000; fax (32) 225-2539; e-mail transparencia@directemar.cl; internet www.directemar.cl; maritime admin. of the coast and national waters, control of the merchant navy; ship registry; Dir-Gen. Rear-Adm. HUMBERTO RAMÍREZ NAVARRO.

Cargo-handling Companies

Empresa Portuaria Antofagasta (EPA): Avda Grecia s/n, Puerto Antofagasta, Casilla 190, Antofagasta; tel. (55) 256-3756; fax (55) 256-3735; e-mail epa@puertoantofagasta.cl; internet www.puertoantofagasta.cl; f. 1998; Pres. WALDO MORA LONGA; Gen. Man. CARLOS ESCOBAR OLGUIN.

Empresa Portuaria Arica: Máximo Lira 389, Arica; tel. (58) 220-2080; fax (58) 220-2090; e-mail puertoarica@puertoarica.cl; internet www.puertoarica.cl; f. 1998; Pres. FRANCISCO JAVIER GONZÁLEZ SILVA; Gen. Man. ALDO SIGNORELLI BONOMO.

Empresa Portuaria Austral: Avda Bernardo O'Higgins 1385, Punta Arenas; tel. (61) 271-1200; fax (61) 271-1231; e-mail info@australport.cl; internet www.australport.cl; Pres. JULIO COVARRUBIAS FERNÁNDEZ; Gen. Man. IGNACIO FUGELLIE.

Empresa Portuaria Chacabuco (EMPORCHA): Avda Bernardo O'Higgins s/n, Puerto Chacabuco, XI Región; tel. (67) 235-1139; fax (67) 235-1174; e-mail info@chacabucoport.cl; internet www.chacabucoport.cl; f. 1998; Pres. GUILLERMO MARTÍNEZ BARROS; Gen. Man. ENRIQUE RUNÍN ZUÑIGA.

Empresa Portuaria Coquimbo: Melgarejo 676, Casilla 10D, Coquimbo; tel. (51) 231-3606; fax (51) 232-6146; e-mail ptoqq@entelchile.net; internet www.puertocoquimbo.cl; Pres. HUGO GRISANTI ABOGABIR.

Empresa Portuaria Iquique: Avda Jorge Barrera 62, Casilla 47D, Iquique; tel. (57) 240-0100; fax (57) 241-3176; e-mail epi@epi.cl; internet www.epi.cl; f. 1998; Pres. ANGEL CABRERA VENEGAS; Gen. Man. ALFREDO LEITON ARBEA.

Empresa Portuaria Puerto Montt: Avda Angelmó 1673, Puerto Montt, Región de los Lagos; tel. (65) 236-4500; fax (65) 236-4517; e-mail gerencia@empormontt.cl; internet www.empormontt.cl; Pres. CARLOS GUILLERMO GEISSE MACEVOY; Gen. Man. ALEX WINKLER RIETZSCH.

Empresa Portuaria San Antonio (EPSA): Alan Macowan 0245, San Antonio; tel. (35) 258-6000; fax (35) 258-6015; e-mail correo@saiport.cl; internet www.sanantonioport.cc.cl; f. 1998; Pres. PATRICIO ARRAU PONS; Gen. Man. ALVARO ESPINOSA ALMARZA.

Empresa Portuaria Talcahuano-San Vicente: Avda Blanco Encalada 547, Talcahuano; tel. (41) 272-0300; fax (41) 272-0326; e-mail eportuaria@puertotalcahuano.cl; internet www.puertotalcahuano.cl; Pres. EUGENIO GUSTAVO CANTUARIAS LARRONDO; Gen. Man. LUIS ALBERTO ROSENBERG NESBET.

Empresa Portuaria Valparaíso: Avda Errázuriz 25, 4°, Of. 1, Valparaíso; tel. (2) 2244-8800; fax (2) 2222-4190; e-mail comercial@epv.cl; internet www.epv.cl; Pres. ALFONSO MUJÍCA VIZCAYA; Gen. Man. HARALD JAEGER KARL.

Principal Shipping Companies

Santiago

Agencias Universales, SA (AGUNSA): Edif. del Pacífico, 15°, Avda Andrés Bello 2687, Casilla 2511, Las Condes, Santiago; tel. (2) 2460-2700; fax (2) 2203-9009; e-mail agunsascl@agunsa.cl; internet www.agunsa.cl; f. 1960; maritime transportation and shipping, port and docking services; owned by Empresas Navieras, SA; Chair. JOSÉ MANUEL URENDA SALAMANCA; Gen. Man. LUIS MANCILLA PÉREZ.

Empresa Marítima, SA (Empremar Chile): Encomenderos 260, Piso 7°, Las Condes, Santiago; tel. (2) 2469-6100; fax (2) 2469-6199; internet www.empremar.cl; f. 1953; international and coastal services; Chair. LORENZO CAGLEVIC; Gen. Man. CRISTIÁN BERNALES.

Navimag Ferries, SA (NAVIMAG): Avda El Bosque, Norte 0440, 11°, Of. 1103/1104, Las Condes, Santiago; tel. (2) 2442-3150; fax (2) 2203-4025; e-mail sales@navimag.cl; internet www.navimag.com; f. 1979; part of Nisa Navegación, SA; Gen. Man. HÉCTOR HENRÍQUEZ NEGRÓN.

Ultragas Ltda: Avda El Bosque Norte 500, 20°, Las Condes, Santiago; tel. (2) 2630-1009; fax (2) 2232-8856; e-mail ultragas@ultragas.cl; internet www.ultragasgroup.com; f. 1960; part of Ultragas Group; tanker services; Chair. DAG VON APPEN BUROSE; CEO CHRISTIAN CSASZAR.

Valparaíso

Broom Valparaíso: Errázuriz 629, 3° y 4°, Valparaíso; tel. (32) 226-8200; fax (32) 221-3308; e-mail info@ajbroom.cl; internet www.broomgroup.com; f. 1920; shipowners and brokers; Pres. JAMES C. WELLS M.; CEO ANDRÉS NUÑEZ SORENSEN.

Cía Chilena de Navegación Interoceánica, SA (CCNI): Plaza de la Justicia 59, Valparaíso; tel. (32) 227-5500; fax (32) 225-5949; e-mail info@ccni.cl; internet www.ccni.cl; f. 1930; regular sailings to Japan, Republic of Korea, Taiwan, Hong Kong, USA, Mexico, South Pacific, South Africa and Europe; bulk and dry cargo services; owned by Empresas Navieras, SA; Chair. JOSÉ MANUEL URENDA SALAMANCA; CEO FELIPE IRARRÁZAVAL OVALLE.

Cía Sud Americana de Vapores (CSAV): Plaza Sotomayor 50, Casilla 49V, Valparaíso; tel. (32) 220-3000; fax (32) 320-3333; e-mail info@csav.com; internet www.csav.com; f. 1872; regular services worldwide; bulk and container carriers, tramp and reefer services; Chair. FRANCISCO PÉREZ MACKENNA; Gen. Man. JUAN ANTONIO ALVAREZ AVENDAÑO.

Naviera Chilena del Pacífico, SA (Nachipa): Almirante Señoret 70, 6°, Casilla 370, Valparaíso; tel. (32) 250-0300; e-mail valparaiso@nachipa.com; internet www.nachipa.cl; cargo; Pres. PABLO SIMIAN ZAMORANO; Gen. Man. FELIPE SIMIAN FERNÁNDEZ.

Sudamericana Agencias Aéreas y Marítimas, SA (SAAM): Blanco 895, Valparaíso; tel. (32) 220-1000; fax (32) 220-1481; e-mail servicioalcliente@saamsa.com; internet www.saam.cl; f. 1961; cargo services; Gen. Man. ALEJANDRO GARCÍA-HUIDOBRO.

Punta Arenas

Transbordadora Austral Broom, SA: Avda Juan Williams 06450, Punta Arenas; tel. (61) 272-8100; fax (61) 272-8109; e-mail correo@tabsa.cl; internet www.tabsa.cl; f. 1968; ferry services in Chilean Antarctica; Pres. PEDRO LECAROS; Gen. Man. ALEJANDRO KUSANOVIC.

Puerto Montt

Transmarchilay, SA (Transporte Marítimo Chiloé-Aysén): Angelmo 2187, Puerto Montt; tel. (65) 227-0700; fax (65) 227-0730; e-mail transporte@tmc.cl; internet www.transmarchilay.cl; f. 1971; Pres. HARALD ROSENQVIST; Gen. Man. ALVARO CONTRERAS.

CIVIL AVIATION

There are 330 airfields in the country, of which eight have long runways. Arturo Merino Benítez, 20 km north-east of Santiago, and Chacalluta, 14 km north-east of Arica, are the principal international airports.

Regulatory Authority

Dirección General de Aeronática Civil (DGAC): Miguel Claro 1314, Providencia, Santiago; tel. (2) 2439-2000; fax (2) 2436-8143; internet www.dgac.gob.cl; f. 1930; Dir-Gen. Gen. JAIME ALARCÓN PÉREZ.

Principal Airlines

Aerocardal: Aeropuerto Internacional Arturo Merino Benítez, Avda Diego Barros Ortiz 2065, Pudahuel, Santiago; tel. (2) 2377-7400; fax (2) 2377-7405; e-mail ventas@aerocardal.com; internet www.aerocardal.com; f. 1990; executive, charter and tourist services; Gen. Man. RICARDO REAL.

Aerovías DAP: Avda Bernardo O'Higgins 891, Casilla 406, Punta Arenas; tel. (61) 261-6100; fax (61) 261-6159; e-mail ventas@aeroviasdap.cl; internet www.aeroviasdap.cl; f. 1980; domestic services; CEO ALEX PISCEVIC.

LAN Airlines (Línea Aérea Nacional de Chile): Avda Presidente Riesco 5711, 20°, Las Condes, Santiago; tel. (2) 2565-2525; fax (2) 2565-3890; internet www.lan.com; f. 1929; merged with TAM Linhas Aéreas, SA in 2012 to form LATAM Airlines Group, SA, although still operates under LAN brand; operates scheduled domestic and international passenger and cargo (LAN Cargo) services; CEO, LATAM Airlines ENRIQUE CUETO PLAZA; CEO, LAN Airlines IGNACIO CUETO PLAZA.

Tourism

Chile has a wide variety of attractions for the tourist, including fine beaches, ski resorts in the Andes, lakes, rivers and desert scenery. Isla de Pascua (Easter Island) may also be visited by tourists. In 2012 there were 3,554,279 tourist arrivals and receipts from tourism totalled US $2,201m.

Servicio Nacional de Turismo (SERNATUR): Avda Providencia 1550, 2°, CP 7500548, Santiago; tel. (2) 2731-8419; fax (2) 2236-1417; e-mail contacto@sernatur.cl; internet www.sernatur.cl; f. 1975; Nat. Dir ALVARO CASTILLA FERNÁNDEZ.

Asociación Chilena de Empresas de Turismo (ACHET): Avda Providencia 2019, Of. 42B, Santiago; tel. (2) 2439-9100; fax (2) 2439-9118; e-mail achet@achet.cl; internet www.achet.cl; f. 1945; 155 mems; Pres. GUILLERMO CORREA SANFUENTES; Sec.-Gen. LORENA ARRIAGADA GÁLVEZ.

Defence

As assessed at November 2013, Chile's armed forces numbered 61,400: army 34,650, navy 18,700 and air force 8,050. There were also paramilitary forces of 44,700 *carabineros*. Reserve troops numbered 40,000. Compulsory military service was ended in 2005.

Defence Expenditure: Expenditure was budgeted at 2,250,000m. pesos in 2013.

Chief of Staff of National Defence: Rear-Adm. JOSÉ MIGUEL ROMERO AGUIRRE.

Commander-in-Chief of the Army: Gen. HUMBERTO OVIEDO ARRIAGADA.

Commander-in-Chief of the Navy: Adm. ENRIQUE LARRAÑAGA MARTÍN.

Commander-in-Chief of the Air Force: Gen. JORGE ROJAS AVILA.

Education

Primary education in Chile is free and compulsory for eight years, beginning at six or seven years of age. It is divided into two cycles: the first lasts for four years and provides a general education; the second cycle offers a more specialized schooling. There were 1,976,176 pupils in primary education in 2012. Secondary education is divided into the humanities-science programme (lasting four years), with the emphasis on general education and possible entrance to university, and the technical-professional programme (lasting for up to six years). In 2012 there were 1,044,233 students in secondary education. There are three types of higher education institution: universities, professional institutes and centres of technical information. In 2012 there were 1,127,181 students in higher education. The 2013 central government budget allocated 6,712,290m. pesos to the Ministry of Education.

THE PEOPLE'S REPUBLIC OF CHINA

Introductory Survey

LOCATION, CLIMATE, LANGUAGE, RELIGION, FLAG, CAPITAL

The People's Republic of China covers a vast area of eastern Asia, with Mongolia and Russia to the north, Tajikistan, Kyrgyzstan and Kazakhstan to the north-west, Afghanistan and Pakistan to the west, and India, Nepal, Bhutan, Myanmar (formerly Burma), Laos and Viet Nam to the south. The country borders the Democratic People's Republic of Korea (North Korea) in the north-east, and has a long coastline on the Pacific Ocean. The climate ranges from subtropical in the far south to an annual average temperature of below 10°C (50°F) in the north, and from the monsoon climate of eastern China to the aridity of the north-west. The principal language is Northern Chinese (Mandarin, known as Putonghua or common speech); in the south and south-east local dialects are spoken. The Xizangzu (Tibetans), Wei Wuer (Uygurs), Menggus (Mongols) and other groups have their own languages. The traditional religions and philosophies of life are Confucianism, Buddhism and Daoism. There are also Muslim and Christian minorities. The national flag (proportions 2 by 3) is plain red, with one large five-pointed gold star and four similar but smaller stars, arranged in an arc, in the upper hoist. The capital is Beijing (Peking).

CONTEMPORARY POLITICAL HISTORY

Historical Context

The People's Republic of China was proclaimed on 1 October 1949, following the victory of Communist forces over the Kuomintang (KMT) Government, which fled to the island province of Taiwan. The new Communist regime received widespread international recognition, but it was not until 1971 that the People's Republic was admitted to the United Nations, in place of the KMT regime, as the representative of China. Most countries subsequently recognized the People's Republic, with the 'Republic of China' being confined to Taiwan.

With the establishment of the People's Republic, the leading political figure was Mao Zedong, who was Chairman of the Chinese Communist Party (CCP) from 1935 until his death in 1976. Chairman Mao, as he was known, also became head of state in October 1949, but he relinquished this post in December 1958. His successor was Liu Shaoqi, First Vice-Chairman of the CCP, who was elected head of state in April 1959. Liu was dismissed in October 1968, during the Cultural Revolution, and died in prison in 1969. The post of head of state was left vacant, and was formally abolished in January 1975, when a new Constitution was adopted. The first Premier (Head of Government) of the People's Republic was Zhou Enlai, who held this office from October 1949. Zhou was also Minister of Foreign Affairs from 1949 to 1958.

The economic progress of the early years of Communist rule enabled China to withstand the effects of the industrialization programmes of the late 1950s (the 'Great Leap Forward', which is variously estimated to have caused the death by starvation of between 14m. and 48m. people, mainly in rural areas), the drought of 1960–62 and the withdrawal of Soviet aid in 1960. To prevent the establishment of a ruling class, Chairman Mao launched the Great Proletarian Cultural Revolution in 1966. The ensuing excesses of the Red Guards prompted the army to intervene; Liu Shaoqi and Deng Xiaoping, General Secretary of the CCP, were disgraced. In 1971 an attempted coup by the Minister of National Defence, Marshal Lin Biao, was unsuccessful, and by 1973 it was apparent that Chairman Mao and Premier Zhou Enlai had retained power. In 1975 Deng Xiaoping re-emerged as first Vice-Premier and Chief of the General Staff. Zhou Enlai died in January 1976. Hua Guofeng, hitherto Minister of Public Security, was appointed Premier, and Deng was dismissed. Mao died in September. His widow, Jiang Qing, tried unsuccessfully to seize power, with the help of three radical members of the CCP's Political Bureau (Politburo). This 'Gang of Four' and six associates of Lin Biao were tried in November 1980. All were found guilty and were given long terms of imprisonment. The 10th anniversary of Mao's death was marked in September 1986 by an official reassessment of his life; while his accomplishments were praised, it was acknowledged that he had made mistakes, although most of the criticism was directed at the 'Gang of Four'.

Domestic Political Affairs

In October 1976 Hua Guofeng succeeded Mao as Chairman of the CCP and Commander-in-Chief of the People's Liberation Army (PLA). The 11th National Congress of the CCP, held in August 1977, restored Deng Xiaoping to his former posts. Deng initiated a series of economic reforms, which included replacing collective farms by individually managed units, allowing greater autonomy to state-owned enterprises, permitting the establishment of businesses by entrepreneurs, and opening the country to foreign investment, particularly through the formation (from 1980) of Special Economic Zones, initially on China's south-east coast. In September 1980 Hua Guofeng resigned as Premier, but retained his chairmanship of the CCP. The appointment of Zhao Ziyang, a Vice-Premier since April 1980, to succeed Hua as Premier confirmed the dominance of the moderate faction of Deng Xiaoping. In June 1981 Hua Guofeng was replaced as Chairman of the CCP by Hu Yaobang, former Secretary-General of the Politburo, and as Chairman of the party's Central Military Commission by Deng Xiaoping. A sustained campaign by Deng to eradicate 'leftist' elements from the Politburo led to Hua's demotion to a Vice-Chairman of the CCP and, in September 1982, to his exclusion from the Politburo.

In September 1982 the CCP was reorganized and the post of Party Chairman was abolished. Hu Yaobang became, instead, General Secretary of the CCP. A year later a 'rectification' of the CCP was launched, aimed at expelling 'Maoists', who had risen to power during the Cultural Revolution, and those opposed to the pragmatic policies of Deng. China's new Constitution, adopted in December 1982, restored the office of head of state, and in June 1983 Li Xiannian, a former Minister of Finance, became President of China. In September 1986 a session of the 12th CCP Central Committee adopted a detailed resolution on the 'guiding principles for building a socialist society', which redefined the general ideology of the CCP, to provide a theoretical basis for the programme of modernization and the 'open door' policy of economic reform.

In January 1986 investigations began into reports that many officials had exploited the programme of economic reform for their own gain (see The Campaign against Corruption for subsequent offensives). A significant cultural liberalization took place in 1986, with a revival of the 'Hundred Flowers' movement of 1956–57, which had encouraged the development of intellectual debate. However, a series of student demonstrations in major cities in late 1986 was regarded by China's leaders as an indication of excessive 'bourgeois liberalization'. In January 1987 Hu Yaobang unexpectedly resigned as CCP General Secretary, being accused of 'mistakes on major issues of political principles'. Zhao Ziyang became acting General Secretary. At the 13th National Congress of the CCP, which opened in October, Deng Xiaoping retired from the Central Committee, but amendments to the Constitution of the CCP permitted him to retain the influential positions of Chairman of the State Military Commission and of the CCP Central Military Commission. A new Politburo was appointed by the Central Committee in November. The majority of its 18 members were relatively young supporters of Deng Xiaoping's policies. The membership of the new Politburo also indicated a decline in military influence in Chinese politics. The newly appointed Standing Committee of the Politburo (the highest decision-making body) was regarded, on balance, as being 'pro-reform'. In late November Li Peng was appointed Acting Premier of the State Council, in place of Zhao Ziyang. At the first session of the Seventh National People's Congress (NPC), convened in March 1988, Li Peng was confirmed as Premier, and Yang Shangkun (a member of the CCP Politburo) was elected President.

Following the death of Hu Yaobang in April 1989, students criticized the alleged prevalence of corruption and nepotism within the Government, seeking a limited degree of Soviet-style *glasnost* (openness) in public life. When negotiations between government officials and the students' leaders had failed to satisfy the protesters' demands, workers from various professions joined the demonstrations in Tiananmen Square, Beijing, which had now become the focal point of the protests. At one stage more than 1m. people congregated in the Square, as demonstrations spread to more than 20 other Chinese cities. In mid-May some 3,000 students began a hunger strike in Tiananmen Square, while protesters demanded the resignation of both Deng Xiaoping and Li Peng. The students ended their hunger strike at the request of Zhao Ziyang. On 20 May martial law was declared in Beijing. Within days, some 300,000 troops had assembled.

On 3 June 1989 a further unsuccessful attempt was made to dislodge the demonstrators, but on the following day troops of the PLA attacked protesters in and around Tiananmen Square, killing an unspecified number of people. Television evidence and eye-witness accounts suggested a death toll of between 1,000 and 5,000. The Government immediately rejected these figures, claiming that a counter-revolutionary rebellion had been taking place. Arrests and executions ensued, although some student leaders eluded capture and fled to Hong Kong. Zhao Ziyang was dismissed from all his party posts and replaced as General Secretary of the CCP by Jiang Zemin, hitherto the secretary of the Shanghai municipal party committee. Zhao was accused of participating in a conspiracy to overthrow the CCP and placed under house arrest. In November Deng resigned as Chairman of the CCP Central Military Commission, his sole remaining party position, and was succeeded by Jiang Zemin, who was hailed as the first of China's 'third generation' of communist leaders (Mao being representative of the first, and Deng of the second). In January 1990 martial law was removed in Beijing, and it was announced that a total of 573 prisoners, detained following the demonstrations, had been freed. Further groups of detainees were released subsequently. In March Deng Xiaoping resigned from his last official post, that of Chairman of the State Military Commission, and was succeeded by Jiang Zemin. An extensive military reorganization ensued. At the CCP's 14th National Congress, held in October 1992, a new 319-member Central Committee was elected. The Politburo was expanded and a new Secretariat was chosen by the incoming Central Committee. Many opponents of Deng Xiaoping's reforms were replaced.

At the first session of the Eighth NPC, convened in March 1993, Jiang Zemin was elected as the country's President, remaining CCP General Secretary. Li Peng was reappointed as Premier, and an extensive reorganization of the State Council was announced. The Congress also approved amendments to the 1982 Constitution, which included confirmation of the State's practice of a 'socialist market economy'. During 1993, however, the Government became concerned at the growing disparity between urban and rural incomes. In June thousands of peasants took part in demonstrations in Sichuan Province to protest against excessive official levies. In response to the ensuing riots, the central Government banned the imposition of additional local taxes.

In March 1995, at the third session of the Eighth NPC, the appointment of Wu Bangguo and of Jiang Chunyun as Vice-Premiers of the State Council was approved. However, in an unprecedented display of opposition neither nominee received the NPC's full endorsement. Nevertheless, the position of Jiang Zemin appeared to have been strengthened. Personnel changes in the military hierarchy later in the year were also viewed as favourable to the President. In April 1996 the Government initiated 'Strike Hard', a new campaign against crime, executing hundreds of people.

The death of Deng Xiaoping in February 1997 precipitated a period of uncertainty regarding China's future direction. President Jiang Zemin declared that the economic reforms would continue, and this was reiterated in Premier Li Peng's address to the NPC in March. Delegates at the Congress approved legislation reinforcing the CCP's control over the PLA, and revisions to the criminal code were also promulgated, whereby statutes concerning 'counter-revolutionary' acts (under which many of the pro-democracy demonstrators had been charged in 1989) were removed from the code, but were replaced by 11 crimes of 'endangering state security'. Financial offences were also included for the first time.

At the 15th National Congress of the CCP, convened in September 1997, emphasis was placed on radical reform of the 370,000 state-owned enterprises (SOEs). Delegates approved amendments to the party Constitution, enshrining the 'Deng Xiaoping Theory' of socialism with Chinese characteristics alongside 'Mao Zedong Thought' as the guiding ideology of the CCP. The Congress elected a new 344-member Central Committee, which in turn re-elected Jiang Zemin as General Secretary of the CCP and appointed a 22-member Politburo. Qiao Shi, a reformist and Jiang's most influential rival, who was ranked third in the party hierarchy, was excluded from the Politburo, reportedly because of his age, as was Gen. Liu Huaqing, China's most senior military official. Zhu Rongji, a former mayor of Shanghai, replaced Qiao Shi. Gen. Liu was replaced by a civilian, Wei Jinxiang, who was responsible for combating corruption within the CCP. The absence of the military from the Politburo, and the composition of the new Central Military Commission, confirmed Jiang's increased authority over the PLA.

At the first session of the Ninth NPC, which was held in March 1998, the number of ministry-level bodies was reduced from 40 to 29, mainly through mergers. Jiang Zemin was re-elected as President, and Hu Jintao, a member of the Standing Committee of the Politburo, was elected Vice-President. Li Peng resigned as Premier and was replaced by Zhu Rongji, who received overwhelming support from the NPC delegates. Li Peng replaced Qiao Shi as Chairman of the NPC. Zhu's appointments to a new 39-member State Council included a number of associates of Jiang Zemin.

In March 1999 the NPC ratified a number of constitutional amendments. These included the elevation of private sector and other non-state enterprises to 'important components of the socialist market economy'; a recommendation for adherence to the rule of law; and the incorporation of Deng Xiaoping's ideology into the Constitution alongside Marxism-Leninism and 'Mao Zedong Thought'. At celebrations of the 50th anniversary of the foundation of the People's Republic of China in October, a picture of Jiang Zemin was paraded alongside portraits of Mao Zedong and Deng Xiaoping: the first time that the current President had been publicly placed on a par with his predecessors. In the same month Hu Jintao was appointed a Vice-Chairman of the Central Military Commission.

In February 2000 Jiang Zemin had launched a new political theory entitled 'The Three Represents', which declared that the CCP would 'always represent the development needs of China's advanced social productive forces, always represent the onward direction of China's advanced culture and always represent the fundamental interests of the largest number of Chinese people'. However, it appeared that with the advent of social change the CCP was finding it increasingly difficult to maintain control over its members. In the following months there was harsh repression of provincial labour unrest.

At its session in March 2000, the NPC focused mainly on economic issues. In October the CCP announced a new five-year plan, under which China was to concentrate on rural development, the creation of employment, economic modernization and combating corruption. When the NPC convened in March 2001, Premier Zhu Rongji outlined plans for economic restructuring in preparation for China's membership of the World Trade Organization (WTO). The authorities renewed their action against dissent. In a report released in June, the CCP acknowledged that its rule might be undermined by social discontent arising from the country's free-market reforms, warning that inequality and corruption were issues of increasing importance. In July President Jiang urged the modernization of the CCP and for the first time stated that business people would be welcome as party members. However, left-wing forces, which included orthodox Communists, supporters of moderate socialism, the agricultural lobby and liberals, opposed the transformation of the CCP into a more business-orientated party.

'Fourth generation' leadership

The 16th CCP Congress was held in early November 2002, when the long-awaited transfer of power to the 'fourth generation' leadership headed by the incoming General Secretary, Hu Jintao, was effected. A new 356-member Central Committee was elected, as well as a 24-member Politburo, the Standing Committee of which was expanded from seven to nine members, of whom Hu was the only incumbent to be retained. Jiang retained the chairmanship of the CCP Central Military Commission, which again contained several important military allies of his. Another associate of Jiang, Gen. Liang Guanglie, hitherto Commander of the Nanjing Military Region, was appointed Chief of the PLA's General Staff. The Congress stressed continuity in policy, but introduced some economic reforms. Although state ownership would remain dominant, private businesses would be able to compete on a more equal basis. Discriminatory regulations on investment, financing, taxation, land use and foreign trade would be revised, and private property would be granted greater legal protection.

The final stage of the transfer of power to the 'fourth generation' of Chinese leadership took place during the 10th NPC, held in March 2003. Hu Jintao replaced Jiang Zemin as President, and Zeng Qinghong, who had become a full member of the Politburo in December 1999, was appointed Vice-President. Wen Jiabao, hitherto a Vice-Premier, succeeded Zhu Rongji as Premier. The new State Council also included Ma Kai as Minister of State Development and Reform Commission and Jin Renqing as Minister of Finance, both of whom had expertise in economics. Li Zhaoxing, a former ambassador to the USA and the UN, was appointed Minister of Foreign Affairs, and Gen. Cao Gangchuan became Minister of National Defence. The incoming leadership immediately confronted a new challenge with the outbreak of Severe Acute Respiratory Syndrome (SARS), a previously unknown illness (see Health and Environmental Concerns).

In August 2003 government directives banning media discussion of political and constitutional reform were issued. There were, none the less, some signs of reform. At district elections in Beijing in December two seats were secured by independent candidates. In March 2004 a constitutional amendment to provide legal protection of private property rights was approved by the NPC. Another important constitutional change approved at the NPC session was a new reference to the 'Three Represents' theory (see above) as a guiding ideology. Premier Wen Jiabao also outlined plans for eliminating agricultural taxation and reducing economic inequalities. In September former President Jiang Zemin relinquished his last official post, that of Chairman of the CCP Central Military Commission, to Hu Jintao.

In March 2007, following several years of discussion, the NPC finally approved new legislation affording greater protection for private property and assets. In April President Hu effected a reorganization of the State Council. The Minister of Foreign Affairs, Li Zhaoxing, was replaced by Yang Jiechi, a former ambassador to the USA, while Chen Lei succeeded Wang Shucheng as Minister of Water Resources. Also of note was the appointment of Wan Gang, a non-member of the CCP, as Minister of Science and Technology. (A second non-member, Chen Zhu, joined the State Council in June as Minister of Health, following the departure of Gao Qiang.) Further changes were announced in August, including the appointment of Xie Xuren as successor to Minister of Finance Jin Renqing, and the selection of Ma Wen as Minister of Supervision, following Li Zhilun's death in April.

At the 17th CCP Congress, held in October 2007, President Hu outlined plans to address the disparity between rich and poor and to amend property laws; Hu also acknowledged continuing problems such as corruption. Elections to the CCP Central Committee were followed by a plenary session of the new Committee, during which President Hu was re-elected General Secretary of the party and the composition of the Politburo and Standing Committee was determined. New appointees to the latter included Xi Jinping and Li Keqiang, senior CCP officials in Shanghai and Liaoning, respectively.

At the first session of the 11th NPC, held in March 2008, President Hu Jintao was re-elected for a second five-year term of office. Xi Jinping was elected as Vice-President, in succession to Zeng Qinghong. Wen Jiabao was confirmed as Premier for a further five-year term, while Li Keqiang became First Vice-Premier. A subsequent reorganization of the State Council included the appointment of Gen. Liang Guanglie as Minister of National Defence, and the elevation of the State Environmental Protection Agency to the status of ministry (one of five so-called 'super-ministries'), under Zhou Shengxian.

In May 2008 a devastating earthquake caused the loss of at least 69,000 lives and widespread damage in Sichuan Province. A massive relief effort, supported by international rescue groups, was organized by the Government, which was relatively candid about the disaster. In view of the large number of child fatalities, the safety of building construction and regulatory frameworks, particularly for schools, was called into question. However, activists who subsequently campaigned on behalf of bereaved parents were brought to trial on charges of subversion (see Human Rights and Media Freedom).

Meanwhile, in April 2008 the journey of the Olympic torch, the traditional prelude to the Olympic Games, was beset with difficulties as protesters disrupted ceremonies around the world in an attempt to highlight the Chinese Government's alleged human rights violations, particularly in relation to Tibet. Nevertheless, the Olympic Games, which took place in Beijing in August, were widely deemed a major success. On the 60th anniversary of the foundation of the People's Republic in October 2009, mass celebrations in Beijing included a parade of 8,000 soldiers and extensive displays of missiles and other military equipment.

The second session of the 11th NPC, convened in March 2009, focused largely on the repercussions of the global economic crisis. Substantial increases in expenditure on health services and education facilities were among the various initiatives announced. Issues relating to economic recovery dominated the next session of the NPC, held in March 2010. In October, at the closing session of a meeting of the Central Committee of the CCP, it was announced that Vice-President Xi Jinping had been appointed a Vice-Chairman of the party's Central Military Commission.

In early 2011, meanwhile, the Chinese leadership began to acknowledge the need for a slower pace of economic growth. An increasing focus on household consumption and quality of life, particularly with regard to the environment, was envisaged, in place of the recent emphasis on investment in infrastructural projects and in manufacturing for the export market as the main sources of rapid, but uneven, economic growth. In his opening address to the annual session of the NPC in March 2011, Premier Wen Jiabao stressed the importance of social stability, emphasizing the need to reduce inflation and to curb corruption. The NPC endorsed the country's 12th Five-Year Plan, encompassing the period 2011–15. In an address to the nation on 1 July 2011, the 90th anniversary of the founding of the CCP, President Hu also identified corruption as a major threat to the party.

In 2012, during the months preceding the expected change in national leadership to be effected by the 18th CCP Congress, there were indications (according to some analysts) of a power struggle at senior party level. Bo Xilai, a member of the Politburo and a former Minister of Commerce, who had been the secretary of the CCP's Chongqing committee since 2007, had been widely expected to be promoted to the Politburo Standing Committee in 2012. Bo was the son of one of the revolutionary associates of Mao Zedong, and had achieved national prominence with an aggressive campaign against corruption and organized crime in Chongqing, redistributive social policies and the revival of the use of Maoist songs: his openly ambitious style of leadership, however, was controversial, and critics alleged that his anti-crime campaign had involved extrajudicial methods, including torture. In February Bo's appointee as chief of police in Chongqing and vice-mayor of the city, Wang Lijun, who had been responsible for implementing the campaign against organized crime, sought refuge in the US consulate in Chengdu, days after losing his police post: Wang reportedly claimed that Bo's wife, Gu Kailai, had been responsible for the death in November 2011 of a British expatriate businessman, Neil Heywood, who had social and business links with Bo's family. Wang was reported to have attempted to claim asylum on the grounds that his life was endangered by his rift with Bo, but was later released to the Chinese authorities. In March 2012 Bo was relieved of the party leadership in Chongqing, and in April his membership of the CCP Central Committee and Politburo was suspended pending his investigation for 'serious disciplinary violations'. In the same month it was announced that Gu Kailai and a family employee, Zhang Xiaojun, were under investigation in connection with the death of Heywood, and in July they were formally charged with his murder. At her one-day trial in August Gu did not contest the charge, and following her conviction she received a suspended death sentence, while Zhang received a prison sentence. In September Wang Lijun stood trial on charges of defection, bribe-taking, abuse of power and 'bending the law to selfish ends' by initially concealing evidence of Gu's involvement in Heywood's death: he was found guilty and received a 15-year prison sentence. Later in September it was announced that Bo, who had reportedly not been seen in public since March, had been expelled from the CCP, and was to be charged with criminal offences, including abuse of power, accepting bribes and improper relations with women: although apparently not accused of direct involvement in the murder of Heywood, Bo was described as having 'major responsibility' in the case. In late October Bo was formally expelled from the NPC, thereby forfeiting his immunity from prosecution.

Recent developments: Xi Jinping as President

The 18th CCP Congress, in November 2012, duly brought about a change in China's leadership, following the completion of the terms of office of Hu Jintao, Wen Jiabao and other senior members of the Politburo. Some 2,300 Congress delegates elected the party's Central Committee, with 205 full members (of whom about one-half were new, and only 10 were female) and 171 alternate members. At its first plenary session the Central Committee then appointed Vice-President Xi Jinping to replace Hu as the party's General Secretary, as had been widely expected, and appointed a new Politburo (with 25 members, of whom two were women) and a new Politburo Standing Committee. Membership of the latter was reduced from nine to seven, of whom only Xi and Li Keqiang, the First Vice-Premier, had been members previously: the new members were Vice-Premier Zhang Dejiang (who had replaced Bo Xilai earlier in the year as CCP committee secretary in Chongqing); Vice-Premier Wang Qishan; Yu Zhengsheng and Zhang Gaoli (CCP committee secretaries in Shanghai and Tianjin, respectively); and Liu Yunshan, director of the party's propaganda department. Meng Jianzhu, the new Secretary of the Commission for Political and Legal Affairs, (an extremely powerful position supervising all internal security matters) was not appointed to the Politburo Standing Committee, unlike his predecessor, Zhou Yongkang (who had reportedly been criticized by veteran party members for reviving Maoist policies). Except for Xi and Li, the Standing Committee members were all well into their sixties and would therefore be ineligible for a further term of office after five years; observers also noted that the members were reputed to hold relatively conservative political views, and that most were associates of former President Jiang, who still appeared to wield a strong influence. The Central Committee immediately appointed Xi Jinping to replace Hu as Chairman of the CCP Central Military Commission. In a speech immediately after his appointment as CCP General Secretary, Xi identified particular problems affecting the party, namely corruption, bribe-taking, being out of touch with the people, and undue formality and bureaucracy.

At the first session of the 12th NPC, in March 2013, Xi was duly elected as President of China and Li Keqiang was approved to replace Wen as Premier in a new State Council. Four longstanding party officials were appointed Vice-Premiers: Zhang Gaoli, Liu Yandong, Wang Yang and Ma Kai. The number of ministries was reduced by two to 25, with responsibility for the railways being transferred to the Ministry of Transport and responsibility for health and for family planning, hitherto separate, entrusted to a single National Health and Family Planning Commission. Sixteen ministers retained their posts; new appointments included Wang Yi (hitherto in charge of the Taiwan Affairs Office) as Minister of Foreign Affairs, Lou Jiwei (hitherto chairman of the China Investment Corporation) as Minister of Finance, and Gen. Chang Wanquan (a member of the CCP Central Military Commission) as Minister of National Defence, while Xu Shaoshi (hitherto Minister of Land and Resources) replaced Ma Kai at the head of the National Development and Reform Commission. The State Food and Drug Administration was elevated to ministry level. Several maritime agencies were amalgamated into a single National Oceanic Administration; the electricity regulatory commission was merged with the National Energy Administration; and the two state administrations for the press, publications, radio, film and television were amalgamated into one supervisory body.

In September 2013, after a brief trial held in Jinan, Shandong Province, Bo Xilai was found guilty of bribery, embezzlement and abuse of power, and sentenced to life imprisonment; an appeal was rejected in October by the Shandong High Court. State media portrayed the trial as an example of the struggle against corruption, but supporters of Bo viewed the accusations as politically motivated. Numerous other public figures were accused of and/or tried for corruption during 2013 (see The Campaign against Corruption). Although not officially confirmed, the most senior person under investigation was reported to be Zhou Yongkang, believed to be an ally of Bo: until November 2012 Zhou (a former general manager of the China National Petroleum Corporation—CNPC) had been a member of the Politburo Standing Committee and secretary of the CCP Central Political and Legislative Committee, i.e. in charge of the police and domestic security. A number of other officials under investigation during 2013 for alleged corruption (see below) were reported to be associates of Zhou. During 2013 Xi also initiated a vigorous campaign against 'hedonism and extravagance' among party officials, but it became evident that the state would not tolerate citizens who were perceived as over-zealous in demanding the exposure of official abuses at a senior level (see Human Rights and Media Freedom).

In November 2013, following the third plenary session ('Third Plenum') of the 18th CCP Central Committee, various economic and social reforms were announced. It was stated, *inter alia*, that the market was to be given a decisive role in the allocation of resources; rules on the financial markets, prices and foreign investment were to be revised; the fiscal system was to be improved, with changes in budget management and taxation at both central and local government levels; the system of residency permits was to be liberalized; and farmers' property rights were to be increased. The rule limiting families to one child was to be modified to allow two children per family if one parent was an only child (it had already been relaxed in some cities to allow two children for parents who were both only children). 'Re-education through labour' camps were to be abolished, and a reduction was to be made in the number of crimes subject to the death penalty. Officials were to be held accountable for environmental damage. These changes were to be implemented by a 'leading group for overall reform', which was convened for the first time in January 2014, under the chairmanship of President Xi. The formation of a National Security Commission, to co-ordinate decision-making on matters of national security, was also approved by the Third Plenum, and this likewise held its inaugural meeting in January, chaired by Xi.

In a speech given at the close of the second session of the 12th NPC, in March 2014, Premier Li Keqiang warned of the likelihood of a spate of bankruptcies and debt defaults among Chinese companies over the following year as the rate of growth of the economy decelerated (notably within the industrial sector). Premier Li also reiterated the Government's 'zero tolerance' approach towards tackling corruption, stated that deeper reforms of the systems of governance, justice, tax and finance were to be a priority during the year ahead, and pledged to continue to combat organized crime, terrorism and pollution.

The Campaign against Corruption

From the 1990s there was increasing disquiet over persistent corruption within the CCP, the state bureaucracy and economic enterprises. In August 1993 the CCP initiated a major anti-corruption campaign. Hundreds of executions of officials were subsequently reported. In October 1998, following a two-year investigation, government auditors reported the embezzlement or serious misuse of the equivalent of more than US $11,000m. of public funds by government officials.

In May 2003 the Governor of Yunnan Province, Li Jiating, received a suspended death sentence for accepting bribes, and in October China's Minister of Land and Natural Resources, Tian Fengshan, was removed from office as a result of allegations of corruption. Senior banking officials were also revealed as having been involved in corruption, bribery, money-laundering and fraudulent dealings. In February 2004 the CCP announced the introduction of new regulations for the supervision of its officials. It was officially announced that 30,788 government officials were prosecuted in 2004 for work-related offences such as corruption, embezzlement and abuse of power.

In September 2007 several senior officials received lengthy prison sentences for their involvement in a scandal involving the misappropriation of large sums from the Shanghai pension fund. In the same month the Minister of Supervision, Ma Wen, was appointed to chair the newly formed National Corruption Prevention Bureau. One of the most significant trials in 2007 was that of Zheng Xiaoyu, the former director of the State Food and Drug Administration, who was convicted of accepting bribes and of dereliction of duty; he was executed in July. The case drew attention to other important issues, such as product safety and the inadequacies of food and pharmaceutical regulations in China. By October, in response to several international scandals involving the safety standards of Chinese exports, an extensive government campaign had resulted in hundreds of arrests. Following a scandal exposed in September 2008 over the deliberate contamination of infant milk with melamine, stringent legislation governing food safety, in particular the use of additives, was approved, and a national food safety commission was established in early 2010. In November, however, Zhao Lianhai, who had campaigned on behalf of those affected by the contaminated milk and established a website to support parents, was convicted on charges of inciting social disorder.

Following an investigation into the finances of Guangdong Province, in January 2009 53 CCP officials were charged in connection with the misappropriation of a total of 22m. yuan of public funds, which were alleged to have been used to finance the pursuit of personal gambling activities in Macao and Hong Kong. Several senior officials were convicted. Others convicted of corruption in 2009 and 2010 included senior executives of Sinopec, the state petrochemical corporation, China National Nuclear Corporation and China Mobile. In May 2010 Huang Guangyu, reputedly one of the country's wealthiest entrepreneurs, was found guilty of bribery, insider trading and market manipulation; he was sentenced to 14 years' imprisonment. In the same month Guo Jingyi, a senior official in the Ministry of Commerce, was sentenced to death with a two-year reprieve, having been found guilty of accepting bribes totalling more than 8m. yuan.

In January 2010, at a session of the CCP's Central Commission for Discipline Inspection (CCDI), President Hu Jintao reiterated the importance of more effectively addressing issues such as the abuse of power, corruption, embezzlement and dereliction of duty. With public anger rising, particularly in view of the lack of any independent supervision of government and party officials, a new code of conduct for CCP members was issued by the party in February. A major investigation into allegations of bribery in Chongqing, which began in mid-2009, resulted in nearly 800 prosecutions. In July 2010 the city's most senior judicial official, Wen Qiang, was executed following his conviction on charges that included rape and the protection of criminal gangs, as well as bribery. The activities of 783 judges (of whom 540 were disciplined and 113 received criminal penalties for bribery, embezzlement and abuse of power) and of 267 procurators were investigated during the course of 2010. In total it was reported that more than 146,500 officials had been penalized for disciplinary violations during 2010.

In February 2011 the Minister of Railways, Liu Zhijun, became the most senior official to be dismissed and placed under investigation, following an inquiry into allegations of widespread corruption at the Ministry. Having served as Minister of Railways since 2003, Liu was alleged to have misappropriated more than 800m. yuan, reportedly having taken substantial bribes in exchange for the allocation of contracts for the upgrading of the Chinese rail network. (Liu was found guilty in July 2013, and received a suspended death sentence.) In addition to the seemingly rampant corruption, the case also drew attention to sub-standard construction work and attendant safety concerns, in particular following the collision of two trains in July. The accident, and the Government's apparent subsequent attempts to reduce adverse publicity, provoked unusually outspoken criticism in the state media, as well as thousands of outraged comments by domestic internet users. Other senior officials convicted of corruption in 2011 included the former mayor of Shenzhen, the deputy mayors of Hangzhou and Suzhou, and the former executive director of Beijing's principal airport. Less prominent cases of malpractice on the part of more junior officials were believed to have been the cause of numerous local protests and 'mass incidents' in recent years (see Human Rights and Media Freedom).

During 2012 the most conspicuous investigation into alleged corruption was that concerning Bo Xilai (see Recent developments: Xi Jinping as President). In October a Chinese government spokesman dismissed as a 'smear' reports in a US newspaper that relatives of Premier Wen Jiabao had amassed assets worth US $2,700m. Upon taking office as CCP General Secretary in November 2012, and as President in March 2013, Xi Jinping reiterated his predecessor's emphasis on combating corruption, warning that both 'tigers' and 'flies' (senior and junior officials) should expect retribution if they abused their position; he also initiated a vigorous campaign to reduce excessive expenditure by officials. As well as Zhou Yongkang (see above), the most senior officials reported to be under investigation for corruption during 2013 included Liu Tienan, a deputy director of the National Development and Reform Commission, dismissed from his post in May; Jiang Jiemin, until his dismissal in September director of the state-owned Assets Supervision and Administration Commission and former chairman of the state petroleum corporation, CNPC; several other current or former senior executives of CNPC and its subsidiary Petrochina; Li Dongsheng, former Vice-Minister of Public Security; and Lt-Gen. Gu Junshan, a former senior PLA officer. In September the CCDI opened a special website on which citizens were encouraged to report instances of corruption, and during the first month it reported that more than 800 such reports had been received per day. During 2013, however, a number of activists who campaigned for senior CCP members to reveal their assets were arrested on charges of disrupting public order (see Human Rights and Media Freedom). In March 2014 a military court formally charged Lt-Gen. Gu Junshan, who had allegedly enjoyed a very lavish lifestyle, with embezzlement, bribery, misuse of state funds and abuse of power.

Human Rights and Media Freedom

The suppression of dissident activity continued during the 1990s and the early 21st century, and the issue of media freedom remained an area of much contention. In January 1991 the trials of many of those arrested during the pro-democracy protests of 1989 commenced. Most activists received relatively short prison sentences. In February 1994 Asia Watch, an independent human rights organization based in New York, issued a highly critical report of the situation in China, detailing the cases of more than 1,700 detainees, imprisoned for their political, ethnic or religious views. In July the trial on charges of counter-revolutionary activity of 14 members of a dissident group, in detention since 1992, commenced. In December 1994 nine of the defendants received lengthy prison sentences.

In mid-1997 the Chinese Government repudiated reports by the human rights organization Amnesty International that several pro-democracy activists remained among the numerous political prisoners in China: the Government classified as criminals the estimated 2,000 detainees imprisoned on charges of 'counter-revolution'. In September 1998 Amnesty International released a report stating that China had executed 1,876 people in 1997, more than the rest of the world combined. Attempts during 1998 by dissidents in Beijing and the provinces to create and register an opposition party, the Chinese Democratic Party (CDP), were suppressed by the Government, and in December at least 30 members of the CDP were detained. Three democracy activists, Xu Wenli (who had been released in 1993 after 12 years' imprisonment for pro-democracy activities), Qin Yongmin and Wang Youcai, were sentenced to imprisonment, provoking strong international condemnation. (Xu and Wang were later permitted to leave for the USA on medical grounds, in December 2002 and March 2004, respectively.) By November 1999 a further 18 CDP leaders had been convicted of subverting state power and sentenced to long prison terms.

Attempts were made by the Government in February and in November 2000 to regulate the publication of material on the internet, with the issuing of new rules first granting the regime the right to 'reorganize' or close down offending websites, and then requiring government approval prior to the posting of news bulletins. Between April and November 2001 some 17,000 internet cafés were closed down. In June 2002 three leading internet providers were punished for disseminating harmful content and were forced to suspend a number of services. Press freedom was further restricted from mid-2003, with lists of banned topics being issued to journalists, and in August an order was issued restraining public debate on political reform and on constitutional amendments, as well as on reassessment of historical events. Despite increasing privatization of the media sector, with newspapers being required to become financially independent of the state, there were few signs that the Government was relinquishing its control over the reporting of sensitive issues. The Government also continued to exercise strict control over the internet, reportedly employing a large force to monitor web activities. In February 2004 it was announced that foreign investment in Chinese media companies was to be allowed, on condition that foreign investors agreed to adhere to government regulations on media content. In March the NPC approved an amendment to the Constitution that introduced an explicit reference to human rights. In July a new campaign for censorship of text messages was announced, with telephone companies being required to use filtering technology to identify suspicious material. In December three leading intellectuals, Yu Jie, Liu Xiaobo and Zhang Zuhua, who were known to have expressed critical views, were detained for questioning.

In February 2005 it was reported that some 12,500 internet cafés had been closed by the authorities in the last three months of 2004. In June 2005 the Government ordered all websites and blogs in the country to register with the authorities or risk fines and possible closure. In October the Government announced a general ban on internet material inciting 'illegal demonstrations', apparently in response to the increasing number of public protests around the country. In January 2006 the internet search company Google (which had obtained a licence to operate in China in May 2005) provoked widespread criticism when it announced that it would comply with the Chinese Government's demands to restrict access to certain websites from its Chinese-language search engine. In June 2009 the Government undertook to install filtering software on all new computers. In January 2010 Google revealed that the e-mail accounts of numerous users, primarily advocates of human rights in China, had been subjected to external interference. Google then threatened to withdraw from the country, stating that it was no longer willing to censor its Chinese search engine. From March, therefore, mainland users of the Google search engine were automatically redirected to the company's Hong Kong website, which remained uncensored. In a 'new approach' in June, however, the automatic link to Hong Kong was removed, and in the following month it was announced that Google's operating licence had been renewed by the Chinese Government, thereby permitting the company to continue providing web services. The number of internet users in China was estimated to have exceeded 400m. by the end of 2010.

China's human rights situation came under increased international scrutiny prior to the holding of the Olympic Games in Beijing in 2008. In March 2007 activist Zhang Jianhong was sentenced to six years' imprisonment on charges of incitement to subversion of the state's authority, in relation to articles posted on the internet. The following month CCP officials were reportedly instructed to combat the 'spread of decadent and backward ideological and cultural material online'. In April 2008 Hu Jia, another prominent activist, was sentenced to imprisonment, having been convicted of 'inciting subversion of state power'; his cause attracted widespread media attention when he was awarded the annual Sakharov Prize for Freedom of Thought by the European Parliament in October. He was released, as scheduled, in June 2011, but was reported to remain under close surveillance at his home.

In November 2008 Huang Qi, who had given advice to Sichuan families who had lost children after the collapse of poorly constructed school buildings in the earthquake earlier in that year, with a view to instigating a legal case against the Government, was found guilty of 'illegally holding state secrets', and received a three-year prison sentence. (In 2003 he had been sentenced to five years' imprisonment for his hosting of an online discussion forum.) Another campaigner on behalf of the earthquake victims, Tan Zuoren, was found guilty of subversion in February 2010 and sentenced to five years' imprisonment.

In February 2009, as the 20th anniversary of the Tiananmen Square protests approached, a group of activist mothers reiterated their request that the Chinese leadership show greater openness and conduct a full investigation into the events surrounding the deaths of 1989. At the end of May 2009 the expiring licences to practise of about 20 civil rights lawyers were not renewed by the authorities: they included Jiang Tianyong, who had recently become the first independent lawyer to be appointed to represent a defendant in Tibet, charged with involvement in the recent protests (see Events in Tibet).

In September 2010 a blind human rights activist, Chen Guangcheng, was released after four years' imprisonment for allegedly 'damaging property and organizing a mob to disturb traffic'. In 2005 Chen had accused family-planning officials in Shandong Province of forcing at least 7,000 women to have late-term abortions or sterilizations. After his release his activities were closely monitored by the authorities, in conditions tantamount to house arrest. In April 2012 Chen took refuge in the US embassy in Beijing. He was granted permission to study in the USA and left China in late May. In November Chen's nephew was given a prison sentence for assaulting officials who had raided relatives' homes after Chen's escape.

Liu Xiaobo was rearrested in December 2008 after he and more than 300 other dissidents, on the 60th anniversary of the Universal Declaration of Human Rights, signed Charter 08, an online petition demanding democratic reform in China. In December 2009 Liu was placed on trial on charges of 'inciting subversion of state power'. His conviction and immediate sentencing to a prison term of 11 years aroused international criticism. In October 2010 the announcement in Norway of the award of the annual Nobel Peace Prize to Liu Xiaobo, in recognition of his 'long and non-violent struggle for fundamental human rights in China', led to renewed demands for the dissident's release from prison. The Chinese Government submitted a formal protest to the Norwegian Government, and Liu's wife was placed under house arrest. More than 100 activists, including eminent lawyers and academics, issued a public letter demanding Liu's release. Also in October, shortly before an annual plenary meeting of the CCP Central Committee, it was reported that 23 party veterans, including a former secretary of Mao Zedong, had issued an appeal to the NPC for greater freedom of speech in China. Although the details of the party elders' letter were promptly removed from the internet, the audacious initiative none the less represented a significant action in support of the ending of censorship.

Meanwhile, social unrest continued to offer a challenge to the authorities. Official statistics released in 2005 estimated that in the previous year 3.7m. people had taken part in 74,000 'mass incidents' of one form or another, including labour strikes and riots. Many protests were related to land disputes; the number of illegal land seizure cases was officially estimated to have reached 31,700 in 2008. In March of that year an activist who had campaigned against the removal of land from farmers was sentenced to five years' imprisonment on subversion charges, and in the following month a protester was killed by the police at a demonstration against land seizures perpetrated by a mining company. As internet forums became an increasingly popular method of sharing information, the deaths in separate 'accidents' in December 2010 and in January 2011, respectively of a man who had led a campaign against the construction of a power station in the vicinity of his village and of a woman who had opposed the relocation of a canal, aroused much scepticism.

Despite the introduction in 2008 of new legislation providing for better mediation and arbitration, reports of labour unrest continued to emerge. In 2010 Chinese workers at Japanese-owned manufacturing plants were reported to have secured substantial pay increases as a result of strike action. In August Premier Wen Jiabao urged Japanese companies to address the issue of low wages. Other protests in that year related to working conditions at Foxconn, a Taiwanese manufacturer of electronics and a major supplier of equipment to foreign firms, including the US-based company Apple: several employees had committed suicide. Independent reports published in 2012 described poor conditions and excessive working hours at factories owned by Foxconn, the South Korean firm Samsung, and other companies manufacturing in China.

In early 2011 Jiang Tianyong was among dozens of lawyers and activists reported to have been detained in what appeared to be a new campaign of suppression. In March pro-democracy activist Liu Xianbin was sentenced to 10 years' imprisonment, having been found guilty of inciting subversion (his third such conviction since the protests of 1989). The detention of the internationally renowned artist Ai Weiwei in April 2011, ostensibly on suspicion of economic crimes, was widely deplored. Ai had criticized human rights abuses and supported the rights of alleged victims of official incompetence or corruption. He was released in June, but the authorities claimed that he had admitted tax evasion and demanded payment of 15m. yuan.

In May 2011 it was announced that a new State Internet Information Office was to assume control of internet content, replacing several other government agencies. It had become evident that, despite censorship, the internet (in particular social network sites such as Sina Weibo, which claimed in August to have 250m. registered users) was providing a major outlet for outspoken comments and criticism of the authorities. 'Cultural development guidelines' published in October ordered stricter regulation of the internet to prevent the spread of rumours and 'harmful information'. In December it was announced that internet users' real names had to be registered when participating in online forums or issuing blogs, and in June 2012 stricter enforcement of this rule was announced, with penalties for internet companies that failed to comply. In July it was reported that some 10,000 people had been arrested in an official campaign against 'cyber-crime', but some observers expressed concern that, as well as targeting genuine criminals, the campaign could be used to censor critics of the Government. In January 2013 journalists on an influential newspaper based in Guangdong Province, the *Southern Weekend*, attracted widespread support when they went on strike for several days after the suppression of an editorial demanding constitutional rights.

In December 2011 two activists, Chen Wei and Chen Xi, were given prison sentences after posting allegedly subversive material on the internet, and in January 2012 a writer, Li Tie, was also convicted of subversion and imprisoned. Also in January the prominent author Yu Jie left China for the USA, claiming that he had undergone surveillance and physical abuse. In June the death of the pro-democracy campaigner Li Wangyang (who had been released in the previous year after spending a total of 22 years in prison for taking part in the Tiananmen Square protests in 1989 and for subsequently 'assaulting state organs') was officially described as suicide, but the verdict was rejected by many and large demonstrations took place in Hong Kong demanding further investigation.

During 2011 reports continued of numerous local protests at the confiscation of farmland or houses to make way for redevelopment, often aimed at local officials who were perceived to be corrupt. In July legislation was adopted imposing limits on forced evictions and the compulsory demolition of houses, to come into effect in 2012. Protests that erupted in September 2011 in the village of Wukan in Guangdong Province, against the sale of communal land by an allegedly corrupt local official, received widespread publicity, and were later represented in the official media as demonstrating the need for reform in the rules on expropriation of land. In April 2012 the Supreme People's Court ruled that the compulsory demolition of homes could be halted by the courts if compensation was not considered adequate. In November 2013 the major reforms announced at the 'Third Plenum' of the CCP Central Committee included the improvement of farmers' property rights.

Many other protests during 2011 and 2012 were related to the grievances of migrant workers in China's cities (believed to number some 260m.): under the system of household registration known as *hukou*, these workers and their families, often originally from rural areas of China, were not entitled to the same housing, educational and social care provisions as permanent local residents, a situation which was described as a serious threat to stability in a report by a government research centre published in 2011. In December 2012 the Government announced that it would expedite the reform of household registration and improve facilities for urban residents, and the 'Third Plenum' of November 2013 confirmed that limitations on settlement in cities would be gradually relaxed to allow improved rights for migrant workers.

In October 2012 a senior official stated that China was to reform its system of 're-education through labour' under which alleged offenders could be detained for up to four years without trial in labour camps (numbering 350, with 150,000 inmates, according to official figures issued in 2008). In November 2013 it was announced that the re-education camps were to be abolished and replaced by an already existing 'community correction' programme for minor offenders.

In January 2013 Liu Hui, the brother-in-law of the jailed Nobel laureate Liu Xiaobo, was arrested on charges of fraud, and in June he was given an 11-year prison sentence; his supporters asserted that the conviction was politically motivated. In March it was announced that a single regulatory authority was to replace the two official bodies supervising the press and broadcasting, namely the State General Administration of Press, Publication, Radio, Film and Television. New rules for China's internet users (officially estimated to number 618m. at the end of the year) were announced in September, including the possibility of a prison sentence for anyone posting 'slanderous' comments or 'false rumours' that were viewed by at least 5,000 users or reposted at least 500 times. Hundreds of internet commentators were reportedly detained during 2013. Several members of the New Citizens' Movement, an informal grouping of activists which campaigned for migrant workers' rights and for the disclosure of assets accrued by senior officials, were also detained, even though their demands appeared to be compatible with the Government's campaign against corruption. In January 2014 Xu Zhiyong, a lawyer who was a leading member of the movement, was convicted of disrupting public order and sentenced to four years in prison. His appeal against the conviction was rejected in April; in the same month four other activists linked to the New Citizens' Movement also received prison sentences for disrupting public order. Meanwhile, in March, having reportedly earlier been denied medical treatment for several months while being held in government detention in Beijing, the human rights activist Cao Shunli died in hospital.

Religious Affairs

China's Constitution ostensibly guarantees freedom of religious belief, but religious practice is subject to government supervision, under the State Administration for Religious Affairs (SARA). Five principal religious groupings are officially recognized: the Buddhist Association of China, the China Daoist (Taoist) Association, the China Islamic Association, the Three-Self Patriotic Movement (of Protestant Christian churches) and the Chinese Patriotic Catholic Association (CPCA, linking Catholic Christian churches). Estimates of the numbers of adherents vary considerably, particularly with regard to Buddhism and Daoism, which lack formal structures but retain an enduring cultural influence. In 2010, according to the SARA, there were 16m. officially recognized Protestant Christians and 6m. officially recognized Catholic Christians in China (but the number of members of 'unofficial' churches was believed to be much larger); the same source stated that the number of Muslims was more than 23m. (some 10m. of whom were Uygurs living in Xinjiang: see Events in Xinjiang).

Diplomatic relations with the Holy See were severed in 1951. The state-controlled CPCA continued to operate independently of the Vatican, co-existing with a clandestine, Vatican-linked Roman Catholic church. In January 2000 five Catholic bishops were consecrated after being appointed by the CPCA, despite the opposition of the Vatican; the arrest of an archbishop belonging to the 'underground' Catholic Church in February further undermined any prospect of an improvement in China's relations with the Vatican. By early 2003 China and the Vatican had held several sessions of informal discussions on improving bilateral relations. However, China was in confrontation with Bishop Joseph Zen Ze-kiun, the head of the Roman Catholic Church in Hong Kong, who had become increasingly critical of the central Government's administration in Hong Kong and its religious policies on the mainland. In June 2005, according to the US-based China Aid Association, police forcibly entered 100 'underground' churches in Jilin Province, detaining some 600 worshippers. The detention of members of the unofficial Catholic church in Hebei Province, apparently the most significant 'underground' church in China, also continued in 2005. Relations with the Vatican were further strained in 2006 when the Chinese Catholic church consecrated three bishops, two of whom were subsequently excommunicated by the Vatican.

In January 2007 Pope Benedict XVI announced that he would make efforts to restore full diplomatic relations with the People's Republic; he also expressed a willingness to enter negotiations with the Chinese Government over issues such as the appointment of bishops. In September Father Joseph Li Shan was consecrated as Bishop of Beijing, although formal approval by the Vatican was not given. In November 2010 Joseph Guo Jincai, the vice-president of the CPCA, was consecrated Bishop of Chengde, an action described by the Vatican as harmful to relations. Two more bishops were appointed by the CPCA, in April and July 2011, respectively: the second of these, Joseph Huang Bingzhang, was excommunicated by the Vatican shortly after his consecration as Bishop of Shantou. In July 2012 a bishop was consecrated in Harbin without Vatican approval, and in the same month another bishop, Thaddeus Ma Daquin (whose appointment had been approved by both the Vatican and the Chinese authorities) was reported to be in detention after publicly announcing his resignation from the CPCA during his consecration ceremony in Shanghai; in December it was reported that Ma's appointment as bishop had been revoked, and one year later he was reportedly still virtually confined to a local seminary. The Chinese Government congratulated Pope Francis on his election to the papacy in March 2013, but declared that the Vatican must 'stop interfering in China's internal affairs', while urging the Holy See (the only European state still to accord diplomatic recognition to Taiwan) to sever diplomatic relations with Taiwan before normal relations with the People's Republic could be resumed.

The 'official' Protestant churches are jointly supervised by the Three-Self Patriotic Association and the China Christian Council, but there are also large numbers of unaffiliated, informal churches which have frequently come into conflict with the authorities. Hundreds of arrests were reported during 2008, and numerous illegal churches were demolished by the authorities, but worshippers continued to meet in private homes and other clandestine venues. However, in an indication of a more conciliatory approach on the part of the Government, secret discussions were reportedly held with representatives of unofficial Protestant groups. In April 2011 members of the large Shouwang unofficial Protestant church in Beijing were detained when they attempted to hold outdoor services. In July a senior Protestant pastor, Shi Enhao, the deputy chairman of the Chinese House Church Alliance, was sentenced to two years' re-education in a labour camp, for conducting illegal meetings; he was released, however, in January 2012. Further police raids on 'house churches' in Beijing were reported in October 2013, and in November the pastor and members of an officially recognized Protestant church in Henan Province were detained in connection with a land dispute.

The emergence of the religious movement Falun Gong in the late 1990s was perceived as a threat to the supremacy of the CCP; following widespread demonstrations protesting at the arrest of more than 100 adherents, the authorities banned the popular sect in July 1999 on the grounds that it constituted a threat to society. The group, which was also known as Falun Dafa and embraced elements of Buddhism, mysticism and *qigong* (traditional exercise), had been established in 1992 by Li Hongzhi, who was based in the USA, and claimed tens of millions of adherents, mainly in China. Particularly concerned by the high level of Falun Gong membership among CCP and PLA officials, the authorities embarked on a campaign of harsh persecution of those who refused to renounce their faith. In August 2001 the authorities sentenced 45 members to long prison terms for organizing resistance, and in September 2002 15 members were sentenced to between four and 20 years' imprisonment for violating anti-cult laws and damaging broadcasting equipment. In 2005 the US-based Falun Gong Information Center asserted that 2,300 practitioners had died in custody in China since the banning of the sect in 1999. The suppression of Falun Gong continued. In early 2009 it was reported that in the previous year as many as 8,000 practitioners had been detained, of whom at least 100 had died in custody.

Health and Environmental Concerns

In the early 21st century the Chinese Government confronted several serious issues of public health. First, there was increasing concern about the spread of HIV/AIDS in China. In June 2001 it was reported that as many as 500,000 people in Henan Province had been infected with HIV after selling their blood plasma to companies that had employed unhygienic practices during the 1990s. The authorities announced an increase in funds to counter the spread of the virus and to improve the safety of blood banks. The Government began to provide improved access to health information and to affordable health care; measures included the supply of free drugs to HIV/AIDS patients on low incomes. At the end of October 2012, according to the Ministry of Health, a total of 492,191 mainland Chinese were living with HIV/AIDS.

By the end of April 2003 the outbreak of SARS, a hitherto unknown virus, had affected almost 3,500 people and resulted in more than 300 deaths in the People's Republic alone. The Minister of Public Health, Zhang Wenkang, and the mayor of Beijing, Meng Xuenong, were accused of having concealed the extent of the disease and were relieved of their party and state positions. The SARS epidemic was officially declared to have ended in mid-June, and the World Health Organization (WHO) removed its ban on travel to Beijing.

In November 2005 China became the fifth country to register human fatalities resulting from the epidemic of avian influenza ('bird flu') that had spread across East Asia since 2003; in the same month the central Government announced that it would endeavour to vaccinate all of China's 14,000m. poultry, following a series of outbreaks throughout the year. A more serious threat to public health emerged during 2009, with the appearance of a new variant of swine influenza, the A(H1N1) virus, following which the Government initiated a major vaccination programme. By March 2010 the number of cases of 'swine flu' in China was reported to have reached 127,427, and nearly 800 people had died. A new outbreak of avian influenza, known as H7N9, began in eastern China in March and April 2013, and resulted in the banning of markets selling live poultry; by January 2014 219 cases had been recorded, of which 55 were fatal, but no instances of person-to-person transmission had been confirmed.

In April 2009, meanwhile, the Government responded to public disquiet with regard to the difficulties of access to health care, particularly in rural areas, by announcing plans for a major reform of the health service. With projected expenditure of 850,000m. yuan during 2009–11, thousands of new hospitals and health centres were to be built, while many existing facilities were to be upgraded. In the longer term, a programme of universal health insurance was envisaged.

Particularly after the discovery of the deliberate contamination of infant formula milk with melamine in 2008, leading to six deaths and making thousands of babies ill, there was widespread concern about food safety and the quality of other products manufactured in China. Health problems arising from the lack of adequate environmental controls also drew public attention. In August 2009 two separate cases of serious environmental contamination by metal smelters, causing lead poisoning, were reported. Similar cases were subsequently reported from elsewhere in China. During 2011 and 2012 large demonstrations resulted in the abandonment of several industrial projects that local people regarded as harmful to the environment, such as the building of a copper alloy plant in Sichuan Province and the expansion of a petrochemical plant in the east coast city of Ningbo. In November 2013 the official media criticized the state petrochemical corporation Sinopec after an explosion caused by a leaking oil pipeline killed at least 55 people in Shandong Province.

China's rapid industrial expansion, largely dependent on coal as a source of energy, led to a doubling of carbon dioxide emissions in the decade to 2012; by 2006 China was estimated to have superseded the USA as the world's largest emitter of greenhouse gases. Efforts to develop renewable sources of energy included major investment in hydroelectric power, most conspicuously the controversial Three Gorges Dam on the River Yangtze: construction of the dam began in 1994, necessitating the displacement of some 1.3m. people, and the final turbine began operating in July 2012. The dam was expected to provide 11% of the country's hydroelectric capacity. A government paper issued in October envisaged the further development of hydroelectric, solar and wind-derived power, with the aim of deriving 30% of installed generating capacity from non-fossil fuels by the end of 2015. In October 2011 the Government announced that it would use stricter criteria for measuring air pollution, a major problem in many Chinese cities, caused by fumes from coal-burning power stations and industrial plants, and by the increasing number of vehicles on the streets. During 2013 the official press repeatedly expressed concern at air pollution in Beijing, which often reached levels considerably above those viewed as hazardous to health. In September the Government announced a five-year plan for reducing coal consumption and pollution by factories within and around major cities, and in November it was declared that environmental considerations were to be given greater weight in the evaluation of officials' achievements. In January 2014 the Government announced targets for all provinces to reduce air pollution by up to 25% by 2017.

Events in Tibet

Tibet (Xizang), hitherto a semi-independent region of western China, was occupied in October 1950 by Chinese Communist forces. In March 1959 there was an unsuccessful armed uprising by Tibetans opposed to Chinese rule. The Dalai Lama, the head of Tibet's Buddhist clergy and thus the region's spiritual leader, fled with some 100,000 supporters to Dharamshala, in northern India, where a government-in-exile was established. Thousands of Tibetans, including many lamas (Buddhist monks), were killed, and monasteries were destroyed. Tibet became an 'Autonomous Region' of China in September 1965. In October 1987 violent clashes occurred in Lhasa (the regional capital) between the Chinese authorities and Tibetans seeking independence; similar demonstrations followed.

Between March 1989 and May 1990 martial law was imposed in Lhasa for the first time since 1959, after further violent clashes between separatists and the Chinese police, which resulted in the deaths of 16 protesters. In October 1989 the Chinese Government condemned as an interference in its internal affairs the award of the Nobel Peace Prize to the Dalai Lama. Human rights groups claimed that during the last six months of the period of martial law as many as 2,000 people had been executed. In May 1992 a report issued by Amnesty International was critical of the Chinese authorities' violations of the human rights of the monks and nuns of Tibet. In May 1993 several thousand Tibetans were reported to have demonstrated in Lhasa against Chinese rule. A number of protesters were believed to have been killed.

In May 1995 the Dalai Lama's nomination of the 11th incarnation of the Panchen Lama (the second position in the spiritual hierarchy, the 10th incumbent having died in 1989) was condemned by the Chinese authorities, which banned the six-year old nominee, Gedhun Choekyi Nyima, from travelling to Dharamshala. In September 1995 China lodged a strong protest following an informal meeting between the Dalai Lama and US President Bill Clinton in Washington, DC. In November the Chinese Government announced Gyaltsen (Gyaincain) Norbu as its own nominee as Panchen Lama. There were violent confrontations in Tibet in May 1996, following the banning of any public display of images of the Dalai Lama. In November Jigme Gyatso, the leader of a youth movement advocating independence for Tibet, was convicted on charges of separatism and endangering state security, and sentenced to 15 years in prison (later extended to 18 years): he was designated a prisoner of conscience by Amnesty International. A series of minor explosions during 1996 culminated in late December with the detonation of a powerful bomb outside a government office in Lhasa.

In May 1997 it was reported that Chadrel Rinpoche, an official in the Tibetan administration and one of Tibet's most senior monks, had been sentenced to six years' imprisonment for allegedly revealing information to the Dalai Lama about the Chinese Government's search for the new Panchen Lama. In October the Dalai Lama appealed to the Chinese Government to reopen negotiations over the status of Tibet, confirming that he did not seek full independence for the region. In December the International Commission of Jurists (see p. 472) published a report accusing China of suppressing nationalist dissent and Tibetan culture, and appealed for a referendum, under the auspices of the UN, to decide the territory's future status.

During his visit to China and Hong Kong in June 1998, US President Clinton discussed the issue of Tibet with the Chinese leadership. The Government proclaimed its readiness to open negotiations if the Dalai Lama first declared both Tibet and Taiwan to be inalienable parts of China. In October the Dalai Lama admitted that since the 1960s he had received US $1.7m. annually from the US Central Intelligence Agency (CIA) to support the Tibetan separatist movement. While visiting the USA in November, the Dalai Lama had an unofficial meeting with President Clinton, and in January 1999 a new US special co-ordinator for Tibetan affairs was appointed.

In January 2000 the Chinese Government was embarrassed by the flight of the third-ranking Lama, the Karmapa, from Tibet to Dharamshala, where he requested political asylum. Ugyen Trinley Dorjie had been enthroned in 1992 at the age of seven; in an unusual development, the Karmapa had been recognized by both the Dalai Lama and the Chinese Government. In April 2001 the Dalai Lama paid a 10-day visit to Taiwan, where he met President Chen Shui-bian and addressed the island's legislature, thus antagonizing China, which opposed any co-operation between the two 'renegade provinces'. In May the 50th anniversary of the 'peaceful liberation' of Tibet was officially commemorated. In August Chinese troops seized the largest Tibetan monastery, Serthar, and forced thousands of monks and nuns to denounce the Dalai Lama.

In January 2002 Ngawang Choephel, a Tibetan music scholar serving an 18-year sentence on spying charges, was released, and in April the authorities freed, on medical grounds, Tanag Jigme Sangpo, who had endured a total of 32 years in detention for campaigning against Chinese rule. In June CCP officials in Tibet formally welcomed Gyaltsen Norbu as the new Panchen Lama. In September 2002 exiled Tibetan officials visited China (including Tibet—the first such visit there since 1985): during the tour, the Dalai Lama's envoy to the USA, Lodi Gyaltsen Gyari, and the envoy to Europe, Kelsang Gyaltsen, held the first meetings with government officials since 1993. In 2003 discussions between Chinese officials and envoys of the Dalai Lama were held. The delegation to Beijing was led by Lodi Gyaltsen Gyari. In June the Indian Prime Minister acknowledged Tibet as part of China in writing for the first time.

In September 2005 celebrations were held in Lhasa to commemorate the 40th anniversary of the establishment of the Tibet Autonomous Region. In October the construction of the 1,118-km railway link from Golmud in Qinghai Province to Lhasa was completed, thereby compounding fears that such development schemes and the considerable influx of Han Chinese (the majority ethnic group, which dominated the new economy) from neighbouring provinces were irreversibly transforming the character and culture of Tibet. By October 2006 services to Lhasa were also being offered from Shanghai and Guangzhou. In March 2007 the central Government announced that 100,000m. yuan was to be spent on various projects in Tibet, including the construction of an airport and the extension of the Lhasa railway line. In October the presentation of the Congressional Gold Medal to the Dalai Lama in the USA precipitated violent confrontations in Tibet, between monks celebrating the occasion and the police. In March 2008, in the largest protests against Chinese rule since 1989, hundreds of monks attended rallies in Lhasa. In the ensuing violence the Chinese Government claimed that some 19 fatalities had been caused by protesters, while activists asserted that as many as 100 people had been killed by government forces. As the international community urged the Chinese Government to moderate its response, which had involved the deployment of thousands of troops, the Dalai Lama described the Government's actions as 'cultural genocide'. Further sporadic protests took place in the region and elsewhere as the Olympic torch made its symbolic journey around the world. In June 2008 Amnesty International expressed concern at the uncertain fate and treatment of a large number of detainees. In May, meanwhile, representatives of the Government and the Dalai Lama attended discussions in Beijing. During his tour of Europe later in the month, the Dalai Lama indicated that some sections of the Tibetan community were dissatisfied with the lack of progress towards greater autonomy through non-violent means.

In March 2009 the central Government released a document entitled 'Fifty Years of Democratic Reform in Tibet', which emphasized the ending of the system of 'feudal serfdom' in 1959. In April 2009 several death sentences were meted out, as those charged in connection with the rioting of 2008 were brought to trial and convicted. Although some death sentences were commuted to life imprisonment, the Government confirmed the execution of two Tibetan prisoners in October 2009. In March 2010 the government-appointed Panchen Lama, who in the previous year had begun to make public appearances, became a member of the influential National Committee of the Chinese People's Political Consultative Conference (CPPCC). As the second anniversary of the protests of 2008 approached, a major security operation was mounted. Hundreds of Tibetans were reported to have been detained, and the authorities announced the seizure of numerous weapons. Also in March 2010 the new Governor of Tibet, Padma Choling, who in January had replaced Qiangba Puncog upon the latter's resignation, stated that Gedhun Choekyi Nyima (the Dalai Lama's choice as Panchen Lama) continued to reside in Tibet. A report released by the US-based non-governmental organization Human Rights Watch in July, based on the testimony of more than 200 Tibetan refugees, was highly critical of the Chinese authorities' use of excessive force to suppress the protests of 2008.

In March 2011 the Dalai Lama (now 76 years of age) formally announced his decision to relinquish his political responsibilities, which were to be transferred to an elected representative of the Tibetan people. However, the Dalai Lama confirmed his intention to retain his role of spiritual leader, and to determine the method whereby his eventual successor in that role would be chosen. In April it was announced that Lobsang Sangay, a research fellow at Harvard Law School in the USA, had won 55% of the votes cast by the Tibetan diaspora to defeat two other candidates and thus secure election as Prime Minister of the Tibetan government-in-exile. In July the Chinese Government announced further major investment in Tibet, amounting to 138,400m. yuan, for transport, public services and hydroelectricity. The death in March in Sichuan Province of a Tibetan monk who had set himself on fire was reported to have caused tension between local residents and security forces. By January 2012 there had been reports of at least 16 incidents of self-immolation by Tibetans in Sichuan and in Tibet itself (several of whom had died), demanding freedom and the return of the Dalai Lama from exile. The Chinese Government accused the Dalai Lama of encouraging such actions, which he denied. In late January at least three Tibetans were reported to have been killed in violent confrontations between protesters and security forces in areas of Sichuan largely inhabited by ethnic Tibetans. The Chinese authorities responded by ordering stricter controls on Tibetan Buddhist monasteries and on road transport.

In April 2013 the activist Jigme Gyatso (see above) was released from prison. In June Human Rights Watch reported that more than 2m. Tibetans, including 300,000 who had been following a traditional nomadic way of life, had been forcibly resettled by the Chinese authorities over the past seven years. In December Tibetans in exile also claimed that up to 2m. pastoralists had been forcibly displaced and the pastoral land exploited for mining, while the Chinese Government argued that resettlement had been necessary owing to environmental degradation caused by over-grazing. Although reports of self-immolation were less frequent in 2013, by the end of the year 120 Tibetans were reported to have set themselves on fire (of whom at least 100 were believed to have died), while during the year a number of people accused of encouraging them to do so were sentenced to prison terms.

Events in Xinjiang

Anti-Chinese sentiment in the Xinjiang Uygur Autonomous Region, the westernmost region of China, intensified in the 1990s, resulting in the instigation of a new campaign by the authorities to repress the Islamist separatist movement, whose goal was to establish an independent 'East Turkestan'. Since 1949 Han Chinese had been encouraged or forced to move to the region by the central Government, thereby reducing the proportion of the indigenous Uygur population. Separatist movements such as the Xinjiang Liberation Front and the Uygur Liberation Organization (ULO) often had the support of the Uygur diaspora in Kyrgyzstan and Uzbekistan. Suppression of separatism increased in 1996, following a number of violent incidents.

Hundreds of people were detained for their part in rioting and bomb attacks, and many were subsequently executed or imprisoned. Reports in late 1997 indicated that there had been a renewal of armed separatist activity, in which more than 300 people had been killed. In January 1998 13 people were executed in Xinjiang, allegedly for robbery and murder, although unofficial reports suggested that those executed were Muslim separatist demonstrators. Muslim separatists were believed to be responsible for an incendiary device deposited on a bus in Wuhan in February, which killed 16 people. At least 12 separatists were reportedly executed in 1999, while others received long prison sentences. In October 2000 Abduhelil Abdulmejit, a leading organizer of resistance to Chinese rule in Xinjiang who had been imprisoned three years previously, was reported to have died of pneumonia while in custody; international groups alleged that he had been tortured and murdered.

During 2001 the authorities continued the 'Strike Hard' campaign against separatists, with multiple executions reported. In August the PLA conducted large-scale military exercises involving 50,000 troops in the region. China's fears of Islamist separatism were heightened after the terrorist attacks in the USA on 11 September 2001. China stated that as many as 1,000 Uygur Islamist fighters had been trained in terrorist camps in Afghanistan operated by the al-Qa'ida network of the Saudi-born militant Osama bin Laden. Stability in Xinjiang remained crucial to China's 'go west' programme of developing the country's remote inner regions, and in late September Chinese troops began anti-guerrilla operations in the Afghan border region of Xinjiang, aimed at preventing Islamist infiltration.

In January 2002 the Government released a new report alleging links between the separatists and Osama bin Laden. In March Amnesty International reported that thousands of Muslim Uygurs had been detained since 11 September 2001, and that up to 8,000 had been given 'political education' courses. In June 2002 the authorities announced that from September Xinjiang University would no longer teach courses in the Uygur language; for 50 years students had had a choice of studying in Uygur or Mandarin. In August the USA designated the East Turkestan Islamic Movement (ETIM, founded in the 1990s) a terrorist group and froze the organization's assets, in a conciliatory gesture towards the Chinese Government. The UN also added the organization to its list of terrorist organizations in September. In December 2003 China issued a 'terrorist' list that named the Eastern Turkestan Liberation Organization, the World Uygur Youth Congress and the East Turkestan Information Center, as well as the ETIM, as 'terrorist' organizations. Of these, only the ETIM was considered a terrorist movement by the USA.

During 2004 Erkin Alptekin (son of Isa Yusuf Alptekin, who had been head of a brief Uygur government in the 1940s) reportedly emerged as leader of a Uygur exile movement committed to achieving independence for Xinjiang by peaceful means. In September 2004 an East Turkestan government-in-exile was proclaimed by Anwar Yusuf Turani, head of the East Turkestan National Freedom Center. However, many Uygur groups did not recognize the government-in-exile.

Tension in the Xinjiang region recurred in January 2007 when 18 terrorist suspects were killed in a police operation against an alleged militants' training camp close to the Chinese border with Afghanistan and Pakistan, reportedly supervised by members of the ETIM. A few days previously the Vice-Secretary of the region's Communist Party Committee had denounced Rebiya Kadeer (a Uygur businesswoman and human rights activist who had been imprisoned in 1999–2005) as a separatist, determined to 'destroy the peace and stability of Chinese society'. Kadeer, who was in exile in the USA, had been nominated for the 2006 Nobel Peace Prize. In February 2007 Ismail Semed, a Uygur activist who had previously been accused of ETIM membership, was executed, having been convicted in 2005 of trying to 'split the motherland' and possession of weapons. In January 2008 two militants, suspected of planning an attack on the Beijing Olympic Games to be held in August, were killed in a police operation in the regional capital, Urumqi, and 15 others were arrested. About 100 Uygurs were arrested following a protest in late March, and a further 45 were detained in April, on suspicion of planning attacks to disrupt the Olympic Games. In July, after five Uygurs were killed by security forces, bomb explosions on two buses in Kunming caused two fatalities; the attacks were reportedly linked with Uygur militants. Two Uygurs attacked and killed 16 police officers, injuring a further 16, in Kashgar in early August. Suicide bombings and further outbreaks of violence were reported in the region later in the month. The two Uygur militants subsequently received the death sentence and were executed in April 2009.

In early July 2009 a protest by Uygur youths in Urumqi, apparently in response to an altercation between Han and Uygur workers in a factory in southern China in which two Uygurs had died, developed into a major confrontation between the two communities in Xinjiang. In the ensuing violence, nearly 200 people were killed and 1,700 injured. Hundreds of Han-owned shops and other buildings were attacked and seriously damaged, while numerous vehicles were destroyed by arson, in what was reported to be the worst civil unrest witnessed in China since 1989. Thousands of troops were deployed to the area, a curfew was imposed and order was swiftly restored. More than 1,500 people were believed to have been detained. State media immediately accused Rebiya Kadeer and other exiled Uygurs of inciting the attacks, declaring that the majority of those killed were Han Chinese; other sources claimed that police brutality had resulted in many Uygur deaths. Several more deaths occurred in September 2009, when thousands of Han demonstrators protested on the streets of Urumqi. About 80 people were prosecuted in connection with the July unrest; nine executions were carried out in November. In a major security operation in December, a further 94 suspects were apprehended. During the first half of 2010 two Uygur journalists and three Uygur website owners were sentenced to imprisonment after being found guilty of 'endangering state security'. In August eight people (including two alleged attackers) were killed and 15 injured in a bombing incident in the city of Aksu, reportedly perpetrated by a Uygur activist. In February and March 2011 seven death sentences, in connection with three attacks in the latter part of 2010, were confirmed by the authorities.

As part of the central Government's investment in the development of Xinjiang, during 2010 the city of Kashgar was designated a Special Economic Zone, intended to emulate the prospering equivalent zones in eastern China, with an emphasis on improving railway connections and on supporting local enterprises. In January 2011 the construction of four new airports in Xinjiang, and the improvement of existing ones, was announced.

In July 2011 fresh outbreaks of violence in the city of Hotan and in Kashgar reportedly caused the deaths of 36 police officers and civilians. In August the regional authorities announced a two-month 'Strike Hard' campaign to investigate and suppress suspicious activities. In September four Uygurs were sentenced to death for their part in the recent unrest. In December seven alleged kidnappers and a police officer were killed in another confrontation in southern Xinjiang. In February 2012 13 people were reportedly killed in a shopping street near Kashgar, together with eight of their attackers; an ethnic Uygur, described as the leader of the terrorist group that had perpetrated the attack, was sentenced to death in March. In April the authorities published a list of six ETIM members who had allegedly incited attacks in Xinjiang. In May the Chinese Minister of Foreign Affairs, visiting Pakistan, urged that country's Government to expel Uygur militants who were believed to be operating from within Pakistan.

During 2013 there were further serious outbreaks of violence in Xinjiang, attributed by the authorities to attacks on the police by terrorists: 21 deaths were reported during a confrontation in Kashgar prefecture in April, and 35 during violence in Lukqun in June; five men subsequently received death sentences for the respective alleged attacks. Between June and August more than 100 people were reported to have been detained in Xinjiang for 'spreading rumours' on the internet. Between November and mid-February 2014 several separate confrontations in Xinjiang claimed at least 56 lives. In October 2013 an apparently deliberate car crash in Tiananmen Square, Beijing, caused the deaths of five people, including the vehicle's occupants, who were Uygurs: the state media described the incident as a 'violent terror attack' and attributed it to the ETIM. In January 2014 the Chairman of the regional government, Nur Bekri, declared that Xinjiang was to play a central role in transport, logistics and finance for the proposed 'Silk Road' economic belt linking China with the countries of Central Asia; in the same month cargo trains began travelling from Zhejiang Province through Xinjiang to Kazakhstan and beyond. The arrest by the Chinese authorities in February of the renowned Uygur economics professor, Ilham Tohti, on charges of separatism provoked widespread international condemnation.

In early March 2014 Chinese officials claimed that a mass knife attack by eight assailants at a railway station in Kunming in the south-western province of Yunnan, which left 29 dead and more than 140 injured, had been carried out by Uygur separatists from Xinjiang as a politically motivated act of terrorism. Four of the attackers were shot dead by police officers at the scene, an injured female suspect was reportedly detained and the three remaining suspects were captured two days later.

Hong Kong, Macao and Taiwan

In September 1984, following protracted negotiations, China reached agreement with the British Government over the terms of the future administration of Hong Kong upon the territory's return to Chinese sovereignty, scheduled for mid-1997. The transfer of Hong Kong from British to Chinese administration was effected at midnight on 30 June 1997, whereupon some 4,000 troops of the PLA were deployed in the territory. In December 36 deputies from Hong Kong were directly elected to the Ninth NPC in Beijing. In June 2007 President Hu Jintao travelled to Hong Kong to attend the celebration of the 10th anniversary of the territory's transfer to Chinese sovereignty. However, tensions with regard to the pace of democratic reform in Hong Kong remained (see Hong Kong).

In June 1986 China and Portugal opened formal negotiations for the return of the Portuguese overseas territory of Macao to full Chinese sovereignty, and agreement was reached in January 1987. The agreement was based upon the 'one country, two systems' principle, which had formed the basis of China's negotiated settlement regarding the return of Hong Kong. China duly resumed sovereignty of Macao at midnight on 19 December 1999, and a PLA garrison was established in the territory. President Hu Jintao visited Macao in December 2009 on the 10th anniversary of the territory's return to Chinese rule (see Macao).

Taiwan has continued to reject China's proposals for reunification, whereby the island would become a 'special administrative region' along the lines of Hong Kong and Macao. China has never relinquished its claim to sovereignty over the island and has repeatedly threatened to use military force against Taiwan in the event of any formal declaration of independence from the mainland. In March 2005 the NPC approved anti-secession legislation aimed at preventing Taiwan from declaring independence. In April–May, during an historic visit to the mainland by Lien Chan, leader of the opposition KMT, President Hu Jintao and the former Premier of Taiwan agreed to uphold their opposition to Taiwanese independence. Despite intermittent political tensions, cross-Straits business links flourished as Taiwanese investment continued to flow to the mainland. Relations between the People's Republic and Taiwan improved considerably following the election of Ma Ying-jeou of the KMT as President of Taiwan in March 2008. In a major development in June 2010, a bilateral preferential trade agreement, the Economic Co-operation Framework Agreement (ECFA), was signed in the mainland city of Chongqing. Ma's re-election to the presidency in January 2012 was welcomed by the official Chinese media (see Taiwan). The two countries signed an agreement in June 2013 which would allow both sides to invest more freely in each other's services market; however, the proposed accord provoked mass protests in Taiwan when it reached the legislature in March 2014, with opponents claiming that it would make Taiwan overly reliant in economic terms on China and that it would harm small businesses and local employment. At April the service trade agreement had not yet been approved by the Taiwanese legislature. There was a further significant development in relations between China and Taiwan in February 2014 when the two sides held their first formal, direct intergovernment talks since the end of the Chinese civil war in 1949. The talks, which were held in Nanjing over four days, were attended by Zhang Zhijun, the head of the Chinese Taiwan Affairs Office, and Wang Yu-chi, the Minister of the Taiwanese Mainland Affairs Council. As a result of their historic meeting, the two officials agreed to increase economic ties and to establish representative offices for their respective organizations 'as early as possible'.

Foreign Affairs

Relations with Japan

Japan recognized the People's Republic in 1972, and a bilateral treaty of peace and friendship was signed in 1978. However, historical issues and territorial disputes continued to affect China's relations with Japan. In 1982 China complained that passages in Japanese school textbooks sought to justify the Japanese invasion of China in 1937. In June 1989 Japan criticized the Chinese Government's suppression of the pro-democracy movement and suspended (until late 1990) a five-year aid programme to China. In April 1992 Jiang Zemin travelled to Japan, the first visit by the General Secretary of the CCP for nine years. In October Emperor Akihito made the first ever imperial visit to the People's Republic. Japan was one of many countries to criticize China's resumption of underground nuclear testing, at Lop Nor in Xinjiang Province, in October 1993. Relations were seriously strained in May 1994, when the Japanese Minister of Justice referred to the 1937 Nanjing massacre (in which more than 300,000 Chinese citizens were killed by Japanese soldiers) as a 'fabrication', and again in August, when a second Japanese minister was obliged to resign, following further controversial remarks about his country's war record. In May 1995, during a visit to Beijing, the Japanese Prime Minister expressed his deep remorse for the wartime atrocities, but offered no formal apology.

China's continuation of its nuclear-testing programme, in defiance of international opinion, prompted Japan to announce a reduction in financial aid to China. In August 1995 Japan suspended most of its grant aid to China. Following China's 'final' nuclear test in July 1996, and the declaration of a moratorium, Japan resumed grant aid in March 1997. (China signed the Comprehensive Nuclear Test Ban Treaty in September 1996.) In July 1996, however, Sino-Japanese relations were affected by a territorial dispute relating to the Diaoyu (or Senkaku) Islands, a group of Japanese-administered uninhabited islets in the East China Sea, which China had claimed as its own since ancient times, and Japan since 1895, and to which Taiwan also laid claim; the islands adjoin important shipping lanes and fishing grounds, in an area believed to be potentially rich in deposits of petroleum and natural gas. The construction of a lighthouse on one of the islands by a group of Japanese nationalists led to strong protests from the Governments of both the People's Republic and Taiwan. At a meeting with President Jiang Zemin during the Asia-Pacific Economic Cooperation (APEC, see p. 201) conference in November 1996, the Japanese Prime Minister apologized for Japanese aggression during the Second World War, and emphasized his desire to resolve the dispute over the Diaoyu/Senkaku Islands.

During a visit by President Jiang Zemin to Japan in November 1998, the first by a head of state from the People's Republic, the Japanese Government failed to issue an unequivocal apology for its invasion and occupation of China during 1937–45. The Japanese Prime Minister, Keizo Obuchi, undertook a reciprocal visit to the People's Republic in July 1999, when various co-operation agreements were reached.

By mid-2001 China and Japan had become embroiled in trade disputes involving tariffs on imported goods. China was further antagonized by the visit of the Japanese Prime Minister, Junichiro Koizumi, to the Yasukuni Shrine, a controversial war memorial in Tokyo that revered Japan's war dead, including several prominent war criminals. In August 2002 a Tokyo court finally admitted that Japan had conducted biological warfare in China during the Second World War, but rejected the demands by 180 Chinese plaintiffs for individual compensation.

In January 2003 the Diaoyu/Senkaku Islands dispute re-emerged when Japan announced plans to lease the islands to a private owner. In March 2004 there were protests in China following the arrest by Japanese police of seven Chinese activists who had landed on the islands. In April 2005 violent demonstrations took place across China in protest at Japan's bid for a permanent seat on the UN Security Council, as well as at the Japanese Government's approval for use in schools of history textbooks reportedly omitting mention of Japanese atrocities in China (and also Korea) during the Second World War. In June 2006 Japan agreed to resume low-interest loans to China, which had earlier been suspended as a result of the Chinese Government's criticisms of the Yasukuni Shrine visits. Sino-Japanese relations sharply deteriorated in August, however, following the publication of a Japanese defence policy document that was deemed to have exaggerated China's military strength, and after Prime Minister Koizumi's visit to the Yasukuni Shrine on 15 August (the anniversary of Japan's surrender in the Second World War). The appointment of Shinzo Abe as Japanese Prime Minister in the following month led to a marked improvement in relations.

In April 2007 Wen Jiabao became the first Chinese Premier to address the Japanese legislature. Wen emphasized the suffering caused by the Japanese occupation and the need for amends; he also looked forward to increased co-operation between the two countries. Discussions between Wen and Abe resulted in an agreement to co-operate in economic matters, defence, energy and the environment. President Hu Jintao visited Japan in May 2008, attending discussions with the Japanese Prime Minister, Yasuo Fukuda. The two leaders agreed to hold annual summit meetings, and to resolve the matter of resource development in the East China Sea. In October 2009 it was reported that China and Japan had entered exploratory discussions with a view to the eventual establishment of an East Asian community, similar to the EU: it was also agreed that joint studies would begin on the feasibility of a free trade agreement between China, Japan and the Republic of Korea (South Korea). Ongoing bilateral issues included the disputed development of gas reserves in the East China Sea, the North Korean nuclear programme and the need for closer co-operation on matters of food safety.

A major diplomatic dispute arose in September 2010 after a Chinese fishing vessel collided with a Japanese patrol boat near the Diaoyu/Senkaku Islands, and the trawler's captain was detained for questioning by the Japanese authorities. Bilateral exchanges were abruptly suspended. Although the captain was released a fortnight later, in the same month tensions were exacerbated by China's purchase of unusually large amounts of Japanese government bonds, prompting Japan to request a clarification of the Chinese Government's strategy. China rejected a US offer of mediation in the dispute over the Diaoyu/Senkaku Islands. In August 2011 the Chinese Government expressed 'strong dissatisfaction' with a report published by the Japanese Ministry of Defence: the document described China as increasing its regional naval capabilities and stated that Japan's coastal defences would be strengthened in response. In December, none the less, the two countries concluded a currency swap agreement, allowing the direct exchange of their respective currencies to facilitate bilateral trade.

In May 2012 the heads of government of China, Japan and South Korea, meeting in Beijing, concluded an agreement on investment, and undertook to begin formal negotiations on a trilateral free trade agreement. In July the Japanese Government protested at the entry of three Chinese patrol boats into the disputed waters near the Diaoyu/Senkaku Islands, and in August tensions increased when successive groups of activists from both sides landed temporarily on the islands; anti-Japanese demonstrations ensued in several Chinese cities, including attacks on Japanese-owned businesses. In September the Japanese Government bought three of the islands from their private Japanese owner, forestalling a still more controversial attempt to buy them by the nationalist mayor of Tokyo. Discussions between representatives of both Governments took place during the remainder of the year, but successive incursions into the disputed waters by Chinese vessels served to reinforce hostile public attitudes in both countries. The Chinese media criticized joint naval exercises conducted in the East China Sea by Japan and the USA in November. In December Shinzo Abe, newly elected as Japanese Prime Minister for a second time, undertook to 'stop the challenge' of China's claim to the disputed islands, while still emphasizing the importance of good relations.

In February 2013 the Japanese Government made a formal protest alleging that in January Chinese naval vessels had directed weapon-targeting radar at a Japanese ship and helicopter near the Diaoyu/Senkaku Islands: this was denied by the Chinese Ministry of Defence. The Chinese official media criticized senior Japanese government ministers and members of the legislature for visiting the Yasukuni Shrine in April and again in August, and a visit to the shrine by Abe himself in December was condemned as completely unacceptable. Meanwhile, numerous patrols near the disputed East China Sea islands by coastguard vessels and military aircraft of both countries served to exacerbate tension. In November the Chinese Government declared an air defence identification zone (ADIZ) around the islands, threatening emergency defensive measures against any aircraft that entered the zone without first reporting its intentions and identifying itself. Japan responded with an official protest, while the US and Australian Governments also expressed opposition to the ADIZ. In December Japan announced a new national security strategy, involving increased defence expenditure, the acquisition of advanced aircraft and the formation of a new amphibious unit; the Chinese Government denounced the plan as likely to increase regional tensions. Despite these difficulties, between March 2013 and March 2014 China and Japan (with South Korea) took part in four sessions of negotiations on the proposed trilateral free trade agreement.

Other regional relations

During the 1990s and the early 21st century China's neighbours in South-East Asia, while benefiting from Chinese investment and trade, also displayed unease, in some cases, at China's perceived expansionism in the region. A particular source of friction was the question of sovereignty over the South China Sea, especially over the Paracel (Xisha or Hoang Sa) Islands (seized by China from Vietnamese forces in 1974) and the Spratly (Nansha, Kalayaan or Truong Sa) Islands, as well as a number of reefs and shoals. The Paracel and Spratly groups were claimed by China, Taiwan and Viet Nam, while the Philippines also claimed part of the Spratly Islands; in addition, Malaysia claimed three of the Spratly Islands, while Brunei's exclusive economic zone also included some of the area under dispute. This strategic area, which was traversed by major international shipping routes, was believed to possess deposits of petroleum and gas, in addition to rich fishing resources. By 1994 both China and Viet Nam (which had re-established normal diplomatic relations in 1991, following many years of mutual hostility) had awarded petroleum exploration concessions to US companies, leading to increased tension among the claimants. In February 1995 it emerged that Chinese forces had occupied a reef to which the Philippines laid claim, resulting in a formal diplomatic protest from the Philippine Government. Following consultations in August, China and the Philippines declared their intention to resolve their claims by peaceful means. In May 1996 China declared an extension of its maritime boundaries in the South China Sea. In November 1998 China antagonized the Philippines by building permanent structures on a disputed reef in the Spratly Islands. Discussions between the two countries in April 1999 proved fruitless, and relations deteriorated further later in the year when two Chinese fishing boats sank following collisions with a Philippine navy vessel. In November 2002, in Cambodia, Prime Minister Zhu Rongji signed a significant 'declaration on the conduct of parties in the South China Sea' with members of the Association of Southeast Asian Nations (ASEAN), which aimed to avoid conflict in the area. Under this agreement, claimants would practise self-restraint in the event of potentially hostile action (such as inhabiting the islands), effect confidence-building measures and give advance notice of military exercises in the region. However, the agreement did not include the Paracel Islands. In September 2003 China proposed a joint development and petroleum exploration strategy for the Spratly Islands. In March 2005 the China National Offshore Oil Corporation (CNOOC), the Philippine National Oil Company and the Vietnam Oil and Gas Corporation (Petrovietnam) signed an agreement to conduct joint marine seismic experiments in the Spratly Islands region.

Reports that China had established a new, city-level administrative division for the Spratly Islands and the Paracel Islands prompted protests in Viet Nam in December 2007. Tensions rose in May 2009 when the deadline for applications under the UN Convention on the Law of the Sea (UNCLOS) expired and the various countries formally submitted their respective claims (with the exception of Taiwan, which was not a signatory). China strengthened its patrols in the South China Sea, ostensibly in an attempt to counter illegal fishing activities. In various incidents during 2009–10 the Chinese navy intercepted several Vietnamese fishing vessels, operating in the area of the Paracels, and detained the crews. In January 2010 China announced plans to promote tourism on the Paracel Islands. In March 2011 the Philippine Government protested after a survey vessel, undertaking seismic testing in the South China Sea, was challenged by two Chinese patrol boats. In July the two countries' ministers responsible for foreign affairs reaffirmed their commitment to the 2002 declaration concerning the South China Sea. In the same month, however, a visit to one of the disputed Spratly Islands by a group of members of the Philippine legislature was condemned by the Chinese Government as an infringement of its sovereignty. President Benigno Aquino paid an official visit to China in August 2011, accompanied by a large delegation of business leaders, one of the principal aims of the visit being to attract Chinese investment.

In June 2011 the Vietnamese navy conducted exercises in the South China Sea, claiming that the Chinese navy had been harassing Vietnamese survey vessels in the Spratlys area. In October the two countries concluded an agreement to hold meetings twice a year concerning the maritime dispute, and established emergency procedures for consultation in the event of a confrontation. The launching of China's first aircraft carrier in August was widely viewed as a further sign of China's regional assertiveness, although the vessel was not expected to be fully operational for several years.

In March 2012 Viet Nam accused China of violating Vietnamese sovereignty by allowing companies to bid for petroleum exploration near the Paracel Islands, and in the same month the Chinese authorities arrested 21 Vietnamese fishermen, alleging that they had been fishing illegally in the waters around the Paracels: the men were released in April. Between April and June there was also a prolonged confrontation between Chinese and Philippine vessels in the area of the disputed Scarborough Shoal (or Huangyan Island, north of the Spratly Islands), each side accusing the other of trespassing in its territorial waters: the Philippine vessels eventually withdrew, citing bad weather as the reason. In July a meeting of ASEAN ministers of foreign affairs failed to agree on a joint statement concerning the South China Sea, with the members divided over China's insistence that the territorial disputes should only be considered on a bilateral basis. Later in July the Chinese Government incurred protests by the Philippines and Viet Nam when it formally inaugurated a local administrative centre for the Spratly and Paracel Islands, based in the newly developed Sansha City on one of the Paracel Islands, and including a legislative body and a military garrison. The Government expressed 'strong dissatisfaction' at a comment by the US State Department that these actions risked escalating regional tensions. In November the ASEAN Secretary-General condemned as provocative China's recent announcement that its border patrol police were to be empowered to board, seize and expel vessels in the disputed waters; Viet Nam responded to the announcement by stating that it would provide its own patrols to protect its vessels, and anti-Chinese demonstrations took place in Viet Nam in early December. In January 2013 the Philippine Government announced that it was to submit its South China Sea claims to an UNCLOS tribunal. In March confrontations between Vietnamese fishing boats and Chinese patrol vessels in the disputed waters provoked an official complaint by Viet Nam. In June, however, the Vietnamese President, Truong Tan San, paid an official visit to China, and in October Premier Li Keqiang visited Viet Nam and concluded an agreement with his Vietnamese counterpart, Nguyen Tan Dung, to establish three working groups to further co-operation in maritime affairs, infrastructure development, and finance. New regulations requiring foreign vessels to seek permission to fish in the South China Sea, declared by the Chinese authorities with effect from the beginning of 2014, were declared invalid by Viet Nam and appeared likely to increase the prospect of confrontation. In February 2014 the Philippines lodged an official protest with China regarding an alleged incident near the Scarborough Shoal in the previous month in which a Chinese coastguard vessel fired a water cannon at two Filipino fishing boats.

Myanmar's increasing international isolation from 1988 resulted in China assuming an important role, becoming Myanmar's principal aid donor, supplier of weapons and source of investment, largely for the exploitation of Myanmar's natural resources. In June 2010 an agreement was concluded on the construction by a Chinese company of an oil and gas pipeline linking Yunnan Province to Myanmar's energy resources, due to be completed in 2013. In April 2011 an agreement was announced whereby a railway was to be constructed between western Myanmar and Yunnan, over a three-year period. Amid increasing resentment at Chinese projects that appeared to be of little benefit to the local economy, in September the Myanma Government suspended work on the construction of the controversial Myitsone Dam on the upper Ayeyarwady river, which had begun in 2009 as part of a major hydroelectric scheme financed by a Chinese state corporation, primarily for exporting electricity to China; because of its environmental and social impact, the dam had provoked considerable opposition and anti-Chinese feeling in Myanmar. In February 2013 Chinese mediation was reported to have resulted in an agreement between the Myanma Government and ethnic Kachin rebels to hold discussions with a view to ending their long-standing conflict in the north-east of Myanmar, near the Chinese border. The pipeline supplying natural gas to China from Myanmar was inaugurated in July and became fully operational in October.

China was accorded the status of 'dialogue partner' with ASEAN in 1996. At the ASEAN summit meeting held in Cambodia in November 2002, an agreement to establish a free trade area by 2010 was signed with China. In October 2003 relations with ASEAN were further strengthened by the signing of a Declaration on Strategic Partnership for Peace and Prosperity, to be implemented by subsequent five-year action plans; in the same month China also signed the Association's Treaty of Amity and Co-operation, a pact for the promotion of regional stability. The free trade agreement entered into force in January 2010, and by 2015 the policy of a zero tariff for 90% of traded goods was expected to extend between China and four additional ASEAN members, namely Cambodia, Laos, Myanmar and Viet Nam. Regular joint ASEAN-China ministerial meetings take place, and a Chinese delegation attended the first ASEAN Defence Ministers' Meeting-Plus (ADMM-Plus), convened in Viet Nam in December 2010, when topics of discussion included China's territorial claims in the South China Sea: this subject became a matter of controversy at subsequent meetings (see above).

In April 2011 the Chinese Premier, Wen Jiabao, paid official visits to Malaysia and Indonesia, during which agreements were concluded on bilateral economic co-operation and investment by China in the two countries' infrastructure. In November 2012 it was announced that China and Malaysia were to implement a five-year economic co-operation plan. President Xi Jinping visited Indonesia and Malaysia in October 2013, concluding a number of agreements on trade and investment, and attending an APEC meeting of heads of state and government at which he urged greater regional economic co-ordination, particularly through the establishment of an Asian infrastructure investment bank.

In the late 1990s China, as one of the few allies of the isolated regime in the Democratic People's Republic of Korea (DPRK—North Korea) participated in quadripartite negotiations, together with the USA, North Korea and South Korea, to resolve the continuing tension on the Korean peninsula. The North Korean leader, Kim Jong Il, paid frequent visits to China, the principal source of aid for the DPRK. Chinese diplomatic efforts played a major role in ensuring North Korean participation in the six-party talks on the DPRK's nuclear programme, held in Beijing in August 2003 and attended by representatives of North and South Korea, China, the USA, Japan and Russia. Following the North Korean Government's declaration in February 2005 that it possessed nuclear weapons, the delayed fourth round of six-party disarmament talks was hosted by China, with discussions commencing in Beijing in July. China was credited with having played an important part in the conclusion of a framework agreement at the talks in September, under which North Korea agreed to disarm in exchange for various concessions; however, the agreement subsequently faltered. Throughout 2006 the Chinese Government continued to urge the DPRK to revoke its nuclear weapons programme, but in July North Korea proceeded with a test of a long-range missile; in October the country carried out its first test of a nuclear device. Embarrassed by North Korea's disregard for its entreaties, China surprised observers by agreeing, albeit with reservations, to the imposition of UN sanctions against the regime of Kim Jong Il. In February 2007 the resumed six-party talks, with considerable Chinese input, resulted in an agreement that included the closure of North Korea's Yongbyon nuclear site in exchange for substantial aid. In April 2009, however, the DPRK announced its withdrawal from the six-party talks and the resumption of its nuclear programme. In the following month China joined Russia and the USA in condemning North Korea's second underground nuclear test.

Following an artillery attack on South Korean territory by North Korea in November 2010, China came under renewed international pressure, notably from the USA, to exert greater influence over the North Korean Government. In June 2011 Chinese and North Korean officials announced the formation of two new economic development zones, to be created within the DPRK with Chinese assistance. After Kim's death in December, the Chinese Government described him as a 'close friend', and endorsed his son, Kim Jong Un, as his successor.

Following the failed launch of a North Korean rocket-mounted satellite in April 2012 (an operation generally suspected, as on previous occasions, to be the testing of a long-range missile banned under UN resolutions), China did not veto condemnation of the launch by the UN Security Council. However, it called for restraint from all interested parties, and subsequently President Hu Jintao reaffirmed his country's close ties to North Korea. In August, during a visit to China by a senior North Korean official, Jang Song Thaek (uncle of Kim Jong Un), new agreements on economic co-operation, including the joint development of two special economic zones, were concluded. In December the official Chinese media welcomed the election of Park Geun-Hye as the new South Korean President, expressing the hope that she would contribute to regional harmony. In that month China expressed 'regret' at the successful testing of another long-range rocket by the DPRK, and in January 2013 it agreed to a UN Security Council resolution condemning the launch and expanding the scope of economic sanctions against North Korea. In the same month China declared that it would reduce its aid to North Korea if the latter proceeded, as it threatened to do, with a third nuclear test. When the test duly took place, in February, China expressed 'firm opposition'. In April the ministers responsible for foreign affairs in China and the USA announced that they would work together to persuade North Korea to halt its nuclear weapons programme. In May Chinese banks ceased transactions with the Foreign Trade Bank of the DPRK. Negotiations with South Korea and Japan on a proposed trilateral free trade agreement opened in March, and in June Park Geun-Hye received a cordial welcome from the official Chinese media when she paid a state visit to China. In November, however, the South Korean Government formally protested at China's declaration of an ADIZ above the East China Sea (see Relations with Japan). The execution in December of Jang Song Thaek, denounced as a traitor by the DPRK Government, was described as an 'internal matter' by the Chinese Government, which urged the maintenance of stability in North Korea: Jang had been perceived as playing an important role in relations between the two countries. In March 2014 China dismissed a UN report cataloguing extensive human rights abuses in North Korea as lacking any real credibility, thereby confirming fears that any subsequent attempt to pass a resolution through the UN Security Council condemning the alleged atrocities would almost definitely be blocked by China (as well as by a number of other nations).

In the early 21st century there was increasing competition between China and Taiwan for influence in the Pacific Islands, a region in which several countries accorded diplomatic recognition to Taiwan. China continued to provide substantial aid and investment to those Pacific nations with which it maintained diplomatic relations. In April 2005 China began negotiations on a free trade agreement with Australia, a major source of vital mineral commodities (particularly coal and iron ore). The announcement in November 2011 that US troops were to be stationed in northern Australia was greeted with guarded disapproval by the Chinese Government. In March 2012 it was announced in Australia that the major Chinese telecommunications firm Huawei had been excluded from bidding for work on the country's national broadband network, owing to security concerns because of the company's alleged links to the Chinese armed forces. In the same month, however, the two countries concluded a currency swap agreement, allowing the exchange of their respective currencies between the two central banks so as to facilitate bilateral trade and investment, and in April 2013 the Australian dollar became the third currency (joining those of the USA and Japan) to trade directly with the Chinese yuan. In November the Australian Government expressed its disapproval of China's declaration of an ADIZ over the East China Sea (see Relations with Japan), saying that the action was unhelpful in view of current regional tensions.

In China's relations with South Asia, the long-standing border dispute with India, which gave rise to a short military conflict in 1962, remains unresolved. Discussions on the issue were held in 1988 and 1991, and in September 1993 China and India signed an agreement to reduce their troops along the frontier and to resolve the dispute by peaceful means. In August 1995 it was confirmed that the two countries were to disengage their troops from four border posts in Arunachal Pradesh. Other Indian concerns included the increasing levels of imports of cheap Chinese goods and the question of China's nuclear co-operation with Pakistan, while China resented India's continued hosting of Tibetan separatist organizations.

In June 2003 the Indian Prime Minister, Atal Bihari Vajpayee, visited Beijing: he officially recognized Tibet as part of China, and China agreed to trade with India's north-eastern state of Sikkim, thus implicitly recognizing India's control of that area. In November China and India held their first joint naval exercises. Further border-related negotiations took place in 2004, and during a visit to India in March 2005 the Chinese Premier, Wen Jiabao, signed an agreement aimed at resolving the border dispute. In July 2006 the reopening of the Nathu La border pass connecting the Indian state of Sikkim with Tibet represented a formal recognition by India of China's claim to Tibet and by China of India's claim to Sikkim.

In December 2010 Premier Wen Jiabao led a large delegation (including 400 representatives of the Chinese business sector) to India, where he had discussions with his Indian counterpart. In January 2012 renewed discussions on the two countries' border disputes resulted in an agreement to establish a joint border management mechanism to prevent the escalation of incidents into major confrontations. In September the two countries announced that they would resume joint military exercises (which had been suspended since 2008). In April 2013 the Chinese Government denied violating Indian territory, following reports that Chinese troops had entered the disputed border area of Ladakh. In May the Chinese Premier, Li Keqiang, paid a visit to India, during which he described China and India as 'strategic partners': it was agreed that the two countries should continue discussions on a mutually acceptable boundary settlement, and a number of agreements on investment and trade were concluded. Further confrontations in Ladakh were reported in July and August. In October, during a visit to Beijing by the Indian Prime Minister, Manmohan Singh, a formal accord on border defence co-operation was signed, together with further economic agreements.

Extensive Chinese assistance to Pakistan includes the development of its nuclear energy programme, and in May 2004 an agreement for the construction of a second nuclear plant in Pakistan was signed. In November 2006, during a visit to Pakistan, President Hu Jintao signed a free trade agreement with the Pakistani President, Pervez Musharraf. The visit was widely regarded as an attempt to reassure Pakistan of the continuing strength of bilateral links, particularly in view of China's growing relationship with India. In October 2008 the Pakistani President, Asif Ali Zardari, visited China, securing China's assistance with the construction of a further two nuclear power stations. In December 2010, during a visit to Pakistan, the Chinese Premier Wen Jiabao and his Pakistani counterpart agreed further to expand bilateral trade. Wen also expressed his support for Pakistan's attempts to combat terrorist activities. In May 2012 the Chinese Minister of Foreign Affairs, Yang Jiechi, was reported to have asked the Pakistan Government to take more effective action against Uygur militants who were believed to be based in Pakistan (see Events in Xinjiang). In May 2013 the new Chinese Premier, Li Keqiang, visited Pakistan, initiating plans for an 'economic corridor' between the two countries.

During 2000–01 China began improving relations with the Taliban regime in Afghanistan, signing several economic and technical agreements in the expectation that the Taliban would cease supporting Islamist Uygur fighters in Xinjiang. Following the collapse of the Taliban regime in late 2001 China continued to support the reconstruction process. In 2009 Chinese corporations began developing the Aynak copper mine, the largest foreign investment project in Afghanistan. In October 2011 it was announced that the China National Petroleum Corporation had become the first foreign company to obtain a licence for exploration of Afghanistan's unexploited petroleum reserves, which were believed to be large. In June 2012 the Afghan President, Hamid Karzai, attended a meeting of the Shanghai Cooperation Organization in Beijing, when Afghanistan was admitted as an observer member (see Relations with the USSR and successor states). In September representatives of the Chinese and Afghan Governments signed agreements on security (including Chinese assistance for police training) and economic co-operation.

Relations with the USA

For many years the USA refused to recognize the People's Republic, continuing to regard the Taiwanese administration as the legitimate Chinese Government. In February 1972, however, US President Richard Nixon visited the People's Republic and acknowledged that 'Taiwan is a part of China'. In January 1979 the USA formally recognized the People's Republic and severed diplomatic relations with Taiwan. Following the suppression of the pro-democracy movement in China in 1989, all senior-level government exchanges were suspended by the USA, and the export of weapons to China was prohibited. In September 1992 the announcement of the sale of US fighter aircraft to Taiwan caused a further deterioration in Sino-US relations. Between August 1993 and October 1994 the USA imposed sanctions on China, in response to the latter's sales of technology for nuclear-capable missiles to Pakistan. In June 1995, following President Bill Clinton's highly controversial decision to grant him a visa, President Lee Teng-hui of Taiwan embarked upon an unofficial visit to the USA, where he met members of the US Congress. The visit resulted in the withdrawal of the Chinese ambassador from the USA. In October, at a meeting in New York,

Presidents Jiang Zemin and Clinton agreed to resume dialogue on various issues, the USA reaffirming its commitment to the 'one China' policy (that Taiwan is part of the People's Republic of China). In November the two countries reached agreement on the resumption of bilateral military contacts.

President Jiang Zemin visited the USA in October 1997, the first such visit by a Chinese head of state since 1985. Measures to reduce the US trade deficit with China and to accelerate China's entry into the World Trade Organization (WTO) were negotiated. In addition, the Chinese Government agreed to control the export of nuclear-related materials, in return for the removal of sanctions on the sale of nuclear-reactor technology to the People's Republic. In November 1999, after 13 years of negotiations, a bilateral trade agreement was concluded, thus facilitating China's eventual accession to the WTO. In February 2000 the US House of Representatives approved legislation establishing direct military links between the USA and Taiwan.

In early September 2001 the USA sought to reduce China's fears over its national missile defence (NMD) programme by undertaking to keep China informed of its development and by abandoning its objections to China's build-up of its nuclear forces, in return for China's acceptance of the NMD. The attacks against the USA on 11 September 2001 were strongly condemned by China, which pledged its co-operation in the US-led 'war on terror'. In October President George W. Bush made his first official visit to China to attend the summit meeting of APEC, which was dominated by the issue of terrorism. However, the USA did not endorse China's view that Uygur and Tibetan separatists in Xinjiang and Tibet respectively were terrorists. China formally became a member of the WTO in December. At the end of 2001 President Bush signed proclamations granting China permanent normal trading relations status commencing on 1 January 2002.

On visiting Beijing in February 2002, Bush's discussions with Jiang revealed disagreements on the issues of human rights, China's close relations with Iran, Iraq and North Korea (countries the US President had described as forming an 'axis of evil'), the USA's planned missile defence system, China's export of nuclear technology to Pakistan and US support for Taiwan. A report issued in mid-July by the US Department of Defense warned that China was increasing its defence spending in order to intimidate Taiwan, while in the same month a report published by a US congressional commission stated that China had become a leading proliferator of missile technology to countries opposed to the USA, and that US corporations and their investments in China were assisting its emergence as a major economic power, to the detriment of the US trade balance. In late August China introduced regulations to curb the export of missiles and related technology. In return, the USA designated the East Turkestan Islamic Movement a terrorist group (see Events in Xinjiang).

There was strong opposition in China to the US military intervention in Iraq in March 2003. Tensions over trade issues also increased, and during a visit to Beijing in September the US Secretary of the Treasury criticized China's refusal to revalue its currency, amid concerns that undervaluation of the yuan was having an adverse effect on the US economy by making China's exports artificially cheap. China in turn expressed strong criticism of the USA's imposition of quotas on Chinese textile exports in November 2003. US concerns over China's economic strength and the trade deficit between the two countries (to the detriment of the USA) were illustrated in mid-2005 when a bid by the China National Offshore Oil Corporation to take control of a California-based oil and gas company encountered strong opposition in the US House of Representatives. The bid was regarded as potentially damaging to the security of the USA, and the company in question accepted a lower offer from a US firm. Diplomatic tension likewise arose over the huge increase in Chinese textile exports to the USA following the expiry of the WTO's Multi-Fibre Arrangement (MFA) at the end of 2004. Negotiations resulted in an agreement in November 2005 whereby limits were imposed on the rate at which the volume of Chinese clothing exports to the USA could expand.

In October 2008 a US military agreement with Taiwan, envisaging the sale of defence equipment to the value of US $6,000m., resulted in China's suspension of diplomatic and military exchanges with the USA. Following the election in November of Barack Obama as President of the USA, the Chinese Government urged him to halt the sale of US weapons to Taiwan. In February 2009 the new US Secretary of State, Hillary Clinton, visited Beijing, urging bilateral co-operation on various issues, including the deterioration in the global economic situation, climate change and security concerns. During a visit by the Chinese Minister of Foreign Affairs, Yang Jiechi, to the USA in March the two sides agreed to collaborate more closely in order to avoid the recurrence of a recent confrontation between a US navy surveillance vessel and Chinese ships in the South China Sea. In April the two Governments initiated an annual Strategic and Economic Dialogue for bilateral discussions at a senior ministerial level. In a joint action with the EU in June, the USA lodged a formal complaint at the WTO in relation to China's imposition of restrictions on the country's exports of various raw materials, which the complainants argued were distorting international markets for certain commodities.

In November 2009 President Obama undertook his first official visit to China and discussed greater bilateral co-operation in trade, global security and climate change. Obama's decision to receive the Dalai Lama in Washington, DC, in February 2010 drew unusually strong condemnation from the Chinese Government. Other sources of ongoing tension in Sino-US relations in 2010 included the US Administration's decision to proceed with a major sale of defence equipment to Taiwan (a matter over which Sino-US military contacts were briefly suspended), China's continuing refusal to implement any significant revaluation of its currency, and its less than rigorous enforcement of intellectual property rights.

During 2011 China (the US Government's largest foreign creditor) repeatedly expressed concern at the size of the US budget deficit. In August China accused the US Government of exaggeration in the latter's annual report on Chinese military capabilities, particularly with reference to China's expanding naval presence in the South China Sea: China had launched its first aircraft carrier in August and was, according to the report, predicted to be planning to construct more. In September China issued an official protest at the US Government's decision to give assistance towards the modernization of Taiwan's air force, although the USA had not complied with Taiwan's request for the sale of new military aircraft. In November President Obama declared that the Asia-Pacific region was a 'top priority' in terms of US security, and announced that US military personnel were to be stationed in northern Australia: China's official response was that the deployment might not be 'appropriate'.

In May 2012, during the two Governments' annual dialogue, the US Secretary of the Treasury, Timothy Geithner, urged China to reduce its dependence on exports for economic growth and to increase domestic consumption instead, and reiterated previous demands for China to allow the appreciation of its currency. In the same month a meeting of the two countries' ministers responsible for defence agreed to co-operate more fully on cyber-security, particularly in view of recent US intelligence reports that illegal access to sensitive information had been gained by Chinese computer users. In July the US Government made a complaint to the WTO concerning duties imposed by China on imports of US vehicles, and in September a further US complaint to the WTO alleged that China was illegally subsidizing its own vehicle exports; in October the WTO reiterated a recent ruling that China was illegally imposing tariffs on some US steel imports. Also in October a US Congress committee concluded that the major Chinese telecommunications firms Huawei and ZTE represented a threat to US security, owing to their alleged links with the Chinese state and armed forces, and recommended that US government departments and companies should avoid using equipment manufactured by them. During 2012 and 2013 the US Government repeatedly urged China to reach a peaceful settlement with its neighbours over the territorial disputes in the South China Sea and the East China Sea (see Relations with Japan, and Other regional relations).

Following North Korea's third nuclear test, in February 2013, the ministers responsible for foreign affairs in China and the USA announced that they would work together to persuade North Korea to halt its nuclear weapons programme. In May the annual report issued by the US Department of Defense stated that instances of cyber-espionage affecting commercial and defence-related organizations in the USA appeared to be directly attributable to the Chinese Government and armed forces; the accusation was dismissed as groundless by the official Chinese media. In turn, the Chinese media strongly criticized clandestine US internet and telephone surveillance activities, details of which were revealed in June by a former contractor of the US National Security Agency, Edward Snowden. In the same month President Xi Jinping visited the USA for informal discussions with President Obama. In July a joint working group on cybersecurity held its first meeting, and in the same month, following the two countries' annual dialogue, it was announced that negotiations were to take place on a bilateral investment treaty, to cover all economic sectors. In November the US Government expressed concern at China's establishment of an ADIZ above a disputed area of the East China Sea (see Relations with Japan), and refused to recognize its validity. In December the Chinese Government submitted a formal complaint to the WTO concerning US allegations that Chinese products were being 'dumped' on the US market at unfairly low prices, while in January 2014 the US Government accused China of failing to comply with the WTO's ruling (in 2012: see above) on steel imports. During his visit to China—as part of an Asian tour—in February 2014, US Secretary of State John Kerry stated that he had received reassurances from the Chinese authorities that they would work towards reining in North Korea's nuclear ambitions. The following week, however, Sino-US relations were put under renewed strain as a result of China's strong disapproval of President Obama's third meeting with the Dalai Lama in Washington, DC.

Relations with the USSR and successor states

Following the establishment of the People's Republic in 1949, China was dependent on the USSR for economic and military aid. However, as China began to develop its own form of socialism, the USSR withdrew all technical aid in 1960. In what became known as the 'Sino-Soviet Split', Chinese hostility to the USSR increased, and ideological differences were exacerbated by territorial disputes, by the Soviet invasion of Afghanistan and by the Soviet-supported Vietnamese intervention in Cambodia in the late 1970s. In 1987, however, China and the USSR signed a partial agreement concerning the exact demarcation of the disputed common border at the Amur River (Heilong Jiang). In May 1989 a full summit meeting was held in Beijing, at which normal state and party relations between China and the USSR were formally restored. During the next two years senior Chinese officials visited the USSR. In December 1991, upon the dissolution of the USSR, China recognized the newly independent states of the former union. The President of Russia, Boris Yeltsin, visited China in December 1992. In September 1994 President Jiang Zemin travelled to Moscow, the first visit to Russia by a Chinese head of state since 1957. The two sides reached agreement on the formal demarcation of the western section of the border (the eastern section having been delimited in May 1991), and each pledged not to aim nuclear missiles at the other. In June 1995 the Chinese Premier, Li Peng, paid an official visit to Russia, where several bilateral agreements were signed.

In April 1996, together with their counterparts from Kazakhstan, Kyrgyzstan and Tajikistan, the Chinese and Russian Presidents signed a treaty aimed at reducing tension along their respective borders. A further treaty on military co-operation and border demilitarization was signed by these five heads of state in April 1997. An agreement signed during President Yeltsin's visit to Beijing in November formally ended the border dispute. In November 1998, in Moscow, representatives from Russia, China and North Korea signed an inter-governmental agreement on the delimitation of their borders along the Tumannaya River. In June 1999 it was announced that a final accord on the demarcation of a common border between China and Russia had been agreed.

Vladimir Putin, who succeeded Boris Yeltsin as Russian President in December 1999, visited Beijing in July 2000, and in July 2001 Presidents Jiang and Putin signed a new 20-year Sino-Russian 'Good-neighbourly Treaty of Friendship and Co-operation' in Moscow and reaffirmed their opposition to the USA's plans for the NMD system. The Chinese Premier signed several trade agreements during a visit to Russia in September.

Russian Prime Minister Mikhail Kasyanov visited Beijing in August 2002 to discuss strategic issues, and President Putin travelled to China for discussions in December. The two countries issued a joint declaration on various global issues; they also sought to increase bilateral trade and economic co-operation. Hu Jintao visited Russia during his first foreign visit in his capacity as China's President in May 2003. Presidents Hu and Putin discussed the use of Siberian oil resources in China. President Putin's visit to China in October 2004 was dominated by the Chinese Government's wish to reach agreement on the route of a new oil pipeline, which, China hoped, would export Russian oil to Daqing, in north-eastern China. During a visit to Beijing in March 2006 President Putin appeared to favour the Daqing route, rather than a pipeline giving Japan priority.

In August 2005 the Chinese and Russian armed forces conducted joint military exercises for the first time. In November 2006 Russian Prime Minister Mikhail Fradkov paid an official visit to China, where he signed eight agreements to expand bilateral investment, trade and technical co-operation, particularly in the energy sector. President Hu paid an official visit to Russia in March 2007, concluding a major agreement on bilateral trade, and also undertaking to increase co-operation in a number of other fields, including technology and security. The new President of Russia, Dmitrii A. Medvedev, visited China in May 2008, signing an agreement on nuclear co-operation with President Hu. The two countries resolved a 40-year border dispute in mid-2008, when Russia recognized China's sovereignty over all of the island of Yinlong and half of the island of Heixiazi. In February 2009 China and Russia signed an agreement whereby, in exchange for Siberian oil supplies, the China Development Bank was to provide loans totalling US $25,000m. to two Russian companies—Rosneft, the state oil producer, and Transneft, holder of the country's pipeline monopoly. During a visit to Beijing by Putin (now the Russian Prime Minister) in October 2009, trade agreements valued at $3,500m. were signed. The Chinese and Russian Presidents met several times in the course of 2010, and during a visit by Medvedev to Beijing in September the two leaders celebrated the completion of their largest bilateral project, the 999-km oil pipeline between Daqing and the Russian city of Angarsk. They also signed various agreements providing for further co-operation in the field of energy.

In April 2012 the Chinese and Russian navies undertook a joint exercise in the Yellow Sea, the first time they had co-operated in this way. During a visit to Beijing in June Putin (re-elected President of Russia in the previous March) emphasized the importance of maintaining the recent increase in bilateral trade, and, with Hu, he signed agreements that included co-operation in energy, industry, banking and aviation. Following his formal accession to the Chinese presidency, Xi Jinping's first foreign visit was to Russia in March 2013, and it reportedly resulted in a resolution of differences on the supply of Russian natural gas to China, with effect from 2018 (originally agreed in 2009 but delayed by a dispute over pricing); it was also agreed that Russian exports of petroleum to China were to increase threefold.

During the 1990s China steadily consolidated its relations with the former Soviet republics of Central Asia, and in 1996 China, Russia, Kazakhstan, Kyrgyzstan, and Tajikistan established the 'Shanghai Five', which became the Shanghai Cooperation Organization (SCO) at the group's annual meeting in June 2001 (when Uzbekistan became the sixth member). Both China and Russia apparently hoped that the SCO would help to counter US influence in Central Asia. At a meeting of SCO heads of state in June 2012, in Beijing, Afghanistan was admitted to the organization as an observer member, a status already accorded to India, Iran, Mongolia and Pakistan. During the meeting there was an emphasis on regional economic co-operation, and the Chinese Government announced that it would make available loans to member states amounting to US $10,000m. The establishment of an SCO development bank was reported to be under discussion at the meeting of member countries' heads of state in September 2013, together with the establishment of modern-day 'silk roads' linking China with Central Asia, and measures to combat terrorism and illegal trade in narcotics.

Other external relations

Frequently expressed concerns about China's human rights record did not prevent European governments from greatly increasing trade and commercial links with China during the early 21st century. Trade between the European Union (EU) and China increased fourfold between 2000 and 2012, and in 2006 it became the EU's largest source of imports. The first China-EU summit meeting, which was scheduled to become an annual event, took place in London in April 1997, prior to the Asia-Europe Meeting (ASEM). China and the EU committed themselves to greater mutual co-operation in the area of trade and economic relations. At the fourth annual China-EU summit meeting, in September 2000, discussions encompassed the issue of access by EU companies to China's insurance market, the last obstacle to China's admission to the WTO (which took place in December 2001).

In late November 2008 the Chinese Government postponed the 11th EU-China summit meeting, scheduled to be held in the French city of Lyon in the following month, citing opposition to a forthcoming meeting between the French President, Nicolas

Sarkozy, and the Dalai Lama. In late January 2009 Premier Wen Jiabao embarked on a five-day visit to Europe, where his agenda included discussions on the worsening global financial crisis: he visited Switzerland, Germany, Belgium, Spain and the United Kingdom. In April 2010 President Sarkozy paid an official visit to China, one of his objectives being to reverse the recent decline in bilateral trade. President Hu Jintao visited France in November, when various bilateral co-operation agreements, encompassing areas such as energy, finance and environmental protection, were signed. In November, during an official visit to Portugal, the Chinese President offered support for the troubled Portuguese economy.

In November 2010 David Cameron, the British Prime Minister, undertook an official visit to China, at the head of a large delegation incorporating cabinet ministers and business representatives. Discussions with Chinese leaders included the topics of trade, finance and energy. Cameron was also reported to have raised the issue of imprisoned dissident Liu Xiaobo. In June 2011 a visit to Europe by Wen Jiabao included a visit to the United Kingdom, where agreements were reached on major investments in China by, among others, a British energy company; Wen rebuked the British Government, however, for its insistence on referring to human rights abuses in China. He then proceeded to Germany, China's largest European trading partner, where, as well as concluding important trade agreements, Wen expressed support for the eurozone members in their current economic difficulties, and gave an undertaking that China would be willing to purchase European sovereign debt. In April 2012 Wen visited Iceland, Germany, Sweden and Poland; while in Poland he met leaders from other central and eastern European countries and proposed initiatives for developing the region's relations with China, including an investment co-operation fund and a line of credit amounting to US $10,000m. for infrastructure and technology projects. In June the EU asked the WTO to arbitrate in a dispute with China over the latter's restrictions on its exports of 'rare earth' minerals, while in November China lodged an official complaint with the WTO, alleging that European governments were unfairly subsidizing manufacturers of solar panels (after the EU began investigating claims that Chinese solar panel manufacturers were 'dumping' their products on the European market).

In April 2013 President François Hollande of France paid a state visit to China, accompanied by a large trade delegation, securing a major order for the supply of 60 Airbus aircraft to China. A free trade agreement with Iceland was concluded in April, China's first such agreement with a European country. In May the EU announced that it was preparing to open an 'anti-dumping' investigation into imports of mobile telecommunications equipment from China, in addition to a number of current investigations into the alleged unfairly low pricing of, among other Chinese exports to Europe, steel, paper, ceramics and bicycles; the dispute over the pricing of imports of Chinese solar panels was resolved, however, in July. In May the Chinese Premier, Li Keqiang, visited Switzerland, with which another free trade agreement was concluded, and Germany. In June the United Kingdom and China achieved a three-year currency swap agreement worth 200,000m. yuan, and a similar arrangement worth 350,000m. yuan was made with the European Central Bank in October, with the aim of facilitating trade and investment and expanding the global use of the Chinese currency. British Prime Minister Cameron paid a second official visit to China in December; it was reported that trade between China and the United Kingdom reached a record level in 2013, while Chinese investment in the United Kingdom was twice as large as its investment in any other European country. The first session of negotiations on a Sino-EU investment treaty took place in January 2014. In March President Xi Jinping undertook a 10-day visit to Europe; the tour, which incorporated France, Germany and Belgium (including the EU headquarters in Brussels), focused primarily on trade negotiations.

China continued to maintain good relations with various Middle Eastern nations, despite its establishment of diplomatic links with Israel in 1992. China did not support the US-led military action against Iraq in March 2003. As international concerns over Iran's nuclear programme intensified from 2005, China participated in discussions on the matter by the permanent members of the UN Security Council and Germany (the 'P5+1' group), but consistently opposed the imposition of sanctions against the country, and refused to agree to US recommendations that countries should reduce their imports of petroleum from Iran, one of China's principal suppliers of crude petroleum; negotiations between Iran and 'P5+1' reached an agreement in November 2013 on limits to Iran's nuclear development, in exchange for a reduction in sanctions. In March 2011, meanwhile, having abstained from the UN vote on the issue, China expressed its opposition to the multinational military intervention in Libya, following a popular uprising there.

In February 2012 China imposed its veto (as did Russia) on a UN Security Council resolution that condemned the recent violent suppression of anti-Government protests in Syria, and in July it again imposed a veto on a resolution that proposed increased sanctions against Syria: throughout the year it refused to withdraw its support for the existing Syrian Government, while urging a peaceful solution to the conflict. After the apparent use of chemical weapons by the Syrian Government against its own citizens in August 2013, China continued to refuse to support outside military intervention, but agreed to give practical assistance (including a naval escort) in dismantling Syria's chemical weapons arsenal, in accordance with a UN Security Council resolution adopted in September. China was represented at a conference which began in Geneva, Switzerland, in January 2014, with the aim of resolving the Syrian conflict.

Following the conflict between Lebanon and Israel in mid-2006, in September of that year China announced that it was to increase its force in Lebanon to 1,000 peacekeepers, its largest single such deployment since China first began contributing to UN-mandated peacekeeping forces in the 1980s. By 2009 China had become an important contributor of personnel to UN peacekeeping operations. In addition to its deployment in Lebanon, Chinese troops were also serving in the Democratic Republic of the Congo, Liberia and Sudan. In December 2013 there were 2,078 Chinese uniformed personnel taking part in UN peacekeeping operations, and in 2012 China contributed 3.9% of the UN budget for such operations.

China continued to pursue closer economic relations with African nations, while adhering to the principle of non-interference in other countries' political affairs. The first Forum on China-Africa Co-operation (FOCAC) was held in Beijing in October 2000, when the People's Republic announced its decision to reduce or cancel outstanding debt totalling US $1,200m. In November 2005 Beijing hosted the first summit meeting of FOCAC, which was attended by senior representatives from 48 African nations. China pledged to ensure that by 2010 its trade with Africa would more than double to reach $100,000m. China also announced the immediate implementation of various trade and investment agreements, including plans for major projects in Egypt, Nigeria and Zambia. However, many international critics accused China of depleting Africa's mineral resources, and it was alleged that the rapid expansion in Africa's imports from China was having an adverse effect on local manufacturing activities, while Chinese investment in African agricultural land was also controversial. At the fourth ministerial meeting of FOCAC, convened in Egypt in November 2009, Premier Wen Jiabao committed China to the provision of low-interest loans totalling $10,000m. over a three-year period. Special concessions to the poorest African nations included China's cancellation of their debts and the introduction of a zero-tariff arrangement on nearly all Chinese imports from those countries.

In May 2007 Liu Guijin was appointed as China's envoy to Africa, specifically to engage in attempts to resolve conflict in the Sudanese province of Darfur, China's support for the Sudanese Government having drawn widespread opprobrium. In June 2011 China received a visit by the President of Sudan, Omar al-Bashir, despite the fact that a warrant had been issued by the International Criminal Court for his arrest on charges of war crimes. In August the Chinese Minister of Foreign Affairs, Yang Jiechi, visited Sudan and the newly independent South Sudan, which together constituted an important source of China's petroleum, offering to mediate between the two in their outstanding differences, particularly concerning petroleum shipments; in April 2012 the South Sudan Government announced that China had offered US $8,000m. in loans for various infrastructure projects, although this did not include a pipeline that would allow South Sudan to export petroleum independently of its neighbour. In December 2013 China sent an envoy to South Sudan in an attempt to mediate in the civil conflict that had recently erupted there.

In January 2012, meanwhile, the new headquarters of the African Union opened in Addis Ababa, Ethiopia, funded entirely by China. At a FOCAC summit meeting in July the Chinese Government undertook to provide US $20,000m. in loans for

African countries over the next three years, supporting infrastructure, agricultural development and small enterprises, and Wen Jiabao offered assurances that the social and environmental consequences of Chinese investment would receive greater attention. In March 2013 President Xi Jinping paid visits to Tanzania, South Africa and the Republic of the Congo, during which he announced the provision of Chinese aid for, among other things, health care and port improvements. In July, during a visit to China by the Nigerian President, Goodluck Jonathan, the Chinese Government agreed to provide a low-interest loan of $1,100m. to Nigeria (another major source of petroleum for China) for infrastructure development, while in August, during a visit by the Kenyan President, Uhuru Kenyatta, China agreed to finance and undertake the construction of a major new railway that would link Kenya to neighbouring countries.

China is a major market for the exports of many Latin American countries, particularly hydrocarbons, copper and iron ore, and one of the region's principal sources of investment in mining, energy production and infrastructure. China's first free trade agreement with a Latin American country was concluded with Chile, taking effect in October 2006, with the objective of giving China access to the latter's natural resources, particularly copper. In November 2008 President Hu Jintao visited Costa Rica, Cuba and Peru, where he signed trade and investment contracts, and concluded a bilateral free trade agreement with Peru. Venezuela was one of several Latin American countries visited by then Vice-President Xi Jinping in February 2009, when various co-operation and investment agreements were signed, including arrangements for a substantial increase in Chinese imports of Venezuelan petroleum. Latin America reportedly received 50% of all Chinese overseas investment in the two years 2008–09. During a visit to Brazil in April 2010 President Hu signed various bilateral trade accords; agreement was also reached on the construction by China of a steel plant in Brazil. In May 2011 negotiations took place on the diversification of Brazil's exports to China: Brazil requested that more processed agricultural goods should be included, rather than raw materials. In June 2012 the Chinese Premier, Wen Jiabao, visited Argentina, Brazil, Chile and Uruguay and proposed a feasibility study for a free trade agreement between China and the Latin American 'common market', Mercosur, also offering to provide US $10,000m. in loans for regional infrastructure projects. In March 2013 China and Brazil concluded a currency swap agreement, allowing the exchange of up to $30,000m. in their respective currencies to facilitate bilateral trade. In June President Xi Jinping visited Trinidad and Tobago, where he signed co-operation agreements and held discussions with the leaders of several other Caribbean nations; he also visited Costa Rica, where Chinese finance for road-building was announced; and Mexico, where discussions were held on balancing the two countries' trade relationship (hitherto heavily in China's favour) and encouraging Chinese investment in Mexico.

CONSTITUTION AND GOVERNMENT

China is a unitary state. Directly under the Central Government there are 22 provinces, five autonomous regions, including Xizang (Tibet), and four municipalities (Beijing, Chongqing, Shanghai and Tianjin). The highest organ of state power is the National People's Congress (NPC), which is indirectly elected for five years by the people's congresses of the provinces, autonomous regions, municipalities directly under the Central Government, and the People's Liberation Army. The NPC elects a Standing Committee to be its permanent organ. The current Constitution, adopted by the NPC in December 1982 and subsequently amended, is China's fourth since 1949. It restored the office of head of state (President of the Republic). Executive power is exercised by the State Council (Cabinet), comprising the Premier, Vice-Premiers and other ministers heading ministries and commissions. The State Council is appointed by, and accountable to, the NPC.

Political power is held by the Chinese Communist Party (CCP). The CCP's highest authority is the Party Congress, which is convened every five years. In November 2012 the CCP's 18th National Congress elected a Central Committee of 205 full members and 171 alternate members. To direct policy, the Central Committee elected a 25-member Politburo. The incoming Standing Committee of the Politburo comprised seven members.

Provincial people's congresses are the local organs of state power. Provincial people's governments are responsible for local affairs.

REGIONAL AND INTERNATIONAL CO-OPERATION

China is a member of the Asian Development Bank (ADB, see p. 207) and of Asia-Pacific Economic Cooperation (APEC, see p. 201). In 1996 the secretariat of the Tumen River Economic Development Area (TREDA) was established in Beijing by the Governments of China, North and South Korea, Mongolia and Russia. China became an observer member of the South Asian Association for Regional Co-operation (SAARC, see p. 420) in 2005. In 2001 China was a founder member of the Shanghai Cooperation Organization (SCO—formerly known as the 'Shanghai Five'). China is also a member of the UN's Economic and Social Commission for Asia and the Pacific (ESCAP, see p. 28).

China was admitted to the UN in place of the 'Republic of China' in 1971. It is a permanent member of the UN Security Council. The country became a full member of the World Trade Organization (WTO, see p. 434) in 2001. China is also a member of the Association of Tin Producing Countries (ATPC) and of the Bank for International Settlements (BIS, see p. 221). China participates in the Group of 20 (G20, see p. 456) major industrialized and systemically important emerging market nations.

ECONOMIC AFFAIRS

In 2012, according to estimates by the World Bank, China's gross national income (GNI), measured at average 2010–12 prices, was US $7,671,547m., equivalent to some $5,680 per head (or $9,060 on an international purchasing-power parity basis). During 2003–12, it was estimated, the population increased at an average annual rate of 0.5%, while gross domestic product (GDP) per head increased, in real terms, at an average annual rate of 9.9%. Overall GDP increased, in real terms, at an average annual rate of 10.5% in 2003–12. GDP grew by 7.7% in 2013, according to official figures.

Agriculture (including forestry and fishing) contributed 10.0% of GDP in 2013, and accounted for 33.6% of total employment in 2012. China's principal crops are rice (production of which accounted for an estimated 28.6% of the total world harvest in 2012), maize, sugar cane, wheat, potatoes, sweet potatoes, soybeans, tobacco, cotton and jute. According to the World Bank, agricultural GDP increased at an average annual rate of 4.8%, in real terms, in 2003–11. In comparison with the previous year, the sector grew by 4.0% in 2013, according to official figures.

Industry (including mining, manufacturing, construction and power) contributed 43.9% of GDP in 2013, and engaged 30.3% of the employed labour force in 2012. According to the World Bank, industrial GDP increased at an average annual rate of 11.7%, in real terms, in 2003–11. Compared with the previous year, industrial GDP expanded by 7.8% in 2013, according to official figures.

The mining sector accounted for less than 0.9% of total employment in 2002. Output in the sector accounted for some 5.3% of total industrial production in that year. China has enormous mineral reserves and is the world's largest producer of natural graphite, antimony, tungsten and zinc. Other important minerals include coal, iron ore, molybdenum, tin, lead, mercury, bauxite, phosphate rock, diamonds, gold, manganese, crude petroleum and natural gas. Proven reserves of petroleum at the end of 2012 amounted to 17,335m. barrels, sufficient to sustain production at that year's levels (averaging 4.2m. barrels per day) for nearly 11 years.

According to the World Bank, the manufacturing sector contributed an estimated 29.5% of GDP in 2010. It accounted for 13.0% of total employment in 2002. China is a leading world producer of chemical fertilizers, cement and steel. Textiles, paper and paperboard, and motor vehicles are also important, while the information technology and electronics sectors have expanded extremely rapidly; high- and new-technology products accounted for 29.9% of total exports in 2013. The GDP of the manufacturing sector increased at an average annual rate of 10.6%, in real terms, during 2003–10, according to the World Bank. Growth in the GDP of the manufacturing sector was 9.0% in 2010, compared with the previous year.

The construction sector accounted for 6.9% of GDP in 2013. The sector engaged 4.7% of the working population in 2009. In comparison with the previous year, the construction sector's GDP grew by 9.5% in 2013.

Energy is derived principally from coal (76.5% in 2012); other sources are petroleum (8.9%), hydroelectric, nuclear and wind power (10.3%), and natural gas (4.3%). Although China is a significant oil producer, it is a major importer of crude petroleum. The 22,500-MW Three Gorges Dam hydroelectric power project on the River Yangtze (Changjiang), the world's largest hydro-electric complex, was fully operational by July 2012; its 32 generators have a potential annual output of 84,700m. kWh, or about 1.8% of national electric energy production at 2011 levels (in comparison with the original projection of 10%, owing to the unexpectedly rapid rise in total energy demand). The rapid development from the mid-2000s of China's nuclear power industry was temporarily affected by the accident in March 2011 at the Fukushima nuclear power plant, Japan, after which approvals for any further reactors in China were suspended. However, later that year the country's commitment to a greater reliance on nuclear energy was reaffirmed. At March 2013 17 nuclear reactors were operating in China and 28 new reactors were under construction. Imports of mineral fuels comprised 18.4% of the cost of total merchandise imports in 2012.

Services contributed 46.1% of GDP in 2013, and engaged 36.1% of the employed labour force in 2012. Along with retail and wholesale trade, the tourism sector, especially domestic travel, has expanded rapidly. Receipts from international tourism were estimated to have increased by 3.4%, compared with the previous year, to reach US $51,700m. in 2013. In 2013 a total of 129.1m. tourists visited China (a decline of 2.5% compared with 2012), of whom 26.3m. (a decrease of 3.3%) were classified as foreign visitors, the remainder being travellers from Hong Kong, Macao and Taiwan. During 2003–11, according to the World Bank, the GDP of the services sector increased at an average annual rate of 11.3% in real terms. Compared with the previous year, growth in the GDP of the services sector was 8.3% in 2013, according to official figures.

In 2012, according to IMF figures, China recorded a merchandise trade surplus of US $317,598m., and there was a surplus of $193,139m. on the current account of the balance of payments. In 2013 the principal source of imports was the Republic of Korea (which provided 9.4% of total imports). Other important suppliers were Japan, Taiwan, the USA and Australia. The principal market for exports in that year was Hong Kong (17.4% of total exports). Other important purchasers were the USA and Japan. Most of the goods exported to Hong Kong are subsequently re-exported. The principal imports in 2013 were crude petroleum (accounting for 11.3% of total imports), iron ore (5.4%), plastics in primary form, soybean, and copper and copper alloys. The principal exports in that year were automatic data processing machines and components (accounting for 8.2% of total exports), clothing and accessories (8.0%), textiles, mobile and car telephones, and rolled steel.

In 2013 China's official budget deficit was equivalent to 1.9% of GDP (slightly higher than in 2012, but still within the government target of 2.0%). China's general government gross debt was 1,354,743m. yuan in 2012, equivalent to 26.1% of GDP. According to the Asian Development Bank, the country's total external debt at the end of 2013 was US $810,000m. In that year the cost of debt-servicing was equivalent to 2.2% of the value of exports of goods and services. China's foreign exchange reserves totalled $3,821,300m. at the end of 2013. Consumer prices increased at an average annual rate of 3.0% during 2004–13, and rose by 2.6% in 2013. The official rate of urban unemployment stood at 4.1% at the end of 2013. However, as these statistics did not include workers who had been made redundant through reform of state-owned enterprises, or unemployed persons from rural areas who had migrated to urban areas in search of work, many observers estimated the urban unemployment rate to be significantly higher. In 2012 the total number of migrant workers was 268.9m.

Following the introduction in 1978 of the 'open door' policy of reform, which reduced state control of agriculture and industry and permitted foreign investment in Chinese enterprises (particularly through the newly established Special Economic Zones), the Chinese economy became one of the fastest-growing in the world, and by 2010 it had surpassed Japan to become the world's second largest economy (after the USA), and a major overseas investor. China's foreign exchange reserves were estimated at US $3,300,000m. at the beginning of 2013, by far the largest in the world: of this a major proportion was invested in US government bonds, making China the USA's principal official creditor. The value of the Chinese currency remained a contentious issue in 2013, with trading partners (especially the USA) asserting that the Chinese currency was undervalued and that the country's exporters were thus being afforded an unfair advantage. According to official figures published in early 2014, in 2013 China for the first time overtook the USA as the world's largest trading nation in goods. The 12th Five-Year Plan (2011–15), confirmed in March 2011, envisaged average annual GDP expansion at 7.0% over that period: it gave priority to the achievement of a more equitable distribution of China's wealth, the raising of standards of living, increased domestic consumption, improvements in social services, energy efficiency and the reduction of carbon emissions, and environmental protection. To control inflation the People's Bank of China, the central bank, raised interest rates five times between October 2010 and the end of 2011. Consumer price increases reached 6.5% in July 2011, but the rate of increase slowed thereafter, and remained well below the Government's preferred limit of 4% during 2012 and 2013; property prices rose steadily, however, despite measures to limit speculation. China's GDP expanded by 9.3% in 2011, but the rate of growth slowed to 7.8% in 2012 and to 7.7% in 2013, with industrial production for export affected by falling demand worldwide, particularly as a result of continuing economic difficulties in the European Union and the USA. The Government undertook to rebalance the economy by focusing on domestic consumption rather than exports. During late 2011 and early 2012 the People's Bank made three reductions in the reserve ratio requirement (the amount banks are obliged to keep in reserve), thus increasing the amount available for loans to businesses, and in June and July 2012 the Bank twice reduced interest rates (for the first time since 2008) and also announced that domestic banks were to be given more flexibility in setting their lending rates, so as to encourage businesses to borrow and invest. A major stimulus to the domestic economy was provided by the Government's announcement in September 2012 of about 60 infrastructure projects, to be undertaken at a cost of some $150,000m. In April quotas were increased for access to the Chinese financial markets by foreign institutions, and in November it was announced that the procedures for foreign direct investment were to be simplified. Shanghai's pilot Free Trade Zone (FTZ) was officially opened in September 2013, with the aim of attracting both foreign and domestic companies, and in January 2014 state media reported that a further 12 FTZs were being planned. A series of currency swap agreements with major trading partners (including Japan in December 2011, Australia and Brazil in March and June 2012, respectively, the United Kingdom in June 2013 and the European Central Bank in October 2003) aimed to stimulate trade and increase the role of the yuan in international transactions. During 2013 the level of debt incurred by local governments and companies became a matter of concern, particularly that resulting from credit provided by 'shadow banking', i.e. less-regulated non-bank institutions. In November the 'Third Plenum' of the 18th CCP Central Committee (see Domestic Political Affairs) envisaged a 'decisive role' for the market system: among numerous economic reforms approved, state-owned enterprises, while remaining central to the economy, were to increase efficiency and productivity, with participation by private investors; the formation of small and medium-sized privately-funded banks was to be permitted; budgetary management and taxation systems of both central and local governments were to be modernized; interest rates and exchange rates were to be liberalized; and a greater role was to be permitted for foreign investment. In response to a slowdown in manufacturing output, in April 2014 the Government announced further economic stimulus measures, including increased expenditure on infrastructure and business tax reductions. According to World Bank predictions released in the same month, GDP growth in 2014 was forecast to diminish slightly, to 7.6%.

PUBLIC HOLIDAYS

2015: 1 January (Solar New Year), 19–25 February* (Lunar New Year), 8 March (International Women's Day), 5 April (Qingming Festival), 1 May (Labour Day), 20 June (Dragon Boat Festival), 1 August (Army Day), 27 September (Mid-Autumn Festival), 1–7 October (National Days).

* From the first to the fourth day of the first moon of the lunar calendar.

Various individual regional holidays are also observed.

Statistical Survey

Source (unless otherwise stated): National Bureau of Statistics of China, 38 Yuetan Nan Jie, Sanlihe, Beijing 100826; tel. (10) 68515074; fax (10) 68515078; e-mail service@stats.gov.cn; internet www.stats.gov.cn/english/.

Note: Wherever possible, figures in this Survey exclude Taiwan. In the case of unofficial estimates for China, it is not always clear if Taiwan is included or excluded. Where a Taiwan component is known, either it has been deducted from the all-China figure or its inclusion is noted. Figures for the Hong Kong Special Administrative Region (SAR) and for the Macao SAR are listed separately. Transactions between the SARs and the rest of the People's Republic continue to be treated as external transactions.

Area and Population

AREA, POPULATION AND DENSITY

Area (sq km)	9,572,900*
Population (census results)	
1 November 2000	1,242,612,226
1 November 2010	
Males	682,329,104
Females	650,481,765
Total	1,332,810,869
Population (official estimates at 31 December)†	
2012	1,354,040,000
2013	1,360,720,000
Density (per sq km) at 31 December 2013	142.1

* 3,696,100 sq miles.

† Figures rounded to the nearest 10,000 persons.

Note: Data for population census do not include adjustment for under-enumeration (estimated at 0.12% for 2010); adjusted total for 2000 was 1,265,830,000.

POPULATION BY AGE AND SEX
('000 at 2010 census)

	Males	Females	Total
0–14	119,794.5	101,528.1	221,322.6
15–64	505,329.1	487,232.0	992,561.1
65 and over	57,205.5	61,721.6	118,927.2
Total	682,329.1	650,481.8	1,332,810.9

Note: Totals may not be equal to the sum of components, owing to rounding.

PRINCIPAL ETHNIC GROUPS
(at census of 1 November 2010)

	Number	%
Han (Chinese)	1,220,844,520	91.59
Zhuang	16,926,381	1.27
Hui	10,586,087	0.79
Manchu	10,387,958	0.78
Uygur (Uighur)	10,069,346	0.76
Miao	9,426,007	0.71
Yi	8,714,393	0.65
Tujia	8,353,912	0.63
Tibetan	6,282,187	0.47
Mongolian	5,981,840	0.45
Dong	2,879,974	0.22
Bouyei	2,870,034	0.22
Yao	2,796,003	0.21
Bai	1,933,510	0.15
Korean	1,830,929	0.14
Hani	1,660,932	0.12
Li	1,463,064	0.11
Kazakh	1,462,588	0.11
Dai	1,261,311	0.09
She	708,651	0.05
Lisu	702,839	0.05
Dongxiang	621,500	0.05
Gelao	550,746	0.04
Others	3,856,056	0.29
Unknown	640,101	0.05
Total	1,332,810,869	100.00

ADMINISTRATIVE DIVISIONS
(previous or other spellings given in brackets)

	Area ('000 sq km)	Population at 1 November 2010: Total	Density (per sq km)	Capital of province or region	Estimated population ('000) at mid-2000*
Provinces					
Sichuan (Szechwan)	487.0	80,417,528	165.1	Chengdu (Chengtu)	3,294
Henan (Honan)	167.0	94,029,939	563.1	Zhengzhou (Chengchow)	2,070
Shandong (Shantung)	153.3	95,792,719	624.9	Jinan (Tsinan)	2,568
Jiangsu (Kiangsu)	102.6	78,660,941	766.7	Nanjing (Nanking)	2,740
Guangdong (Kwangtung)	197.1	104,320,459	529.3	Guangzhou (Canton)	3,893
Hebei (Hopei)	202.7	71,854,210	354.5	Shijiazhuang (Shihkiachwang)	1,603
Hunan	210.5	65,700,762	312.1	Changsha	1,775
Anhui (Anhwei)	139.9	59,500,468	425.3	Hefei (Hofei)	1,242
Hubei (Hupeh)	187.5	57,237,727	305.3	Wuhan (Hankow)	5,169
Zhejiang (Chekiang)	101.8	54,426,891	534.6	Hangzhou (Hangchow)	1,780
Liaoning	151.0	43,746,323	289.7	Shenyang (Mukden)	4,828
Jiangxi (Kiangsi)	164.8	44,567,797	270.4	Nanchang	1,722
Yunnan	436.2	45,966,766	105.4	Kunming	1,701
Heilongjiang (Heilungkiang)	463.6	38,313,991	82.6	Harbin	2,928
Guizhou (Kweichow)	174.0	34,748,556	199.7	Guiyang (Kweiyang)	2,533
Shaanxi (Shensi)	195.8	37,327,379	190.6	Xian (Sian)	3,123
Fujian (Fukien)	123.1	36,894,217†	299.7	Fuzhou (Foochow)	1,397
Shanxi (Shansi)	157.1	35,712,101	227.3	Taiyuan	2,415
Jilin (Kirin)	187.0	27,452,815	146.8	Changchun	3,093
Gansu (Kansu)	366.5	25,575,263	69.8	Lanzhou (Lanchow)	1,730
Hainan	34.3	8,671,485	252.8	Haikou	438‡
Qinghai (Tsinghai)	721.0	5,626,723	7.8	Xining (Hsining)	692
Autonomous regions					
Guangxi Zhuang (Kwangsi Chuang)	220.4	46,023,761	208.8	Nanning	1,311
Nei Monggol (Inner Mongolia)	1,177.5	24,706,291	21.0	Hohhot (Huhehot)	978

—continued		Population at 1 November 2010			
—continued	Area ('000 sq km)	Total	Density (per sq km)	Capital of province or region	Estimated population ('000) at mid-2000*
Xinjiang Uygur (Sinkiang Uighur)	1,646.9	21,815,815	13.2	Urumqi (Wulumuqi)	1,415
Ningxia Hui (Ninghsia Hui)	66.4	6,301,350	94.9	Yinchuan (Yinchuen)	592
Tibet (Xizang)	1,221.6	3,002,165	2.5	Lhasa	134
Municipalities					
Shanghai	6.2	23,019,196	3,712.8	—	12,887
Beijing (Peking)	16.8	19,612,368	1,167.4	—	10,839
Tianjin (Tientsin)	11.3	12,938,693	1,145.0	—	9,156
Chongqing (Chungking)	82.0	28,846,170	351.8	—	4,900
Total	9,572.9	1,332,810,869§	139.2		

* UN estimates, excluding population in counties under cities' administration.
† Excluding islands administered by Taiwan, mainly Jinmen (Quemoy) and Mazu (Matsu), with 49,050 inhabitants according to figures released by the Taiwan authorities at the end of March 1990.
‡ December 1998 figure.
§ Including 2,300,000 military personnel and 4,649,985 persons with unregistered households.

PRINCIPAL TOWNS
(incl. suburbs, UN estimates, population at mid-2010)

Shanghai	19,554,059	Kunming	3,388,025
Beijing (Peking, the capital)	14,999,554	Dalian (Dairen)	3,305,435
Guangzhou (Canton)	10,485,570	Suzhou	3,248,306
Shenzhen	10,222,493	Wuxi	3,222,086
Chongqing (Chungking)	9,732,286	Changsha	3,212,091
Wuhan (Hankow)	8,904,018	Urumqi (Wulumuqi)	2,954,226
Tianjin (Tientsin)	8,535,265	Hefei (Hofei)	2,829,545
Dongguan	7,159,504	Fuzhou (Foochow)	2,799,438
Chengdu (Chengtu)	6,397,335	Shijiazhuang (Shihkiachwang)	2,740,568
Foshan	6,207,756	Xiamen	2,701,535
Nanjing (Nanking)	5,664,951	Zhongshan	2,694,989
Harbin	5,496,375	Taipei	2,654,039
Shenyang (Mukden)	5,468,771	Wenzhou	2,635,149
Hangzhou (Hangchow)	5,189,275	Ningbo	2,632,375
Xi'an (Sian), Shaanxi	4,845,821	Lanzhou (Lanchow)	2,487,187
Shantou	4,062,449	Guiyang	2,457,594
Zhengzhou (Chengchow)	3,796,482	Zibo	2,456,098
Qingdao (Tsingtao)	3,679,853	Nanchang	2,331,101
Changchun	3,597,815	Changzhou	2,322,650
Jinan (Tsinan)	3,581,356	Xuzhou	2,143,975
Taiyuan	3,392,059	Nanning	2,095,797

Note: Alternative names or spellings are given in parentheses.

Mid-2011 (incl. suburbs, UN estimate): Shanghai 20,207,600; Beijing 15,594,400; Guangzhou 10,848,500; Shenzhen 10,629,700; Chongqing 9,977,000.

Source: UN, *World Urbanization Prospects: The 2011 Revision*.

BIRTHS AND DEATHS
(sample surveys)

	2011	2012	2013
Birth rate (per 1,000)	11.93	12.10	12.08
Death rate (per 1,000)	7.14	7.15	7.16

2013 (rounded data): Births 16,400,000; Deaths 9,720,000.

Marriages (number registered, rounded data): 1,236,100 in 2010; 1,297,480 in 2011; 1,318,270 in 2012.

Life expectancy (years at birth): 73.5 (males 71.8; females 75.3) in 2011 (Source: World Bank, World Development Indicators database).

EMPLOYMENT*
('000 persons at 31 December, official estimates)

	2000	2001	2002
Agriculture, forestry and fishing	333,550	329,740	324,870
Mining	5,970	5,610	5,580
Manufacturing	80,430	80,830	83,070
Electricity, gas and water	2,840	2,880	2,900
Construction	35,520	36,690	38,930
Geological prospecting and water conservancy	1,100	1,050	980
Transport, storage and communications	20,290	20,370	20,840
Wholesale and retail trade and catering	46,860	47,370	49,690
Banking and insurance	3,270	3,360	3,400
Real estate	1,000	1,070	1,180
Social services	9,210	9,760	10,940
Health care, sports and social welfare	4,880	4,930	4,930
Education, culture, art, radio, film and television broadcasting	15,650	15,680	15,650
Scientific research and polytechnic services	1,740	1,650	1,630
Government agencies, etc.	11,040	11,010	10,750
Others	56,430	58,520	62,450
Total	629,780	630,520	637,790

* In addition to employment statistics, sample surveys of the economically active population are conducted. On the basis of these surveys, the number of employed persons ('000 at 31 December) was: 758,280 (agriculture, etc. 288,900, industry 210,800, services 258,570) in 2009; 761,050 (agriculture, etc. 279,310, industry 218,420, services 263,320) in 2010; 764,200 (agriculture, etc. 265,940, industry 225,440, services 272,820) in 2011; 767,040 (agriculture, etc. 257,730, industry 232,410, services 276,900) in 2012.

Health and Welfare

KEY INDICATORS

Total fertility rate (children per woman, 2011)	1.6
Under-5 mortality rate (per 1,000 live births, 2011)	15
HIV/AIDS (% of persons aged 15–49, 2012)	<0.1
Physicians (per 1,000 head, 2010)	1.5
Hospital beds (per 1,000 head, 2009)	4.2
Health expenditure (2010): US $ per head (PPP)	373
Health expenditure (2010): % of GDP	5.0
Health expenditure (2010): public (% of total)	54.3
Access to water (% of persons, 2011)	92
Access to sanitation (% of persons, 2011)	65
Total carbon dioxide emissions ('000 metric tons, 2010)	8,286,892.0
Carbon dioxide emissions per head (metric tons, 2010)	6.2
Human Development Index (2012): ranking	101
Human Development Index (2012): value	0.699

For sources and definitions, see explanatory note on p. vi.

Agriculture

(FAO data are assumed to include Hong Kong, Macao and Taiwan; may include official, semi-official or estimated data)

PRINCIPAL CROPS
('000 metric tons)

	2010	2011	2012
Wheat	115,186	117,414	120,583
Rice, paddy	197,212	202,667	205,985
Barley	2,520*	1,637	1,800*
Maize	177,541	192,904	208,235
Rye†	570	680	659
Oats	525†	490†	600*
Millet	1,573	1,568	1,601†
Sorghum	2,460	2,054	2,004*
Buckwheat†	500	680	700
Triticale (wheat-rye hybrid)†	350	500	460
Potatoes	81,594	88,354	85,920*
Sweet potatoes	74,382	75,567	73,361*
Cassava (Manioc)†	4,565	4,514	4,575
Taro (Cocoyam)†	1,769	1,697	1,810
Sugar cane	111,501	115,124	124,038
Sugar beet	9,296	10,731	11,469
Beans, dry*	1,339	1,583	1,461
Broad beans, horse beans, dry*	1,400	1,550	1,400
Peas, dry*	911	1,190	1,114
Chestnuts†	1,620	1,600	1,650
Walnuts, with shell	1,284	1,656	1,700†
Soybeans (Soya beans)	15,083	14,485	12,800
Groundnuts, with shell	15,709	16,114	16,857
Coconuts	266	269	282†
Oil palm fruit†	660	650	660
Sunflower seed	2,298	2,313	2,369*
Rapeseed	13,082	13,426	14,000
Sesame seed	588	606	601*
Linseed	353	359	350*
Cabbages and other brassicas	31,189*	32,334*	33,391†
Asparagus†	7,003	7,253	7,353
Lettuce and chicory†	13,005	13,434	14,005
Spinach	18,130*	18,783*	19,513†
Tomatoes	46,876*	48,573*	50,125†
Cauliflowers and broccoli†	8,713	9,025	9,596
Pumpkins, squash and gourds†	6,732	6,965	7,063
Cucumbers and gherkins	45,711*	47,358*	48,049†
Aubergines (Eggplants)	26,766*	27,723*	28,825†
Chillies and peppers, green†	15,001	15,542	16,024
Onions and shallots, green†	901	924	965
Onions, dry†	21,748	22,065	22,667
Garlic	18,549*	19,234*	20,082†
Beans, green	15,171*	15,717*	16,212†
Peas, green	9,917*	10,274*	11,507†
Carrots and turnips	15,662*	16,220*	16,907†
Mushrooms and truffles	4,834*	5,009*	5,159†
Watermelons	68,407	69,140	70,243†
Cantaloupes and other melons	17,254	17,263	17,569†
Grapes	8,652	9,174	9,699†
Apples	33,265	35,987	37,002†
Pears	15,232	15,945	16,266†
Peaches and nectarines†	10,828	11,530	12,028
Plums and sloes†	5,665	5,874	6,023
Oranges	5,603*	6,014*	6,662†
Tangerines, mandarins, clementines and satsumas	11,133*	12,679*	13,788†
Lemons and limes	2,059*	2,319*	2,322†
Grapefruit and pomelos	2,885*	3,611*	3,878†
Guavas, mangoes and mangosteens†	4,135	4,519	4,567
Pineapples†	1,420	1,351	1,392
Persimmons†	3,046	3,290	3,386
Bananas	9,849	10,706	10,845†
Tea	1,467	1,640	1,715†
—continued			
Chillies and peppers, dry†	265	282	290
Ginger†	400	457	463
Other spices†	91	97	98
Tobacco, unmanufactured	3,006	3,159	3,202
Jute	40*	44*	45†
Natural rubber	691	751	780†

* Unofficial figure(s).
† FAO estimate(s).

Aggregate production ('000 metric tons, may include official, semi-official or estimated data): Total cereals 498,468.3 in 2010, 520,630.2 in 2011, 542,642.8 in 2012; Total vegetable fibres 6,301.8 in 2010, 6,894.4 in 2011, 7,141.7 in 2012; Total treenuts 3,120.5 in 2010, 3,526.2 in 2011, 3,625.8 in 2012; Total oilcrops (primary) 16,691.2 in 2010, 17,186.5 in 2011, 17,437.2 in 2012; Total pulses 3,890.7 in 2010, 4,610.5 in 2011, 4,260.7 in 2012; Total roots and tubers 162,328.5 in 2010, 170,149.3 in 2011, 165,683.1 in 2012; Total vegetables (incl. melons) 545,437.6 in 2010, 562,710.6 in 2011, 576,658.8 in 2012; Total fruits (excl. melons) 124,618.6 in 2010, 134,477.2 in 2011, 139,680.9 in 2012.

Source: FAO.

LIVESTOCK
('000 head at 31 December)

	2010	2011	2012*
Horses	6,787	6,773	6,802
Asses	6,484	6,397	7,000
Cattle	121,431†	114,899†	115,140
Buffaloes	23,602†	23,382†	23,254
Camels	248	256	260
Pigs	476,267	470,961	471,875
Sheep	176,900†	185,120†	187,000
Goats	195,650†	184,705†	185,000
Chickens*	5,302,720	5,330,988	5,398,000
Ducks*	796,569	818,724	824,800
Geese and guinea fowls*	327,136	328,754	331,700

* FAO estimates.
† Unofficial figure.

Source: FAO.

LIVESTOCK PRODUCTS
('000 metric tons)

	2010	2011	2012
Cattle meat	6,244*	6,182*	6,266†
Buffalo meat	310*	308*	310†
Sheep meat	2,070*	2,050*	2,080†
Goat meat	1,922*	1,890*	1,902†
Pig meat	49,581*	49,396*	50,004†
Horse meat†	178	193	193
Rabbit meat	690	731	735†
Chicken meat*	12,153	12,170	13,237
Duck meat*	2,738	2,818	2,988
Goose and guinea fowl meat*	2,434	2,440	2,665
Other meat†	717	728	732
Cows' milk	36,036	36,929	37,768
Buffaloes' milk†	3,050	3,050	3,080
Sheep's milk	1,724	1,529	1,580†
Goats' milk†	277	282	293
Hen eggs	23,990	24,232	24,832†
Other poultry eggs	4,176*	4,244	4,327†
Honey	409	446	452†
Wool, greasy	387	393	400†

* Unofficial figure(s).
† FAO estimate(s).

Source: FAO.

Forestry

ROUNDWOOD REMOVALS
('000 cubic metres, excl. bark)

	2010	2011	2012
Sawlogs, veneer logs and logs for sleepers	58,920	58,823	58,823*
Pulpwood*	46,048	46,752	46,752
Other industrial wood*	38,460	38,460	38,460
Fuel wood*	188,823	185,430	182,100
Total*	332,251	329,466	326,135

* FAO estimate(s).

Source: FAO.

Timber production (official figures, '000 cubic metres): 72,720 in 2011; 80,880 in 2012; 83,670 in 2013.

SAWNWOOD PRODUCTION
('000 cubic metres, incl. railway sleepers)

	2010	2011	2012
Coniferous (softwood)	14,911	17,918	22,318
Broadleaved (hardwood)	22,320	26,720	33,420
Total	37,231	44,638	55,738

Source: FAO.

Fishing

('000 metric tons, live weight)

	2009	2010	2011
Capture	14,919.6	15,417.0	15,772.1
Freshwater fishes	1,526.3	1,614.7	1,582.5
Aquaculture*	34,779.9	36,734.2	38,621.3
Common carp	2,462.3	2,538.5	2,718.2
Crucian carp	2,055.5	2,216.1	2,296.8
Bighead carp	2,434.6	2,550.8	2,668.3
Grass carp (White amur)	4,081.5	4,222.2	4,442.2
Silver carp	3,484.4	3,607.5	3,713.9
Pacific cupped oyster	3,503.8	3,642.8	3,756.3
Japanese carpet shell	3,192.5	3,538.9	3,613.3
Total catch*	49,699.5	52,151.2	54,393.3

* FAO estimates.

Note: Figures exclude aquatic plants ('000 metric tons, wet weight): 10,775.5 (capture 276.2, aquaculture 10,499.3) in 2009; 11,342.0 (capture 246.6, aquaculture 11,095.4) in 2010; 11,826.0 (capture 274.1, aquaculture 11,551.9) in 2011.

Source: FAO.

Mining

('000 metric tons unless otherwise indicated)

	2010	2011	2012
Coal*	3,235,000	3,520,000	3,650,000
Crude petroleum*	202,414	202,876	207,478
Natural gas (million cu m)*	94,848	102,689	107,153
Iron ore: gross weight	1,070,000	1,330,000	1,310,000
Copper ore†	1,160	1,270	1,550
Nickel ore (metric tons)†	80,000	90,000	93,300
Bauxite	44,000	45,000	47,000
Lead ore†	1,980	2,400	2,800
Zinc ore†	3,840	4,050	4,900
Tin concentrates (metric tons)†	149,000	156,000	148,000
Manganese ore†	2,600	2,800	2,900
—continued			
Tungsten concentrates (metric tons)†	59,000	61,800	64,000
Molybdenum ore (metric tons)†	96,600	103,000	105,000
Vanadium (metric tons)†	58,000	65,000	70,000
Antimony ore (metric tons)†	193,000	200,000	230,000
Cobalt ore (metric tons)†	6,380	6,800	6,800
Mercury (metric tons)†	1,600	1,500	1,350
Silver (metric tons)†	3,500	3,700	3,900
Uranium (metric tons)†‡	827	1,500	1,500
Gold (metric tons)†	345	362	403
Magnesite	14,000	19,000	16,000
Phosphate rock§	20,400	24,000	28,500
Potash‖	3,600	3,800	4,100
Native sulphur	1,100	1,100	1,200
Fluorspar	4,600	4,200	4,600
Barite (Barytes)	4,000	4,100	4,200
Salt (unrefined)*	70,378	67,422	69,118
Gypsum (crude)	4,700	4,800	4,900
Graphite (natural)	700	800	820
Asbestos	400	440	420
Talc and related materials	2,000	2,200	2,200

* Official figures. Figures for coal include brown coal and waste. Figures for petroleum include oil from shale and coal. Figures for natural gas refer to gross volume of output.

† Figures refer to the metal content of ores, concentrates or (in the case of vanadium) slag.

‡ Data are estimates from the World Nuclear Association (London, United Kingdom).

§ Figures refer to phosphorous oxide (P_2O_5) content.

‖ Potassium oxide (K_2O) content of potash salts mined.

2013 ('000 metric tons unless otherwise indicated): Coal 3,680,000; Crude petroleum 209,000; Natural gas (million cu m) 117,050.

Source: mainly US Geological Survey.

Industry

SELECTED PRODUCTS

Unofficial Figures
('000 metric tons unless otherwise indicated)*

	2008	2009	2010
Plywood ('000 cu m)†‡	35,578	44,681	44,681§
Mechanical wood pulp†‡§	865	865	865
Chemical and semi-chemical wood pulp†‡§	6,223	5,015	6,585
Other fibre pulp†‡	12,970	11,748	12,970
Sulphur§‖¶(a)	3,350	4,000	4,100
Sulphur§‖¶(b)	4,300	4,370	4,400
Kerosene	11,589	14,803	19,217
Residual fuel oil	17,374	13,534	15,074
Paraffin wax	2,990	3,389	1,601
Petroleum coke	10,108	11,458	16,245
Petroleum bitumen (asphalt)	10,303	11,679	19,639
Liquefied petroleum gas	19,148	18,317	20,455
Refined aluminium (primary and secondary)‖	15,900	16,000	20,200
Refined copper (primary and secondary)‖	3,900	4,150	4,650

—continued	2008	2009	2010
Refined lead (primary and secondary)‖	3,200	3,780	4,160
Tin (unwrought, Sn content)‖	110	97	115
Refined zinc (primary and secondary)‖	4,040	4,290	5,210

* Figures include Hong Kong and Macao SARs, but exclude Taiwan, except where otherwise specified.

† Data from FAO.

‡ Including Taiwan.

§ Provisional or estimated figure(s).

‖ Data from the US Geological Survey.

¶ Figures refer to: (a) sulphur recovered as a by-product in the purification of coal-gas, in petroleum refineries, gas plants and from copper, lead and zinc sulphide ores; and (b) the sulphur content of iron and copper pyrites, including pyrite concentrates obtained from copper, lead and zinc ores.

Lubricating oils: 5,326,000 metric tons in 2004.

Source: mainly UN Industrial Commodity Statistics Database.

2011 ('000 metric tons unless otherwise indicated): Plywood ('000 cu m) 44,681 (estimate); Mechanical wood pulp 865 (estimate); Chemical and semi-chemical wood pulp 7,837 (estimate); Other fibre pulp 12,400; Refined aluminium (primary and secondary) 22,200; Refined copper (primary and secondary) 5,240; Refined lead (primary and secondary) 4,600; Tin (unwrought, Sn content) 120; Refined zinc (primary and secondary) 5,210 (Sources: FAO; US Geological Survey).

2012 ('000 metric tons unless otherwise indicated): Plywood ('000 cu m) 44,681 (estimate); Mechanical wood pulp 865 (estimate); Chemical and semi-chemical wood pulp 7,609 (estimate); Other fibre pulp 10,738; Refined aluminium (primary and secondary) 24,500; Refined copper (primary and secondary) 5,880; Refined lead (primary and secondary) 4,700; Tin (unwrought, Sn content) 110; Refined zinc (primary and secondary) 4,890 (Sources: FAO; US Geological Survey).

Official Figures

('000 metric tons unless otherwise indicated)

	2010	2011	2012
Edible vegetable oils	38,785.4	43,318.0	51,730.0
Refined sugar	11,175.9	11,874.3	14,094.7
Beer (million litres)	44,901.6	48,345.0	47,785.8
Cigarettes ('000 million)	2,375.3	2,447.4	2,516.1
Cotton yarn (pure and mixed)	27,170	27,179	29,840
Woven cotton fabrics (pure and mixed—million metres)	80,000	81,414	84,894
Chemical fibres	30,900.0	33,900.7	38,373.7
Paper and paperboard	98,326.3	110,108.9	109,565.4
Rubber tyres ('000)	776,118.3	835,662.2	893,704.9
Sulphuric acid	70,904.7	74,827.0	78,766.3
Caustic soda (Sodium hydroxide)	22,283.9	24,735.2	26,968.2
Soda ash (Sodium carbonate)	20,348.2	22,940.3	23,959.3
Nitrogenous fertilizers (a)*	44,586.7	45,009.7	48,655.8
Phosphate fertilizers (b)*	15,329.1	15,612.2	15,644.1
Potash fertilizers (c)*	3,462.8	3,572.0	4,021.1
Synthetic rubber	3,195.2	3,671.3	3,973.9
Plastics	44,325.9	49,923.1	53,309.2
Motor spirit (gasoline)	76,760.4	81,580.6	89,760.7
Distillate fuel oil (diesel oil)	158,881.5	166,763.1	170,638.1
Coke	388,640.3	432,707.8	447,788.7
Cement	1,881,912	2,099,259	2,209,840
Pig-iron	597,333.4	640,508.8	663,544.0
Crude steel	637,229.9	685,283.1	723,882.2
Internal combustion engines ('000 kw)	1,385,920.3	1,370,994.3	1,361,114.8
Tractors—over 20 horse-power (number)	3,368,000	4,019,000	4,633,000
Railway freight wagons (number)	48,100	66,900	59,200
Road motor vehicles ('000)	18,265.3	18,416.4	19,276.2
Bicycles ('000)	68,194.8	71,691.1	76,128.5
Electric fans ('000)	180,679.2	188,458.9	165,935.9

—continued	2010	2011	2012
Mobile telephones ('000 units)	998,273.6	1,132,577.1	1,181,545.7
Microcomputers ('000)	245,845	320,369	354,110
Integrated circuits (million)	65,250	71,952	82,328
Colour television receivers ('000)	118,300	122,313	128,235
Cameras ('000)	93,277.0	82,413.4	88,017.1
Electric energy (million kWh)	420,716	471,302	498,755

* Production in terms of: (a) nitrogen; (b) phosphorous oxide; or (c) potassium oxide.

2013 ('000 metric tons unless otherwise indicated): Cigarettes ('000 million) 2,560.4; Cotton yarn (pure and mixed) 32,000; Crude steel 779,041.0; Sulphuric acid 81,226.0; Caustic soda (Sodium hydroxide) 28,590.0; Soda ash (Sodium carbonate) 24,349.0; Colour television receivers ('000) 127,761.0; Chemical fibres 41,219.0; Chemical fertilizers 70,370.0; Cement 2,420,000; Road motor vehicles ('000) 12,104.0; Integrated circuits (million) 86,650.0; Microcomputers ('000) 336,610.0; Tractors—over 20 horse-power (number) 5,870,000; Electric energy (million kWh) 539,759.

Finance

CURRENCY AND EXCHANGE RATES

Monetary Units

100 fen = 10 jiao = 1 yuan; the currency is officially known as the renminbi (people's currency).

Sterling, Dollar and Euro Equivalents (31 December 2013)

£1 sterling = 10.049 yuan;
US $1 = 6.102 yuan;
€1 = 8.416 yuan;
100 yuan = £9.95 = $16.39 = €11.88.

Average Exchange Rate (yuan per US $)

2011 6.4615
2012 6.3123
2013 6.1958

Note: Since 1994 the official rate has usually been based on the prevailing rate in the interbank market for foreign exchange. Between 1997 and 2005 the currency was pegged to the US dollar at a rate of 8.27 yuan = 1 US dollar, but in recent years the exchange rate has been allowed to float within a managed band (2.0% of the prevailing interbank rate in 2014).

STATE BUDGET

(million yuan)*

Revenue	2010	2011	2012†
Taxes	7,321,079	8,973,839	10,061,428
Personal income tax	483,727	605,411	582,028
Company income tax	1,284,354	1,676,964	1,965,453
Tariffs	202,783	255,912	278,393
Business tax	1,115,791	1,367,900	1,574,764
Consumption tax	607,155	693,621	787,558
Value-added tax	2,109,348	2,426,663	2,641,551
Non-tax revenue	989,072	1,413,604	1,663,924
Total	8,310,151	10,387,443	11,725,352
Central government	4,248,847	5,132,732	5,617,523
Local authorities	4,061,304	5,254,711	6,107,829

Expenditure	2010	2011	2012†
General public services	933,716	1,098,778	1,270,046
Foreign affairs	26,922	30,958	33,383
External assistance	13,614	15,909	—
National defence	533,337	602,791	669,192
Public security	551,770	630,427	711,160
Armed police	93,384	108,202	—
Education	1,255,002	1,649,733	2,124,210
Science and technology	325,018	382,802	445,263
Culture, sport and media	154,270	189,336	226,835
Social safety net and employment effort	913,062	1,110,940	1,258,552
Medical and health care	480,418	642,951	724,511
Environment protection	244,198	264,098	296,346
Urban and rural community affairs	598,738	762,055	907,912
Agriculture, forestry and water conservancy	812,958	993,755	1,197,388
Transportation	548,847	749,780	819,616
Purchase of vehicles	154,182	231,460	—

Expenditure—*continued*	2010	2011	2012†
Mining and quarrying, electricity and information technology	348,503	401,138	440,768
Commerce and services	141,314	142,172	137,180
Financial supervision	63,704	64,928	45,928
Post-earthquake recovery and reconstruction	113,254	17,445	10,381
Land and weather department	133,039	152,135	166,567
Housing security	237,688	382,069	447,962
Management of grain and oil reserves	117,196	126,957	137,629
Interest payments on domestic and foreign debt	184,424	238,408	263,574
Other expenditure	270,038	291,124	260,894
Total	8,987,416	10,924,779	12,595,297
Central government	1,598,973	1,651,411	1,876,463
Local authorities	7,388,443	9,273,368	10,718,834

* The data exclude extrabudgetary transactions, totalling (in million yuan): *Revenue:* 579,442 in 2010; n.a. in 2011–12. *Expenditure:* 575,469 in 2010; n.a. in 2011–12.

† Preliminary.

Note: Omissions in data for expenditure reflect changes in classification of expenditure type during 2010–12.

2012 (incl. central government stabilization fund transfers, million yuan, actual figures): *Revenue:* 11,990,975 (Central government 5,883,242, Local government 6,107,733); *Expenditure:* 12,790,975 (Central government 6,433,242, Local government 6,357,733).

2013 (incl. central government stabilization fund transfers, '000 million yuan, budget proposals): *Revenue:* 12,763 (Central government 6,106, Local government 6,657); *Expenditure:* 13,825 (Central government 6,956, Local government 6,869).

INTERNATIONAL RESERVES

(US $ million at 31 December)

	2010	2011	2012
Gold (national valuation)	9,815	9,815	9,815
IMF special drawing rights	12,344	11,856	11,356
Reserve position in IMF	6,397	9,785	8,175
Foreign exchange*	2,847,338	3,181,148	3,311,589
Total*	2,875,894	3,212,604	3,340,935

* Excluding the Bank of China's holdings of foreign exchange.

Source: IMF, *International Financial Statistics*.

MONEY SUPPLY

(million yuan at 31 December)*

	2010	2011	2012
Currency outside banking institutions	4,462,820	5,074,850	5,465,980
Demand deposits at banking institutions	22,199,340	23,909,920	25,400,450
Total money	26,662,160	28,984,770	30,866,430

* Figures are rounded to the nearest 10 million yuan.

Source: IMF, *International Financial Statistics*.

COST OF LIVING

(General Consumer Price Index; base: previous year = 100)

	2011	2012	2013
Food (incl. non-alcoholic beverages)	111.8	104.8	104.7
Alcoholic beverages and tobacco	102.8	102.9	100.3
Clothing	102.1	103.1	102.3
Housing*	105.3	102.1	102.8
Household goods and furnishings	102.4	101.9	101.5
Health	103.4	102.0	101.3
Transport and communication	100.5	99.9	99.6
Education, recreation and culture	100.4	100.5	101.8
All items	105.4	102.6	102.6

* Including water, electricity and fuels.

NATIONAL ACCOUNTS

('000 million yuan at current prices)

Expenditure on the Gross Domestic Product

	2010	2011	2012
Government final consumption expenditure	5,335.6	6,315.5	7,140.9
Private final consumption expenditure	14,075.9	16,895.7	19,042.4
Increase in stocks	998.9	1,266.2	1,101.6
Gross fixed capital formation	18,361.5	21,568.2	24,175.7
Total domestic expenditure	38,771.9	46,045.6	51,460.6
Exports of goods and services *Less* Imports of goods and services	1,509.8	1,216.3	1,463.2
Sub-total	40,281.7	47,261.9	52,923.8
Statistical discrepancy*	–130.4	48.5	–976.9
GDP in purchasers' values	40,151.3	47,310.4	51,947.0

* Referring to the difference between the sum of the expenditure components and official estimates of GDP, compiled from the production approach.

Gross Domestic Product by Economic Activity

	2011	2012	2013
Agriculture, forestry and fishing	4,748.6	5,237.4	5,695.7
Construction	3,194.3	3,549.1	3,899.5
Other industry*	18,847.0	19,967.1	21,068.9
Transport, storage and communications	2,243.3	2,466.0	2,728.3
Wholesale and retail trade	4,344.5	4,939.4	5,567.2
Hotels and restaurants	917.3	1,046.4	1,149.4
Financial intermediation	2,495.8	2,872.3	3,353.5
Real estate	2,678.4	2,936.0	3,329.5
Other services	7,841.2	8,933.4	10,092.5
Total	47,310.4	51,947.0	56,884.5

* Includes mining, manufacturing, electricity, gas and water.

BALANCE OF PAYMENTS

(US $ million)

	2010	2011	2012
Exports of goods	1,476,226	1,805,900	1,970,945
Imports of goods	–1,230,687	–1,569,850	–1,653,347
Balance on goods	245,539	236,050	317,598
Exports of services	171,490	184,763	196,302
Imports of services	–194,005	–238,909	–282,055
Balance on goods and services	223,024	181,904	231,845
Primary income received	142,424	144,268	160,441
Primary income paid	–168,324	–214,585	–202,581
Balance on goods, services and primary income	197,125	111,586	189,705
Secondary income received	49,521	55,570	51,167
Secondary income paid	–8,835	–31,060	–47,733
Current balance	237,810	136,097	193,139
Capital account (net)	4,630	5,446	4,272
Direct investment assets	–87,237	–99,940	–116,762
Direct investment from liabilities	272,987	331,592	307,887
Portfolio investment assets	–7,643	6,248	–6,391
Portfolio investment liabilities	31,681	13,391	54,170
Other investment assets	–116,262	–183,604	–231,600
Other investment liabilities	188,708	192,338	–28,388
Net errors and omissions	–53,016	–13,768	–79,773
Reserves and related items	471,659	387,799	96,555

Source: IMF, *International Financial Statistics*.

External Trade

PRINCIPAL COMMODITIES
(distribution by HS, US $ million)

Imports c.i.f.	2011	2012	2013
Vegetables and vegetable products	40,199.6	50,967.5	55,946.2
Mineral products	432,216.3	453,141.4	469,133.9
Ores, slag and ash	150,655.6	133,728.0	148,447.3
Iron ores and concentrates	112,408.9	95,619.2	105,114.6
Mineral fuels, oils, distillation products, etc.	275,766.3	313,067.0	314,700.2
Crude petroleum oils	196,770.6	220,793.8	219,634.1
Chemicals and related products	117,920.1	118,062.5	125,495.3
Organic chemicals	63,132.0	60,864.3	65,953.2
Plastics and articles thereof; rubber and articles thereof	93,261.6	90,076.3	92,304.3
Plastics and articles thereof	70,198.7	69,424.5	72,409.5
Iron and steel, other base metals and articles of base metals	118,847.7	111,242.8	104,322.2
Copper and articles thereof	54,251.5	54,516.3	50,380.7
Machinery and mechanical appliances	550,268.0	563,481.0	609,987.5
Machinery, boilers, etc.	199,313.8	181,960.0	170,669.1
Electrical, electronic equipment	350,954.3	381,521.0	439,318.4
Electronic integrated circuits, etc.	171,142.2	192,967.2	232,007.8
Vehicles, aircraft, vessels and other transport equipment	83,004.7	91,174.9	100,363.8
Vehicles other than railway, tramway	65,438.6	70,596.7	74,145.8
Optical instruments and appliances	102,676.3	110,597.7	111,933.7
Optical, photo, technical, medical, etc. apparatus	99,140.7	106,145.6	107,738.3
Liquid crystal devices, lasers and other optical instruments	53,140.4	55,867.7	55,521.1
Total (incl. others)	1,743,394.9	1,818,199.2	1,949,934.7

Exports f.o.b.	2011	2012	2013
Chemicals and related products	97,087.1	94,447.0	97,760.0
Plastics and articles thereof; rubber and articles thereof	66,345.8	77,345.7	84,912.3
Textiles and textile articles	240,539.6	246,058.2	274,047.8
Articles of apparel, accessories, knitted or crocheted	80,164.6	87,045.2	96,810.4
Articles of apparel, accessories, not knitted or crocheted	63,073.9	61,224.4	68,271.9
Footwear, headgear, umbrellas, walking sticks, etc.	52,464.5	58,811.9	64,083.9
Iron and steel, other base metals and articles of base metals	144,923.7	149,073.4	156,048.1
Machinery and mechanical appliances	799,520.6	863,221.9	945,014.1
Machinery, boilers, etc.	353,763.9	375,899.5	383,310.5
Automatic data processing machines, optical readers, etc.	152,029.0	163,436.8	161,707.8
Electrical, electronic equipment	445,756.7	487,322.5	561,703.6
Electric appliances for line telephony, etc.	133,413.9	153,185.3	174,974.9
Electronic integrated circuits, etc.	32,900.3	53,745.3	88,039.4

Exports f.o.b.—*continued*	2011	2012	2013
Vehicles, aircraft, vessels and other transport equipment	109,110.8	108,381.5	100,561.2
Optical instruments and appliances	65,996.5	79,396.9	81,927.3
Optical, photo, technical, medical, etc. apparatus	60,685.0	72,631.4	74,689.7
Miscellaneous manufactured articles	103,789.6	125,685.8	135,409.3
Furniture, lighting, signs, prefabricated buildings	59,336.4	77,886.2	86,435.7
Total (incl. others)	1,898,388.4	2,048,782.2	2,210,522.7

Source: Trade Map-Trade Competitiveness Map, International Trade Centre, www.intracen.org/marketanalysis.

PRINCIPAL TRADING PARTNERS
(US $ million)*

Imports c.i.f.	2011	2012	2013
Angola	24,922.2	33,561.9	31,955.2
Australia	82,667.5	84,568.2	98,593.1
Brazil	52,386.8	52,281.1	53,747.5
Canada	22,167.1	23,209.1	25,219.2
Chile	20,578.3	20,631.6	20,801.4
France (incl. Monaco)	22,078.8	24,124.5	23,116.4
Germany	92,726.2	91,933.1	94,242.3
India	23,372.3	18,797.2	17,043.7
Indonesia	31,337.1	31,936.0	31,486.2
Iran	30,333.0	24,869.4	25,404.9
Italy	17,578.8	16,065.7	17,580.5
Japan	194,567.9	177,832.3	162,378.7
Korea, Republic	162,716.8	168,728.4	183,024.0
Malaysia	62,136.6	58,304.9	60,071.1
Oman	14,876.7	16,975.0	21,003.8
Philippines	17,992.3	19,643.2	18,236.8
Russia	40,362.6	44,138.3	39,617.3
Saudi Arabia	49,467.5	54,861.1	53,488.6
Singapore	28,139.6	28,529.6	29,966.6
South Africa	32,095.2	44,653.7	48,352.5
Switzerland	27,287.2	22,884.2	56,127.6
Taiwan	124,910.6	132,199.3	156,586.9
Thailand	39,039.8	38,551.2	38,521.9
USA	123,124.0	133,765.8	153,606.9
Total (incl. others)	1,743,394.9	1,818,199.2	1,949,934.7

Exports f.o.b.	2011	2012	2013
Australia	33,910.0	37,734.9	37,563.5
Brazil	31,836.7	33,413.6	36,192.0
Canada	25,266.6	28,125.2	29,224.0
France (incl. Monaco)	30,245.9	27,196.0	26,948.5
Germany	76,400.0	69,212.7	67,365.0
Hong Kong†	267,983.7	323,445.3	384,854.0
India	50,536.4	47,677.5	48,449.3
Indonesia	29,220.9	34,285.2	36,948.2
Italy	33,694.6	25,657.5	25,757.4
Japan	148,268.7	151,626.6	150,388.8
Korea, Republic	82,920.3	87,673.8	91,196.7
Malaysia	27,886.0	36,525.7	45,931.1
Mexico	23,975.9	27,518.0	28,971.2
Netherlands	59,499.7	58,898.8	60,328.8
Russia	38,903.0	44,056.6	49,601.2
Singapore	35,570.1	40,750.2	45,879.9
Spain	19,723.6	18,240.2	18,938.7
Taiwan	35,109.1	36,777.4	40,665.0
Thailand	25,694.6	31,196.8	32,739.4
United Arab Emirates	26,812.8	29,568.3	33,403.4
United Kingdom	44,122.1	46,296.7	50,957.4
USA	325,011.0	352,438.2	369,111.2
Viet Nam	29,091.6	34,212.6	48,594.3
Total (incl. others)	1,898,388.4	2,048,782.2	2,210,522.7

* Imports by country of origin; exports by country of consumption.
† The majority of China's exports to Hong Kong are re-exported.

Source: Trade Map-Trade Competitiveness Map, International Trade Centre, www.intracen.org/marketanalysis.

Transport

SUMMARY

	2011	2012	2013
Freight (million ton-km):			
railways	2,946,579	2,918,710	2,917,390
roads	5,137,474	5,999,200	6,711,450
waterways	7,542,384	8,065,450	8,652,060
Passenger-km (million):			
railways	961,229	981,230	1,059,560
roads	1,676,024	1,846,840	1,970,560
waterways	7,453	7,740	7,630

ROAD TRAFFIC
('000 motor vehicles in use)*

	2011	2012	2013
Passenger cars and buses	74,783.7	89,430.1	108,920.0
Goods vehicles	17,879.9	18,947.5	n.a.
Total (incl. others)	93,563.2	109,330.9	137,410.0

* Excluding military vehicles.

SHIPPING

Flag Registered Fleet
(at 31 December)

	2011	2012	2013
Number of vessels	3,661	3,670	3,864
Total displacement ('000 grt)	40,958.9	42,423.5	46,400.3

Source: Lloyd's List Intelligence (www.lloydslistintelligence.com).

Sea-borne Shipping
(freight traffic, '000 metric tons)

	2010	2011	2012
Goods loaded and unloaded	5,483,580	6,162,920	6,652,450

CIVIL AVIATION

	2011	2012	2013
Passenger traffic (million)	293.2	320.0	350.0
Passenger-km (million)	453,696.3	501,070.0	565,850.0
Freight traffic ('000 metric tons)	5,574.8	5,416.0	5,576.0
Freight ton-km (million)	17,391.3	16,220.0	16,860.0
Total ton-km (million)	57,744.3	n.a.	n.a.

Tourism

FOREIGN VISITORS
(arrivals, '000)

Country of origin	2010	2011	2012
Australia	661.3	726.2	774.3
Canada	685.3	748.0	708.3
Germany	608.6	637.0	659.6
India	549.3	606.5	610.2
Indonesia	573.4	608.7	622.0
Japan	3,731.2	3,658.2	3,518.2
Korea, Republic	4,076.4	4,185.4	4,069.9
Malaysia	1,245.2	1,245.1	1,235.5
Mongolia	794.4	994.2	1,010.5
Philippines	828.3	894.3	962.0
Russia	2,370.3	2,536.3	2,426.1
Singapore	1,003.7	1,063.0	1,027.7
Thailand	635.5	608.0	647.6
United Kingdom	575.0	595.7	618.4
USA	2,009.6	2,116.1	2,118.1
Total (incl. others)*	26,126.9	27,112.0	27,191.5

* Excluding visitors from Hong Kong and Macao ('000): 102,498.8 in 2010; 103,048.5 in 2011; 99,873.5 in 2012, and from Taiwan ('000): 5,140.6 in 2010; 5,263.0 in 2011; 5,340.2 in 2012.

Total foreign visitors ('000): 26,290.0 in 2013 (excluding 102,790.0 visitors from Hong Kong, Macao and Taiwan).

Tourism receipts (US $ million): 48,464 in 2011; 50,000 in 2012; 51,700 in 2013.

Communications Media

	2011	2012	2013
Telephones ('000 main lines in use)	285,098	278,153	266,990
Mobile cellular telephones ('000 subscribers)	986,253	1,112,155	1,229,110
Internet subscribers ('000)	513,100	564,000	618,000
Broadband subscribers ('000)	156,487	530,000	500,000
Book production:			
titles	369,523	414,005	n.a.
copies (million)	7,700	8,100	8,300
Newspaper production:			
titles	1,928	1,918	n.a.
copies (million)	46,740	48,230	47,800
Magazine production:			
titles	9,849	9,867	n.a.
copies (million)	3,385	3,400	3,400

Education

(2013 unless otherwise indicated)

	Institutions*	Full-time teachers ('000)*	Students ('000)
Kindergartens	181,251	1,479	38,947
Primary schools	255,400	5,616	93,605
Secondary schools	81,662	5,994	88,362
Junior secondary schools	54,794	3,512	44,401
Senior secondary schools	14,205	1,601	24,359
Vocational secondary schools	12,663	881	19,602
Special schools	1,853	44	368
Higher education	2,442	1,440	24,681

* Data for 2012.

Pupil-teacher ratio (primary education, UNESCO estimate): 16.8 in 2010/11 (Source: UNESCO Institute for Statistics).

Adult literacy rate (UN estimate): 95.1% (males 97.5%; females 92.7%) in 2010 (Source: UNESCO Institute for Statistics).

Directory

The Government

HEAD OF STATE

President: XI JINPING (elected by the 12th National People's Congress on 14 March 2013).

Vice-President: LI YUANCHAO.

STATE COUNCIL

(April 2014)

The Government is formed by the Chinese Communist Party.

Premier: LI KEQIANG.

Vice-Premiers: ZHANG GAOLI, LIU YANDONG, WANG YANG, MA KAI.

State Councillors: YANG JING, CHANG WANQUAN, YANG JIECHI, GUO SHENGKUN, WANG YONG.

Secretary-General: YANG JING.

Minister of Foreign Affairs: WANG YI.

Minister of National Defence: CHANG WANGQUAN.

Minister of National Development and Reform Commission: XU SHAOSHI.

Minister of Education: YUAN GUIREN.

Minister of Science and Technology: WAN GANG.

Minister of Industry and Information Technology: MIAO WEI.

Minister of State Ethnic Affairs Commission: WANG ZHENGWEI.

Minister of Public Security: GUO SHENGKUN.

Minister of State Security: GENG HUICHANG.

Minister of Supervision: HUANG SHUXIAN.

Minister of Civil Affairs: LI LIGUO.

Minister of Justice: WU AIYING.

Minister of Finance: LOU JIWEI.

Minister of Human Resources and Social Security: YIN WEIMIN.

Minister of Land and Resources: JIANG DAMING.

Minister of Environmental Protection: ZHOU SHENGXIAN.

Minister of Housing and Urban-Rural Construction: JIANG WEIXIN.

Minister of Transport: YANG CHUANTANG.

Minister of Water Resources: CHEN LEI.

Minister of Agriculture: HAN CHANGFU.

Minister of Commerce: GAO HUCHENG.

Minister of Culture: CAI WU.

Minister of National Health and Family Planning Commission: LI BIN.

Governor of the People's Bank of China: ZHOU XIAOCHUAN.

Auditor-General of the National Audit Office: LIU JIAYI.

MINISTRIES

Ministry of Agriculture: 11 Nongzhanguan Nanli, Chaoyang Qu, Beijing 100125; tel. (10) 59193366; fax (10) 59192468; e-mail webmaster@agri.gov.cn; internet www.agri.gov.cn.

Ministry of Civil Affairs: 147 Beiheyan Dajie, Dongcheng Qu, Beijing 100721; tel. (10) 58123114; internet www.mca.gov.cn.

Ministry of Commerce: 2 Dongchangan Dajie, Dongcheng Qu, Beijing 100731; tel. (10) 65121919; fax (10) 65677512; e-mail webmaster@mofcom.gov.cn; internet www.mofcom.gov.cn.

Ministry of Culture: 10 Chaoyang Men Bei Dajie, Chaoyang Qu, Beijing 100020; tel. (10) 59881114; e-mail webmaster@ccic.gov.cn; internet www.ccnt.gov.cn.

Ministry of Education: 37 Damucang Hutong, Xidan, Beijing 100816; tel. (10) 66096114; e-mail english@moe.edu.cn; internet www.moe.edu.cn.

Ministry of Environmental Protection: 115 Xizhimennei Nan Xiao Jie, Xicheng Qu, Beijing 100035; tel. (10) 66556006; fax (10) 66556010; e-mail mailbox@mep.gov.cn; internet www.mep.gov.cn.

Ministry of Finance: 3 Nansanxiang, Sanlihe, Xicheng Qu, Beijing 100820; tel. (10) 68551114; e-mail webmaster@mof.gov.cn; internet www.mof.gov.cn.

Ministry of Foreign Affairs: 2 Chaoyang Men Nan Dajie, Chaoyang Qu, Beijing 100701; tel. (10) 65961114; e-mail webmaster@mfa.gov.cn; internet www.fmprc.gov.cn.

Ministry of Housing and Urban-Rural Construction: 9 Sanlihe Lu, Haidian Qu, Beijing 100835; tel. (10) 58933575; e-mail cin@mail.cin.gov.cn; internet www.mohurd.gov.cn.

Ministry of Human Resources and Social Security: 12 Hepinglizhong Jie, Dongcheng Qu, Beijing 100716; tel. (10) 84201114; fax (10) 64218350; internet www.mohrss.gov.cn.

Ministry of Industry and Information Technology: 13 Xichangan Dajie, Beijing 100804; tel. (10) 68208025; e-mail mail@miit.gov.cn; internet www.miit.gov.cn.

Ministry of Justice: 10 Chaoyangmen, Nan Dajie, Chaoyang Qu, Beijing 100020; tel. (10) 84772882; fax (10) 84772883; e-mail pfmaster@legalinfo.gov.cn; internet www.moj.gov.cn.

Ministry of Land and Resources: 64 Funei Dajie, Xisi, Beijing 100812; tel. (10) 66558407; fax (10) 66127247; e-mail mhwz@mail.mlr.gov.cn; internet www.mlr.gov.cn.

Ministry of National Defence: 20 Jingshanqian Jie, Beijing 100009; tel. (10) 66730000; fax (10) 65962146; e-mail chinamod@chinamil.com.cn; internet www.mod.gov.cn.

Ministry of Public Security: 14 Dongchangan Dajie, Dongcheng Qu, Beijing 100741; tel. (10) 66262114; e-mail gabzfwz@mps.gov.cn; internet www.mps.gov.cn.

Ministry of Science and Technology: 15B Fuxing Lu, Haidian Qu, Beijing 100862; tel. (10) 58881888; e-mail officemail@mail.most.gov.cn; internet www.most.gov.cn.

Ministry of State Security: 14 Dongchangan Dajie, Dongcheng Qu, Beijing 100741; tel. (10) 65244702.

Ministry of Supervision: 2 Guanganmen Nan Jie, Xuanwu Qu, Beijing 100053; tel. (10) 59595320; e-mail jcbfwxx@mos.gov.cn; internet www.mos.gov.cn.

Ministry of Transport: 11 Jianguomennei Dajie, Beijing 100736; tel. (10) 65292327; fax (10) 65292345; e-mail jtbweb@moc.gov.cn; internet www.mot.gov.cn.

Ministry of Water Resources: 2 Baiguang Lu, Xiang 2, Xuanwu Qu, Beijing 100053; tel. (10) 63202114; e-mail webmaster@mwr.gov.cn; internet www.mwr.gov.cn.

STATE COMMISSIONS

National Development and Reform Commission (NDRC): 38 Yuetannan Jie, Xicheng Qu, Beijing 100824; tel. (10) 68504409; fax (10) 68512929; e-mail ndrc@ndrc.gov.cn; internet www.ndrc.gov.cn.

National Health and Family Planning Commission: 14 Zhichun Lu, Haidian Qu, Beijing 100088; tel. (10) 62046622; fax (10) 62051865; e-mail sfpcdfa@public.bta.net.cn; internet www.npfpc.gov.cn.

State Ethnic Affairs Commission: 252 Taipingqiao Dajie, Xicheng Qu, Beijing 100800; tel. and fax (10) 66080952; fax (10) 66057719; e-mail webmaster@seac.gov.cn; internet www.seac.gov.cn.

People's Governments

PROVINCES

Governors: WANG XUEJUN (Anhui), SHU SHULIN (Fujian), LIU WEIPING (Gansu), ZHU XIAODAN (Guangdong), CHEN MINER (Guizhou), JIANG DINGZHI (Hainan), ZHANG QINGWEI (Hebei), LU HAO (Heilongjiang), XIE FUZHAN (Henan), WANG GUOSHENG (Hubei), DU JIAHAO (Hunan), LI XUEYONG (Jiangsu), LU XINSHE (Jiangxi), BAYANQOLU (Jilin), CHEN ZHENGGAO (Liaoning), HAO PENG (Qinghai), LOU QINJIAN (Shaanxi), GUO SHUQING (Shandong), LI XIAOPENG (Shanxi), WEI HONG (Sichuan), LI JIHENG (Yunnan), LI QIANG (Zhejiang).

SPECIAL MUNICIPALITIES

Mayors: WANG ANSHUN (Beijing), HUANG QIFAN (Chongqing), YANG XIONG (Shanghai), HUANG XINGGUO (Tianjin).

AUTONOMOUS REGIONS

Chairmen: CHEN WU (Guangxi Zhuang), BAGATUR (Inner Mongolia—Nei Monggol), LIU HUI (Ningxia Hui), LOSANG GYALTSEN (Tibet—Xizang), NUR BEKRI (Xinjiang Uygur).

Legislature

NATIONAL PEOPLE'S CONGRESS

(Quanguo Renmin Daibiao Dahui)

The National People's Congress (NPC) is the highest organ of state power, and is indirectly elected for a five-year term. The first plenary session of the 12th NPC was convened in Beijing in March 2013, and was attended by nearly 3,000 deputies. The first session of the 12th National Committee of the Chinese People's Political Consultative Conference (CPPCC, www.cppcc.gov.cn, Chair. YU ZHENGSHENG), a revolutionary united front organization led by the Communist Party, took place simultaneously. The CPPCC holds discussions and consultations on the important affairs in the nation's political life. Members of the CPPCC National Committee or of its Standing Committee may be invited to attend the NPC or its Standing Committee as observers.

Standing Committee

In March 2013 161 members were elected to the Standing Committee, in addition to the following:

Chairman: ZHANG DEJIANG.

Vice-Chairmen: LI JIANGUO, WANG SHENGJUN, CHEN CHANGZHI, YAN JUNQI, WANG CHEN, SHEN YUEYUE, JI BINGXUAN, ZHANG PING, QIANGBA PUNCOG, ARKEN IMIRBAKI, WAN EXIANG, ZHANG BAOWEN, CHEN ZHU.

Secretary-General: WANG CHEN.

Political Organizations

COMMUNIST PARTY

Zhongguo Gongchan Dang (Chinese Communist Party—CCP): Zhongnanhai, Beijing; internet cpc.people.com.cn; f. 1921; 80.3m. mems (Dec. 2010); at the 18th Nat. Congress of the CCP in Nov. 2012, a new Cen. Cttee of 205 full mems and 171 alternate mems was elected; at its first plenary session the 18th Cen. Cttee elected a new Political Bureau.

Eighteenth Central Committee

General Secretary: XI JINPING.

Political Bureau (Politburo)

Members of the Standing Committee: XI JINPING, LI KEQIANG, ZHANG DEJIANG, YU ZHENGSHENG, LIU YUNSHAN, WANG QISHAN, ZHANG GAOLI.

Other Full Members: MA KAI, WANG HUNING, LIU YANDONG, LIU QIBAO, Gen. XU QILIANG, SUN CHUNLAN, SUN ZHENGCAI, LI JIANGUO, LI YUANCHAO, WANG YANG, ZHANG CHUNXIAN, Gen. FAN CHANLONG, MENG JIANZHU, ZHAO LEJI, HU CHUNHUA, LI ZHANSHU, GUO JINLONG, HAN ZHEN, DU QINGLIN, ZHAO HONGZHU, YANG JING.

Secretariat: LIU YUNSHAN, LIU QIBAO, ZHAO LEJI, LI ZHANSHU, DU QINGLIN, ZHAO HONGZHU, YANG JING.

OTHER POLITICAL ORGANIZATIONS

China Association for Promoting Democracy: Bldg 7, Xiao Yun Li, Xiao Yun Lu, Chao Yang Qu, Beijing 100125; tel. (10) 64033452; e-mail webmaster@mj.org.cn; internet www.mj.org.cn; f. 1945; 128,000 mems, drawn mainly from literary, cultural and educational circles; 45-mem. Cen. Cttee; Chair. of Cen. Cttee YAN JUNQI.

China Democratic League: 1 Beixing Dongchang Hutong, Dongcheng Qu, Beijing 100006; tel. (10) 65232757; fax (10) 65232852; e-mail webmaster@mmzy.org.cn; internet www.dem-league.org.cn; f. 1941; formed from reorganization of League of Democratic Parties and Organizations of China; 230,000 mems, mainly intellectuals active in education, science and culture; Chair. ZHANG BAOWEN.

China National Democratic Construction Association: 208 Jixiangli, Chaowai Lu, Chaoyang Qu, Beijing 100020; tel. (10) 85698008; fax (10) 85698007; e-mail bgt@cndca.org.cn; internet www.cndca.org.cn; f. 1945; 112,698 mems, mainly industrialists and business executives; Chair. CHEN CHANGZHI.

China Zhi Gong Dang (Party for Public Interests): 11 Dongbinghe Lu, Deshengmen, Xicheng Qu, Beijing; tel. (10) 51550800; fax (10) 51550900; e-mail czgpwz@zg.org.cn; internet www.zg.org.cn; f. 1925; reorg. 1947; 15,000 mems, mainly returned overseas Chinese and scholars; Chair. WAN GANG; Sec.-Gen. QIU GUOYI.

Chinese Communist Youth League: 10 Qianmen Dong Dajie, Beijing 100051; tel. (10) 67018132; fax (10) 67018131; e-mail gqt@gqt.org.cn; internet www.gqt.org.cn; f. 1922; 68.5m. mems; First Sec. of Cen. Cttee LU HAO.

Chinese Peasants' and Workers' Democratic Party: 55 An Wai Dajie, Beijing; tel. and fax (10) 84125629; e-mail info@ngdzy.org.cn; internet www.ngd.org.cn; f. 1930; est. as the Provisional Action Cttee of the Kuomintang; took present name in 1947; more than 102,000 mems, active mainly in public health and medicine; Chair. CHEN ZHU.

Jiu San (3 September) Society: 14 Wan Quan Xinxin Jiayuan, Wanliu Donglu, Haidian Qu, Beijing 100089; tel. (10) 82552001; fax (10) 82552002; e-mail bwww@93.gov.cn; internet www.93.gov.cn; f. 1946; fmrly Democratic and Science Soc; more than 105,000 mems, mainly scientists and technologists; Chair. HAN QIDE.

Revolutionary Committee of the Chinese Kuomintang: 84 Donghuang Chenggen Nan Jie, Dongcheng Qu, Beijing 100006; tel. (10) 65595873; fax (10) 65125886; e-mail webmaster@minge.gov.cn; internet www.minge.gov.cn; f. 1948; over 53,000 mems, mainly fmr Kuomintang mems, and those in cultural, educational, health and financial fields; Chair. WAN EXIANG; Sec.-Gen. QI XUCHUN.

Taiwan Democratic Self-Government League: 20 Jingshan Dongjie, Beijing 100009; tel. and fax (10) 64043293; e-mail webmaster@taimeng.org.cn; internet www.taimeng.org.cn; f. 1947; 1,600 mems; recruits Taiwanese living on the mainland; Chair. LIN WENYI.

Diplomatic Representation

EMBASSIES IN THE PEOPLE'S REPUBLIC OF CHINA

Afghanistan: 8 Dong Zhi Men Wai Dajie, Chaoyang Qu, Beijing 100600; tel. (10) 65321582; fax (10) 65322269; e-mail afgemb_beijing@gmail.com; Ambassador SULTAN AHMAD BAHEEN.

Albania: 28 Guang Hua Lu, Jian Guo Men Wai, Beijing 100600; tel. (10) 65321120; fax (10) 65325451; e-mail embassy.beijing@mfa.gov.al; Ambassador KUJTIM XHANI.

Algeria: 7 San Li Tun Lu, Beijing; tel. (10) 65321231; fax (10) 65321648; e-mail algpek@ymail.com; internet www.algeriaembassychina.net; Ambassador HASSANE RABEHI.

Angola: 1-8-1 Tayuan Diplomatic Office Bldg, Chaoyang Qu, Beijing 100600; tel. (10) 65326968; fax (10) 65326992; e-mail angolaembassy-china@hotmail.com; Ambassador JOÃO GARCIA BIRES.

Argentina: Bldg 11, 5 Dong Wu Jie, San Li Tun, Beijing 100600; tel. (10) 65322090; fax (10) 65322319; e-mail echin@mrecic.gov.ar; Ambassador GUSTAVO ALBERTO MARTINO.

Armenia: 4-1-61 Tayuan Diplomatic Office Bldg, Chaoyang Qu, Beijing 100600; tel. (10) 65325677; fax (10) 65325654; e-mail armchinaembassy@mfa.am; Ambassador ARMEN SARGSYAN.

Australia: 21 Dong Zhi Men Wai Dajie, San Li Tun, Beijing 100600; tel. (10) 51404111; fax (10) 51404204; e-mail pubaff.beijing@dfat.gov.au; internet www.china.embassy.gov.au; Ambassador FRANCES ADAMSON.

Austria: 5 Xiu Shui Nan Jie, Jian Guo Men Wai, Beijing 100600; tel. (10) 65322061; fax (10) 65321505; e-mail peking-ob@bmeia.gv.at; internet www.bmeia.gv.at/botschaft/peking; Ambassador Dr IRENE GINER-REICHL.

Azerbaijan: Qijiayuan Diplomatic Compound, Villa No. B-3, Beijing 100600; tel. (10) 65324614; fax (10) 65324615; e-mail mailbox@azerbembassy.org.cn; internet www.azerbembassy.org.cn; Ambassador YASHAR TOFIGI ALIYEV.

Bahamas: 2-4 Tayuan Diplomatic Office Bldg, 14 Liang Ma He Lu, Beijing 100600; tel. (10) 65322922; fax (10) 65322304; e-mail info@bahamasembassy.cn; internet www.bahamasembassy.cn; Ambassador ELMA CHASE CAMPBELL.

Bahrain: 10-06 Liang Ma Qiao Diplomatic Residence Compound, 22 Dong Fang Dong Lu, Chaoyang Qu, Beijing 100600; tel. (10) 65326483; fax (10) 65326393; e-mail kingdombahrain@yahoo.cn; internet www.mofa.gov.bh/beijing; Ambassador BIBI SHARAF AL-ALAWI.

Bangladesh: 42 Guang Hua Lu, Beijing 100600; tel. (10) 65322529; fax (10) 65324346; e-mail bdemb@public3.bta.net.cn; internet www.bangladeshembassy.com.cn; Ambassador MUHAMMAD AZIZUL HAQUE.

Barbados: Villa 09-02, Block A, Liang Ma Qiao Diplomatic Compound, 22 Dong Fang Dong Lu, Chaoyang Qu, 100600 Beijing; tel. (10) 85325404; fax (10) 85325437; e-mail beijing@foreign.gov.bb; Ambassador Dr CHELSTON BRATHWAITE.

Belarus: 1 Dong Yi Jie, Ri Tan Lu, Beijing 100600; tel. (10) 65321691; fax (10) 65326417; e-mail china@belembassy.org; internet china.mfa.gov.by; Ambassador VIKTOR BURYA.

Belgium: 6 San Li Tun Lu, Beijing 100600; tel. (10) 65321736; fax (10) 65325097; e-mail beijing@diplobel.fed.be; internet www.diplomatie.be/beijing; Ambassador MICHEL MALHERBE.

Benin: 38 Guang Hua Lu, Jian Guo Men Wai, Beijing 100600; tel. (10) 65322741; fax (10) 65325103; e-mail ambeninbj@yahoo.fr; Ambassador SEDOZAN APITHY.

Bolivia: 2-3-2 Tayuan Diplomatic Office Bldg, Chaoyang Qu, Beijing 100600; tel. (10) 65323074; fax (10) 65324686; e-mail embolchin@gmail.com; internet www.embolchina.com; Ambassador Gen. GUILLERMO CHALUP.

Bosnia and Herzegovina: 1-5-1 Tayuan Diplomatic Office Bldg, Chaoyang Qu, Beijing 100600; tel. (10) 65326587; fax (10) 65326418; e-mail ambbhdip@public.bta.net.cn; internet www.bhembassychina.com; Ambassador BORISLAV MARIĆ.

Botswana: 1 Dong San Jie, San Li Tun, Chaoyang Qu, Beijing 100600; tel. (10) 65326898; fax (10) 65326896; e-mail botchin@gov.bw; internet www.botswanaembassy.com; Ambassador SASARA CHASALA GEORGE.

Brazil: 27 Guang Hua Lu, Jian Guo Men Wai, Chaoyang Qu, Beijing 100600; tel. (10) 65322881; fax (10) 65322751; e-mail brasemb.pequim@itamaraty.gov.br; internet pequim.itamaraty.gov.br; Ambassador VALDEMAR CARNEIRO LEAO.

Brunei: 1 Liang Ma Qiao Bei Jie, Chaoyang Qu, Beijing 100600; tel. (10) 65329773; fax (10) 65324097; e-mail beb@public.bta.net.cn; Ambassador Datin Paduka MAGDALENE TEO CHEE SIONG.

Bulgaria: 4 Xiu Shui Bei Jie, Jian Guo Men Wai, Beijing 100600; tel. (10) 65321946; fax (10) 65324502; e-mail embassy.beijing@mfa.bg; internet www.mfa.bg/embassies/china; Ambassador PLAMEN SHUKYURLIEV.

Burundi: 25 Guang Hua Lu, Jian Guo Men Wai, Beijing 100600; tel. (10) 65321801; fax (10) 65322381; e-mail ambbubei@yahoo.fr; Ambassador PASCAL GASUNZU.

Cambodia: 9 Dong Zhi Men Wai Dajie, Beijing 100600; tel. (10) 65321889; fax (10) 65323507; e-mail cambassy@public2.bta.net.cn; Ambassador KHEK CAI MEALY SYSODA.

Cameroon: 7 Dong Wu Jie, San Li Tun, Beijing 100600; tel. (10) 65321828; fax (10) 65321761; e-mail acpk71@hotmail.com; Ambassador MARTIN MPANA.

Canada: 19 Dong Zhi Men Wai Dajie, Chaoyang Qu, Beijing 100600; tel. (10) 51394000; fax (10) 51394454; e-mail beijing-pa@international.gc.ca; internet www.canadainternational.gc.ca/china-chine; Ambassador GUY SAINT-JACQUES.

Cape Verde: 6-2-121 Tayuan Diplomatic Office Bldg, Chaoyang Qu, Beijing 100600; tel. (10) 65327547; fax (10) 65327546; e-mail cvembassych@chinaembassy.ch; internet www.cvembassy.com; Ambassador JULIO CESAR FREIRE DE MORAIS.

Central African Republic: 1-1-132 Tayuan Diplomatic Office Bldg, 1 Xin Dong Lu, Chaoyang Qu, Beijing; tel. 65327353; fax 65327354; e-mail ambrcapk@yahoo.fr; Ambassador EMMANUEL TOUABOY.

Chad: 2-2-102 Tayuan Diplomatic Compound, Xin Dong Lu, Chaoyang Qu, Beijing 100600; tel. (10) 85323822; fax (10) 85322783; e-mail ambatchad.beijing@yahoo.fr; Ambassador AHMED SOUNGUI.

Chile: 1 Dong Si Jie, San Li Tun, Beijing 100600; tel. (10) 65321591; fax (10) 65323179; e-mail embachile@echilecn.com; internet chileabroad.gov.cl/china; Ambassador LUIS SCHMIDT MONTES.

Colombia: 34 Guang Hua Lu, Jian Guo Men Wai, Beijing 100600; tel. (10) 65323377; fax (10) 65321969; e-mail ebeijing@cancilleria.gov.co; internet www.embcolch.org.cn; Ambassador CARMENZA JARAMILLO.

Congo, Democratic Republic: 6 Dong Wu Jie, San Li Tun, Beijing 100600; tel. (10) 65323224; fax (10) 65321360; Ambassador CHARLES MUMBALA NZANKU.

Congo, Republic: 7 Dong Si Jie, San Li Tun, Beijing 100600; tel. (10) 65321658; fax (10) 65322915; e-mail chine@yahoo.fr; Ambassador DANIEL OWASSA.

Costa Rica: Jian Guo Men Wai, 1-5-41 Jiao Gong Lu, Beijing 100600; tel. (10) 65324157; fax (10) 65324546; e-mail info@embajadacrchina.org; internet www.costaricaembassycn.com; Ambassador MARCO VINICIO RUIZ GUTIÉRREZ.

Côte d'Ivoire: 9 San Li Tun, Bei Xiao Jie, Beijing 100600; tel. (10) 65321223; fax (10) 65322407; Ambassador COFFIE ALAIN NICAISE PAPATCHI.

Croatia: 2-72 San Li Tun Diplomatic Office Bldg, Beijing 100600; tel. (10) 65326241; fax (10) 65326257; e-mail croemb.beijing@mvep.hr; internet cn.mfa.hr; Ambassador NEBOJSA KOHAROVIC.

Cuba: 1 Xiu Shui Nan Jie, Jian Guo Men Wai, Beijing 100600; tel. (10) 65321714; fax (10) 65322870; e-mail embajada@embacuba.cn; internet embacuba.cubaminrex.cu/china; Ambassador ALBERTO J. BLANCO SILVA.

Cyprus: 2-13-2 Tayuan Diplomatic Office Bldg, 14 Liang Ma He Nan Lu, Chaoyang Qu, Beijing 100600; tel. (10) 65325057; fax (10) 65324244; e-mail cyembpek@public3.bta.net.cn; Ambassador IOANNA MALLIOTIS.

Czech Republic: 2 Ri Tan Lu, Jian Guo Men Wai, Beijing 100600; tel. (10) 85329500; fax (10) 65325653; e-mail beijing@embassy.mzv.cz; internet www.mzv.cz/beijing; Ambassador LIBOR SEČKA.

Denmark: 1 Dong Wu Jie, San Li Tun, Beijing 100600; tel. (10) 85329900; fax (10) 85329999; e-mail bjsamb@um.dk; internet www.ambbeijing.um.dk; Ambassador FRIIS ARNE PETERSEN.

Djibouti: 1-1-122 Tayuan Diplomatic Office Bldg, Chaoyang Qu, Beijing; tel. (10) 65327857; fax (10) 65327858; e-mail espoir@vip.sina.com; Ambassador ABDALLAH ABDILLAHI MIGUIL.

Dominica: LA-06 Liang Ma Qiao Diplomatic Residence Compound, 22 Dong Fang Dong Lu, Chaoyang Qu, Beijing 100600; tel. (10) 65320848; fax (10) 65320838; e-mail dominica@dominicaembassy.com; Ambassador DAVID K. HSIU.

Ecuador: 2-62 San Li Tun Office Bldg, Chaoyang Qu, 100600 Beijing; tel. (10) 65320489; fax (10) 65324371; e-mail eecuchina@mmrree.gob.ec; internet www.ecuadorenchina.org.ec; Ambassador JOSÉ MARÍA BORJA LOPEZ.

Egypt: 2 Ri Tan Dong Lu, Jian Guo Men Wai, Beijing 100600; tel. (10) 65321825; fax (10) 65325365; e-mail eg_emb_bj@yahoo.com; internet www.mfa.gov.eg/Beijing_Emb; Ambassador AHMED REZK M. REZK.

Equatorial Guinea: 2 Dong Si Jie, San Li Tun, Beijing; tel. (10) 65323679; fax (10) 65323805; e-mail emguies@yahoo.com; Ambassador MARCOS MBA ONDO.

Eritrea: 2-10-1 Tayuan Diplomatic Office Bldg, Chaoyang Qu, Beijing 100600; tel. (10) 65326534; fax (10) 65326532; Ambassador TSEGGAI TESFAZION SEREKE.

Estonia: C-617–618 Office Bldg, Beijing Lufthansa Center, 50 Liang Ma Qiao Lu, Chaoyang Qu, Beijing 100125; tel. (10) 64637913; fax (10) 64637908; e-mail embassy.beijing@mfa.ee; internet www.peking.vm.ee; Ambassador TOOMAS LUKK.

Ethiopia: 3 Xiu Shui Nan Jie, Jian Guo Men Wai, Beijing 100600; tel. (10) 65325258; fax (10) 65325591; e-mail eth.beijing@mfa.gov.et; internet www.ethiopiaemb.org.cn; Ambassador SEYOUM MESFIN.

Fiji: 1-15-2 Tayuan Diplomatic Office Bldg, 14 Liang Ma He Nan Lu, San Li Tun, Chaoyang Qu, Beijing 100600; tel. (10) 65327305; fax (10) 65327253; e-mail info@fijiembassy.org.cn; internet www.fijiembassy.org.cn; Ambassador Cdre ESALA TELENI.

Finland: Beijing Kerry Centre, 26/F South Tower, 1 Guanghua Lu, Beijing 100020; tel. (10) 85198300; fax (10) 85198301; e-mail sanomat.pek@formin.fi; internet www.finland.cn; Ambassador JARI GUSTAFSSON.

France: 3 Dong San Jie, San Li Tun, Chaoyang Qu, Beijing 100600; tel. (10) 85312000; fax (10) 85312090; e-mail presse@ambafrance-cn.org; internet www.ambafrance-cn.org; Ambassador SYLVIE-AGNÈS BERMANN.

Gabon: 36 Guang Hua Lu, Jian Guo Men Wai, Beijing 100600; tel. (10) 65322810; fax (10) 65322621; Ambassador JEAN-ROBERT GOULONGANA.

Georgia: G-38 King's Garden Villas, 18 Xiao Yun Lu, Chaoyang Qu, Beijing; tel. (10) 64681203; fax (10) 64681202; e-mail china.emb@mfa.gov.ge; internet www.china.mfa.gov.ge; Ambassador DAVID APTSIAURI.

Germany: 17 Dong Zhi Men Wai Dajie, Chaoyang Qu, Beijing 100600; tel. (10) 85329000; fax (10) 65325336; e-mail embassy@peking.diplo.de; internet www.peking.diplo.de; Ambassador Dr MICHAEL CLAUSS.

Ghana: 8 San Li Tun Lu, Beijing 100600; tel. (10) 65321319; fax (10) 65323602; e-mail ghmfa85@yahoo.com; Ambassador HELEN MAMLE KOFI.

Greece: 17/F The Place Tower, 9 Guang Hua Lu, Jian Guo Men Wai, Chaoyang Qu, Beijing 100020; tel. (10) 65872838; fax (10) 65872839; e-mail gremb.pek@mfa.gr; internet www.grpressbeijing.com; Ambassador VASSILIOS COSTIS.

Grenada: T5-2-52 Tayuan Diplomatic Office Bldg, Chaoyang Qu, Beijing 100600; tel. (10) 65321208; fax (10) 65321015; e-mail public@pek.gov.gd; Ambassador KARL HOOD.

Guinea: 2 Xi Liu Jie, San Li Tun, Beijing 100600; tel. (10) 65323649; fax (10) 65324957; Ambassador DIARE MAMADY.

Guinea-Bissau: 2-2-101 Tayuan Diplomatic Compound, Chaoyang Qu, Beijing; tel. (10) 65327393; fax (10) 65327106; e-mail egb.beijing2010@yahoo.com; Ambassador MALAM SAMBU.

Guyana: 1 Xiu Shui Dong Jie, Jian Guo Men Wai, Beijing 100600; tel. (10) 65321337; fax (10) 65325741; e-mail guyemb@public3.bta.net.cn; Ambassador DAVID DABYDEEN.

Hungary: 10 Dong Zhi Men Wai Dajie, San Li Tun, Beijing 100600; tel. (10) 65321431; fax (10) 65325053; e-mail mission.pek@mfa.gov.hu; internet www.mfa.gov.hu/kulkepviselet/CN; Ambassador SÁNDOR KUSAI.

Iceland: Landmark Tower 1, 802, 8 Dongsanhuan Bei Lu, Beijing 100004; tel. (10) 65907795; fax (10) 65907801; e-mail emb.beijing@mfa.is; internet www.iceland.is/cn; Ambassador STEFAN SKJALDARSON.

India: 5 Liang Ma Qiao Bei Jie, Chaoyang Qu, Beijing 100600; tel. (10) 65321908; fax (10) 65324684; e-mail hoc@indianembassy.org.cn; internet www.indianembassy.org.cn; Ambassador ASHOK K. KANTHA.

Indonesia: 4 Dong Zhi Men Wai Dajie, Beijing 100600; tel. (10) 65325486; fax (10) 65325368; e-mail set.beijing.kbri@kemlu.go.id; internet www.kemlu.go.id/beijing; Ambassador SOEGENG RAHARDJO.

Iran: 13 Dong Liu Jie, San Li Tun, Beijing 100600; tel. (10) 65322040; fax (10) 65321403; e-mail iranembassyinchina@yahoo.com; internet www.iranembassy-china.org; Ambassador Mehdi Safari.

Iraq: 25 Xiu Shui Bei Jie, Jian Guo Men Wai, Beijing 100600; tel. (10) 65323385; fax (10) 65321599; e-mail bknemb@iraqmofamail.net; internet www.iraqembassy.cn; Ambassador Abdul Karim Hashim Mustafa.

Ireland: 3 Ri Tan Dong Lu, Jian Guo Men Wai, Beijing 100600; tel. (10) 65322691; fax (10) 65326857; e-mail beijing@dfa.ie; internet www.embassyofireland.cn; Ambassador Declan Kelleher.

Israel: 17 Tian Ze Lu, Chaoyang Qu, Beijing 100600; tel. (10) 85320500; fax (10) 85320555; e-mail info@beijing.mfa.gov.il; internet beijing.mfa.gov.il; Ambassador Matan Vilnai.

Italy: 2 Dong Er Jie, San Li Tun, Beijing 100600; tel. (10) 85327600; fax (10) 65324676; e-mail ambasciata.pechino@esteri.it; internet www.ambpechino.esteri.it; Ambassador Alberto Bradanini.

Jamaica: 6-2-72 Jian Guo Men Wai Diplomatic Compound, 1 Xiu Shui Jie, Beijing 100600; tel. (10) 65320667; fax (10) 65320669; e-mail embassy@jamaicagov.cn; internet www.jamaicagov.cn; Ambassador Ralph Thomas.

Japan: 7 Ri Tan Lu, Jian Guo Men Wai, Beijing 100600; tel. (10) 65322361; fax (10) 65324625; e-mail info@eoj.cn; internet www.cn.emb-japan.go.jp; Ambassador Masato Kitera.

Jordan: 5 Dong Liu Jie, San Li Tun, Beijing 100600; tel. (10) 65323906; fax (10) 65323283; e-mail beijing@fm.gov.jo; Ambassador Yahya Eslayyem Salman Qaralleh.

Kazakhstan: 9 Dong Liu Jie, San Li Tun, Beijing 100600; tel. (10) 65324189; fax (10) 65326183; e-mail kz@kazembchina.org; internet www.kazembchina.org; Ambassador Nurlan Yermekbayev.

Kenya: 4 Xi Liu Jie, San Li Tun, Beijing 100600; tel. (10) 65323381; fax (10) 65321770; e-mail info@kenyaembassy.cn; internet www.kenyaembassy.cn; Ambassador (vacant).

Korea, Democratic People's Republic: 11 Ri Tan Bei Lu, Jian Guo Men Wai, Beijing 100600; tel. (10) 65321186; fax (10) 65326056; Ambassador Ji Jae Ryong.

Korea, Republic: 20 Dong Fang Dong Lu, Chaoyang Qu, Beijing 100600; tel. (10) 85310700; fax (10) 85320726; e-mail chinawebmaster@mofat.go.kr; internet chn.mofat.go.kr; Ambassador Kwon Young-Se.

Kuwait: 23 Guang Hua Lu, Jian Guo Men Wai, Beijing 100600; tel. (10) 65322216; fax (10) 65321607; e-mail beijing@mofa.gov.kw; Ambassador Muhammad Saleh al-Thuwaikh.

Kyrgyzstan: H-10-11 King's Garden Villas, 18 Xiao Yun Lu, Chaoyang Qu, Beijing 100125; tel. (10) 64681297; fax (10) 64681291; e-mail kyrgyz.embassy.china@gmail.com; internet www.kyrgyzstanembassy.net; Ambassador Jeenbek Kulubayev.

Laos: 11 Dong Si Jie, San Li Tun, Chaoyang Qu, Beijing 100600; tel. (10) 65321224; fax (10) 65326748; e-mail laoemcn@public.east.cn.net; Ambassador Somdy Bounkhoum.

Latvia: Unit 71, Green Land Garden, 1A Green Land Rd, Chaoyang Qu, Beijing 100016; tel. (10) 64333863; fax (10) 64333810; e-mail embassy.china@mfa.gov.lv; internet www.mfa.gov.lv/en/china; Ambassador Ingrida Levrence.

Lebanon: 10 Dong Liu Jie, San Li Tun, Beijing 100600; tel. (10) 65323281; fax (10) 65322770; e-mail lebanon@public.bta.net.cn; Ambassador Dr Farid Abboud.

Lesotho: 302 Dong Wai Diplomatic Office Bldg, 23 Dong Zhi Men Wai Dajie, Chaoyang Qu, Beijing 100600; tel. (10) 65326843; fax (10) 65326845; e-mail lesotho-brussels@foreign.gov.ls; Ambassador Lebohang Ntsinyi.

Liberia: Rm 013, Gold Island Diplomatic Compound, 1 Xi Ba He Nan Lu, Beijing 100028; tel. (10) 64403007; fax (10) 64403918; Ambassador Jarjar M. Kamara.

Libya: 3 Dong Liu Jie, San Li Tun, Beijing 100600; tel. (10) 65323666; fax (10) 65323391; Ambassador Taher E. Jehaimi.

Lithuania: A-18 King's Garden Villas, 18 Xiaoyun Lu, Chaoyang Qu, Beijing 100125; tel. (10) 84518520; fax (10) 84514442; e-mail amb.cn@urm.lt; internet cn.mfa.lt; Ambassador Lina Antanaviciene.

Luxembourg: 1701, Tower B, Pacific Century Place, 2A Gong Ti Bei Lu, Chaoyang Qu, Beijing 100027; tel. (10) 85880900; fax (10) 65137268; e-mail pekin.amb@mae.etat.lu; internet pekin.mae.lu; Ambassador Paul Steinmetz.

Macedonia, former Yugoslav republic: 1-32 San Li Tun Diplomatic Office Bldg, Beijing 100600; tel. (10) 65327846; fax (10) 65327847; e-mail beijing@mfa.gov.mk; Ambassador Oliver Sambevski.

Madagascar: 3 Dong Jie, San Li Tun, Beijing 100600; tel. (10) 65321353; fax (10) 65322102; Ambassador Victor Sikonina.

Malawi: 503 Dong Wai Diplomatic Office Bldg, 23 Dong Zhi Men Wai Dajie, Beijing 100600; tel. (10) 65325889; fax (10) 65326022; Ambassador Ernest Makawa.

Malaysia: 2 Liang Ma Qiao Bei Jie, Chaoyang Qu, San Li Tun, Beijing 100600; tel. (10) 65322531; fax (10) 65325032; e-mail mwbjing@kln.gov.my; internet www.kln.gov.my/web/chn_beijing; Ambassador Datuk Iskandar bin Sarudin.

Maldives: 1-5-31 Jian Guo Men Wai Diplomatic Compound, Jianwai Xiushui Lu, Chaoyang Qu, Beijing 100600; tel. (10) 85323847; fax (10) 85323746; e-mail admin@maldivesembassy.cn; internet www.maldivesembassy.cn; Ambassador Mohamed Rasheed.

Mali: 8 Dong Si Jie, San Li Tun, Beijing 100600; tel. (10) 65321704; fax (10) 65321618; e-mail ambamali@163bj.com; Ambassador Lansina Boua Kone.

Malta: 1-51 San Li Tun Diplomatic Compound, Gong Ti Bei Lu, Beijing 100600; tel. (10) 65323114; fax (10) 65326125; e-mail maltaembassy.beijing@gov.mt; internet www.mfa.gov.mt/china; Ambassador Clifford Borg-Marks.

Mauritania: 9 Dong San Jie, San Li Tun, Beijing 100600; tel. (10) 65321346; fax (10) 65321685; e-mail ambarim@ambarim-beijing.com; internet ambarim-beijing.com; Ambassador Bal Mohamed El Habib.

Mauritius: 202 Dong Wai Diplomatic Office Bldg, 23 Dong Zhi Men Wai Dajie, Chaoyang Qu, Beijing 100600; tel. (10) 65325695; fax (10) 65325706; e-mail beijing@mail.gov.mu; internet www.gov.mu/portal/sites/mfamission/beijing/index.htm; Ambassador Paul Reynold Lit Fong Chong Leung.

Mexico: 5 Dong Wu Jie, San Li Tun, Beijing 100600; tel. (10) 65321717; fax (10) 65323744; e-mail embmxchn@public.bta.net.cn; internet www.sre.gob.mx/china; Ambassador Julian Ventura.

Micronesia, Federated States: 1-1-11 Jian Guo Men Wai Diplomatic Compound, Chaoyang Qu, Beijing 100010; tel. (10) 65324738; fax (10) 65324609; e-mail embassy@fsmembassy.cn; Ambassador Akillino H. Susaia.

Moldova: 2-9-1 Tayuan Diplomatic Office Bldg, Chaoyang Qu, Beijing 100600; tel. (10) 65325494; fax (10) 65325379; e-mail beijing@mfa.md; Ambassador Anatol Urecheanu.

Mongolia: 2 Xiu Shui Bei Jie, Jian Guo Men Wai, Beijing 100600; tel. (10) 65321203; fax (10) 65325045; e-mail mail@mongolembassychina.org; Ambassador Tsedenjavyn Sükhbaatar.

Montenegro: 3-1-12 San Li Tun Diplomatic Compound, Beijing 100600; tel. (10) 65327610; fax (10) 65327662; e-mail china@mfa.gov.me; Ambassador Branko Perović.

Morocco: 16 San Li Tun Lu, Beijing 100600; tel. (10) 65321489; fax (10) 65321453; e-mail sifama.beijing@moroccoembassy.org.cn; internet www.moroccoembassy.cn; Ambassador Jaafar Alj Hakim.

Mozambique: 1-7-2 Tayuan Diplomatic Office Bldg, Chaoyang Qu, Beijing 100600; tel. (10) 65323664; fax (10) 65325189; e-mail embamoc@embmoz.org; Ambassador António Inácio Júnior.

Myanmar: 6 Dong Zhi Men Wai Dajie, Chaoyang Qu, Beijing 100600; tel. (10) 65320351; fax (10) 65320408; e-mail info@myanmarembassy.com; internet www.myanmarembassy.com; Ambassador Tin Oo.

Namibia: 2-9-2 Tayuan Diplomatic Office Bldg, Chaoyang Qu, Beijing 100600; tel. (10) 65324810; fax (10) 65324549; e-mail namemb@eastnet.com.cn; Ambassador Leonard Nambahu.

Nepal: 1 Xi Liu Jie, San Li Tun Lu, Beijing 100600; tel. (10) 65322739; fax (10) 65323251; e-mail beijing@nepalembassy.org.cn; internet www.nepalembassy.org.cn; Ambassador Mahesh Kumar Maskey.

Netherlands: 4 Liang Ma He Nan Lu, Beijing 100600; tel. (10) 85320200; fax (10) 85320300; e-mail pek@minbuza.nl; internet www.hollandinchina.org; Ambassador Aart Jacobi.

New Zealand: 3 Dong San Jie, San Li Tun, Chaoyang Qu, Beijing 100600; tel. (10) 85312700; fax (10) 65324317; e-mail beijing.enquiries@mft.net.nz; internet www.nzembassy.com/china; Ambassador Carl Robinson Worker.

Niger: 1-21 San Li Tun, Beijing 100600; tel. (10) 65324279; fax (10) 65327041; e-mail nigerbj@public.bta.net.cn; Ambassador Dambina Bawa.

Nigeria: 2 Dong Wu Jie, San Li Tun, Beijing; tel. (10) 65323631; fax (10) 65321650; e-mail info@nigeriaembassy.cn; internet www.nigeriaembassy.cn; Ambassador Aminu Bashir Wali.

Norway: 1 Dong Yi Jie, San Li Tun, Beijing 100600; tel. (10) 85319600; fax (10) 65322392; e-mail emb.beijing@mfa.no; internet www.norway.cn; Ambassador Svein Ole Sæther.

Oman: 6 Liang Ma He Nan Lu, San Li Tun, Beijing 100600; tel. (10) 65323692; fax (10) 65327185; e-mail omnbeijing@chnmail.com; Ambassador Abdullah Saleh al-Saadii.

Pakistan: 1 Dong Zhi Men Wai Dajie, San Li Tun, Beijing 100600; tel. (10) 65322504; fax (10) 65322715; e-mail info@pakembassy.cn; internet www.pakbj.org.pk; Ambassador Masood Khalid.

Papua New Guinea: 2-11-2 Tayuan Diplomatic Office Bldg, Chaoyang Qu, Beijing 100600; tel. (10) 65324312; fax (10)

65325483; e-mail kundu_beijing@pngembassy.org.cn; Ambassador CHRISTOPHER SIAOA MERO.

Peru: 1-91 San Li Tun, Chaoyang Qu, Beijing 100600; tel. (10) 65323477; fax (10) 65322178; e-mail info@embaperuchina.com.cn; internet www.embperuchina.com; Ambassador GONZALO GUTIERREZ.

Philippines: 23 Xiu Shui Bei Jie, Jian Guo Men Wai, Beijing 100600; tel. (10) 65321872; fax (10) 65323761; e-mail beijing.pe@dfa.gov.ph; internet www.philembassychina.org; Ambassador ERLINDA BASILIO.

Poland: 1 Ri Tan Lu, Jian Guo Men Wai, Chaoyang Qu, Beijing 100600; tel. (10) 65321235; fax (10) 65321745; e-mail pekin.amb.sekretariat@msz.gov.pl; internet www.pekin.msz.gov.pl; Ambassador TADEUSZ CHOMICKI.

Portugal: 8 San Li Tun Dong Wu Jie, Beijing 100600; tel. (10) 65323242; fax (10) 65324637; e-mail pequim@mne.pt; internet www.portugalembassychina.com; Ambassador JORGE RYDER TORRES-PEREIRA.

Qatar: A-7 Liang Ma Qiao Diplomatic Compound, Chaoyang Qu, Beijing 100600; tel. (10) 6522233; fax (10) 65325274; e-mail beijing@mofa.gov.qa; Ambassador SULTAN S. AL-MANSOURI.

Romania: Ri Tan Lu, Dong Er Jie, Beijing 100600; tel. (10) 65323442; fax (10) 65325728; e-mail ambasada@roamb.link263.com; internet www.beijing.mae.ro; Ambassador DORU ROMULUS COSTEA.

Russia: 4 Dong Zhi Men Nei, Bei Zhong Jie, Beijing 100600; tel. (10) 65322051; fax (10) 65324851; e-mail embassy@russia.org.cn; internet www.russia.org.cn; Ambassador ANDREI DENISOV.

Rwanda: 30 Xiu Shui Bei Jie, Jian Guo Men Wai, Beijing 100600; tel. (10) 65322193; fax (10) 65322006; e-mail ambabeijing@minaffet.gov.rw; internet www.china.embassy.gov.rw; Ambassador CHARLES KAYONGA.

Samoa: 2-72 Tayuan Diplomatic Office Bldg, 14 Liang Ma He Nan Lu, Chaoyang Qu, Beijing 100600; tel. (10) 65321673; fax (10) 65321642; e-mail info@samoaembassy.cn; internet www.samoaembassy.cn; Ambassador TAPUSALAIA TERRY TOOMATA.

Saudi Arabia: 1 Bei Xiao Jie, San Li Tun, Beijing 100600; tel. (10) 65324825; fax (10) 65325324; Ambassador YAHYA AL-ZAID.

Senegal: 305 Dong Wai Diplomatic Office Bldg, 23 Dong Zhi Men Wai Dajie, Beijing 100600; tel. (10) 65325035; fax (10) 65323730; Ambassador Gen. ABDOULAYE FALL.

Serbia: 1 Dong Liu Jie, San Li Tun, Beijing 100600; tel. (10) 65323516; fax (10) 65321207; e-mail embserbia@embserbia.cn; internet www.embserbia.cn; Chargé d'affaires a.i. TATJANA PANAJOTOVIĆ-CVETKOVIĆ.

Seychelles: Rm 1105, The Spaces International Center, 8 Dong Da Qiao, Chaoyang Qu, Beijing 100020; tel. (10) 58701192; fax (10) 58701219; e-mail amb.legall@yahoo.com; Ambassador PHILIPPE LE GALL.

Sierra Leone: 7 Dong Zhi Men Wai Dajie, Beijing 100600; tel. (10) 65322174; fax (10) 65323752; e-mail slbeijing@foreignaffairs.gov.sl; Ambassador VICTOR BOCKARIE FOH.

Singapore: 1 Xiu Shui Bei Jie, Jian Guo Men Wai, Chaoyang Qu, Beijing 100600; tel. (10) 65321115; fax (10) 65329405; e-mail singemb_bej@sgmfa.gov.sg; internet www.mfa.gov.sg/beijing; Ambassador STANLEY LOH KA LEUNG.

Slovakia: Ri Tan Lu, Jian Guo Men Wai, Beijing 100600; tel. (10) 65321531; fax (10) 65324814; e-mail emb.beijing@mzv.sk; internet www.mzv.sk/peking; Ambassador FRANTISEK DLHOPOLCEK.

Slovenia: Block F, King's Garden Villas, 18 Xiao Yun Lu, Chaoyang Qu, Beijing 100016; tel. (10) 64681030; fax (10) 64681040; e-mail vpe@gov.si; internet beijing.embassy.si; Ambassador MARIJA ADANJA.

Somalia: 2 San Li Tun Lu, Beijing 100600; tel. and fax (10) 65321651; fax (10) 65321752; e-mail somaliaemb.beij@yahoo.com; Ambassador YUSUF HASSAN IBRAHIM.

South Africa: 5 Dong Zhi Men Wai Dajie, Chaoyang Qu, Beijing 100600; tel. (10) 85320000; fax (10) 65327319; e-mail embassy@saembassy.org.cn; internet www.saembassy.org.cn; Ambassador W. J. LANGA.

South Sudan: House 1-2, King's Garden Villas, 18 Xiao Yun Lu, Beijing; tel. (10) 64649921; fax (10) 64649928; e-mail southsudanembassy.beijing@live.com; Ambassador YOKWE ELUZAI MOGA.

Spain: 9 San Li Tun Lu, Beijing 100600; tel. (10) 65323629; fax (10) 65323401; e-mail emb.pekin@maec.es; internet www.exteriores.gob.es/Embajadas/Pekin; Ambassador MANUEL MARIA VALENCIA ALONSO.

Sri Lanka: 3 Jian Hua Lu, Jian Guo Men Wai, Beijing 100600; tel. (10) 65321861; fax (10) 65325426; e-mail lkembj@slemb.com; internet www.slemb.com; Ambassador RANJITH UYANGODA.

Sudan: 1 Dong Er Jie, San Li Tun, Beijing 100600; tel. (10) 65323715; fax (10) 65321280; e-mail info@sudanembassybeijing.com; internet www.sudanembassybeijing.com; Ambassador MIRGHANI MOHAMED SALIH.

Suriname: 2-2-22 Jian Guo Men Wai Diplomatic Compound, Beijing 100600; tel. (10) 65322938; fax (10) 65322941; e-mail amb.china@foreignaffairs.gov.sr; internet www.surinameembassy.cn; Ambassador LLOYD LUCIEN PINAS.

Sweden: 3 Dong Zhi Men Wai Dajie, San Li Tun, Beijing 100600; tel. (10) 65329790; fax (10) 65325008; e-mail ambassaden.peking@foreign.ministry.se; internet www.swedenabroad.com/peking; Ambassador LARS FREDÉN.

Switzerland: 3 Dong Wu Jie, San Li Tun, Beijing 100600; tel. (10) 85328888; fax (10) 65324353; e-mail bei.vertretung@eda.admin.ch; internet www.eda.admin.ch/beijing; Ambassador JEAN-JACQUES DE DARDEL.

Syria: 6 Dong Si Jie, San Li Tun, Beijing 100600; tel. (10) 65321372; fax (10) 65321575; e-mail sy@syria.org.cn; internet www.syrembassy.cn; Ambassador Dr IMAD MOUSTAPHA.

Tajikistan: LA-01-04 Liang Ma Qiao Diplomatic Compound, Chaoyang Qu, Beijing; tel. (10) 65322598; fax (10) 65323039; e-mail tajikistanchina@yahoo.com; internet www.tajikembassychina.com; Ambassador RASHID ALIMOV.

Tanzania: 8 Liang Ma He Nan Lu, San Li Tun, Beijing 100600; tel. (10) 65321719; fax (10) 65324351; e-mail tanrep@tanzaniaembassy.org.cn; internet www.tanzaniaembassy.org.cn; Ambassador ABDULRAHMAN A. SHIMBO.

Thailand: 40 Guang Hua Lu, Jian Guo Men Wai, Beijing 100600; tel. (10) 65321749; fax (10) 65321748; e-mail thaibej@eastnet.com.cn; internet www.thaiembbeij.org; Ambassador WIBOON KHUSAKUL.

Timor-Leste: D-15 King's Garden Villas, 18 Xiao Yun Lu, Beijing 100028; tel. (10) 64681316; fax (10) 64684360; e-mail embassy@embtimorleste-beijing.com; internet www.embtimorleste-beijing.com; Ambassador VICKY FUN HA TCHONG.

Togo: 11 Dong Zhi Men Wai Dajie, Beijing 100600; tel. (10) 65322202; fax (10) 65325884; e-mail ambatogochine@yahoo.fr; Ambassador NOLANA TA-AMA.

Tonga: 1-3-22 Jian Guo Men Wai Diplomatic Compound, Chaoyang Qu, Beijing 100600; tel. (10) 65327203; fax (10) 65327204; e-mail info@tongaembassycn.com; internet www.tongaembassycn.com; Ambassador SIAMELIE LATU.

Tunisia: 1 Dong Jie, San Li Tun, Chaoyang Qu, Beijing 100600; tel. (10) 65322435; fax (10) 65325818; e-mail at_beijing@netchina.com.cn; internet www.embassyoftunisia.com; Ambassador TAREK AMRI.

Turkey: 9 Dong Wu Jie, San Li Tun, Beijing 100600; tel. (10) 65321715; fax (10) 65325480; e-mail embassy.beijing@mfa.gov.tr; internet beijing.emb.mfa.gov.tr; Ambassador ALI MURAT ERSOY.

Turkmenistan: D-1 King's Garden Villas, 18 Xiao Yuan Lu, Beijing; tel. (10) 65326975; fax (10) 65326976; e-mail embturkmen@netchina.com.cn; internet www.turkmenembassy.cn; Ambassador CHINAR RUSTEMOVA.

Uganda: 5 Dong Jie, San Li Tun, Beijing 100600; tel. (10) 65321708; fax (10) 65322242; e-mail ugembssy@public.bta.net.cn; Ambassador CHARLES MADIBO WAGIDOSO.

Ukraine: 11 Dong Liu Jie, San Li Tun, Beijing 100600; tel. (10) 65326359; fax (10) 65326765; e-mail emb_cn@mfa.gov.ua; internet www.mfa.gov.ua/china; Ambassador OLEG DYOMIN.

United Arab Emirates: LA-10-04 Liang Ma Qiao Diplomatic Compound, 22 Dong Fang Dong Lu, Beijing; tel. (10) 65327651; fax (10) 65327652; e-mail info@uaeembassy.cn; internet www.uaeembassy.cn; Ambassador OMAR AHMED OUDAI NASEEB AL-BETAR.

United Kingdom: 11 Guang Hua Lu, Jian Guo Men Wai, Beijing 100600; tel. (10) 51924000; fax (10) 51924239; e-mail consular.beijing@fco.gov.uk; internet www.ukinchina.fco.gov.uk; Ambassador SEBASTIAN WOOD.

USA: 55 An Jia Lou Lu, Beijing 100600; tel. (10) 85313000; fax (10) 85314200; e-mail beijingwebmaster@state.gov; internet beijing.usembassy-china.org.cn; Ambassador MAX SIEBEN BAUCUS.

Uruguay: 1-11-2 Tayuan Diplomatic Office Bldg, Chaoyang Qu, Beijing 100600; tel. (10) 65684772; fax (10) 65684773; e-mail urubei@urubei.org; Ambassador ROSARIO PORTELL.

Uzbekistan: 11 Bei Xiao Jie, San Li Tun, Beijing 100600; tel. (10) 65326305; fax (10) 65326304; e-mail uzbekistan@embassy-uz.cn; internet www.embassy-uz.cn; Ambassador DANIYAR KURBANOV.

Vanuatu: 3-1-11 San Li Tun Diplomatic Compound, Chaoyang Qu, Beijing 100600; tel. (10) 65320337; fax (10) 65320336; e-mail info@vanuatuembassy.org.cn; internet www.vanuatuembassy.org.cn; Ambassador SELA MOLISA.

Venezuela: 14 San Li Tun Lu, Beijing 100600; tel. (10) 65321295; fax (10) 65323817; e-mail embvenez@public.bta.net.cn; internet www.venezuela.org.cn; Ambassador IVAN ZERPA ANTONIO GUERRERO.

Viet Nam: 32 Guang Hua Lu, Jian Guo Men Wai, Beijing 100600; tel. (10) 65321155; fax (10) 65325720; internet www.vnemba.org.cn; Ambassador NGUYEN VAN THO.

Yemen: 5 Dong San Jie, San Li Tun, Beijing 100600; tel. (10) 65321558; fax (10) 65327997; e-mail info@embassyofyemen.net; internet www.embassyofyemen.net; Chargé d'affaires a. i. ALI ATEF.

Zambia: 5 Dong Si Jie, San Li Tun, Chaoyang Qu, Beijing 100600; tel. (10) 65321554; fax (10) 65321891; e-mail admin@zambiaembassy-beijing.com; internet www.zambiaembassy-beijing.com; Ambassador GERTRUDE KASUBA MWAPE.

Zimbabwe: 7 Dong San Jie, San Li Tun, Beijing 100600; tel. (10) 65323795; fax (10) 65325383; e-mail zimbei@163.bj.com; Ambassador FREDERICK M. SHAVA.

Judicial System

According to the Constitution and under the Organic Law of the People's Courts (revised 1983), the People's Courts serve as the main trial organs of the state. A system of local courts and special courts is supervised by the Supreme Court. Local courts are established in line with administrative divisions and special courts are set up where necessary.

Supreme People's Court: 27 Dongjiaomin Xiang, Beijing 100745; tel. (10) 67550114; e-mail info@court.gov.cn; internet www.court.gov.cn; f. 1949; the highest judicial organ of the state; handles first instance cases of national importance; handles cases of appeals and protests lodged against judgments and orders of higher people's courts and special people's courts, and cases of protests lodged by the Supreme People's Procuratorate in accordance with the procedures of judicial supervision; reviews death sentences meted out by local courts, supervises the administration of justice by local people's courts; interprets issues concerning specific applications of laws in judicial proceedings; its judgments and rulings are final; Pres. ZHOU QIANG (five-year term of office coincides with that of National People's Congress, by which the President is elected).

Local People's Courts: comprise higher courts, intermediate courts and basic courts.

Special People's Courts: include military courts, maritime courts and railway transport courts.

Supreme People's Procuratorate: 147 Beiheyan Dajie, Beijing 100726; tel. (10) 65209114; e-mail web@spp.gov.cn; internet www.spp.gov.cn; acts for the National People's Congress in examining govt depts, civil servants and citizens, to ensure observance of the law; prosecutes in criminal cases; Procurator-Gen. CAO JIANMING (elected by the National People's Congress for a five-year term).

Local People's Procuratorates: undertake the same duties at the local level; ensure that the judicial activities of the people's courts, the execution of sentences in criminal cases and the activities of departments in charge of reform through labour conform to the law; institute, or intervene in, important civil cases that affect the interest of the state and the people.

Religion

The 1982 Constitution states that citizens enjoy freedom of religious belief and that legitimate religious activities are protected. All religious organizations are required to register with the State Administration for Religious Affairs. In the late 1990s a new religious sect, Falun Gong (also known as Falun Dafa, and incorporating elements of Buddhism and Daoism) emerged and quickly gained new adherents. However, the authorities banned the group in 1999.

State Administration for Religious Affairs: 32 Beisantiao, Jiaodaokou, Dongcheng Qu, Beijing 100007; tel. (10) 64023355; fax (10) 66013565; Dir WANG ZUOAN.

ANCESTOR WORSHIP

Ancestor worship is believed to have originated with the deification and worship of all important natural phenomena. The divine and human were not clearly defined; all the dead became gods and were worshipped by their descendants. The practice has no code or dogma, and the ritual is limited to sacrifices made during festivals and on birth and death anniversaries.

BUDDHISM

Buddhism was introduced into China from India in AD 67, and flourished during the Sui and Tang dynasties (6th–8th centuries), when eight sects were established. The Chan and Pure Land sects are the most popular. The dominant religion of Tibet (Xizang) is Tibetan Buddhism or Lamaism, a branch of Vajrayana Buddhism.

Buddhist Association of China (BAC): f. 1953; Pres. YIN CHUAN; Sec.-Gen. XUE CHENG.

Tibetan Institute of Lamaism: Pres. BUMI JANGBALUOZHU; Vice-Pres. CEMOLIN DANZENGCHILIE.

14th Dalai Lama: His Holiness the Dalai Lama TENZIN GYATSO; spiritual leader of Tibet; fled to India following the failure of the Tibetan national uprising in 1959; resident at: Thekchen Choeling, McLeod Ganj, Dharamsala 176 219, Himachal Pradesh, India; tel. (91) 1892-21343; fax (91) 1892-21813; e-mail ohhdl@cta.unv.ernet.ind; internet www.tibet.com.

CHRISTIANITY

In the early 21st century there was a revival of interest in the Christian faith. The official Catholic Church in China operates independently of the Vatican. The 'underground' Catholic Church is recognized by the Vatican. Various Christian sects have continued to expand in China. By 2009 the number of Chinese Christians had reached an estimated 130m. Of these, 100m. were believed to be independent worshippers, with only 21m. adhering to the official Protestant Church and 5m. to the approved Catholic Church.

Three-Self Patriotic Movement Committee of Protestant Churches of China: 219 Jiujiang Lu, Shanghai 200002; tel. (21) 63210806; fax (21) 63232605; e-mail tspmccc@online.sh.cn; Chair. Rev. FU XIANWEI; Gen. Sec. Rev. XU XIAOHONG.

Catholic Church: Catholic Mission, Si-She-Ku, Beijing; Bishop of Beijing JOSEPH LI SHAN.

China Christian Council: 219 Jiujiang Lu, Shanghai 200002; tel. (21) 63210806; fax (21) 63232605; e-mail tspmccc@online.sh.cn; f. 1980; comprises provincial Christian councils; Pres. Rev. K. H. TING; Gen. Sec. Rev. KAN BAOPING.

Chinese Patriotic Catholic Association (CPCA): f. 1957; Pres. JOHN FANG XINGYAO; Sec.-Gen. LIU BAINIAN.

CONFUCIANISM

Confucianism is a philosophy and a system of ethics, without ritual or priesthood. The respect that adherents accord to Confucius is not bestowed on a prophet or god, but on a great sage whose teachings promote peace and good order in society and whose philosophy encourages moral living.

DAOISM

Daoism was founded by Zhang Daoling during the Eastern Han dynasty (AD 125–144). Lao Zi, a philosopher of the Zhou dynasty (born 604 BC), is its principal inspiration, and is honoured as Lord the Most High by Daoists. According to unofficial sources, there were 1,600 Daoist temples in China in 2005.

China Daoist Association: Temple of the White Cloud, Xi Bian Men, Beijing 100045; tel. (10) 63406670; e-mail chinadaosim@yahoo.com.cn; internet www.taoist.org.cn; f. 1957; Pres. REN FARONG; Sec.-Gen. YUAN BINGDONG.

ISLAM

Islam was introduced into China in AD 651. There were some 20.3m. adherents in China in 2000, according to official sources, mainly among the Wei Wuer (Uygur) and Hui people, although unofficial sources estimate that the total is far higher.

Beijing Islamic Association: Dongsi Mosque, Beijing; f. 1979; Chair. Imam Al-Hadji CHEN GUANGYUAN.

China Islamic Association: Beijing 100053; tel. (10) 63546384; fax (10) 63529483; internet www.chinaislam.net.cn; f. 1953; Chair. Imam Al-Hadji CHEN GUANGYUAN; Sec.-Gen. YU ZHENGUI.

The Press

In 2012 about 2,000 newspaper titles (including those below provincial level) and 9,000 magazines were published in China. Each province publishes its own daily newspaper. The major newspapers and periodicals are listed below.

PRINCIPAL NEWSPAPERS

Anhui Ribao (Anhui Daily): 1469 Zhongshan Lu, Hefei, Anhui 230071; tel. (551) 5179860; fax (551) 2832534; e-mail ahch2005@163.com; internet www.anhuinews.com; Pres. WANG JIASI.

Beijing Ribao (Beijing Daily): 20 Jian Guo Men Nei Dajie, Beijing 100734; tel. (10) 85201843; fax (10) 65136522; e-mail beijingbjd@gmail.com; internet www.bjd.com.cn; f. 1952; organ of the Beijing municipal cttee of the CCP; Dir WAN YUNLAI; Editor-in-Chief LIU ZONGMING; circ. 700,000.

Beijing Wanbao (Beijing Evening News): 20 Jian Guo Men Nei Dajie, Beijing 100734; tel. 8008108440 (mobile); fax (10) 65126581; internet www.ben.com.cn; f. 1958; Editor-in-Chief REN HUANYING; circ. 800,000.

Beijing Youth Daily: Beijing; tel. (10) 65901655; e-mail jubao@ynet.com; internet bjyouth.ynet.com; f. 1949; national and local news; promotes ethics and social service; circ. 3m.–4m.

Changsha Wanbao (Changsha Evening News): 161 Caie Zhong Lu, Changsha, Hunan 410005; tel. (731) 4424457; fax (731) 4445167.

Chengdu Wanbao (Chengdu Evening News): Qingyun Nan Jie, Chengdu 610017; tel. (28) 664501; fax (28) 666597; circ. 700,000.

China Economic Times: Palace St, Changping Qu, Beijing 102209; tel. (10) 81785100; fax (10) 81785121; e-mail info@cet.com.cn; internet www.cet.com.cn; economic news; publ. by the Development Research Centre of the State Council.

China Times: Wanda Plaza, 93 Jianguo Lu, Chaoyang Qu, Beijing 100022; tel. (10) 59250005; internet www.chinatimes.cc; f. 1989; finance; weekly.

Chongqing Ribao (Chongqing Daily): Chongqing; Dir and Editor-in-Chief LI HUANIAN.

Dazhong Ribao (Dazhong Daily): Dazhong News Bldg, 4/F, 6 Luoyuan Dajie, Jinan, Shandong 250014; tel. (531) 85193202; fax (531) 2962450; internet www.dzwww.com; f. 1939; Pres. LIN ZHONGLI; Editor-in-Chief ZHU DEQUAN; circ. 2.1m.

Fujian Ribao (Fujian Daily): 84 Hualin Lu, Fuzhou, Fujian; tel. (591) 87079319; e-mail fjnet.cn@163.com; internet www.fjsen.com; daily; Dir HUANG SHIYUN; Editor-in-Chief HUANG ZHONGSHENG.

Gansu Ribao (Gansu Daily): Gansu; tel. (931) 8157213; fax (931) 8158955; e-mail gansudaily@163.com; internet www.gansudaily.com.cn.

Global Times: 7/F Topnew Tower, 15 Guanghua Lu, Chaoyang Ou, Beijing 100026; tel. (10) 52937633; e-mail editor@globaltimes.com.cn; internet www.globaltimes.cn; English; Editor-in-Chief HU XIJIN.

Gongren Ribao (Workers' Daily): Dongcheng Qu, Beijing 100718; tel. (10) 84151567; fax (10) 84151516; e-mail news@workercn.cn; internet www.workercn.cn; f. 1949; trade union activities and workers' lives; also major home and overseas news; Dir LIU YUMING; Editor-in-Chief SHENG MINGFU; circ. 2.5m.

Guangming Ribao (Guangming Daily): 5 Dong Lu, Chongwen Qu, Zhushikou, 100062; tel. (10) 67078855; fax (10) 67078854; e-mail webmaster@gmw.cn; internet www.gmw.cn; f. 1949; literature, art, science, education, history, economics, philosophy; circ. 920,000.

Guangxi Ribao (Guangxi Daily): Guangxi Region; tel. (771) 5690995; fax (771) 5690933; e-mail newgx@gxrb.com.cn; internet www.gxnews.com.cn; Dir and Editor-in-Chief CHENG ZHENSHENG; circ. 650,000.

Guangzhou Ribao (Canton Daily): 10 Dongle Lu, Renmin Zhonglu, Guangzhou, Guangdong; tel. (20) 81919191; fax (20) 81862022; internet gzdaily.dayoo.com; f. 1952; daily; social, economic and current affairs; Editor-in-Chief LI YUANJIANG; circ. 600,000.

Guizhou Ribao (Guizhou Daily): Guiyang, Guizhou; tel. (851) 6793333; fax (851) 6625615; internet gzrb.gog.com.cn; f. 1949; Dir GAO ZONGWEN; Editor-in-Chief GAN ZHENGSHU; circ. 300,000.

Hainan Ribao (Hainan Daily): News Bldg, 9/F, Haikou, Hainan 570001; tel. (898) 66810815; fax (898) 66810545; e-mail hnrb@hndaily.com.cn; internet hnrb.hinews.cn; Dir ZHOU WENZHANG; Editor-in-Chief CHANG FUTANG.

Harbin Ribao (Harbin Daily): Harbin; internet www.harbindaily.com.

Hebei Ribao (Hebei Daily): 210 Yuhuazhong Lu, Shijiazhuang, Hebei 050013; tel. (311) 88631054; fax (311) 6046969; e-mail webmaster@hebeidaily.com; internet hebnews.cn; f. 1949; Dir GUO ZENGPEI; Editor-in-Chief PAN GUILIANG; circ. 500,000.

Heilongjiang Ribao (Heilongjiang Daily): Heilongjiang Province; tel. (451) 84656368; e-mail hljnews@hljnews.cn; internet www.hljnews.cn; Dir JIA HONGTU; Editor-in-Chief AI HE.

Henan Ribao (Henan Daily): Henan Newspaper Network Center, 10/F, 28 East Agriculture Rd, Zhengzhou, Henan 450008; tel. and fax (371) 65795870; e-mail dahenews@dahe.cn; internet www.dahe.cn; f. 1949; Dir YANG YONGDE; Editor-in-Chief GUO ZHENGLING; circ. 390,000.

Huadong Xinwen (Eastern China News): f. 1995; published by Renmin Ribao.

Huanan Xinwen (South China News): Guangzhou; f. 1997; published by Renmin Ribao.

Hubei Ribao (Hubei Daily): Metropolis Media Bldg, 13/F, 181 Wuchang Dong Wu Lu, Wuhan, Hubei 430077; tel. (27) 88567711; e-mail webmaster@cnhubei.com; internet www.cnhubei.com; f. 1949; Editor-in-Chief YAN SITIAN; circ. 800,000.

Hulunbeir Ribao (Hulunbeir Daily): 28 Victory Ave, Hahilar, Hulunbeir; tel. (470) 8252039; fax (470) 8258035; e-mail hlbrdaily@163.com; internet www.hlbrdaily.com.cn.

Hunan Ribao (Hunan Daily): 18 Furong Zhong Lu, Changsha, Hunan 410071; tel. (731) 4312999; fax (731) 4314029; Dir JIANG XIANLI; Editor-in-Chief WAN MAOHUA.

Jiangxi Ribao (Jiangxi Daily): 175 Yangming Jie, Nanchang, Jiangxi; tel. (791) 6849868; fax (791) 6849008; internet www.jxnews.com.cn/jxrb; f. 1949; Dir ZHOU JINGUANG; circ. 300,000.

Jiefang Ribao (Liberation Daily): 300 Han Kou Lu, Shanghai 200001; tel. (21) 63521111; fax (21) 63516517; e-mail info@jfdaily.com; internet www.jfdaily.com.cn; f. 1949; Editor-in-Chief JIA SHUMEI; circ. 1m.

Jiefangjun Bao (Liberation Army Daily): 34 Fuchengmenwai Dajie, Xicheng Qu, Beijing 100832; tel. (10) 68577779; fax (10) 68577779; e-mail feedback@jfjb.com.cn; internet www.chinamil.com.cn; f. 1956; official organ of the Central Military Commission; Dir Maj.-Gen. ZHANG SHIGANG; Editor-in-Chief WANG MENGYUN; circ. 800,000.

Jilin Ribao (Jilin Daily): Changchun, Jilin Province; tel. (431) 88600621; fax (431) 88600622; e-mail news@chinajilin.com.cn; internet www.chinajilin.com.cn; Dir and Editor-in-Chief YI HONGBIN.

Jingji Ribao (Economic Daily): 2 Bai Zhi Fang Dong Jie, Xuanwu Qu, Beijing 100054; tel. (10) 83512266; fax (10) 83543336; e-mail en_feedback@mail.ce.cn; internet www.ce.cn; f. 1983; financial affairs, domestic and foreign trade; administered by the State Council; Editor-in-Chief TUO ZHEN; circ. 1.2m.

Jinrong Shibao (Financial News): 18 Zhongguancun Nan Dajie, 18–22/F, Blk D, Haidan Qu, Beijing 100081; tel. (10) 82198111; fax (10) 82198029; e-mail fnweb@126.com; internet www.financialnews.com.cn.

Liaoning Ribao (Liaoning Daily): Shenyang, Liaoning Province; tel. (10) 22698539; e-mail lnd@lndaily.com.cn; internet www.lndaily.com.cn; Dir XIE ZHENGQIAN.

Nanfang Ribao (Nanfang Daily): 289 Guangzhou Da Lu, Guangzhou, Guangdong 510601; tel. (20) 87373998; fax (20) 87375806; internet nf.nfdaily.cn; f. 1949; Nanfang Daily Group also publishes *Nanfang Dushi Bao* (Southern Metropolis Daily), *Ershiyi Shiji Jingji Baodao* (21st Century Economic Herald), and weekly edn *Nanfang Zhoumo* (Southern Weekend); Dir YANG XINFENG; Editor WANG FU; circ. 1m.

Nanjing Ribao (Nanjing Daily): 223 Nanjing Lu, Shanghai 210002; tel. (25) 84499000; internet office@njdaily.cn; Editor ZHAO LIANG.

Nongmin Ribao (Peasants' Daily): Shilipu Beili, Chaoyang Qu, Beijing 100029; tel. (10) 85831572; fax (10) 85832154; e-mail zbs@farmer.com.cn; internet www.farmer.com.cn/wlb/nmrb; f. 1980; 6 a week; circulates in rural areas nationwide; Dir ZHANG DEXIU; Editor LIU ZHENYUN; circ. 1m.

Renmin Ribao (People's Daily): 2 Jin Tai Xi Lu, Chaoyang Qu, Beijing 100733; tel. (10) 65363470; fax (10) 65363689; e-mail info@peopledaily.com.cn; internet www.people.com.cn; f. 1948; organ of the CCP; also publishes overseas edn; Pres. ZHANG YANNONG; Editor-in-Chief YANG ZHENWU; circ. 3m.

Shaanxi Ribao (Shaanxi Daily): 1 East Ring Rd, Xian, Shaanxi Province 710054; tel. (29) 82267114; fax (29) 82267082; e-mail sxdaily@tom.com; internet www.sxdaily.com.cn; Dir LI DONGSHENG; Editor-in-Chief DU YAOFENG.

Shanghai Daily: 38/F Wenhui-Xinmin United Press Tower, 755 Weihai Lu, Shanghai 200041; e-mail editor@shanghaidaily.com; internet www.shanghaidaily.com; f. 1999.

Shanxi Ribao (Shanxi Daily): 124 Shuangtasi Jie, Taiyuan, Shanxi; tel. (351) 4281494; fax (351) 4283320; internet www.sxrb.com; CEO LIU XINYU; Editor-in-Chief HU KAIMIN; circ. 300,000.

Shenzhen Tequ Bao (Shenzhen Special Economic Zone Daily): 4 Shennan Zhonglu, Shenzhen 518009; tel. (755) 83518877; e-mail sznews@sznews.com; internet www.sznews.com; f. 1982; reports on special economic zones, as well as mainland, Hong Kong and Macao; Editor-in-Chief HUANG YANGLUE.

Sichuan Ribao (Sichuan Daily): Sichuan Daily Press Group, 70 Hongxing Zhong Lu, Erduan, Chengdu, Sichuan 610012; tel. and fax (28) 86968000; e-mail 028@scol.com.cn; internet www.sichuandaily.com.cn; f. 1952; Chair. of Bd YU CHANGQIU; Editor-in-Chief LUO XIAOGANG; circ. 8m.

Tianjin Ribao (Tianjin Daily): Tianjin Bldg, 10/F, 873 Dagu Nan Lu, Heri Qu, Tianjin 300211; tel. (22) 28201063; fax (22) 28201064; e-mail tjw@tjrb.com.cn; internet www.tianjinwe.com; f. 1949; Editor-in-Chief WANG HONG; circ. 600,000.

Wenhui Bao (Wenhui Daily): 50 Huqiu Lu, Shanghai 200002; tel. (21) 63211410; fax (21) 63230198; internet wenhui.news365.com.cn; f. 1938; Editor-in-Chief WU ZHENBIAO; circ. 500,000.

Xin Jing Bao (The Beijing News): 37 Xingfu Bei Lu, Dongcheng Qu, Beijing 100061; tel. (10) 67106666; fax (10) 67106777; e-mail shepingbj@vip.sina.com; internet www.bjnews.com.cn; f. 2003 as jt venture by owners of Guangming Ribao and Nanfang Ribao.

Xin Min Wan Bao (Xin Min Evening News): 839 Yan An Zhong Lu, Shanghai 200040; tel. (21) 62791234; fax (21) 62473220; e-mail newmedia@wxjt.com.cn; internet xmwb.news365.com.cn; f. 1929;

specializes in public policy, education and social affairs; Editor-in-Chief HU JINGJUN; circ. 1.8m.

Xinhua Ribao (New China Daily): Dacheng Plaza, 20/F, 127 Xuanwumen Xi Lu, Beijing 100031; tel. (10) 63070950; fax (10) 63070938; e-mail xhszbs@xinhuanet.com; internet www.xinhuanet.com; Editor-in-Chief HE PING; circ. 900,000.

Xinjiang Ribao (Xinjiang Daily): Daily News Bldg, 11/F, Yangtze River Rd, Urumqi, Xinjiang 830051; tel. (991) 5593345; fax (991) 5859962; e-mail info@xjdaily.com; internet www.xjdaily.com; Editor-in-Chief HUANG YANCAI.

Xizang Ribao (Tibet Daily): Lhasa, Tibet; Editor-in-Chief LI ERLIANG.

Yangcheng Wanbao (Yangcheng Evening News): 7/F, Yangcheng Wanbao Bldg, 733 Dongfeng Dong Lu, Guangzhou, Guangdong 510085; tel. (20) 87319116; fax (20) 87133836; e-mail kefu@ycwb.net; internet www.ycwb.com; f. 1957; Editor-in-Chief PAN WEIWEN; circ. 1.3m.

Yunnan Ribao (Yunnan Daily): 51 Xinwen Lu, Kunming 650032; tel. (871) 4160447; fax (871) 4156165; e-mail ynrb-zbs@yndaily.com; internet www.yndaily.com; Editor-in-Chief LUO JIE.

Zhejiang Ribao (Zhejiang Daily): Zhejiang Province; tel. (571) 85310961; e-mail zjrb@zjnews.com.cn; internet zjdaily.zjol.com.cn; f. 1949; Pres. GAO HAIHAO; Editor-in-Chief YANG DAJIN.

Zhongguo Qingnian Bao (China Youth Daily): 2 Haiyuncang, Dong Zhi Men Nei, Dongcheng Qu, Beijing 100702; tel. (10) 64098088; fax (10) 64098077; e-mail cehuabu@cyol.com; internet www.cyol.com; f. 1951; daily; aimed at 14–40 age-group; Dir XU ZHUQING; Editor-in-Chief CHEN XIAOCHUAN; circ. 1m.

Zhongguo Ribao (China Daily): 15 Huixin Dong Jie, Chao Yang Qu, Beijing 100029; tel. (10) 64995000; fax (10) 64918377; internet www.chinadaily.com.cn; f. 1981; English; China's political, economic and cultural developments; world, financial and sports news; also publishes *Business Weekly* (f. 1985), *Beijing Weekend* (f. 1991), *Shanghai Star* (f. 1992), *Reports from China* (f. 1992), *21st Century* (f. 1993), *China Daily Hong Kong Edition* ; Editor-in-Chief ZHU LING; circ. 400,000.

Zhongguo Xinwen (China News): 12 Baiwanzhuang Nan Jie, Beijing 100037; tel. (10) 87826688; fax (10) 68327649; e-mail gaojian@chinanews.com.cn; internet www.chinanews.com; f. 1952; daily; current affairs; Editor-in-Chief WANG XIJIN.

SELECTED PERIODICALS

Ban Yue Tan (China Comment): Shijingshan Qu, Beijing 100043; tel. (10) 63074102; fax (10) 63074105; e-mail news_byt@xinhua.org; internet www.xinhuanet.com/banyt; f. 1980; in Chinese and Wei Wuer (Uygur); Editor-in-Chief DONG RUISHENG; circ. 6m.

Beijing Review: 24 Baiwanzhuang Lu, Xicheng Qu, Beijing 100037; tel. (10) 68996288; fax (10) 68328738; e-mail contact@bjreview.com.cn; internet www.bjreview.com.cn; f. 1958; weekly; English; also *Chinafrica* (monthly in English and French); Publr WANG GANGYI; Editor-in-Chief LII HAIBO.

BJ TV Weekly: 2 Fu Xing Men Wai Zhenwumiao Jie, Beijing 100045; tel. (10) 6366036; fax (10) 63262388; circ. 1m.

Caijing: 19/F, Prime Tower, 22 Chaoyangmenwai Lu, Beijing 100020; tel. (10) 65885047; fax (10) 65885046; e-mail newsroom@caijing.com.cn; internet www.caijing.com.cn; f. 1998; business and finance; 2 a month; Editor WANG BOMING.

China TV Weekly: 15 Huixin Dong Jie, Chaoyang Qu, Beijing 100013; tel. (10) 64214197; circ. 1.7m.

Chinese Literature Press: 24 Baiwanzhuang Lu, Beijing 100037; tel. (10) 68326010; fax (10) 68326678; e-mail chinalit@public.east.cn.net; f. 1951; monthly (bilingual in English); quarterly (bilingual in French); contemporary and classical writing, poetry, literary criticism and arts; Exec. Editor LING YUAN.

Chinese National Geography: Rm 200, Jia 11, Datun Rd, Chaoyang Qu, Beijing 100101; tel. (10) 64865566; fax (10) 64859755; e-mail bjb@cng.com.cn; internet cng.dili360.com; f. 1950; monthly; world geography, anthropology and nature; Editor LI SHUAN.

Dianying Xinzuo (New Films): 796 Huaihai Zhong Lu, Shanghai; tel. (21) 64379710; f. 1979; bi-monthly; introduces new films.

Dianzi yu Diannao (Compotech China): Beijing; tel. (10) 82563704; fax (10) 82563744; e-mail jane_ma@compotech.com.cn; internet www.compotech.com.cn; f. 1985; monthly; popular information on computers and microcomputers; Editor-in-Chief CAROL LIAO; circ. 20,000.

Elle (China): 14 Lane 955, Yan'an Zhong Lu, Shanghai; tel. (21) 62790974; fax (21) 62479056; internet www.ellechina.com; f. 1988; monthly; fashion; Publr and Editor-in-Chief XIAO XUE; circ. 300,000.

Guoji Xin Jishu (New International Technology): Zhanwang Publishing House, Beijing; f. 1984; also publ. in Hong Kong; international technology, scientific and technical information.

Guowai Keji Dongtai (Recent Developments in Science and Technology Abroad): 15 Fuxing Lu, Haidian Qu, Beijing 100038; tel. (10) 58882628; fax (10) 58882288; e-mail kjdt@istic.ac.cn; internet www.wanfang.com.cn; f. 1962; monthly; scientific journal; Editor-in-Chief GUO YUEHUA; circ. 40,000.

Huasheng Monthly (Voice for Overseas Chinese): 12 Bai Wan Zhuang Nan Jie, Beijing 100037; tel. and fax (10) 68315039; e-mail huaren@chinanews.com.cn; internet www.chinaqw.com; f. 1995; monthly; intended mainly for overseas Chinese and Chinese nationals resident abroad; Editor-in-Chief FAN DONGSHENG.

Jianzhu (Construction): Baiwanzhuang, Beijing; tel. (10) 68992849; f. 1956; monthly; Editor FANG YUEGUANG; circ. 500,000.

Jinri Zhongguo (China Today): 24 Baiwanzhuang Lu, Beijing 100037; tel. (10) 68996376; fax (10) 68328338; e-mail chinatodaynews@yahoo.com.cn; internet www.chinatoday.com.cn; f. 1952; fmrly China Reconstructs; monthly; edns in English, Spanish, French, Arabic and Chinese; economic, social and cultural affairs; illustrated; Pres. HU BAOMIN.

Liaowang (Outlook): 57 Xuanwumen Xijie, Beijing; tel. (10) 63073049; internet news.sohu.com/liaowang; f. 1981; weekly; current affairs; Editor-in-Chief JI BIN; circ. 500,000.

Luxingjia (Traveller): Beijing; tel. (10) 6552631; e-mail info@luxingjia.com; internet www.luxingjia.com; f. 1955; monthly; Chinese scenery, customs, culture; Editor DAZHEN WU.

Meishu Zhi You (Friends of Art): 32 Beizongbu Hutong, East City Region, Beijing; tel. and fax (10) 5122583; f. 1982; every 2 months; art review journal, also providing information on fine arts publs in China and abroad; Editors ZONGYUAN GAO, PENG SHEN.

Nanfang Zhuomo (Southern Weekend): 289 Guangzhou Da Lu, Guangzhou, Guangdong 510601; tel. (20) 83000300; fax (20) 87375806; e-mail service@infzm.com; internet www.infzm.com; f. 1984; weekly; liberal; Editor-in-Chief HUANG CAN; circ. 1.5m.

Nongye Zhishi (Agricultural Knowledge): 21 Ming Zi Qian Lu, Jinan, Shandong 250100; tel. (531) 88935267; fax (531) 88550734; e-mail sdnyzs@jn-public.sd.cninfo.net; internet www.sdny.com.cn; f. 1950; fortnightly; popular agricultural science; Dir YANG LI JIAN; circ. 410,000.

Qiushi (Seeking Truth): 83 Beiheyan Dajie, Dongcheng Qu, Beijing 100727; tel. (10) 64037005; fax (10) 64022727; e-mail qiushi@qstheory.com; internet www.qsjournal.com.cn; f. 1988; succeeded Hong Qi (Red Flag); 2 a month; theoretical journal of the CCP; Editor-in-Chief LI BAOSHAN; circ. 1.83m.

Renmin Huabao (China Pictorial): 33 Chegongzhuang Xilu, Haidian Qu, Beijing 100044; tel. (10) 88417467; fax (10) 68412601; e-mail cnpictorial@gmail.com; internet www.chinapictorial.com.cn; f. 1950; monthly; edns: two in Chinese, one in Tibetan and 12 in foreign languages; Dir and Editor-in-Chief YU TAO.

Shufa (Calligraphy): 81 Qingzhou Nan Lu, Shanghai 200233; tel. (21) 64519008; fax (21) 64519015; f. 1977; every 2 months; journal on ancient and modern calligraphy; Chief Editor LU FUSHENG.

Stories: 74 Shaoxing Lu, Shanghai 200020; tel. and fax (21) 64677160; e-mail storychina@gmail.com; internet www.storychina.cn; f. 1963; bi-monthly; short stories, fiction, comics; Editor HE CHENGWEI.

Tiyu Kexue (Sports Science): 11 Tiyuguan Lu, Beijing 100061; tel. (10) 87182588; fax (10) 67181293; f. 1981; sponsored by the China Sports Science Soc; monthly; in Chinese; summary in English; Chief Officer TIAN YE; circ. 5,000.

Wenxue Qingnian (Youth Literature Journal): 27 Mu Tse Fang, Wenzhou, Zhejiang; tel. (577) 3578; f. 1981; monthly; Editor-in-Chief CHEN YUSHEN; circ. 80,000.

Window of the South: Guangzhou; tel. (20) 61036188; fax (20) 61036195; e-mail window@vip.163.com; internet www.nfcmag.com; bi-monthly; politics and current affairs; Exec. Editor YANG JUN.

Women of China English Monthly: Rm 814, 15 Jianguonei Dajie, Beijing, 100730; tel. (10) 65103405; fax (10) 65225376; e-mail service@womenofchina.cn; internet www.womenofchina.com.cn; f. 1956; monthly; in English; administered by All-China Women's Federation; women's rights and status, views and lifestyle, education and arts, etc.; Dep. Editor-in-Chief WEI LIANG.

Xian Dai Faxue (Modern Law Science): Southwest University of Political Science and Law, Chongqing, Sichuan 400031; tel. (23) 67258823; fax (23) 67258826; e-mail xiandaifaxue@126.com; internet www.swupl.edu.cn; f. 1979; bi-monthly; with summaries in English; Editor-in-Chief SUN CHANGYONG.

Zhongguo Sheying (Chinese Photography): South Tower Bldg, Rm 502, 67 Campbell St, Dongheng Qu, Dongdan, Beijing 100005; tel. (10) 65280529; fax (10) 65257623; e-mail cphotoeditor@sina.com;

internet www.cphoto.com.cn; f. 1957; monthly; photographs and comments; Editor CHEN ZHONGYUAN.

Zhongguo Zhenjiu (Chinese Acupuncture and Moxibustion): China Academy of Traditional Chinese Medicine, 16 Nan Xiao Jie, Dongzhimen Nei, Beijing 100700; tel. (10) 84014607; fax (10) 84046331; e-mail zhenjiubj@vip.sina.com; internet www.cjacupuncture.com; f. 1981; monthly; publ. by Chinese Soc. of Acupuncture and Moxibustion; abstract in English; Editor-in-Chief Prof. HUANG LONGXIANG.

Other popular magazines include *Gongchandang Yuan* (Communists, circ. 1.63m.) and *Nongmin Wenzhai* (Peasants' Digest, circ. 3.54m.).

NEWS AGENCIES

Xinhua (New China) News Agency: 57 Xuanwumen Xi Dajie, Beijing 100803; tel. (10) 63071114; fax (10) 63071210; e-mail xhszbs@xinhuanet.com; internet www.xinhuanet.com; f. 1931; offices in all Chinese provincial capitals, and about 100 overseas bureaux; news service in Chinese, English, French, Spanish, Portuguese, Arabic and Russian, feature and photographic services; CNC World (China Xinhua News Network Corporation) commenced television broadcasts in Jan. 2010; 24-hour English-language news channel began broadcasting in July 2010; Pres. LI CONGJUN; Editor-in-Chief HE PING.

Zhongguo Xinwen She (China News Service): 12 Baiwanzhuang Nan Jie, Beijing 100037; tel. (10) 87826688; fax (10) 68327649; e-mail hezuo@chinanews.com.cn; internet www.chinanews.com; f. 1952; office in Hong Kong; supplies news features, special articles and photographs for newspapers and magazines in Chinese printed overseas; services in Chinese; Pres. LIU BEIXIAN.

PRESS ORGANIZATIONS

All China Journalists' Association: Xijiaominxiang, Beijing 100031; tel. (10) 66023981; fax (10) 66014658; Chair. TIAN CONG MING.

China Newspapers Association: Beijing; Chair. WANG CHEN.

State Administration of Press, Publication, Radio, Film and Television (see Broadcasting and Communications).

Publishers

A total of 414,005 titles were published in China in 2012.

Beijing Chubanshe Chuban Jituan (Beijing Publishing House Group): 6 Bei Sanhuan Zhong Lu, Beijing 100011; tel. (10) 58572219; fax (10) 58572220; e-mail public@bphg.com.cn; internet www.bph.com.cn; f. 1956; politics, history, law, economics, geography, science, literature, art, etc.; Dir ZHU SHUXIN; Editor-in-Chief TAO XINCHENG.

Beijing Daxue Chubanshe (Peking University Press): 205 Chengfu Lu, Zhongguancun, Haidian Qu, Beijing 100871; tel. (10) 62752033; fax (10) 62556201; e-mail zpup@pup.cn; internet www.pup.cn; f. 1979; academic and general; Pres. WANG MINGZHOU.

China International Book Trading Corpn: 35 Chegongzhuang Xilu, Beijing 100044; tel. (10) 68412045; fax (10) 68412023; e-mail cibtc@mail.cibtc.com.cn; internet www.cibtc.com.cn; f. 1949; foreign trade org. specializing in publs, including books, periodicals, art and crafts, microfilms, etc.; import and export distributors; Pres. QI PINGJIN.

China Publishing Group (CPG): 55A Dajie, Dongcheng Qu, Beijing; tel. and fax (10) 59757238; e-mail zq@cnpubg.com; internet www.cnpubg.com; f. 2002; aims to restructure and consolidate publishing sector; comprises 29 major publishing houses, including the People's Publishing House, the Commercial Press, Zhonghua Book Co, Encyclopaedia of China Publishing House, China Fine Arts Publishing Group, People's Music Publishing House, SDX Joint Publishing Co, China Translation and Publishing Corpn, Orient Publishing Centre; Pres. NIE ZHENNING.

CITIC Publishing House: 8–10/F, Fusheng Bldg, Tower 2, Huixindong Jie 4, Chaoyang Qu, Beijing 100029; tel. (10) 84849555; fax (10) 84849000; e-mail liyinghong@citicpub.com; internet www.publish.citic.com; f. 1988; finance, investment, economics and business; Pres. WANG BIN.

Dianzi Gongye Chubanshe (Publishing House of the Electronics Industry—PHEI): 288 Jin Jia Cun, Wanshou Nan Lu, Beijing 100036; tel. (10) 88258888; fax (10) 68159025; internet www.phei.com.cn; f. 1982; electronic sciences and technology; Pres. LIANG XIANGFENG; Vice-Pres. WANG MINGJUN.

Dolphin Books: 24 Baiwanzhuang Lu, Beijing 100037; tel. (10) 68997480; fax (10) 68993503; e-mail dolphin_books@sina.cn; internet www.dolphin-books.com.cn; f. 1986; children's books in Chinese and foreign languages; Dir WANG YANRONG.

Falü Chubanshe (Law Publishing House): Lianhuachi Xili, Fengtai Qu, Beijing 100073; tel. (10) 63939796; fax (10) 63939622; e-mail info@lawpress.com.cn; internet www.lawpress.com.cn; f. 1980; current laws and decrees, legal textbooks, translations of important foreign legal works; Pres. MIN HUANG.

Foreign Languages Press: 19 Chegongzhuang Xi Lu, Fu Xing Men Wai, Beijing 100044; tel. (10) 68413344; fax (10) 68424931; e-mail wwdinggou@cipg.org.cn; internet www.flp.com.cn; f. 1952; books in 20 foreign languages reflecting political and economic devts in China and features of Chinese culture; Pres. HU BAOMIN; Editor-in-Chief LI ZHENGUO.

Gaodeng Jiaoyu Chubanshe (Higher Education Press): 4 Dewai Dajie, Xicheng Qu, Beijing 100011; tel. (10) 82085550; fax (10) 82085552; e-mail international@hep.edu.cn; internet www.hep.edu.cn; f. 1954; academic, textbooks; Pres. LIU ZHIPENG; Editor-in-Chief ZHANG ZENGSHUN.

Gongren Chubanshe (Workers' Publishing House): Liupukeng, Andingmen Wai, Beijing; tel. (10) 64215278; f. 1949; labour movement, trade unions, science and technology related to industrial production.

Guangdong Keji Chubanshe (Guangdong Science and Technology Press): 11 Shuiyin Lu, Huanshidong Lu, Guangzhou, Guangdong 510075; tel. and fax (20) 37607770; e-mail gdkjzbb@21cn.com; internet www.gdstp.com.cn; f. 1978; natural sciences, technology, agriculture, medicine, computing, English language teaching; Dir HUANG DAQUAN.

Heilongjiang Kexue Jishu Chubanshe (Heilongjiang Science and Technology Press): 41 Jianshe Jie, Nangang Qu, Harbin 150001, Heilongjiang; tel. and fax (451) 3642127; f. 1979; industrial and agricultural technology, natural sciences, economics and management, popular science, children's and general.

Huashan Wenyi Chubanshe (Huashan Literature and Art Publishing House): 45 Bei Malu, Shijiazhuang, Hebei; tel. (311) 22501; f. 1982; novels, poetry, drama, etc.

Kexue Chubanshe (Science Press): 16 Donghuangchenggen Beijie, Beijing 100717; tel. (10) 64034313; fax (10) 64020094; e-mail webmaster@mail.sciencep.com; internet www.sciencep.com; f. 1954; books and journals on science and technology.

Lingnan Meishu Chubanshe (Lingnan Art Publishing House): 11 Shuiyin Lu, Guangzhou, Guangdong 510075; tel. (20) 87771044; fax (20) 87771049; f. 1981; works on classical and modern painting, picture albums, photographic, painting techniques; Pres. CAO LIXIANG.

Minzu Chubanshe (The Ethnic Publishing House): 14 Anwai Hepingli Beijie, Beijing 100013; tel. and fax (10) 64211126; e-mail e56@e56.com.cn; internet www.e56.com.cn; f. 1953; books and periodicals in minority languages, e.g. Mongolian, Tibetan, Uygur, Korean, Kazakh, etc.; Editor-in-Chief HUANG ZHONGCAI.

Qunzhong Chubanshe (Masses Publishing House): Bldg 15, Part 3, Fangxingyuan, Fangzhuan Lu, Beijing 100078; tel. (10) 67633344; f. 1956; politics, law, judicial affairs, criminology, public security, etc.

Renmin Chubanshe (People's Publishing House): 8 Hepinglidongjie, Andingmenwai, Beijing; tel. (10) 4213713; f. 1950; publishes works on Marxism-Leninism, Mao Zedong Thought and Deng Xiaoping Theory, collected works and biographies of Chinese leaders, academic works in philosophy, social sciences, arts and culture, biography, etc.; Dir and Editor-in-Chief XUE DEZHEN.

Renmin Jiaoyu Chubanshe (People's Education Press): 17-1 Zhongguancun Nan Dajie, Haidian Qu, Beijing 100081; tel. (10) 58758866; fax (10) 58758877; e-mail pep@pep.com.cn; internet www.pep.com.cn; f. 1950; school textbooks, guidebooks, teaching materials, etc.

Renmin Meishu Chubanshe (People's Fine Arts Publishing House): Beijing; tel. (10) 65122371; fax (10) 65122370; f. 1951; works by Chinese and foreign painters, sculptors and other artists, picture albums, photographic, painting techniques; Dir GAO ZONGYUAN; Editor-in-Chief CHENG DALI.

Renmin Weisheng Chubanshe (People's Medical Publishing House): 19 Panjia Yuan Xi Lu, Nan Li, Chaoyang Qu, Beijing 100021; tel. (10) 59780011; fax (10) 59787588; e-mail pmphsales@pmph.com; internet www.pmph.com; f. 1953; medicine (Western and traditional Chinese), pharmacology, dentistry, public health; Pres. HU GUOCHEN.

Renmin Wenxue Chubanshe (People's Literature Publishing House): 166 Chaoyangmen, Nei Dajie, Beijing 100705; tel. (10) 65287513; fax (10) 65138394; e-mail rwbq@sina.com; internet www.rw-cn.com; f. 1951; largest publr of literary works and translations into Chinese; Pres. PAN KAIXIONG; Editor-in-Chief GUAN SHIGUANG.

Shanghai Guji Chubanshe (Shanghai Classics Publishing House): 272 Ruijin Erlu, Shanghai 200020; tel. (21) 64370011; fax (21) 64339287; e-mail guji1@guji.com.cn; internet www.guji.com.cn;

f. 1956; classical Chinese literature, history, art, philosophy, geography, linguistics, science and technology.

Shanghai Jiaoyu Chubanshe (Shanghai Education Publishing House): 123 Yongfu Lu, Shanghai 200031; tel. (21) 64377165; fax (21) 64339995; e-mail webmaster@seph.com.cn; internet www.seph.com.cn; f. 1958; academic; Dir and Editor-in-Chief BAO NANLIN.

Shanghai Yiwen Chubanshe (Shanghai Translation Publishing House): 193 Fujian Lu, Shanghai 200001; tel. (21) 53594508; fax (21) 63914291; e-mail info@yiwen.com.cn; internet www.yiwen.com.cn; f. 1978; translations of foreign classic and modern literature; philosophy, social sciences, dictionaries, etc.

Shangwu Yinshuguan (The Commercial Press): 36 Wangfujing Dajie, Beijing 100710; tel. (10) 65258899; fax (10) 65134942; e-mail xxzx@cp.com.cn; internet www.cp.com.cn; f. 1897; dictionaries and reference books in Chinese and foreign languages, translations of foreign works on social sciences; Editor HU LONGBIAO; Pres. YU DIANLI.

Shaonian Ertong Chubanshe (Juvenile and Children's Publishing House): 1538 Yan An Xi Lu, Shanghai 200052; tel. (21) 62823025; fax (21) 62821726; e-mail forwardz@public4.sta.net.cn; f. 1952; children's educational and literary works, teaching aids and periodicals; Gen. Man. ZHOU SHUNPEI.

Wenwu Chubanshe (Cultural Relics Publishing House): 2 Dongzhimen Bei Dajie, Beijing 100007; tel. (10) 64027424; fax (10) 64010698; e-mail web@wenwu.com; internet www.wenwu.com; f. 1956; books and catalogues of Chinese relics in museums and those recently discovered; Dir SU SHISHU.

Wuhan Daxue Chubanshe (Wuhan University Press): Luojia Hill, Wuhan, Hubei; tel. (27) 68756075; fax (27) 68754094; e-mail epd@whu.edu.cn; internet www.wdp.com.cn; f. 1981; reference books, academic works, maps, audio-visual works, etc.; Pres. Prof. CHEN QINGHUI.

Xiandai Chubanshe (Modern Press): 504 Anhua Li, Andingmenwai, Beijing 100011; tel. (10) 64263515; fax (10) 64214540; f. 1981; directories, reference books, etc.; Dir ZHOU HONGLI.

Xinhua Chubanshe (Xinhua Publishing House): 8 Jungyuan Lu, Shijingshan, Beijing 100000; tel. (10) 63074407; fax (10) 63073880; e-mail wjybox@xinhuanet.com; f. 1979; social sciences, economy, politics, history, geography, directories, dictionaries, etc.; Dir LUO HAIYUAN.

Xuelin Chubanshe (Scholar Books Publishing House): 120 Wenmiao Lu, Shanghai 200010; tel. and fax (21) 63768540; f. 1981; academic, including personal academic works at authors' own expense; Dir LEI QUNMING.

Zhongguo Caizheng Jingji Chubanshe (China Financial and Economic Publishing House): 28 Fu Cheng Lu, Haidian Qu, Beijing 100142; tel. (10) 64011805; e-mail cfeph@cfeph.cn; internet www.cfeph.cn; f. 1961; finance, economics, commerce and accounting.

Zhongguo Dabaike Quanshu Chubanshe (Encyclopaedia of China Publishing House): 17 Fu Cheng Men Bei Dajie, Beijing 100037; tel. (10) 68338370; fax (10) 88390680; e-mail jxh@ecph.com.cn; internet www.ecph.com.cn; f. 1978; specializes in encyclopaedias; Dir SHAN JIFU.

Zhongguo Ditu Chubanshe (SinoMaps Press): 57 Nan Lu, Xuanwu Qu, Beijing 100055; tel. (10) 63529243; fax (10) 63529403; e-mail webmaster@sinomaps.com; internet www.sinomaps.com; f. 1954; cartographic publr; Dir ZHAO XIAOMING.

Zhongguo Funü Chubanshe (China Women Publishing House): 24A Shijia Hutong, Beijing 100010; tel. (10) 65228814; fax (10) 65133162; e-mail service@womenbooks.com.cn; internet www.womenbooks.com.cn; f. 1981; women's movement, marriage and family, child care, etc.; Editor-in-Chief YANG GUANGHUI.

Zhongguo Qingnian Chubanzongshe (China Youth Publishing Group): 21 Dongsi Shiertiao, Beijing 100708; tel. (10) 84039659; fax (10) 64031803; e-mail cyp_webmaster@126.com; internet www.cyp.com.cn; f. 1950; state-owned; literature, social and natural sciences, youth work, autobiography; also periodicals; Pres. ZHANG JINGYAN; Editor-in-Chief WEN YUXIN.

Zhongguo Shehui Kexue Chubanshe (China Social Sciences Publishing House): 158A Gulou Xidajie, Beijing 100720; tel. (10) 84029453; fax (10) 84002041; e-mail duzhe-cbs@cass.org.cn; internet www.csspw.com.cn; f. 1978; Dir MENG ZHAOYU.

Zhongguo Xiju Chubanshe (China Theatrical Publishing House): 52 Dongsi Batiao Hutong, Beijing; tel. (10) 64015815; f. 1957; traditional and modern Chinese drama.

Zhongguo Youyi Chuban Gongsi (China Friendship Publishing Corpn): Beijing; e-mail tmdoxu@public.east.cn.net; Dir YANG WEI.

Zhonghua Shuju (Zhonghua Book Co): 38 Taipingqiao Xili, Fenglai Qu, Beijing; tel. (10) 63458226; f. 1912; general; Pres. LI YAN.

PUBLISHERS' ASSOCIATION

Publishers' Association of China: 22 East St, Beijing Art Museum, Dongcheng Qu, Beijing 100010; tel. and fax (10) 65246062; e-mail cbanxie@163.com; internet www.pac.org.cn; f. 1979; arranges academic exchanges with foreign publrs; Chair. YU YOUXIAN.

Broadcasting and Communications

TELECOMMUNICATIONS

The telecommunications industry in the People's Republic of China is regulated by the Ministry of Industry and Information Technology. There were 1,229.1m. mobile telephone users at the end of 2013, with 116.9m. new subscribers in that year. In the same year there were 618m. internet users. Internet coverage stood at 42.1% in 2012.

China Mobile Communications Corpn (China Mobile): 53A Xibianmen Nei Dajie, Xuanwu Qu, Beijing 100053; tel. (10) 63604988; fax (10) 63600364; internet www.chinamobile.com; headquarters in Hong Kong; controlling shareholder in China Mobile (Hong Kong) Ltd; f. 2000; Pres. LI YUE.

China Satellite Communications Corpn Ltd (CHINA SATCOM): International Finance Centre, Haidian Qu, Beijing 100089; tel. (10) 59718188; fax (10) 59718199; internet www.chinasatcom.com; f. 2001; satellite telecommunications, radio and television services; Chair. RUI XIAOWU.

China Telecom Corpn Ltd: 31 Jinrong Jie, Xicheng Qu, Beijing 100032; tel. (10) 66428166; fax (10) 66010728; e-mail ir@chinatelecom.com.cn; internet www.chinatelecom-h.com; f. 1997; est. as a vehicle for foreign investment in telecommunications sector; restructured as a jt-stock ltd company in 2002 with responsibility for fixed-line networks, via its subsidiaries, in 20 provinces, municipalities and autonomous regions; Chair. and CEO WANG XIAOCHU; Pres. YANG JIE.

China United Network Communications Co Ltd (China Unicom): 21 Financial St, Xicheng Qu, Beijing 100140; fax (10) 66110009; e-mail webmaster@chinaunicom.com.cn; internet www.chinaunicom.com.cn; f. 1994; fixed-line and mobile telephone services; fmrly China United Telecommunications Corpn; above name adopted after merger with China Netcom Group in 2009; Chair. and CEO CHANG XIAOBING.

Netease.com: SP Tower D, 26th Floor, Tsinghua Science Park Bldg 8, 1 Zhongguancun Dong Lu, Haidian Qu, Beijing 100084; tel. (10) 82558163; fax (10) 82618163; e-mail bjsales@service.netease.com; internet www.netease.com; f. 1997; Nasdaq-listed internet portal; Founder and CEO WILLIAM DING LEI.

Sina.com: Jinmao Tower, 37th Floor, 88 Century Blvd, Pudong, Shanghai 200121; tel. (21) 50498666; fax (21) 50498806; e-mail ir@staff.sina.com.cn; internet www.sina.com.cn; Nasdaq-listed internet portal; Pres. and CEO CHARLES CHAO; Chair. YAN WANG.

Sohu.com: Sohu Internet Plaza, Park 1, Zhongguancun Dong Lu, Haidian Qu, Beijing 100084; tel. (10) 62726666; fax (10) 62726988; e-mail webmaster@contact.sohu.com; internet www.sohu.com; Nasdaq-listed internet portal; Chair. and CEO CHARLES ZHANG.

BROADCASTING

At the end of 2012 radio and television broadcasting coverage rates were 97.5% and 98.2%, respectively.

Regulatory Authority

State Administration of Press, Publication, Radio, Film and Television: 2 Fu Xing Men Wai Dajie, POB 4501, Beijing 100866; tel. (10) 68513409; fax (10) 68512174; e-mail sarft@chinasarft.gov.cn; internet www.sarft.gov.cn; f. 2013 through a merger of the State Administration of Radio, Film, and Television with the General Administration of Press and Publication; executive branch of the State Council; controls the Central People's Broadcasting Station, the Central TV Station, China Radio International, China Record Co, Beijing Broadcasting Institute, Broadcasting Research Institute, the China Broadcasting Art Troupe, etc.; Dir CAI FUCHAO.

Radio

Radio broadcasting is largely under state control; China National Radio operates the largest radio network in the country.

China National Radio (CNR): 2 Fu Xing Men Wai Dajie, Beijing 100866; tel. (10) 86093114; fax (10) 63909751; e-mail cn@cnr.cn; internet www.cnr.cn; f. 1941; domestic service in Chinese, Zang Wen (Tibetan), Min Nan Hua (Amoy), Ke Jia (Hakka), Hasaka (Kazakh), Wei Wuer (Uygur), Menggu Hua (Mongolian) and Chaoxian (Korean); Dir-Gen. YANG BO.

Radio Tianjin: 143 Weijin Rd, Heping, Tianjin; tel. (22) 23601782; e-mail radiotjworld@gmail.com; internet www.radiotj.com; f. 1949; Pres. FENG XUIFEI.

Shaanxi Radio: 336 Chang An Nan Jie, Xian 710061; tel. (29) 85231660; e-mail sxradio6105@126.com; internet www.sxradio.com.cn.

Zhongguo Guoji Guangbo Diantai (China Radio International): 16A Shijingshan Lu, Beijing 100040; tel. (10) 68891123; fax (10) 68891232; e-mail crieng@cri.com.cn; internet www.cri.cn; f. 1941; fmrly Radio Beijing; foreign service in 61 languages and dialects, incl. Arabic, Burmese, Czech, English, Esperanto, French, German, Hindi, Indonesian, Italian, Japanese, Lao, Malay, Polish, Portuguese, Russian, Spanish, Turkish and Vietnamese; Dir WANG GENGNIAN.

Television

In addition to the state-run television network, there are a number of regional and privately owned television stations. China announced the switch to digital television services in 2006, and was expected to shut down the analogue signal between 2015 and 2018.

China Central Television (CCTV): Media Centre, 11B Fuxing Lu, Haidian Qu, Beijing 100038; tel. (10) 68508381; fax (10) 68513025; e-mail cctv-9@cctv.com; internet www.cntv.com; operates under Bureau of Broadcasting Affairs of the State Council, Beijing; f. 1958; operates 8 networks; 24-hour global satellite service commenced in 1996; Pres. HU ZHANFAN.

Anhui Television (AHTV): 38 Ma On Shan Rd, Heifei 230009; tel. (551) 2615582; fax (551) 2615582; e-mail webmaster@ahtv.cn; internet www.ahtv.cn; f. 1960; broadcasts eight television channels.

China Beijing Television Station (BTV): 98 Jianguo Lu, Chaoyang Qu, Beijing 100022; tel. (10) 68419922; fax (10) 68429120; e-mail btvsuggest@btv.com.cn; internet www.btv.com.cn; broadcasts 14 television channels; state-owned; Dir WANG XIAODONG.

Chongqing Television (CTV): 60 Futuguang, Chongqing 630042; tel. (23) 68812609; fax (23) 63850485; e-mail webmaster@ccqtv.com; internet www.cbg.cn; f. 1961; broadcasts nine television channels.

Fujian Television: 2 Gu Tian Lu, Fuzhou 350001; tel. (591) 83310941; fax (591) 83311945; internet www.fjtv.net; f. 1960; broadcasts 10 television channels; part of the Fujian Media Group.

Gansu Television (GSTV): 226 Dong Gang Xi Lu, Lanzhou 370000; tel. (931) 8416419; fax (931) 8416499; internet www.gstv.com.cn; f. 1970; broadcasts three television channels.

Guangdong Television: Guangdong Television Centre, 331 Huan Shi Dong Lu, Guangzhou 510066; tel. (20) 83355188; e-mail gdtv@gdtv.com.cn; internet www.gdtv.com.cn; f. 1959; programmes in Mandarin, Cantonese and English; state-owned; broadcasts 14 channels.

Guangxi Television (GXTV): 73 National Rd, Nanning 530022; tel. (771) 2196666; fax (771) 5854039; e-mail gxtv@gxtv.com.cn; internet www.gxtv.cn; f. 1970; broadcasts six television channels.

Guizhou Television (GZTV): 261 Qingyun Lu, Nanming, Guiyang, Guizhou 550002; tel. (851) 5376221; e-mail webmaster@gztv.com; internet www.gztv.com; f. 1968; broadcasts three television channels.

Hainan Television (HNTV): Haixiu Rd, Haikou, Hainan 570206; tel. (898) 6778691; fax (898) 6772453; e-mail hninf@hq.cninfo.net; internet www.channel.bluehn.com; f. 1982; broadcasts three television channels.

Hebei Television (HEBTV): internet www.hebtv.com; f. 1969; broadcasts two television channels.

Henan Television (HNTV): 2 Jing Wu Lu, Zhengzhou 450008; tel. (371) 5726212; fax (371) 5726285; e-mail hntv@hntv.ha.cn; internet www.hntv.ha.cn; f. 1969; broadcasts three television channels.

Hubei Television (HBTV): 1 Zi Jin Cun Liang Dao Jie, Wuchang, Wuhan 430071; tel. (27) 87139710; fax (27) 87139706; e-mail webmaster@hbtv.com.cn; internet www.hbtv.com.cn; f. 1960; broadcasts two television channels.

Hunan Television (HNTV): Hunan International Convention & Exhibition Center, 4th Floor, Changsha 410003; tel. (731) 82871680; fax (731) 82871686; e-mail media@hunantv.com; internet www.hunantv.com; f. 1960; broadcasts two television channels; CEO ZHANG RUOBO.

Jiangsu Broadcasting Corpn: 4 East Beijing Rd, Nanjing, Jiangsu; tel. (25) 83188185; fax (25) 83188187; e-mail info@vip.jsbc.com; internet www.jstv.com/jsbc_en/index.shtml; f. 1960; broadcasts 14 television channels; Pres. ZHOU LI.

Liaoning Television (LNTV): 10 Guang Rong Jie, Shenyang 110003; tel. (24) 23232945; fax (24) 22913733; e-mail lntv@lntv.com.cn; internet www.lntv.com.cn; f. 1959; broadcasts two television channels.

Nei Monggol Television (NMGTV): 71 Xinhua Dajie, Hohhot 010058; tel. (471) 6953000; fax (471) 6630600; e-mail info@nmtv.cn; internet www.nmtv.cn; f. 1969; broadcasts two television channels; Dir FANG GUAN.

Ningxia Television (NXTV): 66 Ningxia Lu, Beijing 750001; tel. (951) 6130011; e-mail nxtvweb@nxtv.cn; internet www.nxtv.com.cn; f. 1970; broadcasts two television channels.

Shaanxi Television (SXTV): 336 Chang An Nan Jie, Xian 710061; tel. (29) 85257538; fax (29) 5218553; e-mail webmaster@sxtvs.com; internet www.sxtvs.com; f. 1970; broadcasts seven television channels.

Shandong Television (SDTV): 81 Jingshi Lu, Jinan 250062; tel. (531) 2951295; fax (531) 2953809; e-mail webmaster@sdtv.com.cn; internet www.sdtv.com.cn; f. 1960; broadcasts six television channels.

Shanghai Media Group: 298 Weihai Lu, Shanghai; tel. (21) 62565899; internet www.smg.cn; f. 2001; est. by merger of Radio Shanghai, Eastern Radio Shanghai, Shanghai Television, Oriental Television Station and Shanghai Cable TV; broadcasts 15 television channels and 11 radio channels; Pres. LI RUIGANG.

Shanxi Television (SXTV): 318 Ying Chak Lu, Taiyuan, Shanxi 030001; tel. and fax (351) 4066178; e-mail mail@sxrtv.com; internet www.sxrtv.com; f. 1960; broadcasts two television channels; Dir DONG YUZHONG.

Sichuan Television (SCTV): 40 Dong Sheng Jie, Chengdu 610015; tel. (28) 86636065; fax (28) 86635195; e-mail webmaster@sctv.com; internet www.sctv.com; f. 1960; broadcasts nine television channels.

Xinjiang Television (XJTV): Xinjiang Television Centre 84B, 8th Floor, Urumqi 830044; tel. (991) 2577531; fax (991) 2871947; e-mail XJTVS@96669.net; internet www.xjtvs.com.cn; f. 1970; broadcasts 15 television channels; broadcasts in Mandarin, Uygur and Kazakh.

Xizang Television (XZTV): 11 Xi Lu, Lhasa; tel. (891) 6814522; internet www.xztv.net.cn; f. 1993; broadcasts two television channels; Mandarin and Tibetan.

Yunnan Television: 182 Renmin Xi Lu, Kunmin, Yunnan 650031; tel. (871) 5357842; fax (871) 5350586; e-mail webmaster@yntv.com.cn; internet www.yntv.cn; f. 1969; broadcasts nine television channels.

Zhejiang Satellite Television (ZJSTV): 111 Mo Gan Shan Lu, Hangzhou 310005; internet www.zjstv.com; f. 1960; broadcasts two television channels.

Finance

(cap. = capital; auth. = authorized; p.u. = paid up; res = reserves; dep. = deposits; m. = million; amounts in yuan, unless otherwise stated)

BANKING

Regulatory Authority

China Banking Regulatory Commission: 15 Financial St, Xicheng Qu, Beijing 100140; tel. (10) 66279113; e-mail cbrclib@cbrc.gov.cn; internet www.cbrc.gov.cn; f. 2003; Chair. SHANG FULIN.

Central Bank

People's Bank of China (PBC): 32 Chengfang Jie, Xicheng Qu, Beijing 100800; tel. (10) 66194114; fax (10) 66195370; e-mail webbox@pbc.gov.cn; internet www.pbc.gov.cn; f. 1948; bank of issue; decides and implements China's monetary policies; Gov. ZHOU XIAOCHUAN; 2,204 brs.

Other Banks

Agricultural Bank of China: 69 Jianguomen Nei Dajie, Dongcheng Qu, Beijing 100005; tel. (10) 85109619; fax (10) 85108557; e-mail 95599@abchina.com; internet www.abchina.com; f. 1951; serves mainly China's rural financial operations, providing services for agriculture, industry, commerce, transport, etc. in rural areas; sale of shares commenced in mid-2010; cap. 324,794m., res 216,533m., dep. 11,838,762m. (Dec. 2012); Chair. JIANG CHAOLIANG; Pres. ZHANG YUN; 23,472 brs (domestic).

Agricultural Development Bank of China: 2A Yuetanbei Jie, Xicheng Qu, Beijing 100045; tel. (10) 68081557; fax (10) 68081773; internet www.adbc.com.cn; f. 1994; cap. 20,000m., res 4,174m., dep. 422,375m. (Dec. 2012); Pres. ZHENG HUI.

Bank of Beijing Co Ltd: 17C Financial St, Xicheng Qu, Beijing 100140, Beijing 100031; tel. (10) 66426928; fax (10) 66426691; internet www.bankofbeijing.com.cn; f. 1996; est. as Beijing City United Bank Corpn, changed name to Beijing City Commercial Bank Corpn Ltd in 1998, assumed present name in 2004; cap. 8,800.1m., res 44,618.8m., dep. 964,966.2m. (Dec. 2012); Chair. YAN BINGZHU; Pres. YAN XIAOYAN.

Bank of Changsha: 433 Furong Zhong Lu, Section 1, Changsha, Hunan 410005; tel. (731) 96511; fax (731) 4305560; e-mail cscb@hnccb.com; internet www.cscb.cn; f. 1997; fmrly Changsha City Commercial Bank, name changed as above in 2008; cap. 1,807.8m., res 2,136.5m., dep. 103,837.2m. (Dec. 2011); Chair. ZHI YONG ZHANG.

Bank of China Ltd: 1 Fu Xing Men Nei Dajie, Beijing 100818; tel. (10) 66596688; fax (10) 66594568; e-mail bocir@bank-of-china.com; internet www.boc.cn; f. 1912; handles foreign exchange and international settlements; operates Orient AMC (asset management corporation) since 1999; fmrly Bank of China; became shareholding co in Aug. 2004; cap. 279,147m., res 234,199m., dep. 10,594,367m. (Dec. 2011); Chair. TIAN GUOLI; Pres. LI LIHUI; over 2,000 brs.

Bank of Chongqing: 153 Zou Rong Lu, Zou Rong Sq., Yu Zhong Qu, Chongqing 400010; tel. (23) 63836229; fax (23) 63792176; e-mail webmaster@cqcbank.com.cn; internet www.cqcbank.com.cn; f. 1996; fmrly Chongqing Commercial Bank; cap. 2,020.6m., res 1,671.6m., dep. 127,889.3m. (Dec. 2012); Chair. GAN WEIMIN; Pres. RAN HAILING.

Bank of Communications Ltd: 188 Yin Cheng Lu, Pudong Qu, Shanghai 200120; tel. (21) 58766688; fax (21) 58798398; e-mail investor@bankcomm.com; internet www.bankcomm.com; f. 1908; commercial bank; 19.9% stake was acquired by HSBC in Aug. 2004; cap. 74,262m., res 163,082m., dep. 3,962,264m. (Dec. 2011); Chair. NIU XIMING; Pres. PENG CHUN; 93 brs.

Bank of Hebei Co Ltd: 28 Ping An Bei Lu, Shijiazhuang, Hebei 050011; tel. (11) 88627003; fax (11) 88627075; internet www.hebbank.com; f. 1996; fmrly Shijiazhuang City Commercial Bank, name changed as above in 2009; cap. 2,000m., res 1,543.3m., dep. 86,667.2m. (Dec. 2011); Chair. QIAO ZHIQIANG.

Bank of Jiangsu Co Ltd: 55 Hongwu Lu, Nanjing, Jiangsu Province 210005; tel. (25) 58588050; fax (25) 58588055; internet www.jsbchina.cn; f. 2007; est. by merger of 13 banks; cap. 9,100m., res 16,434.3m., dep. 578,166.7m. (Dec. 2012); Chair. XIA PING; Pres. HU CHANGZHENG.

Bank of Ningbo Co Ltd: 700 Ningnan Dong Lu, Ningbo 315040, Zhejiang; tel. (574) 87050028; fax (574) 87050027; e-mail dsh@nbcb.com.cn; internet www.nbcb.com.cn; f. 1997; cap. 2,883m., res 10,885.4m., dep. 252,120.8m. (Dec. 2012); Chair. LU HUAYU; Pres. LUO MENG-BO.

Bank of Shanghai Co Ltd: 585 Zhongshan Lu (E2), Shanghai 200010; tel. (21) 68475888; fax (21) 68476111; e-mail webmaster@bankofshanghai.com.cn; internet www.bankofshanghai.com; f. 1995; est. as Shanghai City United Bank, assumed present name in 1998; cap. 4,234m., res 18,160.7m., dep. 577,805.5m. (Dec. 2011); Chair. FAN YIFEI; Pres. CHEN XIN; 209 brs.

Bank of Shaoxing Co Ltd: 20 Lao Dong Lu, Shaoxing, Zhejiang 312000; tel. (575) 85129734; fax (575) 85131190; e-mail sxsyyh@mail.sxptt.zj.cn; internet www.sxccb.com; f. 1997; fmrly Shaoxing City Commercial Bank Co Ltd, name changed as above in 2009; cap. 983.6m., res 1,176.5m., dep. 37,807.5m. (Dec. 2012); Pres. CHEN FANG XIAO; Chair. CHEN JUN QUAN; 43 brs.

Bank of Weifang Co Ltd: 5139 Shengli Dong Lu, Weifang 261041; tel. (536) 8106161; internet www.wfccb.com; f. 1997; fmrly Weifang City Commercial Bank, name changed as above in 2009; cap. 1,744.4m., res 822.4m., dep. 38,191.8m. (Dec. 2011); Pres. WANG ZHONGUA.

BNP Paribas (China) Ltd: World Financial Center, 25/F, 100 Century Ave, Pudong Nan Lu, Shanghai 200120; tel. (21) 28962888; fax (21) 28962800; internet www.bnpparibas.com.cn; f. 1992; fmrly Int. Bank of Paris and Shanghai; name changed as above 2004; 100% owned by BNP Paribas SA (France); cap. US $653.1m., res US $79.6m., dep. US $2,581.8m. (Dec. 2012); Chair. LAURENT COURAUDON; CEO CLARENCE T'AO.

Changshu Rural Commercial Bank: 58 Century Blvd, Changshu, Jiangsu; tel. (512) 52909020; fax (512) 52909157; e-mail jscsxhc@sina.com; internet www.csrcbank.com; f. 1953; cap. 1,520.1m., res. 3,030.4m., dep. 66,871.1m. (Dec. 2012); Chair. SONG JIANMING; Pres. QIN WEIMING.

China Bohai Bank: 201–205 Machang Lu, Hexi Qu, Tianjin 300204; tel. (22) 58316666; fax (22) 58316528; e-mail enquiry@cbhb.com.cn; internet www.cbhb.com.cn; f. 2004; 20% stake owned by Standard Chartered Bank; cap. 13,855m., res 3,484.3m., dep. 339,408.3m. (Dec. 2012); Chair. LIU BAOFENG; Pres. ZHAO SHIGANG.

China Citic Bank Corpn Ltd: Blk C, Fuhua Mansion, 8 Chaoyang Men Bei Dajie, Dongcheng Qu, Beijing 100027; tel. (10) 65558000; fax (10) 65550809; e-mail ir@citicbank.com; internet bank.ecitic.com; f. 1987; est. as Citic Industrial Bank; name changed as above in April 2007; cap. 46,787m., res 77,087m., dep. 2,516,849m. (Dec. 2011); Chair. TIAN GUOLI; Pres. CHEN XIAOXIAN; 26 brs.

China Construction Bank Corpn (CCBC): 25 Jinrong Jie, Xicheng Qu, Beijing 100033; tel. (10) 67597114; fax (10) 66212862; e-mail ccb@bj.china.com; internet www.ccb.com; f. 1954; fmrly People's Construction Bank of China; makes payments for capital construction projects; issues loans to construction enterprises and others, incl. housing loans; handles foreign-exchange business; cap. 250,011m., res 271,864m., dep. 11,080,855m. (Dec. 2011); Chair. WANG HONGZHANG; Pres. ZHANG JIANGUO; 44 brs.

China Development Bank (CDB): 29 Fuchengmenwai Dajie, Xicheng Qu, Beijing 100037; tel. (10) 68306688; fax (10) 68306699; e-mail webmaster@cdb.cn; internet www.cdb.com.cn; f. 1994; merged with China Investment Bank 1998; handles low-interest loans for infrastructural projects and basic industries; cap. 306,711m., res 98,098m., dep. 1,112,841m. (Dec. 2012); Chair. HU HUAIBANG; Pres. ZHENG ZHIJIE; 32 BRS.

China Everbright Bank: Everbright Centre, 25 Tai Ping Qiao Dajie, Xicheng Qu, Beijing 100033; tel. (10) 63636363; fax (10) 63639066; e-mail eb@cebbank.com; internet www.cebbank.com; f. 1992; est. as Everbright Bank of China; acquired China Investment Bank and assumed present name in 1999; cap. 40,434.7m., res 54,881.0m., dep. 1,954,502m. (Dec. 2012); Pres. GUO YOU; Chair. TANG SHUANGNING; 30 brs.

China Guangfa Bank Co Ltd: 713 Dongfeng Dong Lu, Guangzhou, Guangdong 510080; tel. (20) 38323832; fax (20) 87310779; internet www.cgbchina.com.cn; f. 1988; fmrly Guangdong Development Bank; name changed as above in 2011; cap. 15,402.3m., res 28,651.4m., dep. 1,034,786.7m. (Dec. 2012); Chair. DONG JIANYUE; Pres. MORRIS LI; 30 brs.

China International Capital Corporation (CICC): 28th Floor, China World Tower 2, 1 Jian Guo Men Wai Dajie, Beijing 100004; tel. (10) 65051166; fax (10) 65051156; e-mail info@cicc.com.cn; internet www.cicc.com.cn; f. 1995; international investment bank; 43.4% owned by China Jianyin Investment Ltd, 34.3% owned by Morgan Stanley; registered cap. US $125m.; Chair. LI JIANGE; Pres. and CEO LEVIN ZHU.

China Merchants Bank: China Merchants Bank Tower, 49/F, 7088 Shennan Blvd, Shenzhen 518040; tel. (755) 83198888; fax (755) 83105109; e-mail cmb@cmbchina.com; internet www.cmbchina.com; f. 1987; cap. 21,577m., res 107,425m., dep. 2,917.7m. (Dec. 2012); Chair. Dr FU YUNING; Pres. and CEO TIAN HUIYU; 82 brs.

China Minsheng Banking Corporation: 8/F, 2 Fuxingmen Nei Dajie, Xicheng Qu, Beijing 100031; tel. (10) 58560666; fax (10) 58560635; internet www.cmbc.com.cn; first non-state national commercial bank, opened Jan. 1996; cap. 28,336m., res 97,096m., dep. 2,703.4m. (Dec. 2012); Chair. DONG WENBIAO; Pres. QI HONG; 30 brs.

China Zheshang Bank Co Ltd: 288 Qingchun Lu, Hangzhou, Zhejiang 310006; tel. (571) 95105665; fax (571) 87659108; e-mail zcbho@mail.nbptt.zj.cn; internet www.czbank.com; f. 1993; fmrly Zhejiang Commercial Bank; cap. 10,007m., res 8,043.4m., dep. 329,048.4m. (Dec. 2012); Chair. ZHANG DAYANG; 68 brs.

Chinese Mercantile Bank: Ground and 23rd Floors, Dongfeng Bldg, 2010 Shennan Lu, Futian Qu, Shenzhen 518031; tel. (755) 83786833; fax (755) 83257955; e-mail service@cmbcn.com.cn; internet www.cmbcn.com.cn; f. 1993; wholly owned by ICBC (Asia) Ltd; cap. 3,150m., res 421.3m., dep. 33,887.1m. (Dec. 2011); CEO WAN HAI SONG.

CITIC Group: Capital Mansion, 6 Xin Yuan Nan Lu, Chaoyang Qu, Beijing 100004; tel. (10) 64660088; fax (10) 64661186; e-mail g-office@citic.com.cn; internet www.citicgroup.com.cn; f. 1979; name changed from China International Trust and Investment Corporation in 2003; economic and technological co-operation; finance, banking, investment and trade; total assets 3,227,100m. (Dec. 2011); Chair. CHANG ZHENMING; Pres. TIAN GUOLI.

Export and Import Bank of China (China Exim Bank): 30 Fu Xin Men Nei Lu, Xicheng Qu, Beijing 100031; tel. (10) 83579988; fax (10) 66060636; internet www.eximbank.gov.cn; f. 1994; provides trade credits for export of large machinery, electronics, ships, etc.; cap. 5,000m., res 10,697.5m., dep 336,246.7m. (Dec. 2012); Chair. and Pres. LI RUOGU.

Fujian Haixia Bank Co Ltd: 158 Liuyi Bei Lu, Fuzhou; tel. (591) 87593778; fax (591) 87585341; e-mail gyb@fuzhoubank.com; internet www.fjhxbank.com; fmrly Fuzhou City Commercial Bank Co Ltd, name changed as above in 2009; cap. 2,965.4m., res 1,890.6m., dep. 56,908.4m. (Dec. 2012); Chair. YUNLIAN GUO; Pres. JIEHONG JIANG; 30 brs.

Guangdong Shunde Rural Commercial Bank Co Ltd: 38 Fengshan Zhong Lu, Guangdong, Shunde 528300; tel. (757) 22388888; fax (757) 22388226; e-mail lsbgs@sdebank.com; internet www.sdebank.com; fmrly The Rural Credit Cooperatives Union of Shunde, name changed to Foshan Shunde Rural Commercial Bank in 2009 and as above in 2012; cap. 2,227.7m., res 5,378.4m., dep. 137,744.2m. (Dec. 2012).

Guangxi Beibu Gulf Bank Co Ltd: 10 Qing Xiu Lu, Nanning, Guangxi Zhuang 530028; tel. (771) 6115338; fax (771) 6115383; internet www.bankofbbg.com; cap. 2,500m., res 3,753.9m., dep. 70,398.8m. (Dec. 2012); Chair. TENG CHONG; Pres. ZHAO XIJUN.

Hua Xia Bank: Hua Xia Bank Mansions, 22 Jianguomennei Dajie, Dongcheng Qu, Beijing 100005; tel. (10) 85238000; fax (10) 85239000; e-mail zhgjb@hxb.com.cn; internet www.hxb.com.cn; f. 1992; est. as part of Shougang Corpn; cap. 6,849.7m., res 49,935.5m., dep. 1,265,255m. (Dec. 2012); Chair. WU JIAN; Pres. FAN DAZHI; 47 brs.

Industrial and Commercial Bank of China: 55 Fu Xing Men Nei Dajie, Xicheng Qu, Beijing 100140; tel. (10) 66106070; fax (10) 66106053; e-mail webmaster@icbc.com.cn; internet www.icbc.com.cn; f. 1984; handles industrial and commercial credits and international business; operates Huarong AMC (asset management corporation) since 1999; cap. 349,084m., res 294,324m., dep. 13,816,008m. (Dec. 2011); Chair. JIANG JIANQING; Pres. YANG KAISHENG.

Industrial Bank Co Ltd: Zhong Shang Bldg, 154 Hudong Lu, Hualin, Fuzhou, Fujian 350003; tel. (591) 87839338; fax (591) 87841932; e-mail irm@cib.com.cn; internet www.cib.com.cn; f. 1982; fmrly Fujian Industrial Bank; cap. 12,702m., res 85,592m., dep. 2,707,702m. (Dec. 2012); Chair. GAO JIANPING; Pres. LI RENJIE; 79 brs.

Laishang Bank Co Ltd: 137 Longtan Dong Dajie, Laiwu, Shandong 271100; tel. (634) 8861182; fax (634) 8681177; e-mail lsyhbgs@163.com; internet www.lsbankchina.com; f. 1987; cap. 1,000m., res 2,578.4m., dep. 35,979.7m. (Dec. 2012); Chair LI MINSHI; Pres. TAN LEQING.

Linshang Bank Co Ltd: 336 Yimeng Lu, Linyi, Shandong; tel. (539) 8311353; fax (539) 8309052; e-mail lypfboy@sohu.com; internet www.lsbchina.com; f. 1998; fmrly Linyi City Commercial Bank Co Ltd, name changed as above in 2008; cap. 2,514.2m., res 1,395.8m., dep. 43,540.7m. (Dec. 2012); Chair. WANG JIAYU; Gen. Man. QIANG ZHAO.

PingAn Bank Co Ltd: 5047 Shennan Dong Lu, Shenzhen, Guangdong 518001; tel. (755) 22168113; e-mail callcenter@pingan.com.cn; internet bank.pingan.com; f. 1995; fmrly Ping An Bank; merged with Shenzhen Development Bank and renamed as above in 2012; Chair. XIAO SUINING; Pres. SHAO PING; 45 brs.

QiLu Bank Co Ltd: 176 Shun He Lu, Jinan 250001; tel. (531) 86075850; fax (531) 81915514; e-mail boardoffice@qlbchina.com; internet www.qlbchina.com; f. 1996; fmrly Jinan City Commercial Bank Co Ltd, above name adopted in 2009; cap. 2,368.7m., res 2,524m., dep. 71,605.4m. (Dec. 2012); Chair. QIU YUNZHANG.

Shanghai Pudong Development Bank: 12 Zhongshan Dong Yi Lu, Shanghai 200002; tel. (21) 63296188; fax (21) 63232036; e-mail bdo@spdb.com.cn; internet www.spdb.com.cn; f. 1993; cap. 18,653.4m., res 109,858m., dep. 2,681,044m. (Dec. 2012); Chair. JI XIAOHUI; Pres. FU JIANHUA; 28 brs.

Xiamen Bank Co Ltd: 101 Hubin Bei Lu, Siming, Xiamen 361012; tel. (592) 2275219; fax (592) 2275173; e-mail xmcbgc@public.xm.fj.cn; internet www.xmccb.com; f. 1996; cap. 1,372.8m., res 2,843.8m., dep. 66,849.4m. (Dec. 2012); Pres. WU SHIQUN.

Xiamen International Bank: 8–10 Jiang Lu, Xiamen, Fujian 361001; tel. (592) 2078888; fax (592) 2988788; e-mail xib@xib.com.cn; internet www.xib.com.cn; f. 1985; cap. 1,807.8m., res 7,238.8m., dep. 179,869.8m. (Dec. 2012); Chair. WENG RUO TONG; Pres. LU YAO MING; 3 brs.

Zhejiang Chouzhou Commercial Bank Co Ltd: Jiangbin Lu, Yiwu Leyuan, Zhejiang 322000; tel. (579) 85337701; fax (579) 85337706; e-mail intl@czcb.com.cn; internet www.czcb.com.cn; f. 2006; cap. 1,337m., res 4,308m., dep. 66,335.4m. (Dec. 2012); Chair. JIN ZIJUN; Pres. ZHOU RUIGU.

STOCK EXCHANGES

Stock Exchange Executive Council (SEEC): Beijing; tel. (10) 64935210; f. 1989; oversees the development of financial markets in China; mems comprise leading non-bank financial institutions authorized to handle securities; Vice-Pres. WANG BOMING.

Securities Association of China (SAC): Focus Plaza, 2/F, Tower B, 19 Financial St, Xicheng Qu, Beijing 100032; tel. (10) 66575800; fax (10) 66575827; e-mail bgs@sac.net.cn; internet www.sac.net.cn; f. 1991; 332 mems; Chair. HUANG XIANGPING.

Beijing Securities Exchange: 5 Anding Lu, Chao Yang Qu, Beijing 100029; tel. (10) 64939366; fax (10) 64936233.

Shanghai Stock Exchange (SSE): 528 Pudong Nan Lu, Shanghai 200120; tel. (21) 68808888; fax (21) 68804868; e-mail webmaster@secure.sse.com.cn; internet www.sse.com.cn; f. 1990; 975 listed cos (Dec. 2012); Chair. GUI MINJIE; Pres. HANG HONGYUAN.

Shenzhen Stock Exchange (SZSE): 5045 Shennan Dong Lu, Shenzhen, Guangdong 518010; tel. (755) 82083333; fax (755) 82083947; e-mail cis@szse.cn; internet www.szse.cn; f. 1991; 1,536 listed cos (Sept. 2013); Chair. CHEN DONGZHENG; Pres. SONG LIPING.

Regulatory Authorities

Operations are regulated by the State Council Securities Policy Committee and by the following:

China Securities Regulatory Commission (CSRC): 19 Focus Plaza, Jinrong Lu, Xicheng Qu, Beijing 100033; tel. (10) 66210182; fax (10) 66210205; e-mail consult@csrc.gov.cn; internet www.csrc.gov.cn; f. 1993; Chair. XIAO GANG.

INSURANCE

At the end of 2010 the number of insurance institutions operating in China totalled 142, of which eight were insurance group corporations, 53 were joint venture corporations and 81 were domestically funded insurance corporations.

Aegon-CNOOC Life Insurance Co Ltd: 15/F, Pufa Tower, 588 Pudong Nan Lu, Shanghai 200120; internet www.aegon-cnooc.com; f. 2002; jt venture between Aegon (The Netherlands) and China Nat. Offshore Oil Corpn.

Anbang Property and Casualty Insurance Co Ltd: Beijing; tel. (10) 65309999; e-mail webmaster@ab-insurance.com; internet www.ab-insurance.com; f. 2004.

AXA-Minmetals Assurance Co: 19/F China Merchants Tower, 166 Jia Zui Dong Lu, Pudong, Shanghai 200120; tel. (21) 58792288; fax (21) 58792299; internet www.axa-minmetals.com.cn; f. 1999; jt venture by Groupe AXA (France) and China Minmetals Group; CEO MA ZHEMING.

China Continent Property and Casualty Insurance Co Ltd: Shanghai; tel. (21) 58369588; internet www.ccic-net.com.cn; f. 2003; Chair. DAI FENGJU; CEO JIANG MING.

China Life Insurance Co: China Life Centre, 22–28/F, 17 Financial St, Xicheng Qu, Beijing 100140; tel. (10) 66009999; e-mail serve@e-chinalife.com; internet www.chinalife.com.cn; f. 1999; formed from People's Insurance (Life) Co, division of fmr People's Insurance Co of China—PICC; restructured into a parent company and a shareholding company Aug. 2003; initial public offering Dec. 2003; Chair. YANG MINGSHENG; Exec. Dir WAN FENG.

China Pacific Insurance Co Ltd (CPIC): 1226 Zhongshan Lu (Bei 1), Shanghai; tel. (21) 58767282; fax (21) 68870791; e-mail ir@cpic.com.cn; internet www.cpic.com.cn; f. 1991; jt-stock co; Chair. GAO GUOFU; Pres. YANG XIANGHAI.

China Taiping Insurance Group Co: Beijing; tel. (10) 63600601; fax (10) 63600605; internet www.cntaiping.com; f. 1931; fmrly China Insurance (Holdings) Co Ltd; cargo, hull, freight, fire, life, personal accident, industrial injury, motor insurance, reinsurance, etc.; 20 subsidiaries; Chair. BIN WANG; CEO KENNETH NG YU LAM.

China United Property Insurance Co: 600 Chengdu Bei Lu, Shanghai; tel. (21) 53554600; fax (21) 63276000; internet www.cicsh.com; f. 1986; fmrly Xinjiang Corpn Property Insurance Co; Gen. Man. LU FENG YUAN.

Huatai Insurance Co of China Ltd: International Business Bldg, 18/F, Tower A, 35 Financial St, Xicheng Qu, Beijing 100033; tel. (10) 59371818; fax (10) 63370081; e-mail beijing@ehuatai.com; internet www.ehuatai.com; f. 1996; est. by 63 industrial cos; Chair. and CEO WANG ZIMU.

Manulife Sinochem Life Insurance Co Ltd: Jin Mao Bldg, 21/F, 88 Century Rd, Pudong, Shanghai 200121; tel. (21) 50492288; fax (21) 50491110; e-mail cs@manulife-sinochem.com; internet www.manulife-sinochem.com; f. 1996; jt venture between Manulife (Canada) and Sinochem; Chair. MARC STERLING.

New China Life Insurance: 12 Jian Guo Man Wai Dajie, Chaoyang Qu, Beijing 100073; e-mail e@newchinalife.com; internet www.newchinalife.com; f. 1996; Chair. KANG DIAN.

PICC Property and Casualty Co Ltd: 69 Dongheyan Jie, Xuanwu Men, Beijing 100052; tel. (10) 63156688; fax (10) 63033589; e-mail webmaster@piccnet.com.cn; internet www.picc.com.cn; f. 2003; fmrly the People's Insurance Company of China; Chair. WU YAN; CEO YI WANG.

Ping An Insurance (Group) Co of China (Ping An): Galaxy Development Centre, 3 Fu Hua Lu, Futian District, Shenzhen; tel. (400) 8866338; fax (755) 82431019; e-mail IR@pingan.com.cn; internet www.pingan.com; f. 1988; 15.6% owned by Charoen Pokphand Group (Thailand); total assets 292,519m. (June 2005); Chair. and CEO MA MINGZHE.

Sino Life Insurance: Yi Tian Rd, Fujian Qu, Shenzhen; internet www.sino-life.com; f. 2000; Chair. ZHANG JUN.

Sunlife Everbright Insurance Co Ltd: 37/F, Tianjin International Bldg, 75 Nanjing Lu, Heping Qu, Tianjin 300050; tel. (22) 23391188; fax (22) 23399929; internet www.sunlife-everbright.com; f. 1999; jt venture between Sunlife Financial (Canada) and China Everbright Group; Pres. and CEO JANET DE SILVA.

Sunshine Property and Casualty Insurance Co Ltd: 28/F, Kuntai International Mansion, 12B Chao Wai Dajie, Beijing 100020; tel. (10) 58289999; fax (10) 58289688; e-mail pinpaixuanchuan@ygbx.com; internet yangguang.sinosig.com; Pres. and Dir-Gen. ZHANG WEIGONG.

Taikang Life Insurance Co Ltd: Taikang Life Bldg, 156 Fu Xing Men Nei Dajie, Beijing 100031; tel. (10) 66429988; fax (10) 66426397; internet www.taikang.com; f. 1996; Chair. CHEN DONGSHENG.

Tianan Insurance Co Ltd: 1 Pudong Dajie, Shanghai 200120; tel. (21) 61017878; internet www.tianan-insurance.com; f. 1994; Chair. QIU QIANG.

Yongan Insurance: Jinqiao International Plaza, Tower C, 50 Keji Lu, Xian 710075; tel. (29) 87233888; fax (29) 88231200; internet www.yaic.com.cn; Chair. ZHANG DONG WU.

Regulatory Authority

China Insurance Regulatory Commission (CIRC): 15 Financial St, Xicheng Qu, Beijing 100140; tel. (10) 66286688; fax (10) 66018871; e-mail help@circ.gov.cn; internet www.circ.gov.cn; f. 1998; under direct authority of the State Council; Chair. WU DINGFU.

Trade and Industry

GOVERNMENT AGENCIES

China Council for International Investment Promotion (CCIIP): Rm 406–409, Jing Guang Centre, Hujia Lu, Chao Yang Qu, POB 8806, Beijing 100020; tel. (10) 65978801; fax (10) 65978210; e-mail msc@cciip.org.cn; internet www.cciip.org.cn; f. 2006; est. by State Council; aims to promote China's inward and outward investment; Pres. MIAO GENGSHU; Sec.-Gen. ZHOU MING.

China Investment Corpn (CIC): New Poly Plaza, 1 Chaoyangmen Bei Dajie, Dongcheng Qu, Beijing 100010; tel. (10) 64086277; fax (10) 64086908; e-mail pr@china-inv.cn; internet www.china-inv.cn; f. 2007; sovereign wealth fund; manages China's foreign-exchange reserves; Chair. LOU JIWEI; Pres. GAO XIQING.

China National Light Industry Council: 22B Fuwai Dajie, Beijing 100833; tel. (10) 68396613; fax (10) 68396264; e-mail webmaster@clii.com.cn; internet www.clii.com.cn; under supervision of State Council; Chair. CHEN SHINENG; Sec.-Gen. WANG SHICHENG.

China National Textile Industry Council (CNTIC): 12 Dong Chang An Jie, Beijing 100742; tel. (10) 65129545; under supervision of State Council; Chair. SHI WANPENG.

State Administration of Foreign Exchange (SAFE): Huanrong Hotel, 18 Fucheng Lu, Haidan Qu, Beijing 100048; tel. (10) 68402265; internet www.safe.gov.cn; drafts foreign-exchange regulations, designs and implements balance of payments statistical system, manages foreign-exchange reserves; brs in Hong Kong, Singapore, London and New York; Administrator YI GANG.

State Administration for Industry and Commerce: 8 San Li He Dong Lu, Xicheng Qu, Beijing 100820; tel. (10) 68013447; fax (10) 68010463; e-mail dfa@saic.gov.cn; internet www.saic.gov.cn; responsible for market supervision and administrative execution of industrial and commercial laws; functions under direct supervision of State Council.

State-owned Assets Supervision and Administration Commission: West St, Xuanwu, Beijing 100053; tel. (10) 63192334; e-mail iecc@sasac.gov.cn; internet www.sasac.gov.cn; f. 2003; supervision and administration of state-owned assets, regulation of ownership transfers of state-owned enterprises; Chair. ZHANG YI.

Takeover Office for Military, Armed Police, Government and Judiciary Businesses: Beijing; f. 1998; est. to assume control of enterprises fmrly operated by the People's Liberation Army.

CHAMBERS OF COMMERCE

All-China Federation of Industry and Commerce (All-China General Chamber of Industry and Commerce): 93 Beiheyan Dajie, Beijing 100006; tel. (10) 65136677; fax (10) 65131769; e-mail acfic@acfic.org.cn; internet www.acfic.com.cn (Chinese); www.chinachamber.org.cn (English); f. 1953; Chair. HUANG MENGFU.

China Chamber of Commerce for the Import and Export of Foodstuffs, Native Produce and Animal By-products (CFNA): Talent International Bldg, 80 Guanqumennei Jie, Chongwen Qu, Beijing 100062; tel. (10) 87109883; fax (10) 87109829; e-mail contact@cccfna.org.cn; internet www.cccfna.org.cn; f. 1988; over 5,400 mems; Pres. BIAN ZHENHU.

China Chamber of Commerce for Import and Export of Light Industrial Products and Arts-Crafts (CCCLA): 10/F, Pan Jia Yuan Da Sha Bldg, 12 Pan Jia Yuan Nanli, Chaoyang Qu, Beijing 100021; tel. (10) 67732707; fax (10) 67732698; e-mail xxb@cccla.org.cn; internet www.cccla.org.cn; f. 1988; over 6,000 mems; Chair. WANG ZHONGQI.

China Chamber of Commerce for Import and Export of Machinery and Electronic Products (CCCME): Rm 904, 9/F, Bldg 12, Pan Jia Yuan Nanli, Chaoyang Qu, Beijing; tel. (10) 58280863; fax (10) 58280860; e-mail international@cccme.org.cn; internet www.cccme.org.cn; f. 1988; more than 6,500 mems; Pres. and Sec.-Gen. ZHANG YUJING.

China Chamber of Commerce for Import and Export of Medicines and Health Products (CCCMHPIE): 11–12/F, Bldg 3, 6 Nanzhugan Hutong, Dongcheng Qu, Beijing 100010; tel. (10) 58036282; fax (10) 58036284; internet www.cccmhpie.org.cn; f. 1989; more than 1,500 mems; Pres. ZHOU XIAOMING.

China Chamber of Commerce for Import and Export of Textiles (CCCT): 12 Pan Jia Yuan Nanli, Chaoyang Qu, Beijing 100021; tel. (10) 67739246; fax (10) 67719235; e-mail info@ccct.org.cn; internet www.ccct.org.cn; f. 1988; Chair. WANG SHENYANG; over 6,300 mems.

China Council for the Promotion of International Trade (CCPIT)—China Chamber of International Commerce (CCOIC): 1 Fuxingmenwai Lu, Xicheng Qu, Beijing 100860; tel. (10) 88075000; fax (10) 68011370; e-mail webmaster@ccpit.org; internet www.ccpit.org; Chair. WAN JIFEI.

TRADE AND INDUSTRIAL ORGANIZATIONS

Beijing Urban Construction Group Co Ltd: 62 Xueyuannan Lu, Haidian Qu, Beijing 100081; tel. (10) 62255511; fax (10) 62256027; e-mail cjp@mail.bucg.com; internet www.bucg.com; construction of civil and industrial buildings and infrastructure; Chair. LIU LONGHUA.

China Aerospace Science and Industry Corpn (CASIC): Aerospace Science and Industry Bldg 8, Fu Cheng Men Nei Dajie, Haidian Qu, Beijing 100048; tel. (10) 68373522; fax (10) 68383626; e-mail bgt@casic.com.cn; internet www.casic.com.cn; f. 1999; Gen. Man. XU DAZHE.

China Aerospace Science and Technology Corpn: 16 Fucheng Lu, Haidian Qu, Beijing 100048; tel. (10) 68767492; fax (10) 68372291; e-mail casc@spacechina.com; internet www.spacechina.com; f. 1999; Pres. MA XINGRUI.

China Association of Automobile Manufacturers: 46 San Li He, Xicheng Qu, Beijing 100823; tel. (10) 68594182; fax (10) 68595243; e-mail caam@caam.org.cn; internet www.caam.org.cn; f. 1987; Chair. HU MAOYUAN.

China Aviation Industry Corporation I: AVIC1 Plaza, 128, Jianguo Lu, Beijing 100022; tel. (10) 65665922; fax (10) 65666518; e-mail lixm@avic1.com.cn; internet www.avic1.com.cn; f. 1999; Pres. LIN ZUOMING.

China Aviation Industry Corporation II: 67 Jiao Nan Dajie, Beijing 100712; tel. (10) 64094013; fax (10) 64032109; e-mail international@avic2.com; internet www.avic2.com.cn; Pres. ZHANG HONGBIAO.

China Aviation Supplies Holding Co (CASC): 3 Tianwei Si Jie, Airport Industrial Zone A, Shunyi, Beijing 101312; tel. (10) 89455000; fax (10) 89455018; internet www.casc.com.cn; f. 1980; fmrly China Aviation Supplies Import & Export Group Corpn; aviation equipment supply services; Pres. LI HAI.

China Certification and Inspection Group Co Ltd (CCIC): Sanyuan Bldg, 18 Xibahe Dongli, Chaoyang Qu, Beijing 100028; tel. (10) 84603456; fax (10) 84603333; e-mail ccic@ccic.com; internet www.ccic.com; fmrly China National Import and Export Commodities Inspection Corpn; inspects, tests and surveys import and export commodities for overseas trade, transport, insurance and manufacturing firms; Pres. WANG FENGQING.

China Civil Engineering Construction Corpn (CCECC): 4 Beifeng Wo, Haidian Qu, Beijing 100038; tel. (10) 63263392; fax (10) 63263864; e-mail zongban@ccecc.com.cn; internet www.ccecc.com.cn; f. 1979; general contracting, provision of technical and labour services, consulting and design, etc.; Chair. LIU ZHIMING; Pres. LI YUAN.

China Construction International Inc: 9 Sanlihe Lu, Haidian Qu, Beijing; tel. (10) 68394086; fax (10) 68394097; Pres. FU RENZHANG.

China Electronics Corpn: 27 Wanshou Lu, Haidian Qu, Beijing 100846; tel. (10) 68218529; fax (10) 68213745; e-mail webmaster@cec.com.cn; internet www.cec.com.cn; Chair. XIONG QUNLI; Pres. LIU LIEHONG.

China Garment Industry Corpn: 9A Taiyanggong Beisanhuandong Lu, Chao Yang Qu, Beijing 100028; tel. (10) 64216660; fax (10) 64239134; Pres. DONG BINGGEN.

China General Technology (Group) Holding Ltd (Genertec): 23/F Genertec Plaza, 90 Xi San Huan Zhong Lu, Feng Tai Qu, Beijing 100055; tel. (10) 63348889; fax (10) 63348118; e-mail genertec@genertec.com.cn; internet www.genertec.com.cn; f. 1998; est. by merger of China Nat. Technical Import and Export Corpn, China Nat. Machinery Import and Export Corpn, China Nat. Instruments Import and Export Corpn and China Nat. Corpn for Overseas

Economic Co-operation; total assets 16,000m. yuan; Chair. HE TONGXIN; Dir and Pres. LI DANG.

China Great Wall Computer Group: 18/F, Great Wall Technology Bldg, 66 East Rd, Haidian Qu, Beijing 100190; tel. (10) 59831188; fax (10) 59831133; e-mail cs@gwssi.com.cn; internet www.gwssi.com.cn; f. 1988; Pres. DU HEPING.

China Great Wall Industry Corpn: 67 Beisihuan Xilu, Haidian Qu, Beijing 100080; tel. (10) 88102000; fax (10) 88102107; e-mail cgwic@cgwic.com; internet www.cgwic.com.cn; f. 1980; international commercial wing of China Aerospace Science and Technology Corpn (CASC); Pres. YIN LIMING.

China Guangdong Nuclear Power Holding Co Ltd (CGNPC): Science Bldg, 1001 Shangbu Zhong Lu, Shenzhen 518028; e-mail webmaster_cgnpc@cgnpc.com.cn; internet www.cgnpc.com.cn; f. 1994; operates nuclear power plants; develops hydropower and wind power stations; more than 20 subsidiaries; Chair. HE YU.

China International Book Trading Corpn: see under PublishersChina International Contractors Association: Dong Zhi Men Wai Dajie, Dongcheng Qu, Beijing 100007; tel. (10) 59765260; fax (10) 59765200; e-mail webmaster@chinca.org; internet www.chinca.org; f. 1988; Chair. DIAO CHUNHE.

China International Futures Co Ltd (CIFCO): Rong Chao Business Centre, 15/F, Bldg A, 6003 Yi Tian Lu, Futian Qu, Shenzhen 518000; tel. (755) 23818333; fax (755) 23818283; e-mail cifco996@hotmail.com; internet www.szcifco.com; f. 1992; Pres. CHEN DONGHUA.

China International Telecommunication Construction Corpn (CITCC): 56 Nan Fang Zhuang, Fengtai Qu, Beijing 100079; tel. (10) 67668269; fax (10) 67668183; e-mail office@citcc.cn; internet www.citcc.cn; f. 1983; Chair. WANG QI; Gen. Man. XU CHUGUO.

China International Water and Electric Corpn (CWE): 3 Liupukang Yiqu Zhongjie, Xicheng Qu, Beijing 100120; tel. (10) 59302288; fax (10) 59302900; e-mail headoffice@cwe.cn; internet www.cwe.cn; f. 1956; est. as China Water and Electric International Corpn, name changed 1983; imports and exports equipment for projects in the field of water and electrical engineering; undertakes such projects; provides technical and labour services; Pres. LU GUOJUN.

China Iron and Steel Industry and Trade Group Corpn (Sinosteel): Sinosteel Plaza, 8 Hai Dian Lu, Beijing 100080; tel. (10) 62686689; fax (10) 62686688; e-mail info@sinosteel.com; internet www.sinosteel.com; f. 1999; formed by merger of China National Metallurgical Import and Export Corpn, China Metallurgical Raw Materials Corpn and China Metallurgical Steel Products Processing Corpn; Pres. HUANG TIANWEN.

China Minmetals Corpn (Minmetals): 5 San Li He, Haidian Qu, Beijing 100044; tel. (10) 68495888; fax (10) 68335570; e-mail support@minmetals.com.cn; internet www.minmetals.com.cn; f. 1950; fmrly China National Metals and Minerals Import and Export Corpn, current name adopted 2004; imports and exports steel, antimony, tungsten concentrates and ferro-tungsten, zinc ingots, tin, mercury, pig-iron, cement, etc.; Pres. ZHOU ZHONGSHU.

China National Aerotechnology Import and Export Corpn: Catic Plaza, 18 Beichen Dong Lu, Chaoyang Qu, Beijing 100101; tel. (10) 84972255; fax (10) 84971088; e-mail master@catic.cn; internet www.catic.com.cn; f. 1979; exports signal flares, electric detonators, tachometers, parachutes, general purpose aircraft, etc.; Pres. MA ZHIPING.

China National Animal Breeding Stock Import and Export Corpn (CABS): 5/F Beijing News Plaza, 26 Jian Guo Men Nei Dajie, Beijing 100005; tel. (10) 65228866; fax (10) 85201555; e-mail cabs@cabs.com.cn; sole agency for import and export of stud animals including cattle, sheep, goats, swine, horses, donkeys, camels, rabbits, poultry, etc., as well as pasture and turf grass seeds, feed additives, medicines, etc.; Gen. Man. LIU XIAOFENG.

China National Arts and Crafts (Group) Corpn (CNACGC): Arts and Crafts Bldg, 103 Jixiangli, Chaoyang Men Wai, Chaoyang Qu, Beijing 100020; tel. (10) 85698808; fax (10) 85698866; e-mail info@cnacgc.com; internet www.cnacgc.com; deals in jewellery, ceramics, handicrafts, embroidery, pottery, wicker, bamboo, etc.; jointly est. by two central enterprises: China National Arts and Crafts Import & Export Corpn and China National Arts & Crafts (Group) Corpn; Pres. ZHOU ZHENGSHENG.

China National Automotive Industry Corpn (CNAIC): 46 Fucheng Lu, Haidian Qu, Beijing 100036; tel. (10) 88123968; fax (10) 68125556; Pres. CHEN XULIN.

China National Automotive Industry Import and Export Corpn (CAIEC): 265 Beisihuan Zhong Lu, Beijing 100083; tel. (10) 82379009; fax (10) 82379088; e-mail info@caiec.cn; internet www.caiec.cn; Pres. ZHANG FUSHENG; 1,100 employees.

China National Cereals, Oils and Foodstuffs Import and Export Corpn (COFCO): COFCO Fortune Plaza, 8 Chaoyang Men Wai Dajie, Chaoyang Qu, Beijing 100020; tel. (10) 85006688; fax (10) 65278612; e-mail cofcointo@cofco.com; internet www.cofco.com; f. 1952; imports, exports and processes grains, oils, foodstuffs, etc.; also hotel management and property development; Chair. NING GAONING; Pres. YU XUBO.

China National Chartering Ltd (SINOCHART): Sinotrans Plaza A, Rm 818, 43 Xi Zhi Men Bei Dajie, Beijing 100044; tel. (10) 62295052; fax (10) 62296859; e-mail sinochart@sinochart.com; internet www.sinochart.com; f. 1950; subsidiary of SINOTRANS (see below); arranges chartering of ships, reservation of space, managing and operating chartered vessels; Gen. Man. GENG CHEN.

China National Chemical Construction Corpn: Bldg No. 15, Songu, Anzhenxili, Chaoyang Qu, Beijing 100029; tel. (10) 64429966; fax (10) 64419698; e-mail cnccc@cnccc.com.cn; internet www.cnccc.com.cn; Pres. CHEN LIHUA.

China National Chemicals Import and Export Corporation (SINOCHEM): SINOCHEM Tower, 6–12/F, 28 Fu Xing Men Nei Dajie, Beijing 100031; tel. (10) 59568888; fax (10) 59568890; internet www.sinochem.com; f. 1950; import and export, domestic trade and entrepôt trade of oil, fertilizer, rubber, plastics and chemicals; Pres. LIU DESHU.

China National Coal Group Corpn: 1 Huangsi Lu, Chaoyang Qu, Beijing 100120; tel. (10) 82256688; fax (10) 82236023; e-mail zgzm@chinacoal.com; internet www.chinacoal.com; f. 1982; imports and exports coal and equipment for coal industry, joint coal development and compensation trade; fmrly known as China National Coal Industry Import and Export Corpn; Chair. and Pres. WU YAOWEN.

China National Coal Mine Corpn: 21 Bei Jie, Heipingli, Beijing 100013; tel. (10) 64217766; Pres. WANG SENHAO.

China National Complete Plant Import and Export Corpn (Group) (Complant): 9 Xi Bin He Lu, An Ding Men, Beijing 100011; tel. (10) 64253388; fax (10) 64211382; e-mail info@complant.com; internet www.complant.com; Chair. LI ZHIMIN; Gen. Man. TANG JIANGUO.

China National Electronics Import and Export Corpn: 8th Floor, Electronics Bldg, 23A Fuxing Lu, Beijing 100036; tel. (10) 68219550; fax (10) 68212352; e-mail webmaster@ceiec.com.cn; internet www.ceiec.com.cn; f. 1980; imports and exports electronics equipment, light industrial products, ferrous and non-ferrous metals; advertising; consultancy; Pres. and CEO CHEN XU.

China National Export Bases Development Corpn: Bldg 16–17, District 3, Fang Xing Yuan, Fang Zhuang Xiaoqu, Fengtai Qu, Beijing 100078; tel. (10) 67628899; fax (10) 67628803; Pres. XUE ZHAO.

China National Foreign Trade Transportation Corpn (Group) (SINOTRANS): 12/F, Sinotrans Plaza A, 43 Xi Zhi Men Bei Dajie, Beijing 100044; tel. (10) 62295900; fax (10) 62295901; e-mail office@sinotrans.com; internet www.sinotrans.com; f. 1950; agents for China's import and export corpns; arranges customs clearance, deliveries, forwarding and insurance for sea, land and air transport; Chair. ZHAO HUXIANG; Pres. LIU XIHAN.

China National Gold Group Corpn (China Gold): 1 South St, Liuyin Park, Dongcheng Qu, Beijing 100011; tel. (10) 84123635; fax (10) 84118355; e-mail cngc@chinagoldgroup.com; internet www.chinagoldgroup.com; gold mining, research and trade; Pres. SUN ZHAOXUE.

China National Instruments Import and Export Corpn (Instrimpex): Instrimpex Bldg, 6 Xi Zhi Men Wai Jie, Beijing 100044; tel. (10) 68330618; fax (10) 68318380; e-mail cnic@cnic.genertec.com.cn; internet www.instrimpex.com.cn; f. 1955; imports and exports; technical service, real estate, manufacturing, information service, etc.; Pres. AN FENGSHOU.

China National Light Industrial Products Import and Export Corpn: 910, 9th Section, Jin Song, Chaoyang Qu, Beijing 100021; tel. (10) 67766688; fax (10) 67747246; e-mail info@chinalight.com.cn; internet www.chinalight.com.cn; imports and exports household electrical appliances, audio equipment, photographic equipment, films, paper goods, building materials, bicycles, sewing machines, enamelware, glassware, stainless steel goods, footwear, leather goods, watches and clocks, cosmetics, stationery, sporting goods, etc.; Pres. PAN WANG.

China National Machine Tool Corpn: World Trade Centre, 23/F, Blk A, Dong San Huan Bei Lu, Dongcheng Qu, Beijing; tel. (10) 58257788; fax (10) 64015657; e-mail zcb@cnmtc.net; internet www.cnmtc.net; f. 1979; imports and exports machine tools and tool products, components and equipment; supplies apparatus for machine-building industry; Pres. QUAN YILU.

China National Machinery and Equipment Import and Export Corpn (Group) (CMEC): 178 Guang An Men Wai Dajie, Beijing 100055; tel. (10) 63451188; fax (10) 63261865; e-mail cmec@mail.cmec.com; internet www.cmec.com; f. 1978; imports and exports machine tools, all kinds of machinery, automobiles, hoisting and transport equipment, electric motors, photographic equipment, etc.; Pres. JIA ZHIQIANG.

China National Medicine and Health Products Import and Export Corpn (Meheco): Meheco Plaza, 18 Guangming Zhong Jie, Chongwen Qu, Beijing 100061; tel. (10) 67116688; fax (10) 67121579; e-mail meheco@meheco.com.cn; internet www.meheco.cn; Pres. ZHANG BEN ZHI.

China National Native Produce and Animal By-products Import and Export Corpn (TUHSU): COFCO Fortune Plaza, 8 Chaoyang Men Wai Dajie, Chaoyang Qu, Beijing 100020; tel. (10) 85018181; fax (10) 85615151; e-mail tuhsu@cofco.com; internet www.tuhsu.com.cn; f. 1949; imports and exports include tea, coffee, cocoa, fibres, etc.; 9 tea brs; 23 overseas subsidiaries; Pres. WANG ZHEN.

China National Non-ferrous Metals Import and Export Corpn (CNIEC): 12B Fuxing Lu, Beijing 100814; tel. (10) 63975588; fax (10) 63964424; Chair. WU JIANCHANG; Pres. XIAO JUNQING.

China National Nuclear Corpn: 1 Nansanxiang, Sanlihe, Beijing 100822; tel. (10) 68512211; fax (10) 68533989; e-mail xxzx@cnnc.com.cn; internet www.cnnc.com.cn; Dir SUN QIN.

China National Oil and Gas Exploration and Development Corpn: 1 Fu Cheng Men Bei Dajie, Xicheng Qu, Beijing 100034; tel. (10) 58551114; fax (10) 58551000; e-mail master@cnpcint.com; internet www.cnpc.com.cn/cnodc; subsidiary of China National Petroleum Corpn (see below); Gen. Man. BO QILIANG.

China National Packaging Import and Export Corpn: Xinfu Bldg B, 3 Dong San Huan Bei Lu, Chaoyang Qu, Beijing 100027; tel. (10) 64616359; fax (10) 64611080; e-mail info@chinapack.net; internet www.chinapack.net; handles import and export of packaging materials, containers, machines and tools; contracts for the processing and converting of packaging machines and materials supplied by foreign customers; Pres. ZHENG CHONGXIANG.

China National Petroleum Corpn (CNPC): 9 Dong Zhi Men Bei Lu, Dongcheng Qu, Beijing 100007; tel. (10) 62094114; fax (10) 62094205; e-mail admin_eng@cnpc.com.cn; internet www.cnpc.com.cn; responsible for petroleum extraction and refining in northern and western China, and for setting retail prices of petroleum products; restructured mid-1998, transferring to PetroChina Co Ltd (a publicly listed subsidiary) domestic operations in the areas of petroleum and gas exploration and devt, petroleum refining and petrochemical production, marketing, pipeline transport, and natural gas sales and utilization; acquired PetroKazakhstan in 2005; Pres. JIANG JIEMIN.

China National Publications Import and Export (Group) Corpn: 16 Gongrentiyuguandong Lu, Chaoyang Qu, Beijing; tel. (10) 65066688; fax (10) 65067100; e-mail cnpeak@cnpiec.com.cn; internet www.cnpeak.com; imports and exports books, newspapers and periodicals, records, CD-ROMs, etc.; Pres. WU JIANGJIANG.

China National Publishing Industry Trading Corpn: POB 782, 504 An Hua Li, An Ding Men Wai, Beijing 100011; tel. (10) 64210403; fax (10) 64214540; e-mail cnpitc@cnpitc.com.cn; internet www.cnpitc.com.cn; f. 1981; imports and exports publications, printing equipment technology; holds book fairs abroad; undertakes joint publication; Pres. ZHOU HONGLI.

China National Seed Group Corpn: Sinochem Tower A, 15/F, 2 Fu Xing Men Wai Dajie, Beijing 100045; tel. (10) 88079999; fax (10) 88079998; e-mail chinaseeds@sinochem.com; internet www.chinaseeds.com.cn; f. 1978; imports and exports crop seeds, including cereals, cotton, oil-bearing crops, teas, flowers and vegetables; seed production for foreign seed companies etc.; Gen. Man. ZHANG WEI.

China National Silk Import and Export Corpn: 105 Bei He Yan Jie, Dongcheng Qu, Beijing 100006; tel. (10) 65123338; fax (10) 65125125; e-mail chinasilk@chinasilk.com; internet www.chinasilk.com; 22 subsidiaries and more than 40 domestic co-operative enterprises; Gen. Man. ZHANG WEIMING.

China National Technical Import and Export Corpn: 16/F, Genertec Plaza, 90 Xi San Huan Zhong Lu, Fengtai Qu, Beijing 100055; tel. (10) 63349206; fax (10) 63373713; e-mail cntic@cntic.genertec.com.cn; internet www.cntic.com.cn; f. 1952; imports all kinds of complete plant and equipment, acquires modern technology and expertise from abroad, undertakes co-production and jt ventures, and technical consultation and updating of existing enterprises; Pres. TANG YI.

China National Textiles Import and Export Corpn: Chinatex Mansion, 19 Jian Guo Men Nei Lu, Beijing 100005; tel. (10) 65281122; fax (10) 65124711; e-mail webmaster@chinatex.com; internet www.chinatex.com; f. 1951; imports synthetic fibres, raw cotton, wool and garment accessories; exports cotton yarn, cotton fabric, knitwear and woven garments; over 30 subsidiaries; Pres. ZHAO BOYA.

China National Tobacco Import and Export Group Corpn: 9 Guang An Men Wai Dajie, Xuan Wu Qu, Beijing 100055; tel. (10) 63605290; fax (10) 63605915; internet www.cntiegc.com.cn; Chair. ZHANG HUI.

China North Industries Group Corpn (CNGC): 44 Sanlihe Lu, Beijing 100821; tel. (10) 68594210; fax (10) 68594232; e-mail webmaster@cngc.com.cn; internet www.cngc.com.cn; exports vehicles and mechanical products, light industrial products, chemical products, opto-electronic products, building materials, military products, etc.; Pres. ZHANG GUOQING.

China Railway Construction Corpn: 40 Fuxing Lu, Beijing 100855; tel. (10) 51888114; fax (10) 68217382; e-mail webmaster@crcc.cn; internet www.crcc.cn; f. 1948; state-owned; over 30 subsidiaries; design, construction, equipment installation and maintenance of railways and highways; Pres. ZHAO GUANGFA.

China Railway Group Ltd: China Railway Tower 9, 69 Fuxing Lu, Haidian Qu, Beijing 100039; tel. (10) 51845225; fax (10) 51841757; e-mail webmaster@crec.cn; internet www.crec.cn; f. 2007; est. as jt stock co; 46 subsidiaries; infrastructure construction, design, survey and consulting services; mfr of engineering equipment; Chair. LI CHANGJIN; Pres. (vacant).

China Road and Bridge Corpn: Zhonglu Bldg, 88C, An Ding Men Wai Dajie, Beijing 100011; tel. (10) 64280055; fax (10) 64285686; e-mail crbc@crbc.com; internet www.crbc.com; overseas and domestic building of highways, urban roads, bridges, tunnels, industrial and residential buildings, airport runways and parking areas; contracts to do surveying, designing, pipe-laying, water supply and sewerage, building, etc., and/or to provide technical or labour services; Chair. ZHANG JIANCHU; Pres. WEN GANG.

China Shipbuilding Trading Co Ltd: 8–12/F, Bldg 1, 9 Shouti Nan Lu, Haidian Qu, Beijing 100048; tel. (10) 88573688; fax (10) 88573600; e-mail webmaster@cstc.com.cn; internet www.cstc.com.cn; f. 1982; Pres. LI ZHUSHI.

China State Construction Engineering Corpn: CSCEC Mansion, 15 San Li He Dajie, Haidian Qu, Beijing 100037; tel. (10) 88082888; fax (10) 88082789; e-mail ir@cscec.com.cn; internet www.cscec.com.cn; f. 1982; Pres. YI JUN.

China State Shipbuilding Corpn (CSSC): 9 Shouti Nan Lu, Haidian Qu, Beijing 100044; tel. (10) 68038833; fax (10) 68034592; e-mail cssc@cssc.net.cn; internet www.cssc.net.cn; f. 1999; naval and civil shipbuilding; Pres. TAN ZUOJUN.

China Tea Import and Export Corpn: South Gate, Chaoyang Qu, Beijing 100020; tel. (10) 64204127; fax (10) 64204101; e-mail info@teachina.com; internet www.chinatea.com.cn; Chair. ZHU FUTANG; Gen. Man. SUN YUEHUA.

China Xinshidai (New Era) Co: Xinshidai Plaza, 26 Ping An Xi Li Dajie, Xicheng Qu, Beijing 100034; tel. (10) 88009999; fax (10) 88009779; e-mail xsd@xsd.com.cn; internet www.xsd.com.cn; f. 1980; imports and exports defence industry and civilian products; Pres. WANG XINGYE.

Daqing Petroleum Administration Bureau: Sartu Qu, Daqing, Heilongjiang; tel. (459) 814649; fax (459) 322845; Gen. Man. WANG YONGCHUN.

Maanshan Iron and Steel Co (Masteel): 8 Hongqibei Lu, Maanshan 243003, Anhui Province; tel. (555) 2888158; fax (555) 2324350; internet www.magang.com.cn; sales 34,319.9m. yuan (2006); Chair. GU JIANGUO.

PetroChina International Co Ltd (China National United Oil Corporation—Chinaoil): 27 Chengfang Lu, Xicheng Qu, Beijing 100032; tel. (10) 66227001; fax (10) 66227002; internet www.chinaoil.com.cn; international trading subsidiary of PetroChina Co Ltd; imports and exports petroleum, natural gas and refined petroleum products; Chair. DUAN WENDE; Pres. WANG LIHUA.

Shanghai International Trust Trading Corpn: 201 Zhaojiabang Lu, Shanghai 200032; tel. (21) 64033866; fax (21) 64034722; f. 1979; present name adopted 1988; handles import and export business, international mail orders, processing, assembling, compensation, trade, etc.

State Bureau of Non-ferrous Metals Industry: 12B Fuxing Lu, Beijing 100814; tel. (10) 68514477; fax (10) 68515360; Dir ZHANG WULE.

Xinxing Oil Co (XOC): Beijing; f. 1997; exploration, development and production of domestic and overseas petroleum and gas resources; Gen. Man. ZHU JIAZHEN.

UTILITIES

Regulatory Authority

State Electricity Regulatory Commission: 86 Xichangan Dajie, Beijing 100031; tel. (10) 66058800; e-mail serc_manager@serc.gov.cn; internet www.serc.gov.cn; f. 2003; Dir. TAN RONGYAO.

Electricity

Anhui Province Energy Group Co Ltd (Wenergy): 76 Ma'anshan Lu, Hefei, Anhui 230001; tel. (551) 2225678; fax (551) 2225959; e-mail webmaster@wenergy.com.cn; internet www.wenergy.com.cn.

Beijing Electric Power Corpn: Qianmen Xi Dajie, Beijing 100031; tel. (10) 63129201.

Central China Electric Power Group Co: 47 Xudong Lu, Wuchang, Wuhan 430077; tel. (27) 6813398.

Changsha Electric Power Bureau: 162 Jiefang Sicun, Changsha 410002; tel. (731) 5912121; fax (731) 5523240; Dir. LIU MEIGUAN.

China Atomic Energy Authority: Jia 8, Fucheng 100048; e-mail webmaster@caea.gov.cn; internet www.caea.gov.cn; Chair. CHEN QUIFA.

China Guodian Corpn: 6–8 Fu Cheng Men Bei Dajie, Xicheng Qu, Beijing 100034; tel. (10) 58682000; fax (10) 58553900; e-mail cgdcb@cgdc.com.cn; internet www.cgdc.com.cn; f. 2002; transfer of Jianbi power plant from fmr State Power Corpn completed Sept. 2003; Pres. ZHU YONGPENG.

China Power Grid Development (CPG): 4 Xueyuang Nanli, Haidian Qu, Beijing; manages transmission and transformation lines for the Three Gorges hydroelectric scheme; Pres. ZHOU XIAOQIAN.

China Power Investment Corpn: Bldg 3, 28 Financial St, Xicheng Qu, Beijing 100140; tel. (10) 66298000; fax (10) 66298095; e-mail engweb@cpicorp.com.cn; internet www.zdt.com.cn; f. 2002; formed from part of the constituent businesses of fmr State Power Corpn; parent company of China Power International; Pres. LU QIZHOU.

China Southern Power Grid Co: 6 Huasui Lu, Zhujiang Xincheng, Tianhe Qu, Guangzhou 510623, Guangdong Province; tel. (20) 38121080; fax (20) 38120189; e-mail international@csg.cn; internet eng.csg.cn; f. 2002; est. from power grids in southern provinces of fmr State Power Corpn; Chair. ZHAO JIANGUO; Pres. JUN ZHONG.

China Three Gorges Project Corpn (CTGPC): 1 Yuyuantan Nan Lu, Haidian Qu, Beijing 100038; tel. (10) 57081999; fax (10) 57082000; e-mail webmaster@ctgpc.com.cn; internet www.ctgpc.com; Chair. CAO GUANGJING; Pres. FI CHEN.

China Yangtze Power Co Ltd: Block B, Focus Place, 19 Financial St, Xicheng Qu, Beijing 100032; tel. (10) 58688999; fax (10) 58688888; e-mail cypc@cypc.com.cn; internet www.cypc.com.cn; f. 2002; generation of power from the Yangtze river; manages power-generating assets on behalf of China Yangtze Three Gorges Project Development Corpn; initial public offering on the Shanghai Stock Exchange Nov. 2003; Gen. Man. ZHANG CHENG.

Chongqing Jiulong Electric Power Co Ltd: 15 Qianjinzhi Lu, Yangjiaping, Jiulongpo Qu, Chongqing 400050; tel. (23) 68787928; fax (23) 68787944; internet www.jiulongep.com; Chair. LIU WEIQING; Gen. Man. LIU YI.

Chongqing Three Gorges Water Conservancy and Electric Power Co Ltd: 85 Gao Suntang, Wanzhou Qu, Chongqing 400040; tel. (23) 87509622; fax (23) 58237588; internet www.cqsxsl.com; Chair. YE JIANQIAO.

Dalian Power Supply Co: 102 Zhongshan Lu, Dalian 116001; tel. (411) 2637560; fax (411) 2634430; Chief Gen. Man. LIU ZONGXIANG.

Datang Huayin Electric Power Co Ltd: 255, Third Section, Central Furong Lu, Changsha 410007; tel. (731) 5388028; internet www.hypower.com.cn; Gen. Man. WEI YUAN.

Datang International Power Generation Co Ltd: 9 Guang Ning Bo Lu, Xicheng Qu, Beijing 100140; tel. (10) 88008800; fax (10) 88008111; internet www.dtpower.com; independent power producer; Pres. CAO JINGSHAN.

Fujian Electric Power Co Ltd: 4 Xingang Dao, Taijrang Qu, Fuzhou 350009; tel. and fax (591) 3268514; Gen. Man. LI WEIDONG.

Fujian Mindong Electric Power Co Ltd: 8–10/F, Hualong Bldg, 143 Huancheng Lu, Jiaocheng Qu, Ningde 352100; tel. (593) 2096666; fax (593) 2096993; internet www.mdep.com.cn; f. 2000; Chair. LUO HONGZHUAN.

Gansu Electric Power Co: 628 Xijin Dong Lu, Qilihe Qu, Lanzhou 730050; tel. (931) 2334311; fax (931) 2331042; e-mail webmaster@gsepc.com; Dir ZHANG MINGXI.

GD Power Development Co Ltd: 19 Anyuan, Anhui Bei Li, Chaoyang Qu, Beijing 100101; tel. (10) 58682200; fax (10) 583553800; e-mail gdd1@600795.com.cn; internet www.600795.com.cn; manufacture and sale of electricity and heat, and the operation of power grids in northern, eastern, north-eastern and north-western China, as well as Yunnan and Sichuan Provinces; Chair. ZHU PENG.

Guangdong Electric Power Bureau: 757 Dongfeng Dong Lu, Guangzhou 510600; tel. (20) 87767888; fax (20) 87770307.

Guangdong Electric Power Development Co Ltd: 23–26/F, South Tower, Yuedian Plaza, 2 Tian He Dong Lu, Guangzhou 510630; tel. (20) 87570251; fax (20) 85138004; internet www.ged.com.cn; Chair. LI PAN.

Guangdong Yudean Group: Yudean Plaza, 2 Tianhe Dong Lu, Guangzhou, Guangdong 510630; tel. (20) 85138888; fax (20) 85136666; e-mail ydxwzx@gdyd.com; internet www.gdyd.com; Chair. LI PAN.

Guangxi Guiguan Electric Power Co Ltd: 126 Minzhu Lu, Nanning 530022; tel. (771) 6118880; fax (771) 6118899; e-mail ggep@ggep.com.cn; internet www.ggep.com.cn; Chair. CAI ZHEFU; Gen. Man. DAI BO.

Guangzhou Electric Power Co: 9th Floor, Huale Bldg, 53 Huale Lu, Guangzhou 510060; tel. (20) 83821111; fax (20) 83808559.

Guodian Changyuan Electric Power Co Ltd: State Power Bldg, Hongshan Qu, Wuhan 430066, Hubei Province; tel. (27) 86610541; fax (27) 88717966; e-mail sec@cydl.com.cn; internet www.cydl.com.cn; Chair. ZHANG YUXIN.

Hainan Electric Power Industry Bureau: 34 Haifu Dadao, Haikou 570203; tel. (898) 5334777; fax (898) 5333230.

Huadian Energy Co Ltd: 209 Dacheng Jie, Harbin 150001; tel. (451) 53685938; fax (451) 53685915; internet www.hdenergy.com; Chair. SHUHUI REN.

Huadian Power International Corpn Ltd: 2 Xuanwumen Jie, Xicheng Qu, Beijing 100031; tel. (10) 83567888; fax (10) 83567963; e-mail hdpi@hdpi.com.cn; internet www.hdpi.com.cn; f. 1994; fmrly Shandong International Power Development, renamed as above 2003; Chair. DA HONGXING; Gen. Man. CHEN JIANHUA.

Huadong Electric Power Group Corpn: 201 Nanjing Dong Lu, Shanghai; tel. (21) 63290000; fax (21) 63290727; power supply.

Huaneng Power International: Huaneng Bldg 4, Fu Xing Men Nei Dajie, Xicheng Qu, Beijing 100031; tel. (10) 63226999; fax (10) 63226888; e-mail zqb@hpi.com.cn; internet www.hpi.com.cn; f. 1998; transfer of generating assets from fmr State Power Corpn completed Sept. 2003; Chair. CAO PEIXI; Pres. LIU GUOYUE.

Huazhong Electric Power Group Corpn: Liyuan, Donghu, Wuhan, Hubei Province; tel. (27) 6813398; fax (27) 6813143; electrical engineering; Gen. Man. LIN KONGXING.

Hunan Chendian International Development Share-holding Ltd Co: 15/F, Wanguo Bldg, Minsheng Lu, Intersection Qingnian Dajie, Chenzhou 423000; tel. (735) 2339233; fax (735) 2339269; internet www.chinacdi.com; f. 2000; electricity and gas supply and generation; Chair. FU GUO.

Inner Mongolia Electric Power Co: 28 Xilin Nan Lu, Huhehaose 010021; tel. (471) 6942222; fax (471) 6924863.

Jiangmen Electric Power Supply Bureau: 87 Gangkou Lu, Jiangmen 529030; tel. and fax (750) 3360133.

Jiangxi Electric Power Corpn: 13 Yongwai Zheng Jie, Nanchang 330006; tel. (791) 6224701; fax (791) 6224830; internet www.jepc.com.cn; f. 1993.

National Grid Construction Co: established to oversee completion of the National Grid.

North China Grid Company Ltd: 482 Guanganmen Nei Dajie, Xuanwu Qu, Beijing 100053; tel. and fax (10) 83583114; internet www.nc.sgcc.com.cn; Chair. MA ZONGLIN.

Northeast China Grid Co Ltd: 11 Shiyiwei Lu, Heping Qu, Shenyang 110003; tel. (24) 3114382; fax (24) 3872665; internet www.ne.sgcc.com.cn; Gen. Man. LI YIFAN.

Northwest Power Construction Group Corpn: 3 Changle Xi Lu, Xian 710032; tel. (29) 82551370; fax (29) 83382405; e-mail nwepc_hr@163.com; internet www.nwepc.cn.

Shandong Electric Power Group Corpn: 150 Jinger Lu, Jinan 250001; tel. (531) 6911919; internet www.sd.sgcc.com.cn; Dir. LI XIAOPENG.

Shandong Rizhao Power Co Ltd: 1st Floor, Bldg 29, 30 Northern Section, Shunyu Xiaoqu, Jinan 250002; tel. (531) 2952462; fax (531) 2942561; subsidiary of Huaneng Power International.

Shanghai Electric Power Co Ltd: China Resource Plaza, Bldg 1, 36/F, 268 Zhongshou Nan Lu, Shanghai 200010; tel. (21) 23108800; fax (21) 23108718; e-mail sepco@shanghaipower.com; internet www.shanghaipower.com; Chair. WANG YUNDAN.

Shanghai Municipal Electric Power Co (SMEPC): 1122 Yuanshen Lu, Shanghai 200122; tel. (21) 28925222; fax (21) 28926512; e-mail smepc@smepc.com; internet www.smepc.com.cn.

Shantou Electric Power Development Co: 23 Zhuchi Lu, Shantou 515041; tel. (754) 8857191; Chair. LIN WEIGUANG.

Shanxi Zhangze Electric Power Co Ltd: 197 Wuyi Lu, Taiyuan 030001; tel. (351) 4265111; fax (351) 4265112; e-mail xww@zdthb.com.cn; internet www.zhangzepower.com; Chair. ZHANG FENG.

Shenergy Co Ltd: 1 Fuxing Zhong Lu, Shanghai 200021; tel. (621) 63900303; fax (621) 63900456; e-mail zhengquan@shenergy.com.cn;

internet www.shenergy.com.cn; f. 1992; supply and distribution of electricity and natural gas; Chair. QIU WEIGUO.

Shenzhen Power Supply Co: 2 Yanhe Xi Lu, Luohu Qu, Shenzhen 518000; tel. (755) 5561920.

Sichuan Electric Power Co: 63 Renmin Nan Lu, Chengdu 610061; tel. (28) 444321; fax (28) 6661888; Gen. Man. WANG SHU CHEUNG.

Sichuan Mingxing Electric Power Co Ltd: 88 Ming Yue Lu, Sui Ning 629000; tel. (825) 2210076; fax (825) 2210017; internet www.mxdl.com.cn; f. 1988; distribution of electric power and gas; Chair. QIN HUAIPING.

State Grid Corpn of China: 86 Chang'an Xi Lu, Xicheng Qu, Beijing 100031; tel. and fax (10) 66597205; e-mail sgcc-info@sgcc.com.cn; internet www.sgcc.com.cn; f. 1997 from holdings of Ministry of Electric Power; fmrly State Power Corpn of China; became a grid co following division of State Power Corpn into 11 independent companies (five generating companies, four construction companies and two transmission companies) in Dec. 2002; generating assets transferred to Huaneng Group, Huadian Group, Guodian Group, China Power Investment Corpn and Datang Group; Pres. and CEO LIU ZHENYA.

Tianjin Electric Power Corpn: 39 Jinbu Dao, Hebei Qu, Tianjin 300010; tel. (22) 24406031; fax (22) 24408615; e-mail tj.sgcc-info@sgcc.com.cn; internet www.tj.sgcc.com.cn; Gen. Man. ZHANG NING.

Top Energy Co Ltd: 272 Changzhi Jie, Taiyuan, Shanxi; tel. (351) 7021857; fax (351) 7021077; f. 1992; Chair. LIU JIANZHONG.

Wuhan Power Supply Co: 1053 Jiefang Dadao, Hankou 430013, Wuhan Province; tel. (27) 82403109.

Wuxi Power Supply Bureau: 8 Houxixi, Wuxi 214001; tel. (510) 2717678; fax (510) 2719182.

Xiamen Power Transformation and Transmission Engineering Co: 67 Wenyuan Lu, Xiamen 361004; tel. (592) 2046763.

Xian Power Supply Bureau: Huancheng Dong Lu, Xian 710032; tel. (29) 7271483.

Xinjiang Tianfu Thermoelectric Co Ltd: 54 Hongxing Lu, Shihezi 832000; tel. (993) 2901108; fax (993) 2901121; e-mail yj@tfrd.com.cn; internet www.tfrd.com.cn; f. 1999; generation and distribution of electricity in Shihezi, Xinjiang Uygur Autonomous Region; Chair. WEI LU.

Zhejiang Southeast Electric Power Co: 152 Tianmushan Lu, Hangzhou, Zhejiang 310007; tel. (51) 85774566; fax (51) 85774321; internet www.zsepc.com; Chair. MAO JIANHONG.

Gas

Beijing Gas Group Co Ltd: Xicheng; tel. (10) 66205589; fax (10) 66205587; e-mail bjgas@bjgas.com; internet www.bjgas.com; owned by the Hong Kong-based Beijing Enterprises Holdings Ltd; Chair. ZHOU SI.

Beijing Natural Gas Co: Bldg 5, Dixingju, An Ding Men Wai, Beijing 100011; tel. (10) 64262244.

Changchun Gas Co: 421 Yan'an Jie, Changchun 130021; tel. (431) 5937850; fax (431) 5954646; e-mail changchunbjb@126.com; internet www.ccrq.com.cn; Chair. ZHANG ZHICHAO.

Changsha Gas Co: 18 Shoshan Lu, Changsha 410011; tel. (731) 4427246.

ENN Energy Holdings Ltd: Bldg A, ENN Industrial Park, Xinyuan Dong Lu, Langfang Economic and Technical Development Zone, Hebei 065001; tel. (316) 2598100; fax (316) 2598585; e-mail xagas_news@enn.cn; internet yw.xinaogas.com; fmrly known as Xinao Gas Holdings Ltd; Chair. WANG YUSUO.

Qingdao Gas Co: 399A Renmin Lu, Qingdao 266032; tel. (532) 4851945; fax (532) 4858653; e-mail gasoffice@qdgas.com.cn; internet www.qdgas.com.cn.

Shanghai Dazhong Public Utilities Group Co Ltd: 8/F, 1515 Zhongshan Xi Lu, Shanghai 200235; tel. (21) 64288888; fax (21) 64288727; internet www.dzug.cn; Chair. YANG GUOPING.

Shenzhen Energy Group Co Ltd: 2068 Shennan Lu, Futian Qu, Shenzhen 518031; tel. (755) 83680288; fax (755) 83680298; e-mail IR@sec.com.cn; internet www.sec.com.cn; f. 1992; Chair. GAO ZIMIN.

Wuhan Gas Co: Qingnian Lu, Hankou, Wuhan 430015; tel. (27) 5866223.

Xiamen Gas Corpn: Ming Gong Bldg, Douxi Lukou, Hubin Nan Lu, Xiamen 361004; tel. (592) 2025937; fax (592) 2033290.

Water

Beijing Water Authority: 5 Yuyuantan Nan Lu, Haidian Qu, Beijing; tel. (10) 68556606; Dir. CHENG JING.

Changchun Water Group Co Ltd: 53 Dajing Lu, Changchun 130000; tel. (431) 88974423; e-mail ccws@changchunwater.com; internet www.changchunwater.com.

Chengdu Municipal Waterworks Co Ltd: Wuhou, Chengdu; tel. (28) 77663122; fax (28) 7776876; internet www.cdwater.chengdu.gov.cn; subsidiary of Chengdu Xingrong Investment Co Ltd.

Guangzhou Water Supply Co: 12 Zhongshan Yi Lu, Yuexiu Qu, Guangzhou 510600; fax (20) 87159099; internet www.gzwatersupply.com; Pres. WANG JIANPING.

Haikou Water Group Co Ltd: 2 Haidian Erxi Lu, Hainan 570208; tel. (898) 66269271; fax (898) 66269696; internet www.haikouwater.com.

Harbin Water Co: 49 Xi Shidao Jie, Daoli Qu, Harbin 150010; tel. (451) 4610522; fax (451) 4611726.

Jiangmen Water Supply Co Ltd: 44 Jianshe Lu, Jiangmen 529000; tel. (750) 3286358; fax (750) 3286368; e-mail jmwtof@163.com; internet www.jmwater.com.

Qinhuangdao Pacific Water Co: 71 West First St, Changli, Hebei 066600; tel. (335) 2022579; fax (335) 2986924; e-mail qpwc@sinofrench.com; internet www.sinofrench.com/Qinhuangdao.htm; f. 1998; Sino-US water supply project.

Sembcorp Utilities Investment Management (Shanghai) Ltd: Unit 3305, Bund Center, 222 Yan An Dong Lu, Shanghai 200002; tel. (21) 33310088; fax (21) 33317100; internet www.sembcorp.com; f. 1996; treatment of waste water, industrial water, potable water and overall water management; fmrly The China Water Co, name changed as above after acquisition by Sembcorp (Singapore) in 2010; Pres. and CEO TANG KIN FEI.

Shanghai Water Authority: 389 Jiangsu Lu, Shanghai 200050; tel. (21) 52397000; e-mail webmaster@shanghaiwater.gov.cn; internet www.shanghaiwater.gov.cn; service provider for municipality of Shanghai; Dir-Gen. ZHANG JIAYI.

Shenzhen Water Group Co: Water Bldg, 7/F, 1019 Shennan Zhong Lu, Shenzhen 518031; tel. (755) 82137618; fax (755) 82137830; e-mail master@waterchina.com; internet www.waterchina.com.

Tianjin Waterworks Group: 54 Jianshe Lu, Heping Qu, Tianjin 300040; tel. (22) 3393887; fax (22) 3306720; e-mail tianjinwater@sohu.com; internet www.jinnanwater.com.

Xian Water Co: Huancheng Xi Lu, Xian 710082; tel. (29) 4244881.

Zhanjiang Water Co: 20 Renmin Dadaonan, Zhanjiang 524001; tel. (759) 2286394.

Zhongshan Water Supply Co: 23 Yinzhu Jie, Zhuyuan Lu, Zhongshan 528403; tel. (760) 8312969; fax (760) 6326429.

Zhoushan Water Supply Co Ltd: 263 Jiefang Xi Lu, Zhoushan 316000; tel. (580) 8812695; e-mail webmaster@zswater.com; internet www.zswater.com.

Zhuhai Water Group Co Ltd: 338 Meihua Dong Lu, Zhuhai 519000; tel. (756) 8899110; internet www.zhuhai-water.com.cn.

TRADE UNIONS

At September 2010 China's 2.24m. trade unions comprised 239m. members.

All-China Federation of Trade Unions (ACFTU): 10 Fu Xing Men Wai Jie, Beijing 100865; tel. (10) 68592114; fax (10) 68562030; e-mail webmaster@acftu.org.cn; internet www.acftu.org.cn; f. 1925; organized on an industrial basis; 15 affiliated national industrial unions, 30 affiliated local trade union councils; 169.94m. mems (2007); Chair. LI JIANGUO; First Sec. SUN CHUNLAN.

Transport

RAILWAYS

The total length of railways in operation in 2012 was 97,625 km, of which 35,486 km were electrified. High-speed links began operating between Beijing and Tianjin in 2008, Shanghai and Hangzhou in 2010, Beijing and Shanghai in 2011, and Shenzhen and Xiamen in December 2013.

In March 2013 the Ministry of Railways was dissolved and its responsibilities divided between three separate bodies: the Ministry of Transport (safety and regulation); the State Railways Administration (inspection); and the China Railway Corporation (construction and service management).

China Railway Corporation: 10 Fuxing Lu, Haidian Qu, Beijing; internet www.china-railway.com.cn; national railway operator; under the Ministry of Transport; Chair. SHENG GUANGZU.

Ministry of Transport: see under Ministries; responsible for safety and regulation of the railways.

State Railways Administration: Beijing; responsible for inspection regime; Dir LU DONGFU.

City Underground Railways

Beijing Mass Transit Railway Operation Corpn Ltd: 2 Beiheyan Lu, Xicheng, Beijing 100044; tel. (10) 62293820; fax (10) 62292074; e-mail dtservice@bjsubway.com; internet www.bjsubway.com; f. 1969; total length 442 km; Gen. Man. RICHARD WONG.

Chengdu Metro Co Ltd: Chengdu; internet www.cdmetro.cn; f. 2004; by 2020 network expected to comprise nine lines and 332 km of track.

Chongqing Metro: Yuzhong Qu, Chongqing; tel. (23) 68002222; e-mail cqmetro@cta.cq.cn; internet www.cqmetro.cn; f. 2005; China's first monorail system; one operating line of 19.15 km, expected by 2020 to expand the network to over 400 km.

Guangzhou Metro: 204 Huanshi Lu, Guangzhou 510010; tel. (20) 83289999; e-mail fuwurexian@gzmtr.com; internet www.gzmtr.com; opened June 1997; total length 236 km; network expected to comprise 10 lines and 600 km of track by 2020; Gen. Man. DING JIANLONG.

Nanjing Metro: Nanjing; internet www.nj-dt.com; f. 2005; one line of 17 km; Line 2 completed in 2009.

Shanghai Shentong Metro Group Co Ltd: Level 31, Jiu Shi Bldg, 28 Zhongshan Nan Lu, Shanghai 200010; tel. (21) 58308595; fax (21) 63300065; e-mail hexieditie@shmetro.com; internet www.shmetro.com; f. 1995; total length 434 km; Chair. YU GUANGYAO; Gen. Man. GU CHENG.

Shenzhen Metro Group Co Ltd: 1016 Metro Bldg, 1 Fuzhong Lu, Futian Qu, Shenzhen; tel. (755) 23992600; fax (755) 23992555; e-mail szmc@shenzhenmc.com; internet www.szmc.net; f. 2004; Chair. LIN MAODE; Dep. Gen. Man. CHEN QI.

Tianjin Metro Group Ltd: 3 Harmony Jiayuan, Hankou Xi Lu, Heping, Tianjin 300051; tel. (22) 87811512; fax (22) 27825588; e-mail master@tjdt.cn; internet www.tjdt.cn; f. 2000; est as Tianjin Metro Corpn; name changed as above in 2008; total network 128.6 km, planned to be extended to 234 km comprising nine lines; Gen. Man. WANG YUJI.

Wuhan Metro Group Co Ltd: Wuhan; tel. (27) 83749024; internet www.whrt.gov.cn; f. 2004; Chair. HEPING TU; Gen. Man. LIU YUHUA.

Xian Metro: 132 Weiyang Lu, Xian 710018; internet www.xametro.gov.cn; f. 2005, first run 2011; operates a single line and 26.4 km of railway track, by 2018 planned to consist of six lines and cover more than 200 km of track.

Construction of the first line of an underground system planned for Qingdao commenced in 2009 and was expected to be completed in late 2015. According to the official plans, Qingdao Metro was eventually to consist of five lines, with a total combined track length of 231.5 km.

ROADS

In 2012 China had 4,237,508 km of highways, including 96,200 km of expressways. The programme of expressway construction to link all main cities continued; the expressway network was projected to total 55,000 km by 2020. Construction work on a bridge connecting Zhuhai with Macao and Hong Kong commenced in December 2009. Spanning nearly 50 km and comprising a six-lane expressway, the project was scheduled for completion in 2015.

INLAND WATERWAYS

In 2012 there were some 124,995 km of navigable inland waterways in China. The main navigable rivers are the Changjiang (Yangtze River), the Zhujiang (Pearl River), the Heilongjiang, the Grand Canal and the Xiangjiang.

SHIPPING

China has a network of more than 2,000 ports, of which more than 130 are open to foreign vessels. With full operation scheduled for 2020, the third stage of the biggest container port in the world, sited on the Yangshan Islands off shore from Shanghai, was completed in 2010. Other major ports include Dalian, Qinhuangdao, Tianjin, Yantai, Qingdao, Rizhao, Lianyungang, Shanghai, Ningbo, Guangzhou and Zhanjiang. In December 2013 China's flag registered fleet comprised 3,864 ships, totalling 46.40m. grt, including 821 general cargo carriers, 563 bulk carriers, 539 tankers and 81 gas tankers.

Bureau of Water Transportation: Beijing; controls rivers and coastal traffic.

China International Marine Containers (Group) Co Ltd (CIMC): 2 Gangwan Dajie, Shekou Industrial Zone, Shenzhen, Guangdong 518067; tel. (755) 26691130; fax (755) 26692707; e-mail email@cimc.com; internet www.cimc.com; f. 1980; jt venture between China Merchants Holdings, the East Asiatic Co Ltd (EAC) and China Ocean Shipping (Group) Co (COSCO); manufacture and supply of containers, trailers and airport equipment; cap. 2,017.0m., res 7,596.8m., sales 30,938.5m. (2005); Chair. LI JIANHONG; Pres. MAI BOLIANG.

China National Chartering Corpn (SINOCHART): see Trade and Industrial Organizations.

China Ocean Shipping (Group) Co (COSCO): 11–12/F, Ocean Plaza, 158 Fu Xing Men Nei, Xi Cheng Qu, Beijing 100031; tel. (10) 66493388; fax (10) 66492288; internet www.cosco.com.cn; f. 1961; reorg. 1993, re-est. 1997; head office transferred to Tianjin late 1997; br. offices: Shanghai, Guangzhou, Tianjin, Qingdao, Dalian; 200 subsidiaries (incl. China Ocean Shipping Agency—PENAVIC) and joint ventures in China and abroad, engaged in ship-repair, container-manufacturing, warehousing, insurance, etc.; merchant fleet of more than 800 vessels; 47 routes; Chair. WEI JIAFU.

China Shipping (Group) Co: 700 Dong Da Ming Lu, Shanghai 200080; tel. (21) 65966666; fax (21) 65966556; e-mail cscas@cnshipping.com; internet www.cnshipping.com/en; f. 1997; state-owned shipping conglomerate; incorporates five specialized shipping fleets of oil tankers, tramps, passenger ships, container vessels and special cargo ships respectively; a total of 440 vessels with an aggregate deadweight of 20.18m. metric tons; Pres. LI SHAODE.

China Shipping Container Lines Co Ltd: 5/F, Shipping Tower, 700 Dong Da Ming Lu, Shanghai 200080; tel. (21) 65966833; fax (21) 65966498; e-mail ir@cnshipping.com; internet www.cscl.com.cn; container shipping company; operates 80 domestic and international container routes; 150 vessels (Sept. 2012); Chair. LI SHAODE; Gen. Man. XU LIRONG.

China Shipping Development Co Ltd: Shanghai Maritime Bldg, 16th Floor, 700 Dong Da Ming Lu, Shanghai 200080; tel. (21) 65967160; fax (21) 65966160; e-mail csd@cnshipping.com; internet www.cnshipping.com/cndev; 50.51% owned by China Shipping (Group) Co; operates oil tankers and dry bulk cargo vessels; Chair. LI SHAODE.

Fujian Shipping Co: 151 Zhong Ping Lu, Fuzhou 350009; tel. (591) 87949702; fax (591) 87949709; e-mail fuscokh@fusco.com.cn; internet www.fusco.com.cn; f. 1950; transport of bulk cargo, crude petroleum products, container and related services; subsidiary of Fujian Provincial Communication Transportation Group Co Ltd; Gen. Man. YANG JINCHANG.

Guangzhou Maritime Transport (Group) Co: 308 Binjiang Zhong Lu, Guangzhou 510220; tel. (20) 84102787; fax (20) 84102187; e-mail gzmaritime@gzmaritime.com; internet www.gzmaritime.com; f. 1949; Gen. Man. ZHANG RONGBIAO.

CIVIL AVIATION

Air travel has continued to expand very rapidly, following the approval of the establishment of private airlines in 2004. At November 2012 China had a total of 182 commercial airports (compared with 94 in 1990 and 135 in 2005). According to the Twelfth Five-Year Plan (2011–15), the number of airports was to expand to 230 by 2015. Plans to construct a second international airport to be located some 46 km south of Beijing were approved in January 2013. The new facility was designed to function as a major hub alongside Beijing Capital International Airport and was scheduled to open in 2018.

Civil Aviation Administration of China (CAAC): POB 644, 155 Dongsixi Jie, Beijing 100710; tel. (10) 64014104; fax (10) 64016918; e-mail webmaster@caac.gov.cn; internet www.caac.gov.cn; f. 1949; restructured in 1988; subsidiary of Ministry of Transport; Dir LI JIAXIANG.

Air China Ltd: Beijing International Airport, POB 644, Beijing 100621; tel. (10) 61462799; fax (10) 9558310; e-mail ir@airchina.com; internet www.airchina.com.cn; f. 1988; 51% owned by state-owned China Nat. Aviation Holding Co (CNAC); international and domestic scheduled passenger and cargo services; Chair. WANG CHANGSHUN; Pres. CAI JIANJIANG.

Chengdu Airways Ltd: Chengdu Shuangliu International Airport, Chengdu 610202, Sichuan Province; tel. (28) 66668888; fax (28) 85706199; internet www.chengduair.cc; f. 2004; privately owned; fmrly United Eagle Airlines; name changed as above in 2010; Chair. WANG WENBIN.

China Eastern Airlines Corpn Ltd: 92 Hongqiao Lu, Hongqiao Airport, Shanghai 200335; tel. (21) 62686268; fax (21) 62686116; e-mail ir@ceair.com; internet www.ceair.com; f. 1988; fmrly China Eastern Airlines, re-est. as above entity in 1995; domestic services; operates flights within Asia and to the USA, Europe and Australia; Chair. LIU SHAOYONG.

China Eastern Airlines Wuhan (CEAW): 435 Jianshe Dajie, Wuhan 430030; tel. (87) 63603888; fax (87) 83625693; e-mail wuhanair@public.wh.hb.cn; f. 1986; fmrly Wuhan Air Lines; became China's first partly privately owned airline upon refounding in 2002; 96% owned by China Eastern Airlines; domestic services; Pres. CHENG YAOKUN.

China Eastern Xi Bei Airlines: Laodong Nan Lu, Xian 710082, Shaanxi Province; tel. (29) 88792299; fax (29) 84261622; e-mail webcnwa@mail.cnwa.com; internet www.cnwa.com; f. 1992; fmrly China Northwest Airlines; renamed following acquisition of assets by China Eastern Airlines in 2005; domestic services and flights to Macao, Singapore and Japan; Pres. GAO JUNQUI.

China Eastern Yunnan Airlines: Wujaba Airport, Kunming 650200; tel. (871) 7113007; fax (871) 7151509; internet www.c3q.com.cn; f. 1992; est. as Yunnan Airlines; renamed following acquisition of assets by China Eastern Airlines in 2005; 49 domestic services; also serves Thailand, Singapore, and Laos; Pres. XUE XIAOMING.

China General Aviation Corpn: Wusu Airport, Taiyuan 030031, Shanxi Province; tel. (351) 7040600; fax (351) 7040094; f. 1989; 34 domestic routes; Pres. ZHANG CHANGJING.

China Southern Airlines: 6 Airport Lu, Guangzhou Baiyun Int. Airport; tel. (20) 86134388; fax (20) 86137318; e-mail webmaster@csair.com; internet www.csair.com; f. 1991; merged with Zhong Yuan Airlines in 2000; acquired operations and assets of China Northern Airlines and China Xinjiang Airlines in 2004; domestic services; overseas destinations include Bangkok, Fukuoka, Hanoi, Ho Chi Minh City, Kuala Lumpur, Penang, Pyongyang, Singapore, Manila, Vientiane, Jakarta and Surabaya; Chair. SI XIANMIN; Gen. Man. XU JIEBO.

Xiamen Airlines: 22 Dai Liao Lu, Xiamen 361006, Fujian Province; tel. (592) 5739888; fax (592) 5739777; e-mail et@xiamenair.com.cn; internet www.xiamenair.com.cn; f. 1992; 51% owned by China Southern Airlines, 34% owned by Xiamen Construction and Devt Corpn and 15% by Hebei Aviation Investment Group; domestic services; also serves Bangkok (Thailand); Pres. CHE SHANGLUN.

China United Airlines: Dong Lu, Fengtai Qu, Beijing 100076; tel. (10) 67978899; internet www.cu-air.com; f. 2005; est. in 1986 as part of the People's Liberation Army civil transport division; closed down in 2002; resumed operations in 2005; 80% owned by Shanghai Airlines; Pres. LAN DINGSHOU.

Hainan Airlines (HNA): 7 Guoxing Dajie, Haikou 570203, Hainan Province; tel. (898) 66739801; fax (898) 68875305; e-mail webmaster@hnair.com; internet www.hnair.com; f. 1993; leading air transport enterprise of HNA Group; 300 domestic services; international services to Korea; 14.8% owned by financier George Soros; Chair. CHEN MING; Pres. LI TIE.

China Xinhua Airlines: 1 Jinsong Nan Lu, Chaoyang Qu, Beijing 100021; tel. (10) 66766027; fax (10) 67740126; e-mail infocxh@homeway.com.cn; internet www.chinaxinhuaair.com; f. 1992; subsidiary of HNA Group; Chair. LIU JIAXU; Pres. YANG JINGLIN.

Grand China Airlines: 7 Guoxing Dajie, Haikou 570203, Hainan Province; tel. (898) 66739801; fax (898) 68875305; internet www.grandchinaair.com; f. 2007; subsidiary of HNA Group; international and domestic passenger services; Chair. CHEN MING; Pres. LI TIE.

Okay Airways: 16 Tianzhu Lu, Tianzhu Airport Industrial Zone, Shunyi Qu, Beijing 101312; tel. (10) 59237777; fax (10) 59237590; internet www.okair.net; f. 2004; inaugural flight 2005; China's first privately owned airline; Chair. WANG SHUSHENG.

Shandong Airlines: Shandong Aviation Mansion, 5746 Er Huan Dong Lu, Lixia Qu, Jinan 250014, Shandong Province; tel. (531) 85698666; fax (531) 85698668; e-mail webmaster@shandongair.com.cn; internet www.shandongair.com.cn; f. 1994; domestic services; Pres. MA CHONGXIAN.

Shanghai Airlines: 212 Jiangning Lu, Shanghai 200041; tel. (21) 62558888; fax (21) 62558885; e-mail service@shanghai-air.com; internet www.shanghai-air.com; f. 1985; domestic services; also serves Phnom Penh (Cambodia); Chair. ZHOU CHI.

Shenzhen Airlines: Lingtian Tian, Lingxiao Garden, Shenzhen Airport, Shenzhen 518128, Guangdong Province; tel. (755) 7771999; fax (755) 7777242; e-mail wm@shenzhenair.com; internet www.shenzhenair.com; f. 1993; owned by Air China (51%), Total Logistics Co (25%) and Shenzhen Huirun Investment (24%); domestic services; Chair. CAI JIANJIANG.

Sichuan Airlines: Chengdu Shuangliu International Airport, Chengdu 610202, Sichuan Province; tel. (28) 85393566; fax (28) 85393045; e-mail scal@scal.com; internet www.scal.com.cn; f. 1986; domestic services; Pres. LAN XINGGUO.

Spring Airlines: 4/F, Bldg 3, 2550 Hongqiao Lu, Shanghai 200335; tel. (21) 62692626; fax (21) 62523734; e-mail cs@air-spring.com; internet www.china-sss.com; privately owned; low-cost airline; inaugural flight July 2005; Chair. and Pres. WANG ZHENGHUA.

Tourism

The tourism sector has continued to develop rapidly. Attractions include dramatic scenery and places of historical interest such as the Temple of Heaven and the Forbidden City in Beijing, the Great Wall, the Ming Tombs and the terracotta warriors at Xian. In 2013 China received a total of nearly 129.1m. visitors, of whom 26.3m. were foreign tourists; visitors from Hong Kong, Macao and Taiwan totalled 102.8m. Revenue from international tourism was estimated to have risen by 3.4% in 2013 to reach US $51,700m., while in 2012 receipts from domestic tourism increased by 17.6% to reach an estimated 2,270.6m. yuan.

China International Travel Service (CITS): 1 Dongdan Bei Dajie, Dongcheng Qu, Beijing; tel. (10) 65222991; fax (10) 65226855; e-mail info@cits.com.cn; internet www.cits.net; f. 1954; makes travel arrangements for foreign tourists; 14 subsidiary overseas cos; Pres. TONG WEI.

China National Tourism Administration (CNTA): 9A Jian Guo Men Nei Dajie, Beijing 100740; tel. (10) 65201114; fax (10) 65137871; e-mail webmaster@cnta.gov.cn; internet www.cnta.gov.cn; parastatal org. charged with co-ordinating devt and regulation of the tourism industry; five subsidiary cos; Chair. SHAO QIWEI.

Chinese People's Association for Friendship with Foreign Countries: 1 Tai Ji Chang Dajie, Beijing 100740; tel. (10) 65122474; fax (10) 65128354; e-mail cpaffcwangzhan@126.com; internet www.cpaffc.org.cn; f. 1954; Chair. LI XIAOLIN.

Defence

China is divided into seven major military administrative units. All armed services are grouped in the People's Liberation Army (PLA). As assessed at November 2013, according to Western estimates, the regular forces totalled up to 2,333,000, of whom 660,000 were paramilitary forces: the army numbered 1,600,000, the navy 235,000 (including a naval air force of 26,000), the air force approximately 398,000, and the strategic missile forces 100,000. Reserves numbered some 510,000, and the People's Armed Police comprised an estimated 660,000. Military service is usually by selective conscription, and is for two years in all services. In support of international peacekeeping efforts, 218 Chinese troops were stationed in the Democratic Republic of the Congo in November 2013, 343 in Lebanon, 564 in Liberia, 340 in South Sudan and 233 in Sudan.

Defence Expenditure: Budgeted at 718,000m. yuan for 2013.

Chairman of the CCP Central Military Commission (Commander-in-Chief): XI JINPING.

Director of the General Political Department (Chief Political Commissar): ZHANG YANG.

Chief of General Staff: Gen. FANG FENGHUI.

Commander, PLA Navy: Adm. WU SHENGLI.

Commander, PLA Air Force: Gen. MA XIAOTIAN.

Director, General Armaments Department: Lt-Gen. ZHANG YOUXIA.

Education

Fees are charged at all levels. Much importance is attached to kindergartens. Primary education begins for most children at seven years of age and lasts for six years. Secondary education usually begins at 12 years of age and lasts for six years. In 2013 some 38.9m. children attended kindergartens (of which there were 181,251 in 2012), and 93.6m. pupils were enrolled at primary schools (which numbered 255,400 in 2012). In 2009/10 enrolment at pre-primary school was equivalent to 54% of pupils in the relevant age-group (males 54%; females 54%). In 2011/12 enrolment in secondary education was equivalent to 89% of the relevant age groups (males 88%; females 90%). In 2012 there were 81,662 secondary schools; secondary school enrolment totalled 88.4m. pupils in 2013. In 2013 368,000 children attended special schools (which numbered 1,853 in 2012), while a total of 24.7m. students were enrolled at higher education institutions (of which there were 2,442 in 2012). Private education developed quickly from the 1980s when it was first permitted. By 2004 the number of private schools was estimated at 70,000. As the Government placed increasing emphasis on higher education, this sector expanded extremely rapidly in the early years of the 21st century and by 2008 higher education establishments included universities, research institutes, specialized institutions, medical schools and colleges, and executive training schools. In the budget for 2012, the state allocated an estimated 2,124,210m. yuan to education, accounting for about 16.9% of total expenditure.

CHINESE SPECIAL ADMINISTRATIVE REGIONS

HONG KONG

Introductory Survey

LOCATION, CLIMATE, LANGUAGE, RELIGION, FLAG, CAPITAL

The Special Administrative Region (SAR) of Hong Kong, as the territory became on 1 July 1997, lies in eastern Asia, off the south coast of the People's Republic of China. The SAR consists of the island of Hong Kong, Stonecutters Island, the Kowloon Peninsula and the New Territories, which are partly on the mainland. The climate is sunny and dry in winter, and hot and humid in summer. The average annual rainfall is 2,214 mm (87 in), of which about 80% falls between May and September. The official languages are Chinese and English. Cantonese is spoken by the majority of the Chinese community, while Putonghua (Mandarin) is widely understood and of increasing significance. The main religion is Buddhism. Confucianism, Islam, Hinduism and Daoism are also practised, and there is a large Christian community. The flag of the Hong Kong SAR (proportions 2 by 3), flown subordinate to the flag of the People's Republic of China, displays a bauhinia flower consisting of five white petals, each bearing a red line and a red five-pointed star, at the centre of a red field. The administrative and business centre is Central District.

CONTEMPORARY POLITICAL HISTORY

Historical Context

Hong Kong Island was ceded to the United Kingdom under the terms of the Treaty of Nanking (Nanjing) in 1842. The Kowloon Peninsula was acquired by the Convention of Peking (Beijing) in 1860. The New Territories were leased from China in 1898 for a period of 99 years. From the establishment of the People's Republic in 1949, the Chinese Government asserted that the 'unequal' treaties giving the British control over Hong Kong were no longer valid.

Japanese forces invaded Hong Kong in December 1941, forcing the British administration to surrender. In August 1945, at the end of the Second World War, the territory was recaptured by British forces. Colonial rule was restored, with a British military administration until May 1946. Upon the restoration of civilian rule, the territory was again administered in accordance with the 1917 Constitution, which vested full powers in the British-appointed Governor. In 1946 the returning Governor promised a greater measure of self-government but, after the communist revolution in China in 1949, plans for constitutional reform were abandoned. Thus, unlike most other British colonies, Hong Kong did not proceed, through stages, to democratic rule.

Between 1949 and 1964 an estimated 1m. refugees crossed from the People's Republic to Hong Kong, imposing serious strains on Hong Kong's housing and other social services. More than 460,000 Chinese immigrants arrived, many of them illegally, between 1975 and 1980. Strict measures, introduced in October 1980, reduced the continuous flow of refugees from China, but the number of legal immigrants remained at a high level.

Domestic Political Affairs

Following a visit to Hong Kong by the British Prime Minister in September 1982, discussions between the United Kingdom and China were held regarding the territory's future status. In 1984 the United Kingdom conceded that in mid-1997, upon the expiry of the lease on the New Territories, China would regain sovereignty over the whole of Hong Kong. In September 1984 British and Chinese representatives met in Beijing and initialled a legally binding agreement, the Sino-British Joint Declaration, containing detailed assurances on the future of Hong Kong. China guaranteed the continuation of the territory's capitalist economy and lifestyle for 50 years after 1997. The territory, as a Special Administrative Region of the People's Republic, would be designated 'Hong Kong, China', and would continue to enjoy a high degree of autonomy, except in matters of defence and foreign affairs. It was agreed that Hong Kong would retain its identity as a free port and separate customs territory, and its citizens would be guaranteed freedom of speech, of assembly, of association, of travel and of religious belief. In December 1984, after being approved by the National People's Congress (NPC—the Chinese legislature) and the British Parliament, the agreement was signed in Beijing by the British and Chinese Prime Ministers, and in May 1985 the two Governments exchanged documents ratifying the agreement. A Joint Liaison Group (JLG), comprising British and Chinese representatives, was established to monitor the provisions of the agreement, and this group held its first meeting in July 1985. A 58-member Basic Law Drafting Committee (BLDC), including 23 representatives from Hong Kong, was formed in Beijing in June, with the aim of drawing up a new Basic Law (Constitution) for Hong Kong.

The majority of the population reportedly accepted the terms of the Joint Declaration, but the sensitive issue of the future nationality of Hong Kong residents proved controversial. The 1981 British Nationality Act had already caused alarm in the territory, where the reclassification of 2.3m. citizens was perceived as a downgrading of their status. As holders of Hong Kong residents' permits, they had no citizenship status under British laws. Following the approval of the Hong Kong agreement, the British Government announced a new form of nationality, to be effective from 1997, designated 'British National (Overseas)', which would not be transferable to descendants and would confer no right of abode in the United Kingdom.

In September 1985 indirect elections were held for 24 new members of an expanded Legislative Council (Legco), to replace the former appointees and government officials. The participation rate among the very small proportion of the population eligible to vote in the elections was low. In March 1986 municipal elections were held for the urban and regional councils, which were thus, for the first time, wholly directly elected. A new Governor, Sir David Wilson (who had played a prominent part in the Sino-British negotiations on the territory's future), formally assumed office in April 1987, following the death of his predecessor, Sir Edward Youde, in December 1986. In May 1987 the Hong Kong Government published proposals regarding the development of representative government during the final decade of British rule. Among the options that it proposed was the introduction, in 1988, of direct elections to the Legislative Council, based upon universal adult suffrage. In spite of the disapproval of the Chinese Government, in February 1988 the Hong Kong Government published, with the support of the majority of the population, a policy document on the development of representative government; the principal proposal was the introduction, in 1991, of 10 (subsequently increased) directly elected members of the Legislative Council.

In April 1988 the first draft of the Basic Law for Hong Kong was published, and a Basic Law Consultative Committee (BLCC) was established in Hong Kong, initially with 176 members, to collect public comments on its provisions, over a five-month period; the draft was to be debated by the Legislative Council and by the Parliament of the United Kingdom, but no referendum was to be held in Hong Kong, and final approval of the Basic Law rested with the NPC of China. The draft offered five options for the election of a chief executive and four regarding the composition of the future Legislative Council; however, none of these proposed that the Council be elected entirely by universal suffrage. Although the legislature would be empowered to impeach the chief executive for wrongdoing, the Chinese Government would have final responsibility for his removal.

In November 1988 the UN Commission on Human Rights criticized the British attitude to the transfer of Hong Kong, with particular reference to the lack of direct elections. A second draft of the Basic Law was approved by the Chinese NPC in February 1989, which ignored all five options previously proposed for the election of a chief executive. In May there were massive demonstrations in Hong Kong in support of the anti-Government protests taking place in China. In June, following the killing of thousands of protesters by the Chinese armed forces in Tiananmen Square in Beijing, further demonstrations and a general strike took place in Hong Kong, expressing revulsion at the massacres. The British Government refused to consider renegotiating the Sino-British Joint Declaration but, in response to demands that the British nationality laws should be changed to allow Hong Kong residents the right to settle in the United Kingdom after 1997, it announced in December 1989 that the British Parliament would be asked to enact legislation enabling as many as 50,000 Hong Kong residents (chosen on a 'points system', which was expected to favour leading civil servants, business executives and professional workers), and an estimated 175,000 dependants, to be given the right of abode in the United Kingdom. The Hong Kong authorities cautiously welcomed the announcement, but China warned prospective applicants that it would not recognize their British nationality after 1997. Despite widespread protests in Hong Kong against the scheme, the relevant legislation was approved in the British Parliament in April 1990.

Among other recommendations made by the parliamentary select committee were the introduction of a Bill of Rights for Hong Kong and an increase in the number of seats subject to direct election in the Hong Kong Legislative Council, to one-half of the total in 1991, leading to full direct elections in 1995. A draft Bill of Rights, based on the UN International Covenant on Civil and Political Rights, was published by the Hong Kong Government in March 1990. The draft was criticized in principle because its provisions would have been subordinate, in the case of conflict, to the provisions of the Basic Law. Nevertheless, the Bill of Rights entered into law in June 1991.

The transition to Chinese sovereignty

In April 1990 China's NPC approved a final draft of the Basic Law for Hong Kong: 24 of the 60 seats in the Legislative Council would be subject to direct election from 1999, and 30 seats from 2003; a referendum, to be held after 2007, would consult public opinion on the future composition of the Council, although the ultimate authority to make any changes would rest with the NPC. The British Government had agreed to co-operate with these measures by offering 18 seats for direct election in 1991 and 20 seats in 1995. Under the Basic Law, the Chief Executive of the Hong Kong Special Administrative Region (SAR), as the territory was to be designated in 1997, would initially be elected for a five-year term by a special 800-member election committee; a referendum was to be held during the third term of office in order to help to determine whether the post should be subject to a general election. However, no person with the right of residence in another country would be permitted to hold an important government post. Particular concern was expressed over a clause in the Law that would 'prohibit political organizations and groups in the Hong Kong SAR from establishing contacts with foreign political organizations or groups'.

Liberal groups founded Hong Kong's first formal political party, the United Democrats of Hong Kong (UDHK), with Martin Lee as its Chairman, in April 1990. The party subsequently became the main opposition to the pro-Beijing 'conservatives', and achieved considerable success in local elections in March and May 1991, and in the territory's first direct legislative elections in September. Of the 18 seats in the Legislative Council subject to election by universal suffrage, 17 were won by members of the UDHK and like-minded liberal and independent candidates. However, only 39% of registered electors reportedly voted. Despite the party's electoral success, the Governor nominated only one of the UDHK's 20 suggested candidates when selecting his direct appointees to the Legislative Council. Changes in the membership of the Executive Council were announced in October, liberal citizens again being excluded by the Governor.

In July 1992 Christopher Patten, hitherto Chairman of the Conservative Party in the United Kingdom, took office as Governor of Hong Kong, replacing Sir David Wilson upon his retirement. Plans for democratic reform in the territory, announced by the Governor in October, included the separation of the Executive Council from the Legislative Council. The former was reorganized to include prominent lawyers and academics. At the 1995 elections to the latter, the number of directly elected members was to be increased to the maximum permissible of 20; the franchise for the existing 21 functional constituencies, representing various occupations and professions, was to be widened and nine additional constituencies were to be established, in order to encompass all categories of workers. Various social and economic reforms were also announced. The proposed electoral changes were denounced by China as a contravention of the Basic Law and of the 1984 Joint Declaration. Although Patten's programme received the general support of the Legislative Council, many conservative business leaders were opposed to the proposals.

In July 1993 the 57-member Preliminary Working Committee (PWC), established to study issues relating to the forthcoming transfer of sovereignty and chaired by the Chinese Minister of Foreign Affairs, held its inaugural meeting in Beijing. In December, no progress in the intermittent bilateral negotiations having been made, proposed electoral reforms were submitted to the Legislative Council. The Governor's decision to proceed unilaterally was denounced by China.

In February 1994 the Legislative Council approved the first stage of the reform programme, which included the lowering of the voting age from 21 to 18 years. The second stage was presented to the Legislative Council in March. In April a British parliamentary report endorsed Patten's democratic reforms. In the same month the UDHK and Meeting Point, a smaller party, merged and formed the Democratic Party of Hong Kong. In April the trial in camera of a Beijing journalist (who worked for a respected Hong Kong newspaper) on imprecise charges of 'stealing state secrets' and his subsequent severe prison sentence aroused widespread concern. Hundreds of journalists took part in a protest march through the streets of Hong Kong.

In June 1994, in an unprecedented development that reflected growing unease with Patten's style of government, the Legislative Council approved a motion of censure formally rebuking the Governor for refusing to permit a debate on an amendment to the budget. Nevertheless, at the end of the month the Legislative Council endorsed further constitutional reforms, entailing an increase in the number of its directly elected members and an extension of the franchise. Despite China's strong opposition to these reforms the People's Republic and the United Kingdom concluded an agreement on the transfer of defence sites, some of which were to be retained for military purposes and upgraded prior to 1997, while others were to be released for redevelopment. At the end of August 1994, following the issuing of a report by the PWC in the previous month, the Standing Committee of the NPC in Beijing approved a decision on the abolition, in 1997, of the current political structure of Hong Kong.

In September 1994, at elections to the 18 District Boards (the first to be held on a fully democratic basis), 75 of the 346 seats were won by the Democratic Party. The pro-Beijing Democratic Alliance for the Betterment of Hong Kong (DAB) won 37 seats, the progressive Association for Democracy and People's Livelihood (ADPL) 29 seats, and the pro-Beijing Liberal Party and Liberal Democratic Foundation 18 seats and 11 seats, respectively. Independent candidates secured 167 seats. The level of voter participation was a record 33.1%. In December 1994 the director of the State Council's Hong Kong and Macao Affairs Office and Secretary-General of the PWC, Lu Ping, formally confirmed that the Legislative Council would be disbanded in 1997. Elections for the 32 seats on the Urban Council and the 27 seats on the Regional Council took place in March 1995. The Democratic Party took 23 seats, the DAB eight seats and the ADPL also eight seats. Fewer than 26% of those eligible voted in the polls. In the same month Donald Tsang Yam-kuen was nominated as Financial Secretary; his predecessor, along with other expatriate senior officials, had been asked to take early retirement to allow for the appointment of a local civil servant. Tsang took office in September.

Following a redrafting of the legislation, in June 1995 the United Kingdom and China reached agreement on the establishment of the Court of Final Appeal. Contrary to the Governor's original wishes, this new body would not now be constituted until after the transfer of sovereignty in mid-1997. The agreement was approved by the Legislative Council in July 1995. In the same month an unprecedented motion of no confidence in the Governor was defeated at a session of the Legislative Council. At elections to the Legislative Council in September, for the first time all 60 seats were determined by election. The Democratic Party won 19 seats in total, including 12 of the 20 seats open to direct election on the basis of geographical constituencies and two of the 10 chosen by an electoral committee. The Liberal Party took nine of the 60 seats, the pro-Beijing DAB six, and the ADPL four. Independent candidates won 17 seats.

The Governor aroused much controversy in September 1995, when he urged the United Kingdom to grant the right of abode to more than 3m. citizens of Hong Kong. The proposals were rebuffed by the British Home Secretary. In October the Chinese Minister of Foreign Affairs visited London, where agreement was reached on the establishment of a liaison office to improve bilateral contacts between civil servants. China's disclosure of a plan to establish a parallel administration six months prior to the transfer of sovereignty provoked outrage in Hong Kong.

In January 1996 the 150-member Preparatory Committee of the Hong Kong SAR was formally established in Beijing to succeed the PWC. The 94 Hong Kong delegates included representatives of the territory's business and academic communities. The Democratic Party was excluded from the new body, which was to appoint a 400-member Selection Committee responsible for the choice of the territory's future Chief Executive. During a visit to the territory in March, the British Prime Minister announced that more than 2m. holders of the forthcoming Hong Kong SAR passports would be granted visa-free access to (but not residency in) the United Kingdom. The Preparatory Committee in Beijing approved a resolution to appoint a provisional body to replace the Legislative Council. As the final deadline approached, thousands of Hong Kong residents rushed to submit applications for British Dependent Territories Citizenship (BDTC), which, although conferring no right of abode in the United Kingdom, would provide an alternative travel document to the new SAR passports. In early July eight pro-democracy politicians from Hong Kong, including five members of the Legislative Council, were refused entry to China to deliver a petition of 60,000 signatures against the proposed establishment of a provisional legislative body for Hong Kong. In mid-August nominations opened for candidacy for the 400-member Selection Committee. In the same month a new pro-democracy movement, The Frontier, comprising teachers, students and trade unionists, was established.

In December 1996 the second ballot for the selection of Hong Kong's Chief Executive (the first having been held in November) resulted in the choice of Tung Chee-hwa, a shipping magnate and former member of the territory's Executive Council, who obtained 320 of the 400 votes. Later in the month the Selection Committee chose the 60 members of the SAR's controversial Provisional Legislative Council (PLC). More than 30 of the new appointees were members of the existing Legislative Council, belonging mainly to the DAB and to the Liberal Party. Despite much criticism of the PLC's establishment, the new body held its inaugural meeting in Shenzhen in January 1997, and elected Rita Fan as its President.

In early 1997 the Chief Executive-designate announced the composition of the Executive Council, which was to comprise three ex-officio members (as previously) and 11 non-official members (the latter subsequently being increased to 15). The Chief Secretary, Anson Chan, was to remain in office, while Donald Tsang was to continue as Financial Secretary; Elsie Leung was to become Justice Secretary, replacing the incumbent Attorney-General. China's approval of Tung Chee-hwa's recommendations that senior civil servants be retained did much to enhance confidence in the territory's future. In February, however, relations with the outgoing administration deteriorated when the Preparatory Committee voted overwhelmingly in favour of proposals to repeal or amend 25 laws.

The inauguration of the SAR and subsequent events

Shortly after the transfer of Hong Kong from British to Chinese sovereignty at midnight on 30 June 1997, the inauguration of the SAR Executive Council, the PLC and members of the judiciary was held. Some 4,000 dignitaries attended the ceremonies, although the British Prime Minister and Foreign Secretary, and the US Secretary of State, did not attend the inauguration of the PLC, to register their disapproval of its undemocratic nature. Pro-democracy groups and members of the former legislature staged peaceful demonstrations in protest at the abolition of the Legislative Council. More than 4,000 Chinese troops of the People's Liberation Army entered Hong Kong shortly after the transfer ceremony, joining the small number of Chinese military personnel that had been deployed in the territory in April; a further 500 had entered on the day of 30 June.

Details of the procedure for elections to a new Legislative Council, which would replace the PLC, were announced by the SAR Government in early July 1997. The elections were scheduled to take place in May 1998 and were to be conducted under a new system of voting. Of the 60 seats in the legislature, 20 were to be directly elected by means of a revised system of proportional representation, 30 were to be elected by functional constituencies (comprising professional and special interest groups) and 10 by an 800-member electoral college. Legislative amendments governing the electoral arrangements were approved by the PLC in late September 1997. The significant reduction of the franchise, by comparison with the 1995 legislative elections, was condemned by the Democratic Party. The appointment by indirect election of 36 Hong Kong delegates to the Chinese NPC, in December 1997, also attracted criticism.

Following the transfer of sovereignty to China, concerns continued about freedom of expression in the SAR. In March 1998 a prominent publisher and a member of the Chinese People's Political Consultative Conference (CPPCC), Xu Simin, challenged the right of the public broadcaster, Radio Television Hong Kong, to criticize government policy, while Tung Chee-hwa stated that government policies should be positively presented by the media. At the same time, Tung denied that Xu's position reflected government policy. In the same month the Secretary of Justice, Elsie Leung, was criticized following the Government's decision not to prosecute another prominent publisher and CPPCC member, Sally Aw Sian, for corruption, despite a ruling against her by the Independent Commission Against Corruption (ICAC). Pro-democracy groups expressed fears regarding the independence of the Justice Department. In May two pro-democracy activists were found guilty of defacing flags of China and the Hong Kong SAR at a rally in January, the first such conviction since Hong Kong's transfer to Chinese sovereignty. In March 1999 the Court of Final Appeal ruled that the law prohibiting the defacing of the SAR flag was an unconstitutional restriction of freedom of expression; in December, however, under pressure from the Chinese Government, the Court rescinded its own decision, and the conviction was confirmed. In June the 10th anniversary of the Tiananmen Square massacre was marked by a peaceful demonstration, attended by 70,000 protesters.

Fears concerning the SAR's autonomy were exacerbated by the rapid adoption by the PLC in April 1998 of the Adaptation of Laws Bill. The Bill was ostensibly simply to replace references to the British crown in existing legislation but in practice it exempted the official Chinese news agency Xinhua, the office of the Chinese Ministry of Foreign Affairs and the garrison of the People's Liberation Army from all laws unless otherwise stated. Concerns about the territory's legal autonomy were also raised in late 1998 by the conviction and execution in the People's Republic of five criminals from Hong Kong.

At the elections to the first Legislative Council of the SAR on 24 May 1998, participation (53.3% of registered voters) was the highest since the introduction of direct elections in Hong Kong. The Democratic Party and other pro-democracy parties suffered a reduction in their overall political strength in the legislature, despite winning 14 of the 20 directly elective seats. A total of 19 seats were secured by pro-democracy candidates, including 13 by the Democratic Party (nine directly elected), led by Martin Lee, which became the largest party in the Legislative Council. Lee advocated direct elections by universal suffrage for all 60 seats in the next poll, to be held in 2000. Pro-Beijing supporters dominated the functional constituencies and the election committee ballot. The pro-business Liberal Party, led by Allen Lee, failed to win a single seat in the direct elections but obtained nine in the other constituencies. The DAB also won nine seats, five of which were directly elective.

The powers of the new legislature were curbed by the Basic Law. Legislative Councillors were not permitted to introduce bills related to political expenditure, the political structure or the operation of the government. The passage of private members' bills or motions also required a majority of votes of both groups of councillors—those elected directly and those returned through functional constituencies and the election committee. At its first session in July 1998 the Legislative Council elected Rita Fan as its President. The division between the Chief Executive, who rarely consulted the legislature, and the Legislative Council became more apparent after Tung Chee-hwa's second annual policy address in October. He announced the abolition of urban and regional councils, a decision opposed by many members of the legislature.

In March 1999 Anson Chan agreed to continue serving as Chief Secretary for Administration for two years beyond her normal retirement age, until 2002, when Tung Chee-hwa's term of office was to end. In April 1999 the administration decided to abolish the municipal and regional councils, while existing district boards were to be replaced by district councils. Although the public had been dissatisfied with the performance of the municipal councils, there was resentment at the restructuring of local democracy, which was perceived as a retrograde development. The first district elections in the Hong Kong SAR took place in late November. The Democratic Party won the largest number of elected seats (86), but the pro-Beijing DAB substantially increased its representation, from 37 seats to 83.

Popular support for the SAR Government declined substantially throughout 2000, and public unrest increased. In May the controversial Elsie Leung was reappointed Secretary of Justice for an additional two years. In June Tung Chee-hwa's administration was embarrassed by the resignation of Rosanna Wong as Secretary for Housing. Three days later the Legislative Council approved a vote of no confidence in Wong and one of her senior officials, holding them responsible for a series of scandals relating to sub-standard construction works. However, Wong remained a member of the Executive Council. This affair appeared to justify the resignation in April of the prominent opposition politician, Christine Loh, from the Legislative Council. Loh had cited her frustration with the Government's reluctance to share power with the legislature.

The second elections to the Legislative Council took place on 10 September 2000. The Democratic Party won the highest number of seats with 12, including nine of the now 24 directly elective seats, while the DAB obtained 11 seats. Thirty seats were elected by functional constituencies and six (reduced from 10) by an 800-member electoral college. The level of voter participation was 43.6%. At the first session of the new Legislative Council, Rita Fan was re-elected President. In January 2001 the widely respected Anson Chan unexpectedly announced that she was to resign, for personal reasons. Chan was succeeded as Chief Secretary for Administration in April by Donald Tsang; the latter was replaced as Financial Secretary by Antony Leung, a former banker and member of the Executive Council, who was known to be a close associate of Tung Chee-hwa.

In March 2001 the Hong Kong Government presented the new Chief Executive Election Bill, proposing the recognition of the powers of the central Government in Beijing to remove the Chief Executive and providing details of the procedure for the next election for that post, scheduled for 24 March 2002 (but see below). The new incumbent was to serve a five-year term commencing on 30 June 2002. The Bill was approved by the Legislative Council by 36 votes to 18 in July 2001 after minor amendments.

In early 2001 the Chinese Government warned that it would not allow Hong Kong to become a centre for the activities of Falun Gong, a religious sect banned on the mainland since mid-1999, and in May 2001 the Hong Kong Government increased its efforts to prevent the movement's followers from congregating in the territory in advance of a business conference, to be attended by President Jiang Zemin. Scores of Falun Gong followers were prevented from entering Hong Kong, although a small demonstration was permitted. More than 100 Hong Kong academics urged the People's Republic to release Chinese scholars detained on the mainland in previous months (some of whom were citizens or residents of the USA, or residents of Hong Kong), including Li Shaomin and Gao Zhan, who had both been convicted for espionage. The two were freed in late July, and Li was allowed to resume his academic duties.

In November 2001 opposition groups and trade unions, led by Emily Lau, announced the formation of a coalition aimed at preventing the re-election of Tung Chee-hwa as Chief Executive. In December Lau criticized the procedures for the election of the Chief Executive as undemocratic. Despite his growing unpopularity, Tung announced his intention to stand for a second five-year term as Chief Executive, and was quickly endorsed by President Jiang Zemin. At the end of February 2002 Tung was nominated for re-election by 714 members of the 800-member Election Committee, thereby securing a second term in office without challenge. He was formally sworn in for a second term on 1 July.

Plans for a major reorganization of government structures were announced in April 2002. The Executive Council was to be expanded into a cabinet-style body consisting of 14 ministers, all appointed by the Chief Executive, and would administer the 184,000-member civil service. Critics of the proposals warned that the new system would strengthen Tung's (and therefore China's) control over the territory and compromise the independence of the professional civil service. The Legislative Council none the less adopted the changes, and a new administration was appointed in late June. The incoming Executive Council incorporated five appointees from the private sector, including Henry Tang Ying-yen, the new Secretary for Commerce, Industry and Technology, and Patrick Ho, the Secretary for Home Affairs. The portfolios of several leading officials, including Donald Tsang, the Chief Secretary for Administration, and Antony Leung, the Financial Secretary, remained unchanged.

In late September 2002 the Government revealed proposals for new anti-subversion laws, which it was required to introduce under Article 23 of the Basic Law, but which had thus far not been implemented. Chinese Vice-Premier Qian Qichen had, in June, urged the SAR Government to enact the legislation. Critics warned that the new laws would undermine civil liberties and freedom of speech. Suspicions were increased by the fact that no draft of the laws was made available to the public. The proposals sought to criminalize treason, secession, sedition and subversion, and would also give police the powers to conduct emergency 'search and entry' acts without a warrant. 'Secession' referred to attempts to break away from China, while 'subversion' was defined as threatening or using force to intimidate or overthrow the Government. The Government would also be able to ban any groups affiliated to a mainland organization that had been proscribed in the mainland by the central authorities on national security grounds. Furthermore, the legislation could also ban any 'seditious publications' that incited treason, secession or subversion, or disclosed state secrets. A maximum penalty of life imprisonment would be imposed on violators of these laws.

In December 2002 Martin Lee retired from the leadership of the Democratic Party, after completing four two-year terms (the maximum allowed), and was succeeded by a former party vice-chairman, Yeung Sum. Lee remained a member of the Legislative Council. The Hong Kong Bar Association condemned the anti-subversion laws, describing them as unacceptable and harmful to the territory's freedoms. In the same month between 20,000 and 60,000 people from a broad section of society demonstrated against the planned anti-subversion laws, and subsequent demonstrations by those in favour of the laws attracted 10,000 people. In early 2003 the Government indicated that, following the end of a three-month public consultation period, some aspects of the laws would be modified, namely provisions dealing with the possession of seditious publications, and a ban on access to state secrets.

The outbreak of Severe Acute Respiratory Syndrome (SARS, a hitherto unknown pneumonia-like illness) in Hong Kong in early 2003, which killed almost 300 people in the territory before the disease was brought under control in June, led to demands for the resignation of the Chief Executive, who was accused of mishandling the crisis. In June the Hong Kong and Beijing Governments concluded a Closer Economic Partnership Arrangement (CEPA), to strengthen co-operation in trade and investment. On the sixth anniversary of Hong Kong's reversion to Chinese sovereignty, 500,000 people took part in a demonstration against the proposed anti-subversion legislation, which was due to be introduced in early July. The Chairman of the Liberal Party, James Tien, resigned from his position in the Government, stating that his party would not support the bill in the Legislative Council vote. Tung Chee-hwa subsequently postponed the introduction of the legislation. In late July two government ministers, the Secretary for Security, Regina Ip, and the Financial Secretary, Antony Leung, resigned from their positions. In early September the controversial anti-subversion bill was withdrawn by Tung Chee-hwa owing to popular opposition; this represented an indirect challenge to the authority of the Chinese Government in Hong Kong. In November, during a visit to Hong Kong, Chinese Vice-Premier Zeng Peiyan expressed China's continuing support for Tung Chee-hwa. At local government elections held in Hong Kong at the end of November the pro-Beijing DAB suffered heavy losses, prompting the resignation of the alliance's chairman, Tsang Yok-sing.

In January 2004 there were further popular protests demanding the direct election of Hong Kong's Chief Executive and of all members of the Legislative Council. In February a group of Hong Kong officials, led by Chief Secretary for Administration Donald Tsang, visited Beijing for discussions with the Chinese Government on the future political development of Hong Kong. In April the Standing Committee of the NPC in Beijing ruled that the SAR's next Chief Executive would not be chosen by direct election in 2007. The introduction of direct elections for all members of the Legislative Council in 2008 was similarly ruled out. The NPC ruling prompted protests by democracy campaigners in Hong Kong, who claimed that the decision contravened Hong Kong's Basic Law. At the end of April 2004 eight Chinese ships entered Hong Kong harbour, representing the strongest display of force by the Chinese navy since 1997.

In May 2004 there were renewed concerns over the freedom of the media after two well-known radio broadcasters, Albert Cheng and Raymond Wong, left Hong Kong, citing attempts to limit their freedom of speech and threats of violence by pro-Beijing groups. A third broadcaster, Allen Lee, subsequently resigned as well, claiming to have been subjected to similar intimidation. Lee also resigned from his position as a Hong Kong delegate to China's NPC. In June Chief Executive Tung held discussions with pro-democracy leaders and reiterated the promise that universal suffrage would eventually be realized in Hong Kong. At the beginning of July, as many as 500,000 people, according to one estimate, took part in a demonstration demanding universal suffrage. In the same month the Secretary for Health, Welfare and Food, Yeoh Eng-kiong, resigned following the publication of a report on the 2003 SARS epidemic.

Elections to the Legislative Council were held on 12 September 2004, when 30 of the total of 60 members were directly elected. Support for the pro-democracy faction was less evident than had been expected. Of the directly elective seats, 18 were won by democratic parties and 12 by pro-Beijing parties. In the Legislative Council as a whole, pro-Beijing parties held 34 of 60 seats after the election, thus retaining their majority. Voter participation in the election was comparatively high, at 55.6%.

The Tsang administration

On 10 March 2005 Tung Chee-hwa resigned from the post of Chief Executive, two years before his term of office was due to end, citing ill health. However, there was speculation that the Chief Executive had been removed from his post by the central Government in Beijing owing to his unpopularity in the SAR and his perceived inadequate response to the pro-democracy movement. Chief Secretary for Administration Donald Tsang occupied the role of acting Chief Executive until 25 May, when he resigned in order to present his candidacy for the election of a new Chief Executive, due to be held in July. Financial Secretary Henry Tang replaced Tsang as acting Chief Executive. Meanwhile, in a controversial ruling in April, the NPC had decreed that Tung's successor would serve out only the remaining two years of his predecessor's second term, rather than being appointed to the position for a full five-year term. The two other contenders for the post, Lee Wing-tat, Chairman of the Democratic Party, and legislator Chim Pui-chung, failed to secure the required 100 nominations from among the 800 members of the Election Committee, and their candidacies were thus rejected. Donald Tsang, who was endorsed by 674 of the 800 Committee members, was therefore elected unopposed to the post of Chief Executive on 16 June. Tsang's experience of public office under both the British and Chinese administrations, and his reputation for decisiveness and financial acumen, were thought to make him a popular choice among Hong Kong residents.

In September 2005 all the members of Hong Kong's Legislative Council, notably including several pro-democracy legislators whose political stance had prompted the central Government to impose a ban preventing them from travelling in mainland China, were invited on a tour of the Zhujiang (Pearl River) Delta region, in what was widely regarded as a conciliatory gesture towards the SAR's pro-democratic movement. In October Elsie Leung, Secretary for Justice since 1997, resigned. Chief Executive Tsang nominated Wong Yan-lung, a barrister with reported links to the pro-democratic Article 45 Concern Group, as her replacement, and the central Government approved the nomination. In the same month various proposals for electoral reform were published, which included the doubling of the membership of the Election Committee from 800 to 1,600 members and increasing the size of the Legislative Council from 60 to 70 members. Chief Executive Tsang endorsed the proposals, which were criticized by the pro-democracy movement for failing to set out a definite timetable for the adoption of universal suffrage. In December 2005 pro-democracy legislators were invited to mainland China to meet with senior representatives of the central Government. Two days later a large pro-democracy march (estimates of attendance varied from 63,000 to more than 250,000) took place in Hong Kong, demanding universal suffrage. Later in the month the Legislative Council voted to reject the electoral reform proposals.

Increasing dissatisfaction with the reform process led, in March 2006, to the establishment of a new political party. Founded by members of the Article 45 Concern Group, intellectuals and democracy activists, the new Civic Party became the fourth largest party in the Legislative Council. According to the leader of the new grouping, Audrey Eu, the Civic Party advocated the early introduction of full democracy to Hong Kong, although the party's manifesto contained no timetable for this process. In May, however, democracy activists were thwarted once again when the Legislative Council endorsed by 31 votes to 22 a bill whereby the term of any Chief Executive who took office prior to the expiry of the mandate of his or her predecessor would end upon the expiry of the predecessor's term. The term of office of Donald Tsang, therefore, would end in 2007 (completing that begun by Tung in 2002), after which he would be eligible to stand for one further term only. Pro-reform activists continued to demand a change in the law to allow the Chief Executive to belong to a political party.

On 1 July 2006 thousands took to the streets of Hong Kong for the fourth annual pro-democracy march. Particularly notable was the participation of former Chief Secretary Anson Chan, who, while stressing that she did not intend to challenge the Government, demanded the introduction of universal suffrage. None the less, there were many in the SAR who opposed the activists' demands; a pro-China rally, conducted earlier on the same day, attracted a similar number of demonstrators.

In August 2006 the Legislative Council approved the Interception of Communications and Surveillance Bill, which authorized the monitoring of e-mails and telephone lines, including private communications in both homes and offices. Under the new legislation, surveillance operations would require approval by judges appointed by the Hong Kong leadership, thus raising concerns about political bias. Pro-democracy legislators (who had tabled proposals for about 200 amendments to the bill, all of which were defeated), believed that the legislation would allow police officers to spy on anyone opposing the Government, in particular politicians, journalists and lawyers. The bill was approved by 32 votes to none, after pro-democracy legislators abandoned the proceedings.

Elections to determine the membership of the committee that would choose the SAR's next Chief Executive were held on 10 December 2006. Once again the ballot was restricted to the business and community sectors, with only about 5% of Hong Kong's registered electorate being eligible to vote and the level of participation being declared at 27.4%. Nevertheless, the results improved the prospects of the pro-reform camp, which unexpectedly secured 114 of the 427 contested seats on the 800-member Election Committee; the remaining 373 seats were uncontested. Having surpassed the threshold of 100 seats required to present an opposition candidate for the post of Chief Executive, the democrats were thus able to nominate Alan Leong of the Civic Party as their candidate for the forthcoming election.

Alan Leong duly received 132 formal nominations in February 2007, while Donald Tsang received 641. The unprecedented challenge mounted by Leong and the reformists, combined with the novelty of two televised debates between the candidates, contributed to an atmosphere of change, albeit marginal. At the same time, members of the pro-democracy movement criticized Leong for participating in an essentially undemocratic process, thereby lending it legitimacy. On 25 March Tsang was re-elected as Chief Executive, by an increased margin of 649 to 123. Leong protested against the outcome, alleging that the system had been manipulated. Meanwhile, Tsang had expressed hopes of establishing a timetable for full democracy in the SAR by 2012, but he acknowledged that he would need the support of China in order to secure this objective.

In April 2007 Tsang was formally appointed to the position of Chief Executive by Chinese Premier Wen Jiabao, and in June the composition of the Executive Council was announced. The new Council, which was sworn in during the following month, retained the former Financial Secretary, Henry Tang, who was promoted to Chief Secretary for Administration. The erstwhile Director of the Chief Executive's Office, John Tsang Chun-wah, was appointed to replace Tang, while Wong Yan-lung remained Secretary for Justice. New appointees included Tsang Tak-sing as Secretary for Home Affairs, and two women members, Secretary for Development Carrie Lam and Secretary for Transport and Housing Eva Cheng.

In mid-July 2007 the Government presented a Green Paper on Constitutional Development, which was to be subject to a three-month public consultation period. Options proposed in the document included the implementation of universal suffrage for elections to the post of Chief Executive, by 2012 at the earliest. Following the completion of the consultation, it was revealed that the majority of those polled supported the introduction of direct elections to the Legislative Council as well as for the post of Chief Executive, upon the expiry of the incumbent Government's term in 2012. Tsang's recommendations to the central Chinese Government in December 2007 were criticized for weakening these proposals to a certain extent, suggesting the holding of elections for the Chief Executive as a preliminary phase in 2012 or, perhaps preferably, 2017. The decision of the Chinese Government to consider Tsang's proposal, albeit with any implementation to be deferred until 2017, followed by the possibility of direct elections for the Legislative Council in 2020, was hailed as a positive development by Tsang, but the slow pace of reform disappointed many.

At district council elections held in November 2007 the Democratic Party and its pro-democracy allies lost more than one-quarter of the seats they had previously held. At a by-election to the Legislative Council in December, however, Anson Chan, the former Chief Secretary, was elected to the seat left vacant by the death in August of Ma Lik, the Chairman of the DAB: the result was seen as a victory for the pro-democracy movement. Ma's successor as Chairman of the DAB was Tam Yiu-chung. After only a year in office, in June 2008 the Secretary for Commerce and Economic Development, Frederick Ma, was compelled to resign for health reasons and was replaced by Rita Lau. In July the long-awaited approval by the Legislative Council of the Race Discrimination Bill, outlawing discrimination, harassment and vilification on the grounds of race, was widely welcomed. However, critics claimed that the protection thus afforded to Hong Kong's various minority groups, as well as to immigrants from mainland China, was inadequate. The Bill provided for numerous exemptions from prosecution on the grounds of discrimination for those serving in government agencies, notably in Hong Kong's immigration service and the police force.

At the elections to the Legislative Council held on 7 September 2008, a total of 200 candidates contested the 60 seats, with 142 candidates from 53 lists standing for 30 seats in the five geographical constituencies; 14 candidates in the functional constituencies were returned to the Legislative Council unopposed. Approximately 45% of the electorate participated in the elections. Pro-democracy candidates won a total of 23 seats, three fewer than previously held and significantly fewer than the number taken by pro-Beijing candidates. The DAB remained the largest single party in the legislature, securing 13 seats. However, the Liberal Party's representation was reduced, its seven seats all being won in functional constituencies only. (Moreover, its representation in the chamber was immediately decreased to six by one legislator's resignation from the party; and further reduced by three departures in October.) James Tien lost his seat in the chamber and announced his resignation as Chairman of the Liberal Party, later being replaced by Miriam Lau. Selina Chow, Vice-Chairwoman of the Liberal Party and a non-official member of the Executive Council, similarly failed to secure re-election to the Legislative Council. In October Jasper Tsang, a founder member of the DAB, was elected President of the Legislative Council, defeating Fred Li of the Democratic Party. The Frontier merged with the Democratic Party in November 2008, and in the following month Albert Ho Chun-yan, Chairman of the Democratic Party, was re-elected to head the grouping. Emily Lau, hitherto leader of The Frontier, was appointed as a Vice-Chairwoman of the expanded Democratic Party. None of the five new members appointed to the Executive Council by Donald Tsang in January 2009 was representative of pro-democracy groups.

In early June 2009, on the 20th anniversary of the Tiananmen Square massacre in Beijing, a record number of demonstrators, estimated to total as many as 150,000, attended a vigil to commemorate the events of 1989. In September 2009, following the detention of Hong Kong journalists who had been reporting on a disturbance in Xinjiang Province in western China, a march in Hong Kong in support of press freedom was attended by 700 demonstrators, who included DAB members of the Legislative Council. In December a demonstration was held to protest against the sentencing in Beijing of Liu Xiaobo, a leading advocate of democratic reform on the mainland, to 11 years' imprisonment after being found guilty of subversion. (Liu was awarded the Nobel Peace Prize in December 2010).

In September 2009 Donald Tsang stated that the election for the Chief Executive in 2017 would be held on the basis of universal suffrage, but pro-democracy groups remained sceptical. In November 2009 various proposals for political reform were presented. The Government's proposed changes, which were to be subject to a three-month public consultation period, included an increase in the number of members of the Election Committee from 800 to 1,200, to incorporate directly elected district councillors, prior to the next election for Hong Kong's Chief Executive in 2012; as before, the approval of one-eighth of the Committee's membership would be required for any nomination for the post. An expansion of the Legislative Council from 60 to 70 members was also envisaged, with one-half being directly elected in the geographical constituencies, while the remainder would continue to be chosen by the various interest groups voting in the functional constituencies. The proposals were criticized as inadequate by pro-democracy groups, which continued to press for full universal suffrage.

In January 2010 five pro-democracy members of the Legislative Council submitted their resignation, stating that the by-elections brought about by their departure would serve as a de facto referendum on the issue of universal suffrage in Hong Kong: two were members of the Civic Party, including Alan Leong, and three belonged to the League of Social Democrats, including Raymond Wong, the group's Chairman. The by-elections took place in May, when all five candidates won back their seats; however, pro-Beijing candidates had refused to contest the elections, criticizing them as a waste of public funds, and the Democratic Party had also refused to take part; participation by the electorate was low (at about 17% of eligible voters). The central Government denounced the 'referendum' as unconstitutional. The Democratic Party, with 10 other pro-democracy organizations (but not the Civic Party or the League of Social Democrats), had, earlier in the year, formed the Alliance for

Universal Suffrage, issuing a detailed 'road map' for progress towards universal suffrage.

In April 2010, meanwhile, the Hong Kong Government formally announced its proposals for electoral reform, following the period of public consultation that had begun in November 2009. The proposals were debated by the Legislative Council in June 2010. Following discussions with Tsang and with a representative of the mainland Chinese Government, the Democratic Party agreed to support the proposals, on condition that candidates for five of the 10 new seats in the Legislative Council, rather than being elected by the existing functional constituencies as originally proposed, should be nominated by members of district councils and elected by all voters who did not have a ballot in the functional constituencies (i.e. more than 90% of the electorate). This concession was accepted by Tsang and approved by the central Government. The proposals were duly adopted by the Legislative Council, with the support of eight members of the Democratic Party; a ninth member resigned from the party in protest. The League of Social Democrats and the Civic Party accused the Democratic Party of having betrayed the principles of the pro-democracy movement by voting for a system that still included functional constituencies and fell far short of universal suffrage. In August the Standing Committee of the Chinese NPC reviewed the reforms and declared them to be compatible with Hong Kong's Basic Law.

In December 2010 about 30 members of the Democratic Party, including several district councillors, resigned from the party in protest at its support for the electoral reforms. Many reportedly joined the NeoDemocrats, a group established in October 2010. The League of Social Democrats was also split by internal disagreements: in January the Chairman, Raymond Wong, resigned, and was replaced by Andrew To. Another new grouping, People Power, was established by former members of the League, including Wong, later in 2011, while in December the (pro-democracy) Labour Party was established, under the leadership of Lee Cheuk-yan, the general secretary of the Hong Kong Confederation of Trade Unions (as distinct from the pro-Beijing Hong Kong Federation of Trade Unions).

In January 2011, meanwhile, the Legislative Council approved the establishment of a statutory minimum wage, amounting to HK $28 per hour, with effect from 1 May of that year; employers had argued against the measure, while trade unions had declared the amount insufficient. The minimum wage applied only to permanent residents and not to foreign workers. In April the Secretary for Commerce and Economic Development, Rita Lau, resigned for reasons of ill-health, and was replaced by Gregory So, hitherto under-secretary in the same department. In June, at the annual commemoration of the Tiananmen Square protests, demonstrators in Hong Kong demanded the release of the internationally renowned artist Ai Weiwei and other mainland activists who had recently been detained during a period of stricter security enforcement. On 1 July, during Hong Kong's annual pro-democracy rally, there were protests at a government proposal to abolish by-elections and fill any vacant seat in accordance with the previous election result: the proposal was intended to avoid the occurrence of 'referendum' by-elections such as had taken place in May 2010. The demonstrators also protested at the high cost of living, particularly with regard to property prices and recent increases in the cost of food. The Hong Kong Government announced later in July 2011 that the proposed electoral revision would be postponed.

In August 2011 the Chinese Vice-Premier, Li Keqiang, visited Hong Kong. At a forum on China's 12th Five-Year Plan (2011–15), Li undertook to liberalize the trade in services between Hong Kong and the mainland; to improve Hong Kong's status as an international centre for finance and trade; and to develop Hong Kong as an offshore centre for the Chinese currency, the yuan (or renminbi). More than 200 people were arrested in the course of a protest rally that took place during Li's visit: participants claimed that the police had used excessive force. In September the Chief Secretary, Henry Tang, resigned in order to consider standing for election as Chief Executive, since Donald Tsang's term of office was to expire in the following year; Tang was replaced as Chief Secretary by Stephen Lam, hitherto Secretary for Constitutional and Mainland Affairs. Lam's previous post was assumed by Raymond Tam, until then the director of the Chief Executive's office. In October the convenor of the Executive Council, Leung Chun-ying, also resigned in order to take part in the election to the post of Chief Executive, due to take place in March 2012.

In October 2011, in his final annual policy address, Tsang, the outgoing Chief Executive, responded to public concern over property prices that were widely perceived as unaffordable, by announcing that the Government would resume a scheme (suspended in 2002) to provide subsidized housing for sale to low- and middle-income families; he also announced the provision of extra units of public rental housing, over several years. Measures were also to be taken to reduce the price of food, another popular grievance, by widening the sources of supply. Tsang identified the ageing of the population as an impending challenge, with one-quarter of Hong Kong's inhabitants expected to be over 65 years of age by 2030, and announced improvements in support and concessions for the elderly. At elections to district councils in November 2011, pro-Beijing candidates were the most successful: the DAB, in alliance with the Hong Kong Federation of Trade Unions, secured 148 of the 412 elective seats. The Democratic Party won 47, out of a total of some 90 seats estimated to have been won by pro-democracy candidates (many candidates had no formal affiliation). The chairman of the League of Social Democrats, Andrew To, resigned after his party failed to win any seats.

The election to the post of Chief Executive took place on 25 March 2012, and was unprecedentedly keenly contested. Tang was initially considered to be the candidate favoured by the Chinese Government, but after embarrassing revelations in the media concerning an extramarital affair and the construction of a luxurious basement complex, without planning permission, at a house belonging to his wife, there were reports that the Liaison Office of the Beijing Government in Hong Kong was exerting its influence in favour of Tang's rival, Leung. Leung was duly elected as Chief Executive, securing 689 votes from the expanded Election Committee of 1,200 members, while Tang received 285 votes, and the pro-democracy candidate Albert Ho, the leader of the Democratic Party, won only 76 votes. The conduct of the election increased pressure by pro-democracy supporters for the direct election of the Chief Executive by universal suffrage.

In March 2012 Tsang, whose term as Chief Executive was to end in June, was criticized for accepting inappropriate favours from business executives. He denied any wrongdoing and undertook to cooperate with an investigation by the ICAC. None the less, the allegations heightened popular anxiety concerning a lack of transparency in business leaders' influence over government policy. In April Tsang survived a motion of no confidence brought against him in the Legislative Council, the first such motion against a leader since the reversion to Chinese rule in 1997. In June 2012 large street protests demanded an investigation into the recent death, officially described as suicide, of the mainland pro-democracy activist Li Wangyang: even the outgoing Chief Executive, Tsang, publicly expressed doubt at the official explanation of Li's death.

Recent developments: Leung Chun-ying

Leung Chun-ying took office as Chief Executive on 1 July 2012, in a ceremony presided over by President Hu Jintao. The traditional pro-democracy demonstrations on this date, the anniversary of the transition from British rule, were estimated to be on a larger scale than usual. New appointments to the Executive Council with effect from the beginning of July included that of Carrie Lam (hitherto Secretary for Development) as Chief Secretary for Administration, and Anthony Cheung as Secretary for Transport and Housing; several members retained their former posts, including those responsible for finance (John Tsang), commerce and economic development (Gregory So), financial services and the Treasury (K. C. Chan) and constitutional and mainland affairs (Raymond Tam). The newly appointed Secretary for Development, Mak Chai-kwong, resigned after less than two weeks in office, when he was arrested in connection with the alleged abuse of official housing allowances; his position was taken by Paul Chan. Mak and another official were charged in October with conspiracy to defraud the Government, and were found guilty in June 2013, receiving suspended prison sentences. Meanwhile, in July 2012 the integrity of the Chief Executive himself was questioned when his electoral rival, Albert Ho, initiated a legal challenge to the election result, on the grounds that Leung had made misleading statements concerning unauthorized building work at his home; the case was rejected by the High Court in October. Also in July, the former Chief Secretary for Administration (in 2005–07), Rafael Hui, was implicated in a major corruption scandal: following an investigation by the ICAC, Hui was charged with misconduct in public office, having allegedly accepted bribes from Thomas and Raymond Kwok, the chairmen of Sun Hung Kai Properties, Hong Kong's largest property development company, during 2000–09. The trials of Hui and of the Kwok brothers were due to commence in May 2014.

In the weeks before the Legislative Council election in September 2012 there were vociferous demonstrations against the proposed introduction of compulsory 'moral and national education' lessons in Hong Kong schools, the curriculum for which, according to opponents, was uncritically in favour of the Communist Government in China. In response, on the day before the election Leung announced that the introduction of the classes would be optional for schools. For the election on 9 September the number of seats in the Legislative Council was increased from 60 to 70, with 35 geographical constituencies, 30 traditional functional constituencies, and five seats under the new 'District Council (Second)' functional constituency, in accordance with the reforms adopted in 2010 (see above). Voter participation, at 52.4%, was relatively high. Pro-Beijing candidates won the majority of seats (43, of which 26 represented functional constituencies) with the DAB securing a total of 13, the Hong Kong Federation of Trade Unions six and the Liberal Party five. Pro-democracy candidates won 27 seats (of which nine represented functional constituencies), fewer than anticipated but enough to defeat future legislation that required a two-thirds' majority (such as constitutional revisions). The Civic Party and the Democratic Party each won six seats, the Labour Party four and People Power three. Albert Ho immediately resigned the leadership of the Democratic Party, citing his failure to increase its representation, and was succeeded by Emily Lau, hitherto the party's Vice-Chairwoman. Miriam Lau, the Chairwoman of the Liberal Party, (which had lost two seats) also resigned, and was replaced by Selina Chow, the party's former Vice-Chairwoman.

In December 2012 the Conference for electing deputies of the Hong Kong SAR to the 12th NPC, comprising 1,621 members from various sectors of Hong Kong society, elected 36 deputies to the Chinese legislature, from among 52 candidates.

In his first annual policy address, in January 2013, Leung gave an assurance that universal adult suffrage was the administration's ultimate aim, and undertook to initiate a 'comprehensive consultation' on the methods of electing the Legislative Council in 2016 and 2020 and the Chief Executive in 2017. His speech also addressed other concerns frequently expressed by Hong Kong residents: it described measures being undertaken to alleviate poverty, increase the quantity and quality of available housing, improve air quality by phasing out the vehicles responsible for most pollution, and limit 'birth tourism' by mainland residents (see Issues of Immigration and Asylum).

In March 2013 pro-democracy representatives in the Legislative Council formed the Alliance for True Democracy (superseding the Alliance for Universal Suffrage that had been formed in 2010: see above) to encourage public discussion on constitutional reform: in particular, it emphasized the need to avoid the possibility that voters electing a future Chief Executive by universal suffrage would be presented only with candidates favoured by the Beijing Government. The Alliance also demanded an end to the system of functional constituencies in elections to the Legislative Council. In April 2013 Anson Chan, the former Chief Secretary for Administration, announced the formation of Hong Kong 2020, a group that undertook to consult as many sections of the community as possible on electoral change. Another pro-democracy group also emerged in early 2013, known as Occupy Central with Love and Peace (or simply Occupy Central): members proposed to hold peaceful demonstrations in Hong Kong's principal business district from July 2014 onwards, if progress were not made on democratic reform. In June 2013 the Chairman of People Power, Christopher Lau, resigned, and was replaced by Erica Yuen, reportedly after disagreements within the party, viewed as one of the more radical elements of the Alliance for True Democracy. In July Zhang Xiaoming, the director of the Beijing Government's Hong Kong Liaison Office, held an unprecedented meeting with pro-democracy members of the Legislative Council, assuring them that the central Government sincerely intended to permit the introduction of universal suffrage in Hong Kong, as long as this was done in accordance with the Basic Law. Visiting Hong Kong in November, Li Fei, the Chairman of the Hong Kong SAR Basic Law Committee (subordinate to the Standing Committee of the NPC) stated that a future Chief Executive 'must love the country and Hong Kong' and that anyone 'opposed to the central Government' could not hold the office.

In early December 2013 the Hong Kong Government formally began a five-month public consultation on constitutional reform. The Chief Secretary for Administration, Carrie Lam, made a statement to the Legislative Council, introducing the consultation document: she quoted the Basic Law as stating that the Chief Executive was ultimately to be chosen 'by universal suffrage upon nomination by a broadly representative nominating committee, in accordance with democratic procedures'. The document gave details of the 'five-step process' whereby proposed changes would have to be submitted to the Standing Committee of the NPC and, if approved, adopted by a two-thirds' majority of Hong Kong's Legislative Council. It described the principal questions relating to the method of selecting the Chief Executive, namely the size and composition of the proposed nominating committee; who should elect this committee and how it should proceed to nominate candidates; what the voting arrangements should be for electing the Chief Executive by universal suffrage; and the political affiliation (if any) of candidates. The document also enumerated the principal decisions to be made relating to the Legislative Council election to be held in 2016, namely the total number of seats; the composition and electorate base of functional constituencies; and the number of geographical constituencies and the number of seats within each. Reacting to the consultation document in January 2014, the Alliance for True Democracy appeared to accept that the nominating committee for elections to the post of Chief Executive might be similar in composition to the existing Election Committee (viewed by many as far from 'broadly representative'), but stipulated that the committee should be obliged to accept nominations by political parties (holding at least 5% of votes for directly elected seats in the Legislative Council) or by signature campaigns (attracting the signatures of at least 1% of registered voters). The Alliance urged the abolition of the existing rule forbidding the Chief Executive to belong to a political party. Also in January the Hong Kong 2020 group, together with the Civic Party, issued a more critical response, demanding the election of a genuinely representative committee for selecting Chief Executive nominees, and urging the abolition of functional constituencies by 2020.

In his second policy address, made in January 2014, Leung Chun-ying announced efforts to reduce the gap between rich and poor in Hong Kong, including a new allowance benefiting more than 200,000 low-income working families, improvements in social security assistance, and greater support for the increasing numbers of elderly people. In response to public concern over the SAR's chronic housing shortage, he undertook to 'rezone' sites for residential use and build 470,000 new units of housing over the next 10 years, of which 60% would be public housing. New measures to reduce air pollution by vehicles and to increase the recycling of waste were also announced in the address. Among various economic measures, particular emphasis was given to the planned development of Lantau Island in readiness for the inauguration of the Hong Kong-Zhuhai-Macao Bridge in 2016.

Issues of Immigration and Asylum

Following the reversion to Chinese sovereignty, various issues relating to immigration from the mainland intermittently came to the fore. Legislation approved by the PLC in July 1997 had included the introduction of measures to restrict the immigration into the territory of mainland-born children of Hong Kong residents. However, in January 1998 a judge ruled that this new legislation contravened the Basic Law, and the ruling was upheld by the Court of Final Appeal in January 1999, arousing fears that the decision would result in an influx of more than 1.6m. mainland Chinese. In June the Standing Committee of the NPC in Beijing stated that the Court of Final Appeal had failed to adhere to the Basic Law in not requesting an interpretation before delivering its judgment. The NPC stipulated that mainlanders were to be granted the right of abode in Hong Kong only if at least one parent had been permanently resident in the territory at the time of their birth and that mainland children of Hong Kong parents who wished to settle in the territory had to apply for mainland approval before entering the SAR.

In February 2003 plans were announced to ease immigration restrictions for skilled workers and business people from the Chinese mainland wishing to enter Hong Kong. The Admission Scheme for Mainland Professionals was introduced in July. Under new regulations introduced in the same month, persons holding a dependant visa were no longer entitled to take up employment in Hong Kong. Meanwhile, 18,621 mainland Chinese were refused entry to Hong Kong in 2003. The total number of illegal immigrants intercepted by the authorities declined from 25,651 in 1995/96 to 3,926 in 2003/04, a reduction of nearly 85%. Reports suggested that as many as 12,000 mainland women gave birth in the SAR in 2006, in order to gain Hong Kong residency rights for their children and to circumvent the mainland's 'one child' policy. In February 2007, therefore, new rules took effect to limit the number of pregnant women from the mainland entering Hong Kong in order to give birth there. Henceforth the immigration authorities were to refuse entry to any mainland woman who appeared to be at least seven months pregnant and who was unable to provide evidence of prior hospital arrangements and advance payment of medical fees. In April 2011 a new regulation was introduced, imposing an annual quota of 10,000 on the number of mainland women allowed to give birth in public hospitals in Hong Kong, in order to reduce pressure on medical facilities: the number of babies born to mainland mothers in Hong Kong was reported to have exceeded 40,000 (or some 45% of total births) in 2010. The quota was reduced to 3,400 for 2012, and in December it was announced that the quota would be reduced to zero from the beginning of 2013, except for mainland mothers whose husbands were Hong Kong residents. Legal action was taken in 2012 against intermediaries assisting pregnant women to travel to Hong Kong from the mainland without authorization. In January 2014 the Chief Executive undertook to alleviate problems caused by the demand for Hong Kong school places by mainland children, following complaints that Hong Kong residents were experiencing difficulties in obtaining school places for their children.

In September 2011 the Court of First Instance declared unconstitutional a law that denied foreign domestic helpers the right to apply for permanent residency after seven years working in Hong Kong (a right that was granted to other categories of non-Chinese nationals). There were estimated to be some 290,000 foreign domestic helpers in Hong Kong, mostly female, the majority from Indonesia and the Philippines. Opponents of the court's decision argued that it would allow domestic workers' families to settle in Hong Kong, placing additional strains on housing and welfare resources. However, in March 2012 the Government won an appeal against the ruling, giving rise to a further challenge from two foreign domestic workers. The Court of Final Appeal issued a final ruling in March 2013, confirming the constitutionality of denying foreign domestic workers eligibility for permanent residency.

Following the end of the Viet Nam War in 1975, the arrival in Hong Kong of numerous Vietnamese refugees became a major issue. The influx of asylum seekers increased substantially during the 1980s. At one stage as many as 60,000 'boat people' were interned in detention camps in Hong Kong where, under a controversial policy, the majority remained for many years with little prospect of resettlement elsewhere. Legislation to distinguish between political refugees and 'economic migrants' took effect in June 1988. In October 1991, following protracted negotiations, it was announced that Viet Nam had agreed to the mandatory repatriation of refugees from Hong Kong. The last remaining detention camp was closed in 2000, with most of the Vietnamese refugees having been resettled in other countries or repatriated.

Foreign Affairs

Despite the tensions surrounding the transfer of sovereignty during the 1990s, many citizens of Hong Kong supported the Government of the People's Republic of China in its territorial dispute with Japan regarding the Diaoyu (or Senkaku) Islands. In September 1996 a Hong Kong activist drowned during a protest against Japan's claim to the islands. As issues of patriotism assumed greater significance in Hong Kong, more than 10,000 people attended a demonstration to mourn the protester's death and to denounce Japan. In October protesters from Hong Kong joined a flotilla of small boats from Taiwan and Macao, which successfully evaded Japanese patrol vessels and raised the flags of China and Taiwan on the disputed islands. Tension between China and Japan over the Diaoyu/Senkaku Islands escalated once again during 2012, and in August 14 Hong Kong activists were temporarily detained by the Japanese after sailing to the islands.

Relations with the USA were strained in November 2007 when a US naval vessel was refused permission to dock in Hong Kong by the Chinese authorities, but such port calls were permitted to resume in January 2008. A nuclear-powered aircraft carrier, along with four other US vessels, was permitted to enter Hong Kong in February 2010, but in the same month the Chinese Government protested against sales of weapons by the USA to Taiwan and suspended official meetings between members of the Chinese and US armed forces. In November, however, a US naval vessel was allowed to make an official port visit in Hong Kong, and another did so in February 2011, when the Commander of the US Seventh Fleet stated that military contacts between the two nations were in the process of being re-established; regular port visits subsequently took place.

In June 2013 Edward Snowden, a US citizen and computer expert formerly contracted to the US National Security Agency, took refuge in Hong Kong, after revealing that the US security services were engaged in widespread surveillance of telephone and internet communications, both within and outside the USA. In the same month the US Government made an official application for Snowden's extradition from Hong Kong, to face charges of espionage. The Hong Kong authorities stated that the application documents did not comply with legal requirements, and allowed Snowden to leave for Russia (where he was granted temporary asylum), a decision described as disappointing by the US Department of Justice. Albert Ho (the former leader of the Democratic Party) acted as Snowden's legal representative while the latter was in Hong Kong. Ho suggested that the Beijing Government had influenced the decision to let Snowden leave, since a lengthy extradition process would have damaged Sino-US relations.

In January 2014 the Chief Executive announced that Hong Kong was to begin formal negotiations on a free trade agreement with the Association of Southeast Asian Nations (ASEAN) later in the year: members of ASEAN are among Hong Kong's principal trading partners.

CONSTITUTION AND GOVERNMENT

Since 1 July 1997 the Hong Kong SAR has been administered by a Chief Executive, who is accountable to the State Council of the People's Republic of China and serves a five-year term, there being a limit of two consecutive terms. The first incumbent was chosen by a 400-member Selection Committee in December 1996. Upon the expiry of his first term in 2002, the Chief Executive was chosen by an 800-member Election Committee, which also oversaw the selection of his successor in 2005. In July 2002 a new government structure was introduced, which expanded the Executive Council into a cabinet-style body comprising 14 ex officio members known as principal officials (each with an individual portfolio) and five non-official members, all accountable to the Chief Executive. In October 2005 the number of non-official Council members was increased to 15. Elections to the third four-year term of the 60-member Legislative Council took place in September 2004; 30 of the seats (compared with 24 in the previous legislature) were directly elective (under a system of proportional representation), with 30 seats being determined by functional constituencies (comprising professional and special interest groups). The same system was retained for the Legislative Council elections of September 2008. In June 2010 electoral reforms were adopted, according to which the Election Committee for choosing the Chief Executive was to be expanded from 800 to 1,200 members, and the Legislative Council was to be expanded from 60 to 70 members: of these, 35 were to be directly elected, and 30 elected by the same functional constituencies as in previous elections, while, in a new development, five were to be nominated by and from among members of district councils, and elected by all the members of the electorate who were not eligible to vote in other functional constituencies (about 90%). Under these new arrangements, elections to the post of Chief Executive and to the Legislative Council took place in March and September 2012, respectively.

REGIONAL AND INTERNATIONAL CO-OPERATION

Hong Kong is a member of the Asian Development Bank (ADB, see p. 207) and an associate member of the UN's Economic and Social Commission for Asia and the Pacific (ESCAP, see p. 28). Hong Kong is also a member of Asia-Pacific Economic Cooperation (APEC, see p. 201).

After 1997 Hong Kong remained a separate customs territory, within the World Trade Organization (WTO, see p. 434), which it joined in 1995. Hong Kong is also a member of the Bank for International Settlements (BIS, see p. 221).

ECONOMIC AFFAIRS

In 2012, according to estimates by the World Bank, Hong Kong's gross national income (GNI), measured at average 2010–12 prices, was US $261,599m., equivalent to US $36,560 per head (or US $53,050 on an international purchasing-power parity basis). During 2003–12, it was estimated, the population increased at an average annual rate of 0.7%; gross domestic product (GDP) per head increased, in real terms, at an average rate of 3.9% per year. Overall GDP increased, in real terms, at an average annual rate of 4.7% in 2003–12. According to the Asian Development Bank (ADB), GDP grew by 2.9% in 2013.

Agriculture, fishing, and mining and quarrying together contributed less than 0.1% of GDP in 2012, according to official preliminary figures, and the sector employed only 0.2% of the working population in 2008. Crop production is largely restricted to vegetables, while cattle, pigs and poultry are the principal livestock. Hong Kong relies heavily on imports for its food supplies. According to figures from the World Bank, the GDP of the agricultural sector decreased at an average annual rate of 2.9% in 2003–12. According to the ADB, the agricultural sector contracted by 3.2% in 2012, but increased by 1.5% in 2013.

Industry (including manufacturing, construction and utilities) provided nearly 6.9% of GDP in 2012, according to official preliminary figures, and employed 13.5% of the working population in 2008. According to the World Bank, industrial GDP declined at an average annual rate, in real terms, of 0.9% in 2003–12. According to the ADB, the industrial sector expanded by 8.8% in 2011, 5.6% in 2012 and only 0.4% in 2013.

Manufacturing contributed an estimated 1.5% of GDP in 2012, according to official preliminary figures, and employed 5.4% of the working population in 2008 (4.8% in 2011). According to World Bank figures, in real terms the GDP of the sector declined at an average annual rate of 0.9% in 2003–12. In 2012, according to chain-linked methodologies, manufacturing GDP decreased by 0.8%. The principal branches of manufacturing include textiles and clothing, plastic products, metal products and electrical machinery (particularly radio and television sets).

Construction contributed nearly 3.7% of GDP in 2012, according to official preliminary figures. In 2011 the sector employed 7.8% of the working population. According to chain-linked methodologies, construction GDP increased by 11.3% in 2012.

Electricity production is derived mainly from coal, which accounted for 71.2% of output in 2011. Total production of electricity reached 38,752m. kWh in 2012. Fuel imports accounted for 3.7% of the cost of Hong Kong's total merchandise imports in 2012.

The services sector plays the most important role in the economy, accounting for 93.0% of GDP in 2012, according to official preliminary figures. The sector employed 86.3% of the working population in 2008 (86.8% in 2011). The value of Hong Kong's invisible exports (notably financial services, tourism and shipping) was US $96,852m. in 2012. Hong Kong is regarded as a major international financial centre. Revenue from tourism totalled an estimated US $32,089m. in 2012. The number of visitors in that year rose by 6.5% to around 23.8m. (of whom more than 15.1m. were from mainland China). According to World Bank figures, the GDP of the services sector increased at an average annual rate, in real terms, of 5.1% in 2003–12. According to the ADB, the sector's GDP increased by 1.8% in 2012 and by 3.0% in 2013.

In 2012, according to the IMF, Hong Kong recorded a visible merchandise trade deficit of US $21,319m., while there was a surplus of US $6,067m. on the current account of the balance of payments. Re-exports constituted 98.3% of total exports in that year. The principal source of Hong Kong's imports in 2012 was the People's Republic of China (63.5%); the principal market for re-exports was also the People's Republic of China (53.3%). Other major trading partners included Japan, Singapore, Taiwan and the USA. In 2012 the principal exports (including re-exports) were machinery and transport equipment, miscellaneous manufactured articles and basic manufactures. The principal imports in that year were machinery and transport equipment, miscellaneous manufactured articles, basic manufactures and chemicals and related products.

The fiscal deficit was equivalent to 0.6% of GDP in 2013. Hong Kong's general government gross debt was HK $663,381m. in 2011, equivalent to 34.8% of GDP. Hong Kong's external debt totalled US $1,166,362m. in 2013, according to the ADB. In that year the cost of debt-servicing was equivalent to 48.0% of the value of exports of goods and services. International reserves stood at US $305,787m. in 2013. Consumer prices decreased at an average annual rate of 2.3% in 2003–12. According to official figures, consumer prices increased by 4.3% in 2013 and the rate of unemployment was 3.2% in the three months to December 2013.

Hong Kong is a major port and one of the world's principal international financial centres, benefiting from a reputation for efficiency, legal probity and relative freedom from corruption. The Closer Economic Partnership Arrangement (CEPA) concluded with the Government of the People's Republic in 2003 and expanded by successive subsequent agreements, allowed the liberalization of trade in goods and services between the SAR and mainland China. Hong Kong's position adjacent to one of China's principal industrial areas, the Pearl River Delta region of Guangdong Province, enables the SAR to handle a significant proportion of the mainland's export and import trade, and has facilitated massive investment by Hong Kong companies in mainland manufacturing activities. The deterioration in global economic conditions in 2008/09 had an adverse impact on the Hong Kong economy, but following the implementation of government measures to maintain and restore confidence, including providing liquidity to banks, protection for small and medium-sized enterprises, a fiscal stimulus and investment in new jobs, the SAR recovered relatively quickly. Unemployment declined from a peak of 5.5% in 2009, averaging 3.2% in the last quarter of 2013. Substantial increases in property prices led to demands for more stringent regulation of the sector, and from 2010 various measures to stabilize the housing market were announced, together with building schemes to increase the supply of public rented and subsidized private housing. In August 2011 the Chinese Government stated that during its 2011–15 Five-Year Plan period it intended to increase the liberalization of trade in services between Hong Kong and the mainland, and to expand Hong Kong's role as an international financial centre, in particular as an offshore centre for the Chinese currency, the yuan. Consumer prices increased by an average of 5.3% in 2011, by 4.1% in 2012 and by 4.3% in 2013. A statutory minimum wage was introduced in May 2011, but the conspicuous disparity between the richest and poorest sectors of society remained a source of public concern. The budget for 2013/14 included help for the poor and the elderly as well as the financial sector and small businesses, following further increases in stamp duty and restrictions on home loans announced earlier in February 2013 in an attempt to slow the swift increase in property prices. Hong Kong's GDP grew by 4.9% in 2011, but growth slowed to 1.4% in 2012, as exports diminished owing to unfavourable economic conditions in the eurozone and the USA; domestic demand, however, remained strong, supported by the administration's fiscal policy, and the construction and tourism sectors continued to flourish. Although exports to the USA and to European countries declined further in 2013, the SAR's GDP increased by 2.9% in that year. The inauguration of the Shanghai free trade zone in October 2013 gave support to speculation that the mainland city might eventually become a major international financial centre, to the detriment of Hong Kong. A bridge and tunnel connection between Hong Kong, Macao and the Guangdong city of Zhuhai, due to be completed in 2015 and to open in 2016, was expected to make access to the mainland considerably quicker for freight and passengers, thereby increasing trade via Hong Kong and stimulating new development in the SAR.

PUBLIC HOLIDAYS

2015: 1 January (New Year), 19–21 February (Chinese Lunar New Year), 3 April (Good Friday), 4 April (Ching Ming), 6 April (Easter Monday), 1 May (Labour Day), 25 May (Buddha's Birthday), 20 June (Tuen Ng, Dragon Boat Festival), 1 July (SAR Establishment Day), 28 September (Chinese Mid-Autumn Festival), 1 October (National Day), 21 October (Chung Yeung Festival), 25–26 December (Christmas).

Statistical Survey

Source (unless otherwise stated): Census and Statistics Department, 19/F, Wanchai Tower, 12 Harbour Rd, Hong Kong; tel. 25825073; fax 28271708; e-mail gen-enquiry@censtatd.gov.hk; internet www.censtatd.gov.hk.

Area and Population

AREA, POPULATION AND DENSITY

Land area (sq km)	1,104*
Population (census and by-census results)†	
14 July 2006	6,864,346
30 June 2011	
Males	3,303,015
Females	3,768,561
Total	7,071,576‡
Population (official estimates at mid-year)	
2012	7,154,600
2013§	7,184,000
Density (per sq km) at mid-2013	6,507.2

* 426 sq miles.

† All residents (including mobile residents) on the census date, including those who were temporarily absent from Hong Kong. In 2006 the census recorded population by place of birth as follows: Hong Kong 4,138,844, China (other than Hong Kong) 2,298,956, Other 426,546.

‡ Comprising 6,859,341 usual residents (present at census 6,635,558, absent at census 223,783) and 212,235 mobile residents (present at census 40,359, absent at census 171,876).

§ Provisional.

POPULATION BY AGE AND SEX

('000, official population estimates at mid-2013, provisional)

	Males	Females	Total
0–14	408.0	382.6	790.6
15–64	2,442.5	2,923.7	5,366.2
65 and over	479.5	547.7	1,027.2
Total	3,330.0	3,854.0	7,184.0

DISTRICTS AND DISTRICT COUNCILS

(population at 2011 census)

	Area (sq km)	Population	Density (per sq km)
Hong Kong Island	81	1,270,876	15,690
Central and Western	13	251,519	19,348
Wanchai	10	152,608	15,261
Eastern	19	588,094	30,952
Southern	39	278,655	7,145
Kowloon	47	2,108,419	44,860
Yau Tsim Mong	7	307,878	43,983
Sham Shui Po	9	380,855	42,317
Kowloon City	10	377,351	37,735
Wong Tai Sin	9	420,183	46,687
Kwun Tong	11	622,152	56,559
New Territories	976	3,691,093	3,782
Kwai Tsing	23	511,167	22,225
Tsuen Wan	63	304,637	4,836
Tuen Mun	85	487,546	5,736
Yuen Long	139	578,529	4,162
North	137	304,134	2,220
Tai Po	148	296,853	2,006
Sha Tin	69	630,273	9,134
Sai Kung	136	436,627	3,210
Islands	176	141,327	803
Total	1,104	7,071,576*	6,405

* Including marine population (1,188).

BIRTHS, MARRIAGES AND DEATHS

	Known live births		Registered marriages		Known deaths	
	Number	Rate (per 1,000)	Number	Rate (per 1,000)	Number	Rate (per 1,000)
2005	57,098	8.4	43,018	6.3	38,830	5.7
2006	65,626	9.6	50,328	7.3	37,457	5.5
2007	70,875	10.2	47,453	6.8	39,476	5.7
2008	78,822	11.3	47,331	6.8	41,796	6.0
2009	82,095	11.7	51,175	7.3	41,175	5.9
2010	88,584	12.6	52,558	7.5	42,194	6.0
2011	95,451	13.5	58,369	8.2	42,346	6.0
2012	91,558	12.8	60,459	8.4	43,917	6.1

Life expectancy (years at birth, 2012): Males 80.7; females 86.4.

ECONOMICALLY ACTIVE POPULATION
('000 persons aged 15 years and over, excl. armed forces)

	2006	2007	2008
Agriculture and fishing	8.2	6.4	8.3
Manufacturing	216.9	202.4	191.2
Electricity, gas and water	14.6	15.2	14.1
Construction	269.2	274.7	268.6
Wholesale, retail and import/export trades, restaurants and hotels	1,104.8	1,143.8	1,145.5
Transport, storage and communications	369.2	372.2	377.9
Financing, insurance, real estate and business services	525.7	548.0	580.0
Community, social and personal services	892.1	921.1	933.1
Total employed	3,400.8	3,483.8	3,518.8
Unemployed	171.1	145.7	130.1
Total labour force	3,571.9	3,629.5	3,648.9
Males	1,950.6	1,958.2	1,949.4
Females	1,621.2	1,671.3	1,699.5

Source: ILO.

2011 (persons aged 15 years and over, excl. armed forces): Manufacturing 170,797; Construction 275,517; Wholesale, retail and import/export trades, restaurants and hotels 1,067,763; Transport, storage and communications 376,065; Financing, insurance, real estate and business services 620,486; Community, social and personal services 1,013,859; Others (incl. Agriculture and fishing, Mining and quarrying, Electricity, gas and water) 23,294; *Total employed* 3,547,781; Unemployed 179,626; *Total labour force* 3,727,407.

Health and Welfare

KEY INDICATORS

Total fertility rate (children per woman*, 2012)	1.2
Under-5 mortality rate (per 1,000 live births, provisional, 2007)	1.6
HIV/AIDS (% of persons aged 15–49, 2003)	0.1
Physicians (per 1,000 head, provisional, 2012)†	2.2
Hospital beds (per 1,000 head, provisional, 2012)	5.1
Total carbon dioxide emissions ('000 metric tons, 2010)	36,288.6
Carbon dioxide emissions per head (metric tons, 2010)	5.2
Human Development Index (2012): ranking	13
Human Development Index (2012): value	0.906

* Excluding female domestic helpers.

† Including dentists and dental hygienists and excluding practitioners of Chinese medicine.

For sources and definitions, see explanatory note on p. vi.

Agriculture

PRINCIPAL CROPS
('000 metric tons, FAO estimates)

	2010	2011	2012
Lettuce	5.0	4.5	5.0
Spinach	12.5	13.0	13.0
Onions and shallots (green)	4.5	4.7	5.0
Other vegetables	10.0	10.2	11.0
Fruit	4.7	4.7	5.0

Source: FAO.

LIVESTOCK
('000 head, unless otherwise indicated, year ending September, FAO estimates)

	2009	2010	2011
Cattle (head)	1,500	1,600	1,600
Pigs	160	170	175
Chickens	1,200	1,250	1,300
Ducks	250	250	250

2012: Figures assumed to be unchanged from 2011 (FAO estimates).

Source: FAO.

LIVESTOCK PRODUCTS
('000 metric tons, FAO estimates)

	2010	2011	2012
Beef and veal	8.5	8.5	9.0
Pig meat	129.0	116.7	118.0
Poultry meat	31.5	27.5	28.3
Game meat	7.4	7.4	7.4
Cattle hides (fresh)	1.3	1.3	1.3

Source: FAO.

Fishing

('000 metric tons, live weight)

	2009	2010	2011
Capture*	159.0	168.0	170.7
Lizardfishes*	5.9	6.2	6.3
Threadfin breams*	17.1	18.1	18.4
Shrimps and prawns*	4.7	5.0	5.0
Squids*	7.4	7.9	8.0
Aquaculture	4.8	4.3	3.4
Total catch*	163.8	172.3	174.2

* FAO estimates.

Source: FAO.

Industry

SELECTED PRODUCTS
('000 metric tons unless otherwise indicated)

	2005	2006	2007
Cotton yarn (other than sewing thread)	62.2	70.5	39.8
Cotton woven fabrics (million sq m)	199.8	n.a.	n.a.
Women's and girls' blouses ('000)	29,706.0	2,077.0	7,401.0
Women's and girls' dresses, not knitted or crocheted ('000)	2,609.0	n.a.	n.a.
Women's and girls' skirts, slacks and shorts ('000)	43,426.0	83,756.0	45,504.0
Men's or boys' shirts, not knitted or crocheted ('000)	72,360.0	5,702.0	21,052.0
Watches ('000)	6,099.0	9,455.0	5,029.0

2008: Women's and girls' blouses ('000) 2,011.0; Women's and girls' skirts, slacks and shorts ('000) 42,922.0; Men's or boys' shirts, not knitted or crocheted ('000) 7,627.0.

Uncooked macaroni and noodle products (instant macaroni and noodles only, '000 metric tons): 62 in 2001; 20 in 2002; 99 in 2003.

Knitted sweaters ('000): 151,965 in 2001; 113,685 in 2002; 143,143 in 2003.

Men's and boys' jackets ('000): 1,838 in 2001; 1,285 in 2002; 1,087 in 2003.

Men's and boys' trousers ('000): 14,139 in 2001; 22,696 in 2002; 11,293 in 2003.

Source: UN, *Industrial Commodity Statistics Yearbook* and Industrial Commodity Statistics Database.

Cement ('000 metric tons): 1,005 in 2005; 1,255 in 2006; 1,300 in 2007 (Source: Asian Development Bank).

Electric energy (million kWh): 38,292 in 2010; 39,026 in 2011; 38,752 in 2012 (Source: Asian Development Bank).

Finance

CURRENCY AND EXCHANGE RATES

Monetary Units
100 cents = 1 Hong Kong dollar (HK $).

Sterling, US Dollar and Euro Equivalents (31 December 2013)
£1 sterling = HK $12.768;
US $1 = HK $7.754;
€1 = HK $10.693;
HK $100 = £7.83 = US $12.90 = €9.35.

Average Exchange Rate (HK $ per US $)
2011 7.7840
2012 7.7564
2013 7.7560

BUDGET
(HK $ million, year ending 31 March)

Revenue	2010/11	2011/12	2012/13
Direct taxes:			
Earnings and profits tax	143,007	176,822	182,442
Indirect taxes:			
Bets and sweeps tax	14,759	15,761	16,565
Duties on petroleum products, beverages, tobacco and cosmetics	7,551	7,725	8,977
General rates (property tax)	8,956	9,722	11,204
Motor vehicle taxes	6,657	7,070	7,466
Royalties and concessions	2,452	4,849	2,736
Others (stamp duties, hotel accommodation tax and air passenger departure tax)	52,818	46,303	44,909
Fines, forfeitures and penalties	1,159	2,660	1,208
Receipts from properties and investments	15,806	16,971	19,268
Loans, reimbursements, contributions and other receipts	2,887	3,425	3,404

Revenue—*continued*	2010/11	2011/12	2012/13
Operating revenue from utilities	3,483	3,573	3,687
Fees and charges	11,363	13,219	11,590
Investment income:			
General revenue account	17,824	20,105	20,024
Land Fund	11,078	11,216	11,126
Capital Works Reserve Fund (land sales and interest)	68,342	88,466	74,238
Capital Investment Fund	1,357	1,386	1,482
Loan Fund	2,238	2,389	2,240
Other capital revenue	4,744	6,061	19,584
Total government revenue	376,481	437,723	442,150

Expenditure	2010/11	2011/12	2012/13
Operating expenditure	239,293	296,446	302,942
Recurrent expenditure	135,093	145,798	156,213
Personal emoluments	51,018	54,690	58,218
Pensions	18,027	19,737	21,843
Departmental expenses	21,005	22,614	23,926
Other recurrent expenditure	45,043	48,757	52,226
Subventions	88,080	96,698	106,108
Education	29,616	32,097	34,067
Health	33,800	38,227	42,478
Universities and polytechnics	11,016	11,633	13,550
Other subventions	13,648	14,741	16,013
Non-recurrent operating expenditure	16,120	53,950	40,621
Capital expenditure	62,067	67,591	74,382
Plant, equipment and works	1,303	1,488	1,583
Subventions	1,697	1,585	1,562
Capital Works Reserve Fund	53,537	60,837	66,527
Loan fund	1,987	2,061	2,304
Other funds	3,543	1,620	2,406
Total government expenditure	301,360	364,037	377,324

INTERNATIONAL RESERVES
(US $ million at 31 December)

	2010	2011	2012
Gold (national valuation)	94	105	111
Foreign exchange*	268,649	285,266	317,189
Reserve position in the fund	—	36	62
Total	268,743	285,407	317,362

* Including the foreign-exchange reserves of the Hong Kong Special Administrative Region Government's Land Fund.

Source: IMF, *International Financial Statistics*.

MONEY SUPPLY
(HK $ '000 million at 31 December)

	2010	2011	2012
Currency outside banks	218.6	248.1	281.6
Demand deposits at banking institutions	420.4	444.3	510.5
Total money	639.0	692.4	792.1

Source: IMF, *International Financial Statistics*.

COST OF LIVING
(Consumer Price Index; base: 2000 = 100)

	2010	2011	2012
Food	119.3	127.7	135.0
All items (incl. others)	104.4	109.9	114.3

Source: ILO.

NATIONAL ACCOUNTS
(HK $ million at current prices)

Expenditure on the Gross Domestic Product

	2010	2011	2012
Government final consumption expenditure	157,371	168,487	185,380
Private final consumption expenditure	1,098,564	1,240,842	1,320,264
Change in stocks	37,522	11,742	–7,728
Gross fixed capital formation	386,852	455,048	538,951
Total domestic expenditure	1,680,309	1,876,119	2,036,867
Exports of goods and services	3,890,747	4,347,901	4,570,925
Less Imports of goods and services	3,794,273	4,287,937	4,565,847
GDP in purchasers' values	1,776,783	1,936,083	2,041,945
GDP in chain linked prices	1,846,505	1,936,083	1,965,153

Gross Domestic Product by Economic Activity

	2010	2011	2012*
Agriculture, fishing, mining and quarrying	948	944	1,114
Manufacturing	30,410	30,578	30,651
Electricity, gas and water	34,486	33,882	35,394
Construction	56,531	65,484	73,927
Wholesale, retail and import/export trades, restaurants and hotels	469,726	559,321	586,412
Transport, storage and communications	192,965	182,986	191,065
Financing, insurance, real estate and business services	472,679	520,752	553,556
Community, social and personal services	295,257	313,612	336,684
Ownership of premises	184,745	195,005	208,012
Gross domestic product at factor cost	1,737,748	1,902,565	2,016,815
Taxes on production and imports	68,707	69,401	64,645
Statistical discrepancy	–29,672	–35,883	–39,515
GDP in purchasers' values	1,776,783	1,936,083	2,041,945

* Preliminary.

BALANCE OF PAYMENTS
(US $ million)

	2010	2011	2012
Exports of goods	388,901	437,661	466,053
Imports of goods	–385,609	–445,143	–487,372
Balance on goods	3,292	–7,482	–21,319
Exports of services	80,599	91,497	97,852
Imports of services	–70,398	–74,259	–73,293
Balance on goods and services	13,493	9,756	3,240
Primary income received	119,668	136,104	137,842
Primary income paid	–114,828	–129,316	–132,237
Balance on goods, services and primary income	18,333	16,544	8,845
Secondary income received	573	881	972
Secondary income paid	–2,835	–3,423	–3,750
Current balance	16,070	14,002	6,067
Capital account (net)	–571	–260	–185
Direct investment assets	–98,431	–95,906	–83,991
Direct investment liabilities	82,709	96,135	74,584
Portfolio investment assets	–80,687	–19,997	–34,739
Portfolio investment liabilities	23,717	18,604	33,090
Financial derivatives and employee stock options (net)	2,403	2,684	1,970
Other investment assets	–69,543	–100,290	–14,608
Other investment liabilities	136,579	95,640	43,385
Net errors and omissions	–4,631	541	–1,213
Reserves and related items	7,616	11,153	24,360

Source: IMF, *International Financial Statistics*.

External Trade

PRINCIPAL COMMODITIES
(HK $ million)

Imports c.i.f.	2010	2011	2012
Food and live animals	117,661	138,870	144,143
Chemicals and related products	180,317	190,233	181,956
Basic manufactures	381,267	433,135	416,875
Textile yarn, fabrics, made-up articles, etc.	87,523	85,950	80,384
Machinery and transport equipment	1,923,525	2,112,822	2,265,143
Office machines and automatic data-processing equipment	322,728	356,601	409,428
Telecommunications and sound recording and reproducing apparatus and equipment	457,229	527,241	626,689
Other electrical machinery, apparatus and appliances, and electrical parts thereof	956,769	1,013,350	1,016,002
Miscellaneous manufactured articles	590,850	683,182	703,105
Clothing (excl. footwear)	129,315	134,089	126,724
Photographic apparatus, equipment and supplies, optical goods, watches and clocks	93,437	112,415	121,298
Total (incl. others)	3,364,840	3,764,596	3,912,163

Exports f.o.b.*	2010	2011	2012
Chemicals and related products	143,153	155,513	151,458
Basic manufactures	320,843	380,645	350,654
Textile yarn, fabrics, made-up articles, etc.	87,848	87,791	81,798
Machinery and transport equipment	1,823,214	1,991,858	2,120,117
Office machines and automatic data-processing equipment	332,819	379,385	427,837
Telecommunications and sound recording and reproducing apparatus and equipment	511,023	562,106	596,479
Other electrical machinery, apparatus and appliances, and electrical parts thereof	843,192	899,977	917,409
Miscellaneous manufactured articles	663,583	717,024	717,868
Clothing (excl. footwear)	186,840	190,592	175,085
Photographic apparatus, equipment and supplies, optical goods, watches and clocks	97,203	107,793	114,116
Baby carriages, toys, games and sporting goods	88,436	91,343	90,596
Total (incl. others)	3,031,019	3,337,254	3,434,346

* Including re-exports (HK $ million): 2,961,507 in 2010; 3,271,592 in 2011; 3,375,516 in 2012.

PRINCIPAL TRADING PARTNERS
(HK $ million, excl. gold)

Imports	2010	2011	2012
China, People's Republic	1,529,751	1,696,807	1,840,862
Germany	57,660	65,688	57,278
India	71,794	86,603	81,831
Japan	308,161	318,601	311,605
Korea, Republic	133,714	149,969	153,527
Malaysia	84,705	89,015	83,649
Philippines	39,713	40,867	40,984
Singapore	237,407	254,556	246,346
Taiwan	224,761	240,916	244,889
Thailand	76,304	76,537	72,873
USA	179,160	211,368	204,459
Total (incl. others)	3,364,840	3,764,596	3,912,163

Domestic exports	2010	2011	2012
Australia	1,148	792	n.a.
China, People's Republic	31,223	30,699	26,026
Germany	861	589	371
Japan	2,032	1,531	1,192
Korea, Republic	1,495	1,444	1,277
Netherlands	2,639	839	180
Singapore	2,866	2,620	2,712
Switzerland	1,683	2,847	3,062
Taiwan	2,815	3,004	2,698
United Kingdom	1,554	1,510	n.a.
USA	8,356	7,165	6,766
Total (incl. others)	69,512	65,662	58,830

Re-exports	2010	2011	2012
China, People's Republic	1,566,999	1,716,656	1,831,732
France	34,582	38,994	36,769
Germany	79,776	88,675	77,441
India	73,481	92,919	76,281
Japan	125,615	133,624	142,778
Korea, Republic	52,174	59,829	57,576
Netherlands	41,482	41,462	41,256
Singapore	48,113	53,624	53,238
Taiwan	65,789	82,266	78,145
United Kingdom	59,226	57,178	54,015
USA	323,733	323,606	331,739
Total (incl. others)	2,961,507	3,271,592	3,375,516

Transport

RAILWAYS
(traffic)

	2008	2009	2010
Freight ('000 metric tons):			
loaded	19	16	7
unloaded	90	68	29

Passenger journeys ('000): 3,188 in 2003.

ROAD TRAFFIC
('000 registered motor vehicles at 31 December)

	2010	2011	2012
Private cars	415	435	455
Buses (private and public)	13	13	13
Light buses (private and public)	6	7	7
Taxis	18	18	18
Goods vehicles	109	111	113
Motorcycles	38	39	40
Government vehicles (excl. military vehicles)	6	6	6
Total (incl. others)	608	630	653

Note: Figures do not include tramcars.

SHIPPING

Flag Registered Fleet
(at 31 December)

	2011	2012	2013
Number of vessels	1,989	2,203	2,375
Total displacement ('000 grt)	68,310.6	78,251.1	86,544.3

Source: Lloyd's List Intelligence (www.lloydslistintelligence.com).

Traffic
(2012 unless otherwise indicated)

	Ocean-going vessels	River vessels
Total capacity (million nrt)	832	194*
Cargo landed ('000 metric tons)	117,448	37,251
Cargo loaded ('000 metric tons)	71,412	43,172

* 2007.

Passenger traffic ('000, arrivals and departures by sea, 2012): Passengers landed 12,647; Passengers embarked 14,732.

Note: Includes passengers travelling to and from Macao by helicopter.

CIVIL AVIATION

	2010	2011	2012
Passengers ('000):			
arrivals	17,030	18,160	19,346
departures	16,241	17,334	18,426
Freight ('000 metric tons):			
landed	1,479	1,442	1,463
loaded	2,649	2,496	2,562

Tourism

TOURIST ARRIVALS BY COUNTRY OF RESIDENCE
(non-resident tourist arrivals at national borders)

	2010	2011	2012
Australia	505,907	500,225	495,441
Canada	290,827	291,454	278,028
China, People's Republic	11,678,055	13,599,768	15,110,372
Germany	170,170	163,975	161,970
Indonesia	340,147	379,915	370,161
Japan	823,575	787,220	774,426
Korea, Republic	587,866	670,835	725,783
Macao	274,616	281,678	291,219
Malaysia	424,491	452,172	434,212
Philippines	493,092	542,967	585,760
Singapore	527,560	585,727	530,561
Taiwan	724,561	778,653	754,190
Thailand	356,060	380,647	388,681
United Kingdom	421,566	413,156	436,392
USA (incl. Guam)	838,752	861,006	841,630
Total (incl. others)	20,085,155	22,316,073	23,770,195

Source: Hong Kong Tourism Board.

Receipts from tourism (US $ million, excl. passenger transport): 22,200 in 2010; 27,665 in 2011; 32,089 in 2012 (provisional) (Source: World Tourism Organization).

Communications Media

	2010	2011	2012
Telephones ('000 in use)	4,361.7	4,342.2	4,361.7
Mobile cellular telephones ('000 subscribers)	13,793.7	15,292.9	16,403.1
Internet subscribers ('000)	2,922.3	3,059.0	n.a.
Broadband subscribers ('000)	2,111.1	2,248.9	2,270.7

Source: International Telecommunication Union.

Education

(2012/13 unless otherwise indicated)

	Institutions	Teachers	Students
Kindergartens	957	11,817	164,764
Primary schools	569	22,173	317,442
Secondary schools	519	29,981	418,787
Special schools	61	1,605	7,946
Institute of Vocational Education	1	2,151	55,328
Approved post-secondary college	5	499	7,542
Other post-secondary colleges	17	n.a.	10,893
University Grants Committee-funded institutions	8	5,813*†	197,117
Open University of Hong Kong	1	130*	20,781
Adult education institutions	2,507	n.a.	218,606

* 2006/07.

† Provisional figure.

Pupil-teacher ratio (primary education, UNESCO estimate): 14.8 in 2010/11 (Source: UNESCO Institute for Statistics).

Adult literacy rate (UNESCO estimates): 94.6% in 2003 (Source: UN Development Programme, *Human Development Report*).

Directory

The Government

Chief Executive: LEUNG CHUN-YING (elected 25 March 2012; inaugurated 1 July 2012).

EXECUTIVE COUNCIL

(April 2014)

Chairman: The Chief Executive.

Ex Officio Members (Principal Officials)

Chief Secretary for Administration: CARRIE LAM CHEUNG YUET-NGOR.

Financial Secretary: JOHN TSANG CHUN-WAH.

Secretary for Justice: RIMSKY YUEN KWOK-KEUNG.

Secretary for Education: EDDIE NG HAK-KIM.

Secretary for Commerce and Economic Development: GREGORY SO KAM-LEUNG.

Secretary for Constitutional and Mainland Affairs: RAYMOND TAM CHI-YUEN.

Secretary for Security: LAI TUNG-KWOK.

Secretary for Food and Health: Dr KO WING-MAN.

Secretary for the Civil Service: PAUL TANG KWOK-WAI.

Secretary for Home Affairs: TSANG TAK-SING.

Secretary for Labour and Welfare: MATTHEW CHEUNG KIN-CHUNG.

Secretary for Financial Services and the Treasury: Prof. K. C. CHAN KA-KEUNG.

Secretary for Development: PAUL CHAN MO-PO.

Secretary for the Environment: WONG KAM-SING.

Secretary for Transport and Housing: Prof. ANTHONY CHEUNG BING-LEUNG.

In addition to the above ex officio members of the Executive Council, there were also 14 non-official members.

GOVERNMENT OFFICES

Executive Council: Low Blk, Central Government Offices, 2 Tim Mei Ave, Tamar, Admiralty; tel. 28102581; fax 28450176; e-mail exco@ceo.gov.hk; internet www.ceo.gov.hk/exco.

Office of the Chief Executive: Low Blk, Central Government Offices, 2 Tim Mei Ave, Tamar, Admiralty; tel. 28783300; fax 25090580; e-mail ceo@ceo.gov.hk; internet www.ceo.gov.hk.

Government Secretariat: Central Government Offices, 2 Tim Mei Ave, Tamar, Admiralty; tel. 28820099; fax 28457895.

Information Services Department: North Point Government Offices, 333 Java Rd, North Point; tel. 28428604; fax 25211046; e-mail internet@isd.gov.hk; internet www.isd.gov.hk.

Legislature

LEGISLATIVE COUNCIL

The fifth Legislative Council since Hong Kong's transfer to Chinese sovereignty was elected on 9 September 2012. The Legislative Council comprises 70 members: 35 chosen by functional constituencies and 35 by direct election in five geographical constituencies. The term of office is four years.

President: JASPER TSANG YOK-SING.

Election, 9 September 2012

Party	Directly elective seats	Functional Constituency seats	Total seats
Democratic Alliance for the Betterment and Progress of Hong Kong	9	4	13
Civic Party	5	1	6
Democratic Party	4	2	6
Hong Kong Federation of Trade Unions	3	3	6
Liberal Party	1	4	5
Labour Party	3	1	4
Economic Synergy	—	3	3
People Power	3	—	3
New People's Party	2	—	2
Association for Democracy and People's Livelihood	—	1	1
Federation of Hong Kong and Kowloon Labour Unions	—	1	1
Kowloon West New Dynamic	1	—	1
League of Social Democrats	1	—	1
Neighbourhood and Worker's Service Centre	1	—	1
NeoDemocrats	1	—	1
New Forum	—	1	1
Independents and others	1	14	15
Total	35	35	70

Election Commission

Electoral Affairs Commission: 10/F, Harbour Centre, 25 Harbour Rd, Wanchai; tel. 28911001; fax 28274644; e-mail eacenq@reo.gov.hk; internet www.eac.gov.hk; f. 1997; Chair. BARNABAS FUNG.

Political Organizations

Alliance for True Democracy (ATD): Hong Kong; e-mail atd@atd.hk; internet www.atd.hk; f. 2013; superseding the Alliance for Universal Suffrage which was suspended in Jan. 2013; coalition of the 12 pro-democracy parties represented in the Legislative Council to promote electoral reform, notably direct elections by universal suffrage; Convenor Prof. JOSEPH CHENG YU-SHEK.

Association for Democracy and People's Livelihood (ADPL): Sun Beam Commercial Bldg, Rm 1104, 469–471 Nathan Rd, Kowloon; tel. 27822699; fax 27823137; e-mail info@adpl.org.hk; internet www.adpl.org.hk; advocates democracy; Chair. BRUCE LIU; Sec.-Gen. YANG ZHENYU.

Civic Party: Unit 202, 2/F, Blk B, Sea View Bldg, 4–6 Watson Rd, North Point; tel. 28657111; fax 28652771; e-mail contact@civicparty.hk; internet www.civicparty.hk; f. 2006; pro-democracy; Chair. AUDREY EU; Leader ALAN LEONG.

Democratic Alliance for the Betterment and Progress of Hong Kong (DAB): SUP Tower, 15/F, 83 King's Rd, North Point; tel. 35821111; fax 35821188; e-mail info@dab.org.hk; internet www.dab.org.hk; f. 2005; formed by merger of Democratic Alliance for the Betterment of Hong Kong (f. 1992, supported return of Hong Kong to the motherland and implementation of the Basic Law) and Hong Kong Progressive Alliance (f. 1994, supported by business and professional community); pro-Beijing; Chair. TAM YIU-CHUNG; Sec.-Gen. CHEN XUEFENG.

Democratic Party: Hanley House, 4/F, 776–778 Nathan Rd, Kowloon; tel. 23977033; fax 23978998; e-mail dphk@dphk.org; internet www.dphk.org; f. 1994; formed by merger of United Democrats of Hong Kong (UDHK—declared a formal political party in 1990) and Meeting Point; merged with The Frontier (f. 1996) in Nov. 2008; liberal grouping; advocates democracy; Chair. EMILY LAU WAI-HING; Sec.-Gen. CHEUNG YIN-TUNG.

Economic Synergy: 3204A, 32/F, Tower 1, Admiralty Centre, 18 Harcourt Rd, Admiralty; tel. 25201112; fax 25279930; e-mail enquiries@economicsynergy.org; internet www.economicsynergy.org; f. 2009; est. by former members of Liberal Party.

Hong Kong Democratic Foundation: POB 35588, King's Road Post Office, North Point; tel. 28696443; fax 28696318; e-mail secretariat@hkdf.org; internet www.hkdf.org; f. 1989; advocates democracy and an open society; Chair. ALAN LUNG KA-LUN.

Hong Kong 2020: Hong Kong; f. 2013; group established to campaign for universal suffrage; Leader ANSON CHAN.

Labour Party: Hong Kong; internet www.labour.org.hk; f. 2011; Chair. LEE CHEUK-YAN; Sec.-Gen. GUO YONGJIAN.

League of Social Democrats: B-2, 4/F, Tai Cheong Factory Bldg, 3 Wing Ming St, Cheung Sha Wan, Kowloon; tel. 23755338; fax 23755732; e-mail lsd@lsd.org.hk; internet www.lsd.org.hk; socialist group; anti-Beijing; Chair. LEUNG KWOK-HUNG; Sec.-Gen. MICHAEL MAK.

Liberal Party: 801–803 Manhattan Place, 23 Wang Tai Rd, Kowloon; tel. 28696833; fax 25334238; e-mail liberal@liberal.org.hk; internet www.liberal.org.hk; f. 1993; est. by mems of Co-operative Resources Centre (CRC); business-orientated; pro-Beijing; Chair. SELINA CHOW LIANG SHUK-YEE; Leader TIEN PEI-CHUN.

Neighbourhood and Worker's Service Centre: Unit 326, 3/F, West Wing, Central Government Offices, 11 Ice House St, Central; tel. 25372101; fax 25372102; e-mail legco@nwsc.org.hk; internet www.nwsc.org.hk; Chair. LEUNG YIU-CHUNG.

NeoDemocrats: Yuk Nga Lane, Tseung Kwan O, New Territories; tel. 81099986; e-mail neodemocrats@gmail.com; internet www.neodemocrats.hk; f. 2010; Leader GARY FAN KWOK WAI.

New People's Party (NPP): Flats D–F, 11/F, China Overseas Bldg, 139 Hennessy Rd, Wanchai; tel. 31000079; fax 31000087; e-mail info@npp.org.hk; internet www.npp.org.hk; f. 2011; pro-Beijing; advocates universal suffrage, economic diversification and reduction in wealth gap; Chair. REGINA IP.

Occupy Central with Love and Peace (Occupy Central): Hong Kong; f. 2013; group proposing civil disobedience in support of universal suffrage; Founder BENNY TAI YIU-TING.

People Power: c/o The Legislative Council; tel. 51731993; fax 23925762; e-mail admin@peoplepower.hk; internet www.peoplepower.hk; f. 2011; est. by fmr mems of League of Social Democrats; pro-democracy; Chair. ERICA YUEN.

At the elections of September 2012, the Hong Kong Federation of Trade Unions and the Federation of Hong Kong and Kowloon Labour Unions (see Trade and Industry), Kowloon West New Dynamic and New Forum also secured seats in the Legislative Council.

The Chinese Communist Party (based in the People's Republic) and the Kuomintang (Nationalist Party of China, based in Taiwan) also maintain organizations in Hong Kong.

Judicial System

Court of Final Appeal: 1 Battery Path, Central, Hong Kong; tel. 21230123; fax 21210300; internet www.judiciary.gov.hk; f. July 1997 upon the commencement of the Hong Kong Court of Final Appeal Ordinance, replacing the Privy Council in London as the highest appellate court in Hong Kong; the Court comprises five judges—the Chief Justice, three permanent judges and one non-permanent Hong Kong judge or one judge from another common-law jurisdiction; Chief Justice GEOFFREY MA TAO-LI.

High Court: 38 Queensway, Hong Kong; tel. 25232212; fax 25249725; e-mail enquiry@judiciary.gov.hk; internet www.judiciary.gov.hk; consists of a Court of Appeal and a Court of First Instance; the Court is presided over by the Chief Judge or a Vice-President of the Court of Appeal with one or two Justices of Appeal; Chief Judge ANDREW CHEUNG KUI-NUNG.

District Court: there are 38 District Judges and a Principal Family Court Judge headed by a Chief District Judge.

Magistrates' Courts: there are four Principal Magistrates, 59 Magistrates and 10 Special Magistrates and a Chief Magistrate, sitting in seven magistracies.

Religion

The population is predominantly Buddhist. The number of active Buddhists is estimated at between 650,000 and 700,000, and there were more than 600 temples in 2005. Confucianism and Daoism are widely practised. The three religions are frequently found in the same temple. In 2005 there were some 660,000 Christians, approximately 90,000 Muslims, 40,000 Hindus, and 8,000 Sikhs. Judaism, the Bahá'í faith and Zoroastrianism are also represented.

BUDDHISM

Hong Kong Buddhist Association: 1/F, 338 Lockhart Rd, Wanchai; tel. 25749371; fax 28340789; e-mail enquiry@hkbuddhist.org; internet www.hkbuddhist.org; Pres. Ven. KOK KWONG.

CHRISTIANITY

Hong Kong Christian Council: 9/F, 33 Granville Rd, Kowloon; tel. 23687123; fax 27242131; e-mail hkcc@hkcc.org.hk; internet www.hkcc.org.hk; f. 1954; 22 mem. orgs; Chair. Rev. NICHOLAS TAI HO-FAI; Sec. Rev. YUEN TIN-YAU.

The Anglican Communion

Primate of Hong Kong Sheng Kung Hui and Bishop of Hong Kong Island and Macao: Most Rev. PETER K. K. KWONG, Bishop's House, 1 Lower Albert Rd, Central; tel. 25265355; fax 25212199; e-mail office1@hkskh.org; internet www1.hkskh.org.

Bishop of Eastern Kowloon: Rt Rev. LOUIS TSUI, 4/F, Holy Trinity Bradbury Centre, 139 Ma Tau Chung Rd, Kowloon; tel. 27139983; fax 27111609; e-mail dek@hkskh.org; internet dek.hkskh.org.

Bishop of Western Kowloon: Rt Rev. THOMAS SOO, 15/F, Ultra Grace Commercial Bldg, 5 Jordan Rd, Kowloon; tel. 27830811; fax 27830799; e-mail dwk@hkskh.org; internet dwk.hkskh.org.

The Lutheran Church

Evangelical Lutheran Church of Hong Kong: 4/F, Lutheran Bldg, Waterloo Rd, Yau Ma Tei, Kowloon; tel. 23885847; fax 23887539; e-mail info@elchk.org.hk; internet www.elchk.org.hk; f. 1954; 16,000 mems (2011); Bishop Rev. JENNY CHAN.

Lutheran Church—Hong Kong Synod: 68 Begonia Rd, Yau Yat Chuen, Kowloon; tel. 23973721; fax 23974826; e-mail hksynod@lutheran.org.hk; internet www.lutheran.org.hk; Pres. Rev. ALLAN YUNG.

The Roman Catholic Church

For ecclesiastical purposes, Hong Kong forms a single diocese, nominally suffragan to the archdiocese of Canton (Guangzhou), China. According to Vatican sources, in December 2007 there were an estimated 352,939 adherents in the territory, representing more than 5% of the total population.

Bishop of Hong Kong: JOHN TONG HON, 12/F, Catholic Diocese Centre, 16 Caine Rd, Central; tel. 28434679; fax 25254707; e-mail bishophk@pacific.net.hk; internet www.catholic.org.hk.

The Press

According to Hong Kong government figures, at July 2013 there were 53 daily newspapers, including 27 Chinese-language and 12 English-language dailies, nine bilingual dailies, five Japanese dailies and 701 periodicals.

PRINCIPAL DAILY NEWSPAPERS

English Language

China Daily: internet www.chinadaily.com.cn/hkedition/hk.html; Hong Kong edn of China's official English-language newspaper; launched 1997; Editor-in-Chief RAY ZHOU; circ. 20,000.

International Herald Tribune: 1201 K Wah Centre, 191 Java Rd, North Point; tel. 29221188; fax 29221190; internet www.iht.com; Man. Dir RANDY WEDDLE.

South China Morning Post: 3/F, 1 Leighton Rd, Causeway Bay; tel. 25652222; fax 28111048; e-mail info@scmp.com; internet www.scmp.com; f. 1903; Editor-in-Chief WANG XIANGWEI; circ. 104,000.

The Standard: 3/F, Sing Tao News Corporation Bldg, 3 Tung Wong Rd, Shau Kei Wan; tel. 27982723; fax 23051765; e-mail editor@thestandard.com.hk; internet www.thestandard.com.hk; f. 1949; publ. as free newspaper since Jan. 2007; Editor-in-Chief IVAN TONG; circ. 231,018.

Target Intelligent Report: Suite 2901, Bank of America Tower, 12 Harcourt Rd, Central; tel. 25730379; fax 28381597; e-mail info@targetnewspapers.com; internet www.targetnewspapers.com; f. 1972; financial news, commentary, politics, property, litigations, etc.; Dir. CECILIA LEE.

Wall Street Journal Asia: 25/F, Central Plaza, 18 Harbour Rd, Wanchai; tel. 25737121; fax 28345291; e-mail wsj.ltrs@wsj.com; internet www.wsj-asia.com; f. 1976; business; Editor-in-Chief ALMAR LATOUR; circ. 83,421.

Chinese Language

Hong Kong Commercial Daily: 1/F, 499 King's Rd, North Point; tel. 25905322; fax 25658947; internet www.hkcd.com.hk; f. 1952; Chair. and CEO HUANG YANG LUE; Editor CHENG XI TIAN.

Hong Kong Daily News: 5/F, CWG Bldg, 3A Kung Ngam Village Rd, Shau Kei Wan; tel. 39216688; fax 39216686; e-mail edit@hkdailynews.com.hk; internet www.hkdailynews.com.hk; f. 1958; morning; CEO RODDY YU; Chief Editor K. K. YEUNG; circ. 120,000.

Hong Kong Economic Journal: 22/F, North Point Industrial Bldg, 499 King's Rd, North Point; tel. 28567567; fax 28111070; e-mail enquiry@hkej.com; internet www.hkej.com; Dir CHO CHI-MING; Chief Editor K. C. CHAN; circ. 63,000.

Hong Kong Economic Times: Kodak House, Block 2, 6/F, 321 Java Rd, North Point; tel. 28802444; fax 25169989; e-mail etp_info@hket.com; internet www.etpress.com.hk; f. 1988; Publr and Man. Dir MAK PING LEUNG; Chief Editor CHAN CHO BIU; circ. 100,000.

Ming Pao Daily News: Blk A, Ming Pao Industrial Centre, 15/F, 18 Ka Yip St, Chai Wan; tel. 25953111; fax 28982534; e-mail mingpao@mingpao.com; internet www.mediachinesegroup.com; f. 1959; morning; Chief Editor CHONG TIEN-SIONG; circ. 130,000.

Oriental Daily News: Oriental Press Centre, 23 Dai Cheong St, Tai Po Industrial Estate, New Territories; tel. 36008811; fax 336008800; e-mail news@oriental.com.hk; internet orientaldaily.on.cc; Chair. C. F. MA; Editor-in-Chief LAM SHUN-CHUEN; circ. 500,000.

Ping Kuo Jih Pao (Apple Daily): 8 Chun Ying St, Industrial Estate West, Tseung Kwan; tel. 29908388; fax 26239132; e-mail adnews@appledaily.com; internet appledaily.atnext.com; f. 1995; published by Next Media; Propr JIMMY LAI; Publr LOH CHAN; circ. 226,816.

Sing Pao Daily News: 3/F, CWG Bldg, 3A Kung Ngam, Village Rd, Shau Kei Wan; tel. 25702201; fax 28062091; e-mail dailynews@singpao.com.hk; internet www.singpao.com; f. 1939; morning; Chief Editor CHENG SI WEI; circ. 100,000.

Sing Tao Daily: 3/F, Sing Tao News Corpn Bldg, 3 Tung Wong Rd, Shau Kei Wan; tel. 27982323; fax 27518634; e-mail info@singtao.com; internet www.singtao.com; f. 1938; morning; Editor-in-Chief LUK KAM WING; circ. 60,000.

The Sun: Oriental Press Centre, 23 Dai Cheong St, Tai Po Industrial Estate, New Territories; tel. 36009911; fax 36009900; e-mail news@the-sun.com.hk; internet the-sun.on.cc; f. 1999; publ. by the Oriental Press Group; circ. 200,000.

Ta Kung Pao: 342 Hennessy Rd, Wanchai; tel. 25757181; fax 28345104; e-mail tkp@takungpao.com; internet www.takungpao.com; f. 1902; morning; pro-Beijing; Editor T. S. TSANG; circ. 150,000.

Wen Wei Po: 2–4 Hing Wai Centre, 3/F, 7 Tin Wan Praya Rd, Aberdeen; tel. 28738288; fax 28730657; e-mail editor@wenhuibao.com.hk; internet www.wenweipo.com; f. 1948; morning; Dir WANG SHUCHENG; Editor-in-Chief WONG BAK YAO; circ. 200,000.

SELECTED PERIODICALS

English Language

Asia Money: 27/F, 248 Queen's Rd East, Wanchai; tel. 29128074; fax 28656225; e-mail richard.morrow@asiamoney.com; internet www.asiamoney.com; 10 a year; Publr ANDREW COVER; Man. Editor MARK BAKER.

Business Traveller Asia–Pacific: Suite 405, 4/F, Chinachem Exchange Square, 1 Hoi Wan St, Quarry Bay; tel. 25949300; fax 25196846; e-mail enquiry@businesstravellerasia.com; internet asia.businesstraveller.com; f. 1982; consumer business travel; 10 a year; Publr PEGGY TEO; Editor-in-Chief TOM OTLEY; circ. 34,098.

Electronics: 38/F, Office Tower, Convention Plaza, 1 Harbour Rd, Wanchai; tel. 1830668; fax 28240249; e-mail hktdc@hktdc.org; internet www.hktdc.com; f. 1985; 4 a year (April, June, Oct. and Dec.); publ. by the Hong Kong Trade Development Council; Exec. Dir FRED LAM; Chief Editor GEOFF PICKEN; circ. 90,000.

Enterprise: 38/F, Office Tower, Convention Plaza, 1 Harbour Rd, Wanchai; tel. 1830668; fax 28240249; e-mail hktdc@hktdc.org; internet www.hktdc.com; f. 1967; monthly; publ. by the Hong Kong Trade Devt Council; Exec. Dir FRED LAM; Chief Editor GEOFF PICKEN; circ. 150,000.

Hong Kong Industrialist: Federation of Hong Kong Industries, 31/F, Billion Plaza, 8 Cheung Yue St, Cheung Sha Wan, Kowloon; tel. 27323188; fax 27213494; e-mail fhki@fhki.org.hk; internet www.industryhk.org; monthly; publ. by the Federation of Hong Kong Industries; Chair. STANLEY LAU; Editor ANTHONY CHAN; circ. 6,000.

Hong Kong Special Administrative Region Government Gazette: Printing Division, Government Logistics Department, 10/F, Government Offices, 333 Java Rd, North Point; tel. 25649500; fax 28876591; e-mail info@gld.gov.hk; internet www.gld.gov.hk; weekly.

Houseware: 38/F, Office Tower, Convention Plaza, 1 Harbour Rd, Wanchai; tel. 1830668; fax 28240249; e-mail hktdc@hktdc.org; internet www.hktdc.com; f. 1983; publ. by the Hong Kong Trade Development Council; household and hardware products; 2 a year; Exec. Dir FRED LAM; Chief Editor GEOFF PICKEN; circ. 90,000.

Official Hong Kong Guide (e-Newsletter): c/o HKTB, Citicorp Centre, 9–11/F, 18 Whitfield Rd, North Point; f. 1982; monthly; information on sightseeing, shopping, dining, etc. for overseas visitors; published by the Hong Kong Tourism Board.

Orientations: 816, 8/F, Zung Fu Industrial Bldg, 1067 King's Rd, Quarry Bay; tel. 25111368; fax 25074620; e-mail office@orientations.com.hk; internet www.orientations.com.hk; f. 1970; 8 a year; arts of East Asia, the Indian subcontinent and South-East Asia; Publr YIFAWN LEE; Editor ANNIE KNIBB.

Reader's Digest (Asia Edn): Reader's Digest Association Far East Ltd, 19/F, Cyber Centre, 3 Tung Wong Rd, Shau Kei Wan; tel. 25681117; fax 96906389; e-mail friends@rdasia.com.hk; internet www.readersdigest.com.hk; f. 1963; general topics; monthly; Editor DORA CHEOK; circ. 332,000.

Sunday Examiner: 11/F, Catholic Diocese Centre, 16 Caine Rd, Central; tel. 25220487; fax 25369939; e-mail sunday@examiner.org.hk; internet sundayex.catholic.org.hk; f. 1946; religious; weekly; Editor-in-Chief Sister TERESA YUEN; Deputy Editor-in-Chief Fr JIM MULRONEY; circ. 9,000.

Textile Asia: c/o Business Press Ltd, California Tower, 11/F, 30–32 D'Aguilar St, GPOB 185, Central; tel. 25233744; fax 28106966; e-mail texasia@biznetvigator.com; internet www.textileasia-businesspress.com; f. 1970; monthly; textile and clothing industry; Publr and Editor-in-Chief MAX W. SUNG; circ. 17,000.

Travel Business Analyst: GPOB 12761, Hong Kong; tel. 25072310; e-mail TBAoffice@gmail.com; internet www.travelbusinessanalyst.com; f. 1982; monthly; travel trade; Editor MURRAY BAILEY.

Chinese Language

Affairs Weekly: Hong Kong; tel. 28950801; fax 25767842; f. 1980; general interest; Editor WONG WAI MAN; circ. 130,000.

Cheng Ming Monthly: Hennessy Rd, POB 20370, Wanchai; tel. 25740664; e-mail editor.chengmingmag@gmail.com; internet www.chengmingmag.com; current affairs; Chief Editor WAN FAI.

City Magazine: 9/F, Zung Fu Industrial Bldg, 1067 King's Rd, Quarry Bay; tel. 22509188; fax 28919719; e-mail hk@modernmedia.com.hk; internet www.cityhowwhy.com.hk; f. 1976; monthly; fashion, wine, cars, society, etc.; Publr JOHN K. C. CHAN; Chief Editor PETER WONG; circ. 82,000.

East Touch: 3/F, Sing Tao News Corpn Bldg, 3 Tung Wong Rd, Shau Kei Wan; tel. 27074471; fax 27074554; e-mail easttouch@singtaonewscorp.com; internet www.easttouch.com.hk; f. 1995; weekly; fashion, celebrity and entertainment news; circ. 85,000.

East Week: 3/F, Sing Tao News Corpn Bldg, 3 Tung Wong Rd, Shau Kei Wan; tel. 31813588; fax 21104209; e-mail info@eastweek.com.hk; internet www.eastweek.com.hk; f. 1992; weekly; publication halted in 2002; relaunched in 2003; general interest; Chair. HE ZHUGUO; circ. 135,000.

Kung Kao Po (Catholic Chinese Weekly): 16/F, 11 Catholic Parish Centre, Caine Rd, Central; tel. 25220487; fax 25213095; internet kkp.org.hk; e-mail kkp@kkp.org.hk; f. 1928; religious; weekly; Editor-in-Chief Sister TERESA YUEN.

Ming Pao Monthly: Ming Pao Industrial Centre, 15/F, Block A, 18 Ka Yip St, Chai Wan; tel. 25953111; fax 28982691; e-mail mpmeditor@mingpao.com; internet www.mingpaomonthly.com; Chief Editor KOO SIU-SUN.

Next Magazine: 8 Chun Ying St, T. K. O. Industrial Estate West, Tseung Kwan O, Kowloon; tel. 27442733; fax 29907210; internet www.nextmedia.com; internet next.atnext.com; f. 1989; weekly; news, business, lifestyle, entertainment; Editor-in-Chief LEE CHI-HO; circ. 80,336.

Open Magazine: POB 20064, Hennessy Rd; tel. 28939197; fax 28915591; e-mail open@open.com.hk; internet www.open.com.hk; f. 1990; monthly; Chief Editor JIN ZHONG; circ. 15,000.

Oriental Sunday: 10/F, Johnson Bldg, 14–16 Lee Chung St, Chai Wan; tel. 29603504; fax 29605701; e-mail anniekwan@newmediagroup.com.hk; internet www.orientalsunday.hk; f. 1991; weekly; leisure magazine; Publr TSO SUET CHUNG; circ. 120,000.

Reader's Digest (Chinese Edn): Reader's Digest Association Far East Ltd, 19/F, Cyber Centre, 3 Tung Wong Rd, Shau Kei Wan; tel. 25681117; fax 25690370; internet www.readersdigest.com.hk; f. 1965; monthly; Editor-in-Chief JOEL POON; circ. 177,306.

Today's Living: 2207, 22/F, Westlands Center, 20 Westlands Rd, Quarry Bay; tel. 28822230; fax 28823949; e-mail magazine@todaysliving.com; internet www.todaysliving.com; f. 1987; monthly; interior design; Publr and Editor-in-Chief KENNETH LI; circ. 42,000.

Yazhou Zhoukan: Blk A, Ming Pao Industrial Centre, 15/F, 18 Ka Yip St, Chai Wan; tel. 25155358; fax 25059662; e-mail yzzk@mingpao.com; internet www.yzzk.com; f. 1987; international Chinese news weekly; Chief Editor YAU LOP-POON; circ. 110,000.

Yuk Long TV Weekly: Hong Kong; tel. 25657883; fax 25659958; f. 1977; entertainment, fashion, etc.; Publr TONY WONG; circ. 82,508.

NEWS AGENCIES

International News Service: 2E Cheong Shing Mansion, 33–39 Wing Hing St, Causeway Bay; tel. 25665668; Rep. AU KIT MING.

Xinhua (New China) News Agency, Hong Kong SAR Bureau: 387 Queen's Rd East, Wanchai; tel. 28314126; f. 2000; est. from fmr news dept of branch office of Xinhua (responsibility for other activities assumed by Liaison Office of the Central People's Govt in the Hong Kong SAR); Dir ZHANG GUOLIANG.

PRESS ASSOCIATIONS

Chinese Language Press Institute: 3/F, Sing Tao News Corpn Bldg, 3 Tung Wong Rd, Shau Kei Wan; tel. 27982501; fax 27953017; e-mail clpi68@yahoo.com.hk; f. 1968; Pres. Sir TIONG HIEW KING.

Hong Kong Chinese Press Association: Rm 2208, 22/F, 33 Queen's Rd, Central; tel. 28613622; fax 28661933; 13 mems; Chair. HUE PUE-YING.

Hong Kong Journalists Association: Henfa Commercial Bldg, Flat 15A, 348–350 Lockhart Rd, Wanchai; tel. 25910692; fax 25727329; e-mail hkja@hkja.org.hk; internet www.hkja.org.hk; f. 1968; over 400 mems; Chair. SHAM YEE-LAN.

Newspaper Society of Hong Kong: Rm 904, 9/F, 75–83 King's Rd, North Point; tel. 25713102; fax 25712676; e-mail secretariat@nshk.com.hk; internet www.nshk.org.hk; f. 1954; Chair. KEITH KAM; Pres. LEE CHO-JAT.

Publishers

Asia 2000 Ltd: Rm 4, 26/F, Global Trade Centre, 15 Wing Kin Rd, Kwai Chung, New Territories; tel. 25301409; fax 25261107; e-mail sales@asia2000.com.hk; internet www.asia2000.com.hk; Asian studies, politics, photography, fiction; Man. Dir MICHAEL MORROW.

Chinese University Press: Sha Tin Galleria, 18–24 Shan Mei St, Fo Tan, New Territories; tel. 39439822; fax 26037355; e-mail cup@cuhk.edu.hk; internet www.chineseupress.com; f. 1977; studies on China and Hong Kong and other academic works; Dir QI GAN.

Commercial Press (Hong Kong) Ltd: Eastern Central Plaza, 8/F, 3 Yiu Hing Rd, Shau Kei Wan; tel. 25651371; fax 25645277; e-mail info@commercialpress.com.hk; internet www.commercialpress.com.hk; f. 1897; trade books, dictionaries, textbooks, Chinese classics, art, etc.; Chair. and Man. Dir CHAN MAN HUNG.

Excerpta Medica Asia Ltd: 1601, 16/F, Leighton Centre, 77 Leighton Rd, Causeway Bay; tel. 29651300; fax 29760778; e-mail emal@excerptahk.com; subsidiary of Elsevier; f. 1980; sponsored medical publications, abstracts, journals, etc.

Hoi Fung Publisher Co: 125 Lockhart Rd, 2/F, Wanchai; tel. 25286246; fax 25286249; Dir K. K. TSE.

Hong Kong University Press: Hing Wai Centre, 14/F, 7 Tin Wan Praya Rd, Aberdeen; tel. 39177815; fax 28581655; e-mail hkupress@hku.hk; internet www.hkupress.org; f. 1956; Publr MICHAEL DUCKWORTH.

Ling Kee Publishing Co Ltd: 14/F, Zung Fu Industrial Bldg, 1067 King's Rd, Quarry Bay; tel. 25616151; fax 28111980; e-mail admin@lingkee.com; internet www.lingkee.com; f. 1956; educational and reference; Chair. B. L. AU; Man. Dir K. W. AU.

Oxford University Press (China) Ltd: Warwick House East, 18/F, 979 King's Rd, Taikoo Place, Quarry Bay; tel. 25163126; fax 25658491; e-mail elt.china.hk@oup.com; internet www.oupchina.com.hk; f. 1961; school textbooks, reference, academic and general works relating to Hong Kong, Macao, Taiwan and China; Regional Dir SIMON LI.

Taosheng Publishing House: Lutheran Bldg, 3/F, 50A Waterloo Rd, Yau Ma Tei, Kowloon; tel. 23887061; fax 27810413; e-mail taosheng@elchk.org.hk; internet www.taosheng.org.hk; Deputy Dir LEUNG MEI YING.

Textile Asia/Business Press Ltd: California Tower, 11/F, 30–32 D'Aguilar St, GPOB 185, Central; tel. 25233744; fax 28106966; e-mail texasia@biznetvigator.com; internet www.textileasia-businesspress.com; f. 1970; textile magazine; Man. Dir KAYSER W. SUNG.

Times Publishing (Hong Kong) Ltd: Seaview Estate, Block C, 10/F, 2–8 Watson Rd, North Point; tel. 25668381; fax 25080255; e-mail abeditor@asianbusiness.com.hk; trade magazines and directories; CEO COLIN YAM; Executive Editor JAMES LEUNG.

The Woods Publishing Co: Li Yuen Bldg, 2/F, 7 Li Yuen St West, Central; tel. 25233002; fax 28453296; e-mail tybook@netvigator.com; Production Man. TONG SZE HONG.

GOVERNMENT PUBLISHING HOUSE

Government Information Services: see Government Offices.

PUBLISHERS' ASSOCIATIONS

Hong Kong Publishers' and Distributors' Association: Flat C, 4/F, 240–246 Nathan Rd, Kowloon; tel. 23674412; 45 mems; Chair. HO KAM-LING; Sec. HO NAI-CHI.

Hong Kong Publishing Federation Ltd: Room 904, SUP Tower, 75–83 King's Rd, North Point; tel. 25786000; fax 25786838.

Hong Kong Publishing Professionals' Society Ltd: 8/F, Eastern Central Plaza, 3 Yiu Hing Rd, Shaukeiwan; tel. 29766804; fax 25645270; Chair. Dr CHAN MAN HUNG.

The Society of Publishers in Asia: 8/F, Win Century Centre, 2A Mong Kok Rd, Mong Kok, Kowloon; tel. 35899778; fax 35899779; e-mail mail@sopasia.com; internet www.sopasia.com; f. 1982; Chair. DAVID E. SMITH.

Broadcasting and Communications

TELECOMMUNICATIONS

All sectors of the Hong Kong telecommunications industry were liberalized by the early 2000s and there are no restrictions on foreign ownership. At August 2013 there were 21 companies licensed to provide local fixed carrier services, 196 internet service providers licensed to provide broadband services, and six mobile network operators: China Mobile (Hong Kong) Company Limited, CSL Limited, PCCW-HKT Telephone Ltd, Hong Kong Telecommunications (HKT) Ltd, Hutchison Telephone Company Ltd and SmarTone Mobile Communications Ltd. At June 2013 there were 16,713,948 mobile subscribers in Hong Kong.

Asia Satellite Telecommunications Co Ltd (AsiaSat): 19/F, Sunning Plaza, 10 Hysan Ave, Causeway Bay; tel. 25000888; fax 25000895; e-mail as-mkt@asiasat.com; internet www.asiasat.com; f. 1988; Pres. and CEO WILLIAM WADE.

China Mobile Ltd: 60/F, The Center, 99 Queen's Rd, Central; tel. 31218888; fax 25119092; internet www.chinamobileltd.com; f. 1997; leading mobile services provider in mainland China, operating through its 31 subsidiaries in all 31 provinces, autonomous regions and municipalities in the People's Republic; 584m. subscribers (December 2010); Chair. and CEO XI GUOHUA.

China Unicom (Hong Kong) Ltd: 75/F, The Center, 99 Queen's Rd, Central; tel. 21262018; fax 21262016; e-mail info@chinaunicom.com.hk; internet www.chinaunicom.com.hk; f. 2000; internet and telephone service provider; operates throughout China; 57.8% shares held by Unicom Group; 303.5m. subscribers (July 2010); Chair. and CEO CHANG XIAOBING.

CSL Limited: Unit 501-8, 5/F Cyberport 3, 100 Cyberport Road; tel. 28834688; fax 29626111; e-mail customerservice@hkcsl.com; internet www.hkcsl.com; f. 1983; CEO JOSEPH O'KONEK.

Hutchison Telecommunications Hong Kong: 22/F, Hutchison House, 10 Harcourt Rd; tel. 21281188; fax 21281778; internet www.hthkh.com; Chair. CANNING FOK KIN-NING.

PCCW-HKT Telephone Ltd: 39/F, PCCW Tower, Taikoo Place, 979 King's Rd, Quarry Bay; tel. 25145084; e-mail ir@hkt.com; internet www.pccw.com; fmrly Cable and Wireless HKT Ltd, acquired by PCCW in Aug. 2000; telecommunications, multimedia, information and communications technology services provider; Chair. RICHARD LI; Group Man. Dir ALEXANDER ARENA.

SmarTone Mobile Communications Limited: 31/F, Millennium City II, 378 Kwun Tong Rd, Kwun Tong, Kowloon; tel. 28802688; fax 28816405; e-mail customer_care@smartone.com; internet www.smartone.com; CEO DOUGLAS LI.

Regulatory Authority

Office of the Communications Authority (OFCA): 29/F, Wu Chung House, 213 Queen's Rd East, Wanchai; tel. 29616333; fax 28035110; e-mail webmaster@ofca.gov.hk; internet www.ofca.gov.hk; f. 2012; est. following merger of Office of the Telecommunications Authority with certain divisions of Television and Entertainment Licensing Authority; executive arm of the Communications Authority and regulator of the broadcasting and telecommunications sectors; Dir-Gen. ELIZA LEE.

BROADCASTING

Radio

Radio Television Hong Kong is the only public broadcaster. Digital audio broadcasting services were launched in November 2011. However, there are 13 analogue radio channels provided by two commercial broadcasters.

Digital Broadcasting Corporation: Unit 302, Level 3, IT St, Cyberport 3, 100 Cyberport Rd; tel. 22971999; e-mail info@dbc.hk; internet www.dbc.hk; Chair. HOI-YING.

Hong Kong Commercial Broadcasting Co Ltd: 3 Broadcast Drive, KCPOB 73000, Kowloon; tel. 23394810; fax 23380021;

e-mail comradio@crhk.com.hk; internet www.881903.com; f. 1959; broadcasts in English and Cantonese on three radio frequencies; Chair. G. J. Ho; Dir and CEO Rita Ching-han Chan.

Metro Broadcast Corpn Ltd (Metro Broadcast): Basement 2, Site 6, Whampoa Garden, Hunghom, Kowloon; tel. 36988000; fax 21239889; e-mail prenquiry@metroradio.com.hk; internet www.metroradio.com.hk; f. 1991; broadcasts on three channels in English, Cantonese and Mandarin; Man. Dir Bianca Ma.

Phoenix U Radio: 2–6 Dai King St, Tai Po Industrial Estate, Tai Po; tel. 22008888; e-mail uradio@phoenixtv.com; internet www.uradiohk.com; f. 2011; owned by the Phoenix Group.

Radio Television Hong Kong: Broadcasting House, 30 Broadcast Drive, Kowloon; tel. 23369314; fax 23380279; e-mail ccu@rthk.org.hk; internet rthk.hk; f. 1928; govt-funded; 24-hour service in English, Cantonese and Mandarin on seven radio channels; Dir Roy Tang Yun-kwong.

Television

Hong Kong has begun the switch to digital television services; analogue broadcasting services were originally scheduled to end in 2012, but in June 2011 this was postponed until 2015. The digital terrestrial television take-up rate was 82% in April 2013. At July 2013 there were over 700 local and overseas television channels in various languages through free-to-air terrestrial and satellite reception or pay television services in Hong Kong.

Asia Television Ltd (ATV): 25–31 Dai Shing St, Tai Po Industrial Estate, Tai Po; tel. 29928888; fax 23380438; e-mail atv@atv.com.hk; internet www.hkatv.com; f. 1973; operates eight commercial television services (English and Chinese) and produces television programmes; Chair. Wong Po-yan.

Hong Kong Cable Television Ltd: Cable TV Tower, 9 Hoi Shing Rd, Tsuen Wan; tel. 21126868; fax 21127878; e-mail info@i-cablecomm.com; internet www.i-cablecomm.com; f. 1993; subsidiary of i-CABLE Communications Ltd; 24-hour subscription service of news, sport and entertainment on 100 channels; carries BBC World Service Television; Chair. and CEO Stephen Ng.

Phoenix Satellite Television: No. 9, Tower 1, Seashore Square, 18 Defeng St, Kowloon; tel. 26219888; fax 26219898; internet www.ifeng.com; f. 1995; partly owned by News Corpn (USA); Mandarin; three domestic and two international channels; CEO Liu Changle.

Radio Television Hong Kong: see Radio; produces drama, documentary and public affairs programmes; also operates an educational service for transmission by two local commercial stations; Dir Roy Tang Yun-kwong.

STAR Group Ltd: One Harbourfront, 8/F, 18 Tak Fung St, Hunghom, Kowloon; tel. 26218888; fax 26213050; e-mail corp_aff@startv.com; internet www.startv.com; f. 1990; subsidiary of News Corpn; broadcasts over 40 channels in English, Hindi, Tamil, Mandarin, Cantonese, Korean and Thai, including a range of sports programmes, music, movies, news, entertainment and documentaries; reaches more than 300m. people in 53 countries across Asia and the Middle East, with a daily audience of about 130m. people; has interests in cable systems in India and Taiwan; services also extend to terrestrial and cable TV, wireless and digital media platforms.

Television Broadcasts Ltd (TVB): TVB City, 77 Chun Choi St, Tseung Kwan O Industrial Estate, Kowloon; tel. 23352288; fax 23581300; e-mail external.affairs@tvb.com.hk; internet www.tvb.com; f. 1967; operates Chinese and English language television programme services; Chair. Norman Leung Nai Pang.

Finance

(cap. = capital; res = reserves; dep. = deposits; m. = million; brs = branches; amounts in Hong Kong dollars, unless otherwise stated)

BANKING

In 2012 there were 153 licensed banks operating in Hong Kong. There were also 20 restricted licence banks (formerly known as licensed deposit-taking companies), 25 deposit-taking companies and 60 foreign banks' representative offices.

Hong Kong Monetary Authority (HKMA): 55/F, Two International Finance Centre, 8 Finance St, Central; tel. 28788196; fax 28788197; e-mail hkma@hkma.gov.hk; internet www.hkma.gov.hk; f. 1993; est. by merger of Office of the Commr of Banking and Office of the Exchange Fund; govt authority responsible for maintaining monetary and banking stability; manages official reserves in the Exchange Fund; Chief Exec. Norman T. Chan.

Banks of Issue

Bank of China (Hong Kong) Ltd (People's Repub. of China): Bank of China Tower, 1 Garden Rd, Central; tel. 28266888; fax 28105963; internet www.bochk.com; f. 1917; became third bank of issue in May 1994; merged in Oct. 2001 with the local branches of 11 mainland banks (incl. Kwangtung Provincial Bank, Sin Hua Bank Ltd, China and the South Sea Bank Ltd, Kincheng Banking Corpn, China State Bank, National Commercial Bank Ltd, Yien Yieh Commercial Bank Ltd, Hua Chiao Commercial Bank Ltd and Po Sang Bank Ltd), to form the Bank of China (Hong Kong); cap. 43,043m., res 31,454m., dep. 1,387,628m. (Dec. 2011); Chair. Tian Guoli; CEO He Guangbei; 270 brs.

The Hongkong and Shanghai Banking Corporation Ltd (HSBC): 1 Queen's Rd, Central; tel. 28221111; fax 28101112; internet www.hsbc.com.hk; f. 1865; personal and commercial banking; cap. 58,969m., res 133,790m., dep. 4,491,312m. (Dec. 2012); Chair. Stuart Gulliver; CEO Anita Fung; more than 600 offices worldwide.

Standard Chartered Bank: Standard Chartered Bank Bldg, 32/F, 4–4A Des Voeux Rd, Central; tel. 28203333; fax 28569129; internet www.standardchartered.com.hk; f. 1859; cap. 97m., res 15,650m., dep. 735,950m. (2011); Chair. Katherine Tsang King Suen; CEO Benjamin Hung; more than 500 offices worldwide.

Other Commercial Banks

Bank of East Asia Ltd: Bank of East Asia Bldg, 16/F, 10 Des Voeux Rd, Central; tel. 36083608; fax 36086000; e-mail chengwcm@hkbea.com; internet www.hkbea.com; inc in Hong Kong in 1918, absorbed United Chinese Bank Ltd in Aug. 2001, and First Pacific Bank (FPB) in April 2002; cap. 5,190m., res 31,658m., dep. 495,001m. (Dec. 2011); Chair. and Chief Exec. Sir David K. P. Li; 91 domestic brs, 23 overseas brs.

China CITIC Bank International Ltd: 232 Des Voeux Rd, Central; tel. 36036633; fax 36034057; e-mail info@citicbankintl.com; internet www.citicbankintl.com; f. 1922; cap. 7,283m., res 700.6m., dep. 149,822.5m. (Dec. 2012); acquired Hong Kong Chinese Bank Ltd Jan. 2002; fmrly CITIC Ka Wah Bank Ltd, name changed to CITIC Bank International Ltd in 2010, as above in 2012; Chair. Dou Jianzhong; CEO Doreen Chan Hui Dor Lam; 30 domestic brs.

Chiyu Banking Corpn Ltd: 78 Des Voeux Rd, Central; tel. 28430111; fax 28104207; e-mail chiyu@chiyubank.com; internet www.chiyubank.com; f. 1947; mem. of Bank of China (Hong Kong); cap. 300m., res 1,195.6m., dep. 40,514m. (Dec. 2012); Chair. He Guangbei; 24 brs.

Chong Hing Bank Ltd: 17–18/F, Chong Hing Bank Centre, 24 Des Voeux Rd, Central; tel. 37681111; fax 37681888; e-mail customerservice@chbank.com; internet www.chbank.com; f. 1948; fmrly Liu Chong Hing Bank; cap. 217.5m., res 3,531.6m., dep. 70,019.8.1m. (Dec. 2012); Chair. Liu Lit-mo; CEO Lau Wai-man; 51 domestic brs, 3 overseas brs.

Dah Sing Bank Ltd: Dah Sing Financial Centre, 36/F, 108 Gloucester Rd, Central; tel. 25078866; fax 28288060; e-mail ops@dahsing.com.hk; internet www.dahsing.com; f. 1947; cap. 5,000m., res 2,512m., dep. 129,192.1m. (Dec. 2012); Chair. David S. Y. Wong; CEO and Man. Dir Gary Wang; 39 domestic brs.

DBS Bank (Hong Kong) Ltd: G/F, The Center, 99 Queen's Rd, Central; tel. 36682000; fax 21678222; e-mail enquiry.hk@dbs.com; internet www.dbs.com.hk; f. 1938; inc in 1954 as Kwong On Bank, name changed 2000; subsidiary of the Development Bank of Singapore; cap. 7,000m., res 3,230m., dep. 230,751m. (Dec. 2012); acquired Dao Heng Bank and Overseas Trust Bank July 2003; Chair. Peter Seah Lim Huat; CEO Juan Sebastian P. Muirragui; 32 brs.

Hang Seng Bank Ltd: 83 Des Voeux Rd, Central; tel. 21983422; fax 28684047; e-mail ccdca@hangseng.com; internet www.hangseng.com; f. 1933; a principal member of the HSBC group, which has an ownership of 62.14%; cap. 9,559m., res 23,081m., dep. 838,644m. (Dec. 2012); Chair. Raymond K. F. Ch'ien; CEO Rose W. M. Lee; 149 brs in Hong Kong, 17 in mainland China and 1 in Macao; also rep. office in Taipei.

Industrial and Commercial Bank of China (Asia): 33/F, ICBC Tower, 3 Garden Rd, Central; tel. 25881188; fax 28051166; e-mail enquiry@icbcasia.com; internet www.icbcasia.com; f. 1964; fmrly Union Bank of Hong Kong; cap. 4,129.4m., res 22,352.6m., dep. 371,472.6m. (Dec. 2012); Chair. Chen Aiping; 42 brs.

Mevas Bank: Suite 3704, 37/F, Dah Sing Financial Centre, 108 Gloucester Rd, Wanchai; tel. 29212485; fax 28401737; e-mail contactus@mevas.com; internet www.mevas.com; cap. 400.0m., res. 2.1m., dep. 82.8m. (Dec. 2011); Chair. David S. Y. Wong; CEO Francesca So.

Nanyang Commercial Bank Ltd: 151 Des Voeux Rd, Central; tel. 28520888; fax 28153333; e-mail nanyang@ncb.com.hk; internet www.ncb.com.hk; f. 1949; cap. 700m., res 28,913.2m., dep. 185,533.7m. (Dec. 2012); Chair. Zhou Zaiqun; 42 domestic brs, 2 overseas brs.

Public Bank (Hong Kong) Ltd: Public Bank Centre, 2/F, 120 Des Voeux Rd, Central; tel. 25419222; fax 25410009; e-mail contact@publicbank.com.hk; internet www.publicbank.com.hk; f. 1934; fmrly Asia Commercial Bank; name changed as above June 2006; cap.

1,481.6m., res 1,873.6m., dep. 30,601.1m. (Dec. 2012); Chair. Tan Sri Dato' Sri Dr TEH HONG PIOW; CEO TAN YOKE KONG; 32 domestic brs, 3 overseas brs.

Shanghai Commercial Bank Ltd: 35/F, Gloucester Tower, The Landmark, 15 Queen's Rd, Central; tel. 28415415; fax 28104623; e-mail contact@shacombank.com.hk; internet www.shacombank.com.hk; f. 1950; cap. 2,000m., res 8,965.2m., dep. 116,520.7m. (Dec. 2012); Chair. LINCOLN CHU KUEN YUNG; CEO, Man. Dir and Gen. Man. DAVID SEK-CHI KWOK; 42 domestic brs, 5 overseas brs.

Standard Bank Plc, Hong Kong Branch: 36/F, Two Pacific Place, 88 Queensway, Central; tel. 28227888; fax 28227999; e-mail tom.chenoweth@standardbank.com.hk; internet www.standardbank.com/cib; f. 1970; est. as Jardine Fleming & Co Ltd; renamed Jardine Fleming Bank Ltd in 1993; absorbed by Standard Bank Investment Corpn Ltd; fmrly Standard Bank Asia Ltd; current name adopted in July 2011; cap. US $1,083.5m., res US $442.3m., dep. US $9,600.7m. (Dec. 2012); Chief Exec. TOM CHENOWETH.

Tai Yau Bank Ltd: 130-132, Des Voeux Rd, Central Tai Tung; tel. 25445011; fax 25455242; internet www.taisangbank.com.hk; f. 1947; cap. 300.0m., res 51.6m., dep. 1,674.2m. (Dec. 2011); Chair. WILLIAM MA CHING WAI; Gen. Man. PATRICK MA CHING HANG.

Wing Hang Bank Ltd: 161 Queen's Rd, Central; tel. 28525111; fax 25410036; e-mail whbpsd@whbhk.com; internet www.whbhk.com; f. 1937; cap. 302.1m., res 6,727.8m., dep. 169,590.4m. (Dec. 2012); acquired Chekiang First Bank Ltd in Aug. 2004; Chair. and Chief Exec. PATRICK Y. B. FUNG; 40 domestic brs, 13 overseas brs.

Wing Lung Bank Ltd: 45 Des Voeux Rd, Central; tel. 28268333; fax 28100592; e-mail wlb@winglungbank.com; internet www.winglungbank.com; f. 1933; cap. 1,160.9m., res 1,348.7m., dep. 151,973.9m. (Dec. 2012); Chair. MA WEIHUA; Exec. Dir and Chief Exec. ZHU QUI; 41 domestic brs, 4 overseas brs, 1 rep. office in China.

Principal Foreign Banks

ABN AMRO Bank NV (Netherlands): 70/F, International Commerce Centre, 1 Austin Rd West, Kowloon; tel. 37633700; fax 37633709; CEO (Asia) HUGUES DELCOURT; 3 brs.

American Express International Inc (USA): 18/F, Cityplaza 4, 12 Taikoo Wan Rd, Taikoo Shing; tel. 22771010; internet www.americanexpress.com/hk; Senior Country Exec. DOUGLAS H. SHORT III; 3 brs.

Australia and New Zealand Banking Group Ltd: 17/F, One Exchange Square, 8 Connaught Place, Central; tel. 21768888; fax 39182211; internet www.anz.com.au/hongkong; CEO SUSAN YUEN.

Bangkok Bank Public Co Ltd (Thailand): Bangkok Bank Bldg, 28 Des Voeux Rd, Central; tel. 28016688; fax 28015679; e-mail bangkokbank@bbl.com.hk; Gen. Man. KHUN SITTHICHAI JIWATTANAKUL; 2 brs.

Bank of Communications, Hong Kong Branch: 20 Pedder St, Central; tel. 28419611; fax 28106993; e-mail enquiry@bankcomm.com.hk; internet www.bankcomm.com.hk; f. 1934; Group Chair. and Pres. NIU XIMING; 41 brs.

Bank of India: Ruttonjee Centre, 2/F, Dina House, 11 Duddell St, Central; tel. 25240186; fax 28771178; e-mail boi.hk@bankofindia.co.in; internet www.bankofindia.com.hk; Chair. and Man. Dir. V. R. IYER.

Bank Negara Indonesia: G/F, Far East Finance Centre, 16 Harcourt Rd; tel. 28618600; fax 28656500; Gen. Man. BRAMONO DWIEDJANTO.

Bank of Tokyo-Mitsubishi UFJ Ltd (Japan): 8/F, AIA Central, 1 Connaught Rd, Central; tel. 28236666; fax 25293821.

Barclays Capital Asia Ltd: 41/F, Cheung Kong Center, 2 Queen's Rd, Central; tel. 29032000; fax 29032999; internet www.barcap.com; f. 1972; Chair. and CEO ROBERT A. MORRICE.

BNP Paribas (France): 63/F, Two International Finance Centre, 8 Finance St, Central; tel. 29098888; fax 28652523; e-mail communication.hk@asia.bnpparibas.com; internet www.bnpparibas.com.hk; f. 1958; Chair. BAUDOUIN PROT; Chief Exec. JEAN-LAURENT BONNAFÉ; 2 brs.

China Construction Bank (Asia) Corpn Ltd: 16/F, York House, The Landmark, 15 Queen's Rd Central, Central; tel. 27795533; fax 37183273; internet www.asia.ccb.com; fmrly Bank of America (Asia); wholly owned subsidiary of China Construction Bank Corpn; commercial banking and retail banking; cap. 6,511m., res 1,293.1m., dep. 115,961.2m. (Dec. 2011); Pres. and CEO MIRANDA KWOK; 41 brs in Hong Kong; 9 brs in Macao.

Citibank, NA (USA): Citibank Tower, 39–40/F and 44–50/F, Citibank Plaza, 3 Garden Rd, Central; tel. 28688888; fax 25230949; internet www.citibank.com.hk; CEO (Asia-Pacific) STEPHEN BIRD; 26 brs.

Commerzbank AG (Germany): 29/F, Two International Finance Centre, 8 Finance St, Central; tel. 39880988; fax 39880990; internet www.commerzbank.com.hk; Man. EBERHARD BRODHAGE; 1 br.

Crédit Agricole Corporate and Investment Bank (France): 27/F, Two Pacific Place, 88 Queensway, Central; tel. 28267338; e-mail human.resources-hk@ca-cib.com; fax 28261270; fmrly Calyon Bank, above name adopted in 2010; Country Officer ELLEN WONG; 1 br.

Crédit Suisse (Switzerland): 88/F, International Commerce Centre, 1 Austin Rd West, Kowloon; tel. 28414888; fax 28414921; internet www.credit-suisse.com/hk; Man. Dir (Asia-Pacific) FRANCESCO DE FERRARI.

Deutsche Bank AG (Germany): 52/F, International Commerce Centre, 1 Austin Rd West, Kowloon; tel. 22038888; fax 22037300; internet www.db.com/hongkong; CEO (Asia-Pacific) ROBERT RANKIN; Gen. Mans Dr MICHAEL THOMAS, REINER RUSCH; 1 br.

Indian Overseas Bank: 3/F, Ruttonjee House, 11 Duddell St, Central; tel. 25227249; fax 28451549; e-mail iobsm@netvigator.com; internet www.iobhongkong.com; f. 1955; CEO and Man. Dir M. NARENDRA; 2 brs.

JP Morgan Bank (USA): 39/F, One Exchange Square, Connaught Place, Central; tel. 28001000; fax 28414396.

Malayan Banking Berhad (Malaysia): 21/F, Man Yee Bldg, 68 Des Voeux Rd, Central; tel. 35188888; fax 35188889; f. 1962; trades in Hong Kong as Maybank; Gen. Man. AMOS ONG SEET JOON; 2 brs.

Mizuho Corporate Bank Ltd (Japan): 17/F, Two Pacific Place, 88 Queensway, Admiralty; tel. 21033000; fax 28101326; Man. Dir and CEO NOBORU AKATSUKA; 1 br.

National Bank of Pakistan: 1801–1805, 18/F, ING Tower, 308–320 Des Voeux Rd, Central; tel. 28507723; fax 28451703; e-mail nbphkkm@netvigator.com; Chair. and Pres. Dr ASIF A. BROHI; 2 brs.

Oversea-Chinese Banking Corpn Ltd (Singapore): 9/F, 9 Queen's Rd, Central; tel. 28406200; fax 28453439; Group CEO SAMUEL N. TSIEN; 3 brs.

Philippine National Bank: Unit 2, 9/F, Tung Wai Commercial Bldg, 109–111 Gloucester Rd, Wanchai; tel. 25431066; fax 25253107; e-mail pnbhkgrp@pnbhk.com; CEO RODEL BICOL; 1 br.

Société Générale Asia Ltd (France): Level 34, Three Pacific Place, 1 Queen's Rd East; tel. 21665388; fax 28682368; internet www.sgcib.hk; Head (Asia-Pacific) HIKARU OGATA.

Sumitomo Mitsui Banking Corpn (SMBC) (Japan): 7–8/F, One International Finance Centre, 1 Harbour View St, Central; tel. 22062000; fax 22062888; Chair. TEISUKE KITAYAMA; 1 br.

UBAF (Hong Kong) Ltd (France): The Sun's Group Centre, 21/F, 200 Gloucester Rd, Wanchai; tel. 25201361; fax 25274256; e-mail larry.yap@ubaf.fr; cap. US $30.4m., dep. US $29.6m. (Dec. 2010); CEO and Man. Dir LARRY S. YAP.

United Overseas Bank Ltd (Singapore): 25/F, Gloucester Tower, The Landmark, 15 Queen's Rd, Central; tel. 29108888; fax 29108899; internet www.uobgroup.com/hk; Sr Vice-Pres. and CEO WEE EE CHEONG; 5 brs.

Banking Associations

Chinese Banks' Association Ltd: South China Bldg, 5/F, 1–3 Wyndham St, Central; tel. 25224789; fax 28775102; e-mail info@cbsa.com.hk; internet www.cbsa.com.hk; 20 mems; chaired by Bank of East Asia.

DTC Association (Hong Kong Association of Restricted Licence Banks and Deposit-taking Companies): Unit 2704, 17/F, Bonham Trade Centre, 50 Bonham Strand East, Sheung Wan; tel. 25264079; fax 25230180; e-mail dtca@dtca.org.hk; internet www.dtca.org.hk; f. 1981; Sec. PUI CHONG LUND; 50 mem. banks.

Hong Kong Association of Banks: Rm 525, Prince's Bldg, Central; tel. 25211169; fax 28685035; e-mail info@hkab.org.hk; internet www.hkab.org.hk; f. 1981; est. to succeed The Exchange Banks' Assn of Hong Kong; all licensed banks in Hong Kong are required by law to be mems of this statutory body, the function of which is to represent and further the interests of the banking sector; 156 mems; chaired by Bank of China (HK) Ltd; Sec. EVA WONG.

STOCK EXCHANGE

Hong Kong Exchanges and Clearing Ltd (HKEx): 12/F, One International Finance Centre, 1 Harbour View St, Central; tel. 25221122; fax 22953106; e-mail info@hkex.com.hk; internet www.hkex.com.hk; f. 2000; est. by merger of the Stock Exchange of Hong Kong, the Hong Kong Futures Exchange and the Hong Kong Securities Clearing Co; Chair. CHOW CHUNG-KONG; CEO CHARLES LI.

SUPERVISORY BODY

Securities and Futures Commission (SFC): 8/F, Chater House, 8 Connaught Rd, Central; tel. 28409222; fax 25217836; e-mail enquiry@sfc.hk; internet www.sfc.hk; f. 1989; regulates the securities and futures markets; Chair. EDDY FONG; CEO ASHLEY ALDER.

INSURANCE

In 2012 there were 163 authorized insurance companies, of which 98 were pure general insurers, 45 were pure long-term insurers and the remaining 20 were composite insurers. The following are among the principal companies:

ACE Insurance Ltd: 25/F, Shui On Centre, 6–8 Harbour Rd, Wanchai; tel. 31916800; fax 25603565; e-mail inquiries.hk@acegroup.com; internet www.aceinsurance.com.hk; Pres. and CEO (Asia-Pacific) DAMIEN SULLIVAN.

American Home Assurance Co: AIA Bldg, 1 Stubbs Rd, Wanchai; tel. 28321800; e-mail cs@aiu.com.hk; internet www.aiu.com.hk.

Asia Insurance Co Ltd: Worldwide House, 16/F, 19 Des Voeux Rd, Central; tel. 36069933; fax 28100218; e-mail mailbox@afh.hk; internet www.asiainsurance.com.hk; Chair. ROBIN CHAN.

Aviva Life Insurance Co Ltd: Suite 1701, Cityplaza One, 1111 King's Rd, Taikoo Shing; tel. 35509600; fax 29071787; e-mail enquiry@aviva-asia.com; internet www.aviva.com.hk; Gen. Man. ELBA TSE.

AXA General Insurance Hong Kong Ltd: 21/F, Manhattan Pl., 23 Wang Tai Rd, Kowloon Bay; tel. 25233061; fax 28100706; e-mail axahk@axa-insurance.com.hk; internet www.axa-insurance.com.hk; CEO BILLY CHAN.

Bank of China Group Insurance Co Ltd: 9/F, Wing On House, 71 Des Voeux Rd, Central; tel. 28670888; fax 25221705; e-mail info_ins@bocgroup.com; internet www.bocgroup.com/bocg-ins.

China Taiping Insurance (HK) Co Ltd: China Taiping Tower, 19/F, 8 Sunning Rd, Causeway Bay; tel. 28151551; fax 25416567; e-mail mai@mingan.com.hk; internet www.mingan.com; f. 1949; fmrly Ming An Insurance Co Ltd, name changed as above in 2009; Chair. LIN FAN; CEO CHENG KWOK PING.

Hong Kong Export Credit Insurance Corpn: South Seas Centre, Tower I, 2/F, 75 Mody Rd, Tsim Sha Tsui East, Kowloon; tel. 27329988; fax 27226277; internet www.hkecic.com; f. 1966; est. by Govt to encourage and support trade; Commr RALPH LAI; Gen. Man. CYNTHIA CHIN.

HSBC Insurance (Asia) Ltd: 18/F, Tower 1, HSBC Centre, 1 Sham Mong Road, Kowloon; tel. 22886688; fax 28277636; e-mail insurance@hsbc.com.hk; internet www.insurance.asiapacific.hsbc.com; Man. Dir JASON SADLER.

MSIG Insurance (Hong Kong) Ltd: 9/F, Cityplaza One, 1111 King's Rd, Taikoo Shing; tel. 28940555; fax 28905741; e-mail hk_hotline@hk.msig-asia.com; internet www.msig.com.hk; CEO KENNETH REID.

Prudential Assurance Co Ltd: 23/F, One Exchange Square, Central; tel. 22811333; fax 29771233; e-mail service@prudential.com.hk; internet www.prudential.com.hk; life and general; CEO DEREK YUNG.

QBE Hongkong and Shanghai Insurance Ltd: 17/F, Warwick House, West Wing, Taikoo Place, 979 King's Rd, Quarry Bay; tel. 28778488; fax 36070300; e-mail info.hk@qbe.com.hk; internet www.qbe.com.hk; Gen. Man. JECKY LUI.

Royal and Sun Alliance (Hong Kong) Ltd: Dorset House, 32/F, Taikoo Place, 979 King's Rd, Quarry Bay; tel. 29683000; fax 29685111; e-mail hotline@hk.rsagroup.com; internet www.rsagroup.com.hk; Chief Exec. SIMON LEE.

Swiss Re Hong Kong Branch: 61/F, Central Plaza, 18 Harbour Rd, Wanchai; tel. 28274345; fax 28276033; acquired Mercantile and General Reinsurance in 1996; Head (Asia) MARTYN PARKER.

Zurich Insurance Group (Hong Kong): 24–27/F, One Island East, 18 Westlands Rd, Island East; tel. 29682222; fax 29680988; e-mail enquiry@hk.zurich.com; internet www.zurich.com.hk; CEO TED RIDGWAY.

Insurance Associations

Hong Kong Federation of Insurers (HKFI): 29/F, Sunshine Plaza, 353 Lockhart Rd, Wanchai; tel. 25201868; fax 25201967; e-mail hkfi@hkfi.org.hk; internet www.hkfi.org.hk; f. 1988; 87 general insurance and 47 life insurance mems; Chair. ALLAN YU.

Insurance Institute of Hong Kong: Rm 1705, Beverly House, 93–107 Lockhart Rd, Wanchai; tel. 25200098; fax 22953939; e-mail enquiry@iihk.org.hk; internet www.iihk.org.hk; f. 1967; Pres. MICHAEL HAYNES.

Trade and Industry

Hong Kong Trade Development Council: 38/F, Office Tower, Convention Plaza, 1 Harbour Rd, Wanchai; tel. 1830668; fax 28240249; e-mail hktdc@hktdc.org; internet www.hktdc.com; f. 1966; Chair. JACK SO CHAK-KWONG; Exec. Dir FREDERICK LAM.

Trade and Industry Department: Learning Resource Centre, Rm 912B, Trade and Industry Department Tower, 700 Nathan Rd, Kowloon; tel. 23985388; fax 23989173; e-mail enquiry@tid.gov.hk; internet www.tid.gov.hk; Dir-Gen. KENNETH MAK.

DEVELOPMENT ORGANIZATIONS

Hong Kong Housing Authority: 33 Fat Kwong St, Homantin, Kowloon; tel. 27122712; fax 26245685; e-mail hkha@housingauthority.gov.hk; internet www.housingauthority.gov.hk; f. 1973; plans, builds and manages public housing; Chair. ANTHONY CHEUNG BING-LEUNG; Dir of Housing D. W. PESCOD.

Hong Kong Productivity Council: HKPC Bldg, 78 Tat Chee Ave, Yau Yat Chuen, Kowloon Tong, Kowloon; tel. 27885678; fax 27885900; e-mail hkpcenq@hkpc.org; internet www.hkpc.org; f. 1967; promotes increased productivity and international competitiveness of industry; Council comprises a Chair. and 22 mems appointed by the Govt, representing managerial, labour, academic and professional interests, and govt depts associated with productivity matters; Chair. CLEMENT CHEN CHENG-JEN.

CHAMBERS OF COMMERCE

Chinese Chamber of Commerce, Kowloon: 2/F, 8–10 Nga Tsin Long Rd, Kowloon; tel. 23822309; f. 1936; 234 mems; Chair. and Exec. Dir YEUNG CHOR-HANG.

Chinese General Chamber of Commerce: 4/F, 24–25 Connaught Rd, Central; tel. 25256385; fax 28452610; e-mail cgcc@cgcc.org.hk; internet www.cgcc.org.hk; f. 1900; over 6,000 mems; Chair. CHARLES YEUNG.

Hong Kong General Chamber of Commerce: United Centre, 22/F, 95 Queensway, POB 852. Admiralty; tel. 25299229; fax 25279843; e-mail chamber@chamber.org.hk; internet www.chamber.org.hk; f. 1861; 4,000 mems; Chair. C. K. CHOW; CEO SHIRLEY YUEN.

Kowloon Chamber of Commerce: KCC Bldg, 3/F, 2 Liberty Ave, Homantin, Kowloon; tel. 27600393; fax 27610166; e-mail kcc02@hkkcc.biz.com.hk; internet www.hkkcc.org.hk; f. 1938; 1,600 mems; Chair. CHENG KWAN SUEN; Sec. of Gen. Affairs CHENG PO-WO.

FOREIGN TRADE ORGANIZATIONS

Hong Kong Chinese Importers' and Exporters' Association: Champion Bldg, 7–8/F, 287–291 Des Voeux Rd, Central; tel. 25448474; fax 25814979; e-mail info@hkciea.org.hk; internet www.hkciea.org.hk; f. 1954; 3,000 mems; Pres. ZHUANG CHENG XIN.

Hong Kong Exporters' Association: Rm 825, Star House, 3 Salisbury Rd, Tsim Sha Tsui, Kowloon; tel. 27309851; fax 27301869; e-mail exporter@exporters.org.hk; internet www.exporters.org.hk; f. 1955; not-for-profit asscn; comprises leading merchants and manufacturing exporters; 520 mems (March 2012); Chair. CHAN WING-KEE; Exec. Dir SHIRLEY SO.

INDUSTRIAL AND TRADE ASSOCIATIONS

Chinese Manufacturers' Association of Hong Kong: CMA Bldg, 64 Connaught Rd, Central; tel. 25456166; fax 25414541; e-mail info@cma.org.hk; internet www.cma.org.hk; f. 1934; promotes and protects industrial and trading interests; operates testing and certification laboratories; 3,700 mems; Pres. IRONS SZE WING-WAI; CEO ADELINE C. WONG.

Communications Association of Hong Kong: 12/F, Suite 1205, 625 King's Rd, North Point; tel. 25042732; fax 25042752; e-mail info@cahk.hk; internet www.cahk.hk; 108 mems; Chair. STEPHEN HO.

Federation of Hong Kong Garment Manufacturers: Unit 401–403, Cheung Lee Commercial Bldg, 25 Kimberley Rd, Tsim Sha Tsui, Kowloon; tel. 27211383; fax 23111062; e-mail info@garment.org.hk; internet www.garment.org.hk; f. 1964; 120 mems; Pres. YEUNG FAN; Sec.-Gen. MICHAEL LEUNG.

Federation of Hong Kong Industries (FHKI): 31/F, Billion Plaza, 8 Cheung Yue St, Cheung Sha Wan, Kowloon; tel. 27323188; fax 27213494; e-mail fhki@fhki.org.hk; internet www.industryhk.org; f. 1960; 3,000 mems; Chair. STANLEY LAU; Dir-Gen. LINDA KA-PIK SO.

Federation of Hong Kong Watch Trades and Industries Ltd: Peter Bldg, Rm 604, 58–62 Queen's Rd, Central; tel. 25233232; fax 28684485; e-mail hkwatch@hkwatch.org; internet www.hkwatch.org; f. 1947; 650 mems; Chair. GABRIEL AU YU FAN.

Hong Kong Association for the Advancement of Science and Technology Ltd: 2A, Tak Lee Commercial Bldg, 113–117 Wanchai Rd, Wanchai; tel. 28913388; fax 28381823; e-mail info@hkaast.org.hk; internet www.hkaast.org.hk; f. 1985; 170 mems; Pres. Dr LOUIS F. S. LOCK.

Hong Kong Biotechnology Association Ltd: Rm 1007, 10/F, Hang Seng Bldg, 77 Des Voeux Rd, Central; tel. 28770222; fax 26201238; e-mail secretary@hkbta.org.hk; internet www.hkbta.org.hk; f. 1999; 100 mems; Chair. FRANK WAN.

Hong Kong Chinese Enterprises Association: Rm 2104–2106, Harbour Centre, 25 Harbour Rd, Wanchai; tel. 28272831; fax

28272606; e-mail info@hkcea.com; internet www.hkcea.com; f. 1991; 960 mems; Chair. SONG LIN.

Hong Kong Chinese Textile Mills Association: 11/F, 38–40 Tai Po Rd, Sham Shiu Po, Kowloon; tel. 27778236; fax 27881836; f. 1921; 150 mems; Pres. Dr ROGER NG KENG-PO.

Hong Kong Construction Association Ltd: 3/F, 180–182 Hennessy Rd, Wanchai; tel. 25724414; fax 25727104; e-mail admin@hkca.com.hk; internet www.hkca.com.hk; f. 1920; 372 mems; Pres. THOMAS HO.

Hong Kong Electronic Industries Association Ltd: Rm 1201, 12/F, Harbour Crystal Centre, 100 Granville Rd, Tsim Sha Tsui, Kowloon; tel. 27788328; fax 27882200; e-mail hkeia@hkeia.org; internet www.hkeia.org; 310 mems; Chair. JOHNNY YEUNG; Sec. ERIC YU.

Hong Kong Footwear Association: Kar Tseuk Bldg, 2/F, Blk A, 185 Prince Edward Rd, Kowloon; internet www.hkfootwear.org; f. 1948; over 300 mems; Pres. TOMMY FONG.

Hong Kong Garment Manufacturers Association: Unit 401–403, Cheung Lee Commercial Bldg, 25 Kimberley Rd, Tsim Sha Tsui, Kowloon; tel. 23052893; fax 23052493; e-mail sec@textilecouncil.com; f. 1987; 40 mems; Chair. PETER WANG.

Hong Kong Information Technology Federation Ltd: KITEC, 1 Trademart Dr., Kowloon Bay, Kowloon; tel. 31018197; fax 30074728; e-mail info@hkitf.com; internet www.hkitf.org.hk; over 300 mems; f. 1980; Pres. FRANCIS FONG.

Hong Kong Jewellery and Jade Manufacturers Association: Flat A, 12/F, Kaiser Estate Phase 1, 41 Man Yue St, Hunghom, Kowloon; tel. 25430543; fax 28150164; e-mail hkjja@hkjja.org; internet www.jewellery-hk.org; f. 1965; 230 mems; Pres. CHARLES CHAN; Chair. BILLY LAU.

Hong Kong Jewelry Manufacturers' Association: Unit G, 2/F, Kaiser Estate Phase 2, 51 Man Yue St, Hunghom, Kowloon; tel. 27663002; fax 23623647; e-mail enquiry@jewelry.org.hk; internet www.jewelry.org.hk; f. 1988; 345 mems; Chair. ADAM LAU.

Hong Kong Knitwear Exporters and Manufacturers Association: Unit 401–403, Cheung Lee Commercial Bldg, 25 Kimberley Rd, Tsim Sha Tsui, Kowloon; tel. 27552621; fax 27565672; f. 1966; 70 mems; Chair. LAWRENCE LEUNG; Exec. Sec. KARINA TSUI.

Hong Kong Optical Manufacturers' Association Ltd: 2/F, 11 Fa Yuen St, Mongkok, Kowloon; tel. 23326505; fax 27705786; e-mail hkoma@biznetvigator.com; internet www.hkoptical.org.hk; f. 1982; 111 mems; Pres. GRACE TAI CHO YEE MUI.

Hong Kong Plastics Manufacturers Association Ltd: Rm 3, 10/F, Asia Standard Tower, 59–65 Queen's Rd, Central; tel. 25742230; fax 25742843; f. 1957; 200 mems; Chair. CLIFF SUN; Pres. JEFFREY LAM.

Hong Kong Printers Association: 1/F, 48–50 Johnston Rd, Wanchai; tel. 25275050; fax 28610463; e-mail printers@hkprinters.org; internet www.hkprinters.org; f. 1939; over 400 mems; Chair. CHIU KWOK CHU.

Hong Kong Sze Yap Commercial and Industrial Association: Cosco Tower, Unit 1205–6, 183 Queen's Rd, Central; tel. 25438095; fax 25449495; e-mail gahk_ltd@hotmail.com; f. 1909; 1,082 mems; Chair. LOUIE CHICK-NAN; Sec. WONG KA CHUN.

Hong Kong Toys Council: 31/F, Billion Plaza, 8 Cheung Yue St, Cheung Sha Wan, Kowloon; tel. 27323188; fax 27213494; e-mail hktc@fhki.org.hk; internet www.toyshk.org; f. 1986; 200 mems; Chair. JOHN TONG SHING JING.

Hong Kong Watch Manufacturers' Association: Fu Hing Bldg, 2/F, 10 Jubilee St, Central; tel. 25225238; fax 28106614; e-mail hkwma@netvigator.com; internet www.hkwma.org; 650 mems; Pres. DAVID H. K. LAI; Sec.-Gen. HUNG HAN SANG.

Information and Software Industry Association Ltd: Unit C, 19/F, 169 Electric Rd, North Point; tel. 26222867; fax 26222731; e-mail info@isia.org.hk; internet www.isia.org.hk; f. 1999; 80 mems; Chair. REGGIE WONG.

New Territories Commercial and Industrial General Association Ltd: Cheong Hay Bldg, 2/F, 107 Hoi Pa St, Tsuen Wan; tel. 24145316; fax 24934130; e-mail ntciga@netvigator.com; f. 1973; 2,663 mems; Pres. YU WAN; Chair. WAN HOK LIM; Sec.-Gen. HUANG JINHUI.

Real Estate Developers Association of Hong Kong: Worldwide House, Rm 1403, 19 Des Voeux Rd, Central; tel. 28260111; fax 28452521; e-mail info@reda.hk; internet www.reda.hk; f. 1965; 829 mems; Pres. KEITH KERR; Chair. STEWART LEUNG; Sec.-Gen. LOUIS LOONG.

Textile Council of Hong Kong Ltd: 401–3, Cheung Lee Commercial Bldg, 25 Kimberley Rd, Tsim Sha Tsui, Kowloon; tel. 23052893; fax 23052493; e-mail sec@textilecouncil.com; internet www.textilecouncil.com; f. 1989; 13 mems; Chair. CLEMENT CHEN; Exec. Dir MICHAEL LEUNG.

Toys Manufacturers' Association of Hong Kong Ltd: Rm 1302, Metroplaza, Tower 2, 223 Hing Fong Rd, Kwai Chung, New Territories; tel. 24221209; fax 31880982; e-mail info@tmhk.net; internet www.tmhk.net; f. 1996; 250 mems; Pres. CHEUNG TAK CHING.

EMPLOYERS' ORGANIZATIONS

Employers' Federation of Hong Kong: 1230, One Island South, 2 Heung Yip Rd, Wong Chuk Hang; tel. 25280033; fax 28655285; e-mail efhk@efhk.org.hk; internet www.efhk.org.hk; f. 1947; 504 mems; Chair. Y. K. PANG; Exec. Dir LOUIS PONG.

Hong Kong Factory Owners' Association Ltd: Wing Wong Bldg, 11/F, 557–559 Nathan Rd, Kowloon; tel. 23882372; fax 23857129; f. 1982; 1,261 mems; Pres. HWANG JEN; Sec. CHA KIT YEN.

UTILITIES

Electricity

CLP Power Ltd: 147 Argyle St, Kowloon; tel. 26788111; fax 27604448; e-mail clp_info@clp.com.hk; internet www.clpgroup.com; f. 1918; fmrly China Light and Power Co Ltd; generation and supply of electricity to Kowloon and the New Territories; Chair. Sir MICHAEL D. KADOORIE; CEO ANDREW BRANDLER.

The Hongkong Electric Co Ltd (HK Electric): 44 Kennedy Rd; tel. 28433111; fax 28100506; e-mail mail@hkelectric.com; internet www.hkelectric.com; Power Assets Holdings Ltd; generation and supply of electricity to Hong Kong Island, and the islands of Ap Lei Chau and Lamma; Chair. CANNING FOK KIN-NING; Group Man. Dir WAN CHI TIN.

Gas

Gas Authority: all gas supply cos, gas installers and contractors are required to be registered with the Gas Authority.

Chinese People Holdings Co Ltd: Unit 2111, 21/F, China Merchants Tower, Shun Tak Centre, 168–200 Connaught Rd, Central; tel. 29022008; fax 28030108; e-mail info@681hk.com; internet www.681hk.com; distributes and supplies natural gas in mainland China; Chair. XU RUIXIN; Man. Dirs JIN SONG, YEUNG PAAK CHING.

The Hong Kong and China Gas Co Ltd (Towngas): 23/F, 363 Java Rd, North Point; tel. 29633388; fax 25616182; e-mail webmaster@towngas.com; internet www.towngas.com; f. 1862; production, distribution and marketing of gas, water and energy related activities in Hong Kong and mainland China; operates two plants; Chair. LEE SHAU KEE; Man. Dir ALFRED CHAN WING KIN.

Water

Drainage Services Department: responsible for planning, designing, constructing, operating and maintaining the sewerage, sewage treatment and stormwater drainage infrastructures.

Water Supplies Department: 48/F, Immigration Tower, 7 Gloucester Rd, Wanchai; tel. 28294500; fax 28240578; e-mail wsdinfo@wsd.gov.hk; internet www.wsd.gov.hk; responsible for water supplies for some 7m. people living within 1,100 sq km of the Hong Kong SAR; Dir ENOCH LAM TIN-SING.

TRADE UNIONS

In December 2011 there were 836 trade unions representing 804,774 workers in Hong Kong, comprising 788 employees' unions, 18 employers' associations and 30 mixed organizations.

Federation of Hong Kong and Kowloon Trade Unions (HKFLU): 6–8 Fu Yao Bldg, 2/F, Tai Po Rd, Sham Shui Po, Kowloon; tel. 27767242; fax 27840044; e-mail flutpd@netvigator.com; internet www.hkflu.org.hk; Chair. POON SIU-PING; Sec.-Gen. XIAN QIMING.

Transport

Transport Department: 41/F Immigration Tower, 7 Gloucester Rd, Wanchai; tel. 28042600; fax 28042652; e-mail tdenq@td.gov.hk; internet www.td.gov.hk; Commr INGRID YEUNG.

RAILWAYS

Kowloon–Canton Railway Corpn: 8/F, Fo Tan Railway House, 9 Lok King St, Fo Tan, New Territories; tel. 26881333; fax 31241073; e-mail admin@kcrc.com; internet www.kcrc.com; f. 1982; operated by the Kowloon–Canton Railway Corpn, a public statutory body; assets controlled by MTR Corpn since 2007; also provides passenger and freight services to and from various cities on the mainland; plans for 17-km railway to link Sha Tin and Central districts via a new cross-harbour tunnel and thus provide the first direct rail route from the Chinese border to Hong Kong Island; Chair. K. C. CHAN; CEO Ir EDMUND LEUNG KWONG-HO.

MTR Corporation: MTR Tower, Telford Plaza, 33 Wai Strip St, Kowloon Bay; tel. 28818888; fax 27959991; internet www.mtr.com

.hk; f. 1975; first section of underground mass transit railway (MTR) system opened in 1979; merged operations with Kowloon–Canton Railway Corpn in 2007; nine railway lines serving Hong Kong Island, Kowloon and New Territories; 26-km Guangzhou–Shenzhen–Hong Kong Express Rail Link to be completed by 2015; CEO JAY WALDER; Chair. Dr RAYMOND K. F. CH'IEN.

TRAMWAYS

Hong Kong Tramways Ltd: Whitty Street Tram Depot, Connaught Rd West, Western District; tel. 21186338; fax 21186038; e-mail enquiry@hktramways.com; internet www.hktramways.com; f. 1904; operates six routes and 161 double-deck trams between Kennedy Town and Shaukeiwan; Man. Dir BRUNO CHARRADE.

ROADS

In 2010 there were 2,076 km of public roads in Hong Kong. Almost all of them are concrete or asphalt surfaced. Owing to the hilly terrain, and the density of building development, the scope for substantial increase in the road network is limited. Work on a bridge linking Hong Kong's Lantau Island with Macao and Zhuhai City, in the Chinese province of Guangdong, commenced in late 2009. Spanning nearly 50 km and comprising a six-lane expressway, the project was scheduled for completion in 2015 (and opening in 2016).

Highways Department: Ho Man Tin Government Offices, 5/F, 88 Chung Hau St, Ho Man Tin, Kowloon; tel. 29264111; fax 27145216; e-mail enquiry@hyd.gov.hk; internet www.hyd.gov.hk; f. 1986; planning, design, construction and maintenance of the public road system; co-ordination of major highway and railway projects; Dir PETER LAU KA-KEUNG.

FERRIES

Conventional ferries, hoverferries, catamarans and jetfoils operate between Hong Kong, China and Macao. There is also an extensive network of ferry services to outlying districts.

Hongkong and Yaumati Ferry Co Ltd: 98 Tam Kon Shan Rd, Ngau Kok Wan, North Tsing Yi, New Territories; tel. 23944294; fax 27869001; e-mail hkferry@hkf.com; internet www.hkf.com; licensed routes on ferry services, incl. excursion, vehicular and dangerous goods; Chair. COLIN K. Y. LAM.

Shun Tak-China Travel Ship Management Ltd (TurboJET): 83 Hing Wah St West, Lai Chi Kok, Kowloon; tel. 23070880; fax 23075083; e-mail enquiry@turbojet.com.hk; internet www.turbojet.com.hk; f. 1999; operates hydrofoil services between Hong Kong, Macao and Shenzhen.

The Star Ferry Co Ltd: Star Ferry Pier, Kowloon Point, Tsim Sha Tsui, Kowloon; tel. 23677065; fax 21186028; e-mail sf@starferry.com.hk; internet www.starferry.com.hk; f. 1898; operates 9 passenger ferries between Tsim Sha Tsui and Central, the main business district of Hong Kong; between Central and Hung Hom; between Tsim Sha Tsui and Wanchai; and between Wanchai and Hung Hom; also a licensed harbour tour ferry service at Victoria Harbour; Man. Dir FRANKIE YICK.

SHIPPING

Hong Kong is one of the world's largest shipping centres and among the busiest container ports. At the end of 2013 the shipping register comprised a fleet of 2,375 vessels, totalling 86.5m. grt which included 673 bulk carriers, 170 general cargo ships, 327 tankers and 32 gas tankers. The container terminals at Kwai Chung are privately owned and operated. The construction of a ninth terminal (CT9) at Kwai Chung was completed in 2004, bringing the total number of berths to 24. Lantau Island has been designated as the site for any future expansion.

Marine Department, Hong Kong Special Administrative Region Government: Harbour Bldg, 22/F, 38 Pier Rd, Central, GPOB 4155; tel. 25423711; fax 25417194; e-mail mdenquiry@mardep.gov.hk; internet www.mardep.gov.hk; Dir FRANCIS LIU.

Shipping Companies

Anglo-Eastern Ship Management Ltd: 23/F, 248 Queen's Rd East, Wanchai; tel. 28636111; fax 28612419; e-mail commercial@angloeasterngroup.com; internet www.aesm.com.hk; f. 1974; merged with Denholm Ship Management in 2001; CEO PETER CREMERS; Man. Dir MARCEL LIEDTS.

COSCO (Hong Kong) Shipping Co Ltd (CHS): 52/F, Cosco Tower, 183 Queen's Rd, Central; tel. 28098865; fax 25485653; internet www.coscochs.com.hk; established by merger of former Ocean Tramping Co Ltd and Yick Fung Shipping and Enterprise Co; owned by COSCO (Hong Kong) Group Ltd; Dep. Gen. Man. CHEN XINCHUAN.

Fairmont Shipping (HK) Ltd: Fairmont House, 21/F, 8 Cotton Tree Dr., Central; tel. 25218338; fax 28104560; e-mail fsahkginfo@fairmontshipping.com; Pres. ROBERT HO.

Hong Kong Ming Wah Shipping Co: Unit 3701, China Merchants Tower, 37/F, Shun Tak Centre, 168–200 Connaught Rd, Central; tel. 25172128; fax 25473482; e-mail mwbs@hkmw.com.hk; internet www.hkmw.com.hk; f. 1980; subsidiary of China Merchants Group; Pres. HUANG SHAO JIE.

Island Navigation Corpn International Ltd: Harbour Centre, 28–29/F, 25 Harbour Rd, Wanchai; tel. 28333222; fax 28270001; Man. Dir M. H. LIANG.

Jardine Shipping Services: 24/F, Devon House, Taikoo Place, 979 King's Rd; tel. 25793001; fax 28569927; e-mail enquiries@jardineshipping.com; internet www.jardine-shipping.com; CEO ERIC VAN DER HOEVEN.

Oak Maritime (HK) Inc Ltd: Rms 703–705, AXA Centre, 151 Gloucester Rd, Wanchai; tel. 25063866; fax 25063563; e-mail mail01@oakhk.com; Chair. STEVE G. K. HSU; Man. Dir JACK HSU.

Orient Overseas Container Line Ltd: 31/F, Harbour Centre, 25 Harbour Rd, Wanchai; tel. 28333888; fax 25318122; e-mail hkgcsd@oocl.com; internet www.oocl.com; mem. of the Grand Alliance of shipping cos (five partners); Chair. C. C. TUNG; CEO ANDY TUNG.

Teh-Hu Cargocean Management Co Ltd: Unit B, Fortis Tower, 15/F, 77–79 Gloucester Rd, Wanchai; tel. 25988688; fax 28249339; e-mail tehhuhk@on-nets.com; f. 1974; Man. Dir KENNETH K. W. LO.

Wah Kwong Shipping Holdings Ltd: Shanghai Industrial Investment Bldg, 26/F, 48–62 Hennessy Rd, POB 283; tel. 28635333; fax 28635338; e-mail admin@wahkwong.com.hk; internet www.wahkwong.com.hk; Chair. GEORGE S. K. CHAO.

Wallem Shipmanagement Ltd: 12/F Warwick House East, Taikoo Place, 979 King's Rd, Quarry Bay; tel. 28768200; fax 28761234; e-mail group@wallem.com; internet www.wallem.com; Man. Dir DEEPAK S. HONAWAR.

Associations

Hong Kong Cargo-Vessel Traders' Association: 21–23 Man Wai Bldg, 2/F, Ferry Point, Kowloon; tel. 23847102; fax 27820342; e-mail info@cvta.com.hk; internet www.cvta.com.hk; 978 mems; Chair. CHOW YAT-TAK; Sec. CHAN BAK.

Hong Kong Shipowners' Association: Queen's Centre, 12/F, 58–64 Queen's Rd East, Wanchai; tel. 25200206; fax 25298246; e-mail hksoa@hksoa.org.hk; internet www.hksoa.org.hk; f. 1957; 202 mems; Chair. ALAN TUNG; Man. Dir ARTHUR BOWRING.

Hong Kong Shippers' Council: Rm 603, Chong Yip St, Kwun Tung, Kowloon; tel. 22112323; fax 28919787; e-mail shippers@hkshippers.org.hk; internet www.hkshippers.org.hk; 63 mems; Chair. (Exec. Cttee) WILLY LIN SUN MO.

CIVIL AVIATION

The international airport on the island of Chek Lap Kok, near Lantau Island, opened in 1998. Construction of a third runway was approved in principle in March 2012 and was expected to be completed by 2020. A new cargo terminal started operations in 2013. Hong Kong was served by over 100 airlines operating nearly 900 daily flights in 2012.

Airport Authority of Hong Kong: HKIA Tower, 1 Sky Plaza Rd, Hong Kong International Airport, Lantau; tel. 21887111; fax 28240717; internet www.hongkongairport.com; f. 1995; state-owned; Chair. MARVIN CHEUNG KIN-TUNG; CEO STANLEY H. C. HUI.

Civil Aviation Department: 1 Tung Fai Rd, Hong Kong International Airport, Lantau; tel. 29106342; fax 29106351; e-mail enquiry@cad.gov.hk; internet www.cad.gov.hk; Dir-Gen. NORMAN LO SHUNG-MAN.

AHK Air Hong Kong Ltd: 4/F, South Tower, Cathay Pacific City, 8 Scenic Rd, Hong Kong International Airport, Lantau; tel. 27618588; fax 27618586; e-mail ahk.hq@airhongkong.com.hk; internet www.airhongkong.com.hk; f. 1986; regional cargo carrier; wholly owned subsidiary of Cathay Pacific Airways Ltd; COO ANNA THOMPSON.

Cathay Pacific Airways Ltd: 7/F, North Tower, Cathay Pacific City, 8 Scenic Rd, Hong Kong International Airport, Lantau; tel. 27471888; fax 25601411; internet www.cathaypacific.com; f. 1946; services to more than 40 major cities in the Far East, Middle East, North America, Europe, South Africa, Australia and New Zealand; Chair. CHRISTOPHER D. PRATT; CEO JOHN SLOSAR.

Hong Kong Airlines Ltd: 7/F, One Citygate, 20 Tat Tung Rd, Tung Chung, Lantau; tel. 31511800; fax 31511838; e-mail crd@hkairlines.com; internet www.hkairlines.com; f. 2004; flights to mainland China, Japan, Philippines, Singapore, Indonesia, Viet Nam, Taiwan, Thailand and Moscow, Russia; Pres. YANG JIANG HONG.

Hong Kong Dragon Airlines Ltd (Dragonair): Dragonair House, 11 Tung Fai Rd, Hong Kong International Airport, Lantau; tel. 31933888; fax 31933889; internet www.dragonair.com; f. 1985; scheduled and charter flights to destinations throughout mainland China and to Bangladesh, Thailand, Cambodia, Brunei, Malaysia, Taiwan and Japan; wholly owned subsidiary of Cathay Pacific Airways Ltd; CEO PATRICK YEUNG.

Sky Shuttle Helicopters Ltd: Rm 1603, 16/F, China Merchants Tower, Shun Tak Centre, 200 Connaught Rd, Central; tel. 21089988; fax 21089938; e-mail reservation@skyshuttlehk.com; internet www.skyshuttlehk.com; f. 1990; fmrly East Asia Airlines; merged with Helicopters Hong Kong Ltd in 1998; renamed as Heli Express Ltd in 2005, and as above in 2008; operates helicopter services between Hong Kong, Macao and Shenzhen (China); CEO CHEYENNE CHAN.

Tourism

Tourism is a major source of foreign exchange. Receipts from tourism totalled an estimated US $32,089m. in 2012. Tourist arrivals totalled 23.8m. in 2012 (of whom 15.1m. came from mainland China). At the end of November 2011 the 189 licensed hotels offered 62,259 rooms, while tourist guest houses totalled 637, with 6,145 rooms available. A Disneyland theme park opened in 2005.

Hong Kong Tourism Board (HKTB): 9–11/F, Citicorp Centre, 18 Whitfield Rd, North Point; tel. 28076543; fax 28060303; e-mail info@hktb.com; internet www.discoverhongkong.com; f. 1957; est. as Hong Kong Tourist Asscn; reconstituted as Hong Kong Tourism Bd in April 2001; co-ordinates and promotes the tourist industry; has govt support and financial assistance; up to 20 mems of the Bd represent the Govt, the private sector and the tourism industry; Chair. JAMES TIEN; Exec. Dir ANTHONY LAU.

Defence

In July 1997 a garrison of 4,800 troops belonging to the Chinese People's Liberation Army (PLA) was established in Hong Kong. The garrison can intervene in local matters only at the request of the Hong Kong Government, which remains responsible for internal security. A total of 7,000 Chinese troops were stationed in Hong Kong in 2007.

Defence Expenditure: Projected expenditure on internal security in 2006/07 totalled HK $92.7m.

Commander of the PLA Garrison in Hong Kong: Lt-Gen. WANG XIAOJUN.

Education

Full-time education is free and compulsory in Hong Kong between the ages of six and 15. In 2008/09 the duration of free education was extended from nine to 12 years. In 2012/13 164,764 children attended kindergartens, which totalled 957. In the same year a total of 317,442 children attended primary schools, while secondary school pupils totalled 418,787. There are three main types of secondary school in Hong Kong: grammar, technical and pre-vocational schools. Primary enrolment in 2011/12 included an estimated 94% of children in the relevant age-group, while the comparable ratio for secondary enrolment in the same year was 89% (males 89%; females 89%). An education reform programme was in progress from 2000, including reform of curriculum and education management, and the establishment of Project Yi Jin, a life-long learning initiative. Budgetary expenditure on general education was an estimated HK $34,067m. in the financial year 2012/13, accounting for 9.0% of total spending.

MACAO

Introductory Survey

LOCATION, CLIMATE, LANGUAGE, RELIGION, FLAG, CAPITAL

The Special Administrative Region (SAR) of Macao comprises the peninsula of Macao, an enclave on the mainland of southern China, and two nearby islands, Taipa, which is linked to the mainland by three bridges, and Coloane. The latter island is connected to Taipa by a causeway and by a large area of reclaimed land. The territory lies opposite Hong Kong on the western side of the mouth of the Xijiang (Sikiang) River. The climate is subtropical, with temperatures averaging 15°C in January and 29°C in July. There are two official languages, Chinese (Cantonese being the principal dialect) and Portuguese. English is also widely spoken. The predominant religions are Roman Catholicism, Chinese Buddhism, Daoism and Confucianism. The flag of the Macao SAR (proportions 2 by 3), introduced upon the territory's reversion to Chinese sovereignty in December 1999 and flown subordinate to the flag of the People's Republic of China, displays a stylized white flower below an arc of one large and four small yellow stars, above five white lines, on a green background. The executive and legislative bodies of Macao are based in the city of Macao, which is situated on the peninsula.

CONTEMPORARY POLITICAL HISTORY

Historical Context

Established by Portugal in 1557 as a permanent trading post with China, Macao became a Portuguese Overseas Province in 1951. After the military coup in Portugal in April 1974, Col José Garcia Leandro was appointed Governor of the province. A new statute, promulgated in February 1976, redefined Macao as a 'Special Territory' under Portuguese jurisdiction, but with a great measure of administrative and economic independence. Proposals to enlarge the Legislative Assembly from 17 to 21 members, thus giving the Chinese population an increased role in the administration of Macao, were abandoned when they did not receive the approval of the Government of the People's Republic of China in March 1980. China and Portugal established diplomatic relations in February 1979.

Domestic Political Affairs

Col Leandro was replaced as the territory's Governor by Gen. Nuno de Melo Egídio, Deputy Chief of Staff of Portugal's armed forces, in February 1979. In June 1981 Gen. Egídio was replaced by Cdre (later Rear-Adm.) Vasco Almeida e Costa, a Portuguese former minister and naval commander. Following a constitutional dispute in March 1984 over the Governor's plans for electoral reform (extending the franchise to the ethnic Chinese majority), the Legislative Assembly was dissolved. Elections for a new Assembly were held in August, at which the Chinese majority were allowed to vote for the first time, regardless of their length of residence in the territory. Following the elections, the Assembly was dominated by ethnic Chinese deputies.

In January 1986 Governor Almeida e Costa resigned. In May he was replaced by Joaquim Pinto Machado, whose appointment represented a departure from the tradition of military governors for Macao. However, his political inexperience placed him at a disadvantage. In May 1987 he resigned, citing 'reasons of institutional dignity' (apparently referring to the problem of corruption in the Macao administration). He was replaced in August by Carlos Melancia, a former Socialist deputy in the Portuguese legislature, who had held ministerial posts in several Portuguese governments.

The first round of negotiations between the Portuguese and Chinese Governments on the future of Macao took place in June 1986 in Beijing. Portugal's acceptance of China's sovereignty greatly simplified the issue. On 13 April 1987, following the conclusion of the fourth round of negotiations, a joint declaration was formally signed in Beijing by the Portuguese and Chinese Governments, during an official visit to China by the Prime Minister of Portugal. According to the agreement (which was formally ratified in January 1988), Macao was to become a 'special administrative region' (SAR) of the People's Republic (to be known as Macao, China) on 20 December 1999. Macao was thus to have the same status as that agreed (with effect from 1997) for Hong Kong, and was to enjoy autonomy in most matters except defence and foreign policy. A Sino-Portuguese Joint Liaison Group (JLG), established to oversee the transfer of power, held its inaugural meeting in the Portuguese capital of Lisbon in April 1988. In 1999 a Chief Executive for Macao was to be appointed by the Chinese Government, following 'elections or consultations to be held in Macao', and the territory's legislature was to contain 'a majority of elected members'. The inhabitants of Macao were to become citizens of the People's Republic of China. The Chinese Government refused to allow the possibility of dual Sino-Portuguese citizenship, although Macao residents in possession of Portuguese passports were apparently to be permitted to retain them for travel purposes. The agreement guaranteed a 50-year period during which Macao would be permitted to retain its free capitalist economy, and to be financially independent of China.

In August 1988 a Macao Basic Law Drafting Committee was formed. Comprising 30 Chinese members and 19 representatives from Macao, the Committee was to draft a law determining the territory's future constitutional status within the People's Republic of China. Elections to the Legislative Assembly were held in October. Low participation (fewer than 30% of the electorate) was recorded, and a 'liberal' grouping secured three of the seats reserved for directly elected candidates, while a coalition of pro-Beijing and conservative Macanese (lusophone Eurasian) groups won the other three.

In January 1989 it was announced that Portuguese passports were to be issued to about 100,000 ethnic Chinese inhabitants, born in

Macao before October 1981, and it was anticipated that as many as a further 100,000 would be granted before 1999. Unlike their counterparts in the neighbouring British dependent territory of Hong Kong, therefore, these (but not all) Macao residents were to be granted the full rights of a citizen of the European Community (EC, now European Union—EU, see p. 273). In February 1989 President Mário Soares of Portugal visited Macao, in order to discuss the transfer of the territory's administration to China.

Following the violent suppression of the pro-democracy movement in China in June 1989, as many as 100,000 residents of Macao participated in demonstrations in the enclave to protest against the Chinese Government's action, which caused great concern in Macao. In August, however, China assured Portugal that it would honour the agreement to maintain the capitalist system of the territory after 1999.

In March 1990 the implementation of a programme to grant permanent registration to parents of 4,200 Chinese residents, the latter having already secured the right of abode in Macao, developed into chaos when other illegal immigrants demanded a similar concession. The authorities decided to declare a general amnesty, but were unprepared for the numbers of illegal residents, some 50,000 in total, who rushed to take advantage of the scheme, thereby revealing the true extent of previous immigration from China. Border security was subsequently increased, in an effort to prevent any further illegal immigration.

In late March 1990 the Legislative Assembly approved the final draft of the territory's revised Organic Law. The Law was approved by the Portuguese Assembly of the Republic in mid-April, and granted Macao greater administrative, economic, financial and legislative autonomy, in advance of 1999. The powers of the Governor and of the Legislative Assembly, where six additional seats were to be created, were therefore increased. The post of military commander of the security forces was abolished, responsibility for the territory's security being assumed by a civilian Under-Secretary.

Meanwhile, in February 1990 it was alleged that Carlos Melancia had accepted a substantial bribe from a foreign company in connection with a contract for the construction of the new airport in Macao. Although he denied any involvement in the affair, the Governor resigned, and was replaced on an acting basis by the Under-Secretary for Economic Affairs, Dr Francisco Murteira Nabo. In September 1991 it was announced that Melancia and five others were to stand trial on charges of corruption. In August 1993 the former Governor was acquitted on the grounds of insufficient evidence.

Meanwhile, many observers believed that the enclave was being adversely affected by the political situation in Lisbon, as differences between the socialist President and centre-right Prime Minister were being reflected in rivalries between officials in Macao. In an attempt to restore confidence, therefore, President Soares visited the territory in November 1990. In January 1991, upon his re-election as head of state, the President appointed Gen. Vasco Rocha Vieira (who had previously served as the territory's Chief of Staff and as Under-Secretary for Public Works and Transport) Governor of Macao. In March 1991 the Legislative Assembly was expanded from 17 to 23 members. All seven Under-Secretaries were replaced in May.

The transition to Chinese sovereignty

Following his arrival in Macao, Gen. Rocha Vieira announced that China would be consulted on all future developments in the territory. The 10th meeting of the Sino-Portuguese JLG took place in Beijing in April 1991. Topics under regular discussion included the participation of Macao in international organizations, progress towards an increase in the number of local officials employed in the civil service (hitherto dominated by Portuguese and Macanese personnel) and the status of the Chinese language. The progress of the working group on the translation of local laws from Portuguese into Chinese was also examined, a particular problem being the lack of suitably qualified bilingual legal personnel. It was agreed that Portuguese was to remain an official language after 1999. The two sides also reached agreement on the exchange of identity cards for those Macao residents who would require them in 1999. Regular meetings of the JLG continued.

In July 1991 the Macao Draft Basic Law was published. Confidence in the territory's future was enhanced by China's apparent flexibility on a number of issues. Unlike the Hong Kong Basic Law, that of Macao did not impose restrictions on holders of foreign passports assuming senior posts in the territory's administration after 1999, the only exception being the future Chief Executive. In November 1991 the Governor of Macao visited China, where it was confirmed that the 'one country, two systems' policy would operate in Macao from 1999. In March 1993 the final draft of the Basic Law of the Macao SAR was ratified by the National People's Congress (NPC) in Beijing, which also approved the design of the future SAR's flag. The adoption of the legislation was welcomed by the Governor of Macao, who reiterated his desire for a smooth transfer of power in 1999. The Chief Executive of the SAR was to be selected by local representatives. The SAR's first Legislative Council was to comprise 23 members, of whom eight would be directly elected. Its term of office would expire in October 2001, when it would be expanded to 27 members, of whom 10 would be directly elected. The Macao Basic Law, unlike that of Hong Kong, did not envisage the eventual adoption of universal suffrage.

Meanwhile, elections to the Legislative Assembly were held in September 1992. The level of participation was higher than on previous occasions, with 59% of the registered electorate (albeit only 13.5% of the population) attending the polls. Fifty candidates contested the eight directly elective seats, four of which were won by members of the main pro-Beijing parties, the União Promotora para o Progresso (UPP, representing neighbourhood associations and the territory's women's association) and the União para o Desenvolvimento (UPD, representing trade unions).

In June 1993 Portugal and China reached agreement on all outstanding issues regarding the construction of the territory's airport and the future use of Chinese airspace. Furthermore, Macao was to be permitted to negotiate air traffic agreements with other countries.

In April 1994, during a visit to China, the Portuguese Prime Minister received an assurance that Chinese nationality would not be imposed on Macanese people of Portuguese descent, who would be able to retain their Portuguese passports. Speaking in Macao itself, the Prime Minister expressed confidence in the territory's future. In July a group of local journalists dispatched a letter, alleging intimidation and persecution in Macao, to President Soares, urging him to intervene to defend the territory's press freedom. The journalists' appeal followed an incident involving the director of the daily *Gazeta Macaense*, who had been fined for reproducing an article from a Lisbon weekly newspaper, and now awaited trial. The territory's press had been critical of the Macao Supreme Court's decision to extradite ethnic Chinese to the mainland (despite the absence of any extradition treaty) to answer criminal charges and risk the possibility of a death sentence.

The draft of the new penal code for Macao did not incorporate the death penalty. In January 1995, during a visit to Portugal, Vice-Premier Zhu Rongji of China confirmed that the People's Republic would not impose the death penalty in Macao after 1999, regarding the question as a matter for the authorities of the future SAR. The new penal code, prohibiting capital punishment, took effect in January 1996.

Visiting the territory in April 1995, President Soares stressed the importance of three issues: the modification of the territory's legislation; the rights of the individual; and the preservation of the Portuguese language. During a visit to Beijing in February 1996, the Portuguese Minister of Foreign Affairs, Jaime Gama (who urged that the rights and aspirations of the people of Macao be protected), met President Jiang Zemin and other senior officials, describing the discussions as positive. While acknowledging the sound progress of recent years, Gama and the Chinese Minister of Foreign Affairs agreed on an acceleration in the pace of work of the Sino-Portuguese JLG. In the same month Gen. Rocha Vieira was reappointed Governor of Macao by the newly elected President of Portugal, Jorge Sampaio. António Guterres, the new Portuguese Prime Minister, confirmed his desire for constitutional consensus regarding the transition of Macao.

At elections to the Legislative Assembly in September 1996 the pro-Beijing UPP received 15.2% of the votes and won two of the eight directly elective seats, while the UPD won 14.5% and retained one of its two seats. The business-orientated groups were more successful: the Associação Promotora para a Economia de Macau took 16.6% of the votes and secured two seats; the Convergência para o Desenvolvimento de Macau (CODEM) and the União Geral para o Desenvolvimento de Macau each won one seat. The pro-democracy Associação de Macau Novo (AMN), presenting candidates through an electoral list under the title of the Associação de Novo Macau Democrático (ANMD), also won one seat. The level of voter participation was 64%. The 23-member legislature was to remain in place beyond the transfer of sovereignty in 1999.

From 1996 there were numerous bomb attacks and brutal assaults, including several serious attacks on local casino staff. Many attributed the alarming increase in organized crime to the opening of the airport in Macao, which was believed to have facilitated the entry of rival gangsters from mainland China, Taiwan and Hong Kong. In May 1997, following the murder of three men believed to have associations with one such group of gangsters, the Chinese Government expressed its concern at the deterioration of public order in Macao and urged Portugal to observe its responsibility to maintain the enclave's social stability during the transitional period, while pledging the enhanced co-operation of the Chinese security forces in the effort to curb organized crime in Macao. In June several Chinese-language newspapers, along with a television station, received threats instructing them to cease reporting on the activities of the notorious 14K triad, a 10,000-member secret society to which much of the violence had been attributed. In August China deployed 500 armed police officers to reinforce the border with Macao in order to intensify its efforts to combat illegal immigration, contraband and the smuggling of arms into the enclave. Despite the approval in July of a law further to restrict activities such as extortion and 'protection rackets', organized crime continued unabated. In October the police forces of Macao and China initiated a joint campaign against illegal immigration.

Meanwhile, the slow progress of the 'three localizations' (civil service, laws and the adoption of Chinese as an official language) continued to concern the Government of China. At mid-1996 almost 50% of senior government posts were still held by Portuguese expatriates. In January 1997 the Governor pledged to accelerate the process with regard to local legislation, the priority being the training of the requisite personnel. In December details of the establishment in Macao of the office of the Chinese Ministry of Foreign Affairs, which was to commence operations in December 1999, were announced. In January 1998 the Macao Government declared that the vast majority of senior civil service posts were now held by local officials.

In March 1998 the Chinese authorities reiterated their concern at the deteriorating situation in Macao. In April, by which month none of the 34 triad-related murders committed since January 1997 had been solved, the Portuguese and Chinese Governments agreed to co-operate in the exchange of information about organized criminal activities. Also in April 1998 the trial, on charges of breaching the gaming laws, of the head of the 14K triad, Wan Kuok-koi ('Broken Tooth'), was adjourned for two months, owing to the apparent reluctance of witnesses to appear in court. In early May Wan Kuok-koi was rearrested and charged with the attempted murder of Macao's chief of police, António Marques Baptista, in a car-bomb attack. The case was dismissed by a judge three days later on the grounds of insufficient evidence. Wan Kuok-koi remained in prison, charged with other serious offences. His renewed detention led to a spate of arson attacks. The Portuguese Government was reported to have dispatched intelligence officers to the enclave to reinforce the local security forces. In June Marques Baptista travelled to Beijing and Guangzhou for discussions on the problems of cross-border criminal activity and drugs-trafficking.

The Preparatory Committee for the Establishment of the Macao SAR, which was to oversee the territory's transfer to Chinese sovereignty and was to comprise representatives from both the People's Republic and Macao, was inaugurated in Beijing in May 1998. Four subordinate working groups (supervising administrative, legal, economic, and social and cultural affairs) were subsequently established. The second plenary session of the Preparatory Committee was convened in July 1998, discussions encompassing issues such as the 'localization' of civil servants, public security and the drafting of the territory's fiscal budget for 2000. In July 1998, during a meeting with the Chinese Premier, the Governor of Macao requested an increase in the mainland's investment in the territory prior to the 1999 transfer of sovereignty.

In August 1998 representatives of the JLG agreed to intensify Luso-Chinese consultations on matters relating to the transitional period. In September, in response to increasing security problems related to criminal gangs, China unexpectedly announced that, upon the transfer of sovereignty, it was to station troops in the territory. This abandonment of a previous assurance to the contrary caused much disquiet in Portugal, where the proposed deployment was deemed unnecessary. Although the Basic Law made no specific provision for the stationing of a mainland garrison, China asserted that it was to be ultimately responsible for the enclave's defence. By October, furthermore, about 4,000 soldiers of the People's Liberation Army (PLA) were on duty at various Chinese border posts adjacent to Macao.

In November 1998 procedures for the election of the 200 members of the Selection Committee were established by the Preparatory Committee. Responsible for the appointment of the members of Macao's post-1999 Government, the delegates of the Selection Committee were required to be permanent residents of the territory: 60 members were to be drawn from the business and financial communities, 50 from cultural, educational and professional spheres, 50 from labour, social service and religious circles, and the remaining 40 were to be former political personages.

In November 1998 raids on casinos believed to be engaged in illegal activities, conducted by the authorities, resulted in several arrests. Further violent incidents took place in December. At the end of that month it was confirmed that Macao residents of wholly Chinese origin would be entitled to full mainland citizenship, while those of mixed Chinese and Portuguese descent would be obliged to decide between the two nationalities. In January 1999 several protesters were arrested during demonstrations to draw attention to the plight of numerous immigrant children, who had been brought illegally from China to Macao to join their legitimately resident parents and whose irregular status precluded entitlement to the territory's education, health and social services.

In January 1999 details of the composition of the future PLA garrison were disclosed. The troops were to comprise solely ground forces, totalling fewer than 1,000 soldiers and to be directly responsible to the Commander of the Guangzhou Military Unit. They would be permitted to intervene to maintain social order in the enclave only if the local police were unable to control major triad-related violence or if street demonstrations posed a threat of serious unrest. In March, during a trip to Macao (where he had discussions with the visiting Portuguese President), Qian Qichen, a Chinese Vice-Premier, indicated that an advance contingent of PLA soldiers would be deployed in Macao prior to the transfer of sovereignty. Other sources of contention between China and Portugal remained the unresolved question of the post-1999 status of those Macao residents who had been granted Portuguese nationality and also the issue of the court of final appeal.

In April 1999, at the first plenary meeting of the Selection Committee, candidates for the post of the SAR's Chief Executive were elected. Edmund Ho received 125 of the 200 votes, while Stanley Au garnered 65 votes. Three other candidates failed to secure the requisite minimum of 20 votes. Edmund Ho and Stanley Au, both bankers and regarded as moderate pro-business candidates, thus proceeded to the second round of voting by secret ballot, held in May. Edmund Ho received 163 of the 199 votes cast, and confirmed his intention to address the problems of law and order, security and the economy. The Chief Executive-designate also fully endorsed China's decision to deploy troops in Macao.

During 1999, in co-operation with the Macao authorities, the police forces of Guangdong Province, and of Zhuhai in particular, initiated a new offensive against the criminal activities of the triads, which had been in regular evidence with further murders throughout the year. China's desire to deploy an advance contingent of troops prior to December 1999, however, reportedly continued to be obstructed by Portugal. Furthermore, the announcement that, subject to certain conditions, the future garrison was to be granted law-enforcement powers raised various constitutional issues. Nevertheless, many Macao residents appeared to welcome the mainland's decision to station troops in the enclave. In a further effort to address the deteriorating security situation, from December Macao's 5,800-member police force was to be restructured.

In July 1999 the penultimate meeting of the JLG took place in Lisbon. In August, in accordance with the nominations of the Chief Executive-designate, the composition of the Government of the future SAR was announced by the State Council in Beijing. Appointments included that of Florinda da Rosa Silva Chan as Secretary for Administration and Justice. In September the Governor urged improved co-operation with the authorities of Guangdong Province in order to combat organized crime, revealing that the majority of the inmates of Macao's prisons were not permanent residents of the territory. In the same month it was reported that 90 former Gurkhas of the British army were being drafted in as prison warders, following the intimidation of local officers. Also in September the Chief Executive-designate announced the appointment of seven new members of the Legislative Council, which was to succeed the Legislative Assembly in December. While the seven nominees of the Governor in the existing Legislative Assembly were thus to be replaced, 15 of the 16 elected members (one having resigned) were to remain in office as members of the successor Legislative Council. (However, in practice the new legislative body continued to be known by its former name.) At the same time the composition of the 10-member Executive Council was also announced.

In October 1999 President Jiang Zemin undertook a two-day visit to Portugal, following which it was declared that the outstanding question of the deployment of an advance contingent of Chinese troops in Macao had been resolved. The advance party was to be restricted to a technical mission, which entered the territory in early December. In November the 37th and last session of the JLG took place in Beijing, where in the same month the Governor of Macao held final discussions with President Jiang Zemin.

Meanwhile, in April 1999 Wan Kuok-koi had been acquitted of charges of coercing croupiers. In November his trial on other serious charges concluded: he was found guilty of criminal association and other illegal gambling-related activities and sentenced to 15 years' imprisonment. Eight co-defendants received lesser sentences. In a separate trial Artur Chiang Calderon, a former police officer alleged to be Wan Kuok-koi's military adviser, received a prison sentence of 10 years and six months for involvement in organized crime. While two other defendants were also imprisoned, 19 were released on the grounds of insufficient evidence. As the transfer of the territory's sovereignty approached, by mid-December almost 40 people had been murdered in triad-related violence since January 1999.

The inauguration of the SAR and subsequent events

In November 1999 representatives of the JLG reached agreement on details regarding the deployment of Chinese troops in Macao and on the retention of Portuguese as an official language. At midnight on 19 December 1999, therefore, in a ceremony attended by the Presidents and heads of government of Portugal and China, the sovereignty of Macao was duly transferred; 12 hours later (only after the departure from the newly inaugurated SAR of the Portuguese delegation), 500 soldiers of the 1,000-strong force of the PLA, in a convoy of armoured vehicles, crossed the border into Macao, where they were installed in a makeshift barracks. However, prior to the ceremony it was reported that the authorities of Guangdong Province had detained almost 3,000 persons, including 15 residents of Macao, suspected of association with criminal gangs. The celebrations in Macao were also marred by the authorities' handling of demonstrations by members of Falun Gong, a religious movement recently outlawed in China. The expulsion from Macao of several members of the sect in the days preceding the territory's transfer and the arrest of 30 adherents on the final day of Portuguese sovereignty prompted strong criticism from President Jorge Sampaio of Portugal. Nevertheless, in an effort to consolidate relations with the EU, in May 2000 the first official overseas visit of the SAR's Chief Executive was to Europe, his itinerary including Portugal. The EU agreed in principle in December to grant residents of Hong Kong and Macao visa-free access to member states, subject to final approval by the European Parliament.

In March 2000, in an important change to the immigration rules, it was announced that children of Chinese nationality whose parents were permanent residents of Macao would shortly be allowed to apply for residency permits. A monthly quota of 420 successful applicants was established, while the youngest children were to receive priority. In May hundreds of demonstrators participated in a march to protest against Macao's high level of unemployment. This shortage of jobs was attributed to the territory's use of immigrant workers, mainly from mainland China and South-East Asia, who were estimated to total 28,000. Trade unions continued to organize protests, and in July (for the first time since the unrest arising from the Chinese Cultural Revolution of 1966) tear gas and water cannon were used to disperse about 200 demonstrators who were demanding that the immigration of foreign workers be halted by the Government. In the same month it was announced that, in early 2001, an office of the Macao SAR was to be established in Beijing, in order to promote links between the two Governments.

Celebrations to mark the first anniversary of the reversion to Chinese sovereignty were attended by President Jiang Zemin, who made a speech praising Macao's local administration, but warning strongly against those seeking to use either of the SARs as a base for subversion. A number of Falun Gong adherents from Hong Kong who had attempted to enter Macao for the celebrations were expelled. The same fate befell two Hong Kong human rights activists who had hoped to petition the Chinese President during his stay in Macao about the human rights situation in the People's Republic. A group of Falun Gong members in Macao, who held a protest the day before President Jiang's arrival, were detained in custody and subsequently alleged that they had suffered police brutality.

In January 2001 China urged the USA to cease interfering in its internal affairs, following the signature by President Bill Clinton of the US Macao Policy Act, which related to the control of Macao's exports and the monitoring of its autonomy. The Governor of Guangdong Province, Lu Ruihua, made an official visit to Macao in February to improve links between the two regions. At the same time, the Legislative Council announced plans to strengthen relations with legislative bodies on the mainland, and the President of the Legislative Council, Susana Chou, visited Beijing, where she held discussions with Vice-Premier Qian Qichen. Edmund Ho visited Beijing in early March to attend the fourth session of the Ninth NPC, and held talks with President Jiang Zemin, who praised the former's achievements since the reversion of Macao to Chinese rule. The EU announced in mid-March that SAR passport holders would, from May 2001, no longer require visas to enter EU countries.

The Macao, Hong Kong and mainland police forces established a working group in March 2001 to combat cross-border crime, with a special emphasis on narcotics, and later that month the Macao, Hong Kong and Guangdong police forces conducted a joint anti-drugs operation, resulting in the arrest of 1,243 suspected traffickers and producers, and the seizure of large quantities of heroin, ecstasy and marijuana. Macao and Portugal signed an agreement in May to strengthen co-operation in the fields of economy, culture, public security and justice. In June Macao's Secretary for Security, Cheong Kuoc Va, visited Beijing and signed new accords aimed at reducing the trafficking of drugs, guns and people. In the same month Chief Executive Edmund Ho made his first official visit to the EU headquarters in the Belgian capital, Brussels, where he sought to promote contacts and exchanges between the SAR and the EU. Another major campaign against illegal activities related to the triads was conducted by the Macao, Hong Kong and Guangdong police forces in July, and in a further sign of co-operation between Macao and the mainland against crime, the two sides signed an agreement on mutual judicial co-operation and assistance in August, the first of its kind.

Elections to the Legislative Council were held on 23 September 2001, the first since Macao's reversion to Chinese rule. The number of seats was increased from 23 to 27: seven members were appointed by the Chief Executive, 10 elected directly and 10 indirectly. Of the 10 directly elective seats, two seats each were won by the business-orientated CODEM, the pro-Beijing UPP and UPD and the pro-democracy AMN (as the ANMD). Two other factions won one seat each. Of the 10 indirectly elective seats, four were taken by representatives of business interests, two by representatives of welfare, cultural, educational and sports interests, two by representatives of labour interests, and two by representatives of professionals.

In October 2001 China appointed Bai Zhijian as director of its liaison office in Macao, its most senior representative in the SAR, replacing the late Wang Qiren. In the same month Edmund Ho attended the summit meeting of Asia-Pacific Economic Cooperation (APEC, see p. 201) in Shanghai, and the EU-Macao Joint Committee held a meeting in the SAR, aimed at improving trade, tourism and legal co-operation between the two entities. During late 2001, meanwhile, Macao increased co-operation with Hong Kong and the mainland in fighting crime and combating terrorism, amid reports that Russian mafias were becoming increasingly active in the SARs.

In December 2001 the Government finally acted to end the 40-year monopoly on casinos and gambling held by Stanley Ho and his long-established company, the Sociedade de Turismo e Diversões de Macau (STDM). Under the new arrangements, some 21 companies, none of which was Chinese-owned, were to be permitted to bid for three new operating licences for casinos in the SAR. On 1 April 2002 Stanley Ho's STDM formally relinquished its long-standing monopoly on casinos. However, Ho retained influence in the gambling sector after his Sociedade de Jogos de Macau (SJM) won an 18-year licence to operate casinos.

In January 2002 Edmund Ho visited the mainland city of Chongqing, seeking to reinforce economic links between the two places, and stating that Macao would play a more active role in developing the region. Also in January, the Government granted permission to the Taipei Trade and Cultural Office (TTCO) to issue visas for Taiwan-bound visitors from Macao and the mainland. In February Li Peng, Chairman of the Standing Committee of the NPC, paid an official visit to Macao, where he held discussions with the Chief Executive of the SAR. During Li's visit, a leading Macao political activist, along with several activists from the Hong Kong-based April Fifth Action group, were arrested for planning to stage protests against Li for his role in the Tiananmen Square suppression of 1989 and in favour of the release of mainland political dissidents. The Hong Kong activists were immediately deported. In March 2002 a new representative office of the Macao SAR was established in Beijing, with the aim of enhancing links between the SAR and the mainland; Wu Beiming was named as its director. At its inaugural ceremony, Edmund Ho and Chinese Vice-Premier Qian Qichen praised the 'one country, two systems' model, and the director of the central Government's Liaison Office in Macao, Bai Zhijian, suggested that Macao might become a model for Taiwan's eventual reunification with the mainland.

In December 2002 Macao selected its 12 candidates for the 10th NPC, convened in Beijing in March 2003. Edmund Ho held a meeting with the new Chinese Premier, Wen Jiabao, in March at which the future development of Macao under the policy of 'one country, two systems' was discussed. In October 2003 Chinese Vice-President Zeng Qinghong visited Macao to attend the signing ceremony of the Closer Economic Partnership Arrangement (CEPA) between Macao and the Chinese mainland.

In November 2003 Edmund Ho outlined plans for administrative reform of Macao's Government, alongside legal reform, to begin in 2004. In June 2004 it was announced that the re-election of the Chief Executive would take place in late August. Edmund Ho began his election campaign in mid-August, and was duly re-elected on 29 August, securing 296 of the 300 votes of the members of the Election Committee.

In mid-2005 it was reported that the number of voters registered for the legislative elections scheduled for September had reached 220,653, almost one-half of the population of the SAR and an increase of some 35% compared with the number registered for the elections of 2001. At the elections, held on 25 September, the number of seats allocated by direct suffrage was increased from 10 to 12, bringing the total number of seats in the Legislative Council to 29. The pro-democracy AMN (ANMD) received the highest proportion of votes cast (18.8%) and secured two of the 12 directly elective seats. The Associação dos Cidadãos Unidos de Macau (ACUM), a citizens' association largely comprising immigrants from Fujian Province and advocating support for the gaming industry, also obtained two seats, while the pro-Beijing UPD and UPP retained their representation of two seats each in the legislature. Angela Leong On Kei, the wife of the influential businessman and casino owner Stanley Ho, was elected on the list of the Aliança para o Desenvolvimento de Macau (ADM). The remaining three seats were divided among Nova Esperança (NE), supported by civil servants and the ethnic Portuguese community, the União Geral para o Bem-querer de Macau (UBM) and CODEM. The turnout was evaluated at 58.4% of registered voters. The 10 indirectly elective seats, meanwhile, were distributed among the same functional constituencies as in 2001.

In September 2005 the US Administration asserted that the Government of the Democratic People's Republic of Korea (North Korea) had been laundering and counterfeiting money through a Macao bank, Banco Delta Asia (BDA). The Macao authorities took control of the bank pending an inquiry into its activities, and the assets held within these accounts, believed to total US $25m., were frozen. A three-month investigation by Chinese officials reportedly concluded in January 2006 that the allegations were accurate. In February it was announced that BDA was terminating its links with North Korea and that independent accountants had been appointed to monitor the bank's clients. In October an audit conducted by Ernst & Young, an international accounting company, reported that it had found no evidence to suggest that the bank had knowingly facilitated money-laundering activities. However, following the completion of an 18-month investigation, in March 2007 US Treasury officials concluded that the bank had deliberately disregarded illicit activities and ordered US banks and companies to terminate all links with BDA. The Monetary Authority of Macao expressed deep regret at this conclusion. The North Korean assets in question were to be released and transferred to a mainland Chinese bank. A Russian bank subsequently agreed to act as intermediary for the transfer of the funds, which was carried out in late June (see the Democratic People's Republic of Korea). In September the Monetary Authority of Macao announced that control of BDA was being restored to its Chairman, Stanley Au, partly because the bank had shown an improvement in its practices. The US Treasury's measures, despite a legal challenge filed by the bank, remained in effect.

Although the next elections for Macao's Legislative Council were not due to take place until the latter part of 2009, it was reported in 2006 that bogus associations were being established in an apparent attempt to influence the outcome of the future poll. The majority of these newly founded nominal organizations were sports groups, part of the category responsible for choosing two of the Legislative Council's 10 indirectly elected members. The legitimacy of the SAR's Election Committee, responsible for choosing Macao's next Chief Executive in 2009, was also believed to be compromised, with 80 of its 300 members due to be selected by the constituency of culture, education and sport. Under electoral rules, associations were required to have been established for at least three years in order to be eligible to vote, hence the proliferation of these organizations prior to the deadline in 2006.

In December 2006 the Chief Executive ordered the arrest of Ao Man Long, Secretary for Transport and Public Works, and that of 11 others. Ao was subsequently charged on 76 corruption-related counts, including accepting bribes and money-laundering; he was alleged to have misappropriated 800m. patacas and to have amassed a considerable personal fortune. Ao was alleged to have collaborated with his relatives to register a number of bogus companies abroad in order to launder the bribes that he had reportedly received. In January 2008, having been found guilty of 57 of the charges against him, Ao was sentenced to 27 years' imprisonment. In June Ao's wife, three members of his family and three business associates were also convicted of various money-laundering and bribery charges. In April 2009 and May 2012 Ao was convicted of additional similar charges.

At a May Day labour rally in 2007, demonstrators protesting against alleged corruption and the use of illegal workers in the SAR demanded the resignation of Edmund Ho as Chief Executive. In this unusual display of civil unrest, there were violent clashes between thousands of protesters and several hundred police officers, armed with batons and pepper spray. Another demonstration took place in October. Amid increasing popular concern about the rapid pace of change and the perceived deterioration in the quality of life in Macao, in December hundreds attended a further protest against corruption, this time coinciding with the eighth anniversary of the establishment of the SAR. Meanwhile, in August 2007 it was alleged in the media that Edmund Ho owned shares in Many Town Company, a Hong Kong-based business with interests in STDM; the Government issued a denial, claiming that Ho's shares had been transferred to his brother in 1995. During 2007 Macao superseded Las Vegas, USA, as the world's most lucrative gambling centre. In April 2008 the Chief Executive introduced new measures that limited the number of gaming licences to six, ruling out the building of any new casinos, as the Chinese Government encouraged a shift in emphasis to other areas of the economy. However, the construction of a new casino was approved in May 2012, while a very gradual increase in the number of gaming tables was being permitted, in an indication that restrictions were being eased. During 2008 the administration attempted to alleviate the rising cost of living by introducing a Wealth Sharing Scheme, which provided annual cash payments to residents.

In December 2008 more than 20 Hong Kong activists, who had planned to attend a demonstration against proposed legislation relating to the security of Macao, were barred from entering the SAR. In February 2009 the Legislative Council overwhelmingly approved the National Security Bill, prohibiting acts of treason, secession, sedition or subversion against the Chinese Government and outlawing the theft of state secrets. The legislation provided for prison sentences of up to 30 years for those convicted of such crimes. Fearing that the law was open to abuse by the authorities, various human rights groups, including Amnesty International, criticized the ambiguous wording of the law, particularly the reference to ill-defined 'preparatory acts'. Furthermore, shortly after the promulgation of the law in early March, various Hong Kong residents, including the dean of the faculty of law at the University of Hong Kong, pro-democracy politicians and a photographer, were prohibited from entering Macao.

Meanwhile, in January 2008 Macao conducted its election of deputies to the mainland Chinese legislature. The electoral conference, comprising more than 300 representatives of various sectors of Macao society, selected 12 deputies, who were to attend the 11th NPC, convened in Beijing in March.

Recent developments: the elections of 2009 and beyond

The election for Edmund Ho's replacement as Chief Executive of the SAR took place in July 2009. Fernando Chui Sai On, the former Secretary for Social Affairs and Culture, was elected unopposed to the post by the Election Committee. The legislative elections were held on 20 September 2009, with the level of participation reported to be 60% of the electorate. The pro-Beijing UPD and the ACUM each won two of the 12 seats determined by direct election, while the pro-democracy AMN, using two electoral lists, namely the ANMD (as before) and the Associação de Próspero Macau Democrático (APMD) took three seats. The remaining five seats were won by: the pro-Beijing UPP; the Nova União para o Desenvolvimento de Macau (NUDM, formerly the ADM), representing the interests of the gaming sector; the pro-democracy NE, representing civil servants; the União Macau-Guangdong (UMG), promoting business links with the mainland; and the Aliança para a Mudança (MUDAR), a business-based alliance advocating public reform. As previously, four of the 10 indirectly elective seats were taken by representatives of business interests; two by representatives of the professional sector; two by representatives of labour interests; and two by members of the welfare, cultural, educational and sports sectors.

Fernando Chui's five-year term of office commenced on 20 December 2009. The incoming Chief Executive retained the four incumbent Secretaries, and Cheong U was appointed as Secretary for Social Affairs and Culture. In his first policy address, delivered in March 2010, the Chief Executive focused on issues of social welfare, announcing the continuation of various measures to provide financial support for the residents of Macao (see Economic Affairs), along with subsidies to assist disadvantaged families and other needy citizens, particularly the elderly. In an acknowledgement of increasing public concern with regard to the issue of corruption in Macao, Chui also pledged to improve the transparency and integrity of the civil service. The probity of public servants was to be more closely supervised by the Commission Against Corruption; in particular, details of the property transactions of government officials were to be made publicly available. The Commission Against Corruption subsequently agreed to establish a permanent working group with its counterparts in neighbouring Guangdong Province and in Hong Kong.

In June 2010 it was announced that, in order to assist the Chief Executive in the area of policy-making, a new government institute was to be established. This policy institute was to be responsible for conducting research on political, economic and legal issues, as well as various other matters.

During an official visit to Portugal in June 2010 Chui had discussions with President Aníbal Cavaco Silva and other senior government members. With the objective of revitalizing bilateral relations and of promoting co-operation in the areas of trade, investment in tourism, education and culture, it was agreed that meetings of a Joint Commission, originally envisaged under the agreement concluded in 2001 (see above), would take place annually.

Amid much public criticism, draft legislation to provide civil servants with financial aid, either if being sued or if pursuing a lawsuit on a matter arising from the performance of their public duty, was under consideration in mid-2010. Critics of the proposed legislation included Susana Chou, former President of the Legislative Assembly, who denounced it as a serious violation of the Basic Law. Media organizations, in particular, expressed concern for the freedom of the press, fearing that such a law might be used to support legal action against newspaper reporters. The most controversial parts of the proposal were subsequently abandoned by the Macao Government.

In November 2010 the Chief Executive announced that, following public consultation, the Government had decided to exclude the development of casino premises from the urban planning for newly reclaimed land; the areas in question were to be used only for the purposes of the development of residential housing, along with local industries that would help to diversify the economy. The SAR's dependence on gambling was becoming a matter of urgent concern: despite recent efforts to promote conventional tourism, conferences and exhibitions, the gambling sector was by far Macao's principal source of income, contributing more than three-quarters of government revenue in 2010. Since casinos were not permitted in mainland China, Macao attracted many mainland gamblers, including not only wealthy entrepreneurs but also senior officials and the managers of state-owned industries, some of whom were suspected of gambling with illicitly obtained funds, at a time when corruption had been identified as a major problem.

In December 2010 it was announced that the wife of the 89-year-old Stanley Ho, Angela Leong (now representing the NUDM in the legislature), had replaced him as managing director of SJM, Macao's principal casino operating company. In early 2011 various disputes were reported between Ho and his numerous relatives concerning the eventual control of the companies that he had founded, which not only dominated the gambling sector but also included major interests in the hotel industry, the SAR's airline and airport, ferry services to Hong Kong, bus services to the Chinese mainland, and the retail sector.

In March 2011 the Chief Executive of Macao and the Governor of the adjacent Guangdong Province signed the Guangdong-Macao Co-operation Framework Agreement, whereby the two areas were to co-operate in the development of local industries, the construction of infrastructural facilities, the provision of public services and in development planning. In July the Beijing Government appointed Hu Zhengyue to replace Lu Shumin as commissioner of the Ministry of Foreign Affairs in the Macao SAR.

To address concerns regarding the adverse affects of gambling on Macao's inhabitants, in August 2012 the Legislative Council approved legislation regulating entry conditions for casinos: with effect from November, the minimum legal age to enter and work in a casino was raised from 18 to 21 years, while individuals who were concerned about their gambling were able to request a ban on their entry to casinos. Some 150 people were arrested in late August, when police raided casinos and hotels in response to a number of violent crimes connected to the gambling industry, including the murders of three Chinese nationals. The notorious criminal Wan Kuok-koi (see above) was released from prison in December, prompting the authorities to warn casinos and hotels to tighten security, but his power was believed to have waned considerably, owing to the transformation of the gambling industry during the period of his incarceration. The gambling sector experienced a marked deceleration in annual revenue growth in 2012, to 13% (compared with 42% in 2011), which was attributed to the slowing of economic growth in mainland China, together with restrictions on credit and measures to combat corruption there. Investment by the six companies licensed to conduct gambling activities in Macao continued, however, with major new 'resorts' planned, particularly in the Cotai area of reclaimed land: despite efforts by the authorities to increase the provision of non-gambling attractions for visitors, casinos continued to feature prominently in these new developments. The completion of the bridge and tunnel link between Hong Kong, Zhuhai, on the mainland, and Macao (due to open in 2016) was expected to provide speedier access to Macao and increase the number of visitors from the mainland (who numbered almost 17m., about 60% of all visitors, in 2012). It was anticipated that 'mass market' gambling would gradually provide a larger share of the sector's revenue, reducing the proportion (some 70% in 2012) provided by 'VIP' gambling, i.e. wealthy individuals betting large amounts of money, sometimes of dubious provenance.

Following the approval of the NPC, the Legislative Council adopted amendments to the Basic Law at the end of August 2012. The number of seats in the Council was to increase from 29 to 33 at the legislative elections due in September 2013, with two additional deputies to be selected by direct election and two by indirect election. Also, with effect from the 2014 election of the Chief Executive, the Election Committee would expand from 300 members to 400.

The election of Macao's deputies to the mainland Chinese legislature took place in December 2012. From 15 candidates, the electoral conference of 359 members selected 12 deputies (10 of whom were re-elected) to attend the 12th NPC, which convened in Beijing in March 2013.

Legislative elections took place in Macao on 15 September 2013. Twenty groups presented a total of 145 candidates for the 14 seats now subject to direct election: some 55% of the registered electorate participated. Reports of benefits being illicitly offered to voters led the Commissioner Against Corruption, Fong Man Chong, to state that in some cases the participants had 'tested the boundary of legality'. The majority of the 14 elective seats were won, as before, by 'pro-establishment' groups supportive of the Beijing Government and/or representing business interests, in particular the gambling sector. Of the business interest groups, the ACUM won three seats (compared with two previously), the UMG two (gaining one), and the NUDM and the MUDAR one each. Of the two groups regarded as particularly pro-Beijing, the UPP won two seats (a gain of one) and the UPD one (a loss of one). Of the pro-democracy groups, the AMN, through its APMD and ANMD electoral lists, won two seats (one fewer than in 2009), and the NE also secured two (an increase of one). The 12 indirectly elective seats (none of which was contested) were allocated to the same functional constituencies as at the previous elections, but representatives of welfare services and education were now given a separate seat (having previously shared two with cultural and sports representatives), and an extra seat was also allocated to professional interests. The remaining seven seats were subject to appointment by the Chief Executive.

In January 2014 Bai Zhijian, the director of the central Government's Liaison Office in Macao, retired, and was replaced by Li Gang (hitherto the deputy director). In February it was announced that a total of 825 associations, representing various sectors (including no fewer than 313 under the category of sports associations), were to choose 344 of the 400 members of the expanded Election Committee for electing the Chief Executive later in the year (the remainder being members of the legislature and deputies to the NPC and the Chinese People's Political Consultative Conference). It was widely expected that Fernando Chui would be elected to a second term of office. In February the leader of the AMN, Jason Chao, declared that the AMN would conduct a parallel 'election' at the same time, and would campaign for universal adult suffrage in the next legislative elections, due to be held in 2017, and in the election to the post of Chief Executive in 2019.

CONSTITUTION AND GOVERNMENT

The Macao Special Administrative Region (SAR) is governed by a Chief Executive, chosen by an Election Committee, which was to comprise 400 members with effect from the election due in 2014 (increased from 300 in an amendment adopted in mid-2012). The Chief Executive is accountable to the State Council of China, the term of office being five years, with a limit of two consecutive terms. Upon the territory's transfer to Chinese sovereignty in December 1999, a 10-member Executive Council, appointed by the Chief Executive to assist in policy-making, assumed office. The Chief Executive is assisted in administration by five Secretaries, who hold individual portfolios. In 2001 the Legislative Council (commonly referred to as the Legislative Assembly) was expanded from 23 to 27 members, of whom 10 were directly elected, 10 indirectly elected and seven appointed by the Chief Executive, all with a mandate of four years. In 2005 the membership of the Legislative Council was increased to 29, to incorporate two additional deputies to be chosen by direct election; the composition remained unchanged at the 2009 legislative elections. At the 2013 legislative elections the membership of the Legislative Council was increased to 33, of whom 14 were directly elected, 12 indirectly elected and seven appointed. For the purposes of local government, the islands of Taipa and Coloane are administered separately. Macao selects 12 deputies to attend the National People's Congress in Beijing.

REGIONAL AND INTERNATIONAL CO-OPERATION

Macao is an associate member of the UN's Economic and Social Commission for Asia and the Pacific (ESCAP, see p. 28).

In 1991 Macao became a party to the General Agreement on Tariffs and Trade (GATT, subsequently superseded by the World Trade Organization—WTO, see p. 434). Macao retained its membership of WTO after December 1999. Macao also remained a 'privileged partner' of the European Union.

ECONOMIC AFFAIRS

In 2011, according to estimates by the World Bank, Macao's gross national income (GNI), measured at average 2009–11 prices, was US $30,440m., equivalent to $55,720 per head (or $68,710 per head on an international purchasing-power parity basis). During 2003–12, it was estimated, the population increased at an average annual rate of 2.4%, while gross domestic product (GDP) per head increased, in real terms, by an average of 11.3% per year. According to the World Bank, overall GDP rose, in real terms, at an average annual rate of 13.9% in 2003–12; GDP increased by 9.9% in 2012.

Agriculture is of minor importance, engaging only 0.4% of the economically active population in 2011. The main crops are rice and vegetables. Cattle, pigs and chickens are reared. Macao is heavily reliant on imports for its food supplies.

Industry (including manufacturing, construction and public utilities) accounted for 4.1% of GDP in 2011. The sector engaged 13.4% of the economically active population in July–September 2013. The mining sector is negligible.

The manufacturing sector contributed 0.4% of GDP in 2011. The sector engaged 2.5% of the economically active population in July–September 2013. The most important manufacturing industry is the production of textiles and garments. Although exports of textile items and garments have continued to decrease, from 1,070m. patacas in 2011 to only 889m. patacas in 2012, the sector nevertheless accounted for 10.9% of the value of total exports in the latter year. The significance of other manufacturing industries, such as footwear, furniture and jewellery, has declined.

In 2011 the construction sector contributed 3.1% of GDP. The sector engaged 10.5% of the economically active population in July–September 2013.

Macao possesses few natural resources. Energy is derived principally from imported petroleum. Imports of petroleum and its products accounted for 5.7% of total import costs in 2012. The territory receives some of its electricity and water supplies from mainland China.

The services sector accounted for 95.9% of GDP in 2011. The sector employed 86.4% of the economically active population in July–September 2013. At the end of June 2013 a total of 54,554 workers were engaged in the gaming sector. Tourism and gambling activities make a substantial contribution to the territory's economy. At the end of

2012 six concessionaires were operating a total of 35 casinos in Macao, 20 of which were managed by the Sociedade de Jogos de Macau (SJM). Gross revenue from games of fortune increased from 46,047m. patacas in 2005 to 304,138m. patacas in 2012. The Government's revenue from gambling taxes reached 113,377m. patacas in 2012, representing 78.2% of total public revenue. Receipts from tourism totalled an estimated US $43,707m. in 2012. Tourist arrivals increased from almost 25m. in 2010 to more than 28m. in 2012. In 2012 60.2% of visitors came from mainland China and 25.2% from Hong Kong.

Legislation regulating offshore banking was introduced in 1987. A law enacted in 1995 aimed to attract overseas investment by offering the right of abode in Macao to entrepreneurs with substantial funds at their disposal. From December 1999, upon the territory's reversion to Chinese sovereignty, Macao continued to administer its own finances and was exempt from taxes imposed by central government. The pataca was retained, remaining freely convertible.

In 2012, according to the IMF, Macao recorded a visible merchandise trade deficit of US $8,794.8m., but registered a surplus of US $19,018.3m. on the current account of the balance of payments. The principal sources of imports in 2012 were China (which supplied 32.7% of the total), followed by Hong Kong, France, Germany, Switzerland, Italy, Japan and the USA. The principal market for exports was Hong Kong (which purchased 50.2%), followed by China and the USA. The main exports were machines and apparatus, tobacco and spirits, and electrical and electronic equipment. The principal imports were beverages and tobacco, chemicals, petroleum products, and clothing and accessories. After December 1999 Macao retained its status as a free port and remained a separate customs territory.

A budget surplus of 90,981.9m. patacas was recorded in 2012. According to ILO, the average annual rate of inflation (including rents) between 2003 and 2012 was 4.5%. Consumer prices rose by 6.1% in 2012. The rate of unemployment was 1.9% in the period from July to September 2013, while underemployment was 0.6% in the period from November 2012 to January 2013.

In accordance with the Closer Economic Partnership Arrangement (CEPA), which came into effect at the beginning of 2004, successive agreements liberalized trade in goods and services between Macao and mainland China, and facilitated investment and travel between the two. Despite various attempts to diversify, gambling-related tourism has continued to dominate the economy of Macao. In November 2008, in response to the global financial crisis and the resultant decline in the SAR's gambling revenues, measures to support the economy were announced. Various new infrastructural projects, including public housing, were initiated, and subsidies were made available to homebuyers, in an effort to stimulate the property market. A Wealth Sharing Scheme was introduced, whereby lump sum payments were to be distributed to all residents: the scheme was continued in subsequent years, with the annual payments announced in November 2013 increasing to 9,000 patacas for permanent residents and 5,400 patacas for non-permanent residents. Macao's GDP grew by only 1.7% in 2009, but a robust recovery took place during 2010, when GDP expanded by 27.0%, with the earnings of the gambling sector increasing by 58%, to US $23,500m., contributing some 41% of GDP. There was further strong GDP growth of 20.7% in 2011, when revenue from gambling increased again, by 42%, to some $33,500m. The economy of Macao slowed in 2012, in tandem with that of mainland China, with GDP growth of 9.9%, while growth in gambling revenue (amounting to $38,000m.) decelerated to 13% and tourist numbers increased by only 0.3%, compared with 12.2% in 2011. In 2013 revenue from gambling increased by 18.6%, totalling $45,000m., while the total number of visitors increased by 4% to 29.3m., of whom 18.6m. were from the mainland. Investment by the six companies licensed to operate casinos in Macao continued, with several new resorts, combining casinos, luxury shopping areas and hotels, under construction in 2012 and 2013. The average rate of unemployment remained low in 2013, at 1.8%, reflecting a shortage of labour. Inflationary pressures persisted, with consumer prices rising by an average of 5.5% during the year. In November 2012, in a continued effort to diversify the economy and reduce dependence on the gambling sector, the Chief Executive pledged support to the 'MICE' sector (meetings, incentives, conventions and exhibitions) and announced the provision of interest-free loans to young entrepreneurs. Construction of a series of bridges linking Macao with Hong Kong and with Zhuhai, on the mainland, was due to be completed in 2015. The new bridges, which were scheduled to be opened in 2016 were expected to increase the speed of access to Macao for tourists and traders.

PUBLIC HOLIDAYS

2015: 1 January (New Year), 19–25 February (Chinese Lunar New Year), 3 April (Good Friday), 5 April (Ching Ming), 6 April (Easter Monday), 1 May (Labour Day), 25 May (Feast of Buddha), 20 June (Dragon Boat Festival), 27 September (Chinese Mid-Autumn Festival), 1–2 October (National Day of the People's Republic of China and day following), 2 October (Festival of Ancestors—Chung Yeung), 2 November (All Souls' Day), 8 December (Immaculate Conception), 20 December (SAR Establishment Day), 22 December (Winter Solstice), 24–25 December (Christmas).

Statistical Survey

Source (unless otherwise indicated): Direcção dos Serviços de Estatística e Censos, Alameda Dr Carlos d'Assumpção 411–417, Dynasty Plaza, 17° andar, Macao; tel. 83995311; fax 28307825; e-mail info@dsec.gov.mo; internet www.dsec.gov.mo.

AREA AND POPULATION

Area (2012): 29.9 sq km (11.54 sq miles), comprising Macao peninsula 9.3, Taipa island 7.4, Coloane island 7.6, Cotai Reclamation Area 5.6.

Population: 502,113 (males 245,167, females 256,946) according to results of by-census of 19 August 2006 (491,482 were classed as usual residents and 10,631 as mobile residents); 552,503 (males 265,144, females 287,359) at census of 12 August 2011 (529,320 were classed as usual residents and 23,183 as mobile residents). *31 December 2012* ('000, official estimates): 582.0 (males 280.3, females 301.7).

Density (at 31 December 2012): 19,464.8 per sq km.

Population by Age and Sex ('000, official estimates at 31 December 2012): *0–14:* 67.4 (males 35.1, females 32.3); *15–64:* 470.0 (males 224.6, females 245.4); *65 and over:* 44.6 (males 20.6, females 24.0); *Total* 582.0 (males 280.3, females 301.7).

Population by Nationality (at 2011 census): Chinese 509,788; Portuguese 5,020.

Population by Parish ('000, official estimates at 31 December 2012): Santo António 127.4; São Lázaro 32.5; São Lourenço 50.6; Sé 50.0; Nossa Senhora de Fátima 231.1; Taipa 84.7; Coloane 5.0; Maritime 0.7; Total 582.0.

Births, Marriages and Deaths (2012): Registered live births 7,315 (birth rate 12.6 per 1,000); Registered marriages 3,783 (marriage rate 6.5 per 1,000); Registered deaths 1,841 (death rate 3.2 per 1,000).

Life Expectancy (years at birth, 2012): 82.4 (males 79.1; females 85.7).

Economically Active Population ('000 persons aged 16 years and over, July–September 2013): Manufacturing 9.1; Production and distribution of electricity, gas and water 1.6; Construction 38.2; Wholesale and retail trade, repair of motor vehicles, motorcycles and personal and household goods 44.0; Hotels, restaurants and similar activities 52.4; Transport, storage and communications 15.6; Financial services 9.8; Real estate, renting and services to companies 28.4; Public administration, defence and compulsory social security 27.1; Education 14.4; Health and social work 9.0; Other community, social and personal service activities 93.8; Private households with employed persons 20.2; Not classifiable by economic activity 0.7; *Total employed* 364.3 (males 186.5, females 177.8); Unemployed 6.9; *Total labour force* 371.2 (males 191.1, females 180.1).

HEALTH AND WELFARE

Key Indicators

Under-5 Mortality Rate (per 1,000 live births, 2012): 2.5.

HIV/AIDS (% persons aged 15–49, 2008): 0.1.

Physicians (per 1,000 head, 2012): 2.5.

Hospital Beds (per 1,000 head, 2012): 2.3.

Human Development Index (2011): value 0.868.

For definitions, see explanatory note on p. vi.

AGRICULTURE, ETC.

(since 2004 no separate data available for livestock—see the chapter on the People's Republic of China)

Livestock ('000 head, 2004): Poultry 700 (FAO estimate).

Livestock Products ('000 metric tons, 2004): Beef and veal 1.1; Pig meat 9.6; Poultry meat 6.5 (FAO estimate); Hen eggs 1.0 (FAO estimate).

Fishing (metric tons, live weight, 2011, FAO estimates): Marine fishes 1,020; Shrimps and prawns 230; Other marine crustaceans 210; Total catch (incl. others) 1,500.

Source: FAO.

INDUSTRY

Production (2003 unless otherwise indicated): Wine 700,745 litres; Knitwear 36.18m. units; Footwear 12.13m. pairs; Clothing 230.73m. units; Furniture 5,253 units; Electric energy 560.9 million kWh (2012).

FINANCE

Currency and Exchange Rates: 100 avos = 1 pataca. *Sterling, Dollar and Euro Equivalents* (31 December 2013): £1 sterling = 13.153 patacas; US $1 = 7.987 patacas; €1 = 11.015 patacas; 100 patacas = £7.60 = $12.52 = €9.08. *Average Exchange Rate* (patacas per US dollar): 8.018 in 2011; 7.990 in 2012; 7.989 in 2013. Note: The pataca has a fixed link with the value of the Hong Kong dollar (HK $1 = 1.030 patacas).

Budget (million patacas, 2012): *Revenue:* Current revenue 130,217.5 (Direct taxes 111,962.7, Indirect taxes 4,956.7, Property income 3,498.7, Transfers 6,523.7, Other current revenue 3,275.6); Capital revenue 14,777.0; Total 144,994.5. *Expenditure:* Payroll 12,090.3; Goods and services 7,835.9; Current transfers 15,088.3; Other current expenditure 1,802.3; Capital expenditure 17,195.8; Total 54,012.6.

International Reserves (million patacas, 2012): Total (all foreign exchange) 132,536.0.

Money Supply (million patacas at 31 December 2012): Currency outside depository corporations 7,068.6; Transferable deposits 40,054.6; Other deposits 326,707.4; Securities other than shares 204.9; *Broad money* 374,035.5. Source: IMF, *International Financial Statistics*.

Cost of Living (Consumer Price Index; base: April 2008–March 2009 = 100): All items 104.25 in 2010; 110.30 in 2011; 117.04 in 2012.

Expenditure on the Gross Domestic Product (million patacas at current prices, 2012): Government final consumption expenditure 23,579.4; Private consumption expenditure 69,376.1; Changes in inventories 4,810.0; Gross fixed capital formation 46,518.0; *Total domestic expenditure* 144,283.5; Exports of goods and services 377,034.1; *Less* Imports of goods and services 173,101.2; *GDP in purchasers' values* 348,216.4.

Gross Domestic Product by Economic Activity (million patacas at current prices, 2011): Mining and quarrying 13.3; Manufacturing 1,321.0; Electricity, gas and water supply 1,596.4; Construction 9,211.3; Wholesale, retail, repair, restaurants and hotels 30,889.2; Transport, storage and communications 6,216.5; Financial intermediation, real estate, renting and business activities 34,827.0; Public administration, other community, social and personal services (incl. gaming services) 210,142.1; *GDP at basic prices* 294,216.7; Taxes on products (net) 411.2; Statistical discrepancy (representing the difference between the expenditure and production approaches) 418.4; *GDP at market prices* 295,046.3.

Balance of Payments (US $ million, 2012): Exports of goods 1,383.8; Imports of goods −10,178.5; *Balance on goods* −8,794.8; Exports of services 45,811.1; Imports of services −11,352.2; *Balance on goods and services* 25,664.1; Primary income received 2,262.0; Primary income paid −7,773.7; *Balance on goods, services and primary income* 20,152.5; Secondary income received 70.0; Secondary income paid −1,204.2; *Current balance* 19,018.3; Direct investment assets −114.6; Direct investment liabilities 4,261.3; Portfolio investment assets −910.6; Portfolio investment liabilities 420.3; Financial derivatives and employee stock options (net) 61.0; Other investment assets −21,339.2; Other investment liabilities 4,258.0; Net errors and omissions −1,883.7; *Reserves and related items* 3,770.7. Source: IMF, *International Financial Statistics*.

EXTERNAL TRADE

Principal Commodities (million patacas, 2012): *Imports c.i.f.* (distribution by SITC): Live animals (excl. marine) 442.2; Vegetables and fruits 644.7; Beverages and tobacco 4,265.8 (Beverages 3,572.6); Petroleum, petroleum products, etc. 4,076.6; Chemicals 4,270.1 (Essential oils, etc. 2,486.3); Textile yarn, fabrics, etc. 564.2; Clothing and accessories 3,691.4; Iron and steel 1,140.1; Office machines 2,703.3; Electrical machinery, apparatus, etc. 1,776.8; Road vehicles 3,048.8; Total (incl. others) 70,927.8. *Exports f.o.b.:* Tobacco and spirits 768.3; Copper and copper articles 371.5; Cotton garments (knitted and crocheted) 316.0; Cotton garments (excl. knitted and crocheted) 300.2; Radios, televisions, image and sound recorders and reproducers 88.5; Electrical and electronic equipment 629.8; Machines and apparatus 1,426.0; Jewellery 246.5; Total (incl. others) 8,159.7 (incl. re-exports 5,874.7).

Principal Trading Partners (million patacas, 2012): *Imports c.i.f.:* China, People's Republic 23,199.4; France 6,196.4; Germany 1,710.7; Hong Kong 8,211.1; Italy 5,386.5; Japan 4,244.0; Korea, Republic 1,695.3; Malaysia 892.4; Singapore 1,470.6; Switzerland 5,608.4; Taiwan 1,403.1; Thailand 930.4; United Kingdom 1,691.5; USA 3,679.6; Total (incl. others) 70,927.8. *Exports f.o.b.:* China, People's Republic 1,369.0; Germany 81.9; Hong Kong 4,095.4; Japan 162.2; USA 507.3; Viet Nam 135.8; Total (incl. others) 8,159.7 (incl. re-exports 5,874.7).

TRANSPORT

Road Traffic (motor vehicles in use, October 2013): Light vehicles 100,239; Heavy vehicles 6,867; Motorcycles 118,318.

Shipping (international sea-borne containerized freight traffic, '000 metric tons, 2012): Goods imported 183.6; Goods exported 17.7.

Civil Aviation (2012 unless otherwise indicated): Passenger arrivals 1,842,074 (2008 figure); Passenger departures 1,934,393 (2008 figure); Goods loaded (metric tons) 16,348; Goods unloaded (metric tons) 6,393.

TOURISM

Visitor Arrivals by Country of Residence (2012): China, People's Republic 16,902,499; Hong Kong 7,081,153; Taiwan 1,072,052; Total (incl. others) 28,082,292.

Receipts from Tourism (US $ million, excl. passenger transport): 27,802 in 2010; 38,453 in 2011; 43,707 in 2012 (provisional) (Source: World Tourism Organization).

COMMUNICATIONS MEDIA

Telephones (2012): 162,500 main lines in use.

Mobile Cellular Telephones (2012): 1,613,500 subscribers.

Internet Subscribers (2011): 138,200.

Broadband Subscribers (2012): 144,400.

Source: International Telecommunication Union.

EDUCATION

(2012/13 unless otherwise indicated)

Kindergarten: 57 schools; 765 teachers; 12,669 pupils.

Primary: 60 schools; 1,622 teachers; 22,231 pupils.

Secondary: 43 schools; 2,587 teachers; 33,921 pupils.

Vocational/Technical (2010/11): 10 schools; 172 teachers; 1,527 pupils.

Higher: 10 institutions; 1,914 teaching staff; 27,776 students.

Pupil-teacher Ratio (primary education, UNESCO estimate): 14.1 in 2011/12 (Source: UNESCO Institute for Statistics).

Adult Literacy Rate: 95.6% (males 97.8%, females 93.7%) in 2011 (Source: UNESCO Institute for Statistics).

Note: for non-tertiary education, figures for schools and teachers refer to all those for which the category is applicable. Some schools and teachers provide education at more than one level. Institutions of higher education refer to those recognized by the Government of Macao Special Administrative Region.

Directory

The Government

Chief Executive: FERNANDO CHUI SAI ON (took office 20 December 2009).

SECRETARIES

(April 2014)

Secretary for Administration and Justice: FLORINDA DA ROSA SILVA CHAN.

Secretary for Economy and Finance: FRANCIS TAM PAK YUEN.

Secretary for Security: CHEONG KUOC VA.

Secretary for Social Affairs and Culture: CHEONG U.

Secretary for Transport and Public Works: LAU SI IO.

GOVERNMENT OFFICES

Office of the Chief Executive: Sede do Governo, Av. da Praia Grande; tel. 28726886; fax 28725468; internet www.gov.mo.

Executive Council: Sede do Governo, Av. da Praia Grande; tel. 28726886; fax 89895704; Sec.-Gen. O LAM.

Office of the Secretary for Administration and Justice: Rua de S. Lourenço 28, Sede do Governo, 4º andar; tel. 28726886; fax 28726880; internet www.gov.mo.

Office of the Secretary for Economy and Finance: Edif. do Banca da China 307–323, Avda Dr Mário Soares, 23º andar; tel. 28787350; fax 28726302; internet www.gov.mo.

Office of the Secretary for Security: Calçada dos Quartéis, Quartel de S. Francisco; tel. 87997501; fax 28580702; internet www.gov.mo.

Office of the Secretary for Social Affairs and Culture: Rua de S. Lourenço 28, Sede do Governo, 2º andar; tel. 28726886; fax 28727594; internet www.gov.mo.

Office of the Secretary for Transport and Public Works: Edif. Banca da China 307–323, Avda Dr Mário Soares, 26º andar; tel. 28786919; fax 28727566; internet www.gov.mo.

Macao Government Information Bureau: Gabinete de Comunicação Social do Governo de Macau, Av. da Praia Grande 762–804, Edif. China Plaza, 15° andar; tel. 28332886; fax 28355426; e-mail info@gcs.gov.mo; internet www.gcs.gov.mo; Dir VICTOR CHAN CHI PING.

Economic Services Bureau: Direção dos Serviços de Economia, Rua Dr Pedro José Lobo 1–3, Edif. Banco Luso Internacional, 6°–7° andares; tel. 28386937; fax 28590310; e-mail info@economia.gov.mo; internet www.economia.gov.mo; Dir SOU TIM PENG.

Legislature

LEGISLATIVE COUNCIL (LEGISLATIVE ASSEMBLY)

The Legislative Assembly was superseded by the Legislative Council under the terms of the Basic Law, implemented in 1999. In practice, however, the legislature continues to be referred to as the Legislative Assembly. It currently comprises 33 members: seven appointed by the Chief Executive, 14 elected directly (geographical constituencies) and 12 indirectly (functional constituencies). Members serve for four years. The Assembly chooses its President from among its members, by secret vote. At the elections held on 15 September 2013 the pro-Beijing Associação dos Cidadãos Unidos de Macau (ACUM), which also supports the gaming industry, received the highest number of votes cast and secured three of the 14 directly elective seats. The pro-democracy Associação de Macau Novo (AMN) won two seats, as did the pro-business União de Macau-Guangdong (UMG). The pro-Beijing União Promotora para o Progresso (UPP) and pro-democracy Nova Esperança (NE), supported by civil servants, also secured two seats each. The following three groupings each took one seat: the Nova União para o Desenvolvimento de Macau (NUDM), which promotes the interests of the gaming sector; the União para o Desenvolvimento (UPD), which is a pro-establishment party; and the Aliança para a Mudança (MUDAR), which advocates public reform. The 12 members of the functional constituency seats were elected uncontested from representatives of five sectors: the business sector (four seats), the professional sector (three), the labour sector (two), the culture and sport sector (two) and the welfare and educational sector (one). Turnout was 55.02% for the directly elective seats.

Legislative Council (Legislative Assembly): Praça da Assembléia Legislativa, Edif. da Assembléia Legislativa, Aterros da Baía da Praia Grande; tel. 28728377; fax 28727857; e-mail info@al.gov.mo; internet www.al.gov.mo.

President: LAU CHEOK VA.

Political Organizations

There are no formal political parties, but various registered civic associations exist and may participate in elections for the Legislative Council by presenting a list of candidates (see Legislature). A total of 20 interest groups, with 145 candidates, contested the directly elected seats in the legislative elections of 15 September 2013.

Judicial System

Formal autonomy was granted to the territory's judiciary in 1993. A new penal code took effect in January 1996. Macao operates its own five major codes, namely the Penal Code, the Code of Criminal Procedure, the Civil Code, the Code of Civil Procedure and the Commercial Code. In 1999 the authority of final appeal was granted to Macao. The judicial system operates independently of the mainland Chinese system.

The judicial system has three tiers: the Court of Final Appeal, the Intermediate Court and the First Trial Court.

Court of Final Appeal (Tribunal de Ultima Instância): Praçeta 25 de Abril, Edif. dos Tribunais de Segunda Instância e Ultima Instância; tel. 83984117; fax 28326744; e-mail ptui@court.gov.mo; internet www.court.gov.mo; Pres. SAM HOU FAI.

Procurator-General: HO CHIO MENG.

Religion

The majority of residents profess Buddhism, and there are numerous places of worship, Daoism and Confucianism also being widely practised. The Christian community numbers about 30,000. There are small Muslim and Hindu communities.

CHRISTIANITY

The Roman Catholic Church

Macao forms a single diocese, directly responsible to the Holy See. At 31 December 2007 there were 28,242 adherents in the territory, comprising nearly 5.6% of the population.

Bishop of Macao: Rt Rev. JOSÉ LAI HUNG SENG, Paço Episcopal, Largo da Sé s/n, POB 324; tel. 28309954; fax 28309861; e-mail jesuitas@macau.ctm.net; internet www.catholic.org.mo.

The Anglican Communion

Macao forms part of the Anglican diocese of Hong Kong (q.v.).

The Press

A new Press Law, prescribing journalists' rights and obligations, was enacted in August 1990.

PORTUGUESE LANGUAGE

O Clarim: Rua Central 26A, 1° andar; tel. 28573860; fax 28307867; e-mail clarim@macau.ctm.net; internet www.oclarim.com.mo; f. 1948; weekly; Editor ALBINO BENTO PAIS; circ. 1,500.

Hoje Macau: Calçada de Santo Agostinho, Centro Comercial Nam Yue, 6° andar, Sala 1408; tel. 28752401; fax 28752405; e-mail info@hojemacau.com.mo; internet www.hojemacau.com; f. 2001; daily; Dir CARLOS MORAIS JOSÉ; circ. 1,500.

Jornal Tribuna de Macau: Av. Almeida Ribeiro 99, Edif. Comercial Nam Wah, 6° andar, Salas 603–05; tel. 28378057; fax 28337305; internet www.jtm.com.mo; f. 1998 through merger of Jornal de Macau (f. 1982) and Tribuna de Macau (f. 1982); daily; Dir JOSÉ FIRMINO DA ROCHA DINIS; circ. 1,000.

Ponto Final: Alameda Dr Carlos d'Assumpção; tel. 28339566; fax 28339563; e-mail editor@pontofinalmacau.com; internet pontofinalmacau.wordpress.com; daily; Publr RICARDO PINTO; Dir MARIA CAETANO; circ. 1,500.

CHINESE LANGUAGE

Cheng Pou: Av. da Praia Grande 57–63, Edif. Heng Chang, 1° andar, Bloco E–F; tel. 28965972; fax 28965741; e-mail chengpou@macau.ctm.net; internet www.chengpou.com.mo; daily; Dir KUNG SU KAN; Editor-in-Chief LEONG CHI CHUN; circ. 5,000.

Jornal Informação (Son Pou): Rua de Francisco 22, Edif. Mei Fun, 1° andar; tel. 28561557; fax 28566575; e-mail sonpou@macau.ctm.net; internet www.sonpou.com.mo; weekly; Dir CHAO CHONG PENG; circ. 8,000.

Jornal San Wa Ou: Av. Venceslau de Morais 231, Edif. Industrial Nam Fong, 15° andar, Bloco E–F; tel. 28717569; fax 28717572; e-mail correiro@macau.ctm.net; internet www.waou.com.mo; daily; Dir LAM CHONG ZHOU HAI YAN; circ. 1,500.

Jornal 'Si-Si': Av. Dr Rodrigues, Edif. Centro Comercial First National, 21° andar, Sala 2103; tel. and fax 28421333; e-mail sisinews@hotmail.com; internet www.jornalsisi.com; weekly; Dir and Editor-in-Chief SZE LEE AH; circ. 3,000.

Jornal Va Kio: Rua da Alfândega 69; tel. 28345888; fax 28513724; e-mail vakiopou@macau.ctm.net; internet www.jornalvakio.com; f. 1937; daily; Publr ALICE CHIANG SAO MENG; circ. 25,000.

Ou Mun Iat Pou (Macao Daily News): Rua Pedro Nolasco da Silva 37; tel. 28371688; fax 28331998; e-mail mcnews@macau.ctm.net; internet www.macaodaily.com; f. 1958; daily; Dir LEI PANG CHU; Editor-in-Chief PO LOK; circ. 50,000.

O Pulso de Macau: Rua 1, 13°, Bloco B, Guang Dong Nan-Gui Jardim, Taipa; tel. 28400194; fax 28400284; e-mail pulsomacau@gmail.com; internet www.pulso.com.mo; weekly; Dir IEONG KUN FO.

Semanário Desportivo de Macau: Av. Venceslau de Morais 231, Edif. Industrial Nam Fong 7C; tel. 28354208; fax 28718285; e-mail macsport@macau.ctm.net; internet www.macausports.com.mo; weekly; sport; Dir FONG NIM LAM; Editor-in-Chief FONG NIM SEONG; circ. 2,000.

Semanário Recreativo de Macau: Av. Sidónio Pais 31D, 3° andar, Bloco A; tel. 28553216; fax 28516792; e-mail srm405@yahoo.com.hk; weekly; Dir IEONG CHEOK KUONG; Editor-in-Chief IEONG CHEOK KUONG.

Seng Pou (Star): Travessa da Caldeira 9; tel. 28938387; fax 28388192; e-mail sengpou@macau.ctn.net; f. 1963; daily; Dir and Editor-in-Chief POLICARPO KOK.

Si Man Pou (Jornal do Cidadão): Rua dos Pescadores, Edif. Indian Ocean, 2° Fase, Bloco 2B; tel. 28722111; fax 28722133; e-mail shemin@macau.ctm.net; internet www.shimindaily.net; f. 1944; daily; Dir and Editor-in-Chief KUNG MAN; circ. 20,000.

Tai Chung Pou: Av. Leste do Hipódromo 25–69, Edif. Fok Tai, 6° andar; tel. 28939888; fax 28282322; e-mail taichung@macau.ctm.net; f. 1933; daily; Dir VONG U. KONG; circ. 8,000.

Today Macau Journal: Pátio da Barca 20, R/C; tel. 28215050; fax 28210478; e-mail todaymac@yahoo.com; internet www.todaymacao.com; daily; Dir LAM IONG CHONG; Editor-in-Chief IU VENG ION; circ. 6,000.

ENGLISH LANGUAGE

Macau Daily Times: Av. do Infante D. Henrique, 2º andar, Centro Comercial Central; tel. 28716082; fax 28716084; e-mail general@macaudailytimes.com; internet www.macaudailytimes.com.mo; daily; Man. Editor PAULO BARBOSA; Dir and Editor-in-Chief PAULO COUTINHO.

Macau Post Daily: Av. de Almeida Ribeiro 99, Edif. Nam Wah Centre, 10° andar; tel. 28331050; fax 28331104; e-mail macaupost@macau.ctm.net; internet www.macaupostdaily.com; f. 2004; Dir HARALD BRUNING.

SELECTED PERIODICALS

Agora Macau: Av. Dr Rodrigo Rodrigues 7B, Edif. Centro Comercial First National, 10° andar, Sala 1005; tel. 66283212; fax 28519236; e-mail agora28@macau.ctn.net; weekly; Chinese; Dir LAO TAT KAO.

Boletim Associação Budista Geral de Macau: Estrada de Lou Lim Ieok 2, Pou Tai Un, Ilha da Taipa; tel. 28811038; bi-monthly; Dir LEI SENG VO.

Business Intelligence: Av. da Amizade, Edif. Chong Yu 12 D; tel. 28331258; fax 28331487; e-mail admin@bizintelligenceonline.com; internet www.bizintelligenceonline.com; monthly; Chinese; Dir PAULO ALEXANDRE TEIXEIRA DE AZEVEDO.

Cáritas Ligação: Largo de Santo Agostinho 1A; tel. 28573297; bimonthly; Dir PUN CHI MENG.

Macau Business: Av. do Dr Francisco Vieira Machado 679, Bloco C, Edif. Industrial Nam Fong, 9° andar H; tel. 28331258; fax 28331487; e-mail editor@macaubusiness.com; internet www.macaubusiness.com; f. 2004; monthly; Publr PAULO A. AZEVEDO; Editor-in-Chief EMANUEL GRAÇA; circ. 35,000.

Macau Manager: Rua de Santa Clara 9, Edif. Ribeiro, 6° andar; tel. 28323233; quarterly; Chinese; published by the Macau Management Asscn; Dir CHUI SAI CHEONG.

Macau Times: Rua Almirante Costa Cabral 11, Edif. Iau Fai, 11° andar A; tel. 28554978; e-mail mail@macautimes.net; internet www.macautimes.net; f. 1994; monthly; Chinese; Dir WONG TAI WAI; circ. 5,000.

Revista Mensal de Macau: Av. Dr Rodrigo Rodrigues 600E, Edif. Centro Comercial First National, 14° andar, Sala 1404; tel. 28323660; fax 28323601; e-mail contacto@revistamacau.com; internet www.revistamacau.com; f. 1987; quarterly; Portuguese; govt publication; Dir VICTOR CHAN CHI PING; Editor FERNANDO SALES LOPES.

x1 Week: Av. do Infante D. Henrique 43–53A, Edif. The Macau Square, 7° andar; tel. 28710566; fax 28710565; e-mail info@x1week.com; internet www.x1week.com; computing; Dir CHAN SAO SEONG.

NEWS AGENCIES

China News Service: Rua de Londres, Edif. Zhu Kuan, 14° andar, Y/Z; tel. 28594585; fax 28594586; Correspondent WANG GUOAN.

Xinhua (New China) News Agency Macao SAR Branch: Av. Gov. Jaime Silvério Marques, Edif. Zhu Kuan, 13° andar V; tel. 28727720; fax 28700548; e-mail xinhua@macau.ctm.net; Dir ZHAO WEI.

PRESS ASSOCIATIONS

Associação de Imprensa de Língua Portuguesa e Inglesa de Macau: Av. do Dr Rodrigo Rodrigues 600E, Centro Comercial First National, 14° andar, Sala 1408; tel. 28752401; fax 28752405; e-mail imprensamacau@gmail.com; f. 2005; Dir PAULO AZEVEDO.

Macao Media Workers Association: Travessa do Matadouro, Edif. 3, 3B; tel. and fax 28939486; e-mail mcju@macau.ctm.net; Pres. LEI PANG CHU.

Macao Journalists Association: Rua de Jorge Alvares 7–7B, Viva Court 17A; tel. and fax 28569819; e-mail macauja@gmail.com; internet hk.myblog.yahoo.com/macaujournalist; f. 1999; Pres. PANG OI CHI.

Macao Journalists Club: Estrada do Repouso, Edif. Tak Fai 18B; tel. and fax 28921395; e-mail cjm@macau.ctm.net; Pres. LO SONG MAN.

Macao Media Club: Rua de Santa Clara 5–7E, Edif. Ribeiro, 4B; tel. 28330035; fax 28330036; e-mail mmedia@macau.ctn.net; Pres. CHEONG CHI SENG.

Macao Sports Press Association: Estrada de D. Maria II 1-E, Edif. Kin Chit 2G; tel. 28838206, ext. 151; fax 28718285; e-mail macsport@macau.ctm.net; Pres. LAO IU KONG.

Publishers

Associação Beneficência Leitores Jornal Ou Mun: Nova-Guia 339; tel. 28711631; fax 28711630.

Fundação Macau: Av. República 6; tel. 28966777; fax 28968658; e-mail info@fm.org.mo; internet www.fmac.org.mo; Chair. WU ZHILIANG.

Instituto Cultural de Macau: publishes literature, social sciences and history; see under Tourism.

Livros do Oriente: Av. Amizade 876, Edif. Marina Gardens, 15E; tel. 28700320; fax 28700423; e-mail livros.macau@loriente.com; internet www.loriente.com; f. 1990; publishes in Portuguese, English and Chinese on regional history, culture, etc.; Gen. Man. ROGÉRIO BELTRÃO COELHO; Exec. Man. CECÍLIA JORGE.

Universidade de Macau—Centro de Publicações: Av. Padre Tomás Pereira, SJ, Taipa; tel. and fax 83978189; e-mail pub_enquiry@umac.mo; internet www.umac.mo/pub; f. 1993; art, economics, education, political science, history, literature, management, social sciences, etc.; Head Dr RAYMOND WONG.

GOVERNMENT PUBLISHER

Imprensa Oficial: Rua da Imprensa Nacional s/n; tel. 28573822; fax 28596802; e-mail info@io.gov.mo; internet www.io.gov.mo; Dir TOU CHI MAN.

Broadcasting and Communications

TELECOMMUNICATIONS

The Government initiated a liberalization of the mobile telecommunications market in 2001. In October 2006 the Government awarded an eight-year licence for 3G operations to Hutchison Telephone (Macau) Co Ltd, and to China Unicom (Macao) Ltd, a subsidiary of the Hong Kong-based China Unicom Ltd. These services commenced in October 2007.

Companhia de Telecomunicações de Macau, SARL (CTM): Rua de Lagos, Edif. Telecentro, Taipa; tel. 28833833; fax 88913031; e-mail helpdesk@macau.ctm.net; internet www.ctm.net; f. 1981; holds local telecommunications monopoly; shareholders include CITIC Telecom International (99%) and Macau Post (1%); 460,000 mobile, 173,000 fixed-line and 142,000 broadband customers at Dec. 2012; CEO VANDY POON; 806 employees.

Hutchison Telephone (Macau) Co Ltd (3 Macau): Av. Xian Xing Hai, Zhu Kuan Bldg, 8/F; tel. 8933388; fax 781282; e-mail feedback@three.com.mo; internet www.three.com.mo; f. 2001; mobile telecommunications operator; subsidiary of Hutchison Whampoa Group (Hong Kong); local capital participation; CEO HO WAI-MING.

SmarTone Mobile (Macau) Ltd: Macao; tel. 28802688; fax 25628229; e-mail customer_care@smartone.com; internet www.smartone.com.mo; f. 2001; mobile telecommunications provider; subsidiary of SmarTone Mobile Communications Ltd (Hong Kong); local capital participation; CEO PATRICK CHAN KAI-LUNG.

Regulatory Authority

Office for the Development of Telecommunications and Information Technology (GDTTI): Av. da Praia Grande 789, 3° andar; tel. 28356328; fax 83969166; e-mail ifx@gdtti.gov.mo; internet www.gdtti.gov.mo; f. 2000.

BROADCASTING

Radio and Television

Cosmos Televisão por Satélite, SARL: Av. do Infante D. Henrique 29, Edif. Va Iong, 4° andar A; tel. 28785731; fax 28788234; satellite TV services; Chair. NG FOK.

Lotus TV Macau: Alameda Dr Carlos D'Assumpção 180, Tong Nam Ah Centro Comércial, 22° andar A–V; tel. 28787606; fax 28787607; e-mail lotustv@lotustv.cc; internet www.lotustv.cc; f. 2008; Dir LI ZI SONG.

Macau Cable TV Ltd: Av. Conselheiro Ferreira de Almeida 71B; tel. 28822866; e-mail enquiry@macaucabletv.com; internet www.macaucabletv.com; f. 2000; offers 70 channels from around the world; CEO ANTONIO AGUIAR.

Macau Satellite Television: c/o Cosmos Televisão por Satélite, Av. do Infante D. Henrique 29, Edif. Va Iong, 4° andar A; commenced transmissions in 2000; operated by Cosmos Televisão por Satélite, SARL; domestic and international broadcasts in Chinese aimed at Chinese-speaking audiences worldwide.

Rádio Vilaverde: Macao Jockey Club, Taipa; tel. 28820338; fax 28820337; e-mail helpdesk@am738.com; internet www.am738.com; private radio station; programmes in Chinese; CEO STANLEY LEI.

Teledifusão de Macau, SARL (TDM): Rua Francisco Xavier Pereira 157A, POB 446; tel. 28335888 (Radio), 28519188 (TV); fax 28519522; e-mail inf@tdm.com.mo; internet www.tdm.com.mo; f. 1982; owned by the Govt of the Macao SAR; radio channels: Rádio Macau (Av. do Dr Rodrigo Rodrigues, Edif. Nam Kwong, 7° andar; tel. 28335888; fax 28343220; rmacau@tdm.com.mo), broadcasting 24 hours per day in Portuguese on TDM Canal 1 (incl. broadcasts from RTP International in Portugal) and 17 hours per day in Chinese on TDM Channel 2; Chair. MANUEL PIRES, Jr.

Finance

(cap. = capital; res = reserves; dep. = deposits; m. = million; brs = branches; amounts in patacas, unless otherwise indicated)

BANKING

Macao has no foreign exchange controls, its external payments system being fully liberalized on current and capital transactions. The Financial System Act, aiming to improve the reputation of the territory's banks and to comply with international standards, took effect in September 1993. A total of 27 registered banks were in operation in 2013.

Issuing Authority

Autoridade Monetária de Macau (AMCM) (Monetary Authority of Macao): Calçada do Gaio 24–26, POB 3017; tel. 28568288; fax 28325432; e-mail general@amcm.gov.mo; internet www.amcm.gov.mo; f. 1989; est. as Autoridade Monetária e Cambial de Macau (AMCM), to replace the Instituto Emissor de Macau; cap. 8,324m., res 4,860m., dep. 132,183.1m. (Dec. 2009); govt-owned; Chair. ANSELMO L. S. TENG.

Banks of Issue

Banco Nacional Ultramarino (BNU), SA: Av. Almeida Ribeiro 22, POB 465; tel. 28335533; fax 28355653; e-mail markt@bnu.com.mo; internet www.bnu.com.mo; f. 1864; est. in Macao 1902; subsidiary of Caixa Geral de Depósitos (Portugal) since 2001; agent of Macao Govt; agreement whereby the Bank remains an agent of the treasury signed with the administration of the Macao SAR in 2000; to remain a note-issuing bank until 2020; cap. 400m., res 1,937m., dep. 26,726m. (Dec. 2011); Chair. Dr JOAQUIM JORGE PERESTRELO NETO VALENTE; Pres. PEDRO MANUEL DE OLIVEIRA CARDOSO; 14 brs.

Bank of China: Av. Dr Mário Soares, Edif. Banco da China, R/C; tel. 28781828; fax 28781833; e-mail bocmo@bocmacao.com; internet www.bocmacau.com; f. 1950 as Nan Tung Bank, name changed 1987; authorized to issue banknotes from Oct. 1995; Gen. Man. YE YIXIN; 24 brs.

Other Commercial Banks

Banco Comercial de Macau, SA: Av. da Praia Grande 572, POB 545; tel. 87910000; fax 28332795; e-mail bcmbank@bcm.com.mo; internet www.bcm.com.mo; f. 1974; cap. 225m., res 215.2m., dep. 11,723.3m. (Dec. 2011); Chair. and Pres. DAVID SHOU-YEH WONG; CEO KONG YIU-FAI; 17 brs.

Banco Delta Asia (BDA), SARL: Largo de Santo Agostinho; tel. 87969600; fax 87969624; e-mail contact@bdam.com; internet www.delta-asia.com.mo; f. 1935; fmrly Banco Hang Sang; cap. 210.0m., res 173.2m., dep. 3,323.1m. (Dec. 2004); Chair. STANLEY AU; Exec. Dir DAVID LAU; 9 brs.

Banco Tai Fung, SA: Av. Alameda Dr Carlos d'Assumpção 418, Edif. Sede Banco Tai Fung; tel. 28322323; fax 28570737; e-mail tfbsecr@taifungbank.com; internet www.taifungbank.com; f. 1971; cap. 1,000m., res 3,658m., dep. 52,674m. (June. 2013); Chair. HO HAO TONG; Pres. LIU DAGUO; 23 brs.

Banco Weng Hang, SA: Av. Almeida Ribeiro 241; tel. 28335678; fax 28576527; e-mail bwhhrd@whbmac.com; internet www.whbmac.com; f. 1973; subsidiary of Wing Hang Bank Ltd, Hong Kong; cap. 120m., res 1,729.3m., dep. 19,157.4m. (Dec. 2011); Chair. PATRICK YUK-BUN FUNG; Gen. Man. TAK LIM LEE; 11 brs.

China Construction Bank (Macau) Corpn Ltd: Av. Almeida Ribeiro 70–76, POB 165; tel. 83969611; fax 83969683; e-mail ccb.macau@asia.ccb.com; internet www.asia.ccb.com; f. 1937; fmrly Banco da América (Macau); cap. 500m., res 102m., dep. 4,290m. (Dec. 2010); Pres. and CEO (Asia) MIRANDA KWOK; 8 brs.

Industrial and Commercial Bank of China (Macau) Ltd (ICBC—Macau): Av. da Amizade 555, Macau Landmark, 18° andar, Torre Banco ICBC; tel. 28555222; fax 28338064; e-mail icbc@icbc.com.mo; internet www.icbc.com.mo; f. 1972; est. as Seng Heng Bank Ltd; present name adopted 2009, following merger with Industrial and Commercial Bank of China; Exec. Dir PATRICK YUEN; 9 brs.

Luso International Banking Ltd: Av. Dr Mário Soares 47; tel. 28725113; fax 28578517; e-mail lusobank@lusobank.com.mo; internet www.lusobank.com.mo; f. 1974; cap. 950m., res 265.8m., dep. 16,571.7m. (Dec. 2010); Chair. LU YAO MING; Gen. Man. IP KAI MING; 11 brs.

Banking Association

Associação de Bancos de Macau (ABM) (Macau Association of Banks): Av. da Praia Grande 575, Edif. 'Finanças', 15/F; tel. 28511921; fax 28346049; e-mail abm@macau.ctm.net; internet www.abm.org.mo; f. 1985; Chair. YE YIXIN.

INSURANCE

ACE Seguradora, SA: Rua Dr Pedro José Lobo 1–3, Luso Bank Bldg, 17° andar, Apt 1701–02; tel. 28557191; fax 28570188; Pres. and CEO (Asia-Pacific) DAMIEN SULLIVAN.

American International Assurance Co (Bermuda) Ltd: Unit 601, AIA Tower, Av. Comercial de Macau 251A–301; tel. 89881817; fax 28315900; e-mail salina-if.ieong@aig.com; life insurance; Rep. ALEXANDRA FOO CHEUK LING.

Asia Insurance Co Ltd: 762 Av. da Praia Grande, Edif. China Plaza, 10° andar, Apt C–D; tel. 28570439; fax 28570438; e-mail asiamc@macau.ctm.net; non-life insurance; Rep. S. T. CHAN.

AXA China Region Insurance Company: Av. do Infante D. Henrique 43–53A, 20° andar, The Macau Square; tel. 28781188; fax 28780022; life insurance; CEO (Asia) MICHAEL BISHOP.

Chartis Insurance Hong Kong Ltd: Av. Comercial de Macau 251A–301, Unit 6, AIA Tower, 5° andar; tel. 28355602; fax 28355299; internet www.chartisinsurance.com.hk/macau; f. 2010; non-life insurance.

China Life Insurance (Overseas) Co Ltd: Alameda Dr Carlos D'Assumpção 263, China Civil Plaza, 22° andar A–B; tel. 28787288; fax 28787287; e-mail info@chinalife.com.mo; Gen. Man. WANG JIAN GUO.

China Taiping Insurance (Macau) Co Ltd: Av. Alameda Dr Carlos d'Assumpção 398, Edif. CNAC, 10° andar; tel. 28785578; fax 28787218; e-mail info@mo.cntaiping.com; internet www.cicmacau.com.mo; non-life insurance.

Companhia de Seguros Delta Asia, SA: Rua do Campo 39–41; tel. 28559898; fax 28921545; e-mail contact@bdam.com; internet www.delta-asia.com/macau; Chair. STANLEY AU.

Companhia de Seguros Fidelidade: Av. da Praia Grande 567, Edif. BNU, 14° andar; tel. 28374072; fax 28511085; e-mail info@fidelidademundial.com.mo; life and non-life insurance; Gen. Man. EDUARDO CLARISSEAU MESQUITA D'ABREU.

Crown Life Insurance Co: Av. da Praia Grande 287, Nam Yuet Commercial Centre, Bl. B, 8° andar; tel. 28570828; fax 28570844; Rep. STEVEN SIU.

HSBC Insurance (Asia) Ltd: Av. da Praia Grande 619, Edif. Comercial Si Toi, 1° andar; tel. 28212323; fax 28217162; non-life insurance; Rep. NORA CHIO.

ING Life Insurance Co (Macao) Ltd: Av. Almeida Ribeiro 61, 11° andar, Units C and D; tel. 9886060; fax 9886100; e-mail customerservice@ing.com.mo; internet www.ing.com.mo; Heads LENNARD YONG, WIM HEKSTRA.

Luen Fung Hang Insurance Co Ltd (Luen Fung Hang Life Ltd): Alameda Dr Carlos d'Assumpção 398, Edif. CNAC, 4° andar; tel. 28700033; fax 28700088; e-mail info@luenfunghang.com; internet www.luenfunghang.com; life (Luen Fung Hang Life Ltd) and non-life insurance; Rep. SI CHI HOK.

Macao Life Insurance Co (Macao Insurance Company): Av. da Praia Grande 594, Edif. BCM, 10–11° andar; tel. 28555078; fax 28551074; e-mail mic@bcm.com.mo; internet www.macauinsurance.com.mo; life and non-life insurance (Macao Insurance Company); Rep. STEVEN CHIK.

Manulife (International) Ltd: Av. da Praia Grande 517, Edif. Comercial Nam Tung, 8° andar, Unit B & C; tel. 3980388; fax 28323312; internet www.manulife.com.hk; CEO MICHAEL HUDDART.

MassMutual Asia Ltd: Av. da Praia Grande 517, Edif. Nam Tung 16° andar, E1–E2; tel. 28322622; fax 28322042; life insurance; Pres. MANLY CHENG.

Min Xin Insurance Co Ltd: Rua do Dr Pedro José Lobo 1–3, Luso International Bank Bldg, 27° andar, Rm 2704; tel. 28305684; fax 28305600; non-life insurance; Rep. PETER CHAN.

MSIG Insurance (Hong Kong) Ltd: Av. da Praia Grande 693, Edif. Tai Wah, 13° andar A–B; tel. 28923329; fax 28923349; internet www.msig.com.hk; wholly owned subsidiary of Mitsui Sumitomo Insurance Group Holdings Inc; CEO KENNETH REID.

QBE Insurance (International) Ltd: Rua do Comandante Mata e Oliveira 32, Edif. Associação Industrial de Macau, 8° andar B–C; tel. 28323909; fax 28323911; e-mail sally.siu@mo.qbe.com; non-life insurance; Rep. SALLY SIU.

Insurers' Associations

Federation of Macao Professional Insurance Intermediaries: Rua de Pequim 244–246, Macao Finance Centre, 6° andar G; tel. 28703268; fax 28703266; Rep. DAVID KONG.

Macao Insurance Agents and Brokers Association: Av. da Praia Grande 309, Nam Yuet Commercial Centre, 8° andar D; tel. 28378901; fax 28570848; Rep. JACK LI KWOK TAI.

Macao Insurers' Association: Av. da Praia Grande 575, Edif. 'Finanças', 15° andar; tel. 28511923; fax 28337531; e-mail info@mia-macau.com; internet www.mia-macau.com; 22 mems; Pres. SI CHI HOK.

Trade and Industry

CHAMBER OF COMMERCE

Associação Comercial de Macau (Macao Chamber of Commerce): Rua de Xangai 175, Edif. ACM, 5° andar; tel. 28576833; fax 28594513; internet www.acm.org.mo; Pres. MA IAO LAI.

INDUSTRIAL AND TRADE ASSOCIATIONS

Associação dos Construtores Civis e Empresas de Fomento Predial de Macau (Macao Association of Building Contractors and Developers): Rua do Campo 103, 5° andar; tel. 28573226; fax 28345710; e-mail info@macaudeveloper.com; internet www.macaudeveloper.com; 145 corp. mems; Pres. FONG CHI KEONG.

Associação dos Exportadores e Importadores de Macau (Macao Importers and Exporters Association): Av. Infante D. Henrique 60–62, Centro Comercial 'Central', 3° andar; tel. 28375859; fax 28512174; e-mail aeim@macau.ctm.net; internet www.macauexport.com; Pres. VITOR NG.

Associação dos Industriais de Tecelagem e Fiação de Lã de Macau (Macao Weaving and Spinning of Wool Manufacturers' Asscn): Av. da Amizade 271B, Edif. Kam Wa Kok, 6° andar A; tel. 28553378; fax 28511105; Pres. WONG SHOO KEE.

Associação Industrial de Macau (Industrial Association of Macao): Rua Dr Pedro José Lobo 34–36, Edif. AIM, 17° andar; tel. 28574125; fax 28578305; e-mail info@madeinmacau.net; internet www.madeinmacau.net; f. 1959; Pres. HO IAT SENG.

Centro de Produtividade e Transferência de Tecnologia de Macau (Macao Productivity and Technology Transfer Centre): Rua de Xangai 175, Edif. ACM, 6° andar; tel. 28781313; fax 28788233; e-mail cpttm@cpttm.org.mo; internet www.cpttm.org.mo; vocational or professional training; Pres. VITOR NG; Dir-Gen. VICTOR KUAN.

Instituto de Promoção do Comércio e do Investimento de Macau (IPIM) (Macao Trade and Investment Promotion Institute): Av. da Amizade 918, World Trade Center Bldg, 1°–4° andares; tel. 28710300; fax 28590309; e-mail ipim@ipim.gov.mo; internet www.ipim.gov.mo; Pres. JACKSON CHANG.

Ponto de Contacto da Rede Portuguesa da Enterprise Europe Network: Alameda Dr Carlos d'Assumpção 263, Edif. China Civil Plaza, 20°andar; tel. 28713338; fax 28713339; e-mail info@ieem.org.mo; internet euinfo.ieem.org.mo; f. 1992; promotes trade with European Union; fmrly Euro-Info Centre Relay of Macao; Man. LORETTA KU; Pres. JOSÉ LUÍS DE SALES MARQUES.

SDPIM (Macao Industrial Parks Development Co Ltd): Av. da Amizade 918, World Trade Center Bldg, 13° andar A & B; tel. 28786636; fax 28785374; e-mail sdpim@macau.ctm.net; internet www.sdpim.com.mo; f. 1993; Pres. of the Bd PAULINA Y. ALVES DOS SANTOS.

World Trade Center Macao, SARL: Av. da Amizade 918, Edif. World Trade Center, 16° andar; tel. 28727666; fax 28727633; e-mail wtcmc@wtc-macau.com; internet www.wtc-macau.com; f. 1995; trade information and business services, office rentals, exhibition and conference facilities; Chair. PETER LAM; Man. Dir ALBERTO EXPEDITO MARÇAL.

UTILITIES

Electricity

Companhia de Electricidade de Macau, SARL (CEM): Estrada D. Maria II 32–36, Edif. CEM; tel. 28339933; fax 28308361; e-mail e-doc@cem-macau.com; internet www.cem-macau.com; f. 1972; sole distributor; Chair. JOÃO MARQUES DA CRUZ; CEO FRANKLIN WILLEMYNS.

Water

Sociedade de Abastecimento de Aguas de Macau, SARL (SAAM) (Macao Water): Av. do Conselheiro Borja 718; tel. 28220088; fax 28234660; e-mail customer.info@macaowater.com; internet www.macaowater.com; f. 1985; jt venture with Suez Lyonnaise des Eaux; Chair. STEPHEN CLARK; Man. Dir CHIN CHEUNG.

TRADE UNIONS

Macao Federation of Trade Unions: Rua Ribeira do Patane 2; tel. 28576231; fax 28553110; Chair. CHIANG CHONG SEK.

Transport

RAILWAYS

There are no railways in Macao. A plan to connect Macao with Zhuhai and Guangzhou (People's Republic of China) by rail is under consideration. Construction of the Zhuhai–Guangzhou section was under way in mainland China in the early 21st century. Construction of the first phase (the Macau–Taipa Line) of a light rail transit system began in February 2012; the line, which was to have a total of 21 stations, was expected to be operational in 2016.

ROADS

In 2010 the public road network extended to 413 km. The peninsula of Macao is linked to the islands of Taipa and Coloane by three bridges and by a 2.2-km causeway, respectively. The first bridge (2.6 km) opened in 1974. In conjunction with the construction of an airport on Taipa (see Civil Aviation), a 4.4-km four-lane bridge to the Macao peninsula was opened in 1994. A third link between Macao and Taipa, a double-deck bridge, opened in 2005. A second connection to the mainland, the 1.5-km six-lane road bridge (the Lotus Bridge) linking Macao with Hengqin Island (in Zhuhai, Guangdong Province), opened to traffic in December 1999. Construction of a new bridge linking Macao with Hong Kong's Lantau Island and Zhuhai City, Guangdong Province, commenced in December 2009. To extend to nearly 50 km and comprising a six-lane expressway, the bridge was scheduled for completion in 2015.

SHIPPING

There are representatives of shipping agencies for international lines in Macao. There are passenger and cargo services to the People's Republic of China. Regular services between Macao and Hong Kong are run by the Hong Kong-based New World First Ferry and Shun Tak-China Travel Ship Management Ltd companies.

Agência de Navegação Ka Fung: Av. da Praia Grande 429, South Bay Centro Comercial, 11° andar, Rm 1101; tel. 28553311; fax 28569233; e-mail info@kafung-shipping.com; internet www.kafung-shipping.com; f. 1984.

CTS Parkview Holdings Ltd: Av. Amizade, Porto Exterior, Terminal Marítimo de Macau, Sala 2006 B; tel. 28726789; fax 28727112; purchased by Sociedade de Turismo e Diversões de Macau (STDM, q.v.) in 1998.

DHC Logistics (Macau) Ltd: Av. de Praia Grande 619, Edif. Comercial Si Toi, 7° andar B; tel. 28788063; fax 28788093; e-mail pollywong@dhclogistics.com; internet www.dhclogistics.com.

New Line Shipping Ltd: Av. do Dr Rodrigo Rodrigues, Centro Comercial First Int., 24° andar, Rm 2404; tel. 28710250; fax 28710252; e-mail newline@macau.ctm.net; internet www.newline.com.mo; f. 2001.

STDM Shipping Dept: Av. da Amizade Terminal Marítimo do Porto Exterior; tel. 28726111; fax 28726234; e-mail shpgdept@macau.ctm.net; affiliated to STDM; Gen. Man. ALAN HO; Office Man. ALAN LI.

Association

Associação de Agências de Navegação e de Logistica de Macau (Macau Shipping and Logistics Association): Rua de Xanghai 175, Edif. ACM, 8F; tel. 28528207; fax 28302667; e-mail secretary@logistics.org.mo; internet www.logistics.org.mo; f. 1981; Pres. VONG KOK SENG.

Port Authority

Capitania dos Portos de Macau: Rampa da Barra, Quartel dos Mouros, POB 47; tel. 28559922; fax 28511986; e-mail info@marine.gov.mo; internet www.marine.gov.mo; Dir WONG SOI MAN.

CIVIL AVIATION

Macau International Airport, constructed on the island of Taipa, was officially opened in 1995. The terminal has the capacity to handle 6m.

passengers a year. At September 2013 a total of 21 airlines operated flights to destinations mostly in mainland China, but also to the Democratic People's Republic of Korea, the Philippines, Singapore, Taiwan and Thailand. Helicopter services between Hong Kong and Macao are available.

Autoridade de Aviação Civil (AACM) (Civil Aviation Authority of Macao): Alameda Dr Carlos d'Assumpção 336–342, Centro Comercial Cheng Feng, 18° andar; tel. 28511213; fax 28338089; e-mail aacm@aacm.gov.mo; internet www.aacm.gov.mo; f. 1991; Pres. SIMON CHAN WENG HONG.

Administração de Aeroportos, Lda (ADA): Macao International Airport, Taipa; tel. 28861111; fax 28862222; e-mail christinapeng@ada.com.mo; internet www.ada.com.mo; f. 1995; CEO PATRICK ONG.

CAM (Sociedade do Aeroporto Internacional de Macau, SARL): CAM Office Bldg, 4/F, Av. Wai Long, Macao International Airport; tel. 5988888; fax 28785465; e-mail mkd@macau-airport.com; internet www.macau-airport.com; f. 1989; airport owner, responsible for design, construction, development and international marketing of Macao International Airport; Chair. DENG JUN.

Air Macau: Macao Unidos Praça, Alameda Dr Carlos d'Assumpção 398, 13°–18° andar; tel. 83966888; fax 83966866; e-mail airmacau@airmacau.com.mo; internet www.airmacau.com.mo; f. 1994; controlled by China National Aviation Corpn (Group) Macao Co Ltd; services to several cities in the People's Republic of China, the Republic of Korea, the Philippines, Taiwan and Thailand; other destinations planned; Chair. ZHENG YAN; CEO ZHOU GUANG QUAN.

Tourism

In addition to the casinos, Macao's attractions include its cultural heritage and museums, dog racing, horse racing, and annual events such as Chinese New Year (January/February), the Macao Arts Festival (February/March), the Dragon Boat Festival (May/June), the Macao International Fireworks Festival (September/October), the International Music Festival (October), the Macao Grand Prix for racing cars and motorcycles (November) and the Macao International Marathon (December). A total of 26,069 hotel rooms were available in Macao in December 2012. Visitor arrivals rose from 25.0m. in 2010 to 28.1m. in 2012, the majority of tourists travelling from mainland China and from Hong Kong. Over the same period, receipts from tourism (excluding passenger transport) increased by more than 57%, from US $27,802m. to an estimated $43,707m.

Macao Government Tourist Office (MGTO): Alameda Dr Carlos d'Assumpção 335–341, Edif. Hot Line, 12° andar; tel. 28315566; fax 28510104; e-mail mgto@macautourism.gov.mo; internet www.macautourism.gov.mo; Dir JOÃO MANUEL COSTA ANTUNES.

Instituto Cultural de Macau: Praça do Tap Seac, Edif. do Instituto Cultural; tel. 28366866; fax 28366899; e-mail postoffice@icm.gov.mo; internet www.icm.gov.mo; f. 1982; organizes performances, concerts, exhibitions, festivals, etc.; library facilities; Pres. HAN XIAOYAN.

Macau Hotel Association: Hotel Lisboa, East Wing 4F, Av. de Lisboa 2–4; tel. 28703416; fax 28703415; e-mail mhacmo@macau.ctm.net; internet www.macauhotel.org; f. 1985; aims to promote and support high quality standards and growth of tourism, in conjunction with MGTO; Dir ANTONIO SAMEIRO.

Sociedade de Turismo e Diversões de Macau (STDM), SA: Hotel Lisboa, 9th Floor, Avda de Lisboa; tel. 28574266; fax 28562285; e-mail stdmmdof@macau.ctm.net; f. 1962; operation of its casinos handled by subsidiary Sociedade de Jogos de Macau after the termination of STDM's monopoly franchise in 2002; other commercial interests include hospitality, real estate, transport, infrastructure and overseas investments; Chair. CHENG KAR SHUN.

Defence

The budget for defence is allocated by the Chinese Government. Upon the territory's reversion to Chinese sovereignty in December 1999, troops of the People's Liberation Army (PLA) were stationed in Macao. The force comprises around 1,000 troops: a maximum of 500 soldiers are stationed in Macao, the remainder in Zhuhai, China, on the border with the SAR. The unit is directly responsible to the Commander of the Guangzhou Military Region and to the Central Military Commission. The Macao garrison is composed mainly of ground troops. Naval and air defence tasks are performed by the naval vessel unit of the PLA garrison in Hong Kong and by the air force unit in Huizhou. Subject to the request of the Macao SAR, the garrison may participate in law enforcement and rescue operations in the SAR.

Commander of the PLA Garrison in Macao: Col. ZHU QINGSHENG.

Education

The education system in Macao is structured as follows: pre-school education (lasting two years); primary preparatory year (one year); primary education (six years); and secondary education (five–six years, divided into junior secondary of three years and senior secondary of two–three years). Schooling is compulsory between the ages of five and 15, but normally lasts from the ages of three to 17. In 2012/13 schools enrolled a total of 12,669 children in kindergarten, 22,231 primary pupils and 33,921 secondary students. Enrolment at primary schools included 86% (males 86%; females 88%) of pupils in the relevant age-group in 2007/08, while enrolment at secondary level included 78% (males 80%; females 77%) of pupils in the relevant age-group in 2010/11. In 2012/13 27,776 students attended courses offered by tertiary institutions, ranging from the bacharelato (three-year courses) to doctorate programmes. In 2011 the Government allocated 8,500m. patacas for the education sector, accounting for 12.4% of the total budget.

COLOMBIA

Introductory Survey

LOCATION, CLIMATE, LANGUAGE, RELIGION, FLAG, CAPITAL

The Republic of Colombia lies in the north-west of South America, with the Caribbean Sea to the north and the Pacific Ocean to the west. Its continental neighbours are Venezuela and Brazil to the east, and Peru and Ecuador to the south, while Panama connects it with Central America. The coastal areas have a tropical rainforest climate, the plateaux are temperate, and in the Andes mountains there are areas of permanent snow. The language is Spanish. Almost all of the inhabitants profess Christianity, and around 87% are Roman Catholics. There are small Protestant and Jewish minorities. The national flag (proportions 2 by 3) has three horizontal stripes, of yellow (one-half of the depth) over dark blue over red. The capital is Bogotá.

CONTEMPORARY POLITICAL HISTORY

Historical Context

Colombia was under Spanish rule from the 16th century until 1819, when it achieved independence as part of Gran Colombia, which included Ecuador, Panama and Venezuela. Ecuador and Venezuela seceded in 1830, when Colombia (then including Panama) became a separate republic. In 1903 the province of Panama successfully rebelled and became an independent country. For more than a century, ruling power in Colombia has been shared between two political parties, the Conservatives (Partido Conservador Colombiano, PCC) and the Liberals (Partido Liberal Colombiano, PL), whose rivalry has often led to violence. President Laureano Gómez of the PCC ruled as a dictator from 1949 until his overthrow by Gen. Gustavo Rojas Pinilla in a coup in June 1953. President Rojas established a right-wing dictatorship but, following widespread rioting, he was deposed in May 1957, when a five-man military junta took power. According to official estimates, lawlessness during 1949–58, known as 'La Violencia', caused the deaths of about 280,000 people.

Domestic Political Affairs

In an attempt to restore peace and stability, the PCC and the PL agreed to co-operate in a National Front. Under this arrangement, the presidency was to be held by the PCC and the PL in rotation, while cabinet portfolios would be divided equally between the two parties and both would have an equal number of seats in each house of the bicameral Congreso (Congress). In December 1957, in Colombia's first vote on the basis of universal adult suffrage, this agreement was overwhelmingly approved by a referendum and was subsequently incorporated in Colombia's Constitution, dating from 1886.

In May 1958 the first presidential election under the amended Constitution was won by the National Front candidate, Alberto Lleras Camargo, a PL member who had been President in 1945–46. As provided by the 1957 agreement, he was succeeded by a member of the PCC, Guillermo León Valencia, who was, in turn, succeeded by a PL candidate, Carlos Lleras Restrepo, in 1966.

At the presidential election in April 1970 the National Front candidate, Misael Pastrana Borrero (PCC), narrowly defeated Gen. Rojas, the former dictator, who campaigned as leader of the Alianza Nacional Popular (ANAPO). At concurrent congressional elections the National Front lost its majority, while ANAPO became the main opposition group in the Congress. The result of the presidential election was challenged by supporters of ANAPO, and an armed wing of the party, the Movimiento 19 de Abril (M-19), began to organize guerrilla activity against the Government. It was joined by dissident members of a pro-Soviet guerrilla group, the Fuerzas Armadas Revolucionarias de Colombia (FARC), established in 1964. (In 1982 the FARC was renamed the Fuerzas Armadas Revolucionarias de Colombia—Ejército del Pueblo, FARC—EP, although it continued to be known by its shorter acronym.)

The bipartisan form of government ended formally with the 1974 elections, although the Cabinet remained subject to the parity agreement. The PCC and the PL together won an overwhelming majority of seats in the Congress, and support for ANAPO was greatly reduced. The presidential election was won by the PL candidate, Alfonso López Michelsen.

The PL won a clear majority in both houses at congressional elections in 1978, and the PL candidate, Julio César Turbay Ayala, won the presidential election. Turbay continued to observe the National Front agreement, and attempted to address the problems of urban terrorism and drugs-trafficking. In 1982 the guerrillas suffered heavy losses after successful counter-insurgency operations, combined with the activities of a new anti-guerrilla group associated with drugs-smuggling enterprises, the Muerte a Secuestradores (MAS, Death to Kidnappers), whose targets later became trade union leaders, academics and human rights activists.

At congressional elections in 1982 the PL maintained its majority in both houses, while the PCC candidate, Belisario Betancur Cuartas, won the presidential election, benefiting from a division within the PL. President Betancur declared a broad amnesty for guerrillas later that year, reconvened the Peace Commission (first established in 1981) and ordered an investigation into the MAS. Despite the Peace Commission's successful negotiation of ceasefire agreements with the FARC, the M-19 (now operating as a left-wing guerrilla movement) and the Ejército Popular de Liberación (EPL) during 1984, factions of all three groups opposed to the truce continued to conduct guerrilla warfare against the authorities. The assassination of the Minister of Justice in May prompted the Government to declare a nationwide state of siege and announce its intention to enforce its hitherto unobserved extradition treaty with the USA.

In June 1985 the M-19 formally withdrew from the ceasefire agreement. In November a dramatic siege by the M-19 at the Palace of Justice in the capital, during which more than 100 people were killed, resulted in severe public criticism of the Government and the armed forces for their handling of events. Negotiations with the M-19 were suspended indefinitely.

At congressional elections in March 1986 the traditional wing of the PL secured a clear victory over the PCC, and the PL's candidate, Virgilio Barco Vargas, was elected President in May. The PL's large majority in both elections obliged the PCC to form the first formal opposition to a government for 30 years.

Hopes that an indefinite ceasefire agreement, concluded between the FARC and the Government in March 1986, would facilitate the full participation of the Unión Patriótica (UP), formed by the FARC, in the political process were largely frustrated by the Government's failure to respond effectively to a campaign of assassinations of UP members, conducted by paramilitary 'death squads'. The crisis was compounded in October 1987 by the decision of six guerrilla groups, including the FARC, the Ejército de Liberación Nacional (ELN) and the M-19, to form a joint front, the Coordinadora Guerrillera Simón Bolívar. Although the Government extended police powers against drugs dealers, its efforts were severely hampered by the Supreme Court's ruling that Colombia's extradition treaty with the USA was unconstitutional.

In September 1989 the M-19 announced that it had reached agreement with the Government on a peace treaty, under which its members were to demobilize and disarm in exchange for a general amnesty, reintegration into civilian life and firm commitments on changes to electoral law and that a referendum would be held to decide the question of constitutional reform. In October the M-19 was formally constituted as a political party, and by March 1990 all M-19 guerrilla forces had surrendered their weapons.

César Gaviria Trujillo

In March 1990 Bernardo Jaramillo, the UP candidate in the upcoming presidential ballot, was assassinated, and in April Carlos Pizarro of the M-19 became the third presidential candidate to be killed by hired assassins since August 1989. César Gaviria Trujillo of the PL was proclaimed the winner of the election in May. Some 90% of voters approved proposals for the creation of a National Constituent Assembly in a de facto referendum held simultaneously. The new President formed a Cabinet of 'national unity', and confirmed his commitment to combating drugs-trafficking.

In October 1990 the creation of the National Constituent Assembly was declared constitutionally acceptable by the Supreme Court. Alianza Democrática (AD)—M-19 candidates secured 19 of the 70 contested Assembly seats, forcing the ruling PL and the Conservatives to seek support from them for the successful enactment of reform proposals. In February 1991 the Assembly was inaugurated and expanded to 74 members in order to incorporate representatives of several former guerrilla groupings. By June an agreement was reached between President Gaviria and representatives of the PL, the AD—M-19 and the conservative Movimiento de Salvación Nacional (MSN) that, in order to facilitate the process of political and constitutional renovation, the Congress should be dissolved prematurely, pending new elections.

The new Constitution became effective on 6 July 1991. The state of siege, imposed in 1984 in response to the escalation in political and drugs-related violence, also was ended. The Constitution placed considerable emphasis upon increased political participation and the eradication of electoral corruption. While the Constitution was welcomed enthusiastically by the majority of the population, reservations were expressed that provisions relating to the armed forces remained largely unchanged and that recognition of the democratic rights of indigenous groups did not extend to their territorial claims.

Relations with the Medellín drugs cartel, believed to be responsible for a series of assassinations of prominent citizens, improved considerably following the release, in May 1991, of its two remaining hostages. In June, Pablo Escobar, the supposed head of the Medellín cartel, surrendered, following the decision to prohibit constitutionally the practice of extradition. Charges brought against Escobar included several of murder, kidnapping and terrorism. In July the cartel announced that its military operations were to be suspended; however, hopes that Escobar's surrender might precipitate a decline in drugs-related violence were frustrated by reports that Escobar was continuing to direct cocaine cartel operations from his purpose-built prison at Envigado, and by the emergence of the powerful Cali drugs cartel.

The Liberals were the most successful party in the congressional elections of October 1991, with a clear majority of seats in both chambers. The traditional Conservative opposition suffered from a division in their support between the PCC, the MSN and the Nueva Fuerza Democrática, which together secured around one-quarter of the seats in each house.

Meanwhile, in February 1990 the Government had established the National Council for Normalization, in an attempt to repeat the success of recent peace initiatives with the M-19 in negotiations with other revolutionary groups. The EPL announced the end of its armed struggle in August and joined the political mainstream (retaining the initials EPL as Esperanza, Paz y Libertad), along with the Comando Quintín Lame and the Partido Revolucionario de Trabajadores, in 1991. Attempts to negotiate with the FARC and the ELN, however, proved fruitless, and violent clashes between the remaining guerrilla groups (now operating jointly as the Coordinadora Nacional Guerrillera Simón Bolívar—CNGSB) and security forces persisted. In November Gaviria declared a 90-day state of internal disturbance, prompting the M-19 to withdraw from the Government.

As the security situation continued to deteriorate, in early 1993 the Government announced a significant increase in its budget allocation for security, and doubled the length of prison terms for terrorist acts. The state of internal disturbance was also extended twice. The intensification of drugs-related violence in the capital was attributed to an attempt by Pablo Escobar (who had escaped from prison in mid-1992) to force the Government to negotiate more favourable conditions for his surrender, and prompted the formation of a vigilante group, Pepe (Perseguidos por Pablo Escobar—those Persecuted by Pablo Escobar), which launched a campaign of retaliatory violence against Escobar's family, associates and property. A simultaneous and sustained assault by Pepe and by the security forces against the remnants of the Medellín cartel resulted in the death or surrender of many notable cartel members, culminating in the death of Escobar himself in December.

Ernesto Samper Pizano

Congressional elections conducted in March 1994 re-established the traditional two-party dominance of the PL and the PCC. The PL candidate, Ernesto Samper Pizano, was elected to the presidency in June. Shortly after taking office, allegations emerged that Samper's election campaign had been funded partly by contributions from the Cali cartel. Tape recordings of conversations were dismissed by the Prosecutor-General as insufficient proof of such contributions having been made, however, emergence of a similar recording, implicating the Colombian Chief of National Police in the payment of a bribe by the Cali cartel, prompted the US Senate to vote to make the disbursement of future aid to Colombia dependent on its co-operation in anti-drugs programmes.

A CNGSB offensive in 1994, resulting in numerous deaths on both sides and considerable damage to infrastructure, intensified after the new administration took office. In September, under intense international pressure, the new Government announced an initiative to address allegations of human rights abuses by the security forces; measures included the reform of the National Police and the dissolution of all paramilitary units. In November Samper complied with a guerrilla request that imprisoned rebel leaders be moved from military installations to civilian prisons.

In February 1995 President Samper reiterated his commitment to combating all illegal drugs-related activities in the country. A number of initiatives were launched in Cali, resulting in the capture of the head of the Cali drugs cartel, Gilberto Rodríguez Orejuela, and four other cartel leaders in mid-1995. Meanwhile, in April nine prominent PL politicians were suspended from the party owing to their alleged links with the Cali cartel. It was subsequently confirmed that the Comptroller-General and the Attorney-General were also to be investigated as a result of similar allegations, while Samper's former election campaign treasurer, Santiago Medina, was arrested on charges related to the processing of drugs cartel contributions through Samper's election fund. In August the Minister of National Defence, Fernando Botero Zea, resigned, having been implicated in the affair.

In December 1995 the congressional accusations committee voted against a full-scale inquiry into allegations of Samper's use of funds proceeding from drugs cartels, on the grounds of insufficient evidence. The repercussions of the scandal, however, severely undermined the political integrity of the Government. In January 1996 the PCC announced an immediate suspension of co-operation with the Government, and two PCC cabinet members resigned. Evidence collected by the Prosecutor-General was submitted in February, together with four formal charges to be brought against the President. In March Samper testified that the Cali cartel had part-financed the campaign, albeit without his knowledge. In June the Congress voted to acquit Samper of charges of having been aware of the part-financing of his election campaign by drugs-traffickers. The US Administration condemned the result and in the following month revoked the President's visa to travel to the USA. During 1996 Botero, Medina and María Izquierdo, a former PL senator, were all sentenced to terms of imprisonment for their involvement in the Samper affair.

Internal unrest continued in 1996 and in April a CNGSB-organized nationwide 'armed industrial strike' resulted in some 40 deaths. A major offensive launched in August by FARC and ELN rebels coincided with large-scale protests by coca growers demanding a review of the coca eradication programme. Legislation approved in November 1997 permitting the extradition of Colombian nationals was strongly criticized by the US Administration as it would be retroactive.

In the months preceding the October 1997 local elections the activities of guerrilla and paramilitary groups intensified. More than 40 candidates were killed, some 200 were kidnapped and as many as 1,900 withdrew after receiving death threats. In May the Government had agreed to the temporary demilitarization of part of the Caquetá department in order to secure the release of 70 members of the armed forces captured by the FARC. Voting was cancelled in numerous municipalities, while reports of secret preliminary peace negotiations between government representatives and the FARC were undermined by a major military offensive in September, in which 652 FARC guerrillas were killed and a further 1,600 were captured.

Andrés Pastrana Arango

The PL retained a narrow overall majority in both chambers of the legislature at congressional elections in March 1998. The ballot was preceded by a period of violent attacks on the security forces by guerrilla groups. At a first round of the presidential election in May the PL candidate, Horacio Serpa Uribe, secured 35% of the vote and the PCC nominee, Andrés Pastrana Arango garnered 34%. Serpa's candidacy had been strongly opposed by the US Administration, owing to his alleged links with drugs-traffickers. Pastrana emerged victorious in the second ballot, and was inaugurated as President in August.

In July 1998 President-elect Pastrana announced that he had held secret talks with Manuel Marulanda Vélez (alias 'Tirofijo'), the FARC leader, and that he had agreed to demilitarize five southern municipalities for a 90-day period in order to facilitate negotiations with the guerrillas. Pastrana subsequently recognized the political status of the FARC, thereby allowing the Government to negotiate with an outlawed group. None the less, FARC attacks on the security forces continued. Shortly before the negotiations began in January 1999, it was revealed that the FARC had held informal talks with government officials from the USA and Colombia. In mid-January the FARC suspended talks until the authorities provided evidence that they were taking action against paramilitary groups. In February Pastrana announced the extension of the period of demilitarization by three months.

In October 1998 representatives of the ELN, Colombian 'civil society' and the Government agreed on a timetable for preliminary peace talks. Despite the Government's recognition of the ELN as a political entity, the group did not cease hostilities and talks were not begun as scheduled, owing to the ELN's request for further demilitarization. In support of its demands the ELN intensified its operations, hijacking an Avianca domestic flight in April 1999, kidnapping all 46 people on board, and abducting some 140 members of the congregation of a church in Cali in May. In June Pastrana withdrew political recognition of the ELN and made the release of hostages a precondition for future peace talks. Following negotiations the ELN freed the last hostage in November 2000.

Meanwhile, in May 1999 talks between FARC leader Marulanda and President Pastrana resulted in an agreement on a comprehensive agenda for future peace negotiations; the period of demilitarization was again extended, but the FARC continued to pursue its military campaign. Pastrana's strategy was not supported entirely by his administration and Rodrigo Lloreda, the Minister of National Defence, resigned in protest at the policy. Demonstrations for peace were attended by some 10m. people throughout the country.

In March 1999 the USA decided to 'certify' Colombia's efforts to combat drugs-trafficking and announced the creation of a new US financed anti-narcotics battalion. Collaboration between the Colombian and US authorities led to the arrest of more than 60 suspected drugs-traffickers in two major operations conducted in late 1999. However, the most important progress in Colombian-US relations came in 2000 with the development of Pastrana's so-called 'Plan Colombia'. This was an ambitious, US $7,500m. project intended to strengthen the Colombian state by increasing the efficiency of the security forces and the judicial system, eliminating drugs production through both crop eradication and crop substitution, and by reducing unemployment. The US Congress approved $1,300m. to support the Plan. Human rights organizations warned of an escalation of human rights abuses following the Plan's implementation, as the main aid component was allocated to strengthening the security forces, whose links to paramilitary groups were, allegedly, yet to be severed. Colombia's Andean neighbours feared that an escalation in violence would force refugees onto their territory, and subsequently reinforced their borders.

During negotiations in September 2000 the FARC threatened to halt the peace process if the US military went ahead with plans to destroy coca plantations in Putumayo under Plan Colombia. The FARC effectively blockaded Putumayo and succeeded in delaying the aerial spraying of coca plantations. In November the FARC withdrew from talks, demanding greater government action to combat the Autodefensas Unidas de Colombia (AUC), an organization representing most of Colombia's paramilitary groups. By the end of the year Pastrana was under increasing pressure to regain control of the demilitarized zone; a report released in December estimated a 30% increase in FARC military capacity since the zone was created. In early 2001 the FARC leadership met the President and agreed to revive the stalled negotiations. The new US Administration of George W. Bush refused an invitation to join the peace process, preferring instead to focus on drugs-eradication policies.

In June 2001 some 300 prisoners were released by the FARC following the signing of a prisoner-exchange agreement with the Government. In October the Government extended the term of the demilitarized zone until January 2002, after the FARC agreed to reduce the number of kidnappings and to begin ceasefire negotiations. However, the Government's refusal to remove military controls around the demilitarized zone prevented any progress being made on negotiations during the rest of the year. On 9 January 2002 Pastrana gave the FARC just 48 hours to leave the demilitarized zone. Hours before the expiry of the deadline the FARC rescinded demands for relaxed security around the zone and agreed to recommence negotiations. However, on 20 February, following the hijacking of an aeroplane and the kidnapping of a prominent senator, Pastrana terminated peace talks and ordered the armed forces to regain control of the demilitarized zone.

In April 2000 an agreement was reached with the ELN on the establishment of a similar demilitarized zone, in southern Bolívar. The agreement was strongly opposed by residents of the region and by the AUC, which began an offensive in order to prevent the establishment of the zone. Talks which faltered in mid-2001 resumed in December in Cuba, but the ELN again withdrew in May 2002. The ELN resumed negotiations in December 2005 in Cuba.

Alvaro Uribe Vélez

At legislative elections in March 2002 the most significant gains were made by independents and parties allied to Alvaro Uribe Vélez, the former Governor of Antioquia, a dissident member of the PL and a candidate in the forthcoming presidential election. The PL remained the largest single party in both chambers, although its representation was substantially reduced. At the presidential election, in May, amid a climate of increased intimidation by both guerrilla and paramilitary groups, Uribe was victorious. Support from the PCC, the PL and a number of independents gave him an overwhelming majority in both parliamentary chambers.

Under the framework of his 'democratic security' plan, Uribe resolved to strengthen the capacity of the Government to achieve a lasting victory over the rebel groups. In September 2002 he issued a decree establishing a 'state of internal disturbance' and introduced a war tax (intended to raise US $750m.). The decree extended police powers to military units and designated two 'Rehabilitation and Consolidation Zones' in the north-eastern departments of Sucre, Bolívar and Arauca, within which media access and civil liberties were to be drastically curtailed. Uribe pledged to double the size of the army (to some 100,000 professional soldiers), recruit a further 100,000 police officers, create localized militias and establish a network of 'informants' to ensure public security along the road network. As a result of the measures, the President's popularity soared. In December the Congress approved labour, pension and fiscal reforms that provided for an increase in military spending. Notwithstanding concerns over reports of human rights infringements by the security forces, throughout 2003 and 2004 the Government achieved apparent progress in its campaign against the rebel groups, with murder, kidnapping, massacre and terrorism rates all declining.

In December 2002 agreement was reached in the Congress on some 15 proposed economic and political reforms, which were to be included in a national referendum. The proposals included: a two-year freeze on public sector salaries, and reductions in civil service pensions; the transfer of responsibility for regional finances to the federal authorities; a reduction in the number of seats in the Congress; and an increase in prison terms for those convicted of corruption. However, participation in the referendum in October 2003 was below the required 25% of the electorate, in part owing to the complexity of the referendum document, but also to widespread fears of violence and to the scheduling of the referendum one day before local elections. The failure of the proposals meant that the Uribe administration had to gain congressional approval for its reforms and in December a series of anti-terrorism measures were approved, although these were subsequently overturned by the Constitutional Court, owing to voting irregularities. A controversial amendment allowing a President to serve two consecutive terms in office was approved by the Congress in December 2004, and by the Constitutional Court in October 2005.

Meanwhile, in July 2003, following the declaration of a ceasefire in December 2002, the leaders of the AUC confirmed their intention to proceed with peace talks and disband by December 2005. In late 2004 AUC leader Salvatore Mancuso began the demobilization of its 30,000 combatants under the Government-sponsored programme of reinsertion to civilian society. In June 2005 the Cámara de Representantes (House of Representatives) approved legislation, the *Ley de Justicia y Paz* (Peace and Justice

Law), according the status of political prisoners to demobilized paramilitaries and allowing for reduced prison sentences for any subsequently convicted of human rights abuses. Although opposition and human rights groups were vociferous in their condemnation of the legislation, the Government maintained that such concessions were necessary to ensure the success of the peace process. Nevertheless, sustained criticism of the law resulted in its amendment by the Constitutional Court to strengthen provisions for the punishment of crimes committed by paramilitaries. In mid-2005 the AUC announced the indefinite suspension of demobilization, owing to concerns over the possible extradition of its leaders to the USA on drugs-trafficking charges. Protracted negotiations led to an extension of the deadline for demobilization. The process was completed in March 2006.

At legislative elections in March 2006 the Partido Social de la Unidad Nacional (Partido de la U), a pro-Uribe group formed by former members of the PL, won significant representation in both houses, as did the two traditional parties. Cambio Radical (CR), another pro-Uribe party also fared well. At the presidential election in May Uribe secured an emphatic victory, winning 64% of the valid votes cast. Carlos Gaviria Díaz of the left-wing Polo Democrático Alternativo (PDA), won a higher than expected 23% of the ballot, while Horacio Serpa, representing the PL, won just 12%. Uribe's new administration included Juan Manuel Santos Calderón, leader of the Partido de la U, as Minister of National Defence.

In November 2006 the Supreme Court ordered the arrest of three pro-Uribe members of the Congress on charges of promoting the creation of paramilitary groups in the department of Sucre to fight left-wing rebels. The following week Salvador Arana, the Governor of Sucre, was also implicated, and later in the month other legislators were questioned over similar allegations, in what became known as the 'parapolitical' scandal. In February 2007 six pro-Uribe members of the legislature were arrested on charges of having links with paramilitary organizations; the Minister of Foreign Affairs, María Consuelo Araújo, was forced to resign from office as her brother was among those arrested. The reputation of the Uribe administration was further damaged after Jorge Noguera, the President's former intelligence adviser and a close ally, was arrested on charges of supplying information on left-wing sympathizers to the AUC. By April 2008 a total of 62 members of the Congress, primarily from pro-Uribe parties, were under judicial investigation in connection with the 'parapolitical' affair.

Relations between the Government and the Supreme Court worsened in June 2008 when the latter convicted a former deputy, Yidis Medina, of accepting bribes in exchange for her decisive vote in December 2004 in favour of the constitutional amendment that allowed President Uribe's re-election. Because Medina's conviction implicitly questioned the legitimacy of Uribe's second term in office, the Constitutional Court was asked to reconsider the amendment. The Court upheld the legality of the amendment in July.

In December 2006 the trial began of Mancuso, who had surrendered under the terms of the Ley de Justicia y Paz. AUC leaders, who had announced their withdrawal from the peace process in protest against their transfer to the high-security Itagüí prison, protested against the Supreme Court ruling in mid-2007 that former paramilitaries should be tried with common crimes rather than the pardonable offence of sedition. Uribe responded by proposing that some 19,000 paramilitaries would be charged with simple criminal conspiracy, thereby making them eligible for early release. However, in May 2008 Uribe announced the extradition of 14 senior AUC leaders to the USA on charges of drugs-trafficking, declaring that they had violated the terms of the *Ley de Justicia y Paz* by failing to tell the truth about their paramilitary activities or to provide compensation to their victims.

The prospect of a further constitutional amendment to allow President Uribe to run for a third consecutive term dominated domestic politics during 2009. Amid allegations of bribery, in September the Congress approved a referendum on the issue, pending final authorization by the Constitutional Court, although questions about the legality of such a plebiscite persisted. The Congress approved a series of much-delayed political reforms in June 2009. Primarily intended to punish those parties with deputies embroiled in the 'parapolitical' scandal, the final bill was criticized for diluting these efforts, particularly as the measure was not retroactive and thus provided protection for deputies currently being investigated, most of whom were allies of Uribe.

Damaging evidence of extra-judicial killings by the military was uncovered in October 2008. Soldiers had murdered civilians and disguised the victims as combatants to meet quotas, attracting domestic and international condemnation. The 'false positives' scandal escalated throughout 2009, and by mid-2010 the Attorney-General was investigating some 1,300 cases involving over 2,000 deaths. The steady imposition during 2010–11 of lengthy prison sentences upon members of the armed forces convicted of 'false positive' murders demonstrated that progress was being made in bringing the perpetrators to justice. In May 2012 four soldiers were given prison sentences of 30 years, and an army major and a lieutenant of 50 years, for their roles in the atrocity.

Meanwhile, in February 2009 allegations emerged that the intelligence service, the Departamento Administrativo del Servicio (DAS—Administrative Department of Security), had carried out illegal surveillance of opposition politicians, trade union leaders, journalists and Supreme Court judges. Although the majority of the victims in the so-called 'chuzadas' (wiretapping) scandal were opponents of the Government, Uribe insisted that the operations were the work of rogue elements within the DAS and were not officially sanctioned. Relations between the Government and the Supreme Court deteriorated further when it was revealed that the judge overseeing the 'parapolitical' affair was among the surveillance targets. The USA revealed in April 2010 that it would cease its financial support of the DAS, while it was reported in the following month that several of Uribe's closest associates had been directly involved in the intelligence-gathering scandal.

Juan Manuel Santos Calderón

In February 2010 the Constitutional Court ruled against a referendum on a third term for Uribe, and in early March Juan Manuel Santos Calderón, a former Minister of National Defence in Uribe's Government, was formally confirmed as the candidate for the ruling Partido de la U in the upcoming presidential election. In the same month Noemí Sanín was elected as the PCC's nominee and former Mayor of Bogotá Antanas Mockus Šivickas won the vote for the candidature of the Partido Verde (PV).

At legislative elections on 14 March 2010 Santos's Partido de la U increased its representation in the House of Representatives to 47 seats and in the Senado (Senate) to 28 seats. The PCC also improved its position, winning 37 lower house seats and 22 senate seats, while the PL's representation remained virtually unaltered at 35 and 17 seats in each chamber, respectively. The Partido de Integración Nacional, formed in 2009 by a number of pro-Uribe parties (which controversially included many members with links to politicians involved in the 'parapolitical' scandal), secured 11 seats in the lower house and nine in the Senate, and the PV, another newcomer to the Congress, won three and five seats, respectively. The ballot was peaceful, but monitors from the Organization of American States (OAS) reported numerous electoral irregularities.

At the presidential election on 30 May 2010 Santos secured 46.7% of the votes cast, followed by Mockus with 21.5%, necessitating a second round run-off, at which.Santos who garnered 69.1% of the ballot, compared with 27.5% for Mockus. The rate of participation by the electorate was recorded at 44.3%. Mockus's anti-corruption campaign had gathered momentum as the election approached and was particularly attractive to younger voters seeking an alternative to the traditional parties, but the popularity of Santos's platform, based on the continuation of the 'Uribismo' project, proved to be insurmountable. Santos assumed the presidency on 7 August and announced that the priorities of his new Government were economic growth, job creation, and the improvement of relations with Venezuela and Ecuador; pledges of congressional support by the PCC, the PL and CR provided Santos with the necessary backing to effect his political agenda.

In October 2010 the Attorney-General ruled that nine high-profile members of the Uribe administration would be prohibited from assuming official positions owing to misconduct. An inquiry into the former President's involvement in the 'chuzadas' scandal was subsequently initiated. In November María del Pilar Hurtado Afanador, Uribe's appointee to head the DAS between 2007 and 2008, was granted asylum in Panama after claiming that her life was at risk in Colombia. Comments by Uribe declaring his support for Hurtado's decision to flee the country attracted criticism from the Attorney-General, the leaders of the PL and the PCC, and, most notably, President Santos. By August 2011 three senior DAS officials had been sentenced to eight-year gaol terms for their involvement in the 'chuzadas' affair, two of whom alleged that they had been following Hurtado's instructions. In December the Government requested Hurtado's extradition from Panama to face charges of organizing illegal surveillance operations. The Agencia Nacional de Inteligencia (ANI) was established on 1 January 2012, to replace the discredited DAS, which Santos had dissolved on the previous day. The ANI was given a much narrower mandate, with many of the DAS's powers and resources being transferred to other government departments and the police.

In February 2011 Santos announced a new security strategy to address the growing problem of the Bandas Criminales Emergentes (Bacrim, or Emerging Criminal Gangs—organized groups involved in the illegal drugs trade, formed mainly by recently demobilized AUC combatants). The Government asserted that the main focus of the security forces would be shifted from defeating the guerrilla insurgency to combating the Bacrim's activities, underlining the severity of the threat posed by these criminal groups.

During 2011 two of Uribe's close associates were convicted of involvement in the 'parapolitical' scandal. Mario de Jesús Uribe Escobar, a cousin of the former President Uribe and an erstwhile Senate President, received a seven-and-a-half-year prison term for his role in the affair, and =Jorge Noguera, the Director of the DAS between 2002 and 2005, given a 25-year prison sentence for the 2004 murder of a left-wing activist, Alfredo Correa de Andreis, having provided the AUC with confidential information that led to his assassination.

Legislation was adopted in May 2011 to facilitate the transfer of reparation payments from the state to the victims of human rights abuses committed by guerrillas, paramilitaries or the security forces during the various post-1985 internal conflicts. Land that had been seized illegally after 1990 (estimated to total at least 2m. ha) was also to be restituted to the original title holders. While UN Secretary-General Ban Ki-Moon welcomed the new legislation, critics argued that the law would be too expensive to implement and claimed that it equated the actions of the armed forces with those of illegal organizations. A further concern was the large number of land restitution campaigners who had been murdered during 2011, presumably targeted by armed groups unwilling to comply with the terms of the victims' law.

In regional elections held on 30 October 2011 the Partido de la U secured four governorships, five departmental capitals and 259 mayoralties, and the PL also performed strongly, winning six, seven and 181 mandates, respectively. Gustavo Francisco Petro Urrego, a former M-19 militant representing the recently formed Movimiento Progresista Colombiano, won the politically significant mayoralty of Bogotá. Right-wing 'Uribista' candidates performed poorly in the elections. Voting was conducted peacefully, although over 40 candidates had been murdered during pre-election campaigning.

Uribe's opposition to President Santos was confirmed at a political rally in July 2012 when the former President announced his intention to back a candidate from a so-called 'convergence coalition' in the 2014 presidential election. Uribe, who had been a persistent critic of Santos's administration, accused the President of weakening national security and squandering state finances. His action prompted speculation that any major division between pro-Uribe and pro-Santos members of the Partido de la U could result in the ruling group becoming ungovernable. Uribe was supported at the rally by the high profile, populist figure, Fernando Londoño Hoyos, a former interior and justice minister responsible for implementing Uribe's hardline security strategy. Londoño had survived an assassination attempt in Bogotá in May, assumed to have been carried out by the FARC, in which two people were killed and 40 injured.

In July 2012 Uribe's former head of security, Gen. Mauricio Santoyo, was arrested by US agents in Bogotá and extradited to the USA on charges of accepting bribes from the AUC and of co-operating with drugs cartels. Drugs-related charges were withdrawn in return for Santoyo's future co-operation with the US authorities. Uribe, who had expressed support for Santoyo when the accusations first arose, condemned his decision as a betrayal of the Uribe administration. Santoyo's admission of guilt, along with the recent extraditions of Uribe's niece and the girlfriend of his brother to the USA on drugs-related charges, made the likelihood of a political comeback for the former President seem remote.

Along with several other South American nations in 2012, Colombia raised the prospect of an alternative to a prohibitionist drugs policy. In April the outgoing police chief, Gen. Oscar Naranjo, urged politicians to enagage in a debate on drugs liberalization, and in July the Colombian legislature promulgated a law that effectively reclassified drugs use as a public health issue, rather than one of security. In June 2013 UN Secretary-General Ban Ki-Moon announced that the organization's Council on Narcotic Drugs would conduct a major review of drugs policy during 2014, in preparation for the UN General Assembly Special Session on the subject that was to take place in 2016 at the request of the Presidents of Colombia, Mexico and Guatemala.

During August and September 2013 small-scale farmers organized a series of strikes and demonstrations across the country. Several thousand farmers gathered in Bogotá to demand greater governmental support for agricultural producers; their ability to make a living had been adversely affected by various factors, the most significant of which had been the recent introduction of free trade agreements with the USA and the European Union that had resulted in an influx of cheap food imports. The farmers received widespread public support for their campaign, although some of the protests became violent, leading to many injuries and at least three deaths. President Santos, who had responded swiftly to the crisis, acknowledged the hardships suffered by the country's agricultural workers and in September announced the introduction of a national agricultural and rural development pact to assist the sector, which included financial assistance for some production costs such as fertilizers and pesticides, as well as the creation a new post of Deputy Minister for Rural Development.

Large-scale public demonstrations also took place in Bogotá in December 2013 in support of the city's Mayor Gustavo Petro, who had been dismissed and banned from holding public office for 15 years, following a dispute about the city's refuse collection services. Petro, a former member of the guerrilla group M-19 (see above), was to be subject to a recall referendum, scheduled for April 2014. In March the Council of State rejected all appeals against Petro's removal from office. On the same day the Inter-American Commission on Human Rights (IACHR) ordered the Government to suspend the dismissal while it reviewed the case; although President Santos ignored the IACHR ruling and dismissed the mayor from office, in late April he reappointed Petro following a local court ruling. As a rare example of a public figure who had made the transition from guerrilla to democratically elected politician, the political fate of Petro was expected to have a significant impact on the ongoing peace process between the Government and the FARC (see below).

Recent developments: the 2014 elections

In November 2013 President Santos formally announced his intention to stand for re-election in the 2014 presidential elections. Oscar Iván Zuluaga was confirmed as the candidate for Uribe's newly formed Centro Democrático (CD). Clara López for the PDA, Aída Abello for the Unión Patriótica and former FARC hostage Ingrid Betancourt for the Partido Alianza Verde. The forthcoming elections were likely to be seen as a test of public support for the peace process with the FARC (see below). Santos himself stated that his re-election would be an endorsement of the process, while Uribe, a fierce opponent of the negotiations and a candidate for the Senate, led the campaign for Zuluaga. In October 2013 Santos had secured approval in the Congress for a referendum on the peace process. This was provisionally set to be held concurrently with the presidential election that was scheduled for 25 May 2014.

At legislative elections held on 9 March 2014 the Partido de la U secured the largest representation overall, with 37 seats in the House of Representatives and 21 in the Senate, according to preliminary results. The PL secured 39 and 17 seats, while the PCC won 27 and 19 seats, respectively. The CR garnered 16 lower house seats and nine senate seats. Uribe's CD performed well with 12 lower house and 19 senate seats, respectively, but not as strongly as had been predicted. Uribe subsequently claimed that irregularities had taken place during the electronic vote counting. However, OAS observers declared that the election had been fairly conducted overall, although the organization expressed concern at the low turnout of just 43.5% of the electorate.

'Democratic security' and the FARC

In 2004 the Government announced the initiation of the so-called Plan Patriota, a largely US-funded military campaign in which some 17,000 troops were to be deployed in the traditional FARC strongholds of Caquetá, Guaviare, Meta and Putumayo. In May the UN Special Envoy to Colombia expressed concerns that Plan

Patriota could lead to increased numbers of internally displaced refugees and human rights abuses. Nevertheless, in September the Government announced the capture of nearly 6,000 alleged insurgents and the death of some 1,500 others as a result of Plan Patriota. In spite of the success of the Plan, in December 2005 President Uribe pledged to demilitarize 180 sq km of a south-eastern department in order to facilitate an exchange of FARC prisoners for hostages held by the guerrillas. (An estimated 3,000 civilians had been kidnapped, among them foreigners and politicians, including Ingrid Betancourt, a former presidential candidate, in February 2002.) However, in the wake of a car bomb attack in Bogotá in late 2006, the Government withdrew from talks and Uribe announced that the hostages would be freed by military means. In July some 450 FARC fighters stormed a police station, killing 17 officials, while in December almost 30 soldiers who had been deployed to destroy coca crops in the south of the country were killed by the group.

In an effort to re-engage the FARC in the peace process, in June 2007 President Uribe ordered the release of some 150 imprisoned members of the group. Weeks later, however, the FARC announced that 11 of 12 deputies from Valle del Cauca, kidnapped in 2002, had been killed in crossfire in a battle with an 'unidentified military group'. Although the FARC appeared to implicate either the armed forces or a paramilitary group in the deputies' deaths, Sigifredo López, the only surviving Valle del Cauca deputy, freed in February 2009, corroborated the Government's claim that the rebels had been responsible for the killings. Two high-profile hostages were released by the FARC in January 2008, and four further captives were freed in February following a series of anti-FARC demonstrations in Colombia and throughout the world, in which several million people participated. In March Colombian armed forces launched a raid on a FARC training camp in Ecuador, killing 17 rebels, including the group's second-in-command, Raúl Reyes; the attack provoked a crisis in relations with Ecuador and Venezuela (see below). The FARC was further debilitated later in that month by the death of its commander-in-chief, Marulanda. In July, moreover, the Government secured a major victory against the FARC when special forces rescued the group's highest-profile hostage, Ingrid Betancourt, along with 14 other captives. A steady stream of hostage releases by the FARC during the first half of 2009, followed in August by a statement of the group's willingness to initiate talks with the Government, raised hopes for fresh dialogue. However, the Government remained sceptical of engaging with the rebels, fearing that any abatement in the operations against the FARC would provide the group with the opportunity to rebuild.

In December 2009 the FARC and the ELN, in spite of a history of conflict and division, announced a ceasefire and revealed that they would henceforth unite forces against the military. Although clearly damaged by the Government's aggressive 'democratic security' initiatives, the FARC still possessed the ability to orchestrate attacks, and in a high-profile incident in December Luis Francisco Cuellar, the Governor of Caquetá, was kidnapped and murdered. Uribe responded by authorizing an air-strike on two FARC bases in Meta, resulting in the deaths of 31 rebels. Guaviare gubernatorial candidate José Alberto Pérez Restrepo was wounded and six of his associates were killed during a failed kidnapping raid carried out by FARC rebels in the following month. Nevertheless, two further hostages were released by the FARC at the end of March.

President Santos made clear his intention to continue Uribe's 'democratic security' policies, and his tough stance on the FARC was symbolized by his refusal to designate a High Commissioner for Peace. In September 2010 the FARC and the ELN initiated a series of co-ordinated attacks. In response, the Government rapidly organized counter-operations against the rebels and established a National Security Council. Santos secured a major victory on 22 September, when senior FARC leader and military commander Víctor Suárez ('Mono Jojoy') was killed during an attack by the security forces on a rebel base in Meta. None the less, FARC activity continued, although fewer direct attacks and a greater use of bombings and ambushes were perceived by Santos as a sign of its declining military capabilities. In May 2011 the Government announced that it intended to end the guerrilla insurgency (and eliminate the major Bacrim groups) by 2014 through the implementation of a new security strategy, the Integral Policy on Security and Defence for Prosperity, essentially an extension of the 'democratic security' campaign. The killing of FARC commander Sáenz Vargas in November 2011 was hailed by Santos as 'the most crushing blow against the FARC in its entire history'. The President's call for the group to disband was firmly rejected, and Rodrigo Londoño Echeverri ('Timochenko') promptly became the new FARC leader. That month the group murdered four members of the security forces, who had been held hostage for over 12 years. In December widely attended anti-FARC protest marches were held in Colombia, the USA and Europe, underlining the deep unpopularity of the guerrilla movement. A FARC proposal to resume negotiations was rejected by Santos in January 2012. In March the Government announced the deaths of 33 FARC members in a military operation in Arauca, carried out in retaliation for an attack in that area in which 11 army personnel had been killed. The FARC released its 10 remaining security force captives at the beginning of April; however, the group still held more than 400 civilians hostage.

In August 2012 Santos confirmed rumours that his Government was engaged in preliminary negotiations with the FARC with the aim of achieving a peace accord. The Governments of Cuba and Norway were to act as guarantors in the process, with assistance from those of Chile and Venezuela. A round of talks began in Oslo, Norway, in October, although their success was threatened by the FARC's request that Simón Trinidad, a FARC leader currently serving a 60-year prison sentence in the USA, be released in order to represent the organization in the negotiations. The FARC's apparent desire to broaden the talks to cover wider political issues resulted in the Government's decision to agree to a discussion of comprehensive agrarian reform. Meanwhile, the Government's military operations continued, despite the FARC's declaration of a ceasefire between 20 November 2012 and 20 January 2013. By the end of the year an estimated 34 FARC guerrillas had been killed by the security forces during the period of the ceasefire. However, peace talks resumed in Cuba in February and by late May it was announced that the two sides had reached an agreement on agrarian reform, one of six items under discussion. The most significant element of the reform was the legal entitlement to land ownership it conferred on peasant farmers who had lost their land as a result of the conflict. In June the lead negotiator for the FARC, Iván Márquez, urged the Government to postpone the legislative elections, scheduled for the following year, in order to create a national popular assembly to ratify and implement any potential peace deal. The demands were dismissed by the Government's lead negotiator, former Vice-President Humberto de la Calle Lombana, who stated that the next round of talks would focus on establishing a framework to allow FARC's transition into an unarmed political force. Agreement on the future political participation of the FARC was reportedly reached in early November. The remaining four items on the agenda for discussion were the end of the conflict, the issue of illicit drugs, reparation to victims of violence and agreement on the implementation, verification and signing process. However, sporadic violent incidents attributed to the FARC during 2013 threatened to undermine the negotiations. The discovery of a FARC plot to assassinate former President Uribe in November was among the most serious of these threats. Without accepting responsibility for any of the incidents the FARC declared a 30-day ceasefire on 15 December. However, according to a report by the Centro de Recursos para el Análisis del Conflicto (a group monitoring the country's armed conflict), the organization had broken the ceasefire on at least seven occasions by 2 January 2014. The report raised questions about the strength of the current leadership of the FARC and its ability to control its various guerrilla operations across the country. The group was also criticized for the continued recruitment of minors to serve in its armed campaigns, and for its ongoing use of anti-personnel mines, the latter having killed an estimated 10,607 people (of which some 1,058 were children) since 1990.

Foreign Affairs

Regional relations

Colombia has a long-standing border dispute with Venezuela. Relations between the countries improved following the signing, in 1989, of a border integration agreement, which included a provision on joint co-operation in the campaign to eradicate drugs-trafficking. Colombia's efforts to improve relations with Venezuela were hampered by the activities of FARC guerrillas in the border region, leading the two countries to sign an agreement to improve border co-operation in 1997 and subsequent agreements to strengthen military co-operation and intelligence sharing. In 2000 relations deteriorated, owing to accusations by Colombia that Venezuela was covertly aiding the guerrilla forces. Following the appointment of President Uribe, relations improved: in 2002 Venezuelan President Hugo Chávez and Uribe agreed on measures to promote bilateral trade and to deal with problems on their common border. However, relations were severely strained in December 2004 following the arrest of Rodrigo Granda Escobar, the supposed international spokesperson of the FARC. It was subsequently alleged by the Venezuelan Government that Granda, although ultimately arrested in Cúcuta, was first kidnapped in Venezuela by Venezuelan and Colombian agents in the pay of the Colombian Government and with the collusion of US intelligence services. Both the Uribe Government and the US Administration denied all accusations of wrongdoing. In August 2007 Chávez was invited to mediate between the Colombian Government and the FARC to effect an exchange of prisoners and hostages, although the initiative was then cancelled by Uribe, reportedly because Chávez had made contact with Colombian military leaders against Uribe's expressed wishes. Bilateral relations again deteriorated and Chávez recalled his ambassador. Furthermore, in March 2008, Uribe's claim that computers taken during a raid on a FARC camp in Ecuador (see below) indicated that Chávez had pledged some US $30m.-worth of petroleum to the rebel group prompted the Venezuelan President to expel the Colombian ambassador in Caracas and to dispatch troops to the border. The two countries restored diplomatic relations after Colombia announced it would not pursue charges against Chávez in the International Criminal Court. Relations, already strained by the impending US base deal (see below), reached a new nadir in July 2009 when Chávez suspended diplomatic ties after Venezuela was accused of supplying weapons to the FARC, a charge vehemently denied. Chávez imposed an informal trade blockade upon Colombia, and cross-border commerce declined sharply. In July 2010, at an OAS summit meeting, Colombian officials publicly accused the Venezuelan Government of providing shelter to large numbers of FARC and ELN guerrillas. Chávez immediately severed diplomatic relations with Colombia. However, tensions eased in August following the inauguration of Santos, who adopted a more conciliatory stance towards Venezuela. Santos and Chávez agreed to restore diplomatic relations and following discussions in November signed several economic accords and formed a commission to combat drugs-trafficking. In a further act of rapprochement, from late 2010 Chávez began to comply with Colombian requests for the extradition of alleged guerrillas sheltering in Venezuela. Moreover, in mid-2011 joint mediation by Santos and Chávez resulted in a breakthrough in the political crisis in Honduras. In May 2013, however, Venezuela's newly elected President Nicolás Maduro announced his intention to 're-evaluate' his country's relations with Colombia following Santos's decision to host an official meeting with Venezuela's opposition leader and defeated presidential candidate Henrique Capriles. Claims by Maduro that President Uribe had conspired with the Venezuelan opposition to plan an assassination attempt on Maduro were dismissed by Uribe as 'irresponsible slanders', but served to exacerbate tensions between the two countries. In September, however, Venezuela's chronic food shortages and Colombia's need to increase its agricultural exports resulted in a bilateral agreement, worth some US $600m., under which Colombia was to supply basic food stuffs to its neighbour.

Ecuador has repeatedly objected to incursions by Colombian combatants into its territory, and to the Colombian Government's policy of aerial spraying of drugs crops in departments on the border between the two countries. The Uribe administration agreed to a temporary cessation of aerial fumigation in border areas from January 2006. In December, however, Colombia resumed its crop-spraying programme, which Ecuador described as a hostile act. Following intervention by the OAS, the diplomatic crisis was resolved after Colombia agreed to give notice of any aerial fumigation conducted in the border area. The raid by Colombian forces on a FARC camp in Ecuador in March 2008 provoked an angry response from the Ecuadorean administration, which expelled the Colombian ambassador in Quito, withdrew its own ambassador from Bogotá, and sent troops to the Colombian–Ecuadorean border. Tensions were further exacerbated by the Colombian Government's claim that documents seized in the raid proved that the Ecuadorean President, Rafael Correa, was seeking to establish official relations with the FARC. Correa dismissed the claims, asserting that his Government's involvement had been solely on humanitarian grounds as part of efforts to secure the release of hostages. In January 2009 Colombia reinforced security along its border with Ecuador by deploying some 27,000 troops and relations deteriorated further in July when a video was made public in which a FARC leader apparently admitted to making financial contributions to Correa's election campaign; both Correa and the FARC dismissed the video as fraudulent. (However, according to documents recovered during the 2008 raid, the FARC had indeed made a US $100,000 campaign contribution.) Nevertheless, partial diplomatic relations were restored in November 2009. Economic concerns played a major role in the rapprochement: Uribe was eager to offset the rapid decline in exports to Venezuela (see above) with increased trade with Ecuador. President Santos made efforts to improve ties with Ecuador. In November 2010 the Government handed over to the Ecuadorean authorities a dossier containing detailed information about the 2008 raid, precipitating the normalization of diplomatic ties. Relations continued to improve with the signing of two bilateral border security agreements in 2011. Moreover, in September 2013 the Ecuadorean authorities abandoned a legal case against Colombia for its programme of aerial spraying along the joint border, which it had launched at the International Court of Justice (ICJ) in 2008. Another long-running legal case, concerning the death of an Ecuadorean national in a cross-border raid by Colombian armed forces, was also abandoned.

In 1980 Nicaragua laid claim to the Colombian-controlled islands of Providencia and San Andrés. Colombia has a territorial dispute with Honduras over cays in the San Andrés and Providencia archipelago. In 1986 Colombia and Honduras agreed a delimitation treaty of marine and submarine waters in the Caribbean Sea. Ratification of the treaty, which strengthened Colombia's claim to the islands of Providencia and San Andrés, in 1999, angered Nicaragua, which filed a complaint with the ICJ. In December 2007 the ICJ dismissed Nicaragua's claim to the San Andrés archipelago, while continuing to consider the jurisdiction of the other disputed waters. In its final ruling in November 2012 the ICJ awarded sovereignty over all the disputed islands and cays to Colombia, but awarded Nicaragua control of an estimated 75,000 sq km of territorial waters hitherto considered Colombian. Colombia announced that it intended to challenge the ruling and ordered its naval forces to remain in the waters to be ceded to Nicaragua. At a meeting of President Santos and his Nicaraguan counterpart, Daniel Ortega, in Mexico in December both leaders sought to downplay bilateral tensions. However, a further ruling by the ICJ in September 2013 supporting Nicaragua's claim to the disputed maritime territory was rejected by Santos, who claimed that any modification to the country's borders would require congressional approval of a bilateral treaty.

Other external relations

The USA renewed and extended the Andean Trade Promotion and Drug Eradication Act (ATPDEA) with Colombia every year since its inception in 2002 (when it succeeded the Andean Trade Preference Act). The ATPDEA offered commercial incentives to those Andean countries deemed co-operative in US counter-narcotics policy. The ATPDEA expired in February 2011, but was renewed again in October. In the same month the Colombia Trade Promotion Agreement, a free trade agreement between the USA and Colombia, signed in November 2006, was finally ratified by the US Congress. The delay was in part owing to concerns over Colombia's human rights record. The agreement finally came into force in May 2012, and was expected to double bilateral trade within three years. Free trade agreements with South Korea and the European Union came into effect in mid- and late 2013, respectively.

CONSTITUTION AND GOVERNMENT

A new 380-article Constitution took effect in July 1991. Executive power is exercised by the President (assisted by a Cabinet), who is elected for a four-year term by universal adult suffrage. A 1995 amendment allowed for the re-election of the President for a second term of office. Legislative power is vested in the bicameral Congress, consisting of the Senado (Senate—102 members elected for four years) and the Cámara de Representantes (House of Representatives—166 members elected for four years). Judicial power is ultimately exercised by the Supreme Court of Justice. The integrity of the state is ensured by the Constitutional Court. The Council of State serves as the supreme consultative body for the Government in matters of legislation and administration. The country is divided into 32 Departments and one Capital District.

REGIONAL AND INTERNATIONAL CO-OPERATION

Colombia has been a member of the UN since its inception in 1945. It acceded to the World Trade Organization (see p. 434) in April 1995. Colombia is a member of the Organization of American States (see p. 394), the Latin American Integration Association (see p. 361), the Andean Community (see p. 193), the Association of Caribbean States (see p. 449), and of the Community of Latin American and Caribbean States (see p. 464), which was formally inaugurated in December 2011. The country belongs to the Inter-American Development Bank (see p. 331). In December 2004 Colombia was one of 12 countries that were signatories to the agreement, signed in Cusco, Peru, creating the South American Community of Nations (Comunidad Sudamericana de Naciones, which was renamed Union of South American Nations—Unión de Naciones Suramericanas, UNASUR, see p. 469, in April 2007), intended to promote greater regional economic integration. In June 2012 the Presidents of Colombia, Chile, Mexico and Peru signed a framework agreement in Antofagasta, Chile, creating a new regional economic bloc, the Pacific Alliance (Alianza del Pacífico, see p. 453). The country participated in the Trans-Pacific Strategic Economic Partnership Agreement (see p. 454), signed in 2006.

ECONOMIC AFFAIRS

In 2012, according to estimates by the World Bank, Colombia's gross national income (GNI), measured at average 2010–12 prices, was US $333,536m., equivalent to $6,990 per head (or $10,110 per head on an international purchasing-power parity basis). During 2003–12, it was estimated, the population increased at an average annual rate of 1.5%. Average annual growth of gross domestic product (GDP) per head, in real terms, was 3.3% in the same period. Colombia's overall GDP increased, in real terms, by an average of 4.8% per year in 2003–12; GDP grew by an estimated 4.2% in 2012.

Agriculture (including hunting, forestry and fishing) contributed 6.5% of GDP in 2012 and employed 17.3% of the labour force in August–October 2013. The principal cash crops are coffee (which accounted for 3.2% of official export earnings in 2012), cocoa, sugar cane, bananas, tobacco, cotton and cut flowers. Plantains, rice, cassava, and potatoes are the principal food crops. Timber and beef production are also important. During 2003–12, according to World Bank estimates, agricultural GDP increased at an average annual rate of 1.8%; the GDP of the sector increased by 2.6% in 2012.

Industry (including mining, manufacturing, construction and power) employed 18.7% of the labour force in August–October 2013 and contributed 37.6% of GDP in 2012. According to the World Bank, during 2003–12 real industrial GDP increased at an estimated average annual rate of 4.7%; sectoral GDP increased by 8.0% in 2011 and increased by only 2.4% in 2012.

Mining employed 0.9% of the labour force in August–October 2013 and contributed 12.3% of GDP in 2012. Petroleum, natural gas, coal, nickel, emeralds and gold are the principal minerals exploited. At the end of 2012 Colombia's proven oil reserves stood at 2,200m. barrels. Silver, platinum, iron, lead, zinc, copper, mercury, limestone and phosphates are also mined. During 2003–12 the real GDP of the mining sector increased at an average annual rate of 6.4%; the GDP of the sector increased by 6.0% in 2012, according to official estimates.

Manufacturing contributed 13.0% of GDP in 2012 and employed 11.4% of the labour force in August–October 2013. According to World Bank estimates, during 2003–12 manufacturing GDP increased at an average annual rate of 3.2%. Manufacturing GDP increased by 5.0% in 2011, but decreased by 0.5% in 2012. Based on the value of output, the most important branches of manufacturing were food products, beverages, chemical products, textiles and transport equipment.

The construction sector contributed 8.6% of GDP in 2012, and engaged 5.9% of the employed labour force in August–October 2013. During 2003–12, according to official figures, the GDP of the sector increased at an annual rate of 7.5%; construction GDP increased by 6.3% in 2012.

Hydroelectricity provided 79.1% of Colombia's electricity requirements in 2011. Natural gas provided a further 13.4% of energy needs. The country is self-sufficient in petroleum and coal, and these minerals together accounted for 65.5% of export revenues in 2012.

The services sector contributed 55.9% of GDP in 2012 and engaged 64.0% of the labour force in August–October 2013. According to the World Bank, during 2003–12 the combined GDP of the services sector increased, in real terms, at an average rate of 5.0% per year; the GDP of the sector increased by 4.8% in 2012.

In 2012 Colombia recorded a visible merchandise trade surplus of US $4,871.6m., but there was a deficit of $11,907.5m. on the current account of the balance of payments. The country's principal market for imports in 2012 was the USA, which provided 24.1% of total imports. The USA was also the biggest market for exports, providing 36.3% of total export revenue in the same year. Other important trading partners were the People's Republic of China and Mexico. The principal exports in 2012 were petroleum and its derivatives, coal, metal manufactures, prepared foodstuffs, beverages and tobacco, and chemicals. The principal imports in the same year were mechanical and electrical equipment, chemical products, vehicles and transport equipment, metals and metal manufactures and prepared foodstuffs, beverages and tobacco. A significant amount of foreign exchange is believed to be obtained from illegal trade in cocaine.

In 2013 there was an estimated budgetary deficit of 15,927m. pesos. Colombia's general government gross debt was 215,013,459m. pesos in 2012, equivalent to 32.6% of GDP. Colombia's external debt amounted to US $76,918m. at the end of 2011, of which $39,040m. was public and publicly guaranteed debt. In that year, the cost of servicing long-term public and publicly guaranteed debt and repayments to the IMF was equivalent to 15.6% of the value of exports of goods, services and income (excluding workers' remittances). During 2003–12 the average annual rate of inflation was 4.8%; consumer prices increased by an annual average of 3.5% in 2012. Some 8.7% of the labour force were unemployed in August–October 2013.

Colombia's economy is viewed as one of the most promising in the regiona situation that was reflected in its relatively rapid recovery from the worldwide financial crisis and subsequent economic slowdown in 2008–09. A government fiscal stimulus programme, combined with rising oil prices, increased investment and output in the mining and manufacturing sectors, led to real GDP growth of some 6.6% in 2011. Oil output rose during that year, with petroleum accounting for 49.1% of total export earnings. The importance of the hydrocarbons sector continued in 2012, attracting significant foreign direct investment (FDI), and the initiation of several large exploratory projects. Oil exports accounted for 52.5% of total export earnings in that year. FDI totalled a record level of US $16,000m. in 2012 (compared with $7,200m. in 2009). Excessive dependence on the hydrocarbons sector, however, has resulted in severe environmental problems, has created few jobs and has left the economy vulnerable to fluctuations in international commodity prices. Legislation approved in December 2012 aimed to reduce inequality in the country's tax system and, although the reforms were not likely to generate additional revenue, they were expected to create around 1m. new jobs. The Santos Government made some progress in its aim to reduce the Gini coefficient (an international measure of income disparity) by 1% per year from 2010 to 2014: reforms to the country's health care system and in a more equitable method of distribution between the regions of revenue from the export of natural resources were introduced. Other issues of importance in 2013 were the need for infrastructural improvements, reforms to the pensions and taxation systems, and measures to address corruption and the ongoing problems caused by the illegal drugs trade. Most significant of all, however, was the peace process with the FARC, initiated by the Santos administration in 2012, which, if successful was likely to make Colombia an even more attractive prospect for foreign investors. According to official sources, GDP growth was estimated at 4.1% in 2013 and predicted at 4.0% in 2014.

PUBLIC HOLIDAYS

2015: 1 January (New Year's Day), 5 January (for Epiphany), 23 March (for St Joseph's Day), 2 April (Maundy Thursday), 3 April (Good Friday), 1 May (Labour Day), 18 May (for Ascension Day), 8 June (for Corpus Christi), 15 June (for Sacred Heart of Jesus), 29 June (SS Peter and Paul), 21 July (for Independence), 7 August (Battle of Boyacá), 17 August (for Assumption), 12 October (Discovery of the Americas), 2 November (for All Saints' Day), 16 November (for Independence of Cartagena), 8 December (Immaculate Conception), 25 December (Christmas Day).

Statistical Survey

Sources (unless otherwise stated): Departamento Administrativo Nacional de Estadística (DANE), Transversal 45 No 26-70, Interior I-CAN, Bogotá, DC; tel. (1) 597-8300; fax (1) 597-8399; e-mail dane@dane.gov.co; internet www.dane.gov.co; Banco de la República, Carrera 7A, No 14-78, 5°, Apdo Aéreo 3551, Bogotá, DC; tel. (1) 343-1111; fax (1) 286-1686; e-mail wbanco@banrep.gov.co; internet www.banrep.gov.co.

Area and Population

AREA, POPULATION AND DENSITY

Area (sq km)	1,141,748*
Population (census results)	
24 October 1993†	37,635,094
30 June 2005‡	
Males	21,169,835
Females	21,718,757
Total	42,888,592
Population (official projections at mid-year)	
2012	46,581,823
2013	47,121,089
2014	47,661,787
Density (per sq km) at mid-2014	41.7

* 440,831 sq miles.

† Revised figure, including adjustment for underenumeration. The enumerated total was 33,109,840 (males 16,296,539, females 16,813,301) in 1993.

‡ A 'census year' was conducted between 22 May 2005 and 22 May 2006, and a 'conciliated' total for 30 June 2005 was finally published in May 2007 (the original enumerated total was 41,298,706) incorporating adjustments for underenumeration, geographical undercoverage and underlying natural growth trends.

POPULATION BY AGE AND SEX
(official projections at mid-2014)

	Males	Females	Total
0–14	6,579,899	6,292,690	12,872,589
15–64	15,390,911	15,911,272	31,302,183
65 and over	1,560,860	1,926,155	3,487,015
Total	23,531,670	24,130,117	47,661,787

DEPARTMENTS
(official population projections at mid-2014)

Department	Area (sq km)	Population	Density (per sq km)	Capital (with population)
Amazonas	109,665	75,388	0.7	Leticia (41,000)
Antioquia	63,612	6,378,132	100.3	Medellín (2,441,123)
Arauca	23,818	259,447	10.9	Arauca (87,242)
Atlántico	3,388	2,432,003	717.8	Barranquilla (1,212,943)
Bolívar	25,978	2,073,004	79.8	Cartagena (990,179)
Boyacá	23,189	1,274,615	55.0	Tunja (184,864)
Caldas	7,888	986,042	125.0	Manizales (394,627)
Caquetá	88,965	471,541	5.3	Florencia (169,336)
Casanare	44,640	350,239	7.8	Yopal (136,484)
Cauca	29,308	1,366,984	46.6	Popayán (275,129)
César	22,905	1,016,533	44.4	Valledupar (443,210)
Chocó	46,530	495,151	10.6	Quibdó (115,517)
Córdoba	25,020	1,683,782	67.3	Montería (434,950)
Cundinamarca	22,623	2,639,059	116.7	Bogotá*
Guainía	72,238	40,839	0.6	Puerto Inírida (19,641)
La Guajira	20,848	930,143	44.6	Riohacha (250,236)
Guaviare	42,327	109,490	2.6	San José del Guaviare (63,493)
Huila	19,890	1,140,539	57.3	Neiva (340,046)
Magdalena	23,188	1,247,514	53.8	Santa Marta (476,385)
Meta	85,635	943,072	11.0	Villavicencio (473,766)
Nariño	33,268	1,722,945	51.8	Pasto (434,486)
Norte de Santander	21,658	1,344,038	62.1	Cúcuta (643,666)
Putumayo	24,885	341,034	13.7	Mocoa (41,304)
Quindío	1,845	562,114	304.7	Armenia (295,143)
Risaralda	4,140	946,632	228.7	Pereira (467,185)
San Andrés y Providencia Islands	44	75,801	1,722.8	San Andrés (70,684)
Santander del Sur	30,537	2,051,022	67.2	Bucaramanga (527,451)
Sucre	10,917	843,202	77.2	Sincelejo (271,375)
Tolima	23,562	1,404,262	59.6	Ibagué (548,209)
Valle del Cauca	22,140	4,566,875	206.3	Cali (2,344,734)
Vaupés	65,268	43,240	0.7	Mitú (31,265)
Vichada	100,242	70,260	0.7	Puerto Carreño (15,505)
Capital District				
Bogotá, DC	1,587	7,776,845	4,900.3	—
Total	1,141,748	47,661,787	41.7	—

* The capital city, Bogotá, exists as the capital of a department as well as the Capital District. The city's population is included only in Bogotá, DC.

PRINCIPAL TOWNS
(official projected population estimates at mid-2014)

Bogotá, DC (capital)	7,776,845	Bello	447,185
Medellín	2,441,123	Valledupar	443,210
Cali	2,344,734	Montería	434,950
Barranquilla	1,212,943	Pasto	434,486
Cartagena	990,179	Manizales	394,627
Cúcuta	643,666	Buenaventura	392,054
Soledad	599,012	Neiva	340,046
Ibagué	548,209	Palmira	302,727
Bucaramanga	527,451	Armenia	295,143
Soacha	500,097	Popayán	275,129
Santa Marta	476,385	Sincelejo	271,375
Villavicencio	473,766	Itagüí	264,775
Pereira	467,185	Floridablanca	264,695

BIRTHS, MARRIAGES AND DEATHS*

	Registered live births	Registered deaths
2005	719,968	189,022
2006	714,450	192,814
2007	709,253	193,936
2008	715,453	196,943
2009	699,775	196,933
2010	654,627	200,524
2011	655,387	193,077
2012†	668,197	194,515

* Data are tabulated by year of registration rather than by year of occurrence, although registration is incomplete. According to UN estimates, the average annual rates in 1995–2000 were: births 24.0 per 1,000, deaths 5.8 per 1,000; in 2000–05: births 22.0 per 1,000, deaths 5.6 per 1,000; and in 2005–10: births 20.6 per 1,000, deaths 5.5 per 1,000 (Source: UN, *World Population Prospects: The 2012 Revision*).

† Preliminary figures.

Registered marriages: 102,448 in 1980; 95,845 in 1981; 70,350 in 1986.

Life expectancy (years at birth): 73.6 (males 70.0; females 77.3) in 2011 (Source: World Bank, World Development Indicators database).

ECONOMICALLY ACTIVE POPULATION
(integrated household survey August–October, '000 persons aged 10 years and over)

	2011	2012	2013
Agriculture, hunting, forestry and fishing	3,772.0	3,673.9	3,726.7
Mining and quarrying	220.2	216.3	186.1
Manufacturing	2,725.9	2,619.9	2,464.7
Electricity, gas and water	130.0	117.0	122.3
Construction	1,203.6	1,236.1	1,261.6
Trade, restaurants and hotels	5,358.2	5,569.9	5,890.5
Transport, storage and communications	1,629.9	1,760.4	1,711.1
Financial intermediation	247.4	252.0	314.3
Real estate, renting and business activities	1,349.1	1,508.0	1,536.4
Community, social and personal services	3,981.2	4,022.5	4,330.0
Sub-total	20,617.5	20,976.0	21,543.7
Activities not adequately described	4.9	2.5	4.7
Total employed	20,622.4	20,978.5	21,548.4
Unemployed	2,187.9	2,204.1	2,045.9
Total labour force	22,810.3	23,182.6	23,594.3

Health and Welfare

KEY INDICATORS

Total fertility rate (children per woman, 2011)	2.3
Under-5 mortality rate (per 1,000 live births, 2011)	18
HIV/AIDS (% of persons aged 15–49, 2012)	0.5
Physicians (per 1,000 head, 2010)	1.5
Hospital beds (per 1,000 head, 2007)	1.0
Health expenditure (2010): US $ per head (PPP)	614
Health expenditure (2010): % of GDP	6.5
Health expenditure (2010): public (% of total)	74.6
Access to water (% of persons, 2011)	93
Access to sanitation (% of persons, 2011)	78
Total carbon dioxide emissions ('000 metric tons, 2010)	75,679.5
Carbon dioxide emissions per head (metric tons, 2010)	1.6
Human Development Index (2012): ranking	91
Human Development Index (2012): value	0.719

For sources and definitions, see explanatory note on p. vi.

Agriculture

PRINCIPAL CROPS
('000 metric tons)

	2010	2011	2012
Rice, paddy	2,011	2,034	1,957
Maize	1,422	1,681	1,826
Sorghum	99	50	30
Potatoes	1,868	1,710	1,847
Cassava (Manioc)	2,082	2,165	2,274
Yams	394	397	361
Sugar cane*	37,000	42,000	38,000
Beans, dry	137	130	133
Soybeans (Soya beans)	54	75	87
Coconuts	101†	102†	102*
Oil palm fruit*	3,100	3,780	3,820
Cabbages and other brassicas*	145	136	135
Tomatoes	513	595	647
Chillies and peppers, green*	50	52	n.a.
Onions, dry	459	379	377

—continued	2010	2011	2012
Carrots and turnips	263	264	261
Watermelons	100	93	117
Bananas	2,020	2,043	1,983
Plantains	2,978	2,946	3,327
Oranges	228	260	269
Mangoes, mangosteens and guavas	201	221	235
Avocados	205	215	219
Pineapples	444	512	551
Papayas	158	153	164
Coffee, green	535	468	464

* FAO estimate(s).
† Unofficial figure.

Aggregate production ('000 metric tons, may include official, semi-official or estimated data): Total cereals 3,564 in 2010, 3,783 in 2011, 3,827 in 2012; Total roots and tubers 4,398 in 2010, 4,348 in 2011, 4,556 in 2012; Total vegetables (incl. melons) 1,854 in 2010, 1,850 in 2011, 1,965 in 2012; Total fruits (excl. melons) 7,936 in 2010, 8,097 in 2011, 8,527 in 2012.

Source: FAO.

LIVESTOCK
('000 head, year ending September)

	2010	2011	2012
Horses	2,126	851	900
Asses	172	134	111
Mules	310	147	183
Cattle	27,329	25,156	23,494
Pigs	5,162	5,127	5,527
Sheep	1,792	1,549	1,045
Goats	2,564	1,694	804
Chickens*	158,000	160,000	160,000

* FAO estimates.

Source: FAO.

LIVESTOCK PRODUCTS
('000 metric tons)

	2010	2011	2012
Cattle meat	766.6	821.0	854.2
Sheep meat*	5.8	11.6	7.7
Goat meat*	14.1	14.2	14.2
Pig meat	196.6	216.2	238.5
Horse meat*	6.7	6.8	6.8
Chicken meat	1,066.9	1,075.1	1,112.2
Cows' milk	6,285	6,284	6,483
Hen eggs	585	640	636

* FAO estimates.

Source: FAO.

Forestry

ROUNDWOOD REMOVALS
('000 cu metres, excl. bark)

	2008	2009	2010
Sawlogs, veneer logs and logs for sleepers	1,062	1,500	1,029
Pulpwood	746	825	932
Other industrial wood	503	1,421	1,589
Fuel wood	8,826	8,826	8,826
Total	11,137	12,572	12,376

2011–12: Production assumed to be unchanged from 2010 (FAO estimates).

Source: FAO.

SAWNWOOD PRODUCTION
('000 cu metres, incl. railway sleepers)

	2008	2009	2010
Coniferous (softwood)	115	163	166
Broadleaved (hardwood)	366	517	527
Total	481	680	693

2011–12: Production assumed to be unchanged from 2010 (unofficial figures).

Source: FAO.

Fishing

('000 metric tons, live weight)

	2009	2010	2011
Capture	106.4	79.7	85.5
Bigeye tuna	1.3	2.0	1.2
Characins	9.4	6.7	10.6
Freshwater siluroids	11.5	11.3	10.5
Other freshwater fishes	1.7	3.1	3.8
Pacific anchoveta	5.7	8.2	7.8
Skipjack tuna	14.1	12.1	19.5
Yellowfin tuna	31.3	22.8	23.3
Aquaculture	80.6*	80.4	83.7
Tilapias	28.2	41.0	38.4
Pirapatinga	8.2*	10.7	14.8
Rainbow trout	5.7	2.9	5.6
Whiteleg shrimp	18.1*	12.6	9.4
Total catch	187.1*	160.1	169.2

* FAO estimate.

Note: Figures exclude crocodiles, recorded by number rather than by weight. The number of spectacled caimans caught was: 405,386 in 2009; 647,565 in 2010; 638,903 in 2011. The number of American crocodiles caught was: 10 in 2009; 200 in 2010; 1,192 in 2011.

Source: FAO.

Mining

('000 metric tons unless otherwise indicated)

	2009	2010	2011
Gold (kg)	47,838	53,606	55,908
Silver (kg)	10,827	15,300	24,045
Salt	612	645	428
Hard coal	72,807	74,350	85,803
Iron ore*	281	77	174

* Figures refer to the gross weight of ore. The estimated iron content was 46%.

† Preliminary figure.

Source: US Geological Survey.

Crude petroleum ('000 metric tons, estimates): 35,320 in 2009; 41,391 in 2010; 48,206 in 2011; 49,863 in 2012 (Source: BP, *Statistical Review of World Energy*).

Natural gas ('000 million cu m): 10.5 in 2009; 11.3 in 2010; 11.0 in 2011; 12.0 in 2012 (Source: BP, *Statistical Review of World Energy*).

Industry

SELECTED PRODUCTS
('000 metric tons unless otherwise indicated)

	2008	2009	2010
Sugar	2,036	n.a.	n.a.
Cement*	10,456	9,100	9,488
Crude steel ingots (incl. steel for casting)*	1,125	1,053	1,213
Semi-manufactures of iron and steel (hot-rolled)*	1,435	1,454	1,614
Gas-diesel (distillate fuel) oils	4,395	3,570	3,501
Residual fuel oils	3,318	3,251	n.a.
Motor spirit (petrol)	3,164	2,964	3,113

* Source: US Geological Survey.

Source: mostly UN Industrial Commodity Statistics Database.

2011 ('000 metric tons): Cement 10,777; Crude steel ingots (incl. steel for casting) 1,290; Semi-manufactures of iron and steel (hot-rolled) 1,500 (estimate) (Source: US Geological Survey).

Finance

CURRENCY AND EXCHANGE RATES

Monetary Units
100 centavos = 1 Colombian peso.

Sterling, Dollar and Euro Equivalents (31 December 2013)
£1 sterling = 3,166.1 pesos;
US $1 = 1,922.6 pesos;
€1 = 2,651.4 pesos;
10,000 Colombian pesos = £3.16 = $5.20 = €3.77.

Average Exchange Rate (pesos per US $)
2011 1,848.14
2012 1,796.90
2013 1,868.79

GOVERNMENT FINANCE
(budgetary central government transactions, non-cash basis, '000 million pesos, provisional figures)

Summary of Balances

	2009	2010	2011
Revenue	79,016	82,319	106,031
Less Expense	92,050	97,497	103,500
Net operating balance	–13,033	–15,178	2,531
Less Net acquisition of non-financial assets	8,567	7,348	625
Net lending/borrowing	–21,600	–22,526	1,906

Revenue

	2009	2010	2011
Taxes	59,587	61,730	85,397
Taxes on income, profits and capital gains	23,061	20,539	23,325
Individuals	23,027	20,502	23,325
Taxes on goods and services	26,310	29,777	33,754
Social contributions	428	405	439
Grants	1,453	185	214
Other revenue	17,548	19,999	19,980
Total	79,016	82,319	106,031

Expense/Outlays

Expense by economic type	2009	2010	2011
Compensation of employees	6,677	7,113	7,609
Use of goods and services	5,990	6,871	6,923
Consumption of fixed capital	750	832	998
Interest	16,205	15,189	16,106
Subsidies	1,741	1,836	1,660
Grants	30,017	31,737	38,331
Social benefits	17,860	23,533	15,112
Other expense	12,808	10,385	16,761
Total	92,050	97,497	103,500

Source: IMF, *Government Finance Statistics Yearbook*.

2013 (budgetary central government transactions, '000 million pesos, 2013, preliminary): *Revenue* Tax revenue 101,685; Non-tax revenue 519; Funds 1,552; Capital revenue 14,559; Total 118,315. *Expenditure* Interest payments 19,019; Investment 20,269; Operational expense 94,808; Total 134,096 (excl. net lending 146) (Source: Ministry of Finance and Public Credit, Bogotá, DC).

Public sector account ('000 million pesos): *Revenue:* 146,896.3 in 2010; 171,213.0 in 2011; 193,798.4 in 2012 (preliminary). *Expenditure (incl. interest payments):* 161,588.6 in 2010; 175,680.1 in 2011; 185,732.9 in 2012 (preliminary).

INTERNATIONAL RESERVES

(US $ million at 31 December)

	2010	2011	2012
Gold (national valuation)	311	524	554
IMF special drawing rights	1,157	1,140	1,131
Reserve position in IMF	260	370	392
Foreign exchange	26,349	29,876	34,920
Total	28,077	31,910	36,997

Source: IMF, *International Financial Statistics*.

MONEY SUPPLY

('000 million pesos at 31 December)

	2010	2011	2012
Currency outside banks	29,674.1	33,366.9	35,063.3
Transferable deposits	29,790.5	33,177.0	36,694.8
Other deposits	78,180.1	95,573.2	109,695.5
Securities other than shares	68,754.7	83,340.9	103,453.4
Broad money	206,399.3	245,457.9	284,907.0

Source: IMF, *International Financial Statistics*.

COST OF LIVING

(Consumer Price Index for low-income families; base: 2000 = 100)

	2010	2011	2012
Food and beverages	191.7	201.0	209.2
All items (incl. others)	177.4	184.2	190.7

Source: ILO.

NATIONAL ACCOUNTS

('000 million pesos at current prices, provisional figures)

Expenditure on the Gross Domestic Product

	2010	2011	2012
Final consumption expenditure	434,319	479,364	518,685
Households*	342,072	379,592	408,897
General government	92,247	99,772	109,788
Gross capital formation	120,570	147,615	156,821
Gross fixed capital formation	119,091	146,522	157,074
Change in inventories	1,480	1,094	–253
Total domestic expenditure	554,890	626,980	675,506
Exports of goods and services	86,839	117,672	121,374
Less Imports of goods and services	96,805	123,037	131,115
GDP in market prices	544,924	621,615	665,765
GDP at constant 2005 prices	424,599	452,815	471,892

* Including non-profit institutions serving households.

Gross Domestic Product by Economic Activity

	2010	2011	2012
Agriculture, hunting, forestry and fishing	35,431	38,925	39,618
Mining and quarrying	45,960	70,145	74,987
Manufacturing	69,527	76,923	78,951
Electricity, gas and water	19,658	21,259	22,763
Construction	39,340	46,419	52,495
Wholesale and retail trade; repair of motor vehicles, motorcycles, and personal and household goods; hotels and restaurants	63,210	69,848	75,199
Transport, storage and communications	34,681	36,154	38,768
Financial intermediation, insurance, real estate, renting and business activities	105,048	114,085	124,176
Other community, social and personal service activities	86,280	93,342	101,910
Gross value added in basic prices	499,135	567,100	608,867
Taxes on products	46,340	55,407	57,852
Less Subsidies on products	551	892	954
GDP in market prices	544,924	621,615	665,765

BALANCE OF PAYMENTS

(US $ million)

	2010	2011	2012
Exports of goods	40,655.1	58,176.1	61,506.1
Imports of goods	–38,405.8	–52,127.0	–56,634.5
Balance on goods	2,249.3	6,049.1	4,871.6
Exports of services	4,322.5	4,749.6	5,152.7
Imports of services	–7,843.8	–9,340.1	–10,587.6
Balance on goods and services	–1,272.0	1,458.5	–563.3
Primary income received	1,439.2	2,709.7	3,816.2
Primary income paid	–13,463.0	–18,748.9	–19,743.7
Balance on goods, services and primary income	–13,295.9	–14,580.6	–16,490.8
Secondary income received	5,342.6	5,673.2	5,498.4
Secondary income paid	–867.9	–735.4	–915.1
Current balance	–8,821.2	–9,642.8	–11,907.5
Direct investment assets	–6,892.8	–8,304.3	302.9
Direct investment liabilities	6,753.4	13,403.5	15,612.2
Portfolio investment assets	–2,290.0	–2,111.3	–1,666.1
Portfolio investment liabilities	3,262.6	8,201.7	7,355.7
Other investment assets	1,187.4	–3,773.3	–2,191.6
Other investment liabilities	9,743.4	5,623.2	–2,479.8
Net errors and omissions	174.5	339.8	295.6
Reserves and related items	3,117.2	3,736.6	5,321.4

Source: IMF, *International Financial Statistics*.

External Trade

PRINCIPAL COMMODITIES

(US $ million)

Imports c.i.f.	2010	2011	2012
Agricultural, livestock, hunting and forestry products	2,000	2,543	2,685
Prepared foodstuffs, beverages and tobacco	2,236	2,873	3,624
Textiles, clothing and leather products	1,723	2,556	2,922
Chemical products	7,387	9,130	9,783
Rubber and plastic goods	1,406	1,842	2,062
Metals and metal manufactures	3,328	4,558	4,572
Mechanical, electrical, office, telecommunications and medical equipment	11,579	14,206	15,534
Vehicles and transport equipment	6,332	9,720	9,005
Total (incl. others)	40,486	54,233	59,111

Exports f.o.b.	2010	2011	2012
Coffee	1,884	2,608	1,910
Coal	6,015	8,397	7,805
Petroleum and its derivatives	16,502	28,421	31,559
Prepared foodstuffs, beverages and tobacco	3,591	4,775	3,988
Textiles, clothing and leather products	1,250	1,364	1,389
Paper and publishing	666	736	727
Chemicals	2,613	3,053	3,149
Metal manufactures	4,115	4,682	5,412
Mechanical, electrical and office equipment	633	735	836
Vehicles and transport equipment	469	457	618
Total (incl. others)	39,713	56,915	60,125

PRINCIPAL TRADING PARTNERS
(US $ million)

Imports c.i.f.	2010	2011	2012
Brazil	2,370	2,740	2,851
China, People's Republic	5,477	8,176	9,822
Ecuador	835	1,066	1,090
Germany	1,611	2,147	2,267
Japan	1,157	1,438	1,677
Mexico	3,857	6,059	6,453
Spain	502	614	789
USA	10,477	13,594	14,242
Venezuela	305	563	533
Total (incl. others)	40,486	54,233	59,111

Exports f.o.b.	2010	2011	2012
Belgium	450	621	488
Ecuador	1,825	1,909	1,910
Germany	250	420	395
Japan	511	528	360
Mexico	638	705	835
Peru	1,132	1,323	1,582
USA	16,764	21,969	21,833
Venezuela	1,423	1,725	2,556
Total (incl. others)	39,713	56,915	60,125

Transport

RAILWAYS
(traffic)

	1996	1997	1998
Freight ('000 metric tons)	321	348	281
Freight ton-km ('000)	746,544	736,427	657,585

Source: Sociedad de Transporte Ferroviario, SA.

ROAD TRAFFIC
(motor vehicles in use at 31 December)

	2007	2008	2009
Passenger cars	1,674,441	1,849,962	2,397,716
Vans and lorries	1,064,513	554,064	619,136
Buses	148,537	197,285	203,938
Motorcycles and mopeds	1,930,978	2,311,652	2,630,391

Source: IRF, *World Road Statistics*.

SHIPPING

Flag Registered Fleet
(at 31 December)

	2011	2012	2013
Number of vessels	569	575	593
Total displacement ('000 grt)	164.9	158.3	176.7

Source: Lloyd's List Intelligence (www.lloydslistintelligence.com).

Domestic Sea-borne Freight Traffic
('000 metric tons)

	1987	1988	1989
Goods loaded and unloaded	772.1	944.8	464.6

International Sea-borne Freight Traffic
('000 metric tons)

	1999	2000	2001
Goods loaded	4,111	3,543	3,832
Goods unloaded	1,274	1,114	1,399

CIVIL AVIATION
(traffic)

	2010	2011
Kilometres flown (million)	163	174
Passengers carried ('000)	16,932	18,769
Passenger-km (million)	16,723	17,832
Total ton-km (million)	2,555	2,687

Source: UN, *Statistical Yearbook*.

Passengers carried ('000): 20,945 in 2012 (Source: World Bank, World Development Indicators database).

Tourism

TOURIST ARRIVALS

Country of origin	2008	2009	2010
Argentina	51,057	61,358	77,495
Brazil	45,506	47,493	63,793
Canada	27,632	28,157	30,388
Chile	29,716	36,168	42,976
Costa Rica	21,179	20,184	22,588
Ecuador	93,452	101,820	116,358
France	27,381	30,366	29,897
Germany	22,133	26,138	24,134
Italy	24,320	26,054	22,706
Mexico	59,107	57,474	64,886
Netherlands	20,576	23,621	12,064
Panama	28,379	30,956	37,822
Peru	66,313	77,733	74,093
Spain	62,176	77,913	76,484
United Kingdom	17,112	18,947	20,055
USA	264,453	314,858	357,460
Venezuela	237,329	238,078	187,618
Total (incl. others)	1,222,966	1,353,700	1,474,863

Tourist arrivals ('000): 2,045 in 2011; 2,175 in 2012 (provisional).

Tourism receipts (US $ million, excl. passenger transport): 2,083 in 2010; 2,201 in 2011; 2,351 in 2012 (provisional).

Source: World Tourism Organization.

Communications Media

	2010	2011	2012
Telephones ('000 main lines in use)	7,186.2	7,126.7	6,290.7
Mobile cellular telephones ('000 subscribers)	44,477.7	46,200.4	49,066.4
Internet subscribers ('000)	2,675.5	3,297.0	n.a.
Broadband subscribers ('000)	2,594.1	3,256.6	3,975.2

Source: International Telecommunication Union.

Education

(2011/12 unless otherwise indicated)

	Institutions	Teachers	Students ('000) Males	Females	Total
Pre-primary	42,450*	54,603	668.9†	640.5†	1,309.4†
Primary	54,993*	189,335	2,461.6	2,280.9	4,742.5
Secondary: general	17,484*	155,926‡	2,249.9	2,335.0	4,584.9
Secondary: technical/vocational		31,198‡	145.5	173.0	318.5
Higher (incl. universities)	32§	110,488‖	935.2	1,023.2	1,958.4

* 2007/08.
† 2010/11.
‡ 2009/10.
§ 2001/02.
‖ 2008/09.

Sources: Ministerio de Educación Nacional and UNESCO Institute for Statistics.

Pupil-teacher ratio (primary education, UNESCO estimate): 25.0 in 2011/12 (Source: UNESCO Institute for Statistics).

Adult literacy rate (UNESCO estimates): 93.6% (males 93.5%; females 93.7%) in 2011 (Source: UNESCO Institute for Statistics).

Directory

The Government

HEAD OF STATE

President: JUAN MANUEL SANTOS CALDERÓN (took office on 7 August 2010).

Vice-President: ANGELINO GARZÓN.

CABINET
(April 2014)

The Government is formed by a coalition led by the Partido Social de la Unidad Nacional.

Minister of the Interior: AURELIO IRAGORRI VALENCIA.

Minister of Foreign Affairs: MARÍA ANGELA HOLGUÍN CUÉLLAR.

Minister of Finance and Public Credit: MAURICIO CÁRDENAS SANTAMARÍA.

Minister of National Defence: JUAN CARLOS PINZÓN BUENO.

Minister of Justice and Law: ALFONSO GÓMEZ MÉNDEZ.

Minister of Agriculture and Rural Development: RUBÉN DARIO LIZARRALDE MONTOYA.

Minister of Health and Social Protection: ALEJANDRO GAVIRIA URIBE.

Minister of Mines and Energy: AMILKAR ACOSTA MEDINA.

Minister of Trade, Industry and Tourism: SANTIAGO ROJAS ARROYO.

Minister of National Education: MARÍA FERNANDA CAMPO SAAVEDRA.

Minister of Housing, Cities and Territorial Development: LUIS FELIPE HENAO CARDONA.

Minister of the Environment and Sustainable Development: LUZ HELENA SARMIENTO VILLAMIZAR.

Minister of Information Technology and Communications: DIEGO MOLANO VEGA.

Minister of Transport: CECILIA ALVAREZ-CORREA.

Minister of Culture: MARIANA GARCÉS CÓRDOBA.

Minister of Labour: RAFAEL PARDO RUEDA.

Minister-Counsellor for Social Dialogue and Citizen Mobilization: LUIS EDUARDO (LUCHO) GARZÓN.

High Commissioner for Peace: SERGIO JARAMILLO CARO.

In addition, there are nine other Minister-Counsellors and five Secretaries in the Cabinet.

MINISTRIES

Office of the President: Palacio de Nariño, Carrera 8, No 7-26, Bogotá, DC; tel. (1) 562-9300; fax (1) 286-8063; internet www.presidencia.gov.co.

Ministry of Agriculture and Rural Development: Avda Jiménez, No 7A-17, Bogotá, DC; tel. (1) 334-1199; fax (1) 284-1775; e-mail despachoministro@minagricultura.gov.co; internet www.minagricultura.gov.co.

Ministry of Culture: Carrera 8, No 8-43, Bogotá, DC; tel. (1) 342-4100; fax (1) 381-6353; e-mail servicioalcliente@mincultura.gov.co; internet www.mincultura.gov.co.

Ministry of the Environment and Sustainable Development: Calle 37, No 8-40, Bogotá, DC; tel. (1) 332-3400; fax (1) 332-3400; e-mail servicioalciudadano@minambiente.gov.co; internet www.minambiente.gov.co.

Ministry of Finance and Public Credit: Carrera 8, No 6C-38, Of. 305, Bogotá, DC; tel. (1) 381-1700; fax (1) 381-2863; e-mail atencioncliente@minhacienda.gov.co; internet www.minhacienda.gov.co.

Ministry of Foreign Affairs: Palacio de San Carlos, Calle 10, No 5-51, Bogotá, DC; tel. (1) 381-4000; fax (1) 381-4747; e-mail cancilleria@cancilleria.gov.co; internet www.cancilleria.gov.co.

Ministry of Health and Social Protection: Carrera 13, No 32-76, Bogotá, DC; tel. (1) 330-5000; fax (1) 330-5050; e-mail atencionalciudadano@minproteccionsocial.gov.co; internet www.minproteccionsocial.gov.co.

Ministry of Housing, Cities and Territorial Development: Calle 18, No 7-59, Bogotá, DC; tel. (1) 332-3434; fax (1) 281-7327; e-mail correspondencia@minvivienda.gov.co; internet www.minvivienda.gov.co.

Ministry of Information Technology and Communications: Edif. Murillo Toro, Carrera 8A entre, Calle 12 y 13, Apdo Aéreo 111711, Bogotá, DC; tel. (1) 344-3460; fax (1) 344-2293; e-mail info@mintic.gov.co; internet www.mintic.gov.co.

Ministry of the Interior: La Giralda, Carrera 8, No 7-83, Bogotá, DC; tel. (1) 242-7400; fax (1) 341-9583; e-mail servicioalciudadano@mininterior.gov.co; internet www.mininterior.gov.co.

Ministry of Justice and Law: Carrera 9, No 12C-10, Bogotá, DC; tel. (1) 444-3100; e-mail reclamos.minjusticia@minjusticia.gov.co; internet www.minjusticia.gov.co.

Ministry of Labour: Carrera 14, No 99-33, Bogotá, DC; tel. (1) 489-3900; fax (1) 489-3100; e-mail contactenostlc@mintrabajo.gov.co; internet www.mintrabajo.gov.co.

Ministry of Mines and Energy: Calle 43, No 57-31, Centro Administrativo Nacional (CAN), Bogotá, DC; tel. (1) 220-0300; fax

(1) 222-3651; e-mail menergia@minminas.gov.co; internet www.minminas.gov.co.

Ministry of National Defence: Carrera 54, No 26-25, Centro Administrativo Nacional (CAN), Bogotá, DC; tel. (1) 266-0296; fax (1) 315-0111; e-mail usuarios@mindefensa.gov.co; internet www.mindefensa.gov.co.

Ministry of National Education: Calle 43, No 57-14, Centro Administrativo Nacional (CAN), Bogotá, DC; tel. (1) 222-2800; fax (1) 222-4953; e-mail dci@mineducacion.gov.co; internet www.mineducacion.gov.co.

Ministry of Trade, Industry and Tourism: Edif. Centro de Comercio Internacional, Calle 28, No 13A-15, 18°, Bogotá, DC; tel. (1) 606-7676; fax (1) 606-7522; e-mail info@mincomercio.gov.co; internet www.mincomercio.gov.co.

Ministry of Transport: Centro Administrativo Nacional (CAN), Of. 409, Avda El Dorado, Transversal 45, No 47-14, Bogotá, DC; tel. (1) 324-0800; fax (1) 428-7054; e-mail mintrans@mintransporte.gov.co; internet www.mintransporte.gov.co.

President and Legislature

PRESIDENT

Presidential Election, First Round, 30 May 2010

	Valid votes	% of votes cast
Juan Manuel Santos Calderón (Partido de la U)	6,802,043	46.68
Antanas Mockus Šivickas (PV)	3,134,222	21.51
Germán Vargas Lleras (CR)	1,473,627	10.11
Gustavo Petro Urrego (PDA)	1,331,267	9.14
Noemí Sanín (PCC)	893,819	6.13
Rafael Pardo Rueda (PL)	638,302	4.38
Others	75,336	0.52
Votos en blanco*	223,977	1.52
Total†	14,572,593	100.00

* Blank, valid votes.
† In addition, there were 208,427 invalid votes.

Presidential Election, Second Round, 20 June 2010

	Valid votes	% of votes cast
Juan Manuel Santos Calderón (Partido de la U)	9,028,942	69.13
Antanas Mockus Šivickas (PV)	3,587,975	27.47
Votos en blanco*	444,274	3.40
Total valid votes†	13,061,191	100.00

* Blank, valid votes.
† In addition, there were 235,732 invalid votes.

CONGRESS

Senate
(Senado)

President: JUAN FERNANDO CRISTO BUSTOS.

General Election, 9 March 2014, preliminary results

	Seats
Partido Social de la Unidad Nacional (Partido de la U)	21
Centro Democrático (CD)	19
Partido Conservador Colombiano (PCC)	19
Partido Liberal Colombiano (PL)	17
Cambio Radical (CR)	9
Alianza Partido Verde (PV)	5
Polo Democrático Alternativo (PDA)	5
Opción Ciudadana	5
Indigenous groups*	2
Total	102

* Under the terms of the Constitution, at least two Senate seats are reserved for indigenous groups.

House of Representatives
(Cámara de Representantes)

President: HERNÁN PENAGOS GIRALDO.

General Election, 9 March 2014, preliminary results

	Seats
Partido Liberal Colombiano (PL)	39
Partido Social de la Unidad Nacional (Partido de la U)	37
Partido Conservador Colombiano (PCC)	27
Cambio Radical (CR)	16
Centro Democrático (CD)	12
Alianza Partido Verde (PV)	6
Opción Ciudadana	6
Polo Democrático Alternativo (PDA)	3
Movimiento MIRA	3
Fundación Ebano de Colombia Funeco	2
Indigenous groups*	2
Others	3
Undecided	10
Total	166

* Under the terms of the Constitution, at least two lower house seats are reserved for indigenous groups.

Governors

DEPARTMENTS
(April 2014)

Amazonas: WILSON MUÑOZ CABRERA (acting).

Antioquia: SERGIO FAJARDO VALDERRAMA.

Arauca: JOSÉ FACUNDO CASTILLO CISNERO.

Atlántico: JOSÉ ANTONIO SEGEBRE BERARDINELLI.

Bolívar: JUAN CARLOS GOSSAÍN ROGNINI.

Boyacá: JUAN CARLOS GRANADOS BECERRA.

Caldas: JULIÁN GUTIÉRREZ BOTERO.

Caquetá: VÍCTOR ISIDRO RAMÍREZ LOAIZA.

Casanare: MARCO TULIO RUIZ RIAÑO.

Cauca: TEMÍSTOCLES ORTEGA NARVÁEZ.

César: LUIS ALBERTO MONSALVO GNECCO.

Chocó: EFRÉN PALACIOS SERNA.

Córdoba: ALEJANDRO LYONS MUSKUS.

Cundinamarca: ALVARO CRÚZ VARGAS.

Guainía: OSCAR ARMANDO RODRÍGUEZ SÁNCHEZ.

La Guajira: SUGEILA OÑATE ROSADO (acting).

Guaviare: JOSÉ OCTAVIANO RIVERA MONCADA.

Huila: CARLOS MAURICIO IRIARTE BARRIOS.

Magdalena: LUÍS MIGUEL COTES HABEYCH.

Meta: ALÁN JESÚS EDMUNDO JARA URZOLA.

Nariño: SEGUNDO RAÚL DELGADO GUERRERO.

Norte de Santander: EDGAR JESÚS DÍAZ CONTRERAS.

Putumayo: JIMMY HAROLD DÍAZ BURBANO.

Quindío: SANDRA PAOLA HURTADO PALACIO.

Risaralda: CARLOS ALBERTO BOTERO LÓPEZ.

San Andrés y Providencia Islands: AURY SOCORRO GUERRERO.

Santander del Sur: RICHARD ALFONSO AGUILAR VILLA.

Sucre: JULIO CÉSAR GUERRA TULENA.

Tolima: LUÍS CARLOS DELGADO PEÑÓN.

Valle del Cauca: UBEIMAR DELGADO BLANDÓN.

Vaupés: ROBERTO JARAMILLO GARCÍA.

Vichada: SERGIO ANDRÉS ESPINOSA FLORES.

Bogotá, DC: GUSTAVO FRANCISCO PETRO URREGO.

Election Commissions

Consejo Nacional Electoral (CNE): Edif. Organización Electoral (CAN), Avda Calle 26 No 51-50, Bogotá, DC; tel. (1) 220-0800; e-mail contactenos.cne@registraduria.gov.co; internet www.cne.gov.co; f. 1888 as Gran Consejo Electoral; refounded under current name in 1985; Pres. PABLO GUILLERMO GIL DE LA HOZ.

Registraduría Nacional del Estado Civil: Avda Calle 26, No 51-50, Bogotá, DC; tel. (1) 220-2880; internet www.registraduria.gov.co; f. 1948; ensures electoral transparency; Registrar CARLOS ARIEL SÁNCHEZ TORRES.

Political Organizations

Alianza Social Independiente: Calle 17, No 5-43, 8°, Bogotá, DC; tel. (1) 283-0616; fax (1) 282-7474; e-mail alianzasocialindependiente@gmail.com; internet www.asicolombia .com; f. 1991; fmrly Alianza Social Indígena; Leader ALONSO TOBON.

Cambio Radical (CR): Carrera 7, No 26-20, 26°, Bogotá, DC; tel. (1) 327-9696; fax (1) 210-6800; e-mail cambioradical@cable.net.co; internet www.partidocambioradical.org; f. 1998; contesting the 2014 elections in coalition with the Partido de la U; Pres. GERMÁN VARGAS LLERAS; Sec.-Gen. ANTONIO ALVAREZ LLERAS.

Centro Democrático (CD) (Centro Democrático Mano Firme Corazón Grande): Bogotá, DC; internet centrodemocratico.com.co; f. 2013 by supporters of fmr Pres. Alvaro Uribe; right-wing; Pres. ALVARO URIBE VÉLEZ.

Compromiso Ciudadano por Colombia: Carrera 36, 8A-46, Of. 201, Medellín; tel. (4) 448-6048; fax (4) 312-7014; e-mail info@ sergiofajardo.com; internet www.sergiofajardo.com; f. 2008; Leader SERGIO FAJARDO.

Fundación Ebano de Colombia Funeco: internet fundacionebanocolombia.jimdo.com; f. 1998; represents those of African descent; Leader CASSIANI HERRERA ALEXI.

Marcha Patriótica: internet www.marchapatriotica.org; f. 2012; left-wing, supports the Fuerzas Armadas Revolucionarias de Colombia—Ejército del Pueblo (q.v.).

Movimiento Apertura Liberal: Avda 3B, 5-70B, Latino, Cúcuta, Norte de Santander; tel. (7) 571-3729; e-mail info@aperturaliberal .com; f. 1993; Nat. Dir Dr MIGUEL ANGEL FLÓREZ RIVERA.

Movimiento de Autoridades Indígenas de Colombia (AICO): Calle 23, No 7-61, Of. 302, Bogotá DC; tel. (1) 286-8233; fax (1) 341-8930; e-mail aico@aicocolombia.org; internet www.aicocolombia.org; f. 1990; Pres. LUIS HUMBERTO CUASPUD.

Movimiento MIRA (Movimiento Independiente de Renovación Absoluta): Transversal 29, No 36-40, Bogotá, DC; tel. (1) 369-3222; fax 369-3210; e-mail contacto@movimientomira.com; internet www .movimientomira.com; f. 2000; Pres. CARLOS ALBERTO BAENA LÓPEZ.

Movimiento Progresista Colombiano: Carrera 15, No 44-18, CP 11001, Bogotá, DC; tel. (1) 289-7895; e-mail progresistascolombia@ etb.net.co; internet www.colombiaprogresistas.com; f. 2011; Leader GUSTAVO FRANCISCO PETRO URREGO.

Opción Ciudadana: Calle 39, No 28A–26, Bogotá, DC; tel. (1) 340-8120; fax (1) 244-0189; internet www.partidoopcionciudadana.com; f. 2009; Sec.-Gen. EDISON BIOSCAR RUIZ VALENCIA.

Partido Colombia Democrática: Calle 41, No 13A-07, 2°, Bogotá, DC; tel. (1) 338-3624; fax (1) 338-2310; e-mail contactenos@ colombiademocratica.com; f. 2003; conservative; Nat. Dir MARIO URIBE ESCOBAR; Sec.-Gen. GABRIEL SIERRA.

Partido Comunista Colombiano (PC): Calle 18A, No 14-56, Apdo Aéreo 2523, Bogotá, DC; tel. (1) 334-1947; fax (1) 281-8259; e-mail notipaco@pacocol.org; internet www.pacocol.org; f. 1930; Marxist-Leninist; Sec.-Gen. JAIME CAYCEDO TURRIAGO.

Partido Conservador Colombiano (PCC): Avda Carrera 24, No 37-09, La Soledad, Bogotá, DC; tel. (1) 597-9630; fax (1) 369-0053; e-mail presidencia@partidoconservador.com; internet www .partidoconservador.com; f. 1849; contesting the 2014 elections in coalition with the Partido de la U; 2.9m. mems; Pres. OMAR YEPES ALZATE; Sec.-Gen. JUAN CARLOS WILLS OSPINA.

Partido de Integración Nacional (PIN): Calle 39, No 28A-26, Barrio La Soledad, Bogotá, DC; tel. (1) 608-8822; fax (1) 244-0189; e-mail convergencia@intercable.net.co; internet partidopin.org; f. 2009; pro-Govt party; Pres. SAMUEL ARRIETA.

Partido Liberal Colombiano (PL): Avda Caracas, No 36-01, Bogotá, DC; tel. (1) 593-4500; fax (1) 323-1070; e-mail direcciondecomunicaciones@partidoliberal.org.co; internet www .partidoliberal.org.co; f. 1848; contesting the 2014 elections in coalition with the Partido de la U; Pres. SIMÓN GAVIRIA MUÑOZ; Sec.-Gen. HÉCTOR OLIMPO ESPINOSA.

Partido de la U (Partido Social de la Unidad Nacional): Carrera 7, No 32-16, 21°, Bogotá, DC; tel. and fax (1) 350-0215; internet www .partidodelau.com; f. 2005; conservative; Pres. JAIME BUENAHORA, AURELIO IRAGORRI; Sec.-Gen. FELIPE CARREÑO.

Partido Alianza Verde (PV): Calle 66, No 7–69, Bogotá, DC; tel. (1) 606-7888; fax (1) 608-1312; e-mail movilizacion@partidoverde.org .co; internet www.partidoverde.org.co; Nat. Dir CARLOS RAMÓN GONZÁLEZ; Sec.-Gen. NÉSTOR DANIEL GARCÍA COLORADO.

Polo Democrático Alternativo (PDA): Carrera 17A, No 37-27, Bogotá, DC; tel. (1) 288-6188; e-mail info@polodemocratico.net; internet www.polodemocratico.net; f. 2002 as electoral alliance, constituted as a political party in July 2003; founded by fmr mems of the Movimiento 19 de Abril; fmrly Polo Democrático Independiente; adopted current name 2006; left-wing; Pres. CLARA LÓPEZ OBREGÓN; Sec.-Gen. GERMÁN ÁVILA.

Unión Patriótica (UP): Carrera 13A, No 38-32, Of. 204, Bogotá, DC; fax (1) 570-4400; f. 1985; Marxist party formed by the Fuerzas Armadas Revolucionarias de Colombia—Ejército del Pueblo (q.v.); declared illegal in 2002; legal status reinstated in 2013; Pres. OMER CALDERÓN.

The following are the principal guerrilla groups in operation in Colombia:

Ejército de Liberación Nacional (ELN): internet www.eln-voces .com; Castroite guerrilla movt; f. 1964; 1,500 mems; political status recognized by the Govt in 1998; Leader NICOLÁS RODRÍGUEZ BAUTISTA (alias Gabino).

Fuerzas Armadas Revolucionarias de Colombia—Ejército del Pueblo (FARC—EP): internet www.farc-ep.co; f. 1964, although mems active from 1949; name changed from Fuerzas Armadas Revolucionarias de Colombia to the above in 1982; fmrly military wing of the Communist Party; composed of 39 armed fronts and 8,000 mems; political status recognized by the Govt in 1998; mem. of the Coordinadora Nacional Guerrilla Simón Bolívar; C-in-C RODRIGO LONDOÑO ECHEVERRI (alias Timochenko).

Diplomatic Representation

EMBASSIES IN COLOMBIA

Algeria: Carrera 11, No 93-53, Of. 302, Bogotá, DC; tel. (1) 635-0520; fax (1) 635-0531; e-mail admin@embargelia-colombia.org; internet www.embargelia-colombia.org; Ambassador MOHAMED ZIANE HASSENI.

Argentina: Carrera 12, 97-80, 5°, Bogotá, DC; tel. (1) 288-0900; fax (1) 384-9488; e-mail embargentina@etb.net.co; internet www.ecolo .mrecic.gov.ar; Ambassador CELSO ALEJANDRO JAQUE.

Belgium: Calle 26, No 4A-45, 7°, Apdo Aéreo 3564, Bogotá, DC; tel. (1) 380-0370; fax (1) 380-0340; e-mail bogota@diplobel.fed.be; internet www.diplomatie.be/bogota; Ambassador SADI PAUL BRANCART.

Bolivia: Carrera 10, No 113-36, Santa Bárbara Central, Bogotá, DC; tel. (1) 619-4701; fax (1) 619-6050; e-mail central@ embajadaboliviacolombia.org; internet www .embajadaboliviacolombia.org; Ambassador MARÍO CARVAJAL LOZANO.

Brazil: Calle 93, No 14-20, 8°, Apdo 90540, Bogotá, DC; tel. (1) 218-0800; fax (1) 218-8393; e-mail embaixada@brasil.org.co; internet bogota.itamaraty.gov.br; Ambassador MARIA ELISA BERENGUER.

Canada: Carretera 7, No 114-33, 14°, Apdo Aéreo 110067, Bogotá, DC; tel. (1) 657-9800; fax (1) 657-9912; e-mail bgota@international.gc .ca; internet www.canadainternational.gc.ca/colombia-colombie; Ambassador CARMEN SILVAIN.

Chile: Calle 100, No 11B-44, Apdo Aéreo 90061, Bogotá, DC; tel. (1) 742-0136; fax (1) 744-1469; e-mail echile.colombia@minrel.gov.cl; internet chileabroad.gov.cl/colombia; Ambassador GUSTAVO AYARES OSSANDÓN.

China, People's Republic: Carrera 16, No 98-30, Bogotá, DC; tel. (1) 622-3215; fax (1) 622-3114; e-mail chinaemb_co@mfa.gov.cn; internet co.china-embassy.org; Ambassador WANG XIAOYUAN.

Costa Rica: Carrera 12, No 114-37, Santa Bárbara Central, Bogotá, DC; tel. (1) 629-5095; fax (1) 691-8558; e-mail embacosta@etb.net.co; internet www.embajadadecostarica.org; Ambassador CIRCE MILENA VILLANUEVA MONGE.

Cuba: Carrera 9, No 92-54, Bogotá, DC; tel. (1) 621-7054; fax (1) 611-4382; e-mail embacuba@cable.net.co; internet www .cubadiplomatica.cu/colombia; Ambassador JORGE IVÁN MORA GODOY.

Dominican Republic: Carrera 18, No 123-43, Bogotá, DC; tel. (1) 601-1670; fax (1) 620-7597; e-mail embajado@cable.net.co; Ambassador BRIUNNY GARABITO.

Ecuador: Edif. Fernando Mazuera, 7°, Calle 72, No 6-30, Bogotá, DC; tel. (1) 212-6512; fax (1) 212-6536; e-mail eecucolombia@mmrree .gov.ec; internet www.ecuadorencolombia.net; Ambassador CÉSAR RAUL VALLEJO CORRAL.

Egypt: Carrera 16, No 101-51, Bogotá, DC; tel. (1) 236-9917; fax (1) 236-9914; e-mail embajadadeegipto@telmex.net.co; Ambassador TAREK MAHMOUD ELKOUNY.

El Salvador: Edif. El Nogal, Of. 503, Carrera 9, No 80-15, Bogotá, DC; tel. (1) 349-6771; fax (1) 349-6670; e-mail elsalvador@supercable .net.co; Ambassador MARCOS GREGORIO SÁNCHEZ TREJO.

France: Carrera 11, No 93-12, Bogotá, DC; tel. (1) 638-1400; fax (1) 638-1430; e-mail amfrabog@andinet.com; internet www .ambafrance-co.org; Ambassador JEAN-MARC LAFORÊT.

Germany: Edif. Torre Empresarial Pacífic, 11°, Calle 110, No 9-25, Bogotá, DC; tel. (1) 423-2600; fax (1) 423-2615; e-mail info@bogota

.diplo.de; internet www.bogota.diplo.de; Ambassador GÜNTER KNIESS.

Guatemala: Calle 87, No 20-27, Of. 302, Bogotá, DC; tel. (1) 257-6133; fax (1) 610-1449; e-mail embcolombia@minex.gob.gt; Ambassador MANILO FERNANDO SESENNA OLIVERO.

Holy See: Carrera 15, No 36-33, Apdo Aéreo 3740, Bogotá, DC (Apostolic Nunciature); tel. (1) 705-4545; fax (1) 285-1817; e-mail nunciatura@cable.net.co; Apostolic Nuncio ETTORE BALESTRERO (Titular Archbishop of Victoriana).

Honduras: Carrera 12, No 119-52, Barrio Multicentro, Bogotá, DC; tel. (1) 629-3302; fax (1) 217-1457; e-mail info@embajadadehonduras.org.co; internet www.embajadadehonduras.org.co; Ambassador FRANCISCO RAMÓN ZEPEDA ANDINO.

India: Calle 116, No 301, Torre Cusezar, Bogotá, DC; tel. (1) 637-3259; fax (1) 637-3451; e-mail central@embajadaindia.org; internet www.embajadaindia.org; Ambassador RIEWARD W. WARJRI.

Indonesia: Carrera 11, No 75-27, Bogotá, DC; tel. (1) 217-2404; fax (1) 326-2165; e-mail eindones@colomsat.net.co; internet bogota.kemlu.go.id; Ambassador TRIE EDI MULYANI.

Iran: Calle 96, No 11A-20, Apdo 93854, Bogotá, DC; tel. (1) 256-2862; fax (1) 256-2842; e-mail emiracol@gmail.com; Chargé d'affaires a.i. ALIREZA SABZALI.

Israel: Calle 35, No 7-25, 14°, Bogotá, DC; tel. (1) 327-7500; fax (1) 327-7555; e-mail info@bogota.mfa.gov.il; internet bogota.mfa.gov.il; Ambassador YOED MAGEN.

Italy: Calle 93B, No 9-92, Apdo Aéreo 50901, Bogotá, DC; tel. (1) 218-7206; fax (1) 610-5886; e-mail ambbogo.mail@esteri.it; internet www.ambbogota.esteri.it; Ambassador GIANNI BARDINI.

Jamaica: Avda 19, No 106A-83, Of. 304, Apdo Aéreo 102428, Bogotá, DC; tel. (1) 612-3389; fax (1) 612-3479; e-mail emjacol@cable.net.com; Chargé d'affaires ELAINE TOWNSEND DE SÁNCHEZ.

Japan: Carrera 7A, No 71-21, 11°, Torre B, Bogotá, DC; tel. (1) 317-5001; fax (1) 317-4989; e-mail info@embjp-colombia.com; internet www.colombia.emb-japan.go.jp; Ambassador KAZUO WATANABE.

Korea, Republic: Calle 94, No 9-39, Bogotá, DC; tel. (1) 616-7200; fax (1) 610-0338; e-mail embcorea@mofat.go.kr; internet col.mofat.go.kr/index.jsp; Ambassador CHOO JONG-YOUN.

Lebanon: Calle 74, No 11-88, CP 51084, Bogotá, DC; tel. (1) 348-1781; fax (1) 347-9106; e-mail info@embajadadellibano.org.co; internet www.embajadadellibano.org.co; Ambassador HASSAN MUSLIMANI.

Mexico: Edif. Teleport Business Park, Calle 113, No 7-21, Of. 204, Torre A, Barrio Santa Ana, Bogotá, DC; tel. (1) 629-4989; fax (1) 629-5121; e-mail emcolmex@etb.net.co; internet www.sre.gob.mx/colombia; Ambassador ARNULFO VALDIVIA MACHUCA.

Morocco: Carrera 23, No 104A-34, Bogotá, DC; tel. (1) 619-3681; fax (1) 619-3685; e-mail embamarruecos@etb.net.co; internet www.embajadamarruecosbogota.com; Ambassador NOUREDDINE KHALIFA.

Netherlands: Carrera 13, No 93-40, 5°, Apdo Aéreo 43585, Bogotá, DC; tel. (1) 638-4200; fax (1) 623-3020; e-mail bog@minbuza.nl; internet colombia.nlembajada.org; Ambassador ROBERT VAN EMBDEN.

Nicaragua: Calle 108A, No 25-42, Bogotá, DC; tel. (1) 703-6450; fax (1) 612-6050; e-mail embnicaragua@007mundo.com; Ambassador JULIO JOSÉ CALERO REYES.

Norway: OXO Centre, Of. 904, Carrera 11A, No 94-45, Bogotá, DC; tel. (1) 651-5500; fax (1) 2395-6902; e-mail emb.bogota@mfa.no; internet colombia.norway.info; Ambassador LARS OLE VAAGEN.

Panama: Calle 92, No 7A-40, Bogotá, DC; tel. (1) 257-5068; fax (1) 257-5067; e-mail embpacol@cable.net.co; internet www.empacol.org; Ambassador RICARDO ANGUIZOLA.

Paraguay: Calle 72, No 10-51, 10°, Of. 1001, Bogotá, DC; tel. (1) 235-6987; fax (1) 212-7552; e-mail embparaguaycol@gmail.com; internet www.mre.gov.py/embaparcolombia; Ambassador RICARDO LAVIERO SCAVONE YEGROS.

Peru: Calle 80A, No 6-50, Bogotá, DC; tel. (1) 257-0505; fax (1) 249-8581; e-mail embaperu@embajadadelperu.org.co; internet www.embajadadelperu.org.co; Ambassador NESTOR FRANCISCO POPOLIZIO BARDALES.

Poland: Carrera 21, Calle 104A, No 23-48, Apdó Aéreo 101363, Bogotá, DC; tel. (1) 214-0400; fax (1) 214-0854; e-mail bogota.amb.sekretariat@msz.gov.pl; internet www.bogota.polemb.net; Ambassador MACIEJ ZIĘTARA.

Portugal: Carrera 2, No 109-92, Barrio Santa Ana, Bogotá, DC; tel. (1) 215-6430; fax (1) 637-0042; e-mail embporbog@cable.net.co; Ambassador JOÃO MANUEL RIBEIRO DE ALMEIDA.

Romania: Carrera 7A, No 92-58, Chico, Bogotá, DC; tel. (1) 256-6438; fax (1) 256-6158; e-mail ambrombogota@etb.net.co; internet bogota.mae.ro; Chargé d'affaires a.i. RADU SARBU.

Russia: Carrera 4, No 75-02, Apdo Aéreo 90600, Bogotá, DC; tel. (1) 212-1881; fax (1) 210-4694; e-mail embajadaderusiaencolombia@gmail.com; internet www.colombia.mid.ru; Ambassador PÁVEL SÉRGIEV.

Spain: Calle 92, No 12-68, Apdo 90355, Bogotá, DC; tel. (1) 593-0370; fax (1) 621-0809; e-mail informae@maec.es; internet www.mae.es/embajadas/bogota; Ambassador NICOLÁS MARTIN CINTO.

Sweden: Edif. Avenida Chile, 8°, Calle 72, No 5-83, Apdo Aéreo 52966, Bogotá, DC; tel. (1) 325-6100; fax (1) 325-6101; e-mail embsueca@cable.net.co; internet www.swedenabroad.com/bogota; Ambassador MARIE ANDERSSON DE FRUTOS.

Switzerland: Carrera 9, No 74-08, Of. 1101, 11°, Apdo Aéreo 251957, Bogotá, DC; tel. (1) 349-7230; fax (1) 349-7195; e-mail bog.vertretung@eda.admin.ch; internet www.eda.admin.ch/bogota; Ambassador DORA RAPOLD.

Turkey: Calle 76, No 8-47, Bogotá, DC; tel. (1) 321-0073; fax (1) 321-0076; e-mail turkemb.bogota@hotmail.com; Ambassador ENGIN YÜRUR.

United Kingdom: Edif. ING Barings, Carrera 9, No 76-49, 9°, Bogotá, DC; tel. (1) 326-8300; fax (1) 326-8302; e-mail ppa.bogota@fco.gov.uk; internet ukincolombia.fco.gov.uk; Ambassador LINDSAY CROISDALE-APPLEBY.

USA: Calle 24-bis, No 48-50, Apdo Aéreo 3831, Bogotá, DC; tel. (1) 275-2000; fax (1) 275-4600; e-mail AmbassadorB@state.gov; internet bogota.usembassy.gov; Chargé d'affaires a.i. BENJAMIN ZIFF.

Uruguay: Edif. El Nogal, Carrera 9A, No 80-15, 11°, Apdo Aéreo 101466, Bogotá, DC; tel. (1) 235-2748; fax (1) 248-3734; e-mail urucolom@etb.net.co; Ambassador DUNCAN CAYRÚS CROCI DE MULA.

Venezuela: Edif. Horizonte, 5°, Carrera 11, No 87-51, 5°, Bogotá, DC; tel. (1) 644-5555; fax (1) 640-1242; e-mail correspondencia.colombia@mppre.gob.ve; internet colombia.embajada.gob.ve; Ambassador IVÁN GUILLERMO RINCÓN URDANETA.

Judicial System

CONSTITUTIONAL COURT

The constitutional integrity of the State is ensured by the Constitutional Court. The Constitutional Court is composed of nine judges who are elected by the Senate for eight years. Judges of the Constitutional Court are not eligible for re-election.

Corte Constitucional: Edif. del Palacio de Justicia, Calle 12, No 7-65, Bogotá, DC; tel. (1) 350-6200; fax (1) 336-6822; internet www.corteconstitucional.gov.co; f. 1991; Pres. JORGE IVÁN PALACIO PALACIO.

SUPREME COURT OF JUSTICE

The ordinary judicial integrity of the State is ensured by the Supreme Court of Justice. The Supreme Court of Justice is composed of the Courts of Civil and Agrarian, Penal, and Labour Cassation. Judges of the Supreme Court of Justice, of which there are 23, are selected from the nominees of the Higher Council of Justice and serve an eight-year term of office, which is not renewable.

Corte Suprema de Justicia: Edif. de Palacio de Justicia, Calle 12, No 7-65, Bogotá, DC; tel. (1) 562-2000; internet www.cortesuprema.gov.co; Pres. Dr LUÍS GABRIEL MIRANDA BUELVAS.

Court of Civil Cassation (seven judges): Pres. Dr JESÚS VALL DE RUTEN RUIZ.

Court of Penal Cassation (nine judges): Pres. Dr FERNANDO ALBERTO CASTRO CABALLERO.

Court of Labour Cassation (seven judges): Pres. Dr RIGOBERTO ECHEVERRI BUENO.

Attorney-General: EDUARDO MONTEALEGRE LYNETT.

COUNCIL OF STATE

The Council of State serves as the supreme consultative body to the Government in matters of legislation and administration. It also serves as the supreme tribunal for administrative litigation (*Contencioso Administrativo*). It is composed of 27 magistrates, including a President.

Council of State: Edif. del Palacio de Justicia, Calle 12, No 7-65, Bogotá, DC; tel. (1) 350-6700; internet www.consejodeestado.gov.co; Pres. Dr MARIA CLAUDIA ROJAS LASSO.

Religion

CHRISTIANITY

The Roman Catholic Church

Colombia comprises 13 archdioceses, 52 dioceses and 10 apostolic vicariates. Some 87% of the population are Roman Catholics.

Bishops' Conference: Conferencia Episcopal de Colombia, Carrera 58, No 80-87, Apdo Aéreo 7448, Bogotá, DC; tel. (1) 437-5540; fax (1) 311-5575; e-mail colcec@cec.org.co; internet www.cec.org.co; f. 1978; statutes approved 1996; Pres. Cardinal JESÚS RUBÉN SALAZAR GÓMEZ (Archbishop of Bogotá).

Archbishop of Barranquilla: JAIRO JARAMILLO MONSALVE, Carrera 45, No 53-122, Apdo Aéreo 1160, Barranquilla 4, Atlántico; tel. (5) 360-0047; fax (5) 349-1530; e-mail contactenos@arquidiocesisbaq.org; internet www.arquidiocesisbaq.org.

Archbishop of Bogotá: Cardinal JESÚS RUBÉN SALAZAR GÓMEZ, Carrera 7A, No 10-20, Bogotá, DC; tel. (1) 350-5511; fax (1) 350-7290; e-mail sistemas@arquidiocesisbogota.org.co; internet www.arquidiocesisbogota.org.co.

Archbishop of Bucaramanga: ISMAEL RUEDA SIERRA, Calle 33, No 21-18, Bucaramanga, Santander del Sur; tel. (7) 630-4698; fax (7) 642-1361; e-mail sarqdbu@col1.telecom.com; internet www.arquidiocesisbucaramanga.com.

Archbishop of Cali: DARJÍO DE JESÚS MONSALVE MEJÍA, Carrera 4, No 7-17, Apdo Aéreo 8924, Cali, Valle del Cauca; tel. (2) 889-0562; fax (2) 883-7980; e-mail jsarasti@andinet.com; internet www.arquidiocesiscali.org.

Archbishop of Cartagena: JORGE ENRIQUE JIMÉNEZ CARVAJAL, Carerra 5, No 34–55, Apdo Aéreo 400, Cartagena; tel. (5) 664-5308; fax (5) 664-4974; e-mail buzonvirtual@arquicartagenadeindias.org; internet www.arquicartagenadeindias.org.

Archbishop of Ibagué: FLAVIO CALLE ZAPATA, Calle 10, No 2-58, Plaza de Bolivar, Ibagué, Tolima; tel. (8) 261-1680; fax (8) 263-2681; e-mail info@arquidiocesisdeibague.org; internet www.arquidiocesisdeibague.org.

Archbishop of Manizales: GONZALO RESTREPO RESTREPO, Carrera 23, No 19-22, Manizales, Caldas; tel. (6) 884-2933; fax (6) 884-3344; e-mail administrador@arquidiocesisdemanizales.com; internet www.arquidiocesisdemanizales.com.

Archbishop of Medellín: RICARDO ANTONIO TOBÓN RESTREPO, Calle 57, No 49-44, 3°, Medellín; tel. (4) 251-7700; fax (4) 251-9395; e-mail arquidiomed@epm.net.co; internet www.arqmedellin.com.

Archbishop of Nueva Pamplona: LUIS MADRID MERLANO, Carrera 5, No 4-87, Nueva Pamplona; tel. (7) 568-2816; fax (7) 568-4540; e-mail gumafri@hotmail.com; internet www.arquipamplona.org.

Archbishop of Popayán: IVÁN ANTONIO MARÍN LÓPEZ, Calle 5, No 6-71, Apdo Aéreo 593, Popayán; tel. (2) 824-1710; fax (2) 824-0101; e-mail ivanarzo@emtel.net.co; internet www.arquidiocesisdepopayan.org.

Archbishop of Santa Fe de Antioquia: ORLANDO ANTONIO CORRALES GARCÍA, Plazuela Martínez Pardo, No 12-11, Santa Fe de Antioquia; tel. (4) 853-1155; fax (4) 853-1144; e-mail arquistafe@edatel.net.co; internet www.arquisantioquia.org.co.

Archbishop of Tunja: LUIS AUGUSTO CASTRO QUIROGA, Carrera 2, No 59-390, Apdo Aéreo 1019, Tunja, Boyacá; tel. (8) 742-2093; fax (8) 743-3130; e-mail arquidio@telecom.com.co; internet www.arquidiocesisdetunja.org.

Archbishop of Villavicencio: OSCAR URBINA ORTEGA, Carrera 39, No 34-19, Apdo Aéreo 2401, Villavicencio, Meta; tel. (8) 663-0337; fax (8) 665-3200; e-mail diocesisvillavicencio@andinet.com.

The Anglican Communion

Anglicans in Colombia are members of the Episcopal Church in the USA.

Bishop of Colombia: Rt Rev. FRANCISCO JOSÉ DUQUE GÓMEZ, Carrera 6, No 49-85, 2°, Apdo Aéreo 52964, Bogotá, DC; tel. (1) 288-3187; fax (1) 288-3248; e-mail iec@iglesiaepiscopal.org.co; internet www.iglesiaepiscopal.org.co.

Other Christian Churches

Church of Jesus Christ of Latter-Day Saints (Mormons): Carrera 46, 127-45, Bogotá, DC; tel. (1) 625-8000; internet www.lds.org; 180,526 mems.

Iglesia Evangélica Luterana de Colombia: Calle 75, No 20-54, Apdo Aéreo 51538, Bogotá, DC; tel. (1) 212-5735; fax (1) 212-5714; e-mail ofcentral@ielco.org; internet www.ielco.org; 1,519 mems; Pres. Bishop EDUARDO MARTINEZ.

BAHÁ'Í FAITH

National Spiritual Assembly of the Bahá'ís of Colombia (Comunidad Bahá'í de Colombia): Apdo Aéreo 51387, Bogotá, DC; tel. and fax (1) 268-1658; internet www.bahai.org.co; Gen. Sec. XIMENA OSORIO V.; adherents in 1,013 localities.

JUDAISM

There is a community of about 4,200 Jews.

The Press

DAILIES

Bogotá, DC

El Espectador: Avda El Dorado 69-76, Bogotá, DC; tel. and fax (1) 423-2300; e-mail servicioalcliente@elespectador.com; internet www.elespectador.com; f. 1887; Editor LEONARDO RODRÍGUEZ.

El Nuevo Siglo: Calle 25B, No 101-04, Apdo Aéreo 5452, Bogotá, DC; tel. (1) 413-9200; fax (1) 413-8547; e-mail contacto@elnuevosiglo.com.co; internet www.elnuevosiglo.com.co; f. 1936; conservative; Dir JUAN GABRIEL URIBE; Editor ALBERTO ABELLO; circ. 68,000.

Portafolio: Avda Calle 26, No 68B-70, Apdo Aéreo 3633, Bogotá, DC; tel. (1) 294-0100; e-mail sugerenciasysolicitudes@portafolio.co; internet www.portafolio.co; f. 1993; economics and business; Dir RICARDO AVILA PINTO.

La República: Calle 25D Bis, 102A-63, Bogotá, DC; tel. (1) 422-7600; fax (1) 413-3725; e-mail diario@larepublica.com.co; internet www.larepublica.com.co; f. 1954; morning; finance and economics; Dir FERNANDO QUIJANO; circ. 55,000.

El Tiempo: Avda Calle 26, No 68B-70, Bogotá, DC; tel. (1) 294-0100; fax (1) 410-5088; e-mail servicioalcliente@eltiempo.com; internet www.eltiempo.com; f. 1911; morning; liberal; Editor ERNESTO CORTÉS; Dir ROBERTO POMBO; circ. 265,118 (weekdays), 536,377 (Sun.).

Barranquilla, Atlántico

El Heraldo: Calle 53B, No 46-25, Barranquilla, Atlántico; tel. (5) 371-5000; fax (5) 371-5091; internet www.elheraldo.com.co; f. 1933; morning; liberal; Dir MARCO SCHWARTZ; circ. 70,000.

La Libertad: Carrera 53, No 55-166, Barranquilla, Atlántico; tel. (5) 349-1175; fax (5) 349-1298; e-mail libertad@lalibertad.com.co; internet www.lalibertad.com.co; f. 1979; liberal; Dir ROBERTO ESPER REBAJE; Editor LUZ MARINA ESPER FAYAD; circ. 25,000.

Bucaramanga, Santander del Sur

Vanguardia Liberal: Calle 34, No 13-42, Bucaramanga, Santander del Sur; tel. (7) 680-0700; fax (7) 630-2443; e-mail ogonzalez@vanguardialiberal.com.co; internet www.vanguardia.com; f. 1919; morning; liberal; Sunday illustrated literary supplement and women's supplement; Editor PABLO BUITRAGA; circ. 48,000.

Cali, Valle del Cauca

Diario Occidente: Calle 8, No 5-70, 2°, Apdo Aéreo 5262, Cali, Valle del Cauca; tel. (2) 486-0555; e-mail opinion@diariooccidente.com.co; internet www.diariooccidente.com.co; f. 1961; morning; conservative; Editor ROSA MARÍA AGUDELO AYERBE; Dir LUIS OSWALDO VENEGAS CABRERA; circ. 25,000.

El País: Carrera 2A, No 24-46, Apdo Aéreo 4766, Cali, Valle del Cauca; tel. (2) 898-7000; e-mail diario@elpais.com.co; internet www.elpais.com.co; f. 1950; conservative; Dir and Gen. Man. MARÍA ELVIRA DOMÍNGUEZ; circ. 60,000 (weekdays), 120,000 (Sat.), 108,304 (Sun.).

Cartagena, Bolívar

El Universal: Pie del Cerro Calle 30, No 17-36, Cartagena, Bolívar; tel. (5) 650-1050; fax (5) 650-1057; e-mail director@eluniversal.com.co; internet www.eluniversal.com.co; f. 1948; daily; liberal; Editor GERMÁN MENDOZA; Dir PEDRO LUIS MOGOLLÓN VÉLEZ; circ. 167,000.

Cúcuta, Norte de Santander

La Opinión: Avda 4, No 16-12, Cúcuta, Norte de Santander; tel. (7) 582-9999; fax (7) 571-7869; e-mail gerencia@laopinion.com.co; internet www.laopinion.com.co; f. 1960; morning; Editor Dr JOSÉ EUSTORGIO COLMENARES OSSA; circ. 16,000.

Manizales, Caldas

La Patria: Carrera 20, No 46-35, Manizales, Caldas; tel. (6) 878-1700; e-mail lapatria@lapatria.com; internet www.lapatria.com; f. 1921; morning; ind; Dir NICOLÁS RESTREPO ESCOBAR; circ. 22,000.

Medellín, Antioquia

El Colombiano: Carrera 48, No 30 sur-119, Apdo Aéreo 80636, Medellín, Antioquia; tel. (4) 331-5252; fax (4) 331-4858; e-mail elcolombiano@elcolombiano.com.co; internet www.elcolombiano.com; f. 1912; morning; conservative; Dir ANA MERCEDES GÓMEZ MARTÍNEZ; circ. 90,000.

El Mundo: Calle 53, No 74-50, Apdo Aéreo 53874, Medellín, Antioquia; tel. (4) 264-2800; fax (4) 264-3729; e-mail elmundo@elmundo.com; internet www.elmundo.com; f. 1979; Dir GUILLERMO GAVIRIA

ECHEVERRI; Editor IRENE GAVIRIA CORREA; circ. 37,200 (Mon.–Sat.), 55,000 (Sun.).

Neiva, Huila

Diario del Huila: Calle 8A, No 6-30, Neiva, Huila; tel. (8) 871-2458; fax (8) 871-2543; e-mail prensa@diariodelhuila.com; internet www.diariodelhuila.com; f. 1966; Dir MARÍA PÍA DUQUE RENGIFO; Editor GERMÁN HERNÁNDEZ VERA; circ. 12,000.

Pasto, Nariño

Diario del Sur: Calle 18, No 47-160, Torobajo, San Juan de Pasto, Nariño; tel. (2) 731-0048; e-mail diariodelsur@diariodelsur.com.co; internet www.diariodelsur.com.co; f. 1983; Dir HERNANDO SUÁREZ BURGOS.

Pereira, Risaralda

El Diario del Otún: Carrera 8A, No 22-75, Apdo Aéreo 2533, Pereira, Risaralda; tel. (6) 335-1313; fax (6) 325-4878; e-mail luiscramirez@eldiario.com.co; internet www.eldiario.com.co; f. 1982; Administrative Dir JAVIER IGNACIO RAMÍREZ MÚNERA; Editor-in-Chief JOHANNA MOLANO; circ. 30,000.

La Tarde: Parque Empresarial La Tarde, Km 3, Vía Armenia, Pereira, Risaralda; tel. (6) 313-7676; fax (6) 335-5187; internet www.latarde.com; f. 1975; morning; Dir SONIA DÍAZ MANTILLA; circ. 30,000.

Popayán, Cauca

El Liberal: Carrera 3, No 2-60, Apdo Aéreo 538, Popayán, Cauca; tel. (28) 24-2418; fax (28) 23-3888; e-mail gerencia@elliberal.com.co; internet www.elliberal.com.co; f. 1938; Man. ANA MARIA LONDOÑO R.; Dir ISMENIA ARDILA DÍAZ; circ. 6,500.

Santa Marta, Magdalena

El Informador: Avda Libertador 12A-37, Santa Marta, Magdalena; tel. (5) 421-7736; e-mail mensajes@elinformador.com.co; internet www.elinformador.com.co; f. 1958; liberal; Dir ALFONSO VIVES CAMPO; circ. 26,000.

PERIODICALS

ART NEXUS/Arte en Colombia: Carrera 5, No 67-19, Apdo Aéreo 90193, Bogotá, DC; tel. (1) 312-9435; fax (1) 312-9252; e-mail info@artnexus.com; internet www.artnexus.com; f. 1976; quarterly; Latin American art, photography, visual arts; editions in English and Spanish; Pres. and Chief Editor CELIA SREDNI DE BIRBRAGHER; CEO SUSANNE BIRBRAGHER; circ. 26,000.

Coyuntura Económica: Calle 78, No 9-91, Apdo Aéreo 75074, Bogotá, DC; tel. (1) 325-9777; fax (1) 325-9770; e-mail coyuntura@fedesarrollo.org.co; internet www.fedesarrollo.org.co; f. 1971; twice yearly; economics; published by Fundación para Educación Superior y el Desarrollo; Editor DANIEL GÓMEZ GAVIRIA; circ. 300.

Cromos Magazine: Avda El Dorado 69-76, Bogotá, DC; tel. (1) 423-2300; fax (1) 423-7641; e-mail internet@cromos.com.co; internet www.cromos.com.co; f. 1916; weekly; illustrated; general news; Dir JAIRO DUEÑAS VILLAMIL; circ. 102,000.

Dinero: Calle 93B, No 13-47, Bogotá, DC; tel. (1) 646-8400; fax (1) 621-9526; e-mail correo@dinero.com; internet www.dinero.com; f. 1993; fortnightly; economics and business; Dir SANTIAGO GUTIÉRREZ VIANA.

Gerente: Edif. Oficenter, Carrera 16, No 96-64, Santa Fe de Bogotá, DC; tel. (1) 636-9136; fax (1) 636-9638; e-mail ndelahoz@gmail.com; internet www.gerente.com; current affairs; Editor NARCISO DE LA HOZ.

El Malpensante: Calle 35, No 14-27, Bogotá, DC; tel. (1) 320-0120; fax (1) 340-2808; e-mail info@elmalpensante.com; internet www.elmalpensante.com; f. 1996; monthly; literature; Dir MARIO JURSICH DURÁN; Editor ANGEL UNFRIED.

Revista Credencial: Carrera 10, No 28-49, 23°, Bogotá, DC; tel. (1) 353-8307; fax (1) 353-8320; e-mail direccionrc@revistacredencial.com; internet www.revistacredencial.com; current affairs; Dir MARÍA ISABEL RUEDA; Editor ANDRÉS ARIAS.

Revista Escala: Calle 30, No 17-752, Bogotá, DC; tel. (1) 287-8200; fax (1) 285-9882; e-mail escala@revistaescala.com; internet www.revistaescala.com; f. 1962; fortnightly; architecture; Dir DAVID SERNA CÁRDENAS; circ. 18,000.

Revista Fucsia: Calle 93B, No 13-47, Bogotá, DC; tel. (1) 646-8400; fax (1) 621-9526; e-mail correo@fucsia.com; internet www.revistafucsia.com; fortnightly; women's interest; Dir LILA OCHOA.

Semana: Calle 93B, No 13-47, Bogotá, DC; tel. (1) 646-8400; fax (1) 621-9526; e-mail director@semana.com; internet www.semana.com; f. 1982; general; weekly; Dir ALEJANDRO SANTOS RUBINO; Editor ALVARO SIERRA RESTREPO.

Tribuna Médica: Calle 8B, No 68A-41, y Calle 123, No 8-20, Bogotá, DC; tel. (1) 262-6085; fax (1) 262-4459; e-mail editor@tribunamedica.com; internet www.tribunamedica.com; f. 1961; monthly; medical and scientific; Dir JOSÉ RIOS RODRIGUEZ; circ. 50,000.

Tribuna Roja: Calle 39, No 21-30, Bogotá, DC; tel. (1) 245-9647; e-mail tribojar@moir.org.co; internet tribunaroja.moir.org.co; f. 1971; quarterly; organ of the MOIR (pro-Maoist Communist party); Dir CARLOS NARANJO; circ. 300,000.

PRESS ASSOCIATIONS

Asociación Nacional de Diarios Colombianos (ANDIARIOS): Calle 61, No 5-20, Apdo Aéreo 13663, Bogotá, DC; tel. (1) 345-8011; fax (1) 212-7894; e-mail andiarios@andiarios.com; internet www.andiarios.com; f. 1962; 32 affiliated newspapers; Pres. JON RUIZ ITUARTE; Exec. Dir NORA SANÍN DE SAFFON.

Asociación Nacional de Medios de Comunicación (ASOMEDIOS): see Broadcasting and Communications.

Círculo de Periodistas de Bogotá (CPB): Diagonal 33A, Bis No 16-56, Bogotá, DC; tel. (1) 340-0883; e-mail contactenos@circulodeperiodistasdebogota.com; internet circulodeperiodistasdebogota.com; f. 1946; Pres. WILLIAM GIRALDO CEBALLOS; Sec.-Gen. MARTHA LUCÍA DÍAZ.

Publishers

Cengage Learning de Colombia, SA: Edif. Seguros Aurora, 8°, Carrera 7, No 74-21, Bogotá, DC; tel. (1) 212-3340; fax (1) 211-3995; e-mail clientes.pactoandino@cengage.com; internet www.cengage.com.co; Country Man. LILIANA GUTIERREZ.

Ecoe Ediciones Ltda: Carrera 19, No 63C-32, Bogotá, DC; tel. (1) 248-1449; fax (1) 346-1741; e-mail oswaldo@ecoeediciones.com; internet www.ecoeediciones.com; science, medical and general interest; Gen. Man. OSWALDO PEÑUELA CARRIÓN.

Ediciones Gaviota: Carrera 62, No 98B-13, Bogotá, DC; tel. (1) 613-6650; fax (1) 613-9117; e-mail gaviotalibros@edicionesgaviota.com.co; internet www.edicionesgaviota.com; Rep. FABIOLA RAMOS MONDRAGÓN.

Ediciones Modernas: Carrera 41A, No 22F-22, Bogotá, DC; tel. (1) 269-0072; fax (1) 244-0706; e-mail edimodernas@edimodernas.com.co; internet www.empresario.com.co/edimodernas; f. 1991; juvenile; Gen. Man. JORGE SERRANO GARCES.

Editorial Cypres Ltda: Carrera 15, No 80-36, Of. 301, Bogotá, DC; tel. (1) 618-0657; fax (1) 691-0578; e-mail cypresad@etb.net.co; general interest and educational; Gen. Man. JOHANNA VALENZUELA GONZÁLEZ.

Editorial El Globo, SA: Calle 25D, Bis 102A-63, Bogotá, DC; tel. (1) 606-1290; fax (1) 210-4900; e-mail rhumanos@larepublica.com.co; Gen. Man. OLGA LUCIA LONDOÑO M.

Editorial Kinesis: Carrera 25, No 18-12, Armenia; tel. (6) 740-9155; fax (6) 740-1584; e-mail informacion@kinesis.com.co; internet www.kinesis.com.co; physical education, recreation and sport; Dir DIÓGENES VERGARA LARA.

Editorial Leyer Ltda: Carrera 4, No 16-51, Bogotá, DC; tel. (1) 282-1903; fax (1) 282-2373; e-mail contacto@edileyer.com; internet www.edileyer.com; f. 1991; law; Dir HILDEBRANDO LEAL PÉREZ.

Editorial Paulinas: Calle 161A, No 15-50, Bogotá, DC; tel. (1) 528-7444; fax (1) 671-0992; e-mail comunicaciones@paulinas.org.co; internet www.paulinas.org.co; Christian and self-help.

Editorial San Pablo (Sociedad de San Pablo): Carrera 46, No 22A-90, Quintaparedes, Apdo Aéreo 080152, Bogotá, DC; tel. (1) 368-2099; fax (1) 244-4383; e-mail editorial@sanpablo.com.co; internet www.sanpablo.com.co; f. 1914; religion (Catholic); Editorial Dir Fr VICENTE MIOTTO; Editor AMPARO MAHECHA.

Editorial Temis, SA: Calle 17, No 68D, Apdo Aéreo 46, Bogotá, DC; tel. (1) 424-7855; fax (1) 292-5801; e-mail editorial@editorialtemis.com; internet www.editorialtemis.com; f. 1951; law, sociology, politics; Gen. Man. ERWIN GUERRERO PINZÓN.

Editorial Voluntad, SA: Avda El Dorado, No 90-10, Bogotá, DC; tel. (1) 410-6355; fax (1) 295-2994; e-mail voluntad@voluntad.com.co; internet www.voluntad.com.co; f. 1930; school books; Pres. GASTÓN DE BEDOUT.

Fondo de Cultura Económica: Calle de la Enseñanza 11, No 5–60, La Candelaria, Zona C, Bogotá, DC; tel. (1) 283-2200; fax (1) 337-4289; e-mail caguilar@fce.com.co; internet www.fce.com.co; f. 1934; academic; Gen. Man. CÉSAR ANGEL AGUILAR ASIAIN.

Fundación Centro de Investigación y Educación Popular (CINEP): Carrera 5A, No 33B -02, Apdo Aéreo 25916, Bogotá, DC; tel. (1) 245-6181; fax (1) 287-9089; e-mail cinep@cinep.org.co; internet www.cinep.org.co; f. 1972; education and social sciences; Exec. Dir LUIS GUILLERMO GUERRERO GUEVARA.

Instituto Caro y Cuervo: Calle 10, No 4-69, Bogotá, DC; tel. (1) 342-2121; fax (1) 284-1248; e-mail direcciongeneral@caroycuervo.gov.co; internet www.caroycuervo.gov.co; f. 1942; philology, general linguistics and reference; Dir-Gen. GENOVEVA IRIARTE.

Inversiones Cromos, SA: Avda El Dorado, No 69-76, Bogotá, DC; tel. (1) 423-2300; fax (1) 423-7641; e-mail jduenas@cromos.com.co; internet www.cromos.com.co; f. 1916; Dir JAIRO DUEÑAS VILLAMIL; Editor LEONARDO RODRÍGUEZ.

Legis, SA: Avda Calle 26, No 82–70, Apdo Aéreo 98888, Bogotá, DC; tel. (1) 425-5200; e-mail servicio@legis.com.co; internet www.legis.com.co; f. 1952; economics, law, general; Pres. LUIS ALFREDO MOTTA VENEGAS.

McGraw Hill Interamericana, SA: Carrera 85D, No 46A–65, Bodegas 9, 10 y 11, Complejo Logístico San Cayetano, Urb. San Cayetano Norte, Bogotá, DC; tel. (1) 600-3800; fax (1) 600-3855; e-mail info_colombia@mcgraw-hill.com; internet www.mcgraw-hill.com.co; university textbooks; Dir-Gen. MARTÍN RENÉ CHUECO.

Publicar, SA: Avda 68, No 75A-50, 2°, 3° y 4°, Centro Comercial Metrópolis, Apdo Aéreo 8010, Bogotá, DC; tel. (1) 646-5555; fax (1) 646-5523; e-mail e-hamburger@publicar.com; internet www.publicar.com; f. 1959; owned by the Carvajal Group; directories; Pres. ERIC HAMBURGER.

Siglo del Hombre Editores, SA: Carrera 31A, No 25B-50, Bogotá, DC; tel. (1) 337-7700; fax (1) 337-7665; e-mail info@siglodelhombre.com; internet www.siglodelhombre.com; f. 1992; arts, politics, anthropology, history, humanities; Gen. Man. EMILIA FRANCO DE ARCILA.

Tercer Mundo Editores, SA: Grupo TM, SA, Calle 25B, No 31A-34, Bogotá, DC; tel. (1) 368-8645; e-mail grupotmsa@etb.net.co; internet grupotmsa.blogspot.com; f. 1963; social sciences.

Thomson PLM: Calle 106, No 54–81, Apdo Aéreo 52998, Barrio Puente Largo, Bogotá, DC; tel. (1) 613-1111; fax (1) 624-2335; e-mail contactoco@plmlatina.com; internet www.plmlatina.com; medical; Regional Dir CONSTANZA RIAÑO RODRÍGUEZ.

Tragaluz Editores: Edif. Lugo, Of. 108, Calle 6 Sur, No 43A-200, Medellín, Antioquia; tel. (4) 312-0295; fax (4) 268-4366; e-mail info@tragaluzeditores.com; internet tragaluzeditores.com; literature and graphics; Editorial Dir PILAR GUTIÉRREZ LLANO.

Villegas Editores: Avda 82, No 11-50, Interior 3, Bogotá, DC; tel. (1) 616-1788; fax (1) 616-0020; e-mail informacion@villegaseditores.com; internet www.villegaseditores.com; f. 1986; illustrated and scholarly; Pres. BENJAMÍN VILLEGAS JIMÉNEZ.

ASSOCIATIONS

Asociación de Editoriales Universitarias de Colombia (ASEUC): Carrera 13A, No 38-82, Of. 901, Bogotá, DC; tel. (1) 805-2357; fax (1) 287-9257; e-mail asistente@aseuc.org.co; internet www.aseuc.org.co; Pres. NICOLÁS MORALES THOMAS; Sec.-Gen. LORENA RUIZ SERNA.

Cámara Colombiana del Libro: Calle 35, No 5A-05, Bogotá, DC; tel. (1) 323-0111; fax (1) 285-1082; e-mail camlibro@camlibro.com.co; internet www.camlibro.com.co; f. 1951; Pres. GUSTAVO RODRÍGUEZ GARCÍA; Exec. Dir ENRIQUE GONZÁLEZ VILLA; 95 mems.

Fundalectura: Avda Diagonal 40A Bis, No 16-46, Bogotá, DC; tel. (1) 320-1511; fax (1) 287-7071; e-mail contactenos@fundalectura.org.co; internet www.fundalectura.org; f. 1990; Pres. ALFONSO OCAMPO GAVIRIA; Exec. Dir CARMEN BARVO.

Broadcasting and Communications

TELECOMMUNICATIONS

Avantel, SAS: Carrera 11, No 93-92, Bogotá, DC; tel. (1) 634-3434; e-mail contactenos@avantel.com.co; internet www.avantel.com.co; f. 1996; telecom operator, wireless broadband; subsidiary of Axtel (Mexico); Pres. JORGE ANDRÉS PALACIO BECERRA.

Claro Colombia: Calle 90, No 14-37, Bogotá, DC; tel. (1) 616-9797; fax (1) 256-0538; e-mail servicioalcliente@claro.com.co; internet www.claro.com.co; f. 1994 as Occidente y Caribe Celular, SA (Occel); present name adopted in 2012 following the merger of Comcel and Telmex; owned by América Móvil, SA de CV (Mexico); cellular mobile telephone operator; Pres. JUAN CARLOS ARCHILA.

Colombia Móvil, SA (Tigo): Edif. Citibank, 5°, Carrera 9A, No 99-02, Bogotá, DC; tel. (1) 330-3000; fax (1) 618-2712; internet www.tigo.com.co; f. 2003; subsidiary of Millicom International Cellular, SA since 2006; mobile telephone services; Pres. ESTEBAN IRIARTE.

Empresa de Telecomunicaciones de Bogotá, SA (ETB): Carrera 8, No 20-56, 3°–9°, Bogotá, DC; tel. (1) 242-3483; fax (1) 242-2127; e-mail adrimara@etb.com.co; internet www.etb.com.co; Bogotá telephone co; partially privatized in 2003; Pres. SAÚL KATTAN COHEN; Sec.-Gen. JAVIER GUTIÉRREZ AFANADOR.

Telefónica Móviles Colombia (Movistar): Edif. Capital Tower, 17°, Calle 100, No 7-33, Bogotá, DC; tel. (1) 650-0000; fax (1) 650-1852; internet www.movistar.co; f. 2004 following acquisition of BellSouth's operations by Telefónica Móviles, subsidiary of Telefónica, SA of Spain; CEO ARIEL PONTÓN.

Telefónica Telecom: Carrera 70, No 108-84, Bogotá, DC; tel. (1) 593-5399; fax (1) 593-1252; internet www.telefonica.co; f. 2003 following dissolution of state-owned Empresa Nacional de Telecomunicaciones (TELECOM, f. 1947); subsidiary of Telefónica, SA (Spain); Pres. ALFONSO GÓMEZ PALACIO.

UNE EPM Telecomunicaciones, SA (Une): Edif. EEPPM, Carrera 16, No 11, Sur 100, Medellín; tel. (4) 382-2020; fax (4) 515-5050; e-mail une@une.com.co; internet www.une.com.co; broadband and telecom services provider; Pres. MARC EICHMANN PERRET.

Regulatory Authority

Comisión de Regulación de Comunicaciones (CRC): Edif. LINK Siete Sesenta, 9°, Calle 59A bis, No 5-53, Bogotá, DC; tel. (1) 319-8300; fax (1) 319-8314; e-mail atencioncliente@crcom.gov.co; internet www.crcom.gov.co; f. 2000; regulatory body; Exec. Dir CARLOS PABLO MÁRQUEZ.

BROADCASTING

Radio

Cadena Melodía de Colombia: Calle 45, No 13-70, Bogotá, DC; tel. (1) 323-1500; fax (1) 288-4020; e-mail presidencia@cadenamelodia.com; internet www.cadenamelodia.com; Pres. EFRAÍN PÁEZ ESPITIA; Gen. Man. ELVIRA MEJÍA DE PÁEZ.

CARACOL, SA (Primera Cadena Radial Colombiana, SA): Edif. Caracol Radio, Calle 67, No 7-37, Bogotá, DC; tel. (1) 348-7600; fax (1) 337-7126; internet www.caracol.com.co; f. 1948; 107 stations; Pres. JOSÉ MANUEL RESTREPO FERNÁNDEZ DE SOTO.

Circuito Todelar de Colombia: Avda 13, No 84-42, Apdo Aéreo 27344, Bogotá, DC; tel. (1) 616-1011; fax (1) 616-0056; e-mail dircomercial@todelar.com; internet www.todelar.com; f. 1953; 74 stations; Dir SANDRA PATRICIA BARBOSA.

Colmundo Radio, SA ('La Cadena de la Paz'): Diagonal 61D, No 26A-29, Apdo Aéreo 36750, Bogotá, DC; tel. (1) 217-9220; fax (1) 348-2746; e-mail direcciongeneral@colmundoradio.com.co; internet colmundoradio.com.co; f. 1989; Pres. ZAIDY MORA QUINTERO; Dir-Gen. MIRIAM QUINTERO.

Organización Radial Olímpica, SA (ORO, SA): Calle 72, No 48-37, 2°, Apdo Aéreo 51266, Barranquilla; tel. (5) 358-0500; fax (5) 345-9080; e-mail ventasbarranquila@oro.com.co; internet www.oro.com.co; programmes for the Antioquia and Atlantic coast regions; Pres. MIGUEL CHAR; Production Dir RAFAEL PÁEZ.

Radio Cadena Nacional, SA (RCN Radio): Calle 37, No 13A-19, Apdo Aéreo 4984, Bogotá, DC; tel. (1) 314-7070; fax (1) 288-6130; e-mail rcn@impsat.net.co; internet www.rcn.com.co; 116 stations; official network; Pres. FERNANDO MOLINA SOTO.

Radio Nacional de Colombia: Carrera 45, No 26-33, Bogotá, DC; tel. (1) 597-8111; fax (1) 597-8011; e-mail contactoradionacional@rtvc.gov.co; internet www.radionacionaldecolombia.gov.co; f. 1940; national public radio; Dir GABRIEL GÓMEZ MEJÍA.

Radio Regional Independiente: Carrera 19A, No 98-12, Of. 801, Bogotá, DC; tel. (1) 691-9724; fax (1) 691-9725; e-mail info@reiltda.com; internet www.reiltda.com; f. 1995; Gen. Man. JUAN MANUEL ORTIZ NOGUERA.

Sistema Super de Columbia: Calle 39A, No 18-12, Bogotá, DC; tel. (1) 234-7777; fax (1) 287-8678; e-mail gerencia@cadenasuper.com; internet www.cadenasuper.com; f. 1971; stations include Radio Super and Super Stereo FM; Gen. Man. JUAN CARLOS PAVA CAMELO.

Television

Canal Institutional: Avda El Dorado, Carrera 45, No 26-33, Bogotá, DC; tel. (1) 597-8000; fax (1) 597-8011; e-mail contactoinstitucional@rtvc.gov.co; internet www.institucional.gov.co; f. 2004; govt-owned; Co-ordinator LENNART RODRÍGUEZ.

Canal RCN Televisión: Avda Américas, No 65-82, Bogotá, DC; tel. (1) 426-9292; e-mail quienessomos@canalrcn.com; internet www.canalrcnmsn.com; f. 1998; Pres. GABRIEL REYES.

Caracol Televisión, SA: Calle 103, No 69B-43, Apdo Aéreo 26484, Bogotá, DC; tel. (1) 643-0430; fax (1) 643-0444; internet www.caracoltv.com; f. 1969; Pres. PAULO LASERNA PHILLIPS.

Fox Telecolombia: Carrera 50, No 17-77, Bogotá, DC; tel. (1) 417-4200; fax (1) 341-6198; e-mail john.ahumada@foxtelecolombia.com; internet www.foxtelecolombia.com; formerly Cadena Uno; f. 1992; acquired by Fox International Channels and changed name as above in 2007; Pres. SAMUEL DUQUE ROZO.

Señal Colombia: Avda El Dorado, Carrera 45, No 26-33, Bogotá, DC; tel. (1) 597-8132; fax (1) 597-8062; e-mail senalencontacto@rtvc

.gov.co; internet www.senalcolombia.tv; govt-owned; Co-ordinator ADRIAN FRANCISCO COMAS.

Teleantioquia: Calle 44, No 53A–11, Apdo Aéreo 8183, Medellín, Antioquia; tel. (4) 356-9900; fax (4) 356-9909; e-mail comunicaciones@teleantioquia.com.co; internet www.teleantioquia.com.co; f. 1985; Gen. Man. SELENE BOTERO GIRALDO.

Telecafé: Carrera 19A, Calle 43, Barrio Sacatín contiguo Universidad Autónoma, Manizales, Caldas; tel. (6) 872-7100; fax (6) 872-7610; e-mail info@telecafe.tv; internet www.telecafe.tv; f. 1986; govt-owned; broadcasts to the 'Eje Cafetero' (departments of Caldas, Quindío and Risaralda); Gen. Man. JORGE EDUARDO URREA GIRALDO.

TeleCaribe: Carrera 54, No 72-142, 4°, Barranquilla, Atlántico; tel. (5) 368-0184; fax (5) 360-7300; e-mail info@telecaribe.com.co; internet www.telecaribe.com.co; f. 1986; Pres. ARTURO SARMIENTO; Gen. Man. IVÁN GUILLERMO BARRIOS MASS.

Telepacífico (Sociedad de Televisión del Pacifico Ltda): Calle 5, No 38A-14, 3°, esq. Centro Comercial Imbanaco, Cali, Valle del Cauca; tel. (2) 518-4000; fax (2) 588-281; e-mail gerenciatp@telepacifico.com; internet www.telepacifico.com; Gen. Man. LORENA IVETTE MENDOZA MARMOLEJO.

TV Cúcuta: tel. (7) 574-7874; fax (7) 575-2922; f. 1992; Pres. JOSÉ A. ARMELLA.

Regulatory Authority

Autoridad Nacional de Televisión: Edif. Link Siete Sesenta, Of. 405, Calle 59A Bis, No 5–53, Bogotá, DC; tel. (1) 795-7000; e-mail informacion@antv.gov.co; internet www.antv.gov.co; f. 2012; successor to Comisión Nacional de Televisión; Dir TATIANA ANDREA RUBIO L.

Association

Asociación Nacional de Medios de Comunicación (ASOMEDIOS): Carrera 19C, No 85-72, Bogotá, DC; tel. (1) 611-1300; fax (1) 621-6292; e-mail asomedios@asomedios.com; internet www.asomedios.com; f. 1978; Exec. Pres. TITULO ANGEL ARBELAEZ.

Finance

(cap. = capital; res = reserves; dep. = deposits; m. = million; brs = branches; amounts in pesos unless otherwise indicated)

Contraloría General de la República: Edif. Gran Estación II, Carrera 60, No 24-09, Bogotá, DC; tel. (1) 353-7700; fax (1) 353-7616; e-mail mesaportal@contraloriagen.gov.co; internet www.contraloriagen.gov.co; f. 1923; Comptroller-Gen. SANDRA MORELLI RICO.

BANKING

Supervisory Authority

Superintendencia Financiera de Colombia: Calle 7, No 4-49, 11°, Apdo Aéreo 3460, Bogotá, DC; tel. (1) 594-0200; fax (1) 350-7999; e-mail super@superfinanciera.gov.co; internet www.superfinanciera.gov.co; f. 2006 following merger of the Superintendencia Bancaria and the Superintendencia de Valores; Supt GERARDO HERNÁNDEZ CORREA.

Central Bank

Banco de la República: Carrera 7A, No 14-78, 5°, Apdo Aéreo 3551, Bogotá, DC; tel. (1) 343-1111; fax (1) 286-1686; e-mail wbanco@banrep.gov.co; internet www.banrep.gov.co; f. 1923; sole bank of issue; cap. 12,711m., res 13,671,591.5m., dep. 11,092,426.6m. (Dec. 2009); Gov. JOSÉ DARÍO URIBE ESCOBAR; 17 brs.

Commercial Banks

Banco Agrario de Colombia (Banagrario): Carrera 8, No 15-43, Bogotá, DC; tel. (1) 382-1400; fax (1) 599-5509; e-mail servicio.cliente@bancoagrario.gov.co; internet www.bancoagrario.gov.co; f. 1999; state-owned; Pres. FRANCISCO ESTUPIÑÁN HEREDIA; 732 brs.

Banco de Bogotá: Calle 36, No 7-47, 15°, Apdo Aéreo 3436, Bogotá, DC; tel. (1) 332-0032; fax (1) 338-3302; internet www.bancodebogota.com.co; f. 1870; cap. 2,868m., res 5,900,206m., dep. 28,107,976m. (Dec. 2011); Pres. Dr ALEJANDRO AUGUSTO FIGUEROA JARAMILLO; 556 brs.

Banco Colpatria Red Multibanca Colpatria SA: Torre Colpatria, Carrera 7A, No 24-89, Bogotá, DC; tel. (1) 745-6300; e-mail serviciocliente@colpatria.com; internet www.colpatria.com; f. 1969 as Banco Colpatria; name changed as above in 1998; merged with Scotiabank Colombia SA (Canada) in 2012 following Scotiabank's purchase of 51% of shares; cap. 233,878.1m., res 477,061.7m., dep. 7,634,726.1m. (Dec. 2009); Pres. LUIS SANTIAGO PERDOMO MALDONADO.

Banco de Comercio Exterior de Colombia, SA (BANCOLDEX): Calle 28, No 13A-15, 37°–42°, Apdo Aéreo 240092, Bogotá, DC; tel. (1) 486-3000; fax (1) 286-2451; e-mail contactenos@bancoldex.com; internet www.bancoldex.com; f. 1992; provides financing alternatives for Colombian exporters; affiliate trust co FIDUCOLDEX, SA, manages PROEXPORT (Export Promotion Trust); cap. 855,669.6m., res 477,018.1m., dep. 2,156,357.2m. (Dec. 2011); Pres. SANTIAGO ROJAS ARROYO.

Banco Davivienda, SA: Edif. Torre Bolívar, 68B-31, 1°, Avda El Dorado, Bogotá, DC; tel. (1) 338-3838; e-mail contactenos@davivienda.com; internet www.davivienda.com; f. 1972 as Corporación Colombiana de Ahorro y Vivienda (Coldeahorro), current name adopted in 1997; merged with Banco Superior in 2006, with Bancafé in 2010; cap. 55,479.7m., res 4,109,510.2m., dep. 23,024,263.2m. (Dec 2011); Pres. EFRAÍN ENRIQUE FORERO FONSECA.

Banco GNB Sudameris, SA: Carrera 7, No 71-52, 19°, Torre B, Bogotá, DC; tel. (1) 325-5000; fax (1) 313-3259; internet www.sudameris.com.co; f. 2005 following merger of Banco Sudameris Colombia, SA and Banco Tequendama; cap. 44,649.4m., res 445,474.6m., dep. 4,953,116.9m. (Dec. 2010); Pres. and Chair. CAMILO VERÁSTEGUI CARVAJAL; 6 brs.

Banco de Occidente: Carrera 4, No 7-61, 12°, Apdo Aéreo 7607, Cali, Valle del Cauca; tel. (2) 886-1111; fax (2) 886-1298; e-mail dinternacional@bancodeoccidente.com.co; internet www.bancodeoccidente.com.co; f. 1965; cap. 4,676.9m., res 2,798,947.2m., dep. 12,422,643.9m. (Dec. 2011); 78.2% owned by Grupo Aval Acciones y Valores; Pres. EFRAÍN OTERO ÁLVAREZ; 194 brs.

Banco Popular, SA: Calle 17, No 7-43, 3°, Bogotá, DC; tel. (1) 339-5449; fax (1) 281-9448; e-mail vpinternacional@bancopopular.com.co; internet www.bancopopular.com.co; f. 1950; cap. 77,253m., res 1,423,380m., dep. 9,256,874m. (Dec. 2011); Pres. JOSÉ HERNÁN RINCÓN GÓMEZ; 216 brs.

Bancolombia, SA: Carrera 48, Avda Los Industriales 26-85, Medellín, Antioquia; tel. (4) 404-0000; fax (4) 404-5105; e-mail angospin@bancolombia.com.co; internet www.bancolombia.com; f. 1998 by merger of Banco Industrial Colombiano and Banco de Colombia; cap. 393,914m., res 5,792,394m., dep. 52,434,492m. (Dec. 2011); Chair. DAVID EMILIO BOJANINI GARCÍA; Pres. CARLOS RAÚL YEPES JIMÉNEZ; 992 brs.

BBVA Colombia (Banco Bilbao Vizcaya Argentaria Colombia, SA): Carrera 9, No 72-21, 11°, Bogotá, DC; tel. (1) 312-4666; fax (1) 347-1600; internet www.bbva.com.co; f. 1956 as Banco Ganadero; assumed current name 2004; 95.2% owned by Banco Bilbao Vizcaya Argentaria, SA (Spain); cap. 89,779m., res 307,020m., dep. 18,643,976m. (Dec. 2011); Exec. Pres. OSCAR CABRERA IZQUIERDO; 279 brs.

Citibank Colombia, SA: Carrera 9A, No 99-02, 3°, Bogotá, DC; tel. (1) 638-2420; fax (1) 618-2606; internet www.citibank.com.co; wholly owned subsidiary of Citibank (USA); cap. 144,123m., res 1,049,325m., dep. 5,359,712m. (Dec. 2011); Pres. BERNARDO NOREÑA OCAMPO; 23 brs.

Corpbanca Colombia: Carrera 7, No 99-53, Bogotá, DC; tel. (1) 644-8028; fax (1) 644-8344; internet www.bancocorpbanca.com.co; f. 1961 as Banco Comercial Antioqueño; bought by Grupo Santander (Spain) in 1997 and name changed to Banco Santander Colombia, present name adopted 2011 following acquisition by Corpbanca (Chile), which was bought by Itaú Unibanco (Brazil) in 2014; dep. 7,077,000m. (March 2013); Pres. JAIME MUNITA.

GNB Colombia, SA: Carrera 7, No 71-21, Of. 1601, Torre B, 16°, Apdo Aéreo 3532, Bogotá, DC; tel. (1) 334-5088; fax (1) 341-9433; e-mail colombia.contactenos@bancognb.com.co; internet www.bancognb.com.co; f. 1976 as Banco Anglo Colombiano; changed name to HSBC Colombia in 2007; present name adopted in 2012; cap. 233,096m., res 16,893m., dep. 1,483,765m. (Dec. 2011); Pres. HANS JUERGEN THEILKUHL; 52 brs.

Helm Bank SA: Carrera 7, No 27-18, 19°, Bogotá, DC; tel. (1) 581-8181; e-mail servicio.empresarial@grupohelm.com; internet www.grupohelm.com; f. 1963 as Banco de Crédito; renamed Banco de Credito—Helm Financial Services in 2000; present name adopted in 2009; bought by Corpbanca in 2012; cap. 218,623.1m., res 912,991.6m., dep. 7,945,649.8m. (Dec. 2011); Pres. CARMIÑA FERRO IRIARTE; 26 brs.

Development Bank

Banco Caja Social: Torre BCSC, Carrera 7, No 77-65, 11°, Bogotá, DC; tel. (1) 313-8000; fax (1) 321-6912; e-mail csgarzon@fundacion-social.com.co; internet www.bancocajasocial.com; f. 1911; cap. 204,678m., res 510,445m., dep. 6,300,449m. (Dec. 2009); Pres. CARLOS EDUARDO UPEGUI CUARTAS; 260 brs.

Banking Associations

Asociación Bancaria y de Entidades Financieras de Colombia (Asobancaria): Carrera 9A, No 74-08, 9°, Bogotá, DC; tel.

(1) 326-6612; fax (1) 326-6604; e-mail info@asobancaria.com; internet www.asobancaria.com; f. 1936; 56 mem. banks; Pres. MARÍA MERCEDES CUÉLLAR LÓPEZ.

Asociación Nacional de Instituciones Financieras (ANIF): Calle 70A, No 7-86, Bogotá, DC; tel. (1) 310-1500; fax (1) 235-5947; e-mail anif@anif.com.co; internet anif.co; f. 1974; Pres. DR SERGIO CLAVIJO.

STOCK EXCHANGE

Bolsa de Valores de Colombia: Edif. Bancafé, Torre B, Of. 1201, Carrera 7, No 71-21, Bogotá, DC; tel. (1) 313-9800; fax (1) 313-9766; internet www.bvc.com.co; f. 2001 following merger of stock exchanges of Bogotá, Medellín and Occidente; Pres. JUAN PABLO CÓRDOBA GARCÉS; Sec.-Gen. ANGEL ALBERTO VELANDIA RODRÍGUEZ.

INSURANCE

Principal Companies

ACE Seguros, SA: Calle 72, No 10-51, 7°, Apdo Aéreo 29782, Bogotá, DC; tel. (1) 319-0300; fax (1) 319-0304; e-mail ace.servicioalcliente@acegroup.com; internet www.acelatinamerica.com; fmrly Cigna Seguros de Colombia, SA; Pres. PILAR LOZANO.

Aseguradora Colseguros, SA: Carrera 13A, No 29-24, Parque Central Bavaria, Apdo Aéreo 3537, Bogotá, DC; tel. (1) 560-0600; fax (1) 561-6695; internet www.colseguros.com; subsidiary of Allianz AG, Germany; f. 1874; Pres. ALBA LUCIA GALLEGO NIETO.

Aseguradora Solidaria de Colombia: Calle 100, No 9A-45, 8° y 12°, Bogotá, DC; tel. (1) 646-4330; fax (1) 296-1527; e-mail eguzman@solidaria.com.co; internet www.aseguradorasolidaria.com.co; Pres. CARLOS ARTURO GUZMÁN PÉREZ.

BBVA Seguros: Carrera 11, No 87-51, Bogotá, DC; tel. (1) 219-1100; fax (1) 640-7995; internet www.bbvaseguros.com.co; f. 1994; Pres. JORGE MANUEL SEIJAS RUMBRO; Sec.-Gen. HERNÁN FELIPE GUZMÁN ALDANA.

Chartis Seguros Colombia, SA: Calle 78, No 9–57, Apdo Aéreo 9281, Bogotá, DC; tel. (1) 317-2193; fax (1) 310-1014; e-mail servicioal.cliente@chartisinsurance.com; internet www.chartisinsurance.com; fmrly AIG Colombia Seguros Generales, SA; Pres. ANDRES HÉCTOR BOULLÓN.

Chubb de Colombia Cía de Seguros, SA: Carrera 7A, No 71-52, Torre B, 10°, Bogotá, DC; tel. (1) 326-6200; fax (1) 326-6210; e-mail informaciongeneral@chubb.com; internet www.chubb.com.co; f. 1972; Pres. MANUEL OBREGÓN; 4 brs.

Cía Aseguradora de Fianzas, SA (Confianza): Calle 82, No 11-37, 7°, Apdo Aéreo 056965, Bogotá, DC; tel. (1) 644-4690; fax (1) 610-8866; e-mail correos@confianza.com.co; internet www.confianza.com.co; f. 1979; Pres. LUIS ALEJANDRO RUEDA RODRÍGUEZ; Exec. Vice-Pres. ANDRÉS EDUARDO MONTOYA SOTO.

Cía Mundial de Seguros, SA: Calle 33, No 6B-24, 2° y 3°, Bogotá, DC; tel. (1) 285-5600; fax (1) 285-1220; e-mail mundial@mundialseguros.com.co; internet www.mundialseguros.com.co; f. 1995; Pres. JUAN ENRIQUE BUSTAMANTE MOLINA.

Cía de Seguros Bolívar, SA: Avda El Dorado, No 68B-31, 10°, Casilla 4421 y 6406, Bogotá, DC; tel. (1) 341-0077; fax (1) 283-0799; internet www.segurosbolivar.com.co; f. 1939; Pres. JORGE ENRIQUE URIBE MONTAÑO.

Cía de Seguros Colmena, SA: Calle 26, No 69C-03, Torre A, 4°–6°, Apdo Aéreo 5050, Bogotá, DC; tel. (1) 324-1111; fax (1) 324-0866; internet www.colmena-arp.com.co; Pres. SILVIA CAMARGO.

Cía de Seguros de Vida Aurora, SA: Carrera 7, No 74-21, 1°–3°, Bogotá, DC; tel. (1) 319-2930; fax (1) 345-5980; e-mail soporte@segurosaurora.com; internet www.segurosaurora.com; f. 1967; Pres. EUDORO CARVAJAL IBAÑEZ; Sec.-Gen. ANDREA MORA SÁNCHEZ.

Condor, SA, Cía de Seguros Generales: Carrera 7, No 74-21, 2°, Bogotá, DC; tel. (1) 319-2930; fax (1) 345-4980; e-mail orlandolugo@condorsa.com.co; internet www.seguroscondor.com.co; f. 1957 as Cía de Seguros del Pacífico, SA; changed name as above as above 1983; Pres. JOSÉ ANCÍZAR JIMÉNEZ GUITÍERREZ.

La Equidad Seguros, Organización Cooperativa: Edif. Torre La Equidad Seguros, 13° y 14°, Carrera 9A, 99-07, Apdo Aéreo 30261, Bogotá, DC; tel. (1) 592-2929; fax (1) 520-0169; e-mail equidad@laequidadseguros.coop; internet www.laequidadseguros.coop; Exec. Pres. DR CLEMENTE AUGUSTO JAIMES PUENTES.

Generali Colombia—Seguros Generales, SA: Edif. Generali, Carrera 7A, No 72-13, 8°, Apdo Aéreo 076478, Bogotá, DC; tel. (1) 346-8888; fax (1) 319-8280; e-mail generali_colombia@generali.com.co; internet www.generali.com.co; f. 1937; Pres. EDUARDO SARMIENTO PULIDO.

Global Seguros, SA: Carrera 9, No 74-62, Bogotá, DC; tel. (1) 313-9200; fax (1) 317-5376; e-mail rodrigo.uribe@globalseguroscolombia.com; internet www.globalseguroscolombia.com; Pres. RODRIGO URIBE BERNAL.

Liberty Seguros, SA: Calle 72, No 10-07, 6°–8°, Apdo Aéreo 57227 y 57243, Bogotá, DC; tel. (1) 376-5330; fax (1) 217-9917; e-mail lhernandez@impsat.net.co; internet www.libertycolombia.com.co; f. 1954; fmrly Latinoamericana de Seguros, SA; Pres. MAURICIO GARCÍA ORTIZ.

Mapfre Seguros de Crédito, SA (Mapfre Crediseguro, SA): Edif. Forum II, 8°, Calle 7 Sur, No 42-70, Antioquia; tel. (4) 444-0145; fax (4) 314-1990; e-mail adritoac@crediseguro.com.co; internet www.crediseguro.com.co; f. 1999; subsidiary of Mapfre; Pres. ALEJANDRO CALCEDO.

Mapfre Seguros Generales de Colombia, SA: Carrera 14, No 96-34, Bogotá, DC; tel. (1) 650-3300; fax (1) 650-3400; e-mail mapfre@mapfre.com.co; internet www.mapfre.com.co; f. 1995; Pres. VICTORIA EUGENIA BEJARANO DE LA TORRE.

Metlife Colombia Seguros de Vida, SA: Carrera 7, No 99-53, 17°, Bogotá, DC; tel. (14) 358-1258; fax (14) 638-1299; e-mail cliente@metlife.com.co; internet www.metlife.com.co; fmrly American Life Insurance Co (Alico); sold to MetLife in 2010; Pres. SANTIAGO OSORIO; Sec.-Gen. CONSUELO GONZÁLEZ.

Pan American de Colombia Cía de Seguros de Vida, SA: Carrera 7A, No 75-09, Apdo Aéreo 76000, Bogotá, DC; tel. (1) 326-7400; fax (1) 326-7390; e-mail servicioalclienteco@panamericanlife.com; internet www.panamericanlife.com; f. 1974; Gen. Man. MANUEL LEMUS.

La Previsora, SA, Cía de Seguros: Calle 57, No 9-07, Apdo Aéreo 52946, Bogotá, DC; tel. (1) 348-5757; fax (1) 540-5294; e-mail contactenos@previsora.gov.co; internet www.previsora.gov.co; f. 1914; Exec. Pres. DIEGO BARRAGÁN CORREA.

QBE Seguros, SA: Carrera 7, No 76-35, 7°–9°, Apdo Aéreo 265063, Bogotá, DC; tel. (1) 319-0730; fax (1) 319-0749; e-mail sylvia.rincon@qbe.com.co; internet www.qbe.com.co; subsidiary of QBE Insurance Group, Australia; Pres. SYLVIA LUZ RINCÓN LEMA.

RSA Colombia: Edif. Royal & Sun Alliance, Avda 19, No 104-37, Apdo Aéreo 4225, Bogotá, DC; tel. (1) 488-1000; fax (1) 214-0440; e-mail servicioalcliente@co.rsagroup.com; internet www.rsagroup.com.co; fmrly Seguros Fénix, SA, then Royal and Sun Alliance Seguros; Pres. LILIAN PEREA RONCO.

Segurexpo de Colombia, SA: Calle 72, No 6-44, 12°, Apdo Aéreo 75140, Bogotá, DC; tel. (1) 326-6969; fax (1) 211-0218; e-mail segurexpo@segurexpo.com; internet www.segurexpo.com; f. 1993; Gen. Man. JESÚS URDANGARAY LÓPEZ.

Seguros Alfa, SA: Carrera 13, No 27-47, 22° y 23°, Apdo Aéreo 27718, Bogotá, DC; tel. (1) 743-5333; fax (1) 344-6770; e-mail presidencia@segurosalfa.com.co; internet www.segurosalfa.com.co; Pres. ROBERTO VERGARA ORTIZ.

Seguros Colpatria, SA: Carrera 7A, No 24-89, 27°, Apdo Aéreo 7762, Bogotá, DC; tel. (1) 336-4677; fax (1) 286-9998; e-mail servicioalcliente@ui.colpatria.com; internet www.seguroscolpatria.com; f. 1955; Pres. FERNANDO QUINTERO ARTURO.

Seguros del Estado, SA: Carrera 13, No 96-66, Apdo Aéreo 6810, Bogotá, DC; tel. (1) 218-0903; fax (1) 218-0913; e-mail luis.correa@segurosdelestado.com; internet www.segurosdelestado.com; f. 1956 as Cía Aliadas de Seguros, SA; changed name as above in 1973; Pres. JORGE MORA SÁNCHEZ.

Seguros Generales Suramericana, SA (Sura): Centro Suramericana, Carrera 64B, No 49A-30, Apdo Aéreo 780, Medellín, Antioquia; tel. (4) 260-2100; fax (4) 260-3194; e-mail contactenos@suramericana.com; internet www.sura.com; f. 1944; Pres. GONZALO ALBERTO PÉREZ ROJAS.

Seguros de Riesgos Profesionales Suramericana, SA (ARP Sura): Centro Suramericana, Edif. Torre Suramericana, 7°, Calle 49A, No 63-55, Medellín, Antioquia; tel. (4) 430-7100; fax (4) 231-8080; e-mail scliente@sura.com.co; internet www.arpsura.com; f. 1996; fmrly SURATEP; name changed as above in 2009; subsidiary of Cía Suramericana de Seguros (Sura); Gen. Man. IVÁN IGNACIO ZULUAGA LATORRE.

Skandia Seguros de Vida, SA: Avda 19, No 109A-30, Apdo Aéreo 100327, Bogotá, DC; tel. (1) 658-4000; fax (1) 658-4123; e-mail servicioempresa@skandia.com.co; internet www.skandia.com.co; Pres. MARÍA CLAUDIA CORREA ORDÓÑEZ.

Insurance Association

Federación de Aseguradores Colombianos (FASECOLDA): Carrera 7A, No 26-20, 11° y 12°, Apdo Aéreo 5233, Bogotá, DC; tel. (1) 344-3080; fax (1) 210-7041; e-mail fasecolda@fasecolda.com; internet www.fasecolda.com; f. 1976; 32 mems; Chair. FERNANDO QUINTERO ARTURO; Exec. Pres. ROBERTO JUNGUITO BONNET.

Trade and Industry

GOVERNMENT AGENCIES

Agencia Nacional de Hidrocarburos (ANH): Calle 26, No 59-65, 2°, Bogotá, DC; tel. (1) 593-1717; fax (1) 593-1718; e-mail info@anh.gov.co; internet www.anh.gov.co; f. 2003; govt agency responsible for regulation of the petroleum industry; Pres. ORLANDO CABRALES SEGOVIA; Dir-Gen. JOSÉ ARMANDO ZAMORA REYES.

Departamento Nacional de Planeación: Edif. Fonade, Calle 26, No 13-19, 14°, Bogotá, DC; tel. (1) 381-5000; fax (1) 282-7080; e-mail tmendoza@dnp.gov.co; internet www.dnp.gov.co; f. 1958; supervises and administers devt projects; approves foreign investments; Dir-Gen. TATIANA OROZCO DE LA CRUZ; Sec.-Gen TATIANA MILENA MENDOZA LARA.

Superintendencia de Industria y Comercio (SUPERINDUSTRIA): Carrera 13, No 27-00, 5°, Bogotá, DC; tel. (1) 382-0840; fax (1) 382-2696; e-mail contactenos@sic.gov.co; internet www.sic.gov.co; supervises chambers of commerce; controls standards and prices; Supt JOSÉ ALEJANDRO BERMÚDEZ DURANA.

Superintendencia de Sociedades (SUPERSOCIEDADES): Avda El Dorado, No 51-80, Apdo Aéreo 4188, Bogotá, DC; tel. (1) 324-5777; fax (1) 324-5000; e-mail webmaster@supersociedades.gov.co; internet www.supersociedades.gov.co; f. 1931; oversees activities of local and foreign corpns; Supt LUIS GUILLERMO VÉLEZ CABRERA.

DEVELOPMENT AGENCIES

Agencia Presidencial para la Acción Social y la Cooperación Internacional: Calle 7, No 6-54, Bogotá, DC; tel. (1) 352-6666; fax (1) 284-4120; internet www.accionsocial.gov.co; f. 2005 following merger of Red de Solidaridad Social (RSS) and Agencia Colombiana de Cooperación Internacional (ACCI); govt agency intended to channel domestic and international funds into social programmes; Dir BRUCE MAC MASTER.

Asociación Colombiana de Ingeniería Sanitaria y Ambiental (ACODAL): Calle 39, No 14-75, Bogotá, DC; tel. (1) 245-9539; fax (1) 323-1408; e-mail gerencia@acodal.org.co; internet www.acodal.org.co; f. 1956 as Asociación Colombiana de Acueductos y Alcantarillados; assen promoting sanitary and environmental engineering projects; Pres. MARYLUZ MEJÍA DE PUMAREJO; Man. ALBERTO VALENCIA MONSALVE.

Asociación Colombiana de las Micro, Pequeñas y Medianas Empresas (ACOPI): Carrera 15, No 36-70, Bogotá, DC; tel. and fax (1) 320-4783; e-mail prensa@acopi.org.co; internet www.acopi.org.co; f. 1951; promotes small and medium-sized industries; Exec. Pres. MAURICIO RAMÍREZ MALAVER.

Centro Internacional de Educación y Desarrollo Humano (CINDE): Calle 77, Sur 43A-27 Sabaneta, Antioquia, Medellín; tel. (4) 444-8424; fax (4) 288-3991; e-mail cinde@cinde.org.co; internet www.cinde.org.co; education and social devt; f. 1977; Dir-Gen. MARTA ARANGO MONTOYA.

Corporación para la Investigación Socioeconómica y Tecnológica de Colombia (CINSET): Carrera 48, No 91-94, La Castellana, Bogotá, DC; tel. (1) 256-0961; fax (1) 218-6416; e-mail cinset@cinset.org.co; internet www.cinset.org.co; f. 1987; social, economic and technical devt projects; Pres. RAFAEL DARIO ARIAS DURÁN; Exec. Dir JUAN CARLOS GUTIÉRREZ ARIAS.

Corporación Región: Calle 55, No 41-10, Medellín; tel. (4) 216-6822; fax (4) 239-5544; e-mail admonregion@region.org.co; internet www.region.org.co; f. 1989; environmental, political and social devt; Exec. Dir MAX YURI GIL RAMÍREZ.

Fondo Financiero de Proyectos de Desarrollo (FONADE): Calle 26, No 13-19, 19°-22°, Apdo Aéreo 24110, Bogotá, DC; tel. (1) 594-0407; fax (1) 282-6018; e-mail fonade@fonade.gov.co; internet www.fonade.gov.co; f. 1968; responsible for channelling loans towards economic devt projects; administered by a cttee under the head of the Departamento Nacional de Planeación; FONADE works in close assen with other official planning orgs; Gen. Man. NATALIA ARIAS ECHEVERRY.

Instituto Colombiano de Desarrollo Rural: Centro Administrativo Nacional (CAN), Avda El Dorado, Calle 43, No 57-41, Bogotá, DC; tel. (1) 383-0444; e-mail incoder@incoder.gov.co; internet www.incoder.gov.co; rural devt agency; Gen. Man. MIRIAM VILLEGAS.

CHAMBERS OF COMMERCE

Confederación Colombiana de Cámaras de Comercio (CONFECAMARAS): Edif. Banco de Occidente, Of. 502, Carrera 13, No 27-47, Apdo Aéreo 29750, Bogotá, DC; tel. (1) 381-4100; fax (1) 346-7026; e-mail confecamaras@confecamaras.org.co; internet www.confecamaras.org.co; f. 1969; 56 mem. orgs; Exec. Pres. JULIÁN DOMÍNGUEZ RIVERA.

Cámara Colombo China de Inversión y Comercio: Of. 214, Carrera 10, No 96-25, Bogotá, DC; tel. (1) 616-6164; e-mail info@camaracolombochina.com; internet www.camaracolombochina.com; f. 2010; Pres. RICARDO DUARTE.

Cámara Colombo Japonesa de Comercio e Industria: Calle 72, No 7-82, 7°, Bogotá, DC; tel. (1) 210-0383; fax (1) 349-0736; e-mail camcoljapon@etb.net.co; internet www.ccjci.com.co; f. 1988; Colombian-Japanese trade asscn; Pres. JUAN CARLOS MONDRAGÓN A.

Cámara Colombo Venezolana: Edif. Suramericana, Of. 503, Calle 72, No 8-24, Bogotá, DC; tel. (1) 211-6224; fax (1) 211-6089; e-mail info@comvenezuela.com; internet www.comvenezuela.com; f. 1977; Colombian-Venezuelan trade asscn; 19 mem. cos; Pres. MAGDALENA PARDO DE SERRANO.

Cámara de Comercio de Bogotá: Avda Eldorado, 68D-35, Bogotá, DC; tel. (1) 383-0300; fax (1) 284-7735; e-mail webmaster@ccb.org.co; internet www.ccb.org.co; f. 1878; 3,650 mem. orgs; Pres. JUAN DIEGO TRUJILLO MEJÍA.

Cámara de Comercio Colombo Americano: Of. 1209, Calle 98, No 22-64, Bogotá, DC; tel. (1) 587-7828; fax (1) 621-6838; e-mail website@amchamcolombia.com.co; internet www.amchamcolombia.com.co; f. 1955; Colombian-US trade asscn; Exec. Dir CAMILO REYES RODRÍGUEZ.

Cámara de Comercio Colombo Británica: Of. 301, Calle 104, No 14A-45, Bogotá, DC; tel. (1) 256-2833; fax (1) 256-3026; e-mail comunicaciones@colombobritanica.com; internet www.colombobritanica.com; Colombian-British trade asscn; Pres. SANTIAGO ECHAVARRIA; Dir PATRICIA TOVAR.

INDUSTRIAL AND TRADE ASSOCIATIONS

Corporación de la Industria Aeronáutica Colombiana, SA (CIAC SA): Avda Calle 26, No 103-08, Entrada 1, Bogotá, DC; tel. (1) 413-8312; e-mail atencion@ciac.gov.co; internet www.ciac.gov.co; Gen. Man. HUGO ENRIQUE ACOSTA TELLEZ.

Industria Militar (INDUMIL): Calle 44, No 51-11, Apdo Aéreo 7272, Bogotá, DC; tel. (1) 220-7800; fax (1) 222-4889; e-mail indumil@indumil.gov.co; internet www.indumil.gov.co; attached to Ministry of National Defence; Gen. Man. Gen. (retd) GUSTAVO MATAMOROS CAMACHO.

Instituto Colombiano Agropecuario (ICA): Carrera 41, No 17-81, Bogotá, DC; tel. (1) 288-4800; fax (1) 332-3700; e-mail info@ica.gov.co; internet www.ica.gov.co; f. 1962; attached to the Ministry of Agriculture and Rural Devt; institute for promotion, co-ordination and implementation of research into and teaching and devt of agriculture and animal husbandry; Gen. Man. TERESITA BELTRÁN OSPINA.

Instituto Colombiano de Geología y Minería (INGEOMINAS): Diagonal 53, No 34-53, Apdo Aéreo 4865, Bogotá, DC; tel. (1) 222-1811; fax (1) 220-0797; e-mail director@ingeominas.gov.co; internet www.ingeominas.gov.co; f. 1968; responsible for mineral research, geological mapping and research including hydrogeology, remote sensing, geochemistry, geophysics and geological hazards; attached to the Ministry of Mines and Energy; Dir OSCAR PAREDES ZAPATA.

EMPLOYERS' AND PRODUCERS' ORGANIZATIONS

Asociación Colombiana de Cooperativos (ASCOOP): Transversal 29, No 36-29, Bogotá, DC; tel. (1) 368-3500; fax (1) 369-5475; e-mail ascoop@ascoop.coop; internet www.ascoop.coop; promotes co-operatives; Exec. Dir CARLOS ERNESTO ACERO SÁNCHEZ.

Asociación de Cultivadores de Caña de Azúcar de Colombia (ASOCAÑA): Calle 58N, No 3N-15, Apdo Aéreo 4448, Cali, Valle del Cauca; tel. (2) 664-7902; fax (2) 664-5888; internet www.asocana.com.co; f. 1959; sugar planters' asscn; Pres. LUIS FERNANDO LONDOÑO CAPURRO.

Asociación Nacional de Comercio Exterior (ANALDEX): Edif. UGI, Calle 40, No 13-09, 10°, Bogotá, DC; tel. (1) 570-0600; fax (1) 284-6911; e-mail analdex@analdex.org; internet www.analdex.org; exporters' asscn; Pres. JAVIER DÍAZ MOLINA.

Asociación Nacional de Empresarios de Colombia (ANDI): Carrera 43A, No 1-50, San Fernando Plaza, Torre 2, 9º, Apdo Aéreo 997, Medellín, Antioquia; tel. (4) 326-5100; fax (4) 326-0068; e-mail servicioalcliente@andi.com.co; internet www.andi.com.co; f. 1944; Pres. LUIS CARLOS VILLEGAS ECHEVERRI; 9 brs; 756 mems.

Asociación Nacional de Exportadores de Café de Colombia (Asoexport): Calle 72, No 10-07, Of. 1101, Bogotá, DC; tel. (1) 347-8419; fax (1) 347-9523; e-mail asoexport@asoexport.org; internet www.asoexport.org; f. 1933; private asscn of coffee exporters; Pres. JORGE ENRIQUE VÁSQUEZ.

Federación Colombiana de Ganaderos (FEDEGAN): Calle 37, No 14-31, Apdo Aéreo 9709, Bogotá, DC; tel. (1) 245-3041; fax (1) 578-2020; e-mail fedegan@fedegan.org.co; internet www.fedegan.org.co; f. 1963; cattle raisers' asscn; about 350,000 affiliates; Exec. Pres. JOSÉ FÉLIX LAFAURIE RIVERA.

Federación Nacional de Cacaoteros: Carrera 17, No 30-39, Apdo Aéreo 17736, Bogotá, DC; tel. (1) 327-3000; fax (1) 288-4424; e-mail info@fedecacao.com.co; internet www.fedecacao.com.co; fed. of cocoa growers; Gen. Man. Dr JOSÉ OMAR PINZÓN USECHE.

Federación Nacional de Cafeteros de Colombia (FEDERACAFE) (National Federation of Coffee Growers): Calle 73, No 8-13, Apdo Aéreo 57534, Bogotá, DC; tel. (1) 217-0600; fax (1) 217-1021; internet www.federaciondecafeteros.org; f. 1927; totally responsible for fostering and regulating the coffee economy; Gen. Man. LUIS GENARO MUÑOZ ORTEGA; 203,000 mems.

Federación Nacional de Comerciantes (FENALCO): Carrera 4, No 19-85, 7°, Bogotá, DC; tel. (1) 350-0600; fax (1) 350-9424; e-mail fenalco@fenalco.com.co; internet www.fenalco.com.co; Pres. GUILLERMO BOTERO NIETO.

Federación Nacional de Cultivadores de Cereales y Leguminosas (FENALCE): Km 1, Via Cota Siberia, vereda El Abra Cota, Bogotá, Cundinamarca; tel. (1) 592-1092; fax (1) 592-1098; e-mail fenalce@cable.net.co; internet www.fenalce.org; f. 1960; fed. of grain growers; Pres. MAXÍMO CUBILLOS; Gen. Man. HENRY VANEGAS ANAGARITA; 30,000 mems.

Sociedad de Agricultores de Colombia (SAC) (Colombian Farmers' Society): Carrera 7, No 24-89, Of. 4402, Bogotá, DC; tel. (1) 281-0263; fax (1) 284-4572; e-mail sac@sac.org.co; internet www.sac.org.co; f. 1871; Pres. RAFAEL MEJÍA LÓPEZ.

UTILITIES

Electricity

Corporación Eléctrica de la Costa Atlántica, SA ESP (Corelca): Centro Ejecutivo II, 5°, Calle 55, No 72-109, 9°, Barranquilla, Atlántico; tel. (5) 330-3000; fax (5) 330-3011; e-mail presidencia@corelca.com.co; internet www.corelca.com.co; responsible for supplying electricity to the Atlantic departments; generates more than 2,000m. kWh annually from thermal power stations; Gen. Man. DANIEL ALSINA GALOFRE.

Empresa de Energía de Bogotá, SA ESP (EEB): Of. Principal, 6°, Carrera 9A, No 73-44, Bogotá, DC; tel. (1) 326-8000; fax (1) 226-8010; e-mail webmaster@eeb.com.co; internet www.eeb.com.co; provides electricity for Bogotá area by generating capacity of 680 MW, mainly hydroelectric; Pres. MÓNICA DE GREIFF; Man. Dir ASTRID MARTÍNEZ ORTIZ.

Instituto de Planificación y Promoción de Soluciones Energéticas para las Zonas No Interconectadas (IPSE): Edif. 100 Street, Torre 3, 13°-15°, Calle 99, No 9A-54, Bogotá, DC; tel. (1) 639-7888; fax (1) 622-3461; e-mail ipse@ipse.gov.co; internet www.ipse.gov.co; f. 1999; attached to the Ministry of Mines and Energy; coordinates and develops energy supply in rural areas; Dir-Gen. CARLOS EDUARDO NEIRA ESTRADA.

Interconexión Eléctrica, SA (ISA): Calle 12 Sur, No 18-168, El Poblado, Apdo Aéreo 8915, Medellín, Antioquia; tel. (4) 325-2270; fax (4) 317-0848; e-mail isa@isa.com.co; internet www.isa.com.co; f. 1967; created by Colombia's principal electricity production and distribution cos to form a national network; operations in Brazil, Ecuador, Peru, Bolivia and Central America; 52.9% state-owned; Pres. ORLANDO CABRALES MARTÍNEZ; Gen. Man. LUIS FERNANDO ALARCÓN MANTILLA.

Isagen: Avda El Poblado, Carrera 43A, No 11A-80, Apdo Aéreo 8762, Medellín, Antioquia; tel. (4) 316-5000; fax (4) 268-4646; e-mail isagen@isagen.com.co; internet www.isagen.com.co; f. 1995 following division of ISA (q.v.); 57.7% state-owned; generates electricity from 3 hydraulic and 2 thermal power plants; Gen. Man. LUIS FERNANDO RICO PINZÓN.

Gas

Empresa Colombiana de Gas (Ecogás): Of. 209, Centro Internacional de Negocios La Triada, Calle 35, No 19-41, Bucaramanga, Santander del Sur; tel. (7) 642-1000; fax (7) 642-6446; e-mail correspondencia@ecogas.com.co; internet www.ecogas.com.co; f. 1997; operation and maintenance of gas distribution network; sold in 2006 to Empresa de Energía de Bogotá, SA; Dir GERONIMO MANUEL GUERRA CÁRDENAS.

Gas Natural, SA ESP: Calle 71A, No 5-38, Bogotá, DC; tel. (1) 338-1199; fax (1) 288-0807; internet portal.gasnatural.com; f. 1987; owned by Gas Natural of Spain; distributes natural gas in Bogotá and Soacha; Dir-Gen. (Latin America) SERGIO ARANDA MORENO; Pres. MARÍA EUGENIA CORONADO.

TRADE UNIONS

Central Unitaria de Trabajadores de Colombia (CUT): Calle 35, No 7-25, 9°, Apdo Aéreo 221, Bogotá, DC; tel. and fax (1) 323-7550; e-mail comunicaciones@cut.org.co; internet www.cut.org.co; f. 1986; comprises 50 feds and 80% of all trade union members; Pres. TARCISIO HORA GODOY; Sec.-Gen. DOMINGO TOVAR ARRIETA.

Confederación General del Trabajo (CGT): Calle 39A, No 14-52, Bogotá, DC; tel. (1) 288-1504; fax (1) 573-4021; e-mail cgtprensa2010@gmail.com; internet www.cgtcolombia.org; Pres. JULIO ROBERTO GÓMEZ ESGUERRA; Sec.-Gen. MIRYAM LUZ TRIANA ALVIS.

Confederación de Trabajadores de Colombia (CTC) (Colombian Confederation of Workers): Calle 39, No 26A-23, Barrio La Soledad, Apdo Aéreo 4780, Bogotá, DC; tel. (1) 269-7117; fax (7) 268-8576; e-mail ctc1@etb.net.co; internet www.ctc-colombia.com.co; f. 1934; mainly liberal; 600 affiliates, including 6 national orgs and 20 regional feds; admitted to the International Trade Union Confederation; Pres. LUIS MIGUEL MORANTES ALFONSO; Sec.-Gen. ROSA ELENA FLÉREZ; 400,000 mems.

Transport

Land transport in Colombia is rendered difficult by high mountains, so the principal means of long-distance transport is by air.

Superintendencia de Puertos y Transporte: Ministerio de Transporte, Edif. Estación de la Sabana, 2° y 3°, Calle 63, No 9A–45, Bogotá, DC; tel. and fax (2) 352-6700; e-mail atencionciudadano@supertransporte.gov.co; internet www.supertransporte.gov.co; f. 1992 as Superintendencia General de Puertos, present name adopted in 1998; part of the Ministry of Transport; oversees transport sector; Supt Dr JUAN MIGUEL DURÁN PRIETO.

Agencia Nacional de Infraestructura (ANI): Edif. Ministerio de Transporte, Centro Administrativo Nacional (CAN), 3°, Avda El Dorado, Bogotá, DC; tel. (1) 379-1720; fax (1) 324-0800; e-mail contactenos@ani.gov.co; internet www.ani.gov.co; fmrly Instituto Nacional de Concesiones; changed name as above in 2011; govt agency charged with contracting devt of transport infrastructure to private operators; part of the Ministry of Transport; Pres. LUIS FERNANDO ANDRADE MORENO.

Instituto Nacional de Vías (INVIAS): Edif. INVIAS, Centro Administrativo Nacional (CAN), Carrera 59, No 26-60, Bogotá, DC; tel. and fax (1) 705-6000; e-mail atencionciudadano@invias.gov.co; internet www.invias.gov.co; govt agency responsible for non-contracted transport infrastructure; Dir-Gen. CARLOS ALBERTO ROSADO ZÚÑIGA.

RAILWAYS

In 2008 there were 1,663 km of track. The Agencia Nacional de Infraestructura (q.v.) operates the Red Férrea del Atlántico and the Red Férrea del Pacífico. Construction of Ferrocarril del Carare, which would connect mining sites in the departments of Santander del Sur, Boyacá and Cundinamarca with ports on the Atlantic coast, was proceeding in 2013. The cost of the proposed project was US $2,700m.

El Cerrejón Mine Railway: Cerrejón, Calle 100, No 19-54, Bogotá, DC; tel. (1) 595-5555; e-mail comunica@cerrejon.com; internet www.cerrejon.com; f. 1989 to link the mine and the port at Puerto Bolívar; 150 km.

Ferrocarriles del Norte de Colombia, SA (FENOCO, SA): Calle 94A, No 11A-27, 3°, Bogotá, DC; tel. (1) 622-0505; fax (1) 622-0440; e-mail contactenos@fenoco.com.co; internet www.fenoco.com.co; f. 1999; operates the Concesión de la Red Férrea del Atlántico; 226 kms; Pres. PETER BURROWES.

Metro de Medellín (Empresa de Transporte Masivo del Valle de Aburrá Ltda): Calle 44, No 46-001, Apdo Aéreo 9128, Bello, Medellín, Antioquia; tel. (4) 444-9598; fax (4) 452-4450; e-mail contactenos@metrodemedellin.gov.co; internet www.metrodemedellin.gov.co; f. 1995; 5-line metro system; Gen. Man. RAMIRO MÁRQUEZ RAMÍREZ.

Tren de Occidente, SA: Avda Vásquez Cobo, No 23N-27, Of. 308, Santiago de Cali, Valle del Cauca; tel. (2) 667-7733; e-mail contacto.cali@trendeoccidente.com; internet www.trendeoccidente.com; f. 1998; operates the Concesión de la Red Férrea del Pacífico; Gen. Man. ALFONSO PATIÑO FAJARDO.

ROADS

In 2009 there were 129,485 km of roads, of which 13,386 km were under the national road network and 27,577 km formed the regional road network. A part of the Pan-American Highway, the Western Trunk Highway, connects the country with Ecuador. Other major highways include the Buenaventura Transverse and the Caribbean Transverse which connects major cities and ports with the Venezuelan highway network. In 2013 the Government initiated an ambitious US $7,200m. project to build more than 1,000 km of roads.

Instituto Nacional de Vías (INVIAS): Edif. INVIAS, Carrera 59, No 26-60, Bogotá, DC; tel. (1) 705-6000; fax (1) 315-6713; e-mail lnarvaezm@invias.gov.co; internet www.invias.gov.co; f. 1966; reorganized 1994; responsible to the Ministry of Transport; maintenance and construction of national road network; Gen. Man. JOSÉ LEONIDAS NARVÁEZ MORALES.

Transmilenio: Edif. Ministerio de Transporte, Centro Administrativo Nacional (CAN), 3°, Avda El Dorado, No 66-63, Bogotá, DC; tel. (1) 220-3000; fax (1) 324-9870; e-mail marthal.gutierrez@transmilenio.gov.co; internet www.transmilenio.gov.co; f. 2000; bus-based mass transit system in Bogotá; Gen. Man. JAIRO FERNANDO PAÉZ MENDIETA.

INLAND WATERWAYS

The Magdalena–Cauca river system is the centre of river traffic and is navigable for 1,500 km, while the Atrato is navigable for 687 km. The Orinoco system has more than five navigable rivers, which total more than 4,000 km of potential navigation (mainly through Venezuela); the Amazon system has four main rivers, which total 3,000 navigable km (mainly through Brazil).

SHIPPING

The four most important ocean terminals are Buenaventura on the Pacific coast and Santa Marta, Barranquilla and Cartagena on the Atlantic coast. The port of Tumaco on the Pacific coast is gaining in importance and there are plans for construction of a deep-water port at Bahía Solano. In December 2013 Colombia's flag registered fleet comprised 593 vessels, with a total displacement of some 176,739 grt.

Port Authorities

Sociedad Portuaria Regional de Barranquilla: Carrera 38, Calle 1A, Barranquilla, Atlántico; tel. (5) 371-6200; fax (5) 371-6310; e-mail servicioalcliente@sprb.com.co; internet www.sprb.com.co; privatized in 1993; Man. ENRIQUE CARVAJALES MARULANDA.

Sociedad Portuaria Regional de Buenaventura: Edif. de Administración, Avda Portuaria, Apdo 478-10765, Buenaventura; tel. 241-0700; fax 242-2700; e-mail servicioalaccionista@sprbun.com; internet www.puertobuenaventura.com; Pres. PEDRO JOSÉ GUTIÉRREZ HELO; Gen. Man. DOMINGO CHINEA BARRERA.

Sociedad Portuaria Regional de Cartagena: Manga, Terminal Marítimo, Cartagena, Bolívar; tel. (5) 660-7781; fax (5) 650-2239; e-mail comercial@sprc.com.co; internet www.puertocartagena.com; f. 1993; Gen. Man. ALFONSO SALAS TRUJILLO.

Sociedad Portuaria de Santa Marta: Carrera 1, 10A-12, Apdo 655, Santa Marta; tel. (5) 421-7970; fax (5) 421-2161; e-mail spsm@spsm.com.co; internet www.spsm.com.co; Dir ARMANDO DUARTE-PELÁEZ; Gen. Man. MAURICIO SUÁREZ.

Private shipping companies include the following:

NAVESCO, SA: Torre Cusezar, No 7-15, 17°, Avda Calle 116, Bogotá, DC; tel. (1) 657-5868; fax (1) 657-5869; e-mail gsolano@navesco.com.co; internet www.navesco.com.co; f. 1980; Pres. RUBEN ESCOBAR; Gen. Man. GUILLERMO SOLANO.

CIVIL AVIATION

Colombia has 11 international airports: Bogotá, DC (El Dorado International Airport), Medellín, Cali, Barranquilla, Bucaramanga, Cartagena, Cúcuta, Leticia, Pereira, San Andrés and Santa Marta.

Regulatory Authority

Aeronáutica Civil (Aerocivil): Nuevo Edif. Aerocivil, Avda El Dorado 103–15, 4°, Bogotá, DC; tel. (1) 425-1000; fax (1) 413-5000; e-mail quejasyreclamos@aerocivil.gov.co; internet www.aerocivil.gov.co; f. 1967 as Departamento Administrativo de Aeronáutica Civil, reorganized in 1992; part of the Ministry of Transport; develops and regulates the civil aviation industry; Dir-Gen. SANTIAGO CASTRO.

National Airlines

Avianca (Aerovías Nacionales de Colombia, SA): Avda El Dorado, No 93-30, 5°, Bogotá, DC; tel. (1) 413-9862; fax (1) 413-8716; internet www.avianca.com; f. 1919; operates domestic services to all cities in Colombia and international services to the USA, France, Spain, and throughout Central and Southern America; allied with TACA of El Salvador (q.v.) in 2009; Exec. Pres. FABIO VILLEGAS RAMÍREZ.

Copa Airlines Colombia: Edif. Citibank, Calle 100, Carrera 9A, No 99–02, Bogotá, DC; tel. (1) 320-9090; fax (1) 320-9095; internet www.copaair.com; f. 1992 as Aero República; changed name as above in 2010; subsidiary of Copa Holdings (Panama); Pres. ROBERTO JUNGUITO POMBO.

LAN Colombia (Aires Colombia): El Dorado International Airport, Bogotá, DC; internet www.lan.com; f. 1980 as Aerovías de Integración Regional (AIRES); acquired by LAN Airlines, SA (Chile) and rebranded as above in 2010; domestic and international passenger services, domestic cargo services; CEO HERNÁN PASMAN.

Líneas Aéreas Suramericanas (LAS): Avda El Dorado, No 103-22, Entrada 2, Interior 7, Bogotá, DC; tel. (1) 413-9515; fax (1) 413-5356; internet www.lascargo.com; f. 1972 as AeroNorte, present name adopted 1986; charter cargo services.

Satena (Servicio de Aeronavegación a Territorios Nacionales): Avda El Dorado, No 103-08, Apdo Aéreo 11163, Bogotá, DC; tel. (1) 423-8530; e-mail info@satena.com; internet www.satena.com; f. 1962; commercial enterprise attached to the Ministry of National Defence; internal services; Pres. Brig.-Gen. CARLOS EDUARDO MONTEALEGRE RODRIGUEZ.

Tampa Cargo, SA: Aeropuerto José María Córdova, Terminal Internacional de Carga, Rionegro, Medellín, Antioquia; tel. (4) 569-9200; fax (4) 562-2847; e-mail laura.herzberg@aviancataca.com; internet www.tampacargo.com.co; f. 1973; operates international cargo services to destinations throughout the Americas; acquired by AviancaTaca Holdings in 2010; Dir LUÍS FELIPE GOMÉZ TORO.

Tourism

The principal tourist attractions are the Caribbean coast (including the island of San Andrés), the 16th-century walled city of Cartagena, the Amazonian town of Leticia, the Andes mountains, the extensive forests and jungles, pre-Columbian relics and monuments of colonial art. In 2012 there were a provisional 2,175,000 visitors, most of whom came from the USA and Venezuela. In the same year tourism receipts totalled a provisional US $2,351m.

Asociación Colombiana de Agencias de Viajes y Turismo (ANATO): Carrera 19B, No 83-49, 4°, Apdo Aéreo 7088, Bogotá, DC; tel. (1) 610-7099; fax (1) 236-2424; e-mail anato@anato.org; internet www.anato.org; f. 1949; Pres. PAULA CORTÉS CALLE; Exec. Dir ISMAEL ENRIQUE RAMIREZ.

Defence

As assessed at November 2013, Colombia's armed forces numbered 281,400, of whom the army comprised 221,500, the navy 46,150 (including 27,000 marines and 7,200 conscripts) and the air force 13,750. In addition, there were some 61,900 reservists, of whom 54,700 were in the army, 4,800 in the navy, 1,200 in the air force and 1,200 in the joint services. There was also a paramilitary National Police Force numbering 159,000. Military service is compulsory for men (except for students) and lasts for 12–24 months.

Defence Budget: 12,600,000m. pesos in 2013.

Commander of the Armed Forces: Maj.-Gen. JUAN PABLO RODRÍGUEZ BARRAGÁN.

Chief of Staff of the Armed Forces: Maj.-Gen. JAVIER ALBERTO FLÓREZ ARISTIZÁBAL.

Commander of the Army: Maj.-Gen. JAIME ALFONSO LASPRILLA VILLAMIZAR.

Commander of the Navy: Rear-Adm. HERNANDO WILLS VÉLEZ.

Commander of the Air Force: Maj.-Gen. GUILLERMO LEÓN.

Education

Education in Colombia commences at nursery level for children under six years of age. Primary education is free and compulsory for five years. Admission to secondary school is conditional upon the successful completion of these five years. Secondary education is for four years. Following completion of this period, pupils may pursue a further two years of vocational study. In 2011/12 a total of 4,742,500 students were in primary education and some 4,584,900 attended secondary schools. In 2012 enrolment at primary and secondary schools included 84% and 74% of the school-age population, respectively. In 2013 there were 32 public universities in Colombia. The proposed central Government expenditure on education for 2013 was 24.9m. pesos.

THE COMOROS*

Introductory Survey

LOCATION, CLIMATE, LANGUAGE, RELIGION, FLAG, CAPITAL

The Union of the Comoros (formerly the Federal Islamic Republic of the Comoros) is an archipelago in the Mozambique Channel, between the island of Madagascar and the east coast of the African mainland. The group comprises four main islands (Ngazidja, Nzwani and Mwali—formerly Grande-Comore, Anjouan and Mohéli, respectively—and Mayotte, which is a French overseas possession) and numerous islets and coral reefs. The climate is tropical, with average temperatures ranging from 23°C (73.4°F) to 28°C (82.4°F). Average annual rainfall is between 1,500 mm (59 ins) and 5,000 mm (197 ins). The official languages are Comorian (a blend of Swahili and Arabic), French and Arabic. Islam is the state religion. The flag (proportions 2 by 3) has four equal horizontal stripes, of yellow, white, red and blue, with a green triangle at the hoist depicting a white crescent moon and a vertical row of four five-pointed white stars. The capital, which is situated on Ngazidja, is Moroni.

CONTEMPORARY POLITICAL HISTORY

Historical Context

Formerly attached to Madagascar, the Comoros became a separate French Overseas Territory in 1947. The islands achieved internal self-government in December 1961, with a Government Council responsible for local administration. On 6 July 1975 the legislature voted for immediate independence, elected the President of the Government Council, Ahmed Abdallah, to be first President of the Comoros and reconstituted itself as the Assemblée Nationale (National Assembly). Although France made no attempt to intervene, it maintained control of the island of Mayotte. Abdallah was deposed in August, and the National Assembly was abolished. A National Executive Council was established, with Prince Saïd Mohammed Jaffar, leader of the opposition party, the Front National Uni, as its head, and Ali Soilih, leader of the coup, among its members. In November the Comoros was admitted to the UN, as a unified state comprising the whole archipelago. In December France officially recognized the independence of Ngazidja, Nzwani and Mwali, but relations between France and the Comoros were effectively suspended. In February 1976 Mayotte voted overwhelmingly to retain its links with France.

Soilih, who had been elected Head of State in January 1976, was killed in May 1978, following a coup by a group of European mercenaries, led by a Frenchman, Col Robert Denard, on behalf of Abdallah. The Comoros was proclaimed a Federal Islamic Republic and diplomatic relations with France were restored. In October a new Constitution was approved in a referendum, on the three islands excluding Mayotte, by 99.3% of the votes cast. Abdallah was elected President in the same month, and in December elections for a new legislature, the Assemblée Fédérale (Federal Assembly), took place. In January 1979 the Federal Assembly approved the formation of a one-party state (although unofficial opposition groups continued to operate). In September 1984 Abdallah was re-elected President.

Domestic Political Affairs

In November 1989 a constitutional amendment permitting Abdallah to remain in office for a third six-year term was approved by 92.5% of votes cast in a popular referendum. The result of the referendum, however, was disputed by the President's opponents. Violent demonstrations followed, and opposition leaders were detained. On the night of 26–27 November Abdallah was assassinated by members of the presidential guard, under the command of Denard. The President of the Supreme Court, Saïd Mohamed Djohar, was appointed interim Head of State; however, Denard and his supporters defeated the regular army in a coup, which attracted international condemnation. (In May 1999 Denard stood trial in Paris, France, in connection with the assassination. Both Denard and his co-defendant, Dominique Malacrino, were acquitted of the murder charge.) In December 1989 Denard agreed to relinquish power and, following the arrival of French paratroops in Moroni, was transported to South Africa, together with the remaining mercenaries.

At the end of December 1989 the main political groups formed a provisional Government of National Unity. An amnesty for all political prisoners was proclaimed, and an inquiry into the death of Abdallah was instigated. In March 1990 Djohar, the official candidate for the Union Comorienne pour le Progrès (Udzima), secured victory at a multi-candidate presidential election, taking 55.3% of the votes cast and defeating Mohamed Taki Abdulkarim, the leader of the Union Nationale pour la Démocratie aux Comores (UNDC).

In November 1991 agreement was reached between Djohar and the principal opposition leaders to initiate a process of national reconciliation, which would include the convening of a constitutional conference. The accord also guaranteed the legitimacy of Djohar's election as President. In January 1992 a new transitional Government of National Unity was formed, pending legislative elections.

At a constitutional referendum, held on 7 June 1992, reform proposals, which had been submitted in April, were approved by 74.3% of the votes cast. The new Constitution limited the presidential tenure to a maximum of two five-year terms of office and provided for a bicameral legislature, comprising a Federal Assembly, elected for a term of four years, and a 15-member Sénat (Senate), selected for a six-year term by the regional Councils.

The first round of voting in legislative elections took place on 22 November 1992. Numerous electoral irregularities and violent incidents were reported and several opposition parties demanded that the results be declared invalid. Election results in six constituencies were subsequently annulled, while the second round of voting on 29 November took place in only 34 of the 42 constituencies. Following partial elections on 13 and 30 December, reports indicated that candidates supporting Djohar—including seven members of the Union des Démocrates pour la Démocratie (UDD), a pro-Government organization based on Nzwani—had secured a narrow majority in the Federal Assembly. The leader of the UDD, Ibrahim Abdérémane Halidi, was appointed Prime Minister on 1 January 1993 and formed a new Council of Ministers.

In May 1993 eight supporters of the Minister of Finance, Commerce and Planning (and Djohar's son-in-law), Mohamed Saïd Abdallah M'Changama, allied with a number of opposition deputies, proposed a motion of no confidence in the Government (apparently with the tacit support of Djohar), which was approved by 23 of the 42 deputies. Shortly afterwards, Djohar appointed an associate of M'Changama, Saïd Ali Mohamed, as Prime Minister, and a new Council of Ministers was formed. In June, in view of the continued absence of a viable parliamentary majority, Djohar dissolved the Federal Assembly and announced legislative elections. He subsequently dismissed Mohamed and appointed a former presidential adviser, Ahmed Ben Cheikh Attoumane, as Prime Minister. Shortly afterwards an interim Council of Ministers was formed.

Following the dissolution of the Federal Assembly, opposition parties declared Djohar unfit to hold office, in view of the increasing political confusion, and demanded that legislative elections take place within the period of 40 days stipulated in the Constitution. In July 1993, however, Djohar announced that the legislative elections (which were to take place concurrently with local elections) were to be postponed until October. In October Djohar established a political organization, the Rassemblement pour la Démocratie et le Renouveau (RDR). In November the legislative elections were rescheduled for December, while the local elections were postponed indefinitely. Later in November Djohar reorganized the Council of Ministers and established a

*Some of the information contained in this chapter refers to the whole Comoros archipelago, which the independent Comoran state claims as its national territory. However, the island of Mayotte (Mahoré) is, in fact, administered by France. Separate information on Mayotte may be found in the chapter on French Overseas Possessions.

new national electoral commission, in response to opposition demands.

At the first round of the legislative elections, which took place on 12 December 1993, four opposition candidates secured seats in the Federal Assembly. Following a second round of voting on 20 December, the electoral commission declared the results in several constituencies to be invalid. Opposition candidates refused to participate in further elections in these constituencies, on the grounds that voting was again to be conducted under the supervision of the authorities, rather than that of the commission; RDR candidates consequently won all 10 contested seats, and 22 seats overall, thereby securing a narrow majority in the Federal Assembly.

In September 1995 about 30 European mercenaries, led by Denard, staged a military coup, seizing control of the garrison at Kandani and capturing Djohar. The mercenaries, who were joined by some 300 members of the Comoran armed forces, released a number of prisoners and installed a former associate of Denard, Capt. Ayouba Combo, as leader of a Transitional Military Committee. The French Government denounced the coup and suspended economic aid to the Comoros. In October Combo announced that he had transferred authority to Taki and the leader of CHUMA (Islands' Fraternity and Unity Party), Saïd Ali Kemal, (who had both welcomed the coup) as joint civilian Presidents. However, following appeals for intervention from the Prime Minister, Mohamed Caabi El Yachroutu, who invoked a defence co-operation agreement that had been established between the two countries in 1978, some 900 French military personnel landed on the Comoros and surrounded the mercenaries at Kandani. Shortly afterwards Denard and his associates, together with the disaffected members of the Comoran armed forces, surrendered to the French troops. (In October 1996, following his release from imprisonment in France in July, Denard claimed that the coup attempt had been planned at the request of several Comoran officials, including Taki. In mid-2006 Denard was given a suspended sentence of five years by a French court for his involvement in the coup. Denard died in France in October 2007.)

Following the French military intervention, El Yachroutu declared himself interim President, in accordance with the Constitution, and formed a Government of National Unity. Djohar (who had been transported to Réunion by the French in order to receive medical treatment) rejected El Yachroutu's assumption of power and announced the reappointment of Mohamed as Prime Minister. Later in October 1995 a National Reconciliation Conference decided that El Yachroutu would remain interim President, pending the forthcoming election, which was provisionally scheduled for early 1996. At the end of October 1995 El Yachroutu granted an amnesty to all Comorans involved in the coup attempt and appointed representatives of the UNDC and Udzima (which had supported the coup) to the new Council of Ministers. In November Djohar announced the formation of a rival government, headed by Mohamed. El Yachroutu, who was supported by the Comoran armed forces, refused to recognize the legitimacy of Djohar's appointments, while opposition parties equally opposed his return to power; only elements of the RDR continued to support Djohar's authority. Political leaders on Mwali rejected the authority of both rival governments, urged a campaign of civil disobedience and established a 'citizens' committee' to govern the island; discontent with the central administration also emerged on Nzwani.

A presidential election took place in March 1996 in which Taki was elected to the presidency. He appointed a new Council of Ministers, which included five of the presidential candidates who had supported him in the second round of the election, and in April he dissolved the Federal Assembly. New Governors, all belonging to the UNDC, were appointed to each of the three islands. In August Taki issued a decree awarding himself absolute powers. This measure was widely criticized in the media and by opposition groups as being in violation of the Constitution.

In September 1996 Taki established a constitutional consultative committee, comprising 42 representatives of political parties and other organizations, which was to provide advice concerning the drafting of a new constitution. Also in that month the legislative elections were postponed until November. A national referendum to endorse a new draft Constitution was scheduled for 20 October. In order to comply with a constitutional proposal, which effectively restricted the number of political parties to a maximum of three, 24 pro-Taki political organizations merged to form one presidential party, the Rassemblement National pour le Développement (RND). The new Constitution, which was approved by 85% of votes cast, extended the presidential term to six years, with an unrestricted number of consecutive mandates. Political parties were required to have two parliamentary deputies from each island (following legislative elections) to be considered legal; organizations that did not fulfil these stipulations were to be dissolved. Extensive executive powers were vested in the President, who was to appoint the Governors of the islands and who acquired the right to initiate constitutional amendments.

Following unsuccessful negotiations with the Government, the opposition parties (having formed a new alliance) refused to participate in the electoral process. Consequently, the legislative elections, which took place in two rounds in December 1996, were only contested by the RND and the Front National pour la Justice (FNJ), a fundamentalist Islamist organization, together with 23 independent candidates. The RND secured 36 of the 43 seats in the expanded Federal Assembly, while the FNJ won three, with four seats taken by independent candidates. Taki nominated Ahmed Abdou, who had served in the administration of former President Ahmed Abdallah, as Prime Minister to head a new Council of Ministers.

The separatist movement

During early 1996 separatist leaders declared their intention to seek the restoration of French rule and in March established a 'political directorate' on Nzwani, chaired by Abdallah Ibrahim, the leader of the Mouvement Populaire Anjouanais, a grouping of separatist movements on Nzwani. (The relative prosperity of neighbouring Mayotte appeared to have prompted the demand for a return to French rule; it was reported that up to 200 illegal migrants a day attempted to enter Mayotte from Nzwani.) Military reinforcements were sent to Nzwani and the Governor of the island was replaced once again.

On 3 August 1997 the 'political directorate' unilaterally declared Nzwani's secession from the Comoros. The separatists subsequently elected Ibrahim as president of a 13-member 'politico-administrative co-ordination', which included Abdou Madi as spokesperson. France, while denouncing the secession, refused to mediate in the crisis and declared itself in favour of the intervention of the Organization of African Unity (OAU, now the African Union—AU, see p. 186), which dispatched a special envoy to the Comoros. Meanwhile, separatist agitation intensified on Mwali, culminating on 11 August, when secessionists declared Mwali's independence from the Comoros, appointed a president and government, and called for re-attachment to France.

As OAU mediation efforts proceeded, Taki dispatched some 300 troops to Nzwani in early September 1997 in an attempt forcibly to suppress the separatist insurrection. As it emerged that some 40 Comoran soldiers and 16 Nzwani residents had been killed in the fighting, with many more injured, demonstrators demanding Taki's resignation clashed violently with the security forces in Moroni. The separatists on Nzwani reaffirmed their independence and empowered Ibrahim to rule by decree. Taki subsequently declared a state of emergency, assumed absolute power and dismissed the Government of Ahmed Abdou and his military and civilian advisers. (Abdou had reportedly resigned from his position in late August, although this had not been announced publicly.) Shortly afterwards, Taki established a State Transition Commission, which included representatives from Nzwani and Mwali. The League of Arab States (Arab League, see p. 362) agreed to a request from Taki for assistance, and following talks with the OAU, all three islands hosted discussions in late September, which were convened by envoys from both organizations.

In September 1997 Ibrahim announced his decision to hold a referendum on self-determination for Nzwani on 26 October, prior to a reconciliation conference sponsored by both the OAU and the Arab League. Despite international opposition, the referendum was conducted as scheduled; according to separatist officials, 99.9% of the electorate voted in favour of independence for Nzwani. The following day Ibrahim dissolved the 'politico-administrative co-ordination' and appointed a temporary government, which was charged with preparing a constitution and organizing a presidential election. Taki responded by severing Nzwani's telephone and transport links.

In early December 1997 Taki formed a new Council of Ministers, appointing Nourdine Bourhane as Prime Minister. An inter-Comoran reconciliation conference was held later that month; some agreement was reached on proposals for the establishment of an international commission of inquiry to investigate September's military intervention and on the holding of a

Comoran inter-island conference to discuss institutional reform. In January 1998 the OAU announced that both the Comoran Government and the Nzwani separatists had agreed to a number of conciliatory measures, including the restoration of air and maritime links and the release of federal soldiers still detained on Nzwani.

In July 1998, as social unrest on Nzwani escalated, a dispute over the future aims of the secessionist movement led to the dismissal of the island's government, provoking violent clashes between islanders loyal to Ibrahim, who favoured independence within the framework of an association of the Comoran islands, and supporters of the outgoing prime minister of the island, Chamassi Saïd Omar, who continued to advocate re-attachment to France.

On 6 November 1998 President Taki died unexpectedly, reportedly having suffered a heart attack, although several senior officials expressed serious doubts about the cause of death. Tadjidine Ben Saïd Massoundi, the President of the High Council of the Republic and a former Prime Minister, was designated acting President, in accordance with the Constitution, pending an election which would be held after 30–90 days. In January 1999 Massoundi extended his presidential mandate, which was soon to expire, pending a resolution of the crisis dividing the islands. Also in that month Ibrahim agreed to relinquish some of his powers to a five-member 'politico-administrative directorate', as meetings commenced between the rival separatist factions. No consensus was reached in the following months, however, and when Ibrahim replaced the directorate with a 'committee of national security' in March, the new administration was immediately rejected by rival leaders.

At an OAU-sponsored inter-island conference, held in Antananarivo, Madagascar, in April 1999, an agreement was reached that envisaged substantial autonomy for Nzwani and Mwali, the changing of the country's name to the Union of the Comoran Islands and the rotation of the presidency among the three islands. However, the delegates from Nzwani refused to sign the agreement, insisting on the need to consult the Nzwani population prior to a full endorsement. On 30 April the Chief of Staff of the Comoran armed forces, Col Assoumani Azali, seized power in a bloodless coup, deposing Massoundi and dissolving the Government, the Federal Assembly and all other constitutional institutions. Azali promulgated a new constitutional charter and proclaimed himself head of state and of government, and Commander-in-Chief of the armed forces. Full legislative functions were also vested in Azali, who announced his intention to stay in power for one year only, during which time he pledged to oversee the creation of the new institutions envisaged in the Antananarivo accord. The appointment of a State Committee (composed of six members from Ngazidja, four from Mwali and two from Nzwani) was followed by that of a State Council, which was to supervise the activities of the State Committee and comprised eight civilians and 11 army officers. The coup was condemned by the OAU; the UN, however, sent representatives to Azali's inauguration.

In June 1999 Lt-Col Saïd Abeid Abdérémane, who had previously held the role of 'national mediator' on Nzwani, formed a government of national unity on the island and assumed the role of 'national co-ordinator'. In July delegates from the three islands, including Azali and Abeid, met on Mwali for talks aimed at resolving the political crisis (in the most senior-level contact between the islands since the secessions of August 1997).

In December 1999 the OAU threatened to impose sanctions on Nzwani should its leaders not have signed the peace accord by 1 February 2000. In response, Abeid announced that a referendum would be held on Nzwani in January 2000 regarding the signing of the Antananarivo accord. According to the separatist authorities of Nzwani, the results of the referendum revealed an overwhelming majority (94.5%) in favour of full independence for the island; the OAU, however, announced that it did not recognize the outcome of the ballot, following allegations of intimidation and repression of those in favour of reconciliation. Meanwhile, following a series of meetings between Azali and a number of political parties from all three islands regarding the establishment of a more representative and decentralized government in Moroni, the State Committee underwent an extensive reorganization in December 1999, including the appointment of a Prime Minister, Bianrifi Tarmidi (from Mwali).

In February 2000, as threatened, the OAU imposed economic sanctions on Nzwani; the overseas assets of the separatist leaders were frozen and they themselves were confined to the island. Furthermore, as part of the OAU sanctions, the federal Government suspended sea and air transport links, as well as telephone communications, with Nzwani. In May the OAU announced that the lifting of sanctions against Nzwanian separatists was dependent on a return to constitutional order on the Comoros. The possibility of armed intervention on Nzwani was rejected at an OAU summit, held in July, although the establishment of a total maritime blockade of the island was agreed.

Towards a new constitution

Following negotiations in Fomboni, the administrative centre of Mwali, in August 2000 Azali and Abeid reached an agreement, known as the Fomboni Accord, which provided for the establishment of a new Comoran entity and granted the three islands considerable control over internal matters. A new constitution was to be drafted and approved, by referendum, within 12 months. Moreover, Abeid and Azali appealed for the sanctions imposed on Nzwani to be lifted. The declaration was rejected by the OAU, however, on the grounds that it contravened the Antananarivo accord and threatened the integrity of the Comoros. Nevertheless, a tripartite commission, comprising delegates from Ngazidja, Nzwani and Mwali, was established to define the terms of the new constitution. In November Bianrifi Tarmidi was replaced as Prime Minister by Hamada Madi 'Boléro', who subsequently formed a new Government. However, opposition members refused to participate in the new authorities, instead presenting to international mediators their own proposals for a resolution to the crisis.

With the mediation of the OAU and the Organisation Internationale de la Francophonie (OIF), negotiations between opposition and government members continued throughout late 2000 and early 2001. In February the Framework Agreement for Reconciliation in the Comoros was signed in Fomboni by representatives of the Comoran Government, the Nzwani administration, opposition parties and civil society. The OAU, the OIF and the European Union (EU, see p. 273) were to be guarantors of the peace accord, which provided for the establishment of a new Comoran entity. Under the provisions of the agreement, an independent tripartite commission (comprising equal numbers of delegates from each of the islands, representing all the signatory groups) was to draft a new constitution, which would be subject to approval in a national referendum. The new constitution was to define the areas of jurisdiction of the new entity and the individual islands, although the central administration would retain control over religion, nationality, currency, foreign affairs and defence. An independent national electoral commission was also to be created. Following the constitutional referendum, a transitional government of national union was to be formed and charged with creating the new institutions by 31 December. However, in March, following disagreements over the composition of a follow-up committee intended to monitor the implementation of the Fomboni Accord, the opposition withdrew from the reconciliation process. Despite this, the OAU suspended sanctions against Nzwani in May.

On 8–9 August 2001 a bloodless military coup on Nzwani resulted in the removal from power of Abeid, who was replaced by a collective presidency, comprising Maj. Mohamed Bacar, Maj. Hassane Ali Toihili and Maj. Charif Halidi; a government of eight civilian commissioners (none of whom had been members of the previous administration) was appointed. The new leadership stated its commitment to the Fomboni Accord. However, on 24 September a further bloodless military coup was instigated by the deputy head of the Comoran army and close ally of Col Azali, Maj. Ayouba Combo. Although Combo was initially declared leader of the army, and Ahmed Aboubakar Foundi was installed as leader of Nzwani, they were captured the following day, before subsequently escaping the island. In November Abeid attempted unsuccessfully to regain control of Nzwani, but was defeated by forces loyal to Bacar and fled the island; the attempted coup was strongly condemned by the Government, which reaffirmed its support for the island's authorities.

At the constitutional referendum, which took place on 23 December 2001, 76.4% of the electorate voted in favour of the proposed new constitution. The country, which was to change its name to the Union of the Comoros, was to be led by the President of the Union, at the head of a Council of the Union, and governed by a legislative assembly, the Assemblée de l'Union (Assembly of the Union). The position of President was to rotate between the islands, while the Vice-Presidents, who were also members of the Council of the Union, were to be inhabitants of the two remaining islands; the first President was to come from Ngazidja. Each of the three islands was to become financially autonomous and was to be ruled by its own local government and institutions. The Union was to be responsible for matters of religion, nationality, currency, foreign affairs and external defence, while shared responsibilities between the Union and the islands were to be determined at a later date. A transitional government was to be established to monitor the installation of the new institutions.

In January 2002 a transitional Government of National Unity (GNU) was installed, with 'Boléro' reappointed as Prime Minister; the new administration included members of the former Government, opposition representatives and two of Nzwani's separatist leaders. However, on the following day the GNU collapsed, after the withdrawal of the opposition representatives, as a result of a disagreement over the allocation of ministerial portfolios. Meanwhile, Col Azali resigned as Head of State and announced his intention to stand as an independent candidate in the forthcoming presidential election; 'Boléro' was to serve as acting President. In February the GNU was re-established.

Azali elected Federal President

In March and April 2002 voters on Nzwani, Mwali and Ngazidja approved new local Constitutions. In a first round of voting in the federal presidential election on 17 March, contested by nine candidates, Col Azali secured 39.8% of the vote. Mahamoud Mradabi won 15.7% and Saïd Ali Kemal 10.7%; however, both Mradabi and Kemal boycotted the second round. Consequently, on 14 April Col Azali was elected unopposed as Federal President of the Union of the Comoros, reportedly securing more than 75% of the votes cast. Although the result was declared invalid by the electoral commission, on the grounds that the election had not been free and fair, following the dissolution of the electoral commission and the appointment of an independent electoral body, Col Azali was declared Federal President. Meanwhile, in late March and early April, Maj. Mohamed Bacar and Mohamed Saïd Fazul were elected as regional Presidents of Nzwani and Mwali, respectively; on 19 May Abdou Soulé Elbak was elected regional President of Ngazidja. The regional Presidents subsequently formed local Governments. Col Azali appointed a new federal Government in early June.

Elections to the three island assemblies were held on 14 and 21 March 2004. Pro-Azali candidates won an overall total of only 12 seats in the assemblies, while candidates allied to Elbak secured 14 of the 20 seats in the Ngazidja assembly, supporters of Bacar were reported to have won 19 of the 25 seats available on Nzwani, and nine allies of Fazul were elected to the 10-member assembly on Mwali. Elections to the Assembly of the Union took place on 18 and 25 April. According to final results, declared on 28 April, Azali's party, the Convention pour le Renouveau des Comores (CRC) won only six of the 18 directly elected seats, while a loose coalition supporting the three island Presidents secured 11 seats and CHUMA took one seat. The rate of participation by eligible voters at the second round was 68.5%. The remaining 15 seats in the 33-member Assembly of the Union were taken by five nominees from each of the island legislatures. The inauguration of the Assembly, at which Saïd Dhiuffur Bounou was elected Speaker, took place on 4 June. In mid-July President Azali announced his new Government, granting responsibility for co-ordinating Union affairs on their home islands to the two Vice-Presidents. The new cabinet comprised the two Vice-Presidents, seven ministers of state and two secretaries of state, and included a member of CHUMA, and representatives nominated by the Presidents of Nzwani and Mwali. President Bacar declined to participate in the creation of the Government.

Despite the submission of draft legislation in April 2005 that would have permitted President Azali to stand for a second term as President of the Union, in June the Assembly of the Union officially approved the rotation of the presidency between the three islands, thus ensuring that the next President of the Union would be from Nzwani. In October the Assembly of the Union approved legislation granting Comorans living abroad the right to vote.

The system of the rotational presidency took effect upon the 2006 presidential elections. In the first round of the elections, held on 16 April, three of the 13 candidates from the island of Nzwani received sufficient votes cast to proceed to the nationwide second ballot; this took place on 14 May and resulted in Ahmed Abdallah Sambi, a businessman and the founder of the Islamist FNJ, securing 99,112 (58.0%) of the votes cast. The conduct of the elections was endorsed by international monitors. The former Prime Minister, Ibrahim Halidi, was placed second with 48,378 (28.3%) of the votes, while Mohammad Djaanfari received 23,322 votes (13.7%). Sambi officially assumed the presidency on 26 May and a new Government was appointed within three days, considerably reduced in size, and consisting of two Vice-Presidents and six ministers. Notably, the defence portfolio was allocated to the President's office and the army was to be reunified under single command. National troops were confined to barracks for the duration of the elections and the AU contributed over 400 troops to ensure the first peaceful transition of power since independence.

The new Government was swift to pursue corruption charges against former officials, to recommence the payment of salaries to civil servants (which had been suspended from the beginning of the year), and to reduce the price of rice (a staple food). However, conflicts over the competencies of the Union and island Governments persisted.

In March 2007 President Sambi carried out a reorganization of the Government, creating four new portfolios. Most notably, Mohamed Ali Solihi was appointed Minister of Finance, Budget and Planning, while the newly created departments included the Ministry of Energy and the Ministry of Islamic Affairs, Human Rights and Information.

Instability on Nzwani

The period prior to the island presidential elections in mid-2007 was marred by violence and allegations of corruption and intimidation. Elections took place on Ngazidja and Mwali on 10 June as scheduled, while the election on Nzwani was postponed until 17 June at the request of President Sambi and the AU. However, Bacar proceeded to hold the election despite its rescheduling and subsequently claimed victory with 73.2% of the vote, declaring himself President of Nzwani for a second term. Both the AU and the Union Government announced that the election was null and void. While unrest continued on Nzwani, a second round of voting took place on Ngazidja and Mwali on 25 June. Mohamed Abdouloihabi was elected to the presidency on Ngazidja and Mohamed Ali Said secured victory on Mwali in what were largely deemed to be free and fair elections.

The impasse on Nzwani persisted and in October 2007 the AU imposed sanctions on Nzwani, including restrictions on the movements of the self-proclaimed President and his supporters and the freezing of their assets. These attempts to regain control of the island and restore peace failed and Bacar dismissed threats of military force. Following the failure of further negotiations aimed at breaking the deadlock, in February 2008 the AU Peace and Security Council mandated the deployment of a Mission d'Assistance Électorale et Sécuritaire (MAES) to 'facilitate the restoration of the authority of the Union' on Nzwani. The MAES was to comprise some 1,500 members, including troops from Senegal, Sudan and Tanzania, as well as logistical support staff from Libya, and represented the first occasion that the AU had approved military intervention to enforce peace in a member country. On 25 March some 450 Sudanese, Tanzanian and Comoran troops landed on Nzwani and succeeded in regaining control of the island. The following day President Sambi announced that Union Vice-President Ikililou Dhoinine had been appointed interim President of Nzwani, pending the formation of a transitional regional government, and confirmed that the presidential election on the island would be re-held within two months. On 31 March Laili Zamane Abdou, hitherto President of the Nzwani Court of Appeal, was sworn in as interim President. In the mean time, Bacar was reported to have fled Nzwani, initially taking refuge on Mayotte from where the Comoran authorities immediately sought his extradition; however, on 28 March Bacar was transported by the French military to Réunion where he was, according to French officials, to be investigated for landing illegally on Mayotte in possession of weapons. Initially that charge was dismissed, although Bacar and 22 of his supporters remained in custody on Réunion, and in June the Réunion Court of Appeal sentenced Bacar to a three-month suspended prison term for importing weapons. Bacar's application for political asylum in France had been rejected in May, but that country also ruled that he could not be sent back to the Comoros. In July the Beninois Government agreed to a request by the French authorities that Bacar be transported to Benin, where he took up exile.

Meanwhile, in June 2008 a presidential election was held in Nzwani to establish a permanent replacement for Bacar. Five candidates contested the first round on 15 June, including Djaanfari, who had unsuccessfully challenged for the Union presidency in May 2006, and Moussa Toybou, a former minister under Djohar. Toybou and Djaanfari won 42.5% and 42.3% of the votes, respectively, and contested a second round of voting on

29 June, at which Toybou secured 52.4% of the votes cast. Local and international monitors declared the election to have been free and fair.

In July 2008 President Sambi announced a reorganization of the Union Government, in which five new ministers were appointed. In December further governmental changes were made and the number of ministries was reduced from 15 to 10. The reduction in cabinet posts was a condition imposed by the IMF as part of an Emergency Post-conflict Assistance Programme.

In mid-April 2009 Sambi declared that a constitutional referendum was to be held on 17 May, the aim of which was to 'harmonize' the Constitution: Sambi's term of office was to be extended by one year, the mandates of the Ngazidja and Mwali Presidents were to be reduced by one year and that of the President of Nzwani by two years. Although Sambi had declared that opposition parties were free to campaign against the plan, the security forces prevented the holding of an opposition rally in Moroni and arrested a number of protesters. Despite a low rate of participation in the referendum, which opposition parties claimed to be a consequence of their call to boycott the vote, the right to reduce the size of the Government and the powers of the three autonomous island Presidents by restyling them as Governors was approved by 92.3% of those who voted, according to official figures. These stated that the rate of voter participation was 44.8%; however, opposition estimates claimed that less than 20% of the electorate voted. In a joint declaration at the end of May, a coalition of 20 opposition parties announced that they would present single candidates in each constituency in the legislative elections scheduled for 2 August, in order to increase the chances of defeating Sambi's Mouvance Présidentielle.

The legislative elections were postponed until 29 November 2009 and were subsequently delayed by a further week. Of the 33 seats available in the Assembly of the Union, 24 were to be decided by direct universal suffrage, while the remaining nine were to be allocated by the island assemblies at a rate of three per island. On 12 November the Constitutional Court rejected the candidature of former Prime Minister Ibrahim Halidi due to his failure to produce his police record, and on 17 November the leader of the opposition party, the Rassemblement pour une Initiative de Développement avec une Jeunesse Avertie (RIDJA), was arrested and put on trial for 'insulting the head of state' at a political meeting. The Mouvance Présidentielle secured three seats in the first round of voting, which took place on 6 December. In the second round on 20 December, the Mouvance Présidentielle took a further 14 seats, while three seats were won by allies of the President and four by opposition candidates.

The 2010 presidential and gubernatorial elections

Under the rotating presidential system, Sambi (from Nzwani) was to hand over power to a leader from Mwali upon the expiry of his term on 26 May 2010. However, legislation approved on 1 March by the Assembly of the Union provided for the postponement of the presidential election until November 2011, thus effectively extending Sambi's tenure by 18 months and depriving Mwali of its turn to hold the presidency. The opposition denounced such a major reform being passed without consultation and protests took place in Fomboni, where army reinforcements had been deployed under orders to disperse any public gathering. Libyan troops were also dispatched to bolster local forces, and several protesters were arrested. On 8 May 2010 the Constitutional Court ruled the extension of Sambi's presidential mandate as illegal; however, on 25 May, the eve of the formal expiration of his mandate, Sambi announced the appointment of an interim administration, prompting the formation of a national Union Government-in-exile in France with the stated aim of expediting Sambi's deposition. In mid-June Sambi announced a further reorganization and tasked the new Government with the planning of fresh Union elections within six months. Presidential and gubernatorial elections were subsequently scheduled to take place on 7 November, with a second round due to be held on 26 December.

Meanwhile, media reports emerged concerning disagreement between senior officials in the Comoran army, particularly surrounding Chief of General Staff Gen. Salimou Mohamed Amiri. In June 2010 Lt-Col Ayouba Combo, Chief of Staff of the Comoran Defence Force, was assassinated outside his home; Gen. Amiri was subsequently arrested in connection with the incident (he was replaced as Chief of General Staff by Lt-Col Abdallah Gamil Solihi). In April 2011 charges of rebellion held against Gen. Amiri were withdrawn, although accusations of his complicity in Combo's murder were upheld and he remained under house arrest.

A total of 10 candidates contested the first round of the presidential election, which was held as scheduled on 7 November 2010. According to results confirmed by the Constitutional Court on 13 November, Dhoinine, the Union Vice-President with responsibility for Land Settlement, Infrastructure, Town Planning and Housing, won 28.2% of the votes cast, while Mohamed Saïd Fazul and Dr Abdou Djabir took 22.9% and 9.9% of the votes, respectively. The three candidates contested a second round on 26 December, at which Dhoinine secured victory with 60.9% of the votes. The rate of participation was recorded by the Commission Electorale Nationale Indépendante at 52.8% of the electorate. Gubernatorial polls held concurrently with the presidential ballots resulted in the re-election of Ali Said to the governorship of Mwali, while Anissi Chamsidine and Mouigni Baraka Saïd Soilih became Governors of Nzwani and Ngazidja, respectively.

On 13 January 2011 the Constitutional Court confirmed the election of Dhoinine (and those of the three island Governors). On 26 May Dhoinine was officially inaugurated as President—the country's first Head of State from the island of Mwali. Dhoinine's 10-member Government, which included seven new ministers, was formed on 31 May. A government decision to increase substantially the market price of petroleum products led to social unrest in September. The protests, which were supported by the political opposition, employers' and consumer associations and trade unions, culminated in the closure of all businesses and transport services in Moroni for two days at the beginning of October. The Government subsequently established a commission to consider a new price structure for petroleum products and dismissed the Director-General of the Société Comorienne des Hydrocarbures.

A new law regulating religious practices in the Comoros, which had been adopted by the Assembly of the Union in June 2008, was signed into force by President Dhoinine on 8 January 2013; the legislation provided for the imposition of short custodial sentences and other penalties for any religious propaganda or campaign that caused social unrest or endangered national unity.

Recent developments: thwarted coup attempt

In April 2013 the Comoran authorities announced that 15 people had been detained by the security forces on suspicion of involvement in an attempted coup. Among those arrested was the son of former President Abdallah, while it was reported that a former associate of French mercenary Denard, Patrick Klein, was one of the leaders of the conspiracy to overthrow the Government. Later that month some 1,000 people representing both government and opposition political parties, and civil groups demonstrated in Moroni against the alleged attempt to destabilize the country.

In July 2013 President Dhoinine carried out a government reorganization in which six new ministers were appointed, including El-Anrif Saïd Hassane as the new Minister of External Relations and Co-operation, with responsibility for the Diaspora, and for Francophone and Arab Relations. Amid renewed pledges issued by Dhoinine to combat official corruption, in October a former head of national security, Abou Achirafi, was arrested on suspicion of complicity in the sale of false documentation. In November two journalists and a radio presenter were detained, after reporting the denouncement by a former public prosecutor of alleged corruption within the island's judiciary. Small anti-corruption protests were staged in Moroni in November and December.

Foreign Affairs

In November 1978 the Comoros and France signed agreements on military and economic co-operation, apparently deferring any decision on the future of Mayotte. In subsequent years, however, member countries of the UN General Assembly repeatedly voted in favour of a resolution affirming the Comoros' sovereignty over Mayotte, with only France dissenting. In November 2008 the Comoran authorities objected strongly to the announcement by the French Government that it intended to hold a referendum over the future status of Mayotte. At the referendum, which was held on 29 March 2009, 95.2% of voters approved of Mayotte attaining the status of an Overseas Department within the French Republic (in contradiction to the AU's and the Comoran Government's recognition of the island as an inseparable part of the Comoran state). Some 61% of those eligible to vote cast their ballots. The Comoran Government denounced the referendum and declared it 'null, void and without effect'. None the less, on 31 March 2011 Mayotte was officially granted departmental status.

In September 2002 France resumed military co-operation with the Comoros, which had been suspended following the military coup of 1999. In November 2006 a framework partnership agreement was signed by the French Minister-Delegate for Co-operation, Development and La Francophonie, allocating a grant of €88m. to the Union for 2006–10. Relations between the Comoros and France significantly worsened following Bacar's removal as President of Nzwani in March 2008 (see above). Many Comorans believed that the French Government had helped Bacar to escape from Nzwani, leading to widespread anti-French sentiment and the staging of demonstrations outside the French embassy in Moroni. Nevertheless, later that year the French Government supported the IMF's allocation of US $5.1m. in emergency post-conflict assistance to the Comoros.

On the occasion of the UN General Assembly in New York, USA, in September 2012, President Dhoinine reiterated the Comoran claim to Mayotte (see Foreign Affairs), and denounced the visa requirement imposed by the French Government for citizens of the Comoros as being contributory to the death of migrants attempting to reach Mayotte. In October it was reported that the Comoran Government was in the process of establishing a coastguard to replace French officials, as part of efforts to counter piracy activities and illegal immigration to Mayotte. During a visit by President Dhoinine to France in June 2013, a co-operation agreement was signed with French President François Hollande, and the leaders pledged to establish a joint high council in order to improve political dialogue between the two countries. The first meeting of the council was duly convened in November, when further agreements on judicial and police co-operation were concluded.

Following Djohar's accession to power, diplomatic relations were established with the USA in June 1990. In September 1993 the Comoros' application was accepted and it became a member of the Arab League. In mid-2004 a joint commission with Sudan was created. In September 2004 the USA claimed that the Comoros was harbouring members of a militant Islamist group, Al Haramain. The USA conducts an International Military Education and Training programme in the Comoros, which was increased in 2008. In January 2013 the new Indian Ocean Commission (see p. 451) Secretary-General, Jean-Claude de l'Estrac, made his first official visit to the Comoros.

CONSTITUTION AND GOVERNMENT

Under the Constitution of 23 December 2001 (and as amended on 23 May 2009), each of the islands in the Union of the Comoros is headed by a local government and is partially autonomous. The Head of State of the Union of the Comoros is the President, who appoints the members of the Government and heads the Council of the Union, which also includes the Vice-Presidents. The President is elected for a five-year term, and the position of President rotates between the islands, while the Vice-Presidents are inhabitants of the two remaining islands. The President appoints the members of the Government (ministers of the Union) and determines their respective portfolios. The composition of the Government must represent all of the islands equally. Federal legislative power is vested in the Assemblée de l'Union (Assembly of the Union), which serves a five-year term and is composed of 33 deputies, 24 of whom are directly elected, with the remaining 9 seats divided equally among representatives of the three islands. Each island also elects its own legislative local assembly and Governor.

REGIONAL AND INTERNATIONAL CO-OPERATION

In 1985 the Comoros joined the Indian Ocean Commission (IOC, see p. 451). The country is also a member of the Common Market for Eastern and Southern Africa (COMESA, see p. 233), of the Franc Zone (see p. 329) and the African Union (see p. 186).

The Comoros became a member of the UN in 1975, and a Working Party was established in 2007 to examine the country's application to join the World Trade Organization (WTO, see p. 434).

ECONOMIC AFFAIRS

In 2012, according to estimates from the World Bank, the gross national income (GNI) of the Comoros (excluding Mayotte), measured at average 2010–12 prices, was US $605m., equivalent to $840 per head (or $1,230 per head on an international purchasing-power parity basis). During 2003–12, it was estimated, the population increased at an average annual rate of 2.6%, while gross domestic product (GDP) per head decreased, in real terms, by an average of 0.8% per year. Overall GDP grew, in real terms, at an average annual rate of 1.7% in 2003–12; it increased by 3.0% in 2012.

Agriculture (including hunting, forestry and fishing) contributed an estimated 42.9% of GDP in 2010, according to the African Development Bank (AfDB). Approximately 67.6% of the labour force, according to FAO estimates, were employed in the agricultural sector in mid-2014. In 2004 the sector accounted for some 98% of export earnings. The principal cash crops are cloves, ylang ylang and vanilla; the Comoros produces an estimated 80% of the ylang ylang consumed globally, and in 2011 export earnings for this crop totalled 6,361m. Comoros francs. Cassava, rice, taro, maize, pulses, coconuts and bananas are also cultivated. In late 2005 an agreement on fishing rights in Comoran waters, which would extend until 2010, was reached with the European Union (EU). The agreement was renewed for a further three years in late 2010, and for a further three years in 2014. (Moroni was selected to host a new Indian Ocean Commission Centre for Fishing Surveillance, largely funded by the EU.) According to the World Bank, the real GDP of the agricultural sector increased at an average annual rate of 0.9% in 2003–09. Agricultural GDP declined by 0.7% in 2010, but grew by 4.1% in 2011, according to the AfDB.

According to the AfDB, industry (including manufacturing, construction and power) contributed an estimated 10.5% of GDP in 2010. Some 9.4% of the labour force were employed in the industrial sector in 1990. According to the World Bank, the Comoros' industrial GDP increased at an average annual rate of 1.6% in 2003–09; industrial GDP grew by 4.6% in 2009.

The manufacturing sector contributed an estimated 3.7% of GDP in 2010, according to the AfDB. The sector consists primarily of the processing of agricultural produce, particularly of vanilla and essential oils. Manufacturing GDP increased at an average annual rate of 2.1% in 2003–09, according to the World Bank. Manufacturing GDP expanded by 2.0% in 2011, according to the AfDB.

The construction sector contributed an estimated 5.4% of GDP in 2010, according to estimates by the AfDB; the sector's GDP increased by 4.2% in 2011.

Electrical energy is derived from wood (some 80%) and from thermal installations. Imports of petroleum products comprised 22.7% of the total cost of imports in 2011 and approximately 43m. kWh of electricity were produced in the Comoros in 2009. In March 2012 the Government announced that it had awarded its first oil exploration and production licence to a private Kenyan exploration company.

The services sector contributed an estimated 46.6% of GDP in 2010, according to the AfDB. Strong growth in tourism from 1991 led to a significant expansion in trade, restaurant and hotel activities, although political instability inhibited subsequent growth and there remained much potential for development. In 2007 a new facility at Moroni airport was completed; the project was financed by the Government of the People's Republic of China and was expected to precipitate a three-fold increase in annual passenger turnover. However, in 2009 Comoro Islands Airline closed its operations after only five months, and although Air Mohéli International made its first flight in July 2011 it failed to comply with government regulations and by September it also was no longer in operation. According to the World Bank, the GDP of the services sector increased at an average rate of 2.0% per year in 2003–09. It contracted by 2.3% in 2009.

In 2011 the Comoros recorded an estimated merchandise trade deficit of 61,466m. Comoros francs and there was a deficit of 20,064m. Comoros francs on the current account of the balance of payments. In 2011, according to the AfDB, the principal source of imports was the United Arab Emirates (accounting for some 19.2% of the total); the other major sources were France, South Africa, India and Pakistan. Turkey was the principal market for exports (30.5%) in that year; the other major purchasers were France, the Netherlands, India and Saudi Arabia. The leading exports in 2011 were cloves and ylang ylang. The principal imports in that year were petroleum products, vehicles, rice, cement, meat and meat products, and iron and steel.

The Comoran budget registered an estimated surplus of 2,027m. Comoros francs in 2012. The Comoros' general government gross debt was 97,074m. Comoros francs in 2012, equivalent to 42.6% of GDP. The Comoros' external public debt at the end of that year totalled US $278m., of which $246m. was public and publicly guaranteed debt. The annual rate of inflation averaged 4.1% during 2003–12. In 2012 consumer prices rose by 5.6%. According to the IMF, an estimated 13.3% of the labour force were unemployed in 2005.

The economy of the Comoros is dominated by agricultural activity, with a shortage of natural resources and heavy dependence on foreign aid. Although membership of the Franc Zone was credited with maintaining relatively low levels of inflation and fiscal deficit, a large public wage bill and weak institutional capacity has inhibited economic growth. In 2009 the Comoran Government implemented structural reforms recommended by the IMF, which in September approved a three-year credit arrangement amounting to US $20.6m. In June 2010 the IMF and World Bank declared that the Comoros had reached the decision point under the Enhanced Heavily Indebted Poor Countries (HIPC) Initiative, and hence had become eligible for comprehensive debt relief. After a slowdown in reform progress during 2011, the IMF and World Bank announced in December 2012 that the Comoros had reached the HIPC completion point, and under the Multilateral Debt Relief Initiative had secured debt relief of $176m. In early 2013 the partial privatization of Comores Télécom was initiated in accordance with IMF recommendations. In September the World Bank approved a grant of $5m. to support reforms in the management and performance of the state power utility, with the aim of reducing power costs and improving the supply of electricity (its limited availability being regarded as a main impediment to growth). In December the IMF completed its sixth performance review under an Extended Credit Facility programme and approved the final disbursement of $2.4m. Although GDP growth was projected to increase slightly, to 3.5%, in 2013, the Board also noted a deterioration in fiscal performance, which was attributed to higher imports necessitated by ongoing investment projects; the fiscal primary balance, having recorded a surplus in 2012, had moved into deficit. In January 2014 the Comoran authorities announced a new growth and poverty reduction strategy programme for 2015–19, which emphasized diversification and improvement of the business climate. Later in January it was reported that the Government of Oman was to provide financing of $10m. for infrastructure development in the Comoros, while the US Carlyle Group consortium announced that it was to invest $200m. in a three-year oil exploration project.

PUBLIC HOLIDAYS

2015: 1 January (New Year's Day), 2 January*† (Mouloud, Birth of the Prophet), 1 May (International Labour Day), 15 May* (Leilat al-Meiraj, Ascension of the Prophet), 6 July (Independence Day), 17 July* (Id al-Fitr, end of Ramadan), 23 September* (Id al-Adha, Feast of the Sacrifice), 14 October* (Muharram, Islamic New Year), 23 October* (Ashoura), 27 November (Anniversary of President Abdallah's assassination), 23 December*† (Mouloud, Birth of the Prophet).

* These holidays are dependent on the Islamic lunar calendar and may differ by one or two days from the dates given.

† This festival occurs twice (in the Islamic years AH 1436 and 1437) within the same Gregorian year.

Statistical Survey

Sources (unless otherwise stated): *Rapport Annuel*, Banque Centrale des Comores, place de France, BP 405, Moroni; tel. 7731814; fax 7730349; e-mail bancecom@comorestelecom.km; internet www.banque-comores.km.

Note: Unless otherwise indicated, figures in this Statistical Survey exclude data for Mayotte.

AREA AND POPULATION

Area: 1,862 sq km (719 sq miles). *By Island:* Ngazidja (Grande-Comore) 1,146 sq km, Nzwani (Anjouan) 424 sq km, Mwali (Mohéli) 290 sq km.

Population: 446,817, at census of 15 September 1991; 575,660, at census of 1 September 2003. *Mid-2014* (UN estimate): 752,440 (Source: UN, *World Population Prospects: The 2012 Revision*). *By Island* (1991 census): Ngazidja (Grande-Comore) 233,533; Nzwani (Anjouan) 188,953; Mwali (Mohéli) 24,331.

Density (at mid-2014): 404.1 per sq km.

Population by Age and Sex (UN estimates at mid-2014): *0–14:* 315,240 (males 160,585, females 154,655); *15–64:* 415,911 (males 208,944, females 206,967); *65 and over:* 21,289 (males 9,608, females 11,681); *Total* 752,440 (males 379,137, females 373,303). Source: UN, *World Population Prospects: The 2012 Revision*.

Principal Town (incl. suburbs, mid-2011, UN estimate): Moroni (capital) 53,819. Source: UN, *World Urbanization Prospects: The 2011 Revision*.

Births and Deaths (incl. figures for Mayotte, UN estimates, 2005–10): Average annual birth rate 38.3 per 1,000; Average annual death rate 9.6 per 1,000. Source: UN, *World Population Prospects: The 2012 Revision*.

Life Expectancy (years at birth, including Mayotte): 60.4 (males 59.1; females 61.8) in 2011. Source: World Bank, World Development Indicators database.

Economically Active Population (ILO estimates, '000 persons at mid-1980, including figures for Mayotte): Agriculture, forestry and fishing 150; Industry 10; Services 20; Total 181 (males 104, females 77) (Source: ILO, *Economically Active Population Estimates and Projections, 1950–2025*). *1991 Census* (persons aged 12 years and over, excluding Mayotte): Total labour force 126,510 (males 88,034, females 38,476) (Source: UN, *Demographic Yearbook*). *Mid-2014* (official estimates in '000): Agriculture, etc. 246; Total labour force 364 (Source: FAO).

HEALTH AND WELFARE

Key Indicators

Total Fertility Rate (children per woman, 2011): 4.9.

Under-5 Mortality Rate (per 1,000 live births, 2011): 79.

HIV/AIDS (% of persons aged 15–49, 2012): 2.1.

Physicians (per 1,000 head, 2004): 0.15.

Hospital Beds (per 1,000 head, 2006): 2.2.

Health Expenditure (2010): US $ per head (PPP): 58.

Health Expenditure (2010): % of GDP: 5.3.

Health Expenditure (2010): public (% of total): 57.2.

Access to Water (% of persons, 2010): 95.

Access to Sanitation (% of persons, 2010): 36.

Total Carbon Dioxide Emissions ('000 metric tons, 2010): 139.3.

Carbon Dioxide Emissions Per Head (metric tons, 2010): 0.2.

Human Development Index (2012): ranking: 169.

Human Development Index (2012): value: 0.429.

For sources and definitions, see explanatory note on p. vi.

AGRICULTURE, ETC.

Principal Crops ('000 metric tons, 2012, FAO estimates): Rice, paddy 27.0; Maize 7.2; Potatoes 0.8; Sweet potatoes 7.0; Cassava (Manioc) 68.5; Taro 12.0; Yams 5.0; Pulses 13.13.5; Groundnuts, with shell 1.5; Coconuts 90.0; Tomatoes 0.8; Bananas 66.0; Vanilla (dried, metric tons) 42; Cloves 2.2. *Aggregate Production* ('000 metric tons, may include official, semi-official or estimated data): Total vegetables (incl. melons) 7.1; Total fruits (excl. melons) 70.3.

Livestock ('000 head, year ending September 2012, FAO estimates): Asses 5.0; Cattle 50.0; Sheep 23.5; Goats 118.0; Chickens 520.

Livestock Products (metric tons, 2012, FAO estimates): Cattle meat 1,265; Sheep and goat meat 469; Chicken meat 536; Cows' milk 5,250; Hen eggs 784.

Fishing ('000 metric tons, live weight of capture, 2011): Total catch 25.1 (Sardines 1.0; Sardinellas 1.2; Anchovies, etc. 1.1; Seerfishes 0.8; Skipjack tuna 4.5; Yellowfin tuna 8.0; Chub mackerel 0.05; Jack and horse mackerels 1.7; Carangids 0.7).

Source: FAO.

INDUSTRY

Electric Energy (million kWh): 47.0 in 2007; 45.0 in 2008; 43.0 in 2009 (Source: UN Industrial Commodity Statistics Database).

FINANCE

Currency and Exchange Rates: 100 centimes = 1 Comoros franc. *Sterling, Dollar and Euro Equivalents* (31 December 2013): £1 sterling = 587.465 Comoros francs; US $1 = 356.731 Comoros francs; €1 = 491.968 Comoros francs; 1,000 Comoros francs = £1.70 = $2.80 = €2.03. *Average Exchange Rate* (Comoros francs per US $): 353.900 in 2011; 382.708 in 2012; 370.530 in 2013. Note: The Comoros franc was introduced in 1981, replacing (at par) the CFA franc. The fixed link to French currency was retained, with the exchange rate set at 1 French franc = 50 Comoros francs. This remained in effect until January 1994, when the Comoros franc was devalued by 33.3%, with the exchange rate adjusted to 1 French franc = 75 Comoros francs. This relationship to French currency remained in effect with the introduction of the euro on 1 January 1999. From that date, accordingly, a fixed exchange rate of €1 = 491.968 Comoros francs has been in operation.

Budget (million Comoros francs, 2012, estimates): *Revenue:* Tax revenue 26,871; Non-tax revenue 4,976; Total 31,847 (excluding grants received 25,912). *Expenditure:* Current expenditure 37,710 (Wages and salaries 18,288); Capital expenditure 18,022; Total 55,732.

International Reserves (US $ million at 31 December 2012): IMF special drawing rights 17.44; Gold (national valuation) 1.06; Reserve position in IMF 0.89; Foreign exchange 175.73; Total 195.12. Source: IMF, *International Financial Statistics*.

Money Supply (million Comoros francs at 31 December 2012): Currency outside depository corporations 21,755; Transferable deposits 34,770; Other deposits 30,871; *Broad money* 87,396. Source: IMF, *International Financial Statistics*.

Cost of Living (Consumer Price Index; base: 2000 = 100): All items 144.9 in 2010; 154.8 in 2011; 163.5 in 2012. Source: African Development Bank.

Expenditure on the Gross Domestic Product (million Comoros francs at current prices, 2010, provisional): Government final consumption expenditure 41,199; Private final consumption expenditure 197,940; Gross fixed capital formation 20,452; Changes in inventories 4,123; *Total domestic expenditure* 263,714; Exports of goods and services 4,624; *Less* Imports of goods and services 71,282; *GDP in purchasers' values* 197,056. Source: African Development Bank.

Gross Domestic Product by Economic Activity (million Comoros francs at current prices, 2010, provisional): Agriculture, hunting, forestry and fishing 77,983; Manufacturing 10,292; Electricity, gas and water 3,027; Construction 9,942; Wholesale and retail trade, restaurants and hotels 54,153; Transport and communications 9,062; Finance, insurance, real estate and business services 12,552; Public administration and defence 24,372; Other services 994; *Sub-total* 202,377; Indirect taxes –5,321; *GDP in purchasers' values* 197,056. Source: African Development Bank.

Balance of Payments (million Comoros francs, 2011, provisional): Exports of goods f.o.b. 9,128; Imports of goods f.o.b. –70,594; *Trade balance* –61,466; Services (net) –11,621; *Balance on goods and services* –73,087; Income (net) –277; *Balance on goods, services and income* –73,364; Current transfers (net) 53,301; *Current balance* –20,064; Capital and financial account 20,972; Net errors and omissions 4,474; *Overall balance* 5,383.

EXTERNAL TRADE

Principal Commodities (million Comoros francs, 2011): *Imports c.i.f.:* Rice 12,168; Meat and meat products 5,285; Petroleum products 22,190; Cement 6,812; Vehicles 17,988; Iron and steel 3,406; Total (incl. others) 97,935. *Exports f.o.b.:* Vanilla 350; Cloves 6,361; Ylang ylang 745; Total (incl. others) 8,908.

Principal Trading Partners (million Comoros francs, 2011): *Imports:* France (incl. Monaco) 18,332; India 6,183; Pakistan 5,776; South Africa 7,178; United Arab Emirates 18,764; Total (incl. others) 97,935. *Exports:* France (incl. Monaco) 1,883; India 833; Netherlands 839; Saudi Arabia 833; Turkey 2,719; Total (incl. others) 8,908. Source: African Development Bank.

TRANSPORT

Road Traffic (motor vehicles in use, 2007): Passenger cars 19,245; Vans and lorries 1,790; Motorcycles and mopeds 1,343; Total 22,378. Source: International Road Federation, *World Road Statistics*.

Shipping: *Flag Registered Fleet* (at 31 December 2013): Number of vessels 250; Total displacement (grt) 1,006,612 (Lloyd's List Intelligence—www.lloydslistintelligence.com). *International Sea-borne Freight Traffic* (estimates, '000 metric tons, 1991): Goods loaded 12; Goods unloaded 107 (Source: UN Economic Commission for Africa, *African Statistical Yearbook*).

Civil Aviation (traffic at Prince Said Ibrahim international airport, 1999): Passengers carried ('000) 130.4; Freight handled 1,183 metric tons.

TOURISM

Tourist Arrivals (2007): France 8,975; Madagascar 818; Réunion 1,286; South Africa 409; Total (incl. others) 14,582. *2010:* 15,300.

Receipts from Tourism (US $ million, excl. passenger transport): 32.0 in 2009; 35.0 in 2010; 42 in 2011.

Source: World Tourism Organization.

COMMUNICATIONS MEDIA

Telephones (2012): 24,000 main lines in use.

Mobile Cellular Telephones (2012): 250,000 in use.

Internet Subscribers (2009): 1,600.

Broadband Subscribers (2012): 200.

Source: International Telecommunication Union.

EDUCATION

Pre-primary (2007/08 unless otherwise indicated): 483 teachers (2004/05); 14,058 pupils (males 7,280, females 6,778). Source: UNESCO Institute for Statistics.

Primary (2011/12 unless otherwise indicated): 348 schools (1998); 4,201 teachers (2010/11); 133,023 pupils (males 70,866; females 62,157). Sources: UNESCO Institute for Statistics and IMF, *Comoros: Statistical Appendix* (August 2005).

Secondary (2011/12 unless otherwise indicated): Teachers: general education 2,812 (2006/07); teacher training 11 (1991/92); vocational 20 (2004/05). Pupils: 75,158 (males 38,945, females 36,213). Sources: UNESCO Institute for Statistics and IMF, *Comoros: Statistical Appendix* (August 2005).

Post-secondary Vocational (2004/05): 51 teachers (males 41, females 10); 734 pupils (males 399, females 335). Source: UNESCO Institute for Statistics.

Tertiary (2011/12 unless otherwise indicated): 130 teachers (males 111, females 19) (2003/04); 7,054 pupils (males 3,880, females 3,174). *2010/11:* 431 teachers. Source: UNESCO Institute for Statistics.

Pupil-teacher Ratio (primary education, UNESCO estimate): 27.7 in 2010/11. Source: UNESCO Institute for Statistics.

Adult Literacy Rate: 75.5% (males 80.5%; females 70.6%) in 2011. Source: UNESCO Institute for Statistics.

Directory

The Government

HEAD OF STATE

Federal President: Dr IKILILOU DHOININE (elected 26 December 2010).

REGIONAL GOVERNORS

(April 2014)

Mwali: MOHAMED ALI SAID.

Ngazidja: MOUIGNI BARAKA SAÏD SOILIH.

Nzwani: ANISSI CHAMSIDINE.

GOVERNMENT OF THE UNION OF THE COMOROS

(April 2014)

Vice-President, with responsibility for Health, Solidarity, Social Cohesion and Gender Empowerment: Dr FOUAD MOHADJI.

Vice-President, with responsibility for Finance, the Economy, the Budget and Investments and External Trading (Privatization): MOHAMED ALI SOILIHI.

Vice-President, with responsibility for Land Settlement, Infrastructure, Town Planning and Housing: NOURDINE BOURHANE.

Minister of External Relations and Co-operation, with responsibility for the Diaspora, and for Francophone and Arab Relations: EL-ANRIF SAÏD HASSANE.

Minister of Post and Telecommunications, Communication and the Promotion of New Information Technology, with responsibility for Transport and Tourism: BAHIAT MASSOUND.

Keeper of the Seals, Minister of Justice, the Civil Service, Administrative Reforms, Human Rights and Islamic Affairs: Dr ABDOU OUSSENI.

Minister of National Education, Research, Culture and the Arts, with responsibility for Youth and Sports: ABDOULKARIM MOHAMED.

Minister of Production, the Environment, Energy, Industry and Crafts: ABDOU NASSUR MADI.

Minister of Employment, Labour, Professional Training and Female Entrepreneurship, Government Spokesperson: SITI KASSIM.

Minister of the Interior, Information and Decentralization, with responsibility for Relations with the Institutions: HOUSSEN HASSAN IBRAHIM.

MINISTRIES

Office of the Head of State: Palais de Beit Salam, BP 521, Moroni; tel. 7744808; fax 7744829; e-mail presidence@comorestelecom.km; internet www.beit-salam.km.

Ministry of Employment, Professional Training, Labour and Female Entrepreneurship: Moroni.

Ministry of External Relations and Co-operation: BP 428, Moroni; tel. 7732306; fax 7732108; e-mail mirex@snpt.km; internet www.diplomatie.gouv.km.

Ministry of Finance, the Economy, the Budget and Investments and External Trading (Privatization): BP 324, Moroni; tel. 7744140; fax 7744141.

Ministry of Health, Solidarity, Social Cohesion and Gender Empowerment: Moroni.

Ministry of the Interior, Information and Decentralization: Moroni.

Ministry of Justice, the Civil Service, Administrative Reforms, Human Rights and Islamic Affairs: BP 2028, Moroni; tel. 7744040; fax 7734045; e-mail ministre@ministerejustice.gouv.km; internet www.ministerejustice.gouv.km.

Ministry of Land Settlement, Infrastructure, Town Planning and Housing: BP 12, Moroni; tel. 7744500; fax 7732222.

Ministry of National Education, Research, Culture and the Arts: BP 73, Moroni; tel. 7744180; fax 7744181.

Ministry of Post and Telecommunications, Communication and the Promotion of New Information Technology: BP 1315, Moroni; tel. 7734266; fax 7732222.

Ministry of Production, the Environment, Energy, Industry and Crafts: BP 41, Moroni; tel. 7750001; fax 7750003.

President

Presidential Election, First Round, 7 November 2010

Candidate	Votes	% of votes
Dr Ikililou Dhoinine	3,785	28.19
Mohamed Saïd Fazul	3,080	22.94
Dr Abdou Djabir	1,327	9.88
Bianrifi Tarmidi	1,250	9.31
Saïd Dhiuffur Bounou	1,154	8.59
Hamada Madi Boléro	1,060	7.89
Mohamed Larif Oukacha	977	7.28
Mohamed Hassanaly	523	3.90
Abdoulhakime Said Allaoui	208	1.55
Zahariat Said Ahmed	63	0.47
Total	13,427	100.00

Presidential Election, Second Round, 26 December 2010

Candidate	Votes	% of votes
Dr Ikililou Dhoinine	106,890	60.91
Mohamed Saïd Fazul	57,587	32.81
Dr Abdou Djabir	11,018	6.28
Total	175,495	100.00

Legislature

Assembly of the Union: BP 447, Moroni; tel. 7744000; fax 7744011.

President: BOURHANE HAMIDOU.

Elections, 6 and 20 December 2009

Party	Seats
Mouvance Présidentielle	17
Opposition Candidates	4
Allies of the Mouvance Présidentielle	3
Total	33*

* The remaining nine seats were filled by nominees from the islands' local assemblies, each of which selected three members.

Election Commission

Commission Electorale Nationale Indépendante aux Comores (CENI): Moroni; f. 2007 to succeed the Commission Nationale des Elections aux Comores; 10–13 mems; each island has a Commission Electorale Insulaire, consisting of 7 mems; Pres. MMADI LAGUERA.

Political Organizations

CHUMA (Islands' Fraternity and Unity Party): Moroni; e-mail chuma@pourlescomores.com; f. 1985; Leader SAÏD ALI KEMAL.

Convention pour le Renouveau des Comores (CRC): f. 2002; Leader Col ASSOUMANI AZALI; Sec.-Gen. HOUMED M'SAIDIE.

Djawabu: Leader YOUSSOUF SAÏD SOILIHI.

Faliki: Pres. KAAMBI ROUBANI.

Front Démocratique (FD): BP 758, Moroni; tel. 7733603; e-mail idriss@snpt.km; f. 1982; Chair. MOUSTOIFA SAÏD CHEIKH; Sec.-Gen. MOHAMED ISSIMAILA.

Front National pour la Justice (FNJ): Islamist fundamentalist orientation; Leader AHMED RACHID.

Mouvement Populaire Anjouanais (MPA): f. 1997 by merger of Organisation pour l'Indépendance d'Anjouan and Mouvement Séparatiste Anjouanais; principal separatist movement on Nzwani (Anjouan).

Mouvement pour la République, l'Ouverture et l'Unité de l'Archipel des Comores (Mouroua) (Movement for the Republic, Openness and the Unity of the Comoran Archipelago): Moroni; f. 2005; advocates institutional reform; Pres. SAÏD ABBAS DAHALANI.

Mouvement pour le Socialisme et la Démocratie (MSD): Moroni; f. 2000 by splinter group of the FD; Leader ABDOU SOEFOU.

Parti Comorien pour la Démocratie et le Progrès (PCDP): route Djivani, BP 179, Moroni; tel. 7731733; fax 7730650; Leader ALI MROUDJAÉ.

Parti pour l'Entente Comorienne (PEC): Moroni; f. 2007; Pres. FAHMI SAÏD IBRAHIM.

Parti pour le Renouveau et le Développement (PRD): Pres. MOHAMED SAÏD DJAFFAR.

Parti Républicain des Comores (PRC): BP 665, Moroni; tel. 7733489; fax 7733329; e-mail prc@online.fr; internet www.chez.com/prc; f. 1998; Leader MOHAMED SAÏD ABDALLAH M'CHANGAMA.

Parti Social Démocrate des Comores (PSDC-Dudja): Ngazidja; f. 2008; Leader ABDOU SOULÉ ELBAK; Sec.-Gen. Dr SOULE AHAMADA.

Parti Socialiste des Comores (Pasoco): tel. 7731328; Leader MOHAMED ALI MBALIYA.

Rassemblement pour une Initiative de Développement avec une Jeunesse Avertie (RIDJA): BP 1905, Moroni; tel. and fax 7733356; f. 1999; Leader SAÏD LARIFOU; Sec.-Gen. AHAMED ACHIRAFI.

Rassemblement National pour le Développement (RND): f. 1996; Chair. OMAR TAMOU; Sec. Gen. ABDOULHAMID AFFRAITANE.

Shawiri: Moroni; Leader Col MAHAMOUD MRADABI.

Union Nationale pour la Démocratie aux Comores (UNDC): Moroni; f. 1986; Pres. KAMAR EZZAMANE MOHAMED.

Diplomatic Representation

EMBASSIES IN THE COMOROS

China, People's Republic: Coulée de Lave, C109, BP 442, Moroni; tel. 7732521; fax 7732866; e-mail ambassadechine@snpt.km; Ambassador WANG LEYOU.

France: blvd de Strasbourg, BP 465, Moroni; tel. 7730615; fax 7730922; e-mail cad.moroni-ambassade@diplomatie.gouv.fr; internet ambafrance-km.org; Ambassador PHILIPPE LACOSTE.

Libya: Moroni; Chargé d'affaires HUSSEIN ALI AL-MIZDAWI.

Saudi Arabia: Hotel Retaj, ave Ali Soilih, Moroni; tel. 7735261; fax 7735264; Chargé d'affaires ABDULLAH BIN FALEH AL-ARJANI.

South Africa: BP 2589, Moroni; tel. 7734783; fax 7734786; e-mail moroni@foreign.gov.za; Ambassador G. H. ASMAL.

Judicial System

Under the terms of the Constitution, the President is the guarantor of the independence of the judicial system, and is assisted by the Higher Council of the Magistracy. The highest ruling authority in judicial, administrative and fiscal matters is the Supreme Court, which comprises a President, a Vice-President, an Attorney-General, at least nine councillors, at least one law commissioner, a general advocate, a chief clerk and other clerks. The High Council considers constitutional matters. A Constitutional Court, comprising eight members—appointed by the President of the Union of the Comoros, the Vice-Presidents and the three regional Governors—was established in 2004.

Constitutional Court: Moroni; e-mail mohamedyoussouf@hotmail.com; 8 mems; Pres. SOULAIMANE LOUTFI.

Supreme Court: Moroni; e-mail prescoursup@ministerejustice.gouv.km; f. 2011; Pres. CHEIKH SALIM SAÏD ATTOUMANI.

Religion

The majority of the population are Muslims, mostly Sunni.

ISLAM

Organisation Islamique des Comores: BP 596, Coulée, Moroni; tel. 7732071.

CHRISTIANITY

The Roman Catholic Church

Adherents comprise just 1% of the total population.

Office of Vicariate Apostolic of the Comoros: Mission Catholique, BP 46, Moroni; tel. and fax 7631996; fax 7730503; e-mail mcatholique@comorestelecom.km; f. 1975; Vicar Apostolic Bishop CHARLES MAHUZA YAVA.

The Press

Albalad: Bacha ancien SOCOCOM, route Asgaraly, BP 7702, Moroni; tel. 7739471; e-mail amoindjie@albaladcomores.com; internet www.albaladcomores.com; daily; Dir of Publication ALI MOINDJIÉ.

Al Watwan: Nagoudjou, BP 984, Moroni-Coulée; tel. 3494448; e-mail contact@alwatwan.net; internet www.alwatwan.net; f. 1985; weekly; state-owned; Dir-Gen. HASSANE MOINDJIÉ; Editor-in-Chief MOHAMED SOILIHI AHMED; circ. 1,500.

La Gazette des Comores: BP 2216, Moroni; tel. 7632620; e-mail elhad.omar@lagazettedescomores.com; internet www.lagazettedescomores.com; weekly; Publication Dir EL-HAD SAÏD OMAR.

Kashkazi: BP 5311, Moroni; internet www.kashkazi.com; f. 2005; weekly; French.

Le Matin des Comores: BP 1040, Moroni; tel. 7732995; fax 7732939; daily; Dir ALILOIAFA MOHAMED SAÏD.

NEWS AGENCY

Agence Comorienne de Presse (HZK-Presse): BP 2216, Moroni; tel. and fax 7632620; e-mail hzk_presse2@yahoo.fr; internet www.hzkpresse.com; f. 2004; Dir EL-HAD SAID OMAR.

PRESS ASSOCIATION

Organisation Comorienne de la Presse Ecrite (OCPE): Moroni; f. 2004; Pres. ABOUBACAR MCHANGAMA.

Publisher

KomEdit: BP 535, Moroni; tel. 7738178; e-mail edition@komedit.com; internet www.komedit.net; f. 2000; general.

Broadcasting and Communications

TELECOMMUNICATIONS

Autorité Nationale de Régulation des TIC (ANRTIC): BP 1183, Moroni; tel. 7738761; fax 7738762; e-mail contact@anrtic.km; internet www.anrtic.km; f. 2009; Dir-Gen. MOHAMED HASSANE ALFEINE.

Comores Télécom (Comtel): BP 7000, Moroni; tel. 7631031; fax 7732222; e-mail marketing@comorestelecom.km; internet www.comorestelecom.km; formerly Société Nationale des Postes et des Télécommunications; post and telecommunications operations separated in 2004; also operates mobile cellular telephone network (HURI); Dir-Gen. MAHAMOUDOU ABIAMRI.

BROADCASTING

Transmissions to the Comoros from Radio France Internationale commenced in early 1994. A number of privately owned radio and television stations also broadcast in the Comoros.

Office de la Radio Télévision des Comores (ORTC): Moroni; internet www.radiocomores.km; Comoran state broadcasting company; broadcasts Radio Comoros (f. 1960) and Télévision Nationale Comorienne (TNC, f. 2006); Dir-Gen. SOILIH MOHAMED SOILIH.

Radio-Télévision Anjouanaise (RTA): Mbouyoujou-Ouani, Nzwani; tel. 7710124; e-mail contact@rtanjouan.org; internet www.rtanjouan.org; f. 1997; television station f. 2003; owned by the Nzwani regional government; Dir (Radio) FAHARDINE ABDOULBAY; Dir (Television) AMIR ABDALLAH.

Radio

Radio Dzialandzé Mutsamudu (RDM): Mutsamudu, Nzwani; f. 1992; broadcasts on Nzwani; Co-ordinator SAÏD ALI DACAR MGAZI.

Radio Ngazidja: Moroni; internet radiongazidja.com; broadcasts on Ngazidja; also known as Radio Mdjidjengo; represents Ngazidja regional government; Man. MOHAMED ABDELKADER.

Radio Ocean Indien: Mkazi, BP 2398, Ngazidja; tel. 7731291; fax 7750101; e-mail radio.mrv@hotmail.fr; internet www.radioceanindien.fr; govt-controlled; Dir-Gen. SAID YOUSSOUFALI-BOUROI MROIVILI.

Television

Djabal TV: Iconi, BP 675, Moroni; tel. 7736767.

TV—SHA: Shashagnogo; tel. 7733636.

Finance

In 2013 there were four banking institutions in the Comoros: one central bank, one commercial bank, one development bank and one savings bank.

BANKING

(cap. = capital; res = reserves; dep. = deposits; m. = million; brs = branches; amounts in Comoros francs)

Central Bank

Banque Centrale des Comores: pl. de France, BP 405, Moroni; tel. 7731814; fax 7730349; e-mail bancecom@comorestelecom.com; internet www.bancecom.com; f. 1981; bank of issue; cap. 1,100m., res 10,305m., dep. 17,606m. (Dec. 2006); Gov. MZÉ ABOUDOU MOHAMED CHANFIOU.

Commercial Bank

Banque pour l'Industrie et le Commerce—Comores (BIC): pl. de France, BP 175, Moroni; tel. 7730243; fax 7731229; e-mail bic@bnpparibas.com; f. 1990; 51% owned by BNP Paribas-BDDI Participations (France); 34% state-owned; cap. 300.0m., res 1,676.5m., dep. 17,059.9m. (Dec. 2011); Dir-Gen. CHRISTIAN GOULT; 6 brs.

Savings Bank

Société Nationale de la Poste et des Services Financiers (SNPSF): BP 5000, Moroni; tel. 734327; fax 730304; internet www.lapostecomores.com; f. 2005; Dir-Gen. IBRAHIM ABDALLAH.

Development Bank

Banque de Développement des Comores: pl. de France, BP 298, Moroni; tel. 7730818; fax 7730397; e-mail info@bdevcom.net; internet www.bdevcom.net; f. 1982; provides loans, guarantees and equity participation for small- and medium-scale projects; 20% state-owned; cap. and res 1,610.0m., total assets 6,142.5m. (Dec. 2012); Pres. HASSAN MOHAMED; Gen. Man. MARC ATHIEL.

Trade and Industry

GOVERNMENT AGENCIES

Office National d'Importation et de Commercialisation du Riz (ONICOR): BP 748, Itsambouni, Moroni; tel. 7735566; fax 7730144; e-mail onicor_moroni@snpt.km; Dir-Gen. ALADINE DAROUMI.

Société de Développement de la Pêche Artisanale des Comores (SODEPAC): Moroni; state-operated agency overseeing fisheries development programme.

DEVELOPMENT ORGANIZATION

Centre Fédéral d'Appui au Développement Rural (CEFADER): Moroni; rural development org. with branches on each island.

CHAMBER OF COMMERCE

Union des Chambres de Commerce, d'Industrie et d'Agriculture des Comores: BP 763, Moroni; tel. 7730958; fax 7731983; e-mail secretariat@uccia.km; internet www.uccia-comores.com; privatized in 1995; Pres. AHMED ALI BAZI.

TRADE ASSOCIATIONS

Organisation Comorienne de la Vanille (OCOVA): BP 472, Moroni; tel. 7732709; fax 7732719.

There is a further association, the **Fédération du Secteur Privé Comorien** (FSPC).

EMPLOYERS' ORGANIZATIONS

Club d'Actions des Promoteurs Economiques: Moroni; f. 1999; Head SAÏD HASSANE DINI.

Organisation Patronale des Comores (OPACO): Oasis, BP 981, Moroni; tel. 7730848; internet www.opaco.km; f. 1991; Pres. MOHAMED ABDALLAH HALIFA.

UTILITIES

MA-MWE—Gestion de l'Eau et de l'Electricité aux Comores: BP 1762, Moroni; tel. 7733130; fax 7732359; e-mail cee@snpt.km; f. as Electricité et Eau des Comores; transferred to private management and renamed Comorienne de l'Eau et de l'Electricité in 1997; renationalized and renamed Service Public de l'Eau et de l'Electricité in 2001; reprivatized in Jan. 2002 and renamed as above; responsible for the production and distribution of electricity and water; Dir-Gen. IBRAHIM MZÉ ABDALLAH.

Société d'Electricité d'Anjouan (EDA): BP 54, 98113 Mutsamudu, Nzwani; tel. 3321318; fax 7710209; e-mail yabdulmadjid@gmail.com; f. 2001; Technical Dir YOUSSOUF ALI OICHEI ABDULMADJID.

STATE-OWNED ENTERPRISE

Societé Comorienne des Hydrocarbures (SCH): BP 28, Moroni; tel. 7730486; fax 7731883; imports petroleum products; Dir-Gen. HOUSSEINE CHEIKH SOILIH.

TRADE UNION

Confédération des Travailleurs des Comores (CTC): BP 1199, Moroni; tel. and fax 7633439; e-mail syndicatctcomores@yahoo.fr; f. 1996; Sec.-Gen. IBOUROI ALI TABIBOU; 5,000 mems.

Transport

ROADS

In 2000 there were an estimated 880 km of classified roads. About 76.5% of the network was paved in that year.

SHIPPING

The port of Mutsamudu, on Nzwani, can accommodate vessels of up to 11 m draught. Goods from Europe are routed via Madagascar, and coastal vessels connect the Comoros with the east coast of Africa. The country's flag registered fleet at 31 December 2013 numbered 250 vessels, totalling 1.01m. grt.

Autorité Portuaire des Comores (APC): Moroni; f. 2001.

Société de Représentation et de Navigation (SORNAV): M.Z.I. Mavouna, BP 2493, Moroni; tel. 7730590; fax 7730377; e-mail sornav.moroni@comorestelecom.km; internet www.sornav.com; f. 1996; shipping agents; responsible for handling, unloading and shipping of goods; Dir-Gen. Capt. MANSOUR IBRAHIM.

CIVIL AVIATION

The international airport is at Moroni-Hahaya on Ngazidja. Each of the other islands has a small airfield. International services are operated by Air Austral (Réunion), Air Mayotte, Air Tanzania, Sudan Airways, Precision Air (Tanzania) and Yemenia. Kenya Airways commenced flying to the Comoros and Mayotte in November 2006.

Agence Nationale de l'Aviation Civile et de la Météorologie (ANACM): Moroni; tel. 7730948; e-mail transport@anacm-comores.com; internet www.anacm-comores.com; f. 2008; Dir-Gen. MOHAMED ATTOUMANE (acting).

AB Aviation: Hadoudja, Moroni; tel. and fax 7739570; internet www.flyabaviation.com; f. 2010.

Air Service Comores (ASC): Moroni; tel. 7733366; internet www.airservicecomores.com; internal services and international flights to Madagascar.

Comores Aviation International: route Corniche, Moroni; tel. 7733400; fax 7733401; internet www.comoresaviation.com; f. 1999; twice-weekly charter flights between Moroni and Mayotte; Dir JEAN-MARC HEINTZ.

Tourism

The principal tourist attractions are the beaches, underwater fishing and mountain scenery. Increasing numbers of Comorans resident abroad are choosing to visit the archipelago; in 2004 it was estimated that 58.3% of visitors to the Comoros were former Comoran residents. In 2005 hotel capacity amounted to an estimated 836 beds. Tourist arrivals totalled some 15,300 in 2010. Receipts from tourism amounted to US $42m. in 2011.

Defence

The national army, the Armée Nationale de Développement, comprised about 1,100 men in early 2009. In December 1996 an agreement was ratified with France, which provided for the permanent presence of a French military contingent in the Comoros. Following the military coup in April 1999, French military co-operation with the Comoros was suspended, but resumed in September 2002.

Defence Expenditure: Estimated at US $3m. in 1994.

Chief of General Staff of the Comoran Armed Forces: Lt-Col ABDALLAH GAMIL SOLIHI.

Education

Education is officially compulsory for 10 years between six and 16 years of age. Primary education begins at the age of six and lasts for six years. Secondary education, beginning at 12 years of age, lasts for seven years, comprising a first cycle of four years and a second of three years. According to UNESCO estimates, enrolment at primary schools in 2007 included 83% of children in the relevant age-group (males 86%; females 80%), while enrolment at secondary schools in 2012 was equivalent to 73% of children in the relevant age-group (males 75%; females 72%). In 2011/12 a total of 7,054 pupils were enrolled in tertiary education. Children may also receive a basic education through traditional Koranic schools, which are staffed by Comoran teachers. The Comoros' first university opened in December 2003, and in 2004/05 there were 2,187 students enrolled at that institution. In 2008 spending on education was equivalent to 7.6% of GDP.

THE DEMOCRATIC REPUBLIC OF THE CONGO

Introductory Survey

LOCATION, CLIMATE, LANGUAGE, RELIGION, FLAG, CAPITAL

The Democratic Republic of the Congo (formerly Zaire) lies in central Africa, bordered by the Republic of the Congo to the north-west, by the Central African Republic and South Sudan to the north, by Uganda, Rwanda, Burundi and Tanzania to the east and by Zambia and Angola to the south. There is a short coastline at the outlet of the River Congo. The climate is tropical, with an annual average temperature of 27°C (80°F) and annual rainfall of 150 cm–200 cm (59 in–97 in). French is the official language. More than 400 Sudanese and Bantu dialects are spoken; Kiswahili, Kiluba, Kikongo and Lingala being the most widespread. An estimated 51% of the population is Roman Catholic, and there is a smaller Protestant community. Many inhabitants follow traditional (mostly animist) beliefs. The national flag (proportions 2 by 3) is light blue, with a yellow star in the upper left corner and a diagonal red stripe edged in yellow. The capital is Kinshasa.

CONTEMPORARY POLITICAL HISTORY

Historical Context

The Democratic Republic of the Congo (DRC), formerly the Belgian Congo, became independent from Belgium as the Republic of the Congo on 30 June 1960. Five days later the armed forces mutinied, and the UN subsequently dispatched troops to the region to maintain order. In July 1964 President Joseph Kasavubu appointed Moïse Tshombe, the former leader of a group supporting the secession of the Katanga region, as interim Prime Minister, pending elections, and in August the country was renamed the Democratic Republic of the Congo. In November 1965 Col (subsequently Marshal) Joseph-Désiré Mobutu seized power and proclaimed himself head of the 'Second Republic'. In late 1970 Mobutu, as sole candidate, was elected President. (From January 1972, as part of a national policy of 'authenticity', he became known as Mobutu Sese Seko.) In October 1971 the DRC was renamed the Republic of Zaire, and one year later the Government of Zaire and the Executive Committee of the Mouvement Populaire de la Révolution (MPR), the sole legal political party, merged into the National Executive Council (NEC).

Legislative elections took place in October 1977, and, at a presidential election in December, Mobutu (again the sole candidate) was re-elected for a further seven-year term. In early 1982 opponents of Zaire's one-party system of government formed the Union pour la Démocratie et le Progrès Social (UDPS).

In April 1990 Mobutu declared the inauguration of the 'Third Republic' and announced that a plural political system, initially to comprise three parties, would be introduced after a transitional period of one year; the UDPS was immediately granted legal status. The NEC was dissolved and Prof. Lunda Bululu, previously an adviser to Mobutu, was appointed First State Commissioner (Prime Minister). In May a new, smaller, transitional NEC was formed, and in June Mobutu relinquished presidential control of the NEC and of foreign policy. Legislation permitting the establishment of a full multi-party political system was introduced in November.

Domestic Political Affairs

By early 1991 a large number of new parties had emerged. However, none of the major opposition parties agreed to join a new Government, headed by Prof. Mulumba Lukoji as First State Commissioner, which was installed in March. A National Conference, initially convened that August, elected Etienne Tshisekedi Wa Mulumba, the leader of the UDPS, as First State Commissioner in August 1992, pending the promulgation of a new constitution. Later that month Tshisekedi appointed a transitional 'Government of National Union', which included opponents of Mobutu.

In November 1992 the National Conference adopted a draft Constitution, providing for the establishment of a 'Federal Republic of the Congo', the introduction of a bicameral legislature and the direct election of a President. In early December the Conference dissolved itself and was succeeded by a 453-member Haut Conseil de la République (High Council of the Republic—HCR), headed by Archbishop Laurent Monsengwo Pasinya and empowered to amend and adopt the new Constitution and to organize elections. With support from the USA, Belgium and France, Monsengwo reiterated the HCR's recognition of Tshisekedi as head of Zaire's Government.

In January 1993 the HCR declared Mobutu to be guilty of treason, on account of his mismanagement of state affairs, and threatened impeachment proceedings unless he recognized the legitimacy of the 'Government of National Union'. In March Mobutu convened a special 'conclave' of political forces to debate the country's future, which appointed Faustin Birindwa, a former UDPS member and adviser to Tshisekedi, as Prime Minister, charged with the formation of a 'Government of National Salvation'. Birindwa's Cabinet, which was established in April, failed to receive official international recognition.

In January 1994 an agreement to form a government of national reconciliation was signed by all major political parties, with the exception of Tshisekedi's UDPS. Later that month Mobutu announced the dissolution of the HCR, the dismissal of the Government of National Salvation and the creation of a transitional legislature, to be known as the Haut Conseil de la République—Parlement de Transition (Transitional Parliament—HCR—PT). In April the HCR—PT endorsed a new Transitional Constitution Act, reiterating the provisions of previous accords for the organization of a constitutional referendum, and presidential and legislative elections. The Government, to be accountable to the HCR—PT, was to assume some presidential powers, including control of the security forces.

In June 1995 the HCR—PT adopted a constitutional amendment (approved by Mobutu), whereby the period of national transition (due to end on 9 July) was to be extended by two years, owing to a shortage of government resources. A draft of the new Constitution, which provided for a federal state with a parliamentary system of government and a president with limited powers, was approved by the Government in late May 1996.

In the mid-1990s existing ethnic tensions in eastern Zaire were heightened by the inflow of an estimated 1m. Hutu refugees from Rwanda. The plight of the region's Zairean Tutsis (Banyamulenge) aroused international concern in late 1996, following reports of the organized persecution of Banyamulenge communities by elements of the Zairean security forces and by extremist Hutu refugees. In October the Sud-Kivu regional administration ordered all Banyamulenge to leave the area within one week or risk internment or forced expulsion. Although the order was subsequently rescinded, this threat provoked the mobilization of armed Banyamulenge rebels, who launched a violent counter-offensive, reportedly supported by the Tutsi-dominated authorities in Rwanda and Burundi. Later in October the rebels announced the formation of the Alliance des Forces Démocratiques pour la Libération du Congo-Zaïre (AFDL), under the leadership of Laurent-Désiré Kabila (hitherto leader of the Parti de la Révolution Populaire, and a long-standing opponent of the Mobutu regime). In November the HCR—PT urged the expulsion of all Tutsis from the country; following attacks on Tutsis and their property, many Tutsi residents of Kinshasa fled to Brazzaville (Republic of the Congo). However, AFDL forces made rapid territorial gains, and the movement developed into a national rebellion aimed at overthrowing Mobutu. AFDL troops entered the strategically important northern town of Kisangani in March 1997, and Lubumbashi in early April. The Zairean Government protested that the AFDL offensive was being supported by government troops from Rwanda, Uganda, Burundi and Angola, while the AFDL, in turn, claimed that the Zairean army had been reinforced by forces of the União Nacional para a Independência Total de Angola (UNITA).

The continued exclusion of Tshisekedi from the Government prompted his supporters to mount a campaign of civil disobedience, and in January 1997 his faction of the UDPS announced its support for the AFDL. On 8 April Mobutu declared a national state of emergency, dissolving the Government and ordering the deployment of security forces throughout Kinshasa. Gen. Likulia Bolongo was appointed Prime Minister at the head of a 'Government of National Salvation'.

Kabila assumes power

Peace talks between Mobutu and Kabila ended in failure in early May 1997, and on 16 May Mobutu left Kinshasa (travelling to Togo, and then to Morocco, where he died in September), while many of his supporters and family fled across the border to Brazzaville. On 17 May AFDL troops entered Kinshasa and Kabila declared himself President of the DRC (the name in use during 1964–71), which swiftly gained international recognition. On 23 May 1997 Kabila formed a transitional Government, which was dominated by members of the AFDL, but also included UDPS representatives. All political parties and public demonstrations were banned and on 28 May Kabila issued an interim constitutional decree, investing the President with virtually absolute legislative and executive power, as well as control over the armed forces and the treasury. All existing state institutions, except for the judiciary, were dissolved. On 29 May Kabila was inaugurated as President of the DRC. In October he appointed a 42-member Constitutional Commission, which was to draft a new constitution by March 1998.

In July 1998 Kabila issued a decree expelling Rwandan troops from the country. In August an armed insurrection was launched in Nord-Kivu province, in the east of the DRC, reportedly with Rwandan and French support. The rebels advanced quickly in the east of the country and were soon reported to have captured Bukavu and Goma. Shortly afterwards a second front was opened from Kitona, in the west of the country, where the rebels also made territorial gains. At that time the rebel forces announced that they had formed a political organization, the Rassemblement Congolais Démocratique (RCD), with the aim of introducing political democracy in the DRC.

Other countries in the region were, meanwhile, becoming involved in the conflict. While Rwanda had initially denied accusations that it was supporting the rebels, it quickly became evident that the anti-Kabila insurgents had the support of both Rwanda and Uganda, and that Kabila was receiving support from Angola, Namibia and Zimbabwe. Efforts by the Southern African Development Community (SADC, see p. 424) to reach a political solution to the civil conflict took place in August and September 1998. The Government refused to negotiate with the RCD and a newly formed rebel grouping, the Mouvement de Libération du Congo (MLC), however, on the grounds that their activities were supported by Rwanda and Uganda, respectively.

In May 1999 the RCD announced changes to its executive committee; Wamba dia Wamba was replaced as President by Dr Emile Ilunga. However, a number of the RCD's founding members opposed this move, and dia Wamba denounced it as a coup. Following clashes in Kisangani between supporters of dia Wamba and those of Ilunga, two factions emerged: Ilunga's group, known as RCD—Goma, was based in Goma and received support from Rwanda, while the other, led by dia Wamba, RCD—Mouvement de Libération (RCD—ML), was based in Kisangani and supported by Uganda.

Ceasefire agreement

Despite a number of regional initiatives to end the civil war in late 1998 and early 1999, no lasting ceasefire was negotiated, largely owing to Kabila's continued insistence that the rebels were supported by Rwanda and Uganda, and that they, therefore, be excluded from any talks. Although Col Muammar al-Qaddafi, the Libyan leader, hosted two rounds of regional talks in Sirte (Libya), it was in Lusaka, Zambia, under the mediation of Zambia's President Frederick Chiluba, that the rebels were first accorded a place at the negotiations, during a summit held in late June. Following this meeting, a ceasefire agreement was signed by the heads of state of the DRC, Angola, Namibia, Zimbabwe, Rwanda and Uganda on 10 July, by the leader of the MLC, Jean-Pierre Bemba Gombo, on 1 August and eventually by the RCD on 31 August. The agreement provided for an immediate ceasefire, the establishment of a Joint Military Commission (JMC) and the deployment of a UN peacekeeping force. In July a general amnesty for rebels within the DRC was announced, and in that month the JMC was formed, comprising representatives of the rebel groups and the six Lusaka signatory states (the DRC, Angola, Namibia, Rwanda, Uganda and Zimbabwe). In mid-August the UN military liaison mission received official approval.

In August 1999 further fighting erupted in Kisangani between forces from Rwanda and Uganda and their respective factions of the RCD. A ceasefire was negotiated in late August. However, in November both factions of the RCD announced that they no longer respected the ceasefire (having previously denied violations), and RCD—Goma accused the Government of openly breaching the agreement. In that month the UN Security Council voted to extend the mandate of the military liaison mission until mid-January 2000, owing to the difficulties experienced in obtaining security assurances and permission to deploy throughout the DRC. On 30 November 1999 the Council approved the establishment of a UN Mission in the Democratic Republic of the Congo (MONUC), to comprise some 5,000 troops, with an initial mandate until March 2000. At a meeting of the UN Security Council concerning the conflict in the DRC, which took place in New York, USA, in January 2000, regional Heads of State expressed support for the rapid deployment of MONUC forces to support the Lusaka peace accord. In February the UN Security Council authorized the expansion of MONUC to number 5,537 and the extension of its mandate to the end of August.

In July 2000 240 deputies of a new 300-member transitional Parlement (Parliament) were elected by a commission under the supervision of the Ministry of Internal Affairs, while the remaining 60 were nominated by Kabila. A presidential decree, adopted in that month, provided for the decentralization of the Government, with the transferral of the legislature to Lubumbashi. The new transitional Parliament was inaugurated in Lubumbashi on 22 August.

In October 2000, in a reorganization of the RCD—Goma leadership, Ilunga was replaced by Adolphe Onusumba. In the same month an attempt to oust dia Wamba from the leadership of the RCD—ML was suppressed by Ugandan troops. The RCD—ML subsequently divided, following the establishment of a dissident breakaway faction, led by Roger Lumbala, which became known as RCD—National (RCD—N). In December the six countries and three rebel groups involved in the conflict signed an agreement in Harare, Zimbabwe, pledging to withdraw forces 15 km from positions of military engagement, prior to the deployment of MONUC troops (which was scheduled to take place within 45 days). Nevertheless, hostilities continued at Pweto, and in other eastern regions, while RCD—Goma refused to withdraw its forces in accordance with the agreement until the Government entered into bilateral discussions with the rebels and permitted the complete deployment of MONUC troops. In mid-December (following a previous extension in August) the UN Security Council adopted a resolution extending the mandate of MONUC to mid-June 2001.

Assassination of Kabila

On 16 January 2001 Kabila was assassinated by a member of his presidential guard at his private residence in Kinshasa. The transitional Parliament approved the nomination by the political leadership of his son, Maj.-Gen. Joseph Kabila Kabange (hitherto Chief of Staff), as interim President. Following his inauguration on 26 January, Joseph Kabila immediately engaged in international diplomatic efforts to resolve the conflict and urged rebel leaders to attend peace discussions with him. At a meeting of the UN Security Council in February, attended by representatives of the six countries and three rebel factions involved in the conflict, it was agreed that the 15 km withdrawal of forces was to commence by mid-March.

The withdrawal from positions of military engagement duly commenced in mid-March 2001, in accordance with the UN-sponsored agreement, with the retreat from Pweto of the RCD—Goma and allied Rwandan troops. The first contingents of MONUC troops arrived in the DRC, and by the end of the month were stationed in the north-east of the country. At the beginning of April, however, the Ugandan-supported Forces pour la Libération du Congo (FLC, which had been formed by breakaway members of the MLC and the RCD—ML) refused to proceed with the withdrawal from military positions near Kisangani until MONUC guaranteed security in the region. The deployment of MONUC troops in the east of the country was delayed, after RCD forces initially prevented the peacekeeping forces from entering Kisangani.

In May 2001 representatives of the DRC Government and the rebel factions, meeting in Lusaka, under the aegis of the

Organization of African Unity (OAU, now the African Union, see p. 186—AU), SADC and the UN, signed a declaration establishing the principles for an 'Inter-Congolese National Dialogue' (a formal process of national consultation, with the aim of reaching a permanent peace settlement). Later that month Kabila ended the remaining restrictions on political activity and ordered the release of a number of detained human rights activists.

In late May 2001 a report by the state prosecutor claimed that forces opposing the Government (the RCD factions, and Rwandan and Ugandan troops) had conspired in the assassination of Laurent-Désiré Kabila, with the aim of seizing power. In June the UN Security Council approved a resolution extending the mandate of MONUC until mid-2002, while urging all foreign forces to complete their withdrawal from the country. In August, however, the President of Rwanda, Maj.-Gen. Paul Kagame insisted that Kabila fulfil pledges to demobilize Rwandan Hutu militia, known as Interahamwe (who had become allied with DRC government forces, after participating in the genocide in Rwanda in 1994), as a precondition to withdrawing the Rwandan troops deployed in the country. Also in August dia Wamba was ousted as the RCD—ML leader by Mbusa Nyamwisi.

Preparatory discussions between Kabila and the leaders of the FLC and the RCD factions, which were for the first time attended by unarmed opposition groups and civic associations, were conducted in Gaborone, Botswana, in August 2001. The Inter-Congolese National Dialogue commenced in the Ethiopian capital, Addis Ababa, in October, and, having been suspended in late 2001, was reconvened in Sun City, South Africa, in February 2002. In April it was announced that the Government and the MLC had reached a compromise agreement, providing for the establishment of an administration of national unity: Kabila was to remain President and Bemba became Prime Minister for a transitional period, prior to general elections. Signatories to the agreement commenced discussions in Matadi in May to draft a new constitution, while RCD—Goma and the UDPS announced their intention to form a political alliance to oppose the accord between Kabila and Bemba. At the end of July a peace agreement was signed by Kabila and President Kagame in Pretoria, South Africa. Under the accord, Kabila pledged to arrest and disarm the Interahamwe militia in the DRC, while the Rwandan Government was to withdraw all troops from the country (thereby also providing for the integration of RCD—Goma into the peace process). President Robert Mugabe of Zimbabwe subsequently announced his intention of withdrawing the remaining Zimbabwean troops supporting the DRC Government. In early September the DRC and Uganda reached an accord in the Angolan capital, Luanda, providing for the normalization of relations between the two countries, and the full withdrawal of Ugandan troops in the DRC. The Ugandan and Zimbabwean Governments subsequently commenced the withdrawal of forces from the DRC (although the UN permitted some Ugandan troops provisionally to remain near Bunia to assist in the maintenance of security). At the end of September the withdrawal of Rwandan forces commenced, and it was announced that all 23,400 Rwandan troops had left the country by early October.

Following the convening of a peace conference in early December 2002 in Pretoria, the Government and rebels signed an extensive power-sharing agreement later that month. Under the terms of this accord, Kabila was to remain as President, while four vice-presidential posts were to be allocated, respectively, to the incumbent Government, opposition parties, RCD—Goma and the MLC. The new 36-member transitional administration, to remain in power for a two-year period, was to comprise representatives of the Government, all three RCD factions, the MLC, the opposition and civil society. At the end of December the MLC and the RCD factions signed a ceasefire agreement in Gbadolite, which was to allow the transportation of humanitarian assistance in the region. (However, all rebel factions subsequently failed to observe the ceasefire, and continued hostilities near the border with Uganda were reported.)

Transitional government

Further discussions on constitutional and security issues for the transitional period were conducted in Pretoria in early 2003; agreement was reached on the adoption of a draft constitution and the deployment of a neutral international force in the country, pending the establishment of a new national army (which would include former rebel combatants). At the final peace conference, which was convened at Sun City on 2 April, government and rebel representatives endorsed the establishment of the two-year transitional administration. The official adoption of the Constitution on 4 April was followed by Kabila's inauguration as interim Head of State on 7 April. Despite the deployment of some 700 (mainly Uruguayan) MONUC troops at Bunia to compensate for the Ugandan withdrawal, Hema militia forces recaptured the town following intensive fighting, during which large numbers of civilians were massacred. On 30 May, in response to the developing humanitarian crisis, the UN Security Council authorized the establishment of a 1,500-member Interim Emergency Multinational Force, with a three-month mandate to restore order. Deployment of the contingent (which comprised troops from several European Union—EU, see p. 273—nations, principally France) commenced in early June.

In May 2003 the nomination of the four Vice-Presidents to the new transitional Government was announced: these included Bemba and the new leader of RCD—Goma, Azarias Ruberwa. On 29 June all former combatant groups finally signed an agreement on power-sharing in the future integrated transitional armed forces. On the following day Kabila nominated a transitional Government, in which portfolios were divided between representatives of the former rebel factions, the incumbent administration, political opposition and civil society organizations. The four Vice-Presidents were inaugurated on 17 July and the new power-sharing Government was installed on 24 July. At the end of that month the UN Security Council approved a one-year extension of MONUC's mandate, and increased the contingent's military strength significantly. The new International Criminal Court (ICC, see p. 340), which had been established on 1 July 2002 in The Hague, Netherlands, announced that it was to initiate investigations into alleged atrocities committed in the Ituri region. On 20 August 2003 Kabila announced nominations to the military leadership of the new unified armed forces, which was to incorporate elements of all the former rebel groups and the local Mai-Mai militia; former RCD—Goma and MLC commanders were appointed to senior posts. On 22 August the inaugural session of the new bicameral transitional Parlement (Parliament) was conducted in Kinshasa; representation in the 500-member Assemblée Nationale (National Assembly) and 120-member Sénat (Senate) was likewise divided between the former rebel groups, the Mai-Mai, the incumbent Government, political opposition and civil society. At the beginning of September the Interim Emergency Multinational Force officially transferred control of the Ituri region to MONUC reinforcements; the remaining French troops belonging to the Force were finally withdrawn by the end of that month. In November, following the final report by the Panel of Experts, the UN Security Council issued a statement condemning the widespread illicit exploitation of the DRC's natural resources, which had financed the activities of former combatant groups.

At the end of May 2004 some 2,000 dissident troops, led by Banyamulenge former RCD—Goma commanders who had been integrated into the national army, Brig.-Gen. Laurent Nkunda and Col Jules Mutebutsi, attacked forces loyal to the Government deployed in Bukavu, and by 2 June had seized control of the town. Rebel forces began to retreat about two days later, and troops loyal to Kabila succeeded in regaining control of the town by 9 June. Following the massacre of some 160 Banyamulenge refugees from the DRC in Burundi in August, Nkunda warned that he would take further action if the DRC Government failed to protect the refugees. In September the UN Security Council authorized the expansion of MONUC to 16,700, while renewing the contingent's mandate for a further six months. After MONUC troops confirmed the presence of Rwandan forces in the DRC, Kabila requested in December that the UN Security Council impose sanctions against Rwanda; Kagame protested that Rwandan forces had responded to rebel bombardments launched from DRC territory. Heavy fighting continued in Nord-Kivu between government forces and dissident army units reportedly supported by Rwanda.

At the end of March 2005 the mandate of MONUC was extended for a further six months, while in April the UN Security Council voted to adopt the recommendation of the UN panel of experts investigating implementation of the armaments embargo in eastern DRC, that the embargo be extended to the entire country, and provided for the imposition of a travel ban and 'freeze' of assets on those who violated the sanctions. On 13 May the transitional National Assembly finally approved a new Constitution, which was to be submitted for endorsement at a national referendum. The new Constitution provided for the direct election of a President for a maximum of two five-year terms, a balanced distribution of power between the executive and legislature and the granting of citizenship to members of all ethnic groups resident in the country since 1960. In June

Parliament approved the extension of the transitional period for six months (in accordance with the provisions of the April 2003 Constitution). In September 2005, in response to the continuing instability in eastern DRC, the UN Security Council authorized the temporary reinforcement of MONUC, and the mandate of the contingent was subsequently extended until the end of September 2006.

According to official results of the national referendum, which was conducted on 18 December 2005, the draft Constitution was adopted by 84.3% of votes cast, subject to its approval by the country's Supreme Court of Justice. The minimum age for a presidential candidate was reduced from 35 to 30 years, thereby allowing Kabila to contest the forthcoming elections. (Kabila was subsequently officially nominated as the candidate of the Parti du Peuple pour la Reconstruction et la Démocratie—PPRD, which he had formed in 2002.) The new Constitution also provided for an increase in the number of provinces from 11 to 26 (including Kinshasa), and granted them significant powers of self-government. The Supreme Court endorsed the results of the referendum on 3 February 2005, having rejected a number of legal challenges by opposition parties and non-governmental organizations (NGOs). The new Constitution was signed into effect by Kabila on 18 February. New electoral legislation was approved by Parliament on 21 February, when the Commission Electorale Indépendante (CEI) also announced that the presidential and legislative elections were again to be postponed, to 18 June, to allow further preparations, including voter registration. In March Thomas Lubanga of the Union des Patriotes Congolais was transferred from MONUC custody to the ICC on charges of war crimes, becoming the first indictee to be extradited to the Court.

In an attempt to ensure that the elections were conducted peacefully, on 26 April 2006 the UN Security Council authorized the temporary establishment of an EU military force (EUFOR RD Congo), which began deployment in the country on 30 July (remaining until the end of November). Meanwhile, in May government and MONUC troops intensified operations against militia activity in the Ituri region. On 27 July the Government reached a UN-mediated peace agreement with a local militia group, the Mouvement Révolutionnaire Congolais, which, in return for an amnesty from prosecution, undertook to end hostilities in Ituri, to allow the free movement of displaced civilians for the elections and to become integrated into the armed forces.

The July 2006 elections

The presidential and legislative elections finally took place on 30 July 2006. Although a South African observer mission announced that the elections had been conducted fairly, a number of presidential candidates subsequently accused the authorities of perpetrating mass falsification of the results, and in early August six poll officials were arrested on suspicion of malpractice. According to the CEI, Kabila secured 44.8% and Bemba 20.0% of votes cast; about 70.5% of the electorate had participated in the ballot. Consequently, a second round of the presidential election was scheduled for 29 October (when deputies were also to be elected to the provincial Assemblies).

Results of the legislative elections were released in early September 2006; the PPRD secured 111 seats, Bemba's MLC won 64, the revived Parti Lumumbiste Unifié (PALU) 34, the Mouvement Social pour le Renouveau (MSR) 27, the Forces du Renouveau (FR) 26 and the RCD 15. More than 70 other parties also secured parliamentary representation. The new National Assembly was officially inaugurated on 22 September; however, in December petitions were raised against the election of 18 deputies and in July 2007 the results of those seats were annulled. Meanwhile, Kabila conclusively won the second presidential round on 29 October 2006 by 58.1% of votes cast, according to official results.

Kabila was inaugurated as President on 6 December 2006. At the end of that month the leader of PALU, Antoine Gizenga, was nominated Prime Minister-Designate. Meanwhile, following negotiations mediated by the Rwandan Government, the DRC authorities reached a peace agreement with Nkunda, whereby his forces, now grouped together as the Congrès National pour la Défense du Peuple (CNDP), were to be integrated into the national army. On 19 January 2007 the provincial Assemblies elected the 108-member Senate. According to official results, the PPRD secured 22 seats in the chamber, the MLC 14, while the FR and the RCD each received seven seats. A further 22 parties were represented in the Senate, while Bemba himself became one of eight senators representing the capital. Gubernatorial elections took place later in January. The Senate was installed on 3 February and two days later the establishment of a 60-member coalition Government was announced.

In February 2007 the peace agreement ended, following violent clashes in the west of the country. Bemba was threatened with an arrest warrant for failing to command his troops to withdraw from the capital and he subsequently sought refuge in the South African embassy in Kinshasa. In April he was granted permission to leave the country to receive medical treatment in Portugal. (In May 2008 Bemba was arrested and detained in Brussels, Belgium, on charges of war crimes, and in July he was transferred to the ICC to await trial.)

Fighting escalated in Nord-Kivu in mid-2007, prompting the UN to extend the mandate of MONUC until the end of that year. Nkunda had consolidated his influence over the region and withdrew his forces from the national army just months after they had been integrated into it. In September the UN brokered a fragile ceasefire under which Nkunda ordered the withdrawal of CNDP troops to areas outside Kivu, while President Kabila entered into talks with Nkunda to negotiate the reintegration of his fighters into the national army. However, Nkunda claimed that his troops had been attacked by Interahamwe and Hutu militia groups and fighting resumed soon afterwards.

At a meeting on 9 November 2007 in Nairobi, Kenya, mediated by the UN, the USA and the EU, the Governments of the DRC and Rwanda reached an agreement on their commitments to ending the violence in eastern DRC. However, renewed attacks by Nkunda's forces on the national army were launched shortly afterwards, and in December the UN Security Council extended MONUC's mandate for a further year. Meanwhile, in late November Kabila announced a major government reorganization, in which the number of ministers was reduced from 60 to 32.

Overthrow of Nkunda

Following a peace conference, which was convened in early January 2008, an official ceasefire was signed on 23 January; under the peace accord, the DRC Government pledged not to renew an arrest warrant for war crimes charges against Nkunda. In February, however, Nkunda announced the CNDP's withdrawal from the ceasefire agreement, reportedly in protest against UN accusations of his faction's involvement in the killing of some 30 Hutu civilians during the peace negotiations the previous month. In March one of the principal rebel factions to sign the January ceasefire agreement also withdrew from the accord, amid complaints over the composition of monitoring bodies to be established to oversee the implementation of the peace process.

In September 2008 Prime Minister Gizenga announced his resignation citing health concerns, although there had been reports of a planned vote of no confidence in his administration in the Parliament. In October President Kabila named Adolphe Muzito, hitherto Minister of the Budget, as Gizenga's successor, and a new Cabinet was appointed. Later that month heavy fighting resumed when Nkunda's CNDP advanced within Nord-Kivu to Goma, gaining control of a large part of the province before declaring a ceasefire. The DRC Government accused Rwanda of deploying troops in Nord-Kivu to support Nkunda's forces. Former Nigerian President Gen. (retd) Olusegun Obasanjo was appointed the UN Secretary-General's Special Envoy to the Eastern DRC, and on 7 November he mediated an emergency summit meeting in Nairobi. On 9 November SADC leaders, meeting at a summit in Sandton, South Africa, endorsed a joint statement on an immediate ceasefire in Nord-Kivu, the guarantee of safe passage for international humanitarian personnel and the implementation of the previous peace agreements. However, the CNDP continued to advance; the UN approved the deployment of further MONUC troops, bringing the strength of the peacekeeping mission to some 20,000, and in December renewed its mandate for a further year. In December Ugandan government troops, supported by DRC and southern Sudanese forces, launched an offensive against bases of Ugandan rebel movement the Lord's Resistance Army (LRA) in northern DRC; it was reported that more than 600 Congolese civilians were subsequently killed in reprisal attacks by LRA combatants.

Divisions within the CNDP emerged in January 2009 when a breakaway faction, led by the movement's military commander, Bosco Ntaganda, announced Nkunda's dismissal and support for the Governments of the DRC and Rwanda, which had unexpectedly formed an alliance and agreed to conduct a joint operation to suppress rebel activity in the Kivu provinces (principally involving Rwandan rebel group the Forces Démocratiques de Libération du Rwanda—FDLR). Nkunda denied that he had been removed from the leadership of the CNDP; however, in late January, after refusing to support the operation by DRC and Rwandan troops, he sought to escape arrest and fled to Rwanda where he was captured and detained. In February 2009 it was announced that a five-week joint operation conducted by DRC and Rwandan troops against the FDLR and forces loyal to Nkunda in Nord-Kivu had severely weakened the rebels; Rwandan troops commenced withdrawal from the country. Former CNDP combatants under the command of Ntaganda became integrated into the DRC armed forces, and in March it was announced that an agreement had been reached with the Government whereby the CNDP was to be reconstituted as a political party, chaired by Desiré Kamanzi, while prisoners belonging to the former rebel movement were to be released. The President of the National Assembly, Vital Kamerhe, resigned in March, owing to pressure from supporters of Kabila, after he criticized the agreement between the DRC and Rwandan Governments; he was succeeded by Evariste Boshab of the PPRD in April. In May both chambers of the Parliament approved legislation providing for the amnesty of rebel combatants (excluding those suspected of acts of genocide or other war crimes). Following the opening of Lubanga's trial at the ICC (on charges relating to the conscription and use of child soldiers during 2002 and 2003) in January, the trial of two militia leaders, Germain Katanga and Mathieu Ngudjolo Chui, began in November. In December the UN Security Council extended the mandate of MONUC for only five months, envisaging a reconfiguration of the mission, while Kabila favoured a full withdrawal.

In February 2010 Kabila effected a major reorganization of the Government, including the appointment of two new Deputy Prime Ministers. In accordance with a UN Security Council resolution on 28 May, MONUC was reconstituted as the UN Organization Stabilization Mission in the Democratic Republic of Congo (MONUSCO), with a maximum authorized strength of about 22,000 personnel, and an initial one-year mandate. In addition to stabilization and peace consolidation in the DRC, MONUSCO was tasked with monitoring the implementation of the UN armaments embargo, and providing support in the organization of forthcoming elections. In June a prominent human rights activist, Floribert Chebeya, was found dead in Kinshasa after he had been summoned to a meeting with police. Following widespread allegations of police involvement in Chebeya's death, the Inspector-General of the police, John Numbi, was suspended from his post shortly afterwards. As a result of an investigation, eight police officers were subsequently placed on trial at a military court on charges relating to the killing of Chebeya. (In June 2011 four of the defendants were sentenced to death, three *in absentia*; one was sentenced to life imprisonment and three were acquitted.)

In October 2010 the appeals chamber of the ICC reversed an earlier decision by the Court that proceedings against Lubanga be abandoned (after the prosecution failed to disclose information identifying witnesses), and his trial resumed. The trial of Bemba, in connection with atrocities allegedly perpetrated by the MLC in the Central African Republic during 2002 and 2003, began at the ICC in November 2010. At the end of that month the UN Security Council renewed the armaments embargo and other sanctions in force against the DRC for a further year.

On 15 January 2011 both legislative chambers approved a number of significant amendments to the Constitution, which, *inter alia*, stipulated that the presidential election be conducted in just one round, granted the President the right to dissolve provincial assemblies and remove provincial governors, and provided for an increase in the number of provinces (from 11 to 26). The parliamentary vote was boycotted by over 100 opposition members, and the constitutional amendments were widely denounced as undemocratic. (They were signed into law by Kabila in June 2012.) On 27 February 2011 an attack by armed combatants against Kabila's presidential palace in Kinshasa was repelled by the Republican Guard. The Government subsequently accused Gen. Faustin Munene, a former army chief of staff, who had established a rebel movement, of involvement in the attack, and requested his extradition from Brazzaville, where he had been detained in January. (However, the authorities of the Republic of the Congo refused to extradite Munene.) In March Kabila removed François Joseph Mobutu Nzanga Ngbangawe (the son of the former President), from his government post as Deputy Prime Minister, owing to his absence from the country since November 2010. Mobutu's party, the Union des Démocrates Mobutistes, subsequently withdrew from Kabila's presidential alliance. In April 2011 a new Commission Electorale Nationale Indépendante (CENI), headed by Daniel Ngoy Mulunda, a pastor with close ties to Kabila, announced that the presidential and legislative elections would be conducted on 28 November. In June MONUSCO's mandate was extended for a further year.

Presidential and legislative elections

The pre-election period in November 2011 was marred by violent incidents, which included clashes between supporters of rival political parties (resulting in the deaths of at least eight people) and the shooting of a prominent MLC politician. In early November the UN Security Council denounced human rights violations committed by the police. The presidential and legislative elections were conducted on 28 November, as scheduled, but were disrupted by continuing violent incidents and by rioting at polling centres; voting was extended for a further day in some regions, owing to severe logistical difficulties, including shortages of voting materials. An EU monitoring mission and US observers reported widespread electoral irregularities, and three opposition presidential candidates demanded that the elections be annulled on the grounds of malpractice. On 9 December the CENI declared that Kabila (under the amended system) had been re-elected with about 49% of the votes cast, while Tshisekedi had received 32.3% of the votes; the participation rate was estimated at 58% of the electorate. The announcement of the results prompted further rioting in Kinshasa and the official figures were strongly rejected by Tshisekedi's UDPS. On 16 December, however, the Supreme Court dismissed an opposition appeal against the official electoral results. The US Administration criticized the Supreme Court's ruling and described the conduct of the elections as severely flawed. Kabila was inaugurated for a new term on 20 December. Tshisekedi, who continued to contest the legitimacy of Kabila's election, was prevented by police from publicly conducting his own 'swearing-in' ceremony, which instead took place at his residence, amid protests by his supporters. Later in December the Government pledged to order an investigation into post-election killings (which were reported to number at least 24) by security forces. Following delays in the vote-counting process for the legislative elections, on 1 February 2012 the CENI announced provisional results for 162 of the 169 electoral districts, recommending that the results for the remaining seven electoral districts be annulled. The provisional results represented a significant decline in support for the PPRD; opposition parties, however, demanded a full recount of the presidential and parliamentary votes.

In early March 2012 Muzito resigned from his position as Prime Minister and was replaced on an interim basis by Louis Alphonse Koyagialo Gbase te Gerengbo, hitherto Deputy Prime Minister, Minister of Posts, Telephones and Telecommunications. A total of 22 ministers in the outgoing Muzito Government had been elected to the National Assembly and thus were to be replaced. In April Augustin Matata Ponyo, hitherto Minister of Finance, was appointed Prime Minister and shortly afterwards the composition of his Government was finally announced. Ponyo retained the finance portfolio, while Daniel Mukoko Samba was appointed Deputy Prime Minister, Minister of the Budget, and Alexandre Luba Ntambo became Deputy Prime Minister, Minister of National Defence and War Veterans. On 25 April the Supreme Court upheld complaints regarding the election of 32 deputies, and declared the results for 482 seats. In June the CENI announced the final results for 492 of the 500 seats in the National Assembly: the PPRD won 69 seats, while the UDPS received 42 seats, the Parti du Peuple pour la Paix et la Démocratie (PPPD) 30 seats, the MSR 28 seats and the MLC 21 seats. Meanwhile, in mid-March Lubanga was found guilty by the ICC on charges relating to the conscription and use of child soldiers during 2002 and 2003, thereby becoming the first person to be convicted by the Court since its inception in 2002. (On 10 July 2012 Lubanga was sentenced to 14 years' imprisonment.)

Conflict with the M23 rebel movement

Violence erupted once more in Nord-Kivu in April 2012, following a mutiny by former members of the CNDP, led by Ntaganda, who defected from the army, complaining of unpaid salaries and poor living conditions. The rebels later formed a new armed group, March 23 (M23—named after the date in 2009 on which the CNDP had signed a ceasefire agreement with the DRC Government). The UN Security Council on 27 June 2012 approved a resolution extending the mandate of MONUSCO for a further year and again condemned the M23 rebellion. In the same month a report by a UN Group of Experts on the DRC stated that senior

Rwandan military officials had financed and supported M23. The Rwandan Government strenuously denied the allegations.

In July 2012 a second ICC arrest warrant was issued against Ntaganda, who was sought for three counts of crimes against humanity and four counts of war crimes. After making progressive territorial advances, M23 forces seized Goma on 20 November, but under international pressure withdrew from the town by the end of that month, following pledges by the Government to release some of their supporters in detention. On 9 December the Government and the M23 leaders began peace negotiations, mediated by the Ugandan Minister of Defence, in Kampala, Uganda. Meanwhile, on 28 November a UN Security Council resolution renewed the armaments embargo and other sanctions in force against the DRC. At the end of December the UN Security Council additionally imposed travel sanctions and asset freezes against the leadership of M23 (as well as against FDLR rebels).

Peace negotiations between the Government and M23 continued in January 2013, but failed to result in the signature of an agreement owing to differences over the proposed regional force. Meanwhile, Mai-Mai and associated militias staged attacks in Oriental and Katanga provinces, and the UN announced that it intended to introduce the use of surveillance drone aircraft for peacekeeping operations. On 6 February the Government reached an agreement with the M23 rebels on implementation of their March 2009 peace accord. On 24 February 11 regional states, under the auspices of the UN, the AU, SADC and the International Conference on the Great Lakes Region, signed a Peace and Security Co-operation Framework in Addis Ababa, pledging not to support rebel operations in the DRC; the agreement provided for the creation of an additional military brigade force within MONUSCO. Shortly afterwards, however, it was reported that M23 President Jean-Marie Runiga had been removed by its military commander, Gen. Sultani Makenga, and clashes between the rival M23 factions erupted in the region of Rutshuru. In early March the Government announced that it had reoccupied the towns of Rutshuru and Kiwanja, after M23 operations were diverted by internal conflict. Later that month Makenga's M23 faction selected Bertrand Bisimwa as its new President.

On 18 March 2013 Ntaganda unexpectedly surrendered to officials at the US embassy in Kigali, Rwanda, and was swiftly transferred to the custody of the ICC, appearing before the Court later that month. Also in March a UN Security Council resolution extended the mandate of MONUSCO for a further year, and approved the deployment of the special intervention brigade, which was authorized to conduct 'targeted offensive operations' against rebel forces. Bisimwa denounced the prospective establishment of the brigade, which was to comprise more than 3,000 Tanzanian, Malawian and South African troops, and issued warnings to the Tanzanian and South African Governments that their soldiers would be killed in the event of its deployment. By the end of April M23 had abandoned the peace dialogue, principally owing to the Government's failure to extend an offer of an amnesty for senior rebel commanders. In June Apollinaire Malu Malu, who had headed the electoral commission at the time of the 2006 elections, was appointed President of a new CENI.

The contingents of the special intervention brigade began to arrive in the country in May 2013, and in July the UN announced that they were to be mobilized near Goma, following further clashes between M23 and government troops in the region. Also in July the armed forces repelled an offensive by the Ugandan rebel Allied Democratic Forces-National Army for the Liberation of Uganda (ADF-NALU), which briefly occupied two border towns in Nord-Kivu. Government forces and MONUSCO, with the support of the special brigade, launched an operation against M23 at the beginning of August, and by the end of the month Bisimwa announced the rebels' withdrawal from the region of Goma. M23 denied responsibility for a mortar attack against the town of Goma that killed five civilians in late August, prompting further allegations of Rwandan involvement. Peace negotiations between the Government and M23 resumed in early September, when President Kabila also convened a national dialogue between representatives of the main political parties and civil society groups in Kinshasa. In mid-October, following the conclusion of the national dialogue at the end of September, Kabila promulgated legislation (originally approved by Parliament in 2010) that provided for the establishment of a Constitutional Court. The peace negotiations were again suspended in late October; by the end of the month the government and MONUSCO offensive had succeeded in expelling M23 forces, including Bisimwa, from eastern border towns into Uganda.

Recent developments: peace agreement with M23

M23 declared an end to its armed rebellion in early November 2013 to allow the resumption of peace negotiations (although it was reported that fighting continued, despite Bisimwa's appeal for a ceasefire). The DRC Government withdrew from the signature of a peace agreement with M23 on 11 November, demanding revisions to the text. On 12 December, however, Bisimwa and government representatives signed a peace agreement in Nairobi, under which an amnesty was to be extended to combatants not responsible for war crimes, crimes against humanity and genocide, while M23 was to be dissolved and its forces demobilized. In the same month government and MONUSCO troops launched an offensive against the FDLR in Nord-Kivu, and it was announced that the special brigade would be deployed against other militia groups, including the ADF-NALU.

On 30 December 2013 armed youths briefly seized control of the state television centre in Kinshasa, where they broadcast a statement claiming to be followers of a self-styled religious leader (and former presidential candidate), Paul Joseph Mukungubila Mutombo; attacks were also staged at the airport and army headquarters, and in Lubumbashi. The DRC authorities announced that government troops had repelled the insurgents, killing 95 (with the loss of eight soldiers) and subsequently arresting some 150 suspected rebels. In January 2014 a popular army commander who had led the successful offensive against M23 was killed in an ambush in Nord-Kivu; the attack was initially attributed to the ADF-NALU, although it was reported that several senior military officers had been arrested shortly afterwards. A UN Security Council resolution at the end of that month extended the mandate of MONUSCO and renewed the sanctions in force against the DRC for a further year. On 12 February Kabila declared an amnesty (covering 'acts of insurgency, acts of war and political offences') for former M23 combatants. His announcement coincided with a visit to Kinshasa by the UN Secretary-General's Special Envoy for the Great Lakes Region, Mary Robinson, who met Kabila and other government officials to urge the fulfilment of commitments to the February 2013 regional peace accord. In February 2014 an opposition rally staged by supporters of former parliamentary speaker Kamerhe in Bukavu was violently dispersed by security forces. In the same month the UN announced that MONUSCO troops would be reinforced in the southern Katanga province, after some 400,000 civilians were displaced there in fighting between local militia groups, including the Bakata Katanga movement which demanded secession for the region.

Foreign Affairs

The DRC Government has maintained strong relations with its former allies in the civil conflict, Zimbabwe, Angola and Namibia, while South Africa's political and economic influence increased, owing to former President Thabo Mbeki's strong involvement in the domestic and regional peace process. Following Joseph Kabila's agreement with Rwandan President Kagame in Pretoria, South Africa, in July 2002, relations improved between the Rwandan and DRC Governments, although the two continued to support opposing forces engaged in hostilities in Nord-Kivu. The DRC Government's relations with Uganda also improved, despite ongoing tensions between Kabila and Uganda's main ally in the DRC, the MLC. Following the massacre of Banyamulenge refugees from the DRC in Burundi in August 2004, MONUC confirmed later that year that Rwandan troops had re-engaged in hostilities in DRC territory. In December 2005 the International Court of Justice (ICJ, see p. 24) upheld an appeal by the DRC against Uganda, submitted in April, and ordered the Ugandan Government to pay reparations for violations of international law perpetrated by its forces deployed in the country during 1998–2003. In February 2006, however, the ICJ ruled that it was unable to issue a decision in a similar case brought by the DRC against the Rwandan Government (which had refused to accept the jurisdiction of the Court). The renewal of hostilities in Nord-Kivu in October 2008 (see above) prompted further accusations by the DRC that Rwandan government troops were supporting rebel activity, and international diplomatic efforts to ease tensions ensued. Intensive ministerial negotiations resulted in an agreement between the DRC and Rwandan Governments in December, whereby Kabila officially permitted Rwandan troops to enter the country in a counter-rebel action. In early 2009 the DRC and Rwandan Governments conducted an unprecedented joint operation to suppress rebel activity in Nord-Kivu. However, relations with Rwanda deteriorated dramatically in June 2012 after the DRC Government accused the Rwandan authorities of aiding a mutiny in eastern DRC, led by the M23 militia group (see Domestic Political Affairs). Kagame strongly denied the allegations; however, reports issued by the international NGO Human Rights Watch and the UN both presented evidence of Rwandan support for M23. At the end of August the Rwandan Government announced that it was withdrawing special forces, which had been supporting the DRC troops in joint operations against the FDLR in the Rutshuru region of Nord-Kivu.

In October 2009 it was reported that Kabila had ordered the expulsion of some 30,000 Angolans, in response to Angola's deportation campaign of economic migrants from the DRC (under which some 160,000 DRC nationals had been expelled since December 2008); both Governments subsequently agreed to suspend forcible expulsions, pending a formal agreement. However, in 2010 the deportation of migrants from Angola resumed on a smaller scale. According to estimates by the Office of the UN High Commissioner for Refugees (UNHCR), conflict in the Central African Republic precipitated the flight of 50,000 refugees to the DRC during 2013, when a total of 203,570 (principally Rwandan) refugees were based in the country. Although some 56,500 refugees were repatriated to the DRC in that year, about 450,000 remained in neighbouring states, while 2.6m. civilians were internally displaced, amid continuing hostilities in the east of the country.

CONSTITUTION AND GOVERNMENT

According to the new Constitution, which entered into effect in February 2006, the President is the Head of State and Commander-in-Chief of the armed forces and is elected by direct universal suffrage for a term of five years, which is renewable once. Legislative power is vested in a bicameral Parlement (Parliament), comprising a lower chamber, the Assemblée Nationale (National Assembly), and an upper chamber, the Sénat (Senate). The 500 members of the National Assembly are elected by direct universal suffrage for a renewable term of five years, while the 108 members of the Senate are indirectly elected by the Assemblies of each of the country's 26 provinces for a renewable term of five years.

REGIONAL AND INTERNATIONAL CO-OPERATION

The DRC maintains economic co-operation agreements with neighbouring states, Burundi and Rwanda, through the Economic Community of the Great Lakes Countries (see p. 450). The DRC is a member of the Common Market for Eastern and Southern Africa (COMESA, see p. 233), and in September 1997 the DRC became a member of the Southern African Development Community (SADC, see p. 424). In September 2009 Kabila held the chairmanship of SADC for a one-year term.

The DRC joined the UN in 1960, and was admitted to the World Trade Organization (WTO, see p. 434) in 1997. The DRC is also a member of the International Coffee Organization (see p. 446).

ECONOMIC AFFAIRS

In 2012, according to estimates by the World Bank, the gross national income (GNI) of the DRC, measured at average 2010–12 prices, was US $14,761m., equivalent to $220 per head (or $370 per head on an international purchasing-power parity basis). During 2003–12, it was estimated, the population increased at an average annual rate of 2.9%, while gross domestic product (GDP) per head grew, in real terms, by an average of 3.3% per year. Overall GDP increased, in real terms, at an average annual rate of 6.3% in 2003–12; it rose by an estimated 7.2% in 2012.

According to the African Development Bank (AfDB), agriculture (including forestry, livestock, hunting and fishing) contributed an estimated 38.9% of GDP in 2011. According to FAO estimates, about 55.2% of the working population were employed in agriculture at mid-2014. The principal cash crops are coffee (which accounted for 8.8% of export earnings in 1999, although its contribution declined to an estimated 0.9% in 2008, owing largely to the dramatic increase in exports of copper and cobalt), palm oil and palm kernels, sugar, tea, cocoa, rubber and cotton. According to World Bank estimates, agricultural GDP increased at an average annual rate of 2.8% in 2003–11; the sector's GDP grew by 3.0% in 2011, according to World Bank estimates.

According to the AfDB, industry (including mining, manufacturing, construction and public works, and power) contributed an estimated 26.7% of GDP in 2011. Some 15.9% of the working population were employed in industry in 1991. According to World Bank estimates, industrial GDP increased at an average annual rate of 9.0% in 2003–11. The sector's GDP expanded by 11.0% in 2011.

According to the AfDB, mining (including mineral processing) contributed an estimated 12.0% of GDP in 2011. Copper accounted for 43.3% of total export earnings in 2011, while cobalt (of which the country has 65% of the world's reserves) is another important source of foreign exchange, accounting for 39.0% of export earnings in that year. Other important minerals are diamonds, of which the DRC has rich deposits, and zinc. Cadmium, cassiterite, gold and silver are also mined on a small scale. Columbite-tantalite (coltan) has become a principal export in eastern regions previously under rebel control. By the mid-2000s the partial restoration of peace and the adoption of new mining and investment codes had prompted renewed investment interest in the sector. There are extensive offshore reserves of petroleum (revenue from crude petroleum accounted for 10.4% of export earnings in 2011). According to the IMF, the GDP of the mining sector grew at an average annual rate of 8.8% during 2003–08. The sector's GDP increased by some 13.4% in 2011, according to the AfDB.

According to the AfDB, manufacturing contributed an estimated 5.4% of GDP in 2011. The most important sectors are textiles, building materials, agricultural processing and industrial chemicals. According to World Bank estimates, manufacturing GDP increased at an average annual rate of 8.9% in 2002–07. According to the AfDB, the GDP of the sector grew by an estimated 2.0% in 2011.

According to the AfDB, construction contributed an estimated 6.0% of GDP in 2011. The IMF estimated that the GDP of the construction sector increased at an average annual rate of 13.5% in 2003–08; the sector's GDP increased by an estimated 13.1% in 2011, according to the AfDB.

Energy is derived almost exclusively from hydroelectric power. In 2011 an estimated 99.6% of electricity production was generated by hydroelectric plants. In 2011 imports of petroleum and petroleum products comprised 4.5% of the value of total merchandise imports.

According to the AfDB, the services sector contributed an estimated 34.3% of GDP in 2011. Some 19.0% of the working population were engaged in the sector in 1991. The GDP of the services sector increased at an average annual rate of 7.6% in 2003–12, and grew by an estimated 6.7% in 2011, according to World Bank estimates.

According to IMF figures, in 2012 the DRC recorded a merchandise trade surplus of US $178.5m., while there was a deficit of $1,696.3m. on the current account of the balance of payments. In 2010 the principal source of imports (accounting for 18.7% of the total) was South Africa; other major suppliers were the People's Republic of China, Zambia and Belgium. In that year China was the principal market for exports (taking 28.1% of the total); Zambia was also an important market for exports. According to the AfDB, the principal exports in 2011 were copper (43.3%), cobalt (39.0%), crude petroleum and diamonds. The principal imports included road vehicles, specialized machinery, cereals and petroleum.

In 2011 the estimated overall budget deficit was 253,000m. new Congolese francs, equivalent to 1.7% of GDP. The DRC's general government gross debt was 5,137,919m. new Congolese francs in 2012, equivalent to 35.5% of GDP. In 2011 external debt totalled US $5,448m., of which $3,940m. was public and publicly guaranteed debt. In that year the cost of servicing long-term public and publicly guaranteed debt and repayments to the IMF was equivalent to 2.4% of the value of exports of goods, services and income (excluding workers' remittances). According to the IMF, consumer prices increased at an average annual rate of 14.1% during 2002–08. Consumer prices expanded by 17.3% in 2008.

Potentially one of Africa's richest states, the DRC has extensive agricultural, mineral and energy resources. However, prolonged civil conflict from August 1997 resulted in a serious deterioration in the financial situation, and rebel factions systematically exploited mineral resources. Following the succession to the presidency of Joseph Kabila in 2001, a UN embargo on trade in unlicensed diamonds was imposed. In December 2009 the IMF approved a three-year Extended Credit Facility (ECF) arrangement (totalling US $551m.), and $73m. in interim assistance under the Heavily Indebted Poor Countries (HIPC) Initiative for the DRC. In June 2010 the IMF and World Bank stated that the DRC had implemented the measures required to reach completion point under the HIPC Initiative, and approved debt relief totalling $12,300m., thereby significantly reducing the country's external debt burden. In November the 'Paris Club' of creditor nations, in accordance with IMF and World Bank recommendations, cancelled a large part of the DRC's foreign debt. In late 2011, however, the release of funds was suspended by the IMF, after state-owned mining company GÉCAMINES failed to publish contracts relating to the sale of its share in a joint venture in accordance with the stipulated transparency programme. In December 2012 the IMF pronounced that notes published by the Government on the 2011 sale were insufficient and halted the ECF-funded programme (thereby withholding three loan disbursements totalling about $225m.), citing the authorities' continued lack of accountability and transparency in the operations of state-owned enterprises in extractive industries. Meanwhile, the Government introduced a 16% value-added tax in January 2012. However, conflict in the east of the DRC continued to deter business investment and to divert government attention from structural reforms. A peace agreement reached between the Government and the M23 rebel movement in November 2013 (see Domestic Political Affairs) appeared to improve economic prospects, although hostilities with other militia groups continued. The Government indicated that it had no plans to negotiate a resumption of the ECF credit arrangement with the IMF, which estimated that GDP growth in the DRC had increased to 8.5% in 2013, and projected a further rise to 10.5% in 2014. However, in January 2014 the World Bank approved a International Development Association grant of $5m. to support improvements in public finances and allocation of resources to social services. In the mean time, negotiations continued in early 2014 on international financing for a $12,000m. hydroelectric power project on the Congo River (Inga 3).

PUBLIC HOLIDAYS

2015: 1 January (New Year's Day), 4 January (Commemoration of the Martyrs of Independence), 16–17 January (National Hero's Day), 1 May (Labour Day), 17 May (National Liberation Day), 30 June (Independence Day), 1 August (Parents' Day), 25 December (Christmas Day).

Statistical Survey

Sources (unless otherwise stated): Département de l'Economie Nationale, Kinshasa; Institut National de la Statistique, Office Nationale de la Recherche et du Développement, BP 20, Kinshasa; tel. (12) 31401.

Area and Population

AREA, POPULATION AND DENSITY

Area (sq km)	2,344,885*
Population (census result)	
1 July 1984	
Males	14,543,800
Females	15,373,000
Total	29,916,800
Population (UN estimates at mid-year)†	
2012	65,705,093
2013	67,513,676
2014	69,360,118
Density (per sq km) at mid-2014	29.6

* 905,365 sq miles.

† Source: UN, *World Population Prospects: The 2012 Revision*.

POPULATION BY AGE AND SEX
(UN estimates at mid-2014)

	Males	Females	Total
0–14	15,555,372	15,474,504	31,029,876
15–64	18,024,354	18,324,783	36,349,137
65 and over	874,829	1,106,276	1,981,105
Total	34,454,555	34,905,563	69,360,118

Source: UN, *World Population Prospects: The 2012 Revision*.

REGIONS*

	Area (sq km)	Population (31 Dec. 1985)†
Bandundu	295,658	4,644,758
Bas-Zaïre	53,920	2,158,595
Équateur	403,293	3,960,187
Haut-Zaïre	503,239	5,119,750
Kasaï Occidental	156,967	3,465,756
Kasaï Oriental	168,216	2,859,220
Kivu	256,662	5,232,442
Shaba (formerly Katanga)	496,965	4,452,618
Kinshasa (city)‡	9,965	2,778,281
Total	2,344,885	34,671,607

* In October 1997 a statutory order redesignated the regions as provinces. Kivu was divided into three separate provinces, and several of the other provinces were renamed. The Constitution of February 2006 increased the existing 11 provinces to 26: Bas-Uele, Équateur, Haut-Lomami, Haut-Katanga, Haut-Uele, Ituri, Kasaï, Kasaï Oriental, Kongo Central, Kwango, Kwilu, Lomami, Lualaba, Lulua, Mai-Ndombe, Maniema, Mongala, Nord-Kivu, Nord-Ubangi, Sankuru, Sud-Kivu, Sud-Ubangi, Tanganyika, Tshopo, Tshuapa and Kinshasa (city).

† Provisional.

‡ Including the commune of Maluku.

Source: Département de l'Administration du Territoire.

PRINCIPAL TOWNS
(population at census of July 1984)

Kinshasa (capital)	2,664,309	Likasi	213,862
Lubumbashi	564,830	Boma	197,617
Mbuji-Mayi	486,235	Bukavu	167,950
Kolwezi	416,122	Kikwit	149,296
Kisangani	317,581	Matadi	138,798
Kananga	298,693	Mbandaka	137,291

Source: UN, *Demographic Yearbook*.

Mid-2011: (incl. suburbs, UN estimate) Kinshasa (capital) 8,797,730 (Source: UN, *World Urbanization Prospects: The 2011 Revision*).

BIRTHS AND DEATHS
(annual averages, UN estimates)

	1995–2000	2000–05	2005–10
Birth rate (per 1,000)	48.3	46.8	45.1
Death rate (per 1,000)	19.3	17.8	16.9

Source: UN, *World Population Prospects: The 2012 Revision*.

Life expectancy (years at birth): 49.3 (males 47.6; females 51.1) in 2011 (Source: World Bank, World Development Indicators database).

Economically Active Population ('000, estimates, mid-2014): Agriculture, etc. 15,191; Total labour force 27,499 (Source: FAO).

Health and Welfare

KEY INDICATORS

Total fertility rate (children per woman, 2011)	5.7
Under-5 mortality rate (per 1,000 live births, 2011)	168
HIV/AIDS (% of persons aged 15–49, 2012)	1.1
Physicians (per 1,000 head, 2004)	0.1
Hospital beds (per 1,000 head, 2006)	0.8
Health expenditure (2010): US $ per head (PPP)	26
Health expenditure (2010): % of GDP	7.5
Health expenditure (2010): public (% of total)	28.4
Access to water (% of persons, 2011)	46
Access to sanitation (% of persons, 2011)	31
Total carbon dioxide emissions ('000 metric tons, 2010)	3,039.9
Carbon dioxide emissions per head (metric tons, 2010)	<0.1
Human Development Index (2012): ranking	186
Human Development Index (2012): value	0.304

For sources and definitions, see explanatory note on p. vi.

Agriculture

PRINCIPAL CROPS
('000 metric tons)

	2010	2011	2012*
Rice, paddy	318	319	350
Maize	1,156	1,156	1,200
Millet	38	39	48
Sorghum	6	6	8
Potatoes	95	95	100
Sweet potatoes	247	251	265
Cassava (Manioc)	15,014	15,024	16,000
Taro (Cocoyam)	67	67	70
Yams	90	91	100
Sugar cane*	1,950	1,950	1,950
Beans, dry	115	116	125
Peas, dry	1	1	2
Groundnuts, with shell	388	394	371
Oil palm fruit	1,164	1,200*	1,250
Melonseed*	52	61	62
Cabbages and other brassicas*	26	27	28
Tomatoes*	50	52	53
Onions, dry*	60	62	65
Pumpkins, squash and gourds*	31	32	33
Bananas	316	317	322
Plantains	491	492	510
Oranges	181	182	182
Avocados	67	68	70
Mangoes, mangosteens and guavas	212	314	325
Pineapples	201	202	205
Papayas	226	228	230
Coffee, green	32	32	33

* FAO estimate(s).

Aggregate production ('000 metric tons, may include official, semi-official or estimated data): Total cereals 1,528 in 2010, 1,529 in 2011, 1,615 in 2012; Total roots and tubers 16,272 in 2010, 16,376 in 2011, 17,400 in 2012; Total vegetables (incl. melons) 557 in 2010, 575 in 2011,600 in 2012; Total fruits (excl. melons) 1,782 in 2010, 1,906 in 2011, 1,954 in 2012.

Source: FAO.

LIVESTOCK
('000 head, year ending September)

	2010	2011	2012*
Cattle	750	748	745
Sheep	904	905	906
Goats	4,052	4,058	4,065
Pigs	977	981	1,000
Chickens	20,067	20,128	20,500

* FAO estimates.

Source: FAO.

LIVESTOCK PRODUCTS
('000 metric tons)

	2010	2011	2012*
Cattle meat	12.2	12.3	12.0
Goat meat	18.7	18.7	19.0
Pig meat	24.1	24.2	25.0
Chicken meat	10.8	10.8	11.5
Game meat*	110.1	110.1	110.1
Sheep meat	2.9	2.8	2.9
Cows' milk*	7.5	8.0	9.0
Hen eggs*	8.9	8.9	9.0

* FAO estimates.

Source: FAO.

Forestry

ROUNDWOOD REMOVALS
('000 cubic metres, excl. bark, FAO estimates)

	2010	2011	2012
Sawlogs, veneer logs and logs for sleepers	310	304	304
Other industrial wood	4,282	4,282	4,282
Fuel wood	76,602	77,736	78,894
Total	81,194	82,322	83,480

Source: FAO.

SAWNWOOD PRODUCTION
('000 cubic metres, incl. railway sleepers, unofficial figures)

	2006	2007	2008
Total (all broadleaved)	92	92	150

2009–2012: Production assumed to be unchanged from 2008 (FAO estimates).

Source: FAO.

Fishing

('000 metric tons, live weight, FAO estimates)

	2005	2006	2007
Capture	236.6	236.6	236.0
Aquaculture	3.0	3.0	3.0
Total catch	239.6	239.6	239.0

2008–11: Catch assumed to be unchanged from 2007 (FAO estimates).

Source: FAO.

Mining

(metric tons unless otherwise indicated)

	2009	2010	2011
Hard coal	120,000*	120,000*	n.a.
Crude petroleum ('000 barrels)	9,382	8,628	8,558
Copper ore*†	340,000	430,000	540,000
Tantalum and niobium (columbium) concentrates	468	397	380*
Cobalt concentrates*†	40,000	60,000	60,000
Gold (kg)*	3,500	3,500	3,500
Silver (kg)	n.a.	6,446	10,080
Germanium (kg)*	2,500	2,500	2,500
Diamonds ('000 carats)‡	18,275	16,900*	19,700*

* Estimated production.

† Figures refer to the metal content of mine output.

‡ An estimated 20% of the diamond output is gem quality; the majority of production is from artisanal mining.

Source: US Geological Survey.

Industry

SELECTED PRODUCTS

('000 metric tons unless otherwise indicated)

	2006	2007	2008*
Maize flour	14	15	15
Wheat flour	186	179	184
Sugar	91	94	96
Cigarettes ('000 cartons)	3,048	3,433	3,536
Beer (million litres)	301	295	304
Soft drinks (million litres)	162	130	140
Soaps	24	8	25
Acetylene	10	7	19
Tyres ('000 units)	53	55	56
Cement	530	539	411
Steel	104	110	113
Explosives	26	27	—
Bottles ('000 units)	18	19	21
Cotton fabrics ('000 sq m)	852	267	—
Printed fabrics ('000 sq m)	6,411	5,616	—
Footwear ('000 pairs)	1,432	21,178	21,814
Blankets ('000 units)	12	12	13
Electric energy (million kWh)	7,633	7,543	7,495

* Estimates.

Source: IMF, *Democratic Republic of the Congo: Statistical Appendix* (January 2010).

2009 ('000 metric tons unless otherwise indicated): Electric energy (million kWh) 7,830; Sugar 70 (Source: UN Industrial Commodity Statistics Database).

2010 ('000 metric tons unless otherwise indicated): Electric energy (million kWh) 7,884; Sugar 70 (Source: UN Industrial Commodity Statistics Database).

Finance

CURRENCY AND EXCHANGE RATES

Monetary Units

100 centimes = 1 new Congolese franc.

Sterling, Dollar and Euro Equivalents (31 December 2013)

£1 sterling = 1,524.12 new Congolese francs;
US $1 = 925.50 new Congolese francs;
€1 = 1,276.36 new Congolese francs;
10,000 new Congolese francs = £6.56 = $10.80 = €7.83.

Average Exchange Rate (new Congolese francs per US $)

2011	919.491
2012	919.755
2013	919.793

Note: In June 1967 the zaire was introduced, replacing the Congolese franc (CF) at an exchange rate of 1 zaire = CF 1,000. In October 1993 the zaire was replaced by the new zaire (NZ), equivalent to 3m. old zaires. On 30 June 1998 a new Congolese franc, equivalent to NZ 100,000, was introduced. The NZ was withdrawn from circulation on 30 June 1999.

BUDGET

('000 million new Congolese francs)*

Revenue†	2006	2007	2008‡
Taxes on income and profits	128,774	161,371	253,100
Corporations and enterprises	79,076	89,408	147,790
Individuals	40,756	58,107	85,601
Taxes on goods and services	146,301	192,774	282,866
Turnover taxes	110,056	150,917	221,628
Selective excises	35,543	40,406	59,431
Beer	13,804	16,911	26,771
Tobacco	11,040	11,985	20,146
Taxes on international trade	163,805	239,333	342,528
Import duties and taxes	154,045	230,596	326,240
Export duties and taxes	9,630	8,679	16,288
Others	129	58	0
Other revenue	89,818	167,509	326,795
Total	528,698	760,987	1,205,289

Expenditure	2006	2007	2008‡
Wages and salaries	218,898	300,984	452,220
Goods and services (incl. off-budget)	133,194	203,685	277,694
Interest on domestic debt	22,921	28,721	34,225
Interest on external debt	72,995	155,413	169,550
Transfers and subsidies	87,102	111,730	226,871
Exceptional expenditure	171,706	45,034	74,417
Investment	134,050	121,085	243,706
Total	840,866	966,653	1,478,682

* Figures refer to the consolidated accounts of the central Government.

† Excluding grants received ('000 million new Congolese francs): 328,507 in 2006; 76,014 in 2007; 121,484 in 2008 (estimate).

‡ Estimates.

Source: IMF, *Democratic Republic of the Congo: Statistical Appendix* (January 2010).

2010 ('000 million new Congolese francs, estimates): *Revenue:* Taxes on income, profits, and capital gains 582; Taxes on goods and services 742; Taxes on international trade 309; Other taxes 22; Non-tax revenues 598; Total revenue 2,253 (excl. grants 1,676). *Expenditure:* Wages and salaries 697; Purchase of goods and services 607; Interest 263; Other expenditure 506; Capital expenditure 1,269; Total expenditure 3,342 (Source: IMF, see below).

2011 ('000 million new Congolese francs, estimates): *Revenue:* Taxes on income, profits, and capital gains 708; Taxes on goods and services 971; Taxes on international trade 418; Other taxes 12; Non-tax revenues 606; Total revenue 2,715 (excl. grants 1,226). *Expenditure:* Wages and salaries 1,091; Purchase of goods and services 733; Interest 381; Other expenditure 735; Capital expenditure 1,253; Total expenditure 4,194 (Source: IMF, see below).

2012 ('000 million new Congolese francs, projections): *Revenue:* Taxes on income, profits, and capital gains 855; Taxes on goods and services 1,356; Taxes on international trade 598; Other taxes 1; Non-tax revenues 854; Total revenue 3,664 (excl. grants 1,408). *Expenditure:* Wages and salaries 1,227; Purchase of goods and services 1,027; Interest 386; Other expenditure 655; Capital expenditure 2,205; Total expenditure 5,500 (Source (2010–12): IMF, *2012 Article IV Consultation—Staff Report; Public Information Notice on the Executive Board Discussion; and Statement by the Executive Director for the Democratic Republic of the Congo*—April 2013).

INTERNATIONAL RESERVES

(excluding gold, US $ million at 31 December)

	2010	2011	2012
IMF special drawing rights	543.93	541.20	541.47
Foreign exchange	755.72	726.30	1,091.09
Total	1,299.65	1,267.50	1,632.55

Source: IMF, *International Financial Statistics*.

MONEY SUPPLY
(million new Congolese francs at 31 December)

	2010	2011	2012
Currency outside banks	489,377	615,345	595,164
Demand deposits at deposit money banks	212,909	166,100	300,651
Total money (incl. others)	706,164	789,829	902,768

Source: IMF, *International Financial Statistics*.

COST OF LIVING
(Consumer Price Index for Kinshasa at 31 December; base: August 1995 = 100)

	2005	2006	2007
Food	546,165	697,790	762,946
Rent	622,109	736,670	817,241
Clothing	930,811	1,077,902	1,128,393
All items (incl. others)	644,137	798,297	877,842

Source: IMF, *Democratic Republic of the Congo: Statistical Appendix* (January 2010).

Cost of living (Consumer Price Index; base: 2005 = 100): 113.1 in 2006; 132.2 in 2007; 155.1 in 2008 (Source: IMF, *International Financial Statistics*).

NATIONAL ACCOUNTS
('000 million new Congolese francs at current prices)

Expenditure on the Gross Domestic Product

	2009	2010	2011*
Government final consumption expenditure	868	1,046	1,272
Private final consumption expenditure	6,993	9,183	11,196
Gross fixed capital formation	1,398	1,735	2,107
Change in inventories	73	71	98
Total domestic expenditure	9,332	12,035	14,673
Exports of goods and services	3,218	3,686	4,166
Less Imports of goods and services	3,517	3,770	4,025
GDP in purchasers' values	9,032	11,949	14,815

Gross Domestic Product by Economic Activity

	2009	2010	2011*
Agriculture, forestry, livestock, hunting, and fishing	3,715	5,027	5,525
Mining	801	1,254	1,697
Manufacturing	456	571	772
Construction and public works	454	632	855
Electricity and water	271	347	469
Wholesale and retail trade; restaurants and hotels	1,575	1,841	2,413
Finance, insurance, real estate, etc.	500	641	867
Transport and telecommunications	407	521	705
Public administration, defence and other services	511	653	886
Sub-total	8,690	11,487	14,189
Taxes, less subsidies, on imports	440	595	805
Less Imputed bank service charge	98	133	180
GDP at market prices	9,032	11,949	14,815

* Provisional figures.

Source: African Development Bank.

BALANCE OF PAYMENTS
(US $ million)

	2010	2011	2012
Exports of goods	8,477.9	9,471.9	8,534.2
Imports of goods	−8,042.5	−8,915.6	−8,355.7
Balance on goods	435.4	556.3	178.5
Exports of services	388.6	739.4	287.7
Imports of services	−2,662.7	−2,889.3	−2,289.0
Balance on goods and services	−1,838.7	−1,593.6	−1,822.9
Primary income received	48.3	168.2	18.3
Primary income paid	−1,225.8	−1,266.1	−1,057.9
Balance on goods, services and primary income	−3,016.2	−2,691.5	−2,862.5
Secondary income received	1,688.0	2,430.4	2,844.0
Secondary income paid	−845.3	−1,019.5	−1,677.8
Current balance	−2,173.5	−1,280.6	−1,696.3
Capital account (net)	−160.7	932.7	94.0
Direct investment assets	6.3		
Direct investment liabilities	2,728.8	1,596.0	2,891.6
Portfolio investment assets	−3,237.4	−2,136.9	−1,942.6
Other investment assets	216.4	1,803.4	2,172.9
Other investment liabilities	−9,178.1	−989.9	−762.9
Net errors and omissions	1,148.4	−82.3	−142.0
Reserves and related items	−10,649.8	−157.5	614.7

Source: IMF, *International Financial Statistics*.

External Trade

PRINCIPAL COMMODITIES
('000 million new Congolese francs)

Imports c.i.f.	2009	2010	2011
Cereals and cereal preparations	189.4	223.8	229.0
Petroleum, petroleum products and related materials	257.6	292.5	219.0
Specialized machinery	155.5	182.6	345.5
Other industrial machinery and parts	130.8	192.5	n.a.
Road vehicles	190.2	268.0	391.6
Total (incl. others)	3,158.2	4,076.6	4,878.8

Exports f.o.b.	2009	2010	2011
Crude petroleum	450.7	594.5	903.9
Timber	n.a.	58.2	60.0
Copper	n.a.	2,816.1	3,772.7
Cobalt	n.a.	3,438.3	3,395.2
Diamonds	175.1	281.4	335.2
Total (incl. others)	4,601.8	7,679.7	8,708.9

Source: African Development Bank.

SELECTED TRADING PARTNERS
('000 million new Congolese francs)

Imports c.i.f.	2008	2009	2010
Belgium	221.1	282.2	329.8
China, People's Repub.	132.8	280.7	441.4
France	104.1	200.6	211.6
South Africa	642.3	535.0	761.8
Zambia	186.0	290.4	441.4
Total (incl. others)	2,405.0	3,158.2	4,076.6

Exports f.o.b.	2008	2009	2010
Belgium	329.7	235.0	253.5
China, People's Repub.	1,024.3	1,138.4	2,160.5
Finland	210.8	102.1	112.5
USA	175.0	339.5	470.9
Zambia	368.8	522.9	1,115.1
Total (incl. others)	3,658.0	4,601.8	7,679.7

2011: *Imports* Belgium 543.3; France 303.0; Total (incl. others) 4,878.8. *Exports* Belgium 423.7; Finland 103.7; USA 723.0; Total (incl. others) 8,708.9.

Source: African Development Bank.

Transport

RAILWAYS
(traffic)*

	1999	2000	2001†
Passenger-km (million)	145.2	187.9	222.1
Freight (million ton-km)	386.5	429.3	459.1

* Figures refer to Société Nationale des Chemins de Fer du Congo (SNCC) services only.
† Estimates.

Source: IMF, *Democratic Republic of the Congo: Selected Issues and Statistical Appendix* (June 2003).

ROAD TRAFFIC
(motor vehicles in use at 31 December)

	1994	1995*	1996*
Passenger cars	698,672	762,000	787,000
Buses and coaches	51,578	55,000	60,000
Lorries and vans	464,205	495,000	538,000
Total vehicles	1,214,455	1,312,000	1,384,000

* Estimates.

2007: Total vehicles 311,781.

Source: IRF, *World Road Statistics*.

1999: Passenger cars 172,600; Commercial vehicles 34,600 (Source: UN, *Statistical Yearbook*).

SHIPPING

Flag Registered Fleet
(at 31 December)

	2011	2012	2013
Number of vessels	17	18	19
Total displacement ('000 grt)	12.7	13.0	13.2

Source: Lloyd's List Intelligence (www.lloydslistintelligence.com).

International Sea-borne Freight Traffic
(estimates, '000 metric tons)

	1988	1989	1990
Goods loaded	2,500	2,440	2,395
Goods unloaded	1,400	1,483	1,453

Source: UN, *Monthly Bulletin of Statistics*.

CIVIL AVIATION
(traffic on scheduled services)

	1992	1993	1994
Kilometres flown (million)	4	4	6
Passengers carried ('000)	116	84	178
Passenger-km (million)	295	218	480
Total ton-km (million)	56	42	87

Source: UN, *Statistical Yearbook*.

Passengers carried ('000): 211 in 2010; 252 in 2011; 161 in 2012 (Source: World Bank, World Development Indicators database).

Tourism

FOREIGN TOURIST ARRIVALS BY REGION OF NATIONALITY

	2009	2010	2011
Africa	31,328	30,620*	43,765
Congo, Republic	805	3,995	5,426
East Asia and Pacific	5,540	3,884	14,272
India	—	2,767	5,668
Middle East	—	1,650	6,060
Europe	13,101	35,012	67,895
Belgium	4,087	12,047	15,631
France	2,654	10,038	14,734
Italy	1,182	2,012	4,053
Central America	3,433	7,184	2,585
North America			12,386
South America			5,536
Others	—	—	27,833
Total	53,402	81,117	186,000

* Including 10,319 nationals of the Democratic Republic of Congo permanently resident abroad.

Tourism receipts (US $ million): 11 in 2010; 11 in 2011.

Source: World Tourism Organization.

Communications Media

	2010	2011	2012
Telephones ('000 main lines in use)	42.0	57.0	58.2
Mobile cellular telephones ('000 subscribers)	11,820.3	15,644.9	19,487.1
Internet subscribers ('000)	75.7	30.0	n.a.
Broadband subscribers ('000)	8.7	15.2	n.a.

Source: International Telecommunication Union.

Education

(2011/12 unless otherwise indicated)

	Teachers	Students		
		Males	Females	Total
Pre-primary	10,676	133,671	140,518	274,189
Primary	345,486	6,413,860	5,590,944	12,004,804
General secondary	253,929	1,968,172	1,193,169	3,161,341
Technical and vocational		484,805	247,878	732,683
Tertiary	23,116*	330,050	181,201	511,251

* 2010/11.

Institutions (1998/99): Primary 17,585; Secondary 6,007.

Source: UNESCO Institute for Statistics.

Pupil-teacher ratio (primary education, UNESCO estimate): 34.7 in 2011/12 (Source: UNESCO Institute for Statistics).

Adult literacy rate (UNESCO estimates): 66.8% (males 76.9%; females 57.0%) in 2010 (Source: UNESCO Institute for Statistics).

Directory

The Government

HEAD OF STATE

President: Maj.-Gen. JOSEPH KABILA KABANGE (inaugurated 26 January 2001, re-appointed 7 April 2003, elected 6 December 2006, re-elected 28–29 November 2011).

CABINET
(April 2014)

Prime Minister: AUGUSTIN MATATA PONYO.

Deputy Prime Minister, Minister of the Budget: DANIEL MUKOKO SAMBA.

Deputy Prime Minister, Minister of National Defence and War Veterans: ALEXANDRE LUBA NTAMBO.

Minister of Foreign Affairs, International Co-operation and the Francophonie: RAYMOND TSHIBANDA N'TUNGAMULONGO.

Minister of the Interior, Security, Decentralization and Traditional Affairs: RICHARD MUYEJ MANGEZ.

Minister of Justice and Human Rights: WIVINE MUMBA MATIPA.

Minister of Media, in charge of Relations with Parliament and Initiation of New Citizenship: LAMBERT MENDE OMALANGA.

Minister of Planning, Implementation and Modernization: CÉLESTIN VUNABANDI KANYAMIHIGO.

Minister of Portfolio: LOUISE MUNGA MESOZI.

Minister of the Economy and Commerce: JEAN PAUL NEMOYATO BEGEPOLE.

Minister of Land Settlement, Town Planning, Housing, Infrastructure, Public Works and Reconstruction: FRIDOLIN KASWESHI MUSOKA.

Minister of Transport and Communication Routes: JUSTIN KALUMBA MWANA NGONGO.

Minister of the Environment, Conservation of Nature and Tourism: BAVON N'SA MPUTU ELIMA.

Minister of Mines: MARTIN KABWELULU LABILO.

Minister of Water Resources and Electricity: BRUNO KAPANJI KALALA.

Minister of Hydrocarbons: CRISPIN ATAMA TABE.

Minister of Industry and Small and Medium-sized Enterprises: REMY MUSUNGAYI BAMPALE.

Minister of Posts, Telecommunications and New Information and Communication Technologies: TRIPHON KIN KIEY MULUMBA.

Minister of Employment, Labour and Social Security: MODESTE BAHATI LUKWEBO.

Minister of Public Health: FÉLIX KABANGE NUMBI MUKWAMPA.

Minister of Higher and University Education and Scientific Research: CHELO LOTSIMA.

Minister of Primary and Secondary Education and Professional Training: MAKER MWANGU FAMBA.

Minister of Agriculture and Rural Development: JEAN CHRISOSTOME VAHAMWITI MUKESYAYIRA.

Minister of Land Affairs: ROBERT MBWINGA BILA.

Minister of Social Affairs, Humanitarian Action and National Solidarity: CHARLES NAWEJ MUNDELE.

Minister of Gender Equality, the Family and Children: GENEVIÈVE INAGOSI KASSONGO.

Minister of the Civil Service: JEAN CLAUDE KIBALA.

Minister of Youth, Sport, Culture and the Arts: BANZA MUKALAYI NSUNGU.

Minister-delegate to the Prime Minister, in charge of Finance: PATRICE KITEBI KIBOL MVUL.

There were also eight deputy ministers.

MINISTRIES

Office of the President: Hôtel du Conseil Exécutif, ave de Lemera, Kinshasa-Gombe; tel. (12) 30892; internet www.presidentrdc.cd.

Office of the Prime Minister: Kinshasa.

Ministry of Agriculture and Rural Development: Kinshasa.

Ministry of the Budget: blvd du 30 juin, Immeuble Alhadeff, Kinshasa; internet www.ministeredubudget.cd.

Ministry of the Civil Service: Kinshasa.

Ministry of the Economy and Commerce: ave PUMBU 42, Kinshasa; tel. 812693500 (mobile); e-mail mincomrdc@gmail.com; internet www.mincommerce.cd.

Ministry of Employment, Labour and Social Security: blvd du 30 juin, BP 3840, Kinshasa-Gombe.

Ministry of the Environment, Conservation of Nature and Tourism: 76 ave des Cliniques, Kinshasa-Gombe; tel. 8802401 (mobile); internet www.minenv.itgo.com.

Ministry of Finance: blvd du 30 juin, BP 12998 KIN I, Kinshasa-Gombe; tel. (12) 33232; internet www.minfinrdc.cd.

Ministry of Foreign Affairs, International Co-operation and the Francophonie: Kinshasa.

Ministry of Gender Equality, the Family and Children: Kinshasa.

Ministry of Higher and University Education and Scientific Research: Kinshasa.

Ministry of Hydrocarbons: Kinshasa.

Ministry of Industry and Small and Medium-sized Enterprises: Kinshasa.

Ministry of the Interior, Security, Decentralization and Traditional Affairs: ave de Lemera, Kinshasa-Gombe; tel. (12) 23171.

Ministry of Justice and Human Rights: 228 ave de Lemera, BP 3137, Kinshasa-Gombe; tel. (12) 32432.

Ministry of Land Affairs: Kinshasa.

Ministry of Land Settlement, Town Planning, Housing, Infrastructure, Public Works and Reconstruction: Kinshasa.

Ministry of Media: Immeuble RATELESCO, 83 ave Tombalbaye, Kinshasa; tel. 818134753 (mobile); e-mail mincomedia.rdc@gmail.com; internet www.comediardc.org.

Ministry of Mines: Kinshasa; internet www.miningcongo.cd.

Ministry of National Defence and War Veterans: BP 4111, Kinshasa-Gombe; tel. (12) 59375.

Ministry of Planning, Implementation and Modernization: 4155 rue des Côteaux, BP 9378, Kinshasa-Gombe 1; tel. 812675558 (mobile); e-mail plcom@plan.gouv.cd; internet www.plan.gouv.cd.

Ministry of Posts, Telecommunications and New Information and Communication Technologies: Immeuble Kilou, 4484 ave des Huiles, BP 800 KIN I, Kinshasa-Gombe; tel. (12) 24854.

Ministry of Primary and Secondary Education and Professional Training: Enceinte de l'Institut de la Gombe, BP 3163, Kinshasa-Gombe; tel. (12) 30098; internet www.eduquepsp.org.

Ministry of Public Health: blvd du 30 juin, BP 3088 KIN I, Kinshasa-Gombe; tel. (12) 31750.

Ministry of Social Affairs, Humanitarian Action and National Solidarity: Kinshasa.

Ministry of Transport and Communication Routes: Immeuble ONATRA, blvd du 30 juin, BP 3304, Kinshasa-Gombe; tel. (12) 23660.

Ministry of Water Resources and Electricity: Immeuble SNEL, 239 ave de la Justice, BP 5137 KIN I, Kinshasa-Gombe; tel. (12) 22570.

Ministry of Youth, Sport, Culture and the Arts: 77 ave de la Justice, BP 8541 KIN I, Kinshasa-Gombe.

President

Presidential Election, 28–29 November 2011

Candidate	Votes	% of votes
Joseph Kabila Kabange (Ind.)	8,880,944	48.95
Etienne Tshisekedi Wa Mulumba (UDPS)	5,864,775	32.33
Vital Kamerhe Lwa-Kanyiginyi (UNC)	1,403,372	7.74
Léon Kengo Wa Dondo (UFC)	898,362	4.95
Others	1,095,651	6.04
Total	18,143,104*	100.00

* In addition, there were 768,468 blank or invalid votes.

Legislature

The bicameral Parliament (Parlement) of the Democratic Republic of the Congo comprises a lower chamber, or National Assembly (Assemblée Nationale), and an upper chamber, or Senate (Sénat), members of which are elected by the deputies of the provincial Assemblies.

NATIONAL ASSEMBLY

President: AUBIN MINAKU.

General Election, 28–29 November 2011

Party	Seats
Parti du Peuple pour la Reconstruction et la Démocratie	69
Union pour la Démocratie et le Progrès Social	42
Parti du Peuple pour la Paix et la Démocratie	30
Mouvement Social pour le Renouveau	28
Mouvement de Libération du Congo	21
Alliance des Forces Démocratiques du Congo	17
Parti Lumumbiste Unifié	17
Union pour la Nation Congolaise	16
Alliance pour le Renouveau au Congo	15
Rassemblement pour la Reconstruction du Congo	12
Parti Démocrate Chrétien	9
Avenir du Congo	8
Eveil de la Conscience pour le Travail et le Développement	8
Mouvement pour l'Intégrité du Peuple	8
Union des Nationalistes Fédéralistes du Congo	8
Rassemblement Congolais pour la Démocratie—Kisangani Mouvement de Libération	7
Union Congolaise pour le Progrès	6
Union pour le Développement du Congo	6
Others*	152
Independents	13
Total	492†

* Comprising political parties that won fewer than six seats.

† A total of eight seats were declared vacant.

SENATE

President: LÉON KENGO WA DONDO.

Election, 19 January 2007

Party	Seats
Parti du Peuple pour la Reconstruction et la Démocratie	22
Mouvement de Libération du Congo	14
Forces du Renouveau	7
Rassemblement Congolais pour la Démocratie	7
Parti Démocrate Chrétien	6
Convention des Démocrates Chrétiens	3
Mouvement Social pour le Renouveau	3
Parti Lumumbiste Unifié	2
Others*	18
Independents	26
Total	108

* Comprising 18 political parties that each won one seat.

Election Commission

Commission Electorale Nationale Indépendante (CENI): 4471 blvd du 30 juin, Kinshasa; tel. 818110613 (mobile); e-mail info@cei-rdc.org; internet www.ceni.gouv.cd; f. 2010 to replace the Commission Electorale Indépendante; 7 mems; Pres. Fr APOLLINAIRE MALU MALU.

Political Organizations

In January 1999 a ban on the formation of political associations was officially ended, and in May 2001 remaining restrictions on the registration and operation of political parties were removed. At August 2011 some 417 political parties were registered with the Ministry of the Interior.

Alliance des Forces Démocratiques du Congo (AFDC): Kinshasa; Pres. PLACIDE TSHISUMPA TSHIAKATUMBA; Sec.-Gen. PASCAL RUKENGWA.

Congrès National pour la Défense du Peuple (CNDP): Bukavu; tel. 993456427 (mobile); e-mail cndpadmin@cndp-congo.org; f. 2006; Pres. LAURENT NKUNDA MIHIGO; Sec. G. KAMBASU NGEVE.

Convention des Démocrates Chrétiens: Kinshasa; Leader FLORENTIN MOKONDA BONZA.

Démocratie Chrétienne Féderaliste—Convention des Féderalistes pour la Démocratie Chrétienne (DCF—COFEDEC): 2209 ave des Etoiles, Kinshasa-Gombe; Leader VENANT TSHIPASA VANGI.

Eveil de la Conscience pour le Travail et le Développement (ECT): Kinshasa; Pres. Dr FÉLIX KABANGE NUMBI.

Forces du Renouveau: Kinshasa; Leader ANTIPAS MBUSA NYAMWIS.

Alliance pour le Renouveau du Congo (ARC): 1165-1175 ave Tombalbaye, Kinshasa-Gombe; tel. 998911096 (mobile); fax 815947347 (mobile); e-mail arc_secgen@yahoo.fr; f. 2006; Leader OLIVIER KAMITATU ETSU.

Forces Novatrices pour l'Union et la Solidarité (FONUS): 13 ave de l'Enseignement, Kasa-Vubu, Kinshasa; f. 2004; advocates political pluralism; Pres. JOSEPH OLENGHANKOY; Sec.-Gen. EMERY OKUNDJI.

Mouvement pour l'Intégrité du Peuple (MIP): Kinshasa.

Mouvement de Libération du Congo (MLC): 6 ave du Port, Kinshasa-Gombe; f. 1998; fmr Ugandan-supported rebel movement; incl. in Govt in July 2003; Leader JEAN-PIERRE BEMBA GOMBO; Sec.-Gen. THOMAS LUHAKA.

Mouvement Social pour le Renouveau (MSR): Kinshasa; f. 2006; Leader YVES MOBANDO YOGO.

Parti Démocrate Chrétien (PDC): Leader JOSÉ ENDUNDO BONONGE.

Parti Démocrate et Social Chrétien (PDSC): 3040 route de Matadi, C/Ngaliema, Kinshasa; tel. (12) 21211; f. 1990; centrist; Pres. ANDRÉ BOBOLIKO; Sec.-Gen. TUYABA LEWULA.

Parti Lumumbiste Unifié (PALU): 9 rue Cannas, C/Limete, Kinshasa; Leader ANTOINE GIZENGA.

Parti du Peuple pour la Paix et la Démocratie (PPPD): Kinshasa.

Parti du Peuple pour la Reconstruction et la Démocratie (PPRD): Croisement des aves Pumbu et Batetela, Kinshasa-Gombe; f. March 2002 by Pres. Joseph Kabila; Sec.-Gen. ÉVARISTE BOSHAB.

Rassemblement Congolais pour la Démocratie (RCD—Goma): 26 ave Lukusa, Kinshasa-Gombe; f. 1998; rebel movement until Dec. 2002 peace agreement; incl. in Govt July 2003; main Ilunga faction; supported by Rwanda; Leader AZARIAS RUBERWA; Sec.-Gen. FRANCIS BEDY MAKHUBU MABELE.

Rassemblement Congolais pour la Démocratie—National (RCD—N): blvd du 30 juin, S.V./64 Haut-Uélé (Isiro); broke away from RCD—ML in Oct. 2000; Leader ROGER LUMBALA.

Rassemblement des Forces Sociales et Fédéralistes (RSF): 98 rue Poto-poto, Kimbanseke; Leader VINCENT DE PAUL LUNDA BULULU.

Rassemblement pour une Nouvelle Société (RNS): 1 bis rue Lufu, C/Bandalungwa; e-mail info@congozaire.org; Leader Dr ALAFUELE M. KALALA.

Rassemblement pour la Reconstruction du Congo (RRC): Kinshasa.

Union des Démocrates Mobutistes (UDEMO): f. by son of fmr Pres. Mobutu; Leader FRANÇOIS JOSEPH MOBUTU NZANGA NGBANGAWE.

Union des Forces du Changement (UFC): Kinshasa; Pres. LÉON KENGO WA DONDO.

Union Nationale des Démocrates Féderalistes (UNADEF): Kinshasa; Leader CHARLES MWANDO NSIMBA.

Union des Nationalistes Fédéralistes du Congo (UNAFEC): 5 ave Citronniers, Kinshasa-Gombe; Leader GABRIEL KYUNGA WA KUMWANZA.

Union des Patriotes Congolais (UPC): 25 blvd de la Libération, Bunia; rebel group of Hema ethnic group, fmrly in conflict with Lendu in north-east; registered as political org. 2004, after peace agreement with Govt; Leader THOMAS LUBANGA.

Union pour la Démocratie et le Progrès Social (UDPS): 546 ave Zinnia, Limete, Kinshasa; tel. 813140685 (mobile); e-mail udps@udps.net; internet www.udps.net; f. 1982; Leader Dr ETIENNE TSHISEKEDI WA MULUMBA; Sec.-Gen. BRUNO MAVUNGU.

Union pour le Développement du Congo (UDCO): Kinshasa; Pres. BAUDOUIN BANZA MUKALAYI NSUNGU.

Union pour la Nation Congolaise (UNC): ave Croix-Rouge 3, Commune de Barumbu, Kinshasa; tel. 999915385 (mobile); e-mail unc_sg@yahoo.fr; internet www.unc-rdc.com; Pres. VITAL KAMERHE LWA-KANYIGINYI.

Union pour la Reconstruction du Congo (UREC): Leader OSCAR LUKUMWENA KASHALA.

Union pour la République—Mouvement National (UNIR—MN): Immeuble VeVe center, 2 rue de Bongandanga, c/Kasa-Vubu, Kinshasa; tel. 812431078 (mobile); e-mail info@unir-mn.org; internet www.unir-mn.org; f. 2001; officially registered as a political party in 2005; Pres. FRÉDÉRIC BOYENGA-BOFALA; Sec.-Gen. OLIVIER MESKENS NTAMBU KUFUANGA.

Diplomatic Representation

EMBASSIES IN THE DEMOCRATIC REPUBLIC OF THE CONGO

Algeria: 50–52 ave Col Ebeya, Gombe, Kinshasa; tel. 818803717 (mobile); fax 813010577 (mobile); Ambassador (vacant).

Angola: 4413–4429 blvd du 30 juin, BP 8625, Kinshasa; tel. (12) 32415; fax (13) 98971; e-mail consangolakatanga@voila.fr; Ambassador EMILIO DE CARVALHO GUERRA.

Belgium: Immeuble Le Cinquantenaire, pl. du 27 octobre, BP 899, Kinshasa; tel. (12) 20110; fax (12) 21058; e-mail kinshasa@diplobel.fed.be; internet diplomatie.belgium.be/rd_congo; Ambassador MICHEL LASTSCHENKO.

Benin: 3990 ave des Cliniques, BP 3265, Kinshasa-Gombe; tel. 98128659 (mobile); e-mail abkin@raga.net; Ambassador OUSSOU-EDOUARDS AHO-GLELE.

Cameroon: 171 blvd du 30 juin, BP 10998, Kinshasa; tel. (12) 34787; Ambassador MARTIN CHUNGONG AYAFOR.

Canada: 17 ave Pumbu, Commune de la Gombe, BP 8341, Kinshasa 1; tel. 898950310 (mobile); fax 999975403 (mobile); e-mail knsha@international.gc.ca; internet www.canadainternational.gc.ca/congo; Chargé d'affaires a.i. ALAIN LATULIPPE.

Central African Republic: 11 ave Pumbu, BP 7769, Kinshasa; tel. (12) 30417; Ambassador ELIE OUEIFIO.

Chad: 67–69 ave du Cercle, BP 9097, Kinshasa; tel. (12) 22358; Ambassador (vacant).

Congo, Republic: 179 blvd du 30 juin, BP 9516, Kinshasa; tel. (12) 34028; Ambassador GUSTAVE ZOULA.

Côte d'Ivoire: 68 ave de la Justice, BP 9197, Kinshasa; tel. 773477664 (mobile); Ambassador JOACHIM ANVIRE DJABIA.

Cuba: 4660 ave Cateam, BP 10699, Kinshasa; tel. (12) 8803823; Ambassador LUIS CASTILLO.

Egypt: 519 ave de l'Ouganda, BP 8838, Kinshasa; tel. (51) 10137; fax (88) 03728; Ambassador ACHRAF IBRAHIM.

Ethiopia: BP 8435, Kinshasa; tel. (12) 23327; Ambassador DIEUDEONNE A. GANGA.

France: 1 ave du Colonel Mondjiba, BP 3093, Kinshasa; tel. 815559999 (mobile); fax 815559937 (mobile); e-mail presse.kinshasa-amba@diplomatie.gouv.fr; internet www.ambafrance-cd.org; Ambassador LUC HALLADE.

Gabon: ave du 24 novembre, BP 9592, Kinshasa; tel. (12) 68325; Ambassador CHRISTOPHE ELLA EKOGHA.

Germany: 82 ave Roi Baudouin, BP 8400, Kinshasa-Gombe; tel. 815561380 (mobile); e-mail amballemagne@ic.cd; internet www.kinshasa.diplo.de; Ambassador Dr WOLFGANG MANIG.

Greece: Immeuble de la Communauté Hellénique, 3ème étage, blvd du 30 juin, BP 478, Kinshasa; tel. 815554941 (mobile); fax 815554945 (mobile); e-mail gremb.kin@mfa.gr; Ambassador KATRANIS ALEXANDROS.

Holy See: 81 ave Goma, BP 3091, Kinshasa; tel. (88) 08814; fax (88) 48483; e-mail nuntius@raga.net; Apostolic Nuncio Most Rev. ADOLFO TITO YLLANA (Titular Archbishop of Montecorvino).

India: 18B, ave Batetela, Commune de la Gombe, Kinshasa; tel. 815559770 (mobile); fax 815559774 (mobile); e-mail amb.indembkin@gbs.cd; Ambassador MANOHAR RAM.

Iran: 78 blvd du 30 juin, BP 16599, Kinshasa; tel. 817005298 (mobile); Ambassador ALI AMIR EMAM JOMEH SHAHIDI.

Japan: Immeuble La Rosée, 7e étage, 7 ave de l'OUA, BP 1810, Kinshasa; tel. 815554731 (mobile); fax 870-7639-59668 (satellite); e-mail ambjaponrdc@yahoo.fr; internet www.rdc.emb-japan.go.jp; Ambassador TOMINAGA YOSHIMASA.

Kenya: 4002 ave de l'Ouganda, BP 9667, Kinshasa; tel. 815565935 (mobile); fax 815565939 (mobile); e-mail info@kenyaembassy.cd; Chargé d'affaires a.i. ABDISHAKUR HUSSEIN.

Korea, Democratic People's Republic: 168 ave de l'Ouganda, BP 16597, Kinshasa; tel. 8801443 (mobile); fax 815300194 (mobile); e-mail kenem-drc@jobantech.cd; Ambassador RI MYONG-CHOL.

Korea, Republic: 65 blvd Tshatshi, BP 628, Kinshasa; tel. 819820302 (mobile); e-mail amb-rdc@mofat.go.kr; Ambassador LEE HO-SUNG.

Lebanon: 3 ave de l'Ouganda, Kinshasa; tel. (12) 82469; Ambassador SAAD ZAKHIA.

Liberia: 3 ave de l'Okapi, BP 8940, Kinshasa; tel. (12) 82289; Ambassador JALLA D. LANSANAH.

Mauritania: BP 16397, Kinshasa; tel. (12) 59575; Ambassador Lt-Col M'BARECK OULD BOUNA MOKHTAR.

Morocco: POB 912, ave Corteaux et Vallée No. 40, Kinshasa 1; tel. (12) 34794; Ambassador MOHAMED BEN KADDOUR.

Namibia: 138 blvd du 30 Juin, BP 8934, Kinshasa; tel. 815559840 (mobile); fax 813010546 (mobile); Ambassador WILBARD HELLAO.

Netherlands: 11 ave Zongontolo, 55 Immeuble Residence, BP 10299, Kinshasa; tel. 996050600 (mobile); fax 996050629 (mobile); e-mail kss@minbuza.nl; internet drcongo.nlambassade.org; Ambassador COR VAN HONK.

Nigeria: 141 blvd du 30 juin, BP 1700, Kinshasa; tel. 817005142 (mobile); fax 812616115 (mobile); e-mail nigemb@jobantech.cd; Ambassador GRANT EHIOBUCHE.

Portugal: 279 ave des Aviateurs, BP 7775, Kinshasa; tel. 815161277 (mobile); e-mail ambassadeportugal@vodanet.net; Ambassador JOÃO MANUEL PINA PERESTRELLO CAVACO.

Russia: 80 ave de la Justice, BP 1143, Kinshasa 1; tel. 998743189 (mobile); fax 873761322071 (mobile); e-mail ambrus_drc@mail.ru; internet www.drc.mid.ru; Ambassador IGOR EVDOKIMOV.

Rwanda: 80 ave Uvira, Commune de la Gombe, Kinshasa; e-mail arugira@minaffet.gov.rw; Ambassador AMANDIN RUGIRA.

South Africa: 77 ave Ngongo Lutete, BP 7829, Kinshasa-Gombe; tel. 814769100 (mobile); fax 815554322 (mobile); e-mail pearces@foreign.gov.za; Ambassador JOSEPH NTSHIKIWANE MASHIMBYE.

Spain: blvd du 30 juin, Bldg Communauté Hellénique, Commune de la Gombe, BP 8036, Kinshasa; tel. 818843195 (mobile); fax 813010396 (mobile); e-mail emb.kinshasa@mae.es; Ambassador (vacant).

Sudan: 24 ave de l'Ouganda, Kinshasa; tel. 999937396 (mobile); Ambassador GAAFAR BABIKER EL-KHALIFA EL-TAYEB.

Sweden: 93 ave Roi Baudouin, Commune de la Gombe, BP 11096, Kinshasa; tel. 999301102 (mobile); fax 870-600-147849 (satellite); e-mail ambassaden.kinshasa@foreign.ministry.se; internet www.swedenabroad.com/sv-SE/Ambassader/Kinshasa; Ambassador ANNIKA BEN DAVID.

Switzerland: 654 blvd Col Tshatshi, BP 8724, Gombe, Kinshasa; tel. 898946800 (mobile); e-mail kin.vertretung@eda.admin.ch; internet www.eda.admin.ch/kinshasa; Ambassador JACQUES GREMAUD.

Tanzania: 142 blvd du 30 juin, BP 1612, Kinshasa; tel. 815565850 (mobile); fax 815565852 (mobile); e-mail tanzanrepkinshasa@yahoo.com; Ambassador GORDON LUHWANO NGILANGWA.

Togo: 3 ave de la Vallée, BP 10117, Kinshasa; tel. (12) 30666; Ambassador YAWO ADOMAYAKPOR.

Tunisia: 67–69 ave du Cercle, BP 1498, Kinshasa; tel. 818803901 (mobile); e-mail atkinshasa@yahoo.fr; Ambassador EZZEDDINE ZAYANI.

Uganda: ave des Cocotiers, Plot no. 15, pl. Wenge, Commune de la Gombe, BP 8804, Kinshasa; tel. 810507179 (mobile); e-mail ugambassy@simbatel.com; Ambassador Maj. JAMES KINOBE.

United Kingdom: 83 ave Roi Baudouin, BP 8049, Kinshasa; tel. 813300252 (mobile); fax 813464291 (mobile); e-mail ambrit@ic.cd; internet ukindrc.fco.gov.uk; Ambassador DIANE CORNER.

USA: 310 ave des Aviateurs, BP 397, Kinshasa; tel. 815560151 (mobile); fax 815560173 (mobile); e-mail AEKinshasaConsular@state.gov; internet kinshasa.usembassy.gov; Ambassador JAMES C. SWAN.

Zambia: 54–58 ave de l'Ecole, BP 1144, Kinshasa; tel. 819999437 (mobile); fax (88) 45106; e-mail ambazambia@ic.cd; Ambassador FIDELIS MULENGA KAPOKA.

Judicial System

Under the Constitution that entered into effect in February 2006, the judicial system is independent. Members of the judiciary are under the authority of the High Council of the Judiciary. The Court of Cassation has jurisdiction over legal decisions and the Council of State over administrative decisions. The Constitutional Court interprets the provisions of the Constitution and ensures the conformity of new legislation. The judicial system also comprises a Military High Court, and lower civil and military courts and tribunals. The High Council of the Judiciary has 18 members, including the Presidents and Chief Prosecutors of the main courts. The Constitutional Court comprises nine members, who are appointed by the President (including three nominated by the legislature and three by the High Council of the Judiciary for a term of nine years. The Head of State appoints and dismisses magistrates, on the proposal of the High Council of the Judiciary.

Court of Cassation (Cour de Cassation): cnr ave de la Justice and ave de Lemera, BP 3382, Kinshasa-Gombe; tel. (12) 25104; Pres. BENOÎT LWAMBA BINDU.

Supreme Court of Justice (Cour Suprême de Justice): ave de la Justice 2, BP 13, Kinshasa-Gombe; Pres. BENOÎT LWAMBA BINDU.

Procurator-General of the Republic: FLORY KABANGE NUMBI.

Religion

Many of the country's inhabitants follow traditional beliefs, which are mostly animistic. A large proportion of the population is Christian, predominantly Roman Catholic, and there are small Muslim, Jewish and Greek Orthodox communities.

CHRISTIANITY

The Roman Catholic Church

The Democratic Republic of the Congo comprises six archdioceses and 41 dioceses. Some 51% of the population are Roman Catholics.

Bishops' Conference: Conférence Episcopale Nationale du Congo, BP 3258, Kinshasa-Gombe; tel. (12) 34528; fax (88) 44948; e-mail conf.episc.rdc@ic.cd; internet www.cenco.cd; Pres. Most Rev. NICOLAS DJOMO LOLA (Bishop of Tshumbe).

Archbishop of Bukavu: FRANÇOIS-XAVIER MAROY RUSENGO, Archevêché, ave Mbaki 18, BP 3324, Bukavu; tel. 813180621 (mobile); e-mail archevechebk@yahoo.fr.

Archbishop of Kananga: Most Rev. MARCEL MADILA BASANGUKA, Archevêché, BP 70, Kananga; tel. 815013942 (mobile); e-mail archidiocesekananga@yahoo.fr.

Archbishop of Kinshasa: Cardinal LAURENT MONSENGWO PASINYA, Archevêché, ave de l'Université, BP 8431, Kinshasa 1; tel. (12) 3723546; e-mail archikin@ic.cd.

Archbishop of Kisangani: Most Rev. MARCEL UTEMBI TAPA, Archevêché, ave Mpolo 10B, BP 505, Kisangani; tel. 812006715 (mobile); fax (761) 608336.

Archbishop of Lubumbashi: Most Rev. JEAN-PIERRE TAFUNGA MBAYO, Archevêché, BP 72, Lubumbashi; tel. 997031991 (mobile); e-mail archidiolub@mwangaza.cd.

Archbishop of Mbandaka-Bikoro: Most Rev. JOSEPH KUMUONDALA MBIMBA, Archevêché, BP 1064, Mbandaka; tel. 817301027 (mobile); e-mail mbandakabikoro@yahoo.fr.

The Anglican Communion

The Church of the Province of the Congo comprises eight dioceses.

Archbishop of the Province of the Congo and Bishop of Kinshasa: Most Rev. Dr DIROKPA BALUFUGA FIDÈLE, 11 ave Basalakala, Quartier Immocongo, Commune de Kalamu, BP 16482, Kinshasa; tel. 998611180 (mobile); e-mail dirokpa1@hotmail.com.

Bishop of Arua: Rt Rev. Dr GEORGE TITRE ANDE, POB 226, Arua, Uganda; tel. 810393071 (mobile); e-mail revdande@yahoo.co.uk.

Bishop of Boga: Rt Rev. HENRY KAHWA ISINGOMA, CAC- Boga, Congo Liaison Office, POB 25586, Kampala, Uganda; e-mail peac_isingoma@yahoo.fr.

Bishop of Bukavu: Rt Rev. SYLVESTRE BALI-BUSANE BAHATI, CAC-Bukavu, POB 53435, Nairobi, Kenya.

Bishop of Katanga: Rt Rev. MUNO KASIMA, c/o UMM, POB 22037, Kitwe, Zambia; tel. 97047173 (mobile); fax (88) 46383; e-mail peac_isingoma@yahoo.fr.

Bishop of Kindu: Rt Rev. ZACHARIE MASIMANGO KATANDA, c/o ESCO Uganda, POB 7892, Kampala, Uganda; e-mail angkindu@yahoo.fr.

Bishop of Kisangani: Rt Rev. LAMBERT FUNGA BOTOLOME, c/o Congo Liaison Office, POB 25586, Kampala, Uganda; e-mail lambertfunga@hotmail.com.

Bishop of Nord-Kivu: Rt Rev. METHUSELA MUSUBAHO MUNZENDA, CAZ-Butembo, POB 506, Bwera-Kasese, Uganda; fax 870-166-1121 (satellite); e-mail munzenda_eac@yahoo.fr.

Kimbanguist

Eglise de Jésus Christ sur la Terre par le Prophète Simon Kimbangu: BP 7069, Kinshasa; tel. (12) 68944; f. 1921; officially est. 1959; c. 5m. mems (1985); Spiritual Head HE SALOMON DIALUNGANA KIANGANI; Sec.-Gen. Rev. LUNTADILLA.

Protestant Churches

Eglise du Christ au Congo (ECC): ave de la Justice 75, BP 4938, Kinshasa-Gombe; internet congodisciples.org; f. 1902; a co-ordinating agency for all the Protestant churches, with the exception of the Kimbanguist Church; 62 mem. communities and a provincial org. in each province; Pres. Bishop MARINI BODHO; includes:

Communauté Baptiste du Congo-Ouest: BP 4728, Kinshasa 2; f. 1970; 450 parishes; Gen. Sec. Rev. LUSAKWENO-VANGU.

Communauté des Disciples du Christ: BP 178, Mbandaka; tel. 31062; f. 1964; 250 parishes; Gen. Sec. Rev. Dr ELONDA EFEFE.

Communauté Episcopale Baptiste en Afrique: 2 ave Jason Sendwe, BP 2809, Lubumbashi 1; tel. and fax (2) 348602; e-mail kitobokabwe@yahoo.fr; f. 1956; 1,300 episcopal communions and parishes; 150,000 mems (2001); Pres. Bishop KITOBO KABWEKA-LEZA.

Communauté Evangélique: BP 36, Luozi; f. 1961; 50 parishes; Pres. Rev. K. LUKOMBO NTONTOLO.

Communauté Lumière: BP 10498, Kinshasa 1; f. 1931; 150 parishes; Patriarch KAYUWA TSHIBUMBU WA KAHINGA.

Communauté Mennonite: BP 18, Tshikapa; f. 1960; Gen. Sec. Rev. KABANGY DJEKE SHAPASA.

Communauté Presbytérienne: BP 117, Kananga; f. 1959; Gen. Sec. Dr M. L. TSHIHAMBA.

Eglise Missionaire Apostolique: 375 ave Commerciale, BP 15859, Commune de N'Djili, Kinshasa 1; tel. 988165927 (mobile); e-mail buzi4@hotmail.com; f. 1986; 5 parishes; 2,600 mems; Apostle for Africa Rev. LUFANGA-AYIMOU NANANDANA.

Evangelical Lutheran Church in Congo: 150 ave Kasaï, Lumbabashi; tel. (2) 22396; fax (2) 24098; e-mail bnationaleelco@yahoo.fr; 136,000 mems (2010); Pres. Bishop RENÉ MWAMBA SUMAILI.

The Press

DAILIES

L'Avenir: Immeuble Ruzizi, 873 ave Bas-Congo, Kinshasa-Gombe; tel. 999942485 (mobile); internet www.groupelavenir.cd; owned by Groupe de l'Avenir; Chair. PIUS MUABILU.

Elima: 1 ave de la Révolution, BP 11498, Kinshasa; tel. (12) 77332; f. 1928; evening; Dir and Editor-in-Chief ESSOLOMWA NKOY EA LINGANGA.

Mjumbe: BP 2474, Lubumbashi; f. 1963; Dir and Editor TSHIMANGA KOYA KAKONA.

Le Palmarès: Kinshasa.

Le Phare: bldg du 29 juin, ave Col Lukusa 3392, BP 2481, Kinshasa; tel. 813330195 (mobile); e-mail info@le-phare.com; internet www.lepharerdc.com; f. 1983; Editor POLYDOR MUBOYAYI MUBANGA; circ. 5,000 (2012).

Le Potentiel: Immeuble Ruzizi, 873 ave du Bas-Congo, BP 11338, Kinshasa; tel. 98135483 (mobile); e-mail lepotentiel@lepotentiel.com; internet www.lepotentiel.com; f. 1982; Editor MODESTE MUTINGA MUTUISHAYI; circ. 8,000.

La Prospérité: Kinshasa; tel. 818135157 (mobile); e-mail marcelngo@yahoo.fr; internet www.laprosperiteonline.net; f. 2001; Dir-Gen. MARCEL NGOYI.

PERIODICALS

Afrique Editions: Kinshasa; tel. (88) 43202; e-mail bpongo@raga.net.

Allo Kinshasa: 3 rue Kayange, BP 20271, Kinshasa-Lemba; monthly; Editor MBUYU WA KABILA.

Cahiers des Religions Africaines: Faculté de Théologie Catholique de Kinshasa, BP 712, Kinshasa/Limete; tel. (12) 78476; f. 1967; English and French; religion; 2 a year; circ. 1,000.

Congo-Afrique: Centre d'Etudes pour l'Action Sociale, 9 ave Père Boka, BP 3375, Kinshasa-Gombe; tel. 898912981 (mobile); e-mail congoafrique@yahoo.fr; internet www.congo-afrique.org; f. 1961; economic, social and cultural; monthly; Editors FRANCIS KIKASSA MWANALESSA, RENÉ BEECKMANS; circ. 2,500.

Documentation et Informations Africaines (DIA): BP 2598, Kinshasa 1; tel. (12) 33197; fax (12) 33196; e-mail dia@ic.cd; internet www.peacelink.it/dia/index.html; Roman Catholic news agency reports; 3 a week; Dir Rev. Père VATA DIAMBANZA.

Etudes d'Histoire Africaine: National University of the Congo, BP 1825, Lubumbashi; f. 1970; French and English; history; annually; circ. 1,000.

KYA: 24 ave de l'Équateur, BP 7853, Kinshasa-Gombe; tel. (12) 27502; f. 1984; weekly for Bas-Congo; Editor (vacant).

Le Moniteur de l'Economie (Economic Monitor): Kinshasa; Man. Editor FÉLIX NZUZI.

Mutaani Magazine: Goma; tel. 995652115 (mobile); f. 2012.

Mwana Shaba: Générale des Carrières et des Mines, BP 450, Lubumbashi; monthly; circ. 25,000.

Njanja: Société Nationale des Chemins de Fer du Congo, 115 pl. de la Gare, BP 297, Lubumbashi; tel. (2) 23430; fax (2) 61321; railways and transportation; annually; circ. 10,000.

NUKTA: 14 chaussée de Kasenga, BP 3805, Lubumbashi; weekly; agriculture; Editor NGOY BUNDUKI.

Post: Immeuble Linzadi, 1538 ave de la Douane, Kinshasa-Gombe; e-mail thepostrdc@yahoo.com; internet www.congoonline.com/thepost; 2 a week; Editor-in-Chief MUKEBAYI NKOSO.

Problèmes Sociaux Zaïrois: Centre d'Exécution de Programmes Sociaux et Economiques, Université de Lubumbashi, 208 ave

Kasavubu, BP 1873, Lubumbashi; f. 1946; quarterly; Editor N'KASHAMA KADIMA.

Promoteur Congolais: Centre du Commerce International du Congo, 119 ave Colonel Tshatshi, BP 13, Kinshasa; f. 1979; international trade news; 6 a year.

Telema: Faculté Canisius, Kimwenza, BP 3724, Kinshasa-Gombe; f. 1974; religious; quarterly; edited by the Central Africa Jesuits; circ. 1,200.

La Voix des Sans-Voix: ave des Ecuries 3858, commune de Ngaliema, BP 11445, Kinshasa-Gombe; tel. (88) 40394; fax (88) 01826; e-mail vsv@ic.cd; internet www.congonline.com/vsv.

La Voix du Paysan Congolais: 1150 ave Tabora, C/Barumbu, BP 14582, Kinshasa; tel. 999982097 (mobile); e-mail lavoixdupaysan_rdc@yahoo.fr; internet lavoixdupaysancongolais.com; f. 2008; agricultural issues; 4 a year; Dir of Publication JEAN BAPTISTE LUBAMBA.

NEWS AGENCIES

Agence Congolaise de Presse (ACP): 44–48 ave Tombalbaye, BP 1595, Kinshasa 1; tel. 816573788 (mobile); e-mail info@acpcongo.cd; internet www.acpcongo.cd; f. 1957; state-controlled; Dir-Gen. JEAN-MARIE VIANNEY LONGONYA.

Digital Congo: 21 ave Kabasele Tshiamala, Kinshasa-Gombe; tel. 8941010; e-mail lettres@digitalcongo.net; internet www.digitalcongo.net; news service owned by Multimedia Congo.

Documentation et Informations Africaines (DIA): BP 2598, Kinshasa 1; tel. (12) 34528; f. 1957; Roman Catholic news agency; Dir Rev. Père VATA DIAMBANZA.

Publishers

Aequatoria Centre: BP 276, Mbandaka; f. 1980; anthropology, biography, ethnicity, history, language and linguistics, social sciences; Dir HONORÉ VINCK.

CEEBA Publications: BP 246, Bandundu; f. 1965; humanities, languages, fiction; Man. Dir (Editorial) Dr HERMANN HOCHEGGER.

Centre de Documentation Agricole: BP 7537, Kinshasa 1; tel. (12) 32498; agriculture, science; Dir PIERTE MBAYAKABUYI; Chief Editor J. MARCELLIN KAPUKUNGESA.

Centre de Linguistique Théorique et Appliquée (CELTA): BP 4956, Kinshasa-Gombe; tel. 818129998 (mobile); e-mail anyembwe@yahoo.fr; f. 1971; language, arts and linguistics; Dir-Gen. ANDRÉ NYEMBWE NTITA.

Centre de Recherches Pédagogiques: BP 8815, Kinshasa 1; f. 1959; accounting, education, geography, language, science; Dir P. DETIENNE.

Centre de Vulgarisation Agricole: BP 4008, Kinshasa 2; tel. (12) 71165; fax (12) 21351; agriculture, environment, health; Dir-Gen. KIMPIANGA MAHANIAH.

Centre Protestant d'Editions et de Diffusion (CEDI): 209 ave Kalémie, BP 11398, Kinshasa 1; tel. (12) 22202; fax (12) 26730; f. 1935; fiction, poetry, biography, religious, juvenile; Christian tracts, works in French, Lingala, Kikongo, etc.; Dir-Gen. HENRY DIRKS.

Connaissance et Pratique du Droit Congolais Editions (CDPC): BP 5502, Kinshasa-Gombe; f. 1987; law; Editor DIBUNDA KABUINJI.

Editions Lokole: BP 5085, Kinshasa 10; state org. for the promotion of literature; Dir BOKEME SHANE MOLOBAY.

Editions Paulines: BP 8505, Kinshasa; tel. 998859777 (mobile); e-mail libanga.c@gmail.com; f. 1988; fiction, general non-fiction, poetry, religion, education; Dir CATTANEO PIERA; Sec. Sister M. ROSARIO ZAMBELLO.

Facultés Catholiques de Kinshasa: 2 ave de l'Université, Kinshasa-Limete; tel. and fax (12) 46965; e-mail facakin@ic.cd; f. 1957; anthropology, art, economics, history, politics, computer science; Rector Prof. Mgr HIPPOLYTE NGIMBI NSEKA.

Les Editions du Trottoir: BP 1800, Kinshasa; tel. (12) 9936043; e-mail smuyengo@yahoo.fr; f. 1989; communications, fiction, literature, drama; Pres. CHARLES DJUNJU-SIMBA.

Librairie les Volcans: 22 ave Pres. Mobutu, BP 400, Goma, Nord-Kivu; f. 1995; social sciences; Man. Dir RUHAMA MUKANDOLI.

Presses Universitaires du Congo (PUC): 290 rue d'Aketi, BP 1800, Kinshasa 1; tel. (12) 9936043; e-mail smuyengo@yahoo.fr; f. 1972; science, arts and communications; Dir Abbé SÉBASTIEN MUYENGO.

GOVERNMENT PUBLISHING HOUSE

Imprimerie du Gouvernement Central: BP 3021, Kinshasa-Kalina.

Broadcasting and Communications

TELECOMMUNICATIONS

Airtel Congo: croisement des aves Tchad et Bas-Congo, Kinshasa; tel. 996000121 (mobile); e-mail info.airteldrc@cd.airtel.com; internet africa.airtel.com/drc; acquired by Bharti Airtel (India) in 2010; mobile cellular telephone network; fmrly Celtel Congo, subsequently Zain Congo, present name adopted in 2010; Dir-Gen. LOUIS LUBALA; 1.83m. subscribers (Dec. 2006).

Congo Chine Telecom (CCT): ave du Port, Kinshasa; tel. 8400085 (mobile); e-mail admin@cct.cd; internet www.cct.cd; mobile cellular telephone network; covers Kinshasa and Bas-Congo, Kasaï, Katanga and Oriental provinces; 100% owned by France Télécom; Dir-Gen. WANG XIANGGUO; 1.5m. subscribers (Sept. 2011).

Oasis Telecom (Tigo): 372 ave Col Mondjiba, Kinshasa; tel. 898901000 (mobile); fax 898901001 (mobile); internet www.tigo.cd; 100% owned by Millicom; 50,000 subscribers (Dec. 2006).

Supercell: 99 ave des Tulipiers, BP 114, Goma; tel. 808313010 (mobile); e-mail rogern@supercell.cd; 69,000 subscribers.

Vodacom Congo: Immeuble Mobil–Oil, 2ème étage, 3157 blvd du 30 juin, BP 797, Kinshasa 1; tel. 813131000 (mobile); fax 813131351 (mobile); e-mail vodacom@vodacom.cd; internet www.vodacom.cd; 51% owned by Vodacom (South Africa); 2.33m. subscribers (Dec. 2006).

Regulatory Authority

Autorité de Régulation de la Poste et des Télécommunications du Congo (ARPTC): blvd du 30 juin, BP 3000, Kinshasa 1; tel. (13) 92491; e-mail info.arptc@arptc.cd; Pres. OSCAR MANIKUNDA.

BROADCASTING

Radio-Télévision Nationale Congolaise (RTNC): ave Kabinda, Lingwala, Kinshasa; tel. 9999256200 (mobile); e-mail info@radiotele-rdc.net; internet www.radiotele-rdc.net; state radio, terrestrial and satellite television broadcasts; Dir-Gen. JOSE KAJANGUA.

Radio

Several private radio broadcasters operate in Kinshasa. Radio France Internationale broadcasts via FM in nine localities.

Radio Candip: Centre d'Animation et de Diffusion Pédagogique, BP 373, Bunia.

Mutaani FM: Goma; tel. 995652115 (mobile); internet mutaani.com/la_radio_en_direct; f. 2011.

Radio Okapi: 12 ave des Aviateurs, Gombe, Kinshasa; tel. 818906747 (mobile); e-mail contact@radiookapi.net; internet radiookapi.net; f. 2002; owned by the Fondation Hirondelle (Switzerland).

La Voix du Congo: Station Nationale, BP 3164, Kinshasa-Gombe; tel. (12) 23175; state-controlled; operated by RTNC; broadcasts in French, Swahili, Lingala, Tshiluba, Kikongo; regional stations at Kisangani, Lubumbashi, Bukavu, Bandundu, Kananga, Mbuji-Mayi, Matadi, Mbandaka and Bunia.

Television

Several private television broadcasters operate in Kinshasa.

Antenne A: Immeuble Forescom, 2ème étage, ave du Port 4, POB 2581, Kinshasa 1; tel. (12) 21736; private and commercial station; Dir-Gen. IGAL AVIVI NEIRSON.

Canal Z: ave du Port 6, POB 614, Kinshasa 1; tel. (12) 20239; commercial station; Dir-Gen. FRÉDÉRIC FLASSE.

Tele Kin Malebo (TKM): 32B route de Matadi, Ngaliema, Kinshasa; tel. (12) 2933338; e-mail malebokin@hotmail.com; Dir-Gen. NGONGO LUWOWO.

Télévision Congolaise: ave Kabinda, Lingwala, Kinshasa; tel. 9999256200 (mobile); e-mail info@radiotele-rdc.net; govt commercial station; operated by RTNC; broadcasts 2 channels.

Regulatory Authority

Conseil Supérieur de l'Audiovisuel et de la Communication: Kinshasa; f. 2011; Pres. JEAN BOSCO BAHALA OKW' IBALE.

Finance

(cap. = capital; res = reserves; dep. = deposits; m. = million; br(s). = branch(es); amounts in new Congolese francs, unless otherwise indicated)

BANKING

Central Bank

Banque Centrale du Congo: 563 blvd Colonel Tshatshi au nord, BP 2697, Kinshasa; tel. 818105970 (mobile); fax (12) 8805152; e-mail webmaster@bcc.cd; internet www.bcc.cd; f. 1964; dep. 254,133m., total assets 2,174,871m. (Dec. 2009); Gov. DEOGRATIAS MUTOMBO MWANA NYEMBO; 8 brs.

Commercial Banks

Advans Banque Congo: ave du Bas Congo 4, Commune de la Gombe, Kinshasa; tel. 995904466 (mobile); internet www.advansgroup.com; f. 2008; Dir-Gen. BRUNO DEGOY; 2 brs.

Afriland First Bank: 767 blvd du 30 juin, BP 10470, Kinshasa-Gombe; tel. 810775359 (mobile); e-mail jtoubi@afrilandfirstbank.com; internet www.afrilandfirstbank.com; f. 2004; 2 brs.

Bank of Africa: 22 ave des Aviateurs, Kinshasa-Gombe; tel. 993004600 (mobile); e-mail infos@boa-rdc.com; internet www.bank-of-africa.net; f. 2010; Pres. PAUL DERREUMAUX.

Banque Commerciale du Congo SARL (BCDC): blvd du 30 juin, BP 2798, Kinshasa 1; tel. 818845704 (mobile); fax 99631048 (mobile); e-mail dir@bcdc.cd; internet www.bcdc.cd; f. 1952 as Banque du Congo Belge; name changed as above 1997; cap. 4,975.7m., res 41,728.6m., dep. 270,024.8m. (Dec. 2011); Pres. GUY-ROBERT LUKAMA NKUNZI; Man. Dir YVES CUYPERS; 16 brs.

Banque Internationale de Crédit SARL (BIC): 191 ave de l'Équateur, BP 1299, Kinshasa 1; tel. 999921624 (mobile); fax 812616000 (mobile); e-mail bic@ic.cd; internet www.bic.cd; f. 1994; cap. and res 946.2m., dep. 12,352.7m. (Dec. 2003); Pres. PASCAL KINDUELO LUMBU; Dir-Gen. FREDERIC PULULU MANGONDA; 23 brs.

Banque Internationale pour l'Afrique au Congo (BIAC): 87 blvd du 30 juin, BP 8725, Kinshasa; tel. 815554000 (mobile); fax 8153010681 (mobile); e-mail contact@biac.cd; internet www.biac.cd; f. 1970; cap. 6,140.5m., res 14,185.4m., dep. 317,409.8m. (Dec. 2011); Pres. CHARLES SANLAVILLE; 30 brs.

Citigroup (Congo) SARL Congo: 657 Immeuble Citibank Congo, angle aves Col Lukusa et Ngongo Lutete, BP 9999, Kinshasa 1; tel. 815554808 (mobile); fax 813017070 (mobile); e-mail singa.boyenge@citicorp.com; f. 1971; cap. 7,140.0m., res 7,139.2m., dep. 47,518.7m. (Dec. 2009); Man. Dir MICHAEL LOSEMBE; 1 br.

La Cruche Banque: 37 rue Kinshasa, Ville de Butembo, Nord-Kivu; tel. 815203045 (mobile); e-mail lacruchebank@yahoo.fr; internet www.lacruchebank.com; Pres. KATEMBO MBANGA.

Ecobank DRC: Immeuble Future Tower, 3642 blvd du 30 Juin, BP 7515, Kinshasa; tel. 996016000 (mobile); fax 996016070 (mobile); internet www.ecobank.com; cap. 6,148.0m., res 16,789.4m., dep. 93,597.6m. (Dec. 2011); Pres. JEAN-PIERRE KIWAKANA KIMAYALA; Dir Gen. SERGE ACKRE; 14 brs.

Rawbank Sarl: 3487 blvd du 30 juin, Immeuble Concorde, POB 2499, Kinshasa; tel. 998320000 (mobile); fax 89240224 (mobile); e-mail contact@rawbank.cd; internet www.rawbank.cd; f. 2002; cap. 46,515m., res 14,956m., dep. 453,590m. (Dec. 2012); Pres. MAZHAR RAWJI; Dir-Gen. THIERRY TAEYMANS; 19 brs.

Société Financière de Développement SARL (SOFIDE): Immeuble SOFIDE, 9–11 angle aves Ngabu et Kisangani, BP 1148, Kinshasa 1; tel. 816601531 (mobile); e-mail sofide2001@yahoo.fr; f. 1970; partly state-owned; provides tech. and financial aid, primarily for agricultural devt; cap. and res 285.3m., total assets 1,202.0m. (Dec. 2003); Pres. and Dir-Gen. RAPHAËL SENGA KITENGE; 4 brs.

Standard Bank RDC: 12 ave de Mongala, BP 16297, Kinshasa 1; tel. 817006000 (mobile); fax 813013848 (mobile); e-mail stanbiccongoinfo@stanbic.com; internet www.standardbank.cd; f. 1973; subsidiary of Standard Bank Investment Corpn (South Africa); cap. 1,768.0m., res –1,163.6m., dep. 19,160.1m. (Dec. 2005); Chair. CLIVE TASKER; CEO ERIC MBOMA; 4 br.

Banking Association

Association Congolaise des Banques: 1 pl. du Marché, Kinshasa 1; tel. 817562771 (mobile); internet acb-asso.com; fax 999940863 (mobile); Pres. MICHEL LOSEMBE; 20 mems.

Trade and Industry

GOVERNMENT AGENCY

Bureau Central de Coordination (BCECO): ave Colonel Mondjiba 372, Complexe Utex Africa, Kinshasa; tel. 815096430 (mobile); e-mail bceco@bceco.cd; internet www.bceco.cd; f. 2001; manages projects funded by the African Development Bank and the World Bank; Dir-Gen. THÉOPHILE MATONDO MBUNGU.

DEVELOPMENT ORGANIZATIONS

Agence Congolaise des Grands Travaux: 1 blvd du 30 juin, Commune de la Gombe, Kinshasa; tel. and fax 816909241 (mobile); e-mail contact@acgt.cd; internet acgt.cd; f. 2008; Dir-Gen. CHARLES MÉDARD ILUNGA MWAMBA.

Caisse de Stabilisation Cotonnière (CSCo): BP 3058, Kinshasa-Gombe; tel. (12) 31206; f. 1978 to replace Office National des Fibres Textiles; acts as an intermediary between the Govt, cotton ginners and textile factories, and co-ordinates international financing of cotton sector.

Centre National d'Appui au Développement et à la Participation Populaire (CENADEP): 1150 ave Tabora, Barumbu, BP 14582, Kinshasa; tel. 819982097; fax 17754027683; e-mail info@cenadep.net; internet www.cenadep.net; f. 1999; Pres. BAUDOUIN HAMULI; Dir-Gen. DANNI SYNGOMA.

La Générale des Carrières et des Mines (GÉCAMINES): 419 blvd Kamanyola, BP 450, Lubumbashi; tel. (2) 341105; fax (2) 341041; e-mail info@gecamines.cd; internet www.gecamines.cd; f. 1967 to acquire assets of Union Minière du Haut-Katanga; engaged in mining and marketing of copper, cobalt, zinc and coal; also has interests in agriculture; Pres. ALBERT YUMA MULIMBI; Dir-Gen. AHMED KALEJ NKAND.

Institut National pour l'Etude et la Recherche Agronomiques (INERA): BP 1513, Kisangani; internet www.inera-drc.org; f. 1933; agricultural research.

Office National du Café: ave Général Bobozo 1082, BP 8931, Kinshasa 1; tel. (12) 77144; internet www.onc-rdc.cd; f. 1979; state agency for coffee and also cocoa, tea, quinquina and pyrethrum; Dir-Gen. ALBERT KASONGO.

CHAMBER OF COMMERCE

Chambre de Commerce, d'Industrie et d'Agriculture du Congo: 10 ave des Aviateurs, BP 7247, Kinshasa 1; tel. (12) 22286; Pres. ILUNGA KONYA.

EMPLOYERS' ASSOCIATIONS

Fédération des Entreprises du Congo: 10 ave des Aviateurs, BP 7247, Kinshasa; tel. 812488890 (mobile); fax 812488909 (mobile); e-mail fec@ckt.cd; internet www.fec.cd; f. 1972 as the Association Nationale des Entreprises du Zaïre; name changed as above in 1997; represents business interests for both domestic and foreign institutions; Pres. ALBERT YUMA MULIMBI.

Confédération Nationale de Producteurs Agricoles du Congo (CONAPAC): 4746 ave de la Gombe, Kinshasa; tel. 998286456 (mobile); e-mail conapacrdc@yahoo.fr; f. 2011; Pres. PALUKU MIVIMBA.

UTILITIES

Electricity

Société Nationale d'Electricité (SNEL): 2831 ave de la Justice, BP 500, Kinshasa; tel. 815041639 (mobile); e-mail cco@snel.cd; internet www.snel.cd; f. 1970; state-owned; Pres. MAKOMBO MONGA MAWAWI; Dir-Gen. ERIC MBALA MUSANDA.

Water

Régie de Distribution d'Eau (REGIDESO): 59–63 blvd du 30 juin, BP 12599, Kinshasa; tel. (88) 45125; e-mail courrier@regidesordc.com; internet www.regidesordc.com; f. 1978; water supply admin; Pres. ROMBEAU FUMANI GIBANDI; Dir-Gen. JACQUES MUKALAY MWEMA.

TRADE UNIONS

The Union Nationale des Travailleurs du Congo was founded in 1967 as the sole organization. In 1990 the establishment of independent trade unions was legalized.

Confédération Démocratique du Travail: BP 10897, Quartier Industriel, C/Limete, Kinshasa 1; tel. (88) 0457311; e-mail cdtcongo@yahoo.fr; Pres. LIÉVIN KALUBI.

Confédération Syndicale du Congo: 81 ave Tombalbaye, Kinshasa-Gombe; tel. 898922090 (mobile); fax (13) 98126; e-mail csc_congo@hotmail.com; internet www.csc.cd; f. 1991; Pres. GUY KOLELA TSHIBANGU.

Union Nationale des Travailleurs du Congo: 5 ave Mutombo Katshi, Commune de la Gombe, BP 8814, Kinshasa; tel. 998616193 (mobile); e-mail untcrdc@yahoo.fr; internet www.untc-congo.org; f. 1967; comprises 14 unions; Pres. MODESTE AMÉDÉE NDONGALA N'SIBU.

Transport

Office National des Transports (ONATRA): BP 98, Kinshasa 1; tel. (12) 21457; fax (12) 1398632; e-mail onatradf@ic.cd; f. 1935; operates 12,674 km of waterways, 366 km of railways, and road and air transport; administers ports of Matadi, Boma and Banana; Man. Dir RAYMOND GEORGES.

RAILWAYS

In 2008 the rail network totalled 4,007 km, of which 858 km were electrified. The main line runs from Lubumbashi to Ilebo. International services run to Dar es Salaam (Tanzania) and Lobito (Angola), and also connect with the Zambian, Zimbabwean, Mozambican and South African systems. In 1997 the railway system was nationalized. Under a major investment programme agreed with the People's Republic of China in the late 2000s, the rail network was to be extensively modernized.

Kinshasa–Matadi Railway: BP 98, Kinshasa 1; 366 km operated by ONATRA; Pres. JACQUES MBELOLO BITWEMI.

Société Nationale des Chemins de Fer du Congo (SNCC): 115 pl. de la Gare, BP 297, Lubumbashi; tel. (2) 346306; fax (2) 342254; e-mail sncc01@ic-libum.cd; f. 1974; 3,641 km (including 858 km electrified); administers all internal railway sections as well as river transport and transport on Lakes Tanganyika and Kivu; management contract concluded with a Belgian-South African corpn, Sizarail, in 1995 for the management of the Office des Chemins de Fer du Sud (OCS) and the Société des Chemins de Fer de l'Est (SFE) subsidiaries, with rail networks of 2,835 km and 1,286 km, respectively; assets of Sizarail nationalized and returned to SNCC control in May 1997; CEO FREDDY STRUMANE.

ROADS

In 2004 there were an estimated 154,000 km of roads, of which some 42,000 km were highways. Following the installation of transitional authorities in July 2003, an extensive infrastructure rehabilitation programme, financed by external donors, including the World Bank, was initiated. Work on a principal road, connecting the south-western town of Moanda with Kinshasa and Lubumbashi, commenced late that year. Under a major investment programme agreed with the People's Republic of China in the late 2000s, modernization of the road network (which remained in a very poor state of repair) was to be undertaken, including the construction of a major highway linking Katanga to the Kisangani river port and the building of a new ring road around Kinshasa.

Office des Routes: 1 ave Office des Routes, BP 10899, Kinshasa-Gombe; tel. (12) 32036; e-mail info@officedesroutes.cd; internet www.officedesroutes.cd; construction and maintenance of roads; Man. Dir MUTIMA BATRIMU HERMAN.

INLAND WATERWAYS

The River Congo is navigable for more than 1,600 km. Above the Stanley Falls the Congo becomes the Lualaba, and is navigable along a 965-km stretch from Ubundu to Kindu and Kongolo to Bukama. The River Kasaï, a tributary of the River Congo, is navigable by shipping as far as Ilebo, at which the line from Lubumbashi terminates. The total length of inland waterways is 14,935 km.

Régie des Voies Fluviales: 109 ave Lumpungu, Kinshasa-Gombe, BP 11697, Kinshasa 1; tel. (12) 26526; fax (12) 42580; f. 1971; administers river navigation; Pres. BENJAMIN MUKULUNGU; Dir-Gen. RUFFIN NGOMPER ILUNGA.

Société Congolaise des Chemins de Fer des Grands Lacs: River Lualaba services: Bubundu–Kindu and Kongolo–Malemba N'kula; Lake Tanganyika services: Kamina–Kigoma–Kalundu–Moba–Mpulungu; Pres. and Gen. Man. KIBWE MBUYU KAKUDJI.

SHIPPING

The principal seaports are Matadi, Boma and Banana on the lower Congo. The port of Matadi has more than 1.6 km of quays and can accommodate up to 10 deep-water vessels. Matadi is linked by rail with Kinshasa. At 31 December 2013 the DRC's flag registered fleet comprised 19 vessels, totalling 13,244 grt.

Lignes Maritimes Congolaises SA: Immeuble AMICONGO-LMC, 6ème étage, ave des Aviateurs 13, pl. de la Poste, Gombe, BP 9496, Kinshasa; tel. 856485395 (mobile); e-mail info@lmc.cd; internet www.lmc.cd; f. 1974; fmrly Compagnie Maritime du Congo, name changed as above in 2009; services: North Africa, Europe, North America and Asia to West Africa, East Africa to North Africa; Dir-Gen. CAROLINE MAWANDJI MASALA.

CIVIL AVIATION

International airports are located at Ndjili (for Kinshasa), Luano (for Lubumbashi), Bukavu, Goma and Kisangani. There are smaller airports and airstrips dispersed throughout the country.

Blue Airlines: BP 1115, Barumbu, Kinshasa 1; tel. (12) 20455; f. 1991; regional and domestic charter services for passengers and cargo; Man. T. MAYANI.

Congo Express: Kinshasa; f. 2010; operates from Kinshasa to Lubumbashi and Mbuji-Mayi; Man. Dir DIDIER KINDAMBU.

Fly Congo: 1928 ave Kabambare, BP 1284, Kinshasa; tel. 817005015 (mobile); f. 2012 to replace Hewa Bora Airways; international, regional and domestic scheduled services for passengers and cargo; Dir-Gen. JEAN-MARC PAJOT.

Korongo Airlines: 1939 ave M'siri, Lubumbashi; tel. 996030101 (mobile); internet www.flykorongo.com; f. 2010; commenced operations in April 2012; majority owned by Brussels Airlines (Belgium); Dir-Gen. CHRISTOPHE ALLARD.

Lignes Aériennes Congolaises (LAC): 4 ave du Port, Kinshasa-Gombe, BP 8552, Kinshasa 1; tel. 815042422 (mobile); e-mail info@lacrdc.com; internet www.lacrdc.com; f. 1961; Pres. LOUISE L. LONGANGE; Man. Dir PAUL KYAMBALE.

Malila Airlift: ave Basoko 188, BP 11526, Kinshasa-Gombe; tel. (88) 46428; fax 1-5304817707 (satellite); e-mail malila.airlift@ic.cd; internet malift.isuisse.com; f. 1996; regional services; Man. VÉRONIQUE MALILA.

Tourism

The country offers extensive lake and mountain scenery, although tourism remains largely undeveloped. In 2011 tourist arrivals totalled 186,000. Receipts from tourism amounted to an estimated US $11m. in that year.

Office National du Tourisme: 2A/2B ave des Orangers, BP 9502, Kinshasa-Gombe; tel. (12) 30070; f. 1959; Man. Dir BOTOLO MAGOZA.

Société Congolaise de l'Hôtellerie: Immeuble Memling, BP 1076, Kinshasa; tel. (12) 23260; Man. N'JOLI BALANGA.

Defence

The total strength of the armed forces of the Democratic Republic of the Congo, as assessed at November 2013, was estimated at 134,250 (central staff 14,000; army 103,000; Republican Guard 8,000; navy 6,700; air force 2,550). The UN Organization Stabilization Mission in the Democratic Republic of Congo (MONUSCO) has a maximum authorized strength of about 22,000 personnel. MONUSCO has a mandate to remain in the country until the end of March 2015 and in March 2013 was the first ever UN peacekeeping mission to be authorized to carry out 'offensive combat operations'. To this end, a specialized 'intervention brigade' was created within the operation's existing 19,815-strong force.

Defence Expenditure: Estimated at CF 393,000m. in 2013.

Commander-in-Chief: Maj.-Gen. JOSEPH KABILA KABANGE.

Chief of Staff of the Armed Forces: Lt-Gen. DIEUDONNE KAYEMBE MBANDAKULU.

Chief of Staff of the Army: Lt-Gen. DIDIER ETUMBA.

Chief of Staff of the Navy: Vice-Adm. DIDIER LONGILA.

Chief of Staff of the Air Force: Maj.-Gen. RIGOBERT MASAMBA MUSUNGUI.

Education

Primary education, beginning at six years of age and lasting for six years, is officially compulsory and is available free of charge in public institutions. Secondary education, which is not compulsory, begins at 12 years of age and lasts for up to six years, comprising a first cycle of two years and a second of four years. In 2012, according to UNESCO estimates, primary enrolment was equivalent to 111% of pupils (118% of boys; 104% of girls), while the comparable ratio for secondary enrolment was 43% (54% of boys; 32% of girls). There are four universities, located at Kinshasa, Kinshasa/Limete, Kisangani and Lubumbashi. In 2011/12 there were a total of 511,251 students (330,050 males, 181,201 females) enrolled in tertiary education. In 2010 spending on education represented 8.9% of total budgetary expenditure.

THE REPUBLIC OF THE CONGO

Introductory Survey

LOCATION, CLIMATE, LANGUAGE, RELIGION, FLAG, CAPITAL

The Republic of the Congo is an equatorial country on the west coast of Africa. It has a coastline of about 170 km on the Atlantic Ocean, from which the country extends northward to Cameroon and the Central African Republic. The Republic of the Congo is bordered by Gabon to the west and the Democratic Republic of the Congo to the east, while in the south there is a short frontier with the Cabinda exclave of Angola. The climate is tropical, with temperatures averaging 21°C–27°C (70°F–80°F) throughout the year. The average annual rainfall is about 1,640 mm (65 ins). The official language is French; Kituba, Lingala and other African languages are also used. Some 40% of the population follow traditional animist beliefs and about 57% are Roman Catholics. There are small Protestant and Muslim minorities. The national flag (proportions 2 by 3) comprises a yellow stripe running diagonally from lower hoist to upper fly, separating a green triangle at the hoist from a red triangle in the fly. The capital is Brazzaville.

CONTEMPORARY POLITICAL HISTORY

Historical Context

Formerly part of French Equatorial Africa, Middle Congo became the autonomous Republic of the Congo, within the French Community, in November 1958, with Abbé Fulbert Youlou as Prime Minister, and subsequently as President when the Congo became fully independent on 15 August 1960. Youlou relinquished office in August 1963, following a period of internal unrest, and was succeeded by Alphonse Massamba-Débat, initially as Prime Minister, and from December as President. In July 1964 the Mouvement National de la Révolution (MNR) was established as the sole political party. In August 1968 Massamba-Débat was overthrown in a military coup, led by Capt. (later Maj.) Marien Ngouabi, who was proclaimed President in January 1969. A new Marxist-Leninist party, the Parti Congolais du Travail (PCT), replaced the MNR, and in January 1970 the country was renamed the People's Republic of the Congo. In March 1977 Ngouabi was assassinated, and in April Col (later Brig.-Gen.) Jacques-Joachim Yhombi-Opango, the head of the armed forces, became the new Head of State. In February 1979 Yhombi-Opango surrendered his powers to a Provisional Committee appointed by the PCT. In March the head of the Provisional Committee, Col (later Gen.) Denis Sassou-Nguesso, became Chairman of the PCT Central Committee and President of the Republic. In July 1989 Sassou-Nguesso, the sole candidate, was re-elected Chairman of the PCT and President of the Republic for a third five-year term. At legislative elections in September the PCT-approved list of 133 candidates (which included, for the first time, non-party candidates) was endorsed by 99.2% of voters.

Progress towards political reform dominated the latter half of 1990. In August several political prisoners were released, among them Yhombi-Opango, and in September the Central Committee of the PCT agreed to the immediate registration of new political parties. The party formulated constitutional amendments legalizing a multi-party system, which took effect in January 1991. Gen. Louis Sylvain Goma was appointed Prime Minister (a position he had held in 1975–84), to lead an interim Government.

A National Conference, chaired by the Roman Catholic Bishop of Owando, Ernest N'Kombo, was convened in February 1991; opposition movements were allocated seven of the 11 seats on the Conference's governing body. Having voted to establish itself as a sovereign body, in April the Conference announced proposals to abrogate the Constitution and dissolve the legislature. In June a 153-member legislative Haut Conseil de la République (High Council of the Republic—HCR) was established, chaired by N'Kombo. From June the Prime Minister replaced the President as Chairman of the Council of Ministers, and the country's official name reverted to the Republic of the Congo. A new Prime Minister, André Milongo (a former World Bank official), was appointed in June.

Domestic Political Affairs

In March 1992 a new Constitution, which provided for legislative power to be vested in an elected Assemblée Nationale (National Assembly) and Sénat (Senate) and for executive power to be held by an elected President, was approved by 96.3% of voters at a national referendum. At elections to the National Assembly, held in June and July, the Union Panafricaine pour la Démocratie Sociale (UPADS) won 39 of the 125 seats, the Mouvement Congolais pour la Démocratie et le Développement Intégral (MCDDI) 29 seats and the PCT 18 seats. At indirect elections to the Senate, held in July, the UPADS won the largest share (23) of the 60 seats, followed by the MCDDI, with 13 seats. At the first round of presidential voting in August, Pascal Lissouba, the leader of the UPADS (and Prime Minister in 1963–66), won the largest share of the votes cast (35.9%); of the 15 other candidates, his closest rival was Bernard Kolélas of the MCDDI (22.9%). Sassou-Nguesso took 16.9% of the votes cast. At a second round of voting two weeks later, Lissouba defeated Kolélas, with 61.3% of the votes cast.

Lissouba took office as President in August 1992. Maurice-Stéphane Bongho-Nouarra, of the UPADS, was appointed as Prime Minister. Meanwhile, the Union pour le Renouveau Démocratique (URD), a new alliance of seven parties, including the MCDDI, formed a coalition with the PCT (thereby establishing a parliamentary majority), which succeeded in winning a vote of no confidence against the Government in October. In November the Government resigned, and shortly afterwards Lissouba dissolved the National Assembly and announced that fresh legislative elections would be held. In December Claude Antoine Dacosta, a former World Bank official, was appointed Prime Minister and formed a transitional Government, comprising members of all the main political parties.

At the first round of elections to the National Assembly, which took place in May 1993, the Mouvance Présidentielle (MP), an electoral coalition of the UPADS and its allies, won 62 of the 125 seats, while the URD-PCT coalition secured 49. Protesting that serious electoral irregularities had occurred, the URD-PCT refused to contest the second round of elections in June, after which the MP held an absolute majority (69) of seats in the legislature. President Lissouba appointed a new Council of Ministers, with Yhombi-Opango as Prime Minister. Later in June the Supreme Court ruled that electoral irregularities had occurred at the first round of elections, and in August, following external mediation, the Government and the opposition agreed to repeat the second round of elections.

Following the repeated elections, held in October 1993, the MP retained its majority in the National Assembly, with 65 seats. In September six opposition parties formed an alliance, the Forces Démocratiques Unies (FDU), headed by Sassou-Nguesso and affiliated with the URD. In December Lissouba and the two main opposition leaders—Sassou-Nguesso and Kolélas—signed an agreement seeking a permanent end to hostilities between their supporters.

In February 1997 some 19 opposition parties issued a number of demands, including the expedited establishment of republican institutions, the creation of an independent electoral commission, the disarmament of civilians and the deployment of a multinational peacekeeping force. A fierce national conflict along ethnic and political lines developed and, despite mediation, none of the numerous ceasefire agreements signed during mid-1997 endured. In June French troops assisted in the evacuation of foreign residents from Brazzaville, and later in the month themselves departed. In September Lissouba appointed a Government of National Unity, under the premiership of Kolélas.

Sassou-Nguesso takes power

In October 1997 Sassou-Nguesso's forces, assisted by Angolan government troops, won control of Brazzaville and the strategic port of Pointe-Noire. Lissouba and Kolélas both found refuge abroad. Sassou-Nguesso was inaugurated as President on 25 October; he appointed a new transitional Government in November. It was later announced that a Conseil National de Transition (National Transitional Council—CNT) was to hold legislative power, pending the approval of a new constitution by referendum (scheduled for 2001), and subsequent elections.

Throughout 1998 clashes continued in the southern Pool region, a stronghold of the militia loyal to Kolélas. In December a battle for control of Brazzaville broke out between forces loyal to Kolélas (who remained in exile), reputedly supported by Angolan rebel groups, and Congolese government forces. Later that month government forces, aided by Angolan troops, also launched offensives against Kolélas' forces in the south and west of the country. By March 1999 the rebel militias had been obliged to withdraw to Pool. Following discussions in Libreville, Gabon, mediated by Gabonese President Omar Bongo, representatives of the armed forces and of the rebel militias signed a peace agreement in December. In May 2000 Kolélas and his nephew, Col Philippe Bikinkita, the Minister of the Interior in the previous Lissouba administration, were convicted, *in absentia*, of operating personal prisons in Brazzaville and of mistreating prisoners and causing their deaths during the 1997 civil war. Kolélas and Bikinkita, both in exile abroad, were sentenced to death and ordered to pay compensation to their victims.

In November 2000 the Government adopted a draft Constitution, which included provisions for the institution of an executive presidency and a bicameral legislature. The Head of State would be elected for a term of seven years, renewable only once. In December it was announced that some 13,000 weapons had been surrendered and 12,000 militiamen disarmed in the past year, although UN sources suggested that this represented less than one-half of the total number of militiamen in the Congo. Some 2,200 delegates from public institutions, civic associations and political parties attended a series of regional debates during March 2001, reportedly reaching a consensus on the draft Constitution.

A new Constitution was approved by 84.5% of votes cast at the referendum that took place on 20 January 2002, with a participation rate of 77.5% of the electorate. In February the Supreme Court approved 10 presidential candidates, including Sassou-Nguesso and Milongo. In March three opposition candidates, including Milongo, who had been widely regarded as the sole credible challenger to Sassou-Nguesso, and who now headed the Union pour la Démocratie et la République (UDR—Mwinda), withdrew from the election. Milongo urged his supporters to boycott the poll, stating that his concerns about the transparency of electoral procedures and the impartiality of the Commission Nationale d'Organisation des Elections (CONEL) remained unresolved. With all the major opposition candidates thereby excluded, Sassou-Nguesso won an overwhelming victory at the presidential election, which was held on 10 March, securing 89.4% of the votes cast. According to official figures, 69.4% of the electorate participated in the election.

Conflict in the Pool region

Meanwhile, in late March 2002 renewed violence erupted in the Pool region, apparently instigated by members of a 'Ninja' militia group, led by Rev. Frédéric Bitsangou (Ntumi), which attacked the town of Kindamba, prompting several thousand civilians to flee. By mid-April the unrest had spread to southern Brazzaville. Later that month government forces announced that they had regained control of the railway, allowing a normalization in the supply of fuel and food to Brazzaville, although fighting continued in Pool. At the end of May government troops regained control of the rebel stronghold of Vindza.

The first round of elections to the 137-member National Assembly took place on 26 May 2002. As a result of the unrest in Pool, voting was postponed indefinitely in eight constituencies, while disruption caused by protesters and administrative irregularities necessitated a rerun of polling in a further 12 constituencies on 28–29 May. Turnout in the first round, at which the PCT and its allies in the FDU won 38 of the 51 seats decided, was around 65%. Prior to the second round, the security situation in Brazzaville deteriorated markedly. In mid-June, while Sassou-Nguesso was in Italy, Ninja troops attacked the capital's main military base resulting in the deaths of 72 rebels, three army officers and 15 civilians. Despite requests by the UDR—Mwinda for a postponement of the elections in those areas where fighting had occurred, voting went ahead on 23 June, although the rate of participation, at an estimated 30% nationwide, was appreciably lower than in the first round, and was as low as 10% in some constituencies in Brazzaville and in Pointe-Noire. Following the polls, supporters of Sassou-Nguesso held an absolute majority in the new Assembly; the PCT emerged as the largest party, with 53 seats, while the FDU alliance, by this stage comprising some 29 parties, held a total of 30 seats. The UDR—Mwinda became the largest opposition party, with six seats, while the UPADS held four seats. Notably, the MCDDI failed to secure parliamentary representation.

Following local and municipal elections, held on 30 June 2002, the Senate comprised 56 supporters of the President (44 from the PCT and 12 from the FDU), two representatives of civil society organizations, one independent and one member of the opposition. In early August Jean-Pierre Thystère Tchicaya, the leader of the Rassemblement pour la Démocratie et le Progrès Social, one of the constituent parties of the FDU, was elected as President of the National Assembly, and the Secretary-General of the PCT, Ambroise-Edouard Noumazalay, was elected as President of the Senate. Sassou-Nguesso was inaugurated as elected President on 14 August; later in the month he announced the formation of a new Government, which, notably, included no representatives of the opposition (although several representatives from civil society were appointed to ministerial positions).

During the second half of 2002 sporadic attacks by 'Ninja' militias in the Pool region, in particular against freight trains on the Congo–Océan railway, intensified. In November Sassou-Nguesso announced that a 'safe passage' would be provided from Pool to Brazzaville until mid-December for fighters who surrendered their arms, reiterating that the terms of the peace agreement concluded in 1999 remained valid. Despite an extension of the amnesty offered by Sassou-Nguesso, fewer than 500 rebels had surrendered by January 2003, and in February the first outbreak of violence in the neighbouring Bouenza region since 1999 was reported. None the less, in March 2003 the Government and Ntumi's 'Ninja' militia group signed a peace agreement. It was reported that at least 2,300 rebels had surrendered their weapons by April. In August the National Assembly formally approved an amnesty for former 'Ninja' fighters, to cover the period from January 2000. By September 2003 the situation in Pool had stabilized sufficiently to allow an electoral commission to be formed in the region; the delayed local and legislative elections were due to be held in 2005.

In October 2004 the rail service between Brazzaville and Pointe-Noire was suspended following a series of attacks on trains in the Pool region. Ntumi denied claims that the attacks had been perpetrated by his Ninja rebel group, by now also known as the Conseil National de la Résistance (CNR), and demanded an independent inquiry into the incidents. Meanwhile, displaced persons who had fled hostilities in Pool continued to return gradually during 2004 with government assistance, although reports suggested that armed fighters continued to intimidate civilians, despite the peace agreement signed in March 2003. (It was estimated that between 100,000 and 147,000 people had fled Pool between 1998 and 2002, and that by late 2004 most towns and villages in the region had regained no more than two-thirds of their original populations.)

Towards conciliation

In January 2005 President Sassou-Nguesso effected a reorganization of the Council of Ministers. The new post of Prime Minister was awarded to Isidore Mvouba, hitherto Minister of State, Minister of Transport and Privatization, responsible for the Coordination of Government Action, and a native of the Pool region, while the hitherto deputy Governor of the Banque des Etats de l'Afrique Centrale, Pacifique Issoïbeka, was appointed as Minister of the Economy, Finance and the Budget. Opposition figures criticized the creation of the post of Prime Minister, claiming that it was in violation of the 2002 Constitution, which had enshrined presidential control over the executive.

In March 2005 the Government initiated a new programme for the disarmament, demobilization and reintegration of former combatants in Pool, where instability persisted. In May it was announced that the Government had commenced power-sharing talks with the CNR, with the aim of bringing members of the movement into 'all national institutions' (although the holding of legislative elections in the region was again postponed).

Indirect partial elections to renew one-half of the seats in the Senate were held, as scheduled, on 2 October 2005, after which the PCT continued to hold an absolute majority of seats in the chamber, although its representation was reduced from 44 senators to 39. Most opposition parties boycotted these elections, and, partly in consequence, several independent representatives were elected.

In mid-October 2005 at least six people were killed in clashes in southern Brazzaville between 'Ninja' fighters and pro-Government troops. The outbreak of violence followed the return of Kolélas to the Congo, to attend the funeral of his wife (who had died in Paris, France). President Sassou-Nguesso subsequently requested that the legislature grant amnesty to Kolélas, in the interests of national reconciliation; legislation to that end was duly approved on 6 December, and the death sentence issued *in absentia* against the former Prime Minister in May 2000 was overturned. The Minister of Justice and Human Rights, Gabriel Entcha Ebia, stated that private citizens would, none the less, retain the right to file lawsuits against Kolélas. Several days after the granting of amnesty, Kolélas issued an apology to the Congolese people for his role in instigating the 1997 civil conflict.

Unrest in the south of the country continued into 2006. In March Ntumi insisted on the creation of an agreement on 'political partnership' between the Government and the CNR (which, as a political force, was subsequently renamed the Conseil National des Républicains) as a condition for complete disarmament of his troops. In March the acting President of the UPADS, Pascal Gamassa, asked that the party be pardoned, in the name of former President Lissouba, for its role in the 1997 civil war.

The 2007 legislative elections

In January 2007 Sassou-Nguesso resigned from the presidency of the PCT, citing Article 72 of the Constitution which rendered incompatible the functions of the Head of State with those of a party leader. In February it was announced that the first and second rounds of legislative elections would be held on 24 June and 22 July, respectively.

The first round of the legislative elections (which was boycotted by several opposition parties) took place as scheduled on 24 June 2007; the PCT took 23 of the initial 44 seats available. However, allegations of widespread malpractice and procedural irregularities threatened to undermine the legitimacy of the poll and the results in 19 constituencies were annulled. A new ballot was held in those areas, although the announcement of the results was delayed until 19 July, prompting the postponement (until 5 August) of the second round of the elections. Following the second round of voting, the PCT held 46 of the 137 seats in the National Assembly, according to official results; the MCDDI and the UPADS each secured 11 seats.

In early December 2007 André Obami Itou was elected President of the Senate, following the death the previous month of Noumazalay. Also in December 58 political parties loyal to the President formed an alliance, the Rassemblement de la Majorité Présidentielle (RMP), led by the PCT, to contest local and senatorial elections in 2008 and the presidential election in July 2009. At elections for 42 of the 72 seats in the enlarged Senate (membership of that body had been increased from 66 following the creation of Pointe-Noire département), held on 5 August 2008, the RMP secured 33 seats, while independent candidates won seven seats and the UPADS two.

The 2009 presidential election

In December 2008 13 opposition parties, including the UPADS, signed a declaration requesting the suspension of the revision of electoral lists, and stating that dialogue regarding the organization of the presidential election planned for July 2009 had not been held prior to the revision of the lists. In April a 'Republican dialogue' between the Government, clergy, diplomatic corps and deputies of the ruling parties was boycotted by opposition parties which also demanded the dissolution of the CONEL (which had been mandated at the four-day meeting in Brazzaville to organize the elections) and the establishment of a joint and inclusive electoral commission.

The presidential election, held on 12 July 2009, was contested by 13 candidates. (Former Prime Minister Ange Edouard Poungui had been selected as the presidential candidate of the UPADS, but his candidature was rejected by the Constitutional Court on the grounds that he had not been resident in the country for two years prior to the election.) According to provisional figures, Sassou-Nguesso was re-elected to the presidency with 78.6% of the votes, independent candidate Joseph Kignoumbi Kia Mbougou was placed second with 7.5% of the ballot, followed by Nicéphore Fylla de Saint-Eudes of the Parti Républicain et Libéral, who took 7.0% of the votes.

The African Union (AU, see p. 186) issued a joint statement with the Communauté Economique des Etats de l'Afrique Centrale (CEEAC, see p. 450) that endorsed the conduct of the elections. However, a national human rights organization, the Observatoire Congolais des Droits Humains, reported 'fraud and irregularities'. Independent observers claimed that the electoral register had been inflated by 458,000 'ghost' voters and that opposition press conferences had been prevented from taking place on the grounds that they were unauthorized public rallies. The election results were validated in late July 2009 by the Constitutional Court, which also rejected five applications from opposition candidates for the outcome to be annulled. Travel restrictions were imposed on several opposition leaders, due to their participation in post-election protest rallies, all of which had been banned by the authorities.

President Sassou-Nguesso carried out a major government reorganization in September 2009: the position of Prime Minister was abolished and Isidore Mvouba took over as Minister of State, Co-ordinator of Basic Infrastructures, and Minister of Civil Aviation and of Maritime Trade, the most senior position in the Government. In addition to that of basic infrastructures, a further three principal portfolios were created (economy, sovereignty and socio-cultural issues). Meanwhile, in Paris the Congolese opposition in exile formed a parallel 'government' led by Tony Gilbert Moudilou, a former adviser to Kolélas (who died in November), and appealed for the dismantling of the Sassou-Nguesso 'dictatorship'.

In October 2010 Congolese security forces commenced operations to restore civil order in the Pool region and to prepare for the rehabilitation of basic infrastructures, including the construction of a road linking the main town of Kinkala to Brazzaville. Police officers and members of the armed forces were initially to identify areas where they could safely establish bases, before taking steps to reduce incidences of banditry and disruption to the Brazzaville–Point Noire railway line.

On 9 October 2011 the PCT and allied parties of the RMP overwhelmingly won partial elections to the Senate that were held in six of the country's 12 départments, securing 33 of the 36 contested seats. (The UPADS held only four seats overall in the Senate.) In November the Congolese Government announced that it had initiated a dialogue with opposition parties and civil society groups over the conduct of forthcoming legislative elections in 2012, with discussions focusing on revision of the electoral register and the restructuring of the CONEL, following demands from opposition parties, civil society organizations and international observers for the adoption of reforms.

The 2012 legislative elections

A series of explosions caused by a fire in a munitions depot at an army barracks in Brazzaville in March 2012 resulted in some 300 deaths, severe infrastructural damage and the displacement of some 14,000 people. The Government, which suggested that the incident was related to an attempted coup, pledged to pay compensation to those affected. Of 32 soldiers subsequently charged (with arson, breach of state security and the illegal possession of armaments) at the Brazzaville criminal court in connection with the munitions depot fire, in September 2013 one officer was sentenced to 15 years' imprisonment, while a further five received short terms; the remaining 26 defendants were acquitted.

As had been agreed during the consultations conducted by the Government with political parties and civil society groups in late 2011, legislation that, *inter alia*, provided for an increase in the number of deputies in the National Assembly from 137 to 139 was adopted in May 2012. Elections to the National Assembly took place on 15 July and 5 August, following a slight delay owing to the explosions at the arms depot in March. The PCT consolidated its position as the largest party in the lower chamber, securing an absolute majority, with 89 of the 136 seats contested, followed by the MCDDI and the UPADS, which each won only seven seats (both parties recording a poorer performance than in the 2007 polls); 12 independent candidates were elected. The PCT and allied parties secured a total of 117 seats in the National Assembly. (The term of three previous parliamentary deputies was extended, since voting was not conducted in three Brazzaville constituencies affected by the March 2012 explosions.) Opposition parties accused the PCT of malpractice, while AU and Communauté Economique et Monétaire de l'Afrique Centrale (CEMAC, see p. 330) observers reported irregularities in the conduct of the elections. In September President Sassou-Nguesso reorganized the Government, appointing Charles Richard Mondjo as Minister at the Presidency, responsible for National Defence. In October a group of opposition parties dispatched a public letter to Sassou-Nguesso denouncing a perceived crisis in the country, particularly with regard to a lack of personal freedom, and demanding that a national sovereign dialogue be convened.

Recent developments: hostilities in Brazzaville

In December 2013 at least 22 people were killed in a military confrontation in Brazzaville when an attempt by government forces to search the residence of a former deputy head of the National Security Council, Colonel Marcel Ntsourou, was resisted by his security personnel. Ntsourou subsequently surrendered to the authorities and was detained. It was reported that President Sassou-Nguesso had suspected Ntsourou, who in September had received a five-year suspended sentence in connection with the fire at the munitions depot, of planning dissident activity; Ntsourou had denounced the charges against him as having been politically motivated.

Foreign Affairs

Since the 1997 civil war the principal aims of Congolese foreign policy have been to gain international recognition for the legitimacy of the Sassou-Nguesso Government and to ensure the continued support of the country's bilateral and multilateral donors. During the war President Lissouba accused France of favouring the rebel forces of Sassou-Nguesso (who was reported to have allied himself with French petroleum interests) over the elected administration. In May 1998 France extended its formal recognition to the Sassou-Nguesso Government, and in June resumed aid payments that had been suspended since the 1997 conflict. Relations between France and the Congo deteriorated from mid-2002, as a result of an investigation by a French court into several Congolese officials, including Sassou-Nguesso, in connection with the reported disappearance of 353 Congolese citizens, following their return from asylum in the Democratic Republic of the Congo (DRC) in 1999. In December 2002 the Congo filed a case against France at the International Court of Justice (ICJ) in The Hague, Netherlands, claiming that the investigations represented a violation of Congolese sovereignty and disregarded Sassou-Nguesso's immunity as a Head of State. In November 2010 the French Court of Cassation ruled that investigations into the financial transactions of Sassou-Nguesso in France could proceed. Charges had been brought by Transparency International, which maintained that Sassou-Nguesso and members of his family had used Congolese public funds in order to purchase property in France and had opened as many as 112 bank accounts in that country.

Relations between the Republic of the Congo and the DRC steadily improved from the late 1990s. In December 1998 the two countries signed a non-aggression pact and agreed to establish a joint force to guarantee border security. In December 1999 Sassou-Nguesso met President Laurent-Désiré Kabila in order to discuss bilateral co-operation and the implementation of the tripartite Luanda accord, and further discussion on issues of common interest subsequently took place regularly between the two countries. In May 2001 some 19 DRC nationals suspected of involvement in the assassination of Laurent-Désiré Kabila in January were extradited from the Congo to Kinshasa, DRC. In April 2005 the repatriation of some 57,000 refugees from the Congo to the DRC's Equateur province commenced under an agreement signed in September 2004 between the two countries and the office of the UN High Commissioner for Refugees (UNHCR); by October 2007 a total of 36,000 refugees had returned to Equateur province since the programme began. However, persistent instability in the east of the DRC from late 2009 resulted in further influxes of refugees. According to UNHCR estimates, more than 66,000 refugees remained in the Congo at the end of 2013, of whom 57,350 were from the DRC.

By the mid-2000s Sassou-Nguesso's attempts to obtain international legitimacy for his regime had been largely successful. In 2003 Sassou-Nguesso chaired the CEEAC (see p. 450) and also the CEMAC. In January 2006 Sassou-Nguesso was elected as head of the AU for a one-year term. The Republic of the Congo contributed troops to a CEEAC peacekeeping force deployed in the Central African Republic (CAR) from 2008. In May 2013 Brazzaville hosted the inaugural meeting of an international contact group that was established to address the mounting instability in the CAR, after its President had been forced to flee the country in March. Later in May Sassou-Nguesso announced that the Congolese contingent of the CEEAC force in the CAR was to be enlarged from some 150 troops to 350.

The Republic of the Congo's relations with the People's Republic of China have expanded, particularly following a visit to the Congo by Chinese Premier Wen Jiabao in 2006, when a strategic co-operation accord was signed. A visit to the Congo by Chinese President Xi Jinping in March 2013 (as part of his overseas tour after taking office earlier that month) was the first by a Chinese President since the establishment of diplomatic relations between the two countries in 1964. Xi pledged to strengthen co-operation further and a series of agreements were signed, which provided, *inter alia*, for the construction of a river port at the central town of Oyo and a seaport at Pointe-Noire. In December 2013 the Congolese Government and the China Railway Construction Corporation signed an agreement on the rehabilitation of the state railway.

CONSTITUTION AND GOVERNMENT

Under the terms of the 2002 Constitution, executive power is vested in a President, who is directly elected for a seven-year term, renewable only once. The President appoints a Council of Ministers. (The President appointed a Prime Minister in early 2005, although no explicit constitutional provision for such a post existed; in 2010 he abolished the role.) Legislative power is vested in a bicameral Parliament, comprising a 139-member Assemblée Nationale (National Assembly), which is directly elected for a five-year term, and a 72-member Sénat (Senate), which is indirectly elected by local councils for a six-year term (with one-half of the membership renewable every three years).

For administrative purposes, the country is divided into 12 départements, consisting of 86 districts (sous-préfectures) and seven municipalities (communes urbaines).

REGIONAL AND INTERNATIONAL CO-OPERATION

The Republic of the Congo is a member of the African Union (see p. 186), the Central African organs of the Franc Zone (see p. 329) and of the Communauté Economique des Etats de l'Afrique Centrale (CEEAC, see p. 450).

The Republic of the Congo became a member of the UN in 1960, and was admitted to the World Trade Organization (WTO, see p. 434) in 1997.

ECONOMIC AFFAIRS

In 2012, according to estimates by the World Bank, the Congo's gross national income (GNI), measured at average 2010–12 prices, was US $11,070m., equivalent to $2,550 per head (or $3,510 on an international purchasing-power parity basis). During 2003–12, it was estimated, the population increased at an average annual rate of 2.9%, while gross domestic product (GDP) per head increased, in real terms, by an average of 2.0% per year. Overall GDP increased, in real terms, at an average annual rate of 4.9% in 2003–12; it grew by 3.8% in 2012.

Agriculture (including forestry and fishing) contributed an estimated 3.3% of GDP in 2011, according to the African Development Bank (AfDB), and employed about 28.9% of the total labour force in mid-2014, according to FAO estimates. The staple crops are cassava, bananas and plantains, while the major cash crops are sugar cane and oil palm. In the mid-2000s cassava production declined owing to the spread of the cassava mosaic disease, leading to fears of widespread hunger in the country. Thousands of varieties created by the International Institute of Agricultural Technologies to be resistant to the disease were brought in from the Democratic Republic of the Congo and distributed throughout five départements in an attempt to improve food security. In 2012 the total production of cassava was estimated by FAO at 1.2m. metric tons, compared with some 800,000 tons in the mid-2000s. Forests cover about 66% of the country's total land area, and forestry is a major economic activity. In 2012 exports of wood provided 0.8% of export earnings. In 2009 Voluntary Partnership Agreement (VPA) on Forest Law Enhancement, Governance and Trade was signed with the European Union, which provided for the strict control of timber exportation and the prevention of illegal logging. According to the World Bank, during 2003–11 agricultural GDP increased at an average annual rate of 4.5%; in 2011 agricultural GDP grew by 8.4%.

Industry (including mining, manufacturing, construction and power) contributed an estimated 77.7% of GDP in 2011, according to the AfDB, and employed an estimated 14.7% of the labour force in 1990. During 2003–11, according to the World Bank, industrial GDP increased at an average annual rate of 4.7%; it grew by 11.6% in 2010, but contracted by 1.0% in 2011.

Mining contributed an estimated 70.5% of GDP in 2011, according to AfDB estimates. The hydrocarbons sector is the only significant mining activity. In 2012 sales of petroleum and petroleum products provided 78.9% of export earnings. Petroleum production (an estimated 295,708 barrels per day in 2012, according to the BP Statistical Review of World Energy) was expected to continue to increase, as a result of major exploration and development planned at various offshore deposits, in particular near to the maritime border with Angola. At the end of 2012 the Congo had estimated petroleum reserves of 1,600m. barrels, sufficient to sustain production at current levels for some

15 years. Deposits of natural gas are also exploited. Lead, zinc, gold and copper are produced in small quantities. According to the AfDB, the mining sector grew by 13.2% in 2010, but declined by 5.0% in 2011. There are also exploitable reserves of diamonds, phosphate, iron ore and bauxite. A joint venture with a Canadian company commenced in 2009 for the construction of a potash mining plant in Kouilou region aimed at placing the Congo among the world's leading producers of that commodity and which would create some 4,000 jobs.

Manufacturing contributed 2.8% of GDP in 2011, according to AfDB estimates. The most important industries, the processing of agricultural and forest products, were adversely affected by the civil conflict in the late 1990s, but recovered in the early 2000s, as political stability was restored. The textile, chemical and construction materials industries are also significant. According to the World Bank, during 2003–11 manufacturing GDP increased at an average annual rate of 7.5%; growth of 8.0% was recorded in 2011.

The construction sector contributed an estimated 3.9% of GDP in 2011. According to the AfDB, the sector grew by 15.0% in 2011.

In 2011 61.2% of the country's electricity production was generated by hydroelectric plants, with the remainder generated by natural gas and petroleum. The construction of a new hydroelectric dam at Imboulou, some 200 km north of Brazzaville, commenced in 2003; the dam was inaugurated in 2011.

The services sector contributed 19.0% of GDP in 2011, according to AfDB estimates. During 2003–11, according to the World Bank, the GDP of the services sector increased at an average annual rate of 5.6%; the GDP of the sector grew by 6.8% in 2011.

In 2007 the Congo recorded a visible merchandise trade surplus of an estimated US $2,949.9m., while there was an estimated deficit of $2,181.0m. on the current account of the balance of payments. In 2012 the principal source of imports (contributing 25.5% of the total) was Angola. Other major import providers were Gabon, France and Brazil. In 2012 the People's Republic of China was the principal market for exports (accounting for 21.7% of the total). The Netherlands, France, the USA, Australia and Portugal were also important purchasers. The principal exports in 2012 were mineral fuels, oils, distillation products, etc., and ships, boats and other floating structures. The principal imports in that year were ships, boats and other floating structures, and machinery, nuclear reactors, boilers, etc.

According to IMF estimates, in 2012 there was a budget surplus of 450,000m. francs CFA, equivalent to 6.2% of GDP. The Congo's general government gross debt was 2,059,100m. francs CFA in 2011, equivalent to 30.3% of GDP. The country's external debt totalled US $2,523m. in 2011, of which $2,157m. was public and publicly guaranteed debt. In 2009, the cost of servicing long-term public and publicly guaranteed debt and repayments to the IMF was equivalent to 6.8% of the value of exports of goods, services and income (excluding workers' remittances). The average annual rate of inflation in Brazzaville during 2003–12 was 3.8%. Consumer prices increased by an average of 3.0% in 2010.

The Republic of the Congo is one of the largest producers of petroleum in sub-Saharan Africa; nevertheless, the World Bank estimates that more than one-half of the population lives under the poverty threshold. Thus, the country has remained dependent upon significant external assistance, including the initiative for heavily indebted poor countries (HIPC) debt relief scheme, under which it has achieved cancellation of a substantial proportion of its external debt. In July 2010 the USA agreed to cancel the Congo's total debt to that country, of some US $33.4m., after the 'Paris Club' of creditors agreed that the Congo had reached completion point of the HIPC initiative. In October a contract signed with France allowed repaid debt, totalling an estimated €80m., to be redirected towards development projects. The Congo's membership of the Communauté Economique et Monétaire de l'Afrique Centrale (CEMAC), with a common regional exchange rate, was considered to have promoted stability. In 2012 it was announced that four specialized economic zones were to be established (in Brazzaville and three other main cities) as part of government efforts to attract investment. Further integration between the six member countries of CEMAC was envisaged, and CEMAC's Central Africa Stock Exchange (based in Gabon) was intended to assist private investment financing. The National Development Plan 2012–16 emphasized the Government's priority to improve the business environment as part of its poverty reduction strategy, in conjunction with continued public infrastructure investment. Nevertheless, the Congo remained one of the lowest placed countries in the World Bank's 2013 *Doing Business* report (ranking 183rd out of 185 countries). In late 2013 the IMF reported that production at the Congo's oil fields was in decline, although non-oil growth was expected to be strengthened in the agricultural and construction sectors, and by a large increase in government spending related to reconstruction work (following explosions at a munitions depot in the capital, Brazzaville in early 2012) and significant public investment; overall GDP growth for 2013 was projected to fall slightly, to 3.4%. In December the Government announced plans to raise tax rates in the following year to compensate for the rise in expenditure. Increased co-operation with the People's Republic of China resulted in the signature of a number of joint economic agreements during 2013 (see Foreign Affairs); proposed Chinese-financed projects included rehabilitation of the state railway and the construction of a seaport at the southern town of Pointe-Noire.

PUBLIC HOLIDAYS

2015: 1 January (New Year's Day), 6 April (Easter Monday), 1 May (Labour Day), 14 May (Ascension Day), 25 May (Whit Monday), 10 June (Reconciliation Day), 15 August (Independence Day), 1 November (All Saints' Day), 28 November (Republic Day), 25 December (Christmas).

Statistical Survey

Source (unless otherwise stated): Direction Générale, Centre National de la Statistique et des Etudes Economiques, Immeuble du Plan, Rond point du Centre Culturel Français, BP 2031, Brazzaville; tel. and fax 22-281-59-09; e-mail cnsee@hotmail.com; internet www.cnsee.org.

Area and Population

AREA, POPULATION AND DENSITY

Area (sq km)	342,000*
Population (census results)	
30 July 1996	2,591,271
28 April 2007	
Males	1,821,357
Females	1,876,133
Total	3,697,490
Population (UN estimates at mid-year)†	
2012	4,337,052
2013	4,447,630
2014	4,558,592
Density (per sq km) at mid-2014	13.3

* 132,047 sq miles.

† Source: UN, *World Population Prospects: The 2012 Revision*.

POPULATION BY AGE AND SEX

(UN estimates at mid-2014)

	Males	Females	Total
0–14	975,287	961,985	1,937,272
15–64	1,233,015	1,234,242	2,467,257
65 and over	70,589	83,474	154,063
Total	2,278,891	2,279,701	4,558,592

Source: UN, *World Population Prospects: The 2012 Revision*.

ETHNIC GROUPS

1995 (percentages): Kongo 51.4; Téké 17.2; Mbochi 11.4; Mbédé 4.7; Punu 2.9; Sanga 2.5; Maka 1.8; Pygmy 1.4; Others 6.7 (Source: La Francophonie).

REGIONS AND MUNICIPALITIES
(official population estimates at 2009)

	Area (sq km)	Population	Capital
Bouenza	12,268	320,835	Madingou
Brazzaville	100	1,425,663	Brazzaville
Cuvette	74,850	161,983	Owando
Cuvette ouest		75,777	Ewo
Kouilou	13,695	95,457	Pointe-Noire
Lékoumou	20,950	100,061	Sibiti
Likouala	66,044	159,982	Impfondo
Niari	25,943	240,074	Loubomo (Dolisie)
Plateaux	38,400	181,235	Djambala
Pool	33,955	245,600	Kinkala
Sangha	55,795	89,002	Ouesso
Total	342,000	3,838,238	

PRINCIPAL TOWNS
(population at 2007 census)

Brazzaville (capital)	1,373,382	Loubomo (Dolisie)	83,798
Pointe-Noire	715,334	Nkayi	71,620

Mid-2011 (incl. suburbs, UN estimate): Brazzaville 1,610,760 (Source: UN, *World Urbanization Prospects: The 2011 Revision*).

BIRTHS AND DEATHS
(annual averages, UN estimates)

	1995–2000	2000–05	2005–10
Birth rate (per 1,000)	38.9	39.3	39.1
Death rate (per 1,000)	13.6	13.5	11.9

Source: UN, *World Population Prospects: The 2012 Revision*.

Life expectancy (years at birth): 57.8 (males 56.4; females 59.2) in 2011 (Source: World Bank, World Development Indicators database).

EMPLOYMENT
('000 persons at 1984 census)

	Males	Females	Total
Agriculture, etc.	105	186	291
Industry	61	8	69
Services	123	60	183
Total	289	254	543

Mid-2014 (estimates in '000): Agriculture, etc. 530; Total labour force 1,834 (Source: FAO).

Health and Welfare

KEY INDICATORS

Total fertility rate (children per woman, 2011)	4.5
Under-5 mortality rate (per 1,000 live births, 2011)	99
HIV/AIDS (% of persons aged 15–49, 2012)	2.8
Physicians (per 1,000 head, 2007)	0.1
Hospital beds (per 1,000 head, 2005)	1.6
Health expenditure (2010): US $ per head (PPP)	97
Health expenditure (2010): % of GDP	2.3
Health expenditure (2010): public (% of total)	60.5
Access to water (% of persons, 2011)	72
Access to sanitation (% of persons, 2011)	18
Total carbon dioxide emissions ('000 metric tons, 2010)	2,027.9
Carbon dioxide emissions per head (metric tons, 2010)	0.5
Human Development Index (2012): ranking	142
Human Development Index (2012): value	0.534

For sources and definitions, see explanatory note on p. vi.

Agriculture

PRINCIPAL CROPS
('000 metric tons)

	2010	2011*	2012*
Maize	10.5	12.0	13.0
Sweet potatoes	7.7*	8.2	8.5
Cassava (Manioc)	1,148.5	1,150.0	1,200.0
Yams	14.0*	14.5	15.0
Sugar cane	650.0*	650.0	650.0
Groundnuts, with shell	29.1	28.5	32.0
Oil palm fruit	141.3*	142.0	143.5
Bananas	85.0*	92.0	100.0
Plantains	81.1	82.0	84.0
Guavas, mangoes and mangosteens	39.0*	38.0	40.0
Avocados	8.0*	8.1	9.0

* FAO estimate(s).

Aggregate production ('000 metric tons, may include official, semi-official or estimated data): Total cereals 25.0 in 2010, 27.1 in 2011, 29.0 in 2012; Total roots and tubers 1,230.3 in 2010, 1,233.9 in 2011, 1,286.0 in 2012; Total vegetables (incl. melons) 138.2 in 2010, 139.3 in 2011, 143.4 in 2012; Total fruits (excl. melons) 262.0 in 2010, 272.3 in 2011, 284.3 in 2012.

Source: FAO.

LIVESTOCK
('000 head, year ending September, FAO estimates)

	2010	2011	2012
Cattle	330	335	336
Pigs	88	92	920
Sheep	120	122	122
Goats	320	323	325
Chickens	2,600	2,700	2,780

Source: FAO.

LIVESTOCK PRODUCTS
('000 metric tons, FAO estimates)

	2010	2011	2012
Cattle meat	6.2	6.4	6.6
Pig meat	1.9	1.9	1.9
Chicken meat	6.3	6.5	6.6
Game meat	39.6	41.0	41.0
Sheep and goat meat	1.5	1.5	1.5
Cows' milk	1.3	1.3	1.4
Hen eggs	1.6	1.6	1.6

Source: FAO.

Forestry

ROUNDWOOD REMOVALS
('000 cubic metres, excluding bark, FAO estimates)

	2010	2011	2012
Sawlogs, veneer logs and logs for sleepers	1,314	1,463	1,405
Pulpwood	361	361	361
Other industrial wood	370	370	370
Fuel wood	1,336	1,357	1,378
Total	3,381	3,551	3,514

Source: FAO.

SAWNWOOD PRODUCTION
('000 cubic metres, including railway sleepers, FAO estimates)

	2009	2010	2011
Total (all broadleaved)	199	179	228

2012: Production assumed to be unchanged from 2011 (FAO estimate).

Source: FAO.

Fishing

('000 metric tons, live weight)

	2009	2010	2011
Capture	61.2	65.2	73.2
Freshwater fishes	28.4	30.5	33.4
West African croakers	3.2	3.8	4.6
Sardinellas	12.2	9.3	19.7
Aquaculture*	0.1	0.1	0.1
Total catch*	61.3	65.2	73.3

* FAO estimates.

Source: FAO.

Mining

	2010	2011	2012
Crude petroleum ('000 metric tons)	15,136	15,119	15,287
Gold (kg)*	150	150	n.a.

* Estimated metal content of ore.

Sources: US Geological Survey; BP, *Statistical Review of World Energy*.

Industry

SELECTED PRODUCTS

('000 metric tons unless otherwise indicated)

	2008	2009	2010
Raw sugar	67.0	70.0	n.a.
Veneer sheets ('000 cu metres)	14	n.a.	n.a.
Jet fuels	31.0	56.0	47.0
Motor gasoline (petrol)	46.0	68.0	98.0
Kerosene	17	21	34
Distillate fuel oils	109	172	n.a.
Residual fuel oils	327	349	227
Electric energy (million kWh)	461	539	559

Source: UN Industrial Commodity Statistics Database.

Finance

CURRENCY AND EXCHANGE RATES

Monetary Units

100 centimes = 1 franc de la Coopération Financière en Afrique Centrale (CFA).

Sterling, Dollar and Euro Equivalents (31 December 2013)

£1 sterling = 783.286 francs CFA;
US $1 = 475.641 francs CFA;
€1 = 655.957 francs CFA;
10,000 francs CFA = £12.77 = $21.02 = €15.24.

Average Exchange Rate (francs CFA per US $)

2011	471.866
2012	510.527
2013	494.040

Note: The exchange rate of 1 French franc = 50 francs CFA, established in 1948, remained in force until January 1994, when the CFA franc was devalued by 50%, with the exchange rate adjusted to 1 French franc = 100 francs CFA. The relationship to French currency remained in effect with the introduction of the euro on 1 January 1999. From that date, accordingly, a fixed exchange rate of €1 = 655.957 francs CFA has been in operation.

BUDGET

(central government operations, '000 million francs CFA)

Revenue*	2011	2012†	2013‡
Oil revenue	2,283	2,291	2,462
Non-oil revenue	571	663	726
Investment income	5	12	46
Total	2,859	2,966	3,233

Expenditure	2011	2012†	2013‡
Current expenditure	691	1,023	968
Wages and salaries	207	248	270
Other current expenditure	430	723	636
Interest payments	11	13	18
External	11	13	18
Domestic	0	0	0
Local authorities	44	38	44
Capital expenditure	1,084	1,503	1,325
Externally financed	216	1,207	1,000
Domestically financed	868	296	325
Total	1,774	2,526	2,293

* Excluding grants received ('000 million francs CFA): 35 in 2011; 10 in 2012 (estimate); 75 in 2013 (projection).

† Estimates.

‡ Projections.

Source: IMF, *Republic of Congo: 2013 Article IV Consultation* (September 2013).

INTERNATIONAL RESERVES

(US $ million at 31 December)

	2010	2011	2012
Gold (national valuation)	17.82	17.01	18.73
IMF special drawing rights	107.89	107.56	107.94
Reserve position in IMF	0.89	0.88	0.89
Foreign exchange	4,338.07	5,532.70	5,440.74
Total	4,464.67	5,658.15	5,568.30

Source: IMF, *International Financial Statistics*.

MONEY SUPPLY

('000 million francs CFA at 31 December)

	2010	2011	2012
Currency outside depository corporations	449.83	524.63	582.24
Transferable deposits	715.98	1,103.06	1,359.15
Other deposits	165.15	209.74	260.48
Broad money	1,330.96	1,837.42	2,201.87

Source: IMF, *International Financial Statistics*.

COST OF LIVING

(Consumer Price Index for Brazzaville; base: 2000 = 100)

	2010	2011	2012
Food	143.3	145.5	161.4
All items (incl. others)	139.2	n.a.	145.2

Source: ILO.

NATIONAL ACCOUNTS

('000 million francs CFA at current prices)

Expenditure on the Gross Domestic Product

	2009	2010	2011*
Government final consumption expenditure	417	451	466
Private final consumption expenditure	1,280	1,364	1,453
Gross fixed capital formation	1,900	1,892	2,205
Changes in inventories	5	5	5
Total domestic expenditure	3,602	3,712	4,129
Exports of goods and services	3,139	4,858	5,809
Less Imports of goods and services	2,624	2,706	2,529
GDP at purchasers' values	4,117	5,863	7,409

Gross Domestic Product by Economic Activity

	2009	2010	2011*
Agriculture, hunting, forestry and fishing	202	221	242
Mining and quarrying	2,342	3,883	5,118
Manufacturing	194	202	206
Electricity, gas and water	30	28	31
Construction	179	232	285
Trade, restaurants and hotels	326	371	428
Finance, insurance and real estate	290	317	375
Transport and communications	254	277	312
Public administration and defence	210	225	264
GDP at factor cost	4,027	5,755	7,260
Indirect taxes	91	109	149
GDP in purchasers' values	4,117	5,863	7,409

* Estimates.

Note: Deduction for imputed bank service charge assumed to be distributed at origin.

Source: African Development Bank.

BALANCE OF PAYMENTS

(US $ million)

	2005	2006	2007
Exports of goods f.o.b.	4,745.3	6,065.7	5,808.0
Imports of goods f.o.b.	–1,305.5	–2,003.5	–2,858.1
Trade balance	3,439.8	4,062.2	2,949.9
Exports of services	220.5	266.0	319.4
Imports of services	–1,417.1	–2,425.9	–3,527.7
Balance on goods and services	2,243.2	1,902.3	–258.3
Other income received	17.6	20.1	23.4
Other income paid	–1,595.5	–1,772.6	–1,908.1
Balance on goods, services and income	665.3	149.7	–2,143.1
Current transfers received	87.2	37.9	43.0
Current transfers paid	–56.9	–63.5	–81.0
Current balance	695.6	124.1	–2,181.0
Capital account (net)	11.2	9.6	31.7
Direct investment from abroad	513.6	1,487.7	2,638.4
Portfolio investment assets	–1.1	–1.3	–1.5
Other investment assets	–246.5	–228.9	266.2
Other investment liabilities	–492.7	–831.5	–356.4
Net errors and omissions	30.5	142.5	–201.1
Overall balance	510.5	702.1	196.4

Source: IMF, *International Financial Statistics*.

External Trade

PRINCIPAL COMMODITIES

(distribution by HS, US $ million)

Imports c.i.f.	2010	2011	2012
Mineral products	320.5	251.5	189.2
Mineral fuels, oils, distillation products, etc.	248.6	157.3	81.1
Petroleum oils, not crude	221.9	147.7	71.4
Iron and steel, other base metals and articles of base metal	178.4	215.9	323.0
Machinery and mechanical appliances; electrical equipment; parts thereof	463.6	616.5	872.7
Machinery, boilers, etc.	329.5	451.9	678.5
Electrical, electronic equipment	134.1	164.6	194.2
Vehicles, aircraft, vessels and associated transport equipment	2,785.9	5,168.2	4,856.7
Vehicles other than railway, tramway	99.7	143.2	235.6
Ships, boats and other floating structures	2,667.8	4,978.4	4,560.9
Cruise ships, cargo ships, barges	773.9	2,729.8	2,836.3
Light vessels, dredgers; floating docks; floating/submersible drill platforms	1,824.9	2,163.6	1,655.7
Total (incl. others)	4,369.4	7,154.7	7,464.4

Exports f.o.b.	2010	2011	2012
Mineral products	4,684.8	11,048.5	5,979.1
Mineral fuels, oils, distillation products, etc.	4,684.6	11,047.7	5,978.4
Crude petroleum oils	4,481.1	10,799.7	5,888.9
Vehicles, aircraft, vessels and associated transport equipment	1,866.1	2,799.6	1,325.9
Ships, boats and other floating structures	1,851.2	2,743.9	1,300.6
Cruise ships, cargo ships, bargess	679.7	1,876.9	628.0
Light vessels, dredgers; floating docks; floating/submersible drill platforms	1,107.3	860.9	623.9
Total (incl. others)	6,917.6	14,216.5	7,574.8

Source: Trade Map-Trade Competitiveness Map, International Trade Centre, www.intracen.org/marketanalysis.

PRINCIPAL TRADING PARTNERS

(US $ million)

Imports c.i.f.	2010	2011	2012
Angola	656.8	875.1	1,902.1
Australia	7.6	17.6	252.8
Belgium	163.7	276.1	367.4
Brazil	15.2	141.9	461.4
Cameroon	63.9	234.5	206.7
China, People's Rep.	152.2	296.1	322.3
Côte d'Ivoire	135.4	47.5	148.0
Equatorial Guinea	269.3	441.7	54.4
France (incl. Monaco)	533.8	546.8	613.3
Gabon	206.6	1,020.0	896.7
Italy	124.5	198.8	264.5
Liberia	0.0	71.6	47.9
Malaysia	15.8	38.2	97.5
Namibia	60.5	90.8	147.8

Imports c.i.f.—*continued*	2010	2011	2012
Netherlands	168.2	69.6	57.4
Nigeria	123.4	815.3	224.3
Panama	0.0	84.2	0.0
Singapore	441.0	595.4	132.1
South Africa	141.6	447.5	181.7
Spain	27.7	14.5	188.9
United Arab Emirates	39.9	55.2	101.0
United Kingdom	289.3	40.8	53.0
USA	156.8	151.7	185.0
Total (incl. others)	4,369.4	7,154.7	7,464.4

Exports f.o.b.	2010	2011	2012
Angola	903.4	1,255.5	375.7
Australia	0.6	781.8	450.2
Benin	6.7	54.0	104.3
Brazil	163.3	116.0	0.7
Canada	64.3	410.4	102.0
China, People's Rep.	1,446.7	4,006.7	1,640.7
Côte d'Ivoire	58.5	166.4	42.5
Egypt	0.8	0.9	124.5
France (incl. Monaco)	867.7	1,048.1	941.7
Gabon	327.4	417.6	175.3
Iceland	69.3	82.6	0.0
India	70.2	169.8	142.8
Italy	53.4	287.8	152.1
Korea, Rep.	134.7	1.9	0.9
Malaysia	0.3	96.9	215.5
Namibia	1.6	48.8	143.5
Netherlands	197.0	706.1	1,063.0
Nigeria	11.4	134.3	265.5
Portugal	159.4	218.4	436.1
Singapore	193.6	80.4	44.8
Spain	73.2	358.8	274.0
Switzerland	105.4	6.8	4.9
Taiwan	513.9	824.9	0.3
United Kingdom	29.1	416.2	111.3
USA	716.3	1,932.0	470.5
Total (incl. others)	6,917.6	14,216.5	7,574.8

Source: Trade Map-Trade Competitiveness Map, International Trade Centre, www.intracen.org/marketanalysis.

Transport

RAILWAYS
(traffic)

	2007	2008	2009
Passengers carried ('000)	727	770	592
Passenger-km (million)	199	233	207
Freight carried ('000 metric tons)	614	630	593
Freight ton-km (million)	224	253	257

ROAD TRAFFIC
(estimates, '000 motor vehicles in use)

	1999	2000	2001
Passenger cars	26.2	29.7	29.7
Commercial vehicles	20.4	23.1	23.1

Source: UN, *Statistical Yearbook*.

2007 ('000 motor vehicles in use at 31 December): Passenger cars 56; Vans and lorries 36; Motorcycles and mopeds 3; Total (incl. others) 100 (Source: IRF, *World Road Statistics*).

SHIPPING

Flag Registered Fleet
(at 31 December)

	2011	2012	2013
Number of vessels	7	7	8
Total displacement ('000 grt)	1,281	1,281	1,320

Source: Lloyd's List Intelligence (www.lloydslistintelligence.com).

Freight Traffic
(ports of Brazzaville and Pointe-Noire, '000 metric tons)

	2007	2008	2009
Goods loaded	11,666.3	12,859.9	15,146.1
Goods unloaded	2,859.3	3,883.9	3,745.3

CIVIL AVIATION
(traffic on scheduled services)*

	2001	2002	2003
Kilometres flown (million)	3	1	1
Passengers carried ('000)	95	47	52
Passenger-km (million)	157	27	31
Total ton-km (million)	22	3	3

* Including an apportionment of the traffic of Air Afrique.

Source: UN, *Statistical Yearbook*.

Passengers carried ('000): 311.6 in 2010; 399.6 in 2011; 477.1 in 2012 (Source: World Bank, World Development Indicators database).

Tourism

FOREIGN VISITORS BY COUNTRY OF RESIDENCE*

	2008	2009	2010
Angola	2,134	3,193	3,352
Belgium	1,056	1,149	1,518
Cameroon	2,792	3,182	3,954
Congo, Democratic Rep.	5,224	7,052	8,712
France	22,473	30,343	30,181
Gabon	1,629	1,763	2,116
Italy	1,617	3,097	2,945
United Kingdom	819	2,565	3,607
USA	1,371	2,156	2,149
Total (incl. others)	62,016	93,797	100,691

* Arrivals at hotels and similar establishments.

2011: Total arrivals 218,000.

Receipts from tourism (US $ million, excl. passenger transport): 40 in 2005; 45 in 2006; 54 in 2007.

Source: World Tourism Organization.

Communications Media

	2010	2011	2012
Telephones ('000 main lines in use)	9.8	14.2	14.9
Mobile cellular telephones ('000 subscribers)	3,798.6	3,884.8	4,283.1
Internet users ('000)	2.0	2.1	n.a.
Broadband subscribers	200	300	400

Source: International Telecommunication Union.

Education

(2011/12 unless otherwise indicated)

	Institutions*	Teachers	Students		
			Males	Females	Total
Pre-primary	95	2,101	27,308	26,612	53,920
Primary	1,168	16,527	356,221	378,272	734,493
Secondary	n.a.	18,165	182,429	156,821	339,250
Tertiary	n.a.	3,317	24,187	15,116	39,303

* 1998/99.

Sources: mostly UNESCO Institute for Statistics.

Pupil-teacher ratio (primary education, UNESCO estimate): 44.4 in 2011/12 (Source: UNESCO Institute for Statistics).

Adult literacy rate (UNESCO estimates): 86.8% (males 92.1%; females 81.7%) in 2007 (Source: UNESCO Institute for Statistics).

Directory

The Government

HEAD OF STATE

President: Gen. DENIS SASSOU-NGUESSO (assumed power 15 October 1997; inaugurated 25 October 1997; elected 10 March 2002; re-elected 12 July 2009).

COUNCIL OF MINISTERS
(April 2014)

Minister of State, Minister of Industrial Development and the Promotion of the Private Sector: ISIDORE MVOUBA.

Minister of State, Keeper of the Seals, Minister of Justice and Human Rights: AIMÉ EMMANUEL YOKA.

Minister of State, Minister of Transport, Civil Aviation and Maritime Trade: RODOLPHE ADADA.

Minister of State, Minister of Labour and Social Security: FLORENT NTSIBA.

Minister of State, Minister of the Economy, Finance, Planning, the Public Portfolio and Integration: GILBERT ONDONGO.

Minister of Foreign Affairs and Co-operation: BASILE IKOUÉBÉ.

Minister of the Interior and Decentralization: RAYMOND ZÉPHYRIN MBOULOU.

Minister of Mining and Geology: Gen. PIERRE OBA.

Minister of the Forest Economy and Sustainable Development: HENRI DJOMBO.

Minister of the Civil Service and State Reform: GUY-BRICE PARFAIT KOLÉLAS.

Minister of Construction, Town Planning and Housing: CLAUDE ALPHONSE NSILOU.

Minister of Agriculture and Stockbreeding: RIGOBERT MABOUNDOU.

Minister of Energy and Water Resources: HENRI OSSEBI.

Minister of Equipment and Public Works: EMILE OUOSSO.

Minister of Health and Population: FRANÇOIS IBOVI.

Minister of Small and Medium-sized Enterprises and Crafts: ADÉLAÏDE YVONNE MOUGANY.

Minister at the Presidency, responsible for Territorial Management and Grand Projects: JEAN-JACQUES BOUYA.

Minister of Scientific Research and Technological Innovation: BRUNO JEAN-RICHARD ITOUA.

Minister at the Presidency, responsible for National Defence: CHARLES RICHARD MONDJO.

Minister of Hydrocarbons: ANDRÉ RAPHAËL LOEMBA.

Minister of Culture and the Arts: JEAN-CLAUDE GAKOSSO.

Minister of Trade and Supplies: CLAUDINE MOUNARI.

Minister of Posts and Telecommunications: THIERRY MOUNGALLA.

Minister of Social Affairs, Humanitarian Action and Solidarity: EMILIENNE RAOUL.

Minister of Higher Education: GEORGES MOYEN.

Minister of Primary and Secondary Education and Literacy: HELLOT MATSON MAMPOUYA.

Minister at the Presidency, responsible for the Special Economic Zones: ALAIN AKOUALA ATIPAULT.

Minister of Communication and Relations with Parliament: BIENVENUE OKIEMY.

Minister of Land Reform and the Preservation of the Public Domain: PIERRE MABIALA.

Minister of Sports and Physical Education: LÉON-ALFRED OPIMBAT.

Minister of Fisheries and Aquaculture: BERNARD TCHIBAMBELELA.

Minister of Technical Education, Vocational Training and Employment: SERGE BLAISE ZONIABA.

Minister of Tourism and the Environment: JOSUÉ RODRIGUE NGOUONIMBA.

Minister of Youth and Civic Education: ANATOLE COLLINET MAKOSSO.

Minister of the Promotion of Women and the Integration of Women into Development: CATHÉRINE EMBONDZA LIPITI.

Minister-delegate to the Minister of Transport, Civil Aviation and Maritime Trade, responsible for Maritime Trade: MARTIN PARFAIT AIMÉ COUSSOUD MAVOUNGOU.

Minister-delegate to the Minister of Transport, Civil Aviation and Maritime Trade, responsible for Navigable Paths and the River Economy: GILBERT MOKOKI.

Minister-delegate to the Minister of State, Minister of the Economy, Finance, Planning, the Public Portfolio and Integration: RAPHAËL MOKOKO.

MINISTRIES

Office of the President: Palais du Peuple, Brazzaville; tel. 22-281-17-11; internet www.presidence.cg.

Office of the Minister at the Presidency, responsible for National Defence: Brazzaville; tel. 22-281-22-31.

Office of the Minister at the Presidency, responsible for the Special Economic Zones: Brazzaville.

Ministry of Agriculture and Stockbreeding: BP 2453, Brazzaville; tel. 22-281-41-31; fax 22-281-19-29.

Ministry of the Civil Service and State Reform: BP 12151, Brazzaville; tel. 22-281-41-68; fax 22-281-41-49.

Ministry of Communication and Relations with Parliament: BP 114, Brazzaville; tel. 22-281-41-29; fax 22-281-41-28; e-mail depcompt@congonet.cg.

Ministry of Construction, Town Planning and Housing: BP 1580, Brazzaville; tel. 22-281-34-48; fax 22-281-12-97.

Ministry of Culture and the Arts: BP 20480, Brazzaville; tel. 22-281-02-35; fax 22-281-40-25.

Ministry of the Economy, Finance, Planning, the Public Portfolio and Integration: ave de l'Indépendance, croisement ave Foch, BP 2083, Brazzaville; tel. 22-281-45-24; fax 22-281-43-69; e-mail mefb-cg@mefb-cg.net; internet www.mefb-cg.org.

Ministry of Energy and Water Resources: Brazzaville.

Ministry of Equipment and Public Works: BP 2099, Brazzaville; tel. 22-281-59-41; fax 22-281-59-07.

Ministry of Fisheries and Aquaculture: Brazzaville.

Ministry of Foreign Affairs and Co-operation: BP 2070, Brazzaville; tel. 22-281-10-89; fax 22-281-41-61.

Ministry of the Forest Economy and Sustainable Development: Immeuble de l'Agriculture, face à Blanche Gomez, BP 98, Brazzaville; tel. 22-281-41-37; fax 22-281-41-34; e-mail ajdbosseko@minifor.com.

Ministry of Health and Population: BP 20101, Brazzaville; tel. 22-281-30-75; fax 22-281-14-33.

Ministry of Higher Education: Ancien Immeuble de la Radio, BP 169, Brazzaville; tel. 22-281-08-15; fax 22-281-52-65.

Ministry of Hydrocarbons: BP 2120, Brazzaville; tel. 22-281-10-86; fax 22-281-10-85; internet www.congopetrole.fr.

Ministry of Industrial Development and the Promotion of the Private Sector: Centre Administratif, Quartier Plateau, BP 2117, Brazzaville; tel. 22-281-30-09; fax 22-281-06-43.

Ministry of the Interior and Decentralization: BP 880, Brazzaville; tel. 22-281-40-60; fax 22-281-33-17.

Ministry of Justice and Human Rights: BP 2497, Brazzaville; tel. and fax 22-281-41-49.

Ministry of Labour and Social Security: Immeuble de la BCC, ave Foch, BP 2075, Brazzaville; tel. 22-281-41-43; fax 22-281-05-50.

Ministry of Land Reform and the Preservation of the Public Domain: Brazzaville; tel. 22-281-34-48.

Ministry of Mining and Geology: BP 2124, Brazzaville; tel. 22-281-02-64; fax 22-281-50-77.

Ministry of Posts and Telecommunications: BP 44, Brazzaville; tel. 22-281-41-18; fax 22-281-19-34.

Ministry of Primary and Secondary Education and Literacy: BP 5253, Brazzaville; tel. 22-281-24-52; fax 22-281-25-39.

Ministry of the Promotion of Women and the Integration of Women into Development: Brazzaville; tel. 22-281-19-29.

Ministry of Scientific Research and Technological Innovation: Ancien Immeuble de la Radio, Brazzaville; tel. 22-281-03-59.

Ministry of Security and Public Order: BP 2474, Brazzaville; tel. 22-281-41-73; fax 22-281-34-04.

Ministry of Small and Medium-sized Enterprises and Crafts: Brazzaville.

Ministry of Social Affairs, Humanitarian Action and Solidarity: Brazzaville.

Ministry of Sports and Physical Education: BP 2061, Brazzaville; tel. 06-660-89-24 (mobile).

Ministry of Technical Education, Vocational Training and Employment: BP 2076, Brazzaville; tel. 22-281-17-27; fax 22-281-56-82; e-mail metp_cab@yahoo.fr.

Ministry of Tourism and the Environment: Brazzaville.

Ministry of Trade and Supplies: BP 2965, Brazzaville; tel. 22-281-41-16; fax 22-281-41-57; e-mail mougany@yahoo.fr.

Ministry of Transport, Civil Aviation and Maritime Trade: Immeuble Mafoua Virgile, BP 2066, Brazzaville; tel. 22-281-53-39; fax 22-281-57-56.

Ministry of Youth and Civic Education: Brazzaville.

President

Presidential Election, 12 July 2009

Candidate	Votes	% of votes
Denis Sassou-Nguesso	1,055,117	78.61
Joseph Kignoumbi Kia Mbougou	100,181	7.46
Nicéphore Fylla de Saint-Eudes	93,749	6.98
Mathias Dzon	30,861	2.30
Joseph Hodjuila Miokono	27,060	2.02
Guy-Romain Kinfoussia	11,678	0.87
Jean François Tchibinda Kouangou	5,475	0.41
Anguios Nganguia-Engambé	4,064	0.30
Bonaventure Mizidy Bavouéza	3,594	0.27
Clément Miérassa	3,305	0.25
Bertin Pandi-Ngouari	2,749	0.20
Marion Michel Madzimba Ehouango	2,612	0.19
Jean Ebina	1,797	0.13
Total	1,342,242	100.00

Legislature

The legislature, Parliament, comprises two chambers: a directly elected lower house, the National Assembly; and an indirectly elected upper house, the Senate.

NATIONAL ASSEMBLY

National Assembly: Palais du Parlement, BP 2106, Brazzaville; tel. 22-281-11-12; fax 22-281-41-28; e-mail dsancongo@yahoo.fr.

President: JUSTIN KOUMBA.

General Election, 15 July and 5 August 2012

Party	Seats
Parti Congolais du Travail (PCT)	89
Mouvement Congolais pour la Démocratie et le Développement Intégral (MCDDI)	7
Union Panafricaine pour la Démocratie Sociale (UPADS)	7
Rassemblement pour la Démocratie et le Progrès Social (RDPS)	5
Mouvement d'Action et pour le Renouveau (MAR)	4
Rassemblement Citoyen (RC)	3
Mouvement pour l'Unité, la Solidarité et le Travail (MUST)	2
Union Patriotique pour la Démocratie et le Progrès (UPDP)	2
Club 2002-Parti pour l'Unité et la République (Club 2002 PUR)	1
Club Perspectives et Réalités (CPR)	1
Parti Républicain et Libéral (PRL)	1
Union des Forces Démocratiques (UFD)	1
Union pour la République (UR)	1
Independents	12
Total	136*

* Voting in three constituencies did not take place.

SENATE

Senate: Palais du Parlement, BP 2642, Brazzaville; tel. and fax 22-281-18-34; fax 02-281-00-18 (mobile); e-mail foutysoungou@yahoo.fr; internet www.senat.cg.

President: ANDRÉ OBAMI ITOU.

The upper chamber comprises 72 members, elected by representatives of local, regional and municipal authorities for a six-year term. After elections to the Senate held on 9 October 2011 the strength of the parties was as follows:

Party	Seats
Rassemblement de la Majorité Présidentielle*	38
PCT	12
UPADS	4
Club 2002 PUR	2
MCDDI	2
Mouvement pour la Solidarité et la Démocratie	1
PRL	1
Independents	12
Total	72

* An alliance of parties and associations supporting Pres. Denis Sassou-Nguesso.

Elections to renew 36 seats were held on 9 October 2011, at which the PCT secured 12 seats, the RMP 11 seats, the UPADS two, the MCDDI two, the Club 2002 PUR two, the PRL and the MSD one seat each, and independent candidates won five seats.

Election Commission

Commission Nationale d'Organisation des Elections (CONEL): Brazzaville; f. 2001; reorganized in 2007; mems appointed by President of the Republic; Pres. HENRI BOUKA.

Advisory Council

Economic and Social Council (Conseil Economique et Social): Brazzaville; f. 2003; 75 mems, appointed by the President of the Republic; Pres. AUGUSTE-CÉLESTIN GONGARAD NKOUA.

Political Organizations

In early 2004 there were more than 100 political parties and organizations in the Republic of the Congo. The following were among the most important of those believed to be active in 2014:

Action pour le Congo (APC): Brazzaville.

Alliance pour la Démocratie et le Développement National (ADDN): Brazzaville; f. 2005; supports Govt of Pres. Sassou-Nguesso; Pres. BRUNO MAZONGA.

Alliance pour la République et la Démocratie (ARD): Brazzaville; f. 2007.

Union Patriotique pour le Renouveau National (UPRN): Brazzaville; Leader MATHIAS DZON.

Club 2002-Parti pour l'Unité et la République (Club 2002 PUR): Brazzaville; f. 2002; Pres. WILFRID NGUESSO.

Conseil National des Républicains (CNR): formed as political wing of 'Ninja' rebel group, the Conseil National de la Résistance; Leader Rev. FRÉDÉRIC BITSANGOU (NTUMI).

Jeunesse en Mouvement (JEM): Brazzaville; f. 2002.

Mouvement d'Action pour le Renouveau (MAR): BP 1287, Pointe-Noire; Pres. ROLAND BOUITI VIAUDO.

Mouvement Congolais pour la Démocratie et le Développement Intégral (MCDDI): 744 route de Djoué, Brazzaville; e-mail info@mcddi.net; f. 1990; Interim Pres. GUY-BRICE PARFAIT KOLÉLAS.

Mouvement pour la Démocratie et le Progrès (MDP): Brazzaville; f. 2007; Leader JEAN-CLAUDE IBOVI.

Mouvement pour la Solidarité et la Démocratie (MSD): Brazzaville; Leader RENÉ SERGE BLANCHARD OBA.

Parti Congolais du Travail (PCT): BP 80, Brazzaville; internet particongolaisdutravail.com; f. 1969; sole legal political party 1969–90; Pres. DENIS SASSOU-NGUESSO; Sec.-Gen. PIERRE NGOLO.

Parti Républicain et Libéral (PRL): Brazzaville; Pres. NICÉPHORE FYLLA DE SAINT-EUDES.

Parti Social Démocrate Congolais (PSDC): Brazzaville; Pres. CLÉMENT MIÉRASSA.

Parti pour l'Unité et la République (PUR): Brazzaville.

Parti la Vie: Brazzaville.

Rassemblement Citoyen (RC): route du Djoué, face Centre Sportif de Bacongo, Brazzaville; Pres. CLAUDE ALPHONSE NSILOU.

Rassemblement pour la Démocratie et le Progrès Social (RDPS): Pointe-Noire; f. 1990; Pres. BERNARD MBATCHI.

Rassemblement de la Majorité Présidentielle (RMP): Brazzaville; f. 2007; org. of some 100 political parties and associations supporting Pres. Sassou-Nguesso.

Union pour la Démocratie et la République—Mwinda (UDR—Mwinda): Brazzaville; e-mail journalmwinda@presse-ecrite.com; f. 1992; Leader GUY ROMAIN KIMFOUSSIA.

Union des Forces Démocratiques (UFD): Brazzaville; supports Govt; Pres. DAVID CHARLES GANOU.

Union Panafricaine pour la Démocratie Sociale (UPADS): BP 1370, Brazzaville; e-mail courrier@upads.org; Pres. PASCAL LISSOUBA; Sec.-Gen. PASCAL TSATY MABIALA.

Union Patriotique pour la Démocratie et le Progrès (UPDP): 112 rue Lamothe, Brazzaville; Pres. GONGARA KOUA.

Union pour le Progrès (UP): 965 rue Sounda, pl. des 15 ans, Brazzaville; Pres. JEAN-MARTIN MBEMBA; Sec.-Gen. OMER DEFOUNDOUX.

Diplomatic Representation

EMBASSIES IN THE REPUBLIC OF THE CONGO

Algeria: rue Col Brisset, BP 2100, Brazzaville; tel. 22-281-17-37; fax 22-281-54-77; Ambassador ABDELOUAHAB OSMANE.

Angola: ave Fourneau, BP 388, Brazzaville; tel. 22-281-47-21; fax 22-283-52-96; e-mail miranotom@yahoo.fr; Ambassador Dr PEDRO FERNANDO MAVUNZA.

Belgium: blvd Sassou Nguesso, BP 225, Brazzaville; tel. 22-281-07-65; e-mail brazzaville@diplobel.fed.be; internet www.diplomatie.be/brazzaville; Ambassador HERMAN MERCKX.

Cameroon: ave Bayardelles, Brazzaville; tel. 22-281-10-08; fax 22-281-56-75; Ambassador HAMIDOU KOMIDOR NJIMOLUH.

Central African Republic: BP 10, Brazzaville; tel. 05-526-75-55 (mobile); Ambassador MARIE-CHARLOTTE FAYANGA.

Chad: BP 386, Brazzaville; tel. 05-558-92-06 (mobile); Ambassador KALZEUBE KINGAR.

China, People's Republic: blvd du Marechal Lyauté, BP 213, Brazzaville; tel. 22-281-11-32; fax 22-281-11-35; e-mail amba_chine@yahoo.fr; internet cg.chineseembassy.org; Ambassador GUAN JIAN.

Congo, Democratic Republic: ave Nelson Mandela, Brazzaville; tel. 22-281-30-52; Ambassador CHRISTOPHE MUZUNGU.

Cuba: 28 rue Lacien Fourneaux, BP 80, Brazzaville; tel. 22-281-03-79; e-mail embacuba@congonet.cg; Ambassador ALBA BEATRIZ SOTO PIMENTAL.

Egypt: 7 bis ave Bayardelle, BP 917, Brazzaville; tel. 22-281-07-94; fax 22-281-15-33; Ambassador KHALED EZZAT OMRAH.

Equatorial Guinea: Brazzaville; Ambassador ELA EBANG MBANG.

France: rue Alfassa, BP 2089, Brazzaville; tel. 05-361-24-06 (mobile); e-mail webmestre@mail.com; internet www.ambafrance-cg.org; Ambassador JEAN-PIERRE VIDON.

Gabon: BP 20336, Brazzaville; tel. 22-281-56-20; Ambassador BARTHÉLEMY ONGAYE.

Holy See: rue Col Brisset, BP 1168, Brazzaville; tel. 06-950-56-66 (mobile); e-mail nonapcg@yahoo.com; Apostolic Nuncio JAN ROMEO PAWLOWSKI.

Italy: 2 ave Auxence Ickonga, BP 2484, Brazzaville; tel. 22-281-58-41; fax 22-283-52-70; e-mail ambasciata.brazzaville@esteri.it; internet www.ambbrazzaville.esteri.it; Ambassador NICOLÒ TASSONI ESTENSE DI CASTELVECCHIO.

Libya: BP 920, Brazzaville; tel. 22-281-56-35; Chargé d'affaires a.i. IBRAHIM TAHAR EL-HAMALI.

Nigeria: 11 blvd Lyauté, BP 790, Brazzaville; tel. 22-281-10-22; fax 22-281-55-20; e-mail embnigbra@yahoo.co.uk; Ambassador VICTORIA JOLAADE BOSEDE ONIPEDE.

Russia: ave Félix Eboué, BP 2132, Brazzaville; tel. 22-281-19-23; fax 22-281-50-85; e-mail amrussie@yandex.ru; internet www.congo.mid.ru; Ambassador YOURI ALEKSANDROVICH ROMANOV.

Senegal: Brazzaville; Ambassador BATOURA KANE NIANG.

South Africa: 82 ave Marechal Lyautey, Brazzaville; tel. 22-281-08-49; e-mail brazzaville@foreign.gov.za; Ambassador RICHARD BALOYI.

USA: blvd Maya-Maya, BP 1015, Brazzaville; tel. 06-612-20-00 (mobile); e-mail BrazzavilleHR@state.gov; internet brazzaville.usembassy.gov; Ambassador STEPHANIE S. SULLIVAN.

Judicial System

The 2002 Constitution provides for the independence of the judiciary from the legislature. Judges are accountable to the Higher Council of Magistrates, under the chairmanship of the President of the Republic. The constituent bodies of the judiciary are the Supreme Court, the Revenue and Budgetary Discipline Court and the appeal courts. The High Court of Justice is chaired by the First President of the Supreme Court and is competent to try the President of the Republic in case of high treason, and to try members of the legislature, the Supreme Court, the Constitutional Court and government ministers for crimes or offences committed in the execution of their duties.

Supreme Court: Palais de Justice, BP 597, Brazzaville; tel. 22-283-01-32; e-mail ndallaa@yahoo.fr; First Pres. PLACIDE LENGA; Chief Prosecutor GEORGES AKIERA MOUANDZIBI.

High Court of Justice: BP 595, Brazzaville; tel. 02-281-45-17; fax 02-281-18-30; f. 2003; Pres. PLACIDE LENGA.

Constitutional Court: blvd Alfred Raoul (ex blvd des Armées), BP 543, Brazzaville; tel. 02-283-01-32; fax 02-281-18-28; e-mail courconstitutionnelle@yahoo.fr; Pres. AUGUSTE ILOKI; Vice-Pres. PIERRE PASSI.

Religion

More than 40% of the population follow traditional animist beliefs. Most of the remainder are Christians (of whom a majority are Roman Catholics).

CHRISTIANITY

The Roman Catholic Church

The Congo comprises one archdiocese and seven dioceses. An estimated 57% of the population are Roman Catholics.

Bishops' Conference: Conférence Episcopale du Congo, BP 200, Brazzaville; tel. 06-663-83-91 (mobile); fax 22-281-18-28; e-mail confepiscongo@yahoo.fr; f. 1992; Pres. Most Rev. LOUIS PORTELLA MBUYU (Bishop of Kinkala).

Archbishop of Brazzaville: Most Rev. ANATOLE MILANDOU, Archevêché, BP 2301, Brazzaville; tel. 05-538-20-84 (mobile); fax 22-281-26-15; e-mail archibrazza@yahoo.fr.

Protestant Church

Eglise Evangélique du Congo: BP 3205, Bacongo-Brazzaville; tel. and fax 22-281-04-54; internet eeccongo.org; f. 1909; Presbyterian; autonomous since 1961; 150,000 mems (2007); 120 parishes (2007); Pres. Rev. Dr Patrice N'Souami.

Eglise Evangélique Luthérienne du Congo: 137 rue Osselé-Mougali, BP 1456, 00242 Brazzaville; tel. 05-557-15-00 (mobile); e-mail evlcongo@yahoo.fr; Pres. Rev. Joseph Tchibinda Mavoungou; 1,828 mems (2010).

ISLAM

In 1997 an estimated 2% of the population were Muslims.

Comité Islamique du Congo: 77 Makotipoko Moungali, BP 55, Brazzaville; tel. 22-282-87-45; f. 1988; Leaders Habibou Soumare, Bachir Gatsongo, Bouilla Guibidanesi.

BAHÁ'Í FAITH

Assemblée Spirituelle Nationale: BP 2094, Brazzaville; tel. 22-281-36-93; e-mail congolink1@aol.com.

The Press

In July 2000 legislation was adopted on the freedom of information and communication. The legislation, which confirmed the abolition of censorship and reduced the penalty for defamation from imprisonment to a fine, specified three types of punishable offence: the encouragement of social tension (including incitement to ethnic conflict), attacks on the authorities (including libels on the Head of State or on the judiciary) and libels against private individuals. The terms of the legislation are guaranteed by a regulatory body, the Higher Council for the Freedom of Communication.

DAILIES

ACI Actualité: BP 2144, Brazzaville; tel. and fax 22-281-01-98; publ. by Agence Congolaise d'Information; Dir-Gen. Théodore Kiamossi.

Les Dépêches de Brazzaville: 84 ave Denis Sassou N'Guesso, Immeuble Les Manguiers (Mpila), Brazzaville; tel. 05-532-01-09 (mobile); internet www.brazzaville-adiac.com; Dir of Publication Jean-Paul Pigasse.

PERIODICALS

L'Arroseur: Immeuble Boulangerie ex-Léon, BP 15021, Brazzaville; tel. 05-558-65-51 (mobile); fax 05-558-37-60 (mobile); e-mail larroseur@yahoo.fr; f. 2000; weekly; satirical; Dir Gerry-Gérard Mangondo; Editor-in-Chief Jean-Marie Kanga.

L'Autre Vision: 48 rue Assiéné-Mikalou, BP 5255, Brazzaville; tel. 05-551-57-06 (mobile); e-mail lautrevision@yahoo.fr; 2 a month; Dir Jean Paulin Itoua.

Capital: 3 ave Charles de Gaulle, Plateau Centre Ville, BP 541, Brazzaville; tel. 05-558-95-10 (mobile); fax 05-551-37-48 (mobile); e-mail capital@hotmail.com; 2 a month; economics and business; Dir Serge-Denis Matondo; Editor-in-Chief Hervé Sampa.

Le Choc: BP 1314, Brazzaville; tel. 06-666-42-96 (mobile); fax 22-282-04-25; e-mail groupejustinfo@yahoo.fr; internet www.lechoc.info; weekly; Dir-Gen. and Publr Asie Dominique de Marseille; Dir of Publication Marien Ngapili.

Le Coq: Brazzaville; e-mail sosolecoq@yahoo.fr; f. 2000; weekly; Editor-in-Chief Malonga Bouka.

Le Défi Africain: Brazzaville; f. 2002; Dir of Publication Jean Romuald Mbepa.

Les Echos du Congo: Immeubles Fédéraux 036, Centre-ville, Brazzaville; tel. 05-551-57-09 (mobile); e-mail wayiadrien@yahoo.fr; weekly; pro-govt; Dir-Gen. Adrien Wayi-Lewy; Editor-in-Chief Innocent Olivier Taty.

Le Flambeau: BP 1198, Brazzaville; tel. 06-666-35-23 (mobile); e-mail congolink1@aol.com; weekly; independent; supports Govt of Pres. Sassou-Nguesso; Dir and Man. Editor Prince-Richard Nsana.

La Lettre de Brazzaville: Résidence Méridien, BP 15457, Brazzaville; tel. and fax 22-281-28-13; e-mail redaction@adiac.com; f. 2000; weekly; publ. by Agence d'Information d'Afrique Centrale; Man. Dir Jean-Paul Pigasse; Editor-in-Chief Belinda Ayessa.

Le Nouveau Stade: BP 2159, Brazzaville; tel. 06-668-45-52 (mobile); 2 a month; sports; Dir-Gen. Louis Ngami; Editor-in-Chief S. F. Kimina Makumbu.

La Nouvelle République: 3 ave des Ambassadeurs, BP 991, Brazzaville; tel. 22-281-00-20; state-owned; weekly; Dir-Gen. Gaspard Nwan; Editorial Dir Henri Boukoulou.

L'Observateur: 165 ave de l'Amitié, BP 13370, Brazzaville; tel. 06-666-33-37 (mobile); fax 22-281-11-81; e-mail lobservateur_2001@yahoo.fr; f. 1999; weekly; independent; opposes Govt of Pres. Sassou-Nguesso; Dir Gislin Simplice Ongouya; circ. 2,000 (2004).

Le Pays: BP 782, Brazzaville; tel. 06-661-06-11 (mobile); fax 22-282-44-50; e-mail heblepays@yahoo.fr; f. 1991; weekly; Editorial Dir Sylvère-Arsène Samba.

La Référence: BP 13778, Brazzaville; tel. 05-556-11-37 (mobile); fax 06-662-80-13 (mobile); 2 a month; supports Govt of Pres. Sassou-Nguesso; Dir Philippe Richet; Editor-in-Chief R. Assebako Amaidjore.

La Rue Meurt (Bala-Bala): BP 1258, Brazzaville; tel. 06-666-39-80 (mobile); fax 22-281-02-30; e-mail laruemeurt@yahoo.fr; f. 1991; weekly; satirical; opposes Govt of Pres. Sassou-Nguesso; Publr Matthieu Gayele; Editorial Dir Jean-Claude Bongolo; circ. 2,000 (2004).

La Semaine Africaine: blvd Lyautey, face Chu, BP 2080, Brazzaville; tel. 06-678-76-94 (mobile); e-mail contact@lasemaineafricaine.com; internet www.lasemaineafricaine.com; f. 1952; 2 a week; Roman Catholic; general news and social comment; circulates widely in francophone equatorial Africa; Editor-in-Chief Joachim Mbanza; circ. 7,500.

Le Stade: BP 114, Brazzaville; tel. 22-281-47-18; f. 1985; weekly; sports; Dir Hubert-Trésor Madouaba-Ntoualani; Editor-in-Chief Lelas Paul Nzolani; circ. 6,500.

Tam-Tam d'Afrique: 97 rue Moussana, Ouenzé, BP 1675, Brazzaville; tel. 05-551-03-95 (mobile); e-mail gouala@yahoo.fr; weekly; economics, finance; circ. 1,500 (2004).

Le Temps: BP 2104, Brazzaville; e-mail kiala_matouba@yahoo.fr; weekly; owned by supporters of former Pres. Lissouba; Editor-in-Chief Henri Boukoulou.

Vision pour Demain: 109 rue Bakongo Poto-Poto, BP 650, Brazzaville; tel. 04-441-14-22 (mobile); 6 a year; Dir Saint Eudes Mfumu Fylla.

NEWS AGENCIES

Agence Congolaise d'Information (ACI): ave E. P. Lumumba, BP 2144, Brazzaville; tel. and fax 22-281-01-98; e-mail agencecongoinfo@yahoo.fr; internet www.agencecongoinfo.net; f. 1961; Gen. Man. Auguste Kinzonzi-Kitoumou.

Agence d'Information d'Afrique Centrale (ADIAC): Les Manguiers, 76 ave Paul Doumer, Brazzaville; tel. 05-532-01-09 (mobile); fax 05-532-01-10 (mobile); e-mail belie@congonet.cg; internet www.brazzaville-adiac.com; f. 1997; Dirs Jean-Paul Pigasse, Belinda Ayessa; br. in Paris (France).

Publishers

Editions ADIAC—Agence d'Information d'Afrique Centrale: Hôtel Méridien, BP 15457, Brazzaville; tel. and fax 22-281-28-13; e-mail redaction@brazzaville-adiac.com; internet www.brazzaville-adiac.com; f. 1997; publishes chronicles of current affairs; Dir Jean-Paul Pigasse.

Editions 'Héros dans l'Ombre': BP 1678, Brazzaville; e-mail leopold_mamo@yahoo.fr; f. 1980; literature, criticism, poetry, essays, politics, drama, research; Chair. Léopold Pindy Mamonsono.

Editions Lemba: 20 ave des Emetteurs, Sangolo-OMS, Malèkélé, BP 2351, Brazzaville; tel. 06-667-65-58 (mobile); fax 22-281-00-17; e-mail editions_lemba@yahoo.fr; literature; Dir Apollinaire Singou-Basseha.

Editions PAARI—Pan African Review of Innovation: BP 1622, Brazzaville; tel. 05-551-86-49 (mobile); e-mail edpaari@yahoo.fr; internet www.cafelitteraire.fr; f. 1991; social and human sciences, philosophy; Dir Mâwa-Kiese Mawawa.

Imprimerie Centrale d'Afrique (ICA): ave du Gen. de Gaulle, BP 162, Pointe-Noire; f. 1949; Man. Dir M. Schneider.

Mokandart: BP 939, Brazzaville; tel. 06-668-46-69 (mobile); e-mail mokandart@yahoo.fr; adult and children's literature; Pres. Annick Veyrinaud Makonda.

GOVERNMENT PUBLISHING HOUSE

Imprimerie Nationale du Congo (INC): BP 58, Brazzaville; Dir Jules Ondzeki.

Broadcasting and Communications

TELECOMMUNICATIONS

In 2013 there were four mobile telephone operators in the country, providing services to 4.73m. of subscribers. SOTELCO, operating under the brand name Congo Télécom, held a monopoly on fixed-line services.

Airtel Congo: blvd Charles de Gaulle, angle allée Makimba, BP 1267, Pointe-Noire; tel. 05-520-00-00 (mobile); fax 22-294-88-75; e-mail info.africa@airtel.com; internet africa.airtel.com/congob; f. 1999 as Celtel Congo and fmrly Zain Congo; acquired by Bharti Airtel (India) in 2010; mobile cellular telephone operator; network covers Brazzaville, Pointe-Noire, Loubomo (Dolisie), Ouesso, Owando and other urban areas; Dir-Gen. JOHN NDEGO.

AMC Telecom: Immeuble CNSS, ave Alphonse, Brazzaville; tel. 05-545-07-60 (mobile); fax 22-281-18-30; e-mail amc@amc-telecom.com; internet www.amc-telecom.com; internet service provider.

Equateur Telecom Congo: 35 William Guynet, Poto-Poto, Brazzaville; e-mail info@azur-congo.com; internet www.azur-congo.com; f. 2010; provides mobile cellular telephone services under the brand name Azur; Dir-Gen. STÉPHANE BEUVELET.

MTN Congo: 36 ave Amílcar Cabral, face City-Center, Brazzaville; tel. 06-669-15-40 (mobile); e-mail yellonews@mtncongo.net; internet www.mtncongo.net; f. 2000; mobile cellular telephone operator; Dir-Gen. MATHIEU FREDDY TCHALA ABINA.

Société des Télécommunications du Congo (SOTELCO): blvd Denis Sassou-Nguesso, BP 2027, Brazzaville; tel. 22-281-00-00; fax 22-281-07-52; e-mail sotelco@congonet.cg; f. 2001 by division of postal and telecommunications services of the fmr Office National des Postes et Télécommunications; mobile cellular telephone system introduced in 1996; operates under the brand name Congo Telecom; majority govt-owned, part-owned by Atlantic TeleNetwork; further transfer to private ownership pending; Dir-Gen. CÉDRIC BEN CABINE AKOUALA.

Warid Congo SA: Immeuble Monte Cristo, croisement ave Orsy, ave Paul Doumer, Centre ville, BP 238, Brazzaville; tel. 04-400-01-23 (mobile); e-mail serviceclient@waridtel.cg; internet waridtel.cg; mobile cellular telephone operator; Pres. Sheikh NAHAYAN MABARAK AL NAHAYAN; Dir-Gen. MICHEL OLIVIER ELAMÉ.

Regulatory Authority

Agence de Régulation des Postes et des Communications Electroniques (ARPCE): Immeuble ARPCE, 91 bis ave de l'Amitié, BP 2490, Mpila, Brazzaville; tel. 05-510-72-72 (mobile); e-mail contact@arpce.net; internet www.arpce.cg; f. 2009; Dir-Gen. YVES CASTANOU.

RADIO AND TELEVISION

Canal FM: BP 60, Brazzaville; tel. 22-283-03-09; f. 1977 as Radio Rurales du Congo; present name adopted 2002; community stations established by the Agence de Coopération Culturelle et Technique; transmitters in Brazzaville, Sembé, Nkayi, Etoumbi and Mossendjo; Dir ETIENNE EPAGNA-TOUA.

Digital Radio Télévision: BP 1974, Brazzaville; internet drtvcongo@drtvcongo.com; f. 2002; Dir-Gen. PAUL SONI-BENGA.

Radio Brazzaville: face Direction Générale, SOTELCO, Brazzaville; tel. 05-551-60-73 (mobile); f. 1999; official station; Man. JEAN-PASCAL MONGO SLYM.

Radio Liberté: BP 1660, Brazzaville; tel. 22-281-57-42; f. 1997; operated by supporters of Pres. Sassou-Nguesso.

Radio Magnificat: Centre Interdiocésain des Oeuvres (CIO), Brazzaville; tel. 05-531-12-60 (mobile); e-mail radio.magnificat@yahoo.fr; f. 2006; Man. MAURICE MILANDOU.

Radiodiffusion-Télévision Congolaise (RTC): BP 2241, Brazzaville; tel. 22-281-24-73; state-owned; Pres. JEAN-GILBERT FOUTOU; Dir-Gen. GILBERT-DAVID MUTAKALA.

Radio Congo: BP 2241, Brazzaville; tel. 22-281-50-60; radio programmes in French, Lingala, Kikongo, Subia, English and Portuguese; transmitters at Brazzaville and Pointe-Noire; Gen. Man. ALPHONSE BOUYA DIMI; Dir of Broadcasting THÉOPHILE MIETE LIKIBI.

Télé Pointe-Noire: BP 769, Pointe-Noire; tel. 22-294-02-65; f. 1988.

Télé Congo: Brazzaville; f. 1960; operated by Radiodiffusion-Télévision Congolaise; Dir-Gen. JEAN OBAMBI.

Regulatory Authority

Conseil Supérieur de la Liberté de la Communication (Higher Council for the Freedom of Communication): Brazzaville; tel. 06-668-93-49 (mobile); e-mail jacques_banas@yahoo.fr; f. 2003; 11 mems, nominated by the President of the Republic; Pres. PHILIPPE MVOUO.

Finance

(cap. = capital; res = reserves; dep. = deposits; m. = million; br(s). = branch(es); amounts in francs CFA)

BANKING

In 2008 there were seven commercial banks and one other financial institution in the Republic of the Congo.

Central Bank

Banque des Etats de l'Afrique Centrale (BEAC): BP 126, Brazzaville; tel. 22-281-10-73; fax 22-281-10-94; e-mail beacbzv@beac.int; internet www.beac.int; HQ in Yaoundé, Cameroon; f. 1973; bank of issue for mem. states of the Communauté Economique et Monétaire de l'Afrique Centrale (CEMAC, fmrly Union Douanière et Economique de l'Afrique Centrale) comprising Cameroon, the Central African Repub., Chad, the Repub. of the Congo, Equatorial Guinea and Gabon; cap. 88,000m., res 227,843m., dep. 4,110,966m. (Dec. 2007); Gov. LUCAS ABAGA NCHAMA; Dir in Repub. of the Congo CÉDRIC JOVIAL ONDAYE EBAUH; br. at Pointe-Noire.

Commercial Banks

Banque Commerciale Internationale: ave Amílcar Cabral, BP 147, Brazzaville; tel. 22-281-58-34; fax 22-281-03-73; internet www.bci.banquepopulaire.com; f. 2001 on privatization of Union Congolaise de Banques; renamed as above in 2006; cap. and res 2,868.2m., total assets 57,523.9m. (Dec. 2003); Pres. DOMINIQUE MARTINIE; Dir-Gen. DOMINIQUE BILYNSKI; 16 brs.

Banque Congolaise de l'Habitat (BCH): ave Amílcar Cabral, BP 987, Brazzaville; tel. 22-281-25-88; fax 22-281-33-56; e-mail audriche.elenga@bch.cg; internet www.bch.cg; f. 2008; Pres. JEAN ALFRED ONANGA; Dir-Gen. FADHEL GUIZANI.

BGFI Bank Congo: angle rue Reims, face à paierie de France, BP 14579, Brazzaville; tel. 22-281-40-50; fax 22-281-50-89; e-mail agence_brazzaville@bgfi.com; internet www.bgfi.com; subsidiary of BGFIBANK Group (Gabon); cap. 5,000m. (2007); Dir-Gen. NARCISSE OBIANG ONDO; 2 brs.

La Congolaise de Banque (LCB): ave Amílcar Cabral, BP 2889, Brazzaville; tel. 22-281-09-79; fax 22-281-09-77; internet lacongolaisedebanque.com; f. 2004 on privatization of Crédit pour l'Agriculture, l'Industrie et le Commerce (CAIC); cap. 4,000m. (2005); Dir-Gen. YOUNÈS EL MASLOUMI; 17 brs.

Crédit du Congo (CDCo): ave Emmanuel Daddet, BP 1312, Pointe-Noire; tel. 22-294-24-00; fax 22-294-16-65; e-mail svpinfos@creditducongo.com; internet www.creditducongo.com; f. 2002 to replace Banque Internationale du Congo; fmrly Crédit Lyonnais Congo; name changed as above in 2007; 91% owned by Attijariwafa bank (Morocco), 9% state-owned; cap. and res 2,868.2m., total assets 116,550.0m. (Dec. 2007); Pres. BOUBKER JAÏ; Dir-Gen. ABDELAHAD KETTANI; 4 brs.

Ecobank Congo: rond point de la Coupole, BP 2485, Brazzaville; tel. 05-547-00-35 (mobile); e-mail ecobankcg@ecobank.com; internet www.ecobank.com; cap. 5,000.0m., dep. 67,243.4m.; Pres. GERVAIS BOUITI-VIAUDO; Dir-Gen. LAZARE KOMI NOULEKOU.

Société Congolaise de Financement (SOCOFIN): BP 899, Pointe-Noire; tel. 06-667-10-44 (mobile); fax 22-294-37-93; e-mail socofin.pnr@celtelplus.com; f. 2001; acquired by BGFI Bank in 2008; cap. 1,000m., res 109.5m., total assets 6,434.3m. (Dec. 2005); Dir-Gen. THIERRY SANSONNAT.

Co-operative Banking Institution

Mutuelle Congolaise d'Epargne et de Crédit (MUCODEC): ave Paul Doumer, BP 13237, Brazzaville; tel. 22-281-07-57; fax 22-281-01-68; e-mail contact@mucodec.com; internet www.mucodec.com; f. 1994; cap. and res 2,080m., total assets 29,000m. (Dec. 2003); Pres. BIENVENU MAZIÉZOULA; Dir-Gen. GÉRARD LEGIER; 45 brs.

Development Bank

Banque de Développement des Etats de l'Afrique Centrale: BP 1177, Brazzaville; tel. 22-281-18-85; fax 22-281-18-80; e-mail bdeac@bdeac.org; internet www.bdeac.org; cap. 38,013.1m., res 33,320.8m., dep. 6,624.1m. (Dec. 2010); Pres. MICHAËL ANDADÉ.

Financial Institution

Caisse Congolaise d'Amortissement (CCA): ave Foch, BP 2090, Brazzaville; tel. 22-281-57-35; fax 22-281-52-36; f. 1971; management of state funds; Dir-Gen. GEORGES NGUEKOUMOU.

INSURANCE

Assurances Générales du Congo: Brazzaville; tel. 22-918-93-00; fax 22-281-55-57; e-mail agccongo@yahoo.fr; f. 1999; Dir-Gen. (Non-Life) RAYMOND IBATA; Dir-Gen. (Life) AÏSSATA MOUSSA.

Assurances et Réassurances du Congo (ARC): ave du Camp, BP 14524, Brazzaville; tel. 22-281-35-08; f. 1973; 50% state-owned; privatization pending; Dir-Gen. WILFRIED ALBERT OSSIE; brs at Brazzaville, Loubomo and Ouesso.

Gras Savoye Congo: 13 rue Germain Bikouma, angle route de la Radio, Immeuble Guenin, BP 1901, Pointe-Noire; tel. 22-294-79-72; fax 22-294-79-74; e-mail grassavoye.congo@cg.celtelplus.com; affiliated to Gras Savoye (France); insurance brokers and risk managers; Man. PHILIPPE BAILLÉ.

Nouvelle Société Interafricaine d'Assurances: 1 ave Foch, angle rue Sergent Malamine, face hôtel de ville, BP 1151, Brazzaville; tel. 22-281-13-34; fax 22-281-21-70; f. 2004; life and non-life; Dir-Gen. ALFRED YAMEOGO.

Trade and Industry

GOVERNMENT AGENCY

Comité des Privatisations et de Renforcement des Capacités Locales: Immeuble ex-SCBO, 7ème étage, BP 1176, Brazzaville; tel. 22-281-46-21; fax 22-281-46-09; e-mail privat@aol.com; oversees and co-ordinates transfer of state-owned enterprises to the private sector.

DEVELOPMENT ORGANIZATIONS

Agence Française de Développement (AFD): rue Béhagle, BP 96, Brazzaville; tel. 22-281-53-30; fax 22-281-29-42; e-mail afdbrazzaville@afd.fr; internet www.afd.fr; French fund for economic co-operation; Country Dir PATRICK DAL BELLO.

Service de Coopération et d'Action Culturelle: BP 2175, Brazzaville; tel. 22-283-15-03; f. 1959; administers bilateral aid from France; Dir RICHARD MOUTHUY.

CHAMBERS OF COMMERCE

Chambre de Commerce, d'Industrie, d'Agriculture et des Métiers de Brazzaville (CCIAMB): ave Amílcar Cabral, Centre Ville, BP 92, Brazzaville; tel. 05-521-70-04; fax 22-281-16-08; internet cciambrazza.com; f. 1935; Pres. PAUL OBAMBI; Sec.-Gen. ALPHONSE MFOURGA.

Chambre de Commerce, d'Industrie, d'Agriculture et des Métiers de Pointe-Noire: 3 blvd Général Charles de Gaulle, BP 665, Pointe-Noire; tel. 22-294-12-80; fax 22-294-07-13; e-mail infos@cciampnr.org; internet www.cciampnr.com; f. 1948; Chair. SYLVESTRE DIDIER MAVOUENZELA; Sec.-Gen. JEAN-BAPTISTE SOUMBOU.

EMPLOYERS' ORGANIZATIONS

Confédération Générale du Patronat Congolais (COGEPACO): Brazzaville; Pres. JEAN GALESSAMY-IBOMBOT.

Forum des Jeunes Entreprises du Congo (FJEC): Quartier Milice, Villa 43B, ave de l'OUA, BP 13700, Makélékélé, Brazzaville; tel. 06-666-26-06 (mobile); e-mail fjecbrazza@fjec.org; internet www.fjec.org; f. 1990; Sec.-Gen. PAUL KAMPAKOL.

Union Nationale des Opérateurs Economiques du Congo (UNOC): BP 5187, Brazzaville; tel. 22-281-54-32; e-mail unoc_patronat@yahoo.fr; f. 1985; operates a professional training centre; Pres. El Hadj DJIBRIL ABDOULAYE BOPAKA.

Union Patronale et Interprofessionnelle du Congo (UNICONGO): Immeuble CAPINFO, 1er étage, ave Paul Doumer, BP 42, Brazzaville; tel. 06-629-79-06 (mobile); fax 22-281-47-66; e-mail unicongobvz@unicongo.net; internet www.unicongo.org; f. 1958; Nat. Pres. CHRISTIAN BARROS; Sec.-Gen. JEAN-JACQUES SAMBA; membership of 20 feds (2008).

UTILITIES

Electricity

Agence Nationale d'Électrification Rurale du Congo (ANER): BP 2120, Brazzaville; tel. 05-570-19-52 (mobile); fax 22-281-50-77; e-mail aner_congo@yahoo.fr; f. 2003.

Société Nationale d'Electricité (SNE): 95 ave Paul Doumer, BP 95, Brazzaville; tel. 22-281-05-66; fax 22-281-05-69; e-mail snecongo@caramail.com; f. 1967; transfer to private management proposed; operates hydroelectric plants at Bouenza and Djoué; Dir-Gen. LOUIS KANOHA-ELENGA.

Water

Société Nationale de Distribution d'Eau (SNDE): rue du Sergent Malamine, BP 229, Brazzaville; tel. 22-294-22-16; fax 22-294-28-60; internet www.sndecongo.com; f. 1967; transferred to private sector management by Bi-Water (United Kingdom) in 2002; water supply and sewerage; holds monopoly over wells and import of mineral water; Dir-Gen. EMILE MOKOKO.

TRADE UNION FEDERATIONS

Independent trade unions were legalized in 1991.

Confédération Nationale des Syndicats Libres (CNASYL): Brazzaville; f. 1994; Sec.-Gen. MICHEL KABOUL MAOUTA.

Confédération Syndicale Congolaise (CSC): BP 2311, Brazzaville; tel. 22-283-19-23; f. 1964; 80,000 mems; Sec.-Gen. DANIEL MONGO.

Confédération Syndicale des Travailleurs du Congo (CSTC): BP 14743, Brazzaville; tel. 06-661-47-35 (mobile); f. 1993; fed. of 13 trade unions; Chair. ELAULT BELLO BELLARD; 40,000 mems.

Confédération des Syndicats Libres Autonomes du Congo (COSYLAC): BP 14861, Brazzaville; tel. 22-282-42-65; fax 22-283-42-70; e-mail b.oba@congonet.cg; Sec.-Gen. JEAN BERNARD.

Transport

RAILWAYS

In 2008 there were 795 km of railway track in the Congo. Rail traffic was severely disrupted by the 1997 civil war. The main line (of some 518 km) between Brazzaville and Pointe-Noire reopened briefly in November 1998 for freight traffic, but was subsequently closed following further unrest and sabotage. In early 2000 the Government signed two agreements with the Société Nationale des Chemins de Fer Français (France) relating to the repair of the line and associated infrastructure, and to the management of the network. Freight services resumed in August 2000, followed by passenger services in January 2001, although there was further disruption to the railways during unrest in mid-2002. In May 2004 the rail service linking Brazzaville to the Pool region resumed operations. In 2008 work started on a 1,000-km railway project to link Pointe-Noire with Ouesso.

Chemin de Fer Congo-Océan (CFCO): ave Charles de Gaulle, BP 651, Pointe-Noire; tel. 05-559-91-24 (mobile); fax 22-294-04-47; internet www.cfco.cg; f. 1969; entered partnership with Rail Afrique International in June 1998; transfer to private management proposed; Dir-Gen. SAUVEUR JOSEPH EL BEZ.

ROADS

In 2006 there were an estimated 17,289 km of roads. Only about 7.1% of the total network was paved. The principal routes link Brazzaville with Pointe-Noire, in the south, and with Ouesso, in the north. A number of major construction projects initiated by President Sassou-Nguesso in 2000 and 2001 have involved the highways from Brazzaville to Kinkala, and from Brazzaville to the Pool region.

Régie Nationale des Transports et des Travaux Publics: BP 2073, Brazzaville; tel. 22-283-35-58; f. 1965; civil engineering, maintenance of roads and public works; Man. Dir HECTOR BIENVENU OUAMBA.

INLAND WATERWAYS

The Congo and Oubangui rivers form two axes of a highly developed inland waterway system. The Congo river and seven tributaries in the Congo basin provide 2,300 km of navigable river, and the Oubangui river, developed in co-operation with the Central African Republic, an additional 2,085 km.

Coordination Nationale des Transports Fluviaux: BP 2048, Brazzaville; tel. 22-283-06-27; Dir MÉDARD OKOUMOU.

Transcap—Congo: BP 1154, Pointe-Noire; tel. 22-294-01-46; f. 1962; Chair. J. DROUAULT.

SHIPPING

The deep-water Atlantic seaport at Pointe-Noire is the most important port in Central Africa, and Brazzaville is one of the principal ports on the Congo river. A major rehabilitation programme began in 1999, with the aim of establishing Pointe-Noire as a regional centre for container traffic and as a logistics centre for offshore petroleum exploration. At 31 December 2013 the Congo's flag registered fleet comprised eight vessels, totalling 1,320 grt.

La Congolaise de Transport Maritime (COTRAM): Pointe-Noire; f. 1984; national shipping co; state-owned.

Maersk Congo: 10 rue Massabi, Zone Portuaire, Pointe-Noire; tel. 22-294-21-41; fax 22-294-23-25; f. 1997; represents Maersk Sealand (Denmark).

Port Autonome de Brazzaville et des Ports Secondaires (PABPS): BP 2048, Brazzaville; tel. 22-283-00-42; f. 2000; port authority; Dir MARTIN BLAISE BOYAMBA.

Port Autonome de Pointe-Noire (PAPN): BP 711, Pointe-Noire; tel. 22-294-00-13; fax 22-294-02-87; e-mail info@papn-cg.org; internet www.papn-cg.org; f. 2000; port authority; Pres. JEAN LOUIS OSSO; Dir-Gen. JEAN-MARIE ANIÉLÉ.

SAGA Congo: 18 rue du Prophète Lasse Zephirin, BP 674, Pointe-Noire; tel. 22-294-10-16; fax 22-294-34-04; e-mail emmanuelle.peillon@bollore.com; acquired by Bolloré Africa Logistics au Congo in Oct. 2013; Dir-Gen. PIERRE BELLEROSE.

Société Congolaise de Transports Maritimes (SOCOTRAM): BP 4922, Pointe-Noire; tel. 22-294-49-21; fax 22-294-49-22; e-mail info@socotram.com; internet www.socotram.fr; f. 1990; Dir JUSTE MONDELE.

CIVIL AVIATION

There are international airports at Brazzaville (Maya-Maya), Oyo (Oyo Ollombo) and Pointe-Noire (Agostinho Neto). There are also five regional airports, at Loubomo (Dolisie, Ngot-Nzounzoungou), Nkayi, Owando, Ouesso and Impfondo, as well as 12 smaller airfields.

Agence Nationale de l'Aviation Civile: rue de la Libération de Paris, Camp Clairon, BP 128, Brazzaville; e-mail courrier@anac-congo.org; internet anaccongo.org; Dir-Gen. MICHEL AMBENDÉ.

Aéro-Service: ave Charles de Gaulle, BP 1138, Pointe-Noire; tel. 05-556-41-41 (mobile); fax 22-294-14-41; e-mail info@aero-service.net; f. 1967; scheduled and charter passenger and freight services; operates nationally and to regional destinations; Pres. and Dir-Gen. R. GRIESBAUM.

Equatorial Congo Airlines SA (ECAir): 1604 ave des Trois Martyrs, Quartier Batignolles, Brazzaville; tel. 06-509-05-09 (mobile); e-mail info@flyecair.com; internet www.flyecair.com; f. 2011; operates flights between Brazzaville and Pointe-Noire; Dir-Gen. FATIMA BEYNA MOUSSA.

Trans Air Congo: Immeuble City Center, ave Amílcar Cabral, BP 2422, Brazzaville; tel. 22-281-10-46; fax 22-281-10-57; e-mail info@flytransaircongo.com; internet www.flytransaircongo.com; f. 1994; private airline operating internal scheduled and international charter flights; Pres. and Dir-Gen. BASSAM ELHAGE.

Tourism

Tourist visitors numbered some 218,000 in 2011 (compared with tourist arrivals of 21,611 in 2002) and the industry has been identified as having considerable potential for growth by the Government. In 2007 earnings from tourism were estimated at US $54m.

Office National du Tourisme: BP 456, Brazzaville; tel. 22-283-09-53; f. 1980; Dir-Gen. ANTOINE KOUNKOU-KIBOUILOU.

Defence

As assessed at November 2012, the army numbered 8,000, the navy about 800 and the air force 1,200. In addition, there was a 2,000-strong gendarmerie. National service is voluntary for men and women, and lasts for two years.

Defence Expenditure: Estimated at 108,000m. francs CFA for 2011.

Supreme Commander of the Armed Forces: Gen. DENIS SASSOU-NGUESSO.

Chief of General Staff of the Congolese Armed Forces: Gen. NORBERT ROBERT MONDJO.

Chief of Staff of the Air Force: Col JEAN-BAPTISTE FÉLIX TCHIKAYA.

Chief of Staff of the Navy: Col FULGOR ONGOBE.

Commander of the Ground Forces: Gen. NOËL LEONARD ESSONGO.

Sec.-Gen. of the National Security Council: Col JEAN-DOMINIQUE OKEMBA.

Education

Education is officially compulsory for 10 years between six and 16 years of age and is provided free of charge in public institutions. Primary education begins at the age of six and lasts for six years. Secondary education, from 12 years of age, lasts for seven years, comprising a first cycle of four years and a second of three years. According to UNESCO estimates, in 2012 enrolment at primary schools included 90% of children in the relevant age-group (boys 86%; girls 94%), while enrolment at secondary schools was equivalent to 54% of children in the relevant age-group (boys 57%; girls 50%). In 2011/12 39,303 students (24,187 males; 15,116 females) were attending tertiary institutions. In 2004 the World Bank approved a grant of US $20m. to assist with the reconstruction of the country's educational sector, which had been severely damaged by years of civil conflict. In 2005 spending on education represented 8.1% of total budgetary expenditure.

COSTA RICA

Introductory Survey

LOCATION, CLIMATE, LANGUAGE, RELIGION, FLAG, CAPITAL

The Republic of Costa Rica lies in the Central American isthmus, with Nicaragua to the north, Panama to the south, the Caribbean Sea to the east and the Pacific Ocean to the west. The climate is warm and damp in the lowlands (average temperature 27°C (81°F)) and cooler on the Central Plateau (average temperature 22°C (72°F)), where two-thirds of the population live. The language spoken is Spanish. Almost all of the inhabitants profess Christianity, and the majority adhere to the Roman Catholic Church, the state religion. The national flag (proportions 3 by 5) has five horizontal stripes, of blue, white, red, white and blue, the red stripe being twice the width of the others. The state flag, in addition, has on the red stripe (to the left of centre) a white oval enclosing the national coat of arms, showing three volcanic peaks between the Caribbean and the Pacific. The capital is San José.

CONTEMPORARY POLITICAL HISTORY

Historical Context

Costa Rica was ruled by Spain from the 16th century until 1821, when independence was declared. The only significant interruption in the country's constitutional government since 1920 occurred in February 1948, when the victory of the opposition candidate, Otilio Ulate Blanco, in the presidential election was disputed. The legislature annulled the election but a civil war ensued. The anti-Government forces, led by José Figueres Ferrer, were successful, and a revolutionary junta took power in April. Costa Rica's army was abolished in December. After the preparation of a new Constitution, Ulate took office as President in January 1949.

Figueres, who founded the socialist Partido Liberación Nacional (PLN), dominated national politics for decades, holding presidential office in 1953–58 and 1970–74. Under his leadership, Costa Rica became one of the most democratic countries in Latin America. Since the 1948 revolution, there have been frequent changes of power, all achieved by constitutional means.

Domestic Political Affairs

Figueres's first Government nationalized the banks and instituted a comprehensive social security system. The presidential election of 1958, however, was won by a conservative, Mario Echandi Jiménez, who reversed many PLN policies. His successor, Francisco Orlich Bolmarich (President from 1962 to 1966), was supported by the PLN but continued the encouragement of private enterprise. Another conservative, José Joaquín Trejos Fernández, held power in 1966–70. In 1974 the PLN candidate, Daniel Oduber Quirós, was elected President. He continued the policies of extending the welfare state and of establishing amicable relations with communist states. In 1978 Rodrigo Carazo Odio of the conservative Partido Unidad Opositora coalition (subsequently the Coalición Unidad) was elected President. During Carazo's term of office increasing instability in Central America led to diplomatic tension, and the President was criticized for his alleged involvement in illegal arms-trafficking between Cuba and El Salvador.

At elections in February 1982, Luis Alberto Monge Alvarez and his party, the PLN, won a comfortable majority. The new President announced a series of emergency economic measures, in an attempt to rescue the country from near-bankruptcy. A policy of neutrality towards the left-wing Sandinista Government of Nicaragua was continued. However, following a number of cross-border raids, a national alert was declared in May. The rebel Nicaraguan leader, Edén Pastora Gómez, was expelled. Relations with Nicaragua deteriorated as guerrilla activity spread to San José. In November 1983 Monge declared Costa Rica's neutrality in an attempt to elicit foreign support for his country. This declaration was opposed by the USA and led to the resignation of the Minister of Foreign Affairs.

In 1984 there were increasing reports of incursions into Costa Rica by the Sandinista forces. An attempt was made to defuse the tension with the establishment of a commission, supported by the Contadora group (Colombia, Mexico, Panama and Venezuela), to monitor the border area. In May, however, the attempted assassination of Pastora exacerbated the inter-government differences on policy towards Nicaragua. Reports of clashes along the joint border became increasingly frequent and in 1985 the Government's commitment to neutrality was disputed when it decided to establish an anti-guerrilla battalion, trained by US military advisers.

At presidential and legislative elections in February 1986 Oscar Arias Sánchez, the PLN candidate, was elected President. The PLN also obtained a clear majority in the Asamblea Legislativa (Legislative Assembly). The new Government was committed to the development of a welfare state, the renegotiation of the country's external debt, and the reinforcement of Costa Rica's policy of neutrality. Diplomatic relations with Nicaragua were fully restored, and the Government embarked on a series of arrests and expulsions of Contras resident in Costa Rica. A degree of Costa Rican complicity in anti-Sandinista activity became apparent, however, when the existence of a secret air-strip in Costa Rica, used as a supply base for the Contras, was made public.

Arias became increasingly involved in the quest for peace in Central America. In 1987 the Presidents of El Salvador, Nicaragua, Guatemala, Honduras and Costa Rica signed a peace agreement based on proposals presented by Arias, who was subsequently awarded the Nobel Peace Prize. In 1988 Arias brought Nicaraguan government officials and Contra leaders together in San José for their first discussions concerning the implementation of a ceasefire.

Industrial unrest

At presidential and legislative elections in February 1990, Rafael Angel Calderón Fournier, the candidate of the Partido Unidad Social Cristiana (PUSC), was elected President. The PUSC also obtained a clear majority in the Legislative Assembly. Calderón inherited a large fiscal deficit and was therefore forced to renege on his pre-election promise of improvements in welfare and income distribution. The Government introduced an adjustment programme of austerity measures, but this was abandoned in November 1991 in response to public pressure.

Presidential and legislative elections were held in February 1994. The presidential ballot was narrowly won by José María Figueres Olsen, the PLN candidate. The PLN failed to obtain an outright majority in the Legislative Assembly, however. Industrial unrest increased in 1994, and government proposals for the deregulation and privatization of state enterprises prompted a 100,000-strong demonstration in the capital in August. The Government agreed to establish a commission to debate proposed reforms of the pension system and other government policies.

The PUSC in power

At the presidential election of February 1998 Miguel Angel Rodríguez Echeverría, the candidate of the PUSC, secured a narrow victory. The PUSC failed to obtain an outright majority in the Legislative Assembly. The new President's attempts to alleviate the budget deficit through economic reform met with considerable opposition. In May 2000 the Government was forced to withdraw proposed legislation on the privatization of the telecommunications and energy sectors, after the largest popular protests in the country in 30 years.

Presidential and legislative elections were held in February 2002. As no candidate gained 40% of the votes cast, for the first time a further round of voting was held in April between the two leading candidates, Abel Pacheco de la Espriella of the ruling PUSC and Rolando Araya of the PLN. Pacheco won the second round ballot.

In August 2004 the deteriorating economic situation prompted public sector unions to organize a week-long general strike. The unrest escalated after drivers' associations also began protests against the monopoly on vehicle inspections held by the Spanish company Riteve SyC. At the end of the month the Government agreed to increase salaries and to review Riteve SyC's contract. The concessions provoked the resignations of the Ministers of Finance and of the Presidency.

In September 2004 former President Calderón was charged with accepting illegal payments. His apprehension came just one week after another former PUSC President, Miguel Angel Rodríguez, was accused of accepting payments from a French company in connection with a contract with the Instituto Costarricense de Electricidad (ICE—the state electricity and telecommunications company). Furthermore, in the same month President Pacheco admitted to having received an illegal campaign contribution of US $100,000. The corruption scandals prompted a protest march, attended by thousands of people, in the capital in October. Later that month another former President, this time from the PLN, José María Figueres, was accused of receiving illegal payments totalling US $900,000. Pacheco was beleaguered by further accusations of corrupt practices in 2005: in June of that year he submitted to a parliamentary inquiry into a number of undisclosed gifts. Calderón was convicted of embezzlement and sentenced to five years' imprisonment in 2009. In April 2011 Rodríguez was found guilty of accepting bribes and also received a five-year prison sentence; however, following an appeal, he was acquitted in December 2012.

The PLN in power

In presidential and legislative elections in February 2006 Oscar Arias Sánchez, representing the PLN, reattained the presidency. The PLN also performed well in the concurrently held legislative election, winning 25 of the 57 seats in the Legislative Assembly. Upon assuming office, Arias negotiated an alliance with the Movimiento Libertario (ML) and the Partido Acción Ciudadana (PAC) to secure a legislative majority. In return for their support, the new President undertook to grant property rights to residents in marginal urban areas, and to restrict political patronage.

Intermittent protests against the proposed Dominican Republic-Central American Free Trade Agreement (CAFTA-DR) were organized in 2006 and 2007. In October 2006 ICE employees were joined by workers from the health, education and finance sectors to participate in two days of industrial action. Some 9,000 people gathered in San José to signal their opposition to the putative trade agreement with the USA. Protesters were particularly opposed to the proposed liberalization of the telecommunications and insurance industries, as well as the privatization of the ICE. In April 2007, in what many viewed as a delaying tactic, the opposition submitted a request to the Supreme Electoral Tribunal that a referendum on implementation of CAFTA-DR be held; the request was granted, provided the opposition could obtain 132,000 signatures (equivalent to 5% of the electorate) in favour of a vote. The time limit for the collection of signatures was 10 months, which would have made implementation of the accord almost impossible before the 1 March 2008 deadline. However, President Arias pre-empted the tactic by successfully petitioning the Assembly to hold a binding plebiscite on ratification within 90 days instead.

The referendum on CAFTA-DR was held on 7 October 2007. The campaign was bitterly fought: in September the Second Vice-President, Kevin Casas Zamora, resigned after recommending aggressive tactics be used by the 'yes' campaign to win the plebiscite. Supporters of the free trade agreement secured a narrow victory, winning 51.6% of the total votes cast, compared with 48.4% garnered by the 'no' campaign, led by the PAC. Turnout was estimated at 59.2% of the electorate. At the end of November President Arias signed into law the proposed CAFTA-DR. However, the legislature still had to approve the 13 measures necessary to implement the treaty by the March 2008 deadline. Although it agreed not to obstruct passage of the enabling laws, the PAC refused to attend congressional sessions to discuss the reforms, rendering many sessions inquorate. By February 2008 less than one-half of the necessary laws had been approved, forcing Arias to seek an extension of the deadline until 1 October. One of the most significant enabling laws was passed in May when the 50-year state monopoly on telecommunications by the ICE was ended. By September 12 of the enabling laws had been approved, but the final piece of legislation, concerning intellectual property and biodiversity, was rejected by the Constitutional Court, and a further extension of the deadline was necessary. The final law required for implementation of CAFTA-DR was approved on 12 November, and the agreement took effect from 1 January 2009.

The Chinchilla Government

A presidential election was held on 7 February 2010. The candidate of the ruling PLN, Laura Chinchilla Miranda, won with a substantial 47% of the votes cast. Ottón Solís Fallas of the PAC won 25% of the ballot, followed by the ML's Otto Guevara Guth, with 21%. The PLN also remained the largest party in the Legislative Assembly, with 24 of the 57 seats. The PAC and ML secured 11 and nine seats, respectively, while the PUSC won six seats and the Partido Accesibilidad Sin Exclusión (PASE) four. The remaining three seats were distributed between the Frente Amplio (FA), the Partido Renovación Costarricense (PRC) and the Partido Restauración Nacional.

Rising crime rates had been a dominant theme of the electoral campaign and Chinchilla had pledged to increase spending on security by 50%. Following a public consultation, in February 2011 a 10-year security policy was announced; an additional 4,000 police officers were to be recruited by 2014, and there was also to be increased training. There was to be greater co-operation between security forces and local government and efforts made to keep young people within the education system. Chinchilla also took steps to address the growing problem of drugs-trafficking and in May 2010 established an anti-narcotics commission. The USA provided US $1m. in funding for the national coastguard service and in July the Legislative Assembly approved the largest ever number of US vessels and personnel on Costa Rican territory. Despite these measures, in September the USA included Costa Rica for the first time on its list of major illicit drugs-producing and -trafficking countries. Following widespread dissatisfaction with the Government's often vague security plans, in May 2011 Chinchilla appointed a new Minister of Governance, Police and Public Security, Mario Zamora Cordero.

The Chinchilla administration's other main priority was fiscal reform. By introducing new taxes and increasing existing levies, Chinchilla planned to generate some US $900m. in additional annual revenues, which could then be used to lower the fiscal deficit and fund her policy agenda. However, the Government's attempts to restructure the tax system were repeatedly obstructed by the opposition parties, which in May 2011 had formed a fragile coalition (comprising the PAC, the ML, the PUSC, the PASE and the FA), giving them a parliamentary majority. The ruling PLN had also been undermined by internal divisions, and in April almost one-half of the party's deputies had briefly established a separate voting bloc in the Asamblea. In September the PAC, the main opposition party, entered into negotiations with the Government on a compromise fiscal reform plan. The revised tax reform bill was approved by the Asamblea in March 2012, but in the following month the Constitutional Court overturned the legislation. The Government thus pursued a number of less ambitious measures, overseeing a minor restructuring of the tax system in mid-2012 and modest spending reductions, and a $1,000m. bond was issued in November.

Meanwhile, in July 2011 René Castro was replaced as Minister of Foreign Relations by Enrique Castillo Barrantes. Earlier in July the President had dismissed 27 diplomats following allegations that they had acquired their positions through nepotism, although Chinchilla denied that there was any connection between the two events; Castro's critics claimed that he had been replaced after being outmanoeuvred by the Nicaraguan authorities in relation to the San Juan territorial dispute (see Regional relations). Also in that month, the Minister of Public Health, María Luisa Ávila, resigned amid a funding crisis in the national social security scheme; she was replaced by Daisy Corrales Díaz. The Minister of Public Works and Transport, Francisco Jiménez, was replaced by Luis Llach in May 2012 following the discovery of alleged corruption within his ministry. Also in May, the PLN established an alliance with the PASE, thus restoring the ruling party's control of the legislature and precipitating the disintegration of the opposition coalition. Chinchilla reorganized the Cabinet again in October, appointing new heads of the public works, labour, and housing ministries. The Minister of Communications and Public Relations, Francisco Chacón Gonzalez, resigned in May 2013 amid accusations that he had chartered a private aircraft for Chinchilla from a businessman with alleged ties to the illegal drugs trade. Chacón was replaced by Carlos Roverssi in June. Also in that month Ana Isabel Garita was appointed as the new Minister of Justice and Peace.

Recent developments: the 2014 elections

Luis Guillermo Solís Rivera of the PAC secured 30.6% of the valid votes cast at the presidential election conducted on 2 February 2014. Johnny Araya Monge, the nominee of the governing PLN, was his closest rival, with 29.7% of the ballot, while the FA's José María Villalta Florez-Estrada attracted 17.3% and Otto Guevara

Guth of the ML 11.3%. A run-off election between Solís and Araya was scheduled to take place on 6 April; however, in early March Araya announced he was withdrawing from the contest, owing to the closeness of the first round result. As electoral rules prohibited a candidate's withdrawal, Araya declared he would not campaign for the second round of voting, although his name would still appear on ballot papers. Predictably, Solís won a landslide victory on 6 April, garnering 77.8% of the ballot, according to preliminary results. Araya won 22.2% of the vote. Although the rate of abstention was high, Solís still attracted more than 1.3m. votes, giving him a strong mandate to govern. He was scheduled to take office on 8 May.

Legislative polls were held concurrently with the first round of the presidential election. The PLN's representation in the Legislative Assembly declined to 18 seats, while the PAC and the FA performed strongly, increasing the number of seats under their control to 14 and nine, respectively. The PUSC won eight seats and the ML retained three, with the remaining five mandates allocated to smaller parties.

Foreign Affairs

Regional relations

Relations with Nicaragua became strained in 1995 after Costa Rica began expelling previously tolerated illegal immigrants. In 1998 Nicaragua prohibited Costa Rican civil guards from carrying arms while navigating the San Juan river, part of Nicaraguan territory. In 2009 the International Court of Justice (ICJ) decreed that Costa Rica had navigational rights on the San Juan river for commercial purposes only. Tensions increased again in 2010 after Costa Rica accused Nicaragua of violating Costa Rican territory during a dredging operation. In March 2011, pending a definitive ruling, the ICJ ordered military and civilian personnel from both sides to leave the disputed area, although it did not halt Nicaraguan dredging. In December Nicaragua began legal proceedings at the ICJ against Costa Rica over the environmental impact of a planned road along the river. The Central American Court of Justice, the legal authority of which was not recognized by Costa Rica, ruled in favour of Nicaragua in relation to the San Juan highway dispute in July 2012; Chinchilla rejected this judgment as 'illegitimate'. Meanwhile, Costa Rica submitted formal complaints to the Nicaraguan authorities in 2012 and 2013 owing to concerns over, respectively, a potential new shipping lane and petroleum exploration in the border region. Chinchilla also took steps to increase security along the shared frontier. The Costa Rican ambassador to Nicaragua was recalled in August 2013 after Nicaraguan President Daniel Ortega intimated that he might file a legal challenge with the ICJ regarding Costa Rica's long-standing sovereignty over the province of Guanacaste. In September Costa Rica, Colombia and Panama raised the matter of Nicaragua's 'expansionist' policies with UN Secretary-General Ban Ki-Moon. In November, in response to a Costa Rican appeal, the ICJ demanded that Nicaragua desist from dredging and canal-building operations in the contested San Juan region while the relevant case was still being considered; all Nicaraguan personnel were again instructed to disengage from the area. Costa Rica secured another favourable ruling in the following month, when the ICJ adjudged the environmental impact of the San Juan highway to be negligible. In February 2014 Costa Rica submitted a further protest to the ICJ, claiming that the Nicaraguan Government was offering oil concessions that fell within Costa Rican maritime territory.

Other external relations

Costa Rica severed diplomatic relations with Taiwan in 2007 in favour of establishing relations with the People's Republic of China, which provided US $20m. in immediate aid for victims of severe floods that occurred in September, and a further $27m. for longer-term projects. In 2008 President Hu Jintao of China visited Costa Rica and signed a series of co-operation accords, which included assurances to invest in the state petroleum refinery, Refinadora Costarricense de Petróleo, and to fund a national stadium. In 2011 a bilateral free trade agreement was ratified by Costa Rica. President Chinchilla travelled to China in August 2012 and concluded a number of additional bilateral economic and security accords. In the following month the Costa Rican Government announced that China had also agreed to provide a $400m. credit line to finance a road construction project. In 2012 Costa Rica, with other Central American countries, concluded a free trade agreement with the European Union.

CONSTITUTION AND GOVERNMENT

Under the Constitution of 1949, executive power is vested in the President and an appointed Cabinet. The President is elected for a four-year term by compulsory adult suffrage, and a successful candidate must receive at least 40% of the votes. The legislative organ is the unicameral Legislative Assembly, with 57 members who are similarly elected for four years. Judicial power is vested in the Supreme Court, the justices of which are elected by the Legislative Assembly.

REGIONAL AND INTERNATIONAL CO-OPERATION

Costa Rica was a founder member of the UN. As a contracting party to the General Agreement on Tariffs and Trade, Costa Rica joined the World Trade Organization (see p. 434) on its establishment in 1995. Costa Rica is a member of the Organization of American States (see p. 394), the Central American Common Market (CACM, see p. 229), the Association of Caribbean States (see p. 449), the Inter-American Development Bank (see p. 331), and the Community of Latin American and Caribbean States (see p. 464), which was formally inaugurated in December 2011.

ECONOMIC AFFAIRS

In 2012, according to estimates by the World Bank, Costa Rica's gross national income (GNI), measured at average 2010–12 prices, was US $42,001m., equivalent to $8,740 per head (or $12,580 per head on an international purchasing-power parity basis). During 2003–12, it was estimated, the population increased by an average of 1.6% per year, while gross domestic product (GDP) per head increased, in real terms, by an average of 3.1% per year. According to official preliminary figures, overall GDP increased, in real terms, by an average annual rate of 4.8% in 2003–12; GDP increased by a preliminary 5.1% in 2012.

Agriculture (including hunting, forestry and fishing) contributed an estimated 5.9% of GDP in 2012 and employed 12.7% of the economically active population in 2013. The principal cash crops are pineapples (which accounted for 7.1% of export earnings in 2012), bananas (6.3%) and coffee (3.8%). Sugar cane is also cultivated. According to official preliminary figures, the real GDP of the agricultural sector increased at an average annual rate of 3.1% during 2003–12; real agricultural GDP increased by an estimated 3.5% in 2012.

Industry (including mining, manufacturing, construction and power) employed 19.0% of the economically active population in 2013 and provided an estimated 23.8% of GDP in 2012. According to official preliminary figures, real industrial GDP increased at an average annual rate of 4.4% during 2003–12; the real GDP of the sector increased by an estimated 6.0% in 2012.

Mining employed 0.1% of the economically active population in 2011 and contributed an estimated 0.1% of GDP in 2012. According to official preliminary figures, real mining GDP increased at an estimated average annual rate of 1.1% during 2003–12; the sector's GDP decreased by an estimated 3.2% in 2011, but increased by 5.3% in 2012.

Manufacturing and mining employed 11.7% of the employed workforce in 2013 and manufacturing alone contributed an estimated 16.1% of GDP in 2012. The principal branches of manufacturing were food products, chemical products, beverages, and paper and paper products. Production of computer components was also important. According to official preliminary figures, the real GDP of the manufacturing sector increased at an average annual rate of 4.3% during 2003–12; the sector's GDP increased by an estimated 6.3% in 2012.

Construction employed 5.7% of the economically active population in 2013 and provided an estimated 5.3% of GDP in 2012. According to official preliminary figures, the real GDP of the construction sector increased at an average annual rate of 5.7% during 2003–12; the sector's GDP decreased by an estimated 3.8% in 2011, but increased by 5.7% in 2012.

Energy is derived principally from petroleum and hydroelectric power. In 2012 the state petroleum company Refinadora Costarricense de Petróleo, its Chinese counterpart, the China National Petroleum Corporation, and the Chinese Development Bank signed a memorandum of understanding to seek financing for a joint refinery, although problems with the feasibility study in 2013 led to delays in the project. The Chinese firm was also scheduled to commence oil and gas exploration in areas off the country's Caribbean coast. In 2011 hydroelectric power accounted for 72.6% of total electrical energy generation. Imports of mineral products accounted for an estimated 12.8% of the total value of imports in 2012.

The services sector employed 68.3% of the economically active population in 2013 and provided an estimated 70.2% of GDP in 2012. According to official preliminary figures, the real GDP of this sector increased at an average annual rate of 5.5% during 2003–12; sectoral GDP increased by an estimated 5.1% in 2012. Tourism is the country's most important source of foreign-exchange earnings. Receipts from tourism totalled a provisional US $2,425m. in 2012. Tourist arrivals totalled 2,192,059 in 2011, a 4.4% increase on the previous year's total. Some 39.2% of the 2011 total came from the USA.

In 2012 Costa Rica recorded a visible merchandise trade deficit of US $7,427.2m. and there was a deficit of $2,376.2m. on the current account of the balance of payments. In 2012 the principal source of imports (51.7%) was the USA; other major suppliers were the People's Republic of China and Mexico (with whom Costa Rica signed an amended free trade agreement in early 2013). The USA was also the principal market for exports (37.0%); other significant purchasers were the Netherlands and Panama. The principal exports in 2012 were food and live animals (particularly bananas), machinery and electrical equipment (particularly computer components), optical and topographical equipment, basic manufactures, plastic materials, and chemical and chemical products. The principal imports in that year were machinery and electrical equipment, mineral products, chemicals and related products, common metals, transport equipment, plastic materials and manufactures, and food and live animals.

In 2012 there was an estimated budgetary deficit of 1,001,191m. colones (equivalent to some 4.4% of GDP). Costa Rica's general government gross debt was an estimated 8,014,510m. colones in 2012, equivalent to 35.3% of GDP. Costa Rica's total external debt in 2011 was US $10,291m., of which $3,925m. was public and publicly guaranteed debt. In that year, the cost of servicing long-term public and publicly guaranteed debt and repayments to the IMF was equivalent to 13.5% of the value of exports of goods, services and income (excluding workers' remittances). According to ILO, annual rate of inflation averaged 9.2% in 2003–12. Consumer prices increased by 4.5% in 2012. Some 8.5% of the labour force were unemployed in 2012.

The incoming Government of Laura Chinchilla inherited a substantial fiscal deficit in 2010, and the new administration's fiscal reform proposals were repeatedly blocked by the opposition. Nevertheless, the economy recovered well from the international downturn from 2008, and grew by 5.0% in 2010, and by 4.4% in 2011. Exports and foreign direct investment both increased markedly in both years. These positive economic trends continued into 2012, with GDP growth of 5.1%, supported by robust levels of domestic demand and increased activity in the tourism and manufacturing sectors. Chinchilla's expansive fiscal reform plans were rejected by the Constitutional Court in April, forcing the President to pursue smaller-scale measures. However, these proved insufficient to stabilize the Government's financial position, and public debt and the fiscal deficit continued to rise during 2012–13. Economic growth moderated to 3.5% in 2013, according to the IMF, following a disappointing agricultural season and a slowdown in both internal and external demand. The IMF forecast that real GDP would increase by 3.8% in 2014, although the country's fiscal indicators were expected to deteriorate further.

PUBLIC HOLIDAYS

2015: 1 January (New Year's Day), 19 March (Feast of St Joseph, San José only), 2 April (Maundy Thursday), 3 April (Good Friday), 11 April (Anniversary of the Battle of Rivas), 1 May (Labour Day), 25 July (Anniversary of the Annexation of Guanacaste Province), 2 August (Our Lady of the Angels), 15 August (Mothers' Day), 15 September (Independence Day), 12 October (Columbus Day), 25 December (Christmas Day), 28–31 December (San José only).

Statistical Survey

Sources (unless otherwise stated): Instituto Nacional de Estadística y Censos, Edif. Ana Lorena, Calle Los Negritos, de la Rotonda de la Bandera 450 m oeste, Mercedes de Montes de Oca, San José; tel. 2280-9280; fax 2224-2221; e-mail informacion@inec.go.cr; internet www.inec.go.cr; Banco Central de Costa Rica, Avdas Central y Primera, Calles 2 y 4, Apdo 10058, 1000 San José; tel. 2233-4233; fax 2223-4658; internet www.bccr.fi.cr.

Area and Population

AREA, POPULATION AND DENSITY

Area (sq km)	
Land	51,060
Inland water	40
Total	51,100*
Population (census results)	
28 June 2000	3,810,179
30 May–3 June 2011	
Males	2,106,188
Females	2,195,524
Total	4,301,712
Population (official estimates at mid-year)	
2012	4,652,459
2013	4,713,168
2014	4,773,130
Density (per sq km) at mid-2014	93.4

* 19,730 sq miles.

POPULATION BY AGE AND SEX

('000 persons, official estimates at mid-2014)

	Males	Females	Total
0–14	573.2	544.7	1,117.9
15–64	1,676.1	1,637.9	3,314.1
65 and over	161.0	180.1	341.1
Total	2,410.3	2,362.8	4,773.1

Note: Totals may not be equivalent to components, owing to rounding.

PROVINCES

(population at 2011 census)

	Area (sq km)	Population	Density (per sq km)	Capital (with population)
Alajuela	9,757.5	847,660	86.9	Alajuela (254,567)
Cartago	3,124.7	491,425	157.3	Cartago (147,882)
Guanacaste	10,140.7	326,821	32.2	Liberia (62,987)
Heredia	2,657.0	433,975	163.3	Heredia (123,067)
Limón	9,188.5	386,954	42.1	Limón (94,420)
Puntarenas	11,265.7	410,914	36.5	Puntarenas (115,009)
San José	4,965.9	1,403,963	282.7	San José (287,619)
Total	51,100.0	4,301,712	84.2	—

PRINCIPAL TOWNS

(population at 2011 census)

San José	287,619	Pérez Zeledón	135,429
Alajuela	254,567	Pococí	125,847
Desamparados	207,082	Heredia	123,067
San Carlos	163,751	Puntarenas	115,009
Cartago	147,882	Goicoechea	114,736

BIRTHS, MARRIAGES AND DEATHS

	Registered live births		Registered marriages		Registered deaths	
	Number	Rate (per 1,000)	Number	Rate (per 1,000)	Number	Rate (per 1,000)
2005	71,548	16.8	25,631	6.0	16,139	3.8
2006	71,291	16.5	26,575	6.1	16,766	3.9
2007	73,144	16.7	26,010	5.9	17,071	3.9
2008	75,187	16.9	25,034	5.6	18,021	4.1
2009	75,000	16.6	23,920	5.3	18,560	4.1
2010	70,922	15.5	23,955	5.3	19,077	4.2
2011	73,459	17.1	25,013	5.8	18,801	4.4
2012*	73,326	15.7	26,112	5.6	19,200	4.1

* Preliminary.

Life expectancy (years at birth): 79.5 (males 77.3; females 81.8) in 2011 (Source: World Bank, World Development Indicators database).

ECONOMICALLY ACTIVE POPULATION*
(household survey at July, '000 persons aged 12 years and over)

	2011	2012	2013
Agriculture, hunting, forestry and fishing	271.49	269.54	256.43
Mining and manufacturing	237.36	228.00	235.31
Electricity, gas and water supply	40.08	36.90	33.98
Construction	118.95	127.25	114.64
Wholesale and retail trade	361.20	354.75	364.27
Hotels and restaurants	88.21	98.04	96.86
Transport, storage and communications	125.94	142.17	140.41
Financial intermediation	52.37	51.99	48.04
Real estate, renting and business activities	149.55	174.71	186.10
Public administration activities	102.97	93.63	110.18
Education	128.11	132.50	129.78
Health and social work	67.35	66.34	71.02
Other community, social and personal service activities	86.51	89.48	100.67
Private households with employed persons	150.28	139.84	131.20
Extra-territorial organizations and bodies	2.73	2.93	0.91
Sub-total	1,983.12	2,008.10	2,019.79
Not classifiable by economic activity	6.41	4.15	2.68
Total employed	1,989.53	2,012.25	2,022.47
Unemployed	165.02	169.49	188.10
Total labour force	2,154.55	2,181.75	2,210.57

* Figures for activities are rounded to the nearest 10 persons, and totals may not be equivalent to the sum of component parts as a result.

Health and Welfare

KEY INDICATORS

Total fertility rate (children per woman, 2011)	1.8
Under-5 mortality rate (per 1,000 live births, 2011)	10
HIV/AIDS (% of persons aged 15–49, 2012)	0.3
Physicians (per 1,000 head, 2000)	1.3
Hospital beds (per 1,000 head, 2010)	1.2
Health expenditure (2010): US $ per head (PPP)	1,197
Health expenditure (2010): % of GDP	10.3
Health expenditure (2010): public (% of total)	68.9
Access to water (% of persons, 2011)	96
Access to sanitation (% of persons, 2011)	94
Total carbon dioxide emissions ('000 metric tons, 2010)	7,770.4
Carbon dioxide emissions per head (metric tons, 2010)	1.7
Human Development Index (2012): ranking	62
Human Development Index (2012): value	0.773

For sources and definitions, see explanatory note on p. vi.

Agriculture

PRINCIPAL CROPS
('000 metric tons)

	2010	2011	2012
Rice, paddy	267.8	279.0	214.3
Potatoes	55.8	60.0	69.3
Cassava (Manioc)*	529.1	788.0	560.0
Sugar cane	4,150.0*	4,000.0*	4,005.8
Watermelons	49.7	44.4	52.4
Cantaloupes and other melons	198.9	160.8	132.0
Oil palm fruit	985.8	1,050.0	1,111.3
Bananas†	2,020	2,125	2,136
Plantains	90.0	90.0	80.0
Oranges	252.0	170.0*	280.0
Pineapples	1,976.8	2,269.0	2,484.7
Coffee, green	97.2	100.1	125.1

* FAO estimate(s).
† Unofficial figures.

Aggregate production ('000 metric tons, may include official, semi-official or estimated data): Total cereals 286.5 in 2010, 297.5 in 2011, 231.6 in 2012; Total roots and tubers 653.9 in 2010, 919.6 in 2011, 694.1 in 2012; Total vegetables (incl. melons) 431.1 in 2010, 394.0 in 2011, 366.2 in 2012; Total fruits (excl. melons) 4,732.9 in 2010, 5,078.5 in 2011, 5,435.3 in 2012.

Source: FAO.

LIVESTOCK
('000 head, year ending September, FAO estimates)

	2010	2011	2012
Horses	124	125	126
Asses	8	8	8
Cattle	1,350	1,380	1,400
Pigs	438	432	436
Sheep	3	3	3
Goats	5	5	5
Chickens	23,900	22,900	23,600

Source: FAO.

LIVESTOCK PRODUCTS
('000 metric tons)

	2010	2011	2012
Cattle meat	97.5	96.0	87.5
Pig meat	46.1	51.8	55.4
Chicken meat	105.1	100.2	103.9
Cows' milk	951.7	966.3	1,014.6
Hen eggs	53.5	50.8	59.2
Honey*	1.1	1.1	1.2

* FAO estimates.

Source: FAO.

Forestry

ROUNDWOOD REMOVALS
('000 cubic metres, excl. bark)

	2010	2011	2012
Sawlogs, veneer logs and logs for sleepers	1,080*	1,080†	1,080†
Other industrial wood†	246	246	246
Fuel wood†	3,377	3,364	3,352
Total†	4,703	4,690	4,678

* Unofficial figure.
† FAO estimate(s).

Source: FAO.

SAWNWOOD PRODUCTION
('000 cubic metres, incl. railway sleepers, unofficial figures)

	2008	2009	2010
Broadleaved (hardwood)	615	524	540
Total	615	524	540

2011–12: Production assumed to be unchanged from 2010 (FAO estimates).

Source: FAO.

Fishing

('000 metric tons, live weight)

	2009	2010	2011
Capture*	20.7	21.0	20.5
Clupeoids	2.6	2.6*	2.6*
Tuna-like fishes	1.4	1.4	1.4
Common dolphinfish	3.8	3.9	3.8
Sharks, rays, skates, etc.	2.9	2.8*	2.6*
Other marine fishes	3.9	4.2*	4.1*
Aquaculture	24.7	26.8	27.8*
Tilapias	20.6	23.0	24.0
Whiteleg shrimp	3.5	3.2	3.0
Total catch*	45.4	47.8	48.3

* FAO estimate(s).

Source: FAO.

Industry

SELECTED PRODUCTS
('000 metric tons unless otherwise indicated)

	2008	2009	2010
Raw sugar	351	305	n.a.
Kerosene	2	2	2
Distillate fuel oils	244	127	n.a.
Residual fuel oils	201	91	196
Bitumen	9	14	2
Electric energy (million kWh)	9,474	9,290	9,583

Source: UN Industrial Commodity Statistics Database.

Cement ('000 metric tons): 2,100 in 2009; 1,276 in 2010; 1,600 in 2011 (estimate) (Source: US Geological Survey).

Finance

CURRENCY AND EXCHANGE RATES

Monetary Units

100 céntimos = 1 Costa Rican colón.

Sterling, Dollar and Euro Equivalents (31 December 2013)

£1 sterling = 825.714 colones;
US $1 = 501.405 colones;
€1 = 691.488 colones;
10,000 Costa Rican colones = £12.11 = $19.94 = €14.46.

Average Exchange Rate (colones per US $)

2011 505.664
2012 502.901
2013 499.767

GOVERNMENT FINANCE
(central government operations, '000 million colones)

Revenue	2010	2011	2012
Current revenue	2,741.6	3,024.1	3,270.4
Taxation	2,552.8	2,836.1	3,082.0
Income tax	934.6	828.7	891.7
Taxes on property	125.3	121.0	161.3
Taxes on goods and services	1,444.4	1,626.4	1,752.6
Taxes on international trade	170.1	187.7	197.6
Non-tax revenue	27.4	22.7	22.2
Current transfers	161.4	165.3	166.2
Capital revenue	1.6	0.3	3.9
Total	2,743.2	3,024.4	3,274.3

Expenditure	2010	2011	2012
Current expenditure	3,281.7	3,566.6	3,943.9
Wages and salaries	1,134.1	1,268.2	1,380.1
Social security contribution	154.7	172.6	188.8
Goods and services	120.7	135.6	142.9
Current transfers	1,470.7	1,540.8	1,760.4
Interest payments	401.5	449.4	471.8
Domestic	336.6	390.9	424.8
External	64.9	58.5	47.0
Capital expenditure	442.9	303.2	331.6
Real investment	61.5	65.3	50.2
Financial investment	2.9	6.8	1.3
Capital transfers	378.5	231.1	280.1
Total	3,724.6	3,869.8	4,275.5

Source: Ministerio de Hacienda, San José.

Public Sector Accounts ('000 million colones): *Total revenue:* 6,275.7 in 2010; 7,039.1 in 2011; 7,675.0 in 2012. *Total expenditure:* 7,199.1 in 2010; 7,783.7 in 2011; 8,550.3 in 2012.

INTERNATIONAL RESERVES
(excl. gold, US $ million at 31 December)

	2010	2011	2012
IMF special drawing rights	204.20	203.49	203.68
Reserve position in IMF	30.83	30.73	30.77
Foreign exchange	4,392.20	4,521.58	6,622.22
Total	4,627.23	4,755.81	6,856.67

Source: IMF, *International Financial Statistics*.

MONEY SUPPLY
('000 million colones at 31 December)

	2010	2011	2012
Currency outside depository corporations	473.7	545.7	590.9
Transferable deposits	4,286.8	4,731.5	5,013.6
Other deposits	78.5	78.9	98.6
Securities other than shares	4,743.3	4,927.7	5,512.1
Broad money	9,582.3	10,283.8	11,215.2

Source: IMF, *International Financial Statistics*.

COST OF LIVING
(Consumer Price Index at July; base: July 2006 = 100)

	2011	2012	2013
Food and non-alcoholic beverages	170.5	178.5	184.5
Clothing and footwear	103.3	103.3	102.8
Housing	160.8	166.7	206.1
Medical care	156.1	163.3	173.0
Transport	140.3	144.0	149.2
Education	167.3	180.0	193.4
All items (incl. others)	147.6	153.4	162.3

NATIONAL ACCOUNTS

('000 million colones at current prices)

National Income and Product

	2010	2011*	2012*
GDP in purchasers' values	19,086.7	20,748.0	22,684.6
Net primary incomes from abroad	–515.8	–496.6	–624.0
Gross national income	18,570.9	20,251.4	22,060.6
Less consumption of fixed capital	1,123.2	1,223.6	1,337.8
Net national income	17,447.7	19,027.8	20,722.8
Net current transfers	192.5	163.2	154.3
Gross national disposable income	17,640.2	19,191.0	20,877.2

* Preliminary figures.

Expenditure on the Gross Domestic Product

	2010	2011*	2012*
Government final consumption expenditure	3,369.1	3,726.9	4,058.0
Private final consumption expenditure	12,302.5	13,555.4	14,758.1
Increase in stocks	158.0	377.0	221.8
Gross fixed capital formation	3,783.3	4,104.9	4,584.5
Total domestic expenditure	19,613.0	21,764.2	23,622.4
Exports of goods and services	7,285.4	7,766.6	8,545.5
Less Imports of goods and services	7,811.7	8,782.8	9,483.4
GDP in purchasers' values	19,086.7	20,748.0	22,684.6
GDP at constant 1991 prices	2,179.1	2,275.8	2,392.5

* Preliminary figures.

Gross Domestic Product by Economic Activity

	2010	2011*	2012*
Agriculture, hunting, forestry and fishing	1,250.0	1,227.8	1,291.9
Mining and quarrying	27.6	29.3	31.7
Manufacturing	3,055.7	3,250.1	3,498.2
Electricity, gas and water	459.5	462.2	495.3
Construction	1,012.3	1,028.8	1,155.4
Trade, restaurants and hotels	2,972.5	3,257.1	3,545.0
Transport, storage and communications	1,693.9	1,877.0	2,082.5
Finance and insurance	1,194.4	1,298.4	1,463.1
Real estate	531.7	579.7	638.1
Other business services	1,214.7	1,417.9	1,642.2
Public administration	856.8	956.7	1,032.6
Other community, social and personal services	4,006.8	4,435.7	4,860.9
Sub-total	18,275.9	19,820.7	21,736.6
Less Imputed bank service charge	861.8	972.8	1,105.2
GDP at basic prices	17,414.0	18,848.0	20,631.4
Taxes on products	1,721.4	1,948.8	2,104.7
Less Subsidies	48.7	48.8	51.6
GDP in purchasers' values	19,086.7	20,748.0	22,684.6

* Preliminary figures.

BALANCE OF PAYMENTS

(US $ million)

	2010	2011	2012
Exports of goods	4,457.1	4,932.3	5,314.0
Imports of goods	–9,819.1	–11,867.7	–12,741.1
Balance on goods	–5,362.0	–6,935.4	–7,427.2
Exports of services	6,140.7	6,644.4	7,418.6
Imports of services	–1,681.1	–1,668.3	–1,886.0
Balance on goods and services	–902.5	–1,958.8	–1,894.6
Primary income received	199.3	484.1	664.3
Primary income paid	–944.5	–1,051.1	–1,479.1
Balance on goods, services and primary income	–1,647.6	–2,525.8	–2,709.4
Secondary income received	605.7	593.5	628.5
Secondary income paid	–239.3	–270.6	–295.3

—continued	2010	2011	2012
Current balance	–1,281.2	–2,202.9	–2,376.2
Capital account (net)	53.5	21.6	37.5
Direct investment assets	–24.8	–57.8	–776.8
Direct investment liabilities	1,465.6	2,155.6	2,636.2
Portfolio investment assets	218.6	258.9	192.5
Portfolio investment liabilities	—	–102.2	1,180.6
Other investment assets	–376.5	–243.8	–324.4
Other investment liabilities	495.4	417.2	548.7
Net errors and omissions	–144.0	–220.8	244.0
Reserves and related items	406.7	25.7	1,362.2

Source: IMF, *International Financial Statistics*.

External Trade

PRINCIPAL COMMODITIES

(US $ million)

Imports c.i.f.	2010	2011	2012
Food and live animals	736.0	959.3	955.8
Mineral products	1,733.2	2,338.8	2,358.2
Basic manufactures	554.7	688.5	1,106.6
Chemicals and related products	1,575.5	1,792.4	1,861.0
Plastic materials and manufactures	1,017.0	1,380.0	1,259.6
Leather, hides and furs	77.5	59.2	44.8
Paper, paperboard and manufactures	50.8	125.2	81.0
Wood pulp and other fibrous materials	597.4	727.7	690.8
Silk, cotton and textile fibres	512.2	609.1	628.0
Footwear, hats, umbrellas, etc.	118.5	143.8	155.4
Stone manufactures, etc.	144.4	204.1	192.4
Natural and cultured pearls	51.6	46.5	54.6
Common metals and manufactures	1,088.3	1,521.7	1,512.9
Machinery and electrical equipment	3,959.6	5,201.1	5,098.5
Transport equipment	733.5	1,556.4	1,402.5
Optical and topographical apparatus and instruments, etc.	365.2	537.4	635.8
Total (incl. others)	13,920.2	18,263.8	18,371.5

Exports f.o.b.	2010	2011	2012
Food and live animals	2,476.3	2,821.5	2,993.3
Mineral products	76.8	66.4	39.7
Basic manufactures	857.4	966.3	1,043.3
Chemicals and related products	573.8	640.0	567.5
Plastic materials and manufactures	443.2	563.6	596.4
Leather, hides and furs	27.6	34.7	23.9
Paper, paperboard and manufactures	45.4	73.6	86.8
Wood pulp and other fibrous materials	221.8	240.7	161.4
Silk, cotton and textile fibres	205.4	220.7	269.1
Stone manufactures, etc.	93.1	101.5	164.5
Natural and cultured pearls	68.3	90.6	105 8
Common metals and manufactures	318.1	404.4	538.6
Machinery and electrical equipment	2,380.2	2,652.2	2,987.4
Transport equipment	47.9	74.9	122.0
Optical and topographical apparatus and instruments, etc.	1,102.2	1,198.0	1,364.7
Total (incl. others)	9,044.8	10,223.5	11,266.0

PRINCIPAL TRADING PARTNERS
(US $ million)

Imports c.i.f.	2010	2011	2012
Brazil	294.6	351.7	424.2
China, People's Rep.	990.7	1,528.5	1,446.0
Colombia	499.2	655.9	342.7
Germany	310.3	421.3	318.4
Guatemala	324.0	457.3	416.9
Japan	499.5	688.7	560.6
Korea, Republic	152.2	n.a.	n.a.
Mexico	895.6	1,220.6	1,187.1
USA	6,477.1	8,296.6	9,493.7
Total (incl. others)	13,920.2	18,263.8	18,371.5

Exports f.o.b.	2010	2011	2012
China, People's Rep.	268.8	n.a.	326.7
El Salvador	269.2	285.8	305.0
Germany	138.6	n.a.	n.a.
Guatemala	361.7	407.5	432.5
Honduras	292.2	336.2	349.4
Hong Kong	438.0	517.0	533.4
Mexico	254.4	307.1	314.9
Netherlands	633.7	686.2	850.0
Nicaragua	378.9	455.8	501.3
Panama	430.2	560.0	584.0
USA	3,269.0	3,764.4	4,167.0
Total (incl. others)	9,044.8	10,223.5	11,266.0

Transport

ROAD TRAFFIC
(motor vehicles in use at 31 December)

	2009	2010	2011
Passenger cars	594,192	598,021	611,175
Buses and coaches	13,999	14,182	13,969
Lorries and vans	153,492	175,380	174,017
Motorcycles and mopeds	141,470	144,681	130,500

SHIPPING

Flag Registered Fleet
(at 31 December)

	2011	2012	2013
Number of vessels	6	6	8
Total displacement (grt)	2,760	2,760	6,977

Source: Lloyd's List Intelligence (www.lloydslistintelligence.com).

International Sea-borne Freight Traffic
('000 metric tons)

	1996	1997	1998
Goods loaded	3,017	3,421	3,721
Goods unloaded	3,972	4,522	5,188

Source: Ministry of Public Works and Transport.

CIVIL AVIATION
(scheduled services)

	2010	2011
Kilometres flown (million)	28	31
Passengers carried ('000)	1,678	1,862
Passenger-km (million)	2,761	2,950
Total ton-km (million)	251	268

Source: UN, *Statistical Yearbook*.

Passengers carried ('000): 1,905 in 2012 (Source: World Bank, World Development Indicators database).

Tourism

FOREIGN TOURIST ARRIVALS BY COUNTRY OF ORIGIN

	2009	2010	2011
Canada	102,471	119,654	133,033
Colombia	32,014	32,999	33,121
El Salvador	44,185	53,669	61,257
France	30,737	35,266	38,290
Germany	40,918	44,539	49,225
Guatemala	40,340	48,682	54,759
Honduras	31,324	34,043	35,598
Italy	18,497	19,658	20,225
Mexico	47,771	54,662	52,707
Netherlands	25,006	26,373	27,731
Nicaragua	413,713	427,362	432,766
Panama	58,202	77,918	n.a.
Spain	46,457	48,492	47,782
United Kingdom	28,882	34,745	35,689
USA	770,129	830,993	858,829
Venezuela	21,138	24,586	28,237
Total (incl. others)	1,922,579	2,099,829	2,192,059

Tourism receipts (US $ million, excl. passenger transport): 1,999 in 2010; 2,152 in 2011; 2,425 in 2012 (provisional) (Source: World Tourism Organization).

Communications Media

	2010	2011	2012
Telephones ('000 main lines in use)	1,269.2	1,233.7	1,017.6
Mobile cellular telephones ('000 subscribers)	3,035.0	4,358.1	6,151.3
Internet subscribers ('000)	n.a.	452.9	n.a.
Broadband subscribers ('000)	481.7	429.5	481.3

Source: International Telecommunication Union.

Education

(2012/13 unless otherwise indicated)

	Institutions	Teachers	Students		
			Males	Females	Total
Pre-primary	2,862	7,693*	60,097	57,233	117,330
Primary	4,069	29,233*	247,085	233,040	480,125
Secondary	951	28,111*	222,801	226,234	449,035
Special	2,420	n.a.	8,843	5,911	14,754
Tertiary	52†	4,494‡	92,353§	110,822§	203,175§

* 2005.
† 1999.
‡ 2002/03.
§ 2011/12.

Source: mainly Ministry of Public Education, San José.

Pupil-teacher ratio (primary education, UNESCO estimate): 17.3 in 2010/11 (Source: UNESCO Institute for Statistics).

Adult literacy rate (UNESCO estimates): 96.3% (males 96.0%; females 96.5%) in 2011 (Source: UNESCO Institute for Statistics).

Directory

The Government

HEAD OF STATE

President: LAURA CHINCHILLA MIRANDA (took office 8 May 2010).

President-elect: LUIS GUILLERMO SOLÍS RIVERA (scheduled to assume office on 8 May 2014).

First Vice-President: DR ALFIO PIVA MESÉN.

Second Vice-President: LUIS LIBERMAN GINSBURG.

THE CABINET

(April 2014)

The Government was formed by the Partido Liberación Nacional. A new Government was scheduled to take office in May 2014 following the inauguration as President of Luis Guillermo Solís Rivera of the Partido Acción Ciudadana.

Minister of the Presidency: CARLOS RICARDO BENAVIDES JIMÉNEZ.

Minister of Justice and Peace: ANA ISABEL GARITA.

Minister of National Planning and Economic Policy: ROBERTO JAVIER GALLARDO NUÑEZ.

Minister of Finance: EDGAR AYALES ESNA.

Minister of Foreign Relations: ENRIQUE CASTILLO BARRANTES.

Minister of Foreign Trade: ANABEL GONZÁLEZ CAMPABADAL.

Minister of Governance, Police and Public Security: MARIO ZAMORA CORDERO.

Minister of Economy, Industry and Commerce: MAYI ANTILLÓN GUERRERO.

Minister of Decentralization and Local Government: JUAN MARÍN QUIRÓS.

Minister of Social Welfare: FERNANDO MARÍN ROJAS.

Minister of the Environment, Energy and Telecommunications: RENÉ CASTRO SALAZAR.

Minister of Labour and Social Security: OLMAN SEGURA BONILLA.

Minister of Public Education: LEONARDO GARNIER RIMOLO.

Minister of Public Health: DAISY CORRALES DÍAZ.

Minister of Housing and Settlements: GUIDO ALBERTO MONGE FERNÁNDEZ.

Minister of Public Works and Transport: PEDRO CASTRO FERNÁNDEZ.

Minister of Science and Technology: ALEJANDRO CRUZ MOLINA.

Minister of Culture and Youth: MANUEL OBREGÓN LÓPEZ.

Minister of Tourism: ALLAN FLORES.

Minister of Agriculture and Livestock: GLORIA ABRAHAM PERALTA.

Minister of Communications and Public Relations: CARLOS ROVERSSI.

Minister of Sport: WILLIAM CORRALES ARAYA.

President of the National Women's Institute: MARÍA ISABEL CHAMORRO SANTAMARÍA.

MINISTRIES

Ministry of Agriculture and Livestock: Antigüo Colegio La Salle, Sabana Sur, Apdo 10094, 1000 San José; tel. 2231-2344; fax 2232-2103; e-mail sunii@mag.go.cr; internet www.mag.go.cr.

Ministry of Communications and Public Relations: San José.

Ministry of Culture and Youth: Avdas 3 y 7, Calles 11 y 15, frente al parque España, San José; tel. 2255-3188; fax 2233-7066; e-mail mincjd@mcjd.go.cr; internet www.mcjdcr.go.cr.

Ministry of Decentralization and Local Government: San Vicente de Moravia, del Antigüo Colegio Lincoln 2000 este, 100 sur y 200 oeste, contiguo a Sinfónica Juvenil, San José; tel. 2507-1070; e-mail webmaster@ifam.go.cr; internet www.ifam.go.cr.

Ministry of Economy, Industry and Commerce: 400 m oeste de la Contraloría General de la República, Sabana Sur, Apdo 10216-1000, San José; tel. 2249-1400; fax 2291-2059; e-mail informacion@meic.go.cr; internet www.meic.go.cr.

Ministry of the Environment, Energy and Telecommunications: Edif. Vista Palace, Avdas 8 y 10, Calle 25, Apdo 10104, 1000 San José; tel. 2233-4533; fax 2257-0697; e-mail dgpcc.dir@gmail.com; internet www.minae.go.cr.

Ministry of Finance: Edif. Antigüo Banco Anglo, Avda 2a, Calle 3a, San José; tel. 2284-5000; fax 2255-4874; e-mail webmaster1@hacienda.go.cr; internet www.hacienda.go.cr.

Ministry of Foreign Relations: Avda 7 y 9, Calle 11 y 13, Apdo 10027, 1000 San José; tel. 2223-7555; fax 2257-6597; e-mail despacho.ministro@rree.go.cr; internet www.rree.go.cr.

Ministry of Foreign Trade: Edif. Centro Comercio Exterior, Avda 1 y 3, Calle 40, Apdo 297, 1007 Centro Colón, San José; tel. 2299-4700; fax 2255-3281; e-mail pep@comex.go.cr; internet www.comex.go.cr.

Ministry of Governance, Police and Public Security: Apdo 55, 4874 San José; tel. 2227-4866; fax 2226-6581; internet www.msp.go.cr.

Ministry of Housing and Settlements: Of. Mall San Pedro, 7°, Costado Norte, Apdo 1753, 2050 San Pedro de Montes de Oca; tel. 2202-7900; fax 2202-7910; e-mail info@mivah.go.cr; internet www.mivah.go.cr.

Ministry of Justice and Peace: 50 m norte de la Clínica Bíblica, frente a la Escuela M. García Flamenco, 1000 San José; tel. 2256-6700; fax 2234-7959; e-mail justicia@gobnet.go.cr; internet www.mjp.go.cr.

Ministry of Labour and Social Security: Edif. Benjamín Núñez, 4°, Barrio Tournón, Apdo 10133, 1000 San José; tel. 2542-0000; fax 2256-2061; e-mail walter.villalobos@mtss.go.cr; internet www.mtss.go.cr.

Ministry of National Planning and Economic Policy: De Autos Subarú 200 m al norte, Barrio Dent, San Pedro de Montes de Oca, Apdo 10127, 1000 San José; tel. 2281-2700; fax 2253-6243; e-mail despacho@mideplan.go.cr; internet www.mideplan.go.cr.

Ministry of the Presidency: Casa Presidencial, Zapote, Apdo 520, 2010 San José; tel. 2207-9100; fax 2253-9078; e-mail sugerencias@presidencia.go.cr; internet www.presidencia.go.cr.

Ministry of Public Education: Edif. Rofas, frente al Hospital San Juan de Dios, Apdo 10087, 1000 San José; tel. 2258-3745; fax 2248-1763; e-mail contraloriaservicios@mep.go.cr; internet www.mep.go.cr.

Ministry of Public Health: Calle 16, Avda 6 y 8, Apdo 10123, 1000 San José; tel. 2223-0333; fax 2255-2636; e-mail prensams@netsalud.sa.cr; internet www.ministeriodesalud.go.cr.

Ministry of Public Works and Transport: Plaza González Víquez, Calles 9 y 11, Avda 20 y 22, Apdo 10176, 1000 San José; tel. 2523-2000; fax 2257-7405; e-mail ofprensa@mopt.go.cr; internet www.mopt.go.cr.

Ministry of Science and Technology: 50 m Este del Museo Nacional, Avda Segunda, Calles 19 y 17, Apdo 5589, 1000 San José; tel. 2248-1515; fax 2257-8895; e-mail micit@micit.go.cr; internet www.micit.go.cr.

Ministry of Social Welfare: San José; tel. 2202-4000; fax 2202-4069; e-mail informatica@imas.go.cr; internet www.imas.go.cr.

Ministry of Sport: Parque Metropolitano, La Sabana, Estadio Nacional, Apdo 5009, 1000 San José; tel. 2549-0700; e-mail gabriela.azofeifa@icoder.go.cr; internet www.icoder.go.cr.

Ministry of Tourism: Costado Este del Puente Juan Pablo II, sobre Autopista General Cañas, Apdo 777, 1000 San José; tel. 2299-5800; fax 2220-0243; internet www.ict.go.cr.

National Women's Institute (Instituto Nacional de las Mujeres—INAMU): 100 m este Taller Wabe, Granadilla Norte, Curridabat, San José; tel. (506) 2253-8066; fax (506) 2283-0657; e-mail despacho@inamu.go.cr; internet www.inamu.go.cr.

President and Legislature

PRESIDENT

Election, First Round, 2 February 2014

Candidate	Valid votes cast	% of valid votes
Luis Guillermo Solís Rivera (PAC)	629,866	30.64
Johnny Araya Monge (PLN)	610,634	29.71
José María Villalta Florez-Estrada (FA)	354,479	17.25
Otto Guevara Guth (ML)	233,064	11.34
Rodolfo Piza Rocafort (PUSC)	123,653	6.02
José Miguel Corrales Bolaños (PPN)	30,816	1.50
Carlos Luis Avendaño Calvo (PREN)	27,691	1.35
Others	45,269	2.20
Total valid votes*	2,055,472	100.00

* In addition there were 43,747 invalid or blank votes.

Election, Second Round, 6 April 2014

Candidate	Valid votes cast	% of valid votes
Luis Guillermo Solís Rivera (PAC)	1,338,321	77.77
Johnny Araya Monge (PLN)	382,600	22.23
Total valid votes*	1,720,921	100.00

* In addition there were 18,314 invalid or blank votes.

LEGISLATIVE ASSEMBLY

President: LUIS FERNANDO MENDOZA JIMÉNEZ (PLN).

General Election, 2 February 2014, preliminary results

Party	Votes cast	% of votes cast	Seats
Partido Liberación Nacional (PLN)	432,772	25.54	18
Partido Acción Ciudadana (PAC)	403,845	23.84	14
Frente Amplio (FA)	221,780	13.09	9
Partido Unidad Social Cristiana (PUSC)	169,675	10.01	8
Movimiento Libertario (ML)	134,235	7.92	3
Partido Restauración Nacional (PRN)	69,712	4.11	5 (jointly with PRC and PASE)
Partido Renovación Costarricense (PRC)	67,315	3.97	
Partido Accesibilidad sin Exclusión (PASE)	66,953	3.95	
Partido Patria Nueva (PPN)	35,019	2.07	—
Partido Nueva Generación (PNG)	21,113	1.25	—
Others	71,791	4.23	
Total valid votes*	1,695,623	100.00	57

* In addition, there were 10,815 blank and 27,609 invalid votes cast.

Election Commission

Tribunal Supremo de Elecciones (TSE): Avda 1 y 3, Calle 15, Apdo 2163, 1000 San José; tel. 2287-5555; fax 2255-0213; e-mail secretariatse@tse.go.cr; internet www.tse.go.cr; f. 1949; independent; Pres. LUIS ANTONIO SOBRADO GONZÁLEZ; Exec. Dir FRANCISCO RODRÍGUEZ SILES.

Political Organizations

Alianza Patriótica: Edif. Rojo, 2°, de la esquina sureste del Museo Nacional, 1 cuadra este a mano derecha, San José; tel. 2223-9595; fax 2223-9596; e-mail adrianj.zuniga@gmail.com; Pres. MARIANO FIGUERES OLSEN; Sec.-Gen. ARNOLDO MORA VAGLIO.

Avance Nacional: Barrio Colonia del Río, detrás del Centro Comercial Guadalupe, Guadalupe, Goicoechea, San José; tel. 2256-7375; fax 2223-6714; e-mail contactenos@partidoavancenacional.com; internet partidoavancenacional.com; Pres. JOSÉ MANUEL ECHANDI MEZA; Sec.-Gen. SHIRLEY MARÍA ARAYA CASTILLO.

Centro Democrático y Social: 75 m sur del Restaurante Rostipollos, Barrio Jiménez, Goicoechea, Guadalupe, San José; tel. 2245-7522; fax 2256-6274; e-mail guivarsa@gmail.com; f. 2012; Pres. GUILLERMO VARGAS SALAZAR; Sec.-Gen. JUAN RAFAEL LIZANO SÁENZ.

Frente Amplio (FA): Barrio Amón, costado suroeste del INVU, 25 m sur, Apdo 280, Moravia, San José; tel. 2258-5641; fax 2243-2830; e-mail info@frenteamplio.org; internet www.frenteamplio.org; f. 2004; Pres. PATRICIA MORA CASTELLANOS; Sec.-Gen. RODOLFO ULLOA BONILLA.

Movimiento Libertario (ML): Of. de Cabinas San Isidro, Barrio Los Yoses Sur, Apdo 4674, 1000 San José; tel. 2283-8600; fax 2283-9600; internet www.movimientolibertario.com; f. 1994; Pres. OTTO GUEVARA GUTH; Sec.-Gen. VÍCTOR DANILO CUBERO CORRALES.

Partido Accesibilidad Sin Exclusión (PASE): San José; tel. 2214-6110; internet partidopase.blogspot.in; f. 2004; Leader OSCAR LÓPEZ ARIAS; Sec. ERIC RAMÓN CHACÓN VALERIO.

Partido Acción Ciudadana (PAC): 25 San Pedro, 425 m sur del Templo Parroquial, San José; tel. 2281-2727; fax 2280-6640; e-mail accionciudadana@pac.or.cr; internet www.pac.or.cr; f. 2000; centre party; Pres. OLIVIER PÉREZ; Sec.-Gen. OLGA MARTES SÁNCHEZ.

Partido Integración Nacional (PIN): Edif. de Imágenes Médicas, 2°, Apdo 219, 2050 San Pedro de Montes de Oca, San José; tel. 2221-3300; fax 2500-0729; e-mail partidointegracionnacionalcr@gmail.com; f. 1996; Pres. Dr WALTER MUÑOZ CÉSPEDES; Sec.-Gen. HEINER ALBERTO LEMAITRE ZAMORA.

Partido Liberación Nacional (PLN): Mata Redonda, 125 m oeste del Ministerio de Agricultura y Ganadería, Casa Liberacionista José Figueres Ferrer, Apdo 10051, 1000 San José; tel. 2232-5133; fax 2231-4097; e-mail secregeneralpln@ice.co.cr; internet www.pln.or.cr; f. 1952; social democratic party; affiliated to the Socialist International; 500,000 mems; Pres. BERNAL JIMÉNEZ MONGE; Sec.-Gen. ANTONIO CALDERÓN CASTRO.

Partido Nueva Generación (PNG): 250 m al este y 125 m norte de la POPs, contiguo al Parque Infantil, Cinco Esquinas, Llorente, Tibás, San José; tel. 2253-3193; fax 2253-3180; e-mail contacto@partidonuevageneracion.net; internet www.partidonuevageneracion.net; f. 2010; Pres. SERGIO MENA DÍAZ; Sec.-Gen. LUZ MARY ALPÍZAR LOAIZA.

Partido Patria Nueva (PPN): Edif. Amalia, 3°, Of. 4B, del Templo de la Música del Parque Morazán, 100 m sur y 25 m oeste, San José; tel. 2256-3298; e-mail partidopatrianueva@gmail.com; f. 2012; Pres. ALVARO EDUARDO MONTERO MEJÍA; Sec.-Gen. CÉLIMO GUIDO CRUZ.

Partido Renovación Costarricense (PRC): Centro Educativo Instituto de Desarrollo de Inteligencia, Hatillo 1, Avda Villanea, Apdo 31, 1300 San José; tel. 2254-3651; fax 2252-3270; e-mail jimmysos@costarricense.cr; f. 1995; Pres. JUSTO OROZCO ALVAREZ; Sec. JIMMY SOTO SOLANO.

Partido Restauración Nacional (PRN): Del Restaurante la Princesa Marina, 75 m norte, portón amarillo, casa al fondo, contiguo al local de pinturas Protecto, Moravia, San Vicente; tel. 2243-2851; fax 2243-2855; e-mail restauracion.sol@gmail.com; f. 2005; provincial party; Pres. CARLOS LUIS AVENDAÑO CALVO; Sec.-Gen. CÉSAR ALEXANDER ZÚÑIGA RAMÍREZ.

Partido de los Trabajadores (PT): Edif. de Ladrillos en medio de la cuadra, Avda 10, entre Calle 1 y 3, San José; tel. 2222-0442; e-mail secretariado@ptcostarica.org; internet ptcostarica.org; Pres. HÉCTOR ENRIQUE MONESTEL HERRERA; Sec. JAVIER FERNÁNDEZ BARRERO.

Partido Unidad Social Cristiana (PUSC): 100 m al oeste del Hospital de Niños, Paseo Colón, Apdo 10095, 1000 San José; tel. 2280-2920; fax 2248-3678; e-mail alvarado-w@hotmail.com; internet www.pusc.cr; f. 1983; Pres. GERARDO VARGAS ROJAS; Sec.-Gen. WILLIAM ALVARADO BOGANTES.

Unión Nacional: Frente a la Asociación China, Barrio Francisco Peralta, San José; tel. 2289-4670; fax 2234-3207; e-mail partidounionnacional@yahoo.com; f. 2004; Pres. ARTURO ACOSTA MORA; Sec.-Gen. HERNÁN RICARDO ZAMORA ROJAS.

Diplomatic Representation

EMBASSIES IN COSTA RICA

Argentina: McDonald's de Curridabat, 700 m sur y 25 m este, Apdo 1963, 1000 San José; tel. 2234-6520; fax 2283-9983; e-mail erica@mrecic.gov.ar; Ambassador MARTÍN ANTONIO BALZA.

Bolivia: Del Centro Comercial Plaza del Sol, 200 m al sur y 50 metros al este, Curridabat, San José; tel. 2524-3491; fax 2280-0320; e-mail embocr@racsa.co.cr; Chargé d'affaires a.i. JOSÉ ENRRIQUE COLODRO BALDIVIEZO.

Brazil: Edif. Torre Mercedes, 6°, Paseo Colón, Apdo 10132, 1000 San José; tel. 2295-6875; fax 2295-6874; e-mail brasemb.saojose@itamaraty.gov.br; internet www.brasilcostarica.tk; Ambassador MARIA DULCE SILVA BARROS.

Canada: Oficentro Ejecutivo La Sabana, Edif. 5, 3°, detrás de la Contraloría, Centro Colón, Apdo 351, 1007 San José; tel. 2242-4400; fax 2242-4410; e-mail sjcra@international.gc.ca; internet www.canadainternational.gc.ca/costa_rica; Ambassador WENDY DRUKIER.

Chile: Casa 225, Los Yoses, del Automercado Los Yoses 225 m sur, Calle 39, Avdas 10 y 12, Apdo 10102, 1000 San José; tel. 2280-0037; fax 2253-7016; e-mail infocr@minrel.gov.cl; internet chileabroad.gov.cl/costa-rica; Ambassador MIGUEL ÁNGEL GONZÁLEZ MORALES.

China, People's Republic: De la casa de Don Oscar Arias, 100 m sur y 50 m este, Rohrmoser, Pavas, Apdo 1518, 1200 San José; tel. 2291-4811; fax 2291-4820; e-mail embchina_costarica@yahoo.com.cn; internet cr.chineseembassy.org/esp; Ambassador SONG YANBIN.

Colombia: Barrio Dent de Taco Bell, San Pedro, Apdo 3154, 1000 San José; tel. 2283-6871; fax 2283-6818; e-mail esanjose@cancilleria.gov.co; internet www.embajadaencostarica.gov.co; Ambassador HERNANDO HERRERA VERGARA.

Cuba: Sabana Norte, del restaurante El Chicote 100 norte, 50 este y 200 norte, Casa esquinera, costado izquierdo, San José; tel. 2231-6812; fax 2232-2985; e-mail oficinapolitica@consulcubacr.com; internet www.cubadiplomatica.cu/costarica; Ambassador LEDA ELVIRA PEÑA HERNÁNDEZ.

Dominican Republic: McDonald's de Curridabat 400 sur, 100 m este, Apdo 4746, 1000 San José; tel. 2283-8103; fax 2280-7604; e-mail embdominicanacr@ice.co.cr; Ambassador NESTOR JUAN CERÓN SUERO.

Ecuador: Sabana sur de la Contraloría-General de la República, 400 m sur y 75 m este, San José; tel. and fax 2232-1562; e-mail eecucostarica@mmrree.gov.ec; internet www.consuladoecuadorsj.com; Ambassador DAISY TULA ESPINEL DE ALVARADO.

El Salvador: Del Restaurante McDonald's de Plaza del Sol, 7 c. sur y 50 m. este, Curridabat, San José; tel. 2257-7855; fax 2258-1234; e-mail embasacr@amnet.co.cr; internet embajadacostarica.rree.gob.sv/; Ambassador SEBASTIÁN VAQUERANO LÓPEZ.

France: Carretera a Curridabat, de Mitsubishi 200 m sur y 25 m oeste, Apdo 10177, 1000 San José; tel. 2234-4167; fax 2234-4195; e-mail sjfrance@sol.racsa.co.cr; internet www.ambafrance-cr.org; Ambassador JEAN-BAPTISTE CHAUVIN.

Germany: Edif. Torre la Sabana, 8°, Sabana Norte, Apdo 4017, 1000 San José; tel. 2290-9091; fax 2231-6403; e-mail info@san-jose.diplo.de; internet www.san-jose.diplo.de; Ambassador Dr ERNST MARTENS.

Guatemala: De Sabana Sur, del Gimnasio Fitsimons 100 sur y 50 m oeste, Apdo 328, 1000 San José; tel. 2291-6172; fax 2290-4111; e-mail embaguat@ice.co.cr; Ambassador HECTOR ROLANDO PALACIOS LIMA.

Holy See: Barrio Rohrmoser, Centro Colón, Apdo 992, 1007 San José (Apostolic Nunciature); tel. 2232-2128; fax 2231-2557; e-mail nuncio@nunciocr.org; Apostolic Nuncio Rt Rev. PIERRE NGUYÊN VAN TOT (Titular Archbishop of Rusticiana).

Honduras: De la Esq. norte de Telética, 175 m. oeste, por el Estadio Nacional, Sabana Oeste,San José; tel. 2232-9506; fax 2291-5147; e-mail embhoncr@embajadahonduras.co.cr; internet www.embajadahonduras.co.cr; Ambassador JUAN ALBERTO LARA BUESO.

Israel: Edif. Centro Colón, 11°, Calle 38 Paseo Colón, Apdo 5147, 1000 San José; tel. 2221-6444; fax 2257-0867; e-mail admin-sec@sanjose.mfa.gov.il; internet sanjose.mfa.gov.il; Ambassador ABRAHAM HADDAD.

Italy: Los Yoses, 5a entrada, Apdo 1729, 1000 San José; tel. 2225-6396; fax 2225-8200; e-mail ambasciata.sanjose@esteri.it; internet www.ambsanjose.esteri.it; Ambassador FRANCESCO CALOGERO.

Japan: Edif. Torre La Sabana, 10°, Sabana Norte, Apdo 501, 1000 San José; tel. 2232-1255; fax 2231-3140; e-mail embjapon@racsa.co.cr; internet www.cr.emb-japan.go.jp; Ambassador MAMORU SHINOHARA.

Korea, Republic: 400 m. norte y 200 m. oeste del Restaurante Rostipollos, Urb. Trejos Montealegre, San Rafael de Escazú, San José; tel. 2220-3160; fax 2220-3168; e-mail koco@mofat.go.kr; internet cri.mofat.go.kr; Ambassador HONG JO CHUN.

Mexico: Avda 7A, No 1371, Apdo 10107, 1000 San José; tel. 2257-0633; fax 2258-2437; e-mail rmision@embamexico.or.cr; internet embamex.sre.gob.mx/costarica; Ambassador FERNANDO BAEZA MELÉNDEZ.

Netherlands: Oficentro Ejecutivo La Sabana (detrás de la Contraloría), Edif. 3, 3°, Sabana Sur, Apdo 10285, 1000 San José; tel. 2296-1490; fax 2296-2933; e-mail sjo@minbuza.nl; internet costarica.nlembajada.org; Ambassador METTE GONGGRIJP.

Nicaragua: Avda Central 2540, Calle 25 bis, Barrio la California, Apdo 1382, 1000 San José; tel. 2233-8747; fax 2221-3036; e-mail embanic@racsa.co.cr; Ambassador HAROLD FERNANDO RIVAS REYES.

Panama: Del Antigüo Higuerón de San Pedro 200 m sur y 25 m este, Barrio La Granja, San Pedro de Montes de Oca, Apdo 103, 2050 San José; tel. 2280-1570; fax 2281-2161; e-mail panaembacr@racsa.co.cr; internet www.embajadadepanamaencostarica.org; Ambassador JOSÉ JAVIER MULINO QUINTERO.

Paraguay: De la Kentucky de Plaza del Sol 600 m al sur y 50 m al este, 12 Curridabat, San Pedro de Montes de Oca, Apdo 2420, 2050 San José; tel. 2234-2932; fax 2234-0891; e-mail embapar@racsa.co.cr; Ambassador OSCAR BUENAVENTURA LLANES TORRES.

Peru: De McDonald's de Plaza del Sol, 500 m al sur y 175 m al este, Curridabat, San José; tel. 2225-9145; fax 2253-0457; e-mail embaperu@amnet.co.cr; Ambassador LUIS WILFREDO SANDIGA CABRERA.

Russia: Barrio Escalante, 100 m norte y 150 m este de la Iglesia Santa Teresita, Apdo 6340, 1000 San José; tel. 2256-9181; fax 2221-2054; e-mail rusemb.costarica@mail.ru; internet www.costarica.mid.ru; Ambassador VLADIMIR T. KURAEV.

Spain: Calle 32, entre Paseo Colón y Avda 2, Apdo 10150, 1000 San José; tel. 2222-1933; fax 2257-5126; e-mail Emb.SanJose@maec.es; internet www.maec.es/subwebs/embajadas/sanjosecostarica; Ambassador ELENA MADRAZO HEGEWISCH.

Switzerland: Edif. Centro Colón, 10°, Paseo Colón, Apdo 895, 1007 San José; tel. 2221-4829; fax 2255-2831; e-mail sjc.vertretung@eda.admin.ch; internet www.eda.admin.ch/sanjose; Ambassador YASMINE CHATILA ZWAHLEN.

United Kingdom: Edif. Centro Colón, 11°, Paseo Colón, Apdo 815, 1007 San José; tel. 2258-2025; fax 2233-9938; e-mail britemb@racsa.co.cr; internet www.ukincostarica.fco.gov.uk; Ambassador SHARON ISABEL CAMPBELL.

Uruguay: Trejos Monte Alegre, Escazú, del Vivero Exótica 900 m oeste y 100 m sur, Apdo 3448, 1000 San José; tel. 2288-3424; fax 2288-3070; e-mail embajrou@sol.racsa.co.cr; Ambassador FERNANDO DANIEL ALEJANDRO MARR MERELLO.

USA: Calle 98, Vía 104, Pavas, San José; tel. 2519-2000; fax 2220-2305; e-mail info@usembassy.or.cr; internet sanjose.usembassy.gov; Chargé d'affaires a.i. GONZALO GALLEGOS.

Venezuela: De la Casa de Don Oscar Arias, 100 m al sur, 400 m al oeste y 25 m al sur, Barrio Rohrmoser, Apdo 10230, 1000 San José; tel. 2220-3102; fax 2290-3806; e-mail embve.crsjo@mre.gob.ve; internet embavenezuelacr.org; Ambassador AURA MAHUAMPI RODRÍGUEZ DE ORTIZ.

Judicial System

Ultimate judicial power is vested in the Supreme Court, the justices of which are elected by the Legislative Assembly for a term of eight years, and are automatically re-elected for an equal period, unless the Assembly decides to the contrary by a two-thirds' vote. The Supreme Court justices sit in four courts: the First Court (civil, administrative, agrarian and commercial matters), the Second Court (employment and family), the Third Court (penal) and the Fourth, or Constitutional, Court. There are, in addition, appellate courts, criminal courts, civil courts and special courts. The jury system is not used.

Supreme Court: Sala Constitucional de la Corte Suprema de Justicia, Apdo 5, 1003 San José; tel. 2295-3000; fax 2295-3712; e-mail sala4-informacion@poder-judicial.go.cr; internet www.poder-judicial.go.cr; Pres. ZARELA VILLANUEVA.

Attorney-General: JORGE CHAVARRÍA.

Religion

Under the Constitution, all forms of worship are tolerated. Roman Catholicism is the official religion of the country. Various Protestant churches are also represented.

CHRISTIANITY

The Roman Catholic Church

Costa Rica comprises one archdiocese and seven dioceses. Roman Catholics represent some 82% of the total population.

Bishops' Conference: Conferencia Episcopal de Costa Rica, Apdo 7288, 1000 San José; tel. 2221-3053; fax 2221-6662; e-mail seccecor@racsa.co.cr; internet www.iglesiacr.org; f. 1977; Pres. Most Rev. JOSÉ RAFAEL QUIROS QUIROS (Archbishop of San José de Costa Rica).

Archbishop of San José de Costa Rica: Most Rev. JOSÉ RAFAEL QUIROS QUIROS, Arzobispado, Apdo 497, 1000 San José; tel. 2258-1015; fax 2221-2427; e-mail arzobispo@arquisanjose.org; internet www.arquisanjose.org.

The Anglican Communion

Costa Rica comprises one of the five dioceses of the Iglesia Anglicana de la Región Central de América.

Bishop of Costa Rica: Rt Rev. HÉCTOR MONTERROSO GONZALEZ, Apdo 10520, 1000 San José; tel. 2225-0790; fax 2253-8331; e-mail hmonterroso@episcopalcostarica.org; internet www.episcopalcostarica.org.

Other Churches

Church of Jesus Christ of Latter-Day Saints (Mormons): Del Hotel Marriott, 600m oeste, La Ribera de Belén, 40702 Heredia, San José; tel. 2293-6681; internet www.lds.org; Bishop SAAVEDRA BRIONES; 41,353 mems.

Federación de Asociaciones Bautistas de Costa Rica: Apdo 1631, del Banco Nacional en Guadalupe centro, 100 norte y 75 este, San José; tel. 2253-5820; fax 2253-4723; e-mail fabcr@fabcr.com; internet www.fabcr.com; f. 1946; represents Baptist churches; Pres. NIDIA RODRÍGUEZ JIMÉNEZ.

Iglesia Evangélica Metodista de Costa Rica (Evangelical Methodist Church of Costa Rica): Apdo 5481, 1000 San José; tel. 2227-3321; fax 2227-3243; e-mail oficinacentral@iglesiametodistacr.org; internet iglesiametodistacr.org; autonomous since 1973; affiliated to the United Methodist Church; 6,000 mems; Pres. Bishop LUIS F. PALOMO.

Iglesia Luterana Costarricense (Lutheran Church of Costa Rica): Apdo 1890, Paseo de los Estudiantes, 1002 San José; tel. 2226-1792; fax 2227-1984; e-mail direccionejecutiva@ilco.cr; f. 1955; German congregation; 220 mems; Bishop MELVIN JIMÉNEZ; Exec. Dir XINIA CHACÓN RODRÍGUEZ.

BAHÁ'Í FAITH

National Spiritual Assembly of the Bahá'ís of Costa Rica: Apdo 553, 1150 La Uruca; tel. 2520-2127; fax 2296-1033; e-mail info@bahaicr.org; internet www.bahaicr.org; f. 1942.

The Press

DAILIES

Al Día: Llorente de Tibás, Apdo 10138, 1000 San José; tel. 2247-4647; fax 2247-4665; e-mail redacccionad@aldia.co.cr; internet www.aldia.co.cr; f. 1992; morning; independent; Dir GUSTAVO JIMÉNEZ; Editor ANTONIO ALFARO; circ. 60,000.

Diario Extra: Edif. de La Prensa Libre, Calle 4, Avda 4, Apdo 177, 1009 San José; tel. 2223-6666; fax 2223-6101; e-mail redaccion@diarioextra.com; internet www.diarioextra.com; f. 1978; morning; independent; Dir IARY GOMÉZ; circ. 157,000.

La Gaceta: La Uruca, Apdo 5024, San José; tel. 2296-9570; e-mail direccion@imprenta.go.cr; internet www.gaceta.go.cr; f. 1878; official gazette; Dir JORGE LUIS VARGAS ESPINOZA; circ. 5,300.

La Nación: Llorente de Tibás, Apdo 10138, 1000 San José; tel. 2247-4747; fax 2247-5022; e-mail agonzales@nacion.com; internet www.nacion.com; f. 1946; morning; independent; Dir YANANCY NOGUERA; Editor ARMANDO MAYORGA; circ. 90,000.

La Prensa Libre: Edif. Borrasé, Calle 4, Avda 4, Apdo 10121, 1000 San José; tel. 2547-9300; fax 2223-4671; e-mail plibre@prensalibre.cr; internet www.prensalibre.cr; f. 1889; evening; independent; Dir WILLIAM GÓMEZ VARGAS; Editor SANDRA GONZALEZ VARGAS; circ. 56,000.

La República: Barrio Tournón, Guadalupe, Apdo 2130, 1000 San José; tel. 2522-3300; fax 2257-0401; e-mail redaccion@larepublica.net; internet www.larepublica.net; f. 1950; reorganized 1967; morning; independent; Editor DANIEL CHACÓN; circ. 61,000.

PERIODICALS

Abanico: Calle 4, Avda 4, Apdo 10121, 1000 San José; tel. 2223-6666; fax 2223-4671; e-mail abanico@prensalibre.co.cr; internet www.prensalibre.cr; weekly supplement of La Prensa Libre; women's interests; Editor EFRÉN LÓPEZ; circ. 50,000.

Actualidad Económica: San José; tel. 2226-6483; fax 2224-1528; e-mail contacto@actualidad.co.cr; internet www.actualidad.co.cr; Dir NORA RUIZ.

Eco Católico: Calle 22, Avdas 3 y 5, Apdo 1064, San José; tel. 2222-8391; fax 2256-0407; e-mail info@ecocatolico.org; internet www.ecocatolico.org; f. 1883; Catholic weekly; Dir MARTÍN RODRÍGUEZ GONZÁLEZ; circ. 20,000.

El Financiero: Grupo Nación, Edif. Subsidiarias, Llorente de Tibás, 185-2120 Guadalupe; tel. 2247-5555; fax 2247-5177; e-mail redaccion@elfinancierocr.com; internet www.elfinancierocr.com; f. 1995; Dir JOSÉ DAVID GUEVARA MUÑOZ.

INCAE Business Review: Apdo 960-4050, Alajuela; tel. 2258-6834; fax 2258-2874; e-mail info@revistaincae.com; internet www.revistaincae.com; f. 1982; publ. by INCAE business school; Dir MARLENE DE ESTRELLA LÓPEZ; circ. 18,000.

Perfil: Llorente de Tibás, Apdo 1517, 1100 San José; tel. 2247-4345; fax 2247-5110; e-mail perfil@nacion.co.cr; internet www.perfilcr.com; f. 1984; fortnightly; women's interests; Dir ISABEL OVARES; Man. Editor THAIS AGUILAR ZÚÑIGA; circ. 16,000.

The Tico Times: Calle 15, Avda 8, Apdo 4632, 1000 San José; tel. 2258-1558; fax 2223-6378; e-mail info@ticotimes.net; internet www.ticotimes.net; f. 1956; weekly; in English; Editor STEVE MACK; circ. 15,210.

PRESS ASSOCIATIONS

Colegio de Periodistas de Costa Rica: Sabana Este, Calle 42, Avda 4, Apdo 5416, San José; tel. 2233-5850; fax 2223-8669; e-mail direccion@colper.or.cr; internet www.colper.or.cr; f. 1969; 1,447 mems; Pres. Dr MARLON MORA JIMÉNEZ; Exec. Dir CLARIBET MORERA.

Sindicato Nacional de Periodistas de Costa Rica: Edif. Colegio de Periodistas de Costa Rica, 2°, diagonal al Gimnasio Nacional, San José; tel. 2222-7589; fax 2258-3229; e-mail info@sindicatodeperiodistas.org; internet sindicatodeperiodistas.org; f. 1970; 220 mems; Sec.-Gen. SANTIAGO ORTÍZ.

Publishers

Caribe-Betania Editores: Apdo 1.307, San José; tel. 2222-7244; e-mail info@editorialcaribe.com; internet www.caribebetania.com; f. 1949 as Editorial Caribe; present name adopted 1992; division of Thomas Nelson Publrs; religious textbooks; Exec. Vice-Pres. TAMARA L. HEIM; Dir JOHN STROWEL.

Editorial Costa Rica: Calle 1, entre avda 8 y 10, esq. suroeste del Banco Popular, 250 m al sur, Apdo 10010-1000, San José; tel. 2233-0812; fax 2233-1949; e-mail difusion@editorialcostarica.com; internet www.editorialcostarica.com; f. 1959; govt-owned; cultural; Pres. LUIS ENRIQUE ARCE NAVARRO; Gen. Man. MARÍA ISABEL BRENES ALVARADO.

Editorial Fernández Arce: 50 este de Sterling Products, la Paulina de Montes de Oca, Apdo 2410, 1000 San José; tel. 2224-5201; fax 2225-6109; e-mail ventas@fernandez-arce.com; internet www.fernandez-arce.com; f. 1967; textbooks for primary, secondary and university education; Dir Dr MARIO FERNÁNDEZ ARCE.

Editorial INBio de Costa Rica: San José; tel. 2507-8183; e-mail editorial@inbio.ac.cr; internet www.inbio.ac.cr/editorial; f. 2000; part of Instituto Nacional de Biodiversidad; Man. FABIO ROJAS.

Editorial Legado: Apdo 2160, 2050 San José; tel. 2280-8007; fax 2280-0945; e-mail legado@editlegado.com; internet www.editlegado.com; f. 1976; Gen. Man. SEBASTIÁN VAQUERANO.

Editorial Tecnológica de Costa Rica: 1 km al sur de la Basílica de Los Angeles, Apdo 159-7050, Cartago; tel. 2550-2297; fax 2552-5354; e-mail editorial@tec.ac.cr; internet www.tec.ac.cr; f. 1978; Dir ANA RUTH VÍLCHEZ RODRÍGUEZ.

Editorial de la Universidad Autónoma de Centro América (UACA): Apdo 7637, 1000 San José; tel. 2272-9100; fax 2271-2046; e-mail info@uaca.ac.cr; internet www.uaca.ac.cr; f. 1981; Editor JULISSA MÉNDEZ MARÍN.

Editorial Universidad de Costa Rica: Ciudad Universitaria Rodrigo Facio, San Pedro, Montes de Oca, 2060 San José; tel. 2511-5310; fax 2511-5257; e-mail direccion.siedin@ucr.ac.cr; internet www.editorial.ucr.ac.cr; Dir ALBERTO MURILLO-HERRERA.

Editorial de la Universidad Estatal a Distancia (EUNED): Mercedes de Montes de Oca, Apdo 474-2050, San José; tel. 2527-2440; fax 2234-9138; e-mail euned@uned.ac.cr; internet www.uned.ac.cr/editorial; f. 1979; Pres. Dr LUIS ALBERTO CAÑAS ESCALANTE; Dir RENÉ MUIÑOS GUAL.

Editorial Universidad Nacional: Campus Universitario, Frente Escuela de Ciencias Ambientales, Apdo 86, 3000 Heredia; tel. 2277-3204; fax 2277-3825; e-mail editoria@una.ac.cr; internet www.una.ac.cr/euna; f. 1976; Pres. CARLOS FRANCISCO MONGE.

Grupo Editorial Norma: Zona Franca Metropolitana Local 7B, Barreal de Heredia, Heredia, Apdo 592, 1200 Pavas; tel. 2293-1333; fax 2239-3947; e-mail gerencia@farben.co.cr; internet www.norma.com; fmrly Ediciones Farben; Man. Editor ALEXANDER OBONAGA.

Grupo Santillana: La Uruca 78, 1150 San José; tel. 2220-4242; fax 2220-1320; e-mail santilla@santillana.co.cr; internet www.gruposantillana.co.cr; f. 1993; Editorial Dir ELSA MORALES CORDERO.

Imprenta Nacional: La Uruca, San José; tel. 2296-9570; e-mail direccion@imprenta.go.cr; internet www.imprentanacional.go.cr; Dir-Gen. JORGE VARGAS ESPINOZA.

Librería Lehmann, Imprenta y Litografía, Ltda: Calles 1 y 3, Avda Central, Apdo 10011, 1000 San José; tel. 2522-4848; fax 2233-0713; e-mail servicio@librerialehmann.com; internet www.librerialehmann.com; f. 1896; general fiction, educational, textbooks; Man. Dir ANTONIO LEHMANN GUTIÉRREZ.

Océcor de CR: Edif. Océano, Sabana Norte, del ICE 300m al Noreste, San José; tel. 2210-2000; fax 2210-2061; e-mail ocecor@racsa.co.cr; internet www.oceano.com; Gen. Man. JORGE ROJAS.

PUBLISHING ASSOCIATION

Cámara Costarricense del Libro: Paseo de los Estudiantes, Apdo 1571, 1002 San José; tel. 2225-1363; fax 2253-4297; e-mail ccl@libroscr.com; internet www.libroscr.com; f. 1978; Pres. DUNIA SOLANO AGUILAR.

Broadcasting and Communications

TELECOMMUNICATIONS

Cabletica: Sabana Oeste, 25 m al sur del Estadio Nacional, contiguo a Canal 7, San José; tel. 2210-1450; fax 2520-7777; e-mail servicioalcliente@cabletica.com; internet www.cabletica.com; cable television and internet services; Gen. Man. HILDA MORENO.

Claro CR Telecomunicaciones, SA: Ruta 27, Salida de Santa Ana hacia Lindora, 500 m norte y 400 m este, Pozos de Santa Ana, San José; tel. 2296-3136; e-mail clientes@claro.cr; internet www.claro.cr;

f. 2011; subsidiary of América Móvil, Mexico; Exec. Dir RICARDO TAYLOR.

Instituto Costarricense de Electricidad (ICE): govt agency for power and telecommunications (see Utilities). ICE's monopoly over the telecommunications sector was ended in 2010.

Kölbi: Sabana Norte, San José; tel. 2000-7720; e-mail tuserviciokolbi@ice.go.cr; cellular and internet services; owned by ICE; Gen. Man. CARLOS MECUTCHEN AGUILAR.

Radiográfica Costarricense, SA (RACSA): Avda 5, Calle 1, frente al Edif. Numar, Apdo 54, 1000 San José; tel. 2287-0087; fax 2287-0379; e-mail racsaenlinea@racsa.co.cr; internet www.racsa.co.cr; f. 1921; state telecommunications co, owned by ICE; Gen. Man. ORLANDO CASCANTE.

Telefónica de Costa Rica TC, SA (Movistar): Edif. Los Balcones, 4°, Centro de Negocios Plaza Roble, Escazú, San José; internet www.movistar.co.cr; f. 2011 in Costa Rica; subsidiary of Telefónica, Spain; Dir-Gen. JORGE ABADÍA.

Tigo: Edif. Sabana Real, Sabana Sur, del MAG 200 m este, San José; tel. 4030-9000; internet www.tigo.cr; f. 2004 as Amnet Cable; adopted present name in 2012; cable television, cellular and internet services; subsidiary of Millicom International Cellular (Luxembourg); Gen. Man. ANGELO IANNUZZELLI.

Regulatory Authority

Superintendencia de Telecomunicaciones (SUTEL): Edif. Tapantí, 3°, Complejo Multipark, 100 m norte Construplaza, Guachipelín de Escazú, San José; tel. 4000-0000; fax 2215-6821; e-mail info@sutel.go.cr; internet www.sutel.go.cr; f. 2008; regulatory body for the telecommunications sector; forms part of the Autoridad Reguladora de los Servicios Públicos (ARESEP—see Trade and Industry—Utilities); Pres. CARLOS RAÚL GUTIÉRREZ.

BROADCASTING

Radio

Cadena Radial Costarricense: 75 m oeste de la Pozuelo, La Uruca, San José; tel. 2220-1001; fax 2255-4483; e-mail aguevara@crc.cr; internet www.crc.cr; operates nine AM and FM radio stations; Dir ANDRÉS QUINTANA CAVALLINI.

Faro del Caribe: Apdo 2710, 1000 San José; tel. 2286-1755; fax 2227-1725; e-mail info@farodelcaribe.org; internet www.farodelcaribe.org; f. 1948; religious and cultural programmes in Spanish and English; non-commercial; Dir LUIS SERRANO.

FCN Radio Internacional (Family Christian Network): Apdo 60-2020, Zapote, San José; tel. 2209-8000; fax 2293-7993; e-mail info@fcnradio.com; internet www.fcnradio.com; non-commercial; Dir Dr DECAROL WILLIAMSON.

Grupo Centro: Tibás, 100 norte y 125 oeste de la Municipalidad, Apdo 6133, 1000 San José; tel. 2240-7591; fax 2236-3672; e-mail info@radiocentrocr.com; internet www.radiocentrocr.com; f. 1971; operates Radio Centro 96.3 FM, Radio 820 AM, Televisora Guanacasteca Channels 16 and 28; Dir ROBERTO HERNÁNDEZ RAMÍREZ.

Grupo Columbia: 400 m oeste de la Casa Presidencial, Zapote, Apdo 168-2020, San José; tel. 2224-0707; fax 2225-9275; e-mail columbia@columbia.co.cr; internet www.columbia.co.cr; operates Radio Columbia, Radio Dos, Radio 955 Jazz; Dir YASHÍN QUESADA ARAYA; Gen. Man. MIGUEL MONGE.

Radio 16: Centro Comercial San Francisco, Calle 5 y 6, Grecia 16-4100, Alajuela; tel. 2494-5356; fax 2494-2031; e-mail gerencia@radio16.com; internet www.radio16.com; Dir LUIS GUSTAVO JIMÉNEZ RAMÍREZ.

Radio América: Sociedad Periódistica Extra Ltda, Edif. Borrasé de la Prensa Libre, Calle 4, Avda 4, Fecosa 177, 1009 San José; tel. 2223-6666; fax 2255-3712; e-mail radioamerica@780am.com; internet www.780america.com; f. 1948 as Radio América Latina; changed name as above in 1996; Dir ADRIÁN MARRERO REDONDO.

Radio Chorotega: Conferencia Episcopal de Costa Rica, Casa Cural de Santa Cruz, Apdo 92, 5175 Guanacaste; tel. and fax 2680-0447; e-mail ugiocr@hotmail.com; internet www.radiochorotega1100am.com; f. 1983; Roman Catholic station; Co-Ordinator-Gen. JOSÉ MARCELINO MAYORGA CASTILLO.

Radio Emaús: Edif. CENAP, contiguo a la Of. Parroquial, Parroquia de Nuestra Señora de Lourdes, San Vito, Coto Brus; tel. and fax 2773-3101; fax 2773-4035; e-mail radioemaus@racsa.co.cr; internet radioemaus.org; f. 1962; Roman Catholic station; religious programmes; Dir Rev. WILLIAM RODRGUEZ LÉON.

Radio Fides: Avda 4, 2°, costado sur de la Catedral Metropolitana, Curia Metropolitana, Apdo 5079, 1000 San José; tel. 2258-1415; fax 2233-2387; e-mail programas@radiofides.co.cr; internet www.radiofides.co.cr; f. 1952; Roman Catholic station; non-commercial; Dir JASON GRANADOS SÁNCHEZ.

Radio Monumental: Avda Central y 2, Calle 2, Apdo 800, 1000 San José; tel. 2296-6093; fax 2296-0413; e-mail ventas@monumental.co.cr; internet www.monumental.co.cr; f. 1929; operates 8 radio stations: Radio Monumental, Radio ZFM, Radio Reloj, Punto Cinco, EXA FM, Radio Fabulosa, Radio Favorita and 670 AM; Gen. Man. HERNAN AZOFEIFA.

Radio Musical: 1 km al este Hipermás, Carretera a 3 Ríos, Apdo 854, 1000 San José; tel. 2518-2290; fax 2518-2270; e-mail cabina@radiomusical.com; internet www.radiomusical.com; f. 1951; Gen. Man. JAVIER CASTRO.

Radio Nacional: 1 km oeste del Parque Nacional de Diversiones, La Uruca, Apdo 7, 1980 San José; tel. 2231-3331; fax 2220-0070; e-mail sdiaz@sinart.go.cr; internet www.sinart.go.cr; f. 1978; non-commercial; Dir FREDDY GÓMEZ HERNÁNDEZ.

Radio Santa Clara: Edif. CENCO, Santa Clara, San Carlos, Apdo 221, Ciudad Quesada, Alajuela; tel. 2460-6666; fax 2460-2151; e-mail radio@radiosantaclara.org; internet www.radiosantaclara.org; f. 1984; Roman Catholic station; non-commercial; Dir Rev. MARCO ANTONIO SOLÍS V.

Sistema Radiofónico de la Universidad de Costa Rica: Ciudad Universitaria Rodrigo Facio, San Pedro, Montes de Oca, Apdo 2060, 1000 San José; tel. 2511-6850; fax 2511-4832; e-mail radiosucr@gmail.com; internet radios.ucr.ac.cr; f. 1949; stations include Radio Universidad (96.7 FM), Radio U (101.9 FM) and Radio 870 UCR (870 AM); Dir GISELLE BOZA SOLANO.

Television

Cablevision de Costa Rica, SA: Edif. CableVision, Calle Privada, esq. noreste del colegio San Francis, 75 m este y 25 m sur, Moravia, San José; tel. 2545-1111; fax 2236-8801; e-mail mbarboza@cablevision.co.cr; internet www.cablevision.co.cr; more than 100 channels; digital television; Gen. Man. LEYDA ELIZABETH LOMBANA.

Representaciones Televisivas Repretel (Canales 4, 6 y 11): Edif. Repretel, La Uruca del Hospital México, 300 m al oeste, Apdo 2860, 1000 San José; tel. 2299-7200; fax 2232-4203; e-mail info@repretel.com; internet www.repretel.com; f. 1993; Pres. FERNANDO CONTRERAS LÓPEZ; News Dir MARCELA ANGULO.

Sistema Nacional de Radio y Televisión Cultural (SINART): 1 km al oeste del Parque Nacional de Diversiones La Uruca, Apdo 7, 1980 San José; tel. 2231-3333; fax 2231-6604; e-mail secretariapresidencia@sinart.go.cr; internet www.sinart.go.cr; f. 1977; cultural; Dir-Gen. RODRIGO ARIAS CAMACHO.

Telefides (Canal 40): detrás de la Imprenta Nacional, de La Kia Motors, 200 m sur y 200 m oeste, La Uruca, San José; tel. 2520-1112; fax 2290-5346; e-mail info@telefides.com; internet www.telefides.com; f. 1992; Man. SARAY AMADOR.

Televisora de Costa Rica (Canal 7), SA (Teletica): Costado oeste Estadio Nacional, Apdo 3876, San José; tel. 2290-6245; fax 2231-6258; e-mail escribanos@teletica.com; internet www.teletica.com; f. 1960; operates Channel 7; Pres. OLGA COZZA DE PICADO; Gen. Man. RENÉ PICADO COZZA.

Regulatory Authorities

Asociación Costarricense de Información y Cultura (ACIC): Apdo 365, 1009 San José; tel. 2227-4694; f. 1983; independent body; controls private radio stations; Pres. MIGUEL ANGEL AGÜERO ALFARO.

Cámara Nacional de Radio (CANARA): Paseo de los Estudiantes, Apdo 1583, 1002 San José; tel. 2256-2338; fax 2255-4483; e-mail info@canara.org; internet www.canara.org; f. 1947; Pres. GUSTAVO PIEDRA GUZMÁN; Sec. CARLOS LAFUENTE CHRYSSOPOULOS.

Control Nacional de Radio (CNR): Edif. García Pinto, 2°, Calle 33, Avdas Central y Primera, Barrio Escalante, Apdo 1344, 1011 San José; tel. 2524-0455; fax 2524-0454; e-mail controlderadio@ice.co.cr; internet www.controlderadio.go.cr; f. 1954; governmental supervisory department; Dir FERNANDO VÍCTOR.

Finance

(cap. = capital; res = reserves; dep. = deposits; m. = million; brs = branches; amounts in colones, unless otherwise indicated)

BANKING

Central Bank

Banco Central de Costa Rica: Avdas Central y Primera, Calles 2 y 4, Apdo 10058, 1000 San José; tel. 2243-3333; fax 2243-4566; internet www.bccr.fi.cr; f. 1950; cap. and res –1,276,176.5m., dep. 3,991,482.1m. (Dec. 2009); state-owned; Pres. Dr RODRIGO BOLAÑOS ZAMORA; Gen. Man. FÉLIX DELGADO QUESADA.

State-owned Banks

Banco de Costa Rica (BCR): Avdas Central y 2da, Calles 4 y 6, Apdo 10035,1000 San José; tel. 2287-9000; fax 2255-0911; e-mail ServiciosBancaElectronica@bancobcr.com; internet www.bancobcr.com; f. 1877; responsible for industry; cap. 96,571.5m., res 139,846.3m., dep. 1,766,243.4m. (Dec. 2009); Pres. ALBERTO RAVEN ODIO; Gen. Man. MARIO RIVERO TURCIOS; 260 brs.

Banco Crédito Agrícola de Cartago (BANCREDITO): Costado sur de la Catedral de Cartago (Iglesia del Carmen), 7050 Cartago; tel. 2550-0202; fax 2222-1911; e-mail zailyn.espinoza@bancreditocr.com; internet www.bancreditocr.com; f. 1918; cap. 14,039.1m., res 24,088.0m., dep. 563,611.1m. (Dec. 2011); Pres. THELVIN CABEZAS GARITA; CEO GERARDO PORRAS SANABRIA.

Banco Nacional de Costa Rica: Avda 1–3, Calle 4, Apdo 10015, 1000 San José; tel. 2212-2000; fax 2255-0270; e-mail bncr@bncr.fi.cr; internet www.bncr.fi.cr; f. 1914; responsible for the agricultural sector; cap. 133,013.0m., res 423,766.7m., dep. 5,711,636.9m. (Dec. 2011); Pres. ALFREDO VOLIO PÉREZ; Gen. Man. FERNANDO NARANJO VILLALOBOS; 150 brs.

Banco Popular y de Desarrollo Comunal: Calle 1, Avda 2, Apdo 10190, 1000 San José; tel. 2211-7000; fax 2258-5259; e-mail popularenlinea@bp.fi.cr; internet www.bancopopular.fi.cr; f. 1969; cap. 130,000m., res 84,348.3m., dep. 1,099,489.1m. (Dec. 2011); Pres. Dr FRANCISCO ANTONIO PACHECO; Gen. Man. GERARDO PORRAS SANABRIA.

Private Banks

Banca Promérica, SA: Centro Corporativo El Cedral, Trejos Montealegre, Escazú, Costado Oeste del Hipermás, Apdo 1289, 1200 San José; tel. 2505-7000; fax 2290-1991; e-mail solucion@promerica.fi.cr; internet www.promerica.fi.cr; cap. 19,929.3m., res 1,974.1m., dep.198,951.5m. (Dec. 2011); Pres. EDGAR ZURCHER GURDIÁN; 21 brs.

Banco BAC San José, SA: Calle Central, Avdas 3 y 5, Apdo 5445, 1000 San José; tel. 295-9797; fax 256-7200; e-mail info@bacsanjose.com; internet www.bacsanjose.com; f. 1986; fmrly Bank of America, SA; cap. 104,050m., res 17,084.3m., dep. 968,070.3m. (Dec. 2011); Pres. ERNESTO CASTEGNARO ODIO; Gen. Man. GERARDO CORRALES BRENES; 38 brs.

Banco BCT, SA: 150 m norte de la Catedral Metropolitana, San José; tel. 2212-8000; fax 2222-3706; e-mail info@corporacionbct.com; internet www.bancobct.com; f. 1984; cap. 13,250m., res 2,861.2m., dep. 143,306.4m. (Dec. 2011); merged with Banco del Comercio, SA, in 2000; Gen. Man. ALVARO SABORIO DE ROCAFORT.

Banco CMB (Costa Rica), SA: Oficentro Plaza Roble, Edif. El Patio, 4°, Guachipelín de Escazú, San José; tel. 2201-0800; fax 2201-8311; e-mail citibab@sol.racsa.co.cr; internet www.bancocmb.fi.cr; f. 1984 as Banco de Fomento Agrícola; changed name to Banco BFA in 1994 and became Cuscatlan in 2000; current name adopted in 2008 after acquisition by Citi; cap. 10,917m., res 1,247.1m., dep. 135,849.6m. (Dec. 2011); Pres. JUAN ANTONIO MIRÓ.

Banco Davivienda (Costa Rica), SA: Barrio Tournón, Diagonal a Ulacit, Apdo 7983, 1000 San José; tel. 2257-1155; fax 2257-1167; internet www.davivienda.cr; f. 1981 as Banco Agroindustrial y de Exportaciones, SA; became Banco Banex SA in 1987; incorporated Banco Metropolitano in 2001 and Banco Bancrecen in 2002, became Banco HSBC in 2007; bought by Banco Davivienda (Colombia) in 2012; cap. 57,597.2m., res 7,509.6m., dep. 475,206.3m. (Dec. 2011); CEO EFRAÍN FORERO; 33 brs.

Banco Improsa, SA: Barrio Tournón, costado sur del Periódico La República, San José; tel. 2284-4000; fax 2284-4009; e-mail cramirez@improsa.com; internet www.improsa.com; cap. 18,443.2m., res 4,120.2m, dep. 106,217.6m. (Dec. 2011); Pres. MARIANELA ORTUÑO PINTO; Gen. Man. FÉLIX ALPÍZAR LOBO.

Banco Lafise: Fuente de la Hispanidad 50 m este, San Pedro, Montes de Oca; tel. 2246-0800; fax 2280-5090; e-mail info@lafise.fi.cr; internet www.lafise.fi.cr; f. 1974; owned by Grupo Lafise; cap. 11,157.7m., res 1,714.7m., total assets 143,755m. (Dec. 2011); Pres. ROBERTO J. ZAMORA LLANES; Gen. Man. GILBERTO SERRANO.

Bansol (Banco de Soluciones de Costa Rica, SA): Montes de Oca, frente al costado norte del Mall San Pedro, Apdo 10882, 1000 San José; tel. 2528-1800; fax 2528-1880; e-mail info@bansol.fi.cr; internet www.bansol.fi.cr; f. 2010; owned by Grupo Financiera Acobo; internet banking; cap. 8,772.5m., res 295.9m, dep. 62,380.4m. (Dec. 2011); Pres. JACK LOEB CASANOVA; Gen. Man. FERNANDO VÍQUEZ SALAZAR; 5 brs.

Scotiabank de Costa Rica (Canada): Frente a la esquina noroeste de La Sabana, Edif. Scotiabank, Apdo 5395, 1000, San José; tel. 2210-4000; fax 2233-13766; e-mail scotiacr@scotiabank.com; internet www.scotiabankcr.com; f. 1995; cap. 64,314.2m., res 40,906.3m, dep. 673,312m. (Dec. 2011); Pres. JUAN CARLOS GARCÍA VIZCAÍNO; Gen. Man. BRIAN W. BRADY; 13 brs.

Banking Associations

Asociación Bancaria Costarricense: Apdo 7-0810, 1000 San José; tel. 2253-2898; fax 2225-0987; e-mail ejecutiva@abc.fi.cr; internet www.abc.fi.cr; Pres. GILBERTO SERRANO G.; Exec. Dir MARÍA ISABEL CORTÉS C.

Cámara de Bancos e Instituciones Financieras de Costa Rica (CBF): Edif. Torre Mercedes, 2°, Paseo Colón, San José; tel. 2256-4652; fax 2221-9444; e-mail info@camaradebancos.fi.cr; internet www.camaradebancos.fi.cr; f. 1968; Pres. GUILLERMO QUESADA O.; Exec. Dir ANNABELLE ORTEGA A.

STOCK EXCHANGE

Bolsa Nacional de Valores, SA: Parque Empresarial FORUM (Autopista Próspero Fernández), Santa Ana, Apdo 03-6155, 1000 San José; tel. 2204-4848; fax 2204-4749; e-mail servicioalcliente@bolsacr.com; internet www.bolsacr.com; f. 1976; Pres. Dr GILBERTO SERRANO GUTIÉRREZ; Gen.Man. JOSÉ RAFAEL BRENES.

INSURANCE

State monopoly of the insurance sector was ended in 2008.

Supervisory Authorities

Instituto Nacional de Seguros: Avdas 7 y 9, Calles 9 y 9B, Apdo 10061, 1000 San José; tel. 2287-6000; fax 2255-3381; e-mail contactenos@ins-cr.com; internet www.ins-cr.com; f. 1924; Exec. Pres. Dr GUILLERMO CONSTENLA UMAÑA; Vice-Pres. LUIS ALBERTO CASAFONT FLORES.

Superintendencia General de Seguros (SUGESE): San José; tel. 2243-5108; fax 2243-5151; e-mail sugese@sugese.fi.cr; internet www.sugese.fi.cr; f. 2010; regulates the insurance sector; Supt TOMÁS SOLEY PÉREZ.

Principal Companies

ALICO Costa Rica, SA (American Life Insurance Co): Oficentro Fuentes del Obelisco, 2°, Of. 18, San Rafael de Escazú, San José; tel. 2288-0960; fax 2288-0931; e-mail servicioalcliente@alico.co.cr; internet www.alico.co.cr; f. 2010; part of MetLife Inc; Pres. RICARDO RODOLFO GARCÍA HOLTZ; Gen. Man. LUIS YOUNG VIRZI.

Aseguradora del Istmo (ADISA), SA: Edif. Stewart Title, 4°, San Rafael de Escazú, San José; tel. 2228-4850; fax 2228-0483; e-mail info@adisa.cr; internet www.adisa.cr; f. 2010; Gen. Man. KEVIN MARK LUCAS.

ASSA Cía de Seguros, SA: Edif. F, Centro Empresarial Fórum I, 1°, Santa Ana, San José; tel. 2503-2700; fax 2503-2797; e-mail contacto@assanet.com; internet www.assanet.cr; f. 2009; subsidiary of Grupo ASSA, Argentina; Pres. STANLEY MOTTA; Gen. Man. SERGIO RUÍZ.

Caja Costarricense de Seguro Social: Avda 2da, entre calles 5 y 7, Apdo 10105, San José; tel. 2539-0000; fax 2222-1217; e-mail ibalmace@ccss.sa.cr; internet www.info.ccss.sa.cr; accident and health insurance; state-owned; Exec. Pres. Dr ILEANA BALMACEDA ARIAS.

Mapfre Seguros Costa Rica, SA: Edif. Alvasa, 2°, Barrio Tournón, Ruta 32, San José; tel. 2010-3000; e-mail servicioalcliente@mapfre.co.cr; internet www.mapfrecr.com; f. 2010; fmrly Aseguradora Mundial, SA; Pres. MANUEL JOSÉ PAREDES LEFEVRE; Gen. Man. CARLOS GRANGEL LOIRA.

Pan-American Life Insurance de Costa Rica, SA: Edif. Los Balcones B, 3°, Centro Corporativo Plaza Roble, Guachipelín de Escazú, San José; tel. 2505-3600; e-mail servicioalclientecr@panamericanlife.com; internet www.panamericanlife.com; f. 2010; Country Man. ALFREDO RAMÍREZ.

Sociedad de Seguros de Vida del Magisterio Nacional, SA: Costado Sur de la Sociedad de Seguros del Vida del Magisterio Nacional, Calle 1, Avda 10, San José; tel. 2523-6767; fax 2222-5332; e-mail info@segurosdelmagisterio.com; internet www.segurosdelmagisterio.com; f. 1920; insurance for teachers; Pres. JOSÉ ANTONIO CASTILLO ARAYA; Gen. Man. RAFAEL MONGE CHINCHILLA.

Trade and Industry

GOVERNMENT AGENCIES

Instituto Nacional de Vivienda y Urbanismo (INVU): Avda 9, Calles 3 bis y 5, Apdo 2534-1000, San José; tel. 2256-5265; fax 2223-4006; internet www.invu.go.cr; housing and town planning institute; Exec. Pres. EUGENIA VARGAS GURDIÁN; Gen. Man. MARÍA DEL CARMEN REDONDO SOLÍS.

Promotora del Comercio Exterior de Costa Rica (PROCOMER): Edif. Centro de Comercio Exterior, Avdas 3, Calle 40, Centro Colón, Apdo 1278, 1007 San José; tel. 2299-4700; fax 2233-5755;

e-mail info@procomer.com; internet www.procomer.com; f. 1997 to improve international competitiveness by providing services aimed at increasing, diversifying and expediting international trade; Pres. Anabel González Campabadal; Gen. Man. Jorge Sequeira.

DEVELOPMENT ORGANIZATIONS

Cámara de Azucareros: Calle 3, Avda Fernández Güell, Apdo 1577, 1000 San José; tel. 2221-2103; fax 2222-1358; e-mail crazucar@racsa.co.cr; internet www.laica.co.cr; f. 1949; sugar growers; 16 mems; Pres. Federico Chavarría K; Exec. Dir Nidia Alfaro.

Cámara Nacional de Bananeros: Edif. Urcha, 3°, Calle 11, Avda 6, Apdo 10273, 1000 San José; tel. 2222-7891; fax 2233-1268; e-mail canaba@ice.co.cr; internet canabacr.com; f. 1967; banana growers; Pres. Jorge Osborne; Exec. Dir María de los Angeles Vindas.

Cámara Nacional de Cafetaleros: Condominio Oroki 4D, La Uruca, Apdo 1310, San José; tel. and fax 2296-8334; fax 2296-8334; e-mail camcafe@ice.co.cr; f. 1948; 30 mems; coffee millers and growers; Pres. Rodrigo Vargas Ruíz; Exec. Dir Gabriela Lobo H.

Coalición Costarricense de Iniciativas de Desarrollo (CINDE) (Costa Rican Investment Promotion Agency): Edif. Los Balcones, Plaza Roble, 4°, Guachipelin, Ezcazú; tel. 2201-2800; fax 2201-2867; e-mail invest@cinde.org; internet www.cinde.org; f. 1983; coalition for development of initiatives to attract foreign investment for production and export of new products; Pres. José Rossi; CEO Gabriela Llobet.

Corporación Bananera Nacional, SA (CORBANA): Zapote frente Casa Presidencial, Apdo 6504-1000 San José; tel. 2202-4700; fax 2234-9421; e-mail corbana@racsa.co.cr; internet www.corbana.co.cr; f. 1971; public co; cultivation and wholesale of agricultural produce, incl. bananas; Pres. Jorge Sauma; Man. Romano Orlich.

InfoAgro (Sistema de Información del Sector Agropecuario): Ministerio de Agricultura y Ganadería, Antigüo Colegio La Salle, Sabana Sur, San José; tel. 2296-2579; fax 2296-1652; e-mail infoagro@mag.go.cr; internet www.infoagro.go.cr; state agency; dissemination of information to promote the agricultural sector; Nat. Co-ordinator Ana Isabel Gómez de Miguel.

Instituto del Café de Costa Rica: Calle 1, Avdas 18 y 20, Apdo 37, 1000 San José; tel. 2222-6411; fax 2222-2838; internet www.icafe.go.cr; e-mail promo@icafe.cr; internet www.icafe.cr; f. 1933 to develop the coffee industry, to control production and to regulate marketing; Exec. Dir Ronald Peters Seevers.

CHAMBERS OF COMMERCE

Cámara de Comercio de Costa Rica: Urb. Tournón, 125 m noroeste del parqueo del Centro Comercial El Pueblo, Goicochea, Apdo 1114, 1000 San José; tel. 2221-0005; fax 2223-1157; e-mail camara@camara-comercio.com; internet www.camara-comercio.com; f. 1915; 900 mems; Pres. Arnoldo André Tinoco; Exec. Dir Alonso Elizondo Bolaños.

Cámara de Industrias de Costa Rica: 350 m sur de la Fuente de la Hispanidad, San Pedro de Montes de Oca, Apdo 10003, San José; tel. 2202-5600; fax 2234-6163; e-mail cicr@cicr.com; internet www.cicr.com; Pres. Marco Meneses Granados; Exec. Vice-Pres. Martha Castillo Díaz.

Unión Costarricense de Cámaras y Asociaciones de la Empresa Privada (UCCAEP): De McDonald's en Sabana Sur, 400 m al sur, 100 m al este, 25 m al sur, San José; tel. 2290-5595; fax 2290-5596; e-mail uccaep@uccaep.or.cr; internet www.uccaep.or.cr; f. 1974; business fed; Pres. Manuel H. Rodríguez Peyton; Exec. Dir Shirley Saborío Marchena.

INDUSTRIAL AND TRADE ASSOCIATIONS

Asociación de Empresas de Zonas Francas (AZOFRAS): Plaza Mayor, 2°, Pavas, San José; tel. 2520-1635; fax 2520-1636; e-mail azofras@racsa.co.cr; internet www.azofras.com; f. 1990; Pres. Jorge Brenes; Exec. Dir Alvaro Valverde Palavicini.

Cámara Nacional de Agricultura y Agroindustria: 300 m sur y 50 m este de McDonald's, Plaza del Sol, Curridabat, Apdo 1671, 1000 San José; tel. 2280-0996; fax 2280-0969; e-mail camaradeagricultura@cnaacr.com; internet www.cnaacr.com; f. 1947; Pres. Alvaro Sáenz Saborío; Exec. Dir Martín Calderón Chaves; 23 mems.

Cámara de Tecnología de Información y Comunicación (CAMTIC): Apdo 2101, San Pedro de Montes de Oca, 2050 San José; tel. 2283-2205; fax 2280-4691; e-mail info@camtic.org; internet www.camtic.org; Pres. Alexander Mora Delgado; Exec. Dir Otto Rivera Valle.

Consejo Nacional de Producción: Avda 10, Calle 36, Apdo 2205, San José; tel. 2257-9355; fax 2256-9625; e-mail soporte@cnp.go.cr; internet www.cnp.go.cr; f. 1948 to encourage agricultural and fish production and to regulate production and distribution of basic commodities; state-run; Exec. Pres. William Barrantes Sáenz; Gen. Man. Zoraida Fallas Cordero.

Instituto de Desarrollo Agrario (IDA): Ofs Centrales IDA, Moravia, Residencial Los Colegios, frente al IFAM, Apdo 5054, 1000 San José; tel. 2247-7400; fax 2241-4891; internet www.ida.go.cr; Exec. Pres. Rolando González Ulloa; Gen. Man. Víctor Julio Carvajal Garro.

Instituto Mixto de Ayuda Social (IMAS): Calle 29, Avdas 2 y 4, Apdo 6213, San José; tel. 2202-4066; fax 2224-8930; e-mail gerencia_general@imas.go.cr; internet www.imas.go.cr; Exec. Pres. Fernando Marín Rojas; Gen. Man. Margarita Fernández Garita.

Instituto Nacional de Fomento Cooperativo: Avdas 5 y 7, Calle 20 Norte, Apdo 10103, 1000 San José; tel. 2256-2944; fax 2255-3835; e-mail info@infocoop.go.cr; internet www.infocoop.go.cr; f. 1973 to encourage the establishment of co-operatives and to provide technical assistance and credit facilities; Pres. Freddy González Rojas; Exec. Dir Martín Robles Robles.

UTILITIES

Regulatory Body

Autoridad Reguladora de los Servicios Públicos (ARESEP): Edif. Turrubares, Complejo Multipark, 100 m norte Construplaza, Guachipelín de Escazú, Apdo 936, 1000 San José; tel. 2506-3200; fax 2215-6052; e-mail cmora@aresep.go.cr; internet www.aresep.go.cr; f. 1996; oversees telecommunications, public utilities and transport sectors; Regulator Gen. Dennis Meléndez Howell.

Electricity

Instituto Costarricense de Electricidad (ICE): Apdo 10032, 1000 San José; tel. 2220-7720; fax 2220-1555; e-mail ice-si@ice.co.cr; internet www.ice.co.cr; f. 1949; govt agency for power and telecommunications; Exec. Pres. Teófilo de la Torre Arguello; Gen. Man. Alejandro Soto Zúñiga.

Cía Nacional de Fuerza y Luz, SA (CNFL): Calle Central y 1, Avda 5, Apdo 10026, 1000 San José; tel. 2296-4608; fax 2296-3950; e-mail info@cnfl.go.cr; internet www.cnfl.go.cr; f. 1941; electricity co; mem. of ICE Group; Gen. Man. Pablo Cob Saborío.

JASEC (Junta Administrativa del Servicio Eléctrico Municipal de Cartago): Apdo 179, 7050 Cartago; tel. 2550-6800; fax 2551-1683; e-mail agomez@jasec.co.cr; internet www.jasec.co.cr; f. 1964; Pres. Alfonso Víquez Sánchez.

Water

Instituto Costarricense de Acueductos y Alcantarillados: Edif. Central, Pavas, 1000 San José; tel. 2242-5591; fax 2222-2259; e-mail centrodoc@aya.go.cr; internet www.aya.go.cr; water and sewerage; Pres. Yessenia Calderón; Gen. Man. Heibel Antonio Rodríguez Araya.

TRADE UNIONS

Central del Movimiento de Trabajadores Costarricenses (CMTC) (Costa Rican Workers' Union): Calle 20, 200 m norte del Hospital de Niños, 1000 San José; tel. 2221-7701; fax 2221-3353; e-mail info@cmtccr.org; internet www.cmtccr.org; f. 1994; Pres. Olman Chincilla; 108,000 mems (2011).

Confederación de Trabajadores Rerum Novarum (CTRN): Barrio Escalante, de la Rotonda el Farolito 250 m este, Apdo 31100, San José; tel. 2283-4244; fax 2234-2282; e-mail ctrn@ice.co.cr; internet www.rerumnovarum.or.cr; Pres. Rodrigo Aguilar Arce; Sec.-Gen. Sergio Saborío Brenes.

Transport

Autoridad Reguladora de los Servicios Públicos (ARESEP): regulatory body for the telecommunications industry, public utilities and transport (see Trade and Industry—Utilities).

RAILWAYS

AmericaTravel: Edif. INCOFER, Estación al Pacífico, Avda 20, Calle 2, Apdo 246, 1009 San José; tel. 2233-3300; fax 2223-3311; e-mail americatravel@ice.co.cr; operates weekend tourist trains between San José and Caldera; Gen. Man. Juan Paniagua Zeledón.

Instituto Costarricense de Ferrocarriles (INCOFER): Calle Central, Avda 22 y 24, Apdo 1, 1009 San José; tel. 2222-8857; fax 2222-6998; e-mail incofer@sol.racsa.co.cr; f. 1985; govt-owned; 471 km, of which 388 km are electrified; in 1995 INCOFER suspended most operations, pending privatization, although some cargo transport continued; by 2012 a wide range of rail lines had reopened; Pres. Miguel Carabaguíaz.

ROADS

In 2010 there were 39,018 km of roads, of which 26% were paved. In 2009 the Government and the Andean Promotion Corporation signed a US $60m. loan agreement for the Atlantic Corridor Investment Program. The project included construction of a new highway between the Atlantic ports of Costa Rica and Nicaragua, as well as a new bridge over the Sixaola river on the border with Panama. In 2010 the Central American Bank for Economic Integration approved a loan of $140m. for the San José–San Carlos highway, intended to improve access between the capital and the north of the country.

Consejo Nacional de Vialidad (CONAVI): 50 m este y 10 m norte de la Rotonda Betania, Apdo 616, Zapote, 2010 San José; tel. 2202-5300; e-mail contraloria@conavi.go.cr; internet www.conavi.go.cr; f. 1998; Exec. Dir CARLOS ACOSTA MONGE.

SHIPPING

Local services operate between the Costa Rican ports of Puntarenas and Limón and those of Colón and Cristóbal in Panama and other Central American ports. Caldera on the Gulf of Nicoya is the main Pacific port. The Caribbean coast is served by the port complex of Limón/Moín, which was being expanded in 2014. In December 2013 the flag registered fleet comprised eight vessels, with a total displacement of some 6,977 grt.

Instituto Costarricense de Puertos del Pacífico (INCOP): Calle 36, Avda 3, Apdo 543, 1000 San José; tel. 2634-9100; fax 2634-9101; e-mail info@incop.go.cr; internet www.incop.go.cr; f. 1972; state agency for the development of Pacific ports; Exec. Pres. URIAS UGALDE VARELA; Gen. Man. WITMAN CRUZ MÉNDEZ.

Junta de Administración Portuaria y de Desarrollo Económico de la Vertiente Atlántica (JAPDEVA): Calle 17, Avda 7, Apdo 5.330, 1000 San José; tel. 2795-4747; fax 2795-0728; e-mail cthomas@japdeva.go.cr; internet www.japdeva.go.cr; f. 1963; state agency for the devt of Atlantic ports; Exec. Pres. ALLAN HIDALGO CAMPOS; Gen. Man. CARLOS THOMAS ARROYO.

Principal Shipping Companies

Inter-Moves SG Global de Costa Rica: Apdo 11990, 1000 San José; tel. 2241-2147; fax 2241-2260; e-mail info@intermoves-sgcr.com; internet www.intermoves-sgcr.com; shipping, freight forwarding and logistics; Gen. Man. JOSÉ ANTONIO SUEIRAS.

Maersk Costa Rica, SA: San José; tel. 2543-5100; fax 2543-5150; e-mail crics@maersk.com; internet www.maerskline.com; f. 1994; subsidiary of Maersk Line (Denmark); Man. PAOLO JIMENEZ.

Puerto Limón Agency: 800 este y 100 sur Plaza del Sol, San José; tel. 2758-2062; fax 2758-2022; e-mail info@limonagency.com; internet www.limonagency.com.

CIVIL AVIATION

Costa Rica has four international airports: Juan Santamaría Airport, the largest, 16 km from San José at El Coco, Tobías Bolaños Airport in Pavas, Daniel Oduber Quirós Airport, at Liberia, and Limón International.

Fly Latin America: San José; tel. 2256-3222; e-mail info@flylatinamerica.net; internet www.flylatinamerica.com; operates services to 9 destinations in Central and South America; Pres. CHARLES STRATFORD; Man. RICHARD KRUG.

Nature Air: Juan Santamaría Main Airport, San José; tel. 2299-6000; fax 2232-2516; e-mail info@natureair.com; internet www.natureair.com; f. 2000; flights from San José to 13 domestic destinations; international destinations include Nicaragua and Panama; carbon-neutral airline; CEO ALEX KHAJAVI.

Servicios Aéreos Nacionales, SA (SANSA): Edif. TACA, La Uruca, San José; tel. 2290-3543; fax 2290-3538; e-mail infosansa@taca.com; internet www.flysansa.com; subsidiary of TACA; international, regional and domestic scheduled passenger and cargo services; Man. Dir CARLOS MANUEL DELGADO AGUILAR.

Tourism

Costa Rica boasts a system of nature reserves and national parks unique in the world, covering one-third of the country. Some 2,192,059 tourists visited Costa Rica in 2011, while tourism receipts totalled a provisional US $2,425m. in 2012. Most visitors came from the USA (39% in 2011).

Cámara Nacional de Turismo de Costa Rica (CANATUR): Zapote, de la Universidad Veritas, 200 m hacia el este, San José; tel. 2234-6222; fax 2253-8102; e-mail supervisor@canatur.org; internet www.canatur.org; f. 1974; Pres. JUAN CARLOS RAMOS TORRES; Exec. Dir MAURICIO CÉSPEDES.

Instituto Costarricense de Turismo (ICT): La Uruca, Costado Este del Puente Juan Pablo II, Apdo 777, 1000 San José; tel. 2299-5876; fax 2220-3559; e-mail info@visitcostarica.com; internet www.visitcostarica.com; f. 1931; Exec. Pres. ALLAN RENE FLORES MOYA; Gen. Man. JUAN CARLOS BORBÓN MARKS.

Defence

Costa Rica has had no armed forces since 1948. As assessed at November 2013, Rural and Civil Guards totalled 2,000 and 4,500 men and women, respectively. In addition, there were 2,500 Border Security Police. There was also a Coast Guard Unit numbering 400 and an Air Surveillance Unit of 400.

Security Budget: an estimated 202,000m. colones in 2013.

Minister of Governance, Police and Public Security: MARIO ZAMORA CORDERO.

Education

Education in Costa Rica is free, and is compulsory between six and 13 years of age. Primary education begins at the age of six and lasts for six years. Official secondary education consists of a three-year basic course, followed by a more specialized course lasting two years in academic schools and three years in technical schools. In 2012/13 a total of 480,125 students attended primary schools and 449,035 attended secondary schools. In 2013 there were 57 universities, of which five were state-run, with, in 2011/12, 203,175 students. The provision for education in the 2013 government budget was US $3.479m., equivalent to 9.3% of total government spending.

CÔTE D'IVOIRE

(THE IVORY COAST)

Introductory Survey

LOCATION, CLIMATE, LANGUAGE, RELIGION, FLAG, CAPITAL

The Republic of Côte d'Ivoire lies on the west coast of Africa, between Ghana to the east and Liberia to the west, with Guinea, Mali and Burkina Faso to the north. Average temperatures vary between 21°C and 30°C (70°F and 86°F). The main rainy season, May–July, is followed by a shorter wet season in October–November. The official language is French, and a large number of African languages are also spoken. At the time of the 1998 census it was estimated that some 34% of the population were Christians (mainly Roman Catholics), 27% Muslims, 15% followed traditional indigenous beliefs, and 3% practised other religions, while 21% had no religious affiliation. (However, it was thought that the proportion of Muslims was, in fact, significantly higher, as the majority of unregistered foreign workers in Côte d'Ivoire were believed to be Muslims.) The national flag (proportions 2 by 3) has three equal vertical stripes, of orange, white and green. The political and administrative capital is Yamoussoukro, although most government ministries and offices remain in the former capital, Abidjan, which is the major centre for economic activity.

CONTEMPORARY POLITICAL HISTORY

Historical Context

Formerly a province of French West Africa, Côte d'Ivoire achieved self-government, within the French Community, in December 1958. Dr Félix Houphouët-Boigny, leader of the Parti Démocratique de la Côte d'Ivoire—Rassemblement Démocratique Africain (PDCI—RDA), became Prime Minister in 1959. The country became fully independent on 7 August 1960; a new Constitution was adopted in October 1960, and Houphouët-Boigny became President in November.

Until 1990 the PDCI—RDA was Côte d'Ivoire's only legal political party, despite constitutional provision for the existence of other political organizations. A high rate of economic growth, together with strong support from France, contributed, until the late 1980s, to the stability of the regime. However, the announcement in early 1990 of austerity measures precipitated an unprecedented level of unrest. In April Houphouët-Boigny appointed Alassane Ouattara, the Governor of the Banque Centrale des Etats de l'Afrique de l'Ouest (BCEAO, the regional central bank), to chair a special commission to formulate economic and political reforms. From May it was announced that hitherto unofficial political organizations were to be formally recognized.

Domestic Political Affairs

Côte d'Ivoire's first contested presidential election was held on 28 October 1990. Houphouët-Boigny—challenged by Laurent Gbagbo, the candidate of the socialist Front Populaire Ivoirien (FPI)—was re-elected for a seventh term with 81.7% of votes cast. In November the legislature, the Assemblée Nationale (National Assembly), approved two constitutional amendments. The first authorized the President of the legislature to assume the functions of the President of the Republic, in the event of the presidency becoming vacant, until the expiry of the previous incumbent's mandate. The second amendment provided for the appointment of a Prime Minister, who would be accountable to the President; Ouattara was subsequently designated premier. At legislative elections that month the PDCI—RDA returned 163 deputies to the 175-member National Assembly; the FPI won nine seats, the Parti Ivoirien des Travailleurs (PIT) one, and two independent candidates were elected. The incoming legislature re-elected Henri Konan Bédié, who had held the presidency of the legislature since 1980, to that post.

The Government's response to the report of a commission of inquiry into student disturbances in May–June 1991, in which one student died, provoked renewed violence in early 1992, led by the outlawed Fédération Estudiantine et Scolaire de Côte d'Ivoire (FESCI). Houphouët-Boigny refused to subject the armed forces Chief of General Staff, Brig.-Gen. Robert Gueï, to disciplinary proceedings, despite the commission's conclusion that Gueï was ultimately responsible for violent acts perpetrated by forces under his command. In February Gbagbo was among more than 100 people arrested during a violent anti-Government demonstration in Abidjan, and he was one of nine opposition leaders imprisoned in March under a new presidential ordinance that rendered political leaders responsible for violent acts committed by their supporters.

Houphouët-Boigny left Côte d'Ivoire in May 1993 to receive medical treatment in Europe. As the President's health failed, controversy arose over the issue of succession. Many senior politicians, including Ouattara and Gbagbo (both of whom were known to have presidential aspirations), asserted that the process defined in the Constitution effectively endorsed a 'hereditary presidency', since Bédié, like Houphouët-Boigny, was a member of the Akan ethnic group. Houphouët-Boigny died on 7 December, and Bédié assumed the duties of President of the Republic with immediate effect. Ouattara, who refused to recognize Bédié's right of succession, tendered his resignation two days later. Daniel Kablan Duncan, hitherto Minister-delegate, responsible for the Economy, Finance and Planning, was subsequently appointed Prime Minister. Bédié's position was consolidated by his election to the chairmanship of the PDCI—RDA in April 1994. Disaffected members of the governing party left in June to form what they termed a moderate, centrist organization, the Rassemblement des Républicains (RDR); Ouattara formally announced his membership of the RDR in early 1995.

A new electoral code, adopted in December 1994, imposed new restrictions on eligibility for public office, notably stipulating that candidates for the presidency or for the National Assembly be of direct Ivorian descent. The RDR protested that these restrictions would prevent Ouattara from contesting the presidency, since the former Prime Minister was of Burkinabè descent and would also, as a former senior official of the IMF, be affected by the code's requirement that candidates had been continuously resident in Côte d'Ivoire for five years prior to seeking election. At the presidential election, which took place, as scheduled, on 22 October 1995, Bédié, with 95.3% of the valid votes cast, secured an overwhelming victory

In December 1999 a mutiny by soldiers demanding salary increases, the payment of outstanding arrears and the reinstatement of Gueï (who had been replaced in October 1995) as armed forces Chief of General Staff rapidly escalated into a coup. Gueï announced that he had assumed power at the head of a Comité National de Salut Public (National Committee for Public Salvation—CNSP), and that the Constitution and its institutions had been suspended. Bédié left Côte d'Ivoire in January 2000, subsequently seeking refuge in France. A revised Constitution was endorsed by 86.5% of votes cast in a referendum on 23–24 July. Notably, the new document required that presidential candidates be of solely Ivorian nationality and parentage. Also under its terms, all those involved in the coup, and members of the CNSP, were granted immunity from prosecution.

Gbagbo becomes President

Preliminary results of the presidential election held on 22 October 2000 indicated that Gbagbo had received a larger share of votes cast than Gueï; however, on 24 October the Ministry of the Interior and Decentralization dissolved the national electoral commission and declared Gueï to have won the election. The Government alleged fraud on the part of certain, unspecified, political parties, and announced that, following the readjustment of the results, Gueï had defeated Gbagbo. Following clashes between rival army factions in Abidjan, and a declaration of support for Gbagbo by the Chief of Staff of the Armed Forces, Gueï fled, and Gbagbo declared himself President.

According to official figures released by the electoral commission, and confirmed by the Supreme Court, Gbagbo had secured

59.4% of the valid votes cast, and Gueï 32.7%. However, a low rate of participation (an estimated 33.2% overall, but markedly lower in the largely Muslim and RDR-supporting regions in the north, as well as in the political capital, Yamoussoukro, and other strongholds of the PDCI—RDA) cast doubt on the legitimacy of Gbagbo's victory. Concern was raised that Gbagbo had voiced support, during his campaign, for the notion of strengthening national identity, or '*ivoirité*', in potentially inflammatory terms, similar to those used previously by Bédié. Gbagbo was inaugurated as President on 26 October 2000. The following day he appointed a new Council of Ministers, comprising members of the FPI, the PDCI—RDA and the PIT. (The RDR stated that it would await legislative elections before participating in a coalition government.) Pascal Affi N'Guessan, the manager of Gbagbo's electoral campaign and a minister in the outgoing Government, was named as Prime Minister.

Legislative elections proceeded on 10 December 2000, although violent clashes between RDR supporters and the security forces delayed voting in 28 northern constituencies. Electoral turn-out was low, at 31.5%. The FPI won 96 of the 225 seats in the National Assembly, the PDCI—RDA 77, the PIT four, and independent candidates 17, while a 'moderate' faction of the RDR secured one seat. At the outstanding elections, held in January 2001, the PDCI—RDA secured 17 of the 26 contested seats, increasing its overall representation in the legislature to 94 seats, only two less than the FPI. Independent candidates won five seats, and the 'moderate' RDR faction four. Only 13.3% of eligible voters participated. The balance of power in the Assembly remained unclear, and it soon emerged that seven of the 22 nominally independent deputies had been financed by the PDCI—RDA and were to return to that party. A further 14 independents formed an alliance with the FPI, and subsequently created a new centre-right party with some 50 other former members of the PDCI—RDA, the Union pour la Démocratie et pour la Paix de la Côte d'Ivoire (UDPCI).

Attempted coup

On 19 September 2002, while Gbagbo was on a state visit to Italy, there was a co-ordinated armed rebellion in Bouaké, Korhogo and Abidjan. The unrest in Abidjan culminated in the death of Gueï and the assassination of Emile Boga Doudou, the Minister of State, Minister of the Interior and Decentralization. In all, some 300 people were killed in the city. Although government troops rapidly regained control of Abidjan, two ministers were held hostage for several days in the north, which remained under rebel control. Gbagbo, on his return to Côte d'Ivoire on 20 September, implied that an unnamed foreign country (widely understood to refer to Burkina Faso) was implicated in the insurgency, which he described as an attempted *coup d'état*. In late September an emergency summit of the Economic Community of West African States (ECOWAS, see p. 260) resolved to dispatch a military mission to act as a 'buffer' between government and rebel troops, and mandated a 'contact group' of six regional heads of state, to undertake negotiations between Gbagbo and the insurgents. Master-Sgt Tuo Fozié emerged as a spokesman for the rebels, who identified themselves as the Mouvement Patriotique de la Côte d'Ivoire (MPCI) and stated as their principal demand the removal of Gbagbo from the presidency and the holding of fresh elections. The Coordination des Jeunes Patriotes (CJP), a movement led by Charles Blé Goudé, a former leader of the FESCI and an ally of Gbagbo, was vocal in demanding that there be no compromise with rebel groups. Nevertheless, at the end of October the Government and the MPCI entered into negotiations in Lomé, Togo, under the aegis of ECOWAS; another former leader of the FESCI, Guillaume Kigbafori Soro, now the Secretary-General of the recently formed political wing of the MPCI, led the rebel delegation.

National security deteriorated further in November 2002, with the emergence of two new rebel groups, apparently unconnected to the MPCI, in western regions. By the end of the month the Mouvement Populaire Ivoirien du Grand Ouest (MPIGO) and the Mouvement pour la Justice et la Paix (MJP) had taken gained control of Man and Danane, near the border with Liberia. In December the French Government announced that its troops in Côte d'Ivoire were henceforth to be authorized to use force to maintain the ceasefire; France was to increase its contingent of troops in the country to number some 2,500, while the deployment of the ECOWAS mission remained in abeyance. In January 2003 representatives of the Ivorian Government, seven political parties and the three rebel groups travelled to France for negotiations at Marcoussis, outside Paris. On 18 January the first contingent of the ECOWAS military mission (ECOMICI) arrived in Côte d'Ivoire. Although unrest continued, on 24 January agreement on a peace plan was reached by all parties to the Marcoussis talks. Under its terms, Gbagbo was to remain as President until the expiry of his term of office in 2005, but was to share power with a new consensus Prime Minister (who would be debarred from contesting the subsequent presidential election). Rebel groups and opposition parties were to receive posts in a government of national reconciliation.

The poor security situation meant that the formation of the new government was delayed, but on 8 March 2003 an ECOWAS-brokered summit in Accra, Ghana, reached agreement on the share of ministerial portfolios; the FPI was to be given 10 posts, the PDCI—RDA eight, the RDR and the MPCI seven each, and the MJP and the MPIGO one each, while four smaller parties were to receive a total of six posts. Separately, a 15-member Conseil de la Securité Nationale (Council of National Security—CSN), comprising the President, the Prime Minister, the Chief of Staff of the Armed Forces, the leaders of the gendarmerie and the police force, and representatives of the political parties and groups in the Government of National Reconciliation, was to be established to monitor the operations of the defence and security ministries, and to approve Prime Minister Seydou Diarra's nominees to these portfolios.

Prior to the inaugural session of the Council of Ministers, in mid-March 2003, the MPCI, the MPIGO and the MJP refused to attend meetings at which ministerial posts were to be allocated. Later that month Gbagbo issued a decree confirming the decision of the CSN that two existing ministers, from the FPI and the RDR, were to assume additional interim responsibility for the security and defence ministries. However, the MPCI denied that its representative on the CSN had consented to the interim appointments. In mid-April the first full meeting of the Council of Ministers took place. Among the former rebels appointed to the Government were Soro, as Minister of State, Minister of Communication, and Fozié, as Minister of Youth and Public Service. The military leader of the MPCI, Col Michel Gueu, became Minister of Sports and Leisure.

In May 2003 Gueu and the Chief of Staff of the Armed Forces, Gen. Mathias Doué, signed a ceasefire agreement, covering all rebel groups. In June the UN Mission in Côte d'Ivoire (MINUCI), which had been authorized by the UN Security Council in May, charged with overseeing the implementation of the Marcoussis Accords, commenced operations in Abidjan, and on 4 July MPCI leaders formally announced the end of the conflict. In August the National Assembly approved legislation providing for an amnesty for those involved in political unrest between 17 September 2000 and 19 September 2002, excluding persons accused of abuses of human rights or violations of international humanitarian law. By the end of August 2003 more than 50 political prisoners had been released. Meanwhile, the MPCI effectively absorbed the MPIGO and MJP, and announced that the organization was henceforth to be known as the Forces Nouvelles (FN).

Effective division of the country

In early December 2003 Gbagbo announced that the former rebel forces in the north of the country would shortly commence disarmament, several months later than had been initially planned. In the event, the disarmament process was further delayed, although some 40 government soldiers who had been held as prisoners of war in FN-controlled areas were released. Also in December the Council of Ministers approved legislation that required a presidential candidate to have at least one parent of Ivorian origin, rather than both parents as previously specified by the Constitution.

In February 2003 the UN Security Council authorized establishment of the UN Operation in Côte d'Ivoire (UNOCI, see p. 90); with a military strength of 6,240, the peacekeeping operation was deployed for an initial period of 12 months from early April, when authority was transferred from MINUCI and ECOMICI to UNOCI. Nevertheless, the process of national reconciliation appeared to be stalling with Soro's announcement that former rebel fighters would not disarm prior to legislative and presidential elections scheduled for 2005.

In March 2004 clashes occurred between members of the security forces and protesters following a demonstration in Abidjan, organized by seven of the 10 signatory parties to the Marcoussis Accords (known collectively as the G7). According to official figures, 37 people were killed, although opposition sources put the number of deaths at more than 300. An inquiry conducted by the Office of the UN High Commissioner for Human Rights (OHCHR, see p. 13) concluded that the security forces had been responsible for the death of at least 120 civilians in a 'carefully planned operation' organized by 'the highest authorities of the state'. In response to the violence, the RDR, the FN and the Mouvement des Forces d'Avenir (MFA) announced that they were to suspend their participation in the Government. In April President Gbagbo acceded to the G7's principal demands, agreeing to allow equal access to the state media to all political organizations, to respect the right to demonstrate and to ensure the security of the people. The peace process remained stalled, however, and in May Gbagbo dismissed three opposition ministers, including Soro, replacing them in an acting capacity with members of the FPI.

All parties to the Ivorian conflict attended a meeting of West African heads of state in Accra in July 2004, convened by the UN Secretary-General and the President of Ghana, at which they signed an agreement on implementation of the Marcoussis Accords. The agreement, which was to be monitored by UNOCI, ECOWAS and the African Union (AU, see p. 186), stated that disarmament of the rebels was to commence by 15 October. In August, as agreed in Accra, Gbagbo reinstated the three government ministers dismissed in May, and all ministers from opposition parties and rebel groups resumed participation in the Government. Shortly afterwards Gbagbo delegated some of his powers to the Prime Minister, pending the presidential election scheduled for October 2005. However, the disarmament deadline was not observed by the former rebels, who declared that insufficient progress had been made towards political reform.

In November 2004 the 18-month ceasefire was broken when the Ivorian air force launched bombing raids on Bouaké and other targets in the north of the country, reportedly resulting in the death of nine French peacekeeping troops and a US aid consultant. In response, French forces, acting on the direct orders of French President Jacques Chirac, destroyed the Ivorian air force on the ground. This provoked several days of violence in Abidjan and elsewhere, with thousands of Ivorians—in particular members of Blé Goudé's CJP—rioting, looting and attacking French and other foreign targets. French troops intervened to take control of Abidjan's airport and major thoroughfares, and to protect French and other foreign nationals, clashing with rioters and protesters in the process. In mid-November the UN Security Council voted unanimously to impose a 13-month arms embargo on Côte d'Ivoire. (The embargo was reinforced by a further Security Council resolution in February 2005.) Meanwhile, Soro and eight other opposition ministers announced that they would not attend meetings of the Government, on the grounds that their security in Abidjan could not be guaranteed.

Efforts towards rebel disarmament

President Thabo Mbeki of South Africa, in his capacity as AU mediator, conducted talks with the Ivorian Government and the FN in November–December 2004, aimed at re-establishing the Marcoussis Accords as the basis for solution of the crisis. Despite a number of concessions by Gbagbo, unrest intensified in February–March 2005. In early April Mbeki hosted a summit in Pretoria, South Africa, attended by Bédié, Diarra, Gbagbo, Ouattara and Soro, as a result of which an agreement was signed, on 6 April, committing all parties to the disbandment of militia groups and to the disarmament of the former rebel troops. Subsequently, following consultation with the UN Secretary-General, Kofi Annan, and the Chairman of the AU, President Olusegun Obasanjo of Nigeria, regarding conditions for eligibility of presidential candidates at the election due to be held in October, Mbeki determined that the Ivorian Constitutional Council should confirm the candidate of any party that had signed the Marcoussis Accords. This was interpreted as permitting Ouattara's eventual candidacy. Two FN ministers subsequently resumed participation in the Government. Later in April Gbagbo declared that he would accept Ouattara as a legitimate candidate at the presidential election.

In May 2005 the FN and the Ivorian armed forces agreed that disarmament of former rebel forces would commence on 27 June and be completed by 10 August, and that a new republican army would be established to incorporate members of the existing armed forces and former rebel fighters. Later that month the PDCI—RDA, the RDR, the MFA and the UDPCI formed a new alliance, the Rassemblement des Houphouëtistes pour la Démocratie et la Paix (RHDP), and agreed that, in the event of the presidential election progressing to a second round (i.e. should no candidate receive an absolute majority of votes cast in the first round), the four parties would support a common candidate in opposition to Gbagbo.

In June 2005 the UN Security Council extended the mandate of UNOCI and the French peacekeeping forces until January 2006. The terms of UNOCI operations were broadened to include an active role in disarmament, and support for the organization of elections and the establishment of the rule of law. At the end of June 2005, following two days of talks in Pretoria, it was agreed that the dismantling of pro-Government militias would commence immediately and be completed by 20 August, and that legislation providing for the establishment of an independent electoral commission would be enacted by mid-July. Following further negotiations, the timetable for disarmament was again revised: some 40,500 former rebels and 15,000 pro-Government troops were to assemble at cantonment sites from 31 July and surrender their weapons between 26 September and 3 October. Later in July Gbagbo approved a number of legislative changes, notably concerning nationality, citizenship rights and the establishment of an independent electoral commission, using exceptional constitutional powers to override the requirement for parliamentary approval.

The FN refused to begin the disarmament process on 31 July 2005, stating that the terms of the legislation recently adopted by decree by Gbagbo differed from those that had been agreed in Pretoria. In August, however, South African mediators judged that the legislation conformed to the provisions of the peace agreement, prompting the FN to express doubts about Mbeki's impartiality. Later that month the FN and the main opposition parties declared that it would be impossible for a free and fair election to be held within two months, demanding that Gbagbo resign to allow a transitional administration to organize a deferred poll. At the beginning of September the FN rejected South Africa's mediation, after the South African Government, in a briefing to the UN Security Council, blamed the movement for hindering the peace process. Later that month Annan acknowledged that it was no longer feasible to hold the presidential election on 30 October, given that the electoral commission had yet to be established and the voters' register updated.

In early October 2005 the Peace and Security Council (PSC) of the AU proposed the extension by up to 12 months of President Gbagbo's term of office, following its scheduled expiry at the end of the month; it also recommended the appointment of a new Prime Minister, acceptable to all signatories of the Marcoussis Accords, with enhanced powers. The PSC supported the continued involvement of South Africa in mediation efforts, and also proposed the establishment of an International Working Group (IWG) to monitor the implementation of the peace plan. The working group was to comprise senior officials from Benin, Ghana, Guinea, Niger, Nigeria, South Africa, France, the United Kingdom, the USA, the UN, the AU, ECOWAS, the European Union (EU, see p. 273), La Francophonie, the World Bank and the IMF. The UN Security Council adopted a resolution endorsing the AU proposals later that month.

Banny appointed Prime Minister

In November 2005 President Obasanjo of Nigeria led efforts to reach a consensus on the nomination of a new Ivorian Prime Minister. The FN insisted that, as a precondition to Gbagbo's remaining in office as President, Soro or one of his deputies should assume the premiership on the grounds that the FN controlled one-half of the country. Nevertheless, in early December Charles Konan Banny, hitherto Governor of the BCEAO, was designated interim Prime Minister. The new Prime Minister was to be responsible for ensuring the disarmament of former rebel fighters and pro-Gbagbo militias, and for the organization of a presidential election (which he would not be permitted to contest) by October 2006.

In mid-December 2005 the UN Security Council unanimously adopted a resolution to ban imports of uncut diamonds from Côte d'Ivoire, and to renew for a further year the arms embargo and the possibility of imposing sanctions on individuals deemed to have impeded the peace process. Later that month, after three weeks of negotiations, Banny announced the formation of a 32-member transitional Council of Ministers, including seven ministers from the FPI, six from the FN, five from each of the PDCI—RDA and the RDR, and one each from the MFA, the PIT, the UDPCI and the Union Démocratique Citoyenne, as well as four representatives of civil society. Banny assumed personal responsibility for the economy and finance, and communication, while Soro was appointed as Minister of State for the Programme of Reconstruction and Reintegration—the most senior position in the Government after that of Prime Minister. Antoine Bohoun Bouabré, an FPI ally of Gbagbo and hitherto Minister of State, Minister of the Economy and Finance, became Minister of State for Planning and Development. The defence and interior portfolios were, notably, allocated to independents.

The term of the National Assembly formally expired in December 2005. In January 2006 the IWG issued a statement rejecting an extension of the legislative term. Apparently considering the statement as constituting a dissolution of the National Assembly (although the IWP was not empowered to effect this), CJP militias loyal to President Gbagbo seized control of main roads and government buildings in Abidjan and the south-west of the country, and clashed with UN peacekeepers. At the end of the month Banny issued a decree prolonging the mandate of the legislature.

In early February 2006 the UN Security Council, which had in late January extended the mandate of UNOCI and the French military presence until 15 December, approved the imposition of sanctions against three individuals: Blé Goudé and Eugène Djué of the CJP, and Martin Kouakou Fofié, an FN commander accused of human rights abuses, were to be subject to a 12-month travel ban and a freeze on their assets. In late February Banny chaired negotiations in Yamoussoukro between Gbagbo, Soro, Bédié and Ouattara; this was the first occasion on which the four leaders had met in Côte d'Ivoire since the de facto division of the country in late 2002. It was agreed, in principle, that further discussions between the parties would take place, with a particular view to establishing a new schedule for the disbanding of the rival militia and paramilitary groups. In March Soro returned to Abidjan, after more than a year, to take up his ministerial responsibilities.

In May 2006, despite strong opposition from Gbagbo, Banny announced that a one-week pilot phase of voter identification would begin in seven areas across the country in mid-May, to be followed by a national programme of identification and disarmament. Meanwhile, the military authorities on both sides took the first steps towards redeploying their forces in preparation for disarmament. However, the disarmament, initially scheduled to take place in early June, was further delayed until mid-July. At the beginning of September a further meeting between Banny, Gbagbo, Soro, Bédié and Ouattara failed to reach agreement on issues of disarmament, the elections and voter identification.

The Government resigned in September 2006, in response to a public health crisis arising from the illegal unloading of toxic waste from a Panamanian-registered vessel, operated by the multinational Trafigura, at Abidjan in August; the waste had been deposited at numerous sites around the city. In mid-September, at Gbagbo's request, Banny formed a new Council of Ministers. The key positions remained unaltered, but the Ministers of Transport and of the Environment, Water and Forestry were both replaced. Some 17 people were reported to have been killed as a result of the dumping of the toxic waste, and more than 100,000 required medical treatment. In February 2007 Trafigura agreed to pay US $160m. to the Government of Côte d'Ivoire, without admission of liability, in respect of the 2006 incident. This was followed, in September 2009, by an undertaking by Trafigura, again without admitting liability, to pay a further $45m., to be shared among some 30,000 victims, on whose behalf a class action was pending in the United Kingdom. In October 2008 the Nigerian head of the company responsible for unloading the toxic waste on behalf of Trafigura was sentenced to 20 years' imprisonment, and an Ivorian shipping agent received a five-year term, for their respective roles in the incident. Eventually, in July 2010 a court in the Netherlands found Trafigura, which continued to deny wrongdoing, culpable of having illegally exported hazardous waste to Côte d'Ivoire in 2006.

Meanwhile, following a meeting in New York, USA, involving parties to the IWG and various Ivorian interest groups, the UN confirmed in September 2006 that the presidential election would not take place in October. Gbagbo, who had refused to attend the talks, subsequently stated that he intended to remain as President upon the expiry of his mandate at the end of October.

Following a meeting in Addis Ababa, Ethiopia, in mid-October 2006, the AU's PSC recommended that a new transitional period, with a maximum duration of 12 months, should commence on 1 November. The mandates of Gbagbo and Banny were to be extended until 31 October 2007, and the Prime Minister was to assume 'all the necessary powers, and all appropriate financial, material and human resources', to ensure, *inter alia*, that credible electoral rolls were compiled, and that the disarmament, demobilization and reintegration (DDR) programme was carried out, with a view to holding transparent elections by the expiry of his mandate. The Prime Minister was granted the power to introduce legislation by decree (contrary to the 2000 Constitution, which vested legislative authority in the President), and was also to take control of the country's defence and security forces. The FN stated that it would refuse to recognize any arrangement whereby Gbagbo remained head of state, while Gbagbo, for his part, was reported to have maintained that any recommendation that did not comply with the Constitution would not be applied. Nevertheless, on 1 November 2006 the UN Security Council adopted a resolution endorsing the PSC programme. On 15 December the Security Council extended the mandate of UNOCI until January 2007, further to which UNOCI's mandate was again extended until 30 June.

The Ouagadougou Agreement

Meanwhile, in December 2006 President Gbagbo announced a new initiative to resolve the impasse in the peace process, offering to commence direct dialogue with the FN. Under Gbagbo's proposals, the 'buffer zone' dividing the country would be removed, and a new amnesty law would be enacted. At an ECOWAS summit held in Ouagadougou, Burkina Faso, in January 2007, the Burkinabè President and Chairman of ECOWAS, Blaise Compaoré, was tasked with facilitating dialogue between Gbagbo and the FN. Both Soro, on behalf of the FN, and Gbagbo attended separate meetings with Compaoré in Burkina Faso later that month, and representatives from both sides attended discussions with the Burkinabè President in early February. Ouattara, on behalf of the RDR, and Alphonse Djédjé Mady, the Secretary-General of the PDCI—RDA, met with Compaoré later that month.

Meeting in Ouagadougou on 4 March 2007, Gbagbo and Soro signed an agreement defining a detailed timetable for the resolution of the political crisis. According to the schedule, a joint armed forces command, the Centre de Commandement Integré (Integrated Command Centre—CCI), was to be formed within two weeks, made up of an equal number of troops from both sides, while a power-sharing government was to be formed by mid-April. The signatories to the accord also agreed to undertake a nationwide identification programme, lasting up to three months, which would result in the issuing of identity cards and the compilation of a definitive electoral list to replace the 2000 register. The DDR programme would commence two weeks after the formation of the new administration. In mid-March President Gbagbo formally announced the establishment of the CCI, and on 29 March Soro was appointed Prime Minister. A 33-member Government, including six new appointees, was installed on 7 April. On 16 April the buffer zone was officially revoked.

However, ongoing disagreements between the signatories to the Ouagadougou Agreement meant that the reconciliation and disarmament process progressed only slowly. In August 2007 it was announced that elections, previously scheduled to be held in January 2008, were to be postponed until later that year. In September 2007 the much-delayed process of issuing identification papers to Ivorians without documents was officially launched, thus granting all citizens the right to enrol on the electoral register. This was deemed the precursor to establishing a full electoral list in preparation for the legislative and presidential elections. In November the country's major political parties adopted a new electoral code, under the aegis of the Commission Electorale Indépendante (CEI), which aimed to ensure the free and fair conduct of future polls. A draft agreement aimed at accelerating the reconciliation process and scheduling elections for mid-2008 was presented at the end of November 2007, but Gbagbo abandoned talks with the FN. None the less, he subsequently agreed to the holding of elections in June 2008.

The disarmament process finally began in December 2007. It was anticipated that some 5,000 government soldiers and 33,000 members of the rebel forces were to assemble at disarmament sites and barracks by the end of March 2008. In January 2008 the UN Security Council again approved the extension of UNOCI's mandate until 30 July; the mandate was thereafter extended, at intervals, to December 2010.

Delays in the election process

In March 2008 it became apparent that preparations for the forthcoming presidential election, including the provision of identification documents, would not be complete in time for the ballot to take place as scheduled in June. In April, as recommended by the CEI, a new date was set for the election to be held on 30 November. Legislative elections would be held at a later, unspecified date. Registration for the postponed presidential election began in mid-September. In October, however, the UN issued a report stating that the process of disarming former rebels had stalled, and that unrest in Bouaké in June had presented a renewed threat to national security. Earlier, in April, the UN had accused the Ivorian armed forces and the FN of engaging in military training that contravened the arms embargo imposed in 2004. The UN asserted that inspection officials had been denied access to several bases; both the armed forces and the FN denied the allegations. In November 2008, following a meeting in Burkina Faso of the main political parties to discuss security concerns and delays in voter registration, the presidential election was again postponed, and the CEI was instructed to draw up a new electoral schedule by the end of December.

On 24 December 2008 Gbagbo and Soro signed a fourth complementary peace accord to the Ouagadougou Agreement, termed 'Ouaga IV'. The agreement created the framework for the demobilization of 36,000 FN troops and an unspecified number of militia forces, for the integration of 9,000 former rebels into the national army and police force, and for the extension of central government administration into rebel-held areas. In April 2009 the CCI announced that a mixed force of 8,000 troops would redeploy into the north of the country, as part of the process of reunification agreed under Ouaga IV. The force would comprise 2,000 personnel from the national army, 2,000 gendarmes and 4,000 FN troops, with a mandate to re-establish the Government's authority across the national territory and provide security for the electoral process. The first contingents of this force were deployed to Bouaké in May, and late that month a ceremony was held there to mark the transfer of power from the FN's 10 regional commanders to central government prefects. However, the implementation of the CCI's security force proceeded slowly, with only 500 FN troops having deployed to Bouaké by the end of May.

In May 2009 Soro announced that the presidential election would take place on 29 November. Compilation of the electoral lists was to be completed by 30 June; and publication of the provisional electoral list was scheduled for September. Owing to logistical problems (including industrial action by electoral agents demanding payment of salary arrears), the provisional list of voters was not delivered to Soro until October, after which it was submitted to Gbagbo for approval. In mid-October the CEI announced that it had received 20 candidatures for the presidential election. A final list of 5.3m. voters, from the provisional list of 6.38m., was validated by the CEI in early November. In mid-November, however, the commission announced that there would be a 'slight delay' in the electoral timetable. In early December Compaoré, in his capacity as 'facilitator' of the inter-Ivorian dialogue, stated that it was intended to hold the presidential election in late February or early March 2010. He also expressed concern about the delay encountered by the CCI in establishing the mixed units responsible for election security—at this time less than one-half of the proposed force had been assembled—and requested the provision of further security reinforcements.

The disputed 2010 presidential election

In January 2010 Gbagbo accused the President of the CEI, Robert Mambé, of having allowed as many as 429,000 ineligible voters to register to participate in the election. In mid-February, following violent protests across the country, most notably in Man, Divo and Katiola, Gbagbo dissolved both the Government and the CEI, describing the peace process as 'broken'. The examination of appeals concerning voter registration was immediately suspended, and a further delay to the electoral schedule appeared inevitable. Soro was reappointed as Prime Minister and requested to form a new administration. Opposition parties denounced Gbagbo's action as undemocratic and unconstitutional, and the RHDP coalition urged the population to mobilize against the President. Two weeks of mainly non-violent protests followed; however, police were reported to have fired on protesters in Gagnoa, killing five, and two people were killed during demonstrations in Daloa.

Soro named his new Government in late February 2010. However, only 16 of the 27 ministerial posts were confirmed, as both the RDR and the PDCI—RDA refused to join the Government until the CEI had been reconstituted. At the end of the month Youssouf Bakayoko, a representative of the PDCI—RDA and former government minister, was sworn in as President of the CEI, and Ouattara announced that the RDR would take up its allocated posts in the Government. The new Government thus included members of the PIT, the RDR, the PDCI—RDA, the UDPCI and the MFA.

A new electoral list was published in mid-July 2010, and verification was completed in early August. The Council of Ministers subsequently announced that the presidential election would take place on 31 October. In September the FN marked the completion of the demobilization process in a ceremony in Dabakala. It was reported at this time that 5,000 fighters had been reintegrated into the national armed forces, with a further 5,000 scheduled to return to barracks before being reintegrated.

A total of 14 candidates contested the first round of the presidential election, which proceeded according to the latest revised schedule on 31 October 2010. Results released by the CEI on 3 November, and confirmed by the Constitutional Council on 6 November, showed that no candidate had secured an outright majority. A second round of voting was thus scheduled for 21 November, to be contested by the two leading candidates: Gbagbo, who had won 38.0% of the votes cast; and Ouattara, with 32.1%. The rate of voter participation was officially recorded at 83.7%.

Additional security measures, including the deployment of supplementary UN peacekeepers and the imposition of a night-time curfew, were enforced prior to the second round. Following a one-week postponement, the run-off took place on 28 November 2010. On 1 December a representative of the CEI was prevented from announcing initial results by a supporter of Gbagbo, who destroyed the documents that the official was preparing to read to members of the press. The following day the CEI proclaimed Ouattara to have won the run-off, with 54.1% of the votes cast. On 3 December, however, the President of the Constitutional Council, Paul Yao N'Dré, declared the CEI's announcement null and void; he subsequently issued results showing that Gbagbo had won the election, having received 51.5% of votes cast. The Special Representative of the UN Secretary-General for Côte d'Ivoire, Choi Young-Jin, described N'Dré's decision as 'having no factual basis'. In his capacity as certifier of the Ivorian elections, Choi declared Ouattara to have won the presidential election. Ouattara was also recognized as the legitimate head of state by, *inter alia*, the EU, France, the USA, the IMF and ECOWAS—this last announced the suspension of Côte d'Ivoire from its membership on 7 December. Shortly thereafter the AU also announced that Côte d'Ivoire's participation in its activities had been suspended.

In separate ceremonies on 4 December 2010, both Gbagbo and Ouattara were sworn in as President, and each subsequently named a government. Ouattara's administration, which rapidly gained legitimacy, was headed by Soro as Prime Minister and Minister of Defence, and retained a number of senior ministers from the cabinet appointed in March. The armed forces announced the closure of Côte d'Ivoire's borders, and there were violent clashes in numerous parts of the country. Ouattara, blockaded in a hotel in Abidjan, received protection from UN peacekeepers and members of the FN. Gbagbo demanded that all UN and French troops leave the country, but UNOCI's mandate was extended for a further six months in late December. Also in late December the BCEAO (which recognized Ouattara as the elected President) announced that it would deny Gbagbo access to state funds at the bank, and that only officials designated by the legitimate Government could access the country's deposits and represent it within the Union Economique et Monétaire Ouest-Africaine (UEMOA, see p. 330). A delegation of West African leaders, comprising the Presidents of Cape Verde, Benin and Sierra Leone, subsequently held meetings with Gbagbo in Abidjan on behalf of ECOWAS, amid reports that ECOWAS was considering the use of force to remove him, but were unable to secure a resolution to the crisis.

Several major international banking groups had suspended their operations in Côte d'Ivoire by February 2011, and there was further economic disruption after Ouattara urged a ban on the export of cocoa and requested that Ivorian companies withhold the payment of taxes. There were violent clashes in the suburbs of Abidjan in late February and early March—most notably in the Abobo district, where it was reported that soldiers had shot and killed six Ouattara supporters. In retaliation, four vehicles of the security forces were ambushed, and their occupants killed. Meanwhile, Gbagbo used state media to accuse the UN and French forces of plotting to depose him, and in mid-March supporters of Ouattara marched on the national broadcasting headquarters. The protest was violently suppressed by troops loyal to Gbagbo, and reports followed of 30–48 deaths. The office of the UN High Commissioner for Refugees (UNHCR) estimated at this time that as many as 450,000 Ivorians had fled their homes in the post-election violence.

By late March 2011 Ouattara's forces had captured Yamoussoukro, and were reported to have reached Abidjan and surrounded Gbagbo. There were heavy assaults on Gbagbo's residence, and violence persisted across the country: in the western town of Duékoué alone, according to subsequent UN figures, some 536 people were killed. In early April it was confirmed that UN and French forces had fired on military camps operated by Gbagbo, although the UN Secretary-General insisted that any engagement had been in order to prevent attacks on civilians by Gbagbo loyalists. On 11 April Gbagbo was captured by forces loyal to Ouattara, with the assistance of French troops and UN peacekeeping forces. The UN welcomed the detention of Gbagbo, and offered its support to the new Government. Government forces had regained control of Abidjan by early May.

On 5 May 2011 the Constitutional Council formally confirmed Ouattara as the winner of the presidential election, and he was officially sworn in as President the following day. (An inauguration ceremony, attended by many heads of state, followed in Yamoussoukro on 21 May.) Ouattara requested that the International Criminal Court (ICC) investigate allegations of serious human rights crimes committed in the post-election violence; ICC prosecutors subsequently reported that at least 3,000 people had been killed. On 1 June Ouattara appointed a new Government, again under the premiership of Soro, retaining several senior ministers from the previous administration. The new administration subsequently announced the establishment of a national commission of inquiry into human rights abuses in the post-election period, together with the formation of a special investigative unit within the Ministry of Justice to identify, and expedite proceedings against, alleged perpetrators of atrocities committed in the post-election period. In September President Ouattara formally established a Commission Dialogue, Vérité et Réconciliation (Commission on Dialogue, Truth and Reconciliation—CDVR), led by former Prime Minister Banny, with a two-year mandate. Also in September it was announced that legislative elections would be held on 11 December.

In July 2011 Gen. Soumaila Bakayoko, a former rebel commander loyal to President Ouattara, was appointed as the Chief of Staff of the Armed Forces; Bakayoko was to be responsible for the new, integrated Forces Républicaines de Côte d'Ivoire (FRCI). In late July the UN Security Council adopted a resolution extending the mandate of UNOCI until the end of July 2012. The UNOCI mandate was thereafter extended for a further year, to July 2013.

In mid-August 2011 Laurent Gbagbo and his wife, Simone Gbagbo, who had been under house arrest at separate locations since April, were charged in connection with what were termed economic crimes, including looting, armed robbery and embezzlement, related to the violence that had followed the presidential election. Earlier in August 12 of Gbagbo's associates, including his son, Michel, and former Prime Minister and FPI leader N'Guessan, had been charged in connection with the post-election violence.

Meanwhile, although the humanitarian situation had improved significantly, 247,000 civilians remained internally displaced in Côte d'Ivoire at September 2011, according to UNHCR. At mid-2013 UNHCR put the number of internally displaced persons (IDPs) at 24,000, and returned IDPs at 21,000.

Recent developments: the 2011 legislative elections

In November 2011 Gbagbo was extradited to the ICC in The Hague, Netherlands. Gbagbo, who was to be the first former head of state to come under ICC custody, was indicted on four counts of crimes against humanity in connection with atrocities committed between December 2010 and April 2011.

In response to the former President's extradition, three parties loyal to Gbagbo announced their withdrawal from the forthcoming legislative elections; the FPI had already announced a boycott, in protest at Gbagbo's detention. Only about 36.6% of the electorate participated in the elections, which proceeded as scheduled on 11 December 2011. According to provisional results, announced by the CEI on 16 December, Ouattara's RDR won 127 of the 255 seats contested in the National Assembly, and the PDCI—RDA 77. It was subsequently reported that several independent candidates had also joined the RDR-led alliance. In February 2012 the results of voting in 11 constituencies were annulled after the Constitutional Council upheld complaints of irregularities. Polls were repeated for those seats (and held in a further constituency where the vote had been postponed owing to the death of a candidate) on 26 February. According to final results published by the CEI on 8 March (with two seats undeclared), the RDR held 138 of the 253 declared seats, the PDCI—RDA 86, independent candidates 17, and the UDPCI eight.

Soro, who had announced the resignation of his Government, was elected President of the National Assembly in mid-March 2012. The following day Jeannot Kouadio Ahoussou of the PDCI, hitherto Minister of State, Keeper of the Seals, Minister of Justice, was appointed Prime Minister; he also retained the justice portfolio. Ouattara assumed personal responsibility for defence. All other members of the outgoing administration were reappointed to their previous positions. In late May Adama Bictogo was dismissed as Minister of African Integration, following allegations of the misappropriation of more than US $1m. from the fund intended to compensate victims of the illegal dumping of hazardous waste in 2006 (see above). Bictogo, who denied any wrongdoing, was subsequently replaced by Ally Coulibaly, hitherto the country's ambassador to France.

Moïse Lida Kouassi, who had held the defence portfolio under Gbagbo at the time of the 2002 coup attempt, was extradited to Côte d'Ivoire from Togo in June 2012, having been subject to an international arrest warrant issued one year earlier. It was reported that Kouassi, who was taken into custody in Abidjan, was to be questioned in connection with the violence that had followed the 2010 presidential election. Shortly after his arrest the Ivorian authorities announced that a plot against the Government had been uncovered: in a televised confession, Kouassi stated that documents seized at his house in the Togolese capital contained information about a conspiracy against the Ouattara administration earlier in the year. The Government stated that those involved in the plot had connections with Liberian mercenaries and Ivorian militias loyal to Gbagbo who were held responsible for recent violent raids in the south-west, near the border with Liberia. In one such incident, a few days previously, at least eight civilians and seven members of the UN peacekeeping force had been killed. One of the alleged leaders of the plot, a senior officer in Gbagbo's presidential guard, who had been apprehended while entering the country some months previously, was purported also to have admitted to the involvement of Gbagbo's security entourage in the assassination of Robert Gueï in 2002.

The national commission of inquiry that had been established in mid-2011 to examine the post-election violence submitted its report to President Ouattara in August 2012. The commission, which found that there had been mass violations of human rights and of international humanitarian law, officially recorded 3,248 deaths in the post-election violence in 2010–11, although the head of the commission, Paulette Badjo, acknowledged that it was likely that the actual number was significantly higher. The commission attributed 1,452 deaths, of which 1,009 were summary executions, to forces loyal to Gbagbo; and 727 deaths, including 545 summary executions, to pro-Ouattara forces. In response, Ouattara affirmed his commitment to combat impunity in respect of the violence, and gave assurances that all those responsible for crimes committed during the post-election crisis would be brought to justice.

Also in August 2012 the Secretary-General of the FPI, Laurent Akoun, was sentenced to six month's imprisonment, having been convicted of public order offences. Akoun, who had been arrested north of Abidjan a few days earlier, was one of three former associates of Gbagbo to have been detained apparently in connection with recent violence in the city, in which armed Gbagbo loyalists had clashed with members of the Ivorian military.

The first trial in connection with the violence that had followed the 2010 presidential election took place in October 2012 in Abidjan. Gen. Brunot Dogbo Blé, the former commander of the republican guard, was one of several members of Gbagbo's security forces accused in connection with the death of a senior military official in March 2011. Blé, who denied the charges against him, was sentenced to 15 years' military detention, having been found guilty of complicity in abduction, illegal detention and murder; four co-defendants received custodial sentences of between five and 15 years. (Three others were charged *in absentia*.) Blé was also charged separately in connection with Gueï's death in 2002.

Ouattara dissolved the Government in mid-November 2012, in response to a dispute among its members regarding legislation that would give women equal rights with men within the family: members of the PDCI—RDA opposed to the measure had attempted to block the introduction of the new family law in the National Assembly. Ahoussou was replaced as Prime Minister by Daniel Kablan Duncan, the premier in 1993–99, who had latterly held the post of Minister of State, Minister of Foreign Affairs. Duncan also assumed responsibility for the economy and finance within the new Council of Ministers, while Charles Koffi Diby took the foreign affairs portfolio. Raymonde Goudou Coffie, of the PDCI—RDA, who, as Minister of Solidarity, the Family, Women and Children, had sponsored the family law that was opposed by members of her own party, was transferred to the post of Minister of Health and the Fight against AIDS; she was replaced in her former position by Anne Désirée Ouloto. Hamed Bakayoko remained in post as Minister of State, Minister of the Interior and Security, and Ouattara retained the defence portfolio. A report issued by the non-governmental organization Human Rights Watch in late November 2012 drew attention to what it alleged were widespread abuses of human rights by the Ivorian military in August–September in suppressing violent assaults against military installations by Gbagbo loyalists. Human Rights Watch warned that the force of the response to security threats 'recalled the grave crimes' that had followed the 2010 presidential election, and urged the Ouattara administration to ensure that members of the armed forces responsible for 'torture, inhuman treatment, and criminality' be brought swiftly to account.

In December 2012 the Appeals Chamber of the ICC dismissed a submission by Gbagbo's defence counsel that the Court lacked jurisdiction with regard to the post-2010 election period. The lawyers acting for Gbagbo had argued that Côte d'Ivoire, which is not a party to the ICC's founding Rome Statute, accepted its jurisdiction only in relation to events in 2002–03. (In February 2012, meanwhile, the ICC had announced that it would extend the scope of its investigations to include alleged war crimes committed since September 2002.) A confirmation of charges hearing subsequently proceeded in the second half of February 2013. In early June, however, the ICC announced its decision to adjourn the hearing, and requested that the prosecution consider providing further evidence or conducting further investigations with respect to the charges against Gbagbo: the pre-trial judges deemed that the evidence hitherto presented by the prosecution was neither sufficiently strong to allow a move to trial, nor weak enough for the charges to be dismissed. Later in June the Court rejected a defence challenge that the case against Gbagbo was inadmissible because he was subject to prosecution in Côte d'Ivoire, having concluded that there was no tangible proof of active steps at the national level to bring proceedings against him. The prosecution's appeal against the adjournment was rejected in mid-December.

In November 2012, meanwhile, the ICC formally issued its warrant for the arrest of Simone Gbagbo, in respect of her alleged role in crimes against humanity in the 2010–11 post-election crisis. The Court confirmed the full co-operation of the Ivorian authorities, and stated that it expected the extradition of Simone Gbagbo to ICC jurisdiction. In late September 2013, however, the Ivorian Government declared its decision to seek the dismissal of the ICC warrant and to try Simone Gbagbo under national jurisdiction.

In mid-January 2013 the former head of the CJP, Charles Blé Goudé, was apprehended in Ghana in a joint operation involving Ivorian and Ghanaian police forces. Blé Goudé, who had been in hiding since April 2011, and who denied leading militia attacks on northerners and non-Ivorians during the violence that had followed the 2010 presidential election, was subsequently extradited to Côte d'Ivoire and detained on charges including war crimes, murder, economic crimes and kidnapping. At the end of September 2013 the ICC formally released its arrest warrant for Blé Goudé, first issued in December 2011, in respect of alleged crimes against humanity in Côte d'Ivoire in the 2010–11 post-election violence.

There were violent protests in various towns and cities in late April 2013, following the announcement by the CEI of the partial results of regional and municipal elections. At least one person was reported to have been killed in the violence in Abidjan. The elections had been notably boycotted by the FPI, which maintained that the conditions were not in place for a fair and transparent vote, and which continued to dispute the legitimacy of the CEI. Final results showed that the RDR had control of 95 of the country's 197 communes in the municipal elections, and of 11 of the 31 regional councils. According to the CEI, the rate of participation was 44.0% for the regional elections and 36.4% for the municipal elections, although the FPI claimed that turnout was substantially lower than officially stated.

At the end of July 2013 the UN Security Council adopted Resolution 2112, extending to the end of June 2014 the mandate of UNOCI. The revised mandate prioritized the protection of civilians, and, *inter alia*, charged the mission with supporting the Ivorian authorities in the processes of disarmament, demobilization and reintegration, weapons collection, security sector reform, monitoring of the arms embargo and supporting compliance with international humanitarian and human rights law. It was envisaged that the military component of the mission would be reduced to a maximum of 7,137 personnel by the end of the mandate, and, based on the security situation, that a further reduction to 5,437 by mid-2015 would be considered thereafter. At November 2013 the military strength of UNOCI was 9,915 personnel.

In early August 2013 a court in Abidjan ordered the provisional release from custody of 14 former members of Gbagbo's entourage, among them N'Guessan, Kouassi and Michel Gbagbo. The UN Independent Expert on the human rights situation in Côte d'Ivoire, Doudou Diène, welcomed their release, pending trial, as significant in the process of justice and national reconciliation, although a senior official of the FPI, Michel Amani N'Guessan, urged the release of all party members, including Gbagbo, as a prerequisite for national reconciliation. In a report to the UN Human Rights Council in June, Diène stated that Côte d'Ivoire must address what he termed its profound political fragmentation, and emphasized political dialogue as being fundamental to effective reconciliation. Diène acknowledged the Ivorian authorities' efforts to reinforce the country's justice system, which he regarded as central to democratic reconstruction and national reconciliation. He suggested that the mandate of the CDVR be extended beyond the scheduled expiry of its term in September. Diène furthermore recommended that the arms embargo applied against Côte d'Ivoire since 2004 be removed, in the interests of reinforcing internal security. (The embargo had in April been extended for a further 12-month period by the UN Security Council, on the grounds that the country remained vulnerable to instability fuelled by the availability of weapons.)

In late August 2013 the National Assembly approved new laws considered to be important factors in addressing deep-seated tensions concerning citizenship and land ownership in Côte d'Ivoire. Two pieces of legislation were adopted with regard to citizenship: one allowing foreigners to acquire citizenship upon marriage to an Ivorian national; and one granting citizenship rights to foreign-born residents who were living in Côte d'Ivoire at the time of independence in 1960, as well as foreign nationals born in the country in 1961–73, and to their descendants. In addition, deputies adopted legislation extending by 10 years the grace period under a 1998 law for the codification of land ownership. A new population and housing census, the first since 1998, took place in late 2013, although the FPI declared its opposition to the process.

In a minor reorganization of the Council of Ministers in mid-November 2013, Abdourahmane Cissé was appointed to the position of Minister-delegate to the Prime Minister, in charge of the Budget. Ouattara also appointed René Kouassi Aphing-Kouassi, a lawyer and former defence minister, to the presidency of a new High Authority for Good Governance, charged with countering corruption in state and parastatal institutions. At the same time, Brig.-Gen. Vagondo Diomandé was named as the President's personal Chief of General Staff, in place of Gen. Michel Gueu.

The CDVR presented its report to President Ouattara in late November 2013. Among its recommendations to promote national reconciliation were: the application of the 1998 law on land registration; acceleration of the disarmament and reintegration of former combatants into the FRCI; legislative scrutiny of the appointment of senior state officials; the adoption of a national plan to promote good governance and counter corruption; and media engagement in civic and moral education. Critics of the CDVR's work considered that its mandate had been inadequately defined, and that it had achieved little in two years beyond identifying causes of conflict since the 1990s that were already well known and making basic recommendations for future actions. Concerns were expressed, furthermore, that the CDVR had yet to facilitate public hearings or reparation for the victims of the political violence, and that its president, Charles Konan Banny, was not a politically impartial figure. It remained unclear at this time whether the mandate of the CDVR, which had yet to produce its final, edited report, would be extended.

In early December 2013 the UN published a report, compiled by UNOCI in co-operation with OHCHR, that urged the Ivorian authorities to investigate serious abuses of human rights allegedly committed in security operations by Dozo traditional hunters: according to the report, at least 228 people had been killed in security activities by Dozos between March 2009 and May 2013. The High Commissioner for Human Rights notably appealed to the Ivorian Government to deploy appropriate security forces throughout the country, and to end the impunity granted to the Dozos. Having supported Ouattara's forces following the disputed 2010 presidential election, the Dozos had continued to conduct proxy security operations mainly in western Côte d'Ivoire.

A presidential decree issued at the end of December 2013 provided for the extension of the mandate and scope of the special investigative unit that had been established within the justice ministry in mid-2011. Meanwhile, human rights organizations continued to urge the Ivorian authorities to pursue an even-handed approach in respect of bringing to justice persons suspected of acts of political violence, and to avoid any culture of impunity or 'victors' justice'. In late October 2013, notably, a report by the International Federation for Human Rights Leagues (FIDH) emphasized that there was an apparently disproportionate number of cases involving charges against Gbagbo loyalists, despite the judiciary also being in possession of witness statements detailing alleged offences by members of the FRCI. According to figures reported by Human Rights Watch in early January 2014, investigations hitherto had resulted in charges being brought against more than 150 pro-Gbagbo civilian and military leaders, and nine members of Gbagbo-loyalist forces had been convicted by military court. Human Rights Watch noted, however, that no significant arrests had been made from within forces loyal to Ouattara in relation to serious crimes committed during the post-election crisis, despite the findings of the national commission of inquiry conducted in 2011–12.

Foreign Affairs

Regional relations

The emphasis on '*ivoirité*', or Ivorian national identity, in domestic policy has at times strained Côte d'Ivoire's relations with other West African states, particularly Burkina Faso; Burkinabè migrants in Côte d'Ivoire increasingly suffered from discrimination and became the victims of inter-ethnic violence, causing several thousand to flee the country in early 2001. Thousands of citizens of Burkina and Mali left Côte d'Ivoire after September 2002, and the border between Côte d'Ivoire and Burkina Faso remained closed until September 2003. In July 2004, at a meeting in Abidjan, representatives of the two countries pledged to combat 'destabilizing acts' against their respective countries, and agreed to increase co-operation in security and defence matters.

The protracted civil war in neighbouring Liberia resulted in the presence of large numbers of Liberian refugees in Côte d'Ivoire in the 1990s; UNHCR estimated the total number at 327,288 at the end of 1996. The possible infiltration of refugee groups by Liberian fighters, together with sporadic incursions into Côte d'Ivoire by Liberian armed factions, proved a significant security concern to the Ivorian authorities at this time. By 2002, following the installation of elected organs of state in Liberia in 1997, and the outbreak of civil conflict in Côte d'Ivoire in September 2002, the number of Liberian refugees in the country registered with UNHCR had been reduced to 43,000, although it rose again to more than 74,000 during 2003 with the deterioration of the security situation in eastern Liberia. Some 25,000 Ivorian nationals were estimated by UNHCR to have fled to Liberia in 2002 to escape fighting in western Côte d'Ivoire, and in 2004 some 10,000 Ivorians were reported to have sought refuge in Liberia following the renewed outbreak of violence in Côte d'Ivoire in November. UNHCR estimated that some 224,000 Ivorian refugees were in Liberia in July 2011. In the following month UNHCR signed an agreement with the Governments of Côte d'Ivoire and Liberia to facilitate the voluntary repatriation of refugees from Liberia. At late 2013 UNHCR put the registered population of Ivorian refugees in Liberia at some 58,000, and stated that it had exceeded its target for that year of assisting 16,000 voluntary repatriations. Meanwhile, a series of violent incidents in south-west Côte d'Ivoire in 2012 were believed to have involved Liberian mercenaries acting with Ivorian armed elements loyal to Gbagbo who were operating from Liberia (see Recent developments, above). In October, during a visit to Abidjan by President Ellen Johnson Sirleaf of Liberia, a joint communiqué was signed concerning the promotion of security in the border region; among other measures, the two countries sought the reactivation of their bilateral commission, which had been established in the 1970s but later rendered inactive by the civil war in Liberia. It was reported in April 2013 that Côte d'Ivoire's permanent representative to the UN had requested that the planned reduction in the military strength of the UNOCI peacekeeping force be offset by measures such as the deployment of surveillance drones to monitor the border with Liberia.

In October 2011, meanwhile, an agreement was reached regarding the repatriation of Ivorian refugees from Ghana, estimated by UNHCR to number some 18,000 at that time. At December 2013 UNHCR put the number of refugees remaining in Ghana at 9,800. In September 2012 Côte d'Ivoire closed its land, sea and air frontiers with Ghana, with the stated aim of halting all cross-border incursions from that country. The action was prompted by an assault on an Ivorian military checkpoint near the border, in which several people were killed. Air links were resumed shortly after, but the land and sea borders remained closed for more than two weeks. Although Ivorian and Ghanaian police notably co-operated in the arrest of Charles Blé Goudé in Ghana in January 2013 (see Recent developments, above), there was a deterioration in relations between the two countries in subsequent months. It was reported in late 2013 that in submissions to the UN the Ghanaian Government had expressed concern regarding Côte d'Ivoire's intentions and actions with regard to former officials of the Gbagbo regime who were currently resident in Ghana: it had been alleged during a visit to Ghana by UN officials in July that at least two missions by Ivorian agents to assassinate or abduct pro-Gbagbo figures had been foiled by the Ghanaian authorities earlier in the year. (It was noted, however, that the UN had not independently verified these allegations.) In August a request made by the Government of Côte d'Ivoire for the extradition of a former spokesman and minister for the budget under Gbagbo, Justin Koné Katinan, was rejected by a Ghanaian judge on the grounds that charges against him had some element of political motivation. Katinan had first been arrested in Ghana in August 2012 under an international arrest warrant for economic crimes, and a subsequent warrant on murder charges had been issued by Côte d'Ivoire.

CONSTITUTION AND GOVERNMENT

Under the terms of the Constitution of July 2000, executive power is vested in the President, as Head of State, who is appointed by direct universal suffrage for a term of five years, renewable only once. (The mandate of former President Laurent Gbagbo expired in October 2005, but was periodically extended as a result of the failure of the Côte d'Ivoire authorities to hold presidential elections.) The President appoints a Prime Minister, and on the latter's recommendation, a Council of Ministers. Legislative power is held by the National Assembly, which is elected for a term of five years. The country is divided into 31 regions, and further sub-divided into 107 departments and 197 communes, each with its own elected council.

REGIONAL AND INTERNATIONAL CO-OPERATION

Côte d'Ivoire is a member of numerous regional organizations, including the West African organs of the Franc Zone (see p. 330) and the African Petroleum Producers' Association (APPA, see p. 445). Côte d'Ivoire is also a member of the Economic Community of West African States (ECOWAS, see p. 260) and the African Union (see p. 186). In June 2013 the African Development Bank (AfDB, see p. 183), which had in 2003 relocated to Tunisia because of the political instability in Côte d'Ivoire, formally announced its plan to return to its headquarters in Abidjan.

Côte d'Ivoire became a member of the UN in 1960. As a contracting party to the General Agreement on Tariffs and Trade, Côte d'Ivoire joined the World Trade Organization (WTO, see p. 434) on its establishment in 1995. Côte d'Ivoire is also a member of the International Cocoa Organization (ICCO, see p. 446), the International Coffee Organization (see p. 446) and the Conseil de l'Entente (see p. 450).

ECONOMIC AFFAIRS

In 2012, according to estimates by the World Bank, Côte d'Ivoire's gross national income (GNI), measured at average 2010–12 prices, was US $24,249m., equivalent to $1,220 per head (or $1,960 on an international purchasing-power parity basis). During 2003–12, it was estimated, the population increased at an average annual rate of 1.8%, while gross domestic product (GDP) per head increased, in real terms, by an average of 0.2% per year. Overall GDP increased, in real terms, by an average annual rate of 2.0% in 2003–12; real GDP declined by 4.7% in 2011, but grew by 9.5% in 2012.

Agriculture (including forestry and fishing) contributed 30.0% of GDP in 2012, according to the African Development Bank (AfDB). The sector employed about 33.8% of the labour force in mid-2014, according to FAO estimates. Côte d'Ivoire is the world's foremost producer of cocoa, accounting for some 30% of global cocoa bean output in 2010. In 2012 cocoa and related products contributed 25.6% of the country's total export earnings. Political developments in Côte d'Ivoire are a significant factor influencing global prices for cocoa. Côte d'Ivoire also produces and exports coffee, although output declined markedly during the early 2000s and the maintenance of coffee plantations was adversely affected by political unrest at the end of the decade. Other major cash crops include cotton, rubber, bananas and pineapples. The principal subsistence crops are yams, cassava, plantains, rice (although large quantities of the last are still imported) and maize. Excessive exploitation of the country's forest resources has led to a decline in the importance of this sector. Abidjan is among sub-Saharan Africa's principal fishing ports; however, the participation of Ivorian fishing fleets is minimal. According to the World Bank estimates, during 2002–11 agricultural GDP increased at an average annual rate of 2.6%. According to the AfDB, agricultural GDP grew by 0.7% in 2012.

Industry (including mining, manufacturing, construction and power) contributed 26.4% of GDP in 2012, according to the AfDB. According to UN estimates, 11.5% of the labour force were employed in the sector in 1994. During 2002–11 industrial GDP increased by an average annual rate of 1.7%, according to the World Bank estimates; industrial GDP grew by 5.5% in 2011.

Mining and quarrying contributed 4.7% of GDP in 2012, according to the AfDB. Commercial exploitation of important offshore reserves of petroleum and natural gas commenced in the mid-1990s, and output of crude petroleum amounted to some 14.8m. barrels in 2011. Gold and diamonds are also mined, although illicit production of the latter has greatly exceeded commercial output. There is believed to be significant potential for the development of nickel deposits, and there are also notable reserves of manganese, iron ore and bauxite. According to UN estimates, during 2002–11 mining GDP (combined with utilities) increased at an average annual rate of 1.6%. According to the AfDB, the real GDP of the mining sector increased by 5.9% in 2011, but declined by 6.1% in 2012.

The manufacturing sector, which, according to the AfDB contributed 13.1% of GDP in 2012, is dominated by agro-industrial activities (such as the processing of cocoa, coffee, cotton, palm kernels, pineapples and fish). Crude petroleum is refined at Abidjan, while the tobacco industry uses mostly imported tobacco. According to World Bank estimates, during 2002–11 manufacturing GDP increased by an average of 0.6% per year. The GDP of the sector decreased by 4.6% in 2011, but increased by 5.8% in 2012, according to the AfDB.

Construction contributed 6.0% of GDP in 2012, according to the AfDB. According to 1988 census figures, the sector employed 7.6% of the labour force. According to UN estimates, construction GDP increased at an average annual rate of 1.6% during 2002–11. According to the AfDB, the GDP of the sector declined by 11.6% in 2011, but increased by 30.0% in 2012.

Some 69.3% of Côte d'Ivoire's electricity generation in 2011 was derived from natural gas, while 29.1% was derived from hydroelectric installations, and a negligible portion from petroleum (a major decline from 1994, when 50.3% of the country's electricity had been generated from oil combustion). Since 1995 the country has exploited its reserves of natural gas, with the intention of becoming not only self-sufficient in energy, but also a regional exporter; the first stage of a major gas-powered turbine and power station in Abidjan commenced operations in 1999. Imports of petroleum and petroleum products accounted for 35.1% of the value of total merchandise imports in 2012.

According to the AfDB, the services sector contributed 43.6% of GDP in 2012, and (according to UN estimates) employed 37.4% of the labour force in 1994. The transformation of Abidjan's stock market into a regional exchange for the member states of the Union Economique et Monétaire Ouest-Africaine was expected to enhance the city's status as a centre for financial services. However, Abidjan's position as a major hub of regional communications and trade has been threatened by political unrest since the late 1990s, most recently by the instability that followed the 2010 presidential election. According to the World Bank estimates, the GDP of the services sector increased by an average of 1.9% per year in 2002–11; the GDP of the sector increased by 6.0% in 2011.

In 2010 Côte d'Ivoire recorded a visible merchandise trade surplus of US $3,621.6m., and there was a surplus of $464.5m. on the current account of the balance of payments. In 2011 the principal source of imports was Nigeria (which supplied 20.6% of total imports); France and the People's Republic of China were also notable suppliers. The Netherlands was the principal market for exports in 2011 (taking 10.4% of total exports), followed by the USA, the Netherlands, Nigeria and France. The principal exports in 2012 were cocoa and related products, and petroleum products. The principal imports in the same year were petroleum products, rice, electrical machinery, vehicles and fish products.

According to IMF estimates, Côte d'Ivoire recorded an estimated overall budget deficit of 432,700m. francs CFA in 2012, equivalent to 3.5% of GDP. Côte d'Ivoire's general government gross debt was 8,083.9m. francs CFA in 2011, equivalent to 94.9% of GDP. The country's total external debt was US $12,012m. at the end of 2011, of which $9,800m. was public and publicly guaranteed debt. In 2010, the cost of servicing long-term public and publicly guaranteed debt and repayments to the IMF was equivalent to 4.7% of the value of exports of goods, services and income (excluding workers' remittances). According to the AfDB, the annual rate of inflation averaged 2.9% in 2003–12. Consumer prices increased by 2.1% in 2012. An estimated 216,158 persons were registered as unemployed in 2006, representing 2.7% of the labour force.

Protracted instability in Côte d'Ivoire from the late 1990s resulted in an economic decline that reduced living standards and increased poverty. The effective division of the country arising from the 2002 rebellion disrupted international trade and inhibited economic growth. International donor confidence increased with the signing of the Ouagadougou Agreement in 2007, but the 2010–11 post-election crisis resulted in severe economic disruption, particularly to the cocoa sector and banking operations. Following the eventual removal of former President Laurent Gbagbo, in April 2011, the administration of President Alassane Ouattara initiated a programme of recovery, with the assistance of the international community, and business activity rapidly normalized. In November of that year the IMF approved a three-year Extended Credit Facility (ECF) arrangement for Côte d'Ivoire totalling SDR 390.24m.; and also approved interim assistance equivalent to some US $8m. under the enhanced Heavily Indebted Poor Countries (HIPC) initiative. This was followed, in 2012, by the approval by the IMF and the International Development Association of debt relief of $3,100m., representing a reduction of 24% in the country's external debt, upon attaining HIPC completion point, together with additional relief of $1,300m. under the Multilateral Debt Relief Initiative. The Government's national development plan for 2012–15 prioritized sectors including agriculture, security, transport infrastructure, energy, health and education; and, to address the problem of youth unemployment, envisaged the creation of 250,000 jobs annually over four years in the private sector; it was aimed to achieve emerging market status by 2020. Under the new Conseil du Café-Cacao, established in 2012, minimum prices were guaranteed to producers of cocoa and coffee; mechanisms were also introduced to guarantee minimum prices for cotton and for cashews. At the end of 2014, in its fourth assessment under the ECF, the IMF noted that Côte d'Ivoire had made considerable progress towards its objective of achieving high levels of medium-term growth in order to raise living standards, but considered that the challenge remained to meet the population's expectation of improved living standards. Progress towards the achievement of the country's Millennium Development Goals had been slow. The rate of recovery in 2012 was stronger than expected, and real GDP growth of 8.7% was expected for 2013. In large part reflecting the strength of the economic recovery, an acceleration in investment-related imports and improved business confidence, the current account of the balance of payments, which had moved into deficit in 2012, after many years of surplus, was expected to remain in deficit in 2013 and thereafter. Inflation was projected to remain at a moderate level in 2013, below 3%, while the overall fiscal deficit was forecast to narrow to 2.7%. Concern was expressed at continuing high levels of unemployment, particularly among young people and women, and in

Abidjan in general, and the IMF cautioned that efforts towards political reconciliation and social cohesion, while ongoing, remained difficult.

PUBLIC HOLIDAYS

2015: 1 January (New Year's Day), 2 January*† (Mouloud, Birth of the Prophet), 3 April (Good Friday), 6 April (Easter Monday), 1 May (Labour Day), 14 May (Ascension Day), 25 May (Whit Monday), 17 July* (Id al-Fitr, end of Ramadan), 7 August (National Day), 15 August (Assumption), 23 September* (Id al-Adha, Feast of the Sacrifice), 1 November (All Saints' Day), 15 November (National Peace Day), 23 December*† (Mouloud, Birth of the Prophet), 25 December (Christmas).

* These holidays are dependent on the Islamic lunar calendar and may vary by one or two days from the dates given.

† This festival occurs twice (in the Islamic years AH 1436 and 1437) within the same Gregorian year.

Statistical Survey

Source (unless otherwise stated): Institut National de la Statistique, BP V55, Abidjan; tel. 20-21-05-38; fax 20-21-44-01; e-mail site-ins@globeaccess.net; internet www.ins.ci.

Area and Population

AREA, POPULATION AND DENSITY

Area (sq km)	322,462*
Population (census results)	
1 March 1988	10,815,694
20 December 1998	
Males	7,844,621
Females	7,522,050
Total	15,366,671
Population (UN estimates at mid-year)†	
2012	19,839,749
2013	20,316,087
2014	20,804,775
Density (per sq km) at mid-2014	64.5

* 124,503 sq miles.

† Source: UN, *World Population Prospects: The 2012 Revision*.

ETHNIC GROUPS

1998 census (percentages, residents born in Côte d'Ivoire): Akan 42*; Voltaïque 18†; Mandé du nord 17‡; Krou 11; Mandé du sud 10§; Naturalized Ivorians 1; Others 1.

* Comprising the Baoulé, Agni, Abrou, Ebrié, Abouré, Adioukrou and Appollonien groupings.

† Comprising the Sénoufo, Lobi and Koulango groupings.

‡ Comprising the Malinké and Dioula groupings.

§ Comprising the Yacouba and Gouro groupings.

POPULATION BY AGE AND SEX
(UN estimates at mid-2014)

	Males	Females	Total
0–14	4,306,344	4,254,372	8,560,716
15–64	5,928,239	5,658,873	11,587,112
65 and over	360,913	296,034	656,947
Total	10,595,496	10,209,279	20,804,775

Source: UN, *World Population Prospects: The 2012 Revision*.

NATIONALITY OF POPULATION
(numbers resident in Côte d'Ivoire at 1998 census)

Country of citizenship	Population	%
Côte d'Ivoire	11,366,625	73.97
Burkina Faso	2,238,548	14.57
Mali	792,258	5.16
Guinea	230,387	1.50
Ghana	133,221	0.87
Liberia	78,258	0.51
Other	527,375	3.43
Total	15,366,672	100.00

POPULATION BY REGION
(1998 census)

Region	Population
Centre	1,001,264
Centre-Est	394,758
Centre-Nord	1,189,424
Centre-Ouest	2,169,826
Nord	929,686
Nord-Est	696,292
Nord-Ouest	740,175
Ouest	1,445,279
Sud	5,399,220
Sud-Ouest	1,400,748
Total	15,366,672

Note: In January 1997 the Government adopted legislation whereby Côte d'Ivoire's regions were to be reorganized. Further minor reorganizations were effected in April and July 2000. The new regions (with their regional capitals) are: Agnéby (Agboville), Bas-Sassandra (San-Pédro), Bafing (Touba), Denguélé (Odienné), 18 Montagnes (Man), Fromager (Gagnoa), Haut-Sassandra (Daloa), Lacs (Yamoussoukro), Lagunes (Abidjan), Marahoué (Bouaflé), Moyen-Cavally (Guiglo), Moyen-Comoé (Abengourou), N'zi-Comoé (Dimbokro), Savanes (Korhogo), Sud-Bandama (Divo), Sud-Comoé (Aboisso), Vallée du Bandama (Bouaké), Worodougou (Mankono) and Zanzan (Bondoukou).

PRINCIPAL TOWNS
(population at 1998 census)

Abidjan*	2,877,948	Korhogo	142,093
Bouaké	461,618	San-Pédro	131,800
Yamoussoukro*	299,243	Man	116,657
Daloa	173,107	Gagnoa	107,124

* The process of transferring the official capital from Abidjan to Yamoussoukro began in 1983.

2008 ('000 at December, official estimate): Abidjan 3,899.

Mid-2011 (incl. suburbs, UN estimates): Abidjan 4,288,820; Yamoussoukro 966,394 (Source: UN, *World Urbanization Prospects: The 2011 Revision*).

BIRTHS AND DEATHS
(annual averages, official estimates)

	2007	2008	2009
Birth rate (per 1,000)	37.5	37.1	36.7
Death rate (per 1,000)	13.8	13.6	13.3

2012: Birth rate 35.2 per 1,000; Death rate 12.6 per 1,000 (Source: African Development Bank).

Life expectancy (years at birth): 50.0 (males 49.3; females 50.9) in 2011 (Source: World Bank, World Development Indicators database).

ECONOMICALLY ACTIVE POPULATION*
(persons aged 6 years and over, 1988 census)

	Males	Females	Total
Agriculture, hunting, forestry and fishing	1,791,101	836,574	2,627,675
Mining and quarrying } Manufacturing	78,768	6,283	85,051
Electricity, gas and water	13,573	1,092	14,665
Construction	82,203	2,313	84,516
Trade, restaurants and hotels	227,873	302,486	530,359
Transport, storage and communications	114,396	3,120	117,516
Other services	434,782	156,444	591,226
Sub-total	2,742,696	1,308,312	4,051,008
Activities not adequately defined	998	297	1,295
Total labour force	2,743,694	1,308,609	4,052,303

* Figures exclude persons seeking work for the first time, totalling 210,450 (males 142,688; females 67,762).

Source: UN, *Demographic Yearbook*.

2006 (official estimates): Total employed 7,787,952; Unemployed 216,158; Total labour force 8,004,110.

Mid-2014 ('000, estimates): Agriculture, etc. 2,811; Total labour force 8,317 (Source: FAO).

Health and Welfare

KEY INDICATORS

Total fertility rate (children per woman, 2011)	4.3
Under-5 mortality rate (per 1,000 live births, 2011)	115
HIV/AIDS (% of persons aged 15–49, 2012)	3.2
Physicians (per 1,000 head, 2008)	0.14
Hospital beds (per 1,000 head, 2009)	0.54
Health expenditure (2010): US $ per head (PPP)	115
Health expenditure (2010): % of GDP	6.2
Health expenditure (2010): public (% of total)	24.5
Access to water (% of persons, 2011)	80
Access to sanitation (% of persons, 2011)	24
Total carbon dioxide emissions ('000 metric tons, 2010)	5,804.9
Carbon dioxide emissions per head (metric tons, 2010)	0.3
Human Development Index (2012): ranking	168
Human Development Index (2012): value	0.432

For sources and definitions, see explanatory note on p. vi.

Agriculture

PRINCIPAL CROPS
('000 metric tons)

	2010	2011	2012
Rice, paddy	722.6	702.4	725.0*
Maize	641.6	621.8	654.7
Millet	48.8	48.8	49.3
Sorghum	47.7	46.5	48.8
Sweet potatoes	47.0	45.1	46.5
Cassava (Manioc)	2,306.8	2,359.0	2,412.4
Taro (Cocoyam)	70.6	69.7	71.8
Yams	5,392.4	5,531.9	5,674.7
Sugar cane	1,800.5	1,940.5	1,866.7
Cashew nuts, with shell	380.0	393.0	450.0
Kolanuts	67.0	79.8*	79.8*
Groundnuts, with shell	90.2	91.8	93.4
Coconuts	150.8	153.5*	154.0*
Oil palm fruit	1,566.7	1,636.0	1,841.8
Cottonseed*	91.0	170.0	140.0
Tomatoes	31.2	32.4	33.5
Aubergines (Eggplants)	84.0	85.7	88.3

—continued	2010	2011	2012
Chillies and peppers, green*	25.0	25.7	26.5
Maize, green*	185.0	190.2	200.0
Bananas	314.3	317.0*	240.0
Plantains	1,541.6	1,559.2	1,577.0
Oranges*	40.0	40.4	42.5
Pineapples	68.2	77.0*	78.0*
Guavas, mangoes and mangosteens	45.2	47.0	49.0
Coffee, green	94.4	32.3	50.0*
Cocoa beans	1,301.3	1,559.4	1,650.0*
Natural rubber (dry weight)	235.0	238.7	256.0

* FAO estimate(s).

Aggregate production ('000 metric tons, may include official, semi-official or estimated data): Total cereals 1,478.2 in 2010, 1,436.8 in 2011, 1,495.6 in 2012; Total roots and tubers 7,828.8 in 2010, 8,018.0 in 2011, 8,217.9 in 2012; Total vegetables (incl. melons) 643.3 in 2010, 661.4 in 2011, 685.3 in 2012; Total fruits (excl. melons) 2,190.0 in 2010, 2,218.4 in 2011, 2,171.2 in 2012.

Source: FAO.

LIVESTOCK
('000 head, year ending September)

	2010	2011	2012
Cattle	1,582	1,583	1,584
Pigs	349	350	353
Sheep	1,692	1,700	1,708
Goats	1,324	1,332	1,339
Poultry*	45,052	43,133	43,856

* FAO estimates.

Source: FAO.

LIVESTOCK PRODUCTS
('000 metric tons)

	2010	2011	2012
Cattle meat	34.9	29.2	31.1
Sheep meat*	8.3	8.4	8.7
Goat meat*	3.7	4.0	4.0
Pig meat	6.9	7.2	7.2
Chicken meat	34.9	33.7	33.8
Game meat*	140.4	142.0	144.0
Cows' milk	31.3	31.3	31.4
Hen eggs*	32.0	33.0	34.0

* FAO estimates.

Source: FAO.

Forestry

ROUNDWOOD REMOVALS
('000 cubic metres, excluding bark, FAO estimates)

	2010	2011	2012
Sawlogs, veneer logs and logs for sleepers	1,469	1,469	1,469
Fuel wood	8,947	8,989	9,035
Total	10,416	10,458	10,504

Source: FAO.

SAWNWOOD PRODUCTION
('000 cubic metres, including railway sleepers, unofficial figures)

	2008	2009	2010
Total (all broadleaved)	600	700	700

2011–12: Production assumed to be unchanged from 2010 (unofficial figures).

Source: FAO.

Fishing

('000 metric tons, live weight)

	2009	2010	2011
Capture	44.2	69.5	71.7
Freshwater fishes	5.6	6.8	6.3
Bigeye grunt	1.7	1.6	1.8
Round sardinella	4.2	9.6	3.2
Skipjack tuna	2.8	2.6	2.1
Aquaculture*	1.3	1.7	3.4
Total catch*	45.5	71.2	75.1

* FAO estimates.

Source: FAO.

Mining

	2009	2010	2011
Gold (kg)	6,947	5,310	9,871
Natural gas (million cu m)	1,540	1,666	1,600*
Crude petroleum ('000 barrels)	19,882	16,400	14,800
Manganese ore (metric tons)	161,300	87,400	43,600

* Estimated figure.

Source: US Geological Survey.

Industry

SELECTED PRODUCTS
('000 metric tons unless otherwise indicated)

	2008	2009	2010
Beer of barley*†	306	315	344
Palm oil—unrefined*	285	345	330
Raw sugar	150	150	n.a.
Plywood ('000 cu m)*‡	81	81	81
Jet fuel	53	53	40
Motor gasoline (petrol)	466	526	392
Kerosene	750	826	616
Gas-diesel (distillate fuel) oils	1,174	1,088	n.a.
Residual fuel oils	657	438	408
Cement§	360	283	188
Electric energy (million kWh)	5,800	5,905	5,993

Cotton yarn (pure and mixed, '000 metric tons): 24.7† in 1989.

Canned fish ('000 metric tons): 121.8 in 2002 (Source: FAO).

Beer of barley ('000 metric tons): 344† in 2011 (Source: FAO).

Palm oil—unrefined ('000 metric tons): 400.0‡ in 2011 (Source: FAO).

Plywood ('000 cu m): 81‡ in 2011 (Source: FAO).

Cement ('000 metric tons): 99 in 2011 (Source: US Geological Survey).

* Data from FAO.

† Estimated figure(s).

‡ Unofficial figure(s).

§ Data from the US Geological Survey.

Source: mainly UN Industrial Commodity Statistics Database.

Finance

CURRENCY AND EXCHANGE RATES

Monetary Units

100 centimes = 1 franc de la Communauté Financière Africaine (CFA).

Sterling, Dollar and Euro Equivalents (31 December 2013)

£1 sterling = 783.286 francs CFA;
US $1 = 475.641 francs CFA;
€1 = 655.957 francs CFA;
10,000 francs CFA = £12.77 = $21.02 = €15.24.

Average Exchange Rate (francs CFA per US $)

2011	471.87
2012	510.53
2013	494.04

Note: An exchange rate of 1 French franc = 50 francs CFA, established in 1948, remained in force until January 1994, when the CFA franc was devalued by 50%, with the exchange rate adjusted to 1 French franc = 100 francs CFA. This relationship to French currency remained in effect with the introduction of the euro on 1 January 1999. From that date, accordingly, a fixed exchange rate of €1 = 655.957 francs CFA has been in operation.

BUDGET
('000 million francs CFA)

Revenue*	2011	2012†	2013‡
Tax revenue	1,493.2	2,213.0	2,409.6
Direct taxes	507.9	720.4	692.3
Indirect taxes§	985.3	1,492.5	1,717.3
Social security contributions	130.9	235.9	269.8
Other	68.9	91.3	63.0
Total	1,693.0	2,540.2	2,742.4

Expenditure¶	2011	2012†	2013‡
Current expenditure	1,923.9	2,436.0	2,355.3
Wages and salaries	719.7	934.6	1,038.9
Social security benefits	181.8	229.2	232.6
Subsidies and other current transfers	314.6	410.6	328.7
Crisis-related expenditure	75.4	56.5	7.6
Other current expenditure	413.1	572.1	534.8
Interest due	219.3	233.0	212.7
Internal	89.6	79.6	106.7
External	129.7	153.4	106.1
Capital expenditure	285.7	615.8	1,031.9
Domestically funded	237.2	510.3	581.5
Funded from abroad	48.5	105.5	450.4
Total	2,209.6	3,051.8	3,387.2

* Excluding grants received ('000 million francs CFA): 32.9 in 2011; 81.2 in 2012 (estimate); 246.1 in 2013 (programmed figure).

† Estimates.

‡ Programmed figures.

§ Excluding taxes on petroleum products.

¶ Excluding net lending ('000 million francs CFA): –0.9 in 2011; 2.3 in 2012 (estimate); 0.0 in 2013 (programmed figure).

Source: IMF, *Côte d'Ivoire: Third Review Under the Three-Year Arrangement Under the Extended Credit Facility, Requests for Modifications of Performance Criteria and Waiver of Nonobservance of Performance Criterion* (June 2013).

INTERNATIONAL RESERVES
(excluding gold, US $ million at 31 December)

	2010	2011	2012
IMF special drawing rights	420.5	418.9	419.3
Reserve position in IMF	1.3	1.4	1.5
Foreign exchange	3,202.6	3,895.6	3,507.4
Total	3,624.4	4,316.0	3,928.1

Source: IMF, *International Financial Statistics*.

MONEY SUPPLY
('000 million francs CFA at 31 December)

	2010	2011	2012
Currency outside banks	1,638.2	1,555.3	1,590.5
Demand deposits at deposit money banks*	1,091.1	1,555.6	1,597.8
Total money (incl. others)	2,736.6	3,142.0	3,257.3

* Excluding the deposits of public establishments of an administrative or social nature.

Source: IMF, *International Financial Statistics*.

COST OF LIVING
(Consumer Price Index for African households in Abidjan; base: 2000 = 100)

	2009	2010	2011
Food, beverages and tobacco	142.3	109.1	120.5
All items (incl. others)	131.3	132.9	139.4

Source: ILO.

NATIONAL ACCOUNTS
(million francs CFA at current prices)

Expenditure on the Gross Domestic Product

	2010	2011	2012
Government final consumption expenditure	1,640,082	1,581,540	1,620,789
Private final consumption expenditure	7,490,233	7,515,062	8,319,511
Change in inventories	144,927	–719,938	192,791
Gross fixed capital formation	1,025,493	928,030	1,553,166
Total domestic expenditure	10,300,735	9,304,693	11,686,257
Exports of goods and services	5,558,691	5,742,316	5,921,845
Less Imports of goods and services	4,507,244	3,687,052	5,148,102
GDP in purchasers' values	11,352,181	11,359,956	12,460,000

Gross Domestic Product by Economic Activity

	2010	2011	2012
Agriculture, forestry and fishing	3,003,878	3,376,316	3,453,445
Mining and quarrying	511,289	488,172	534,660
Manufacturing	1,377,779	1,375,770	1,502,748
Electricity, gas and water	272,438	278,976	309,943
Construction	556,430	515,987	684,869
Wholesale and retail trade, restaurants and hotels	1,550,787	1,511,805	1,690,155
Finance, insurance, real estate and business services	1,219,634	1,093,109	1,291,551
Transport and communications	428,761	365,118	433,682
Public administration and defence	1,432,601	1,482,957	1,559,196
Other services	30,641	32,033	32,904
Sub-total	10,384,237	10,520,242	11,493,154
Indirect taxes (net)	967,944	839,714	966,846
GDP in purchasers' values	11,352,181	11,359,956	12,460,000

Source: African Development Bank.

BALANCE OF PAYMENTS
(US $ million)

	2008	2009	2010
Exports of goods	10,251.4	11,168.0	11,410.2
Imports of goods	–6,882.2	–6,911.2	–7,788.6
Balance on goods	3,369.2	4,256.8	3,621.6
Exports of services	1,155.2	1,171.8	1,183.0
Imports of services	–2,838.3	–2,775.1	–2,986.8
Balance on goods and services	1,686.1	2,653.4	1,817.9
Primary income received	236.6	221.9	217.3
primary income paid	–1,138.7	–1,159.0	–1,131.3
Balance on goods, services and primary income	784.0	1,716.3	903.9
Secondary income received	582.3	790.0	432.8
Secondary income paid	–914.8	–888.7	–872.1
Current balance	451.6	1,617.6	464.5
Capital account (net)	89.3	224.9	1,178.3
Direct investment assets	–20.3	–9.4	–44.1
Direct investment liabilities	466.5	396.0	358.1
Portfolio investment assets	–28.6	–18.6	–22.1
Portfolio investment liabilities	76.6	–11.8	486.5
Financial derivatives employee stock options (net)	–6.2	–7.5	–7.3
Other investment assets	–369.9	–1,234.5	–1,383.4
Other investment liabilities	–322.0	167.1	449.9
Net errors and omissions	–106.5	–37.1	–53.1
Reserves and related items	230.5	1,086.6	1,427.3

Source: IMF, *International Financial Statistics*.

External Trade

PRINCIPAL COMMODITIES
(distribution by SITC, US $ million)

Imports c.i.f.	2008	2009	2010
Food and live animals	1,376.8	1,442.3	1,273.8
Fish, crustaceans and molluscs, and preparations thereof	394.0	360.6	286.3
Fish, frozen, excl. fillets	385.9	353.5	278.3
Cereals and cereal preparations	657.8	787.0	648.8
Rice	468.3	597.3	460.2
Rice, semi-milled or wholly milled	468.3	597.3	460.1
Rice, semi-milled or wholly milled (unbroken)	332.0	458.7	348.7
Mineral fuels, lubricants, etc.	2,815.2	1,739.7	1,860.4
Petroleum, petroleum products, etc.	2,806.4	1,712.2	1,809.0
Crude petroleum and oils obtained from bituminous materials	2,669.0	1,622.9	1,689.7
Petroleum products, refined	119.1	76.5	106.0
Chemicals and related products	898.0	916.3	925.6
Medical and pharmaceutical products	228.5	251.2	238.5
Medicaments (incl. veterinary medicaments)	209.8	213.9	213.0
Basic manufactures	886.6	816.2	837.9
Iron and steel	259.3	207.0	205.1
Non-metallic mineral manufactures	191.1	162.2	174.4
Machinery and transport equipment	1,317.6	1,442.9	2,310.8
Road vehicles	404.4	341.3	407.7
Other transport equipment	25.4	55.3	864.4
Miscellaneous manufactured articles	261.9	277.8	267.8
Total (incl. others)*	7,883.7	6,959.9	7,849.3

Exports f.o.b.	2008	2009	2010
Food and live animals	3,715.2	4,646.5	4,759.6
Fish, crustaceans and molluscs, and preparations thereof	196.5	170.2	24.0
Fish, prepared or preserved	174.8	135.7	16.5
Vegetables and fruit	344.7	335.3	16.5
Fruit and nuts, fresh, dried	338.0	321.9	488.1
Coffee, tea, cocoa, spices and manufactures thereof	3,016.0	3,944.5	4,058.6
Coffee and coffee substitutes	204.5	217.3	230.3
Coffee, not roasted; coffee husks and skins	132.5	134.4	170.7
Cocoa	2,644.1	3,606.1	3,699.1
Cocoa beans, raw, roasted	1,754.1	2,596.1	2,492.5
Cocoa butter and paste	282.5	323.3	302.2
Crude materials (inedible) except fuels	910.9	609.2	1,014.9
Cork and wood	260.6	148.6	158.7

Exports f.o.b.—*continued*	2008	2009	2010
Wood, simply worked and railway sleepers of wood	220.6	109.1	118.5
Wood, non-coniferous species, sawn, planed, tongued, grooved, etc.	193.5	90.0	90.6
Textile fibres (not wool tops) and their wastes (not in yarn)	80.7	68.8	126.5
Raw cotton, excl. linters, not carded or combed	79.7	68.1	125.9
Mineral fuels, lubricants, etc.	3,627.9	3,019.2	2,432.7
Petroleum, petroleum products, etc.	3,625.4	3,016.7	2,430.0
Crude petroleum and oils obtained from bituminous materials	1,524.5	1,141.1	1,091.3
Petroleum products, refined	2,036.4	1,409.3	1,206.6
Chemicals and related products	369.7	405.2	320.5
Basic manufactures	376.3	346.8	287.1
Machinery and transport equipment	315.8	630.0	875.4
Road vehicles	41.4	86.5	26.6
Other transport equipment	194.4	423.3	744.7
Ships, boats and floating structures	96.8	338.8	726.4
Total (incl. others)†	9,778.8	10,280.1	10,283.5

* Including commodities and transactions not classified elsewhere in SITC (US $ million): 33.6 in 2008; 47.8 in 2009; 9.1 in 2010.

† Including commodities and transactions not classified elsewhere in SITC (US $ million): 94.9 in 2008; 220.7 in 2009; 185.5 in 2010.

Source: UN, *International Trade Statistics Yearbook*.

2011 (million francs CFA): *Imports:* Petroleum products 1,274; Electrical machinery 196; Fish, crustaceans, molluscs 190; Rice 268; Vehicles (incl. trucks) 96; Total (incl. others) 3,596. *Exports:* Cocoa beans 1,429; Cocoa manufactures 541; Petroleum products 1,740; Lumber 84; Cotton mass 65; Total (incl. others) 5,920 (Source: African Development Bank).

2012 (million francs CFA): *Imports:* Petroleum products 1,783; Electrical machinery 316; Fish, crustaceans, molluscs 235; Rice 295; Vehicles (incl. trucks) 238; Total (incl. others) 5,073. *Exports:* Cocoa beans 1,059; Cocoa manufactures 512; Petroleum products 1,588; Lumber 105; Cotton mass 71; Total (incl. others) 6,138 (Source: African Development Bank).

PRINCIPAL TRADING PARTNERS
(US $ million)

Imports c.i.f.	2008	2009	2010
Belgium	75.9	96.9	24.8
Brazil	86.4	67.7	59.5
China, People's Republic	542.1	501.0	545.7
Columbia	93.6	72.9	265.0
France (incl. Monaco)	999.6	991.5	931.4
Germany	224.5	205.2	216.4
India	131.5	127.7	—
Italy	160.9	152.7	169.4
Japan	204.6	146.7	176.1
Korea, Republic	108.9	99.3	97.7
Mauritania	114.7	117.2	163.4
Morocco	85.0	62.7	67.7
Netherlands	155.8	163.5	140.2
Nigeria	2,313.4	1,434.8	2,064.4
South Africa	89.3	98.9	135.6
Spain	193.9	182.3	153.9
Thailand	356.2	355.2	331.8
United Kingdom	158.8	103.1	119.2
USA	209.1	228.3	235.7
Venezuela	284.2	126.5	—
Viet Nam	82.0	144.6	105.9
Total (incl. others)	7,883.7	6,959.9	7,849.3

Exports f.o.b.	2008	2009	2010
Algeria	103.3	97.3	92.4
Belgium	204.6	238.6	5.1
Benin	104.2	96.9	110.6
Burkina Faso	412.0	381.4	360.4
Canada	36.6	144.8	242.9
Equatorial Guinea	148.4	112.6	249.4
Estonia	166.3	132.0	232.5
France (incl. Monaco)	1,357.8	1,123.1	715.9
Germany	694.6	738.0	521.7
Ghana	450.9	563.9	783.1
India	178.3	281.4	—
Italy	380.5	328.1	319.7
Malaysia	58.9	133.1	154.8
Mali	326.0	267.0	226.1
Netherlands	1,100.3	1,428.2	1,462.0
Nigeria	625.2	715.6	668.6
Poland	95.7	97.0	113.6
Senegal	163.8	146.3	113.0
Spain	223.6	191.1	253.2
Switzerland-Liechtenstein	74.3	218.1	170.3
Togo	138.5	70.4	66.8
United Kingdom	278.1	259.3	279.7
USA	945.1	800.3	1,060.1
Total (incl. others)	9,778.8	10,280.1	10,283.5

Source: UN, *International Trade Statistics Yearbook*.

2011 (million francs CFA): *Imports* China, People's Republic 217.4; France 374.7; Germany 86.7; Nigeria 741.5; USA 60.5; Total (incl. others) 3,596.0. *Exports* France 297.9; Italy 148.0; Netherlands 613.9; Nigeria 314.4; USA 624.3; Total (incl. others) 5,920.0 (Source: African Development Bank).

2012 (million francs CFA): Total imports 5,073; Total exports 6,138 (Source: African Development Bank).

Transport

RAILWAYS
(traffic)

	2001	2002	2003
Passengers ('000)	399.5	320.0	87.5
Freight carried ('000 metric tons)	1,016.3	900.7	149.7

Passenger-km (million): 93.1 in 1999 (Source: SITARAIL—Transport Ferroviaire de Personnel et de Marchandises, Abidjan).

Freight ton-km (million): 537.6 in 1999 (Source: SITARAIL—Transport Ferroviaire de Personnel et de Marchandises, Abidjan).

ROAD TRAFFIC
('000 motor vehicles in use)

	1998	1999	2000
Passenger cars	98.4	109.6	113.9
Commercial vehicles	45.4	54.1	54.9

2001–02 ('000 motor vehicles in use): Figures assumed to be unchanged from 2000.

Source: UN, *Statistical Yearbook*.

2007 (motor vehicles in use): Passenger cars 314,165; Buses and coaches 17,512; Vans and lorries 78,575; Motorcycles and mopeds 38,105 (Source: IRF, *World Road Statistics*).

SHIPPING

Flag Registered Fleet
(at 31 December)

	2010	2011	2012
Number of vessels	18	19	19
Total displacement ('000 grt)	3.1	3.9	3.9

Source: Lloyd's List Intelligence (www.lloydslistintelligence.com).

International Sea-borne Freight Traffic
(freight traffic at Abidjan, '000 metric tons)

	2001	2002	2003
Goods loaded	5,787	5,710	6,108
Goods unloaded	9,858	9,018	8,353

Source: Port Autonome d'Abidjan.

Freight traffic at San-Pédro ('000 metric tons, 2000): Goods loaded 1,102; Goods unloaded 251.

CIVIL AVIATION
(traffic on scheduled services)*

	1999	2000	2001
Kilometres flown (million)	6	3	1
Passengers carried ('000)	260	108	46
Passenger-km (million)	381	242	130
Total ton-km (million)	50	34	19

* Including an apportionment of the traffic of Air Afrique.

Source: UN, *Statistical Yearbook*.

Passengers carried ('000): 516.1 in 2010; 89.8 in 2011; 39.5 in 2012 (Source: World Bank, World Development Indicators database).

Tourism

ARRIVALS BY COUNTRY OF RESIDENCE
('000)

	1996*	1997†	1998†
Belgium	4.3	4.2	4.5
Benin	12.5	11.1	14.3
Burkina Faso	11.0	11.9	17.1
Congo, Repub.	6.0	n.a.	7.6
France	66.7	69.0	73.2
Gabon	3.0	n.a.	5.4
Germany	3.2	3.8	3.9
Ghana	5.4	n.a.	6.7
Guinea	8.1	n.a.	12.5
Italy	5.0	14.0	7.6
Mali	10.7	n.a.	15.2
Niger	5.0	n.a.	5.4
Nigeria	7.9	n.a.	14.1
Senegal	13.0	12.1	16.6
Togo	8.7	8.2	10.8
United Kingdom	5.1	4.5	5.6
USA	15.3	17.0	18.8
Total (incl. others)	236.9	274.1	301.0

* Figures refer only to air arrivals at Abidjan—Félix Houphouët-Boigny airport.

† Figures refer to air arrivals at Abidjan—Félix Houphouët-Boigny airport and to arrivals at land frontiers.

Receipts from tourism (US $ million, excl. passenger transport): 151 in 2009; 201 in 2010; 141 in 2011.

Source: World Tourism Organization.

Communications Media

	2010	2011	2012
Telephones ('000 main lines in use)	283.3	268.2	268.0
Mobile cellular telephones ('000 subscribers)	15,599.0	17,344.2	19,826.8
Internet users ('000)	n.a.	49.8	n.a.
Broadband subscribers ('000)	7.9	49.5	49.5

Source: International Telecommunication Union.

Education

(2011/12 unless otherwise indicated)

		Students		
	Teachers	Males	Females	Total
Pre-primary	4,941	45,898	45,495	91,393
Primary	70,016	1,586,356	1,334,435	2,920,791
Secondary	31,109	474,203*	262,446*	736,649*
Tertiary†	n.a.	95,566	48,704	144,270

* 2001/02.

† 2009/10.

Institutions: 207 pre-primary in 1995/96; 7,599 primary in 1996/97.

Source: mostly UNESCO Institute for Statistics.

Pupil-teacher ratio (primary education, UNESCO estimate): 41.7 in 2011/12 (Source: UNESCO Institute for Statistics).

Adult literacy rate (UNESCO estimates): 56.9% (males 65.6%; females 47.6%) in 2011 (Source: UNESCO Institute for Statistics).

Directory

The Government

HEAD OF STATE

President of the Republic, Minister of Defence: ALASSANE DRAMANE OUATTARA (elected 28 November 2010; sworn in 6 May 2011).

COUNCIL OF MINISTERS
(April 2014)

Prime Minister, Minister of the Economy, Finance and the Budget: DANIEL KABLAN DUNCAN.

Minister of State in the Office of the President of the Republic: JEANNOT KOUADIO AHOUSSOU.

Minister of State, Minister of the Interior and Security: HAMED BAKAYOKO.

Minister of State, Minister of Foreign Affairs: CHARLES KOFFI DIBY.

Minister of State, Minister of Planning and Development: ALBERT TOIKESSE MABRI.

Minister of State, Minister of Employment, Social Affairs and Professional Training: MOUSSA DOSSO.

Keeper of the Seals, Minister of Justice, Human Rights and Public Liberties: GNÉNÉMA MAMADOU COULIBALY.

Minister-delegate to the Prime Minister, in charge of the Economy and Finance: NIALÉ KABA.

Minister-delegate to the Prime Minister, in charge of the Budget: ABDOURAHMANE CISSÉ.
Minister of African Integration and Ivorians Abroad: ALLY COULIBALY.
Minister of Petroleum and Energy: ADAMA TOUNGARA.
Minister of the Environment, Urban Hygiene and Sustainable Development: RÉMI ALLAH KOUADIO.
Minister of Economic Infrastructure: PATRICK ACHI.
Minister of the Civil Service and Administrative Reform: KONAN GNAMIEN.
Minister of National and Technical Education: KANDIA KAMISSOKO CAMARA.
Minister of Trade, Handicrafts and the Promotion of Small and Medium-sized Enterprises: JEAN-LOUIS BILLON.
Minister of Higher Education and Scientific Research: IBRAHIMA CISSÉ BACONGO.
Minister of Transport: GAOUSSOU TOURÉ.
Minister of Animal and Fishing Resources: KOBENA KOUASSI ADJOUMANI.
Minister of Health and the Fight Against AIDS: RAYMONDE GOUDOU COFFIE.
Minister of Agriculture: MAMADOU SANGAFOWA COULIBALY.
Minister of Construction, Housing, Sanitation and Town Planning: MAMADOU SANOGO.
Minister of Industry and Mines: JEAN-CLAUDE BROU.
Minister of Solidarity, the Family, Women and Children: ANNE DÉSIRÉE OULOTO.
Minister of Culture and Francophone Affairs: MAURICE KOUAKOU BANDAMA.
Minister of Posts and Information and Communication Technologies, Government Spokesperson: BRUNO NABAGNÉ KONÉ.
Minister of Water and Forests: MATHIEU BABAUD DARRET.
Minister of Communication, Deputy Government Spokesperson: AFFOUSSIATA BAMBA LAMINE.
Minister of Tourism: ROGER KAKOU.
Minister of the Promotion of Youth, Sport and Leisure: ALAIN MICHEL LOBOGNON.
Minister-delegate to the President of the Republic, in charge of Defence: PAUL KOFFI KOFFI.

MINISTRIES

Office of the President: 01 BP 1354, Abidjan 01; tel. 20-22-02-22; fax 20-21-14-25; internet www.cotedivoirepr.ci.

Office of the Prime Minister: blvd Angoulvant, 01 BP 1533, Abidjan 01; tel. 20-31-50-00; fax 20-22-18-33; internet www.premierministre.ci.

Ministry of African Integration and Ivorians Abroad: 08 BP 1816, Abidjan 08; tel. 22-41-71-46; e-mail info@integration.gouv.ci; internet www.integration.gouv.ci.

Ministry of Agriculture: 25e étage, Immeuble Caisse de Stabilisation, BP V82, Abidjan; tel. 20-21-08-33; fax 20-21-46-18; e-mail minagra@cimail.net; internet www.agriculture.gouv.ci.

Ministry of Animal and Fishing Resources: 11e étage, Immeuble Caisse de Stabilisation, Plateau, Abidjan; tel. 20-21-33-94; internet www.ressourcesanimales.gouv.ci.

Ministry of the Civil Service and Administrative Reform: Immeuble Fonction Public, blvd Angoulvand, BP V93, Abidjan; tel. 20-21-42-90; fax 20-21-12-86; internet www.fonctionpublique.gouv.ci.

Ministry of Communication: 22e étage, Tour C, Tours Administratives, Plateau, Abidjan; tel. 20-21-07-84; internet www.communication.gouv.ci.

Ministry of Construction, Housing, Sanitation and Town Planning: 26e étage, Tour D, Tours Administratives, 20 BP 650, Abidjan; tel. 20-21-82-35; fax 20-21-35-68; internet www.construction.gouv.ci.

Ministry of Culture and Francophone Affairs: 22e étage, Tour E, Tours Administratives, BP V39, Abidjan; tel. 20-21-40-34; fax 20-21-33-59; e-mail culture.ci@ci.refer.org; internet www.mcf-culture.ci.

Ministry of Defence: Camp Galliéni, côté Bibliothèque Nationale, BP V241, Abidjan; tel. 20-21-02-88; fax 20-22-41-75.

Ministry of Economic Infrastructure: 23e étage, Immeuble Postel 2001, BP V6, Plateau, Abidjan; tel. 20-34-73-01; fax 20-21-20-43; e-mail minie@aviso.ci; internet www.infrastructures.gouv.ci.

Ministry of the Economy, Finance and the Budget: 16e étage, Immeuble SCIAM, ave Marchand, BP V163, Abidjan; tel. 20-20-08-42; fax 20-21-32-08; internet www.finances.gouv.ci.

Ministry of Employment, Social Affairs and Professional Training: Abidjan; tel. 20-22-39-24; e-mail info@formation.gouv.ci; internet www.formation.gouv.ci.

Ministry of the Environment, Urban Hygiene and Sustainable Development: 10e étage, Tour D, Tours Administratives, BP V06, Abidjan; tel. 20-22-61-35; fax 20-22-20-50; internet www.environnement.gouv.ci.

Ministry of Foreign Affairs: Bloc Ministériel, blvd Angoulvant, BP V109, Abidjan; tel. 20-22-71-50; fax 20-33-23-08; e-mail infos@mae.ci; internet www.mae.ci.

Ministry of Health and the Fight Against AIDS: 16e étage, Tour C, Tours Administratives, Plateau, Abidjan; tel. 20-21-08-71; fax 20-22-22-20; internet www.sante.gouv.ci.

Ministry of Higher Education and Scientific Research: 20e étage, Tour C, Tours Administratives, BP V151, Abidjan; tel. 20-21-57-73; fax 20-21-22-25; internet www.enseignement.gouv.ci.

Ministry of Industry and Mines: 15e étage, Immeuble CCIA, rue Jean-Paul II, BP V65, Abidjan; tel. 20-21-64-73; fax 20-21-64-74; e-mail mipsp@industrie.gouv.ci; internet www.industrie.gouv.ci.

Ministry of the Interior and Security: Immeuble SETU, en face de la préfecture, BP V241, Abidjan; tel. 20-22-38-16; fax 20-22-36-48; internet www.interieur.gouv.ci.

Ministry of Justice, Human Rights and Public Liberties: Bloc Ministériel, blvd Angoulvand A-17, BP V107, Plateau, Abidjan; tel. 20-21-17-27; fax 20-33-12-59; internet www.justice.gouv.ci.

Ministry of National and Technical Education: 28e étage, Tour D, Tours Administratives, BP V120, Abidjan; tel. 20-21-85-27; fax 20-22-93-22; e-mail menfb@ci.refer.org; internet education-ci.org.

Ministry of Petroleum and Energy: 15e étage, Immeuble SCIAM, ave Marchand, BP V40, Abidjan; tel. 20-21-66-17; fax 20-21-37-30; internet www.energie.gouv.ci.

Ministry of Planning and Development: 16e étage, Immeuble SCIAM, Plateau, Abidjan; tel. 20-20-08-42; fax 20-20-08-65; e-mail gvode@plan.gouv.ci; internet www.plan.gouv.ci.

Ministry of Posts and Information and Communication Technologies: 21e étage, Immeuble Postel 2001, BP V138, Abidjan; tel. 22-34-73-65; fax 22-44-78-47; internet www.telecom.gouv.ci.

Ministry of the Promotion of Youth, Sport and Leisure: 8e étage, Tour B, Tours Administratives, BP V136, Abidjan; tel. 20-21-92-64; fax 20-22-48-21; internet www.jeunesse.gouv.ci.

Ministry of Solidarity, the Family, Women and Children: Tour E, Tours Administratives, BP V200, Abidjan; tel. 20-21-76-26; fax 20-21-44-61; internet www.famille.gouv.ci.

Ministry of Tourism: 15e étage, Tour D, Tours Administratives, BP V184, Abidjan 01; tel. 20-34-79-13; fax 20-44-55-80; internet www.tourisme.gouv.ci.

Ministry of Trade, Handicrafts and the Promotion of Small and Medium-sized Enterprises: 26e étage, Immeuble CCIA, rue Jean-Paul II, BP V65, Abidjan; tel. 20-21-76-35; fax 20-21-64-74; internet www.commerce.gouv.ci.

Ministry of Transport: 14e étage, Immeuble Postel 2001, BP V06, Abidjan; tel. 20-34-48-58; fax 20-34-48-54; internet www.transports.gouv.ci.

Ministry of Water and Forests: BP 650, Abidjan; tel. 20-21-94-06; fax 20-21-05-12; internet www.eauxetforets.gouv.ci.

President

Presidential Election, First Round, 31 October 2010

Candidate	Votes	% of votes
Laurent Gbagbo (FPI)	1,756,504	38.04
Alassane Dramane Ouattara (RDR)	1,481,091	32.07
Henri Konan Bédié (PDCI—RDA)	1,165,532	25.24
Albert Toikesse Mabri (UDPCI)	118,671	2.57
Others*	96,023	2.08
Total†	4,617,821	100.00

* There were 10 other candidates.
† Excluding invalid votes (225,624).

Presidential Election, Second Round, 28 November 2010

Candidate	Votes	% of votes
Alassane Dramane Ouattara (RDR)	2,483,164	54.10
Laurent Gbagbo (FPI)	2,107,055	45.90
Total	4,590,219	100.00

The above results were released by the Commission Electorale Indépendant on 2 December 2010. However, later on 2 December the President of the Constitutional Council, Paul Yao N'Dré, declared the CEI's announcement null and void and the following day released results indicating that Gbagbo had won the election, having received 51.45% of votes cast to Ouattara's 48.55%. The

Special Representative of the UN Secretary-General for Côte d'Ivoire, Choi Young-Jin, described N'Dré's decision as 'having no factual basis'; furthermore, in his role as certifier of the Ivorian elections Choi declared Ouattara the winner. On 8 December the UN Security Council released a statement confirming its endorsement of Ouattara as the President-elect of Côte d'Ivoire.

Legislature

National Assembly: 01 BP 1381, Abidjan 01; tel. 20-20-82-00; fax 20-20-82-33; e-mail admin@anci.ci; internet www.anci.ci.

President: GUILLAUME SORO.

General Election, 11 December 2011*

Party	Seats
Rassemblement des Républicains (RDR)	127
Parti Démocratique de la Côte d'Ivoire—Rassemblement Démocratique Africain (PDCI—RDA)	77
Union pour la Démocratie et la Paix de la Côte d'Ivoire (UDPCI)	7
Rassemblement des Houphouëtistes pour la Démocratie et la Paix (RHDP)	4
Mouvement des Forces d'Avenir (MFA)	3
Union pour la Côte d'Ivoire (UPCI)	1
Independents	35
Total	254‡

* The election was boycotted by the Front Populaire Ivoirien (FPI).
‡ Voting in one constituency did not take place owing to the death of a candidate. On 31 January 2012 the Constitutional Council annulled the results of voting in 12 constituencies owing to irregularities. Subsequently, by-elections were held on 26 February in the 13 constituencies, at which the RDR won four seats, the UDPCI two seats, the PDCI—RDA one seat and independent candidates secured four seats. The results in the remaining two constituencies remained undeclared. According to final results published by the Commission Electorale Indépendant on 8 March, the RDR held 138 of the 253 declared seats, the PDCI—RDA held 86 seats, independent candidates held 17 seats and the UDPCI held eight seats. Other party representations remained unchanged.

Election Commission

Commission Electorale Indépendant: 08 BP 2648, Abidjan; tel. 21-30-58-01; internet www.ceici.org; f. 2001; 30 mems; Pres. YOUSSOUF BAKAYOKO.

Advisory Councils

Constitutional Council (Conseil Constitutionnel): 22 blvd Carde, BP 4642, Abidjan 01; tel. 20-21-31-64; fax 20-21-21-68; internet www.gouv.ci/conconst.php; f. 2000; Pres. FRANCIS WODIÉ.

Economic and Social Council: blvd Carde, angle ave Terrasson de Fougère, 04 BP 304, Abidjan 04; tel. 20-21-14-54; internet ces-ci.org; f. 1961; Pres. MARCEL ZADI KESSY; 120 mems.

Political Organizations

In 2007 there were more than 100 registered political organizations.

Alliance pour la Paix, le Progrès et la Souveraineté (APS): Abidjan; f. 2003 by fmr members of the UDPCI; Pres. HILAIRE DIGBEU ANI.

Forces Nouvelles (FN): Bouaké; tel. 20-20-04-04; e-mail senacom@fnci.info; internet www.fninfo.ci; f. 2003 by the Mouvement Patriotique de Côte d'Ivoire (MPCI), following its absorption of the Mouvement Populaire Ivoirien du Grand Ouest (MPIGO) and the Mouvement pour la Justice et la Paix (MJP), both of which were based in Man, in the west of Côte d'Ivoire.

Front Populaire Ivoirien (FPI): Marcory Zone 4C, 22 BP 302, Abidjan 22; tel. 21-24-36-76; fax 21-35-35-50; internet www.fpi.ci; f. 1990; socialist; Pres. PASCAL AFFI N'GUESSAN.

Liberté et Démocratie pour la République (Lider): Abidjan; f. 2011; Leader MAMADOU COULIBALY.

Mouvement des Forces d'Avenir (MFA): 15 BP 794, Abidjan 15; tel. 21-24-42-02; e-mail contact@mfa-ci.com; internet www.mfa-ci.com; f. 1995; Pres. INNOCENT KOBENA ANAKY; Sec.-Gen. DAKPA PHILIPPE LEGRE.

Parti Démocratique de la Côte d'Ivoire—Rassemblement Démocratique Africain (PDCI—RDA): 05 BP 36, Abidjan 05; e-mail sg@pdcirda.org; internet www.pdcirda.org; f. 1946; Pres. HENRI KONAN BÉDIÉ; Sec.-Gen. ALPHONSE DJÉDJÉ MADY.

Parti Ivoirien des Travailleurs (PIT): Adjamé 220 logements, face Cinéma Liberté, Immeuble Mistral Appartement 602, 20 BP 43, Abidjan 20; tel. 20-37-79-42; fax 20-37-29-00; e-mail pit.ci@aviso.ci; internet www.pit-ci.org; social-democratic; f. 1990; First Nat. Sec. FRANCIS WODIÉ.

Rassemblement du Peuple de Côte d'Ivoire (RPCI): Abidjan; f. 2012; Pres. MORIFERÉ BAMBA.

Parti pour le Progrès et le Socialisme (PPS): Abidjan; f. 1993; Sec.-Gen. Prof. MORIFÉRÉ BAMBA.

Union des Sociaux-Démocrates (USD): 08 BP 1866, Abidjan 08; tel. 22-44-06-70; Pres. BERNARD ZADI ZAOUROU; Sec.-Gen. Me JÉRÔME CLIMANLO COULIBALY.

Rassemblement des Républicains (RDR): 8 rue Lepic, Cocody, 06 BP 111, Abidjan 06; tel. 22-44-33-51; fax 22-41-55-73; e-mail le-rdr@yahoo.fr; internet www.le-rdr.org; f. 1994 following split from PDCI—RDA; Pres. Dr ALASSANE DRAMANE OUATTARA; Sec.-Gen. AMADOU SOUMAHORO.

Union Démocratique Citoyenne (UDCY): 37 bis rue de la Canebière—PISAM, 01 BP 1410, Abidjan 01; tel. 22-47-12-94; e-mail udcy_ci@hotmail.com; f. 2000 following split from PDCI—RDA; Pres. THÉODORE MEL-EG.

Union pour la Démocratie et pour la Paix de la Côte d'Ivoire (UDPCI): 06 BP 1481, Abidjan 06; tel. 22-41-60-94; e-mail info@udpci.org; internet www.udpci.org; f. 2001 following split from PDCI—RDA by supporters of fmr Head of State Gen. Robert Gueï; mem. of alliance, Rassemblement des Houphouëtistes pour la Démocratie et la Paix, formed in advance of proposed (but subsequently postponed) presidential elections in 2005; Pres. ALBERT TOIKESSE MABRI; Sec.-Gen. ALASSANE SALIF N'DIAYE.

Diplomatic Representation

EMBASSIES IN CÔTE D'IVOIRE

Algeria: 53 blvd Clozel, 01 BP 1015, Abidjan 01; tel. 20-21-23-40; fax 20-22-37-12; Ambassador BOUMEDIENE GUENNAD.

Angola: Lot 2461, rue des Jardins, Cocody-les-Deux-Plateaux, 01 BP 1734, Abidjan 01; tel. 22-44-45-91; fax 22-44-46-52; Ambassador GILBERTO BUTA LUTUKUTA.

Belgium: Cocody Ambassades, angle rue de Bélier et rue A56, 01 BP 1800, Abidjan 01; tel. 22-48-33-60; fax 22-44-16-40; e-mail abidjan@diplobel.fed.be; internet www.diplomatie.be/abidjan; Ambassador PETER HUYGHEBAERT.

Benin: rue des Jardins, Lot 1610, Cocody-les-Deux-Plateaux, 09 BP 283, Abidjan 09; tel. 22-41-44-13; fax 22-41-27-89; e-mail ambabenin@aviso.ci; Ambassador DAOUDA WABI.

Brazil: Immeuble Alpha 2000, 22ème étage, 01 BP 3820, Abidjan; tel. 20-22-74-83; fax 20-22-64-01; Ambassador ALFREDO JOSÉ CAVALCANTI JORDA DE CAMARGO.

Burkina Faso: Immeuble SIDAM, 5e étage, 34 ave Houdaille, 01 BP 908, Plateau, Abidjan 01; tel. 20-21-15-01; fax 20-21-66-41; e-mail amba.bf@africaonline.ci; Ambassador JUSTIN KOUTABA.

Cameroon: Immeuble le Général, blvd Botreau Roussel, 06 BP 326, Abidjan 06; tel. 20-21-33-31; fax 20-21-66-11; Ambassador ALFRED NGUINI.

Canada: Immeuble Trade Center, 23 ave Nogues, 01 BP 4104, Abidjan 01; tel. 20-30-07-00; fax 20-30-07-20; e-mail abdjn@international.gc.ca; internet www.canadainternational.gc.ca/cotedivoire; Ambassador CHANTAL DE VARENNES.

Central African Republic: 9 rue des Jasmins, Cocody Danga Nord, 01 BP 3387, Abidjan 01; tel. 20-21-36-46; fax 22-44-85-16; Ambassador YAGAO-N'GAMA LAZARE.

China, People's Republic: Lot 45, ave Jacques Aka, Cocody, 01 BP 3691, Abidjan 01; tel. 22-44-59-00; fax 22-44-67-81; e-mail ambchine@aviso.ci; internet ci.chineseembassy.org/chn; Ambassador ZHANG GUOQING.

Congo, Democratic Republic: Carrefour France-Amérique, RAN Treichville, ave 21, 01 BP 541, Abidjan 01; tel. 21-24-69-06; Ambassador ISABELLE IBOULA NGANGELLI.

Egypt: Immeuble El Nasr, 17e étage, rue du Commerce, 01 BP 2104, Abidjan 01; tel. 20-22-62-31; fax 20-22-30-53; e-mail amegypteci@afnet.net; Ambassador USAMA SAEED MAHMOUD KHALIL.

Ethiopia: Immeuble Nour Al-Hayat, 8e étage, 01 BP 3712, Abidjan 01; tel. 20-21-33-65; fax 20-21-37-09; e-mail ambethio@gmail.com; Ambassador ABDULAZIZ AHMED ADEM.

France: 17 rue Lecoeur, 17 BP 175, Abidjan 17; tel. 20-20-04-04; fax 20-20-04-47; e-mail scac.abidjan-amba@diplomatie.gouv.fr; internet www.ambafrance-ci.org; Ambassador GEORGE SERRE.

Gabon: Immeuble Les Heveas, blvd Carde, 01 BP 3765, Abidjan 01; tel. 22-44-51-54; fax 22-44-75-05; Ambassador FAUSTIN MOUNGUENGUI NZIGOU.

Germany: 39 blvd Hassan II, Cocody, 01 BP 1900, Abidjan 01; tel. and fax 22-44-20-30; fax 22-44-20-41; e-mail info@abidjan.diplo.de; internet www.abidjan.diplo.de; Ambassador KARL PRINZ.

Ghana: Lot 2393, rue J 95, Cocody-les-Deux-Plateaux, 01 BP 1871, Abidjan 01; tel. 20-33-11-24; fax 20-22-33-57; Ambassador Lt-Col (retd) ENOCH KWAME TWENEBOAH DONKOR.

Guinea: Immeuble Duplessis, 08 BP 2280, Abidjan 08; tel. 20-22-25-20; fax 20-32-82-45; Ambassador OLGA SYRADIN.

Holy See: Apostolic Nunciature, rue Mgr. René Kouassi 18, 08 BP 1347, Abidjan 08; tel. 22-40-17-70; fax 22-40-17-74; e-mail nuntius .ci@gmail.com; Apostolic Nuncio JOSEPH SPITERI (Titular Archbishop of Serta).

India: Cocody Danga Nord, 06 BP 318, Abidjan 06; tel. 22-42-37-69; fax 22-42-66-49; e-mail amb.office@eoiabidjan.org; Ambassador (vacant).

Iran: blvd de France, en Face de Campus Université de Cocody, rue Belier, Villa No. 1, Abidjan; tel. 22-48-75-48; fax 22-48-75-47; Ambassador NOBAKHTI SEYED REZA.

Israel: Immeuble Nour Al-Hayat, 9th Floor, ave Chardy, 01 BP 1877, Abidjan 01; tel. 20-21-31-78; fax 20-21-87-04; e-mail info@abidjan .mfa.gov.il; internet abidjan.mfa.gov.il; Ambassador ISI YANOUKA.

Italy: 16 rue de la Canebière, Cocody, 01 BP 1905, Abidjan 01; tel. 22-44-61-70; fax 22-44-35-87; e-mail ambasciata.abidjan@esteri.it; internet www.ambabidjan.esteri.it; Ambassador ALFONSO DI RISO.

Japan: Immeuble Alpha 2000, ave Chardy, 01 BP 1329, Abidjan 01; tel. 20-21-28-63; fax 20-21-30-51; internet www.ci.emb-japan.go.jp; Ambassador SUSUMU INOUE.

Korea, Democratic People's Republic: Abidjan; Ambassador JONG HAKE.

Korea, Republic: Immeuble le Mans, 8e étage, 01 BP 3950, Abidjan 01; tel. 20-32-22-90; fax 20-22-22-74; e-mail ambcoabj@mofat.go.kr; internet civ.mofat.go.kr; Ambassador SURH SUNG-YOL.

Lebanon: Immeuble Trade Center, ave Noguès, 01 BP 2227, Abidjan 01; tel. 20-33-28-24; fax 20-32-11-37; e-mail ambliban@hotmail.com; Ambassador Dr ALI AJAMI.

Liberia: Immeuble La Symphonie, ave Général de Gaulle, 01 BP 2514, Abidjan 01; tel. 20-22-23-59; fax 22-44-14-75; Ambassador VIVIENNE TITI WREH.

Libya: Immeuble Shell, 01 BP 5725, Abidjan 01; tel. 20-22-01-27; fax 20-22-01-30; Chargé d'affaires TAHER A. S. BAKIR.

Mali: 46 blvd Lagunaire, 01 BP 2746, Abidjan 01; tel. 20-32-31-47; fax 20-21-55-14; Ambassador AMADOU OUSMANE TOURÉ.

Mauritania: rue Pierre et Marie Curie, 01 BP 2275, Abidjan 01; tel. 22-41-16-43; fax 22-41-05-77; Ambassador MOHAMED ABDELLAHI EL BOUKHARY EL VILALY.

Morocco: 24 rue de la Canebière, 01 BP 146, Cocody, Abidjan 01; tel. 22-44-58-73; fax 22-44-60-58; e-mail sifmaabj@aviso.ci; Ambassador MUSTAPHA JEBARI.

Niger: 23 ave Angoulvant, 01 BP 2743, Abidjan 01; tel. 21-26-28-14; fax 21-26-41-88; Ambassador MOUSSA ALOUA.

Nigeria: Immeuble Maison du Nigéria, 35 blvd de la République, 01 BP 1906, Abidjan 01; tel. 20-22-30-82; fax 20-21-30-83; e-mail info@nigeriaembassyci.org; internet www.nigeriaembassyci.org; Ambassador IFEOMA AKABOGU-CHINWUBA.

Russia: BP 583, Riviera, Abidjan 01; tel. 22-43-09-59; fax 22-43-11-66; e-mail ambrci@yandex.ru; internet www.cotedivoire.mid.ru; Ambassador LEONID ROGOD.

Saudi Arabia: Villa No. 15, rue Victor Scheolcher, Abidjan 08; tel. 22-44-24-80; fax 22-44-24-03; e-mail ciemb@mofa.gov.sa; internet embassies.mofa.gov.sa/sites/IvoryCoast; Ambassador SAUD AL-THEBAITY.

Senegal: Immeuble Nabil Choucair, 6 rue du Commerce, 08 BP 2165, Abidjan 08; tel. 20-33-28-76; fax 20-32-50-39; Ambassador ABDOU LAHAD SOURANG.

South Africa: Villa Marc André, rue Mgr René Kouassi, Cocody, 08 BP 1806, Abidjan 08; tel. 22-44-59-63; fax 22-44-74-50; e-mail Abidjan@dirco.gov.za; internet www.dirco.gov.za/Abidjan; Ambassador VUSUMUZI LAWRENCE SINDANE.

Spain: Impasse Abla Pokou, Cocody Danga Nord, 08 BP 876, Abidjan 08; tel. 22-44-48-50; fax 22-44-71-22; e-mail embespci@correo.mae .es; Ambassador FERNANDO MORAN CALVO-SOTELO.

Switzerland: Immeuble Botreau Roussel, 28 ave Delafosse, Plateau, 01 BP 1914, Abidjan 01; tel. 20-21-17-21; fax 20-21-27-70; e-mail abi.vertretung@eda.admin.ch; internet www.eda.admin.ch/abidjan; Ambassador THOMAS LITSCHER.

Tunisia: Immeuble Shell, ave Lamblin, 01 BP 3906, Abidjan 01; tel. 20-22-61-23; fax 20-22-61-24; Ambassador NACEUR BOU ALI.

Turkey: Immeuble N'Zarama, 3ème étage, blvd Lagunaire Charles de Gaulle, Plateau, 01 BP 5137, Abidjan 01; tel. 20-25-51-10; fax 20-25-51-11; e-mail ambassade.abidjan@mfa.gov.tr; internet www .abidjan.be.mfa.gov.tr; Ambassador YALÇIN KAYA ERENSOY.

United Kingdom: Cocody Quartier Ambassades, rue l'Impasse du Belier, 01 BP 2581, Abidjan 01; tel. 22-44-26-69; fax 22-48-95-48; e-mail uk_abidjan@yahoo.fr; Ambassador SIMON DAVID TONGE.

USA: Cocody Riviera Golf, 01 BP 1712, Abidjan 01; tel. 22-49-40-00; fax 22-49-43-23; e-mail abjpress@state.gov; internet abidjan .usembassy.gov; Ambassador TERENCE PATRICK MCCULLEY, III.

Judicial System

Since 1964 all civil, criminal, commercial and administrative cases have come under the jurisdiction of the courts of first instance, the assize courts and the Courts of Appeal, with the Supreme Court (referred to in the Constitution of 2000 as the Court of Cassation) as the highest court of appeal.

Supreme Court: rue Gourgas, Cocody, BP V30, Abidjan; tel. 20-22-73-72; fax 20-21-63-04; internet www.gouv.ci/coursupreme_1.php; comprises three chambers: judicial, administrative and auditing; Pres. MAMADOU KONÉ; Pres. of the Judicial Chamber CHANTAL NANABA CAMARA; Pres. of the Administrative Chamber PIERRE CLAVER KOBO.

Courts of Appeal: Abidjan: First Pres. MATHURIN KANGAN BENON YAO; Bouaké: First Pres. BLAISE SIMPLICE MOULARÉ; Daloa: First Pres. AKISSI JEANNE YAO.

Courts of First Instance: Abengourou: Pres. SORO DRISSA; Abidjan: Pres. AHMED SOULEYMANE COULIBALY; Bouaké: Pres. DEMBÉLÉ TAHIROU; Daloa: Pres. KOUAMÉ AUGUSTIN YAO; Korhogo, Vice-Pres. HERMANN KOUA KADJO; Gagnoa: Pres. KOUAMÉ TÉHUA; Yopougon: Pres. KOUADIO KOFFI BERNARD; Man: Pres. CISSOKO AMOUROULAYE; there are a further 25 courts in the principal centres.

Tribunal de Commerce d'Abidjan: Cocody, aux deux Plateau, derrière la fondation Donwahi, Abidjan; tel. 46-04-87-92; e-mail infos@tribunalcommerceabidjan.org; internet tribunalcommerceabidjan.org; f. 2012; Pres. FRANÇOIS KOMOIN.

High Court of Justice: composed of deputies elected from and by the National Assembly; has jurisdiction to impeach the President or other mems of the Govt.

Constitutional Council: 22 blvd Carde, BP 4642, Abidjan 01; tel. 20-21-31-64; fax 20-21-21-68; internet www.gouv.ci/conconst.php; f. 2000 to replace certain functions of the fmr Constitutional Chamber of the Supreme Court; Pres. FRANCIS WODIÉ.

Religion

The Constitution guarantees religious freedom, and this right is generally respected. Religious groups are required to register with the authorities, although no penalties are imposed on a group that fails to register. At the 1998 census it was estimated that about 34% of the population were Christians (mainly Roman Catholics), 27% of the population were Muslims, 15% followed traditional indigenous beliefs, 3% practised other religions, while 21% had no religious affiliation. It is, however, estimated that the proportion of Muslims is in fact significantly higher, as the majority of unregistered foreign workers are Muslims. Muslims are found in greatest numbers in the north of the country, while Christians are found mostly in the southern, central, western and eastern regions. Traditional indigenous beliefs are generally prevalent in rural areas.

ISLAM

Conseil National Islamique (CNI): Mosquée d'Aghien les deux Plateaux, BP 174 Cédex 03, Abidjan 08; tel. and fax 22-42-67-79; e-mail infos@cnicosim.org; f. 1993; groups more than 5,000 local communities organized in 13 regional and 78 local organizations; Chair. Imam El Hadj IDRISS KOUDOUSS KONÉ.

Conseil Supérieur des Imams (COSIM): 05 BP 2092, Abidjan 08; tel. 21-35-87-51; fax 05-79-61-04; e-mail contact@cosim-ci.org; internet www.cosim-ci.org; Pres. CHEICK BOIKARY FOFANA.

Conseil Supérieur Islamique (CSI): 11 BP 71, Abidjan 11; tel. 21-25-24-70; fax 21-24-28-04; f. 1978; Pres. MOUSTAPHA SY FADIGA.

Other Islamic organizations include the Association des Musulmans Sunnites, Conseil des Imams Sunnites, Front de la Oummat Islamique and Haut Conseil des Imamats et Oulémas.

CHRISTIANITY

The Roman Catholic Church

Côte d'Ivoire comprises four archdioceses and 11 dioceses. An estimated 20% of the total population are Roman Catholics.

Bishops' Conference: Conférence Episcopale de la Côte d'Ivoire, BP 713 Cédex 03, Abidjan-Riviera; tel. 22-47-20-00; fax 22-47-60-65; Pres. Most Rev. JOSEPH YAPO AKÉ (Archbishop of Gagnoa).

Archbishop of Abidjan: Cardinal JEAN-PIERRE KUTWA, Archevêché, ave Jean-Paul II, 01 BP 1287, Abidjan 01; tel. 20-21-23-08; fax 20-21-40-22.

Archbishop of Bouaké: Most Rev. PAUL-SIMÉON AHOUANAN DJRO, Archevêché, 01 BP 649, Bouaké 01; tel. and fax 31-63-24-59; e-mail archebke@aviso.ci.

Archbishop of Gagnoa: Most Rev. JOSEPH YAPO AKÉ, Archevêché, BP 527, Gagnoa; tel. and fax 32-77-25-68; e-mail evechegagnoa@aviso.ci.

Archbishop of Korhogo: Most Rev. MARIE-DANIEL DADIET, BP 1581, Yamoussoukro; tel. 36-86-01-18; fax 36-86-08-31; e-mail dieulesauve@yahoo.fr.

Protestant Churches

Conseil National des Eglises Protestantes et Evangéliques de Côte d'Ivoire (CNEPECI): Abidjan; Pres. PAUL AYOH.

Eglise Evangélique des Assemblées de Dieu de Côte d'Ivoire: 26 BP 1396, Abidjan 26; tel. 21-35-55-48; fax 21-24-94-65; e-mail itpk2006@yahoo.fr; internet www.eeadci.org; f. 1960; Pres. BÉCHIÉ DÉSIRÉ GNANCHOU; Sec.-Gen. CHARLES ATTOUA GBANDA.

Eglise Harriste: 01 BP 3620, Abidjan 01; tel. 22-42-31-03; internet egliseharriste.org; f. 1913 by William Wadé Harris; affiliated to World Council of Churches 1998; allows polygamous new converts; 100,000 mems, 1,400 preachers, 7,000 apostles; Sec.-Gen. DOGBO JULES.

Eglise Méthodiste Unie de Côte d'Ivoire: 41 blvd de la République, 01 BP 1282, Abidjan 01; tel. 20-21-17-97; fax 20-22-52-03; e-mail emuciconf@yahoo.fr; internet www.emu-ci.org; f. 1924; publ. *Le Méthodiste* (monthly); autonomous since 1985; c. 800,000 mems; Pres. BENJAMIN BONI.

Eglise du Nazaréen (Church of the Nazarene): 22 BP 623, Abidjan 22; tel. 22-41-07-80; fax 22-41-07-81; e-mail awfcon@compuserve.com; internet www.nazarenemissions.org; f. 1987; active in evangelism, ministerial training and medical work; 4,429 mems; Dir JOHN SEAMAN.

Eglise Protestante Baptiste Oeuvres et Mission Internationale: 03 BP 1032, Abidjan 03; tel. 23-45-20-18; fax 23-45-56-41; e-mail epbomi@yahoo.com; internet www.epbomi.net; f. 1975; active in evangelism, teaching and social work; medical centre, 6,000 places of worship, 400 missionaries and 193,000 mems; Pres. Rev. Dr YAYE ROBERT DION.

Eglise Protestante Evangélique CMA de Côte d'Ivoire: BP 685, Abidjan 27; tel. 22-41-09-81; e-mail eglisecma_ci@ymail.com; internet www.eglisecma-ci.org; f. 1930; 350,000 mems; Nat. Pres. Rev. BROU PIERRE ALONLE; Sec.-Gen KOUASSI EMMANUEL KOUADIO.

Mission Evangélique de l'Afrique Occidentale (MEAO): 08 BP 1873, Abidjan 08; tel. and fax 22-47-59-95; e-mail hebohl@gmx.net; f. 1934; Team Leaders BRUCE PINKE, CAROLYN PINKE; affiliated church: Alliance des Eglises Evangéliques de Côte d'Ivoire (AEECI); 3 MEAO missionaries, 4 AEECI missionaries, 400 churches, 104 full-time pastors; Pres. ALAINGBRÉ PASCAL KOUASSI.

Union des Eglises Evangéliques, Services et Œuvres de Côte d'Ivoire: 08 BP 20, Abidjan 08; tel. 40-22-75-00; e-mail ueesoci63@yahoo.fr; internet www.ueeso-ci.org; f. 1927; c. 250 places of worship; Pres. GILBERT GOUENTOUEU; Sec.-Gen. MICHEL LOH.

WorldVenture: BP 109, Korhogo; tel. 36-86-01-07; fax 36-86-11-50; internet www.worldventure.com; f. 1947; fmrly Conservative Baptist Foreign Mission Society, subsequently CB International; active in evangelism, medical work, translation, literacy and theological education in the northern area and in Abidjan.

The Press

Conseil National de la Presse (CNP): Cocody-les-Deux-Plateaux, 1ère tranche, Villa 224 bis, BP V 106, Abidjan; tel. 22-40-53-53; fax 22-41-27-90; e-mail info@lecnp.ci; internet www.lecnp.com; f. 1991; Pres. DÉBY DALLI GBALAWOULOU; Sec.-Gen. RENÉ BOURGOIN.

DAILIES

24 Heures: rue St Jean, duplex 65, Cocody–Val Doyen I, 10 BP 3302, Abidjan 10; tel. 22-41-29-53; fax 22-41-37-82; e-mail infos@24heures.net; internet www.24heuresci.com; f. 2002; Dir-Gen. ABDOULAYE SANGARÉ; Dir of Publication and Editor-in-Chief JOACHIM BEUGRÉ; circ. 21,000 (2005).

Côte d'Ivoire Economie: Cocody-les-Deux-Plateaux, rue K24, 28 BP 1473, Abidjan 28; tel. 22-41-77-50; fax 22-41-76-16; e-mail info@cotedivoire-economie.com; internet www.cotedivoire-economie.com; f. 2010; Dir-Gen. and Dir of Publication MARION N'GOUAN EZZEDINE; Editor-in-Chief JEAN-PIERRE PONT.

Le Courrier d'Abidjan: Riviera Bonoumin, 25 BP 1682, Abidjan 25; tel. 22-43-38-22; fax 22-43-30-46; internet www.lecourrierdabidjan.info; f. 2003.

Douze: rue Louis Lumière, Zone 4C, 10 BP 2462, Abidjan 10; tel. 21-25-54-00; fax 21-24-47-27; e-mail douze@afnet.net; publ. by Editions Olympe; f. 1994; sport; Dir MAZÉ SOUMAHORO; Editor-in-Chief FRANÇOIS BINI.

Fraternité Matin: blvd du Général de Gaulle, 01 BP 1807, Abidjan 01; tel. 20-37-06-66; fax 20-37-25-45; e-mail contact@fratmat.info; internet www.fratmat.info; f. 1964; official newspaper; state-owned; Dir-Gen. JEAN-BAPTISTE AKROU; Editorial Dir ALFRED DAN MOUSSA; circ. 26,000 (2011).

L'Intelligent d'Abidjan: Villa 12S, Bâtiment Star 4, 19 BP 1534, Abidjan 19; tel. 22-42-71-61; fax 22-42-11-70; e-mail Editeur@lintelligentdabidjan.org; internet www.lintelligentdabidjan.org; f. 2003; Dir-Gen. W. ALAFÉ ASSÉ.

L'Inter: 10 BP 2462, Abidjan 10; tel. 21-21-28-00; fax 21-21-28-05; e-mail linter@linter-ci.com; internet www.linter-ci.com; f. 1998; publ. by Editions Olympe; national and international politics and economics; Dir RAYMOND N'CHO NIMBA; Editor-in-Chief CHARLES A. D'ALMÉIDA; circ. 18,000 (2002).

Le Jour Plus: 26 Cocody-les-Deux-Plateaux, 25 BP 1082, Abidjan 25; tel. 20-21-95-78; fax 20-21-95-80; f. 1994; publ. by Editions Le Nere; independent; Dir of Publication COULIBALY SEYDOU; Editor-in-Chief FRÉDÉRIC KOFFI; circ. 15,000 (2002).

Le Libéral: 01 BP 6938, Abidjan 01; tel. and fax 22-52-21-41; e-mail leliberal@aviso.ci; f. 1997; Dir YORO KONÉ; Editor-in-Chief BAKARY NIMAGA; circ. 15,000.

Le Matin d'Abidjan: Deux Plateaux Vallon 06, BP 2853, Abidjan 06; tel. 22-42-74-57; fax 22-42-59-06; e-mail info@lematindabidjan.com; internet www.lematindabidjan.com; Dir KOUAMENAN G. LAURENT.

Nord-Sud: Abidjan; internet nordsudquotidien.net; f. 2005; Dir TOURÉ MOUSSA; circ. 18,000 (2005).

Notre Voie: Cocody-les-Deux-Plateaux, 06 BP 2868, Abidjan 06; tel. 22-42-63-31; fax 22-42-63-32; e-mail gnh@africaonline.co.ci; internet www.notrevoie.com; f. 1978; organ of the FPI; Dir and Editor-in-Chief LAHOUA SOUANGA ETIENNE; circ. 20,000 (2002).

Le Nouveau Courrier: Abidjan; Editor-in-Chief SAINT-CLAVER OULA.

Le Nouveau Réveil: Adjamé Sud 80 Logements, Tours SICOGI, face Frat-Mat, Bâtiment A, 2e étage, porte 6, 01 BP 10684, Abidjan 01; tel. 20-38-42-00; fax 20-38-67-91; e-mail lenouveaureveil@yahoo.fr; internet www.lenouveaureveil.com; f. 2001 to replace weekly *Le Réveil-Hebdo*; supports PDCI—RDA; Dir-Gen. DENIS KAH ZION; Dir of Publication PATRICE YAO; circ. 18,000 (2005).

Le Patriote: 23 rue Paul Langevin, Zone 4C, 22 BP 509, Abidjan 22; tel. 21-21-19-45; fax 21-35-11-83; e-mail info@lepatriote.net; internet www.lepatriote.net; organ of the RDR; Dir of Publication CHARLES SANGA; Editor-in-Chief KORÉ EMMANUEL; circ. 40,000 (2002).

Soir Info: 10 BP 2462, Abidjan 10; tel. 21-21-28-00; fax 21-21-28-06; e-mail quotidiensoirinfo@yahoo.fr; internet www.soirinfo.com; f. 1994; publ. by Editions Olympe; independent; Dir VAMARA COULIBALY; Editor-in-Chief NAZAIRE KIKIÉ; circ. 22,000 (2002).

Le Sport: Cocody Attoban, face au Groupe Scolaire Jules Ferry, 09 BP 3685, Abidjan 09; tel. 22-43-92-54; fax 22-43-01-90; internet www.lesport.ci; Dir of Publication ASSI ADON AMÉDÉE.

Supersport: Abidjan; internet www.supersport.ci; f. 2006; Dir-Gen. HAMIDOU FOMBA.

La Voie: face Institut Marie-Thérèse Houphouët-Boigny, 17 BP 656, Abidjan 17; tel. 20-37-68-23; fax 20-37-74-76; organ of the FPI; Dir ABOU DRAHAMANE SANGARÉ; Man. MAURICE LURIGNAN.

SELECTED BI-WEEKLIES AND WEEKLIES

L'Agora: Immeuble Nana Yamoussou, ave 13, rue 38, Treichville, 01 BP 5326, Abidjan 01; tel. 21-34-11-72; f. 1997; weekly; Dir FERNAND DÉDÉ; Editor-in-Chief BAMBA ALEX SOULEYMANE.

Le Démocrate: Maison du Congrès, ave 2, Treichville, 01 BP 1212, Abidjan 01; tel. 21-24-45-88; fax 21-24-25-61; f. 1991; weekly; organ of the PDCI—RDA; Dir NOËL YAO.

Le Front: Immeuble Mistral, 3e étage, 220 Logements, 11 BP 11 2678, Abidjan 11; tel. 20-38-13-24; fax 20-38-70-83; e-mail quotidienlefront@yahoo.fr; internet www.lefront.com; two a week; Editorial Dir FATOUMATA COULIBALY; Editor KPOKPA BLÉ.

Gbich!: 10 BP 399, Abidjan 10; tel. and fax 21-26-31-94; e-mail gbich@assistweb.net; internet www.gbichonline.com; weekly; satirical; Editor-in-Chief MATHIEU BLEDOU.

Le Nouvel Horizon: 220 Logements, blvd du Général de Gaulle, Adjamé, 17 BP 656, Abidjan 17; tel. 20-37-68-23; f. 1990; weekly; organ of the FPI; Dir ABOU DRAHAMANE SANGARÉ; circ. 15,000.

La Nouvelle Presse: rue des Jardins, Cocody-les-Deux-Plateaux, 01 BP 8534, Abidjan 01; tel. 22-41-04-76; fax 22-41-04-15; e-mail jvieyra@africaonline.co.ci; f. 1992; weekly; publ. by Centre Africain de Presse et d'Edition; current affairs; Editors JUSTIN VIEYRA, JÉRÔME CARLOS; circ. 10,000.

Le Repère: 220 Logements, Adjamé Sud-Tours SICOGI, face Frat-Mat, Bâtiment A, 2e étage P6, 04 BP 1947, Abidjan 04; tel. and fax 20-38-67-91; supports PDCI—RDA; two a week; Dir of Publication DENIS KAH ZION; circ. 10,000 (2004).

Téré: 220 Logements, blvd du Général de Gaulle, Adjamé-Liberté, 20 BP 43, Abidjan 20; tel. and fax 20-37-79-42; weekly; organ of the PIT; Dir ANGÈLE GNONSOA.

Top-Visages: rue du Commerce, 23 BP 892, Abidjan 23; tel. 20-33-72-10; fax 20-32-81-05; e-mail contact@topvisages.net; internet www.topvisages.net; weekly; Editor-in-Chief E. TONGA BÉHI; circ. 40,000 (2004).

SELECTED PERIODICALS

Juris-Social: Centre National de Documentation Juridique (CNDJ), Villa 381, ilôt 43, face Polyclinique Saint Jacques, blvd Latrille, Cocody-les-Deux-Plateaux, 01 BP 2757, Abidjan 01; tel. 20-22-74-85; fax 20-22-74-86; e-mail cndj@aviso.ci; internet www.cndj.ci; monthly; jurisprudence; CNDJ also publishes quarterly periodical *Juris OHADA*.

La Lettre de l'Afrique de l'Ouest: rue des Jardins, Cocody-les-Deux-Plateaux, 01 BP 8534, Abidjan 01; tel. 22-41-04-76; fax 22-41-04-15; f. 1995; publ. by Centre Africain de Presse et d'Edition; six a year; politics, economics, regional integration; Editors JUSTIN VIEYRA, JÉRÔME CARLOS.

News&Co: Cocody 2 Plateaux Vallons, 28 BP 580, Abidjan 28; tel. 22-51-04-72; fax 22-51-04-73; e-mail info@newseco-ci.com; internet www.newseco-ci.com; monthly; financial and economic affairs; publ. by Publi Services Editions; Dir of Publication MARION N'GOUAN EZZEDINE; Editor-in-Chief ELODIE VERMEIL; circ. 10,000.

PME Magazine: Abidjan; tel. 22-48-80-76; fax 22-44-17-80; e-mail info@pmemag.ci; internet www.pmemag.ci; economics.

Roots-Rock Magazine: Abidjan; tel. 22-42-84-74; f. 1998; monthly; music; Dir DIOMANDÉ DAVID.

RTI-Mag: 08 BP 663, Abidjan 08; tel. 20-33-14-46; fax 20-32-12-06; publ. by Radiodiffusion-Télévision Ivoirienne; listings magazine.

Sentiers: 26 ave Chardy, 01 BP 2432, Abidjan 01; tel. 20-21-95-68; fax 20-21-95-80; e-mail redaction@aviso.ci; Editor-in-Chief DIÉGOU BAILLY.

Stades d'Afrique: blvd du Général de Gaulle, 01 BP 1807, Abidjan 01; tel. 20-37-06-66; fax 20-37-25-45; f. 2000; sports; monthly; Dir-Gen. EMMANUEL KOUASSI KOKORÉ; Editor-in-Chief HÉGAUD OUATTARA.

Le Succès: 21 BP 3748, Abidjan 21; tel. 20-37-71-64; monthly; Dir AKPLA PLAKATOU.

NEWS AGENCY

Agence Ivoirienne de Presse (AIP): ave Chardy, 04 BP 312, Abidjan 04; tel. 20-22-64-13; fax 20-21-35-99; e-mail aip@aip.ci; internet www.aip.ci; f. 1961; Dir OUMOU BARRY-SAN.

PRESS ASSOCIATIONS

Association de la Presse Démocratique Ivoirienne (APDI): Abidjan; tel. 20-37-06-66; f. 1994; Chair. JEAN-BAPTISTE AKROU.

Conseil National de la Presse: Cocody les Deux Plateaux 1ère tranche, No. 224 bis; BP V 106, Abidjan; tel. 22-40-53-53; fax 22-41-27-90; e-mail info@lecnp.ci; internet www.lecnp.com; f. 1991; Pres. RAPHAËL LAPKE.

Union Nationale des Journalistes de Côte d'Ivoire (UNJCI): 06 BP 1675, Plateau, Abidjan 06; tel. 20-21-61-07; e-mail prunjci@unjci.org; f. 1991; Pres. MAMERY CAMARA.

Publishers

Centre Africain de Presse et d'Edition (CAPE): rue des Jardins, Cocody-les-Deux-Plateaux, 01 BP 8534, Abidjan 01; tel. 22-41-04-76; fax 22-41-04-15; Man. JUSTIN VIEYRA.

Centre d'Edition et de Diffusion Africaines (CEDA): 17 rue des Carrossiers, 04 BP 541, Abidjan 04; tel. 20-24-65-10; fax 21-25-05-67; e-mail infos@ceda-ci.com; internet www.ceda-ci.com; f. 1961; 20% state-owned; general non-fiction, school and children's books, literary fiction; Pres. and Dir-Gen. VENANCE KACOU.

Centre de Publications Evangéliques: 08 BP 900, Abidjan 08; tel. 22-44-48-05; fax 22-44-58-17; e-mail cpe@aviso.ci; internet www.editionscpe.com; f. 1967; evangelical Christian; Dir JULES OUOBA.

Editions Bognini: 06 BP 1254, Abidjan 06; tel. 20-41-16-86; social sciences, literary fiction.

Editions Eburnie: 01 BP 1984, 01 Abidjan; tel. 20-21-64-65; fax 20-21-45-46; e-mail eburnie@aviso.ci; f. 2001; illustrated books for children, social sciences, poetry.

Editions Neter: 01 BP 7370, Abidjan 01; tel. 22-52-52-68; f. 1992; politics, culture, history, literary fiction; Dir RICHARD TA BI SENIN.

Nouvelles Editions Ivoiriennes: 1 blvd de Marseille, 01 BP 1818, Abidjan 01; tel. 21-24-07-66; fax 21-24-24-56; e-mail edition@nei-ci.com; internet www.nei-ci.com; f. 1972; literature, criticism, essays, drama, social sciences, history, in French and English; Dir GUY LAMBIN.

Presses Universitaires et Scolaires d'Afrique (PUSAF—Editions Cissé): 08 BP 177, Abidjan 08; tel. 22-41-12-71; mathematics, economics, medicine.

Université Nationale de Côte d'Ivoire: 01 BP V34, Abidjan 01; tel. 22-44-08-59; f. 1964; academic and general non-fiction and periodicals; Publications Dir GILLES VILASCO.

GOVERNMENT PUBLISHING HOUSE

Imprimerie Nationale: BP V87, Abidjan; tel. 20-21-76-11; fax 20-21-68-68; Dir-Gen. EMILE BOY KOUASSI.

Broadcasting and Communications

TELECOMMUNICATIONS

In 2011 there were six operators in the Côte d'Ivoire telecommunications market. Four of these provided mobile cellular telephone services, one provided fixed-line services and one provided both mobile and fixed-line services. A new mobile company, Aircom, commenced operations in April 2012 under the brand name Café Mobile.

Atlantique Telecom—Moov (Moov): Immeuble Karrat, rue du Commerce, 01 BP 2347, Abidjan 01; tel. 20-25-01-01; fax 20-25-26-62; e-mail moovcontact@moov.com; internet www.moov.com; f. 2005 as jt venture by Atlantique Télécom (Côte d'Ivoire) and Etisalat (United Arab Emirates); 80% owned by Etisalat (United Arab Emirates); mobile cellular telecommunications; CEO NAGI ABBOUD; 3.8m. subscribers (April 2012).

Comium: Blvd VGE Marcory, cnr rue Lumière, BP 2591, Abidjan 11; tel. 21-35-90-41; internet www.koz.ci; f. 2009; Pres. NIZAR DALLOUL; Dir-Gen MICHEL HEBERT; 1.8m. subscribers (April 2012).

Côte d'Ivoire-Télécom (CI-Télécom): Immeuble Postel 2001, rue Lecoeur, 17 BP 275, Abidjan 17; tel. 20-34-40-00; fax 20-21-28-28; internet www.citelecom.ci; f. 1991; 51% owned by France Télécom, 49% state-owned; Pres. Gen. MICHEL GUEU; Man. Dir MAMADOU BAMBA; 327,000 subscribers (June 2002).

Green Network (GreenN): Abidjan; tel. 60-00-60-60; internet www.greenn.ci; f. 2009; owned by Libya Africa Portfolio; operates under name of Oricel; Dir-Gen. ABDULGHANI RAMADAN; 2.9m. subscribers (April 2012).

MTN Côte d'Ivoire: Immeuble Loteny, 12 rue Crossons Duplessis, 01 BP 3685, Abidjan 01; tel. 20-31-63-16; fax 20-31-84-50; internet www.mtn.ci; f. 1996 as Loteny Télécom-Télécel; present name adopted 2005; mobile cellular telephone operator in more than 110 urban centres and on principal highway routes; 51% owned by Mobile Telephone Network International (South Africa); Chief Exec. WIM VAN HELLEPUTTE; 5.7m. subscribers (April 2012).

Orange Côte d'Ivoire: Immeuble Saha, blvd Valéry Giscard d'Estaing, Zone 4C, 11 BP 202, Abidjan 11; tel. 21-23-90-07; fax 21-23-90-11; internet www.orange.ci; f. 1996 as Ivoiris, present name adopted 2002; mobile cellular telephone operator in more than 60 urban centres; 85% owned by France Télécom; Man. Dir MAMADOU BAMBA; 6.2m. subscribers (April 2012).

Regulatory Authorities

Agence des Télécommunications de Côte d'Ivoire (ATCI): Immeuble Postel 2001, 4e étage, rue Lecoeur, 18 BP 2203, Abidjan 18; tel. 20-34-43-74; fax 20-34-43-75; e-mail courrier@atci.ci; internet www.atci.ci; f. 1995; Pres. LASSINA KONÉ; Dir-Gen. ARTHUR ALLOCO KOUASSI.

Conseil des Télécommunications de Côte d'Ivoire (CTCI): 17 BP 110, Abidjan 17; tel. 20-34-43-04; f. 1995; deals with issues of arbitration; Pres. LEMASSOU FOFANA.

BROADCASTING

Regulatory Authority

Haute Autorité de la Communication Audiovisuelle: Pl. de la République, 05 BP 56, Abidjan; tel. 20-31-15-80; internet www.haca.ci; f. 2011 to replace Conseil National de la Communication Audiovisuelle (CNCA); Pres. IBRAHIM SY SAVANÉ.

Radio

In 1993 the Government permitted the first commercial radio stations to broadcast in Côte d'Ivoire; of the five licences initially granted, four were to foreign stations. Between 1998 and early 2001, a further 52 licences were granted.

Radiodiffusion-Télévision Ivoirienne (RTI): blvd des Martyrs, Cocody, 08 BP883, Abidjan 08; tel. 22-48-61-62; fax 22-44-78-23; e-mail info.rti@rti.ci; internet www.rti.ci; f. 1962; state-owned; two national TV channels, La Première and TV2, and two national radio channels, La Nationale and Fréquence II; Pres. PASCAL BROU AKA; Dir-Gen. LAZARE AKA SAYÉ; Dir, La Première VICTOR DEBASS KPAN; Dir, TV2 ADÈLE DJEDJE; Dir, Radiodiffusion ELOI OULAÏ.

Abidjan 1: Deux Plateaux Hayat, au dessus de la pharcie des jardins, Abidjan; tel. 22-41-29-03; e-mail info@radioabidjan1.com; internet www.radioabidjan1.com; Dir JULIEN ADAYE.

City FM: Immeuble Alpha Cissé, avant la piscine d'Etat, Treichville, 01 BP 7207, Abidjan 01; tel. 21-25-10-28; f. 1999; Pres. and Man. Dir Me ALIOU SIBI.

Radio Espoir: 12 BP 27, Abidjan 12; tel. 21-75-68-01; fax 21-75-68-04; e-mail respoir@aviso.ci; internet www.radioespoir.ci; f. 1990; Roman Catholic; broadcasts in French, local and sub-regional languages; Dir Fr BASILE DIANÉ KOGNAN.

Radio JAM: Abidjan; tel. 21-25-08-73; e-mail radiojamofficiel@yahoo.fr; internet www.radiojam.biz; Dir FRANÇOIS KONIAN.

Radio Nostalgie: Immeuble Le Paris, ave Chardy, 01 BP 157, Abidjan 01; tel. 20-21-10-52; fax 20-21-85-53; e-mail contact@nostalgie.ci; internet www.nostalgie.ci; f. 1993; Dir-Gen. HERVÉ CORNUEL.

Radio Notre Dame: BP 1555, Yamoussoukro; tel. 30-64-41-55; e-mail nfo@radionotredame-yakro.com; internet www.radionotredame-yakro.com; broadcasts religious programmes; Dir-Gen. JEAN-CLAUDE ATSAIN.

Radio Peleforo Gbon: route Ferké km 2, BP 841, Korhogo; tel. 21-86-22-62; fax 21-86-20-33.

Radio Soleil: 16 BP 1179, Abidjan 16; tel. 21-99-17-64; fax 21-79-12-48; e-mail badouel_jeannette@yahoo.fr; f. 2001; Dir JEANNETTE BADOUEL.

Côte d'Ivoire also receives broadcasts from the Gabon-based Africa No 1 radio station, from the French-language Africa service of the BBC (United Kingdom), and from Radio France Internationale.

Television

Radiodiffusion-Télévision Ivoirienne (RTI): see Radio section.

Canal+ Côte d'Ivoire: Immeuble Alpha 2000, 01 BP 1132, Abidjan 01; tel. 20-31-99-97; fax 20-22-72-22; e-mail abonne@canalhorizons.ci; internet www.canalplus-afrique.com; broadcasts commenced 1994; subsidiary of Canal Plus (France); Dir-Gen. SERGE AGNÉRO.

Finance

(cap. = capital; res = reserves; dep. = deposits; m. = million; brs = branches; amounts in francs CFA, unless otherwise indicated)

BANKING

In early 2013 there were 24 commercial banks and one financial institution in Côte d'Ivoire. Following the disputed presidential election of 28 November 2010, a number of commercial banking institutions announced the suspension of their operations. Of these, the Banque Internationale pour le Commerce et l'Industrie de la Côte d'Ivoire, Citibank, the Société Générale de Banques en Côte d'Ivoire and the Standard Chartered Bank Côte d'Ivoire were later forcibly nationalized by Laurent Gbagbo, who refused to relinquish the presidency. The Bourse Régionale des Valeurs Mobilières also suspended its operations, but subsequently resumed them from a new base in Bamako, Mali. Gbagbo was detained in April 2011, and in early May the legitimately-elected President, Alassane Ouattara, confirmed that banking operations in the country would recommence.

Central Bank

Banque Centrale des Etats de l'Afrique de l'Ouest (BCEAO): blvd Botreau-Roussel, angle ave Delafosse, 01 BP 1769, Abidjan 01; tel. 20-20-85-00; fax 20-22-28-52; e-mail webmaster@bceao.int; internet www.bceao.int; f. 1962; HQ in Dakar, Senegal; bank of issue for the mem. states of the Union Economique et Monétaire Ouest-Africaine (UEMOA, comprising Benin, Burkina Faso, Côte d'Ivoire, Guinea-Bissau, Mali, Niger, Senegal and Togo); cap. 134,120m., res 1,474,195m., dep. 2,124,051m. (Dec. 2009); Gov. KONÉ TIÉMOKO MEYLIET; Dir in Côte d'Ivoire JEAN-BAPTISTE AMAN AYAYE; 7 brs in Côte d'Ivoire.

Commercial Banks

Access Bank Cote d'Ivoire: 6e étage, Immeuble Alliance, 17 ave Terrasson de Fougères, 01 BP 6928, Abidjan 01; tel. 20-21-42-08; fax 20-21-42-58; e-mail info.cotedivoire@accessbankplc.com; internet subs.accessbankplc.com; f. 1996; name changed as above in 2008; 88% owned by Access Bank (Nigeria); cap. 3,000m. (Dec. 2005); Pres. JACOB AWUKU AMEMATEKPO; Dir-Gen. AMADOU LY.

Bank of Africa-Côte d'Ivoire (BOA-CI): ave Terrasson de Fougères, angle Rue Gourgas, 01 BP 4132, Abidjan 01; tel. 20-30-34-00; fax 20-30-34-01; e-mail boaci@bkofafrica.com; internet www.bank-of-africa.net; f. 1996; 68.1% owned by BOA Group (Luxembourg); cap. 7,200m., res 7,142m., dep. 186,325m., total assets 213,900m. (Dec. 2010); Dir-Gen. LALA MOULAYE; 18 brs.

Banque Atlantique Côte d'Ivoire (BACI): Immeuble Atlantique, ave Noguès, Plateau, 04 BP 1036, Abidjan 04; tel. 20-31-59-50; fax 20-21-68-52; e-mail kone.dossongui@banqueatlantique.net; internet www.banqueatlantique.net; f. 1979; merged with Compagnie Bancaire de l'Atlantique Côte d'Ivoire in 2009; cap. and res 13,230m., dep. 224,832m. (Dec. 2007); Pres. SOULEYMANE DIARRASSOUBA; Dir-Gen. HABIB KONÉ; 3 brs.

Banque de l'Habitat de Côte d'Ivoire (BHCI): 22 ave Joseph Anoma, 01 BP 2325, Abidjan 01; tel. 20-25-39-39; fax 20-22-58-18; e-mail info@bhci.ci; internet www.bhci.ci; f. 1993; cap. and res 1,755m., total assets 16,834m. (Dec. 1999); Chair. DAVID AMUAH; Man. Dir SOULEYMANE DOGONI; 3 brs.

Banque pour le Financement de l'Agriculture (BFA): Immeuble Alliance B, 2e étage, rue Lecoeur, BP 103 Poste Entreprise, Cedex 1, Abidjan; tel. 20-25-61-61; fax 20-25-61-99; e-mail info@bfa.ci; internet www.bfa.ci; Dir-Gen. WENCESLAS APPIA; 4 brs.

Banque Internationale pour le Commerce et l'Industrie de la Côte d'Ivoire SA (BICI-CI): ave Franchet d'Espérey, 01 BP 1290, Abidjan 01; tel. 20-20-16-00; fax 20-20-17-00; e-mail michel.lafont@africa.bnpparibas.com; internet www.bicici.com; f. 1962; 67.5% owned by BNP Paribas (France); absorbed BICI Bail de Côte d'Ivoire in 2003 and Compagnie Financière de la Côte d'Ivoire in 2004; cap. 16,666.6m., res 15,643.8m., dep. 314,370.7 (Dec. 2011); Chair. ANGE KOFFY; 39 brs.

Banque Nationale d'Investissement (BNI): Immeuble SCIAM, ave Marchand, Plateau, 01 BP 670, Abidjan 01; tel. 20-20-98-00; fax 20-21-35-78; e-mail info@bni-ci.net; internet www.bni.ci; f. 1959 as Caisse Autonome d'Amortissement de Côte d'Ivoire (CAA); name and operations changed as above in 2004; cap. and res 28,408m., total assets 253,668m. (Dec. 2003); Dir-Gen. EUGÈNE NDA KASSI.

BIAO-Côte d'Ivoire (BIAO-CI): 8–10 ave Joseph Anoma, 01 BP 1274, Abidjan 01; tel. 20-20-07-20; fax 20-20-07-00; e-mail info@biao.co.ci; internet www.biao.co.ci; f. 1980; fmrly Banque Internationale pour l'Afrique de l'Ouest—Côte d'Ivoire; 20% state-owned; cap. 20,000m., res 729m., dep. 118,135m. (Dec. 2009); Pres. SEYDOU ELIMANE DIARRA; Dir-Gen. PHILIPPE ATTOBRA; 31 brs.

La Caisse d'Epargne de Côte d'Ivoire: 11 ave Joseph Anoma, 01 BP 6889, Abidjan 01; tel. 20-25-43-00; fax 20-25-53-11; e-mail info@caissepargne.ci; internet www.caissepargne.ci; f. 1998; Pres. KOUMAN MOISE YAO; Dir-Gen. MAMAH DIABAGATÉ.

Citibank Côte d'Ivoire: Immeuble Botreau-Roussel, 28 ave Delafosse, 01 BP 3698, Abidjan 01; tel. 20-20-90-00; fax 20-21-76-85; e-mail citibank@odaci.net; f. 1976; total assets US $198.7m. (2003); Dir-Gen. KEVIN MURRAY.

COFIPA Investment Bank CI: Immeuble Botreau Roussel, 5e étage, ave Delafosse, 04 BP 411, Abidjan 04; tel. 20-30-23-00; fax 20-30-23-01; e-mail Info@cofipa.ci; internet www.cofipa.ci; cap. and res 2,382.5m., total assets 19,171.2m. (Dec. 2002); Chair. MACAULEY OVIA; Man. Dir and CEO GUY KOIZAN; 49 brs.

Ecobank Côte d'Ivoire: Immeuble Alliance, 1 ave Terrasson de Fougères, 01 BP 4107, Abidjan 01; tel. 20-31-92-00; fax 20-21-88-16; e-mail ecobankci@ecobank.com; internet www.ecobank.com; f. 1989;

94% owned by Ecobank Transnational Inc (Togo); cap. 21,438.2m, res 10,269.6m, dep. 463,284.7m, total assets 639,488.3m. (Dec. 2012); Chair. PIERRE RENÉ MAGNE; Dir-Gen. CHARLES DABOIKO; 16 brs.

Guaranty Trust Bank Côte d'Ivoire SA: 11 ave du Senateur Lagarosse, Plateau, 01 BP 13141, Abidjan 01; tel. 20-31-15-00; fax 20-31-15-15; e-mail informations.ci@gtbank.com; internet www.gtbankci.com; f. 2012; Dir-Gen. OULIMATA NDIAYE.

Orabank Côte d'Ivoire: ave Joseph Anoma, angle blvd République, BP 312, Abidjan; tel. 20-25-55-54; fax 20-21-07-68; fmrly Banque Régionale de Solidarité Côte d'Ivoire; name changed as above in 2014; owned by Oragroup SA (Togo).

Société Générale de Banques en Côte d'Ivoire (SGBCI): 5–7 ave Joseph Anoma, 01 BP 1355, Abidjan 01; tel. 20-20-12-34; fax 20-20-14-92; e-mail info.sgbci@socgen.com; internet www.sgbci.ci; f. 1962; 66.8% owned by Société Générale (France); cap. 15,556m., res 57,153m., dep. 230,082m. (Dec. 2011); Pres. TIÉMOKO YADÉ COULIBALY; Dir-Gen. BERNARD LABADENS; 41 brs.

Société Ivoirienne de Banque (SIB): Immeuble Alpha 2000, 34 blvd de la République, 01 BP 1300, Abidjan 01; tel. 20-20-00-00; fax 20-20-01-19; e-mail info@sib.ci; internet www.sib.ci; f. 1962; 51% owned by Calyon, Paris La Défense (France), 49% state-owned; reduction of state holding to 19% proposed; cap. 10,000m., res 4,803m., dep. 174,683m., total assets 234,963m. (Dec. 2009); Pres. LAMBERT FEH KESSE; Administrator and Dir-Gen. MOUNIR OUDGHIRI; 15 brs.

Standard Chartered Bank Côte d'Ivoire (SCBCI): 23 blvd de la République, face Commissariat du 1er arrondissement, 17 BP 1141, Abidjan 17; tel. 20-30-32-00; fax 20-30-32-01; e-mail info.CDI@sc.com; internet www.standardchartered.com/ci; f. 2001; subsidiary of Standard Chartered Bank (United Kingdom); cap. and res 9,218m., total assets 76,289m. (Dec. 2003); Pres. EBENEZER ESSOKA; CEO SERGES BAILLY; 4 brs.

United Bank for Africa Côte d'Ivoire: blvd Botreau-Roussel, Plateau, 01 BP 1874, Abidjan; tel. 20-31-22-22; fax 20-31-22-26; e-mail ubacotedivoire@ubagroup.com; internet www.ubagroup.com/ubacotedivoire; f. 2008; Dir-Gen. FRANKLIN EREBOR.

Versus Bank: Immeuble CRAAE-UMOA, blvd Botreau Roussel, angle ave Joseph Anoma, 01 BP 1874, Abidjan 01; tel. 20-25-60-60; fax 20-25-60-99; e-mail infos@versusbank.com; internet www.versusbank.com; f. 2004; cap. 3,000m.; Pres. DANO DJÉDJÉ; Dir-Gen. GUY KOIZAN.

Credit Institution

Société Africaine de Crédit Automobilier (SAFCA): 1 rue des Carrossiers, Zone 3, 04 BP 27, Abidjan 04; tel. 21-21-07-07; fax 21-21-07-00; e-mail cotedivoire@alios-finance.com; internet www.alios-finance.com; f. 1956; also known as Alios Finance Côte d'Ivoire; cap. and res 5,681.8m., total assets 22,511.1m. (Dec. 2001); Pres. JAN-ALBERT VALK; Dir-Gen. THIERRY PAPILLION.

Bankers' Association

Association Professionnelle des Banques et Etablissements Financiers de Côte d'Ivoire (APBEFCI): Immeuble Aniaman, ave Lamblin, 01 BP 3810, Abidjan 01; tel. 20-32-20-08; fax 20-32-69-60; internet www.apbef-ci.org; affiliated to Confédération Générale des Entreprises de Côte d'Ivoire (q.v.); Pres. SOULEYMANE DIARRASSOUBA.

STOCK EXCHANGE

Bourse Régionale des Valeurs Mobilières (BRVM): 18 ave Joseph Anoma, 01 BP 3802, Abidjan 01; tel. 20-32-66-85; fax 20-32-66-84; e-mail brvm@brvm.org; internet www.brvm.org; f. 1998 to succeed Bourse des Valeurs d'Abidjan; regional stock exchange serving mem. states of UEMOA; Pres. GABRIEL FAL; Dir-Gen. EDOH KOSSI AMENOUNVE.

INSURANCE

In 2009 there were 32 insurance companies in Côte d'Ivoire, of which 21 provided non-life insurance and 11 provided life insurance.

Alliance Africaine d'Assurances (3A): Immeuble Le Mans, 6e étage, ave Botreau Roussel, 01 BP 11944, Abidjan 01; tel. 20-33-85-07; fax 20-33-88-14; e-mail aaavie@aaavie.com; internet www.3a-vie.com; Dir-Gen. DRAMANE CISSE.

Allianz Côte d'Ivoire: 2 blvd Roume, 01 BP 1741, Abidjan 01; tel. 20-30-40-00; fax 20-30-40-01; e-mail groupe-safarriv@safarriv.ci; internet www.agf-ci.com; f. 1975; affiliated to AGF Afrique; Dir-Gen. RENÉ BUCAIONI.

AMSA Assurances: 19 ave Delafosse, 01 BP 1333, Abidjan 01; tel. 20-30-05-00; fax 20-30-05-45; e-mail amsa-ci@amsa-group.com; internet amsa-group.com; f. 1972; fmrly Compagnie Nationale d'Assurances; cap. 400m.; insurance and reinsurance; Dir-Gen. IBRAHIM CHERIF.

Atlantique Assurances Côte d'Ivoire: Immeuble MACI, 2e étage, 15 ave Joseph Anoma, Plateau, 01 BP 1841, Abidjan 01; tel. 20-31-78-00; fax 20-33-18-37; e-mail atlantiqueassurances@atlantiqueassurances.net; f. 1956; Dir-Gen. ROSALIE LOGON.

AXA Assurances Côte d'Ivoire: ave Lamine Fadiga Prolongée, 01 BP 378, Abidjan 01; tel. 20-31-88-88; fax 20-31-88-00; e-mail axarci@africaonline.co.ci; f. 1981; fmrly l'Union Africaine-IARD; insurance and reinsurance; Dir-Gen. ROGER BOA.

Colina: Immeuble Colina, blvd Roume 3, 01 BP 3832, Abidjan 01; tel. 20-25-36-00; fax 20-22-59-05; e-mail colinaci@groupecolina.com; internet www.groupecolina.com; f. 1980; life and non-life; Chair. MOULAY HAFID ELALAMY; Dir-Gen. (non-life) ALFRED JOËL ACKAH; Dir-Gen. (life) RAOUL MOLOKO.

Génération Nouvelle d'Assurances Côte d'Ivoire (GNA-CI): Ground Floor, Immeuble l'Ebrien, rue du commerce, 04 BP 1522, Abidjan 04; tel. 20-25-98-00; fax 20-33-60-65; internet www.gnassurances.com; f. 2006; Pres. BARTHÉLEMY VIDJANNANGNI; Dir-Gen. FÉLIX KOUAME ZEGBE N'GUESSAN.

Gras Savoye Côte d'Ivoire: Immeuble Trade Center, ave Noguès, 01 BP 5675, Abidjan 01; tel. 20-25-25-00; fax 20-25-25-25; e-mail grassavoyeci@ci.grassavoye.com; affiliated to Gras Savoye (France); Man. JEAN-FRANÇOIS ALAUZE.

Nouvelle Société Africaine d'Assurances (NSIA—CI): Immeuble Manci, rue A43, 01 BP 1571, Abidjan 01; tel. 20-31-75-00; fax 20-31-98-00; e-mail nsia@africaoline.co.ci; f. 1995; Pres. and Dir-Gen. JANINE DIAGOU WODIÉ.

NSIA-Vie: Immeuble Zandaman, ave Noguès, 01 BP 4092, Abidjan 01; tel. 20-31-98-00; fax 20-33-25-79; f. 1988; fmrly Assurances Générales de Côte d'Ivoire-Vie (AGCI-Vie); life; Pres. and Dir-Gen. JEAN KACOU DIAGOU.

Serenity: 41 blvd Général de Gaulle (face gare sud), Immeuble Ex-Monoprix, 01 BP 10244, Abidjan 01; tel. 20-32-16-52; fax 20-32-16-63; e-mail serenity@serenity-sa.com; internet www.serenity-sa.com; f. 2009; Pres. and Dir-Gen. MAURICE KIPRÉ DIGBEU.

Union des Assurances de Côte d'Ivoire (UA-Vie): 9 ave Houdaille, 01 BP 2016, Abidjan 01; tel. 20-31-04-00; fax 20-22-37-60; e-mail info@uavie.ci; internet www.uavie.ci; f. 1985; fmrly Union Africaine Vie, subsequently AXA Vie Côte d'Ivoire; present name adopted 2005; life assurance and capitalization; Dir-Gen. MOHAMED LAMINE BAH.

Trade and Industry

GOVERNMENT AGENCIES

Agence Nationale d'Appui au Développement Rural (-ANADER): blvd de la paix Abidjan, BP V183, Abidjan; tel. 21-35-46-99; fax 21-35-46-74; e-mail anader@anader.ci; internet www.anader.ci; f. 1993 to replace CIDV, SATMACI and SODEPRA; Man. Dir SIDIKI CISSÉ.

Autorité pour la Régulation du Café et du Cacao (ARCC): blvd Botreau Roussel, Immeuble Caistab 17ème–19ème étages, Plateau, 25 BP 1501, Abidjan 25; tel. 20-20-29-87; fax 20-20-27-05; e-mail courrier@arcc.ci; internet www.arcc.ci; f. 2000; implements regulatory framework for coffee and cocoa trade; Pres. GILBERT N'GUESSAN.

Bureau National d'Etudes Techniques et de Développement (BNETD): blvd Hassan II, Cocody, 04 BP 945, Abidjan 04; tel. 22-48-34-00; fax 22-44-56-66; e-mail info@bnetd.ci; internet www.bnetd.ci; f. 1978 as Direction et Contrôle des Grands Travaux; management and supervision of major public works projects; Dir-Gen. KRA KOFFI PASCAL.

Comité de Privatisation: 6 blvd de l'Indénié, 01 BP 1141, Abidjan 01; tel. 20-22-22-31; fax 20-22-22-35; f. 1990; state privatization authority; Pres. PAUL AGODIO; Dir-Gen. AHOUA DON MELLO.

Conseil de Régulation, de Stabilisation et de Développement de la Filière Café-Cacao (Conseil du Café-Cacao): Immeuble Caistab, 23e étage, 17 BP 797, Abidjan 17; tel. 20-25-69-69; fax 20-21-83-30; e-mail info@conseilcafecacao.ci; internet www.conseilcafecacao.ci; f. 2012 to replace the Comite de Gestion de la Filière Café-Cacao; comprises the Autorité pour la Régulation du Café et du Cacao (ARCC), the Bourse du Café et du Cacao (BCC), the Fonds de Régulation et de Contrôle du Café et du Cacao (FRCC) and the Fonds de Développement et de Promotion des Activités des Producteurs de Café et de Cacao (FDPCC); Pres. LAMBERT KOUASSI KONAN; Dir-Gen. MASSANDJÉ TOURÉ-LITSE.

Conseil Economique et Social: angle blvd Carde et ave Terrason de Fougère, 04 BP 304, Abidjan 04; tel. 20-21-14-54; internet ces-ci.org; f. 1961; Pres. MARCEL ZADI KESSY.

Fonds de Régulation et de Contrôle du Café et du Cacao (FRCC): Immeuble Caistab, 17 BP 797, Abidjan 17; tel. 20-20-27-11; fax 20-21-83-30; e-mail frc@frc.ci; internet www.frc.ci; f. 2002; assists small-scale producers and exporters of coffee and cocoa; administrative bd comprises five representatives of producers, two of exporters, three of banks and insurance cos, two of the state; Pres. ANGELINE KILI; Dir-Gen. FIRMIN KOUAKOU.

PETROCI: Immeuble les Hévéas, 14 blvd Carde, BP V194, Abidjan 01; tel. 20-20-25-00; fax 20-21-68-24; e-mail info@petroci.ci; internet www.petroci.ci; f. 1975 as Société Nationale d'Opérations Pétrolières de la Côte d'Ivoire (PETROCI); restructured 2000 to comprise three companies—Petroci Exploration Production, SA, Petroci Gaz and Petroci Industries Services; all aspects of hydrocarbons devt; Pres. PAUL GUI DIBO; Dir-Gen. DANIEL GNAGNI.

Société de Développement des Forêts (SODEFOR): blvd François Mitterrand, 01 BP 3770, Abidjan 01; tel. 22-48-30-00; fax 22-44-02-40; e-mail info@sodefor.ci; internet www.sodefor.ci; f. 1966; establishment and management of tree plantations, sustainable management of state forests, marketing of timber products; Dir-Gen. SANGARÉ MAMADOU.

Société pour le Développement Minier de la Côte d'Ivoire (SODEMI): 31 blvd des Martyrs, 01 BP 2816, Abidjan 01; tel. 22-44-29-94; fax 22-44-08-21; e-mail sodemidg@aviso.cg; internet www.sodemi.ci; f. 1962; geological and mineral research; Man. Dir KOUAMÉ KADIO.

DEVELOPMENT AGENCIES

Agence Française de Développement (AFD): blvd François Mitterrand, 01 BP 1814, Abidjan 01; tel. 22-40-70-40; fax 22-44-21-78; e-mail afdabidjan@afd.fr; internet www.afd.fr; Country Dir BRUNO LECLERC.

Association pour la Promotion des Exportations de Côte d'Ivoire (Apex-CI): Immeuble Tropique 3, Mezzanine 1 et 2, blvd de la République, 01 BP 3485, Abidjan 01; tel. 20-30-25-30; fax 20-21-75-76; e-mail info@apex-ci.org; internet www.apex-ci.org; Dir-Gen. GUY M'BENGUE.

Centre de Promotion des Investissements en Côte d'Ivoire (CEPICI): Immeuble Belle-Rive, 16ème étage, BP V152, Abidjan 01; tel. 20-31-14-00; fax 20 31 14 09; e-mail infos-cepici@cepici.ci; internet www.cepici.gouv.ci; f. 1993; investment promotion authority; Dir-Gen. EMMANUEL ESSIS ESMEL.

France Volontaires: 01 BP 2532, Abidjan; tel. 20-22-85-09; fax 20-22-05-96; internet www.france-volontaires.org; f. 1965; name changed as above in 2009; Nat. Representative ALEXIS K. SOUNGALO.

Institut de Recherche pour le Développement: Quartier Marcory Zone 4C, rue Dr Alexander Fleming, 15 BP 917, Abidjan 15; tel. 21-35-96-03; fax 21-35-40-15; e-mail cote-ivoire@ird.fr; internet www.ird.ci; Admin. SÉKOU YEO.

CHAMBERS OF COMMERCE

Chambre Nationale d'Agriculture: 11 ave Lamblin, 01 BP 1291, Abidjan 01; tel. 20-32-92-13; fax 20-32-92-20; Pres. BAMBA SINDOU.

Chambre de Commerce et d'Industrie de Côte d'Ivoire (CCI-CI): 6 ave Joseph Anoma, 01 BP 1399, Abidjan 01; tel. 20-33-16-00; fax 20-30-43-42; e-mail info@cci.ci; internet www.cci.ci; f. 1992; Pres. NICOLAS YOUSSOUF DJIBO; Dir-Gen. MARIE-GABRIELLE BOKA-VARLET.

TRADE ASSOCIATIONS

Association Nationale des Organisations Professionnelles Agricoles de Côte d'Ivoire (ANOPACI): Cocody Cité des Arts, Derrière la Cité BAD, rue C7, 20 BP 937, Abidjan 20; tel. 22-44-11-76; e-mail anopaci@yahoo.fr; f. 1998; Pres. MATHIAS N'GOAN.

Bourse du Café et du Cacao (BCC): 04 BP 2576, Abidjan 04; tel. 20-20-27-20; fax 20-20-28-14; e-mail info@bcc.ci; internet www.bcc.ci; f. 2001 to replace marketing, purchasing and certain other functions of La Nouvelle Caistab (Caisse de Stabilisation et de Soutien des Prix des Productions Agricoles); Pres. LUCIEN TAPÉ DOH; Dir-Gen. TANO KASSI KADIO.

Fédération Ivoirienne des Producteurs de Café et de Cacao (FIPCC): Yamoussoukro; f. 1998; coffee and cocoa growers' asscn; Chair. CISSÉ LOCINÉ; c. 3,000 mems.

Organisation de Commercialisation de l'Ananas et de la Banane (OCAB): Abidjan; pineapple and banana growers' asscn; Pres. MICHEL GNUI; Exec. Sec. EMMANUEL DOLI.

EMPLOYERS' ORGANIZATIONS

Association Nationale des Paysans de Côte d'Ivoire (ANAPA-CI): Bouaké; Pres. KONÉ WAYARAGA.

Association Nationale des Producteurs de Café-Cacao de Côte d'Ivoire (ANAPROCI): BP 840, San-Pédro; tel. 34-71-20-98; fax 34-71-14-65; Pres. BOTI BI ZOUA; Sec.-Gen. THOMAS EYIMIN.

Confédération Générale des Entreprises de Côte d'Ivoire: 01 BP 8666, Abidjan 01; tel. 20-30-08-21; fax 20-22-28-25; e-mail cgeci@cgeci.org; internet www.cgeci.org; f. 1993 as Conseil National du Patronat Ivoirion; current name adopted 2005; Pres. JEAN KACOU DIAGOU; Dir-Gen. LAKOUN OUATTARA; nine affiliated federations, including the following:

Fédération Maritime de Côte d'Ivoire (FEDERMAR): Treichville, ave Christiani, 01 BP 4082, Abidjan 01; tel. 21-22-08-09; fax 21-22-07-90; e-mail issouf.fadika@ci.dti.bollore.com; f. 1958; Pres. ISSOUF FADIKA; Sec.-Gen. VACABA TOURÉ DE MOVALY.

Fédération Nationale des Industries et Services de Côte d'Ivoire (FNISCI): Immeuble Les Harmonies, 1er étage, Plateau, Abidjan 01; tel. 20-31-90-70; fax 20-21-72-56; e-mail infos@fnisci.net; internet www.fnisci.net; f. 1993; Pres. JOSEPH-DESIRÉ BILEY; Dir-Gen. LOUIS S. AMÉDÉ; 180 mems.

Groupement Ivoirien du Bâtiment et des Travaux Publics (GIBTP): 25 rue des Carrossiers, Concession SIDELAF, zone 3, 01 BP 464, Abidjan 01; tel. 21-25-29-46; fax 21-25-29-57; f. 1934 as Syndicat des Entrepreneurs et des Industriels de la Côte d'Ivoire; present name adopted 1997; Pres. KONGO KOUADIO KOUASSI.

Syndicat Autonome des Producteurs de Café-Cacao de Côte d'Ivoire (SYNAPROCI): Abidjan; f. 2003; Pres. BANNY KOFFI GERMAIN (acting).

Syndicat des Exportateurs et Négociants en Bois de Côte d'Ivoire: route du Lycée Technique, Cocody Danga, Villa No. 4, 01 BP 1979, Abidjan 01; tel. 22-44-44-80; fax 22-44-44-74; e-mail unemaf@africaonline.co.ci; f. 1960; Pres. SOULEYMANE COULIBALY.

Syndicat des Producteurs Industriels du Bois (SPIB): route du Lycée Technique, Cocody Danga, Villa No. 4, 01 BP 318, Abidjan; tel. 22-44-44-80; fax 22-44-44-74; e-mail unemaf@africaonline.co.ci; internet www.spib.ci; f. 1943; Pres. BOUBARCAR BEN SALAH.

Union des Entreprises Agricoles et Forestières: route du Lycée Technique, Cocody Danga, Villa No. 4, 01 BP 2300, Abidjan 01; tel. 22-44-44-80; fax 22-44-44-74; e-mail unemaf@aviso.ci; internet www.unemaf.org; f. 1952; Pres. YORO BI TRAZIÉ.

UTILITIES

Electricity

Compagnie Ivoirienne d'Electricité (CIE): 1 ave Christiani, 01 BP 6932, Abidjan 01; tel. 21-23-34-70; fax 21-23-63-22; e-mail info@cie.ci; internet www.groupecie.net; f. 1990; 71% controlled by Société Bouygues group (France); Pres. OUSMANE DIARRA; Dir-Gen. DOMINIQUE KACOU.

Compagnie Ivoirienne de Production d'Electricité (CIPREL): Tour Sidom, 12e étage, ave Houdaille, 01 BP 4039, Abidjan 01; tel. 20-22-60-97; independent power production; Dir-Gen. BERNARD KOUASSI N'GUESSAN.

Gas

Gaz de Côte d'Ivoire (GDCI): 01 BP 1351, Abidjan; tel. 22-44-49-55; f. 1961; transfer to majority private ownership pending; gas distributor; Man. Dir LAMBERT KONAN.

Water

Société de Distribution d'Eau de la Côte d'Ivoire (SODECI): 1 ave Christiani, Treichville, 01 BP 1843, Abidjan 01; tel. 21-23-30-00; fax 21-24-30-06; e-mail sodeci@sodeci.ci; internet www.sodeci.com; f. 1959; production, treatment and distribution of drinking water; 46% owned by Groupe Bouygues (France), 51% owned by employees; Pres. FIRMIN AHOUNÉ; Dir-Gen. BASILE EBAH.

TRADE UNIONS

Fédération des Syndicats Autonomes de la Côte d'Ivoire (FESACI): Abidjan; breakaway group from the Union Générale des Travailleurs de Côte d'Ivoire; Sec.-Gen. KOUAMÉ KRA FÉLIX.

Union Générale des Travailleurs de Côte d'Ivoire (UGTCI): Bourse du Travail de Treichville, 05 BP 1203, Abidjan 05; tel. and fax 21-24-09-78; fax 20-24-08-83; e-mail ugtcisg@yahoo.fr; internet www.ugtci.org; f. 1962; Sec.-Gen. JOSEPH LÉON EBAGNERIN; 108,000 individual mems; 157 affiliated unions.

Transport

RAILWAYS

The rail network in Côte d'Ivoire totalled 1,316 km in 2000, including 660 km of track from Abidjan to Niangoloko, on the border with Burkina Faso; from there, the railway extends to Kaya, via the Burkinabè capital, Ouagadougou. Work on a 737-km railway project linking San-Pédro with the western parts of the country was expected to begin in 2014.

SITARAIL—Transport Ferroviaire de Personnel et de Marchandises: Résidence Memanou, blvd Clozel, Plateau, 16 BP 1216, Abidjan 16; tel. 20-20-80-00; fax 20-22-48-47; f. 1995 to operate services on Abidjan–Ouagadougou–Kaya (Burkina Faso) line; Man. Dir JOËL HOUNSINOU.

ROADS

In 2007 there were about 81,996 km of roads, of which some 6,500 km were paved. Tolls were introduced on some roads in the mid-1990s, to assist in funding the maintenance of the network. In December 2013 a 230-km highway connecting Abidjan with Yamoussoukro was inaugurated.

Fonds d'Entretien Routier (FER): Immeuble FER, ave Chardy, Plateau, 04 BP 3089, Abidjan 04; tel. 20-31-13-05; e-mail fer@aviso.ci; f. 2001; Dir-Gen. SIANDOU FOFANA.

Société des Transports Abidjanais (SOTRA): 01 BP 2009, Abidjan 01; tel. 21-24-90-80; fax 21-25-97-21; e-mail infos@sotra.ci; internet www.sotra.ci; f. 1960; 60% state-owned; urban transport; Dir-Gen. BOUAKÉ MÉITÉ.

SHIPPING

Côte d'Ivoire has two major ports, Abidjan and San-Pédro, both of which are industrial and commercial establishments with financial autonomy. Abidjan, which handled some 14.5m. metric tons of goods in 2003, is the largest container and trading port in West Africa. Access to the port is via the 2.7-km Vridi Canal. The port at San-Pédro remains the main gateway to the south-western region of Côte d'Ivoire. At 31 December 2013 the country's flag registered fleet comprised 19 vessels, with a total displacement of 3,858 grt.

Port Autonome d'Abidjan (PAA): BP V85, Abidjan; tel. 21-23-80-00; fax 21-23-80-80; e-mail info@paa-ci.org; internet www.paa-ci.org; f. 1992; transferred to private ownership in 1999; Pres. KANTÉ KOLY; Man. Dir HIEN SIÉ.

Port Autonome de San-Pédro (PASP): BP 339/340, San-Pédro; tel. 34-71-72-00; fax 34-71-72-15; e-mail pasp@pasp.ci; internet www.sanpedro-portci.com; f. 1971; Pres. JEAN-BAPTISTE KOUAMÉ; Man. Dir HILAIRE MARCEL LAMIZANA.

CIVIL AVIATION

There are three international airports: Abidjan–Félix Houphouët-Boigny, Bouaké and Yamoussoukro. In addition, there are 25 domestic and regional airports, including those at Bouna, Korhogo, Man, Odienné and San-Pédro.

Autorité Nationale de l'Aviation Civile (ANAC): blvd de l'Aéroport, 07 BP 148, Abidjan 07; tel. 21-58-69-00; fax 21-27-63-46; e-mail info@anac.ci; internet www.anac.ci; civil aviation authority; Dir JEAN KOUASSI ABONOUAN.

Air Côte d'Ivoire: Immeuble République, pl. de la République, 01 BP 7782, Abidjan 01; tel. 20-25-15-61; fax 20-32-04-90; internet www.aircotedivoire.com; f. 2012 to replace Air Ivoire (f. 1960); 50% state-owned; 20% owned by Air France; Pres. ABDOULAYE COULIBALY; Dir-Gen. RENÉ DÉCUREY; 180 employees.

Tourism

The game reserves, forests, lagoons, coastal resorts, rich ethnic folklore and the lively city of Abidjan are tourist attractions; Côte d'Ivoire also has well-developed facilities for business visitors, including golfing centres. Some 301,000 tourists visited Côte d'Ivoire in 1998; receipts from tourism in that year totalled US $331m. In 2011 receipts from tourism totalled $141m. Tourism was negatively affected by instability from the late 1990s, most recently as a result of the violence that followed the disputed presidential run-off election of November 2010.

Office Ivoirien du Tourisme et de l'Hôtellerie: Immeuble ex-EECI, pl. de la République, 01 BP 8538, Abidjan 01; tel. 20-25-16-00; fax 20-32-03-88; internet oith@tourismeci.org; internet tourismeci.org; f. 1992; Dir CAMILLE KOUASSI.

Defence

As assessed at November 2010, Côte d'Ivoire's active armed forces comprised an army of 6,500 men, a navy of about 900, an air force of 700, a paramilitary presidential guard of 1,350 and a gendarmerie of 7,600. There was also a 1,500-strong militia, and reserve forces numbered 10,000 men. Military service is by selective conscription and lasts for 18 months. Following the disputed presidential election of November 2010 and a subsequent increase in violence in the country, the mandate of the UN Operation in Côte d'Ivoire (UNOCI) (originally deployed in April 2004) was extended until 30 June 2011 and in January the Security Council approved the deployment of an additional 2,000 military personnel, bringing the total authorized strength of UNOCI to 10,650. In August 2013 the UN Security Council extended the mandate of the operation until 30 June 2014 and reduced its strength to 7,137.

Defence Expenditure: Estimated at 324,000m. francs CFA in 2012.

Chief of Staff of the Armed Forces: Gen. SOUMAILA BAKAYOKO.

Commander of Land-based Forces: Col SÉKOU TOURÉ.

Commander of the Navy: Frigate Capt. DJAKARIDJA KONATÉ.

Commander of the Air Force: Maj.-Col JEAN-JACQUES RÉNÉ OUEGNIN.

Education

Education at all levels is available free of charge. Primary education, which is officially compulsory for six years between the ages of seven and 13 years. According to UNESCO estimates, enrolment at primary schools in 2009 included 62% of children in the relevant age-group (males 67%; females 56%). Secondary education, from the age of 12, lasts for up to seven years, comprising a first cycle of four years and a second cycle of three years. In 2001/02 total enrolment at secondary level was equivalent to 27% of children in the relevant age-group (males 35%; females 19%), according to UNESCO estimates. The Université Félix Houphouët-Boigny (as the Université de Cocody was renamed in 2012), in Abidjan, has six faculties, and there are two other universities, at Abodo-Adjamé (also in Abidjan) and at Bouaké. In 2006 there were 18 private universities and 120 private grande écoles in the country. The country's first Islamic university, Université Musulmane de Côte d'Ivoire (UMCI), was opened in 2009. Some 144,270 students (95,566 males; 48,704 females) were enrolled at tertiary-level institutions in 2009/10. In 2008 spending on education represented 24.6% of total budgetary expenditure.

CROATIA

Introductory Survey

LOCATION, CLIMATE, LANGUAGE, RELIGION, FLAG, CAPITAL

The Republic of Croatia is situated in south-eastern Europe and has a long western coastline on the Adriatic Sea. It is bordered to the north-west by Slovenia, to the north-east by Hungary and to the east by Serbia (the province of Vojvodina). Bosnia and Herzegovina abuts into Croatia, forming a southern border along the Sava river and an eastern border within the Dinaric Alps. The Croatian territory of Dubrovnik, which is situated at the southern tip of the narrowing stretch of Croatia (beyond a short coastal strip of Bosnia and Herzegovina), has a short border with Montenegro. The climate is continental in the hilly interior and Mediterranean on the coast. There is steady rainfall throughout the year, although summer is the wettest season. The average annual rainfall in Zagreb is 890 mm (35 ins). Both the ethnic Croats (who comprised 89.6% of the total population according to the 2001 census) and the Serb minority (4.5%) speak closely related languages of the Southern Slavonic group formerly referred to as variants of Serbo-Croat, but known, since the early 1990s, as Croatian and Serbian. Croatian is written in the Latin script, while Serbian is more commonly written in the Cyrillic script. There are, in addition, a number of small minority communities in Croatia, notably the Slav Muslim (Bosniak) community (which comprised 0.5% of the total population in 2001). The national flag (proportions 1 by 2) consists of three horizontal stripes, of red, white and dark blue, with the arms of Croatia (a shield of 25 squares, alternately red and white, below a blue crown composed of five shields) fimbriated in red and white and set in the centre of the flag, overlapping all three stripes. The capital is Zagreb.

CONTEMPORARY POLITICAL HISTORY

Historical Context

From the 16th century the territory of what is now Croatia was divided between the Osmanlı (Ottoman—Turkish) and Habsburg (Austrian) Empires (although Dalmatia and Istria were dominated at different times by Venice and by France, while Ragusa—Dubrovnik—was formerly an independent republic). After the Hungarian revolution of 1848–49, Croatia and Slavonia (the north-eastern region of present-day Croatia) were made Austrian crown-lands. The Habsburg Empire became the Dual Monarchy of Austria-Hungary in 1867, and the territories were restored to the Hungarian Crown in the following year. Croatia gained its autonomy and was formally joined with Slavonia in 1881. Following the collapse of the Austro-Hungarian Empire at the end of the First World War in October 1918, a Kingdom of Serbs, Croats and Slovenes (under the Serbian monarchy) was proclaimed on 4 December. The new Kingdom united Serbia, including Macedonia and Kosovo, with Montenegro and the Habsburg lands (modern-day Croatia, Slovenia and Vojvodina). However, increasing unrest within the Kingdom culminated in the meeting of a separatist Croat assembly in Zagreb in 1928. King Aleksandar imposed a royal dictatorship in January 1929, formally renaming the country Yugoslavia in October. In 1934 the King was assassinated in France by Croat extremists.

After German and Italian forces invaded Yugoslavia in 1941, the Independent State of Croatia (NDH), incorporating all of Bosnia and Herzegovina and parts of Serbia and Slovenia as well as much of modern-day Croatia, was established on 9 April. The NDH was led by the leader of the Fascist Ustaša (Rebel) movement, Ante Pavelić. During the Ustaša regime fierce armed resistance was waged by the Partisans, led by Josip Broz (Tito), the Croat-Slovene leader of the Communist Party of Yugoslavia (KPJ). The NDH collapsed in 1945, and Croatia was restored to Yugoslavia as one unit of a federal communist republic, which became the Socialist Federal Republic of Yugoslavia (SFRY) in 1963.

Following an increase in nationalism in Croatia, including among Croatian members of the ruling League of Communists (as the KPJ had been renamed), in December 1971 the Croatian communist leaders were obliged to resign, and were arrested; a purge of the League of Communists of Croatia (SKH) followed. In 1974, however, Tito introduced a new Constitution, which enshrined the federal and collective nature of the Yugoslav state. When the power of the LCC began to decline, particularly from 1989, Croatian nationalism re-emerged as a significant force. Dr Franjo Tuđman formed the Hrvatska demokratska zajednica (HDZ—Croatian Democratic Union) in 1990, which rapidly became the main challenger to the ruling party, by then called the League of Communists of Croatia—Party of Democratic Reform (SKH—SDP). Tuđman campaigned as a nationalist for multi-party elections to the republican legislature, advocating a 'Greater Croatia' (to include Bosnia).

At the elections to the tricameral republican Assembly (Sabor), which took place on 24 April and 6–7 May 1990, the HDZ obtained an absolute majority in each of the three chambers, with 205 out of 351 seats in total, while the SKH—SDP took 73 seats. Tuđman was elected President of Croatia. However, Serb-dominated areas remained alienated by Tuđman's nationalism. A 'Serb National Council', based at Knin (in the south-western Krajina region), formed in July, organized a referendum on autonomy for the Croatian Serbs, which, despite attempts by the Croatian authorities to prohibit it, took place in late August–early September. In October the 'Serb National Council', announcing the results of the referendum, declared autonomy for the Krajina areas as the 'Serb Autonomous Region (SAR) of Krajina'.

Meanwhile, in August 1990 the Socialist Republic of Croatia was renamed the Republic of Croatia. In that month the Assembly voted to dismiss the republican member of the federal State Presidency, Dr Stjepan Šuvar, and replace him with Stjepan (Stipe) Mesić, then President of the Government (premier) of Croatia. In December the Assembly enacted a new republican Constitution, which declared Croatia's sovereignty, its authority over its own armed forces and its right to secede from the SFRY. Tensions increased when, in January 1991, the Croatian authorities refused to comply with an order by the federal State Presidency to disarm all paramilitary groups, and subsequently boycotted negotiations on the future of the federation. On 21 February Croatia asserted the primacy of its Constitution and laws over those of the SFRY. Later that month the self-proclaimed SAR of Krajina declared its separation from Croatia and its intention of uniting with Serbia. In April a Croatian National Guard was formed, replacing the Territorial Defence Force. On 19 May some 94% of the voters participating in a referendum (largely boycotted by the Serb population) favoured Croatia's becoming a sovereign entity, while 92% rejected a federal Yugoslavia.

On 25 June 1991 Croatia and Slovenia declared independence, beginning the process of dissociation from the SFRY. Two days later the SAR of Krajina declared its unification with the self-proclaimed Serb 'Community of Municipalities of Bosnian Krajina', based in Banja Luka, in Bosnia and Herzegovina. Amid escalating fighting between the Croat and Serb communities in Croatia, in August an SAR of West Slavonia (in north-eastern Croatia) was declared; the SAR of Slavonia, Baranja and Western Srem (Sirmium) also proclaimed its autonomy later that month. In the same month Tuđman appointed a coalition Government, dominated by the HDZ. In October the Croatian Government refused to extend the three-month moratorium on the process of dissociation from the SFRY that had been agreed during peace negotiations sponsored by the European Community (EC—later European Union, EU, see p. 273) in The Hague, Netherlands, in July. By November the Yugoslav People's Army (JNA), supported by Serbian irregular troops, had secured about one-third of Croatian territory. The main area of conflict was Slavonia, although Serbian and JNA attacks were also concentrated on the port of Zadar, in central Dalmatia. Meanwhile, in October principally Montenegrin units of the JNA attacked and besieged Dubrovnik. The eastern Slavonian town of Vukovar (where particularly intense fighting had taken place) finally surrendered on 18 November, after the 13th ceasefire agreement negotiated by the EC, which supervised the subsequent civilian evacuation. (At least 260 civilians were massacred by JNA troops during the evacuation.) After both parties indicated readiness to accept a UN peacekeeping force, in December UN Security Council Resolution 724 provided for observers to be sent to the SFRY, in addition to a small team of civilian and military personnel. In the same month a 'Republic of Serb Krajina' (RSK), formed by the union of the three SARs, was proclaimed.

Domestic Political Affairs

In November 1991 the Supreme Council (a special war cabinet, chaired by Tuđman) ordered all Croats to vacate any federal posts that they held. On 5 December Mesić resigned as Yugoslavia's nominal head of state; the federal Prime Minister, Ante Marković, resigned on 19 December. On 23 December Germany announced its recognition of Croatia, and on 15 January 1992 the other members of the EC initiated general international recognition of Croatia, which culminated in its accession to the UN in May.

The re-election of Franjo Tuđman

With more than 6,000 dead and 400,000 internally displaced in Croatia, the Croatian National Guard and the JNA signed a UN-sponsored, unconditional ceasefire on 2 January 1992. In February a 14,000-strong UN Protection Force (UNPROFOR) was entrusted with ensuring the withdrawal of the JNA from Croatia and the demilitarization of the three Serb-held enclaves, which were designated UN Protected Areas (UNPAs). In the same month UNPROFOR's mandate in Croatia was extended to cover those areas occupied by JNA troops and with majority Serb populations, but outside the official UNPAs. In May the JNA began to withdraw from Croatia. However, sporadic shelling continued, and UNPROFOR failed to prevent the expulsion of over 1,000 Croats by Serbian forces from East Slavonia. In June Croat forces launched a series of offensives in Serb-held areas. This development provoked UN Security Council Resolution 762, adopted on 30 June, which required the Croatian forces to withdraw to the positions that they had held prior to 21 June and to refrain from entering Serb-controlled areas. In July a military court in Split convicted 19 leading figures from the RSK of threatening the territorial integrity of Croatia. Shortly afterwards, the leaders of the RSK renounced their claims to independence.

Presidential and legislative elections (the latter to a new bicameral legislature comprising a directly elected Zastupnički dom—Chamber of Representatives—and an indirectly elected Županijski dom—Chamber of Counties) were held in Croatia on 2 August 1992. Tuđman was re-elected President, with 56% of the votes cast, defeating Dražen Budiša of the Hrvatska socijalno-liberalna stranka (HSLS—Croatian Social Liberal Party), while at the legislative elections the ruling HDZ obtained a majority, securing 85 of the 138 seats contested in the lower Chamber of Representatives. A new Government, under the premiership of Hrvoje Šarinić, was appointed shortly thereafter. Elections to the Chamber of Counties were held on 7 February. The HDZ won 37 of the elective 63 seats, while the HSLS, together with allied parties, obtained 16 seats.

Meanwhile, in late January 1993 Croatian troops launched an offensive across UN peacekeeping lines into Serb-held Krajina, subsequently succeeding in regaining control of the Maslenica bridge, a vital communications link between northern Croatia and the Dalmatian coast and Zemunik airport. The Serb forces in Krajina reclaimed weapons that they had earlier surrendered to UNPROFOR, while President Dobrica Ćosić of the Federal Republic of Yugoslavia (comprising Serbia and Montenegro) warned the UN that, if UNPROFOR did not intervene, Yugoslavia would dispatch troops to defend the Serbs in Croatia. At local elections in Istria in February, the Istarski demokratski sabor (IDS—Istrian Democratic Assembly), a party advocating Istrian autonomy, obtained 72% of the total votes cast. In March Šarinić's Government resigned, and a former executive of the Croatian state petroleum company, Nikica Valentić, was appointed Prime Minister.

In July 1993 the UN negotiated the Erdut Agreement between the leaders of Croatia and Serbia, whereby Croat forces were to leave the Maslenica area by the end of the month, which would be returned to UNPROFOR administration. However, the Croats failed to withdraw and fighting resumed. In August the Croatian Minister of Foreign Affairs, Dr Mate Granić, declared the Erdut Agreement invalid. In September a full-scale mobilization was undertaken among the Serbs of East Slavonia, Baranja and West Sirmium. Following worsening Serb–Croat hostilities, a UN-mediated ceasefire was agreed in mid-September. On 4 October the UN Security Council voted unanimously to extend UNPROFOR's mandate by Resolution 871, which also required the return to Croatian sovereignty of all remaining areas occupied by JNA troops outside the UNPAs, and the disarmament of Serb paramilitary groups; UNPROFOR forces were empowered to act in self-defence. The Croatian administration accepted the Resolution, but it was rejected by the Assembly of the RSK, which proceeded to order the mobilization of all Serb conscripts in Krajina. Multi-party elections held in the RSK in December were declared illegal by the Constitutional Court of Croatia. In January 1994 Milan Martić, a candidate supported by President Slobodan Milošević of Serbia, was elected 'President' of the RSK.

In January 1994 Croatia and Yugoslavia announced their intention to begin the normalization of relations, including the establishment of representative offices in their respective capitals. In the same month, however, the Croatian Government indicated the possibility of direct Croatian intervention in central Bosnia and Herzegovina, prompting the US Permanent Representative to the UN, Madeleine Albright, to threaten the imposition of international sanctions against Croatia. (Croatian army units had from 1992 supported the self-styled breakaway Croat state in western Bosnia and Herzegovina, the 'Croat Community of Herzeg-Bosna'.) In February Tuđman approved proposals, advanced by the USA, for a Bosniak (Muslim)-Croat federation within Bosnia and Herzegovina, known as the Federation of Bosnia and Herzegovina. Following the repeated extension of a ceasefire in the RSK, at the end of March 1994 it was agreed that an UNPROFOR-monitored 'buffer' zone would be established there.

In April 1994 long-standing public dissension between Tuđman and Josip Manolić, the President of the Chamber of Counties, and other prominent liberals in the HDZ, led to a division in the party. After Tuđman suspended Manolić from his position within the HDZ, the latter, together with Mesić (by this time the President of the Chamber of Representatives), left the HDZ to form a new party, the Croatian Independent Democrats (CID). The CID, led by Mesić, became the largest opposition party in the Assembly, with 18 deputies.

Meanwhile, the ceasefire in the RSK continued precariously. In September 1994 the UN Security Council renewed the UNPROFOR mandate in Croatia for a further six months. In October a new negotiating forum, the Zagreb Group, was established with the aim of resolving the Krajina question; it comprised two representatives of the EU, and the US and Russian ambassadors to Croatia. The RSK rejected the Group's initial proposal that it be reintegrated into Croatia, with extensive autonomy. In January 1995 the Zagreb Group presented a fresh peace plan, which envisaged the return of one-half of Serb-controlled territory to Croatia, in exchange for extensive regional autonomy for the Krajina Serbs. In March Tuđman reversed a decision to expel UNPROFOR from Croatian territory, two weeks before the UN troops were due to begin their withdrawal. Croatia had agreed to a revised peacekeeping plan, following intensive diplomatic negotiations conducted with the international community, as a result of which a compromise UN mandate was to provide for a reduced peacekeeping force (to be known as the UN Confidence Restoration Operation—UNCRO) until October, including several hundred troops to be deployed along Croatia's frontiers with Bosnia and Herzegovina and Yugoslavia.

In early March 1995 a formal military alliance was announced between the Herzeg-Bosna and the (by that time predominantly Bosniak) Bosnian government armies. In April Bosnian Serb artillery attacked Dubrovnik and its airport. On 1–2 May Croatian government forces regained control of West Slavonia; large numbers of Serb troops fled the area. The Croatian Serbs launched artillery attacks on Zagreb (where six civilians were killed), Karlovac and Sisak. On 3 May, under the mediation of the UN Special Envoy, the warring parties agreed a ceasefire, according to which Serb artillery was to be surrendered to the UN, in exchange for the safe passage of all Serb civilians and troops from West Slavonia into Bosnia and Herzegovina.

'Operation Storm' and the reintegration of East Slavonia

In July 1995 a joint offensive by Croatian government forces and Herzeg-Bosna troops resulted in the seizure of the Serb-held town of Bosansko Grahovo, in western Bosnia and Herzegovina, thereby blocking the principal supply route from Serb-held areas of northern Bosnia and Herzegovina to Serb-held Krajina. On 4 August Croatian government troops launched a massive military operation ('Operation Storm') and rapidly recaptured the Krajina enclave, as a result of which about 150,000 Croatian

Serbs fled or were expelled to Serb-held areas in Bosnia and Herzegovina or to Serbia. In early September the UN announced that some 10,500 peacekeeping troops were to be withdrawn from Croatia, in view of the restoration of government authority over Krajina. On 20 September the Chamber of Representatives voted to suspend sections of the law on minorities, which had provided the Krajina Serbs with special rights in areas where they had been a majority; this decision had been preceded two days earlier by a new electoral law reducing the reserved representation of the Serb minority in the Croatian legislature from 13 seats to three. The law also provided for 12 seats in the Chamber of Representatives to represent some 470,000 Croatian emigrés.

On 3 October 1995 Croatian government officials and Serb leaders in East Slavonia signed an 'agreement on basic principles', following talks in the Serb-held town of Erdut. The 11-point agreement provided for a 'transitional period', during which authority over the enclave would be invested in an interim administration established by the UN, demilitarization of the area and creation of a joint Serb-Croat police force, and the safe return of refugees.

Following a campaign that was marred by widespread allegations of state media bias, the HDZ secured about 45% of votes cast in elections to the Chamber of Representatives on 29 October 1995. A new Government was appointed in early November, headed by the erstwhile Minister of the Economy, Zlatko Matesa.

In November 1995 representatives of Croatia and the East Slavonian Serbs signed an agreement on the reintegration of the East Slavonian enclave. Under the terms of the accord, East Slavonia was to be placed under the authority of a UN-appointed transitional administration for a period of up to two years prior to its full reintegration into Croatia. The interim administration and UN peacekeeping forces would supervise the demilitarization of the area and the return of refugees and displaced persons. In January 1996, under Resolution 1037, the UN Security Council established the UN Transitional Administration for Eastern Slavonia, Baranja and Western Sirmium (UNTAES), with an initial one-year mandate. The UN Security Council also authorized the establishment of a UN Mission of Observers in Prevlaka (UNMOP), comprising 28 military observers, to assume responsibility for monitoring the demilitarization of the Prevlaka peninsula, south-east of Dubrovnik, which was claimed by Yugoslavia.

In April 1996 the Regional Executive Council of East Slavonia appointed a former RSK 'President' (1992–94), Goran Hadžić, as President of the region. A new Regional Assembly (comprising representatives of Krajina and the five East Slavonian municipalities) and Executive Council were subsequently established. In the same month the Chamber of Representatives approved legislation on co-operation between Croatia and the UN International Criminal Tribunal for the Former Yugoslavia (ICTY—based in The Hague), which provided for the transfer of authority to conduct criminal proceedings to the Tribunal and the extradition of the accused. In May the Chamber of Representatives adopted legislation granting amnesty for crimes (but not war crimes) committed during the civil conflict in East Slavonia from August 1990. Later in May 1996 a 30-day process for the demilitarization of East Slavonia commenced, and was completed as scheduled. In July an international security force was installed in East Slavonia for the transitional period.

In August 1996 an agreement, providing for the establishment of full diplomatic relations between Croatia and Yugoslavia was signed; remaining issues of contention, most notably the territorial dispute over Prevlaka, were to be resolved by further negotiations. In October the Council of Europe (see p. 252) agreed to accept Croatia's application for membership, after the Government undertook to ratify the European Convention on Human Rights within one year of admission.

In early April 1997 Serb officials in East Slavonia conducted a referendum (which the Croatian Government and UN officials declared to be illegitimate) regarding the future of the enclave; about 99.5% of the participating electorate voted in favour of East Slavonia remaining a single administrative unit under Serb control after its return to Croatia. In mid-April elections to the Chamber of Counties and to a number of municipal and regional councils took place. Election monitors from the Organization for Security and Co-operation in Europe (OSCE, see p. 387) declared that the elections had been largely free and fair. The HDZ secured 42 of the 63 elective seats in the Chamber of Counties, while the Hrvatska seljačka stranka (HSS—Croatian Peasants' Party) took nine, the HSLS six, the Socijaldemokratska partija Hrvatske (SDP—Social Democratic Party of Croatia, which had been constituted from the former LCC–PDR) four, and the IDS two seats. (A further five deputies were nominated by Tuđman, of whom two were to be members of the Serb community in East Slavonia.)

On 15 June 1997 Tuđman was re-elected as President, obtaining 61.4% of the votes cast. Although OSCE monitors declared that the election had not been conducted fairly, on the grounds that opposition parties had not been permitted coverage in the state-controlled media, the Constitutional Court endorsed the results of the election later in the month. Tuđman was officially inaugurated for a second term on 5 August. In November the legislature approved constitutional amendments, proposed by Tuđman, which, notably, prohibited the re-establishment of a union of Yugoslav states.

Meanwhile, in July 1997 the Government had announced the initiation of the programme for the return of some 80,000 Croat refugees to East Slavonia. In the same month the UN Security Council adopted a resolution extending the mandate of UNTAES (which had already been renewed for an additional six months) until January 1998, owing to UN concern over the continued stability of East Slavonia. After East Slavonia was returned to Croatian authority in January, an increase in the number of Serbs leaving the region was reported. In May the Government announced a programme that relaxed conditions for the return of Serb refugees to Croatia, following pressure from the international community.

In May 1998 Andrija Hebrang became Minister of Defence. In June Croatia submitted to the UN a proposal for a settlement of the status of the Prevlaka peninsula; it was envisaged that a joint Croatian-Yugoslav commission would demarcate the borders between the two countries and that a demilitarized zone would be established for a period of five years. In October, following a disagreement with Tuđman, Hebrang resigned as Minister of Defence and Vice-President of the HDZ.

In August 1999 the Croatian Government complied with a request by the ICTY for the extradition of a Bosnian Croat commander, Vinko Martinović, who had been indicted for crimes committed during the Croat–Muslim conflict in Bosnia and Herzegovina. However, the authorities' reluctance to extradite Mladen Naletilić, who had been indicted on similar charges, prompted severe criticism from the ICTY. (Naletilić's extradition was facilitated in March 2000.)

The death of Tuđman and the defeat of the HDZ

On 26 November 1999 the Assembly provisionally transferred the powers of Head of State to the parliamentary Speaker, Vlatko Pavletić, after Tuđman underwent emergency medical treatment. Pavletić rescheduled elections to the Chamber of Representatives, due to take place on 22 December, for 3 January 2000. Six opposition parties—the HSS, the Croatian People's Party, the HSLS, the IDS, the Liberal Party and the SDP—formed a loose alliance, known as the Opposition Six, prior to the parliamentary elections. Tuđman died on 10 December 1999, and the Government announced that the election for his successor would take place on 24 January 2000.

Some 55 political associations contested the elections to the Chamber of Representatives, held on 3 January 2000. A coalition of the SDP and the HSLS (together with two minor parties) secured 47.0% of the votes cast and 71 of the 151 seats, followed by the HDZ, which obtained 30.5% of the votes cast and 45 seats; the four other Opposition Six parties, together with the Croatian Social Democrats' Action, won 15.9% of the total votes cast and 25 seats. Later in January nine candidates emerged to contest the presidential election, including the HSLS leader, Budiša (who was to represent the SDP-HSLS alliance), and Mesić, who was the joint candidate of the four other principal opposition parties. The HDZ selected Mate Granić, hitherto Deputy Prime Minister and Minister of Foreign Affairs, as its presidential candidate. In the first round of the election, held on 24 January, Mesić secured 41.1% of the votes cast, while Budiša won 27.7% and Granić 22.5%. On 27 January Pavletić formally appointed the Chairman of the SDP, Ivica Račan, as Prime Minister. Račan announced the establishment of a coalition Government, comprising members of the Opposition Six parties. In the second round of voting in the presidential election, on 7 February, Mesić secured 56.2% of the votes cast. On 9 February the Assembly adopted a motion expressing confidence in Račan's Government. Following his inauguration as President on 18 February, Mesić pledged to support the return of Serb refugees to Croatia.

In April 2000 Granić left the HDZ to form a new party, the Demokratski Centar (DC—Democratic Centre). In that month

Ivo Sanader was elected as leader of the HDZ at a party congress. In May the Chamber of Representatives approved constitutional amendments guaranteeing representation in the legislature for those ethnic groups constituting more than 8% of the total population. On 25 May Croatia officially joined the 'Partnership for Peace' programme of the North Atlantic Treaty Organization (NATO, see p. 370).

In November 2000 the Chamber of Representatives adopted constitutional amendments reducing the powers of the President and increasing those of the legislature, which, henceforth, was to appoint the Government. In March 2001 the Government submitted a proposal to the Chamber of Representatives for the abolition of the Chamber of Counties. Despite the strenuous opposition of the HDZ, which held a majority of seats in the upper house, the Chamber of Representatives accordingly approved a constitutional amendment converting the Assembly into a unicameral legislature. At local government elections on 20 May, the SDP-led coalition obtained control of 14 of the 21 County Assemblies. The HDZ secured a majority in only four County Assemblies (compared with the 16 it controlled after the 1997 elections). In early June the IDS (which had held the European integration portfolio) withdrew from the Government.

In June 2001 the County Court in Rijeka indicted a prominent former rebel Bosniak, Fikret Abdić, for crimes against humanity, including the killing of civilians in a detention camp in 1993. In accordance with a bilateral agreement between Croatia and Bosnia and Herzegovina, the trial of Abdić, who had obtained Croatian citizenship in 1995, commenced in the Croatian town of Karlovac in July 2001. (He was sentenced to 20 years' imprisonment in July 2002.) In July 2001 the Government voted to extradite two Croat generals suspected of war crimes to the ICTY, precipitating the resignation in protest of four HSLS ministers. In mid-July Račan's administration won a motion of confidence in the Assembly, which also approved a statement reaffirming the Government's policy of co-operation with the ICTY. Following the forced resignation of Budiša (who had strongly opposed the extradition) from the leadership of the HSLS, the four representatives of that party rejoined the Government. Later in July one of the indicted suspects, Gen. (retd) Rahim Ademi, surrendered to the ICTY. The other suspect, Gen. (retd) Ante Gotovina, who had been indicted on similar charges, pertaining to having led 'Operation Storm' in 1995, remained at large.

In September 2001 Milošević, who had been extradited to the ICTY in June on charges relating to the province of Kosovo, was formally indicted for crimes against humanity and violations of the Geneva Convention; he was held responsible for the killing of Croat civilians and the expulsion of 170,000 non-Serbs from Croatian territory by Serb forces in 1991–92. (Milošević died in March 2006, while on trial at the ICTY.) In October 2001 Croatia (after having been deemed to have co-operated with the ICTY) signed a Stabilization and Association Agreement with the EU, which was ratified by the Assembly on 5 December.

In February 2002 Budiša was re-elected to the presidency of the HSLS. At the end of the month the HSLS leadership decided to remove the First Deputy Prime Minister, Goran Granić, and a further two of its ministers from the Government, reportedly owing to their failure to support Budiša in opposing co-operation with the ICTY. The remaining three HSLS members in the Government subsequently tendered their resignations to demonstrate disagreement with the party leadership. As part of a cabinet reorganization in March, Budiša became First Deputy Prime Minister, while Granić (henceforth an independent) and three of the HSLS representatives were reappointed to the Government.

In May 2002 Milan Martić, the former 'President' of the RSK, who had been indicted in 1996 for war crimes, in particular his alleged responsibility for the bombardment of Zagreb in 1995, surrendered to the ICTY. In early July 2002 Budiša finally withdrew the HSLS from the government coalition, after an agreement on Croatian-Slovenian joint ownership of the Krško nuclear power installation in Slovenia was ratified in the Assembly, despite the opposition of 17 of the HSLS's 23 deputies. On 5 July Račan submitted his resignation to Mesić, following the collapse of his administration. Five days later, however, Račan was returned to the office of Prime Minister, after his nomination by Mesić was supported by 84 deputies in the Assembly. On 28 July Račan and the leaders of the other political parties belonging to the ruling coalition reached agreement on a new Council of Ministers, which was approved by the Assembly two days later.

In July 2002 the Presidents of Croatia and Yugoslavia met the members of the collective State Presidency of Bosnia and Herzegovina in Sarajevo (the first such trilateral summit meeting since the dissolution of the SFRY). In December the Ministers of Foreign Affairs of Croatia and Yugoslavia reached a provisional accord on Prevlaka, thereby allowing the UN Security Council to end the mandate of UNMOP; the peninsula was to remain demilitarized and joint maritime patrols were to be introduced. In February 2003 Croatia submitted a formal application for membership of the EU, having pledged commitment to full co-operation with the ICTY.

In March 2003 a former army commander, Gen. (retd) Mirko Norac (the most senior officer to be convicted by a Croatian court), was sentenced to 12 years' imprisonment for his involvement in the killing of some 50 Croatian Serb civilians in 1991; a further two defendants received terms of 15 years and 10 years, respectively. (In May 2004 the ICTY issued an indictment against Norac on a further five charges relating to an attack by Croatian troops in 1993.) In November 2003 the former leader of the self-proclaimed SAR of Krajina, Milan Babić, appearing before the ICTY, was charged with war crimes and crimes against humanity in connection with the 'ethnic cleansing' of Croats from regions under his control in 1991–92. Babić was sentenced to 13 years' imprisonment in June 2004 (he committed suicide in March 2006).

The HDZ regains power

Legislative elections were conducted on 23 November 2003. The HDZ obtained 66 of the 152 elective seats in the Assembly, while the SDP, led by Račan, won a total of 43 seats, including 28 in coalition with other parties, among them the IDS. The HDZ negotiated coalition agreements with the HSLS and the DC (which, in coalition, had received three seats) and the HSS (which held 10 seats), and obtained the support of several other deputies, in order to command a narrow parliamentary majority. On 23 December a new Government, headed by Sanader and principally comprising members of his HDZ, was approved by 88 votes in the Assembly. The administration included former members of the Tuđman administration, notably Hebrang, as Deputy Prime Minister and Minister of Health and Social Welfare; and a former ambassador to the USA, Miomir Žužul, as Minister of Foreign Affairs. The newly elected President of the DC, Vesna Škare-Ožbolt, was appointed as Minister of Justice.

In March 2004, following continued international pressure on Croatia, two retired generals, Ivan Čermak and Mladen Markač, surrendered to the ICTY, charged with crimes relating to the seizure of Krajina by Croatian government forces in 1995. In April 2004 the European Commission announced that it favoured the opening of accession negotiations with Croatia, subject to its continued compliance with the ICTY. In June Croatia was awarded the official status of EU candidate country.

In early January 2005 Žužul, who had been implicated by media reports concerning corrupt financial practices during the Tuđman regime, announced his resignation. Meanwhile, at the first round of a presidential election on 2 January, Mesić, supported by an alliance of centre-left parties led by the SDP, secured 48.9% of the votes cast; his principal opponent, Jadranka Kosor, a Deputy Prime Minister and the HDZ representative, won 20.3% of the votes. At the second round on 16 January, Mesić was re-elected to the presidency, receiving 65.9% of the votes cast.

In January 2005 Lt-Gen. (retd) Pavle Strugar, a former commander of the Yugoslav navy, was sentenced by the ICTY to eight years' imprisonment for his involvement in the military campaign by the JNA against the Dubrovnik region in 1991. (Strugar was released in February 2009, after his sentence was commuted on grounds of his deteriorating health.) In February 2005 Sanader reorganized the Government, after Hebrang resigned from the Council of Ministers. A prominent business executive, Damir Polančec, replaced Hebrang as Deputy Prime Minister, while the Ministries of Foreign Affairs and of European Integration were merged. Mesić was inaugurated as President on 18 February. In March, following an official report by the ICTY Prosecutor, Carla Del Ponte, stating that the Croatian authorities had failed to demonstrate full co-operation with the ICTY (with regard to Gotovina), the EU postponed accession negotiations, which had been scheduled to begin that month. Elections for local and regional governments were conducted in May: the HDZ lost significant support to centre-left coalitions led by the SDP and to the extreme nationalist Hrvatska stranka prava (HSP—Croatian Party of Rights). On 3 October Croatia was declared eligible to enter into accession negotiations with the EU (which officially opened the following day), after Del Ponte, despite reiterating dissatisfaction at the end of September, issued an assessment stating that the Government's co-operation with the ICTY had improved.

In December 2005 Gotovina was apprehended in the Canary Islands, Spain, reportedly as a result of information received by ICTY investigators from the Croatian authorities; his arrest was perceived as removing the main obstacle to the country's NATO and EU membership. On 10 December Gotovina was extradited to the Tribunal, where he pleaded not guilty to charges relating to the killing and forcible expulsion of Serbs from the Krajina region in August–November 1995. Several thousand nationalist supporters of Gotovina staged demonstrations in Zagreb and Split, to demand the transfer of his trial to Croatian jurisdiction.

In February 2006 Sanader announced that Škare-Ožbolt had been removed from the post of Minister of Justice, and the DC withdrew from the Government. In October an HDZ parliamentary deputy, Branimir Glavaš, who had been charged with involvement in the killing of Serbs in Slavonia in 1991, surrendered to the Croatian authorities, following the removal of his parliamentary immunity. In January 2007 Račan resigned as SDP Chairman. (Račan died in April, and Zoran Milanović was elected Chairman of the party in June.) In June Martić, the former 'President' of the RSK, was sentenced to 35 years' imprisonment at the ICTY on 16 charges of war crimes. In the same month the trials of Norac and Ademi (who had both been transferred to Croatia by the ICTY in November 2005) began.

On 25 November 2007 elections to the Assembly took place. The HDZ secured 66 of the 153 seats, and the SDP obtained 56. Glavaš, of the Hrvatski demokratski savez Slavonije i Baranje (HDSSB—Croatian Democratic Alliance of Slavonia and Baranja), secured one of the eight seats reserved for representatives of national minorities. In December the Minister of the Interior, Ivica Kirin, tendered his resignation, after it emerged that he and other senior government officials had participated in a hunting expedition with Mladen Markač (in violation of the conditions for Markač's provisional pre-trial release from the ICTY); Markač was returned to The Hague. In January 2008, following lengthy negotiations, the HDZ signed a coalition agreement with the HSS and HSLS (which, as part of an electoral alliance, had won eight seats in the Assembly), and seven of the eight parliamentary parties representing minority ethnic groups. On 12 January the Assembly voted to approve a new Government, comprising representatives of the HDZ, the HSS, the HSLS and the Samostalna demokratska srpska stranka (SDSS—Independent Democratic Serb Party).

The trial of Gotovina, together with those of Markač and Čermak, commenced at the ICTY in March 2008. In May, following the conclusion of their trials at Zagreb County Court, Norac was sentenced to seven years' imprisonment, while Ademi was acquitted of all charges. In October, after the daughter of a prominent lawyer was shot dead in Zagreb, Sanader dismissed the Minister of the Interior, Berislav Rončević, and the Minister of Justice, Ana Lovrin, together with the national chief of police. Tomislav Karamarko, hitherto the head of the Security and Intelligence Agency, received the interior portfolio, while Ivan Šimonović, an independent former Deputy Minister of Foreign Affairs, was appointed to succeed Lovrin. Later that month the editor of independent newspaper *Nacional*, Ivo Pukanić, and another journalist were killed by a car bomb in Zagreb. In November the authorities announced the establishment of four special courts for cases of corruption and organized crime. In May 2009 Glavaš fled to Bosnia and Herzegovina, after being convicted by a Zagreb court of atrocities against Serb civilians in Osijek in 1991 and sentenced to 10 years' imprisonment.

Election of President Josipović

On 1 July 2009 Sanader announced his resignation as Prime Minister, and stated that he was to withdraw from political life; he named the Deputy Prime Minister and Minister of the Family, Veterans' Affairs and Intergenerational Solidarity, Jadranka Kosor, as his successor to the premiership and to the chairmanship of the HDZ. The nomination of Kosor (the country's first female Prime Minister) was approved by the Assembly on 6 July. A reorganized Government was subsequently formed. Following her appointment, Kosor, as part of her stated commitment to suppress corruption, encouraged investigations into the suspected involvement of senior HDZ members in corrupt practices within state-controlled enterprises. In October the Deputy Prime Minister and Minister of Economy, Labour and Entrepreneurship, Damir Polančec, resigned, following allegations of corruption relating to fraudulent transactions by managers of a local food producer, Podravka. In November Đuro Popijač, hitherto the President of the Croatian Employers' Association, became Minister of Economy, Labour and Entrepreneurship; the Minister of Health and Social Welfare, Darko Milinović, and the Minister of Finance, Ivan Šuker, were appointed by Kosor as deputy premiers (while retaining their portfolios).

The first round of a presidential election was conducted on 27 December 2009; of the 12 candidates contesting the ballot, Ivo Josipović of the SDP, a university professor, secured 32.4% of the votes cast, the mayor of Zagreb and independent candidate Milan Bandić, obtained 14.8% of the votes, and former member of the Tuđman administration and Deputy Prime Minister, Andrija Hebrang of the HDZ, 12.1% of the votes. On 3 January 2010 Sanader announced his intention to return to active politics, criticizing the poor performance of the HDZ in the presidential election. On the following day, however, he was expelled from the HDZ, following his criticism of Kosor's administration and consequent concern at the prospect of divisions within the party. In the second round of the presidential election, which took place on 10 January, Josipović was elected to the presidency, with 60.3% of the votes cast, according to official results. Josipović was inaugurated on 18 February. On 16 June Croatia approved constitutional amendments that allowed the implementation of a number of EU regulations and facilitated the organization of a referendum on accession to the Union. On 10 July the HSLS withdrew from the ruling coalition, which, however, retained sufficient parliamentary support for stability.

In September 2010 Glavaš was detained in Bosnia and Herzegovina at the request of the Croatian authorities after his conviction had been confirmed, with a reduced sentence of eight years, by the Croatian Supreme Court in July. In late September the head of the Customs Administration and a close associate of Sanader, Mladen Barišić, was arrested on suspicion of corrupt practices. In October Polančec (who in March had been arrested over the allegations relating to Podravka) was sentenced to 15 months' imprisonment on further charges of abuse of office. In November six men were sentenced by a court in Zagreb, one *in absentia*, to terms of imprisonment ranging from 15 to 40 years, after being convicted of the killing of Pukanić in October 2008. In early December 2010 Berislav Rončević was sentenced to four years' imprisonment, after being convicted on charges of abuse of office while Minister of Defence in Sanader's administration. On 9 December Sanader (who in October had been permitted to return to the Assembly as an independent deputy) left the country shortly before his parliamentary immunity from prosecution was suspended. He was subsequently detained in Austria, following an arrest warrant issued by Croatia relating to corruption charges.

Centre-left coalition Government

In December 2010, in an stated effort to assist economic recovery efforts, Kosor effected an extensive government reorganization, which included the appointment of Domagoj Milošević to the newly created post of Deputy Prime Minister in charge of investments. In February 2011 anti-Government demonstrations were organized in protest at a deterioration in living standards; a number of demonstrators were arrested in Zagreb, following clashes with police.

On 15 April 2011 the ICTY convicted Gotovina and Markač of war crimes against the Serb population of the Krajina region in 1995, sentencing them to 24 years' and 18 years' imprisonment, respectively. (Čermak was acquitted of the charges.) The announcement of their sentences precipitated large protests in Zagreb and other main towns. On 20 July 2011 the arrest of Goran Hadžić, the final indicted war crimes suspect to remain at large, was announced by the Serbian authorities; two days later he was extradited to the ICTY to be brought to trial on 14 charges of war crimes and crimes against humanity. In the same month Sanader was extradited by the Austrian authorities in compliance with Croatia's arrest warrant. Sanader's parliamentary immunity was formally removed in September, and his trial on charges of corruption began on 3 November.

In October 2011 Prime Minister Kosor pledged that the HDZ would co-operate with an official inquiry into allegations that the party had raised illicit funds to finance undisclosed activities. In legislative elections, which took place on 4 December, the centre-left Kukuriku coalition, comprising the SDP, the Croatian People's Party—Liberal Democrats (HNS), the IDS and the Croatian Pensioners' Party, secured about 45.7% of the votes cast and 80 of the 151 seats in the Assembly, decisively defeating the HDZ, which obtained 18.4% of votes and 47 seats. Josipović appointed SDP and Kukuriku leader Milanović as Prime Minister; his new Government, comprising members of the four coalition parties, was approved in the Assembly on 23 December.

Anti-corruption efforts continued (under the supervision of the European Commission) during 2012; in August a joint investigation by Croatia and Slovenia resulted in the arrest of the head of the Croatian branch of principal Slovenian bank Nova Kreditna banka Maribor, on accusations of fraud. In November the President of the HNS, Radimir Čačić, resigned from his position as Deputy Prime Minister and Minister of the Economy, after being sentenced to 22 months' imprisonment for causing a car crash in which two people died. Minister of Foreign and European Affairs Vesna Pusić succeeded him as deputy premier, while Ivan Vrdoljak, hitherto Minister of Construction and Physical Planning, received the economy portfolio.

Acquittal of Gotovina and Markač

On 16 November 2012 the Appeals Chamber of the ICTY overturned the convictions of Gotovina and Markač (by the decision of three judges to two), reversing the previous verdict that artillery bombardments ordered by them (which were more than 200 metres from a military target) had constituted unlawful attacks on civilians, and that they had participated in the forcible expulsion of the Serb population in the Krajina region. The announcement was widely welcomed in Croatia, while prompting outrage in Serbia (which denounced the Tribunal for perceived bias). The two former indictees were immediately released and returned to Croatia. On 20 November Sanader was sentenced to 10 years' imprisonment for having received bribes while in office from the Hungarian Oil and Gas Company and Hypo Alpe-Adria Bank of Austria, in exchange for preferential contracts; further corruption cases against him continued.

Following Čačić's departure from the Government, instability increased within the ruling coalition in December 2012, exacerbated by the smaller government parties' opposition to the planned introduction of a property tax in 2013. In February 2013 the presidency of the HNS confirmed that Čačić had resigned from its leadership, and endorsed the candidacy of Pusić for the post; Pusić was elected as HNS leader on 25 March. In the same month Croat war veteran groups began to organize protests in Vukovar against government plans to erect road signs there in Cyrillic (as well as Latin) script, under a constitutional requirement to introduce use of the Serbian language in areas where Serbs comprised more than one-third of the population. In April the Government announced that the introduction of the property tax had been postponed indefinitely.

Recent developments: Croatia's EU accession

Upon Croatia's scheduled accession to the EU on 1 July 2013 (see Regional Affairs), the country's nominee to the European Commission, the hitherto Deputy Prime Minister responsible for Domestic, Foreign and European Affairs and a close associate of Prime Minister Milanović, Neven Mimica, took office as the Commissioner for Consumer Protection. In August controversy arose over legislation adopted the day before Croatia's admission to the EU, which prevented those suspected of having committed crimes before August 2002 from being extradited (thereby protecting war veterans from prosecution abroad). A threat against the life of Prime Minister Milanović was apparently prompted by Croatia's failure to extradite to Germany a former head of intelligence, Josip Perković, in connection with the murder of a Yugoslav defector in 1983, and the European Commission strongly criticized the added restriction to the EU's extradition regulations, and warned of possible financial sanctions. Consequently, in late September the Minister of Justice issued assurances that Croatia's extradition legislation would be amended to conform with EU requirements from the beginning of 2014.

At the beginning of December 2013 a nationwide referendum organized by conservative groups with the support of the Roman Catholic Church, and with the approval of 104 of the votes cast in the Assembly, resulted in about 66% of voters favouring the prohibition of same-sex marriage. The Government, which had declared its opposition to the proposal, confirmed that the Constitution would be amended accordingly, but indicated that legislation granting same-sex couples equivalent rights to married couples would be adopted. Meanwhile, war veteran groups continued their opposition to the use of the Cyrillic script in Vukovar, and in December submitted a petition to the Assembly for a referendum to be conducted on the issue.

Perković was arrested on 1 January 2014, when the amended extradition legislation duly entered into force, and the Supreme Court subsequently dismissed an appeal by him against his extradition to Germany. In the same month the Velika Gorica County Court ruled against the extradition of a head of secret service, Zdravko Mustac, in connection with the same killing; however, the decision was overturned by the Supreme Court in March. On 11 March Sanader and three other former HDZ officials were convicted of misappropriating funds from state companies for party activities during 2003–09; Sanader was sentenced to a further nine years' imprisonment and ordered to repay US $2.8m., while the HDZ was to be liable for nearly $5.3m.

Regional Affairs

In early 2007 a longstanding dispute between Croatia and Slovenia over their joint maritime boundary was revived with a diplomatic protest by Slovenia that the Croatian Government had pre-empted a border demarcation by extending concessions for petroleum exploration in the disputed region. The Croatian Government demanded that the dispute be referred to international arbitration (a measure that the Slovenian Government strongly opposed). In early 2008 Croatia implemented legislation enforcing an environmental fishing zone in the Adriatic Sea, which the Government had declared in 2003; Italy and Slovenia opposed the measure, on the grounds that it would result in significant financial damage for their fleets, and the EU repeatedly warned that the legislation would adversely affect Croatia's application for entry. In March, following continued pressure from the EU, the Government agreed to postpone the implementation of the environmental fishing zone until Croatia's entry into the Union, a decision that was subsequently approved in the Assembly.

At a NATO summit meeting, convened in Bucharest, Romania, on 2 April 2008, it was announced that an official invitation to begin accession negotiations was to be extended to Croatia. Croatia's accession protocol to NATO was officially signed on 9 July. In December the Slovenian Government announced that it would veto Croatia's EU accession process, after Croatia presented documentation to the European Commission, which was considered by Slovenia to predetermine the common maritime border that remained under dispute. However, in February 2009 Slovenia's legislature ratified the protocols for Croatia's accession to NATO, and on 1 April Croatia was admitted as a member of the Alliance. Following discussions between new Prime Minister Jadranka Kosor and her Slovenian counterpart, Borut Pahor, it was finally agreed in September that the border dispute should not present an obstacle to the resumption of Croatia's EU accession negotiations, and that the dispute would be resolved through international arbitration. Croatia resumed negotiations with the EU in early October. On 4 November the Governments of Croatia and Slovenia signed an agreement whereby international arbitrators were to delineate the joint border, and the agreement was ratified by the Assembly on 20 November. After the arbitration agreement was narrowly supported by 51.5% of the participating electorate in a national referendum, held in Slovenia in June 2010, it officially became binding in November. On 30 June 2011 the EU confirmed that Croatia had complied with the requirements of the final outstanding negotiating chapters of the *acquis communautaire*, the EU's body of law. The Croatian Government officially signed the EU Accession Treaty on 9 December; subject to ratification of the Treaty by all EU states, Croatia's official entry into the Union was scheduled to take effect in July 2013. Croatia's membership of the EU was submitted for approval at a national referendum on 22 January 2012, when it was endorsed by about 66.3% of votes cast (with a participation rate of only about 44%). US Secretary of State Hillary Clinton made an official visit to Zagreb in October, during which she welcomed the increased US investment enabled by Croatia's anticipated entry into the EU. In March 2013 the Croatian and Slovenian Governments signed a memorandum of understanding on a longstanding dispute over the reimbursement of Croatian depositors of Slovenia's former Ljubljanska Banka, under which Croatia was to suspend all associated legal proceedings and settlement was to be determined by international arbitration. Resolution of the outstanding issue allowed parliamentary ratification of Croatia's Accession Treaty by Slovenia on 2 April (the final EU member state to do so). Elections to the European Parliament took place in Croatia for the first time on 14 April, with a rate of participation of only about 21% of the electorate. The HDZ won six of the 12 seats available, while the SDP took five; the remaining seat was secured by Hrvatski Laburisti—Stranka Rada (Croatian Labourists—Party of Labour). On 1 July Croatia became the 28th member of the EU, as scheduled.

During a visit to Zagreb in June 2007, the President of Serbia, Boris Tadić, issued an unprecedented apology to the Croatian people for atrocities committed by Serbs during the war. In November 2008 the International Court of Justice (ICJ, see p. 24) ruled that it had jurisdiction to hear a case of genocide brought by Croatia against Serbia (as the successor state to the State Union of Serbia and Montenegro, and Yugoslavia), pertaining to crimes allegedly committed by Yugoslav forces in Croatia in 1991–95, which had been submitted to the Court in 1999. In January 2010 Serbia submitted a genocide counter-case against Croatia for alleged war crimes committed during 'Operation Storm' in 1995. In April 2009 the Bosnian presidency threatened to institute legal proceedings against Croatia unless a settlement was negotiated on a continued dispute over the delineation of a small border area on the Adriatic Sea, including the status of Neum, in Bosnian territory, and the Croatian port of Ploče. In June 2010 the Croatian and Serbian Ministers of Defence signed a military co-operation agreement between the two countries in Zagreb, and in July President Josipović met Tadić in Belgrade to discuss outstanding issues of contention. In May 2012 the newly elected President of Serbia, Tomislav Nikolić, prompted protests from the Croatian Government after he referred to Vukovar as 'a Serbian town' during a media interview. Nikolić and other Serbian politicians reacted with outrage to the acquittal of former war crimes indictees Gotovina and Markač in November (see above). In January 2013 an official visit by Croatian Prime Minister Zoran Milanović to Belgrade, where he met his Serbian counterpart, was regarded as an initial move towards improving bilateral relations. However, following strenuous opposition to the use of the Cyrillic script in Vukovar and a proposed referendum on the issue (see above), in December Serbia's Ministry of Foreign Affairs formally protested to all countries with Serbian embassy representation that Serb minority rights in Croatia were endangered. Hearings on Croatia's genocide case against Serbia began at the ICJ on 3 March 2014. Meanwhile, following violent protests in the Federation entity of Bosnia and Herzegovina in February, Milanović visited the town of Mostar, declaring that he supported a peaceful resolution of the unrest.

CONSTITUTION AND GOVERNMENT

According to the 1990 Constitution (as subsequently amended), legislative power is vested in the unicameral Sabor (Assembly), which has between 100 and 160 members and is elected for a four-year term. Executive power is held by the President, who is elected by universal adult suffrage for a period of five years. The Assembly appoints the Prime Minister and (upon the recommendation of the Prime Minister) the ministers. Judicial power is vested in the courts and is autonomous and independent. Croatia is divided, for administrative purposes, into 20 counties and the City of Zagreb, 429 municipalities and 127 towns.

REGIONAL AND INTERNATIONAL CO-OPERATION

Croatia was admitted to the Organization for Security and Co-operation in Europe (OSCE, see p. 387) in 1992, and became a member of the Council of Europe (see p. 252) in 1996. Croatia joined the Central European Free Trade Agreement (CEFTA, see p. 449) in 2003. In February 2003 Croatia made a formal application for membership of the European Union (EU, see p. 273), following the signature of a Stabilization and Association Agreement in 2001, and EU entry negotiations officially opened in October 2005; Croatia acceded to the EU on 1 July 2013. Croatia formally acceded to the North Atlantic Treaty Organization (NATO, see p. 370) on 1 April 2009.

Croatia was admitted to the UN in 1992, and became a member of the World Trade Organization (see p. 434) in 2000.

ECONOMIC AFFAIRS

In 2012, according to estimates by the World Bank, Croatia's gross national income (GNI), measured at average 2010–12 prices, was US $56,718m., equivalent to $13,290 per head (or $19,760 per head on an international purchasing-power parity basis). During 2003–12, it was estimated, while the population decreased at an average rate of 0.4%, gross domestic product (GDP) per head increased, in real terms, by an average of 1.5% per year. Overall GDP increased, in real terms, at an average annual rate of 1.1% in 2003–12; real GDP remained constant in 2011, but decreased by 2.0% in 2012.

Agriculture (including hunting, forestry and fishing) contributed 5.0% of GDP and engaged 4.5% of the employed labour force in 2012. The principal crops are maize, sugar beet, wheat, barley and potatoes. According to World Bank estimates, the GDP of the agricultural sector increased by 1.2%, in real terms, during 2003–12; real agricultural GDP decreased by 1.2% in 2011, but increased by 1.0% in 2012.

Industry (including mining, manufacturing, construction and power) contributed 26.3% of GDP in 2012, when it engaged 27.8% of the employed labour force. According to World Bank estimates, industrial GDP decreased, in real terms, at an average annual rate of 0.1% during 2003–12; real GDP in the industrial sector decreased by 2.9% in 2012.

The mining sector contributed 5.5% of GDP in 1998, and engaged only 0.4% of the employed labour force in 2012. Croatia has many exploitable mineral resources, including petroleum, coal and natural gas. In March 2010 Croatia signed an agreement with Russia, according to which it was to join the South Stream project, which is to carry natural gas under the Black Sea from Russia to Western Europe.

According to World Bank estimates, the manufacturing sector contributed 16.2% of GDP in 2012. The sector, along with mining and utilities, engaged 17.3% of the employed labour force in 2012. The GDP of the manufacturing sector remained constant, in real terms, during 2003–12; real manufacturing GDP decreased by 2.8% in 2012.

The construction sector contributed 5.4% of GDP in 2012, when it engaged 7.3% of the employed labour force.

Of total electricity production in 2011, some 42.0% was provided by hydroelectric power, 24.5% by natural gas, 4.1% by coal and 7.0% by petroleum. However, the country remains dependent on imported fuel. In 2012 mineral fuels accounted for 23.2% of total imports.

Services provided 68.8% of GDP in 2012, and the sector engaged 67.6% of the employed labour force in the same year. According to World Bank estimates, the GDP of the services sector increased, in real terms, at an average annual rate of 1.6% in 2003–12; real GDP in the sector increased by 1.2% in 2011, but decreased by 1.6% in 2012.

In 2012 Croatia recorded a visible merchandise trade deficit of US $7,862.3m., while there was a deficit of $130.5m. on the current account of the balance of payments. In 2012 the principal source of imports was Italy (supplying 16.8% of total imports); other major sources were Germany, Russia, the People's Republic of China and Slovenia. Italy was also Croatia's principal market for exports (accounting for 15.3% of the total); other important purchasers were Bosnia and Herzegovina, Germany, Slovenia and Austria. The main imports in 2012 were mineral fuels and lubricants (particularly petroleum and petroleum products). Other significant imports were machinery and transport equipment, basic manufactures, chemical products, miscellaneous manufactured articles, and food and live animals. The principal exports in that year were machinery and transport equipment. Other important exports were basic manufactures, mineral fuels and lubricants, miscellaneous manufactured articles, chemical products, food and live animals, and transport equipment.

According to official figures, Croatia's overall budgetary deficit for 2012 was 6,281m. kuna (equivalent to 1.9% of GDP). Croatia's general government gross debt was 177,310m. in 2012, equivalent to 53.7% of GDP. The country's total external debt at the end of 2007 amounted to US $48,584m., of which $14,212m. was public and publicly guaranteed debt. In that year the cost of servicing long-term public and publicly guaranteed debt and repayments to the IMF was equivalent to 33.0% of the value of exports of goods, services and income (excluding workers' remittances). Consumer prices increased at an average annual rate of 3.0% in 2003–12. The rate of consumer price inflation was 3.4% in 2012. In that year 18.9% of the labour force were registered as unemployed.

Croatia's relations with the international community improved markedly following the installation of a pro-reform Government in early 2000, and financial aid increased. Croatia again became a popular tourist destination, and the tourism sector an increasingly significant source of income. A European Union (EU, see p. 273) Stabilization and Association Agreement for Croatia was signed in 2001 and entered into force in February 2005; EU accession negotiations officially opened in October. Despite reform efforts by the Government during 2009, however, domestic consumption and investment failed to recover from the adverse effects of the international financial crisis. The deterioration in economic conditions, particularly the sharp rise in unemployment and decline in living standards, prompted a series of anti-Government demonstrations from early 2011. On 30 June the EU declared that Croatia had fulfilled the final requirements for accession to the Union. The new, centre-left Government that was installed in December inherited high levels of foreign debt and budget deficit; in August 2012 it adopted a structural reform programme, which, in addition to measures to improve competitiveness prior to EU entry, entailed further privatization of state-owned enterprises, and retrenchment in the pension and health care systems. Following dissension within the ruling coalition, however, in April 2013 the Government announced that the introduction of a new property tax, which had been designed to replace the more bureaucratic system of taxes, had been postponed indefinitely. Croatia's accession to the EU, which officially took place on 1 July, was expected significantly to improve the business environment and provide increased investment opportunities, particularly in the transport, energy and environmental sectors, as well as facilitating trade. In 2013 GDP registered negative growth, and the IMF forecast that GDP would again contract slightly in 2013, although progress had been made in implementing structural reforms, particularly privatization measures. In January 2014 the European Commission began disciplinary proceedings against Croatia, under its excessive deficit procedure, imposing a deadline of 2016 for the reduction of the budget deficit from some 5.5% to 3.0% of GDP, in accordance with EU criteria, and urging the adoption of revised expenditure plans. In April 2014 the Government adopted a National Reform Programme and a Convergence Programme for 2014–17, in response to EU recommendations, which identified the need for reform in the areas of public finance, the financial sector, labour and competition.

PUBLIC HOLIDAYS

2015: 1 January (New Year's Day), 6 January (Epiphany), 6 April (Easter Monday), 1 May (Labour Day), 4 June (Corpus Christi), 22 June (Anti-Fascism Day), 25 June (Statehood Day), 5 August (National Day), 15 August (Assumption), 8 October (Independence Day), 1 November (All Saints' Day), 25–26 December (Christmas).

Statistical Survey

Source (unless otherwise stated): Central Bureau of Statistics of the Republic of Croatia, 10000 Zagreb, Ilica 3; tel. (1) 4806111; fax (1) 4806148; e-mail stat.info@dzs.hr; internet www.dzs.hr.

Area and Population

AREA, POPULATION AND DENSITY

Area (sq km)	56,594*
Population (census results)	
31 March 2001	4,437,460
31 March 2011	
Males	2,066,335
Females	2,218,554
Total	4,284,889
Population (official estimate at mid-year)	
2012	4,267,558
Density (per sq km) at mid 2012	75.4

* 21,851 sq miles.

POPULATION BY AGE AND SEX

(official estimates at mid-2012)

	Males	Females	Total
0–14	328,363	311,725	640,088
15–64	1,428,603	1,429,776	2,858,379
65 and over	301,735	467,356	769,091
Total	2,058,701	2,208,857	4,267,558

POPULATION BY ETHNIC GROUP

(2011 census)

	Number ('000)	% of total population
Croat	3,874.3	90.4
Serb	186.6	4.4
Muslim	31.5	0.7
Italian	17.8	0.4
Albanian	17.5	0.4
Roma	17.0	0.4
Hungarian	14.0	0.2
Slovene	10.5	0.2
Czech	9.6	0.4
Others*	106.0	2.5
Total	4,284.8	100.0

* Including other groups, ethnically non-declared persons and those of unknown ethnicity.

ADMINISTRATIVE DIVISIONS

(population estimates at mid-2012)

	Area (sq km)	Population	Density (per sq km)
Counties (Županije)			
Bjelovar-Bilogora	2,640	118,083	44.7
Dubrovnik-Neretva	1,781	122,337	68.7
Istria	2,813	207,719	73.8
Karlovac	3,626	126,997	35.0
Koprivnica-Križevci	1,748	114,846	65.7
Krapina-Zagorje	1,229	131,734	107.2
Lika-Senj	5,353	49,942	9.3
Međimurje	729	113,561	155.8
Osijek-Baranja	4,155	302,751	72.9
Požega-Slavonia	1,823	76,651	42.0
Primorje-Gorski kotar	3,588	295,300	82.3
Sisak-Moslavina	4,468	169,379	37.9
Slavonski Brod-Posavina	2,030	157,086	77.4
Split-Dalmatia	4,540	454,777	100.2
Šibenik-Knin	2,984	107,595	36.1
Varaždin	1,262	175,150	138.8
Virovitica-Podravina	2,024	83,820	41.4
Vukovar-Sirmium	2,454	177,583	72.4
Zadar	3,646	170,955	46.9
Zagreb	3,060	318,235	104.0
Capital City			
Zagreb	641	793,057	1,237.2
Total	56,594	4,267,558	75.4

PRINCIPAL TOWNS

(population at 2011 census)

Zagreb (capital)	790,017	Sisak	47,768
Split	178,102	Varaždin	46,946
Rijeka	128,624	Šibenik	46,332
Osijek	108,048	Dubrovnik	42,615
Zadar	75,062	Bjelovar	40,276
Velika Gorica	63,517	Kaštela	38,667
Slavonski Brod	59,141	Samobor	37,633
Pula	57,460	Vinkovci	35,312
Karlovac	55,705	Koprivnica	30,854

BIRTHS, MARRIAGES AND DEATHS

	Registered live births		Registered marriages		Registered deaths	
	Number	Rate (per 1,000)	Number	Rate (per 1,000)	Number	Rate (per 1,000)
2005	42,492	9.6	22,138	5.0	51,790	11.7
2006	41,446	9.3	22,092	5.0	50,378	11.3
2007	41,910	9.4	23,140	5.2	52,367	11.8
2008	43,753	9.9	23,373	5.3	52,151	11.8
2009	44,577	10.1	22,382	5.1	52,414	11.8
2010	43,361	9.8	21,294	4.8	52,096	11.8
2011	41,197	9.4	20,211	4.6	51,019	11.6
2012	41,771	9.8	20,323	4.8	51,710	12.1

Life expectancy (years at birth, official estimates): 77.0 (males 73.9; females 80.1) in 2012.

IMMIGRATION AND EMIGRATION

	2010	2011	2012
Immigrants	4,985	8,534	8,959
Emigrants	9,860	12,699	12,877

ECONOMICALLY ACTIVE POPULATION
(annual averages, '000 persons)

	2010	2011	2012
Agriculture, hunting, forestry and fishing	65.5	64.8	63.3
Mining and quarrying	7.5	6.5	5.8
Manufacturing	256.8	248.8	240.5
Electricity, gas and water supply	38.8	39.0	39.3
Construction	120.0	109.8	102.2
Wholesale and retail trade; repair of motor vehicles, motorcycles and personal and household goods	225.0	220.6	216.1
Hotels and restaurants	83.5	83.5	84.6
Transport, storage and communications	110.1	110.0	110.1
Financial intermediation	37.7	37.8	38.2
Real estate, renting and business activities	113.3	113.0	115.5
Public administration and defence; compulsory social security	115.5	116.5	116.1
Education	105.4	107.2	108.3
Health and social work	94.0	95.4	96.8
Other community, social and personal service activities	52.2	52.3	53.2
Private households with employed persons	5.9	5.0	4.3
Sub-total	1,431.2	1,410.2	1,394.3
Activities not classified	1.2	1.0	0.8
Total employed	1,432.5	1,411.2	1,395.1
Registered unemployed	302.4	305.3	324.3
Total labour force	1,734.9	1,716.5	1,719.4

Health and Welfare

KEY INDICATORS

Total fertility rate (children per woman, 2011)	1.5
Under-5 mortality rate (per 1,000 live births, 2011)	5
HIV/AIDS (% of persons aged 15–49, 2011)	<0.1
Physicians (per 1,000 head, 2009)	2.7
Hospital beds (per 1,000 head, 2009)	5.4
Health expenditure (2010): US $ per head (PPP)	1,475
Health expenditure (2010): % of GDP	7.8
Health expenditure (2010): public (% of total)	84.8
Access to water (% of total population, 2011)	99
Access to sanitation (% of total population, 2011)	98
Total carbon dioxide emissions ('000 metric tons, 2010)	20,883.6
Carbon dioxide emissions per head (metric tons, 2010)	4.7
Human Development Index (2012): ranking	47
Human Development Index (2012): value	0.805

For sources and definitions, see explanatory note on p. vi.

Agriculture

PRINCIPAL CROPS
('000 metric tons)

	2010	2011	2012
Wheat	681.0	782.5	999.7
Barley	172.4	194.0	235.8
Maize	2,067.8	1,733.7	1,297.6
Oats	48.2	77.2	94.5
Potatoes	178.6	167.5	151.3
Sugar beet	1,249.2	1,168.0	960.0
Beans, dry	1.6	1.1	0.5
Soybeans (Soya beans)	153.6	147.3	96.0
Sunflower seed	61.8	85.0	89.8
Rapeseed	33.0	49.5	26.4
Cabbages and other brassicas	36.6	38.9	23.1
Tomatoes	33.6	35.8	25.4
Cucumbers and gherkins	10.9	11.1	6.7
Chillies and peppers, green	18.6	20.0	14.6
Onions, dry	26.1*	25.5*	22.9
Garlic	4.3*	4.1*	4.6
Beans, green	5.3	4.8	2.9
Peas, green	3.7	6.1	3.5
Carrots and turnips	13.0	10.8	15.3
Watermelons	23.3	21.1	21.5*
Apples	106.9	112.9	42.4*
Pears	8.7	8.9	2.1*
Peaches and nectarines	8.9	11.8	6.2*
Plums and sloes	40.9	36.9	14.6*
Grapes	207.7	204.4	183.5
Tobacco, unmanufactured	8.5	10.6	11.8

* Unofficial figure.

Aggregate production ('000 metric tons, may include official, semi-official or estimated data): Total cereals 3,008.9 in 2010, 2,829.3 in 2011, 2,688.3 in 2012; Total roots and tubers 178.6 in 2010, 167.5 in 2011, 151.3 in 2012; Total vegetables (incl. melons) 215.1 in 2010, 225.4 in 2011, 182.9 in 2012; Total fruits (excl. melons) 449.2 in 2010, 446.5 in 2011, 317.5 in 2012.

Source: FAO.

LIVESTOCK
('000 head at 31 December)

	2010	2011	2012
Horses	19	20	20
Cattle	444	446	452
Pigs	1,231	1,233	1,182
Sheep	630	639	679
Goats	75	70	72
Chickens	5,041	4,222	4,415
Ducks	201	172	210
Geese and guinea fowls	46	39	46
Turkeys	726	609	471

Source: FAO.

LIVESTOCK PRODUCTS
('000 metric tons)

	2010	2011	2012
Cattle meat*	37.5	36.2	28.3
Sheep meat*	2.2	1.9	2.0
Pig meat*	121.0	120.1	104.1
Chicken meat*	22.4	28.0	27.2
Cows' milk	769.0	780.0	786.0
Sheep's milk	6.1	11.2	5.5
Hen eggs	42.3	41.5	35.1
Honey	2.1	2.8	2.8†

* Unofficial figures.
† FAO estimate.

Source: FAO.

Forestry

ROUNDWOOD REMOVALS
('000 cubic metres)

	2010	2011	2012
Sawlogs and veneer logs	2,068	2,461	2,961
Pulpwood	1,205	1,302	1,117
Other industrial wood	148	73	79
Fuel wood	1,056	1,422	1,557
Total	4,477	5,258	5,714

Source: FAO.

SAWNWOOD PRODUCTION
('000 cubic metres)

	2010	2011	2012
Coniferous (softwood)	93	110	115
Broadleaved (hardwood)	584	644	736
Total	677	754	851

Source: FAO.

Fishing

(metric tons, live weight)

	2009	2010	2011
Capture	55,750	52,828	70,953
European pilchard (sardine)	32,191	29,600	46,051
European anchovy	15,456	15,224	14,387
Atlantic bluefin tuna	619	388	372
Aquaculture	14,229	13,991	12,846*
Common carp	2,058	1,816	2,891
Rainbow trout	1,982	2,482	2,481
European seabass	2,800	2,800	2,775
Mediterranean mussel	2,000	2,000	400
Total catch	69,979	66,819	83,799*

* FAO estimate.

Mining

('000 metric tons unless otherwise indicated)

	2009	2010	2011
Crude petroleum ('000 barrels)	5,760*	5,340*	5,616
Natural gas (million cu m)	2,705	2,727	2,471
Ceramic clay	300.0*	300.0*	n.a.
Salt (unrefined)*	30.0	30.0	30.0
Gypsum (crude)	221.9	248.7	231.0

* Estimate(s).

Source: US Geological Survey.

Industry

SELECTED PRODUCTS
('000 metric tons unless otherwise indicated)

	2007	2008	2009
Beer ('000 hectolitres)	3,810	3,880	3,674
Spirits ('000 hectolitres)	136	53	49
Cigarettes (million)	14,415	15,586	11,382
Leather footwear ('000 pairs)	4,026	3,713	3,332
Motor spirit (petrol)	1,202	1,001	1,207
Gas-diesel oil (distillate fuel oil)	1,673	1,395	1,488
Cement	3,587	3,636	2,904
Tractors (number)	12,645	15,136	7,981
Tankers ('000 gross registered tons)	476	377	146
Electric energy (million kWh)	12,245	12,326	12,777

2003: Cotton fabrics and blankets ('000 sq metres) 12,321; Ready-to-wear clothing ('000 sq metres) 17,710; Tankers ('000 gross registered tons) 262; Cargo ships ('000 gross registered tons) 83; Chairs ('000) 2,059.

2010: Electric energy (million kWh) 14,105; Motor spirit (petrol) 1,094,000 metric tons.

Source: UN Industrial Commodity Statistics Database.

Finance

CURRENCY AND EXCHANGE RATES

Monetary Unit
100 lipa = 1 kuna.

Sterling, Dollar and Euro Equivalents (31 December 2013)
£1 sterling = 9.138 kuna;
US $1 = 5.549 kuna;
€1 = 7.653 kuna;
100 kuna = £10.94 = $18.02 = €13.07.

Average Exchange Rate (kuna per US $)
2011 5.344
2012 5.850
2013 5.705

Note: The Croatian dinar was introduced on 23 December 1991, replacing (and initially at par with) the Yugoslav dinar. On 30 May 1994 the kuna, equivalent to 1,000 dinars, was introduced.

CONSOLIDATED BUDGET
(general government accounts, million kuna)

Revenue

	2011	2012	2013*
Taxes	70,228	74,118	75,963
Taxes on income, profits and capital gains	16,561	17,574	17,117
Taxes on property	886	803	756
Taxes on goods and services	50,637	53,608	56,675
General taxes on goods and services	37,899	40,834	43,146
Excises	11,215	11,206	11,798
Taxes on international trade and transactions	1,766	1,754	1,143
Other taxes	378	380	272
Social contributions	38,605	37,846	37,635
Grants	880	995	2,702
Other revenue	13,311	13,173	13,919
Total	123,025	126,132	130,218

Expense by Economic Category

	2011	2012	2013*
Compensation of employees	35,608	35,381	33,495
Use of goods and services	15,362	14,996	15,616
Interest	7,571	8,849	10,261
Subsidies	7,606	6,801	7,001
Grants	1,639	1,832	3,791
Social benefits	57,136	56,881	56,665
Other expense	8,023	7,674	8,403
Total	132,945	132,413	135,232

Expense by Government Division

	2011	2012	2013*
Budgetary Central Government	116,163	115,318	118,074
Extrabudgetary users	4,152	3,838	4,228
Croatian Waters	1,437	1,440	1,601
Fund for Environmental Protection and Energy Efficiency	884	934	927
Croatian Roads Ltd	1,321	1,277	1,558
State Agency for Deposit Insurance and Bank Rehabilitation	409	89	23
Croatian Privatization Fund	16	0	0
Agency for Management of the Public Property	85	98	120
Budgetary Local Government	12,630	13,257	12,929
Total	132,945	132,413	135,232

* Projected figures.

Source: Ministry of Finance, Zagreb.

INTERNATIONAL RESERVES

(US $ million at 31 December)

	2010	2011	2012
IMF special drawing rights	466.9	465.5	467.6
Reserve position in IMF	0.2	0.2	0.2
Foreign exchange	13,665.4	14,018.1	14,339.3
Total	14,132.5	14,483.8	14,807.1

Source: IMF, *International Financial Statistics*.

MONEY SUPPLY

(million kuna at 31 December)

	2010	2011	2012
Currency outside depository corporations	15,262.7	16,689.1	16,947.1
Transferable deposits	35,325.3	37,330.1	42,818.7
Other deposits	183,755.5	187,677.3	205,477.2
Securities other than shares	1,018.7	1,769.1	1,121.0
Broad money	235,362.2	243,465.6	266,363.9

Source: IMF, *International Financial Statistics*.

COST OF LIVING

(Consumer Price Index; base: 2010 = 100)

	2011	2012
Food and non-alcoholic beverages	103.5	107.4
Alcohol and tobacco	106.8	111.2
Clothing and footwear	96.7	92.4
Housing and utilities	102.8	113.6
Health	100.8	102.8
Transport	106.0	109.5
Communications	96.0	91.1
Recreation and culture	97.9	100.2
Education	92.7	92.0
Restaurants and hotels	100.8	102.1
Miscellaneous goods and services	101.7	104.0
All items	102.3	105.8

NATIONAL ACCOUNTS

(million kuna at current prices)

Expenditure on the Gross Domestic Product

	2010	2011	2012
Final consumption expenditure	257,473	263,141	263,996
Household	189,314	194,518	195,355
Non-profit institutions serving households	3,126	3,325	3,340
Government	65,033	65,298	65,301
Change in inventories*	536	3,962	3,221
Gross fixed capital formation	67,254	63,286	60,740
Total domestic expenditure	325,263	330,389	327,957
Exports of goods and services	128,693	139,549	143,245
Less Imports of goods and services	130,149	139,768	140,971
GDP in purchasers' values	323,807	330,171	330,232
GDP at constant 2005 prices	275,325	275,289	n.a.

* Including statistical discrepancy.

Gross Domestic Product by Economic Activity

	2010	2011	2012
Agriculture, hunting, forestry and fishing	13,649	13,771	13,991
Mining and quarrying; manufacturing; electricity, gas and water supply	55,935	58,422	58,450
Construction	18,594	17,076	15,180
Wholesale and retail trade; transportation and storage, accommodation and food service activities	55,746	57,719	57,125
Information and communication	14,060	13,770	13,302
Financial intermediation; real estate, renting and business activities	68,805	70,859	70,313
Public administration and defence; compulsory social security; education; health and social work; other community, social and personal services; private households with employed persons	50,264	51,578	52,044
Gross value added in basic prices *	277,053	283,195	280,405
Taxes, *less* subsidies, on products	46,754	46,976	49,827
GDP in market prices	323,807	330,171	330,232

* Deduction for financial intermediation services indirectly measured assumed to be distributed by sector.

BALANCE OF PAYMENTS

(US $ million)

	2010	2011	2012
Exports of goods	11,914.1	13,452.8	12,449.0
Imports of goods	–19,583.8	–22,126.4	–20,311.3
Balance on goods	–7,669.7	–8,673.6	–7,862.3
Exports of services	11,354.6	12,796.0	12,023.8
Imports of services	–3,861.8	–3,898.3	–3,793.2
Balance on goods and services	–176.9	224.1	368.3
Primary income received	1,179.2	1,378.5	1,297.6
Primary income paid	–3,251.7	–3,587.7	–3,264.6
Balance on goods, services and primary income	–2,249.4	–1,985.1	–1,598.7
Secondary income received	2,192.8	2,307.3	2,185.8
Secondary income paid	–790.9	–727.0	–717.6
Current balance	–847.5	–404.8	–130.5

—*continued*	2010	2011	2012
Capital account (net)	45.1	42.3	35.6
Direct investment assets	–185.7	240.0	96.6
Direct investment liabilities	786.8	1,288.0	1,395.3
Portfolio investment assets	–469.5	612.0	–439.5
Portfolio investment liabilities	1,012.6	130.9	2,690.8
Financial derivatives and employee stock options (net)	–333.6	–80.5	123.9
Other investment assets	904.9	405.5	944.6
Other investment liabilities	15.7	–122.2	–3,950.8
Net errors and omissions	–921.1	–1,523.1	–626.6
Reserves and related items	7.7	588.1	139.3

Source: IMF, *International Financial Statistics*.

External Trade

PRINCIPAL COMMODITIES
(distribution by SITC, € million)

Imports c.i.f.	2010	2011	2012
Food and live animals	1,360.0	1,539.0	1,618.3
Mineral fuels, lubricants, etc.	2,843.5	3,553.1	3,767.3
Petroleum and petroleum products	2,211.9	2,719.2	2,609.2
Chemicals and related products	2,137.2	2,247.0	2,195.8
Basic manufactures	2,725.0	2,930.7	2,696.9
Machinery and transport equipment	3,880.4	3,623.2	3,603.4
Electrical machinery, apparatus etc. (excl. telecommunications and sound equipment)	709.0	682.4	645.1
Road vehicles and parts*	737.7	801.0	671.3
Other transport equipment and parts*	357.0	177.6	337.1
Miscellaneous manufactured articles	1,736.1	1,889.5	1,819.5
Clothing and accessories (excl. footwear)	435.2	504.1	479.5
Total (incl. others)	15,137.0	16,281.1	16,214.4

Exports f.o.b.	2010	2011	2012
Food and live animals	760.3	851.7	958.9
Crude materials (inedible) except fuels	601.5	746.7	757.0
Cork and wood	277.0	318.3	335.1
Mineral fuels, lubricants, etc.	1,113.1	1,154.7	1,320.1
Petroleum and petroleum products	865.4	952.1	1,052.9
Chemicals and related products	1,013.5	1,097.0	1,050.1
Medicinal and pharmaceutical products	328.2	375.9	426.0
Plastics in primary forms	235.8	160.6	43.7
Basic manufactures	1,260.8	1,432.2	1,372.9
Non-metallic mineral manufactures	306.8	323.2	330.0
Machinery and transport equipment	2,819.5	2,845.7	2,582.0
Electrical machinery, apparatus etc. (excl. telecommunications and sound equipment)	732.1	692.0	675.4
Transport equipment and parts (excl. road vehicles)*	1,143.6	1,108.0	719.9
Miscellaneous manufactured articles	1,120.1	1,211.0	1,205.1
Clothing and accessories (excl. footwear)	368.1	415.0	401.2
Total (incl. others)	8,905.2	9,582.2	9,628.7

* Data on parts exclude tyres, engines and electrical parts.

PRINCIPAL TRADING PARTNERS
(€ million)

Imports c.i.f.	2010	2011	2012
Austria	720.9	726.0	730.1
Belgium	204.8	195.2	218.4
Bosnia and Herzegovina	461.7	544.0	567.8
China, People's Republic	1,085.0	1,152.6	1,156.7
Czech Republic	288.7	314.1	293.0
France	409.7	479.7	503.6
Germany	1,893.1	2,049.2	2,057.1
Hungary	421.6	489.8	494.6
Italy	2,308.2	2,676.1	2,732.9
Japan	184.4	168.9	141.5
Korea, Republic	128.2	120.5	107.2
Netherlands	325.3	315.0	337.5
Russia	1,365.8	1,184.6	1,239.2
Slovenia	886.0	1,012.3	947.9
Spain	226.8	256.3	279.2
Sweden	128.7	132.1	173.1
Switzerland	260.0	285.0	362.3
United Kingdom	241.9	241.3	237.9
USA	327.2	372.7	358.7
Total (incl. others)	15,137.0	16,281.1	16,214.4

Exports f.o.b.	2010	2011	2012
Austria	471.4	547.3	628.2
Bosnia and Herzegovina	1,033.9	1,173.6	1,228.9
France	121.7	280.1	142.5
Germany	922.7	967.2	981.3
Greece	66.7	35.2	73.5
Hungary	199.8	240.8	242.9
Italy	1,660.4	1,511.1	1,472.7
Liberia	36.4	141.9	48.4
Macedonia, former Yugoslav republic	84.7	96.0	97.1
Malta	154.6	179.6	123.9
Netherlands	128.3	128.9	161.9
Poland	89.7	103.3	98.4
Russia	175.0	229.9	331.2
Serbia	349.2	375.0	418.2
Slovenia	697.1	794.0	828.2
United Kingdom	132.2	143.1	151.7
USA	222.0	255.6	281.9
Total (incl. others)	8,905.2	9,582.2	9,628.7

Transport

RAILWAYS
(traffic)

	2010	2011	2012
Passenger journeys ('000)	69,564	49,983	27,669
Passenger-kilometres (million)	1,742	1,486	1,104
Freight carried ('000 metric tons)	12,203	11,794	11,088
Freight net ton-km (million)	2,618	2,438	2,332

ROAD TRAFFIC
(registered motor vehicles at 31 December unless otherwise indicated)

	2010*	2011	2012
Passenger cars	1,515,449	1,518,278	1,445,220
Buses	4,877	4,841	4,655
Registered goods vehicles	157,731	154,884	141,567
Motorcycles and mopeds	176,773	176,948	156,981

* Data at 30 September.

INLAND WATERWAYS
(vessels and traffic)

	2010	2011	2012
Barges, tanker and cargo vessels	45	50	47
Goods unloaded (million metric tons)	0.2	0.1	0.3

Tugs: 24 in 2009.

SHIPPING

Flag Registered Fleet
(at 31 December)

	2011	2012	2013
Number of vessels	242	237	420
Total displacement ('000 grt)	1,543.3	1,410.5	1,354.2

Source: Lloyd's List Intelligence (www.lloydslistintelligence.com).

International Sea-borne Freight Traffic

	2002	2003	2004
Vessels entered (million grt)	33.1	43.1	51.5
Goods loaded ('000 metric tons)	4,597	4,053	4,809
Goods unloaded ('000 metric tons)	6,705	7,364	7,757
Goods in transit ('000 metric tons)	4,443	5,618	7,582

CIVIL AVIATION

	2010	2011	2012
Kilometres flown ('000)	19,058	19,527	17,865
Passengers carried ('000)	1,861	2,078	1,961
Passenger-km (million)	1,510	1,591	1,451
Freight carried (metric tons)	3,197	3,347	3,567
Ton-km ('000)	2,167	2,293	2,515

Tourism

FOREIGN TOURIST ARRIVALS BY COUNTRY OF ORIGIN
('000)

	2010	2011	2012
Austria	810	892	946
Bosnia and Herzegovina	217	223	220
Czech Republic	606	638	647
France	388	395	418
Germany	1,525	1,661	1,853
Hungary	298	328	308
Italy	1,018	1,150	1,051
Poland	454	495	544
Slovakia	310	335	337
Slovenia	1,017	1,100	1,054
United Kingdom	241	256	307
USA	133	151	173
Total (incl. others)	9,111	9,927	10,369

Receipts from tourism (US $ million, excl. passenger transport): 8,259 in 2010; 9,211 in 2011; 8,744 in 2012 (provisional) (Source: World Tourism Organization).

Communications Media

	2010	2011	2012
Telephones ('000 main lines in use)	1,865.7	1,760.9	1,640.0
Mobile cellular telephones ('000 subscribers)	4,928.4	5,115.1	4,971.4
Internet subscribers ('000)	1,496.6	1,191.6	n.a.
Broadband subscribers ('000)	803.8	861.3	90.3

Source: International Telecommunication Union.

Education

(2012/13 unless otherwise indicated)

	Institutions	Teachers	Students
Pre-primary	1,534	10,591	128,046
Primary schools	2,140	32,310	334,070
Secondary schools	724	25,023	184,793
Higher education	134*	16,975	157,289*

* 2011/12.

Pupil-teacher ratio (primary education, UNESCO estimate): 13.8 in 2010/11 (Source: UNESCO Institute for Statistics).

Adult literacy rate (UNESCO estimates): 98.3% (males 99.5%; females 98.9%) in 2011 (Source: UNESCO Institute for Statistics).

Directory

The Government

HEAD OF STATE

President of the Republic: IVO JOSIPOVIĆ (elected 10 January 2010; inaugurated 18 February 2010).

GOVERNMENT
(April 2014)

A coalition comprising representatives of the Socijaldemokratska partija Hrvatske (SDP—Social Democratic Party of Croatia), Hrvatska narodna stranka—Liberalni demokrati (HNS—Croatian People's Party—Liberal Democrats), Istarski demokratski sabor (IDS—Istrian Democratic Assembly) and the Hratska stranka umirovljenika (HSU—Croatian Pensioners' Party).

Prime Minister: ZORAN MILANOVIĆ (SDP).

First Deputy Prime Minister and Minister of Foreign and European Affairs: Prof. VESNA PUSIĆ (HNS).

Deputy Prime Minister and Minister of Social Policy and Youth: MILANKA OPAČIĆ (SDP).

Deputy Prime Minister and Minister of Regional Development and EU Funds: Prof. BRANKO GRČIĆ (SDP).

Deputy Prime Minister and Minister of Internal Affairs: RANKO OSTOJIĆ (SDP).

Minister of Finance: SLAVKO LINIĆ (SDP).

Minister of Defence: ANTE KOTROMANOVIĆ (SDP).

Minister of Justice: ORSAT MILJENIĆ (Independent).

Minister of Public Administration: ARSEN BAUK (SDP).

Minister of the Economy: IVAN VRDOLJAK (HNS).

Minister of Entrepreneurship and Crafts: GORDAN MARAS (SDP).

Minister of Labour and Pensions: MIRANDO MRSIĆ (SDP).

Minister of Maritime Affairs, Transport and Infrastructure: SINIŠA HAJDAŠ DONČIĆ (SDP).

Minister of Agriculture: TIHOMIR JAKOVINA (SDP).

Minister of Tourism: DARKO LORENCIN (IDS).

Minister of Environmental Protection and Nature: MIHAEL ZMAJLOVIĆ (SDP).

Minister of Construction and Physical Planning: ANKA MRAK-TARITAŠ (HNS).

Minister of Veterans Affairs: PREDRAG MATIĆ (Independent).

Minister of Health: Prof. RAJKO OSTOJIĆ (SDP).

Minister of Science, Education and Sport: ŽELJKO JOVANOVIĆ (SDP).

Minister of Culture: Prof. ANDREA ZLATAR VIOLIĆ (HNS).

MINISTRIES

Office of the President: 10000 Zagreb, Pantovčak 241; tel. (1) 4565191; fax (1) 4565299; e-mail ured@predsjednik.hr; internet www.predsjednik.hr.

Office of the Prime Minister: 10000 Zagreb, trg sv. Marka 2; tel. (1) 4569239; fax (1) 6303022; e-mail press@vlada.hr; internet www.vlada.hr.

Ministry of Agriculture: 10000 Zagreb, ul. grada Vukovara 78; tel. (1) 6106111; fax (1) 6109201; e-mail office@mps.hr; internet www.mps.hr.

Ministry of Construction and Physical Planning: 10000 Zagreb, ul. Republike Austrije 20; tel. (1) 3782444; fax (1) 3772822; internet www.mgipu.hr.

Ministry of Culture: 10000 Zagreb, Runjaninova 2; tel. (1) 4866308; fax (1) 4816755; e-mail kabinet@min-kulture.hr; internet www.min-kulture.hr.

Ministry of Defence: 10000 Zagreb, Sarajevska cesta 7; tel. (1) 4567111; fax (1) 3104613; e-mail infor@morh.hr; internet www.morh.hr.

Ministry of the Economy: 10000 Zagreb, ul. grada Vukovara 78; tel. (1) 6106111; fax (1) 6109110; e-mail ministar@mingo.hr; internet www.mingorp.hr.

Ministry of Entrepreneurship and Crafts: 10000 Zagreb, ul. grada Vukovara 78; tel. (1) 6106111; fax (1) 6106921; e-mail pitanja@minpo.hr; internet www.minpo.hr.

Ministry of Environmental Protection and Nature: 10000 Zagreb, ul. Republike Austrije 14; tel. (1) 3717111; fax (1) 3717149; e-mail ministar@mzoip.hr; internet www.mzoip.hr.

Ministry of Finance: 10000 Zagreb, ul. Katančićeva 5; tel. (1) 4591333; fax (1) 4922583; e-mail kabinet@mfin.hr; internet www.mfin.hr.

Ministry of Foreign and European Affairs: 10000 Zagreb, trg Nikole Šubića Zrinskog 7–8; tel. (1) 4569964; fax (1) 4551795; e-mail ministrica@mvep.hr; internet www.mvep.hr.

Ministry of Health: 10000 Zagreb, Ksaver 200A; tel. (1) 4607555; fax (1) 4677076; e-mail pitajtenas@miz.hr; internet www.miz.hr.

Ministry of Internal Affairs: 10000 Zagreb, ul. grada Vukovara 33; tel. (1) 6122111; fax (1) 6122771; e-mail pitanja@mup.hr; internet www.mup.hr.

Ministry of Justice: 10000 Zagreb, ul. grada Vukovara 49; tel. (1) 3714000; fax (1) 3714507; e-mail ministar@pravosudje.hr; internet www.mprh.hr.

Ministry of Labour and Pensions: 10000 Zagreb, ul. grada Vukovara 78; tel. (1) 6106835; fax (1) 6109638; e-mail info@mrms.hr; internet www.mrms.hr.

Ministry of Maritime Affairs, Transport and Infrastructure: 10000 Zagreb, Prisavlje 14; tel. (1) 3784520; fax (1) 3784580; e-mail ministar@mmpi.hr; internet www.mmpi.hr.

Ministry of Public Administration: 10000 Zagreb, Maksimirska 63; tel. (1) 2357555; fax (1) 2357607; e-mail kontakt-uprava@uprava.hr; internet www.uprava.hr.

Minister of Regional Development and EU Funds: 10000 Zagreb, Kralja Petra Krešimira IV 1; tel. (1) 6400660; fax (1) 6400644; e-mail kabinet@mrrfeu.hr; internet www.mrrfeu.hr.

Ministry of Science, Education and Sport: 10000 Zagreb, Donje Svetice 38; tel. (1) 4569000; fax (1) 4594301; e-mail ministar@mzos.hr; internet public.mzos.hr.

Ministry of Social Policy and Youth: 10000 Zagreb, Savska cesta 66; tel. (1) 5557111; fax (1) 5557222; e-mail ministarstvo@mspm.hr; internet www.mspm.hr.

Ministry of Tourism: 10000 Zagreb, Prisavlje 14; tel. (1) 6169180; fax (1) 6169181; e-mail ministar@mint.hr; internet www.mint.hr.

Ministry of Veterans Affairs: 10000 Zagreb, Savska 66; tel. (1) 2308888; fax (1) 2308855; e-mail ministarstvo@branitelji.hr; internet www.branitelji.hr.

President

Presidential Election, First Ballot, 27 December 2009

	Votes	% of votes
Ivo Josipović (Socijaldemokratska partija Hrvatske)	640,594	32.43
Milan Bandić (Independent)	293,068	14.84
Andrija Hebrang (Hrvatska demokratska zajednica)	237,998	12.05
Nadan Vidošević (Independent)	223,892	11.33
Vesna Pusić (Hrvatska narodna stranka—Liberalni demokrati)	143,190	7.25
Dragan Primorac (Independent)	117,154	5.93
Others	298,545	15.11
Total*	1,975,331	100.00

* Including 20,890 invalid votes (1.06% of the total).

Second Ballot, 10 January 2010

	Votes	% of votes
Ivo Josipović (Socijaldemokratska partija Hrvatske)	1,339,385	60.26
Milan Bandić (Independent)	883,222	39.74
Total*	2,222,607	100.00

* Excluding 30,547 invalid votes.

Legislature

Assembly (Sabor)

10000 Zagreb, trg sv. Marka 6; tel. (1) 4569444; fax (1) 6303010; e-mail gradjani@sabor.hr; internet www.sabor.hr.

The unicameral Sabor comprises a minimum of 100 and a maximum of 160 members, who are elected directly for a term of four years. Eight seats are reserved for representatives of minority ethnic groups. Of these, three seats are elected by Serbs, one by Hungarians and one by Italians. One representative is elected by Czechs and Slovaks; one by a constituency comprising Austrians, Bulgarians, Germans, Jews, Poles, Roma, Romanians, Russians, Ruthenians, Turks, Ukrainians and Vlachs; and one by Albanians, Bosniaks, Macedonians, Montenegrins and Slovenes.

President: JOSIP LEKO.

General Election, 4 December 2011

Parties/coalitions	% of votes	Seats
Kukuriku*	45.65	80
Hrvatska demokratska zajednica†	18.39	47
Hrvatski Laburisti—Stranka Rada	7.68	6
Hrvatski demokratski savez Slavonije i Baranje	4.45	6
Independent List–Ivan Grubišić	2.35	2
Hrvatska stranka prava—Dr Ante Starčević‡	2.86	1
Hrvatska seljačka stranka‖	1.24	1
Others	17.38	0
Total	100.00	151§

* Coalition comprising the Socijaldemokratska partija Hrvatske, the Hrvatska narodna stranka—Liberalni demokrati, Istarski demokratski sabor and Hratska stranka umirovljenika.

† In coalition with the Hrvatska građanska stranka and Demokratski Centar.

‡ In coalition with the Hrvatska čista stranka prava.

‖ In coalition with the Green Party and Hratska stranka umirovljenika.

§ Including eight seats reserved for representatives of minority ethnic groups.

Election Commission

Državno izborno povjerenstvo Republike Hrvatske (State Electoral Commission of the Republic of Croatia): 10000 Zagreb,

Visoka 15; tel. (1) 4569712; fax (1) 6303509; e-mail dip@izbori.hr; internet www.izbori.hr; Pres. BRANKO HRVATIN.

Political Organizations

Demokratski Centar (DC) (Democratic Centre—DC): 10000 Zagreb, Ilica 48/1; tel. (1) 4831111; fax (1) 4831045; e-mail tajnistvo@demokratski-centar.hr; internet www.demokratski-centar.hr; f. 2000 by mems of Hrvatska demokratska zajednica; pro-European, moderate; Pres. VESNA ŠKARE OŽBOLT; 14,000 mems (2004).

Hrvatska čista stranka prava (HČSP) (Croatian Pure Party of Rights): 10000 Zagreb, Tratinska 2; tel. and fax (1) 3864059; e-mail hcsp.hr@gmail.com; internet www.hcsp.hr; f. 1992; Pres. JOSIP MILJAK.

Hrvatski demokratski savez Slavonije i Baranje (HDSSB) (Croatian Democratic Alliance of Slavonia and Baranja): 31000 Osijek, trg Lava Mirskog 1; tel. (31) 250910; fax (31) 250919; e-mail info@hdssb.hr; internet www.hdssb.hr; f. 2006; Pres. VLADIMIR ŠIŠLJAGIĆ.

Hrvatska demokratska zajednica (HDZ) (Croatian Democratic Union): 10000 Zagreb, trg Žrtava fašizma 4; tel. (1) 4553000; fax (1) 4552600; e-mail hdz@hdz.hr; internet www.hdz.hr; f. 1989; Christian Democrat; Chair. TOMISLAV KARAMARKO; 220,000 mems (2005).

Hrvatska građanska stranka (HGS) (Croatian Civic Party): 21000 Split, Zrinsko frankopanska 68; tel. and fax (21) 381023; e-mail hgs@hgs.com.hr; internet www.hgs.com.hr; f. 2009; Pres. ŽELJKO KERUM.

Hrvatski Laburisti—Stranka Rada (Croatian Labourists—Party of Labour): 10000 Zagreb, Ilica 108; tel. (1) 8890750; e-mail info@laburisti.com; internet www.laburisti.hr; f. 2010; left-wing; Pres. DRAGUTIN LESAR.

Hrvatska narodna stranka—Liberalni demokrati (HNS) (Croatian People's Party—Liberal Democrats): 10000 Zagreb, Kneza Mislava 8; tel. (1) 4629111; fax (1) 4629110; e-mail ured@hns.hr; internet www.hns.hr; f. 1990; fmrly Croatian People's Party; Chair. VESNA PUSIĆ; 45,000 mems (2013).

Hrvatska pučka stranka (Croatian Popular Party): 10000 Zagreb, Ozaljska 93/2; tel. (1) 3633569; fax (1) 3633749; e-mail hps@hps.hr; f. 1997; Pres. TOMISLAV MERČEP; 23,700 mems (2006).

Hrvatska seljačka stranka (HSS) (Croatian Peasants' Party): 10000 Zagreb, ul. Kralja Zvonimira 17; tel. (1) 4553624; fax (1) 4553631; e-mail hss@hss.hr; internet www.hss.hr; f. 1989; Pres. BRANKO HRG; 43,000 mems (2005).

Hrvatska socijalno-liberalna stranka (HSLS) (Croatian Social Liberal Party): 10000 Zagreb, trg N. Š. Zrinskog 17/1; tel. (1) 4810401; fax (1) 4810404; e-mail hsls@hsls.hr; internet www.hsls.hr; f. 1989; Pres. DARINKO KOSOR; 25,000 mems (2011).

Hrvatska stranka prava (HSP) (Croatian Party of Rights): 10000 Zagreb, Primorska 5; tel. (1) 3778016; fax (1) 3778736; e-mail hsp@hsp.hr; internet www.hsp.hr; f. 1990 as revival of group originally founded in 1861; extreme right-wing nationalist; Pres. DANIEL SRB; 30,979 mems (2006).

Hrvatska stranka prava—Dr Ante Starčević (Croatian Party of Rights—Dr Ante Starčević): 10000 Zagreb, Čulinečka 119; tel. (1) 2865261; fax (1) 2865264; e-mail hspas@hspas.hr; internet www.hsp-ante-starcevic.hr; f. 2009 as splinter group from the HSP; Pres. RUŽA TOMAŠIĆ.

Hratska stranka umirovljenika (HSU) (Croatian Pensioners' Party): 10000 Zagreb, Frankopanska 7/1; tel. (1) 4840058; fax (1) 4815324; e-mail strankahsu@hsu.hr; internet www.hsu.hr; f. 1996; Pres. SILVANO HRELJA.

Hrvatska socijalno-liberalna stranka (HSLS) (Croatian Social Liberal Party): 10000 Zagreb, trg N. Š. Zrinskog 17/1; tel. (1) 4810401; fax (1) 4810404; e-mail hsls@hsls.hr; internet www.hsls.hr; f. 1989; Pres. DARINKO KOSOR; 25,000 mems (2011).

Istarski demokratski sabor (IDS) (Istrian Democratic Assembly): 52100 Pula, Splitska 3; tel. (52) 210588; fax (52) 223316; e-mail pula@ids-ddi.com; internet www.ids-ddi.com; f. 1990; Pres. BORIS MILETIĆ; 5,000 mems (2011).

Primorsko Goranski Savez (Primorje-Gorski kotar Alliance): 51000 Rijeka, Ciottina 19; tel. (51) 335418; fax (51) 335359; e-mail pgs@optinet.hr; internet www.pgs.hr; f. 1990; regionalist; Pres. DARUO VASILIĆ.

Samostalna demokratska srpska stranka (SDSS) (Independent Democratic Serb Party): 32000 Vukovar, trg Drvena Pijaca 28; tel. (32) 423211; fax (32) 416654; e-mail predsjednik@sdss.hr; internet www.sdss.hr; f. 1995 by Serbs in Eastern Slavonia; liberal, social democratic; Pres. Dr VOJISLAV STANIMIROVIĆ; 8,000 mems (2009).

Socijaldemokratska partija Hrvatske (SDP) (Social Democratic Party of Croatia): 10000 Zagreb, Iblerov trg 9; tel. (1) 4552055; fax (1) 4557509; e-mail sdp@sdp.hr; internet www.sdp.hr; f. 1990; fmrly the ruling League of Communists of Croatia (Party of Democratic Reform), renamed as above in 1993; Chair. ZORAN MILANOVIĆ.

Stranka demokratske akcije Hrvatske (SDA Hrvatske) (Party of Democratic Action of Croatia): 10000 Zagreb, Mandaličina 17; tel. (1) 4569472; fax (1) 3771288; e-mail sdah@sdah.hr; f. 1990; represents interests of Bosniaks and Muslims; Pres. Prof. ŠEMSO TANKOVIĆ; 4,877 mems (2011).

Zagorska demokratska stranka (ZDS) (Democratic Party of Zagorje): 49210 Zabok, Matije Gupce 53/1; tel. and fax (49) 222359; e-mail zds@kr.t-com.hr; internet www.zds.hr; f. 1997; Pres. Dr BELINA STANKO; 5,500 mems (2002).

Zagorska Stranka (Zagorje Party): 49210 Zabok, M. Gupca 53; tel. and fax (49) 221224; e-mail info@zagorskastranka.hr; internet www.zagorskastranka.hr; f. 2004; Pres. MILJENKO JERNEIĆ.

Diplomatic Representation

EMBASSIES IN CROATIA

Albania: 10000 Zagreb, Boškovićeva 7A; tel. (1) 4810679; fax (1) 4810682; e-mail embassy.zagreb@mfa.gov.al; Ambassador PËLLUMB QAZIMI.

Algeria: 10000 Zagreb, Bosanska 26; tel. (1) 3780333; fax (1) 3780344; e-mail info@ambalgzagreb.com; internet www.ambalgzagreb.com; Ambassador FARIDA AÏOUAZE.

Australia: 10000 Zagreb, Nova Ves 11/III; tel. (1) 4891200; fax (1) 4891216; e-mail austemb.zagreb@dfat.gov.au; internet www.croatia.embassy.gov.au; Ambassador SUSAN COX.

Austria: 10000 Zagreb, Radnička cesta 80/IX; tel. (1) 4881050; fax (1) 4834461; e-mail agram-ob@bmaa.gv.at; internet www.aussenministerium.at/zagreb; Ambassador ANDREA IKIĆ-BÖHM.

Belgium: 10000 Zagreb, Pantovčak 125/B1; tel. (1) 4578901; fax (1) 4578902; e-mail zagreb@diplobel.fed.be; internet www.diplomatie.be/zagreb; Ambassador NANCY ROSSIGNOL.

Bosnia and Herzegovina: 10000 Zagreb, Josipa Torbara 9; tel. (1) 4501070; fax (1) 4501071; e-mail amb.zagreb@mvp.gov.ba; Ambassador AZRA KALAJDŽISALIHOVIĆ.

Brazil: 10000 Zagreb, Trg Nikole Šubića Zrinskog 10/I; tel. (1) 4002250; fax (1) 4002266; e-mail info@brazilembassy.hr; internet www.brazilembassy.hr; Ambassador LUIZ FERNANDO GOUVÊA DE ATHAYDE.

Bulgaria: 10000 Zagreb, Nike Grškovića 31; tel. (1) 4646609; fax (1) 46446625; e-mail embassy.zagreb@mfa.bg; internet www.mfa.bg/embassies/croatia; Ambassador TANYA DIMITROVA.

Canada: 10000 Zagreb, prilaz Gjure Deželića 4; tel. (1) 4881200; fax (1) 4881230; e-mail zagrb@international.gc.ca; internet www.canadainternational.gc.ca/croatia-croatie; Ambassador LOUISE LAROCQUE.

Chile: 10000 Zagreb, Smičiklasova 23/II; tel. (1) 4611958; fax (1) 4610328; e-mail embajada@echile.hr; Ambassador GERMÁN ORLANDO IBARRA MORÁN.

China, People's Republic: 10000 Zagreb, Mlinovi 132; tel. (1) 4637011; fax (1) 4637012; e-mail chnemb@zg.tel.hr; internet hr.china-embassy.org; Ambassador DENG YING.

Czech Republic: 10000 Zagreb, Radnička cesta 47/6, Romeo Tower; tel. (1) 6177246; fax (1) 6176630; e-mail zagreb@embassy.mzv.cz; internet www.mzv.cz/zagreb; Ambassador MARTIN KOŠATKA.

Denmark: 10000 Zagreb, Trg Nikole Šubića Zrinskog 10; tel. (1) 4924530; fax (1) 4924554; e-mail zagreb@um.dk; internet www.kroatien.um.dk; Ambassador POUL ERIK DAM KRISTENSEN.

Egypt: 10000 Zagreb, Babonićeva 58; tel. (1) 2310781; fax (1) 2310619; e-mail embassy.zagreb@mfa.gov.eg; internet www.mfa.gov.eg/english/embassies/egyptian_embassy_croatia; Ambassador IMAN MOHAMED MEDHAT ELFARR.

Finland: 10000 Zagreb, Miramarska 23; tel. (1) 6312080; fax (1) 6312090; e-mail sanomat.zag@formin.fi; internet www.finland.hr; Ambassador TIMO RAJAKANGAS.

France: 10000 Zagreb, Hebrangova 2; tel. (1) 4893600; fax (1) 4893660; internet www.ambafrance-hr.org; Ambassador MICHÈLE BOCCOZ.

Germany: 10000 Zagreb, ul. grada Vukovara 64; tel. (1) 6300100; fax (1) 6155536; e-mail info@zagreb.diplo.de; internet www.zagreb.diplo.de; Ambassador HANS PETER ANNEN.

Greece: 10000 Zagreb, Opatička 12; tel. (1) 4810444; fax (1) 4810419; e-mail greece-embassy@grembassy.hr; internet www.grembassy.hr; Ambassador ELENI GEROKOSTOPOULOU.

Holy See: 10000 Zagreb, Ksaverska cesta 10 A; tel. (1) 4673996; fax (1) 4673997; e-mail apostolska.nuncijatura.rh@inet.hr; Apostolic

Nuncio H. E. Mgr. ALESSANDRO D'ERRICO (Titular Archbishop of Truentum).

Hungary: 10000 Zagreb, Pantovčak 255–257; tel. (1) 4890906; fax (1) 4579301; e-mail mission.zgb@mfa.gov.hu; internet www.mfa.gov.hu/emb/zagreb; Ambassador GÁBOR IVÁN.

India: 10000 Zagreb, ul. Kulmerska 23A; tel. (1) 4873239; fax (1) 4817907; e-mail info@indianembassy.hr; internet www.indianembassy.hr; Ambassador LAL THLA MUANA.

Iran: 10000 Zagreb, Pantovčak 125C; tel. (1) 4578980; fax (1) 4578987; e-mail iran.embassy@zg.t-com.hr; Ambassador MOHSEN SHARIF KHODAEI.

Israel: 10000 Zagreb, ul. grada Vukovara 271/11; tel. (1) 6169500; fax (1) 6169555; e-mail info@zagreb.mfa.gov.il; internet www.embassies.gov.il/zagreb; Ambassador YOSEF AMRANI.

Italy: 10000 Zagreb, Medulićeva 22; tel. (1) 4846386; fax (1) 4846384; e-mail amb.zagabria@esteri.it; internet www.ambzagabria.esteri.it; Ambassador EMANUELA D'ALESSANDRO.

Japan: 10000 Zagreb, Boškovićeva 2; tel. (1) 4870650; fax (1) 4667334; e-mail politics_economy@japan.t-com.hr; internet www.hr.emb-japan.go.jp; Ambassador KEIJI IDE.

Kazakhstan: 10000 Zagreb, Pantovčak 142; tel. (1) 4839255; fax (1) 4573796; e-mail embassy@kazembassy.hr; Ambassador ASLAN MUSIN.

Korea, Republic: 10000 Zagreb, Ksaverska cesta 111A–B; tel. (1) 4821282; fax (1) 4821274; e-mail croatia@mofat.go.kr; internet hrv.mofat.go.kr; Ambassador SUH HYUNG-WON.

Kosovo: 10000 Zagreb, Trg Nikole Šubića Zrinskog 1; tel. (1) 4827741; fax (1) 4827721; e-mail embassy.croatia@ks-gov.net; Ambassador SHKENDIJE GECI SHERIFI.

Libya: 10000 Zagreb, Gornje Prekrižje 51B; tel. (1) 4629250; fax (1) 4629279; e-mail libya-embassy.zg@email.t-com.hr; Chargé d'affaires a.i. YOSEF ALASWAD.

Macedonia, former Yugoslav republic: 10000 Zagreb, Kralja Zvonimira 6/1; tel. (1) 4620261; fax (1) 4617369; e-mail zagreb@mfa.gov.mk; Ambassador DANIELA KARAGJOZOSKA.

Malaysia: 10000 Zagreb, Slavujevac 4A; tel. (1) 4834346; fax (1) 4834348; e-mail malzagreb@kln.gov.my; Ambassador YEAN YOKE HENG.

Montenegro: 10000 Zagreb, Trg Nikole Šubića Zrinskog 1/IV; tel. (1) 4573362; fax (1) 4573423; e-mail croatia@mfa.gov.me; Ambassador IGOR GRAĐEVIĆ.

Netherlands: 10000 Zagreb, Medveščak 56; tel. (1) 4642200; fax (1) 4642211; e-mail zag@minbuza.nl; internet kroatie.nlambassade.org; Ambassador STELLA RONNER-GRUBAČIĆ.

Norway: 10000 Zagreb, Hektorovićeva 2/3; tel. (1) 6273800; fax (1) 6273899; e-mail emb.zagreb@mfa.no; internet www.norwegianembassy.hr; Ambassador HENRIK OFSTAD.

Poland: 10000 Zagreb, Krležin Gvozd 3; tel. (1) 4899444; fax (1) 4834577; e-mail hrzagamb@msz.gov.pl; internet www.zagrzeb.msz.gov.pl; Ambassador MACIEJ SZYMAŃSKI.

Portugal: 10000 Zagreb, Trg ban J. Jelačića 5/2; tel. (1) 4882210; fax (1) 4920663; e-mail emb.port.zagreb@zg.htnet.hr; Ambassador PAULO TIAGO FERNANDES JERÓNIMO DA SILVA.

Romania: 10000 Zagreb, Mlinarska 43; tel. (1) 4677550; fax (1) 4677854; e-mail veleposlanstvo.rumunjske@zg.t-com.hr; internet zagreb.mae.ro; Ambassador COSMIN-GEORGE DINESCU.

Russia: 10000 Zagreb, Bosanska 44; tel. (1) 3755038; fax (1) 3755040; e-mail veleposlanstvo-ruske-federacije@zg.htnet.hr; internet www.zagreb.mid.ru; Ambassador ROBERT MARKARIAN.

Serbia: 10000 Zagreb, Pantovčak 245; tel. (1) 4579067; fax (1) 4573338; e-mail ambasada@ambasada-srbije.hr; internet www.ambasada-srbije.hr; Chargé d'affaires a. i. BOSA PRODANOVIĆ.

Slovakia: 10000 Zagreb, prilaz Gjure Deželića 10; tel. (1) 4877070; fax (1) 4877078; e-mail emb.zagreb@mzv.sk; internet www.mzv.sk/zahreb; Ambassador JURAJ PRIPUTEN.

Slovenia: 10000 Zagreb, Alagovićeva 30; tel. (1) 6311000; fax (1) 6177236; e-mail vzg@gov.si; internet www.zagreb.embassy.si; Ambassador VOJKO VOLK.

Spain: 10000 Zagreb, Tuškanac 21A; tel. (1) 4848950; fax (1) 4848711; e-mail emb.zagreb@mae.es; Ambassador RODRIGO AGUIRRE DE CÁRCER.

Sweden: 10000 Zagreb, Frankopanska 22; tel. (1) 4925100; fax (1) 4925125; e-mail ambassaden.zagreb@gov.se; internet www.swedenabroad.com/zagreb; Ambassador LARS SCHMIDT.

Switzerland: 10000 Zagreb, Bogovićeva 3; tel. (1) 4810800; fax (1) 4810890; e-mail zag.vertretung@eda.admin.ch; internet www.eda.admin.ch/zagreb; Ambassador DENIS KNOBEL.

Turkey: 10000 Zagreb, Masarykova 3/II; tel. (1) 4864660; fax (1) 4864670; e-mail turkishemb@zg.t-com.hr; internet zagreb.emb.mfa.gov.tr; Ambassador BURAK ÖZÜGERGIN.

Ukraine: 10000 Zagreb, Voćarska 52; tel. (1) 4616296; fax (1) 4633726; e-mail emb_hr@mfa.gov.ua; internet www.mfa.gov.ua/croatia; Ambassador OLEKSANDR M. LEVCHENKO.

United Kingdom: 10000 Zagreb, Ivana Lučića 4; tel. (1) 6009100; fax (1) 6009111; e-mail british.embassyzagreb@fco.gov.uk; internet www.gov.uk/government/world/croatia; Ambassador DAVID SLINN.

USA: 10010 Zagreb, Thomasa Jeffersona 2; tel. (1) 6612200; fax (1) 6658933; e-mail irczagreb@state.gov; internet zagreb.usembassy.gov; Ambassador KENNETH MERTEN.

Judicial System

The Supreme Court is the highest judicial body in the country, comprising 26 judges, elected for a period of eight years. The Constitutional Court consists of 11 judges, elected by the Sabor for a period of eight years.

Supreme Court: 10000 Zagreb, trg Nikole Šubića Zrinskog 3; tel. (1) 4862222; fax (1) 4810035; e-mail vsrh@vsrh.hr; internet www.vsrh.hr; Pres. BRANKO HRVATIN.

Constitutional Court: 10000 Zagreb, Marka trg 4; tel. (1) 6400251; fax (1) 4551055; e-mail ustavni_sud@usud.hr; internet www.usud.hr; f. 1991; Pres. Prof. JASNA OMEJEC.

State Judicial Council: 10000 Zagreb, trg Nikole Šubića Zrinskog 3; tel. and fax (1) 4811501; Pres. MILAN GUDELJ.

Office of the Public Prosecutor: 10000 Zagreb, Gajeva 30A; tel. (1) 4591888; fax (1) 4591854; e-mail dorh@zg.htnet.hr; Public Prosecutor MLADEN BAJIĆ.

Religion

Most of the population are Christian, the largest denomination being the Roman Catholic Church, of which most ethnic Croats are adherents. The Archbishop of Zagreb is the most senior Roman Catholic prelate in Croatia. There is a significant Orthodox minority. According to the 2001 census, 87.8% of the population of Croatia were Roman Catholics, 4.4% were Eastern Orthodox, 1.3% Muslim, and there were small communities of Protestants and Jews.

CHRISTIANITY

The Roman Catholic Church

For ecclesiastical purposes, Croatia comprises five archdioceses (including one, Zadar, directly responsible to the Holy See) and 12 dioceses, including one for Catholics of the Byzantine rite. The dioceses of Srijem, in Serbia, and Kotor, in Montenegro, are also suffragan to the Croatian hierarchy. There are an estimated 4.1m. adherents, equivalent to 91.5% of the total population.

Bishops' Conference: 10000 Zagreb, Kaptol 22; tel. (1) 4811893; fax (1) 4811894; Pres. Most Rev. MARIN SRAKIĆ (Archbishop of Đakovo-Osijek).

Latin Rite

Archbishop of Đakovo-Osijek: Most Rev. MARIN SRAKIĆ, 31400 Đakovo, Strossmayerov trg 6; tel. (31) 802200; fax (31) 812310; e-mail biskupski-ordinarijat-djakovo@os.t-com.hr.

Archbishop of Split-Makarska: Most Rev. MARIN BARIŠIĆ, 21000 Split, Poljana kneza Trpimira 7, POB 328; tel. (21) 407501; fax (21) 407538; e-mail marin.barisic@hbk.hr.

Archbishop of Zadar: Most Rev. ŽELIMIR PULJIĆ, 23000 Zadar, trg Jurja Bijankinija 2; tel. (23) 208650; fax (23) 208640; e-mail nadbiskupija.zadarska@zd.htnet.hr.

Archbishop of Zagreb: Cardinal JOSIP BOZANIĆ, 10001 Zagreb, Kaptol 31; tel. (1) 4894808; fax (1) 4816104; e-mail kancelar@zg-nadbiskupija.hr.

Byzantine Rite

Bishop of Križevci: Most Rev. SLAVOMIR MIKLOVŠ, 10000 Zagreb, Kaptol 20; tel. (1) 4811872; fax (1) 4811873; 21,467 adherents (2004).

Serbian Orthodox Church

Metropolitan of Zagreb and Ljubljana: Bishop JOVAN, 10000 Zagreb, Srpska Biskupija.

The Press

In 2010 a total of 267 newspaper titles and 2,676 periodicals were published in Croatia.

PRINCIPAL NEWSPAPERS

24 Sata (24 Hours): 10000 Zagreb, Oreškovićeva 3D; tel. (1) 6069500; fax (1) 6069660; e-mail redakcija@24sata.hr; internet www.24sata.hr; f. 2005; Editor-in-Chief RENATO IVANUŠ; circ. 163,505 (2009).

Business.hr: 10000 Zagreb, F. Andrašeca 14; tel. (1) 8992600; fax (1) 8992800; e-mail redakcija@business.hr; internet www.business.hr; f. 2005 as weekly; published daily since 2008; Editor-in-Chief PLAMENKO CVITIĆ.

Glas Istre (Voice of Istria): 52100 Pula, Riva 10; tel. (52) 591500; fax (52) 591544; e-mail portal@glasistre.hr; internet www.glasistre.hr; morning; Dir ŽELJKO ŽMAK; Editor-in-Chief RANKO BOROVČKI; circ. 20,000.

Glas Slavonije (Voice of Slavonia): 31000 Osijek, Hrvatske Republike 20; tel. (31) 223200; fax (31) 223203; e-mail glas@glas-slavonije.hr; internet www.glas-slavonije.hr; f. 1920; morning; independent; Editor-in-Chief MARIO MIHALJEVIĆ; circ. 25,000.

Jutarnji list: 10000 Zagreb, Koranska 2; tel. (1) 6103100; fax (1) 6103148; e-mail redakcija@jutarnji.hr; internet www.jutarnji.hr; Editor-in-Chief GORDANA JANKOSKA VRANIĆ.

Novi List (New Paper): 51001 Rijeka, Zvonimirova 20A, POB 130; tel. (51) 650011; fax (51) 672114; e-mail redakcija@novilist.hr; internet www.novilist.hr; morning; Editor-in-Chief BRANKO MIJIĆ; circ. 60,000.

Poslovni Dnevnik (Business News): 10000 Zagreb, Savska 66/10; tel. (1) 6326000; fax (1) 6326060; e-mail redakcija@poslovni.hr; internet www.poslovni.hr; Editor-in-Chief DARKO MARKUŠIĆ.

Slobodna Dalmacija (Free Dalmatia): 21000 Split, ul. Hrvatske mornarice 4; tel. (21) 352888; fax (21) 383102; e-mail redakcija@slobodnadalmacija.hr; internet www.slobodnadalmacija.com; morning; Editor-in-Chief KRUNOSLAV KLJAKOVIĆ.

Sportske novosti (Sports News): 10000 Zagreb, Koranska 2; tel. (1) 6103100; fax (1) 6103148; e-mail sn@sn.t-com.hr; internet www.sportske.jutarnji.hr; morning; Editor-in-Chief DANIJET BRAČUN; circ. 55,000.

Večernji list (Evening Paper): 10000 Zagreb, Oreškovićeva 6H/1; tel. (1) 6300605; fax (1) 6300676; e-mail vecernji@vecernji.hr; internet www.vecernji.hr; evening; Editor-in-Chief GORAN OGURLIĆ; circ. 200,000.

La Voce del Popolo (Voice of the People): 51000 Rijeka, Zvonimirova 20A; tel. (51) 672119; fax (51) 672112; e-mail lavoce@edit.hr; internet www.edit.hr/lavoce; f. 1944; morning; Italian; Editor-in-Chief ERROL SUPERINA; circ. 4,000.

PERIODICALS

Arena: 10000 Zagreb, Koranska 2; tel. (1) 6103400; fax (1) 6103404; f. 1957; illustrated weekly; Editor MARK CIGOJ; circ. 135,000.

DuList (Dubrovnik News): 20000 Dubrovnik, Ćira Carića 3; tel. (20) 350670; fax (20) 350675; e-mail info@dulist.hr; internet www.dulist.hr; weekly; Editor BARBARA DJURASOVIĆ.

Eukonomist: 10000 Zagreb, Savska 28; tel. (1) 4882582; fax (1) 4843860; e-mail veceslav.kocijan@eukonomist.com; internet www.eukonomist.com; monthly; business and economy; Editor-in-Chief VEĆESLAV KOCIJAN.

Glas Koncila (The Voice of the Council): 10000 Zagreb, Kaptol 8/216; tel. (1) 4874300; fax (1) 4874303; e-mail redakcija@glas-koncila.hr; internet www.glas-koncila.hr; f. 1962; weekly; Catholic; Editor-in-Chief IVAN MIKLENIĆ.

Globus: 10000 Zagreb, Koranska 2; tel. (1) 6103200; fax (1) 6103204; e-mail redakcija@jutarnji.hr; internet www.globus.jutarnji.hr; f. 1990; political weekly; Editor-in-Chief GORDANA JANKOSKA VRANIĆ; circ. 110,000.

Gloria: 10000 Zagreb, Koranska 2; tel. (1) 6103250; fax (1) 6103252; e-mail web@gloria.hr; internet www.gloria.hr; f. 1994; weekly; popular culture; owned by Europa Press Holding; Editor ANTONIJA BILIĆ ARAR; circ. 110,000.

Hrvatsko slovo (Croatian Letter): 10000 Zagreb, Hrvatske bratske zajednice 4; tel. (1) 4814965; fax (1) 6190111; e-mail hkz@zg.htnet.hr; internet www.hkz.hr; f. 1995; weekly; culture; Editor NENAD PISKAČ.

Informator: 10000 Zagreb, ul. Pavla Hatza 26; tel. (1) 5612295; fax (1) 5604440; e-mail informator@informator.hr; internet www.informator.hr; f. 1952; economic and legal matters; Dir and Editor NATAŠA HREN.

Karlovački tjednik (The Karlovac Weekly): 47000 Karlovac, ul. J. Križanića 30; tel. (47) 611855; fax (47) 615011; e-mail zdenko@karlovacki-tjednik.hr; internet www.karlovacki-tjednik.hr; f. 1944; weekly; news from Karlovac County; Editor-in-Chief ZDENKO ŽIVČIĆ.

Lider (The Leader): 10144 Zagreb, Savska cesta 41; tel. (1) 6333500; fax (1) 6333599; e-mail miodrag.sajatovic@liderpress.hr; internet www.liderpress.hr; f. 2005; weekly; business; Man. Editor MIODRAG ŠAJATOVIĆ.

Majstor: 10000 Zagreb, Ivanićgradska 64; tel. (1) 6055777; fax (1) 2450163; e-mail majstor@majstor.hr; internet www.majstor.hr; f. 1992; monthly; trade-related technology; Editor-in-Chief TOMISLAV TOTH.

Međimurje: 40000 Čakovec, Zrinsko frankopanska 10/75; tel. (40) 310822; fax (40) 638995; e-mail urednik@medjimurje.hr; internet www.medjimurje.hr; weekly, Tue.; regional; Editor-in-Chief IVICA JURGEC.

Nacional (The National): 10000 Zagreb, Kneza Branimira 29; tel. (1) 5555000; fax (1) 5555092; e-mail nacional@nacional.hr; internet www.nacional.hr; f. 1995; independent weekly; also daily online edn, in Croatian and English; Chief Editor ROBERT BAJRUŠI.

Narodni list (The People's Paper): 23000 Zadar, Poljana Zemaljskog odbora 2; tel. (23) 224810; fax (23) 224824; e-mail angela.juricic@narodni-list.hr; internet www.narodni-list.hr; f. 1862; weekly; Editor-in-Chief ANĐELA JURIČIĆ.

Novi Plamen (A New Flame): 10000 Zagreb, Pavla Hatza 14; tel. (1) 4835340; fax (1) 6679518; e-mail redakcija@noviplamen.org; internet www.noviplamen.org; f. 2007; every four months; democratic socialist; Editors-in-Chief IVICA MLADENOVIĆ, MLADEN JAKOPOVIĆ, GORAN MARKOVIĆ.

Privredni vjesnik (Economic Herald): 10000 Zagreb, Kačićeva 9; tel. (1) 4846233; fax (1) 4846232; e-mail redakcija@privredni.hr; internet www.privredni.hr; f. 1953; weekly; economics, finance; Chief Editor DARKO BUKOVIĆ.

Republika: 10000 Zagreb, trg bana Josipa Jelačića 7; tel. (1) 4816931; fax (1) 4816959; e-mail dhk@dhk.hr; internet www.dhk.hr; f. 1945; monthly; publ. by Društvo hrvatskih književnika; literary review; Editor-in-Chief ANTE STAMAĆ.

Školske Novine: 10000 Zagreb, Andrije Hebranga 40; tel. (1) 4855720; fax (1) 4855712; e-mail info@skolskenovine.hr; internet www.skolskenovine.hr; f. 1950; educational weekly; Editor-in-Chief MARIJAN ŠIMEG.

NEWS AGENCIES

HINA News Agency—Hrvatska izvještajna novinska agencija (Croatian Information and News Agency): 10000 Zagreb, trg Marulidev 16; tel. (1) 4808600; fax (1) 4808822; e-mail hina@hina.hr; internet www.hina.hr; f. 1990; Dir BRANKA GABRIELA VALENTIĆ.

IKA—Informativna katolička agencija (Catholic Press Agency): 10000 Zagreb, Kaptol 4; tel. (1) 4814951; fax (1) 4814957; e-mail ika-zg@zg.htnet.hr; internet www.ika.hr; f. 1993; Dir ENCO RODINIS.

STINA: 21000 Split, Šetaliste Bačvice 10; tel. (21) 488945; fax (21) 321421; e-mail stina@st.htnet.hr; internet www.stina.hr; f. 1991; Dir GORAN VEŽIĆ; Editor-in-Chief STOJAN OBRADOVIĆ.

Publishers

AGM Publisher: 10000 Zagreb, Mihanovićeva 28; tel. (1) 4856307; fax (1) 4856316; e-mail agm@agm.hr; internet www.agm.hr; Croatian and foreign literature, arts, economics, science; Gen. Dir BOŽE ĆOVIĆ.

Algoritam: 10000 Zagreb, Harambašićeva 19; tel. (1) 2359333; fax (1) 2335956; e-mail info@algoritam.hr; internet www.algoritam.hr; international bestsellers; Pres. NEVEN ANTIČEVIĆ.

Ceres: 10000 Zagreb, Tomašićeva 13; tel. (1) 4558501; fax (1) 4550387; e-mail ceres@zg.tel.hr; poetry, fiction, and philosophical and scientific writings; Gen. Dir DRAGUTIN DUMANČIĆ.

Croatian Academy of Sciences and Arts Publishing Dept (Hrvatska akademija znanosti i umjetnosti, Odjel za izdavačku djelatnost): 10000 Zagreb, Zrinski trg 11; tel. (1) 4895111; fax (1) 4819979; e-mail naklada@hazu.hr; internet info.hazu.hr; f. 1861; Sec.-Gen. Dr PAVAO RUDAN.

Egmont: 10000 Zagreb, Višnjevac 3; tel. (1) 3040555; fax (1) 3091713; e-mail info@cro.egmont.com; internet www.egmont.hr; f. 1995; children's books.

Erasmus Publishing: 10000 Zagreb, Rakušina 4; tel. and fax (1) 433114; Croatian literature; Gen. Dir SREĆKO LIPOVČAN.

Europa Press: 10000 Zagreb, Koranska 2; tel. (1) 6173760; fax (1) 6173704; f. 1990; Pres. NINOSLAV PAVIĆ.

Fraktura: 10290 Zaprešić, Bregovita 7; tel. (1) 3357863; fax (1) 3358320; e-mail fraktura@fraktura.hr; internet www.fraktura.hr; f. 2002; literary fiction.

Golden Marketing-Tehnička Knjiga: 10000 Zagreb, Jurišićeva 10; tel. (1) 4810820; fax (1) 4810821; e-mail gmtk@gmtk.net; tel. www.gmtk.net; f. 1947; academic publisher; Dir ANA REŠETAR.

Hena Com: 10000 Zagreb, Gosposvetska 28; tel. and fax (1) 3750206; fax (1) 3756037; e-mail hena-com@hena-com.hr; internet www.hena-com.hr; children's books; Gen. Man. UZEIR HUSKOVIĆ.

Izvori: 10000 Zagreb, Trnjanska 64; tel. (1) 6112576; fax (1) 6112321; e-mail info@izvori.com; internet www.izvori.com; f. 1990; scientific journalism, literature, classics, popular fiction, comic books.

Kršćanska Sadašnjost: 10000 Zagreb, ul. Vukovara 271/XI; tel. (1) 6349010; fax (1) 4666815; e-mail uprava@ks.hr; internet www.ks.hr; theological publications.

Masmedia: 10000 Zagreb, ul. Baruna Trenka 11–13; tel. (1) 4577400; fax (1) 4577769; e-mail mm@masmedia.hr; internet www.masmedia.hr; f. 1990; business and professional literature; Gen. Dir STJEPAN ANDRAŠIĆ.

Matica Hrvatska: 10000 Zagreb, trg Strossmayerov 4; tel. (1) 4878360; fax (1) 4819319; e-mail matica@matica.hr; internet www.matica.hr; f. 1842; arts and science, fiction, popular science, politics, economics, sociology, history; Chair. Prof. IGOR ZIDIĆ.

Miroslav Krleža Institute of Lexicography (Leksikografski zavod Miroslav Krleža): 10000 Zagreb, Frankopanska 26; tel. (1) 4800398; fax (1) 4800399; e-mail lzmk@lzmk.hr; internet www.lzmk.hr; f. 1950; encyclopedias, lexicons, bibliographies and dictionaries; Dir-Gen. ANTUN VUJIĆ.

Mozaik Knjiga: 10000 Zagreb, Karlovačka 24A; tel. (1) 6315124; fax (1) 6315222; e-mail info@mozaik-knjiga.hr; internet www.mozaik-knjiga.hr; f. 1991; Gen. Dir BOJAN VIDMAR.

Naprijed-Ljevak: 10000 Zagreb, trg Josipa Jelačića 17; tel. (1) 4812992; fax (1) 3887886; e-mail ljevak@ljevak.hr; internet www.naklada-ljevak.hr; f. 1957; philosophy, psychology, religion, sociology, medicine, dictionaries, children's books, art, politics, economics, tourist guides; Exec. Dir PETRA LJEVAK.

Školska Knjiga (Schoolbooks): 10001 Zagreb, Masarykova 28, POB 1039; tel. (1) 4830511; fax (1) 4830505; e-mail ante.zuzul@skolskaknjiga.hr; internet www.skolskaknjiga.hr; education, textbooks, art; Dir Prof. ANTE ŽUŽUL.

SysPrint: 10020 Zagreb, Medarska 69; tel. (1) 6558740; fax (1) 6558741; e-mail info@sysprint.hr; internet www.sysprint.hr; fiction, textbooks, journals and manuals; Dir ROBERT ŠIPEK.

Verbum: 21000 Split, Trumbićeva obala 12; tel. (21) 340260; fax (21) 340270; e-mail naklada@verbum.hr; internet www.verbum.hr; f. 1992; religion, philosophy and humanism; Gen. Man. MIRO RADALJ.

Znanje (Knowledge): 10000 Zagreb, Mandićeva 2; tel. (1) 3689534; fax (1) 3689531; e-mail znanje@znanje.hr; internet www.znanje.hr; f. 1958; popular science, agriculture, fiction, poetry, essays; Dir ZVONIMIR CIMIĆ.

PUBLISHERS' ASSOCIATION

Croatian Publishers' and Booksellers' Assn (Poslovna Zajednica Izdavača i Knjižara Hrvatske): 10000 Zagreb, Klaićeva 7; fax (1) 171624; f. 1996; Pres. ZDENKO LJEVAK; 187 mem. orgs.

Broadcasting and Communications

TELECOMMUNICATIONS

The mobile cellular communications sector in Croatia was liberalized in 1998, and competition in fixed telephony has been permitted since 2005. At 2012 the penetration rates for fixed-line and mobile telecommunications services were 37% and 117% of the population, respectively.

B.net Hrvatska: 10000 Zagreb, Vrtni put 1; tel. and fax (1) 6566372; e-mail sluzba.za.korisnike@bnet.hr; internet www.bnet.hr; f. 2007; provides fixed-line and mobile telephone and internet services.

Optima Telekom: 10010 Zagreb, Bani 75A; tel. (1) 5005001; fax (1) 5005003; e-mail info@optima-telekom.hr; internet www.optima.hr; f. 2004; fixed-line telephone and internet services; Pres. GORAN JOVIČIĆ.

T-Hrvatski Telekom (T-HT): 10110 Zagreb, Roberta Frangeša Mihanovića 9; tel. (1) 4911000; fax (1) 4911011; e-mail info@t.ht.hr; internet www.t.ht.hr; f. 1999; 51% owned by Deutsche Telekom (Germany); offers services under two brands: T-Com (fixed network telephony and online services) and T-Mobile (mobile cellular telecommunications); Pres. DAVOR TOMAŠKOVIĆ.

Tele2 Croatia: 10000 Zagreb, ul. grada Vukovara 269D; internet www.tele2.com.hr; f. 2005; wholly owned by Tele2 AB (Sweden); mobile cellular telecommunications and internet services; CEO VIVEK SHARMA.

VIPnet: 10000 Zagreb, Put Vrtni 1; tel. (1) 4691091; fax (1) 4691099; e-mail sluzba.za.korisnike@vipnet.hr; internet www.vipnet.hr; wholly owned by Mobilkom Austria; f. 1998; provides mobile cellular telecommunications services; CEO MLADEN PEJKOVIĆ.

BROADCASTING

In 2007, in addition to the publicly owned broadcaster Croatian Television (HRT), which operated two terrestrial television networks, a satellite channel and a radio station, there were two private broadcasters operating national terrestrial networks and 15 private regional television stations. There were additionally two private national radio stations and numerous regional, country and community radio stations at that time.

Radio

Croatian Radio (HRT): 10000 Zagreb, Prisavlje 3; tel. (1) 6343258; fax (1) 6343936; e-mail hrt@hrt.hr; internet www.hrt.hr; f. 1926; 3 radio stations; 8 regional stations (Sljeme, Osijek, Pula, Rijeka, Split, Zadar, Dubrovnik and Knin); broadcasts in Croatian, English and Spanish; Dir-Gen. GORAN RADMAN.

Otvoreni Radio: 10010 Zagreb, Cebini 28; tel. (1) 6623700; fax (1) 6623800; e-mail otvoreni@otvoreni.hr; internet www.otvoreni.hr; broadcasts popular music and entertainment programmes nationwide; Dirs ROBERT MILIČEVIĆ, DANIEL BERDAIS.

Radio 101: 10000 Zagreb, Ljudevita Gaja 10; tel. (1) 4891120; fax (1) 4891190; e-mail apr.radio101@gmail.com; internet www.radio101.hr; independent; Dir THOMAS ALEXANDER THIMME.

Radio Baranja: 31300 Beli Manastir, trg Slobode 32/3; tel. (31) 705111; fax (31) 701700; e-mail zlata@radio-baranja.hr; internet www.radio-baranja.hr; f. 1992; independent; Dir ZLATA MARŠIĆ.

Television

Croatian Television (HRT): 10000 Zagreb, Prisavlje 3; tel. (1) 675370; fax (1) 6343712; e-mail program@hrt.hr; internet www.hrt.hr; f. 1956; 2 channels; Dir-Gen. GORAN RADMAN; Dir MARIJA NEMČIĆ.

Finance

(cap. = capital; res = reserves; dep. = deposits; m. = million; amounts in kuna; brs = branches)

BANKING

In April 2012 some 31 commercial banks, one savings banks, and five housing savings banks (building societies) were operating in Croatia.

Central Bank

Croatian National Bank (HNB) (Hrvatska Narodna Banka): 10002 Zagreb, trg Hrvatskih velikana 3; tel. (1) 4564555; fax (1) 4610551; e-mail info@hnb.hr; internet www.hnb.hr; in 1990 assumed the responsibilities of a central bank empowered as the republic's bank of issue; cap. 2,500.0m., res 5,846.5m., dep. 46,470.8m. (Dec. 2009); Gov. BORIS VUJČIĆ.

Selected Banks

Banco Popolare Croatia d.d.: 10000 Zagreb, Petrovaradinska 1; tel. (1) 4653400; fax (1) 4653799; e-mail info@bpc.hr; internet www.bpc.hr; f. 1992 as Stedionica Sonic d.d.; renamed as Banka Sonic d.d. Zagreb in 2001; current name adopted in 2007; owned by Banco Popolare Soc Coop (Italy); cap. 89m., res 250m., dep. 2,027m. (Dec. 2012); Pres. ANDREA MARABINI; 4 brs.

Croatian Bank for Reconstruction and Development (Hrvatska Banka za Obnovu i Razvoj—HBOR): 10000 Zagreb, Strossmayerov trg 9; tel. (1) 4591666; fax (1) 4591721; e-mail hbor@hbor.hr; internet www.hbor.hr; f. 1992; name changed in 1995; state-owned; cap. 5,944.0m., res 37.3m., dep. 466.0m. (Dec. 2012); CEO ANTON KOVAČEV; 7 brs.

Erste & Steiermärkische Bank d.d.: 51000 Rijeka, Jadranski trg 3A; tel. (72) 371000; fax (72) 372000; e-mail erstebank@erstebank.hr; internet www.erstebank.hr; f. 2000 by merger of Bjelovarska Banka, Cakoveka Banka and Trgovačka Banka; owned by ESB Holding (Austria); cap. 1,698m., res 2,082m., dep. 32,419m. (Dec. 2012); CEO PETAR RADAKOVIĆ; 132 brs.

Hrvatska Poštanska Banka (Croatian Post Bank): 10000 Zagreb, Jurišićeva 4; tel. (62) 472472; fax (1) 4810773; e-mail hpb@hpb.hr; internet www.hpb.hr; f. 1991; 51.46% state owned, 27.49% Croatian Post, 20.18% Croatian Pension Insurance Institute; cap. 967.0m., res 279.0m., dep. 13,634.3m. (Dec. 2012); Chair. ČEDO MALETIĆ; 26 brs.

Hypo Alpe-Adria-Bank d.d.: 10000 Zagreb, Slavonska Ave 6; tel. (1) 6030000; fax (1) 6036001; e-mail bank@hypo.hr; internet www.hypo-alpe-adria.hr; f. 1996; cap. 5,209.0m., res 197.5m., dep. 22,398.0m. (Dec. 2012); CEO MARKUS FERSTL; 45 brs.

Istarska Kreditna Banka Umag (Istria Credit Bank Umag): 52470 Umag, Ernesta Miloša 1; tel. (52) 702300; fax (52) 702388; e-mail callcentar@ikb.hr; internet www.ikb.hr; f. 1956; commercial and joint-stock bank; cap. 163m., res 38m., dep. 2,310m. (Dec. 2012); Chair. MIRO DODIĆ; 25 brs.

Jadranska Banka d.d.: 22000 Šibenik, Ante Starčevića 4; tel. (22) 242100; fax (22) 335881; e-mail idzapo@jaba.hr; internet www.jadranska-banka.hr; f. 1957; cap. 239.2m., res 86.0m., dep. 2,348.3m. (Dec. 2012); Pres. IVICA DŽAP.

Kreditna Banka Zagreb (Credit Bank Zagreb): 10000 Zagreb, ul. grada Vukovara 74; tel. (1) 6167333; fax (1) 6116466; e-mail kbz-uprava@kbz.hr; internet www.kbz.hr; f. 1994; cap. 187.0m., res 44.0m., dep. 2,606.4m. (Dec. 2012); Pres. ANTE GAŠPAROVIĆ; 18 brs.

OTP Banka Hrvatska d.d.: 23000 Zadar, Domovinskog rata 3; tel. (62) 201555; fax (62) 201950; e-mail info@otpbanka.hr; internet www.otpbanka.hr; f. 1957 as Komunalna Banka Zadar; merged with Dubrovačka Banka Dubrovnik in 2004; acquired by OTP Bank (Hungary) (q.v.) and name changed from Nova Banka in 2005; cap. 822.3m., res 375.3m., dep. 10,692.0m. (Dec. 2012); Pres. BALÁZS BÉKEFFY; 8 brs.

Podravska Banka d.d.: 48000 Koprivnica, Opatička 3; tel. (62) 655000; fax (62) 655266; e-mail info@poba.hr; internet www.poba.hr; cap. 268.0m., res 117.1m., dep. 2,346.2m. (Dec. 2012); Pres. JULIO KURUC; 35 brs.

Privredna Banka Zagreb d.d.: 10000 Zagreb, Račkoga 6, POB 1032; tel. (1) 6360000; fax (1) 6360063; e-mail uuzkk@pbz.hr; internet www.pbz.hr; f. 1966; commercial bank; 76.59% owned by Intesa Sanpaolo Holding International SA (Luxembourg), and 20.86% by European Bank for Reconstruction and Development (UK); absorbed Međimurska banka Cakovec in Nov. 2012; cap. 1,907m., res 1,842m., dep. 48,870m. (Dec. 2012); Pres. and CEO BOŽO PRKA.

Raiffeisenbank Austria d.d.: 10000 Zagreb, ul. Petrinjska 59; tel. (1) 4566466; fax (1) 4811624; e-mail info@rba.hr; internet www.rba.hr; f. 1994; 75% owned by Raiffeisen Bank International AG (Austria), and 25% by Raiffeisen-Zagreb Beteiligungs (Austria); cap. 3,621m., res 204m., dep. 23,230m. (Dec. 2012); Chair. ZDENKO ADROVIĆ; 36 brs.

Sberbank d.d.: 10000 Zagreb, Varšavska 9; tel. (1) 4801300; fax (1) 4801365; e-mail info@sberbank.hr; internet www.sberbank.hr; f. 2012; cap. 616.0m., res 944.0m., dep. 5,137.4m. (Dec. 2012); Chair. ANDREA KOVACS-WOEHRY; 23 brs.

Société Générale-Splitska Banka d.d.: 21000 Split, Ruđera Boškovića 16; tel. (21) 304539; fax (21) 304652; e-mail info@splitskabanka.hr; internet www.splitskabanka.hr; f. 1966; cap. 491m., res 687m., dep. 15,988m. (Dec. 2012); Pres. ANDRE-MARC PRUDENT; 124 brs.

Štedbanka d.d.: 10000 Zagreb, Slavonska Ave 3; tel. (1) 6306666; fax (1) 6187014; e-mail stedbanka@stedbanka.hr; internet www.stedbanka.hr; f. 1994; cap. 250.0m., res 14.0m., dep. 743.3m. (Dec. 2012); Pres. ANTE BABIĆ.

Zagrebačka Banka d.d. (Bank of Zagreb): 10000 Zagreb, Paromlinska 2; tel. (1) 6104000; fax (1) 6110533; e-mail zaba@zaba.hr; internet www.zaba.hr; f. 1914; 84.47% owned by UniCredit Bank Austria AG (Austria), 13.67% by Allianz SE (Germany); cap. 6,405m., res 4,017m., dep. 85,283m. (Dec. 2011); Chair. FRANJO LUKOVIĆ; 129 brs.

Bankers' Organization

Croatian Banking Asscn (Hrvatska udruga banaka): 10000 Zagreb, Centar Kaptol, Nova Ves 17; tel. (1) 4860080; fax (1) 4860081; e-mail info@hub.hr; internet www.hub.hr; Man. Dir Dr ZORAN BOHACEK.

Supervisory Authority

Croatian Financial Services Supervisory Agency (HANFA) (Hrvatska Agencija za Nadzor Financijskih Usluga): 10000 Zagreb, Miramarska 24B; tel. (1) 6173200; fax (1) 4811406; e-mail info@hanfa.hr; internet www.hanfa.hr; Chair. PETAR-PIERRE MATEK.

STOCK EXCHANGE

Zagreb Stock Exchange (Zagrebačka Burza): 10000 Zagreb, Ivana Lučića 2A; tel. (1) 4686800; fax (1) 4677680; e-mail pitanja@zse.hr; internet www.zse.hr; f. 1990; Gen. Man. IVANA GAŽIĆ.

INSURANCE

In mid-2009 there were 29 licensed insurance companies operating in Croatia; of these, eight specialized in life insurance, 10 in non-life insurance and the remainder covered both life and non-life insurance.

Agram životno osiguranje d.d.: 10000 Zagreb, Trnjanska cesta 108; tel. (1) 6004400; fax (1) 6004940; e-mail zagreb@agramlife.hr; internet www.agramlife.hr; f. 1997; CEO TOMISLAV NOVAČIĆ.

Allianz: 10000 Zagreb, Heinzelova 70; tel. (1) 3670466; fax (1) 3670411; e-mail osiguranje@allianz.hr; internet www.allianz.hr; life insurance, annuity, property, motor vehicle and transport insurance, personal accident insurance, health insurance, liability insurance; CEO and Chair. of Bd BORIS GALIĆ.

Basler Osiguranje Zagreb: 10000 Zagreb, Radnička cesta 37B; tel. (1) 6405000; fax (1) 6405003; e-mail info@basler-oz.hr; internet www.basler-oz.hr; CEO DARKO CESAR.

Croatia Osiguranje: 10000 Zagreb, Miramarska 22; tel. (1) 6332000; fax (1) 6332020; e-mail info@crosig.hr; internet www.crosig.hr; f. 1884; privatized in 2002; Chair. of Bd KREŠIMIR STARČEVIĆ.

Erste Osiguranje: 10000 Zagreb, Miramarska 23; tel. (72) 372748; fax (62) 372710; e-mail kontakt@erste-osiguranje.hr; internet www.erste-osiguranje.hr; mem. of Vienna Insurance Group (Austria); CEO SNJEŽANA BERTONCELJ; 10 mems.

Euroherc Osiguranje: 10000 Zagreb, ul. grada Vukovara 282; tel. (1) 6004601; fax (1) 6004999; e-mail euroherc@euroherc.hr; internet www.euroherc.hr; f. 1992; CEO DAMIR ZORIĆ; 14 brs.

Grawe Hrvatska d.d.: 10000 Zagreb, ul. grada Vukovara 5; tel. (1) 3034000; fax (1) 3034500; e-mail info@grawe.hr; internet www.grawe.hr; CEO IGOR PURETA.

Jadransko Osiguranje: 10000 Zagreb, Listopadska 2; tel. (1) 3036666; fax (1) 3036000; e-mail zg@jadransko.hr; internet www.jadransko.hr; Chair. of Bd ŽARKO BUBALO.

Merkur Osiguranje: 10000 Zagreb, ul. Ljudevita Posavskog 31; tel. (1) 6308333; fax (1) 6157130; e-mail info@merkur.hr; internet www.merkur.hr; f. 1996; Exec. Dir MILAN KRIZMANIĆ.

Triglav Osiguranje d.d.: 10000 Zagreb, Antuna Heinza 4; tel. (1) 5632777; fax (1) 5632799; e-mail centrala@triglav-osiguranje.hr; internet www.triglav-osiguranje.hr; subsidiary of Triglav Insurance Co (Slovenia); CEO MARIN MATIJACA.

Wiener Osiguranje VIG: 10000 Zagreb, ul. Slovenska 24; tel. (1) 3718600; fax (1) 3718601; e-mail kontakt@wiener.hr; internet www.helios.hr; f. 2013; by merger of Helios VIG and Kvarner Vienna Insurance Group; Pres. WALTER LEONHARTSBERGER.

Trade and Industry

GOVERNMENT AGENCIES

Croatian Agency for Small Business (Hrvatska agencija za malo gospodarstvo): 10000 Zagreb, Prilaz Gjure Deželića 7; tel. (1) 4881003; fax (1) 4881009; e-mail hamag@hamag.hr; internet www.hamag.hr; Pres. of Man. Bd TOMISLAV KOVAČEVIĆ.

Croatian Competition Agency (Agencija za zaštitu tržišnog natjecanja): 10000 Zagreb, Savska cesta 41/XIV; tel. (1) 6176448; fax (1) 6176450; e-mail agencija.ztn@aztn.hr; internet www.aztn.hr; Pres. OLGICA SPEVEC.

Government Asset Management Agency (AUDIO) (Agencija za upravljanje državnom imovinom): 10000 Zagreb, Ivana Lučića 6; tel. (1) 6346111; fax (1) 6346102; e-mail ravnatelj@audio.hr; internet www.audio.hr; f. 2011 to replace Croatian Privatization Fund; Chair. of Bd NEVEN MIMICA; Dir ERIK MOHOROVIĆ.

Trade and Investment Promotion Agency (Agencija za promicanje izvoza i ulaganja): 10000 Zagreb, Andrije Hebranga 34/II; tel. (1) 4866000; fax (1) 4866008; Man. Dir SANI LJUBUNČIĆ.

CHAMBERS OF COMMERCE

Croatian Chamber of Economy (Hrvatska Gospodarska Komora): 10000 Zagreb, trg Rooseveltov 2; tel. (1) 4561555; fax (1) 4828380; e-mail hgk@hgk.hr; internet www.hgk.hr; Pres. NADAN VIDOŠEVIĆ.

Croatian Chamber of Economy—Zagreb Chamber: 10000 Zagreb, Draškovićeva 45, POB 238; tel. (1) 4606777; fax (1) 4606813; e-mail hgkzg@hgk.hr; internet www.zg.hgk.hr; f. 1852; Pres. Dr ZLATAN FRÖHLICH.

Croatian Chamber of Trades and Crafts (Hrvatska obrtnička komora—HOK): 10000 Zagreb, Ilica 49/2, POB 166; tel. (1) 4806666; fax (1) 4846610; e-mail hok@hok.hr; internet www.hok.hr; Pres. DRAGUTIN RANOGAJEC.

EMPLOYERS' ASSOCIATION

Croatian Employers' Association (Hrvatska udruga poslodavaca—HUP): 10000 Zagreb, Pavla Hatza 12; tel. (1) 4897555; fax (1) 4897556; e-mail hup@hup.hr; internet www.hup.hr; Gen. Dir DAVOR MAJETIĆ.

UTILITIES

Regulatory Authority

Croatian Energy Regulatory Agency (Hrvatska energetska regulatorna agencija—HERA): 10000 Zagreb, ul. grada Vukovara

14; tel. (1) 6323777; fax (1) 6115344; e-mail hera@hera.hr; internet www.hera.hr; Pres. TOMISLAV JUREKOVIĆ.

Electricity

HEP—Hrvatska Elektroprivreda (Croatian Electricity): 10000 Zagreb, ul. grada Vukovara 37; tel. (1) 6322111; fax (1) 6170430; e-mail leo.begovic@hep.hr; internet www.hep.hr; f. 1990; production and distribution of electricity; Dir LEO BEGOVIĆ.

Gas

Gradska Plinara d.o.o.: 10000 Zagreb, Radnička cesta 1; tel. (1) 6302333; fax (1) 6302587; e-mail info@plinara-zagreb.hr; internet www.plinara-zagreb.hr; f. 1862; municipal and regional distribution of natural gas; Dir MLADEN PEJNOVIĆ.

Plinacro Ltd: 10000 Zagreb, Savska cesta 88 A; tel. (1) 6301777; fax (1) 6301787; e-mail plinacro@plinacro.hr; internet www.plinacro.hr; f. 2001; gas transmission system operator; 100% state-owned; Pres. MARIN ZOVKO.

Water

Hrvatske Vode (Croatian Water): 10000 Zagreb, ul. grada Vukovara 220; tel. (1) 6307333; fax (1) 6155910; e-mail voda@voda.hr; internet www.voda.hr; f. 1995; state water-management organization; Dir-Gen. JADRANKO HUSARIĆ.

TRADE UNIONS

Independent Trade Unions of Croatia (Nezavisni Hrvatski Sindikati—NHS): 10000 Zagreb, trg Francuske Republike 9/V; tel. (1) 3908620; fax (1) 3908621; e-mail nhs@nhs.hr; internet www.nhs.hr; f. 1992; 87,313 mems (2007); Pres. KREŠIMIR SEVER.

Union of Autonomous Trade Unions of Croatia—UATUC (Savez samosalnih sindikata hrvatske—SSSH): 10000 Zagreb, trg kralja Petra Krešimira IV 2; tel. (1) 4655013; fax (1) 4655040; e-mail sssh@sssh.hr; internet www.sssh.hr; f. 1990; 17 br. unions with 100,000 mems (2010); Pres. MLADEN NOVOSEL.

Workers' Trade Union Asscn of Croatia (Udruga radničkih sindikata Hrvatske—URSH): 10000 Zagreb, ul. Kralja Držislava 4/1; tel. (1) 4617791; fax (1) 4612896; e-mail ursh@inet.hr; internet www.ursh.hr; 45 affiliated member unions; Pres. DAMIR JAKUŠ.

Transport

RAILWAYS

In 2012 there were an estimated 2,722 km of railway lines in Croatia.

Croatian Railways (Hrvatske Željeznice): 10000 Zagreb, Mihanovićeva 12; tel. (1) 3783061; fax (1) 4577604; e-mail informacije@hzpp.hr; internet www.hzpp.hr; f. 1990; state-owned; public railway transport, construction, modernization and maintenance of railway vehicles; Pres. DRAŽEN RATKOVIĆ.

ROADS

In 2012 there were 26,690 km of roads in Croatia, of which 1,254 km were motorways and 6,581 km were main roads.

SHIPPING

The principal ports are located at Rijeka, Šibenek, Split, Ploče, Omišalj, Dubrovnik and Zadar. At the end of 2013 Croatia's registered fleet had 420 vessels, with a total displacement of 1.35m. grt.

Atlantska Plovidba: 20000 Dubrovnik, od sv. Mihajla 1; tel. (20) 352333; fax (20) 356148; e-mail atlant@atlant.hr; internet www.atlant.hr; f. 1974; Pres. PERO KULAŠ.

Jadrolinija Adriatic Shipping Line: 51000 Rijeka, Riva 16; tel. (51) 666111; fax (51) 213116; e-mail passdept_h@jadrolinija.hr; internet www.jadrolinija.hr; f. 1947 as a continuation of various smaller shipping companies which had operated along the Croatian coast since 1872; regular passenger and car-ferry services between Croatian and Italian ports, and along the Adriatic coast of Dalmatia; Pres. SLAVKO LONČAR.

Jadroplov: 21000 Split, Obala kneza Branimira 16; tel. (21) 302777; fax (21) 398380; e-mail branimir.kovacic@jadroplov.com; internet www.jadroplov.com; f. 1984; fleet of 17 vessels and 1,500 containers engaged in linear and tramping service; Pres. BRANIMIR KOVAČIĆ.

Tankerska Plovidba: 23000 Zadar, Božidara Petranovića 4; tel. (23) 202202; fax (23) 202375; e-mail info@tankerska.hr; internet www.tankerska.hr; f. 1976; Gen. Dir MARIO PAVIĆ.

CIVIL AVIATION

There are 10 international airports in Croatia.

Croatia Airlines: 10000 Zagreb, Bani 75B; tel. (1) 6676555; fax (1) 6160152; e-mail contact@croatiaairlines.hr; internet www.croatiaairlines.com; f. 1989 as Zagreb Airlines; name changed 1990; operates domestic and international services; Pres. KREŠIMIR KUČKO.

Tourism

The attractive Adriatic coast and the country's 1,185 islands make Croatia a popular tourist destination. In 2012 there were 10.4m. foreign tourist arrivals, and revenue from tourism (excluding passenger transport) totalled US $8,744m., according to provisional figures.

Croatian Tourist Board (Hrvatska turistička zajednica): 10000 Zagreb, Ilberov trg 10/4; tel. (1) 4699333; fax (1) 4557827; e-mail info@htz.hr; internet www.croatia.hr; Pres. DARKO LORENCIN.

Defence

As assessed at November 2013, the estimated total strength of the armed forces was 16,550, comprising an army of 11,250, a navy of 1,600 and an air force of 1,850, and 1,850 general staff. There were, in addition, 3,000 armed military police. In May 2000 Croatia was admitted to the 'Partnership for Peace' programme of the North Atlantic Treaty Organization (NATO), and it acceded to NATO in April 2009. Compulsory military service was abolished from the beginning of 2008.

Defence Expenditure: Budgeted at 4,280m. kuna for 2014.

Chief of the General Staff: Lt-Gen. DRAGO LOVRIĆ.

Commander of the Army: DRAGUTIN REPINC.

Commander of the Navy: ROBERT HRANJ.

Education

Pre-school education, for children aged from three to six years, is available free of charge. Education is compulsory for eight years, between seven and 15 years of age. Primary education continues for four years. Secondary education lasts for up to eight years, comprising two cycles of four years each. There are various types of secondary school: grammar, technical and specialized schools, and mixed-curriculum schools. In 2010/11 the pre-primary education enrolment ratio included 64% of children in the relevant age-group. In the same year 88% of children in the relevant age-group were enrolled at primary schools, when the ratio for secondary enrolment included 93%. In 2011/12 a total of 157,289 students were enrolled at 134 institutions of higher education. Government expenditure on education totalled 7,244.7m. kuna (8.5% of total spending) in 2004.

CUBA

Introductory Survey

LOCATION, CLIMATE, LANGUAGE, RELIGION, FLAG, CAPITAL

The Republic of Cuba is an archipelago of two main islands, Cuba and the Isla de la Juventud (Isle of Youth), formerly the Isla de Pinos (Isle of Pines), and about 1,600 keys and islets. It lies in the Caribbean Sea, 145 km (90 miles) south of Florida, USA. Other nearby countries are the Bahamas, Mexico, Jamaica and Haiti. The climate is tropical, with the annual rainy season from May to October. The average annual temperature is 25°C (77°F) and hurricanes are frequent. The language spoken is Spanish. Most of the inhabitants are Christians, of whom the great majority are Roman Catholics. The national flag (proportions 1 by 2) has five equal horizontal stripes, of blue, white, blue, white and blue, with a red triangle, enclosing a five-pointed white star, at the hoist. The capital is Havana (La Habana).

CONTEMPORARY POLITICAL HISTORY

Historical Context

Cuba was ruled by Spain from the 16th century until 1898, when the island was ceded to the USA following Spain's defeat in the Spanish–American War. Cuba became an independent republic on 20 May 1902, but the USA retained its naval bases on the island and, until 1934, reserved the right to intervene in Cuba's internal affairs. In 1933 an army sergeant, Fulgencio Batista Zaldívar, came to power at the head of a military revolt. Batista ruled the country until 1944, when he retired after serving a four-year term as elected President.

Domestic Political Affairs

In March 1952, however, Gen. Batista (as he had become) seized power again, deposing President Carlos Prío Socarrás in a bloodless coup. Batista's new regime soon proved to be unpopular and became harshly repressive. In July 1953 a radical opposition group, led by Dr Fidel Castro Ruz, attacked the Moncada army barracks in Santiago de Cuba. Castro was captured, with many of his supporters, but was later released. He went into exile and formed a revolutionary movement committed to Batista's overthrow. In December 1956 Castro landed in Cuba with a small group of followers, most of whom were captured or killed. However, 12 survivors, including Castro and the Argentine-born Dr Ernesto ('Che') Guevara, escaped into the hills of the Sierra Maestra, where they formed the nucleus of the guerrilla forces which, after a prolonged struggle, forced Batista to flee from Cuba on 1 January 1959. The Batista regime collapsed, and Castro's forces occupied Havana.

The assumption of power by the victorious rebels was initially met with great popular acclaim. The 1940 Constitution was suspended in January 1959 and replaced by a new 'Fundamental Law'. Executive and legislative power was vested in the Council of Ministers, with Fidel Castro as Prime Minister and his brother Raúl as his deputy and Minister of the Revolutionary Armed Forces. The new regime ruled by decree but promised to hold elections within 18 months. The Castro Government adopted a radical economic programme, including agrarian reform and the nationalization of industrial and commercial enterprises. These drastic reforms, combined with the regime's authoritarian nature, provoked opposition from some sectors of the population, including former supporters of Castro, and many Cubans went into exile.

All US business interests in Cuba were expropriated, without compensation, in October 1960, and the USA severed diplomatic relations in January 1961. A US-sponsored force of anti-Castro Cuban émigrés landed in April 1961 at the Bahía de Cochinos (Bay of Pigs), in southern Cuba, but the invasion was thwarted by Castro's troops. Later in the year all pro-Government groups were merged to form the Organizaciones Revolucionarias Integradas (ORI). In December 1961 Fidel Castro announced that Cuba had become a communist state, and he proclaimed a 'Marxist-Leninist' programme for the country's future development. In January 1962 Cuba was excluded from active participation in the Organization of American States (OAS). The USA instituted a full economic and political embargo against Cuba. Hostility to the USA was accompanied by increasingly close relations between Cuba and the USSR. In October the USA revealed the presence of Soviet missiles in Cuba but, after the imposition of a US naval blockade, the weapons were withdrawn. The missile bases, capable of launching nuclear weapons against the USA, were dismantled, thus resolving one of the most serious international crises since the Second World War. In 1964 the OAS imposed diplomatic and commercial sanctions against Cuba.

The ORI was replaced in 1962 by a new Partido Unido de la Revolución Socialista Cubana (PURSC), the country's sole legal party. In October 1965 the PURSC was renamed the Partido Comunista de Cuba (PCC). Although ostracized by most other Latin American countries, the PCC Government consolidated its internal authority. Supported by considerable aid from the USSR, the regime made significant progress in social and economic development, including improvements in education and public health. At the same time, Cuba continued to give active support to left-wing revolutionary movements in Latin America and elsewhere. Guevara was killed in Bolivia, following an unsuccessful guerrilla uprising under his leadership, in October 1967. In 1972 Cuba's links with the Eastern bloc were strengthened when the country became a full member of the Council for Mutual Economic Assistance (dissolved in 1991), a Moscow-based organization linking the USSR and other communist states, receiving preferential trade terms from these countries as a result.

Cuba's first 'socialist' Constitution was submitted to the First Congress of the PCC, held in December 1975, and came into force in 1976, after being approved by popular referendum. As envisaged by the new Constitution, elections for 169 municipal assemblies were held in October. These assemblies later elected delegates to provincial assemblies and deputies to the Asamblea Nacional del Poder Popular (National Assembly of People's Power), 'the supreme organ of state'. The National Assembly chose the members of a new Council of State, with Fidel Castro as President.

Cuba continued to be excluded from the activities of the OAS, although the Organization voted in favour of allowing members to normalize their relations with Cuba in 1975. The relaxation of restrictions on emigration in 1980 resulted in the departure of more than 125,000 Cubans for Florida, USA. High-level talks between Cuba and the USA took place in November 1981, but US hostility increased. Economic sanctions were strengthened, the major air link was closed, and tourism and investment by US nationals was prohibited in 1982. Cuba's support of Argentina during the 1982 crisis concerning the Falkland Islands improved relations with the rest of Latin America, and the country's legitimacy was finally acknowledged when it was elected to the chair of the UN General Assembly Committee on Decolonization in September of that year.

An increase in US military activity in Honduras and the Caribbean region led President Castro to declare a 'state of national alert' in August 1983. The US invasion of Grenada in October, and the ensuing short-lived confrontation between US forces and Cuban personnel on the island, severely damaged relations, and left Cuba isolated in the Caribbean, following the weakening of its ties with Suriname in November.

In July 1984 official negotiations were begun with the USA on the issues of immigration and repatriation, and in December agreement was reached on the resumption of Cuban immigration to the USA. The repatriation of Cuban 'undesirables' began in February 1985, but, following the inauguration of Radio Martí (a radio station sponsored by the 'Voice of America' radio network, which began to broadcast Western-style news and other programmes to Cuba from Florida), the Cuban Government suspended its immigration accord with the USA. Subsequently, all visits to Cuba by US residents of Cuban origin were banned. In September 1986, as a result of mediation by the Roman Catholic Church, more than 100 political prisoners and their families were permitted to leave Cuba for the USA. Relations with the USA continued to deteriorate in 1987 when the US Government launched a campaign to direct public attention to human rights violations in Cuba. In 1988 the Cuban Government released some 250 political prisoners.

President Castro was confronted by Cuba's most serious political crisis since the 1959 Revolution in June 1989. It was discovered that a number of senior military personnel were not only involved in smuggling operations in Angola but were also aiding Colombian drugs-traffickers by enabling them to use Cuban airstrips. Gen. Arnaldo Ochoa Sánchez, who had led the military campaign in Angola, as well as three other officers, were found guilty of high treason and were executed. A further purge led to the imposition of harsh sentences on 14 senior officials.

Post-Cold War Cuba

In September 1991 the USSR announced that it intended to withdraw the majority of its military personnel (some 3,000 troops and advisers) from Cuba. The decision, condemned by Cuba as a threat to its national security, came as the result of US demands that the USSR reduce its aid to Cuba as a precondition to the provision of US aid to the USSR. Cuba's subsequent demands that the USA withdraw its troops from the naval base at Guantánamo were rejected. The withdrawal of Russian troops was completed in June 1993. Meanwhile, the collapse of the USSR in late 1991, and the resulting termination of Soviet subsidies to Cuba, initiated a period of severe economic decline.

In 1992 President Castro's efforts to quiet internal dissent revealed an increasingly militant attitude, as several death sentences were imposed on Cuban dissidents. In the same year the USA strengthened its economic blockade against Cuba. In April US President George Bush barred ships that were engaged in trade with Cuba from entering US ports. In October the Cuban Democracy Act, also known as the 'Torricelli Law', was adopted, making it illegal for foreign subsidiaries of US companies to trade with Cuba. These measures encountered widespread international criticism and in November the UN General Assembly adopted a non-binding resolution demanding the cessation of the trade embargo. The General Assembly continued to adopt similar resolutions on an annual basis, most recently in October 2013.

In July 1992 the National Assembly approved a number of amendments to the Constitution: the President was granted the authority to declare a state of emergency and, in such an event, to assume full control of the armed forces. The constitutional revisions also legitimized foreign investment in approved state enterprises and recognized foreign ownership of property in joint ventures. Elections to the National Assembly were also to be conducted by direct vote. The first such elections were held in 1993. Only candidates nominated by the PCC were permitted to contest the elections. According to official results, 87% of the electorate cast a 'united' ballot (a vote for the entire list of candidates). In the following month Fidel Castro and Raúl Castro were unanimously re-elected by the National Assembly to their respective posts as President and First Vice-President of the Council of State.

With the economic crisis deepening and international reserves exhausted, in July 1993 Castro announced that a 30-year ban on Cuban citizens possessing foreign currency was to be lifted. The measure was intended to attract the large sums of foreign currency (principally US dollars) in circulation on the black market into the economy, and to encourage remittances from Cuban exiles. Restrictions on Cuban exiles travelling to Cuba were also to be relaxed. Later in the year the Government authorized limited individual private enterprise in a range of occupations. Plans were announced for the introduction of agricultural reforms allowing for the decentralization and reorganization of state farms into 'Units of Basic Co-operative Production', to be managed and financed by the workers themselves.

In August 1994 increasing discontent at deteriorating economic conditions resulted in rioting in the capital. The surge of Cubans attempting to reach the USA by sea reached crisis proportions, and US President Bill Clinton was forced to revoke the automatic refugee status conferred on Cubans to deter them; in addition, cash remittances from Cuban exiles in the USA were halted. However, these measures failed to stem the flow of Cubans seeking refuge in the USA, and in September the US and Cuban Governments held bilateral talks to resolve the crisis. The USA promised to grant visas allowing for the migration of a minimum of 20,000 Cubans annually; in return, Cuba reintroduced border restrictions. A further immigration accord was signed in 1995, officially ending the automatic refugee status that had been revoked in the previous August. The accord also stated that all Cuban refugees intercepted at sea by the USA would thenceforth be repatriated. In addition, the USA agreed to grant visas to the majority of the approximately 20,000 Cuban refugees detained at Guantánamo, although the figure was to be deducted from the annual quota of visas granted under the 1994 accord.

The Helms-Burton bill

In early 1995 legislative proposals seeking to tighten the US embargo against Cuba were introduced to the US Congress. The proposals, referred to as the Helms-Burton bill after its proposers, sought to impose sanctions on countries trading with or investing in Cuba, and threatened to reduce US aid to countries providing Cuba with financial assistance, notably Russia. The proposed law provoked international criticism, and a formal complaint was registered by the European Union (EU, see p. 273). The bill was approved by the House of Representatives in September but was considerably modified by the Senate.

In February 1996 Cuban MiG fighters shot down two US light aircraft piloted by members of the Cuban-American exile group Brothers to the Rescue, killing all four crew members. The action was vigorously condemned by the USA, which implemented further sanctions, including the indefinite suspension of charter flights to Cuba. President Clinton reversed his previous opposition to certain controversial elements of the Helms-Burton bill, and in March he signed the legislation, officially entitled the Cuban Liberty and Democratic Solidarity (LIBERTAD) Act. However, Clinton was empowered to issue executive orders postponing the implementation of a section of the law, Title III, which allowed US citizens, including naturalized Cuban exiles, to prosecute through US courts any foreign corporation or investor with business dealings involving property that had been expropriated during the Castro regime. Approval of the Helms-Burton Act prompted strenuous criticism from Cuba's major trading partners and Canada, Mexico and the EU adopted legislation to protect companies against the Act.

In December 1996 agreement was reached by the members of the EU to make the extent of economic co-operation with Cuba contingent upon progress towards democracy in the country. In that month the Cuban Government adopted legislation to counteract the application of the Helms-Burton Act in an attempt to protect foreign investment in the country. The Government also expressed its readiness to negotiate with the USA regarding the compensation of US citizens with property claims in Cuba. In April 1997 the EU and the USA reached an agreement on a resolution of the dispute whereby the USA was to continue deferring the implementation of Title III indefinitely, while negotiations continued towards a multilateral accord defining investment principles. In March 1998 it was agreed that shipments of food and medicines from the USA to Cuba were to be permitted. In addition, the USA ended the ban on direct flights between the two countries and on the transfer of cash remittances from the USA to Cuba. However, the Cuban Government was extremely critical of a further outline agreement on extra-territorial legislation drafted by the US Government and the EU in May, which it considered to be highly concessionary on the part of the EU, at the expense of Cuban interests. Under the terms of the agreement, in return for a commitment from the US President to seek congressional consensus for a relaxation of the application of the Helms-Burton Act, EU member states would participate in the compilation of a register of former US assets in Cuba (considered to have been illegally expropriated) and would observe firm US recommendations regarding their exclusivity. The USA continued to suspend the implementation of Title III at six-monthly intervals.

Strained Cuban–US relations

In October 2000 legislation was adopted by the US Congress easing some aspects of the trade embargo, including the export of food and medicine. However, the Cuban Government declared that the conditions attached to the lifting of the restrictions were such that the legislation would tighten, rather than ease, the US embargo. In response, Cuba imposed a 10% tax on all telephone calls between the two countries and, in December, suspended telephone links with the USA, following the refusal of US telecommunications companies to pay the levy.

An alleged plot to assassinate President Castro in Panama was uncovered in November 2000. Anti-Castro activist Luis Posada Carriles was arrested, along with three others. Posada Carriles had escaped from custody in Venezuela, where he was indicted for the bombing of a Cuban aeroplane near Barbados in 1976, and was also implicated in a series of hotel bombings in Havana in 1997. In April 2004 Posada Carriles was sentenced in Panama to an eight-year prison term. However, in August of that year, having been pardoned by the Panamanian President, Posada Carriles fled the country. In the following year he filed a request for political asylum in the USA and was subsequently arrested on the charge of illegal entry into the USA. Castro conceded that extradition to Venezuela would be acceptable. However, the US Government refused to co-operate, citing the threat posed to, and lack of evidence against, Posada Carriles. In April 2009 an indictment was filed against him in the USA for allegedly lying when questioned about the 1997 Havana hotel bombings. In April 2011 Posada Carriles was acquitted of all charges by a court in Texas. The Cuban Government condemned the verdict.

Continuing repression

In May 2002 an 11,000-signature petition—part of a dissident initiative known as the Varela Project—was submitted to the National Assembly; it called for a referendum on basic civil and political liberties. (The Constitution allowed legislative proposals that were supported by at least 10,000 registered voters to be submitted to the National Assembly for consideration.) In the following month the Government responded by initiating a drive to mobilize popular support for an amendment to the Constitution, declaring the socialist system to be 'untouchable' and ratifying that 'economic, diplomatic and political relations with any other state can never be negotiated in the face of aggression, threat or pressure from a foreign power'. The National Assembly subsequently voted unanimously to adopt a constitutional amendment declaring socialism in Cuba to be permanent and 'irrevocable'.

Relations with the USA worsened in March 2003 when James Cason, Principal Officer of the US Interests Section in Havana, was accused by the Cuban Government of attempting to incite a counter-revolution, having met with opponents of Fidel Castro and, allegedly, disseminated anti-Government propaganda. Castro subsequently ordered that all those dissidents who had met with Cason be arrested, and imposed strict travel restrictions on all US diplomatic personnel resident in Cuba. In April 75 of the dissidents (who included many of the leaders of the Varela Project) were found guilty of charges of subversion and treason and sentenced to prison terms of up to 28 years, and three men found guilty of hijacking a ferry in an attempt to reach the USA were convicted of terrorism and executed. In July, after the EU suspended Cuba's application to join its Cotonou Agreement (see below) in protest at the country's recent human rights record, President Castro announced that his Government would reject any aid offered by the EU and would terminate all political contact with the organization. Meanwhile, the EU imposed 'diplomatic sanctions' on Cuba, announcing that its member states would officially welcome Cuban dissidents into their embassies while restricting contact with the Government.

The Government continued to operate in an increasingly repressive manner. In January 2004 new regulations concerning internet usage were announced, further enforcing state control over access to information. In April the UN Commission on Human Rights adopted a motion condemning human rights violations in Cuba and mandating the Commission to send a mission to the country. In response, the Cuban Government declared that it would not permit any human rights monitors to enter the country. In May the USA announced further restrictions on remittances into the country. In addition, Cuban Americans resident in the USA were only to be permitted to visit their relatives in Cuba once every three years. In response, President Castro restricted the quantity of goods available for purchase in US dollars within Cuba. In October the Government announced that circulation of the US dollar in Cuba would not be permitted from the following month; a commission of 10% would also be imposed henceforth when changing US dollars into Cuban convertible pesos.

In April 2005 the UN Human Rights Commission approved a resolution condemning the imprisonment of political dissidents and journalists in Cuba and calling for the renewal of the mandate of a UN envoy to investigate alleged human rights abuses in the country. In July, in the largest crackdown on dissidents since March 2003, 26 people were arrested during a protest outside the French embassy in Havana. The demonstrators were opposed to France's decision to normalize relations with Cuba.

After Hurricane Dennis struck the island in July 2005, killing 16 Cubans and causing damage estimated at US $1,400m., President Castro rejected an offer of US financial aid, insisting that Cuba would not accept any assistance from the USA while the US trade embargo remained in place. In the wake of Hurricane Wilma in October, Cuba did accept a US offer of an assessment team from the Office of US Foreign Disaster Assistance. However, in November the US Department of State withdrew the offer after Castro announced he wanted to discuss regional co-operation with the team. In September President George W. Bush had rejected an offer by the Cuban Government to send doctors, medical supplies and field hospitals to the US city of New Orleans following the destruction wrought by Hurricane Katrina.

Raúl Castro assumes power

In July 2006 it was announced that, owing to ill health, President Castro was temporarily to cede power to his brother, Raúl. At the National Assembly's end-of-year session in December, the acting President urged the legislature to strive for greater transparency. Earlier in December, in an apparent manifestation of a more pragmatic approach to relations with the USA, Castro had expressed his amenability to negotiations. In July 2007 Castro acknowledged Cuba's severe economic difficulties, including under-production, low wages and high prices, and declared that 'structural and conceptual changes' were necessary to overcome them.

In December 2007 it was announced that Cuba would subscribe to two of the UN's seven conventions on human rights, as well as allowing the recently constituted UN Human Rights Council to scrutinize the status of human rights in the country. Cuba had previously opposed any monitoring of its affairs by the UN. The conventions, which were signed by Cuba in February 2008, covered civil and political and social, economic and cultural rights, respectively, including freedom of expression and association and the right to travel. Dissident groups expressed scepticism of the Government's commitment to the accords.

Elections to the National Assembly (enlarged from 609 to 614 seats) were held on 20 January 2008. All of the 614 candidates were elected with the requisite 50% of valid votes. The participation rate was 96.9%, of whom some 4.8% cast blank or spoiled ballots. Fidel Castro was re-elected to the National Assembly, a necessary condition to his remaining as Head of State, but in mid-February he announced that he would not aspire to nor accept re-election to the presidency of the Council of State. On 24 February the Assembly unanimously elected Raúl Castro to succeed his brother as President of the Council of State and of the Council of Ministers. Raúl Castro was replaced as First Vice-President by José Ramón Machado Ventura, a senior member of the PCC's Politburo and a veteran of the Revolution; Machado Ventura's election surprised many observers, who had expected a younger member of the Government to accede to the position. The new President obtained the Assembly's approval to consult his brother on major issues of state.

In his inaugural address to the National Assembly, Raúl Castro indicated an imminent relaxation of some of the island's more restrictive economic and social policies. Accordingly, restrictions on the sale of computers and various other electronic appliances were removed, while the sale of mobile telephones to the public was also permitted. Reforms of the agricultural sector were announced in March, which were to include the distribution of unused state-owned land to private farmers. (Following concerns that the redistributed land was being underutilized, partly owing to a lack of resources and drought conditions, from December 2012 the maximum size of the leasable plots was increased and individuals were permitted to build homes on the land.) Wage reform was announced in June 2008, whereby upper limits on salaries were abolished and employees would be able to earn bonuses for meeting production quotas.

In March 2009 President Castro carried out an extensive government reorganization. Most notably, Felipe Pérez Roque and Carlos Lage Dávila, both regarded as close allies of Fidel Castro and possible successors to Raúl Castro, were dismissed as Minister of Foreign Relations and Secretary of the Council of Ministers, respectively. Brig.-Gen. José Amado Ricardo Guerra replaced Lage as cabinet secretary, and Bruno Rodríguez Parrilla was awarded the foreign relations portfolio.

Relations between Raúl Castro and Barack Obama

In April 2009 the new US President, Barack Obama, relaxed restrictions on US residents making family visits to Cuba and on the transfer of remittances to family members in Cuba. Furthermore, Obama removed constraints preventing US telecommunications companies from operating within Cuba, although this also required Cuban approval. The new US President expressed his willingness to talk to the Cuban Government, but emphasized that the trade embargo, which continued to be renewed annually, would only be eased following democratic reform and an improvement in human rights. The Cuban response to these developments was lukewarm: Castro announced that he was open to fresh dialogue with the Obama Administration, but stressed that talks would only take place if there were no preconditions attached and that the Cuban political system was non-negotiable. In July migration talks between Cuba and the USA, suspended since 2003, resumed. However, this amelioration in relations began to falter in November, following the publication of a report by Human Rights Watch that censured the ongoing repression of dissenters by the Cuban leadership. Cuban–US relations were further strained in December when a US government contractor, Alan Gross, was arrested in Havana for allegedly supplying computers and mobile telephones to dissident organizations. In March 2011 Gross was convicted of acts against 'the integrity and territorial independence' of the state and sentenced to 15 years' imprisonment. Nevertheless, Obama further eased restrictions on travel and the transfer of remittances to Cuba by US residents in January, notably allowing religious organizations and higher education institutions to sponsor visits to the country. In March the USA increased the number of US airports permitted to operate charter flights to Cuba from three to 11; further authorizations followed. In September 2012 the Cuban Government declared its willingness to hold talks with US officials on the case of Gross. (In January 2014, following an appeal by Gross to the US President, it was reported that US Secretary of State John Kerry had sought the assistance of the Vatican in securing his release.) Following Obama's re-election in November 2012, in a statement to the UN General Assembly, the Cuban Minister of Foreign Relations, Bruno Rodríguez Parrilla, proposed a draft agenda for bilateral negotiations, which suggested areas in which agreements on co-operation could be concluded, but otherwise largely reiterated previous demands. These included the withdrawal of the trade embargo and other US sanctions against Cuba, compensation for damage caused by such sanctions, the return of the territory occupied by the US naval base in Guantánamo and the release of the four remaining Cubans who had been convicted of spying-related charges in the USA in 2001 (one of the prisoners, René González, was released in 2011; a second detainee, Fernando González, was freed in March 2014).

Economic crisis and reforms

In response to a growing liquidity crisis that had left the country struggling to pay for its energy imports, emergency restrictions on electricity usage were announced in June 2009. This was followed by the rationing of several staple food items and the closure of some subsidized workers' canteens, while in August the Government revealed that there would be a decrease in public spending on health and education, sectors that the Cuban leadership had previously regarded as immune from spending reductions.

In July 2010 the Roman Catholic Church announced that, following negotiations also involving the Spanish Government, President Castro had agreed to release 52 of the 75 political dissidents detained in March 2003 (the other 23 having been previously freed). All 52 had been freed by the end of March 2011, together with a number of additional prisoners not included in the agreement with the Church, most going into exile in Spain.

Amid continuing economic difficulties, during the second half of 2010 the Government announced a series of reforms aimed at increasing productivity and reducing the size of the public sector. In an attempt to improve agricultural production, farmers were allowed to purchase a limited range of supplies directly from local shops, rather than being allocated such resources centrally by the state. Moreover, under new legislation adopted in July and specifically aimed at facilitating foreign participation in the development of the tourism sector, foreign investors were permitted to lease state-owned land for a period of up to 99 years (compared with 50 years previously). Addressing the National Assembly in August, President Castro pledged to reduce the role of the state in some areas of the economy, to cut the state payroll and to ease restrictions on self-employment and the creation of small businesses, but ruled out major market reforms. A decree taking effect that month legalized the sale at unregulated prices of agricultural produce from roadside stands, subject to a 5% sales tax. In September it was confirmed that 500,000 people would be removed from the state payroll by March 2011, followed by a further 500,000 at a later date. (A revised target emerged in April 2012: 500,000 state employees would be removed by 2015.) The Government hoped that 465,000 non-state jobs would be created in 2011, with 250,000 new licences for self-employment to be issued. The number of products available to Cubans at subsidized prices was to be gradually reduced.

In advance of the long-delayed sixth congress of the PCC (the fifth congress had taken place in 1997), to be held in April 2011, the Government distributed a 32-page consultation document, *Draft Guidelines for the Economic and Social Policy of the Party*, and a three-month national debate on the proposals commenced in December 2010. The guidelines reaffirmed the Government's commitment to retaining a centrally planned socialist economic model, but defined socialism as equality of rights and of opportunity for all citizens rather than egalitarianism, and emphasized that the focus of central planning would be on regulating and taxing state businesses rather than administering them. Foreign investment would be encouraged, while the two Cuban currencies would eventually be unified. In March 2011 Adel Izquierdo Rodríguez was appointed as Minister of Economy and Planning, succeeding Marino Murillo Jorge, who was designated Chairman of the Economic Policy Commission of the Sixth Party Congress, responsible for supervising the implementation of the ongoing economic reforms.

The changes to the economic system proposed by President Castro—which numbered more than 300 and were expected to be implemented over a period of at least five years—were approved at the sixth congress of the PCC in April 2011. In late March Fidel Castro had announced that he had relinquished the post of First Secretary of the Central Committee of the PCC in favour of his brother when he fell ill in July 2006. President Raúl Castro was thus confirmed as First Secretary at the congress, while First Vice-President José Ramón Machado Ventura became Second Secretary, and three new members were elected to the Politburo: Adel Izquierdo, Marino Murillo and Mercedes López Acea, the head of the party in Havana. In addition, President Castro notably proposed a limit of two consecutive five-year terms for senior political and state officials. Significant progress in the implementation of some of the economic reforms had already been achieved, with more than 200,000 licences for the establishment of privately run businesses having been issued since October 2010, although the process of reducing the public sector work-force had suffered delays, partly as a result of disagreements between trade unions and administrators at the state-run bodies affected. (A total of 365,000 state jobs were cut in 2011–12.)

In May 2011, as part of wider efforts by the Cuban authorities to curb corruption, a former Minister of the Food Industry, Alejandro Francisco Roca Iglesias, who had been dismissed from the Council of Ministers in March 2009, was sentenced to 15 years' imprisonment after being found guilty of accepting bribes. His erstwhile deputy, Celio Hernández, and 10 other senior officials were convicted on similar charges in June and received prison sentences of between three and five years.

The economic reforms approved by the sixth PCC congress were endorsed by the National Assembly in August 2011. Their introduction was to be monitored by an Implementation and Development Permanent Commission. The Minister of the Revolutionary Armed Forces, Gen. Julio Casas Regueiro, who was also a member of the Politburo and a close ally of the President, died in September; he was succeeded in the Council of Ministers by his deputy, Lt-Gen. Leopoldo Cintra Frías. Also in September, reflecting the Government's policy of decentralizing economic power, it was decided that the Ministry of Sugar would be replaced by the Grupo Empresarial de la Agroindustria Azucarera, a public holding company comprising 13 provincial state-owned enterprises. Legislation allowing and regulating the sale and purchase of cars and property by Cuban residents entered into force in October and November, respectively. Under further reforms announced in November, moreover, from December farmers were permitted to sell their produce directly to state-run hotels and restaurants, rather than through government agencies, while bank loans were made available to self-employed people (who numbered some 436,000 in September 2013). In late December 2011 President Castro announced that 2,900 prisoners, including some convicted of crimes against 'the security of the state', would be pardoned for humanitarian reasons.

Pope Benedict XVI visited Cuba in March 2012, his visit facilitated by the release of prisoners in 2010–11. He spoke of the need for 'authentic freedom', but also indirectly criticized the US trade embargo, asserting that Cubans 'should not be hampered by limitations on basic freedoms or a lack of material resources, a situation which is worsened when restrictive economic measures, imposed from outside the country, unfairly burden its people'. Dissidents were divided in their opinions on the visit, and a number were temporarily detained prior to the Pope's arrival.

A number of changes to the Government were effected in March 2012, including the replacement of two of its oldest members, José Ramón Fernández Alvarez, a Vice-President of the Council of Ministers, and José Miyar Barrueco, the Minister of Science, Technology and the Environment, who were succeeded by Miguel Díaz-Canel Bermúdez (hitherto Minister of Higher Education) and Elba Rosa Perez Montoya, respectively. The Minister of Information Technology and Communications and the Minister of Basic Industry were replaced by their deputies in June. In August 12 officials from the state-owned nickel company, Cubaniquel, and the Ministry of Basic Industry, including three former deputy ministers, were convicted of corruption and sentenced to between four and 12 years' imprisonment. The Ministry of Basic Industry was abolished in November, with most of its functions being transferred to a new Ministry of Energy and Mines.

The founder of the Varela Project (see above), prominent dissident Oswaldo Payá, and a human rights campaigner, Harold Cepero, were killed in a car crash in July 2012. Also in the vehicle were two European politicians, Jens Aron Modig from Sweden and Angel Carromero from Spain, who survived the crash and admitted being in Cuba to deliver funds to dissident groups. In October Carromero, the driver, was convicted of 'vehicular manslaughter' and sentenced to four years' imprisonment (later being permitted to serve this sentence in Spain), although Payá's family demanded an official investigation into the incident, claiming that the dissident had received numerous death threats and suggesting that the car had been forced off the road.

Restrictions on travel abroad were eased during 2012. From March those leaving the country were permitted to take up to US $5,000 of foreign currency and up to 2,000 convertible pesos with them without government approval (the export of hard currency having hitherto required the consent of the central bank). In October, moreover, the Government announced that from January 2013 most travellers would no longer be required to purchase an exit visa and to obtain a written invitation from the Cuban Embassy in their destination country, although some highly qualified professionals would still require permission to leave the country. The length of time that Cubans were permitted to spend outside Cuba without losing their rights as Cuban citizens was extended from 11 to 24 months, with the possibility of a further 24-month extension. In November 2012 the Government also decided to allow visits to Cuba by people who had emigrated from the country without authorization as long as their departure had occurred more than eight years earlier.

Meanwhile, in an attempt to discourage the sale on the commercial market of food sent by Cubans abroad, customs duty was reimposed on food imports in June 2012 (having been removed in 2008, after a series of hurricanes led to food shortages). Moreover, a substantial increase in import duties on a wider range of consumer goods was announced in July in a continued effort to curb informal shipments of merchandise to Cuba. The new measures were expected adversely to affect the private businesses that had recently emerged, but to compensate to some extent for the corresponding decline in public revenue from state-run retail activities. In March 2013 it was announced that a state-run wholesale company would be established to sell food, industrial and other consumer goods to both state and private businesses.

Hurricane Sandy caused 11 deaths, damaged more than 188,000 homes and destroyed almost 100,000 ha of crops when it hit Cuba in October 2012, raising renewed concerns regarding food security. The UN's World Food Programme provided emergency aid for the most afflicted areas in the south-east of the country, while assistance was also forthcoming from countries including Japan, Russia and Venezuela. The Government reduced the price of construction materials and offered interest-free loans to those affected, to repair damage.

A final term for Castro

Addressing the PCC's Central Committee in December 2012, President Castro emphasized the urgency of renewing the leadership of the party with younger members. The Minister of Foreign Relations, Bruno Rodríguez Parrilla, was elected to the Politburo, becoming only the fourth member aged under 65 years. Also that month, in a continuation of the implementation of the economic reforms approved by the PCC in April 2011, the establishment of non-agricultural co-operatives was authorized. The new co-operatives, which were to comprise an unlimited number of members, could be formed through the rental of state property or the transfer of state businesses to their employees.

At elections to the National Assembly, held on 3 February 2013, all of the 614 candidates were elected with the requisite 50% of valid votes. A participation rate of 90.9% was recorded; 5.8% of votes cast were blank or spoiled. Fidel Castro was among those re-elected to the Assembly. Ricardo Alarcón de Quesada, President of the National Assembly since 1993, notably did not stand for re-election; he was replaced as the head of the legislature on 24 February by Juan Esteban Lazo Hernández. (Alarcón and four other members of the PCC Central Committee retired from their posts in July.) On the same day, the Assembly re-elected Raúl Castro to a second term as President of the Council of State and of the Council of Ministers. Upon being sworn in, Castro announced that he intended to step down in 2018 at the end of the five-year term. The legislature also appointed Miguel Díaz-Canel Bermúdez, a 52-year old Politbureau member, as First Vice-President. Díaz-Canel replaced 82-year old José Ramón Machado Ventura (who remained a Vice-President). In his speech to the National Assembly Castro announced his commitment to a gradual economic reform programme and to combating 'indiscipline and lawlessness of all kinds', including corruption.

In May 2013 it was reported that senior government officials had reaffirmed their commitment to anti-corruption that was an integral part of the reform plan approved at the sixth congress in April 2011, in particular in the areas of business deals with foreign companies and petroleum distribution. Meanwhile, later that month four foreign businessmen were tried secretly on corruption charges after spending more than one year in custody. A number of Cuban senior officials were also thought to have been involved in the two cases. While the British citizens, Amado Fakhre and Stephen Purvis, who worked for British investment fund Coral Capital Group, were released the following month for time served, having been found guilty of minor charges, Krikor Bayassalian, a Lebanese citizen, received a four-year term. His cousin and associate, Canadian-born Sarkis Yacoubian (of Tri-Star Caribbean) was sentenced to nine years' imprisonment, although he was freed and expelled from Cuba in February 2014. The trial of a second Canadian businessman, Cy Tokmakjian, was still pending.

The most challenging stage of Cuba's economic reform process, namely the unification of its dual currency system (in which the convertible peso used in the tourism sector and in foreign trade was worth much more than the Cuban peso, in which most workers were paid) and the deregulation of the majority of state-run companies, was announced to the National Assembly in mid-July 2013. Plans to eliminate the dual currency system were set out in October; the process was expected to take around 18 months to implement. Meanwhile, a series of other measures to accelerate economic growth were put in place during that year, mainly involving the reform of the agricultural sector; private intermediaries were to be permitted to supply and purchase from farmers and farmers would be able to sell directly to hotels and tourism-oriented restaurants. In addition, a pilot scheme, involving the privatization of a number of state-run restaurants, was announced in September. In October the Government reiterated that its economic reforms were not concerned with the privatization of state-owned assets but with increasing Cuba's productivity and efficiency.

Recent developments: negotiations with the USA

On 18–19 June 2013, in Washington, DC, USA, talks were held on resuming the direct mail service between Cuba and the USA which had been terminated in 1963. (Discussions on the issue had been initiated in September 2009 but suspended following the arrest of Alan Gross. A further round of talks was held in Havana in mid-September.) In July 2013 a North Korean ship with a cargo of sugar was detected by the US Administration departing from a port in Cuba. Not wishing to risk a bilateral incident, US officials reported their sighting to their Panamanian counterparts, who found the vessel to be carrying a consignment of obsolete defensive weapons bound for North Korea for repair and eventual return to Cuba. Following a search of the ship by UN weapons inspectors, Cuba was declared to be in contravention of UN arms sanctions against North Korea; this was confirmed by a UN report published in March 2014, which also suggested that other such violations by Cuba may have occurred in 2012. Despite this incident, on 17 July 2013 the first bilateral migration talks since the beginning of 2011 took place in Washington between Cuban and US officials. The discussions, according to Cuban sources held in 'a climate of respect', related to the implementation of the US immigration accords of 1994 and 1995; during the meeting the US delegation reiterated its demand for the release of Gross. In early August it was announced that Cubans wanting to travel to the USA for personal reasons would be granted a non-immigrant multiple entry visa valid for five years.

In mid-2013 allegations emerged that a number of Cuban migrants detained in a detention centre in the Bahamas had been physically and sexually abused, prompting a hunger strike by US-based Cuban advocacy group Democracy Movement. Three detainees in particular gained notoriety when a video was broadcast on a Spanish-language television channel in Florida, USA that depicted their alleged beating by Bahamanian officers following their attempted escape from the centre in May. Bahamanian foreign minister Fred Mitchell claimed that the events in the video were staged; none the less an investigation into the affair was completed at the end of September. On 26 November Cuban consular services in the USA were suspended by the Interests Section of the country's diplomatic mission after it failed to find a replacement for a bank that was terminating its services to foreign diplomatic missions; on 9 December, however, services were temporarily resumed in early December, but suspended again in February 2014.

In November 2013, at a fundraising event in Miami, Florida, USA, President Obama expressed a willingness to revise US foreign policy towards Cuba; this was confirmed later that month in a speech by US Secretary of State John Kerry, in which he announced that Obama was seeking a pragmatic approach with Cuba without political pre-conditions. The following month, at the memorial service for former South African President Nelson Mandela, President Obama publicly shook the hand of Raúl Castro, a move which many Cubans saw as a further sign of hope for improved relations between the two countries, particularly after Castro subsequently proposed a relationship based on 'mutual respect'. In April 2014 reports emerged of a secret US government programme to establish a social network in Cuba with the aim of destabilizing the regime.

Foreign Affairs

Regional relations

The OAS voted overwhelmingly in 2009 to abolish its 1962 suspension of Cuba's membership. Although the Cuban Government announced that it had no intention of rejoining the organization, which was viewed with suspicion in Cuba, it expressed satisfaction with this diplomatic victory. The USA, the only OAS member without diplomatic relations with Cuba, had pressed for Cuban membership to be contingent upon political reform and an improvement in human rights, but was forced to compromise; a 'process of dialogue', conforming to the OAS's democratic values, was agreed as a less stringent precondition to Cuban re-entry. Cuba's exclusion from the next Summit of the Americas, held in Colombia in April 2012, was condemned by most OAS members, but the USA remained resolutely opposed to Cuban participation.

Cuba traditionally enjoyed good relations with Mexico (which was the only Latin American country not to suspend diplomatic relations with the Castro regime in 1961). However, in 2002 bilateral relations were strained when Mexico supported a UN resolution condemning Cuba's human rights record. Meanwhile, diplomatic relations with Argentina, severed in 2001 following Argentina's support of a UN vote condemning Cuba's human rights record, were restored in 2003. In 2004 Cuba broke off diplomatic relations with Panama following that country's pardon of four Cuban exiles suspected of involvement in an attempt to assassinate Fidel Castro in 2000 (see above). The two countries restored diplomatic links in 2005. A bilateral co-operation agreement with Bolivia came into effect in January 2006, with the accession of Evo Morales to the Bolivian presidency. In October 2011, after 15 years of negotiations, Cuba and the Bahamas reached agreement on the delimitation of their maritime border. From November 2012 Cuba hosted a series of formal peace negotiations between the Colombian Government and the rebel Fuerzas Armadas Revolucionarias de Colombia.

Relations between Cuba and Venezuela were bolstered considerably following Hugo Chávez's accession to the Venezuelan presidency in 1999. Venezuelan aid was crucial in allowing the Cuban economy to recover from its post-Soviet era economic depression, and numerous military exchanges were conducted between the two countries. In 2004 Presidents Castro and Chávez signed the Bolivarian Alliance for the Peoples of our America-People's Trade Treaty (Alianza Bolivariana para los Pueblos de Nuestra América-Tratado de Comercio de los Pueblos—ALBA-TCP, see p. 463), which was intended as an alternative to the US-supported proposed Free Trade Area of the Americas, from which Cuba had been excluded. Cuba agreed to provide skilled workers, particularly doctors, to Venezuela, in return for oil at preferential rates. In 2005 some 182 new co-operative agreements were signed between Cuba and Venezuela. In 2008 Raúl Castro attended the inaugural Latin America and the Caribbean Integration and Development Summit in Sauípe, Brazil, the first meeting of all of the region's heads of government without the presence of the USA or members of the EU, and was regarded as an important step in Cuba's reintegration with other Latin American and Caribbean states. Meanwhile, in December 2009 Castro and Chávez concluded a significant trade agreement worth some US $3,200m., confirming Venezuela's position as Cuba's principal commercial partner. The deal also granted Venezuela further petroleum exploration rights in Cuban waters. In November 2010 Castro and Chávez renewed a bilateral economic co-operation agreement first signed in 2000 for a further 10-year period. Chávez's death in March 2013 raised concerns in Cuba regarding a potential future loss of financial assistance from Venezuela, notably the preferential oil supplies. However, economic co-operation between the two countries was strengthened by the announcement in early November that import duties would be gradually eliminated.

Cuba's relations with Brazil were strengthened during 2012 after Brazilian President Dilma Rousseff made her first official visit to Cuba. Economic co-operation was the main focus of discussions, with a Brazilian company, Odebrecht, notably undertaking the expansion of the port of Mariel; the project, which was also largely being financed by Brazil and was completed in early 2014, included the creation of a 'special development zone' intended to attract foreign investment and promote exports. Brazilian involvement in efforts to revive Cuba's sugar industry was also agreed in November 2012. In May 2013 Brazil agreed to finance a project to expand and modernize Cuba's airports. In September, in return for several thousand Cuban doctors deploying their services in Brazil, talks were held in Cuba with a Brazilian delegation regarding the transfer of technology and machinery to improve Cuba's food security.

Other external relations

In 2001 Cuba signed an agreement with the Caribbean Community and Common Market (CARICOM, see p. 223) designed to promote trade and co-operation, and the country hosted a CARICOM summit meeting for the first time in the following year. Cuba enjoyed observer status to the Cotonou Agreement (see p. 324) between the EU and the African, Caribbean and Pacific countries. In 2003 the EU opened a legation office in Havana. The EU initially declared its support for Cuba's application to join the Cotonou Agreement; however, following the Government's imprisonment of a large number of dissidents in April, it subsequently downgraded relations with Cuba and indefinitely postponed the country's application to join the Agreement. Following the release of some of the dissidents, the EU ended its 'diplomatic sanctions' in June 2008. In October co-operation between Cuba and the EU was formally revived when the EU agreed to provide financial assistance towards reconstruction efforts following a series of hurricanes. In March 2014 EU and Cuban representatives announced that they were to begin negotiations towards restoring full bilateral relations with Cuba.

Cuba strengthened its relations with the Far East in the 2000s. Several bilateral agreements were signed between Cuba and Viet Nam in 2005, including a memorandum of understanding on health care co-operation and a co-operation agreement on science, technology and the environment. A memorandum on marine biodiversity was signed between Cuba and the People's Republic of China in November. The commencement in 2006 of Sino-Cuban joint oil and gas explorations, following the signing of a bilateral energy accord in 2005, heightened already sizeable US concerns about the burgeoning relationship between the two communist states. Sino-Cuban relations were further boosted by the signature of a bilateral economic and technical co-operation agreement during a visit to Havana by the Chinese Minister of Foreign Affairs in July 2010, and by the conclusion of several further agreements during a visit by the Chinese Vice-President, Xi Jinping, in June 2011. China notably pledged to invest some US $6,000m. in the expansion of Cuba's Cienfuegos oil refinery and the construction of a new liquefied natural gas plant, while a new accord on joint oil and gas explorations in Cuban waters was also signed. President Castro visited China and Viet Nam in July 2012, further strengthening co-operation with both countries.

Relations with Russia, which went into sharp decline after the collapse of the USSR in 1991, were strengthened following Raúl Castro's assumption of office in 2008. Cuba and Russia signed 10 economic co-operation agreements in that year. Russian President Dmitrii A. Medvedev visited Cuba in November, and in early 2009 Castro paid a return visit to Russia as part of his second foreign tour as President. Russian oil executive Igor Sechin visited Cuba in July and signed an agreement granting the Russian oil company Zarubezhneft petroleum exploration rights in the Gulf of Mexico. As part of the deal, Cuba secured a US $150m. loan for the purchase of Russian agricultural and construction supplies. On a visit in February 2013 President Medvedev signed a number of agreements which would result in 90% of Cuban debt to the former USSR being written off by 2014 (with the rest refinanced over 10 years) and would develop co-operation for joint research in industrial, pharmaceutical and energy projects.

CONSTITUTION AND GOVERNMENT

Under the 1976 Constitution (the first since the 1959 Revolution, amended in July 1992), the supreme organ of state, and the sole legislative authority, is the Asamblea Nacional del Poder Popular (National Assembly of People's Power), with deputies (614 following the general election of 2008) elected for five years by direct vote. The National Assembly elects 31 of its members to form the Council of State, the Assembly's permanent organ. The Council of State is the highest representative of the State, and its President is both Head of State and Head of Government. Executive and administrative authority is vested in the Council of Ministers, appointed by the National Assembly on the proposal of the Head of State. Municipal, regional and provincial assemblies have also been established. The Partido Comunista de Cuba (PCC), the only authorized political party, is 'the leading force of society and the State'. The PCC's highest authority is the Party Congress, which elects a Central Committee and a Secretariat to supervise the Party's work. To direct its policy, the Central Committee elects a Politburo.

REGIONAL AND INTERNATIONAL CO-OPERATION

Cuba has been a member of the UN since its inception in 1945. The country acceded to the World Trade Organization (see p. 434) in 1995. Cuba is a member of the Latin American Economic System (see p. 452), the Association of Caribbean States (see p. 449), and of the Community of Latin American and Caribbean States (CELAC, see p. 464), which was formally inaugurated in December 2011; Raúl Castro assumed the chairmanship of CELAC in January 2013 for a one-year term. In 1998 Cuba became the 12th full member of the Latin American Integration Association (LAIA, see p. 361), having enjoyed observer status since 1986. Cuba was afforded observer status to the European Union's (EU) Cotonou Agreement (see p. 324), which guaranteed access to EU markets. Cuba became a member of Venezuela's Bolivarian Alliance for the Peoples of our America-People's Trade Treaty (Alianza Bolivariana para los Pueblos de Nuestra América-Tratado de Comercio de los Pueblos—ALBA-TCP, see p. 463) in 2004.

ECONOMIC AFFAIRS

In 2011, according to UN estimates, Cuba's gross national income (GNI), measured at average 2009–11 prices, was US $67,715m., equivalent to $6,017 per head. According to estimates by the World Bank, during 2003–12, the population remained constant with a negligible growth, while gross domestic product (GDP) per head increased, in real terms, at an average annual rate of 6.2% during 2003–10. According to official figures, during 2005–12 GDP increased, in real terms, at an average annual rate of 4.0%; real GDP increased by 3.0% in 2012.

Agriculture (including hunting, forestry and fishing) contributed 3.6% of GDP in 2011 and employed 19.7% of the employed labour force in the same year. The principal cash crop was traditionally sugar cane; however, as the industry became increasingly unprofitable, the Government closed many sugar mills. By 2012 sugar and its derivatives accounted for 8.5% of export earnings, compared with 27.4% in 2000. In 2011 sugar cane production was estimated at just 15.8m. metric tons, an improvement on the 11.5m. tons recorded the previous year, but still lower than the 36.4m. tons produced in 2000. In 2011 Cuba produced some 19,900 tons of tobacco, when 391.6m. cigars were made. Other important crops are plantains, rice, cassava, sweet potatoes, citrus fruits, maize and bananas. Fishing exports contributed 1.2% of the value of total exports in 2012. In real terms, the GDP of the agricultural sector increased at an average rate of 1.1% per year during 2005–12; agricultural GDP increased by 4.4% in 2011, but decreased by 1.1% in 2012.

Industry (including mining, manufacturing, construction and power) contributed 22.5% of GDP and employed 17.1% of the employed labour force in 2011. Industrial GDP increased, in real terms, at an average rate of 3.8% per year in 2005–12; sectoral GDP increased by 6.2% in 2012.

Mining contributed 1.3% of GDP and employed 0.8% of the employed labour force in 2011. Nickel is the principal mineral export. Production totalled an estimated 2.4m. metric tons in 2011. Cuba also produces considerable amounts of chromium and copper, some iron and manganese, and there are workable deposits of gold and silver. The GDP of the mining sector increased by an average of 3.0% per year in 2005–12; sectoral GDP increased by 2.0% in 2012.

Manufacturing contributed 14.9% of GDP in 2011. In the same year the sector engaged 10.1% of the employed labour force. The principal branches of manufacturing were food products, beverages and tobacco, machinery and industrial chemicals. During 2005–12 manufacturing GDP increased, in real terms, at an average annual rate of 3.9%; the sector's GDP increased by 2.3% in 2012.

Construction contributed 4.8% of GDP and engaged 4.4% of the employed labour force in 2011. During 2005–12 construction GDP increased, in real terms, at an average annual rate of 4.0%; the sector's GDP decreased by 7.3% in 2011, but increased by 18.0% in 2012.

Energy is derived principally from petroleum and natural gas. Cuba produced approximately 3.0m. metric tons of crude petroleum in 2011 and 1,034.5m. cu m of natural gas in 2012. Imports of mineral fuels accounted for 46.9% of the total cost of imports in 2012. Cuba was one of the signatories to the Petrocaribe accord, under which Caribbean nations could purchase petroleum from Venezuela at reduced prices. In 2011 the country generated 43.3% of its electricity requirement from petroleum. Efforts to reduce dependence on energy imports from Venezuela received a setback in 2012, when exploratory drilling at three sites off the Cuban coast failed to discover commercially exploitable quantities of petroleum or natural gas.

Services accounted for 73.8% of GDP and engaged 63.2% of the total employed force in 2011. Tourism is one of the country's principal sources of foreign exchange, earning an estimated 2,613m. pesos in 2012, and development of the sector remained a priority of the Government. In 2012 tourist arrivals reached 2.8m., a slight increase on the 2.7m. recorded in the previous year. In real terms, the GDP of the services sector increased at an average rate of 5.2% per year during 2005–12; the GDP of the services sector increased by 2.4% in 2012.

In 2009 Cuba recorded a merchandise trade deficit of 5,917.4m. pesos, and a deficit of 162.4m. pesos on the current account of the balance of payments. In 2012 the principal source of imports was Venezuela (44.0%), followed by the People's Republic of China and Spain. Venezuela was also the principal market for exports, accounting for 44.5% of the total, followed by the Netherlands, Canada and China. The principal imports in 2012 were mineral fuels, lubricants and related products, machinery and transport equipment, food and live animals, basic manufactures, and chemicals and related products. The principal exports in that year were crude materials (inedible) except fuels, metalliferous ores and metal scrap (mainly nickel), chemicals and related products, food and live animals, medicinal and pharmaceutical products, and beverages and tobacco.

In 2012 Cuba recorded a budget deficit of 2,670m. pesos. The country's external debt totalled US $19,440m. at the end of 2009, according to media reports. In December 2013 an accord was reached between Cuba and Russia on the settlement and restructuring of Cuba's debt to Russia (as the successor state to the USSR), estimated at $32,000m.; some 90% of the debt was to be pardoned, and Cuba given 10 years to pay the remaining balance. However, the agreement was still to be ratified by the Russian parliament. According to official figures, 3.8% of the labour force were unemployed in 2012.

In April 2011 the sixth congress of the PCC approved some 313 measures aimed at improving Cuba's productivity, reducing the role of the state and expanding the private sector (see Contemporary Political History): 500,000 public sector employees were to be made redundant by March 2011 (later extended until 2015), while self-employment and the creation of small businesses was encouraged. The number of self-employed people had increased to more than 436,000 by August 2013, a rise of some 150,000 since October 2010, while 137,000 state jobs were cut in 2011 and a further 228,000 in 2012. The Government intended that the contribution of non-state economic activity to GDP would increase from some 5% in 2012 to 40%–45% by 2017. Further reforms took effect in 2011, including the legalization of trade in cars and property, the provision of loans to privately run businesses and, with the aim of increasing domestic agricultural production amid a sharp rise in the cost of food imports, a further easing of restrictions on farmers (in 2012 47% of agricultural goods were sold on the open market). The creation of non-agricultural co-operatives was legalized in December in an effort further to expand the private sector. In June 2013, in response to the USA's continuing designation of Cuba as a state sponsor of terrorism, the central bank began imposing new banking regulations designed to detect and prevent money-laundering, terrorist-financing and illicit capital movements. The easing of restrictions on remittances from the USA by President Barack Obama had a significant effect on the economy; a report published in mid-2013 estimated that cash remittances sent to Cuba in 2012 were worth an estimated US $2,600m., representing an increase of 13% on 2011 and 100% on 2006. Two major economic reforms were announced in 2013 that, if successful, would significantly improve the country's economic performance: first, a move to make state enterprises more efficient by allowing them to retain 50% of their post-tax profits and to give their managers more autonomy; and second, the unification of the dual currency, which would allow wages to rise and stimulate those sectors of the economy that produce goods and services for export and the substitution of imports. According to official estimates, GDP growth amounted to 2.7% in 2013, down from 3.0% in 2012 and far short of the 3.6% target. At the end of March 2014 a far-reaching law on foreign investment was approved which was to allow foreign investment in all sectors with the exception of health, education and defence, and would offer tax exemptions to overseas companies.

PUBLIC HOLIDAYS

2015: 1 January (Liberation Day), 2 January (Armed Forces' Victory Day), 3 April (Good Friday), 1 May (Labour Day), 25–27 July (Anniversary of the 1953 Revolution), 10 October (Wars of Independence Day), 25 December (Christmas Day), 31 December (New Year's Eve).

Statistical Survey

Sources (unless otherwise stated): Cámara de Comercio de la República de Cuba, Calle 21, No 661/701, esq. Calle A, Apdo 4237, Vedado, Havana; tel. (7) 830-4436; fax (7) 833-3042; e-mail pdcia@camara.com.cu; internet www.camaracuba.cu; Oficina Nacional de Estadísticas, Calle Paseo 60, entre 3 y 5, Plaza de la Revolución, Vedado, Havana, CP 10400; tel. (7) 830-0053; fax (7) 833-3083; e-mail oneweb@one.gov.cu; internet www.one.cu.

Area and Population

AREA, POPULATION AND DENSITY

Area (sq km)	109,884*
Population (census results)	
7–16 September 2002	11,177,743
15–24 September 2012	
Males	5,570,825
Females	5,596,500
Total	11,167,325
Density (per sq km) at 2012 census	101.6

* 42,426 sq miles.

POPULATION BY AGE AND SEX
(population at 2012 census, preliminary)

	Males	Females	Total
0–14	985,894	931,052	1,916,946
15–64	3,905,994	3,876,229	7,782,223
65 and over	679,759	785,006	1,464,765
Total	5,571,647	5,592,287	11,163,934

PROVINCES
(population at 2012 census)

	Area (sq km)	Population	Density (per sq km)	Capital (population)
Artemisa	4,003.2	494,631	123.6	Artemisa (82,873)
Camagüey	15,386.2	771,905	50.2	Camagüey (323,309)
Ciego de Avila	6,971.6	426,054	61.1	Ciego de Avila (147,745)
Cienfuegos	4,188.6	404,228	96.5	Cienfuegos (171,946)
Granma	8,374.2	834,380	99.6	Bayamo (235,107)
Guantánamo	6,168.0	515,428	83.6	Guantánamo (228,436)
La Habana	728.3	2,106,146	2,891.9	—
Holguín	9,215.7	1,035,072	112.3	Holguín (346,195)
Isla de la Juventud	2,419.3	84,751	35.0	Nueva Gerona (56,214)*
Matanzas	11,791.8	694,476	58.9	Matanzas (151,624)
Mayabeque	3,743.8	376,825	100.7	San Jose de las Lajas (73,136)
Pinar del Río	8,883.7	587,026	66.1	Pinar del Río (188,614)
Sancti Spíritus	6,777.3	463,458	68.4	Sancti Spíritus (138,504)
Santiago de Cuba	6,227.8	1,049,084	168.5	Santiago de Cuba (506,037)
Las Tunas	6,592.7	532,645	80.8	Las Tunas (202,105)
Villa Clara	8,411.8	791,216	94.1	Santa Clara (240,543)
Total	109,884.0	11,167,325	101.6	—

* Preliminary figure.

PRINCIPAL TOWNS
(population at 2012 census)

La Habana (Havana, capital)	2,106,146	Guantánamo	228,436
Santiago de Cuba	506,037	Las Tunas	202,105
Holguín	346,195	Pinar del Río	188,614
Camagüey	323,309	Cienfuegos	171,946
Santa Clara	240,543	Matanzas	151,624
Bayamo	235,107	Ciego de Avila	147,745

BIRTHS, MARRIAGES AND DEATHS*

	Registered live births†		Registered marriages‡		Registered deaths	
	Number	Rate (per 1,000)	Number	Rate (per 1,000)	Number	Rate (per 1,000)
2005	120,716	10.7	51,831	4.6	84,824	7.5
2006	111,323	9.9	56,377	5.0	80,831	7.2
2007	112,472	10.0	56,781	5.1	81,927	7.3
2008	122,569	10.9	61,852	5.5	86,423	7.7
2009	130,036	11.6	54,969	4.9	86,940	7.7
2010	127,746	11.4	58,490	5.2	91,065	8.1
2011	133,067	11.8	59,676	5.3	87,040	7.7
2012	125,674	11.3	55,759	5.0	89,371	4.6

* Data are tabulated by year of registration rather than by year of occurrence.

† Births registered in the National Consumers Register, established on 31 December 1964.

‡ Including consensual unions formalized in response to special legislation.

Life expectancy (years at birth): 78.9 (males 76.9; females 81.0) in 2011 (Source: World Bank, World Development Indicators database).

ECONOMICALLY ACTIVE POPULATION
('000 persons aged 15 years and over, official estimates)

	2009	2010	2011
Agriculture, hunting, forestry and fishing	945.6	921.5	986.5
Mining and quarrying	27.0	33.7	40.2
Manufacturing	530.8	486.6	507.9
Electricity, gas and water	90.3	101.6	91.5
Construction	239.1	224.5	219.2
Trade, restaurants and hotels	628.2	641.9	647.3
Transport, storage and communications	297.1	304.5	310.1
Financing, insurance, real estate and business services	118.5	116.2	125.2
Community, social and personal services	2,195.8	2,154.0	2,082.3
Total employed	5,072.4	4,984.5	5,010.2
Unemployed	86.1	128.0	164.3
Total labour force	5,158.5	5,112.5	5,174.5

Health and Welfare

KEY INDICATORS

Total fertility rate (children per woman, 2011)	1.5
Under-5 mortality rate (per 1,000 live births, 2011)	6
HIV/AIDS (% of persons aged 15–49, 2012)	<0.1
Physicians (per 1,000 head, 2010)	6.7
Hospital beds (per 1,000 head, 2010)	5.9
Health expenditure (2010): US $ per head (PPP)	414
Health expenditure (2010): % of GDP	10.2
Health expenditure (2010): public (% of total)	95.2
Access to water (% of persons, 2011)	94
Access to sanitation (% of persons, 2011)	92
Total carbon dioxide emissions ('000 metric tons, 2010)	38,364.2
Carbon dioxide emissions per head (metric tons, 2010)	3.4
Human Development Index (2012): ranking	59
Human Development Index (2012): value	0.780

For sources and definitions, see explanatory note on p. vi.

Agriculture

PRINCIPAL CROPS
('000 metric tons)

	2010	2011	2012
Rice, paddy	454.4	566.4	641.6
Maize	324.5	354.0	360.4
Potatoes	191.5	165.6	130.9
Sweet potatoes	384.7	311.9	335.3
Cassava (Manioc)	405.9	485.7	465.8
Yautia (Cocoyam)	137.4	132.1	153.8
Sugar cane	11,500.0	15,800.0	14,400.0
Beans, dry	80.4	133.0	127.1
Groundnuts, in shell*	5.8	5.3	5.8
Coconuts	72.1	65.5	70.9
Cabbages and other brassicas	134.6	162.9	123.3
Tomatoes	517.0	601.0	494.4
Pumpkins, squash and gourds	347.1	340.3	361.4
Cucumbers and gherkins	92.7	94.1	95.5
Chillies and peppers, green	44.5	55.1	62.2
Onions, dry	111.7	143.5	118.2
Garlic	33.8	26.0	21.8
Watermelons	52.0	53.1	48.9
Cantaloupes and other melons*	46.8	48.1	50.0
Bananas	249.2	250.0	195.5
Plantains	485.8	585.0	689.5
Oranges	178.3	122.9	93.8
Tangerines, mandarins, clementines and satsumas	23.0	23.0	18.6
Lemons and limes	6.1	6.6	6.5
Grapefruit and pomelos	137.7	112.0	84.7
Guavas, mangoes and mangosteens	275.2	270.0	389.6
Pineapples	64.8	76.9	84.1
Papayas	135.7	135.0	178.6
Coffee, green	8.4†	10.2†	11.0*
Tobacco, unmanufactured	20.5	19.9	19.5

* FAO estimate(s).

† Unofficial figure.

Aggregate production ('000 metric tons, may include official, semi-official or estimated data): Total cereals 779.1 in 2010, 920.7 in 2011, 1,002.3 in 2012; Total roots and tubers 1,515.0 in 2010, 1,445.0 in 2011, 1,452.0 in 2012; Total vegetables (incl. melons) 2,187.8 in 2010, 2,248.1 in 2011, 2162.0 in 2012; Total fruits (excl. melons) 1,870.5 in 2010, 1,966.4 in 2011, 2,014.3 in 2012.

Source: FAO.

LIVESTOCK
('000 head, year ending September)

	2010	2011	2012
Cattle	3,992.5	4,059.1	4,084.0
Horses	613.6	642.7	681.9
Mules	20.3	20.0	20.3
Pigs	1,591.0	1,518.0	1,545.1
Sheep	2,361.9	2,125.7	2,102.3
Goats	938.1	844.3	651.0
Chickens	30,950	33,663	30,182

Source: FAO.

LIVESTOCK PRODUCTS
('000 metric tons)

	2010	2011	2012
Cattle meat	63.5	66.5	67.1
Pig meat	172.3	176.2	166.3
Chicken meat	33.6	35.4	35.0
Cows' milk	629.5	599.5	604.3
Hen eggs	106.9	115.3	110.5
Honey	4.7	6.7	6.8

Source: FAO.

Forestry

ROUNDWOOD REMOVALS
('000 cubic metres, excl. bark, FAO estimates)

	2008	2009	2010
Sawlogs, veneer logs and logs for sleepers	278	258	358
Other industrial wood	361	361	361
Fuel wood	1,273	1,743	1,141
Total	1,912	2,362	1,860

2011–12: Production assumed to be unchanged from 2010 (FAO estimates).

Source: FAO.

SAWNWOOD PRODUCTION
('000 cubic metres, incl. railway sleepers)

	2008*	2009	2010
Coniferous (softwood)	115	145	125
Broadleaved (hardwood)	51	44	32
Total	166	189	157

* Unofficial figures.

2011–12: Production assumed to be unchanged from 2010 (FAO estimates).

Source: FAO.

Fishing

('000 metric tons, live weight)

	2009	2010	2011
Capture	28.8	24.0	24.0
Blue tilapia	2.5	2.0	1.3
Lane snapper	1.3	1.5	1.2
Caribbean spiny lobster	4.1	4.5	5.0
Aquaculture	36.0	31.4	24.6
Silver carp	17.4	16.2	14.6
Total catch	64.8	55.4	48.6

Note: Figures exclude sponges (metric tons): 46 in 2009; 45 in 2010; 49 in 2011.

Source: FAO.

Mining

('000 metric tons unless otherwise indicated)

	2009	2010	2011
Crude petroleum	2,731.3	3,024.8	3,011.7
Natural gas (million cu m)	1,155.3	1,072.5	1,019.8
Nickel (metal content)	3,949.0	2,511.0	2,442.8

2012: Natural gas 1,034.5 million cu m.

Industry

SELECTED PRODUCTS
('000 metric tons unless otherwise indicated)

	2010	2011	2012
Crude steel	277.6	282.1	277.0
Grey cement	1,631.4	1,730.7	1,824.8
Corrugated asbestos-cement tiles	5,430.8	5,316.3	4,290.8
Colour television sets ('000)	46.5	57.2	7.0
Fuel oil	2,435.9	2,321.9	2,520.4
New tyres ('000)	57.4	58.3	49.3
Recapped tyres ('000)	90.2	111.1	119.4
Woven textile fabrics (million sq metres)	25.6	24.8	27.5
Cigarettes ('000 million)	13.1	13.0	13.0
Cigars (million)	376.4	391.6	391.2
Alcoholic beverages (excl. wines, '000 litres)	1,102.8	1,111.2	1,146.8
Beer ('000 hectolitres)	2,586.3	2,589.0	2,533.0
Soft drinks ('000 hectolitres)	3,669.9	3,781.3	3,773.1
Bicycles ('000)	28.2	54.3	61.0
Fishing vessels	14	4	12
Electric energy (million kWh)	17,395.5	17,754.1	18,431.5

Finance

CURRENCY AND EXCHANGE RATES

Monetary Units

100 centavos = 1 Cuban peso.
1 Cuban peso = 1 convertible peso (official rate).

Sterling, Dollar and Euro Equivalents (31 December 2013)

£1 sterling = 1.647 convertible pesos;
US $1 = 1.000 convertible pesos;
€1 = 1.379 convertible pesos;
100 convertible pesos = £60.72 = $100.00 = €72.51.

Note: The foregoing information relates to official exchange rates. For the purposes of foreign trade, the peso was at par with the US dollar during each of the 10 years 1987–96. In addition, a 'convertible peso' was introduced in December 1994. Although officially at par with the Cuban peso, in March 2005 the 'unofficial' exchange rate prevailing in domestic exchange houses was adjusted to 24 pesos per convertible peso.

STATE BUDGET
(million pesos)

Revenue	2010	2011	2012
Tax revenue	24,201	26,508	29,068
Road and sales tax	10,525	11,819	14,511
Taxes on services	1,758	1,876	1,721
Taxes on utilities	3,049	3,742	3,662
Taxes on labour	4,414	4,235	4,108
Personal income tax	554	762	873
Other taxes	927	1,078	1,150
Social security contributions	2,974	2,996	3,043
Non-tax revenue	17,546	17,551	18,867
Transfers from state enterprises	2,886	4,664	5,629
Other non-tax revenue	14,660	12,887	13,238
Capital revenue	1,228	1,189	1,097
Restitution payments	–252	–388	–396
Total	42,723	44,861	48,635

Expenditure	2010	2011	2012
Current expenditure	41,118	42,048	44,876
Education	8,282	8,817	8,776
Public health and social assistance	6,930	7,314	6,236
Administration, defence and public order	3,586	5,148	5,566
Social security	4,886	5,074	5,346
Community services	1,718	1,323	1,306
Industry	791	393	550
Culture, art and sport	2,117	1,970	1,664
Science and technology	613	212	188
Other activities	2,588	477	268
Subsidies, etc. to state enterprises	7,710	9,679	10,826
Financial operations	1,897	1,641	4,150
Investment expenditure	3,895	3,966	6,430
Total	45,013	46,015	51,305

2013 (million pesos, approved budget proposals): *Revenue:* Tax revenue 29,584.5 (Road and sales tax 15,602.4, Taxes on services 1,656.2, Taxes on utilities 3,694.9, Taxes on labour 3,656.1, Personal income tax 956.1, Other taxes 1,035.9, Social security contributions 2,982.9); Non-tax revenue 18,459.5 (Transfers from state enterprises 5,592.6, Other non-tax revenue 12,866.9); Restitution payments –420.0; Total revenue 47,624.0. *Expenditure:* Current expenditure 45,300.5 (Education 9,115.6, Public health and social assistance 7,184.8, Administration, defence and public order 7,159.9, Social security 5,308.0, Community services 1,615.9, Industry 283.3, Culture, art and sport 1,735.7, Science and technology 167.6, Subsidies, etc. to state enterprises 11,126.9, Financial operations 1,302.8, Provisions for disasters 300.0); Investment expenditure 4,052.6; Reserves 400.0; Development fund 532.0; Total expenditure 50,285.1.

INTERNATIONAL RESERVES

(million pesos at 31 December)

	1987	1988
Gold and other precious metals	17.5	19.5
Cash and deposits in foreign banks (convertible currency)	36.5	78.0
Sub-total	54.0	97.5
Deposits in foreign banks (in transferable roubles)	142.5	137.0
Total	196.5	234.5

MONEY SUPPLY

(million pesos)

	2010	2011	2012
Currency in circulation	10,362.1	10,646.0	12,480.4
Savings	15,726.2	16,436.1	17,567.6
Total	26,088.3	27,082.1	30,048.0

NATIONAL ACCOUNTS

(million pesos at current prices)

Composition of Gross National Product

	2007	2008	2009
Compensation of employees	20,385.7	21,729.1	23,006.1
Operating surplus } Consumption of fixed capital	24,295.1	25,077.8	25,514.2
Gross domestic product (GDP) at factor cost	44,680.8	46,806.9	48,520.3
Indirect taxes, less subsidies	13,923.1	13,999.4	13,558.3
GDP in purchasers' values	58,603.9	60,806.3	62,078.6
Less Factor income paid abroad (net)	959.7	1,055.2	1,643.0
Gross national product	57,644.2	59,751.1	60,435.6

Expenditure on the Gross Domestic Product

	2009	2010	2011
Government final consumption expenditure	24,187.1	22,359.6	24,436.3
Private final consumption expenditure	29,857.7	32,368.6	36,468.9
Increase in stocks	1,402.3	1,229.8	407.2
Gross fixed capital formation	5,385.9	5,561.4	5,319.6
Total domestic expenditure	60,833.0	61,519.4	66,632.0
Exports of goods and services	10,838.9	14,209.5	17,157.1
Less Imports of goods and services	9,593.4	11,400.6	14,799.0
GDP in purchasers' values	62,078.6	64,328.2	68,990.1
GDP at constant 1997 prices	46,352.0	47,459.0	48,789.3

Gross Domestic Product by Economic Activity

	2009	2010	2011
Agriculture, hunting, forestry and fishing	2,439.5	2,324.8	2,487.6
Mining and quarrying	594.1	861.3	895.1
Manufacturing	9,060.5	9,623.1	10,129.4
Electricity, gas and water	1,000.3	1,031.7	1,067.1
Construction	3,377.0	3,211.1	3,265.2
Wholesale and retail trade, restaurants and hotels	14,432.8	15,156.0	16,170.2
Transport, storage and communications	5,150.6	5,314.3	5,594.7
Finance, insurance, real estate and business services	2,598.3	2,802.2	2,854.5
Community, social and personal services	22,797.5	23,345.6	25,745.7
Sub-total	61,450.6	63,670.1	68,209.5
Import duties	628.0	658.1	780.6
Total	62,078.6	64,328.2	68,990.1

BALANCE OF PAYMENTS

(million pesos)

	1999	2000	2001
Exports of goods	1,456.1	1,676.8	1,661.5
Imports of goods	–4,365.4	–4,876.7	–4,838.3
Trade balance	–2,909.3	–3,117.2	–3,076.2
Services (net)	2,162.7	2,223.0	2,212.8
Balance on goods and services	–746.6	–894.2	–863.4
Other income (net)	–514.1	–622.2	–502.2
Balance on goods, services and income	–1,260.7	–1,516.4	–1,365.6
Current transfers (net)	798.9	740.4	812.9
Current balance	–461.8	–776.0	–552.7
Direct investment (net)	178.2	448.1	38.9
Other long-term capital (net)	31.7	570.3	328.3
Other capital (net)	275.0	–213.0	227.3
Overall balance	23.1	29.4	41.8

2007 (million pesos): Exports of goods 3,685.7; Imports of goods –10,079.2; Goods acquired at seaports and airports 128.5; *Trade balance* –6,265.0; Services (net) 7,824.3; *Balance on goods and services* 1,559.3; Income (net) –959.7; Current transfers (net) –199.0; *Current balance* 400.6.

2008 (million pesos): Exports of goods 3,664.2; Imports of goods –14,234.1; Goods acquired at seaports and airports 197.2; *Trade balance* –10,372.7; Services (net) 8,637.2; *Balance on goods and services* –1,735.5; Income (net) –1,055.2; Current transfers (net) 481.9; *Current balance* –2,308.8.

2009 (million pesos): Exports of goods 2,863.0; Imports of goods –8,906.0; Goods acquired at seaports and airports 125.6; *Trade balance* –5,917.4; Services (net) 7,163.0; *Balance on goods and services* 1,245.6; Income (net) –1,643.0; Current transfers (net) 235.0; *Current balance* –162.4.

External Trade

PRINCIPAL COMMODITIES
('000 pesos)

Imports c.i.f.	2010	2011	2012
Food and live animals	1,467,094	1,863,194	1,644,877
Cereals and cereal preparations	670,547	906,073	755,850
Mineral fuels, lubricants, etc.	4,529,660	6,369,886	6,475,033
Chemicals and related products	966,239	1,254,433	1,225,362
Basic manufactures	1,100,435	1,396,452	1,415,344
Manufactures of metal	245,328	297,530	320,507
Machinery and transport equipment	1,668,506	1,954,198	1,939,893
General industrial machinery and equipment and machine parts	372,870	543,631	495,864
Electrical machinery, appliances and apparatus	321,428	427,161	451,230
Miscellaneous manufactured articles	595,396	732,055	666,543
Total (incl. others)	10,644,338	13,952,403	13,800,851

Exports f.o.b.	2010	2011	2012
Food and live animals	355,850	482,568	570,329
Sugar, sugar preparations and honey	266,038	378,606	471,490
Beverages and tobacco	284,724	315,703	316,992
Tobacco and snuff products	202,070	222,987	224,381
Crude materials (inedible) except fuels	1,206,917	1,479,788	1,082,279
Metalliferous ores and metal scrap	1,198,538	1,465,513	1,060,178
Chemicals and related products	538,407	582,706	620,141
Medicinal and pharmaceutical products	489,574	523,281	553,676
Basic manufactures	123,347	145,148	144,599
Machinery and transport equipment	111,380	136,110	104,699
Total (incl. others)	4,549,533	5,870,090	5,577,268

PRINCIPAL TRADING PARTNERS
('000 pesos)

Imports c.i.f.	2010	2011	2012
Algeria	213,271	308,756	330,979
Argentina	129,110	148,613	119,539
Brazil	444,354	643,863	648,177
Canada	331,398	478,784	387,253
China, People's Republic	1,223,245	1,281,415	1,236,840
France	189,629	343,975	359,705
Germany	269,417	286,259	311,463
Italy	292,133	387,799	380,512
Korea, Republic	94,455	128,819	110,185
Mexico	359,970	449,711	486,694
Russia	227,220	224,366	251,674
Spain	785,376	1,019,560	1,006,294
USA	406,118	433,795	508,656
Venezuela	4,301,862	5,902,075	6,078,898
Viet Nam	266,260	308,747	190,459
Total (incl. others)	10,644,338	13,952,403	13,800,851

Exports f.o.b.	2010	2011	2012
Brazil	57,843	82,069	108,053
Canada	604,024	718,645	551,042
China, People's Republic	680,564	778,196	459,060
Côte d'Ivoire	93,465	n.a.	n.a.
Cyprus	28,669	39,400	n.a.
Dominican Republic	23,218	29,360	84,128
France	106,664	23,479	28,021
Netherlands	353,154	655,009	697,605
Nigeria	20,386	100,934	111,745
Panama	12,295	7,002	111,750
Russia	57,472	55,792	89,554
Singapore	186,227	26,553	31,913
Spain	160,746	164,868	149,792
Venezuela	1,716,739	2,273,109	2,483,951
Total (incl. others)	4,549,533	5,870,090	5,577,268

Transport

RAILWAYS

	2010	2011	2012
Passenger-kilometres (million)	925	934	922
Freight ton-kilometres (million)	1,852	1,913	2,714

ROAD TRAFFIC
(motor vehicles in use at 31 December)

	1996	1997
Passenger cars	216,575	172,574
Buses and coaches	28,089	28,861
Lorries and vans	246,105	156,634

2007–08: Passenger cars 236,881; Buses and coaches 197,740; Lorries and vans 171,081; Motorcycles and mopeds 217,141.

Source: IRF, *World Road Statistics*.

SHIPPING

Flag Registered Fleet
(at 31 December)

	2011	2012	2013
Number of vessels	66	65	66
Total displacement ('000 grt)	97	87	95

Source: Lloyd's List Intelligence (www.lloydslistintelligence.com).

International Sea-borne Freight Traffic
('000 metric tons)

	2010	2011	2012
Goods loaded	2,521	2,336	2,297
Goods unloaded	8,348	7,782	7,314

CIVIL AVIATION
(traffic on scheduled services)

	2010	2011	2012
Passengers carried (million)	1.2	1.1	1.2
Passenger-kilometres (million)	2,574	2,545	2,610
Freight carried ('000 metric tons)	10.5	8.6	9.6
Total ton-kilometres (million)	50	43	33

Kilometres flown (million): 16 in 2010; 17 in 2011 (Source: UN, *Statistical Yearbook*).

Tourism

ARRIVALS BY COUNTRY OF RESIDENCE*

	2010	2011	2012
Argentina	58,612	75,968	94,691
Canada	945,248	1,002,318	1,071,696
France	80,470	94,370	101,522
Germany	93,136	95,124	108,712
Italy	112,298	110,432	103,290
Mexico	66,650	76,326	78,289
Russia	56,245	78,554	86,944
Spain	104,948	101,631	81,354
United Kingdom	174,343	175,822	153,737
USA	63,046	73,566	98,050
Total (incl. others)	2,531,745	2,716,317	2,838,607

* Figures include same-day visitors (excursionists).

Tourism receipts (million pesos, incl. passenger transport): 2,218 in 2010; 2,503 in 2011: 2,613 in 2012.

Communications Media

	2010	2011	2012
Telephones ('000 main lines in use)	1,163.6	1,193.4	1,216.5
Mobile cellular telephones ('000 subscribers)	1,003.0	1,315.1	1,681.6
Internet subscribers ('000)	40.1	41.1	n.a.
Broadband subscribers ('000)	3.7	4.4	5.0

Source: International Telecommunication Union.

Education

(2012/13 unless otherwise indicated)

	Institutions	Teachers	Students
Pre-primary	1,086	7,645	106,629
Primary	6,921	106,930	732,683
Secondary	1,802	99,535	794,588
Tertiary	58	53,891*	261,468

* 2011/12.

Pupil-teacher ratio (primary education, UNESCO estimate): 9.1 in 2011/12 (Source: UNESCO Institute for Statistics).

Adult literacy rate (UNESCO estimates): 99.8% (males 99.8%; females 99.8%) in 2011 (Source: UNESCO Institute for Statistics).

Directory

The Government

Head of State: Gen. Raúl Castro Ruz (took office 24 February 2008, re-elected 24 February 2013).

COUNCIL OF STATE

President: Gen. Raúl Castro Ruz.

First Vice-President: Miguel Díaz-Canel Bermúdez.

Vice-Presidents: José Ramón Machado Ventura, Ramiro Valdés Menéndez, Gladys Bejerano Portela, Lázara Mercedes López Acea, Salvador Antonio Valdés Mesa.

Secretary: Homero Acosta Alvarez.

Members: Inés María Chapman Waugh, Lt-Gen. Leopoldo Cintra Frías, Abelardo Colomé Ibarra, Guillermo García Frías, Tania León Silveira, Lt-Gen. Alvaro López Miera, Marino Alberto Murillo Jorge, Sergio Juan Rodrígiez Morales, Lester Alain Alemán Hurtado, Teresa María Amarelle Boué, Yaramis Armenteros Medina, Miguel Angel Barnet Lanza, Yuniasky Crespo Baquero, Ileana Amparo Flores Morales, Félix González Viego, Carmen Rosa López Rodríguez, Martha del Carmen Mesa Valenciano, Carlos Rafael Miranda Martínez, Miriam Nicado García, Miladys Orraca Castillo, Bruno Rodríguez Parilla, Liz Belkys Rosabal Ponce, Adel Onofre Yzquierdo Rodríguez.

COUNCIL OF MINISTERS
(April 2014)

The Government is formed by the Partido Comunista de Cuba.

President: Gen. Raúl Castro Ruz.

Secretary: Brig.-Gen. José Amado Ricardo Guerra.

First Vice-President: Miguel Díaz-Canel Bermúdez.

Vice-Presidents: Ricardo Cabrisas Ruiz, Ramiro Valdés Menéndez, Gen. Ulises Rosales del Toro, Marino Alberto Murillo Jorge, Gen. Antonio Enrique Lussón Batlle, Adel Onofre Yzquierdo Rodríguez.

Minister of Agriculture: Gustavo Rodríguez Rollero.

Minister of Construction: René Mesa Villafaña.

Minister of Culture: Rafael Bernal Alemany.

Minister of Domestic Trade: Mary Blanca Ortega Barredo.

Minister of Economy and Planning: Adel Onofre Yzquierdo Rodríguez.

Minister of Education: Ena Elsa Velázquez Cobiella.

Minister of Energy and Mines: Alfredo López Valdés.

Minister of Finance and Prices: Lina Pedraza Rodríguez.

Minister of the Food Industry: María del Carmen Concepción González.

Minister of Foreign Relations: Bruno Eduardo Rodríguez Parilla.

Minister of Foreign Trade and Investment: Rodrigo Malmierca Díaz.

Minister of Higher Education: Rodolfo Alarcon Ortiz.

Minister of Industries: Salvador Pardo Cruz.

Minister of Information Technology and Communications: Maimir Mesa Ramos.

Minister of the Interior: Lt-Gen. Abelardo Colomé Ibarra.

Minister of Justice: María Esther Reus González.

Minister of Labour and Social Security: Margarita Marlene González Fernández.

Minister of Public Health: Roberto Morales Ojeda.

Minister of the Revolutionary Armed Forces: Lt-Gen. Leopoldo Cintra Frías.

Minister of Science, Technology and the Environment: Elba Rosa Perez Montoya.

Minister of Tourism: Manuel Marrero Cruz.

Minister of Transportation: César Ignacio Arocha Masid.

Minister, President of the Banco Central de Cuba: Ernesto Medina Villaveirán.

MINISTRIES

Ministry of Agriculture: Edif. MINAG, Avda Conill, esq. Carlos M. Céspedes, Nuevo Vedado, Plaza de la Revolución, 10600 Havana; tel. (7) 884-5370; fax (7) 881-2837; e-mail armando@minag.cu; internet www.minag.cu.

Ministry of Construction: Avda Carlos Manuel de Céspedes, Calle 35, Plaza de la Revolución, 10600 Havana; tel. (7) 881-4745; fax (7) 855-5303; e-mail sitio@micons.cu; internet www.micons.cu.

Ministry of Culture: Calle 2, No 258, entre 11 y 13, Plaza de la Revolución, Vedado, CP 10400, Havana; tel. (7) 838-2246; e-mail secretarias@min.cult.cu; internet www.min.cult.cu.

Ministry of Domestic Trade: Calle Habana 258, entre Empedrado y San Juan de Dios, Havana; tel. (7) 867-0133; fax (7) 867-0094; e-mail estadistica@cinet.cu.

Ministry of Economy and Planning: 20 de Mayo, entre Territorial y Ayestarán, Plaza de la Revolución, Havana; tel. (7) 881-9354; fax (7) 855-5371; e-mail mep@ceniai.inf.cu.

Ministry of Education: Calle 17, esq. O, Vedado, Havana; tel. (7) 838-2930; fax (7) 838-3105; e-mail despacho@mined.rimed.cu; internet www.rimed.cu.

Ministry of Energy and Mines: Avda Salvador Allende 666, entre Oquendo y Soledad, Havana; tel. (7) 878-7840; fax (7) 873-5345.

Ministry of Finance and Prices: Calle Obispo 211, esq. Cuba, Habana Vieja, Havana; tel. (7) 867-1800; fax (7) 833-8050; e-mail bhcifip@mfp.gov.cu; internet www.mfp.cu.

Ministry of the Food Industry: Avda 41, No 4455, entre 48 y 50, Playa, Havana; tel. (7) 203-6801; fax (7) 204-0517; e-mail minal@minal.get.cma.net; internet www.minal.cubaindustria.cu.

Ministry of Foreign Relations: Calzada 360, esq. G, Vedado, Plaza de la Revolución, Havana; tel. (7) 836-4500; e-mail cubaminrex@minrex.gov.cu; internet www.cubaminrex.cu.

Ministry of Foreign Trade and Investment: Infanta y 23, Plaza de la Revolución, Miramar, Havana; tel. (7) 838-0436; fax (7) 204-3496; e-mail secretariataller@mincex.cu; internet www.mincex.cu.

Ministry of Higher Education: Calle 23, No 565, esq. F, Vedado, Plaza de la Revolución, Havana; tel. (7) 830-3674; e-mail sitio_mes@reduniv.edu.cu; internet www.mes.edu.cu.

Ministry of Industries: Avda Independencia y Calle 100, Havana; tel. (7) 265-3606; fax (7) 267-0501.

Ministry of Information Technology and Communications: Avda Independencia No 2, entre 19 de Mayo y Aranguren, Plaza de la Revolución, Havana; tel. (7) 882-8000; fax (7) 885-4048; e-mail dircom@mic.cu; internet www.mic.gov.cu.

Ministry of the Interior: Sitio Minint, Plaza de la Revolución, Havana; tel. (7) 30-1566; fax (7) 855-6621; e-mail correominint@mn.mn.co.cu.

Ministry of Justice: Calle O, No 216, entre 23 y 25, Plaza de la Revolución, Apdo 10400, Havana 4; tel. (7) 838-3450; e-mail apoblacion@oc.minjus.cu; internet www.minjus.cu.

Ministry of Labour and Social Security: Calle 23, esq. Calles O y P, Vedado, Municipio Plaza de la Revolución, Havana; tel. (7) 838-0022; e-mail webmaster@mtss.cu; internet www.mtss.cu.

Ministry of Public Health: Calle 23, No 201, entre M y N, Vedado, Plaza de la Revolución, Havana; tel. (7) 835-2767; fax (7) 833-2195; e-mail apoblacion@infomed.sld.cu; internet www.sld.cu.

Ministry of the Revolutionary Armed Forces: Plaza de la Revolución, Havana; internet www.cubagob.cu/otras_info/minfar/far/minfar.htm.

Ministry of Science, Technology and the Environment: Industria y San José, Habana Vieja, Havana; tel. (7) 860-3411; fax (7) 866-8654; e-mail comunicacion@citma.cu.

Ministry of Tourism: Calle 3, No 6, entre F y G, Vedado, Plaza de la Revolución, Havana; tel. (7) 836-3245; fax (7) 836-4086; e-mail dircomunicacion@mintur.tur.cu; internet www.cubatravel.cu.

Ministry of Transportation: Avda Carlos Manuel de Céspedes s/n, entre Tulipán y Lombillo, Plaza de la Revolución, 10600 Havana; tel. (7) 855-5030; fax (7) 884-1105; e-mail mitrans@mitrans.transnet.cu; internet www.transporte.cu.

Legislature

NATIONAL ASSEMBLY OF PEOPLE'S POWER
(Asamblea Nacional del Poder Popular)

The National Assembly of People's Power was constituted on 2 December 1976. In 1992 the National Assembly adopted a constitutional amendment providing for legislative elections by direct vote. Only candidates nominated by the Partido Comunista de Cuba (PCC) were permitted to contest the elections. At elections to the National Assembly conducted on 3 February 2013, all 614 candidates succeeded in obtaining the requisite 50% of valid votes cast. Of the 8.7m. registered voters, 90.88% participated in the elections. Only 5.83% of votes cast were blank or spoiled.

President: Juan Esteban Lazo Hernández.

Vice-President: Ana María Mari Machado.

Secretary: Miriam Brito Sarroca.

Political Organizations

Partido Comunista de Cuba (PCC) (Communist Party of Cuba): Havana; e-mail root@epol.cipcc.inf.cu; internet www.pcc.cu; f. 1961 as the Organizaciones Revolucionarias Integradas (ORI) from a fusion of the Partido Socialista Popular (Communist), Fidel Castro's Movimiento 26 de Julio and the Directorio Revolucionario 13 de Marzo; became the Partido Unido de la Revolución Socialista Cubana (PURSC) in 1962; adopted current name in 1965; youth wing, the Unión de Jóvenes Comunistas (Union of Young Communists, First Sec. Yuniaski Crespo), comprises c. 500,000 mems; 150-member Central Committee, Political Bureau, 12-member Secretariat and five Commissions.

Political Bureau

Gen. Raúl Castro Ruz (First Sec.), José Ramón Machado Ventura (Second Sec.), Ramiro Valdés Menéndez, Juan Esteban Lazo Hernández, Lt-Gen. Abelardo Colomé Ibarra, Lt-Gen. Leopoldo Cintra Frías, Lt-Gen. Ramón Espinosa Martín, Miguel Mario Díaz-Canel Bermúdez, Salvador Antonio Valdés Mesa, Lt-Gen. Alvaro López Miera, Adel Onofre Yzquierdo Rodríguez, Marino Alberto Murillo Jorge, Mercedes López Acea, Bruno Eduardo Rodríguez Parilla.

There are a number of dissident groups operating in Cuba. Among the most prominent of these are the following:

Arco Progresista: tel. 763-0912; e-mail arcoprogresista.gl@gmail.com; internet www.cuba-progresista.org; f. 2003 as an alliance of three social-democratic groups in and outside Cuba: Corriente Socialista Democrática, Partido del Pueblo and Coordinadora Socialdemócrata en el Exilio; merged into a single party in 2008; Spokesperson Manuel Cuesta Morúa.

Asamblea para Promover la Sociedad Civil en Cuba: e-mail asambleacivil@bellsouth.net; internet www.asambleasociedadcivilcuba.info; f. 2002; alliance of 365 civil society asscns; Leader Martha Beatriz Roque Cabello.

Movimiento Cristiano Liberación (MCL): e-mail info@oswaldopaya.org; internet www.oswaldopaya.org; f. 1988; campaigns for peaceful democratic change and respect for human rights; associated with the Varela Project, established 1998 to petition the Govt for democratic freedoms; Leader Ofelia Acevedo.

Partido Demócrata Cristiano de Cuba (PDC): 1236 SW 22 Ave, Miami, FL 33135, USA; tel. (305) 644-3395; fax (305) 644-3311; e-mail miyares@pdc-cuba.org; internet www.pdc-cuba.org; f. 1959 as Movimiento Demócrata Cristiano; adopted current name in 1991; Pres. Marcelino Miyares Sotolongo; Vice-Pres José Vázquez, René Hernández, Yaxys Cires.

Partido Liberal de Cuba: 20 de Mayo 531, Apto B-14, entre Marta Abreu y Línea del Ferrocarril, Cerro, 10600 Havana; tel. and fax (7) 878-4010; f. 1991 as Partido Liberal Democrático de Cuba; mem. of Liberal International; Pres. Héctor Maseda Gutiérrez; Sec. Reinaldo Hernández Cardona.

Partido Liberal Nacional Cubano (PLNC): Calle 148, No 4116 entre 41 y 43, Apto 1, La Lisa, Havana; tel. 3445927; e-mail fernandopalacio3@gmail.com; internet cubadesdeadentro.com; f. 2004 as Movimiento Liberal Cubano; adopted present name in 2009; part of Convergencia Liberal Cubana; Pres. Fernando Edgardo Palacio Mogar; Exec. Nat. Sec. Ronaldo Mendoza Mendez.

Partido Pro-Derechos Humanos de Cuba (PPDHC): e-mail rene.montesdeoca@yahoo.es; internet www.partidoproderechoshumanosdecuba.com; f. 1988 to defend human rights in Cuba; Pres. Julián Enrique Martínez Báez (arrested in Dec. 2009); Nat. Sec. Ricardo Rubén Barreto Fuentes.

Partido Social Revolucionario Democrático de Cuba: 5900 Starlite Lane, Milton, FL 32570, USA; tel. and fax (305) 541-2334; e-mail psrdc@psrdc.org; internet www.psrdc.org; f. 1992; executive committee of 15 members; Pres. Jorge Valls; Exec. Sec. Roberto Simeon.

Partido Socialdemócrata de Cuba (PSC): Calle 36, No 105, Nuevo Vedado, 10600 Havana; tel. (7) 881-8203; e-mail vroca@pscuba.org; internet pscuba.org; f. 1996; Pres. Vladimiro Roca Antúnez; Exec. Sec. Carlos J. Menéndez Cervera; Sec.-Gen. Antonio Santiago Ruiz.

Partido Solidaridad Democrática (PSD): Calle Trocadero 414 bajos, entre Galiano y San Nicolás, Municipio Pio-Centro, 10200 Havana; tel. (7) 866-8306; e-mail gladyperez@aol.com; f. 1993; mem. of Liberal International; Pres. Fernando Sánchez López.

Unión Liberal Cubana: Paseo de la Retama 97, 29600 Marbella, Spain; tel. (91) 4340201; fax (91) 5011342; e-mail cubaliberal@mercuryin.es; internet www.cubaliberal.org; mem. of Liberal International; Pres. Antonio Guedes.

Diplomatic Representation

EMBASSIES IN CUBA

Algeria: Avda 5, No 2802, esq. 28, Miramar, Havana; tel. (7) 204-2835; fax (7) 204-2702; e-mail embhav@argelia.sytes.net; Ambassador Abdellah Laouari.

Angola: Avda 5, No 1012, entre 10 y 12, Miramar, Havana; tel. (7) 204-2474; fax (7) 204-0487; e-mail embangol@ceniai.inf.cu; Ambassador JOSÉ CÉSAR AUGUSTO.

Antigua and Barbuda: Avda 5, esq. 66, No 6407, Miramar, Havana; tel. (7) 207-9756; fax (7) 207-9757; e-mail anubarembassy@enet.cu; Ambassador BRUCE GOODWIN.

Argentina: Calle 36, No 511, entre 5 y 7, Miramar, Havana; tel. (7) 204-2565; fax (7) 204-2140; e-mail embajador@ecuba.co.cu; Ambassador JULIANA ISABEL MARINO.

Austria: Avda 5A, No 6617, esq. 70, Miramar, Havana; tel. (7) 204-2825; fax (7) 204-1235; e-mail havanna-ob@bmeia.gv.at; Ambassador ANDREAS RENDL.

Bahamas: Avda 5, No 3006, entre 30 y 32, Miramar, Playa, Havana; tel. (7) 206-9918; fax (7) 206-9921; e-mail embahamas@enet.cu; Ambassador ALMA ADAMS.

Belarus: Avda 5, No 6405, entre 64 y 66, Miramar, Havana; tel. (7) 204-7330; fax (7) 204-7332; e-mail cuba@mfa.gov.by; internet www.cuba.mfa.gov.by; Ambassador VLADZIMIR A. ASTAPENKA.

Belgium: Calle 8, No 309, entre 3 y 5, Miramar, Havana; tel. (7) 204-4806; fax (7) 204-6516; e-mail havana@diplobel.fed.be; internet www.diplomatie.be/havana; Ambassador LUC DEVOLDER.

Belize: Avda 5, No 3606, esq. 36 y 36, AMiramar, Havana; tel. (7) 204-3504; fax (7) 204-3506; e-mail belizecuba@yahoo.es; Chargé d'affaires a.i. EFRAIN RAVEY NOVELO.

Benin: Calle 20, No 119, entre 1 y 3, Miramar, Havana; tel. (7) 204-2179; fax (7) 204-2334; e-mail ambencub@ceniai.inf.cu; Ambassador ANTOINE DIMON AFOUDA.

Bolivia: Calle 36A, No 3601, entre Avdas 3 y 5, Miramar, Havana; tel. (7) 209-7513; fax (7) 204-2739; e-mail emboliviacuba@gmail.com; Ambassador PALMIRO LEÓN SORIA SAUCEDO.

Brazil: Centro de Negocios Miramar, Edif. Beijing, 2°, Of. 206, Calle 3, entre 76 y 79, Miramar, Havana; tel. (7) 214-4713; fax (7) 866-2912; e-mail brasemb.havana@itamaraty.gov.br; Ambassador JOSÉ E. MARTINS FELICIO.

Bulgaria: Calle B, No 252, entre 11 y 13, Vedado, Havana; tel. (7) 833-3125; fax (7) 833-3297; e-mail embassy.havana@mfa.bg; internet www.mfa.bg/embassies/kuba; Ambassador SVETLA T. STEFANOVA.

Burkina Faso: Calle 40, No 516, entre Avdas 5 y 7, Miramar, Havana; tel. (7) 204-2217; fax (7) 204-1942; e-mail ambfaso@ceniai.inf.cu; Ambassador DANIEL OUÉDRAOGO.

Cambodia: Avda 5, No 7001, entre 70 y 72, Miramar, Havana; tel. (7) 204-1496; fax (7) 204-6400; e-mail cambohav@enet.cu; Ambassador HAY SONNARIN.

Canada: Calle 30, No 518, esq. 7, Miramar, Havana; tel. (7) 204-2516; fax (7) 204-2044; e-mail havan@international.gc.ca; internet www.canadainternational.gc.ca/cuba; Ambassador YVES GAGNON.

Cape Verde: Calle 20, No 2001, esq. a 7, Miramar, Havana; tel. (7) 204-2979; fax (7) 204-1072; e-mail emb.caboverde.cuba@gmail.com; Ambassador MANUEL AVELINO COUTO DA SILVA MATOS.

Chile: Calle 33, No 1423, entre 14 y 18, Miramar, Havana; tel. (7) 204-1222; fax (7) 204-1694; e-mail echile.cuba@minrel.gov.cl; Ambassador ROLANDO DRAGO RODRÍGUEZ.

China, People's Republic: Calle C, entre 13 y 15, Vedado, Havana; tel. (7) 833-3005; fax (7) 833-3092; e-mail chinaemb_cu@mfa.gov.cn; Ambassador ZHANG TUO.

Colombia: Calle 14, No 515, entre 5 y 7, Miramar, Havana; tel. (7) 204-1248; fax (7) 204-0464; e-mail ecuba@cancilleria.gov.co; internet cuba.embajada.gov.co; Ambassador GUSTAVO ADOLFO BELL LEMUS.

Congo, Republic: Avda 5, No 1003, Miramar, Havana; tel. and fax (7) 204-9055; fax (7) 204-9055; e-mail ambacohavane@yahoo.fr; Ambassador PASCAL ONGEMBY.

Costa Rica: Avda 5, No 6604, esq. 66 y 68, Miramar, Havana; tel. (7) 204-6938; fax (7) 204-6937; e-mail embajada@costaricacuba.org; Ambassador HUBERT GERARDO MÉNDEZ ACOSTA.

Cyprus: Avda 5, No 8409, entre 84 and 86, Miramar, Havana; tel. (7) 212-5229; fax (7) 212-5227; e-mail chancery@cyprusembassycuba.org; internet www.cyprusembassycuba.org; Ambassador STAVROS LOIZIDES.

Czech Republic: Avda Kohly, No 259, entre 41 y 43, Nuevo Vedado, CP 10600, Havana; tel. (7) 883-3201; fax (7) 883-3596; e-mail havana@embassy.mzv.cz; internet www.mzv.cz/havana; Chargé d'affaires a.i. JAROSLAV ZAJÍC.

Dominica: Calle 36, No 507, entre 5 y 7, Miramar, Havana; tel. (7) 214-1096; fax (7) 214-1097; e-mail embcwdom@enet.cu; Ambassador CHARLES J. CORBETTE.

Dominican Republic: Avda 5, No 9202, entre 92 y 94, Miramar, Havana; tel. (7) 204-8429; fax (7) 204-8431; e-mail edc@enet.cu; Ambassador JOSÉ MANUEL CASTILLO BETANCES.

Ecuador: Avda 7, No 3804, esq. a 40, Miramar, Havana; tel. (7) 204-2868; e-mail embecuador@yahoo.com; Ambassador EDGAR PONCE ITURRIAGA.

Egypt: Avda 5, No 1801, esq. 18, Miramar, Havana; tel. (7) 204-2441; fax (7) 204-0905; e-mail emegipto@enet.cu; Ambassador TAREK MOHEY ELDIN ELWASSIMY.

El Salvador: Calle 24, No 307, esq. 3ra y 5ta, Miramar, Havana; tel. (7) 212-5612; e-mail embajadaencuba@rree.gob.sv; Ambassador DOMINGO SANTACRUZ CASTRO.

Equatorial Guinea: Calle 20, No 713, entre 7 y 9, Miramar, Havana; tel. (7) 204-1720; fax (7) 204-1724; Ambassador LOURDES MBA AYECABA.

Ethiopia: Avda 5, No 6604, Apto 3, entre 66 y 68, Miramar, Havana; tel. (7) 206-9905; fax (7) 206-9907; e-mail info@embaethi.co.cu; Ambassador BOGALE TOLESSA MARU.

France: Calle 14, No 312, entre 3 y 5, Miramar, Havana; tel. (7) 201-3131; fax (7) 201-3107; e-mail internet.la-havane-amba@diplomatie.fr; internet www.ambafrance-cu.org; Ambassador JEAN MENDELSON.

The Gambia: Calle 40A, No 301, esq. a 3, Miramar, Havana; tel. and fax (7) 212-5626; e-mail gambia.secretariat@mail.com; Ambassador MASANNEH NYUKU KINTEH.

Germany: Calle 13, No 652, esq. B, Vedado, Havana; tel. (7) 833-2569; fax (7) 833-1586; e-mail info@havanna.diplo.de; internet www.havanna.diplo.de; Ambassador PETER RUDOLF SCHOLZ.

Ghana: Avda 5, No 1808, esq. 20, Miramar, Havana; tel. (7) 204-2153; fax (7) 204-2317; e-mail embassyofghanahavgh@gmail.com; Ambassador DAVID SARPONG BOATENG.

Greece: Avda 5, No 7802, esq. 78, Miramar, Havana; tel. (7) 204-2995; fax (7) 204-9770; e-mail gremb@enet.cu; Ambassador APOSTOLOS-PAUL CHARALAMPOUS.

Grenada: Avda 5, No 2006, entre 20 y 22, Miramar, Havana; tel. (7) 204-6764; fax (7) 204-6765; e-mail embgranada@ip.etecsa.cu; Ambassador CLARICE CHARLES.

Guatemala: Calle 20, No 301, entre 3 y 5, Miramar, Havana; tel. (7) 204-3417; fax (7) 204-8173; e-mail cuba@minex.gob.gt; internet www.cuba.minex.gob.gt; Ambassador JUAN LEÓN ALVARADO.

Guinea: Calle 20, No 504, entre 5 y 7, Miramar, Havana; tel. (7) 292-9212; fax (7) 204-1894; e-mail ambaguineehav@yahoo.com; Ambassador HADIATOU SOW.

Guinea-Bissau: Avda 5, No 8203, entre 82 y 84, Miramar, Havana; tel. (7) 204-5742; fax (7) 204-2794; e-mail embaguib@enet.cu; Ambassador ABEL COELHO MENDONÇA.

Guyana: Calle 18, No 506, entre 5 y 7, Miramar, Havana; tel. (7) 204-2094; fax (7) 204-2867; e-mail embguyana@enet.cu; Ambassador MITRADEVI ALI.

Haiti: Avda 7, No 4402, esq. 44, Miramar, Havana; tel. (7) 204-5421; fax (7) 204-5423; e-mail embhaiti@enet.cu; Ambassador JEAN VICTOR GENEUS.

Holy See: Calle 12, No 514, entre 5 y 7, Miramar, Havana (Apostolic Nunciature); tel. (7) 204-2700; fax (7) 204-2257; e-mail csa@pcn.net; Apostolic Nuncio BRUNO MUSARÒ (Titular Archbishop of Abari).

Honduras: Edif. Santa Clara, 1°, Of. 121 Centro de Negocios Miramar, Calle 3a No 123, entre 78 y 80 Calles, Miramar, Havana; tel. (7) 204-5496; fax (7) 204-5497; e-mail embhondcuba@yahoo.com; Ambassador ALAMS ARMANDO ESPINAL ZUNIGA.

Hungary: Calle G, No 458, entre 19 y 21, Vedado, Havana; tel. (7) 833-3365; fax (7) 833-3286; e-mail mission.hav@kum.hu; internet www.mfa.gov.hu/kulkepviselet/cu/hu; Ambassador ANDRÁS GÁBOR DREXLER.

India: Calle 21, No 202, esq. K, Vedado, Havana; tel. (7) 833-3777; fax (7) 833-3287; e-mail hoc@indembassyhavana.cu; internet www.indembassyhavana.cu; Ambassador CHINTHAPALLY RAJASEKHAR.

Indonesia: Avda 5, No 1607, esq. 18, Miramar, Havana; tel. (7) 204-9618; fax (7) 204-9617; e-mail indonhav@ceniai.inf.cu; internet www.deplu.go.id/havana; Ambassador TEISERAN FOUN CORNELIS.

Iran: Avda 5, No 3002, esq. 30, Miramar, Havana; tel. (7) 204-2675; fax (7) 204-2770; e-mail embassy_iran_havana@yahoo.com; Ambassador ALI CHEGENI.

Italy: Avda 5, No 402, esq. 4, Miramar, Havana; tel. (7) 204-5615; fax (7) 204-5659; e-mail ambasciata.avana@esteri.it; internet www.amblavana.esteri.it; Ambassador CARMINE ROBUSTELLI.

Jamaica: Calle 22, No 503, entre 5 y 7, Miramar, Havana; tel. (7) 204-2908; fax (7) 204-2531; e-mail embjmcub@enet.cu; Ambassador A'DALE GEORGE ROBINSON.

Japan: Centro de Negocios Miramar, Avda 3, Edif. 1, 5°, esq. 80, Miramar, Havana; tel. (7) 204-3355; fax (7) 204-8902; e-mail taisi@ceniai.inf.cu; internet www.cu.emb-japan.go.jp; Ambassador HIROSHI SATO.

Korea, Democratic People's Republic: Calle 17 y Paseo, No 752, Vedado, Havana; tel. (7) 833-2313; fax (7) 833-3073; e-mail dprkorcuba@enet.cu; Ambassador (vacant).

Laos: Avda 5, No 2808, esq. 30, Miramar, Havana; tel. (7) 204-1057; fax (7) 204-9622; e-mail embalao@enet.cu; Ambassador KHAMPO KYAKHAMPHITOUNE.

Lebanon: Calle 17A, No 16403, entre 164 y 174, Siboney, Havana; tel. (7) 208-6220; fax (7) 208-6432; e-mail lbcunet@ceniai.inf.cu; Ambassador ROBERT NAOUM.

Libya: Avda 7, No 1402, esq. 14, Miramar, Havana; tel. (7) 204-2192; fax (7) 204-2991; e-mail oficinalibia@ip.etecsa.cu.

Malaysia: Avda 5, No 6612, entre 66 y 68, Miramar, Havana; tel. (7) 204-8883; fax (7) 204-6888; e-mail malhavana@kln.gov.my; internet www.kln.gov.my/perwakilan/havana; Ambassador JOJIE SAMUEL.

Mali: Calle 36A, No 704, entre 7 y 42, Miramar, Havana; tel. (7) 204-5321; fax (7) 204-5320; e-mail ambamali@ceniai.inf.cu; Ambassador MODIBO DIARRA.

Mexico: Calle 12, No 518, esq. Avda 7, Miramar, Playa, Havana; tel. (7) 204-2553; fax (7) 204-2717; e-mail embamex@embamexcuba.org; internet www.sre.gob.mx/cuba; Ambassador JUAN JOSÉ BREMER DE MARTINO.

Mongolia: Calle 66, No 505, esq. 5A, Miramar, Havana; tel. (7) 204-2763; fax (7) 204-0639; e-mail embahavana@ceniai.inf.cu; Ambassador OTGONBAYARYN DAVAASAMBUU.

Mozambique: Avda 7, No 2203, entre 22 y 24, Miramar, Havana; tel. (7) 204-2443; fax (7) 204-2232; e-mail tsocotsinha@gmail.com; Ambassador MIGUEL COSTA MKAIMA.

Namibia: Calle 36, No 504, entre 5 y 5A, Miramar, Havana; tel. (7) 204-1430; fax (7) 204-1431; e-mail namembassycuba@hotmail.com; Ambassador JEROBEAM SHAANIKA.

Netherlands: Calle 8, No 307, entre 3 y 5, Miramar, Havana; tel. (7) 204-2511; fax (7) 204-2059; e-mail hav@minbuza.nl; internet cuba.nlambassade.org; Ambassador NORBERT W.M. BRAAKHUIS.

Nicaragua: Calle 20, No 709, entre 7 y 9, Miramar, Havana; tel. (7) 204-1025; fax (7) 204-5387; e-mail nicaragua@embnicc.co.cu; Ambassador LUIS CABRERA GONZÁLEZ.

Nigeria: Avda 5, No 1401, entre 14 y 16, Miramar, Havana; tel. (7) 204-2898; fax (7) 204-2202; e-mail chancery@nigeria-havana.com; Ambassador LARABA ELSIE BINTA BHUTTO.

Norway: Calle 30, No 315, entre 3 y 5, Miramar, Havana; tel. (7) 204-0696; fax (7) 204-0699; e-mail emb.havana@mfa.no; internet www.noruega-cuba.org; Ambassador JOHN PETTER OPDAHL.

Pakistan: Avda 5, No 2606, entre 26 y 28, Miramar, Havana; tel. (7) 214-1151; fax (7) 214-1154; e-mail parephavana@hotmail.com; internet www.mofa.gov.pk/cuba; Ambassador QAZI M. KHALILULLAH.

Panama: Calle 26, No 109, entre 1 y 3, Miramar, Havana; tel. (7) 204-0858; fax (7) 204-1674; e-mail panaemba_cuba@panaemba.co.cu; Ambassador MARIO RAFAEL GÁLVEZ EVERS.

Paraguay: Calle 34, No 503, entre 5 y 7, Miramar, Havana; tel. (7) 204-0884; fax (7) 204-0883; e-mail cgphav@enet.cu; Chargé d'affaires a.i. VÍCTOR BENÍTEZ.

Peru: Calle 30, No 107, entre 1 y 3, Miramar, Havana; tel. (7) 204-2632; fax (7) 204-2636; e-mail embaperu@embaperu.org; Ambassador VÍCTOR RICARDO MAYORGA MIRANDA.

Philippines: Avda 5, No 2207, esq. 24, Miramar, Havana; tel. (7) 204-1372; fax (7) 204-2915; e-mail philhavpe@enet.cu; Ambassador GEORGE B. REYES.

Poland: Calle G, No 452, esq. 19, Vedado, Havana; tel. (7) 833-2439; fax (7) 833-2442; e-mail hawana.amb.sekretariat@msz.gov.pl; Ambassador MALGORZATA GALINSKA-TOMASZEWSKA.

Portugal: Avda 7, No 2207, esq. 24, Miramar, Havana; tel. (7) 204-0149; fax (7) 204-2593; e-mail embpthav@embporthavana.org; Ambassador FERNANDO ANTONIO ALBERTY TAVARES DE CARVALHO.

Qatar: Avda 3, No 3407, entre 34 y 36, Miramar, Havana; tel. (7) 204-0587; fax (7) 204-0003; e-mail embajada@qatar.co.cu; Ambassador RASHID MIRZA AL-MULLA.

Romania: Avda 5, No 4407, entre 44 y 46, Miramar, Havana; tel. (7) 214-4922; fax (7) 214-4949; e-mail havana@mae.ro; Ambassador DUMITRU PREDA.

Russia: Avda 5, No 6402, entre 62 y 66, Miramar, Havana; tel. (7) 204-2686; fax (7) 204-1038; e-mail embrusia@newmail.ru; internet www.cuba.mid.ru; Ambassador MIKHAIL L. KAMYNIN.

Saint Lucia: Centro de Negocios Miramar, Edif. Jerusalén, Calle 3, No 403, entre 78 y 80, Miramar, Havana; tel. (7) 206-9609; fax (7) 206-9610; Ambassador CHARLES ISAAC.

Saint Vincent and the Grenadines: Centro de Negocios Miramar, Edif. Jerusalén, Of. 403, Avda 3 y Calle 80, Miramar, Havana; tel. (7) 206-9783; fax (7) 206-9782; e-mail embsvg@mtc.co.cu; Ambassador DEXTER E. M. ROSE.

Saudi Arabia: Avda 5, No 4605, Miramar, Havana; tel. (7) 214-4590; fax (7) 214-4587; e-mail haemb@mofa.gov.sa; Ambassador SAEED HASSAN SAEED AL-JOMAE.

Serbia: Avda 5, No 4406, entre 44 y 46, Miramar, Havana; tel. (7) 204-2488; fax (7) 204-2982; e-mail ambsrbhav@embajadaserbia.co.cu; internet havana.mfa.gov.rs; Ambassador MARINA PEROVIĆ PETROVIĆ.

Slovakia: Calle 66, No 521, entre 5B y 7, Miramar, Havana; tel. (7) 204-1884; fax (7) 204-1883; e-mail embeslovaca@mzv.sk; Ambassador ZDENEK ROZHOLD.

South Africa: Avda 5, No 4201, esq. 42, Miramar, Havana; tel. (7) 204-9671; fax (7) 204-1101; e-mail mision@sudafrica.cu; Ambassador NAPHTAL MANANA.

Spain: Calle Cárcel No 51, esq. a Zulueta, Havana; tel. (7) 866-8025; fax (7) 866-8006; e-mail emb.lahabana@maec.es; Ambassador JUAN FRANCISCO MONTALBAN CARRASCO.

Sri Lanka: Avda 5, No 3004, entre 30 y 32, Miramar, Havana; tel. (7) 204-2562; fax (7) 204-2183; e-mail sri.lanka@enet.cu; Ambassador K. S. C. DISSANAYAKE.

Suriname: Edif. Jerusalén, Of. 106, Centro de Negocios de Miramar, Calle 3, entre 78 y 80, Playa, Havana; tel. (7) 207-9559; fax (7) 207-9561; e-mail secembsur@mtc.co.cu; Ambassador IKE DESMOND ANTONIUS.

Sweden: Calle 34, No 510, entre 5 y 7, Miramar, Havana; tel. (7) 204-2831; fax (7) 204-1194; e-mail ambassaden.havanna@foreign.ministry.se; internet www.swedenabroad.com/havanna; Ambassador ELISABETH EKLUND.

Switzerland: Avda 5, No 2005, entre 20 y 22, Miramar, Havana; tel. (7) 204-2611; fax (7) 204-1148; e-mail hav.vertretung@eda.admin.ch; internet www.eda.admin.ch/havana; Ambassador ANNE PASCALE KRAUER MÜLLER.

Syria: Calle 20, No 514, entre 5 y 7, Miramar, Havana; tel. (7) 204-2266; fax (7) 204-9754; e-mail embsiria@ceniai.inf.cu; Ambassador (vacant).

Timor-Leste: Calle 40A, No 301, esq. 3, Miramar, Havana; tel. (7) 206-9911; e-mail embtimor@enet.cu; Ambassador OLIMPIO BRANCO.

Trinidad and Tobago: Avda 5, No 6603, entre 66 y 68, Miramar, Havana; tel. (7) 207-9603; fax (7) 207-9604; e-mail ttmissionscuba@enet.cu; Ambassador JENNIFER JONES-KERNAHAN.

Turkey: Avda 5, No 3805, entre 36 y 40, Miramar, Havana; tel. (7) 204-1204; fax (7) 204-2899; e-mail turkemb@gmail.com; internet havana.be.mfa.gov.tr; Ambassador HASAN SERVET OKTEM.

Ukraine: Avda 5, No 4405, entre 44 y 46, Miramar, Havana; tel. (7) 204-2586; fax (7) 204-2341; e-mail emb_cu@mfa.gov.ua; internet www.mfa.gov.ua/cuba; Chargé d'affaires a.i. VOLODYMYR KOZLOV.

United Kingdom: Calle 34, No 702/4, esq. 7 y 17, Miramar, Havana; tel. (7) 214-2200; fax (7) 214-2218; e-mail embrit@ceniai.inf.cu; internet ukincuba.fco.gov.uk; Ambassador TIM COLE.

USA (Relations severed in 1961): Interests Section in the Embassy of Switzerland: Calzada, entre L y M, Vedado, Havana; tel. (7) 833-3551; fax (7) 833-1084; e-mail irchavana@state.org; internet havana.usint.gov; Principal Officer JOHN CAULFIELD.

Uruguay: Calle 36, No 716, entre 7 y 17, Miramar, Havana; tel. (7) 204-2311; fax (7) 206-9683; e-mail urucub@rou.co.cu; Ambassador ARIEL ARTURO BERGAMINO SOSA.

Venezuela: Edif. Beijing, 2°, Centro de Negocios Miramar, Avda 3, entre 74 y 76, Miramar, Havana; tel. (7) 204-2612; fax (7) 204-9790; e-mail embajada@venezuela.co.cu; Ambassador EDGARDO ANTONIO RAMÍREZ.

Viet Nam: Avda 5, No 1802, esq. 18, Miramar, Havana; tel. (7) 204-1525; fax (7) 204-5333; e-mail embavina@embavicu.org; internet www.vietnamembassy-cuba.org; Ambassador DUONG MIHN.

Yemen: Avda 5, No 8201, entre 82 y 84, Miramar, Havana; tel. (7) 204-1506; fax (7) 204-1131; e-mail gamdan-hav@enet.cu; Ambassador YAHYA MOHAMED AHMED AL-SYAGHI.

Zimbabwe: Avda 3, No 1001, entre 10 y 12, Miramar, Havana; tel. (7) 204-2857; fax (7) 204-2720; e-mail zimhavan@enet.cu; Ambassador JOHN SHUMBA MVUNDURA.

Judicial System

The judicial system comprises the People's Supreme Court, the People's Provincial Courts and the People's Municipal Courts. The People's Supreme Court exercises the highest judicial authority.

Tribunal Supremo Popular (TSP) (People's Supreme Court): Nuevo Veodad, CP 10600, Havana; tel. (7) 881-2124; fax (7) 881-2245; e-mail ravelo@tsp.cu; internet www.tsp.cu; comprises the Plenum, six Courts of Justice in joint session and the Council of Govt, which comprises the President and Vice-Presidents of the TSP, the

Presidents of each Court of Justice, and the Attorney-General; Pres. Dr RUBÉN REMIGIO FERRO.

Religion

There is no established Church, and all religions are permitted, though Roman Catholicism predominates. The Afro-Cuban religions of Regla de Ocha (Santería) and Regla Conga (Palo Monte) also have numerous adherents.

CHRISTIANITY

Consejo de Iglesias de Cuba (CIC) (Cuban Council of Churches): Calle 14, No 304, entre 3 y 5, Miramar, Playa, Havana; tel. (7) 204-2878; fax (7) 204-1755; e-mail iglesias@enet.cu; internet www.consejodeiglesias.co.cu; f. 1941; 25 mem. churches; Pres. Rev. JOEL ORTEGA DOPICO.

The Roman Catholic Church

Cuba comprises three archdioceses and eight dioceses. Adherents represent some 53% of the total population.

Conferencia de Obispos Católicos de Cuba (COCC) (Bishops' Conference): Calle 26, No 314, entre 3 y 5, Miramar, Apdo 635, 11300 Havana; tel. (7) 204-0165; fax (7) 204-2168; e-mail cocc@iglesiacatolica.cu; internet www.iglesiacubana.org; f. 1983; Pres. DIONISIO GUILLERMO GARCÍA IBÁÑEZ (Archbishop of Santiago de Cuba).

Archbishop of Camagüey: JUAN DE LA CARIDAD GARCÍA RODRÍGUEZ, Calle Luaces, No 55, Apdo 105, 70100 Camagüey; tel. (32) 229-2268; fax (32) 228-7143; e-mail info@arzcamaguey.co.cu.

Archbishop of San Cristóbal de la Habana: Cardinal JAIME LUCAS ORTEGA Y ALAMINO, Calle Habana No 152, esq. a Chacón, Apdo 594, 10100 Havana; tel. (7) 862-4000; fax (7) 866-8109; e-mail info@arquidiocesisdelahabana.org; internet www.arquidiocesisdelahabana.org.

Archbishop of Santiago de Cuba: DIONISIO GUILLERMO GARCÍA IBÁÑEZ, Calle Sánchez Hechevarría 607, entre Barnada y Paraíso, Apdo 26, 90100 Santiago de Cuba; tel. (22) 62-5480; fax (22) 68-6186; e-mail info@arzsantiago.co.cu; internet www.arzobispadosantiagodecuba.org.

The Anglican Communion

Anglicans are adherents of the Iglesia Episcopal de Cuba (Episcopal Church of Cuba).

Bishop of Cuba: Rt Rev. MIGUEL TAMAYO ZALDÍVAR, Calle 6, No 273, entre 11 y 13, Vedado, 10400 Havana; tel. (7) 832-1120; fax (7) 834-3293; e-mail episcopal@ip.etecsa.cu; internet www.cuba.anglican.org.

Other Christian Churches

Iglesia Metodista en Cuba (Methodist Church in Cuba): Calle K, No 502, 25 y 27, Vedado, 10400 Havana; tel. (7) 832-2991; fax (7) 832-0770; e-mail imecu@enet.cu; internet www.imecu.com; autonomous since 1968; 215 churches, 17,000 mems (2005); Bishop RICARDO PEREIRA DÍAZ.

Iglesia Presbiteriana Reformada en Cuba (Presbyterian-Reformed Church in Cuba): Salud 222, entre Lealtad y Campanario, 10200 Havana; tel. (7) 862-1219; fax (7) 866-8819; e-mail presbit@enet.cu; internet www.prccuba.org; f. 1890; 8,000 mems; Moderator Rev. Dr HÉCTOR MÉNDEZ RODRÍGUEZ.

Other denominations active in Cuba include the Apostolic Church of Jesus Christ, the Bethel Evangelical Church, the Christian Pentecostal Church, the Church of God, the Church of the Nazarene, the Free Baptist Convention, the Holy Pentecost Church, the Pentecostal Congregational Church and the Salvation Army. Membership of evangelical churches increased from the late 20th century—in 2010 there were an estimated 800,000 adherents, according to the Consejo de Iglesias de Cuba.

The Press

DAILIES

Granma: Avda Gen. Suárez y Territorial, Plaza de la Revolución, Apdo 6187, CP 10699, Havana; tel. (7) 881-3333; fax (7) 881-9854; e-mail correo@granma.cip.cu; internet www.granma.cubaweb.cu; f. 1965, to replace *Hoy* and *Revolución*; official Communist Party organ; Editor-in-Chief PELAYO TERRY CUERVO; circ. 400,000.

Juventud Rebelde: Avda Territorial y Gen. Suárez, Plaza de la Revolución, Apdo 6344, CP 10600, Havana; tel. (7) 882-0155; fax (7) 883-8959; e-mail digital@jrebelde.cip.cu; internet www.juventudrebelde.cu; f. 1965; organ of the Young Communist League; Editor-in-Chief MARINA MENÉNDEZ; circ. 250,000.

PERIODICALS

Adelante: Salvador Cisneros Betancourt 306, entre Ignacio Agramonte y General Gómez, Camagüey; tel. (32) 284432; e-mail cip222@cip.enet.cu; internet www.adelante.cu; f. 1959; Dir Dr DAICAR SALADRIGAS GONZÁLEZ; Editor YANEXIS ESTRADA TORRES; circ. 42,000.

Ahora: Salida a San Germán y Circunvalación, Holguín; e-mail director@ahora.cu; internet www.ahora.cu; f. 1962; Dir JORGE LUIS CRUZ BERMÚDEZ; circ. 50,000.

Alma Mater: Prado 553, esq. Teniente Rey, Habana Vieja, Havana; e-mail almamater@editoraabril.co.cu; internet www.almamater.cu; f. 1922; aimed at a student readership; Dir YOERKY SÁNCHEZ CUÉLLAR.

Bohemia: Avda Independencia y San Pedro, Apdo 6000, Havana; tel. (7) 81-9213; fax (7) 33-5511; e-mail bohemia@bohemia.co.cu; internet www.bohemia.cu; f. 1908; fortnightly; politics; Dir JOSÉ FERNÁNDEZ VEGA; circ. 100,000.

El Caimán Barbudo: Casa Editora Abril, Prado 553, entre Dragones y Teniente Rey, Vedado, Havana; tel. (7) 860-4237; e-mail rgrillo@enet.cu; internet www.caimanbarbudo.cu; f. 1966; 6 a year; cultural; Dir FIDEL DÍAZ CASTRO; Editor RAFAEL GRILLO; circ. 20,000.

Cinco de Septiembre: Avda 54, No 3516, entre 35 y 37, CP 55100, Cienfuegos; tel. (43) 52-2144; e-mail arosell@enet.cu; internet www.5septiembre.cu; f. 1980; Dir ALINA ROSELL CHONG; circ. 18,000.

Cubadebate: Unión de Periodistas de Cuba, Avda 23, No 452, esq. I, Vedado, Havana; e-mail editor@cubadebate.cu; internet www.cubadebate.cu; Dir RANDY ALONSO FALCÓN.

Dedeté: Territorial y Gen. Suárez, Plaza de la Revolución, Apdo 6344, Havana; tel. (7) 882-0155; fax (7) 81-8621; e-mail contacto@dedete.cu; internet dedete.cu; f. 1969; weekly; humorous supplementary publ. of Juventud Rebelde; Dir ADÁN IGLESIAS TOLEDO; circ. 70,000.

La Demajagua: Amado Estévez, esq. Calle 10, Rpto R. Reyes, Bayamo; tel. (23) 42-4221; e-mail cip225@cip.enet.cu; internet www.lademajagua.co.cu; f. 1977; Dir LUIS CARLOS FRÓMETA AGÜERO; Editor GISLANIA TAMAYO CEDEÑO; circ. 21,000.

El Economista de Cuba: Asociación Nacional de Economistas y Contadores de Cuba, Calle 22, No 901 esq. a 901, Miramar, Havana; tel. (7) 209-3303; fax (7) 202-3456; e-mail eleconomista@cibercuba.com; internet www.eleconomista.cubaweb.cu; monthly; business; Dir-Gen. DANILO GUZMAN DOVAO; Editor MAGALI GARCÍA MORÉ.

Escambray: Adolfo del Castillo 10, Sancti Spíritus; tel. (41) 32-3003; e-mail cip220@cip.enet.cu; internet www.escambray.cu; f. 1979 as daily; weekly from 1992; serves Sancti Spíritus province; Dir JUAN ANTONIO BORREGO DÍAZ; circ. 21,000.

Girón: Avda Camilo Cienfuegos No 10505, P. Nuero, Matanzas; e-mail cip217@cip.enet.cu; internet www.giron.co.cu; f. 1960; organ of the Communist Party in Matanzas province; Dir CLOVIS ORTEGA CASTAÑEDA; circ. 25,000.

Guerrillero: Colón 12 entre Juan Gualberto Gómez y Adela Azcuy, CP 20100, Pinar del Río; e-mail cip216@cip.enet.cu; internet www.guerrillero.cu; f. 1969; organ of Communist Party in Pinar del Río province; Dir ERNESTO OSORIO ROQUE; Editor IDALMA MENÉNDEZ FEBLES; circ. 33,000.

Invasor: Avda de los Deportes s/n, Ciego de Avila; e-mail cip221@cip.enet.cu; internet www.invasor.cu; f. 1979; provincial periodical; Editor RIGOBERTO TRIANA MARTÍNEZ; circ. 10,500.

La Jiribilla: Havana; e-mail lajiribilla@enet.cu; internet www.lajiribilla.cu; f. 2001; cultural; weekly; Dir IROEL SÁNCHEZ ESPINOSA.

Juventud Técnica: Prado 553, esq. Teniente Rey, Habana Vieja, Havana; tel. (7) 862-9264; e-mail jtecnica@editoraabril.co.cu; internet www.juventudtecnica.cu; f. 1965; every 2 months; scientific-technical; Editor-in-Chief IRAMIS ALONSO PORRO; Editor BÁRBARA MASEDA; circ. 20,000.

Mar y Pesca: Calle Línea 10, esq. N, Vedado, Plaza de la Revolución, Havana; tel. (7) 835-0883; fax (7) 835-0084; e-mail revist@marypesca.cu; internet www.marypesca.cu; f. 1965; bi-monthly; fishing; Dir PEDRO E. PÉREZ BORDÓN; circ. 23,500.

Mujeres: Galiano 264, entre Neptuno y Concordia, CP 10200, Havana; tel. (7) 861-5919; e-mail mujeres@teleda.get.tur.cu; internet www.mujeres.co.cu; f. 1961; weekly; organ of the Federación de Mujeres Cubanas; Dir IVETTE VEGA HERNÁNDEZ; circ. 270,000.

El Nuevo Fenix: Independencia 52, esq. Honorato del Castillo, Sancti Spíritus; tel. (41) 327902; e-mail plss@ip.etecsa.cu; internet www.fenix.co.cu; f. 1999; published by Sancti Spíritus bureau of Prensa Latina (see News Agencies); Editor-in-Chief RAÚL I. GARCÍA ALVAREZ.

Opciones: Territorial esq. Gen. Suárez, Plaza de la Revolucíon, Havana; tel. (7) 881-8934; fax (7) 881-8621; e-mail chabela@opciones

.cu; internet www.opciones.cu; f. 1994; weekly; finance, commerce and tourism; Chief Editor ISABEL FERNÁNDEZ GARRIDO.

Palante: Calle 21, No 954, entre 8 y 10, Vedado, Havana; tel. (7) 833-5098; e-mail cip319@cip.enet.cu; internet www.palante.co.cu; f. 1961; weekly; humorous; Dir MERCEDES AZCANO TORRES; circ. 235,000.

Periódico 26: Avda Carlos J. Finlay s/n, CP 75100, Las Tunas; e-mail cip224@cip.enet.cu; internet www.periodico26.cu; f. 2000; provincial periodical; Dir RAMIRO SEGURA GARCÍA; Editor MARYLA GARCÍA SANTOS.

Pionero: Calle 17, No 354, Havana; tel. (7) 32-4571; e-mail pionero@editoraabril.co.cu; internet www.pionero.cu; f. 1961; monthly; children's magazine; Dir LUCÍA SANZ ARAUJO; circ. 210,000.

Revista Casa: 3 y G, Vedado, CP 10400, Havana; tel. (7) 838-2706; fax (7) 834-4554; e-mail revista@casa.cult.cu; internet www.casa.cult.cu/revistacasa.php; f. 1960; 6 a year; Latin American theatre; Dir ROBERTO FERNÁNDEZ RETAMAR; Editor XENIA RELOBA.

Sierra Maestra: Avda de Los Desfiles, Santiago de Cuba; e-mail cip226@cip.enet.cu; internet www.sierramaestra.cu; f. 1957; weekly; organ of the PCC in Santiago de Cuba; Dir OLGA THAUREAUX PUERTAS; circ. 45,000.

Somos Jóvenes: Calle Prado, esq. a Teniente Rey, Havana; tel. (7) 862-5031; e-mail abadell@gmail.com; internet www.somosjovenes.cu; f. 1977; weekly; Dir MARIETTA MANSO MARTÍN; Editor ALICIA CENTELLES; circ. 200,000.

Temas: Calle 23, No 1155, 5° entre 10 y 12, CP 10400, El Vedado, Havana; tel. and fax (7) 838-3010; e-mail temas@iciaic.cu; internet www.temas.cult.cu; f. 1995; quarterly; cultural, political; Dir RAFAEL HERNÁNDEZ; Chief Editor JUANA MARÍA MARTÍNEZ.

Trabajadores: Territorial esq. Gen. Suárez, Plaza de la Revolución, CP 10698, Havana; tel. (7) 79-0819; fax (7) 55-5927; e-mail editor@trabaja.cip.cu; internet www.trabajadores.cu; f. 1970; organ of the trade union movt; Dir ALBERTO NÚÑEZ BETANCOURT; circ. 150,000.

Tribuna de la Habana: Territorial esq. Gen. Suárez, Plaza de la Revolución, Havana; tel. (7) 881-8021; e-mail redac@tribuna.cip.cu; internet www.tribuna.co.cu; f. 1980; weekly; Dir JESÚS ALVAREZ FERRER; circ. 90,000.

Vanguardia: Calle Céspedes 5, esq. Plácido, Santa Clara, CP 50100, Matanzas; e-mail contacto@vanguardia.cip.cu; internet www.vanguardia.co.cu; f. 1962; weekly; Dir F. A. CHANG L.; circ. 45,000.

Venceremos: Avda Ernesto Che Guevara, Km 1½, CP 95400, Guantánamo; tel. (7) 32-7398; e-mail cip227@cip.enet.cu; internet www.venceremos.co.cu; f. 1962; economic, political and social publ. for Guantánamo province; Dir YAMILKA ALVAREZ RAMOS; Editor-in-Chief ARIANNY TÉLLEZ LAMOTHE; circ. 33,500.

Victoria: Carretera de la Fe, Km 1½, Plaza de la Revolución, Nueva Gerona, Isla de la Juventud; tel. (46) 32-4210; e-mail cip228@cip.enet.cu; internet www.victoria.co.cu; f. 1967; Dir MATILDE CAMPOS JOA; Chief Editor OLGA L. MORALES VILAÚ; circ. 9,200.

Zunzún: Prado 553, CP 10500, Havana; e-mail zunzun@eabril.jovenclub.cu; internet www.zunzun.cu; f. 1980; children's magazine; Dir ADELA MORO; Chief Editor HÉCTOR QUINTERO.

PRESS ASSOCIATIONS

Unión de Escritores y Artistas de Cuba: Calle 17, No 354, entre G y H, Vedado, Havana; tel. (7) 838-3158; e-mail presidencia@uneac.co.cu; internet www.uneac.org.cu; f. 1961; Pres. MIGUEL BARNET LANZA.

Unión de Periodistas de Cuba (UPEC): Avda 23, No 452, esq. a I, Vedado, CP 10400, Havana; tel. (7) 832-4550; fax (7) 33-3079; e-mail vpetica@upec.co.cu; internet www.cubaperiodistas.cu; f. 1963; Pres. ANTONIO MOLTÓ MARTORELL.

NEWS AGENCIES

Agencia de Información Nacional (AIN): Calle 23, No 358, esq. J, Vedado, Havana; tel. (7) 881-6423; fax (7) 66-2049; e-mail edda@ain.cu; internet www.ain.cu; f. 1974; national news agency; Gen. Dir EDDA DIZ GARCÉZ REALIZACIÓN.

Prensa Latina (Agencia Informativa Latinoamericana, SA): Calle 23, No 201, esq. N, Vedado, Havana; tel. (7) 838-3496; fax (7) 33-3068; e-mail difusion@prensa-latina.cu; internet www.prensa-latina.cu; f. 1959; Pres. LUIS ENRIQUE GONZÁLEZ.

Publishers

Artecubano Ediciones: Calle 3, No 1205, entre 12 y 14, Playa, Havana; tel. (7) 203-8581; fax (7) 204-2744; e-mail cnap@cubarte.cult.cu; attached to the Ministry of Culture; Dir RAFAEL ACOSTA DE ARRIBA.

Casa de las Américas: Calle 3 y Avda G, Plaza de la Revolución, Vedado, 10400 Havana; tel. (7) 838-2706; fax (7) 834-4554; e-mail presidencia@casa.cult.cu; internet www.casadelasamericas.com; f. 1959; Latin American literature and social sciences; Dir ROBERTO FERNÁNDEZ RETAMAR.

Casa Editora Abril: Prado 553, esq. Teniente Rey y Dragones, Habana Vieja, 10200 Havana; tel. (7) 862-5031; fax (7) 862-4330; e-mail webeditora@editoraabril.co.cu; internet www.editoraabril.cu/editora; f. 1980; attached to the Union of Young Communists; cultural, children's literature; Dir NIURKA DUMÉNIGO GARCÍA.

Ediciones Creart: Calle 4, No 205, entre Línea y 11, Plaza de la Revolución, Vedado, Havana; tel. (7) 55-3496; fax (7) 33-3069; e-mail creart@cubarte.cult.cu; f. 1994; Dir TOMÁS VALDÉS BECERRA.

Ediciones Unión: Calle 17, No 354, entre G y H, Plaza de la Revolución, Vedado, 10400 Havana; tel. (7) 55-3112; fax (7) 33-3158; e-mail editora@uneac.co.cu; internet www.uneac.org.cu; f. 1962; publishing arm of the Unión de Escritores y Artistas de Cuba; Cuban literature, art; Dir OLGA MARTA PÉREZ RODRÍGUEZ.

Ediciones Vigía: Magdalena 1, Plaza de la Vigía, 40100 Matanzas; tel. (452) 44845; e-mail vigia@cult.cu; internet www.atenas.cult.cu/?q=editorialedicionesvigia; f. 1985; Dir AGUSTINA PONCE.

Editora Atril (Ediciones Musicales—ABDALA): Producciones Abdala, SA, Calle 32, No 318, esq. 5 Avda, Miramar, Playa, Havana; tel. (7) 204-5213; fax (7) 204-4006; e-mail atril.abdalal@cimex.com.cu; internet www.abdala.cu; Dir TERESA TORRES PÁEZ.

Editora Política: Belascoaín No 864, esq. Desagüe, Centro Habana, 10300 Havana; tel. (7) 879-8553; fax (7) 55-6836; e-mail editora@epol.cc.cu; internet www.editpolitica.cu; f. 1963; publishing institution of the Communist Party of Cuba; Dir SANTIAGO DÓRQUEZ PÉREZ.

Editorial Academia: Industria y Barcelona, Capitolio Nacional, 4°, Centro Habana, 10200 Havana; tel. and fax (7) 863-0315; e-mail editorial@gecyt.cu; f. 1962; attached to the Ministry of Science, Technology and the Environment; scientific and technical; Dir GLADYS HERNÁNDEZ HERRERA.

Editorial Arte y Literatura: Calle O'Reilly, No 4, esq. Tacón, Habana Vieja, 10100 Havana; tel. (7) 862-4326; fax (7) 833-8187; e-mail publicaciones@icl.cult.cu; internet www.cubaliteraria.cu/editorial/Arte_y_Literatura; f. 1967; traditional Cuban literature and arts; Dir LOURDES GONZÁLEZ CASAS.

Editorial Ciencias Médicas: Edif. Soto, 2°, Calle 23, No 177, entre N y O, Plaza de la Revolución, Vedado, 10400 Havana; tel. (7) 833-0311; fax (7) 33-3063; e-mail ecimed@infomed.sld.cu; internet www.sld.cu/sitios/ecimed; f. 1988; publishing arm of the Centro Nacional de Información de Ciencias Médicas de Cuba; attached to the Ministry of Public Health; books and magazines specializing in the medical sciences; Dir DAMIANA MARTÍN LAURENCIO.

Editorial Félix Varela: San Miguel No 1011, entre Mazón y Basarrate, Plaza de la Revolución, Vedado, 10400 Havana; tel. (7) 877-5617; fax (7) 73-5419; e-mail elsa@enpses.co.cu; Dir ELSA RODRÍGUEZ.

Editorial Gente Nueva: Calle 2, No 58, entre 3 y 5, Plaza de la Revolución, Vedado, 10400 Havana; tel. (7) 833-7676; fax (7) 33-8187; e-mail gentenueva@icl.cult.cu; f. 1967; books for children; Dir ENRIQUE PÉREZ DÍAZ.

Editorial José Martí: Calzada 259, entre I y J, Apdo 4208, Plaza de la Revolución, Vedado, 10400 Havana; tel. (7) 835-1921; fax (7) 33-3441; e-mail editjmal@icl.cult.cu; internet www.cubaliteraria.cu/editorial/editora_marti; f. 1982; attached to the Ministry of Culture; foreign-language publishing; Dir ANA MARÍA DÍAZ CANALS.

Editorial Letras Cubanas: Calle O'Reilly, No 4, esq. Tacón, Habana Vieja, 10100 Havana; tel. (7) 862-4378; fax (7) 66-8187; e-mail elc@icl.cult.cu; internet www.letrascubanas.cult.cu; f. 1977; attached to the Ministry of Culture; general, particularly classic and contemporary Cuban literature and arts; Dir ROGELIO RIVERÓN.

Editorial de la Mujer: Calle Galiano, No 264, esq. Neptuno, Havana; tel. (7) 862-4905; e-mail mujeres@enet.cu; f. 1995; female literature; publishing house of the Cuban Women's Fed; Dir-Gen. ISABEL MOYA RICHARD.

Editorial Nuevo Milenio: Calle 14, No 4104, entre 41 y 43, Playa, Havana; tel. (7) 203-6090; fax (7) 833-3441; e-mail nuevomil@cubarte.cult.cu; internet www.cubaliteraria.cu/editorial/Nuevo Milenio; f. 1967 as Editorial de Ciencias Sociales and Editorial Científico-Técnica; merged and name changed as above in 1999; attached to the Ministry of Culture; technical, scientific and social sciences literature; Dir SONIA ALMAGUER DARNA.

Editorial Oriente: Santa Lucía 356, 90100 Santiago de Cuba; tel. (226) 22496; fax (226) 86111; e-mail edoriente@cultstgo.cult.cu; internet www.editorialoriente.cult.cu; f. 1971; fiction, history, female literature and studies, art and culture, practical books, and books for children; Dir AIDA BAHR.

Editorial Pablo de la Torriente Brau: Calle 11, No 160, entre K y L, Plaza de la Revolución, Vedado, 10400 Havana; tel. (7) 832-7581; fax (7) 33-3079; e-mail pbagenda@ip.etecsa.cu; f. 1985; publishing arm of the Unión de Periodistas de Cuba; Dir IRMA DE ARMAS FONSECA.

Editorial Pueblo y Educación: Avda 3A, No 4601, entre 46 y 60, Playa, Havana; tel. (7) 202-1490; fax (7) 204-0844; e-mail epe@ceniai.inf.cu; f. 1971; textbooks and educational publs; publishes Revista Educación (3 a year, circ. 2,200); Dir CATALINA LAJUD HERRERO.

Editorial Sanlope: Calle Gonzalo de Quesada, No 121, entre Lico Cruz y Lucas Ortiz, Las Tunas; tel. (31) 48191; fax (31) 47380; e-mail librolt@tunet.cult.cu; internet www.tunet.cult.cu/pagsec/institut/sanlope/index.html; f. 1991; attached to the Ministry of Culture; Dir VERENA GARCÍA MIRABAL.

GOVERNMENT PUBLISHING HOUSES

Instituto Cubano del Libro: Palacio del Segundo Cabo, Calle O'Reilly, No 4, esq. Tacón, Habana Vieja, Havana; tel. (7) 862-8091; fax (7) 33-8187; e-mail promocion@icl.cult.cu; internet www.cubaliteraria.cu; f. 1967; printing and publishing org. attached to the Ministry of Culture, which combines several publishing houses and has direct links with others; presides over the National Editorial Council (CEN); organizes the annual Havana International Book Fair; Pres. ZULEICA ROMAY GUERRA.

Oficina Publicaciones del Consejo de Estado: Calle 17, No 552, esq. D, Plaza de la Revolución, Vedado, 10400 Havana; tel. (7) 55-1406; fax (7) 57-5258; e-mail palvarez@ip.etecsa.cu; f. 1972; attached to the Council of State; books, pamphlets and other printed media on historical and political matters; Dir PEDRO ALVAREZ TABÍO.

Broadcasting and Communications

TELECOMMUNICATIONS

Empresa de Telecomunicaciones de Cuba, SA (ETECSA): Edif. Beijing, 5°, Avda 3, entre 76 y 78, Centro de Negocios Miramar, 11300 Havana; tel. (7) 266-8500; fax (7) 860-5144; e-mail atencion_usuarios@etecsa.cu; internet www.etecsa.cu; f. 1991; merged with Empresa de Telecomunicaciones Celulares del Caribe, SA (C-Com) and Teléfonos Celulares de Cuba, SA (CUBACEL) in 2003; Exec. Pres. MAIMIR MESA RAMOS.

Instituto de Investigación y Desarrollo de Comunicaciones (LACETEL): Avda Independencia, No 34515, Km 14½, Reparto 1 de Mayo, Rancho Boyeros, CP 19210, Havana; tel. (7) 683-9180; fax (7) 649-5828; e-mail glauco@lacetel.cu; internet www.lacetel.cu; f. 1964; Dir-Gen. GLAUCO GUILLÉN NIETO.

Telecomunicaciones Móviles, SA (MOVITEL): Avda 47, No 3405, Reparto Kohly, Playa, Havana; tel. (7) 204-8400; fax (7) 204-4264; e-mail movitel@movitel.co.cu; internet www.movitel.co.cu; mobile telecommunications; Dir-Gen. ASELA FERNÁNDEZ LORENZO.

Regulatory Authority

Ministerio de la Informática y las Comunicaciones (Dirección de Regulaciones y Normas): Avda Independencia y 19 de Mayo, Plaza de la Revolución, Havana; tel. (7) 81-7654; e-mail infosoc@mic.cu; internet www.mic.gov.cu; Dir WILFREDO REINALDO LÓPEZ RODRÍGUEZ.

BROADCASTING

Radio

In 2011 there were seven national networks and one international network, 16 provincial radio stations and 25 municipal radio stations.

Habana Radio: Edif. Lonja del Comercio, Lamparilla 2, Plaza de San Francisco de Asís, Habana Vieja, Havana; tel. (7) 866-2706; e-mail sitioweb@habradio.ohc.cu; internet www.habanaradio.cu; f. 1999; run by the Oficina del Historiador de la Ciudad de La Habana; cultural and factual programmes; Dir MAGDA RESIK.

Radio Cadena Agramonte: Calle Cisneros, No 310, entre Ignacio Agramonte y General Gómez, 70100 Camagüey; tel. (322) 29-8673; e-mail cip240@cip.enet.cu; internet www.cadenagramonte.cu; f. 1957; serves Camagüey; Dir ONELIO CASTILLO CORDERÍ.

Radio Cubana: Calle 23, No 258, entre L y M, 10°, Vedado, Plaza de la Revolución, Havana; tel. (7) 832-2477; e-mail pavon@radio.icrt.cu; internet www.radiocubana.cu; Vice-Pres. GUILLERMO PAVÓN PACHECO.

Radio Enciclopedia: Edif. N, Calle N, No 266, entre 21 y 23, Vedado, 10400 Havana; tel. (7) 838-4586; e-mail lmarquez@renciclopedia.icrt.cu; internet www.radioenciclopedia.cu; f. 1962; national network; instrumental music programmes; 24 hours daily; Dir-Gen. LUISA MÇARQUEZ ECHEVARRIA.

Radio Habana Cuba: Infanta 105, Apdo 6240, Havana; tel. (7) 877-6628; e-mail radiohc@enet.cu; internet www.radiohc.cu; f. 1961; shortwave station; broadcasts in Spanish, English, French, Portuguese, Arabic, Esperanto, Quechua, Guaraní and Creole; Dir-Gen. ISIDRO FARDALES GONZÁLEZ.

Radio Musical Nacional (CBMF): Edif. N, Calle N, No 266, entre 21 y 23, Vedado, 10400 Havana; tel. (7) 832-8893; e-mail rmusical@cmbf.icrt.cu; internet www.cmbfradio.cu; f. 1948; national network; classical music programmes; 17 hours daily; Dir OTTO BRAÑA GONZÁLEZ.

Radio Progreso: Infanta 105, esq. a 25, 6°, Apdo 3042, Havana; tel. (7) 877-5519; e-mail paginaweb@rprogreso.icrt.cu; internet www.radioprogreso.cu; f. 1929; national network; mainly entertainment and music; 24 hours daily; Dir-Gen. JOSÉ ANTONIO GUERRA GARCÍA.

Radio Rebelde: Calle 23, No 258, entre L y M, Plaza de la Revolución, Vedado, Apdo 6277, 10400 Havana; tel. (7) 838-4365; fax (7) 33-4270; e-mail smabel@radiorebelde.icrt.cu; internet www.radiorebelde.com.cu; f. 1958; merged with Radio Liberación in 1984; national network; 24-hour news and cultural programmes, music and sports; Dir-Gen. SOFÍA MABEL MANSO DELGADO.

Radio Reloj: Edif. Radiocentro, Calle 23, No 258, entre L y M, Plaza de la Revolución, Vedado, 10400 Havana; tel. (7) 838-4185; fax (7) 838-4225; e-mail relojmailj@rreloj.icrt.cu; internet www.radioreloj.cu; f. 1947; national network; 24-hour news service; Dir OMAIDA ALONSO DIEZCABEZA.

Radio Revolución: Aguilera No 554, entre San Agustín y Barnada, 90100 Santiago de Cuba; tel. (226) 28038; e-mail cip233@cip.enet.cu; internet www.cmkc.cu; serves Santiago de Cuba; Dir ROSA ILEANA NAVARRO PUPO.

Radio Taino: Edif. Radiocentro, Calle 23, No 258, Plaza de la Revolución, entre L y M, Vedado, 10400 Havana; tel. (7) 838-4157; e-mail sitioweb@rtaino.icrt.cu; internet www.radiotaino.icrt.cu; f. 1985; broadcasts in English and Spanish; Dir FERNANDO PÉREZ RICARDO.

Television

The Cuban Government holds a 19% stake in the regional television channel Telesur, based in Caracas, Venezuela.

Televisión Cubana: Avda 23, No 258, entre L y M, Vedado, 10400 Havana; tel. (7) 55-4059; fax (7) 33-3107; e-mail tvcubana@icrt.cu; internet www.tvcubana.icrt.cu; f. 1950; broadcasts through five national channels—Canal Educativo, Canal Educativo 2, Cubavisión, Multivisión, Tele Rebelde—and 15 provincial channels; Pres. DANIEL SIRIO; Dir-Gen. FABIO FERNÁNDEZ QUEZZEL.

Canal Educativo: Calle P, entre Humbolt y 23, Plaza de la Revolución, Vedado, 10400 Havana; tel. (7) 831-4653; fax (7) 831-4654; e-mail canaleducativo@cedu.icrt.cu; internet www.canaleducativo.cu; f. 2002; broadcasts on channel 13; educational; Dir IVÁN BARRETO.

Cubavisión: Calle M, No 313, Vedado, Havana; e-mail info@cubavision.icrt.cu; internet www.cubavision.cubaweb.cu; broadcasts on channel 6.

Multivisión: f. 2008; broadcasts programmes from foreign networks.

Tele Rebelde: Mazón, No 52, Vedado, Havana; tel. (7) 32-3369; broadcasts on channel 2; Dir MAURICIO NÚÑEZ RODRÍGUEZ.

Regulatory Authorities

Empresa de Radiocomunicación y Difusión de Cuba (RADIOCUBA): Calle Habana 406, entre Obispo y Obrapía, Habana Vieja, Havana; tel. (7) 860-0796; fax (7) 860-3107; e-mail radiocuba@radiocuba.cu; f. 1995; controls the domestic and international broadcast transmission networks; Dir-Gen. AMADO HERNÁNDEZ.

Instituto Cubano de Radio y Televisión (ICRT): Edif. Radiocentro, Avda 23, No 258, entre L y M, Vedado, Havana 4; tel. (7) 32-1568; fax (7) 33-3107; e-mail icrt@cecm.get.tur.cu; internet www.cubagob.cu/des_soc/icrt; f. 1962; Vice-Pres. OMAR OLAZÁBAL.

Finance

(cap. = capital; res = reserves; dep. = deposits; m. = million; brs = branches, amounts in convertible pesos)

BANKING

All banks were nationalized in 1960. Legislation establishing the national banking system was approved by the Council of State in 1984. A restructuring of the banking system, initiated in 1995, to accommodate Cuba's transformation to a more market-orientated economy, was proceeding. A new central bank, the Banco Central de Cuba (BCC), was created in 1997 to supersede the Banco Nacional de Cuba (BNC). The BCC was to be responsible for issuing currency, proposing and implementing monetary policy, and the regulation of financial institutions. The BNC was to continue functioning as a commercial bank and servicing the country's foreign debt. The restructuring of the banking system also allowed for the creation of an investment bank, the Banco de Inversiones, to provide medium- and long-term financing for investment, and the Banco Financiero Internacional, SA, to offer short-term financing. A new agro-industrial and commercial bank was also to be created to provide services for farmers and co-operatives. The new banking system is under the control of Grupo Nueva Banca, which holds a majority share in each institution. In 2010 there were nine commercial banks, 12 non-banking financial institutions, nine representative offices of foreign banks and two representative offices of non-banking financial institutions operating in Cuba.

Central Bank

Banco Central de Cuba (BCC): Calle Cuba, No 402, Aguiar 411, Apdo 746, Habana Vieja, Havana; tel. (7) 860-4811; fax (7) 863-4061; e-mail cibe@bc.gov.cu; internet www.bc.gov.cu; f. 1997; sole bank of issue; Pres. ERNESTO MEDINA VILLAVEIRÁN.

Commercial Banks

Banco de Crédito y Comercio (BANDEC): Amargura 158, entre Cuba y Aguiar, Habana Vieja, Havana; tel. (7) 861-4533; fax (7) 833-8968; e-mail ileana@oc.bandec.cu; f. 1997; cap. 700m., res 671.9m., dep. 14,684m. (Dec. 2010); Pres. ILEANA ESTÉVEZ.

Banco Exterior de Cuba: Calle 23, No 55, esq. P, Vedado, Municipio Plaza, Havana; tel. (7) 55-0795; fax (7) 55-0794; e-mail bec@bec.co.cu; f. 1999; cap. 486m., res 22.7m., dep. 898.2m. (Dec. 2010); Pres. JACOBO PEISON WEINER.

Banco Financiero Internacional, SA: Avda 5, No 9009, esq. 92, Miramar, Municipio Playa, Havana; tel. (7) 267-5000; fax (7) 267-5002; e-mail bfi@bfi.com.cu; f. 1984; autonomous; finances Cuba's foreign trade; Pres. MARCOS A. DÍAZ SOPEÑA; 29 brs.

Banco Industrial de Venezuela-Cuba, SA (BIVC): Edif. Jerusalén, 2°, Of. 202, Centro de Negocios Miramar, Sector Miramar, Havana; tel. (7) 206-9650; fax (2) 206-9651; f. 2005 as a subsidiary of state-owned Banco Industrial de Venezuela, SA; Pres. RODOLFO PORRO ALETTI.

Banco Internacional de Comercio, SA: 20 de Mayo y Ayestarán, Apdo 6113, 10600 Havana; tel. (7) 883-6038; fax (7) 883-6028; e-mail bicsa@bicsa.co.cu; f. 1993; cap. 401.4m., res 49m., dep. 4,305.5m. (Dec. 2010); Chair. and Pres. JOSÉ JULIO RODRÍGUEZ FALCÓN.

Banco Metropolitano, SA: Avda 5 y Calle 112, Miramar, Municipio Habana Vieja, 11600 Havana; tel. (7) 204-3869; fax (7) 204-9193; e-mail bm@banco-metropolitano.com; internet www.banco-metropolitano.com; f. 1996; offers foreign currency and deposit account facilities; cap. 415.6m., res 158.4m., dep. 12,226.1m. (Dec. 2010); Pres. MANUEL ANTONIO VALE MARRERO.

Banco Nacional de Cuba (BNC): Aguiar 456, entre Amargura y Lamparilla, Habana Vieja, Havana; tel. (7) 862-8896; fax (7) 866-9390; e-mail bancuba@bnc.cu; f. 1950; reorganized 1997; Pres. RENÉ LAZO FERNÁNDEZ.

Savings Bank

Banco Popular de Ahorro: Calle 16, No 306, entre 3ra y 5ta, Playa, Miramar, Havana; tel. (7) 204-2545; fax (7) 204-1180; e-mail presidencia@mail.bpa.cu; f. 1983; savings bank; cap. 249.3m., res 278.7m., dep. 11,059.2m. (Dec. 2010); Pres. JOSÉ LÁZARO ALARI MARTÍNEZ; 520 brs.

Investment Bank

Banco de Inversiones, SA: Avda 5, No 6802 esq. a 68, Miramar, Havana; tel. (7) 204-3374; fax (7) 204-3377; e-mail inversiones@bdi.cu; internet www.bdi.cu; f. 1996; cap. 31.5m., res 4.7m., dep. 33.1m. (Dec. 2010); Exec. Pres. ARMINDA GARCÍA GONZÁLEZ.

INSURANCE

The Superintendencia de Seguros (f. 1997) is the regulatory authority supervising the entities engaged in insurance, reinsurance and auxiliary services of brokers and insurance agents. The insurance market consists of two direct insurance companies, two auxiliary service agencies, two insurance brokers and over 2,000 individual agents.

State Organizations

Grupo Caudal, SA (Grupo de Seguros y Servicios Financieros de Cuba): Calle 43, No 2210, entre 22 y 24, Playa, Havana; tel. (7) 204-8822; fax (7) 204-8813; e-mail caudal@caudal.cu; management and development of insurance, brokerage and insurance auxiliary services; includes Agencia Internacional de Inspección, Ajuste de Averías y Otros Servicios Conexos (INTERMAR, SA), Asistencia al Turista (ASISTUR), Consultorías y Avalúos (CONAVANA, SA), Empresa Grafica de Finanzas y Precios (EGRAFIP) and INTERAUDIT, SA; Pres. JOSÉ M. ESCANDELL CÁMBARA.

Empresa del Seguro Estatal Nacional (ESEN): Calle 5, No 306, entre C y D, Vedado, Havana; tel. (7) 832-2500; fax (7) 833-8717; e-mail rfo@esen.com.cu; internet www.ain.cu/publicidad/sitio esen/index.htm; f. 1978; motor and agricultural insurance; Dir-Gen. RAFAEL J. GONZÁLEZ PÉREZ.

Seguros Internacionales de Cuba, SA (Esicuba): Cuba No 314, entre Obispo y Obrapía, Habana Vieja, Havana; tel. (7) 862-8031; fax (7) 866-8038; e-mail esicuba.clientes@esicuba.cu; internet www.esicuba.cu; f. 1963; reorganized 1986; all classes of insurance except life; Dir-Gen. JOSÉ CARLOS MEIJIDES ALFONSO.

Trade and Industry

GOVERNMENT AGENCIES

Centro para la Promoción del Comercio Exterior de Cuba (CEPEC): Infanta 16, esq. 23, 2°, Vedado, Municipio Plaza, Havana; tel. (7) 838-0428; fax (7) 833-2220; e-mail cepecdir@mincex.cu; internet www.cepec.cu; f. 1995; Dir-Gen. RAYSA COSTA BLANCO.

Grupo Empresarial de la Agroindustria Azucarera (AZCUBA): Of. de Comunicación Institucional, Calle 23, No 171, entre N y O, Vedado, Havana; tel. (7) 832-9356; e-mail liobel@ocentral.minaz.cu; f. 2011 to replace the Ministry of Sugar; 13 provincial brs managing 56 sugar mills; Pres. ORLANDO CELSO GARCÍA.

CHAMBER OF COMMERCE

Cámara de Comercio de la República de Cuba: Calle 21, No 661/701, esq. Calle A, Apdo 4237, Vedado, Havana; tel. (7) 830-4436; fax (7) 833-3042; e-mail pdcia@camara.com.cu; internet www.camaracuba.cu; f. 1963; mems include all Cuban foreign trade enterprises and the most important agricultural and industrial enterprises; Pres. ESTRELLA MADRIGAL VALDÉS; Sec.-Gen. OMAR DE JESÚS FERNÁNDEZ JIMÉNEZ.

AGRICULTURAL ORGANIZATION

Asociación Nacional de Agricultores Pequeños (ANAP) (National Association of Small Farmers): Calle I, No 206, entre Linea y 13, Vedado, Havana; tel. (7) 32-4541; fax (7) 33-4244; f. 1961; 200,000 mems; Pres. FÉLIX GONZÁLEZ VIEGO; 331,874 mems.

STATE IMPORT-EXPORT BOARDS

Alimport (Empresa Cubana Importadora de Alimentos): Infanta 16, 3°, Apdo 7006, Havana; tel. (7) 54-2501; fax (7) 33-3151; e-mail precios@alimport.com.cu; f. 1962; controls import of foodstuffs and liquors; Pres. IGOR MONTERO.

Aviaimport (Empresa Cubana Importadora y Exportadora de Aviación): Calle 182, No 126, entre 1 y 5, Rpto Flores, Playa, Havana; tel. (7) 273-0077; fax (7) 273-6365; e-mail dcom@aviaimport.avianet.cu; import and export of aircraft and components; Man. Dir MARCOS LAGO MARTÍNEZ.

Caribex (Empresa Comercial Caribe): Avda La Pesquera y Atarés, Puerto Pesquero de La Habana, 3°, Habana Vieja, Havana; tel. (7) 864-4135; fax (7) 864-4144; e-mail caribex@caribex.cu; internet www.caribex.cu; export of seafood and marine products; Dir ESTHER ALEJO.

Catec (Empresa Cubana Exportadora y Comercializadora de Productos y Servicios de la Ciencia y la Técnica Agraria): Calle 148, No 905, entre 9 y 9A, Rpto Cubanacán, Playa, Havana; tel. (7) 208-2164; fax (7) 204-6071; e-mail alina@catec.co.cu; internet www.catec.cu; exports, imports and markets scientific and technical products relating to the farming and forestry industries; Dir-Gen. OSVALDO CARVEJAL GABELA.

Construimport (Empresa Exportadora e Importadora de Equipos de Construcción): Carretera de Varona, Km 1½, Capdevila, Havana; tel. (7) 645-2567; fax (7) 646-8943; e-mail equipo@construimport.co.cu; internet www.construimport.cubaindustria.cu; f. 1969; controls the import and export of construction machinery and equipment; Gen. Dir DEYSI ROMAY.

Consumimport (Empresa Cubana Importadora de Artículos de Consumo General): Calle 23, No 55, 9°, Apdo 6427, Vedado, Plaza de Revolución, Havana; tel. (8) 36-7717; fax (8) 33-3847; e-mail comer@consumimport.infocex.cu; f. 1962; imports and exports general consumer goods; Dir MERCEDES REY HECHAVARRÍA.

Copextel (Corporación Productora y Exportadora de Tecnología Electrónica): Avda 11, entre 222B y 222C, Siboney, Playa, Havana; tel. (7) 273-0820; fax (7) 273-6540; e-mail copextel@copextel.com.cu; internet www.copextel.com.cu; f. 1985; exports LTEL personal computers and micro-computer software; Dir ADOLFO CEPERO BARROSO.

Cubaexport (Empresa Cubana Exportadora de Alimentos y Productos Varios): Calle 23, No 55, entre Infanta y P, 8°, Vedado, Apdo 6719, Havana; tel. (7) 838-0595; fax (7) 833-3587; e-mail cubaexport@cexport.mincex.cu; f. 1965; export of foodstuffs and industrial products; Man. Dir FRANCISCO SANTIAGO PICHARDO.

Cubahidráulica (Empresa Central de Equipos Hidráulicos): Carretera Vieja de Guanabacoa y Linea de Ferrocarril, Rpto Mañana, Guanabacoa, Havana; tel. (7) 797-0821; fax (7) 797-1627; e-mail cubahidraulica@enet.cu; internet www.cubahidraulica.com; f. 1995; imports and exports hydraulic and mechanical equipment, parts and accessories; Dir-Gen. OSMUNDO PAZ PAZ.

Cubametales (Empresa Cubana Importadora de Metales, Combustibles y Lubricantes): Infanta 16, 4°, entre 23 y Humboldt, Apdo 6917, Vedado, Havana; tel. (7) 838-0531; fax (7) 838-0530; e-mail mcarmen@cubametal.mincex.cu; f. 1962; controls import of metals (ferrous and non-ferrous), crude petroleum and petroleum products; also engaged in the export of petroleum products and ferrous and non-ferrous scrap; Dir-Gen. MARY CARMEN ARENCIBIA VÁZQUEZ.

Cubaniquel (Empresa Cubana Exportadora de Minerales y Metales): Carretera Moa, Sagua Km 1½, Moa, CP 83330, Holguín; tel. (24) 60-8283; fax (24) 60-2156; e-mail cceac@cubaniquel.moa.minbas.cu; f. 1961; sole exporter of minerals and metals; operates 2 nickel plants; Man. Dir ANGEL ROBERTO HERNÁNDEZ.

Cubatabaco (Empresa Cubana del Tabaco): Calle Nueva 75, entre Universidad y Pedroso, Cerro, Havana; tel. (7) 879-0253; fax (7) 33-8214; e-mail cubatabaco@cubatabaco.cu; internet www.cubatabaco.cu; f. 1962; controls export of leaf tobacco, cigars and cigarettes to France; Dir ALFREDO S. CALERO ACOSTA.

Ediciones Cubanas (Empresa de Comercio Exterior de Publicaciones): Obispo 527, esq. Bernaza, Apdo 47, Habana Vieja, Havana; tel. (7) 863-1989; fax (7) 33-8943; e-mail edicuba@cubarte.cult.cu; controls import and export of books and periodicals; Dir ROLANDO VERDÉS PINEDA.

Egrem (Estudios de Grabaciones y Ediciones Musicales): Calle 3, No 1008, entre 10 y 12, Miramar, Playa, Havana; tel. (7) 204-1925; fax (7) 204-2519; e-mail director@egrem.co.cu; internet www.egrem.com.cu; f. 1964; controls the import and export of CDs, printed music and musical instruments; Gen. Dir MARIO ESCALONA SERRANO.

Emiat (Empresa Importadora y Exportadora de Suministros Técnicos): Avda 47, No 2828, entre 28 y 34, Rpto Kohly, Havana; tel. (7) 203-0345; fax (7) 204-9353; e-mail emiat@enet.cu; f. 1983; imports technical materials, equipment and special products; exports furniture, kitchen utensils and accessories.

Emidict (Empresa Especializada Importadora, Exportadora y Distribuidora para la Ciencia y la Técnica): Calle 16, No 102, esq. Avda 1, Miramar, Playa, 13000 Havana; tel. (7) 203-5316; fax (7) 204-1768; e-mail emidict@ceniai.inf.cu; internet www.emidict.com.cu; f. 1982; controls import and export of scientific and technical products and equipment, live animals; scientific information; Dir-Gen. CALIXTO A. RODRÍGUEZ DIAGO.

Energoimport (Empresa Importadora de Objetivos Electro-energéticos): Amenidad No 124, entre Nueva y 20 de Mayo, Municipio Cerro, 10600 Havana; tel. (7) 70-2501; fax (7) 66-6079; f. 1977; controls import of equipment for electricity generation; Dir-Gen. RAFAEL ERNESTO.

Eprob (Empresa de Proyectos para las Industrias de la Básica): Avda 31A, No 1805, entre 18 y 20, Edif. Las Ursulinas, Miramar, Playa, Apdo 12100, Havana; tel. (7) 202-5562; fax (7) 204-2146; e-mail direccion@eprob.cu; f. 1967; exports consulting services, processing of engineering construction projects and supplies of complete industrial plants and turnkey projects; Man. Dir GLORIA EXPÓSITO DÍAZ.

Eproyiv (Empresa de Proyectos para Industrias Varias): Calle 31A, No 1815, entre 18 y 20, Playa, Havana; tel. (7) 202-7097; fax (7) 204-2149; e-mail dg-eproyiv@eproyiv.cu; internet www.eproyiv.cu; f. 1967; consulting services, feasibility studies, devt of basic and detailed engineering models, project management and turnkey projects; Dir MARTA ELENA HERNÁNDEZ DÍAZ.

Fondo Cubano de Bienes Culturales: Calle 36, No 4702, esq. Avda 47, Rpto Kohly, Playa, Havana; tel. (7) 204-6428; fax (7) 204-0391; e-mail fcbc@fcbc.cult.cu; f. 1978; controls export of fine handicrafts and works of art; Dir-Gen. GUILLERMO SOLENZAL MORALES.

Habanos, SA: Avda 3, No 2006, entre 20 y 22, Miramar, Havana; tel. (7) 204-0524; fax (7) 204-0491; e-mail habanos@habanos.cu; internet www.habanos.com; f. 1994; controls export of leaf and pipe tobacco, cigars and cigarettes to all markets; jt venture with Altadis, SA (Spain); Pres. JORGE LUIS FERNÁNDEZ MAIQUE.

ICAIC (Instituto Cubano del Arte e Industria Cinematográficos): Calle 23, No 1155, Vedado, Havana 4; tel. (7) 55-3128; fax (7) 33-3032; e-mail webmaster@icaic.cu; internet www.cubacine.cu; f. 1959; production, import and export of films and newsreel; Dir CAMILO VIVES PALLÉS.

Maprinter (Empresa Cubana Importadora y Exportadora de Materias Primas y Productos Intermedios): Edif. MINCEX, Calle 23, No 55, entre P e Infanta, 8°, Plaza de la Revolución, Vedado, Havana; tel. (7) 878-0711; fax (7) 833-3535; e-mail direccion@maprinter.mincex.cu; internet www.maprinter.cu; f. 1962; controls import and export of raw materials and intermediate products; Dir-Gen. ODALYS ALDAMA VALDÉS.

Maquimport (Empresa Comercializadora de Objetivos Industriales, Maquinarias, Equipos y Artículos de Ferretería): Calle 23, No 55, 6°, entre P e Infanta, Vedado, Apdo 6052, Havana; tel. (7) 838-0635; fax (7) 838-0632; e-mail direccion@maquimport.mincex.cu; imports industrial goods and equipment; Dir ESTHER VERA GONZALEZ.

Medicuba (Empresa Cubana Importadora y Exportadora de Productos Médicos): Máximo Gómez 1, esq. Egido, Habana Vieja, Havana; tel. (7) 862-4061; fax (7) 866-8516; e-mail dirgeneral@medicuba.sld.cu; f. 1962; enterprise for the export and import of medical and pharmaceutical products; Dir-Gen. JORGE LUIS MECÍAS CUBILLA.

Quimimport (Empresa Cubana Importadora y Exportadora de Productos Químicos): Calle 23, No 55, entre Infanta y P, Apdo 6088, Vedado, Havana; tel. (7) 33-3394; fax (7) 33-3190; e-mail global@quimimport.infocex.cu; internet www.quimimport.cu; controls import and export of chemical products; Dir ARMANDO BARRERA MARTÍNEZ.

Tecnoazúcar (Empresa de Servicios Técnicos e Ingeniería para la Agro-industria Azucarera): Calle 12, No 310, entre 3 y 5, Miramar, Playa, Havana; tel. (7) 29-5441; fax (7) 33-1218; e-mail tecno@tecnoazucar.cu; internet www.tecnoazucar.cu; imports machinery and equipment for the sugar industry; provides technical and engineering assistance for the sugar industry; exports equipment and spare parts for sugar machinery; provides engineering and technical assistance services for sugar-cane by-product industry; Dir-Gen. HÉCTOR COMPANIONI ECHEMENDÍA.

Tractoimport (Empresa Central de Abastecimiento y Venta de Maquinaria Agrícola y sus Piezas de Repuesto): Avda Rancho Boyeros y Calle 100, Apdo 7007, Havana; tel. (7) 45-2166; fax (7) 267-0786; e-mail direccion@tractoimport.co.cu; f. 1962; import of tractors and agricultural equipment; also exports pumps and agricultural implements; Dir-Gen. ABDEL GARCÍA GONZÁLEZ.

Transimport (Empresa Central de Abastecimiento y Venta de Equipos de Transporte Pesados y sus Piezas): Calle 102 y Avda 63, Marianao, Apdo 6665, 11500 Havana; tel. (7) 260-0329; fax (7) 267-9050; e-mail direccion@transimport.co.cu; internet www.transimport.co.cu; f. 1968; controls import and export of vehicles and transportation equipment; Dir-Gen. JESÚS JOSÉ DE HOMBRE MARCIAL.

UTILITIES

Electricity

Unión Nacional Eléctrica (UNE): Havana; public utility; Dir-Gen. RAÚL GARCÍA BARREIRO.

Water

Aguas de la Habana: Calle Fomento, esq. Recreo, Rpto Palatino, Cerro, Havana; tel. (7) 643-4950; fax (7) 642-4961; e-mail jmtura@ahabana.co.cu; internet www.ahabana.co.cu; water supplier; Dir-Gen. JOSEP OLLER HERNÁNDEZ.

Instituto Nacional de Recursos Hidráulicos (INRH) (National Water Resources Institute): Calle Humbolt, No 106, esq. a P, Plaza de la Revolución, Vedado, Havana; tel. (7) 836-5571; e-mail gisel@hidro.cu; internet www.hidro.cu; regulatory body; Pres. INÉS MARÍA CHAPMAN WAUGH.

TRADE UNIONS

All workers have the right to become members of a national trade union according to their industry and economic branch.

The following industries and labour branches have their own unions: Agriculture, Chemistry and Energetics, Civil Workers of the Revolutionary Armed Forces, Commerce and Gastronomy, Communications, Construction, Culture, Defence, Education and Science, Food, Forestry, Health, Light Industry, Merchant Marine, Mining and Metallurgy, Ports and Fishing, Public Administration, Sugar, Tobacco, and Transport.

Central de Trabajadores de Cuba (CTC) (Confederation of Cuban Workers): Palacio de los Trabajadores, San Carlos y Peñalver, Havana; tel. (7) 78-4901; fax (7) 55-5927; e-mail cubasindical@ctc.cu; internet www.cubasindical.cu; f. 1939; 19 national trade unions affiliated; Gen. Sec. SALVADOR ANTONIO VALDÉS MESA.

Transport

RAILWAYS

The total length of railways in 2009 was 5,076 km.

Ferrocarriles de Cuba: Edif. Estación Central, Egido y Arsenal, Havana; tel. (7) 70-1076; fax (7) 33-1489; f. 1960; operates public services; Dir-Gen. MIGUEL ACUÑA FERNÁNDEZ; divided as follows:

División Camilo Cienfuegos: serves part of Havana province and Matanzas.

División Centro: serves Villa Clara, Cienfuegos and Sancti Spíritus.

División Centro-Este: serves Camagüey, Ciego de Avila and Las Tunas.

División Occidente: serves Pinar del Río, Ciudad de la Habana, Havana province and Matanzas.

División Oriente: serves Santiago de Cuba, Granma, Guantánamo and Holguín.

ROADS

There were an estimated 60,856 km of roads, of which 4,353 km were highways or main roads. Nearly 50% of the total road network is paved. The Central Highway runs from Pinar del Río in the west to Santiago de Cuba, for a length of 1,144 km. In addition to this highway, there are a number of secondary and 'farm-to-market' roads. Some of these secondary roads are paved, but many can be used by motor vehicles only during the dry season.

SHIPPING

Cuba's principal ports are Havana (which handles 60% of all cargo), Santiago de Cuba, Cienfuegos, Nuevitas, Matanzas, Antilla, Guayabal and Mariel. A US $800m. expansion of the Port of Mariel was completed in early 2014, funded by a loan from the Brazilian Government. The upgraded facilities would be able to handle 3m. containers annually. In 2010 a project to expand the port of Cienfuegos, including the construction of a super-freighter terminal, was announced. At December 2013 the flag registered fleet comprised 66 vessels, totalling 94,897 grt.

Regulatory Authority

Administración Portuaria Nacional (APN): Calle Oficios 170, entre Teniente Rey y Amargura, Habana Vieja, Havana; tel. (7) 860-5383; internet www.apn.transnet.cu; f. 2005; Dir LUIS MEDINA SOÑARA.

Principal Companies

Consignataria Marítima Caribeña, SA: Quinta Avda, No. 4001, entre 40 y 42, Miramar, Playa, Havana; tel. (7) 204-1226; fax (7) 204-1227; e-mail info@cmc.com.cu; internet www.cmc.com.cu; f. 1996; Pres. ALEJANDRO GONZÁLEZ NEIRA.

Coral Container Lines, SA: Of. 170, 1°, POB 6755, Habana Vieja, Havana; tel. (7) 33-8261; fax (7) 33-8970; e-mail info@coral.com.cu; internet fis.com/coralcontainer; f. 1994; liner services to Europe, Canada, Brazil and Mexico; 11 containers; Dir LUIS RODRÍGUEZ HERNÁNDEZ.

Empresa Consignataria Mambisa: San José No 65, entre Prado y Zulueta, Habana Vieja, Havana; tel. (7) 862-2061; fax (7) 66-8111; e-mail mercedes@mambisa.transnet.cu; shipping agent, bunker suppliers; Man. Dir MERCEDES PÉREZ NEWHALL.

Empresa de Navegación Caribe (Navecaribe): Calle San Martín, No 65, 4°, entre Agramonte y Pasco de Martí, Habana Vieja, Havana; tel. (7) 861-8611; fax (7) 866-8564; e-mail navcar@transnet.cu; f. 1966; operates Cuban coastal fleet; Dir LUIS IRENE RODRÍGUEZ HERNÁNDEZ.

Expedimar, SA: Avda 1, no 1404, entre Calle 14 y 16, 3°, Playa, Havana; tel. (7) 204-2440; fax (7) 204-0080; e-mail expedimar@expedimar.cu; Dir-Gen. FRANCISCO A. PIEDRA SANSARIG.

Waterfront AUSA: Centro de Negocios AUSA, Of. 513, Desamparados 166, entre Habana y Compostela, Habana Vieja, Havana; tel. (7) 866-4976; fax (7) 863-5814; e-mail ariel@waterfrontshipping.com; internet www.waterfrontshipping.com; jt venture between Waterfront Shipping Ltd and Almacenes Universales, SA.

CIVIL AVIATION

There are a total of 21 civilian airports, with 11 international airports, including Havana, Santiago de Cuba, Camagüey, Varadero and Holguín. In 2003 the King's Gardens International Airport in Cayo Coco was opened. The airport formed part of a new tourist 'offshore' centre. In 2013 Brazil agreed to finance a project to expand and modernize Cuba's airports.

Instituto de Aeronáutica Civil de Cuba (IACC): Calle 23, No 64, Plaza de la Revolución, Vedado, Havana; tel. (7) 834-4949; fax (7) 834-4553; e-mail webmaster@iacc.gov.cu; internet www.iacc.gov.cu; f. 1985; responsible for directing, implementing and monitoring air transport and other related services; Pres. RAMÓN MARTÍNEZ ECHEVARRÍA.

Aero Caribbean: Calle 23, No 64, esq. P, Vedado, Havana; tel. (7) 832-7584; fax (7) 336-5016; e-mail reserva@cacsa.avianet.cu; f. 1982; international and domestic scheduled and charter services; state-owned; Chair. JULIÁN ALVAREZ INFIESTA.

Aerogaviota: Aeropuerto de Playa Baracoa, Carretera Panamericana. Km. 15 ½, Caimito, Artemisa; tel. (7) 203-0668; fax (7) 204-2621; e-mail vpcom@aerogaviota.avianet.cu; internet www.aerogaviota.com; f. 1994; Exec. Pres. VÍCTOR MANUEL AGUILAR OSORIA.

Empresa Consolidada Cubana de Aviación (Cubana): Aeropuerto Internacional José Martí, Terminal 1, Avda Rancho Boyeros, Havana; tel. (7) 266-4644; fax (7) 33-4056; e-mail comunicacion@cubana.avianet.cu; internet www.cubana.cu; f. 1929; international services to North America, Central America, the Caribbean, South America and Europe; internal services from Havana to 14 other cities; Pres. RICARDO SANTILLÁN MIRANDA.

Tourism

Tourism began to develop after 1977, with the easing of travel restrictions by the USA, and Cuba subsequently attracted European tourists. In 2011 the number of hotel rooms had reached 65,878. In 2012 receipts from tourism totalled an estimated 2,613m. pesos. Tourist arrivals stood at an estimated 2,838,607 in 2012, compared with 2,716,317 in 2011.

Cubanacán: Calle 23, No 156, entre O y P, Vedado, 10400 Havana; tel. (7) 833-4090; fax (7) 22-8382; e-mail com_electronic@cubanacan.cyt.cu; internet www.cubanacan.cu; f. 1987; Pres. JUAN JOSÉ VEGA.

Empresa de Turismo Internacional (Cubatur): Calle 15, No 410, entre F y G, Plaza, Vedado, Havana; tel. (7) 836-2076; fax (7) 836-3170; e-mail casamatriz@cubatur.cu; internet www.cubatur.cu; f. 1963 as Empresa de Turismo Nacional e Internacional; changed name as above in 1969; Dir BÁRBARA CRUZ.

Defence

As assessed at November 2013, according to Western estimates, Cuba's Revolutionary Armed Forces numbered 49,000 (including ready reserves serving 45 days a year, to complete active and reserve units): Army 38,000, Navy 3,000 and Air Force 8,000. There were an additional 39,000 army reserves. Cuba's paramilitary forces included 20,000 State Security troops, 6,500 border guards, a civil defence force of 50,000 and a Youth Labour Army of some 70,000. There was also a Territorial Militia, comprising an estimated 1m. men and women. Conscription for military service is for a two-year period from 17 years of age, and conscripts also work on the land. Despite Cuban hostility, the USA maintains a base at Guantánamo Bay, which comprised 950 armed forces personnel.

Defence Expenditure: The proposed state budget for 2013 allocated 7,159.9m. pesos to administration, defence and public order.

Minister of the Revolutionary Armed Forces: Lt-Gen. LEOPOLDO CINTRA FRÍAS.

Head of the Joint Chiefs of Staff: Lt-Gen. ALVARO LÓPEZ MIERA.

Education

Education is universal and free at all levels. Education is based on Marxist-Leninist principles and combines study with manual work. Day nurseries are available for all children after their 45th day, and national schools at the pre-primary level are operated for children of five years of age. Primary education, from six to 11 years of age, is compulsory, and secondary education lasts from 12 to 17 years of age, comprising two cycles of three years each. In 2012 enrolment at primary and secondary schools included 96% and 87% of the school-age population, respectively. There were 261,468 students in higher education in 2012/13. Workers attending university courses receive a state subsidy to provide for their dependants. Courses at intermediate and higher levels lay an emphasis on technology, agriculture and teacher training. In 2013 proposed budgetary expenditure on education was 9,115.6m. pesos (18.1% of total spending).

CYPRUS

Introductory Survey

LOCATION, CLIMATE, LANGUAGE, RELIGION, FLAG, CAPITAL

The island of Cyprus is located in the eastern Mediterranean Sea, about 75 km south of Turkey and around 100 km west of Syria. The climate is mild, although snow falls in the mountainous south-west between December and March. Temperatures in Nicosia are generally between 5°C (41°F) and 36°C (97°F). About 75% of the population speak Greek and almost all of the remainder Turkish. The Greek-speaking community is overwhelmingly Christian, and nearly all Greek Cypriots adhere to the Orthodox Church of Cyprus, while most of the Turkish Cypriots are Muslims. Since 1974 the island has been divided into separately Greek Cypriot- and Turkish Cypriot-administered areas by a UN-monitored demilitarized zone, which extends for more than 180 km across the island. The two-thirds of the island to the south of the UN zone constitute the Republic of Cyprus, which is recognized internationally as the legitimate authority for the whole island. The national flag of the Republic of Cyprus (proportions 3 by 5) is white, with a gold map of Cyprus, above two crossed green olive branches, in the centre. The capital is Nicosia.

CONTEMPORARY POLITICAL HISTORY

Historical Context

A guerrilla war against British rule in Cyprus was begun in 1955 by Greek Cypriots seeking unification (*Enosis*) with Greece. Their movement, the National Organization of Cypriot Combatants (EOKA), was led politically by Archbishop Makarios III, the head of the Greek Orthodox Church in Cyprus, and militarily by Gen. George Grivas. Archbishop Makarios was suspected by the British authorities of being involved in EOKA's campaign of violence, and in March 1956 he and three other *Enosis* leaders were deported. After a compromise agreement between the Greek and Turkish communities, a Constitution for an independent Cyprus was finalized in 1959. Makarios returned from exile and was elected the country's first President in December 1959. Cyprus became independent on 16 August 1960, although the United Kingdom retained sovereignty over two military base areas.

A constitutional dispute resulted in the withdrawal of the Turks from the central Government in December 1963 and serious intercommunal violence. In March 1964 a UN Peacekeeping Force in Cyprus (UNFICYP, see p. 93) was established to prevent a recurrence of fighting between the Greek and Turkish Cypriot communities. The effective exclusion of the Turks from political power led to the creation of separate administrative, judicial and legislative organs for the Turkish community. Discussions with a view to establishing a more equitable constitutional arrangement began in 1968; these continued intermittently for six years without achieving any agreement.

In 1971 Gen. Grivas returned to Cyprus, revived EOKA and began a terrorist campaign for *Enosis*, directed against the Makarios Government and apparently supported by the military regime in Greece. Grivas died in January 1974, and in June Makarios ordered a purge of EOKA sympathizers from the police, National Guard and civil service, accusing the Greek regime of subversion. On 15 July Makarios was deposed in a military coup led by Greek officers of the National Guard, who appointed as President Nikos Sampson, an extremist Greek Cypriot politician and former EOKA militant. Makarios escaped from the island the following day and travelled to the United Kingdom. At the request of Rauf Denktaş, the Turkish Cypriot leader, the Turkish army intervened to protect the Turkish community and to prevent Greece from using its control of the National Guard to take over Cyprus. Turkish troops landed on 20 July and rapidly occupied the northern third of Cyprus, dividing the island along what became the Green Line (also known as the Attila Line), which runs from Morphou through Nicosia to Famagusta. Sampson resigned on 23 July, and Glavkos Klerides, the President of the House of Representatives, became acting head of state. The military regime in Greece collapsed the same day. In December Makarios returned to Cyprus and resumed the presidency.

Events surrounding the Turkish Cypriots' declaration of independence

Makarios died in August 1977. He was succeeded as President by Spyros Kyprianou. Following a government reorganization in September 1980, the powerful communist party, the Anorthotiko Komma Ergazomenou Laou (AKEL—Progressive Party of the Working People), withdrew its support from the ruling Dimokratiko Komma (DIKO—Democratic Party), and Kyprianou lost his overall majority in the legislature. At the next general election, held in May 1981, AKEL and the Dimokratikos Synagermos (DISY—Democratic Rally) each won 12 seats in the House. DIKO, however, won only eight seats, so the President remained dependent on AKEL's support.

In September 1980 UN-sponsored intercommunal peace talks resumed. The constitutional issue remained the main problem: the Turkish Cypriots demanded equal status for the two communities, with equal representation in government, while the Greek Cypriots favoured a strong central government and objected to any disproportionate representation for the Turkish Cypriot community, which constituted less than 20% of the population. Discussions on a UN plan involving a federal council, an alternating presidency and the allocation of 70% of the island to the Greek Cypriot community faltered in February 1982, when the Greek Prime Minister, Andreas Papandreou, proposed the withdrawal of all Greek and Turkish troops and the convening of an international conference to replace the intercommunal talks. Meanwhile, in April 1981 it was agreed to establish a Committee on Missing Persons in Cyprus, comprising one representative of each community and a representative of the International Committee of the Red Cross, to investigate the fate of 1,619 Greek Cypriots and 803 Turkish Cypriots listed as missing since the 1974 invasion. In May 1983 the UN General Assembly voted in favour of the withdrawal of Turkish troops from Cyprus, whereupon Denktaş threatened to boycott any further intercommunal talks and to seek recognition for the 'Turkish Federated State of Cyprus' ('TFSC'—which had been established in 1975) as a sovereign state; simultaneously it was announced that the Turkish lira was to replace the Cyprus pound as legal tender in the 'TFSC'. On 15 November 1983 the 'TFSC' made a unilateral declaration of independence as the 'Turkish Republic of Northern Cyprus' ('TRNC'). The announcement prompted condemnation by the UN Security Council and, like the 'TFSC', the 'TRNC' was recognized only by Turkey.

In February 1983 Kyprianou was returned to the presidency for a second term. In November 1985, following a debate on his leadership, the House of Representatives was dissolved. Legislative elections proceeded in December: Kyprianou's DIKO secured 16 seats in the chamber (which, under a constitutional amendment, had been enlarged to 56 Greek Cypriot deputies), while DISY, which won 19 seats, and AKEL, with 15, failed to reach the two-thirds' majority required to amend the Constitution and thus challenge the President's tenure of power. However, in February 1988 the presidential election was won at a second round of voting by Georghios Vassiliou, an independent candidate who nevertheless enjoyed unofficial support from AKEL and the Socialistiko Komma Kyprou EDEK (EDEK—EDEK Socialist Party of Cyprus). Vassiliou undertook to restore a multi-party National Council (originally convened by President Makarios) to address the Cyprus issue.

Settlement plans proposed by the UN Secretary-General in July 1985 and in April 1986 were rejected by the Turkish Cypriots and the Greek Cypriots, respectively. Further measures concerning the demilitarization of the island, reportedly proposed by the Greek Cypriot Government, were rejected by Denktaş, who maintained that negotiations on the establishment of a two-zone, federal republic should precede any demilitarization. However, following a meeting with the revived National Council in June 1988, Denktaş and Vassiliou agreed to a proposal by the UN Secretary-General that they should resume intercommunal talks without pre-conditions. A UN-sponsored summit meeting between the two leaders took place in Geneva, Switzerland, in August; direct negotiations began in September. However, despite resuming negotiations at the UN in February 1990, these were abandoned in March, chiefly because Denktaş demanded recognition of the right to self-determination for Turkish Cypriots.

Initiatives for reconciliation following Cyprus's application for European Community membership

In July 1990 the Government of the Republic of Cyprus formally applied to join the European Community (EC, now European Union—EU, see p. 273). Denktaş condemned the application, on the grounds that the Turkish Cypriots had not been consulted, and stated that the action would prevent the resumption of intercommunal talks. In June 1993, none the less, the European Commission approved the eligibility of Cyprus for EC membership, although it insisted that the application should be linked to progress in the latest UN-sponsored talks.

At the May 1991 elections to the House of Representatives, the conservative DISY, in alliance with the Komma Phileleftheron (Liberal Party), received 35.8% of the votes cast, thereby securing 20 of the 56 seats in the legislature. AKEL unexpectedly made the most significant gains, obtaining 30.6% of the votes and 18 seats.

Following unsuccessful attempts to promote the resumption of discussions between Vassiliou and Denktaş by the UN, the EC and the USA during 1990–91, the new UN Secretary-General, Boutros Boutros-Ghali, made the resolution of the Cyprus problem a priority. Boutros-Ghali held two rounds of separate meetings in New York, USA, with Vassiliou and Denktaş in early and mid-1992, followed by direct discussions. The talks aimed to arrive at a draft settlement based on his proposals and endorsed by UN Security Council Resolution 750, advocating 'uninterrupted negotiations' until a settlement was reached. The UN proposals centred on the demarcation of Greek Cypriot and Turkish Cypriot areas of administration under a federal structure. However, after it was revealed that the proposed area of Turkish administration was some 25% smaller than the 'TRNC', Denktaş asserted that the UN's territorial proposals were totally unacceptable to the 'TRNC' Government, and the discussions ended in August.

At an election to the presidency in February 1993, the DISY leader, Glavkos Klerides, narrowly defeated the incumbent Vassiliou at a second round of voting. Vassiliou subsequently formed a new party, the Kinema ton Eleftheron Dimokraton (KED—Movement of Free Democrats). UN-sponsored negotiations were reconvened in New York in May, focusing on the Secretary-General's plan to introduce a series of 'confidence-building measures', which included the proposed reopening, under UN administration, of the international airport at Nicosia. However, the talks were abandoned in June, when the Turkish Cypriot negotiators declined to respond to the proposals.

In July 1994 the UN Security Council adopted Resolution 939, advocating a new initiative on the part of the Secretary-General to formulate a solution for peace, based on a single nationality, international identity and sovereignty. The 'TRNC' authorities responded by asserting that no settlement based on the concept of a federation would be acceptable, and demanding political and sovereign status equal to that of Greek Cyprus. The issue of Cyprus's bid to accede to the EU had greatly disrupted the progress of negotiations. Denktaş remained adamant that any approach by the Greek Cypriots to the EU would prompt the 'TRNC' to seek further integration with Turkey.

Elections to the House of Representatives on 26 May 1996 produced little change in the chamber's composition. DISY retained 20 seats, with 34.5% of the votes cast; AKEL took 19 seats, with 33.0% of the votes, while DIKO secured 10 seats, with 16.4%. Meanwhile, in April 1996 the UN Security Council endorsed a US initiative to promote a federal-based settlement for Cyprus. In June, in advance of a visit to the island by the UN Secretary-General's newly appointed Special Representative in Cyprus, Han Sung-Joo, Boutros-Ghali held separate discussions with Denktaş and Klerides. In October a UN-mediated military dialogue, involving senior commanders of the Greek and Turkish Cypriot armed forces, was initiated to consider proposals for reducing intercommunal tension. However, further mediation efforts were undermined in November by alleged violations of Greek Cypriot airspace by Turkish military aircraft, as well as by Greek Cypriot efforts to prevent tourists from visiting the 'TRNC' and the latter's continued opposition to Cyprus's application to join the EU.

In January 1997 an agreement signed by the Republic of Cyprus Government and Russia regarding the purchase of an advanced anti-aircraft missile system was condemned by the 'TRNC' as an 'act of aggression'. The potential for conflict over the issue increased when Turkey declared its willingness to use military force to prevent the deployment of the system. Greece in turn reiterated that it would defend Cyprus against any Turkish attack. However, US mediators were assured by the Government that deployment would not take place until at least May 1998 and would be dependent upon the progress made in talks. In addition, both sides approved UN-supported measures to reduce tension in the border area, although the Greek Cypriots rejected a US proposal for a ban on all military flights over the island. Later in January 1997 Turkey threatened to establish air and naval bases in the 'TRNC' if Greece continued to promote plans for the establishment of military facilities in the south, and at the end of the month Turkish military vessels arrived in the 'TRNC' port of Famagusta.

In July 1997 Klerides and Denktaş took part in direct UN-sponsored negotiations in the USA, under the chairmanship of the UN Special Envoy for Cyprus, Diego Córdovez. The discussions were held under the auspices of the new UN Secretary-General, Kofi Annan, and with the participation of Richard Holbrooke, the newly appointed US Special Envoy to Cyprus. During further private direct talks in Nicosia at the end of July, agreement was reached to co-operate in efforts to trace persons missing since the hostilities of 1974. However, a second formal round of UN-sponsored negotiations, convened in Switzerland in August 1997, collapsed without agreement, after Denktaş demanded the suspension of Cyprus's application for EU membership.

At the second round of voting in the presidential election, held on 15 February 1998, Klerides defeated Georghios Iacovou, an independent candidate supported by AKEL and DIKO, securing 50.8% of the votes cast. A new coalition Government, composed of members of DISY, EDEK, the Enomeni Dimokrates (EDI—United Democrats—formed in 1996 by a merger of the KED and the Ananeotiko Dimokratiko Socialistiko Kinima—Democratic Socialist Reform Movement) and independents, was sworn in at the end of the month. The new Government began accession talks with the EU in March 1998. In August Denktaş rejected a UN plan for reunification, proposing instead a confederation of equal status; this was deemed unacceptable by Klerides on the grounds that it would legitimize the status of the 'TRNC'.

It was formally announced in December 1998 that the contentious Russian missile system would not be deployed in Cyprus, following diplomatic pressure from Greece, the EU (which threatened to suspend Cypriot accession talks if the deployment proceeded), the USA and the UN. The missiles were reportedly deployed in Crete, Greece, in March 1999, following an agreement by the Greek and Republic of Cyprus Governments to the effect that Cyprus would own the missiles although they would be under Greek operational control. Klerides's reversal of policy regarding the missiles' deployment provoked intense domestic criticism, and prompted the withdrawal of EDEK (to which party the Minister of Defence belonged) from the governing coalition. (In 2000 Kinima Sosialdimokraton EDEK, KISOS—Movement of Social Democrats, was established as a successor movement to EDEK.)

In December 1999 Denktaş and Klerides attended proximity talks in New York under UN auspices; however, the indirect talks were undermined by a decision taken that month at a summit meeting of EU Heads of State and Government in Helsinki, Finland, that a political settlement for Cyprus was not a precondition to the accession of the Republic of Cyprus to the EU. This decision was widely acknowledged to be a response to Greece's reversal of its opposition to Turkey's EU membership application, and the summit thus accorded Turkey formal status as an EU candidate.

A third round of proximity talks, mediated by the UN Special Adviser on Cyprus, Álvaro de Soto, took place in Geneva in July–August 2000. A further round of UN-sponsored indirect negotiations began in New York in September. Klerides boycotted the early stages of the talks, in protest at a statement in which Secretary-General Annan had, in his view, implied that the 'TRNC' was equal in authority to the internationally recognized Republic of Cyprus Government; however, the President resumed attendance after receiving assurances that the UN would act in accordance with earlier Security Council resolutions on the Cyprus issue. Nevertheless, the Greek and Turkish Cypriots remained apparently irreconcilable on the issue of a future structure for Cyprus, with the former advocating a reunified, bicommunal federation and the latter a looser confederation based on equal sovereignty. A fifth round of proximity talks was convened in Geneva in November, and Annan invited Klerides and Denktaş to attend further discussions in January 2001. Later in November 2000, however, Denktaş stated that he would not return to the talks until the 'TRNC' was accorded international recognition.

At elections to the House of Representatives on 27 May 2001, AKEL secured a narrow victory over DISY, taking 20 seats (with 34.7% of the votes cast), compared with the latter's 19 (34.0%); DIKO held nine seats (14.8%). In June the AKEL leader, Demetris Christofias, was elected as the new President of the legislature, defeating DISY's Nikos Anastasiades, with support from the DIKO deputies.

EU accession and the 'Annan Plan'

In early December 2001 Presidents Klerides and Denktaş met briefly for the first time in four years; following the meeting, Alvaro de Soto stated that the two leaders had agreed to recommence direct talks on the future of the island in January 2002 'without preconditions'. On 5 December 2001 Klerides became the first Greek Cypriot leader to visit the 'TRNC' since the island's partition, holding a meeting with Denktaş. The 'TRNC' President made a reciprocal visit at the end of December. Formal direct negotiations, mediated by de Soto, commenced on 21 January 2002, with a view to reaching agreement by the end of June.

In September 2002 Kofi Annan hosted talks between Klerides and Denktaş in Paris, France. On 11 November the UN presented a comprehensive new peace plan (which became known as the 'Annan Plan') to Klerides and Denktaş. The plan envisaged the creation of a common federal state with two equal components, but a single international legal personality. The state would have a joint six-member presidential council, with members holding a 10-month rotating presidency, and a bicameral legislature, comprising a 48-member senate with an equal number of deputies from both sides, and a 48-member proportionally composed chamber of deputies. A common supreme court would have three judges from both sides, and three non-Cypriots. Dispossessed property owners would receive compensation, and the 'TRNC' would return territory to the Greek side, reducing the former's share of the island from 36% to 28.5%. Cyprus would be demilitarized, but Greece and Turkey would each be permitted to station up to 9,999 troops on the island, and UNFICYP would retain its presence. The two leaders initially agreed to use the plan as a basis for future negotiations, but in early December Denktaş rejected a revised version of it.

The progress of EU accession talks meant that the need for a settlement to the Cyprus problem was increasingly urgent. At the EU summit held in Copenhagen, Denmark, in December 2002, Cyprus was formally invited to join the EU in 2004. However, it was reiterated that in the absence of a peace agreement, only the Greek part of the island would be admitted. Meanwhile, Greece, which assumed the presidency of the EU in January 2003, had earlier emphasized that it would veto the admission of other EU candidate countries if Cyprus was not admitted at the next round of expansion. Turkey, for its part, had warned in November 2001 that it might annex northern Cyprus if a divided island was admitted to the EU.

In the presidential election held on 16 February 2003, the DIKO leader, Tassos Papadopoulos (who was also supported by AKEL), was elected outright, with 51.5% of the votes cast. Klerides won 38.8% of the votes. Papadopoulos appointed a new Government, which for the first time included four AKEL representatives. The new President, who favoured a less compromising approach towards the Turkish Cypriots than his predecessor, immediately demanded changes to the Annan Plan that would allow all Greek Cypriot refugees to return to the north. Annan extended, to 10 March, a deadline previously set at 28 February for agreement on the island's future, which would thus allow a unified Cyprus to accede to the EU, and Papadopoulos and Denktaş held discussions in The Hague, Netherlands. However, the new deadline passed without agreement: Denktaş denounced the Annan Plan as unacceptable, and refused to continue discussions. The office of the UN Secretary-General's Special Adviser on Cyprus was subsequently closed down. In early April the Government rejected an offer by Denktaş to return the eastern town of Varosha, stating that the UN plan should be the principal basis for negotiation.

On 16 April 2003 President Papadopoulos signed Cyprus's Treaty of Accession to the EU in Athens, Greece, thereby confirming that Cyprus would join the organization on 1 May 2004. On 23 April 2003 the Turkish Cypriot authorities announced that they would open the 'TRNC' border for the first time in 30 years, allowing Turkish Cypriots to visit that area for one-day trips and permitting Greek Cypriots to visit the north for up to three nights. The Republic of Cyprus Government stated that the opening of the border should not be regarded as a substitute for a settlement in accordance with UN resolutions. By July more than 900,000 people were reported to have crossed the border. The Treaty of Accession was unanimously approved by the House of Representatives on 14 July and ratified by Papadopoulos on 28 July.

The formation of a new 'TRNC' Government in January 2004 gave renewed impetus to the search for a political settlement. On 13 February, following a further round of UN-sponsored talks between Denktaş and Papadopoulos in New York, agreement was reached for the resumption of bilateral negotiations based on the Annan Plan (providing for a federation of two politically equal states). It was hoped that a settlement would be reached prior to the island's accession to the EU on 1 May. In late February 2004 Papadopoulos and Denktaş resumed intensive UN-sponsored negotiations in Nicosia, in an effort to finalize the details of a settlement, which was to be submitted for approval by both the Greek and Turkish Cypriot communities at concurrent referendums scheduled for 24 April. The discussions were relocated to Bürgenstock, Switzerland, in late March 2004, where the Greek and Turkish Prime Ministers also joined the process. However, Denktaş, who continued to reject the UN plan, withdrew from the negotiations and was replaced by Mehmet Ali Talat, the Turkish Cypriot Prime Minister, as head of the 'TRNC' delegation.

At the end of March 2004 Annan presented a finalized version of the peace plan, which was accepted by the 'TRNC' leadership and by the Greek and Turkish Governments; however, Papadopoulos (in a reversal of previous government policy) campaigned against this final settlement, which he strongly opposed on the grounds that it provided for the establishment of a recognized Turkish Cypriot state. At the referendums held on 24 April the Annan Plan was endorsed by Turkish Cypriots by 64.9% of votes cast, but rejected by Greek Cypriots by 75.8% of the votes. Consequently, only the Greek Cypriot-administered part of the island was admitted to the EU on 1 May; the *acquis communautaire* (the body of EU legislation, treaties and case law) was suspended in the 'TRNC', pending a future political settlement. Following appeals by Talat, the EU proposed measures for the resumption of direct trade between the two sides of the island, and consequently for the export of commodities produced in the 'TRNC' to EU member states.

The Cyprus question after EU accession

In October 2004 the UN Security Council renewed the mandate of UNFICYP until June 2005, but significantly reduced the size of the contingent. On 9 March 2005 AKEL Secretary-General Demetris Christofias met with Talat, in the first discussions between Greek Cypriot and 'TRNC' leaders since the April 2004 referendums. In April 2005—in which month Talat was elected to succeed Denktaş as the 'TRNC' President—the European Court of Human Rights (ECHR) issued a significant decision upholding a Greek Cypriot property claim against Turkey and rejecting the contention that the 'TRNC' authorities had provided adequate restitution for such claims by establishing a property commission. The case reflected Greek Cypriot concerns over increasing sales of property in the 'TRNC' involving houses and land owned legally by Greek Cypriots.

Meanwhile, the EU's provisional invitation to Turkey, issued on 17 December 2004, to open accession negotiations in October 2005 again focused international attention on the necessity of reaching a political settlement in Cyprus. The Turkish Prime Minister, Recep Tayyip Erdoğan, accepted a condition to extend Turkey's customs accord with the EU to cover the 10 new member states that had joined the organization in May 2004, including Cyprus. However, Erdoğan insisted that the customs protocol (which the Turkish Government signed in July 2005) would not constitute official Turkish recognition of the authorities of Greek Cypriot-administered Cyprus, instead agreeing to a compromise arrangement whereby Turkey made a commitment for future recognition. In September 2005 EU member states declared that Turkish recognition of Cyprus was necessary to the accession process, but, in the absence of a specific deadline, accession negotiations were officially approved on 3 October.

In January 2006 the Turkish Government proposed a resumption of dialogue concerning reunification, and presented an 'action plan' to the UN Secretary-General, under which Turkish ports and airports would be opened to Cypriot traffic in exchange for the ending of trade restrictions against the 'TRNC'. The Republic of Cyprus Government immediately rejected the proposals, emphasizing that the Turkish authorities were required to open ports and airports to all EU member states by the end of 2006 as a condition to progress in the accession negotiations. Following a UN-mediated meeting in July, Papadopoulos and Talat reached a framework agreement on an initiative—known as 'the 8 July process'—to resolve technical issues between the two communities, with the objective of resuming the formal peace process.

Elections conducted to the House of Representatives on 21 May 2006 resulted in no major changes to its composition. AKEL and DISY both won 18 seats, attracting 31.1% and 30.3% of the votes cast, respectively, while DIKO secured 11 seats, with 17.9% of the ballot. Also securing representation were KISOS, with five seats (8.9%), a new party called the Evropaiko Komma (Evro.Ko—European Party), with three seats (5.8%), and the Kinima Oikologon Perivallontiston (KOP—Cyprus Green Party), with one seat (2.0%).

Following the onset of hostilities between the militant Shi'a organization Hezbollah and Israeli armed forces in July 2006 (see the chapter on Lebanon), Cyprus became the main transit point for refugees fleeing southern Lebanon by sea, and applied to the EU for financial assistance in managing the influx. By 14 August, upon which date a UN-imposed ceasefire agreement entered into effect, some 60,000 civilians (mainly foreign nationals) fleeing the fighting in Lebanon had been evacuated through Cyprus. The Minister of Finance announced that the cost to the authorities had been equivalent to US $223,000 per day, and the EU pledged some $8.9m. towards meeting the expense.

In November 2006 the European Commission published a critical report on Turkey's accession progress, in which it issued an ultimatum demanding that the Turkish Government open ports and airports in accordance with the 2005 customs protocol by early December 2006, prior to a meeting of EU foreign ministers. In early December, following indications that the continuing impasse would result in the partial suspension of Turkey's accession negotiations, the Turkish Government offered to open one port and one airport, in exchange for the resumption of international flights to the 'TRNC' airport of Ercan and direct trade to the port of Famagusta. The Republic of Cyprus Government rejected the proposal and, together with Greece and Austria, continued to demand a total cessation of EU discussions with Turkey. In mid-December EU ministers of foreign affairs agreed to a suspension of negotiations on eight of the 35 policy areas (concerning trade and external relations).

At the end of December 2006, following a meeting between Demetris Christofias and Ferdi Sabit Soyer, the 'TRNC' Prime Minister, in the northern part of Nicosia, it was announced that both sides had expressed willingness to enter into further dialogue concerning a resolution for Cyprus. In February 2007 Archbishop Chrysostomos of the Greek Orthodox Church of Cyprus and Ahmet Yonluer, head of the 'TRNC' Religious Affairs Directorate, met for the first time since 1974, and discussed methods of fostering dialogue between the two communities with a view to increasing inter-religious tolerance. In the following month the Republic of Cyprus Government orchestrated the demolition of a wall at Ledra Street in Nicosia, which formed part of the barrier that had divided the city into Greek and Turkish sectors for more than four decades. Since 2004 five crossing-points had been opened along the Green Line, although, thus far, none had been opened in the capital.

AKEL announced in July 2007 that it was withdrawing from the governing coalition, thereby enabling party leader Christofias to stand in the presidential election scheduled to take place in early 2008. The four government portfolios relinquished by AKEL were awarded later that month to independents, including Eratou Kozakou-Marcoullis as the Minister of Foreign Affairs.

The 2008 presidential election and resumption of reunification talks

In the first round of the presidential election, held on 17 February 2008, Papadopoulos was unexpectedly eliminated from the running, a result attributed by many to increasing levels of popular frustration at his perceived intractability with regard to the Cyprus problem. The DISY-backed independent Ioannis Kasoulides garnered 33.5% of the ballot, and Demetris Christofias secured 33.4%, relegating Papadopoulos, with 31.8% of the vote, into third place among a total of nine candidates. The run-off election between the two highest-polling candidates, held on 24 February, was a relatively close contest, from which Christofias emerged victorious, with 240,604 votes (53.4% of the ballot), compared with 210,195 votes cast in favour of Kasoulides (46.6%). DIKO had transferred its backing from Papadopoulos to Christofias before the second round of voting, although the former President remained officially neutral. During his electoral campaign Christofias had expressed a desire to 'reunite the state, the people, the institutions and the economy', and pledged his firm commitment to the holding of reunification negotiations with the 'TRNC'.

Christofias was formally inaugurated as President on 28 February 2008, and a new Council of Ministers was sworn in on the following day. The allocation of portfolios effectively, though unofficially, restored the tripartite coalition that had been in power prior to AKEL's withdrawal in July 2007: four ministries were headed by AKEL, and two each by DIKO and KISOS, with responsibility for the remaining two being awarded to AKEL-backed independents. Notable appointments included those of Markos Kyprianou (DIKO—hitherto EU Commissioner for Health) as Minister of Foreign Affairs and Charilaos Stavrakis (independent—Chief Executive of the Bank of Cyprus) as Minister of Finance.

During discussions between Christofias and Talat in Nicosia in March 2008 the two leaders agreed to: open the Ledra Street crossing in central Nicosia as a symbol of reconciliation between their two communities (this occurred in early April); devise a precise agenda for the reunification negotiations to take place; and establish a number of working groups and technical committees. This latter objective was achieved in mid-April, when six bicommunal working groups and seven technical committees were set up to consider a number of issues pertinent to the success of further talks. The working groups were to consider: governance and power-sharing; EU matters; security and guarantees; territory; property; and economic matters; while the technical committees would oversee: crime/criminal matters; economic and commercial matters; cultural heritage; crisis management; humanitarian matters; health; and the environment.

In May 2008 Christofias and Talat conducted a second meeting in Nicosia, hosted by the UN Secretary-General's newly appointed Special Representative in Cyprus and head of UNFICYP, Tayé-Brook Zerihoun of Ethiopia. At the close of the meeting, which reviewed the progress achieved thus far by the working groups and technical committees, the two leaders reiterated their 'commitment to a bizonal, bicommunal federation with political equality, as defined by relevant Security Council resolutions'. A third bilateral meeting was held in early July, and later that month it was announced that Alexander Downer, hitherto the Australian Minister for Foreign Affairs, had been appointed as the UN Secretary-General's Special Adviser on Cyprus. Christofias and Talat subsequently reconvened in Nicosia in late July, where they undertook a final review of the working groups and technical committees. They subsequently agreed to hold weekly talks, in a development seen as indicative of their desire to accelerate efforts to achieve a comprehensive solution to the Cyprus problem.

Christofias and Talat met in Nicosia in mid-September 2008, in the presence of Zerihoun and Downer. This marked the first of a series of substantive negotiations held between the two leaders over successive months, which were intended to facilitate consensus on matters ranging from power-sharing and governance to security, property and the environment. However, in spite of the considerable optimism generated by the commencement of these long-awaited reunification talks, familiar tensions—principally with regard to issues of power-sharing—soon began to hamper the progress of the meetings.

President Christofias officially resigned as Secretary-General of AKEL in December 2008. In January 2009, AKEL political bureau member (in charge of international relations) Andros Kyprianouwas elected as his successor.

The withdrawal of KISOS from the Government

In April 2009 the European Court of Justice (ECJ) upheld a ruling, first issued by a Republic of Cyprus court in 2004, that ordered the restoration of a property in the 'TRNC' to its original Greek Cypriot owner. The property in question, which had been vacated following the 1974 invasion, had subsequently been sold to a British couple who had constructed a holiday villa on the site. The couple were ordered to relinquish their claim on the land, restore the site to its original state, and pay rent and damages to the owner. Owing to the Cypriot court's lack of jurisdiction in northern Cyprus, the original verdict had not been enforced. However, the plaintiff's legal team subsequently petitioned the High Court of Justice in the United Kingdom, from where the case was referred to the ECJ. The latter concluded that, as the defendants were EU citizens, the ruling could be enforced by EU law, raising fears that the judgment could form a legal precedent for similar cases. The 'TRNC' authorities stated that all property disputes should be resolved solely through the ongoing political negotiations and declared that they would not enforce the decision, despite an appeal by the defendants being rejected by the British Court of Appeal in January 2010.

By early June 2009 Christofias and Talat had held over 30 meetings since their first substantive negotiations on reunification in September of the previous year. At the 32nd meeting, in mid-June, discussions on economic matters—at least at the presidential level—were concluded and talks on territorial issues commenced. In late June it was announced that agreement had been reached on the opening of an additional crossing-point at Limnitis (Yeşilırmak), near the island's north-eastern coast; this occurred on 14 October 2010. Meanwhile, following a 40th meeting, on 6 August 2009, the first round of negotiations was concluded. A second round of talks, encompassing power-sharing, property rights, economic affairs and the EU, began on 10 September. Many observers believed that the talks were entering a critical period, as both leaders were confronting increasing domestic pressure over their handling of the negotiations, with hardline elements on both sides opposed to the granting of concessions. In late September the two leaders agreed to intensify negotiations, with meetings scheduled to take place twice weekly from October. In November the British Government promised to transfer into Cypriot control around one-half of the territory currently under British military jurisdiction, upon the successful conclusion of a settlement. On 14 December the UN Security Council adopted Resolution 1898, which urged the leaders to redouble their efforts to exploit the existing opportunity to reach a settlement, and extended the mandate of the UN force until June 2010. (UNFICYP's mandate had been consistently renewed at six-monthly intervals since its inception in 1964.)

Following the conclusion of the second round of talks on 29 January 2010, Downer announced that 'significant progress' had been made in the negotiations concerning governance. In an attempt to bolster the protracted negotiations, UN Secretary-General Ban Ki-Moon arrived in Cyprus on 30 January for his first official visit. The Secretary-General held separate talks with Christofias and Talat. However, his meeting with Talat resulted in criticism from numerous Greek Cypriot politicians, who maintained that the decision to hold the meeting at Talat's presidential office was tantamount to UN recognition of the 'TRNC'. Four parties, including DIKO and KISOS, subsequently boycotted an official reception in honour of the Secretary-General.

In February 2010 KISOS announced its withdrawal from the governing coalition, citing its dissatisfaction with the strategy implemented by President Christofias in the reconciliation talks. However, the party's two ministers agreed to remain in their respective posts until a new government could be formed. Later in February the leader of DIKO, Marios Karoyian, announced that his party would remain in the Government, having obtained greater representation within the Greek Cypriot negotiating party. In March President Christofias appointed two independents to the Council of Ministers, in place of the two outgoing KISOS representatives: former Minister of Foreign Affairs Kozakou-Marcoullis became the Minister of Communications and Works, and Demetris Eliades was appointed Minister of Agriculture, Natural Resources and the Environment.

UN efforts to accelerate the reunification talks

After a two-month break, the UN-led reunification talks resumed in May 2010, with the newly elected 'TRNC' President, Dr Derviş Eroğlu, leading the Turkish Cypriot negotiating team. Although Eroğlu stated his commitment to continuing the reconciliation talks begun by his predecessor, there were fears that the dominance of 'TRNC' politics by his nationalist party would undermine efforts to achieve a political settlement. In June Lisa Buttenheim of the USA was appointed to succeed Zerihoun as the UN Secretary-General's Special Representative in Cyprus and head of UNFICYP, the mandate of which was extended until December. Both Ban Ki-Moon and the UN Security Council assessed that a settlement of the Cyprus issue was now 'well within reach', and the UN resolution urged the two sides to seize the opportunity and accelerate the peace process, citing in particular the need to introduce further confidence-building measures. However, hopes that the Greek and Turkish Cypriots would agree a settlement by the end of 2010—the target date outlined by the two leaders at their 59th meeting on 21 December 2009—were not realized. The discussions since the resumption of negotiations had focused on the controversial issue of property rights, which the UN Secretary-General described as 'seemingly irreconcilable'. In late June 2010 a ruling by the ECHR had condemned the Turkish authorities for having denied nine Greek Cypriots access to the properties that they had owned in northern Cyprus prior to the 1974 invasion; Turkey was reportedly required to pay between €10,000 and €400,000 in compensation to the claimants.

Ban Ki-Moon invited Christofias and Eroğlu to hold a further meeting in New York in November 2010, amid concern that the reunification negotiations were losing momentum. The UN Secretary-General urged the two leaders to identify the core issues in all of the chapters yet to be resolved and to formulate a practical plan to overcome these differences. In December the UN Security Council approved Resolution 1953, which renewed the UNFICYP mandate until June 2011. In this resolution the UN was noticeably critical of the way in which the fully fledged negotiations were being conducted, noting the recent lack of progress in the discussions. However, after a bilateral meeting in Geneva in January 2011, Ban expressed his satisfaction at the efforts made by both leaders to formulate a practical plan for resolving specific issues and asserted that progress had been made on several chapters, particularly those concerning the economy, the EU, and governance and power-sharing. Nevertheless, he urged Christofias and Eroğlu to do more to resolve outstanding differences. In June the UN Security Council adopted Resolution 1986, extending the mandate of UNFICYP until December; in the resolution the UN again urged the acceleration of reunification talks and also the implementation of confidence-building measures, including the opening of further crossing points.

The 2011 parliamentary elections

Elections to the 56-seat House of Representatives were held on 22 May 2011. The opposition DISY increased its parliamentary representation to 20 seats, while AKEL increased its own representation to 19 seats; AKEL's coalition partner, DIKO, secured nine seats, while KISOS won five seats and Evro.Ko two, with the remaining seat secured by KOP. Turnout was recorded at 78.7% of the registered electorate.

A series of explosions at a naval base in southern Cyprus in July 2011 resulted in the deaths of 13 people—including the head of the Cypriot naval force, Andreas Ioannides, and the base commander, Lambros Lambrou—while more than 60 others were injured. The incident, which caused severe damage to the nearby Vassiliko power station (providing more than one-half of Cyprus's electricity), prompted the resignations of both the Minister of Defence, Costas Papacostas, and the commander of the National Guard, Brig.-Gen. Petros Tsaliklides. The explosions were later found to have been caused by a small fire igniting improperly stored containers of Iranian munitions that had been confiscated from a Syria-bound vessel in 2009. Public anger in response to the Government's apparent failure adequately to dispose of the munitions precipitated the staging of popular protests in the capital, with an estimated 10,000 people amassing outside the presidential palace in mid-July 2011 to demand the resignation of President Christofias. However, the Government claimed that it had requested several times that the UN remove the munitions from Cyprus but that the organization had declined. A few days later Minister of Foreign Affairs Kyprianou tendered his resignation, and in late July the entire Council of Ministers resigned at the request of the President.

A new Council of Ministers, comprising members of AKEL and independents, was inaugurated in early August 2011. Among notable changes, Eratou Kozakou-Marcoullis was appointed Minister of Foreign Affairs for the second time, while the incumbent Minister of Agriculture, Demetris Eliades, was transferred to the defence portfolio. Kikis Kazamias joined the Government as Minister of Finance. Two days previously DIKO had announced that it was to withdraw from the ruling coalition, citing irreconcilable differences with Christofias and AKEL regarding the ongoing reunification talks. DIKO's withdrawal left Christofias even more isolated in the House of Representatives, and threatened to undermine the Government's efforts to pass key austerity measures and economic reforms intended to address the country's increasingly precarious situation as a result of the ongoing financial crisis within the eurozone (see Economic Affairs).

In early October 2011 the findings of an inquiry into the munitions explosion in July were published in a report by Polys Polyviou, a lawyer appointed by the Government to investigate the incident. Polyviou concluded that President Christofias bore 'a serious and very heavy personal responsibility' for the disaster, having ignored warnings prior to the explosion that the confiscated munitions were in an unstable condition. Nevertheless, the President dismissed the report's findings, insisting that he was in no way culpable. In early March 2012 police formally charged Papacostas and Kyprianou with 'negligent manslaughter' as a result of the explosion at the southern naval base in July 2011. Six other military or emergency services personnel also faced similar charges, including Brig.-Gen. Tsaliklides, who was resident in his home country of Greece. However, one man was subsequently acquitted of the charges, and officials instead decided to prosecute Tsaliklides in Greece. Trial proceedings against the two former ministers, together with four other defendants, began in early July 2012; all denied the charges. Following the trial's conclusion in early July 2013, Papacostas was found guilty of manslaughter and sentenced to five years in gaol; Kyprianou and a military official were cleared of all charges, while three senior members of the fire brigade were found guilty of causing death through negligence, and each given a two-year prison term.

Following a break in negotiations owing to the elections in May 2011, together with those in Turkey (q.v.) in June, the reunification talks between Christofias and Eroğlu resumed at the end of October in Manhasset, USA, under the auspices of the UN Secretary-General. In December the UN Security Council renewed UNFICYP's mandate until July 2012. Following a further meeting at the end of January 2012 between the two leaders and Ban, Christofias noted that 'significant differences on governance, property and territory as well as details of other issues that may prove significant are still pending'. The negotiations subsequently stalled; Eroğlu stated in early February that reunification talks could not continue while the Republic of Cyprus held the rotating EU presidency (scheduled for the second half of 2012) and the UN Secretary-General informed the Security Council in late March 2012 that discussions on the core issues were approaching deadlock. Meanwhile, the resignation in mid-March of Minister of Finance Kazamias on the grounds of ill health prompted a reorganization of the Government. AKEL's Eleni Mavrou, a former mayor of Nicosia, took office as Minister of the Interior in place of Neoklis Sylikiotis, who was appointed as Minister of Commerce, Industry and Tourism, and Vasos Shiarlis, an independent former banker, became Minister of Finance.

Following consultations with Downer, in late April 2012 Ban Ki-Moon announced that a proposed international conference on Cyprus would not take place, owing to the continued lack of agreement between the Greek and Turkish Cypriot sides on the key issues of contention—principally property, territory and security measures. Ban's Special Adviser subsequently told both Christofias and Eroğlu that the UN was henceforth to restrict its mediatory role between northern and southern Cyprus to negotiations on technical issues and confidence-building measures. Any immediate progress in the reunification talks was then delayed by the Republic of Cyprus's assumption of the EU presidency and the 2013 presidential election (see The 2013 presidential election and Cyprus's international bailout).

Tensions arising from a dispute over the exploration and development of potentially lucrative reserves of natural gas in the waters surrounding the island, particularly in the absence of a political settlement of the Cyprus issue, intensified in late April 2012. The state-owned Türkiye Petrolleri Anonim Ortaklığı (Turkish Petroleum Corpn) began drilling for oil and gas near Famagusta, in the Turkish-controlled part of the island, as a direct response to the start of exploratory work by the Republic of Cyprus authorities in late 2011. The Republic of Cyprus Government claimed that the action was unlawful since some of the waters being explored fell within its exclusive economic zone. A memorandum of co-operation reached in July 2012 between the Republic of Cyprus and Israel concerning their respective maritime boundaries and use of any hydrocarbons discoveries, and, in March of that year, the confirmation of plans to construct, with Greece, an underwater cable to transport electricity from Israel to Greece via Cyprus by 2016 were denounced by the Turkish Government.

With his five-year term as President scheduled to end in February 2013, in mid-May 2012 Christofias announced that he would not seek re-election, citing his lack of optimism regarding a reunification of the island being achieved by that time. On 1 July the Republic of Cyprus assumed the rotating EU presidency of the EU for a six-month period; the Government of Turkey responded by freezing all high-level contacts with the EU. In mid-July the UN Security Council adopted a resolution extending the UNFICYP mandate until the end of January 2013; another six-month extension was agreed in late January 2013. Among the recommendations in the latter document, Resolution 2089, were the need for further military and social confidence-building measures to be implemented.

On 25 June 2012 the Government confirmed that it would apply to the European Financial Stability Facility for financial assistance to recapitalize the commercial banking sector—amid significant exposure to the debt-laden Greek economy—and towards its growing budget deficit (for further details, see Economic Affairs). The total value of the financial package being sought was thought to be in the region of €17,000m. Cyprus had, on 12 June, requested a €5,000m. loan from Russia, having secured a €2,500m. loan in late 2011; this request was, however, turned down. It was reported in November 2012 that a deal 'in principle' had been agreed between the so-called 'troika' of international lenders—the European Commission, the European Central Bank and the IMF—regarding the terms under which any such assistance would be provided, but that the exact amount of the bailout was to be dependent on the outcome of an official review into Cyprus's banking sector.

The 2013 presidential election and Cyprus's international bailout

At the presidential election, which was held on 17 February 2013, Nikos Anastasiades emerged as the leading candidate, winning 45.5% of the valid votes cast. His closest rival, Stavros Malas, a former Minister of Health who was supported by AKEL, garnered 26.9% of the vote. Giorgos Lillikas, a former Minister of Foreign Affairs whose candidacy had been endorsed by KISOS, took 24.9%. None of the eight remaining candidates secured more than 1.0% of the votes cast. Anastasiades and Malas proceeded to a second ballot on 24 February, at which Anastasiades secured an overwhelming victory, winning some 57.5% of the vote. The leader of DISY was duly sworn in as President upon the expiry of Christofias's term on 28 February. In his inaugural speech, Anastasiades pledged to seek a 'just' solution to the negotiations with the EU over Cyprus's financial situation, and to implement measures to promote economic growth; to continue negotiations over reunification; to expand diplomatic relations with the countries of the Middle East and with the USA, Russia and China; and to increase efforts to eliminate corruption. On 1 March a new Council of Ministers, comprising members of DISY, DIKO and Evro.Ko, took office. Ioannis Kasoulides of DISY was appointed as Minister of Foreign Affairs, in which role he had served in 1997–2003, while Michalis Sarris regained the finance portfolio he previously held in 2005–08. DIKO General Secretary Kyriakos Kenevezos became Minister of Education and Culture, while party colleague Fotis Fotiou assumed the post of Minister of Defence. Nikos Kouyalis of Evro.Ko entered the Government as Minister of Agriculture, Natural Resources and the Environment.

In mid-March 2013 it was announced that the Government and the troika had reached agreement on the provision of a €10,000m. bailout for Cyprus. However, the terms of the bailout prompted widespread public criticism, owing to the perceived severity of the terms. Cyprus was expected to raise an additional €5,800m. of funds, principally via a levy of 6.7% on all bank deposits below €100,000, and one of 9.9% on deposits over that amount. Protests erupted outside the parliament building and presidential palace in Nicosia, amid fears that significant withdrawals of funds by ordinary bank depositors could precipitate a collapse of the banking system. However, on 19 March the proposed terms of the bailout were overwhelmingly rejected by the House of Representatives. Three days later a plan for the managed liquidation of the Cyprus Popular Bank (also known as Laiki Bank—the country's second largest bank after the Bank of Cyprus) was approved by the legislature. The former was subsequently to be closed, after some of its assets were merged into the latter institution. On 25 March President Anastasiades announced the terms of a revised bailout plan. A levy of up to 40% was to be charged against deposits of more than €100,000 in the Bank of Cyprus and Laiki Bank, while smaller, insured deposits were to remain unaffected. To allay fears of a run on the country's banks, the Government imposed strict controls on financial transactions, including limits on daily withdrawals of funds and restrictions on transfers of money out of the country. The plan was formally approved by the eurozone ministers of finance in mid-April. Meanwhile, in early April, following the completion of negotiations over the bailout, Sarris resigned as Minister of Finance. He had been widely criticized both for the manner in which he had conducted the negotiations—the process of which was to be subject to a judicial inquiry—and for his role as Chairman of the failed Laiki Bank prior to August 2012. The recently appointed Minister of Labour and Social Insurance, Haris Georgiades, assumed the finance portfolio in his place, while Zeta Emilianidou, a former civil servant, joined the Government in Georgiades's former post. The imposition of a levy on bank deposits was expected to damage relations with Russia, as significant numbers of Russian individuals and businesses were thought to retain large deposits in Cypriot banks.

The terms of Cyprus's bailout agreement were narrowly approved by the House of Representatives (by 29 votes to 27) on 30 April 2013, and the first instalment (of some €3,000m.) was received by the Government in two stages in May and June. At the end of August the Russian Government agreed to extend the terms of the €2,500m. loan it had provided to the Republic of Cyprus over a five-year period in late 2011, to allow them to repay the debt in eight six-monthly instalments from 2016; the interest rate was also to be reduced to ease Cyprus's financial burden. After the legislature on 5–6 September 2013 adopted 14 legislative bills required, *inter alia*, to raise revenue and bring Cyprus's co-operative banks under the direct supervision of the Bank of Cyprus, the troika of international lenders commended the Government for the measures it had taken thus far to stabilize and reform the financial sector. On 13 September the eurozone finance ministers agreed to release the second instalment of the bailout, totalling €1,500m.

The UN Security Council extended the UNFICYP mandate for a further six-month period on 30 July 2013, and again on 30 January 2014. In its latest document, Resolution 2135, the Security Council expressed disappointment that formal negotiations on a settlement for the island remained stalled, and urged both sides to achieve substantive progress to enable a resumption of the talks as soon as possible. Since the election of President Anastasiades in February 2013, the Republic of Cyprus authorities had been largely preoccupied with negotiations concerning the international bailout; it was also feared that the new Government would adopt a more hardline approach towards the peace talks. In September the UN Secretary-General, Ban Ki-Moon, held discussions with both Anastasiades and Eroğlu in New York in an effort to break the deadlock between the two sides. However, despite the UN expressing hopes in July 2013 that reunification negotiations would resume in October, a failure by the two leaders to agree on the wording of a joint statement hampered any such progress being made. On 16 July 2013 Andreas Mavroyiannis was appointed as the leading Greek Cypriot negotiator in any forthcoming talks, a role which had previously been held by the President.

Recent developments: resumption of reunification talks under President Anastasiades

Finally, after months of protracted discussions, it was announced on 7 February 2014 that the two leaders had reached agreement on a joint communiqué which would enable them formally to restart the peace process. The roadmap for a resolution to the Cyprus problem reaffirmed their mutual intention to create a bizonal, bicommunal federation with political equality, and with a single sovereignty and international legal personality. Both Anastasiades and Eroğlu declared that the current political situation in Cyprus was 'unacceptable'. Following the announcement, Alexander Downer declared that he was to resign as the UN Secretary-General's Special Adviser on Cyprus. A meeting conducted between Anastasiades and Eroğlu, under UN auspices, in Nicosia on 11 February marked the formal resumption of reunification negotiations after a hiatus of almost two years; Mavroyiannis and the Secretary-General's Special Representative in Cyprus, Lisa Buttenheim, also attended the talks. Meanwhile, the newly elected leader of DIKO, Nicolas Papadopoulos, raised speculation that his party might seek to withdraw its four ministers from the governing coalition, strongly criticizing Anastasiades for having granted too many concessions to the Turkish Cypriots in the joint communiqué. In early March DIKO did indeed withdraw from the coalition. In the subsequent reorganization of the Council of Ministers on 14 March, DIKO's three ministers were replaced by appointees from DISY and independents. DISY's Tasos Mitsopoulos (hitherto the Minister of Communications and Works) was appointed as Minister of Defence, while Marios Demetriades, an independent, joined the cabinet in Mitsopoulos' previous post. Independents Costas Kadis and Philippos Patsalis, respectively, became Minister of Health and Minister of Education and Culture. However, on 22 March it was announced that Mitsopoulos had died, following an unexpected illness. Christoforos Fokaides, also of DISY, assumed responsibility for the defence portfolio on 7 April.

CONSTITUTION AND GOVERNMENT

The 1960 Constitution provided for a system of government in which power would be shared by the Greek and Turkish communities in proportion to their numbers. This Constitution officially remains in force, but since the ending of Turkish participation in the Government in 1963, and particularly since the creation of a separate Turkish area in northern Cyprus in 1974, each community has administered its own affairs, refusing to recognize the authority of the other's Government. The Greek Cypriot administration of the Republic of Cyprus is internationally recognized as the Government of all Cyprus, although it has no Turkish participation and no de facto control over the northern part of the island. The President is elected for a term of five years and appoints a Council of Ministers. (Under the 1960 Constitution, the position of Vice-President and three posts in the Council of Ministers were reserved for Turkish Cypriots.) The House of Representatives comprises 56 deputies, who are elected for a five-year term. (Following amendments to the Constitution in 1985, the House of Representatives officially comprised 80 seats, of which 24 were allocated to Turkish Cypriots).

REGIONAL AND INTERNATIONAL CO-OPERATION

Following an application by the Government in July 1990, the Republic of Cyprus officially acceded to the European Union (EU, see p. 273) on 1 May 2004 (see Contemporary Political History). Cyprus also participates in the Council of Europe (see p. 252) and the Organization for Security and Co-operation in Europe (OSCE, see p. 387).

Cyprus became a member of the UN on 20 September 1960 and, as a contracting party to the General Agreement on Tariffs and Trade, it joined the World Trade Organization (WTO, see p. 434) on its establishment in 1995. Cyprus is also a member of The Commonwealth (see p. 236).

ECONOMIC AFFAIRS

In 2012, according to estimates by the World Bank, Cyprus's gross national income (GNI), measured at average 2010–12 prices, was US $22,708m., equivalent to $26,000 per head (or $29,400 per head on an international purchasing-power parity basis). During 2003–12, it was estimated, the population increased at an average annual rate of 1.4%, while gross domestic product (GDP) per head decreased, in real terms, by an average of 0.1% per year. Overall GDP increased, in real terms, at an average annual rate of 2.0% in 2003–12; it grew by an estimated 0.5% in 2011, but declined by 2.4% in 2012, according to both constant price data and chain-linked methodology.

Agriculture (including hunting, forestry and fishing) contributed 2.5% of GDP in 2012, according to provisional figures. An estimated 2.9% of the employed labour force were engaged in the sector in that year. The principal crops are citrus fruit, potatoes and vegetables; grapes are cultivated notably for the wine industry, and barley is the principal cereal crop. Prepared foodstuffs, vegetable and vegetable products contributed 14.4% of total export earnings in 2012. In an effort to offset Cyprus's vulnerability to drought, during the 1990s the Government granted concessions for the construction and operation of several desalination plants. According to the World Bank, the GDP of the agricultural sector declined by an average of 4.2% per year in 2003–08. In 2012, according to chain-linked methodologies, agricultural GDP increased by 0.5%, according to provisional figures.

Industry (comprising mining, manufacturing, construction and power) accounted for 14.9% of GDP in 2012, according to provisional figures, and engaged an estimated 20.1% of the employed labour force. According to the World Bank, industrial GDP increased by an average of 2.8% per year in 2003–08.

Mining and quarrying, principally the extraction of material for the construction industry, provided only 0.2% of GDP in 2012, according to provisional figures, and engaged about 0.2% of the employed labour force in the same year. In 2001 it was announced that 25 foreign oil companies had expressed interest in acquiring exploration rights for potential petroleum and gas deposits in the eastern Mediterranean within Cyprus's exclusive economic zone. The Government signed respective agreements with Egypt and Lebanon in 2006 and 2007 concerning the joint exploration of potential offshore oil- and gasfields, and a similar deal with Israel in 2010 to develop natural gas reserves. These agreements have provoked a strong response from the Turkish authorities, which in April 2012 began exploring the Famagusta area of the 'TRNC' for potential hydrocarbons fields (see Contemporary Political History). The Republic of Cyprus Government concluded a second licensing round for its own exploratory work in May, although a new survey revealed in late 2013 that Cyprus's offshore gasfield was actually smaller than initial estimates had shown. According to chain-linked methodologies, mining GDP declined by 27.9% in 2012, according to provisional figures.

Manufacturing accounted for 5.7% of GDP in 2012, according to provisional figures, and engaged about 7.5% of the employed labour force. The GDP of the manufacturing sector remained constant during 2003–08, according to the World Bank. According to chain-linked methodologies, the sector's GDP decreased by a provisional 7.4% in 2012.

Construction accounted for 5.8% of GDP in 2012, and engaged about 10.5% of the employed labour force in that year, according to provisional figures. According to chain-linked methodologies, construction GDP decreased by an estimated 9.8% in 2011 and further by a provisional 19.5% in 2012.

Energy is derived almost entirely from imported petroleum, and mineral fuels and lubricants comprised 30.2% of total imports (including goods for re-export) in 2012. The Government is encouraging the development of renewable energy sources, including solar, wind and hydroelectric power. Cyprus suffered from power shortages during 2011–12, as a result of the July 2011 explosion (see Contemporary Political History), which caused severe damage to the Vassiliko power station. Following extensive repairs, the power plant was fully operational again in August 2013.

The services sector contributed 82.6% of GDP in 2012, according to provisional figures, and engaged 76.9% of the employed labour force. Within the sector, financial and business services provided a provisional 28.6% of total GDP in 2012, and generated 15.1% of employment. The Government has also attempted to enhance Cyprus's status as an entrepôt for shipping and trade throughout the eastern Mediterranean. In 2012 tourism arrivals were recorded at 2.46m., while receipts from tourism in that year amounted to an estimated €1,927.7m. The GDP of the services sector increased at an average annual rate of 4.7% in 2003–08, according to the World Bank.

According to the IMF, in 2012 Cyprus recorded a visible merchandise trade deficit of US $4,154m. and a deficit of $1,577m. on the current account of the balance of payments. In 2012 the principal source of imports was Greece (21.2%), followed by Israel, Italy, the United Kingdom, Germany, the Netherlands and France. Greece was also the principal purchaser of exports in that year, taking 20.3% of the total; the United Kingdom was also an important market. The principal exports in 2012 were chemicals and related products, mineral fuels and lubricants, machinery, mechanical and electrical appliances and their parts, iron and steel base metals and their articles, prepared foodstuffs, live animals and animal products, and vegetables and vegetable products. Among the principal imports in that year were mineral fuels and lubricants, machinery, mechanical and electrical appliances and their parts, chemical and related products, and vehicles, aircraft, vessels and associated transport equipment.

In 2012 the Government recorded a budget deficit of an estimated C£874.6m., equivalent to 4.9% of GDP. General government gross debt was C£15,350m. in the same year, equivalent to 85.8% of GDP. Cyprus's annual rate of inflation averaged 2.6% in 2005–12, with consumer prices increasing by 2.4% in 2012. The rate of unemployment was some 11.8% of the labour force in 2012.

The economy of Cyprus and its future development are inextricably linked to the continuing division of the island, which intensive efforts by the UN and the European Union (EU) have failed to resolve. The Republic of Cyprus adopted the European single currency on 1 January 2008. Negative growth was recorded in 2009, principally due to declining activity in the construction, tourism and financial services sectors as a result of financial turmoil in the global credit markets from late 2008. Following a sharp increase in the budget deficit, to 6.1% of GDP, in 2009, and an anticipated rise in public debt to 62.3% of GDP in 2010, Cyprus was placed under the EU's excessive deficit procedure in July 2010; the authorities' target was to reduce the fiscal deficit to below 3% by 2012. Amid the ongoing financial crisis within the eurozone, new economic measures approved by parliament in December 2011 included a 2% increase in the standard rate of value-added tax from 1 March 2012, while public sector salaries were frozen until the end of 2013. However, despite efforts to restore confidence in Cyprus's financial system, the banking sector (in particular the two largest banks, the Bank of Cyprus and Laiki Bank) had been heavily exposed to sovereign debt in Greece. As a consequence of this and the failure of the authorities to borrow money owing to a successive lowering of Cyprus's sovereign rating by international credit ratings agencies since 2010, in June 2012 the Government began negotiations with the 'troika' of international lenders concerning the terms of a bailout. An agreement was reached in March 2013, under the terms of which Cyprus was to raise €5,800m. in addition to the €10,000m. disbursed by the troika. Initial proposals to raise the sum through a levy of 6.7% on insured bank deposits (amounts below €100,000) and 9.9% on sums above €100,000 prompted demonstrations in Nicosia, and were subsequently rejected by the legislature. Finally, a revised plan to impose a levy of up to 40% on deposits of more than €100,000 held in the Bank of Cyprus and Laiki Bank was approved. Additionally, the latter was to be closed and some of its assets transferred to the former. GDP contracted by 2.4% in 2012, and by some 6.0% in 2013. Meanwhile, unemployment increased from 11.8% in mid-2012 to around 17% in late 2013. Following a budget deficit of 6.0% of GDP in 2011, a deficit of 4.9% was recorded in 2012—still above the Government's revised target of 4.5%. The Ministry of Finance forecast a deficit of 7% for 2014, lower than the target figure of 8.25% set by the troika, as a result of significant reductions in public expenditure. In April 2013 President Nikos Anastasiades announced a series of measures which were intended to precipitate an economic recovery. There were positive results: tourism receipts during the first 10 months of 2013 exceeded those for the whole of 2012, and by early 2014 the Government was planning to ease the strict capital controls imposed in March 2013. Following a third review of the €10,000m. economic adjustment programme by the troika in early February 2014, the Government was praised for significantly exceeding its fiscal targets and for stabilizing the financial sector. Although the IMF anticipated a contraction in GDP of 4.8% in 2014, a return to growth was expected in 2015. The troika raised concerns, however, over Cyprus's rising unemployment rate and the decline in disposable incomes.

PUBLIC HOLIDAYS

2015: 1 January (New Year's Day), 6 January (Epiphany), 3 March (Green Monday), 25 March (Greek Independence Day), 1 April (Anniversary of Cyprus Liberation Struggle), 10–13 April (Easter), 1 May (May Day), 31 May (Pentecost), 15 August (Assumption), 1 October (Independence Day), 28 October (Greek National Day), 24–26 December (Christmas).

Statistical Survey

Source (unless otherwise indicated): Statistical Service of Cyprus (CYSTAT), Ministry of Finance, Michalakis Karaolis St, 1444 Nicosia; tel. 22602102; fax 22661313; e-mail enquiries@cystat.mof.gov.cy; internet www.cystat.gov.cy.

Note: Since July 1974 the northern part of Cyprus has been under Turkish occupation. As a result, the majority of statistics relating to subsequent periods do not cover the whole island. See section on the 'Turkish Republic of Northern Cyprus' for detailed data on the Turkish-occupied region.

AREA AND POPULATION

Area: 9,251 sq km (3,572 sq miles), incl. Turkish-occupied region; 5,896 sq km (2,276 sq miles), government-controlled area only.

Population: 703,529, excl. Turkish-occupied region, at census of 1 October 2001 (adjusted figures); 867,600, incl. 88,900 in Turkish-occupied region, at 31 December 2006 (official estimate); 840,407 (males 408,780, females 431,627), excl. Turkish-occupied region, at census of 1 October 2011. Note: Figures for the Turkish-occupied region exclude settlers from Turkey, estimated at 115,000 in 2001.

Density (at 2011 census): 90.8 per sq km.

Population by Age and Sex (excl. Turkish-occupied region, population at 2011 census): *0–14:* 134,948 (males 69,161, females 65,787); *15–64:* 593,593 (males 287,904, females 305,689); *65 and over:* 111,866 (males 51,715, females 60,151); *Total* 840,407 (males 408,780, females 431,627).

Ethnic Groups (31 December 2001, estimates): Greeks 639,400 (80.6%), Turks 87,600 (11.1%), Others 66,100 (8.3%); Total 793,100.

Districts (excl. Turkish-controlled region, population at 2011 census): Ammochostos 46,629; Larnaka (Larnaca) 143,192; Lefkosia 326,980; Lemesos (Limassol) 235,330; Pafos (Paphos) 88,276; *Total* 840,407.

Principal Towns (population at 31 December 2011): Nicosia (capital) 244,500 (excl. Turkish-occupied portion); Limassol 183,555; Larnaca 85,874; Paphos 63,541.

Births, Marriages and Deaths (government-controlled area, 2011): Registered live births 9,622 (birth rate 11.3 per 1,000); Registered marriages 13,248 (incl. 6,210 residents of Cyprus); Registered deaths 5,504 (death rate 6.5 per 1,000).

Life Expectancy (years at birth): 79.5 (males 77.5; females 81.6) in 2011. Source: World Bank, World Development Indicators database.

Economically Active Population (government-controlled area, '000 persons aged 15 years and over, excl. armed forces, labour force survey 2012): Agriculture, forestry and fishing 11.3; Mining and quarrying 0.9; Manufacturing 29.1; Electricity, gas and water 7.6; Construction 40.7; Wholesale and retail trade; repair of motor vehicles, motor cycles and personal and household goods 72.7; Restaurants and hotels 30.0; Transport, storage and communications 25.4; Financial intermediation 23.3; Real estate, renting and business activities 35.3; Public administration and defence 25.0; Education 28.8; Health and social work 16.2; Other community, social and personal service activities 17.1; Private households 23.7; Extra-territorial organizations 1.4; *Total* 388.6; Unemployed 52.0; *Total labour force* 440.6.

HEALTH AND WELFARE

Key Indicators

Total Fertility Rate (children per woman, 2011): 1.5.

Under-5 Mortality Rate (per 1,000 live births, 2011): 3.

HIV/AIDS (% of persons aged 15–49, 2007): 0.25.

Physicians (per 1,000 head, 2008): 2.6.

Hospital Beds (per 1,000 head, 2008): 3.8.

Health Expenditure (2010): US $ per head (PPP): 2,218.

Health Expenditure (2010): % of GDP: 7.4.

Health Expenditure (2010): public (% of total): 43.3.

Total Carbon Dioxide Emissions ('000 metric tons, 2010): 7,708.0.

Carbon Dioxide Emissions Per Head (metric tons, 2010): 7.0.

Human Development Index (2012): ranking: 31.

Human Development Index (2012): index: 0.848.

For sources and definitions, see explanatory note on p. vi.

AGRICULTURE

Principal Crops (government-controlled area, '000 metric tons, 2012): Wheat 19.4; Barley 40.7; Potatoes 113.3; Olives 14.9; Cabbages and other brassicas 2.3; Tomatoes 14.3; Cucumbers and gherkins 9.5; Onions, dry 6.6; Bananas 6.9; Oranges 22.1; Tangerines, mandarins, etc. 40.2; Lemons and limes 14.1; Grapefruit and pomelos 26.0; Apples 6.4; Grapes 47.0; Cantaloupes and other melons 7.7.

Livestock (government-controlled area, '000 head, 2012): Cattle 56.9; Sheep 346.8; Goats 271.2; Pigs 394.7; Chickens 3,103.0.

Livestock Products (government-controlled area, '000 metric tons, 2012): Sheep meat 3.1; Goat meat 2.7; Pig meat 51.7; Chicken meat 25.1; Cows' milk 153.0; Hen eggs 8.5.

Forestry (government-controlled area, '000 cubic metres, 2012): Roundwood removals (excl. bark) 11.0; Sawnwood production (incl. railway sleepers) 2.6.

Fishing (government-controlled area, metric tons, live weight, 2011): Capture 1,184 (FAO estimate—Bogue 109; Picarels 82); Aquaculture 4,745 (European seabass 1,517; Gilthead seabream 3,113); *Total catch* 5,929 (FAO estimate).

Source: FAO.

MINING

Selected Products (government-controlled area, '000 metric tons, 2010): Sand and gravel 12,525.0; Gypsum 227.7; Bentonite 157.4; Umber 6.3.

INDUSTRY

Selected Products (government-controlled area, 2012 unless otherwise indicated): Wine 14.2m. litres (2011); Beer 33.5m. litres; Soft drinks 32.1m. litres; Cigarettes 3,803m. (2001); Footwear 89,974 pairs (2011); Bricks 35.0m (2011); Floor and wall tiles 40,000 sq m (2011); Cement 1,080,019 metric tons; Electric energy 4,929.1m. kWh (2011).

FINANCE

Currency and Exchange Rates: 100 cent = 1 euro (€). *Sterling and Dollar Equivalents* (31 December 2013): £1 sterling = €1.194; US $1 = €0.725; €10 = £8.37 = US $13.79. *Average Exchange Rate* (euros per US dollar): 0.7550 in 2010; 0.7194 in 2011; 0.7779 in 2012. Note: The Cyprus pound (C£) was formerly in use. On 1 January 2008 the government-controlled area of Cyprus adopted the euro, which became the sole legal tender in that area from the end of the same month.

Budget (government-controlled area, € million, 2012): *Revenue:* Taxation 5,585.4 (Direct taxes 2,072.7, Indirect taxes 2,499.9, Social security contributions 1,012.7); Other current revenue 911.0; Total 6,496.4, excl. grants from abroad (105.7). *Expenditure:* Current expenditure 7,100.0 (Wages and salaries 1,907.2, Other goods and services 513.7, Social security payments 1,497.1, Subsidies 95.5, Interest payments 652.6, Pensions and gratuities 635.8, Social pension 64.4, Other current transfers 1,664.0, Unallocated 69.8); Capital expenditure (investments) 376.7; Total 7,476.7. Source: Budgets and Fiscal Control Directorate, Ministry of Finance, Nicosia.

International Reserves (government-controlled area, US $ million at 31 December 2012): Gold (national valuation) 742.1; IMF special drawing rights 177.2; Reserve position in IMF 127.9; Foreign exchange 142.5; Other reserve assets 1.3; Total 1,191.0. Source: IMF, *International Financial Statistics*.

Money Supply (incl. shares, government-controlled area, € million at 31 December 2012): Currency issued 1,739 (Currency issued by the Central Bank of Cyprus 1,739); Demand deposits 10,081; Other deposits 33,145; Securities other than shares 1,758; Shares and other equity 16,078; Other items (net) –862; *Total* 61,939. Source: IMF, *International Financial Statistics*.

Cost of Living (government-controlled area, Retail Price Index; base: 2005 = 100): 112.9 in 2010; 116.6 in 2011; 119.4 in 2012.

Gross Domestic Product (government-controlled area, € million at current prices): 17,406.0 in 2010; 17,878.0 in 2011; 17,720.2 in 2012 (provisional figure).

Expenditure on the Gross Domestic Product (government-controlled area, € million at current prices, 2012, provisional figures): Government final consumption expenditure 3,438.2; Private final consumption expenditure 12,087.3; Increase in stocks 234.6; Gross fixed capital formation 2,430.0; *Total domestic expenditure* 18,190.1; Exports of goods and services 7,710.2; *Less* Imports of goods and services 8,180.1; *GDP in market prices* 17,720.2.

Gross Domestic Product by Economic Activity (government-controlled area, € million at current prices, 2012, provisional figures): Agriculture, forestry and fishing 407.6; Mining and quarrying 28.5; Manufacturing 915.9; Electricity, gas and water supply 515.8; Construction 942.1; Wholesale and retail trade 1,910.9; Restaurants and hotels 1,119.2; Transport, storage and communications 1,450.2; Financial intermediation 1,542.4; Real estate, renting and business activities 3,059.0; Public administration and defence 1,726.0; Education 1,106.6; Health and social work 687.4; Other community, social and personal services 510.5; Private households with employed persons 194.4; *Sub-total* 16,116.5; Import duties 57.4; Value-added tax 1,546.3; *GDP in market prices* 17,720.2.

Balance of Payments (government-controlled area, US $ million, 2012): Exports of goods 2,591; Imports of goods −6,745; *Balance on goods* −4,154; Exports of services 7,166; Imports of services −3,724; *Balance on goods and services* −712; Primary income received 3,428; Primary income paid −4,015; *Balance on goods, services and primary income* −1,300; Secondary income received 663; Secondary income paid −940; *Current balance* −1,577; Capital account (net) 30; Direct investment assets 311; Direct investment liabilities 1,233; Portfolio investment assets 8,519; Portfolio investment liabilities −1,584; Financial derivatives and employee stock options assets −464; Financial derivatives and employee stock options liabilities −669; Other investment assets −5,669; Other investment liabilities −663; Net errors and omissions 463; *Reserves and related items* −71. Source: IMF, *International Financial Statistics*.

EXTERNAL TRADE

Principal Commodities (distribution by HS, government-controlled area, US $ million, 2012): *Imports c.i.f.:* Vegetable and vegetable products 277.8; Prepared foodstuffs; beverages, spirits, vinegar; tobacco and articles thereof 780.8; Mineral products 2,233.4 (Mineral fuels, oils, distillation products, etc. 2,224.6); Chemicals and related products 699.0 (Pharmaceutical products 285.3); Plastics, rubber, and articles thereof 260.5; Textiles and textile articles 359.9; Iron and steel, other base metals and articles of base metal 346.3; Machinery and mechanical appliances; electrical equipment; parts thereof 795.9 (Machinery, boilers, etc. 396.0; Electrical and electronic equipment 399.9); Vehicles, aircraft, vessels and associated transport equipment 418.0 (Vehicles other than railway, tramway 385.9); Miscellaneous manufactured articles 222.6; Total (incl. others) 7,376.9. *Exports f.o.b.:* Live animals and animal products 122.2 (Dairy products, eggs, honey and edible animal products 83.2); Vegetables and vegetable products 100.6; Prepared foodstuffs; beverages, spirits, vinegar; tobacco and articles thereof 128.7 (Tobacco and tobacco products 59.3); Mineral products 366.5 (Mineral fuels, oils, distillation products, etc. 335.4); Chemicals and related products 451.2 (Organic chemicals 144.3; Medicinal and pharmaceutical products 283.6); Pearls, precious or semi-precious stones, precious metals, and articles thereof 77.8; Iron and steel, other base metals and articles of base metal 146.7 (Copper and articles thereof 57.8); Machinery and mechanical appliances; electrical equipment; parts thereof 171.3 (Machinery, boilers, etc. 63.4; Electrical and electronic equipment 107.8); Vehicles, aircraft, vessels and associated transport equipment 80.1; Total (incl. others) 1,826.0. Source: Trade Map-Trade Competitiveness Map, International Trade Centre, www.intracen.org/marketanalysis.

Principal Trading Partners (government-controlled area, US $ million, 2012): *Imports c.i.f.:* Belgium 179.9; Brazil 111.7; China, People's Republic 339.7; France (incl. Monaco) 434.7; Germany 515.1; Greece 1,567.3; Israel 868.6; Italy 603.1; Netherlands 486.1; Russia 77.1; Spain 274.3; United Kingdom 529.4; USA 94.0; Total (incl. others) 7,376.9. *Exports f.o.b.* (incl. re-exports): China, People's Republic 36.2; Egypt 27.2; Germany 42.2; Greece 369.9; Hong Kong 30.0; India 18.7; Israel 51.0; Italy 50.9; Jordan 21.1; Lebanon 64.6; Netherlands 20.9; Romania 20.3; Russia 26.0; Sweden 21.5; United Arab Emirates 44.9; United Kingdom 163.3; USA 59.1; Total (incl. others) 1,826.0. Source: Trade Map-Trade Competitiveness Map, International Trade Centre, www.intracen.org/marketanalysis.

TRANSPORT

Road Traffic (government-controlled area, licensed motor vehicles, 31 December 2011): Private passenger cars 460,085; Taxis and self-drive cars 9,458; Buses and coaches 3,461; Lorries and vans 118,003; Motorcycles 39,803; Total (incl. others) 651,671.

Shipping (government-controlled area, freight traffic, '000 metric tons, 2011): Goods loaded 1,693, Goods unloaded 5,842. *Flag Registered Fleet:* At 31 December 2013 a total of 1,210 merchant vessels (combined displacement 21,365,427 grt) were registered in Cyprus (Source: Lloyd's List Intelligence, www.lloydslistintelligence.com).

Civil Aviation (government-controlled area, 2011): Overall passenger traffic 7,233,428; Total freight transported 38,503 metric tons.

TOURISM

Foreign Tourist Arrivals (government-controlled area, '000): 2,173.0 in 2010; 2,392.2 in 2011; 2,464.9 in 2012 (estimate).

Arrivals by Country of Residence (government-controlled area, '000, 2012, estimates): Germany 144.4; Greece 133.0; Norway 69.4; Russia 474.4; Sweden 117.3; United Kingdom 959.5; Total (incl. others) 2,464.9.

Tourism Receipts (government-controlled area, € million): 1,549.8 in 2010; 1,749.3 in 2011; 1,927.7 in 2012.

COMMUNICATIONS MEDIA

Telephones (main lines in use, 2012): 373,196.

Mobile Cellular Telephones (subscribers, 2012): 1,110,935.

Personal Computers: 324,000 (383.4 per 1,000 persons) in 2006.

Internet Subscribers (2011): 212,100.

Broadband Subscribers (2012): 217,072.

Source: International Telecommunication Union.

EDUCATION

2011/12 (government-controlled area): Pre-primary: 672 institutions, 2,250 teachers, 28,687 pupils; Primary: 365 institutions, 4,699 teachers, 53,955 pupils; Secondary (Gymnasiums and Lyceums): 168 institutions, 7,560 teachers, 62,740 pupils; Tertiary (incl. University of Cyprus): 44 institutions, 1,826 teachers, 31,772 students (of whom 8,540 were foreign students). Note: 19,199 Cypriot students were studying abroad in 2010/11.

Pupil-teacher Ratio (primary education): 11.5 in 2011/12.

Adult Literacy Rate (2011 census): 98.7% (males 99.3%; females 98.1%).

Directory

The Government

HEAD OF STATE

President: NIKOS ANASTASIADES (took office 28 February 2013).

COUNCIL OF MINISTERS

(April 2014)

A coalition Government formed by the Democratic Rally (DISY), the European Party (Evro.Ko) and independents (Ind.).

Minister of Foreign Affairs: IOANNIS KASOULIDES (DISY).

Minister of Finance: HARIS GEORGIADES (DISY).

Minister of the Interior: SOCRATES HASIKOS (DISY).

Minister of Defence: CHRISTOFOROS FOKAIDES (DISY).

Minister of Education and Culture: COSTAS KADIS (Ind.).

Minister of Communications and Works: MARIOS DEMETRIADES (Ind.).

Minister of Commerce, Industry and Tourism: GEORGIOS LAKKOTRYPIS (DIKO).

Minister of Agriculture, Natural Resources and the Environment: NIKOS KOUYALIS (Evro.Ko).

Minister of Labour and Social Insurance: GEORGIA (ZETA) EMILIANIDOU (Ind.).

Minister of Justice and Public Order: IONAS NICOLAOU (DISY).

Minister of Health: PHILIPPOS PATSALIS (Ind.).

Government Spokesman: CHRISTOS STYLIANIDES (DISY).

MINISTRIES

Office of the President: Presidential Palace, Demosthenis Severis Ave, 1400 Nicosia; tel. 22867400; fax 22663799; e-mail info@presidency.gov.cy; internet www.presidency.gov.cy.

Ministry of Agriculture, Natural Resources and the Environment: Loukis Akritas Ave, 1411 Nicosia; tel. 22408305; fax 22408352; e-mail registry@moa.gov.cy; internet www.moa.gov.cy.

Ministry of Commerce, Industry and Tourism: 6 Andreas Araouzos St, 1421 Nicosia; tel. 22867100; fax 22375120; e-mail perm.sec@mcit.gov.cy; internet www.mcit.gov.cy.

Ministry of Communications and Works: 28 Achaeon St, Agios Andreas, 1424 Nicosia; tel. 22800288; fax 22776266; e-mail ipiresia.politi@mcw.gov.cy; internet www.mcw.gov.cy.

Ministry of Defence: 4 Emmanuel Roides Ave, 1432 Nicosia; tel. 22807724; fax 22429392; e-mail othellos4@cytanet.com.cy; internet www.mod.gov.cy.

Ministry of Education and Culture: Kimonos and Thoukididis, 1434 Nicosia; tel. 22800600; fax 22426349; e-mail moec@moec.gov.cy; internet www.moec.gov.cy.

Ministry of Finance: Cnr Michalakis Karaolis St and Gregoriou Afxentiou St, 1439 Nicosia; tel. 22601104; fax 22602741; e-mail registry@mof.gov.cy; internet www.mof.gov.cy.

Ministry of Foreign Affairs: Presidential Palace Ave, 1447 Nicosia; tel. 22651000; fax 22661881; e-mail minforeign1@mfa.gov.cy; internet www.mfa.gov.cy.

Ministry of Health: 1 Prodomou and 17 Chilonos, 1448 Nicosia; tel. 22605300; fax 22605487; e-mail perm.sec@moh.gov.cy; internet www.moh.gov.cy.

Ministry of the Interior: Demosthenis Severis Ave, Ex Secretariat Compound, 1453 Nicosia; tel. 22867800; fax 22671465; e-mail cgregoriades@moi.gov.cy; internet www.moi.gov.cy.

Ministry of Justice and Public Order: 125 Athalassa Ave, 1461 Nicosia; tel. 22805950; fax 22518356; e-mail registry@mjpo.gov.cy; internet www.mjpo.gov.cy.

Ministry of Labour and Social Insurance: 7 Byron Ave, 1463 Nicosia; tel. 22401600; fax 22670993; e-mail administration@mlsi.gov.cy; internet www.mlsi.gov.cy.

President

Presidential Election, First Ballot, 17 February 2013

Candidate	Valid votes	%
Nikos Anastasiades (DISY)	200,591	45.46
Stavros Malas (Ind., with AKEL support)	118,755	26.91
Giorgos Lillikas (Ind., with KISOS support)	109,996	24.93
Georgios Charalambous (ELAM)	3,899	0.88
Praxoula Antoniadou Kyriakou (EDI)	2,678	0.61
Makaria-Andri Stylianou (Ind.)	1,898	0.43
Lakis Ioannou (LASOK)	1,278	0.29
Solon Gregoriou (Ind.)	792	0.18
Kostas Kyriacou (Ind.)	722	0.16
Andreas Efstratiou (Ind.)	434	0.10
Loukas Stavrou (Ind.)	213	0.05
Total	441,256*	100.00

* Excluding 12,278 blank or invalid votes (2.7% of the total votes cast).

Presidential Election, Second Ballot, 24 February 2013

Candidate	Votes	%
Nikos Anastasiades (DISY)	236,965	57.48
Stavros Malas (Ind., with AKEL support)	175,267	42.52
Total*	412,232	100.00

* Excluding 32,777 blank or invalid votes (7.36% of total votes cast).

Legislature

The House of Representatives originally consisted of 50 members, 35 from the Greek community and 15 from the Turkish community, elected for a term of five years. In January 1964 the Turkish members withdrew and set up the 'Turkish Legislative Assembly of the Turkish Cypriot Administration'. At the 1985 elections the membership of the House was expanded to 80 members, of whom 56 were to be from the Greek community and 24 from the Turkish community (according to the ratio of representation specified in the Constitution).

House of Representatives: 1402 Nicosia; tel. 22407300; fax 22668611; e-mail vouli@parliament.cy; internet www.parliament.cy.

President: Yiannakis Omirou.

Elections for the Greek Representatives, 22 May 2011

Party	Votes	% of Votes	Seats
Democratic Rally (DISY)	138,682	34.28	20
Progressive Party of the Working People (AKEL)	132,171	32.67	19
Democratic Party (DIKO)	63,763	15.76	9
Movement of Social Democrats EDEK (KISOS)	36,113	8.93	5
European Party (Evro.Ko)	15,711	3.88	2
Cyprus Green Party (KOP)	8,960	2.21	1
Others	9,177	2.27	—
Total*	404,577	100.00	56

* Excluding 8,701 invalid votes and 4,969 blank votes.

Political Organizations

Agonistiko Dimokratiko Kinima (ADIK) (Fighting Democratic Movement): POB 216095, 80 Archbishop Makarios III Ave, 2085 Nicosia; tel. 22765353; fax 22375737; e-mail info@adik.org.cy; internet www.adik.org.cy; f. 1999; centre-right; supports independent and united Cyprus and a settlement based on UN resolutions; Pres. Dinos Michaelides; Gen. Sec. Spyros Stefou.

Anorthotiko Komma Ergazomenou Laou (AKEL) (Progressive Party of the Working People): POB 21827, 4 E. Papaioannou St, 1075 Nicosia; tel. 22761121; fax 22761574; e-mail k.e.akel@cytanet.com.cy; internet www.akel.org.cy; f. 1941; successor to the Communist Party of Cyprus (f. 1926); Marxist-Leninist; supports united, sovereign, independent, federal and demilitarized Cyprus; over 14,000 mems; Sec.-Gen. Andros Kyprianou.

Dimokratiko Komma (DIKO) (Democratic Party): POB 23979, 50 Grivas Dhigenis Ave, 1080 Nicosia; tel. 22873800; fax 22873801; e-mail diko@diko.org.cy; internet www.diko.org.cy; f. 1976; absorbed Enosi Kentrou (Centre Union, f. 1981) in 1989; supports settlement of the Cyprus problem based on UN resolutions; Pres. Nicolas Papadopoulos; Gen. Sec. Kyriakos Kenevezos.

Dimokratikos Synagermos (DISY) (Democratic Rally): POB 25305, 25 Pindarou St, 1308 Nicosia; tel. 22883000; fax 22753821; e-mail disy@disy.org.cy; internet www.disy.org.cy; f. 1976; absorbed Democratic National Party (DEK) in 1977, New Democratic Front (NEDIPA) in 1988 and Liberal Party in 1998; advocates the reunification of Cyprus on the basis of a bizonal federation; also advocates market economy with restricted state intervention and increased state social role; 40,000 mems; Pres. Averof Neophytou; Dir-Gen. Demetris Stylianou.

Enomeni Dimokrates (EDI) (United Democrats): POB 23494, 1683 Nicosia; tel. 22663030; fax 22664747; e-mail edicy@spidernet.com.cy; internet www.edi.org.cy; f. by merger of Ananeotiko Dimokratiko Socialistiko Kinima (ADISOK—Democratic Socialist Reform Movement) and Kinima ton Eleftheron Dimokraton (KED—Movement of Free Democrats); Pres. Praxoula Antoniadou Kyriakou; Gen. Sec. Dr George D. Christodoulides.

Epalxi Anasygrotisis Kentrou (EPALXI) (Political Forum for the Restructuring of the Centre): 1 Lambousa St, 1095 Nicosia; POB 22119, 1517 Nicosia; tel. 22777000; fax 22779939; e-mail info@epalxi.com; internet www.epalxi.com; f. 1998; aims to achieve a wider grouping of all centrist social-democratic movements; supports a settlement to the Cyprus problem based on the principles of the Rule of Law, international law and respect for human rights for all citizens, and the establishment of a democratic federal system of govt; Pres. Kypros Chrysostomides.

Ethniko Laiko Metopo (ELAM) (National People's Front): Nicosia; tel. 96645264; e-mail ethnikolaikometwpo@gmail.com; internet www.elamcy.com; right-wing, nationalist; Leader Christos Christou.

Evropaiko Komma (Evro.Ko) (European Party): Stasandrou 27, 1060 Nicosia; tel. 22460033; fax 22761144; e-mail evropaiko.komma@cytanet.com.cy; internet www.evropaikokomma.org; f. 2005 by fmr mems of Neoi Orizontes (NEO) and other political orgs; Pres. Demetris Syllouris.

Kinima Oikologon Perivallontiston (KOP) (Cyprus Green Party): POB 29682, 1722 Nicosia; tel. 22518787; fax 22512710; e-mail greenparty@cytanet.com.cy; internet www.greenpartycy

.com; f. 1996; advocates the reunification of Cyprus; promotes the principles of sustainable devt; Sec.-Gen. GEORGE PERDIKIS.

Kinima Sosialdimokraton EDEK (KISOS) (Movement of Social Democrats EDEK): POB 21064, 40 Byron Ave, 1096 Nicosia; tel. 22476000; fax 22678894; e-mail tipos@edek.org.cy; internet www.edek.org.cy; f. 2000 as successor to Socialistiko Komma Kyprou (EDEK—Socialist Party of Cyprus, f. 1969); supports independent, non-aligned, unitary, demilitarized Cyprus; Pres. YIANNAKIS OMIROU; Hon. Pres. Dr VASSOS LYSSARIDES.

Diplomatic Representation

EMBASSIES AND HIGH COMMISSIONS IN CYPRUS

Australia: 27 Pindarou St, Blk A, Alpha Business Centre, 7th Floor, 1060 Nicosia; tel. 22753001; fax 22766486; e-mail nicosia.ahc@dfat.gov.au; internet www.cyprus.embassy.gov.au; High Commr TREVOR PEACOCK.

Austria: POB 23961, 34 Demosthenis Severis Ave, 1080 Nicosia; tel. 22410151; fax 22680099; e-mail nicosia-ob@bmeia.gv.at; internet www.bmeia.gv.at/botschaft/nikosia; Ambassador Dr KARL MÜLLER.

Belgium: 2A Chilonos St, Office 102, 1101 Nicosia; tel. 22449020; fax 22774717; e-mail nicosia@diplobel.fed.be; internet www.diplomatie.be/nicosia; Ambassador ALPHONSE CREUSEN.

Brazil: 14 Acheon St, Ayios Andreas, 1101 Nicosia; tel. 22592300; fax 22354538; e-mail brasemb.nicosia@itamaraty.gov.br; internet nicosia.itamaraty.gov.br; Chargé d'affaires a.i. ANTENOR AMÉRICO MOURÃO BOGÉA FILHO.

Bulgaria: POB 24029, 13 Konst. Paleologos St, 2406 Engomi, Nicosia; tel. 22672486; fax 22676598; e-mail bulgaria@cytanet.com.cy; internet www.mfa.bg/embassies/cyprus; Ambassador VESSELIN VALCHEV.

China, People's Republic: POB 24531, 30 Archimedes St, 2411 Engomi, Nicosia; tel. 22352182; fax 22353530; e-mail chinaemb_cy@mfa.gov.cn; internet cy.china-embassy.org; Ambassador LIU XINSHENG.

Cuba: POB 28173, 51-A Kratinou St, 2040 Strovolos, 1st Floor, Nicosia; tel. 22769743; fax 22753820; e-mail embacuba@spidernet.com.cy; Ambassador ARAMIS FUENTE HERNÁNDEZ.

Czech Republic: POB 25202, 48 Arsinois St, 1307 Nicosia; tel. 22421118; fax 22421059; e-mail nicosia@embassy.mzv.cz; internet www.mzv.cz/nicosia; Chargé d'affaires a.i. PETR KAVÁN.

Denmark: POB 23322, 34 Demosthenis Severis Ave, 1st Floor, 1080 Nicosia; tel. 22377417; fax 22377472; e-mail nicamb@um.dk; internet cypern.um.dk; Ambassador CASPER KLYNGE.

Egypt: POB 21752, 14 Ayios Prokopios St, Engomi, 1512 Nicosia; tel. 22449050; fax 22449081; e-mail info@egyptianembassy.org.cy; Ambassador MENHA MAHROUZ BAKHOUM.

Finland: POB 21438, 9 Arch. Makarios III Ave, 1508 Nicosia; tel. 22458020; fax 22477880; e-mail sanomat.nic@formin.fi; internet www.finland.org.cy; Ambassador ANU SAARELA.

France: 14–16 Saktouri St, 2nd Floor, Agioi Omologitai, 1080 Nicosia; tel. 22585353; fax 22585350; e-mail ambafrance@cytanet.com.cy; internet www.ambafrance-cy.org; Ambassador JEAN-LUC FLORENT.

Georgia: 46 Themistocles Dervis St, Medcon Tower, 5th Floor, 1066 Nicosia; tel. 22357327; fax 22357307; e-mail geoembassy@cytanet.com.cy; internet cyprus.mfa.gov.ge; Chargé d'affaires ZURAB BEKAIA.

Germany: 10 Nikitaras St, Ay. Omoloyitae, 1080 Nicosia; POB 25705, 1311 Nicosia; tel. 22451145; fax 22665694; e-mail info@nikosia.diplo.de; internet www.nikosia.diplo.de; Ambassador Dr GABRIELA GUELLIL.

Greece: POB 21799, 8–10 Byron Ave, 1096 Nicosia; tel. 22445111; fax 22680649; e-mail grembnicosia@cytanet.com.cy; internet www.mfa.gr/cyprus; Ambassador VASSILIS PAPAIOANNOU.

Holy See: POB 21964, Holy Cross Catholic Church, Paphos Gate, 1010 Nicosia (Apostolic Nunciature); tel. 22662132; fax 22660767; e-mail holcross@logos.cy.net; Apostolic Nuncio Most Rev. GIUSEPPE LAZZAROTTO (Titular Archbishop of Numana—also Apostolic Delegate to Jerusalem and Palestine and Apostolic Nuncio to Israel, resident in Jerusalem).

Hungary: 2 Prodromou and Demetrakopoulou, Zenios Tower, 3rd Floor, 1090 Nicosia; tel. 22459132; fax 22459134; e-mail huembnic@cytanet.com.cy; internet www.mfa.gov.hu/emb/nicosia; Ambassador BALÁZS BOTOS.

India: POB 25544, 3 Indira Gandhi St, Engomi, 2413 Nicosia; tel. 22351741; fax 22352062; e-mail hicomind@spidernet.com.cy; internet www.hcinicosia.gov.in; High Commr RAVI BANGAR.

Iran: POB 28908, 42 Armenias St, 2003 Acropolis, Nicosia; tel. 22314459; fax 22315446; e-mail iranemb@cytanet.com.cy; Ambassador Dr ALI AKBAR REZAEI.

Ireland: 7 Aiantas St, Ayios Omoloyites, 1082 Nicosia; POB 23848, 1686 Nicosia; tel. 22818183; fax 22660050; e-mail nicosiaembassy@dfa.ie; internet www.embassyofireland.com.cy; Ambassador NICHOLAS TWIST.

Israel: POB 25159, 4 Ioanni Grypari St, 1090 Nicosia; tel. 22369524; fax 22369555; e-mail ambass-sec@nicosia.mfa.gov.il; internet nicosia.mfa.gov.il; Ambassador MICHAEL HARARI.

Italy: POB 27695, 11 25th March St, Engomi, 2408 Nicosia; tel. 22357635; fax 22357616; e-mail ambnico.mail@esteri.it; internet www.ambnicosia.esteri.it; Ambassador GUIDO CERBONI.

Kuwait: 38 Armenias St, Strovolos, 2003 Nicosia; tel. 22466656; fax 22454424; e-mail kuwait.emb@cytanet.com.cy; Ambassador AHMAD SALEM AL-WEHAIB.

Lebanon: POB 21924, 6 Chiou St, Ayios Dhometios, 1515 Nicosia; tel. 22878282; fax 22878293; e-mail lebanon.emb@cytanet.com.cy; Ambassador YOUSSEF SADAKA.

Libya: POB 22487, 7 Stassinos Ave, 1060 Nicosia; tel. 22460055; fax 22452710; e-mail info@libyanembassy.com.cy; Chargé d'affaires a.i. NUR AL-DIN M. S. EJLEDI.

Netherlands: POB 23835, 34 Demosthenis Severis Ave, 1080 Nicosia; tel. 22873666; fax 22872399; e-mail nic@minbuza.nl; internet www.cyprus.nlembassy.org; Ambassador BRECHJE SCHWACHÖFER.

Oman: Hilton Cyprus Hotel, Nicosia; tel. 22376064; fax 22374436; e-mail embassyofoman@cytanet.com.cy; Ambassador Sheikh AHMAD BIN SALEM BIN AHMAD AL-SHANFARI.

Poland: POB 22743, 12–14 Kennedy Ave, 1087 Nicosia; tel. 22751980; fax 22751981; e-mail nikozja.amb.sekretariat@msz.gov.pl; internet nikozja.msz.gov.pl; Charge d'affaires. a.i. MARIUSZ TOMASZEWSKI.

Portugal: 9 Arch. Makarios III Ave, Severis Bldg, 5th Floor, POB 27407, 1645 Nicosia; tel. 22375131; fax 22756456; e-mail embportugal@nicosia.dgaccp.pt; Ambassador JOÃO MANUEL PINA PERESTRELLO (designate).

Qatar: 10 Agathonos St, Lykavittos, 1070 Nicosia; tel. 22466864; fax 22466893; e-mail qatarembassy@cytanet.com.cy; Ambassador HUSSEIN BIN AHMAD MUHAMMAD IBRAHIM AL-HMEID.

Romania: POB 22210, 27 Pireos St, Strovolos, 2023 Nicosia; tel. 22495333; fax 22517383; e-mail embrom@cytanet.com.cy; internet nicosia.mae.ro; Ambassador ION PASCU.

Russia: POB 21845, Ayios Prokopias St and Archbishop Makarios III Ave, Engomi, 2406 Nicosia; tel. 22774622; fax 22774854; e-mail russia1@cytanet.com.cy; internet www.cyprus.mid.ru; Ambassador STANISLAV V. OSADCHII.

Serbia: 2 Vasilissis Olgas St, Engomi, 1101 Nicosia; tel. 22777511; fax 22775910; e-mail nicosia@serbia.org.cy; Ambassador SAVO DJURICA.

Slovakia: POB 21165, 4 Kalamatas St, 2002 Strovolos, Nicosia; tel. 22879681; fax 22311715; e-mail skembassy@cytanet.com.cy; Ambassador Dr OKSANA TOMOVA.

Spain: POB 28349, 2093 Strovolos, Nicosia; tel. 22450410; fax 22491291; e-mail emb.nicosia@maec.es; internet www.exteriores.gob.es/embajadas/nicosia; Ambassador ANA MARÍA SÁLOMON PÉREZ.

Sweden: POB 21621, 9 Archbishop Makarios Ave, Severis Bldg, 2nd Floor, 1065 Nicosia; tel. 22458088; fax 22374522; e-mail ambassaden.nicosia@gov.se; internet www.swedenabroad.se/nicosia; Ambassador KLAS GIEROW.

Switzerland: 46 Themistocles Dervis St, Medcon Tower, 1066 Nicosia; POB 20729, 1663 Nicosia; tel. 22466800; fax 22766008; e-mail nic.vertretung@eda.admin.ch; internet www.eda.admin.ch/nicosia; Ambassador GABRIELA NUTZI SULPIZO.

Syria: POB 21892, 24 Nikodimos Mylona St, Ayios Antonios, 1071 Nicosia; tel. 22817333; fax 22756963; e-mail syrianembassy@cytanet.com.cy; Chargé d'affaires a.i. ZOUHEIR JABBOUR.

Ukraine: 10 Andrea Miaouli St, Makedonitissa, Engomi, 2415 Nicosia; tel. 22464380; fax 22464381; e-mail emb_cy@mfa.gov.ua; internet www.mfa.gov.ua/cyprus; Ambassador BORYS HUMENIUK.

United Kingdom: POB 21978, Alexander Pallis St, 1587 Nicosia; tel. 22861100; fax 22861125; e-mail brithc.2@cytanet.com.cy; internet ukincyprus.fco.gov.uk; High Commr MATTHEW KIDD.

USA: Metochiou and Ploutarchou St, Engomi, 2407 Nicosia; POB 24536, 1385 Nicosia; tel. 22393939; fax 22780944; e-mail info@americanembassy.org.cy; internet cyprus.usembassy.gov; Ambassador JOHN M. KOENIG.

Venezuela: POB 23367, 12 Andrea Zakou St, Engomi, 2402 Nicosia; tel. 22445332; fax 22662975; e-mail embaven_chipre@hotmail.com; Chargé d'affaires a.i. JEANPIER ANAYA SALAS.

Judicial System

As required by the Constitution, a law was adopted in 1960 providing for the establishment, jurisdiction and powers of courts of civil and criminal jurisdiction, i.e. of six District Courts and six Assize Courts. In accordance with the provisions of new legislation, approved in 1991, a permanent Assize Court, with powers of jurisdiction in all districts, was established.

In addition to a single Military Court, there are specialized courts concerned with cases relating to industrial disputes, rent control and family law.

Supreme Council of Judicature: Nicosia; tel. 22865716; fax 22304500; The Supreme Council of Judicature is composed of the President and Judges of the Supreme Court. It is responsible for the appointment, promotion, transfer, etc., of the judges exercising civil and criminal jurisdiction in the District Courts, the Assize Courts, the Family Courts, the Military Court, the Rent Control Courts and the Industrial Dispute Court.

Supreme Court: Charalambos Mouskos St, 1404 Nicosia; tel. 22865741; fax 22304500; e-mail chief.reg@sc.judicial.gov.cy; internet www.supremecourt.gov.cy; f. 1964; final appellate court and adjudicator in matters of constitutional and administrative law, including recourses on conflict of competence between state organs on questions of the constitutionality of laws, etc. It deals with appeals from Assize Courts, District Courts and other inferior courts as well as from the decisions of its own judges when exercising original jurisdiction in certain matters such as prerogative orders of *habeas corpus, mandamus, certiorari*, etc., and in admiralty cases; Pres. DEMETRIOS H. HADJIHAMBIS.

Attorney-General: COSTAS CLERIDES.

Religion

The majority of the Greek Cypriot community are adherents of the Orthodox Church, although there are also adherents of the Armenian Apostolic Church, the Anglican Communion and the Roman Catholic Church (including Maronites).

CHRISTIANITY

The Orthodox Church of Cyprus

The Autocephalous Orthodox Church of Cyprus, founded in AD 45, is part of the Eastern Orthodox Church; the Church is independent, and the Archbishop, who is also the Ethnarch (national leader of the Greek community), is elected by representatives of the towns and villages of Cyprus. The Church comprises 16 dioceses, and in 1995 had an estimated 600,000 members.

Archbishop of Nova Justiniana and all Cyprus: Archbishop CHRYSOSTOMOS II, POB 1130, Archbishop Kyprianos St, Nicosia; tel. 22554600; fax 22431796; e-mail office@churchofcyprus.org.cy; internet www.churchofcyprus.org.cy.

Metropolitan of Kitium: Bishop CHRYSOSTOMOS.

Metropolitan of Kyrenia: Bishop KYKKOTIS.

Metropolitan of Limassol: Bishop ATHANASIOS.

Metropolitan of Morphou: Bishop NEOPHYTOS.

Metropolitan of Paphos: Bishop GEORGIOS.

The Roman Catholic Church

Latin Rite

The Patriarchate of Jerusalem covers Israel, Jordan and Cyprus. The Patriarch is resident in Jerusalem (see the chapter on Israel).

Vicar Patriarchal for Cyprus: Fr UMBERTO BARATO, Holy Cross Catholic Church, Paphos Gate, POB 21964, 1010 Nicosia; tel. 22662132; fax 22660767; e-mail holcross@logos.cy.net.

Maronite Rite

Most of the Roman Catholics in Cyprus are adherents of the Maronite rite. Prior to June 1988 the Archdiocese of Cyprus included part of Lebanon. At 31 December 2006 the archdiocese contained an estimated 10,000 Maronite Catholics.

Archbishop of Cyprus: Most Rev. JOSEPH SOUEIF, POB 22249, Maronite Archbishop's House, 8 Ayios Maronas St, Nicosia; tel. 22678877; fax 22668260; e-mail archmar@cytanet.com.cy.

The Anglican Communion

Anglicans in Cyprus are adherents of the Episcopal Church in Jerusalem and the Middle East, officially inaugurated in January 1976. The Church has four dioceses. The diocese of Cyprus and the Gulf includes Cyprus, Iraq and the countries of the Arabian peninsula.

Bishop in Cyprus and the Gulf, President Bishop of the Episcopal Church in Jerusalem and the Middle East: Right Rev. MICHAEL LEWIS, c/o POB 22075, Diocesan Office, 2 Grigoris Afxentiou St, 1516 Nicosia; tel. 22671220; fax 22674553; e-mail cygulf@spidernet.com.cy; internet www.cypgulf.org; Archdeacon in Cyprus Very Rev. STEPHEN COLLIS.

Other Christian Churches

Among other denominations active in Cyprus are the Armenian Apostolic Church and the Greek Evangelical Church.

The Press

DAILIES

Alithia (Truth): 26A Pindaros and Androklis St, 1060 Nicosia; POB 21695, 1512 Nicosia; tel. 22763040; fax 22763945; e-mail news@alithia-news.com; internet www.alithia.com.cy; f. 1952 as a weekly, 1982 as a daily; morning; Greek; right-wing; Man. Dir FRIXOS N. KOULERMOS; Editor-in-Chief PAMBOS CHARALAMBOUS; circ. 11,000.

Cyprus Mail: 24 Vassilios Voulgaroktonos St, 1010 Nicosia; POB 21144, 1502 Nicosia; tel. 22818585; fax 22676385; e-mail mail@cyprus-mail.com; internet www.cyprus-mail.com; f. 1945; morning; English; independent; Man. Dir KYRIACOS IAKOVIDES; Editor JEAN CHRISTOU; circ. 6,000.

Haravgi (Dawn): ETAK Bldg, 6 Ezekia Papaioannou St, 1075 Nicosia; POB 21556, 1510 Nicosia; tel. 22766666; fax 22765154; e-mail haravgi@spidernet.com.cy; internet www.haravgi.com.cy; f. 1956; morning; Greek; organ of AKEL; Dir and Chief Editor ANDROULLA GIOUROV; Publr KYPROS KOURTELLARIS; circ. 10,000.

MAXH (Combat): POB 27628, 1st Floor, Block D, 109 office, 2113 Engomi, Nicosia; tel. 22356676; fax 22356701; e-mail newsmaxi@spidernet.com.cy; internet www.maxhnews.com; f. 1960; weekly; Greek; right-wing; Gen. Man. MINA SAMPSON; Chief Editor FROSSO GEORGIOU; circ. 5,000.

O Phileleftheros (Liberal): POB 21094, 1501 Nicosia; tel. 22744000; fax 22590122; e-mail mailbox@phileleftheros.com; internet www.phileleftheros.com.cy; f. 1955; morning; Greek; independent; moderate; Exec. Dir MYRTO MARKIDOU-SELIPA; Sr Editor ARISTOS MICHAELIDES; circ. 28,000.

Politis (Citizen): 8 Vassilios Voulgaroktonos St, 1010 Nicosia; POB 22894, 1524 Nicosia; tel. 22861861; fax 22861871; e-mail info@politis-news.com; internet www.politis.com.cy; f. 1999; morning; Greek; independent; Publr YIANNIS PAPADOPOULOS; Chief Editors GEORGE KASKANIS, SOTIRIS PAROUTIS.

Simerini (Today): POB 21836, 31 Archangelos Ave, Strovolos, 2054 Nicosia; tel. 22580580; fax 22580570; e-mail mail@simerini.com; internet www.simerini.com; f. 1976; morning; Greek; right-wing; supports DISY; Pres. KOSTAS HADJIKOSTIS; Publr PETROS ZACHARIADES; circ. 17,000.

WEEKLIES

Athlitiki tis Kyriakis (Sunday Sports News): 53 Demosthenis Severis Ave, 9th Floor, 1080 Nicosia; tel. 22664344; fax 22664543; e-mail fellouka@cytanet.com.cy; f. 1996; Greek; athletics; Dir PANAYIOTIS FELLOUKAS; Chief Editor NICOS NICOLAOU; circ. 4,000.

Cyprus Weekly: POB 24977, 1 Diogenous St, Engomi, 2404 Nicosia; tel. 22744400; fax 22744440; e-mail info@cyprusweekly.com.cy; internet www.cyprusweekly.com.cy; f. 1979; English; independent; Publishing Dirs ALEX EFTHYVOULOS, ANDREAS HADJIPAPAS; Chief Editor MARTYN HENRY; circ. 17,000.

Dimosios Ypallilos (Civil Servant): 3 Demosthenis Severis Ave, 1066 Nicosia; tel. 22844445; fax 22668639; e-mail pasydy@spidernet.com.cy; internet www.pasydy.org; f. 1927; Greek; publ. by the Cyprus Civil Servants' Trade Union (PASYDY); circ. 15,000.

Ergatiki Phoni (Workers' Voice): POB 25018, SEK Bldg, 23 Alkeou St, Engomi, 2018 Nicosia; tel. 22849849; fax 228498508; f. 1947; Greek; organ of SEK trade union; Dir NICOS MOYSEOS; Chief Editor XENIS XENOFONTOS; circ. 10,000.

Ergatiko Vima (Workers' Tribune): POB 21185, 1514 Nicosia; tel. 22866400; fax 22349381; e-mail ergatiko-vima@peo.org.cy; f. 1956; Greek; organ of PEO trade union; Chief Editor LEFTERIS GEORGIADIS; circ. 14,000.

Financial Mirror: POB 16077, 2085 Nicosia; tel. 22678666; fax 22678664; e-mail info@financialmirror.com; internet www.financialmirror.com; f. 1993; English (with Greek-language supplement); independent; Publr and Dir MASIS DER PARTHOGH; circ. 4,000.

Official Gazette: Printing Office of the Republic of Cyprus, 1445 Nicosia; tel. 22405811; fax 22303175; e-mail entorzi@gpo.mof.gov.cy; internet www.mof.gov.cy/gpo; f. 1960; Greek; publ. by the Govt of the Republic of Cyprus; circ. 5,000.

Selides (Pages): POB 21094, 1 Diogenous St, Engomi, 2404 Nicosia; POB 21094, 1501 Nicosia; tel. 22744000; fax 22590516; e-mail mailbox@phileleftheros.com; internet www.phileleftheros.com; f. 1991; Greek; Exec. Dir MYRTO MARKIDOU-SELIPA; Chief Editor MARIA MENIKOU; circ. 16,500.

Tharros (Courage): POB 27628, 14A Danaes St, Engomi, Nicosia; tel. 22356676; fax 22356701; e-mail newsmaxi@spidernet.com.cy; internet www.maxinewspaper.com; f. 1961; Greek; right-wing; Gen. Man. MINA SAMSON; circ. 5,500.

To Periodiko: POB 21836, 23 Alkeou St, 4th Floor, 2404 Nicosia; tel. 22580670; fax 22662247; e-mail psillidesc@toperiodiko.com; f. 1986; Greek; general interest; Dir ANTIS HADJIKOSTIS; Chief Editor POPI VAKI; circ. 16,000.

OTHER WEEKLIES

The Blue Beret: POB 21642, HQ UNFICYP, 1590 Nicosia; tel. 22614550; fax 22614461; e-mail unficyp-blue-beret@un.org; internet www.unficyp.org; bi-monthly journal of the UN Peacekeeping Force in Cyprus (UNFICYP); English; f. 1965; circ. 1,500; Editor JOSÉ DIAZ.

The Cyprus Lion: 55 AEC Episkopi, BFPO 53; tel. 25962052; fax 25963181; e-mail lioncy@cytanet.com.cy; distributed to British Sovereign Base Areas, UN Forces and principal Cypriot towns; includes British Forces Broadcasting Services programme guide; Editor LOUISE CARRIGAN; circ. 5,000.

Middle East Economic Survey: Middle East Petroleum and Economic Publications (Cyprus), POB 24940, 23 Alkeos St, Politica Business Centre, 1355 Nicosia; tel. 22665431; fax 22671988; e-mail info@mees.com; internet www.mees.com; f. 1957 (in Beirut, Lebanon); review and analysis of petroleum, finance and banking, and political devts; Publr Dr SALEH S. JALLAD; Editor-in-Chief DAVID KNOTT.

PERIODICALS

Cool: POB 8205, 86 Iphigenias St, 2091 Nicosia; tel. 22378900; fax 22378916; f. 1994; Greek; youth magazine; Chief Editor PROMETHEAS CHRISTOPHIDES; circ. 4,000.

Cypria (Cypriot Woman): POB 28506, 56 Kennedy Ave, 11th Floor, Strovolos, 2080 Nicosia; tel. 22494907; fax 22427051; e-mail pogo@spidernet.com.cy; f. 1983; every 2 months; Greek; Owner MARO KARAYIANNI; circ. 7,000.

Cyprus P.C.: POB 24989, 6th Floor, 1 Kyriakou Matsi St, 1306 Nicosia; tel. 22765999; fax 22765909; e-mail pc@infomedia.cy.net; f. 1990; monthly; Greek; computing magazine; Dir LAKIS VARNAVA; circ. 5,000.

Cyprus Time Out: POB 3697, 4 Pygmalionos St, 1010 Nicosia; tel. 22472949; fax 22360668; f. 1978; monthly; English; Dir ELLADA SOPHOCLEOUS; Chief Editor LYN HAVILAND; circ. 8,000.

Cyprus Today: c/o Ministry of Education and Culture, Cultural Services, Ifighenias 27, 2007 Strovolos, Nicosia; tel. 22809845; fax 22809876; e-mail plyssioti@pio.moi.gov.cy; f. 1963; quarterly; English; cultural and information review; publ. and distributed by Press and Information Office; Chair. PAVLOS PARASKEVAS; circ. 15,000.

Cyprus Tourism: POB 51697, Limassol; tel. 25337377; fax 25337374; f. 1989; bi-monthly; Greek and English; tourism and travel; Man. Dir G. EROTOKRITOU; circ. 250,000.

Enosis (Union): 71 Piraeus & Tombazis, Nicosia; tel. 22756862; fax 22757268; f. 1996; monthly; Greek; satirical; Chief Editor VASOS FTOCHOPOLILOS; circ. 2,000.

Eva: 6 Psichikou St, Strovolos, Nicosia; tel. 22322959; fax 22322940; f. 1996; Greek; Dir DINOS MICHAEL; Chief Editors CHARIS PONTIKIS, KATIA SAVVIDOU; circ. 4,000.

Hermes International: POB 24512, Nicosia; tel. 22570570; fax 22581617; f. 1992; quarterly; English; lifestyle, business, finance, management; Chief Editor JOHN VICKERS; circ. 8,500.

I Kypros Simera (Present Day Cyprus): 1 Apellis St, 1456 Nicosia; tel. 22801186; fax 22666123; e-mail kvrahimis@pio.moi.gov.cy; f. 1983; fortnightly; Greek; publ. by the Press and Information Office of the Ministry of the Interior; Principal Officers MILTOS MILTIADOU, MICHALAKIS CHRISTODOULIDES; circ. 3,500.

Nicosia This Month: POB 20365, 2 Agathokleous St, Strovolos, Nicosia; tel. 22441922; fax 22519743; e-mail info@gnora.com; internet www.gnora.com; f. 1984; monthly; English; Publr MARINOS MOUSHIOTTAS; Man. Dir ANDREAS HADJKYRIACOS; circ. 4,000.

Omicron: POB 21094,1 Diogenous St, Engomi, 1501 Nicosia; tel. 22744000; fax 22590516; f. 1996; Greek; Dir NIKOS CHR. PATTICHIS; Chief Editor MARIANNA KARAVALI; circ. 10,000.

Paediki Chara (Children's Joy): POB 136, 18 Archbishop Makarios III Ave, 1065 Nicosia; tel. 22817585; fax 22817599; e-mail poed@cytanet.com.cy; f. 1962; monthly; for pupils; publ. by the Pancyprian Union of Greek Teachers; Dir FILIOS FILAKTOU; circ. 15,000.

Synergatiko Vima (The Co-operative Tribune): Kosti Palama 5, 1096 Nicosia; tel. 22680757; fax 22660833; e-mail coop.confeder@cytanet.com.cy; internet confederation.coop.com.cy; f. 1983; monthly; Greek; official organ of Pancyprian Co-operative Confed. Ltd; circ. 5,000; Pres. ANDREAS MOUSKALLIS.

Synthesis (Composition): 6 Psichikou St, Strovolos, Nicosia; tel. 22322959; fax 22322940; f. 1988; every 2 months; Greek; interior decorating; Dir DINOS MICHAEL; circ. 6,000.

Tele Ores: POB 28205, 4 Acropoleos St, 1st Floor, 2091 Nicosia; tel. 22513300; fax 22513363; f. 1993; fortnightly; Greek; television guide; Chief Editor PROMETHEAS CHRISTOPHIDES; circ. 17,000.

TV Kanali (TV Channel): POB 25603, 5 Aegaleo St, Strovolos, Nicosia; tel. 22353603; fax 22353223; f. 1993; Greek; Dirs A. STAVRIDES, E. HADJIEFTHYMIOU; Chief Editor CHARIS TOMAZOS; circ. 13,000.

NEWS AGENCY

Cyprus News Agency: 21 Akademias Ave, 2107 Aglantzia, Nicosia; tel. 22556009; fax 22556103; e-mail director@cna.org.cy; internet www.cna.org.cy; f. 1976; Greek, Turkish and English; Acting Dir and Editor-in-Chief GEORGE PENINTAEX; Chair. of Bd LARKOS LARKOU.

Publishers

Andreou Chr. Publishers: POB 22298, 67A Regenis St, 1520 Nicosia; tel. 22666877; fax 22666878; e-mail andreou2@cytanet.com.cy; f. 1979; biography, literature, history, regional interest.

KY KE M (Cyprus Research Centre): POB 22687, 1523 Nicosia; tel. 22668848; fax 22667816; e-mail kykem@cytanet.com.cy; Pres. TONIS TOUMAZIS.

Anastasios G. Leventis Foundation: 40 Gladstonos St, POB 22543, 1095 Nicosia; tel. 22667706; fax 22675002; e-mail leventcy@zenon.logos.cy.net; internet www.leventisfoundation.org; f. 1980; Dir CHARALAMBOS BAKIRTZIS.

MAM Ltd (The House of Cyprus and Cyprological Publications): POB 21722, 1512 Nicosia; tel. 22753536; fax 22375802; e-mail mam@mam.com.cy; internet www.mam.com.cy; f. 1965.

Nikoklis Publishing House: POB 20300, 2150 Nicosia; tel. 22334918; fax 22330218; history, geography, culture, travel; Man. Dr ANDREAS SOPHOCLEOUS.

Pierides Foundation: POB 40025, 6300 Larnaca; tel. 24814555; fax 24817868; e-mail centrart@spidernet.com.cy; internet www.pieridesfoundation.com.cy; f. 1974.

Broadcasting and Communications

TELECOMMUNICATIONS

Cyprus Telecommunications Authority (CYTA): POB 24929, Telecommunications St, Strovolos, 1396 Nicosia; tel. 22701000; fax 22494940; e-mail enquiries@cyta.com.cy; internet www.cyta.com.cy; provides fixed-line telecommunications services and broadband internet access; signed partnership agreement with Vodafone PLC (United Kingdom) in 2004 to offer mobile cellular telecommunications services under brand name Cytamobile-Vodafone; Chair. CHRISTOS PATSALIDES; CEO ARISTOS RIRIS.

MTN Cyprus: Nicosia; e-mail contactus@mtn.com.cy; internet www.mtn.com.cy; f. 2004 as Areeba; wholly owned by MTN Group (South Africa); provides mobile cellular telecommunications services; CEO, MTN Cyprus PHILLIP VAN DALSEN.

PrimeTel PLC: POB 51490, The Maritime Center, 141 Omonia Ave, 3506 Limassol; tel. 22027300; fax 22102211; e-mail info@prime-tel.com; internet www.prime-tel.com; f. 2003; provides fixed-line telecommunications services, broadband internet access and cable television to domestic customers under brand name PrimeHome; Man. Dir HERMES N. STEPHANOU.

BROADCASTING

Radio

British Forces Broadcasting Service, Cyprus: Akrotiri, BFPO 57; tel. 25278518; fax 25278580; e-mail cyprus@bfbs.com; internet www.bfbs.com/radio/online/cyprus; f. 1948; broadcasts daily radio and television services in English; Station Man. CHRIS PEARSON.

Cyprus Broadcasting Corporation (CyBC): POB 24824, CyBC St, 2120 Nicosia; tel. 22862000; fax 22314050; e-mail rik@cybc.com.cy; internet www.cybc.com.cy; f. 1952; four 24-hour radio channels, two of which are mainly Greek; channel 2 broadcasts programmes in Turkish, English and Armenian; Pres. ALECOS MICHAELIDES; Dir-Gen. THEMIS THEMISTOCLEOUS.

Kanali Exi: POB 54845, 69 Irinis St, 3041 Limassol; tel. 25820500; fax 25820550; e-mail info@kanali6.com; internet www.kanali6.com.cy; Dir MICHALIS PAPAEVAGOROU.

Logos: Church of Cyprus, POB 27400, 1644 Nicosia; tel. 22580400; fax 22352349; e-mail a.lambrou@logosradio.com.cy; internet www.logosradio.com.cy; Pres. PANIKOS HADJIPANTELI; Dir-Gen. LOUCAS A. PANAYIOTOU.

Radio Astra: Arch. Makarios III Ave 33, 2220 Latsia, Nicosia; tel. 22368888; fax 22319262; e-mail astra@cytanet.com.cy; internet www.astra.com.cy; Chair. YIANNAKIS KOLOKASIDES; Dir GEORGE PAVLIDES.

Radio Proto: POB 21836, 31 Archangelos St, Parissinos, 2057 Nicosia; tel. 22580400; fax 22580425; e-mail news@radioproto.com; internet www.radioproto.com; Chair. KOSTAS HADJIKOSTIS; Gen. Man. MANOS MOYSEOS.

Super FM: POB 22795, 4 Annis Komninis St, Solea Court, 6th Floor, 1060 Nicosia; tel. 22460150; fax 22769516; e-mail info@superfmradio.com; internet www.superfmradio.com; Gen. Man. MANOS MOYSEOS.

Super Sport FM: 5 Archibishop Kyprianou, Latsia, 2235 Nicosia; tel. 22471472; fax 22571901; e-mail papageorgiou@alfamedia.press.cy; internet www.sport-fm.com.cy; Gen. Man. GEORGE TSALAKOS.

Television

Greek Cypriot viewers have access to Greek television channels via satellite. Digital Video Broadcasting replaced analogue transmission networks in Cyprus in July 2011.

Antenna TV Cyprus (ANT1 Cyprus): POB 20923, 1665 Nicosia; tel. 22200200; fax 22200210; e-mail info@antenna.com.cy; internet www.antenna.com.cy; f. 1983; Chair. LOUKIS PAPAPHILIPPOU; Gen. Man. STELIOS MALEKOS.

British Forces Broadcasting Service, Cyprus: BFPO 57, Akrotiri; tel. 25952009; fax 25278580; e-mail dusty.miller@bfbs.com; internet www.bfbs.com/tv; f. 1948; broadcasts a daily TV service; Station Man. IAN NOAKES; Engineering Man. ADRIAN ALMOND.

Cyprus Broadcasting Corporation (CyBC): POB 24824, CyBC St, 1397 Nicosia; tel. 22862000; fax 22314050; e-mail rik@cybc.com.cy; internet www.cybc.com.cy; f. 1957; Pik 1 (CyBC 1) one Band III 100/10-kW transmitter on Mount Olympus; Pik 2 (CyBC 2) one Band IV 100/10-kW ERP transmitter on Mount Olympus; ET1 one Band IV 100/10-kW ERP transmitter on Mount Olympus for transmission of the ETI Programme received, via satellite, from Greece; the above three TV channels are also transmitted from 80 transposer stations; Dir of Television GREGORIS MALIOTIS.

Lumiere TV Public Co Ltd: POB 25614, 1311 Nicosia; tel. 22357272; fax 22354638; e-mail administration@ltv.com.cy; internet www.ltv.tv; f. 1992; encoded signal; Exec. Chair. AKIS AVRAAMIDES; Man. Dir GEORGE XINARIS.

MEGA TV: POB 27400, 1644 Nicosia; tel. 22477777; fax 22477737; e-mail newsdpt@megatv.com.cy; internet www.megatv.com; Gen. Man. GEORGE CHOULIARAS.

Music TV: 49 Archbishop Makariou Ave, Office 101, Latsia, 2222 Nicosia; tel. 22210001; fax 22210002; e-mail info@musictv.com; internet www.musictv.com.cy; Man. MARIOS AHAS.

Sigma Radio TV Ltd: POB 21836, 2054 Nicosia; tel. 22580100; fax 22580308; e-mail programme@sigmatv.com; internet www.sigmatv.com; f. 1995; island-wide coverage; Chair. and Dir KOSTAS HADJICOSTIS.

Finance

(br.(s) = branches; cap. = capital; res = reserves; dep. = deposits; m. = million; amounts in euros unless otherwise indicated)

BANKING

Central Bank

Central Bank of Cyprus: POB 25529, 80 Kennedy Ave, 1076 Nicosia; tel. 22714100; fax 22714959; e-mail cbcinfo@centralbank.gov.cy; internet www.centralbank.gov.cy; f. 1963; became fully independent from govt control in July 2002; cap. 30m., res 33m., dep. 3,713m. (Dec. 2009); Gov. CHRYSTALLA GEORGHADJI.

Principal Commercial Banks

Alpha Bank Cyprus Ltd: POB 21661, 3 Lemesos Ave, 1596 Nicosia; tel. 22888888; fax 22334868; e-mail secretariat@alphabank.com.cy; internet www.alphabank.com.cy; f. 1960 as Lombard Banking (Cyprus) Ltd; name changed to Lombard NatWest Banking Ltd in 1989 and as above in 1998; locally incorporated although foreign-controlled; 100% owned by Alpha Bank (Greece); cap. 118m., res 17m., dep. 4,134m. (Dec. 2012); Chair. SPYROS N. FILARETOS; Man. Dir GEORGE GEORGIOU; 35 brs and three international units.

Bank of Cyprus Public Company Ltd: POB 21472, 51 Stassinos St, Ayia Paraskevi, 2002 Strovolos 140, 1599 Nicosia; tel. 22842100; fax 22378111; e-mail info@cy.bankofcyprus.com; internet www.bankofcyprus.com; f. 1899; reconstituted 1943 by the amalgamation of Bank of Cyprus, Larnaca Bank Ltd and Famagusta Bank Ltd; cap. 899m., res 2,030m., dep. 30,654m. (Dec. 2011); Chair. CHRISTIS HASSAPIS; 143 brs in Cyprus, 452 brs abroad.

Co-operative Central Bank Ltd: POB 24537, 8 Gregoris Afxentiou St, 1389 Nicosia; tel. 22743000; fax 22670261; e-mail coopbank.gm@ccb.com.cy; internet www.ccb.coop.com.cy; f. 1937 under the Co-operative Societies Law; banking and credit facilities to mem. societies, importer and distributor of agricultural requisites, insurance agent; cap. 100m., res 31m., dep. 3,943m. (Dec. 2012); Chair. NICHOLAS HATZIGIANNIS; CEO and Gen. Man. MARIOS CLERIDES; 4 brs.

Cyprus Popular Bank Public Co Ltd (Laiki Bank): POB 22032, Laiki Bank Bldg, 154 Limassol Ave, 1598 Nicosia; tel. 22552000; fax 22811496; e-mail laiki.telebank@laiki.com; internet www.laiki.com; f. 1901 as People's Savings Bank of Limassol; fmrly Marfin Popular Bank; name changed as above in Apr. 2012; full commercial banking; cap. 1,369m., res 2,132m., dep. 29,786m. (Dec. 2011); Chair. ANDREAS PHILLIPOU; Group CEO CHRISTOS STYLIANIDIS; 114 brs in Cyprus, 5 brs abroad.

Hellenic Bank Public Company Ltd: 200 cnr Limassol and Athalassa Ave, 2025 Nicosia; tel. 22500000; fax 22500050; e-mail hellenic@hellenicbank.com; internet www.hellenicbank.com; f. 1974; financial services group; cap. 266m., res 204m., dep. 7,813m. (Dec. 2012); Chair. Dr ANDREAS P. PANAYIOTOU; CEO MAKIS KERAVNOS; 70 brs in Cyprus, 27 abroad.

National Bank of Greece (Cyprus) Ltd: 15 Arch. Makarios III Ave, 1597 Nicosia; tel. 22840000; fax 22840010; e-mail cloizou@nbg.com.cy; internet www.nbg.com.cy; f. 1994 by incorporating all local business of the National Bank of Greece SA; full commercial banking; Chair. ALEXANDROS TOURKOLIAS; Man. Dir NICHOLAOS BEIS; 24 brs.

USB Bank PLC: 83 Dhigenis Akritas Ave, 1070 Nicosia; tel. 22883333; fax 22875899; e-mail usbmail@usb.com.cy; internet www.usbbank.com.cy; f. 1925 as Yialousa Savings Ltd (closed 1974, reopened 1990), renamed Universal Savings Bank Ltd 2001, became Universal Bank Public Ltd 2004, restyled as above 2009; cap. 56m., res 26m., dep. 699m. (Dec. 2012); Chair. MAURICE SEHNAOUI; 16 brs.

Investment Organization

The Cyprus Investment and Securities Corpn Ltd: POB 20597, 1660 Nicosia; tel. 22881700; fax 22338488; e-mail info@cisco.bankofcyprus.com; internet www.cisco-online.com.cy; f. 1982 to promote the devt of capital market; brokerage services, fund management, investment banking; mem. of Bank of Cyprus Group; issued cap. 22m. (2004); Chair. DEMETRIS IOANNOU; Gen. Man. ANNA SOFRONIOU.

Development Bank

The Cyprus Development Bank Public Company Ltd: POB 21415, Alpha House, 50 Archbishop Makarios III Ave, 1065 Nicosia; tel. 22846500; fax 22846600; internet www.cyprusdevelopmentbank.com; f. 1963; cap. 21m., res 19m., dep. 304m. (Dec. 2009); aims to accelerate the economic devt of Cyprus by providing medium- and long-term loans for productive projects, developing the capital market, encouraging jt ventures, and providing technical and managerial advice to productive private enterprises; Chair. RENA ROUVITHA PANOU; CEO ANDRI GEORGHIOU; 1 br.

STOCK EXCHANGE

Cyprus Stock Exchange: POB 25427, 71–73 Lordou Vyronos Ave, 1309 Nicosia; tel. 22712300; fax 22570308; e-mail info@cse.com.cy; internet www.cse.com.cy; f. 1996; official trading commenced in March 1996; 135 cos listed in Feb. 2009; Chair. GIORGOS KOUFARIS; Dir-Gen. NONDAS METAXAS.

INSURANCE

Insurance Companies Control Service: Ministry of Finance, POB 23364, 1682 Nicosia; tel. 22602952; fax 22660135; e-mail insurance@mof.gov.cy; internet www.mof.gov.cy; f. 1969 to control insurance cos, insurance agents, brokers and agents for brokers in Cyprus; Superintendent VICTORIA NATAR.

Insurance Companies

Atlantic Insurance Co Public Ltd: POB 24579, 15 Espiridon St, 1301 Nicosia; tel. 22886000; fax 22886111; e-mail atlantic@atlantic.com.cy; internet www.atlantic.com.cy; f. 1983; general, non-life; Chair. and Man. Dir EMILIOS PYRISHIS.

Cosmos Insurance Co Public Ltd: Cosmos Tower, 46 Griva Digeni St, 1080 Nicosia; POB 21770, 1513 Nicosia; tel. 22796000; fax 22022000; e-mail info@cosmosinsurance.com.cy; internet www

.cosmosinsurance.com.cy; f. 1981; present name adopted 2004; general; Pres. ANDREAS P. EROTOKRITOU; Man. Dir ANDREAS K. TYLLIS.

Eurolife Ltd: POB 21655, Eurolife House, 4 Evrou, 1511 Nicosia; tel. 22474000; fax 22341090; e-mail info@eurolife.bankofcyprus.com; internet www.eurolife.com.cy; wholly owned subsidiary of Bank of Cyprus; life, accident and health; CEO ARTEMIS PANTELIDOU.

General Insurance of Cyprus Ltd: POB 21668, 2–4 Themistoklis Dervis St, 1511 Nicosia; tel. 22128705; fax 22676682; e-mail general@gic.bankofcyprus.com; internet www.gic.com.cy; f. 1951; wholly owned subsidiary of Bank of Cyprus; general, non-life; CEO STELIOS CHRISTODOULOU.

Hellenic Alico Life Insurance Ltd: POB 20672, 38 Kennedy Ave, 1662 Nicosia; tel. 22450650; fax 22450750; e-mail life@hellenicalico.com; internet www.hellenicbank.com; f. by merger of Hellenic Bank PCL and Alico AIG Life; 72.5% stake owned by Hellenic Bank PCL; Chair. and Man. Dir CHRISTOS A. ANTONIOU.

Laiki Cyprialife Ltd: POB 20819, 64 Archbishop Makarios III Ave and 1 Karpenisiou St, 1077 Nicosia; tel. 22887300; fax 22374460; e-mail pmichaelides@laiki.com; internet www.laiki.com; f. 1995; wholly owned subsidiary of Marfin Popular Bank; life, accident and health; CEO POLIS MICHAELIDES.

Laiki Insurance Co Ltd: POB 25218, 45 Vyzantiou St, Strovolos, 1307 Nicosia; tel. 22887600; fax 22887501; e-mail anstylianou@cnpmarfin.com; internet www.laiki.com; f. 1981; subsidiary of Marfin Popular Bank and CNP Assurances; general; Gen. Man. ANDREAS STYLIANOU.

Minerva Insurance Co Public Ltd: POB 23544, 1684 Nicosia; tel. 22551616; fax 22551717; f. 1970; general and life; CEO COSTAKIS KOUTSOKOUMNIS.

Pancyprian Insurance Ltd: POB 21352, Pancyprian Tower, 66 Grivas Dhigenis Ave, 1095 Nicosia; tel. 22743743; fax 22677656; e-mail pancyprian@hellenicbank.com; internet www.pancyprianinsurance.com; f. 1992; wholly owned subsidiary of Hellenic Bank PCL; general, non-life; CEO SOCRATES DEMETRIOU.

Prime Insurance Co Ltd: POB 22475, 1522 Nicosia; tel. 22896000; fax 22767768; e-mail info@primeinsurance.eu; internet www.primeinsurance.eu; acquired by Demco Insurance Ltd (Greece) May 2011; fmrly Interlife Insurance Co; present name adopted Sept. 2011; life and general; Man. Dir MICHALIS MICHAELIDES.

Universal Life Insurance Public Company Ltd: POB 21270, Universal Tower, 85 Dhigenis Akritas Ave, 1505 Nicosia; tel. 22882222; fax 22882200; e-mail info@unilife.com.cy; internet www.universallife.com.cy; f. 1970; life, accident, health and general; Chair. PHOTOS PHOTIADES; CEO and Man. Dir ANDREAS GEORGHIOU.

Insurance Association

Insurance Association of Cyprus: POB 22030, Insurance Centre, 23 Zenon Sozos St, 1st Floor, 1516 Nicosia; tel. 22452990; fax 22374288; e-mail info@iac.org.cy; internet www.iac.org.cy; 28 mem. cos; Chair. POLYS MICHAELIDES; Dir-Gen. STEPHIE DRACOS.

Trade and Industry

CHAMBERS OF COMMERCE AND INDUSTRY

Cyprus Chamber of Commerce and Industry: POB 21455, 38 Grivas Dhigenis Ave, 1509 Nicosia; tel. 22889800; fax 22669048; e-mail chamber@ccci.org.cy; internet www.ccci.org.cy; f. 1927; Pres. MANTHOS MAVROMMATIS; Sec.-Gen. PANAYIOTIS LOIZIDES; 8,000 mems, 120 affiliated trade asscns.

Famagusta Chamber of Commerce and Industry: POB 53124, 339 Ayiou Andreou St, Andrea Chambers Bldg, 2nd Floor, Office No. 201, 3300 Limassol; tel. 25370165; fax 25370291; e-mail chamberf@cytanet.com.cy; internet www.famagustachamber.org.cy; f. 1952; Pres. GEORGE MICHAELIDES; Sec. and Dir IACOVOS HADJIVARNAVAS; 400 mems and 200 assoc. mems.

Larnaca Chamber of Commerce and Industry: POB 40287, 12 Gregoriou Afxentiou St, Skouros Bldg, Apt 43, 4th Floor, 6302 Larnaca; tel. 24655051; fax 24628281; e-mail lcci@spidernet.com.cy; f. 1954; Pres. ANDREAS LOUROUTZIATIS; Sec. GEORGE PSARAS; 600 mems and 25 assoc. mems.

Limassol Chamber of Commerce and Industry: 170 Franklin Roosevelt Ave, 3045 Limassol; POB 55699, 3781 Limassol; tel. 25877350; fax 25661655; e-mail info@limassolchamber.eu; internet www.limassolchamber.eu; f. 1962; Pres. PHILOKYPROS ANDREOU; Sec. and Dir CHRISTOS ANASTASSIADES; 800 mems.

Nicosia Chamber of Commerce and Industry: POB 21455, 38 Grivas Dhigenis Ave, Chamber Bldg, 1509 Nicosia; tel. 22889600; fax 22667433; e-mail reception@ncci.org.cy; internet www.ncci.org.cy; f. 1952; Pres. COSTAS GEORGALLIS; Dir SOCRATES HERACLEOUS; 1,520 mems.

Paphos Chamber of Commerce and Industry: POB 82, Tolmi Court, 1st Floor, cnr Athinon Ave and Alexandrou Papayou Ave, 8100 Paphos; tel. 26818173; fax 26944602; e-mail evepafos@cytanet.com.cy; internet www.pcci.org.cy; Pres. THEODOROS ARISTODEMOU; Sec. KENDEAS ZAMPIRINIS; 530 mems and 6 assoc. mems.

EMPLOYERS' ORGANIZATION

Cyprus Employers' & Industrialists' Federation: POB 21657, 2 Acropoleos Ave, 1511 Nicosia; tel. 22665102; fax 22669459; e-mail info@oeb.org.cy; internet www.oeb.org.cy; f. 1960; 64 mem. trade asscns, 500 direct and 4,500 indirect mems; Chair. PHILIOS ZACHARIADES; Dir-Gen. MICHAEL PILIKOS; the largest of the trade asscn mems are: Cyprus Building Contractors' Asscn; Land and Building Developers' Asscn; Asscn of Cyprus Tourist Enterprises; Cyprus Shipping Asscn; Cyprus Footwear Mfrs' Asscn; Cyprus Metal Industries Asscn; Cyprus Bankers Employers' Asscn; Cyprus Asscn of Business Consultants; Mechanical Contractors Asscn of Cyprus; Union of Solar Energy Industries of Cyprus.

UTILITIES

Electricity

Electricity Authority of Cyprus (EAC): POB 24506, 1399 Nicosia; tel. 22201000; fax 22201020; e-mail eac@eac.com.cy; internet www.eac.com.cy; generation, transmission and distribution of electric energy in govt-controlled area; also licensed to install and commercially exploit wired telecommunication network; total installed capacity 1,118 MW in 2008; Chair. CHARALAMBOS TSOURIS; Gen. Man. STELIOS STYLIANOU.

Water

Water Development Department: 100–110 Kennenty Ave, 1047 Pallouriotissa, Nicosia; tel. 22609000; fax 22675019; e-mail eioannou@wdd.moa.gov.cy; internet www.moa.gov.cy/wdd; f. 1939; owned by Ministry of Agriculture, Natural Resources and the Environment; dam storage capacity 331.9m. cu m; Dir Dr KYRIACOS KYROU.

TRADE UNIONS

Pankypria Ergatiki Omospondia (PEO) (Pancyprian Federation of Labour): POB 21885, 31–35 Archermos St, Nicosia 1045; tel. 22886400; fax 22349382; e-mail peo@peo.org.cy; internet www.peo.org.cy; f. 1946; regd 1947; previously the Pancyprian Trade Union Cttee (f. 1941, dissolved 1946); 8 unions and 176 brs with a total membership of 75,000; affiliated to WFTU; Gen. Sec. PAMBIS KYRITSIS.

Synomospondia Ergazomenon Kyprou (SEK) (Cyprus Workers' Confederation): POB 25018, 11 Strovolos Ave, 2018 Strovolos, 1306 Nicosia; tel. 22849849; fax 22849850; e-mail sek@sek.org.cy; internet www.sek.org.cy; f. 1944; regd 1950; 7 federations, 5 labour centres, 47 unions, 12 brs with a total membership of 65,000; affiliated to ITUC and the European Trade Union Confed.; Gen. Sec. NIKOS MOYSEOS.

Transport

RAILWAYS

There are no railways in Cyprus.

ROADS

According to the International Road Federation, in 2010 there were 12,483 km of roads in the government-controlled areas, of which 2,186 km were motorways, 257 km were highways and main or national roads, and 3,226 km were secondary or regional roads. The Nicosia–Limassol four-lane dual carriageway, which was completed in 1985, was subsequently extended with the completion of the Limassol and Larnaca bypasses. Highways also connect Nicosia and Larnaca, Nicosia and Anthoupolis-Kokkinotrimithia, Larnaca and Kophinou, Aradippo and Dhekelia, Limassol and Paphos, and Dhekelia and Ammochostos (Famagusta). The north and south are now served by separate transport systems, and there are no services linking the two sectors.

SHIPPING

Until 1974 Famagusta, a natural port, was the island's most important harbour, handling about 83% of the country's cargo. Since its capture by the Turkish army in August of that year the port has been officially declared closed to international traffic. However, it continues to serve the Turkish-occupied region.

The main ports that serve the island's maritime trade at present are Larnaca and Limassol. There is also an industrial port at Vassiliko, and there are three specialized petroleum terminals, at

Larnaca, Dhekelia and Moni. In August 2012 the Government awarded a contract for a three-phase redevelopment (on a build-operate-transfer basis) of Larnaca port and its subsequent management to the international Zenon Consortium. Construction was expected to commence in 2013, and to cost an estimated €700m.

In addition to serving local traffic, Limassol and Larnaca ports act as transshipment load centres and as regional warehouse and assembly bases.

At 31 December 2013 the Greek Cypriot shipping registry comprised 1,210 flag registered vessels, with an aggregate displacement of 21.3m. grt, of which 244 were bulk carriers, five were fish carriers, 11 were gas tankers and 178 were general cargo ships.

Port and Regulatory Authorities

Department of Merchant Shipping: POB 56193, Kylinis St, Mesa Geitonia, 4007 Limassol; tel. 25848100; fax 25848200; e-mail maritimeadmin@dms.mcw.gov.cy; internet www.shipping.gov.cy; f. 1977; Dir SERGHIOS S. SERGHIOU.

Cyprus Ports Authority: POB 22007, 23 Crete St, 1516 Nicosia; tel. 22817200; fax 22765420; e-mail cpa@cpa.gov.cy; internet www.cpa.gov.cy; f. 1973; Chair. CHRYSIS PRENTZAS.

Shipping Companies

Ahrenkiel Shipmanagement (Cyprus) Ltd: POB 53594, 4th Floor, O & A Tower, 25 Olympion St, 3033 Limassol; tel. 25854000; fax 25854001; e-mail infocy@ahrenkiel.net; internet www.ahrenkiel.net; f. 1977; Man. Dir VASSOS STAVROU.

Amer Shipping Ltd: POB 27363, 701 Ghinis Bldg, 58–60 Dhigenis Akritas Ave, 1644 Nicosia; tel. 22875188; fax 22756556; e-mail ateam@amershipping.com; internet www.amershipping.com; f. 1989; Man. Dir ANIL DESHPANDE.

Bernhard Schulte Shipmanagement (Cyprus) Ltd: Hanseatic House, 111 Spyrou Araouzou St, POB 50127, 3036 Limassol; tel. 25846400; fax 25745245; e-mail cy-sdc-man@bs-shipmanagement.com; internet www.bs-shipmanagement.com; f. 1972; CEO ANDREAS J. DROUSSIOTIS.

Columbia Shipmanagement Ltd: Dodekanissou St, 4043 Limassol; tel. 25843100; fax 25320325; e-mail marketing@csmcy.com; internet www.columbia.com.cy; f. 1978; Man. Dir DIRK FRY.

Cyprus Shipping Chamber: POB 56607, City Chambers, 1st Floor, 6 Regas Fereos St, 3309 Limassol; tel. 25360717; fax 25358642; e-mail csc@csc-cy.org; internet www.csc-cy.org; f. 1989; Dir-Gen. THOMAS A. KAZAKOS.

Interorient Navigation Co Ltd: POB 51309, 142 Franklin Roosevelt Ave, 3504 Limassol; tel. 25840300; fax 25575895; e-mail management@interorient.com.cy; internet www.interorient.com; Man. Dir JAN LISSOW.

Louis Cruise Lines: 11 Lemessos Ave, 2112 Nicosia; tel. 22588168; fax 22442957; e-mail investors@louisgroup.com; internet www.louisgroup.com; f. 1935; Exec. Chair. COSTAKIS LOIZOU.

Marlow Navigation Co Ltd: POB 54077, 13 Alexandrias St, 3720 Limassol; tel. 25882588; fax 25882599; e-mail marlow@marlow.com.cy; internet www.marlownavigation.com.cy; f. 1982; Chair. HERMANN EDEN; Man. Dirs ANDREAS NEOPHYTOU, JAN MEYERING.

Oldendorff Ltd, Reederei 'Nord' Klaus E: POB 56345, Libra Tower, 23 Olympion St, 3306 Limassol; tel. 25841400; fax 25345077; e-mail mail@rnkeo.com.cy; internet www.rnkeo.com; f. 1964; Chair. and Man. Dir CHRISTIANE E. OLDENDORFF; Gen. Man. Capt. KEITH V. OBEYESEKERA.

CIVIL AVIATION

There is an international airport at Nicosia, which has been closed since 1974, following the Turkish invasion. A new international airport was constructed at Larnaca, from which flights operate to Europe, the USA, the Middle East and Asia. Another international airport at Paphos began operations in 1983. A project to expand and modernize Larnaca and Paphos airports commenced in June 2006; by November 2008 the new terminal at Paphos airport was fully operational, and the new Larnaca airport, with an annual capacity of 7.5m. passengers, was inaugurated in November 2009.

Cyprus Airways: POB 21903, 21 Alkeou St, Engomi, 2404 Nicosia; tel. 22661800; fax 22663167; e-mail webcenter@cyprusairways.com; internet cyprusair.com; f. 1947; jointly owned by Cyprus Govt (93.67%) and local interests; services throughout Europe and the Middle East; Chair. STAVROS STAVROU; CEO GEORGE MAVROCOSTAS.

Tourism

In 2012 an estimated 2.5m. foreign tourists visited the Greek Cypriot area, while receipts from tourism amounted to some €1,927.7m.

Cyprus Tourism Organisation (CTO): POB 24535, 19 Leoforos Lemesou, Aglantzia, 1390 Nicosia; tel. 22691100; fax 22334696; e-mail cytour@visitcyprus.com; internet www.visitcyprus.com; Chair. ALECOS OROUNTIOTIS.

Defence

The House of Representatives authorized the formation of the National Guard in 1964, after the withdrawal of the Turkish members. Men aged between 18 and 50 years are liable to 24 months' conscription. As assessed at November 2013, the National Guard comprised an army of 12,000 regulars, mainly composed of Cypriot conscripts (some 10,700) but with an estimated 200 seconded Greek Army officers and NCOs, and 50,000 reserves. A further 950 Greek army personnel were stationed in Cyprus at that time. There is also a Greek Cypriot paramilitary police force of some 750. A UN peacekeeping force is also based in Cyprus, and there are British military bases at Akrotiri, Episkopi, Ayios Nikolaos and Dhekelia.

Commander of the National Guard: Lt-Gen. STYLIANOS NASIS.

UNITED NATIONS PEACEKEEPING FORCE IN CYPRUS (UNFICYP)

POB 21642, 1590 Nicosia; tel. 22464000; e-mail unficyp-public-information-office@un.org; internet www.unficyp.org.

UNFICYP was established for a three-month period in March 1964 by a UN Security Council resolution (subsequently extended at intervals of three or six months by successive resolutions) to keep the peace between the Greek and Turkish communities and help to solve outstanding issues between them. In mid-1993, following an announcement by troop-providing countries that they were to withdraw a substantial number of troops, the Security Council introduced a system of financing UNFICYP by voluntary and assessed contributions. Following a significant reduction in the size of UNFICYP, as prescribed by a UN Security Council resolution adopted in October 2004, the contingent numbered 924 uniformed personnel (857 troops, 67 police), supported by 149 local and international civilian staff, at the end of February 2014.

Commander: Maj.-Gen. CHAO LIU (People's Republic of China).

Special Representative of the UN Secretary-General and Head of Mission: LISA M. BUTTENHEIM (USA).

See also the section on UN Peacekeeping Operations in the Regional Organizations section of Part Three.

BRITISH SOVEREIGN BASE AREAS

Akrotiri and Dhekelia

Headquarters British Forces Cyprus, Episkopi 3370, BFPO 53; tel. 25967295; fax 25963521; e-mail cosba@cytanet.com.cy; internet www.sba.mod.uk.

Under the Cyprus Act 1960, the United Kingdom retained sovereignty in two base areas and this was recognized in the Treaty of Establishment signed between the United Kingdom, Greece, Turkey and the Republic of Cyprus in August 1960. The base areas cover 99 sq miles. The Treaty also conferred on Britain certain rights within the Republic, including rights of movement and the use of specified training areas. As assessed at November 2013, military personnel in the sovereign base areas numbered 2,620.

Administrator: Maj.-Gen. RICHARD J. CRIPWELL.

Education

Until 1965 each community in Cyprus managed its own schooling through a Communal Chamber. In March, however, the Greek Communal Chamber was dissolved and a Ministry of Education was established to take its place. Intercommunal education has been placed under this Ministry. Public expenditure on education by the central Government in the Greek Cypriot area was €1.390,9m. (equivalent to 8.0% of GDP) in 2010, according to official figures.

Primary education is compulsory and is provided free in six grades to children between five-and-a-half and 12 years of age. In some towns and large villages there are separate junior schools consisting of the first three grades. Apart from schools for the deaf and blind, there are also seven schools for handicapped children. In 2011/12 there were 672 kindergartens, with 2,250 teachers and 28,687 pupils. There were 365 primary schools, with 4,699 teachers and 53,955 pupils in that year. According to UNESCO estimates, enrolment in primary education in 2011 included 99% of children in the relevant age-group.

Secondary education is also free for all years of study and lasts for six years, with three compulsory years at a general secondary school (gymnasium) being followed by three non-compulsory years at a technical school or lyceum. Pupils at the lyceums may choose one of five main fields of specialization: humanities, science, economics, commercial/secretarial and foreign languages. At technical schools students may undertake one of several specializations offered within two categories of courses—technician and craft; the school-leaving certificate awarded at the end of the course is equivalent to that of the lyceums. In 2011/12 there were 168 secondary schools (gymnasiums and lyceums), with 7,560 teachers and 62,740 pupils. In addition, there were numerous privately operated secondary schools, where instruction is in English. According to UNESCO estimates, in 2011 enrolment in secondary education included 90% of children in the relevant age-group.

Post-secondary education was provided at a total of 44 tertiary institutions in 2011/12, including schools in the humanities and social sciences, pure and applied sciences, and economics and management. The University of Cyprus was established in 1992. The Higher Technical Institute offers sub-degree courses, leading to a diploma, in civil, electrical, mechanical and marine engineering and in computer studies. Other specialized training is provided at the Cyprus Forestry College, the Higher Hotel Institute, the Mediterranean Institute of Management and the School of Nursing. In 2011/12 31,772 students (including 8,540 foreign pupils) were enrolled in tertiary education, while in 2010/11 a total of 19,199 students from the Greek Cypriot area were studying at universities abroad, mainly in Greece, the USA and the United Kingdom.

CYPRIOT SECESSIONIST TERRITORY

The northern one-third of the island of Cyprus has been administered as a separate territory since the invasion of Cyprus by Turkey on 20 July 1975. On 15 November 1983 the 'Turkish Federated State of Cyprus' (as the de facto governing authority had hitherto referred to itself) issued a unilateral declaration of independence as the 'Turkish Republic of Northern Cyprus' ('TRNC'). While the 'TRNC' has enjoyed de facto political and military support from, and full diplomatic relations with, Turkey, the territory is not formally recognized by any other state.

'TURKISH REPUBLIC OF NORTHERN CYPRUS'

Introductory Survey

LANGUAGE, RELIGION, FLAG, CAPITAL

Turkish is the official language of the de facto 'Turkish Republic of Northern Cyprus' ('TRNC'). The population of the Turkish-occupied area to the north of the UN-monitored demilitarized zone is overwhelmingly Muslim. The flag of the 'TRNC' (proportions 2 by 3) has a white field, with a red crescent and star to the left of centre between two narrow horizontal bands of red towards the upper and lower edges. The capital is Lefkoşa (Nicosia).

CONTEMPORARY POLITICAL HISTORY

Historical Context

Cyprus achieved independence from British rule on 16 August 1960. There was serious fighting between the Greek and Turkish Cypriot communities following a constitutional dispute, which resulted in the withdrawal of the Turks from the central Government in December 1963. Consequently, separate political and judicial institutions were established for the Turkish community. Meanwhile, in March 1964 a UN Peacekeeping Force in Cyprus (UNFICYP) was formed in an effort to stem the intercommunal violence.

Following a Greek-led military coup which had led to the replacement of Cyprus's President Makarios by an extremist Greek Cypriot politician who sought a union with Greece, on 20 July 1974 Turkish armed forces invaded Cyprus to protect the Turkish community and prevent Greece from taking over the island. This action resulted in the division of Cyprus along the so-called Green Line (or Attila Line), extending from Morphou through Nicosia to Famagusta. The Turkish Cypriots subsequently established a de facto Government in the northern third of the island, and in February 1975 declared a 'Turkish Federated State of Cyprus' ('TFSC'), with Rauf Denktaş as President.

In the 'TFSC' a new Council of Ministers was formed in December 1978, under Mustafa Çağatay of the Ulusal Bırlık Partisi (UBP—National Unity Party). Peace negotiations between the Greek and Turkish Cypriot sides were relaunched in September 1980, under UN auspices, with the Turkish Cypriots demanding equal status for the two communities and equal representation in government (despite constituting less than 20% of the island's population). At elections held in June 1981 President Denktaş was returned to office, but his party, the UBP, lost its legislative majority, and the Government that was subsequently formed by Çağatay was defeated in December. In March 1982 Çağatay formed a coalition Government, comprising the UBP, the Demokratik Halk Partisi (Democratic People's Party) and the Türkiye Bırlık Partisi (Turkish Unity Party). In May 1983 the UN General Assembly adopted a resolution demanding the removal of Turkish forces from Cyprus. Denktaş responded, on 15 November, by making a unilateral declaration of independence for the 'TFSC' (which had already adopted the Turkish lira as its currency); it was designated the 'Turkish Republic of Northern Cyprus' ('TRNC').

Events following the establishment of the 'TRNC'

After Denktaş's announcement, Çağatay resigned the premiership and as leader of the UBP; an interim Government was formed in December 1983 under Nejat Konuk. Like the 'TFSC', the 'TRNC' was recognized only by Turkey, and the declaration of independence was condemned by the UN Security Council. The 'TRNC' and Turkey established diplomatic relations in April 1984, and the 'TRNC' formally rejected UN proposals for a suspension of its declaration prior to further talks.

During 1984 a 'TRNC' Constituent Assembly drafted a new Constitution, which was approved by 70% of voters at a referendum in May 1985. At a presidential election held on 9 June, Denktaş was returned to office. A general election followed on 23 June, at which the UBP, led by Derviş Eroğlu, won 24 of the 50 seats in the legislature, the Assembly of the Republic. In July Eroğlu became Prime Minister, leading a coalition Government comprising the UBP and the Toplumcu Kurtuluş Partisi (TKP—Communal Liberation Party).

Following an agreement between Denktaş and the new Greek Cypriot President, Georghios Vassiliou, to resume intercommunal talks without pre-conditions, UN-sponsored direct negotiations began in September 1988. However, the intermittent talks were abandoned in March 1990; the principal reason cited was the insistence by the Turkish Cypriot President that his community be granted the right to self-determination.

In April 1988 Eroğlu resigned as Prime Minister, following a disagreement between the UBP and its coalition partner since September 1986, the Yeni Doğuş Partisi (New Dawn Party), which was demanding greater representation in the Government. At the request of Denktaş, in May 1988 Eroğlu formed a new, UBP-dominated Council of Ministers, which also included independents. In April 1990 Denktaş secured re-election in an early presidential poll. Eroğlu remained Prime Minister, after the UBP won 34 of the 50 seats in the Assembly of the Republic at elections in May. (Following by-elections for 12 seats in October 1991, the UBP increased its representation in the Assembly to 45 members.)

Settlement proposals following Cyprus's application to join the European Community

In July 1990 Denktaş condemned a formal application by the Government of Cyprus for European Community (EC, now European Union—EU) membership, since the 'TRNC' leadership had not been consulted. Direct discussions between Vassiliou and Denktaş, brokered by the new UN Secretary-General, Boutros Boutros-Ghali, finally resumed in mid-1992. The purpose of the talks was to achieve a draft settlement based on the Secretary-General's proposals, which outlined a federal structure for the island with separate Greek and Turkish Cypriot areas of administration. However, after it became apparent that the proposed Turkish administrative area was around 25% smaller than the 'TRNC', Denktaş firmly rejected the UN plans.

An early general election was held in December 1993, partly in response to increasing disagreement between President Denktaş and Prime Minister Eroğlu over the handling of the peace talks. The UBP lost its majority in the Assembly, retaining only 17 of the 50 seats, and at the end of the month a coalition Government was formed by the Demokrat Parti (DP—Democrat Party), which had been supported by Denktaş, and the left-wing Cumhuriyetçi Türk Partisi (CTP—Republican Turkish Party). Together the DP and the CTP won 53.4% of the votes cast and 28 seats. The leader of the DP, Hakkı Atun, was appointed as Prime Minister of the new administration.

In response to the adoption in July 1994 by the UN Security Council of Resolution 939, the 'TRNC' legislature approved measures seeking to co-ordinate future foreign and defence policies with those of Turkey, demanding political and sovereign status equal to that of Greek Cyprus in any future settlement. Meanwhile, after the European Commission had, in June 1993, endorsed Cyprus's application to join the EU, Denktaş insisted that the 'TRNC' would integrate further with Turkey if the accession became a reality.

At a presidential election held on 15 April 1995, Denktaş received a mere 40.4% of votes cast in the first poll, only securing a conclusive victory against Eroğlu, with 62.5% of the votes, at a second round on 22 April. A new coalition of the DP and the CTP, under Atun's premiership, took office in June. In August the Assembly adopted legislation concerning compensation for Greek-owned property in the north. However, in November Atun submitted the resignation of his entire Government, after Denktaş rejected a new list of CTP ministers. A new DP-CTP coalition, again under Atun's leadership and with Mehmet Ali Talat (of the CTP) as Deputy Prime Minister, took office in December.

Persistent policy differences within the coalition caused the Government to resign in July 1996, and in August the DP and the UBP signed a coalition agreement whereby UBP leader Eroğlu became Prime Minister of a new administration. In December the European Court of Human Rights ruled that Turkey was in breach of the European Convention on Human Rights by denying a woman access to her property as a result of its occupation in the north. The ruling implicated Turkey as fully responsible for activities in the 'TRNC' and for the consequences of the military action in 1974.

Direct negotiations took place during July 1997 between Denktaş and the Greek Cypriot President, Glavkos Klerides, in the presence of the UN's new Secretary-General, Kofi Annan. However, a second round of UN-sponsored talks, held in August 1997 in Switzerland, collapsed after Denktaş demanded the suspension of Cyprus's application to join the EU. Cyprus's accession talks with the EU began in March 1998. In August the Turkish Cypriot President rejected a UN plan for Cyprus's reunification, instead suggesting a confederation of equal status; however, Klerides immediately dismissed this proposal since it would legitimize the status of the 'TRNC'.

At legislative elections held on 6 December 1998, the UBP increased its representation to 24 seats, while the DP held only 13 seats. The TKP won seven seats and the CTP the remaining six. At the end of the month a new UBP-TKP Council of Ministers received presidential approval. Eroğlu remained as Prime Minister, and the TKP leader, Mustafa Akıncı, became Minister of State and Deputy Prime Minister. At a first round of presidential voting, conducted on 15 April 2000, Denktaş won 43.7% of the votes cast, thus failing to secure the majority necessary for outright victory. However, on 19 April his closest contender, Eroğlu, announced his withdrawal from the process and Denktaş was consequently proclaimed President.

Resolution 1303, which was adopted by the UN Security Council in mid-June 2000 and extended the mandate of UNFICYP for a further six months, notably excluded any reference to the authority of the 'TRNC'. At the end of the month the 'TRNC' instituted a number of retaliatory measures against UNFICYP, including measures to impede the movement of UN forces and new tariffs for UN vehicles and for the use of utilities supplied by the north. 'TRNC' and Turkish forces also crossed into the buffer zone and established a checkpoint at a village inhabited by Greek Cypriots. During UN-sponsored proximity talks held by Klerides and Denktaş between July and September 2000, no agreement was reached on the issue of a future structure for Cyprus. The Greek Cypriot leader continued to advocate a reunified, bicommunal federation, while his Turkish Cypriot counterpart insisted on a looser confederation based on equal sovereignty. Indeed, Denktaş stated in November that he would not return to the talks until the 'TRNC' was granted international recognition. His decision, taken with the support of the Turkish Government, apparently reflected anger in the 'TRNC' that Annan had emphasized that any agreement on Cyprus must be based on the premise of a single sovereign entity, and in Turkey that the European Commission had recently stipulated among preconditions for Turkish admission to the EU Turkey's willingness to promote a settlement for Cyprus based on UN resolutions. (Turkey had been accorded formal status as an EU candidate in December 1999.)

The governing coalition collapsed in late May 2001, following disagreement between the UBP and the TKP on the issue of whether to rejoin talks on the future status of the island. In June the UBP and the DP agreed to form a new coalition administration, with Eroğlu continuing as Prime Minister. The new Government was expected to be more supportive than its predecessor of President Denktaş's policy on the Cyprus question.

The 'Annan Plan'

Amid signs of an improvement in bilateral relations, on 11 November 2002 the UN presented the Turkish and Greek Cypriot leaders with a comprehensive new peace plan (the 'Annan Plan'). This included proposals for the creation of a common federal state with two equal components, but with a single international legal identity. It required the 'TRNC' to return territory to the Greek side, reducing the former's share of the island from 36% to 28.5%, and pledged to compensate dispossessed property owners. However, Denktaş rejected a revised version of the Annan Plan in early December.

At the EU summit held in Copenhagen, Denmark, in December 2002, Cyprus was formally invited to join the EU in 2004. However, the prospect of only the Greek part of the island being admitted increased following the election, in February 2003, of the more hardline Tassos Papadopoulos as Greek Cypriot President. Upon taking office, Papadopoulos demanded that the Annan Plan be amended to allow all Greek Cypriot refugees to return to northern Cyprus. Despite a concerted effort by Annan to persuade Denktaş and Papadopoulos to agree a settlement that would allow a unified Cyprus to accede to the EU, the Turkish Cypriot President denounced the Annan Plan as unacceptable, and refused to continue discussions. Following confirmation that Cyprus would join the EU on 1 May 2004, on 23 April the 'TRNC' Government declared that it would open its border to the Greek part of the island for the first time in 30 years. Henceforth Turkish Cypriots would be permitted to visit the south for one-day trips, while Greek Cypriots could visit the north for up to three nights.

Legislative elections held on 14 December 2003 proved inconclusive with regard to the issue of EU accession: the pro-EU CTP narrowly defeated the ruling UBP; however, parliamentary seats were distributed equally between pro-EU parties and parties that opposed the terms of the Annan Plan. Two days later Eroğlu resigned and Talat was appointed as Prime Minister, and in early January 2004 Talat agreed to enter into a coalition with the DP (led by the President's son, Serdar Denktaş), despite differences of opinion between the CTP and the DP over reunification. On 13 January President Denktaş approved a new coalition Government nominated by Talat, comprising six CTP ministers and four DP ministers. Serdar Denktaş was appointed Deputy Prime Minister and Minister of Foreign Affairs in the new administration.

There was an intensification of efforts to finalize the details of a settlement from late February 2004; discussions in Switzerland from late March also involved the Turkish and Greek premiers. However, Denktaş withdrew from the negotiations and was replaced as head of the Turkish Cypriot delegation by Talat. At the end of March the UN Secretary-General presented a finalized version of his peace plan, which was accepted by the 'TRNC', Turkish and Greek Governments; however, Papadopoulos rejected this final settlement since it provided for the creation of a recognized Turkish Cypriot state. At concurrent referendums held in both parts of the island on 24 April, the Annan Plan was approved by Turkish Cypriots by 64.9% of votes cast, but rejected by Greek Cypriots by 75.8% of the votes. Consequently, only the Greek Cypriot-administered part of the island was admitted to the EU on 1 May. The EU subsequently proposed measures for the resumption of direct trade between the north and south of the island, and consequently for the export to member states of goods produced in the 'TRNC'.

Domestic developments after Cyprus's EU accession

At the end of April 2004 the coalition Government lost its parliamentary majority, after two DP deputies withdrew their support and resigned from the legislature. On 20 October Talat tendered his resignation, having failed to form a new administration. President Denktaş subsequently invited Eroğlu to nominate a new government, with his UBP now the largest party in the Assembly; at the end of the month, however, Eroğlu returned the mandate to the President, after being unable to secure sufficient support from other parties. Following a further failure by Talat to reach a coalition agreement, the President subsequently announced that early legislative elections would be conducted in February 2005.

At the elections to the Assembly of the Republic on 20 February 2005, Talat's CTP secured 44.5% of votes cast and 24 of the chamber's 50 seats, while the UBP won 31.6% of the votes (19 seats). The CTP was thus obliged to seek a renewed parliamentary alliance with the anti-reunification DP, which had secured 13.4% of the vote (six seats), to enable Talat to command a parliamentary majority. On 8 March President Denktaş approved a new, largely unchanged coalition Government, formed by Talat under a slightly amended power-sharing arrangement. Soon after the referendums of April 2004, Denktaş had announced his retirement from public office; he stood down after the 2005 presidential election, and died in January 2012.

Nine candidates contested the presidential election, held on 17 April 2005: Mehmet Ali Talat was elected outright, with 55.6% of votes cast, while Eroğlu, his closest rival, secured 22.7%. Talat, who pledged his commitment to achieving reunification, was inaugurated on 24 April. He duly nominated the Secretary-General of the CTP, Ferdi Sabit Soyer, as Prime Minister, and a new CTP-DP coalition Government was approved by the Legislative Assembly on 28 April.

Eroğlu resigned as UBP leader in November 2005, and in February 2006 Hüseyın Özgürgün was elected as his successor. In the same month the EU approved an aid disbursement of €139m. for the 'TRNC', after agreeing to a Greek Cypriot demand that the financial assistance be addressed separately to the proposed trade measures. Meanwhile, the start of Turkey's accession negotiations with the EU had been approved on 3 October 2005, although member states declared that Turkish recognition of Cyprus was necessary to the accession process.

Three parliamentary deputies resigned from the UBP and one from the DP in early September 2006, and collectively established a new organization, the Özgürlük ve Reform Partisi (ORP—Freedom and Reform Party). Soyer subsequently dissolved the Government, citing prolonged disagreements within the coalition over a reallocation of ministerial positions and policy regarding the reunification of Cyprus. Having received the necessary mandate, on 13 September Soyer formed a new coalition administration with the ORP, which was approved by Talat on 25 September. Three ORP representatives were included within the administration, including the party leader, Turgay Avcı, who became Deputy Prime Minister and Minister of Foreign Affairs. On 5 October the new Government secured a motion of confidence in the legislature by 28 of the 50 deputies; however, the DP and the UBP refused to recognize its legitimacy.

In order to make progress in its talks on EU accession, Turkey was required to open ports and airports to all EU member states by the end of 2006. However, in early December the Turkish Government offered to open only one port and one airport to the Republic of Cyprus, in exchange for the resumption of international flights to the 'TRNC' airport of Ercan and direct trade to the port of Famagusta. The Greek Cypriot leadership rejected the proposal, and in mid-December EU foreign ministers agreed to a partial suspension of Turkey's accession negotiations. On 22 January 2007 EU foreign ministers urged immediate action towards the ending of trade restrictions against the 'TRNC', in accordance with the EU's commitment made in 2004. In March 2007 the demolition by the Greek Cypriot authorities of a wall at Ledra Street in Nicosia was hailed as a significant step towards ending the division of the city.

The resumption of reunification talks and elections during 2009–10

In a sign that Greek Cypriots were becoming frustrated by Papadopoulos's hardline stance towards the 'TRNC', he was defeated by the (nominally) communist Demetris Christofias in the Republic of Cyprus's presidential election of February 2008. Christofias had pledged to hold further reunification negotiations with a view to reaching a permanent settlement. During talks between Talat and Christofias in Nicosia in March 2008, the two leaders agreed to: open the Ledra Street crossing in central Nicosia (this was achieved in early April); formulate an agenda for future negotiations; and establish working groups and technical committees to consider issues pertinent to the success of further talks (this occurred in mid-April).

At a meeting held in May 2008 under UN auspices, the two leaders again emphasized their 'commitment to a bizonal, bicommunal federation with political equality, as defined by relevant Security Council resolutions'. They subsequently agreed to hold weekly meetings in an effort to accelerate the peace process. Long-awaited, fully fledged negotiations finally commenced in September, but issues of contention such as power-sharing prevented any immediate breakthrough.

It was announced in February 2009 that the 'TRNC' would hold an early parliamentary election in April—a year ahead of schedule. This proposal was reportedly an effort by the Government to ensure that the Assembly of the Republic was able to offer adequate support in ongoing reunification talks with Greek Cypriots. At the election held on 19 April, the UBP secured 44.0% of the votes cast, increasing its representation to 26 seats and securing an overall majority in the legislature, while President Talat's CTP garnered only 15 seats and 29.3% of the votes. The DP won five seats, and the ORP and the Toplumcu Demokrasi Partisi (TDP—Communal Democracy Party) each secured two seats. (The TDP had been established in 2007 following a merger between the TKP and the Bariş ve Demokrasi Hareketi—Peace and Democracy Movement). A new Council of Ministers was approved by Talat in May. Eroğlu, who had been re-elected as UBP leader in November 2008, reassumed the post of Prime Minister; Özgürgün was accorded the foreign affairs portfolio. Eroğlu pledged his Government's support for the reunification talks between Talat and Christofias. None the less, it was widely felt that the election victory by the UBP, which had long favoured the establishment of the 'TRNC' as an independent nation, would almost certainly undermine negotiations, which were widely believed to be entering a critical period.

In mid-June 2009, at the 32nd meeting between the Turkish and Greek Cypriot leaders since the resumption of fully fledged negotiations in September 2008, discussions on economic matters were concluded and talks on territorial issues commenced. In late June an agreement was reached on the opening of an additional crossing-point at the north-eastern village of Limnitis (Yeşilırmak); this occurred on 14 October 2010. Following a 40th meeting between Talat and Christofias on 6 August 2009, the first round of reunification negotiations was concluded. A second round of talks ended on 29 January 2010, after the two leaders had agreed to conduct twice-weekly meetings from October 2009.

At a presidential election, held on 18 April 2010, Eroğlu emerged victorious, having secured 50.4% of the valid votes cast. The incumbent, Talat, received 42.9% of the vote, while five other independent candidates all achieved less than 4.0%. The rate of voter participation was recorded at 76.4%. Eroğlu was sworn in as President on 23 April, and on 10 May he nominated the new leader of the UBP, İrsen Küçük, as Prime Minister. A new, minority Government—in which the main portfolios remained unchanged—was endorsed by President Eroğlu on 17 May and won a vote of confidence in the Assembly on 27 May, having obtained the support of DP and ORP deputies.

Eroğlu led the Turkish Cypriot negotiating team when the UN-led reunification talks resumed in May 2010. However, despite considerable optimism on the part of the UN concerning the progress of the talks, hopes that the Turkish and Greek Cypriots would agree a settlement by the end of 2010—the target date outlined by the two leaders at their 59th meeting on 21 December 2009—were not realized. In December 2010 the UN Secretary-General, Ban Ki-Moon, insisted that a settlement based on a bicommunal, bizonal federation with political equality must be reached in the coming months and that the two sides must concentrate on the measures required to settle outstanding differences.

Protests against austerity measures and the stalling of reunification negotiations

In January 2011 tens of thousands of Turkish Cypriot public sector workers went on strike and staged a mass protest in Nicosia against the package of economic austerity measures that the Government had imposed at the beginning of the month. These measures included significant reductions in the salaries of civil servants and the divestment to private Turkish companies of several public sector institutions in the 'TRNC'. There were fears that the changes might encourage an even greater number of Turkish Cypriots to emigrate. The protesters also claimed that the austerity measures were in fact being imposed by Turkey, which was seeking to reduce its expenditure on financing the budget deficit of the 'TRNC'. Further general strikes and rallies against the austerity measures took place in March and April. In the latter month Küçük effected an extensive reorganization of the Government; most notably, Nazım Çavuşoğlu (hitherto Minister of National Education, Youth and Sport) replaced İrkay Kamil as Minister of Interior Affairs and Local Administrations.

The UN-sponsored reunification talks between Presidents Eroğlu and Christofias were restarted at the end of October 2011. In a report published in the same month, the European Commission urged the 'TRNC' to do more to normalize relations with the Greek Cypriot administration, noting with concern that the territory's EU accession negotiations had 'regrettably not moved into any new areas for a year'. In early February 2012 the reunification discussions stalled, with Eroğlu stating that they could not continue while Greek Cyprus held the rotating presidency of the EU (scheduled for the second half of 2012). In late March 2012 Ban Ki-Moon informed the UN Security Council that discussions on the core issues were approaching deadlock, and in late April the UN decided to restrict its role as a mediator between the Turkish and Greek Cypriot Governments to negotiations on technical issues and confidence-building measures.

The Republic of Cyprus's assumption of the rotating EU presidency for a six-month period starting on 1 July 2012 led the Government of Turkey to freeze all high-level contacts with EU member states, stating that Cyprus had assumed this role in the absence of a settlement with the 'TRNC' on the island's reunification. The impasse in the reunification negotiations continued, and by late January 2013 no further direct meetings had been held between Eroğlu and Christofias.

Recent developments: The collapse of the Küçük Government and early legislative elections

After eight deputies from Küçük's UBP had, on 26 May 2013, chosen to join the opposition DP, on 5 June the Assembly held a vote of no confidence in the Prime Minister. Having lost the parliamentary vote (with the CTP, the TDP and DP all opposing him), Küçük's Government resigned on 6 June. On 11 June Eroğlu appointed Sibel Siber of the CTP at the head of an interim Council of Ministers; she was sworn into office on 14 June, becoming the territory's first female premier. The new interim Government was endorsed by the legislature on 23 June and was to remain in office until after early elections scheduled for the following month.

The elections to the Assembly held on 28 July 2013 resulted in a victory for the CTP, which secured 21 seats (with 38.4% of the votes cast). President Eroğlu's UBP won only 14 seats (27.3%), the DP 12 (23.2%) and the TDP three (7.4%). The election result appeared to demonstrate widespread public disillusionment with the austerity measures imposed by the Küçük administration.

President Eroğlu designated the CTP leader, Özkan Yorgancıoğlu, as Prime Minister on 15 August 2013. A new coalition Government, formed by the CTP and the DP, took office on 2 September. The DP leader, Serdar Denktaş, became Deputy Prime Minister and Minister of Economy, Tourism, Culture and Sport. Among the other notable appointments were those of Özdil Nami (of the CTP) as Minister of Foreign Affairs, Teberrüken Uluçay (of the CTP) as Minister of Interior Affairs and Local Administrations, and Mustafa Arabacıoğlu (of the DP) as Minister of National Education. The CTP's Zeren Mungan retained the post of Minister of Finance that he had held in Siber's interim administration. The new 'TRNC' Government secured a motion of confidence in the Assembly on 11 September. In early November the EU agreed to restart negotiations with Turkey on one of the chapters relating to the country's application to join the Union, despite EU officials expressing ongoing concerns about Turkey's democratic credentials and its Government's record on human rights.

CONSTITUTION AND GOVERNMENT

The northern area of Cyprus is under the de facto control of the 'Turkish Republic of Northern Cyprus' ('TRNC'—for which a new Constitution was approved by a referendum in May 1985). The 'TRNC' is recognized only by Turkey. The 'TRNC' elects its own 50-member legislature for a term of five years and has an independent judicial system. The President of the 'TRNC' is elected for a five-year term and appoints a Prime Minister, who forms a 10-member Council of Ministers.

REGIONAL AND INTERNATIONAL CO-OPERATION

The 'TRNC' is only recognized by Turkey, and as such has no formal relations with other countries or organizations. Following the accession of the Republic of Cyprus to the European Union (see p. 273) in 2004, the *acquis communautaire* (the body of EU legislation, treaties and case law) was suspended in the 'TRNC' until such time as a final settlement on reunification could be achieved. However, the 'TRNC' has been granted special guest status at the Economic Cooperation Organization (ECO, see p. 265).

ECONOMIC AFFAIRS

Gross national product (GNP) in the 'TRNC' was officially estimated at US $5,649.5m., or $14,703 per head, in 2010. Real GDP increased at an average annual rate of 2.0% in 2005–10. GDP declined by 5.5% in 2009, before increasing by 3.7% in 2010, according to the State Planning Organization.

The agricultural sector contributed 6.5% of GDP in 2010, and engaged 3.7% of the employed labour force in October 2011. The principal crops are citrus fruit, vegetables, potatoes, barley and wheat. The 'TRNC' imports water from Turkey in order to address the problem of drought. The GDP of the agricultural sector declined by an average of 1.1% per year in 2005–10. However, agricultural GDP increased by 10.0% in 2010.

The industrial sector contributed 17.0% of GDP in 2010, and engaged 18.5% of the employed labour force in the same year. Industrial GDP increased at an average annual rate of 3.0% in 2005–10. The GDP of the industrial sector declined by some 14.6% in 2009, before increasing by 2.0% in 2010.

Mining and quarrying contributed 0.7% of GDP, and engaged 0.1% of the employed labour force in 2010. The GDP of the mining sector increased by an average of 2.7% per year in 2005–10; however, mining GDP declined by 15.5% in 2009, and remained constant in 2010.

The manufacturing sector provided 2.6% of GDP, and engaged 9.0% of the employed labour force in 2010. Manufacturing GDP declined at an average annual rate of 2.2% in 2005–10; it decreased by 1.6% in 2010.

The construction sector provided 6.1% of GDP, and engaged 8.3% of the employed labour force in 2010. The GDP of the construction sector increased at an average annual rate of 6.7% in 2005–10; sectoral GDP declined by some 18.5% in 2009, before increasing by 3.8% in 2010.

Mineral fuels and lubricants comprised 20.5% of total imports in the 'TRNC' in 2010.

The services sector contributed 76.5% of GDP, and engaged 75.9% of the employed labour force in 2010. In that year a total of 902,390 tourists (741,925 of whom were from Turkey) visited the 'TRNC', and net tourism receipts were estimated at US $405.8m. Services GDP increased by an average of 1.7% per year in 2005–10; sectoral GDP declined by 3.1% in 2009, before increasing by 1.0% in 2010.

The 'TRNC' recorded a visible merchandise trade deficit in 2010 of US $1,507.8m., and there was a deficit of $275.8m. on the current account of the balance of payments. In 2010 the principal imports were machinery and transport equipment, basic manufactures, mineral fuels and lubricants, food and live animals, and miscellaneous manufactured products; the principal exports were industrial products, agricultural products and minerals. Turkey is by far the territory's principal trading partner, supplying 70.9% of imports and taking 46.4% of exports in 2010.

A budgetary deficit of 566.1m. Turkish lira was estimated in the 'TRNC' in 2010, equivalent to 10.1% of GDP. The average increase in prices for the 12 months to December averaged 18.2% in 2000–09; the annual average rate of inflation was 8.0% in 2012. The unemployment rate was recorded at 9.7% in October 2011.

The Turkish Cypriot economy has continued to suffer from its international isolation and has consequently remained heavily dependent on financial aid from Turkey. In December 2012 the Turkish Government agreed to provide the 'TRNC' with an estimated TL 3,000m. for 2013–16. Furthermore, the construction of an 80 km-long undersea pipeline to transport some 75m. cu m of water each year from southern Turkey to the 'TRNC' was reported to be close to completion in mid-2013, with the transfer of water expected from early 2014. Meanwhile, proposals to end international trade restrictions against the 'TRNC' were not realized, owing to continued Greek Cypriot opposition, while goods produced in the north must also be re-exported via Turkey, making them more costly and therefore less competitive in global markets. Austerity measures introduced by the 'TRNC' Government in January 2011, in an effort to improve its fiscal position, have led to mass protests by state employees in Nicosia. A programme involving the privatization of many state-owned companies, notably in the electricity, transport and telecommunications sectors, also resulted in industrial unrest during 2011–12. The defeat of President Derviş Eroğlu's National Unity Party (UBP) at legislative elections held in July 2013 (see Contemporary Political History) was widely attributed to the unpopularity of the austerity measures recently imposed by his administration in tandem with the Turkish Government, notably the significant reductions in public spending.

PUBLIC HOLIDAYS

2015: 2 January (Birth of the Prophet)*, 23 April (National Sovereignty and Children's Day), 19 May (Youth and Sports Day), 17 July (Ramazam Bayram—end of Ramadan)*, 20 July (Peace and Freedom Day, anniversary of the Turkish invasion of Cyprus in 1974), 1 August (Communal Resistance Day), 30 August (Victory Day), 23 September (Kurban Bayram—Feast of the Sacrifice)*, 29 October (Turkish Republic Day), 15 November ('TRNC' Day), 23 December (Birth of the Prophet)*.

* These holidays are dependent on the Islamic lunar calendar and may vary by one or two days from the dates given.

Statistical Survey

Source: Statistics and Research Dept, State Planning Organization, Prime Ministry, Lefkoşa (Nicosia), Mersin 10, Turkey; tel. (22) 83141; fax (22) 85988; e-mail trnc-spo@management.emu.edu.tr; internet www.devplan.org.

AREA AND POPULATION

Area: 3,242 sq km (1,251 sq miles).

Population: 256,644 at census of 30 April 2006; 286,257 (males 150,483, females 135,774) at census of 4 December 2011.

Density (at 2011 census): 88.3 per sq km.

Population by Age and Sex (at census of 4 December 2011): *0–14:* 52,710 (males 27,158, females 25,552); *15–64:* 210,286 (males 112,823, females 97,463); *65 and over:* 23,261 (males 10,502, females 12,759); *Total* 286,257 (males 150,483, females 135,774).

Population by Country of Nationality (self-declaration at census of 4 December 2011): 'TRNC' 136,362; Turkey 80,550; Joint 'TRNC' and other 54,132 (with Turkey 38,085, with Other 16,047); United Kingdom 3,691; Turkmenistan 1,760; Nigeria 1,279; Iran 1,152; Pakistan 1,075; Bulgaria 920; Azerbaijan 835; Other 4,501; *Total* 286,257.

Districts (population at census of 4 December 2011): Lefkoşa 94,824; Mağusa 69,741; Girne 69,163; Güzelyurt 30,037; İskele 22,492; *Total* 286,257.

Principal Towns (population within the municipal boundary at census of 4 December 2011): Lefkoşa (Nicosia) 61,378 (Turkish-occupied area only); Gazi Mağusa (Famagusta) 40,920; Girne (Kyrenia) 33,207; Güzelyurt 18,946.

Births, Marriages and Deaths (registered, 2001): Live births 2,550 (birth rate 15.0 per 1,000); Marriages 1,090 (marriage rate 5.2 per 1,000); Deaths 781 (death rate 8.0 per 1,000). *2010:* Birth rate 15.2 per 1,000; Death rate 6.9 per 1,000.

Life Expectancy (years at birth, 2010): Males 72.0; Females 76.7.

Economically Active Population (labour force survey, October 2010): Agriculture, forestry and fishing 5,300; Mining and quarrying 73; Manufacturing 8,393; Construction 7,746; Electricity, gas and water 1,051; Wholesale and retail trade 16,547; Hotels and restaurants 7,470; Transport, storage and communications 5,026; Financial institutions 3,498; Real estate and renting 4,686; Public administration 15,669; Education 9,149; Health 2,481; Other community services 6,408; *Total employed* 93,498; Unemployed 12,619; *Total labour force* 106,117. *2011* (labour force survey at October): Agriculture, forestry and fishing 3,614; Non-agricultural 93,489; Total employed 97,103; Unemployed 10,411; Total labour force 107,514.

HEALTH AND WELFARE

Key Indicators

Total Fertility Rate (children per woman, 2010): 1.9.

Under-5 Mortality Rate (per 1,000 live births, 2006): 13.9.

Physicians (per 1,000 head, 2010): 2.7.

Hospital Beds (per 1,000 head, 2010): 5.6.

AGRICULTURE

Principal Crops ('000 metric tons, 2001): Wheat 7.6; Barley 102.1; Potatoes 14.0; Legumes 2.5; Tomatoes 8.3; Onions 1.7; Artichokes 1.2; Watermelons 9.7; Melons 3.0; Cucumbers 2.1; Carobs 2.8; Olives 3.1; Lemons 10.7; Grapefruit 15.8; Oranges 61.6; Tangerines 2.0.

Livestock ('000 head, 2001): Cattle 34.2; Sheep 202.7; Goats 54.8; Chickens 4,238.

Livestock Products ('000 metric tons, unless otherwise indicated, 2001): Sheep's and goats' milk 11.4; Cows' milk 66.5; Sheep meat 3.3; Goat meat 0.8; Cattle meat 2.1; Chicken meat 6.8; Wool 0.2; Eggs (million) 13.4.

Fishing (metric tons, 2001): Total catch 400.

FINANCE

Currency and Exchange Rates: Turkish currency: 100 kuruş = 1 Turkish lira. *Sterling, Dollar and Euro Equivalents* (31 December 2013): £1 sterling = 3.518 liras; US $1 = 2.136 liras; €1 = 2.946 liras; 100 Turkish liras = £28.43 = $46.81 = €33.94. Note: A new currency, the new Turkish lira, equivalent to 1,000,000 of the former units, was introduced on 1 January 2005. Figures in this survey have been converted retrospectively to reflect this development. (The name of the currency reverted to Turkish lira on 1 January 2009, although new Turkish lira banknotes and coins were to remain in circulation for a further year.) *Average Exchange Rate* (liras per US dollar): 1.503 in 2010; 1.675 in 2011; 1.796 in 2012.

Budget ('000 Turkish liras, 2010): *Revenue:* Local revenue 1,791,246.8 (Direct taxes 584,146.9, Indirect taxes 687,951.4, Other income 170,387.4, Fund revenues 348,761.0); Foreign aid 303,637.3; Total 2,094,884.1. *Expenditure:* Personnel 947,401.5; Other goods and services 192,648.5; Transfers 1,169,441.2; Investments 188,138.6; Defence 163,327.2; Total 2,660,957.0.

Cost of Living (Consumer Price Index, annual averages; base: 2008 = 100): 110.3 in 2010; 120.9 in 2011; 130.6 in 2012.

Expenditure on the Gross Domestic Product ('000 Turkish liras at current prices, 2003, provisional figures): Government final consumption expenditure 482,674; Private final consumption expenditure 1,071,916; Increase in stocks 30,900; Gross fixed capital formation 300,218; *Total domestic expenditure* 1,885,707; Net exports of goods and services −56,763; *GDP in purchasers' values* 1,828,944; *GDP at constant 1977 prices* (million liras) 9,523.6.

Gross Domestic Product by Economic Activity ('000 Turkish liras, 2010): Agriculture, forestry and fishing 330,292.7; Mining and quarrying 35,628.4; Manufacturing 130,888.7; Electricity and water 386,319.1; Construction 312,118.7; Wholesale and retail trade 598,030.0; Restaurants and hotels 302,003.6; Transport and communications 525,213.2; Finance 404,371.0; Ownership of dwellings 220,581.2; Business and personal services 652,317.3; Government services 1,180,064.6; *Sub-total* 5,077,828.4; Import duties 536,308.5; *GDP in purchasers' values* 5,614,136.9.

Balance of Payments (US $ million, 2008): Merchandise exports f.o.b. 83.7; Merchandise imports c.i.f. −1,680.7; *Trade balance* −1,597.0; Services and unrequited transfers (net) 1,206.7; *Current balance* −390.3; Foreign aid and loans from Turkey 337.1; Other short-term capital movements 73.4; Net errors and omissions −289.7; *Overall balance* −269.5.

EXTERNAL TRADE

Principal Commodities (US $ million, 2010): *Imports c.i.f.:* Food and live animals 176.9; Beverages and tobacco 86.7; Mineral fuels, lubricants, etc. 328.1; Basic manufactures 331.1; Machinery and transport equipment 362.2; Miscellaneous manufactured articles 149.8; Total (incl. others) 1,604.2. *Exports f.o.b.:* Food and live animals 36.8; Industrial products 52.1; Minerals 7.5; Total 96.4.

Principal Trading Partners (US $ million, 2010): *Imports c.i.f.:* Turkey 1,137.4; United Kingdom 74.7; USA 11.7; Total (incl. others) 1,604.2. *Exports f.o.b.:* Turkey 44.7; United Kingdom 4.8; Total (incl. others) 96.4.

TRANSPORT

Road Traffic (registered motor vehicles, 2001): Saloon cars 76,850; Estate cars 9,168; Pick-ups 3,825; Vans 9,131; Buses 2,077; Trucks 1,593; Lorries 6,335; Motorcycles 16,424; Agricultural tractors 6,594; Total (incl. others) 134,454.

Shipping (2001): Freight traffic ('000 metric tons): Goods loaded 247.2, Goods unloaded 898.1; Vessels entered 3,220.

Civil Aviation (2001): Passenger arrivals and departures 691,431; Freight landed and cleared (metric tons) 4,297.

TOURISM

Visitors (2010): 902,390 (including 741,925 Turkish visitors).

Tourism Receipts (US $ million, 2010): 405.8.

COMMUNICATIONS MEDIA

Radio Receivers (2001, provisional): 82,364 in use.

Television Receivers (2001, provisional): 70,960 in use.

Telephones (2010): 359,000 subscribers.

Mobile Cellular Telephones (2010): 1,832,000 subscribers.

EDUCATION

2010/11: *Pre-primary schools:* 145 institutions, 487 teachers, 6,229 pupils; *Primary schools:* 94 institutions, 1,567 teachers, 18,053 pupils; *Secondary Schools:* 36 institutions, 1,108 teachers, 10,487 students; *General High Schools:* 27 institutions, 973 teachers, 7,786 students; *Vocational Schools:* 11 institutions, 524 teachers, 3,080 students; *Universities:* 8 institutions, 41,230 students (of which 12,666 Turkish Cypriots, 24,319 from Turkey, 4,245 from other countries). Note: 2,620 'TRNC' students were studying abroad.

Pupil-teacher Ratio (primary education): 12.6 in 2010/11.

Adult Literacy Rate (at census of 15 December 1996): 93.5%.

Directory

The Government of the 'Turkish Republic of Northern Cyprus'

HEAD OF STATE

President of the 'Turkish Republic of Northern Cyprus': Dr DERVIŞ EROĞLU (inaugurated 23 April 2010).

COUNCIL OF MINISTERS

(April 2014)

A coalition Government formed by the Republican Turkish Party (CTP) and the Democrat Party (DP).

Prime Minister: ÖZKAN YORGANCIOĞLU (CTP).

Deputy Prime Minister and Minister of Economy, Tourism, Culture and Sport: SERDAR DENKTAŞ (DP).

Minister of Interior Affairs and Local Administrations: TEBERRÜKEN ULUÇAY (CTP).

Minister of Finance: ZEREN MUNGAN (CTP).

Minister of Foreign Affairs: ÖZDIL NAMI (CTP).

Minister of Health: Dr AHMET GÜLLE (CTP).

Minister of Food, Agriculture and Energy: ÖNDER SENNAROĞLU (CTP).

Minister of Public Works and Transport: Dr AHMET KAŞIF (DP).

Minister of National Education: Dr MUSTAFA ARABACIOĞLU (DP).

Minister of Labour and Social Security: AZIZ GÜRPINAR (CTP).

Minister of Environment and Natural Resources: HAMIT BAKIRCI (DP).

MINISTRIES

Office of the President: Şht Selahattin Sonat Sok., Lefkoşa (Nicosia), Mersin 10, Turkey; tel. 2283444; fax 2272252; internet www.kktcb.eu.

Prime Minister's Office: Selçuklu Rd, Lefkoşa (Nicosia), Mersin 10, Turkey; tel. 2283141; fax 2287280; e-mail info@kktcbasbakanlik.org; internet www.kktcbasbakanlik.org.

Ministry of Economy, Tourism, Culture and Sport: Lefkoşa (Nicosia), Mersin 10, Turkey; tel. 2289629; fax 2273976.

Ministry of Environment and Natural Resources: Selçuklu Rd, Lefkoşa (Nicosia), Mersin 10, Turkey; tel. 2275032; fax 2283776.

Ministry of Finance: Lefkoşa (Nicosia), Mersin 10, Turkey; tel. 2283116; fax 2278230; e-mail bim@kktcmaliye.com; internet www.kktcmaliye.com.

Ministry of Food, Agriculture and Energy: Salih Mecit Sok. 16, Lefkoşa (Nicosia), Mersin 10, Turkey; tel. 2283735; fax 2286945.

Ministry of Foreign Affairs: Selçuklu Rd, Lefkoşa (Nicosia), Mersin 10, Turkey; tel. 2283241; fax 2284290; e-mail bakanlik@trncinfo.org; internet www.trncinfo.org.

Ministry of Health: Lefkoşa (Nicosia), Mersin 10, Turkey; tel. 2283173; fax 2283893; e-mail saglik@kktc.net; internet www.saglikbakanligi.com.

Ministry of Interior Affairs and Local Administrations: Lefkoşa (Nicosia), Mersin 10, Turkey; tel. 2283344; fax 2283043.

Ministry of Labour and Social Security: 7 İplik Pazarı Sok., Lefkoşa (Nicosia), Mersin 10, Turkey; tel. 2275032; fax 2283776; e-mail calismadairesi@gmail.com.

Ministry of National Education: Lefkoşa (Nicosia), Mersin 10, Turkey; tel. 2284505; fax 2282334; e-mail info@mebnet.net; internet www.mebnet.net.

Ministry of Public Works and Transport: Lefkoşa (Nicosia), Mersin 10, Turkey; tel. 2283666; fax 2281891; e-mail info@kktculastirma.com; internet bub.gov.ct.tr.

President

Election, 18 April 2010

Candidates	Votes	%
Dr Derviş Eroğlu (National Unity Party)	61,422	50.35
Mehmet Ali Talat (Ind.)	52,294	42.87
Tahsin Ertuğruloğlu (Ind.)	4,647	3.81
Zeki Besiktepeli (Ind.)	1,967	1.61
Mustafa Kemal Tümkan (Ind.)	964	0.79
Arif Salih Kirdag (Ind.)	520	0.43
Ayhan Kaymak (Ind.)	168	0.14
Total*	121,982	100.00

* Excluding 3,312 invalid votes.

Legislature

Assembly of the Republic: Osmanpaşa Cad., Lefkoşa (Nicosia), Mersin 10, Turkey; internet cm.gov.nc.tr.

Speaker: Dr SIBEL SIBER.

General Election, 28 July 2013

Party	Votes	% of votes	Seats
Republican Turkish Party (CTP)	477,209	38.38	21
National Unity Party (UBP)	339,864	27.33	14
Democrat Party (DP)	288,021	23.16	12
Communal Democracy Party (TDP)	92,110	7.41	3
United Cyprus Party (BKP)	39,127	3.15	—
Total (incl. others)	1,243,441	100.00	50

Election Commission

Yüksek Seçim Kurulu (YSK) (Higher Council of Elections): Lefkoşa (Nicosia), Mersin 10, Turkey; internet ysk.mahkemeler.net; Pres. METIN A. HAKKI.

Political Organizations

Communal Democracy Party (Toplumcu Demokrasi Partisi—TDP): 11 Selim Cad., 44 Köşklüçiftlik, Lefkoşa (Nicosia), Mersin 10, Turkey; tel. 2272555; fax 2287539; e-mail tdp@kktc.net; internet www.toplumcudemokrasipartisi.com; f. 2007, by merger between the Bariş ve Demokrasi Hareketi (Peace and Democracy Movement) and the Toplumcu Kurtuluş Partisi (Communal Liberation Party); Pres. MEHMET ÇAKICI.

Cyprus Justice Party (Kıbrıs Adalet Partisi—KAP): 1 Osman Paşa Ave, Köşklüçiftlik, Lefkoşa (Nicosia), Mersin 10, Turkey; tel. 2270274; fax 2289938; Leader OĞUZ KALEIOĞLU.

Cyprus Socialist Party (Kıbrıs Sosyalist Partisi—KSP): Lefkoşa (Nicosia), Mersin 10, Turkey; tel. 2270680; fax 2270681; e-mail ksp@kibrissosyalistpartisi.org; internet www.kibrissosyalistpartisi.org; Gen. Sec. MEHMET BIRINCI.

Democrat Party (Demokrat Parti—DP): Hasane Ilgaz Sok. 13A, Lefkoşa (Nicosia), Mersin 10, Turkey; tel. 2283795; fax 2287130; e-mail basin@demokratparti.net; f. 1992 by disaffected representatives of the Ulusal Bırlık Partisi; merged with the Yeni Doğuş Partisi (New Dawn Party; f. 1984) and Sosyal Demokrat Partisi (Social Democrat Party) in May 1993; Leader SERDAR DENKTAŞ; Gen. Sec. ERTUĞRUL HASIPOĞLU.

Freedom and Reform Party (Özgürlük ve Reform Partisi—Özgür Parti—ORP): Lala Mustafa Paşa Sok. 18, Köşklüçiftlik, Lefkoşa (Nicosia), Mersin 10, Turkey; tel. 2274797; fax 2270537; f. 2006 by breakaway parliamentary deputies; Leader Dr TURGAY AVCI.

National Unity Party (Ulusal Bırlık Partisi—UBP): 9 Atatürk Meydanı, Lefkoşa (Nicosia), Mersin 10, Turkey; tel. 2279252; fax 2288732; e-mail iletisim@ulusalbirlikpartisi.com; internet www.ulusalbirlikpartisi.com; f. 1975; right of centre; opposes reunification of Cyprus; Pres. HÜSEYIN ÖZGÜRGÜN; Sec.-Gen. SUNAT ATUN.

New Cyprus Party (Yeni Kıbrıs Partisi—YKP): Tahir Hussain Bldg, Lefkoşa (Nicosia), Mersin 10, Turkey; tel. 2274917; fax 2288931; e-mail ykp@ykp.org.cy; internet www.ykp.org.cy; f. 1989; operated as Patriotic Unity Movement (Yurtsever Bırlık Hareketi) between 1998–2004; publishes weekly newsletter *Yeniçag*; Gen. Sec. MURAT KANATLI.

New Party (Yeni Partisi): Lefkoşa (Nicosia), Mersin 10, Turkey; f. 2004; Leader NURI ÇEVIKEL.

Republican Turkish Party (Cumhuriyetçi Türk Partisi—CTP): 99 Şehit Salahi, Şevket Sok., Lefkoşa (Nicosia), Mersin 10, Turkey; tel. 2273300; fax 2281914; e-mail info@ctp-bg.org; internet www.ctp-bg.org; f. 1970 by mems of the Turkish community in Cyprus; district orgs at Gazi Mağusa (Famagusta), Girne (Kyrenia), Güzelyurt (Morphou) and Lefkoşa (Nicosia); Leader ÖZKAN YORGANCIOĞLU; Gen. Sec. KUTLAY ERK.

United Cyprus Party (Birleşik Kıbrıs Partisi—BKP): Ali Paşa Sok. 4, Çağlayan, Lefkoşa (Nicosia), Mersin 10, Turkey; tel. 2281845; fax 2281617; e-mail bkp@birlesikkibris.com; internet birlesikkibrispartisi.net; f. 2002; Marxist-Leninist; Sec.-Gen. İZZET İZCAN.

Diplomatic Representation

Turkey is the only country officially to have recognized the 'Turkish Republic of Northern Cyprus'.

Turkey: Bedrettin Demirel Cad., T. C. Lefkoşa Büyükelçisi, Lefkoşa (Nicosia), Mersin 10, Turkey; tel. 2272314; fax 2282209; e-mail buyukelcilik.lefkosa@mfa.gov.tr; internet www.tclefkosabe.org; Ambassador HALIL İBRAHIM AKÇA.

Judicial System

Supreme Court: Lefkoşa (Nicosia), Mersin 10, Turkey; tel. 2285185; fax 2285265; e-mail erkancoskun@kamunet.net; internet www.mahkemeler.net; The Supreme Court is the highest court in the 'TRNC', and functions as the Constitutional Court, the Court of Appeal and the High Administrative Court. The Supreme Court, sitting as the Constitutional Court, has exclusive jurisdiction to adjudicate finally on all matters prescribed by the Constitution. The Supreme Court, sitting as the Court of Appeal, is the highest appellate court in the 'TRNC' in both civil and criminal cases. It also has original jurisdiction in certain matters of judicial review. The Supreme Court, sitting as the High Administrative Court, has exclusive jurisdiction on matters relating to administrative law. The Supreme Court is composed of a President and seven judges; Pres. NEVVAR NOLAN.

Subordinate Courts: Judicial power other than that exercised by the Supreme Court is exercised by the Assize Courts, District Courts and Family Courts.

Supreme Council of Judicature: The Supreme Council of Judicature, composed of the president and judges of the Supreme Court, a member appointed by the President of the 'TRNC', a member appointed by the Assembly of the Republic, the Attorney-General and a member elected by the Bar Association, is responsible for the appointment, promotion, transfer and matters relating to the discipline of all judges. The appointments of the president and judges of the Supreme Court are subject to the approval of the President of the 'TRNC'.

The Attorney-General's Office: The office of the Attorney-General is not attached to any Ministry. The Deputy Attorney-General acts for the Attorney-General in case of his absence; Attorney-General ASKAN ILGEN.

Religion

Most adherents of Islam in the 'TRNC' are Sunni Muslims of the Hanafi sect. The religious head of the Muslim community in the 'TRNC' is the Grand Mufti.

Grand Mufti of the 'TRNC': Sheikh AL-SAYYID MUHAMMAD NAZIM ADIL AL-QUBRUSI AL-HAQQANI, PK 142, Lefkoşa (Nicosia), Mersin 10, Turkey.

The Press

DAILIES

Afrika: Lefkoşa (Nicosia), Mersin 10, Turkey; tel. 2271338; fax 2274585; e-mail avrupa@kktc.net; internet www.afrikagazetesi.net; fmrly *Avrupa*; Turkish; independent; Editor ŞENER LEVENT; circ. 3,000.

Halkın Sesi (Voice of the People): 172 Girne Cad., Lefkoşa (Nicosia), Mersin 10, Turkey; tel. 22856453141; fax 2272612; e-mail halkinsesi@superonline.com; internet www.halkinsesi.org; f. 1942; morning; Turkish; independent Turkish nationalist; Editor SEFA KARAHASAN.

Kıbrıs (Cyprus): Dr Fazıl Küçük Bul., Yeni Sanayi Bölgesi, Lefkoşa (Nicosia), Mersin 10, Turkey; tel. 2252555; fax 2255176; e-mail kibris@kibrisgazetesi.com; internet www.kibrisgazetesi.com; Turkish; Editor BAŞARAN DÜZGÜN; circ. 13,000.

Ortam (Political Conditions): 7 Cengiz Han Sok, Köşklüçiflik, Lefkoşa (Nicosia), Mersin 10, Turkey; tel. 2280852; fax 2283784; e-mail ortam@north-cyprus.net; internet www.ortamgazetesi.com; f. 1981; Turkish; organ of the TDP; Editor-in-Chief MEHMET DAVULCU; circ. 1,250.

Vatan (Homeland): 46 Müftü Ziyai Sok., PK 842, Lefkoşa (Nicosia), Mersin 10, Turkey; tel. 2277557; fax 2277558; e-mail atekman@vatangazetesi.net; internet www.vatangazetesi.com; f. 1991; Turkish; Editor ALI TEKMAN.

Yeni Düzen (New System): Organize Sanayi Bölgesi, Lefkoşa (Nicosia), Mersin 10, Turkey; tel. 2256658; fax 2253240; e-mail yeniduzen@defne.net; internet www.yeniduzengazetesi.com; f. 1975; Turkish; organ of the CTP; Chief Editor CENK MUTLUYAKALI; circ. 1,250.

WEEKLIES

Cyprus Observer: 18 Aytekin Zekai Sok., Kyrenia (Girne), Mersin 10, Turkey; POB 29085, Nicosia; tel. 8155387; fax 8155585; e-mail news@observercyprus.com; internet www.observercyprus.com; f. 2005; English; Exec. Editor HASAN ERCAKICA; Editor UMUT URAS.

Cyprus Today: Dr Fazıl Küçük Bul., PK 831, Lefkoşa (Nicosia), Mersin 10, Turkey; tel. 2252555; fax 2253708; e-mail cyprustoday@yahoo.com; f. 1991; English; political, social, cultural and economic; Editor GILL FRASER; circ. 10,000.

Ekonomi (The Economy): 90 Bedrettin Demirel Cad., Lefkoşa (Nicosia), Mersin 10, Turkey; tel. 2283760; fax 2283089; f. 1958; Turkish; publ. by the Turkish Cypriot Chamber of Commerce; Editor-in-Chief SAMI TAŞARKAN; circ. 3,000.

Safak: PK 228, Lefkoşa (Nicosia), Mersin 10, Turkey; tel. 2271472; fax 2287910; f. 1992; Turkish; circ. 1,000.

Yeniçağ: 28 Ramadan Cad., Lefkoşa (Nicosia), Mersin 10, Turkey; tel. 2274917; fax 2271476; e-mail irtibat@yenicaggazetesi.com.tr; internet www.yenicaggazetesi.com.tr; f. 1990; Turkish; organ of the YKP; Editor MURAT KANATLI; circ. 600.

PERIODICALS

Güvenlik Kuvvetleri Magazine: Lefkoşa (Nicosia), Mersin 10, Turkey; tel. 2275880; publ. by the Security Forces of the 'TRNC'.

Halkbilimi (Folklore): Hasder, PK 199, Lefkoşa, Mersin 10, Turkey; tel. 8534983; fax 2287798; e-mail hasder@hasder.org; internet www.hasder.org; f. 1986; annual; publ. of Hasder Folk Arts Foundation; academic, folkloric; Turkish, with a short summary in English; Chief Editor ALI NEBIH; circ. 750.

Kıbrıs—Northern Cyprus Monthly: Ministry of Foreign Affairs, Lefkoşa (Nicosia), Mersin 10, Turkey; tel. 2283365; fax 2287641; e-mail pio@trncpio.org; internet www.trncpio.org; f. 1963; Editor GÖNÜL ATANER.

Kıbrısli Türkün Sesi: 44 Mecidiye St, Lefkoşa (Nicosia), Mersin 10, Turkey; tel. 2278520; fax 2287966; monthly; political; Exec. Dir DOGAN HARMAN; Gen. Co-ordinator CEVDET ALPARSLAN.

Kuzey Kıbrıs Kültür Dergisi (North Cyprus Cultural Journal): PK 157, Lefkoşa (Nicosia), Mersin 10, Turkey; tel. 2231298; f. 1987; monthly; Turkish; Chief Editor GÜNSEL DOĞASAL.

NEWS AGENCY

TürkAjansı-Kıbrıs (TAK) (Turkish News Agency of Cyprus): PK 355, 30 Mehmet Akif Cad., Lefkoşa (Nicosia), Mersin 10, Turkey; tel. 2282773; fax 2271213; e-mail tak@emu.edu.tr; internet kktc.gov.nc.tr/tak; f. 1973; Dir EMIR HÜSEYN ERSOY.

Publishers

Action Global Communications: 6 Kondilaki St, 1090 Lefkoşa (Nicosia), Mersin 10, Turkey; tel. 22818884; fax 22873633; e-mail action@actionprgroup.com; internet www.actionprgroup.com; f. 1971; affiliate of Weber Shandwick; has 44 offices in the emerging markets; travel, aviation and hospitality; Man. Dir TONY CHRISTODOULOU.

Bolan Matbaası: 35 Pençizade Sok., Lefkoşa (Nicosia), Mersin 10, Turkey; tel. 2274802.

Devlet Basımevi (Turkish Cypriot Government Printing House): Şerif Arzik Sok., Lefkoşa (Nicosia), Mersin 10, Turkey; tel. 2272010; Dir SONGUC KÜRŞAD.

Güneş Gazetesi: Yediler Sok., Lefkoşa (Nicosia), Mersin 10, Turkey; tel. and fax 2272959; e-mail gunesgazetesi@kibris.net; f. 1980; Dir EROL ÖNEY.

Halkın Sesi Ltd: 172 Girne Cad., Lefkoşa (Nicosia), Mersin 10, Turkey; tel. 2285645; fax 2272612; e-mail halkinsesi@superonline.com; internet www.halkinsesi.org.

Kıbrıs Araştırma ve Yayın Merkezi (North Cyprus Research and Publishing Centre—CYREP): PK 327, Lefkoşa (Nicosia), Mersin 10, Turkey; tel. 8555179; fax 2272592; e-mail gazioglu@kktc.net; Dir AHMET C. GAZIOĞLU.

K. Rüstem & Bro.: 22–24 Girne Cad., Lefkoşa (Nicosia), Mersin 10, Turkey; tel. 2271418; fax 2283641.

Tezel Matbaası: 35 Şinasi Sok., Lefkoşa (Nicosia), Mersin 10, Turkey; tel. 2271022.

Broadcasting and Communications

TELECOMMUNICATIONS

Kıbrıs Mobile Telekomünikasyon Ltd (Kuzey Kıbrıs Turkcell): Salih Mecit Sok. 1, Kızılay, Lefkoşa (Nicosia), Mersin 10, Turkey; tel. 6001030; internet www.kktcell.com; f. 1999; subsidiary of Turkcell; provides mobile cellular telecommunications services; Gen. Man. AYBARS KARAATMACA; 318,000 subscribers (March 2009).

KKTC Telekomünikasyon Dairesi (KKTC Telekom): Şehit Arif Salih Sok. 1, Lefkoşa (Nicosia), Mersin 10, Turkey; tel. 4441444; e-mail telekombilgi@telekom.kktc.net; internet www.telekom.kktc.net; f. 1963; state-owned; fixed-line telephone and internet services; Gen. Man. MUSTAFA BERKTUĞ.

KKTC Telsim: Girne Cad. 81, Lefkoşa (Nicosia), Mersin 10, Turkey; tel. 4440542; fax 2280181; e-mail info@kktctelsim.com; internet www.kktctelsim.com; f. 1995; provides mobile cellular telecommunications services; subsidiary of Vodafone Turkey.

BROADCASTING

Radio

Bayrak Radio and TV Corpn (BRTK): BRTK Sitesi, Dr Fazıl Küçük Bul., Lefkoşa (Nicosia), Mersin 10, Turkey; tel. 2255555; fax 2254581; e-mail mete.tumerkan@brtk.net; internet www.brtk.net; f. 1963 as Bayrak Radio; became independent Turkish Cypriot corpn, partly financed by the 'TRNC' Govt, in July 1983; now has five radio stations on air: Radio Bayrak, Bayrak International (international music, 24-hour, and news in English, Greek, Russian, Arabic and German), Bayrak FM (popular music, 24-hour), Bayrak Classic (classical music, 24-hour) and Bayrak Turkish Music (Turkish classical and folk music, 18-hour); Gen. Man. METE TÜMERKAN.

First FM and Interfirst FM: Lefkoşa (Nicosia), Mersin 10, Turkey; tel. 2289308; fax 2276363; f. 1996.

Kıbrıs FM / Kıbrıs TV: Dr Fazıl Küçük Blvd, Yeni Sanayi Bolgesi, Lefkoşa (Nicosia), Mersin 10, Turkey; tel. 2252555; fax 2253707; e-mail kibris@kibrisgazetesi.com; Dir ERDINÇ GÜNDÜZ.

Radio Emu: Eastern Mediterranean University, Gazi Mağusa (Famagusta), Mersin 10, Turkey; e-mail radio@emu.edu.tr; internet www.emu.edu.tr.

Television

In addition to those listed below, several Turkish channels are also transmitted to the 'TRNC'.

Bayrak Radio and TV Corpn (BRTK): BRTK Sitesi, Dr Fazıl Küçük Bul., Lefkoşa (Nicosia), Mersin 10, Turkey; tel. 2255555; fax 2254581; e-mail tvhaber@brtk.net; internet www.brtk.net; f. 1976; in July 1983 it became an independent Turkish Cypriot corpn, partly financed by the 'TRNC' Govt; Bayrak TV; transmits programmes in Turkish, Greek and English; Gen. Man. METE TÜMERKAN.

Kanal T: Şehit Üsteğmen Mustafa Orhan Sok. 10, Lefkoşa (Nicosia), Mersin 10, Turkey; tel. 2280750; fax 2280773; e-mail info@kanalt.com; internet www.kanalt.com; Owner ERSIN TATAR.

Kıbrıs Genç TV: Dr Fazıl Küçük Bul., Meral Birinci Sok. 1, Lefkoşa (Nicosia), Mersin 10, Turkey; e-mail habermerkezi@kibrisgenctv.com; internet www.kibrisgenctv.com; Dir ERTAN BIRINCI.

Finance

(br.(s) = branches; cap. = capital; res = reserves; dep. = deposits; m. = million; amounts in Turkish liras)

BANKING

Central Bank

Central Bank of the 'Turkish Republic of Northern Cyprus': POB 857, Bedreddin Demirel Ave, Lefkoşa (Nicosia), Mersin 10, Turkey; tel. 2283216; fax 2285240; e-mail ileti@kktcmerkezbankasi.org; internet www.kktcmerkezbankasi.org; f. 1984; Pres. Dr BILAL SAN.

Principal Commercial Banks

Asbank Ltd: 8 Mecidiye Sok., PK 448, Lefkoşa (Nicosia), Mersin 10, Turkey; tel. 2283023; fax 2287790; e-mail info@asbank.com.tr; internet www.asbank.com.tr; f. 1986; cap. 17m., res 4m., dep. 424m. (Dec. 2012); Chair. ALTAY ADADEMIR; Gen. Man. BÜLENT BERKAY; 8 brs.

CreditWest Bank Ltd: Şehit Mustafa A. Ruso Cad. 27, Lefkoşa (Nicosia), Mersin 10, Turkey; tel. 6780000; fax 6780029; e-mail info@creditwestbank.com; internet www.creditwestbank.com; f. 1993 as Kıbrıs Altinbaş Bank Ltd; name changed as above Oct. 2006; cap. 8m., res 41m., dep. 719m. (Dec. 2012); Pres. NUSRET ALTINBAŞ; Gen. Man. Dr SÜLEYMAN EROL; 13 brs.

Kıbrıs Continental Bank Ltd: 35–37 Girne Cad., Lefkoşa (Nicosia), Mersin 10, Turkey; tel. 2273220; fax 2286334; e-mail info@kibriscontinentalbank.net; internet www.kibriscontinentalbank.net; f. 1998; cap. 10m., res –5m., dep. 47m. (Dec. 2009); Chair. OSMAN KARAISMAILOĞLU; Gen. Man. SERACETTIN BAKTAY.

Kıbrıs Iktisat Bankasi Ltd (Cyprus Economy Bank Ltd): 151 Bedreddin Demiral Cad., Lefkoşa (Nicosia), Mersin 10, Turkey; tel. 6004000; fax 2281311; e-mail info@iktisatbank.com; internet www.iktisatbank.com; f. 1990; cap. 43m., res 6m., dep. 835m. (Dec. 2012); Chair. METE OZMERTER; 17 brs.

Kıbrıs Türk Kooperatif Merkez Bankası Ltd (Cyprus Turkish Co-operative Central Bank): PK 823, 49–55 Mahmut Paşa Sok., Lefkoşa (Nicosia), Mersin 10, Turkey; tel. 2273398; fax 2276787; e-mail info@koopbank.com; internet www.koopbank.com; f. 1959; cap. 18m., res 121m., dep. 1,870m. (Dec. 2009); banking and credit facilities to mem. societies and individuals; Chair. ZEKI ERKUT; Gen. Man. GÜLHAN ALP; 20 brs.

Kıbrıs Vakiflar Bankası Ltd (Cyprus Vakiflar Bank Ltd): PK 212, Atatürk Cad. 66, Yenisehir, Lefkoşa (Nicosia), Mersin 10, Turkey; tel. 6006020; fax 2275169; e-mail halklailiskiler@vakiflarbankasi.com; internet www.vakiflarbankasi.com; f. 1982; cap. 40m., res 20m., dep. 853m. (Dec. 2012); Chair. OSMAN BAYHANLI; Gen. Man. Cengiz ERCAĞ; 13 brs.

Limasol Türk Kooperatif Bankası Ltd (LKTB) (Limasol Turkish Co-operative Bank Ltd): Atatürk Cad. 38, Yenişehir, Lefkoşa (Nicosia), Mersin 10, Turkey; tel. 2280333; fax 2281350; e-mail info@limasolbank.com.tr; internet www.limasolbank.com.tr; f. 1939; cap. 13m., res 667,286, dep. 342m. (Dec. 2012); Chair. HÜSEYIN KEMALER; Gen. Man. İLKIN YOĞURTCUOĞLU.

Türk Bankası Ltd (Turkish Bank Ltd): 92 Girne Cad., PK 242, Lefkoşa (Nicosia), Mersin 10, Turkey; tel. 6003333; fax 2279447; e-mail info@turkishbank.net; internet www.turkishbank.com; f. 1901; cap. 61m., res 34m., dep. 773m. (Dec. 2012); Chair. IBRAHIM HAKAN BÖRTEÇENE; CEO YUNUS RAHMIOĞLU; 21 brs.

Viyabank Ltd: Atatürk Cad., 16 Muhtar Yusuf Galleria, Lefkoşa (Nicosia), Mersin 10, Turkey; tel. 2285286; fax 2285878; e-mail gm@viyabank.com; internet www.viyabank.com; f. 1998; cap. 40m., res 3m., dep. 16m. (Dec. 2012); Pres. and Chair. SALVO TARAGANO; 1 br.

Yakin Doğu Bank Ltd (Near East Bank Ltd): POB 47, 1 Girne Cad., Lefkoşa (Nicosia), Mersin 10, Turkey; tel. 2283834; fax 2284180; e-mail iletisim@neareastbank.com; internet www.yakindogubank.com; cap. 31m., res 2m., dep. 327m. (Dec. 2012); Chair. Dr SUAT İRFAN GÜNSEL; Gen. Man. KOZAN KARAKURT; 12 brs.

Yeşilada Bank Ltd: POB 626, 11 Atatürk Ave, Lefkoşa (Nicosia), Mersin 10, Turkey; tel. 2281789; fax 2277106; e-mail info@yesilada-bank.com; internet www.yesilada-bank.com; cap. 8m., res –8m., dep. 28m. (Dec. 2009); Chair. and Pres. ISMET KOTAK; Gen. Man. MUSTAFA UZUN.

INSURANCE

Akfinans Sigorta Insurance Ltd: 16 Osman Paşa Cad., Lefkoşa (Nicosia), POB 451, Mersin 10, Turkey; tel. 2284506; fax 2285713; e-mail akfinans@akfinans.com; internet www.akfinans.com; f. 1996; Gen. Man. MEHMET KADER.

Anadolu Anonim: Memduh Asaf Sokak 8, Lefkoşa (Nicosia), Mersin 10, Turkey; tel. 2279595; fax 2279596; e-mail bolge50@anadolusigorta.com.tr; internet www.anadolusigorta.com.tr.

Ankara Sigorta: PK 551, Bedrettin Demirel Cad., Lefkoşa (Nicosia), Mersin 10, Turkey; tel. 2285815; fax 2283099; internet www.ankarasigorta.com.tr.

ERGOİSVİÇRE Sigorta AŞ: Şehit Mustafa Ahmet Ruso Cad. Küçükkaymaklı, Lefkoşa (Nicosia), Mersin 10, Turkey; tel. 2282125; fax 2288236; internet www.ergoisvicre.com.tr; acquired by ERGO Versicherungsgruppe AG (Germany) in 2008.

Gold Insurance Ltd: Salih Mecit Sok. 9, Lefkoşa (Nicosia), Mersin 10, Turkey; tel. and fax 2286500; fax 2286300; e-mail info@gold-insurance.com; internet www.gold-insurance.com; f. 1996; Man. Dir ULKER FAHRI.

Groupama Sigorta: Mehmet Akif Cad. 95, Lefkoşa (Nicosia), Mersin 10, Turkey; tel. 2280208; fax 2286160; e-mail n.kural@groupama.com.tr; internet www.groupama.com.tr; Man. NAMIK KEMAL KURAL.

Güneş Sigorta AŞ: Şehit Mustafa Ahmet Ruso Cad., Küçükkaymaklı, Galeria Muhtar İş Merkezi 218, Lefkoşa (Nicosia), Mersin 10, Turkey; tel. 2286690; fax 2292657; internet www.gunessigorta.com.tr.

Kıbrıs Sigorta STI Ltd (Cyprus Insurance Co Ltd): Abdi İpekçi Cad., Eti Binaları, Lefkoşa (Nicosia), Mersin 10, Turkey; tel. 2283022; fax 2279277; e-mail info@kibris-sigorta.com; internet www.kibris-sigorta.com; Man. Dir MEHMET UĞUR KIRAZ.

Ray Sigorta AŞ: Bedrettin Demirel Cad., Arabacıoğlu Apt 7, Lefkoşa (Nicosia), Mersin 10, Turkey; tel. 2270380; fax 2270383; internet www.raysigorta.com.tr.

Şeker Sigorta (Kıbrıs) Ltd: Mahmut Paşa Sok. 14/A, PK 664, Lefkoşa (Nicosia), Mersin 10, Turkey; tel. 2285883; fax 2274074; e-mail bilgi@sekersigorta-kibris.com; internet www.sekersigorta-kibris.com; Man. Dir AHMET ERASLAN.

Insurance Association

Kuzey Kıbrıs Sigorta ve Reasürans Şirketleri Birliği (Insurance and Reinsurance Association of Northern Cyprus): Selim Cad. 49, Arca Apartment No. 3, Lefkoşa (Nicosia), Mersin 10, Turkey; tel. 2280937; fax 2286483; e-mail info@kksrsb.org; internet www.kksrsb.org; 32 mem. cos; Pres. ÜLKER FAHRI.

Trade and Industry

CHAMBERS OF COMMERCE AND INDUSTRY

Turkish Cypriot Chamber of Commerce: 90 Bedrettin Demirel Cad., PK 718, Lefkoşa (Nicosia), Mersin 10, Turkey; tel. 2283645; fax 2283089; e-mail ktto@ktto.net; internet www.ktto.net; f. 1958; Pres. GÜNAY ÇERKEZ; Sec.-Gen. JANEL BURCAN; more than 9,000 mems.

Turkish Cypriot Chamber of Industry: 126 Mehmet Akif Cad., Lefkoşa (Nicosia), Mersin 10, Turkey; tel. 2258131; fax 2258130; e-mail info@kibso.org; internet www.kibso.org; f. 1977; Pres. ALI ÇIRALI; Sec.-Gen. DOĞA DÖNMEZER; 600 mems.

EMPLOYERS' ORGANIZATION

Kıbrıs Türk İşverenler Sendikası (Turkish Cypriot Employers' Association): PK 674, Lefkoşa (Nicosia), Mersin 10, Turkey; tel. 2273673; fax 2277479; Chair. HASAN SUNGUR.

UTILITIES

Cyprus Turkish Electricity Corpn: Lefkoşa (Nicosia), Mersin 10, Turkey; tel. 2282472; fax 2283851; e-mail info@kibtek.com; internet www.kibtek.com; Chair. ERKAN OKANDAN.

TRADE UNIONS

Devrimci İşçi Sendikaları Federasyonu (Dev-İş) (Revolutionary Trade Unions' Federation): 6 Serabioğlu Sok., 748 Lefkoşa (Nicosia), Mersin 10, Turkey; tel. 2272640; fax 2286463; e-mail dev-is@defne.net; internet www.dev-is.org; f. 1976; 4 unions with a total membership of 1,850 (2002); affiliated to WFTU; Pres. MEHMET SEYIS; Gen. Sec. HASAN FELEK.

Kıbrıs Türk İşçi Sendikaları Federasyonu (TÜRK-SEN) (Turkish Cypriot Trade Union Federation): POB 829, 7–7A Şehit Mehmet R. Hüseyin Sok., Lefkoşa (Nicosia), Mersin 10, Turkey; tel. 2272444; fax 2287831; e-mail erkan.birer@turk-sen.org; internet www.turk-sen.org; f. 1954; regd 1955; affiliated to ITUC, the European Trade Union Confed., the Commonwealth Trade Union Council and the Confed. of Trade Unions of Turkey (Türk-İş); Pres. ARSLAN BIÇAKLI; Gen. Sec. ERKAN BIRER.

Transport

SHIPPING

Until 1974 Gazi Mağusa (Famagusta), a natural port, was the island's most important harbour, handling about 83% of the country's cargo. Since its capture by the Turkish army in August of that year the port has been officially declared closed to international traffic. However, it continues to serve the Turkish-occupied region. Girne (Kyrenia) has also been declared closed to international traffic. A hydrofoil service operates between there and Mersin on the Turkish mainland.

Ak-Günler Co Ltd: Girne (Kyrenia), Mersin 10, Turkey; tel. 8156002; fax 8153268; e-mail denizcilik@akgunler.com.tr; internet www.akgunler.com.tr; f. 1978; operates a fleet of 8 passenger and cargo vessels; Man. Dir İÇIM KAVUKLU; Gen. Man. HAMIT GÖRGÜN.

Armen Shipping Ltd: Altun Tabya, St 10/1, Gazi Mağusa (Famagusta), Mersin 10, Turkey; tel. 3664086; fax 3665860; e-mail armen@armenshipping.com; internet www.armenshipping.com; provides transportation services, shipping agency services and customer clearance facilities; Dir VARGIN VARER.

Fergün Shipping Co: Girne Yeni Liman Yolu, Fergün Apt 1, Girne (Kyrenia), Mersin 10, Turkey; tel. 8151770; fax 8151989; e-mail info@fergun.ne; internet www.fergun.net; ferries to Turkish ports; Owner FEHIM KÜÇÜK.

Kıbrıs Türk Denizcilik Ltd, Şti (Turkish Cypriot Maritime Co Ltd): 3 Bülent Ecevit Bul., Gazi Mağusa (Famagusta), Mersin 10, Turkey; tel. 3665995; fax 3667840; e-mail cypship@superonline.com.

Tahsin Transtürk ve Oğlu Ltd: 11 Kizilkule Yolu, Gazi Mağusa (Famagusta), Mersin 10, Turkey; tel. 3665409; fax 3660330.

CIVIL AVIATION

In 1975 the Turkish authorities opened Ercan (fmrly Tymbou) airport, and a second airport was opened at Geçitkale (Lefkoniko) in 1986. However, only Turkey and Azerbaijan recognize the airports as legitimate points of entry; flights from all other countries involve a preliminary stopover at one of Turkey's airports.

Tourism

In 2010 some 902,390 tourists, 741,925 of whom were from Turkey, visited the Turkish Cypriot area, while revenue from tourism amounted to US $405.8m.

North Cyprus Tourism Centre: Ministry of Economy, Tourism, Culture and Sport, Selçuklu Rd, Lefkoşa (Nicosia), Mersin 10, Turkey; tel. 2289629; fax 2285625; e-mail info@northcyprus.cc; internet www.northcyprus.cc; headquarters based in London, United Kingdom.

Defence

As assessed at November 2013, the 'TRNC' had an army of an estimated 3,500 regulars and 26,000 reserves. There was also a paramilitary armed police force of about 150. Men between 18 and 50 years of age are liable to 24 months' conscription. The 'TRNC' forces were being supported by an estimated 43,000 Turkish troops. In 2010 the defence budget for the 'TRNC' was TL 163.3m.

Commander of 'TRNC' Security Forces: Brig.-Gen. BAKI KAVUN.

Education

With the exception of private kindergartens, a vocational school of agriculture attached to the Ministry of Food, Agriculture and Energy, a training school for nursing and midwifery attached to the Ministry of Health, and a school for hotel catering attached to the Ministry of Economy, Tourism, Culture and Sport, all schools and educational institutes are administered by the Ministry of National Education.

Education in the Turkish Cypriot zone is divided into two sections, formal and adult (informal) education. Formal education covers nursery, primary, secondary and higher education. Adult education caters for special training outside the school system.

Formal education is organized into four categories: pre-primary, primary, secondary and higher education. Pre-primary education is provided by kindergartens for children between the ages of 5 and 6. Primary education lasts for five years and caters for children aged 7–11. In 2010/11 there were 239 pre-primary and primary schools, with 2,054 teachers and 24,282 pupils. Secondary education is provided in two stages. The first stage (junior), lasting three years, is intended for pupils aged 12–14. In 2010/11 there were 36 secondary schools, with 1,108 teachers and 10,487 pupils. The second stage consists of a three-year programme of instruction for pupils aged 15–17. Pupils elect either to prepare for higher education, to prepare for higher education with vocational training, or to prepare for vocational training only. This stage of education is free, but not compulsory. In 2010/11 there were 27 general high schools, with 973 teachers and 7,786 pupils. There were also 11 vocational schools, with 524 teachers and 3,080 pupils.

The Eastern Mediterranean University, which is located near Gazi Mağusa (Famagusta), was opened in 1986. A total of 13,255 students attended the university in 2008/09. Other institutions providing higher education in the Turkish Cypriot zone are: the Near East University in Lefkoşa (Nicosia); the Girne (Kyrenia) American University; the Anadolu University; the European University of Lefke (Levka); the International American University; the Cyprus International University; and the Teachers' Training College in Lefkoşa (Nicosia), which trains teachers for the elementary school stage. In 1982 an International Institute of Islamic Banking and Economics was opened to provide postgraduate training. In 2010/11 some 41,230 students were studying at universities in the 'TRNC', while 2,620 students were pursuing higher education studies abroad, mainly in Turkey, the USA and the United Kingdom.

THE CZECH REPUBLIC

Introductory Survey

LOCATION, CLIMATE, LANGUAGE, RELIGION, FLAG, CAPITAL

The Czech Republic lies in central Europe and comprises the Czech Lands of Bohemia and Moravia, and part of Silesia. Its neighbours are Poland to the north, Germany to the north-west and west, Austria to the south, and Slovakia to the east. The climate is continental, with warm summers and cold winters. The average mean temperature is 9°C (49°F). Czech, a member of the west Slavonic group, is the official language. There is a sizeable Slovak minority and also small Polish, German, Silesian, Roma, Hungarian and other minorities. The major religion is Christianity. The national flag (proportions 2 by 3) has two equal horizontal stripes, of white and red, on which is superimposed a blue triangle (half the length) at the hoist. The capital is Prague (Praha).

CONTEMPORARY POLITICAL HISTORY

Historical Context

In October 1918, following the collapse of the Austro-Hungarian Empire, the Republic of Czechoslovakia was established. The new state united the Czech Lands of Bohemia and Moravia, which had been incorporated into the Austrian Empire in the 16th and 17th centuries, and Slovakia, which had been under Hungarian rule for almost 1,000 years. After the Nazis came to power in Germany in 1933, there was increased agitation in the Sudetenland (an area in northern Bohemia inhabited by 3m. German speakers) for autonomy within, and later secession from, Czechoslovakia. In 1938, to appease German demands, the British, French and Italian Prime Ministers concluded an agreement with the German Nazi leader, Adolf Hitler, whereby the Sudetenland was ceded to Germany, and other parts of Czechoslovakia were transferred to Hungary and Poland. Nazi armed forces invaded and occupied the remainder of Czechoslovakia in March 1939, and a German protectorate was established in Bohemia and Moravia. In Slovakia, which had been granted self-government in late 1938, a separate state was formed, under the pro-Nazi regime of Jozef Tiso.

After Germany's defeat in the Second World War in 1945, the pre-1938 frontiers of Czechoslovakia were restored, although a small area in eastern Slovakia was ceded to the USSR. Almost all of the German-speaking inhabitants of the country were expelled, and the Sudetenland was settled by Czechs from other parts of Bohemia. In response to Slovakian demands for greater autonomy, a legislature (the Slovenská národná rada—Slovakian National Council) and an executive Board of Commissioners were established in Bratislava, the principal Slovakian city. At elections in 1946, the Communist Party of Czechoslovakia (KSČ) emerged as the leading party. The party's leader, Klement Gottwald, became Prime Minister in a coalition Government. After ministers of other parties resigned, communist control became complete on 25 February 1948. A People's Republic was established on 9 June. Gottwald succeeded Eduard Beneš as President, a position that he held until his death in 1953. The country aligned itself with the Soviet-led Eastern European bloc, joining the Council for Mutual Economic Assistance and the Warsaw Pact, and there were many political trials. Although these ended under Gottwald's successors, Antonín Zápotocký and, from 1956, Antonín Novotný, there was no relaxation of policy until 1963, when a new Government, with Jozef Lenárt as Prime Minister, was formed. Meanwhile, the country was renamed the Czechoslovak Socialist Republic, under a new Constitution, proclaimed in 1960.

In January 1968 Alexander Dubček succeeded Novotný as First Secretary of the KSČ, and in March Gen. Ludvík Svoboda succeeded Novotný as President. Oldřich Černík became Prime Minister in April. The new Government envisaged widespread reforms, including the introduction of a federal system of government, a more democratic electoral system, and a greater degree of separation between party and state. In August, however, in order to inhibit these reforms, an estimated 600,000 Warsaw Pact forces invaded Czechoslovakia, occupying Prague and other major cities. Mass demonstrations in protest at the invasion were held throughout the country, and many people were killed in clashes with occupation troops. The Soviet Government exerted heavy pressure on the Czechoslovak leaders to suppress their reformist policies, and in April 1969 Dubček was replaced by a fellow Slovak, Dr Gustáv Husák, as First (subsequently General) Secretary of the KSČ. Under Husák's leadership, there was a severe purge of the KSČ membership and most of Dubček's supporters were removed from the Government. The 1968 reforms were duly abandoned, with the exception of the federalization programme. This was implemented in January 1969, when the unitary Czechoslovak state was transformed into a federation, with separate Czech and Slovakian Republics, each having its own legislature and government. A Federal Government was established as the supreme executive organ of state power, and the legislature was transformed into a bicameral Federální shromáždění (Federal Assembly). The first legislative elections since 1964 were held in November 1971, and 99.8% of the votes cast were in favour of candidates of the National Front (the communist-dominated organization embracing all the legal political parties in Czechoslovakia).

In May 1975 Husák was appointed to the largely ceremonial post of President of Czechoslovakia, retaining his positions of Chairman of the National Front and General Secretary of the KSČ. He held the latter post until December 1987, when he was replaced by Miloš Jakeš, an economist and member of the Presidium of the party's Central Committee. However, Husák remained as President of the Republic.

Although Jakeš affirmed his commitment to the moderate programme of reform initiated by Husák, repressive measures continued against the Catholic Church and dissident groups, such as Charter 77, which had been established in January 1977 by intellectuals and former politicians to campaign for the observance of civil and political rights. Despite continued attempts to suppress the movement, it played a leading role in anti-Government demonstrations, which began in 1988. In February 1989 the Czech playwright Václav Havel (a leader of Charter 77) was sentenced to nine months' imprisonment. (He was released in May, following international condemnation.)

In November 1989 the protest actions evolved into a process of largely peaceful political change, which subsequently became known as the 'velvet revolution'. On 17 November an anti-Government demonstration in Prague, the largest public protest for 20 years, was violently dispersed by the police; large numbers of demonstrators (mainly students) were injured. Large-scale protests continued in Prague and in other towns. Later that month several opposition and human rights organizations, including Charter 77, were united in an informal alliance, Civic Forum, which rapidly attracted widespread popular support. On 24 November it was announced that Jakeš and the entire membership of the Presidium of the Central Committee had resigned. Karel Urbánek succeeded Jakeš as General Secretary, and a new Presidium was elected. Opposition demands for the ending of censorship and the release of all political prisoners were accepted by the authorities, and at the end of November the articles guaranteeing the KSČ's predominance were deleted from the Constitution.

In December 1989 Civic Forum and its Slovakian counterpart, Public Against Violence (VPN), denounced the composition of the reorganized Government, which included only five non-communists. Ladislav Adamec subsequently resigned as Prime Minister, and was replaced by Marián Čalfa. In the following week a new interim Federal Government was formed, with a majority of non-communist members, including seven non-party supporters of Civic Forum. Husák resigned as Federal President and, at the end of December, was replaced by Havel. Dubček was elected Chairman of the Federal Assembly. Meanwhile, at an emergency congress of the KSČ the position of General Secretary of the Central Committee was abolished. Adamec was appointed to the new post of Chairman of the party.

In April 1990 the Federal Assembly voted to rename the country the Czech and Slovak Federative Republic (CzSFR), thereby satisfying Slovakian demands that the new title should reflect the equal status of Slovakia within the federation. On 8–

9 June the first democratic legislative elections since 1946 were held in Czechoslovakia. A total of 27 political associations contested elections to the Federal Assembly and to each republican legislature, with the participation of some 97% of the electorate. In the elections at federal level, the highest proportion of the votes cast (about 46%) was secured by Civic Forum, in the Czech Lands, and by VPN in Slovakia. The KSC, with about 14% of the votes, obtained the second highest representation in the Federal Assembly. The Christian Democratic Union (a coalition of the Czechoslovak People's Party, the Christian Democratic Party—KDS—and the Slovakian-based Christian Democratic Movement—KDH) received some 12% of the votes. Two parties that had campaigned for regional autonomy or secession, the Movement for Autonomous Democracy–Society for Moravia and Silesia (HSD–SMS) and the separatist Slovak National Party (SNS), also secured parliamentary representation. The newly elected Federal Assembly was to serve a transitional two-year term, during which time it was to draft new federal and republican constitutions and elect a new Federal President. In late June Dubček was re-elected Chairman of the Federal Assembly. A new Federal Government, announced in that month, comprised four representatives of Civic Forum, three of VPN, one of the KDH and eight independents. In early July Havel was re-elected to the post of President.

In the latter half of 1990 a widening division emerged between the moderate Slovakian movements, such as VPN and the KDH, and more radical parties, which campaigned for full independence. In March 1991 Vladimír Mečiar, the Slovakian Prime Minister and a founding member of VPN, announced the formation of a minority faction within VPN. known as the Movement for a Democratic Slovakia (HZDS), in support of greater autonomy. Meanwhile, a split had occurred within Civic Forum, with conservatives and economic liberals forming the Civic Democratic Party (ODS), led by Václav Klaus. Mečiar's policies and aggressive style of leadership were seen by many as detrimental to the future of Czech-Slovakian relations, and in April the Slovakian National Council voted to remove him from the Slovakian premiership. Following this, the HZDS was established as a separate political group. The constitutional debate in the Federal Assembly continued in the first half of 1992, with increasing Slovakian support for a loose confederation. The majority of Czech politicians, however, were in favour of preserving the existing state structure, and rejected such proposals. In March it was agreed that constitutional negotiations would be postponed until after forthcoming legislative elections.

The legislative elections of 5–6 June 1992 resulted in the emergence of Mečiar's HZDS as the dominant political force in Slovakia. With about 34% of the total votes cast in Slovakia, the party obtained 57 seats (the second largest representation) in the 300-member Federal Assembly. The leading party in the Slovakian Government, the KDH (which advocated a continued federation), won only 9% of the votes cast in Slovakia, securing 14 seats, one seat fewer than the separatist SNS. Václav Klaus's party, the ODS (in coalition with the KDS), won about 34% of the votes cast in the Czech Lands. The ODS was one of only two parties to contest the elections in both republics, and in Slovakia it received 4% of the votes in Slovakia, becoming the largest party in the Federal Assembly, with a total of 85 seats. Two other splinter groups of the former Civic Forum, including the Civic Democratic Alliance (ODA), failed to win representation in the Federal Assembly, as did the Civic Democratic Union (formerly VPN), in Slovakia. The successor organizations to the communist parties of the two republics achieved considerable success: the Left Bloc (which included the Communist Party of Bohemia and Moravia—KSČM) won a total of 34 seats in the Federal Assembly, while the Slovakian-based Party of the Democratic Left secured 23 seats. The representation of parties in the new republican legislatures was generally similar to that in the Federální shromáždění.

In late June 1992 a new Slovakian Government was announced, with Mečiar as Prime Minister. All but one of the ministers were members of the HZDS. A transitional Federal Government, dominated by members of the ODS and the HZDS, was appointed in early July. The new Prime Minister was Jan Stráský of the ODS. A new coalition Czech Government, dominated by the ODS and with Klaus as Prime Minister, was also appointed in early July. Following three unsuccessful attempts to elect a President in the Federal Assembly, in which the HZDS and the SNS had prevented Havel's re-election, in mid-July he resigned.

The events of June and July 1992 had ensured that the emergence of two independent states was inevitable. On 17 July the Slovakian National Council approved a (symbolic) declaration of Slovakian sovereignty, and in the following week the Czech and Slovakian Prime Ministers agreed to the dissolution of the CzSFR, which was to take effect from 1 January 1993. In October 1992 the Czech and Slovakian Governments ratified a number of accords, including a customs union treaty to abolish trade restrictions between the two republics following their independence. Finally, on 25 November the Federal Assembly adopted legislation providing for the constitutional disbanding of the federation, having secured the necessary three-fifths' majority. Accordingly, the Federal Government accelerated the process of dividing the country's assets and liabilities as well as its armed forces (mainly in the ratio of 2 to 1—the proportion of the Czech and Slovak populations within Czechoslovakia).

Domestic Political Affairs

In anticipation of the establishment of the Czech Republic as an independent state, the existing legislature was replaced by a bicameral body under a new Constitution, which was adopted on 16 December 1992; the 200-member Česká národní rada (Czech National Council) was transformed into a Poslanecká sněmovna (Chamber of Deputies—lower house), while an upper house, the Senát (Senate), was to be elected at a later date. On 17 December a treaty pledging cordial relations and co-operation was signed, followed by the establishment of diplomatic relations between the two republics. At midnight on 31 December all federal structures were dissolved and the Czech Republic and the Slovak Republic were officially established. The two republics were quickly recognized by the states that had maintained diplomatic relations with the CzSFR, as well as by those international bodies of which the CzSFR had been a member. Existing treaties and agreements to which the CzSFR had been a party were to be honoured by both republics.

The Presidency of Václav Havel

On 26 January 1993 the Chamber of Deputies elected Havel as the Czech Republic's first President. The composition of the Government remained largely unchanged. It included among its principal objectives the pursuance of the former Federal Government's economic reforms, including its programme of large-scale privatization. Central banks for each state were established, and in February two separate currencies were introduced.

In April 1994 the Chamber of Deputies adopted legislation permitting the restitution of property expropriated from Czech Jews during the period of Nazi occupation. Renewed controversy emerged in 1995 over the so-called 'lustration', or screening, law, which had been adopted by the Czechoslovak Federal Assembly in October 1991. The law effectively banned former communist functionaries, as well as members of the former state security service, from holding senior political, economic and judicial posts. Despite opposition from Havel, in October 1995 the Chamber of Deputies approved an extension of the lustration law (which had been due to expire in 1996) until 2000.

The first general election since the dissolution of the CzSFR took place on 31 May and 1 June 1996. The ODS (which had merged with the KDS in April) won 68 of the 200 seats in the Chamber of Deputies (with 29.6% of the total votes cast), while the Czech Social Democratic Party (ČSSD), which had become a major force of the centre-left under the leadership of Miloš Zeman, greatly increased its parliamentary representation, winning 61 seats (26.4%). As a result, the coalition of the ODS, the Christian Democratic Union-Czechoslovak People's Party (KDU-ČSL, which obtained 18 seats) and the ODA (13 seats) lost its overall majority, achieving a total of 99 seats. The KSČM and the Association for the Republic—Republican Party of Czechoslovakia secured 22 and 18 seats, respectively. Despite losing its parliamentary majority, the governing coalition remained intact. In July Klaus formed a new Government; in a concession to the ČSSD (which had agreed to support the minority administration), Zeman was appointed Chairman of the Chamber of Deputies. The ruling coalition won 52 of the 81 seats in elections to the Senate, held in November.

Tension within the ODS and the ruling coalition intensified in October 1997, and Josef Zieleniec resigned as both Minister of Foreign Relations and ODS Deputy Chairman. In November allegations of impropriety in the funding of the ODS led to the resignation of the Klaus administration, following the withdrawal of the KDU-ČSL and the ODA from the coalition. Josef Tošovský, hitherto Governor of the Czech National Bank, was designated Prime Minister in December, and a new interim Government, comprising seven non-partisan ministers, four from the ODS members, and three each from the KDU-ČSL and the ODA, was appointed in January 1998. The ODS was divided over its participation in the new administration, and the party's ministers subsequently defected to the Freedom Union (US), a newly established breakaway party, which held 31 seats in the Chamber of Deputies by mid-February. Meanwhile, on 20 January Havel was narrowly re-elected to the presidency. In April the Czech Republic's proposed membership of the North Atlantic Treaty Organization (NATO, see p. 370) was formally approved by the legislature, after the ČSSD withdrew its demand for a referendum on the issue.

Early elections to the Chamber of Deputies were held on 19–20 June 1998. The ČSSD retained its position (held since the earlier defection of the ODS deputies to the US) as the largest party in the Chamber of Deputies, winning 74 seats (with 32.3% of the votes cast), while the ODS secured 63 seats (with 27.7% of the votes). The remaining seats were divided between the KSČM (with 24 seats), the KDU-ČSL (20) and the US (19). The rate of voter participation was 74%. In July Zeman and Klaus signed an agreement whereby the ODS pledged not to initiate or support a motion expressing no confidence in a minority ČSSD government, in exchange for a number of senior parliamentary posts, including the chairmanship of the Chamber of Deputies (to which Klaus was later elected), and a commitment to early constitutional reform. On 17 July Zeman was appointed Prime Minister, and a new Council of Ministers was subsequently formed.

In July 1999 Ivo Svoboda was dismissed as Minister of Finance. (In May 2002 he was charged with embezzlement during his term in office, and he was sentenced to five years' imprisonment in March 2004.) In September 1999 the Council of Ministers approved a number of proposals for constitutional change, which had been drafted by a joint ČSSD-ODS commission. The amendments aimed to restrict presidential powers, including the right to appoint the Prime Minister and the heads of principal state institutions, and the right to grant amnesty. (The Chamber of Deputies approved the changes in January 2000, despite an opposition boycott of the vote.) In November 1999 celebrations commemorating the 10th anniversary of the 'velvet revolution' coincided with a protest against the existing political system, organized by a group of former student leaders.

In April 2001 Vladimír Špidla, the Deputy Prime Minister and Minister of Labour and Social Affairs, was elected unopposed to the chairmanship of the ČSSD; Zeman had agreed to relinquish the party leadership (although he was to remain Prime Minister pending legislative elections).

In February 2002 it was announced that the electoral alliance of the KDU-ČSL, ODA and US-DEU (formed by a merger of the US with a small party, the Democratic Union) had been dissolved, owing to inter-party disagreement; however, the KDU-ČSL and US-DEU subsequently formed a new alliance, known as the Coalition. At elections to the Chamber of Deputies on 14–15 June, the ČSSD was the most successful party (with 30.2% of the votes cast). President Havel invited Špidla to form a government, and on 9 July an agreement establishing a new administration was signed by the leaders of the ČSSD and the Coalition. A new multi-party Government, headed by Špidla and dominated by the ČSSD, was approved by the Chamber of Deputies in August.

Václav Klaus elected President

Prior to the expiry of Havel's second term on 2 February 2003, voting took place in both legislative chambers to select a successor. Following several inconclusive rounds of voting, Klaus (who had relinquished the chairmanship of the ODS) was elected President on 28 February, defeating the candidate of the ruling coalition, Jan Sokol, with 142 of the 281 votes cast in both chambers. Klaus was inaugurated on 7 March. Four days later the Government won a vote of confidence in the Chamber of Deputies (which had been requested by the Prime Minister) by one vote. In mid-June the results of a referendum approved the Czech Republic's proposed accession to the European Union—EU (see p. 273). Klaus, notably, did not urge voters to support accession. In September, after the Government narrowly survived a vote of no confidence, the Chamber of Deputies adopted its reform proposals. In the following month the Minister of Finance, Bohuslav Sobotka, was also appointed Deputy Prime Minister, with responsibility for implementing the public finance reform programme.

At the end of June 2004 Špidla resigned as head of the Government and as leader of the ČSSD, despite surviving a vote of confidence in his party leadership. The vote followed a defeat for the ČSSD in the Czech Republic's first elections to the European Parliament earlier in the month (following the country's accession to the EU on 1 May), in which the ČSSD had obtained only two of the 24 seats contested. In August Stanislav Gross, the acting leader of the ČSSD and hitherto the First Deputy Prime Minister and Minister of the Interior, formed a Government that included six new ministers and again comprised members of the KDU-ČSL and the US-DEU, as well as members of the ČSSD. Later that month the new administration narrowly won a vote of confidence in the Chamber of Deputies.

Gross was re-elected as Chairman of the ČSSD in March 2005. At the end of that month the KDU-ČSL (which demanded Gross's resignation, after he had become the subject of allegations of financial impropriety) withdrew from the governing coalition, as a result of which the Government lost its majority in the Chamber of Deputies. Following Gross's resignation on 25 April, Klaus appointed the Minister of Regional Development, Jiří Paroubek, the deputy leader of the ČSSD, as Prime Minister. The new, largely unchanged Council of Ministers (with the renewed participation of the KDU-ČSL) was confirmed in office on 13 May by the Chamber of Deputies. In late September Gross resigned as leader of the ČSSD. In May 2006 Paroubek was elected Chairman of the ČSSD. Later that month he took legal action for defamation against the Chairman of the ODS, Mirek Topolánek, who had accused him of having connections with organized crime.

Elections to the Chamber of Deputies took place on 2–3 June. The ODS won 81 of the 200 seats, with 35.4% of the votes cast; the ČSSD secured 74 seats, with 32.3% of the votes, the KSČM obtained 26 seats (12.8%), the KDU-ČSL 13 seats (7.2%) and the Green Party (SZ) six (6.3%). Some 64% of the electorate participated in the elections. Topolánek was invited by Klaus to form a new administration, and a coalition agreement between the ODS, the KDU-ČSL and the SZ was signed on 26 June. The ČSSD, however, refused to support Topolánek's proposed coalition government, which, with 100 seats in the Chamber of Deputies, had the support of one deputy fewer than the 101 required to hold a majority. A protracted impasse ensued, with six failed attempts to elect a new Chairman of the Chamber of Deputies. Finally, on 14 August 2006 a member of the ČSSD, Miloslav Vlček, was elected provisionally as Chairman. Two days later Klaus accepted the resignation of Paroubek's Government and officially appointed Topolánek as Prime Minister. After a coalition proposed by Topolánek again failed to secure support, he formed a minority ODS-led administration, which, after approval by Klaus, was installed on 4 September. In early October, however, the Government lost a vote of confidence in the Chamber of Deputies, and Topolánek subsequently tendered his resignation. In November Klaus redesignated Topolánek as Prime Minister, with a mandate to form a new coalition administration.

Political uncertainty

On 9 January 2007 Klaus officially appointed a coalition administration formed by Topolánek, comprising eight members of the ODS, five of the KDU-ČSL and four of the SZ. The new Government was narrowly endorsed by a motion of confidence in the Chamber of Deputies on 19 January, receiving 100 votes, after two ČSSD deputies abstained from voting. Jiří Čunek (who had been elected Chairman of the KDU-ČSL) received the post of Deputy Prime Minister and Minister of Regional Development, while the leader of the SZ, Martin Bursík, became Deputy Prime Minister and Minister of the Environment. In August Topolánek narrowly succeeded in securing approval in the Chamber of Deputies for an extensive programme of fiscal reforms. Controversy over Čunek, who was subject to a criminal investigation into his alleged acceptance of a bribe from a real estate company in 2002, was also perceived to be damaging to the Government; Čunek resigned in early November 2007.

An inconclusive presidential ballot was conducted in both legislative chambers on 8–9 February 2008. Klaus, representing the ODS, was opposed by Jan Švejnar, an economics professor, who was supported by the ČSSD. In a further ballot on 15 February, again contested by Klaus and Švejnar, Klaus was narrowly elected in a third round of voting, with 141 votes. On 7 March Klaus was inaugurated for a second term. In early April Čunek, who had been cleared of the charges against him, was reappointed to the Government, assuming his former position as Deputy Prime Minister and Minister of Regional Development.

Prior to senatorial and local elections, divisions emerged within the ODS owing to policy differences between Klaus and Topolánek with regard to the EU and plans by the USA to establish a military base near Prague (see Foreign Affairs). Elections to one-third of the seats in the Senate, conducted in two rounds on 17–18 October and 24–25 October, resulted in significant gains for the ČSSD, which increased its representation to 23 of the 81 seats, although the ODS remained the largest faction in the chamber, with 33 seats. In local elections, which also took place on 17–18 October, the ČSSD secured control of all 13 regional assemblies, with 35.9% of the votes cast; the ODS (which had previously held 12 of the regional assemblies) received 23.6% of votes. However, later that month the Government narrowly survived a motion of no confidence in the Chamber of Deputies. In January 2009, following controversy over a planned ministerial reorganization, Čunek announced his resignation from the Government; he and three other ministers were subsequently replaced. The incumbent Minister of Defence, Vlasta Parkanová, also of the KDU-ČSL, also became Deputy Prime Minister. On 26 March Topolánek's Government submitted its resignation, after a motion of no confidence was adopted in the Chamber of Deputies. On 9 April President Klaus nominated Jan Fischer, a non-partisan candidate and hitherto the head of the Czech Statistical Office, as Prime Minister, with a mandate to form an interim administration.

On 9 May 2009 a new Government, headed by Fischer and comprising new, mainly technocratic ministers nominated by the principal parties, was installed, with the intention that early legislative elections would be held. At elections to the European Parliament on 5–6 June, the ODS secured 31.5% of votes cast and nine seats, the ČSSD 22.4% of votes and seven seats, the KSČM 14.2% of votes and four seats, and the KDU-ČSL 7.6% of votes and two seats; voter turnout was estimated at some 28.2% of the electorate. Also in June a former Chairman of the KDU-ČSL, Miroslav Kalousek, established a new party, Tradition, Responsibility, Prosperity 09 (TOP 09), headed by former Minister of Foreign Affairs Karel Schwarzenberg, which subsequently gained support at the expense of the KDU-ČSL. In July the presidential office announced that the early elections to the Chamber of Deputies were to be conducted on 9–10 October. In early September 2009 the Constitutional Court, upholding a legal challenge by an independent deputy, declared the legislation allowing early elections to be invalid. President Klaus subsequently endorsed a constitutional amendment providing for the dissolution of the Chamber of Deputies and an amendment to the electoral code that permitted the shortening of election terms. However, in mid-September the ČSSD and the KSČM withdrew their support for the self-dissolution of the chamber, with the consequence that the parliamentary term was to continue until its originally intended date of expiry.

The 2010 legislative elections

In February 2010 Klaus announced that the elections to the Chamber of Deputies would be conducted on 28–29 May. In March Jan Dusík of the SZ resigned as Minister of the Environment, in protest at government proposals concerning the modernization of the Prunéřov coal-fired power station. The other representative of the SZ in the Council of Ministers, Michael Kocáb, resigned as Minister, responsible for Human Rights later in March, after the party announced that it had withdrawn its support for the Government. In April Rut Bízková of the ODS (who had previously been employed at the České energetické závody Skupina—ČEZ—company that owned the Prunéřov power station) was appointed Minister of the Environment. In the same month Topalánek announced his resignation as Chairman of the ODS, after the publication of an interview in which he had made various controversial remarks. His hitherto deputy, Petr Nečas, was appointed to lead the party's election campaign. At the end of April the Chairman of the Chamber of Deputies, Miloslav Vlček of the ODS, also resigned, following allegations suggesting that he had misused public funds.

At the elections to the Chamber of Deputies on 28–29 May 2010, the ČSSD obtained the largest share of the votes, with 22.1% and 56 seats, while the ODS was placed second, with 20.2% and 53 seats, followed by TOP 09 (16.7% and 41 seats), the KSČM (11.3% and 26 seats) while Public Affairs (VV), which had a platform of combating corruption, obtained 10.9% and 24 seats. The KDU-ČSL, which obtained only 4.4% of the votes, failed to obtain representation in the chamber for the first time since the restoration of democracy. On 29 May Paroubek resigned as Chairman of the ČSSD, acknowledging that the party would be unable to form a governing coalition, and was replaced in an interim capacity by Sobotka. On 24 June Miroslava Němcová of the ODS was elected Chairman of the Chamber of Deputies. On 28 June President Klaus nominated Nečas (who had been elected ODS Chairman earlier in the month) as Prime Minister. Following lengthy negotiations, an agreement was signed between the ODS, TOP 09 and VV, which together held 118 of the 200 legislative seats, and a new coalition Government, headed by Nečas, was appointed on 13 July. Among the principal appointments were Schwarzenberg as Deputy Prime Minister and Minister of Foreign Affairs, and Radek John, the leader of VV, as Deputy Prime Minister and Minister of the Interior. On 10 August the new administration won a vote of confidence in the Chamber of Deputies.

Elections to one-third of the seats in the Senate were conducted in two rounds, on 15–16 October and 22–23 October 2010: the ČSSD, winning 12 of the 27 contested seats, gained the highest representation in the chamber, with 41 seats overall, while the ODS took eight seats, its total representation falling to 25 seats. In concurrent local elections on 15–16 October, the ODS secured 18.8% of votes cast and 5,181 seats; the ČSSD, with 19.7% of the votes, won 4,633 seats. On 20 December Pavel Drobil resigned as Minister of the Environment, after concerns about alleged corruption within the State Environmental Fund had led the ČSSD to demand a vote of no confidence in the Government (which was, however, defeated). Tomáš Chalupa, also a member of the ODS, was appointed Minister of the Environment in January 2011.

Corruption allegations

In April 2011 a former director of the police organized crime division, Jan Kubice (an independent candidate), was appointed as Minister of the Interior. His predecessor, John, retained his position as a Deputy Prime Minister, and was additionally appointed to head a new anti-corruption committee. Also in April Vít Bárta of VV resigned as Minister of Transport, after it was alleged that he had bribed parliamentary deputies of the party. He was succeeded by an independent, Radek Šmerda. On 20 May Nečas accepted John's resignation as Deputy Prime Minister, which he had tendered earlier in the month expressing discontent with the level of support shown towards his anti-corruption policies by the Government. John announced that he was to seek re-election to the post of Chairman of VV, with the aim of strengthening his mandate within the party, and at a congress later that month was duly endorsed as Chairman. On 1 July two new appointments of VV representatives were made to the Government, including that of Karolína Peake, who succeeded John as Deputy Prime Minister (and additionally assumed the office of Chairman of the Government Legislative Council). On the same date Šmerda was dismissed as Minister of Transport; he was replaced by the other new VV appointee, Pavel Dobeš. In November the Minister of Industry and Trade, Martin Kocourek of the ODS, was obliged to tender his resignation, owing to the revelation of fraudulent transactions in his personal finances. In December the Minister of Culture, Jiři Besser of TOP 09, also resigned from his post, after it emerged that he had failed to list his partial ownership of a US company in asset declarations.

On 14 December 2011 the Chamber of Deputies approved a constitutional amendment initiated by the Government providing for the introduction of direct elections to the presidency; this was endorsed by the Senate in February 2012, and would thereby enter into effect from the end of Klaus's mandate in 2013. In late March Josef Dobeš of VV resigned as Minister of Education, Youth and Sports; he was succeeded by a non-partisan academic, Petr Fiala. In April Bárta was found guilty of bribery and given an 18-month suspended sentence. In response to the ruling, Peake announced her resignation from VV, and the formation of a new parliamentary faction, which was joined by a number of other VV deputies, including the government members nominated by the party. A mass anti-Government demonstration was subsequently staged in Prague. On 22 April the ruling coalition was ended, with a declaration by the ODS and TOP 09 that they would instead co-operate with the former VV members. On 27 April the Government won a parliamentary vote of confidence, which Nečas had requested to secure endorsement for the reconstituted coalition and for his proposed economic austerity measures. The group of defected VV members led by Peake was officially registered as a new political party, LIDEM—Liberal Democrats, in May. (Consequently, LIDEM became part of the ruling coalition, while the remaining section of VV went into opposition.) On 1 August Klaus (who declared his opposition to the measure) endorsed legislation allowing the adoption of the system of direct presidential elections, which entered into effect on 1 October. Presidential candidates were required to collect 50,000 signatures, or to secure the support of 20 deputies or 10 senators.

Elections to one-third of the seats in the Senate, which were conducted in two rounds on 12–13 October and 19–20 October 2012, demonstrated the increasing unpopularity of the Government: the ODS's representation fell by 10 seats to 15, while that of the ČSSD fell by one seat to 41, although it remained by far the largest faction in the 81-member chamber. The ODS also performed badly in the concurrent local elections, with only 12.3% of the votes cast and a decline in 78 seats, losing support to the KSČM, which increased its share of the vote to 20.4% and gained 68 seats; the ČSSD secured 23.6% of the votes, but lost 75 seats. Later in October Nečas failed to secure sufficient parliamentary support for the approval of tax increases, owing to the dissent of six deputies from his ruling coalition (who were supported by President Klaus). Nevertheless, on 4 November Nečas secured re-election as ODS Chairman at a party congress, defeating a challenge by Fuksa. Meanwhile, at the end of October Jaromír Drábek of TOP 09 resigned as Minister of Labour and Social Affairs, in response to revelations of corruption in the ministry, as a result of which the First Deputy Minister had recently been detained and charged. Drábek was succeeded in office by another member of TOP 09, Ludmila Müllerová. Following an agreement between Nečas and the party dissenters, on 7 November the Government narrowly won, by 101 deputies in the Chamber of Deputies, a vote of confidence that was linked to approval of the tax increases. Klaus signed the measures into law on 22 December. In early December Pavel Dobeš resigned as Minister of Transport; he was succeeded later in the month by Zbyněk Stanjura of the ODS. Meanwhile, concerns that the Government would collapse increased in December, after Nečas dismissed Peake as Minister of Defence (in which capacity she had replaced the dismissed Alexandr Vondra) eight days after her appointment to the post, owing to administrative disagreements. However, she agreed that LIDEM would not withdraw from the ruling coalition and remained in the Government as Deputy Prime Minister.

The country's first direct election to the presidency was contested by a total of nine candidates on 11–12 January 2013. The first-placed candidate was former Prime Minister Zeman, with 24.2% of votes cast, narrowly defeating Schwarzenberg, who obtained 23.4%; former premier Fischer took 16.4%, followed by the ČSSD candidate, Jiří Dienstbier, with 16.1%. Zeman and Schwarzenberg proceeded to a second round on 25–26 January, which Zeman won with 54.8% of the votes. On 4 March, shortly before the expiry of his presidential tenure, the (ČSSD-dominated) Senate approved a motion to impeach Klaus, on the grounds that he had violated the Constitution by granting an extensive amnesty to prisoners in January, and referred charges of high treason against him to the Constitutional Court. Zeman was inaugurated as President on 8 March. Later in the month Gen. Vlastimil Picek, a former Chief of the General Staff, was appointed Minister of Defence. At the end of March the Constitutional Court dismissed the accusations of treason again Klaus.

Recent Developments: Collapse of the Government

On 17 June 2013 Nečas and his Government resigned, before being reappointed in an acting capacity by President Miloš Zeman, as attempts to reconstitute a ruling coalition commenced. The resignation followed the arrest of Nečas's Chief of Staff and several other senior officials on charges of having abused the state security apparatus, allegedly to spy on several people, including the Prime Minister's estranged wife, and of receiving bribes. On 25 June President Zeman nominated the non-partisan Jiří Rusnok, a former Minister of Finance, as Prime Minister-designate, pending attempts to form a new administration, although the two largest parties in the outgoing Government, the ODS and TOP 09 favoured the appointment of an alternative candidate, the Chairman of the Chamber of Deputies, Miroslava Němcová. A new interim Government headed by Rusnok, principally comprising non-partisan technocrats was appointed by the President on 11 July. However, on 7 August the administration lost a vote of confidence in the Chamber of Deputies, with the ODS, TOP 09 and LIDEM deputies rejecting the motion (except for two ODS deputies, who were subsequently expelled from the party, and Peake, who resigned as leader of LIDEM). On 20 August the Chamber of Deputies voted in favour of its dissolution, and later that month Zeman scheduled pre-term elections for 25–26 October.

None of the parties contesting the legislative elections on 25–26 October 2013 secured a parliamentary majority: the ČSSD won 20.5% of votes cast and 50 seats, followed by a recently emerged liberal, anti-corruption party, Action of Dissatisfied Citizens (ANO, with 18.7% and 47 seats), the KSČM (14.9% and 33 seats), TOP 09 (12.0% and 26 seats), the ODS (7.7% and 16 seats), a new populist party, Dawn of Direct Democracy (6.9% and 14 seats), and the KDU-ČSL (6.8% and 14 seats). Following lengthy negotiations between the ČSSD, ANO and the KDU-ČSL, a coalition agreement was signed in early January 2014. On 17 January 2014 President Zeman designated ČSSD Chairman Sobotka as the new Prime Minister. A new administration headed by Sobotka, which included the leader of ANO, the wealthy industrialist Andrej Babiš, as First Deputy Prime Minister, responsible for the Economy, and Minister of Finance, was approved by the Chamber of Deputies on 29 January. Considerable controversy surrounded the appointment of Babiš, who had taken legal action against a Slovakian state archival institution owing to allegations that he had co-operated with the secret services during the communist era; he attended court proceedings in Bratislava on the following day, when the trial was adjourned until April.

Roma Affairs

In August 1997 the Government began to address the issues affecting the Roma population (unofficially estimated at some 300,000), after hundreds of Roma, claiming to have suffered persecution in the Czech Republic, attempted to obtain political asylum in Canada and the United Kingdom. The Government established an interministerial commission for Roma community affairs in October. In early 1998 the Government formed a second commission, headed by Roma, to address issues affecting the Roma population, and a 40-year law restricting their nomadic way of life was revoked. None the less, a large number of Roma continued to seek political asylum abroad. In November 2007 the European Court of Human Rights found the Czech Republic to be in breach of the European convention on human rights for educational discrimination against the Roma population, owing to the practice of placing Roma children in 'special schools' for children with learning difficulties. In February 2013 a report by the Council of Europe Commissioner for Human Rights criticized the continued territorial and educational segregation of the Roma population. In August Czech nationalist activists staged anti-Roma protests in towns nationwide, with ensuing counter-demonstrations and large numbers of arrests; human rights organization Amnesty International warned of an increase in anti-Roma sentiment in the country.

In late 2008 increasing activity by extreme nationalist groups was reported; the most significant of these was the Workers' Party (DS). In March 2009 the Supreme Administrative Court rejected a request by the Ministry of the Interior that the DS be prohibited, on grounds of insufficient evidence. In May a political broadcast by the National Party (NS) prior to the elections to the European Parliament, which advocated the expulsion of the country's Roma population, was withdrawn, and was subsequently condemned by the Minister responsible for Human Rights as incitement to racial hatred (many senior NS members left the party later in the year). In February 2010 the Supreme Administrative Court upheld an appeal by the Government and imposed a ban on the DS, ruling that it posed a threat to democracy. Following the proscription of the party, some of its former members joined an existing nationalist grouping, the Workers' Party for Social Justice.

Foreign Affairs

Regional relations

The Czech Republic is a member, with Slovakia, Hungary and Poland, of the Visegrad Group (established, following the collapse of communist rule, to promote economic, defence and other co-operation in the region). Relations with Slovakia were strained in the 1990s, mainly because of disagreements over the division of former federal property. In September 1998, however, it was announced that a joint Czech-Slovakian committee would meet to discuss unresolved issues. Measures providing for dual Czech-Slovakian citizenship became fully effective in October 1999, and in November an agreement on the division of former federal property was signed in Bratislava. The agreement provided for the exchange of shares between the Czech Republic's Komerční banka and Slovakia's Všeobecná úverová banka, and the restitution of gold reserves to Slovakia, which had been held by the Czech National Bank as collateral for debts owed by Slovakia. The Czech Government consequently opted effectively to relieve Slovakia of its debts by buying the National Bank's claim for a symbolic one koruna, despite the opposition of several Czech politicians. In May 2000 the two Governments signed an agreement that resolved the remaining problems associated with the division of jointly held assets.

Since the end of the Second World War Czech-German relations have been dominated by two issues: the question of compensation for Czech victims of Nazism, and demands for the restitution of property to the Sudeten Germans who were driven from Czechoslovakia in 1945–46. A joint declaration was finally signed by the Czech and German Ministers of Foreign Affairs in December 1996, and by Prime Minister Klaus of the Czech Republic and Federal Chancellor Helmut Kohl of Germany in January 1997: Germany admitted that it was to blame for the Nazi occupation and the partition of Czechoslovakia in 1938–39, while the Czech Republic apologized for the abuses of human rights that were committed during the deportation of ethnic Germans. The declaration did not, however, entitle the expelled Sudeten Germans to make claims for compensation. A Czech-German fund was established in January 1998 to finance joint projects, in particular benefiting victims of the Nazis.

In February 2002 Zeman and Dzurinda announced that they would not attend a summit meeting of the Visegrad countries, scheduled to take place on 1 March, following a demand by their Hungarian counterpart, Viktor Orbán, for the abolition of the Beneš Decrees, which had provided for the expulsion of ethnic Germans, as well as Hungarians, from the Sudetenland. In April the Chamber of Deputies unanimously approved a resolution stipulating the inviolability of the Beneš Decrees. In August 2005 the Czech Government formally apologized to Sudeten Germans actively opposed to Nazism who had experienced persecution after the Second World War. In July 2009 Liechtenstein agreed to establish diplomatic relations with the Czech Republic, having failed to recognize it after independence, in protest at the seizure of land belonging to Liechtenstein citizens in the former Czechoslavakia under the Beneš Decrees. The two countries formally established diplomatic relations in September, also deciding to create a commission of historians in an effort to resolve outstanding matters of concern.

The question of the nuclear power installation at Temelín, in southern Bohemia, has impeded good relations between the Czech Republic and Austria. Despite pressure from the Austrian Government, which suspended imports of Czech electricity, the nuclear power plant began production in October 2000. In December the Czech Republic and Austria signed an agreement, whereby the plant was not to operate at commercial capacity until its safety and its environmental impact had been fully evaluated. In August 2001, however, the Czech authorities declared that a controversial report issued by the European Commission demonstrated the safety of the plant and immediately commenced its reconnection with the national power network; the resumption of operations at the plant was strongly criticized by the Austrian authorities. Further safety issues were eventually agreed, and in April 2003 the Temelín installation began production at full capacity, following the commencement of operations of a second reactor. In late 2011 the Czech Government formally announced a tender for the construction of a further two nuclear reactors at the Temelín installation. In 2013 it was reported that two energy concerns, a Russian-led consortium and the US-based Westinghouse, had submitted bids for the construction contract; owing to subsequent political uncertainty, however, an agreement was not expected to be finalized until 2015.

The Czech Republic was one of a number of central and eastern European states invited to commence negotiations in March 1998 on possible entry to the EU. In December 2002, at a summit meeting in Copenhagen, Denmark, the Czech Republic was one of 10 nations formally invited to join the EU in May 2004. A plebiscite on EU membership was held in the Czech Republic on 13–14 June 2003. Of the 55.2% of the electorate who took part in the referendum, 77.3% voted in support of Czech membership of the EU. The Czech Republic became a full member on 1 May 2004. In December 2007 the Czech Republic implemented the EU's Schengen Agreement, enabling its citizens to travel to and from other member states without border restrictions. In February 2009 President Klaus, who had attracted controversy for his Eurosceptic stance, at a session of the European Parliament criticized the bureaucratization of EU decision-making and reiterated his opposition to the institutional Lisbon Treaty. On 18 February the Lisbon Treaty was approved in the Chamber of Deputies. The Lisbon Treaty was approved in the Senate on 6 May; however, 17 members of the Senate subsequently submitted a legal challenge against it at the Constitutional Court. On 3 November the Court rejected the appeal; the Lisbon Treaty was signed by Klaus on the same day (although he continued to express opposition to it), the Czech Republic becoming the last EU member state to ratify the treaty. Amid an ongoing debt crisis in the eurozone, in early 2012 the Czech Republic and the United Kingdom were the only member states of the Union that refused to enter into the EU's Treaty on Stability, Co-ordination and Governance in the Economic and Monetary Union (the 'fiscal compact'); the decision of Prime Minister Nečas, which was strongly supported by Klaus, drew criticism from Minister of Foreign Affairs Schwarzenberg. The new, ČSSD-led Government established in January 2014 (see above) indicated that it favoured signature of the 'fiscal compact' and adoption of the euro.

Other external relations

In August 1993 the Czech Republic and Russia signed a treaty of friendship and co-operation (replacing the Russian-Czechoslovak treaty of 1992). In March 1994 the Czech Republic joined the 'Partnership for Peace' programme of the North Atlantic Treaty Organization (NATO, see p. 370). In 1996 the Chamber of Deputies approved legislation prohibiting the storage of nuclear weapons on Czech territory, except where international treaties are concerned, thereby allowing for full membership of NATO. In July 1997 the Czech Republic, together with Hungary and Poland, was invited to commence membership negotiations. A protocol providing for the accession of the three states to NATO was signed in December, and in March 1999 the Czech Republic, Hungary and Poland became full members of the alliance.

In January 2007 Prime Minister Topolánek entered into negotiations with the USA regarding the establishment of a military base in the Czech Republic as part of the proposed US National Missile Defence programme. Domestic opposition to the plans had resulted in the establishment of a group comprising some 40 Czech and international civic organizations, which organized a campaign of protests. (Russia strenuously opposed the proposed installation of military bases in the Czech Republic and Poland.) At a NATO summit meeting, which took place in Bucharest, Romania, in April 2008, member states endorsed US plans to position missile defence bases in the Czech Republic and Poland. On 8 July an accord providing for the installation of a US anti-missile radar system in the Czech Republic was officially signed in Prague.

Following the election of US President Barack Obama in November 2008, however, the US Administration announced in September 2009 that the plans for the deployment of part of a long-range missile defence system on Czech Republic and Polish territory had been abandoned. The declaration was welcomed by Russia but prompted criticism from politicians in Central Europe who had supported the system. In response to concerns expressed by the Czech Republic and Polish Governments, the USA indicated that both countries would continue to be involved in revised defence plans. Nevertheless, in June 2011 the Czech Government announced the Czech Republic's withdrawal from the US missile defence system, owing to dissatisfaction with the country's downgraded participation under the revised proposals. In January 2013 a transit gas pipeline that connected with Russia's Nord Stream pipeline and eastern Germany was officially opened.

In July 2009 Canada reintroduced visa requirements for Czech citizens, following a dramatic increase in asylum applications from members of the Czech Roma community since visa restrictions were ended in 2007; the Czech Government responded by reimposing visa requirements for Canadian citizens and recalling its ambassador to Canada for consultations. In September 2009 a Canadian-Czech Working Group was established and convened in Ottawa, Canada, to examine the issue. Although the EU Justice and Home Affairs Council urged the restoration of visa-free travel for Czech nationals to Canada, the visa requirements subsequently remained in force.

CONSTITUTION AND GOVERNMENT

Under the Constitution, which entered into force on 1 January 1993, and as subsequently revised, legislative power is vested in the 200-member Poslanecká sněmovna (Chamber of Deputies) and the 81-member Senát (Senate). Members of the Chamber of Deputies and the Senate are elected for terms of four and six years, respectively, by universal adult suffrage. (One-third of the seats in the Senate are renewable every two years.) Since 2013 the President of the Republic (Head of State) has been directly elected by popular vote for a term of five years (previously the position was elected by a joint session of the legislature). The President, who is also Commander of the Armed Forces, may not be elected for more than two consecutive terms. He appoints the Prime Minister and, on the latter's recommendation, the other members of the Council of Ministers (the highest organ of executive power). The judiciary consists of the Supreme Court, the Supreme Administrative Court, and high, regional and district courts. For administrative purposes, the Czech Republic is divided into 14 self-governing regions.

REGIONAL AND INTERNATIONAL CO-OPERATION

The Czech Republic became a member of the Council of Europe (see p. 252) in 1993. In 1995 the Czech Republic became the first post-communist state in Eastern Europe to be admitted to the Organisation for Economic Co-operation and Development (OECD, see p. 379). The Czech Republic was admitted to the North Atlantic Treaty Organization (NATO, see p. 370) in 1999. In 2004 the country became a full member of the European Union (EU, see p. 273).

The Czech Republic was admitted to the UN following independence in 1993 and, as a contracting party to the General Agreement on Tariffs and Trade, joined the World Trade Organization (WTO, see p. 434) on its establishment in 1995.

ECONOMIC AFFAIRS

In 2012, according to estimates by the World Bank, the Czech Republic's gross national income (GNI), measured at average 2010–12 prices, was US $190,597m., equivalent to $18,130 per head (or $24,710 per head on an international purchasing-power parity basis). During 2003–12, it was estimated, the population increased at an average annual rate of 0.3%, while gross domestic product (GDP) per head increased, in real terms, by an average of 2.5% per year. According to official figures, overall GDP increased, in real terms, at an average annual rate of 2.8% in 2003–12; real GDP grew by 1.8% in 2011, but declined by 1.0% in 2012.

Agriculture (including hunting, forestry and fishing) contributed 2.4% of GDP and engaged 3.1% of the employed labour force in 2012. The principal crops are wheat, sugar beet, barley, rapeseed, maize, potatoes and hops (the Czech Republic is a major producer and exporter of beer). According to official estimates, the GDP of the agricultural sector decreased, in real terms, at an average annual rate of 2.3% in 2003–12; agricultural GDP decreased by 4.1% in 2012.

Industry (including manufacturing, mining, construction and power) contributed 37.3% of GDP and engaged 38.1% of the employed labour force in 2012. According to official estimates, the GDP of the industrial sector increased, in real terms, at an average annual rate of 5.0% in 2003–12; real industrial GDP increased by 4.8% in 2011, but decreased by 1.2% in 2012.

Mining and quarrying contributed 1.2% of GDP and engaged 0.9% of the employed labour force in 2012. The principal minerals extracted are coal and lignite. According to official estimates, the GDP of the mining and quarrying sector decreased, in real terms, at an average annual rate of 4.2% in 2003–12; GDP of the sector decreased by 3.1% in 2012.

The manufacturing sector contributed 24.7% of GDP and engaged 26.6% of the employed labour force in 2012. According to official estimates, the GDP of the manufacturing sector increased at an average annual rate of 7.3%, in real terms, in 2003–12; sectoral GDP increased by 8.6% in 2011, and remained constant in 2012.

The construction sector contributed 6.3% of GDP and engaged 8.7% of the employed labour force in 2012. According to official estimates, the GDP of the construction sector increased at an average annual rate of 0.8%, in real terms, in 2003–12; sectoral GDP decreased by 5.8% in 2012.

In 2012 coal provided 53.8% of total electricity production and nuclear power 34.9%. In 2012 the Czech Republic's proven coal reserves were estimated at about 1,100m. metric tons. Production of coal amounted to 57.8m. metric tons in 2011. Imports of mineral fuels comprised 11.1% of the value of total imports in 2012.

The services sector contributed 60.4% of GDP and engaged 58.8% of the employed labour force in 2012. According to official estimates, the GDP of the services sector increased, in real terms, at an average annual rate of 2.0% in 2003–12; real GDP in the services sector increased by 1.1% in 2011, but decreased by 0.2% in 2012.

In 2012 the Czech Republic recorded a visible merchandise trade surplus of US $6,129.5m., while there was a deficit of $4,731.1m. on the current account of the balance of payments. In 2012 the principal source of imports (accounting for 25.3% of the total) was Germany; other major sources were the People's Republic of China, Poland, Slovakia and Russia. Germany was also the principal market for exports (taking 31.4% of the total) in that year; other important purchasers were Slovakia, Poland and France. The principal imports in 2012 were machinery and transport equipment, basic manufactures, mineral fuels and lubricants, and chemical products. The principal exports in that year were machinery and transport equipment, basic manufactures, miscellaneous manufactured articles, and chemical products.

In 2012 there was a budgetary deficit of 92,883m. koruna (equivalent to 2.4% of GDP). The Czech Republic's general government gross debt was 1,758,872m. koruna in 2012, equivalent to 45.9% of GDP. According to IMF estimates, the country's gross external debt was equivalent to 52.1% of GDP in 2012. The annual rate of inflation averaged 2.7% in 2003–12 and consumer prices increased by 3.1% in 2012, according to ILO. The official rate of unemployment was 7.0% in 2012.

Following the negative impact of the international financial crisis, a programme of austerity measures was adopted in October 2009. In an assessment published in early 2011, the IMF confirmed the Czech Republic's recovery from the economic downturn, with a return to positive GDP growth in 2010, and a reduction in the budgetary deficit (which had remained persistently high) to below 5% of GDP. In January 2012 the Government agreed to contribute €1,500m. to an IMF emergency stabilization fund for the eurozone. In March the Czech Republic refused (together with the United Kingdom) to sign the EU's new 'fiscal compact' treaty that committed EU member states to fiscal discipline measures. Legislation providing for, notably, a 1% increase in value-added tax rates, together with a 7% rise in income tax for higher earners, which entered into effect in January 2013, were intended to raise revenue of 22,000m. koruna, and, under a revised budget, enable the Government to reduce the budget deficit to less than 3% of GDP in accordance with EU criteria. However, amid continued sovereign debt crisis in the eurozone, by the end of 2012 the Czech Republic's economy was again in recession, having contracted by 1.0% overall in that year, with a decline in four consecutive quarters. Following the collapse of the Government, owing to corruption allegations, in mid-2013 and the organization of pre-term elections (see Domestic Political Affairs), a centre-left coalition administration was installed in January 2014. The new Government announced plans to reverse some of the previous austerity measures, envisaging a rise in pensions and the minimum wage, and favouring signature of the 'fiscal compact' and adoption of the euro; however, policy differences between the coalition parties had already emerged. Meanwhile, following the revelation of malpractice at the regional level, in January it was announced that the European Commission had frozen funding of 100,000m. koruna designated for two development programmes, owing to concerns regarding corruption and lack of supervision. However, after a further GDP contraction in 2013, estimated at an overall rate of 1.4%, a return to modest growth was predicted by analysts for 2014, as a result of improved conditions in the eurozone.

PUBLIC HOLIDAYS

2015: 1 January (New Year's Day), 6 April (Easter Monday), 1 May (Labour Day), 8 May (Liberation Day), 5 July (Day of the Apostles SS Cyril and Methodius), 6 July (Anniversary of the Martyrdom of Jan Hus), 28 September (Czech Statehood Day), 28 October (Independence Day), 17 November (Freedom and Democracy Day), 24–25 December (Christmas), 26 December (St Stephen's Day).

Statistical Survey

Source: mainly Czech Statistical Office, Na padesátém 81, 100 82 Prague 10; tel. 274051111; internet www.czso.cz.

Area and Population

AREA, POPULATION AND DENSITY

Area (sq km)	78,867*
Population (census results)	
1 March 2001	10,230,060
26 March 2011	
Males	5,109,766
Females	5,326,794
Total	10,436,560
Population (official estimate at 31 December) 2012	10,516,125
Density (per sq km) at 31 December 2012	133.3

* 30,451 sq miles.

POPULATION BY AGE AND SEX

(official estimates at 31 December 2012)

	Males	Females	Total
0–14	800,529	759,767	1,560,296
15–64	3,640,265	3,547,946	7,188,211
65 and over	723,555	1,044,063	1,767,618
Total	5,164,349	5,351,776	10,516,125

NATIONALITY OF THE POPULATION

(2011 census)

Country of citizenship	Number	%
Czech Republic	9,924,044	95.1
Ukraine	116,139	1.1
Slovakia	82,251	0.8
Viet Nam	52,612	0.5
Russia	31,545	0.3
Germany	14,907	0.1
Poland	16,800	0.2
Others and unknown	198,262	1.9
Total	10,436,560	100.0

REGIONS

(official population estimates at 31 December 2012)

	Area (sq km)	Population	Density (per sq km)
Central Bohemia (Středočeský)	11,014	1,291,816	117.3
Highlands (Vysočina)	6,796	511,207	75.2
Hradec Králové (Královéhradecký)	4,758	552,946	116.2
Karlovy Vary (Karlovarský)	3,315	301,726	91.0
Liberec (Liberecký)	3,163	438,594	138.7
Moravia-Silesia (Moravskoslezský)	5,427	1,226,602	226.0
Olomouc (Olomoucký)	5,267	637,609	121.1
Pardubice (Pardubický)	4,519	516,440	114.3
Plzeň (Plzeňský)	7,561	572,687	75.7
Prague City (Pražský)	496	1,246,780	2,513.7
South Bohemia (Jihočeský)	10,057	636,611	63.3
South Moravia (Jihomoravský)	7,196	1,168,650	162.4
Ústí nad Labem (Ústecký)	5,335	826,764	155.0
Zlín (Zlínský)	3,964	587,693	148.3
Total	78,868	10,516,125	133.3

PRINCIPAL TOWNS

(population estimates at December 2012)

Praha (Prague, capital)	1,246,780	Pardubice	89,467
Brno	378,327	Havířov	77,371
Ostrava	297,421	Zlín	75,555
Plzeň (Pilsen)	167,472	Kladno	68,551
Liberec	102,113	Most	67,490
Olomouc	99,471	Opava	58,054
Ústí nad Labem	93,747	Karviná	57,842
České Budějovice (Budweis)	93,467	Frýdek-Místek	57,523
Hradec Králové	93,035		

BIRTHS, MARRIAGES AND DEATHS

	Registered live births		Registered marriages		Registered deaths	
	Number	Rate (per 1,000)	Number	Rate (per 1,000)	Number	Rate (per 1,000)
2005	102,211	10.0	51,829	5.1	107,938	10.5
2006	105,831	10.3	52,860	5.1	104,441	10.2
2007	114,632	11.1	57,157	5.5	104,636	10.1
2008	119,570	11.5	52,457	5.0	104,948	10.1
2009	118,348	11.3	47,862	4.6	107,421	10.2
2010	117,153	11.1	46,746	4.4	106,844	10.2
2011	108,673	10.4	45,137	4.3	106,848	10.2
2012	108,576	10.3	45,206	4.3	108,189	10.3

Life expectancy (years at birth): 77.9 (males 74.8; females 81.1) in 2011 (Source: World Bank, World Development Indicators database).

IMMIGRATION AND EMIGRATION

	2010	2011	2012
Immigrants	30,515	22,590	30,298
Emigrants	14,867	5,701	10,293

ECONOMICALLY ACTIVE POPULATION

('000 persons aged 15 years and over)

	2010	2011	2012
Agriculture, hunting, forestry and fishing	151.2	145.6	149.2
Mining and quarrying	47.9	46.1	43.3
Manufacturing	1,235.9	1,287.6	1,299.1
Electricity, gas and water	107.0	108.6	96.9
Construction	464.9	431.0	425.0
Wholesale and retail trade, repair of motor vehicles, motorcycles and personal household goods	593.8	597.4	601.9
Hotels and restaurants	190.1	185.0	177.5
Transport, storage and communications	465.2	467.6	434.2
Financial intermediation	115.3	122.5	136.7
Real estate, renting and business activities	355.1	355.0	373.9
Public administration, defence and compulsory social security	329.3	314.8	305.5
Education	295.6	295.5	318.9
Health and social welfare	339.9	324.8	333.4
Other community, social and personal services	176.6	170.8	172.4
Households with employed persons	17.4	20.1	22.1
Total employed	4,885.2	4,872.4	4,890.0
Registered unemployed	383.7	350.6	366.9
Total labour force	5,268.9	5,223.0	5,256.9

Health and Welfare

KEY INDICATORS

Total fertility rate (children per woman, 2011)	1.5
Under-5 mortality rate (per 1,000 live births, 2011)	4.0
HIV/AIDS (% of persons aged 15–49, 2011)	<0.1
Physicians (per 1,000 head, 2009)	3.7
Hospital beds (per 1,000 head, 2009)	7.1
Health expenditure (2010): US $ per head (PPP)	1,885
Health expenditure (2010): % of GDP	7.5
Health expenditure (2010): public (% of total)	83.8
Total carbon dioxide emissions ('000 metric tons, 2010)	111,751.8
Carbon dioxide emissions per head (metric tons, 2010)	10.6
Human Development Index (2012): ranking	28
Human Development Index (2012): value	0.873

For sources and definitions, see explanatory note on p. vi.

Agriculture

PRINCIPAL CROPS

('000 metric tons)

	2010	2011	2012
Wheat	4,162	4,913	3,519
Barley	1,585	1,814	1,616
Maize	693	761	928
Rye*	118	105	147
Oats	138	164	172
Potatoes	665	805	662
Sugar beet	3,065	3,899	3,869
Peas, dry	48	52	31
Rapeseed	1,042	1,046	1,109
Cabbages and other brassicas	36	58	50
Tomatoes	7	16	13
Cauliflowers and broccoli	5	5	4
Cucumbers and gherkins	11	10	7
Onions, dry	35	46	32
Carrots and turnips	19	24	21
Apples	100	85	119
Pears	4	6	5
Peaches and nectarines	2	2	2
Plums and sloes	4	6	4
Grapes	46	91	60
Hops	8	6	4

* Including mixed crops of wheat and rye.

Aggregate production ('000 metric tons, may include official, semi-official or estimated data): Total cereals 6,882 in 2010, 7,973 in 2011, 6,600 in 2012; Total roots and tubers 665 in 2010, 805 in 2011, 662 in 2012; Total vegetables (incl. melons) 161 in 2010, 219 in 2011, 181 in 2012; Total fruits (excl. melons) 190 in 2010, 231 in 2011, 228 in 2012.

Source: FAO.

LIVESTOCK

('000 head at 1 March)

	2010	2011	2012
Horses	31	31	33
Cattle	1,329	1,344	1,354
Pigs	1,908	1,749	1,579
Sheep	206	209	221
Goats	22	23	24
Chickens	24,284	20,577	20,107
Ducks	374	289	249
Turkeys	389	365	320

Source: FAO.

LIVESTOCK PRODUCTS

('000 metric tons unless otherwise indicated)

	2010	2011	2012
Cattle meat	74	72	66
Pig meat	291	275	250
Chicken meat	185	169	151
Cows' milk (million litres)	2,683	2,736	2,815
Hen eggs	127	130	115

Source: FAO.

Forestry

ROUNDWOOD REMOVALS

('000 cubic metres, FAO estimates)

	2009	2010	2011
Sawlogs, veneer logs and logs for sleepers	8,852	9,427	8,838
Pulpwood	4,827	5,245	4,538
Other industrial wood	90	99	91
Fuel wood	1,733	1,965	1,914
Total	15,502	16,736	15,381

2012: Production assumed to be unchanged from 2011 (FAO estimates).

Source: FAO.

SAWNWOOD PRODUCTION

('000 cubic metres)

	2009	2010	2011
Coniferous (softwood)	3,800	4,492	4,153
Broadleaved (hardwood)	248	252	301
Total	4,048	4,744	4,454

2012: Production assumed to be unchanged from 2011 (FAO estimates).

Source: FAO.

Fishing

(metric tons)

	2009	2010	2011
Common carp	20,472	20,907	21,195
Others	3,711	3,503	3,674
Total catch	24,183	24,410	24,869

Source: FAO.

Mining

('000 metric tons unless otherwise indicated)

	2009	2010	2011
Hard coal	10,621	11,193	10,967
Brown coal and lignite	45,616	43,931	46,848
Crude petroleum ('000 barrels)	1,500	1,173	1,105
Kaolin	2,886	3,493	3,606

Source: US Geological Survey.

Industry

SELECTED PRODUCTS
('000 metric tons unless otherwise indicated)

	2010	2011	2012
Wheat flour	745	756	755
Refined sugar	446	517	550
Wine ('000 hectolitres)	463	n.a.	n.a.
Beer ('000 hectolitres)	16,896	17,127	18,028
Cotton yarn (metric tons)	12,535	7,526	5,632
Woven cotton fabrics ('000 metres)	53,166	57,534	70,364
Woven flax fabrics ('000 metres)	638	819	481
Paper and paperboard	121	96	91
Footwear ('000 pairs)	1,137	973	710
Nitrogenous fertilizers*†‡	200	200	n.a.
Soap	29	25	23
Cement	3,559	4,053	n.a.
Pig-iron†	3,987	4,137	n.a.
Crude steel†	5,180	5,583	n.a.
Electric energy (million kWh)	85,910	87,561	87,573§
Motor spirit (petrol)	1,463	n.a.	n.a.
Residual fuel oils	239	n.a.	n.a.

* Estimated.
† Source: US Geological Survey.
‡ Production in terms of nitrogen.
§ Preliminary.

2008: Woollen fabrics ('000 metres) 14,013; Coke 3,645; Bicycles (number) 304,630.

2009: Gas-diesel (distillate fuel) oil ('000 metric tons) 3,131.

Source: partly UN Industrial Commodity Statistics Database.

Finance

CURRENCY AND EXCHANGE RATES

Monetary Units

100 haléřů (singular: haléř—heller) = 1 Czech koruna (Czech crown or Kč.).

Sterling, Dollar and Euro Equivalents (31 December 2013)

£1 sterling = 32.761 koruna;
US $1 = 19.894 koruna;
€1 = 27.436 koruna;
1,000 koruna = £30.52 = $50.27 = €36.45.

Average Exchange Rate (koruna per US $)

2011	17.696
2012	19.578
2013	19.571

CONSOLIDATED BUDGET
(general government transactions, million koruna)

Revenue	2010	2011	2012
Tax revenue	690,797	705,598	727,774
Taxes on income, profits, and capital gains	260,864	257,242	270,889
Taxes on property	16,351	20,344	20,711
Taxes on goods and services	413,422	427,880	435,988
Value-added tax	263,879	269,255	272,962
Excises	138,261	146,586	146,773
Social contributions	517,475	533,166	540,768
Social security contributions	503,431	518,891	526,329
Non-tax revenue	107,970	105,392	105,785
Sales of non-financial assets	21,650	11,536	12,320
Grants	84,910	73,897	111,647
Total	1,422,802	1,429,589	1,498,294

Expenditure	2010	2011	2012
Compensation of employees	145,889	135,970	136,254
Wages and salaries	110,687	102,816	102,515
Use of goods and services	142,101	129,116	122,469
Interest	42,073	47,753	44,548
Subsidies	300,039	307,562	313,900
Grants	30,560	34,260	32,795
Social benefits	670,740	686,944	704,160
Other expense	163,654	166,173	152,363
Purchases of non-financial assets	107,265	93,198	84,690
Total (incl. others)	1,602,321	1,600,976	1,591,179

Source: Ministry of Finance, Prague.

INTERNATIONAL RESERVES
(US $ million at 31 December)

	2010	2011	2012
Gold (national value)	584	620	618
IMF special drawing rights	1,224	1,152	1,154
Reserve position in IMF	349	664	700
Foreign exchange	40,335	37,854	42,412
Total	42,492	40,290	44,884

Source: IMF, *International Financial Statistics*.

MONEY SUPPLY
('000 million koruna at 31 December)

	2010	2011	2012
Currency outside depository corporations	357.5	377.9	388.9
Transferable deposits	1,664.2	1,771.8	1,947.4
Other deposits	698.7	673.1	629.7
Securities other than shares	39.6	14.5	7.7
Broad money	2,760.0	2,837.4	2,973.6

Source: IMF, *International Financial Statistics*.

COST OF LIVING
(Consumer Price Index; base: 2000 = 100)

	2010	2011	2012
Food	115.7	121.0	129.1
All items (incl. others)	128.6	131.0	135.1

Source: ILO.

NATIONAL ACCOUNTS
('000 million koruna at current prices)

Expenditure on the Gross Domestic Product

	2010	2011	2012
Final consumption expenditure	2,724.1	2,727.7	2,733.0
Households	1,889.2	1,907.7	1,916.2
General government	807.5	792.5	788.8
Non-profit institutions serving households	27.4	27.5	28.0
Gross capital formation	939.7	937.1	897.6
Gross fixed capital formation	930.5	922.6	887.9
Changes in inventories	5.6	10.8	4.9
Net acquisition of valuables	3.5	3.6	4.7
Total domestic expenditure	3,663.8	3,664.8	3,630.6
Exports of goods and services	2,554.4	2,818.9	3,032.6
Less Imports of goods and services	2,427.3	2,660.3	2,817.3
GDP in purchasers' values	3,790.9	3,823.4	3,845.9
GDP at constant 2005 prices	3,557.2	3,621.9	3,584.9

Gross Domestic Product by Economic Activity

	2010	2011	2012
Agriculture, forestry and fishing	56.7	79.8	81.4
Mining and quarrying	44.0	46.3	40.5
Manufacturing	785.5	825.3	852.9
Electricity, gas and water supply	186.0	178.6	176.4
Construction	250.8	233.9	216.8
Wholesale and retail trade	379.2	386.1	391.6
Hotels and restaurants	64.7	64.9	63.3
Transport, storage and communications	393.8	384.6	390.5
Financial intermediation	157.9	167.7	151.0
Real estate, renting and business activities	491.9	468.9	481.7
Public administration and defence	238.4	227.3	226.3
Education	142.5	146.2	148.0
Health and social work	145.2	150.5	152.8
Other community, social and personal service activities	83.7	84.3	78.6
Sub-total	3,420.3	3,444.5	3,451.7
Taxes on products	417.5	436.2	452.4
Less Subsidies on products	46.9	57.3	58.2
GDP in purchasers' values	3,790.9	3,823.4	3,845.9

BALANCE OF PAYMENTS
(US $ million)

	2010	2011	2012
Exports of goods	108,282.4	129,414.6	125,179.4
Imports of goods	−106,144.7	−125,196.6	−119,049.9
Balance on goods	2,137.8	4,218.0	6,129.5
Exports of services	21,373.8	23,729.1	23,406.7
Imports of services	−16,778.3	−19,517.0	−19,525.3
Balance on goods and services	6,733.3	8,430.1	10,010.9
Primary income received	6,158.9	7,106.8	6,709.2
Primary income paid	−19,874.7	−20,887.7	−20,411.9
Balance on goods, services and primary income	−6,982.6	−5,350.9	−3,691.8
Secondary income received	3,273.1	3,301.0	2,670.8
Secondary income paid	−3,892.4	−4,063.9	−3,710.2
Current balance	−7,601.9	−6,113.7	−4,731.1
Capital account (net)	1,685.7	799.3	2,653.4
Direct investment assets	−1,200.7	343.6	−1,337.0
Direct investment liabilities	6,119.1	2,248.9	10,580.8
Portfolio investment assets	632.0	−817.8	−1,381.9
Portfolio investment liabilities	7,098.5	1,179.9	3,539.0
Financial derivatives and employee stock options (net)	−162.7	−131.8	443.3
Other investment assets	−4,379.0	−2,836.4	−3,326.9
Other investment liabilities	946.6	3,571.4	−2,291.8
Net errors and omissions	−1,061.4	756.5	38.8
Reserves and related items	2,076.2	−1,000.2	4,186.5

Source: IMF, *International Financial Statistics*.

External Trade

COMMODITY GROUPS
(distribution by SITC, million koruna)

Imports f.o.b.	2010	2011	2012
Food and live animals	112,559	123,162	136,784
Beverages and tobacco	14,373	16,345	18,539
Crude materials (inedible) except fuels	64,648	80,072	79,306
Mineral fuels, lubricants, etc.	231,447	286,233	307,576
Chemicals and related products	257,351	293,700	307,017
Basic manufactures	430,281	490,123	493,687
Machinery and transport equipment	1,046,030	1,126,862	1,143,512
Miscellaneous manufactured articles	247,443	259,514	267,494
Total (incl. others)	2,411,556	2,687,563	2,766,888

Exports f.o.b.	2010	2011	2012
Food and live animals	76,266	91,355	108,057
Beverages and tobacco	16,781	17,120	19,873
Crude materials (inedible) except fuels	75,908	80,854	86,439
Mineral fuels, lubricants, etc.	93,874	109,585	118,705
Chemicals and related products	164,213	180,176	189,474
Basic manufactures	435,348	507,775	532,504
Machinery and transport equipment	1,382,306	1,576,337	1,663,416
Miscellaneous manufactured articles	280,531	307,201	340,363
Total (incl. others)	2,532,797	2,878,691	3,072,598

PRINCIPAL TRADING PARTNERS
(million koruna)

Imports f.o.b.	2010	2011	2012
Austria	81,227	88,521	88,513
Azerbaijan	22,877	30,549	32,024
Belgium	44,013	47,983	46,985
China, People's Republic	295,799	334,528	306,522
France	79,800	86,730	86,263
Germany	613,698	689,590	699,619
Hungary	52,342	59,162	64,855
Italy	94,228	104,900	106,818
Japan	58,667	54,933	55,887
Korea, Republic	40,492	47,839	60,676
Netherlands	77,764	87,636	96,049
Norway	19,833	23,519	28,819
Poland	154,241	176,664	196,377
Russia	130,121	142,960	154,900
Slovakia	125,944	153,068	167,057
Spain	43,919	44,067	43,534
Switzerland	25,656	28,458	28,970
United Kingdom	49,152	50,797	52,186
USA	54,000	52,377	59,339
Total (incl. others)	2,411,556	2,687,563	2,766,888

Exports f.o.b.	2010	2011	2012
Austria	119,667	130,678	141,646
Belgium	62,587	71,227	73,511
China, People's Republic	23,179	29,517	32,712
France	135,194	156,392	155,152
Germany	819,245	927,060	966,190
Hungary	58,266	64,663	70,643
Italy	112,244	119,133	110,329
Netherlands	93,354	101,642	99,312
Poland	154,644	181,475	187,115
Romania	28,565	31,671	34,732
Russia	67,337	92,648	118,025
Slovakia	217,292	257,555	277,491
Spain	60,495	61,390	61,420
Sweden	41,163	47,452	46,428
Switzerland	41,812	48,570	49,904
Turkey	19,823	23,982	33,263
Ukraine	17,875	24,422	33,365
United Kingdom	124,923	130,176	147,084
USA	44,269	55,897	70,093
Total (incl. others)	2,532,797	2,878,691	3,072,598

Transport

RAILWAYS
(traffic)

	2010	2011	2012
Passengers carried ('000)	164,801	167,932	172,801
Passenger-km (million)	6,591	6,714	7,265
Freight carried ('000 metric tons)	82,900	87,096	82,968
Freight net ton-km (million)	13,770	14,316	14,266

ROAD TRAFFIC
(motor vehicles in use at 31 December)

	2010	2011	2012*
Passenger cars†	4,496,232	4,581,642	4,706,325
Buses and coaches	19,653	19,674	19,882
Commercial vehicles	584,921	585,729	595,438
Trailers	278,137	299,546	336,914
Motorcycles	924,291	944,171	976,911

* Data as of 1 July 2013.
† Including vans.

INLAND WATERWAYS
(freight carried, '000 metric tons)

	2010	2011	2012
Imports	167	193	159
Exports	276	205	257
Internal	371	510	411
Total (incl. others)	1,642	1,895	1,767

CIVIL AVIATION

	2010	2011	2012
Kilometres flown ('000)	105,926	105,372	107,996
Passengers carried ('000)	7,466	7,525	6,420
Freight carried (metric tons)	13,572	11,845	9,025
Passenger-km ('000)	10,902	11,586	10,612
Freight ton-km ('000)	22,379	21,966	16,574

Tourism

FOREIGN TOURIST ARRIVALS*

Country of origin	2010	2011	2012
Austria	189,886	185,719	203,891
Denmark	109,292	96,311	103,816
France	251,468	283,480	275,449
Germany	1,348,482	1,386,976	1,420,698
Italy	332,551	337,645	353,165
Japan	133,052	121,663	136,557
Netherlands	194,138	197,975	198,687
Poland	350,637	371,127	370,910
Russia	414,671	559,021	694,138
Slovakia	307,192	344,101	382,595
Spain	196,011	225,778	201,537
United Kingdom	368,643	327,951	346,527
USA	312,883	314,950	366,910
Total (incl. others)	6,333,996	6,715,067	7,164,576

* Figures refer to visitors staying for at least one night at registered accommodation facilities.

Tourism receipts (US $ million, excl. passenger transport): 7,121 in 2010; 7,628 in 2011; 7,035 in 2012 (provisional) (Source: World Tourism Organization).

Communications Media

	2010	2011	2012
Telephones ('000 main lines in use)*	2,405.5	2,289.0	2,100.0
Mobile cellular telephones ('000 subscribers)*	12,972.9	13,285.1	12,973.1
Internet subscribers ('000)*	1,529.1	1,668.8	n.a.
Broadband subscribers ('000)*	1,530.0	1,668.8	1,754.0
Book production (titles)	17,054	18,985	17,247
Other periodicals (number)	5,265	5,098	5,028

* Source: International Telecommunication Union.

Education

(2012/13 unless otherwise indicated)

	Institutions	Teachers	Students
Pre-primary	5,011	27,739	354,340
Basic (primary and lower secondary)	4,095	57,669	807,950
Upper secondary:			
general	368	41,789	131,013
technical and vocational	1,048		309,575
Tertiary:			
higher professional schools	178	1,876	28,980
universities	73	15,449	381,397

Pupil-teacher ratio (primary education, UNESCO estimate): 18.8 in 2010/11 (Source: UNESCO Institute for Statistics).

Directory

The Government

HEAD OF STATE

President: MILOŠ ZEMAN (elected 25–26 January 2013, inaugurated 8 March).

COUNCIL OF MINISTERS
(April 2014)

A coalition of the Czech Social Democratic Party (ČSSD), the Action of Dissatisfied Citizens (ANO) and the Christian Democratic Union-Czechoslovak People's Party (KDU-ČSL).

Prime Minister: BOHUSLAV SOBOTKA (ČSSD).

First Deputy Prime Minister, responsible for the Economy, and Minister of Finance: ANDREJ BABIŠ (ANO).

Deputy Prime Minister, responsible for Science, Research and Innovation: PAVEL BĚLOBRÁDEK (KDU-ČSL).

Minister of Foreign Affairs: LUBOMÍR ZAORÁLEK (ČSSD).

Minister of Defence: MARTIN STROPNICKÝ (ANO).

Minister of the Interior: MILAN CHOVANEC (ČSSD).

Minister of Industry and Trade: JAN MLÁDEK (ČSSD).

Minister of Justice: HELENA VÁLKOVÁ (ANO).

Minister of Labour and Social Affairs: MICHAELA MARKSOVÁ (ČSSD).

Minister of Transport: ANTONÍN PRACHAŘ (ANO).

Minister of Agriculture: MARIAN JUREČKA (KDU-ČSL).

Minister of Health: SVATOPLUK NĚMEČEK (ČSSD).

Minister of Education, Youth and Sports: MARCEL CHLÁDEK (ČSSD).

Minister of Regional Development: VĚRA JOUROVÁ (ANO).

Minister of the Environment: RICHARD BRABEC (ANO).

Minister of Culture: DANIEL HERMAN (KDU-ČSL).

Minister of Human Rights and Chairman of the Government Legislative Council: JIŘÍ DIENSTBIER (ČSSD).

MINISTRIES

Office of the President: Pražský hrad, 119 08 Prague 1; tel. 224371111; fax 224373300; e-mail ladislav.jakl@hrad.cz; internet www.hrad.cz.

Office of the Government: náb. E. Beneše 4, 118 01 Prague 1; tel. 224002111; fax 257531283; e-mail posta@vlada.cz; internet www.vlada.cz.

Ministry of Agriculture: Těšnov 65/17, 110 00 Prague 1; tel. 221811111; fax 224810478; e-mail info@mze.cz; internet www.eagri.cz.

Ministry of Culture: Maltéské nám. 1, 118 11 Prague 1; tel. 257085111; fax 224318155; e-mail epodatelna@mkcr.cz; internet www.mkcr.cz.

Ministry of Defence: Tychonova 1, 160 01 Prague 6; tel. 973201111; fax 973200149; e-mail info@army.cz; internet www.army.cz.

Ministry of Education, Youth and Sports: Karmelitská 7, 118 12 Prague 1; tel. 234811111; fax 234811753; e-mail posta@msmt.cz; internet www.msmt.cz.

Ministry of the Environment: Vršovická 1442/65, 100 10 Prague 10; tel. 267121111; fax 267310308; e-mail info@mzp.cz; internet www.mzp.cz.

Ministry of Finance: Letenská 15, 118 00 Prague 1; tel. 257041111; fax 257042788; e-mail podatelna@mfcr.cz; internet www.mfcr.cz.

Ministry of Foreign Affairs: Loretánské nám. 101/5, 118 00 Prague 1; tel. 224181111; fax 224182048; e-mail epodatelna@mzv.cz; internet www.mzv.cz.

Ministry of Health: Palackého nám. 4, 128 01 Prague 2; tel. 224971111; fax 224972111; e-mail mzcr@mzcr.cz; internet www.mzcr.cz.

Ministry of Industry and Trade: Na Františku 32, 110 15 Prague 1; tel. 224851111; fax 224811089; e-mail posta@mpo.cz; internet www.mpo.cz.

Ministry of the Interior: Nad Štolou 3, POB 21, 170 34 Prague 7; tel. 974811111; fax 974833582; e-mail posta@mvcr.cz; internet www.mvcr.cz.

Ministry of Justice: Vyšehradská 16, 128 10 Prague 2; tel. 221997111; fax 224919927; e-mail posta@msp.justice.cz; internet www.justice.cz.

Ministry of Labour and Social Affairs: Na poříčním právu 1/376, 128 01 Prague 2; tel. 221921111; fax 224918391; e-mail posta@mpsv.cz; internet www.mpsv.cz.

Ministry of Regional Development: Staroměstské nám. 6, 110 15 Prague 1; tel. 224861111; fax 224861333; e-mail info@mmr.cz; internet www.mmr.cz.

Ministry of Transport: nábř. L. Svobody 12/1222, POB 9, 110 15 Prague 1; tel. 225131184; fax 225131112; e-mail posta@mdcr.cz; internet www.mdcr.cz.

President

Presidential Election, First Ballot, 11–12 January 2013

Candidates	Votes	%
Miloš Zeman (SPO—Z)	1,245,848	24.22
Karel Schwarzenberg (TOP 09)	1,204,195	23.41
Jan Fischer (Independent)	841,437	16.36
Jiří Dienstbier (ČSSD)	829,297	16.12
Prof. Vladimír Franz (Independent)	351,916	6.84
Zuzana Roithová (KDU-ČSL)	255,045	4.96
Taťana Fischerová (Key Movement)	166,211	3.23
Přemysl Sobotka (ODS)	126,846	2.47
Jana Bobošíková (Sovereignty Bloc of Jana Bobošíková)	123,171	2.39
Total	5,143,966	100.00

Second Ballot, 25–26 January 2013

Candidates	Votes	%
Miloš Zeman (SPO—Z)	2,717,405	54.80
Karel Schwarzenberg (TOP 09)	2,241,171	45.20
Total	4,958,576	100.00

Legislature

The Czech Constitution, which was adopted in December 1992, provides for a bicameral legislature as the highest organ of state authority in the Czech Republic (which was established as an independent state on 1 January 1993, following the dissolution of the Czech and Slovak Federative Republic). The lower house, the Poslanecká sněmovna (Chamber of Deputies), retained the structure of the Czech National Council (the former republican legislature). The upper chamber, the Senát (Senate), was first elected in November 1996.

Chamber of Deputies (Poslanecká sněmovna)

Sněmovní 4, 118 26 Prague 1; tel. 257171111; fax 257534469; e-mail posta@psp.cz; internet www.psp.cz.

Chairman: MIROSLAVA NĚMCOVÁ.

General Election, 25–26 October 2013

Party	Votes	% of votes	Seats
Czech Social Democratic Party	1,016,829	20.45	50
Action of Dissatisfied Citizens	927,240	18.65	47
Communist Party of Bohemia and Moravia	741,044	14.91	33
Traditions, Responsibility, Prosperity 09	596,357	11.99	26
Civic Democratic Party	384,174	7.72	16
Dawn of Direct Democracy	342,339	6.88	14
Christian Democratic Union-Czechoslovak People's Party	336,970	6.78	14
Others	625,031	12.62	—
Total	4,969,984	100.00	200

Senate (Senát)

Valdštejnské nám. 4, 118 01 Prague 1; tel. 257071111; fax 257075700; e-mail epodatelna@senat.cz; internet www.senat.cz.

Chairman: MILAN ŠTĚCH.

One-third of the 81 seats of the Senát are renewed every two years. Following a partial election, which was conducted in two rounds on 12–13 October and 19–20 October 2012, the strength of the parties was as follows:

Party	Seats
Czech Social Democratic Party	40
Civic Democratic Party	14
Christian Democratic Union-Czechoslovak People's Party	3
Communist Party of Bohemia and Moravia	2
Independents	18
Others	4
Total	81

Election Commission

Státní volební komise, Český statistický úřad (State Electoral Commission, Czech Statistical Office): Na padesátém 81, 100 82 Prague 10; tel. 274051111; e-mail krausova@mvcr.cz; internet www.volby.cz; Chair. Minister of the Interior.

Political Organizations

In early March 2014 some 93 active political parties and 74 active political movements were officially registered with the Ministry of the Interior. The following are among the most significant:

Action of Dissatisfied Citizens (ANO) (Akce Nespokojených Občanů): Pyšelská 2361/4, 149 00 Prague 4; tel. 296827401; e-mail ano2011@ano2011.cz; internet www.anobudelip.cz; f. 2011; liberal; Leader ANDREJ BABIŠ.

Christian Democratic Union-Czechoslovak People's Party (KDU-ČSL) (Křestanská a demokratická unie-Československá strana lidová): Palác Charitas, Karlovo nám. 5, 128 00 Prague 2; tel. 226205111; fax 226205333; e-mail info@kdu.cz; internet www.kdu.cz; f. 1991; Chair. PAVEL BĚLOBRÁDEK.

Civic Democratic Party (ODS) (Občanská demokratická strana): Polygon House, Doudlebská 1699/5, 140 00 Prague 4; tel. 234707111; fax 234707103; e-mail hk@ods.cz; internet www.ods.cz; f. 1991 following a split in Civic Forum (f. 1989); merged with Christian Democratic Party in 1996; 33,916 mems (April 2009); liberal-conservative; Leader MIROSLAVA NĚMCOVÁ.

Communist Party of Bohemia and Moravia (KSČM) (Komunistická strana Čech a Moravy): Politických vězňů 9, 111 21 Prague 1; tel. 222897111; fax 222897207; e-mail info@kscm.cz; internet www.kscm.cz; f. 1990 as a result of the reorganization of the fmr Communist Party of Czechoslovakia; c. 66,627 mems (2010); Chair. VOJTĚCH FILIP.

Czech Social Democratic Party (ČSSD) (Česká strana sociálně demokratická): Lidový dům, Hybernská 7, 110 00 Prague 1; tel. 296522111; fax 224222190; e-mail info@socdem.cz; internet www.socdem.cz; f. 1878; prohibited 1948; re-established 1990; fmrly the Czechoslovak Social Democratic Party; Chair. BOHUSLAV SOBOTKA.

Dawn of Direct Democracy (UPD) (Úsvit Přímé Demokracie): Papírenská 6B, 160 00 Prague 6; e-mail info@hnutiusvit.cz; internet www.hnutiusvit.cz; Leader TOMIO OKAMURA.

Green Party (SZ) (Strana zelených): Nové Město, 110 00 Prague 1; tel. and fax 734388936; e-mail info@zeleni.cz; internet www.zeleni.cz; f. 1990; Pres. ONDŘEJ LIŠKA.

LIDEM—Liberal Democrats (LIDEM—liberální demokraté): Štěpánská 611/14, 110 00 Prague; tel. 777756704; e-mail info@lidem.cz; internet www.lidem.cz; f. 2012 by fmr mems of Public Affairs (q.v.); Leader DAGMAR NAVRÁTILOVÁ (acting).

Mayors and Independents (STAN) (Starostové a nezávislí): V Rovinách 40, 140 00 Prague 4; tel. 241412091; e-mail info@starostove-nezavisli.cz; internet www.starostove-nezavisli.cz; f. 2004; localism; Pres. PETR GAZDÍK.

NorthBohemians.cz (Severočeši.cz): tř. Čs. armády 1766, 434 01 Most; tel. 476146187; e-mail sekretariat@severocesi.cz; internet www.severocesi.cz; Chair. RYBA FRANTIŠEK.

Party of Citizens' Rights—Zemanovci (SPO—Z) (Strana práv občanů—Zemanovci): Opletalova 1418/23, 110 00 Prague 1; tel. 296515321; e-mail info@spoz.cz; internet www.spoz.cz; f. 2009; social democratic; Chair. ZDENĚK ŠTENGL.

Public Affairs (VV) (Věci veřejné): Štefánikova 23/203, 150 00 Prague 5; tel. 800879709; e-mail info@veciverejne.cz; internet www.veciverejne.cz; f. 2002; supports the use of referendums and other forms of direct democracy to increase public involvement in politics; Pres. VÍT BÁRTA.

Tradition, Responsibility, Prosperity 09 (TOP 09) (Tradice, Odpovědnost, Prosperita 09): Michnův palác, budova č. 2, Újezd 450/40, Malá Strana, 118 00 Prague 1; tel. 255790999; fax 255790899; e-mail info@top09.cz; internet www.top09.cz; conservative; f. 2009; Chair. KAREL SCHWARZENBERG.

Diplomatic Representation

EMBASSIES IN THE CZECH REPUBLIC

Afghanistan: Komornická 1852/25, Dejvice, 160 00 Prague 6; tel. 233544228; fax 233542009; e-mail afg.prague@centrum.cz; Ambassador ZIAUDDIN MOJADEDI.

Albania: Kaprova 42/14, 110 00 Prague 1; tel. 233370594; fax 233313655; e-mail embassy.prague@mfa.gov.al; internet www.albanianembassy-prague.com; Chargé d'affaires a.i. GENC PECANI.

Algeria: V Tišině 10/483, POB 204, 160 41 Prague 6; tel. 233101770; fax 233371144; e-mail ambalger@volny.cz; internet www.algerie.cz; Ambassador BELAID HADJEM.

Argentina: Panská 6, 110 00 Prague 1; tel. 224212449; fax 222241246; e-mail eches@mrecic.gov.ar; internet www.eches.mrecic.gov.ar; Chargé d'affaires a.i. GUILLERMO FEDERICO KRECKLER.

Armenia: Na Pískách 1411/95, Dejvice, 160 00 Prague 6; tel. 220518175; fax 220517686; e-mail armembassy.cz@mfa.am; internet www.cz.mfa.am; Ambassador TIGRAN SEYRANIAN.

Austria: Viktora Huga 10, Smíchov, 151 15 Prague 5; tel. 257090511; fax 257316045; e-mail prag-ob@bmeia.gv.at; internet www.bmeia.gv.at/prag; Ambassador FERDINAND TRAUTTSMANDORFF.

Azerbaijan: Na Zátorce 783/17, 160 00 Prague 6; tel. 246032422; fax 246032423; e-mail prague@mission.mfa.gov.az; internet www.azembassyprague.az; Ambassador TAHIR TAGHIZADE.

Belarus: Sádky 626, 171 00 Prague 7; tel. 233540899; fax 233540925; e-mail czech@belembassy.org; internet czech.mfa.gov.by; Ambassador VASIL MARKOVICH.

Belgium: Valdštejnská 6, Malá Strana, 118 01 Prague 1; tel. 257533525; fax 257533750; e-mail prague@diplobel.fed.be; internet www.diplomatie.be/prague; Ambassador FRANÇOISE GUSTIN.

Bosnia and Herzegovina: Opletalova 27, 110 00 Prague 1; tel. 224422510; fax 222210183; e-mail embbh@iol.cz; Ambassador DANKA SAVIĆ.

Brazil: Panská 5, 110 00 Prague 1; tel. 224321910; fax 224312901; e-mail brasemb.praga@itamaraty.gov.br; internet praga.itamaraty.gov.br; Ambassador GEORGE MONTEIRO PRATA.

Bulgaria: Krakovská 6, 110 00 Prague 1; tel. 222211258; fax 222211728; e-mail bulvelv@volny.cz; Ambassador LATCHEZAR PETKOV.

Canada: Ve struhách 95/2, 160 00 Prague 6; tel. 272101800; fax 272101890; e-mail canada@canada.cz; internet www.canada.cz; Ambassador OTTO JELINEK.

Chile: U Vorlíků 4/623, Bubeneč, 160 00 Prague 6; tel. 224315064; fax 224316069; e-mail embachile@embachile.cz; Ambassador PABLO RODRIGO GAETE VIDAL.

China, People's Republic: Pelléova 18, Bubeneč, 160 00 Prague 6; tel. 224311323; fax 233028847; e-mail chinaembassy@seznam.cz; internet www.chinaembassy.cz; Chargé d'affaires a.i. YAN YUQING.

Congo, Democratic Republic: Soukenická 34, 110 00 Prague 1; tel. 222316762; fax 222312218; e-mail ambardcprague@yahoo.fr; Chargé d'affaires a.i. CATHY MULAMBA MUHOMA.

Croatia: V Průhledu 9, 162 00 Prague 6; tel. 235090801; fax 233343464; e-mail velrhprag@vol.cz; internet cz.mvp.hr; Ambassador TROHA BRDAR.

Cuba: Jinonická 14, 150 00 Prague 5; tel. 224311253; fax 233341029; e-mail consul@cz.embacuba.cu; internet www.cubadiplomatica.cu/republicacheca/en/Mission/Embassy.aspx; Chargé d'affaires a.i. FERMÍN GABRIEL QUIÑONES SÁNCHEZ.

Denmark: Maltézské nám. 5, POB 25, Malá Strana, 118 01 Prague 1; tel. 257531600; fax 257531410; e-mail prgamb@um.dk; internet www.ambprag.um.dk; Ambassador CHRISTIAN HOPPE.

Egypt: Pelléova 14, Bubeneč, 160 00 Prague 6; tel. 224311506; fax 224311157; e-mail embassyegypt@centrum.cz; Ambassador MOHAMED IBRAHIM ABDEL HAKAM.

Estonia: Na Kampě 1, 118 00 Prague 1; tel. 257011180; fax 257011181; e-mail embassy.prague@estemb.cz; internet www.estemb.cz; Ambassador LAMBIT UIBO.

Finland: Hellichova 1, 118 00 Prague 1; tel. 251177251; fax 251177241; e-mail sanomat.pra@formin.fi; internet www.finland.cz; Ambassador PÄIVI HILTUNEN-TOIVIO.

France: Velkopřevorské nám. 2, 118 00 Prague 1; tel. 251171711; fax 251171720; e-mail ambapresse@france.cz; internet www.france.cz; Ambassador JEAN-PIERRE ASVAZADOURIAN.

Georgia: Mlýnská 22/4, 160 00 Prague 6; tel. 233311749; fax 233311752; e-mail prague.emb@mfa.gov.ge; internet www.czech.mfa.gov.ge; Ambassador ZAAL GOGSADZE.

Germany: Vlašská 19, 118 01 Prague 1; tel. 257113111; fax 257113318; e-mail zreg@prag.diplo.de; internet www.prag.diplo.de; Ambassador DETLEF LINGEMANN.

Ghana: V Tišině 4, Bubeneč, 160 00 Prague 6; tel. 233377236; fax 233375647; e-mail ghanaemb@gmail.com; Ambassador SAMUEL M. QUARTEY.

Greece: Na Ořechovce 19, Střešovice, 162 00 Prague 2; tel. 222250943; fax 222253686; e-mail gremb.pra@mfa.gr; Ambassador PANAIOTIS SARRIS.

Holy See: Voršilská 12, 110 00 Prague 1; tel. 224999811; fax 224999833; e-mail nunciatgc@mbox.vol.cz; Apostolic Nuncio Most Rev. GIUSEPPE LEANZA (Titular Archbishop of Lilybaeum).

Hungary: Pod Hradbami 17, Střešovice, 160 00 Prague 6; tel. 220317200; fax 233322104; e-mail mission.prg@mfa.gov.hu; internet www.mfa.gov.hu/emb/prague; Ambassador TIBOR PETŐ.

India: Milady Horákové 60/93, 170 00 Prague 7; tel. 257533490; fax 257533378; e-mail hoc@india.cz; internet www.india.cz; Ambassador V. ASHOK.

Indonesia: Nad Buďánkami II/7, 150 21 Prague 5; tel. 257214388; fax 257212105; e-mail embassy@indonesia.cz; internet www.indonesia.cz; Ambassador EMERIA WILUJENG AMIR SIREGAR.

Iran: Na Hřebenkách 2371/70, 150 00 Prague 5; tel. 257090233; fax 257090257; e-mail info@iranemb.cz; internet www.iranemb.cz; Chargé d'affaires GHOLAM REZA DERIKVAND.

Iraq: Mongolská 607/3, 160 00 Prague 6; tel. 224326976; fax 224326975; e-mail iraqembassy60@yahoo.com; Ambassador HUSSAIN SALEH MAJEED MUALLA.

Ireland: Tržiště 13, 118 00 Prague 1; tel. 257011280; fax 257531387; e-mail pragueembassy@dfa.ie; internet www.embassyofireland.cz; Ambassador ALISON KELLY.

Israel: Badeniho 2, 170 06 Prague 7; tel. 233097500; fax 233097519; e-mail info@prague.mfa.gov.il; internet prague.mfa.gov.il; Ambassador GARY KOREN.

Italy: Nerudova 20, Malá Strana, 118 00 Prague 1; tel. 233080111; fax 257531522; e-mail ambasciata.praga@esteri.it; internet www.ambpraga.esteri.it; Ambassador PASQUALE D'AVINO.

Japan: Maltézské nám. 6, Malá Strana, 118 01 Prague 1; tel. 257533546; fax 257532377; e-mail ryoji@japanembassy.cz; internet www.cz.emb-japan.go.jp; Ambassador TETSUO YAMAKAWA.

Kazakhstan: Pod Hradbami 662/9, 160 00 Prague 6; tel. 233375642; fax 233371019; e-mail kzembas@gmail.com; internet www.kazembassy.cz; Ambassador ANARBEK B. KARASHEV.

Korea, Democratic People's Republic: Na Větru 395/18, 162 00 Prague 6; tel. 235362210; fax 235355000; e-mail vel.kldr@seznam.cz; Ambassador KWANG II RI.

Korea, Republic: Slavíčkova 5, Bubeneč, 160 00 Prague 6; tel. 2234090411; fax 2234090450; e-mail czech@mofat.go.kr; internet cze.mofat.go.kr; Ambassador YONG MOON.

Kosovo: Tržiště 366/13, 118 00 Prague 1; tel. 257217775; fax 257310229; e-mail embassy.cz.republic@ks-gov.net; Chargé d'affaires a.i. ARIANA ZHERKA-HOXHA.

Kuwait: Na Zátorce 26, 160 00 Prague 6; tel. 220570781; fax 220570787; e-mail kuwaiti@volny.cz; Ambassador AYMAN MOHAMED YOUSSEF AL-ADSSANI.

Latvia: Hradešínská 3, POB 54, 101 00 Prague 10; tel. 255700881; fax 255700880; e-mail embassy.czech@mfa.gov.lv; internet www.latvia.cz; Ambassador ALBERTS SARKANIS.

Lebanon: Lazarská 6, 120 00 Prague 2; tel. 224930495; fax 224934534; e-mail prague.leb@gmail.com; Chargé d'affaires a.i. ROLA HAMDAN.

Libya: Nad Šárkou 781/56, 160 00 Prague 6; tel. 220515979; fax 220515974; e-mail embassylibyaprg@gmail.com; Chargé d'affaires a.i. ISSAM M. M. SHWEHDI.

Lithuania: Pod Klikovkou 1916/2, 150 00 Prague 5; tel. 257210122; fax 257210124; e-mail amb.cz@urm.lt; internet cz.mfa.lt; Ambassador AURIMAS TAURANTAS.

Luxembourg: Apolinářská 439/9, 128 00 Prague 2; tel. 257181800; fax 257532537; e-mail prague.amb@mae.etat.lu; internet www.ambalux.cz; Ambassador MICHÈLE PRANCHÈRE-TOMASSINI.

Macedonia, former Yugoslav republic: Na Větru 4, 162 00 Prague 6; tel. 222521093; fax 222521108; e-mail prague@mfa.gov.mk; internet www.missions.gov.mk/prague/home; Ambassador PASKAL STOJČESKI.

Malaysia: Na Zátorce 675/30, Bubeneč, 160 00 Prague 6; tel. 234706611; fax 296326192; e-mail mwprague@mwprague.cz; internet www.kln.gov.my/perwakilan/prague; Chargé d'affaires a.i. NIK MUHAMMAD NIK DAUD.

Mexico: V Jirchářích 151/10, 110 00 Prague 1; tel. 283061530; fax 233550477; e-mail embamex@rep-checa.cz; internet www.rep-checa.cz; Ambassador PABLO MACEDO RIBA.

Moldova: Juárezova 14, Bubeneč, 160 00 Prague 6; tel. 233323762; fax 233323765; e-mail praga@mfa.md; internet www.cehia.mfa.md; Ambassador STEFAN GORDA.

Mongolia: Na Marně 5, 160 00 Prague 6; tel. 224311198; fax 224314827; e-mail prague@mfa.gov.mn; Ambassador DORJDAMBYN ZÜMBERELLKHAM.

Morocco: Mickiewiczova 254/6, Dejvice, 160 00 Prague 6; tel. 233325656; fax 233322634; Ambassador SORAYA OTHMANI.

Netherlands: Gotthardská 6/27, Bubeneč, 160 00 Prague 6; tel. 233015200; fax 233015256; e-mail pra@minbuza.nl; internet www.netherlandsembassy.cz; Ambassador EDUARD W. V. M. HOEKS.

Nigeria: Na Čihadle 917/32, 160 00 Prague 6; tel. 220561165; e-mail info@nigeriaembassyprague.org; internet www.nigeriaembassyprague.org; Ambassador CATHERINE UYOK OKON.

Norway: Hellichova 1/458, Malá Strana, 118 00 Prague 1; tel. 257111500; fax 257111501; e-mail emb.prague@mfa.no; internet www.noramb.cz; Ambassador JENS EIKAAS.

Pakistan: Střešovice 56/854, 162 00 Prague 6; tel. 233312868; fax 233312885; e-mail parepprague@gmail.com; internet www.mofa.gov.pk/czechrepublic; Ambassador TAJAMMUL ALTAF CHUGHTAI.

Peru: Muchova 9, Dejvice, 160 00 Prague 6; tel. 224316210; fax 224314749; e-mail embajada@peru-embajada.cz; internet www.peru-embajada.cz; Ambassador MARÍA SUSANA LANDAVERI PORTURAS.

Philippines: Senovážné nám. 8, 110 00 Prague 1; tel. 224216397; fax 224216390; e-mail praguepe@gmail.com; internet www.philembassy-prague.net; Ambassador VICTORIANO LECAROS.

Poland: Valdštejnská 8, 118 01 Prague 1; tel. 257099500; fax 257530399; e-mail praga.amb.sekretariat@msz.gov.pl; internet www.praga.msz.gov.pl; Ambassador GRAŻYNA BERNATOWICZ.

Portugal: Pevnostní 9, 160 00 Prague 6; tel. 257311230; fax 257311234; e-mail embport@mbox.vol.cz; internet www.embportugal.cz; Ambassador JOSÉ JÚLIO PEREIRA GOMES.

Romania: Nerudova 5, POB 87, 118 01 Prague 1; tel. 257534210; fax 257531017; e-mail office@rouemb.cz; internet www.rouemb.cz; Ambassador DANIELA ANDA GRIGORE-GITMAN.

Russia: nám. Pod Kaštany 1, Bubeneč, 160 00 Prague 6; tel. 233374100; fax 233377235; e-mail embrus@bluetone.cz; internet www.czech.mid.ru; Ambassador SERGEI KISELEV.

Saudi Arabia: Korunovační 622/35, 160 00 Prague 6; tel. 257316606; fax 257316593; e-mail resa@saudiembassy.cz; Ambassador ABDULLAH A. AL-ALSHEIKH.

Serbia: Mostecká 15, 118 00 Prague 1; tel. 257532075; fax 257533948; e-mail srbambacz@grbox.cz; internet www.prague.mfa.gov.rs; Ambassador MAJA MITROVIĆ.

Slovakia: Pelléova 87/12, 160 00 Prague 6; tel. 233113051; fax 233113054; e-mail emb.prague@mzv.sk; internet www.mzv.sk/praha; Ambassador PETER WEISS.

Slovenia: Pod Hradbami 15, 160 41 Prague 6; tel. 233081211; fax 224314106; e-mail vpr@gov.si; internet praga.veleposlanistvo.si; Ambassador SMILJANA KNEZ.

South Africa: Ruská 65, POB 133, Vršovice, 100 00 Prague 10; tel. 267311114; fax 267311395; e-mail prague.ambassador@foreign.gov.za; internet www.saprague.cz; Ambassador FRANKI VERWEY.

Spain: Badeniho 401/4, 170 00 Prague 7; tel. 233097211; fax 233341770; e-mail emb.praga@maec.es; internet www.embajada-esp-praga.cz; Ambassador PASCUAL IGNACIO NAVARRO RIOS.

Sweden: Úvoz 13, POB 35, 160 12 Prague 612; tel. 220313200; fax 220313240; e-mail ambassaden.prag@foreign.ministry.se; internet www.swedenabroad.com/prague; Ambassador ANNIKA JAGANDER.

Switzerland: Pevnostní 588/7, POB 84, Střešovice, 162 01 Prague 6; tel. 220400611; fax 224311312; e-mail pra.vertretung@eda.admin.ch; internet www.eda.admin.ch/prag; Ambassador MARKUS-ALEXANDER ANTONIETTI.

Syria: Českomalínská 20/7, 160 00 Prague 6; tel. 224310952; fax 224317911; e-mail souria@volny.cz; internet www.syrianembassy.cz; Chargé d'affaires a.i. IBRAHIM IBRAHIM.

Thailand: Romaina Rollanda 3, Bubeneč, 160 00 Prague 6; tel. 220571435; fax 220570049; e-mail info@thaiembassy.cz; internet www.thaiembassy.cz; Ambassador VITAVAS SRIVIHOK.

Tunisia: Nad Výšinkou 1325/7, 150 00 Prague 5; tel. 244460652; fax 244460825; e-mail amt.prague@volny.cz; Ambassador MONCEF HAJERI.

Turkey: Na Ořechovce 69, 162 00 Prague 6; tel. 224311402; fax 224311279; e-mail embassy.prague@mfa.gov.tr; internet prag.be.mfa.gov.tr; Ambassador CIHAD ERGINAY.

Ukraine: Charlese de Gaulla 29, 160 00 Prague 6; tel. 227020200; fax 233344366; e-mail emb_cz@mfa.gov.ua; internet www.czechia.mfa.gov.ua; Ambassador BORYS ZAYCHUK.

United Kingdom: Thunovská 14, 118 00 Prague 1; tel. 257402111; fax 257402296; e-mail ukinczechrepublic@fco.gov.uk; internet ukinczechrepublic.fco.gov.uk; Ambassador JAN THOMPSON.

Uruguay: Muchova 9, 160 00 Prague 6; tel. 224314755; fax 224313780; e-mail urupra@urupra.cz; Ambassador DIANA MAGDALENA ESPINO PUGLIESE DE PAPANTONAKIS.

USA: Tržiště 15, 118 01 Prague 1; tel. 257022000; fax 257022809; e-mail consprague@state.gov; internet prague.usembassy.gov; Ambassador NORMAN EISEN.

Venezuela: Šafaříkova 201/17, 120 00 Prague 2; tel. 226254100; fax 257534253; e-mail embaven@grbox.cz; internet www.embajada-venezuela.cz; Ambassador VÍCTOR JULIÁN HERNÁNDEZ LEÓN.

Viet Nam: Plzeňská 214/2578, 150 00 Prague 5; tel. 257211540; fax 257211792; e-mail dsqvietnamcz@yahoo.com; Chargé d'affaires a.i. TRUONG MANH SON.

Yemen: Pod Hradbami 5, 160 00 Prague 6; tel. 233331568; fax 233332204; e-mail yemb-prague@mofa.gov.ye; Ambassador ABDULRAHMAN MOHAMED AL-HAMDI.

Judicial System

The judicial system comprises the Supreme Court, the Supreme Administrative Court, and high, regional and district courts. There is also a 15-member Constitutional Court.

Supreme Court (Nejvyšší soud): Burešova 20, 657 37 Brno; tel. 541593111; fax 541213493; e-mail podatelna@nsoud.cz; internet www.nsoud.cz; Chair. IVA BROŽOVÁ.

Supreme Administrative Court (Nejvyšší správní soud): Moravské nám. 6, 657 40 Brno; tel. 542532311; fax 542532361; e-mail podatelna@nssoud.cz; internet www.nssoud.cz; Pres. JOSEF BAXA.

Office of the Chief Prosecutor: Náměstí Hrdinů 1300, 140 65 Prague 4; tel. 261196111; fax 261196550; e-mail podatelna@vsz.pha.justice.cz; internet portal.justice.cz; Chief Prosecutor RENÁTA VESECKÁ.

Constitutional Court (Ústavní soud): Joštova 8, 660 83 Brno 2; tel. 542162111; fax 542161309; e-mail podani@usoud.cz; internet www.concourt.cz; Chair. PAVEL RYCHETSKÝ.

Religion

At the March 2011 national census some 34.2% of the population declared themselves to have no religious belief, while 45.2% did not respond to the census question about religious adherence. Among believers, the principal religion is Christianity, and the largest denomination is Latin-rite Catholicism.

CHRISTIANITY

Ecumenical Council of Churches in the Czech Republic (Ekumenická rada církví v České republice): Donská 5/370, 101 00 Prague 10; tel. and fax 271742850; e-mail erc@ekumenickarada.cz; internet www.ekumenickarada.cz; f. 1955; 11 mem. churches; Pres. DANIEL FAJFR; Gen. Sec. SANDRA SILNÁ.

The Roman Catholic Church

The Czech Republic comprises two archdioceses and six dioceses. There is also an Apostolic Exarchate for Catholics of the Byzantine Rite. The Catholic Church estimated a total of 3,289,836 adherents in the country at 31 December 2008, equivalent to 32.0% of the total population. Of this number, some 178,150 were adherents of the Byzantine Rite.

Latin Rite

Bishops' Conference: Thákurova 3, 160 00 Prague 6; tel. 223315421; fax 224310144; e-mail cbk2@ktf.cuni.cz; Pres. Most Rev. JAN GRAUBNER (Archbishop of Olomouc).

Archbishop of Olomouc: Most Rev. JAN GRAUBNER, Archibiskupský Ordinát, Biskupské nám. 2, POB 193, 771 01 Olomouc; tel. 587405111; fax 585222244; e-mail arcibol@arcibol.cz; internet www.ado.cz.

Archbishop of Prague: Most Rev. DOMINIK DUKA, Hradčanské nám. 56/16, 119 02 Prague 1; tel. 220392123; fax 220515396; e-mail apha@apha.cz; internet www.apha.cz.

Byzantine Rite

Apostolic Exarch for Catholics of the Byzantine Rite Resident in the Czech Republic: Most Rev. Dr LADISLAV HUČKO (Titular Bishop of Orea), Haštalské nám. 4, 110 00 Prague 1; tel. 221778491; fax 222312817; e-mail exarchat@volny.cz; internet www.exarchat.cz.

The Eastern Orthodox Church

Orthodox Church in the Czech Lands and Slovakia (Pravoslavná církev v Českých zemích a na Slovensku): Resslova 9A, 120 00 Prague 2; tel. 224920686; fax 224916100; e-mail cilova@pravoslavnacirkev.cz; internet www.pravoslavnacirkev.cz; divided into two eparchies in the Czech Republic: Prague and Olomouc-Brno; and two eparchies in Slovakia: Prešov and Michalovce; Archbishop of Prague, Metropolitan of the Czech Lands and Slovakia His Beatitude Dr ROSTISLAV.

Protestant Churches

Brethren Evangelical Free Church (Církev bratrská): Soukenická 15, 110 00 Prague 1; tel. and fax 222318131; e-mail sekretariat@cb.cz; internet www.cb.cz; f. 1880; 10,000 mems, 76 churches; mem. of the Ecumenical Council of Churches in the Czech Republic and the International Federation of Free Evangelical Churches; Pres. DANIEL FAJFR; Sec. PETR GRULICH.

Czechoslovak Hussite Church (Církev československá husitská): Wuchterlova 5, 166 26 Prague 6; tel. 220398114; fax 220398123; e-mail external.affairs@ccsh.cz; internet www.ccsh.cz; f. 1920; 70,000 mems (2011); six dioceses, 292 parishes; Chair. Patriarch TOMÁŠ BUTTA.

Evangelical Church of Czech Brethren (Českobratrská církev evangelická): Jungmannova 9, 111 21 Prague 1; tel. 224999211; fax 224999219; e-mail e-cirkev@e-cirkev.cz; internet www.e-cirkev.cz; f. 1781; united since 1918; Presbyterian; active in Bohemia, Moravia and Silesia; 94,000 adherents and 256 parishes (2010); Pres. JOEL RUML; Moderator LIA VALKOVÁ.

Unity of Brethren of the Czech Republic—Unitas Fratrum (Jednota bratrská v České republice): B. Němcové 54/9, 460 05 Liberec; tel. 484847916; e-mail jbcr@jbcr.info; internet www.jbcr.info; f. 1457, reorganized 1862; widely known as the 'Moravian Church'; 4,543 mems in 28 parishes (2012); Rt Rev. Rev. Mgr EVALD RUCKÝ.

JUDAISM

Federation of Jewish Communities in the Czech Republic (Federace židovských obcí v ČR): Maiselova 18, 110 00 Prague 1; tel. 224800824; fax 224810912; e-mail sekretariat@fzo.cz; internet www.fzo.cz; 3,000 mems in 10 registered communities; Pres. PETR PAPOUSEK; Chief Rabbi EPHRAIM KAROL SIDON.

The Press

PRINCIPAL DAILIES

There were 116 national and regional daily newspapers published in 2005.

Blesk (Lightning): Komunardů 1548/42, 170 00 Prague 7; tel. 225977478; fax 225977473; e-mail blesk@blesk.cz; internet www.blesk.cz; popular; Editor-in-Chief RADEK LAIN; circ. 394,225 (Nov. 2010).

Brněnský deník—Rovnost (Brno Daily—Equality): Milady Horákové 9, 602 00 Brno; tel. 545212884; fax 545212873; e-mail tomas.herman@denik.cz; internet brnensky.denik.cz; f. 1885; fmrly *Rovnost* (Equality); morning; Editor-in-Chief TOMÁŠ HERMAN; circ. 62,000.

České noviny/Czech Happenings: Neris s.r.o. Opletalova 5, 110 00 Prague 1; tel. 222098439; fax 222098113; e-mail cn@ctk.cz; internet www.ceskenoviny.cz; f. 1996; online only; in Czech and English; also produces *Finanční noviny* (Financial News) and *Sportovní noviny* (Sport News); Editor-in-Chief KAREL PETRÁK.

Českobudějovický deník (České Budějovice Daily): Přemysla Otakara II 8/5, 370 01 České Budějovice; tel. 386100721; fax 386100770; e-mail redakce.ceskobudejovicky@denik.cz; internet ceskobudejovicky.denik.cz; f. 1992; morning; Editor-in-Chief HANA SVÍTILOVÁ; circ. 53,000.

Českokrumlovský deník: Zámek 57, 381 01 Český Krumlov; tel. 380709211; fax 380711265; e-mail redakce.ceskokrumlovsky@denik.cz; internet www.ceskokrumlovsky.denik.cz; f. 1994; Chief Editor ZUZANA KYSELOVÁ.

Haló noviny: Politických vězňů 9, 111 21 Prague 1; tel. 222897111; fax 224224822; e-mail halonoviny@halonoviny.cz; internet www3.halonoviny.cz; f. 1991; communist; published by Futura; Editor-in-Chief PAVEL ŠAFRÁNEK.

Hospodářské noviny (Economic News): Dobrovského 25, 170 55 Prague 7; tel. 233073001; fax 233072009; e-mail redakce@ihned.cz; internet hn.ihned.cz; f. 1957; morning; Editor-in-Chief PETR ŠIMŮNEK; circ. 44,340 (Nov. 2010).

Hradecký deník (Hradec Králové Daily): Kladská 17, 500 03 Hradec Králové; tel. 495800838; fax 495800875; e-mail jitka.hodasova@denik.cz; internet hradecky.denik.cz; f. 1992; fmrly *Hradecké noviny* (Hradec Králové News); Editor-in-Chief JITKA HODASOVÁ; circ. 30,000.

Lidové noviny (People's News): Karla Engliše 519/11, 150 00 Prague 5; tel. 225067111; fax 225067399; e-mail redakce@lidovky.cz; internet www.lidovky.cz; f. 1893, re-established 1988; morning; Man. Editor DALIBOR BALŠÍNEK; circ. 47,002 (Nov. 2010).

Mladá fronta Dnes (The Youth Front Today): Anděl Media Centrum, POB 43, Karla Engliše 519/11, 150 00 Prague 5; tel. 225061111; fax 225066229; e-mail mfdnes@mfdnes.cz; internet www.zpravy.idnes.cz/mfdnes.asp; f. 1990; morning; independent; Editor-in-Chief ROBERT ČÁSENSKÝ; circ. 245,862 (Nov. 2010).

Moravskoslezský deník (Moravia-Silesia Daily): Mlýnská 10, 701 11 Ostrava; tel. 596176311; fax 596176312; e-mail redakce.moravskoslezsky@denik.cz; internet moravskoslezsky.denik.cz; f. 1991; Editor-in-Chief TOMÁŠ ŠIŘINA; circ. 130,000.

Plzeňský deník (Plzeň Daily): Kovářská 4, 301 00 Plzeň; tel. 3377168321; fax 377221875; e-mail redakce.plzensky@denik.cz; internet www.plzensky.denik.cz; f. 1992; Editor-in-Chief EVA PLEVKOVÁ; circ. 50,000.

Prague Daily Monitor: Václavské nám. 846/1, 110 00 Prague 1; tel. 725412565; e-mail info@praguemonitor.com; internet praguemonitor.com; Man. Editor KRISTINA ALDA.

Právo (Right): Slezská 2127/13, 121 50 Prague 2; tel. 221001111; fax 541616160; e-mail pravo@cpost.cz; internet www.pravo.cz; f. 1920 as

Rudé právo ; present name adopted 1995; morning; Editor-in-Chief ZDENĚK PORYBNÝ; circ. 124,151 (Nov. 2010).

Šíp (The Arrow): Přátelství 986, 104 00 Prague 10; tel. 272015109; fax 221999304; e-mail info@astrosat.cz; internet sip.denik.cz; f. 2005; popular; also weekly edn, *Síp Plus* (f. 2009); Editor-in-Chief MICHAL BROŽ; circ. 130,000.

Ústecký deník (Ústí nad Labem Daily): Klíšská 1702/25, 400 01 Ústí nad Labem; tel. 475246850; fax 475246814; e-mail ustecky@denik.cz; internet ustecky.denik.cz; f. 1993; Editor-in-Chief HANA VOJTOVÁ; circ. 95,000.

PRINCIPAL PERIODICALS

21. Století (The 21st Century): Bohdalecká 6/1420, 101 00 Prague 10; tel. 281090610; fax 281090623; e-mail 21.stoleti@rf-hobby.cz; internet www.21stoleti.cz; science and technology; monthly; Editor-in-Chief Dr PAVEL ŠMEJKAL; circ. 60,251 (2009).

Ateliér (Studio): Londýnská 81, 120 00 Prague 2; tel. 222322316; e-mail atelier.art@volny.cz; internet www.atelier-journal.cz; f. 1988; contemporary fine arts; fortnightly; Editor-in-Chief BLANKA JIRÁČKOVÁ.

Divadelní noviny (Theatre News): Celetná 17, 110 00 Prague 1; tel. 224809114; fax 222315912; e-mail divadelni.noviny@divadlo.cz; internet www.divadelni-noviny.cz; f. 1992; fortnightly; Editor-in-Chief JAN KOLÁŘ.

Ekonom (Economist): Dobrovského 25, 170 55 Prague 7; tel. 233071301; fax 233072002; e-mail ekonom@economia.cz; internet ekonom.ihned.cz; weekly; Editor-in-Chief ONDŘEJ NEUMANN; circ. 19,682 (2009).

Euro: Holečkova 103/31, 150 00 Prague 5; tel. 251026107; fax 257325905; e-mail vydavatelstvi@euro.cz; internet www.euro.cz; weekly; finance, business, economics; f. 1999; Editor PAVEL PÁRAL; circ. 22,567 (Nov. 2010).

History Revue: Bohdalecká 6/1420, 101 00 Prague 10; tel. 281090610; fax 281090623; e-mail sekretariat@rf-hobby.cz; internet www.historyrevue.cz; history magazine; monthly; Editor-in-Chief ILONA KUČEROVÁ; circ. 65,370 (2009).

Instinkt (Instinct): Mikuleckého 1309/4, 147 00 Prague 4; tel. 222994110; fax 296827292; e-mail instinkt@instinkt-online.cz; internet instinkt.tyden.cz; fmrly *Mladý svět* (The Young World); illustrated weekly; Man. Editor JANA VÍŠKOVÁ; circ. 24,509 (Nov. 2010).

Katolický týdeník (Catholic Weekly): Londýnská 44, 120 00 Prague 2; tel. 224250395; fax 224257041; e-mail sekretariat@katyd.cz; internet www.katyd.cz; f. 1989; weekly; Editor-in-Chief ANTONÍN RANDA; circ. 70,000.

LandesZeitung: Vocelova 602/3, 120 00 Prague 2; tel. 235354282; fax 235365903; e-mail redaktion@landeszeitung.cz; internet www.landeszeitung.cz; f. 1994; German; expressing the interests of the German minority in the Czech Republic; fortnightly; Man. Editor ALEXANDRA MOSTÝN.

Pestrý Svět (Colourful World): Moulíkova 1B/3286, 150 00 Prague 5; tel. 225008366; fax 225008103; e-mail pcerna@bauermedia.cz; internet www.bauermedia.cz/casopisy/pestry-svet; f. 2004; weekly; women, social; Editor-in-Chief BARBORA ŠTENGLOVÁ; circ. 262,104 (2009).

Prager Zeitung: Jeseniova 51, 130 00 Prague 3; tel. 222250125; fax 222253379; e-mail info@pragerzeitung.cz; internet www.pragerzeitung.cz; f. 1991; in German; politics, economy, culture and sport; weekly; Thursdays; Editor-in-Chief MARCUS HUNDT.

Prague Post: Štěpánská 1677/20, 110 00 Prague 1; tel. 296334400; fax 296334450; e-mail info@praguepost.com; internet www.praguepost.com; f. 1991; political, economic and cultural weekly in English; Editor-in-Chief MARKÉTA HULPACHOVÁ; circ. 15,000.

Prague Tribune: Na Maninách 876/7, 170 00 Prague 7; tel. 220400121; fax 220400123; e-mail praguetribune@explorer.cz; internet www.prague-tribune.cz; in English; business and lifestyle; monthly; Gen. Man. GIRGIT RECHBERGEROVÁ; circ. 22,800.

Profit: Francouzská 94, 110 00 Prague 10; tel. 234071377; fax 225010377; e-mail redakce@profit.cz; internet www.profit.cz; business, investment; weekly; f. 1990; Man. Dir TOMÁŠ VYŠOHLÍD; Editor-in-Chief MARTIN ZIKA; circ. 19,184 (2009).

Raport: Ottova 418, 269 01 Rakovník; tel. 313512601; fax 313512992; e-mail raport@raport.cz; internet www.raport.cz; f. 1991; focus on people and events of Central Bohemia; weekly; Editor PAVEL SKLENIČKA.

Reflex: Komunardů 1584/42, 170 00 Prague 7; tel. 225977458; fax 225977420; e-mail reflex@ringier.cz; internet www.reflex.cz; f. 1990; general; weekly; Thursdays; Editor-in-Chief PAVEL ŠAFR; circ. 60,571 (Oct. 2010).

Respekt (Respect): Dobrovského 25, 170 00 Prague 1; tel. 233074520; fax 233074545; e-mail redakce@respekt.cz; internet www.respekt.ihned.cz; f. 1990; political and cultural weekly; Editor-in-Chief ERIK TABERY; circ. 27,267 (Nov. 2010).

Revue Sondy (Revue Soundings): W. Churchilla 2, 113 59 Prague 3; tel. 234462328; fax 234462313; e-mail sondy@cmkos.cz; internet www.e-sondy.cz; f. 2008 to replace *Sondy* (weekly); 18 a year; journal of the Czech (Bohemian)-Moravian Confederation of Trade Unions; Chief Editor JANA KAŠPAROVÁ; circ. 30,000 (2009).

Romano Hangos/Romský hlas (Romany Voice): Bratislavská 65A, 602 00 Brno; tel. 728916007; fax 545246674; e-mail rhangos@volny.vz; internet www.srnm.cz/cz/romanohangos.htm; f. 1999; every two weeks; in Romany and Czech; Editor-in-Chief ROMANO HANGOS.

Rytmus života (Rhythm of Life): Moulíkova 1B/3286, 150 00 Prague 5; tel. 225008111; fax 225008103; e-mail info@bauermedia.cz; internet www.bauermedia.cz/casopisy/7-rytmus-zivota; f. 1996; weekly; Mondays; social; Editor-in-Chief VERONIKA HRACHOVCOVÁ; circ. 257,116 (Nov. 2010).

Týden (The Week): Mikuleckého 1309/4, 147 00 Prague 4; tel. 222994110; fax 222994042; e-mail dopisy@tyden.cz; internet www.tyden.cz; f. 1994; general; Editor-in-Chief FRANTIŠEK NACHTIGALL; circ. 39,417 (Nov. 2010).

Žena a Život (Woman and Life): Moulíkova 1B/3286, 150 00 Prague 5; tel. 225008260; fax 257323287; e-mail zenaazivot@bauermedia.cz; internet www.zenaazivot.cz; f. 1994; fortnightly; lifestyle, women; Editor-in-Chief MICHAELA KRAMÁROVÁ; circ. 70,434 (2009).

NEWS AGENCY

Česká tisková kancelář (ČTK) (Czech News Agency): Opletalova 5/7, 111 44 Prague 1; tel. 222098111; e-mail ctk@ctk.cz; internet www.ctk.cz; f. Nov. 1992, assuming control of all property and activities (in the Czech Lands) of the former Czechoslovak News Agency; news and photo-exchange service with all international and many national news agencies; maintains network of foreign correspondents; Czech and English general and economic news service; publishes daily bulletins in English; Gen. Dir JIŘÍ MAJSTR.

PRESS ASSOCIATION

Syndicate of Journalists of the Czech Republic (Syndikát novinářů České republiky): Senovážné náměstí 23, 110 00 Prague 1; tel. 224142455; fax 224142458; e-mail kancelar@syndikat-novinaru.cz; internet www.syndikat-novinaru.cz; f. 1877; reorganized 1990; 5,000 mems; Chair. ADAM ČERNÝ.

Publishers

Academia: Vodičkova 40, 110 00 Prague 1; tel. 221403820; fax 224941982; e-mail padevet@academia.cz; internet www.academia.cz; f. 1953; scientific books, periodicals; Dir JIŘÍ PADEVĚT.

Akropolis: Na Bělidle 1, 150 00 Prague 5; tel. 251560234; e-mail tomas.akropolis@worldonline.cz; internet www.akropolis.info; f. 1990; Dir JIŘÍ TOMÁŠ.

Argo: Milíčova 13, 130 00 Prague 3; tel. 222782262; e-mail argo@argo.cz; internet www.argo.cz; f. 1992; literature, translations, history, social sciences; Dir MILAN GELNAR.

BB Art: Bořivojova 85, 130 00 Prague 3; tel. 222721538; fax 222720525; e-mail info@bbart.cz; internet www.bbart.cz; fiction, history, biography, poetry, children's books.

Brio: Osadní 12A, 170 00 Prague 7; tel. 224236286; fax 224228533; e-mail heger@slovart.sk; internet www.briopublishing.cz; children's; Man. Dir JIŘÍ ŠTĚPÁN.

Ekopress: U Líhní 100, 142 00 Prague 4; tel. and fax 244471676; e-mail nakladatelstvi@ekopress.cz; internet www.ekopress.cz; f. 1992; economics, information technology, languages.

Epocha: Kaprova 12/40, 110 00 Prague 1; tel. 224810353; e-mail epocha@epocha.cz; internet www.epocha.cz; non-fiction, military and other history, biography, fiction; f. 1996; Editor-in-Chief Dr PETR HOFMAN.

Fragment: Pujmanové 1221/4, 140 00 Prague 4; tel. 241004011; fax 241004071; e-mail prijmeni@fragment.cz; internet www.fragment.cz; children's; f. 1991; Dirs JAN EISLER, PAVEL NÝČ.

Fraus: Edvarda Beneše 72, 301 00 Plzeň; tel. 377226102; fax 377224594; e-mail info@fraus.cz; internet www.fraus.cz; f. 1991; textbooks, languages and dictionaries; Dir and CEO JIŘÍ FRAUS.

Grada Publishing: U Průhonu 22, 170 00 Prague 7; tel. 234264411; fax 234264400; e-mail info@gradapublishing.cz; internet www.grada.cz; f. 1991; Dir MILAN BRUNÁT.

Host: Radlas 5, 602 00 Brno; tel. and fax 545212747; e-mail redakce@hostbrno.cz; internet www.nakladatelstvi.hostbrno.cz; f. 1990; fiction, literary criticism and theory; Editor-in-Chief MIROSLAV BALAŠTÍK.

Karolinum: Ovocný trh 3/5, 116 36 Prague 1; tel. 224491276; fax 224212041; e-mail cupress@cuni.cz; internet cupress.cuni.cz; f. 1990; publishing house of the Charles University in Prague; Dir PETR VALO.

Labyrint (Labyrinth): Jablonecká 715, POB 52, 190 00 Prague 9; tel. and fax 224922422; e-mail labyrint@labyrint.net; internet www.labyrint.net; publishing house and cultural magazine; prose, poetry, the arts, children's illustrated books and comics; f. 1991; Dir and Editor-in-Chief JOACHIM DVOŘÁK.

Libri: Neklanova 109/27, 128 00 Prague 2; tel. 252541632; e-mail libri@libri.cz; internet www.libri.cz; f. 1992; encyclopedias, specialist literature; Editor-in-Chief Dr FRANTIŠEK HONZÁK.

Mladá fronta (The Youth Front): Mezi Vodami 1952/9, 143 00 Prague 4; tel. 225276411; e-mail mf@mf.cz; internet www.mf.cz; f. 1945; science fiction and fantasy literature, philosophy, sociology; CEO DAVID HURTA.

Nakladatelství Lidové noviny: Dykova 15, 101 00 Prague 10; tel. 222522350; fax 222514012; e-mail nln@nln.cz; internet www.nln.cz; fiction, history, languages, guide-books, popular science; Dir EVA PLEŠKOVÁ.

Olympia: Werichova 973, 252 67 Velké Přílepy; tel. 233089999; e-mail info@iolympia.cz; internet www.iolympia.cz; f. 1954; sports, tourism, encyclopedias, fiction, illustrated books; Editor-in-Chief Dr JAROSLAV KOTOUČ.

Paseka: Chopinova 4, 120 00 Prague 2; tel. 222710751; fax 222718886; e-mail paseka@paseka.cz; internet www.paseka.cz; f. 1989; Owner LADISLAVA HORÁČKA.

SPN pedagogické nakladatelství (SPN Pedagogical Publishing House): Ostrovní 30, 110 00 Prague 1; tel. and fax 224931447; e-mail spn@spn.cz; internet www.spn.cz; f. 1775; fmrly Státní pedagogické nakladatelství (State Pedagogical Publishing House); school and university textbooks, dictionaries, literature; Dir VÁCLAV HOLICKÝ.

Vyšehrad: Víta Nejedlého 15, 130 00 Prague 3; tel. and fax 224221703; e-mail info@vysehrad.cz; internet www.ivysehrad.cz; f. 1934; religion, philosophy, history, fiction; Dir PRAVOMIL NOVÁK.

PUBLISHERS' ASSOCIATION

Association of Czech Booksellers and Publishers (Svaz českých knihkupců a nakladatelů): Mariánské nám. 190/5, 110 01 Prague 1; tel. 224219944; fax 224219942; e-mail sckn@sckn.cz; internet www.sckn.cz; f. 1879; Sec. MARCELA TUREČKOVÁ.

Broadcasting and Communications

TELECOMMUNICATIONS

In 2009 24 telecommunications services providers were active in the Czech Republic.

České Radiokomunikace: Skokanská 2117/1, 169 00 Prague 6; tel. 242411111; e-mail info@radiokomunikace.cz; internet www.radiokomunikace.cz; f. 1963; privatized 2000; owned by Macquarie Infrastructure and Real Assets (United Kingdom); CEO MICHAL ČUPA.

T-Mobile Czech Republic: Tomíčkova 2144/1, 149 00 Prague 4; tel. 603601111; e-mail info@t-mobile.cz; internet www.t-mobile.cz; f. 1996; fmrly RadioMobil; 60.8% owned by C-Mobil, 39.2% by České Radiokomunikace, a.s.; mobile telecommunications and internet service provider; Gen. Dir MILAN VAŠINA.

Telefónica Czech Republic: Za Brumlovkou 266/2, 140 22 Prague 4; tel. 840114114; e-mail jobs.cz@o2.com; internet www.o2.cz; f. 1992; fmrly Český Telecom; present name adopted 2011; mobile telecommunications and internet service provider; monopoly operator of long-distance and international services; 51.1% owned by Telefónica (Spain); Chair. and CEO LUIS A. MALVIDO.

U:fon: PO Box 116, 130 11 Prague 3; tel. 811811811; e-mail info@ufon.cz; internet www.ufon.cz; f. 2007; owned by Air Telecom; mobile telecommunications and internet service provider.

UPC Czech Republic: POB 53, 130 11, Prague 3; tel. 241005100; fax 241005105; internet www.upc.cz; provides broadband internet, telephone, digital television and radio services; Man. Dir FRANS-WILLEM DE KLOET.

Vodafone Czech Republic: Vinohradská 167, 100 00 Prague 10; tel. 776977100; internet www.vodafone.cz; f. 2000; mobile telecommunications and internet service provider; CEO MURIEL ANTON.

Regulatory Authority

Český Telekomunikační Úřad (Czech Telecommunication Office—ČTU): Sokolovská 219, Prague 9; tel. 224004111; fax 224004830; e-mail podatelna@ctu.cz; internet www.ctu.cz; f. 2005; monitoring and regulatory authority; Pres. JAROMÍR NOVÁK.

RADIO

The Czech Republic has a dual state and private broadcasting system, with one publicly owned radio broadcaster, Český rozhlas (Czech Radio), and two private, nationwide radio broadcasters, Frekvence 1 and Rádio Impuls.

Local stations broadcast from Prague, Brno, České Budějovice, Hradec Králové, Ostrava, Plzeň, Ústí nad Labem and other towns. At the end of 2013 some 63 radio broadcasters were registered in Czech Republic.

Český rozhlas (Czech Radio): Vinohradská 12, 120 99 Prague 2; tel. 221551111; fax 224222223; e-mail info@rozhlas.cz; internet www.rozhlas.cz; broadcasts nationwide programmes (incl. ČRo 1 Radiožurnál, ČRo 2 Praha, ČRo 3 Vlava) and Radio Praha's programme to foreign countries (ČRo 7); Dir-Gen. PETER DUHAN.

Country Radio: Říčanská 3, 101 00 Prague 10; tel. 251024111; fax 251024224; e-mail info@countryradio.cz; internet www.countryradio.cz; f. 1991; commercial station; Dir MIREK ALBRECHT.

Evropa 2: Wenzigova 4, 120 00 Prague 2; tel. 257001111; internet www.evropa2.cz; commercial station; Pres. MICHAEL FLEISCHMANN.

Frekvence 1: Wenzigova 4, 120 00 Prague 2; tel. 257001111; fax 257001150; e-mail info@frekvence1.cz; internet www.frekvence1.cz; commercial station; Pres. MICHAEL FLEISCHMANN.

Hitrádio FM Plus: Koperníkova 794/6, 120 00 Prague 2; tel. 377422222; fax 377422221; e-mail redakce.fmplus@hitradio.cz; internet www.hitradiofmplus.cz; commercial station; Dir VÁCLAV JEŽEK.

Radio Free Europe/Radio Liberty: Vinohradská 159A, 110 00 Prague 10; tel. 221121111; fax 221123010; e-mail hokuvovaj@rferl.org; internet www.rferl.org; f. 1950; non-profit corpn financed by the federal Govt of the USA; broadcasts c. 1,000 hours weekly in 28 languages to Eastern Europe, Eurasia and the Middle East; Pres. and CEO KEVIN KLOSE.

Rádio Impuls: Ortenovo nám. 15A, 170 00 Prague 7; tel. 255700700; fax 255700721; e-mail impuls@impuls.cz; internet www.impuls.cz; f. 1999; Man. Dir JIŘÍ HRABÁK.

TELEVISION

The gradual transition from terrestrial analogue broadcasting to terrestrial digital broadcasting commenced in the second half of 2008, and the process was completed in Prague and Plzeň in 2009. At the end of 2009 the two state-run channels, ČT1 and ČT2, reached 89.1% and 46.4% of the population, respectively, while two private commercial stations, Nova TV and Prima TV, were received by 92.0% and 47.2%, respectively.

Česká televize (Czech Television): Kavčí hory, 140 70 Prague 4; tel. 261131111; fax 26927202; e-mail info@ceskatelevize.cz; internet www.ceskatelevize.cz; f. 1992; state-owned; six channels (ČT1, ČT2, ČT24, ČT sport, ČT :D and ČT art); studios in Prague, Brno and Ostrava; Gen. Dir PETR DVOŘÁK.

Nova TV: Kříženeckého nám. 1078/5, 152 00 Prague 5; tel. 242464111; e-mail dopisove@nova.cz; internet tv.nova.cz; f. 1994, through a joint venture with Central European Media Enterprises Ltd (CME), of the USA, as the Czech Republic's first independent commercial station; majority owned by CME; Gen. Dir and CEO JAN ANDRUŠKO.

Prima TV: Na Žertvách 24/132, 180 00 Prague 8; tel. and fax 266700111; e-mail informace@iprima.cz; internet www.iprima.cz; f. 1993; Gen. Dir MARTIN KONRÁD.

Finance

(cap. = capital; res = reserves; dep. = deposits; m. = million; brs = branches; amounts in Czech koruna)

BANKING

With the establishment of independent Czech and Slovak Republics on 1 January 1993, the State Bank of Czechoslovakia was divided and its functions were transferred to the newly created Czech National Bank and National Bank of Slovakia. The Czech National Bank is independent of the Government. At 30 June 2008 35 banks were operating in the Czech Republic, 13 of which were branches of foreign banks.

Central Bank

Czech National Bank (Česká národní banka): Na Příkopě 28, 115 03 Prague 1; tel. 224411111; fax 224412404; e-mail monestat@cnb.cz; internet www.cnb.cz; f. 1993; bank of issue, the central authority of the Czech Republic in the monetary sphere, legislation and foreign exchange permission; central bank for directing and securing monetary policy, supervision of the financial market; cap. 1,400.0m., res –155,872m., dep. 491,213m. (Dec. 2009); Gov. MIROSLAV SINGER; 7 brs.

Commercial Banks

Česká exportní banka, a.s. (Czech Export Bank): Vodičkova 34, POB 870, 111 21 Prague 1; tel. 222841100; fax 224226162; e-mail ceb@ceb.cz; internet www.ceb.cz; f. 1995; cap. 4,000m., res 159m., dep. 13,223m. (Dec. 2012); Chair. JIŘÍ KLUMPAR.

Česká spořitelna, a.s. (Czech Savings Bank): Olbrachtova 1929/62, 140 00 Prague 4; tel. 956777956; fax 224640663; e-mail csas@csas.cz; internet www.csas.cz; f. 1825; 98% holding owned by Erste Bank AG (Austria); cap. 15,200m., res 4,861m., dep. 744,663m. (Dec. 2012); Chair. and CEO PAVEL KYSILKA; 659 brs.

Československá obchodní banka, a.s. (ČSOB) (Czechoslovak Commercial Bank): Radlická 333/150, 150 57 Prague 5; tel. 224111111; fax 495819531; e-mail info@csob.cz; internet www.csob.cz; f. 1965; owned by KBC Bank NV (Belgium); commercial and foreign trade transactions; cap. 5,855m., res 35,464m., dep. 703,017m. (Dec. 2012); Chair. and CEO PAVEL KAVÁNEK; 319 brs.

GE Money Bank, a.s.: Vyskočilova 1422/1A, BB Centrum, 140 28 Prague 4; tel. 224441111; fax 224448199; internet www.gemoney.cz; f. 1998; present name adopted 2005; 100% owned by GE Capital International Holdings Corpn (USA); cap. 510.0m., res 4,809.2m., dep. 97,441.9m. (Dec. 2012); Chair. SEAN MORRISSEY; 260 brs.

J&T Banka, a.s.: Pobřežní 14/297, 186 00 Prague 8; tel. 221710111; fax 221710211; e-mail info@jtbank.cz; internet www.jtbank.cz; f. 1998; cap. 3,858.1m., res 706.5m., dep. 75,169.8m. (Dec. 2012); Chair. PATRIK TKÁČ.

Komerční banka, a.s.: Na Příkopě 33, POB 839, 114 07 Prague 1; tel. 955512230; fax 955534300; e-mail mojebanka@kb.cz; internet www.kb.cz; f. 1990; 60.4% owned by Société Générale (France); cap. 19,005m., res 40,514m., dep. 617,970m. (Dec. 2012); Chair. and CEO ALBERT LE DIRAC'H; 399 brs.

LBBW Bank CZ: Vitězná 126/1, 150 00 Prague 5; tel. 233233233; fax 233233299; e-mail info@lbbw.cz; internet www.lbbw.cz; f. 1991; 100% owned by LBBW—Landesbank Baden-Württemberg (Germany); present name adopted 2008; cap. 1,708.7m., res 990.6m., dep. 25,994.4m. (Dec. 2012); Chair. of Bd GERNOT DAUMANN.

Raiffeisenbank, a.s.: Hvězdova 1716/2B, City Tower, 140 78 Prague 4; tel. 417941444; fax 225542111; e-mail info@rb.cz; internet www.rb.cz; f. 1993; 51% owned by Raiffeisenbank (Austria); merged with eBanka 2008; cap. 9,357m., res 721.1m., dep. 153,044.9m. (Dec. 2012); Chair. and CEO MARIO DROSC; 120 brs.

Sberbank CZ, a.s.: Na Pankráci 129, 140 00 Prague 4; tel. 800133444; fax 221969951; e-mail mail@sberbankcz.cz; internet www.sberbankcz.cz; f. 1993; 100% owned by Sberbank Europa AG (Austria), a subsidiary co of Sberbank (Russia); name changed as above in 2013; cap. 2,005m., res 2,813m., dep. 47,729m. (Dec. 2012); f. 1993; Chair., Management Bd VLADIMÍR ŠOLC; Chair., Supervisory Bd MARK ARNOLD; 24 brs.

UniCredit Bank Czech Republic and Slovakia, a.s.: Želetavská 1525/1, POB 421, 140 92 Prague 4; tel. 955911111; e-mail info@unicreditgroup.cz; internet www.unicreditbank.cz; f. 2007 by merger of HVB Bank Czech Republic and Živnostenská banka; name changed as above in 2013; owned by Bank Austria Creditanstalt AG; cap. 8,750m., res 10,716m., dep. 205,599m. (Dec. 2012); Chair. and CEO JIŘÍ KUNERT.

Bankers' Organization

Czech Banking Association (Česká bankovní asociace): Vodičkova 30, 110 00 Prague 1; tel. 224422080; fax 224422090; e-mail cba@czech-ba.cz; internet www.czech-ba.cz; f. 1990; present name adopted 1992; Pres. PAVEL KAVÁNEK; 37 mem. banks.

STOCK EXCHANGE

Prague Stock Exchange (Burza cenných papírů Praha): Rybná 14, 110 05 Prague 1; tel. 221831111; fax 221833040; e-mail info@pse.cz; internet www.pse.cz; f. 1992; CEO PETR KOBLIC.

INSURANCE

There were 52 companies providing insurance services in the Czech Republic in 2009, including seven foreign-owned institutions. Of these, 29 provided non-life insurance, seven provided life insurance and 16 provided universal insurance.

Allianz pojišťovna, a.s.: Ke Štvanici 656/3, 186 00 Prague 8; tel. 224405111; fax 242455555; e-mail klient@allianz.cz; internet www.allianz.cz; f. 1993; owned by Allianz AG (Germany); Chair. JAKUB STRNAD.

Česká pojišťovna a.s. (Czech Insurance Corpn): Na Pankráci 123, 140 00 Prague 4; tel. 224557111; internet www.ceskapojistovna.cz; f. 1827; mem. of financial group PPF Group; issues life, accident, fire, aviation, industrial and marine insurance and all classes of reinsurance; CEO and Chair. of Bd LUCIANO CIRINÁ.

ČSOB pojišťovna (ČSOB Insurance): Masarykovo nám. 1458, Zelené předměstí, 532 18 Pardubice; tel. 467007111; fax 467007444; e-mail info@csobpoj.cz; internet www.csobpoj.cz; life and non-life; Chair. and Gen. Dir JEROEN KAREL VAN LEEUWEN.

Generali pojišťovna a.s. (Generali Insurance): Bělehradská 132, 120 84 Prague 2; tel. 221091101; fax 221091507; e-mail servis@generali.cz; internet www.generali.cz; f. 1832; life and non-life; Chair. of Bd and Gen. Dir STEFAN TILLINGER.

ING pojišťovna: Nádražní 344/25, 150 00 Prague 5; tel. 257473111; fax 257473555; e-mail klient@ing.cz; internet www.ing.cz; f. 1992; owned by ING (Netherlands); financial and investment insurance, life and health insurance; Gen. Dir DICK OKHUIJSEN.

Kooperativa pojišťovna, a.s. (Co-operative Insurance Co): Pobřežní 665/21, 186 00 Prague 8; tel. 956421111; fax 956449000; e-mail info@koop.cz; internet www.koop.cz; f. 1991; 96.32% owned by Wiener Städtische Versicherung AG (Austria); life and non-life insurance; Chair. and Gen. Dir MARTIN DIVIŠ.

Uniqa pojišťovna, a.s.: Evropská 136, 160 12 Prague 6; tel. 225393111; fax 225393777; e-mail info@uniqa.cz; internet www.uniqa.cz/uniqa_cz; f. 1993; owned by Uniqa Versicherungen AG (Austria); Chair. MARTIN ŽÁČEK; 180 brs.

Trade and Industry

GOVERNMENT AGENCIES

CzechInvest—Investment and Business Development (Agentura pro podporu podnikání a investic): Štěpánská 15, 120 00 Prague 2; tel. 296342500; fax 296342502; e-mail info@czechinvest.org; internet www.czechinvest.org; f. 1992; foreign investment agency; incorporates fmr Agency for the Development of Industry (CzechIndustry); Dir-Gen. ALEXANDRA RUDYŠAROVÁ.

Czech Trade Promotion Agency (Česká agentura na podporu obchodu): Dittrichova 21, POB 76, 128 01 Prague 2; tel. 224907820; fax 224913440; e-mail info@czechtrade.cz; internet www.czechtrade.cz; Gen. Dir IVAN JUKL.

CHAMBER OF COMMERCE

Economic Chamber of the Czech Republic (Hospodářská komora ČR): Freyova 27, 190 00 Prague 9; tel. 266721300; fax 266721690; e-mail office@komora.cz; internet www.komora.cz; f. 1850; has almost 15,000 members (trading corpns, industrial enterprises, banks and private enterprises); Pres. PETR KUŽEL.

EMPLOYERS' ORGANIZATIONS

Association of Entrepreneurs of the Czech Republic (Sdružení podnikatelů ČR): Na strži 1837/9, 140 00 Prague 2; tel. 733669180; fax 261104262; e-mail info@sppz.cz; internet www.sdruzenispcr.cz; Chair. BEDŘICH DANDA.

Confederation of Industry of the Czech Republic (Svaz průmyslu a dopravy ČR): Freyova 948/11, 190 05 Prague 9; tel. 225279111; fax 225279100; e-mail spcr@spcr.cz; internet www.spcr.cz; f. 1990; Pres. JAROSLAV HANÁK.

UTILITIES

Electricity

České energetické závody Skupina (ČEZ) (Czech Power Co Group): Duhová 2/1444, 140 53 Prague 4; tel. 211041111; fax 211042001; e-mail cez@cez.cz; internet www.cez.cz; f. 1992; production and distribution co; 69.37% owned by National Property Fund; merged with five regional distribution cos in 2003; also operates two nuclear energy plants at Dukovany and Temelín; Gen. Dir Dr MARTIN ROMAN; 8,770 employees.

Dalkia Česká republika: 28 října 3123/152, 709 74 Ostrava; tel. 596609111; fax 596609300; e-mail info@dalkia.cz; internet www.dalkia.cz; f. 1992; Chair. of Bd ZDENĚK DUBA; CEO LAURENT BARRIEUX; 2,500 employees (2010).

E.ON Česká republika: F. A. Gerstnera 2151/6, 370 49 České Budějovice; tel. 387861111; fax 545142584; e-mail info@eon.cz; internet www.eon.cz; f. 2005; comprises three subsidiary cos: E.ON Energie; E.ON Distribuce; and E.ON Trend; Chair. of Management and Chair. of Supervisory Bd MICHAEL FEHN.

International Power Opatovice: Pardubice 2, 532 13 Opatovice nad Labem; tel. 466843111; fax 466536030; e-mail info@ipplc.cz; internet www.eop.cz; f. 1992; fmrly Opatovice Electricity (Elektrarny Opatovice); present name adopted 2005; generation and distribution co; 100% owned by East Bohemia Energy Holding Ltd; Chair. of Bd JAN ŠPRINGL.

Pražská energetika (Prague Energy Co): Na Hroudě 1492/4, 100 05 Prague 10; tel. 267051111; fax 267310817; e-mail pre@pre.cz; internet www.pre.cz; distribution co to Prague city and surrounding area; Chair. and Man. Dir PAVEL ELIS.

Gas

RWE Transgas (Czech Republic): Limuzská 12, 100 98 Prague 10; tel. 267971111; fax 267976965; e-mail info@rwe.cz; internet www.rwe.cz; majority-owned by RWE Energie AG (Germany); subsidiaries incl. 4 regional distribution cos, 4 trading cos, transmission, storage, and import and distribution cos; Chair. of Bd MARTIN SCHMITZ.

Water

Pražské vodovody a kanalizace (PVK) (Prague Water Supply and Sewerage Co): Pařížská 11, 110 00 Prague 1; tel. 840111112; fax 272172379; e-mail info@pvk.cz; internet www.pvk.cz; f. 1998; owned by Veolia Voda (France); CEO MILAN KUCHAR.

TRADE UNIONS

Czech (Bohemian)-Moravian Confederation of Trade Unions (Českomoravská konfederace odborových svazů): W. Churchilla nám. 2, 113 59 Prague 3; tel. 224461111; fax 222718994; e-mail info@cmkos.cz; internet www.cmkos.cz; f. 1990; 32 affiliated unions (2011); Pres. JAROSLAV ZAVADIL.

Transport

RAILWAYS

In 2012 the total length of the Czech railway network was 9,570 km of which 3,217 km were electrified.

ČD Cargo: Jankovcova 1569/2C, 170 00 Prague 7; tel. 972242255; fax 972242103; e-mail info@cdcargo.cz; internet www.cdcargo.cz; f. 2007; freight transportation co; merger with Železničná spoločnost Cargo Slovakia, a.s. (Slovakia) announced 2008; Chair. of Bd of Dirs and Dir-Gen. OLDŘICH MAZÁNEK.

České dráhy (Czech Railways): nábř. L. Svobody 1222, 110 15 Prague 1; tel. 972111111; fax 222328784; e-mail info@cd.cz; internet www.cd.cz; f. 1993; Gen. Dir DALIBOR ZELENÝ.

Prague Public Transport Co (Dopravní podnik hl. m. Prahy): Sokolovska 217/42, 190 22 Prague 9; tel. 222611111; e-mail doslyj@dpp.cz; internet www.dpp.cz; f. 1991; operates public transport services in Prague, including buses, trams, funicular cars, suburban train services and Prague underground railway (59 km and 57 stations operational in 2013); Chief Exec. JAROSLAV ĎURIŠ.

ROADS

In 2010 there were an estimated 130,671 km of roads in the Czech Republic, including 734 km of motorways and 6,255 km of national roads.

INLAND WATERWAYS

In 2012 the total length of navigable waterways in the Czech Republic was 676 km. The Elbe (Labe) and its tributary, the Vltava, connect the Czech Republic with the North Sea via the port of Hamburg (Germany). The Oder provides a connection with the Baltic Sea and the port of Szczecin (Poland). There are river ports at Prague-Holešovice, Prague-Radotín, Kolín, Mělník, Ústí nad Labem and Děčín.

ČSPL Děčín: K. Čapka 211/1, 405 91 Děčín 1; tel. 412561111; fax 412511599; e-mail info@cspl.cz; internet www.cspl.cz; f. 1922; fmrly Czechoslovak Elbe Navigation Co (Československá plavba labská); river transport of goods to Germany, Poland, the Netherlands, Belgium, Luxembourg, France and Switzerland; Dir Gen. MILAN RABA.

CIVIL AVIATION

There are main civil airports at Prague (Ruzyně), Brno, Karlovy Vary and Ostrava, operated by the Czech Airport Administration.

ČSA—České aerolinie (Czech Airlines): Ruzyně Airport, 160 08 Prague 6; tel. 239007007; fax 224314273; e-mail call.centre@csa.cz; internet www.csa.cz; f. 1923; services to destinations in Europe, the Near, Middle and Far East, North Africa and North America; Pres. and Chair. PHILLIPE MOREELS.

Smart Wings: K letišti 1068/30, 160 08 Prague 6; tel. 255700827; internet www.smartwings.net; f. 2005; low-cost airline to various European destinations.

Tourism

The Czech Republic has magnificent scenery, with summer and winter sports facilities. Prague, Kutna Hora, Olomouc, Český Krumlov and Telč are among the best-known of the historic towns, and there are famous castles and cathedrals, and numerous resorts, as well as spas with natural mineral springs at Karlovy Vary (Carlsbad) and Mariánské Lázně (Marienbad). In 2012 a total of 7,164,576 tourist arrivals were recorded. In 2012 receipts from tourism (excluding passenger transport) totalled US $7,035m., according to provisional figures.

CzechTourism: Vinohradská 46, POB 32, 120 41 Prague 2; tel. 221580111; fax 224247516; e-mail info@czechtourism.cz; internet www.czechtourism.com; f. 1993; Dir ROSTISLAV VONDRUSKA.

Defence

As assessed at November 2013, the total active armed forces numbered 23,650, including an army of 13,000 and an air force of 5,950. There were additionally 4,850 civilian Ministry of Defence staff. Paramilitary forces totalled 3,100. In March 1994 the Czech Republic joined the North Atlantic Treaty Organization's (NATO) 'Partnership for Peace' programme of military co-operation, and it was formally admitted to the Alliance in March 1999.

Defence Expenditure: Budgeted at 42,000m. koruna in 2014.

Chief of the General Staff of the Armed Forces: Lt-Gen. PETR PAVEL.

Education

Pre-school education is available for children aged between three and six years. In 2012/13 354,340 children attended pre-primary educational establishments. Education is compulsory for children aged six to 15 years, who attend basic school, covering both primary and lower secondary levels. There are three types of upper secondary schools: gymnasia (academic); vocational; and technical. In 2011/12 enrolment in secondary education was equivalent to 97% of children in the relevant age-group. The combined enrolment in primary and secondary education in the same year was equivalent to 98% of children in the relevant age-group. Tertiary education comprises higher professional schools and universities. In 2012/13 some 807,950 children attended basic schools and 440,588 attended upper secondary schools. In that year 381,397 students attended 73 universities. In 2009 expenditure on education was 9.8% of total budgetary expenditure.

DENMARK

Introductory Survey

LOCATION, CLIMATE, LANGUAGE, RELIGION, FLAG, CAPITAL

The Kingdom of Denmark is situated in northern Europe. Metropolitan Denmark consists of the peninsula of Jutland, the islands of Zealand (Sjælland), Funen (Fyn), Lolland, Falster and Bornholm, and more than 400 smaller named islands (many of which are not populated). The country lies between the North Sea, to the west, and the Baltic Sea, to the east. Denmark's only land frontier is with Germany, to the south. Norway lies to the north of Denmark, across the Skagerrak strait, while Sweden, the most southerly region of which is separated from Zealand by the narrow Øresund strait, lies to the north-east. The Kingdom of Denmark also includes the self-governing territories of Greenland and the Faroe Islands, both of which are situated in the North Atlantic Ocean. Denmark is low-lying and the climate is temperate, with mild summers and cold, rainy winters. The language is Danish. Almost all of the inhabitants profess Christianity: the Evangelical Lutheran Church, to which some 79.1% of the population belong, is the established Church, and there are also small communities of other Protestant groups and of Roman Catholics. The national flag (proportions 28 by 37) displays a white cross on a red background, the upright of the cross being to the left of centre. The capital is Copenhagen (København).

CONTEMPORARY POLITICAL HISTORY

Historical Context

In 1945, following the end of German wartime occupation, Denmark recognized the independence of Iceland, which had been declared in the previous year. Home rule was granted to the Faroe Islands in 1948 and to Greenland in 1979. Denmark was a founder member of the North Atlantic Treaty Organization (NATO, see p. 370) in 1949 and of the Nordic Council (see p. 467) in 1952. In January 1973, following a referendum, Denmark entered the European Community (EC), now European Union (EU, see p. 273).

In 1947 King Frederik IX succeeded to the throne on the death of his father, Christian X. Denmark's Constitution was radically revised in 1953: new provisions allowed for female succession to the throne, abolished the upper house of the Folketing (parliament) and amended the franchise. King Frederik died in January 1972, and his eldest daughter, Margrethe II, became the first queen to rule Denmark for nearly 600 years.

Domestic Political Affairs

The system of proportional representation, which is embodied in the 1953 Constitution, makes it difficult for a single party to gain a majority in the Folketing. The minority Government of Venstre (Liberals), formed in 1973 and led by Poul Hartling, was followed in 1975 by a minority Government of the Socialdemokraterne (Social Democrats) under Anker Jørgensen. Jørgensen led various coalitions and minority Governments until 1982. General elections in 1977, 1979 and 1981 were held against a background of growing unemployment and attempts to tighten control of the economy.

In September 1982 divisions within the Cabinet over Jørgensen's economic policy led the Government to resign. Det Konservative Folkeparti (the Conservative People's Party), which had been absent from Danish coalitions since 1971, formed a centre-right four-party Government—with Venstre, the Centrum-Demokraterne (Centre Democrats) and the Kristeligt Folkeparti (Christian People's Party)—led by Poul Schlüter, who became Denmark's first Conservative Prime Minister since 1894. The coalition narrowly avoided defeat over its economic programme in October 1982 and September 1983, when larger reductions in public spending were proposed. In December 1983 the right-wing Fremskridtspartiet (Progress Party) withdrew its support for further cuts, and the Government was defeated. Following a general election in January 1984, Schlüter's Government remained in office, with its component parties relying on the support of members of Det Radikale Venstre (Social Liberals).

At a general election held in September 1987 Schlüter's coalition retained 70 seats in the Folketing, while the opposition Socialdemokraterne lost two of their 56 seats. Jørgensen resigned as leader of the latter party later that year. Several smaller and extremist parties made considerable gains, thus weakening the outgoing coalition, while the main opposition parties were unable to command a working majority. Schlüter eventually formed a new Cabinet comprising representatives of the former governing coalition. However, Det Radikale Venstre had earlier declared that they would not support any administration that depended on the support of the Fremskridtspartiet.

In April 1988 the Folketing adopted an opposition-sponsored resolution requiring the Government to inform visiting warships of the country's ban on nuclear weapons. The British and US Governments were highly critical of the resolution. Schlüter consequently announced an early general election for May, on the issue of Denmark's membership of NATO and defence policy. In June a new minority coalition, comprising members of Det Konservative Folkeparti, Venstre and Det Radikale Venstre, formed a Cabinet under Schlüter. The new Government restored good relations with its NATO allies by adopting a formula that requested all visiting warships to respect Danish law in its territorial waters, while making no specific reference to nuclear weapons.

The Government proposed large reductions in social welfare provision for 1989, and attacked demands by the Fremskridtspartiet for less taxation as unrealistic. The Fremskridtspartiet, however, continued to increase in popularity, and in November 1989 its share of the vote rose significantly in municipal elections, while Det Konservative Folkeparti lost support. An early general election was scheduled for December 1990. Although the Socialdemokraterne retained the largest share of the vote (winning 69 seats), Schlüter formed a minority coalition Government, comprising Det Konservative Folkeparti, which had lost five seats in the election, and Venstre, which had gained an additional seven seats. Det Radikale Venstre, while no longer part of the Government, continued to support the majority of the new coalition Government's policies.

In January 1993 Schlüter resigned from the premiership after a judicial inquiry found that he had misled the Folketing in April 1989 over a scandal that had its origin in 1987, when the Minister of Justice had illegally ordered civil servants to delay issuing entry visas to the families of Tamil refugees from Sri Lanka. In late January 1993 the leader of the Socialdemokraterne, Poul Nyrup Rasmussen, formed a majority, four-party coalition Government with Det Radikale Venstre, the Centrum-Demokraterne and the Kristeligt Folkeparti.

At an early general election held in September 1994, the Socialdemokraterne won a reduced number of seats, although they retained the largest share of the vote. Venstre gained an additional 13 seats, but the Kristeligt Folkeparti failed to secure representation in the new legislature. None the less, Nyrup Rasmussen was able to form a minority Government with Det Radikale Venstre and the Centrum-Demokraterne, and denied that the Government would be dependent for support on the left-wing Socialistisk Folkeparti (Socialist People's Party). In December 1996, however, the Centrum-Demokraterne withdrew from the coalition, following the Government's decision to seek support from left-wing parties in order to achieve parliamentary approval for legislation relating to the 1997 budget.

At an early general election conducted in March 1998, Nyrup Rasmussen's Government was returned to office with a narrow majority: the Socialdemokraterne, together with their coalition partner Det Radikale Venstre and other informal allies, secured a total of 90 seats, compared with the 89 won by the centre-right opposition. The right-wing Dansk Folkeparti (Danish People's Party), which campaigned, *inter alia*, for stricter immigration controls, won 13 seats.

At an early general election held on 20 November 2001, the Socialdemokraterne won 52 seats in the Folketing, compared with 56 seats for Venstre; thus, for the first time since 1920, the Socialdemokraterne no longer had the largest representation in the legislature. Venstre, led by Anders Fogh Rasmussen, formed a minority coalition Government with Det Konservative Folkeparti, which had secured 16 seats. The Dansk Folkeparti performed well, winning 22 seats. Although the leaders of Venstre stressed that the far-right, anti-immigration party would not exert any influence over government policy, by the end of November 2001 the Government had announced proposals to remove the legal right of refugees to bring their families to Denmark, to extend the period of residence required to obtain a residence permit from three to seven years, and to deport immediately all immigrants convicted of crimes. A new Ministry of Refugee, Immigration and Integration Affairs was also created. The proposed legislation came into force, with the support of the Dansk Folkeparti, in July 2002. Divisions within the Socialdemokraterne following the 2001 election culminated in Nyrup Rasmussen's resignation as party leader in November 2002 and his replacement by Mogens Lykketoft.

The Government, with the support of the Dansk Folkeparti, proposed controversial legislation in June 2004 to replace the 14 county authorities with five new administrative regions and to reduce the number of municipalities from 271 to 98. In January 2005 Fogh Rasmussen announced that the impending general election would be held early, on 8 February, to precede the parliamentary vote on the proposed municipal reforms. In the election, both Venstre and the Socialdemokraterne lost support to the other, smaller parties. Nevertheless, with 52 seats, Venstre remained the largest party in the Folketing; Fogh Rasmussen renewed his party's governing coalition with Det Konservative Folkeparti (which won 18 seats). The Socialdemokraterne secured 47 seats; Lykketoft subsequently resigned as party leader and was replaced by Helle Thorning-Schmidt. The Dansk Folkeparti increased its representation in the legislature to 24 seats, while Det Radikale Venstre made the largest gain, winning 17 seats. The legislation on municipal reform was adopted in 2005, and entered into force on 1 January 2007.

Events following the 2005 election

As a minority coalition, the Government continued to rely on the parliamentary support of the populist, anti-immigrant Dansk Folkeparti. In May 2007 a prominent member of the Folketing for Det Radikale Venstre, Naser Khader, resigned from that party and announced the formation of a new party, the Ny Alliance (New Alliance), which aimed to reduce the influence of the Dansk Folkeparti on government policy. Following a period of internal conflict within Det Radikale Venstre, in June the party leader, Marianne Jelved, resigned. She was replaced by Margrethe Vestager. In October Fogh Rasmussen announced that legislative elections were to take place in mid-November, some two years before the scheduled end of the parliamentary term, in order to facilitate forthcoming cross-party negotiations over welfare reform.

At the general election, the two main parties again lost support to smaller rivals. None the less, Venstre remained the strongest party in the Folketing, winning 46 seats, while its partner in the outgoing coalition Government, Det Konservative Folkeparti, retained its 18 seats in the legislature. The Socialdemokraterne lost one seat, winning 45 seats. The Dansk Folkeparti increased its representation in the Folketing to 25 seats, while the Socialistisk Folkeparti made the most significant gains of any party, winning 23 seats. However, the Ny Alliance secured only five seats, and was outperformed by Det Radikale Venstre, which nevertheless lost almost one-half of its seats, winning only nine. Fogh Rasmussen subsequently announced the renewal of the minority coalition between Venstre and Det Konservative Folkeparti and reorganized the Cabinet. Among the most notable changes was the appointment of Venstre's Lars Løkke Rasmussen (hitherto Minister of the Interior and Health) as Minister of Finance.

The coalition parties' failure to increase their representation at the general election required the Government to continue to rely upon parliamentary support from the Dansk Folkeparti. In January 2008 the Government concluded an agreement with the Dansk Folkeparti over asylum policy reform. Opposition parties were excluded from the talks and subsequently accused the Government of reneging on a promise to hold cross-party talks after the election. Nevertheless, later in that month Khader announced that his party would vote in favour of the proposals, stating that the Ny Alliance was a centre-right party and would thus support the governing coalition. This statement prompted one of the party's co-founders to resign from the party at the end of that month, citing her opposition to the Ny Alliance's implicit co-operation with the Dansk Folkeparti. In August the Ny Alliance was renamed the Liberal Alliance. In January 2009 Khader resigned from the Liberal Alliance, citing declining support for the party and personal disillusionment with its failure effectively to counter the Dansk Folkeparti; Leif Mikkelsen was appointed as the new party leader.

Following the resignation of Bendt Bendtsen as leader of Det Konservative Folkeparti in September 2008, the government portfolios allocated to members of that party were reorganized. Lene Espersen (hitherto Minister of Justice), who had succeeded Bendtsen as party leader, replaced him as Deputy Prime Minister and Minister of Economic and Business Affairs.

Lars Løkke Rasmussen's premiership

On 5 April 2009 Fogh Rasmussen resigned both as Prime Minister and leader of Venstre after his official nomination as Secretary-General of NATO. Lars Løkke Rasmussen, the deputy leader of Venstre, was sworn in as Prime Minister later that day, following pledges of continued parliamentary support for the coalition Government from the Dansk Folkeparti and the Liberal Alliance. Two days later Løkke Rasmussen effected a reorganization of the Cabinet, in which Claus Hjort Frederiksen (hitherto the Minister of Employment) succeeded the new Prime Minister as Minister of Finance. Løkke Rasmussen was formally confirmed as leader of Venstre at a special party congress in May.

In June 2009 a national referendum (held concurrently with elections to the European Parliament) approved a constitutional amendment—by 85.4% of valid votes cast—allowing the monarch's eldest child, regardless of gender, to inherit the throne.

In November 2009 Connie Hedegaard of Det Konservative Folkeparti resigned as Minister of Climate and Energy, having been nominated for membership of the European Commission. Hedegaard remained a member of the Government until December in order to chair the UN Climate Change Conference, which was held in Copenhagen. Despite high international expectations, the conference failed to reach a legally binding international agreement on limiting the emission of gases widely held to cause global warming. Løkke Rasmussen carried out a wide-ranging cabinet reorganization in February 2010. In order to secure the Dansk Folkeparti's support, in May, for a fiscal consolidation agreement and, later that year, for the 2011 budget, the Government agreed to a further tightening of immigration regulations.

Following a marked decline in support for Det Konservative Folkeparti during 2010 (according to opinion polls), Espersen resigned as party leader in January 2011, although she remained Minister of Foreign Affairs; she was succeeded as party leader by the Minister of Justice, Lars Barfoed.

The Minister of Refugee, Immigration and Integration Affairs, Birthe Rønn Hornbech, was dismissed in March 2011, following a report on the ministry's failure to grant citizenship to stateless Danish-born Palestinians, which was in violation of UN conventions. Hornbech was replaced by the Minister of Development Co-operation, Søren Pind, who also retained his existing portfolio. Hornbech's responsibility for ecclesiastical affairs was transferred to the Minister of Culture, Per Stig Møller.

Political agreement was reached in May 2011 on a series of economic reforms aimed at achieving a balanced budget by 2020, with the Government notably securing the approval of the opposition Det Radikale Venstre for its proposed changes to the pensions system, including a phasing out of the early retirement benefit and an accelerated increase in the retirement age. However, a concession made to the Dansk Folkeparti in return for its support, to reintroduce permanent customs inspections at Denmark's borders with Germany and Sweden, provoked considerable controversy. Although the Government insisted that the controls, which were ostensibly aimed at countering rising cross-border crime, would not contravene its commitments under the EU's Schengen Agreement on internal borders, the European Commission questioned their compatibility with EU law, as did Germany. Nevertheless, the enhanced customs checks commenced in July, having been approved by the Folketing.

Recent developments: Helle Thorning-Schmidt's administration

In August 2011 Løkke Rasmussen announced that the general election, due to be held by November, would take place in September. Economic concerns dominated the electoral campaign, amid stagnant growth, a rising budget deficit and difficulties in the banking sector. Løkke Rasmussen pledged to continue with the implementation of his Government's planned reductions in public expenditure if re-elected, while Helle

Thorning-Schmidt of the Socialdemokraterne proposed raising taxes on the financial services sector and high earners, increasing spending on health, education and infrastructure, and lengthening the working week by one hour with the aim of boosting productivity and reviving growth.

At the general election on 15 September 2011, the four centre-left opposition parties, the Socialdemokraterne, the Socialistisk Folkeparti, Det Radikale Venstre and the far-left Enhedslisten—de Rød-Grønne (Red-Green Alliance), won a narrow majority of seats in the Folketing, ending 10 years of minority government by the centre-right parties supported by the Dansk Folkeparti. However, the legislative representation of both the Socialdemokraterne and the Socialistisk Folkeparti declined (although only marginally so for the former), to 44 seats and 16 seats, respectively, while there was a considerable rise in support for Det Radikale Venstre, which secured 17 seats, and for the Enhedslisten—de Rød-Grønne, which secured 12. Of the parties in the outgoing coalition Government, Venstre retained its position as the largest single party in the legislature, obtaining 47 seats, but its partner, Det Konservative Folkeparti, performed particularly poorly, securing only eight seats, constituting a loss of 10 seats, and the representation of its ally, the Dansk Folkeparti, also decreased, to 22 seats. The only other party to win parliamentary representation was the Liberal Alliance, with nine seats. Turnout was recorded at 87.7%.

A minority coalition Government of the Socialdemokraterne, Det Radikale Venstre and the Socialistisk Folkeparti took office on 3 October 2011, with Thorning-Schmidt as Denmark's first female Prime Minister. Vestager, the leader of Det Radikale Venstre, was appointed as Minister of Economics and of the Interior, and Villy Søvndal, the leader of the Socialistisk Folkeparti, was allocated the foreign affairs portfolio. The minority Government would require the support of the Enhedslisten—de Rød-Grønne to secure the approval of legislation, while three of the four deputies elected to represent the Faroe Islands and Greenland were also allied to the new administration, which thus controlled a five-seat majority in the Folketing. The new Prime Minister announced that the previous Government's restoration of border controls was to be reversed. However, plans to phase out the early retirement benefit would be retained, at the insistence of Det Radikale Venstre, as would the target of achieving a balanced budget by 2020. In the area of immigration policy, many of the restrictions introduced during the previous decade, largely at the behest of the Dansk Folkeparti, were to be removed or eased, and the Ministry of Refugee, Immigration and Integration Affairs was abolished.

During its first year in power the new Government was faced with considerable difficulties, many of which arose from the problems created by the stagnating economy. Opponents of Thorning-Schmidt's administration accused the Government of reneging on its electoral pledges and of generally lacking political expertise. Others claimed that the Government was betraying its supporters by adopting right-wing economic policies. The Government's waning popularity suffered a further setback in December 2012 when the Minister of Culture, Uffe Elbæk, was forced to resign amid allegations of nepotism and conflict of interest. In an apparent effort to reverse the decline in the standing of her administration, Thorning-Schmidt carried out a cabinet reorganization in August 2013.

The Prime Minister's position was seriously weakened in late January 2014 when the Socialistisk Folkeparti withdrew from the coalition in protest at the Government's decision to sell part of an ailing state-owned utility company, DONG Energy, to a private consortium headed by the US investment bank Goldman Sachs. The Chairman of the Socialistisk Folkeparti, Annette Vilhelmsen, who had supported the proposed sale of the state assets, stood down as leader of the party following its defection (which left the two remaining parties in the coalition in control of only around one-third of the seats in the Folketing). Public opposition to the controversial divestment was uncharacteristically vehement: an online petition against the deal was signed by nearly 200,000 people. Thorning-Schmidt effected a ministerial reorganization in early February. While many senior posts remained unchanged, among the notable new appointments was that of Martin Lidegaard as the new Minister of Foreign Affairs; in addition, the European affairs portfolio was abolished.

Controversy over press freedom

In September 2005 one of Denmark's principal newspapers, *Jyllands-Posten*, provoked considerable anger among Muslim communities by printing cartoons depicting the Prophet Muhammad, in order to draw attention to perceived self-censorship in the Danish press. Protests against the publication of the caricatures took place in Denmark and a number of predominantly Muslim countries. During January and February 2006 Iran, Libya, Saudi Arabia and Syria temporarily withdrew their ambassadors from Copenhagen. At the end of January the editors of *Jyllands-Posten* finally apologized for causing offence (although not for publishing the caricatures). Fogh Rasmussen welcomed the apology, but defended the freedom of the press, repudiating demands by Islamic states that the Danish Government should punish those responsible for the cartoons and their publication. Muslim outrage over the images continued to escalate in February, as they were reprinted by publications in several other European countries to show solidarity with *Jyllands-Posten*. Many Muslims boycotted Danish goods and violent anti-Danish protests took place in several countries; in mid-February the Danish embassies in Indonesia, Iran, Lebanon, Pakistan and Syria were temporarily closed owing to security concerns. In February 2008 three people were arrested on charges of planning to murder one of the cartoonists, Kurt Westergaard, who had contributed arguably the most contentious cartoon to *Jyllands-Posten*, which depicted the Prophet Muhammad wearing a bomb-shaped turban. In January 2010 an intruder at Westergaard's home was arrested; he was convicted of attempted murder and terrorism in February 2011, and sentenced to nine (later increased to 10) years' imprisonment. The offices of *Jyllands-Posten* were believed to have been the intended target of two planned attacks that were discovered in the second half of 2010. In September a Chechen asylum seeker was arrested in Copenhagen following the premature explosion of a letter bomb he was allegedly preparing; he was convicted on charges of terrorism and illegal weapons possession in June 2011, and sentenced to 12 years' imprisonment. In the second case, in December 2010, four suspected Islamist militants (three of whom were Swedish citizens and the fourth a Tunisian citizen) were arrested on suspicion of planning an armed attack on the newspaper's offices. In June 2012 the four defendants were each sentenced to 12 years' imprisonment. In mid-2012 five men were arrested in connection with two further alleged terrorist plots.

Foreign Affairs

Regional relations

The extent of Denmark's commitment to its membership of the EU has frequently been a matter of debate within the country. In January 1986 the left-wing parties in the Folketing combined to reject the ratification by Denmark of the Single European Act (which amended the Treaty of Rome—the agreement that founded the EC—in order to establish the EC's single market and allow the EC Council of Ministers to take decisions by a qualified majority vote if unanimity was not achieved). Opponents of ratification argued that it would lead to a diminution of Denmark's power to maintain strict environmental controls. In a national referendum in February, however, 56.2% of the votes cast were in favour of ratification of the Act, and the Folketing formally approved it in May.

In May 1992 the Folketing voted, by 130 votes to 25, to approve the Treaty on European Union (the Maastricht Treaty), which further expanded the scope of the Treaty of Rome. In a national referendum held in June, however, 50.7% of the votes cast were against ratification of the Treaty. In December EC heads of government agreed that Denmark should be allowed exemption from certain provisions of the Treaty, namely the final stage of European Monetary Union (including the adoption of a single currency); participation in a common defence policy; common European citizenship; and co-operation in legal and home affairs. This agreement was endorsed by seven of the eight parties represented in the Folketing (the exception being the Fremskridtspartiet), and in a second referendum in May 1993, 56.7% of the votes cast were in favour of ratification.

In May 1998 Danish voters narrowly endorsed the ratification of the Amsterdam Treaty on European integration. In September 2000 the Government held a national referendum regarding adoption of the single European currency, the euro. Approval for the euro had declined in the run-up to the vote, despite the support of the Government, the majority of the major political parties, the industrial sector, banks, trade unions and the media. In the event, 53.1% of the votes cast were opposed to membership of the single currency; turnout was 87.5%.

In February 2005 Fogh Rasmussen, following Venstre's re-election to office, announced that a draft treaty outlining a constitution of the EU would be presented for ratification in a public referendum. However, the referendum, which was scheduled for September, was postponed following the treaty's rejection by voters in France and the Netherlands. A new treaty to replace the rejected constitutional treaty was signed by the heads of state and of government of the EU member states during a summit meeting held in Lisbon, Portugal, in December. The Folketing ratified the Treaty of Lisbon in May 2008, a referendum having been deemed unnecessary by the Government in a decision supported by the Socialdemokraterne and Det Radikale Venstre. The treaty entered into force in December 2009, following its ratification by all of the then 27 EU member states.

Following its assumption of power in September 2011, the new Government of Helle Thorning-Schmidt announced its intention to conduct referendums during the next parliamentary term on abolishing two of the four exemptions from the provisions of the Maastricht Treaty that had been negotiated in 1992: participation in a common defence policy and co-operation in legal and home affairs. In 2010–12 Danish public support for the adoption of the euro notably weakened, amid persistent instability in the eurozone.

Other external relations

The Danish Government contributed a warship, a submarine and 160 troops to the US-led military operation in Iraq to remove the regime of Saddam Hussain in early 2003, despite deep public divisions over the Government's support for the invasion. Following the collapse of Saddam Hussain's regime in April, a 410-strong Danish peacekeeping force was dispatched to Iraq and the Government was involved in plans for the post-war redevelopment of that country. In April 2004 the Minister of Defence, Svend Aage Jensby, resigned amid opposition allegations that the Danish military authorities had exaggerated the threat posed by Saddam Hussain in an attempt to justify the military action in Iraq. On 1 August 2007 the withdrawal of Danish troops from Iraq was completed as planned and in September 2012 Denmark ended its participation in the UN Assistance Mission for Iraq.

In January 2006 the Folketing approved a government proposal to send an additional 200 soldiers to participate in the NATO-led International Security Assistance Force (ISAF) in Afghanistan, bringing the number of Danish troops deployed in that country to some 360; the size of the contingent was further increased to more than 500 in 2007; however, by October 2013 the Danish contingent had decreased to 249 military personnel. NATO combat forces were scheduled to be withdrawn from Afghanistan by the end of 2014. Meanwhile, in April 2012 the Government of Helle Thorning-Schmidt announced that a special commission was to be set up to investigate the Danish authorities' justification for supporting the US-led invasion of Iraq in 2003 and to investigate the treatment of detainees by Danish soldiers in both Iraq and Afghanistan. The opposition claimed that the establishment of the commission, which was to present its findings in 2017, was politically motivated and that it represented an attempt by the Government to discredit its political opponents.

Following the outbreak of civil conflict in Libya in early 2011, Danish military forces participated in the enforcement of an air exclusion zone over Libya (as endorsed by a UN Security Council resolution in March). NATO military action in Libya ended in October, following the death of the Libyan leader, Col Muammar al-Qaddafi.

In October 2004 the Danish Government announced that, in co-operation with the Governments of the Faroe Islands and Greenland, it would attempt to prove that the seabed beneath the North Pole (the Polar Basin) was a natural continuation of Greenland and that Denmark could thus claim legal ownership of any natural resources discovered there. Other claimants to the Pole (currently considered international territory) included Canada, Norway, Russia and the USA. In July 2005 the Danish Government made a formal protest to the Canadian ambassador in Copenhagen after the Canadian Minister of National Defence landed on Hans Island without first notifying the Danish Government. The sovereignty of the small uninhabited island, in the Nares Strait between Ellesmere Island (Canada) and north-west Greenland, had been disputed for more than 30 years, and would affect Denmark's claim for ownership of the North Pole. Moreover, control of Hans Island has assumed greater importance in recent years as global warming has raised the issue of the potential opening of the disputed North-west Passage to shipping. In September the foreign ministers of both countries agreed to hold talks on sovereignty and to inform each other of any activities around the island. In 2012 Canada and Denmark were in negotiations over the island and had embarked on a joint mapping exercise. Two possible solutions to the dispute were shared jurisdiction or the drawing up of a border through the middle of the island. Tensions were further eased in September of that year by a decision by the Canadian military to cease any activity by its armed forces on or around the island, with the exception of search and rescue or emergency operations. Meanwhile, in May 2008 the Danish Minister of Foreign Affairs and the Prime Minister of Greenland co-hosted a meeting in Ilulissat, Greenland, of the countries bordering the Arctic Ocean in an attempt to address issues arising from conflicting territorial interests and increased use of Arctic waters, notably for tourism and shipping, as a result of diminishing sea ice. The resultant Ilulissat Declaration, which was agreed by Canada, Denmark, Norway, Russia and the USA, confirmed the five nations' commitment to compliance with the UN's Convention on the Law of the Sea and ruled out the creation of any new comprehensive legal framework for the governance of the Arctic region. The signatories also committed those countries to 'the orderly settlement' of any disputes over the delineation of borders along the continental shelf. At a ministerial meeting held in Nuuk, the capital of Greenland, in May 2011, Denmark and the seven other states comprising the Arctic Council (see p. 448) (Canada, Finland, Iceland, Norway, Russia, Sweden and the USA), which was formally established in 1996, notably signed their first legally binding agreement, which concerned co-operation in search and rescue efforts in the Arctic. In August 2011, in a joint document detailing their strategy for the Arctic during 2011–20, the Governments of Denmark, Greenland and the Faroes stated that, as the Kingdom of Denmark, they had already submitted evidence to the UN Commission on the Limits of the Continental Shelf for their claim to sovereignty over two areas near the Faroes and, by 2014, planned to do the same for three areas near Greenland, one of which included the North Pole (two partial submissions—for the Southern Continental Shelf of Greenland and for the North-eastern Continental Shelf of Greenland—were presented to the Commission in June 2012 and November 2013, respectively). The document also confirmed plans to establish a non-permanent Arctic Response Force from existing armed forces units and to merge the Greenland and Faroese military commands to form a joint service Arctic Command (this new defence body was officially inaugurated in Nuuk in October 2012).

CONSTITUTION AND GOVERNMENT

The Constitutional Act (Grundlov) was adopted on 5 June 1953, replacing the Constitutional Acts of 1849, 1866 and 1915. Denmark is a constitutional monarchy. Legislative power is held jointly by the hereditary monarch (who has no personal political power) and the unicameral Folketing (parliament), which has 179 members, including 175 from metropolitan Denmark and two each from the Faroe Islands and Greenland. Members are elected for four years (subject to dissolution) on the basis of proportional representation. Executive power is exercised by the monarch through a Cabinet, which is led by the Prime Minister and is responsible to the Folketing. Following municipal reforms which came into effect on 1 January 2007, Denmark comprises five administrative regions, one city and one borough, all with elected regional councils, and 98 municipalities.

REGIONAL AND INTERNATIONAL CO-OPERATION

Denmark is a member of the European Union (EU, see p. 273), although it did not participate in Economic and Monetary Union and thus remains outside of the single currency. Denmark is a member of the Nordic Council (see p. 467) and the Nordic Council of Ministers (see p. 467), which are based in Copenhagen. It is member of the Arctic Council (see p. 448), and was a founder member of both the Council of Europe (see p. 252) and the Council of the Baltic Sea States (see p. 250).

Denmark was a founder member of the UN in 1945. As a contracting party to the General Agreement on Tariffs and Trade, Denmark joined the World Trade Organization (WTO, see p. 434) on its establishment in 1995. It is a member of the North Atlantic Treaty Organization (NATO, see p. 370), and participates in the Organization for Security and Co-operation in Europe (OSCE, see p. 387). Denmark is also a member of the Organisation for Economic Co-operation and Development (OECD, see p. 379).

ECONOMIC AFFAIRS

In 2012, according to estimates by the World Bank, Denmark's gross national income (GNI), measured at average 2010–12 prices, was US $334,135m., equivalent to $59,770 per head (or $43,340 per head on an international purchasing-power parity basis). During 2003–12, Denmark's population grew at an average annual rate of 0.4%, while gross domestic product (GDP) per head increased, in real terms, at an average rate of 0.2% per year. According to World Bank figures, overall GDP grew, in real terms, at an average annual rate of 0.6% in 2003–12. In 2011 real GDP increased by 1.1%, but decreased by 0.5% in 2012, measured at constant prices; according to chain-linked methodologies, GDP increased by 1.1% in 2011, but decreased by 0.4% in 2012.

Agriculture (including forestry and fishing) contributed 1.4% of GDP and employed 2.6% of the economically active population in 2012. The principal activities are pig farming and dairy farming; Denmark is a major exporter of pork products, and exports of meat and meat preparations accounted for 5.1% of total export revenue in 2012. Most of Denmark's agricultural production is exported, and the sector accounted for 16.4% of total exports in 2012. The fishing industry accounted for 2.7% of total export earnings in 2012. According to World Bank estimates, agricultural GDP increased, in real terms, at an average annual rate of 1.4% in 2003–10. According to chain-linked methodologies, the GDP of the sector declined by 2.8% in 2012.

Industry (including mining, manufacturing, construction, power and water) provided 21.8% of GDP and employed 17.9% of the working population in 2012. According to World Bank estimates, industrial GDP declined by an average of 1.2% per year, in real terms, during 2003–10; the sector's GDP contracted by 0.3% in 2010.

Mining provided 3.6% of GDP in 2012, and accounted for only 0.1% of employment in 2008. Denmark has few natural resources, but exploration for petroleum reserves in the Danish sector of the North Sea in the 1970s proved successful. Natural gas has also been extensively exploited. There is a significant reserve of sand in north-western Jutland which could potentially be exploited for rich yields of titanium, zirconium and yttrium. The GDP of the mining sector increased, in real terms, at an average annual rate of 1.0% in 2002–05. The sector's GDP declined by 10.0% in 2012, according to chain linked-methodologies.

Manufacturing contributed 11.0% of GDP in 2012, and employed 15.1% of the working population in 2008. Measured by value of turnover, in 2012 the most important manufacturing industries were food products (accounting for 24.6% of the total), machinery equipment (19.1%), chemicals and oil refineries (13.7%), furniture (7.6%), metal products (7.3%), pharmaceuticals (7.1%), and plastic, glass and concrete (6.3%). According to World Bank estimates, manufacturing GDP increased, in real terms, at an average annual rate of 0.4% during 2003–10. In 2011, according to chain-linked methodologies, the sector's GDP increased by 6.5% and by 3.0% in 2012.

The construction sector contributed 4.8% of GDP and employed 5.8% of the working population in 2012. According to chain-linked methodologies, the GDP of the construction sector increased by 7.1% in 2011, but declined by 1.4% in 2012.

Energy is derived principally from petroleum and natural gas. Since 1997 Denmark has produced enough energy to satisfy its domestic consumption, owing to the extraction of crude petroleum and natural gas from the North Sea and the production of renewable energy. In 2012 crude petroleum production amounted to 207,000 barrels per day and total annual gas output was 6,416m. cu m. In 2012, according to official figures, imports of mineral fuels accounted for 10.8% of the total cost of imports, while exports of mineral fuels contributed 11.3% of total export revenue. In 2012 34.7% of electricity was produced from coal, 14.0% from natural gas and 1.2% from petroleum. At the end of 2012 Denmark's proven oil reserves stood at 700m. barrels, while natural gas reserves were 38,000m. cu m. The use of renewable sources of energy (including wind power) has been encouraged. In 2011 Denmark derived about 24% of its electricity consumption from renewable sources (mostly wind turbines), and planned to increase the share to one-third by 2020.

Services provided 76.8% of GDP and engaged 79.5% of the employed population in 2012. Shipping is an important sector in Denmark. According to World Bank estimates, the combined GDP of the service sectors increased, in real terms, at an average rate of 1.0% per year in 2003–10; the GDP of the sector increased by 1.6% in 2010.

In 2012, according to the IMF, Denmark recorded a visible merchandise trade surplus of US $8,502m. and a surplus of $18,750m. on the current account of the balance of payments. Most Danish trade is with the other member states of the European Union (EU, see p. 273), which accounted for 70.7% of imports and 61.9% of exports in 2012. The principal source of imports in 2012 was Germany (contributing 20.8% of the total); other major suppliers were Sweden, the Netherlands, the People's Republic of China, the United Kingdom and Norway. Germany was also the principal market for exports (accounting for 15.1% of the total); other major purchasers included Sweden, the United Kingdom, the USA and Norway. The principal exports in 2012 were machinery and transport equipment, chemicals and related products, food and live animals, miscellaneous manufactured articles, mineral fuels and lubricants, and basic manufactures. Pork, pharmaceutical products, gas, petroleum and wind turbines are among the key exports. The principal imports in 2012 were machinery and transport equipment, miscellaneous manufactured articles, basic manufactures, chemicals and related products, food and live animals, and mineral fuels and lubricants.

In 2012 there was a general government deficit of an estimated 75,408m. kroner, equivalent to 4.1% of GDP. Denmark's general government gross debt was 832,455m. kroner in 2012, equivalent to 45.6% of GDP. The average annual rate of inflation was 2.1% in 2003–12. Consumer prices increased by 2.4% in 2012. The rate of unemployment was 4.4% in 2012.

Denmark is a small open economy, which is highly dependent on trade with other countries. Denmark did not participate in Stage III of the EU's programme of Economic and Monetary Union (EMU), although it has maintained a stable rate of exchange with the common European currency, the euro. As a result of reforms introduced in the 1980s, Denmark enjoyed a long period of sustained economic growth, low unemployment and generous social welfare provisions. As in many other EU countries, however, demographic changes posed a challenge to Denmark's economy, resulting in a smaller labour force and a larger elderly population. An agreement to reform the welfare system was reached in 2006, which included the gradual increase in the retirement and early retirement ages to 67 and 62 years, respectively. In 2011, moreover, it was agreed to bring forward the increase in the retirement age and to phase out the early retirement benefit. Economic growth began to decelerate in 2007 as a result of the slowing of the housing market and declining investment. This coincided with the effects of the global financial crisis, causing Denmark to be the first country in the EU to enter recession. Despite government initiatives to improve liquidity and stability in the banking sector, a total of nine banks were taken into state control in 2008–11. The recession worsened in 2009, with GDP contracting by 5.8%. Exports and imports declined, and there was an increase in business bankruptcies and in the unemployment rate, which reached 7.5% in 2010 (compared with 1.4% at July 2008). The economy began to recover gradually in the second half of 2009, and GDP increased by 1.3% in 2010. However, quarter-on-quarter contractions were recorded in the final quarter of 2010 and the first quarter of 2011, technically signifying a return to recession, and overall annual growth in 2011 slowed to 1.1%, amid declining private consumption, continued difficulties in the banking sector and a stagnant property market. Rather than focusing solely on austerity, the new centre-left Government that took office in October 2011 announced measures designed to stimulate growth and create employment, including investment of 18,750m. kroner in 2012–13 in public works projects. Despite a recovery in exports, real GDP contracted by 0.5% in 2012; this was caused by a number of factors, including a stagnation in private consumption, collapsing house prices, a decline in investment and the ongoing debt crisis in several European countries (although Denmark's own government debt was notably relatively low). The unemployment rate remained an issue of considerable concern, rising from 6.1% in December 2011 to some 8.0% in December 2012 (fuelled in particular by large rises in unemployment among the country's youth). The general government deficit rose from 2.0% of GDP in 2011 to 4.1% of GDP in 2012, partly owing to the Government's stimulus measures and the need to repay early retirement contributions, but, according to IMF predictions, was forecast to narrow to 1.4% of GDP in 2013 (thus returning to within the 3% limit mandated by the EU's Stability and Growth Pact). Mainly as a result of continuing fiscal prudence (underpinned by the krone being pegged to the euro), GDP was forecast to return to positive growth, of an estimated 0.4%, in 2013; however, this remained well below levels of growth recorded in the years preceding the financial crisis.

PUBLIC HOLIDAYS

2015: 1 January (New Year's Day), 2 April (Maundy Thursday), 3 April (Good Friday), 6 April (Easter Monday), 1 May (General Prayer Day), 14 May (Ascension Day), 25 May (Whit Monday), 5 June (Constitution Day), 24–26 December (Christmas).

Statistical Survey

Source (unless otherwise stated): Danmarks Statistik, Sejrøgade 11, POB 2550, 2100 Copenhagen Ø; tel. 39-17-39-17; fax 39-17-39-99; e-mail dst@dst.dk; internet www.dst.dk.

Note: The figures in this survey relate only to metropolitan Denmark, excluding the Faroe Islands (see p. 1558) and Greenland (see p. 1565), figures for which are dealt with in separate chapters.

Area and Population

AREA, POPULATION AND DENSITY

Area (sq km)	42,895*
Population (census results)	
1 January 2001	5,349,212
1 January 2011	
Males	2,756,582
Females	2,804,046
Total	5,560,628
Population (official estimates at 1 January)	
2012	5,580,516
2013	5,602,628
Density (per sq km) at 1 January 2013	130.6

* 16,562 sq miles.

POPULATION BY AGE AND SEX
(official estimates at 1 January 2013)

	Males	Females	Total
0–14	500,720	476,876	977,596
15–64	1,826,180	1,799,051	3,625,231
65 and over	451,952	547,849	999,801
Total	2,778,852	2,823,776	5,602,628

ADMINISTRATIVE DIVISIONS
(official estimates at 1 January 2013)

Region	Area (sq km)	Population	Density (per sq km)
Hovedstaden	2,546.3	1,732,068	680.2
Midtjylland	13,000.2	1,272,510	97.9
Nordjylland	7,874.0	580,272	73.7
Sjælland	7,217.8	816,359	113.3
Syddanmark	12,256.5	1,201,419	98.0
Total	42,894.8	5,602,628	130.6

PRINCIPAL MUNICIPALITIES
(official estimates at 1 January 2013)

København (Copenhagen, the capital)	558,254	Horsens	84,850
Århus (Aarhus)	318,824	Roskilde	83,545
Ålborg (Aalborg)	203,363	Næstved	81,146
Odense	193,314	Slagelse	77,135
Esbjerg	114,957	Sønderborg	75,707
Vejle	108,790	Gentofte	73,300
Frederiksborg (Frederiksberg)	101,777	Holbæk	69,259
Randers	95,999	Gladsaxe	66,005
Viborg	94,286	Hjørring	65,763
Kolding	89,521	Helsingør	61,562
Silkeborg	89,333	Guldborgsund	61,303
Herning	86,571	Frederikshavn	60,772

BIRTHS, MARRIAGES AND DEATHS

	Registered live births		Registered marriages		Registered deaths	
	Number	Rate (per 1,000)	Number	Rate (per 1,000)	Number	Rate (per 1,000)
2005	64,282	11.9	36,148	6.7	54,962	10.1
2006	64,984	12.0	36,452	6.7	55,477	10.2
2007	64,082	11.8	36,576	6.7	55,604	10.2
2008	65,038	11.8	37,376	6.8	54,591	9.9
2009	62,818	11.4	32,934	6.0	54,872	9.9
2010	63,411	11.5	30,949	5.6	54,368	9.8
2011	58,998	10.6	27,198	5.0	52,516	9.4
2012	57,916	10.3	28,235	5.0	52,325	9.3

Life expectancy (years at birth): 79.8 (males 77.8; females 81.9) in 2011 (Source: World Bank, World Development Indicators database).

ECONOMICALLY ACTIVE POPULATION
(annual averages, '000 persons aged 15–66 years, 2012)

	Male	Female	Total
Agriculture, hunting and forestry	56.0	13.7	69.7
Manufacturing, mining and utilities	227.2	94.1	321.3
Construction	139.7	14.3	154.0
Wholesale and retail trade and transport	378.2	255.3	633.5
Information and communications	68.7	30.0	98.7
Financial intermediation	40.7	40.5	81.2
Real estate, renting and business activities	177.2	137.8	314.9
Public administration, education and health	248.8	617.6	866.5
Arts, entertainment and recreation activities	50.5	67.6	118.1
Sub-total	1,387.0	1,270.9	2,657.9
Activities not adequately defined	9.4	6.3	15.7
Total employed	1,396.4	1,277.2	2,673.6
Unemployed	65.7	56.6	122.2
Total labour force	1,462.1	1,333.7	2,795.8

Note: Employment includes salaried employees, self-employed persons and assisting spouses.

Health and Welfare

KEY INDICATORS

Total fertility rate (children per woman, 2011)	1.9
Under-5 mortality rate (per 1,000 live births, 2011)	4
HIV/AIDS (% of persons aged 15–49, 2011)	0.2
Physicians (per 1,000 head, 2009)	3.4
Hospital beds (per 1,000 head, 2009)	3.5
Health expenditure (2010): US $ per head (PPP)	4,467
Health expenditure (2010): % of GDP	11.1
Health expenditure (2010): public (% of total)	85.1
Total carbon dioxide emissions ('000 metric tons, 2010)	46,303.2
Carbon dioxide emissions per head (metric tons, 2010)	8.3
Human Development Index (2012): ranking	15
Human Development Index (2012): value	0.901

For sources and definitions, see explanatory note on p. vi.

Agriculture

PRINCIPAL CROPS
('000 metric tons)

	2010	2011	2012
Wheat	5,059.9	4,831.0	4,525.1
Barley	2,981.3	3,264.1	4,058.7
Rye	254.7	294.3	384.4
Oats	274.4	224.8	302.5
Triticale (wheat-rye hybrid)	177.4	136.8	114.6
Potatoes	1,357.8	1,620.0	1,664.2
Sugar beet	2,356.0	2,700.0	2,772.0
Peas, dry	28.0	20.2	17.6
Other pulses	5.7	6.9	8.9
Rapeseed	579.8	508.3	484.6
Cabbages and other brassicas	22.7	26.1	29.3
Lettuce and chicory	11.1	11.5	12.6
Tomatoes	15.0	13.2	13.3
Cucumbers and gherkins	15.4	18.3	18.3
Onions, dry	52.3	62.9	47.8
Peas, green	13.8	19.8	19.8
Carrots and turnips	104.8	107.2	84.9
Apples	24.2	25.7	18.7

Aggregate production ('000 metric tons, may include official, semi-official or estimated data): Total cereals 8,818 in 2010, 8,767 in 2011, 9,410 in 2012; Total roots and tubers 1,358 in 2010, 1,620 in 2011, 1,664 in 2012; Total vegetables (incl. melons) 287 in 2010, 317 in 2011, 281 in 2012; Total fruits (excl. melons) 67 in 2010, 87 in 2011, 51 in 2012.

Source: FAO.

LIVESTOCK
(at May)

	2010	2011	2012
Horses	60,000	61,000	68,000
Cattle	1,571,050	1,567,971	1,606,826
Pigs	13,173,060	12,931,678	12,330,879
Sheep	159,626	143,890	153,691
Chickens ('000 head)	14,114	14,325	14,137
Turkeys ('000 head)	201	212	435
Ducks ('000 head)	224	230	103
Geese ('000 head)	7	7	4

Source: FAO.

LIVESTOCK PRODUCTS
('000 metric tons)

	2010	2011	2012
Cattle meat	133	134	127
Pig meat	1,668	1,720	1,669
Chicken meat	186	187	177
Cows' milk	4,909	4,881	5,008
Butter	34	37	39
Cheese	292	275	303
Hen eggs	76	79	78

Source: FAO.

Forestry

ROUNDWOOD REMOVALS
('000 cu m, excl. bark, FAO estimates)

	2009	2010	2011
Sawlogs, veneer logs and logs for sleepers	906	844	779
Pulpwood	705	656	606
Other industrial wood	96	90	83
Fuel wood	1,106	1,080	1,115
Total	2,813	2,669	2,583

2012: Production assumed to be unchanged from 2011 (FAO estimates).

Source: FAO.

SAWNWOOD PRODUCTION
('000 cu m, incl. railway sleepers, unofficial figures)

	2009	2010	2011
Coniferous (softwood)	250	239	248
Broadleaved (hardwood)	191	209	124
Total	441	448	372

2012: Production assumed to be unchanged from 2011 (FAO estimates).

Source: FAO.

Fishing

('000 metric tons, live weight)

	2009	2010	2011
Capture	777.8	828.0	716.3
Norway pout	19.8	71.3	4.1
Blue whiting (Poutassou)	0.2	0.1	0.1
Sandeels (Sandlances)	305.6	292.5	282.5
Atlantic herring	92.0	77.4	85.9
European sprat	195.2	187.0	163.2
Blue mussel	37.4	27.9	34.4
Aquaculture	34.1	39.5*	34.9
Rainbow trout	29.4	34.5	32.6
Total catch	811.9	867.5*	751.2

* FAO estimate.

Source: FAO.

Mining

('000 metric tons unless otherwise indicated)

	2009	2010	2011
Crude petroleum	12,903	12,157	10,940
Natural gas (million cu m)	8,428	8,215	7,063
Limestone (agricultural)	700	n.a.	n.a.
Limestone (industrial)	250	n.a.	n.a.
Chalk	2,735	2,600	2,600
Salt	511	601	600
Peat	145	145	145

2012: Crude petroleum ('000 metric tons) 10,094; Natural gas (million cu m) 6,416.

Sources: BP, *Statistical Review of World Energy*; US Geological Survey.

Industry

SELECTED PRODUCTS
('000 metric tons unless otherwise indicated)

	2007	2008	2009
Wheat flour	247	254	254
Pig meat	1,278	1,281	1,585
Poultry meat	163	145	173
Fish fillets, etc.: fresh, chilled, frozen	10	114	14
Fish salted, dried or smoked	25	29	25
Refined sugar	357	466	395
Beer ('000 hectolitres)	8,016	6,474	6,038
Cigarettes (million)	15,274	15,473	13,102
Cement	2,871	2,539	1,579
Motor gasoline (petrol)	1,962	1,924	2,092
Distillate fuel oils	3,198	3,095	3,308
Residual fuel oils	1,415	1,379	1,265
Washing powders, detergents, softeners, etc.	237	202	192
Electric energy (million kWh)	39,316	36,638	36,364

Source: UN Industrial Commodity Statistics Database.

Finance

CURRENCY AND EXCHANGE RATES

Monetary Units
100 øre = 1 Danish krone (plural: kroner).

Sterling, Dollar and Euro Equivalents (31 December 2013)
£1 sterling = 8.914 kroner;
US $1 = 5.413 kroner;
€1 = 7.465 kroner;
100 Danish kroner = £11.22 = $18.48 = €13.40.

Average Exchange Rate (kroner per US $)
2011 5.3687
2012 5.7925
2013 5.6163

GENERAL BUDGET
(million kroner)

Revenue	2012	2013	2014*
Current taxes on income and wealth	551,664	561,711	589,967
Taxes on production and imports	304,769	318,118	318,212
Social security contributions	16,956	16,600	16,100
Interest and dividends	28,095	29,522	21,926
Other current revenue	93,096	85,818	86,378
Capital revenue (incl. taxes)	9,629	11,616	11,621
Total	1,004,209	1,023,385	1,044,204

Expenditure	2012	2013	2014*
General public services	167,107	134,160	134,689
Defence	27,306	27,805	23,925
Public order and safety	20,366	23,080	22,024
Education	142,676	144,275	148,003
Health	152,263	154,766	158,445
Social protection	459,520	474,663	480,967
Housing and community amenities	6,560	7,086	10,295
Religious, recreational and cultural services	29,340	28,935	28,666
Economic services	66,199	67,091	67,571
Environmental protection	8,280	8,414	7,975
Total	1,079,617	1,070,276	1,082,559

* Forecasts.

INTERNATIONAL RESERVES
(US $ million at 31 December)

	2010	2011	2012
Gold (national valuation)	3,017	3,368	3,560
IMF special drawing rights	2,343	2,244	2,256
Reserve position in IMF	826	1,327	1,513
Foreign exchange	70,334	78,109	82,368
Total	76,520	85,048	89,697

Source: IMF, *International Financial Statistics*.

MONEY SUPPLY
('000 million kroner at 31 December)

	2010	2011	2012
Currency outside depository corporations	52.81	52.47	54.58
Transferable deposits	771.60	722.89	796.97
Other deposits	216.02	212.35	178.00
Securities other than shares	457.02	338.52	331.47
Broad money	1,497.45	1,326.22	1,361.02

Source: IMF, *International Financial Statistics*.

COST OF LIVING
(Consumer Price Index; base: 2000 = 100)

	2010	2011	2012
Food and non-alcoholic beverages	124.2	129.1	134.6
Alcoholic beverages and tobacco	115.9	120.5	129.7
Clothing and footwear	98.0	99.2	100.9
Housing, water, electricity, gas and other fuels	132.5	137.6	141.2
Furnishings, household, etc.	116.8	118.3	119.4
Health	115.2	118.5	118.6
Transport	125.3	129.1	131.5
Communications	82.7	84.6	81.0
Recreation and culture	104.4	103.9	103.8
Education	173.6	181.7	188.0
Restaurants and hotels	129.4	132.7	137.7
Miscellaneous goods and services	134.5	137.9	143.4
All items	122.4	125.8	128.8

NATIONAL ACCOUNTS
(million kroner at current prices)

National Income and Product

	2010	2011	2012
Compensation of employees	985,366	996,583	1,007,670
Gross operating surplus and mixed income	530,602	544,375	564,802
Gross domestic income at factor cost	1,515,968	1,540,958	1,572,473
Taxes, less subsidies, on production	–320	–250	142
Gross value added	1,515,648	1,540,708	1,572,615
Taxes on products	260,034	266,110	269,067
Less Subsidies on products	15,631	15,044	16,099
GDP in purchasers' values	1,760,051	1,791,773	1,825,582
Factor income from abroad	154,620	169,782	164,479
Less Factor income paid abroad	113,977	121,273	109,363
Gross national income	1,800,694	1,840,282	1,880,698
Current taxes on income, wealth, etc. abroad (net)	3,699	3,906	3,993
Other current transfers to and from abroad (net)	–39,141	–39,805	–42,697
Gross national disposable income	1,765,251	1,804,383	1,841,995

Expenditure on the Gross Domestic Product

	2010	2011	2012
Government final consumption expenditure	509,600	508,173	519,475
Private final consumption expenditure	855,352	872,420	895,639
Changes in inventories	–3,176	3,538	–2,309
Gross fixed capital formation	300,659	313,718	320,024
Total domestic expenditure	1,662,435	1,697,849	1,732,829
Exports of goods and services	887,815	961,581	1,000,444
Less Imports of goods and services	790,199	867,657	907,690
GDP in purchasers' values	1,760,051	1,791,773	1,825,582

Gross Domestic Product by Economic Activity

	2010	2011	2012
Agriculture, forestry and fishing	21,622	21,733	22,696
Mining and quarrying	47,848	59,844	56,372
Manufacturing	170,992	170,656	173,516
Electricity, gas and water supply	41,277	37,212	38,212
Construction	69,025	75,235	74,706
Wholesale and retail trade and transport	297,380	296,324	305,260
Information and communication	67,428	67,200	67,080
Finance and insurance	95,418	98,164	107,623
Real estate and renting activities	161,220	167,173	168,779
Business services	117,681	123,642	128,385
Public administration, education, health and welfare	372,702	370,167	375,316
Other community, social and personal service activities	53,055	53,357	54,670
Gross value added at basic prices	1,515,648	1,540,708	1,572,615
Taxes, less subsidies, on products	244,403	251,065	252,968
GDP in purchasers' values	1,760,051	1,791,773	1,825,582

BALANCE OF PAYMENTS
(US $ million)

	2010	2011	2012
Exports of goods	95,030	111,245	105,450
Imports of goods	–85,905	–101,102	–96,947
Balance on goods	9,125	10,143	8,502
Exports of services	61,211	66,494	65,999
Imports of services	–52,310	–58,643	–58,180
Balance on goods and services	18,026	17,995	16,322
Primary income received	26,782	30,919	27,722
Primary income paid	–21,022	–23,124	–19,333
Balance on goods, services and primary income	23,786	25,789	24,711
Secondary income received	3,871	4,334	4,090
Secondary income paid	–9,474	–10,248	–10,052
Current balance	18,183	19,875	18,750
Capital account (net)	83	1,090	91
Direct investment assets	266	–12,795	–7,964
Direct investment liabilities	–11,766	13,556	2,754
Portfolio investment assets	–17,325	989	–26,138
Portfolio investment liabilities	15,943	–89	10,128
Financial derivatives and employee stock options assets	4,854	990	7,091
Other investment assets	–8,152	8,513	–1613
Other investment liabilities	21,507	–19,051	–1,604
Net errors and omissions	–19,313	–2,524	357
Reserves and related items	4,280	10,554	1,852

Source: IMF, *International Financial Statistics*.

External Trade

PRINCIPAL COMMODITIES
(distribution by SITC, million kroner)

Imports c.i.f.	2010	2011	2012
Food and live animals	51,377.2	56,168.8	59,022.4
Crude materials (inedible) except fuels	14,314.7	16,294.0	15,856.8
Mineral fuels, lubricants, etc.	38,787.3	53,570.0	57,817.6
Petroleum, petroleum products, etc.	32,847.9	43,466.6	49,617.5
Chemicals and related products	53,236.3	59,307.0	64,628.2
Medical and pharmaceutical products	18,964.3	20,545.5	23,143.0
Basic manufactures	66,540.2	75,163.4	74,459.7
Iron and steel	13,474.5	17,290.5	16,238.4
Machinery and transport equipment	147,049.2	154,826.0	159,476.9
General industrial machinery, equipment and parts	23,082.3	25,032.9	25,888.6
Office machines and automatic data-processing equipment	17,595.2	19,552.3	20,344.9
Telecommunications and sound equipment	17,740.5	19,305.5	20,884.9
Electrical machinery and parts	24,267.6	26,519.9	28,702.2
Road vehicles (incl. air-cushion vehicles) and parts	27,877.1	33,936.3	31,770.3
Miscellaneous manufactured articles	80,339.1	83,997.0	84,508.6
Clothing and accessories (excl. footwear)	24,227.3	26,129.4	26,608.1
Total (incl. others)	467,472.8	517,248.5	534,301.0

Exports f.o.b.	2010	2011	2012
Food and live animals	90,886.4	97,204.9	101,035.0
Meat and meat preparations	28,341.5	30,834.2	31,395.3
Crude materials (inedible) except fuels	24,049.7	27,581.9	28,975.0
Mineral fuels, lubricants, etc.	52,898.8	64,520.7	69,627.7
Petroleum, petroleum products, etc.	41,078.1	52,131.1	59,617.5
Chemicals and related products	86,624.7	94,802.1	105,096.2
Medicinal and pharmaceutical products	50,390.0	56,407.4	66,750.7
Basic manufactures	49,873.0	57,461.1	55,262.5
Machinery and transport equipment	134,705.7	152,037.3	148,805.9
Power-generating machinery and equipment	21,510.3	22,909.9	23,273.3
Machinery specialized for particular industries	17,970.2	19,101.1	19,674.7
General industrial machinery, equipment and parts	36,003.2	38,869.8	41,765.1
Electrical machinery and parts	20,357.9	22,400.0	23,027.3
Miscellaneous manufactured articles	84,936.4	91,576.8	90,451.4
Clothing and accessories (excl. footwear)	20,844.4	23,306.4	22,369.7
Total (incl. others)	538,321.2	600,069.1	614,673.8

PRINCIPAL TRADING PARTNERS
(million kroner)

Imports c.i.f.	2010	2011	2012
Belgium	15,403.9	16,406.5	16,183.6
China, People's Republic	36,293.9	36,291.9	37,730.2
Czech Republic	5,367.5	6,124.7	6,725.2
Finland	7,707.6	8,828.8	8,753.7
France (incl. Monaco)	15,112.0	16,847.4	16,034.2
Germany	96,579.2	106,456.4	111,032.4
India	4,116.1	5,319.4	4,447.7
Ireland	5,479.2	5,745.4	6,242.6
Italy	16,018.7	17,859.0	19,284.9
Netherlands	33,102.0	36,825.9	39,306.9
Norway	18,698.2	23,593.8	28,603.9
Poland	14,064.0	15,970.5	17,139.7
Russia	6,570.6	11,858.9	7,468.5
Spain	6,669.4	7,531.3	7,936.9
Sweden	61,967.6	69,105.8	71,699.5
Switzerland	4,777.2	4,744.1	4,634.7
Turkey	4,441.9	4,901.2	5,629.3
United Kingdom	28,136.9	32,327.9	29,860.9
USA	15,122.6	14,740.9	14,933.3
Total (incl. others)	467,472.8	517,248.5	534,301.0

Exports f.o.b.	2010	2011	2012
Australia	4,766.9	6,843.0	6,298.7
Belgium	7,460.8	8,276.1	8,514.3
Canada	6,822.6	6,335.8	4,495.4
China, People's Republic	13,389.9	15,141.5	17,370.2
Finland	13,017.0	13,910.8	14,495.2
France (incl. Monaco)	21,770.0	22,415.9	20,361.5
Germany	86,627.9	95,509.4	93,076.1
Hong Kong	8,022.1	9,165.2	10,844.7
Ireland	5,655.9	5,001.9	4,171.3
Italy	14,996.6	16,306.4	15,503.1
Japan	10,652.6	10,437.4	12,059.3
Netherlands	23,976.2	27,383.1	26,604.2
Norway	34,368.1	38,889.3	41,656.9
Poland	13,247.5	15,684.8	14,917.0
Russia	9,720.3	12,056.7	11,721.9
Singapore	2,175.0	7,356.5	3,757.2
Spain	12,325.8	13,073.6	11,360.1
Sweden	73,415.1	77,065.8	80,663.6
United Kingdom	43,438.9	57,510.7	59,603.1
USA	35,313.4	37,702.5	45,231.7
Total (incl. others)	538,321.2	600,069.1	614,673.8

Transport

RAILWAYS
(traffic)

	2010	2011	2012
Passengers carried ('000)	237,973	248,775	256,199
Passenger-km (million)	6,577	6,890	7,026
Goods carried ('000 tons)	8,121	9,277	7,983
Ton-km (million)	2,240	2,614	2,278

ROAD TRAFFIC
(motor vehicles in use at 1 January)

	2011	2012	2013
Private cars	2,163,676	2,197,831	2,237,122
Vans	441,455	426,688	417,016
Buses, coaches	14,496	14,014	13,485
Lorries	30,820	29,698	29,952
Tractors	12,891	12,862	12,589
Motorcycles and mopeds	203,608	200,597	199,243

SHIPPING

Flag Registered Fleet
(all registers, at 31 December)

	2011	2012	2013
Number of vessels	966	981	1,008
Total displacement ('000 grt)	11,781.2	11,803.4	12,721.7

Source: Lloyd's List Intelligence (www.lloydslistintelligence.com).

International Sea-borne Shipping*
(freight traffic, '000 metric tons)

	2010	2011	2012
Goods loaded	20,578	19,916	18,965
Goods unloaded	26,681	30,359	30,066

* Excluding international ferry traffic.

CIVIL AVIATION
(scheduled and charter traffic)

	2010	2011	2012
Aircraft movements ('000)	344	356	331
Passengers carried ('000)	13,335	14,045	n.a.
Passenger-km (million)	470	459	367
Cargo carried ('000 metric tons)	151	156	167

Tourism

FOREIGN TOURIST ARRIVALS
(at accommodation establishments)

Country of residence	2009	2010	2011
France	234,620	241,755	243,695
Germany	2,538,209	2,526,299	2,055,025
Netherlands	319,267	323,513	267,568
Norway	1,628,381	1,665,429	1,481,569
Sweden	1,241,798	1,336,600	1,176,246
United Kingdom	711,362	722,124	653,979
USA	512,034	505,805	531,196
Total (incl. others)	9,264,870	9,425,096	7,969,792

Tourism receipts (US $ million, excl. passenger transport): 5,853 in 2010; 6,580 in 2011; 6,162 in 2012 (provisional).

Source: World Tourism Organization.

Communications Media

	2010	2011	2012
Book production: titles*	12,593	12,859	n.a.
Daily newspapers:			
number	35	33	33
average circulation ('000 copies)†	1,471	1,402	1,248
Telephones ('000 main lines in use)	2,613.8	2,514.8	2,431.3
Mobile cellular telephones ('000 subscribers)	6,981.0	7,158.9	6,597.0
Internet subscribers ('000)	2,167.0	2,39.9	n.a.
Broadband subscribers ('000)	2,092.4	2,095.5	2,137.4

* Including pamphlets.
† On weekdays.

Source: partly International Telecommunication Union.

Education

(2011)

		Students		
	Institutions	Males	Females	Total
General schools	2,672	406,397	407,917	814,314
Basic schools, public	1,704	301,316	281,218	582,534
Basic schools, private	536	50,512	52,215	102,727
Continuation schools	261	13,477	13,444	26,921
Upper secondary schools	171	41,092	61,040	102,132
Vocational institutions of education	266	30,023	68,989	99,012
Social and health schools	45	5,443	35,000	40,443
Schools of teacher training and education science	25	8,935	23,428	32,363
Transport and navigation schools	9	887	64	951
Institutions of education within police and defence	6	1,656	352	2,008
Academies of fine art and music, library schools etc.	27	2,489	3,238	5,727
—continued				
Institutions of education within agriculture and food science	14	3,280	1,065	4,345
Colleges of social work	6	1,088	3,760	4,848
Engineering colleges and schools of architecture	11	6,245	2,082	8,327
Universities	14	68,903	78,415	147,318
Other schools	109	101,235	62,442	163,677
Total	2,938	606,558	617,763	1,224,321

Students (2012): Basic schools, public 574,743; Basic schools, private 107,401; Continuation schools 26,500; Upper secondary schools 102,464; *General schools total:* 811,108.

Teachers (basic schools, rounded figures, 2008): 62,000 (public/municipal 50,000, private 8,000, continuation 4,000) (Source: Ministry of Education, Copenhagen).

Directory

The Government

HEAD OF STATE

Queen of Denmark: HM Queen MARGRETHE II (succeeded to the throne 14 January 1972).

THE CABINET
(April 2014)

The Government is formed of the Socialdemokraterne (SD—Social Democrats) and Det Radikale Venstre (DRV—Social Liberals).

Prime Minister: HELLE THORNING-SCHMIDT (SD).

Minister of Economics and of the Interior: MARGRETHE VESTAGER (DRV).

Minister of Finance: BJARNE CORYDON (SD).

Minister of Foreign Affairs: MARTIN LIDEGAARD (DRV).

Minister of Taxation: MORTEN ØSTERGAARD (DRV).

Minister of Employment: METTE FREDERIKSEN (SD).

Minister of Justice: KAREN HÆKKERUP (SD).

Minister of Higher Education and Science: SOFIE CARSTEN NIELSEN (DRV).

Minister of Culture and of Ecclesiastical Affairs: MARIANNE JELVED (DRV).

Minister of Housing, Urban and Rural Affairs and of Nordic Co-operation: CARSTEN HANSEN (SD).

Minister of Education: CHRISTINE ANTORINI (SD).

Minister of Health: NICK HÆKKERUP (SD).

Minister of Defence: NICOLAI WAMMEN (SD).

Minister of Children, Gender Equality, Integration and Social Affairs: MANU SAREEN (DRV).

Minister of Business and Growth: HENRIK SASS LARSEN (SD).

Minister of Climate, Energy and Building: RASMUS HELVEG PETERSEN (DRV).

Minister of Food, Agriculture and Fisheries: DAN JØRGENSEN (SD).

Minister of Trade and Development Co-operation: MOGENS JENSEN (SD).

Minister of Transport: MAGNUS HEUNICKE (SD).

Minister of the Environment: KIRSTEN BROSBØL (SD).

MINISTRIES

Prime Minister's Office: Christiansborg, Prins Jørgens Gård 11, 1218 Copenhagen K; tel. 33-92-33-00; fax 33-11-16-65; e-mail stm@stm.dk; internet www.stm.dk.

Ministry of Business and Growth: Slotsholmsgade 10–12, 1216 Copenhagen K; tel. 33-92-33-50; fax 33-12-37-78; e-mail evm@evm.dk; internet www.evm.dk.

Ministry of Children, Gender Equality, Integration and Social Affairs: Holmens Kanal 22, 1060 Copenhagen K; tel. 33-92-93-00; fax 33-932-25-18; e-mail sikkermail@sm.dk; internet www.sm.dk.

Ministry of Climate, Energy and Building: Stormgade 2–6, 1470 Copenhagen K; tel. 33-92-28-00; fax 33-92-28-01; e-mail kebmin@kebmin.dk; internet www.kemin.dk.

Ministry of Culture: Nybrogade 2, 1203 Copenhagen K; tel. 33-92-33-70; fax 33-91-33-88; e-mail kum@kum.dk; internet www.kum.dk.

Ministry of Defence: Holmens Kanal 42, 1060 Copenhagen K; tel. 33-92-33-20; fax 33-32-06-55; e-mail fmn@fmn.dk; internet www.fmn.dk.

Ministry of Ecclesiastical Affairs: Frederiksholms Kanal 21, 1220 Copenhagen; tel. 33-92-33-90; internet www.km.dk/kirkeministeriet.

Ministry of Economic Affairs and the Interior: Slotsholmsgade 10–12, 1216 Copenhagen K; tel. 72-28-24-00; fax 72-28-24-01; e-mail oim@oim.dk; internet oim.dk.

Ministry of Education: Frederiksholms Kanal 21, 1220 Copenhagen K; tel. 33-92-50-00; fax 33-92-55-67; e-mail uvm@uvm.dk; internet www.uvm.dk.

Ministry of Employment: Ved Stranden 8, 1061 Copenhagen K; tel. 72-20-50-00; fax 33-12-13-78; e-mail bm@bm.dk; internet www.bm.dk.

Ministry of the Environment: Børsgade 4, 1215 Copenhagen K; tel. 72-54-60-00; fax 33-32-22-27; e-mail mim@mim.dk; internet www.mim.dk.

Ministry of Finance: Christiansborg Slotspl. 1, 1218 Copenhagen K; tel. 33-92-33-33; fax 33-32-80-30; e-mail fm@fm.dk; internet www.fm.dk.

Ministry of Food, Agriculture and Fisheries: Slotsholmsgade 12, 1216 Copenhagen K; tel. 33-92-33-01; fax 33-14-50-42; e-mail fvm@fvm.dk; internet www.fvm.dk.

Ministry of Foreign Affairs: Asiatisk Pl. 2, 1448 Copenhagen K; tel. 33-92-00-00; fax 32-54-05-33; e-mail um@um.dk; internet www.um.dk; incorporates Development Co-operation.

Ministry of Health: Holbergsgade 6, 1057 Copenhagen K; tel. 72-26-90-00; fax 72-26-90-01; e-mail sum@sum.dk; internet www.sum.dk.

Ministry of Higher Education and Science: Slotsholmsgade 10, 1216 Copenhagen K; tel. 33-92-97-00; fax 33-32-35-01; e-mail fivu@fivu.dk; internet fivu.dk.

Ministry of Housing, Urban and Rural Affairs: Gammel Mønt 4, 1117 Copenhagen K; tel. 33–92–93–00; e-mail mbbl@mbbl.dk; internet www.mbbl.dk.

Ministry of Justice: Slotsholmsgade 10, 1216 Copenhagen K; tel. 72-26-84-00; fax 33-93-35-10; e-mail jm@jm.dk; internet www.jm.dk.

Ministry of Taxation: Nicolai Eigtveds Gade 28, 1402 Copenhagen K; tel. 33-92-33-92; fax 33-14-91-05; e-mail skm@skm.dk; internet www.skm.dk.

Ministry of Transport: Frederiksholms Kanal 27, 1220 Copenhagen K; tel. 41-71-27-00; fax 33-12-38-93; e-mail trm@trm.dk; internet www.trm.dk.

Legislature

Folketing

Christiansborg, 1240 Copenhagen K; tel. 33-37-55-00; fax 33-32-85-36; e-mail folketinget@folketinget.dk; internet www.folketinget.dk.

President of the Folketing: MOGENS LYKKETOFT.

General Election, 15 September 2011

Party	Votes	% of votes	Seats
Venstre (Liberals)	947,725	26.73	47
Socialdemokraterne (Social Democrats)	879,615	24.81	44
Dansk Folkeparti (Danish People's Party)	436,726	12.32	22
Det Radikale Venstre (Social Liberals)	336,698	9.50	17
Socialistisk Folkeparti (Socialist People's Party)	326,192	9.20	16
Enhedslisten—de Rød-Grønne (Red-Green Alliance)	236,860	6.68	12
Liberal Alliance	176,585	4.98	9
Det Konservative Folkeparti (Conservative People's Party)	175,047	4.94	8
Kristendemokraterne (Christian Democrats)	28,070	0.79	—
Total (incl. others)	3,545,368*	100.00	179†

* Metropolitan Denmark only.

† Includes two members from the Faroe Islands and two from Greenland.

Political Organizations

Dansk Folkeparti (Danish People's Party): Christiansborg, 1240 Copenhagen K; tel. 33-37-51-99; fax 33-37-51-91; e-mail df@ft.dk; internet www.danskfolkeparti.dk; f. 1995 by defectors from the Progress Party; right-wing, populist; Leader KRISTIAN THULESEN DAHL.

Enhedslisten—de Rød-Grønne (Red-Green Alliance): Studiestræde 24, 1455 Copenhagen K; tel. 33-93-33-24; e-mail landskontoret@enhedslisten.dk; internet www.enhedslisten.dk; f. 1989 as an alliance of three left-wing parties: Danmarks Kommunistiske Parti, Socialistisk Arbejderparti and Venstresocialisterne; 25-mem. collective leadership; Spokesperson JOHANNE SCHMIDT-NIELSEN; 9,483 mems (2013).

Folkebevægelsen mod EU (People's Movement against the European Union): Tordenskjoldsgade 21, 1055 Copenhagen K; tel. 35-36-37-40; fax 35-82-18-06; e-mail fb@folkebevaegelsen.dk; internet www.folkebevaegelsen.dk; f. 1972; opposes membership of the EU, in favour of democracy and co-operation in Nordic and European regions, and worldwide; 21-mem. collective leadership; Sec.-Gen. POUL GERHARD KRISTIANSEN; 3,500 mems (2012).

Fremskridtspartiet (Progress Party): Stationsmestervej 11, 9200 Aalborg SV; tel. 70-26-20-27; fax 70-26-23-27; e-mail frp@frp.dk; internet www.frp.dk; f. 1972; right-wing; advocates deportation of Muslims from Denmark, gradual abolition of income tax, disbandment of most of the civil service, and abolition of diplomatic service and about 90% of all legislation; Leader NIELS HØJLAND.

Det Konservative Folkeparti (Conservative People's Party): Christiansborg, 1240 Copenhagen K; tel. 33-37-43-44; e-mail info@konservative.dk; internet www.konservative.dk; f. 1916; advocates free initiative and the maintenance of private property, but recognizes the right of the state to take action to keep the economic and social balance; Leader LARS BARFOED.

Kristendemokraterne (Christian Democrats): Skindergade 24, 1159 Copenhagen K; tel. 33-27-78-10; fax 33-21-31-16; e-mail kd@kd.dk; internet www.kd.dk; f. 1970 as Kristeligt Folkeparti (Christian People's Party); present name adopted 2003; emphasizes the need for political decisions based on Christian ethics; Chair. STIG GRENOV.

Liberal Alliance: Christiansborg, 1240 Copenhagen K; tel. 33-37-49-95; e-mail leif.mikkelsen@ft.dk; internet liberalalliance.dk; f. 2007 as Ny Alliance by former members of Det Radikale Venstre and Det Konservative Folkeparti; present name adopted 2008; centrist, advocates liberalization of immigration policy and is pro-EU; Chair. LEIF MIKKELSEN.

Det Radikale Venstre (Social Liberals): Christiansborg, 1240 Copenhagen K; tel. 33-37-47-47; fax 33-13-72-51; e-mail radikale@radikale.dk; internet www.radikale.dk; f. 1905; supports international détente and co-operation within regional and world orgs, social reforms without socialism, income policy, workers' participation in industry, state intervention in industrial disputes, state control of trusts and monopolies, strengthening private enterprise; Nat. Chair. KLAUS FRANDSEN; Parliamentary Leader MARGRETHE VESTAGER.

Schleswigsche Partei/Slesvigsk Parti (SP) (Schleswig Party): Vestergade 30, 6200 Aabenraa; tel. 74-62-38-33; fax 74-62-79-39; e-mail sp@bdn.dk; internet www.schleswigsche-partei.dk; f. 1920; represents the German minority in North Schleswig; Chair. CARSTEN LETH SCHMIDT.

Socialdemokraterne (Social Democrats): Danasvej 7, 1910 Frederiksberg C; tel. 72-30-08-00; fax 72-30-08-50; e-mail partikontoret@partikontoret.dk; internet www.socialdemokraterne.dk; f. 1871; finds its chief adherents among workers, employees and public servants; c. 55,000 mems; Leader HELLE THORNING-SCHMIDT; Party Sec. LARS MIDTIBY.

Socialistisk Folkeparti (SF) (Socialist People's Party): Christiansborg, 1240 Copenhagen K; tel. 33-37-44-44; fax 33-32-72-48; e-mail sf@sf.dk; internet www.sf.dk; f. 1959; Chair. PIA OLSEN DYHR.

Venstre, Danmarks Liberale Parti (V) (Liberals): Søllerødvej 30, 2840 Holte; tel. 45-80-22-33; fax 45-80-38-30; e-mail venstre@venstre.dk; internet www.venstre.dk; f. 1870; supports free trade, a minimum of state interference, and the adoption, in matters of social expenditure, of a modern general social security system; Pres. LARS LØKKE RASMUSSEN; Sec.-Gen. CLAUS SØGAARD-RICHTER; 42,132 mems (Dec. 2011).

Diplomatic Representation

EMBASSIES IN DENMARK

Albania: Fredriksholms Kanal 4, 1220 Copenhagen K; tel. 33-91-79-79; fax 33-91-79-69; e-mail embassy.copenhagen@mfa.gov.al; internet www.albanian-embassy.dk; Ambassador ARBEN CICI.

Algeria: Hellerupvej 66, 2900 Hellerup; tel. 33-11-94-40; fax 33-11-58-50; e-mail ambalda@mail.tele.dk; internet www.algerianembassy.dk; Ambassador ABDELHAMID BOUBAZINE.

Argentina: Borgergade 16, 4th Floor, 1300 Copenhagen K; tel. 33-15-80-82; fax 33-15-55-74; e-mail edina@mrecic.gov.ar; Chargé d'affaires a.i. MARCELO JOAQUÍN PUJO.

Armenia: Ryvangs Allé 50, 2900 Hellerup; tel. 35-82-29-00; e-mail armembdk@mfa.am; Ambassador HRACHYA AGHAJANYAN.

Australia: Dampfærgevej 26, 2nd Floor, 2100 Copenhagen Ø; tel. 70-26-36-76; fax 70-26-36-86; e-mail genen.cpgn@dfat.gov.au; internet www.denmark.embassy.gov.au; Ambassador DAMIEN PATRICK MILLER.

Austria: Sølundsvej 1, 2100 Copenhagen Ø; tel. 39-29-41-41; e-mail kopenhagen-ob@bmeia.gv.at; Ambassador ERNST-PETER BREZOVSZKY.

Belgium: Øster Allé 7, 2100 Copenhagen Ø; tel. 35-25-02-00; e-mail copenhagen@diplobel.fed.be; internet www.diplomatie.be/copenhagen; Ambassador POL JEAN MARIE MARC DE WITTE.

Benin: Skelvej 2, 2900 Hellerup; tel. 39-68-10-30; fax 39-68-10-32; e-mail ambabenin@c.dk; internet www.ambabenin.dk; Ambassador ARLETTE DAGNON VIGNIKIN.

Bolivia: Store Kongensgade 81, 2nd Floor, 1264 Copenhagen K; tel. 33-12-49-00; fax 33-12-49-03; e-mail embocopenhagen@mail.dk; internet www.embassyofbolivia.dk; Ambassador (vacant).

Bosnia and Herzegovina: H. C. Andersens Blvd 48, 2nd Floor, 1553 Copenhagen V; tel. 33-33-80-40; fax 33-33-80-17; e-mail info@embassybh.dk; internet www.embassybh.dk; Ambassador KEMAL MUFTIĆ.

Brazil: Christian IX's Gade 2, 1st Floor, 1111 Copenhagen K; tel. 39-20-64-78; fax 39-27-36-07; e-mail brasemb.copenhague@itamaraty.gov.br; internet copenhague.itamaraty.gov.br; Ambassador MARCOS CAMACHO DE VICENZI.

Bulgaria: Gamlehave Allé 7, 2920 Charlottenlund; tel. 39-64-24-84; fax 39-63-49-23; e-mail embassy@bgemb.dk; internet www.mfa.bg/embassies/denmark; Ambassador ROUSSI IVANOV BOGOLUBOV (designate).

Burkina Faso: Svanemøllevej 20, 2100 Copenhagen Ø; tel. 39-18-40-22; fax 39-27-18-86; e-mail mail@ambaburkina.dk; internet www.ambaburkina.dk; Ambassador MONIQUE ILBOUDO.

Canada: Kr. Bernikows Gade 1, 1105 Copenhagen K; tel. 33-48-32-00; fax 33-48-32-20; e-mail copen@international.gc.ca; internet www.canadainternational.gc.ca; Ambassador ANDRÉ FRANÇOIS GIROUX.

Chile: Kastelsvej 15, 3rd Floor, 2100 Copenhagen Ø; tel. 35-38-58-34; fax 35-38-42-01; e-mail embassy@chiledk.dk; internet www.chiledk.dk; Ambassador JUAN SALAZAR SPARKS.

China, People's Republic: Øregårds Allé 25, 2900 Hellerup; tel. 39-46-08-89; fax 39-62-54-84; e-mail mail@chinaembassy.dk; internet www.chinaembassy.dk; Ambassador LIU BIWEI.

Côte d'Ivoire: Gersonsvej 8, 2900 Hellerup; tel. 39-62-88-22; fax 39-62-01-62; e-mail ambaivoire@mail.tele.dk; internet www.ambacotedivoire.org; Ambassador MINA MARIA LAURENT BALDÉ.

Croatia: Søtorvet 5, 1st Floor, 1371 Copenhagen K; tel. 33-91-90-95; fax 33-91-71-31; e-mail denmark@mvep.hr; internet dk.mvp.hr; Ambassador (vacant).

Cuba: Kastelsvej 19, 3rd Floor, 2100 Copenhagen Ø; tel. and fax 39-40-15-06; e-mail embacuba@dk.embacuba.cu; internet www.cubaembassy.dk; Ambassador CARIDAD YAMIRA CUETO MILIÁN.

Cyprus: H. C. Andersens Blvd 38, 1st Floor, 1553 Copenhagen V; tel. 33-91-58-88; fax 33-32-30-37; e-mail copenhagenembassy@mfa.gov.cy; internet www.cyprus-embassy.dk; Chargé d'affaires a.i. DEMETRIS SAMUEL.

Czech Republic: Ryvangs Allé 14–16, 2100 Copenhagen Ø; tel. 39-10-18-10; fax 39-29-09-30; e-mail copenhagen@embassy.mzv.cz; internet www.mfa.cz/copenhagen; Ambassador JIŘÍ BRODSKÝ.

Egypt: Kristianiagade 19, 2100 Copenhagen Ø; tel. 35-43-70-70; fax 35-25-32-62; e-mail embassy.copenhagen@mfa.gov.eg; Ambassador SALWA MOUFID KAMEL MAGHARIOUS.

Estonia: Frederiksgade 19, 4th Floor, 1265 Copenhagen K; tel. 39-46-30-70; fax 39-46-30-76; e-mail embassy.copenhagen@mfa.ee; internet www.estemb.dk; Ambassador KATRIN KIVI.

Finland: Skt Annæ Pl. 24, 1250 Copenhagen K; tel. 33-13-42-14; fax 33-32-47-10; e-mail sanomat.kob@formin.fi; internet www.finlandsambassade.dk; Ambassador ANN-MARIE NYROOS.

France: Kongens Nytorv 4, 1050 Copenhagen K; tel. 33-67-01-00; fax 33-93-97-52; e-mail cad.copenhague-amba@diplomatie.gouv.fr; internet www.ambafrance-dk.org; Ambassador FRANÇOIS ZIMERAY.

Georgia: Nybrogade 10, 1st Floor, 1203 Copenhagen K; tel. 39-11-00-00; fax 39-11-00-01; e-mail copenhagen.emb@mfa.gov.ge; internet www.denmark.mfa.gov.ge; Ambassador NIKOLOZ RTVELIASHVILI.

Germany: Stockholmsgade 57, POB 2712, 2100 Copenhagen Ø; tel. 35-45-99-00; fax 35-26-71-05; e-mail info@kope.diplo.de; internet www.kopenhagen.diplo.de; Ambassador MICHAEL ZENNER.

Ghana: Egebjerg Allé 13, 2900 Hellerup; tel. 39-62-82-22; fax 39-62-16-52; e-mail ghana@mail.dk; internet www.ghanaembassy.dk; Chargé d'affaires YAKUBU AL-HASSAN.

Greece: Hammerensgade 4, 3rd Floor, 1267 Copenhagen K; tel. 33-11-45-33; fax 33-93-16-46; e-mail gremb.cop@mfa.gr; internet www.greekembassy.dk; Ambassador ELENI SOURANI.

Hungary: Strandvejen 170, 2920 Charlottenlund; tel. 39-63-16-88; fax 39-63-00-52; e-mail mission.cph@mfa.gov.hu; internet www.mfa.gov.hu/emb/copenhagen; Ambassador LASZLO HELLEBRANDT.

Iceland: Strandgade 89, 1401 Copenhagen K; tel. 33-18-10-50; fax 33-18-10-59; e-mail icemb.coph@utn.stjr.is; internet www.iceland.org/dk; Ambassador STURLA SIGURJÓNSSON.

India: Vangehusvej 15, 2100 Copenhagen Ø; tel. 39-18-28-88; fax 39-27-02-18; e-mail hoc.copenhagen@mea.gov.in; internet www.indian-embassy.dk; Ambassador NIRAJ SRIVASTAVA.

Indonesia: Ørehøj Allé 1, 2900 Hellerup; tel. 39-62-44-22; fax 39-62-44-83; e-mail unitkomkph@kbricph.dk; internet www.kbricph.dk; Ambassador BOMER PASARIBU.

Iran: Svanemøllevej 48, 2100 Copenhagen Ø; tel. 39-16-00-03; fax 39-16-00-01; e-mail info@iran-embassy.dk; internet www.iran-embassy.dk; Ambassador HAMID BAYAT.

Iraq: Ehlersvej 9, 2900 Hellerup; tel. 39-45-02-70; fax 39-40-69-97; e-mail kbnemb@iraqmofamail.net; Ambassador Dr ALBERT ISSA NADHAR.

Ireland: Østbanegade 21, 2100 Copenhagen Ø; tel. 35-47-32-00; fax 35-43-18-58; e-mail copenhagenembassy@dfa.ie; internet www.embassyofireland.dk; Ambassador BRENDAN SCANNELL.

Israel: Lundevangsvej 4, 2900 Hellerup; tel. 88-15-55-00; fax 88-15-55-55; e-mail administration@copenhagen.mfa.gov.il; internet copenhagen.mfa.gov.il; Ambassador BARUKH BINAH.

Italy: Gammel Vartov Vej 7, 2900 Hellerup; tel. 39-62-68-77; fax 39-62-25-99; e-mail info.copenaghen@esteri.it; internet www.ambcopenaghen.esteri.it; Ambassador STEFANO QUEIROLO PALMAS.

Japan: Havneholmen 25, 9F, 1561 Copenhagen V; tel. 33-11-33-44; fax 33-11-33-77; e-mail km@ch.mofa.go.jp; internet www.dk.emb-japan.go.jp; Ambassador SEISHI SUEI.

Korea, Republic: Svanemøllevej 104, 2900 Hellerup; tel. 39-46-04-00; fax 39-46-04-22; e-mail korembdk@mofat.go.kr; internet dnk.mofat.go.kr; Ambassador BYUNG-HO KIM.

Latvia: Rosbæksvej 17, 2100 Copenhagen Ø; tel. 39-27-60-00; fax 39-27-61-73; e-mail embassy.denmark@mfa.gov.lv; internet www.am.gov.lv/copenhagen; Ambassador KASPARS OZOLINS.

Lithuania: Bernstorffsvej 214, 2920 Charlottenlund; tel. 39-63-62-07; fax 39-63-65-32; e-mail amb.dk@urm.lt; internet dk.mfa.lt; Ambassador VYTAUTAS PINKUS.

Luxembourg: Fridtjof Nansens Pl. 5, 1st Floor, 2100 Copenhagen Ø; tel. 35-26-82-00; fax 35-26-82-08; e-mail copenhague.amb@mae.etat.lu; internet copenhague.mae.lu; Ambassador GÉRARD LÉON PIERRE PHILIPPS.

Macedonia, former Yugoslav republic: Skindergade 28A, 1st Floor, 1159 Copenhagen K; tel. 39-76-69-20; fax 39-76-69-23; e-mail copenhagen@mfa.gov.mk; Ambassador ASAF ADEMI.

Malta: Lille Strandstræde 14B, 1254 Copenhagen K; tel. 33-15-30-90; fax 33-15-30-91; e-mail maltaembassy.copenhagen@gov.mt; Chargé d'affaires a.i. ELAINE CUTAJAR.

Mexico: Bredgade 65, 1st Floor, 1260 Copenhagen K; tel. 39-61-05-00; fax 39-61-05-12; e-mail info@mexican-embassy.dk; internet www.sre.gob.mx/dinamarca; Ambassador MARTHA JOSÉ IGNACIO MADRAZO BOLÍVAR.

Morocco: Øregårds Allé 19, 2900 Hellerup; tel. 39-62-45-11; fax 39-62-24-49; e-mail sifamaeco@yahoo.fr; Ambassador RAJA GHANNAM.

Nepal: Esplanaden 46, 2nd Floor, 1256 Copenhagen Ø; tel. 44-44-40-26; fax 44-44-40-27; e-mail embdenmark@gmail.com; internet www.nepalembassydenmark.org; Ambassador MUKTI NATH BHATTA.

Netherlands: Toldbodgade 33, 1253 Copenhagen K; tel. 33-70-72-00; fax 33-14-03-50; e-mail kop@minbuza.nl; internet denmark.nlembassy.org; Ambassador EDUARD JOHANNES MARIA MIDDELDORP.

Norway: Amaliegade 39, 1256 Copenhagen K; tel. 33-14-01-24; fax 33-14-06-24; e-mail emb.copenhagen@mfa.no; internet www.norsk.dk; Ambassador INGVARD HAVNEN.

Pakistan: Valeursvej 17, 2900 Hellerup; tel. 39-62-11-88; fax 39-40-10-70; e-mail parepcopenhagen@pakistanembassy.dk; internet www.pakistanembassy.dk; Ambassador MASROOR AHMED JUNEJO.

Poland: Richelieus Allé 12, 2900 Hellerup; tel. 39-46-77-00; fax 39-46-77-66; e-mail copenhagen.info@msz.gov.pl; internet www.copenhagen.polemb.net; Ambassador RAFAŁ WIŚNIEWSKI.

Portugal: Toldbodgade 31, 1st Floor, 1253 Copenhagen K; tel. 33-13-13-01; fax 33-14-92-14; e-mail embport@get2net.dk; Ambassador (vacant).

Romania: Strandagervej 27, 2900 Hellerup; tel. 39-40-71-77; fax 39-62-78-99; e-mail roemb@mail.tele.dk; internet copenhaga.mae.ro; Ambassador MATEI VIOREL ARDELEANU.

Russia: Kristianiagade 5, 2100 Copenhagen Ø; tel. 35-42-55-85; fax 35-42-37-41; e-mail embrus@mail.dk; internet www.denmark.mid.ru; Ambassador MIKHAIL VANIN.

Saudi Arabia: Omøgade 8, 2100 Copenhagen; tel. 39-62-12-00; fax 39-62-60-09; e-mail embassy@saudiemb.dk; Ambassador ABD AL-RAHMAN SAAD AL-HADLAG.

Serbia: Svanevænget 36, 2100 Copenhagen Ø; tel. 39-29-77-84; fax 39-29-79-19; e-mail serbianemb@city.dk; internet www.serbianembassy.dk; Ambassador DRAGANA IVANOVIĆ.

Slovakia: Vesterled 26–28, 2100 Copenhagen Ø; tel. 39-20-99-11; fax 39-20-99-13; e-mail emb.copenhagen@mzv.sk; internet www.mzv.sk/copenhagen; Ambassador RADOMÍR BOHÁC.

Slovenia: Amaliegade 6, 2nd Floor, 1256 Copenhagen K; tel. 33-73-01-20; fax 33-15-06-07; e-mail vkh@gov.si; internet kopenhagen.veleposlanistvo.si; Ambassador TONE KAJZER.

South Africa: Gammel Vartov Vej 8, POB 128, 2900 Hellerup; tel. 39-18-01-55; fax 39-18-40-06; e-mail copenhagen.general@dirco.gov.za; internet www.southafrica.dk; Ambassador SAMKELISIWE MHLANGA.

Spain: Kristianiagade 21, 2100 Copenhagen Ø; tel. 35-42-47-00; fax 35-42-47-26; e-mail emb.copenhague@maec.es; internet www.maec.es/embajadas/copenhague; Ambassador DIEGO MUÑIZ LOVELACE.

Sweden: Skt Annæ Pl. 15B, 1250 Copenhagen K; tel. 33-36-03-70; fax 33-36-03-95; e-mail ambassaden.kopenhamn@foreign.ministry.se; internet www.swedenabroad.com/copenhagen; Ambassador INGA ERIKSSON FOGH.

Switzerland: Richelieus Alle 14, 2900 Hellerup; tel. 33-14-17-96; fax 33-33-75-51; e-mail cop.vertretung@eda.admin.ch; internet www.eda.admin.ch/copenhagen; Ambassador DENIS FELDMEYER.

Thailand: Norgesmindevej 18, 2900 Hellerup; tel. 39-62-50-10; fax 39-96-06-80; e-mail info@thaiembassy.dk; internet www.thaiembassy.dk; Ambassador VIMON KIDCHOB.

Turkey: Rosbæksvej 15, 2100 Copenhagen Ø; tel. 39-20-27-88; fax 39-20-51-66; e-mail turkembassy@internet.dk; internet copenhagen.emb.mfa.gov.tr/; Ambassador MEHMET DÖNMEZ.

Uganda: Sofievej 15, 2900 Hellerup; tel. 39-62-09-66; fax 39-61-01-48; e-mail info@ugandaembassy.dk; internet www.ugandaembassy.dk; Ambassador WANUME KIBEDI ZAAKE.

Ukraine: Toldbodgade 37A, 1st Floor, 1253 Copenhagen K; tel. 33-18-56-20; fax 33-16-00-74; e-mail embassy.ua@mail.tele.dk; internet www.mfa.gov.ua/denmark; Ambassador MYKHAJLO V. SKURATOVSKYI.

United Kingdom: Kastelsvej 36–40, 2100 Copenhagen Ø; tel. 35-44-52-00; fax 35-44-52-93; e-mail enquiry.copenhagen@fco.gov.uk; internet ukindenmark.fco.gov.uk; Ambassador VIVIEN LIFE.

USA: Dag Hammarskjölds Allé 24, 2100 Copenhagen Ø; tel. 33-41-71-00; fax 35-43-02-23; e-mail usembassycopenhagen@state.gov; internet denmark.usembassy.gov; Ambassador JOHN RUFUS GIFFORD.

Venezuela: Toldbodgade 31, 3rd Floor, 1253 Copenhagen K; tel. 33-93-63-11; fax 33-37-76-59; e-mail emvendk@mail.dk; internet www.ve-ambassade.dk; Chargé d'affaires a.i. Dr ROGER CORBACHO MORENO.

Viet Nam: Bernstorffsvej 30C, 2900 Hellerup; tel. 39-18-39-32; fax 39-18-41-71; e-mail embvndk@hotmail.com; internet www.vietnamembassy-denmark.vn; Ambassador LAI NGOC DOAN.

Judicial System

In Denmark the judiciary is independent of the Government. Judges are appointed by the Crown on the recommendation of the Minister of Justice and cannot be dismissed except by judicial sentence.

The ordinary courts are divided into three instances, the District Courts, the High Courts and the Supreme Court. There is one District Court for each of the 24 judicial districts in the country. These courts must have at least one judge trained in law and they hear all criminal and civil cases. The two High Courts serve Jutland (West High Court) and the islands (East High Court), respectively. They serve as appeal courts for cases from the District Courts. Each case must be heard by at least three judges. The Supreme Court, at which at least five judges must sit, is the court of appeal for cases from the High Courts. Usually only one appeal is allowed from either court, but in special instances the Appeals Permission Board may give leave for a second appeal, to the Supreme Court, from a case that started in a District Court. Furthermore, in certain minor cases, appeal from the District Courts to the High Courts is allowed only by leave of appeal from the Appeals Permission Board.

There is a special Maritime and Commercial Court in Copenhagen, consisting of a President and two Vice-Presidents with legal training and a number of commercial and nautical assessors. The Land Registration Court, which was established in 2007, deals with disputes regarding the registration of titles to land, marriage settlements and mortgage payments. The West High Court serves as the appeal court for cases from the Land Registration Court.

An ombudsman is appointed by the Folketing (parliament) after each general election, and is concerned with the quality and legality of the administration of the laws and administrative provisions. Although the ombudsman holds no formal power to change decisions taken by the administration, he may, on a legal basis, express criticism of acts and decisions of administrative bodies. He is obliged to present an annual report to the Folketing.

Supreme Court: Prins Jørgens Gård 13, 1218 Copenhagen K; tel. 33-63-27-50; fax 33-15-00-10; e-mail post@hoejesteret.dk; internet www.domstol.dk/hojesteret; Pres. BØRGE DAHL; Pres. of the East High Court BENT CARLSEN; Pres. of the West High Court BJARNE CHRISTENSEN; Pres. of the Maritime and Commercial Court HENRIK ROTHE; Pres. of the Land Registration Court SØRUP HANSEN; Ombudsman JØRGEN STEEN SØRENSEN.

Religion

At 1 January 2013 some 79.1% of the population belonged to the Evangelical Lutheran Church in Denmark. In 2002 the second largest religion was Islam, constituting approximately 3% of the population (170,000 persons), followed by communities of Roman Catholics (36,000), Jehovah's Witnesses (15,000), Jews (7,000), Baptists (5,500), Pentecostalists (5,000) and the Church of Jesus Christ of Latter-day Saints (Mormons—4,500). The German minority in South Jutland and other non-Danish communities (particularly Scandinavian groups) have their own religious communities.

CHRISTIANITY

National Council of Churches in Denmark (Danske Kirkers Råd): Peter Bangs Vej 1, 2000 Frederiksberg; tel. 35-43-29-43; fax 38-87-14-93; e-mail dkr@danskekirkersraad.dk; internet www.danskekirkersraad.dk; f. 1939; associate council of the World Council of Churches; Chair. ANDERS GADEGAARD; Gen. Sec. MADS CHRISTOFFERSEN; 15 mem. churches.

The National Church

Evangelical Lutheran Church in Denmark (Den evangelisk-lutherske Folkekirke i Danmark): Nørregade 11, 1165 Copenhagen K; tel. 33-47-65-00; fax 33-14-39-69; e-mail folkekirken@folkekirken.dk; internet www.folkekirken.dk; the established Church of Denmark, supported by the state; no bishop exercises a presiding role, but the Bishop of Copenhagen is responsible for certain co-ordinating roles; the Council on International Relations of the Evangelical Lutheran Church in Denmark is responsible for ecumenical relations; membership at 1 January 2013 was 4,430,643 (79.1% of the population).

Bishop of København (Copenhagen): PETER SKOV-JAKOBSEN.

Bishop of Helsingør: LISE LOTTE REBEL.

Bishop of Roskilde: PETER FISCHER-MØLLER.

Bishop of Lolland-Falster: STEEN SKOVSGAARD.

Bishop of Odense: KRESTEN DREJERGAARD.

Bishop of Ålborg (Aalborg): HENNING TOFT BRO.

Bishop of Viborg: KARSTEN NISSEN.

Bishop of Århus (Aarhus): KJELD HOLM.

Bishop of Ribe: ELISABETH DONS CHRISTENSEN.

Bishop of Haderslev: NIELS HENRIK ARENDT.

The Roman Catholic Church

Denmark comprises a single diocese, directly responsible to the Holy See. At 31 December 2006 there were an estimated 36,707 adherents in the country (around 0.7% of the population). The Bishop participates in the Scandinavian Episcopal Conference (based in Sweden).

Bishop of København (Copenhagen): Rt Rev. CZESLAW KOZON, Katolsk Bispekontor, Gl. Kongevej 15, 1610 Copenhagen V; tel. 33-55-60-80; fax 33-55-60-18; e-mail biskop@katolsk.dk; internet www.katolsk.dk.

Other Churches

Apostolic Church in Denmark: Holbergsvej 45, 6000 Kolding; tel. 79-32-16-00; fax 79-32-16-01; e-mail servicecenter@apostolic.dk; internet www.apostolskkirke.dk; f. 1924; Nat. Leader JACOB VIFTRUP.

Baptistkirken i Danmark (Baptist Union of Denmark): Købnerhus, Lærdalsgade 7, 2300 Copenhagen S; tel. 32-59-07-08; fax 98-11-68-50; e-mail info@baptist.dk; internet www.baptistkirken.dk; f. 1839; Pres. MOGENS ANDERSEN; 5,100 mems.

Church of England: St Alban's Church, Churchill Parken 6, 1263 Copenhagen K; tel. 39-62-77-36; fax 39-62-77-35; e-mail chaplain@st-albans.dk; internet www.st-albans.dk; f. 1728; Chaplain Rev. JONATHAN LLOYD.

Church of Jesus Christ of Latter-day Saints (Mormons): Borups Allé 128, 2000 Frederiksberg; tel. 38-11-18-50; e-mail martin@wpmail.dk; internet www.mormon.dk; f. in Denmark 1850; Dir, Public Affairs MARTIN STOKHOLM; c. 4,500 mems in 22 congregations.

Danish Mission Covenant Church (Det Danske Missionsforbund): Rosenlunden 17, 5000 Odense C; tel. 66-14-83-31; fax 66-

14-83-00; e-mail ddm@email.dk; internet www.missionsforbundet.dk; Sec. MARIANNE MØRCH.

Methodist Church: Frederikshaldsgade 7, 8200 Århus N; tel. 86-16-69-16; internet www.metodistkirken.dk; f. 1910; Chair. JØRGEN THAARUP.

Moravian Brethren: The Moravian Church, Lindegade 26, 6070 Christiansfeld; tel. 74-56-14-20; fax 74-56-14-21; e-mail boeytler@post7.tele.dk; internet brødremenigheden.dk; f. in Denmark 1773; Pastor Rev. Dr JØRGEN BØYTLER.

Reformed Church: Reformed Synod of Denmark, Dronningensgade 87, 7000 Fredericia; tel. and fax 75-92-05-51; e-mail s.hofmeister@reformert.dk; internet www.reformert.dk; Moderator Rev. SABINE HOFMEISTER.

Religious Society of Friends (Quakers): Danish Quaker Centre, Drejervej 15, 4th Floor, 2400 Copenhagen NV; e-mail post@kvaekerne.dk; internet www.kvaekerne.dk; Clerk MOGENS CLAUSEN.

Russian Orthodox Church: Alexander Nevski Church, Bredgade 53, 1260 Copenhagen K; tel. 33-13-60-46; e-mail ruskirke@ruskirke.dk; internet www.ruskirke.dk; f. 1883; Rector Archpriest SERGY PLEKHOV.

Seventh-day Adventists: Syvende Dags Adventistkirken, Concordiavej 16, POB 15, 2850 Nærum; tel. 45-58-77-77; fax 45-58-77-78; e-mail adventistkirken@adventist.dk; internet www.adventist.dk; f. 1863; Pres. BJØRN OTTESEN.

ISLAM

The Muslim Faith Society (Det Islamiske Trossamfund i Danmark): Dortheavej 45–47, 2400 Copenhagen NV; tel. 38-11-22-25; fax 38-11-22-26; e-mail wakf@wakf.com; internet www.wakf.com; f. 1995.

JUDAISM

The Jewish Community (Det Mosaiske Troessamfund): Krystalgade 12, 1st Floor, 1172 Copenhagen K; tel. 33-12-88-68; e-mail mt@mosaiske.dk; internet www.mosaiske.dk; Chief Rabbi BENT LEXNER; Pres. FINN SCHWARZ; c. 2,400 mems.

The Press

There are more than 220 separate newspapers, including some 35 principal dailies. The average total circulation of daily newspapers in 2012 was 1,248,000 on weekdays.

Most newspapers and magazines are privately owned and published by joint concerns, co-operatives or limited liability companies. The main concentration of papers is held by the Berlingske Group, which owns *Berlingske Tidende*, *B.T.* and *Weekendavisen*, and the provincial *Jydskevestkysten* and *Århus Stiftstidende*.

The largest-selling newspaper in Denmark is *Jyllands-Posten*, published in Viby, a suburb of Århus. Its main competitors are *Berlingske Tidende* and *Politiken*, both published in Copenhagen, but there is no truly national press. Copenhagen accounts for 20% of the national dailies and about one-half of the total circulation.

PRINCIPAL DAILIES

(circulation figures refer to Jan.–June 2011, unless otherwise indicated)

Aabenraa

Der Nordschleswiger: Storegade 30, POB 1041, 6200 Aabenraa; tel. 74-62-38-80; fax 74-62-94-30; e-mail redaktion@nordschleswiger.dk; internet www.nordschleswiger.dk; f. 1946; German; Editor-in-Chief GWYN NISSEN; circ. 2,230.

Ålborg
(Aalborg)

Nordjyske Stiftstidende: Langagervej 1, POB 8000, 9220 Ålborg Øst; tel. 99-35-33-00; fax 99-35-33-75; e-mail redaktion@nordjyske.dk; internet www.nordjyske.dk; f. 1767; adopted present name in 1999, following the merger of six regional dailies; mornings; Publr and Editor-in-Chief PER LYNGBY; circ. weekdays 51,980, Sundays 57,312.

Århus
(Aarhus)

Århus Stiftstidende: Banegårdspladsen 11, POB 3, 8000 Århus C; tel. 87-40-10-10; fax 87-40-13-21; e-mail red@stiften.dk; internet www.stiften.dk; f. 1794; evening and weekend mornings; Editor-in-Chief TURID FENNEFOSS NIELSEN; circ. weekdays 20,329, Sundays 24,754.

Esbjerg

Jydskevestkysten: Norgesgade 1, 6700 Esbjerg; tel. 79-12-45-00; fax 75-13-22-07; e-mail jydskevestkysten@jv.dk; internet www.jv.dk; f. 1917 as *Vestkysten*; merged with *Jydske Tidende* in 1991 to form present daily; morning; Editor-in-Chief MIKAEL KAMBER; circ. weekdays 60,312, Sundays 67,044.

Helsingør

Helsingør Dagblad: Klostermosevej 101, 3000 Helsingør; tel. 49-22-21-10; fax 49-26-65-05; e-mail redaktionen@hdnet.dk; internet www.helsingordagblad.dk; f. 1867; Editor-in-Chief KLAUS DALGAS; circ. 5,625.

Herning

Herning Folkeblad: Østergade 21, 7400 Herning; tel. 96-26-37-00; fax 97-22-36-00; e-mail hk@herningfolkeblad.dk; internet www.aoh.dk; f. 1869; evening; Editor-in-Chief VIBEKE LARSEN; circ. 11,880.

Hillerød

Dagbladet/Frederiksborg Amts Avis: Slotsgade 1, 3400 Hillerød; tel. 48-24-41-00; fax 48-25-48-40; e-mail frederiksborg@sn.dk; internet www.sn.dk; f. 1874; morning; Editor TORBEN DALBY LARSEN; circ. weekdays 39,025.

Holbæk

Holbæk Amts Venstreblad: Ahlgade 1C, 4300 Holbæk; tel. 88-88-43-03; fax 59-44-50-34; e-mail red.hol@nordvest.dk; internet www.nordvestnyt.dk; f. 1905; evening; Editor-in-Chief MOGENS FLYVHOLM; circ. 13,288 (2009).

Holstebro

Dagbladet Holstebro-Struer: Lægårdvej 86, 7500 Holstebro; tel. 99-12-83-00; fax 97-42-62-94; e-mail holstebro@bergske.dk; internet www.dagbladet-holstebro-struer.dk; evening; Editor-in-Chief HANS KRABBE; circ. 12,230.

Horsens

Horsens Folkeblad: Søndergade 47, 8700 Horsens; tel. 76-27-20-00; fax 75-61-07-97; e-mail redaktionen@hsfo.dk; internet hsfo.dk; f. 1866; evening; Editor ALEX PEDERSEN; circ. 13,571.

Kalundborg

Kalundborg Folkeblad: Skibbrogade 40–42, 4400 Kalundborg; tel. 88-88-44-00; fax 59-51-02-80; e-mail red.kf@nordvest.dk; internet www.nordvestnyt.dk; circ. 5,602.

København
(Copenhagen)

Berlingske Tidende: Pilestræde 34, 1147 Copenhagen K; tel. 33-75-75-75; fax 33-75-20-20; e-mail redaktionen@berlingske.dk; internet www.berlingske.dk; f. 1749; morning; Editor-in-Chief LISBETH KNUDSEN; circ. weekdays 100,811, Sundays 118,309.

Børsen: Møntergade 19, 1140 Copenhagen K; tel. 33-32-01-02; fax 33-12-24-45; e-mail redaktionen@borsen.dk; internet www.borsen.dk; f. 1896; morning; business news; Editor-in-Chief ANDERS KRAB-JOHANSEN; circ. 73,330.

B.T.: Pilestræde 34, 1147 Copenhagen; tel. 33-75-75-33; fax 33-75-20-33; e-mail osa@bt.dk; internet www.bt.dk; f. 1916; morning; independent; Editor-in-Chief OLAV ANDERSEN; circ. weekdays 66,547, Sundays 88,898.

Dagbladet Arbejderen: Ryesgade 3F, 2200 Copenhagen N; tel. 35-35-21-93; fax 35-37-20-39; e-mail redaktion@arbejderen.dk; internet www.arbejderen.dk; Editor-in-Chief BIRTHE SØRENSEN.

Dagbladet Information: Store Kongensgade 40C, POB 188, 1264 Copenhagen K; tel. 33-69-60-00; fax 33-69-60-79; e-mail inf-dk@information.dk; internet www.information.dk; f. 1943 (illicitly during occupation by Nazi Germany and then legally in 1945); morning; independent; Editor-in-Chief CHRISTIAN JENSEN; circ. 21,763.

Ekstra Bladet: Rådhuspladsen 37, 1785 Copenhagen V; tel. 33-11-13-13; fax 33-14-10-00; e-mail redaktionen@eb.dk; internet www.eb.dk; f. 1904; evening; Editor-in-Chief POUL MADSEN; circ. weekdays 66,764, Sundays 94,370.

Kristeligt Dagblad: Vimmelskaftet 47, 1161 Copenhagen K; tel. 33-48-05-00; fax 33-48-05-01; e-mail kristeligt-dagblad@kristeligt-dagblad.dk; internet www.kristeligt-dagblad.dk; f. 1896; morning; independent; Editor-in-Chief ERIK BJERAGER; circ. 26,952.

Politiken: Politikens Hus, Rådhuspladsen 37, 1785 Copenhagen V; tel. 33-11-85-11; fax 33-15-41-17; e-mail politiken.dk@pol.dk; internet www.politiken.dk; f. 1884; morning; Editor-in-Chief BO LIDEGAARD; circ. weekdays 98,973, Sundays 124,603.

Næstved

Sjællandske: Dania 38, 4700 Næstved; tel. 72-45-11-00; fax 72-45-11-17; e-mail red@sn.dk; internet www.sn.dk; f. 2005 by merger of *Næstved Tidende* (f. 1866) and *Sjællands Tidende* (f. 1815); Editor HELJE WEDEL; circ. 16,308.

Nykøbing

Lolland-Falsters Folketidende: Tværgade 14, 4800 Nykøbing F; tel. 54-88-02-00; fax 54-88-02-96; e-mail redaktion@folketidende.dk; internet www.folketidende.dk; f. 1873; evening; Editor LARS HOVGAARDHOV; circ. 17,072.

Morsø Folkeblad: Elsøvej 105, 7900 Nykøbing M; tel. 97-72-10-00; fax 97-72-10-10; e-mail mf@mf.dk; internet www.mf.dk; f. 1877; daily except Sun; Senior Editor LEIF KRISTIANSEN; circ. 4,936.

Odense

Fyens Stiftstidende: Banegårdspladsen, 5100 Odense C; tel. 66-11-11-11; fax 65-45-52-88; e-mail redaktion@fyens.dk; internet www.fyens.dk; f. 1772; adopted current name in 1852; morning; independent; Editor-in-Chief PER WESTERGÅRD; circ. weekdays 45,516, Sundays 53,452.

Randers

Randers Amtsavis: Nørregade 7, 8900 Randers; tel. 87-12-20-00; fax 87-12-21-21; e-mail redaktion@amtsavisen.dk; internet www.amtsavisen.dk; f. 1810; evening; independent; Editor-in-Chief TURID FENNEFOSS NIELSEN; circ. 8,211.

Ringkøbing

Dagbladet Ringkøbing-Skjern: Skt Blichersvej 5, POB 146, 6950 Ringkøbing; tel. 99-75-73-00; fax 99-75-74-30; e-mail ringkoebing@bergske.dk; internet www.dagbladetringskjern.dk; evening; Editor SØREN CHRISTENSEN; circ. 8,488.

Rønne

Bornholms Tidende: Nørregade 11–19, 3700 Rønne; tel. 56-90-30-00; fax 56-90-30-91; e-mail redaktion@bornholmstidende.dk; internet www.bornholmstidende.dk; f. 1866; evening; Editor-in-Chief DAN QVITZAU; circ. 9,960.

Silkeborg

Midtjyllands Avis: Papirfabrikken 18, 8600 Silkeborg; tel. 86-82-13-00; fax 86-81-35-77; e-mail slang@mja.dk; internet www.midtjyllandsavis.dk; f. 1857; daily except Sun.; Editor-in-Chief STEFFEN LANGE; circ. 12,364.

Skive

Skive Folkeblad: Gemsevej 7, 7800 Skive; tel. 97-51-34-11; fax 97-51-28-35; e-mail redaktion@skivefolkeblad.dk; internet www.skivefolkeblad.dk; f. 1880; Editor OLE DALL; circ. 10,268.

Svendborg

Fyns Amts Avis: Skt Nicolai Gade 3, POB 40, 5700 Svendborg; tel. 62-21-46-21; fax 62-22-06-10; e-mail post@faa.dk; internet www.fynsamtsavis.dk; f. 1863; Editor-in-Chief TROELS MYLENBERG; circ. weekdays 12,253, Sundays 12,544.

Vejle

Vejle Amts Folkeblad: Bugattivej 8, 7100 Vejle; tel. 75-85-77-88; fax 76-41-48-82; e-mail vaf@vejleamtsfolkeblad.dk; internet www.vejleamtsfolkeblad.dk; f. 1865; evening; Editor ALEX PEDERSON; circ. 12,547.

Viborg

Viborg Stifts Folkeblad: Vesterbrogade 8, 8800 Viborg; tel. 89-27-63-00; fax 89-27-64-80; e-mail viborg@bergske.dk; internet www.viborg-folkeblad.dk; f. 1877; evening; also publishes: *Viborg Nyt* (weekly); Editor LARS NORUP; circ. 9,084.

Viby

Jyllands-Posten: Grøndalsvej 3, 8260 Viby J; tel. 87-38-38-38; fax 87-38-31-99; internet www.jp.dk; f. 1871; independent; Editor-in-Chief JØRN MIKKELSEN; circ. weekdays 104,195, Sundays 135,038.

OTHER NEWSPAPERS

Den Blå Avis (East edition): Generatorvej 8D, 2730 Herlev; tel. 44-85-44-44; fax 44-85-44-15; e-mail rubrik.ost@dba.dk; internet www.dba.dk; 2 a week; circ. 73,000 (July–Dec. 2007).

Den Blå Avis (West edition): Axel Kiers Vej 11, 8270 Højbjerg; tel. 87-31-31-31; fax 86-20-20-02; e-mail rubrik.vest@dba.dk; internet www.dba.dk; Thur.; circ. 46,160 (July–Dec. 2007).

Weekendavisen: Pilestræde 34, 1147 Copenhagen K; tel. 33-75-25-33; fax 33-75-20-50; e-mail bwa@weekendavisen.dk; internet www.weekendavisen.dk; f. 1749; present name adopted in 1972; Fri.; Editor-in-Chief ANNE KNUDSEN; circ. 56,625.

POPULAR PERIODICALS

(circulation figures refer to July–Dec. 2012, unless otherwise indicated)

Ældre Sagen NU: Nørregade 49, 1165 Copenhagen K; tel. 33-96-86-86; fax 33-96-86-87; e-mail aeldresagen@aeldresagen.dk; internet www.aeldresagen.dk; 6 a year; members' magazine for senior citizens; Editor-in–Chief SANNA KJÆR HANSEN; circ. 460,000 (2013).

Alt for damerne: Hellerupvej 51, 2900 Hellerup; tel. 39-45-75-00; fax 39-45-74-80; e-mail alt@altfordamerne.dk; internet www.altfordamerne.dk; f. 1946; weekly; publ. by Egmont Magasiner; women's magazine; Editor-in-Chief TINA NIKOLAISEN; circ. 49,415.

Anders And & Co: Vognmagergade 11, 1148 Copenhagen K; tel. 70-20-50-35; fax 33-30-57-60; e-mail redaktion@andeby.dk; internet www.andeby.dk; weekly; children's magazine; Man. Editor FRANK KNAU; circ. 30,233.

Basserne: Vognmagergade 11, 1148 Copenhagen K; tel. 70-20-50-35; fax 33-30-57-60; e-mail basserne@tsf.egmont.com; internet www.basserne.dk; f. 1972; fortnightly; children and youth; Editor MARTIN BLEMSTED; circ. 12,363.

Billed-Bladet: Havneholmen 33, 1561 Copenhagen V; tel. 72-34-20-00; e-mail annemette.krakau@billed-bladet.dk; internet www.billedbladet.dk; f. 1938; weekly; publ. by Aller Press A/S; royal family and celebrity pictures; Editor-in-Chief ANNEMETTE KRAKAU; circ. 150,293.

Bo Bedre: Finsensvej 6D, 2000 Frederiksberg; tel. 70-22-02-55; e-mail bobedre@bobedre.dk; internet www.bobedre.dk; monthly; publ. by Bonnier Pub. A/S; homes and gardens; Editor-in-Chief ERIK RIMMER; circ. 73,663.

Familie Journal: Havneholmen 33, 1561 Copenhagen V; tel. 72-34-22-22; e-mail redaktionen@familiejournal.dk; internet www.familiejournal.dk; f. 1877; weekly; publ. by Aller Press A/S; Editor-in-Chief ANETTE KOKHOLM; circ. 163,048.

Femina: Havneholmen 33, 1561 Copenhagen V; tel. 72-34-23-23; e-mail redaktionen@femina.dk; internet www.femina.dk; f. 1873; weekly; publ. by Aller Press A/S; Editor-in-Chief CAMILLA KJEMS; circ. 47,576.

Gør Det Selv: Strandboulevarden 130, 2100 Copenhagen Ø; tel. 39-17-20-00; fax 39-21-23-07; e-mail gds@bonnier.dk; internet www.goerdetselv.dk; f. 1975; every 3 weeks; publ. by Bonnier Pub. A/S; home improvements; Editor RUNE MICHAELSEN; circ. 25,596.

Helse: Porschevej 12, 7100 Vejle; tel. 75-84-12-00; fax 75-84-12-29; e-mail info@helse.dk; internet www.helse.dk; f. 1955; 10 a year; social, mental and physiological health; Editor-in-Chief JESPER BO BENDTSEN; circ. 102,630 (2010).

Hendes Verden: Hellerupvej 51, 2900 Hellerup; tel. 39-45-75-52; fax 39-45-75-99; e-mail hv@hendesverden.dk; internet www.hendesverden.dk; f. 1937; weekly; publ. by Egmont Magasiner; for women; Editor IBEN NIELSEN; circ. 33,276.

Her & Nu: Hellerupvej 51, 2900 Hellerup; tel. 39-45-77-00; fax 39-45-77-17; e-mail herognu@herognu.com; internet www.herognu.com; weekly (Wed.); publ. by Egmont Magasiner; illustrated television and film guide; news about the royal family and celebrities; Editor-in-Chief MICHAEL RASMUSSEN; circ. 95,381.

Hjemmet (The Home): Hellerupvej 51, 2900 Hellerup; tel. 39-45-76-02; fax 39-45-76-60; e-mail red@hjemmet.dk; internet www.hjemmet.dk; weekly; publ. by Egmont Magasiner; Editor-in-Chief MARIANNE GRAM; circ. 112,265.

I form: Strandboulevarden 130, 2100 Copenhagen Ø; tel. 39-17-20-00; fax 39-17-23-11; e-mail iform@iform.dk; internet www.iform.dk; f. 1987; 17 a year; publ. by Bonnier Pub. A/S; sport, health, nutrition, sex, psychology; Editor KAREN LYAGER HORVE; circ. 37,223.

Idé-nyt: Gl. Klausdalsbrovej 495, 2730 Herlev; tel. 44-53-40-00; fax 44-92-11-21; e-mail idenyt@idenyt.dk; internet www.idenyt.dk; f. 1973; 10 a year; free magazine (regional editions); homes and gardens; Editor-in-Chief ANNA-LISE AAEN; circ. 1,609,373.

Illustreret Videnskab: Strandboulevarden 130, 2100 Copenhagen Ø; tel. 39-17-20-00; fax 39-17-23-12; e-mail sebastian.relster@illvid.dk; internet www.illvid.dk; f. 1984; 15 a year; publ. by Bonnier Pub. A/S; popular science; Chief Editor SEBASTIAN RELSTER; circ. 46,812.

Kig Ind: Havneholmen 33, 1561 Copenhagen V; tel. 72-34-20-00; e-mail redaktionen@ki.aller.dk; internet www.kigind.com; weekly (Wed.); publ. by Aller Press A/S; fashion and celebrity news; Editor-in-Chief KATRINE MEMBORG; circ. 33,963.

Mad og Bolig: Havneholmen 33, 1561 Copenhagen V; tel. 72-34-27-61; e-mail mb@madogbolig.dk; internet www.madogbolig.dk; f. 1991; 12 a year; publ. by Aller Press A/S; gastronomy, wine, interiors and travel; Editor CHARLOTTE RIPARBELLI; circ. 27,689.

Modemagasinet IN: Havneholmen 33, 1561 Copenhagen V; tel. 72-34-20-50; fax 72-34-20-03; e-mail trine.nygaard@in.dk; internet www.in.dk; monthly; publ. by Aller Press A/S; fashion; Editor-in-Chief TRINE NYGAARD; circ. 30,094.

Motor: Firskovvej 32, 2800 Kgs Lyngby; tel. 45-27-07-07; fax 45-27-09-89; e-mail fdm@fdm.dk; internet www.fdm.dk; f. 1906; monthly; cars and motoring; Editor-in-Chief BO CHRISTIAN KOCH; circ. 242,862.

Samvirke: Høgevej 5D, 3400 Hillerød; tel. 48-22-44-50; fax 48-22-43-47; e-mail samvirke.redaktionen@fdb.dk; internet www.samvirke.dk; f. 1928; consumer monthly; Editor-in-Chief PIA THORSEN JACOBSEN; circ. 488,267 (2008/09).

Se og Hør: Havneholmen 33, 1561 Copenhagen V; tel. 72-34-20-00; e-mail redaktionen@seoghoer.dk; internet www.seoghoer.dk; f. 1940; weekly (Thur.); publ. by Aller Press A/S; news and TV; Editor-in-Chief KIM HENNINGSEN; circ. 124,414.

Søndag: Havneholmen 33, 1561 Copenhagen V; tel. 72-34-20-00; fax 72-34-20-05; e-mail soendag@soendag.dk; internet www.soendag.dk; f. 1921; weekly (Mon.); publ. by Aller Press A/S; women's magazine; Editor STINNE BJERRE; circ. 70,065.

Tipsbladet: Tomsgårdsvej 19, st. tv., 2400 Copenhagen NV; tel. 49-70-89-00; fax 49-70-88-30; e-mail redaktion@tipsbladet.dk; internet www.tipsbladet.dk; f. 1948; weekly (Fri.); sport; Editor-in-Chief TROELS BAGER THØGERSEN.

Ud og Se: DSB, Sølvgade 40, 1349 København K; tel. 70-13-14-15; e-mail udogse@dsb.dk; internet www.dsb.dk/om-dsb/dsb-i-medierne/ud-og-Se; monthly; travel; publ. by DSB (Danish State Railways); circ. 183,394 (2010).

Ude og Hjemme: Havneholmen 33, 1561 Copenhagen V; tel. 72-34-20-00; e-mail redaktionen@udeoghjemme.dk; internet www.udeoghjemme.dk; f. 1926; family weekly; publ. by Aller Press A/S; Editor-in-Chief KAJ ELGAARD; circ. 117,733.

Vi Unge: Havneholmen 33, 1561 Copenhagen V; tel. 72-34-20-00; e-mail redaktionen@viunge.dk; internet www.viunge.dk; 17 a year; publ. by Aller Press A/S; for teenage girls; Editor-in-Chief TINA DINES APPELT; circ. 35,075.

SPECIALIST PERIODICALS

ABF-Nyt: Vester Farimagsgade 1, 8 sal, POB 239, 1501 Copenhagen V; tel. 33-86-28-30; e-mail abf@abf-rep.dk; internet www.abf-rep.dk; for members of Andelsboligforeningernes Fællesrepræsentation (ABF, Co-operative Housing Association); 4 a year; Editor LISE CLEMMENSEN; circ. 93,669 (2011/12).

Aktuel Elektronik: Naverland 35, 2600 Glostrup; tel. 43-24-26-28; fax 43-24-26-26; e-mail rsh@techmedia.dk; internet www.techmedia.dk; 16 a year; computing and information technology; Editor-in-Chief ROLF SYLVESTER-HVID; circ. 6,502 (July–Dec. 2007).

Alt om Data: Sejrøgade 7–9, 2100 Copenhagen Ø; tel. 33-74-71-03; fax 33-74-71-91; e-mail redaktion@altomdata.dk; internet www.altomdata.dk; f. 1983; 17 a year; Editor-in-Chief METTE EKLUND ANDERSEN; circ. 7,054.

Automatik: Glostrup Torv 6, 2600 Glostrup; tel. 43-46-67-00; fax 43-43-15-13; e-mail elo@folkebladet.dk; internet www.automatik.nu; engineering; 10 a year; Editor ELO THORNDAHL; circ. 20,256 (Jan.–June 2011).

Bådnyt: Dortheavej 59, 2400 Copenhagen NV; tel. 32-71-12-00; e-mail redaktionen@baadnyt.dk; internet www.baadnyt.dk; monthly; boats and sailing; Editor MORTEN BRANDT; circ. 10,381 (July–Dec. 2008).

Beboerbladet: Studiestræde 50, 1554 København V; tel. 33-76-20-00; e-mail beboerbladet@bl.dk; internet www.beboerbladet.dk; quarterly; for tenants in public housing; Man. Editor BENT MADSEN; circ. 559,231 (2011/12).

Beredskab: Hedelykken 10, 2640 Hedehusene; tel. 35-24-00-00; fax 35-24-00-01; e-mail bf@beredskab.dk; internet www.beredskab.dk; f. 1934; 6 a year; civil protection and preparedness; publ. by the Danish Civil Protection League; circ. 13,039 (2011/12).

Boligen: Studiestræde 50, 1554 Copenhagen V; tel. 33-76-20-00; fax 33-76-20-01; e-mail blboligen@bl.dk; internet www.blboligen.dk; 11 a year; publ. by BL—Danmarks Almene Boliger; housing asscns, architects; Editor BENT MADSEN; circ. 32,054 (2011/12).

BygTek: Stationsparken 25, 2600 Glostrup; tel. 45-43-29-00; fax 45-43-13-28; e-mail redaktion@odsgard.dk; internet www.odsgard.dk; 10 a year; building and construction; Editor-in-Chief PETER ODSGARD; circ. 21,396 (2009/10).

Computerworld: IDG Danmark A/S, Hørkær 18, 2730 Herlev; tel. 77-30-03-00; fax 77-30-03-01; e-mail redaktionen@computerworld.dk; internet www.cw.dk; f. 1981; 22 a year; computing; Editor-in-Chief LINE ØRSKOV; circ. 4,759 (Jan.–June 2012).

Cyklister: Dansk Cyklist Forbund, Rømersgade 5, 1362 Copenhagen K; tel. 33-32-31-21; e-mail cyklister@cyklistforbundet.dk; internet www.cyklistforbundet.dk; f. 1905; 4 a year; organ of Danish Cyclist Federation; Editor RIKKE RAVN FABER; circ. 12,182.

DLG Nyt: Axelborg, Vesterbrogade 4A, 1620 Copenhagen V; tel. 33-68-30-00; fax 33-68-30-00; e-mail information@dlg.dk; internet www.dlg.dk; 11 a year; farming; Editor-in-Chief ELSE DAMSGAARD.

Diabetes: Rytterkasernen 1, 5000 Odense C; tel. 66-12-90-06; fax 65-91-49-08; e-mail info@diabetes.dk; internet www.diabetes.dk; f. 1940; 4 a year; diabetes; Editor HELEN H. HEIDEMANN; circ. 73,000 (2012/13).

Effektivt Landbrug: Odensevej 29, 5550 Langeskov; tel. 70-15-12-37; fax 65-38-33-37; e-mail redaktion@effektivtlandbrug.dk; internet www.landbrugnet.dk; 21 a year; farming; Editor BØJE ØSTERLUND; circ. 31,407 (July–Dec. 2006).

Finans: Applebys Pl. 5, POB 1960, 1411 Copenhagen K; tel. 32-96-46-00; e-mail cjo@finansforbundet.dk; internet www.finansforbundet.dk; 11 a year; for employees in the financial sector; Editor-in-Chief CARSTEN JØRGENSEN; circ. 53,848 (Jan.–June 2013.

Folkeskolen: Vandkunsten 12, POB 2139, 1015 Copenhagen K; tel. 33-69-63-00; e-mail folkeskolen@dlf.org; internet www.folkeskolen.dk; f. 1883; 22 a year; teaching; publ. by Danish Teachers' Union; Editor HANNE B. JØRGENSEN; circ. 84,782 (Jan.–June 2012).

Havebladet: Frederikssundsvej 304A, 2700 Brønshøj; tel. 38-28-87-50; fax 32-28-83-50; e-mail info@kolonihave.dk; internet www.kolonihave.dk; 5 a year; publ. by Kolonihaveforbundet for Danmark; gardening; Editor PREBEN JACOBSEN; circ. 40,000 (2011/12).

Hunden: Parkvej 1, 2680 Solrød; tel. 56-18-81-00; fax 56-18-81-91; e-mail post@dansk-kennel-klub.dk; internet www.dansk-kennel-klub.dk; f. 1891; 10 a year; organ of Dansk Kennel Klub.

Ingeniøren: Skelbækgade 4, POB 373, 1503 Copenhagen V; tel. 33-26-53-00; fax 33-26-53-01; e-mail redaktion@ing.dk; internet www.ing.dk; f. 1892; weekly engineers' magazine; Editor-in-Chief ARNE R. STEINMARK; circ. 64,574 (Jan.–June 2012).

Jaeger: Hojnæsvej 56, 2610 Rødovre; tel. 88-88-75-00; fax 36-72-09-11; e-mail post@jaegerne.dk; internet www.jaegerforbundet.dk; monthly except July; hunting; Editor STIG TJELLEGAARD MØLLER; circ. 75,126 (Jan.–June 2012).

Jern og Maskinindustrien: Marielundvej 46E, POB 358, 2730 Herlev; tel. 70-11-37-00; fax 44-85-10-13; e-mail jm@jernindustri.dk; internet www.jernindustri.dk; 36 a year; iron and metallic industries; owned by Ofin A/S; Editor-in-Chief JESPER BERNSTORF JENSEN; circ. 15,952 (Jan.–June 2012).

Kommunalbladet: Weidekampsgade 8, 0900 Copenhagen C; tel. 33-30-49-00; fax 33-30-44-49; e-mail kommunalbladet@hk.dk; internet www.hk.dk/kommunal/kommunalbladet; 21 a year; municipal administration, civil servants; Editor LENE LUNDGAARD; circ. 59,864 (2008/09).

Komputer for Alle: Strandboulevarden 130, 2100 Copenhagen Ø; tel. 39-17-20-00; e-mail red@komputer.dk; internet www.komputer.dk; 18 a year; publ. by Bonnier Publications A/S; computers; Editor-in-Chief LEIF JONASSON; circ. 22,901 (July–Dec. 2012).

Kvæg: Vesterbrogade 6D, 2. sal, 1620 Copenhagen V; tel. 33-39-47-00; fax 33-39-47-49; e-mail kvaeg@dlmedier.dk; monthly; for cattle breeders and dairy farmers; Editor HENRIK LISBERG; circ. 3,870 (Jan.–June 2012).

Lederne: Vermlandsgade 65, 2300 Copenhagen S; tel. 32-83-32-83; fax 32-83-32-84; e-mail lh@lederne.dk; internet www.lederne.dk/magasinet; 11 a year; for managers; Editor-in-Chief ULLA BECHSGAARD; circ. 100,710 (2011/12).

Metal: Nyropsgade 38, 1602 Copenhagen V; tel. 33-63-20-00; e-mail metal@danskmetal.dk; internet www.danskmetal.dk; 4 a year; metal industries; Editor-in-Chief ANDERS F. GJESING; circ. 127,264 (2011/12).

Spejdersnus: Det Danske Spejderkorps, Arsenalvej 10, 1436 Copenhagen K; tel. 32-64-00-50; e-mail dds@dds.dk; internet www.dds.dk; 6 a year; organ of the Danish Guide and Scout Association; circ. 14,500.

Stat & Kommune Indkøb: Thyrasvej 33, 4684 Holmegaard; tel. 43-43-31-21; fax 45-65-05-99; e-mail saki@saki.dk; internet www.saki.dk; 6 a year; public works and administration; Editor DAN MORRISON; circ. 7,196 (2008/09).

STRIKKE Magasin: Nørregyde 3, 6000 Kolding; tel. 70-11-70-80; fax 73-99-66-22; internet www.altomhaandarbejde.dk; knitting; publ. by Jacobsen Publishers; Editor-in-Chief LENE VINHOLT.

Sygeplejersken: Skt Annæ Pl. 30, POB 1084, 1008 Copenhagen K; tel. 33-15-15-55; e-mail redaktionen@dsr.dk; internet www.sygeplejersken.dk; 14 a year; nursing; Editor-in-Chief SIGURD NISSEN-PETERSEN; circ. 73,184.

Ugeskrift for Læger: Kristianiagade 12, 2100 Copenhagen Ø; tel. 35-44-85-00; fax 35-44-85-02; e-mail ufl@dadl.dk; internet www

.ugeskriftet.dk; weekly; medical; Editor-in-Chief TORBEN KITAJ; circ. 24,373.

VieW: Park Allé 355, 2605 Brøndby; tel. 43-28-82-00; fax 43-63-27-22; e-mail redaktion@bilsnak.dk; f. 1976; 4 a year; cars; Editor SØS RIGHOLT ILUM; circ. 170,000 (2012).

NEWS AGENCY

Ritzaus Bureau I/S: Store Kongensgade 14, 1264 Copenhagen K; tel. 33-30-00-00; fax 33-30-00-01; e-mail ritzau@ritzau.dk; internet www.ritzau.dk; f. 1866; general, financial and commercial news; owned by all Danish newspapers; Chair. ERIK BJERAGER; Man. Editor LARS VESTERLØKKE.

PRESS ASSOCIATIONS

Danske Medier (Association of the Danish Media): Pressens Hus, Skindergade 7, 1159 Copenhagen K; tel. 33-97-40-00; fax 33-91-26-70; e-mail mail@danskemedier.dk; internet danskemedier.dk; f. 2012; formed by the merger of Danske Dagblades Forening, Dansk Magasinpresses Udgiverforening, Danske Specialmedier, Radioerne, Ugeaviserne and Digitale Publicister; Chair. EBBE DAL.

Publishers

Aarhus Universitetsforlag: Langelandsgade 177, 8200 Aarhus N; tel. 87-15-39-63; fax 87-15-38-75; e-mail unipress@au.dk; internet www.unipress.dk; reference, non-fiction and educational; Dir CARSTEN FENGER-GRØNDAHL.

Forlaget åløkke A/S: Porskærvej 15, Nim, 8740 Brædstrup; tel. 75-67-11-19; fax 75-67-10-74; e-mail alokke@get2net.dk; internet www.alokke.dk; f. 1977; modern languages and history; Man. Dir BERTIL TOFT HANSEN.

Akademisk Forlag A/S (Danish University Press): Vognmagergade 11, 4. sal, 1148 Copenhagen K; tel. 36-15-66-10; fax 33-43-40-99; e-mail info@akademisk.dk; internet www.akademisk.dk; f. 1962; history, health, linguistics, university textbooks, educational materials; Dir EBBE DAM NIELSEN.

Forlaget Apostrof ApS: Vognmagergade 11, 1148 Coepnhagen K; tel. 33-69-50-00; fax 36-15-67-26; e-mail kundeservice@lindhardtogringhof.dk; internet www.apostrof.dk; f. 1980; bought by Forlaget Carlsen A/S in 2013; psychotherapy and contemporary psychology, fiction and non-fiction for children; Dir CAMILLA SCHIERBECK.

Arkitektens Forlag: Pasteursvej 14, 6. sal, 1799 Copenhagen K; tel. 32-83-69-70; fax 32-83-69-41; e-mail arkfo@arkfo.dk; internet www.arkfo.dk; f. 1949; architecture, planning; Man. Dir SANNE WALL-GREMSTRUP.

Peter Asschenfeldt's nye Forlag A/S: Ny Adelgade 6–10, 1104 Copenhagen K; tel. 33-37-07-60; fax 33-91-03-04; e-mail asschenfeldt@dk-online.dk; fiction; Publr PETER ASSCHENFELDT.

Thomas Blom Forlag ApS: Skovenggaardsvej 8, 9490 Pandrup; tel. 98-24-85-25; fax 98-24-80-60; e-mail thomas@thomasblom.dk; internet www.thomasblom.dk; fiction, non-fiction, children's books, talking books; Publrs CONNIE BLOM, THOMAS BLOM.

Bogans Forlag: Egholmvej 5A, 8883 Gjern; tel. 86-27-65-00; fax 86-27-65-37; e-mail mail@hovedland.dk; f. 1974; imprint of Forlaget Hovedland; general paperbacks, popular science, non-fiction, humour, health; Publr EVAN BOGAN.

Borgens Forlag A/S: Mosedalvej 15, 3. sal, 2500 Valby, Copenhagen; tel. 30-37-05-05; fax 36-15-36-29; e-mail post@borgen.dk; internet www.borgen.dk; f. 1948; fiction, poetry, children's books, humour, general non-fiction; Man. Dir NIELS BORGEN.

Carit Andersens Forlag A/S: Kirke Værløsevej 38, 3500 Værløse; tel. 35-43-62-22; fax 35-43-51-51; e-mail info@caritandersen.dk; internet www.caritandersen.dk; Publr ERIK ALBRECHTSEN.

Forlaget Carlsen A/S: Vognmagergade 11, 1148 Copenhagen K; tel. 33-69-50-00; fax 36-16-04-27; e-mail carlsen@carlsen.dk; internet www.carlsen.dk; children's books.

Cicero (Rosinante&Co): Købmagergade 62, 1019 Copenhagen; tel. 33-41-18-00; fax 33-41-18-01; e-mail niels@cicero.dk; internet www.cicero.dk; f. 1902; fiction, non-fiction, art, culture; Man. Dir JAKOB MALLING LAMBERT.

DA-Forlag/Dansk Arbejdsgiverforening: Vester Voldgade 113, 1790 Copenhagen V; tel. 33-38-92-24; fax 33-91-09-32; e-mail forlagshop@da.dk; internet www.daforlag.dk; non-fiction and reference; Dir BRITT KARDEL HETTING.

Dafolo A/S: Suderbovej 22–24, 9900 Frederikshavn; tel. 96-20-66-66; fax 98-42-97-11; e-mail dafolo@dafolo.dk; internet www.dafolo.dk; educational books; Dir HANS CHRISTIAN HØJSLET.

Dansk BiblioteksCenter A/S (DBC): Tempovej 7–11, 2750 Ballerup; tel. 44-86-77-77; fax 44-86-76-93; e-mail dbc@dbc.dk; internet www.dbc.dk; f. 1991; bibliographic data, information services; CEO MOGENS BRABRAND JENSEN.

Dansk Psykologisk Forlag: Knabrostraede 3, 1st Floor, 1210 Copenhagen; tel. 45-46-00-50; e-mail info@dpf.dk; internet www.dpf.dk; f. 1949; educational books, health, psychology; Man. Dir HENRIK SKOVDAHL HANSEN.

Det Danske Bibelselskab/Det Kongelige Vajsenhus' Forlag: Frederiksborggade 50, 1360 Copenhagen K; tel. 33-12-78-35; e-mail bibelselskabet@bibelselskabet.dk; internet www.bibelselskabet.dk; bibles, religious and liturgical books, children's books; Dir MORTEN THOMSEN HØJSGAARD.

Dansklæreforeningens Forlag: Rathsacksvej 7, 1862 Frederiksberg C; tel. 33-79-00-10; fax 33-27-60-79; e-mail dansklf@dansklf.dk; internet www.dansklf.dk; art, culture, school books, non-fiction; Editor-in-Chief HELLE SVANE.

Forlaget Flachs: Holte Midtpunkt 20, 2. sal, 2840 Holte; tel. 45-42-48-30; fax 45-42-48-29; e-mail flachs@flachs.dk; internet www.flachs.dk; f. 1986; fiction, non-fiction, reference, educational and children's books; Publrs ALLAN FLACHS, ANETTE FLACHS.

Forlaget Palle Fogtdal A/S: Østergade 22, 1100 Copenhagen K; tel. 33-15-39-15; fax 33-93-35-05; e-mail pallefogtdal@pallefogtdal.dk; Danish history, photography; Man. Dir PALLE FOGTDAL.

Forum (Rosinante&Co): Købmagergade 62, 1019 Copenhagen K; tel. 33-41-18-00; fax 33-41-18-01; f. 1940; history, fiction, biographies, quality paperbacks and children's books; Man. Dir JAKOB MALLING LAMBERT.

G.E.C. Gad Forlag A/S: Fiolstræde 31–33, 1171 Copenhagen K; tel. 77-66-60-00; fax 77-66-60-01; e-mail reception@gad.dk; internet www.gad.dk; f. 1855; biographies, history, reference, educational materials; Publ. Dir ULRIK HVILSHØJ.

Gyldendalske Boghandel, Nordisk Forlag A/S (Gyldendal): Klareboderne 3, 1001 Copenhagen K; tel. 33-75-55-55; fax 33-75-55-56; e-mail gyldendal@gyldendal.dk; internet www.gyldendal.dk; f. 1770; fiction, non-fiction, reference books, paperbacks, children's books, textbooks; Man. Dir STIG ANDERSEN.

Haase & Søns Forlag A/S: Løvstræde 8, 2nd Floor, 1152 Copenhagen K; tel. 33-14-41-75; fax 33-11-59-59; e-mail haase@haase.dk; internet www.haase.dk; f. 1877; educational books, audio-visual aids, non-fiction; imprints: Natur og Harmoni, Rasmus Navers Forlag; Man. Dir MICHAEL HAASE.

Edition Wilhelm Hansen A/S: Bornholmsgade 1A, 1266 Copenhagen K; tel. 33-11-78-88; fax 33-14-81-78; e-mail ewh@ewh.dk; internet www.ewh.dk; f. 1857; music books, school and educational books; Man. Dir LOUI TÖRNQVIST.

Høst & Søns Forlag (Rosinante&Co): Købmagergade 62, POB 2252, 1019 Copenhagen K; tel. 33-41-18-00; fax 33-41-18-01; e-mail info@rosinante-co.dk; internet www.hoest.dk; f. 1836; fiction, crafts and hobbies, languages, books on Denmark, children's books; Man. Dir JAKOB MALLING LAMBERT.

Forlaget Hovedland: Egholmvej 5A, 8883 Gjern; tel. 86-27-65-00; fax 86-27-65-37; e-mail mail@hovedland.dk; internet www.hovedland.dk; f. 1984; fiction, non-fiction, environment, sport, health, crafts; Publr STEEN PIPER.

Karnov Group Denmark A/S: Sankt Petri Passage 5, 1165 Copenhagen K; tel. 33-74-07-00; e-mail post.dk@karnovgroup.com; internet www.karnovgroup.dk; print and online publications for legal, auditing and accounting professionals; Man. Dir NEIL STORY.

Forlaget Klematis A/S: Østre Skovvej 1, 8240 Risskov; tel. 86-17-54-55; fax 86-17-59-59; e-mail klematis@klematis.dk; internet www.klematis.dk; f. 1987; fiction, non-fiction, crafts, children's books; Dir CLAUS DALBY.

Forlaget Per Kofod ApS: Strandgade 32A, 3000 Helsingør; tel. 33-32-70-27; e-mail info@per-kofod.com; internet www.per-kofod.com; f. 1986; fiction, non-fiction, art and culture; Publr PER KOFOD.

Kroghs Forlag A/S: Chr Hansensvej 3, 7100 Vejle; tel. 75-82-39-00; e-mail kf@kroghsforlag.dk; internet www.kroghsforlag.dk; education, management.

Lindhardt og Ringhof A/S: Vognmagergade 11, 1148 Copenhagen K; tel. 33-69-50-00; fax 33-69-50-01; e-mail info@lindhardtogringhof.dk; internet www.lindhardtogringhof.dk; f. 1971; merged with Aschehoug Dansk Forlag A/S in 2007; general fiction and non-fiction; imprints: Akademisk Forlag, Børsens Forlag, Sesam, Athene, Alinea, Forlag Malling Beck, Alfabeta, Carlsen, Aschehoug; Man. Dir LARS BOESGAARD.

Forlagsgruppen Lohse: Korskærvej 25, 7000 Fredericia; tel. 75-93-44-55; fax 75-92-42-75; e-mail info@lohse.dk; internet www.lohse.dk; f. 1868; imprints: Credo, Fokal, Kolon, Lohse, LogosMedia, Refleks; religion, children's books, biographies, devotional novels; Editorial Dir THOMAS B. MIKKELSEN.

Forlaget Lotus: Bryggervangen 76, 2100 Copenhagen Ø; tel. 29-61-20-01; e-mail fialotus@post7.tele.dk; internet www.forlagetlotus.dk;

management, health, religion, the occult, educational; Publr FINN ANDERSEN.

Magnus Informatik A/S: Nyhavn 16, 1051 Copenhagen K; tel. 70-20-33-14; fax 33-96-01-01; e-mail magnus@magnus.dk; internet www.magnus.dk; f. 1962; guidebooks, journals, law; Man. Dir PETER ALNOR.

Medicinsk Forlag ApS: Rønnebærvej 20, 4500 Nykøbing Sj; tel. and fax 40-81-80-60; e-mail anni@mediciniskforlag.dk; internet www.medicinskforlag.dk; astrology, medical and scientific books; Man. Dir ANNI LINDELØV.

Forlaget Modtryk: Anholtsgade 4–6, 8000 Århus C; tel. 87-31-76-00; fax 86-19-91-38; e-mail forlaget@modtryk.dk; internet www.modtryk.dk; f. 1972; children's and school books, fiction, thrillers and non-fiction; Man. Dir ILSE NØRR.

Nyt Nordisk Forlag-Arnold Busck A/S: Pilestræde 52, 3rd Floor, 1112 Copenhagen K; tel. 33-43-20-00; fax 33-14-01-15; e-mail nnf@nytnordiskforlag.dk; internet www.nytnordiskforlag.dk; f. 1896; textbooks, school books, guidebooks, fiction and non-fiction; Man. Dir JESPER T. FENSVIG; Dir JOAKIM WERNER.

Nyt Teknisk Forlag A/S: Ny Vestergade 17, 1471 Copenhagen K; tel. 63-15-17-00; fax 63-15-17-33; e-mail info@nyttf.dk; internet www.nyttf.dk; f. 1948; owned by Erhvervsskolernes Forlag; technical books, reference, educational, science, popular science; Man. Dir THOMAS SKYTTE.

Hans Reitzels Forlag A/S: Klareboderne 5, 1001 Copenhagen K; tel. 33-75-55-60; fax 33-38-28-08; e-mail hrf@hansreitzel.dk; internet www.hansreitzel.dk; f. 1949; education, philosophy, psychology, sociology; Publ. Dir HENRIETTE THIESEN.

Forlaget Rhodos A/S: Holtegaard, Hørsholmvej 17, 3050 Humlebæk; tel. 32-54-30-20; fax 32-54-30-22; e-mail rhodos@rhodos.dk; internet www.rhodos.dk; f. 1959; university books, art, science, fiction, poetry; Dir RUBEN BLAEDEL.

Samleren (Rosinante&Co): Købmagergade 62, POB 2252, 1019 Copenhagen K; tel. 33-41-18-00; fax 33-41-18-01; e-mail samleren@samleren.dk; internet www.samleren.dk; Danish and foreign fiction, contemporary history and politics, biographies; Man. Dir JAKOB MALLING LAMBERT.

Scandinavia: Drejervej 15, 3. sal, 2400 Copenhagen NV; tel. 31-23-33-80; fax 35-31-03-34; e-mail knud@scanpublishing.dk; internet www.scanpublishing.dk; f. 1973; children's books, religion, Hans Christian Andersen; Publr JØRGEN VIUM OLESEN.

Det Schønbergske Forlag A/S: Pilestræde 52, 3rd Floor, 1112 Copenhagen K; tel. 33-43-20-00; fax 33-14-01-15; e-mail schoenberg@nytnordiskforlag.dk; f. 1857; division of Nyt Nordisk Forlag-Arnold Busck A/S; fiction, humour, psychology, biography, children's books, paperbacks, textbooks; Man. Dir JESPER TOFT FENSVIG.

Special-pædagogisk Forlag: Birk Centerpark 32, 7400 Herning; tel. 97-12-84-33; fax 97-21-01-07; e-mail forlag@spf-herning.dk; internet www.spf-herning.dk/; textbooks; Dir TORBEN THUESEN.

Strandbergs Forlag ApS: Skodsborgparken 12, 2942 Skodsborg; tel. 45-89-47-60; fax 45-89-47-01; e-mail niels@strandbergsforlag.dk; internet www.strandbergsforlag.dk; f. 1861; cultural history, travel; Publr NIELS NØRGAARD.

Tiderne Skifter: Læderstræde 5, 1. sal, 1201 Copenhagen K; tel. 33-18-63-90; fax 33-18-63-91; e-mail tiderneskifter@tiderneskifter.dk; internet www.tiderneskifter.dk; f. 1973; fiction, sexual and cultural politics, psychology, science, religion, arts; Man. Dir CLAUS CLAUSEN.

Unitas Forlag: Frederiksberg Alle 10, 1820 Frederiksberg; tel. 33-24-92-50; fax 33-25-06-07; e-mail unitas@unitasforlag.dk; internet www.unitasforlag.dk; religion, spirituality, education, children's books.

Forlaget Vindrose A/S: Mosedalvej 15, 3rd Floor, 2500 Valby, Copenhagen; tel. 30-37-05-05; fax 36-15-36-29; e-mail post@borgen.dk; internet www.borgen.dk; f. 1980; acquired by Borgens Forlag in 1989; general trade, fiction and non-fiction; Man. Dir NIELS BORGEN.

Forlag Wiboltts: POB 2587, 2100 Copenhagen Ø; tel. 31-39-11-21; e-mail info@wiboltt.com; internet wiboltt.com; f. 2003; spirituality.

Wisby & Wilkens–Mikro: Vesterled 45, 8300 Odder; tel. 70-23-46-22; fax 70-23-47-22; e-mail mikro@wisby-wilkens.com; f. 1986; children's books, crafts, fiction, health, humour, science, religion; imprint: Mikro (drama, poetry, humour); Publr JACOB WISBY.

PUBLISHERS' ASSOCIATION

Forlæggerforeningen: Børsen, 1217 Copenhagen K; tel. 33-15-66-88; e-mail danishpublishers@danishpublishers.dk; internet www.danskeforlag.dk; f. 1837; formerly Den danske Forlæggerforening; 56 mems, 2 associate mems; Chair. PER HEDEMAN; Man. Dir ULRIK HVILSHØJ.

Broadcasting and Communications

TELECOMMUNICATIONS

Hi3G Denmark ApS (3 DK): Scandiagade 8, 2450 Copenhagen SV; tel. 33-33-01-35; fax 33-33-01-55; internet www.3.dk; f. 2003; mobile cellular and other telecommunications services; 60% owned by Hutchison Whampoa Ltd (Hong Kong) and 40% owned by Investor AB (Sweden); CEO MORTEN CHRISTIANSEN.

TDC A/S: Teglholmsgade 1, 0900 Copenhagen; tel. 66-63-76-80; fax 66-60-32-39; e-mail investorrelations@tdc.dk; internet www.tdc.dk; f. 1995 as Tele Danmark A/S; present name adopted 2000; fixed-line and mobile cellular telecommunications, digital television and broadband internet access; fmrly state-owned telecommunications co; transferred to private ownership 1998; Chair. VAGN OVE SØRENSEN; Pres. and CEO CARSTEN DILLING.

Telenor A/S: Frederikskaj, 1780 Copenhagen V; tel. 72-10-01-00; fax 72-12-70-70; internet www.telenor.dk; f. 2009 following the merger of Sonofon (f. 1991) and Cybercity (f. 1995); subsidiary of Telenor ASA (Norway); mobile cellular telecommunications services; Man. Dir MAREK SLACIK; 1.7m. subscribers (2008).

Telia Nattjanster Norden A/B (Telia DK): Holmbladsgade 139, 2300 Copenhagen S; tel. 82-33-70-00; fax 82-33-70-09; internet www.telia.dk; subsidiary of Telia Sonera AB (Sweden); f. 1995; fixed-line and mobile cellular telecommunications, broadband internet access; Man. Dir SØREN ABILDGAARD.

BROADCASTING

Regulatory Authority

Kulturstyrelsen (Danish Agency for Culture): H. C. Andersens Blvd 2, 1553 Copenhagen V; tel. 33-73-33-73; fax 33-73-33-72; e-mail post@kulturstyrelsen.dk; internet www.kulturstyrelsen.dk; f. 2012 by merger of the Danish Arts Agency, the Heritage Agency of Denmark and the Danish Agency for Libraries and Media; under Ministry of Culture; Dir JENS THORHAUGE.

Radio

Digital audio broadcasting (DAB) began in Denmark in 2002, with 10 transmitters in operation covering the main cities of Copenhagen, Aarhus, Odense and Aalborg. The transmitter network has since expanded to cover 90% of the population. The main DAB operator is DR RADIO, which offers eight music channels (DR Boogieradio, DR Dansktop, DR Hit, DR Jazz, DR Klassisk, DR Pop DK, DR Rock and P5000), two news channels (DR Erhverv, DR Nyheder and DR Politik) and a dedicated children's channel (DR Oline), as well as simulcasts of P1, P2, P3, P4 and P5). The private operators, Radio 100FM, Radio Soft and Nova FM, also offer DAB services.

DR RADIO: DR Byen, Emil Holms Kanal 20, 0999 Copenhagen C; tel. 35-20-30-40; fax 35-20-26-44; e-mail drkommunikation@dr.dk; internet www.dr.dk; fmrly Danmarks Radio; independent statutory corpn; Dir-Gen. MARIA RØRBYE RØNN; Exec. Dir of DR Media MIKAEL KAMBER; operates 4 FM stations, 17 DAB stations and nearly 30 channels on the internet

The four FM stations are as follows:

P1: broadcasts for 110 hours per week on FM, in Danish (Greenlandic programmes weekly); simulcast on DAB; Head FINN SLUMSTRUP.

P2: specializes in classical music, jazz, opera and culture, broadcasts on FM for 45 hours per week nationally, in Danish, as well as regional and special (for foreign workers) programmes; Head OLE DAMGAARD.

P3: popular music channel, broadcasts on FM for 24 hours per day, in Danish; also broadcasts news in Greenlandic, Faroese and English; simulcast on DAB; Head OLE DAMGAARD.

P4: popular music, news and regional programmes; 11 regional stations; broadcasts on FM for about 97 hours per week; simulcast on DAB; Head OLE DAMGAARD.

Radio 100: Rådhuspladsen 45, 1550 Copenhagen V; tel. 33-37-89-00; fax 33-37-89-67; e-mail info@radio100.dk; internet www.radio100.dk; f. 2003; commercial channel, specializing in popular music; owned by Talpa Radio International (Netherlands); Dir BJØRN KRISTENSEN.

There are also some 250 operators licensed for low-power FM transmissions of local and community radio, etc.

Television

Digital transmission in Denmark began in March 2006, and the analogue network ceased transmission in November 2009.

Canal Digital Danmark: Stationsparken 25, 2600 Glostrup; tel. 70-13-19-19; fax 70-27-27-61; e-mail cma@canaldigital.dk; internet www.canaldigital.dk; f. 1997; owned by Telenor ASA (Norway); operates 11 TV channels; Man. Dir JARL SØRDERMAN.

DR TV: DR Byen, Emil Holms Kanal 20, 0999 Copenhagen C; tel. 35-20-30-40; fax 35-20-26-44; e-mail dr-kommunikation@dr.dk; internet www.dr.dk; operates 2 services, DR 1 (terrestrial channel) and DR 2 (satellite channel); operates 4 more TV channels; Dir-Gen. MARIA RØRBYE RØNN; Dir of Programmes MIKAEL KAMBER; Exec. Dir of DR Media MIKAEL KAMBER.

TV 2 | DANMARK A/S: Rugaardsvej 25, 5100 Odense C; tel. 65-91-91-91; fax 65-91-33-22; e-mail tv2@tv2.dk; internet www.tv2.dk; began broadcasts in 1988; Denmark's first national commercial and public service TV station; changed to a state share co in 2003; part-privatization pending; Dir-Gen. MERETE ELDRUP; Dir of Programmes PALLE STRØM.

TV3 Viasat: Wildersgade 8, 1408 Copenhagen K; tel. 77-30-55-00; fax 77-30-55-10; e-mail tv3@viasat.dk; internet www.tv3.dk; began broadcasts in 1987; reaches 71% of the country via cable and satellite; Man. Dir LARS BO ANDERSEN; Dir of Programmes HENRIK RAVN.

Broadcasting Association

Forenede Danske Antenneanlæg (FDA) (Danish Cable Television Asscn): Annebergparken 21, 4500 Nykøbing Sjælland; tel. 59-96-17-00; fax 59-96-17-17; e-mail fda@fda.dk; internet www.fda.dk; f. 1983; organizes 236 local networks, representing c. 250,000 connected households; Chair. CARSTEN KARLSEN.

Finance

(cap. = capital; res = reserves; dep. = deposits; m. = million; brs = branches; amounts in kroner, unless otherwise indicated)

BANKING

The first Danish commercial bank was founded in 1846. In 1975 restrictions on savings banks were lifted, giving commercial and savings banks equal rights and status, and restrictions on the establishment of full branches of foreign banks were removed. In 1988 all remaining restrictions on capital movements were ended. In 2012 there were 96 banks and savings banks in operation. All banks are under government supervision, and public representation is obligatory on all bank supervisory boards.

Supervisory Authority

Finanstilsynet (Danish Financial Supervisory Authority): Århusgade 110 2100, Copenhagen Ø; tel. 33-55-82-82; fax 33-55-82-00; e-mail finanstilsynet@ftnet.dk; internet www.ftnet.dk; f. 1988; agency of the Ministry of Business and Growth; Man. Dir ULRIK NØDGAARD.

Central Bank

Danmarks Nationalbank: Havnegade 5, 1093 Copenhagen K; tel. 33-63-63-63; fax 33-63-71-03; e-mail nationalbanken@nationalbanken.dk; internet www.nationalbanken.dk; f. 1818; name changed as above 1936; self-governing; sole right of issue; conducts monetary policy; administers reserves of foreign exchange; cap. 50m., res 60,425.6m., dep. 410,247.1m. (Dec. 2009); Chair. LARS ROHDE; Govs HUGO FREY JENSEN, PER CALLESEN.

Commercial Banks

Alm. Brand Bank: Midtermolen 7, 2100 Copenhagen Ø; tel. 35-47-47-47; fax 35-47-47-35; e-mail bank@almbrand.dk; internet www.almbrand.dk; f. 1983; present name adopted 2003; cap. 1,021m., res 78.7m., dep. 14,721.8m. (Dec. 2012); Chair. JØRGEN HESSELBJERG MIKKELSEN; Pres. and CEO SØREN BOE MORTENSEN; 25 brs.

Arbejdernes Landsbank A/S: Vesterbrogade 5, 1502 Copenhagen V; tel. 38-48-48-48; fax 38-48-50-50; e-mail info@al-bank.dk; internet www.al-bank.dk; f. 1919; present name acquired 1938; cap. 300m., res 784.8m., dep. 26,936.5m. (Dec. 2012); Chair. POUL ERIK SKOV CHRISTENSEN; Man. Dir GERT R. JONASSEN; 68 brs.

Danske Andelskassers Bank A/S: Baneskellet 1, Hammershøj, 8830 Tjele; tel. 87-99-30-00; fax 87-99-30-98; e-mail foreign@dabank.dk; internet www.dabank.dk; f. 1970; owned by 22 co-operative banks; cap. 550.6m., res 0.2m., dep. 9,466.5m. (Dec. 2013); Chair. JAKOB FASTRUP; CEO JAN PEDERSEN; 37 brs.

Danske Bank A/S: Holmens Kanal 2–12, 1092 Copenhagen K; tel. 33-44-00-00; fax 70-12-10-80; e-mail danskebank@danskebank.com; internet www.danskebank.com; f. 1871 as Danske Landmandsbank; merged with Copenhagen Handelsbank and Provinsbanken in 1990 to form Den Danske Bank A/S; present name adopted 2000; cap. 10,086m., res 1,178m., dep. 1,147,658m. (Dec. 2013); Chair. OLE ANDERSEN; CEO THOMAS BORGEN; 252 brs.

Jyske Bank A/S: Vestergade 8–16, 8600 Silkeborg; tel. 89-89-89-89; fax 89-89-19-99; e-mail jyskebank@jyskebank.dk; internet www.jyskebank.dk; f. 1967 by merger of Silkeborg Bank, Kjellerup Bank, Kjellerup Handels- og Landbrugsbank and Handels- og Landbrugsbanken i Silkeborg; cap. 713m., res 361m., dep. 193,858m. (Dec. 2013); Chair. SVEN BUHRKALL RØDDING; CEO ANDERS DAM; 124 brs.

Nordea Bank Danmark A/S: Christiansbro, Strandgade 3, 0900 Copenhagen C; tel. 33-33-33-33; fax 33-33-63-63; internet www.nordea.dk; f. 1990 as Unibank A/S by merger of Andelsbanken, Privatbanken and SDS; in 1999 the bank merged with the insurance co Tryg-Baltica Forsikring A/S, but remained part of the Unidanmark A/S group, which became part of Nordea Group (Finland) in 2000; acquired Fionia Bank A/S in 2010; cap. 5,000m., res 1,972m., dep. 489,929m. (Dec. 2013); Chair. ARI KAPERI; 344 brs.

Nordjyske Bank A/S: Jernbanegade 4–8, POB 701, 9900 Frederikshavn; tel. 96-33-50-00; fax 96-33-50-03; e-mail email@nordjyskebank.dk; internet www.nordjyskebank.dk; f. 2002 by merger of Egnsbank Nord A/S and Vendsyssel Bank A/S; cap. 77.2m., res 45m., dep. 7,432.7m. (Dec. 2013); Chair. HANS JØRGEN KAPTAIN; Dirs CLAUS ANDERSEN, MIKAEL JAKOBSEN; 21 brs.

Nørresundby Bank A/S: Torvet 4, 9400 Nørresundby; tel. 98-70-37-00; fax 98-70-37-19; e-mail post@nrsbank.dk; internet www.nrsbank.dk; f. 1898 as Banken for Nörresundby og Omegn A.S.; name changed as above 1976; cap. 46m., res 30.1m., dep. 7,811.2m. (Dec. 2012); Chair. MADS HVOLBY; Man. Dirs ANDREAS RASMUSSEN, FINN ØST ANDERSSON; 16 brs.

Nykredit Bank A/S: Kalvebod Brygge 1–3, 1780 Copenhagen V; tel. 70-10-90-00; fax 70-10-90-01; e-mail kundeservice@nykredit.dk; internet www.nykreditbank.dk; f. 1986 as Sankt Annae Bank A/S; present name adopted 1994; mem. of Nykredit Group; cap. 6,045m., dep. 156,620m. (Dec. 2013); Chair. STEEN E. CHRISTENSEN; Group CEO PETER ENGBERG JENSEN.

Ringkjøbing Landbobank A/S: Torvet 1, 6950 Ringkøbing; tel. 97-32-11-66; fax 97-32-18-00; e-mail post@landbobanken.dk; internet www.landbobanken.dk; f. 1886; cap. 24.2m., res 121.7m., dep. 14,117.5m. (Dec. 2013); Chair. JENS LYKKE KJELDSEN; CEO JOHN BULL FISKER; 16 brs.

Sydbank A/S: Peberlyk 4, POB 169, 6200 Aabenraa; tel. 74-37-37-37; fax 74-36-35-49; e-mail info@sydbank.dk; internet www.sydbank.com; f. 1970 by merger of 4 regional banks in southern Jutland; cap. 742m., res 509m., dep. 113,932m. (Dec. 2013); Chair. ANDERS THOUSTRUP; CEO KAREN FRØSIG; 100 brs.

vestjyskBANK A/S: Torvet 4–5, 7620 Lemvig; tel. 96-63-20-00; fax 96-63-21-39; e-mail post@vestjyskbank.dk; internet www.vestjyskbank.dk; f. 2008 by merger of vestjyskBANK A/S and Ringkjøbing Bank A/S; cap. 85.9m., res 607m., dep. 17,894.9m. (Dec. 2013); Chair. STEEN HEMMINGSEN; CEO VAGN THORSAGER; 18 brs.

Savings Banks

Lån & Spar Bank A/S: Højbro Pl. 9–11, POB 2117, 1014 Copenhagen K; tel. 33-78-20-00; fax 33-78-23-09; e-mail lsb@lsb.dk; internet www.lsb.dk; f. 1880; present name adopted 1990; cap. 271m., res 65.2m., dep. 11,085.9m. (Dec. 2013); Chair. ANDERS BECH; Man. Dir and CEO FRANK KRISTENSEN; 16 brs.

Spar Nord Bank A/S: Skelagervej 15, POB 162, 9100 Ålborg; tel. 96-34-40-00; fax 96-34-45-60; e-mail sparnord@sparnord.dk; internet www.sparnord.dk; f. 1967; name changed as above 1998 following merger; cap. 1,255.3m., res 596.2m., dep. 59,264.1m. (Dec. 2013); Chair. STEFFEN NØRGAARD; CEO BJARNE DAMM JOHANSEN; 90 brs.

Bankers' Organization

Finansrådet: Finansrådets Hus, Amaliegade 7, 1256 Copenhagen K; tel. 33-70-10-00; fax 33-93-02-60; e-mail mail@finansraadet.dk; internet www.finansraadet.dk; f. 1990; 92 mems; Chair. MICHAEL RASMUSSEN; Man. Dir JØRGEN A. HORWITZ.

STOCK EXCHANGE

NASDAQ OMX Nordic Exchange Copenhagen: Nikolaj Pl. 6, POB 1040, 1007 Copenhagen K; tel. 33-93-33-66; fax 33-12-86-13; internet www.nasdaqomx.com; f. 2005 by merger of Københavns Fondsbørs and OMX (Sweden); became part of OMX Nordic Exchange with Helsinki (Finland) and Stockholm (Sweden) exchanges in 2006; acquired by NASDAQ Stock Market, Inc (USA) in 2008; Group CEO ROBERT GREIFELD.

INSURANCE

In 2012 there were 85 non-life insurance companies in operation and 27 companies offering life insurance.

Principal Companies

Alm. Brand Forsikring A/S: Midtermolen 7, 2100 Copenhagen Ø; tel. 35-47-47-47; e-mail almbrand@almbrand.dk; internet www.almbrand.dk; f. 1792; life, non-life and pensions; CEO SØREN BOE MORTENSEN.

AP Pension Liv: Østbanegade 135, 2100 Copenhagen Ø; tel. 39-16-50-00; e-mail email@appension.dk; internet www.appension.dk; f. 1919; as Cooperative Pension asscn; name changed as above in 1989; pensions, life; CEO SØREN DAL THOMSEN.

Codan A/S: Codanhus, Gl. Kongevej 60, 1790 Copenhagen V; tel. 33-55-55-50; e-mail codan@codan.dk; internet www.codan.dk; f. 1915 as Forsikringsselskabet Codan A/S; adopted present name 2000; mem. of RSA Insurance Group PLC (UK); accident, life; Chair. LARS NØRBY JOHANSEN; CEO MIKE HOLLIDAY-WILLIAMS.

Danica Pension: Parallelvej 17, 2800 Lyngby; tel. 70-11-25-25; fax 45-14-96-16; e-mail kontakt@danicapension.dk; internet www.danicapension.dk; f. 1842 as state insurance co; privatized 1991; acquired by Danske Bank 1995; pensions, life; CEO PER KLITGÅRD.

If: Stamholmen 159, 2650 Hvidovre; tel. 70-12-12-12; fax 70-12-24-25; internet www.if.dk; f. 1999; property and accident; subsidiary of Sampo PLC (Finland); Man. Dir TORBJÖRN MAGNUSSON.

Industriens Pensionsforsikring: Nørre Farimagsgade 3, 1364 Copenhagen K; tel. 70-33-70-70; fax 33-66-80-90; e-mail kundeservice@industrienspension.dk; internet www.industrienspension.dk; f. 1992; by Confed. of Danish Industries (DI) and CO, representing 7 unions, with 35% and 65% ownership respectively; life; CEO LAILA MORTENSEN.

Lærestandens Brandforsikring G/S (LB): Farvergade 17, 1463 Copenhagen K; tel. 33-11-77-55; fax 33-15-77-55; internet www.lb.dk; f. 1880; specializes in vehicle, home and accident insurance; Man. Dir JØRN ANKER-SVENDSEN.

Nordea Liv & Pension: Klausdalsbrovej 615, 2750 Ballerup; tel. 43-33-99-99; fax 43-33-98-98; e-mail Nordealivogpension@nordea.dk; internet www.nordealivogpension.dk; life; CEO STEEN MICHAEL ERICHSEN.

Pension Denmark: Kongens Vænge 8, 3400 Hillerød; tel. 70-12-13-30; e-mail service@pension.dk; internet www.pension.dk; f. 1993; owned by the Pension Denmark Holding A/S; life, health, pensions; Chair. POUL ERIK SKOV CHRISTENSEN; CEO TORBEN MÖGER PEDERSEN.

PFA Pension: Marina Park, Sundkrogsgade 4, 2100 Copenhagen Ø; tel. 39-17-50-00; fax 39-17-59-50; e-mail pension@pfa.dk; internet www.pfa.dk; f. 1917 as Pensionsforsikringsanstalten; present name adopted 1987; life, health, pensions; Chair. SVEND ASKÆR; Pres. and CEO HENRIK HEIDEBY.

Topdanmark Forsikring A/S: Borupvang 4, 2750 Ballerup; tel. 44-68-33-11; fax 44-74-46-50; e-mail kundeservice@topdanmark.dk; internet www.topdanmark.dk; f. 1985; all classes, with subsidiaries; CEO CHRISTIAN SAGILD.

Tryg A/S: Klausdalsbrovej 601, 2750 Ballerup; tel. 70-11-20-20; fax 44-20-66-00; e-mail tryg@tryg.com; internet www.tryg.com; f. 1995 by merger of Tryg Forsikring A/S and Baltica Forsikring A/S; general; Chair. JØRGEN HUNO RASMUSSEN; CEO MORTEN HÜBBE.

Insurance Association

Forsikring & Pension: Philip Heymans Allé 1, 2900 Hellerup; tel. 41-91-91-91; e-mail fp@forsikringogpension.dk; internet www.forsikringogpension.dk; f. 1918 as Assurandør-Societetet; present name adopted 1999; Man. Dir PER BREMER RASMUSSEN; 126 mems.

Trade and Industry

GOVERNMENT AGENCY

Invest in Denmark: Asiatisk Pl. 2, 1448 Copenhagen K; tel. 33-92-11-11; e-mail indk@um.dk; internet www.investindk.com; part of the Ministry of Foreign Affairs; promotes setting up of foreign offices in the country; Dir SUSANNE HYLDELUND.

DEVELOPMENT ORGANIZATION

Det Økonomiske Råd (Danish Economic Council): Amaliegade 44, 1256 Copenhagen K; tel. 33-44-58-00; fax 33-32-90-29; e-mail dors@dors.dk; internet www.dors.dk; f. 1962; supervises national economic development and helps to co-ordinate the actions of economic interest groups; 26 members representing industry, the Government and independent economic experts; Co-Chairs Prof. HANS JØRGEN WHITTA-JACOBSEN, Prof. MICHAEL SVARER, Prof. CLAUS THUSTRUP KREINER, Prof. EIRIK SCHRØDER AMUNDSEN.

CHAMBER OF COMMERCE

Dansk Erhverv (Danish Chamber of Commerce): Børsen, 1217 Copenhagen K; tel. 33-74-60-00; fax 33-74-60-80; e-mail info@danskerhverv.dk; internet www.danskerhverv.dk; f. 1742; Pres. MICHAEL KJÆR; Man. Dir JENS KLARSKOV; approx. 17,000 mem. cos.

INDUSTRIAL AND TRADE ASSOCIATIONS

Bryggeriforeningen (Danish Brewers' Asscn): Faxehus, Gamle Carlsberg Vej 16, 1799 Copenhagen V; tel. 72-16-24-24; fax 72-16-24-44; e-mail contact@bryggeriforeningen.dk; internet www.bryggeriforeningen.dk; f. 1899; Dir NIELS HALD; 46 mems.

Dansk Energi (Danish Energy Asscn): Rosenørns Allé 9, 1970 Frederiksberg C; tel. 35-30-04-00; fax 35-30-04-01; e-mail de@danskenergi.dk; internet www.danskenergi.dk; f. 1923; fmrly Dansk Elvaerkers Forening (Asscn of Danish Energy Cos); promotes the interests of Danish producers and suppliers of electricity; Man. Dir LARS AAGAARD; 100 mem. cos.

Dansk Vand- og Spildevandsforening (DANVA) (Danish Water and Wastewater Association): Vandhuset, Godthåbsvej 83, 8660 Skanderborg; tel. 70-21-00-55; fax 70-21-00-56; e-mail danva@danva.dk; internet www.danva.dk; f. 2002; asscn of water and waste water utilities; Chair. LARS THERKILDSEN.

Danske Maritime (Danish Maritime): Amaliegade 33B, 4th Floor, 1256 Copenhagen K; tel. 33-13-24-16; fax 33-11-10-96; e-mail info@danishmaritime.org; internet www.danishmaritime.org; f. 1919; fmrly Skibsværftsforeningen (Asscn of Danish Shipbuilders); meeting place for Danish producers of maritime equipment and ships; Pres. THOMAS S. KNUDSEN; Man. Dir JENNY N. BRAAT.

Energi- og olieforum (EOF) (Danish Oil Industry Asscn): Landemærket 10, 5th Floor, POB 120, 1004 Copenhagen K; tel. 33-45-65-10; fax 33-45-65-11; e-mail eof@eof.dk; internet www.eof.dk; f. 1968; representative org. for petroleum industry; Pres. STEFFEN PEDERSEN; Dir PETER STIGSGAARD.

Kopenhagen Fur: Langagervej 60, 2600 Glostrup; tel. 43-26-10-00; fax 43-26-11-26; e-mail mail@kopenhagenfur.com; internet www.kopenhagenfur.com; fmrly Dansk Pelsdyravlerforening (Danish Fur Breeders' Asscn); co-operative of 2,300 mems; Chair. TAGE PEDERSEN.

Landbrug & Fødevarer (Danish Agriculture & Food Council): Axeltorv 3, 1609 Copenhagen V; tel. 33-39-40-00; fax 33-39-41-41; e-mail info@lf.dk; internet www.lf.dk; f. 2009 by merger of 5 agricultural and food orgs; Pres. MARTIN MERRILD; CEO. SØREN GADE.

Mejeriforeningen (Danish Dairy Board): Sønderhøj 1, 8260 Viby J; tel. 87-31-20-00; fax 87-31-20-01; e-mail info@mejeri.dk; internet www.mejeri.dk; f. 1912; Chair. STEEN NØRGAARD MADSEN; Man. Dir JØRGEN HALD CHRISTENSEN; 34 mems.

Vindmølleindustrien (Danish Wind Energy Association): Rosenørns Allé 9, 1970 Frederiksberg C; tel. 33-73-03-30; e-mail danish@windpower.org; internet www.windpower.org; CEO JAN HYLLEBERG; 250 mems.

EMPLOYERS' ORGANIZATIONS

Dansk Arbejdsgiverforening (DA) (Confederation of Danish Employers): Vester Voldgade 113, 1790 Copenhagen V; tel. 33-38-90-00; fax 33-12-29-76; e-mail da@da.dk; internet www.da.dk; f. 1896; Chair. TORBEN DALBY LARSEN; 14 mem. orgs.

Dansk Industri (DI) (Confederation of Danish Industries): H. C. Andersens blvd 18, 1787 Copenhagen V; tel. 33-77-33-77; fax 33-77-33-00; e-mail di@di.dk; internet www.di.dk; f. 1992; Dir-Gen. and CEO KARSTEN DYBVAD.

Håndværksrådet (Danish Federation of Small and Medium-sized Enterprises): Islands Brygge 26, POB 1990, 2300 Copenhagen S; tel. 33-93-20-00; fax 33-32-01-74; e-mail hvr@hvr.dk; internet www.hvr.dk; f. 1879; Chair. NIELS TECHEN; Man. Dir ANE BUCH; 110 asscns with 23,000 mems.

Industriens Arbejdsgivere i København (The Copenhagen Employers' Federation): 1787 Copenhagen V; tel. 33-77-39-16; fax 33-77-33-00; e-mail iak@di.dk; internet foreninger.di.dk/iak; mem. of Confed. of Dansk Industri; Chair. NIELS JACOBSEN; Sec. SUSANNE ANDERSEN; 370 mems.

Provinsindustriens Arbejdsgiverforening (Federation of Employers in Provincial Industry): 1787 Copenhagen V; tel. 33-77-33-77; fax 33-77-33-00; e-mail pfo@di.dk; internet foreninger.di.dk/pa; f. 1895; mem. of Dansk Industri (q.v.); Chair. BO STÆRMOSE; Sec. PETER FOSDAL; 558 mem. orgs.

Sammenslutningen af Landbrugets Arbejdsgiverforeninger (SALA) (Danish Confederation of Employers' Asscns in Agriculture): Axelborg, Axeltorv 3, 1. sal, POB 367, 1504 Copenhagen V; tel. 33-13-46-55; fax 33-39-41-41; e-mail info@sala.dk; internet www.sala.dk; Chair. PEJTER SØNDERGAARD; 2 mem. orgs.

UTILITIES

Energistyrelsen (Danish Energy Agency): Amaliegade 44, 1256 Copenhagen K; tel. 33-92-67-00; fax 33-11-47-43; e-mail ens@ens.dk; internet www.ens.dk; f. 1976; govt agency under Ministry of Climate, Energy and Building; Dir-Gen. IB LARSEN.

Energitilsynet (DERA) (Danish Energy Regulatory Authority): Nyropsgade 30, 1780 Copenhagen V; tel. 72-26-80-70; fax 33-18-14-

27; e-mail et@dera.dk; internet www.energitilsynet.dk; f. 2000; independent authority; regulates prices and access to transmission networks for electricity, gas and heating supply cos; bd mems appointed by Minister of Climate, Energy and Building; Chair. UFFE BUNDGAARD-JØRGENSEN.

Electricity

DONG Energy A/S: Kraftværksvej 53, Skærbæk, 7000 Fredericia; tel. 99-55-11-11; e-mail info@dongenergy.com; internet www.dongenergy.com; f. 2006 by merger of 6 energy cos: DONG, Elsam, E2, Nesa, Copenhagen Energy and Frederiksberg Forsyning; petroleum and natural gas exploration, production, storage and distribution; production and sale of electricity, wind power and geothermal energy; CEO HENRIK POULSEN.

EnergiMidt A/S: Tietgensvej 2–4, 8600 Silkeborg; tel. 70-15-15-60; fax 87-22-87-11; internet www.energimidt.dk; co-operative society; 176,000 customers; energy supplier; Chair. JENS JØRN JUSTESEN; Man. Dir HOLGER BLOK.

Energinet.dk: Tonne Kjærsvej 65, 7000 Fredericia; tel. 70-10-22-44; fax 76-24-51-80; e-mail info@energinet.dk; internet www.energinet.dk; f. 2005 by merger of Eltra, Elkraft System, Elkraft Transmission and Gastra; state-owned; co-ordinates supply of electricity, gas and co-generated heat; Pres. and CEO PEDER ØSTERMARK ANDREASEN.

Vattenfall A/S: Støberigade 14, 2450 Copenhagen SV; tel. 88-27-50-00; e-mail marianne.grydgaard@vattenfall.com; internet www.vattenfall.dk; f. 1996; owned by Vattenfall AB (Sweden); generation and supply of thermal and wind energy; acquired assets of Elsam and E2 in 2006; Group CEO ØYSTEIN LØSETH.

Gas

Dansk Gas Forening (Danish Gas Asscn): c/o Dansk Gasteknisk Center a/s, Dr Neergaards Vej 5B, 2970 Hørsholm; tel. 20-16-96-00; fax 45-16-11-99; e-mail dgf@dgc.dk; internet www.gasteknik.dk; f. 1911; promotes the use of gas; Chair. OLE ALBÆK PEDERSEN; Sec. PETER I. HINSTRUP; 450 mems.

DONG Energy A/S: see Electricity.

HMN Naturgas I/S: Gladsaxe Ringvej 11, 2860 Søborg; tel. 39-54-70-00; fax 39-67-23-98; e-mail hmn@naturgas.dk; internet www.hng.dk; f. 2010 by merger between Hovedstadsregionens Naturgas I/S and Naturgas Midt-Nord I/S; distribution and sale of gas in Greater Copenhagen region; Chair. JENS GRØNLUND; Man. Dir SUSANNE JUHL.

Københavns Energi A/S (Copenhagen Energy): Ørestads Blvd 35, 2300 Copenhagen S; tel. 33-95-33-95; fax 33-95-20-20; e-mail ke@ke.dk; internet www.ke.dk; f. 1857 as Københavns Belysningsvæsen; present name adopted 1999; merger with Københavns Vand 2001; supplier of gas, heating and water in Copenhagen and surrounding area; Chair. LEO LARSEN; Man. Dir LARS THERKILDSEN.

Naturgas Fyn A/S: Ørbækvej 260, 5220 Odense SØ; tel. 63-15-64-15; fax 66-15-51-27; e-mail info@ngf.dk; internet www.ngf.dk; distribution of gas on island of Funen; Chair. ANKER BOYE; Man. Dir BJARKE PÅLSSON.

Water

Water provision in Denmark is highly decentralized. Local councils are responsible for the maintenance of water supply infrastructure and the supervision of suppliers. Water supply utilities, of which there were some 2,740 in 2001, are owned either by municipal administrations or by local consumer co-operative organizations.

CO-OPERATIVE

FDB Co-op amba (Danish Co-operative Societies): Vallensbæk Torvevej 9, 2620 Albertslund; tel. 39-47-00-00; internet coop.dk; f. 2013 following merger of Fællesforeningen for Danmarks Brugsforeninger (f. 1896) and Co-op Danmark A/S; c. 1.7m. mems.

TRADE UNIONS

National Confederations

Akademikerne (Danish Confederation of Professional Asscns): Nørre Voldgade 29, POB 2192, 1017 Copenhagen K; tel. 33-69-40-40; e-mail ac@ac.dk; internet www.ac.dk; f. 1972; Pres. ERIK JYLLING; 23 affiliated unions, with a total of 219,000 mems (2012).

FTF (Confederation of Professionals in Denmark): Niels Hemmingsens Gade 12, POB 1169, 1100 Copenhagen K; tel. 33-36-88-00; fax 33-36-88-80; e-mail ftf@ftf.dk; internet www.ftf.dk; f. 1952; affiliated to ITUC and ETUC; Pres. BENTE SORGENFREY; 81 affiliated unions, with c. 450,000 mems.

Landsorganisationen i Danmark (LO) (Danish Confederation of Trade Unions): Islands Brygge 32D, 2300 Copenhagen S; tel. 35-24-60-00; fax 35-24-63-00; e-mail lo@lo.dk; internet www.lo.dk; Pres. HARALD BØRSTING; Vice-Pres. LIZETTE RISGAARD; 18 affiliated unions, with a total of 1.1m. mems.

Transport

In June 1998 an 18-km combined tunnel-and-bridge road and rail link between the islands of Zealand and Funen was completed; the project incorporated the world's second longest suspension bridge. A 16-km road and rail link (incorporating a 4-km tunnel, an artificial island and an 8-km suspension bridge) across the Øresund strait, between Copenhagen and Malmö, Sweden, was completed in July 2000. Construction of a road and rail tunnel across the 19 km Fehmarn Belt, linking eastern Denmark with Germany, was expected to begin in 2015 and be completed by 2021.

DANISH TRANSPORT AUTHORITY

Danish Transport Authority: Edvard Thomsens Vej 14, 2300 Copenhagen K; tel. 72-21-88-00; fax 72-62-67-90; e-mail info@trafikstyrelsen.dk; internet www.trafikstyrelsen.dk; f. 2010 following merger of the Public Transport Authority (Trafikstyrelsen) and the Civil Aviation Administration (Statens Luftfartsvæsen); Dir-Gen. CARSTEN FALK HANSEN.

RAILWAYS

Banedanmark (Rail Net Denmark): Amerika Pl. 15, 2100 Copenhagen Ø; tel. 82-34-00-00; fax 82-34-45-72; e-mail banedanmark@bane.dk; internet www.bane.dk; f. 1997 as Banestyrelsen to assume, from the DSB, responsibility for the maintenance and development of the national rail network; controls 2,349 km of line, of which 602 km are electrified; also manages signalling and train control; CEO JESPER HANSEN.

DSB (Danish State Railways): Sølvgade 40, 1307 Copenhagen K; tel. 70-13-14-15; internet www.dsb.dk; wholly owned by Ministry of Transport; became an independent public corpn in Jan. 1999; privatization pending; operates passenger services; Chair. PETER SCHÜTZE; CEO JESPER T. LOK.

A total of 495 km, mostly branch lines, is run by 15 private companies.

METROPOLITAN TRANSPORT

Metroselskabet I/S: Metrovej 5, 2300 Copenhagen S; tel. 33-11-17-00; e-mail m@m.dk; internet www.m.dk; f. 2002; operates 21-km, 22-station underground light rail network in Copenhagen; construction of 2 new lines due to be completed in 2018; 50% owned by Copenhagen city council, 41.7% by Ministry of Transport and 8.3% by Frederiksberg city council; Chair. HENNING CHRISTOPHERSEN; Man. Dir HENRIK PLOUGMANN OLSEN.

ROADS

In 2010, according to the International Road Federation, Denmark had an estimated 74,054 km of paved roads, including 1,122 km of motorways and 2,705 km of national roads. A 3 km road connecting Nordhavn in Copenhagen with Helsingørmotorvejen (the Elsinore Highway) to the north of the city was expected to be completed by 2015. This new link was expected to ease the flow of traffic in densely populated city areas.

SHIPPING

The Port of Copenhagen is the largest port in Denmark and the only one to incorporate a Free Port Zone. The other major ports are Aarhus, Fredericia, Aalborg, Hirtshals, and Esbjerg, all situated in Jutland. There are petroleum terminals, with adjacent refineries, at Kalundborg, Stigsnæs and Fredericia. Ferry services are provided by Scandlines and by various private companies. At 31 December 2013 the flag registered fleet numbered 1,008 vessels, with a combined displacement of 12.7m. grt,of which 153 were fishing vessels and 33 were passenger ships.

Port Authorities

Århus: Port Authority of Århus, Mindet 2, POB 130, 8100 Århus C; tel. 86-13-32-66; fax 86-12-76-62; e-mail port@aarhus.dk; internet www.aarhushavn.dk; Port Dir JACOB F. CHRISTENSEN.

Associated Danish Ports A/S (ADP): Vesthavnsvej 33, 7000 Fredericia; tel. 79-21-50-00; fax 79-21-50-05; e-mail post@adp-as.dk; internet www.adp-as.dk; has authority for ports of Middelfart, Fredericia and Nyborg; Man. Dir JENS PETER PETERS.

Copenhagen: Copenhagen Malmö Port AB, Containervej 9, POB 900, 2150 Copenhagen Ø; tel. 35-46-11-11; fax 35-46-11-64; e-mail cmport@cmport.com; internet www.cmport.com; f. 2001 by merger of ports of Copenhagen and Malmö; owned by Malmö Municipality (27%), City & Port Development (50%) and pvt. investors (23%); CEO JOHAN RÖSTIN; Port Capt. SØREN F. ANDERSEN.

Esbjerg: Port of Esbjerg, Hulvejen 1, 6700 Esbjerg; tel. 76-12-40-00; fax 75-13-40-50; e-mail adm@portesbjerg.dk; internet www.portesbjerg.dk; Port Dir OLE INGRISCH; Head of Maritime Dept TORBEN JENSEN.

Frederikshavn Havn A/S: Oliepieren 7, POB 129, 9900 Frederikshavn; tel. 96-20-47-00; fax 96-20-47-11; e-mail info@frederikshavnhavn.dk; internet www.frederikshavnhavn.dk; Man. Dir MIKKEL SEEDORFF SØRENSEN; Maritime Chief HELLE BRANDT.

Kalundborg: Kalundborg Port Authority, Baltic Pl., POB 54, 4400 Kalundborg; tel. 59-53-40-00; fax 59-53-40-03; e-mail info@portofkalundborg.dk; internet www.portofkalundborg.dk; Harbour Dir BENT RASMUSSEN.

Sønderborg: Sønderborg Havn, Nørrebro 1, 6400 Sønderborg; tel. 74-42-27-65; fax 74-43-30-19; e-mail havnen@sonderborg.dk; internet www.sonderborg.dk/havn; Port Controller FINN HANSEN.

Principal Shipping Companies

Corral Line A/S: Havnevej 18, 6320 Egernsund; tel. 74-44-14-35; fax 74-44-14-75; e-mail info@corralline.com; internet www.corralline.com; fmrly Sønderborg Rederiaktieselskab; 8 livestock carriers of 19,302 grt; shipowners, managers, chartering agents; worldwide; Man. Dir B. CLAUSEN.

Rederiet Otto Danielsen: Kongevejen 272A, 2830 Virum; tel. 45-83-25-55; fax 45-83-17-07; e-mail od@ottodanielsen.com; internet www.ottodanielsen.com; f. 1944; 7 general cargo vessels, totalling 20,793 grt, under foreign flags; general tramp trade, chartering, ship sales; Man. Dir SØREN ANDERSEN.

Dannebrog Rederi A/S: Rungsted Strandvej 113, 2960 Rungsted Kyst; tel. 45-17-77-77; fax 45-17-77-70; e-mail dbrog@dannebrog.com; internet www.dannebrog.com; f. 1883; 3 ro-ro vessels, product chemical tanker services; liner service USA–Europe, US Gulf–Caribbean, Mediterranean–Caribbean; Man. Dir JOHAN WEDELL-WEDELLSBORG.

DFDS A/S: Sundkrogsgade 11, 2100 Copenhagen Ø; tel. 33-42-33-42; fax 33-42-33-41; internet www.dfds.com; f. 1866; 5 car/passenger ships and 60 freight vessels; passenger and car ferry services between Denmark, Belgium, Finland, France, Germany, Ireland, Latvia, Lithuania, the Netherlands, Norway, Poland, Sweden and the United Kingdom; Pres. and CEO NIELS SMEDEGAARD.

H. Folmer & Co: Fredericiagade 57, 1310 Copenhagen K; tel. 33-36-09-00; fax 33-13-54-64; e-mail folmer@folmer.dk; internet www.folmer.dk; f. 1955; 13 general cargo vessels of 14,100 grt; worldwide tramping; Man. Owners J. J. FOLMER, UFFE MARTIN JENSEN.

J. Lauritzen A/S: Skt Annæ Pl. 28, POB 2147, 1291 Copenhagen K; tel. 33-96-80-00; fax 33-96-80-01; internet www.j-lauritzen.com; f. 1884; operates reefer ships, LPG/C carriers and bulk ships; Pres. and CEO TORBEN JANHOLT.

A. P. Møller—Mærsk A/S: Esplanaden 50, 1098 Copenhagen K; tel. 33-63-33-63; fax 33-63-41-08; e-mail cphinfo@maersk.com; internet www.maersk.com; f. 1904; fleet of 113 container vessels, 19 products tankers, 3 crude petroleum tankers, 5 gas carriers, 10 car carriers, 59 offshore vessels and 22 drilling rigs; further tonnage owned by subsidiary cos in Singapore and the UK; worldwide liner and feeder services under the name of Maersk Line, and worldwide tanker, bulk, offshore and rig services; CEO NILS SMEDEGAARD ANDERSEN.

Dampskibsselskabet Norden A/S: 52 Strandvejen, 2900 Hellerup; tel. 33-15-04-51; fax 33-15-09-56; e-mail direktion@ds-norden.com; internet www.ds-norden.com; f. 1871; operates about 45 tankers and bulk carriers; worldwide tramping; Pres. and CEO CARSTEN MORTENSEN.

Scandlines Danmark A/S: Havneholmen 29, 1561 Copenhagen V; tel. 33-15-15-15; fax 72-68-60-58; e-mail scandlines@scandlines.dk; internet www.scandlines.dk; f. 1998 by merger of Scandlines A/S and Deutsche Fährgesellschaft Ostsee GmbH (Germany); maintains offices in Germany and Sweden; acquired by Deutsche Seereederei GmbH in 2007; operates 12 ferry routes around Denmark and throughout the Baltic; Chair. SØREN POULSGAARD JENSEN; CEO STIG DAMBMANN.

Svitzer A/S: Pakhus 48, Sundkaj 9, 2100 Copenhagen Ø; tel. 39-19-39-19; fax 39-19-39-09; e-mail info@svitzer.com; internet www.svitzer.com; f. 1833; wholly owned subsidiary of A. P. Møller—Mærsk Group; 22 tugs and salvage vessels and a barge fleet; salvage, towage and barge services; Gen. Man. ROBERT MÆRSK UGGLA.

Torm A/S: Tuborg Havnevej 18, 2900 Hellerup; tel. 39-17-92-00; fax 39-17-93-93; e-mail mail@torm.com; internet www.torm.com; f. 1889; more than 121 tankers and bulk carriers; operator of a time-chartered fleet; Chair. FLEMMING IPSEN; CEO JACOB MELDGAARD.

Shipping Association

Danmarks Rederiforening (Danish Shipowners' Asscn): Amaliegade 33, 1256 Copenhagen K; tel. 33-11-40-88; fax 33-11-62-10; e-mail info@shipowners.dk; internet www.shipowners.dk; f. 1884; 49 mems (2010); Chair. of the Bd CARSTEN MORTENSEN; Man. Dir (vacant).

CIVIL AVIATION

The main international airport is Copenhagen Airport, situated about 10 km from the centre of the capital. The following domestic airports have scheduled flights to European and Scandinavian destinations: Ålborg, Århus and Billund in Jutland. Other domestic airports include: Roskilde (30 km south-west of Copenhagen); Esbjerg, Karup, Skrydstrup, Stauning, Sønderborg and Thisted in Jutland; Odense in Funen; and Bornholm Airport on the island of Bornholm.

Statens Luftfartsvæsen (SLV) (Civil Aviation Administration): Luftfartshuset, Ellebjergvej 50, POB 744, 2450 Copenhagen SV; tel. 36-18-60-00; fax 36-18-60-01; e-mail dcaa@slv.dk; internet www.slv.dk; Dir-Gen. KURT LYKSTOFT LARSEN.

Airlines

Scandinavian Airlines System (SAS): SAS Huset, Lufthavnsboulevarden 14, POB 150, 2770 Kastrup; tel. 32-32-00-00; fax 32-32-21-49; internet www.sas.dk; f. 1946; the national carrier of Denmark, Norway and Sweden. It is a consortium owned two-sevenths by SAS Danmark A/S, two-sevenths by SAS Norge ASA and three-sevenths by SAS Sverige AB. Each parent org. is a limited co owned 50% by its respective govt and 50% by private shareholders. The SAS group includes the consortium and the subsidiaries in which the consortium has a majority or otherwise controlling interest; the Board consists of 2 members from each of the parent cos and the chairmanship rotates among the 3 national chairmen on an annual basis; strategic alliance with Lufthansa (Germany) formed in 1995; Chair. FRITZ H. SCHUR; Pres. and CEO RICKARD GUSTAFSON.

SUN-AIR of Scandinavia A/S: Cumulusvej 10, 7190 Billund; tel. 76-50-01-00; fax 75-33-86-18; e-mail info@sunair.dk; internet www.sunair.dk; f. 1978; also maintains offices at Ålborg, Århus, Billund and Thisted Airports; operates charter flights, sells and leases aircraft and operates aircraft maintenance services, operates a franchise of scheduled flights throughout northern Europe in co-operation with British Airways since 1996; CEO NIELS SUNDBERG.

Thomas Cook Airlines Scandinavia A/S: Copenhagen Airport South, Hangar 276, 2791 Dragør; tel. 32-47-72-00; fax 32-45-02-22; e-mail thomascookairlines@thomascook.dk; internet www.thomascookairlines.dk; f. 2008 by merger of MyTravel Airways A/S and Premiair; part of the Thomas Cook Group PLC; flights to major destinations in Europe; Man. Dir TORBEN ØSTERGAARD.

Tourism

In 2011 foreign tourist arrivals in Denmark totalled some 7.9m. Receipts from tourism totalled an estimated US $6,162m. in 2012.

VisitDenmark: Islands Brygge 43, 2300 Copenhagen S; tel. 32-88-99-00; fax 32-88-99-01; e-mail contact@visitdenmark.com; internet www.visitdenmark.com; f. 1967; fmrly Danmarks Turistråd (Danish Tourist Board); Chair. JENS WITTRUP WILLUMSEN; Admin. Dir JAN OLSEN.

Defence

As assessed at November 2013, Denmark maintained total armed forces of 17,200, comprising an army of 7,950 (including 1,000 conscripts), a navy of 3,000 (including 150 conscripts), an air force of 3,150 (including 100 conscripts), and joint forces of 3,100. There was, in addition, a volunteer Home Guard (Hjemmeværnet) numbering some 40,800. Military service is compulsory and lasts for 4–12 months. Denmark abandoned its neutrality after the Second World War and has been a member of the North Atlantic Treaty Organization (NATO) since 1949. In November 2012 Denmark, Finland, Iceland, Sweden and Norway agreed to operate military transport aircraft jointly.

Defence Expenditure: Budget forecast at 23,925m. kroner for 2014.

Chief of Defence: Brig. Gen. PETER BARTRAM.

Education

Primary and lower secondary education at Folkeskole is the joint responsibility of the Ministry of Education and the municipal councils. The Ministries of Education, of Culture and of Science, Innovation and Higher Education are collectively responsible for providing higher education. Education is compulsory for ten years between six and 16 years of age. The state is obliged to offer a pre-school class and an 11th voluntary year. State-subsidized private schools are available, but in 2008/09 81.6% of pupils attended municipal schools. Pre-primary education between the ages of three and seven years at a

Kindergarten (Børnehave) is optional, except for the compulsory pre-primary class, Børnehaveklasse, for children aged six to seven years. In 2010/11 enrolment at pre-primary level included 96% of children in the relevant age-group. Primary and lower secondary education begins at seven years of age and lasts for nine years (with the option of an additional year). This includes at least six years at primary school. Enrolment at primary level, according to UNESCO figures, included 96% of children in the relevant age-group in 2010/11. Secondary education is divided into two cycles of three years, the first beginning at 13 years of age, the second at the age of 16 or 17. At the end of the lower secondary cycle students must take a final exam in seven subjects. Students then progress to one of four options, all of which may lead to higher education: an academically orientated three-year course, Studentereksamen (STX), at a Gymnasium; a two-year course at a Højere Forberedelseseksamen (HF), which follows the voluntary 10th year of the Folkeskole; a three-year higher commercial examination course, Højere Handelseksamen (HHX), or a higher technical examination course, Højere Teknisk Eksamen (HTX). Alternatively students may transfer to vocational courses at this stage. A new vocational programme at the upper secondary level, named Eksamen i Forbindelse med en Erhvervsuddannelse (EUX), was launched in August 2010. This programme is combined with an upper secondary education examination to give access to higher education. Total enrolment at secondary level in 2010/11 included 90% of those in the relevant age-group. There are eight universities or long-cycle education (Lange Videregående Uddannelser) and other institutions of further and higher education: university colleges, medium-cycle non-university education (Mellemlange Videregäende Uddannelser), and academies of higher education, short-cycle non-university education (Korte Videregäende Uddannelser). The first degree course in the university sector is the Bachelor of Arts or Science (BA or BSc) and lasts for three years. In 2005/06 enrolment at tertiary level was equivalent to 81% of those in the relevant age-group. The government budget for 2014 forecast an allocation of 148,003m. kroner to education, representing 13.7% of total budgeted spending.

DANISH EXTERNAL TERRITORIES

THE FAROE ISLANDS

Introductory Survey

LOCATION, CLIMATE, LANGUAGE, RELIGION, FLAG, CAPITAL

The Faroe (Faeroe) Islands are a group of 18 islands (of which 17 are inhabited) in the Atlantic Ocean, between the United Kingdom and Iceland. The main island is Streymoy, where more than one-third of the population resides. The climate is mild in winter and cool in summer, with a mean temperature of 7°C (45°F). Most of the inhabitants profess Christianity: 82.1% of Faroese were Lutherans belonging to the Faroes National Church in 2012. The principal language is Faroese, but Danish is widely spoken and is a compulsory subject in all schools. The flag (proportions 16 by 22) displays a red cross, bordered with blue, on a white background, the upright of the cross being to the left of centre. The capital is Tórshavn, which is situated on Streymoy.

CONTEMPORARY POLITICAL HISTORY

The Faroe Islands have been under Danish administration since Queen Margrethe I of Denmark inherited Norway in 1380. The islands were occupied by the United Kingdom while Denmark was under German occupation during the Second World War, but they were restored to Danish control immediately after the war. The Home Rule Act of 1948 gave the Faroese control over all their internal affairs. The Faroe Islands did not join the European Community (now European Union—EU, see p. 273) with Denmark in 1973. There is a local parliament (the Løgting—Lagting in Danish), but the Danish Folketing (parliament), to which the Faroese send two members, is responsible for defence and foreign policy, constitutional matters, and the judicial and monetary systems. The transfer of competency in some areas from Denmark to the Faroe Islands began in 2005. The Faroes control fishing resources within their fisheries zone, and in September 1992 a long-standing dispute between Denmark and the Faroes was settled when the Danish Government agreed to give the Faroese authorities legislative and administrative power over mineral resources, including those beneath the seabed in the area adjacent to the islands. This agreement removed one of the major obstacles to exploration for hydrocarbons off the Faroe Islands, where geologists considered that prospects for discovering reserves of petroleum and natural gas were favourable. In 1994 the Faroe Islands awarded a US company a licence to begin exploratory surveys, despite the existence of a long-standing dispute between Denmark and the United Kingdom over the demarcation of the continental shelf west of the Shetland Islands and south-east of the Faroe Islands, which had threatened to delay prospecting. This dispute was resolved in mid-1999 when representatives of the Faroese Government (the Landsstýri) signed an agreement with the Danish and British Governments regarding the location of the boundaries of the area concerned.

Following the general election of November 1990, in January 1991 a centre-left coalition Government was formed between the Social Democratic Party (SDP—Javnaðarflokkurin) and the conservative People's Party (Fólkaflokkurin), with the SDP's Atli Dam as Prime Minister (Løgmaður). Marita Petersen (also of the SDP) replaced Dam in January 1993. In April the People's Party withdrew from the coalition, and was replaced by the Republican Party (Tjóðveldisflokkurin) and the Home Rule Party (Sjálvstýrisflokkurin). At a general election held in July 1994, the Union Party (Sambandsflokkurin) became the largest party in the Løgting, winning eight seats, while the SDP's allocation was reduced to five seats. In September a coalition of the Union Party, the SDP, the Home Rule Party and the newly formed Labour Front (Verkmannafylkingin) took office. The Union Party's Edmund Joensen became Prime Minister.

At a general election held in April 1998, both the Republican Party and the People's Party increased their representation to eight seats, while the SDP secured seven; the representation of the Union Party was reduced to six seats. In May a coalition Government was formed by the People's Party, the Republican Party and the Home Rule Party, with Anfinn Kallsberg of the People's Party as Prime Minister.

Tensions with the Danish Government in the early 1990s, the nationalistic persuasion of the new Government and the prospect of offshore petroleum discoveries revived Faroese ambitions for political and economic independence. (The Faroese had narrowly favoured independence from Denmark in a referendum in 1946, but the decision had been overturned by the Danish Folketing.) In October 1998 the Løgting adopted a resolution in support of the Government's intention to seek status for the Faroe Islands as a 'sovereign nation' under the Danish monarchy. A commission charged with the development of a proposal for a Faroese constitution was established by the Government in February 1999, and submitted its conclusions to the Løgting in June 2000. The Faroese envisaged retaining Queen Margrethe II of Denmark as their Head of State and maintaining the link between their local currency and the Danish krone. The islands would seek to continue to co-operate with Denmark in social affairs, justice, health and air traffic control, and would also maintain present arrangements such as mutual rights of residence, employment and education. The Faroes would also seek to join the North Atlantic Treaty Organization (NATO, see p. 370) and the UN.

Negotiations between the Danish and Faroese administrations concerning the future independence of the Faroe Islands began in March 2000, but swiftly stalled after the Danish Government confirmed that, although it would not oppose Faroese independence, it would terminate annual subsidies (of about 1,000m. kroner) to the Faroes within four years should secession take place, compared with the 15 years proposed by the Faroese. Discussions were resumed later in the year, but finally collapsed in October, prompting Kallsberg to announce a plan to hold a referendum on independence in 2001. The referendum, which was scheduled to be held on 26 May, was to include four issues: the full transfer of authority to the Faroese by 2012; the establishment of an economic fund to guarantee financial security during the transitional period; the gradual elimination of subsidies from Denmark; and the holding of a further referendum establishing the Faroe Islands as an independent state by 2012. However, the Danish Government stated that Denmark would regard the referendum as a de facto referendum on sovereignty and that a vote in favour of the proposals for independence would result in the halting of Danish aid within four years. The reluctance of the Faroese population to lose Danish subsidies and disagreement within the Faroese coalition Government resulted in the cancellation of the referendum in March 2001.

At the general election held in April 2002, the People's Party won seven seats in the Løgting; it subsequently formed a coalition Government, headed again by Kallsberg and including the Republican Party (which had secured eight seats), and the Home Rule Party and the Centre Party (Miðflokkurin) (with one seat apiece); the Union Party secured eight seats in the Løgting and the SDP seven.

During an official visit to the Faroe Islands by the Danish Prime Minister, Anders Fogh Rasmussen, in June 2003, he and Kallsberg signed a bill providing a legal basis for the transfer of competencies from the Danish Government to the Faroese Government. The legislation did not in itself transfer any powers (this was to be done subsequently, with a separate resolution required in the Løgting for each power to be transferred), but it did detail those powers that would remain with the Danish Folketing, namely: the Danish Constitution; Danish citizenship; the Danish Supreme Court; currency and monetary policy; and foreign, security and defence policy. As with other bilateral agreements, identical versions of the bill, in both Faroese and Danish, were to pass before the Løgting and the Folketing, respectively.

In December 2003 the Government collapsed, following the withdrawal of the Republican Party from the coalition in response to allegations of Kallsberg's past involvement in accounting fraud. At the ensuing early election, held in January 2004, the Republican Party won eight seats, while the Union Party, the SDP and the People's Party each won seven seats. A new coalition Government was formed in February, with Jóannes Eidesgaard of the SDP as Prime Minister. Whereas the previous coalition had been composed of only pro-independence parties, the new administration comprised the People's Party, which supported independence, and the Union Party and the SDP, which both favoured continued union with Denmark.

In March 2004 the Government proposed a resolution recognizing that, despite the Faroes' long-standing policy of neutrality, they were a de facto member of NATO and had been so for some 50 years. In August the Danish Minister of Foreign Affairs, Per Stig Møller, paid a visit to the Faroes, during which he promised the islanders greater influence over Faroese foreign policy issues. Faroese representatives would also be permitted to attend NATO meetings whenever relevant issues were under discussion.

Following the enactment on 29 July 2005 (the Faroese National Day) of the legislation on the transfer of competencies, the Faroese Government announced its intention to transfer to its control powers covering civil emergency preparedness, company law, copyright law and industrial property rights, and the established church—all before its mandate expired in 2008. Areas that remained to be transferred at a later stage were the regulation of immigration and border control; criminal law; legislation and administration of the financial sector; health care; the judicial courts (excluding the Danish Supreme Court); the issuing of passports; the police and prosecution service; the prison service; and public pensions. Adopted and enacted concurrently with the transfer of competencies bill was an additional piece of new legislation, which granted the Faroese Government authority to negotiate and conclude agreements under international law with other states and international organizations, and allowed (under certain circumstances) the Faroe Islands to become a member of international organizations in their own right. In July 2006 Eidesgaard and Fogh Rasmussen signed an agreement for the Faroese Government to assume ownership of Vágar Airport from Denmark.

At the general election held in January 2008 the Republican Party retained its eight seats in the Løgting, while the Union Party and People's Party each won seven seats. The SDP secured just six seats, prompting speculation over the continuation of Eidesgaard's premiership. Following a change in the electoral law in late 2007, the number of seats in the Løgting was fixed at 33—membership had formerly varied from 27 to 32. In February a new coalition Government, comprising the SDP, the Republican Party and the Centre Party (which had won three seats at the election), took office. Eidesgaard remained as Prime Minister, while Høgni Hoydal assumed the newly created role of Minister of Foreign Affairs.

In mid-September 2008 the coalition Government collapsed, following the resignation of Eidesgaard as a result of a series of disagreements with Hoydal. A new coalition administration, comprising the Union Party, the People's Party and the SDP, took office later that month. The Chairman of the Union Party, Kaj Leo Johannesen, was appointed Prime Minister, while Eidesgaard became Minister of Finance.

In March 2010 a committee of the Løgting agreed on the text of a draft constitution for the Faroe Islands. The text aroused controversy in Denmark, particularly owing to its assertion that 'all power' in the Faroes resided with the Faroese people and the absence of any reference to the islands' status within the Danish Kingdom. In June the Danish Ministry of Justice declared that the text was contrary to the Danish Constitution and that it would place the islands' constitutional status in doubt. A revised version of the draft constitution, which addressed some of the Danish Government's concerns, was approved by the Løgting in May 2011. However, Denmark maintained that the revised document could still be interpreted as a de facto declaration of independence from the Kingdom, and in June the Danish Prime Minister, Lars Løkke Rasmussen, warned Johannesen that, were the constitution to be promulgated in its existing form, Denmark would expect the Faroe Islands formally to declare their independence. In response, Johannesen stated that the islands had no intention of seeking immediate independence, and that he would seek to resolve the Danish Government's concerns before the Løgting began further work on the document.

Meanwhile, in January 2011 Jørgen Niclasen resigned as Minister of Foreign Affairs, citing his wish to focus on his role as Chairman of the People's Party ahead of the next general election. The Minister of Fisheries, Jacob Vestergaard, also of the People's Party, was subsequently allocated additional responsibility for the foreign affairs portfolio. However, the People's Party withdrew its support from the coalition in April; the portfolios previously held by members of the People's Party were redistributed between ministers from the other two parties.

At an early general election held on 29 October 2011, the Union Party and the People's Party both increased their representation in the Løgting to eight seats, while the Republican Party and the SDP each secured six seats, the former losing its position as the party with the largest parliamentary representation. The newly formed pro-independence Progress Party (Framsókn) won two seats, as did the Centre Party, with the remaining seat taken by the Home Rule Party. Turnout was 86.6%. A new centre-right coalition Government, composed of the Union Party, the People's Party, the Centre Party and the Home Rule Party, took office in November, again headed by Johannesen, who also became Minister of Foreign Affairs. Annika Olsen of the People's Party was appointed as Deputy Prime Minister and Minister of Social Affairs, while the party's leader, Niclasen, assumed responsibility for the finance portfolio. The Home Rule Party withdrew from the coalition in September 2013.

In international affairs, the Faroe Islanders attracted opprobrium for their traditional slaughter of pilot whales (historically, an important source of food). After foreign journalists publicized the whaling in 1986, stricter regulations were imposed on such operations. In July 1992 the Faroese Government threatened to leave the International Whaling Commission (IWC, see p. 442), following the latter's criticism of whaling methods practised in the Faroe Islands. It was, however, claimed that the Faroese did not have the legal right to withdraw from the Commission independently of Denmark. Earlier in 1992 the Faroe Islands, Greenland, Norway and Iceland had agreed to establish the North Atlantic Marine Mammal Commission, in protest at what they viewed as the IWC's preoccupation with conservation. The Faroe Islands resumed commercial hunting of the minke whale in 1993 and, following a break of 14 years, recommenced trading in whale meat in 2002.

Agreements on free trade were concluded between the Faroe Islands and Iceland, Norway, Sweden, Finland and Austria in 1992–93 and between the Faroe Islands and the EU in January 2004. A new free trade agreement between the Faroe Islands and Iceland, known as the Hoyvík Agreement, was signed in August 2005. The agreement, which received legislative approval in April 2006, allowed for the free movement of all goods, services, capital and persons—effectively creating a common market between the two countries. A trade delegation led by the Icelandic Prime Minister, Halldór Ásgrímsson, visited the Faroe Islands in that month in order to explore new business opportunities facilitated by the agreement. Eidesgaard and Ásgrímsson discussed the two countries' relations with the EU and the possibility of the Faroe Islands joining the European Free Trade Association (EFTA, see p. 451), for which Ásgrímsson pledged Iceland's support. In May Eidesgaard sought and obtained the Løgting's approval for the initiation of membership negotiations with EFTA.

In September 2006 the Government signed an interim agreement with Denmark, Iceland and Norway regarding the demarcation of the continental shelf north of the Faroe Islands. In February 2007 Eidesgaard and the Icelandic Minister of Foreign Affairs signed a bilateral maritime boundary agreement, thereby ending a dispute that had lasted for more than three decades regarding overlapping claims to an area of around 3,650 sq km.

Faroese relations with the EU and Norway were strained during 2010–13 by a dispute over fishing quotas in the north-east Atlantic Ocean, amid concerns regarding the sustainability of stock. In July 2010 the Faroe Islands unilaterally increased their mackerel quota for 2010 from 25,000 metric tons to 85,000 tons. (Iceland had similarly decided to raise its quota.) The Faroe Islands and Iceland maintained that they had been forced to take this action having been excluded from a bilateral quota arrangement between the EU and Norway, and that stocks of mackerel had become more plentiful in their waters as a result of changing migration patterns. Seven rounds of negotiations between officials from the four parties, held between October 2010 and March 2011, ended without agreement on quotas for 2011. In April 2011 the Faroe Islands unilaterally announced that their mackerel quota for that year would be 150,000 tons. Several further rounds of negotiations, concerning quotas for 2012, took place between October 2011 and February 2012, but again ended without agreement. In February 2012 the Faroes announced a mackerel quota of 148,375 tons for that year. In response, the EU and Norway claimed that the Faroe Islands and Iceland were endangering mackerel stocks by setting their quotas too high. Following the withdrawal of the Faroe Islands from talks over internationally-agreed herring quotas in London, United Kingdom, in January 2013, in May the EU threatened the imposition of sanctions against the islands unless they ceased their overfishing of the Atlanto-Scandian herring stocks; the Faroes had unilaterally increased their herring quota from 31,000 tons in 2012 to 105,230 tons in 2013 (claiming a greater distribution and abundance of the fish in Faroese waters in recent years). In July the EU member states voted (by a qualified majority) to impose the sanctions, which were duly introduced in late August. The sanctions included restrictions on Faroese-flagged trawlers entering EU ports and an import ban on both Faroese herring and mackerel, since the two are often caught in the same nets (in March 2013 the Faroes had increased their mackerel quota for that year to 159,000 tons). In response, Faroese Prime Minister Johannesen accused the EU of introducing these punitive measures in order simply to protect the interests of its own fishing industry.

GOVERNMENT

Under the Home Rule Act of 1948 the Faroe Islands became a self-governing community in the Kingdom of Denmark. Under the Act, so-called Joint Matters (the judiciary, defence and foreign affairs) are under the authority of the Danish Government, whereas Special Matters (financial, economic and cultural matters, industry, foreign trade, natural resources in the subsoil) are under the control of the Faroese Government. A new Act in 2005 increased the areas of unilateral competence for the Faroese Government (see Contemporary Political History).

The legislative body is the Løgting (Lagting in Danish), which consists of 33 members, who are elected for four years on a basis of proportional representation. Following reforms implemented in 2007, the seven electoral constituencies that comprised the Faroe Islands were merged into a single constituency. All Faroese over the age of 18 years have the right to vote. Based on the strength of the parties in the Løgting, a Government (Landsstýri) is formed. This is the administrative body in certain spheres, chiefly relating to Faroese economic affairs. The Prime Minister (Løgmaður) has to ratify all laws approved by the Løgting. Power is decentralized and there are about 50 local authorities. The High Commissioner

(Ríkisumboðsmaður) represents the Danish Government, and has the right to address the Løgting and to advise on joint affairs. All Danish legislation must be submitted to the Landsstýri before becoming law in the Faroe Islands. The Faroese send two members to the Danish Folketing (parliament).

The Faroe Islands have 30 municipal councils.

REGIONAL CO-OPERATION

The Faroe Islands did not join the European Community (now the European Union—EU, see p. 273) with Denmark in 1973, but did secure favourable terms of trade with Community members and special concessions in Denmark and the United Kingdom. The Faroe Islands and Iceland form a free trade area under the Hoyvík Agreement. In international fisheries organizations, where Denmark is represented by the EU, the Kingdom maintains separate membership in respect of the Faroe Islands (and Greenland). In 1970 the Faroes were granted separate representation (of two members) within the Danish delegation to the Nordic Council (see p. 467).

ECONOMIC AFFAIRS

In 2011, according to official figures, gross national income (GNI) was 13,908m. kroner (at current prices). The population increased at an average annual rate of 0.1% per year in 2003–12. Gross domestic product (GDP) increased, in real terms, by an estimated 9.3% in 2007. GDP at current prices increased by 1.9% in 2012.

According to preliminary official figures, agriculture (principally sheep farming) and fishing contributed 17.5% of GDP in 2011. In March 2013 the sector provided 10.4% of employment. Potatoes and other vegetables are the main crops. Only about 6% of the land surface is cultivated.

Fishing is the dominant industry; the sector (excluding fish-processing) engaged 6.8% of the employed labour force in March 2013. Fish products accounted for 86.6% of exports in 2012. Most fishing takes place within the 200-nautical-mile (370-km) fisheries zone imposed around the Faroes in 1977. Fish farming, principally of salmon and trout, began in the 1980s. The traditional hunting of pilot whales continues to provide an important source of meat for the Faroese. The Faroe Islands began trading in whale meat in 2002 after a hiatus of 14 years.

Industry (including mining, manufacturing, construction and power) contributed 17.3% of GDP in 2012, according to preliminary official figures. In March 2013 the sector provided 18.0% of employment. The dominant sectors are fishing-related industries, such as fish-drying and -freezing, and ship maintenance and repairs.

Mining and quarrying contributed only 0.3% of GDP in 2000, and engaged 0.4% of the employed labour force in March 2013. 'Brown coal' (lignite) is mined on Suðuroy. The potential for petroleum production around the islands was initially believed to be significant. However, drilling undertaken during 2000–10 did not uncover hydrocarbons on a commercial scale, thus moderating expectations.

Manufacturing contributed 7.2% of GDP in 2012, according to preliminary official figures. The sector provided 10.7% of employment in March 2013. Technical repairs and shipyards are also significant: exports of vessels accounted for 5.6% of exports in 2012. A small textile industry exports traditional Faroese woollens.

According to preliminary official figures, the construction sector contributed 5.5% of GDP in 2012. The sector engaged 6.2% of the employed labour force in March 2013.

In 2012 62.1% of the islands' electricity production was provided by thermal energy, 34.2% by hydroelectric power and 3.7% by wind power. Imports of fuels and related products accounted for 19.6% of imports in 2012.

The services sector accounted for 67.8% of GDP in 2012, according to preliminary official figures. In March 2013 the sector provided 71.7% of employment. In 2003 an independent Faroese securities market was launched in co-operation with the Icelandic stock market.

In 2011 the Faroe Islands recorded a merchandise trade surplus of 305.8m. kroner and there was a surplus of 1,043.2m. kroner on the current account of the balance of payments. Norway was the Faroes' principal source of imports (27.2%) in 2012; other major suppliers were Denmark, Germany and Iceland. The United Kingdom was the principal market for exports (11.5%) in that year; other major purchasers were Nigeria, the Netherlands, Denmark, France, Germany, the USA and Iceland. In 2012 the European Union (EU, see p. 273) as a whole took 57.1% of exports and supplied 50.6% of imports. The principal import in 2012 was machinery and transport equipment, followed by mineral fuels and lubricants, food and live animals, basic manufactures, and chemical and related products. Fish and fish products accounted for 86.6% of total exports in the same year; other notable exports included ships.

Danish subsidies are an important source of income to the islands and account for about 6% of annual Faroese GDP. In 2012 the Faroese Government recorded a budget deficit of 273m. kroner, equivalent to 2.0% of GDP. In 2006 the public sector debt was 405m. kroner. The average annual rate of inflation was 2.0% in 2003–12; consumer prices rose by 2.2% in 2012. Unemployment was 11.3% of the labour force (including both registered and full-time unemployed) in March 2013.

The Faroe Islands' economy is heavily dependent on the fishing industry for its principal source of income. Depletion of stocks and the resulting decline in catches, together with a fall in export prices, led to a reduction in export earnings and a financial crisis in the early 1990s. From the end of the 1990s until the late 2000s the Faroe Islands experienced a period of economic prosperity (notwithstanding a downturn in 2003–04), with high levels of growth—driven by increases in private consumption and investment—and low unemployment. However, despite public sector investment and tax cuts in 2008, the Faroes were affected by the global financial crisis, which had an adverse impact on the cost and availability of borrowing, and thus on investment, as well as on consumer confidence. By 2009 over-fishing had led to a notable decline in stocks (particularly of cod and haddock), which, combined with lower international fish prices, led to a sharp fall in export revenues and an increase in unemployment. These factors were responsible for an estimated total contraction in real GDP of some 8% in 2008–09. The economy returned to growth in 2010; according to the Government Bank (Landsbanki Føroya), nominal GDP (i.e. GDP at current prices) grew by 7.0% in 2010, 2.5% in 2011 and by 3.6% in 2012. Nominal GDP was forecast to expand by 4.9% in 2013 and by 1.4% in 2014, mainly as a result of an improved outlook for the fisheries sector, particularly salmon-farming and mackerel fisheries, and a projected small rise in private consumption. In the early 2010s the aquaculture sub-sector accounted for some 35% of total annual fish exports. However, the unemployment rate increased significantly in 2008–11, from a low of 1.1% in June 2008 to a peak of 7.9% in February 2011 (a level comparable to those recorded during the economic downturn in the early 1990s), partly owing to significant job losses resulting from the bankruptcy of Faroe Seafood in late 2010. According to the Government Bank, the number of full-time unemployed decreased from 6.8% of the workforce at January 2012 to 5.3% of the workforce at March 2013; this fall was partly owing to a rise in net emigration (as larger numbers of young Faroese sought higher education overseas). In accordance with a parliamentary ruling adopted in December 2012, the Government Bank ceased operations on 1 April 2013; a number of the bank's former functions were transferred to other government institutions (responsibility for loan management and investment management was passed on to the Føroya Gjaldstova). The Government aimed to achieve a balanced budget by 2016 by reducing expenditure, raising greater revenue (primarily through increased charges for fishing rights), and by stimulating both domestic demand and productivity growth in the private and public sectors.

PUBLIC HOLIDAYS

Public holidays in the Faroe Islands are the same as those for Denmark. In addition, the Faroese also celebrate Flag Day on 25 April and Ólavsøka (St Olav's Day) on 28–29 July each year. Various regional holidays are also observed in May–July.

Statistical Survey

Sources (unless otherwise stated): Statistics Faroe Islands, Traðagøta 39, POB 2068, 165 Argir; tel. 352028; fax 352038; e-mail hagstova@hagstova.fo; internet www.hagstova.fo; Faroese Government Office, Hovedvagtsgade 8, 2, 1103 Copenhagen K; tel. 33-14-08-66; fax 33-93-85-75; Landsbanki Føroya (Faroese Government Bank), Staravegur 5, POB 229, 110 Tórshavn; tel. 308120; fax 318537; e-mail landsbank@landsbank.fo; internet landsbankin.fo.

AREA AND POPULATION

Area: 1,396 sq km (539 sq miles).

Population: 48,197 at 1 January 2013 (males 25,019, females 23,178).

Density (1 January 2013): 34.5 per sq km.

Population by Age and Sex (official estimates at 1 January 2013): *0–14:* 10,257 (males 5,309, females 4,948); *15–64:* 30,296 (males 16,034, females 14,262); *65 and over:* 7,644 (males 3,676, females 3,968); *Total* 48,197 (males 25,019, females 23,178).

Principal Towns (population at 1 January 2013): Tórshavn (capital) 12,245; Klaksvík 4,585; Hoyvík 3,730; Argir 1,998; Fuglafjørður 1,503; Vágur 1,330; Vestmanna 1,166; Miðvágur 1,057.

Births, Marriages and Deaths (2012): Registered live births 617 (birth rate 12.7 per 1,000); Registered marriages 237 (marriage rate 4.9 per 1,000); Registered deaths 407 (death rate 8.4 per 1,000).

Life Expectancy (years at birth, 2012): 81.9 (males 79.6; females 84.6).

Immigration and Emigration (2012): *Immigration:* Denmark 1,009; Greenland 20; Iceland 39; Norway 40; Sweden 24; Total (incl. others) 1,301. *Emigration:* Denmark 1,329; Greenland 23; Iceland 18; Norway 52; Sweden 17; Total (incl. others) 1,524.

Economically Active Population (persons aged 16–74 years with at least seven hours' paid work per month, at March 2013): Agriculture 44; Fishing 1,584; Aquaculture 788; Mining 96; Fish-processing 1,208; Shipyards and machine shops 533; Other production 743; Construction 1,452; Energy supply 144; Wholesale and retail trade 2,883; Restaurants and hotels 575; Sea transport 838; Other transport 679; Communication 416; Finance and insurance 755; Business services 693; Household services 315; Public administration (incl. municipal services) 3,781; Education 1,605; Health and social work 3,488; Other services 643; *Sub-total* 23,263; Activities not adequately defined 85; *Total employed* 23,348; Unemployed 2,984; *Total labour force* 26,332 (males 13,302, females 13,030).

HEALTH AND WELFARE

Key Indicators

Physicians (per 1,000 head, 2012): 1.7.

Hospital Beds (per 1,000 head, 2012): 4.7.

Total Carbon Dioxide Emissions ('000 metric tons, 2010): 711.4.

Carbon Dioxide Emissions Per Head (metric tons, 2010): 14.3.

AGRICULTURE, ETC.

Principal Crop (2012, FAO estimate): Potatoes 1,500 metric tons. Source: FAO.

Livestock ('000 head, year ending September 2012, FAO estimates): Cattle 2; Sheep 68. Source: FAO.

Livestock Products (metric tons, 2012, FAO estimates): Cattle meat 78; Sheep meat 528. Source: FAO.

Fishing ('000 metric tons, live weight, 2012): Capture 360.5 (Argentines 12.6; Atlantic cod 29.7; Atlantic mackerel 107.1; Saithe—Pollock 39.3; Blue whiting—Poutassou 43.0; Atlantic herring 51.4; Capelin 29.7); Aquaculture 62.8 (Atlantic salmon 62.8); *Total catch* 423.3.

INDUSTRY

Selected Products ('000 metric tons, 1996): Frozen or chilled fish 123; Salted and processed fish products 15; Aquaculture products 13; Oils, fats and meal of aquatic animals 124; *2006:* Soft drinks ('000 litres) 1,974; Beer ('000 litres) 2,326. *2012:* Electric energy (million kWh) 291.6.

FINANCE

(Danish currency is in use)

Budget (general government budget, million kroner, 2006): *Revenue:* Taxes and duties 3,482; Interest, dividends 156; Transfers from the Danish Government 658; Loan repayments 101; Total (incl. others) 4,088. *Expenditure:* Salaries 1,775; Purchase of goods and services 874; Construction and fixed assets production 238; Transfers to households 1,164; Total (incl. others) 3,946. *2012:* Total revenue 7,263 (Taxes 6,041, Interest and dividends 275, Other current transfers 940, Capital revenue 7); Total expenditure 7,506 (Interest and other property expenditure 201, Subsidies 144, Other current transfers 1,984, Final consumption expenditure 4,213, Capital expenditure 964).

Cost of Living (Consumer Price Index at July–September; base: January–March 2001 = 100): All items 118.4 in 2011; 121.3 in 2012; 120.0 in 2013.

Gross Domestic Product (million kroner at current prices): 12,942 in 2010; 13,254 in 2011; 13,502 in 2012.

Expenditure on the Gross Domestic Product (million kroner at current prices, 2011): Government final consumption expenditure 4,174; Private final consumption expenditure 7,348; Gross capital formation 2,433; *Total domestic expenditure* 13,955; Exports of goods and services 6,511; *Less* Imports of goods and services 7,211; *GDP in purchasers' values* 13,255.

Gross Domestic Product by Sector (million kroner at current prices, 2012): Agriculture, hunting, forestry, fishing and mining 1,753; Manufacture of food products and beverages 844; Electricity, gas and water supply 145; Construction 653; Other industry 400; Wholesale and retail trade, hotels and restaurants 1,157; Transport and communications 1,173; Financial intermediation, insurance and pension funding 439; Real estate and business activities 1,456; Public administration 748; Education 764; Health and social work 1,362; Other service activities 893; *Gross value added in basic prices* 11,788; Taxes on products (net) 1,714; *GDP in market prices* 13,502. Note: Financial intermediation services indirectly measured assumed to be distributed at source.

Balance of Payments (million kroner, 2011): Exports of goods f.o.b. 5,400.9; Imports of goods c.i.f. –5,095.0; *Trade balance* 305.8; Exports of services 1,110.3; Imports of services –2,116.4; *Balance on goods and services* –700.2; Net transfers and income 1,743.4; *Current balance* 1,043.2.

EXTERNAL TRADE

Principal Commodities (million kroner, 2012): *Imports c.i.f.:* Food and live animals 920.8; Mineral fuels, lubricants and related materials 1,303.9 (Petroleum and petroleum products 1,301.9); Chemicals and related products 454.7; Manufactured goods classified chiefly by material 593.1; Machinery and transport equipment 2,364.3 (General industrial machinery and equipment 199.9; Road vehicles 260.6; Other transport equipment 1,390.7); Miscellaneous manufactured articles 526.3; Total (incl. others) 6,660.4. *Exports f.o.b.:* Fish products (chilled, frozen and salted) 4,756.2 (Cod 452.5; Haddock 62.3; Saithe 419.2; Salmon 1,821.6; Trout 0.2; Blue whiting 160.5; Herring 324.6; Atlantic mackerel 826.8; Prawns 102.6); Vessels 306.3; Total (incl. others) 5,493.4.

Principal Trading Partners (million kroner, 2012): *Imports c.i.f.:* Brazil 93.8; China, People's Rep. 259.4; Denmark 1,569.9; France 94.7; Germany 642.1; Iceland 546.2; Netherlands 96.4; Norway 1,811.0; Peru 168.7; Poland 228.4; Russia 72.7; Sweden 210.6; United Kingdom 172.1; Total (incl. others) 6,660.4. *Exports f.o.b.:* China, People's Rep. 197.5; Denmark 393.6; France 397.5; Germany 383.9; Iceland 344.2; Italy 172.4; Lithuania 97.4; Netherlands 403.1; Nigeria 479.4; Norway 221.3; Poland 292.0; Russia 463.0; Spain 186.2; Sweden 93.5; Taiwan 56.8; United Kingdom 630.0; USA 365.5; Total (incl. others) 5,493.4.

TRANSPORT

Road Traffic (registered motor vehicles, 1 January 2013): Private motor cars 20,338 (incl. 99 taxis); Buses 215; Lorries and vans 4,113; Motorcycles 915; Mopeds 1,659.

Shipping: *Flag Registered Fleet* (31 December 2013): 220 vessels, Total displacement 403,998 grt (Source: Lloyd's List Intelligence—www.lloydslistintelligence.com). *International Sea-borne Freight Traffic* (1996, '000 metric tons): Goods loaded 223, Goods unloaded 443.

TOURISM

Nationality of Overnight Guests at Guesthouses (2006): Faroe Islands 30,383; Denmark 44,147; Iceland 7,793; Norway 11,423; Sweden 2,249; Finland 1,285; United Kingdom and Ireland 4,842; Germany 3,922; USA and Canada 1,583; Austria and Switzerland 906; Total (incl. others) 116,236.

COMMUNICATIONS MEDIA

Book Production (2012): 262 titles.

Newspapers (2012): 9 titles per week (circulation 16,800).

Telephones ('000 main lines in use, 2012): 24.0 (Source: International Telecommunication Union).

Mobile Cellular Telephones ('000 subscribers, 2012): 61.0 (Source: International Telecommunication Union).

Internet Subscribers ('000, 2010): 16.4 (Source: International Telecommunication Union).

Broadband Subscribers ('000, 2010): 16.3 (Source: International Telecommunication Union).

EDUCATION

Institutions (2000/01): Basic schools 61 (Secondary schools 21); Upper secondary schools 3; Higher preparatory institutions 3.

Teachers (2002/03): 697 (full-time equivalent) in primary and secondary schools.

Students (2002/03, unless otherwise indicated): Pre-primary (1998/99) 59; Primary 5,567; Secondary 2,131; Upper secondary 600; Higher preparatory 165; Business schools 351; Fishery college 31; Social and health care school 60; Technical schools 108; University 154; Total further education (1996/97) 2,166.

Directory

The Government

The legislative body is the Løgting (Lagting in Danish), which consists of 33 members, who are elected for four years on a basis of proportional representation. Following reforms implemented in 2007, the seven electoral constituencies that comprised the Faroe Islands were merged into a single constituency. All Faroese over the age of 18 years have the right to vote. Based on the strength of the parties in the Løgting, a Landsstýri (Government) is formed. This is the administrative body in certain spheres, chiefly relating to Faroese economic affairs. The Prime Minister (Løgmaður) has to ratify all laws approved by the Løgting. Power is decentralized and there are about 50 local authorities. The High Commissioner (Ríkisumboðsmaður) represents the Danish Government, and has the right to address the Løgting and to advise on joint affairs. All Danish legislation must be submitted to the Landsstýri before becoming law in the Faroe Islands.

The Danish Folketing (parliament), to which the Faroese send two members, is responsible for defence and foreign policy, constitutional matters and the judicial and monetary systems.

HEAD OF STATE

Queen of Denmark: HM Queen MARGRETHE II.

LANDSSTÝRI

(April 2014)

A coalition of the Union Party (UP), the People's Party (PP) and the Centre Party.

Prime Minister and Minister of Foreign Affairs: KAJ LEO JOHANNESEN.

Deputy Prime Minister and Minister of Social Affairs: ANNIKA OLSEN.

Minister of Finance: JØRGEN NICLASEN.

Minister of Health: KARSTEN HANSEN.

Minister of Education, Research and Culture: BJØRN KALSØ.

Minister of Trade and Industry: JOHAN DAHL.

Minister of Fisheries: JACOB VESTERGAARD.

Government Offices

Rigsombudsmanden på Færøerne (Danish High Commission): Amtmansbrekkan 6, POB 12, 110 Tórshavn; tel. 201200; fax 201220; e-mail ro@fo.stm.dk; internet www.rigsombudsmanden.fo; High Commissioner DAN MICHAEL KNUDSEN.

Løgmansskrivstovan (Prime Minister's Office): Tinganes, POB 64, 110 Tórshavn; tel. 306000; fax 351015; e-mail info@tinganes.fo; internet www.tinganes.fo.

Ministry of Education, Research and Culture: Hoyvíksvegur 72, POB 3279, 110 Tórshavn; tel. 306500; fax 306555; e-mail mmr@mmr.fo; internet www.mmr.fo.

Ministry of Finance: Kvíggjartún 1, POB 2039, 165 Argir; tel. 352020; fax 352025; e-mail fmr@fmr.fo; internet www.fmr.fo.

Ministry of Fisheries: Yviri við Strond 15, POB 347, 110 Tórshavn; tel. 353030; fax 353035; e-mail fisk@fisk.fo; internet www.fisk.fo.

Ministry of Health: Eirargarður 2, 100 Tórshavn; tel. 304050; fax 304025; e-mail hmr@hmr.fo; internet www.hmr.fo.

Ministry of the Interior: POB 159, 110 Tórshavn; tel. 306800; fax 306885; e-mail imr@imr.fo; internet www.imr.fo.

Ministry of Trade and Industry: Tinganes, POB 377, 110 Tórshavn; tel. 306600; fax 306665; e-mail vmr@vmr.fo; internet www.vmr.fo.

Representation of the Faroes in Copenhagen: North Atlantic House, Strandgade 91, 4th Floor, 1401 Copenhagen K, Denmark; tel. 32-83-37-70; fax 32-83-37-75; e-mail copenhagen@tinganes.fo; internet www.faroesrep.dk.

LØGTING

The Løgting has 33 members, elected by universal adult suffrage.

Løgtingsskrivstovan (Parliament Office): Tinghúsvegur 1–3, POB 208, 110 Tórshavn; tel. 363900; fax 363901; e-mail logting@logting.fo; internet www.logting.fo.

Speaker: JÓGVAN LAKJUNI.

Election, 29 October 2011

Party	Votes	% of votes	Seats
Sambandsflokkurin (Union Party)	7,545	24.71	8
Fólkaflokkurin (People's Party)	6,882	22.54	8
Tjóðveldi (Republican Party)	5,584	18.29	6
Javnaðarflokkurin (Social Democratic Party)	5,417	17.74	6
Framsókn (Progress Party)	1,933	6.33	2
Miðflokkurin (Centre Party)	1,882	6.16	2
Sjálvstýrisflokkurin (Home Rule Party)	1,289	4.22	1
Total	30,532	100.00	33

Political Organizations

Fólkaflokkurin (People's Party): Jónas Broncksgøta 29, 100 Tórshavn; tel. 318210; fax 322091; e-mail folkaflokkurin@logting.fo; internet folkaflokkurin.fo; f. 1940; conservative-liberal party, favours free enterprise and wider political and economic autonomy for the Faroes; Chair. JØRGEN NICLASEN.

Framsókn (Progress Party): Tórshavn; e-mail framsokn@framsokn.fo; internet www.framsokn.fo; centre-right, liberal, separatist party.

Javnaðarflokkurin (Social Democratic Party—SDP): Áarvegur 2, POB 208, 100 Tórshavn; tel. 312493; fax 319397; e-mail javnadarflokkarin@logting.fo; internet www.j.fo; f. 1925; Leader AKSEL JOHANNESEN.

Miðflokkurin (Centre Party): Áarvegur 2, POB 3237, 110 Tórshavn; tel. 310599; fax 312206; e-mail midflokkurin@olivant.fo; internet www.midflokkurin.fo; f. 1992; Christian principles; Chair. JENIS AV RANA.

Sambandsflokkurin (Union Party): Áarvegur 2, POB 208, 110 Tórshavn; tel. 318870; fax 312496; e-mail sambandsflokkurin@logting.fo; internet www.samband.fo; f. 1906; favours the maintenance of close relations between the Faroes and the Kingdom of Denmark; conservative in internal affairs; Chair. KAJ LEO JOHANNESEN.

Sjálvstýrisflokkurin (Home Rule Party): Áarvegur 2, 100 Tórshavn; tel. 596062; e-mail post@sjalvstyrisflokkurin.fo; internet www.sjalvstyri.fo; f. 1906; social-liberal; advocates eventual political independence for the Faroes within the Kingdom of Denmark; Chair. KÁRI P. HØJGAARD.

Tjóðveldi (Republican Party): POB 143, 110 Tórshavn; tel. 312200; fax 312262; e-mail loysing@post.olivant.fo; internet www.tjodveldi.fo; f. 1948 as Tjóðveldisflokkurin; adopted current name 2007; left-wing, advocates the secession of the Faroes from Denmark; Chair. HØGNI HOYDAL.

Religion

CHRISTIANITY

The Faroes National Church (Fólkakirkjan) is the established church in the islands. Formerly a diocese of the Evangelical Lutheran Church of Denmark, it gained independence in July 2007 as part of an agreement signed in 2005 between the Faroese and Danish authorities regarding the transfer of competencies to the Faroese Government. The Church had 39,560 members in 2012, accounting for 82.1% of the population. The largest independent group is the Plymouth Brethren. There is also a small Roman Catholic community.

Evangelical Lutheran Church

Føroyska Fólkakirkjan (Faroes National Church): Føroya Stiftsstjórn, J. Paturssonargøta 20, 100 Tórshavn; tel. 311995; fax 315889; e-mail stift@folkakirkjan.fo; internet www.folkakirkjan.fo; f. 2007; 39,560 mems (2012); Bishop JÓGVAN FRÍÐRIKSSON.

Christian Brethren Assemblies (Plymouth Brethren)

Around 10% of the population of the Faroe Islands are adherents of the Christian Brethren Assemblies, of which there are 35 in total. The first assembly on the Islands was established in 1878 by a Scottish missionary.

Ebenezer Samkoman (Ebenezer Evangelical Church): N. Finsensgøta 6, POB 168, 100 Tórshavn; tel. 311804; e-mail ebenezer@ebenezer.fo; internet www.ebenezer.fo; f. 1879.

The Roman Catholic Church

Catholic Church in the Faroe Islands: Mariukirkjan (St Mary's Church), Mariugøta 4, 100 Tórshavn; tel. and fax 310380; e-mail sktmaria@post.olivant.fo; internet www.katolsk.fo; 150 adherents; Parish Priest Fr PAUL MARX.

The Press

In 2012 there was one daily newspaper in the Faroe Islands, *Dimmalætting*.

Dimmalætting: Niels Finsensgøta. 10, POB 3019, 110 Tórshavn; tel. 790200; fax 790201; e-mail redaktion@dimma.fo; internet www.dimma.fo; f. 1878; 5 a week; Wed. edn distributed free of charge; Editor ÁRNI GREGERSEN; circ. 7,500 (18,500 on Wed.).

Norðlýsið: Rygsvegur 3, POB 58, 700 Klaksvík; tel. 456285; fax 456498; e-mail info@nordlysid.fo; internet www.nordlysid.fo; f. 1915; weekly; Editor JOHN WILLIAM JOENSEN; circ. 1,300.

Oyggjatíðindi: Lýðarsvegur 19, POB 3312, 110 Tórshavn; tel. 314411; fax 316411; e-mail oyggjat@post.olivant.fo; internet www.oyggjatidindi.com; 2 a week; circ. 3,500.

Sosialurin: Vágsbotnur, POB 76, 100 Tórshavn; tel. 341800; fax 341801; e-mail post@sosialurin.fo; internet www.sosialurin.fo; f. 1927; 3 a week; 34% owned by Føroya Tele; Editor EIRIKUR LINDENSKOV; circ. 8,000.

Vikublaðið: Vágsbotnur POB 76, Vágsbotnur, 110 Tórshavn; tel. 359999; fax 359990; e-mail vikublad@vikublad.fo; internet www.vikublad.fo; f. 2001; weekly; distributed free of charge; acquired by Dimmalætting P/F in 2008; Editor ERNST S. OLSEN; circ. 20,000.

Vinnuvitan: Smyrilsvegur 13, POB 3202, 110 Tórshavn; tel. 541200; fax 541201; e-mail info@vinnuvitan.fo; internet www.vinnuvitan.biz; f. 2004; weekly; business issues; acquired by Dimmalætting P/F in 2008; circ. 2,300.

Publishers

Bókadeild Føroya Lærarafelags: Pedda við Steinsgøta 9, 100 Tórshavn; tel. 317644; fax 319644; e-mail bfl@bfl.fo; internet www.bfl.fo; division of Faroese Teachers Asscn; run on a commercial basis, but receives govt grants; children's books, a children's magazine (*Strok*) and a teachers' magazine (*Skúlablaðið*); Editors MARNA JACOBSEN, TURIÐ KJØLBRO.

Nám: Hoyviksegur 72, POB 3084, 110 Tórshavn; tel. 755150; e-mail nam@nam.fo; internet www.fsg.fo; educational; Chair. ÁRNI DAHL.

Broadcasting and Communications

TELECOMMUNICATIONS

The Faroese telecommunications industry, formerly a monopoly under Føroya Tele, was opened to competition in the early 2000s.

Føroya Tele (Faroese Telecom): Klingran 3, POB 27, 110 Tórshavn; tel. 303030; fax 303031; e-mail ft@ft.fo; internet www.tele.fo; f. 1906; owned by Faroese Govt; fixed-line and mobile cellular telecommunications, broadband internet services; Chair. KLAUS PEDERSEN; CEO KRISTIAN R. DAVIDSEN.

Vodafone: Óðinshædd 2, POB 3299, 110 Tórshavn; tel. 202020; fax 202021; e-mail vodafone@vodafone.fo; internet www.vodafone.fo; f. 1999 as Kall P/F; name changed as above 2008; offers mobile cellular telecommunications and broadband internet access; CEO GUDNY LANGGAARD.

Regulatory Authority

Fjarskiftiseftirlitið (Telecommunications Authority of the Faroe Islands): Skálatrøð 20, POB 73, 110 Tórshavn; tel. 356020; fax 356035; e-mail fjarskiftiseftirlitid@fjarskiftiseftirlitid.fo; internet www.fjarskiftiseftirlitid.fo; f. 1997; independent govt agency with regulatory powers; Dir JÓGVAN THOMSEN.

BROADCASTING

Radio

Kringvarp Føroya (Faroese Broadcasting Corpn): Norðari Ringvegur 20, Postboks 1299, 110 Tórshavn; tel. 347500; fax 347501; e-mail netvarp@kringvarp.fo; internet www.kringvarp.fo; f. 2005 by merger of Sjónvarp Føroya (Faroese Television) and Útvarp Føroya (Radio Faroe Islands); Man. ANNIKA MITTÚN JACOBSEN.

Television

P/F Televarpið: Klingran 1, POB 3128, 110 Tórshavn; tel. 340340; fax 340341; e-mail televarp@televarp.fo; internet www.televarp.fo; f. 2002; digital terrestrial broadcaster; provides 28 channels; subsidiary of Føroya Tele; Man. Dir EDVARD Í SKORINI JOENSEN.

Finance

BANKS

(cap. = capital; res = reserves; dep. = deposits; m. = million; brs = branches; amounts in kroner)

Bank Nordik P/F (Faroese Bank): Húsagøta 3, POB 3048, 110 Tórshavn; tel. 330330; fax 316950; e-mail info@banknordik.fo; internet www.banknordik.fo; f. 1994 as Føroya Banki P/F following merger of Føroya Banki (f. 1906) and Sjóvinnubankin (f. 1932); name changed as above 2010; 33.3% owned by Faroese Govt through Finansieringsfonden af 1992 following privatization in June 2007; cap. 1,957m., res 1,757m., dep. 13,032m. (Dec. 2011); Chair. KLAUS RASMUSSEN; CEO JANUS PETERSEN; 24 brs.

Eik Banki P/F: Yviri við Strond 2, POB 34, 110 Tórshavn; tel. 348000; fax 348800; e-mail eik@eik.fo; internet www.eik.fo; f. 1832; cap. 100m., res 122m., dep. 6,519.5m. (Dec. 2012); Chair. TORBEN NIELSEN; CEO SÚNI SCHWARTZ JACOBSEN; 6 brs.

Norðoya Sparikassi: Ósávegur 1, POB 149, 700 Klaksvík; tel. 475000; fax 476000; e-mail ns@ns.fo; internet www.ns.fo; savings bank; Chair. JOHN P. DANIELSEN; Man. Dir MARNER MORTENSEN.

Suðuroyar Sparikassi P/F: POB 2, 900 Vágur; tel. 359870; fax 359871; e-mail sparsu@sparsu.fo; internet www.ss.fo; savings bank; Man. Dir SØREN L. BRUHN.

STOCK EXCHANGE

Virðisbrævamarknaður Føroya P/F (VMF) (Faroese Securities Market): c/o Landsbanki Føroya, Yviri við Strond 15, POB 229, 110 Tórshavn; tel. 350300; fax 350301; internet vmf.fo; f. 2000; lists Faroese securities in co-operation with Nasdaq OMX Iceland; Chair. STEFÁN HALLDÓRSSON; CEO SIGURÐ POULSEN.

INSURANCE

Tryggingareftirlitið (Insurance Authority): Skálatrøð 20, POB 73, 110 Tórshavn; tel. 356020; fax 356035; e-mail tryggingareftirlitid@tryggingareftirlitid.fo; internet www.tryggingareftirlitid.fo; nat. financial supervisory authority with jurisdiction over insurance, pension funds and one mortgage credit institution; Dir JÓGVAN THOMSEN.

Føroya Lívstrygging P/F (Lív) (Faroese Life Assurance Co): Kopargøta, POB 206, 110 Tórshavn; tel. 311111; fax 351110; e-mail liv@liv.fo; internet www.liv.fo; f. 1967; reorg. 2000; owned by Faroese Govt; partial privatization pending; life insurance; Man. Dir POUL CHRISTOFFUR THOMASSEN.

Trygd P/F: Húsagøta 3, POB 44, 110 Tórshavn; tel. 358100; fax 317211; e-mail trygd@trygd.fo; internet www.trygd.fo; f. 1932; activities suspended 1940–97; owned by Bank Nordik P/F; all types of insurance, both marine and non-marine; Man. Dir JANUS THOMSEN.

Tryggingarfelagið Føroyar P/F: Kongabrúgvin, POB 329, 110 Tórshavn; tel. 345600; e-mail tf@trygging.fo; internet www.trygging.fo; f. 1998; all types of insurance, both marine and non-marine; CEO REGIN HAMMER.

Trade and Industry

GOVERNMENT AGENCIES

Jarðfeingi (Faroese Earth and Energy Directorate): Brekkutún 1, POB 3059, 110 Tórshavn; tel. 357000; fax 357001; e-mail jardfeingi@jardfeingi.fo; internet www.jardfeingi.fo; f. 2006 by merger of Oljufyrisitingin (Faroese Petroleum Administration) and Jarðfrøðisavnið (Faroese Geological Survey); responsible for the administration and responsible utilization of all Faroese earth and energy resources, including hydrocarbons; Dir PETUR JOENSEN.

Kappingarráðið (Faroese Competition Authority): Skálatrøð 20, POB 73, 110 Tórshavn; tel. 356040; fax 356055; e-mail terje@kapping.fo; internet www.kapping.fo; f. 1997; consists of a chairman and 3 members, appointed by the Minister of Trade and Industry for a 4-year term; Dir JÓGVAN THOMSEN.

INDUSTRIAL AND TRADE ASSOCIATIONS

L/F Føroya Fiskasøla—Faroe Seafood P/F: Vestara Bryggja, POB 68, 110 Tórshavn; tel. and fax 555500; e-mail simon@faroe.com; internet www.faroe.com; f. 1948; restructured 1995; jt stock co of fish producers; exports all seafood products; CEO SIMUN P. JACOBSEN.

Føroya Reiðarafelag (Faroe Shipowners' Asscn): Gongin 10, POB 361, 110 Tórshavn; tel. 311800; fax 320380; e-mail shipown@olivant.fo; internet www.shipowner-fo.com; f. 1908; Chair. VIBERG SØRENSEN.

Vinnuhúsið (House of Industry): Smærugøta 9A, POB 1038, 100 Tórshavn; tel. 309900; fax 309901; e-mail industry@industry.fo; internet www.industry.fo; confed. of industrial orgs; 15 branches representing all areas of Faroese industry; Chair MAGNUS MAGNUSSEN.

UTILITIES

Electricity

Elfelagið SEV: Landavegur 92, POB 319, 110 Tórshavn; tel. 346800; fax 346801; e-mail sev@sev.fo; internet www.sev.fo; owned by Faroese Govt; Man. Dir HÁKUN DJURHUUS.

Gas

AGA Føroyar Sp/f (Føroya Gassøla): Akranesgøta 2, POB 1088, 110 Tórshavn; tel. 315544; fax 311706; e-mail gassola@gassola.fo; internet gassola.fo; subsidiary of AGA A/S (Denmark); Dir ANNFINN HANNSON.

Water

Local councils are responsible for the provision of water.

EMPLOYERS' ORGANIZATION

Føroya Arbeiðsgevarafelag (Faroese Employers' Asscn): Vinnuhúsið, Smærugøta 9A, POB 1038, 110 Tórshavn; tel. 311864; fax 317278; e-mail industry@industry.fo; internet www.industry.fo; more than 550 mem. cos; owns and manages House of Industry (see Vinnuhúsið); organized in 15 sectoral asscns, including Faroe Trade Masters Asscn, Faroe Fish Producers' Asscn, Faroe Fish Farming Asscn, Fed. of Faroes Industries, Faroe Merchant and Shopkeepers Asscn and Faroe Oil Industries Asscn; Chair. BERGUR POULSEN.

TRADE UNION

Føroya Arbeiðara- og Serarbeiðarafelag (Faroese Labour Organization): Tjarnardeild 5–7, POB 56, 110 Tórshavn; tel. 312101; fax 315374; e-mail fafelag@fafelag.fo; internet www.fafelag.fo; Chair. GEORG F. HANSEN.

Transport

There are about 458 km of roads in the Faroe Islands. A 4.9-km tunnel running under the sea, linking Vágur to Streymoy, was opened in December 2002. A second tunnel, linking Borðoy with Eysturoy, was opened in 2006.

The main harbour is at Tórshavn; the other ports are at Fuglafjørður, Klaksvík, Skálafjørður, Tvøroyri, Vágur and Vestmanna. Between mid-May and mid-September a ferry service links the Faroe Islands with Iceland, Denmark and Norway.

There is an airport on Vágur. There are no railway lines in the Faroe Islands.

Atlantic Airways P/F: Vágur Airport, 380 Sørvágur; tel. 341000; fax 341001; internet www.atlantic.fo; f. 1987; 67% owned by Faroese Govt; part privatized 2007; scheduled and charter passenger and cargo services to Denmark (Copenhagen, Billund and Aalborg), Greenland, Iceland (Reykjavík), Norway (Stavanger and Oslo), Sweden (Stockholm) and the United Kingdom (London, the Shetland Islands and Aberdeen); CEO MAGNI ARGE.

Smyril Line P/F: Yviri við Strond 1, POB 370, 110 Tórshavn; tel. 345900; fax 345901; e-mail office@smyrilline.com; internet www.smyrilline.com; f. 1982; ferry services to Denmark and Iceland; Man. Dir RÚNI VANG POULSEN.

Tourism

Tourism is the Islands' second largest industry after fishing. In 2006 there were 116,236 tourist arrivals.

VisitFaroeIslands: í Gongini 9, POB 118, 100 Tórshavn; tel. 206100; e-mail info@visitfaroeislands.com; internet www.visitfaroeislands.com; f. 2006 by merger of Faroe Islands Tourist Board and Faroe Islands Trade Council; Dir GUÐRIÐ HØJGAARD.

Defence

In October 2012 a joint service Arctic Command, established by the merger of the Greenland and Faroese military commands, was inaugurated. (See also the chapter on Denmark.)

Education

The education system is similar to that of Denmark, except that Faroese is the language of instruction. Danish is, however, a compulsory subject in all schools. Education is compulsory for nine years between seven and 16 years of age. There is one University in the Faroe Islands.

In 2012 government expenditure on education represented 5.7% of gross domestic product.

GREENLAND

Introductory Survey

LOCATION, CLIMATE, LANGUAGE, RELIGION, FLAG, CAPITAL

Greenland (Kalaallit Nunaat) is the world's largest island, with a total area of 2,166,086 sq km, and lies in the North Atlantic Ocean, east of Canada. Around 81% of the territory is permanently covered by ice, the habitable regions being chiefly on the eastern and south-western coasts. The climate is cold, although tempered by maritime influences in the coastal regions. Average monthly temperatures in Nuuk (Godthåb) range from −7.6°C in January to 7.6°C in July. The interior and the northern regions have a much more severe climate. Greenlandic (Kakaallisut), an Inuit language, is the official language, although Danish is also widely spoken. The majority of the population profess Christianity and belong mainly to the Evangelical Lutheran Church of Denmark. There are also small communities of other Protestant groups and of Roman Catholics. The flag (proportions 2 by 3) consists of two equal horizontal stripes (white above red), on which is superimposed a representation of the rising sun (a disc divided horizontally, red above white) to the left of centre. Nuuk (Godthåb) is the capital.

CONTEMPORARY POLITICAL HISTORY

Domestic Political Affairs

Greenland first came under Danish rule in 1380. In the revision of the Danish Constitution in 1953, Greenland became an integral part of the Kingdom and acquired the representation of two members in the Danish Folketing (parliament). In October 1972 the Greenlanders voted, by 9,658 to 3,990, against joining the European Community (EC, now European Union—EU, see p. 273) but, as part of Denmark, were bound by the Danish decision to join. Resentment of Danish domination of the economy, education and the professions continued, taking expression when, in 1977, the nationalist Siumut (Forward) movement formed a left-wing party. In 1975 the Danish Minister for Greenland appointed a commission to devise terms for Greenland home rule, and its proposals were approved, by 73.1% to 26.9%, in a referendum among the Greenland electorate in January 1979. Siumut, led by Jonathan Motzfeldt, secured 13 seats in the 21-member Landsting (parliament—known as Inatsisartut in Greenlandic) at a general election in April, and a five-member Landsstyre (Home Rule Government), with Motzfeldt as Prime Minister, took office in May. By 1989 Greenland had assumed control of a large part of its internal affairs (with the notable exceptions of policing and judicial affairs); constitutional matters, foreign policy and defence remained under Denmark's jurisdiction.

In February 1982 a referendum held to decide Greenland's continued membership of the EC resulted in a 53% majority in favour of withdrawal. In May the Danish Government commenced negotiations on Greenland's behalf, and on 1 January 1985 Greenland left the EC and was accorded the status of an overseas territory in association with the Community, with preferential access to EC markets.

At the April 1983 general election to the Landsting (enlarged, by measures adopted in 1982, to between 23 and 26 seats, depending on the proportion of votes cast), Siumut and the conservative Atassut (Solidarity) party won 12 seats each, while the pro-independence Inuit Ataqatigiit (IA—Inuit Brotherhood) obtained two seats. Siumut once again formed a Government under Motzfeldt, dependent on the parliamentary support of the IA: this support was withdrawn in March 1984, when the IA members voted against the terms of withdrawal from the EC, and Motzfeldt resigned. In the ensuing general election, held in June, Siumut and Atassut won 11 seats apiece, while the IA took three seats. Motzfeldt formed a coalition Government, comprising Siumut and the IA.

In March 1987 the coalition Government collapsed, following a dispute between Siumut and the IA over the modernization of the US radar facility at Thule, which the IA claimed to be in breach of the 1972 US-Soviet Anti-Ballistic Missile Treaty. At the general election in May, Siumut and Atassut retained 11 seats each in the Landsting (which had been enlarged to 27 seats); the IA won four seats, and the remaining seat was secured by the newly formed Issittup Partiia (Arctic Party). Motzfeldt eventually formed a new coalition Government with the IA. In June 1988 the coalition between Siumut and the IA collapsed, and Motzfeldt formed a new Siumut Government, with support from Atassut. In December 1990 Atassut withdrew its support. At an early general election in March 1991 Siumut retained 11 seats in the Landsting, while Atassut's representation decreased to eight seats and the IA's increased to five. A new party, the liberal Akulliit Partiiaat, won two seats, and the remaining place was taken by the Issittup Partiia. Siumut and the IA formed a coalition Government, with the Chairman of Siumut, Lars Emil Johansen, as Prime Minister.

At the general election held in March 1995 Siumut increased its representation in the Landsting (enlarged to 31 seats) to 12 seats, while Atassut won 10 seats and the IA six. A coalition Government was formed between Siumut and Atassut, with Johansen retaining the premiership. In September 1997 Johansen resigned from the Landsstyre and was replaced as Prime Minister by Motzfeldt.

At the general election held in February 1999 Siumut remained the party with the largest representation in the Landsting, winning 11 seats. Atassut obtained eight seats and the IA seven. A coalition Government was subsequently formed between Siumut and the IA. Jonathan Motzfeldt remained as Prime Minister, while Josef Motzfeldt, the Chairman of the IA, was appointed Minister of Economy, Trade and Taxation.

In September 2001 Jonathan Motzfeldt was forced to resign as leader of Siumut, after he was held responsible for a large deficit on the part of Royal Greenland (the island's main fish and seafood export company); however, he retained the post of Prime Minister. In December the IA withdrew from the coalition Government, accusing Siumut of lacking direction in its policies. Siumut subsequently formed a new coalition Government with Atassut.

At the general election held in December 2002 Siumut won 10 seats in the Landsting, compared with eight for the IA and seven for Atassut. Demokraatit (the Democrats, a new party established in October) secured five seats and Kattusseqatigiit (Alliance of Independent Candidates) one seat. Later that month Siumut and the IA formed a coalition Government, under Hans Enoksen of Siumut as Prime Minister. The Government was, however, extremely short-lived: the appointment as head of the civil service of Jens Lybeth, Enoksen's electoral campaign manager and close personal friend, prompted accusations of favouritism. Lybeth then engaged the services of an Inuit 'healer' to 'chase away evil spirits' from government offices. In the ensuing furore, Enoksen was obliged to dismiss Lybeth. Josef Motzfeldt, the Deputy Prime Minister and Chairman of the IA approached Demokraatit to discuss ousting Enoksen and forming a new government. Enoksen, again compelled to act, dissolved the coalition in January 2003 and formed a new Government in coalition with Atassut.

The new Government was dogged by political controversy, most notably the discord between the coalition partners concerning the revision of a commercial fishing agreement with the EU. In early September 2003, following allegations that Augusta Salling, the Minister of Finance and Chairperson of Atassut, was involved in a sizeable accounting discrepancy, Atassut withdrew from the coalition, and the Government collapsed on 9 September. Siumut and the IA subsequently formed a new coalition Government, with Enoksen as Prime Minister.

In January 2004, following negotiations between Enoksen and the Danish Prime Minister, Anders Fogh Rasmussen, it was announced that the Danish Government and the Landsstyre were shortly to appoint a joint commission to explore ways of granting Greenland greater devolution. Greenland was to remain within the Kingdom of Denmark, however, and would continue receiving grants from Denmark. In March 2005, following a request by the joint commission to the Danish Ministry of Justice, Greenlanders were granted recognition as a separate people under international law. Whether this required recognition by the UN, and whether it granted Greenlanders sovereign rights, remained unresolved.

In June 2005 Jens Napâtôk, the Minister of Infrastructure, Housing and the Environment, resigned following revelations that he had used public funds for personal expenses. Tension in the ruling coalition intensified in August, when Rasmus Frederiksen, the Minister of Fisheries and Hunting, was also forced to resign as a result of his misuse of public funds. A further four members of the Government were unable to provide sufficient documentation for their spending. The governing coalition collapsed in September, when Siumut and the IA failed to reach an agreement on the budget. At the general election in November Siumut retained 10 seats in the Landsting, while Demokraatit and the IA each took seven seats. Atassut secured six seats, and the remaining seat was won by the Kattusseqatigiit Partiiat (KP, as the Alliance had been restyled). Siumut, Atassut and the IA formed a coalition Government, with Enoksen as Prime Minister.

In April 2007 the governing coalition collapsed, marking the culmination of an ongoing dispute between the IA and Siumut regarding government policy on the regulation of the prawn fishing industry. In May a new coalition comprising Siumut and Atassut took office, led by Enoksen.

Following extensive negotiations, in May 2008 the Danish-Greenlandic Self-rule Commission on autonomy presented its final report to the Danish and Greenlandic premiers. Notably, the report recommended the division of all future revenues from the exploitation of petroleum reserves in Greenland's waters. Under the proposals, the first 75m. kroner (at 2009 prices) in annual revenue would be allocated solely to Greenland; any further revenue would be divided equally between Denmark and the Self-rule Government (Naalakkersuisut—as the Home Rule Government/Landsstyre was henceforth to be known), and the annual block-grant paid by Denmark would be reduced annually by an amount equivalent to the revenues allocated to Denmark. The proposed reforms also included the establishment of Greenlandic as the sole official language and the gradual assumption of policing and judicial powers by the Greenlandic authorities. Foreign affairs, defence, rulings by the Danish Supreme Court and policies regarding currency remained outside the self-rule agreement, although the Self-rule Government was entitled to negotiate and conclude international agreements on behalf of Denmark in matters exclusively under its jurisdiction. The proposals were welcomed by both Enoksen and Fogh Rasmussen and were incorporated in the draft Act on Greenland Self-rule. At a referendum held in Greenland on 25 November, the new Act was approved by 75.5% of voters; turnout was 72.0%.

An early general election held on 2 June 2009, in advance of the entry into effect of the self-rule Act later that month, resulted in a defeat for the ruling coalition following a strong performance by the IA, which for the first time became the party with the largest number of seats in the Landsting, doubling its representation to 14 seats (two short of an overall majority). Siumut won nine seats, Demokraatit four seats and Atassut three seats. The IA subsequently formed a coalition with Demokraatit and the KP, which held the one remaining seat. Kuupik Kleist, the leader of the IA, became the first Prime Minister from a party other than Siumut. The self-rule arrangements (including the renaming of the Landsting as the Inatsisartut) duly entered into force on 21 June at a ceremony in Nuuk attended by Queen Margrethe II.

In December 2012 the Inatsisartut approved controversial legislation establishing the framework for foreign mining and exploration companies to exploit Greenland's natural resources (which were now more accessible owing to the melting of previously permanent ice), including allowing such companies to use cheap foreign labour. Opponents of the Large-Scale Projects Act, including Siumut and the trade unions, claimed that the legislation conceded too much to foreign companies (at the expense of the Greenlandic workforce) and that the potential influx of hundreds of foreign workers and the development of large-scale mining projects would have a detrimental effect on Greenland's traditional society and already fragile environment. Despite this opposition and amid widespread public apprehension, the Act came into effect on 1 January 2013.

At a general election held on 12 March 2013, which many considered as a vote on the ruling coalition's plans regarding the future exploitation by foreign concerns of Greenland's mineral wealth, the incumbent Government lost its majority. Siumut, chaired by Aleqa Hammond, won the largest number of seats (14 seats) while the IA secured 11. Atassut, the newly established Partii Inuit (PI, founded by IA dissidents opposed to the Large-Scale Projects Act) and Demokraatit each took two seats. Turnout was 74.2%. Hammond was sworn in as Prime Minister on 5 April as Greenland's first female premier, heading a Siumut-led coalition that included ministers from Atassut and the PI. (The PI subsequently left the coalition.) As promised by the new Prime Minister, who also assumed responsibility for the foreign affairs portfolio, the Large-Scale Projects Act was amended in June in order to tighten considerably the regulation of minimum wages. This effectively removed the possibility of companies employing foreign labour on less favourable employment conditions and without any compliance with Greenlandic collective bargaining agreements.

Foreign Affairs

Denmark remains ultimately responsible for Greenland's foreign relations. Greenland does, however, have separate representation on the Nordic Council (see p. 467), and is a member of the Inuit Circumpolar Council (see p. 452). Denmark, a member of the North Atlantic Treaty Organization (NATO, see p. 370), retains its responsibility for defence. Danish-US military co-operation in Greenland began in 1951, when Denmark signed a defence agreement with the US Government to allow four US bases in Greenland, including the newly constructed Thule airbase, near the Inuit settlement of Uummannaq (Dundas). Two years after the establishment of the base the indigenous Inuits, whose hunting grounds had been severely diminished by the development of the base, were forcibly resettled further north in Qaanaaq; they received monetary compensation from the Danish Government in 1999. Following the renewal in 1981 of the 1951 Danish-US agreement on the defence of Greenland, two US radar stations were established on the island, at Thule and at Kangerlussuaq (Søndre Strømfjord). In 1991 the USA agreed to transfer ownership and control of the base at Kangerlussuaq to the Landsstyre the following year, provided it could use it again in the future.

Jonathan Motzfeldt and the Danish Minister of Foreign Affairs, Mogens Lykketoft, agreed in February 2001 not to adopt an official policy on the proposed US missile defence system, which would involve the upgrading of the early-warning radar station at the Thule base, pending an official request by the USA. Motzfeldt did, however, state that Greenland would not accept the US plans if they proved to be in breach of the 1972 Anti-Ballistic Missile Treaty, or if Russia opposed them. Josef Motzfeldt and the opposition parties of the Folketing strongly opposed the proposals, claiming that they risked provoking another 'arms race'. Public opinion in Greenland was also overwhelmingly against the plans; many feared that they would place Greenland at the centre of potential future conflicts.

In September 2002 the USA returned the Uummannaq settlement and its surroundings to Greenland; the USA had incorporated it into the Thule base some 50 years earlier. In December the US Administration formally submitted a request to upgrade the facilities at the Thule base. In May 2003 Prime Minister Enoksen and the Danish Minister of Foreign Affairs, Dr Per Stig Møller, signed a Danish-Greenlandic principle agreement under which Greenland was to gain greater influence in foreign policy relating to the island, in return for its support for the modernization of the Thule base as part of the US missile defence programme. Henceforth, Denmark was to consult Greenland on foreign policy matters in which Greenland was directly involved, and the Landsstyre was to participate in future negotiations with Denmark on Greenland's foreign policy. Furthermore, Greenland was to be a co-signatory to future international agreements, provided they did not compromise local rights.

In May 2004 Greenland, Denmark and the USA reached an agreement on the upgrading of radar facilities at the Thule base as part of the US missile defence programme. The Landsstyre, the Foreign and Security Policy Committee of the Landsting and the Danish Folketing all approved the agreement unanimously, and it was signed in August. Under the agreement both Greenland and Denmark were to have representatives at the base, and Greenland's flag was to be flown there alongside those of the USA and Denmark. The USA was required to consult with both Greenland and Denmark on any further developments at the base and henceforth to notify the Landsstyre of any US aircraft landing outside the regular airports in Greenland. Agreements were also concluded on wider co-operation between Greenland and the USA, in areas such as research, energy, the environment and education.

In June 1980 the Danish Government declared an economic zone extending 200 nautical miles (370 km) off the east coast of Greenland. This extension of territorial waters, however, caused a dispute with Norway, owing to the existence of the small Norwegian island of Jan Mayen, 460 km to the east of Greenland. In 1988 Denmark requested the International Court of Justice (ICJ) to arbitrate on the issue of conflicting maritime economic zones. A delimitation line was established by the ICJ in June 1993. A subsequent accord on maritime delimitation, agreed between the Governments of Norway, Greenland and Iceland in November 1997, established the boundaries of a 1,934-sq km area of Arctic sea that had been excluded from the terms of the 1993 settlement. In January 2002 Greenland and the Faroe Islands renewed an agreement granting the mutual right to fish in each other's waters.

In October 2004 the Danish Government announced that, in co-operation with the Governments of the Faroe Islands and Greenland, it would attempt to prove that the seabed beneath the North Pole (the Polar Basin) was a natural continuation of Greenland and that Denmark could thus claim legal ownership of any natural resources discovered there. Other claimants to the Pole (currently considered international territory) included Canada, Norway, Russia and the USA. In July 2005 the Danish Government made a formal diplomatic protest after the Canadian Minister of National Defence landed on Hans Island (Tartupaluk) without first notifying the Danish Government. The sovereignty of the small uninhabited island, in the Nares Strait between Ellesmere Island (Canada) and north-west Greenland, had been in dispute for more than 30 years, and would affect Denmark's claim for ownership of the North Pole. Moreover, control of Hans Island had assumed greater importance in recent years as global warming had raised the issue of the potential opening of the disputed North-west Passage to shipping. In September the foreign ministers of both countries agreed to hold talks on sovereignty and to inform each other of any activities around the island. In 2012 Canada and Denmark were in negotiations over the island and had embarked on a joint mapping exercise. Two possible solutions to the dispute were shared jurisdiction or the drawing up of a border through the middle of the island. Tensions were further eased in September of that year by a decision by the Canadian military to cease any activity by its armed forces on or around the island, with the exception of search and rescue or emergency operations.

In May 2008 the Danish Minister of Foreign Affairs and the Prime Minister of Greenland co-hosted a meeting in Ilulissat, Greenland, of the countries bordering the Arctic Ocean in an attempt to address issues arising from conflicting territorial interests and increased use of Arctic waters, notably for tourism and shipping, as a result of diminishing sea ice. The resultant Ilulissat Declaration, which was agreed by Canada, Denmark, Norway, Russia and the USA, committed those countries to increased co-operation and to the settlement of disputes over conflicting claims of sovereignty in the Arctic region through existing international legal frameworks. A document issued jointly by the Governments of Denmark, Greenland and the Faroes in August 2011, detailing their strategy for the Arctic during 2011–20, notably stated that they had already submitted evidence to the UN Commission on the Limits of the Continental Shelf for their claim to sovereignty over two areas near the Faroes and, by 2014, planned to do the same for three areas near Greenland, one of which included the North Pole (two partial submissions—for the Southern Continental Shelf of Greenland and for the North-eastern Continental Shelf of Greenland—were presented to the Commission in June 2012 and November 2013, respectively). With regard to defence, the document also confirmed plans to set up a non-permanent Arctic Response Force from existing armed forces units and to merge the Greenland and Faroese military commands to form a joint service Arctic Command (this new defence body was officially inaugurated in Nuuk in October 2012).

Greenland hosted a ministerial meeting of the Arctic Council (see p. 448) in Nuuk in May 2011, at which the eight member states agreed to increase co-operation in search and rescue efforts in the Arctic. Prime Minister Hammond boycotted the biennial meeting of the Arctic Council, held in Kiruna, Sweden, in May 2013, in protest at the divestment from Greenland and the Faroes of voting rights at the negotiating table. The Council's Swedish presidency had given Denmark only one chair rather than the usual three.

In June 2010 the International Whaling Commission (IWC), in which Greenland is represented by Denmark, agreed to allow Greenland to hunt humpback whales for the first time since 1986, setting a quota of nine per year during 2010–12. In July 2012 the IWC rejected a proposal put forward by Denmark to increase aboriginal subsistence whaling catch quotas for Greenland (which would have allowed indigenous Greenlanders to catch up to 1,326 whales—of four species—between 2013 and 2018); the request was turned down owing to Greenland's growing commercial use of whale meat (in the restaurant and retail sectors).

GOVERNMENT

Greenland is part of the Kingdom of Denmark. Since 1979 the Greenlandic authorities have gradually assumed control of the administration of Greenland's internal affairs. At a referendum held in Greenland on 25 November 2008 the Act on Greenlandic Self-rule was adopted. The reforms, which included the establishment of Greenlandic as the sole official language and the assumption of policing and judicial powers by the Greenlandic authorities, entered into effect from 21 June 2009. Foreign affairs, defence, rulings by the Danish Supreme Court and policies regarding currency remain with the Danish Government, the highest representative of which, in Greenland, is the High Commissioner (Rigsombudsmand). Members are elected for a maximum term of four years to the legislature, Inatsisartut (Landsting in Danish), on a basis of proportional representation. Based on the strength of the parties in the legislature, an executive, the Self-rule Government (Naalakkersuisut, or Landsstyre in Danish), is formed. Greenland sends two representatives to the Danish legislature, the Folketing.

For administration purposes, Greenland is divided into four municipalities, of which the largest is Qaasuitsup (which, by area, is also the largest municipality in the world). The merger of the previous 18 municipalities into just four took effect on 1 January 2009.

REGIONAL CO-OPERATION

Greenland, although a part of the Kingdom of Denmark, withdrew from the European Community (now the European Union—EU, see p. 273) in 1985. It remains a territory in association with the EU, however, and has preferential access to European markets. Greenland, the EU and Denmark signed a new partnership agreement in June 2006, allowing Greenland to continue to receive its EU subsidy in return for EU control over policies such as scientific research and climate change. Greenland is a member of the Nordic Council (see p. 467), the Arctic Council (see p. 448) and the Inuit Circumpolar Council (see p. 452).

ECONOMIC AFFAIRS

In 2009, according to World Bank estimates, Greenland's gross national income (GNI), measured at average 2007–09 prices, was US $1,466m., equivalent to $26,020 per head. The population remained almost constant in 2003–11. According to World Bank estimates, overall gross domestic product (GDP) increased, in real terms, at an average annual rate of 1.5% during 2003–09; real GDP increased by 0.3% in 2008, but decreased by 5.4% in 2009, largely as a result of the impact of the global economic slowdown. The economy recovered somewhat over the following two years (aided by a resurgence in export revenue, owing primarily to high fish prices), recording growth of an estimated 1.2% in 2010 and around 3% in 2011.

In 2011 agriculture (including animal husbandry, fishing and hunting) contributed 8.7% of GDP, according to preliminary data, and employed 4.4% of those in paid employment. Fishing dominates the commercial economy, as well as being important to the traditional way of life. In 2012 the fishing industry, including fresh and preserved fish, crustaceans and molluscs, accounted for 90.4% of Greenland's total export revenue. In 2011 214,493 metric tons of fish (excluding aquatic mammals) were landed in Greenland. The traditional occupation of the Greenlanders was seal-hunting (for meat and fur), and this activity remains important in the north. The most feasible agricultural activity in the harsh climate is livestock-rearing, and only sheep-farming has proved to be of any commercial significance. There are also herds of domesticated reindeer. However, owing to the effects of global warming, from the 2000s some farmers began to cultivate crops, including barley and vegetables.

Industry (including mining, manufacturing, construction and public works) contributed 17.7% of GDP, according to preliminary data, and employed some 14.0% of those in paid employment in 2011. Mining earned 13.0% of total export revenue in 1990, but in 2011 contributed a mere 0.1% of GDP, according to preliminary data, and employed only 1.9% of the working population. Lead, zinc and some silver were extracted from the Black Angel mine at Marmorilik in the north-west until its closure in 1990. In May 2008 a British company, Angus & Ross (subsequently renamed Angel Mining), was granted a licence to reopen the mine. In February 2010 a wholly-owned subsidiary of Angel Mining began gold-mining operations at the Nalunaq mine at Kirkspirdalen, in southern Greenland, which it had purchased the previous year. The first gold doré bar was produced at the mine's processing plant in May 2011, and a record 1,305 oz of gold was poured in May 2012. In February 2013, however, having suffered substantial financial losses in 2012, Angel Mining ceased trading and went into administration. Other mineral deposits in Greenland include diamonds, uranium and large reserves of rare earth elements (REEs, used in the manufacture of electronic components). Global warming has facilitated access to deposits through the melting of sheet ice. By April 2011 the Government had granted 94 exclusive licences for mineral exploration to various foreign companies (many from Australia and Canada). In October 2013 the British company London Mining was awarded an exclusive 30-year contract to operate an open-pit iron ore mine at Isua, around 150 km north-east of Nuuk. Another major project under negotiation in early 2014 was the Kvanefjeld project in south-west Greenland, involving the proposed development of vast deposits of REEs and substantial deposits of zinc and uranium by the Australian company Greenland Minerals and Energy Ltd. Despite environmental concerns, in October 2013 the Greenlandic legislature narrowly approved the lifting of the 25-year-old prohibition on the exploitation of uranium as a mining by-product, thus effectively giving the go-ahead to the Kvanefjeld project since the extraction of REEs is impossible without the simultaneous extraction of uranium. Seismic analyses have indicated that there are significant reserves of petroleum and natural gas beneath the sea off the western and north-eastern coasts of Greenland, and petroleum traces have been discovered in rocks in Disko Bay; however, at early 2014 no commercially viable discoveries had yet been made. In July 2010 the British company Cairn Energy commenced the first exploratory drilling operations in Baffin Bay since 2000. Seven new licences for petroleum and gas exploration in Baffin Bay were awarded in December 2010, bringing the total number of hydrocarbon licences awarded in Greenland to 20, covering an area of some 200,000 sq km. Despite having imposed a moratorium on the granting of further drilling rights (in response to environmental concerns) when it assumed power in March 2013, the new Government reversed this policy in December by awarding licences to several oil companies, including a BP-led consortium, Royal Dutch Shell and the Norwegian company Statoil, to carry out exploratory drilling in four blocks off the coast of north-east Greenland.

Manufacturing is mainly dependent upon the fishing industry and is dominated by processing plants for the shrimp (prawn) industry. In 2011 the manufacturing sector contributed 6.4% of GDP, according to preliminary data, and employed 3.1% of those in paid employment. Water power (meltwater from the ice cap and glaciers) is an important potential source of electricity. All mineral fuels are imported. In 2012 petroleum and petroleum products accounted for 25.2% of total imports.

In 2011 the services sector contributed 73.6% of GDP, according to preliminary data, and employed 81.6% of the working population; the sector is dominated by public administration, which alone employed 40.4% of the working population in that year. Tourism is increasingly important, but is limited by the short season and high costs. Since 2003, when harbour fees were abolished, Greenland has experienced a significant rise in visits from cruise ships: the number of cruise passengers visiting the country rose to 30,271 in 2010, compared with 9,655 passengers in 2003, but fell to 23,399 in 2012.

In 2012 Greenland recorded a trade deficit of 2,234m. kroner. Its principal trading partner remains Denmark, although that country's monopoly on trade ceased in 1950. Denmark supplied 66.5% of imports and received 86.8% of exports in 2009. After Denmark, Sweden is the major source of imports and Japan the major export market. Trade is still dominated by companies owned by the Self-rule Government. The principal exports in 2012 were food and live animals, and miscellaneous products. The principal imports in 2012 were machinery and transport equipment, petroleum oils and lubricants, food and live animals, manufactured products, and chemicals and chemical products.

Greenland continues to be dependent upon large grants from the central Danish Government. In 2012 central government expenditure on Greenland included some 4,418m. kroner in the form of a direct grant to the Greenlandic Government. Greenland has few debts, and also receives valuable revenue from the European Union (EU, see p. 273), for fishing licences. The 2012 budget recorded a surplus of 419m. kroner. The annual rate of inflation averaged 2.1% in 2008–13; consumer prices increased by 0.9% in the year to July 2013. In 2011 9.4% of the labour force were unemployed.

Greenland's economy has traditionally been dominated by the fishing industry. Migration to the towns and the rejection of a traditional lifestyle by many young people have, however, created new social and economic problems, while dependence on a single commodity has left the economy vulnerable to the effects of depletion of fish stocks and fluctuating international prices. After significant expansion in the late 1990s, the economy contracted in both 2002 and 2003, owing to a decline in shrimp prices and the high cost of petroleum imports. Economic conditions began to improve in 2004 and 2005, and strong growth was recorded in 2006 and 2007. Following a deceleration in 2008, real GDP contracted by 5.4% in 2009, largely as a result of the impact of the global economic slowdown, with the value of exports declining by more than 20% in that year. Exports reportedly recorded strong growth in 2010 and 2011, however, mainly owing to high fish prices, and annual GDP returned to positive growth, of an estimated 1.2% in 2010 and around 3% in 2011. The annual Danish subsidy remains fundamental to Greenlandic finances. However, it was hoped that exploitation of Greenland's mineral resources would provide a significant new source of income. The Act on Greenland Self-rule, which took effect in June 2009, provided for the allocation of state revenues from future mineral and petroleum exploitation to the Self-rule Government, together with a corresponding reduction in the Danish state subsidy. Tourism was also being promoted, with particular focus on sustainable tourism projects. The melting of the ice sheets due to global warming, while threatening the traditional way of life, was also expected to yield new economic opportunities, including the development of hydroelectric power and the discovery of further mineral deposits.

PUBLIC HOLIDAYS

Public holidays are the same as those for Denmark, with the exception of Constitution Day, which is not celebrated in Greenland. In addition, Greenlanders celebrate Mitaartut on 6 January, and Ullortuneq (Greenland's national day—literally, 'the longest day') on 21 June. Various regional holidays are also held to celebrate the return of the sun following the end of the long polar night; the timing of these vary according to latitude.

Statistical Survey

Sources: Statistics Greenland, *Statistical Yearbook;* Greenland Home Rule Government—Representation in Denmark, Strandgade 91, 3rd Floor, POB 2151, 1016 Copenhagen K; tel. 33-13-42-24; fax 33-13-49-71; Statistics Greenland, Manutooq 1, POB 1025, 3900 Nuuk; tel. 362366; fax 362361; e-mail stat@gh.gl; internet www.stat.gl.

AREA, POPULATION AND DENSITY

Area: Total 2,166,086 sq km (836,330 sq miles); ice-free portion 410,449 sq km (158,475 sq miles).

Population (official figures): 56,483 (males 29,867, females 26,616) at mid-2013.

Density (mid-2013, ice-free portion): 0.14 per sq km.

Population by Age and Sex (official figures at mid-2013): *0–14:* 12,128 (males 6,234, females 5,894); *15–64:* 40,138 (males 21,427, females 18,711); *65 and over:* 4,217 (males 2,206, females 2,011); *Total* 56,483 (males 29,867, females 26,616).

Principal Towns (population at mid-2013): Nuuk (Godthåb, the capital) 16,583; Sisimiut 5,522; Ilulissat 4,616; Qaqortoq 3,240; Aasiaat 3,096.

Births, Marriages and Deaths (2012 unless otherwise indicated): Registered live births 786 (birth rate 13.9 per 1,000); Registered marriages (1999) 253 (marriage rate 4.5 per 1,000); Registered deaths 453 (death rate 8.0 per 1,000). Source: partly UN, *Population and Vital Statistics Report*.

Life expectancy (years at birth, 2012): Males 68.7; Females 73.5.

Immigration and Emigration (2012): Immigrants 2,191 (persons born in Greenland 871, persons born outside Greenland 1,320); Emigrants 2,900 (persons born in Greenland 1,483, persons born outside Greenland 1,417).

Employment (employed persons with annual income exceeding 40,000 kroner, 2011): Agriculture, fishing and hunting 1,248; Quarrying 553; Manufacturing 878; Energy supply 425; Construction 2,139; Trade and repairs 4,965; Hotels and restaurants 941; Transportation and communications 3,012; Financial and insurance services 188; Real estate and rental 1,779; Public administration services 11,480; Education 100; Health and social affairs 162; Other collective and social services 571; *Sub-total* 28,441; Activities not classified (incl. statistical discrepancy) 158; *Total* 28,599.

HEALTH AND WELFARE

Key Indicators

Total Fertility Rate (children per woman, 2012): 2.0.

Physicians (per 1,000 head, 2000): 1.6.

Health Expenditure (general government, million kronor, 2011): 1,323.

Total Carbon Dioxide Emissions ('000 metric tons, 2010): 634.4.

Carbon Dioxide Emissions Per Head (metric tons, 2010): 11.1.

AGRICULTURE, ETC.

Livestock (2011, estimates): Sheep 20,232; Horses 161; Poultry 215; Cattle 79; Reindeer 3,000.

Livestock Products (metric tons, 2012, FAO estimate): Sheep meat 340 (Source: FAO).

Hunting (2011, unless otherwise indicated): Musk ox 2,676; Polar bears 131; Polar fox 1,263 (2009); Polar hare 1,826 (2009); Reindeer 10,989.

Fishing ('000 metric tons, live weight, 2011): Greenland halibut 32.8; Lumpfish (Lumpsucker) 10.7; Capelin 18.1; Northern prawn 117.0; Total catch (incl. others) 214.5. The total excludes aquatic mammals, which are recorded by number rather than by weight. In 2011 the number of aquatic mammals caught was: Minke whale 189; Fin whale 5; Humpback whale 8; Long-finned pilot whale 114; Harbour porpoise 2,453; White whale 138; Narwhal 296; Walrus 97; Harp seal 45,475; Harbour seal 78; Ringed seal 43,519; Bearded seal 995; Hooded seal 1,837. Source: FAO.

INDUSTRY

Selected Products: Frozen fish 25,040 metric tons (2003); Electric energy 401 million kWh (2010); Dwellings completed 274 (2009). Source: partly UN, *Industrial Commodity Statistics Yearbook*.

FINANCE

(Danish currency is in use)

Central Government Current Expenditure (by Ministry, million kroner, 2000): Finance 2,725 (Grant to Home Rule Government 2,725), Defence (incl. Fisheries Inspection) 268, Justice 165, Environment and Energy 58, Transport 38, Research 7, Prime Minister's Office 8, Labour 3, Agriculture and Fisheries 1, Business and Industry 2, Total 3,274. *2003:* Grant to Home Rule Government 2,952m. kroner.

Budget (general government, million kroner, 2012): *Revenue:* Gross operating surplus 545; Interest, etc. 320; Taxes on production and imports 792 (Taxes on imports 531); Taxes on income, wealth, etc. 3,653; Transfers 4,742 (from Danish state 4,418); Total (incl. others) 10,162; *Expenditure:* Final consumption expenditure 6,901 (Compensation of employees 3,952); Income transfers 2,164 (Households 1,465); Non-financial capital accumulation 619; Investment grants and capital transfers 59 (Households 46); Total 9,743.

Cost of Living (Consumer Price Index; at July each year; base: 2008 = 100): All items 108.6 in 2011; 113.3 in 2012; 114.3 in 2013.

Gross Domestic Product (million kroner at current prices, preliminary): 12,125 in 2009; 12,741 in 2010; 13,060 in 2011.

National Income and Product (million kroner at current prices, 2007, provisional): Compensation of employees 8,752; Gross operating surplus 2,172; *GDP at factor cost* 10,924; Indirect taxes 692; *Less* Subsidies 553; *GDP at market prices* 11,063; Net salary transfers –242; *Gross national income* 10,821; Expenditure of Danish Government 3,866; *Gross disposable national income* 14,687 **Expenditure on the Gross Domestic Product** (million kroner at current prices, 2011, preliminary): Government final consumption expenditure 6,867; Private final consumption expenditure 6,216; Gross investment 8,915; *Total domestic expenditure* 21,998; Exports of goods and services 4,184; *Less* Imports of goods and services 13,122; *GDP at market prices* 13,060.

Gross Domestic Product by Economic Activity (million kroner at current prices, 2011, preliminary): Agriculture, hunting, forestry and fishing 1,104; Mining 12; Manufacturing 816; Electricity and water 350; Construction 1,056; Wholesale and retail trade 1,072; Hotels and restaurants 249; Transport and communications 1,886; Financial intermediation 109; Real estate, renting and business activities 1,621; Public administration 1,492; Education 943; Health and social work 1,628; Other service activities 318; *Sub-total* 12,656; Indirect taxes (net) 404; *GDP at market prices* 13,060.

EXTERNAL TRADE

Principal Commodities (million kroner, 2012): *Imports c.i.f.:* Food and live animals 813.0; Beverages and tobacco 146.9; Raw materials, inedible 64.6; Petroleum oils and lubricants 1,257.2; Chemicals and chemical products 305.8; Manufactured goods and products thereof 700.0; Machinery and transport equipment 2,398.5; Manufactured products 585.3; Total (incl. others) 4,995.8. *Exports f.o.b.:* Food and live animals 2,499.4; Raw materials, inedible 7.2; Machinery and transport equipment 23.9; Manufactured products 9.5; Miscellaneous articles and transactions 213.6; Total exports (incl. others) 2,761.1.

Principal Trading Partners (million kroner, 2009): *Imports c.i.f.:* China, People's Republic 73.2; Denmark 2,440.1; Germany 98.5; Japan 34.5; Norway 51.2; Sweden 630.8; USA 49.5; Total (incl. others) 3,668.8. *Exports f.o.b.:* Canada 74.5; Denmark 1,669.7; Iceland 20.0; Japan 835.0; Norway 32.7; Portugal 71.3; United Kingdom 15.3; Total (incl. others) 1,923.4. *2010:* Total imports 4,794.7; Total exports 2,194.5. *2011:* Total imports 5,182.0; Total exports 2,540.5. *2012:* Total imports 4,995.8; Total exports 2,761.1.

TRANSPORT

Road Traffic (registered motor vehicles excl. emergency services, 2013): Private passenger vehicles 5,857; Taxis 205, Buses 83; Vans and trucks 1,358.

Shipping (2000): Number of vessels 162 (passenger ships 7, dry cargo ships 39, fishing vessels 110, others 6); Total displacement 59,938 grt (passenger ships 5,780 grt, dry cargo ships 6,411 grt, fishing vessels 47,046 grt, others 701 grt).

International Sea-borne Freight Traffic ('000 cubic metres, 2011): Goods loaded 300; Goods unloaded 448.

International Transport (passengers conveyed between Greenland, Denmark and Iceland): Ship (1983) 94; Aircraft (2002) 103,562.

TOURISM

Occupancy of Registered Hotel Accommodation (nights, 2012): 210,398.

COMMUNICATIONS MEDIA

Telephones ('000 main lines in use, 2012): 18.9.

Mobile Cellular Telephones ('000 subscribers, 2012): 59.5.

Internet Users ('000, 2011): 11.8.

Broadband Subscribers ('000, 2012): 11.1.

Book Publishing (titles, 2008): 126.

Source: International Telecommunication Union.

EDUCATION

(municipal primary and lower secondary schools only, 2001/02)

Institutions: 87.

Teachers: 1,191 in 2000/01 (incl. 380 temporarily employed teachers and 202 non-Greenlandic-speaking teachers).

Students: 11,368.

2007/08 (Primary schools only): Teachers 1,189; Students 10,255.

Pupil-teacher Ratio (primary education, official estimate): 8.6 in 2007/08.

Directory

The Government

Since 1979 the Greenlandic authorities have gradually assumed control of the administration of Greenland's internal affairs. At a referendum held in Greenland on 25 November 2008 the Act on Greenlandic Self-rule was adopted. The reforms, which included the establishment of Greenlandic as the sole official language and the assumption of policing and judicial powers by the Greenlandic authorities, entered into effect from 21 June 2009. Foreign affairs, defence, rulings by the Danish Supreme Court and policies regarding currency remain with the Danish Government, the highest representative of which, in Greenland, is the High Commissioner (Rigsombudsmand). Based on the strength of the parties in the legislature, an executive, known as Naalakkersuisut (Landsstyre in Danish), is formed. Greenland sends two representatives to the Danish legislature, the Folketing.

HEAD OF STATE

Queen of Denmark: HM Queen MARGRETHE II.

NAALAKKERSUISUT
(Self-rule Government)
(April 2014)

A coalition of Siumut and Atassut.

Prime Minister, responsible for Foreign Affairs: ALEQA HAMMOND (Siumut).

Deputy Prime Minister, responsible for Health and Infrastructure: STEEN LYNGE (Atassut).

Minister for Nature and Environment: KIM KIELSEN (Siumut).

Minister for Finance and Domestic Affairs: VITTUS QUJAUKITSOQ (Siumut).

Minister for Fisheries, Hunting and Agriculture: FINN KARLSEN (Siumut).

Minister for Industry and Mineral Resources: JENS-ERIK KIRKEGAARD (Siumut).

Minister for Family and Legal and Justice Department: MARTHA LUND OLSEN (Siumut).

Minister for Education, Church, Culture and Gender Equality: NICK NIELSEN (Siumut).

Minister for Housing: SIVERTH K. HEILMANN (Attassut).

Government Offices

Rigsombudsmanden i Grønland (High Commission of Greenland): Indaleeqqap Aqq. 3, POB 1030, 3900 Nuuk; tel. 321001; fax 324171; e-mail ro@gl.stm.dk; internet www.rigsombudsmanden.gl; High Commissioner MIKAELA ENGELL.

Grønlands Selvstyre (Naalakkersuisut—Greenland Self-rule Government): Imaneq 4, POB 1015, 3900 Nuuk; tel. 345000; fax 325002; e-mail info@gh.gl; internet www.nanoq.gl.

Representation of Greenland in Copenhagen: Strandgade 91, 3rd Floor, POB 2151, 1016 Copenhagen K; tel. 32-83-38-00; fax 32-83-38-01; e-mail journal@ghsdk.dk.

Legislature

The legislative body, Inatsisartut (Landsting in Danish), has 31 members elected for four years, on a basis of proportional representation. Greenlanders and Danes resident in Greenland for at least six months prior to an election and over the age of 18 years have the right to vote.

Inatsisartut
(Landsting)

POB 1060, 3900 Nuuk; tel. 345000; fax 324606; e-mail inatsisartut@inatsisartut.gl; internet www.inatsisartut.gl.

Chairman: LARS-EMIL JOHANSEN.

General Election, 12 March 2013

	Votes	% of votes	Seats
Siumut (Forward)	12,910	43.22	14
Inuit Ataqatigiit (Inuit Brotherhood)	10,374	34.73	11
Atassut (Solidarity)	2,454	8.21	2
Partii Inuit	1,930	6.46	2
Demokraatit (Democrats)	1,870	6.26	2
Kattusseqatigiit Partiiat (Alliance of Independent Candidates)	326	1.09	—
Total (incl. others)	29,873	100.00	31

Political Organizations

Atassut (Solidarity): POB 399, 3900 Nuuk; tel. 323366; fax 325840; e-mail atassut@atassut.gl; internet www.atassut.gl; f. 1978 and became political party in 1981; supports close links with Denmark and favours EU membership for Greenland; Chair. GERHARDT PETERSEN.

Demokraatit (Democrats): POB 132, 3900 Nuuk; tel. 346281; fax 311084; e-mail demokrat@demokrat.gl; internet www.demokrat.gl; f. 2002; Chair. JENS B. FREDERIKSEN.

Inuit Ataqatigiit (IA) (Inuit Brotherhood): POB 321, 3900 Nuuk; tel. 323702; fax 323232; e-mail ia@greennet.gl; internet www.ia.gl; f. 1978; socialist party, demanding that Greenland citizenship be restricted to those of Inuit parentage; advocates Greenland's eventual independence from Denmark; Leader KUUPIK KLEIST.

Kattusseqatigiit Partiiat (KP) (Alliance of Independent Candidates): POB 74, 3952 Ilulissat; tel. 944653; fax 944753; e-mail afr@ilulissat.gl; internet www.kattusseqatigiit.gl; Chair. ANTHON FREDERIKSEN.

Partii Inuit (PI): 3900 Nuuk; internet www.partiiinuit.gl; f. 2012; left-wing environmentalist; established by dissident mems of the IA (q.v.); Chair. NIKKU OLSEN.

Siumut (Forward): POB 357, 3900 Nuuk; tel. 322077; fax 322319; e-mail siumut@siumut.gl; internet www.siumut.gl; f. 1971 and became political party in 1977; aims to promote collective ownership and co-operation, and to develop greater reliance on Greenland's own resources; favours greatest possible autonomy within the Kingdom of Denmark; social democratic party; Chair. ALEQA HAMMOND.

Judicial System

The island is divided into 18 court districts and these courts all use lay assessors. For most cases these lower courts are for the first instance and appeal is to the Landsret, the higher court in Nuuk, which is the only one with a professional judge. This court hears the more serious cases in the first instance and appeal in these cases is to the East High Court (Østre Landsret) in Copenhagen.

Landsret (High Court): POB 1040, 3900 Nuuk; tel. 363900; fax 325141; e-mail post.landsret@domstol.gl; internet www.domstol.dk/gronland.

Religion

CHRISTIANITY

The Greenlandic Church, of which most of the population are adherents, forms an independent diocese of the Evangelical Lutheran Church in Denmark and comes under the jurisdiction of the Self-rule Government and of the Bishop of Greenland. There are 17 parishes and in 2007 there were 26 ministers serving in Greenland. There are also small groups of other Protestant churches and of Roman Catholics.

Biskoppen over Grønlands Stift (Bishop of Greenland): SOFIE PETERSEN, Evangelical Lutheran Church, Hans Egedesvej 9, POB 90, 3900 Nuuk; tel. 321134; fax 321061; e-mail biskop@ilagiit.gl; internet www.groenlandsstift.dk.

The Press

There are no daily newspapers in Greenland.

Arnanut: Spindlersbakke 10B, POB 150, 3900 Nuuk; tel. 343570; fax 322499; e-mail arnanut@sermitsiaq.gl; internet www.arnanut.gl; f. 2003; quarterly; women's magazine; Editor IRENE JEPPSON.

Atuagagdliutit (AG): POB 1050, 3900 Nuuk; tel. 383940; fax 322499; e-mail administration@sermitsiaq.ag; internet www.sermitsiaq.gl; f. 1861; weekly; Editor-in-Chief HEIDI MØLLER.

Niviarsiaq: POB 357, 3900 Nuuk; tel. 322077; fax 322319; e-mail siumut@siumut.gl; organ of Siumut party; annually; Editor KENNETH RASMUSSEN.

Sermitsiaq: POB 150, 3900 Nuuk; tel. 383940; fax 322499; e-mail administration@sermitsiaq.ag; internet sermitsiaq.ag; f. 1958; weekly; published by Mediahouse Sermitsiaq; Editor-in-Chief POUL KRARUP.

Publishers

Ilinniusiorfik Undervisningsmiddelforlag: H. J. Rinksvej 35, 1st Floor, POB 1610, 3900 Nuuk; tel. 349889; fax 326236; e-mail ilinniusiorfik@ilinniusiorfik.gl; internet www.ilinniusiorfik.gl; govt-owned; textbooks and teaching materials; non-profit-making org.; Man. CARLA ROSING OLSEN.

Milik Publishing: POB 7017, 3905 Nuussuaq; tel. 322602; e-mail milik@greennet.gl; internet www.milik.gl; f. 2003; children's, culture and society; Publr LENE THERKILDSEN.

Broadcasting and Communications

TELECOMMUNICATIONS

TELE Greenland A/S: Farip Aqqutaa 8, POB 1002, 3900 Nuuk; tel. 341255; fax 325955; e-mail tele@tele.gl; internet www.tele.gl; f. 1994; govt-owned; also owner of Greenland's postal service; Chair. AGNER MARK; CEO MICHAEL BINZER.

BROADCASTING

Radio

Kalaallit Nunaata Radioa: Kissarneqqortuunnguaq 15, POB 1007, 3900 Nuuk; tel. 361500; fax 361502; e-mail info@knr.gl; internet www.knr.gl; f. 1958; 5 AM stations, 45 FM stations; bilingual programmes in Greenlandic and Danish, 17 hours a day; Chair. HANS-PETER POULSEN.

KNR Avannaa: Kussangajaannguaq 20 1. sal, POB 1708, 3952 Ilulissat; tel. 943633; fax 943618; e-mail knr-avannaa@knr.gl; regional station in north Greenland.

KNR Kujataa: Havnevej B 1338, POB 158, 3920 Qaqortoq; tel. 383800; fax 641334; e-mail kujataa@knr.gl; regional station in south Greenland.

Radio—5 OZ 20: SPE BOX 139, 3970 Pituffik; tel. and fax 976680; FM/stereo, non-commercial station; broadcasts 21 hours a day; news, music, etc.; Station Man. INGRID KRISTENSEN.

Television

Kalaallit Nunaata Radioa—Greenlandic Broadcasting Corporation: see Radio section; broadcasts by VHF transmitter to all of Greenland; public service; most programmes in Danish.

Finance

BANK

(cap. = capital; res = reserves; dep. = deposits; m. = million; brs = branches; amounts in kroner)

Bank of Greenland—GrønlandsBANKEN A/S: Imaneq 33, POB 1033, 3900 Nuuk; tel. 701234; fax 347706; e-mail banken@banken.gl; internet www.banken.gl; f. 1967 as Bank of Greenland A/S; present name adopted following merger with Nuna Bank A/S in 1997; cap. 180m., res 16.9m., dep. 4,044.6m. (Dec. 2013); Chair. GUNNAR Í LIÐA; Gen. Man. MARTIN KVIESGAARD; 5 brs.

Trade and Industry

GOVERNMENT AGENCY

Råstofdirektoratet (Bureau of Minerals and Petroleum): Imaneq 29, POB 930, 3900 Nuuk; tel. 346800; fax 324302; e-mail bmp@gh.gl; internet www.bmp.gl; f. 1998; performs the central administrative co-ordinating and regulatory tasks regarding exploration and production of mineral resources in Greenland; Dep. Min. JØRN SKOV NIELSEN.

GOVERNMENT-OWNED COMPANIES

KNI A/S (Greenland Trade Service): J. M. Jensenip Aqq. 2, POB 50, 3911 Sisimiut; tel. 862444; fax 866263; internet www.pilersuisoq.gl; f. 1992; statutory wholesale and retail trading co, petroleum and fuel supply; Chair. MICHAEL MIKKILI SKOURUP; Man. Dir CLAUS JENSEN.

Pisiffik A/S: J. M. Jensenip Aqq. 2, POB 1009, 3911 Sisimiut; tel. 862900; fax 864171; e-mail mos@pisiffik.gl; internet www.pisiffik.gl; f. 1993; statutory wholesale and retail trading co; co-owned by Dagrofa A/S (Denmark) and Greenlandic Govt; Man. Dir PER STEEN LARSEN.

Royal Greenland A/S: Qasapi 4, POB 1073, 3900 Nuuk; tel. 361300; fax 323349; e-mail info@royalgreenland.com; internet www.royalgreenland.com; f. 1774; trade monopoly ended 1950; Govt assumed control 1986; established as share co 1990 (all shares owned by Govt); fishing group based in Greenland with subsidiaries in Japan, the United Kingdom, Scandinavia, the USA, Italy, France and Germany; main products are coldwater prawns and halibut; 5 trawlers; factories in Greenland, China, Denmark, Germany and Poland; Chair. NIELS HARALD DE CONNICK-SMITH; CEO MIKAEL THINGUUS.

EMPLOYERS' ASSOCIATION

Grønlands Arbejdsgiveforening (GA) (Greenland Employers' Assen): Jens Kreutzmannip Aqq. 3, POB 73, 3900 Nuuk; tel. 321500; fax 324340; e-mail ga@ga.gl; internet www.ga.gl; f. 1966; Chair. HENRIK LETH; c. 500 mem. orgs.

TRADE UNION

Sulinermik Inuussutissarsiuteqartut Kattuffiat (SIK) (Greenland Workers' Union): POB 9, 3900 Nuuk; tel. 322133; fax 324939; e-mail sik@sik.gl; internet www.sik.gl; f. 1956 as Grønlands Arbejeder Sammenslutning (GAS); Pres. JESS G. BERTHELSEN; c. 6,000 mems.

Transport

Owing to the long distances and harsh conditions there are no railways, inland waterways or roads connecting towns in Greenland. Domestic traffic is mainly by aircraft (fixed-wing and helicopter) for long distances, and by boat, snowmobile and dog-sled for shorter distances. There are airports or heliports in all towns for domestic flights. The main international airport is located on a former US military base at Kangerlussuaq (Søndre Strømfjord). There are smaller international airports at Narsarsuaq and Kulusuk. Air Greenland offers year-round flights from Copenhagen (Denmark) to Kangerlussuaq and Narsarsuaq; Air Iceland also offers year-round flights from Keflavík (Iceland) to Kulusuk and Nerlerit Inaat in eastern Greenland.

The main port is at Nuuk; there are also all-year ports at Paamiut (Frederikshåb), Maniitsoq (Sukkertoppen) and Sisimiut (Holsteinsborg). There are shipyards at Nuuk, Qaqortoq, Paamiut, Maniitsoq, Sisimiut and Aasiaat. Coastal motor vessels operate passenger services along the west coast from Upernavik to Nanortalik.

SHIPPING COMPANY

Royal Arctic Line A/S: Aqqusinersuaq 52, POB 1580, 3900 Nuuk; tel. 349100; fax 322450; e-mail kundeservice@aral.gl; internet www.ral.gl; f. 1993; govt-owned; 5 container vessels of 49,230 grt and 1 general cargo vessel of 1,171 grt; Chair. MARTHA LABANSEN; Man. Dir KRISTIAN LENNERT.

AIRLINE

Air Greenland: POB 1012, Nuuk Airport, 3900 Nuuk; tel. 343434; fax 327288; e-mail info@airgreenland.gl; internet www.airgreenland.gl; f. 1960 as Grønlandsfly A/S; air services to the 24 principal centres in Greenland, to Copenhagen (Denmark), Keflavik (Iceland) and Iqaluit (Canada); supply, survey, ice-reconnaissance services and helicopter/fixed-wing charters; owned by Danish Govt, Greenlandic Govt and SAS; Chair. JENS WITTRUP WILLUMSEN; CEO MICHAEL HØJGAARD.

Tourism

The national tourist board of Greenland, Greenland Tourism (which changed its name to Visit Greenland in 2012), was established in 1992 in order to develop tourism in Greenland, and concentrates primarily on developing sustainable tourism projects. In 2012 a total of 210,398 accommodation nights were recorded at registered hotels.

Visit Greenland Ltd: Hans Egedesvej 29, POB 1615, 3900 Nuuk; tel. 342820; fax 322877; e-mail info@greenland.com; internet www.greenland.com; f. 1992; owned by the Greenland Govt; Chair. KARIN EGEDE; CEO ANDERS STENBAKKEN.

Defence

The Danish Government, which is responsible for Greenland's defence, co-ordinates military activities through its Greenland Command. The Greenland Command, which also undertakes fisheries control and sea rescues, is based at the Grønnedal naval base, in south-west Greenland. In October 2012 a joint service Arctic Command, established by the merger of the Greenland and Faroese military commands, was inaugurated. Greenlanders are not liable for military service. As part of the Kingdom of Denmark, Greenland belongs to the North Atlantic Treaty Organization (NATO). The USA operates an airbase at Thule. In 2011 the Government spent 93m. kroner on the territory's defence.

Education

The education system is based on that of Denmark, except that the main language of instruction is Greenlandic. Danish is, however, widely used. There is a school in every settlement. In 2001/02 there were 87 municipal primary and lower-secondary schools, with 11,368 pupils and 1,191 teachers (including 380 temporarily employed teachers). In 2007/08 there were 10,255 pupils at primary schools. In 1999/2000 there were three secondary schools, with 571 pupils. There is a teacher-training college in Nuuk, and a university centre opened in 1987. In 2005 the Greenlandic Parliament adopted the Greenland Education Program (GEP), in order to improve levels of academic attainment in Greenland. The GEP aimed to ensure that two-thirds of the working population had academic qualifications or vocational skills by 2020. Expenditure on the GEP was projected at €51.5m. in 2009. In 2011 expenditure on education by the Government amounted to 1,863m. kroner (representing 19.9% of total budget spending).

DJIBOUTI

Introductory Survey

LOCATION, CLIMATE, LANGUAGE, RELIGION, FLAG, CAPITAL

The Republic of Djibouti is in the Horn of Africa, at the southern entrance to the Red Sea. It is bounded on the north by Eritrea, on the north, west and south-west by Ethiopia, and on the south-east by Somalia. The land is mainly volcanic desert, and the climate hot and arid. There are two main ethnic groups, the Issa, who are of Somali origin and comprise 50% of the population, and the Afar, who comprise 40% of the population and are of Ethiopian origin. Both groups are Muslims, and they speak related Cushitic languages. The official languages are Arabic and French. The flag has two equal horizontal stripes, of light blue and light green, with a white triangle, enclosing a five-pointed red star, at the hoist. The capital is Djibouti.

CONTEMPORARY POLITICAL HISTORY

Historical Context

In 1945 the area now comprising the Republic of Djibouti (then known as French Somaliland) was proclaimed an overseas territory of France, and in 1967 was renamed the French Territory of the Afars and the Issas. The Afar and the Issa have strong connections with Ethiopia and Somalia, respectively. The Issa community led demands for independence, and, under pressure from the Organization of African Unity (OAU, now the African Union—AU, see p. 186) to grant full independence to the territory, France acted to improve relations between the two communities. Following a referendum in May 1977, the territory became independent on 27 June. Hassan Gouled Aptidon, a senior Issa politician, became the first President of the Republic of Djibouti.

Domestic Political Affairs

In March 1979 Gouled formed a new political party, the Rassemblement Populaire pour le Progrès (RPP), which was declared the sole legal party in October 1981. In June 1981 Gouled had been elected to a further six-year term as President. Legislative elections were held in May 1982, when candidates were chosen from a single list approved by the RPP. At the next presidential and legislative elections, held in April 1987, Gouled was re-elected, while RPP-sponsored candidates for all 65 seats in the legislature were elected unopposed.

In November 1991 the Front pour la Restauration de l'Unité et de la Démocratie (FRUD), formed by a merger of three insurgent Afar movements, launched a full-scale insurrection against the Government and by the end of that month controlled many towns and villages in the north of the country. The Government requested military assistance from France (see below) to repel what it described as 'external aggression' by soldiers loyal to the deposed President Mengistu Haile Mariam of Ethiopia. The FRUD denied that it constituted a foreign aggressor, claiming that its aim was to secure fair political representation for all ethnic groups in Djibouti.

In January 1992, under pressure from France to accommodate opposition demands for democratic reform, President Gouled appointed a commission to draft a new constitution, which was to restore the multi-party system and provide for free elections. The FRUD stated its willingness to negotiate with Gouled and undertook to observe a ceasefire, subject to satisfactory progress on democratic reforms. Gouled, however, reasserted that the FRUD was controlled by 'foreign interests' and accused France of failing to honour its defence agreement. By late January most of northern Djibouti was under FRUD control, although armed conflict between the FRUD and the Government continued. In June Ahmed Dini Ahmed, who had been Djibouti's first Prime Minister after independence, assumed the leadership of the FRUD.

President Gouled's constitutional plan, which was announced in April 1992, conceded the principle of political pluralism, but proposed few other changes and retained a strong executive presidency. The plan was rejected by the opposition parties and by the FRUD, although cautiously welcomed by France. All the opposition groups boycotted a constitutional referendum, which was held in September; the Government, however, stated that, with 75.2% of the electorate participating, 96.8% of voters had endorsed the new Constitution. At the 30 September deadline for party registration, only the RPP and the Parti du Renouveau Démocratique (PRD), an opposition group formed earlier in 1992 under the leadership of Mohamed Djama Elabe, were granted legal status. The application for registration by the opposition Parti National Démocratique (PND) was initially rejected, although it was allowed in October. Elections to the Assemblée Nationale (National Assembly) were held on 18 December, and the RPP won all 65 seats. However, turnout was less than 50%, prompting complaints from the PND that the legislature was unrepresentative.

Five candidates stood in Djibouti's first contested presidential election, which was held on 7 May 1993: Gouled, Elabe, Aden Robleh Awalleh (for the PND) and two independents. The election was again notable for a low turnout (49.9%), but resulted in a clear victory for Gouled, who, according to official results, obtained 60.8% of the valid votes cast.

In March 1994 serious divisions emerged within the FRUD leadership. It was reported that the political bureau, led by Ahmed Dini, had been dissolved and that dissident members had formed an 'executive council', headed by Ougoureh Kifleh Ahmed. This dissident leadership (Ali Mohamed Daoud was subsequently declared President) sought support within the movement for a negotiated political settlement of the conflict. In June Kifleh Ahmed and the Government agreed terms for a ceasefire, and formal negotiations for a peace settlement began in July. In December an agreement signed by Kifleh Ahmed and the Minister of the Interior, Idris Harbi Farah, provided for a permanent cessation of hostilities, the incorporation of FRUD armed forces into the national force, the recognition of the FRUD as a legal political party, and the multi-ethnic composition of a new government. In accordance with the peace agreement, 300 members of the FRUD armed forces were integrated into the national army in March 1995. However, there was little further implementation of the accord, and the radical faction of the FRUD (which, under the leadership of Ahmed Dini, favoured a continuation of military operations and launched a number of small-scale attacks against government targets in late 1995) and other opposition groups remained critical of the agreement. Nevertheless, Ali Mohamed Daoud and Kifleh Ahmed were appointed to posts in the Government in June. In March 1996 the Government granted legal recognition to the FRUD, which became the country's fourth and largest political party. However, Ibrahim Chehem Daoud, a former high-ranking official in the FRUD, who opposed reconciliation with the Government, formed a new group, FRUD-Renaissance.

In early 1996 President Gouled's prolonged hospitalization in France prompted a succession crisis within the RPP, between the President's nephew and principal adviser, Ismaïl Omar Guelleh, and his private secretary, Ismaël Guedi Hared. In March the Minister of Justice and Islamic Affairs, Bahdon Farah, who was opposed to Guelleh, was dismissed from the Council of Ministers, together with Ahmed Bulaleh Barreh, the Minister of Defence. In April Bahdon Farah established a splinter group of the RPP, the Groupe pour la Démocratie de la République (RPP—GDR), which included 13 of the 65 members of the National Assembly. The President of the Assembly subsequently claimed that the RPP—GDR would remain banned while Bahdon Farah continued to hold his position as Secretary-General of the RPP. In May Gouled expelled Guedi Hared from the RPP's executive committee, together with Bahdon Farah and former ministers Barreh and Ali Mahamade Houmed, all of whom opposed Guelleh. In June Guedi Hared formed an opposition alliance, the Coordination de l'Opposition Djiboutienne, embracing the PND, the Front Uni de l'Opposition Djiboutienne (a coalition of internal opposition groups) and the RPP—GDR.

In April 1997 the FRUD faction led by Ali Mohamed Daoud announced its intention to participate in the forthcoming legislative elections and to present joint electoral lists with the RPP. At the legislative elections, held on 19 December, the RPP-FRUD alliance won all the seats in the National Assembly. The rate of voter participation was officially recorded at 63.8%. In late December President Gouled formed a new Council of Ministers.

The Guelleh presidency

In February 1999 President Gouled confirmed that he would not contest the forthcoming presidential election and the RPP named Guelleh as its presidential candidate. At the election, held on 9 April, Guelleh won 74.4% of the votes cast, convincingly defeating his sole opponent, Moussa Ahmed Idris, who represented an opposition coalition, the Opposition Djiboutienne Unifiée (ODU), including the PND, the PRD and the Dini wing of the FRUD. Electoral participation was estimated at 60%. Following his inauguration as President on 7 May, Guelleh reappointed Barkad Gourad Hamadou as Prime Minister of a new Council of Ministers.

In February 2000 the Government and the Dini wing of the FRUD signed a peace agreement in Paris, France. The accord provided for an end to hostilities, the reciprocal release of prisoners, the return of military units to positions held before the conflict, freedom of movement for persons and goods, the reintegration of FRUD insurgents into their previous positions of employment, and an amnesty for the rebels. In March Ahmed Dini returned to Djibouti from a self-imposed nine-year exile and announced his intention to assist in the implementation of the peace agreement. Also that month the RPP had convened its eighth congress, at which Gouled officially announced his retirement from active politics. Guelleh was elected to succeed him as party President.

In February 2001 Hamadou resigned as Prime Minister on the grounds of ill health. Dileita Mohamed Dileita was appointed as Hamadou's replacement in March. In May it was announced that an agreement bringing an official end to hostilities between the Government and the FRUD had been signed. The Government pledged to establish a number of more representative local bodies and to introduce an 'unrestricted multi-party system' by September 2002. In July 2001 President Guelleh effected a minor reorganization of the Council of Ministers, with moderate FRUD members allocated two portfolios.

On 4 September 2002, to coincide with the 10th anniversary of the approval of the new Constitution, the limit on the number of permitted political parties (previously fixed at four) was lifted. Henceforth, all parties would be recognized, subject to approval by the Ministry of the Interior and Decentralization, and, during the following months, a number of new parties registered with the intention of participating in the forthcoming legislative elections. At the elections, held on 10 January 2003, the Union pour la Majorité Présidentielle (UMP), a coalition comprising the RPP, the FRUD, the PND and the Parti Populaire Social Démocrate, won 62.7% of the total votes cast; in accordance with the electoral laws, as it had won the majority of votes in each of the five constituencies, the UMP secured all 65 seats in the National Assembly. Therefore, despite receiving 37.3% of votes cast, the opposition coalition, the Union pour l'Alternance Démocratique (UAD), comprising the Alliance Républicaine pour le Développement (ARD), the PRD (which in November was renamed the Mouvement pour le Renouveau Démocratique et Développement—MRD), the Parti Djiboutien pour la Démocratie and the Union Djiboutienne pour la Démocratie et la Justice (UDJ), failed to attain any legislative representation. According to official figures, the rate of voter participation was 48.4%.

In July 2003 the Djibouti Government announced that owing to 'security and economic' reasons all illegal immigrants would be required to leave Djibouti by the end of August. The deadline was subsequently extended until mid-September, by which time more than 80,000 immigrants, predominantly from Ethiopia and Somalia, had voluntarily left the country. The USA, which in August had warned of the possibility of terrorist attacks against Western targets in Djibouti, denied allegations that it had exerted pressure on the Government to expel the illegal immigrants. Following the expiry of the deadline, security forces commenced operations to arrest and expel any remaining immigrants not in possession of identity papers.

At the presidential election held on 8 April 2005 Guelleh, who was unopposed following the withdrawal of the sole challenger, the Parti Djiboutien pour le Développement (PDD) President Mohamed Daoud Chehem, was returned for a second term of office. Numerous opposition groups had appealed for a boycott of the election; however, official figures put the rate of voter participation at 78.9% and confirmed that Guelleh had received 100% of the votes cast.

Legislative elections were held on 8 February 2008. The opposition parties had announced their intention to boycott the ballot, and thus the elections were contested solely by candidates from the UMP, which, according to official results, took 94.1% of the total votes cast and secured all 65 seats in the National Assembly. The rate of voter participation was estimated at 72.6%. President Guelleh named a new, 21-member Council of Ministers in March. Dileita was reappointed as Prime Minister.

The 2011 presidential election

In March 2009 delegates at the RPP's annual conference adopted a resolution requesting constitutional changes that would allow Guelleh to stand for a third term of office. On 19 April 2010, as expected, the National Assembly unanimously approved an amendment to the Constitution removing the presidential two-term limit, thereby permitting Guelleh to contest the presidential election scheduled to be held on 8 April 2011. Other constitutional revisions included the imposition of a 75-year age limit for an incoming President, the reduction of the presidential mandate by one year (to five years) and the abolition of the death penalty.

Conflicting reports emerged in February 2011 regarding the number of participants in demonstrations against Guelleh's candidature in the presidential election. Opposition sources claimed that at least 30,000 people took part in the protests, while the Government maintained that the number of people involved totalled less than 1,000. The security forces were reported to have forcibly dispersed the protesters, resulting in the deaths of at least two people, and the brief detention of three opposition leaders, Daoud Chehem of the PDD, Robleh Awalleh of the PND and Guedi Hared of the Union Djiboutienne pour la Démocratie et la Justice.

The presidential election was held as scheduled on 8 April 2011, but was boycotted by the main opposition parties. According to results released by the Minister of the Interior and Decentralization, Guelleh was re-elected having secured 80.6% of the votes cast. His only challenger, the independent candidate Mohamed Warsama Ragueh, received 19.4%. The rate of voter participation was officially recorded at 69.7% of the registered electorate and international observers described the elections as free, fair and transparent. In May Guelleh announced a new Government, which included 11 newly appointed ministers, under the leadership of the incumbent Prime Minister Dileita.

Local elections, which were again boycotted by the main opposition, were held on 20 January and 10 February 2012. For the first time, an opposition party, the newly established Rassemblement pour l'Action, la Démocratie et le Développement, was successful in the second round, with its leader, Abdourahman Mohamed Guelleh, becoming the new mayor of Djibouti town. (However, the long-term opposition parties dismissed Mohamed Guelleh, a former adviser of Prime Minister Dileita, as being affiliated to the ruling party.) In November the National Assembly approved a proposed revision to the electoral system under which 13 of the 65 parliamentary seats would for the first time be elected on the basis of proportional representation. Consequently, the opposition parties agreed to end their electoral boycott, and in December, in preparation for forthcoming legislative elections, the ARD, the MRD, the PDD, and the UDJ formed an alliance known as the Union pour le Salut National (USN).

Recent developments: the 2013 legislative elections

In February 2013 the USN, which attracted widespread popular support, and a further alliance, the Centre des Démocrates Unifiés (CDU), as well as the ruling UMP coalition, organized pre-election rallies; however, the USN withdrew from the country's first televised political debates between the three groupings, claiming pro-Government bias on the part of the state broadcaster. The elections to the National Assembly took place peacefully on 22 February. According to final results released by the Constitutional Council on 12 March, the UMP won 61.5% of the valid votes cast and 55 seats, while the USN obtained 35.7% of the votes and the remaining 10 seats. (The CDU won just 2.8% of the votes and one seat.) Domestic and international observers declared that the elections had been conducted legitimately. However, the USN parties, despite securing parliamentary representation for the first time, accused the authorities of perpetrating malpractice during the voting process and rejected the election results. Ensuing protests by opposition supporters, which were violently suppressed by security forces, continued in early March; demonstrators also demanded the release of several prominent opposition leaders, including Mohamed Guelleh, and MRD President and USN leader Daher Ahmed Farah, following the arrest of large numbers of activists.

On 1 April 2013 Abdoulkader Kamil Mohamed (hitherto Minister of Defence) took office as Prime Minister, following the resignation of Dileita. Mohamed, who had also replaced Dileita as Vice-President of the RPP in September 2012, was appointed to head a 24-member Government, in which the most senior positions remained unaltered. The hitherto Minister of the Interior, Hassan Darar Houffaneh, assumed the vacated defence portfolio, while Hassan Omar Mohamed Bourhan (formerly the Minister of Housing, Urban Planning and the Environment) became the new interior minister.

Although the UMP and the USN in August 2013 agreed to engage in political dialogue, within one month these talks had resulted in deadlock, with the USN complaining of the repeated detention and imprisonment of Ahmed Farah, party supporters and journalists.

Foreign Affairs

Regional relations

Separate treaties of friendship and co-operation were signed in 1981 with Ethiopia, Somalia, Kenya and Sudan, with the aim of resolving regional conflicts. Djibouti's interest in promoting regional co-operation was exemplified by the creation, in February 1985, of the Intergovernmental Authority on Drought and Development (now the Intergovernmental Authority on Development, see p. 335), with six (now seven) member states; Djibouti was chosen as the site of its permanent secretariat, and President Gouled became the first Chairman.

In November 1997 Djibouti granted official recognition to the self-proclaimed 'Republic of Somaliland', which declared independence in 1991. Relations deteriorated in April 2000 when the 'Somaliland' authorities closed the common border with Djibouti, claiming that Djibouti was encouraging ethnic violence and had been responsible for a series of bomb attacks in Hargeisa. In response, Djibouti expelled three 'Somaliland' diplomats and closed the 'Somaliland' liaison office in Djibouti town. Furthermore, in May the 'Somaliland' authorities issued a ban on all flights from Djibouti to its territory; the Djibouti Government responded by prohibiting all flights to and from 'Somaliland'. The Djibouti-sponsored Somali national reconciliation conference, chaired by Guelleh, opened in May in Arta, south-west of Djibouti town, and in August resulted in the creation of the Somali Transitional National Assembly, which elected Abdulkasim Salad Hasan President of Somalia. Relations between Djibouti and 'Somaliland' were further strained in April 2001 after the Djibouti authorities closed the common border and outlawed the transport of all goods and people between the two territories. In October a delegation from 'Somaliland', led by its minister responsible for foreign affairs, held talks with Djibouti officials in an attempt to improve relations; although several bilateral agreements were concluded, the common border remained closed. Following the death of President Mohamed Ibrahim Egal in May 2002, Guelleh sought to establish cordial relations with the new President of 'Somaliland', Dahir Riyale Kahin.

Djibouti re-established an embassy in Somalia in December 2010, and Somalian Prime Minister Mohamed Abdullahi Mohamed made his first official visit to Djibouti shortly afterwards. In December 2011 Djibouti dispatched a contingent of troops to strengthen the AU Mission in Somalia, which was engaged in fighting the Islamist al-Shabaab insurgents (see the chapter on Somalia). Following the continuing violence in Somalia, the Office of the UN High Commissioner for Refugees estimated that Djibouti hosted 27,000 Somalian refugees at December 2013.

In December 1995 the Djibouti Government protested to the Eritrean authorities about alleged incursions by Eritrean troops into north-eastern Djibouti. These allegations were vehemently denied by Eritrea. Relations between the two countries were strained in April 1996, when President Gouled rejected a map of Eritrea submitted by the Eritrean Minister of Foreign Affairs, which reportedly included a 20-km strip of territory belonging to Djibouti. In November 1998 Djibouti suspended diplomatic relations with Eritrea, following accusations by that country that it was supporting Ethiopia in the Eritrea–Ethiopia border dispute. Gouled had been actively involved in an OAU committee mediating on the dispute, which earlier in the month had proposed a peace plan that was accepted by Ethiopia, but not by Eritrea. In November 1999 President Guelleh was praised by the Ethiopian President for his efforts in promoting a peace settlement in Somalia and in December the Djibouti and Ethiopian Governments signed a protocol of understanding on military co-operation, with the aim of establishing a further mutual defence pact. In March 2000, following Libyan mediation, Djibouti and Eritrea announced that they had resumed diplomatic relations. Nevertheless, the border dispute between the two countries remained unresolved, and tensions escalated in early 2008 when Eritrean forces began to mobilize and prepare military positions in the disputed Ras Doumeira region of the common border. In April President Guelleh accused Eritrea of incursions into Djiboutian territory, although the Eritrean Government denied this. Djibouti dispatched troops to the area in response, and, despite diplomatic efforts to settle the dispute, including appeals for restraint from the AU and the League of Arab States (Arab League), fighting broke out in June after Djibouti refused to hand over Eritrean soldiers who had deserted and crossed into Djiboutian territory. Several deaths were reported on both sides and the hostilities elicited strong international condemnation. The UN Security Council launched an investigation into the clashes, and appealed for a normalization in relations between the two countries, warning that further hostility could result in a wider regional conflict. In October Guelleh appealed to the Security Council for mediation, requesting joint demilitarization in the border region, and in January 2009 the Security Council adopted a resolution ordering Eritrea to withdraw its forces from the area, as Djibouti had done following the fighting in June 2008. However, Eritrea refused to comply with this demand and issued a statement to the Security Council in May 2009 denying any involvement in the destabilization of either Djibouti or Somalia. In October the Djibouti Minister of Foreign Affairs and Co-operation accused Eritrea of arming and training militias to carry out acts of sabotage in Djibouti, and of fomenting chaos in the region. Following increasing pressure from numerous East African governments, in December the UN Security Council placed an arms embargo on Eritrea, and imposed sanctions on its political and military leaders. An unexpected settlement in the Djibouti–Eritrea border dispute was reached on 6 June 2010, when both sides signed an accord committing themselves to a peaceful solution, with Qatar acting as mediator. As part of the agreement, Eritrea finally withdrew its troops from the disputed areas, while Qatar deployed a peacekeeping force to patrol the border. It was anticipated that future negotiations would concentrate on the exchange of prisoners and the delineation of the border, paving the way for the re-establishment of cordial relations. The sanctions imposed upon Eritrea remained in place, despite UN acknowledgement of the progress made by both nations.

Following the overthrow of the Ethiopian President, Mengistu Haile Mariam, in May 1991, Djibouti established good relations with the successor transitional Government in that country. However, in December 2000 relations between Djibouti and Ethiopia temporarily deteriorated after plans were announced to increase handling charges at Djibouti port by more than 150%, which the Ethiopian authorities maintained violated a 1999 trade agreement between the two countries. In February 2001 the Dubai Port Authority, which had assumed control of Djibouti port in May 2000, agreed to reduce the tariffs, and bilateral relations subsequently improved. Following lengthy negotiations, in November 2006 Djibouti and Ethiopia signed an agreement allowing for goods imported by Ethiopia to be transported via Djibouti port over the following 20 years. In 2013 efforts to strengthen bilateral economic interaction came to fruition with the commencement of construction of a new railway line connecting Ethiopia with Djibouti town and port, which would reduce journey times significantly. In addition, the two countries agreed on the construction of a cross-border water pipeline.

Djibouti also maintains strong links with the Persian Gulf states, with the Gulf Co-operation Council in December 2013 pledging US $200m. in funding for development projects in the country over the following five years.

Other external relations

In July 2002, as part of a restructuring of the French forces in Djibouti, a new French army base was inaugurated, and in May 2003 the French Government agreed to provide Djibouti with up to €30m. per year of development aid over a 10-year period. In January 2005 relations between the two countries became strained when Djibouti expelled six French aid workers and closed the Radio France Internationale transmitter in the country, apparently in response to France's summoning on 10 January of the Djiboutian chief of security services to appear before an inquiry into the death of Bernard Borrel, a French judge attached to the Djibouti Ministry of Justice, in Djibouti in 1995. (An inquiry conducted by French officials in Djibouti later that year had concluded that Borrel had committed suicide; however, his family had never accepted this verdict.) In January 2006 Djibouti requested that the International Court of Justice (ICJ) in The Hague, Netherlands, intervene in the case after French investigators indicated that Borrel could have been assassinated. Relations further deteriorated in early October when French magistrates issued arrest warrants for the head of Djibouti's security services, Hassan Said, and Chief Prosecutor Djama Souleiman Ali on suspicion of deliberately obstructing the investigation into Borrel's death. Djibouti reacted angrily and refused to accept the warrants. Ali and Said were sentenced *in absentia* to terms of imprisonment of 18 months and one year, respectively, in March 2008 after a French court found them guilty of interfering with witnesses in the Borrel case. In June the ICJ ruled that the French Government's refusal to hand over information from its investigation into the killing of Borrel constituted a violation of its international obligations of co-operation. However, cordial relations between the two countries appeared to have been restored by the decision of a French court in May 2009 to quash the convictions handed down to Said and Ali and to cancel their international arrest warrants. In December 2011 (when some 3,000 French forces were based in Djibouti) President Guelleh and his French counterpart, Nicolas Sarkozy, meeting in Paris, signed a defence co-operation agreement that replaced the existing treaty established in 1977. By 2013 the French military presence in the country stood at some 1,900 personnel.

The attacks on the World Trade Center in New York and the Pentagon in Washington, DC, on 11 September 2001 resulted in a significant enhancement of Djibouti's strategic importance to the USA and its allies. In early October Djibouti demonstrated its support for the US-led coalition against terrorism by establishing a seven-member Comité National de Lutte Contre le Terrorisme to monitor domestic security conditions. Djibouti agreed to grant access to its port and airfields, and coalition members stated their intention to use Djibouti as a base from which to monitor developments in Somalia, Sudan and other countries in the region. In January 2002 Djibouti and Germany signed a memorandum of understanding on the status of German military and civilian personnel in Djibouti. The accord granted German military personnel access to Djibouti's port and airfields to conduct surveillance missions in the region, and some 1,200 German naval personnel were subsequently stationed in Djibouti, although this number had been reduced to 320 by 2005. In December 2002 the US Secretary of Defense, Donald Rumsfeld, visited the 1,500 US troops based off the coast of Djibouti who formed the Combined Joint Task Force-Horn of Africa (CJTF-HOA), which was to monitor ship movements in the Red Sea and along the East African coast. In February 2003 Djibouti and the USA concluded an agreement that allowed US forces to use Djiboutian military installations, and in May CJTF-HOA moved its headquarters onshore to a base in Djibouti. (The base also serves as the headquarters for counter-terrorism efforts throughout East Africa.) Throughout 2004 the US military presence in Djibouti increased further with the construction of a new port at Doraleh. In April 2006 a report published by the human rights organization Amnesty International accused Djibouti of collaborating with US authorities in a practice known as 'rendition'. The report alleged that terrorist suspects detained by the US intelligence services had been held in secret prisons in Djibouti and later transferred to countries where torture was tolerated. In January 2007 Djibouti criticized the USA after US forces based in Djibouti launched a series of air-strikes against suspected members of the radical Islamist al-Qa'ida (Base) organization in southern Somalia. In 2009 the USA announced a major increase in funding for US arms sales to Djibouti through the Foreign Military Financing programme.

As an extension of the above activities, Djibouti also maintains good relations with various representatives of the international community (including India, Japan, Russia and some EU members), and allows them to launch anti-piracy initiatives from its territory further compounding its geostrategic significance. The Japanese maritime force opened its own facility in 2011—the first Japanese overseas military base since the Second World War

CONSTITUTION AND GOVERNMENT

The Djibouti Constitution was approved by national referendum on 4 September 1992 and entered into force on 15 September. Executive power is vested in the President, who is directly elected by universal adult suffrage for a five-year term, initially renewable only once. In April 2010, however, the National Assembly removed the limit on terms served. Legislative power is held by the National Assembly, consisting of 65 members elected for five years. The Council of Ministers, presided over by a Prime Minister, is responsible to the President. The Republic comprises five electoral districts.

REGIONAL AND INTERNATIONAL CO-OPERATION

Djibouti is a member of the African Union (see p. 186), the Intergovernmental Authority on Development (see p. 335) and the Arab Fund for Economic and Social Development (see p. 198).

Djibouti became a member of the UN in 1977, and was admitted to the World Trade Organization (WTO, see p. 434) in 1995.

ECONOMIC AFFAIRS

In 2009, according to estimates by the World Bank, Djibouti's gross national income (GNI), measured at average 2007–09 prices, was US $1,105m., equivalent to $1,270 per head (or $2,450 on an international purchasing-power parity basis). During 2003–12, it was estimated, the population increased at an average annual rate of 1.5%, while gross domestic product (GDP) per head increased, in real terms, by an average of 2.5% per year during 2002–09. Overall GDP increased, in real terms, at an average annual rate of 4.4% during 2002–09; growth of 4.8% was recorded in 2012, according to the African Development Bank (AfDB).

Agriculture (including hunting, forestry and fishing) provided an estimated 3.5% of GDP in 2012, according to official estimates, although some 72.0% of the labour force were estimated to be engaged in the sector in mid-2014, according to FAO. There is little arable farming, owing to Djibouti's unproductive terrain and susceptibility to drought, and the country is able to produce only about 3% of its total food requirements. More than one-half of the population are pastoral nomads, herding goats, sheep and camels. During 2002–06, according to the World Bank, the real GDP of the agricultural sector increased at an average annual rate of 3.7%; agricultural GDP increased by 7.0% in 2010, according to the AfDB. However, these figures are likely to have declined as a result of the worsening in 2011–13 of the drought that had persisted from 2005.

Industry (comprising manufacturing, construction and utilities) provided an estimated 21.1% of GDP in 2012 according to the official estimates, and engaged 11.0% of the employed labour force in 1991. Industrial activity is mainly limited to a few small-scale enterprises. During 2002–06 industrial GDP increased at an average annual rate of 4.9%, according to the World Bank; it increased by 3.7% in 2006.

The manufacturing sector (together with mining) contributed an estimated 2.6% of GDP in 2012, according to the official estimates. Almost all consumer goods have to be imported. According to the World Bank, manufacturing GDP increased by an average of 2.9% per year in 2002–06. According to the AfDB, the GDP of the sector increased by 7.0% in 2010.

According to the official estimates, the construction sector contributed an estimated 13.8% of GDP in 2012. The sector grew by 10.0% in 2010 according to the AfDB.

Total electricity generating capacity rose from 40 MW to 80 MW in 1988, when the second part of the Boulaos power station became operative; this figure continued to rise during the 1990s, and in 2011 Djibouti produced 381.5m. kWh of electricity. Nevertheless, imported fuels continued to satisfy a large proportion of Djibouti's energy requirements. Imports of mineral fuels and lubricants accounted for 6.5% of the value of total imports in 2009. In December 2004 Djibouti and Ethiopia agreed to connect their power generating facilities in an attempt to increase Djibouti's access to electricity; in 2011 a new transmission line became operational to this end. In 2013 seven funding bodies committed to contribute more than US $20m. in concessional financing to assess the commercial viability of geothermal resources in Lake Assal, which could significantly reduce domestic electricity production costs.

Djibouti's economic viability is based on trade through the international port of Djibouti, and on the developing service sector, which accounted for 75.4% of GDP in 2012, according to the official estimates, and engaged 13.8% of the employed labour force in 1991. In May 2000 the Government and Dubai Ports International (DPI—now DP World) signed an agreement providing DPI with a 20-year contract to manage the port of Djibouti. Projects are underway to expand Djibouti's capacity to five ports by 2016; in 2012 construction commenced of a port at Tadjoura and in 2013 of a Chinese-funded livestock port at Damerjog, as well as the development of Doraleh container port into a multi-purpose facility. During 2002–05 the GDP of the services sector increased at an average annual rate of 3.7%. Services GDP increased by 2.5% in 2005.

In 2012 Djibouti recorded a visible merchandise trade deficit of US $426.8m., and there was a deficit of $121.7m. on the current account of the balance of payments. According to the UN, the principal sources of imports in 2009 were France (30.5%), the United Arab Emirates, Saudi Arabia Japan and Ethiopia. The principal markets for exports in that year were Ethiopia (35.4%), France, Somalia, Brazil and Qatar. The principal imports in 2009 were machinery and electrical appliances, food and beverages, vehicles and transport equipment and telecommunication and sound equipment. In that year, the country's principal exports were machinery and transport equipment, and food and live animals.

Djibouti recorded a budget deficit of 6,901m. Djibouti francs in 2012, equal to some 2.9% of GDP in that year. The country's general government gross debt was 103,239m. Djibouti francs in 2012, equivalent to 42.9% of GDP. The country's total external debt was US $767m. at the end of 2011, of which $642m. was public and publicly guaranteed debt. In 2010, the cost of servicing long-term public and publicly guaranteed debt and repayments to the IMF was equivalent to 8.1% of the value of exports of goods, services and income (excluding workers' remittances). According to the IMF, the annual rate of inflation averaged 4.9% during 2003–12. Consumer prices increased by 7.8 in 2012. In 2012 the IMF estimated that unemployment affected some 48% of the labour force.

Djibouti has traditionally relied heavily on foreign assistance, and significant investment in the country's economy has been made by the USA and France, both of which sought to take advantage of Djibouti's strategic location to secure bases for their respective militaries. In the late 2000s the country suffered from the adverse effects of the international economic crisis—experiencing a rapid rise in food and petroleum prices—and from severe drought in the Horn of Africa. However, external price pressures stabilized in 2012 and, according to the IMF, economic growth in that year increased to 4.8%, driven by port activity, transit trade and foreign direct investment (FDI), which also boosted construction. Nevertheless, the volume of transit goods had not yet recovered to its level prior to the 2008 world financial crisis, while FDI was primarily directed into the development of salt mining at Lake Assal and of facilities at Chabelley airport for use by the US military. In 2012 the Government finalized an ambitious infrastructure investment programme, which included the construction of new port facilities to consolidate the country's status as a regional transport hub, and of infrastructure to support the associated increase in cargo transport with Ethiopia. Both the IMF and the AfDB assessed that this domestic and external investment and thriving port activity would sustain economic growth into 2014 and beyond. An IMF Extended Credit Facility to support the Government's economic programme and poverty alleviation strategy ended in May 2012 with a satisfactory performance, including a reduction in inflation. Nevertheless, the IMF maintained notes of caution regarding the country's persistent budget deficits, risk of debt distress and the fact that little of the economic recovery had benefited the general population, among which the rate of those living in poverty remained at some 42%.

PUBLIC HOLIDAYS

2015: 1 January (New Year's Day), 2 January*† (Mouloud, Birth of the Prophet), 1 May (Workers' Day), 27 June (Independence Day), 17 July* (Id al-Fitr, end of Ramadan), 23 September* (Id al-Adha, Feast of the Sacrifice), 14 October* (Muharram, Islamic New Year), 23 December*† (Mouloud, Birth of the Prophet), 25 December (Christmas Day).

* These holidays are dependent on the Islamic lunar calendar and may vary by one or two days from the dates given.

† This festival occurs twice (in the Islamic years AH 1436 and 1437) within the same Gregorian year.

Statistical Survey

Source (unless otherwise stated): Ministère de l'Economie, des Finances et de la Planification, chargé de la Privatisation, Cité Ministérielle, BP 13, Djibouti; tel. 21325105; fax 21356501; e-mail cabmefpp@intnet.dj; internet www.ministere-finances.dj.

AREA AND POPULATION

Area: 23,200 sq km (8,958 sq miles).

Population: 519,900 (including refugees and resident foreigners) at 31 December 1990 (official estimate); 818,159 at the census of 29 May 2009 (official figure). *2014* (UN estimate at mid-year): 886,313 (Sources: UN, *Population and Vital Statistics Report* and *World Population Prospects: The 2012 Revision*).

Density (mid-2014): 38.2 per sq km.

Population by Age and Sex (UN estimates at mid-2014): *0–14:* 297,973 (males 150,936, females 147,037); *15–64:* 552,378 (males 277,512, females 274,866); *65 and over:* 35,962 (males 16,707, females 19,255); *Total* 886,313 (males 445,155, females 441,158) (Source: UN, *World Population Prospects: The 2012 Revision*).

Regions (population at 2009 census): Ali-Sabieh 86,949; Arta 42,380; Dikhil 88,948; Djibouti (ville) 475,322; Obock 37,856; Tadjoura 86,704; *Total* 818,159.

Principal Town (population at 2009 census): Djibouti (capital) 475,322.

Births, Marriages and Deaths (2005–10, UN estimates): Average annual birth rate 28.9 per 1,000; Average annual death rate 9.7 per 1,000 (Source: UN, *World Population Prospects: The 2012 Revision*). *1999* (capital district only): Births 7,898; Marriages 3,808. *2011:* Crude birth rate 28.7 per 1,000; Crude death rate 10.0 per 1,000 (Source: African Development Bank).

Life Expectancy (years at birth): 60.8 (males 59.3; females 62.4) in 2011. Source: World Bank, World Development Indicators database.

Economically Active Population (estimates, '000 persons, 1991): Agriculture, etc. 212; Industries 31; Services 39; *Total* 282 (males 167, females 115) (Source: UN Economic Commission for Africa, *African Statistical Yearbook*). *Mid-2014* ('000 persons, estimates): Agriculture, etc. 309; Total labour force 429 (Source: FAO).

HEALTH AND WELFARE

Key Indicators

Total Fertility Rate (children per woman, 2011): 3.7.

Under-5 Mortality Rate (per 1,000 live births, 2011): 90.

HIV/AIDS (% of persons aged 15–49, 2012): 1.2.

Physicians (per 1,000 head, 2006): 0.2.

Hospital Beds (per 1,000 head, 2010): 1.4.

Health Expenditure (2010): US $ per head (PPP): 184.

Health Expenditure (2010): % of GDP: 7.9.

Health Expenditure (2010): public (% of total): 68.5.

Access to Water (% of persons, 2011): 93.

Access to Sanitation (% of persons, 2011): 61.

Total Carbon Dioxide Emissions ('000 metric tons, 2010): 539.0.

Carbon Dioxide Emissions Per Head (metric tons, 2010): 0.6.

Human Development Index (2012): ranking: 164.

Human Development Index (2012): value: 0.445.

For sources and definitions, see explanatory note on p. vi.

AGRICULTURE, ETC.

Principal Crops ('000 metric tons, 2012, FAO estimates): Beans, dry 2.5; Tomatoes 1.2; Lemons and limes 1.5. *Aggregate Production* ('000 metric tons, may include official, semi-official or estimated data): Vegetables (incl. melons) 36.7; Fruits (excl. melons) 3.4.

Livestock ('000 head, 2012, FAO estimates): Cattle 298; Sheep 470; Goats 514; Asses 8; Camels 71.

Livestock Products ('000 metric tons, 2012, FAO estimates): Cattle meat 6.1; Sheep meat 2.2; Goat meat 2.4; Camel meat 0.7; Cows' milk 9.3; Camels' milk 6.8.

Fishing (metric tons, live weight, 2011,): Groupers 130; Snappers and jobfishes 134; Barracudas 179; Carangids 376; Seerfishes 223; Other tuna-like fishes 122; Total catch (incl. others) 1,667.

Source: FAO.

INDUSTRY

Electric Energy (million kWh): 372.7 in 2010; 367.7 in 2011; 381.5 in 2012. Source: Banque Centrale de Djibouti, *Rapport Annuel 2012*.

FINANCE

Currency and Exchange Rates: 100 centimes = 1 Djibouti franc. *Sterling, Dollar and Euro Equivalents* (31 December 2013): £1 sterling = 292.671 Djibouti francs; US $1 = 177.721 Djibouti francs; €1 = 245.095 Djibouti francs; 1,000 Djibouti francs = £3.42 = $5.63 = €4.08. *Exchange Rate:* Fixed at US $1 = 177.721 Djibouti francs since February 1973.

Budget (million Djibouti francs, 2012): *Revenue:* Tax revenue 44,451 (Direct taxes 21,143, Indirect taxes 21,164, Other taxes 2,144); Other revenue (incl. property sales) 17,547; Total 61,998 (excl. official grants 20,574). *Expenditure:* Current expenditure 58,170 (Salaries and wages 28,995); Capital expenditure 31,303; Total 89,473. Source: Banque Centrale de Djibouti, *Rapport Annuel 2012*.

International Reserves (US $ million at 31 December 2012, excl. gold): IMF special drawing rights 12.75; Reserve position in IMF 1.69; Foreign exchange 234.19; Total 248.63. Source: IMF, *International Financial Statistics*.

Money Supply (million Djibouti francs at 31 December 2012): Currency outside banks 19,919; Demand deposits at commercial banks 123,307; *Total money* 143,226. Source: IMF, *International Financial Statistics*.

Cost of Living (Consumer Price Index; base: 2005 = 100): All items 128.5 in 2010; 134.2 in 2011; 147.2 in 2012. Source: IMF, *International Financial Statistics*.

Expenditure on the Gross Domestic Product (million Djibouti francs at current prices, 2012): Government final consumption expenditure 45,516; Private final consumption expenditure 204,743; Gross capital formation 42,184; *Total domestic expenditure* 292,443; Exports of goods and services 80,086; *Less* Imports of goods and services 131,963; *GDP in purchasers' values* 240,567. Source: African Development Bank.

Gross Domestic Product by Economic Activity (million Djibouti francs at current prices, 2012): Agriculture 7,587; Mining and manufacturing 5,604; Electricity, gas and water 10,399; Construction 30,177; Wholesale and retail trade, restaurants and hotels 41,238; Transport and communications 61,276; Finance, insurance and real estate 30,878; Public administration and defence 27,794; Other services 3,625; *GDP at factor cost* 218,578; Indirect taxes 21,991; *GDP in purchasers' values* 240,569. Note: Deduction for imputed bank service charge assumed to be distributed at origin. Source: Banque Centrale de Djibouti, *Rapport Annuel 2012*.

Balance of Payments (US $ million, 2012): Exports of goods 111.4; Imports of goods −538.1; *Balance on goods* −426.8; Exports of services 330.7; Imports of services −144.6; *Balance on goods and services* −240.7; Primary income received 45.6; Primary income paid −18.0; *Balance on goods, services and primary income* −213.1; Secondary income received 105.3; Secondary income paid −13.9; *Current balance* −121.7; Capital account (net) 52.4; Direct investment liabilities 110.0; Other investment assets −89.6; Other investment liabilities −37.0; Net errors and omissions 49.5; *Reserves and related items* −36.4. Source: IMF, *International Financial Statistics*.

EXTERNAL TRADE

Principal Commodities: *Imports c.i.f.* (US $ million, 2009): Food and beverages 173.0; Mineral fuels and lubricants 41.8; Chemical products 50.3; Basic manufactures 73.6; Telecommunications and sound equipment 57.9; Machinery and electrical appliances 211.2; Vehicles and transport equipment 66.6; Total (incl. others) 647.6. *Exports f.o.b.:* Food and live animals 69.9 (Milk products 29.4; Cereals 10.0); Basic manufactures 61.3; Machinery and transport equipment 177.2 (Road vehicles and parts 105.1); Commodities not classified according to kind 20.7; Total (incl. others) 363.7. Source: UN, *International Trade Statistics Yearbook*.

Principal Trading Partners (US $ million, 2009): *Imports c.i.f.:* Belgium 12.7; China, People's Republic 20.7; Egypt 10.5; Ethiopia 32.5; France 197.5; India 20.6; Italy 18.6; Japan 35.4; Netherlands 4.4; Pakistan 16.7; Saudi Arabia 38.7; Singapore 2.2; Ukraine 13.8; United Arab Emirates 119.7; United Kingdom 3.3; USA 25.6; Yemen 22.2; Total (incl. others) 647.6. *Exports f.o.b.:* Brazil 31.5; Ethiopia 128.6; France 73.0; Pakistan 15.2; Qatar 22.9; Somalia 43.2; Yemen 12.3; Total (incl. others) 363.7. Source: UN, *International Trade Statistics Yearbook*.

TRANSPORT

Railways (traffic, 2002): Passengers ('000) 570; Freight ton-km (million) 201. Source: IMF, *Djibouti: Statistical Appendix* (March 2004).

Road Traffic (motor vehicles in use, 1996, estimates): Passenger cars 9,200; Lorries and vans 2,040. Source: IRF, *World Road Statistics*.

Shipping: *Flag Registered Fleet* (at 31 December 2013): 10 vessels (total displacement 5,283 grt) (Source: Lloyd's List Intelligence—www.lloydslistintelligence.com). *Freight Traffic* ('000 metric tons, 2012): Goods 2,961.2; Fuels 3,911.1 (Source: Banque Centrale de Djibouti, *Rapport Annuel 2012*).

Civil Aviation (international traffic, 2012): *Passengers:* 238,212. *Freight:* 9,158 metric tons. Source: Banque Centrale de Djibouti, *Rapport Annuel 2012*.

TOURISM

Tourist Arrivals ('000): 58 in 2009; 51 in 2010; 32 in 2011 (Source: African Development Bank).

Receipts from Tourism (excl. passenger transport, US $ million): 16.0 in 2009; 18 in 2010; 19 in 2011 (Source: World Tourism Organization).

COMMUNICATIONS MEDIA

Telephones (2012): 18,000 main lines in use.

Mobile Cellular Telephones (2012): 209,000 subscribers.

Personal Computers: 32,000 (37.7 per 1,000 persons) in 2008.

Internet Subscribers (2011): 15,100.

Broadband Subscribers (2012): 15,900.

Sources: International Telecommunication Union.

EDUCATION

Pre-primary (2011/12 unless otherwise indicated): 2 schools (2004/05); 1,595 pupils (males 801, females 794); 75 teaching staff (2008/09).

Primary (2011/12 unless otherwise indicated): 82 schools (2004/05); 63,612 pupils (males 33,868, females 29,744); 1,821 teaching staff.

Secondary (2011/12): 55,082 pupils (males 31,432, females 23,650); 2,074 teaching staff.

Higher (2010/11): 4,705 students (males 2,828, females 1,877); 245 teaching staff.

Sources: UNESCO Institute for Statistics; Ministère de l'éducation nationale et de l'enseignement supérieur; Université de Djibouti.

Pupil-teacher Ratio (primary education, UNESCO estimate): 34.9 in 2011/12. Source: UNESCO Institute for Statistics.

Adult Literacy Rate (UNESCO estimate): 65.5% in 2003. Source: UN Development Programme, *Human Development Report*.

Directory

The Government

HEAD OF STATE

President and Commander-in-Chief of the Armed Forces: ISMAÏL OMAR GUELLEH (inaugurated 7 May 1999, re-elected 8 April 2005 and 8 April 2011).

COUNCIL OF MINISTERS

(April 2014)

The Government is formed by the Rassemblement Populaire pour le Progrès.

Prime Minister: ABDOULKADER KAMIL MOHAMED.

Minister of Justice and Penal Affairs, in charge of Human Rights: ALI FARAH ASSOWEH.

Minister of the Economy and Finance, in charge of Industry: ILYAS MOUSSA DAWALEH.

Minister of Defence: HASSAN DARAR HOUFFANEH.

Minister of Foreign Affairs and International Co-operation, Government Spokesperson: MAHAMOUD ALI YOUSSOUF.

Minister of the Interior: HASSAN OMAR MOHAMED BOURHAN.

Minister of the Budget: BODEH AHMED ROBLEH.

Minister of Health: DR KASSIM ISSAK OSMAN.

Minister of National Education and Professional Training: DR DJAMA ELMI OKIEH.

Minister of Higher Education and Research: DR NABIL MOHAMMED AHMED.

Minister of Agriculture, Water, Fishing, Stockbreeding and Fishing Resources: MOHAMED AHMED AWALEH.

Minister of Equipment and Transport: MOUSSA AHMED HASSAN.

Minister of Muslim Affairs, Culture and Endowments: ADEN HASSAN ADEN.

Minister of Energy, in charge of Natural Resources: ALI YACOUB MAHAMOUD.

Minister of Communication, in charge of Post and Telecommunications: ALI HASSAN BAHDON.

Minister of Labour, in charge of Administrative Reform: ABDI HOUSSEIN AHMED.

Minister of Housing, Urban Planning and the Environment: MOHAMED MOUSSA IBRAHIM BALALA.

Minister of the Promotion of Women and Family Planning, in charge of Relations with Parliament: HASNA BARKAT DAOUD.

Minister-delegate to the Minister of Foreign Affairs, in charge of International Co-operation: AHMED ALI SILAY.

Minister-delegate to the Minister of the Economy and Finance, in charge of Trade, Small and Medium-sized Enterprises, Handicrafts, Tourism and Formalization: HASSAN AHMED BOULALEH.

Secretary of State for National Solidarity: ZAHRA YOUSSOUF KAYAD.

Secretary of State to the Minister of Housing, Urban Planning and the Environment, in charge of Accommodation: AMINA ABDI ADEN.

Secretary of State for Youth and Sports: BADOUL HASSAN BADOUL.

MINISTRIES

Office of the President: Djibouti; e-mail sggpr@intnet.dj; internet www.presidence.dj.

Office of the Prime Minister: BP 2086, Djibouti; tel. 21351494; fax 21355049; internet www.primature.dj.

Ministry of Agriculture, Water, Fishing, Stockbreeding and Fishing Resources: BP 453, Djibouti; tel. 21351297.

Ministry of the Budget: Djibouti.

Ministry of Communication: BP 32, 1 rue de Moscou, Djibouti; tel. 21355672; fax 21353957; e-mail mccpt@intnet.dj; internet www.mccpt.dj.

Ministry of Defence: BP 42, Djibouti; tel. 21352034.

Ministry of the Economy and Finance: BP 13, Djibouti; tel. 21353331; fax 21356501; e-mail sg_mefpp@intnet.dj; internet www.ministere-finances.dj.

Ministry of Energy: BP 175, Djibouti; tel. 21350340.

Ministry of Equipment and Transport: Palais du Peuple, BP 2501, Djibouti; tel. 21350990; fax 21355975.

Ministry of Foreign Affairs and International Co-operation: blvd Cheik Osman, BP 1863, Djibouti; tel. 21352471; fax 21353049; internet www.djibdiplomatie.dj.

Ministry of Health: BP 296, Djibouti; tel. 21353331; fax 21356300.

Ministry of Higher Education and Research: Djibouti.

Ministry of Housing, Urban Planning and the Environment: BP 11, Djibouti; tel. 21350006; fax 21351618.

Ministry of the Interior: BP 33, Djibouti; tel. 21352542; fax 21354862.

Ministry of Justice and Penal Affairs: BP 12, Djibouti; tel. 21351506; fax 21354012; internet www.justice.gouv.dj.

Ministry of Labour: Djibouti.

Ministry of Muslim Affairs, Culture and Endowments: Djibouti.

Ministry of National Education and Professional Training: BP 16, Cité Ministérielle, Djibouti; tel. 21350997; fax 21354234; e-mail education.gov@intnet.dj; internet www.education.gov.dj.

Ministry of the Promotion of Women and Family Planning: BP 458, Djibouti; tel. 21353409; fax 21350439; e-mail minfemme@intnet.dj; internet www.ministere-femme.dj.

Ministry of Youth and Sports: BP 2506, Djibouti; tel. 21355886; fax 21356830.

President

Presidential Election, 8 April 2011

Candidate	% of votes
Ismaïl Omar Guelleh	80.63
Mohamed Warsama Ragueh	19.37
Total	100.00

Legislature

National Assembly (Assemblée Nationale): BP 138, pl. Lagarde, Djibouti; tel. 21350172; internet www.assemblee-nationale.dj.

Speaker: IDRISS ARNAOUD ALI.

General Election, 22 February 2013

Party	Valid votes	% of valid votes	Seats
Union pour la Majorité Présidentielle (UMP)*	74,016	61.53	55
Union pour le Salut National (USN)†	42,894	35.66	10
Centre des Démocrates Unifiés (CDU)	3,392	2.82	—
Total	120,302	100.00	65

* A coalition comprising the FRUD, the PND, the PSD and the RPP.
† A coalition comprising the ARD, the MRD, the PDD, and the UDJ.

Election Commission

Commission Electorale Nationale Indépendante: ave Maréchal Lyautey, Djibouti; tel. 21353654; e-mail ceni@intnet.dj; internet www.ceni.dj; f. 2002; Pres. ABDI ISMAËL HERSI.

Political Organizations

On 4 September 2002, to coincide with the 10th anniversary of the approval of the Constitution, restrictions on the number of legally permitted political parties (hitherto four) were formally removed.

Centre des Démocrates Unifiés (CDU): Djibouti; Pres. OMAR ELMI KHAIREH.

Union pour la Majorité Présidentielle (UMP): Siège de l'UMP, Djibouti; tel. 21340056; e-mail lavictoire@ump.dj; internet www.ump.dj; coalition of major parties in support of Pres. Guelleh; Pres. ABDOULKADER KAMIL MOHAMED.

Front pour la Restauration de l'Unité et de la Démocratie (FRUD): Djibouti; tel. 21250279; f. 1991 by merger of 3 militant Afar groups; advocates fair representation in govt for all ethnic groups; commenced armed insurgency in Nov. 1991; split into 2 factions in March 1994; the dissident group, which negotiated a settlement with the Govt, obtained legal recognition in March 1996 and recognizes the following leaders; Pres. ALI MOHAMED DAOUD; Sec.-Gen. OUGOUREH KIFLEH AHMED; a dissident group, FRUD-Renaissance (led by IBRAHIM CHEHEM DAOUD), was formed in 1996.

Parti National Démocratique (PND): BP 10204, Djibouti; tel. 21342194; f. 1992; Pres. ABDOURAHMAN MOHAMED ALLALEH.

Parti Social Démocrate (PSD): BP 434, route Nelson Mandela, Djibouti; f. 2002; Pres. HASNA MOUMIN BAHDON; Sec.-Gen. HASSAN IDRISS AHMED.

Rassemblement Populaire pour le Progrès (RPP): Djibouti; e-mail rpp@intnet.dj; internet www.rpp.dj; f. 1979; sole legal party 1981–92; Pres. ISMAÏL OMAR GUELLEH; Sec.-Gen. ILYAS MOUSSA DAWALEH.

Union pour la Réforme (UPR): Djibouti; f. 2006; Pres. IBRAHIM CHEHEM DAOUD.

Union pour le Salut National (USN): 2 rue de Pékin, Héron, Djibouti; tel. 21341822; fax 77829999 (mobile); e-mail realite_djibouti@yahoo.fr; coalition of major opposition parties; Pres. AHMAD YOUSSOUF HOUMED.

Alliance Républicaine pour le Développement (ARD): BP 1074, Marabout, Djibouti; tel. 21341822; e-mail realite_djibouti@yahoo.fr; internet www.ard-djibouti.org; f. 2002; Leader AHMAD YOUSSOUF HOUMED; Sec.-Gen. KASSIM ALI DINI.

Mouvement pour le Renouveau Démocratique et le Développement (MRD): BP 3570, ave Nasser, Djibouti; e-mail lerenouveau@mrd-djibouti.org; internet www.mrd-djibouti.com/mrd; f. 1992 as the Parti du Renouveau Démocratique; renamed as above in 2002; Pres. DAHER AHMED FARAH; Sec.-Gen. SOULEIMAN HASSAN FAIDAL.

Parti Djiboutien pour le Développement (PDD): BP 892, Djibouti; tel. 77822860 (mobile); f. 2002; Pres. MOHAMED DAOUD CHEHEM; Sec.-Gen. ABDOULFATAH HASSAN IBRAHIM.

Union pour la Démocratie et la Justice (UDJ): ave Nasser, BP 752, Djibouti; tel. 77829999 (mobile); tel. info@udj-djibouti.com; internet udj-djibouti.com/udj; Chair. ISMAËL GUEDI HARED.

Diplomatic Representation

EMBASSIES IN DJIBOUTI

China, People's Republic: BP 2021, rue Addis Ababa, Lotissement Heron, Djibouti; tel. 21352247; fax 21354833; e-mail chinaemb_dj@mfa.gov.cn; internet dj.chineseembassy.org; Ambassador FU HUAQIANG.

Egypt: BP 1989, Djibouti; tel. 21351231; fax 21356657; e-mail ambegypte2004@gawab.com; Ambassador FARGHALI ABDEL HALIM TAHA.

Eritrea: BP 1944, Djibouti; tel. 21354961; fax 21351831; Ambassador MOHAMED SAÏD MANTAY (recalled in June 2008).

Ethiopia: rue Clochette, BP 230, Djibouti; tel. 21350718; fax 21354803; e-mail ethemb@intnet.dj; Ambassador KHALED AHMED TAHA.

France: 45 blvd du Maréchal Foch, BP 2039, Djibouti; tel. 21350963; fax 21350272; e-mail ambfrdj@intnet.dj; internet www.ambafrance-dj.org; Ambassador RENÉ FORCEVILLE.

Libya: BP 2073, Djibouti; tel. 21350202; Chargé d'affaires HADI WAHECHI.

Qatar: BP 1900, Djibouti; tel. 21322401; fax 21359393; e-mail djibouti@mofa.gov.qa; Ambassador JASSIM JABER JASSIM SOROUR.

Russia: BP 1913, Plateau du Marabout, Djibouti; tel. 21350740; fax 21355990; e-mail russiaemb@intnet.dj; internet www.djibouti.mid.ru; Ambassador VALERII ORLOV.

Saudi Arabia: BP 1921, Djibouti; tel. 21351898; fax 21352284; e-mail djemb@mofa.gov.sa; internet embassies.mofa.gov.sa/sites/djibouti; Ambassador IBRAHIM ABD AL-AZIZ AN-NAOUFAL.

Somalia: BP 549, Djibouti; tel. 21353521; internet www.djibouti.somaligov.net; Ambassador ABDIRAHMAN GULWADE.

Sudan: BP 4259, Djibouti; tel. 21356404; fax 21356662; Ambassador HASSAN EL-TALIB.

USA: Lot No. 350-B, Haramous, Djibouti; tel. 21353995; fax 21353940; e-mail amembadm@bow.intnet.dj; internet djibouti.usembassy.gov; Ambassador GEETA PASI.

Yemen: BP 194, Djibouti; tel. (21) 352975; Ambassador MOHAMMED ABDULLAH HAJAR.

Judicial System

The Supreme Court was established in 1979. There is a high court of appeal and a court of first instance in Djibouti; each of the six administrative districts has a 'tribunal coutumier'.

President of the Court of Appeal: KADIDJA ABEBA.

Constitutional Council: Plateau du Serpent, blvd Foch, BP 4081, Djibouti; tel. 21358662; fax 21358663; e-mail conseil@intnet.dj; f. 1992; Pres. AHMED IBRAHIM ABDI; six mems.

Religion

ISLAM

Almost the entire population are Muslims.

Qadi of Djibouti: MOGUE HASSAN DIRIR, BP 168, Djibouti; tel. 21352669.

High Islamic Council (Haut Conseil Islamique): Djibouti; f. 2004; 7 mems; Pres. Dr CHIKH BOUAMRANE; Sec.-Gen. ALI MOUSSA OKIEH.

CHRISTIANITY

The Roman Catholic Church

Djibouti comprises a single diocese, directly responsible to the Holy See. There were some 7,000 adherents in the country.

Bishop of Djibouti: GIORGIO BERTIN, Evêché, blvd de la République, BP 94, Djibouti; tel. and fax 21350140; e-mail evechcat@intnet.dj.

The Anglican Communion

Within the Episcopal Church in Jerusalem and the Middle East, Djibouti lies within the jurisdiction of the Bishop in Egypt.

Other Christian Churches

Eglise Protestante: blvd de la République, BP 416, Djibouti; tel. 21351820; fax 21350706; e-mail eped@intnet.dj; internet membres.lycos.fr/missiondjibouti; f. 1957; Pastor NATHALIE PAQUEREAU.

Greek Orthodox Church: blvd de la République, Djibouti; tel. 21351325; c. 350 adherents; Archimandrite STAVROS GEORGANAS.

The Ethiopian Orthodox Church is also active in Djibouti.

The Press

Al Qarn: angle rue de Moscou, blvd Cheick Osman, Djibouti; tel. 21355193; fax 21353310; e-mail alqarn@intnet.dj; internet www.alqarn.dj; biweekly; Arabic; Dir YASSIN ABDULLAH BOUH.

Djibouti Post: blvd Bonhoure, près de l'IGAD, BP 32, Djibouti; tel. 21352201; fax 21353937; internet www.lanation.dj/djibpost; fortnightly; English; circ. 500.

La Nation de Djibouti: blvd Bonhoure, près de l'IGAD, BP 32, Djibouti; tel. 21352201; fax 21353937; e-mail lanation@intnet.dj; internet www.lanation.dj; daily; Dir MOHAMED GASS BARKHADLEH; circ. 4,300.

Le Progrès: Djibouti; weekly; publ. by the RPP; Publr ALI MOHAMED HUMAD.

Le Renouveau: BP 3570, ave Nasser, Djibouti; tel. 21351474; weekly; independent; publ. by the MRD; Editor-in-Chief DAHER AHMED FARAH.

Revue de l'ISERT: BP 486, Djibouti; tel. 21352795; twice a year; publ. by the Institut Supérieur d'Etudes et de Recherches Scientifiques et Techniques (ISERT).

Le Temps: Djibouti; independent; fortnightly; Owners AMIN MOHAMED RABLEH, MOHAMED GOUMANEH GUIRREH, ABDOURAHMAN SOULEIMAN BACHIR.

NEWS AGENCY

Agence Djiboutienne d'Information (ADI): 1 rue de Moscou, BP 32, Djibouti; tel. 21354013; fax 21354037; e-mail adi@intent.dj; internet www.adi.dj; f. 1978; Dir YASSER HASSAN BOULLO.

Broadcasting and Communications

TELECOMMUNICATIONS

Djibouti Télécom: 3 blvd G. Pompidou, BP 2105, Djibouti; tel. 21351110; fax 21355757; e-mail djibouti_telecom@intnet.dj; internet www.adjib.dj; f. 1999 to replace Société des Télécommunications Internationales; 100% state-owned; Dir-Gen. MOHAMED ASSOWEH BOUH.

BROADCASTING

Radio and Television

Djibnet: BP 1409, Djibouti; tel. 21354288; e-mail webmaster@djibnet.com; internet www.djibnet.com.

Radiodiffusion-Télévision de Djibouti (RTD): BP 97, 1 ave St Laurent du Var, Djibouti; tel. 21352294; fax 21356502; e-mail rtd@intnet.dj; internet www.rtd.dj; f. 1967; state-controlled; programmes in French, Afar, Somali and Arabic; 17 hours radio and 5 hours television daily; Dir-Gen. Dr KADAR ALI DIRANEH.

Telesat Djibouti: route de l'Aéroport, BP 3760, Djibouti; tel. 21353457.

In the early 2010s a private television operator Djibsat provided a number of foreign channels, including Horn Cable Television (Somalia), TV5, TF1, M6, Canal+, Medsat and BBC.

Finance

(cap. = capital; res = reserves; dep. = deposits; m. = million; br(s) = branch(es); amounts in Djibouti francs)

BANKING

In 2013 there were 11 banks operating in Djibouti, of which four were Islamic banks.

Central Bank

Banque Centrale de Djibouti: BP 2118, ave St Laurent du Var, Djibouti; tel. 21352751; fax 21356288; e-mail bndj@intnet.dj; internet www.banque-centrale.dj; f. 1977 as Banque Nationale de Djibouti; present name adopted 2002; bank of issue; cap. and res 6,056m. (Feb. 2005); Acting Gov. AHMED OSMAN ALI.

Commercial Banks

Bank of Africa—Mer Rouge (BOA—MR): 10 pl. Lagarde, BP 88, Djibouti; tel. 21353016; fax 21351638; e-mail secretariat@bimr-banque.com; f. 1908 as Banque de l'Indochine; present name adopted 2010; cap. 1,500.0m., res 222.8m., dep. 56,954.3m. (Dec. 2011); Chair. and CEO PHILIPPE BOUYAUD; 3 brs.

Banque pour le Commerce et l'Industrie—Mer Rouge (BCI—MR): 11 pl. Lagarde, BP 2122, Djibouti; tel. 21350857; fax 21354260; e-mail contact@bcimr.dj; internet www.bcimr.dj; f. 1977; 51% owned by BRED Banque Populaire (France); cap. 2,092.5m., res 209.2m., dep. 93,583.2m. (Dec. 2011); Pres. ERIC MONTAGNE; Dir-Gen. YAHYA OULD AMAR; 6 brs.

International Commercial Bank (Djibouti) SA: Immeuble 15, pl. du 27 juin, rue d'Ethiopie, Djibouti; tel. 21355006; fax 21355003; e-mail info@icbank-djibouti.com; internet www.icbank-djibouti.com; f. 2007; Dir-Gen. PODILA PHANINDRA; 1 br.

Warka Bank: Djibouti; tel. 21311611; fax 21353693; f. 2010.

Development Bank

Fonds de Développement Economique de Djibouti (FDED): angle ave Georges Clemenceau et rue Pierre Curie, BP 520, Djibouti; tel. 21353391; fax 21355022; internet www.fdeddjibouti.com; f. 2004; Dir-Gen. HIBA AHMED HIBA.

Islamic Banks

Dahabshil Bank International SA: pl. du 27 Juin, BP 2022, Djibouti; tel. 21352233; fax 21355322; e-mail info@dahabshilbank.com; internet www.dahabshilbank.com; f. 2009; Pres. MOHAMED SAID DUALEH.

Saba Islamic Bank (SIB): Immeuble Yassin Yabeh, pl. du 27 juin, BP 1972, Djibouti; tel. 21355777; fax 21357770; e-mail djSaba@SabaBank.com; f. 2006; Dir-Gen. SALEH KARMAN.

Salaam African Bank (SAB): ave Pierre Pascal, BP 2550, Djibouti; tel. 21351544; fax 21351534; e-mail info@banksalaam.com; internet www.banksalaam.com; f. 2008; Pres. OMAR ISMAÏL EGUEH; Dir-Gen. MOHAMED YUSUF AHMED.

Shoura Bank: rue de Marseille, BP 2635, Djibouti; tel. 21343892; fax 21343896; e-mail info@shoura-bank.com; internet shouragroup.com/shoura-bank-djibouti/bank-djibouti.html; f. 2010.

Banking Association

Association Professionnelle des Banques: c/o Banque pour le Commerce et l'Industrie—Mer Rouge, pl. Lagarde, BP 2122, Djibouti; tel. 21350857; fax 21354260; Pres. YAHYA OULD AMAR.

INSURANCE

In 2009 there were two insurance companies in Djibouti.

Les Assureurs de la Mer Rouge et du Golfe Arabe (AMERGA): 8 rue Marchand, BP 2653, Djibouti; tel. 21352510; fax 21355623; e-mail courrier@amerga.com; internet www.amerga.com; f. 2000; Dirs THIERRY MARILL, LUC MARILL, ABDOURAHMAN BARKAT ABDILLAHI, MOHAMED ADEN ABOUBAKER.

GXA Assurances: 3 rue Marchand, BP 200, Djibouti; tel. 21353636; fax 21353056; e-mail accueil@gxaonline.com; internet www.gxaonline.com; Country Man. CHRISTIAN BOUCHER.

Trade and Industry

CHAMBER OF COMMERCE

Chambre de Commerce de Djibouti: pl. Lagarde, BP 84, Djibouti; tel. 21351070; fax 21350096; e-mail ccd@intnet.dj; internet www.ccd.dj; f. 1906; 44 mems, 22 assoc. mems; Pres. YOUSSOUF MOUSSA DAWALEH; First Vice-Pres. MAGDA REMON COUBÈCHE.

UTILITIES

Electricity

Electricité de Djibouti (EdD): 47 blvd de la République, BP 175, Djibouti; tel. 21352851; fax 21354396; e-mail direction-edd@edd.dj; internet www.edd.dj; Pres. RACHID HASSAN SABAN; Dir-Gen. DJAMA ALI GUELLEH.

TRADE UNIONS

Union Djiboutienne pour les Droits Economiques Sociaux et Culturels et Civils et Politiques: rue Pierre Pascal, BP 2767, Djibouti; tel. 77823979 (mobile); e-mail uddesc@yahoo.fr; internet www.uddesc.org; f. 2005; confed. of 21 trade unions; Sec.-Gen. HASSAN CHER HARED.

Union Générale des Travailleurs Djiboutiens (UGTD): Sec.-Gen. HASSAN ALI DOUALEH.

Transport

RAILWAYS

In 2011 the Indian Government announced its intention to provide US $300m. towards the construction of a new railway line connecting Ethiopia with Djibouti town and port.

Chemin de Fer Djibouti–Ethiopien (CDE): BP 2116, Djibouti; tel. 21350280; fax 21351256; e-mail adoches@hotmail.com; f. 1909; adopted present name in 1981; jtly owned by govts of Djibouti and Ethiopia; 781 km of track (121 km in Djibouti) linking Djibouti with Addis Ababa; Pres. ALI HASSAN BAHDON.

ROADS

In 2000 there were an estimated 3,065 km of roads; in 2009 it was estimated that 16% of Djibouti's roads were paved. About one-half of the roads are usable only by heavy vehicles.

SHIPPING

Djibouti, which was established as a free port in 1981, handled 11.3m. metric tons of freight in 2009. At 31 December 2013 Djibouti's flag registered fleet comprised 10 vessels, totalling 5,283 grt.

Djibouti Maritime Management Investment Company (DMMI): BP 1812, Djibouti; f. 2004 to manage Djibouti's fishing port.

Djibouti Ports and Free Zones Authority (DPFZA): POB 198, Djibouti; tel. 359070; fax 359059; e-mail zfd@intnet.dj; internet www.djiboutifz.com; Chair. ABOUBAKER OMAR HADI.

Port Autonome International de Djibouti (PAID): BP 2107, Djibouti; tel. 21357372; fax 21355476; e-mail customer.care@port.dj; internet www.portdedjibouti.com; managed by DP World, UAE, since 2000; Gen. Man. SAAD OMAR GUELLEH.

Principal Shipping Agents

Almis Shipping Line & Transport Co: BP 85, Djibouti; tel. 21356998; fax 21356996; Man. Dir MOHAMED NOOR.

Cie Maritime et de Manutention de Djibouti (COMAD): ave des Messageries Maritimes, BP 89, Djibouti; tel. 21351028; fax 21350466; e-mail hettam@intnet.dj; f. 1990; stevedoring; Man. Dir ALI A. HETTAM.

Global Logistics Services Djibouti: rue Clemenceau, POB 3239, Djibouti; tel. 77839000 (mobile); fax 21352283; e-mail gls.djibouti@gls-logistics.tk; shipping, clearing and freight-forwarding agent; Gen. Man. MOHAMED A. ELMI.

Inchcape Shipping Services & Co (Djibouti) SA: 9–11 rue de Genève, BP 81, Djibouti; tel. 21353844; fax 21353294; e-mail portagencydjibouti@iss-shipping.com; internet www.iss-shipping.com; f. 1942; Man. Dir AHMED OSMAN GELLEH.

J. J. Kothari & Co Ltd: rue d'Athens, BP 171, Djibouti; tel. 21350219; fax 21351778; e-mail ops@kothari.dj; internet www.kotharishipping.net; f. 1957; LLC; shipping agents; also ship managers, stevedores, freight forwarders, project cargo movers; Man. Dir NALIN KOTHARI; Dep. Man. Dir PIERRE VINCIGUERRA.

Smart Logistic Services: BP 1579, Djibouti; tel. 21343950; fax 21340523; e-mail sls@intnet.dj; internet www.smartforwarders.com; f. 2010; Man. Dir FAHMI A. HETTAM.

Société Djiboutienne de Trafic Maritime (SDTM): blvd Cheik Osman, BP 640, Djibouti; tel. 21352351; fax 21351103.

Société Maritime L. Savon et Ries: blvd Cheik Osman, BP 2125, Djibouti; tel. 21352352; fax 21351103; e-mail smsr@intnet.dj; Gen. Man. JEAN-PHILIPPE DELARUE.

CIVIL AVIATION

The international airport is at Ambouli, 6 km from Djibouti. There are six other airports providing domestic services. In late 2009 the European Union banned all Djibouti airlines from flying in its airspace.

Daallo Airlines: BP 2565, Djibouti; tel. 21353401; fax 21351765; e-mail daallo@intnet.dj; internet www.daallo.com; f. 1991; operates services to Somalia, Saudi Arabia, the United Arab Emirates, Kenya and Ethiopia; CEO MOHAMED IBRAHIM YASSIN.

Djibouti Airlines (Puntavia Airline de Djibouti): BP 2240, pl. Lagarde, Djibouti; tel. 21351006; fax 21352429; e-mail djibouti-airlines@intnet.dj; internet www.djiboutiairlines.com; f. 1996; scheduled and charter regional and domestic flights; Man. Dir Capt. MOUSSA RAYALEH WABERI.

Tourism

Djibouti offers desert scenery in its interior and watersport facilities on its coast. A casino operates in the capital. There were about 32,000 tourist arrivals in 2011. Receipts from tourism totalled US $19.0m. in that year.

Office National du Tourisme de Djibouti (ONTD): pl. du 27 juin, BP 1938, Djibouti; tel. 21353790; fax 21356322; e-mail onta@intnet.dj; internet www.office-tourisme.dj; Dir MOHAMED ABDILLAHI WAIS.

Defence

Arrangements for military co-operation exist between Djibouti and France, and in November 2012 there were about 1,400 French military personnel and 200 Japanese military personnel stationed in Djibouti, while the US-led Combined Joint Task Force-Horn of Africa also had its headquarters in the country. Around 1,285 US military, naval and air force personnel were stationed there. In January 2010 Djibouti announced that it would contribute some 450 troops to the African Union Mission in Somalia. As assessed at November 2012, the total armed forces of Djibouti itself, in which all services form part of the army, numbered some 8,450 (including 200 naval and 250 air force personnel). There were also paramilitary forces numbering 2,000 gendarmes, as well as a 2,500-strong national security force. Conscription of all men between 18 and 25 years of age was introduced in 1992.

Defence Expenditure: Budgeted at 1,720m. Djibouti francs in 2011.

Commander-in-Chief of the Armed Forces: Pres. ISMAÏL OMAR GUELLEH.

Chief of Staff of the Army: Gen. ZAKARIA CHEIK IBRAHIM.

Education

The Government has overall responsibility for education. Primary education generally begins at six years of age and lasts for six years. Secondary education, usually starting at the age of 12, lasts for seven years, comprising a first cycle of four years and a second of three years. In 2013 primary enrolment included 58% of pupils in the relevant age-group (61% of boys; 54% of girls), while secondary enrolment was equivalent to 46% of pupils in the relevant age-group (52% of boys; 40% of girls). In 2007 spending on education represented 22.8% of total government expenditure. In 2011/12, according to UNESCO estimates, there were 63,612 primary school pupils and 55,082 pupils receiving general secondary and vocational education. Djibouti's sole university, the Université de Djibouti, was formed in January 2006 as a replacement for the Pôle Universitaire de Djibouti, which opened in 2000 and had 4,705 students in 2010/11.

DOMINICA

Introductory Survey

LOCATION, CLIMATE, LANGUAGE, RELIGION, FLAG, CAPITAL

The Commonwealth of Dominica is situated in the Windward Islands group of the West Indies, lying between Guadeloupe, to the north, and Martinique, to the south. The climate is tropical, though tempered by sea winds, which sometimes reach hurricane force, especially from July to September. The average temperature is about 27°C (80°F), with little seasonal variation. Rainfall is heavy, especially in the mountainous areas, where the annual average is 6,350 mm (250 ins), compared with 1,800 mm (70 ins) along the coast. English is the official language, but a local French patois, or Creole, is widely spoken. In parts of the north-east an English dialect, Cocoy, is spoken by the descendants of Antiguan settlers. There is a small community of Carib Indians on the east coast. Almost all of the inhabitants profess Christianity, and about 62% are Roman Catholics. The national flag (proportions 1 by 2) has a green field, with equal stripes of yellow, white and black forming an upright cross, on the centre of which is superimposed a red disc containing a parrot surrounded by 10 five-pointed green stars (one for each of the island's parishes). The capital is Roseau.

CONTEMPORARY POLITICAL HISTORY

Historical Context

Dominica was first settled by Arawaks and then Caribs. Control of the island was fiercely contested by the Caribs, British and French during the 17th and 18th centuries. The British eventually prevailed and Dominica formed part of the Leeward Islands federation until 1939. In 1940 it was transferred to the Windward Islands and remained attached to that group until the federal arrangement was ended in December 1959. Under a new Constitution, effective from January 1960, Dominica (like each other member of the group) achieved a separate status, with its own Administrator and an enlarged Legislative Council.

Domestic Political Affairs

At the January 1961 elections to the Legislative Council, the ruling Dominica United People's Party was defeated by the Dominica Labour Party (DLP). Edward LeBlanc, the DLP leader, became Chief Minister. In 1967 Dominica became one of the West Indies Associated States, gaining full autonomy in internal affairs, with the United Kingdom retaining responsibility for defence and foreign relations. The House of Assembly replaced the Legislative Council, the Administrator became Governor and the Chief Minister was restyled Premier. At elections to the House in 1970, LeBlanc was returned to power as Premier.

In 1974 LeBlanc retired, and was replaced as DLP leader and Premier by Patrick John. At elections to the enlarged House of Assembly in March 1975 the DLP was returned to power. Following a decision in 1975 by the Associated States to seek independence separately, Dominica became an independent republic within the Commonwealth on 3 November 1978. John became Prime Minister, and Frederick Degazon was eventually elected President.

In May 1979 two people were killed by the Defence Force at a demonstration against the Government's attempts to introduce legislation that would restrict the freedom of trade unions and the press. The deaths fuelled increasing popular opposition to the Government, and a pressure group, the Committee for National Salvation (CNS), was formed to campaign for John's resignation. Government opponents organized a general strike that lasted 25 days, with John relinquishing power only after all his cabinet ministers had resigned and President Degazon had gone into hiding abroad (there was a succession of Acting Presidents; Degazon finally resigned in February 1980). Oliver Seraphin, the candidate proposed by the CNS, was elected Prime Minister, and an interim Government was formed to prepare for a general election after six months.

The Dominica Freedom Party (DFP) achieved a convincing victory in the general election of July 1980. Eugenia Charles, the party's leader, became the Caribbean's first female Prime Minister.

In January 1981 the Government disarmed the Defence Force following reports that weapons were being traded for marijuana. Against a background of increasing violence and the declaration of a state of emergency, however, there were two coup attempts involving former Defence Force members. John, the former Prime Minister, was also implicated and imprisoned. In June 1982 John and his fellow prisoners were tried and acquitted, but the Government secured a retrial in October 1985. John and the former Deputy Commander of the Defence Force each received a prison sentence of 12 years. In 1986 the former Commander of the Defence Force was hanged for the murder of a police officer during the second coup attempt. The death sentences on five other soldiers were commuted to life imprisonment.

By 1985 the DLP, the Democratic Labour Party, the United Dominica Labour Party and the Dominica Liberation Movement had united to form a new left-wing grouping, the Labour Party of Dominica, although in practice the party continued to be known as the DLP. At a general election in July 1985 the DFP was returned to power. Following the election, the DLP began an 18-month boycott of the House, in protest against the Government's decision to curtail live broadcasts of parliamentary proceedings.

Dissatisfaction at continued government austerity measures was offset by the success of the land reform programme. Since independence, the Government had acquired nearly all the large estates, often in an attempt to forestall violence. In 1986 the first of the estates was divided, and tenure granted to the former workers. The DFP was returned for a third term in government at a general election in May 1990.

A programme, introduced in 1991, granting Dominican citizenship to foreigners in return for a minimum investment of US $35,000 in the country caused considerable controversy. The Dominica United Workers' Party (UWP—formed in 1988) expressed opposition to the policy, and in 1992 a pressure group, Concerned Citizens, organized protests demanding that the programme be modified. In response, the Government announced in July that the minimum investment was to be increased substantially, the number of applications was to be limited to 800 and restrictions were to be placed on the investors' right to vote in Dominica.

At a general election in June 1995 the DFP's 15-year tenure was finally ended as the UWP secured a narrow victory. The UWP leader, Edison James, was subsequently appointed Prime Minister, and the DLP and DFP leaders agreed to occupy the position of Leader of the Opposition in alternate years.

In December 1997 the Government's citizenship programme again provoked controversy. It was alleged that, under the scheme, passports were being sold by agents for between US $15,000 and $20,000. The opposition DLP accused the Government of undermining the credibility of Dominican citizenship. In late 1999 it was announced that the Government had stopped granting citizenship to Russians, following reports that up to 300 Russians had paid $50,000 each to obtain a Dominican passport. In addition, there were complaints from the US Government that the trade in passports had increased 'suspicions of money-laundering' in Dominica.

The rise of the DLP

A general election was held in January 2000. The DLP was returned to power after two decades in opposition, albeit one seat short of a majority. Roosevelt (Rosie) Douglas was named as Prime Minister and formed a coalition Government with the DFP (which was allocated two ministerial portfolios). On taking office, the new Government immediately suspended the controversial citizenship programme; however, following changes to ensure that passports would not be granted to those with a criminal record, the programme was relaunched in June 2002, with a fee of US $100,000 for individual applicants.

In October 2000 Prime Minister Douglas died suddenly of a heart attack. Pierre Charles, previously the Minister of Communications and Works, succeeded him as premier. In November Ambrose George, the Minister of Finance, was stripped of his portfolio following the arrest on money-laundering charges of a businessman with whom he was travelling in Puerto Rico. George was instead given the post of Minister of Industry, Physical Planning and Enterprise Development.

Meanwhile, in December 2000 legislation was approved in the House of Assembly making the crime of money-laundering punishable by up to seven years' imprisonment and a fine of EC $1m. At the same time, the Government introduced stricter regulations governing its 'offshore' banking sector, following Dominica's inclusion on a 'black list' published by the Financial Action Task Force earlier in the year. Dominica was removed from the list in 2002 after the Government made progress in improving its anti-money-laundering measures. Part of these measures was the approval, in December 2001, of the Exchange of Information Bill, designed to give foreign authorities greater access to information about Dominica's 'offshore' banks.

In February 2003 the Public Service Union (PSU), objecting to government proposals to reduce the size of the public sector workforce and to compel workers to take two days of unpaid leave every month, organized a six-day strike. The strike ended after the Government agreed to review its proposal to reduce the public sector wage bill (although the Government enforced a 5% reduction in public sector salaries in 2004–05).

Charles died of a heart attack in January 2004. Roosevelt Skerrit, hitherto Minister of Education, Youth and Sports, was sworn in as Prime Minister. On the same day, Skerrit appointed his first Cabinet; notable appointments included the return of Ambrose George (who had left the Cabinet in 2002), as Minister of Agriculture and the Environment. In the following month Skerrit was elected leader of the DLP; George was appointed deputy leader.

In spite of the country's economic difficulties, at the general election on 5 May 2005 the DLP was re-elected with an overall majority of seats (12 of the 21) in the House of Assembly. The UWP secured eight seats, while a close ally of the DLP, standing as an independent candidate, won the remaining seat. The junior coalition partner, the DFP, was defeated in the two constituencies in which it competed; however, its leader, Charles Savarin, was appointed as a senator and retained his place in Skerrit's new administration as Minister of Foreign Affairs, Trade, Labour and the Public Service. In December Earl Williams, a former cabinet minister, succeeded Edison James as leader of the UWP, and proceeded to replace him as Leader of the Opposition in July 2007 when James resigned from office.

In July 2008 Williams was forced to resign as Leader of the Opposition and of the UWP following allegations that he had mishandled clients' money in his capacity as a lawyer. He was succeeded by the party's Deputy Leader, Ron Green. In October Nicholas Liverpool secured a second term as President after receiving the nomination of both the DLP and the UWP. Prime Minister Skerrit reorganized his Cabinet in November, removing Ambrose George from his post as Minister of Public Works following accusations of corruption that included his alleged involvement in an internet fraud operation. His position was reallocated to the hitherto Minister of National Security, Immigration and Labour, Rayburn Blackmoore, while Vince Henderson became Minister of Foreign Affairs, Immigration and Labour. The office of Minister of National Security was assumed by the Prime Minister.

Recent developments: DLP continues in office

In the general election, held on 18 December 2009, the DLP increased its majority in the House of Assembly, securing 18 of the 21 elective seats, while the UWP won the remaining three. Among those to lose their seats were UWP leader Ron Green, who lost to the DLP candidate by two votes, and his deputy, Claudius Sanford. The rate of participation by the electorate was recorded at 59.1%. In the months preceding the election, campaign financing had been a prominent issue: it was alleged that the DLP campaign had been funded by the People's Republic of China and Venezuela, while the UWP was accused of accepting funds from Taiwan. Both parties denied the charges.

Shortly after the release of the election results, Green alleged that the DLP had used bribery to manipulate the outcome of the ballot. He also criticized the DLP's disproportionate access to the state-controlled media. Green announced that the three UWP deputies would boycott the House of Assembly in protest, and appealed to the High Court for a recount in his closely contested constituency. He also demanded that a fresh election be convened within 18 months, despite the fact that monitors from the Caribbean Community and the Organization of American States had declared the ballot to be free and fair. In February 2010, with the parliamentary boycott continuing, the UWP announced that it would instead participate in a separate 'People's Parliament'. Nevertheless, Skerrit's new Cabinet was sworn in on 4 January, which, controversially, included Ambrose George as Minister of Information, Telecommunications and Constituency Empowerment. Skerrit appointed Charles Savarin as Minister of National Security, Labour and Immigration, but retained responsibility for the key portfolios of finance and foreign affairs.

The continuing boycott by two of the three UWP deputies, former Prime Minister Edison James and Hector John, prompted the Speaker of the House of Assembly to designate their seats as vacant in May 2010. By-elections to fill the seats were conducted on 9 July and the two UWP members were re-elected. John became Leader of the Opposition later that month, although he did not announce an end to the UWP's parliamentary boycott until February 2012.

Meanwhile, in August 2010 the High Court, responding to a UWP petition, announced that Skerrit and Minister of Education and Human Resource Development Peter Saint Jean would be required to stand trial to defend themselves against dual-citizenship charges. According to Dominican law, persons maintaining allegiance to a non-Commonwealth country are not permitted to contest elections. Therefore, Skerrit's joint French-Dominican nationality brought into question his eligibility to govern. The Prime Minister asserted that his French citizenship had been attained while he was a child, thereby exempting him from the electoral regulation in question, although the UWP disputed this. In January 2012 the High Court exonerated Skerrit and Saint Jean of any wrongdoing, declaring that there was insufficient evidence to uphold the UWP petition. Following this defeat, Green declined to stand in the UWP leadership election later that month, and Edison James was selected as the party's new leader. In March 2013 the Eastern Caribbean Supreme Court rejected a UWP appeal against the High Court's judgment. Lennox Linton became UWP leader in September.

Following his election by the legislature, Eliud Williams was sworn in as the island's new President in September 2012. The UWP initiated a legal challenge against this move in October, citing alleged procedural violations, although the case was dismissed by the Eastern Caribbean Supreme Court in January 2014. Williams, meanwhile, was succeeded as President by Savarin in October 2013. However, the legality of Savarin's election was also disputed by the UWP.

In November 2013 the Skerrit administration announced it had officially informed the British Government of its intention to establish the Caribbean Court of Justice (CCJ), based in Trinidad and Tobago, as Dominica's final court of appeal, instead of the Privy Council, based in London. In 2003 Dominica had been a signatory to the agreement establishing the CCJ, which was inaugurated in 2005; however, by early 2014 only Barbados, Belize and Guyana had adopted it as a final appellate court. In January 2014 Skerrit announced that the British authorities had not objected to the move, and that legislation allowing for the transition would be put before parliament in that year.

The Government, in February 2014, signed a memorandum of understanding to build a luxury hotel in the north of Dominica. The agreement was facilitated by the recent passage of legislation allowing investment through its Economic Citizenship Programme.

Foreign Affairs

Regional relations

Dominica was one of 13 Caribbean jurisdictions to sign the Petrocaribe accord in 2005, under which Dominica was allowed to purchase petroleum from Venezuela at reduced prices. Owing to insufficient existing petroleum storage and refining capacity on the island, an agreement was signed in 2006 between the Government and PDVSA, the state-managed Venezuelan oil company, for the construction of a 35,000-barrel fuel storage and distribution plant to assist in dissemination of oil under the Petrocaribe initiative.

Other external relations

Dominica has close links with France and the USA. France helped in suppressing the coup attempts against the DFP Government in 1981, and Dominica was the first Commonwealth country to benefit from the French aid agency Fonds d'Aide et de Coopération. In 2005 the USA announced a US $2m. per year aid programme, to help improve Dominica's international competitiveness.

In 2001 Libya granted Dominica, in common with other eastern Caribbean islands, access to a US $2,000m. development fund. In 2005 the Government announced that Libya was paying for the construction of two schools on the island and for 15 scholarships for Dominican students to attend university courses in Libya. The Government refused to sever diplomatic ties with the Libyan regime of Col Muammar al-Qaddafi in 2011 despite the increasingly violent attempts by the Libyan authorities to suppress a popular domestic uprising. Dominica also declined to participate in a UN vote in September that granted recognition to the rebel 'National Transitional Council of Libya'.

In 2004 Dominica established diplomatic relations with the People's Republic of China in place of Taiwan. (China agreed to provide an estimated US $111m. in financial support.) Skerrit was heavily criticized by the opposition over the severing of relations with Taiwan. In 2005 Skerrit accused the UWP of jeopardizing Dominica's nascent relations with China by accepting campaign funds from Taiwan. The Chinese embassy in Roseau condemned the display of Taiwanese flags by UWP supporters and expressed strongly worded dismay at local opposition to the 'one China' principle. In 2009 the Government negotiated an EC $35m. low-interest loan with China to fund a new college on the island. The Chinese Government also agreed to a concessionary loan to finance road rehabilitation and housing projects. China approved an EC $18m. financial aid package in July 2013 and an US $8m. grant in December to support a variety of development programmes in Dominica.

Dominica's perceived attachment to so-called 'chequebook diplomacy' was criticized again in 2004 when Japan provided funding of some EC $33m. for the construction of a fisheries complex on the island, allegedly in return for supporting the Japanese Government's pro-whaling stance at the annual meeting of the International Whaling Commission (IWC) in 2006. Prime Minister Skerrit made an official visit to Japan in 2007, following which he announced that Japanese funding for a further fisheries facility had been secured. Skerrit also stated his intention to renew Dominica's support for the Japanese Government's bid to resume commercial whaling. In 2008, however, Skerrit withdrew his support for the overturning of the whaling ban, citing the island's strict environmental commitments and the importance of its abundant sealife for the tourism industry.

CONSTITUTION AND GOVERNMENT

The Constitution came into effect at the independence of Dominica in November 1978. Legislative power is vested in the unicameral House of Assembly, comprising 30 members (nine nominated and 21 elected for five years by universal adult suffrage). Executive authority is vested in the President, who is elected by the House, but in most matters the President is guided by the advice of the Cabinet and acts as the constitutional Head of State. He appoints the Prime Minister, who must be able to command a majority in the House, and (on the Prime Minister's recommendation) other ministers. The Cabinet is responsible to the House. Justice is administered by the Eastern Caribbean Supreme Court (based in Saint Lucia), although further appeal can, in certain cases, be made to the Privy Council in the United Kingdom. The island is divided into 10 administrative divisions, known as parishes, and there is limited local government in Roseau, the capital, and in the Carib Territory.

REGIONAL AND INTERNATIONAL CO-OPERATION

Dominica is a member of the Organization of American States (see p. 394), the Caribbean Community and Common Market (CARICOM, see p. 223), the Association of Caribbean States (see p. 449), the Organisation of Eastern Caribbean States (OECS, see p. 467), and of the Community of Latin American and Caribbean States (see p. 464), which was formally inaugurated in December 2011. Dominica is also a member of the Eastern Caribbean Central Bank (see p. 455) and the Eastern Caribbean Securities Exchange (both based in Saint Christopher and Nevis). Dominica was a signatory to the Revised Treaty of Basseterre, establishing an Economic Union among OECS member states in 2010. The Cabinet ratified the Treaty in January 2011, and the Economic Union, which involved the removal of barriers to trade and the movement of labour as a step towards a single financial and economic market, came into effect later that month. Freedom of movement between the signatory states was granted to OECS nationals on 1 August. In 2008 Dominica became a member of the Venezuelan-led Bolivarian Alliance for the Peoples of our America-People's Trade Treaty (Alianza Bolivariana para los Pueblos de Nuestra América-Tratado de Comercio de los Pueblos—ALBA-TCP, see p. 463), intended to be an alternative to the proposed Free Trade Area of the Americas advanced by the USA.

Dominica became a member of the UN and of the Commonwealth (see p. 236) upon independence in 1978. As a contracting party to the General Agreement on Tariffs and Trade, Dominica joined the World Trade Organization (see p. 434) on its establishment in 1995. The country is a signatory of the Cotonou Agreement, the successor arrangement to the Lomé Conventions between the African, Caribbean and Pacific (ACP) countries and the European Union (see p. 273).

ECONOMIC AFFAIRS

In 2012, according to estimates by the World Bank, Dominica's gross national income (GNI), measured at average 2010–12 prices, was US $463m., equivalent to $6,460 per head (or $12,190 per head on an international purchasing-power parity basis). Between 2003 and 2012 the population increased at an average annual rate of 0.3%, while gross domestic product (GDP) per head increased, in real terms, by an average of 2.5% per year. According to the Eastern Caribbean Central Bank (ECCB, see p. 455), overall GDP increased, in real terms, by an average of 2.1% per year in 2003–12; GDP increased by 0.2% in 2011, but decreased by 1.2% in 2012.

Agriculture (including forestry and fishing) is the principal economic activity, accounting for 16.0% of GDP in 2012, according to the ECCB. In mid-2014 the sector was expected to engage an estimated 20.0% of the employed labour force, according to FAO estimates. The principal cash crop is bananas, although the industry was adversely affected by the ending of Dominica's preferential access to the European (particularly the British) market from 2010. In 2011 banana output totalled an estimated 23,000 metric tons. Banana production contracted by almost 40% in the first nine months of 2013, partly owing to disease. The value of banana exports also fell in the same period, by 42.2%. In 2010 receipts from banana exports amounted to an estimated US $3.1m., equivalent to only 9.1% of total domestic exports, compared to 20.0% in 2008. Other important crops include taro, yams, coconuts (which provide copra for export as well as edible oil and soap), mangoes, avocados, papayas, ginger, citrus fruits and, mainly for domestic consumption, vegetables. Non-banana crops have rapidly grown in significance during recent years, from one-half of total crop production before 2000 to four-fifths by the late 2000s. Livestock-rearing and fishing are also practised for local purposes. Numerous Japanese-funded fisheries projects have been donated to Dominica in recent years. Dominica has extensive timber reserves (more than 40% of the island's total land area is forest and woodland), and international aid agencies are encouraging the development of a balanced timber industry. According to the ECCB, the GDP of the agricultural sector declined at an average annual rate of 1.4% in 2003–12; however, agricultural GDP increased by 6.7% in 2012.

Industry (comprising mining, manufacturing, construction and utilities) provided 14.4% of GDP in 2012, according to the ECCB, and employed an estimated 22.0% of the employed labour force in 2001. Real industrial GDP increased at an average rate of 3.6% per year during 2003–12; the sector increased marginally, by 0.8%, in 2011, but declined by 2.6% in 2012.

The mining sector contributed only 1.4% of GDP in 2012, according to the ECCB. There is some quarrying of pumice, and there are extensive reserves of limestone and clay. The sector decreased at an annual average rate of 1.0% in 2003–12; mining GDP increased by 10.0% in 2011, but declined by 15.0% in 2012.

In 2012 manufacturing contributed 3.2% of GDP, according to the ECCB, and, in 2001, an estimated 10.6% of the employed workforce were engaged in manufacturing, mining and quarrying activities. The Government has encouraged the manufacturing sector, which is mainly small-scale and dependent upon agriculture, in an attempt to diversify the economy. According to the ECCB, real manufacturing GDP decreased at an average rate of 1.6% per year during 2003–12; the sector decreased by 5.9% in 2011, but increased by 3.8% in 2012. There is a banana-packaging plant, a brewery and factories for the manufacturing and refining of crude and edible vegetable oils, and for the production of soap, canned juices and cigarettes. Furniture, paint, cardboard boxes and candles are also produced.

The construction industry accounted for 4.8% of GDP in 2012, according to the ECCB, and employed 9.8% of the employed labour force in 2001. Extensive infrastructure development by the Government has maintained high levels of activity in the construction sector in recent years. The sector's GDP increased at an average annual rate of 10.3%, in real terms, during 2003–12; sectoral growth of 4.5% was recorded in 2011, but a decline of 6.9% was registered in 2012.

Some 70% of Dominica's energy requirements were supplied by hydroelectric power. A 20-MW electric power plant began production in 2001. Investment in a hydroelectric development scheme and in the water supply system has been partially financed by the export of water, from Dominica's extensive reserves, to drier Caribbean islands such as Aruba. In 2012 Dominica's imports of mineral fuels totalled 22.5% of the cost of total imports. The monopoly enjoyed by Dominica Electricity Services was scheduled to end by 2015. In order to reduce reliance on imported energy, the Government was looking to expand geothermal potential; to this end, in late 2013 construction of a 15 MW power station in Roseau Valley began.

Services engaged an estimated 58.6% of the employed labour force in 2001, and provided 69.6% of GDP in 2012, according to the ECCB. The combined GDP of the services sector increased at an average rate of 1.7% per year during 2003–12; the sector expanded by 1.0% in 2011, but declined by 0.6% in 2012. The tourism industry, which directly contributed an estimated 9.5% of GDP and 8.8% of employment in 2012, according to the World Travel and Tourism Council, is of increasing importance to the economy, and exploits Dominica's natural history and scenery. The majority of tourists are cruise ship passengers. Total visitor arrivals stood at 354,189 in 2012, a 16.4% decrease over the previous year (when there were 423,424 visitors). Tourism receipts totalled EC $307.17 m. in 2012, compared with $313.46m. in the previous year.

In 2012 Dominica recorded an estimated visible merchandise trade deficit of US $142.1m. and a deficit of $54.9m. on the current account of the balance of payments. The principal source of imports in 2012 was the USA, which accounted for 36.8% of total imports, followed by Trinidad and Tobago and the United Kingdom. The principal markets for exports in 2012 were Trinidad and Tobago and Jamaica, both with 18.6% of the total. Saint Christopher and Nevis, Guyana, France, Barbados and Antigua and Barbuda were other important markets. The principal imports in 2012 were mineral products, prepared foodstuffs, beverages, spirits, vinegar, tobacco and articles thereof, machinery and mechanical appliances and electrical equipment, chemicals and related products, live animals and animal products, and iron and steel, other base metals and articles of base metal. The principal exports in the same year were chemicals and related products, pulp of wood, paper and paperboard, and articles thereof, machinery and mechanical appliances, electrical equipment, mineral products, and vegetable products.

In 2012, according to preliminary figures by the ECCB, there was a budget deficit of EC $159.0m., equivalent to 11.9% of GDP. Dominica's general government gross debt was EC $984m. in 2012, equivalent to 74.8% of GDP. At the end of 2011 Dominica's total external debt was US $284m., of which 229m. was public and publicly guaranteed debt. In that year, the cost of servicing long-term public and publicly guaranteed debt and repayments to the IMF was equivalent to 9.8% of the value of exports of goods, services and income (excluding workers' remittances). According to the IMF, the annual rate of inflation averaged 2.7% in 2005–12; consumer prices increased by an average of 1.4% in 2012. An estimated 10.9% of the labour force were unemployed in 2001.

The Dominican economy is heavily dependent on the production of bananas, and is thus vulnerable to adverse weather conditions and price fluctuations. Efforts to expand the country's economic base have been impeded by poor infrastructure and, in terms of tourism, a paucity of desirable beaches. The gradual elimination of the European Union's (see p. 273) tariff system from 2010 brought further insecurity for the banana sector following several years of decline. Dominica was not as badly affected by the global financial crisis as many other nations in the region: expansionary spending policies throughout 2009, and the receipt of a US $5m. IMF grant cushioned the country from the worst effects of the economic crisis. Although banana production declined in 2010, increased activity in the construction sector supported a fragile economic recovery. Economic growth of just 0.2% was achieved in 2011. The IMF estimated that real GDP contracted by 1.2% in 2012, partly caused by sluggish rates of domestic consumption, a decline in tourist arrivals, and the negative effects of Black Sigatoka banana disease. Moreover, the construction industry, which had previously been bolstered by various public works programmes, was negatively affected by the reduction of spending from mid-2011. The economy contracted by a further estimated 0.5% in 2013, according to the ECCB, although growth of 1.2% was forecast for 2014. Meanwhile, drilling operations to assess Dominica's geothermal energy potential in 2012 proved encouraging, lending momentum to the Government's plans to establish a 120-MW geothermal power station on the island, with excess electricity to be exported to Guadeloupe and Martinique. The construction of an initial plant, with an estimated capacity of 15 MW, commenced in late 2013. The Government hoped that the development of a geothermal sector would reinvigorate the island's ailing economy.

PUBLIC HOLIDAYS

2015: 1 January (New Year's Day), 16–17 February (Masquerade, Carnival), 3 April (Good Friday), 6 April (Easter Monday), 4 May (May or Labour Day), 25 May (Whit Monday), 3 August (Emancipation, August Monday), 3 November (Independence Day and Community Service Day), 25–26 December (Christmas).

Statistical Survey

Source (unless otherwise stated): Eastern Caribbean Central Bank; internet www.eccb-centralbank.org.

AREA AND POPULATION

Area: 751 sq km (290 sq miles).

Population: 71,727 at census of 12 May 2001; 71,293 (males 36,411, females 34,882) at census of 14 May 2011 (preliminary).

Density (at 2011 census): 94.9 per sq km.

Population by Age and Sex (31 December 2006): *0–14:* 20,976 (males 10,759, females 10,217); *15–64:* 42,979 (males 22,280, females 20,699); *65 and over:* 7,226 (males 3,200, females 4,026); *Total* 71,180 (males 36,238, females 34,942) (Source: UN, *Demographic Yearbook*).

Principal Town (population at 2011 census, preliminary): Roseau (capital) 15,035.

Births, Marriages and Deaths (registrations, 2002 unless otherwise indicated): Live births 1,081 (birth rate 15.4 per 1,000); Marriages (1998) 336 (marriage rate 4.4 per 1,000); Deaths 594 (death rate 8.4 per 1,000) (Source: UN, *Demographic Yearbook*). *2006:* Live births 1,058 (birth rate 14.9 per 1,000); Deaths 536 (death rate 7.5 per 1,000) (Source: UN, *Population and Vital Statistics Report*). *2010:* Live births 933; Deaths 588.

Life Expectancy (years at birth, WHO estimates): 74 (males 72; females 77) in 2011. Source: WHO, *World Health Statistics*.

Economically Active Population ('000 persons aged 15 years and over, 2001): Agriculture, hunting, forestry and fishing 5.22; Manufacturing (incl. mining and quarrying) 2.10; Utilities 0.41; Construction 2.42; Wholesale and retail trade, restaurants and hotels 5.12; Transport, storage and communications 1.56; Financing, insurance, real estate and business services 1.14; Community, social and personal services 6.77; *Sub-total* 24.73; Activities not adequately defined 0.08; *Total employed* 24.81; Unemployed 3.05; *Total labour force* 27.86 (males 17.03, females 10.83) (Source: ILO). *Mid-2014* (estimates): Agriculture, etc. 6,000; Total labour force 30,000 (Source: FAO).

HEALTH AND WELFARE

Key Indicators

Total Fertility Rate (children per woman, 2011): 2.1.

Under-5 Mortality Rate (per 1,000 live births, 2011): 12.

Physicians (per 1,000 head, 2001): 1.6.

Hospital Beds (per 1,000 head, 2010): 3.8.

Health Expenditure (2010): US $ per head (PPP): 717.

Health Expenditure (2010): % of GDP: 5.9.

Health Expenditure (2010): public (% of total): 71.3.

Access to Water (% of persons, 2004): 97.

Access to Sanitation (% of persons, 2004): 84.

Total Carbon Dioxide Emissions ('000 metric tons, 2010): 135.7.

Total Carbon Dioxide Emissions Per Head (metric tons, 2010): 1.9.

Human Development Index (2012): ranking: 72.

Human Development Index (2012): value: 0.745.

For sources and definitions, see explanatory note on p. vi.

AGRICULTURE, ETC.

Principal Crops ('000 metric tons, 2012, FAO estimates): Sweet potatoes 2.2; Cassava 1.2; Yautia (Cocoyam) 5.0; Taro (Cocoyam) 13.0; Yams 14.0; Sugar cane 4.8; Coconuts 11.5; Cabbages 0.8; Pumpkins 0.9; Cucumbers 1.4; Carrots 0.8; Bananas 24.5; Plantains 5.7; Oranges 6.3; Lemons and limes 1.4; Grapefruit (incl. pomelos) 13.5; Guavas, mangoes and mangosteens 2.1; Avocados 0.4. *Aggregate Production* ('000 metric tons, may include official, semi-official or estimated data): Fruits (excl. melons) 55.0.

Livestock ('000 head, year ending September 2012, FAO estimates): Cattle 14.0; Pigs 5.0; Sheep 7.9; Goats 9.7; Chickens 200.

Livestock Products ('000 metric tons, 2012, FAO estimates): Cattle meat 0.6; Pig meat 0.4; Chicken meat 0.3; Cows' milk 7.6; Hen eggs 0.2.

Fishing (metric tons, live weight, 2011, FAO estimates): Capture 664 (Yellowfin tuna 133; Marlins, sailfishes, etc. 61; Common dolphinfish 149); Aquaculture 35; *Total catch* 699.

Source: FAO.

MINING

Pumice ('000 metric tons, incl. volcanic ash): Estimated production 100 per year in 1988–2004. Source: US Geological Survey.

INDUSTRY

Production (2006, metric tons, unless otherwise indicated, preliminary): Laundry soap 3,605; Toilet soap 4,296; Dental cream 1,376; Liquid disinfectant 1,861; Crude coconut oil 855 (2001); Coconut meal 331 (2001); Electricity 93.0 million kWh (2009). Sources: IMF, *Dominica: Statistical Appendix* (September 2007), and UN Industrial Commodity Statistics Database.

FINANCE

Currency and Exchange Rates: 100 cents = 1 Eastern Caribbean dollar (EC $). *Sterling, US Dollar and Euro Equivalents* (31 December 2013): £1 sterling = EC $4.446; US $1 = EC $2.700; €1 = EC $3.724; EC $100 = £22.49 = US $37.04 = €26.86. *Exchange Rate:* Fixed at US $1 = EC $2.70 since July 1976.

Budget (EC $ million, 2012, preliminary): *Revenue:* Tax revenue 302.7 (Taxes on income and profits 56.8, Taxes on property 6.3, Taxes on domestic goods and services 179.6, Taxes on international trade and transactions 59.9); Other current revenue 46.6; Total 349.3, excl. grants received 1.8. *Expenditure:* Current expenditure 338.0 (Wages and salaries 134.8, Goods and services 91.9, Interest payments 43.3, Transfers and subsidies 68.1); Capital expenditure and net lending 172.1; Total 510.1.

International Reserves (US $ million at 31 December 2012): IMF special drawing rights 2.71; Reserve position in IMF 0.01; Foreign exchange 90.90; Total 93.63. Source: IMF, *International Financial Statistics*.

Money Supply (EC $ million at 31 December 2012): Currency outside depository corporations 45.61; Transferable deposits 226.53; Other deposits 989.49; *Broad money* 1,261.63. Source: IMF, *International Financial Statistics*.

Cost of Living (Retail Price Index, base: 2005 = 100): All items 116.3 in 2010, 119.0 in 2011, 120.8 in 2012. Source: IMF, *International Financial Statistics*.

Gross Domestic Product (EC $ million at constant 2006 prices): 1,179.55 in 2010, 1,181.72 in 2011; 1,167.54 in 2012.

Expenditure on the Gross Domestic Product (EC $ million at current prices, 2012): Government final consumption expenditure 242.03; Private final consumption expenditure 1,103.69; Gross fixed capital formation 199.57; *Total domestic expenditure* 1,545.29; Exports of goods and services 438.18; *Less* Imports of goods and services 645.12; *GDP in purchasers' values* 1,338.36.

Gross Domestic Product by Economic Activity (EC $ million at current prices, 2012): Agriculture, hunting, forestry and fishing 189.55; Mining and quarrying 16.50; Manufacturing 37.56; Electricity and water 60.18; Construction 56.65; Wholesale and retail trade 157.30; Restaurants and hotels 23.76; Transport, storage and communications 158.05; Finance and insurance 77.50; Real estate, housing and business activities 104.65; Government services 287.38; Other services 15.48; *Sub-total* 1,184.57; *Less* Financial intermediation services indirectly measured (FISIM) 62.41; *Gross value added in basic prices* 1,122.16; Taxes, less subsidies, on products 216.20; *GDP in market prices* 1,338.36.

Balance of Payments (US $ million, 2012): Exports of goods 40.6; Imports of goods –182.7; *Balance on goods* –142.1; Services (net) 87.8; *Balance on goods and services* –54.3; Primary income (net) –17.2; *Balance on goods, services and primary income* –71.4; Secondary income (net) 16.5; *Current balance* –54.9; Capital transfers 16.5; Direct investment liabilities 19.6; Portfolio investment (net) 3.7; Other investment (net) 19.2; Net errors and omissions –1.3; *Reserves and related items* 2.7. Source: IMF, *International Financial Statistics*.

EXTERNAL TRADE

Principal Commodities (distribution by HS, US $ million, 2012): *Imports c.i.f.:* Live animals and animal products 13.5 (Meat and edible meat offal 6.7); Vegetables and vegetable products 8.5; Prepared foodstuff, beverages, spirits and vinegar, tobacco, etc. 26.5 (Beverages, spirits and vinegar 7.5); Mineral Products 51.3 (Mineral fuels, oils, distillation products, etc. 47.6); Chemicals and related products 15.3; Plastics, rubbers, and articles thereof 8.9; Pulp of wood, paper and paperboard, and articles thereof 9.2; Iron and steel, other base metals and articles of base metals 12.7; Machinery and mechanical appliances, electrical equipment and parts thereof 25.8 (Machinery, boilers etc. 13.1; Electrical and electronic equipment 12.6); Vehicles, aircraft, vessels and associated transport equipment 10.0 (Vehicles other than railway, tramway 8.6); Total (incl. others) 211.9. *Exports f.o.b.:* Vegetables and vegetable products 3.3 (Vegetables and roots and tubers 1.3; Edible fruit, nuts, peel of citrus fruit, melons etc. 1.9); Mineral products 3.5 (Salt, sulphur, earth, stone, plaster, lime and cement 3.5); Chemicals and related products 18.8 (Tanning, dyeing extracts, pigments, etc. 1.5; Soaps, lubricants, waxes, candles and modelling pastes, etc. 16.5); Pulp of wood, paper and paperboard, and articles thereof 4.5 (Printed books, newspapers and pictures 4.5); Machinery and mechanical appliances, electrical equipment and parts thereof 4.1 (Electrical and electronic equipment 3.8); Total (incl. others) 37.0.

Principal Trading Partners (US $ million, 2012): *Imports c.i.f.:* Antigua and Barbuda 4.5; Barbados 3.8; Brazil 2.2; Canada 4.9; China, People's Republic 5.2; Colombia 4.2; Dominican Republic 3.7; France (incl. Monaco) 4.2; Grenada 2.3; Guyana 2.2; Jamaica 3.8; Japan 5.0; Netherlands 2.7; Saint Lucia 3.5; Saint Vincent and the Grenadines 3.4; Trinidad and Tobago 36.0; United Kingdom 8.4; USA 77.9; Total (incl. others) 211.9. *Exports f.o.b.:* Antigua and Barbuda 2.0; Barbados 2.3; France (incl. Monaco) 3.2; Guyana 3.5; Jamaica 6.9; Saint Christopher and Nevis 5.3; Saint Lucia 0.9; Saint Vincent and the Grenadines 0.4; Suriname 0.7; Trinidad and Tobago 6.9; USA 1.6; Total (incl. others) 37.0.

Source: Trade Map-Trade Competitiveness Map, International Trade Centre, www.intracen.org/marketanalysis.

TRANSPORT

Road Traffic (motor vehicles licensed in 1994): Private cars 6,491; Taxis 90; Buses 559; Motorcycles 94; Trucks 2,266; Jeeps 461; Tractors 24; Total 9,985. *2000* (motor vehicles in use): Passenger cars 8,700; Commercial vehicles 3,400. Source: partly UN, *Statistical Yearbook*.

Shipping: *Flag Registered Fleet* (at 31 December 2013): 79 vessels (total displacement 698,019 grt) (Source: Lloyd's List Intelligence—www.lloydslistintelligence.com); *International Freight Traffic* ('000 metric tons, estimates, 1993): Goods loaded 103.2; Goods unloaded 181.2.

Civil Aviation (1997): Aircraft arrivals and departures 18,672; Freight loaded 363 metric tons; Freight unloaded 575 metric tons.

TOURISM

Visitor Arrivals: 597,935 (70,618 stop-over visitors, 784 excursionists, 517,979 cruise ship passengers, 8,554 yacht passengers) in 2010; 423,424 (70,821 stop-over visitors, 764 excursionists, 341,501 cruise ship passengers, 10,338 yacht passengers) in 2011; 354,189 (74,144 stop-over visitors, 2,104 excursionists, 266,178 cruise ship passengers, 11,763 yacht passengers) in 2012.

Tourism Receipts (EC $ million, estimates): 318.26 in 2010; 313.46 in 2011, 307.17 in 2012.

COMMUNICATIONS MEDIA

Telephones (2012): 14,600 main lines in use.

Mobile Cellular Telephones (2012): 109,300 subscribers.

Personal Computers: 13,000 (181.9 per 1,000 persons) in 2004.

Internet Subscribers (2010): 8,600.

Broadband Subscribers (2012): 8,500.

Source: International Telecommunication Union.

EDUCATION

Institutions (1994/95 unless otherwise indicated): Pre-primary 72 (1992/93); Primary 64; Secondary 14; Tertiary 2.

Teachers (2011/12 unless otherwise indicated): Pre-primary 160; Primary 516; General secondary 503; Secondary vocational 22 (2010/11); Tertiary 34 (1992/93).

Pupils (2011/12 unless otherwise indicated): Pre-primary 1,734 (males 864, females 870); Primary 8,144 (males 4,186, females 3,958); General secondary 6,093 (males 3,090, females 3,003); Secondary vocational 302 (males 93, females 209) (2010/11); Tertiary 229 (males 55, females 174) (2007/08).

Sources: UNESCO, *Statistical Yearbook*, Institute for Statistics; Caribbean Development Bank, *Social and Economic Indicators*; UN Economic Commission for Latin America and the Caribbean, *Statistical Yearbook*.

Pupil-teacher Ratio (primary education, UNESCO estimate): 15.8 in 2011/12 (Source: UNESCO Institute for Statistics).

Adult Literacy Rate (2004): 88.0%. Source: UN Development Programme, *Human Development Report*.

Directory

The Government

HEAD OF STATE

President: Charles Angelo Savarin (assumed office 2 October 2013).

CABINET
(April 2014)

The Government is formed by the Dominica Labour Party.

Prime Minister and Minister of Finance, Foreign Affairs and Information Technology and of National Security, Labour and Immigration: Roosevelt Skerrit.

Attorney-General: Levi Peter.

Minister of Housing, Lands, Settlement and Water Resources: Reginald Austrie.

Minister of Agriculture and Forestry: Matthew Walter.

Minister of Employment, Trade, Industry and Diaspora Affairs: Dr John Colin McIntyre.

Minister of the Environment, Natural Resources, Physical Planning and Fisheries: Dr Kenneth Darroux.

Minister of Education and Human Resource Development: Petter Saint-Jean.

Minister of Social Services, Community Development and Gender Affairs: Gloria Shillingford.

Minister of Culture, Youth and Sports: Justina Charles.

Minister of Tourism and Legal Affairs: Ian Douglas.

Minister of Information, Telecommunications and Constituency Empowerment: Ambrose George.

Minister of Health: Julius Timothy.

Minister of Public Works, Energy and Ports: Rayburn Blackmore.

Minister of Carib Affairs: Ashton Graneau.

Minister of State in the Ministry of Foreign Affairs: Alvin Bernard.

Parliamentary Secretary in the Office of the Prime Minister, responsible for Information Technology: Kelvar Darroux.

Parliamentary Secretary in the Ministry of Public Works: Johnson Drigo.

Parliamentary Secretary in the Ministry of Housing, Lands, Settlement and Water Resources: Ivor Stephenson.

MINISTRIES

Office of the President: Morne Bruce, Roseau; tel. 4482054; fax 4498366; e-mail presidentoffice@cwdom.dm; internet presidentoffice.gov.dm.

Office of the Prime Minister: 6th Floor, Financial Centre, Roseau; tel. 2663300; fax 4488960; e-mail opm@dominica.gov.dm; internet opm.gov.dm.

All other ministries are at Government Headquarters, Kennedy Ave, Roseau; tel. 4482401.

CARIB TERRITORY

This reserve of the remaining Amerindian population is located on the central east coast of the island. The Caribs enjoy a measure of local government and elect their chief.

Chief: Garnet Joseph.

Waitukubuli Karifuna Development Committee (WAIKADA): Salybia, Carib Territory; tel. 4457336; e-mail waikada@cwdom.dm.

Legislature

HOUSE OF ASSEMBLY

Speaker: Alix Boyd-Knight.

Clerk: Vernanda Raymond.

Senators: 9.

Elected Members: 21.

General Election, 18 December 2009

Party	% of votes	Seats
Dominica Labour Party (DLP)	61.2	18
Dominica United Workers' Party (UWP)	34.9	3
Dominica Freedom Party (DFP)	2.4	—
Others	1.5	—
Total	100.0	21

Election Commission

Electoral Office: Cnr Turkey Lane and Independence St, Roseau; tel. 2663336; fax 4483399; e-mail electoraloffice@dominica.gov.dm; internet electoraloffice.gov.dm; Chief Elections Officer Steven La Rocque.

Political Organizations

Dominica Freedom Party (DFP): 37 Great George St, Roseau; tel. 4482104; fax 4481795; e-mail freedompar2@yahoo.com; internet www.thedominicafreedomparty.com; f. 1968; Leader Michael Astaphan.

Dominica Labour Party (DLP): 18 Hanover St, Roseau; tel. 4488511; e-mail dlp@cwdom.dm; internet www.dominicalabourparty.com; f. 1985 as a merger and reunification of left-wing groups, incl. the Dominica Labour Party (f. 1961); Leader Roosevelt Skerrit; Deputy Leader Ambrose George.

Dominica United Workers' Party (UWP): 37 Cork St, POB 00152, Roseau; tel. 6134508; fax 4498448; e-mail secretariat@uwpdm.com; internet www.uwpdm.com; f. 1988; Leader Lennox Linton.

People's Democratic Movement (PDM): 22 Upper Lane, POB 2248, Roseau; tel. 2354171; e-mail para@cwdom.dm; internet www.dapdm.org; f. 2006; Leader Dr William E. 'Para' Riviere.

Diplomatic Representation

EMBASSIES IN DOMINICA

China, People's Republic: Ceckhall, Morne Daniel, POB 2247, Roseau; tel. 4490080; fax 4400088; e-mail chinaemb_dm@mfa.gov.cn; internet dm.chineseembassy.org; Ambassador LI JIANGNING.

Cuba: Morne Daniel, Canefield, POB 1170, Roseau; tel. 4490727; e-mail cubanembassy@cwdom.dm; internet www.cubadiplomatica.cu/dominica; Ambassador JUANA ELENA RAMOS RODRÍGUEZ.

Venezuela: 20 Bath Rd, 3rd Floor, POB 770, Roseau; tel. 4483348; fax 4486198; e-mail embven@cwdom.dm; Ambassador HAYDEN OWANDO PIRELA SÁNCHEZ.

Judicial System

Justice is administered by the Eastern Caribbean Supreme Court (based in Saint Lucia), consisting of the Court of Appeal and the High Court. The final appellate court is the Privy Council in the United Kingdom. Two of the High Court Judges are resident in Dominica and preside over the Court of Summary Jurisdiction. The District Magistrate Courts deal with summary offences and civil offences involving limited sums of money (specified by law).

High Court Judges: ERROL THOMAS, M. E. BIRNIE STEPHENSON-BROOKS.

Registrar: OSSIE WALSH (acting).

Attorney-General: LEVI PETER.

Religion

Most of the population profess Christianity, but there are some Muslims, Bahá'ís and Jews. The largest denomination is the Roman Catholic Church.

CHRISTIANITY

The Roman Catholic Church

Dominica comprises the single diocese of Roseau, suffragan to the archdiocese of Castries (Saint Lucia). According to official figures from 2001, 62% of the population are Roman Catholics. The Bishop participates in the Antilles Episcopal Conference (currently based in Port of Spain, Trinidad and Tobago).

Bishop of Roseau: Rt Rev. GABRIEL MALZAIRE, Bishop Arnold Boghaert Catholic Centre, Turkey Lane, POB 790, Roseau; tel. 4482837; fax 4483404; e-mail bishop@cwdom.dm; internet www.dioceseofroseau.org.

The Anglican Communion

Anglicans in Dominica, representing less than 1% of the population in 2001, are adherents of the Church in the Province of the West Indies. The country forms part of the diocese of the North Eastern Caribbean and Aruba. The Bishop is resident in Antigua and Barbuda, and the Archbishop of the Province is currently the Bishop of Barbados.

Other Christian Churches

According to official figures from 2001, 6% of the population are Seventh-day Adventists, 6% are Pentecostalists, 4% are Baptists and 4% are Methodists. In addition to the Christian Union Church, other denominations include Church of God, Presbyterian, the Assemblies of Brethren and Moravian groups, and the Jehovah's Witnesses.

BAHÁ'Í FAITH

Bahá'ís of the Commonwealth of Dominica: 79 Victoria St, POB 136, Roseau; tel. 4483881; fax 4488460; e-mail monargedom@gmail.com; internet barbadosbahais.org; Sec. MONA GEORGE-DILL.

The Press

The Chronicle: Wallhouse, Loubiere, POB 1764, Roseau; tel. 4487887; fax 4480047; e-mail thechronicle@cwdom.dm; f. 1909; Friday; progressive independent; Man. Dir MICHAEL JONES; circ. 4,500.

Official Gazette: Office of the Prime Minister, Financial Centre, 6th Floor, Kennedy Ave, Roseau; tel. 2363300; fax 4488960; e-mail cabsec@cwdom.dm; weekly; circ. 550.

The Sun: Sun Inc, 50 Independence St, POB 2255, Roseau; tel. 4484501; e-mail info@sundominica.com; internet sundominica.com; f. 1998; weekly; Editor CHARLES JAMES.

Publisher

Andrews Publishing Co Ltd: 25 Independence St, Roseau; tel. 2753196; e-mail dominicanewsonline@gmail.com; internet www.dominicanewsonline.com; publishes Dominica News Online; Man. Dir MERRICK ANDREWS.

Broadcasting and Communications

TELECOMMUNICATIONS

Digicel Dominica: Wireless Ventures (Dominica) Ltd, POB 2236, Roseau; tel. 6161500; fax 4403189; e-mail customercare.dominica@digicelgroup.com; internet www.digiceldominica.com; acquired Cingular Wireless's Caribbean operations and licences in 2005; owned by an Irish consortium; acquired Orange Dominica in 2009; Chair. DENIS O'BRIEN; Country Man. RICHARD STANTON.

LIME: Hanover St, POB 6, Roseau; tel. 2551000; fax 2551111; internet www.lime.com; fmrly Cable & Wireless Dominica; name changed as above 2008; Group CEO TONY RICE; Eastern Caribbean CEO GERARD BORELY; Gen. Man. JEFFREY BAPTISTE.

Marpin 2K4: 5–7 Great Marlborough St, POB 2381, Roseau; tel. 5004107; fax 5002965; e-mail manager@mtb.dm; f. 1982, present name adopted in 1996; jtly owned by WRB Enterprises and the Dominica Social Security; commercial; cable telephone, television and internet services; Man. PERICSON ISIDORE.

SAT Telecommunications: 20 Bath Rd, St George, Roseau; tel. 4485095; fax 4484956; internet www.sat.dm; f. 1999; internet services provider; CEO and Man. Dir MARLON ALEXANDER.

Regulatory Authority

National Telecommunications Regulatory Commission of Dominica (NTRC Dominica): 42-2 Kennedy Ave, POB 649, Roseau; tel. 4400627; fax 4400835; e-mail secretariat@ntrcdm.org; internet www.ectel.int/ntrcdm; f. 2000 as the Dominican subsidiary of the Eastern Caribbean Telecommunications Authority (ECTEL)—established simultaneously in Castries, St Lucia, to regulate telecommunications in Dominica, Grenada, St Christopher and Nevis, St Lucia and St Vincent and the Grenadines; Chair. JULIAN JOHNSON; Exec. Dir CRAIG NESTY.

BROADCASTING

Radio

Dominica Broadcasting Corporation: Victoria St, POB 148, Roseau; tel. 4483283; fax 4482918; e-mail dbsmanager@dbcradio.net; internet www.dbcradio.net; f. 1971; govt station; daily broadcasts in English; 2 hrs daily in French patois; 10 kW transmitter on the medium wave band; FM service; programmes received throughout Caribbean excluding Jamaica and Guyana; Chair. IAN MUNRO.

Kairi FM: 42 Independence St, POB 931, Roseau; tel. 4487331; fax 4487332; e-mail hello@kairifmonline.com; internet www.kairifm.com; f. 1994; CEO FRANKIE BELLOT; Gen. Man. STEVE VIDAL.

Voice of Life Radio (ZGBC): Gospel Broadcasting Corpn, Loubiere, POB 205, Roseau; tel. 4487017; fax 4400551; e-mail volradio@cwdom.dm; internet www.voiceofliferadio.dm; f. 1975; 24 hrs daily FM; Gen. Man. CLEMENTINA MUNRO.

Television

There is no national television service, although there is a cable television network serving 95% of the island.

Finance

(cap. = capital; res = reserves; dep. = deposits; m. = million; brs = branches; amounts in East Caribbean dollars)

The Eastern Caribbean Central Bank, based in Saint Christopher, is the central issuing and monetary authority for Dominica.

Eastern Caribbean Central Bank—Dominica Office: Financial Centre, 3rd Floor, Kennedy Ave, POB 23, Roseau; tel. 4488001; fax 4488002; e-mail eccbdom@cwdom.dm; internet www.eccb-centralbank.org; Country Dir EDMUND ROBINSON.

Financial Services Unit: Ministry of Finance, Kennedy Ave, Roseau; tel. 2663514; fax 4480054; e-mail fsu@cwdom.dm; regulatory authority for banks and insurance cos; Man. AL MONELLE.

BANKS

FirstCaribbean International Bank (Barbados) Ltd: Old St, POB 4, Roseau; tel. 4482571; fax 4483471; internet www.firstcaribbeanbank.com; f. 2002 following merger of Caribbean operations of Barclays Bank PLC and CIBC; Barclays relinquished its stake to CIBC in 2006; Exec. Chair. MICHAEL MANSOOR; CEO RIK PARKHILL; Country Dir PAUL FRAMPTON.

National Bank of Dominica: 64 Hillsborough St, POB 271, Roseau; tel. 2552300; fax 4483982; e-mail customersupport@nbd.dm; internet www.nbdominica.com; f. 1976 as the National Commercial Bank of Dominica; name changed as above following privatization in 2003; cap. 11.0m., res 14.5m., dep. 796.6m. (June 2011); 49% govt-owned; Chair. PATRICK PEMBERTON; Gen. Man. MICHAEL BIRD; 6 brs.

Scotiabank (Canada): 28 Hillsborough St, POB 520, Roseau; tel. 4485800; fax 2551300; e-mail bns.dominica@scotiabank.com; internet www.scotiabank.com/dm/en; f. 1988; Country Man. JIM ALSTON; 1 br.

DEVELOPMENT BANK

Dominica Agricultural, Industrial and Development Bank (AID Bank): cnr Charles Ave and Rawles Lane, Goodwill, POB 215, Roseau; tel. 4484903; fax 4484903; e-mail aidbank@cwdom.dm; internet www.aidbank.com; f. 1971; responsible to Ministry of Finance; provides finance for the agriculture, tourism, housing, education and manufacturing sectors; total assets 125.3m. (June 2006); Chair. MARTIN CHARLES; Gen. Man. KINGSLEY THOMAS.

STOCK EXCHANGE

Eastern Caribbean Securities Exchange: Bird Rock, POB 94, Basseterre, Saint Christopher and Nevis; tel. (869) 466-7192; fax (869) 465-3798; e-mail info@ecseonline.com; internet www.ecseonline.com; f. 2001; regional securities market designed to facilitate the buying and selling of financial products for the eight member territories—Anguilla, Antigua and Barbuda, Dominica, Grenada, Montserrat, St Kitts and Nevis, St Lucia and St Vincent and the Grenadines; Chair. Sir K. DWIGHT VENNER; Gen. Man. TREVOR E. BLAKE.

INSURANCE

First Domestic Insurance Co Ltd: 19–21 King George V St, POB 1931, Roseau; tel. 4498202; fax 4485778; e-mail insurance@cwdom.dm; internet www.firstdomestic.dm; f. 1993; privately owned; Man. Dir and CEO CURTIS TONGE; Gen. Man. ROBERT TONGE.

Windward Islands Crop Insurance Co (Wincrop): Vanoulst House, Goodwill, POB 469, Roseau; tel. 4483955; fax 4484197; f. 1987; regional; coverage for weather destruction of, mainly, banana crops; Man. HERNICA FERREIRA; brs in Grenada, St Lucia and St Vincent.

Trade and Industry

DEVELOPMENT ORGANIZATIONS

Invest Dominica Authority: Financial Centre, 1st Floor, Roseau; tel. 4482045; fax 4485840; e-mail info@investdominica.dm; internet www.investdominica.dm; f. 1988 as National Development Corpn (NDC) by merger of Industrial Development Corpn (f. 1974) and Tourist Board; NDC disbanded in 2007 by act of parliament and replaced by two separate entities, Invest Dominica and Discover Dominica Authority; promotes local and foreign investment to increase employment, production and exports; Chair. PAUL MOSES; Exec. Dir RHODA JOSEPH.

Organisation of the Eastern Caribbean States Export Development Unit (OECS–EDU): Financial Centre, 4th Floor, Kennedy Ave, POB 769, Roseau; tel. 4482240; fax 4485554; e-mail edu@oecs.org; internet www.oecs.org/edu; f. 1997 as Eastern Caribbean States Export Development Agency and Agricultural Diversification Coordination Unit; reformed as above in 2000; OECS Sub Regional Trade Promotion Agency; Head of Unit VINCENT PHILBERT.

INDUSTRIAL AND TRADE ASSOCIATIONS

Dominica Agricultural Producers and Exporters Ltd (DAPEX): Fond Cole Hwy, Fond Cole, POB 1620, Roseau; tel. 4482671; fax 4486445; e-mail dapex@cwdom.dm; f. 1934 as Dominica Banana Growers' Asscn; restructured 1984 as the Dominica Banana Marketing Corpn; renamed Dominica Banana Producers Ltd in 2003; present name adopted in 2010; privatized; Chair. LUKE PREVOST; Gen. Man. ERROL EMANUEL.

Dominica Association of Industry and Commerce (DAIC): 17 Castle St, POB 85, Roseau; tel. and fax 4491962; e-mail daic@cwdom.dm; internet www.daic.dm; f. 1972 by a merger of the Manufacturers' Asscn and the Chamber of Commerce; represents the business sector, liaises with the Govt, and stimulates commerce and industry; 30 mems; Pres. LILIAN PIPER.

Dominica Export-Import Agency (DEXIA): Bay Front, POB 173, Roseau; tel. 4482780; fax 4486308; e-mail info@dexia.dm; internet www.dexia.dm; f. 1986; replaced the Dominica Agricultural Marketing Board and the External Trade Bureau; exporter of Dominican agricultural products, trade facilitator and importer of bulk rice and sugar; Chair. MARGARET GEORGE.

EMPLOYERS' ORGANIZATION

Dominica Employers' Federation: 14 Church St, POB 1783, Roseau; tel. 4482314; fax 4484474; e-mail def@cwdom.dm; f. 1966; Pres. CLEMENT CARTY.

UTILITIES

Regulatory Body

Independent Regulatory Commission (IRC): 42 Cork St, POB 1687, Roseau; tel. 4406634; fax 4406635; e-mail admin@ircdominica.org; internet www.ircdominica.org; f. 2006 to oversee the electricity sector; Exec. Dir LANCELOT MCCARSKY.

Electricity

Dominica Electricity Services Ltd (Domlec): 18 Castle St, POB 1593, Roseau; tel. 2256000; fax 4485397; e-mail support@domlec.dm; internet www.domlec.dm; national electricity service; 52% owned by Light & Power Holdings (Barbados), 21% owned by Dominica Sociak Security; Chair. ROBERT BLANCHARD, Jr; Gen. Man. COLLIN GROVER.

Water

Dominica Water and Sewerage Co Ltd (DOWASCO): POB 185, Roseau; tel. 4484811; fax 4485813; e-mail dowasco@dowasco.dm; internet www.dowasco.dm; state-owned; Chair. LARRY BARDOUILLE; Gen. Man. BERNARD ETTINOFFE.

TRADE UNIONS

Dominica Public Service Union (DPSU): cnr Valley Rd and Windsor Lane, POB 182, Roseau; tel. 4482102; fax 4488060; e-mail dcs@cwdom.dm; internet dpsu.org; f. 1940; registered as a trade union in 1960; representing all grades of civil servants, including firemen, prison officers, nurses, teachers and postal workers; Pres. STEVE JOSEPH; Gen. Sec. THOMAS LETANG; 1,400 mems.

Dominica Trade Union: 70–71 Independence St, Roseau; tel. 4498139; fax 4499060; e-mail domtradun@hotmail.com; f. 1945; Pres. HAROLD SEALEY; Gen. Sec. LEO J. BERNARD NICHOLAS; 400 mems (1995).

National Workers' Union: 102 Independence St, POB 387, Roseau; tel. 4485209; fax 4481934; e-mail icss@cwdom.dm; f. 1977; Pres.-Gen. RAWLINS JEMMOTT; Gen. Sec. FRANKLIN FABIEN; 450 mems (1996).

Transport

ROADS

In 2010 there were an estimated 1,512 km (940 miles) of roads. The West Coast Road Project, estimated to cost some EC $100m. and partly financed by the Government of the People's Republic of China, was completed in 2012. The 45.2 km highway linking Roseau and Portsmouth was one of the four projects agreed when the two countries established diplomatic relations in 2004. There were also plans to improve the Wotten Waven Road, to be financed by the Caribbean Development Bank.

SHIPPING

A deep-water harbour at Woodbridge Bay serves Roseau, which is the principal port. Several foreign shipping lines call at Roseau, and there is a high-speed ferry service between Martinique and Guadeloupe, which calls at Roseau. A ferry service between Dominica and Guadeloupe, Martinique and Saint Lucia began operations in 2011. Ships of the Geest Line call at Prince Rupert's Bay, Portsmouth, to collect bananas, and there are also cruise ship facilities there. There are other specialized berthing facilities on the west coast. In December 2013 Dominica's flag registered fleet comprised 79 vessels, with an aggregate displacement of some 698,019 grt.

Dominica Air and Seaport Authority (DASPA): Woodbridge Bay, Fond Cole, POB 243, Roseau; tel. 4484131; fax 4486131; e-mail daspa@cwdom.dm; f. 1972; air transit, pilotage and cargo handling; Chair. DERMOT SOUTHWELL; Gen. Man. BENOIT BARDOUILLE.

CIVIL AVIATION

Melville Hall Airport, 64 km (40 miles) from Roseau, is the main airport on the island. The first phase of a scheme to rebuild the road from Roseau to the airport at a cost of EC $54m., funded by the French Government, was completed in 2010, and work on the second phase, valued at EC $52m. and also funded by France, was agreed in the same year. The regional airline LIAT (based in Antigua and

Barbuda, and in which Dominica is a shareholder) provides daily services and, together with Air Caraïbes, connects Dominica with all the islands of the Eastern Caribbean. Seaborne Airlines (based in the US Virgin Islands) began services from Puerto Rico to Melville Hall in 2013, and CIT Airways (based in Florida, USA) was expected to begin flights between Dominica and the USA in 2014.

Tourism

The Government has designated areas of the island as nature reserves, to preserve the beautiful, lush scenery and the rich, natural heritage that constitute Dominica's main tourist attractions. Bird life is particularly prolific, and includes several rare and endangered species, such as the imperial parrot. There are also two marine reserves. Tourism is not as developed as it is among Dominica's neighbours, but the country is being promoted as an eco-tourism and cruise destination. There were an estimated 354,189 visitors in 2012 (of whom 266,178 were cruise ship passengers). Efforts were also made to promote tourism to the Carib Territory. Receipts from tourism totalled an estimated EC $307.2m. in 2012.

Discover Dominica Authority: Financial Centre, 1st Floor, Roseau; tel. 4482045; fax 4485840; e-mail tourism@dominica.dm; internet www.discoverdominica.com; f. 1988 following merger of Tourist Board with Industrial Devt Corpn; CEO and Dir of Tourism Colin Piper.

Dominica Hotel and Tourism Association (DHTA): 17 Castle St, POB 384, Roseau; tel. 6161055; fax 4403433; e-mail dhta@cwdom.dm; internet www.dhta.org; Pres. Renee Whitchurch Aird-Douglas (acting); Sec. Daryl Aaron (acting); 98 mems.

Defence

The Dominican Defence Force was officially disbanded in 1982. There is a police force of about 325, which includes a coastguard service. The country participates in the US-sponsored Regional Security System.

Education

Education is free and is provided by both government and denominational schools. There are also a number of schools for the mentally and physically handicapped. Education is compulsory for 10 years between five and 15 years of age. Primary education begins at the age of five and lasts for seven years. Enrolment at primary schools during the academic year 2010 included an estimated 92% of children in the relevant age-group. Secondary education, beginning at 12 years of age, lasts for five years. In 2011/12, according to UNESCO estimates, a total of 6,093 pupils were enrolled at secondary schools in the relevant age-group. The Dominica State College is the main provider of higher education. There is also a teacher-training college, a nursing school and a branch of the University of the West Indies on the island. The Ross University School of Medicine has a campus at Picard for overseas medical students and there is also the All Saints University School of Medicine in the south of the island. The 2013/14 budget allocated EC $59.7m. to the Ministry of Education and Human Resource Development (equivalent to 16% of total recurrent expenditure).

THE DOMINICAN REPUBLIC

Introductory Survey

LOCATION, CLIMATE, LANGUAGE, RELIGION, FLAG, CAPITAL

The Dominican Republic occupies the eastern part of the island of Hispaniola, which lies between Cuba and Puerto Rico in the Caribbean Sea. The country's only international frontier is with Haiti, to the west. The climate is sub-tropical, with an average annual temperature of 27°C (80°F). In Santo Domingo temperatures are generally between 19°C (66°F) and 31°C (88°F). The west and south-west of the country are arid. Hispaniola lies in the path of tropical cyclones. The official language is Spanish. Almost all of the inhabitants profess Christianity, and some 87% are Roman Catholics. There are small Protestant and Jewish communities. The national flag (proportions 5 by 8) is blue (upper hoist and lower fly) and red (lower hoist and upper fly), quartered by a white cross, with the national coat of arms, showing a quartered shield in the colours of the flag (on which are superimposed national banners, a cross and an open Bible) between scrolls above and below, at the centre of the cross. The capital is Santo Domingo.

CONTEMPORARY POLITICAL HISTORY

Historical Context

The Dominican Republic became independent in 1844, although it was occupied by US military forces between 1916 and 1924. General Rafael Leónidas Trujillo Molina overthrew the elected President, Horacio Vázquez, in 1930 and dominated the country until his assassination in 1961. The dictator ruled personally from 1930 to 1947 and indirectly thereafter. His brother, Héctor Trujillo, was President from 1947 until August 1960, when he was replaced by Dr Joaquín Balaguer Ricardo, hitherto Vice-President. After Rafael Trujillo's death, Balaguer remained in office, but in December 1961 he permitted moderate opposition groups to participate in a Council of State, which exercised legislative and executive powers. Balaguer resigned in January 1962, when the Council of State became the Provisional Government. A presidential election in December, the country's first free election for 38 years, was won by Dr Juan Bosch Gaviño, the founder and leader of the Partido Revolucionario Dominicano (PRD), who had been in exile since 1930. President Bosch, a left-of-centre democrat, was overthrown in 1963 by a military coup. The leaders of the armed forces transferred power to a civilian triumvirate, led by Emilio de los Santos. In 1965 a revolt by supporters of ex-President Bosch overthrew the triumvirate. Civil war broke out between pro-Bosch forces and military units headed by Gen. Elías Wessin y Wessin, who had played a leading role in the 1963 coup. The violence was eventually suppressed by the intervention of US troops, who were incorporated into an Inter-American peace force by the Organization of American States (OAS).

Domestic Political Affairs

Following a period of provisional government under Héctor García Godoy, a presidential election in 1966 was won by Balaguer, the candidate of the Partido Reformista Social Cristiano (PRSC). The PRSC also won a majority of seats in both houses of the new Congreso Nacional (National Congress). A new Constitution was promulgated in November. Despite his association with the Trujillo dictatorship, Balaguer initially proved to be a popular leader, and in 1970 he was re-elected for a further four years. In February 1973 a state of emergency was declared when guerrilla forces landed on the coast. Captain Francisco Caamaño Deño, the leader of the 1965 revolt, and his followers were killed. Bosch and other opposition figures went into hiding. Bosch later resigned as leader of the PRD (founding the Partido de la Liberación Dominicana—PLD), undermining hopes of a united opposition in the 1974 elections, when Balaguer was re-elected with a large majority.

In the 1978 presidential election Balaguer was defeated by the PRD candidate, Silvestre Antonio Guzmán Fernández. This was the first occasion in the country's history when an elected President yielded power to an elected successor. President Guzmán undertook to professionalize the armed forces by removing politically ambitious high-ranking officers. Dr Salvador Jorge Blanco, a left-wing PRD senator, was elected President in 1982. In the concurrent congressional election the PRD secured a majority in both the Senado (Senate) and the Cámara de Diputados (Chamber of Deputies). Although a member of the Socialist International, Blanco maintained good relations with the USA (on which the country is economically dependent).

Substantial price increases in 1985 led to violent clashes between demonstrators and the security forces. Public unrest was exacerbated by the Government's decision to accept the IMF's terms for financial aid. More violence preceded the presidential and legislative elections of May 1986. Balaguer of the PRSC was declared the winner of the presidential election by a narrow margin.

Upon taking office as President for the fifth time in August 1986, Balaguer initiated an investigation into alleged corrupt practices by members of the outgoing administration. Blanco was charged with embezzlement and the illegal purchase of military vehicles. (In 1991 he was convicted of abuse of power and misappropriation of public funds, and sentenced to 20 years' imprisonment, although in 1994 he was granted an amnesty.) The financial accounts of the armed forces were examined, and the former Secretary of State for the Armed Forces was subsequently imprisoned. Some 35,000 government posts were abolished; expenditure was redirected to a programme of public works projects. Nevertheless, the civil unrest continued in the remainder of the decade.

In spite of the continuing deterioration of the economy, the initial results of the 1990 presidential election indicated a narrow victory for Balaguer. However, Bosch (the PLD candidate) accused the ruling PRSC and the Junta Central Electoral (JCE—Central Electoral Board) of fraud, necessitating a recount, supervised by monitors from the OAS. Balaguer was eventually declared the official winner. The PRSC also secured a narrow majority in the Senate. No party won an outright majority in the Chamber of Deputies, although this did not threaten seriously to impede government policies, in view of Balaguer's extensive powers to govern by decree.

In an attempt to reduce inflation, the Government announced a programme of austerity measures in August 1990, almost doubling the price of petrol and essential foodstuffs. In response, the trade unions called a 48-hour general strike and in the ensuing conflict with the security forces some 14 people were killed. The price increases were partially offset by an increase of 30% in the salaries of army personnel and civil servants. A stand-by agreement was concluded with the IMF in 1991, in spite of trade union and public opposition.

The interim results of the presidential election of May 1994 indicated a narrow victory for Balaguer. Following a full recount, an investigative commission confirmed that, as a result of serious irregularities, some 73,000 of the registered electorate had been denied a vote. Nevertheless, in August the JCE, having apparently overlooked the commission's findings, proclaimed Balaguer the winner by a margin of less than 1% of the votes cast. Talks aimed at ending the political crisis, mediated by the OAS and the Roman Catholic Church, resulted in the signing of the Pact for Democracy. Under the terms of the accord (agreed by all the major parties), a fresh presidential election was to be held in November 1995 and a series of constitutional reforms would be adopted, providing for the prohibition of the re-election of a president to a consecutive term, a new electoral system for the head of state (see below), and the reorganization of the judiciary. Additionally, the legislative and municipal elections were to be held midway through the presidential term. Nevertheless, in the same month the Congress voted to extend Balaguer's mandate from 18 months to two years. The PRD withdrew from the legislature in protest, and the OAS criticized the Congress for violating the terms of the Pact for Democracy. The constitutional amendments that the Pact envisaged were, however, approved by the Congress. On 16 August Balaguer was inaugurated as President for a seventh term.

A post-Balaguer era

The May 1996 presidential election, the first for some 30 years in which Balaguer was not a candidate, was conducted according to a new system, whereby a second round of voting would be conducted between the two leading candidates should nobody secure an absolute majority in the initial ballot. In the event, a second round of voting—between José Francisco Peña Gómez of the PRD and Leonel Fernández Reyna of the PLD—was held at the end of June. Fernández won 51% of the votes to Peña Gómez's 49%; he was inaugurated in August.

In 1997, as part of a campaign to eliminate deep-seated corruption in the country's institutions, Fernández restructured both the police and the judiciary. He also oversaw a restructuring of the Supreme Court, including the appointment of 15 new judges. Responsibility for appointing judges at all other levels of the judicial system was transferred from the Senate to the Supreme Court, to avoid political appointments. Nevertheless, growing dissatisfaction with the continuing deterioration of public services and Fernández's failure to honour election promises provoked widespread disturbances and strike action in 1997 and 1998, with violent confrontations between demonstrators and the security forces resulting in several deaths. The PRD won a majority of seats in the enlarged 149-seat Chamber of Deputies at legislative elections in 1998.

In the first round of the May 2000 presidential election, Rafael Hipólito Mejía Domínguez, the PRD candidate, narrowly failed to secure the 50% of the ballot required to avoid a second round of voting. Nevertheless, a second ballot was not held and the JCE allowed Mejía to declare himself the winner. With only 73 PRD deputies in the 149-seat lower house (10 of the 83 elected in May 1998 had been expelled from the party), Mejía lacked a parliamentary majority, and was dependent for support on the PRSC.

The Senate approved constitutional amendments in late 2000 to extend the presidential term to five years and the congressional term to six years, and to lower the minimum requirement of votes in a presidential election. In order to appease opposition to the bill, Mejía appointed a Committee on Constitutional Reform to assess the situation. In October 2001 the Committee submitted legislation to the Congress, the principal provision of which was to reduce the proportion of votes needed to win a presidential election to 45% (or 40% if the leading candidate had at least a 10% majority). The Senate subsequently voted to include in the constitutional amendments a clause permitting the re-election of a President. Mejía opposed the inclusion of this reform, and in December the Supreme Court ruled the proposed legislation to be unconstitutional. However, in January 2002 the Chamber of Deputies approved the formation of a National Constituent Assembly and in July, following re-examination, a bill of amendment permitting presidential re-election received legislative assent.

Legislative elections were held in May 2002. The PRD won a majority in the Senate, although its failure to secure a majority in the lower house ensured its continued dependence upon the support of the PRSC for the passage of legislation.

In May 2003 the dissolution of the commercial bank Banco Intercontinental, SA (Baninter), following huge losses owing to fraud, had serious political, as well as economic, implications. The President of Baninter, Ramón Báez Figueroa, allegedly had links to the PLD. Figueroa and two other bank officials were arrested on fraud charges (in 2007 Figueroa was sentenced to 10 years' imprisonment). The Government's subsequent decision to guarantee all the deposits held at Baninter, at a cost of approximately US $2,200m., resulted in the onset of an economic crisis so severe that the Government was forced to request IMF assistance; in August a $618m. stand-by arrangement with the IMF was concluded.

In November 2003 a 24-hour general strike took place, during which violent clashes occurred between the security forces and anti-Government protesters in several cities, resulting in the deaths of at least seven people. The strike was in protest against governmental mismanagement of the economy and, in particular, the failure to resolve the ongoing, and increasingly severe, power shortages. In January 2004 a 48-hour general strike was held, during which at least nine people were killed and many more injured.

At the presidential election in May 2004, former President Fernández of the PLD defeated Mejía by a decisive margin, securing 57% of the votes cast. President Fernández pledged to alleviate the chronic power shortages in the country. Although power supplies initially improved, following the Government's payment of US $50m. towards the debt owed to electricity suppliers, by 2005 the electricity shortages had returned to pre-election levels.

The PLD in power

Legislative elections were held in May 2006. For the first time in its history, the PLD secured a majority in both legislative chambers, winning 96 seats in the Chamber of Deputies (which had been increased from 150 to 178 seats) and 22 seats in the Senate. The PRD's representation was reduced to 60 seats in the Chamber of Deputies and just six seats in the Senate, while the PRSC won 22 in the former and four in the latter.

A series of corruption scandals and continuing labour unrest presented considerable difficulties for the Government in the months preceding the 2008 presidential election. However, a programme of state spending and major public works attracted support for Fernández, who won a third term with 54% of the vote on 16 May. His main rival, Miguel Vargas Maldonado of the PRD, took 41% of the valid votes cast.

In October 2009 the Chamber of Deputies approved changes to more than 40 articles of the Constitution, despite public protests and opposition from civil society groups who were against the more socially conservative provisions. The amendments stipulated a complete ban on abortion and defined marriage as solely between a man and woman. Other measures included making administrative corruption of public officials a constitutional offence and establishing trade unionism, strikes, public education, and swift justice with the presumption of innocence as constitutional rights. The new Constitution came into force on 26 January 2010.

The PLD secured a resounding victory in legislative elections held on 16 May 2010. To facilitate a joint presidential and legislative ballot in 2016, congressional members were elected to an extended six-year term. The ruling party increased its representation in both legislative chambers, winning 105 of the 183 seats in the enlarged Chamber of Deputies and 31 of the 32 Senate seats. The PRD improved its position in the lower house, obtaining 75 seats, but failed to gain representation in the upper chamber. Support for the PRSC, which had organized an electoral pact with the PLD in April 2010, declined dramatically compared with the 2006 election, and the party only managed to win three lower house seats and the remaining Senate seat. The rate of participation by the electorate was a disappointing 56.4%. The PLD argued that the results were a reflection of voter satisfaction with the Government's economic and social policies. However, OAS monitors and the JCE expressed concern regarding the PLD's alleged misuse of public funds to subsidize its election campaign, and the PRD claimed that there had been irregularities in the ballot. The elections were further tarnished by sporadic violence, which left five people dead.

President Fernández reorganized the Cabinet in March 2011. José Ramón Fadul was appointed as Minister of the Interior and Police, Daniel Toribio received the finance portfolio, and Josefina Pimentel became the new Minister of Education. This latter appointment was seemingly made in response to public dissatisfaction with the country's underperforming educational system.

Recent developments: Medina in power

In March 2011 former President Mejía was elected as the PRD's candidate to stand in the upcoming presidential ballot. President Fernández announced in April that he would not seek re-election, which would have required further amendment of the Constitution and, according to the President, may have increased tensions in the country. His wife, Margarita María Cedeño de Fernández, announced shortly thereafter that she would compete in the primary election to select the PLD's presidential candidate. However, she withdrew from the contest later that month, reportedly because of disquiet among factions within the party. In the event, Danilo Medina Sánchez (who had been defeated by Mejía in the 2000 presidential election) won the primary vote in June and was formally named as the ruling party's presidential nominee in August. Despite earlier tensions with Fernández, Medina selected Cedeño to be his vice-presidential candidate in November. The PLD and the PRSC formed an electoral alliance in February 2012.

In the presidential election, held on 20 May 2012, Medina secured a first round victory, winning 51.2% of the valid votes cast compared with 47.0% for Mejía. The rate of participation by the electorate was 70.2%. The opposition accused the ruling party of electoral fraud and the abuse of state resources, although international monitors were generally satisfied with the conduct of the election. In accordance with a constitutional amendment approved in 2009, overseas voters also elected seven additional deputies to the Cámara de Diputados to represent the Dominican diaspora; the PRD won four of these seats and the PLD gained control of the remaining three. Medina was inaugurated on 16 August and the new Cabinet that was installed on the same day included nine ministers from the outgoing administration.

Medina's initial priority was the implementation of fiscal reforms to curtail the public sector deficit, which had grown substantially owing to costly electricity subsidies and the expansionary spending policies of the Fernández administration. Legislation to restructure the tax system received congressional approval in November, and an austerity budget was adopted in the following month. However, the planned tax rises proved to be highly contentious, and anti-Government protests were staged with the support of civil society organizations and the PRD.

In January 2013 the PRD's disciplinary board expelled Mejía from the party for allegedly instigating disunity. His expulsion had ostensibly been orchestrated by the PRD's President, Miguel Vargas Maldonado, who led a rival wing of the party. The PRD had been beset by factional infighting since Mejía's defeat in the presidential election, and outbreaks of violence had been reported on multiple occasions.

The Government announced reform of the police force in early 2013, in order to improve public security. The police service had been widely accused of corruption and human rights abuses. Although a number of senior officers were replaced during that year, no substantive progress was made with the Government's broader objective of effecting a major structural reorganization of the police force. Meanwhile, soldiers were controversially deployed in mid-2013 to assist the police in their patrols.

In March 2014, in its International Narcotics Control Strategy Report, the US Department of State described the Dominican Republic as 'an important transit country' for narcotics, although it stressed that efforts to reduce the flow of narcotics through the country had been 'highly successful'.

Foreign Affairs

Regional relations

The continuing illegal import of plantation labour into the Dominican Republic from Haiti was a major issue for successive Governments. In 1997 the Dominican and Haitian Presidents agreed to put an immediate end to large-scale repatriations of Haitians and for the repatriation process to be monitored by an international body to ensure the observance of human rights. In 1998 agreement was reached on the establishment of joint border patrols to combat the traffic of drugs, arms and other contraband. In 1999, following the summary deportation of some 8,000 Haitians, the two Governments signed a protocol limiting the repatriations.

Following the murder of a Dominican woman in 2005, allegedly by two Haitian men, the Dominican army forcibly repatriated thousands of Haitians. The army insisted that only illegal immigrants had been targeted, but human rights organizations accused the army of acting indiscriminately. In December President Fernández made an official visit to Haiti; however, hopes that the visit would ease tensions were quashed when violent demonstrations erupted outside the presidential palace in protest at the treatment of Haitians in the Dominican Republic. In 2007 a new military border security force, the Cuerpo Especializado de Seguridad Fronteriza (Cesfront), began patrolling the frontier; however, in 2010 the Border Affairs Commission of the Congress asserted that Cesfront was corrupt and that border trafficking had increased since its inception.

In January 2010, following a devastating earthquake in Haiti, the Dominican Government waived visa restrictions for Haitians seeking emergency medical care, authorized nearly 300 flights carrying aid, donated US $11m. and despatched more than 100 soldiers to aid UN forces in stabilizing the country. In an attempt to prevent a cholera outbreak in Haiti from spreading into the Dominican Republic, in October the Government introduced limitations on cross-border travel. However, this failed to prevent the dissemination of the disease, and occurrences of cholera were reported in the country. With thousands of cholera deaths documented in Haiti and anti-Haitian attitudes hardening within the Dominican Republic, in January 2011 the Government restarted the process of deporting illegal Haitian immigrants. Human rights organization Amnesty International criticized the move, but the Government argued that it was necessary in order to prevent the further proliferation of the disease. In March 2012 the two countries signed several co-operation agreements aimed at improving bilateral relations. However, Haiti briefly recalled its ambassador in June, apparently in protest against new work permit regulations that had entered into force in the Dominican Republic earlier that month. The new rules would impact Haitian migrants in particular.

The Constitutional Court, in a hugely contentious decision, proclaimed in September 2013 that children born in the Dominican Republic to undocumented migrants before 2010 were not eligible to receive Dominican citizenship. This premise had already been enshrined in the 2010 Constitution, but it had been assumed that it would not be applied retroactively. Many thousands of ethnic Haitians resident in the Dominican Republic were thus effectively rendered 'stateless' as a consequence of the ruling, which attracted criticism from, *inter alia*, the Office of the UN High Commissioner for Human Rights, the OAS Inter-American Commission on Human Rights, the Caribbean Community and Common Market, and the Organisation of Eastern Caribbean States. Despite this furore, the Dominican Government agreed to respect the Court's judgment. Under increasing regional pressure, however, the Dominican Republic entered into negotiations with Haiti in November in an attempt to resolve the crisis; talks were continuing in early 2014.

CONSTITUTION AND GOVERNMENT

Under the Constitution that was introduced in January 2010, legislative power is exercised by the bicameral Congreso Nacional (National Congress), with a Senado (Senate) of 32 members and a Cámara de Diputados (Chamber of Deputies) comprising 190 members. Members of both houses are elected for four years by universal adult suffrage. Executive power lies with the President, who is also elected by direct popular vote for four years. He is assisted by a Vice-President and a Cabinet. Judicial power is exercised by the Supreme Court of Justice and the other Tribunals. The Dominican Republic comprises 31 provinces, each administered by an appointed governor, and a Distrito Nacional (DN) containing the capital.

REGIONAL AND INTERNATIONAL CO-OPERATION

The Dominican Republic was granted observer status in the Caribbean Community and Common Market (CARICOM, see p. 223) in 1984. An agreement establishing a free trade area between CARICOM countries and the Dominican Republic, came into effect in 2001. In September 2005 the Congress approved the country's membership of the proposed Dominican Republic-Central American Free Trade Agreement with the USA. Implementation of the accord took place in March 2007. The Dominican Republic is a member of the Association of Caribbean States (see p. 449), of the Community of Latin American and Caribbean States (see p. 464), which was formally inaugurated in December 2011, and, from June 2013, of the Central American Integration System (see p. 229).

The Dominican Republic was a founder member of the UN. The country acceded to the World Trade Organization (see p. 434) in 1995. The country was one of the African, Caribbean and Pacific nations covered by the European Union's (EU) Cotonou Agreement (see p. 324), which guaranteed access to EU markets.

ECONOMIC AFFAIRS

In 2012, according to estimates by the World Bank, the Dominican Republic's gross national income (GNI), measured at average 2010–12 prices, was US $56,183m., equivalent to $5,470 per head (or $9,820 per head on an international purchasing-power parity basis). During 2003–12, it was estimated, the population increased by an average of 1.4% per year, while gross domestic product (GDP) per head increased, in real terms, by an average of 4.6% per year. Overall GDP increased, in real terms, by an average of 6.0% per year in 2003–12. Real GDP increased by 3.9% in 2012, according to both constant price data and chain-linked methodologies.

According to official data, agriculture, including hunting, forestry and fishing, contributed 5.9% of GDP in 2012 and employed an estimated 14.3% of the employed labour force in April 2013. The principal cash crops are sugar cane (sugar and sugar derivatives accounted for an estimated 2.2% of total export earnings in 2012), cocoa beans, coffee and tobacco. According to the World Bank, agricultural GDP increased, in real terms, by an average of 4.0% per year during 2003–11. In 2012, according to chain-linked methodologies, real agricultural GDP increased by 4.1%.

Industry (including mining, manufacturing, construction and power) employed an estimated 16.4% of the economically active population in April 2013 and contributed 30.7% of GDP in 2012. According to the World Bank, industrial GDP increased, in real terms, by an average of 3.5% per year during 2003–11. According to chain-linked methodologies, real industrial GDP increased by 1.4% in 2012.

Mining contributed just 0.5% of GDP in 2012, and employed 0.3% of the economically active population in April 2013. The major mineral export is ferro-nickel. Export earnings from ferro-nickel (excluding exports to free trade zones) contributed 20.6% of the total value of exports in 2008; however, the closure of the Falconbridge Dominicana complex in late 2008, owing to falling nickel prices, meant that earnings in 2009 fell dramatically. The mine's owners, Xstrata, reopened the complex in 2011, but export earnings from ferro-nickel (excluding exports to free trade zones) recovered to only 6.5% of the total value of exports in 2012. Gold and silver are also exploited, and there are workable deposits of gypsum, limestone and mercury. Real mining GDP decreased by an annual average of 2.5% during 2000–08. According to chain-linked methodologies, the GDP of the mining sector expanded by 79.7% in 2011 and by 42.0% in 2012, mainly owing to the revival of the ferro-nickel sector.

Manufacturing contributed 22.7% of GDP in 2012 and employed an estimated 9.8% of the economically active population in April 2013. Important branches of manufacturing included beer, cigarettes and cement. At the end of 2012, according to the Consejo Nacional de Zonas Francas de Exportación, there were 584 companies operating in 53 free trade zones in the Dominican Republic, employing some 134,226 people. According to the World Bank, the GDP of the manufacturing sector increased, in real terms, at an average rate of 3.6% per year during 2003–11. In 2012, according to chain-linked methodologies, sectoral GDP increased by only 0.9%.

Construction employed an estimated 5.4% of the economically active population in April 2013 and contributed 5.4% of GDP in 2012. Construction GDP increased, in real terms, by an average of 1.6% per year during 2000–08. According to chain-linked methodologies, construction GDP increased by 0.7% in 2012.

Energy is derived principally from petroleum; however, there is no domestic petroleum production. Imports of crude petroleum and related products accounted for an estimated 21.3% of the total cost of imports in 2012. As part of the Petrocaribe agreement signed in 2005, the Dominican Republic can purchase petroleum from Venezuela at reduced prices. Petroleum provided 47.6% of total energy requirements in 2011, while coal provided a further 15.4% and hydroelectricity 11.8%. In 2009 a hydroelectric plant in Monseñor Nouel province began operations and in 2012 a further plant, Palomino in San Juan, was inaugurated. The administration of Danilo Medina promised to increase generating capacity by at least 1,000 MW by 2017. To this end, in 2013 it offered for tender the construction of two 300 MW coal plants in the south of the country.

The services sector contributed 63.5% of GDP in 2013, and employed an estimated 69.3% of the economically active population in April 2013. The tourism sector was the country's primary source of foreign exchange earnings. In 2012 an estimated 5,047,021 tourists visited the Dominican Republic; receipts from tourism, excluding passenger transport, totalled US $4,549m. in the same year. According to the World Bank, the GDP of the services sector expanded at an average annual rate of 6.8% during 2003–11. According to chain-linked methodologies, real services GDP increased by 3.8% in 2012.

In 2012 the Dominican Republic recorded a visible merchandise trade deficit of US $10,874.1m., and there was a deficit of $4,037.1m. on the current account of the balance of payments. In 2012 the principal source of imports was the USA (38.6%); other major suppliers were the People's Republic of China, Venezuela, Trinidad and Tobago and Mexico. In the same year the USA was also the principal market for exports (56.0% of the total); other significant purchasers were Haiti and China. The principal exports in 2012 were prepared foodstuffs, beverages, spirits, tobacco, etc., textiles and textile articles, optical, photo, cinema, measuring, checking precision equipment, and machinery and mechanical appliances and electrical equipment. Exports from the free trade zones in 2012 amounted to $4,940.0m. The principal imports in 2012 were mineral fuels and related products, machinery and mechanical appliances, electrical equipment, chemical and related products, plastics, rubber and articles thereof, textiles and textile articles, base metals and articles thereof, prepared foodstuffs, beverages, spirits, tobacco, etc., and transport equipment.

In 2012 there was a preliminary budgetary deficit of RD $153,375.3m. (equivalent to 6.6% of GDP). The Dominican Republic's general government gross debt was RD $775,320m. in 2012, equivalent to 33.5% of GDP. The Dominican Republic's total external debt at the end of 2011 was estimated at US $15,395m., of which $10,758m. was public and publicly guaranteed debt. In that year, the cost of debt-servicing long-term public and publicly guaranteed debt and repayments to the IMF was equivalent to 10.4% of the value of exports of goods, services and income (excluding workers' remittances). In 2003–12 the average annual rate of inflation was 10.3%. Consumer prices increased by 3.7% in 2012. An estimated 15.0% of the total labour force was unemployed in April 2013.

In November 2009 the IMF approved a 28-month stand-by arrangement, worth approximately US $1,700m., to support the Government's strategy to stabilize the economy in the wake of the economic global downturn. Expansionary government spending in 2010 precipitated renewed growth in virtually all sectors of the economy. With the recovery under way, the Government began to reduce spending from mid-year in order to stabilize the fiscal position. The restructuring of electricity tariffs formed a central component of the Government's strategy to eliminate the fiscal deficit, and rates were increased in 2010 and 2011 to fund the withdrawal of costly power subsidies. In a complementary move, in 2011 the Congress approved a number of fiscal reforms, including tax increases and the imposition of new levies, in addition to substantial reductions in public expenditure. The IMF stand-by arrangement ended in February 2012; however, negotiations on a replacement facility foundered owing to the authorities' refusal to implement further austerity measures in an election year. President Medina introduced a variety of fiscal reforms, although the country's financial position remained under pressure during 2012. Nevertheless, real GDP expanded by 3.9% in that year as the tourism sector continued to recover and gold production at the Pueblo Viejo mine commenced. It was anticipated that the gold-mining operation, which had attracted $3,800m. of foreign investment, would contribute significantly to future economic growth. Moreover, in September 2013 a new contract was concluded with Barrick Gold (of Canada), the majority shareholder in the Pueblo Viejo development, which would result in the Government receiving a much greater proportion of the mine's revenues than hitherto. According to IMF estimates, real GDP growth slowed to 2.0% in 2013 owing to a decline in domestic consumption (a consequence of the Government's austerity policies), although there was a marked reduction in the public sector deficit. The IMF projected improved growth of 3.6% in 2014 but warned that comprehensive reform of the energy sector was necessary to further alleviate the fiscal burden.

PUBLIC HOLIDAYS

2015: 1 January (New Year's Day), 5 January (for Epiphany), 21 January (Our Lady of Altagracia), 26 January (Birth of Juan Pablo Duarte), 27 February (Independence Day), 3 April (Good Friday), 4 May (for Labour Day), 4 June (Corpus Christi), 16 August (Restoration Day), 24 September (Our Lady of Mercedes), 9 November (for Constitution Day), 25 December (Christmas Day).

Statistical Survey

Sources (unless otherwise stated): Oficina Nacional de Estadística, Edif. de Oficinas Gubernamentales, 9°, Avda México, esq. Leopoldo Navarro, Santo Domingo, DN; tel. 682-7777; fax 685-4424; e-mail info@one.gob.do; internet www.one.gob.do; Banco Central de la República Dominicana, Calle Pedro Henríquez Ureña, esq. Leopoldo Navarro, Apdo 1347, Santo Domingo, DN; tel. 221-9111; fax 686-7488; e-mail info@bancentral.gov.do; internet www.bancentral.gov.do.

Area and Population

AREA, POPULATION AND DENSITY

Area (sq km)	
Land	48,137
Inland water	597
Total	48,734*
Population (census results)	
18–20 October 2002	8,562,541
1–7 December 2010	
Males	4,739,038
Females	4,706,243
Total	9,445,281
Population (official projections)†	
2012	10,135,105
2013	10,257,724
2014	10,378,267
Density (per sq km) at 2014	213.0

* 18,816 sq miles.

† Not adjusted to take account of results of 2010 census.

POPULATION BY AGE AND SEX
(official projections, 2014)

	Males	Females	Total
0–14	1,597,320	1,540,016	3,137,336
15–64	3,262,061	3,317,186	6,579,247
65 and over	315,293	346,391	661,684
Total	5,174,674	5,203,593	10,378,267

PROVINCES
(official population projections, 2014)

	Area (sq km)	Population	Density (per sq km)
Distrito Nacional Region			
Distrito Nacional	104.4	1,168,629	11,193.8
Santo Domingo	1,296.4	2,347,968	1,811.1
Valdesia Region			
Peravia	997.6	213,809	214.3
Monte Plata	2,632.1	220,231	83.7
San Cristóbal	1,265.8	711,209	561.9
San José de Ocoa	650.2	69,366	106.7
Norcentral Region			
Espaillat	839.0	243,505	290.2
Puerto Plata	1,856.9	336,825	181.4
Santiago	2,839.0	1,102,840	388.5
Nordeste Region			
Duarte	1,605.4	305,347	190.2
Hermanas Mirabal	440.4	104,364	237.0
María Trinidad Sánchez	1,271.7	144,183	113.4
Samaná	853.7	102,473	120.0
Enriquillo Region			
Baoruco	1,282.2	120,724	94.2
Barahona	1,739.4	206,980	119.0
Independencia	2,006.4	58,442	29.1
Pedernales	2,074.5	26,980	13.0
Este Region			
El Seibo	1,786.8	110,960	62.1
Hato Mayor	1,329.3	92,613	69.7
La Altagracia	2,474.3	250,665	101.3
La Romana	654.0	258,619	395.4
San Pedro de Macorís	1,255.5	355,646	283.3
El Valle Region			
Azua	2,531.8	252,590	99.8
Elías Piña	1,426.2	74,490	52.2
San Juan	3,569.4	243,463	68.2
—continued			
Noroeste Region			
Dajabón	1,020.7	68,531	67.1
Monte Cristi	1,924.4	125,265	65.1
Santiago Rodríguez	1,111.1	54,242	48.8
Valverde	823.4	200,061	243.0
Cibao Central Region			
La Vega	2,287.0	445,406	194.8
Monseñor Nouel	992.4	204,175	205.7
Sánchez Ramírez	1,196.1	157,666	131.8
Total	48,137.0*	10,378,267	215.6*

* Land area only.

PRINCIPAL TOWNS
(population at census of October 2010)

Santo Domingo DN (capital)	2,806,636	Moca	179,829
Santiago de los Caballeros	691,262	Higuey	168,501
Concepción de la Vega	248,089	Monseñor Nouel	165,224
San Cristóbal	232,769	San Felipe de Puerto Plata	158,756
La Romana	228,875	Baní	157,316
San Pedro de Macorís	195,037	San Juan de la Maguana	132,177
San Francisco de Macorís	188,118	Bajos de Haina	124,193

BIRTHS, MARRIAGES AND DEATHS
(year of registration)

	Registered live births		Registered marriages		Registered deaths	
	Number	Rate (per 1,000)	Number	Rate (per 1,000)	Number	Rate (per 1,000)
2005	183,819	19.9	39,439	4.3	33,949	3.7
2006	174,575	18.7	42,375	4.5	33,060	3.5
2007	193,978	20.4	39,993	4.2	33,009	3.5
2008	196,387	20.4	38,310	4.0	32,991	3.4
2009	210,098	21.5	40,040	4.1	32,826	3.4
2010	196,253	19.9	43,797	4.4	35,244	3.6
2011	194,641	19.4	44,253	4.4	33,995	3.4
2012	193,241	19.1	43,307	4.3	34,198	3.4

Life expectancy (years at birth): 73.0 (males 69.9; females 76.2) in 2011 (Source: World Bank, World Development Indicators database).

ECONOMICALLY ACTIVE POPULATION
(official estimates at April 2013, '000 persons aged 10 years and over)

	Males	Females	Total
Agriculture, hunting, forestry and fishing	537.9	32.1	570.0
Mining and quarrying	11.8	0.7	12.5
Manufacturing	264.4	127.2	391.6
Electricity, gas and water supply	27.5	7.2	34.6
Construction	208.6	8.0	216.5
Wholesale and retail trade	567.2	294.2	861.4
Hotels and restaurants	112.4	132.6	245.0
Transport, storage and communications	287.6	28.8	316.4
Financial intermediation Real estate, renting and business activities	47.7	57.0	104.7
Public administration and defence	114.1	78.3	192.4
Education Health and social work Other community, social and personal service activities	369.0	671.5	1,040.5
Total employed	2,548.1	1,437.6	3,985.6
Unemployed	280.5	422.5	703.0
Total labour force	2,828.6	1,860.1	4,688.6

Health and Welfare

KEY INDICATORS

Total fertility rate (children per woman, 2011)	2.5
Under-5 mortality rate (per 1,000 live births, 2011)	25
HIV/AIDS (% of persons aged 15–49, 2012)	0.7
Physicians (per 1,000 head, 2000)	1.88
Hospital beds (per 1,000 head, 2010)	1.6
Health expenditure (2010): US $ per head (PPP)	509
Health expenditure (2010): % of GDP	5.5
Health expenditure (2010): public (% of total)	50.4
Access to water (% of persons, 2011)	82
Access to sanitation (% of persons, 2011)	82
Total carbon dioxide emissions ('000 metric tons, 2010)	20,964.2
Carbon dioxide emissions per head (metric tons, 2010)	2.1
Human Development Index (2012): ranking	96
Human Development Index (2012): value	0.702

For sources and definitions, see explanatory note on p. vi.

Agriculture

PRINCIPAL CROPS
('000 metric tons)

	2010	2011	2012
Rice, paddy	850.2	874.7	849.7
Maize	36.7	35.4	41.6
Potatoes	51.4	53.6	60.6
Sweet potatoes	53.6	46.5	44.5
Cassava (Manioc)	211.1	184.8	170.0
Yautia (Cocoyam)	30.3	32.9	32.6
Sugar cane	4,577.1	4,644.5	4,865.6
Beans, dry	33.0	34.4	32.4
Coconuts	129.7	150.5	162.5
Oil palm fruit*	236.0	258.5	262.0
Tomatoes	240.3	290.2	258.8
Pumpkins, squash and gourds	40.6	38.3	41.9
Chillies and peppers, green	37.2	36.8	35.6
Onions, dry	48.4	76.4	55.8
Garlic	2.0	3.1	4.3
Carrots and turnips	24.7	44.8	48.0*
Cantaloupes and other melons	18.3	25.1	26.5*
Bananas	735.0	829.8	871.9
Plantains	491.5	503.5	543.5
Oranges	138.0	139.4	170.9
Guavas, mangoes and mangosteens	7.9	9.0	10.0*
Avocados	288.7	295.1	290.0
Pineapples	157.4	221.7	447.4
Papayas	908.5	891.7	815.5
Coffee, green	21.9	27.3	27.0
Cocoa beans	58.3	54.3	72.2
Tobacco, unmanufactured	8.1	10.2	9.1

* FAO estimate(s).

Aggregate production ('000 metric tons, may include official, semi-official or estimated data): Total cereals 888.3 in 2010, 912.4 in 2011, 893.3 in 2012; Total roots and tubers 374.1 in 2010, 346.0 in 2011, 336.3 in 2012; Total vegetables (incl. melons) 527.7 in 2010, 625.5 in 2011, 585.5 in 2012; Total fruits (excl. melons) 2,818.9 in 2010, 2,990.7 in 2011, 3,255.2 in 2012.

Source: FAO.

LIVESTOCK
('000 head, year ending September)

	2010	2011	2012
Horses*	350	350	352
Asses*	151	151	151
Cattle*	2,900.0	2,950.0	3,000.0
Pigs*	620	625	628
Sheep*	240.0	245.0	246.5
Goats*	225.0	230.0	232.0
Chickens	178,433	174,791	173,000*

* FAO estimate(s).

Source: FAO.

LIVESTOCK PRODUCTS
('000 metric tons)

	2010	2011	2012
Cattle meat	113.0	102.0	95.9
Pig meat	89.5	103.8	103.2
Chicken meat	331.8	324.7	299.3*
Cows' milk	521.0	501.6	573.4
Hen eggs*	105.7	97.4	98.1
Honey†	4.9	4.9	5.0

* Unofficial figure(s).
† FAO estimates.

Source: FAO.

Forestry

ROUNDWOOD REMOVALS
('000 cubic metres, excl. bark, FAO estimates)

	2010	2011	2012
Sawlogs, veneer logs and logs for sleepers	7	7	7
Other industrial wood	3	3	3
Fuel wood	913	920	928
Total	922	930	937

Source: FAO.

Fishing

('000 metric tons, live weight)

	2009	2010	2011
Capture	14.2	14.5	14.0
Tilapia	0.3	0.1	0.2
Groupers, seabasses	1.4	1.5	0.7
Common carp	0.03	0.1	0.2
Snappers and jobfishes	1.2	1.3	1.1
King mackerel	0.3	0.8	0.1
Blackfin tuna	0.9	1.0	0.6
Caribbean spiny lobster	1.4	1.0	2.6
Stromboid conchs	2.3	0.3	1.9
Aquaculture	1.2*	1.3*	1.9
Penaeus shrimps	0.5*	0.5*	—
Total catch	15.5*	15.8*	15.9

* FAO estimate.

Source: FAO.

Mining

('000 metric tons)

	2010	2011	2012
Ferro-nickel	—	13.5	15.2
Nickel (metal content of laterite ore)	—	1,143.0	1,301.7
Gypsum	53.8	31.2	102.1

Source: US Geological Survey.

Industry

SELECTED PRODUCTS

('000 metric tons, preliminary, unless otherwise indicated)

	2009	2010	2011
Flour and derivatives ('000 quintales*)	2,409.1	3,714.4	4,747.8
Refined sugar	151.9	147.7	157.8
Cement	3,852.2	4,105.7	3,996.5
Beer ('000 hl)	4,142.1	4,838.0	4,886.9
Cigarettes (million)	2,159.0	2,154.1	2,222.0
Motor spirit (petrol)†‡	3,000	3,000	3,000
Jet fuel†‡	1,900	1,900	2,000
Distillate fuel†‡	2,900	2,900	3,000
Residual fuel oil†‡	4,600	4,600	5,000
Electric energy (million kWh)	11,529.4	12,271.7	12,960.5

* 1 quintale is equivalent to 46 kg.
† Estimated production, '000 barrels.
‡ Source: US Geological Survey.

Finance

CURRENCY AND EXCHANGE RATES

Monetary Units

100 centavos = 1 Dominican Republic peso (RD $ or peso oro).

Sterling, Dollar and Euro Equivalents (31 December 2013)

£1 sterling = 70.467 pesos;
US $1 = 42.790 pesos;
€1 = 59.012 pesos;
1,000 Dominican Republic pesos = £14.19 = $23.37 = €16.95.

Average Exchange Rate (RD $ per US $)

2011 38.232
2012 39.336
2013 41.808

BUDGET

(RD $ million)

Revenue	2010	2011	2012*
Tax revenue	243,942.9	273,132.0	312,064.1
Taxes on income and profits	53,643.5	65,204.9	92,274.4
Taxes on goods and services	151,802.4	167,941.4	175,892.5
Taxes on international trade and transactions	23,408.4	23,003.3	23,444.1
Other current revenue	11,128.1	7,318.2	6,480.7
Capital revenue	14.2	6.7	13.9
Total	255,085.2	280,456.9	318,558.8

Expenditure	2010	2011	2012*
Current expenditure	239,988.3	263,928.7	320,973.4
Wages and salaries	72,254.3	79,113.7	87,846.0
Other goods and services	34,401.1	33,468.7	41,971.5
Current transfers	96,100.5	106,515.5	134,936.7
Interest payments	37,232.5	44,830.6	56,219.3
Capital expenditure	70,373.1	76,454.0	150,960.7
Capital transfers	18,127.9	21,807.1	34,699.4
Total	310,361.4	340,382.7	471,934.1

* Preliminary figures.

INTERNATIONAL RESERVES

(US $ million at 31 December)

	2010	2011	2012
Gold*	25.7	28.0	30.3
IMF special drawing rights	117.7	18.6	20.3
Foreign exchange	3,358.0	4,070.4	3,528.2
Total	3,501.4	4,117.0	3,578.8

* Valued at market-related prices.

Source: IMF, *International Financial Statistics*.

MONEY SUPPLY

(RD $ million at 31 December)

	2010	2011	2012
Currency outside depository corporations	59,559	61,463	65,374
Transferable deposits	106,880	113,917	125,866
Other deposits	279,729	327,857	359,755
Securities other than shares	183,091	205,631	225,552
Broad money	629,259	708,868	776,547

Source: IMF, *International Financial Statistics*.

COST OF LIVING

(Consumer Price Index, annual averages; base: December 2010 = 100)

	2010	2011	2012
Food and non-alcoholic beverages	97.9	106.8	112.2
Alcoholic beverages and tobacco	99.0	103.0	109.0
Clothing	97.8	100.8	100.6
Housing	93.9	106.9	109.0
Furniture	98.8	102.5	105.4
Health	96.9	103.4	108.4
Transport	97.1	111.4	115.1
Communication	98.9	99.1	98.8
Education	95.3	103.7	115.0
Recreation and culture	98.2	100.8	102.1
All items (incl. others)	97.4	105.6	109.5

NATIONAL ACCOUNTS
(RD $ million at current prices)

Expenditure on the Gross Domestic Product

	2010	2011	2012
Final consumption expenditure	1,801,316.4	1,989,712.5	2,149,905.2
Households; Non-profit institutions serving households	1,655,630.9	1,833,739.0	1,962,035.3
General government	145,685.4	155,973.5	187,869.9
Gross capital formation	313,322.3	348,270.3	379,873.6
Gross fixed capital formation	310,751.4	345,404.1	376,738.8
Changes in inventories; Acquisitions, less disposals, of valuables	2,570.9	2,866.1	3,134.8
Total domestic expenditure	2,114,638.7	2,337,982.8	2,529,778.8
Exports of goods and services	438,041.4	530,803.4	574,646.4
Less Imports of goods and services	650,783.4	749,484.4	787,641.6
GDP in market prices	1,901,896.7	2,119,301.8	2,316,783.7

Gross Domestic Product by Economic Activity

	2010	2011	2012
Agriculture, hunting, forestry and fishing	109,084.9	118,040.3	130,860.4
Mining and quarrying	2,698.4	7,528.4	10,197.8
Manufacturing	422,135.1	487,207.0	508,189.4
Local manufacturing	365,955.7	418,444.0	436,114.9
Free trade zones	56,179.4	68,763.0	72,074.5
Electricity and water	39,596.4	44,375.6	48,176.1
Construction	97,324.1	115,921.2	119,956.0
Wholesale and retail trade	171,968.3	194,212.6	212,467.7
Restaurants and hotels	175,214.7	192,250.7	206,338.1
Transport and storage	149,553.7	177,252.9	195,487.9
Communications	54,340.7	53,063.7	54,940.1
Finance, insurance and business activities	120,542.7	142,616.4	170,374.6
Real estate	156,624.2	175,205.5	187,104.2
General government services (incl. defence)	58,504.0	59,666.7	71,123.0
Education	69,759.2	75,496.5	93,159.7
Health	37,812.2	42,757.3	45,008.5
Other services	147,925.4	162,236.2	183,480.0
Sub-total	1,813,084.0	2,047,831.0	2,236,863.5
Less Financial intermediation services indirectly measured	59,567.2	67,614.4	74,235.3
Gross value added in basic prices	1,753,516.9	1,980,216.9	2,162,628.2
Taxes, *less* subsidies	148,379.7	139,084.9	154,155.4
GDP in market prices	1,901,896.7	2,119,301.8	2,316,783.7

BALANCE OF PAYMENTS
(US $ million)

	2010	2011	2012
Exports of goods	2,536.1	3,678.0	4,091.4
Imports of goods	−13,025.3	−14,537.3	−14,965.5
Balance on goods	−10,489.2	−10,859.3	−10,874.1
Exports of services	6,907.5	7,372.7	7,959.9
Imports of services	−2,185.0	−2,235.0	−2,283.5
Balance on goods and services	−5,766.7	−5,721.6	−5,197.7
Primary income received	496.6	505.7	512.6
Primary income paid	−2,183.0	−2,596.3	−2,724.9
Balance on goods, services and primary income	−7,453.1	−7,812.2	−7,410.0
Secondary income received	3,476.1	3,755.5	3,732.8
Secondary income paid	−352.5	−322.2	−359.9

—continued	2010	2011	2012
Current balance	−4,329.5	−4,378.9	−4,037.1
Capital account (net)	81.9	57.8	54.8
Direct investment assets	203.5	79.2	−273.5
Direct investment liabilities	1,692.8	2,195.8	3,857.1
Portfolio investment assets	−10.6	36.9	−800.1
Portfolio investment liabilities	770.1	709.0	−196.1
Other investment assets	694.0	−40.0	−354.3
Other investment liabilities	2,109.7	1,000.4	1,702.5
Net errors and omissions	−1,139.6	501.5	−393.9
Reserves and related items	72.3	161.7	−440.6

Source: IMF, *International Financial Statistics*.

External Trade

PRINCIPAL COMMODITIES
(distribution by HS, US $ million)

Imports f.o.b.	2010	2011	2012
Vegetables and vegetable products	739.8	937.7	781.4
Cereals	394.3	563.0	498.1
Prepared foodstuffs, beverages, spirits, tobacco, etc.	762.0	1,005.3	1,142.7
Mineral products	3,732.4	4,734.2	4,471.6
Mineral fuels, oils, distillation products, etc.	3,710.4	4,669.8	4,407.4
Crude petroleum oils	863.9	979.5	1,030.3
Petroleum oils, not crude	1,993.2	2,508.6	2,233.0
Petroleum gases	627.6	801.4	838.4
Chemicals and related products	1,198.5	1,453.8	1,884.5
Plastics, rubber and articles thereof	859.1	1,228.9	1,395.5
Plastics and articles thereof	711.4	1,053.5	1,168.9
Textiles and textile articles	886.4	1,254.0	1,275.2
Cotton	371.3	664.7	573.3
Base metals and articles thereof	1,030.4	1,324.2	1,180.7
Iron and steel	465.0	677.1	505.6
Machinery and mechanical appliances, electrical equipment	2,566.4	2,599.3	2,958.5
Machinery, boilers, etc.	1,270.7	1,184.5	1,273.9
Electrical and electronic equipment	1,295.8	1,414.9	1,684.6
Transport equipment	974.2	708.3	1,054.6
Vehicles other than railway, tramway	956.5	686.4	942.0
Cars (incl. station wagons)	567.3	373.7	513.6
Total (incl. others)	15,138.2	18,156.1	19,200.5

Exports f.o.b.	2010	2011	2012
Vegetables and vegetable products	355.7	428.2	312.8
Edible fruit, nuts, peel of citrus fruit, melons	194.9	208.0	120.7
Bananas and plantains (fresh or dried)	154.8	153.9	64.8
Prepared foodstuffs, beverages, spirits, tobacco, etc.	930.9	1,023.4	1,103.1
Tobacco and manufactured tobacco substitutes	294.2	407.5	514.2
Cigars, cheroots, cigarillos and cigarettes	290.1	324.4	408.3
Sugars and sugar confectionery	154.7	155.0	182.0
Cocoa and cocoa preparations	178.5	172.7	185.4
Cocoa beans (whole or broken, raw or roasted)	164.5	165.2	178.5
Mineral products	91.8	270.9	219.3

Exports f.o.b.—*continued*	2010	2011	2012
Chemicals and related products	270.1	284.3	554.0
Pharmaceutical products	118.7	125.2	350.5
Pharmaceutical goods and specified sterile products, sutures	7.1	3.3	314.5
Plastics, rubber and articles thereof	153.7	354.9	307.1
Plastics and articles thereof	147.6	342.8	294.5
Textiles and textile articles	826.2	980.1	1,095.9
Cotton	230.8	279.8	234.2
Articles of apparel, accessories, knitted or crocheted	216.8	348.1	463.5
T-shirts, singlets and other vests	68.4	149.0	354.7
Articles of apparel, accessories, not knitted or crocheted	320.7	283.8	285.2
Footwear, headgear, umbrellas, walking sticks, etc.	204.3	259.1	316.4
Footwear, gaiters, etc.	198.7	251.6	307.5
Footwear	164.7	184.9	99.6
Pearls, precious stones, metals, coins, etc.	223.2	223.2	322.2
Articles of jewellery and parts thereof	215.0	197.0	137.5
Base metals and articles thereof	311.1	783.0	604.2
Iron and steel	166.7	584.6	458.2
Ferro-alloys	2.1	277.3	270.1
Machinery and mechanical appliances, electrical equipment	438.9	501.7	615.5
Electrical and electronic equipment	412.3	471.9	513.2
Electrical apparatus for switching, not exceeding 1,000 volts	211.8	40.5	368.4
Optical, photo, cinema, measuring, checking precision equipment	681.7	676.0	712.5
Optical, photo, technical, medical apparatus, etc.	681.6	675.5	711.8
Electro-medical apparatus	670.2	662.4	690.0
Total (incl. others)	4,766.7	6,112.5	6,902.5

Source: Trade Map-Trade Competitiveness Map, International Trade Centre, www.intracen.org/marketanalysis.

PRINCIPAL TRADING PARTNERS
(US $ million)

Imports c.i.f.	2010	2011	2012
Argentina	161.6	243.6	278.6
Bahamas	266.2	161.3	359.2
Brazil	355.4	419.2	524.7
Canada	190.9	180.5	173.1
China, People's Republic	1,615.7	1,787.2	1,928.3
Colombia	578.9	725.1	397.9
Costa Rica	221.7	241.7	253.6
Germany	270.6	287.3	299.7
Italy	195.5	213.4	277.6
Japan	322.0	214.1	347.9
Mexico	908.6	1,084.9	998.0
Spain	271.9	422.7	559.0
Trinidad and Tobago	468.4	835.3	1,165.8
United Kingdom	156.4	129.3	112.2
USA	5,907.3	7,555.2	7,405.9
Venezuela	1,083.9	1,237.2	1,217.5
Total (incl. others)	15,138.2	18,156.1	19,200.5

Exports f.o.b.	2010	2011	2012
Belgium	97.7	84.8	52.0
China, People's Republic	125.5	330.3	355.8
Germany	48.5	59.1	81.5
Guatemala	16.2	47.4	130.0
Haiti	802.0	1,013.6	986.9
Honduras	26.6	54.4	108.2
Jamaica	50.8	51.1	43.5
Korea, Democratic People's Republic	29.6	41.5	82.1
Netherlands	123.5	128.3	120.0
Nigeria	—	73.8	61.0
Spain	98.8	0.4	50.3
United Kingdom	101.8	117.4	63.6
USA	2,750.7	3,330.9	3,867.9
Venezuela	21.3	80.2	37.6
Total (incl. others)	4,766.7	6,112.5	6,902.5

Source: Trade Map-Trade Competitiveness Map, International Trade Centre, www.intracen.org/marketanalysis.

Transport

ROAD TRAFFIC
(motor vehicles in use)

	2010	2011	2012
Passenger cars	914,628	953,542	991,081
Buses and coaches	73,716	76,300	78,888
Vans and lorries	362,323	373,987	382,380
Motorcycles and mopeds	1,352,720	1,481,255	1,566,815
Total (incl. others)	2,734,740	2,917,573	3,052,686

SHIPPING

Flag Registered Fleet
(at 31 December)

	2011	2012	2013
Number of vessels	34	35	38
Total displacement ('000 grt)	13.2	13.4	14.4

Source: Lloyd's List Intelligence (www.lloydslistintelligence.com).

International Sea-borne Freight Traffic
('000 metric tons)

	2010	2011	2012
Goods loaded	2,420	3,570	4,242
Goods unloaded	13,129	15,722	13,766

CIVIL AVIATION
(traffic on scheduled services)

	1997	1998	1999
Kilometres flown (million)	1	1	0
Passengers carried ('000)	34	34	10
Passenger-km (million)	16	16	5
Total ton-km (million)	1	1	0

Source: UN, *Statistical Yearbook*.

Tourism

ARRIVALS BY NATIONALITY

	2010	2011	2012
Argentina	71,461	99,618	103,389
Brazil	38,431	78,083	81,501
Canada	659,063	665,640	685,889
France	244,165	260,289	259,991
Germany	181,682	182,529	183,887
Italy	100,052	104,852	95,030
Russia	79,868	124,319	167,700
Spain	189,724	171,353	157,214
United Kingdom*	169,919	138,816	98,288
USA	1,226,367	1,286,161	1,456,671
Total (incl. others)	4,586,264	4,776,473	5,047,021

* Includes arrivals from England and Scotland only.

Tourism receipts (US $ million, excl. passenger transport): 4,209 in 2010; 4,352 in 2011; 4,549 in 2012 (provisional) (Source: World Tourism Organization).

Communications Media

	2010	2011	2012
Telephones ('000 main lines in use)	1,012.9	1,050.5	1,065.5
Mobile cellular telephones ('000 subscribers)	8,892.8	8,770.8	9,038.1
Internet subscribers ('000)	379.3	436.1	n.a.
Broadband subscribers ('000)	361.1	404.0	450.6

Source: International Telecommunication Union.

Education

(2010/11 unless otherwise indicated)

		Students		
	Teachers	Males	Females	Total
Pre-primary	10,152	120,510	118,889	239,399
Primary	51,615	699,321	610,878	1,310,199
Secondary	31,289	427,398	471,292	898,690
General	27,923	412,457	446,868	859,325
Vocational	3,366	14,941	24,424	39,365
Higher*	11,367	113,520	180,045	293,565

* Estimates for 2003/04.

Institutions: Primary 4,001 (1997/98); General secondary 1,737 (1996/97).

Source: UNESCO, mostly Institute for Statistics.

Pupil-teacher ratio (primary education, estimate): 25.5 in 2010/11 (Source: UNESCO Institute for Statistics).

Adult literacy rate (estimates): 90.1% (males 90.0%; females 90.2%) in 2011 (Source: UNESCO Institute for Statistics).

Directory

The Government

HEAD OF STATE

President: Danilo Medina Sánchez (took office 16 August 2012).

Vice-President: Margarita Cedeño Lizardo.

CABINET
(April 2014)

The Government is formed by the Partido de la Liberación Dominicana.

Minister of the Presidency: Gustavo Montalvo.

Minister of Foreign Affairs: Carlos Morales Troncoso.

Minister of the Interior and Police: José Ramón Fadul.

Minister of the Armed Forces: Vice-Adm. Sigfrido Pared Peréz.

Minister of Finance: Simón Lizardo Mézquita.

Minister of Education: Carlos Amarante Baret.

Minister of Agriculture: Angel Estévez.

Minister of Public Works and Communications: Gonzalo Castillo.

Minister of Public Health and Social Welfare: Lorenzo Wilfredo Hidalgo Núñez.

Minister of Industry and Commerce: José del Castillo Saviñón.

Minister of Labour: Maritza Hernández.

Minister of Tourism: Francisco Javier García.

Minister of Sport and Recreation: Jaime David Fernández Mirabal.

Minister of Culture: José Antonio Rodríguez.

Minister of Higher Education, Science and Technology: Ligia Amada de Melo.

Minister of Women: Alejandrina Germán.

Minister of Youth: Jorge Minaya.

Minister of the Environment and Natural Resources: Dr Bautista Rojas Gómez.

Minister of the Economy, Planning and Development: Juan Temístocles Montás.

Minister of Public Administration: Ramón Ventura Camejo.

Minister of Energy and Mines: Pelegrín Castillo Semán.

Administrative Secretary to the Presidency: José Ramón Peralta.

MINISTRIES

Office of the President: Palacio Nacional, Avda México, esq. Dr Delgado, Gazcue, Santo Domingo, DN; tel. 695-8000; fax 682-4558; e-mail info@presidencia.gob.do; internet www.presidencia.gob.do.

Ministry of Agriculture: Autopista Duarte, Km 6.5, Los Jardines del Norte, Santo Domingo, DN; tel. 547-3888; fax 227-1268; e-mail agricultura@agricultura.gob.do; internet www.agricultura.gob.do.

Ministry of the Armed Forces: Plaza de la Bandera, Avda 27 de Febrero, esq. Avda Luperón, Santo Domingo, DN; tel. 530-5149; fax 531-0461; e-mail directorrev@j2.mil.do; internet www.fuerzasarmadas.mil.do.

Ministry of Culture: Centro de Eventos y Exposiciones, Avda George Washington, esq. Presidente Vicini Burgos, Santo Domingo, DN; tel. 221-4141; fax 688-2908; e-mail accesoainfo@sec.gob.do; internet www.cultura.gob.do.

Ministry of the Economy, Planning and Development: Palacio Nacional, Avda México, esq. Dr Delgado, Bloque B, 2°, Santo Domingo, DN; tel. 688-7000; fax 221-8627; e-mail informacion@economia.gob.do; internet www.economia.gob.do.

Ministry of Education: Avda Máximo Gómez, esq. Santiago 2, Gazcue, Santo Domingo, DN; tel. 688-9700; fax 689-8688; e-mail mlibreacceso@see.gob.do; internet www.see.gob.do.

Ministry of Energy and Mines: Santo Domingo, DN.

Ministry of the Environment and Natural Resources: Avda Luperón, Santo Domingo, DN; tel. 567-4300; fax 683-4774; e-mail contacto@medioambiente.gob.do; internet www.ambiente.gob.do.

Ministry of Finance: Avda México 45, esq. Leopoldo Navarro, Apdo 1478, Santo Domingo, DN; tel. 687-5131; fax 682-0498; e-mail info@hacienda.gov.do; internet www.hacienda.gov.do.

Ministry of Foreign Affairs: Avda Independencia 752, Estancia San Gerónimo, Santo Domingo, DN; tel. 987-7001; fax 987-7002; e-mail relexteriores@serex.gob.do; internet www.serex.gov.do.

Ministry of Higher Education, Science and Technology: Avda Máximo Gómez 31, esq. Pedro Henríquez Ureña, Santo Domingo, DN; tel. 731-1100; fax 535-4694; e-mail info@seescyt.gob.do; internet www.seescyt.gov.do.

Ministry of Industry and Commerce: Edif. de Ofs Gubernamentales Juan Pablo Duarte, 7°, Avda México, esq. Leopoldo Navarro, Apdo 9876, Santo Domingo, DN; tel. 685-5171; fax 686-1973; e-mail info@seic.gob.do; internet www.seic.gov.do.

Ministry of the Interior and Police: Edif. de Ofs Gubernamentales Juan Pablo Duarte, 13°, Avda México, esq. Leopoldo Navarro, Santo Domingo, DN; tel. 686-6251; fax 689-6599; e-mail info@mip.gob.do; internet www.seip.gob.do.

Ministry of Labour: Centro de los Héroes, Avda Jiménez Moya 9, La Feria, Santo Domingo, DN; tel. 535-4404; fax 535-4833; e-mail info@mt.gob.do; internet www.ministeriodetrabajo.gob.do.

Ministry of Public Administration: Edif. de Ofs Gubernamentales Juan Pablo Duarte, 12°, Avda México, esq. Leopoldo Navarro, Apdo 20031, Santo Domingo, DN; tel. 682-3298; fax 686-6652; e-mail seap@seap.gob.do; internet www.map.gob.do.

Ministry of Public Health and Social Welfare: Avda Héctor Homero Hernández, esq. Tiradentes, Ensanche La Fe, Santo Domingo, DN; tel. 541-3121; fax 540-6445; e-mail correo@salud.gob.do; internet www.msp.gov.do.

Ministry of Public Works and Communications: Avda Héctor Homero Hernández, esq. Avda Tiradentes, Ensanche La Fe, Santo Domingo, DN; tel. 565-2811; fax 562-3382; e-mail contacto@mopc.gob.do; internet www.seopc.gov.do.

Ministry of Sport and Recreation: Avda Correa y Cidrón, esq. John F. Kennedy, Estadio Olímpico, Centro Olímpico Juan Pablo Duarte, Santo Domingo, DN; tel. 565-3325; fax 563-6586; e-mail juliomonnadal@miderec.gov.do; internet www.miderec.gov.do.

Ministry of Tourism: Edif. de Ofs Gubernamentales, Bloque D, Avda México, esq. 30 de Marzo, Apdo 497, Santo Domingo, DN; tel. 221-4660; fax 682-3806; e-mail info@sectur.gob.do; internet www.sectur.gob.do.

Ministry of Women: Edif. de Ofs Gubernamentales, Bloque D, 2°, Avda México, esq. 30 de Marzo, Santo Domingo, DN; tel. 685-3755; fax 685-8040; e-mail info@mujer.gob.do; internet www.mujer.gob.do.

Ministry of Youth: Avda Jiménez de Moya 71, esq. Calle Desiderio Arias, Ensanche La Julia, Santo Domingo, DN; tel. 508-7227; fax 508-6686; e-mail info@juventud.gob.do; internet www.juventud.gob.do.

President and Legislature

PRESIDENT

Election, 20 May 2012

Candidate	Votes	% of valid votes cast
Danilo Medina Sánchez (PLD)	2,323,461	51.21
Rafael Hipólito Mejía Domínguez (PRD)	2,130,187	46.95
Guillermo Moreno (ALPAIS)	62,296	1.37
Others	20,962	0.46
Total	4,536,906	100.00

NATIONAL CONGRESS

The Congress comprises a Senate and a Chamber of Deputies.

President of the Senate: Dr Reinaldo Pared Pérez (PLD).

President of the Chamber of Deputies: Abel Martínez Durán (PLD).

General Election, 16 May 2010

	Seats	
	Senate	Chamber of Deputies
Partido de la Liberación Dominicana (PLD)	31	105
Partido Revolucionario Dominicano (PRD)	—	75
Partido Reformista Social Cristiano (PRSC)	1	3
Total	32	183*

* A further seven deputies were elected by overseas voters in an election held on 20 May 2012, increasing the total number of deputies to 190. Of these seven seats, four were won by the PRD and three were secured by the PLD.

Election Commission

Junta Central Electoral (JCE): Avda 27 de Febrero, esq. Gregorio Luperón, Santo Domingo, DN; tel. 539-5419; e-mail webmaster@jce.gob.do; internet www.jce.gob.do; f. 1923; govt-appointed body; Pres. Dr Roberto Rosario Márquez.

Political Organizations

Alianza País (ALPAIS): Calle Pasteur 55, 2°, Gazcue, Santo Domingo, DN; tel. 238-5409; e-mail participa@alianzapais.com.do; internet www.alianzapais.com.do; Pres. Guillermo Moreno.

Alianza por la Democracia (APD): Benito Mención 10, Gazcue, Santo Domingo, DN; tel. 687-0337; fax 687-0360; f. 1992 by breakaway group of the PLD; Pres. Maximiliano Puig; Sec.-Gen. Carlos Luis Sánchez S.

Bloque Institucional Socialdemócrata (BIS): Avda Bolívar 24, esq. Uruguay, Ensanche Lugo, Apdo 5413, Santo Domingo, DN; tel. 682-3232; fax 682-3375; e-mail bloque.institucionalsocialdemocrata@hotmail.com; internet bis.org.do; f. 1989 by breakaway group of the PRD; Pres. José Francisco Peña Guaba.

Fuerza Nacional Progresista (FNP): Calle Emilio A. Morel 17, Ensanche La Fe, Santo Domingo, DN; tel. 732-0849; e-mail fuerza_nacional_progresista@hotmail.com; internet fuerzanacionalprogresista.blogspot.com; right-wing; Pres. Marino Vinicio Castillo (alias Vincho); Sec.-Gen. José Ricardo Taveras Blanco.

Partido de la Liberación Dominicana (PLD): Avda Independencia 401, Santo Domingo, DN; tel. 685-3540; fax 687-5569; e-mail pldorg@pld.org.do; internet www.pld.org.do; f. 1973 by breakaway group of the PRD; left-wing; Leader Leonel Fernández Reyna; Sec.-Gen. Reinaldo Pared Pérez.

Partido Reformista Social Cristiano (PRSC): Avda Tiradentes, esq. San Cristóbal, Ensanche La Fe, Apdo 1332, Santo Domingo, DN; tel. 621-7772; fax 476-9361; e-mail s.seliman@codetel.net.do; internet www.prsc.com.do; f. 1964; centre-right party; Pres. Carlos Morales Troncoso; Sec.-Gen. Ramón Rogelio Genao.

Partido Revolucionario Dominicano (PRD): Avda Dr Comandante Enrique Jiménez Moya 14, Bella Vista, Santo Domingo, DN; tel. 687-2193; e-mail prensa_tribunalp.r.d@hotmail.com; internet www.prd.org.do; f. 1939; democratic socialist; Pres. Miguel Vargas Maldonado; Sec.-Gen. Orlando Jorge Mera.

Partido Revolucionario Independiente (PRI): Edif. Galerías Comerciales, Avda 57, Apdo 509, Santo Domingo, DN; tel. 221-8286; e-mail trajano.s@codetel.net.do; f. 1985 after split by the PRD's right-wing faction; Pres. Dr Trajano Santana; Sec.-Gen. Dr Jorge Montes de Oca.

Partido de los Trabajadores Dominicanos (PTD): Avda Bolívar 101, esq. Dr Báez, Gazcue, Santo Domingo, DN; tel. 685-7705; fax 333-6443; e-mail contacto@ptd.org.do; internet www.ptd.org.do; f. 1979; Communist; Pres. José González Espinoza; Sec.-Gen. Antonio Florián.

Diplomatic Representation

EMBASSIES IN THE DOMINICAN REPUBLIC

Argentina: Avda Máximo Gómez 10, Apdo 1302, Santo Domingo, DN; tel. 682-2977; fax 221-2206; e-mail edomi@mreic.gov.ar; Ambassador Noemi Marcía Gomez.

Belize: Carretera La Isabela, Calle Proyecto 3, Arroyo Manzano 1, Santo Domingo, DN; tel. 567-7146; fax 567-7159; e-mail embassy@embelize.org; internet www.embelize.org; Ambassador R. Eduardo Lama S.

Brazil: Eduardo Vicioso 46A, esq. Avda Winston Churchill, Ensanche Bella Vista, Apdo 1655, Santo Domingo, DN; tel. 532-4200; fax 532-0917; e-mail contacto@embajadadebrasil.org.do; internet www.embajadadebrasil.org.do; Ambassador José Marcus Vinicius de Sousa.

Canada: Avda Winston Churchill 1099, Torre Citigroup en Acrópolis Center, 18°, Ensanche Piantini, Apdo 2054, Santo Domingo, DN; tel. 262-3100; fax 262-3108; e-mail sdmgo@international.gc.ca; internet www.canadainternational.gc.ca/dominican_republic-republique_dominicaine; Ambassador Georges Boissé.

Chile: Avda Anacaona 11, Mirador del Sur, Santo Domingo, DN; tel. 532-7800; fax 530-8310; e-mail embachile1@claro.net.do; internet chileabroad.gov.cl/republica-dominicana; Ambassador Manuel Hinojosa.

Colombia: Calle Andrés Julio Aybar 27, casi esq. Avda Abraham Lincoln, Ensanche Piantini, Santo Domingo, DN; tel. 562-1670; fax 562-3253; e-mail erdomini@cancilleria.gov.co; Ambassador Adm. (retd) ROBERTO GARCÍA MÁRQUEZ.

Costa Rica: Calle Malaquías Gil 11 Altos, entre Abraham Lincoln y Lope de Vega, Ensanche Serralles, Santo Domingo, DN; tel. 683-7209; fax 565-6467; e-mail emb.costarica@codetel.net; Ambassador JOSÉ RAFAEL TORRES CASTRO.

Cuba: Francisco Prats Ramírez 808, El Millón, Santo Domingo, DN; tel. 537-2113; fax 537-9820; e-mail embadom@codetel.net.do; internet www.cubadiplomatica.cu/republicadominicana; Ambassador ALEXIS BANDRICH VEGA.

Ecuador: Edif. Optica Félix, Penthouse 601, Avda Abraham Lincoln 1007, Ensanche Piantini, Santo Domingo, DN; tel. 563-8363; fax 563-8153; e-mail mecuador@verizon.net.do; Ambassador CARLOS LÓPEZ DAMM.

El Salvador: Calle 2da, No 2, esq. Calle Central, Ensanche Bella Vista, Santo Domingo, DN; tel. 565-4311; fax 541-7503; e-mail EmbajadaDominicana@rree.gob.sv; Ambassador CARLOS ALBERTO CALLES CASTILLO.

France: Calle Las Damas 42, esq. El Conde, Zona Colonial, Santo Domingo, DN; tel. 695-4300; fax 695-4311; e-mail ambafrance@ambafrance-do.org; internet www.ambafrance.org.do; Ambassador BLANDINE KREISS.

Germany: Edif. Torre Piantini, 16° y 17°, Calle Gustavo Mejía Ricart 196, esq. Avda Abraham Lincoln, Ensanche Piantini, Santo Domingo, DN; tel. 542-8949; fax 542-8955; e-mail info@santo-domingo.diplo.de; internet www.santo-domingo.diplo.de; Ambassador VICTORIA ZIMMERMANN VON SIEFART.

Guatemala: Edif. Corominas Pepín, 9°, Avda 27 de Febrero 233, Santo Domingo, DN; tel. 381-0249; fax 381-0278; e-mail embrepdominicana@minex.gob.gt; Ambassador ALEJANDRO JOSÉ BUITRÓN PORRAS.

Haiti: Calle Juan Sánchez Ramírez 33, esq. Desiderio Valdez 33, Zona Universitaria, Santo Domingo, DN; tel. 686-8185; fax 686-6096; e-mail embajadahaiti@yahoo.com; Ambassador Dr FRITZ N. CINEAS.

Holy See: Avda Máximo Gómez 27, esq. César Nicolás Penson, Apdo 312, Santo Domingo, DN (Apostolic Nunciature); tel. 682-3773; fax 687-0287; Apostolic Nuncio Most Rev. JUDE THADDEUS OKOLO (Titular Archbishop of Novica).

Honduras: Calle Arístides García Mella, esq. Rodríguez Objío, Edif. El Buen Pastor VI, Apt 1B, 1°, Mirador del Sur, Santo Domingo, DN; tel. 482-7992; fax 482-7505; e-mail e.honduras@codetel.net.do; Ambassador MARÍA EUGENIA BARRIOS ALEMÁN.

Israel: Calle Pedro Henríquez Ureña 80, La Esperilla, Santo Domingo, DN; tel. 920-1500; fax 472-1785; e-mail info@santodomingo.mfa.gov.il; internet santodomingo.mfa.gov.il; Ambassador BAHIJ MANSOUR.

Italy: Calle Rodríguez Objío 4, Gazcue, Santo Domingo, DN; tel. 682-0830; fax 682-8296; e-mail ambsdom.mail@esteri.it; internet www.ambsantodomingo.esteri.it; Chargé d'affaires a.i. OLINDO D'AGOSTINO.

Jamaica: Avda Sarasota 36, Bella Vista, Plaza Kury, Suite 304, Santo Domingo, DN; tel. 567-7770; fax 620-2497; e-mail embjamaica.info@correo.tricom.net; internet www.embajadadejamaica-rd.com; Chargé d'affaires a.i. THOMAS F. ALLAN MARLEY.

Japan: Torre BHD, 8°, Avda Winston Churchill, esq. Luis F. Thomén, Ensanche Evaristo Morales, Apdo 9825, Santo Domingo, DN; tel. 567-3365; fax 566-8013; e-mail embjpn@codetel.net.do; internet www.do.emb-japan.go.jp; Ambassador SOICHI SATO.

Korea, Republic: Torre Forum, 14°, Avda 27 de Febrero 495, Santo Domingo, DN; tel. 482-6505; fax 482-6504; e-mail embcod@mofat.go.kr; internet dom.mofat.go.kr; Ambassador PARK DONG-SIL.

Mexico: Arzobispo Meriño 265, esq. Las Mercedes, Zona Colonial, Santo Domingo, DN; tel. 687-7793; fax 687-7872; e-mail embamex@codetel.net.do; Ambassador JOSÉ IGNACIO PIÑA ROJAS.

Morocco: Avda Abraham Lincoln 1009, Edif. Profesional EFA, 6°, Ensanche Piantini, Santo Domingo, DN; tel. 732-0409; fax 732-1703; e-mail sifamasdomingo@codetel.net.do; Ambassador IBRAHIM HOUSSEIN MOUSSA.

Netherlands: Max Henríquez Ureña 50, entre Avda Winston Churchill y Abraham Lincoln, Ensanche Piantini, Apdo 855, Santo Domingo, DN; tel. 262-0320; fax 565-4685; e-mail std@minbuza.nl; internet www.holanda.org.do; Ambassador MARIJKE A. VAN DRUNEN LITTEL.

Nicaragua: Avda Helios, Calle Corozal, No 6, Bella Vista, Santo Domingo, DN; tel. 535-1120; fax 535-1230; e-mail embanic-rd@codetel.net.do; Ambassador NELSON ARTOLA ESCOBAR.

Panama: Benito Monción 255, Gazcue, Santo Domingo, DN; tel. 688-3789; fax 685-3665; e-mail emb.panam@codetel.net.do; Ambassador ALBERTO MAGNO CASTILLERO PINILLA.

Peru: Calle Mayreni 31, Urb. Los Cacicazgos, Santo Domingo, DN; tel. 482-3300; fax 482-3334; e-mail embaperu@verizon.net.do; Ambassador ENRIQUE ALEJANDRO PALACIOS REYES.

Qatar: Avda Sarasota 7, Santo Domingo, DN; tel. 535-7600; fax 535-7900; internet www.qataremb.com; Ambassador KHAMIS BUTTI AL-SAHOUTI.

Spain: Avda Independencia 1205, Apdo 1468, Santo Domingo, DN; tel. 535-6500; fax 535-1595; e-mail informae@maec.es; internet www.exteriores.gob.es/embajadas/santodomingo; Ambassador JAIME LACADENA HIGUERA.

Switzerland: Edif. Aeromar, 2°, Avda Winston Churchill 71, esq. Desiderio Arias, Bella Vista, Apdo 3626, Santo Domingo, DN; tel. 533-3781; fax 532-3781; e-mail sdd.vertretung@eda.admin.ch; internet www.eda.admin.ch/santodomingo; Ambassador LINE LEON-PERNET.

Taiwan (Republic of China): Avda Rómulo Betancourt 1360, Secto Bella Vista, Santo Domingo, DN; tel. 508-6200; fax 508-6335; e-mail dom@mofa.gov.tw; internet www.taiwanembassy.org/DO; Ambassador TOMÁS PING FU HOU.

United Kingdom: Edif. Corominas Pepin, 7°, Avda 27 de Febrero 233, Santo Domingo, DN; tel. 472-7111; fax 472-7574; e-mail brit.emb.sadom@codetel.net.do; internet ukindominicanrepublic.fco.gov.uk; Ambassador STEVEN FISHER.

USA: Avda César Nicolás Pensón, esq. Leopoldo Navarro, Santo Domingo, DN; tel. 221-2171; fax 686-7437; e-mail irc@usemb.gov.do; internet santodomingo.usembassy.gov; Ambassador JAMES (WALLY) BREWSTER.

Uruguay: Edif. Gapo, Local 401, Avda Luis F. Thomen 110, Ensanche Evaristo Morales, Santo Domingo, DN; tel. 227-3475; fax 472-4231; e-mail urudominicana@mrree.gub.uy; Ambassador RAÚL JUAN POLLAK GIAMPIETRO.

Venezuela: Avda Anacoana 7, Mirador del Sur, Santo Domingo, DN; tel. 537-8882; fax 537-8780; e-mail embvenezuela@codetel.net.do; internet www.embajadavenezuelard.org; Ambassador ALBERTO EFRAÍN CASTELLAR PADILLA.

Judicial System

The Judicial Power resides in the Supreme Court of Justice, the Courts of Appeal, the Tribunals of First Instance, and the municipal courts. The Supreme Court is composed of 16 judges and the Attorney-General, and exercises disciplinary authority over all the members of the judiciary. The National Judiciary Council appoints the members of the Supreme Court, which in turn appoints judges at all other levels of the judicial system.

Suprema Corte de Justicia: Centro de los Héroes, Calle Juan de Dios Ventura Simó, esq. Enrique Jiménez Moya, Apdo 1485, Santo Domingo, DN; tel. 533-3191; fax 532-2906; e-mail suprema.corte@verizon.net.do; internet www.suprema.gov.do; Pres. Dr MARIANO GERMAN MEJÍA.

Attorney-General: FRANCISCO DOMÍNGUEZ BRITO.

Religion

The majority of the inhabitants belong to the Roman Catholic Church, but freedom of worship exists for all denominations. The Baptist, Evangelist, Seventh-day Adventist and Mormon churches and the Jewish faith are also represented.

CHRISTIANITY

The Roman Catholic Church

The Dominican Republic comprises two archdioceses and nine dioceses. Roman Catholics represent about 87% of the population.

Bishops' Conference: Isabel la Católica 55, Apdo 186, Santo Domingo, DN; tel. 685-3141; fax 685-0227; e-mail nicolas.clr@codetel.net.do; internet www.ced.org.do; f. 1985; Pres. Cardinal NICOLÁS DE JESÚS LÓPEZ RODRÍGUEZ (Archbishop of Santo Domingo).

Archbishop of Santiago de los Caballeros: Most Rev. RAMÓN BENITO DE LA ROSA Y CARPIO, Arzobispado, Duvergé 14, Apdo 679, Santiago de los Caballeros; tel. 582-2094; fax 581-3580; e-mail arzobisp.stgo@verizon.net.do.

Archbishop of Santo Domingo: Cardinal NICOLÁS DE JESÚS LÓPEZ RODRÍGUEZ, Arzobispado, Isabel la Católica 55, Apdo 186, Santo Domingo, DN; tel. 685-3141; fax 688-7270; e-mail nicolas.clr@codetel.net.do.

The Anglican Communion

Anglicans in the Dominican Republic are under the jurisdiction of the Episcopal Church in the USA. The country is classified as a missionary diocese, in Province IX.

Bishop of the Dominican Republic: Rt Rev. JULIO CÉSAR HOLGUÍN KHOURY, Santiago 114, Apdo 764, Santo Domingo, DN; tel. 688-6016; fax 686-6364; e-mail iglepidom@verizon.net.do; internet episcopaldominican.org.

Other Christian Churches

Church of Jesus Christ of Latter-Day Saints (Mormons): Avda Bolívar 825, Los Robles, Santo Domingo, DN; tel. 731-2078; internet www.lds.org; 124,435 mems.

BAHÁ'Í FAITH

Bahá'í Community of the Dominican Republic: Cambronal 152, esq. Beller, Santo Domingo, DN; tel. 687-1726; fax 687-7606; e-mail bahai.rd.aen@verizon.net.do; internet www.bahai.org.do; f. 1961; 402 localities.

The Press

DAILIES

El Caribe: Calle Doctor Defilló 4, Los Prados, Apdo 416, Santo Domingo, DN; tel. 683-8100; fax 544-4003; e-mail editora@elcaribe.com.do; internet www.elcaribe.com.do; f. 1948; morning; Pres. FÉLIX M. GARCÍA; Dir OSVALDO SANTANA; circ. 32,000.

El Día: Avda San Martín 236, Santo Domingo, DN; tel. 565-5581; fax 540-1697; e-mail eldia@eldia.com.do; internet www.eldia.com.do; f. 2002; Dir RAFAEL MOLINA MORILLO; Editor FRANKLIN PUELLO.

Diario Libre: Avda Abraham Lincoln, esq. Max Henríquez Ureña, Apdo 20313, Santo Domingo, DN; tel. 476-7200; fax 616-1520; internet www.diariolibre.com; Dir ADRIANO MIGUEL TEJADA.

Dominican Today: Avda Abraham Lincoln 452, Local 220B, Plaza La Francesa, Piantini, Santo Domingo, DN; tel. 334-6386; e-mail jorge.pineda@dominicantoday.com; internet www.dominicantoday.com; online, English language; Editor-in-Chief JORGE PINEDA.

Hoy: Avda San Martín 236, Santo Domingo, DN; tel. 565-5581; fax 567-2424; e-mail periodicohoy@hoy.com.do; internet www.hoy.com.do; f. 1981; morning; Dir ALVAREZ VEGA; Man. Editors CLAUDIO ACOSTA, MARIEN CAPITÁN; circ. 40,000.

La Información: Carretera Licey, Km 3, Santiago de los Caballeros; tel. 581-1915; fax 581-7770; e-mail lainformacion@lainformacion.com.do; internet lainformacion.com.do; f. 1915; morning; Dir EMMANUEL CASTILLO; Editor-in-Chief SERVIO CEPEDA; circ. 15,000.

Listín Diario: Paseo de los Periodistas 52, Ensanche Miraflores, Santo Domingo, DN; tel. 686-6688; fax 686-6595; e-mail info@listindiario.com.do; internet www.listin.com.do; f. 1889; morning; bought in mid-2010; Dir-Gen. MIGUEL FRANJUL; Editor-in-Chief FABIO CABRAL; circ. 60,000.

El Nacional: Avda San Martín 236, Santo Domingo, DN; tel. 565-5581; fax 565-4190; e-mail elnacional@elnacional.com.do; internet www.elnacional.com.do; f. 1966; evening and Sun.; Dir RADHAMÉS GÓMEZ PEPÍN; circ. 45,000.

El Nuevo Diario: Avda Francia 41, Santo Domingo, DN; tel. 687-7450; fax 687-3205; e-mail redaccionnd@gmail.com; internet www.elnuevodiario.com.do; f. 1981; morning; Exec. Dir COSETTE BONNELLY; Editor LUIS BRITO.

PERIODICALS

Arquitexto: Gustavo Mejía Ricart 37, 6°, Ensanche Naco, Apdo 560, Santo Domingo, DN; tel. 732-7674; e-mail arquitexto@arquitexto.com; internet arquitexto.com; f. 1985; 4 a year; architecture; Editor CARMEN ORTEGA.

La Casa: Avda Abraham Lincoln 708, esq. Max Henríquez Ureña, Ensanche Piantini, Apdo 20313, Santo Domingo, DN; tel. 476-3022; e-mail lacasa@revistalacasa.com; internet www.revistalacasa.com; f. 1998; architecture and interior design; Dir BEATRIZ BIENZOBAS.

Gestión: Torre Piantini, Suite 903, Avda Abraham Lincoln, esq. Gustavo Mejía Ricart, Santo Domingo, DN; tel. 542-0126; fax 540-1982; e-mail info@gestion.com.do; internet www.gestion.com.do; f. 2008; Dir-Gen. NEY DIAZ; Editor VIRGINIA DE MOYA.

Novus Dominicana: Calle Gaspar Polanco, 258 Torre Malaquias II, Suite 5-B-Bella Vista, Santo Domingo, DN; tel. 289-2022; fax 341-8877; e-mail info@novusmagazine.com; internet www.novusdominicana.com; Gen. Man DAVIDE VIANELLO.

Pandora: Calle Doctor Defilló 4, Los Prados, Apdo 416, Santo Domingo, DN; tel. 683-8504; fax 544-4003; e-mail pandora@elcaribe.com.do; internet www.pandora.com.do; f. 2003; 2 a month; Dir and Editor AIRAM TORIBIO.

Refugios: Edif. Tres Robles, Calle Freddy Prestol Castillo 23, Apto 1-C, Piantini, Santo Domingo, DN; tel. and fax 732-0421; e-mail info@coralcomunicaciones.com; internet www.refugiosmagazine.com; f. 2007; 6 a year; travel; Pres. LAURA DE LA NUEZ.

Revista Social Sports: Avda Imbert, esq. Pedro Casado, La Vega; tel. 242-4887; e-mail revistasocialsports@gmail.com; internet www.revistasocialsports.com; monthly; Exec. Dir JOSÉ LUIS BAUTISTA.

Visión Agropecuaria: Autopista Duarte, Km 6.5, Los Jardines del Norte, Santo Domingo, DN; tel. 547-1193; e-mail visionagropecuaria27@gmail.com; newsletter of the Ministry of Agriculture; 6 a year; Dir WILFREDO POLANCO; Editor ANTONIO CÁCERES.

Publishers

Editora Alfa y Omega: José Contreras 69, Santo Domingo, DN; tel. 532-5578; e-mail alfayomega.editora@gmail.com; f. 1976.

Editora El Caribe, C por A: Calle Doctor Defilló 4, Los Prados, Apdo 416, Santo Domingo, DN; tel. 683-8100; fax 544-4003; e-mail editora@elcaribe.com.do; internet www.elcaribe.com.do; f. 1948; Pres. FÉLIX GARCÍA.

Editora Hoy, C por A: Avda San Martín 436, Santo Domingo, DN; tel. 566-1147.

Editorama, SA: Calle Eugenio Contreras, No 54, Los Trinitarios, Apdo 2074, Santo Domingo, DN; tel. 596-6669; fax 594-1421; e-mail editorama@editorama.com; internet www.editorama.com; f. 1970; Pres. JUAN ANTONIO QUIÑONES MARTE.

Grupo Editorial Norma: Calle D, Zona Industrial de Herrera, Santo Domingo, DN; tel. 274-3333; e-mail editoranorma@codetel.net.do; internet www.norma.com.do.

Grupo Editorial Oceano: Edif. Calidad a Tiempo, 2°, Calle J, esq. Calle L, Zona Industrial de Herrera, Santo Domingo, DN; tel. 537-0832; fax 537-5187; e-mail info@oceano.com.do; internet www.oceano.com; Pres. JOSÉ LLUIS MONREAL.

Publicaciones Ahora, C por A: Avda San Martín 236, Apdo 1402, Santo Domingo, DN; tel. 565-5580; fax 565-4190; Pres. JULIO A. MORENO.

ASSOCIATIONS

Asociación Dominicana de Libreros y Afines (Asodolibro): Calle Espaillat 201, entre El Conde y Arzobispo Nou, Santo Domingo, DN; tel. 688-8425; fax 689-3865; e-mail asodolibro@codetel.net.do; Pres. DENNIS PEÑA.

Cámara Dominicana del Libro, Inc: Arzobispo Nouel 160, Santo Domingo, DN; tel. 682-1032; fax 686-6110; e-mail camaradominicanadellibro@hotmail.com; internet www.camaradominicanadellibro.com; f. 1970; Pres. URIBE VIRTUES; Sec. JACQUELINE DÍAZ.

Broadcasting and Communications

REGULATORY AUTHORITY

Instituto Dominicano de las Telecomunicaciones (INDOTEL): Avda Abraham Lincoln, No 962, Edif. Osiris, CP 10148, Santo Domingo, DN; tel. 732-5555; fax 732-3904; e-mail info@indotel.gob.do; internet www.indotel.org.do; f. 1998; Chair. GEDEÓN SANTOS; Exec. Dir TERESITA BENCOSME DE UREÑA.

TELECOMMUNICATIONS

Compañía Dominicana de Teléfonos, C por A (Claro—Codetel): Avda John F. Kennedy 54, Apdo 1377, Santo Domingo, DN; tel. 220-1111; fax 543-1301; e-mail servicioalcliente@codetel.net.do; internet www.codetel.net.do; f. 1930; owned by América Móvil, SA de CV (Mexico); operates mobile services as Claro and fixed-line services as Codetel; 51% of mobile market; Pres. OSCAR PEÑA CHACÓN.

Orange Dominicana, SA: Calle Víctor Garrido Puello 23, Edif. Orange, Ensanche Piantini, Santo Domingo, DN; tel. 859-1000; fax 539-8454; e-mail servicio.cliente@orange.com.do; internet www.orange.com.do; f. 2000; mobile cellular telephone operator; subsidiary of Orange, SA (France); 38% of mobile market; Pres. JEAN MARC HARION.

Tricom Telecomunicaciones de Voz, Data y Video: Avda Lope de Vega 95, Ensanche Naco, Santo Domingo, DN; tel. 476-6000; fax 476-6700; e-mail sc@tricom.com.do; internet www.tricom.net; f. 1992; 3% of mobile market; Pres. and CEO HÉCTOR CASTRO NOBOA; Gen. Man. CARLOS ESCOBAR.

VIVA (Trilogy Dominicana, SA): Edif. Carib Alico, 3°, Avda Abraham Lincoln 295, Sector La Julia, Santo Domingo, DN; internet www.viva.com.do; f. 2008; mobile cellular telephone network and internet provider; 7.4% of mobile market.

BROADCASTING

Radio

The government-owned broadcasting network, Corporación Estatal de Radio y Televisión, operates three radio stations. There were some 130 commercial stations in the Dominican Republic.

Asociación Dominicana de Radiodifusoras Inc (ADORA): Calle Paul Harris 3, Centro de los Héroes, Santo Domingo, DN; tel. 535-4057; fax 535-4058; e-mail adora.org.do@gmail.com; internet adora-do.blogspot.com; f. 1967; Pres. Sandra Pons.

Cadena de Noticias (CDN) Radio: Calle Doctor Defilló 4, Los Prados, Apdo 416, Santo Domingo, DN; tel. 683-8100; fax 544-4003; e-mail inforadio@cdn.com.do; internet www.cdn.com.do.

Zulu Radio: Isabel La Católica 7, Santo Domingo 10210, DN; tel. 686-0757; internet www.zulurd.com; f. 2010; Co-owners Auro Loviluz, Juan Carlos García.

Television

Antena Latina, Canal 7: Avda Gustavo Mejía Ricart 45, Ensanche Naco, Santo Domingo, DN; tel. 412-0707; fax 333-0707; e-mail contacto@antenalatina7.com; internet www.antenalatina7.com; f. 1999; owned by Grupo Sin; Pres. José Miguel Bonetti.

Cadena de Noticias (CDN) Televisión: Calle Doctor Defilló 4, Los Prados, Apdo 416, Santo Domingo, DN; tel. 262-2100; fax 567-2671; e-mail direccion@cdn.com.do; internet www.cdn.com.do; broadcasts news on Channel 37; Dir Fernando Hasbún.

Color Visión, Canal 9: Emilio A. Morel, esq. Luis Pérez, Ensanche La Fe, Apdo 30043, Santo Domingo, DN; tel. 566-5875; fax 732-9347; e-mail color.vision@colorvision.com.do; internet www.colorvision.com.do; f. 1969; majority-owned by Corporación Dominicana de Radio y Televisión; commercial station; Dir-Gen. Domingo Octavio Bermudez Madera.

Corporación Estatal de Radio y Televisión (CERTV): Dr Tejada Florentino 8, Apdo 869, Santo Domingo, DN; tel. 689-2120; e-mail rm.colombo@codetel.net.do; internet www.certvdominicana.com; f. 1952; fmrly Radio Televisión Dominicana, Canal 4; changed name as above in 2003; govt station; Channel 4; Pres. Eliseo Pérez; Dir-Gen. Pedro J. Batista Caba.

Teleantillas, Canal 2: Autopista Duarte, Km 7½, Los Prados, Apdo 30404, Santo Domingo, DN; tel. 567-7751; fax 540-4912; e-mail webmaster@tele-antillas.tv; internet www.tele-antillas.tv; f. 1979; Gen. Man. Héctor Valentín Báez.

Telecentro, Canal 13: Avda Luperón 25, Herrera, Santo Domingo, DN; tel. 334-3040; fax 274-0599; e-mail info@rnn.com.do; internet www.telecentro.com.do; f. 1986; Santo Domingo and east region; Pres. Nelson Guillén.

Telemedios Dominicanos, Canal 25: 16 de Agosto, Santo Domingo, DN; tel. 583-2525; internet www.canal25net.tv; f. 1999; Dir César Hernández.

Telemicro, Canal 5: Edif. Telemicro, Calle Mariano Cestero, esq. Enrique Henríquez 1, Gazcue, Santo Domingo, DN; tel. 689-0555; fax 686-6528; e-mail programacion@telemicro.com.do; internet www.telemicro.com.do; f. 1982; Dir Domingo del Pillar.

Telesistema, Canal 11: Avda 27 de Febrero 52, esq. Máximo Gómez, Sector Bergel, Santo Domingo, DN; tel. 563-6661; fax 472-1754; e-mail info@telesistema11.tv; internet www.telesistema11.tv; Pres. José L. Correpio Estrada.

Finance

(cap. = capital; res = reserves; dep. = deposits; m. = million; brs = branches; amounts in pesos)

BANKING

Supervisory Body

Superintendencia de Bancos: 52 Avda México, esq. Leopoldo Navarro, Apdo 1326, Santo Domingo, DN; tel. 685-8141; fax 685-0859; e-mail nmolina@supbanco.gov.do; internet www.supbanco.gov.do; f. 1947; Supt Rafael Camilo Abreu.

Central Bank

Banco Central de la República Dominicana: Calle Pedro Henríquez Ureña, esq. Leopoldo Navarro, Apdo 1347, Santo Domingo, DN; tel. 221-9111; fax 687-7488; e-mail info@bancentral.gov.do; internet www.bancentral.gov.do; f. 1947; cap. 2,371.3m., res 1.0m., dep. 312,156.4m. (Dec. 2009); Gov. Héctor Valdez Albizu; Man. Pedro Silverio Alvarez.

Commercial Banks

Banco BHD, SA: Avda 27 de Febrero, esq. Avda Winston Churchill, Santo Domingo, DN; tel. 243-3232; fax 567-67474949; e-mail servicio@bhd.com.do; internet www.bhd.com.do; f. 1972; cap. 6,964.2m., res 880m., dep. 1,366.5m. (Dec. 2011); Pres. Luis Eugenio Molina Achécar; Dir Jaime Sued; 80 brs.

Banco Dominicano del Progreso, SA (Progreso): Avda John F. Kennedy 3, Apdo 1329, Santo Domingo, DN; tel. 378-3233; fax 227-3107; e-mail informacion@progreso.com.do; internet www.progreso.com.do; f. 1974; merged with Banco Metropolitano, SA, and Banco de Desarrollo Dominicano, SA, in 2000; cap. 4,428.6m., res –408m., dep. 32,351.2m. (Dec. 2011); Pres. Mark Silverman; 20 brs.

Banco Múltiple Leon, SA: Avda John F. Kennedy 135, esq. Tiradentes, Apdo 1502, Santo Domingo, DN; tel. 947-7062; fax 947-7066; e-mail info@leon.com.do; internet www.leon.com.do; f. 1981; fmrly Banco Nacional de Crédito, SA; became Bancrédito, SA, in 2002; adopted current name Dec. 2003; cap. 2,986.3m., res 531m., dep. 36,687.7m. (Dec. 2011); Pres. and CEO Carlos Guillermo León; 56 brs.

Banco Popular Dominicano: Avda John F. Kennedy 20, Torre Popular, Apdo 1441, Santo Domingo, DN; tel. 544-5555; fax 544-5899; e-mail contactenos@bpd.com.do; internet www.bpd.com.do; f. 1963; cap. 9,317.3m., res 3,312.8m., dep. 153,494.4m. (Dec. 2010); Pres., Chair. and Gen. Man. Manuel Alejandro Grullón; 187 brs.

Banco de Reservas de la República Dominicana (Banreservas): Isabel la Católica 201, Apdo 1353, Santo Domingo, DN; tel. 960-2000; fax 685-0602; e-mail mensajeadministrador@banreservas.com; internet www.banreservas.com.do; f. 1941; state-owned; cap. 3,500.0m., res 6,678.5m., dep. 96,012m. (Dec. 2009); Pres. Simón Lizardo Mézquita (Minister of Finance); Administrator Vicente Bengoa Albizu; 195 brs.

Scotiabank (Canada): Avda John F. Kennedy, esq. Lope de Vega, Apdo 1494, Santo Domingo, DN; tel. 567-7268; e-mail drinfo@scotiabank.com; internet www.scotiabank.com.do; f. 1920; Vice-Pres. and Gen. Man. Chiara Borrelli; 74 brs.

Development Banks

Banco ADEMI, SA: Avda Pedro Henríquez Ureña 78, La Esperilla, Santo Domingo, DN; tel. 683-0853; internet www.bancoademi.com.do; f. 1998; Pres. Rondón J. Guillermo.

Banco Agrícola de la República Dominicana: Avda G. Washington 601, Apdo 1057, Santo Domingo, DN; tel. 535-8088; fax 508-6212; e-mail bagricola@bagricola.gov.do; internet www.bagricola.gov.do; f. 1945; govt agricultural devt bank; Gen. Man. and Chair. Carlos Antonio Segura Foster.

Banco BDI, SA: Avda Sarasota 27, esq. La Julia, Santo Domingo, DN; tel. 535-8586; fax 535-8692; internet www.bdi.com.do; f. 1974; cap. 566.4m., res 38.6m., dep. 5,980m. (Dec. 2011); Pres. Juan Carlos Rodriguez Copello.

STOCK EXCHANGE

Bolsa de Valores de la República Dominicana, SA: Edif. Empresarial, 1°, Avda John F. Kennedy 16, Apdo 25144, Santo Domingo, DN; tel. 567-6694; fax 567-6697; e-mail info@bolsard.com; internet www.bolsard.com; Pres. María Antonia Esteva de Bisono; Gen. Man. Darys Estrella.

INSURANCE

Supervisory Body

Superintendencia de Seguros: Ministerio de Finanzas, Avda México 54, esq. Leopoldo Navarro, Apdo 2207, Santo Domingo, DN; tel. 221-2606; fax 685-5096; e-mail info@superseguros.gob.do; internet www.superseguros.gob.do; f. 1969; Supt Euclides Gutiérrez Félix.

Insurance Companies

Angloamericana de Seguros, SA: Avda Gustavo Mejía Ricard 8, esq. Hermanos Roque Martínez, Ensanche El Millón, Santo Domingo, DN; tel. 227-1002; fax 227-6005; e-mail angloseguros@angloamericana.com.do; internet www.angloamericana.com.do; f. 1996; Pres. Nelson Hedi Hernández P.; Vice-Pres. Esteban Betances Fabré.

ARS Palic Salud: Edif. ARS Palic Salud, Avda 27 de Febrero 50, Urb. El Vergel, Santo Domingo, DN; tel. 381-5000; fax 381-4646; e-mail servicios@arspalic.com.do; internet www.arspalic.com.do; fmrly Cía de Seguros Palic, SA; acquired by Centro Financiero BHD in 1998; changed name as above in 2003; Exec. Vice-Pres. Andrés Mejía.

Aseguradora Agropecuaria Dominicana, SA (AGRODOSA): Avda Independencia 455, Gazcue, Santo Domingo, DN; tel. 562-6849; fax 687-4790; e-mail agrodosa@claro.net.do; agricultural sector; Exec. Dir AGRON EMILIO OLIVO TORIBIO.

Atlántica Insurance, SA: Avda 27 de Febrero 365A, 2°, Apdo 826, Santo Domingo, DN; tel. 565-5591; fax 565-4343; e-mail atlanticains@codetel.net.do; Pres. RHINA RAMIREZ; Gen. Man. Lic. GERARDO PERALTA.

BMI Compañía de Seguros, SA: Edif. Alfonso Comercial, Avda Tiradentes 14, Apdo 916, Ensanche Naco, Santo Domingo, DN; tel. 562-6660; fax 562-6849; e-mail reclamos@bmi.com.do; internet www.bmi.com.do; f. 1998; Pres. FRANCISCO GARCÍA; Gen. Man. EFRÉN ORTIZ.

Bupa Dominicana,SA: Avda Lope de Vega 13, casi esq. Avda Roberto Pastoriza, Plaza Progreso Business Center, Suite 310, Santo Domingo, DN; tel. 566-7759; fax 565-6451; e-mail dr@bupalatinamerica.com; internet www.bupalatinamerica.com; fmrly Amedex Insurance Co; Gen. Man. INGRID REYNOSO.

Cía Dominicana De Seguros, C por A: Avda 27 de Febrero 302, Bella Vista, Santo Domingo, DN; tel. 535-1030; fax 533-2576; e-mail dominicana.seg@codetel.net.do; internet www.dominicanadeseguros.com; f. 1960; Pres. RAMÓN MOLINA; CEO VÍCTOR J. ROJAS.

La Colonial, SA: Avda Sarasota 75, Bella Vista, Santo Domingo, DN; tel. 508-8000; fax 508-0608; e-mail luis.guerrero@lacolonial.com.do; internet www.lacolonial.com.do; f. 1971; general; Pres. Dr MIGUEL FERIS IGLESIAS; Exec. Vice-Pres. LUIS EDUARDO GUERRERO ROMÁN.

Confederación del Canadá Dominicana: Calle Salvador Sturla 17, Ensanche Naco, Apdo 30088, Santo Domingo, DN; tel. 544-4144; fax 540-4740; e-mail confedom@codetel.net.do; internet www.confedom.com; f. 1988; Pres. Lic. MOISES A. FRANCO LLENAS.

Cooperativa Nacional De Seguros, Inc (COOP-SEGUROS): Calle Hermanos Deligne 156, Gazcue, Santo Domingo, DN; tel. 682-6118; fax 682-6313; e-mail contacto@coopseguros.coop; internet coopseguros.coop; f. 1990; functions as a co-operative; general and life; Pres. Dr IGNACION VALENZUELA.

Cuna Mutual Insurance Society Dominicana, C. por A: Edif. AIRAC, Avda Aristides Fiallo Cabral 258, Zona Universitaria, Santo Domingo, DN; tel. 682-2862; fax 687-2862; internet www.cunamutual.com.pr/rd; f. 2010; Regional Man. FRANCISCO ANTONIO ESTEPAN GRISANTY.

General de Seguros, SA: Avda Sarasota 55, esq. Pedro A. Bobea, Apdo 2183, Santo Domingo, DN; tel. 535-8888; fax 532-4451; e-mail info@gs.com.do; internet www.lageneraldeseguros.com; f. 1981; general; Pres. Dr FERNANDO A. BALLISTA DÍAZ.

Progreso Compañía de Seguros, SA (PROSEGUROS): Avda John F. Kennedy 1, Ensanche Miraflores, Santo Domingo, DN; tel. 985-5000; fax 985-5187; e-mail carlosro@progreso.com.do; internet www.proseguros.com.do; Pres. GONZALO ALBERTO PÉREZ ROJAS; CEO CARLOS ROMERO.

REHSA Compañía de Seguros y Reaseguros: Avda Gustavo Mejía Ricart, esq. Hermanas Roques Martínez, Ensanche El Millón, Santo Domingo, DN; tel. 548-7171; fax 584-7222; e-mail info@rehsa.com.do; internet www.rehsa.com.do; Pres. NELSON HERNÁNDEZ.

Scotia Seguros: Avda Francia No 141, esq. Máximo Gómez, 3°, Sección 2, Gazcue, Santo Domingo, DN; tel. 730-4031; fax 686-2165; e-mail info@scotiaseguros.com.do; internet www.scotiaseguros.com.do; f. 2006; fmrly BBVA Seguros; Gen. Man. DENIS LISANDRO BERROCAL.

Seguros BanReservas: Avda Jiménez Moya, esq. Calle 4, Centro Technológico Banreservas, Ensanche La Paz, Santo Domingo, DN; tel. 960-7200; fax 960-5148; e-mail serviseguros@segbanreservas.com; internet www.segurosbanreservas.com; Pres. VICENTE BENGOA ALBIZU; Vice-Pres. RAFAEL MEDINA.

Seguros Constitución: Calle Seminario 55, Ensanche Piantini, Santo Domingo, DN; tel. 620-0765; fax 412-2358; e-mail info@segurosconstitucion.com.do; internet www.segurosconstitucion.com.do; fmrly El Sol de Seguros; changed name as above in 2008; Exec. Vice-Pres. SIMÓN MAHFOUD MIGUEL; Gen. Man. JUAN JOSÉ GUERRERO GRILLASCA.

Seguros Pepín, SA: Edif. Corp. Corominas Pepín, Avda 27 de Febrero 233, Ensanche Naco, Santo Domingo, DN; tel. 472-1006; fax 565-9176; e-mail info@segurospepin.com; internet www.segurospepin.com; general; Pres. HÉCTOR COROMINAS PEÑA.

Seguros Universal: Avda Winston Churchill 1100, Evaristo Morales, Apdo 1242, Santo Domingo, DN; tel. 544-7200; fax 544-7999; e-mail servicioalcliente@universal.com.do; internet www.universal.com.do; f. 1964 as La Universal de Seguros; merged with Grupo Asegurador América in 2000; name changed as above in 2006; general; Pres. ERNESTO M. IZQUIERDO; Vice-Pres. MARINO GINEBRA.

Unión de Seguros, C por A: Edif. B 101, Avda John F. Kennedy, Apartamental Proesa, Santo Domingo, DN; tel. 566-2191; fax 542-0065; e-mail r.sanabia@uniondeseguros.com; internet uniondeseguros.com; f. 1964; Pres. JOSÉ A. PADILLA ORTIZ; Exec. Vice-Pres. FERNANDO R. HERNÁNDEZ.

Insurance Association

Cámara Dominicana de Aseguradores y Reaseguradores, Inc: Edif. Torre BHD, 5°, Luis F. Thomen, esq. Winston Churchill, Apdo 601, Santo Domingo, DN; tel. 566-0014; fax 566-2600; e-mail cadoar@codetel.net.do; internet www.cadoar.org.do; f. 1972; Pres. ERNESTO M. IZQUIERDO; Exec. Vice-Pres. MIGUEL VILLAMÁN.

Trade and Industry

GOVERNMENT AGENCIES

Comisión Nacional de Energía (CNE): Avda Rómulo Betancourt 361, Bella Vista, CP 10112, Santo Domingo, DN; tel. 540-9002; fax 547-2073; e-mail info@cne.gov.do; internet www.cne.gov.do; f. 2001; responsible for regulation and devt of energy sector; Pres. ENRIQUE RAMIREZ.

Comisión para la Reforma de la Empresa Pública: Edif. Gubernamental Dr Rafael Kasse Acta, 6°, Gustavo Mejía Ricart 73, esq. Agustín Lara, Ensanche Serrallés, Santo Domingo, DN; tel. 683-3591; fax 683-3114; e-mail info@fonper.gov.do; internet www.fonper.gov.do; commission charged with divestment and restructuring of state enterprises; Pres. JOSÉ AUGUSTO IZQUIERDO.

Consejo Estatal del Azúcar (CEA) (State Sugar Council): Calle Fray Cipriano de Utrera, Centro de los Héroes, Apdo 1256/1258, Santo Domingo, DN; tel. 533-1161; fax 533-1305; f. 1966; Dir-Gen. JOSÉ JOAQUÍN DOMÍNGUEZ PEÑA.

Instituto de Estabilización de Precios (INESPRE): Plaza de la Bandera, Apdo 86-2, Santo Domingo, DN; tel. 621-0020; fax 620-2588; e-mail informacion@inespre.gov.do; internet www.inespre.gov.do; f. 1969; price commission; Exec. Dir RICARDO JACOBO CABRERA.

Instituto Nacional de la Vivienda: Avda Pedro Henríquez Ureña, esq. Avda Alma Mater, Santo Domingo, DN; tel. 732-0600; fax 227-5803; e-mail invi@verizon.net.do; internet www.invi.gob.do; f. 1962; low-cost housing institute; Dir-Gen. ALMA FERNÁNADEZ DURÁN.

DEVELOPMENT ORGANIZATIONS

Centro para el Desarrollo Agropecuario y Forestal, Inc (CEDAF): Calle José Amado Soler 50, Ensanche Paraíso, CP 567-2, Santo Domingo, DN; tel. 565-5603; fax 544-4727; e-mail cedaf@cedaf.org.do; internet www.cedaf.org.do; f. 1987 to encourage the devt of agriculture, livestock and forestry; fmrly Fundación de Desarrollo Agropecuario, Inc; Pres. MARCIAL NAJRI; Exec. Dir JUAN JOSÉ ESPINAL.

Centro de Desarrollo y Competitividad Industrial (PROINDUSTRIA): Avda 27 de Febrero, esq. Avda Luperón, Plaza de las Banderas, Apdo 1462, Santo Domingo, DN; tel. 530-0010; fax 530-1303; e-mail info@proindustria.gov.do; internet www.proindustria.gov.do; f. 1962 as Corporación de Fomento Industrial; restructured and name changed as above in 2007; industrial sector regulator; Dir-Gen. ALEXANDRA IZQUIERDO.

Fundación Dominicana de Desarrollo (Dominican Development Foundation): Mercedes No 4, Apdo 857, Santo Domingo, DN; tel. 688-8101; fax 686-0430; e-mail info@fdd.org.do; internet fdd.org.do; f. 1962 to mobilize private resources for collaboration in financing small-scale devt programmes; 384 mems; Pres. ERNESTO ARMENTEROS CALAC; Exec. Dir FRANCISCO J. ABATE.

Instituto de Desarrollo y Crédito Cooperativo (IDECOOP): Avda Héroes de Luperón 1, Centro de los Héroes, Apdo 1371, Santo Domingo, DN; tel. 533-8131; fax 533-5149; e-mail idecoop@codetel.net.do; internet idecoop.gov.do; f. 1963 to encourage the devt of co-operatives; Pres. PEDRO CORPORÁN CABRERA; Dir CARLOS JUNIOR ESPINAL.

CHAMBERS OF COMMERCE

Cámara Americana de Comercio de la República Dominicana: Torre Empresarial, 6°, Avda Sarasota 20, Apdo 99999, Santo Domingo, DN; tel. 381-0777; fax 381-0286; e-mail amcham@codetel.net.do; internet www.amcham.org.do; Pres. JULIO V. BRACHE ALVAREZ; Exec. Vice-Pres. WILLIAM M. MALAMUD.

Cámara de Comercio y Producción de Santo Domingo: Avda 27 de Febrero 228, Torre Friusa, Sector La Esperilla, CP 10106, Santo Domingo, DN; tel. 682-2688; fax 685-2228; e-mail info@camarasantodomingo.do; internet www.camarasantodomingo.org.do; f. 1910; 1,500 active mems; Pres. PEDRO PEREZ GONZALEZ; Exec. Vice-Pres. FERNANDO FERRAN BRU.

INDUSTRIAL AND TRADE ASSOCIATIONS

Asociación Dominicana de Hacendados y Agricultores (ADHA): 265 Avda 27 de Febrero, al lado de Plaza Central, Santo Domingo, DN; tel. 565-0542; fax 565-8696; farming and agricultural org.; Pres. Ricardo Barceló.

Asociación Dominicana de la Industria Eléctrica (ADIE): Calle Gustavo Mejía Ricart, esq. Avda Abraham Lincoln, Torre Piantini, 5°, Local 502-B, Ensanche Piantini, Santo Domingo, DN; tel. 547-2109; e-mail info@adie.org.do; internet www.adie.org.do; f. 2009; electrical industry asscn; Pres. Otto González.

Asociación Dominicana de Zonas Francas Inc (ADOZONA): Avda Sarasota 20, 4°, Torre Empresarial AIRD, Apdo 3184, Santo Domingo, DN; tel. 472-0251; fax 472-0256; e-mail info@adozona.org; internet www.adozona.org; f. 1988; Pres. Aquíles Bermúdez; Exec. Vice-Pres. José Manuel Torres.

Asociación de Industrias de la República Dominicana, Inc: Avda Sarasota 20, Torre Empresarial AIRD, 12°, Santo Domingo, DN; tel. 472-0000; fax 472-0303; e-mail aird@verizon.net.do; internet www.aird.org.do; f. 1962; industrial org.; Pres. Ligia Bonetti de Valiente; Exec. Vice-Pres. Circe Almánzar Melgén.

Centro de Exportacióne e Inversión de la República Dominicana (CEI-RD): Avda 27 de Febrero, esq. Avda Gregorio Luperón, frente a La Plaza de la Bandera, Apdo 199-2, Santo Domingo, DN; tel. 530-5505; fax 530-8208; e-mail webmaster@cei-rd.gov.do; internet www.cei-rd.gov.do; fmrly Centro Dominicano de Promoción de Exportaciones (CEDOPEX); merged with Oficina para la Promoción de Inversiónes de la República Dominicana (OPI-RD) and changed name as above in 2003; promotion of exports and investments; Exec. Dir Eddy M. Martínez Manzueta.

Consejo Nacional de la Empresa Privada (CONEP): Avda Sarasota 20, Torre Empresarial, 12°, Ensanche La Julia, Santo Domingo, DN; tel. 472-7101; fax 472-7850; e-mail conep@conep.org.do; internet www.conep.org.do; Pres. Manuel Diez Cabral; Exec. Dir Rafael Paz Familia.

Consejo Nacional de Zonas Francas de Exportación (CNZFE): Edif. San Rafael, 5°, Avda Leopoldo Navarro 61, Apdo 21430, Santo Domingo, DN; tel. 686-8077; fax 686-8079; e-mail e.castillo@cnzfe.gob.do; internet www.cnzfe.gov.do; co-ordinating body for the free trade zones; Exec. Dir Luisa Fernández Durán.

Corporación Zona Franca Industrial de Santiago: Avda Mirador del Yaque, Santiago; tel. 575-1290; fax 575-1778; e-mail czfistgo@codetel.net.do; internet www.zonafrancasantiago.com; free zone park; Pres. Miguel Lama.

Dirección General de Minería: Edif. de Ofs Gubernamentales, 10°, Avda México, esq. Leopoldo Navarro, Santo Domingo, DN; tel. 685-8191; fax 686-8327; e-mail direc.mineria@verizon.net.do; internet www.dgm.gov.do; f. 1947; govt mining and hydrocarbon org.; Dir-Gen. Octavio López.

Instituto Agrario Dominicano (IAD): Avda 27 de Febrero, Plaza la Bandera, Santo Domingo, DN; tel. 620-6585; fax 620-1537; e-mail info@iad.gob.do; internet www.iad.gob.do; Exec. Dir Juan Rodríguez Ramírez.

Instituto Azúcarero Dominicano (INAZUCAR): Avda Jiménez Moya, Apdo 667, Santo Domingo, DN; tel. 532-5571; fax 533-2402; e-mail inst.azucar2@codetel.net.do; internet www.inazucar.gov.do; f. 1965; sugar institute; Exec. Dir José Casimiro Ramos Calderón.

Instituto de Innovación en Biotecnología e Industria (INDOTEC): Calle Olof Palme, esq. Núñez de Cáceres, San Gerónimo, Apdo 392-2, Santo Domingo, DN; tel. 566-8121; fax 227-8808; e-mail servicio@iibi.gov.do; internet www.iibi.gov.do; fmrly Instituto Dominicano de Tecnología Industrial (INDOTEC); name changed as above in 2005; Pres. Juan Antonio Ovalles Pérez; Exec. Dir Dra Bernarda A. Castillo.

EMPLOYERS' ORGANIZATIONS

Confederación Patronal de la República Dominicana (COPARDOM): Avda Abraham Lincoln, esq. Avda Gustavo Mejía Ricart 1003, Torre Profesional Biltmore I, Suite 501, Santo Domingo, DN; tel. 683-0013; fax 566-0879; e-mail copardom@copardom.org; internet www.copardom.org; f. 1946; Pres. Jaime O. González; Exec. Dir Pedro R. Rodríguez Velázquez.

Federación Dominicana de Comerciantes: Carretera Sánchez Km 10, Santo Domingo, DN; tel. 533-2666; Pres. Ivan García.

UTILITIES

Regulatory Authority

Superintendencia de Electricidad: Avda John F. Kennedy 3, esq. Erick Leonard Eckman, Arroyo Hondo, Santo Domingo, DN; tel. 683-2500; fax 544-1637; e-mail sie@sie.gov.do; internet www.sie.gov.do; f. 2001; Pres. Eduardo Quincoces Batista.

Electricity

AES Dominicana: Torre Acrópolis, 23°, Santo Domingo, DN; tel. 955–2223; e-mail infoaesdominicana@aes.com; internet www.aesdominicana.com.do; f. 1997; subsidiary of AES Corpn, USA; largest private electricity generator in the Dominican Republic (300 MW); Pres. Marco de la Rosa.

Corporación Dominicana de Empresas Eléctricas Estatales (CDEEE): Edif. Principal CDE, Centro de los Héroes, Avda Independencia, esq. Fray C. de Utrera, Apdo 1428, Santo Domingo, DN; tel. 535-9098; fax 533-7204; e-mail info@cdeee.gov.do; internet www.cdeee.gov.do; f. 1955; state electricity co; partially privatized in 1999, renationalized in 2003; Pres. Armando Peña Castillo; Exec. Vice-Pres. Rubén Bichara.

EDE Este, SA (Empresa Distribuidora de Electricidad del Este): Avda Sábana Larga 1, esq. San Lorenzo, Los Mina, Santo Domingo, DN; tel. 788-2373; fax 788-2595; e-mail infoedeeste@edeeste.com.do; internet www.edeeste.com.do; f. 1999; state-owned electricity distributor; Gen. Man. Francisco Leiva Landabur.

EDENORTE Dominicana, SA (Empresa Distribuidora de Electricidad del Norte): internet www.edenorte.com.do; f. 1999; state-owned electricity distributor; Gen. Man. Eduardo Saavedra Pizarro.

EDESUR Dominicana, SA (Empresa Distribuidora de Electricidad del Sur): Calle Carlos Sánchez y Sánchez, esq. Avda Tiradentes, Torre Serrano, Santo Domingo, DN; tel. 683-9292; internet www.edesur.com.do; f. 1999; state-owned electricity distributor; Man. Marcelo Rogelio Silva Iribarne.

Empresa de Generación Hidroeléctrica Dominicana (EGEHID): Avda Rómulo Betancourt 303, Bella Vista, Santo Domingo, DN; tel. 533-5555; fax 535-7472; e-mail administrador@hidroelectrica.gob.do; internet www.hidroelectrica.gob.do; distributor of hydroelectricity; Pres. Johnny Jones; Dir Victor G. Ventura Hernández.

Unidad de Electrificación Rural y Suburbana (UERS): Avda José Andrés Aybar Castellanos 136, Ensanche La Esperilla, Santo Domingo, DN; tel. 227-7666; e-mail info@uers.gov.do; internet www.uers.gov.do; f. 2006; manages supply of electricity to rural areas; Pres. Julio César Berroa Espaillat; Dir-Gen. Thelma María Eusebio.

Gas

AES Andrés: Santo Domingo, DN; internet www.aes.com; f. 2003; subsidiary of AES Corpn (USA); 3 generation facilities; 1 gas-fired plant and 1 liquefied natural gas terminal, 319-MW in Andrés and 236-MW in Los Mina; 1 coal-fired plant in Itabo; Pres. Andrew Vesey.

Water

Corporación del Acueducto y Alcantarillado de Santo Domingo: Calle Euclides Morillo 65, Arroyo Hondo, Santo Domingo, DN; tel. 562-3500; fax 541-4121; e-mail info@caasd.gov.do; internet www.caasd.gov.do; f. 1973; Dir Freddy Pérez.

Instituto Nacional de Aguas Potables y Alcantarillado (INAPA): Edif. Inapa, Centro Comercial El Millón, Calle Guarocuya, Apdo 1503, Santo Domingo, DN; tel. 567-1241; fax 567-8972; e-mail info@inapa.gob.do; internet www.inapa.gob.do; Exec. Dir Mariano Germán.

Instituto Nacional de Recursos Hidráulicos: Avda Jiménez de Moya, Centro de los Héroes, Santo Domingo, DN; tel. 532-3271; fax 532-2321; internet www.indrhi.gov.do; f. 1965; Exec. Dir Francisco Tomas Rodríguez.

TRADE UNIONS

Confederación Autónoma de Sindicatos Clasistas (CASC) (Autonomous Confederation of Trade Unions): Juan Erazo 14, Villa Juana, 4°, Santo Domingo, DN; tel. 687-8533; fax 689-1439; e-mail cascnacional@codetel.net.do; f. 1962; supports PRSC; Sec.-Gen. Gabriel del Río.

Confederación Nacional de Trabajadores Dominicanos (CNTD) (National Confederation of Dominican Workers): Calle José de Jesús Ravelo 56, Villa Juana, 2°, Santo Domingo, DN; tel. 221-2117; fax 221-3217; e-mail cntd@codetel.net.do; f. 1988 by merger; 11 provincial federations totalling 150 unions are affiliated; Sec.-Gen. Jacobo Ramos; c. 188,000 mems.

Confederación Nacional de Unidad Sindical (CNUS): Edif. Centrales Sindicales, Calle Juan Erazo 14, Villa Juana, Santo Domingo, DN; tel. 221-2158; fax 689-1248; e-mail cnus@verizon.net.do; internet www.cnus.org.do; Pres. Rafael (Pepe) Abreau.

Federación Dominicana de Trabajadores de Zona Francas, Industrias Diversas y de Servicios (FEDOTRAZONAS): Edif. Centrales Sindicales, 1°, Calle Juan Erazo 14, Villa Juana, Santo Domingo, DN; tel. 686-8140; fax 685-2476; e-mail info@

fedotrazonas.org; internet fedotrazonas.org; f. 2002; 10 affiliate trade unions; Sec.-Gen. YGNACIO HERNÁNDEZ HICIANO.

Confederación de Trabajadores Unitaria (CTU) (United Workers' Confederation): Edif. de las Centrales Sindicales, Luis Manuel Caceres (Tunti) 222, 3°, Villa Juana, Santo Domingo, DN; tel. 565-0881; e-mail ctu01@codetel.net.do; internet ctu.com.do; f. 1991; Sec.-Gen. EUGENIO PÉREZ CÉSPEDES.

Transport

Oficina por la Reordenamiento de Transporte (OPRET): Avda Máximo Gómez esq. Reyes Católicos, Antigua Cementera, Santo Domingo, DN; tel. 732-2670; fax 563-0199; internet www.opret.gov.do; f. 2005 to oversee devt and modernization of the transport system.

RAILWAYS

The Government invested US $50m.–$100m. in the installation of an underground railway system in Santo Domingo. The first line—14.5 km in length, between Villa Mella and Centro de los Héroes—entered into service in 2009. The completed network was to have a total length of some 60 km. In 2011 the legislature approved funding for a second line, to run for 32 km between Los Alcarrizos and the Francisco del Rosario Sánchez bridge.

Metro de Santo Domingo: Edif. RS, 1°, Avda 27 de Febrero 328, Santo Domingo, DN; internet metro.gob.do; f. 2008; 1 line currently in operation, north–south between Villa Mella and Centro de los Héroes; second line, east–west between Los Alcarrizos and the Francisco del Rosario Sánchez bridge, under construction.

ROADS

In 2005 there were an estimated 17,000 km of roads, of which about 6,225 km were paved. There is a direct route from Santo Domingo to Port-au-Prince in Haiti. The Coral Highway, a four-lane motorway linking Santo Domingo with Punta Cana, was inaugurated in 2012, at an estimated cost of US $400m. A further 22-km highway between San Pedro and La Romana was opened in late 2013.

Autoridad Metropolitana de Transporte (AMET): Avda Expreso V Centenario, esq. Avda San Martín, Santo Domingo, DN; tel. 686-8469; fax 686-6766; e-mail info@amet.gov.do; internet www.amet.gov.do; Dir-Gen. Maj.-Gen. JOSÉ ANIBAL SANZ JIMINIAN.

Dirección General de Carreteras y Caminos Vecinales: Avda San Cristóbal, esq. Avda Tiradentes, Ensanche la Fe, Santo Domingo, DN; tel. 565-2811; fax 567-5470; f. 1987; operated by the Ministry of Public Works and Communications.

SHIPPING

The Dominican Republic has 14 ports, of which Río Haina is by far the largest, handling about 80% of imports. Other important ports are Boca Chica, Santo Domingo and San Pedro de Macorís on the south coast, and Puerto Plata in the north. The Caucedo port and transshipment centre was specifically for use by free trade zone businesses. In December 2013 the Dominican Republic's flag registered fleet comprised 38 vessels, with an aggregate displacement of some 14,435 grt.

Agencias Navieras B&R, SA: Avda Abraham Lincoln 504, Apdo 1221, Santo Domingo, DN; tel. 793-7000; fax 562-3383; e-mail ops@navierasbr.com; internet www.navierasbr.com; f. 1919; shipping agents and export services; Man. JEFFREY RANNIK.

Autoridad Portuaria Dominicana: Avda Máximo Gómez, Santo Domingo, DN; tel. 687-4772; fax 687-2661; internet www.apordom.gov.do; Pres. VÍCTOR DÍAZ RÚA; Exec. Dir RAMÓN RIVAS.

Frederic Schad, Inc: José Gabriel García 26, Apdo 941, Santo Domingo, DN; tel. 221-8000; fax 688-7696; e-mail mail@fschad.com; internet www.fschad.com; f. 1922; logistics and shipping agent; Pres. FEDERICO SCHAD.

Maersk Dominicana, SA: Calle J. A. Soler 49, Santo Domingo, DN; tel. 732-1234; fax 566-5950; e-mail crbcsegen@maersk.com; internet www.maerskline.com; f. 1995; Gen. Man. MANUEL ALEJANDRO TERRERO.

Naviera Ebenezer, C por A: Los Charamicos, Sosua, Puerto Plata; tel. 875-9704; fax 571-4258; e-mail navieraebenezer@hotmail.com; Pres. MIGUEL A. DÌAZ.

CIVIL AVIATION

There are eight international airports, two at Santo Domingo, and one each at Puerto Plata, Punta Cana, Santiago, La Romana, Samaná and Barahona. The regional airline LIAT (see Antigua and Barbuda) provides scheduled services. Air Europe increased its services to Santo Domingo from mid-2013.

Instituto Dominicano de Aviación Civil: Avda México, esq. Avda 30 de Marzo, Apdo 1180, Santo Domingo, DN; tel. 221-7909; fax 221-6220; e-mail info@idac.gov.do; internet www.idac.gov.do; f. 1955 as Dirección General de Aeronáutica Civil; govt supervisory body; Dir-Gen. DR ALEJANDRO HERRERA RODRIGUEZ.

Aerodomca (Aeronaves Dominicanas): Joaquín Balaguer Int. Airport, El Higuero La Isabela, Santo Domingo, DN; tel. 826-4141; fax 826-4065; e-mail ventas@aerodomca.com; internet www.aerodomca.com; f. 1980; charter flights within the Caribbean.

Caribair (Caribbean Atlantic Airlines): Aeropuerto Internacional La Isabela, Santo Domingo, DN; tel. 826-4444; fax 826-4063; e-mail info@caribair.com.do; internet www.caribair.com.do; f. 1983; scheduled flights to Aruba, Haiti, and domestic and regional charter flights; CEO RAFAEL ROSADO FERMIN.

Servicios Aéreos Profesionales (SAP): Dr Joaquín Balaguer International Airport, La Isabela, Santo Domingo, DN; tel. 826-4117; fax 372-8817; e-mail comercial@sapair.com; internet www.sapair.com; f. 1981; charter flights to Central America, the Caribbean and the USA; Pres. JOSE MIGUEL PATIN.

VOLAIR Líneas Aéreas del Caribe, SA: Dr Joaquín Balaguer International Airport, Santo Domingo, DN; tel. 826-4068; fax 826-4071; e-mail info@govolair.com; internet www.govolair.com; f. 2004; charter flights.

Tourism

The total number of visitors to the Dominican Republic in 2012 was 5,047,021. In that year receipts from tourism, excluding passenger transport, totalled a provisional US $4,549m.

Asociación Dominicana de Agencias de Viajes y Turismo (ADAVIT): Calle Padre Billini 263, Apdo 2097, Santo Domingo, DN; tel. 221-4343; fax 685-2577; e-mail adavit@codetel.net.do; f. 1963; Pres. EDISON UREÑA; Sec. ANA KATINGO SANTELISES DE LATOUR; 126 mems.

Asociación de Hoteles y Turismo de la República Dominicana, Inc (ASONAHORES): Edif. La Cumbre, 8°, Calle Presidente González, esq. Avda Tiradentes, Ensanche Naco, Santo Domingo, DN; tel. 368-4676; fax 368-5566; e-mail asonahores@asonahores.com; internet www.asonahores.com; f. 1962; asscn of private orgs; includes the Consejo de Promoción Turística; Pres. LUIS EMILIO RODRÍGUEZ AMIAMI.

Corporación de Fomento de la Industria Hotelera y Desarrollo del Turismo (CORPHOTELS): Avda México, esq. 30 de Marzo, Ofs Gubernamentales, Santo Domingo, DN; tel. 688-3417; fax 689-3907; internet corphotels.com; f. 1969; promotes the hotel industry and tourism in general; state-run; Dir BIENVENIDO PÉREZ.

Defence

As assessed at November 2013, the Dominican Republic's armed forces numbered an estimated 46,000: army 26,000, navy 10,000 (including naval infantry), air force 10,000. There were also paramilitary forces numbering 15,000. Military service is voluntary and lasts for four years. In February 2012 it was announced that a US naval station was to be constructed on the island of Saona.

Defence Expenditure: The budget allocation for 2013 was an estimated RD $15,100m.

Minister of the Armed Forces and General Chief of Staff: Vice-Adm. SIGFRIDO PARED PERÉZ.

Commander-Gen. of the Army: Maj.-Gen. RUBÉN DARÍO PAULINO SEM.

Commander-Gen. of the Navy: Vice-Adm. EDWIN R. DOMINICI ROSARIO.

Commander-Gen. of the Air Force: Maj.-Gen. RAMÓN M. HERNÁNDEZ Y HERNÁNDEZ.

Education

Education is, where possible, compulsory for children between the ages of six and 14 years. Primary education commences at the age of six and lasts for eight years. Secondary education lasts for four years. In 2012 enrolment at primary level included 87% of children in the relevant age-group, while secondary enrolment included 62% of children in the relevant age-group (males 58%, females 66%). In 2010/11 some 1,310,199 pupils attended primary schools and 898,690 students attended secondary schools. There were 31 higher education institutions recognized by the National Council for Higher Education, Science and Technology. Budgetary expenditure on education in 2012 was RD $43,217m. (9.7% of total expenditure).

ECUADOR

Introductory Survey

LOCATION, CLIMATE, LANGUAGE, RELIGION, FLAG, CAPITAL

The Republic of Ecuador lies on the west coast of South America. It is bordered by Colombia to the north, by Peru to the east and south, and by the Pacific Ocean to the west. The Galápagos Islands, about 960 km (600 miles) off shore, form part of Ecuador. The climate is affected by the Andes mountains, and the topography ranges from the tropical rainforest on the coast and in the Oriente (the eastern region) to the tropical grasslands of the central valley and the permanent snowfields of the highlands. The official language is Spanish, but Quechua, Shuar and other indigenous languages are very common. Almost all of the inhabitants profess Christianity, and some 90% are Roman Catholics. The national flag (proportions 1 by 2) has three horizontal stripes, of yellow (one-half of the depth), blue and red. The state flag has, in addition, the national emblem (an oval cartouche, showing Mount Chimborazo and a steamer on a lake, surmounted by a condor) in the centre. The capital is Quito.

CONTEMPORARY POLITICAL HISTORY

Historical Context

Ecuador was ruled by Spain from the 16th century until 1822, when it achieved independence as part of Gran Colombia. In 1830 Ecuador seceded and became a separate republic. A long-standing division between Conservatives (Partido Conservador), whose support was generally strongest in the highlands, and Liberals (Partido Liberal, subsequently Partido Liberal Radical), based in the coastal region, began in the 19th century. Until 1948 Ecuador's political life was characterized by a rapid succession of presidents, dictators and juntas. Between 1830 and 1925 the country was governed by 40 different regimes. From 1925 to 1948 there was even greater instability, with a total of 22 heads of state.

Domestic Political Affairs

Dr Galo Plaza Lasso, who was elected in 1948 and remained in power until 1952, was the first President since 1924 to complete his term of office. He created a climate of stability and economic progress. Dr José María Velasco Ibarra, who had previously been President in 1934–35 and 1944–47, was elected again in 1952 and held office until 1956. A 61-year history of Liberal Presidents was broken in 1956, when a Conservative candidate, Dr Camilo Ponce Enríquez, took office. He was succeeded in 1960 by Velasco, who campaigned as a non-party Liberal. In the following year, however, Velasco was deposed by a coup, and was succeeded by his Vice-President, Dr Carlos Julio Arosemena Monroy. The latter was himself deposed in 1963 by a military junta, led by Capt. (later Rear-Adm.) Ramón Castro Jijón, the Commander-in-Chief of the Navy, who became President. In 1966 the High Command of the Armed Forces dismissed the junta and installed Clemente Yerovi Indaburu, a wealthy business executive and a former Minister of Economics, as acting President. Yerovi was forced to resign when the Constituent Assembly proposed a new constitution that prohibited the intervention of the armed forces in politics. In November he was replaced as provisional President by Dr Otto Arosemena Gómez, who held office until the election of 1968, when Velasco returned from exile to win the presidency for the fifth time.

In 1970 Velasco, with the support of the army, suspended the Constitution and assumed dictatorial powers to confront a financial emergency. In 1972 he was overthrown for the fourth time by a military coup, led by Brig.-Gen. Guillermo Rodríguez Lara, the Commander-in-Chief of the Army, who proclaimed himself Head of State. In 1976 President Rodríguez resigned, and power was assumed by a three-man military junta, led by Vice-Adm. Alfredo Poveda Burbano. The new junta announced its intention to lead the country to a truly representative democracy. A national referendum approved a newly drafted Constitution in 1978 and Jaime Roldós Aguilera of the Concentración de Fuerzas Populares was elected President, taking office in August, when the Congreso Nacional (National Congress) was inaugurated and the new Constitution came into force. Roldós encountered antagonism from both the conservative sections of the Congress and the trade unions. In 1981 Roldós died and was replaced by the Vice-President, Dr Osvaldo Hurtado Larrea. Hurtado faced opposition from left-wing politicians and trade unions for his efforts to reduce government spending and from right-wing and commercial interests, which feared encroaching state intervention.

In 1983 the Government introduced a series of austerity measures, which met with immediate opposition from the trade unions and private sector employees. Discontent with the Government's performance was reflected in the results of the 1984 elections, when the ruling party, Democracia Popular-Unión Demócrata Cristiana (DP-UDC), lost support. León Febres Cordero, leader of the Partido Social Cristiano (PSC) and presidential candidate of the conservative Frente de Reconstrucción Nacional, unexpectedly defeated Dr Rodrigo Borja Cevallos of the left-wing Izquierda Democrática (ID).

The dismissal of the Chief of Staff of the Armed Forces, Lt-Gen. Frank Vargas Pazzos, brought about a military crisis in 1986. Vargas and his supporters barricaded themselves inside the Manta military base until they had forced the resignation of both the Minister of Defence and the army commander, who had been accused by Vargas of embezzlement. Vargas then staged a second rebellion at the military base where he had been detained. Troops loyal to the President made an assault on the base, captured Vargas and arrested his supporters. In January 1987 President Febres Cordero was abducted and, after being held for 11 hours, was released in exchange for Vargas, who was granted an amnesty. In July 58 members of the air force were sentenced to up to 16 years' imprisonment for involvement in the abduction of the President.

Borja of the ID won the 1988 presidential election, defeating Abdalá Bucaram Ortiz of the Partido Roldosista Ecuatoriano (PRE). Borja's prompt introduction of austerity measures aimed at addressing Ecuador's increasing economic problems, led to protest marches.

In May 1990 about 1,000 indigenous Indians marched into Quito to demand official recognition of the land rights and languages of the indigenous population and compensation from petroleum companies for environmental damage. In the following month the Confederación de Nacionalidades Indígenas del Ecuador (CONAIE) organized an uprising in seven Andean provinces. Roads were blockaded, *haciendas* occupied, and supplies to the cities interrupted. Following the arrest of 30 Indians, the rebels took military hostages. Faltering negotiations were resumed in February 1991, following the seizure by Indian groups in the Oriente of eight oil wells. As a result, the Government promised to consider the Indians' demands for stricter controls on the petroleum industry, and for financial compensation. In April 1992 several thousand Amazon Indians marched from the Oriente to Quito to demand that their historical rights to their homelands be recognized. In May Borja agreed to grant legal title to more than 1m. ha of land in the province of Pastaza to the Indians.

At legislative elections in May 1992 the PSC gained the highest number of seats in the enlarged Congress. The Partido Unidad Republicano (PUR), led by the former PSC presidential candidate, Sexto Durán Ballén, won the second highest number of seats, and was to govern with its ally, the Partido Conservador (PC). In the second round of the presidential election, Durán defeated Jaime Nebot Saadi of the PSC.

In September 1992 the Government's announcement of a programme of economic austerity measures prompted violent demonstrations in Quito and Guayaquil, as well as a general strike in May 1993. Legislation to privatize some 160 state companies and reduce the public sector by 100,000 employees was approved in August. The Government's decision to increase the price of fuel by more than 70% provoked violent demonstrations throughout the country and a general strike in early 1994. The unpopularity of Durán's PUR-PC governing alliance was demonstrated at mid-term congressional elections in May, when it won only nine of the 77 seats.

Environmental concerns regarding the exploitation of the Oriente by the petroleum industry continued during 1993. In November five Amazon Indian tribes began legal proceedings against the international company Texaco to claim compensation totalling US $1,500m. for its part in polluting the rainforest—see below. (It was estimated that some 17m. barrels of oil had been spilled during the company's 25 years of operations in the region.)

In August 1994 a national referendum on constitutional reform took place. All but one of the eight proposed reforms (which included measures to alter the electoral system and the role of the Congress, and the establishment of a bicameral legislature) were approved; however, only some 50% of eligible voters participated, of whom some 20% returned void ballot papers. At a further referendum in November 1995 all of the proposed changes were rejected; the result was widely regarded as a reflection of the Government's continued unpopularity.

In July 1995 the country was plunged into a serious political crisis when Vice-President Alberto Dahik admitted giving budgetary funds to opposition deputies in return for their support for the economic reform programme. Dahik resigned following the initiation of impeachment proceedings in October.

Political instability

An increasingly vocal and politically organized indigenous movement resulted in the strong performance of Freddy Ehlers, the candidate for the newly formed Movimiento Nuevo País—Pachakútik (MNPP), a coalition of Amerindian and labour groups, at the presidential election in May 1996. The MNPP also emerged as a significant new force in the legislature at the concurrent general election. At the second round presidential ballot Abdalá Bucaram Ortiz of the PRE unexpectedly defeated Nebot of the PSC.

Increases of up to 600% in the price of certain commodities and a climate of considerable dissatisfaction with the President's leadership prompted a general strike in January 1997. Unrest intensified in the capital as violent clashes erupted, and Bucaram was barricaded inside the presidential palace. On 6 February, at an emergency session, the Congress voted to dismiss the President on the grounds of mental incapacity (thus evading the normal impeachment requirements of a two-thirds' majority). A state of emergency was declared, and the erstwhile Speaker, Fabián Alarcón Rivera, assumed the presidency in an acting capacity, despite Vice-President Rosalia Arteaga's claim to be the legitimate constitutional successor to Bucaram. Confusion over the correct procedure led to fears of a military coup. Bucaram fled from the presidential palace on 9 February, and on the following day Arteaga was declared interim President. However, by 11 February Arteaga had resigned amid continued constitutional uncertainty, and Alarcón was reinstated as head of state. Alarcón announced a reorganization of cabinet portfolios (which included no members of the two largest parties in the Congress, the PSC and the PRE) and the creation of a commission to investigate allegations of corruption against Bucaram's administration. In March Bucaram's extradition from Panama (where he had been granted political asylum) was requested in order that he face charges of misappropriating some US $90m. of government funds. In May, in response to Bucaram's declaration that he intended to contest Ecuador's next presidential election, the legislature approved a motion to impose an indefinite ban on Bucaram's candidacy in any future ballot. (In 1998 the Supreme Court issued a four-year prison sentence, *in absentia*, to Bucaram for libel, and in 2001 he was indicted on corruption charges.)

At a national referendum in May 1997 some 76% of voters supported the decision to remove Bucaram from office and 68% supported the appointment of Alarcón as interim President. However, Alarcón's success in the plebiscite was undermined by the launch, in the following month, of an official congressional inquiry into allegations that drugs-traffickers had contributed to political party funds, and, particularly, to Alarcón's Frente Radical Alfarista.

In January 1998, following persistent pleas from international environmental and scientific organizations for greater protection of the Galápagos Islands, the Congress approved a law that aimed to preserve the islands' unique environment more effectively. An element of the law, providing for an extension of the marine reserve around the islands from 15 to 40 nautical miles, attracted intense criticism from powerful fishing interests in the country and was vetoed by Alarcón, prompting condemnation by environmentalists and small-scale fishing concerns.

At a presidential election in May 1998 the DP candidate and mayor of Quito, Jamil Mahuad Witt, emerged as the strongest contender and at the second round Mahuad narrowly defeated his closest rival, Alvaro Noboa Pontón of the PRE.

In March 1999 a substantial decrease in the value of the sucre led President Mahuad to declare a week-long bank holiday in an attempt to prevent the withdrawal of deposits and reduce the pressure on the currency. In addition, the Government announced an economic retrenchment programme to restore investor confidence and prevent economic collapse. Measures included an increase in fuel prices of up to 160%, tax rises, the partial freezing of bank accounts, and the planned privatization of certain state-owned companies. These prompted further protests and the resignation of the majority of the board of the Central Bank. The main opposition party, the PSC, refused to endorse the austerity programme, thus compelling the President to dilute the measures. In April the Government announced an economic revival plan, which included US $400m. in initial funding from the IMF.

In January 2000 Mahuad was forced to flee from the presidential palace following large-scale protests in Quito by thousands of mainly Indian demonstrators, supported by sections of the armed forces, who were angered by the President's perceived mismanagement of the economic crisis (especially his controversial decision to replace the sucre with the US dollar). A three-man council was established to oversee the country. However, Gen. Carlos Mendoza, the Chief of Staff of the Armed Forces, swiftly disbanded the council, and announced the appointment of former Vice-President Gustavo Noboa Bejerano as President. This move followed talks with US officials, who had warned that foreign aid to Ecuador would be curtailed if power was not restored to the elected Government. However, Indian activists, who had supported the short-lived council, continued to demonstrate against the assumption of the presidency by Noboa, whom they viewed as ideologically similar to Mahuad. In February four members of the armed forces, who allegedly participated in the events leading to Mahuad's removal from office, were charged with insurrection. The entire military high command was replaced in May, even though later that month the Congress approved an amnesty for military officers and civilians arrested in connection with the coup.

In August 2000 the governing coalition lost its majority in the Congress, endangering the proposed reform (also known as Trole 11) of the labour and petroleum sectors. Noboa resorted to presidential decree to promulgate the legislation, prompting CONAIE and trade unions to claim that the move was illegal. In January 2001 the Constitutional Tribunal upheld almost one-third of the objections against Trole 11, most notably declaring unconstitutional the clause concerning the proposed privatization of state companies.

Popular resentment against the Government erupted in early 2001 following significant increases in fuel prices and transport costs. Thousands of protesters occupied Quito and roadblocks were erected across the Andean highlands and the Amazon lowlands. In early 2002 indigenous and civic groups in the north-east of the country occupied petroleum refineries, halted construction of a new oil pipeline and blocked major roads, prompting President Noboa once again to declare a state of emergency.

No party won an overall majority in the legislative elections of October 2002. In the second round presidential ballot Lucio Gutiérrez Borbua (a former colonel who had been imprisoned for participating in the coup against President Mahuad in 2000), candidate of the Partido Sociedad Patriótica 21 de Enero—PSP and supported by the MNPP, defeated Alvaro Noboa Pontón (unsuccessful candidate in the 1998 presidential election and founder of the right-wing Partido Renovador Institucional Acción Nacional—PRIAN). During 2003 the new Government continuously failed to gain approval for its proposed reforms in the opposition-dominated legislature.

In December 2004 the Congress voted to replace 27 of the 31 members of the Supreme Court, in which, President Gutiérrez alleged, the PSC exerted undue influence. Most of the new judges were allied with, or were sympathetic to, the pro-Government parties. The replacement of the Supreme Court judges was condemned by opposition groups and foreign governments as unconstitutional. In April Bucaram returned to Ecuador after the new President of the Supreme Court, Guillermo Castro, a co-founder of the PRE, annulled his 1998 conviction. Castro claimed that Bucaram had been denied due process during his trial.

Proceedings were also suspended against former President Noboa and former Vice-President Dahik on the same grounds.

In response to a series of protests at the Government's increasingly authoritarian measures, Gutiérrez announced the dissolution of the Supreme Court in April 2005. None the less, shortly afterwards some 30,000 demonstrators surrounded the presidential palace to demand the President's resignation. On the following day the Congress voted almost unanimously to dismiss Gutiérrez from office (Gutiérrez claimed asylum in Brazil). Alfredo Palacio Gonzales, hitherto Vice-President, was subsequently appointed head of state. In late April the Congress voted to dismiss the judges of the Constitutional and Electoral Courts and in November new judges were appointed to the Supreme Court by an ostensibly independent selection panel.

During its first 10 months in office, Palacio's Government was extremely unstable, with 34 ministerial changes. Most notably, in September 2005 Mauricio Gándara resigned as Minister of Government and Police following criticism of his response to the occupation the previous month of petroleum production facilities in the provinces of Sucumbíos and Orellana. Protesters, demanding greater state control over the oil industry and more equitable distribution of its revenues, effectively suspended Ecuador's crude petroleum exports, leading to a state of emergency being declared in the two provinces and the deployment of troops to quell disorder. The occupations ceased at the end of August after Palacio pledged to revise contracts with foreign energy companies in order to increase the state's share of revenue and to allocate more petroleum revenue to social services in the two provinces.

Further unrest affected the petroleum sector in early 2006 when employees at refineries in Napo, Orellana and Sucumbíos began a strike over non-payment of their salaries and reiterated their demands for greater state control of the industry. In response, CONAIE organized a widely supported nationwide protest in solidarity with the oil workers and also to demand a referendum on government plans to negotiate a free trade agreement with the USA. The unrest prompted the resignation of the new Minister of Government and Police, Alfredo Castillo Bujase. Negotiations on the agreement with the USA were suspended in May after the Government revoked the contract of Occidental Petroleum of the USA and announced that it would confiscate its assets in Ecuador. The company announced its intention to seek US $1,000m. in damages by taking the matter to arbitration at the International Center for the Settlement of Investment Disputes in Washington, DC, USA.

The election of Rafael Correa

Presidential and legislative elections were held on 15 October 2006. Alvaro Noboa of the PRIAN, whose electoral pledges included increasing foreign investment and employment, won the largest share of the votes in the presidential ballot, although not enough to win outright. His opponent in the run-off election was former finance minister Rafael Correa, who had pledged to dissolve the Congress and to rewrite the Constitution, as well as to sever Ecuador's ties with the IMF and the World Bank and renegotiate its contracts with foreign petroleum companies. Correa emerged victorious, with 57% of the votes. The new President expressed his commitment to investing in Ecuador's social sector and to strengthening the country's ties with its neighbours, at the expense of its proposed free trade agreement with the USA. He declared that his first act as President would be to promulgate a referendum on the creation of a constituent assembly. PRIAN won the most seats in the congressional ballot. Correa's Alianza País, contesting the elections in alliance with the Partido Socialista—Frente Amplio coalition, failed to win any seats.

Tension between the newly elected Congress and the President emerged in January 2007, principally over Correa's campaign for a constituent assembly. The decision on whether to hold a referendum on the new institution rested with the election commission (Tribunal Supremo Electoral—TSE). However, following a series of protests by government supporters, the TSE handed responsibility for the decision over to the Congress. At the end of January thousands of demonstrators surrounded the legislature to demand that the deputies approve the referendum. In February, after a series of nationwide pro-Government demonstrations, the Congress finally approved Correa's proposal. The plebiscite was approved by the TSE at the beginning of March but without an amendment protecting the position of the Congress and the President demanded by parliament. Four days later the Congress filed a lawsuit against the referendum with the Constitutional Court, and voted to dismiss the President of the TSE, Jorge Acosta. The TSE immediately retaliated by suspending the rights of the 57 deputies who supported the lawsuit, all from the four opposition parties, for one year; as a result, the Congress, which was now inquorate, was forced to suspend its session. On 20 March, however, 21 alternates of the suspended deputies attended the congressional session, giving it a quorum and ending the impasse. In the referendum of 15 April the establishment of a constituent assembly was approved by 81.7% of voters.

A series of demonstrations took place in early 2007 at petroleum installations in the Oriente by community and indigenous groups demanding a greater share of the profits from foreign companies operating in the region. The protesters disrupted production at the facilities, and, consequently, in April Correa granted increased powers to the security forces to suppress further demonstrations around the country's oil installations. The protests continued, however, and in November the Minister of Government, Worship, Police and Municipalities, Gustavo Larrea, and President of PETROECUADOR, Carlos Pareja, were dismissed for failing to prevent further demonstrations, which had resulted in a 20% decrease in daily oil output. A state of emergency was introduced in the province of Orellana in order to safeguard oil production, which was responsible for generating some 35% of government revenue.

Meanwhile, in mid-2007 the Government announced its intention to seek compensation for leaving its petroleum reserves (estimated at some 920m. barrels) in the country's northern Amazonian region untouched. Several concerns, including the state oil companies of Venezuela, Brazil, Chile and the People's Republic of China, had been hoping to secure operating contracts in the Ishpingo-Tiputini-Tambococha (ITT) oil fields, which lie beneath the Yasuní national park, believed by scientists to have the highest biodiversity of any area in the world. Correa declared that, in the interests of the environment and the indigenous communities inhabiting the area, his Government would prefer to leave the reserves unexploited. Under the Yasuní-ITT Initiative, as it was called, Correa's Government requested a total of US $350m. per year (equivalent to some 50% of the estimated revenue of the oil) from the international community as compensation for leaving the oil, which was estimated at 20% of Ecuador's total petroleum reserves, in the ground. Correa's frustration at the alleged mismanagement of the project led to the resignation in early 2010 of the Minister of Foreign Affairs, Fander Falconí, who had been managing the scheme, and of five members of the government committee overseeing the fund. In August Falconí's replacement, Ricardo Patiño, signed an agreement with the UN Development Programme on the establishment of a trust fund for contributions from donor countries. The Government was by this stage seeking a total of $3,600m. over a 13-year period, with Patiño indicating that it would consider exploiting the reserves if an initial funding target of $100m. had not been met within 18 months. By the deadline of December 2011 the initial target had been met, with a total of $116m. received. By late 2012 the fund had reached an estimated $300m in pledges and donations. A poll conducted in that year showed that some 95% of Ecuadoreans believed that Yasuní should be preserved and protected in a similar way to the Galápagos Islands. However, by August 2013 Correa had signed a decree liquidating the fund, claiming it had attracted insufficient financial support, and in early October the National Assembly approved legislation allowing oil exploration to begin in Yasuní. The announcement prompted demonstrations in Quito and condemnation from environmental and indigenous groups. A letter signed by more than 100 scientists from 19 countries imploring the Government not to proceed with its plans to drill in Yasuní was delivered to the National Assembly in September. Campaigners announced their intention to garner the necessary 680,000 signatures on a petition to the Government (equivalent to 5% of the electorate), thereby triggering a national referendum on the issue.

In 2007 UNESCO added the Galápagos Islands to its 'in danger' list, stating that the World Heritage Site was seriously threatened by invasive species, growing tourism and associated immigration. Correa signed an emergency decree aimed at tackling the crisis, which included the expulsion of illegal workers from the islands. By June, however, Correa admitted that Ecuador had failed to protect the Galápagos; his statement followed the discovery of the shells of eight endangered Galápagos giant tortoises, killed by poachers, and led many environmental experts to question the Government's ability to protect the islands adequately. In June 2013 Correa announced the appointment of María Isabel Salvador, Ecuador's former ambassador to the Organization of American States (OAS, see p. 394) and a former senior cabinet member, as President of the Galapagos Provincial Council. Correa stated that Salvador's role would be to address the 'multiple problems' confronting the islands and to increase monitoring and enforcement efforts to ensure compliance with existing regulations aimed at protecting the Galápagos.

Elections to the Constituent Assembly took place on 30 September 2007, and resulted in a significant majority for Correa's Movimiento País. A draft constitution was approved by the Assembly in July 2008. The proposed constitution increased the executive power of the President, who was granted the ability to dissolve the legislature (which was to be renamed the Asamblea Nacional—National Assembly) and call new elections under specified circumstances; conversely, the National Assembly was given similar powers to dismiss the President. The judicial system was to be reformed, with the Supreme Court refounded as the National Court of Justice (Corte Nacional de Justicia) and a new Constitutional Court founded as the supreme judicial authority; moreover, the TSE was to be replaced by two bodies, namely a commission in charge of organizing elections and a court responsible for resolving electoral disputes. Substantial portions of the 444-article draft constitution were dedicated to defining civil rights and shaping economic and social policies; notably, state control of the economy was to be increased, with responsibility for setting monetary policy transferred from the Central Bank to the President. In addition, protection of the environment and natural resources was declared mandatory.

The new Constitution entered into force on 20 October 2008, following its approval by 63.9% of voters in a referendum in the previous month. In accordance with the Constitution's transition regime, on 25 October the Constituent Assembly elected 76 of its members to a Legislative and Supervisory Commission, which was to act as an interim legislature until elections to the new National Assembly (later scheduled, together with a presidential election, for April 2009) were held.

In November 2008 a government commission, established to audit the foreign debt incurred by Ecuador between 1976 and 2006 (reported to total US $10,000m.), reported that a large proportion of the debt had been contracted illegally. The commission's report recommended that the Government halt interest payments on three bond issues worth some $3,860m. issued between 2002 and 2005. In December 2008 Correa announced that the Government would not make a payment of $30.6m. on one of the three bond issues due in the previous month; defaults on the other two issues occurred in early 2009. It was widely reported that Ecuador did not lack the ability to meet its payment obligations, and that this was therefore the first time in recent history that a country had defaulted on its debt for political, rather than fiscal, reasons.

Correa's second term

President Correa won a second term of office at elections in April 2009. In a comfortable first round victory, Correa attracted 52% of the votes, while his nearest rival, former President Lucio Gutiérrez, polled 28%. Correa's victory was the first time since the restoration of civilian democracy in 1979 that a second round had not been required in a presidential contest. Correa also became the first incumbent President to win re-election (President Velasco Ibarra was elected five times between 1934–68, but failed to complete his term on each occasion). The concurrent legislative elections gave the Alianza País 59 seats in the 124-seat National Assembly, while the PSP and PSC secured 19 and 11, respectively.

Correa enjoyed broad popular support for his spending increases on health, education, pensions and infrastructure, and for his defiance in the face of the perceived influence of the USA and international financial institutions. Nevertheless, the Government's efforts to secure the passage of its legislative proposals through the National Assembly were hampered in the first half of 2010 by the Alianza País's lack of a majority, as well as by the divisions within the party. In July Correa threatened to call new elections if the legislature continued to impede the approval of major reforms, and used his constitutional right to promulgate by decree a bill of 'economic urgency', relating to the renegotiation of contracts with foreign companies operating in the oil sector (see Economic Affairs), after the Assembly failed to approve it within a 30-day deadline.

Meanwhile, a truth commission appointed by Correa to investigate government-sponsored human rights violations in Ecuador during 1983–2008 presented its report in June 2010: 457 officials were found to have participated in the perpetration of abuses against 456 people, 310 of whom had suffered under the presidency of Febres Cordero (1984–88) and 17 during Correa's first term in office.

On 30 September 2010 some 800 police officers staged a protest against newly approved legislation that included a reduction in police bonuses. The protest escalated after Correa went to address the disaffected officers at the main police barracks in Quito, when he was attacked with tear gas. After more than 10 hours, during which he claimed that a coup attempt had been made against him and declared a nationwide state of emergency, the President was rescued from the hospital, amid gunfire, by a special army unit. Five people were reportedly killed and more than 16 others seriously injured in the violence. Shortly after the uprising, the Government announced substantial salary increases for the police and armed forces. Some 13 police officers were arrested in connection with the uprising, while Correa continued to insist that he had been the victim of a coup plot, supported by Gutiérrez's PSP. Gutiérrez denied any involvement. In June 2011 six police officers were found guilty of conspiring against state security and were sentenced to between one and three years' imprisonment. In April 2012 the first civilians were found guilty on similar charges over their involvement in the affair.

Correa's authority appeared to have been strengthened by the police mutiny. In October 2010 the National Assembly approved controversial public finance legislation that allowed the Government to increase or reduce budget spending by up to 15% without seeking legislative approval and raised the maximum limit of the level of public debt from 40% of GDP to 50%. Correa issued a decree giving the Ministry of Government, Worship, Police and Municipalities full administrative control over the police force. Meanwhile, the President submitted a proposal for a referendum to the Constitutional Court, comprising the 10 questions that Correa wished to pose to the electorate. These covered a number of areas, including major reforms to the penal code and the judiciary and restrictions on the media and financial institutions. The proposed judicial reforms, provoked particular controversy, prompting criticism from former allies of Correa, who accused Correa of jeopardizing the autonomy of the judiciary. The President, however, maintained that the reforms were necessary to rid the country of corrupt and inefficient judges and to tackle increasing crime rates. Correa's position was further weakened by the withdrawal from the Alianza País of the Ruptura de los 25 movement, which held four seats in the legislature and two government posts.

The referendum took place on 7 May 2011. Allegations by the opposition parties of voting irregularities delayed the release of official results by several weeks. When the results were published they showed a narrow victory for Correa, with an average of 47.1% of the votes in favour of the proposed reforms (between 45.0% and 50.5% depending on the proposal) and an average of 41.1% against (between 39.3% and 42.6%). Although Correa hailed the result as an emphatic success, many observers believed that this latest move to extend executive power was further evidence of an increasingly authoritarian style of leadership that was undermining his support among some sections of the electorate. In October an international advisory commission, composed of senior, well-respected public figures including Spanish judge Baltazar Garzón, former President of Chile Ricardo Lagos, the Secretary-General of the Unión de Naciones Suramericanas (UNASUR), and a former adviser to the Argentine Government, arrived in the country in order to evaluate the judicial reforms approved in the referendum prior to their implementation.

In February 2012 the newly appointed National Court of Justice upheld a ruling made under the new media laws against a journalist and three directors from the *El Universo* newspaper. The defendants, who were charged with defamation of Correa in a report on his handling of the police revolt in 2010, were fined US $40m. and each sentenced to three years' imprisonment. The case attracted international condemnation from media organizations who saw it as an attack on the freedom of the press and damaging to Ecuador's reputation as a democracy.

Legal proceedings begun in 1993 against the US oil company Texaco (later acquired by Chevron) were still ongoing in early 2014. The case, believed to be the largest environmental lawsuit of its kind, had been brought by some 30,000 indigenous people living in the Oriente region of Ecuador who had suffered from large-scale pollution caused by the dumping of toxic waste products and crude oil in the river systems and unlined ground pits in that area of the Amazon. Correa had supported the indigenous people in bringing the case for compensation and decontamination, describing Texaco's actions as 'a crime against humanity'. Chevron countered that any decontamination of the area was the responsibility of the Ecuadorean Government. In February 2011 an international arbitration tribunal ordered Ecuador to suspend enforcement of any judgment against Chevron in the case. In that month Chevron was ordered to pay US $18,000m. (subsequently increased to $19,000m.) in compensation by the Ecuadorean National Court of Justice. Further appeals by Chevron against the ruling were rejected in September 2011, January 2012 and by the US Supreme Court in October 2012. In the following month a legal ruling ordered that Chevron's assets to the value of $19,000m. be frozen in Argentina, as the company had insufficient assets in Ecuador. However, in November 2013 the National Court of Justice reduced the compensation payment to $9,500m., although it upheld the verdict. However, in March 2014 a US court ruled that the original compensation verdict had been obtained through 'corrupt means'. This meant that the indigenous communities affected by Chevron's operations could not seek enforcement of the payment in the USA. The ruling came in spite of a Canadian appeals court decision in December 2013 compelling compensation be paid in Canada; Chevron was believed to have assets totalling some $15,000m. in Canada.

Ongoing dissatisfaction among the indigenous population with Correa's support for large-scale mining projects in the country culminated in a march from the southern Amazonian province of Zamora Chinchipe to Quito in March 2012 organized by CONAIE. Earlier in the month the Government had signed an agreement with a Chinese company to establish the country's first open-cast copper mine in the region. Communities near the proposed mine claimed that the project would entail mass deforestation, contamination of water supplies and other significant environmental damage to the area. Correa dismissed their concerns, however, and accused the 8,000 demonstrators who marched in Quito of colluding with opposition groups in order to destabilize the Government. A similarly controversial project to exploit gold and silver deposits in the ecologically sensitive Amazonian region was granted permission to proceed with Canadian finance in 2012.

Recent developments: Correa's third term

At the presidential election of 17 February 2013 Correa secured a resounding victory with some 57.2% of total votes, thereby obviating the need for a second round ballot. His closest rival, former banker Guillermo Lasso, secured some 22.7% of the vote, and former President Lucio Gutiérrez received just 6.7%. At the concurrent legislative elections the Alianza País secured a critical two-thirds' majority in the National Assembly with some 97 seats, becoming the first single party since 1979 to enjoy a legislative majority. Correa announced his intention to use the increased mandate to accelerate constitutional reform in line with his so-called citizens' revolution.

One of the new Government's first acts, following President Correa's inauguration in late May 2013, was the approval of a controversial bill governing the country's media. The legislation, which Correa had first presented to the Assembly some three years earlier, provided for increased government control and supervision of the media and the reallocation of radio and television frequencies to limit the number of private broadcasters while increasing those reserved for state operators. The opposition claimed that the reforms would erode the influence of Correa's political opponents and described them as an attack on freedom of speech. The Government was similarly criticized for introducing regulations requiring all non-government organizations to undergo a screening process, with powers to disband any that did not meet its criteria. Further accusations that Correa's Government was trying to silence its critics followed the sentencing in August to 12 years' imprisonment of Pepe Luis Acacho, a member of the Shuar indigenous community and leader of the Pachakútik movement, for sabotage and terrorism in his role in the protests against the Government's water policy in the Amazon region in 2009, during which a protester had been shot dead. The unexpectedly harsh sentence prompted expressions of alarm from international human rights groups. Moreover, the environmental charity Fundación Pachamama, which had been involved in the campaign to prevent oil production in the Yasuní national park (see above), was forcibly closed down during a police raid on its premises in December. The action appeared to support accusations that Correa's administration was becoming increasingly authoritarian and less tolerant of dissent.

Efforts to pursue justice for the victims of political violence and human rights abuses continued during 2013. In October three senior military officers were arrested on charges of crimes against humanity, including torture, kidnapping and sexual violence allegedly committed against members of Alfaro Vive ¡Carajo! in 1985, under the presidency of Febres Cordero. A further six retired officers were put under house arrest. In January 2014 former police commander Edgardo Vaca was detained in the USA. Plans were under way for his extradition to Ecuador to face charges of human rights abuses.

Alianza País suffered a serious reversal in the municipal elections of February 2014, losing the mayoralties in nine of the country's 10 most populous cities, most significantly including Quito. Moreover, four of the six Amazonian provinces rejected Correa's party in apparent protests at the President's decision to proceed with oil exploration in the region.

In March 2014 Correa announced that the Asamblea Nacional would begin the process of amending the Constitution with the intention of legitimizing his ambition to seek re-election in 2017.

Foreign Affairs

Regional relations

In April 1999 the World Trade Organization (WTO) upheld a complaint, put forward by the USA, Ecuador and four other Latin American countries, that the European Union (EU) unfairly favoured Caribbean banana producers. A two-tier tariff rate quota arrangement was agreed between Ecuadorean government officials and leaders of Caribbean banana-producing countries in November, easing restrictions on Latin American banana exporters and consequently assisting Ecuadorean producers. Furthermore, EU quotas for Latin American producers were to be phased out by 2006 and replaced by a uniform tariff system. However, in 2005 the Government expressed its strong opposition to the EU's successive proposals of tariff levels of €230 and €187 per metric ton on Latin American banana imports, both of which the WTO subsequently rejected. A challenge to the EU's third proposal, of a tariff of €176 per ton, was upheld by the WTO in 2008. The dispute was finally resolved in December 2009, with the signing of an accord by representatives from the EU, Ecuador and 10 other Latin American countries. Tariff levels were finalized in November 2012 and provided for a gradual reduction from €176 per ton to €114 per ton by 2020.

The long-standing border dispute with Peru over the Cordillera del Cóndor erupted into war in January 1981. A ceasefire was declared a few days later under the auspices of the guarantors of the Rio Protocol of 1942 (Argentina, Brazil, Chile and the USA). The Protocol was not recognized by Ecuador, as it awarded the area, which affords access to the Amazon river system, to Peru. In 1992 discussions on the border dispute were resumed. However, in January 1995 serious fighting broke out between the two sides. Representatives of the two Governments met for negotiations in Rio de Janeiro, Brazil, and a ceasefire agreement was concluded in February. An observer mission, representing the four guarantor nations of the Rio Protocol, was dispatched to the border, to oversee the separation of forces and demilitarization of the border area. Following intensive negotiations, agreement on the delimitation of the demilitarized zone was reached in July, and in October Ecuador finally repealed the state of emergency. The signing of the Santiago Agreement in 1996 provided a framework for a definitive solution to the issue and culminated in the signing of an accord confirming Peru's claim on the delineation of the border, but granting Ecuador navigation and trading rights on the Amazon and its tributaries and the opportunity to establish two trading centres in Peru (although this was not to constitute sovereign access).

Following the initiation in 2004 of the so-called 'Plan Patriota', a US-backed offensive by the Colombian military against the Fuerzas Armadas Revolucionarias de Colombia (FARC) and its source of funding, coca crops, the Ecuadorean Government expressed concern at an increase in illegal incursions into its territory by Colombian combatants. Relations improved after the Colombian Government agreed temporarily to halt aerial fumigation of coca crops in border areas from 2006, but the resumption of the practice led President Correa to cancel a trip to Colombia in 2007. Following intervention by the OAS, an agreement was reached whereby Colombia was to notify Ecuador in advance of any plans to spray the border area and the OAS was to conduct a full investigation into the effects of the herbicide glyphosate on the local population; however, the Ecuadorean authorities accused Colombia of breaching the accord. In February Correa announced the implementation of 'Plan Ecuador', which was intended to counteract the effects of Plan Colombia. As part of Plan Ecuador, Correa declared that the 500,000 Colombian refugees residing in Ecuador would be granted formal asylum status. Relations between the two countries deteriorated significantly following a military incursion by Colombian forces into Ecuadorean territory in March 2008, during which a FARC leader, Raúl Reyes, was killed along with 16 other rebels. The Colombian Government claimed that documents seized during the raid proved that Correa was interested in establishing official relations with the FARC. Correa dismissed the claims, and the Ecuadorean Government responded to the incident by expelling Colombia's ambassador in Quito, withdrawing its own ambassador from Bogotá and sending troops to the border. Relations continued to be strained during 2009, with the Colombian Government alleging that Correa's election campaign had received funding from the FARC. In April 2010 an Ecuadorean court upheld an arrest warrant issued for Colombia's former Minister of National Defence and a candidate in that country's forthcoming presidential election, Juan Manuel Santos, in connection with the 2008 raid. However, following his victory in the election, Santos swiftly sought to improve bilateral relations. Correa and Santos (the warrant for whose arrest had been revoked in August) announced that full diplomatic relations had been restored in November, after the Colombian Government provided Ecuador with information on the 2008 raid. In September 2013 Ecuador formally withdrew from the International Court of Justice its complaint against Colombia for the aerial fumigation of coca crops in border areas. Moreover, in December of that year the two countries collaborated in a joint operation that led to the capture of senior FARC activist Mario Manuel Cabezas Muñoz in Ecuador.

Ecuador's relations with Panama deteriorated significantly in late 2013, following the Ecuadorean authorities' refusal to release a Panama-registered ship seized in Ecuadorean waters in October, which had been found to be carrying 799 kg of cocaine. The Government of Panama claimed that the action was in retaliation for its decision to grant political asylum to a prominent opponent of President Correa. The dispute culminated in December when the Panamanian authorities recalled their ambassador to Ecuador.

Other external relations

In 1999 Ecuador and the USA signed an agreement allowing the USA to establish an air base at Manta, for a period of 10 years, for counter-narcotics surveillance operations in the Andean region. In 2008 the Correa Government gave the USA formal notice to vacate the base by November 2009. Ecuador did sign a new counter-narcotics agreement with the USA in 2009, under which two new élite police units were to be created. The USA's Andean Trade Promotion and Drug Eradication Act (ATPDEA) with Ecuador lapsed in July 2013, following Correa's rejection of a number of conditions the US authorities had attempted to attach to its renewal.

In April 2011 the US ambassador Heather Hodges was expelled from Quito following the publication of leaked diplomatic correspondence on the Wikileaks website in which she claimed that corruption was endemic at all levels of government in Ecuador. Ecuador's relations with the USA and the United Kingdom became strained in June 2012 when the founder of Wikileaks, Julian Assange, who had been resisting extradition to Sweden where he was wanted for questioning on allegations of sexual offences, sought asylum in the Ecuadorean embassy in London. Assange feared that the Swedish authorities would transfer him to the USA where charges against him relating to his organization's activities publishing classified correspondence could carry the death penalty. Ecuador granted asylum to Assange in August; he remained in the embassy in London in early 2014.

In 2012 the Ecuadorean Government suggested that the USA was furthering its interests in the region through the OAS. The accusation followed criticism of Correa's treatment of the media (specifically in the *El Universo* case—see above) under the organization's Inter-American Convention on Human Rights. Correa noted that the USA itself had not ratified the convention and called for the headquarters of the organization to be moved to Latin America from its current base in Washington, DC. Similar accusations against the US aid agency USAID led the organization to announce that it was to cease its work in Ecuador from September 2014.

In 2007 President Correa made an official state visit to China to sign a bilateral agreement covering energy, agriculture, technology and infrastructure. Bilateral economic co-operation increased further in 2010 when Chinese funding for two hydroelectric projects in Ecuador was secured, and an agreement was signed whereby China would provide Ecuador with a loan of US $1,000m. in exchange for the supply of 36,000 barrels per day of crude petroleum over a four-year period. Further loans of $2,000m. and $1,700m. were approved in 2011 and 2012, respectively. It was estimated that Ecuador had accepted a total of $7,250m. in financial assistance from China between 2008 and mid-2012. Since the Government's decision in 2008 to default on its foreign debt and the subsequent withdrawal of substantial amounts of international finance, China had become Ecuador's most important creditor.

CONSTITUTION AND GOVERNMENT

The Constitution of the Republic of Ecuador—the country's 20th—was promulgated on 20 October 2008. Under the terms of the Constitution, executive power is vested in the President, who is directly elected by universal adult suffrage for a four-year term (starting from 24 May following his or her election). The President may be re-elected once only. Legislative power is held by the unicameral Asamblea Nacional (National Assembly), which is also directly elected for a four-year term. For administrative purposes Ecuador is divided into provinces, cantons and parishes. Each province has a Governor, who is appointed by the President.

REGIONAL AND INTERNATIONAL CO-OPERATION

Ecuador became a member of the UN in 1945. Ecuador is a member of the Andean Community (see p. 193), the Organization of American States (OAS, see p. 394), the Asociación Latinoamericana de Integración (ALADI, see p. 361), and of the Community of Latin American and Caribbean States (see p. 464), which was formally inaugurated in December 2011. In 2007 Ecuador rejoined the Organization of the Petroleum Exporting Countries (OPEC, see p. 408), having previously given up membership in 1992. In 1996 Ecuador joined the World Trade Organization (WTO, see p. 434). In 2004 Ecuador was one of 12 countries that were signatories to the agreement, signed in Cusco, Peru, creating the South American Community of Nations (Comunidad Sudamericana de Naciones, which was renamed the Union of South American Nations—Unión de Naciones Suramericanas, UNASUR, see p. 469—in 2007), intended to promote greater regional economic integration. Ecuador was a member of the Bolivarian Alliance for the Peoples of our America-People's Trade Treaty (Alianza Bolivariana para los Pueblos de Nuestra América-Tratado de Comercio de los Pueblos—ALBA-TCP, see p. 463), intended as an alternative to the proposed Free Trade Area of the Americas advanced by the USA. In December 2011 Ecuador formally presented a request for full membership of Mercosur (Mercado Común del Sur, see p. 429).

ECONOMIC AFFAIRS

In 2012, according to estimates by the World Bank, Ecuador's gross national income (GNI), measured at average 2010–12 prices, was US $80,590m., equivalent to $5,200 per head (or $9,700 per head on an international purchasing-power parity basis). During 2003–12, it was estimated, the population increased at an average annual rate of 1.7%, while gross domestic product (GDP) per head increased, in real terms, at an average annual rate of 3.0%. According to the Central Bank, overall GDP increased, in real terms, at an average annual rate of 4.8% in 2003–12; GDP increased by 5.1% in 2012.

Agriculture (including hunting, forestry and fishing) contributed 9.4% of GDP and employed 27.3% of the active labour force in 2012. Ecuador is the world's leading exporter of bananas (earnings were equivalent to 8.7% of the total value of exports in 2012), and coffee and cocoa are also important cash crops. The seafood sector, particularly the shrimp industry, was also a significant contributor to the economy. Ecuador's extensive forests yield valuable hardwoods, and the country is a leading producer of balsawood. Exports of cut flowers were also important, and generated US $771.3m. in earnings in 2012 (equivalent to 3.2% of the total value of exports). According to the Central Bank, during 2003–12 agricultural GDP increased at an average annual rate of 3.1%. Sectoral GDP grew by 1.2% in 2012.

Industry (including mining, manufacturing, construction and power) employed 18.1% of the active labour force and provided

38.5% of GDP in 2012. According to the Central Bank, during 2003–12 industrial GDP increased at an average annual rate of 5.3%. The sector increased by 5.9% in 2012.

Mining contributed an estimated 12.5% of GDP in 2012, although the mining sector employed only 0.5% of the labour force in that year. Petroleum and its derivatives remained the major exports in the early 21st century. Earnings from crude petroleum exports amounted to US $12,711.2m. in 2012, equivalent to 53.3% of the total value of exports. According to the US Energy Information Administration, production averaged 504,500 barrels per day (b/d) in 2012. According to the *Oil and Gas Journal*, Ecuador's proven petroleum reserves were estimated at 8,240m. barrels at the end of 2012 and proven reserves of natural gas were put at 247,000m. cu ft. Gold, silver, copper, antimony and zinc are also mined. In real terms, according to the Central Bank, the GDP of the mining sector increased at an average rate of 4.5% per year during 2003–12; mining GDP increased by 1.5% in 2012.

Manufacturing (excluding petroleum refining) contributed 12.5% of GDP and employed 10.7% of the active labour force in 2012. During 2003–12 manufacturing GDP increased at an average annual rate of 4.6%, according to the Central Bank. Sectoral GDP increased by 5.6% in 2012.

The construction sector contributed 11.8% of GDP and engaged some 6.3% of the employed labour force in 2012. According to the Central Bank, during 2003–12 construction GDP increased at an average annual rate of 7.6%; sectoral GDP increased by 14.0% in 2012.

Energy is derived principally from hydroelectric plants, responsible for 54.9% of total production in 2011, with petroleum accounting for 32.7%. The country had an estimated installed capacity of 5.3m. MW in 2011, of which about one-half was produced domestically, mostly from the 1,075-MW Paute hydroelectric plant. A 160-MW hydroelectric station at Mazar, south of Paute, was inaugurated in 2011, and two further plants, with capacities of 596 MW and 190 MW, were planned in the south and north of the country, respectively, to be built with Russian financing. Imports of mineral fuels and oils comprised 22.8% of the value of total imports in 2012.

The services sector contributed an estimated 52.2% of GDP in 2012. Some 54.7% of the active labour force were employed in services in the same year. The sector's GDP increased at an average annual rate of 5.0% during 2003–12; services GDP increased by 5.1% in 2012.

In 2012 Ecuador recorded a visible merchandise trade surplus of US $69m., and there was a deficit of $177m. on the current account of the balance of payments. In 2012 the principal source of imports was the USA (accounting for 26.9% of the total); that country was also the principal market for exports (44.7%). Other major trading partners were Colombia, the People's Republic of China, Chile, Panama, Peru and Venezuela. In addition to petroleum and derivatives, the principal exports in 2012 were bananas and plantains, shellfish and prepared foodstuffs. The principal imports in 2012 were mineral fuels and oils, nuclear reactors and boilers, machinery and apparatus, vehicles, chemicals and chemical products, aircraft and transport equipment, electrical and electronic equipment, and plastic and rubber articles.

In 2012 there was a provisional budgetary deficit of about US $1,702.8m., equivalent to 1.9% of GDP. In that year some 28.7% of government expenditure was financed by revenue from petroleum. Ecuador's general government gross debt was US $18,652m. in 2012, equivalent to 22.2% of GDP. Ecuador's total external debt was US $16,497m. at the end of 2011, of which $9,929m. was public and publicly guaranteed debt. In that year, the cost of servicing long-term public and publicly guaranteed debt and repayments to the IMF was equivalent to 9.7% of the value of exports of goods, services and income (excluding workers' remittances). The average annual rate of inflation in 2004–12 was 4.3%; the rate averaged 5.1% in 2012. The average rate of unemployment stood at 4.1% in 2012.

The administration of Rafael Correa responded to the recent dramatic increases in proven petroleum reserves in the country by strengthening state intervention in the oil sector. Under new regulations, private oil firms operating in Ecuador were required to pay 99% of 'windfall' profits from rising oil prices to the Government. GDP grew by 7.8% in 2011; the rate slowed to 5.1% in 2012 and further, to an estimated 4.0% in 2013, although growth was predicted at 5.1% in 2014, largely as a result of oil price fluctuations. The upgrade of Ecuador's largest refinery in Esmeraldas in 2014, which would take the facility out of operation for several months, was expected to have an impact on that year's economic growth, as would work on two major hydroelectric projects, scheduled for 2014–15. The economic benefits of increased petroleum-refining capacity and lower energy costs were expected to be noticeable from 2016. In 2013, in an effort to exploit high international prices and increased global demand for cocoa (in addition to reducing the country's dependence on bananas, which are also vulnerable to price fluctuations), the Government announced a 10-year programme to reinvigorate the industry and to double the value of annual cocoa exports to US $1,200m. by 2023. Despite ongoing tensions in the relationship between the two countries, the USA remained Ecuador's most significant trading partner; therefore, the expiry of the ATPDEA trade agreement in 2013 (see above) was expected to cause some hardship for Ecuadorean exporters and the National Assembly consequently approved compensation for their loss of earnings in July. Trade with the European Union was expected to be enhanced with the conclusion of a bilateral agreement in 2014. The Government claimed that a predicted fiscal deficit of $5,275m. for 2014 was 'fully funded', although many observers speculated that funding would take the form of conditional loans and credit from China, fuelling concerns about the country's increasing reliance on Chinese financial assistance.

PUBLIC HOLIDAYS

2015: 1 January (New Year's Day), 16–17 February (Carnival), 3 April (Good Friday), 1 May (Labour Day), 24 May (Battle of Pichincha), 10 August (Independence of Quito), 9 October (Independence of Guayaquil), 2 November (All Souls' Day), 3 November (Independence of Cuenca), 6 December (Foundation of Quito), 25 December (Christmas Day), 31 December (New Year's Eve).

Statistical Survey

Sources (unless otherwise stated): Instituto Nacional de Estadística y Censos, Juan Larrea 534 y Riofrío, Quito; tel. (2) 252-9858; e-mail inec1@ecnet.ec; internet www.inec.gob.ec; Banco Central del Ecuador, Casilla 339, Quito; tel. (2) 257-2522; fax (2) 295-5458; internet www.bce.fin.ec; Ministerio de Industrias y Competitividad, Avda Eloy Alfaro y Amazonas, Quito; tel. (2) 254-6690; fax (2) 250-3818; e-mail info@mic.gov.ec; internet www.mic.gov.ec.

Area and Population

AREA, POPULATION AND DENSITY

Area (sq km)	272,045*
Population (census results)	
25 November 2001	12,156,608
28 November 2010	
Males	7,177,683
Females	7,305,816
Total	14,483,499
Population (official estimates)	
2012	15,520,973
2013	15,774,749
2014	16,027,466
Density (per sq km) at 2014	58.9

* 105,037 sq miles.

POPULATION BY AGE AND SEX

(UN estimates at mid-2014)

	Males	Females	Total
0–14	2,414,440	2,318,794	4,733,234
15–64	5,076,536	5,107,125	10,183,661
65 and over	497,961	567,695	1,065,656
Total	7,988,937	7,993,614	15,982,551

Source: UN, *World Population Prospects: The 2012 Revision*.

2014 (official population estimates): *0–14:* 4,982,359; *15–64:* 9,967,520; *65 and over:* 1,077,587; *Total* 16,027,466 (males 7,939,552, females 8,087,914).

REGIONS AND PROVINCES

(projected population estimates at mid-2007)

	Area (sq km)	Population	Density (per sq km)	Capital
Sierra	63,269	6,111,542	96.6	—
Azuay	8,125	678,746	83.5	Cuenca
Bolívar	3,940	180,293	45.8	Guaranda
Cañar	3,122	226,021	72.4	Azogues
Carchi	3,605	166,116	46.1	Tulcán
Chimborazo	6,072	443,522	73.0	Riobamba
Cotopaxi	6,569	400,411	61.0	Latacunga
Imbabura	4,559	397,704	87.2	Ibarra
Loja	11,027	434,020	39.4	Loja
Pichincha	12,915	2,683,272	207.8	Quito
Tungurahua	3,335	501,437	150.4	Ambato
Costa	67,646	6,720,798	99.4	—
El Oro	5,850	608,032	103.9	Machala
Esmeraldas	15,239	438,576	28.8	Esmeraldas
Guayas	20,503	3,617,504	176.4	Guayaquil
Los Ríos	7,175	742,241	103.4	Babahoyo
Manabí	18,879	1,314,445	69.6	Portoviejo
Amazónica	130,834	662,948	5.1	—
Morona Santiago	25,690	131,337	5.1	Macas
Napo	11,431	96,029	8.4	Tena
Orellana	22,500	110,782	4.9	Puerto Francisco de Orellana (Coca)
Pastaza	29,774	75,782	2.5	Puyo
Sucumbíos	18,328	163,447	8.9	Nueva Loja
Zamora Chinchipe	23,111	85,571	3.7	Zamora
Insular	8,010	22,678	2.8	—
Archipiélago de Colón (Galápagos)	8,010	22,678	2.8	Puerto Baquerizo (Isla San Cristóbal)
Uncharted areas	2,289	87,519	38.2	—
Total	272,045	13,605,485	50.0	

Note: Two new provinces, Santo Domingo de los Tsáchilas and Santa Elena, were created in late 2007.

Source: partly Stefan Helders, *World Gazetteer*.

PRINCIPAL TOWNS

(official population estimates, 2014)

Guayaquil	2,560,505	Manta	247,463
Quito (capital)	2,505,344	Riobamba	246,861
Cuenca	569,416	Loja	243,321
Santo Domingo de los Colorados	411,009	Esmeraldas	206,298
Ambato	360,544	Ibarra	201,237
Portoviejo	304,227	Quevedo	193,308
Eloy Alfaro (Durán)	271,085	Latacunga	188,627
Machala	270,047		

BIRTHS, MARRIAGES AND DEATHS

(excluding nomadic Indian tribes)*

	Registered live births†		Registered marriages		Registered deaths	
	Number	Rate (per 1,000)	Number	Rate (per 1,000)	Number	Rate (per 1,000)
2004	254,362	19.5	63,299	4.9	54,729	4.2
2005	252,725	19.1	66,612	5.0	56,825	4.3
2006	278,591	20.8	74,036	5.5	57,940	4.3
2007	283,984	20.9	76,154	5.6	58,016	4.3
2008	291,055	21.1	76,354	5.5	60,023	4.3
2009	298,337	21.3	76,892	5.5	59,714	4.3
2010	292,375	19.5	74,800	5.3	61,681	4.3
2011	n.a.	n.a.	73,579	4.8	62,304	4.1

* Registrations incomplete.

† Figures include registrations of large numbers of births occurring in previous years. The number of births registered in the year of occurrence was: 168,893 in 2004; 168,324 in 2005; 185,056 in 2006; 195,051 in 2007; 206,215 in 2008; 215,906 in 2009; 219,162 in 2010; 229,780 in 2011.

Life expectancy (years at birth): 75.9 (males 73.1; females 78.9) in 2011 (Source: World Bank, World Development Indicators database).

ECONOMICALLY ACTIVE POPULATION

(ISIC major divisions, December of each year, '000 persons aged 15 years and over)

	2011	2012
Agriculture, hunting and forestry	1,687.6	1,694.8
Fishing	68.6	63.3
Mining and quarrying	32.7	32.3
Manufacturing	672.9	689.6
Electricity, gas and water	27.7	27.7
Construction	382.4	403.2
Wholesale and retail trade; repair of motor vehicles, motorcycles and personal and household goods	1,319.0	1,311.2
Hotels and restaurants	310.7	328.4
Transport, storage and communications	393.6	400.7
Financial intermediation	67.2	58.3
Real estate, renting and business activities	282.7	340.1
Public administration and defence; compulsory social security	237.8	240.2

—continued	2011	2012
Education	325.6	338.0
Health and social work	176.2	177.4
Other community, social and personal service activities	171.7	159.3
Private households with employed persons	147.6	158.0
Extra-territorial organizations and bodies	0.6	2.6
Total employed	6,304.8	6,425.1
Unemployed	276.8	276.2
Total labour force	6,581.6	6,701.3
Males	3,976.3	4,038.5
Females	2,605.4	2,662.8

Source: ILO.

Mid-2014 (estimates in '000): Agriculture, etc. 1,208; Total labour force 7,264 (Source: FAO).

Health and Welfare

KEY INDICATORS

Total fertility rate (children per woman, 2011)	2.4
Under-5 mortality rate (per 1,000 live births, 2011)	23
HIV/AIDS (% of persons aged 15–49, 2012)	0.6
Physicians (per 1,000 head, 2009)	1.7
Hospital beds (per 1,000 head, 2009)	1.5
Health expenditure (2010): US $ per head (PPP)	635
Health expenditure (2010): % of GDP	7.9
Health expenditure (2010): public (% of total)	40.2
Access to water (% of persons, 2011)	92
Access to sanitation (% of persons, 2011)	93
Total carbon dioxide emissions ('000 metric tons, 2010)	32,636.3
Carbon dioxide emissions per head (metric tons, 2010)	2.2
Human Development Index (2012): ranking	89
Human Development Index (2012): value	0.724

For sources and definitions, see explanatory note on p. vi.

Agriculture

PRINCIPAL CROPS

('000 metric tons)

	2010	2011	2012
Rice, paddy	1,706	1,478	1,566
Barley	19	25	11
Maize	906	864	1,243
Potatoes	387	339	285
Cassava (Manioc)	54	52	71
Sugar cane	8,347	8,132	7,379
Beans, dry	15	13	10
Soybeans (Soya beans)	70*	71*	75†
Oil palm fruit	2,850	2,097	2,350†
Tomatoes	54	36	63
Onions and shallots, green†	111	100	105
Carrots and turnips†	28	30	35
Watermelons†	58	60	63
Bananas	7,931	7,428	7,012
Plantains	547	592	559
Oranges	47	37	48
Mangoes†	212	201	202
Pineapples†	124	117	120
Papayas†	41	39	40
Coffee, green	31	24	7
Cocoa beans	132	224	133
Abaca (Manila hemp)†	31	35	35

* Unofficial figure.
† FAO estimate(s).

Aggregate production ('000 metric tons, may include official, semi-official or estimated data): Total cereals 2,654 in 2010, 2,388 in 2011, 2,843 in 2012; Total roots and tubers 465 in 2010, 420 in 2011, 384 in 2012; Total vegetables (incl. melons) 477 in 2010, 447 in 2011, 453 in 2012; Total fruits (excl. melons) 9,325 in 2010, 8,794 in 2011, 8,375 in 2012.

Source: FAO.

LIVESTOCK

('000 head, year ending September)

	2010	2011	2012
Cattle	5,254	5,359	5,236
Sheep	792	743	750*
Pigs	1,490	1,831	1,162
Horses	367	344	338
Goats	135	112	109
Asses	139	131	121
Mules	125	119	120
Chickens	152,926	140,000*	140,000*

* FAO estimate.

Source: FAO.

LIVESTOCK PRODUCTS

('000 metric tons)

	2010	2011	2012
Cattle meat*	260.0	268.0	265.0
Sheep meat*	5.6	5.6	5.6
Pig meat*	184.7	200.0	205.0
Goat meat*	1.2	1.0	1.1
Chicken meat*	340.0	330.0	330.0
Cows' milk	5,709.5	6,375.3	5,675.1
Sheep's milk*	7.1	6.9	7.1
Goats' milk*	2.9	2.9	3.0
Hen eggs*	110.0	130.0	140.0
Wool, greasy*	1.4	1.4	1.4

* FAO estimates.

Source: FAO.

Forestry

ROUNDWOOD REMOVALS

('000 cubic metres, excluding bark, FAO estimates)

	2010	2011	2012
Sawlogs, veneer logs and logs for sleepers	1,280	1,280	1,280
Pulpwood	481	481	481
Other industrial wood	330	330	330
Fuel wood	4,940	4,952	4,965
Total	7,031	7,043	7,056

Source: FAO.

SAWNWOOD PRODUCTION

('000 cubic metres, including railway sleepers)

	2008	2009	2010
Coniferous (softwood)*	107	118	118
Broadleaved (hardwood)	310	310*	401
Total	417	428*	519

* Estimate(s).

2011–12: Production assumed to be unchanged from 2010 (FAO estimates).

Source: FAO.

Fishing

('000 metric tons, live weight)

	2009	2010	2011
Capture	498.7	399.2	508.5
Pacific thread herring	22.5	29.4	20.3
Anchoveta (Peruvian anchovy)	20.2	n.a.	3.0
Pacific anchoveta	7.6	0.7	13.0
Frigate and bullet tunas	35.0	37.7	43.8
Skipjack tuna	143.4	109.6	179.4
Yellowfin tuna	25.4	28.9	33.9
Bigeye tuna	36.6	32.7	32.3
Chub mackerel	36.7	52.8	31.8
Aquaculture	218.4	271.9	308.9*
Whiteleg shrimp	179.1	223.3	260.0*
Nile tilapia	37.5	47.7	48.0*
Total catch	717.0	671.1	817.4*

* Estimate.

Source: FAO.

Mining

	2009	2010	2011
Natural gas (gross, million cu m)	1,200	1,275	1,300
Gold (kg)*	5,392	4,593	4,149

* Metal content of ore only.

Source: US Geological Survey.

Crude petroleum ('000 metric tons, estimates): 26,115 in 2009; 26,116 in 2010; 26,809 in 2011; 27,097 in 2012 (Source: BP, *Statistical Review of World Energy*).

Industry

SELECTED PRODUCTS

('000 barrels unless otherwise indicated)

	2009	2010	2011
Motor spirit (gasoline)	18,635	17,786	17,051
Distillate fuel oils	10,571	9,443	10,027
Residual fuel oils	10,400	7,752	10,670
Liquefied petroleum gas	2,160	1,991	3,788
Crude steel ('000 metric tons)	259	372	525
Cement ('000 metric tons)*	5,000	5,000	5,000

* Estimated figures.

Jet fuels ('000 barrels): 2,913 in 2007.

Source: US Geological Survey.

Electric energy (million kWh): 19,010 in 2008; 18,022 in 2009; 17,688 in 2010 (Source: UN Industrial Commodity Statistics Database).

Finance

CURRENCY AND EXCHANGE RATES

Monetary Units

United States currency is used: 100 cents = 1 US dollar ($).

Sterling and Euro Equivalents (31 December 2013)

£1 sterling = US $1.647;
€1 = US $1.379;
US $100 = £60.72 = €72.51.

Note: Ecuador's national currency was formerly the sucre. From 13 March 2000 the sucre was replaced by the US dollar, at an exchange rate of $1 = 25,000 sucres. Both currencies were officially in use for a transitional period of 180 days, but from 9 September sucres were withdrawn from circulation and the dollar became the sole legal tender.

BUDGET

(consolidated central government accounts, US $ million, provisional)

Revenue	2010	2011	2012
Petroleum revenue	4,411.0	5,971.4	6,085.6
Non-petroleum revenue	10,664.7	11,227.0	13,437.3
Taxation	8,793.8	9,765.3	12,254.7
Taxes on goods and services	4,416.4	4,818.3	6,099.5
Value-added tax	3,886.1	4,200.4	5,415.0
Taxes on income	2,353.1	3,030.2	3,312.9
Import duties	1,152.4	1,156.0	1,261.1
Other non-petroleum revenue	1,511.6	1,209.9	1,128.2
Transfers	359.3	251.8	54.4
Total	15,075.7	17,198.4	19,522.8

Expenditure	2010	2011	2012
Wages and salaries	6,017.2	6,466.2	7,352.9
Purchases of goods and services	1,094.6	1,279.2	1,657.6
Interest payments	529.8	673.0	827.9
Transfers	1,291.3	997.8	1,242.9
Other current expenditure	842.6	983.2	884.1
Capital expenditure	6,431.7	8,035.5	9,260.2
Total	16,207.1	18,434.8	21,225.6

Public Sector Accounts (US $ million): *Total revenue:* 23,185.7 in 2010; 31,189.8 in 2011; 34,529.6 in 2012. *Total expenditure:* 24,122.6 in 2010; 31,194.9 in 2011; 35,478.9 in 2012.

INTERNATIONAL RESERVES

(US $ million at 31 December)

	2010	2011	2012
Gold (national valuation)	1,187.3	1,293.3	1,402.6
IMF special drawing rights	24.9	23.1	24.2
Reserve position in IMF	26.4	43.8	43.8
Foreign exchange	1,383.5	1,597.4	1,011.9
Total	2,622.1	2,957.6	2,482.5

Source: IMF, *International Financial Statistics*.

MONEY SUPPLY

(US $ million at 31 December)

	2009	2010	2011
Currency outside depository corporations	77.4	82.4	83.2
Transferable deposits	6,255.5	7,657.2	8,119.2
Other deposits	10,506.4	12,232.2	15,248.0
Broad money	16,839.3	19,971.8	23,450.4

Source: IMF, *International Financial Statistics*.

COST OF LIVING

(Consumer Price Index; annual averages, base: 2004 = 100)

	2010	2011	2012
Food (incl. non-alcoholic beverages)	145.6	155.4	164.4
Alcoholic beverages and tobacco	165.5	172.4	211.3
Housing, fuel (excl. light)	120.8	123.4	126.5
Clothing	119.0	126.7	132.3
Health	116.4	120.0	125.4
Transport	114.9	117.6	123.6
Communication	96.1	98.1	97.5
Recreation and culture	105.4	105.6	109.5
Education	141.1	147.8	157.1
Hotels and restaurants	129.6	136.0	146.6
All items (incl. others)	127.3	133.0	139.8

NATIONAL ACCOUNTS
(US $ million at current prices)

Expenditure on the Gross Domestic Product

	2010	2011	2012
Government final consumption expenditure	9,181.1	10,092.5	11,507.7
Private final consumption expenditure	44,012.1	48,723.5	53,038.6
Changes in stocks	2,373.6	2,398.9	1,064.1
Gross fixed capital formation	17,127.9	20,769.2	23,779.3
Total domestic expenditure	72,694.6	81,984.2	89,389.8
Exports of goods and services	19,402.4	24,214.3	25,994.3
Less Imports of goods and services	22,541.7	26,418.7	27,889.5
GDP in market prices	69,555.4	79,779.8	87,494.7
GDP in constant 2007 prices	56,481.1	60,882.6	64,009.4

Gross Domestic Product by Economic Activity

	2010	2011	2012
Agriculture, hunting, forestry and fishing	6,769.9	7,544.5	7,838.7
Petroleum and other mining	7,575.5	9,622.0	10,480.0
Manufacturing (excl. petroleum-refining)	8,601.7	9,654.1	10,420.2
Manufacture of petroleum derivatives	720.0	711.2	367.1
Electricity, gas and water	754.1	998.5	1,066.2
Construction	6,501.2	8,347.1	9,833.0
Wholesale and retail trade	7,241.1	8,201.4	8,711.3
Hotels and restaurants	1,312.4	1,576.7	1,852.2
Transport, storage and communications	5,382.7	5,900.4	6,549.5
Financial intermediation	1,947.8	2,318.7	2,557.7
Professional, technical and administrative activities	4,301.6	4,686.5	5,178.5
Public administration, defence and other social services	4,538.6	4,967.4	5,708.4
Education, health and social work	5,750.1	6,336.2	7,170.4
Other services	4,767.9	5,149.3	5,584.5
Private households with domestic services	334.9	348.6	337.5
Gross value added in basic prices	66,499.5	76,362.7	83,655.2
Taxes, less subsidies, on products	3,055.9	3,417.2	3,839.5
GDP in market prices	69,555.4	79,779.8	87,494.7

BALANCE OF PAYMENTS
(US $ million)

	2010	2011	2012
Exports of goods	18,131	23,077	24,648
Imports of goods	−19,635	−23,237	−24,577
Balance on goods	−1,504	−160	69
Exports of services	1,479	1,594	1,816
Imports of services	−3,004	−3,156	−3,223
Balance on goods and services	−3,030	−1,723	−1,338
Primary income received	76	85	105
Primary income paid	−1,118	−1,307	−1,430
Balance on goods, services and primary income	−4,071	−2,946	−2,662
Secondary income received	2,895	2,983	2,762
Secondary income paid	−447	−262	−276
Current balance	−1,623	−225	−177
Capital account (net)	65	82	130
Direct investment liabilities	167	641	591
Portfolio investment assets	−721	48	139
Portfolio investment liabilities	−10	−7	−72
Other investment assets	83	−2,511	−1,343
Other investment liabilities	703	2,174	253
Net errors and omissions	125	72	−149
Reserves and related items	−1,211	273	−627

Source: IMF, *International Financial Statistics*.

External Trade

PRINCIPAL COMMODITIES
(distribution by HS, US $ million)

Imports f.o.b.	2010	2011	2012
Vegetables and vegetable products	751.9	895.0	960.2
Mineral products	4,436.0	5,507.2	5,748.6
Mineral fuels, oils, distillation products, etc.	4,380.4	5,406.6	5,642.6
Oil and other distillation products, etc.	968.5	1,533.7	2,052.8
Non-crude petroleum oils	2,663.2	2,857.3	2,887.1
Petroleum gases	575.4	858.6	644.5
Chemicals and related products	2,465.0	2,874.2	3,046.3
Pharmaceutical products	791.6	953.1	981.8
Medicament mixtures put in dosage	640.2	762.0	788.8
Plastics, rubber, and articles thereof	1,201.9	1,467.5	1,496.0
Plastics and articles thereof	865.2	1,063.6	1,047.3
Textiles and textile articles	590.9	764.7	741.9
Iron and steel, other base metals and articles of base metal	1,544.3	2,047.5	1,969.0
Iron and steel	680.9	901.0	767.0
Machinery and mechanical appliances; electrical equipment; parts thereof	4,445.5	5,072.2	5,618.3
Boilers, machinery, etc.	2,459.5	2,861.2	3,345.6
Electrical, electronic equipment	1,986.0	2,211.0	2,272.7
Vehicles, aircraft, vessels and associated transport equipment	2,407.2	2,352.3	2,348.0
Vehicles other than railway, tramway	2,360.9	2,225.5	2,260.8
Cars, station wagon, etc.	1,068.5	876.9	764.5
Total (incl. others)	20,590.8	24,286.1	25,196.5

Exports f.o.b.	2010	2011	2012
Live animals and animal products	1,107.7	1,507.5	1,657.1
Fish, crustaceans, molluscs, aquatic invertebrates	1,094.1	1,480.8	1,617.9
Crustaceans	850.7	1,176.5	1,279.8
Vegetables and vegetable products	2,911.4	3,314.3	3,187.2
Live trees, plants, bulbs, roots, cut flowers, etc.	611.3	684.3	776.2
Cut flowers and flower buds for bouquets, etc.	607.8	679.9	771.3
Edible fruit, nuts, peel of citrus fruit, melons	2,119.2	2,344.3	2,185.6
Bananas and plantains	2,033.8	2,246.4	2,082.0
Prepared foodstuffs; beverages, spirits, vinegar; tobacco and articles thereof	1,642.5	2,158.9	2,283.9
Food preparations of meat, fish and seafood	603.8	880.0	1,125.8
Prepared or preserved fish, caviar, etc.	598.3	870.3	1,112.8
Mineral products	9,691.9	12,945.8	13,847.6
Mineral fuels, oils, distillation products, etc.	9,672.5	12,909.4	13,797.5
Crude petroleum oils	8,951.9	11,800.0	12,711.2
Non-crude petroleum oils	677.2	1,033.9	863.7
Total (incl. others)	17,489.9	22,342.5	23,852.0

Source: Trade Map-Trade Competitiveness Map, International Trade Centre, www.intracen.org/marketanalysis.

PRINCIPAL TRADING PARTNERS
(US $ million)

Imports c.i.f.	2010	2011	2012
Argentina	584.9	559.2	477.6
Bahamas	253.6	168.0	143.8
Belgium and Luxembourg	297.1	116.2	325.5
Brazil	853.8	949.9	925.3
Canada	265.2	313.8	307.0
Chile	564.3	529.1	625.1
China, People's Republic	1,606.6	3,327.0	2,810.7
Colombia	2,022.3	2,108.1	2,190.2
Germany	475.6	650.3	589.2
India	131.8	258.3	442.5
Italy	274.6	331.6	282.3
Japan	692.7	900.9	727.7
Korea, Republic	896.9	946.7	789.9
Mexico	727.6	1,070.9	888.3
Panama	1,027.2	1,471.6	1,663.0
Peru	1,035.6	915.1	1,128.0
Spain	268.8	322.1	610.8
Thailand	311.5	256.5	313.1
USA	5,736.4	5,138.4	6,774.0
Venezuela	549.8	962.1	239.3
Total (incl. others)	20,590.8	24,286.1	25,196.5

Exports f.o.b.	2010	2011	2012
Belgium and Luxembourg	244.4	265.0	208.4
Chile	846.6	1,105.5	1,993.8
China, People's Republic	328.7	191.9	391.5
Colombia	793.1	1,023.2	1,059.1
El Salvador	183.8	225.7	147.2
France	206.4	211.8	239.8
Germany	320.3	491.9	378.4
Italy	582.4	580.4	489.3
Japan	402.0	348.9	653.7
Netherlands	331.6	349.2	333.5
Netherlands Antilles	131.2	470.7	40.3
Panama	2,139.2	1,041.4	923.5
Peru	1,335.6	1,764.6	1,991.6
Russia	596.7	699.9	706.8
Spain	354.2	467.7	444.0
USA	6,077.5	9,725.7	10,662.6
Venezuela	974.0	1,473.9	1,007.9
Total (incl. others)	17,489.9	22,342.5	23,852.0

Source: Trade Map-Trade Competitiveness Map, International Trade Centre, www.intracen.org/marketanalysis.

Transport

RAILWAYS
(traffic)

	2002	2003	2004
Passenger-km (million)	33	4	2

Source: UN, *Statistical Yearbook*.

ROAD TRAFFIC
(motor vehicles in use at 31 December)

	2007	2009*	2010
Passenger cars	507,469	487,199	597,427
Buses and coaches	10,925	6,518	20,261
Lorries and vans	323,480	285,640	413,073
Motorcycles and mopeds	78,323	106,979	179,855

* Data for 2008 were not available.

Source: IRF, *World Road Statistics*.

SHIPPING

Flag Registered Fleet
(at 31 December)

	2011	2012	2013
Number of vessels	170	176	184
Total displacement ('000 grt)	326.3	331.3	330.6

Source: Lloyd's List Intelligence (www.lloydslistintelligence.com).

International Sea-borne Freight Traffic
('000 metric tons; estimates derived from monthly averages)

	2008	2009	2010
Goods loaded	31,944	31,764	19,944
Goods unloaded	16,680	13,740	10,380

Note: For goods unloaded, data include freight movement at ports of El Salitral, Esmeraldas, Guayaquil, La Libertad, Manta and Puerto Bolívar; data for goods loaded also include movements at the port of Balao.

Source: UN, *Monthly Bulletin of Statistics*.

CIVIL AVIATION
(traffic on scheduled services)

	2010	2011
Kilometres flown (million)	44	45
Passengers carried ('000)	4,818	5,094
Passenger-km (million)	5,421	5,720
Total ton-km (million)	615	63

Source: UN, *Statistical Yearbook*.

Passengers carried ('000): 5,512 in 2012 (Source: World Bank, World Development Indicators database).

Tourism

FOREIGN VISITOR ARRIVALS*

Country of residence	2009	2010	2011
Argentina	22,675	30,653	37,456
Canada	22,489	23,867	24,832
Chile	25,195	28,478	34,854
Colombia	160,116	203,916	265,563
France	19,810	20,272	20,426
Germany	24,841	25,011	26,662
Peru	150,548	154,216	144,968
Spain	56,400	59,030	60,664
United Kingdom	25,030	22,597	22,871
USA	242,096	249,081	241,590
Venezuela	29,416	31,558	38,246
Total (incl. others)	968,499	1,047,098	1,140,978

* Figures refer to total arrivals (including same-day visitors), except those of Ecuadorean nationals residing abroad.

Total visitor arrivals ('000): 1,141 in 2011; 1,272 in 2012 (provisional).

Tourism receipts (US $ million, excl. passenger transport): 781 in 2010; 843 in 2011; 1,026 in 2012 (provisional).

Source: World Tourism Organization.

Communications Media

	2010	2011	2012
Telephones ('000 main lines in use)	2,085.7	2,210.6	2,308.7
Mobile cellular telephones ('000 subscribers)	14,780.7	15,332.7	16,456.7
Internet subscribers ('000)	485.1	639.1	n.a.
Broadband subscribers ('000)	197.9	618.9	806.3

Source: International Telecommunication Union.

Education

(2011/12 unless otherwise indicated)

	Institutions	Teachers	Students ('000)		
			Males	Females	Total
Pre-primary	8,328	39,456	239.5	235.9	475.4
Primary	10,326	116,411	1,079.8	1,038.1	2,117.9
Secondary	34,689	132,867	772.7	758.0	1,530.7
Lower secondary	n.a.	70,605	443.9	414.2	858.1
Upper secondary	n.a.	62,262	328.7	343.8	672.5
Tertiary*	n.a.	26,910	251.9	282.6	534.5

* 2007/08.

Sources: UNESCO Institute for Statistics; Ministerio de Educación.

Pupil-teacher ratio (primary education, UNESCO estimate): 18.2 in 2011/12 (Source: UNESCO Institute for Statistics).

Adult literacy rate: 91.9% (males 93.3%; females 90.5%) in 2010 (Source: UNESCO Institute for Statistics).

Directory

The Government

HEAD OF STATE

President: Rafael Correa Delgado (took office 15 January 2007; re-elected 26 April 2009 and 17 February 2013).

Vice-President: Jorge David Glas Espinel.

CABINET

(April 2014)

The Government is comprised of members of the Alianza País.

Co-ordinating Ministers

Co-ordinating Minister for Social Development: Cecilia Vaca.

Co-ordinating Minister for Cultural and Natural Heritage: María Moncayo.

Co-ordinating Minister for Strategic Sectors: Rafael Poveda.

Co-ordinating Minister for Policy and Autonomous Governance: Viviana Bonilla Salcedo.

Co-ordinating Minister for Economic Policy: Patricio Rivera.

Co-ordinating Minister for Security: Homero Arellano.

Co-ordinating Minister for Production, Competitiveness and Commercialization: Dr Richard Espinosa Guzmán.

Co-ordinating Minister for Human Resources: Guillaume Long.

Ministers

Minister of Foreign Relations, Trade and Integration: Ricardo Armando Patiño Aroca.

Minister of Finance: Fausto Herrera.

Minister of the Interior: José Serrano.

Minister of National Defence: María Fernanda Espinosa Garcés.

Minister of Electricity and Renewable Energy: Esteban Albornoz.

Minister of Transport and Public Works: Paola Carvajal Ayala.

Minister of Telecommunications and Information: Jaime Guerrero Ruiz.

Minister of Agriculture, Livestock, Aquaculture and Fishing: Javier Ponce Cevallos.

Minister of Education: Augusto Espinosa Andrade.

Minister of Justice, Human Rights and Worship: Lenin Lara Rivadeneira.

Minister of Labour Relations: Dr Juan José Francisco Vacas.

Minister of Economic and Social Inclusion: Doris Solis Carrión.

Minister of Public Health: Dr Carina Vance Mafla.

Minister of Urban Development and Housing: Pedro Jaramillo Castillo.

Minister of Culture: Francisco Velasco Andrade.

Minister of Sport: José Francisco Cevallos Villavicencio.

Minister of the Environment: Lorena Tapia.

Minister of Tourism: (vacant).

Minister of Non-Renewable Natural Resources: Pedro Merizalde.

Minister of Industry and Productivity: Ramiro González Jaramillo.

National Secretaries

National Secretary of Public Administration: Vinicio Alvarado Espinel.

National Secretary of Communication: Fernando Alvarado Espinel.

National Secretary of Risk Management: María del Pilar Cornejo.

National Secretary of Management Transparency: Diego Guzmán Espinosa.

National Secretary of Water: Walter Solís.

National Secretary of Planning and Development: Fander Falconí.

National Secretary of Migrants: Lorena Escudero.

National Secretary of the People, Social Movements and Citizen Participation: Mireya Cárdenas.

National Secretary of Higher Education, Science, Technology and Innovation: René Ramírez Gallegos.

National Secretary of Intelligence: Lt-Col Rommy Vallejo Vallejo.

Secretary-General of the Presidency: Omar Simon.

MINISTRIES

Office of the President: Palacio Nacional, García Moreno 10–43, entre Chile y Espejo, Quito; tel. (2) 382-7000; e-mail prensa.externa@secom.gob.ec; internet www.presidencia.gob.ec.

Office of the Vice-President: Calle Benalcázar N4-40, entre Calles Espejo y Chile, Quito; tel. and fax (2) 258-4574; e-mail info@www.vicepresidencia.gob.ec; internet www.vicepresidencia.gob.ec.

Ministry of Agriculture, Livestock, Aquaculture and Fishing: Avda Eloy Alfaro y Amazonas, Quito; tel. (2) 396-0100; fax (2) 396-0200; e-mail webmaster@magap.gob.ec; internet www.magap.gob.ec.

Ministry of Culture: Avda Colón E5-34 y Juan León Mera, Quito; tel. (2) 381-4550; e-mail comunicacion@ministeriodecultura.gob.ec; internet www.ministeriodecultura.gob.ec.

Ministry of Economic and Social Inclusion: Edif. Matríz, Robles E3-33 y Ulpiano Páez, Quito; tel. (2) 398-3000; fax (2) 250-9850; e-mail jantonio.egas@mies.gob.ec; internet www.inclusion.gob.ec.

Ministry of Education: Avda Amazonas N34-451 y Avda Atahualpa, Quito; tel. (2) 396-1300; e-mail info@educacion.gob.ec; internet www.educacion.gob.ec.

Ministry of Electricity and Renewable Energy: Edif. Correos del Ecuador, 6°, Eloy Alfaro N29-50 y 9 de Octubre, Edif. Correos del Ecuador, Quito; tel. (2) 397-6000; e-mail sylvia.abad@meer.gob.ec; internet www.energia.gob.ec.

Ministry of the Environment: Calle Madrid 1159 y Andalusía, Quito; tel. (2) 398-7600; fax (2) 256-3462; e-mail mma@ambiente.gob.ec; internet www.ambiente.gob.ec.

Ministry of Finance: Avda 10 de Agosto 1661 y Bolivia, Quito; tel. (2) 399-8300; fax (2) 250-5256; e-mail mefecuador@finanzas.gob.ec; internet www.finanzas.gob.ec.

Ministry of Foreign Relations, Trade and Integration: Avda 10 de Agosto y Carrión E1-76, Quito; tel. (2) 299-3200; fax (2) 299-3273; e-mail gabminis@mmrree.gob.ec; internet www.mmrree.gob.ec.

Ministry of Industry and Productivity: Avda Eloy Alfaro y Amazonas, Quito; tel. (2) 254-6690; fax (2) 250-3818; e-mail ragama@mipro.gob.ec; internet www.mipro.gob.ec.

Ministry of the Interior: Espejo y Benalcázar N4-24, Quito; tel. (2) 295-5666; fax (2) 295-8360; e-mail informacion@ministeriodelinterior.gob.ec; internet www.ministeriodelinterior.gob.ec.

Ministry of Justice, Human Rights and Worship: Avda Colón, entre Diego de Almagro y Reina Victoria, Quito; tel. (2) 395-5840; fax (2) 246-4914; e-mail sindatos@minjusticia.gob.ec; internet www.justicia.gob.ec.

Ministry of Labour Relations: República del Salvador N34-183 y Suiza, Quito; tel. (2) 381-4000; fax (2) 254-2580; e-mail comunicacion_social@mrl.gob.ec; internet www.relacioneslaborales.gob.ec.

Ministry of National Defence: Calle Exposición S4-71 y Benigno Vela, Quito; tel. (2) 295-1951; fax (2) 258-0941; e-mail comunicacion@midena.gob.ec; internet www.defensa.gob.ec.

Ministry of Non-Renewable Natural Resources: Edif. MTOP, Avda Orellana 26-220 y Juan León Mera (esq.), Quito; tel. (2) 297-7000; fax (2) 290-6350; e-mail Chrystiam_Cevallos@mrnnr.gob.ec; internet www.mrnnr.gob.ec.

Ministry of Public Health: República de El Salvador 36-64 y Suecia, Quito; tel. and fax (2) 381-4400; e-mail comunicacion.social@msp.gob.ec; internet www.salud.gob.ec.

Ministry of Sport: Avda Gaspar de Villaroel E10-122 y 6 de Diciembre, Quito; tel. (2) 396-9200; fax (2) 245-4418; e-mail comunicacion@deporte.gob.ec; internet www.deporte.gob.ec.

Ministry of Telecommunications and Information: Avda 6 de Diciembre N25-75 y Avda Colón, Quito; tel. (2) 220-0200; fax (2) 222-8950; e-mail info@mintel.gob.ec; internet www.telecomunicaciones.gob.ec.

Ministry of Tourism: El Telégrafo E7-58, entre El Tiempo y Avda de los Shyris, Quito; tel. and fax (2) 399-9333; e-mail contactenos@turismo.gob.ec; internet www.turismo.gob.ec.

Ministry of Transport and Public Works: Avda Juan León Mera N26-220 y Orellana, Quito; tel. (2) 397-4600; e-mail comunicacion@mtop.gob.ec; internet www.mtop.gob.ec.

Ministry of Urban Development and Housing: Avda 10 de Agosto y Luis Cordero, Quito; tel. (2) 223-8060; fax (2) 256-6785; e-mail despacho@miduvi.gob.ec; internet www.miduvi.gob.ec.

President and Legislature

PRESIDENT

Election, 17 February 2013

Candidate	Valid votes	% of valid votes
Rafael Correa Delgado (Alianza País)	4,918,482	57.17
Guillermo Alberto Santiago Lasso Mendoza (CREO)	1,951,102	22.68
Lucio Gutiérrez Borbua (PSP)	578,875	6.73
Mauricio Esteban Rodas Espinel (Movimiento SUMA)	335,532	3.90
Alvaro Fernando Noboa Pontón (PRIAN)	319,956	3.72
Alberto Acosta Espinosa (Unidad Plurinacional de las Izquierdas)	280,539	3.26
Others	218,117	2.54
Total*	8,602,603	100.00

* In addition, there were 179,230 blank and 684,027 invalid ballots.

NATIONAL ASSEMBLY
(Asamblea Nacional)

President: GABRIELA RIVADENEIRA.

Election, 17 February 2013

Political parties	Seats
Alianza País (AP)	97
CREO	12
Partido Social Cristiano (PSC)	6
Partido Sociedad Patriótica 21 de Enero (PSP)	6
Unidad Plurinacional de las Izquierdas (UPI)	6
Avanza	5
Independents	3
Partido Roldosista Ecuatoriano (PRE)	1
Sociedad Unida Más Acción (Movimiento SUMA)	1
Total	137

Election Commission

Consejo Nacional Electoral (CNE): Avda 6 de Diciembre N33-122 y Bosmediano, Quito; tel. (2) 381-5410; internet www.cne.gob.ec; f. 2008 to replace the Tribunal Supremo Electoral; independent; Pres. DOMINGO PAREDES CASTILLO.

Political Organizations

Alianza País (Patria Altiva i Soberana—AP): Of. 501, Edif. Torres Whimper, Diego de Almagro 32-27 y Whimper, Quito; tel. (2) 600-0630; fax (2) 600-1029; e-mail galoisho57@yahoo.com; internet movimientoalianzapais.com.ec; f. 2006; electoral alliance mainly comprising the Movimiento País; left-wing; Pres. RAFAEL CORREA DELGADO; Exec. Sec. GALO MORA WITT.

Avanza: Avda Naciones Unidas OE1–108, entre Avda 10 de Agusto y Barón de Carondelet, Quito; tel. (2) 603-6808; e-mail partidoavanza@gmail.com; internet www.avanza.ec; f. 2012; Pres. RAMIRO GONZÁLEZ.

CREO (Creando Oportunidades): Edif. Albra, 6°, Of. 601, Orellana E11-75 y Coruña, Quito; tel. (2) 382-6154; e-mail registro@creo.com.ec; internet creo.com.ec; f. 2012; supported the 2013 presidential election candidacy of Guillermo Alberto Santiago Lasso Mendoza; Nat. Pres. CÉSAR MONGE.

Movimiento Ruptura 25: Quito; f. 2004; left-wing; fmr mem. of Alianza País; Pres. MARÍA PAULA ROMO.

Movimiento SUMA (Sociedad Unida Más Acción): Quito; internet www.suma.ec; f. 2012; Leader MAURICIO ESTEBAN RODAS ESPINEL.

Partido Renovador Institucional Acción Nacional (PRIAN): Quito; internet www.prian.org.ec; right-wing, populist; Leader ALVARO FERNANDO NOBOA PONTÓN.

Partido Roldosista Ecuatoriano (PRE): 1 de Mayo 912 y Tulcán, Quito; tel. (2) 229-0542; fax (2) 269-0250; e-mail dalo-por-hecho@hotmail.com; internet www.dalo10.com; f. 1982; populist; Nat. Dir ABDALÁ BUCARAM PULLEY.

Partido Social Cristiano (PSC): Gerónimo Carrión E6-21 (entre Juan León Mera y Reina Victoria), Casilla 9454, Quito; internet www.la6.ec; f. 1951; centre right; Pres. PASCUAL EUGENIO DEL CIOPPO ARAGUNDI.

Partido Sociedad Patriótica 21 de Enero (PSP): Calle República del Salvador N34-107 y Suiza, Quito; e-mail faustolupera@yahoo.com; internet www.lucio3.com; f. 2002; Leader LUCIO GUTIÉRREZ BORBUA.

Unidad Plurinacional de las Izquierdas (UPI) (Coordinadora Plurinacional de las Izquierdas): Quito; f. 2011; leftist coalition; 2013 presidential election candidate Alberto Acosta Espinosa; constituent political parties and movts include Montecristi Vive, Movimiento Convocatoria por la Unidad Provincial, Poder Popular, Frente Popular and the following:

Movimiento Popular Democrático (MPD): Manuel Larrea N14-70 y Rio Frío, Quito; tel. (2) 250-3580; fax (2) 252-6111; e-mail info@mpd15.org.ec; internet www.mpd15.org.ec; f. 1978; attached to the PCMLE (q.v.); Dir LUIS VILLACÍS; Sec. MARCO CADENA.

Movimiento de Unidad Pluriacional Pachakútik—Nuevo País (MUPP—NP): Calle Lugo 13-04 y Avda Ladrón de Guevara, La Floresta, Quito; tel. (2) 322-7259; fax (2) 256-0422; e-mail info@pachakutik.org.ec; internet www.pachakutik.org.ec; f. 1995 as Movimiento Nuevo País—Pachakútik (MNPP); represents indigenous, environmental and social groups; Nat. Co-ordinator RAFAEL ANTUNÍ; Sec. PATRICIO QUEZADA ORTEGA.

Participación: Quito; f. 2011; Pres. MARCELO LARREA.

Partido Comunista Marxista-Leninista de Ecuador (PCMLE): e-mail pcmle@bigfoot.com; internet www.pcmle.org; f. 1964; contests elections as the MPD; Leader OSWALDO PALACIOS.

Partido Socialista—Frente Amplio (PS—FA): Avda Gran Colombia N15-201 y Yaguachi, Quito; tel. (2) 232-4417; fax (2) 222-2184; e-mail psecuador@andinanet.net; internet psfaecuador .org; f. 1926; Pres. RAFAEL QUINTERO; Sec.-Gen. JOSÉ ROBAYO ZAPATA.

Red Etica y Democracia (RED): Edif. Alemania, 1°, Alemania y Guayanas, Quito; tel. (2) 222-3348; e-mail info@ redeticaydemocracia.com; Leader MARTHA ROLDÓS.

Unión Demócrata Cristiana (UDC): Pradera N30-58 y San Salvador, Quito; tel. (2) 250-2995; e-mail cbonilla@udc.com.ec; internet www.udc.com.ec; f. 1978 as Democracia Popular-Unión Demócrata Cristiana (DP-UDC); adopted current name 2006; deregistered as a pol. party by the CNE in 2013; Pres. SANDRA ALARCÓN.

OTHER ORGANIZATIONS

Confederación de las Nacionalidades Indígenas de la Amazonia Ecuatoriana (CONFENIAE): Union Base, Apdo 17-01-4180, Puyo; tel. (3) 227-644; fax (3) 227-644; e-mail info_confel@ confeniae.org.ec; represents indigenous peoples; mem. of CONAIE; Pres. TITO PUANCHIR.

Confederación de Nacionalidades Indígenas del Ecuador (CONAIE): Avda Los Granados 2553 y 6 de Diciembre, Quito; tel. (2) 245-2335; fax (2) 244-4991; e-mail info@conaie.org; internet www .conaie.org; f. 1986; represents indigenous peoples; MUPP—NP represents CONAIE and related orgs in the legislature; Pres. HUMBERTO CHOLANGO; Vice-Pres. MIGUEL GUATEMAL.

Confederación de los Pueblos de Nacionalidad Kichua del Ecuador (Ecuarunari): Edif. El Conquistador, 1°, Julio Matovelle 128, entre Vargas y Pasaje San Luis, Quito; tel. (2) 258-0700; fax (2) 258-0713; e-mail ecuarunari@ecuarunari.org; internet www .ecuarunari.org; f. 1972; indigenous movt; Pres. DELFÍN TENESACA.

Coordinadora de las Organizaciones Indígenas de la Cuenca Amazónica (COICA): Sevilla N24-358 y Guipuzcoa, La Floresta, Quito; tel. (2) 322-6744; e-mail com@coica.org.ec; internet www.coica .org.ec; f. 1984 in Lima, Peru; moved to Quito in 1993; umbrella group of 9 orgs representing indigenous peoples of the Amazon Basin in Bolivia, Brazil, Colombia, Ecuador, French Guiana, Guyana, Suriname and Venezuela; Gen. Co-ordinator EGBERTO TABO CHIPUNAVI; Vice-Co-ordinator ROSA ALVORADO.

ARMED GROUPS

The following guerrilla organizations were reported to be active in the 2000s.

Ejército de Liberación Alfarista (ELA): f. 2001; extreme left-wing insurrectionist group; formed by fmr mems of disbanded armed groups Alfaro Vive ¡Carajo!, Montoneros Patria Libre and Sol Rojo; Spokesperson SEBASTIÁN SÁNCHEZ.

Grupos de Combatientes Populares (GCP): Cuenca; internet gcp-ecuador.blogspot.com; communist guerrilla grouping; active since 2000.

Izquierda Revolucionaria Armada (IRA): extreme left-wing revolutionary group opposed to international capitalism.

Milicias Revolucionarias del Pueblo (MRP): extreme left-wing grouping opposed to international capitalism.

Diplomatic Representation

EMBASSIES IN ECUADOR

Argentina: Avda Amazonas 447 y Roca, 8°, Apdo 17-12-937, Quito; tel. (2) 256-2292; fax (2) 256-8177; e-mail eecua@cancilleria.gob.ar; Ambassador ALBERTO ÁLVAREZ TUFILLO.

Bolivia: Avda Eloy Alfaro 2432 y Fernando Ayarza, Apdo 17-210003, Quito; tel. (2) 244-4830; fax (2) 224-4833; e-mail embajadabolivia@ embajadabolivia.ec; internet www.embajadabolivia.ec; Ambassador RUSENA MARIBEL SANTAMARÍA MAMANI.

Brazil: Edif. Amazonas Plaza, Avda Amazonas, N39-123 y José Arízaga, 7°, Quito; tel. (2) 227-7300; fax (2) 250-4468; e-mail ebrasil@ embajadadelbrasil.org.ec; internet quito.itamaraty.gov.br/pt-br; Ambassador FERNANDO SIMAS MAGALHÃES.

Canada: Edif. Eurocenter, 3°, Avda Amazonas 4153 y Unión Nacional de Periodistas, Apdo 17-11-6512, Quito; tel. (2) 245-5499; fax (2) 227-7672; e-mail quito@international.gc.ca; internet www .canadainternational.gc.ca/ecuador-equateur; Ambassador PAMELA O'DONNELL.

Chile: Edif. Xerox, 4°, Juan Pablo Sanz 3617 y Amazonas, Apdo 17-17-206, Quito; tel. (2) 245-3327; fax (2) 244-4470; e-mail echile .ecuador@minrel.gov.cl; internet chileabroad.gov.cl/ecuador/; Ambassador GABRIEL ASCENCIO.

China, People's Republic: Avda Atahualpa 349 y Amazonas, Quito; tel. (2) 244-4362; fax (2) 244-4364; e-mail embchina@uio .telconet.net; internet ec.china-embassy.org/chn/; Ambassador WANG SHIXIONG.

Colombia: Edif. World Trade Center, Torre B, 14°, Avda 12 de Octubre No 24-528 y Luis Cordero, Quito; tel. (2) 223-6463; fax (2) 222-1969; e-mail eecuador@cancilleria.gov.co; internet ecuador .embajada.gov.co/; Ambassador RICARDO LOZANO FORERO.

Costa Rica: Javier Aráuz 111 y Germán Alemán, Apdo 17-03-301, Quito; tel. (2) 225-2330; fax (2) 225-4087; e-mail embajcr@uio.satnet .net; Ambassador PAULA MARÍA MIRANDA.

Cuba: Mercurio 365, entre La Razón y El Vengador, Quito; tel. (2) 245-6936; fax (2) 243-0594; e-mail embajada@embacuba.ec; internet www.cubadiplomatica.cu/ecuador; Ambassador JORGE RODRIGUEZ HERNÁNDEZ.

Dominican Republic: German Alemán E12-80 y Juan Ramírez, Sector Megamaxi, Batan Alto, Quito; tel. (2) 243-4232; fax (2) 243-4275; e-mail info@embajadadominicanaecuador.com; internet www .embajadadominicanaecuador.com; Ambassador VÍCTOR REINALDO LORA DÍAZ.

Egypt: Avda Tarqui E4-56 y Avda 6 de Diciembre, Apdo 17-7-9355, Quito; tel. (2) 222-5240; fax (2) 256-3521; e-mail embassy.quito@mfa .gov.eg; internet www.mfa.gov.eg/Quito_Emb; Ambassador MEDHAT K. EL-MELIGY.

El Salvador: Edif. Banco del Litoral, 2°, Calle Japón E5-25 y Avda Amazonas, Quito; tel. (2) 225-4433; fax (2) 225-4431; e-mail embajada@elsalvador.com.ec; internet www.elsalvador.com.ec; Ambassador LUIS ALBERTO CORDOVA.

France: Calle Leonidas Plaza 107 y Avda Patria, Apdo 19-13-536, Quito; tel. (2) 294-3800; fax (2) 294-3809; e-mail chancellerie.quito@ ifrance.com; internet www.ambafrance-ec.org; Ambassador FRANÇOIS GAUTHIER.

Germany: Edif. Citiplaza, 13° y 14°, Avda Naciones Unidas E10-44 y República de El Salvador, Apdo 17-17-536, Quito; tel. (2) 297-0820; fax (2) 297-0815; e-mail info@quito.diplo.de; internet www.quito .diplo.de; Ambassador ALEXANDER OLBRICH.

Guatemala: Edif. Gabriela III, 3°, Of. 301, Avda República de El Salvador 733 y Portugal, Apdo 17-03-294, Quito; tel. (2) 368-0397; fax (2) 368-0397; e-mail embecuador@minex.gob.gt; Ambassador GALO ANDRÉS YÉPEZ HOLGUÍN.

Holy See: Avda Orellana 692 E10-03, Apdo 17-07-8980, Quito; tel. (2) 250-5200; fax (2) 256-4810; e-mail nunzec@uio.satnet.net; Apostolic Nuncio Most Rev. GIACOMO GUIDO OTTONELLO (Titular Archbishop of Sasabe).

Honduras: Edif. Suecia, Avda Shyris y calle Suecia 277, 5° Norte, Apdo 17-03-4753, Quito; tel. (2) 243-8820; fax (2) 244-2476; e-mail embhquito@yahoo.com; Chargé d'affaires a.i. WENDY FABIOLA FLORES GUEVARA.

Indonesia: Avda Portugal E 12-33 y Francisco Cazanova, Quito; tel. (2) 224-7677; fax (2) 333-1967; e-mail lopezmar_indos@yahoo.com; internet www.kemlu.go.id/quito/Pages/default.aspx; Ambassador SAUT MARULI TUA GULTOM.

Iran: José Queri E14-43 y Avda Los Granados, Quito; tel. (2) 334-3450; fax (2) 245-2824; e-mail embiranecuador@gmail.com; Ambassador AHMAD PABARJA.

Israel: Edif. Altana Plaza, Avda La Coruña E25-58 y San Ignacio, Quito; tel. (2) 397-1500; fax (2) 397-1555; e-mail info@quito.mfa.gov .il; internet www.quito.mfa.gov.il; Ambassador ELIYAHU YERUSHALMI.

Italy: Calle La Isla 111 y Humberto Alborñoz, Apdo 17-03-72, Quito; tel. (2) 321-1647; fax (2) 321-0818; e-mail archivio.quito@esteri.it; internet www.ambquito.esteri.it; Ambassador GIANNI MICHELE PICCATO.

Japan: Edif. Amazonas Plaza, 11° y 12°, Avda Amazonas N39-123 y Arízaga, Apdo 17-21-01518, Quito; tel. (2) 227-8700; fax (2) 244-9399; e-mail embapon@qi.mofa.go.jp; internet www.ec.emb-japan.go.jp; Ambassador TORU KODAKI.

Korea, Republic: Edif. World Trade Center, Avda 12 de Octubre 1942 y Cordero, Torre B, 3°, Apdo 17-03-626, Quito; tel. (2) 290-9227; fax (2) 250-1190; e-mail ecuador@mofat.go.kr; internet ecu.mofat.go .kr; Ambassador IN GYUN CHUNG.

Mexico: Avda 6 de Diciembre N36-165 y Naciones Unidas, Apdo 17-11-6371, Quito; tel. (2) 292-3770; fax (2) 244-8245; e-mail embajadamexico@embamex.org.ec; internet www.sre.gob.mx/ ecuador; Ambassador JAIME DEL ARENAL FENOCHIO.

Panama: Germán Alemán No E12-92 y Arroyo, Del Río en el sector Batán Bajo, Quito; tel. (2) 245-1806; fax (2) 245-1825; e-mail panaembaecuador@hotmail.com; internet www

.embajadadepanamaecuador.com; Ambassador JOSÉ NORIEL ACOSTA RODRÍQUEZ.

Paraguay: Edif. Torre Sol Verde, 8°, Avda 12 de Octubre, esq. Salazar, Apdo 17-03-139, Quito; tel. (2) 290-9005; fax (2) 290-9006; e-mail embapar@uio.satnet.net; internet www.embajadadeparaguay.ec/; Ambassador JOSÉ MARÍA ARGANA MATEU.

Peru: Avda República de El Salvador N34-361 e Irlanda, Apdo 17-07-9380, Quito; tel. (2) 246-8410; fax (2) 225-2560; e-mail embaperu-quito@rree.gob.pe; internet www.embajadadelperu.org.ec; Ambassador ESTHER ELIZABETH ASTETE RODRÍGUEZ.

Russia: Reina Victoria 462 y Ramón Roca, Apdo 17-01-3868, Quito; tel. (2) 252-6361; fax (2) 256-5531; e-mail embrusia_ecuador@mail.ru; internet www.ecuador.mid.ru; Ambassador YAN A. BURLIAY.

Spain: General Francisco Salazar E12-73 y Toledo (Sector La Floresta), Apdo 17-01-9322, Quito; tel. (2) 322-6296; fax (2) 322-7805; e-mail emb.quito@mae.es; internet www.maec.es/embajadas/quito; Ambassador VÍCTOR FAGILDE GONZÁLEZ.

Switzerland: Edif. Xerox, 2°, Avda Amazonas 3617 y Juan Pablo Sanz, Apdo 17-11-4815, Quito; tel. (2) 243-4949; fax (2) 244-9314; e-mail qui.vertretung@eda.admin.ch; internet www.eda.admin.ch/quito; Ambassador ROLAND FISCHER.

Turkey: Calle Sebastián de Benalcázar 9-28, entre Oriente y Esmeraldas, Centro Histórico, Quito; tel. (2) 251-1490; fax 251-1493; e-mail embassy.quito@mfa.gov.tr; Ambassador KORKUT GÜNGEN.

United Kingdom: Edif. Citiplaza, 14°, Avda Naciones Unidas y República de El Salvador, Apdo 17-17-830, Quito; tel. (2) 297-0800; fax (2) 297-0809; e-mail britembq@uio.satnet.net; internet ukinecuador.fco.gov.uk; Ambassador PATRICK MULLEE.

USA: Avigiras 12-170 y Eloy Alfaro, Apdo 17-17-1538, Quito; tel. (2) 398-5000; fax (2) 398-5100; e-mail contacto.usembuio@state.gov; internet ecuador.usembassy.gov; Ambassador ADAM E. NAMM.

Uruguay: Edif. Josueth González, 9°, Avda 6 de Diciembre 2816 y Paul Rivet, Apdo 17-12-282, Quito; tel. (2) 256-3762; fax (2) 256-3763; e-mail uruecuador@mrree.gub.uy; Ambassador ENRIQUE DELGADO GENTA.

Venezuela: Edif. COMONSA, 8° y 9°, Avda Amazonas N30-240 y Eloy Alfaro, Apdo 17-01-688, Quito; tel. (2) 255-4032; fax (2) 252-0306; e-mail embve.ecqto@mre.gob.ve; internet ecuador.embajada.gob.ve; Ambassador MARÍA DE LOURDES URBANEJA DURANT.

Judicial System

CONSTITUTIONAL COURT

Tribunal Contencioso Electoral: José Manuel Abascal N37-499 y Portete, Apdo 17-17-949, Quito; tel. (2) 381-5000; e-mail servicio.ciudadano@tce.gob.ec; internet www.tce.gob.ec; f. 2008 by reform of fmr Tribunal Constitucional; Pres. Dr MARÍA CATALINA CASTRO LLERENA; Sec.-Gen. GUILLERMO FALCONÍ.

NATIONAL COURT OF JUSTICE

Corte Nacional de Justicia: Avda Amazonas N37-101, esq. Unión Nacional de Periodistas, Quito; tel. (2) 227-8396; e-mail ramaguai@funcionjudicial-pichincha.gov.ec; internet www.cortenacional.gob.ec; f. 1830 as Corte Suprema de Justicia; reconstituted in 2008 under new Constitution; 21 Justices, including the President; two penal law courts, one administrative litigation court, one fiscal law court, one civil law court and two employment law courts; Pres. Dr CARLOS RAMIREZ ROMERO.

Attorney-General: Dr DIEGO GARCÍA CARRIÓN.

TRANSITIONAL COUNCIL OF THE JUDICIARY

Consejo de la Judicatura: Jorge Washington E4-157, entre Juan León Mera y Avda Río Amazonas, Quito; e-mail webadmin@funcionjudicial.gob.ec; internet www.funcionjudicial.gob.ec; f. 1998; transitional council created by July 2011 referendum charged with reform of the judicial system; Pres. GUSTAVO JALKH.

Religion

There is no state religion, but the vast majority of the population are Roman Catholics. There are representatives of various Protestant Churches and of the Jewish faith in Quito and Guayaquil.

CHRISTIANITY

The Roman Catholic Church

Ecuador comprises four archdioceses, 12 dioceses and eight Apostolic Vicariates. Some 90% of the population are Roman Catholics.

Bishops' Conference: Conferencia Episcopal Ecuatoriana, Avda América 24-59 y La Gasca, Apdo 17-01-1081, Quito; tel. (2) 222-3139; fax (2) 250-1429; e-mail info@iglesiacatolica.ec; internet www.iglesiacatolica.ec; f. 1939; statutes approved 1999; Pres. Most Rev. ANTONIO ARREGUI YARZA (Archbishop of Guayaquil).

Archbishop of Cuenca: LUIS GERARDO CABRERA HERRERA, Arzobispado, Manuel Vega 8-66 y Calle Bolívar, Apdo 01-01-0046, Cuenca; tel. (7) 284-7234; fax (7) 284-4436; e-mail jlcabrera@arquicuencaec.org; internet www.arquicuencaec.org.

Archbishop of Guayaquil: ANTONIO ARREGUI YARZA, Arzobispado, Edif. Promoción Humana, 3°, Of. 302, Diagonal a la Catedral de Guayaquil, Avda 10 de Agosto 541 y Boyacá, Guayaquil; tel. (4) 232-2778; fax (4) 232-9695; e-mail secretaria@rccguayaquil.com; internet www.rccguayaquil.com.

Archbishop of Portoviejo: LORENZO VOLTOLINI ESTI, Arzobispado, Avda Universitaria s/n, Entre Alajuela y Ramos y Duarte, Apdo 13-01-0024, Portoviejo; tel. (5) 263-0404; fax (5) 263-4428; e-mail arzobis@ecua.net.ec; internet arquidiocesisdeportoviejo.org.

Archbishop of Quito: FAUSTO GABRIEL TRÁVEZ TRÁVEZ, Palacio Arzobispal, Calle Chile 1140, Apdo 17-01-106, Quito; tel. (2) 228-4429; fax (2) 252-7898; e-mail info@arquidiocesisdequito.ec; internet www.arquidiocesisdequito.ec.

The Anglican Communion

Anglicans in Ecuador are under the jurisdiction of Province IX of the Episcopal Church in the USA. The country is divided into two dioceses, one of which, Central Ecuador, is a missionary diocese.

Bishop of Central Ecuador: Rt Rev. LUIS FERNANDO RUIZ RESTREPO, Avda Francisco Sarmiento 39-54 y Portete, Apdo 17-03-353, Quito; tel. (2) 254–1735; internet www.episcopalchurch.org/diocese/central-ecuador.

Bishop of Littoral Ecuador: Rt Rev. ALFREDO MORANTE, Amarilis Fuente 603, entre José Vicente Trujillo y la D, Apdo 0901-5250, Guayaquil; tel. (4) 244-6699; e-mail iedl@gu.pro.ec; internet www.episcopalchurch.org/diocese/litoral-ecuador.

Other Churches

Church of Jesus Christ of Latter-Day Saints (Mormons): Calle 6ta y Avda Rodrigo Chávez González, Principado de las Lomas Urdesa Norte, Guayaquil; tel. (4) 288-9388; internet www.lds.org; 211,165 mems.

Convención Bautista Ecuatoriana: Casilla 3236, Guayaquil; tel. (4) 237-5673; fax 245-2319; e-mail julxa@hotmail.com; internet bautistasec.com; f. 1950; Baptist; Pres. Rev. JULIO XAVIER ALVARADO SILVA.

Iglesia Evangélica Metodista Unida del Ecuador: Rumipamba 915, Apdo 17-03-236, Quito; tel. (2) 226-5158; fax (2) 243-9576; Methodist; Bishop SILVIO CEVALLOS PARRA; 800 mems, 2,000 adherents.

BAHÁ'Í FAITH

National Spiritual Assembly of the Bahá'ís: Calle García Moreno 135 y Calle Cumba, Cumbayá, Quito; tel. (2) 256-3484; fax (2) 252-3192; e-mail aelquito@gmail.com; internet www.bahaiecuador.org; mems resident in 1,121 localities.

The Press

PRINCIPAL DAILIES

Quito

El Comercio: Avda Pedro Vicente Maldonado 11515 y el Tablón, Apdo 17-01-57, Quito; tel. (2) 267-0999; fax (2) 267-0214; e-mail contactenos@elcomercio.com; internet www.elcomercio.com; f. 1906; morning; independent; Proprs Compañía Anónima El Comercio; Pres. FABRIZIO ACQUAVIVA MANTILLA; Editor FERNANDO LARENAS; circ. 160,000.

La Hora: Panamericana Norte km 3½, Quito; tel. (2) 247-5724; fax (2) 247-6085; e-mail nacional@lahora.com.ec; internet www.lahora.com.ec; f. 1982; 12 regional edns; Pres. Dr FRANCISCO VIVANCO RIOFRÍO; Gen. Editor JUANA LÓPEZ SARMIENTO.

Hoy: Avda Mariscal Sucre Of. 6-116, Apdo 17-07-09069, Quito; tel. (2) 249-0888; fax (2) 249-1881; e-mail hoy@hoy.com.ec; internet www.hoy.com.ec; f. 1982; morning; independent; Dir JAIME MANTILLA ANDERSON; Editor JUAN TIBANLOMBO; circ. 72,000.

Ultimas Noticias: Avda Pedro Vicente Maldonado 11515 y el Tablón, Apdo 17-01-57, Quito; tel. (2) 267-0999; fax (2) 267-4923; e-mail mivoz@ultimasnoticias.ec; internet www.ultimasnoticias.ec; f. 1938; evening; independent; commercial; Proprs Compañía Anónima El Comercio; Dir JORGE RIBADENEIRA; Gen. Editor CARLOS MORA; circ. 60,000.

Guayaquil

Expreso: Avda Carlos Julio Arosemena km 2½ y Las Mongas, Casilla 5890, Guayaquil; tel. (4) 220-1100; fax (4) 220-0291; e-mail editorgeneral@granasa.com.ec; internet www.diario-expreso.com; f. 1973; morning; independent; Dir GALO MARTÍNEZ MERCHÁN; Gen. Editor RUBÉN DARÍO BUITRÓN; circ. 60,000.

Extra: Avda Carlos Julio Arosemena km 2½, Casilla 5890, Guayaquil; tel. (4) 220-1100; fax (4) 220-0291; e-mail matriz@granasa.com.ec; internet www.diario-extra.com; f. 1974; morning; popular; Dir NICOLÁS ULLOA FIGUEROA; circ. 200,000.

La Razón: Avda Constitución y las Américas, Guayaquil; tel. (4) 228-0100; fax (4) 228-5110; e-mail cartas@larazonecuador.com; internet www.larazonecuador.com; f. 1965; morning; independent; circ. 35,000.

El Telégrafo: Avda Carlos Julio Arosemena, Km 1.5, Guayaquil; tel. (4) 259-5700; fax (4) 232-3265; e-mail info@telegrafo.com.ec; internet www.telegrafo.com.ec; f. 1884; acquired by the state in 2008 and refounded; morning; Dir ORLANDO PÉREZ; Chief Editor OMAR JAEN.

El Universo: Avda Domingo Comín y Alban, Casilla 09-01-531, Guayaquil; tel. (4) 249-0000; fax (4) 249-1034; e-mail redaccion@eluniverso.com; internet www.eluniverso.com; f. 1921; morning; independent; Dir CARLOS PÉREZ BARRIGA; Gen. Editor GUSTAVO CORTEZ; circ. 174,000 (weekdays), 290,000 (Sundays).

Cuenca

El Mercurio: Avda las Américas, Sector El Arenal, Casilla 60, Cuenca; tel. (7) 409-5682; fax (7) 409-5685; e-mail redaccion1@elmercurio.com.ec; internet www.elmercurio.com.ec; f. 1924; morning; Dir NICANOR MERCHÁN LUCO; Editor JORGE DURÁN FIGUEROA.

El Tiempo: Avda Loja y Rodrigo de Triana, Cuenca; tel. (7) 288-2551; fax (7) 288-2555; e-mail redaccion@eltiempo.com.ec; internet www.eltiempo.com.ec; f. 1955; morning; independent; Dir Dr RENÉ TORAL CALLE; Editor MARGARITA TORAL PEÑA; circ. 35,000.

Portoviejo

El Diario: Avda Metropolitana Eloy Alfaro, Km 1½, Vía Manta, Casilla 13-01-050, Portoviejo; tel. (5) 293-3777; fax (5) 293-3151; e-mail redaccion@eldiario.ec; internet www.eldiario.ec; f. 1992; independent; Dir PEDRO ZAMBRANO LAPENTTI; Editor JAIME UGALDE MOREIRA.

Ibarra

El Norte: Avda Juan José Flores 11-55 y Avda Jaime Rivadeneira Imbabura, Ibarra; tel. (6) 295-5495; fax (6) 264-3873; e-mail info@elnorte.ec; internet www.elnorte.ec; Exec. Pres. LUIS MEJÍA MONTESDEOCA; Editor DANILO MORENO.

PERIODICALS

Quito

Chasqui: Avda Diego de Almagro 32-133 y Andrade Marín, Apdo 17-01-584, Quito; tel. (2) 254-8011; fax (2) 250-2487; e-mail chasqui@ciespal.net; internet www.revistachasqui.com; f. 1997; quarterly; media studies; publ. of the Centro Internacional de Estudios Superiores de Comunicación para América Latina (CIESPAL); Dir EDGAR JARAMILLO; Editor GUSTAVO ABAD.

Cosas: Avda 12 de Octubre N26-14 y Avda La Coruña, Quito; tel. and fax (2) 250-2444; e-mail redaccion@cosas.com.ec; internet www.cosas.com.ec; f. 1994; women's interest; Dir PATTY SALAME; Editor MARTHA DUBRAVCIC.

Criterios: Edif. Las Cámaras, 4°, Avda Amazonas y República, Casilla 17-01-202, Quito; tel. (2) 244-3787; fax (2) 243-5862; e-mail criterios@lacamaradequito.com; internet www.lacamaradequito.com; f. 1996; monthly; organ of the Cámara de Comercio de Quito; commerce; Dir-Gen. LOLO ECHEVERRÍA.

Gestión: Edif. Delta, 2°, Avda González Suárez N27-317 y San Ignacio, Quito; tel. (2) 255-9930; e-mail revistagestion@dinediciones.com; internet www.revistagestion.ec; f. 1994; monthly; economy and society; Dir JUANITA ORDOÑEZ; Editor Dr GONZALO ORTIZ; circ. 15,000.

Mundo Diners: Edif. Delta, 2°, Avda González Suárez N27-317 y San Ignacio, Quito; tel. (2) 250-5588; e-mail revistamundodiners@dinediciones.com; internet www.revistamundodiners.com; f. 1986; monthly; culture, politics, society, etc.; Pres. FIDEL EGAS GRIJALVA.

Guayaquil

El Agro: Adace Calle 11 y Calle A, Casilla 09-01-9686, Guayaquil; tel. (4) 269-0019; fax (4) 269-0555; e-mail elagro@uminasa.com; internet www.elagro.com.ec; f. 1991; monthly; agriculture; Pres. EDUARDO PEÑA; Gen. Editor ALEXANDRA ZAMBRANO DE ANDRIUOLI.

Análisis Semanal: Edif. La Mirador, Of. 2, Plaza Lagos, Km. 6.5, Vía Puntilla, Samborondón, Guayaquil; tel. (4) 500-9343; e-mail info@ecuadoranalysis.com; internet www.ecuadoranalysis.com; weekly; economic and political affairs; Editor WALTER SPURRIER BAQUERIZO.

El Financiero: Avda Jorge Pérez Concha (Circunvalación Sur) 201 y Única, Casilla 6666, Guayaquil; tel. (4) 288-0203; fax (4) 288-2950; e-mail redacciong@elfinanciero.com; internet www.elfinanciero.com; weekly; business and economic news; f. 1990; Dir XAVIER PÉREZ MACCOLLUM.

Generación XXI: Aguirre 734 y García Avilés, Guayaquil; tel. (4) 232-7200; fax (4) 232-4870; e-mail g21@vistazo.com; internet www.generacion21.com; f. 1996; youth; Dir SEBASTIAN MÉLIÈRES; Editor CHRISTIAN KALIL CARTER.

Revista Estadio: Aguirre 734 y García Avilés, Casilla 09-01-1239, Guayaquil; tel. (4) 232-7200; fax (4) 232-0499; e-mail estadio@vistazo.com; internet www.revistaestadio.com; f. 1962; fortnightly; sport; Dir-Gen. SEBASTIAN MÉLIÈRES; Editor FABRICIO ZAVALA GARCÍA; circ. 40,000.

Revista Hogar: Aguirre 724 y Boyacá, Apdo 09-01-1239, Guayaquil; tel. (4) 232-7200; fax (4) 232-4870; e-mail rbustap@vistazo.com; internet www.revistahogar.com; f. 1964; monthly; women's interest; Dir-Gen. MARÍA GABRIELA GÁLVEZ VERA; Chief Editor WENDY SALAZAR GUILLÉN; circ. 47,000.

La Verdad: Malecón 502 y Tomás Martínez, Guayaquil; e-mail laverdad@telconet.net; internet www.revista-laverdad.com; f. 1988; monthly; politics and economics; associated with the Partido Renovador Institucional de Acción Nacional; Dir RODOLFO BAQUERIZO BLUM.

Vistazo: Aguirre 734 y García Avilés, Casilla 09-01-1239, Guayaquil; tel. (4) 232-7200; fax (4) 232-4870; e-mail vistazo@vistazo.com; internet www.vistazo.com; f. 1957; fortnightly; general; Gen. Editor PATRICIA ESTUPIÑÁN DE BURBANO; circ. 85,000.

PRESS ASSOCIATION

Asociación Ecuatoriana de Editores de Periódicos (AEDEP): Edif. World Trade Center, 14°, Of. 14-01, Avda 12 de Octubre y Cordero, Quito; tel. (2) 254-7457; fax (2) 254-7404; e-mail aedep@aedep.org.ec; internet www.aedep.org.ec; f. 1985; Pres. CÉSAR PÉREZ BARRIGA; Exec. Dir DIEGO CORNEJO MENACHO.

Publishers

Casa de la Cultura Ecuatoriana: Avdas 6 de Diciembre 16–224 y Patria, El Ejido, Quito; tel. (2) 290-2272; e-mail info@cce.org.ec; internet www.cce.org.ec; Pres. MARCO ANTONIO RODRÍGUEZ.

Centro Interamericano de Artesanías y Artes Populares (CIDAP): Hermano Miguel 3-23, Casilla 01-011-943, Cuenca; tel. (7) 282-9451; fax (7) 283-1450; e-mail cidapl@cidap.org.ec; internet www.cidap.org.ec; art, crafts, games, hobbies; Dir CLAUDIO MALO GONZÁLEZ.

Centro Internacional de Estudios Superiores de Comunicación para América Latina (CIESPAL): Avda Diego de Almagro 32-133 y Andrade Marín, Apdo 17-01-584, Quito; tel. (2) 254-8011; fax (2) 250-2487; e-mail ciespal@ciespal.net; internet www.ciespal.net; f. 1959; communications, technology; Dir FERNANDO CHECA MONTÚFAR.

Centro de Planificación y Estudios Sociales (CEPLAES): Sarmiento N39-198 y Hugo Moncayo, Apdo 17-11-6127, Quito; tel. (2) 225-0659; fax (2) 245-9417; e-mail ceplaes@andinanet.net; internet www.ceplaes.org.ec; f. 1978; agriculture, anthropology, education, health, social sciences, women's studies; Exec. Dir GLORIA CAMACHO.

Corporación Editora Nacional: Roca E9–59 y Tamayo, Apdo 17-12-886, Quito; tel. (2) 255-4358; fax (2) 256-6340; e-mail cen@cenlibrosecuador.org; internet www.cenlibrosecuador.org; f. 1977; archaeology, economics, education, geography, political science, history, law, literature, management, philosophy, social sciences; Pres. SIMÓN ESPINOSA CORDERO.

Corporación de Estudios y Publicaciones: Acuna E2-02 y Juan Agama, entre 10 de Agosto e Inglaterra, Casilla 17-21-00186, Quito; tel. (2) 222-1711; fax (2) 222-6256; e-mail editorial@cep.org.ec; internet www.cep.org.ec; f. 1963; law, public administration; Dir MAURICIO TROYA MENA.

Dinediciones: Avda 12 de Octubre N25-32 y Coruña, esq., Quito; tel. (2) 254-5209; fax (2) 254-5188; e-mail info@dinediciones.com; internet www.portal.dinediciones.com; magazines; Dir HERNÁN ALTAMIRANO.

Ediciones Abya-Yala: Avda 12 de Octubre 1430 y Wilson, Apdo 17-12-719, Quito; tel. (2) 250-6251; fax (2) 250-6255; e-mail editorial@abyayala.org; internet www.abyayala.org; f. 1975; anthropology, environmental studies, languages, education, theology; Pres. Fr JUAN BOTTASSO; Dir-Gen. P. XAVIER HERRÁN.

Edinun: Avda Occidental 10-65 y Manuel Valdivieso, Sector Pinar Alto, Quito; tel. (2) 227-0316; fax (2) 227-0699; e-mail edinun@edinun.com; internet www.edinun.com; f. 1982; Gen. Man. VICENTE VELÁSQUEZ.

Editorial Don Bosco: Vega Muñoz 10-68 y General Torres, Cuenca; tel. (7) 283-1745; fax (7) 284-2722; e-mail edibosco@bosco.org.ec; internet www.lns.com.ec; f. 1920; Gen. Man. MARCELO MEJIA MORALES.

Editorial El Conejo: Edif. Brother, 3°, Avda 6 de Diciembre N26-97 y La Niña, Apdo 17-03-4629, Quito; tel. (2) 222-7948; fax (2) 250-1066; e-mail info@editorialelconejo.com; internet www.editorialelconejo.com; f. 1979; non-profit publr of educational and literary texts; Dir ABDÓN UBIDIA.

Editorial Santillana: Avda Eloy Alfaro N33-347 y Avda 6 de Diciembre, Pichincha, Quito; tel. (2) 244-6656; fax (2) 244-8791; e-mail comunicaciones@santillana.com.ec; internet www.santillana.com.ec; f. 1994; part of Grupo Santillana, Spain; Gen. Man. FERNANDO REVILLA.

Eskeletra Editorial: Edif. Gayal, 1°, Of. 102, Roca 130 y 12 de Octubre, Quito; tel. (2) 255-6691; e-mail eskeletra@hotmail.com; internet www.eskeletra.com; f. 1990; Gen. Man. AZUCENA ROSERO JÁCOME.

Libresa, SA: Murgeón Oe 3–10 y Ulloa, Apdo 17-01-456, Quito; tel. (2) 223-0925; fax (2) 250-2992; e-mail libresa@libresa.com; internet www.libresa.com; f. 1979; education, literature, philosophy; Pres. FAUSTO COBA ESTRELLA; Man. JAIME PEÑA NOVOA.

Manthra Editores: Avda Coruña N31-70 y Whymper, Quito; tel. (2) 600-0998; fax (2) 255-8264; e-mail info@manthra.net; internet www.manthra.net; Gen. Man. JERÓNIMO VILLARREAL.

Maya Ediciones: Avda 6 de Diciembre N40-34 y Los Granados, Quito; tel. (2) 510-2447; e-mail servicioalcliente@mayaediciones.com; internet www.mayaediciones.com; f. 1992; children's books; Gen. Man. FANNY BUSTOS PEÑAHERRERA.

Pontificia Universidad Católica del Ecuador, Centro de Publicaciones: Avda 12 de Octubre, entre Patria y Veintimilla, Apdo 17-01-2184, Quito; tel. (2) 299-1700; fax (2) 256-7117; e-mail puce@edu.ec; internet www.puce.edu.ec; f. 1974; literature, natural science, law, anthropology, sociology, politics, economics, theology, philosophy, history, archaeology, linguistics, languages, business; Dir Dr PATRICIA CARRERA.

Trama Ediciones: Juan de Dios Martínez N34-367 y Portugal, El Batán, Quito; tel. (2) 224-6315; fax (2) 224-6317; e-mail info@trama.ec; internet www.trama.com.ec; f. 1977; architecture, design, art, tourism; Dir-Gen. ROLANDO MOYA TASQUER.

ASSOCIATIONS

Asociación Ecuatoriana de Editores de Libros de Texto: Quito; tel. (2) 227-0285; e-mail revistadidactica@gmail.com; internet www.revistadidactica.blogspot.com; f. 2004; publ. *Revista Didáctica*; Pres. VICENTE VELÁSQUEZ GUZMÁN.

Cámara Ecuatoriana del Libro: Edif. Eloy Alfaro, 9°, entre Inglaterra, Avda Eloy Alfaro 29-61, Quito; tel. (2) 255-3311; fax (2) 222-2150; e-mail celnp@uio.satnet.net; internet www.celibro.org.ec; f. 1978; Pres. FABIÁN LUZURIAGA.

Broadcasting and Communications

REGULATORY AUTHORITIES

Consejo Nacional de Telecomunicaciones (CONATEL): Avda Diego de Almagro 31-95, entre Whymper y Alpallana, Casilla 17-07-9777, Quito; tel. (2) 294-7800; fax (2) 250-5119; e-mail contactanos@conatel.gob.ec; internet www.conatel.gob.ec; f. 1942 as Instituto Ecuatoriano de Telecomunicaciones (IETEL); Pres. JAIME GUERRERO RUIZ.

Secretaría Nacional de Telecomunicaciones (SENATEL): Edif. SENATEL, Avda Diego de Almagro 31-95, entre Whymper y Alpallana, Casilla 17-07-9777, Quito; tel. (2) 294-7800; fax (2) 290-1010; e-mail comunicacion@conatel.gob.ec; internet www.conatel.gob.ec; Nat. Sec. RUBÉN LEÓN.

Superintendencia de Información y Comunicación: Quito; f. 2013; Supt CARLOS OCHOA HERNÁNDEZ.

Superintendencia de Telecomunicaciones (SUPERTEL): Edif. Matriz, Avda 9 de Octubre 1645 (N27-75) y Berlín, Casilla 17-21-1797, Quito; tel. (2) 294-6400; fax (2) 223-2115; e-mail info@supertel.gob.ec; internet www.supertel.gob.ec; f. 1992; Supt FABIÁN LEONARDO JARAMILLO PALACIOS.

TELECOMMUNICATIONS

Claro (CONECEL, SA): Edif. Centrum, Avda Francisco de Orellana y Alberto Borgues, Guayaquil; tel. (4) 269-3693; e-mail callcenter@conecel.com; internet www.claro.com.ec; f. 1993; fmrly Porta; subsidiary of América Móvil group (Mexico); mobile telecommunications provider; Pres. ALFREDO ESCOBAR SAN LUCAS.

Corporación Nacional de Telecomunicaciones EP: Edif. Estudio Zeta, Avda Veintimilla 1149 y Amazonas, Quito; tel. (2) 297-7100; fax (2) 256-2240; e-mail ventalinea@cnt.info.ec; internet www.cnt.gob.ec; f. 2008 by merger of Andinatel and Pacifictel; state-owned; absorbed all services provided by Alegro (Telecomunicaciones Móviles del Ecuador, SA—Telecsa) in 2010; Pres. RODRIGO LÓPEZ; Gen. Man. CÉSAR REGALADO IGLESIAS.

Movistar Ecuador: Avda República y esq. La Pradera, Quito; tel. (2) 222-7700; fax (2) 222-7597; internet www.movistar.com.ec; f. 1997; name changed from BellSouth Ecuador to above in 2004; owned by Telefónica Móviles, SA (Spain); mobile telephone services; CEO JUAN FEDERICO GOULÚ.

Otecel, SA: f. 2004; subsidiary of Movistar Ecuador; mobile cellular telephone network provider.

BROADCASTING

Radio

Radio Católica Nacional: Avda América 1830 y Mercadillo, Casilla 17-03-540, Quito; tel. (2) 254-1557; fax (2) 256-7309; e-mail direccion@radiocatolica.org.ec; internet www.radiocatolica.org.ec; f. 1985; Dir-Gen. RENÉ BRITO.

Radio Centro: Carchi 702, entre 9 de Octubre y 1 de Mayo, 6°, Guayaquil; tel. and fax (4) 288-0500; e-mail noticiero_elobservador@hotmail.com; internet www.radiocentro.com.ec; f. 1979; Dir HERNÁN OVIEDO GUTIERREZ; Gen. Man. JUAN XAVIER BENEDETTI RIPALDA.

Radio CRE Satelital (CORTEL, SA): Edif. El Torreón, 8°, Avda Boyacá 642 y Padre Solano, Apdo 4144, Guayaquil; tel. (4) 256-4290; fax (4) 256-0386; e-mail cre@cre.com.ec; internet www.cre.com.ec; Pres. RAFAEL GUERRERO VALENZUELA; Gen. Man. ANTONIO GUERRERO GÓMEZ.

Radio FM Mundo: Edif. Argentum, 10°, Of. 1001–1002, Avda de los Shyris 1322 y Suecia, Quito; tel. (2) 333-0866; fax (2) 333-2975; e-mail fmmundo@fmmundo.com; internet www.fmmundo.com; Gen. Man. CRISTHIAN DEL ALCÁZAR.

Radio Latina: Quito; internet www.radiolatina.com.ec; f. 1990; Pres. RICARDO GUAMÁN.

Radio La Luna: Avda América 3584, Casilla 17-08-8604, Quito; tel. (2) 226-646; f. 1996; Owner PACO VELASCO; Gen. Man. ATAÚLFO REINALDO TOBAR BONILLA.

Radio Quito (Ecuadoradio, SA): Edif. Aragones, 9°, Avda Coruña 2104 y Whimper, Quito; tel. (2) 250-8301; fax (2) 250-3311; e-mail radioquito@ecuadoradio.com; internet www.ecuadoradio.ec; f. 1940; owned by *El Comercio* newspaper.

Radio Sonorama (RDSR): Moscú 378 y República del Salvador, Quito; tel. (2) 243-5355; fax (2) 227-1555; internet www.sonorama.com.ec; f. 1975; Gen. Man. MAURICIO RIVAS.

Radio Sucre: Ciudadela Albatros, Calle Fragata 203, atrás de la Sociedad Italiana Garibaldi, Guayaquil; tel. (4) 229-2109; fax (4) 229-2119; e-mail info@radiosucre.com.ec; internet www.radiosucre.com.ec; f. 1983; Dir VICENTE ARROBA DITO.

La Voz de los Andes (HCJB): Villalengua OE2-52 y Avda 10 de Agosto, Casilla 17-17-691, Quito; tel. (2) 226-6808; fax (2) 226-4765; e-mail radio@hcjb.org.ec; internet www.radiohcjb.org; f. 1931; operated by World Radio Missionary Fellowship; programmes in 11 languages (including Spanish and English) and 22 Quechua dialects; Evangelical; Dir TATIANA DE LA TORRE; Production Dir DUVAL RUEDA.

Television

EcuadorTV: Edif. Medios Públicos, San Salvador E6-49 y Eloy Alfaro, Quito; tel. (2) 397-0800; internet www.ecuadortv.ec; f. 2007; public service broadcaster; br. in Guayaquil; Gen. Man. ENRIQUE AROSEMANA.

Ecuavisa Guayaquil: Cerro El Carmen, Casilla 1239, Guayaquil; tel. (4) 256-2444; fax (4) 256-2432; e-mail contacto@ecuavisa.com; internet www.ecuavisa.com; f. 1967; Pres. XAVIER ALVARADO ROCA; Gen. Man. RICARDO VAZQUEZ DONOSO.

Ecuavisa Quito: Bosmediano 447 y José Carbo, Bellavista, Quito; tel. (2) 244-8101; fax (2) 244-5488; internet www.ecuavisa.com; commercial; f. 1970; Pres. PATRICIO JARAMILLO; Editor-in-Chief FREDDY BARROS.

TC Televisión: Avda de las Américas, frente al Aeropuerto, Casilla 09-01-673, Guayaquil; tel. (4) 239-7664; fax (4) 228-7544; internet www.tctelevision.com; f. 1969; commercial; seized by the Govt in 2008; Gen. Man. CARLOS COELLO BECEKE.

Teleamazonas Cratel, CA: Antonio Granda Centeno Oeste 429 y Brasil, Casilla 17-11-04844, Quito; tel. (2) 397-4444; fax (2) 244-1620; e-mail abravo@teleamazonas.com; internet www.teleamazonas

.com; f. 1974; commercial; Exec. Dir Luis Cucalón; Gen. Man. Sebastián Corral.

Association

Asociación Ecuatoriana de Radiodifusión (AER): Edif. Atlas, 8°, Of. 802, Calle Justino Cornejo con Francisco de Orellana, Guayaquil; tel. (4) 229-1795; fax (4) 229-1783; internet aer.ec; ind. asscn; Pres. Roberto Manciati Alarcón.

Finance

(cap. = capital; res = reserves; dep. = deposits; m. = million; brs = branches; amounts in US dollars unless otherwise indicated)

SUPERVISORY AUTHORITY

Superintendencia de Bancos y Seguros: Avda 12 de Octubre 1561 y Madrid, Casilla 17-17-770, Quito; tel. (2) 299-6100; fax (2) 250-6812; e-mail webmaster@sbs.gob.ec; internet www.sbs.gob.ec; f. 1927; supervises national banking system, including state and private banks and other financial institutions; Supt Pedro Solines.

BANKING

Central Bank

Banco Central del Ecuador: Avda 10 de Agosto N11-409 y Briceño, Casilla 339, Quito; tel. (2) 257-2522; fax (2) 295-5458; internet www.bce.fin.ec; f. 1927; cap. 2.4m., res 724.9m., dep. 5,300m. (Dec. 2009); Pres. Diego Martinez; Gen. Man. Mateo Villalba; 2 brs.

Other State Banks

Banco Ecuatoriano de la Vivienda: Avda 10 de Agosto 2270 y Luis Cordero, Casilla 3244, Quito; tel. and fax (2) 396-3300; e-mail bevinfo@bev.fin.ec; internet www.bev.fin.ec; f. 1961; Pres. Pedro Jaramillo Castillo; Gen. Man. Luis Efraín Cazar Moncayo.

Banco del Estado (BDE): Avda Atahualpa OE1-109 y Avda 10 de Agosto, Casilla 17-17-1728, Quito; tel. (2) 299-9600; fax (2) 299-9643; e-mail secretaria@bancoestado.com; internet www.bancoestado.com; f. 1979 as Banco de Desarrollo del Ecuador (BEDE); Gen. Man. María Soledad Barrera Altamirano.

Banco Nacional de Fomento: Antonio Ante Oeste 1–15 y Avda 10 de Agosto, Casilla 685, Quito; tel. (2) 294-6500; fax (2) 257-0286; e-mail sugerencias@bnf.fin.ec; internet www.bnf.fin.ec; f. 1928; cap. 254.2m., res 144.1m., dep. 621.9m. (Dec. 2009); Pres. Javier Ponce Cevallos; Gen. Man. José Andrade López; 70 brs.

Corporación Financiera Nacional (CFN): Avda Juan León Mera 130 y Avda Patria, Casilla 17-21-01924, Quito; tel. (2) 256-4900; fax (2) 222-3823; e-mail informatica@q.cfn.fin.ec; internet www.cfn.fin.ec; f. 1964; state-owned bank providing export credits, etc.; Pres. Camilo Samán Salem; Gen. Man. Jorge Wated.

Commercial Banks

Banco Amazonas, SA: Avda Francisco Orellana 238, Guayaquil; tel. (4) 602-1100; fax (4) 602-1090; e-mail ServiciosalCliente@bancoamazonas.com; internet www.bancoamazonas.com; f. 1976; cap. 13.5m., res 1.1m., dep. 106.3m. (Dec. 2011); affiliated to Banque Paribas; CEO Sergio R. Torassa; CFO José Ponce.

Banco del Austro: Sucre y Borrero (esq.), Casilla 01-01-0167, Cuenca; tel. (7) 283-1646; fax (7) 283-2633; internet www.bancodelaustro.com; f. 1977; cap. 54m., res 26.2m., dep. 881.3m. (Dec. 2011); Pres. Juan Eljuri Antón; Gen. Man. Guillermo Tálbot Dueñas; 19 brs.

Banco Bolivariano, CA: Junín 200 y Panamá, Casilla 09-01-10184, Guayaquil; tel. (4) 230-5000; fax (4) 256-6707; e-mail info@bolivariano.com; internet www.bolivariano.com; f. 1978; cap. 102.5m., res 17.7m., dep. 1,402.3m. (Dec. 2010); Pres. José Salazar Barragán; CEO Miguel Babra León; 53 brs.

Banco Comercial de Manabí, SA: Avda 10 de Agosto 600 y 18 de Octubre, Casilla 13-01-038, Portoviejo; tel. and fax (5) 263-2222; fax (5) 263-5527; e-mail info@bcmanabi.com; internet www.bcmanabi.com; f. 1980; Gen. Man. Walter Andrade Castro.

Banco General Rumiñahui: Avda República E6-573 y Avda Eloy Alfaro, Quito; tel. (2) 250-9929; fax (2) 256-3786; e-mail mrodas@bgr.com.ec; internet www.bgr.com.ec; cap. 20.6m., res 2.3m., dep. 354.1m. (Dec. 2010); Gen. Man. Alejandro Ribadeneira Jaramillo.

Banco de Guayaquil, SA: Plaza Ycaza 105 y Pichincha, Casilla 09-01-1300, Guayaquil; tel. (4) 251-7100; fax (4) 251-4406; e-mail servicios@bankguay.com; internet www.bancoguayaquil.com; f. 1923; cap. 181m., res 37.3m., dep. 2,452.2m. (Dec. 2011); Pres. Danilo Carrera Drouet; Exec. Pres. Guillermo Lasso Mendoza; 50 brs.

Banco Internacional, SA: Avda Patria E-421 y 9 de Octubre, Casilla 17-01-2114, Quito; tel. (2) 256-5547; fax (2) 256-5758; e-mail baninteronline@bancointernacional.com.ec; internet www.bancointernacional.com.ec; f. 1973; cap. 110m., res 34.9m., dep. 1,477.6m. (Dec. 2011); Pres. Raúl Guerrero; CEO Enrique Beltrán Mata; 58 brs.

Banco de Loja: esq. Bolívar y Rocafuerte, Casilla 11-01-300, Loja; tel. (7) 257-1682; fax (7) 257-3019; e-mail info@bancodeloja.fin.ec; internet www.bancodeloja.fin.ec; f. 1968; cap. 15m., res 3.8m., dep. 204.3m. (Dec. 2009); Pres. Steve Brown Hidalgo; Man. Leonardo Burneo Muller.

Banco de Machala, SA: Avda 9 de Mayo y Rocafuerte, Casilla 711, Machala; tel. (7) 293-0100; fax (7) 292-2744; e-mail jorejuela@bmachala.com; internet www.bmachala.com; f. 1962; cap. 30m., res 3.4m., dep. 396.7m. (Dec. 2010); Pres. Dr Esteban Quirola Figueroa; 2 brs.

Banco del Pacífico: Francisco de P. Ycaza 200, entre Pichincha y Pedro Carbo, Casilla 09-01-988, Guayaquil; tel. (4) 256-6010; fax (4) 232-8333; e-mail webadmin@pacifico.fin.ec; internet www.bancodelpacifico.com; f. 2000 by merger of Banco del Pacífico and Banco Continental; 100% owned by Banco Central del Ecuador; cap. 223.1m., res 110.9m., dep. 2,347.3m. (Dec. 2009); Exec. Pres. Andrés Baquerizo; 227 brs.

Banco Pichincha, CA: Avda Amazonas 4560 y Pereira, Casilla 261, Quito; tel. (2) 298-0980; fax (2) 298-1226; e-mail sugerencias@pichincha.com; internet www.pichincha.com; f. 1906; cap. 421.5., res 148.7m., dep. 5,572.1m. (Dec. 2011); 61.4% owned by Pres; Exec. Pres. and Chair. Dr Fidel Egas Grijalva; Gen. Man. Aurelio Fernando Pozo Crespo; 267 brs.

Banco Territorial, SA: P. Icaza 115, entre Malecón y Pichincha, Guayaquil; tel. (4) 256-1950; e-mail informacion@grupozunino.com; internet www.bancoterritorial.com; f. 1886; Pres. Pietro Francesco Zuñina Anda; Gen. Man. Raúl Fernando Sánchez Rodríguez.

Produbanco (Banco de la Producción, SA): Avda Amazonas N35-211 y Japón, Quito; tel. (2) 299-9000; fax (2) 244-7319; e-mail bancaenlinea@produbanco.com; internet www.produbanco.com; f. 1978 as Banco de la Producción; adopted current name in 1996; cap. 148m., res 30m., dep. 2,175m. (Dec. 2011); part of Grupo Financiero Producción; Chair. Rodrigo Paz Delgado; Exec. Pres. Abelardo Pachano Bertero; 75 brs.

UniBanco (Banco Universal, SA): República 500 y Pasaje Carrión, Quito; tel. (2) 395-0600; internet unibanco.ec; f. 1964 as Banco de Cooperativas del Ecuador; adopted current name 1994; Pres. Andrés Jervis González.

Associations

Asociación de Bancos Privados del Ecuador: Edif. Delta 890, 7°, Avda República de El Salvador y Suecia, Casilla 17-11-6708, Quito; tel. (2) 246-6670; fax (2) 246-6702; e-mail abpe1@asobancos.org.ec; internet www.asobancos.org.ec; f. 1965; 36 mems; Pres. Ricardo Cuesta Delgado; Exec. Pres. César Robalino Gonzaga.

Asociación de Instituciones Financieras del Ecuador (AIFE): Edif. La Previsora, Torre B, 3°, Of. 308, Avda Naciones Unidas 1084 y Amazonas, Quito; tel. and fax (2) 246-6560; e-mail aife1@punto.net.ec; internet www.aife.com.ec; Pres. Gianni Garibaldi; Exec. Dir Julio Dobronsky Navarro.

STOCK EXCHANGES

Bolsa de Valores de Guayaquil: 9 de Octubre 110 y Pichincha, Guayaquil; tel. (4) 256-1519; fax (4) 256-1871; e-mail rgallegos@bvg.fin.ec; internet www.mundobvg.com; Pres. Rodolfo Kronfle Akel; Dir-Gen. Arturo Bejarano Icaza.

Bolsa de Valores de Quito: Edif. Londres, 8°, Avda Amazonas 21–252 y Carrión, Casilla 17-01-3772, Quito; tel. (2) 222-1333; fax (2) 250-0942; e-mail informacion@bolsadequito.com; internet www.bolsadequito.com; f. 1969; Chair. Patricio Peña Romero; Exec. Pres. Mónica Villagómez de Anderson.

INSURANCE

Principal Companies

Ace Seguros, SA: Edif. Antisana, 4°, Avdas Amazonas 3655 y Juan Pablo Sanz, Quito; tel. (2) 292-0555; fax (2) 244-5817; e-mail serviciocliente@ace-ina.com; internet www.acelatinamerica.com; Exec. Pres. Edwin Astudillo.

AIG Metropolitana Cía de Seguros y Reaseguros, SA: Edifc. IACA, 5°, Avda Brasil 293 y Antonio Granda Centeno, Quito; tel. (2) 395-5000; fax (2) 292-4434; e-mail servicio.cliente@aig.com; internet www.aig.com.ec; part of American International Group, Inc (USA); Exec. Pres. Diana Pinilla Rojas.

Alianza Cía de Seguros y Reaseguros, SA: Avdas 12 de Octubre 24-359 y Baquerizo Moreno, Apdo 17-17-041, Quito; tel. (2) 256-6143; fax (2) 256-4059; e-mail alianzauio@segurosalianza.com; internet www.segurosalianza.com; f. 1982; Gen. Man. Eduardo Barquet Pendón.

Bolívar Cía de Seguros del Ecuador, SA: Edif. Centro Empresarial Las Cámaras, Torre B, 3° y 12°, Planta Baja, Avda Francisco de Orellana, Calle Kennedy Norte, Guayaquil; tel. (2) 602-0700; fax (2) 268-3363; e-mail ssanmiguel@seguros-bolivar.com; internet www.seguros-bolivar.com; f. 1957; Pres. FABIÁN ORTEGA TRUJILLO.

Cía de Seguros Ecuatoriano Suiza, SA: Avda 9 de Octubre 2101 y Tulcán, Apdo 09-01-397, Guayaquil; tel. (4) 373-1515; fax (4) 245-3229; e-mail ecuasuiza@ecuasuiza.com; internet www.ecuasuiza.com; f. 1954; Pres. JOSÉ SALAZAR BARRAGÁN; Gen. Man. LUIS FERNANDO SALAS RUBIO.

Cía Seguros Unidos, SA: Edif. Metrocar, 2°, Avda 10 de Agosto 31–162 y Avda Mariana de Jesús, Quito; tel. (2) 600-7700; fax (2) 245-0920; e-mail quito@sunidos.fin.ec; internet www.segurosunidos.com.ec; f. 1994; part of Grupo Eljuri; Gen. Man. RAFAEL ALBERTO MATEUS PONCE.

Cóndor Cía de Seguros, SA: Edif. Seguros Cóndor, 6°, Francisco de Plaza Ycaza 302, Apdo 09-01-5007, Guayaquil; tel. (4) 256-5300; fax (4) 256-5041; e-mail ochavez@seguroscondor.com; internet www.seguroscondor.com; f. 1966; Gen. Man. OTÓN CHÁVEZ TORRES.

Coopseguros del Ecuador, SA: Edif. Coopseguros, Avda Noruega 210 y Suiza, Casilla 17-15-0084-B, Quito; tel. (2) 292-1669; fax (2) 292-1666; internet www.coopseguros.com; f. 1970; Gen. Man. JUÁN ENRIQUE BUSTAMENTE.

Liberty Seguros: Calle Portugal E-12-72 y Avda Eloy Alfaro, Quito; tel. (2) 298-9600; fax (2) 246-9650; e-mail auto.siniestros@liberty.ec; internet www.panamericana.com.ec; f. 1973; fmrly Panamericana del Ecuador; changed name as above in 2012; Gen. Man. FRANCISCO PROAÑO SALVADOR.

Mapfre Atlas Cía de Seguros, SA: Edif. Torre Atlas, 11°, Kennedy Norte, Justino Cornejo, entre Avda Francisco de Orellana y Avda Luis Orrantia, Casilla 09-04-491, Guayaquil; tel. (4) 269-0430; fax (4) 228-3099; e-mail noticiascorporativas@mapfreatlas.com.ec; internet www.mapfreatlas.com.ec; f. 1984; Gen. Man. RAFAEL SUÁREZ LÓPEZ.

QBE Seguros Colonial: Avda. Eloy Alfaro 40-270 y José Queri, Quito; tel. (2) 399-0500; e-mail info@qbe.com.ec; internet www.qbe.com.ec; f. 1992 as Seguros Colonial, SA; acquired by Grupo QBE (Australia) and changed name as above in 2010; Exec. Pres. FERNANDO MANTILLA.

Seguros Rocafuerte, SA: Edif. Filanbanco, 14°–16°, Plaza Carbo 505 y Avda 9 de Octubre, Apdo 09-04-6491, Guayaquil; tel. (4) 232-6125; fax (4) 232-9353; e-mail segroca@gye.satnet.net; internet www.rocafuerte.com; f. 1967; life and medical; Exec. Pres. PEDRO PICHARDO ZAPAC QUEVEDO.

Seguros Sucre, SA: Edif. San Francisco 300, 6°, Pedro Carbo 422 y Avda 9 de Octubre, Apdo 09-01-480, Guayaquil; tel. (4) 256-3399; fax (4) 231-4163; e-mail pespinel@segurossucre.fin.ec; internet www.segurossucre.fin.ec; f. 1944; part of Grupo Banco del Pacífico; Gen. Man. MAXÍMILIANO DONOSO VALLEJO.

La Unión Cía Nacional de Seguros: Urb. Los Cedros Solares 1–2, Km 5½, Vía a la Costa, Apdo 09-01-1294, Guayaquil; tel. (4) 285-1500; fax (4) 285-1700; e-mail rgoldbaum@seguroslaunion.com; internet www.seguroslaunion.com; f. 1943; state-owned; Pres. ROBERTO GOLDBAUM; Dir DAVID GOLDBAUM.

ASSOCIATIONS

Asociación de Compañías de Seguros del Ecuador (ACOSE): Edif. Carolina Park, 2°, Calle Japón 230 y Avda Amazonas, Quito; tel. (2) 225-6182; fax (2) 246-3057; internet www.acose.org; f. 1978; affiliated to FEDESEG; 15 mems; Pres. RODRIGO CEVALLOS BREIHL; Gen. Man. PATRICIO SALAS GUZMÁN.

Federación Ecuatoriana de Empresas de Seguros (FEDESEG): Edif. Intercambio, 1°, Junín y Malecón Simón Bolivar 105, Guayaquil; tel. (4) 456-5340; fax (4) 430-6208; affiliated to Federación Interamericana de Empresas de Seguros (FIDES); Pres. JOSÉ CÚCALON DE YCAZA; Exec. Sec. LUIS LARREA BENALCÁZAR.

Trade and Industry

GOVERNMENT AGENCIES

Instituto Ecuatoriano de Seguridad Social: Edif. Zarzuela, 6°, Avda 9 de Octubre 20–68 y Jorge Washington, Quito; tel. (2) 396-9300; fax (2) 256-3917; e-mail cdirectivo@iess.gob.ec; internet www.iess.gob.ec; f. 1928; directs the social security system; provides social benefits and medical service; Pres. FERNANDO CORDERO; Dir-Gen. FERNANDO GUIJARRO CABEZAS.

Secretaría Nacional de Planificación y Desarrollo (SENPLADES): Edif. CFN, 8°, Avda Juan León Mera 130 y Avda Patria, Quito; tel. (2) 397-8900; e-mail senplades@senplades.gob.ec; internet www.senplades.gob.ec; f. 1954 as Junta Nacional de Planificación y Coordinación Económica (JUNAPLA); changed name as above 1979; decentralized planning and policy-making; Nat. Sec. FANDER FALCONÍ BENÍTEZ.

Superintendencia de Compañías del Ecuador: Roca 660 y Amazonas, Casilla 687, Quito; tel. (2) 252-9960; fax (2) 256-6685; e-mail comunicacionuio@supercias.gob.ec; internet www.supercias.gob.ec; f. 1964; responsible for the legal and accounting control of commercial enterprises; Supt SUAD RAQUEL MANSSUR VILLAGRÁN; Sec.-Gen. VÍCTOR ANIBAL CEVALLOS VÁSQUEZ.

CHAMBERS OF COMMERCE AND INDUSTRY

Cámara de Agricultura: Edif. La Previsora, Torre B, 8°, Of. 805, Avda Naciones Unidas 1084 y Amazonas, Casilla 17-21-322, Quito; tel. (2) 225-7618; fax (2) 227-4187; e-mail gremios@caiz.org.ec; internet www.agroecuador.com; Pres. VÍCTOR LÓPEZ.

Cámara de Comercio de Ambato: Edif. Las Cámaras, Montalvo 03-31, entre Bolívar y Rocafuerte, Ambato; tel. (3) 242-4773; fax (3) 242-1930; e-mail webmaster@ccomercioambato.org.ec; internet www.ccomercioambato.org.ec; Pres. MIGUEL SUÁREZ JARAMILLO.

Cámara de Comercio de Cuenca: Edif. Cámara de Industrias de Cuenca, 12° y 13°, Avda Florencia Astudillo y Alfonso Cordero, Casilla 4929, Cuenca; tel. (7) 288-5070; fax (7) 281-3100; e-mail cccuenca@etapa.com.ec; internet www.industriascuenca.org.ec; f. 1936; 5,329 mems; Pres. AUGUSTO TOSI LEÓN.

Cámara de Comercio Ecuatoriano-Americana (Amcham Quito-Ecuador): Edif. Multicentro, 4°, Avda 6 de Diciembre y la Niña, Quito; tel. (2) 250-7450; fax (2) 250-4571; e-mail info@ecamcham.com; internet www.ecamcham.com; f. 1974; promotes bilateral trade and investment between Ecuador and the USA; brs in Ambato, Cuenca and Manabí; Pres. XAVIER PONCE VILLAGOMEZ; Gen. Man. JOSÉ RUMAZO.

Cámara de Comercio Ecuatoriano Canadiense (Ecuadorean-Canadian Chamber of Commerce): Torre Centro Ejecutivo, Of. 201, 2°, Inglaterra 1373 y Avda Amazonas, Quito; tel. (2) 244-5972; fax (2) 246-8598; e-mail camara.canadiense@ecucanchamber.org; internet www.ecucanchamber.org; Pres. PAUL HARRIS; Exec. Dir CECILIA PEÑA ODE.

Cámara de Comercio de Guayaquil: Edif. Centro Empresarial 'Las Cámaras', 2° y 3°, Avda Francisco de Orellana y Miguel H. Alcívar, Guayaquil; tel. (4) 268-2771; fax (4) 268-2766; e-mail info@lacamara.org; internet www.lacamara.org; f. 1889; 31,000 affiliates; Pres. EDUARDO PEÑA HURTADO; Sec. JUAN ESTANISLAO LUTYK.

Cámara de Comercio de Machala: Edif. Cámara de Comercio, 2°, Rocafuerte y Buenavista, CP 825, Machala, El Oro; tel. (7) 293-0640; fax (7) 293-4454; e-mail info@ccmachala.org.ec; Pres. FREDDY MONTALVO SALINAS.

Cámara de Comercio de Manta: Edif. Cámara de Comercio, Avda 2, entre Calles 10 y 11, Apdo 13-05-477, Manta; tel. (5) 262-1306; fax (5) 262-6516; e-mail direccion@ccm.org.ec; internet www.ccm.org.ec; f. 1927; Pres. LUCÍA FERNÁNDEZ DE DEGENNA; Exec. Dir AURORA VALLE.

Cámara de Comercio de Quito: Edif. Las Cámaras, 6°, Avda República y Amazonas, Casilla 17-01-202, Quito; tel. (2) 244-3787; fax (2) 243-5862; e-mail ccq@ccq.org.ec; internet www.ccq.org.ec; f. 1906; 12,000 mems; Pres. BLASCO PEÑAHERRERA SOLAH; Exec. Dir GUIDO TOLEDO ANDRADE.

Cámara de Industrias de Cuenca: Edif. Cámara de Industrias de Cuenca, 12° y 13°, Avda Florencia Astudillo y Alfonso Cordero, Cuenca; tel. (7) 284-5053; fax (7) 284-0107; internet www.industriascuenca.org.ec; f. 1936; Pres. AUGUSTO TOSI LEÓN; Exec. Vice-Pres. CAROLA RÍOS DE ANDRADE.

Cámara de Industrias de Guayaquil: Centro Empresarial Las Cámaras, Torre Institucional, 4° y 5°, Avda Francisco de Orellana y M. Alcívar, Casilla 09-01-4007, Guayaquil; tel. (4) 268-2618; fax (4) 268-2680; e-mail caindgye@cig.org.ec; internet www.cig.ec; f. 1936; Pres. HENRY KRONFLE KOZHAYA.

Federación Nacional de Cámaras de Comercio del Ecuador: Avda Amazonas y República, Edif. Las Cámaras, Quito; tel. (2) 244-3787; fax (2) 292-2084; Pres. BLASCO PEÑAHERRERA SOLAH; Vice-Pres. EDUARDO VEÑA.

Federación Nacional de Cámaras de Industrias del Ecuador: Avda República y Amazonas, 10°, Casilla 2438, Quito; tel. (2) 245-2992; fax (2) 244-8118; e-mail fedin@cip.org.ec; internet www.camindustriales.org.ec; f. 1972; Pres. Dr PABLO DÁVILA JARAMILLO.

INDUSTRIAL AND TRADE ASSOCIATIONS

Asociación de la Industria Hidrocarburífera del Ecuador (AIHE): Edif. Puerta del Sol, 8°, Avda Amazonas 4080 y Calle UNP, Quito; tel. (2) 226-1270; fax (2) 226-1272; e-mail aihe@aihe.org.ec; internet www.aihe.org.ec; f. 1997 as Asociación de Compañías Petroleras de Exploración y Explotación de Hidrocarburos del Ecuador (ASOPEC); name changed as above in 2002; asscn of 24 int. and domestic hydrocarbon cos; Exec. Pres. JOSÉ LUIS ZIRITT.

Corporación de Promoción de Exportaciones e Inversiones (CORPEI): Centro de Convenciones Simón Bolivar, 1°, Avda de las Américas 406, Guayaquil; tel. (4) 228-7123; fax (4) 229-2910; internet www.corpei.org; f. 1997 to promote exports and investment; CEO Ricardo Alfredo Estrada.

Federación Ecuatoriana de Exportadores (FEDEXPOR): Edif. Colegio de Economistas, 4°, Iñaquito 3537 y Juan Pablo Sanz, Quito; tel. (2) 225-2426; e-mail fedexpor@fedexpor.com; internet www.fedexpor.com; f. 1976; Pres. Felipe Ribadeneira.

EMPLOYERS' ORGANIZATIONS

Asociación de Compañías Consultoras del Ecuador: Edif. Delta, 4°, Avda República de El Salvador 890 y Suecia, Quito; tel. (2) 246-5048; fax (2) 245-1171; e-mail acce@acce.com.ec; internet www.acce.com.ec; asscn of consulting cos; Pres. Fernando Aguilar García.

Asociación Ecuatoriana de Industriales de la Madera: Edif. de las Cámaras, 7°, República y Amazonas, Quito; tel. (2) 226-0980; fax (2) 243-9560; e-mail director@aima.org.ec; internet www.aima.org.ec; f. 1976; wood mfrs' asscn; Pres. Sebastián Zuquilanda.

Asociación de Exportadores de Banano del Ecuador (AEBE): Edif. World Trade Center, Torre A, 9°, Of. 904, Avda Francisco de Orellana, Calle Kennedy Norte, Guayaquil; tel. (4) 263-1419; fax (4) 263-1485; e-mail eledesma@aebe.com.ec; internet www.aebe.com.ec; banana exporters' asscn; Pres. Jorge Alex Serrano; Exec. Dir Eduardo Ledesma.

Asociación de Industriales Gráficos de Pichincha: Edif. de las Cámaras, 8°, Amazonas y República, Quito; tel. (2) 292-3141; fax (2) 245-6664; e-mail aigquito@aig.org.ec; internet www.aig.org.ec; asscn of the graphic industry; Pres. Mauricio Miranda.

Asociación de Industriales Textiles del Ecuador (AITE): Edif. Las Cámaras, 8°, Avda República y Amazonas, Casilla 2893, Quito; tel. (2) 224-9434; fax (2) 244-5159; e-mail aite@aite.org.ec; internet www.aite.com.ec; f. 1938; textile mfrs' asscn; 40 mems; Pres. José María Ponce; CEO Javier Díaz Crespo.

Asociación Nacional de Empresarios (ANDE): Edif. España, 6°, Of. 67, Avda Amazonas 25–23 y Colón, Casilla 17-01-3489, Quito; tel. (2) 290-2545; fax (2) 223-8507; e-mail info@ande.org.ec; internet www.ande.org.ec; national employers' asscn; Pres. Patricio Donoso Chiriboga; Vice-Pres. Alejandro Ribadeneira.

Asociación Nacional de Exportadores de Cacao y Café (ANECAFE): Edif. Banco Pichincha, 10°, Of. 1001, Avda 2da entre calles 11 y 12, Manta; tel. (5) 261-3337; fax (5) 262-3315; e-mail info@anecafe.org.ec; internet www.anecafe.org.ec; f. 1983; cocoa and coffee exporters' asscn; Pres. Askley Delgado Flor.

STATE HYDROCARBON COMPANY

EP PETROECUADOR (Empresa Pública de Hidrocarburos del Ecuador): Alpallana E8-86 y Avda 6 de Diciembre, Casilla 17-11-5007, Quito; tel. (2) 256-3060; fax (2) 250-3571; e-mail hramirez@petroecuador.com.ec; internet www.eppetroecuador.ec; f. 1989; state petroleum co; Exec. Pres. Marco Calvopiña.

UTILITIES

Regulatory Authorities

Agencia de Control y Regulación Hidrocarburífera (ARCH): Quito; f. 2010; responsible for the regulation and control of the hydrocarbons sector; Dir Carlos Loor.

Centro Nacional de Control de Energía (CENACE): Panamericana Sur Km 17.5, Sector Santa Rosa de Cutuglagua, Casilla 17-21-1991, Quito; tel. (2) 299-2001; fax (2) 299-2031; e-mail pcorporativo@cenace.org.ec; internet www.cenace.org.ec; f. 1999; co-ordinates and oversees national energy system; Exec. Dir Gabriel Argüello Ríos.

Consejo Nacional de Electricidad (CONELEC): Avda Naciones Unidas E7-71 y Avda De Los Shyris, Apdo 17-17-817, Quito; tel. (2) 226-8746; fax (2) 226-8737; e-mail conelec@conelec.gob.ec; internet www.conelec.gob.ec; f. 1999; supervises electricity industry following transfer of assets of the former Instituto Ecuatoriano de Electrificación (INECEL) to the Fondo de Solidaridad; pending privatization as 6 generating cos, 1 transmission co and 19 distribution cos; Exec. Dir Francisco Vergara Ortíz.

Secretaría de Hidrocarburos: Ministerio de Recursos Norenovables, Juan León Mera y Orellana, Quito; f. 2010, fmrly known as the Dirección Nacional de Hidrocarburos; part of the Ministry of Non-Renewable Natural Resources; supervision of the enforcement of laws regarding the exploration and devt of petroleum; also responsible for dispute resolution and imposition of sanctions against oil cos failing industry standards; Dir Ramiro Cazar.

Secretaría Nacional del Agua (SENAGUA): Edif. MAGAP, 3°, Avda Amazonas y Avda Eloy Alfaro, Quito; tel. (2) 381-5640; fax (2) 255-4251; e-mail secretarionacional@senagua.gob.ec; internet www.senagua.gob.ec; Nat. Sec. Walter Solís Valarezo.

Electricity

Eléctrica de Guayaquil: Urb. La Garzota, Sector 3, Manzana 47; tel. (4) 224-8006; fax (4) 224-8040; internet www.electricaguayaquil.gov.ec; f. 2003, as Corporación para la Administración Temporal Eléctrica de Guayaquil (Categ) to administer activities of fmr state-owned Empresa Eléctrica del Ecuador (EMELEC); privatized and changed name as above in 2009; major producer and distributor of electricity, mostly using oil-fired or diesel generating capacity; Admin. Oscar Armijos González-Rubio.

Empresa Eléctrica Quito, SA (EEQ): Avda 10 de Agosto y Las Casas, Casilla 17-01-473, Quito; tel. (2) 396-4700; fax (2) 250-3817; e-mail asoeeq@eeq.com.ec; internet www.eeq.com.ec; f. 1955; produces electricity for the region around Quito, mostly from hydroelectric plants; Gen. Man. Carlos Andrade Faini.

Empresa Eléctrica Regional El Oro, SA (EMELORO): Dir Arízaga 1810 y Santa Rosa, esq. Machala, El Oro; tel. (7) 293-0500; e-mail emeloro@emeloro.gov.ec; internet www.emeloro.gov.ec; electricity production and generation in El Oro province; Chair. Gonzalo Quintana Galvez; Exec. Pres. Washington Moreno Benitez.

Empresa Eléctrica Regional del Sur, SA (EERSSA): internet www.eerssa.com; f. 1973; electricity production and generation in Loja and Zamora Chinchipe provinces; Exec. Pres. Wilson Vivanco Arias.

Empresa Eléctrica Riobamba, SA: Larrea 2260 y Primera Constituyente, Riobamba; tel. (3) 296-0283; fax (3) 296-5257; e-mail e-mail@eersa.com.ec; internet www.eersa.com.ec/eersa.php; state-owned utility; Pres. Mariano Curicama; Gen. Man. Joe Ruales.

TRADE UNIONS

Confederación Sindical de Trabajadoras y Trabajadores del Ecuador (CSE): Pasaje Fray Gerundio E7-19 y el Tiempo (Tras Hotel Crown Plaza), Quito; tel. (2) 246-9547; e-mail cseecuador@cse-ec.org; internet www.gye.cse-ec.org; f. 2010; formed by dissident members of Confederación Ecuatoriana de Organizaciones Sindicales Libres (CEOSL); Pres. Jaime Arciniega.

Frente Unitario de los Trabajadores (FUT): f. 1971; left-wing; 300,000 mems; Pres. Mesías Tatamuez; comprises:

Confederación Ecuatoriana de Organizaciones Clasistas Unitarias de Trabajo (CEDOCUT): Edif. Cedocut, 5°, Flores 846 y Manabí, Quito; tel. (2) 295-4551; fax 295-4013; e-mail presicdocut@cedocut.org; internet www.cedocut.org.ec; f. 1938; humanist; Pres. Mesías Tatamuez Moreno; 1,065 mem. orgs, 86,416 individual mems.

Confederación Ecuatoriana de Organizaciones Sindicales Libres (CEOSL): Avda Tarqui 15-26 (785) y Estrada, 6°, Casilla 17-11-373, Quito; tel. (2) 252-2511; fax (2) 250-0836; e-mail presidencia@ceosl.net; internet ceosl.net; f. 1962; Pres. Pablo Anibal Serrano Cepeda; 110,000 mems (2007).

Confederación de Trabajadores del Ecuador (CTE) (Confederation of Ecuadorean Workers): Avda 9 de Octubre 1248 y Marieta de Veintimilla, Casilla 17-01-4166, Quito; tel. (2) 252-0456; fax (2) 252-0446; e-mail presidencia@cte-ecuador.org; internet www.cte-ecuador.org; f. 1944; Pres. Santiago Yagual Yagual; Vice-Pres. Edgar Sarango Correa.

Transport

RAILWAYS

All railways are government-controlled. In 2000 the total length of track was 960 km. A programme for the rehabilitation of 456 km of disused lines was begun in 2008. By 2011 nine sections had been reopened.

Ferrocarriles del Ecuador Empresa Publica (FEEP): Quilotoa y Sangay, estación Eloy Alfaro (Chimbacalle), Quito; tel. (2) 399-2100; e-mail info@ferrocarrilesdelecuador.gob.ec; internet www.ferrocarrilesdelecuador.gob.ec; fmrly Empresa de Ferrocarriles Ecuatorianos (EFE); presided over by the Co-ordinating Minister for Cultural and Natural Heritage; Gen. Man. Jorge Eduardo Carrera Sánchez.

ROADS

There were 43,670 km of roads in 2007, of which 15.0% were paved. The Pan-American Highway runs north from Ambato to Quito and to the Colombian border at Tulcán, and south to Cuenca and Loja.

Agencia Nacional de Tránsito (ANT): Avda Antonio José de Sucre y José Sánchez, Quito; tel. (2) 382-8890; e-mail contactenos@ant.gob.ec; internet www.ant.gob.ec; govt body, regulates road transport; Exec. Dir Michel Doumet Chedraui.

Comisión de Tránsito del Ecuador: Chile 1710 y Brasil, Guayaquil; tel. (4) 241-1397; internet www.comisiontransito.gob.ec; state-run transit commission; Dir HÉCTOR SOLÓRZANO CAMACHO.

SHIPPING

There are four commercial state-owned ports, which are independently managed. At December 2013 the flag registered fleet comprised 184 vessels, totalling 330,576 grt.

Port Authorities

Autoridad Portuaria de Esmeraldas: Avda Jaime Roldós Aguilera (Recinto Portuario), Esmeraldas; tel. (6) 272-1352; fax (6) 272-1354; e-mail ape@puertoesmeraldas.gob.ec; internet www.puertoesmeraldas.gob.ec; f. 1970; 25-year operating concession awarded to private consortium in 2004; renationalized in 2010; Gen. Man. RAFAEL PLAZA PERDOMO.

Autoridad Portuaria de Guayaquil: Avda de la Marina, Vía Puerto Marítimo, Guayaquil; tel. (4) 248-0120; fax (4) 248-4728; internet www.apg.gob.ec; f. 1958; Pres. RUBÉN MORÁN CASTRO; Man. PUBLIO FRANCISCO FARFÁN BLACIO.

Autoridad Portuaria de Manta: Avda Malecón s/n, Manta; tel. (5) 262-7161; fax (5) 262-1861; e-mail info@puertodemanta.gob.ec; internet www.puertodemanta.gob.ec; Pres. ROBERTO SALAZAR BRACCO.

Autoridad Portuaria de Puerto Bolívar: Avda Bolívar Madero Vargas, Puerto Bolívar; tel. (7) 292-9999; e-mail appb@appb.gob.ec; internet www.appb.gob.ec; f. 1970; Pres. MONTGOMERY SÁNCHEZ REYES; Gen. Man. WILMER ENCALADA LUDEÑA.

Principal Shipping Companies

Andinave, SA: Edif. Previsora, 29°, Of. 2901, Avda 9 de Octubre 100 y Malecon Simon Bolivar, Guayaquil; tel. (4) 232-5555; fax (4) 232-5957; e-mail info@andinave.com; internet www.andinave.com; f. 1983; shipping and port agents, stevedoring and logistics; Gen. Man. RODRIGO VITERI.

BBC Ecuador Andino Cía Ltda: Edif. San Luis, 3°, Suite 6, Avda Tulcán 809 y Hurtado, Casilla 3338, Guayaquil; tel. (4) 236-5585; fax (4) 604-1898; e-mail guayaquil@bbc-chartering.com; internet www.bbc-chartering.com; subsidiary of BBC Chartering & Logistic (Germany); Gen. Man. FEDERICO FERBER.

CMA CGM Ecuador, SA: Parque Empresarial Colón, Corporativo 2, Ofs 501 y 503, Avda Rodrigo Chàvez s/n, Guayaquil; tel. (4) 213-6501; fax (4) 336-5626; e-mail gql.genmbox@cma-cgm.com; internet www.cma-cgm.com; Gen. Man. JAVIER MOREIRA CALDERÓN.

Flota Petrolera Ecuatoriana (FLOPEC): Edif. FLOPEC, Avda Amazonas No 24–196 y Cordero, Casilla 535-A, Quito; tel. (2) 398-3600; fax (2) 250-1428; e-mail planificacion@flopec.com.ec; internet www.flopec.com.ec; f. 1972; Gen. Man. Capt. RAÚL SAMANIEGO GRANJA.

Investamar, SA: Edif. Berlín, 4°, Las Monjas 10 y C. J. Arosemena, Guayaquil; tel. (4) 220-4000; fax (4) 220-6646; e-mail investamar@grupoberlin.com; internet www.investamar.com.ec; Gen. Man. Capt. ROLF BENZ.

J. M. Palau Agencia de Vapores: Edif. Plaza, 6°, Of. 603-604, Baquierzo Moreno 1119 y Avda 9 de Octubre, POB 09019108, Guayaquil; tel. (4) 256-2178; fax (4) 256-3473; e-mail jmpav@ecua.net.ec; internet www.jmpalau-shipagency.com; f. 1956; Gen. Man. NAPOLEON CADENA.

Naviera Marnizam, SA: Edif. El Navio, Avda Malecon y Calle 19, Manta; tel. (5) 262-6445; fax (5) 262-4414; e-mail info@marzam-online.com; internet www.marzam-online.com; f. 1985; Gen. Man. LUCÍA ZAMBRANO SEGOVIA.

CIVIL AVIATION

There are four international airports: Mariscal Sucre in Quito, José Joaquín de Olmedo in Guayaquil, Eloy Alfaro in Manta (Manabí) and Cotopaxi Internacional in Latacunga. In 2009 the total number of airports in Ecuador was 402, of which 103 had paved runways.

Dirección General de Aviación Civil: Avda Buenos Aires Oeste 1-53 y 10 de Agosto, Quito; tel. (2) 223-2184; fax (2) 255-2987; e-mail subdirector.subdac@dgac.gov.ec; internet www.dgac.gob.ec; f. 1946; Dir-Gen. FERNANDO GUERRERO LÓPEZ.

Aerogal (Aerolíneas Galápagos): Amazonas 7797 y Juan Holguín, Quito; tel. (2) 396-0600; fax (2) 243-0487; e-mail customerservice@aerogal.com.ec; internet www.aerogal.com.ec; f. 1985; owned by Avianca (Colombia); domestic flights and also flights to Colombia and USA; Exec. Pres. JULIO GAMERO.

LAN Ecuador, SA: Avda de las Américas s/n, Guayaquil; tel. (4) 269-2850; fax (4) 228-5433; internet www.lan.com; f. 2002; commenced operations in 2003 following acquisition of assets of Ecuatoriana by LAN Chile; scheduled daily flights to Quito, Guayaquil, and the USA; Gen. Man. MAXIMILIANO NARANJO ITURRALDE.

TAME Línea Aérea del Ecuador: Edif. TAME, Avda Amazonas No 24–260 y Avda Colón, 6°, Casilla 17-07-8736, Sucursal Almagro, Quito; tel. (2) 396-6300; fax (2) 255-4907; e-mail tamejefv@impsat.net.ec; internet www.tame.com.ec; f. 1962; fmrly Transportes Aéreos Mercantiles Ecuatorianos, SA; removed from military control in 1990; state-owned; domestic scheduled and charter services for passengers and freight; Pres. FERNANDO MARTÍNEZ DE LA VEGA.

Tourism

Tourism has become an increasingly important industry in Ecuador, with a wide variety of heritage sites, beaches, rainforest reserves and national parks. The main attractions include the Galápagos Islands and the Yasuní National Park. In 2012 foreign arrivals (including same-day visitors) numbered a provisional 1,272,000. In the same year receipts from the tourism industry amounted to a provisional US $1,026m.

Asociación Ecuatoriana de Agencias de Viajes, Operadores de Turismo y Mayoristas (ASECUT): Caldas 340 y Guayaquil, Edif. San Blas, 6°, Ofs 61–62, Quito; tel. (2) 250-0759; fax (2) 250-3669; e-mail asecut@pi.pro.ec; f. 1953; Pres. ALFONSO SEVILLA.

Federación Hotelera del Ecuador (AHOTEC): América No 38–80 y Diguja, Quito; tel. (2) 244-3425; fax (2) 245-3942; e-mail ahotec@interactive.net.ec; internet www.hotelesecuador.com.ec; Pres. JOSÉ OCHOA GARCÍA; Exec. Dir DIEGO UTRERAS.

Defence

As assessed at November 2013, Ecuador's armed forces numbered 58,000: army 46,500, navy 7,300 (including 2,150 marines and 380 in the naval air force) and air force 4,200. Paramilitary forces included 500 coastguards. Military service lasts for one year and is selective for men at the age of 20.

Defence Budget: an estimated US $1,510m. in 2013.

Chief of the Joint Command of the Armed Forces: Gen. CARLOS ANTONIO LEONARDO BARREIRO MUÑOZ.

Chief of Staff of the Army: Gen. JORGE ANÍBAL PEÑA COBEÑA.

Chief of Staff of the Navy: Vice-Adm. LUIS AURELIO JARAMILLO ARIAS.

Chief of Staff of the Air Force: Lt-Gen. ENRIQUE VELASCO DÁVILA.

Education

Education in Ecuador is compulsory between five and 15 years of age. All public schools are free. Private schools feature prominently in the educational system. Primary education lasts for six years. Secondary education, in general and specialized technical or humanities schools, lasts for up to six years, comprising two equal cycles of three years each. In 2012 enrolment at primary schools included 95% of pupils in the relevant age-group, while the comparable ratio for secondary schools in 2012, according to UNESCO estimates, was 74%. In many rural areas, Quechua and other indigenous Amerindian languages are used in education. The total government expenditure on education was estimated at US $23.9m. for 2012.

EGYPT

Introductory Survey

LOCATION, CLIMATE, LANGUAGE, RELIGION, FLAG, CAPITAL

The Arab Republic of Egypt occupies the north-eastern corner of Africa, with an extension across the Gulf of Suez into the Sinai Peninsula, sometimes regarded as lying within Asia. Egypt is bounded to the north by the Mediterranean Sea, to the north-east by Israel, to the east by the Red Sea, to the south by Sudan, and to the west by Libya. The climate is arid, with a maximum annual rainfall of only 200 mm around Alexandria. More than 90% of the country is desert, and some 99% of the population live in the valley and delta of the River Nile. Summer temperatures reach a maximum of 43°C (110°F) and winters are mild, with an average day temperature of about 18°C (65°F). Arabic is the official language. More than 90% of the population are Muslims, mainly of the Sunni sect. The remainder are mostly Christians, principally Copts. The national flag (proportions 2 by 3) has three equal horizontal stripes, of red, white and black; the white stripe has, in the centre, the national emblem (a striped shield superimposed on an eagle, with a cartouche beneath bearing the inscription, in Kufic script, 'Arab Republic of Egypt') in gold. The capital is Cairo (al-Qahirah).

CONTEMPORARY POLITICAL HISTORY

Historical Context

Egypt, a province of Turkey's Ottoman Empire from the 16th century, was occupied by British forces in 1882. The administration was controlled by British officials, although Egypt remained nominally an Ottoman province until 1914, when a British protectorate was declared. The country was granted titular independence in 1922. Fuad I, the reigning Sultan, became King. He was succeeded in 1936 by his son, King Faruq (Farouk). The Anglo-Egyptian Treaty of 1936 recognized full Egyptian sovereignty, although after the Second World War (1939–45) British forces maintained a military presence in the Suez Canal Zone. When the British mandate in Palestine was ended in 1948, Arab armies intervened to oppose the newly proclaimed State of Israel. A ceasefire was agreed in 1949, leaving Egyptian forces occupying the Gaza Strip.

On 23 July 1952 a group of army officers led by Lt-Col (later Col) Gamal Abd al-Nasir (Nasser) instigated a bloodless coup. Farouk abdicated in favour of his infant son, Ahmad Fuad II, and went into exile. Gen. Muhammad Nagib (Neguib) was appointed Commander-in-Chief of the army and Chairman of the Revolution Command Council (RCC), additionally becoming Prime Minister and Military Governor in September. In December the 1923 Constitution was abolished, and in January 1953 all political parties were dissolved. The monarchy was abolished on 18 June, and Egypt was proclaimed a republic, with Neguib as President and Prime Minister. In April 1954 Neguib was succeeded as Prime Minister by his deputy, Nasser; he was relieved of his remaining posts in November, whereupon Nasser became acting head of state.

The establishment of military rule was accompanied by wide-ranging reforms, including the redistribution of land, the promotion of industrial development and the expansion of social welfare services. In foreign affairs, the new regime was strongly committed to Arab unity, and Egypt played a prominent part in the Non-aligned Movement (founded in 1961). In 1955, having failed to secure Western armaments on satisfactory terms, Egypt accepted military assistance from the USSR.

A new Constitution was approved by national referendum in June 1956; Nasser was elected President unopposed, and the RCC was dissolved. In July, following the departure of British forces from the Suez Canal, the US and British Governments withdrew their offers of financial assistance for Egypt's construction of the Aswan High Dam. Nasser responded by nationalizing the Suez Canal Company, so that revenue from Canal tolls could be used to finance the dam's construction. The takeover of the Canal was a catalyst for Israel's invasion of the Sinai Peninsula on 29 October. British and French forces launched military operations against Egypt two days later. Intense pressure from the UN and the USA resulted in a ceasefire on 6 November and UN supervision of the invaders' withdrawal.

Egypt and Syria merged in February 1958 to form the United Arab Republic (UAR), with Nasser as President. The new state strengthened ties with the USSR and other communist countries. In September 1961 Syria seceded from the UAR, but Egypt retained this title until 1971. In December 1962 Nasser established the Arab Socialist Union (ASU) as the country's only recognized political organization. In May 1967 he secured the withdrawal of the UN Emergency Force from Egyptian territory. Egypt subsequently reoccupied Sharm el-Sheikh, on the Sinai Peninsula, and closed the Straits of Tiran to Israeli shipping. This precipitated the so-called Six-Day War (or June War), when Israel quickly defeated neighbouring Arab states, including Egypt, to control the Gaza Strip and a large area of Egyptian territory, including the Sinai Peninsula. The Suez Canal remained closed until June 1975.

Nasser died suddenly in September 1970, and was succeeded by his Vice-President, Col Anwar Sadat. In September 1971 the UAR was renamed the Arab Republic of Egypt, and a new Constitution took effect. In 1976 Egypt terminated its Treaty of Friendship with the USSR. Relations with the USA developed meanwhile, as President Sadat came to rely increasingly on US aid.

In October 1973 Egyptian troops crossed the Suez Canal to recover territory lost to Israel in 1967. After 18 days of fighting a ceasefire was achieved. In 1974–75, following US mediation, disengagement agreements were signed whereby Israel evacuated territory in Sinai, and Israeli and Egyptian forces were separated by a UN-controlled buffer zone. Sadat angered many Arab countries in 1977 by visiting Israel and addressing the Knesset (parliament). In September 1978, following talks held in the USA, Sadat and the Israeli Prime Minister, Menachem Begin, signed two agreements: the first provided for a five-year transitional period during which the inhabitants of the Israeli-occupied West Bank of Jordan and the Gaza Strip would obtain full autonomy and self-government; the second provided for a peace treaty between Egypt and Israel. The latter was signed in March 1979, whereafter Israel made phased withdrawals from the Sinai Peninsula, the last taking place in April 1982. The League of Arab States (the Arab League, see p. 362) expelled Egypt following the signing of the peace treaty, and imposed political and economic sanctions. Nevertheless, in February 1980 Egypt and Israel exchanged ambassadors for the first time.

Domestic Political Affairs

In 1974 Sadat began to introduce a more liberal political and economic regime, allowing political parties to participate in the 1976 elections for the Majlis al-Sha'ab (People's Assembly). In July 1978 Sadat formed the National Democratic Party (NDP), and in 1979 the special constitutional status of the ASU was ended. In October 1981 Sadat was assassinated by members of the militant group Islamic Jihad. He was succeeded by Lt-Gen. Muhammad Hosni Mubarak, his Vice-President and a former Commander-in-Chief of the air force. Meanwhile, a national state of emergency was declared. A new electoral law required parties to receive a minimum of 8% of the total vote in order to secure representation in the People's Assembly. This prompted opposition parties to boycott elections to local councils and to the Majlis al-Shura (Advisory Council). At legislative elections in May 1984 the ruling NDP won 72.9% of the total vote; only the New Wafd Party (or New Delegation Party), in alliance with the Muslim Brotherhood, also achieved representation.

Meanwhile, a division in the Arab world between a 'moderate' grouping (including Jordan and Iraq), which viewed Egypt's participation as indispensable to any diplomatic moves towards solving the problems of the region, and a 'radical' grouping, led by Syria, became increasingly evident. The leader of the Palestinian Liberation Organization (PLO), Yasser Arafat, visited President Mubarak for discussions in December 1983, signifying the end of estrangement between Egypt and the PLO, and in 1984 Jordan resumed diplomatic relations with Egypt. The latter thus became profoundly involved in the pursuit of a negotiated settlement of the Palestinian question. In November 1987, at a summit conference in Jordan, President Hafiz Assad of Syria obstructed proposals to readmit Egypt to the Arab League. However, recognizing Egypt's support for Iraq in the Iran–Iraq War (1980–88) and acknowledging the influence that Egypt could exercise on regional issues, the conference approved a resolution placing the establishment of diplomatic links with Egypt at the discretion of member states. Egypt was readmitted to the League in May 1989.

At the general election held in April 1987 the NDP won 346 of the 448 elective seats in the People's Assembly, the opposition parties together won 95, and independents seven. The Muslim Brotherhood took 37 seats, to become the largest single opposition group in the legislature. At a referendum held in October Mubarak was confirmed as President for a second six-year term of office by 97.1% of voters. In March 1988 the Government renewed the national state of emergency for a further three years, citing the continued threat of internal and external subversion. The legislation was subsequently extended at regular intervals; although the Supreme Council of the Armed Forces (SCAF), which assumed power following Mubarak's resignation as President in February 2011 (see The ouster of President Mubarak), rescinded it in May 2012, the state of emergency was briefly reintroduced following the military's seizure of power from Mubarak's successor, President Muhammad Mursi, in July 2013 (see Military coup brings renewed violence).

Following Iraq's invasion and annexation of Kuwait in August 1990, Egypt convened an emergency summit meeting of Arab leaders at which 12 of the 20 Arab League states supported a resolution demanding the withdrawal of Iraqi forces from Kuwait and, in response to Saudi Arabia's request for international assistance to deter potential aggression by Iraq, voted to send an Arab force to the Persian (Arabian) Gulf region. The Egyptian contingent within the multinational force eventually amounted to 35,000 troops.

Legislative elections in November and December 1990 were boycotted by the principal opposition parties, in protest at the Government's refusal to remove the elections from the supervision of the Ministry of the Interior and repeal the state of emergency. Of the 444 elective seats in the new People's Assembly, the NDP won 348, the National Progressive Unionist Party (NPUP or Tagammu) six, and independent candidates (most of whom were affiliated to the NDP) 83. Voting for the remaining seven seats was suspended. At a national referendum in October 1993, Mubarak was confirmed as President for a third term of office by some 96.3% of the valid votes cast. The opposition parties demanded reforms including: the amendment of the Constitution to allow direct presidential elections; the introduction of a two-term limit to the presidency; and unrestricted formation of political parties.

During the early 1990s violence perpetrated by radical Islamist groups increasingly targeted foreign interests in Egypt, although militants linked to Islamic Jihad attempted to assassinate both the Prime Minister and the Minister of the Interior in 1993. In April 1994 the chief of the anti-terrorist branch of the State Security Investigation Section was assassinated by members of Gama'ah al-Islamiyah (one of Egypt's principal militant Islamist groups). In the mid-1990s the Government arrested several leaders of the Muslim Brotherhood, claiming that there was evidence of links between the movement and Islamist extremists. In June 1995 Mubarak escaped an assassination attempt, apparently carried out by Islamist militants, while he was travelling to a summit meeting of the Organization of African Unity (OAU, now African Union—AU) in Addis Ababa, Ethiopia.

Legislative elections were held in November–December 1995, at which candidates of the NDP won 316 seats and the opposition parties collectively secured just 13 seats. Of the 115 independent candidates elected, 99 were reported to have immediately joined or rejoined the NDP. Allegations of electoral malpractices which favoured the NDP were widespread. A new Council of Ministers was appointed in January 1996, with Kamal Ahmad al-Ganzouri becoming Prime Minister.

In November 1997 the massacre near Luxor of 70 people, including 58 foreign tourists, by members of Gama'ah al-Islamiyah severely undermined both the tourism sector and the claims of the Government to have suppressed Islamist violence. Mubarak responded by dismissing the Minister of the Interior. In December a number of Gama'ah al-Islamiyah's exiled leaders claimed that the Luxor massacre had been perpetrated by a 'rogue' element acting independently of the group's leadership, and announced that those members under their specific authority would no longer target tourists in their conflict with the Government. In March 1998 Gama'ah al-Islamiyah declared a unilateral ceasefire. The Government subsequently accelerated the process of releasing imprisoned Islamist militants, including some 2,400 Gama'ah al-Islamiyah detainees, by the end of the year.

In September 1999 Mubarak's nomination for a fourth presidential term was approved by 93.8% of the valid votes cast in a national referendum. In October Atif Muhammad Obeid succeeded al-Ganzouri as Prime Minister. The Supreme Constitutional Court ruled in July 2000 that the People's Assembly elected in 1995 was illegitimate (as was the Assembly elected in 1990), and that the existing electoral system was invalid since the constitutional requirement that the judiciary have sole responsibility for supervising elections had not been observed. President Mubarak subsequently convened an extraordinary session of the Assembly, at which the electoral legislation was amended to allow judges to monitor voting at both the main and auxiliary polling stations in the impending general election.

Polls for the 444 elective seats in the People's Assembly took place in October–November 2000. The NDP increased its majority, taking 353 seats. Independent candidates secured 72 seats, but 35 of these reportedly joined or rejoined the NDP shortly afterwards. The opposition garnered 17 seats between them. Voting for the two seats in one constituency in Alexandria was postponed following the arrest of some 20 Muslim Brotherhood activists. At least 14 people were killed during the polls.

Meanwhile, in January 2000 three days of violent clashes between Muslims and Copts in the southern village of el-Kosheh resulted in the deaths of an estimated 20 Christians and one Muslim. An inquiry conducted by the Egyptian Organization for Human Rights inferred that the primary cause of the violence was the 'economic inequalities' between the relatively prosperous Coptic majority and the poorer Muslim minority. Following a trial and subsequent retrial, in June 2004 four men convicted of involvement in the violence were given custodial terms, while a further 92 defendants were acquitted.

The Egyptian authorities arrested large numbers of suspected Islamists during late 2001 and 2002. In September 2002 51 militants, who had initially been arrested in May 2001, were sentenced to up to 15 years' imprisonment for conspiring to overthrow the Government. In August 2002, meanwhile, a number of imprisoned senior members of Gama'ah al-Islamiyah announced their complete renunciation of violence. Some 900 members of the organization were released from prison in October 2003.

Limited reform in the early 2000s

At the eighth congress of the NDP in September 2002, Mubarak's second son, Gamal, was elected Secretary-General for Policy, effectively making him the party's third most senior figure and further fuelling speculation that he was being groomed eventually to succeed his father. In June 2003 the People's Assembly approved the creation of a National Council for Human Rights, as well as the closure of a number of the State Security Courts; the punishment of hard labour was also abolished. In September President Mubarak announced that all military orders issued under the emergency laws, which had been in place since the assassination of President Sadat in 1981, would be abolished, except those that were 'necessary to maintain public order and security'. However, a committee established by the Prime Minister to review the existing emergency powers recommended that only six of the 13 military orders could be withdrawn. The Egyptian authorities instigated a massive crackdown on the activities of the Muslim Brotherhood in May 2004, detaining activists and closing down shops and publishing houses.

In July 2004 Prime Minister Obeid announced the resignation of his entire Council of Ministers. Ahmad Mahmoud Muhammad Nazif was appointed Prime Minister. The new technocratic Government included several appointees regarded as having close links with Gamal Mubarak, among them Ahmad Aboul Gheit, hitherto Egypt's Permanent Representative to the UN, who became Minister of Foreign Affairs.

In October 2004 a new political party, Al-Ghad (Tomorrow), was approved after its fourth application. This decision was apparently prompted by criticism from the USA regarding the slow pace of democratic reform in Egypt, which had seen only two new political parties being licensed since 1977. Under the leadership of former New Wafd Party deputy Ayman Abd al-Aziz al-Nour, Al-Ghad brought to 18 the number of officially recognized parties. In January 2005 al-Nour was arrested and charged with having forged signatures required in order to secure his party's registration. His trial commenced in Cairo in June, but was subsequently postponed until late September, thus permitting the Al-Ghad leader to contest the presidential election (see The 2005 presidential and legislative elections). In December al-Nour was given a five-year prison sentence, having been found guilty of forgery. He appealed against the sentence, citing violations of his rights during detention and serious flaws in the original trial; however, in May 2006 the Court of Cassation upheld the original sentence. Al-Nour was finally released from prison on medical grounds in February 2009, with observers suggesting that his release was intended to allow Egypt to forge stronger ties with the USA (see Relations with the USA).

Egypt's first terrorist attack for seven years occurred in early October 2004, when three bombs exploded in the resorts of Taba, Ras Shitan and Nuweiba on the Sinai Peninsula, killing 34 people—many of whom were Israelis. In late October the principal blame for the attacks was placed upon a Palestinian, Ayad Said Salah, who had died in the explosion in Taba. In March 2005 three Egyptians were charged—one *in absentia*—in connection with the bombings, while it was reported that two others suspected of involvement in the attacks had been killed by security forces in the previous month.

In October 2004 more than 650 Egyptian activists, politicians and intellectuals released a statement urging a constitutional amendment to prevent President Mubarak from standing for another term in office. In February 2005 Mubarak did propose altering the Constitution to allow for direct, contested presidential elections. The constitutional amendment, drafted by a parliamentary committee, was overwhelmingly approved by the People's Assembly on 10 May and by some 82.9% of the electorate at a referendum held on 25 May. However, many opposition parties argued that the changes, which stated that political parties required 5% of parliamentary seats in order to field a presidential candidate and that a candidate would need the support of at least 65 members of the Assembly, would prevent non-NDP candidates from standing.

In April 2005 three foreign tourists were killed in a bomb attack in Cairo, and in July at least 60 people, some of them foreigners, were killed following three bomb attacks at hotels in the Red Sea resort of Sharm el-Sheikh. In October it was announced that a security fence would be erected around the resort in order to prevent further attacks. In August 2007 four Egyptian nationals were sentenced to life imprisonment, having been convicted of involvement in the Cairo bombing of April 2005; a further five defendants received terms of between one and 10 years, and four were acquitted.

The 2005 presidential and legislative elections

At the first ever multi-candidate presidential election, held on 7 September 2005, President Mubarak was re-elected for a fifth consecutive six-year term. Mubarak won 88.6% of the vote, while Ayman al-Nour came second, with 7.6%, and No'man Khalil Gomaa of the New Wafd Party secured third place, with 2.9%. Seven other candidates all received less than 0.5% of the vote. Turnout was registered at only 23.0%, attributed in part to an appeal by several opposition parties for a boycott of the poll. The election was marred by accusations of a media bias towards Mubarak and controversy surrounding the newly established Presidential Election Commission's decision to ban independent groups from monitoring the ballot. Mubarak was sworn in on 27 September.

Elections to contest the 444 elective seats in the People's Assembly were conducted on 9 November, 20 November and 1 December 2005 (with run-off elections held six days after each round). The Muslim Brotherhood presented a list of 150 members as independent candidates, after the Egyptian authorities had for the first time allowed the movement to campaign freely. Both prior to and during the elections, however, more than 850 members of the Muslim Brotherhood were arrested amid reports of clashes between NDP and Brotherhood supporters. At least 10 people were killed in rioting during the ballot. Official results issued in mid-December revealed that the NDP had secured 311 of the 432 decided seats. The most notable gains, however, were made by the Brotherhood, which increased its representation from 17 seats to 88. Other independent candidates won 24 seats, while the New Wafd Party took six seats, the NPUP two and Al-Ghad one. Turnout was only 26.2% of the electorate, and voting had to be postponed for 12 seats in six constituencies owing to violence. On 12 December Mubarak appointed five women and five Coptic Christians to the 10 presidentially appointed seats in the People's Assembly in order to increase their level of representation. Mubarak retained Nazif as Prime Minister and asked him to form a new government. The new ministerial appointments were expected to reinforce the position of Gamal Mubarak, who was named as one of three Deputy Secretary-Generals of the NDP in January 2006.

President Mubarak's decision, in February 2006, to postpone local elections scheduled for April of that year until 2008 attracted particular criticism from the Muslim Brotherhood. The amended Constitution required independent candidates standing for the presidency to obtain the support of at least 10 local councillors, and Islamists claimed that the delay in holding the polls would ensure that the NDP retained control over nominations for the presidency. Meanwhile, four senior judges who had persistently criticized government interference in judicial matters and made allegations of vote-rigging in the legislative elections of 2005 were stripped of their immunity and investigated by a state security court. In April–May 2006 the Government's decision to prosecute two of the judges provoked angry demonstrations in Cairo; an estimated 400 Brotherhood protesters were subsequently arrested.

On 24 April 2006 a total of 23 people were killed following three co-ordinated explosions in the Red Sea resort of Dahab. Days later the People's Assembly voted to approve a two-year extension to the national state of emergency, despite earlier indications from Prime Minister Nazif that new anti-terrorism legislation would be implemented in its place.

The 2007 referendum on constitutional reform

In December 2006 the President proposed 34 amendments to the Constitution, including a reduction of presidential powers in favour of the People's Assembly and the Council of Ministers, and steps to ease restrictions on political parties' candidates for presidential elections. However, opposition figures criticized a number of the proposals, in particular the reversal of earlier legislation providing for full judicial supervision of elections. Instead, a government-appointed Higher Election Commission (HEC) was henceforth to monitor the legislative election process. In addition to affirming the fact that Egypt's economy was now based on 'market principles', one of the most significant changes was an increase in the powers of the security forces to monitor, detain and imprison citizens suspected of involvement in terrorist activities. Mubarak also proposed a formal ban on the establishment of political parties based on religion, one of a number of changes aimed at curbing the growing influence of the Muslim Brotherhood. A national referendum on the constitutional amendments, which—despite a boycott by the Islamist movement—were approved by a significant majority of deputies in the People's Assembly in mid-March 2007, took place on 26 March. According to official figures, the amendments were endorsed by 75.9% of voters, although turnout was estimated by the Ministry of Justice at only 27.1%. Opposition parties immediately contested the outcome of the poll.

Concerns about the extent of freedom of expression in Egypt again came to the fore in early 2007, particularly as increasing numbers of dissidents were using blogs to publish articles critical of the Mubarak regime. In May a new liberal political grouping, the Democratic Front Party, was registered by the authorities under the leadership of Osama al-Ghazali Harb, a journalist and former member of the NDP, and former cabinet minister Yahia al-Gamal. By mid-2007 the number of legalized political organizations in Egypt had increased to 24. In August there was a renewed crackdown on the activities of the Muslim Brotherhood, amid reports that the group was preparing to establish a political party.

Partial elections to select 88 members of the Advisory Council were held on 11 and 18 June 2007; 84 seats were secured by the NDP, three by independents aligned to the NDP and one by the NPUP. The Muslim Brotherhood thus failed to win a seat, despite having fielded candidates who stood as independents. A further 44 members of the Council were appointed by President Mubarak. In November Mubarak was re-elected unchallenged as leader of the NDP at the party's ninth congress. There was renewed speculation concerning the likelihood of Gamal Mubarak succeeding his father as President after a reform of the NDP's political structure rendered Gamal eligible to contest future presidential polls. In May 2008 the People's Assembly voted to extend until 2010 the state of emergency in place since 1981—a particularly controversial decision given that Mubarak had pledged to abolish the emergency law during his 2005 presidential campaign.

Increasing political tensions and civil unrest

In June 2009 the People's Assembly approved legislation that increased the number of seats in the Assembly from 454 to 518, with all of the 64 additional seats reserved for female candidates. The changes were to take effect following the legislative elections scheduled for late 2010 and were intended to remain in place for at least two parliamentary terms.

In October 2009 opposition groups began a campaign against the possible candidacy of Gamal Mubarak to succeed his father at the end of the latter's presidential term in 2011. A new opposition movement, Mayihkomsh ('he will not rule'), was formed under the leadership of Ayman al-Nour. Participants at its first conference included representatives of the Muslim Brotherhood, the Democratic Front Party and the Egyptian Movement for Change, also known as Kefaya (Enough). The campaign gained further prominence in February 2010, following an announcement by the former Secretary-General of the International Atomic Energy Agency, Mohammed el-Baradei, that he would be prepared to contest the presidential election. However, despite el-Baradei's possible candidacy being welcomed by opposition activists upon his arrival in Cairo that month, it remained uncertain, as the terms of the Constitution require non-affiliated presidential candidates to obtain the prior support of at least 250 members of parliament or local officials.

Tensions between Egypt's Muslim and Coptic Christian communities escalated following a bomb attack outside a Coptic Christian church in Alexandria at the end of December 2010 while a New Year's Eve service was in progress; 21 people were killed. The authorities subsequently stated that the explosion had been carried out by a lone suicide bomber among the crowd. President Mubarak alleged that the attack had been orchestrated by 'foreign hands' aiming to destabilize Egypt, and appealed to Muslims and Christians to unite against the common threat of terrorism. However, hundreds of Coptic Christians continued to clash with the security forces, accusing them of failing properly to address threats that had recently been issued against their community by Islamist militant groups.

In May 2010 the People's Assembly voted to approve President Mubarak's request to extend the state of emergency for a further two years. Although new limits to the legislation were introduced, whereby the state would have reduced powers to monitor communications, confiscate property and censor publications, critics argued that the emergency law could still be used to stifle opposition to the Government. In June extensive anti-Government protests took place in Alexandria and Cairo, in response to allegations of police brutality which had been sparked by the death—reportedly at the hands of police officers—of a young activist in Alexandria who was apparently seeking to expose corruption in the security forces.

At partial elections to the Advisory Council held on 1 June and 8 June 2010, the NDP secured 80 of the 88 contested seats; Al-Ghad, the NPUP, the Arab Democratic Nasserist Party and the Democratic Generation Party each won one seat, with the remaining four seats being taken by independent candidates. Affiliates of the Muslim Brotherhood, standing as independents, again failed to secure representation. The Brotherhood subsequently pledged its support to a campaign for political reform launched by el-Baradei that included revocation of the emergency legislation, full judicial supervision of elections, and independent candidates being allowed to stand for President. El-Baradei stated that he would only contest the presidential poll then scheduled for 2011 if the Constitution was amended to ensure a 'free and fair election'.

The 2010 legislative elections

In October 2010 President Mubarak announced that elections to the People's Assembly were to be held on 28 November, with run-off elections scheduled for 5 December. In the previous month el-Baradei had urged an electoral boycott, claiming that the ballot was certain to be rigged by the Government. However, the outlawed Muslim Brotherhood subsequently announced its intention to field candidates as independents. In the weeks preceding the poll dozens of candidates who were reportedly affiliated to the Brotherhood were disqualified, and more than 1,000 of the movement's supporters were said to have been arrested. On 26 November administrative courts unsuccessfully ordered the cancellation of the elections in 24 districts after the HEC had ignored previous court orders demanding the reinstatement of disqualified opposition and independent candidates.

In the first round of voting on 28 November 2010, the NDP was reported to have won the vast majority of seats, with independent candidates affiliated to the Muslim Brotherhood failing to secure a single seat. The second round of voting was boycotted by the New Wafd Party and the Brotherhood, both of which alleged widespread voting irregularities during the first round. According to final results released by the HEC, the NDP secured 420 of the 498 contested seats in the People's Assembly, the New Wafd Party six, the NPUP five, and the Democratic Generation Party, Al-Ghad, Al-Salam and the Social Justice Party each garnered one seat; independent candidates won 69 seats, of which just one was taken by an affiliate of the Brotherhood (compared with 88 in 2005). The results appeared to preclude the possibility of any of the opposition parties fielding a candidate at the presidential election scheduled for 2011, since they would require 3% of the total number of seats in the People's Assembly and 5% of seats in the Advisory Council; the chances of an independent candidate being able to stand also appeared remote. The New Wafd Party ordered its six elected legislators to resign from parliament, while the Brotherhood withdrew its support for Magdi Ashour, its sole affiliate in parliament. The Government, meanwhile, denied any allegations of vote-rigging, acknowledging only 'minor irregularities' that it claimed had no bearing on any results. However, election monitors reported widespread electoral violations, while two people were killed during violent clashes between rival supporters.

In mid-December 2010 around 20 opposition party members who had failed to secure election, including members of the Muslim Brotherhood and the New Wafd Party, announced the formation of a shadow parliament, pledging allegiance to the Constitution and 'the will of the people'. There were also widespread popular protests against the perceived fraudulent nature of the elections, although the Brotherhood played an ambivalent role. In mid-January 2011 el-Baradei announced that he would not be seeking election in the presidential poll, and appealed for an election boycott in an attempt to 'erode the regime's legitimacy'. In January 2012, by which time the ballot had been scheduled for June, he repeated that he would not stand for the presidency until such an election was being organized 'within a democratic framework'.

The ouster of President Mubarak

Seemingly inspired by the overthrow of the Tunisian President, Zine al-Abidine Ben Ali, in mid-January 2011 (see the chapter on Tunisia), activists in Egypt called for a 'day of revolt' on 25 January, in protest at state corruption, the alleged practice of torture by state security forces, poverty and unemployment. Thousands of demonstrators gathered in Cairo, Alexandria and other cities, demanding Mubarak's resignation as President and expressing their opposition to the possible candidacy of Gamal Mubarak as his successor. Three protesters were said to have been killed in clashes with the authorities in Suez, while state television reported that a police officer had died in Cairo. On 26 January the Government stated that anyone engaging in public gatherings, protests and marches would be prosecuted, and access to internet sites which had been used by activists to plan protests was blocked. Nevertheless, demonstrators returned to the streets on 26–27 January, during which time a further two people had reportedly been killed and more than 800 people arrested. In anticipation of further mass protests planned for 28 January, the authorities detained a number of senior Muslim Brotherhood members, imposed a total block on internet access and disrupted mobile telephone services. During the protests, which were staged across Cairo, Alexandria, Suez and other major cities, 18 people died and more than 1,000 were injured. A nationwide evening curfew was imposed in an attempt to reduce tensions, and the President stated publicly that he intended to replace the cabinet and to introduce political and economic reforms.

Following an intensification of the protests, on 29 January 2011 Mubarak appointed the chief of the General Intelligence Service, Omar Suleiman, as Vice-President, and announced the dismissal of Prime Minister Nazif and his administration. Later that day Ahmad Muhammad Shafiq, who had served as Minister of Civil Aviation under Nazif, was named as premier and on 31 January a new Council of Ministers was sworn in, including Mahmoud Wagdi as Minister of the Interior, in place of Habib al-Adli, and the replacement of Minister of Information Anas Ahmad al-Fiki. However, demonstrators in Cairo and other cities denounced the new Government as 'illegitimate', citing the reappointment of several unpopular ministers. On 1 February President Mubarak announced in a televised address that neither he nor his son Gamal would contest the presidential election then scheduled for September, but that he would remain in office until the election was concluded. A televised statement earlier that day by a spokesman for the armed forces had indicated that troops would not obey orders to use military force to quell the protests. Violent confrontations between pro- and anti-Government groups erupted on 2 February in Cairo's Tahrir (Independence) Square, which had become the focal point of the demonstrations; the Ministry of Health reported that at least eight people had been killed in the clashes.

On 5 February 2011 Vice-President Suleiman began talks on constitutional reform with representatives of opposition groups, including the Muslim Brotherhood, which on 21 February announced its intention to establish a political party, the Freedom and Justice Party (FJP). The new party, officially founded on 30 April, declared that it would put forward candidates for some 50% of seats in the forthcoming elections to the People's Assembly, and that it would not be contesting the presidential poll. In June the FJP entered into a coalition, the Democratic Alliance, with a diverse group of Islamist and secular parties, including the New Wafd Party, the NPUP and the Al-Nour (Light) Party—an ultra-conservative Salafi Islamist organization established in January. (Some members of the alliance subsequently withdrew in order to contest the legislative ballot independently.) In late February the Al-Wasat (New Centre) Party, a moderate Islamist party established in 1996 by former members of the Muslim Brotherhood, also achieved legal status. Despite the constitutional talks, demands for Mubarak's resignation increased as crowds of demonstrators returned to Tahrir Square. In a second televised address on 10 February 2011, Mubarak promised to transfer unspecified powers to Vice-President Suleiman. However, he again insisted that, for reasons of national security, he would remain in office until September's presidential election. Earlier that day a group of senior military officials, the Supreme Council of the Armed Forces (SCAF), led by the Commander-in-Chief of the Armed Forces, Deputy Prime Minister and Minister of Defence and Military Production, Field Marshal Muhammad Hussein Tantawi, broadcast a communiqué pledging the army's 'support for the legitimate demands of the people'.

Suleiman announced on 11 February 2011 that Mubarak had resigned as President and transferred his powers to the SCAF. On 13 February the SCAF dissolved parliament, suspended the Constitution and declared that it would govern Egypt for a six-month period or 'until the end of parliamentary and presidential elections'. A judicial committee was instructed to formulate amendments to the Constitution in preparation for a national referendum in March. Tantawi was to act as de facto head of state, while the Government of Ahmad Shafiq was requested to remain in office. However, protests against Shafiq's participation in the cabinet continued in Cairo, while police officers and other workers staged separate demonstrations, demanding wage increases. In late February 2011 it was reported that the public prosecution service had begun an investigation into allegations of corruption and money-laundering against a number of senior members of the former regime, including al-Fiki, al-Adli and the businessman Ahmed Ezz, a close associate of Gamal Mubarak who had been an NDP member of the People's Assembly. The judicial committee on constitutional reform published its draft amendments on 28 February, including revisions to those articles regarding political parties and the criteria of eligibility for presidential candidates; on 4 March the SCAF decreed that a referendum was to take place on 19 March. Meanwhile, on 3 March it was announced that Shafiq had resigned as Prime Minister; former Minister of Transport Essam Sharaf was appointed to replace him. Sharaf's new Council of Ministers was sworn in on 7 March. Most notably, Nabil al-Arabi, hitherto Egypt's ambassador to the UN, was appointed as Minister of Foreign Affairs, while Mansour al-Essawi became Minister of the Interior. Also that day the trial of al-Adli on separate charges of money-laundering and unlawful acquisition of public funds began at a court in Cairo.

On 19 March 2011, despite opposition from prominent figures in the anti-Mubarak protest movement, including el-Baradei, the constitutional amendments (which were supported by both the NDP and the Muslim Brotherhood) were approved by some 77.3% of voters; voter turnout was recorded at 41.2%. Accordingly, on 23 March the SCAF issued a Constitutional Declaration which was to usurp the former Constitution until a new document could be formulated. Also included in the draft amendments was the introduction of a two-term limit to the presidency, the judicial monitoring of future polls, and the stipulation that a President must henceforth name a Vice-President.

Hosni Mubarak and his family were placed under house arrest in Sharm el-Sheikh at the end of March 2011, and in early April the Prosecutor-General requested that he and his sons Gamal and Alaa be questioned regarding allegations of corruption and the deaths of protesters during the February uprising. Days later both Gamal and Alaa Mubarak were temporarily detained at a gaol in Cairo, while Hosni Mubarak was held under police custody at a hospital in Sharm el-Sheikh, having reportedly suffered from heart problems. On 17 April the High Administrative Court approved the dissolution of the NDP and the return of its assets to the state, while two days later the Prosecutor-General announced that former Prime Minister Nazif and former Minister of Finance Yousuf Boutros-Ghali had been charged with corruption and misuse of public funds. On 19 April a government committee formed to investigate the deaths of protesters revealed that a total of 846 people had been killed and at least 6,400 injured during the unrest of early 2011. In its report, the committee also accused the security forces of using 'excessive' force in their attempts to quell the protests. On 5 May al-Adli was sentenced to 12 years' imprisonment and fined some £E14m., having been found guilty of money-laundering and of illicitly procuring public funds during his time in office. The postponement of al-Adli's second trial, on charges of murder and attempted murder (he was accused of ordering police to shoot demonstrators during the anti-Mubarak uprising), provoked renewed protests in the capital by demonstrators who sought swift prosecution for former officials accused of wrongdoing. On 24 May it had been officially announced that Hosni, Alaa and Gamal Mubarak would all face trial proceedings over their alleged crimes; the former President's wife, Suzanne, was required to return to the state a list of illegally acquired personal belongings. Meanwhile, on 30 April 2011 Muhammad Mursi was appointed as Chairman of the newly formed FJP by the Muslim Brotherhood leadership, while Muhammad Saad el-Katatni became the party's Secretary-General. In September Ahmed Ezz was imprisoned for 10 years, having been found guilty of corruption. (Ezz received a further seven-year prison term for money-laundering in October 2012.) On 4 June 2011 Boutros-Ghali was sentenced to 30 years' imprisonment, *in absentia*, for corruption, including the use of public funds for personal gain, while serving as Minister of Finance. Nazif was given a three-year gaol term in September.

There was a notable increase in sectarian violence during 2011. In March violence between Coptic Christians and Muslims in a district of Cairo led to more than 13 deaths; the clashes erupted when Copts initiated protests against the burning down of a local church by hardline Muslims. In May further sectarian clashes in the capital, in which 12 people died, resulted from rumours that a female Copt who had married a Muslim man was being forcibly prevented from converting to Islam. In October 25 people (mostly Copts) were reported to have died as a result of renewed fighting between Copts and security forces who, joined by militant Salafi Islamists, reacted forcefully when Coptic protesters held a rally in central Cairo against systematic discrimination towards their religious community.

The trial of Mubarak and Islamist successes in legislative elections

A revised Council of Ministers took office under Prime Minister Sharaf on 21 July 2011; 13 ministers retained their posts, including the Minister of the Interior. Meanwhile, on 28 June 2011 it was announced that 1,750 municipal councils formed under Mubarak's rule would be dissolved. On 13 July the interim Government also declared that up to 700 police officers would be dismissed from their posts for their alleged role in the deaths of protesters earlier in the year.

The trial of Hosni Mubarak, together with his sons Gamal and Alaa, al-Adli and six other former senior officials, commenced at a court in Cairo on 3 August 2011; all the defendants pleaded not guilty to the charges of the unlawful killing of protesters, profiteering and conducting illegal business transactions. The start of the trial proceedings again precipitated a number of violent incidents between supporters and opponents of the former President. On 28 September al-Fiki was convicted of the misuse of public funds in relation to the purchase of television programmes and given a seven-year prison sentence.

In response to the deaths of three protesters at the Israeli embassy in Cairo in early September 2011 (see Egypt and the Middle East peace process), the SCAF announced that, in order to maintain national security, it would be required to reintroduce the emergency legislation that had been in force under Mubarak's presidency. Renewed clashes across Egypt between security forces and protesters demanding the replacement of the SCAF with a civilian administration intensified on 19 November. The following day the Minister of Culture, Emad Abu Ghazi, resigned in protest at the authorities' response to the latest demonstrations. On 22 November Tantawi accepted the resignation of Prime Minister Sharaf and his Council of Ministers. According to the Ministry of Health, at least 40 protesters died in the week prior to 23 November and some 3,500 were wounded. On 25 November Kamal al-Ganzouri (Prime Minister in 1996–99) was instructed to form a new 'national unity' government; he was also given the SCAF's presidential powers, excluding those relating to military and judicial matters. A new Council of Ministers was sworn in on 7 December; Muhammad Youssuf Ibrahim Ahmad (a former Cairo chief of police) was appointed as Minister of the Interior. In November 2011 Tantawi had pledged that a presidential election would take place by the end of June 2012, and that the SCAF would order an independent inquiry into alleged violations by Egypt's security forces against pro-reform activists. In mid-December 2011 thousands of Egyptians again took to the streets of Cairo to protest against such violations; some 18 people were reportedly killed in clashes outside the cabinet building, while military officials were forced to apologize when it was revealed that female demonstrators had been beaten for participating in rallies.

Elections to the 508-member People's Assembly were held in three stages, each of two rounds: on 28–29 November and 5–6 December 2011, on 14–15 December and 21–22 December, and on 3–4 January and 10–11 January 2012. The official results revealed that the FJP had won 235 of the 498 elective seats (47.2% of the vote) and the Salafist Al-Nour Party 123 seats (24.7%); Islamist parties—contesting the elections legally for the first time—had thus garnered at least 70% of the votes. The New Wafd Party secured 38 seats, the Egyptian Bloc (a secular alliance of liberal or left-wing groups) 34 and the Al-Wasat Party 10; independent candidates won 23 seats, while the remaining seats were won by the Reformation and Development Party (nine), the Revolution Continues Alliance (seven), the National Party of Egypt (five), the Freedom Party and the Egyptian Citizen Party (both four), the Union Party (two) and other parties (four). In addition, 10 seats were appointed by the SCAF.

When the new People's Assembly convened on 23 January 2012, Muhammad Saad el-Katatni, the FJP Secretary-General, was elected as Speaker. The chamber's principal task was to select members of a committee to draft Egypt's new constitution, to be voted on in a national referendum before the SCAF was due to transfer power to a government of 'national salvation' after the forthcoming presidential election. On 24 January Tantawi announced that the state of emergency was to be partially lifted on the following day. At elections to the Advisory Council, which took place in two stages on 29 January and 22 February, Islamist parties again secured an overwhelming representation: the FJP took 105 of the 180 elective seats, while the Al-Nour Party garnered 45 seats. Most notably among other parties, the New Wafd Party won 14 seats and the Egyptian Bloc eight seats; four seats were taken by independents. A further 90 members were due to be appointed by the SCAF. At the Council's inaugural session on 29 February, the FJP's Ahmad Fahmi was elected as Speaker. Meanwhile, the electoral commission announced that the first round of the presidential poll would take place in late May.

Muhammad Mursi is elected President and a new Constitution enters effect

On 1 March 2012 Atif Muhammad Obeid (Prime Minister during 1999–2004) and a former Minister of Agriculture, Yousuf Wali, were convicted by a court in Giza on charges of corruption and squandering public funds in relation to the sale of state-owned land for the development of a nature reserve in Luxor; both men were sentenced to 10 years' imprisonment. On 25 March the People's Assembly and Advisory Council elected 100 members—50 parliamentarians and 50 trade union and civil group representatives—to form the Constituent Assembly charged with formulating Egypt's draft constitution. Liberal and secular opposition groups, as well as Coptic Christians, subsequently withdrew their support from the Assembly, complaining that it was unrepresentative and would lead to the pursuit of an Islamist agenda.

Twenty-three people had submitted their candidacy at the deadline for presidential nominations on 8 April 2012. These included former Secretary-General of the Arab League Amr Moussa, former Vice-President and Head of General Intelligence Omar Suleiman, Ahmad Shafiq and a Salafist lawyer, Hazem Abu Ismail. Controversially, having previously stated that it would not contest the elections, the Muslim Brotherhood nominated two candidates: deputy Supreme Guide Khairat al-Shater and FJP leader Muhammad Mursi. However, the final list published by the electoral commission on 26 April confirmed that 10 of the original 23 nominees were to be disqualified, including al-Shater and Ayman al-Nour, owing to previous criminal convictions, and Abu Ismail, following claims that his mother had held dual US and Egyptian citizenship (thus contravening the legal requirement that a candidate be solely of Egyptian parentage). Suleiman was also prevented from contesting the poll, under legislation approved by the People's Assembly in mid-April designed to disbar anyone who had held the roles of Vice-President or Prime Minister during the last 10 years of the Mubarak regime. Nevertheless, Shafiq (who had briefly acted as Prime Minister in early 2011) won an appeal against his disqualification.

At the first round of the presidential election, held on 23–24 May 2012, Mursi narrowly defeated his two closest rivals, Shafiq and Hamdeen Sabbahi—founder of the leftist, nationalist Al-Karama (Dignity) Party—having received 24.8% of the valid votes cast, compared with 23.7% and 20.7%, respectively. Two other independent candidates, Abd el-Monem Aboul Foutouh (a moderate who was expelled from the Muslim Brotherhood for contesting the presidency) and Moussa, received a respective 17.5% and 11.1% of the votes. The remaining eight candidates all received only 1% or fewer of the votes. The rate of voter participation was officially recorded at less than 50%. At the second round of the ballot, which took place on 16–17 June, Mursi secured 51.7% of the vote and Shafiq 48.3%. Voter turnout was reported to be 51.6%. The results of the presidential election were delayed until 24 June, reportedly to allow claims of voting irregularities to be investigated. However, Mursi, who had resigned from the Muslim Brotherhood and as Chairman of the FJP shortly after his victory, was sworn in as President on 30 June. He was replaced as FJP Chairman by el-Katatni.

Meanwhile, the national state of emergency, in place since 1981 and last extended by former President Mubarak in May 2010, expired on 31 May 2012. On 14 June a ruling by the Supreme Constitutional Court invalidated the results of the People's Assembly elections held between November 2011 and January 2012, stating that the electoral legislation in place at the time of voting had been unconstitutional. The Court maintained that one-third of the lower house's 508 seats had been contested by representatives of political parties rather than being reserved for independent candidates. The ruling led to renewed protests being initiated by angry demonstrators in Cairo's Tahrir Square. Also on 14 June the SCAF announced that a new National Defence Council, to be chaired by the incoming president, was to be established to administer the country's military and security affairs. The following day the Islamist-dominated legislature was dissolved by the SCAF, which assumed legislative powers pending the drafting of a new constitution and convening of further elections. The Court also decided that former officials of the Mubarak era should be allowed to contest future polls.

At the conclusion of his trial, on 2 June 2012 Hosni Mubarak was convicted by the Cairo court of failing to protect the 846 protesters who had died during the uprising against his regime, although he was found not to have been responsible for their deaths; both the ex-President and his former interior minister, Habib al-Adli, were sentenced to life imprisonment. Mubarak's opponents expressed dismay at the verdict, since both he and his sons, Gamal and Alaa, had also been acquitted of corruption charges, while the six other former regime officials had been acquitted of charges relating to the deaths of protesters. On 13 January 2013 it was announced that both Hosni Mubarak and al-Adli could face a retrial, after both men had launched appeals against their life sentences (see Military coup brings renewed violence).

Following the presidential vote, al-Ganzouri announced his Government's resignation on 25 June 2012. On 8 July President Mursi defied the SCAF's decree dissolving the People's Assembly by reinstating the newly elected legislature; however, the Supreme Constitutional Court insisted that its decision could not be revoked. On 24 July Mursi named Hisham Qandil, an independent politician who had served as the Minister of Water

Resources and Irrigation in the previous, interim administration, as Prime Minister. A largely non-affiliated Council of Ministers under Qandil was inaugurated on 2 August, with four portfolios being handed to members of the Muslim Brotherhood (including the important Ministry of Information). A notable appointment was that of Ahmed Gamal el-Din as Minister of the Interior, while Muhammad Kamel Amr remained as Minister of Foreign Affairs. Although the Chairman of the SCAF, Tantawi, initially retained the posts of Minister of Defence and Military Production and Commander-in-Chief of the Armed Forces, on 12 August Mursi announced that Tantawi was to retire from public life, along with the Chief of Staff of the Armed Forces, Lt-Gen. Sami Hafez Enan. They were replaced, respectively, by Gen. Abd al-Fatah al-Sisi and Lt-Gen. Sidki Sobhi Sayed Ahmed. Also on 12 August Mahmoud Mekki was named as Vice-President. Mursi concurrently revoked the amendments to the interim Constitutional Declaration approved by the SCAF in June, under which the SCAF had assumed legislative powers. In early September the retirement of a further 70 army generals was announced, following a dramatic deterioration of security in Sinai, where in August 16 Egyptian soldiers had been killed in an attack on their checkpoint by Islamist militants. Egyptian armed forces responded in early September by launching a major security offensive in the region.

On 22 November 2012 President Mursi issued a series of highly controversial decrees with the stated intention of preserving the revolution which had removed Mubarak from office and restoring calm across Egypt. The adopted measures included removing the right of judicial authorities to dissolve either the Constituent Assembly or Advisory Council, and withdrawing all judicial powers to challenge presidential decisions. However, the President insisted that the measures were only temporary, pending the conclusion of the forthcoming national referendum. On 1 December the predominantly Islamist Constituent Assembly approved the final draft of the new constitution. Protests against the President's recent actions subsequently turned violent, leading to further fatalities and attacks on the presidential palace and FJP headquarters in Cairo, as well as on Muslim Brotherhood offices in Suez and Ismailia. In response to the worsening security situation, on 8 December Mursi agreed to annul the decree which had removed his judicial accountability.

The first stage of voting in the nationwide constitutional referendum was held on 15 December 2012. Intense anti-Government demonstrations had preceded the vote, with secular and liberal opposition activists taking to the streets of Cairo and other cities to denounce the proposed constitutional changes. The second stage of the referendum took place on 22 December, when it was announced that Vice-President Mekki had resigned. According to final results issued by the HEC, 63.8% of voters had approved the new Constitution, with turnout recorded at 32.9%. The Constitution entered into effect on 26 December. However, opposition groups complained that the document, in which the role of Islam in the preparation of legislation had been expanded and the powers of parliament strengthened at the expense of those of the President, had been rushed through by Egypt's new authorities. They asserted that the new Constitution limited the rights of women, Christians and secular Egyptians, and restricted freedom of expression. On 6 January 2013 President Mursi carried out a partial reorganization of the Council of Ministers, appointing Maj.-Gen. Muhammad Ibrahim as Minister of the Interior.

Mursi announced on 27 January 2013 that a state of emergency and night-time curfews would be introduced in Port Said, Ismailia and Suez for one month in an effort to restore calm. This followed renewed anti-Government protests across Egypt to mark the second anniversary of the 25 January 2011 uprising, and many fatalities in clashes in the Suez region between demonstrators and security forces as the result of an unpopular legal ruling. A court in Port Said had handed down death sentences to 21 people for their alleged involvement in serious acts of violence inflicted on rival football supporters from Cairo at a match in Port Said in February 2012, which had resulted in 74 deaths. By early February 2013 more than 50 people had been killed in two weeks of intense rioting. In late February Mursi announced that four-stage elections to the People's Assembly were to be held between 22 April and 24 June. The opposition National Salvation Front—led principally by el-Baradei, Moussa and Sabbahi—confirmed that it would boycott the polls, contending that the electoral law favoured Islamist parties. However, in early March the Supreme Administrative Court ruled that the legislation must be referred to the Supreme Constitutional Court for further review, effectively postponing the elections. Further cases concerning the validity of both the 2012 Advisory Council elections and the composition of the Constituent Assembly responsible for drafting the new Constitution were still awaiting the Court's decision (see Military coup brings renewed violence). On 6 April 2013 four Coptic Christians and one Muslim were killed during clashes to the north of Cairo, and the following day a Coptic Christian was killed when violence erupted outside the main Coptic cathedral in the capital after a funeral service to mark the deaths.

Military coup brings renewed violence

Prime Minister Qandil announced a reorganization of the Government on 7 May 2013; the number of ministers affiliated to the Muslim Brotherhood reportedly increased from eight to 10. On 16 June President Mursi appointed 17 new regional governors, including a number of Islamist allies (seven of whom were members of the FJP). The decision to name a politician with close links to Gama'ah al-Islamiyah as the leader of Luxor governorate was widely condemned in view of the terrorist attack against tourists that had been committed by members of that group in 1997 (see Domestic Political Affairs); the new Governor tendered his resignation a week later following protests against his appointment. Meanwhile, after its review of the electoral legislation, on 2 June 2013 the Supreme Constitutional Court declared the elections to the Advisory Council held in 2012 to have been invalid. However, members of the Council were permitted to continue in office until a new People's Assembly was elected. The Court also confirmed the invalidity of the Constituent Assembly that had been responsible for drafting Egypt's new Constitution.

Protests were held across the country during mid-2013, prompted by concerns over President Mursi's perceived authoritarianism and his administration's failure to address Egypt's grave social, economic and security problems. Many Egyptians were also alarmed by the apparent Islamicization of Egyptian society by the Muslim Brotherhood as a result of recent changes to the Constitution and the Brotherhood's hold on the organs of power. On 30 June—the first anniversary of Mursi's inauguration as President—the protests became mass demonstrations by millions of Egyptians who demanded his resignation; the Tamarrud (Rebel) movement, which was formed in late April by members of Kefaya and which had organized the demonstrations, was reported to have gathered some 22m. signatures in support of its demands for Mursi to leave office and an early presidential election be called. On 1 July Egypt's military leaders issued a 48-hour ultimatum to the President that they would intervene with their own 'roadmap' for a peaceful solution to the political crisis if he did not agree to the opposition's demands. On the following day the Minister of Foreign Affairs, Muhammad Kamel Amr, became the most high-profile official to resign in response to the unrest. Following Mursi's refusal to abide by the terms of the ultimatum, the armed forces formally deposed him as President on 3 July. The Commander-in-Chief and Minister of Defence and Military Production, al-Sisi, announced the suspension of the Constitution and the appointment of Adli Mahmoud Mansour, President of the Supreme Constitutional Court, as interim President; Mansour was sworn into office on 4 July.

The Advisory Council was dissolved on 6 July 2013, and two days later the interim President announced a Constitutional Declaration, according to which elections to the People's Assembly were expected to take place in January–February 2014 and presidential elections in February–March. Mansour was to appoint a committee of judges to study amendments to the 2012 Constitution within 25 days of his assumption of office; the committee's recommendations were then to be submitted to a second committee, comprising representatives of the armed forces and of religious institutions, for approval in September. The second committee was to agree on a draft within 30 days, and a national referendum to approve the final draft was due to take place by the end of November 2013. On 8 September 2013 Moussa was elected as Chairman of the 50-member constitutional committee, in which Islamist representation was limited (although the Al-Nour Party was represented).

Meanwhile, Mursi and other senior members of the Muslim Brotherhood were arrested and detained, and on 8 July 2013 at least 51 people were killed in clashes between supporters of Mursi and security forces outside the headquarters of the Republican Guard in Cairo. After Qandil had resigned his post following Mursi's removal from office, on 9 July Hazem al-Biblawi was appointed as Prime Minister. Al-Biblawi was a former member of the now dissolved NDP, who had served as

Deputy Prime Minister for Economic Affairs and Minister of Finance in late 2011. On 14 July 2013 Mohammed el-Baradei took office as Vice-President for International Relations. A new interim Council of Ministers was sworn in on 16 July. Maj.-Gen. Muhammad Ibrahim remained as Minister of the Interior, while Nabil Fahmi was named as Minister of Foreign Affairs.

There was an immediate upsurge of violence across Egypt following the military coup. On 14 August 2013 the interim Government declared a month-long state of emergency and imposed curfews in Cairo and other major cities, following violent clashes between security forces and demonstrators demanding the reinstatement of Mursi as President. (The emergency legislation was extended for a further two months in September, but then lifted on 12 November.) According to official sources, some 525 people were killed in the clashes, which erupted after security forces intervened to remove protesters from an encampment set up in the capital by supporters of Mursi and the Muslim Brotherhood. (Brotherhood officials claimed that more than 2,200 people had died.) Also on 14 August el-Baradei resigned the vice-presidency and left the country, citing his disagreement with the Government's decision forcibly to remove the protesters; he was subsequently charged with 'breaching national trust'. Meanwhile, Muhammad Badie, the Muslim Brotherhood's Supreme Guide, was detained and charged with 'incitement to murder'; trial proceedings against him were ongoing in early 2014. Mahmoud Izzat was subsequently named as the movement's acting Supreme Guide (its deputy leader, Khairat al-Shater, having been detained in early July). On 23 September 2013 an Egyptian court issued a ban on all activities of the Muslim Brotherhood, and ordered its assets to be confiscated by the state. As the military rulers' crackdown on the Brotherhood continued, with thousands of activists being held in detention, on 30 October Essam El-Erian, the FJP's deputy leader, was arrested and charged with the same crime as Badie; his detention provoked particularly violent demonstrations among university students in Cairo, Alexandria and other cities. At the same time, radical Islamists escalated their campaign of violence against Coptic Christian targets, owing to their leadership's backing of Mursi's ouster; churches, schools and other Coptic institutions were systematically burned or destroyed, leading many Copts to seek refuge elsewhere.

The retrial of ex-President Hosni Mubarak and al-Adli on charges relating to the deaths of protesters during the uprising against his regime commenced at Cairo's Criminal Court on 14 September 2013; both men had successfully appealed against the terms of life imprisonment imposed in June 2012. Mubarak had been released from a prison hospital on 22 August 2013 and placed under house arrest while awaiting the retrial. The legal proceedings—which also included Mubarak's two sons, Gamal and Alaa, and six other officials of the Mubarak era—continued into 2014. (On 19 December 2013 Gamal and Alaa Mubarak were acquitted on a number of the corruption charges.) At the same time Ahmad Nazif and Yousuf Boutros-Ghali were also undergoing a retrial on corruption charges, having also submitted appeals against their sentences. Supporters of Mubarak and those of Mursi were involved in clashes outside the court during the former officials' retrial. On 30 September an appeal by Hisham Qandil against a conviction, handed down on 17 April 2013, relating to his failure to adhere to an administration court ruling to re-nationalize a recently privatized firm was rejected by a court in Cairo. The one-year prison sentence given to Qandil was thus validated, although it was not until 24 December that he was arrested while apparently travelling towards the border with Sudan; Qandil subsequently lodged a further appeal against the verdict with the Court of Cassation.

Mursi was charged with having incited violence against protesters opposed to his administration outside the presidential palace in December 2012, as well as having ordered the killing of some protesters; his trial began in Cairo on 4 November 2013. At the initial court session, the ousted leader repeatedly interrupted the proceedings, insisting that he remained 'Egypt's legitimate President'. Fourteen other defendants from the Muslim Brotherhood were to be tried alongside him. The former President was to undergo three other criminal trials in connection with alleged crimes committed during his time in office; these included conspiring with Hamas in espionage on behalf of the Brotherhood, planning terrorist acts, insulting Egypt's judicial authorities and escaping from gaol during the political unrest of early 2011. In late December 2013 the interim Government designated the Brotherhood as a 'terrorist group', after holding the movement responsible for planning a suicide bomb attack at a police headquarters on 24 December in Mansoura, north of Cairo, in which more than 15 people (including at least 12 police officers) died. However, the Muslim Brotherhood leadership condemned the attack and claimed that the Government was using such incidents to justify a further crackdown on its members. Since Mursi's removal from office in July 2013, Egypt had seen a rapid increase in the number of bombings being perpetrated by militant Islamists against government and security targets.

Recent developments: Approval of the draft Constitution and formation of a new Government

Although the original deadline for a national referendum to be held on Egypt's new draft Constitution had been the end of November 2013, the second constitutional committee did not present its final draft of the document to interim President Mansour until 3 December. Supporters of the ousted President Mursi staged a protest in opposition to the proposed constitutional changes in central Cairo, although the security forces acted quickly to maintain order in Tahrir Square. On 24 November Mansour had signed into law a bill that severely restricted the rights of Egyptians to stage protests against the interim authorities. The new law, *inter alia*, made it obligatory for protesters to request police approval three days prior to a proposed demonstration, gave the security forces increased powers to clamp down on such demonstrations, and made it illegal to hold protests in places of worship. The referendum took place on 16–17 January 2014, when—according to the Higher Election Commission—an estimated 98.1% of voters approved the text of the new Constitution. However, the rate of voter participation was reported to be a mere 38.1%. The Muslim Brotherhood immediately declared its opposition to the new document, which included a ban on political parties based on religion and in which the Egyptian military retained considerable powers: for example, the SCAF was still required to approve the appointment of a new Minister of Defence and Military Production. Under the new Constitution, a National Security Council (to be led by the President) was also to be established. Moreover, contrary to the text of the Constitutional Declaration issued by the interim authorities in July 2013, the Constitution effectively granted Mansour the right to choose a schedule for the holding of presidential and parliamentary elections.

On 24 February 2014 Prime Minister al-Biblawi unexpectedly submitted the resignation of his entire administration, without providing any explanation for his action. Later that day the outgoing Minister of Housing and Urban Development, Ibrahim Mehleb (also formerly a senior NDP member), was instructed to form a new government. A new Council of Ministers under Mehleb was sworn into office on 1 March. Some twenty ministers from the previous al-Biblawi Government were reported to have retained their posts, including al-Sisi (who had been promoted to the rank of Field Marshal in January), Fahmi and Maj.-Gen. Ibrahim. Among the 11 new (largely technocratic) appointments were that of Nayer Abd al-Moneim Othman as Minister of Justice and of Hani Qadri Demian as Minister of Finance. Meanwhile, 12 ministries were merged into six: these included the transitional justice and national reconciliation portfolio, which was combined with parliamentary affairs, and the merger of the trade and investment portfolios. Mehleb declared his Government's priorities to be 'maintaining security, combating terrorism and attracting investment'; he also demanded an end to the 'factional protests' being held across Egypt. According to Amnesty International, at least 1,400 people had been killed since the start of clashes between pro-Muslim Brotherhood activists and the security forces in early July 2013. By the end of that year at least 2,000 Brotherhood members had been arrested as part of the government crackdown against the organization. Meanwhile, hundreds more people had died as a result of the violent insurgency being waged by Islamist militants against government and military targets in Sinai. In late March al-Sisi formally declared that he was to contest the forthcoming presidential election, which was scheduled for 26–27 May. He resigned from the Government at the end of that month, and was replaced as Minister of Defence and Commander in Chief of the Armed Forces by the outgoing Chief of Staff, Sidki Sobhi (now promoted to Colonel General). In mid-April the electoral commission announced that only two candidates had been proposed for the presidential election: al-Sisi and Hamdeen Sabbahi was the only other person to submit his candidacy.

Foreign Affairs

Egypt and the Middle East peace process

Egyptian mediators were influential in the secret negotiations between Israel and the PLO that led to the signing of the Declaration of Principles on Palestinian Self-Rule in September 1993. In May 1994 an agreement on Palestinian self-rule in the Gaza Strip and the Jericho area (see the chapter on Israel) was signed in Cairo by the Israeli Prime Minister, Itzhak Rabin, and the PLO Chairman, Yasser Arafat, at a ceremony presided over by President Mubarak. However, relations between Egypt and Israel began to deteriorate, as Egypt hosted summit meetings of Arab leaders in December 1994 and February 1995. Further tension arose when Mubarak reiterated his warning that Egypt would not sign the Treaty on the Non-Proliferation of Nuclear Weapons (or Non-Proliferation Treaty), which was due for renewal in April 1995, unless Israel also agreed to sign it.

Egypt continued its mediatory role in the complex negotiations that eventually led to the signing, in Washington, DC, of the Israeli-Palestinian Interim Agreement on the West Bank and the Gaza Strip in September 1995. In November Mubarak made his first presidential visit to Israel to attend the funeral of Rabin, who had been assassinated at the beginning of that month. Egypt's relations with Israel deteriorated again in April 1996, as a consequence of Israeli military operations in Lebanon (q.v.). In June, in response to the apparently rejectionist stance of the new Israeli administration of Binyamin Netanyahu with regard to the exchange of land for peace, Mubarak convened an emergency summit meeting of the Arab League in Cairo. The summit's final communiqué reaffirmed the Arab states' commitment to peace, but warned that any further rapprochement between them and Israel depended on Israel's returning all the Arab land that it occupied in 1967.

In January 1999 Egypt suspended all contacts with the Israeli Government in protest against its decision to suspend implementation of the Wye River Memorandum signed by Netanyahu and Arafat in October 1998 (see the chapter on Israel). Despite the election, in May 1999, of Ehud Barak to the Israeli premiership, in July the Egyptian Minister of Foreign Affairs emphasized that there could be no normalization of Egyptian-Israeli relations prior to the resumption of comprehensive peace talks. Egyptian mediation was influential in discussions between Israeli and Palestinian negotiators that led to the signing of the Sharm el-Sheikh Memorandum by Barak and Arafat in September (see the chapter on Israel). However, after the failure of the summit held at the US presidential retreat at Camp David, Maryland, in July 2000, Mubarak emphasized that he would not put pressure on Arafat to make concessions regarding the central issue of the status of Jerusalem.

Following the outbreak in September 2000 of violent clashes between Palestinians and Israeli security forces in Jerusalem, which swiftly spread throughout the West Bank and Gaza, President Mubarak assumed an important role in attempting to prevent the violence from escalating into a major regional crisis. A summit meeting held in mid-October at Sharm el-Sheikh, which was brokered by US President Bill Clinton and attended by Barak and Arafat, resulted in an agreement on the establishment of a fact-finding committee to investigate the causes of what had become known as the al-Aqsa *intifada* (uprising). Later that month an emergency meeting of Arab League heads of state was convened in Cairo, at which Arab leaders held Israel solely to blame for the continuing violence. In November Egypt recalled its ambassador to Israel, denouncing Israel's 'deliberate use of force against the Palestinian people'.

Nevertheless, at an Arab League summit on the Palestinian situation, held in Jordan in March 2001, Mubarak deflected demands from more radical Arab states that Egypt and Jordan should entirely sever diplomatic relations with Israel (now under the premiership of the Likud leader, Ariel Sharon). In April a joint Egyptian-Jordanian peace plan urged an immediate halt to Israeli construction of settlements and a withdrawal of Israeli forces to pre-*intifada* positions. The plan was supported by the new US Administration of President George W. Bush, the EU and Arab leaders; however, diplomatic progress subsequently stalled amid escalating violence. At an emergency meeting of Arab League ministers of foreign affairs in Cairo in May, it was agreed to suspend all political contacts with Israel until its attacks on Palestinians were halted; Egypt suspended all non-diplomatic contacts with Israel in April 2002.

Although President Mubarak welcomed the publication, in April 2003, of the 'roadmap' peace plan drafted by the Quartet group (comprising the UN, the USA, the EU and Russia—see the chapter on Israel), Egyptian efforts to secure a ceasefire by armed Palestinian factions made no further progress. In April 2004 the Bush Administration endorsed Sharon's proposals for an Israeli 'disengagement' from Gaza, which also involved the consolidation of six Jewish settlements in the West Bank. In December, after talks held in Jerusalem between the Israeli Minister of Defence, Lt-Gen. Shaul Mofaz, and the Egyptian intelligence chief, Omar Suleiman, it was agreed that 750 Egyptian troops would be stationed on the border with Gaza ahead of the Israeli withdrawal, in a bid to prevent arms from being smuggled into the territory for use by Palestinian militants.

In March 2005 Muhammad Asim Ibrahim assumed the role of ambassador to Israel (the post having been vacant since November 2000). After further talks between Egypt and Israel prior to the latter's unilateral withdrawal from the Gaza Strip in August–September 2005 (see the chapter on Israel), a deal confirming that 750 Egyptian border guards would police the southern border was approved by the Israeli Knesset on 31 August. In October it was announced that the border with Gaza would be reopened at the Rafah checkpoint to allow key crossings, and on 26 November some 1,500 Palestinians passed into Egypt. In February 2006, following the decisive victory of the Islamic Resistance Movement (Hamas) in the first Palestinian legislative elections since 1996, leaders of the organization held discussions in Cairo regarding the formation of a new administration. Egypt subsequently began to exert pressure on Hamas to reconsider its position regarding Israel's right to existence, while urging Israel not to impose sanctions on the Hamas-led administration formed in the West Bank and Gaza in March 2006.

The election of a new Israeli Government under Prime Minister Ehud Olmert in March 2006 led to renewed Egyptian efforts to revive the Middle East peace process. However, in July Mubarak expressed Egypt's solidarity with Lebanon after Israel launched a large-scale offensive against positions held by the Shi'a fundamentalist group Hezbollah in southern Lebanon in response to the kidnapping by Hezbollah militants of two Israeli soldiers and the killing of several others in a cross-border raid, and amid a series of missile attacks on northern Israel (see the chapters on Israel and Lebanon).

After the commencement of serious factional fighting between militias of the rival Hamas and Fatah factions in the Gaza Strip following the formation of the new Palestinian administration in March 2006, Egyptian officials were involved in diplomatic efforts, led principally by Saudi Arabia, to secure a lasting ceasefire between the two sides and establish a Palestinian national unity cabinet. Although a power-sharing administration was formed in March 2007, Hamas militants seized control of Gaza in June, effectively dividing the Palestinian enclaves into two separate entities (see the chapter on the Palestinian Territories). In June President Mubarak hosted a summit meeting of regional leaders in Sharm el-Sheikh, with a view to restarting Middle East peace negotiations based on the 'land-for-peace' plan proposed by Saudi Arabia in 2002.

Despite initial optimism following the international peace conference held in Annapolis, Maryland, USA, in November 2007, Mubarak was highly critical of Israel's continued expansion of Jewish settlements in the West Bank, which was one of the principal factors preventing a comprehensive peace deal being achieved by the US Administration's intended deadline of the end of 2008. The Israeli Deputy Prime Minister and Minister of Defence, Ehud Barak, ordered virtually a complete blockade on the Gaza Strip in mid-January 2008, in an attempt to counter the growing number of Hamas rockets being launched onto Israeli border towns from the Strip. In late January Palestinian fighters succeeded in breaching the Rafah crossing that divides Gaza from Egypt, and hundreds of thousands of Palestinians entered Egypt in search of food, fuel and medical supplies. The crossing had been almost permanently closed since Hamas's takeover of the Strip in June 2007 because the Egyptian Government, as did Israel, refused to recognize Hamas as the legitimate administration there. Egyptian officials responded by offering their backing to a plan proposed by the Executive President of the Palestinian (National) Authority, Mahmud Abbas, that would allow the PA, rather than Hamas, to assume control of the Egypt–Gaza border. The breaches in the border were repaired in February 2008; however, tensions continued between Egyptian security forces and Palestinian militants.

Following several months of negotiations mediated by Egyptian officials, in June 2008 a ceasefire was agreed between Israel and representatives of Hamas in the Gaza Strip. However, in

December Hamas formally declared an end to the truce, and soon afterwards Palestinian militants launched rocket and mortar attacks on northern Israel, while Israel conducted air strikes against Gaza. Following Israel's military response, code-named 'Operation Cast Lead' (see the chapter on the Palestinian Territories), Egypt continued to be involved in international diplomatic efforts to secure a formal, more durable ceasefire between Israel and Hamas.

The appointment of the Likud leader, Binyamin Netanyahu, as Israeli Prime Minister in March 2009 threatened to strain relations between Israel and Egypt. In December, however, Netanyahu proposed a summit meeting hosted by Egypt as a means to recommence Israeli-Palestinian peace talks. Relations between Israel and Egypt were again damaged by the arrest in December 2010 of two Israeli citizens and one Egyptian citizen by the Egyptian authorities on suspicion of spying for Israel since 2008. The three suspects were convicted of the charges of espionage and endangering Egyptian national interests in June 2011, and were each sentenced to 25 years in gaol (the Israelis *in absentia*).

Meanwhile, in 2009–10 Egypt hosted negotiations between representatives of Hamas and Fatah in an effort to secure a lasting reconciliation between the two Palestinian factions. Following the appointment, in March 2011, of Essam Sharaf as Prime Minister (see The ouster of President Mubarak), his Government placed a renewed emphasis on the reconciliation talks, and on 3 May representatives of 13 Palestinian factions signed a so-called 'unity' agreement following a round of negotiations in Cairo. On 4 May President Abbas and Hamas's political leader, Khalid Meshaal, travelled to the Egyptian capital for a ceremony to mark the agreement, which was expected to result in the formation of a joint administration for the West Bank and Gaza pending legislative and presidential elections due to be held in 2012 (see the chapter on the Palestinian Territories). However, the new cabinet had not been formed by late 2013, discussions between Fatah and Hamas having stalled in June 2011. In early January 2013 direct talks on the proposed Palestinian reunification finally resumed between Abbas and Meshaal in Cairo, after the prospects for a reconciliation appeared to have been boosted by the UN's recognition of the Palestinian Territories as a 'non-member observer state' and Hamas's brief conflict with Israel in November 2012, in which Egypt's President Mursi played a prominent role in negotiating a ceasefire (see the chapters on Israel and the Palestinian Territories).

Although the SCAF declared after the overthrow of President Mubarak in February 2011 that it would honour Egypt's peace treaty with Israel, many Israelis feared the implications for their long-term security in the event of an Islamist victory in Egypt's first post-revolution legislative elections. On 28 May, despite Israeli objections, the Egyptian Government allowed the Rafah border crossing with Gaza to reopen for Palestinians; cross-border trade remained prohibited. On 9 September three Egyptian protesters died as violence broke out between Egyptian security forces and militant demonstrators who forced their way into the Israeli embassy in Cairo, prompting Israel to evacuate its ambassador and most diplomatic staff the following day. The protests followed the accidental killing by the Israeli military of five Egyptian security officials in mid-August, as Israeli forces responded to the deaths of eight Israelis in attacks carried out by suspected Palestinian militants in southern Israel, close to the border with Egypt, by targeting Palestinian militants in the Gaza border area. Israel claimed that the attackers had entered Israel from Gaza via Egypt's Sinai Peninsula.

In mid-October 2011, following an agreement reached between Israel and Hamas in Cairo earlier that month as a result of German- and Egyptian-sponsored negotiations, an Israeli soldier kidnapped by Hamas militants in the Gaza Strip in June 2006 was returned to Israel via Egypt. Under the terms of the deal, Israel freed 477 Palestinian prisoners initially to Egypt, with the release of a further 550 to take place two months later. In late October 2011 the Egyptian and Israeli authorities exchanged 25 Egyptians who had been held in Israeli detention for a US-Israeli citizen who had been held by Egypt on charges of spying for Israel. In view of the Muslim Brotherhood's traditionally close links with Hamas, many Israelis expressed concern following the victory of the movement's FJP candidate, Muhammad Mursi, at the second round of the Egyptian presidential election in June 2012. The Israeli authorities also continued with the construction of a fence along Israel's border with Egypt, in response to the worsening security situation in the Sinai region.

In September 2013, two months after the military's removal from power of President Mursi, Egypt's new interim Government launched a large-scale military campaign in Sinai—using both ground forces and an aerial bombardment of militant bases—in an effort to tackle the problem of Islamist militancy there. The Israeli Government supported this military action and the interim authorities' harsh crackdown on the activities of the Muslim Brotherhood, welcoming the fact that the change of Egyptian leadership would undoubtedly result in a weakening of the country's ties with Hamas. This alteration was demonstrated in early March 2014, when an Egyptian court issued a ban on all Hamas activities within the country, ordering the prompt seizure of the group's assets.

Other regional relations

In October 2008 the Egyptian Minister of Foreign Affairs, Ahmad Aboul Gheit, visited Iraq—the first such trip to be undertaken since 1990—in an effort to renew Iraqi-Egyptian relations. In July 2009 Aboul Gheit and his Iraqi counterpart, Hoshyar al-Zibari, signed a memorandum of understanding covering bilateral co-operation in security and commerce, following a meeting in Cairo. In November Sharif Kamal Shahin arrived in Baghdad to take up appointment as Egypt's ambassador to Iraq; the role had been vacant since the abduction and murder in 2005 of the previous ambassador, Ihab al-Sherif, by a militant Islamist group claiming to represent al-Qa'ida in Iraq. Bilateral talks were subsequently held concerning increased Egyptian investment in Iraq's reconstruction effort and its wider economy.

In December 2003 President Mubarak held talks with the Iranian President, Dr Sayed Muhammad Khatami, in Geneva, Switzerland—the first meeting between the leaders of the two countries since diplomatic relations were severed following the Islamic Revolution in Iran of 1979. In December 2004 Iran took the significant step of handing over to Egypt Moustafa Hamzah, a leader of Gama'ah al-Islamiyah and the alleged mastermind of a 1995 assassination attempt on President Mubarak (see Domestic Political Affairs). Khatami's successor, President Mahmoud Ahmadinejad, declared in May 2007 that Iran was prepared to resume diplomatic ties with Egypt and to open an embassy in Cairo. However, despite the evident thaw in bilateral relations, the Egyptian leadership was reluctant to proceed with the normalization until Iran first ended what it deemed to be its interference in the internal affairs of several Arab countries, notably Iraq, Lebanon and the Palestinian territories. In February 2011 Egypt's new caretaker Government after the overthrow of President Mubarak's regime provoked serious concern in Israel by allowing two Iranian naval ships to pass through the Suez Canal for the first time since 1979. In February 2013 Ahmadinejad became the first Iranian President since 1979 to visit Cairo, where he attended a summit of the Organization of Islamic Cooperation. During President Mursi's term in office, tourism links with Iran were opened and the Egyptian Government favoured the inclusion of Iranian officials in regional diplomatic meetings. However, following the replacement of Mursi's pro-Islamist administration by a military-backed one in July 2013, there was a change of policy: in October, for example, visits to Egypt by Iranian tourists were formally suspended for reasons of 'national security'.

Egypt has a long-standing border dispute with Sudan concerning the so-called Halaib triangle. Relations deteriorated sharply in mid-1995, after Egypt accused Sudan of complicity in the attempted assassination of President Mubarak in Addis Ababa. Egypt strengthened its control of the Halaib triangle, and imposed visa and permit requirements on Sudanese nationals visiting or resident in Egypt. In February 1996 the Sudanese authorities introduced permit requirements for Egyptian nationals resident in Sudan. In July Egypt accused Sudan of harbouring Egyptian terrorists. However, in December 1999 Egypt and Sudan agreed to a full normalization of relations, and resolved to co-operate in addressing their border dispute. The new Egyptian ambassador assumed his post in Khartoum in March 2000, and in September a number of bilateral co-operation accords were signed. In January 2004 Mubarak and his Sudanese counterpart, Lt-Gen. Omar Hassan Ahmad al-Bashir, signed what was termed the 'four freedoms' agreement (to take effect in September), which allowed for freedom of movement, residence, work and property ownership between the two countries. During 2006–07 Egyptian mediators attempted to find a regional solution to the conflict in Sudan's Darfur region, and in January 2008 the country deployed 1,200 troops to Darfur as part of a joint African Union-UN peacekeeping force.

Meanwhile, in 2004 Tanzania confirmed that it intended to build a 170-km pipeline to draw water from Lake Victoria. This decision contravened the Nile Water Agreement drawn up in 1929 between Egypt and the United Kingdom, which states that Egypt has the right to veto any work that might threaten the flow of the river and allows the country to inspect the entire length of the Nile. In April 2006 an agreement was reached between the 10 countries that share its waters, whereby a permanent commission was to be established to oversee management, planning and use of the river. In May 2010 Ethiopia, Kenya, Rwanda, Tanzania and Uganda signed a Nile River Basin Co-operative Framework Agreement, which, upon ratification, would create the Nile Basin Commission; Burundi followed suit in February 2011. However, the Egyptian Government refused to sign any accord that affected its share of the Nile's waters; Sudan was also not expected to sign the agreement. In June 2013 the Egyptian Ministry of Water Resources and Irrigation strongly criticized a decision by the Ethiopian Government to proceed with the construction of the Grand Ethiopian Renaissance Dam, which involved diverting one of the Nile's two principal tributaries, before consulting with Egypt and Sudan on the possible effects of the project on their share of the waters.

Relations with the USA

In mid-2002 the Administration of US President George W. Bush announced that it would suspend any additional foreign aid to Egypt in protest at what it considered to be the country's poor treatment of pro-democracy campaigners and human rights organizations. As the likelihood of a US-led military campaign to oust Iraqi President Saddam Hussain increased during late 2002, President Mubarak joined other Arab leaders in expressing his concern at the implications of military intervention in Iraq for both the region as a whole and the unity of Iraq. Following the commencement of US-led hostilities against the Iraqi regime in March 2003, Mubarak warned that the conflict would incite Islamist fanaticism. None the less, the ouster of Saddam Hussain in April was met with ambivalence by Egypt.

The waning importance of US-Egyptian relations to both countries was demonstrated in January 2008, when President Bush visited Egypt only briefly at the end of an eight-day tour of the Middle East. The US leadership had been strongly critical of Egypt for its failure to secure its border with the Gaza Strip following the takeover of the territory by Hamas militants in June 2007. In December the US Congress voted to withhold US $100m. in aid to Egypt until the USA had received assurances that the authorities there had imposed sufficient measures to end the cross-border arms-smuggling being carried out by Palestinian militants, and had taken steps to improve the country's human rights record.

In June 2009 President Obama made a televised speech in Cairo in which he pledged a new beginning in relations between the USA and Muslim countries, and emphasized the importance of a solution to the Israeli–Palestinian conflict. In August Mubarak held talks in Washington, DC, with Obama on proposals to revive peace talks between Israel and the PA. However, relations were strained following widespread allegations of voting irregularities and the intimidation of voters by security forces during Egypt's legislative elections in November–December 2010 (see Domestic Political Affairs). In March 2011, after the resignation of President Mubarak (see Domestic Political Affairs), the US Secretary of State, Hillary Clinton, visited Cairo for talks with leading Egyptian officials and pro-democracy campaigners; during the visit Clinton offered some US $90m. in emergency assistance to the new Government. After Mubarak's successor, President Mursi, helped to negotiate a truce between Israel and Hamas which ended their eight-day conflict in November 2012, President Obama commended his strong leadership during the negotiations. However, Egyptian–US relations were frequently strained during 2012, particularly owing to the perceived harsh treatment of US non-governmental organizations working in Egypt. In October 2013 the US Administration announced that it was suspending part of the $1,300m. in military aid it gives annually to the Egyptian Government, in protest at the authorities' recent harsh clampdown on supporters of the Muslim Brotherhood following Mursi's removal from office by the armed forces in July. In August Obama had cancelled joint exercises due to be held by US and Egyptian armed forces and urged the Government in Cairo to continue the country's transition to democracy.

CONSTITUTION AND GOVERNMENT

A new Constitution for the Arab Republic of Egypt was approved by referendum on 11 September 1971. Amendments to the Constitution were endorsed by the People's Assembly on 30 April 1980, 10 May 2005 and 19 March 2007, and subsequently approved at national referendums. Following the ouster of former President Muhammad Hosni Mubarak in early February 2011, further amendments to the Constitution were approved at a national referendum held on 19 March. A new Constitution entered into effect on 26 December, following approval by 63.8% of participating voters at a two-stage national referendum earlier that month. However, following the removal from office of Mubarak's successor, President Muhammad Mursi, in July 2013, the 2012 Constitution was suspended and a committee appointed to draft a new document. The final draft was presented to interim President Adli Mahmoud Mansour in December 2013, and was approved by some 98.1% of voters at a national referendum held on 16–17 January 2014.

Under the terms of the 2014 Constitution, legislative power is held by a unicameral parliament, which comprises a minimum of 450 directly elected members. The President may appoint no more 5% of the total number of legislative deputies. The legislative term is five years. The President, who is the head of state, has executive powers, and may hold office for no more than two terms of four years. The country is divided into 29 governorates.

REGIONAL AND INTERNATIONAL CO-OPERATION

Egypt is a member of the African Union (AU, see p. 186), the Common Market for Eastern and Southern Africa (COMESA, see p. 233), the Community of Sahel-Saharan States (CEN-SAD, see p. 450) and the Organization of Arab Petroleum Exporting Countries (OAPEC, see p. 400). The League of Arab States (Arab League, see p. 362) has its permanent headquarters in the Egyptian capital, Cairo.

Egypt has been a member of the UN since its foundation in 1945, and, as a contracting party to the General Agreement on Tariffs and Trade, joined the World Trade Organization (WTO) on its establishment in 1995. The country also participates in the Organization of Islamic Cooperation (OIC, see p. 403).

ECONOMIC AFFAIRS

In 2012, according to estimates by the World Bank, Egypt's gross national income (GNI), measured at average 2010–12 prices, was US $241,828m., equivalent to $3,000 per head (or $6,640 per head on an international purchasing-power parity basis). During 2003–12, it was estimated, the population increased at an average annual rate of 1.7%, while gross domestic product (GDP) per head increased, in real terms, by 3.1% per year. Overall GDP increased, in real terms, at an average annual rate of 4.8% in 2003–12. According to Central Bank of Egypt (CBE) figures, real GDP increased by 2.1% in 2012/13.

Agriculture (including forestry and fishing) contributed 14.5% of GDP in 2012/13, and employed an estimated 27.1% of the economically active population in 2012. The principal crops include sugar cane, sugar beet, wheat, tomatoes, maize and rice. Cotton is the principal cash crop. According to the World Bank, during 2003–11 agricultural GDP increased at an average annual rate of 3.2%. Agricultural GDP grew by 3.0% in 2012/13, according to the CBE.

Industry (including mining, manufacturing, construction and power) provided 39.1% of GDP in 2012/13, and engaged an estimated 24.9% of the employed labour force in 2012. According to the World Bank, during 2003–11 industrial GDP expanded at an average annual rate of 5.6%. Industrial GDP increased by 0.6% in 2012/13, according to CBE data.

Mining contributed 17.3% of GDP in 2012/13. Egypt's mineral resources include petroleum, natural gas, phosphates, manganese, uranium, coal, iron ore and gold. Although the mining sector employed only 0.2% of the working population in 2012, petroleum and petroleum products accounted for 30.2% of total export earnings. Petroleum production averaged an estimated 728,200 barrels per day in 2012, and at the end of that year Egypt's oil reserves were estimated to total 4,300m. barrels (sufficient to sustain production at 2012 levels for 16 years). At the end of 2012 Egypt's proven natural gas reserves totalled 2,040,000m. cu m, sustainable for almost 34 years at constant production levels (totalling 60,881m. cu m in 2012). In mid-2003 BP Egypt announced the largest petroleum discovery in the country for 14 years, and there were also major discoveries of natural gas and condensate during the decade. The Government began exporting natural gas in 2003. Exports to Israel and

Jordan were frequently suspended during 2011–13 as a result of repeated militant attacks on the pipeline used to transport the gas. Mining GDP decreased by 2.7% in 2012/13, according to the CBE.

Manufacturing contributed 15.6% of GDP in 2012/13, and engaged an estimated 11.1% of the employed labour force in 2012. Based on the value of output, the main branches of manufacturing are petroleum products, food products, chemicals, pharmaceutical products and textiles. In 2005 the Government initiated a 20-year plan to invest US $10m. in the construction of 14 new petrochemical complexes. Plans to build a $2,000m. petroleum refinery with two Chinese companies were agreed in May 2010, but progressed slowly; the refinery was expected to have an initial annual capacity of 15m. metric tons, with capacity projected ultimately to increase to 30m. tons. According to the World Bank, the real GDP of the manufacturing sector increased by an average of 4.6% per year during 2003–11. Manufacturing GDP increased by 2.3% in 2012/13, according to the CBE.

The construction sector contributed 4.6% of GDP in 2012/13, and engaged an estimated 11.8% of the employed labour force in 2012. Construction GDP increased by 5.9% in 2012/13, according to CBE figures.

Energy is derived principally from natural gas (which provided 74.7% of total electricity output in 2011), petroleum (15.8%) and hydroelectric power (8.3%). In 2012 imports of mineral fuels accounted for 18.7% of the total value of merchandise imports. In 2006 the Government announced that the programme to develop peaceful nuclear technology, which had been suspended in the mid-1980s, was to recommence. A project to construct a 1,000-MW nuclear plant on the Mediterranean coast at Dabaa was proposed as part of a plan to increase capacity by 5,000 MW through the development of four civil nuclear energy plants by 2025. However, the contract for the US $4,000m. project at Dabaa—expected to be awarded in 2011, with completion originally scheduled for 2019—was delayed following the ouster of President Hosni Mubarak in February 2011 (see Contemporary Political History) and amid strong local opposition to the plant's construction. Egypt's first solar energy plant, located in Kuraymat, south of Cairo, commenced operations in December 2010.

Services contributed 46.4% of GDP in 2012/13, and employed an estimated 48.1% of the working population in 2012. Following the campaign of violence aimed by militant Islamists at tourist targets during the 1990s, a recovery in the tourism sector was again hindered by the regional insecurity arising from the Israeli–Palestinian violence from late 2000, the terrorist attacks against the USA in September 2001 and the US-led intervention in Iraq in early 2003. Despite the Sinai bombings in 2004–06, however, the number of visitors to Egypt increased each year in 2005–08. According to the Ministry of Tourism, visitor numbers fell from an estimated 14.5m. in 2010 to some 9.8m. in 2011 as a result of the political unrest. According to the World Bank, in 2003–11 the real GDP of the services sector increased by an average of 4.4% per year. Services GDP increased by 3.0% in 2012/13, according to CBE figures.

In 2012 Egypt recorded a visible merchandise trade deficit of US $25,516m., and there was a deficit of $6,972m. on the current account of the balance of payments. In 2012 the principal source of imports (9.4%) was the People's Republic of China; other major suppliers were the USA, Germany, Russia and Ukraine. The principal market for exports was Italy (7.9%), followed by India, the USA, Saudi Arabia and Turkey. Egypt's principal exports in 2012 were mineral products, chemicals and related products, textile and textile articles, and iron and steel. The principal imports were mineral products, machinery, nuclear reactors and boilers, iron and steel, vegetables and vegetable products, and chemicals and related products.

According to preliminary figures by the Ministry of Finance, there was a deficit of £E237,866m. in the central government budget (equivalent to 15.1% of GDP) for the financial year 2011/12. The deficit was forecast at £E183,828 for the financial year 2012/13. Egypt's general government gross debt was £E1,243,068m. in 2012, equivalent to 80.6% of GDP. Egypt's total external debt in 2011 was US $35,001m. of which $30,580m. was public and publicly guaranteed debt. In that year, the cost of servicing long-term public and publicly guaranteed debt and repayments to the IMF was equivalent to 7.4% of the value of exports of goods, services and income (excluding workers' remittances). According to ILO figures, the annual rate of inflation averaged 10.4% in 2003–12. Consumer prices increased by an average of 7.4% in 2012. An estimated 12.7% of the total labour force were unemployed in that year.

By early 2014, three years after the overthrow of President Mubarak's regime, the Egyptian economy had seen a dramatic decline in GDP growth and a significant rise in the state budget deficit. Between 2004 and the political uprising of 2011 the country experienced impressive rates of GDP growth, principally owing to increased inflows of foreign direct investment (FDI). Despite the global economic slowdown from late 2008, Egypt experienced growth of 5.1% in 2009/10. A non-budgetary stimulus plan and subsequent development plan announced by the Government in December 2010 and April 2011, respectively, were projected to inject much-needed funds into the economy. However, as a result of the uprising, which led to a sharp decline in both FDI and tourism, Egyptian GDP increased by only 2.2% in 2011/12 and 2.1% in 2012/13. In November 2011 the interim Government announced a range of austerity measures to tackle the chronic budget deficit. Nevertheless, in January 2012 the Government resumed discussions with the IMF regarding the terms of a US $4,800m. loan package aimed at reducing the fiscal and trade deficits, and encouraging renewed investment and wider external lending. During 2011–13 Egypt accepted substantial financial support from the IMF and the World Bank, as well as additional loans from the African Development Bank, the Arab Monetary Fund, the Islamic Development Bank and from Saudi Arabia, Qatar, the United Arab Emirates (UAE), Turkey and Libya. In December 2012 President Mursi postponed the introduction of further austerity measures—such as new taxes and the removal of subsidies—as protests against changes to the Constitution provoked significant unrest and renewed violence. The measures had been agreed in November as part of the provisional IMF bailout; the Egyptian authorities thus requested the temporary suspension of the loan negotiations. Egypt's foreign exchange reserves fell from some $35,000m. in June 2010 to $13,600m. in January 2013. Discussions with the IMF proceeded intermittently from March 2013; however, no formal negotiations had begun by early March 2014. In late 2013 the Fund suggested that the interim Government (formed after the overthrow of Mursi's administration in early July 2013) needed to implement structural reforms in order to accelerate Egypt's economic recovery, despite the launch, in August, of a fiscal stimulus package to attract FDI and create jobs for the country's rapidly growing population. By January 2014 international reserves had risen to $17,100m., assisted since July 2013 by further pledges of aid totalling $15,000m. by Kuwait, Saudi Arabia and the UAE. Moreover, a Ministry of Finance report assessing economic performance during the first half of 2013/14 revealed a 2.2% decline in the budget deficit (which stood at around 14% of GDP) and a small increase in tourism GDP. The draft budget for 2013/14, announced by the Government in April 2013, set a GDP growth target of 3.8% for that period, but notably failed to adhere to some of the IMF's loan conditions. The sudden resignation of the al-Biblawi Government in late February 2014 occurred amid serious labour unrest (see Contemporary Political History), shortages of power and cooking oil, and escalating Islamist violence. During the current period of uncertainty, and amid heightened regional tensions, the success of the Government's economic programme and long-term prospects for growth will depend largely on the political landscape that emerges after the legislative and presidential elections scheduled for early 2014.

PUBLIC HOLIDAYS

2015: 1 January (New Year), 2 January* (Mouloud/Yum al-Nabi, Birth of Muhammad), 13 April (Sham al-Nessim, Coptic Easter Monday), 25 April (Sinai Day), 15 May* (Leilat al-Meiraj, Ascension of Muhammad), 17 July* (Id al-Fitr, end of Ramadan), 23 July (Revolution Day), 23 September* (Id al-Adha, Feast of the Sacrifice), 6 October (Armed Forces Day), 14 October* (Muharram, Islamic New Year), 24 October (Popular Resistance Day), 23 December (Victory Day and Mouloud/Yum al-Nabi, Birth of Muhammad).

Coptic Christian holidays include: Christmas (7 January), Palm Sunday (5 April) and Easter Sunday (12 April).

* These holidays are dependent on the Islamic lunar calendar and may vary by one or two days from the dates given.

Statistical Survey

Sources (unless otherwise stated): Central Agency for Public Mobilization and Statistics, POB 2086, Cairo (Nasr City); tel. (2) 4020574; fax (2) 4024099; e-mail misr@capmas.gov.eg; internet www.capmas.gov.eg; Central Bank of Egypt, 31 Sharia Qasr el-Nil, Cairo; tel. (2) 27702770; fax (2) 23925045; e-mail info@cbe.org.eg; internet www.cbe.org.eg.

Area and Population

AREA, POPULATION AND DENSITY

Area (sq km)	1,009,450*
Population (census results)†	
31 December 1996	59,312,914
21 November 2006	
Males	37,219,056
Females	35,578,975
Total	72,798,031
Population (official estimates at 1 January, preliminary)	
2011	79,617,517
2012	81,395,541
2013	83,661,000
Density (per sq km) at 1 January 2013	82.9

* 389,751 sq miles.

† Excluding Egyptian nationals abroad, totalling an estimated 2,180,000 in 1996 and an estimated 3,901,396 in 2006.

POPULATION BY AGE AND SEX

('000, official estimates at 1 January 2013, preliminary)

	Males	Females	Total
0–14	13,509	12,505	26,014
15–64	27,443	26,516	53,959
65 and over	1,821	1,867	3,688
Total	42,773	40,888	83,661

GOVERNORATES

(official estimates at 1 January 2013, preliminary)

	Area (sq km)	Population ('000)	Density (per sq km)	Capital
Cairo*	214.20	8,943	41,750.7	Cairo
Alexandria	2,679.36	4,609	1,720.2	Alexandria
Port Said	72.07	640	8,880.3	Port Said
Ismailia	1,441.59	1,136	788.0	Ismailia
Suez	17,840.42	592	33.2	Suez
Damietta	589.17	1,271	2,157.3	Damietta
Dakahlia	3,470.90	5,668	1,633.0	El-Mansoura
Sharkia	4,179.55	6,163	1,474.6	Zagazig
Kalyoubia	1,001.09	4,881	4,875.7	Banha
Kafr el-Sheikh	3,437.12	3,029	881.3	Kafr el-Sheikh
Gharbia	1,942.21	4,538	2,336.5	Tanta
Menoufia	1,532.13	3,759	2,453.4	Shebien el-Kom
Behera	10,129.48	5,481	541.1	Damanhour
Giza†	85,153.56	7,175	84.3	Giza
Beni-Suef	1,321.50	2,687	2,033.3	Beni-Suef
Fayoum	1,827.10	2,994	1,638.7	El-Fayoum
Menia	2,261.70	4,864	2,150.6	El-Menia
Asyout	1,553.00	4,008	2,580.8	Asyout
Suhag	1,547.20	4,345	2,808.3	Suhag
Qena	1,795.60	2,882	1,605.0	Qena
Luxor	55.00	1,092	19,854.5	Luxor
Aswan	678.45	1,383	2,038.5	Aswan
Red Sea	203,685.00	328	1.6	Hurghada
El-Wadi el-Gidid	376,505.00	215	0.6	El-Kharga
Matruh	212,112.00	404	1.9	Matruh
North Sinai	27,574.00	406	14.7	El-Areesh
South Sinai	33,140.00	168	5.1	El-Tour
Total	997,738.40‡	83,661	83.9‡	—

* Including territory designated as the governorate of Helwan in April 2008 and consisting of 1,713,278 persons at 2006 census.

† Including territory designated as the governorate of Sixth of October in April 2008 and consisting of 2,581,059 persons at 2006 census.

‡ The official, rounded national total is 1,009,450 sq km, producing an overall density figure of 82.9 per sq km.

Note: Totals may not be equal to the sum of components, owing to rounding.

PRINCIPAL TOWNS

(population at 1996 census)*

Cairo (Al-Qahirah, the capital)	6,789,479	Zagazig (Al-Zaqaziq)	267,351
Alexandria (Al-Iskandariyah)	3,328,196	El-Fayoum (Al-Fayyum)	260,964
Giza (Al-Jizah)	2,221,868	Ismailia (Al-Ismailiyah)	254,477
Shoubra el-Kheima (Shubra al-Khaymah)	870,716	Kafr el-Dawar (Kafr al-Dawwar)	231,978
Port Said (Bur Sa'id)	469,533	Aswan	219,017
Suez (Al-Suways)	417,610	Damanhour (Damanhur)	212,203
El-Mahalla el-Koubra (Al-Mahallah al-Kubra)	395,402	El-Menia (Al-Minya)	201,360
Tanta	371,010	Beni-Suef (Bani-Suwayf)	172,032
El-Mansoura (Al-Mansurah)	369,621	Qena (Qina)	171,275
Luxor (Al-Uqsor)	360,503	Suhag (Sawhaj)	170,125
Asyout (Asyut)	343,498	Shebien el-Kom (Shibin al-Kawn)	159,909

* Figures refer to provisional population. Revised figures include: Cairo 6,800,992; Alexandria 3,339,076; Port Said 472,335; Suez 417,527.

Mid-2011 ('000, incl. suburbs, UN estimate): Cairo 11,169 (Source: UN, *World Urbanization Prospects: The 2011 Revision*).

BIRTHS, MARRIAGES AND DEATHS

	Registered live births		Registered marriages		Registered deaths	
	Number ('000)	Rate (per 1,000)	Number	Rate (per 1,000)	Number ('000)	Rate (per 1,000)
2004	1,780	25.7	550,709	7.9	442	6.4
2005	1,801	25.5	522,751	7.4	451	6.4
2006	1,854	25.7	522,887	7.3	452	6.3
2007	1,950	26.5	614,848	8.5	451	6.1
2008	2,051	27.3	660,000	8.8	462	6.1
2009	2,217	28.8	759,004	9.9	477	6.2
2010	2,261	28.7	864,857	11.0	483	6.1
2011	2,442	30.4	894,040	11.1	493	6.1
2012*	2,630	31.9	922,000	11.2	529	6.4

* Preliminary figures.

Life expectancy (official estimates, years at birth, 2013): Males 69.4; Females 72.1.

ECONOMICALLY ACTIVE POPULATION
(labour force sample survey, '000 persons aged 15 years and over, 2012)

	Male	Female	Total
Agriculture, hunting, forestry and fishing	4,633.3	1,752.2	6,385.5
Mining and quarrying	39.7	0.5	40.2
Manufacturing	2,418.8	200.2	2,619.0
Electricity, gas and water supply (incl. water support, drainage and recycling)	374.3	37.9	412.2
Construction	2,776.5	18.3	2,794.8
Wholesale and retail trade; repair of motor vehicles, motorcycles, and personal and household goods	2,262.3	322.5	2,584.8
Hotels and restaurants	504.4	15.6	520.0
Transport, storage and communications	1,775.7	73.7	1,849.4
Financial intermediation	138.2	57.1	195.3
Real estate, renting and business activities	469.9	73.2	543.1
Public administration and defence; compulsory social security	1,413.2	474.9	1,888.1
Education	1,125.3	1,111.4	2,236.7
Health and social work	283.8	383.6	667.4
Other community, social and personal service activities	627.2	42.9	670.1
Private households with employed persons	85.0	98.8	183.8
Extra-territorial organizations and bodies	2.2	0.5	2.7
Sub-total	18,929.8	4,663.3	23,593.1
Activities not adequately defined	1.9	0.3	2.2
Total employed	18,931.9	4,663.8	23,595.7
Unemployed	1,941.7	1,483.1	3,424.8
Total labour force	20,873.6	6,146.9	27,020.5

Note: Totals may not be equal to the sum of components, owing to rounding.

2013 (labour force sample survey, '000 persons aged 15 years and over, July–September): Total employed 23,597 (males 18,961, females 4,636); Unemployed 3,648 (males 2,092, females 1,556); Total labour force 27,245 (males 21,053, females 6,192).

Health and Welfare

KEY INDICATORS

Total fertility rate (children per woman, 2011)	2.7
Under-5 mortality rate (per 1,000 live births, 2011)	21
HIV/AIDS (% of persons aged 15–49, 2012)	0.1
Physicians (per 1,000 head, 2009)	2.8
Hospital beds (per 1,000 head, 2010)	1.7
Health expenditure (2010): US $ per head (PPP)	293
Health expenditure (2010): % of GDP	4.7
Health expenditure (2010): public (% of total)	39.2
Access to water (% of persons, 2011)	99
Access to sanitation (% of persons, 2011)	95
Total carbon dioxide emissions ('000 metric tons, 2010)	204,776.3
Carbon dioxide emissions per head (metric tons, 2010)	2.6
Human Development Index (2012): ranking	112
Human Development Index (2012): value	0.662

For sources and definitions, see explanatory note on p. vi.

Agriculture

PRINCIPAL CROPS
('000 metric tons)

	2010	2011	2012
Wheat	7,177.4	8,407.1	8,795.5
Rice, paddy	4,329.5	5,675.0	5,911.1
Barley	117.1	122.3	108.5
Maize, green	7,041.1	6,876.5	8,093.6
Sorghum	701.6	839.2	757.0
Potatoes	3,643.2	4,338.4	4,500.0*
Sweet potatoes	370.9	274.9	316.0*
Taro (Coco yam)	119.4	103.1	118.8
Sugar cane	15,708.9	15,765.2	16,500.0*
Sugar beet	7,840.3	7,486.1	9,126.1
Broad beans, horse beans, dry	233.5	174.6	140.7
Groundnuts, with shell	202.9	206.6	205.4
Olives	390.9	459.7	465.0*
Cabbages and other brassicas	690.6	626.0	838.3
Artichokes	215.5	202.5	387.8
Lettuce and chicory	97.7	94.3	93.7
Tomatoes	8,545.0	8,105.3	8,625.2
Cauliflowers and broccoli	117.9	201.2	171.1
Pumpkins, squash and gourds	658.2	633.6	559.6
Cucumbers and gherkins	631.4	665.1	613.9
Aubergines (Eggplants)	1,229.8	1,166.4	1,193.9
Chillies and peppers, green	655.8	670.4	650.1
Onions, dry	2,208.1	2,304.2	2,024.9
Garlic	244.6	295.8	309.2
Beans, green	270.7	305.6	251.3
Peas, green	270.7	225.7	180.6
Carrots and turnips	139.0	150.3	179.3
Okra	86.2	84.0	97.1
Bananas	1,029.0	1,054.2	1,129.8
Oranges	2,401.0	2,577.7	2,786.4
Tangerines, mandarins, clementines and satsumas	796.9	848.0	885.4
Lemons and limes	318.1	296.8	300.5
Apples	493.1	455.8	541.2
Peaches and nectarines	273.3	332.5	285.2
Strawberries	238.4	240.3	242.1
Grapes	1,360.3	1,320.8	1,378.8
Watermelons	1,637.1	1,508.9	1,874.7
Cantaloupes and other melons	1,076.8	1,038.4	1,007.8
Figs	185.0	165.5	171.1
Guavas, mangoes and mangosteens	505.7	598.1	786,5
Dates	1,353.0	1,373.6	1,470.0*

* FAO estimate.

Aggregate production ('000 metric tons, may include official, semi-official or estimated data): Total cereals 19,464.7 in 2010, 22,014.9 in 2011, 23,755.7 in 2012; Total roots and tubers 4,137.7 in 2010, 4,721.2 in 2011, 4,939.8 in 2012; Total vegetables (incl. melons) 19,487.1 in 2010, 18,991.8 in 2011, 19,825.3 in 2012; Total fruits (excl. melons) 9,599.5 in 2010, 9,940.7 in 2011, 10,683.1 in 2012.

Source: FAO.

LIVESTOCK
('000 head, year ending September)

	2010	2011	2012*
Cattle	4,729	4,780	4,800
Buffaloes	3,818	3,983	3,985
Sheep	5,530	5,365	5,450
Goats	4,175	4,258	4,340
Pigs	11*	11*	11
Horses	66	71	74
Asses	3,350*	3,355*	3,355
Camels	111	137	137
Chickens	117,500*	125,600*	126,100
Ducks	15,600*	15,600*	15,650
Geese and guinea fowls	7,050*	7,050*	7,055
Turkeys	1,360*	1,400*	1,400

* FAO estimate(s).

Source: FAO.

LIVESTOCK PRODUCTS
('000 metric tons)

	2010	2011	2012*
Cattle meat	457.3	454.5	460.0
Buffalo meat	398.4	395.8	405.0
Sheep meat	75.1	73.6	76.0
Goat meat	52.7	53.5	55.3
Pig meat	1.0	0.5*	0.5
Camel meat	48.0†	47.3*	47.3
Rabbit meat	52.3	53.3	56.3
Chicken meat	744.0	796.0	800.0
Cows' milk	2,995.3	3,107.2	3,250.0
Buffaloes' milk	2,653.2	2,568.1	2,650.0
Sheep's milk	96.0*	95.5*	97.0
Goats' milk	18.2*	18.5*	20.0
Hen eggs	291.2	305.5	310.0
Honey	6.0	6.0	5.7
Wool, greasy	12.0*	12.0*	12.5

* FAO estimate(s).
† Unofficial figure.

Source: FAO.

Forestry

ROUNDWOOD REMOVALS
('000 cubic metres, excluding bark, FAO estimates)

	2010	2011	2012
Sawlogs, veneer logs and logs for sleepers	134	134	134
Other industrial roundwood	134	134	134
Fuel wood	17,511	17,556	17,601
Total	17,779	17,824	17,869

Source: FAO.

SAWNWOOD PRODUCTION
('000 cubic metres, incl. railway sleepers)

	2003	2004	2005
Total (all broadleaved)	3	35	12

2006–12: Output assumed to be unchanged from 2005 (FAO estimates).

Source: FAO.

Fishing

('000 metric tons, live weight)

	2009	2010	2011
Capture	387.4	385.2	375.4
Grass carp	26.1	21.4	32.2
Nile tilapia	105.0	130.3	120.2
Mudfish	37.8	29.2	30.1
Mullets	21.9	31.6	23.5
Aquaculture	705.5	919.6*	986.8*
Cyprinids	62.3	100.0	100.0
Nile tilapia	390.3	557.0	610.6
Flathead grey mullet	210.0	116.0	114.0
Total catch	1,092.9	1,304.8*	1,362.2*

* FAO estimate.

Note: Figures exclude capture data for sponges, estimated by FAO at 1 metric ton per year.

Source: FAO.

Mining

('000 metric tons unless otherwise indicated, year ending 30 June)

	2009	2010	2011
Crude petroleum	35,260	35,030	35,250
Natural gas (million cu m)	62,690	61,320	61,448
Aluminium	265*	359	360*
Iron ore†	195	256	250
Salt (unrefined)	2,666	2,460	2,800
Phosphate rock	6,227	3,435	4,700
Gypsum (crude)	735	942	1,000
Kaolin	523	304	304
Granite (cu m)	59,000	480,000	480,000
Marble (cu m)	284,000	1,400,000	1,400,000

* Estimated production.
† Figures refer to gross weight. The estimated iron content is 50%.

2012: Crude petroleum ('000 metric tons) 35,393; Natural gas (million cu m) 60,881.

Sources: US Geological Survey; BP, *Statistical Review of World Energy*.

Industry

SELECTED PRODUCTS
('000 metric tons unless otherwise indicated)

	2007	2008	2009
Mineral water ('000 hl)	—	2,064	1,547
Cigarettes (million)	—	61,697	59,849
Caustic soda	—	45	155
Jet fuels	2,422	2,319	2,016
Kerosene	143	133	151
Distillate fuel oils	8,803	8,666	8,267
Motor spirit (gasoline)	4,195	4,240	4,384
Residual fuel oil (mazout)	10,989	9,529	9,166
Petroleum bitumen (asphalt)	831	783	871
Electric energy (million kWh)	128,129	134,565	142,690

2010: Jet fuels 1,098; Kerosene 151; Motor spirit (gasoline) 4,089; Petroleum bitumen (asphalt) 726; Electric energy (million kWh) 150,486.

Source: UN Industrial Commodity Statistics Database.

Cement ('000 metric tons): 46,900 in 2009; 44,592 in 2010; 43,884 in 2011 (Source: US Geological Survey).

Finance

CURRENCY AND EXCHANGE RATES

Monetary Units

1,000 millièmes = 100 piastres = 5 tallaris = 1 Egyptian pound (£E).

Sterling, Dollar and Euro Equivalents (31 December 2013)

£1 sterling = £E11.434;
US $1 = £E6.943;
€1 = £E9.575;
£E100 = £8.75 sterling = $14.40 = €10.44.

Note: From February 1991 foreign exchange transactions were conducted through only two markets, the primary market and the free market. With effect from 8 October 1991, the primary market was eliminated, and all foreign exchange transactions are effected through the free market. In January 2001 a new exchange rate mechanism was introduced, whereby the value of the Egyptian pound would be allowed to fluctuate within narrow limits: initially, as much as 1% above or below a rate that was set by the Central Bank of Egypt, but would be adjusted periodically in response to market conditions. The trading band was widened to 3% in August, and in January 2003 the Government adopted a floating exchange rate.

Average Exchange Rate (Egyptian pound per US $)

2011	5.933
2012	6.056
2013	6.870

GOVERNMENT FINANCE

(budgetary central government operations, £E million, year ending 30 June)

Revenue

	2011/12	2012/13*	2013/14†
Tax revenue	207,410	251,119	358,729
Income tax	91,245	117,762	158,951
Property tax	13,089	16,453	24,092
Taxes on goods and services	84,594	92,924	145,184
Taxes on international trade and transactions	14,788	16,771	21,546
Other taxes	3,694	7,208	8,956
Non tax revenue	96,212	99,203	146,770
Grants	10,103	5,208	2,358
Other revenue	86,109	93,996	144,413
Total	303,622	350,322	505,499

Expense

Expense by economic type	2011/12	2012/13*	2013/14†
Compensation of employees	122,818	142,956	171,159
Use of goods and services	26,826	26,652	29,424
Interest payments	104,441	146,995	182,046
Subsidies, grants and social benefits	150,193	197,093	204,739
Other payments	30,796	34,975	38,280
Purchases of non-financial assets	35,918	39,516	63,679
Total	470,992	588,188	689,327

* Preliminary figures.
† Budget figures.

Source: Ministry of Finance, Cairo.

INTERNATIONAL RESERVES

(US $ million at 31 December)

	2010	2011	2012
Gold (national valuation)	2,180	2,743	3,303
IMF special drawing rights	1,261	1,258	1,260
Foreign exchange	32,351	13,658	10,368
Total	35,792	17,659	14,931

Source: IMF, *International Financial Statistics*.

MONEY SUPPLY

(£E million at 31 December)

	2010	2011	2012
Currency outside depository corporations	143,632	176,578	205,020
Transferable deposits	113,895	119,852	133,903
Other deposits	716,434	742,440	828,237
Broad money	973,962	1,038,871	1,167,160

Source: IMF, *International Financial Statistics*.

COST OF LIVING

(Consumer Price Index; base: January 2010 = 100)

	2010	2011	2012
Food and non-alcoholic beverages	109.9	126.5	138.1
Alcoholic beverages and tobacco	121.9	171.2	201.5
Clothing and footwear	101.1	103.6	108.4
Housing and utilities	99.1	102.9	110.1
Health	100.3	102.0	103.7
Education	106.2	127.7	140.8
Transport	100.5	101.6	103.3
Communication	99.9	98.7	95.9
Recreation and culture	102.0	109.8	118.8
All items (incl. others)	105.4	116.4	125.0

NATIONAL ACCOUNTS

(£E million at current prices, year ending 30 June)

Expenditure on the Gross Domestic Product

	2010/11	2011/12	2012/13
Government final consumption expenditure	157,000	179,000	204,800
Private final consumption expenditure	1,036,000	1,271,000	1,423,100
Changes in inventories	5,400	12,000	7,000
Gross fixed capital formation	229,100	246,100	241,600
Total domestic expenditure	1,427,500	1,708,100	1,876,500
Exports of goods and services	282,000	274,600	309,000
Less Imports of goods and services	338,500	407,200	432,200
GDP in purchasers' values	1,371,000	1,575,500	1,753,300

Note: Figures are rounded to the nearest £E hundred million.

Gross Domestic Product by Economic Activity

	2010/11	2011/12	2012/13
Agriculture, hunting, forestry and fishing	190,159	218,216	243,356
Mining and quarrying	195,136	261,671	290,739
Manufacturing	216,184	238,283	262,505
Electricity, gas and water	21,544	23,319	25,904
Construction	60,070	67,382	76,747
Wholesale and retail trade, restaurants and hotels	192,413	212,113	236,592
Transport, storage and communications	122,681	130,386	140,768
Suez Canal	29,311	31,203	32,396
Finance, insurance, real estate and business services	126,527	141,439	157,801
Public administration and defence	133,688	153,984	174,713
Other services	51,503	61,734	68,227
GDP at factor cost	1,309,906	1,508,527	1,677,352
Indirect taxes, *less* subsidies*	61,094	66,973	75,948
GDP in purchasers' values	1,371,000	1,575,500	1,753,300

* Figures obtained as residuals.

BALANCE OF PAYMENTS
(US $ million)

	2010	2011	2012
Exports of goods	25,024	27,913	26,835
Imports of goods	–45,145	–47,312	–52,350
Balance on goods	–20,120	–19,398	–25,516
Exports of services	23,807	19,140	21,767
Imports of services	–14,718	–14,070	–16,450
Balance on goods and services	–11,031	–14,328	–20,200
Primary income received	534	318	232
Primary income paid	–6,446	–6,695	–6,796
Balance on goods, services and primary income	–16,943	–20,705	–26,763
Secondary income received	12,836	15,566	20,136
Secondary income paid	–397	–345	–345
Current balance	–4,504	–5,484	–6,972
Capital account (net)	–39	–45	–119
Direct investment assets	–1,176	–626	–211
Direct investment from liabilities	6,386	–483	2,798
Portfolio investment assets	–445	–220	23
Portfolio investment liabilities	10,887	–10,431	–1,976
Other investment assets	–11,185	2,876	–592
Other investment liabilities	2,003	–2,467	3,417
Net errors and omissions	–2,145	–2,855	–2,160
Reserves and related items	–218	–19,736	–5,792

Source: IMF, *International Financial Statistics*.

External Trade

Note: Figures exclude trade in military goods.

PRINCIPAL COMMODITIES
(distribution by HS, US $ million)

Imports c.i.f.	2010	2011	2012
Live animals and animal products	2,081.8	2,109.3	2,788.7
Vegetables and vegetable products	5,340.7	7,957.5	8,312.4
Cereals	3,483.9	5,452.7	5,349.1
Wheat and meslin	2,181.9	3,199.2	3,196.9
Maize (corn)	1,270.7	2,179.9	1,958.4
Animal, vegetable fats and oils, cleavage products, etc.	1,023.7	2,052.1	1,627.5
Prepared foodstuffs; beverages, spirits, vinegar; tobacco and articles thereof	1,815.2	2,803.6	3,081.4
Mineral products	8,043.6	10,492.8	14,031.2
Mineral fuels, oils, distillation products, etc.	7,130.7	9,280.3	13,061.1
Crude petroleum oils	1,321.2	1,700.2	2,933.3
Non-crude petroleum oils	3,656.7	5,119.3	7,718.7
Petroleum gases	1,806.2	2,055.6	2,230.9
Chemicals and related products	4,399.3	5,150.1	5,820.2
Plastics, rubber, and articles thereof	2,963.0	3,731.8	4,103.6
Plastics and articles thereof	2,296.1	2,915.0	3,112.1
Wood, wood charcoal, cork, and articles thereof	1,205.0	1,342.5	1,672.6

Imports c.i.f.—*continued*	2010	2011	2012
Textiles and textile articles	2,907.4	2,943.3	2,908.1
Iron and steel, other base metals and articles of base metal	7,119.8	8,056.3	8,882.5
Iron and steel	3,125.8	3,600.3	4,307.4
Iron ingots, wastes and scraps	669.4	1,032.9	934.4
Articles of iron or steel	2,787.1	2,598.4	2,583.0
Machinery and mechanical appliances; electrical equipment; parts thereof	8,989.4	9,107.9	9,284.3
Machinery, boilers, etc.	5,613.3	5,452.7	5,570.9
Electrical, electronic equipment	3,376.1	3,655.3	3,713.4
Vehicles other than railway, tramway	3,768.2	3,093.8	3,555.1
Total (incl. others)	53,003.4	62,282.0	69,865.6

Exports f.o.b.	2010	2011	2012
Vegetables and vegetable products	2,843.7	2,749.0	2,498.8
Vegetables, roots and tubers	834.3	986.0	804.3
Fruit, nuts, peel of citrus fruit and melons	955.1	1,020.6	990.3
Prepared foodstuffs; beverages, spirits, vinegar; tobacco and articles thereof	1,273.5	1,330.1	1,223.2
Mineral products	8,027.2	9,903.7	9,616.4
Mineral fuels, oils, distillation products, etc.	7,593.9	9,242.0	8,872.0
Crude petroleum oils	1,777.5	3,014.0	3,022.6
Non-crude petroleum oils	2,962.0	3,507.3	3,150.4
Petroleum gases	2,266.6	2,030.2	2,179.9
Chemicals and related products	2,891.2	3,740.0	3,543.3
Fertilizers	1,152.3	1,443.2	1,284.0
Nitrogenous fertilizers	1,080.8	1,354.5	1,184.9
Plastics, rubber, and articles thereof	955.2	1,202.6	1,354.5
Plastics and articles thereof	886.5	1,098.1	1,266.8
Textiles and textile articles	2,904.6	3,436.2	2,914.8
Non-knitted articles of apparel and accessories	821.0	994.3	770.5
Articles of stone, plaster, cement, asbestos; ceramic and glass products	893.3	823.6	1,107.6
Pearls, precious stones, metals, coins, etc.	1,037.4	1,725.8	1,330.7
Gold, unwrought or semi-manufactured	1,033.8	1,715.2	1,318.7
Iron and steel, other base metals and articles of base metal	2,660.3	3,162.1	2,506.9
Iron and steel	872.9	1,157.6	775.0
Machinery and mechanical appliances; electrical equipment; parts thereof	1,043.3	1,431.3	1,383.3
Electrical and electronic equipment	816.4	1,166.6	1,153.7
Total (incl. others)	26,331.8	31,582.4	29,417.0

Source: Trade Map-Trade Competitiveness Map, International Trade Centre, www.intracen.org/marketanalysis.

PRINCIPAL TRADING PARTNERS
(US $ million)*

Imports c.i.f.	2010	2011	2012
Algeria	412.8	684.0	968.4
Argentina	888.2	1,859.3	1,103.1
Australia	538.5	521.7	457.0
Belgium	861.6	1,336.5	1,692.8
Brazil	1,736.2	2,404.5	2,783.6
China, People's Republic	4,901.8	5,708.3	6,590.7
France (incl. Monaco)	1,886.1	2,053.2	2,278.0
Germany	4,023.9	3,930.0	4,670.0
India	1,557.8	1,642.4	2,251.6
Indonesia	532.6	903.7	774.6

Imports c.i.f.—*continued*	2010	2011	2012
Italy	2,962.6	3,123.8	3,464.6
Japan	1,440.2	1,375.7	1,591.8
Korea, Republic	1,906.0	1,735.3	1,763.2
Kuwait	1,524.1	2,786.8	2,690.9
Malaysia	784.6	768.7	557.7
Malta	1,053.8	208.3	226.2
Netherlands	831.5	1,656.3	1,452.5
Russia	1,835.1	2,634.1	3,988.8
Saudi Arabia	2,120.1	2,546.4	2,722.4
Spain	847.9	1,106.1	1,352.6
Sweden	623.3	707.2	913.3
Switzerland	542.4	657.0	731.3
Thailand	749.1	701.7	911.3
Turkey	1,880.0	2,638.7	3,490.1
Ukraine	1,624.8	1,946.0	3,861.4
United Arab Emirates	730.2	804.7	810.1
United Kingdom	1,269.0	1,270.6	1,265.1
USA	4,961.9	6,470.1	5,276.5
Total (incl. others)	53,003.4	62,282.0	69,865.6

Exports f.o.b.	2010	2011	2012
Algeria	262.4	386.9	391.9
Belgium	351.2	550.9	398.0
China, People's Republic	431.6	623.3	747.1
France (incl. Monaco)	924.1	1,288.6	1,152.5
Germany	573.4	792.5	644.5
Greece	271.9	400.6	225.8
India	1,227.9	2,265.4	2,039.5
Iraq	382.9	450.5	569.9
Italy	2,199.2	2,719.7	2,324.5
Japan	188.9	362.2	1,007.4
Jordan	711.8	864.4	695.0
Korea, Republic	531.3	433.6	278.7
Lebanon	523.9	964.7	843.1
Libya	1,220.4	556.7	1,439.3
Morocco	402.1	492.6	397.3
Netherlands	558.8	701.2	405.6
Russia	213.3	353.2	225.1
Saudi Arabia	1,549.0	1,977.7	1,832.8
South Africa	395.6	1,008.5	526.3
Spain	1,621.4	1,312.9	1,008.2
Sudan	559.2	537.0	452.2
Switzerland	398.1	272.5	344.5
Syria	800.5	762.0	391.7
Taiwan	337.8	377.1	94.8
Turkey	985.3	1,528.8	1,570.2
United Arab Emirates	613.4	867.0	721.7
United Kingdom	813.4	965.9	840.5
USA	1,547.1	1,819.4	2,015.5
Total (incl. others)†	26,331.8	31,582.4	29,417.0

* Imports by country of consignment, exports by country of destination. Totals include trade in free zones, not classifiable by country.

† Including bunkers and ships' stores (US $ million): 948.2 in 2010; 1,114.0 in 2011; 1,236.5 in 2012.

Source: Trade Map-Trade Competitiveness Map, International Trade Centre, www.intracen.org/marketanalysis.

Transport

RAILWAYS
(traffic, year ending 30 June)

	2001/02	2002/03	2003/04
Passenger-km (million)	39,083	46,185	52,682
Net ton-km (million)	4,188	4,104	4,663

Source: UN, *Statistical Yearbook*.

2010/11 (million): Passengers carried (paying passengers only) 224.8; Freight carried (metric tons) 6.2; Passenger-km 27,252; Freight ton-km 1,965.

ROAD TRAFFIC
(licensed motor vehicles in use at 31 December)

	2010	2011	2012
Passenger cars	3,072,047	3,459,477	3,231,513
Buses and coaches	104,131	109,624	107,112
Lorries and vans	956,719	1,000,993	1,042,478
Motorcycles and mopeds	1,374,775	1,525,556	1,674,812
Total (incl. others)	5,714,385	6,321,307	6,552,255

SHIPPING

Flag Registered Fleet
(at 31 December)

	2011	2012	2013
Number of vessels	449	449	445
Displacement ('000 grt)	1,345.9	1,281.4	1,143.9

Source: Lloyd's List Intelligence (www.lloydslistintelligence.com).

International sea-borne freight traffic ('000 metric tons, incl. ships' stores, 2005, figures are rounded): Goods loaded 21,230; Goods unloaded 42,410 (Source: UN, *Monthly Bulletin of Statistics*).

SUEZ CANAL TRAFFIC

	2010	2011	2012
Transits (number)	17,993	17,798	17,298
Displacement ('000 net tons)	846,389	928,879	928,452
Total cargo volume ('000 metric tons)	646,064	691,800	739,911

Source: Suez Canal Port Authority.

CIVIL AVIATION
(traffic on scheduled services)

	2010	2011
Kilometres flown (million)	144	112
Passengers carried ('000)	9,179	6,516
Passenger-km (million)	20,054	13,907
Total ton-km (million)	2,411	1,652

Source: UN, *Statistical Yearbook*.

Passengers carried ('000): 8,366 in 2012 (Source: World Bank, World Development Indicators database).

Tourism

ARRIVALS BY NATIONALITY
('000)

	2009	2010	2011
France	551.7	599.4	344.9
Germany	1,202.3	1,329.0	964.6
Israel	203.3	226.5	177.8
Italy	1,048.0	1,144.4	555.2
Libya	410.2	451.1	524.5
Netherlands	249.0	291.2	206.7
Palestinian Territories	104.7	177.3	229.8
Russia	2,035.3	2,855.7	1,832.4
Saudi Arabia	348.0	374.9	198.3
United Kingdom	1,346.7	1,455.9	1,034.4
USA	321.3	361.5	184.6
Total (incl. others)	12,535.9	14,730.8	9,845.1

Tourism receipts (US $ million, excl. passenger transport): 12,528 in 2010; 8,707 in 2011; 9,940 in 2012 (provisional).

Source: World Tourism Organization.

Total tourist arrivals ('000): 11,532 in 2012.

Communications Media

	2010	2011	2012
Telephones ('000 main lines in use)	9,618.1	8,714.3	8,557.5
Mobile cellular telephones ('000 subscribers)	70,661.0	83,425.1	96,798.8
Internet subscribers ('000)	2,118.2	2,165.8	n.a.
Broadband subscribers ('000)	1,426.1	1,843.6	2,287.2

Source: International Telecommunication Union.

Education

(2011/12 unless otherwise indicated, estimates)

	Schools	Teachers	Students
Pre-primary	8,928	31,768	874,730
Primary	17,249	376,745	9,644,456
Preparatory	10,372	225,861	4,158,845
Secondary:			
general	2,780	96,514	1,324,440
technical	1,892	139,195	1,628,168
University*	42	78,596	1,722,968

* 2010/11 figures.

Source: Ministry of Education.

Al-Azhar (2011/12): *Primary:* 3,465 schools; 1,175,183 students. *Preparatory:* 3,131 schools; 489,703 students. *Secondary:* 2,068 schools; 316,306 students.

Pupil-teacher ratio (primary education, UNESCO estimate): 27.7 in 2009/10 (Source: UNESCO Institute for Statistics).

Adult literacy rate (UNESCO estimates): 73.9% (males 81.7%; females 65.8%) in 2012 (Source: UNESCO Institute for Statistics).

Directory

The Government

HEAD OF STATE

President: ADLI MAHMOUD MANSOUR (ad interim; took office 4 July 2013).

COUNCIL OF MINISTERS
(April 2014)

Prime Minister: IBRAHIM MEHLEB.

Minister of Defence: Col Gen. SIDKI SOBHI SAYED AHMED.

Minister of Higher Education and Scientific Research: WAEL AL-DEGAWI.

Minister of Finance: HANI QADRI DEMIAN.

Minister of Electricity and Energy: Dr MUHAMMAD SHAKER.

Minister of Planning and International Co-operation: ASHRAF AL-ARABI.

Minister of Housing and Urban Development: Dr MUSTAFA MADBOULI.

Minister of Education: MAHMOUD ABUL NASR.

Minister of State for Antiquities: MUHAMMAD IBRAHIM.

Minister of Tourism: MUHAMMAD HISHAM ABBAS ZAAZOU.

Minister of Supply and Internal Trade: KHALID HANAFI.

Minister of the Interior: Maj.-Gen. MUHAMMAD IBRAHIM.

Minister of Manpower and Immigration: NAHED AL-ASHRI.

Minister of Culture: MUHAMMAD SABER ARAB.

Minister of Petroleum and Metallurgical Wealth: SHERIF ISMAIL.

Minister of Information: DORRAYA SHARAF AL-DIN.

Minister of State for Military Production: Maj.-Gen. IBRAHIM YOUNIS.

Minister of Awqaf (Islamic Endowments): MUHAMMAD MOKHTAR GOMAA.

Minister of Foreign Affairs: NABIL FAHMI.

Minister of Civil Aviation: MUHAMMAD HOSSAM KAMAL.

Minister of Agriculture and Land Cultivation: AYMAN FARID ABU HADID.

Minister of Water Resources and Irrigation: MUHAMMAD ABD AL-MUTTALIB.

Minister of Health and Population: ADEL AL-ADAWI.

Minister of Transport: IBRAHIM AL-DOMEIRI.

Minister of Industry, Foreign Trade and Investment: MOUNIR FAKHRI ABD AL-NOUR.

Minister of Communications and Information Technology: ATIF HELMI.

Minister of State for Sports and Youth Affairs: KHALID ABD AL-AZIZ.

Minister of Local and Administrative Development: ADIL LABIB.

Minister of State for Environmental Affairs: Dr LAILA RASHID ISKANDAR.

Minister of Transitional Justice, National Reconciliation and Parliamentary Affairs: MUHAMMAD AMIN AL-MAHDI.

Minister of Social Solidarity: Dr GHADA WALI.

Minister of Justice: NAYER ABD AL-MONEIM OTHMAN.

MINISTRIES

Office of the Prime Minister: 2 Sharia Majlis al-Sha'ab, Cairo; tel. (2) 27935000; fax (2) 27958048; e-mail questions@cabinet.gov.eg.

Ministry of Agriculture and Land Cultivation: 1 Sharia Nadi el-Seid, Cairo (Dokki); tel. (2) 33372970; fax (2) 37498128; e-mail info .malr@agr-egypt.gov.eg; internet www.agr-egypt.gov.eg.

Ministry of Awqaf (Islamic Endowments): Sharia Sabri Abu Alam, Bab el-Louk, Cairo; tel. (2) 23931216; fax (2) 23929828; e-mail mawkaf@idsc1.gov.eg; internet www.awkaf.org.

Ministry of Civil Aviation: Sharia Cairo Airport, Cairo; tel. (2) 22688342; fax (2) 22688341; e-mail info@civilaviation.gov.eg; internet www.civilaviation.gov.eg.

Ministry of Communications and Information Technology: Smart Village, km 28, Sharia Cairo–Alexandria, Cairo; tel. (2) 35341300; fax (2) 35371111; e-mail webmaster@mcit.gov.eg; internet www.mcit.gov.eg.

Ministry of Culture: 2 Sharia Shagaret el-Dor, Cairo (Zamalek); tel. (2) 27485065; fax (2) 27353947; e-mail ecm.gov@gmail.com; internet www.ecm.gov.eg.

Ministry of Defence and Military Production: Sharia 23 July, Kobri el-Kobba, Cairo; tel. (2) 24032158; fax (2) 22916227; e-mail mmc@afmic.gov.eg; internet www.mod.gov.eg.

Ministry of Drinking Water and Sanitation Facilities: Cairo.

Ministry of Education: 12 Sharia el-Falaky, Cairo; tel. (2) 27947363; fax (2) 27962952; e-mail info@mail.emoe.org; internet moe.gov.eg.

Ministry of Electricity and Energy: POB 222, 8 Sharia Ramses, Abbassia Sq., Cairo (Nasr City); tel. (2) 22616317; fax (2) 22616302; e-mail info@moee.gov.eg; internet www.moee.gov.eg.

Ministry of Finance: Ministry of Finance Towers, Cairo (Nasr City); tel. (2) 23428886; fax (2) 26861561; internet www.mof.gov.eg.

Ministry of Foreign Affairs: Corniche el-Nil, Cairo (Maspiro); tel. (2) 25749820; fax (2) 25767967; e-mail contactus@mfa.gov.eg; internet www.mfa.gov.eg.

Ministry of Health and Population: 3 Sharia Majlis al-Sha'ab, Lazoughli Sq., Cairo; tel. (2) 27951821; fax (2) 27953966; e-mail webmaster@mohp.gov.eg; internet www.mohp.gov.eg.

Ministry of Higher Education: 101 Sharia Qasr el-Eini, Cairo; tel. (2) 27920323; fax (2) 27941005; e-mail mohe.info@gmail.com; internet www.egy-mhe.gov.eg.

Ministry of Housing and Urban Development: 1 Sharia Ismail Abaza, 3rd Floor, Qasr el-Eini, Cairo; tel. (2) 27921440; fax (2) 27921423; internet www.moh.gov.eg.

Ministry of Industry and Foreign Trade: 2 Sharia Latin America, Cairo (Garden City); tel. (2) 27921193; fax (2) 27957487; e-mail inquiry@mti.gov.eg; internet www.mti.gov.eg.

Ministry of Information: Radio and TV Bldg, Corniche el-Nil, Cairo (Maspiro); tel. (2) 25748988; fax (2) 25748781; e-mail info@moinfo.gov.eg; internet www.moinfo.gov.eg.

Ministry of the Interior: 25 Sharia Sheikh Rihan, Bab el-Louk, Cairo; tel. (2) 27952300; fax (2) 27960682; e-mail center@iscmi.gov.eg; internet www.moiegypt.gov.eg.

Ministry of International Co-operation: 8 Sharia Adli, Cairo; tel. (2) 23906027; e-mail ministeroffice@moic.gov.eg; internet www.moic.gov.eg.

Ministry of Investment: 3 Salah Salem St, Cairo; tel. (2) 24055628; fax (2) 24055635; e-mail investorcare@gafinet.org; internet www.investment.gov.eg.

Ministry of Local Development: Sharia Nadi el-Seid, Cairo (Dokki); tel. (2) 33067082; fax (2) 37497788; e-mail mld.eg@hotmail.com; internet www.mld.gov.eg.

Ministry of Manpower and Immigration: 3 Sharia Yousuf Abbas, Cairo (Nasr City); tel. (2) 22609366; fax (2) 22618019; e-mail manpower@mome.gov.eg; internet www.manpower.gov.eg.

Ministry of Petroleum and Metallurgical Wealth: 1 Sharia Ahmad el-Zomor, Cairo (Nasr City); tel. (2) 26706401; fax (2) 22746060; e-mail contact@petroleum.gov.eg; internet www.petroleum.gov.eg.

Ministry of Planning: POB 11765, Sharia Salah Salem, Cairo (Nasr City); tel. (2) 24014531; fax (2) 24014627; e-mail contact@mop.gov.eg; internet www.mop.gov.eg.

Ministry of State for Antiquities: Cairo; tel. (2) 27358761; fax (2) 27357239.

Ministry of State for Environmental Affairs: 30 Sharia Misr Helwan el-Zirai, Maadi, Cairo; tel. (2) 25256452; fax (2) 25256490; e-mail eeaa@eeaa.gov.eg; internet www.eeaa.gov.eg.

Ministry of State for Military Production: 5 Sharia Ismail Abaza, Qasr el-Eini, Cairo; tel. (2) 27951428; fax (2) 22634427; e-mail minlog@momp.gov.eg; internet www.momp.gov.eg.

Ministry of State for Scientific Research: 101 Sharia Qasr el-Eini, Cairo; tel. (2) 27944583; fax (2) 27927812; e-mail info@msr.gov.eg.

Ministry of State for Sports: Sharia 26 July, Sphinx Sq., Mohandessin, Cairo (Giza); e-mail info@emss.gov.eg; internet www.emss.gov.eg.

Ministry of State for Youth Affairs: Sharia 26 July, Sphinx Sq., Mohandessin, Cairo (Giza); tel. 33048630; fax 334692025; e-mail support@youth.gov.eg.

Ministry of Social Solidarity: Cairo.

Ministry of Supply and Internal Trade: 99 Sharia Qasr el-Eini, Cairo; tel. (2) 27958481; fax (2) 23365074; internet www.msit.gov.eg.

Ministry of Tourism: Cairo International Conferences Center, Cairo (Nasr City); tel. (2) 22611732; fax (2) 26859551; e-mail mot@idsc.gov.eg; internet www.visitegypt.gov.eg.

Ministry of Transitional Justice and National Reconciliation: Sharia Majlis al-Sha'ab, Cairo.

Ministry of Transport: Nasr Road, Nasr City, Cairo; tel. (2) 2604884; fax (2) 2610510; internet www.mot.gov.eg.

Ministry of Water Resources and Irrigation: Sharia Gamal Abd al-Nasser, Corniche el-Nil, Imbaba, Cairo; tel. (2) 35449420; fax (2) 35449470; e-mail minister@mwri.gov.eg; internet www.mwri.gov.eg.

President

Following the resignation from office of former President Muhammad Hosni Mubarak on 11 February 2011, the Supreme Council of the Armed Forces (SCAF), under the chairmanship of Field Marshal Muhammad Hussein Tantawi, assumed the president's powers on an interim basis, while the Constitution was suspended. A presidential election was held on 23–24 May, at which Muhammad Mursi of the Freedom and Justice Party (with 24.8% of the total valid votes) and former Prime Minister Ahmad Shafiq (23.7%) secured the largest support. At a second round of voting on 16–17 June, Mursi was elected President, securing 51.7% of the valid votes cast, and was sworn into office on 30 June. A new Constitution—which, *inter alia*, formalized the President's powers and term of office—was promulgated on 25 December 2012, following its approval at a national referendum earlier that month.

On 3 July 2013 Mursi was removed from office by the armed forces and the 2012 Constitution was suspended. A new Constitution was approved in January 2014 (see Constitution and Government). It was subsequently announced that a presidential election would be held on 26–27 May. The former Commander-in-Chief of the Armed Forces, First Deputy Prime Minister and Minister of Defence, Field Marshal Abd al-Fatah al-Sisi, and the leftist politician Hamdeen Sabbahi were confirmed as the sole candidates.

Presidential Election, First Ballot, 23–24 May 2012

Candidates	Votes	%
Muhammad Mursi	5,764,952	24.77
Ahmad Shafiq	5,505,327	23.66
Hamdeen Sabbahi	4,820,273	20.71
Abd el-Monem Aboul Foutouh	4,065,239	17.47
Amr Moussa	2,588,850	11.12
Muhammad Salim el-Awwa	235,374	1.01
Khalid Ali	134,056	0.57
Aboul Ezz al-Hariri	40,090	0.17
Hisham al-Bastawisi	29,189	0.12
Mahmoud Hossam	23,992	0.10
Muhammad Fawzi Essa	23,889	0.10
Hossam Khairallah	22,036	0.09
Abdullah al-Ashaal	12,249	0.05
Total*	23,265,516	100.00

* Excluding 406,720 invalid votes (1.74% of total votes cast).

Presidential Election, Second Ballot, 16–17 June 2012

Candidate	Votes	% of votes
Muhammad Mursi	13,230,131	51.73
Ahmad Shafiq	12,347,380	48.27
Total	25,577,511	100.00

Legislature

PEOPLE'S ASSEMBLY

Elections to the People's Assembly were held in three stages, from 28 November–11 January 2012, while elections to a new Advisory Council took place on 29 January–22 February. However, following a ruling by the Supreme Constitutional Court that declared the legislation under which the People's Assembly had been elected to be unconstitutional, on 15 June the Supreme Council of the Armed Forces dissolved the Assembly and assumed legislative powers on an interim basis. Despite a decree issued on 8 July by President Muhammad Mursi that reinstated the Assembly, the Supreme Constitutional Court insisted that its decision could not be revoked. Following the removal from office of Mursi by the armed forces on 3 July 2013, the Constitution was suspended. A new Constitution was approved at a national referendum in January 2014; elections to a new legislature were expected to take place later that year.

People's Assembly: Cairo; tel. (2) 27945000; fax (2) 27943130; e-mail contact-us@parliament.gov.eg; internet www.parliament.gov.eg.

Elections, 28–29 November and 5–6 December 2011, 14–15 December and 21–22 December 2011, 3–4 January and 10–11 January 2012

	Seats
The Freedom and Justice Party (FJP)	235
Al-Nour Party	123
New Wafd Party	38
Egyptian Bloc	34
Al-Wasat Party	10
The Reform and Development Party	9
The Revolution Continues Alliance	7
National Party of Egypt	5
Freedom Party	4
Egyptian Citizen Party	4
Union Party	2
Others	4
Independents	23
Total*	508†

* There were, in addition, 10 representatives appointed by the Supreme Council of the Armed Forces.

† Of the 498 elective seats, 332 seats were allocated to party lists under a system of proportional representation, while the remaining 166 seats were allocated to individual candidates who may or may not be affiliated to political organizations. (List candidates were elected from 46 constituencies and individual candidates from 83 constituencies.).

ADVISORY COUNCIL

In September 1980 elections were held for an advisory body, the **Advisory (Shura) Council**, which replaced the former Central Committee of the Arab Socialist Union. Two-thirds of the 270 members of the Advisory Council are elected by direct suffrage; the remainder are appointed by the Head of State (in 2012, by the Supreme Council of the Armed Forces). The Council's term in office is six years, with one-half of its members being replaced every three years. At a two-stage election held from 29 January to 22 February 2012 the Muslim Brotherhood's Freedom and Justice Party secured 105 of the 180 contested seats, while the Al-Nour Party took 45 seats. The New Wafd Party secured 14 seats and the Egyptian Bloc eight seats. The Freedom Party and the Democratic Peace Party, both offshoots of the defunct National Democratic Party, won three seats and one seat, respectively, while the remaining four seats went to independent candidates. The Advisory Council was dissolved on 6 July 2013, following the removal from office of President Muhammad Mursi by the armed forces and the subsequent suspension of the Constitution.

Advisory Council: Cairo; tel. (2) 27955492; fax (2) 27941980; e-mail gsecretariat@parliament.gov; internet www.shoura.gov.eg.

Election Commissions

Higher Election Commission (HEC): Cairo; tel. (2) 4142613; fax (2) 4142615; e-mail info@elections.gov.eg; internet www.elections.eg; regulates legislative elections; comprises 11 mems; Chair. NABIL SALIB AWADALLAH; Sec.-Gen. Dr HAMDAN HASSAN FAHMI.

Supreme Presidential Election Commission (PEC): 3rd Floor, 117 Sharia Abd al-Aziz Fahmy, Cairo (Heliopolis); f. 2005; independent; comprises 10 mems, presided over by the Chief Justice of the Supreme Constitutional Court and 4 other ex officio mems of the judiciary; of the remaining 5 mems (who are independent, public figures), 3 are appointed by the People's Assembly and 2 by the Advisory Council; Chair. ANWAR AL-RASHAD AL-ASI.

Political Organizations

Following the removal from office of President Hosni Mubarak in February 2011, new legislation governing the licensing of political organizations was promulgated in late March. A number of new parties were granted official recognition—including the Freedom and Justice Party, which was founded in April by the Muslim Brotherhood—and participated in legislative elections held from November. Meanwhile, in mid-April the National Democratic Party of former President Mubarak was dissolved, following a ruling by the High Administrative Court. However, in December 2013 the Muslim Brotherhood was designated as a 'terrorist group' by the interim administration that had taken office in July, following the ouster and detention of Mubarak's successor as President, Muhammad Mursi.

Arab Democratic Nasserist Party: 8 Sharia Talaat Harb, Cairo; f. 1992; advocates maintaining the principles of the 1952 Revolution, achieving a strong national economy and protecting human rights; Chair. SAMIH ASHOUR; Sec.-Gen. AHMED HASSAN.

Democratic Generation Party (Hizb al-Geel al-Dimuqrati): Bldg 26, Ismail Abaza St, Saad Zaghloul Metro Station, Cairo; tel. and fax (2) 27960814; internet www.hzpelgeel.com; f. 2002; advocates improvements in education and youth-based policies; Chair. NAGUI EL-SHEHABY.

Democratic Peace Party: Cairo; f. 2005; Chair. AHMAD MUHAMMAD BAYOUMI AL-FADALI.

Egyptian Arab Socialist Party (Hizb Misr al-Arabi al-Ishtiraki): f. 1976; seeks to maintain principles of the 1952 Revolution and to preserve Egypt's Islamic identity; f. 1985; Leader WAHID FAKHRY AL-UQSURI.

The Egyptian Bloc: e-mail kotla-masreya@info.com; internet www.elkotlaelmasreya.com; f. 2011; originally formed as a coalition of 15 political parties; secular, liberal; currently comprises the Free Egyptians Party, the Egyptian Social Democratic Party and the National Progressive Unionist Party—Tagammu.

Egyptian Citizen Party (Hizb al-Mowaten al-Masri): f. 2011; offshoot of the former National Democratic Party; Leader MUHAMMAD RAGAB.

Egyptian Green Party (Hizb al-Khudr al-Misri): 9 Sharia al-Tahrir, Cairo (Dokki); tel. and fax (2) 33364748; fax (2) 33364748; e-mail awad@egyptiangreens.com; internet www.egyptiangreens.com; f. 1990; Pres. MUHAMMAD AWAD.

Egyptian Islamic Labour Party: 12 Sharia Awali el-Ahd, Cairo; e-mail magdyahmedhussein@gmail.com; internet www.el3amal.net; f. 1978; official opposition party; pro-Islamist; seeks establishment of economic system based on *Shari'a* (Islamic) law, unity between Egypt, Sudan and Libya, and the liberation of occupied Palestinian territory; Sec.-Gen. MUHAMMAD MAGDI AHMAD HUSSEIN.

Freedom Party (Hizb al-Horreya): Center Amwalimomat St, Housing Sheraton, Cairo; tel. (2) 2660325; fax (2) 2660390; internet www.alhoriaparty.com; f. 2011; offshoot of the former National Democratic Party; Chair. MAMDOUH HASSAN; Sec.-Gen MOATAZ HASSAN.

Free Egyptians Party (Hizb al-Masryin al-Ahrar): 281 Sharia Ramsis, Cairo; internet www.fep.org.eg; f. 2011; merged with Democratic Front Party (f. 2007) in Jan. 2014; seeks to promote liberal democracy, the rule of law and a civil society; mem. of the Egyptian Bloc; Pres. AHMAD SAID.

Free Social Constitutional Party: f. 2004; seeks introduction of further political, social and economic reforms; Chair. MAMDOUH QENAWI.

Al-Ghad (Tomorrow) Party: Cairo; e-mail info@elghad.org; f. 2004; aims to combat poverty and to improve the living conditions of Egypt's citizens; Chair. MOUSSA MOUSTAFA MOUSSA.

Misr el-Fatah (Young Egypt Party): f. 1990; pursues a socialist, nationalist and reformist agenda; Chair. ABD AL-HAKIM ABD AL-MAJID KHALIL.

Muslim Brotherhood (Al-Ikhwan al-Muslimun): internet www.ikhwanonline.com; f. 1928, with the aim of establishing an Islamic society; banned in 1954; transnational org.; moderate; advocates the adoption of *Shari'a* (Islamic) law as the sole basis of the Egyptian legal system; founded Freedom and Justice Party to contest at least one-half of the seats at 2011–12 legislative elections; proscribed by the interim Govt in Dec. 2013; Supreme Guide MAHMOUD IZZAT (acting).

Freedom and Justice Party (FJP): Cairo; e-mail info@fjponline.com; internet www.fjponline.com; f. 2011; Islamist party committed to democracy and social equality; member of the Democratic Alliance for Egypt; Chair. MUHAMMAD SAAD EL-KATATNI; Sec.-Gen. MUHAMMAD AL-BELTAGI.

National Party of Egypt (Hizb Masr al-Qawmi): f. 2011; offshoot of the former National Democratic Party.

National Progressive Unionist Party (NPUP) (Hizb al-Tagammu' al-Watani al-Taqadomi al-Wahdawi—Tagammu): 1 Sharia Karim el-Dawlah, Cairo; tel. (2) 5791629; fax (2) 5784867; e-mail khaled@al-ahaly.com; internet www.al-ahaly.com; f. 1976; left-wing; seeks to defend the principles of the 1952 Revolution; Founder KHALED MOHI EL-DIN; Chair. SAYID ABD AL-AAL; 160,000 mems.

New Wafd Party (New Delegation Party): POB 357, 1 Boulos Hanna St, Cairo (Dokki); tel. (2) 3383111; fax (2) 37603060; e-mail info@alwafdparty.com; internet www.alwafd.org; f. 1919 as Wafd Party; banned 1952; re-formed as New Wafd Party Feb. 1978; disbanded June 1978; re-formed 1983; seeks further political, economic and social reforms, greater democracy, the abolition of emergency legislation, and improvements to the health and education sectors; Chair. SAYED EL-BADAWI.

Al-Nour Party: Zezenia, Alexandria; tel. (3) 5741310; fax (3) 5741317; e-mail info@alnourparty.org; internet www.alnourparty.org; f. 2011; Salafist; Chair YOUNIS MAKHYOUN.

The Reform and Development Party (al-Islah wa al-Tanmiya): 28 Samir Mokhtar St, Ard El Golf, Cairo; tel. (2) 4185545; fax (2) 4184920; e-mail info@rdpegypt.org; internet www.rdpegypt.org; f. 2009; was denied licence in 2010; formed by merger of the Reformation and Development Party with the Masrena Party; Chair. MUHAMMAD ANWAR ESMAT EL-SADAT.

The Revolution Continues Alliance (RCA): Cairo; f. 2011; comprises the Socialist Popular Alliance Party, the Egyptian Current Party, the Revolution Youth Coalition, the Egyptian Socialist Party, the Egyptian Alliance Party, the Freedom Egypt Party and the Equality and Development Party.

Solidarity Party (Hizb al-Takaful): f. 1995; advocates imposition of 'solidarity' tax on the rich in order to provide for the needs of the poor; Chair. Dr OSAMA ABD AL-SHAFI SHALTOUT.

Ummah (People's) Party (Hizb al-Umma): f. 1983; social democratic party; Leader AHMAD AL-SABAHI KHALIL.

Union Party (Hizb al-Ittihad): f. 2011; offshoot of the former National Democratic Party; Leader HOSSAM BADRAWI.

Al-Wasat Party: 8 Pearl St, Mokattam, Cairo; tel. (2) 5044151; internet www.alwasatparty.com; f. 2011; originally formed in 1996 but denied licence under rule of former President Hosni Mubarak; Pres. ABUL ELA MADI; Sec.-Gen. MUHAMMAD ABD AL-LATIF.

Diplomatic Representation

EMBASSIES IN EGYPT

Afghanistan: 59 Sharia el-Orouba, Cairo (Heliopolis); tel. (2) 4177236; fax (2) 4177238; e-mail info@afghanembassy-egypt.com; internet www.afghanembassy-egypt.com; Ambassador FAZLURRAHMAN FAZIL.

Albania: Ground Floor, 27 Sharia Gezira al-Wissta, Cairo (Zamalek); tel. (2) 27361815; fax (2) 27356966; e-mail embassy.cairo@mfa.gov.al; Ambassador NURI DOMI.

Algeria: 14 Sharia Bresil, Cairo (Zamalek); tel. (2) 7368527; fax (2) 7364158; e-mail nov54@link.net; Ambassador NAZEER AL-ARBAWI.

Angola: 12 Midan Fouad Mohi el-Din, Mohandessin, Cairo; tel. (2) 3377602; fax (2) 708683; e-mail angola@access.com.eg; internet www.angolaeg.net; Ambassador ANTÓNIO DA COSTA FERNANDES.

Argentina: 1st Floor, 8 Sharia el-Saleh Ayoub, Cairo (Zamalek); tel. (2) 27351501; fax (2) 27364355; e-mail eegip@mrecic.gov.ar; Chargé d'affaires a.i. DIEGO SADOFSCHI.

Armenia: 20 Sharia Muhammad Mazhar, Cairo (Zamalek); tel. (2) 27374157; fax (2) 27374158; e-mail armegyptembassy@mfa.am; internet egypt.mfa.am; Ambassador Dr ARMEN MELKONIAN.

Australia: 11th Floor, World Trade Centre, Corniche el-Nil, Cairo 11111 (Boulac); tel. (2) 27706600; fax (2) 27706650; e-mail cairo.austremb@dfat.gov.au; internet www.egypt.embassy.gov.au; Ambassador Dr RALPH KING.

Austria: 5th Floor, Riyadh Tower, 5 Sharia Wissa Wassef, cnr of Sharia el-Nil, Cairo 11111 (Giza); tel. (2) 35702975; fax (2) 35702979; e-mail kairo-ob@bmeia.gv.at; internet www.bmeia.gv.at/kairo; Ambassador Dr FERDINAND MAULTASCHL.

Azerbaijan: Villa 16/24, Sharia 10, Maadi Sarayat, Cairo; tel. (2) 23583761; fax (2) 23583725; e-mail azsefqahira@link.net; internet www.azembassy.org.eg; Ambassador SHAHIN ABDULLAYEV.

Bahrain: 15 Sharia Bresil, Cairo (Zamalek); tel. (2) 27350642; fax (2) 27366609; e-mail cairo.mission@mofa.gov.bh; internet www.mofa.gov.bh/cairo; Ambassador Sheikh RASHID BIN ABD AL-RAHMAN AL KHALIFA.

Bangladesh: POB 136, 20 Sharia Geziret el-Arab, Mohandessin, Cairo; tel. (2) 37481796; fax (2) 37481782; e-mail bdootcairo@gmail.com; Ambassador MIZANUR RAHMAN.

Belarus: 26 Sharia Gaber Ibn Hayan, Cairo (Dokki); tel. (2) 37499171; fax (2) 33389545; e-mail egypt@mfa.gov.by; internet egypt.mfa.gov.by; Ambassador Dr SERGEI A. RACHKOV.

Belgium: POB 37, 20 Sharia Kamal el-Shennawi, Cairo 11511 (Garden City); tel. (2) 27947494; fax (2) 27943147; e-mail cairo@diplobel.fed.be; internet www.diplomatie.be/cairo; Ambassador GILLES HEYVAERT.

Bolivia: 21 New Ramses Centre, Sharia B. Oman, Cairo 11794 (Dokki); tel. (2) 37624362; fax (2) 37624360; e-mail embolivia_egipto@yahoo.com; Chargé d'affaires a.i. RAÚL PALZA ZEBALLOS.

Bosnia and Herzegovina: 42 Sharia al-Sawra, Cairo (Dokki); tel. (2) 37499191; fax (2) 37499190; e-mail ambbih@link.net; Ambassador BORIVOJ MAROJEVIĆ.

Brazil: Nile City Towers, North Tower, 2005 C, Corniche el-Nil, Cairo; tel. (2) 24619837; fax (2) 24619838; e-mail administ.cairo@itamaraty.gov.br; internet cairo.itamaraty.gov.br; Ambassador MARCO ANTONIO DINIZ BRANDÃO.

Brunei: 14 Sharia Sri Lanka, Cairo (Zamalek); tel. (2) 27366651; fax (2) 27360240; e-mail cairo.egypt@mfa.gov.bn; Ambassador Haji MAHDI PEHIN Dato' Haji ABDULLAH RAHMAN.

Bulgaria: 6 Sharia el-Malek el-Afdal, Cairo (Zamalek); tel. (2) 27363025; fax (2) 27363826; e-mail embassy.cairo@mfa.bg; internet www.mfa.bg/embassies/egypt; Ambassador RUMEN PETROV.

Burkina Faso: POB 306, Ramses Centre, 22 Sharia Wadi el-Nil, Mohandessin, Cairo 11794; tel. (2) 23898056; fax (2) 23806974; Ambassador MOUSSA B. NEBIE.

Burundi: 27 Sharia el-Ryad, Mohandessin, Cairo; tel. (2) 33024301; fax (2) 33441997; Ambassador MUSA SOLEIMANI.

Cambodia: 2 Sharia Tahawia, Cairo (Giza); tel. (2) 3489966; Ambassador IN SOPHEAP.

Cameroon: POB 2061, 15 Sharia Muhammad Sedki Soliman, Mohandessin, Cairo; tel. (2) 3441101; fax (2) 3459208; e-mail ambcam@link.net; Ambassador Dr MOHAMADOU LABARANG.

Canada: POB 57, 26 Kamel el-Shenawy, Cairo (Garden City); tel. (2) 27918700; fax (2) 27918860; e-mail cairo@dfait-maeci.gc.ca; internet www.canadainternational.gc.ca/egypt-egypte; Ambassador DAVID DRAKE.

Central African Republic: 41 Sharia Mahmoud Azmy, Mohandessin, Cairo (Dokki); tel. and fax (2) 38374235; e-mail ambcentrafrique-caire@yahoo.fr; Ambassador ANICET SAULET.

Chad: POB 1869, 12 Midan al-Refaï, Cairo 11511 (Dokki); tel. (2) 37493403; fax (2) 37492733; Ambassador EL HADJ MAHMOUD ADJI.

Chile: 19 Sharia Gabalaya, Apt 92, Cairo (Zamalek); tel. (2) 27358711; fax (2) 27353716; e-mail embchile.eg@gmail.com; internet chileabroad.gov.cl/egipto; Ambassador JOSÉ MIGUEL DE LA CRUZ CROSS.

China, People's Republic: 14 Sharia Bahgat Ali, Cairo (Zamalek); tel. (2) 27380466; fax (2) 27359459; e-mail webmaster_eg@mfa.gov.cn; internet eg.china-embassy.org/eng; Ambassador SONG AIGUO.

Colombia: 6 Sharia Guezira, Cairo (Zamalek); tel. (2) 27364203; fax (2) 27357429; e-mail ccairo@cancilleria.gov.co; internet mre.cancilleria.gov.co/wps/portal/embajada_egipto; Ambassador MARIO GERMÁN IGUARÁN ARANA.

Congo, Democratic Republic: 5 Sharia Mansour Muhammad, Cairo (Zamalek); tel. (2) 3403662; fax (2) 3404342; Ambassador RAFAEL MALONGA.

Côte d'Ivoire: 9 Sharia Shehab, Mohandessin, Cairo; tel. (2) 33034373; fax (2) 33050148; e-mail acieg@ambaci-egypte.org; internet www.ambaci-egypte.org; Ambassador BERNARD TANOH BOUTCHOUE.

Croatia: 3 Sharia Abou el-Feda, Cairo (Zamalek); tel. (2) 27383155; fax (2) 27355812; e-mail croemb.cairo@mvpei.hr; internet eg.mfa.hr; Ambassador DARKO JAVORSKI.

Cuba: Apartment 1, 13th Floor, 10 Sharia Kamel Muhammad, Cairo (Zamalek); tel. (2) 5195762; fax (2) 5213324; e-mail cubaemb@link.net; Ambassador OTTO VAILLANT FRÍAS.

Cyprus: 17 Sharia Omar Tosson, Ahmed Orabi, Mohandessin, Cairo; tel. (2) 33455967; fax (2) 33455969; e-mail cairoembassy@mfa.gov.cy; Ambassador SOTOS A. LIASIDES.

Czech Republic: 1st Floor, 4 Sharia Dokki, Cairo 12511 (Giza); tel. (2) 33339700; fax (2) 37485892; e-mail cairo@embassy.mzv.cz; internet www.mfa.cz/cairo; Ambassador PAVEL KAFKA.

Denmark: 12 Sharia Hassan Sabri, Cairo 11211 (Zamalek); tel. (2) 27396500; fax (2) 27396588; e-mail caiamb@um.dk; internet www.egypten.um.dk; Ambassador PERNILLE DAHLER KARDEL.

Djibouti: 11 Sharia Muhammad Abdou el-Said, Cairo (Dokki); tel. (2) 33366436; fax (2) 33366437; e-mail ambassade@ambdjibouti.com; Ambassador Sheikh MOUSSA MOHAMED AHMED.

Ecuador: 33 Sharia Ismail Muhammad, Cairo (Zamalek); tel. (2) 27372776; fax (2) 27361841; e-mail ecuademb@link.net; Ambassador EDWIN JOHNSON.

Eritrea: 6 Sharia el-Fallah, Mohandessin, Cairo; tel. (2) 3033503; fax (2) 3030516; e-mail eritembe@yahoo.com; Ambassador OSMAN MUHAMMAD OMAR.

Estonia: 8th Floor, Abou el-Feda Bldg, 3 Sharia Abou el-Feda, Cairo 11211 (Zamalek); tel. (2) 27384190; fax (2) 27384189; e-mail embassy.cairo@mfa.ee; internet www.kairo.vm.ee; Ambassador PAUL TEESALU.

Ethiopia: 21 Sharia Sheikh Muhammad el-Gehzali, Cairo (Dokki); tel. (2) 3353693; fax (2) 3353699; e-mail ethio@ethioembassy.org.eg; Ambassador MAHMOUD DRIR.

Finland: 13th Floor, 3 Sharia Abou el-Feda, Cairo 11211 (Zamalek); tel. (2) 27363722; fax (2) 27371376; e-mail sanomat.kai@formin.fi; internet www.finland.org.eg; Ambassador TUULA YRJÖLÄ.

France: POB 1777, 29 Sharia Charles de Gaulle, Cairo (Giza); tel. (2) 35673200; fax (2) 35718498; e-mail questions@ambafrance-eg.org; internet www.ambafrance-eg.org; Ambassador NICOLAS GALEY.

Gabon: 17 Sharia Mecca el-Moukarama, Cairo (Dokki); tel. (2) 3379699; Ambassador JOSEPH MAMBOUNGOU.

Georgia: 11 Sharia Tanta, Aswan Sq., Mohandessin, Cairo; tel. (2) 33044798; fax (2) 33044778; e-mail cairo.emb@mfa.gov.ge; internet www.egypt.mfa.gov.ge; Ambassador ARCHIL DZULIASHVILI.

Germany: 2 Sharia Berlin (off Sharia Hassan Sabri), Cairo (Zamalek); tel. (2) 27282000; fax (2) 27282159; internet www.kairo.diplo.de; Ambassador MICHAEL BOCK.

Ghana: 1 Sharia 26 July, Cairo (Zamalek); tel. (2) 3444455; fax (2) 3032292; Ambassador Alhaji SAID SINARE.

Greece: 18 Sharia Aicha al-Taimouria, Cairo 11451 (Garden City); tel. (2) 27950443; fax (2) 27963903; e-mail gremb.cai@mfa.gr; internet www.mfa.gr/egypt; Ambassador CHRISTODOULOS LAZARIS.

Guatemala: 5th Floor, 17 Sharia Port Said, Maadi, Cairo; tel. (2) 23802914; fax (2) 23802915; e-mail embegipto@minex.gob.gt; internet www.embaguategypt.com; Ambassador LARS PIRA.

Guinea: 46 Sharia Muhammad Mazhar, Cairo (Zamalek); tel. (2) 7358109; fax (2) 7361446; Ambassador El Hadj IBRAHIMA SORI TRAORÉ.

Holy See: Apostolic Nunciature, Safarat al-Vatican, 5 Sharia Muhammad Mazhar, Cairo (Zamalek); tel. (2) 27352250; fax (2) 27356152; e-mail nunteg@yahoo.com; Apostolic Nuncio Most Rev. JEAN-PAUL AIMÉ GOBEL (Titular Archbishop of Calatia).

Honduras: 8th Floor, 5 Sharia el-Israa, Mohandessin, Cairo; tel. (2) 3441337; fax (2) 3441338; e-mail hondemb@idsc.net.eg; Ambassador NELSON VALENCIA.

Hungary: 29 Sharia Muhammad Mazhar, Cairo 11211 (Zamalek); tel. (2) 27358659; fax (2) 27358648; e-mail mission.cai@kum.hu; internet mfa.gov.hu/emb/cairo; Ambassador Dr PÉTER KVECK.

India: 5 Sharia Aziz Abaza, Cairo (Zamalek); tel. (2) 27363051; fax (2) 27364038; e-mail embassy@indembcairo.com; internet www.indembcairo.com; Ambassador NAVDEEP SURI.

Indonesia: POB 1661, 13 Sharia Aicha al-Taimouria, Cairo (Garden City); tel. (2) 27947200; fax (2) 27962495; e-mail pwkcairo@access.com.eg; internet cairo.kemlu.go.id; Ambassador Dr NURFAIZI SUWANDI.

Iraq: 1 Sharia Abd al-Moneim Riad, Thawra Sq., Cairo; tel. (2) 27358087; fax (2) 27365075; e-mail caiemb@iraqmofamail.com; Ambassador ZIA HADI MAHMOUD DABBAS.

Ireland: 22 Sharia Hassan Assem, Cairo (Zamalek); tel. (2) 27358264; fax (2) 27362863; e-mail cairoembassy@dfa.ie; internet www.embassyofireland.org.eg; Ambassador ISOLDE MOYLAN.

Israel: 6 Sharia Ibn el-Malek, Cairo (Giza); tel. (2) 33321500; fax (2) 33321555; Ambassador HAIM KOREN.

Italy: 15 Sharia Abd al-Rahman Fahmi, Cairo (Garden City); tel. (2) 27943194; fax (2) 27940657; e-mail ambasciata.cairo@esteri.it; internet www.ambilcairo.esteri.it; Ambassador MAURIZIO MASSARI.

Japan: POB 500, 2nd Floor, 81 Sharia Corniche el-Nil, Maadi, Cairo; tel. (2) 25285903; fax (2) 25285906; e-mail culture@ca.mofa.go.jp; internet www.eg.emb-japan.go.jp; Ambassador TOSHIRO SUZUKI.

Jordan: 6 Sharia Basem al-Kateb, Cairo (Dokki); tel. (2) 37485566; fax (2) 37601027; e-mail cairo@fm.gov.jo; internet www.jordanembassycairo.gov.jo; Ambassador Dr BISHR KHASAWNEH.

Kazakhstan: 9 Wahib Doss St, Maadi, Cairo; tel. (2) 23809804; fax (2) 23586546; e-mail cairo@mfa.kz; Ambassador BERIK ARYN.

Kenya: POB 362, 29 Sharia al-Quds al-Sharif, Mohandessin, Cairo (Giza); tel. (2) 33453907; fax (2) 33026979; e-mail info@kenemb-cairo.com; internet kenemb-cairo.com; Ambassador DAVE ARUNGA.

Korea, Democratic People's Republic: 6 Sharia al-Saleh Ayoub, Cairo (Zamalek); tel. (2) 3408219; fax (2) 3414615; Ambassador RI HYOK-CHOL.

Korea, Republic: 3 Sharia Boulos Hanna, Cairo (Dokki); tel. (2) 3611234; fax (2) 3611238; e-mail egypt@mofa.go.kr; internet egy.mofat.go.kr; Ambassador KIM YOUNG-SO.

Kuwait: 21 Sharia Muhammad Mazhar, Cairo (Zamalek); tel. (2) 7372120; fax (2) 7371199; Ambassador SALEM GHASSAB AL-ZAMANAN.

Latvia: 8th Floor, Abou el-Feda Bldg, 3 Sharia Abou el-Feda, Cairo (Zamalek); tel. (2) 27384188; fax (2) 27384189; e-mail embassy.egypt@mfa.gov.lv; Ambassador IVETA ŠULCA.

Lebanon: 22 Sharia Mansour Muhammad, Cairo (Zamalek); tel. (2) 7382823; fax (2) 7382818; Ambassador KHALED ZIADEH.

Lesotho: 5 Sharia Ahmed el-Meleby, Cairo (Dokki); tel. (2) 33369161; fax (2) 25211437; e-mail lesotho-cairo@foreign.gov.ls; Ambassador THABO KHASIPE.

Liberia: 4th Floor, 9 Ahmad Samy el-Sayeh Sq., Mohandessin, Cairo; tel. (2) 37626794; fax (2) 37627194; e-mail liberiaembassy1@yahoo.com; Ambassador ALEXANDER WALLACE.

Libya: 4 Sharia Patrice Lumumba, Cairo; tel. (2) 4940286; fax 3934643; Ambassador MUHAMMAD FAYEZ ABD AL-AZIZ JIBRIL.

Lithuania: 23 Muhammad Mazhar, Cairo (Zamalek); tel. (2) 27366461; fax (2) 27365130; e-mail amb.eg@mfa.lt; internet eg.mfa.lt; Ambassador DAINIUS JUNEVIČIUS.

Malaysia: 21 Sharia el-Aanab, Mohandessin, Cairo (Giza); tel. (2) 37610013; fax (2) 37610216; e-mail malcairo@kln.gov.my; internet www.kln.gov.my/web/egy_cairo; Ambassador DATUK KU JAAFAR KU SHAARI.

Mali: POB 844, 3 Sharia al-Kansar, Cairo (Dokki); tel. (2) 33371641; fax (2) 33371841; e-mail ambmalicaire@yahoo.fr; Ambassador MAMADOU KABA.

Malta: 1 Sharia el-Saleh Ayoub, Cairo (Zamalek); tel. (2) 27362368; fax (2) 27362371; e-mail maltaembassy.cairo@gov.mt; internet www.foreign.gov.mt/egypt; Ambassador GEORGE CASSAR.

Mauritania: 114 Mohi el-Din, Abou-el Ezz, Mohandessin, Cairo; tel. (2) 37490671; fax (2) 37491048; Ambassador MOHAMED WELD ABDULAZIZ.

Mauritius: 1st Floor, 33 Sharia Ismail Muhammad, Cairo (Zamalek); tel. (2) 7365208; fax (2) 7365206; e-mail cairoemb@mail.gov.mu; internet cairo.mauritius.gov.mu; Ambassador D. I. FAKIM.

Mexico: 5th Floor, Apt 502–503, 17 Sharia Port Said, Maadi, 11431 Cairo; tel. (2) 23580256; fax (2) 3780059; e-mail oficial@embamexcairo.com; internet www.sre.gob.mx/egipto; Ambassador JORGE ÁLVAREZ FUENTES.

Mongolia: 14 Sharia 152, Maadi, Cairo; tel. and fax (2) 3586012; e-mail monemby@link.net; Ambassador BANZRAGCH ODONJIL.

Morocco: 10 Sharia Salah el-Din, Cairo (Zamalek); tel. (2) 27359849; fax (2) 27361937; e-mail morocemb@link.net; Ambassador MUHAMMAD SAAD AL-ALAMI.

Mozambique: 2 Sharia Tahran, Cairo (Dokki); tel. (2) 7605505; fax (2) 7486378; e-mail embamoc.egipto@minec.gov.mz; Ambassador JOSÉ ANTÓNIO ALBERTO MATSINHA.

Myanmar: 24 Sharia Muhammad Mazhar, Cairo (Zamalek); tel. (2) 27362644; fax (2) 7357712; e-mail me.cairo@gmail.com; Ambassador THET OO MAUNG.

Nepal: 23 Sharia al-Hassan, Mohandessin, Cairo (Dokki); tel. (2) 37612311; fax (2) 33374447; e-mail ne@nepalembassyegypt.com; Ambassador PRAHLAD KUMAR PRASAI.

Netherlands: 18 Sharia Hassan Sabri, Cairo (Zamalek); tel. (2) 27395500; fax (2) 27363821; e-mail kai@minbuza.nl; internet egypt.nlembassy.org; Ambassador GERARD STEEGHS.

New Zealand: North Tower, 8th Floor, Nile City Bldg, Sharia Corniche el-Nil, Cairo (Boulac); tel. (2) 24616000; fax (2) 24616099; e-mail enquiries@nzembassy.org.eg; internet www.nzembassy.com/egypt; Ambassador DAVID STRACHAN.

Niger: 101 Sharia Pyramids, Cairo (Giza); tel. (2) 3865607; fax (2) 33865690; e-mail ambanigercaire@yahoo.fr; Ambassador MOULOUD AL-HOUSSEINI.

Nigeria: 13 Sharia Gabalaya, Cairo (Zamalek); tel. (2) 27356042; fax (2) 27357359; Ambassador LAWAN GANA GUBA.

Norway: 8 Sharia el-Gezirah, Cairo (Zamalek); tel. (2) 27283900; fax (2) 27283901; e-mail emb.cairo@mfa.no; internet www.norway-egypt.org; Ambassador TOR WENNESLAND.

Oman: 52 Sharia el-Higaz, Mohandessin, Cairo; tel. (2) 27350794; fax (2) 27373188; e-mail cairo@mofa.gov.om; Ambassador Sheikh KHALIFA BIN ALI BIN ISSA AL-HARTHY.

Pakistan: 8 Sharia l-Salouli, Cairo (Dokki); tel. (2) 37487806; fax (2) 37480310; e-mail parepcairo@hotmail.com; Ambassador (vacant).

Panama: POB 62, 4A Sharia Ibn Zanki, Cairo 11211 (Zamalek); tel. (2) 27361093; fax (2) 27361092; Chargé d'affaires a.i. ROY FRANCISCO LUNA GONZÁLEZ.

Peru: 41 Sharia el-Nahda, Maadi, Cairo; tel. (2) 23590306; fax (2) 27509011; e-mail info@embaperueg.org; internet embaperueg.org; Ambassador ALBERTO GÁLVEZ DE RIVERO.

Philippines: Villa 28, Sharia 200, Cairo (Degla Maadi); tel. (2) 25213064; fax (2) 25213048; e-mail cairope@dfa.gov.ph; Ambassador CLARO S. CRISTOBAL.

Poland: 5 Sharia el-Aziz Osman, Cairo (Zamalek); tel. (2) 27367456; fax (2) 27355427; e-mail cairo.secretariat@msz.gov.pl; internet www.kair.polemb.net; Ambassador MICHAŁ MURKOCIŃSKI.

Portugal: 1 Sharia el-Saleh Ayoub, Cairo (Zamalek); tel. (2) 27350779; fax (2) 27350790; e-mail embassy@cairo.dgaccp.pt; Ambassador FERNANDO MACHADO.

Qatar: 10 Sharia al-Thamar, Midan al-Nasr, Madinet al-Mohandessin, Cairo; tel. (2) 7604693; fax (2) 7603618; e-mail qa.emb.cai@gmail.com; internet www.qatarembassyegypt.com; Ambassador SAIF BIN MUQADAM AL-BUAINAIN.

Romania: 6 Sharia el-Kamel Muhammad, Cairo (Zamalek); tel. (2) 27359546; fax (2) 27360851; e-mail roembegy@link.net; internet cairo.mae.ro; Ambassador CORNEL ALECSE.

Russia: 95 Sharia Giza, Cairo (Dokki); tel. (2) 37489353; fax (2) 37609074; e-mail rus.egypt@mail.ru; internet www.egypt.mid.ru; Ambassador SERGEI KIRPICHENKO.

Rwanda: 23 Sharia Babel, Mohandessin, Cairo (Dokki); tel. (2) 3350532; fax (2) 3351479; Ambassador (vacant).

Saudi Arabia: 2 Sharia Ahmad Nessim, Cairo (Giza); tel. (2) 7624092; fax (2) 7624091; internet embassies.gov.sa/sites/egypt; Ambassador AHMAD IBN ABD AL-AZIZ QATTAN.

Senegal: 46 Sharia Abd al-Moneim Riad, Mohandessin, Cairo (Dokki); tel. (2) 3460946; fax (2) 3461039; e-mail mamadousow@hotmail.com; Ambassador MAMADOU SOW.

Serbia: 33 Sharia Mansour Muhammad, Cairo (Zamalek); tel. (2) 27354061; fax (2) 27353913; e-mail serbia@serbiaeg.com; Ambassador DRAGAN BISENIĆ.

Singapore: 40 Sharia Adnan Omar Sedki, Cairo 11511 (Dokki); tel. (2) 37490468; fax (2) 37480562; e-mail singemb@link.net; internet www.mfa.gov.sg/cairo; Ambassador PREMJITH SADASIVAN.

Slovakia: 3 Sharia Adel Hussein Rostom, Dokki, Cairo (Giza); tel. (2) 33358240; fax (2) 33355810; e-mail emb.cairo@mzv.sk; Ambassador ANTON PINTER.

Slovenia: 6th Floor, 21 Sharia Soliman Abaza, Mohandessin, Cairo; tel. (2) 37498171; fax (2) 37497141; e-mail vka@gov.si; internet cairo.embassy.si; Ambassador Dr ROBERT KOKALJ.

Somalia: 27 Sharia el-Somal, Cairo (Dokki), Giza; tel. (2) 33374038; fax (2) 33374577; Ambassador ABDULLAHI ALI HASSAN.

South Africa: Bldg 11, Intersection Rd 200 and 203, Maadi, Cairo; tel. (2) 25353000; fax (2) 25213278; e-mail saembcai@tedata.net.eg; internet saembassyinegypt.com; Ambassador NOLUTHANDO MAYENDE-SIBIYA.

Spain: 41 Sharia Ismail Muhammad, Cairo (Zamalek); tel. (2) 27356462; fax (2) 27352132; e-mail emb.elcairo@maec.es; internet www.exteriores.gob.es/embajadas/elcairo; Ambassador FIDEL SENDAGORTA GÓMEZ DEL CAMPILLO.

Sri Lanka: POB 1157, 8 Sharia Sri Lanka, Cairo (Zamalek); tel. (2) 27350047; fax (2) 27367138; e-mail slembare@tedata.net.eg; internet www.slembassyeg.org; Ambassador SUDANTHA GANEGAMA ARACHCHI.

Sudan: 4 Sharia el-Ibrahimi, Cairo (Garden City); tel. (2) 27949661; fax (2) 27942693; Ambassador KAMAL HASSAN ALI.

Sweden: POB 131, 13 Sharia Muhammad Mazhar, Cairo (Zamalek); tel. (2) 27289200; fax (2) 27354357; e-mail ambassaden.kairo@gov.se; internet www.swedenabroad.com/cairo; Ambassador CHARLOTTA SPARRE.

Switzerland: POB 633, 10 Sharia Abd al-Khalek Sarwat, 11511 Cairo; tel. (2) 25758284; fax (2) 25745236; e-mail cai.vertretung@eda.admin.ch; internet www.eda.admin.ch/cairo; Ambassador MARKUS LEITNER.

Syria: 24 Sharia Kamel el-Shnawi, Cairo (Garden City); tel. (2) 27924325; fax (2) 27924326; e-mail syr_emb@syriaenembassyeg.com; Ambassador YOUSUF AL-AHMAD.

Tanzania: 10 Anas Ibn Malek St, Mohandessin, Cairo; tel. (2) 3374155; fax (2) 3374446; e-mail tanrepcairo@infinity.com.eg; Ambassador MUHAMMAD HAJI.

Thailand: 9 Tiba St, Cairo (Dokki); tel. (2) 37603553; fax (2) 37605076; e-mail thaitccairo@depthai.go.eg; internet www.thaiembassy.org/cairo/en; Ambassador PEERASAK CHANTAVARIN.

Tunisia: 26 Sharia el-Jazirah, Cairo (Zamalek); tel. (2) 27368962; fax 27362479; e-mail tunisiacairo@link.net; Ambassador ABDELKADER AL-HAJJAR.

Turkey: 25 Sharia Felaki, Cairo (Bab el-Louk); tel. (2) 27978400; fax (2) 27978477; e-mail embassy.cairo@mfa.gov.tr; internet cairo.emb.mfa.gov.tr; diplomatic relations downgraded to level of chargé d'affaires in late Nov. 2013.

Uganda: 66 Rd 10, Maadi, Cairo; tel. (2) 3802514; fax (2) 3802504; e-mail ugembco@link.net; internet www.uganda-embassy.com; Ambassador RICHARD LAUS ANGUALIA.

Ukraine: 50 Sharia 83, Maadi, Cairo; tel. (2) 23786871; fax (2) 23786873; e-mail emb_eg@mfa.gov.ua; internet mfa.gov.ua/egypt/en; Ambassador YEVHEN KYRYLENKO.

United Arab Emirates: 4 Sharia Ibn Sina, Cairo (Giza); tel. (2) 37766101; fax 35700844; e-mail cairo@mofa.gov.ae; internet uae-embassy.ae/eg; Ambassador MUHAMMAD BIN NAKHIRA AL-DAHERI.

United Kingdom: 7 Sharia Ahmad Ragheb, Cairo (Garden City); tel. (2) 27916000; fax (2) 27916135; e-mail information.cairo@fco.gov.uk; internet ukinegypt.fco.gov.uk; Ambassador JAMES WATT.

USA: 5 Sharia Tawfik Diab, Cairo (Garden City); tel. (2) 27973300; fax (2) 27973200; e-mail pressinfoegypt@state.gov; internet cairo.usembassy.gov; Chargé d'affaires MARC J. SIEVERS.

Uruguay: 6 Sharia Lotfallah, Cairo (Zamalek); tel. (2) 7353589; fax (2) 7368123; e-mail urugemb@idsc.gov.eg; Ambassador CÉSAR WALTER FERRER BURLE.

Uzbekistan: 18 Sharia Sad el-Aali, Cairo (Dokki); tel. (2) 3361723; fax (2) 3361722; e-mail uzembas@internetegypt.com; Ambassador MINOVAROV SHAAZIM SHAISLAMOVICH.

Venezuela: 43, Rd 18, el-Nahda Sq., Maadi, Cairo; tel. (2) 9812141; fax (2) 3809291; e-mail embvenez@tedata.net.eg; internet www.embavenezegypt.com; Ambassador VÍCTOR R. CARAZO.

Viet Nam: Villa 47, Sharia Ahmed Heshmat, Cairo (Zamalek); tel. (2) 7364326; fax (2) 7366091; e-mail vnembcairoeg@yahoo.com.vn; internet www.vietnamembassy-egypt.org; Ambassador DAO THANH CHUNG.

Yemen: 28 Sharia Amean al-Rafai, Cairo (Dokki); tel. (2) 3614224; fax (2) 3604815; e-mail info@yemenembassy-cairo.com; internet www.yemenembassy-cairo.com; Ambassador ABD AL-WALI ABD AL-WALITH AL-SHAMIRI.

Zimbabwe: 40 Sharia Ghaza, Mohandessin, Cairo; tel. (2) 33059742; fax (2) 33059741; e-mail zimcairo@thewayout.net; Ambassador MARGARET MUSKWE (designate).

Judicial System

The Courts of Law in Egypt are principally divided into two juridical court systems: Courts of General Jurisdiction and Administrative Courts. Since 1969 the Supreme Constitutional Court has been at the top of the Egyptian judicial structure.

Supreme Constitutional Court: Corniche el-Nil, Maadi, Cairo; tel. (2) 5246323; fax (2) 7958048; e-mail info@sccourt.gov.eg; has specific jurisdiction over: (i) judicial review of the constitutionality of laws and regulations; (ii) resolution of positive and negative jurisdictional conflicts and determination of the competent court between the different juridical court systems, e.g. Courts of General Jurisdiction and Administrative Courts, as well as other bodies exercising judicial competence; (iii) determination of disputes over the enforcement of two final but contradictory judgments rendered by two courts each belonging to a different juridical court system; (iv) rendering binding interpretation of laws or decree laws in the event of a dispute in the application of said laws or decree laws, always provided that such a dispute is of a gravity requiring conformity of interpretation under the Constitution; Pres. ADLI MAHMOUD MANSOUR.

Court of Cassation: f. 1931; highest court of general jurisdiction. Its sessions are held in Cairo. Final judgments rendered by Courts of Appeal in criminal and civil litigation may be petitioned to the Court of Cassation by the Defendant or the Public Prosecutor in criminal litigation and by any of the parties in interest in civil litigation on grounds of defective application or interpretation of the law as stated in the challenged judgment, on grounds of irregularity of form or procedure, or violation of due process, and on grounds of defective reasoning of judgment rendered. The Court of Cassation is composed of the President, 41 Vice-Presidents and 92 Justices.

Courts of Appeal: Cairo; Each Court of Appeal has geographical jurisdiction over one or more of the governorates of Egypt, and is divided into Criminal and Civil Chambers. The Criminal Chambers try felonies, and the Civil Chambers hear appeals filed against such judgment rendered by the Tribunals of First Instance where the law so stipulates. Each Chamber is composed of three Superior Judges. Each Court of Appeal is composed of the President, and sufficient numbers of Vice-Presidents and Superior Judges.

Tribunals of First Instance: In each governorate there are one or more Tribunals of First Instance, each of which is divided into several Chambers for criminal and civil litigations. Each Chamber is composed of: (a) a presiding judge, and (b) two sitting judges. A Tribunal of First Instance hears, as an Appellate Court, certain litigations as provided under the law.

District Tribunals: Each is a one-judge ancillary Chamber of a Tribunal of First Instance, having jurisdiction over minor civil and criminal litigations in smaller districts within the jurisdiction of such a Tribunal of First Instance.

Public Prosecution: Cairo; represented at all levels of the Courts of General Jurisdiction in all criminal litigations and also in certain civil litigations as required by the law. It also controls and supervises enforcement of criminal law judgments; Prosecutor-General HISHAM BARAKAT.

Administrative Courts System (Conseil d'Etat): has jurisdiction over litigations involving the State or any of its governmental agencies. It is divided into two courts: the Administrative Courts and the Judicial Administrative Courts, at the top of which is the High Administrative Court; Pres. Hon. SAMIR ABD AL-HALIM AHMAD AL-BADAWI.

The State Council: an independent judicial body, which has the authority to make decisions in administrative disputes and disciplinary cases within the judicial system; Chair. MUHAMMAD AHMAD EL-HUSSEINI.

The Supreme Judicial Council: reinstituted in 1984, having been abolished in 1969. It exists to guarantee the independence of the judicial system from outside interference and is consulted with regard to draft laws organizing the affairs of the judicial bodies; Pres. and Chair. HAMAD ABDULLAH.

Religion

According to the 1986 census, some 94% of Egyptians were Muslims (and almost all of these followed Sunni tenets). According to government figures published in the same year, there were about 2m. Copts (a figure contested by Coptic sources, whose estimates ranged between 6m. and 7m.), forming the largest religious minority, and about 1m. members of other Christian groups. A small Jewish minority remains in Egypt.

ISLAM

There is a Higher Council for the Islamic Call, on which sit: the Grand Sheikh of al-Azhar (Chair.); the Minister of Awqaf (Islamic Endowments); the President and Vice-President of Al-Azhar University; the Grand Mufti of Egypt; and the Secretary-General of the Higher Council for Islamic Affairs.

Grand Sheikh of Al-Azhar: Sheikh AHMED MUHAMMAD EL-TAYEB.

Grand Mufti of Egypt: Sheikh ALI GOMAA.

CHRISTIANITY

Orthodox Churches

Armenian Apostolic Orthodox Church: POB 48, 179 Sharia Ramses, Faggalah, Cairo; tel. (2) 25901385; fax (2) 25906671; e-mail armpatrcai@yahoo.com; Prelate Bishop ASHOT MNATSAKANIAN; 7,000 mems.

Coptic Orthodox Church: St Mark's Cathedral, POB 9035, Anba Ruess, 222 Sharia Ramses, Abbassia, Cairo; tel. (2) 2857889; fax (2) 2825683; e-mail coptpope@copticpope.org; internet www.copticpope.org; f. AD 61; Patriarch Pope TAWADROS II; c. 13m. followers in Egypt, Sudan, other African countries, the USA, Canada, Australia, Europe and the Middle East.

Greek Orthodox Patriarchate: POB 2006, Alexandria; tel. (3) 4868595; fax (3) 4875684; e-mail patriarchate@greekorthodox-alexandria.org; internet www.greekorthodox-alexandria.org; f. AD 43; Pope and Patriarch of Alexandria and All Africa THEODOROS II; 3m. mems.

The Roman Catholic Church

Armenian Rite

The Armenian Catholic diocese of Alexandria is suffragan to the Patriarchate of Cilicia. The Patriarch is resident in Beirut, Lebanon.

Bishop of Alexandria: Rt Rev. KRIKOR-OKOSDINOS COUSSA, Patriarcat Arménien Catholique, 36 Sharia Muhammad Sabri Abou Alam, 11121 Cairo; tel. (2) 23938429; fax (2) 23932025; e-mail pacal@tedata.net.eg.

Chaldean Rite

Bishop of Cairo: Rt Rev. YOUSUF IBRAHIM SARRAF, Evêché Chaldéen, Basilique-Sanctuaire Notre Dame de Fatima, 141 Sharia Nouzha, 11316 Cairo (Heliopolis); tel. and fax (2) 26355718; e-mail fatimasarraf@yahoo.com.

Coptic Rite

Egypt comprises the Coptic Catholic Patriarchate of Alexandria and five dioceses.

Patriarch of Alexandria: Cardinal ANTONIOS NAGUIB, Patriarcat Copte Catholique, POB 69, 34 Sharia Ibn Sandar, Koubbeh Bridge, 11712 Cairo; tel. (2) 22571740; fax (2) 24545766; e-mail p_coptocattolico@yahoo.it.

Latin Rite

Egypt comprises the Apostolic Vicariate of Alexandria (incorporating Heliopolis and Port Said).

Vicar Apostolic: Rt Rev. ADEL ZAKY, 10 Sharia Sidi el-Metwalli, Alexandria; tel. (3) 4876065; fax (3) 4878169; e-mail latinvic@link.net.

Maronite Rite

Bishop of Cairo: Rt Rev. FRANÇOIS EID, Evêché Maronite, 15 Sharia Hamdi, Daher, 11271 Cairo; tel. (2) 26137373; fax (2) 25939610; e-mail feid43@yahoo.com.

Melkite Rite

His Beatitude Grégoire III Laham (resident in Damascus, Syria) is the Greek-Melkite Patriarch of Antioch and all the East, of Alexandria, and of Jerusalem.

Patriarchal Exarchate of Egypt and Sudan: Greek Melkite Catholic Patriarchate, 16 Sharia Daher, 11271 Cairo; tel. (2) 25905790; fax (2) 25935398; e-mail grecmelkitecath_egy@hotmail.com; 6,200 adherents (31 December 2007); General Patriarchal Vicar for Egypt and Sudan Most Rev. Archbishop GEORGES BAKAR (Titular Archbishop of Pelusium).

Syrian Rite

Bishop of Cairo: Rt Rev. CLÉMENT-JOSEPH HANNOUCHE, Evêché Syrien Catholique, 46 Sharia Daher, 11271 Cairo; tel. (2) 25901234; fax (2) 25923932.

The Anglican Communion

The Anglican diocese of Egypt, suspended in 1958, was revived in 1974 and became part of the Episcopal Church in Jerusalem and the Middle East, formally inaugurated in January 1976. The Province has four dioceses: Jerusalem, Egypt, Cyprus and the Gulf, and Iran, and its President is the Bishop in Egypt. The Bishop in Egypt has jurisdiction also over the Anglican chaplaincies in Algeria, Djibouti, Eritrea, Ethiopia, Libya, Somalia and Tunisia.

Bishop in Egypt: Rt Rev. Dr MOUNEER HANNA ANIS, Diocesan Office, POB 87, 5 Sharia Michel Lutfalla, 11211 Cairo (Zamalek); tel. (2) 7380829; fax (2) 7358941; e-mail diocese@link.net; internet www.dioceseofegypt.org.

Other Christian Churches

Coptic Evangelical Organization for Social Services: POB 162, 11811 El Panorama, Cairo; tel. (2) 26221425; fax (2) 26221434; e-mail gm@ceoss.org.eg; internet www.ceoss.org.eg; Chair. Dr MERVAT AKHNOUKH ABSAKHROUN; Dir-Gen. Dr NABIL SAMUEL ABADIR.

Other denominations active in Egypt include the Coptic Evangelical Church (Synod of the Nile) and the Union of the Armenian Evangelical Churches in the Near East.

JUDAISM

The 1986 census recorded 794 Jews in Egypt, and there were reported to be around 40 remaining by 2013.

Jewish Community: Main Synagogue, Shaar Hashamayim 17, Adly St, Cairo; tel. (2) 4824613; fax (2) 7369639; e-mail bassatine@yahoo.com; f. 19th century; Pres. MAGDA HAROUN.

The Press

Despite a fairly high illiteracy rate in Egypt, the country's press is well developed. Cairo is one of the region's largest publishing centres.

All newspapers and magazines are supervised, according to law, by the Supreme Press Council. The four major state-owned publishing houses of Al-Ahram Establishment, Dar al-Hilal, Dar Akhbar el-Yom and El-Tahrir Printing and Publishing House operate as separate entities and compete with each other commercially.

DAILIES

Al-Ahram (The Pyramids): Sharia al-Galaa, Cairo 11511; tel. (2) 5801600; fax (2) 5786023; e-mail ahramdaily@ahram.org.eg; internet www.ahram.org.eg; f. 1875; morning, incl. Sun.; Arabic; international edn publ. in London, United Kingdom; North American edn publ. in New York, USA; Chair. ABD EL-MONEIM SAÏD; Chief Editor ABD EL-NASSER SALAMA; circ. 900,000 (weekdays), 1.1m. (Fri.).

Al-Ahram al-Massa'i (The Evening Al-Ahram): Sharia al-Galaa, Cairo 11511; e-mail massai@ahram.org.eg; internet massai.ahram.org.eg; f. 1990; evening; Arabic; Editor-in-Chief MURSI ATALLAH.

Al-Ahrar: 58 Manshyet al-Sadr, Kobry al-Kobba, Cairo; tel. (2) 4823046; fax (2) 4823027; e-mail sawtalahrar@hotmail.com; internet www.sawt-alahrar.net; f. 1977; organ of Liberal Party; Editor-in-Chief SALAH QABADAYA.

Al-Akhbar (The News): Dar Akhbar el-Yom, 6 Sharia al-Sahafa, Cairo; tel. (2) 25782600; fax (2) 25782530; e-mail akhbarelyom@akhbarelyom.org; internet www.elakhbar.org.eg; f. 1952; Arabic; Chair. MUHAMMAD MAHDI FADLI; Editor-in-Chief MUHAMMAD HASSAN EL-BANNA; circ. 850,000.

Arev: 10 Sharia Menouf, Cairo; tel. (2) 24170204; e-mail arev@intouch.com; f. 1915; evening; Armenian; official organ of the Armenian Liberal Democratic Party; Editor ASSBED ARTINIAN.

Al-Dustour (The Constitution): nr Kobri al-Gamaa, Cairo (Giza); tel. (2) 33379008; fax (2) 33379766; internet www.dostor.org; f. 1995; banned by the authorities in 1998; relaunched in 2005; daily and weekly edns; independent; Editor-in-Chief IBRAHIM ISSA.

The Egyptian Gazette: 111–115 Sharia Ramses, Cairo; tel. (2) 5783333; fax (2) 5784646; e-mail ask@egyptiangazette.net.eg; internet www.egyptiangazette.net.eg; f. 1880; morning; English; Chair. MUHAMMAD ABD AL-HADEED; Editor-in-Chief RAMADAN A. KADER; circ. 90,000.

Al-Gomhouriya (The Republic): 24 Sharia Zakaria Ahmad, Cairo; tel. (2) 25781515; fax (2) 25781717; e-mail eltahrir@eltahrir.net; internet www.algomhuria.net.eg; f. 1953; morning; Arabic; mainly economic affairs; Chair. MUHAMMAD ABU HADID; Editor-in-Chief ABD EL-AZIM EL-BABLI; circ. 800,000.

Al-Masry al-Youm: Cairo; tel. (2) 27980100; fax (2) 27926331; e-mail admin@almasry-alyoum.com; internet www.almasry-alyoum.com; f. 2003; Arabic; independent, privately owned; Editor-in-Chief MAGDY AL-GALAD; circ. 100,000.

Al-Misaa' (The Evening): 24 Sharia Zakaria Ahmad, Cairo; tel. (2) 5781010; fax (2) 5784747; e-mail eltahrir@eltahrir.net; internet www.almessa.net.eg; f. 1956; evening; Arabic; political, social and sport; Editor-in-Chief MUHAMMAD FOUDAH; Man. Dir ABD AL-HAMROSE; circ. 450,000.

Le Progrès Egyptien: 24 Sharia Zakaria Ahmad, Cairo; tel. (2) 5783333; fax (2) 5781110; e-mail ask@progres.net.eg; internet www.progres.net.eg; f. 1893; morning incl. Sun.; French; Chair. ALI HACHEM; Editor-in-Chief AHMED AL-BARDISSI; circ. 60,000.

La Réforme: 8 Passage Sherif, Alexandria; French.

Al-Wafd: 1 Sharia Boulos Hanna, Cairo (Dokki); tel. (2) 33383111; fax (2) 33359135; e-mail contact@alwafd.org; internet www.alwafd.org; f. 1984; organ of the New Wafd Party; Editor-in-Chief ABBAS AL-TARABILI; circ. 220,000.

PERIODICALS

Al-Ahaly (The People): Sharia Kareem al-Dawli, Tala'at Harb Sq., Cairo; tel. (2) 7786583; fax (2) 3900412; internet www.al-ahaly.com; f. 1978; weekly; publ. by Nat. Progressive Unionist Party; Chair. LOTFI WAKID; Editor-in-Chief ABD AL-BAKOURY.

Al-Ahram al-Arabi: Sharia al-Galaa, Cairo 11511; tel. (2) 5786100; e-mail arabi@ahram.org.eg; internet arabi.ahram.org.eg; f. 1997; weekly (Sat.); Arabic; political, social and economic affairs; Editor-in-Chief ABD EL-ATTI MUHAMMAD.

Al-Ahram al-Dimouqratiyah (Democracy Review): Sharia al-Galaa, Cairo 11511; tel. (2) 25786960; fax (2) 27705238; e-mail democracy@ahram.org.eg; internet democracy.ahram.org.eg; f. 2001; quarterly; politics; Arabic and English; publ. by Al-Ahram Establishment; Editor-in-Chief HALA MUSTAFA.

Al-Ahram Hebdo: POB 1057, Sharia al-Galaa, Cairo 11511; tel. (2) 27703100; fax (2) 27703314; e-mail hebdo@ahram.org.eg; internet hebdo.ahram.org.eg; f. 1993; weekly (Wed.); French; publ. by Al-Ahram Establishment; Editor-in-Chief MUHAMMAD SALMAWI.

Al-Ahram al-Iqtisadi (The Economic Al-Ahram): Sharia al-Galaa, Cairo 11511; tel. (2) 25786100; fax (2) 25786833; e-mail ik@ahram.org.eg; internet ik.ahram.org.eg; Arabic; weekly (Mon.); economic and political affairs; publ. by Al-Ahram Establishment; Chief Editor ISSAM RIFA'AT; circ. 10,000.

Al-Ahram Weekly (The Pyramids): Al-Ahram Bldg, Sharia al-Galaa, Cairo 11511; tel. (2) 5786100; fax (2) 5786833; e-mail weeklyweb@ahram.org.eg; internet weekly.ahram.org.eg; f. 1989; English; weekly; publ. by Al-Ahram Establishment; Man. Editor GALAL NASSER; Editor-in-Chief ASSEM EL-KERSH; circ. 150,000.

Akhbar al-Adab: 6 Sharia al-Sahafa, Cairo; tel. (2) 5795620; fax (2) 5782510; e-mail akhbarelyom@akhbarelyom.org; internet www.akhbarelyom.org.eg/adab; f. 1993; literature and arts for young people; Editor-in-Chief ABLA AL-RUWAYNI.

Akhbar al-Hawadith: 6 Sharia al-Sahafa, Cairo; tel. (2) 5782600; fax (2) 5782510; e-mail akhbarelyom@akhbarelyom.org; internet www.akhbarelyom.org.eg/hawadeth; f. 1993; weekly; crime reports; Editor-in-Chief MUHAMMAD BARAKAT.

Akhbar al-Nogoom: 6 Sharia al-Sahafa, Cairo; tel. (2) 5782600; fax (2) 5782510; e-mail akhbarelyom@akhbarelyom.org; internet www.akhbarelyom.org.eg/nogoom; f. 1991; weekly; theatre and film news; Editor-in-Chief AMAL OSMAN.

Akhbar al-Riadah: 6 Sharia al-Sahafa, Cairo; tel. (2) 5782600; fax (2) 5782510; e-mail akhbarelyom@akhbarelyom.org; internet www.akhbarelyom.org.eg/riada; f. 1990; weekly; sport; Editor-in-Chief IBRAHIM HEGAZY.

Akhbar al-Sayarat: 6 Sharia al-Sahafa, Cairo; e-mail akhbarelyom@akhbarelyom.org; internet www.akhbarelyom.org.eg/sayarat; f. 1998; car magazine; Editor-in-Chief SOLIMAN QENAWI.

Akhbar el-Yom (Daily News): 6 Sharia al-Sahafa, Cairo; tel. (2) 25782600; fax (2) 25782520; e-mail akhbarelyom@akhbarelyom.org; internet www.akhbarelyom.org.eg; f. 1944; weekly (Sat.); Arabic; Chair. MUHAMMAD MAHDI FADLI; Editor-in-Chief SOLIMAN EL-QENAWI; circ. 1,184,611.

Akher Sa'a (Last Hour): Dar Akhbar el-Yom, Sharia al-Sahafa, Cairo; tel. (2) 5782600; fax (2) 5782530; e-mail akhbarelyom@akhbarelyom.org; internet www.akhbarelyom.org.eg/akhersaa; f. 1934; weekly (Sun.); Arabic; independent; consumer and news magazine; Editor-in-Chief MAHMOUD SALAH; circ. 150,000.

Aqidaty (My Faith): 24–26 Sharia Zakaria Ahmad, Cairo; tel. (2) 5783333; fax (2) 5781110; e-mail eltahrir@eltahrir.net; internet www.aqidati.net.eg; weekly; Arabic; Islamic newspaper; Editor-in-Chief ABD AL-RAOUF EL-SAYED; circ. 300,000.

Business Monthly: 33 Soliman Abaza St, Cairo (Giza); tel. (2) 33381050; fax (2) 33381060; e-mail publications@amcham.org.eg; internet www.amcham.org.eg/resources_publications/publications/business_monthly; f. 1985; English; monthly; business; publ. by the American Chamber of Commerce in Egypt; Editor-in-Chief BERTIL G. PETERSON; circ. 9,000.

Business Today Egypt: 3A Sharia 199, IBA Media Bldg, Degla, Maadi, Cairo; tel. (2) 27555000; fax (2) 27555050; e-mail editor@businesstodayegypt.com; internet www.businesstodayegypt.com; f. 1994; English; monthly; business, economics and politics; publ. by IBA Media Group; Editor PATRICK FITZPATRICK.

Al-Da'wa (The Call): Cairo; monthly; Arabic; organ of the Muslim Brotherhood.

Egypt Today: 3A Sharia 199, IBA Media Bldg, Degla, Maadi, Cairo; tel. (2) 27555000; fax (2) 27555050; e-mail editor@egypttoday.com; internet www.egypttoday.com; f. 1979; monthly; English; current affairs; publ. by IBA Media Group; Editor-in-Chief MADELEINE HARRISON; circ. 11,500–14,500.

Egyptian Cotton Gazette: POB 1772, 12 Muhammad Talaat Nooman St, Ramel Station, Alexandria; tel. (3) 4806971; fax (3) 4873002; e-mail alcotexa@tedata.net.eg; internet www.alcotexa.org; f. 1947; 2 a year; English; organ of the Alexandria Cotton Exporters' Assen; Chief Editor GALAL AL-REFAI.

El-Elm Magazine (Sciences): 24 Sharia Zakaria Ahmad, Cairo; tel. (2) 5781010; fax (2) 5784747; e-mail ask@elm.net.eg; internet www.elm.net.eg; f. 1976; monthly; Arabic; publ. with the Academy of Scientific Research in Egypt; circ. 70,000.

The Employer: Villa 126, 5th Settlement First Zone, First District, New Cairo; tel. and fax (2) 24189939; e-mail info@the-employer.com; internet www.the-employer.net; English; bi-monthly; employment; Man. Dir DINA MAKKAWI.

El-Fagr (The Dawn): Cairo; tel. (2) 33442306; fax (2) 33032344; e-mail info@elfagr.net; internet www.elfagr.org; f. 2005; Arabic; weekly; independent; Editor-in-Chief ADEL HAMMOUDA.

El Gouna Magazine: 66 Abu el-Mahasen el-Shazli St, 4th Floor, Agouza, Cairo; tel. (2) 33034654; e-mail editor@elgounamag.com; internet www.elgounamag.com; f. 2000; English; quarterly; lifestyle; Gen. Man. MARYSE RAAD.

Hawa'a (Eve): Dar al-Hilal, 16 Sharia Muhammad Ezz el-Arab, Cairo 11511; tel. (2) 3625450; fax (2) 3625469; f. 1892; weekly (Sat.); Arabic; women's magazine; Chief Editor EKBAL BARAKA; circ. 210,502.

Al-Hilal: Dar al-Hilal, 16 Sharia Muhammad Ezz el-Arab, Cairo 11511; tel. (2) 3625450; fax (2) 3625469; f. 1895; monthly; Arabic; literary; Editor MAIDI AL-SAYID AL-DAQAQ.

Horreyati: 24 Sharia Zakaria Ahmad, Cairo; tel. (2) 5781010; fax (2) 5784747; e-mail eltahrir@eltahrir.net; internet www.horreyati.net.eg; f. 1990; weekly; social, cultural and sport; Editor-in-Chief MUHAMMAD NOUR EL-DIN; circ. 250,000.

Al-Kawakeb (The Stars): Dar al-Hilal, 16 Sharia Muhammad Ezz el-Arab, Cairo 11511; tel. (2) 3625450; fax (2) 3625469; f. 1952; weekly; Arabic; film magazine; Editor-in-Chief FAWZI MUHAMMAD IBRAHIM; circ. 86,381.

El-Keraza (The Sermon): St Mark's Cathedral, POB 9035, Anba Ruess, 222 Sharia Ramses, Abbassia, Cairo; e-mail coptpope@tecmina.com; internet www.copticpope.org; fortnightly newspaper of the Coptic Orthodox Church; Arabic and English.

Al-Kora wal-Malaeb (Football and Playgrounds): 24 Sharia Zakaria Ahmad, Cairo; tel. (2) 5783333; fax (2) 5784747; internet www.koura.net.eg; f. 1976; weekly; Arabic; sport; circ. 150,000.

Al-Liwa' al-Islami (Islamic Standard): 11 Sharia Sherif Pasha, Cairo; f. 1982; weekly; Arabic; govt paper to promote official view of Islamic revivalism; Propr AHMAD HAMZA; Editor MUHAMMAD ALI SHETA; circ. 30,000.

Magallat al-Mohandessin (The Engineer's Magazine): 30 Sharia Ramses, Cairo; e-mail info@eea.org.eg; internet www.eea.org.eg; f. 1945; publ. by The Engineers' Syndicate; 10 a year; Arabic and English; Editor and Sec. MAHMOUD SAMI ABD AL-KAWI.

Medical Journal of Cairo University: Qasr el-Eini Hospital, Sharia Qasr el-Eini, Cairo; tel. and fax (2) 3655768; internet www.medicaljournalofcairouniversity.com; f. 1933; Qasr el-Eini Clinical Society; quarterly; English; Editor-in-Chief AHMAD SAMEH FARID.

The Middle East Observer: 41 Sharia Sherif, Cairo; tel. and fax (2) 3939732; e-mail info@meobserver.com; internet middleeastobserver.com; f. 1954; weekly; English; specializes in economics of Middle East and African markets; also publishes supplements on law, foreign trade and tenders; agent for IMF, UN and IDRC publs, distributor of World Bank publs; Publr AHMAD FODA; Chief Editor HESHAM A. RAOUF; circ. 20,000.

Al-Mussawar: Dar al-Hilal, 16 Sharia Muhammad Ezz el-Arab, Cairo 11511; tel. (2) 3625450; fax (2) 3625469; f. 1924; weekly; Arabic; news; Chair. and Editor-in-Chief ABD AL-KADER SHUHAYIB; circ. 130,423.

Nesf al-Donia: Sharia al-Galaa, Cairo 11511; tel. (2) 5786100; internet www.ahram.org.eg; f. 1990; weekly; Arabic; women's magazine; publ. by Al-Ahram Establishment; Editor-in-Chief AFKAR EL-KHARADLI.

October: Dar al-Maaref, 1119 Sharia Corniche el-Nil, Cairo; tel. (2) 25777077; fax (2) 25744999; internet www.octobermag.com; f. 1976; weekly; Arabic; Chair. and Editor-in-Chief ISMAIL MUNTASSIR; circ. 140,500.

Al-Omal (The Workers): 90 Sharia al-Galaa, Cairo; internet www.etufegypt.com; weekly; Arabic; publ. by the Egyptian Trade Union Federation; Chief Editor AHMAD HARAK.

Le Progrès Dimanche: 24 Sharia al-Galaa, Cairo; tel. (2) 5781010; fax (2) 5784747; e-mail ask@progres.net.eg; internet leprogresdimanche.newspaperdirect.com; weekly; French; Sun.

edition of *Le Progrès Egyptien*; Editor-in-Chief KHALED ANWAR BAKIR; circ. 35,000.

La Revue d'Egypte: 3A Sharia 199, IBA Media Bldg, Degla, Maadi, Cairo; tel. (2) 27555000; fax (2) 27555050; e-mail courrier@iba-media.com; internet www.larevuedegypte.com; f. 2002; monthly; French; current affairs, culture, lifestyle; publ. by IBA Media Group; Editor-in-Chief FRÉDÉRIC MIGEON.

Rose al-Yousuf: 89A Sharia Qasr el-Eini, Cairo; tel. (2) 7923514; fax (2) 7925540; e-mail info@rosaonline.net; internet www.rosaonline.net; f. 1925; weekly; Arabic; political; circulates throughout all Arab countries; Editor-in-Chief ABDULLAH KAMAL EL-SAYED; circ. 35,000.

Sabah al-Kheir (Good Morning): 89A Sharia Qasr el-Eini, Cairo; tel. (2) 27950367; fax (2) 27923509; e-mail noor@rosaonline.net; internet www.rosaonline.net/Sabah; f. 1956; weekly (Tue.); Arabic; light entertainment; Chief Editor MUHAMMAD ABD AL-NOUR; circ. 70,000.

Al-Shaab (The People): 313 Sharia Port Said, Sayeda Zeinab, Cairo; tel. (2) 3909716; fax (2) 3900283; e-mail elshaab@idsc.gov.eg; internet www.alshaab.com; f. 1979; bi-weekly (Tue. and Fri.); organ of Socialist Labour Party; pro-Islamist; Editor-in-Chief MAGDI AHMAD HUSSEIN; circ. 130,000.

Shashati (My Screen): 24 Sharia Zakaria Ahmad, Cairo; tel. (2) 5781010; fax (2) 5784747; e-mail eltahrir@eltahrir.net; internet www.shashati.net.eg; weekly; art, culture, fashion and television news.

Al-Siyassa al-Dawliya: Al-Ahram Bldg, 12th Floor, Sharia al-Galaa, Cairo 11511; tel. (2) 25786071; fax (2) 25792899; e-mail siyassa@ahram.org.eg; internet www.siyassa.org.eg; f. 1965; quarterly; politics and foreign affairs; publ. by Al-Ahram Establishment; Man. Editor KAREN ABOUL KHEIR; Editor-in-Chief MUHAMMAD ABD EL-SALAM.

Tabibak al-Khass (Family Doctor): Dar al-Hilal, 16 Sharia Muhammad Ezz el-Arab, Cairo; tel. (2) 3625473; fax (2) 3625442; monthly; Arabic.

Watani (My Country): 27 Sharia Abd al-Khalek Sarwat, Cairo; tel. (2) 23927201; fax (2) 23935946; e-mail watani@watani.com.eg; internet www.wataninet.com; f. 1958; weekly (Sun.); Arabic and English, with French supplement; independent newspaper addressing Egyptians in general and the Christian Copts in particular; Editor-in-Chief YOUSSEF SIDHOM; circ. 60,000–100,000.

NEWS AGENCY

Middle East News Agency (MENA): POB 1165, 17 Sharia Hoda Sharawi, Cairo; tel. (2) 3933000; fax (2) 3935055; e-mail newsroom@mena.org.eg; internet www.mena.org.eg; f. 1955; regular service in Arabic, English and French; Chair. and Editor-in-Chief ABDULLAH HASSAN ABD AL-FATTAH.

PRESS ASSOCIATIONS

Egyptian Press Syndicate: Cairo; Chair. MAKRAM MUHAMMAD AHMED.

Foreign Press Association: 2 Sharia Ahmad Ragheb, Cairo (Garden City); tel. (2) 27943727; fax (2) 27943747; e-mail info@fpaegypt.net; internet www.fpaegypt.net; f. 1972; Chair. VOLKHARD WINDFUHR.

Publishers

The General Egyptian Book Organization: POB 235, Sharia Corniche el-Nil, Cairo (Boulac) 11221; tel. (2) 25779283; fax (2) 25789316; e-mail info@egyptianbook.org.eg; internet www.egyptianbook.org.eg; f. 1961; affiliated to the Ministry of Culture; editing, publishing and distribution; organizer of Cairo International Book Fair; Chair. AHMED MEGAHED; Gen. Dir AHMAD SALAH ZAKI.

Al-Ahram Establishment: Al-Ahram Bldg, 6 Sharia al-Galaa, Cairo 11511; tel. (2) 5786100; fax (2) 5786023; e-mail ahram@ahram.org.eg; internet www.ahram.org.eg; f. 1875; state-owned; publishes newspapers, magazines and books, incl. *Al-Ahram*; Chair. ABD EL-MONEIM SAÏD; Dep. Chair. and Gen. Man. ALI GHONEIM.

Dar Akhbar el-Yom: 6 Sharia al-Sahafa, Cairo; tel. (2) 5748100; fax (2) 5748895; e-mail akhbarelyom@akhbarelyom.org; internet www.akhbarelyom.org.eg; f. 1944; state-owned; publs include *Al-Akhbar* (daily), *Akhbar el-Yom* (weekly) and *Akher Sa'a* (weekly); Chair. MUHAMMAD MAHDI FADLI.

American University in Cairo Press: 113 Sharia Qasr el-Eini, POB 2511, Cairo 11511; tel. (2) 27976926; fax (2) 27941440; e-mail aucpress@aucegypt.edu; internet aucpress.com; f. 1960; political history, economics, Egyptology, and Arabic literature in English translation; Dir Dr NIGEL FLETCHER-JONES.

Boustany's Publishing House: 4 Sharia Aly Tawfik Shousha, Cairo (Nasr City) 11371; tel. and fax (2) 2623085; e-mail boustany@link.net; internet www.boustanys.com; f. 1900; fiction, poetry, history, biography, philosophy, language, literature, politics, religion, archaeology and Egyptology; Chief Exec. FADWA BOUSTANY.

Elias Modern Publishing House: 1 Sharia Kenisset al-Rum El-Kathulik, Daher, Cairo 11271; tel. (2) 25903756; fax (2) 25880091; e-mail info@eliaspublishing.com; internet www.eliaspublishing.com; f. 1913; publishing, printing and distribution; publ. dictionaries, children's books, and books on linguistics, poetry and arts; Chair. NADIM ELIAS; Man. Dir LAURA KFOURY.

Dar al-Farouk: 12 Sharia Dokki, 6th Floor, Cairo (Giza); tel. (2) 37622830; fax (2) 33380474; e-mail support@darelfarouk.com.eg; internet www.darelfarouk.com.eg; wide range of books incl. educational, history, science and business; Chair. FAROUK M. AL-AMARY; Gen. Man. Dr KHALED F. AL-AMARY.

Dar al-Gomhouriya: 24 Sharia Zakaria Ahmad, Cairo; tel. (2) 5781010; fax (2) 5784747; e-mail eltahrir@eltahrir.net; internet www.algomhuria.net.eg; state-owned; affiliate of El-Tahrir Printing and Publishing House; publs include the dailies *Al-Gomhouriya*, *Al-Misaa'*, *The Egyptian Gazette* and *Le Progrès Egyptien*; Pres. MUHAMMAD ABOUL HADID.

Dar al-Hilal: 16 Sharia Muhammad Ezz el-Arab, Cairo 11511; tel. (2) 3625450; fax (2) 3625469; f. 1892; state-owned; publs include *Al-Hilal*, *Kitab al-Hilal*, *Tabibak al-Khass* (monthlies); *Al-Mussawar*, *Al-Kawakeb*, *Hawa'a* (weeklies); Chair. ABD AL-KADER SHUHAYIB.

Dar al-Kitab al-Masri: POB 156, 33 Sharia Qasr el-Nil, Cairo 11511; tel. (2) 3922168; fax (2) 3924657; e-mail info@daralkitabalmasri.com; internet www.daralkitabalmasri.com; f. 1929; publishing, printing and distribution; publrs of books on Islam and history, as well as dictionaries, encyclopaedias, textbooks, children's and general interest books; Pres. and Dir-Gen. Dr HASSAN EL-ZEIN.

Dar al-Maaref: 1119 Sharia Corniche el-Nil, Cairo; tel. (2) 25777077; fax (2) 25744999; e-mail maaref@idselgov.eg; internet www.octobermag.com; f. 1890; publishing, printing and distribution of wide variety of books in Arabic and other languages; publrs of *October* magazine; Chair. ISMAIL MUNTASSIR.

Maktabet Misr: POB 16, 3 Sharia Kamal Sidki, Cairo; tel. (2) 5898553; fax (2) 7870051; e-mail info@misrbookshop.com; f. 1932; fiction, biographies and textbooks for schools and universities; Man. AMIR SAID GOUDA EL-SAHHAR.

Dar al-Masri al-Lubnani: 16 Sharia Abd al-Khalek Sarwat, Cairo; tel. (2) 3910250; fax (2) 3909618; e-mail info@almasriah.com; internet www.almasriah.com; Arabic literature, history, sciences, textbooks and children's books; Chair. MUHAMMAD RASHED.

Nahdet Misr Group: al-Nahda Tower, 21 Sharia Ahmad Orabi, Sphinx Sq., Mohandessin, Cairo (Giza); tel. (2) 33464903; fax (2) 33462576; e-mail publishing@nahdetmisr.com; internet www.nahdetmisr.com; f. 1938; fiction, children's literature and educational books; also publishes magazines, incl. *Mickey* (weekly); Chair. MUHAMMAD AHMAD IBRAHIM.

Dar al-Nashr (fmrly Les Editions Universitaires d'Egypte): POB 1347, 41 Sharia Sherif, Cairo 11511; tel. (2) 3934606; fax (2) 3921997; f. 1947; university textbooks, academic works and encyclopaedias.

National Centre for Educational Research and Development: 12 Sharia Waked, el-Borg el-Faddy, POB 836, Cairo; tel. (2) 3930981; f. 1956; fmrly Documentation and Research Centre for Education (Ministry of Education); bibliographies, directories, information and education bulletins; Dir Prof. ABD EL-FATTAH GALAL.

National Library Press (Dar al-Kutub): POB 11638, 8 Sharia al-Sabtteya, Cairo; tel. (2) 5750886; fax (2) 5765634; e-mail info@darelkotob.org; internet www.darelkotob.org; bibliographic works; Chair. Dr MUHAMMAD SABER ARAB.

Safeer Publishing: POB 425, Cairo (Dokki); tel. (2) 37608703; fax (2) 37608650; internet www.safeer.com.eg; f. 1982; children's books; Pres. MUHAMMAD ABD EL-LATIF.

Dar al-Shorouk: 8 Sibaweh al-Masri, Cairo (Nasr City) 11371; tel. (2) 24023399; fax (2) 24037567; e-mail dar@shorouk.com; internet www.shorouk.com; f. 1968; publishing, printing and distribution; publrs of books on current affairs, history, Islamic studies, literature, art and children's books; Chair. IBRAHIM EL-MOALLEM.

El-Tahrir Printing and Publishing House: 24 Sharia Zakaria Ahmad, Cairo; tel. (2) 5781222; fax (2) 2784747; e-mail eltahrir@eltahrir.net; internet www.eltahrir.net; f. 1953; state-owned; Pres. and Chair. of Bd ALI HASHIM.

Dar el-Thaqafa: Coptic Evangelical Organization for Social Services, Sharia Dr Ahmed Zaki, Cairo; tel. (2) 6221425; internet www.darelthaqafa.com; publishing dept of the Coptic Evangelical Org. for Social Services; publishes books on social issues as well as on spiritual and theological topics; Dir Rev. Dr ANDREA ZAKI STEPHANOUS.

Broadcasting and Communications

TELECOMMUNICATIONS

Egyptian Company for Mobile Services (MobiNil): The World Trade Center, 2005c, Corniche el-Nil, Boulaq, Cairo; tel. (2) 25747000; fax (2) 25747111; e-mail customercare@mobinil.com; internet www.mobinil.com; began operation of the existing state-controlled mobile telecommunications network in 1998; owned by France Télécom (93.9%) and Orascom Telecom (5%); 32.2m. subscribers (2012); Chair. ISKANDER N. (ALEX) SHALABY; CEO YVES GAUTHIER.

Etisalat Misr: POB 11, S4 Down Town, Sharia 90, 5th Compound, New Cairo; tel. (2) 35346333; internet www.etisalat.com.eg; f. 2007 as Egypt's third mobile telephone service provider; subsidiary of Etisalat (United Arab Emirates); Chair. GAMAL EL-SADAT; CEO SAEED AL-HAMLI.

Global Telecom Holding: 2005A Nile City Towers, South Tower, Corniche el-Nil, Ramlet Beaulac, 11221 Cairo; tel. (2) 24615050; fax (2) 24615054; internet www.gtelecom.com; fmrly Orascom Telecom, name changed following merger with VimpleCom Ltd (Russia); owns and operates mobile telecommunications providers in North Africa, sub-Saharan Africa, North America and South Asia; approx. 88m. subscribers worldwide; Chair. ANTON KUDRYASHOV; Group CEO AHMED ABU DOMA.

Telecom Egypt: POB 2271, Sharia Ramses, Cairo 11511; tel. (2) 25793444; fax (2) 25744244; e-mail telecomegypt@telecomegypt.com.eg; internet www.telecomegypt.com.eg; f. 1957; provider of fixed-line telephone services; CEO and Man. Dir MUHAMMAD AMIN EL-NAWAWI; Chair. OMAR EL-SHEIKH.

Vodafone Egypt: 7A Corniche el-Nil, Maadi, 11431 Cairo; tel. (2) 25292000; e-mail public.relations@vodafone.com; internet www.vodafone.com.eg; f. 1998 by the MisrFone consortium; mobile telephone service provider; majority-owned by Vodafone Int. (United Kingdom); 36.3m. subscribers (Dec. 2011); Chair. IAN GRAY; CEO HATEM DOWIDAR.

Regulatory Authority

National Telecommunications Regulatory Authority (NTRA): Smart Village, Bldg No. 4, km 28, Sharia Cairo–Alexandria, Cairo; tel. (2) 35344000; fax (2) 35344155; e-mail info@tra.gov.eg; internet www.ntra.gov.eg; f. 2000; Chair. ATIF HELMI (Minister of Communications and Information Technology); Exec. Pres. Dr AMR BADAWI.

BROADCASTING

Radio and Television

Egyptian Radio and Television Union (ERTU): POB 11511, Cairo 1186; tel. (2) 5746881; fax (2) 5746989; e-mail info@ertu.org; internet www.ertu.org; f. 1928; home service radio programmes in Arabic, English and French; foreign services in Arabic, English, French, German, Spanish, Portuguese, Italian, Swahili, Hausa, Urdu, Indonesian, Pashtu, Farsi, Turkish, Somali, Uzbek, Albanian, Afar, Amharic; operates 2 national and 6 regional television channels; also owns the satellite television network Nile TV, which offers 12 specialized channels; Pres. SHOKRI ABU EMARA.

Dreams TV: 23 Polis Hana St, Cairo (Giza); tel. (2) 7492817; fax (2) 7410949; e-mail urquestions@dreams.tv; internet www.dreams.tv; f. 2001; privately owned satellite television station; broadcasts on Dream 1 and Dream 2 networks, providing sports, music and entertainment programmes; Chair. Dr AHMAD BAHGAT.

El-Mehwar TV: Cairo; e-mail ElMehwar@ElMehwar.tv; internet www.elmehwar.tv; f. 2001; privately owned; entertainment and current affairs programmes; Founder Dr HASSAN RATEB.

Middle East Radio: Société Egyptienne de Publicité, 24–26 Sharia Zakaria Ahmad, Cairo; tel. (2) 5781010; fax (2) 5784747; e-mail radioinfo@ertu.org; internet ertu.org/radio/mideast.html.

Nile Radio Productions: Media City Free Zone, 6th of October City; tel. (2) 38555767; fax (2) 38555770; e-mail contactnrp@nileradioproductions.net; internet www.nilefmonline.com; f. 2003; owned by Telemedia Holding; operates radio stations in English (Nile FM) and Arabic (Nogoum FM); Group CEO AYMAN SALEM; Man. Dir and COO HALA HEGAZI.

Finance

(cap. = capital; res = reserves; dep. = deposits; m. = million; brs = branches; amounts in Egyptian pounds, unless otherwise stated)

BANKING

Central Bank

Central Bank of Egypt (CBE): 31 Sharia Qasr el-Nil, Cairo; tel. (2) 27702770; fax (2) 25976081; e-mail info@cbe.org.eg; internet www.cbe.org.eg; f. 1961; controls Egypt's monetary policy and supervises the banking sector; cap. 1,000m., res 1,543.7m., dep. 211,861.5m. (June 2007); Gov. and Chair. HISHAM RAMEZ ABD EL-HAFEZ; 4 brs.

Commercial and Specialized Banks

Abu Dhabi Islamic Bank (Egypt) (ADIB Egypt): 9A Sharia Rostom, Cairo (Garden City); tel. (2) 23959291; fax (2) 23936039; e-mail adibegypt@adib.ae; internet www.adib.eg; f. 1980; fmrly National Development Bank; 51% share bought by Abu Dhabi Islamic Bank in 2007; offers *Shari'a*-compliant banking services; cap. 1,999m., res 2,146m., dep. 13,300m. (Dec. 2012); CEO and Acting Chair. NEVINE LOUTFY; 69 brs.

Bank of Alexandria: 49 Sharia Qasr el-Nil, Cairo; tel. (2) 23913822; fax (2) 23919805; e-mail info@alexbank.com; internet www.alexbank.com; f. 1957; 80% stake acquired by Gruppo Sanpaolo IMI (Italy) in Oct. 2006; cap. 800m., res 1,069m., dep. 33,929m. (Dec. 2012); Chair. and Man. Dir BRUNO GAMBA; 196 brs.

Banque du Caire, SAE: POB 9022, Banque du Caire Tower, 6 Sharia Dr Moustafa Abu Zahra, Nasr City, Cairo 11371; tel. (2) 2647400; fax (2) 403725; e-mail intl.division@bdc.com.eg; internet www.bdc.com.eg; f. 1952; state-owned; privatization pending; cap. 1,600m., res 1,582m., dep. 49,530m. (June 2012); Chair. and CEO MOUNIR ABD EL-WAHAB EL-ZAHID; 216 brs.

Banque Misr, SAE: 151 Sharia Muhammad Farid, Cairo; tel. (2) 27945587; fax (2) 23932495; e-mail staff@banquemisr.com.eg; internet www.banquemisr.com.eg; f. 1920; merger with Misr Exterior Bank in 2004; privatization pending; cap. 11,400m., res 1,914., dep. 194,186m. (June 2013); Chair. MUHAMMAD KAMAL AL-DIN BARAKAT; 438 brs.

Commercial International Bank (Egypt), SAE: POB 2430, Nile Tower Bldg, 21–23 Sharia Charles de Gaulle, Cairo (Giza); tel. (2) 37472000; fax (2) 35703172; e-mail info@cibeg.com; internet www.cibeg.com; f. 1975 as Chase Nat. Bank (Egypt), SAE; adopted present name 1987; Nat. Bank of Egypt has 19.91% interest, Bankers Trust Co (USA) 18.76%, Int. Finance Corpn 5%; cap. 9,002m., res 497m., dep. 98,219m. (Dec. 2013); Chair. and Man. Dir HISHAM EZZ AL-ARAB; 112 brs.

Egyptian Arab Land Bank: 78 Sharia Gameat al-Dowal al-Arabia, Mohandessin, Cairo 12311; tel. (2) 33383579; fax 3383569; e-mail foreign@eal-bank.com; internet www.eal-bank.com; f. 1880; state-owned; Chair. ABD EL-MEGUID MOHIE EL-DIN; 26 brs in Egypt, 15 abroad.

Export Development Bank of Egypt (EDBE): 108 Mohi el-Din Abou al-Ezz, Cairo 12311 (Dokki); tel. (2) 37619006; fax (2) 33385938; e-mail info@edbebank.com; internet www.edbebank.com; f. 1983 to replace Nat. Import-Export Bank; cap. 1,440m., res 417m., dep. 13,495m. (June 2013); Chair. MUHAMMAD ISMAIL AL-SHARIF; 15 brs.

HSBC Bank Egypt, SAE: POB 126, Abou el-Feda Bldg, 3 Sharia Abou el-Feda, Cairo (Zamalek); tel. (2) 27396001; fax (2) 27364010; e-mail hsbcegypt@hsbc.com; internet www.egypt.hsbc.com; f. 1982 as Hong Kong Egyptian Bank; name changed to Egyptian British Bank in 1994, and as above in 2001; 94.5% owned by Hongkong and Shanghai Banking Corpn; cap. 2,078m., res 1,428m., dep. 48,207m. (Dec. 2012); Chair. MUHAMMAD AL-TUWAIJRI; CEO ANDREW LONG; 78 brs.

National Bank of Egypt (NBE): POB 11611, National Bank of Egypt Tower, 1187 Corniche el-Nil, Cairo; tel. (2) 25749101; fax (2) 25762672; internet www.nbe.com.eg; f. 1898; merged with Mohandes Bank and Bank of Commerce and Devt in 2005; privatization pending; handles all commercial banking operations; cap. 7,000m., res 3,789m., dep. 282,570m. (June 2012); Chair. HISHAM AHMAD OKASHA; 401 brs.

Principal Bank for Development and Agricultural Credit (PBDAC): 110 Sharia Qasr el-Eini, 11623 Cairo; tel. (2) 27951229; fax (2) 27948337; e-mail pbdac@pbdac.com.eg; internet www.pbdac.com.eg; f. 1976 to succeed former credit orgs; state-owned; cap. 1,500m., res 314m., dep. 28,464m. (June 2010); Chair. IMAD ABD AL-AZIZ SALIM; 172 brs.

Société Arabe Internationale de Banque (SAIB): 56 Sharia Gamet el-Dowal al-Arabia, Mohandessin, Cairo (Giza); tel. (2) 37602604; fax (2) 33350538; e-mail abdellatif.hassan@saib.com.eg; internet www.saib.com.eg; f. 1976; 46% owned by Arab Int. Bank;

cap. US $150m., res $50m., dep. $2,182m. (Dec. 2012); Chair. and Man. Dir MUHAMMAD NAGUIB IBRAHIM; 20 brs.

Union National Bank-Egypt SAE: el-Gamaa Bldg, 57 Sharia el-Giza, Alexandria 21519; tel. (2) 25780702; fax (2) 25798515; e-mail foreign@acmb.com.eg; internet www.unb-egypt.com; f. 1981 as Alexandria Commercial and Maritime Bank, SAE; adopted present name Dec. 2007; 94.8% owned by Union Nat. (United Arab Emirates); cap. 637m., res 123m., dep. 3,628m. (Dec. 2011); Chair. Sheikh NAHYAN MUBARAK AL NAHYAN; Man. Dir ATIF USMAN IBRAHIM AL-DIB; 25 brs.

The United Bank (UBE): Cairo Center, 106 Sharia Qasr el-Eini, Cairo; tel. (2) 33326010; fax (2) 27920153; e-mail info@ube.net; internet www.theubeg.com; f. 1981 as Dakahlia Nat. Bank for Devt; renamed United Bank of Egypt 1997; current name adopted 2006, when merged with Nile Bank and Islamic Int. Bank for Investment and Devt; privatization mooted in 2008; cap. 1,000.0m., res –11.0m., dep. 10,390.8m. (Dec. 2008); Chair. and Man. Dir MUHAMMAD ASHMAWY; 41 brs.

Social Bank

Nasser Social Bank: POB 2552, 35 Sharia Qasr el-Nil, Cairo; tel. (2) 23924484; fax (2) 23921930; f. 1971; state-owned; interest-free savings and investment bank for social and economic activities, participating in social insurance, specializing in financing co-operatives, craftsmen and social institutions; cap. 20m.; Chair. NASSIF TAHOON.

Multinational Banks

Arab African International Bank: 5 Midan al-Saray al-Koubra, POB 60, Majlis al-Sha'ab, Cairo 11516 (Garden City); tel. (2) 27924770; fax (2) 27925599; e-mail inquiry@aaib.com; internet www.aaib.com; f. 1964 as Arab African Bank; renamed 1978; acquired Misr-America Int. Bank in 2005; cap. US $100m., res $122m., dep. $6,697m. (Dec. 2012); commercial investments and retail banking; shareholders are Central Bank of Egypt, Kuwait Investment Authority (49.37% each), and individuals and Arab institutions; Chair. MAHMOUD A. AL-NOURI; Vice-Chair. and Man. Dir HASSAN E. ABDALLA; 27 brs in Egypt, 3 abroad.

Arab International Bank: POB 1563, 35 Sharia Abd al-Khalek Sarwat, Cairo; tel. (2) 23918794; fax (2) 23916233; e-mail aibweb@aib.com.eg; internet www.aib.com.eg; f. 1971 as Egyptian Int. Bank for Foreign Trade and Investment; renamed 1974; owned by Egypt, Libya, Oman, Qatar, the United Arab Emirates and private Arab shareholders; cap. US $450m., res $229m., dep. $2,326m. (Dec. 2012); 'offshore' bank; aims to promote trade and investment in shareholders' countries and other Arab countries; Chair. GAMAL NEGM; Dep. Chair. and Man. Dir MUHAMMAD IBRAHIM ABD AL-JAWAD; 7 brs.

Commercial Foreign Venture Banks

Ahli United Bank (Egypt): POB 1159, 9th Floor, World Trade Center, 1191 Corniche el-Nil; tel. (2) 26149500; fax (2) 26135160; e-mail info.aube@ahliunited.com; internet www.ahliunited.com; f. 1978 as Delta Int. Bank; name changed as above in 2007; 89.3% stake owned by Ahli United Bank BSC (Bahrain) and other Gulf-based financial institutions; cap. 1,125m., res 180m., dep. 13,691m. (Dec. 2012); Chair. FAHAD AL-RAJAAN; CEO and Man. Dir NEVINE EL-MESSEERI; 28 brs.

alBaraka Bank Egypt, SAE: POB 455, 60 Sharia Mohi el-Din Abu al-Ezz, Cairo (Dokki); tel. (2) 37481777; fax (2) 37611436; e-mail centeral@esf-bank.com; internet www.albaraka-bank.com.eg; f. 1980 as Pyramids Bank; renamed Egyptian-Saudi Finance Bank 1988; current name adopted April 2010; 73.7% owned by Al-Baraka Banking Group (Bahrain); cap. 707m., res 167m., dep. 14,865m. (Dec. 2012); Chair. ADNAN AHMAD YOUSUF ABD AL-MALEK; Vice Chair. and CEO ASHRAF AHMAD MOUSTAFA EL-GHAMRAWY; 23 brs.

Bank Audi SAE: Pyramid Heights Office Park, km 22, Cairo–Alexandria Desert Rd, Cairo; tel. (2) 35343300; fax (2) 35362120; e-mail contactus.egypt@banqueaudi.com; f. 1978 as Cairo Far East Bank SAE; name changed as above in 2006, when acquired by Bank Audi SAL (Lebanon); cap. 1,337m., res 246m., dep. 16,506m. (Dec. 2012); Head MUHAMMAD L. AMAD LABIB; 32 brs.

Barclays Bank Egypt, SAE: POB 110, 12 Midan el-Sheikh Yousuf, Cairo (Garden City); tel. (2) 23662600; fax (2) 23662810; internet www.barclays.com.eg; f. 1975 as Cairo Barclays Int. Bank; renamed Banque du Caire Barclays Int. in 1983 and Cairo Barclays Bank in 1999; name changed as above in 2004; wholly owned by Barclays Bank; acquired 40% stake held by Banque du Caire in 2004; cap. 995m., res 225m., dep. 14,621m. (Dec. 2012); Chair. OMAR EL-SAYEH; Man. Dir KHALID EL-GIBALY; 65 brs.

Blom Bank Egypt: 64 Sharia Mohi el-Din Abou al-Ezz, Cairo (Dokki); tel. (2) 33322770; fax (2) 37494508; e-mail mail@blombankegypt.com; internet www.blombankegypt.com; f. 1977 as Misr Romanian Bank, name changed as above in 2006; 99.7% owned by Blom Bank SAL (Lebanon); cap. 750m., res 121m., dep. 8,572m. (Dec. 2012); Chair. SAAD AZHARI; CEO and Man. Dir MUHAMMAD OZALP; 25 brs.

BNP Paribas SAE: POB 2441, 3 Latin America St, Cairo (Garden City); tel. (2) 27948323; fax (2) 27942218; e-mail bnppegypt@bnpparibas.com; internet www.egypt.bnpparibas.com; f. 1977 as Banque du Caire et de Paris SAE, name changed to BNP Paribas Le Caire in 2001 and as above in 2006; BNP Paribas (France) has 95.2% interest and Banque du Caire 4.8%; cap. 1,700m., res 4m., dep. 13,959m. (Dec. 2012); Chair. BAUDOUIN PROT; Man. Dir JEAN-LAURENT BONNAFÉ; 8 brs.

Crédit Agricole Egypt, SAE: POB 1825, 4 Hassan Sabri St, Cairo 11511 (Zamalek); tel. (2) 27382661; fax (2) 27380450; internet www.ca-egypt.com; f. 2006 by merger of Calyon Bank Egypt (Egyptian affiliate of Crédit Agricole Group—France) and Egyptian American Bank; owned by Crédit Agricole Groupe, Mansour and Maghrabi Investment and Devt, and Egyptian investors; cap. 1,148m., res 215m., dep. 24,521m. (Dec. 2012); Chair. and Man. Dir FRANÇOIS EDOUARD DRION; 44 brs.

Egyptian Gulf Bank: POB 56, El-Orman Plaza Bldg, 8–10 Sharia Ahmad Nessim, Cairo (Giza); tel. (2) 33368357; fax (2) 37490002; e-mail h.r.egb@mst1.mist.com.eg; internet www.egbbank.com.eg; f. 1981; Misr Insurance Co has 19.3% interest; cap. 951m., res 113m., dep. 7,196m. (Dec. 2012); Chair. MUHAMMAD GAMAL EL-DIN MAHMOUD; CEO and Man. Dir MUHAMMAD MAHMOUD AL-ETREBY; 16 brs.

Faisal Islamic Bank of Egypt, SAE: POB 2446, 149 Sharia el-Tahrir, Galaa Sq., Cairo (Dokki); tel. (2) 37621285; fax (2) 37621281; e-mail foreigndept@faisalbank.com.eg; internet www.faisalbank.com.eg; f. 1979; all banking operations conducted according to Islamic principles; cap. 1,059m., res 769m., dep. 37,331m. (Dec. 2012); Chair. Prince MUHAMMAD AL-FAISAL AL-SAOUD; Gov. ABD AL-HAMID ABU MOUSSA; 29 brs.

Piraeus Bank Egypt SAE: POB 92, 4th Floor, Evergreen Bldg, 10 Sharia Talaat Harb, Majlis al-Sha'ab, Cairo; tel. (2) 25764644; fax (2) 25799862; internet www.piraeusbank.com.eg; f. Jan. 2006, following acquisition of Egyptian Commercial Bank by Piraeus Bank Group (Greece) in June 2005; cap. 1,216m., res 98m., dep. 7,295m. (Dec. 2011); Chair. ILIAS MILIS; CEO and Man. Dir CONSTANTINOS LOIZIDES; 49 brs.

Suez Canal Bank, SAE: POB 2620, 7 Abd el-Kader Hamza St, Cairo (Garden City); tel. (2) 27943433; fax (2) 27926476; e-mail info@scbank.com.eg; internet www.scbank.com.eg; f. 1978; cap. 2,000m., res 64m., dep. 14,972m. (Dec. 2012); Chair. and Man. Dir TAREQ KANDIL; 29 brs.

Al-Watany Bank of Egypt: POB 63, 13 Sharia Semar, Dr Fouad Mohi el-Din Sq., Gameat el-Dewal al-Arabia, Mohandessin, Cairo 12655; tel. (2) 33388816; fax (2) 33362763; internet www.alwatany.net; f. 1980; 51% owned by Nat. Bank of Kuwait; cap. 1,000m., res 979m., dep. 14,820m. (Dec. 2012); Chair. ISAM AL-SAGER; Man. Dir Dr YASSER ISMAIL HASSAN; 39 brs.

Non-Commercial Banks

Arab Banking Corporation—Egypt: 1 Sharia el-Saleh Ayoub, Cairo (Zamalek); tel. (2) 27362684; fax (2) 27363643; e-mail abcegypt@arabbanking.com.eg; internet www.arabbanking.com.eg; f. 1982 as Egypt Arab African Bank; acquired by Arab Banking Corpn (Bahrain) in 1999; Arab Banking Corpn has 93% interest, other interests 7%; cap. 600m., res 209m., dep. 4,478m. (Dec. 2011); commercial and investment bank; Chair. HASSAN ALI JUMA; Man. Dir and CEO AKRAM TINAWI; 28 brs.

Arab Investment Bank (Federal Arab Bank for Development and Investment): POB 826, Cairo Sky Center Bldg, 8 Sharia Abd al-Khalek Sarwat, Cairo; tel. (2) 25760031; fax (2) 5770329; e-mail arinbank@mst1.mist.com.eg; internet www.aibegypt.com; f. 1978 as Union Arab Bank for Devt and Investment; Egyptian/Syrian/Libyan jt venture; cap. 500m., res 83m., dep. 3,790m. (Dec. 2012); Chair. and Exec. Man. Dir MUHAMMAD HANI SEIF EL-NASR; 13 brs.

EFG-Hermes: 58 Sharia el-Tahrir, Cairo 12311 (Dokki); tel. (2) 35356499; fax (2) 35370942; e-mail corporate@efg-hermes.com; internet www.efg-hermes.com; f. 1984; offices in Cairo, Alexandria and Mansoura; cap. 2,391m., res 4,848m., dep. 44,750m. (Dec. 2012); Chair. MONA ZULFICAR; CEO YASSER EL-MALLAWANY; 11 brs.

Housing and Development Bank, SAE: POB 234, 12 Sharia Syria, Mohandessin, Cairo (Giza); tel. (2) 37492013; fax (2) 37600712; e-mail hdbank@hdb-egy.com; internet www.hdb-egy.com; f. 1979; cap. 1,150m., res 691m., dep. 8,143m. (Dec. 2012); Chair. and Man. Dir FATHY EL-SEBAIE MANSOUR; 40 brs.

Industrial Development and Workers Bank of Egypt (IDWBE): 110 Sharia al-Galaa, Cairo 11511; tel. (2) 25772468; fax (2) 25751227; e-mail rch@idbe-egypt.com; internet www.idbe-egypt.com; f. 1947 as Industrial Bank; re-established as above in 1976; cap. 500m., res 608m., dep. 2,055m. (Dec. 2009); Chair. and Man. Dir EL-SAYED MUHAMMAD EL-KOSAYER; 19 brs.

Misr Iran Development Bank: POB 219, Nile Tower Bldg, 21 Charles de Gaulle Ave, Cairo 12612 (Giza); tel. (2) 35727311; fax (2) 35701185; e-mail midb@mst1.mist.com.eg; internet www.midb.com.eg; f. 1975; Iran Foreign Investment Co has 40.14% interest, Bank of Alexandria and Misr Insurance Co each have 29.93% interest; cap. 714m., res 567m., dep. 7,559m. (Dec. 2012); Chair. and Man. Dir ISMAIL HASSAN MUHAMMAD; 12 brs.

QNB Al Ahli: POB 2664, 5 Sharia Champollion, 11111 Cairo; tel. (2) 25803800; fax (2) 27707799; e-mail info.qnbaa@qnbalahli.com; internet www.qnbalahli.com; f. 1978; 97.12% of shares held by QNB Group (Qatar), other investors 2.88%; cap. 4,435m., res 2,173m., dep. 54,939m. (Dec. 2012); Chair. and Man. Dir MUHAMMAD OSMAN EL-DIB; 160 brs.

REGULATORY AUTHORITY

Egyptian Financial Supervisory Authority (EFSA): Unit 84B, Bldg 5A, Alexandria Desert Rd, km 28, Cairo 12577; tel. (2) 35370040; fax (2) 35370041; e-mail info@efsa.gov.eg; internet www.efsa.gov.eg; f. 2009, following the merger of the Capital Market Authority, the Egyptian Insurance Supervisory Authority and the Mortgage Finance Authority; also assumed the regulatory functions of the General Authority for Investment and Free Zones, and the Egyptian Exchange; supervision of all non-banking financial markets and institutions, incl. the stock exchange, the capital market, and the insurance and mortgage sectors; Chair. Dr SHARIF SAMIR SAMI.

STOCK EXCHANGE

The Egyptian Exchange (EGX): 4A Sharia el-Sherifein, Cairo 11513; tel. (2) 23928698; fax (2) 23924214; e-mail webmaster@egx.com.eg; internet www.egx.com.eg; f. 1883 as the Cairo and Alexandria Stock Exchanges; present name adopted 2008; Chair. Dr MUHAMMAD OMRAN.

INSURANCE

Allianz Egypt: POB 266, Saridar Bldg, 92 Sharia el-Tahrir, Cairo (Dokki); tel. (2) 37605445; fax (2) 37605446; e-mail info@allianz.com.eg; internet www.allianz.com.eg; f. 1976 as Arab Int. Insurance Co; Allianz AG (Germany) purchased 80% stake in 2000; name changed as above in 2004; general and life insurance; Chair. RAYMOND SEMAAN EL-CHAM.

MetLife Alico: 28th Floor, Nile City Bldg, North Tower, Ramlet Beualac, Cairo; tel. (2) 4619020; fax (2) 4619015; e-mail service-egypt@metlifealico.com; internet www.eg.alico.com; f. 1997; first multinational insurance company to be granted licence to offer life insurance service in Egypt; CEO MICHEL KHALAF.

Misr Insurance Co: POB 950, 7 Sharia Abd al-Latif Boltia, Cairo; tel. (2) 7918300; fax (2) 797041; e-mail quality@misrins.com.eg; internet www.misrins.com.eg; f. 1934; merged with Al-Chark Insurance Co and Egyptian Reinsurance Co in Dec. 2007; scheduled for privatization; all classes of insurance and reinsurance; Chair. Prof. ADEL HAMMAD.

Mohandes Insurance Co: POB 62, 3 el-Mesaha Sq., Cairo (Dokki); tel. (2) 3352547; fax (2) 3361365; e-mail chairman@mohandes-ins.com; internet www.mohandes-ins.com; f. 1980; privately owned; insurance and reinsurance; Chair. and Man. Dir MUHAMMAD AHMED BARAKA.

Al-Mottahida: POB 804, 9 Sharia Sulayman Pasha, Cairo; f. 1957.

National Insurance Co of Egypt, SAE: POB 592, 41 Sharia Qasr el-Nil, Cairo; tel. (2) 3910731; fax (2) 3933051; internet www.ahlya.com; f. 1900; cap. 100m.; scheduled for privatization; Chair. SADEK HASSAN SADEK.

Provident Association of Egypt, SAE: POB 390, 9 Sharia Sherif Pasha, Alexandria; f. 1936; Man. Dir G. C. VORLOOU.

Trade and Industry

GOVERNMENT AGENCIES

Egyptian Mineral Resource Authority (EMRA): 3 Sharia Salah Salem, Abbassia, 11517 Cairo; tel. (2) 6828013; fax (2) 4820128; e-mail info@egsma.gov.eg; f. 1896 as the Egyptian Geological Survey and Mining Authority; state supervisory authority concerned with geological mapping, mineral exploration and other mining activities; Chair. HUSSEIN HAMOUDA.

General Authority for Investment (GAFI): Sharia Salah Salem, 11562 Cairo (Nasr City); tel. (2) 24055452; fax (2) 24055425; e-mail investorcare@gafinet.org; internet www.gafinet.org; Chair. OSAMA SALEH.

CHAMBERS OF COMMERCE

Federation of Egyptian Chambers of Commerce (FEDCOC): 4 el-Falaki Sq., Cairo; tel. (2) 7951136; fax (2) 7951164; e-mail fedcoc@menanet.net; internet www.fedcoc.org.eg; f. 1955; Chair. MUHAMMAD EL-MASRY.

Alexandria

Alexandria Chamber of Commerce: 31 Sharia el-Ghorfa Altogariya, Alexandria; tel. (3) 4837808; fax (3) 4837806; e-mail acc@alexcham.org; internet www.alexcham.org; f. 1922; Chair. AHMAD EL-WAKIL.

Cairo

American Chamber of Commerce in Egypt: 33 Sharia Sulayman Abaza, Cairo (Dokki) 12311; tel. (2) 33381050; fax (2) 33381060; e-mail info@amcham.org.eg; internet www.amcham.org.eg; f. 1981; Pres. OMAR MOHANNA; Exec. Dir HISHAM A. FAHMY.

Cairo Chamber of Commerce: 4 el-Falaki Sq., Cairo; tel. and fax (2) 27962091; f. 1913; Pres. MAHMOUD EL-ARABY; Sec.-Gen. MOSTAFA ZAKI TAHA.

In addition, there are 24 local chambers of commerce.

EMPLOYERS' ORGANIZATION

Federation of Egyptian Industries: 1195 Corniche el-Nil, Ramlet Boulal, Cairo; and 65 Gamal Abd al-Nasir Ave, Alexandria; tel. (2) 25796950; fax (2) 25796953 (Cairo); tel. and fax (3) 34916121 (Alexandria); e-mail info@fei.org.eg; internet www.fei.org.eg; f. 1922; Chair. GALAL ABD AL-MAKSOOD EL-ZORBA.

STATE HYDROCARBONS COMPANIES

Egyptian General Petroleum Corpn (EGPC): POB 2130, 4th Sector, Sharia Palestine, New Maadi, Cairo; tel. (2) 7065358; fax (2) 7028813; e-mail info@egpc.com.eg; state supervisory authority generally concerned with the planning of policies relating to petroleum activities in Egypt with the object of securing the devt of the petroleum industry and ensuring its effective administration; Chair. TARIQ AL-MOLLA.

Arab Petroleum Pipelines Co (SUMED): POB 158, el-Saray, 431 el-Geish Ave, Louran, Alexandria; tel. (3) 5835152; fax (3) 5831295; internet www.sumed.org; f. 1974; EGPC has 50% interest, Saudi Arabian Oil Co 15%, Int. Petroleum Investment Co (United Arab Emirates) 15%, Kuwait Real Estate Investment Consortium 14.22%, Qatar Petroleum 5%, other Kuwaiti cos 0.78%; Suez–Mediterranean crude oil transportation pipeline (capacity: 117m. metric tons per year) and petroleum terminal operators; Chair. and Man. Dir Eng. SHAMEL HAMDI.

Belayim Petroleum Co (PETROBEL): POB 7074, Sharia el-Mokhayam, Cairo (Nasr City); tel. (2) 2621738; fax (2) 2609792; f. 1977; capital equally shared between EGPC and Int. Egyptian Oil Co, which is a subsidiary of Eni of Italy; petroleum and gas exploration, drilling and production; Chair. and Man. Dir MEDHAT EL-SAYED.

Egyptian Natural Gas Co (GASCO): Ring Rd, Exit 12, Sharia el-Tesien, 5th Settlement, Cairo; tel. (2) 6171911; fax (2) 6172824; e-mail gassupplyaffairs@gasco.com.eg; internet www.gasco.com.eg; f. 1997; 70% owned by EGPC, 15% by Petroleum Projects and Technical Consultations Co (PETROJET), 15% by Egypt Gas; transmission and processing of natural gas; operation of the national gas distribution network; Chair. and Man. Dir Eng. YAHIA AL-RIDI.

General Petroleum Co (GPC): POB 743, 8 Sharia Dr Moustafa Abou Zahra, Cairo (Nasr City); tel. (2) 4030975; fax (2) 4037602; f. 1957; wholly owned subsidiary of EGPC; operates mainly in Eastern Desert; Chair. HUSSEIN KAMAL.

Gulf of Suez Petroleum Co (GUPCO): POB 2400, 4th Sector, Sharia Palestine, New Maadi, Cairo 11511; tel. (2) 3520985; fax (2) 3531286; f. 1965; jt venture between EGPC and BP Egypt (United Kingdom/USA); developed the el-Morgan oilfield in the Gulf of Suez, also holds other exploration concessions in the Gulf of Suez and the Western Desert; Chair. Eng. MUHAMMAD ABOUL WAFA; Man. Dir L. D. MCVAY.

Middle East Oil Refinery (MIDOR): POB 2233, 22 Sharia el-Badeya, Cairo (Heliopolis) 11361; tel. (2) 24195501; fax (2) 24145936; e-mail info@midor.com.eg; internet www.midor.com.eg; f. 1994; 78% owned by EGPC, 10% by Engineering for the Petroleum and Process Industries (Enppi), 10% by Petroleum Projects and Technical Consultations Co (PETROJET), 2% by Suez Canal Bank; operation of oil-refining facilities at Ameriya, Alexandria; capacity 100,000 b/d; Chair. and CEO MEDHAT YOUSUF MAHMOUD.

Western Desert Petroleum Co (WEPCO): POB 412, Borg el-Thagr Bldg, Sharia Safia Zagloul, Alexandria; tel. (3) 4928710; fax

(3) 4934016; f. 1967 as partnership between EGPC (50% interest) and Phillips Petroleum (35%) and later Hispanoil (15%); developed Alamein, Yidma and Umbarka fields in the Western Desert and later Abu Qir offshore gasfield in 1978, followed by NAF gasfield in 1987; Chair. MUHAMMAD MOHI EL-DIN BAHGAT.

Egyptian Natural Gas Holding Co (EGAS): POB 8064, 85C Sharia Nasr, 11371 Cairo (Nasr City); tel. (2) 24055845; fax (2) 24055876; e-mail egas@egas.com.eg; internet www.egas.com.eg; f. 2001 as part of a restructuring of the natural gas sector; strategic planning and promotion of investment in the natural gas industry; Chair. Dr SHERIF SOUSA.

UTILITIES

Electricity

In 1998 seven new electricity generation and distribution companies were created, under the direct ownership of the Egyptian Electricity Authority (EEA). In 2000 the EEA was restructured into a holding company (the Egyptian Electricity Holding Co—see below) controlling five generation and seven distribution companies. A specialized grid company was to manage electricity transmission. The Government commenced partial privatizations of the generation and distribution companies in 2001–02, while retaining control of the hydroelectric generation and grid management companies. By 2011/12 the total capacity of the national grid had increased to 27,250 MW, while a governemnt plan was in place to increase capacity still further up to 2020. Nine electricity distribution companies, six generation companies and a transmission company were administered by the Egyptian Electricity Holding Co in 2008.

Egyptian Electricity Holding Co: Sharia Ramses, Cairo (Nasr City); tel. (2) 24030681; fax (2) 24031871; e-mail isats_eehc@yahoo.com; internet www.egelec.com; fmrly Egyptian Electricity Authority; renamed as above 2000; Chair. GABER DSOUKY MUSTAFA IBRAHIM.

Gas

Egypt Gas: Corniche el-Nil, Warak-Imbaba, Cairo; tel. (2) 35406079; fax (2) 35408882; e-mail egyptgas@egyptgas.com.eg; internet www.egyptgas.com.eg; f. 1983; Chair. and Man. Dir NABIL HASHEM.

Egyptian Natural Gas Holding Co (EGAS): 85 Nasr Road, 1st District, Nasr City, Cairo; tel. (2) 24055845; fax (2) 24055876; e-mail egas@egas.com.eg; internet www.egas.com.eg; f. 2001; exploration, production, processing, transmission and distribution of natural gas; Chair. Eng. KHALED ABD EL-BADIE.

Water

Holding Co for Water and Wastewater: Corniche el-Nil, Cairo; tel. (2) 24583590; fax (2) 24583884; e-mail hcww@hcww.com.eg; internet www.hcww.com.eg; f. 2004; operation, maintenance and devt of water and wastewater facilities; oversees the operations of 20 affiliated regional water cos; Chair. Dr ABD EL-KAWI KHALIFA.

National Organization for Potable Water and Sanitary Drainage (NOPWASD): 6th Floor, Mogamma Bldg, el-Tahrir Sq., Cairo; tel. (2) 3557664; fax (2) 3562869; f. 1981; water and sewerage authority; Chair. MUHAMMAD KHALED MOUSTAFA.

TRADE UNIONS

Until early 2011 the Egyptian Trade Union Federation was the sole trade union federation in Egypt. However, following the removal from power of former President Hosni Mubarak in February 2011, two new organizations, the Egyptian Federation of Independent Trade Unions and Egyptian Democratic Labour Congress, were formed.

Egyptian Trade Union Federation (ETUF): 90 Sharia al-Galaa, Cairo; tel. (2) 5740362; fax (2) 5753427; internet www.etufegypt.com; f. 1957; govt-controlled; affiliated to Int. Confed. of Arab Trade Unions and to the Org. of African Trade Union Unity; 23 affiliated unions; 5m. mems; Pres. AHMED ABD AL-ZAHIR; Gen. Sec. MUHAMMAD IBRAHIM AZHARI.

Egyptian Federation of Independent Trade Unions (EFITU): Cairo; f. 2011; Pres. KAMAL ABU EITA; 261 affiliated unions and 2.4m. mems.

Egyptian Democratic Labour Congress (EDLC): 88 Sharia Qasr el-Eini, 1st Floor, Apt no. 7, Downtown, Cairo; tel. (2) 7962564; e-mail edlc.labourcongress@gmail.com; f. 2011; Leader KAMAL ABBAS; 271 affiliated unions and more than 1m. mems.

Transport

RAILWAYS

The area of the Nile Delta is well served by railways. Lines also run from Cairo southward along the Nile to Aswan, and westward along the coast to Salloum. As part of an integrated transport strategy being developed by the Government, up to US $1,500m. was allocated for the upgrading of Egypt's ageing railway infrastructure from 2007. A feasibility study into construction of a high-speed rail connection between Cairo and Alexandria was initiated in mid-2009. In 2010 the total length of Egyptian railways was 5,195 route-km.

Egyptian National Railways: Station Bldg, Midan Ramses, Cairo 11794; tel. (2) 5751000; fax (2) 5740000; e-mail support@enr.gov.eg; internet enr.gov.eg; f. 1852; length over 5,000 km; 42 km electrified; a 346-km line to carry phosphate and iron ore from the Bahariya mines, in the Western Desert, to the Helwan iron and steel works in south Cairo, was opened in 1973, and the Qena–Safaga line (length 223 km) came into operation in 1989; restructured in 2012.

Alexandria Passenger Transport Authority: POB 466, Aflaton, el-Shatby, Alexandria 21111; tel. (3) 5975223; fax (3) 5971187; e-mail apta@link.net; internet www.alexapta.org; f. 1860; controls City Tramways (28 km), Ramleh Electric Railway (16 km), suburban buses and minibuses (1,688 km); 119 tram cars, 519 suburban buses and minibuses; 362 suburban buses and minibuses from private sector; Chair. and Tech. Dir Eng. SHERINE KASSEM.

Cairo Metro: National Authority for Tunnels, POB 466, Ramses Bldg, Midan Ramses, Cairo 11794; tel. (2) 5742968; fax (2) 5742950; e-mail chairman@nat.org.eg; internet www.nat.org.eg; construction of the first electrified, 1,435-mm gauge underground transport system in Africa and the Middle East began in Cairo in 1982; Line 1, which opened to the public in 1987, has a total of 35 stations (5 underground), connects el-Marg el-Gedida with Helwan and is 44 km long with a 4.7-km tunnel beneath central Cairo; Line 2 links Shoubra el-Kheima with Giza, at el-Monib station, totalling 21.6 km (13 km in tunnel), and with 20 stations (12 underground), two of which interconnect with Line 1; the first section of Line 3, which will eventually connect Imbaba and Mohandessin with Cairo International Airport and will total 34.2 km (30.3 km in tunnel) with 29 stations (27 underground), opened in early 2012; the second of four construction phases was due for completion in 2014; Chair. Eng. ATTA A. R. EL-SHERBINY.

Cairo Transport Authority: Sharia Ramses, el-Gabal el-Ahmar, Cairo (Nasr City); tel. (2) 6845712; fax (2) 8654858; owned by the Governorate of Cairo; provider of public transport services in Greater Cairo, incl. tram, surface metro, bus and ferry services; rail system length 78 km (electrified); gauge 1,000 mm; operates 16 tram routes and 24 km of light railway; 720 cars; Chair. SALAH FARAG.

ROADS

The estimated total length of the road network in 2010 was 137,430 km, of which 836 km were motorways, 23,143 km were highways, main or national roads, and 113,451 km were secondary or regional roads. There are good metalled main roads as follows: Cairo–Alexandria (desert road); Cairo–Banha–Tanta–Damanhour–Alexandria; Cairo–Suez (desert road); Cairo–Ismailia–Port Said or Suez; and Cairo–Fayoum (desert road). The Ahmad Hamdi road tunnel (1.64 km) beneath the Suez Canal was opened in 1980. A second bridge over the Suez Canal was completed in 2001. A project to develop the Cairo–Alexandria highway into a 231-km motorway was under way in 2014. Other road projects at the planning or construction stage in 2013 included the Mediterranean coastal highway, linking Port Said with Mersa Matruh, and the Shoubra el-Kheima–Banha and Kafr el-Zayat–Alexandria highways.

General Authority for Roads, Bridges and Land Transport—Ministry of Transport (GARBLT): 105 Sharia Qasr el-Eini, Cairo; tel. (2) 7957429; fax (2) 7950591; e-mail garblt@idsc.gov.eg; Chair. Eng. TAREK EL-ATTAR.

SHIPPING

Egypt's principal ports are Alexandria, Port Said and Suez. A port constructed at a cost of £E315m., and designed to handle up to 16m. metric tons of cargo per year in its first stage of development, was opened at Damietta in 1986. By mid-2008 handling capacity at Damietta had increased to 19.7m. tons. Egypt's first privately operated port was opened in 2002 at Ain Sokhna on the Red Sea coast, near the southern entrance of the Suez Canal. Sokhna's capacity was projected to increase from 6m. tons in 2005 to 90m. tons by 2020. The modernization of the quays at Alexandria port and the construction of two new container terminals at the adjacent Dakahlia port were completed during the first half of 2007. The first phase of a major expansion of the Suez Canal Container Terminal at Port Said, which envisaged a new container terminal with a total capacity of 5.4m. 20-foot equivalent units per year, was inaugurated in August 2010; the second phase was ongoing in early 2014.

At 31 December 2013 Egypt's flag registered fleet totalled 445 vessels, with an aggregate displacement of 1.1m. grt, of which 13 were bulk carriers, three were fish carriers and 17 were general cargo ships.

Port and Regulatory Authorities

Maritime Transport Sector: Ministry of Transport, 4 Sharia Ptolemy, Bab Sharqi, 21514 Alexandria; tel. (3) 4869836; fax (3) 4874674; e-mail mmt@idsc.net.eg; internet www.mts.gov.eg; supervision of the maritime sector; Dir-Gen. Rear-Adm. MUHAMMAD ABD AL-MENEM.

Alexandria Port Authority: 106 Sharia el-Hourriya, Alexandria 26514; tel. (3) 4800359; fax (3) 4807098; e-mail info@apa.gov.eg; internet www.apa.gov.eg; f. 1966; management of Alexandria and Dakahlia ports; Chair. Rear-Adm. AL-SAYED HAMAD SHAKER HEDAYA; Vice-Chair. Rear-Adm. ADEL YASSIN HAMAD.

Damietta Port Authority: POB 13, Damietta; tel. (57) 2290006; fax (57) 2290930; e-mail chairman@damietta-port.gov.eg; internet www.damietta-port.gov.eg; Chair. Adm. IBRAHIM FLAIFEL.

Port Said Port Authority: Intersection Sharia Moustafa Kamel and Sharia Azmy, Port Said; tel. (66) 3348270; fax (66) 3348262; e-mail info@psdports.org; internet www.psdports.org; Chair. Adm. IBRAHIM MUHAMMAD SADEK.

Red Sea Ports Authority: POB 1, Port Tawfik, Suez; tel. (62) 3190731; fax (62) 3191117; e-mail rspsite@emdb.gov.eg; responsible for ports incl. Suez, Sokhna and Hurghada; Chair. Gen. MUHAMMAD ABD EL-KADER.

Principal Shipping Companies

Arab Maritime Petroleum Transport Co (AMPTC): POB 143, 9th Floor, Nile Tower Bldg, 21 Sharia Giza, 12211 Giza; tel. (2) 35701311; fax (2) 33378080; e-mail amptc.cairo@amptc.net; internet www.amptc.net; f. 1973; affiliated to the Org. of Arab Petroleum Exporting Countries; 11 vessels; Gen. Man. SULAYMAN AL-BASSAM.

Canal Shipping Agencies Co: 26 Sharia Palestine, Port Said; tel. (66) 3227500; fax (66) 3239896; e-mail csaagencies@canalshipping.net; internet www.canalshipping.net; f. 1965; shipping agency, cargo and forwarding services; affiliated cos: Assuit Shipping Agency, Aswan Shipping Agency, Damanhour Shipping Agency, El-Menia Shipping Agency; Chair. FOUAD EL-SAYED EL-MULLA.

Egyptian Navigation Co (ENC): 2 el-Nasr St, el-Gomrok, Alexandria; tel. (3) 4800050; fax (3) 4871345; e-mail enc@dataxprs.com.eg; internet www.enc.com.eg; f. 1961; owners and operators of Egypt's mercantile marine; international trade transportation; 12 vessels; Chair. and Man. Dir AMR GAMAL EL-DIN ROUSHDY.

Holding Co for Maritime and Land Transport: POB 3005, Alexandria; tel. (3) 4865547; fax (3) 4872647; e-mail holding@hcmlt.com; internet www.hcmlt.gov.eg; govt-owned; 17 affiliated cos, incl. General Co for River Nile Transportation, Port Said Container and Cargo Handling Co, General Egyptian Warehouses Co; Chair. Adm. MUHAMMAD YOUSUF.

International Maritime Services Co: 20 Sharia Salah Salem, Alexandria; tel. (3) 4840817; fax (3) 4869177; e-mail agency@imsalex.com; internet www.imsalex.com; f. 1986; shipping agency, freight-forwarding, transshipment contractor, marine surveyor; subsidiary: Egyptian Register of Shipping Co; Chair. Capt. MONTASSER EL-SOKKARY.

National Navigation Co: 4 Sharia El-Hegaz, Cairo (Heliopolis); tel. (2) 24525575; fax (2) 24526171; e-mail nnc@nnc.com.eg; internet www.nnc.com.eg; f. 1981; specializes in bulk cargoes; operates passenger services between Egypt and Saudi Arabia; 18 vessels; Chair. and Man. Dir TAMER ABD EL-ALIM.

Pan-Arab Shipping Co: POB 39, 404 ave el-Hourriya, Rushdi, Alexandria; tel. (3) 5468835; fax (3) 5469533; internet www.pan-arab.org; f. 1974; Arab League Co; bulk handling, forwarding and warehousing services; 5 vessels; Chair. Adm. MUHAMMAD SHERIF EL-SADEK; Gen. Man. Capt. MAMDOUH EL-GUINDY.

Red Sea Navigation Co: 10 Gowhar el-Khaled St, Port Tawfik, Suez; tel. (62) 3196971; fax (62) 9136915; e-mail suez@rdnav.com; internet www.rdnav.com; f. 1986; operates a fleet of eight cargo vessels; shipping agency, Suez Canal transit and stevedoring; Chair. ABD EL-MAJID MATAR.

THE SUEZ CANAL

In 2012 a total of 17,225 vessels, with a net displacement of 739.9m. tons, used the Suez Canal, linking the Mediterranean and Red Seas.

Length of canal: 190 km; maximum permissible draught: 20.73 m (68 ft); breadth of canal at water level and breadth between buoys defining the navigable channel at −11 m: 365 m and 225 m, respectively, in the northern section, and 305 m and 205 m in the southern section.

Suez Canal Authority (Hay'at Canal al-Suways): Irshad Bldg, Ismailia; Cairo Office: 6 Sharia Lazoughli, Cairo (Garden City); tel. (64) 3392010; fax (64) 3392834; e-mail info@suezcanal.gov.eg; internet www.suezcanal.gov.eg; f. 1956; govt-owned; Chair. and CEO Vice-Adm. MOHAB MUHAMMAD HUSSEIN MAMISH.

Suez Canal Container Terminal: POB 247, Port Said; tel. (66) 3254960; fax (66) 3254970; e-mail scct@scctportsaid.com; internet www.scctportsaid.com; f. 2000, with 30-year concession to operate the East Port Said container terminal; Man. Dir KLAUS HOLM LAURSEN.

CIVIL AVIATION

The main international airports are at Cairo (located at Heliopolis, 23 km from the centre of the city), Sharm el-Sheikh and Hurghada. A major programme of expansion at Cairo International Airport commenced in 2004: a third terminal was formally inaugurated in December 2008 and became fully operational in June 2009, while a fourth runway was completed in October 2010. Meanwhile, Cairo's Terminal Two was closed in April 2010 in preparation for the commencement of a US $400m. expansion project to increase the terminal's annual capacity to 7.5m. passengers; construction was expected to be completed by 2013. Construction work on a new international airport at Borg el-Arab (40 km south-west of Alexandria) was inaugurated in November 2010. The completion of a second terminal at Sharm el-Sheikh airport in 2007 increased capacity from 3m. to 7.5m. passengers per year; plans for a third terminal, which would increase annual passenger-handling capacity to 15m., were under way in early 2014.

EgyptAir: Administration Complex, Cairo International Airport, Cairo (Heliopolis); tel. (2) 22674700; fax (2) 22663773; e-mail callcenter@egyptair.com; internet www.egyptair.com.eg; f. 1932 as Misr Airwork; known as United Arab Airlines 1960–71; restructured as a holding co with nine subsidiaries 2002; operates internal services in Egypt and external services throughout the Middle East, Far East, Africa, Europe and the USA; Chair. and CEO HUSSEIN MASSOUD (EgyptAir Holding Co); Chair. and CEO Capt. ALAA ASHOUR (EgyptAir Airlines).

Egyptian Civil Aviation Authority: ECAA Complex, Sharia Airport, Cairo 11776; tel. (2) 2677610; fax (2) 2470351; e-mail info@civilaviation.gov.eg; internet www.civilaviation.gov.eg; f. 2000; Pres. Capt. SAMEH EL-HEFNI.

Egyptian Holding Co for Airports and Air Navigation (EHCAAN): EHCAAN Bldg, Airport Rd, Cairo; tel. (2) 6352442; fax (2) 2663440; e-mail info@ehcaan.com; internet www.ehcaan.com; f. 2001; responsible for management and devt of all Egyptian airports; Chair. MUHAMMAD FATHALLAH REFAAT.

Cairo Airport Company: Cairo International Airport, 11776 Cairo (Heliopolis); tel. (2) 2474245; fax (2) 2432522; e-mail cac@cairo-airport.com; internet www.cairo-airport.com; under management of Egyptian Holding Co since 2003; Chair. Dr AHMAD HAFIZ; Exec. Dir PETER DIENSTBACH.

Egyptian Airports Co: Cairo; tel. (2) 22739417; fax (2) 22739416; e-mail info@eac-airports.com; internet www.eac-airports.com; f. 2001; management and devt of 19 regional airports; Chair. and Man. Dir YUSRI GAMAL EL-DIN.

Tourism

Tourism is currently Egypt's second largest source of revenue, generating an estimated US $9,940m. (excluding passenger transport) in 2012. Despite further terrorist attacks in the Sinai region during 2004–06, the number of tourists visiting the country increased significantly in the following years, reaching some 14.7m. by 2010. The industry was severely affected by the political unrest of 2011; according to official estimates, just 9.8m. tourists visited Egypt in that year. The sector recovered somewhat in 2012, with the number of arrivals increasing to 11.5m. However, the outbreak of violence in mid-2013 was expected to prompt a further decline.

Egyptian Tourist Authority: Misr Travel Tower, 32 Sharia Emtidad Ramses, Abbassia Sq., Cairo; tel. (2) 2854509; fax (2) 2854363; e-mail user@egypt.travel; internet www.egypt.travel; f. 1965; brs at Alexandria, Port Said, Suez, Luxor and Aswan; Chair. AMR EL-EZABI.

Egyptian General Co for Tourism and Hotels (EGOTH): 4 Sharia Latin America, 11519 Cairo (Garden City); tel. (2) 27942914; fax (2) 27943531; e-mail info@egoth.com.eg; internet www.egoth.com.eg; f. 1961; affiliated to the Holding Co for Tourism, Hotels and Cinema; Chair. and Man. Dir NABIL SELIM.

Defence

Commander-in-Chief of the Armed Forces: Col Gen. SIDKI SOBHI SAYED AHMED.

Chief of Staff of the Armed Forces: Lt-Gen. MAHMOUD IBRAHIM HEGAZI.

Commander of the Air Force: Lt-Gen. YOUNES HAMED.

Commander of Air Defence Forces: Maj.-Gen. ABD EL-MONEIM BAYOUMI AL-TERRAS.

Commander-in-Chief of the Navy: Vice Adm. OSAMA AHMED EL-GENDI.

Budgeted Defence Expenditure (2013): £E34,300m.

Military service: one–three years, selective.

Total armed forces (as assessed at November 2013): 438,500: army 310,000; air defence command 80,000; navy 18,500 (10,000 conscripts); air force 30,000 (10,000 conscripts). Reserves 479,000.

Paramilitary Forces (as assessed at November 2013): est. 397,000 (Central Security Forces 325,000; National Guard 60,000 and Border Guard 12,000).

Education

Education is compulsory for eight years between six and 14 years of age. Primary education, beginning at six years of age, lasts for five years. Secondary education, beginning at 11 years of age, lasts for a further six years, comprising two cycles (the first being preparatory) of three years each. In 2011, according to UNESCO estimates, primary enrolment included an estimated 95% of children in the relevant age-group, while the comparable ratio for secondary enrolment was estimated at 80%. In 2010/11 there were an estimated 1,722,968 students enrolled at universities. The Al-Azhar University and its various preparatory and associated institutes provide instruction and training in several disciplines, with emphasis on adherence to Islamic principles and teachings. Education is free at all levels. In 2008/09 a total of £E39,880m. (some 11.2% of total expenditure) was allocated to education by the central Government.

EL SALVADOR

Introductory Survey

LOCATION, CLIMATE, LANGUAGE, RELIGION, FLAG, CAPITAL

The Republic of El Salvador lies on the Pacific coast of Central America. It is bounded by Guatemala to the west and by Honduras to the north and east. The climate varies from tropical on the coastal plain to temperate in the uplands. The language is Spanish. About 76% of the population are Roman Catholics, and other Christian churches are represented. The civil flag (proportions 2 by 3) consists of three equal horizontal stripes, of blue, over white, over blue. The state flag differs by the addition, in the centre of the white stripe, of the national coat of arms. The capital is San Salvador.

CONTEMPORARY POLITICAL HISTORY

Historical Context

El Salvador was ruled by Spain until 1821, and became independent in 1839. Since then the country's history has been one of frequent coups and outbursts of political violence. Gen. Maximiliano Hernández Martínez became President in 1931, and ruthlessly suppressed a peasant uprising, with an alleged 30,000 killings (including that of Farabundo Martí, the leader of the rebel peasants), in 1932. Hernández was deposed in 1944, and the next elected President, Gen. Salvador Castañeda Castro, was overthrown in 1948. His successor, Lt-Col Oscar Osorio (1950–56), relinquished power to Lt-Col José María Lemus, who was replaced by a military junta in 1960, which was itself supplanted by another junta in 1961. Under this Junta, the conservative Partido de Conciliación Nacional (PCN) was established and won all 54 seats in elections to the Asamblea Legislativa (Legislative Assembly). Lt-Col Julio Adalberto Rivera, was elected unopposed to the presidency in 1962. He was succeeded by Gen. Fidel Sánchez Hernández in 1967.

Domestic Political Affairs

In the 1972 presidential election Col Arturo Armando Molina Barraza, candidate of the ruling PCN, was elected, despite allegations of massive electoral fraud. Similar allegations were made during the 1977 presidential election, after which the PCN candidate, Gen. Carlos Humberto Romero Mena, took office.

Reports of violations of human rights by the Government were widespread. The polarization of left and right after 1972 was characterized by an increase in guerrilla activity. In 1979 President Romero was overthrown and replaced by a Junta of civilians and army officers. The Junta, which promised to install a democratic system and to organize elections, declared a political amnesty and invited participation from the guerrilla groups, but violence continued between government troops and guerrilla forces, and elections were postponed. In January 1980 an ultimatum from progressive members of the Government resulted in the formation of a new Government, a coalition of military officers and the Partido Demócrata Cristiano (PDC). In March the country moved closer to full-scale civil war following the assassination of the Roman Catholic Archbishop of San Salvador, Oscar Romero, an outspoken supporter of human rights.

In December 1980 José Napoleón Duarte, a member of the Junta, was sworn in as President. In 1981 the guerrillas launched their 'final offensive' and, after initial gains, the opposition front, Frente Democrático Revolucionario—FDR (allied with the guerrilla front, the Frente Farabundo Martí para la Liberación Nacional—FMLN), proposed negotiations with the USA. The US authorities referred them to the Salvadorean Government, which refused to recognize the FDR while it was linked with the guerrillas. The USA affirmed its support for the Duarte Government and provided civilian and military aid. During 1981 the guerrilla forces unified and strengthened their control over the north and east of the country. Attacks on economic targets continued, while the army retaliated by acting indiscriminately against the local population in guerrilla-controlled areas. By December there were an estimated 300,000 Salvadorean refugees, many of whom had fled to neighbouring countries.

At elections to a National Constituent Assembly in March 1982 the PDC failed to win an absolute majority against the five right-wing parties, which formed a Government of National Unity. Major Roberto D'Aubuisson Arrieta, leader of the extreme right-wing Alianza Republicana Nacionalista (ARENA), became President of the National Constituent Assembly. In April a political independent, Alvaro Magaña Borja, was elected interim President. However, the Assembly voted to award itself considerable power over the President.

Following a period of intense activity by 'death squads' in 1983, the US Government urged the removal of several high-level officials. In 1984, following a number of strategic territorial advances, the FDR-FMLN proposed the formation of a broadly based provisional government, as part of a peace plan without preconditions. The plan was rejected by the Government. The guerrillas refused to participate in the 1984 presidential election. As no candidate emerged with a clear majority, a second round of voting was held, when the PDC's José Napoleón Duarte emerged victorious.

Duarte instituted a purge of the armed forces and the disbanding of the notorious Treasury Police. Both the FDR-FMLN and the President expressed their willingness to commence peace negotiations, and the Government opened discussions with guerrilla leaders in Chalatenango in October 1984. A second round of negotiations ended amid accusations of intransigence from both sides. The PDC won a clear majority in the general election of March 1985.

In 1987 the Salvadorean Government's participation in a peace plan for Central America, which was signed in August in Guatemala City, encouraged hopes that a peaceful solution could be found to the conflict. However, the political situation deteriorated in late 1987, following President Duarte's public denunciation of D'Aubuisson's complicity in the murder of Archbishop Romero in 1980. Furthermore, in 1988 there were increasing reports of the resurgence of death squads, and it was suggested that abuses of human rights were rapidly returning to the level reached at the beginning of the internal conflict.

The peace process

By the end of 1988 it was estimated that as many as 70,000 Salvadoreans had died in the course of the civil war, while the US Administration had provided some US $3,000m. in aid to the Government. Moreover, by early 1989 many areas appeared to be without government, following the resignations of some 75 mayors, following death threats by the FMLN. In January, however, radical new peace proposals were announced by the FMLN, which, for the first time, expressed its willingness to participate in the electoral process. However, ceasefire negotiations failed to produce agreement. The FMLN advocated a boycott of the March presidential election, and intensified its campaign of violence. The ballot resulted in victory for the ARENA candidate, Alfredo Cristiani Burkard.

In August 1989 the Heads of State of five Central American countries signed an agreement in Tela, Honduras. The accord included an appeal to the FMLN to abandon its military campaign and to initiate dialogue with the Salvadorean Government. In November the UN Security Council authorized the creation of the UN Observer Group for Central America (ONUCA), a multinational military force, to monitor developments in the region. In the same month the FMLN launched a military offensive, resulting in the fiercest fighting for nine years. The Government declared a state of siege, and stability was further undermined when, on 16 November, gunmen murdered the head of a San Salvador Jesuit university and five other Jesuit priests, along with the Jesuits' housekeeper and her daughter. In January 1990, however, the FMLN announced that it would accept an offer to attend peace talks arranged by the UN Secretary-General, Javier Pérez de Cuéllar. In March President Cristiani announced that he was willing to offer a comprehensive amnesty, territorial concessions and the opportunity to participate fully in political processes to members of the FMLN, as part of a broad-based peace proposal.

Negotiations between the Government and the FMLN continued throughout 1991. In March a new initiative for the negotiation of a peace settlement was presented by the FMLN in Managua, Nicaragua. This new proposal dispensed with previous stipulations put forward by the guerrillas that military and constitutional reforms should be effected prior to any ceasefire. An agreement on human rights (including the creation of a three-member truth commission, to be appointed by the UN Secretary-General) and on judicial and electoral reform was reached, and was swiftly approved by the Assembly. The working structure of a ceasefire and the detailed reform and purge of the armed forces were set aside for negotiation at a later date.

In May 1991 the UN Security Council voted to create an observer mission to El Salvador (ONUSAL), to be charged with the verification of accords reached between the Government and the FMLN, despite protests by right-wing groups. In August both sides attended discussions in New York, USA, where a new framework for peace was agreed. A National Commission for the Consolidation of Peace was to be created, which would supervise the enforcement of guarantees for the political integration of the guerrillas. The FMLN also secured guaranteed territorial rights for peasants settled in guerrilla-controlled areas, and the participation of former FMLN members in a National Civilian Police (Policía Nacional Civil—PNC).

In December 1991 a new peace initiative was announced. Under the terms of the agreement, a formal ceasefire was to be implemented on 1 February 1992, under the supervision of some 1,000 UN personnel. The FMLN was to begin a process of disarmament, to be completed by 31 October. The success of the ceasefire agreement was expected to be dependent upon the adequate implementation, by the Government, of previously agreed reforms to the judiciary, the electoral system, guarantees of territorial rights, human rights, and guerrilla participation in civil defence, and of newly agreed reforms to the armed forces. On 16 January 1992, at Chapultepec Castle in Mexico City, Mexico, the formal peace accord was ratified. In San Salvador on 15 December the conflict was formally concluded. On the same day the FMLN was officially registered and recognized as a legitimate political party.

The Truth Commission

In November 1992, in accordance with the terms of the December 1991 peace accord, the Truth Commission announced the names of more than 200 military personnel alleged to have participated in abuses of human rights during the civil war. The reluctance of the Government to remove those personnel threatened the further successful implementation of the peace process, and prompted the FMLN to delay the demobilization of its forces and the destruction of its remaining arsenals. The situation was exacerbated in March 1993 by the publication of the Commission's report, which attributed responsibility for the vast majority of the war's 75,000 fatalities to the counter-insurgency measures of the armed forces, including the systematic eradication of civilians thought to harbour left-wing sympathies. Some 400 murders were attributed to the FMLN. Among those accused of human rights atrocities was the late ARENA founder Roberto D'Aubuisson Arrieta, who was identified as the authority behind the murder of Archbishop Romero; also implicated were the Minister of Defence and Public Security, Gen. René Emilio Ponce, his deputy, Gen. Orlando Zepeda, and the former air force chief, Gen. Juan Rafael Bustillo, who were believed to have ordered the murder of the six Jesuits in 1989. (In 1991 Col Guillermo Benavides and an army lieutenant were found guilty of murder and sentenced to 30 years' imprisonment; they were controversially released after just two years, however, following the declaration of an amnesty. In 2004 Captain Alvaro Rafael Saravia was found guilty of planning and facilitating the murder of Archbishop Romero in a civil case brought in a US court. He was ordered, *in absentia*, to pay US $2.5m. in compensation and $7.5m. in punitive damages.) The report recommended that the judiciary should be reorganized, and that all individuals identified by the report should be permanently excluded from all institutions of national defence and public security, and should be barred from holding public office for a period of 10 years.

Representatives of the Government and the armed forces challenged the legal validity of the Commission's report, despite the UN's insistence that its recommendations were mandatory under the terms of the peace accord. Nevertheless, the strength of ARENA's representation in the Assembly overcame opposition from the PDC, the Convergencia Democrática (CD, a left-wing alliance comprising two of the leading groups within the FDR-FMLN and the Partido Social Demócrata) and the Movimiento Nacional Revolucionario (MNR), and later in March 1993 secured the approval of an amnesty law to extend to all political crimes committed before 1992, prompting widespread public outrage. In June the Government announced the compulsory retirement of several veteran military officers, including Gen. Ponce, although their immunity from prosecution was still guaranteed.

The findings of the Truth Commission—together with declassified documents relating to the Administrations of former US Presidents Ronald Reagan and George Bush, Sr—suggested that detailed knowledge of abuses of human rights was suppressed by US officials in order to continue to secure congressional funding for the Government in El Salvador in the 1980s. Evidence also emerged that US military training had been provided, in at least one instance, for an El Salvadorean 'death squad'.

The continuing dominance of ARENA

Presidential and legislative elections took place in 1994. ARENA's presidential candidate, Armando Calderón Sol, emerged victorious following two rounds of voting. ARENA candidates also achieved considerable success in the legislative elections. FMLN candidates were also considered to have performed well in the party's first electoral contest, winning 21 seats in the Assembly.

Meanwhile, serious divisions emerged within the FMLN during 1994, and in December two constituent parties, the Resistencia Nacional (RN) and the Expresión Renovadora del Pueblo (ERP—formerly the Fuerzas Armadas de la Resistencia Nacional and the Ejército Revolucionario Popular guerrilla groups, respectively) announced their withdrawal from the party. In 1995 the Secretary-General of the ERP, Joaquín Villalobos, announced the formation of a new centre-left political force, the Partido Demócrata (PD), comprising the ERP, the RN, the MNR and a dissident faction of the PDC.

In May 1994 the UN Security Council extended the ONUSAL mandate for a further six months; two further extensions to the mandate were subsequently approved. A small contingent of UN observers, MINUSAL, was mandated to remain in El Salvador until December 1996, the revised deadline for the fulfilment of the outstanding terms of the peace accord.

The results of the congressional and municipal elections of 1997 demonstrated a significant increase in support for the FMLN and a considerable erosion of ARENA's predominance, with the party securing 29 seats in the Assembly, just one more than the FMLN. Nevertheless, the presidential election of 1999 was won by Francisco Flores Pérez, the ARENA candidate. The Government was subsequently embarrassed by allegations that foreign funds, donated for disaster relief following the impact of Hurricane Mitch in 1998, had been diverted by ARENA to former paramilitaries in an attempt to buy votes for Flores.

Dissatisfaction with the ARENA Government was demonstrated in the results of the legislative elections of March 2000, in which the FMLN became the largest single party in the Assembly. Nevertheless, during 2001 internal divisions deepened between the more orthodox and the reformist elements of the FMLN, culminating in the expulsion of the reformist leader Facundo Guardado. Salvador Sánchez Cerén, from the party's orthodox wing, was elected leader. Following Sánchez's election, in January 2002 six reformist FMLN deputies left the party, thus reducing the FMLN's legislative representation. ARENA became the largest parliamentary bloc.

In a general election held in March 2003 the FMLN garnered 31 seats in the Legislative Assembly. ARENA secured an unexpectedly low 27 seats. Following the election, President Flores announced an initiative, named 'Mano Dura' (Firm Hand), to combat the rising violent crime in the country, particularly that attributed to street gangs, or *maras*.

The ARENA candidate, businessman Elías Antonio (Tony) Saca, secured an overwhelming victory in the March 2004 presidential election. President Saca undertook to reduce gang-related crime. The 'Súper Mano Dura' initiative, launched in September as an extension of the 'Mano Dura' campaign (which the Supreme Court had ruled unconstitutional), gained widespread support. The renewed campaign included proposals to appoint prosecutors dedicated to bringing charges against members of the *maras* and to rehabilitate gang members. In May 2005 Saca introduced extensive house-to-house searches with the stated aims of confiscating illegal firearms and drugs and arresting known murderers; the preventive searches were widely criticized as unconstitutional. In July Saca announced the creation of a new joint task force, intended to reinforce the police presence in the five departments with the highest rates of violent crime.

In the general election of March 2006, ARENA secured 34 parliamentary seats, while the FMLN won 32. The right-wing parties secured a working majority in the Assembly, although the FMLN regained its power to veto proposals that required a two-thirds' majority.

In June 2006 a new strategy to combat violent crime was proposed. The Security Master Plan was designed to increase the judicial conviction rate by improving evidence quality. Moreover, in July the legislature approved reforms to restrict the possession of firearms. In November President Saca announced that the joint task force and the PNC were each to be strengthened by an additional 2,000 recruits.

The FMLN in power

In a general election in January 2009 ARENA lost two seats in congress, reducing its representation to 32 seats, while the FMLN secured 35 seats, an increase of three. The PCN and PDC took 11 and five seats, respectively. Shortly after the legislative elections, both the PDC and the PCN announced their withdrawal from the March presidential ballot. With only the FMLN and ARENA candidates remaining in the contest, it was decided that the election on 15 March would not go to a second round of voting. In the event, Carlos Mauricio Funes Cartagena, from the moderate wing of the FMLN, secured 51.3% and Rodrigo Avila Avilez, representing ARENA, attracted 48.7% of votes, marking the first time that ARENA had lost control of the presidency since the end of the civil war in 1992.

The new President was immediately confronted with a hostile legislature. ARENA, the PCN and the PDC had formed an opposition coalition in May 2009, allowing them to block Funes' proposed legislation. In July Funes was forced to compromise over the composition of the Supreme Court and the appointment of the Procurator-General, which preserved ARENA's domination of the judiciary, thereby undermining the President's pledge to prosecute members of the previous administration for corruption. However, in a dramatic manifestation of the growing disharmony within ARENA, in October 12 deputies announced their withdrawal from the party and formed a new legislative bloc, the Gran Alianza por la Unidad Nacional (GANA). With the loss of its majority in the legislature, the right-wing coalition collapsed. The effects of this upheaval were observed in the following month when GANA, the PCN and the PDC voted with the FMLN to approve Funes' budget, which allocated additional funding for health and education, leaving ARENA politically isolated. Also approved with the help of the GANA deputies, in December, was a fiscal reform bill, intended to increase the low levels of tax collection. As an indication of the continuing discord within ARENA, former President Saca was expelled from the party in the same month; party officials blamed him for the defection of the 12 deputies and the party's lacklustre performance in the presidential election. (Saca was subsequently replaced as ARENA leader by former President Cristiani.)

Meanwhile, official crime figures released in mid-2009 indicated that extortion and murder were on the rise. Funes had espoused the benefits of focusing on the causes of crime, such as poverty and unemployment, but his security strategy, which involved the deployment of the army in high-crime areas to assist police operations, seemed to be a continuation of his right-wing predecessors' 'Mano Dura' campaigns and, although popular with the public, had little effect on crime.

Although Funes had taken advantage of ARENA's internal divisions, tensions within the FMLN also grew steadily throughout 2009. The party was still dominated by hard-liners from the civil war, such as Salvador Sánchez Cerén, the Vice-President. In November, during a visit to Venezuela, Sánchez declared his support for the socialism propounded by Venezuelan head of state Hugo Chávez, and criticized the USA; in December, while visiting Cuba, a country with which Funes had restored diplomatic relations in June, Sánchez proclaimed El Salvador's interest in joining the Venezuelan-led Bolivarian Alliance for the Peoples of our America (Alianza Bolivariana para las Pueblos de Nuestra América—ALBA, see p. 463) grouping. Funes, a moderate, swiftly dismissed Sánchez's remarks and reaffirmed that there would be no radical left-wing shift in El Salvador, a stance that he had painstakingly maintained throughout the year in order to reassure the electorate and business interests.

In January 2010 Funes made the country's first official apology for the human rights violations perpetrated by the right-wing Governments that were in power throughout the civil war period. In a further unprecedented move, Funes issued a similar formal apology in March for the state's role in the murder of Archbishop Romero.

A new security strategy was announced in February 2010 to bolster the police force and increase co-operation with the military. In the same month, the Assembly adopted legislation permitting investigative teams to monitor telephone calls and increasing prison terms for juveniles. In May the Government revealed that further military troops would be deployed to assist in police operations and to maintain order in the country's gaols. However, two brutal attacks on buses in the capital in June, killing 17 people, provoked nationwide outrage. Under intense pressure to address decisively the escalating crime problem, Funes submitted to the Assembly a bill outlawing the *maras* and gang membership, approved in September. However, the new law failed to establish the criteria for proving membership, and it was feared that the overcrowded prison system would not be able to cope with the expected upsurge in inmates. Shortly afterwards, in retaliation for the approval of the legislation, the major *maras* used the threat of violent reprisals to coerce bus operators throughout the country to observe a three-day strike, damaging the economy, generating transport chaos nationwide and prompting the Government to deploy additional military troops onto the streets. None the less, Funes refused to soften his security strategy: a further anti-crime bill was adopted by the legislature later in the month, lengthening gaol sentences for weapons dealers, and the Government introduced new restrictions on prisoners, in an attempt to prevent inmates from organizing criminal acts from behind bars.

The strained relationship between Funes and the FMLN continued during 2010, forcing the President to seek the co-operation of the right-wing blocs in the Legislative Assembly. The Minister of Agriculture and Livestock, Manuel Sevilla, resigned in May, claiming that Funes had instructed him to divert ministry resources to members of GANA and the PCN in order to secure their legislative support. Funes denied the allegation, but the affair exacerbated the tensions. Nevertheless, there was evidence of a rapprochement with the FMLN in October. The improvement of ties with Cuba and Russia and the submission to the Assembly of a proposal to increase pensions and raise the minimum wage for public sector workers were warmly welcomed by left-wing deputies.

In July 2010 the Supreme Court ruled as unconstitutional the requirement that legislative and municipal election candidates must belong to a political party. The Court also eliminated the controversial 'closed list' voting system, whereby the electorate could only vote for parties rather than designated candidates, which placed excessive power in the hands of those political leaders who created the party lists, encouraging parliamentarians to prioritize party interests over those of their constituents. Just before the Court made its announcement, the deputies in the Assembly (all of whom belonged to political parties) attempted to undermine the ruling by pre-emptively adopting a constitutional amendment making party membership compulsory for election candidates. (However, to become law, the amendment would also require the approval of the 2012–15 Assembly.) Nevertheless, in accordance with the Court's judgment, in December 2010 the legislature voted in favour of permitting independents to compete in legislative and municipal ballots.

The Supreme Court, overruling an earlier decision by the legislature, announced the deregistration of the PCN and the PDC in April 2011, on the grounds that during the 2004 presidential poll they had not secured the constitutionally required 3% of the ballot. The PCN and the PDC were reconstituted as the Concertación Nacional (CN) and the Partido de la Esperanza (PES), respectively.

In May 2011 a Spanish court accused 20 former Salvadorean soldiers of perpetrating the 1989 Jesuit massacre in San Salvador, most of the victims of which were Spanish nationals. Nine of the accused, including former Minister of Defence Rafael Humberto Larios, surrendered themselves to the Salvadorean authorities in August. However, since Spain had neglected to submit an official extradition order, the Supreme Court authorized their release later that month, prompting criticism from human rights groups. The Spanish authorities formally requested the extradition of 13 of the accused in December. In the following month Funes notably urged the legislature to abrogate the amnesty law, an unprecedented appeal from a Salvadorean head of state. The Supreme Court ruled against the Spanish extradition request in May 2012, declaring that El

Salvador's extradition laws (adopted in 2000) could not be applied retroactively.

Funes ratified a controversial legislative decree in June 2011 temporarily requiring Constitutional Court decisions to be endorsed by all of the serving judges rather than by a majority. This effectively granted the sole right-wing judge the power of veto over the remaining non-partisan judges, thereby rendering the Court largely inoperable and undermining its independence. The Court regarded this move as an unconstitutional overextension of the legislature's authority and rejected the decree, which had attracted widespread censure. However, the Legislative Assembly appeared reluctant to revoke the decree, ostensibly owing to concerns about the Court's growing assertiveness with respect to party political matters and a consequent desire to exert greater control over the judiciary. This institutional impasse was resolved in July, when the legislature, under intense public pressure, finally abrogated the decree.

Funes announced further anti-crime measures in mid-2011, including an extension of the military's involvement in civil policing activities, the enrolment of additional police recruits and the provision of extra financing for the security forces. Nevertheless, with the murder rate reaching a record high in 2011, Minister of Justice and Public Security Manuel Melgar resigned in November; he was succeeded by Gen. (retd) David Victoriano Munguía Payés, who was replaced as Minister of National Defence by Gen. José Atilio Benítez. Some FMLN members expressed disapproval at Munguía's appointment owing to his military background, while the appointment of Francisco Ramón Salinas, another former general, as chief of police generated further controversy in January 2012.

The 2012 legislative elections

ARENA secured a narrow victory in the legislative elections conducted on 11 March 2012, gaining control of 33 of the 84 seats in the Legislative Assembly. The FMLN won 31 seats, while GANA obtained 11, the CN six, and the PES, the Cambio Democrático (CD) and the CN-PES (the two parties formed a coalition in one department) each received one. Turnout was recorded at approximately 55%. In the concurrent municipal polls, ARENA won 116 mayoralties, including San Salvador, and the FMLN secured 85. Analysts suggested that the FMLN had lost votes because of the country's ongoing economic problems and persistently high crime rates. None the less, Funes was expected to be able to advance his legislative agenda with continuing informal support from GANA and some of the smaller parties in the Assembly.

Armando Flores was appointed as the new Minister of the Economy in April 2012, following the resignation of Héctor Dada Hirezi earlier that month. In July five new Supreme Court judges—nominated by the Assembly in April, despite opposition from ARENA—commenced their duties. However, the incumbent members of the Court rejected the Assembly's judicial appointees, arguing that the legislature had defied constitutional procedures. This fresh institutional conflict, in effect, resulted in the creation of two rival Supreme Courts. The Central American Court of Justice ruled in favour of the Assembly in August, and the dispute was finally resolved later that month when Funes brokered a cross-party compromise agreement on the composition of the Supreme Court. Four of ARENA's representatives in the Assembly were stripped of their party membership in November after endorsing the FMLN's 2013 budget. As a consequence of these expulsions, the FMLN regained its former status as the majority party in the legislature.

In November 2012 Vice-President Sánchez was formally named as the FMLN's candidate in the upcoming presidential election, due to be held in February 2014. Sánchez had resigned as Minister of Education in June 2012 in order that he could concentrate on the forthcoming election campaign, with Franzis Hato Hasbún appointed as his successor. (ARENA had selected Norman Quijano, the mayor of San Salvador, as its presidential nominee in September.) Legislation bestowing enhanced voting privileges upon Salvadoreans resident overseas received congressional approval in January 2013.

The Inter-American Court of Human Rights (an institution of the Organization of American States) adjudged in December 2012 that the Salvadorean state bore responsibility for the massacre of 936 alleged FMLN sympathizers by the military in El Mozote during 1981. The Court demanded that an inquiry be established to investigate this atrocity.

Mara 18 and Mara Salvatrucha, the most prominent of El Salvador's criminal gangs, concluded a truce in March 2012 following mediation efforts by the Roman Catholic Church and the Government. Although the Government's reported involvement provoked controversy, the truce yielded immediate results, with the number of murders decreasing sharply in subsequent months. In October five other *maras* agreed to participate in the truce, the ambit of which was broadened in early 2013. Reported homicides declined from 4,371 in 2011 to 2,576 in 2012. The number of recorded murders decreased further in 2013, to 2,490, but there was a marked upturn in gang-related violence during the second half of that year, and by early 2014, with government support waning, the truce appeared to be on the verge of collapse.

Jorge Velado succeeded Cristiani as ARENA President in February 2013. However, the party's legislative position was seriously undermined in April when it was deprived of the ability to block certain bills in the Legislative Assembly owing to the resignation of one of its parliamentary representatives. The situation was compounded after another ARENA deputy informally disassociated himself from the party in the following month. Also in May, GANA, the CN and the PES established an electoral coalition—the Movimiento Unidad; former President Saca was named as the group's presidential candidate.

The respective appointments of Munguía and Salinas in 2011 and 2012 were adjudged by the Supreme Court in May 2013 to have been unconstitutional as a result of their military backgrounds. Funes was consequently obliged to nominate replacements later that month: José Ricardo Perdomo became Minister of Justice and Public Security and Rigoberto Pleités was selected as the new chief of police. Munguía was appointed as Minister of National Defence in July, while Jaime Miranda Flamenco was assigned the foreign affairs portfolio in August.

Recent developments: Sánchez secures the presidency

At the first round of the presidential election, which took place on 2 February 2014, Sánchez garnered 48.9% of the votes cast, compared with 39.0% for Quijano and 11.4% for Saca. The two leading candidates progressed to a second round run-off election on 9 March, at which Sánchez, with 50.1% of the ballot, narrowly defeated Quijano, who attracted 49.9%. Although the results were sanctioned by the Supreme Electoral Tribunal and international monitors, Quijano alleged that fraudulent activity had taken place and launched an unsuccessful legal challenge, before finally conceded defeat in late March. Sánchez was due to be inaugurated as President on 1 June. His initial priorities included reinvigorating the ailing economy, implementing fiscal reforms, and combating crime, poverty and inequality. Among the early appointments to the new Cabinet, Sánchez retained Carlos Cáceres Chávez as Minister of Finance and Gerson Martínez as Minister of Public Works, Transport, Housing and Urban Development. Tharsis Salomón López was also designated as the incoming Minister of the Economy.

Quijano's image had been tarnished during the pre-election period after accusations of corruption had been directed against one of his campaign advisers, former President Flores. An inquiry was subsequently initiated into the alleged embezzlement of Taiwanese funds by Flores during his presidency, precipitating his resignation from Quijano's campaign team and his suspension from ARENA. In January 2014, apparently in response to this scandal, the Government recalled its ambassador to Taiwan, while later that month Flores attempted unsuccessfully to flee El Salvador.

Foreign Affairs

In 2006 a long-standing dispute between El Salvador and Honduras over three islands in the Gulf of Fonseca and a small area of land on the joint border was ended when the Presidents of both countries met to complete the formal ratification of the border demarcation. The accord followed a 1992 ruling by the International Court of Justice which awarded one-third of the disputed mainland and two of the three disputed islands to El Salvador. The two parties also signed a convention in 1998 specifying the rights and obligations of those affected, including the right to choose between Honduran and Salvadorean citizenship. However, another boundary dispute in the Gulf of Fonseca resurfaced in August 2013 when the Honduran military landed on the tiny Conejo Island, sovereignty over which was asserted by both Honduras and El Salvador, and planted a Honduran flag. The Funes administration submitted a formal complaint to Honduras in September, but Honduran activity on the island increased. El Salvador's acquisition of 10 attack aircraft in October further exacerbated the situation.

Seemingly as a concession to the USA, in August 2011 the Salvadorean Government agreed to send a small military detachment to Afghanistan as part of a training mission. However, in the following month El Salvador was added to the USA's 'black list' of significant drugs-producing and -trafficking nations. El Salvador signed a Partnership for Growth agreement with the USA in November; the five-year programme was intended to boost El Salvador's slow rate of economic development.

CONSTITUTION AND GOVERNMENT

The Constitution came into effect in 1983. Executive power is held by the President, assisted by the Vice-President and the Cabinet. The President is elected for a five-year term beginning and ending on 1 June by universal adult suffrage. Legislative power is vested in the Asamblea Legislativa (Legislative Assembly), with 84 members elected by universal adult suffrage for a three-year term beginning on 1 May. Judicial power is exercised by the Supreme Court and other competent tribunals. Supreme Court judges are elected by the Assembly.

REGIONAL AND INTERNATIONAL CO-OPERATION

El Salvador is a member of the Central American Common Market (CACM, see p. 229), which aims to increase trade within the region and to encourage monetary and industrial co-operation, the Inter-American Development Bank (see p. 331), the Organization of American States (see p. 394), the Association of Caribbean States (see p. 449), the Community of Latin American and Caribbean States (see p. 464), which was formally inaugurated in December 2011, and the Central American Integration System (SICA), which has its headquarters in El Salvador. El Salvador was a founder member of the UN in 1945. It acceded to the World Trade Organization (see p. 434) in 1995.

ECONOMIC AFFAIRS

In 2012, according to estimates by the World Bank, El Salvador's gross national income (GNI), measured at average 2010–12 prices, was US $22,547m., equivalent to $3,580 per head (or $6,810 per head on an international purchasing-power parity basis). In 2003–12 the population increased at an average annual rate of 0.5%, while gross domestic product (GDP) per head increased, in real terms, by an average of 1.4% per year. According to official figures, overall GDP increased, in real terms, at an average annual rate of 1.8% in 2003–12; GDP grew by 1.9% in 2012.

Agriculture (including hunting, forestry and fishing) contributed an estimated 11.4% of GDP and employed some 21.0% of the employed labour force in 2012. The principal cash crops are coffee and sugar cane. Maize, beans, rice and millet are the major subsistence crops. In 2012 coffee output stood at 89,500 metric tons, a slight increase on the 82,100 tons recorded in the previous year. Coffee's share of export earnings has decreased in recent years: in 2000 coffee accounted for 22.4% of export earnings, excluding *maquila* (or assembly sector) zones, but this had fallen to 7.1% in 2012. The fishing catch stood at 59,200 tons in 2011, an increase from the 43,500 tons recorded in 2010. During 2003–12 agricultural GDP increased at an average annual rate of 2.8%. The sector's GDP decreased by an estimated 2.5% in 2011, but increased by 2.5% in 2012.

Industry (including mining, manufacturing, construction and power) contributed an estimated 26.3% of GDP and engaged 21.1% of the employed labour force in 2012. During 2003–12 industrial GDP increased at an average annual rate of 1.0%. The sector's GDP increased by an estimated 1.8% in 2012.

El Salvador has no significant mineral resources. The mining sector employed 0.1% of the economically active population and contributed only 0.3% of GDP in 2012. Small quantities of gold, silver, sea salt and limestone are mined or quarried. During 2003–12 the GDP of the mining sector decreased at an average annual rate of 3.3%; mining GDP increased by 3.1% in 2012.

Manufacturing contributed an estimated 19.6% of GDP and employed 15.5% of the active labour force in 2012. There is an important *maquila* sector, which in 2012 generated about one-fifth (an estimated 20.7%) of the country's total exports. *Maquila* exports increased by 3.5% in 2012, according to the central bank. The most important branches of manufacturing outside the *maquila* industry were petroleum products, food products, chemicals, textiles, apparel (excluding footwear), metal manufactures and beverages. During 2003–12 manufacturing GDP increased at an average annual rate of 1.5%. The sector's GDP increased by an estimated 1.8% in 2012.

Construction contributed an estimated 4.1% of GDP and engaged 5.1% of the employed labour force in 2012. In 2003–12 the sector decreased at an average annual rate of 1.4%; construction expanded by an estimated 1.4% in 2012.

Energy is derived principally from imported fuel. Imports of mineral products accounted for an estimated 20.7% of the cost of merchandise imports in 2012. In 2011 El Salvador derived an estimated 34.6% of its electricity from hydroelectricity. An estimated further 34.1% of total electricity production was contributed by petroleum.

The services sector contributed an estimated 62.3% of GDP and employed 57.9% of the economically active population in 2012. The GDP of the services sector increased by an average of 2.0% per year in 2003–12. The sector grew by an estimated 1.7% in 2012. Receipts from tourism stood at US $544m. in 2012, according to provisional figures by the World Tourism Organization.

In 2012 El Salvador recorded a visible merchandise trade deficit of US $4,939.4m., while there was a deficit of $1,257.4m. on the current account of the balance of payments. Remittances from workers abroad were an important source of income to the Salvadorean economy: remittances in 2013 were an estimated $3,969.1m., an increase of 1.5% on the previous year. The Dominican Republic-Central American Free Trade Agreement (CAFTA-DR) with the USA, which came into effect in 2006, entailed the gradual elimination of tariffs on most industrial and agricultural products over 10 and 20 years, respectively. In 2012 some 37.8% of total imports (including imports into *maquila* zones) was provided by the USA; other major suppliers were Guatemala, Mexico and the People's Republic of China. The USA was the principal market for exports (taking an estimated 46.3% of exports, including exports from the *maquila* sector); other significant purchasers were Honduras, Guatemala and Nicaragua. Free trade agreements with Mexico and the European Union entered into force in 2012. In 2012 the main exports (excluding the *maquila* zones) were clothing, food, beverages and tobacco, and coffee. In the same year the principal imports were mineral products, mechanical and electrical machinery and apparatus, chemicals products, textiles, and live animals and vegetables.

In 2012 there was an estimated budgetary deficit of US $406.7m., equivalent to some 1.7% of GDP. El Salvador's general government gross debt was US $13,229m. in 2012, equivalent to 55.4% of GDP. El Salvador's external debt totalled US $11,995m. at the end of 2011, of which $6,537m. was public and publicly guaranteed debt. In that year, the cost of debt-servicing long-term public and publicly guaranteed debt and repayments to the IMF was equivalent to 21.7% of the value of exports of goods, services and income (excluding workers' remittances). The average annual rate of inflation was 3.7% in 2003–12; consumer prices rose by 1.7% in 2012. Some 6.1% of the labour force were unemployed in 2012.

In January 2009 the IMF approved an US $800m. stand-by arrangement (replaced by a $790m. facility in March 2010) to help the country withstand the effects of the global financial crisis. The economy entered recession in 2009, but there was a resumption of real GDP growth from 2010. The 2011 budget allocated significant funding to social programmes and poverty alleviation, although expansionary spending policies had led to increasing levels of public debt. Exports and remittance inflows continued to rise during 2011, but the economy was negatively affected by severe flooding in October and by the weak economic recovery in the USA. Remittances and foreign direct investment increased during 2012, but exports had registered a decline by the middle of the year. In spite of the Government's fiscal consolidation efforts, high debt levels remained a serious concern throughout 2012, prompting the legislature to authorize an $800m. bond issue in October. The economy expanded by 1.9% in that year. According to provisional economic data, real GDP rose by 1.6% in 2013, supported by modest increases in exports and remittances, although public debt levels were expected to continue their upward trajectory. The IMF projected that the economy would grow by a further 1.6% in 2014. El Salvador's medium-term prospects appeared unfavourable, owing to the constrained fiscal situation, weak demand domestically and internationally, and ongoing uncertainty in the global economy.

PUBLIC HOLIDAYS

2015: 1 January (New Year's Day), 2–5 April (Easter), 1 May (Labour Day), 17 June (Father's Day), 3–5 August (San Salvador Festival), 15 September (Independence Day), 12 October (Discovery of America), 2 November (All Souls' Day), 25 December (Christmas Day), 31 December (New Year's Eve).

Statistical Survey

Sources (unless otherwise stated): Banco Central de Reserva de El Salvador, Alameda Juan Pablo II y 17 Avda Norte, Apdo 01-106, San Salvador; tel. 2281-8000; fax 2281-8011; internet www.bcr.gob.sv; Dirección General de Estadística y Censos, Edif. Centro de Gobierno, Alameda Juan Pablo II y Calle Guadalupe, San Salvador; tel. 2286-4260; fax 2286-2505; internet www.digestyc.gob.sv.

Area and Population

AREA, POPULATION AND DENSITY

Area (sq km)	
Land	20,721
Inland water	320
Total	21,041*
Population (census results)†	
27 September 1992	5,118,599
12 May 2007	
Males	2,719,371
Females	3,024,742
Total	5,744,113
Population (official estimates)	
2012	6,251,494
2013	6,288,899
2014	6,328,196
Density (per sq km) at 2014	300.8

* 8,124 sq miles.

† Excluding adjustments for underenumeration.

POPULATION BY AGE AND SEX
('000, official estimates at 2014)

	Males	Females	Total
0–14	933.5	893.7	1,827.2
15–64	1,822.5	2,191.7	4,014.2
65 and over	211.4	275.4	486.7
Total	2,967.4	3,360.8	6,328.2

Note: Totals may not be equal to the sum of components, owing to rounding.

DEPARTMENTS
(official population estimates at 2014)

	Area (sq km)	Population ('000)	Density (per sq km)
Ahuachapán	1,239.6	337.3	272.1
Santa Ana	2,023.2	577.4	285.4
Sonsonate	1,225.8	464.9	379.2
Chalatenango	2,016.6	206.0	102.2
La Libertad	1,652.9	757.4	458.2
San Salvador	886.2	1,742.5	1,966.3
Cuscatlán	756.2	256.8	339.7
La Paz	1,223.6	330.5	270.1
Cabañas	1,103.5	165.9	150.3
San Vicente	1,184.0	175.7	148.4
Usulután	2,130.4	369.0	173.2
San Miguel	2,077.1	482.0	232.1
Morazán	1,447.4	201.0	138.9
La Unión	2,074.3	261.7	126.2
Total	21,040.8	6,328.2	300.8

PRINCIPAL TOWNS
(official population estimates at 2014)*

San Salvador (capital)	281,870	Santa Tecla†	135,483
Soyapango	275,868	Ciudad Delgado	128,635
Santa Ana	265,518	Tonacatepeque	124,675
San Miguel	249,638	Ilopango	124,522
Apopa	165,897	Colón	120,048
Mejicanos	146,915	Ahuachapán	118,164

* Figures refer to municipios, which may each contain rural areas as well as an urban centre.

† Formerly Nueva San Salvador.

BIRTHS, MARRIAGES AND DEATHS

	Registered live births		Registered marriages		Registered deaths	
	Number	Rate (per 1,000)	Number	Rate (per 1,000)	Number	Rate (per 1,000)
2002	129,363	19.9	26,077	4.0	27,458	4.2
2003	124,476	18.7	25,071	3.8	29,377	4.4
2004	119,710	17.7	25,240	3.7	30,058	4.4
2005	112,769	16.4	24,475	3.6	30,933	4.5
2006	107,111	15.3	24,500	3.5	31,453	4.5
2007	110,730	18.2	28,675	4.0	31,349	4.4
2008	111,278	18.2	27,714	3.8	31,594	4.4
2009	107,880	17.5	28,048	4.6	32,872	5.3

Crude birth rates (annual averages, official estimates): 21.9 per 1,000 in 2000–05; 20.4 per 1,000 in 2005–10.

Crude death rates (annual averages, official estimates): 6.8 per 1,000 in 2000–05; 6.9 per 1,000 in 2005–10.

Life expectancy (years at birth): 71.9 (males 67.3; females 76.7) in 2011 (Source: World Bank, World Development Indicators database).

ECONOMICALLY ACTIVE POPULATION
(sample household surveys, persons aged 16 years and over)

	2010	2011	2012
Agriculture, hunting and forestry	482,195	514,272	518,563
Fishing	16,117	18,163	18,137
Mining and quarrying	1,368	1,068	1,716
Manufacturing	371,372	381,781	397,046
Electricity, gas and water	11,067	13,720	10,921
Construction	129,038	127,875	129,918
Wholesale and retail trade; hotels and restaurants	704,138	700,451	734,113
Transport, storage and communications	102,673	109,502	110,642
Financing, insurance, real estate and business services	128,078	136,920	137,588
Public administration, defence and social security	101,075	107,257	116,297
Education	77,056	76,269	81,379
Health and other community, social and personal services	173,535	175,921	190,074
Private households with employed persons	100,062	102,510	112,688
Other services	704	666	233
Total employed	2,398,478	2,466,375	2,559,315
Unemployed	181,806	174,758	165,439
Total labour force	2,580,284	2,641,133	2,724,754
Males	1,514,123	1,568,675	1,607,819
Females	1,066,161	1,072,458	1,116,935

Health and Welfare

KEY INDICATORS

Total fertility rate (children per woman, 2011)	2.2
Under-5 mortality rate (per 1,000 live births, 2011)	15
HIV/AIDS (% of persons aged 15–49, 2012)	0.6
Physicians (per 1,000 head, 2008)	1.6
Hospital beds (per 1,000 head, 2010)	1.0
Health expenditure (2010): US $ per head (PPP)	456
Health expenditure (2010): % of GDP	6.9
Health expenditure (2010): public (% of total)	61.8
Access to water (% of persons, 2011)	90
Access to sanitation (% of persons, 2011)	70
Total carbon dioxide emissions ('000 metric tons, 2010)	6,248.6
Carbon dioxide emissions per head (metric tons, 2010)	1.0
Human Development Index (2012): ranking	107
Human Development Index (2012): value	0.680

For sources and definitions, see explanatory note on p. vi.

Agriculture

PRINCIPAL CROPS

('000 metric tons)

	2010	2011	2012
Rice, paddy	34.5	25.6	28.3
Maize	768.1	756.4	925.8
Sorghum	106.5	142.0	136.6
Yautia (Cocoyam)*	40.4	43.0	43.0
Sugar cane	5,126.7	9,899.0	9,899.0*
Beans, dry	71.3	64.8	107.8
Coconuts	60.2†	60.3†	63.5*
Watermelons	49.3	52.0*	60.0
Bananas*	39.0	38.4	41.5
Plantains	20.0	11.7	36.8
Oranges	45.7	42.4	94.8
Coffee, green	112.6	82.1	89.5

* FAO estimate(s).

† Unofficial figure.

Aggregate production ('000 metric tons, may include official, semi-official or estimated data): Total cereals 909.1 in 2010, 923.9 in 2011, 1,090.7 in 2012; Total vegetables (incl. melons) 147.3 in 2010, 147.7 in 2011, 160.8 in 2012; Total fruits (excl. melons) 377.4 in 2010, 386.9 in 2011, 473.0 in 2012.

Source: FAO.

LIVESTOCK

('000 head, year ending September)

	2010	2011	2012
Horses*	96	96	98
Asses*	3	3	3
Mules*	24	24	24
Cattle	1,247	1,015	1,123
Pigs	427†	440†	445*
Sheep*	5	5	5
Goats*	15	15	15
Chickens	15,000†	15,500†	15,500*

* FAO estimate(s).

† Unofficial figure.

Source: FAO.

LIVESTOCK PRODUCTS

('000 metric tons)

	2010	2011	2012
Cattle meat	33.0	23.4	26.0
Pig meat	8.3	8.4	9.5
Chicken meat	104.5	108.5	109.5
Cows' milk	457.7	415.7	406.1
Hen eggs	64.7	59.7	62.3

Source: FAO.

Forestry

ROUNDWOOD REMOVALS

('000 cubic metres, excl. bark, estimates)

	2010	2011	2012
Sawlogs, veneer logs and logs for sleepers	682	682	682
Fuel wood	4,225	4,217	4,215
Total	4,907	4,899	4,897

Source: FAO.

SAWNWOOD PRODUCTION

('000 cubic metres, incl. railway sleepers, estimates)

	2002	2003	2004
Total (all broadleaved, hardwood)	68.0	68.0	16.3

2005–12: Figures assumed to be unchanged from 2004 (estimates).

Source: FAO.

Fishing

('000 metric tons, live weight)

	2009	2010	2011
Capture	36.2*	39.0	54.3
Skipjack tuna	18.6	14.3	22.2
Yellowfin tuna	6.3	3.7	9.9
Bigeye tuna	3.1	2.6	4.8
Other marine fishes	0.6	14.9	14.7
Pacific seabobs	0.8	0.9	0.3
Aquaculture*	4.4	4.5	4.9
Total catch*	40.6	43.5	59.2

* FAO estimate(s).

Source: FAO.

Mining

('000 metric tons unless otherwise indicated)

	2006	2007	2008
Gypsum*	5.5	5.5	5.5
Steel (crude)	72.0	73.0	71.0
Limestone*	1,200	1,200	1,200
Salt (marine)*	30.0	30.0	30.0

* Estimates.

2009–11: Limestone 1,200 (estimate).

Steel (crude): 56.0 in 2009 (estimate); 64.0 in 2010; 100.0 in 2011; 102.0 in 2012.

Source: US Geological Survey.

Industry

SELECTED PRODUCTS
('000 metric tons unless otherwise indicated)

	2008	2009	2010
Raw sugar	597	518	n.a.
Motor gasoline (petrol)	111	105	100
Kerosene	2	2	2
Distillate fuel oil	186	197	n.a.
Residual fuel oil	410	399	n.a.
Liquefied petroleum gas (refined)	20	14	13
Cement	1,300	1,212	1,200
Electric energy (million kWh)	5,960	5,788	5,980

Cement ('000 metric tons): 1,200 in 2011–12.

Sources: US Geological Survey; UN Industrial Commodity Statistics Database.

Electric energy (million kWh): 5,722 in 2010; 5,812 in 2011; 5,946 in 2012.

Finance

CURRENCY AND EXCHANGE RATES

Monetary Units
100 centavos = 1 Salvadorean colón.

Sterling, Dollar and Euro Equivalents (31 December 2013)
£1 sterling = 14.410 colones;
US $1 = 8.750 colones;
€1 = 12.067 colones;
100 Salvadorean colones = £6.94 = $11.43 = €8.29.

Note: The foregoing information refers to the principal exchange rate, applicable to official receipts and payments, imports of petroleum and exports of coffee. In addition, there is a market exchange rate, applicable to other transactions. The principal rate was maintained at 8.755 colones per US dollar from May 1995 to December 2000. However, in January 2001, with the introduction of legislation making the US dollar legal tender, the rate was adjusted to $1 = 8.750 colones; both currencies have circulated freely as parallel legal currencies since that date.

CENTRAL GOVERNMENT BUDGET
(US $ million)

Revenue*	2010	2011	2012
Current revenue	3,070.2	3,343.5	3,588.1
Tax revenue	2,881.6	3,193.3	3,433.8
Taxes on earnings	994.8	1,126.8	1,249.8
Import duties	151.0	167.3	179.6
Value-added tax	1,432.8	1,574.1	1,676.9
Non-tax revenue	188.6	150.2	154.3
Public enterprise transfers	24.7	3.3	7.7
Financial public enterprise transfers	28.7	43.0	44.9
Capital revenue	0.2	0.2	0.2
Total	3,070.5	3,343.6	3,588.3

Expenditure†	2010	2011	2012
Current expenditure	3,114.3	3,369.9	3,373.3
Remunerations	1,109.0	1,278.7	1,329.3
Goods and services	587.0	540.7	502.2
Interest payments	496.3	507.9	526.4
Transfers	922.0	1,042.7	1,015.4
To other government bodies	469.6	513.8	526.5
To the private sector	439.6	515.9	481.2
Capital expenditure	682.9	718.4	787.8
Gross investment	392.2	364.8	450.6
Total	3,797.2	4,088.3	4,161.1

* Excluding grants received (US $ million): 142.8 in 2010; 213.9 in 2011; 170.0 in 2012.

† Excluding lending minus repayments (US $ million): –2.8 in 2010; –6.6 in 2011; 3.9 in 2012.

INTERNATIONAL RESERVES
(US $ million at 31 December)

	2010	2011	2012
Gold (national valuation)	313.6	351.3	369.8
IMF special drawing rights	252.3	251.5	252.5
Foreign exchange	2,317.4	1,901.4	2,553.9
Total	2,883.2	2,504.2	3,176.2

Source: IMF, *International Financial Statistics*.

MONEY SUPPLY
(US $ million at 31 December)

	2010	2011	2012
Currency outside depository corporations	4.7	4.5	4.2
Transferable deposits	2,522.5	2,556.7	2,792.2
Other deposits	6,860.8	6,651.8	7,050.8
Securities other than shares	1,023.6	852.8	793.5
Broad money	10,411.5	10,065.8	10,640.7

Source: IMF, *International Financial Statistics*.

COST OF LIVING
(Consumer Price Index; annual averages; base: December 2009 = 100)

	2010	2011	2012
Food and non-alcoholic beverages	104.4	111.6	112.0
Clothing and footwear	100.0	101.7	102.8
Rent, water, electricity, gas and other fuels	98.7	112.3	116.5
Health	100.5	101.5	103.2
Education	101.0	101.8	102.8
Transport	101.8	109.1	113.9
Communications	91.1	89.8	97.0
Recreation and culture	99.2	98.0	97.0
All items (incl. others)	101.1	106.3	108.1

NATIONAL ACCOUNTS
(US $ million at current prices, preliminary)

Expenditure on the Gross Domestic Product

	2010	2011	2012
Final consumption expenditure	22,189.7	24,139.0	24,812.3
Households	19,896.9	21,580.8	22,138.4
General government	2,292.8	2,558.2	2,673.9
Gross capital formation	2,852.5	3,323.2	3,381.3
Total domestic expenditure	25,042.2	27,462.2	28,193.6
Exports of goods and services	5,552.6	6,474.3	6,766.7
Less Imports of goods and services	9,176.5	10,797.4	11,095.9
GDP in purchasers' values	21,418.3	23,139.0	23,864.4
GDP at constant 1990 prices	9,076.0	9,277.2	9,456.2

Gross Domestic Product by Economic Activity

	2010	2011	2012
Agriculture, hunting, forestry and fishing	2,477.9	2,651.4	2,584.0
Mining and quarrying	57.1	65.9	68.6
Manufacturing	4,026.9	4,291.6	4,451.9
Construction	781.7	898.4	934.9
Electricity, gas and water	444.7	479.1	518.9
Transport, storage and communications	1,695.8	1,814.8	1,871.7
Wholesale and retail trade, restaurants and hotels	4,272.5	4,610.9	4,818.4
Finance and insurance	973.2	1,054.1	1,042.7
Real estate and business services	961.8	1,022.6	1,068.1
Owner-occupied dwellings	1,460.0	1,500.4	1,524.3

—*continued*	2010	2011	2012
Community, social, domestic and personal services	1,754.9	1,817.9	1,888.2
Government services	1,626.7	1,851.6	1,939.6
Sub-total	20,533.2	22,058.7	22,711.3
Import duties and value-added tax	1,687.2	1,950.7	2,030.7
Less Imputed bank service charge	802.0	870.3	877.8
GDP in purchasers' values	21,418.3	23,139.0	23,864.4

BALANCE OF PAYMENTS
(US $ million)

	2010	2011	2012
Exports of goods	3,473.2	4,242.6	4,235.6
Imports of goods	–7,495.4	–9,014.8	–9,175.0
Balance on goods	–4,022.2	–4,772.2	–4,939.4
Exports of services	1,498.0	1,636.0	1,849.5
Imports of services	–1,099.7	–1,186.9	–1,239.3
Balance on goods and services	–3,623.9	–4,323.1	–4,329.2
Primary income received	63.4	67.8	57.1
Primary income paid	–607.9	–722.5	–989.2
Balance on goods, services and primary income	–4,168.4	–4,977.8	–5,261.4
Secondary income received	3,670.1	3,919.2	4,104.5
Secondary income paid	–71.6	–78.2	–100.6
Current balance	–569.7	–1,136.8	–1,257.4
Capital account (net)	232.0	266.4	201.4
Direct investment assets	–145.2	113.8	49.0
Direct investment liabilities	247.7	306.2	466.8
Portfolio investment assets	–118.2	99.4	47.0
Portfolio investment liabilities	–3.2	1.0	836.3
Other investment assets	109.1	–111.9	–112.4
Other investment liabilities	–266.5	284.5	604.5
Net errors and omissions	217.6	–238.2	–185.1
Reserves and related items	–296.5	–415.6	650.1

Source: IMF, *International Financial Statistics*.

External Trade

PRINCIPAL COMMODITIES
(US $ million, preliminary)

Imports c.i.f.*	2010	2011	2012
Live animals and animal products; vegetables, crops and related products, primary	660.3	812.2	774.1
Food, beverages (incl. alcoholic) and tobacco manufactures	603.5	682.9	714.2
Mineral products	1,404.2	1,769.8	1,977.9
Crude petroleum oils	473.3	565.7	409.4
Light oils (gasoline, etc.)	209.3	319.4	405.9
Heavy oils (gas oil, diesel oil, fuel oil, etc.)	375.3	506.2	748.8
Chemicals and related products	972.3	1,130.5	1,164.8
Therapeutic and preventative medicines	272.4	325.1	306.0
Plastics, artificial resins, rubbers, and articles thereof	542.2	661.7	663.3
Plastics, artificial resins, and articles thereof	467.0	566.9	564.3
Wood pulp, paper, paperboard and articles thereof	347.9	388.8	397.0
Textile materials and articles thereof	830.9	1,037.9	1,000.0
Base metals and manufactures thereof	478.4	586.0	568.4
Cast iron and steel	226.0	290.6	282.4
Mechanical and electrical machinery and apparatus	1,102.9	1,218.3	1,213.4
Mechanical machinery and apparatus	549.8	638.5	612.2
Electrical machinery and appliances	553.1	579.8	601.2
Radio and television transmitters and receivers, and parts thereof	230.7	226.0	244.1
Transport equipment	243.7	311.6	342.8
Total (incl. others)	7,802.6	9,327.7	9,552.4

* Excluding imports into *maquila* zones (US $ million, preliminary): 613.6 in 2010; 636.8 in 2011; 717.2 in 2012.

Exports f.o.b.*	2010	2011	2012
Vegetables, crops and related products, primary	286.2	580.8	419.7
Coffee, including roasted and decaffeinated	213.2	464.0	300.0
Food, beverages (incl. alcoholic) and tobacco manufactures	616.5	666.3	755.4
Unrefined sugar	127.7	132.6	166.7
Mineral products	144.3	184.9	194.5
Chemical products	225.1	240.4	245.9
Therapeutic and preventative medicines	105.0	104.6	107.1
Plastics, rubber, and articles thereof	241.0	276.5	302.8
Boxes, bags, bottles, stoppers and other plastic containers	117.1	149.2	165.6
Wood pulp, paper, paperboard and articles thereof	232.9	284.2	286.1
Textile materials and articles thereof	1,115.8	1,287.0	1,350.9
Clothing, inner wear	544.8	642.9	694.6
Clothing, outer wear	331.9	362.8	388.9
Base metals and manufactures thereof	224.7	294.9	282.1
Other iron and steel products	96.6	126.7	132.4
Miscellaneous manufactured articles	103.4	124.1	132.0
Total (incl. others)	3,470.5	4,239.6	4,233.1

* Excluding exports from *maquila* zones (US $ million, preliminary): 1,028.7 in 2010; 1,068.6 in 2011; 1,106.0 in 2012.

PRINCIPAL TRADING PARTNERS
(US $ million, preliminary)

Imports c.i.f.*	2010	2011	2012
Brazil	117.4	167.9	218.4
China, People's Republic	477.6	552.2	603.5
Colombia	84.9	182.7	328.9
Costa Rica	261.1	293.2	296.2
Ecuador	254.1	255.8	187.5
Germany	134.2	138.6	151.4
Guatemala	806.9	989.6	997.6
Honduras	373.6	467.3	463.7
Japan	150.6	210.0	172.9
Korea, Republic	86.8	121.4	149.1
Mexico	735.1	740.4	694.6
Netherlands Antilles	158.4	55.2	100.8
Nicaragua	181.9	195.7	209.8
Panama	225.2	203.0	179.4
Taiwan	97.8	139.8	157.4
USA	3,109.2	3,799.9	3,885.2
Venezuela	132.2	232.7	211.6
Total (incl. others)	8,416.2	9,964.5	10,269.6

* Including imports into *maquila* zones (mostly from USA) (US $ million, preliminary): 613.6 in 2010; 636.8 in 2011; 717.2 in 2012.

Exports f.o.b.*	2010	2011	2012
Canada	67.7	70.8	54.4
Costa Rica	161.4	213.6	230.5
Dominican Republic	84.2	68.3	80.0
Germany	81.9	140.3	69.8
Guatemala	628.9	736.3	714.7
Honduras	579.4	698.1	761.0
Mexico	76.2	86.1	83.4
Nicaragua	244.0	294.8	320.2
Panama	102.4	108.7	124.6
Spain	51.7	76.0	79.9
USA	2,161.1	2,425.4	2,469.9
Total (incl. others)	4,499.2	5,308.2	5,339.1

* Including exports from *maquila* zones (mostly to USA) (US $ million, preliminary): 1,028.7 in 2010; 1,068.6 in 2011; 1,106.0 in 2012.

Transport

RAILWAYS
(traffic)

	1999	2000
Number of passengers ('000)	543.3	687.3
Passenger-km (million)	8.4	10.7
Freight ('000 metric tons)	188.6	136.2
Freight ton-km (million)	19.4	13.1

Source: Ferrocarriles Nacionales de El Salvador.

ROAD TRAFFIC
(motor vehicles in use at 31 December)

	2007	2009*	2010
Passenger cars	283,787	302,802	305,856
Buses and coaches	6,306	10,148	26,445
Lorries and vans	n.a.	17,789	n.a.
Motorcycles and mopeds	44,145	51,835	53,637

* Data for 2008 were not available.

Source: IRF, *International Road Statistics*.

SHIPPING

Flag Registered Fleet
(at 31 December)

	2011	2012	2013
Number of vessels	5	6	6
Total displacement ('000 grt)	9.5	9.6	9.6

Source: Lloyd's List Intelligence (www.lloydslistintelligence.com).

CIVIL AVIATION
(traffic on scheduled services)

	2010	2011
Kilometres flown (million)	38	45
Passengers carried ('000)	2,137	2,530
Passenger-km (million)	3,593	4,222
Total ton-km (million)	319	378

Source: UN, *Statistical Yearbook*.

Passengers carried ('000): 1,414.3 (arrivals 702.6, departures 711.7) in 2010; 1,396.7 (arrivals 665.0, departures 731.6) in 2011; 1,461.9 (arrivals 701.1, departures 760.8) in 2012.

Tourism

TOURIST ARRIVALS BY NATIONALITY
(arrivals of non-resident tourists at national borders)

	2009	2010	2011
Canada	26,333	20,432	28,205
Costa Rica	17,714	18,443	20,300
Guatemala	462,944	518,957	535,246
Honduras	138,104	145,868	126,446
Mexico	17,633	17,607	19,699
Nicaragua	42,844	43,488	40,756
Panama	10,107	10,579	10,733
USA	327,314	318,569	320,736
Total (incl. others)	1,090,926	1,149,562	1,184,497

Total tourist arrivals ('000): 1,255 in 2012 (provisional).

Receipts from tourism (US $ million, excl. passenger transport): 390 in 2010; 415 in 2011; 544 in 2012 (provisional).

Source: World Tourism Organization.

Communications Media

	2010	2011	2012
Telephones ('000 main lines in use)	1,000.9	1,029.7	1,059.0
Mobile cellular telephones ('000 subscribers)	7,700.3	8,316.2	8,649.0
Broadband subscribers ('000)	175.3	206.0	242.1

Internet subscribers ('000): 150.5 in 2009.

Source: International Telecommunication Union.

Education

(2010/11 unless otherwise indicated)

		Students		
	Teachers	Males	Females	Total
Pre-primary	9,318	112,913	111,214	224,127
Primary	30,755	470,092	430,589	900,681
Secondary	24,556	302,984	294,839	597,823
Tertiary	9,291	74,386	85,988	160,374

Institutions (2001/02): Pre-primary 4,838; Primary 5,414; Secondary 757; Tertiary 43.

Sources: Ministry of Education and UNESCO Institute for Statistics.

Pupil-teacher ratio (primary education, UNESCO estimate): 29.3 in 2010/11 (Source: UNESCO Institute for Statistics).

Adult literacy rate (UNESCO estimates): 84.5% (males 87.1%; females 82.3%) in 2010 (Source: UNESCO Institute for Statistics).

Directory

The Government

HEAD OF STATE

President: CARLOS MAURICIO FUNES CARTAGENA (assumed office 1 June 2009).

Vice-President: SALVADOR SÁNCHEZ CERÉN.

President-elect: SALVADOR SÁNCHEZ CERÉN (scheduled to assume office on 1 June 2014).

Vice-President-elect: OSCAR SAMUEL ORTIZ.

CABINET
(April 2014)

The Government is formed by the Frente Farabundo Martí para la Liberación Nacional. A new Cabinet was scheduled to take office following the inauguration as President of Salvador Sánchez Cerén on 1 June 2014.

Minister of Finance: JUAN RAMÓN CARLOS ENRIQUE CÁCERES CHÁVEZ.

Minister of Foreign Affairs: JAIME MIRANDA FLAMENCO.

Minister of Internal Affairs: GREGORIO ERNESTO ZELAYANDIA CISNEROS.

Minister of Justice and Public Security: RICARDO PERDOMO.

Minister of the Economy: ARMANDO FLORES.

Minister of Education: FRANZIS HATO HASBÚN.

Minister of National Defence: Gen. (retd) DAVID VICTORIANO MUNGUÍA PAYÉS.

Minister of Labour and Social Security: HUMBERTO CENTENO NAJARRO.

Minister of Public Health: Dra MARÍA ISABEL RODRÍGUEZ.

Minister of Agriculture and Livestock: PABLO ALCIDES OCHOA.

Minister of Public Works, Transport, Housing and Urban Development: GERSON MARTÍNEZ.

Minister of the Environment and Natural Resources: HERMÁN HUMBERTO ROSA CHÁVEZ.

Minister of Tourism: JOSÉ NAPOLEÓN DUARTE DURÁN.

MINISTRIES

Ministry for the Presidency: Alameda Dr Manuel Enrique Araujo 5500, San Salvador; tel. 2248-9000; fax 2248-9370; internet www.presidencia.gob.sv.

Ministry of Agriculture and Livestock: Final 1, Avda Norte, 13 Calle Poniente y Avda Manuel Gallardo, Santa Tecla; tel. 2210-1700; fax 2229-9271; e-mail info@mag.gob.sv; internet www.mag.gob.sv.

Ministry of the Economy: Edif. C1–C2, Centro de Gobierno, Alameda Juan Pablo II y Calle Guadalupe, San Salvador; tel. 2231-5600; fax 2221-5446; e-mail comunicaciones@minec.gob.sv; internet www.minec.gob.sv.

Ministry of Education: Edif. A, Centro de Gobierno, Alameda Juan Pablo II y Calle Guadalupe, San Salvador; tel. 2592-2122; fax 2281-0077; e-mail educacion@mined.gob.sv; internet www.mined.gob.sv.

Ministry of the Environment and Natural Resources: Edif. MARN 2, Calle y Col. Las Mercedes, Carretera a Santa Tecla, Km 5.5, San Salvador; tel. 2132-6276; fax 2132-9420; e-mail medioambiente@marn.gob.sv; internet www.marn.gob.sv.

Ministry of Finance: Blvd Los Héroes 1231, San Salvador; tel. 2244-3000; fax 2244-6408; e-mail info@mh.gob.sv; internet www.mh.gob.sv.

Ministry of Foreign Affairs: Calle El Pedregal, Blvd Cancillería, Ciudad Merliot, Antiguo Cuscatlán; tel. 2231-1000; fax 2289-8016; e-mail webmaster@rree.gob.sv; internet www.rree.gob.sv.

Ministry of Internal Affairs: Centro de Gobierno, Calle Oriente 9 y Avda Norte 15, San Salvador; tel. 2527-7000; fax 2527-7972; e-mail oirmigob@gobernacion.gob.sv; internet www.gobernacion.gob.sv.

Ministry of Justice and Public Security: Complejo Plan Maestro, Edifs B1, B2 y B3, Alameda Juan Pablo II y 17 Avda Norte, San Salvador; tel. 2526-3000; fax 2526-3105; e-mail webmaster@seguridad.gob.sv; internet www.seguridad.gob.sv.

Ministry of Labour and Social Security: Edifs 2 y 3, Alameda Juan Pablo II y 17 Avda Norte, San Salvador; tel. 2209-3700; fax 2209-3756; e-mail asesorialaboral@mtps.gob.sv; internet www.mtps.gob.sv.

Ministry of National Defence: Alameda Dr Manuel E. Araújo, Km 5, Carretera a Santa Tecla, San Salvador; tel. 2250-0100; e-mail oirmdn@faes.gob.sv; internet www.fuerzaarmada.gob.sv/index.html.

Ministry of Public Health: Calle Arce 827, San Salvador; tel. 2205-7000; fax 2221-0991; e-mail atencion@salud.gob.sv; internet www.salud.gob.sv.

Ministry of Public Works, Transport, Housing and Urban Development: Plantel la Lechuza, Carretera a Santa Tecla Km 5.5, San Salvador; tel. 2528-3000; fax 2279-3723; e-mail info@mop.gob.sv; internet www.mop.gob.sv.

Ministry of Tourism: Edif. Carbonel 1, Alameda Dr Manuel Enrique Araujo y Pasaje Carbonel, Col. Roma, San Salvador; tel. 2243-7835; fax 2223-6120; e-mail info@mitur.gob.sv; internet www.mitur.gob.sv.

President and Legislature

PRESIDENT

Election, First Round, 2 February 2014

Candidates	Votes	% of votes
Salvador Sánchez Cerén (FMLN)	1,315,768	48.93
Norman Quijano (ARENA)	1,047,592	38.96
Elías Antonio Saca González (Unidad)*	307,603	11.44
René Rodríguez Hurtado (PSP)	11,314	0.42
Oscar Lemus (FPS)	6,659	0.25
Total valid votes	2,688,936	100.00

* A coalition comprising the Gran Alianza por la Unidad Nacional, the Concertación Nacional and the Partido de la Esperanza.

Election, Second Round, 9 March 2014

Candidates	Votes	% of votes
Salvador Sánchez Cerén (FMLN)	1,495,815	50.11
Norman Quijano (ARENA)	1,489,451	49.89
Total valid votes	2,985,266	100.00

LEGISLATIVE ASSEMBLY

President: OTHON SIGFRIDO REYES MORALES (FMLN).

General Election, 11 March 2012

Party	Valid votes cast	% of valid votes	Seats
Alianza Republicana Nacionalista (ARENA)	892,688	39.84	33
Frente Farabundo Martí para la Liberación Nacional (FMLN)	824,686	36.80	31
Gran Alianza por la Unidad Nacional (GANA)	214,498	9.57	11
Concertación Nacional (CN)	162,083	7.23	6
Partido de la Esperanza (PES)	60,641	2.71	1
Cambio Democrático (CD)	47,797	2.13	1
Coalición CN-PES*	17,580	0.78	1
Others	20,945	0.93	—
Total	2,240,918	100.00	84

* The Concertación Nacional (CN) and the Partido de la Esperanza (PES) formed a coalition in Chalatenango department.

Election Commission

Tribunal Supremo Electoral (TSE): 15 Calle Poniente 4223, Col. Escalón, San Salvador; tel. 2209-4000; fax 2263-4678; e-mail info@tse.gob.sv; internet www.tse.gob.sv; f. 1992; Pres. EUGENIO CHICAS.

Political Organizations

Alianza Republicana Nacionalista (ARENA): Prolongación Calle Arce 2426, Col. Flor Banca, San Salvador; tel. 2260-4400; fax 2260-6260; e-mail infoparena@gmail.com; internet www.arena.com.sv; f. 1981; right-wing; Pres. JORGE VELADO; Exec. Dir ORLANDO CABRERA CANDRAY.

Cambio Democrático (CD): Casa 197, Calle Héctor Silva, Col. Médica, San Salvador; tel. 2225-5978; fax 2281-9636; e-mail comunicaciones@cambiodemocraticosv.org; internet www

.cambiodemocraticosv.org; f. 1987 as Convergencia Democrática (CD); changed name as above in 2005; Sec.-Gen. DOUGLAS AVILÉS; Dep. Sec. JUAN JOSÉ MARTEL.

Fraternidad Patriota Salvadoreña (FPS): 13 Avda Norte, G29, Col. Santa Monica, Santa Tecla; tel. 2288-4211; e-mail fraternidadpatriota@hotmail.com; Pres. OSCAR LEMUS.

Frente Democrático Revolucionario (FDR): Avda Sierra Nevada 926, Col. Miramonte, San Salvador; tel. 2237-8844; fax 2260-1547; e-mail info@fdr.org.sv; internet www.fdr.org.sv; f. 2005; left-wing, reformist; breakaway faction of FMLN; Co-ordinator-Gen. JULIO HERNÁNDEZ.

Frente Farabundo Martí para la Liberación Nacional (FMLN): 27 Calle Poniente, Col. Layco 1316, San Salvador; tel. 2226-7183; e-mail comision.politica@fmln.org.sv; internet www.fmln.org.sv; f. 1980 as the FDR (Frente Democrático Revolucionario—FMLN) as a left-wing opposition front to the Govt; the FDR was the political wing and the FMLN was the guerrilla front; achieved legal recognition 1992; comprised various factions, including Communist (Leader SALVADOR SÁNCHEZ CERÉN), Renewalist (Leader OSCAR ORTIZ) and Terceristas (Leader GERSON MARTÍNEZ); Co-ordinator-Gen. MEDARDO GONZÁLEZ.

Partido Salvadoreño Progresista (PSP): Col. San Benito, Calle 2, Casa 280, entre Calle La Reforma y Avda Loma Linda, San Salvador; tel. 2223-3191; e-mail pspartidopolitico@gmail.com; internet www.psp.org.sv; Pres. RENÉ RODRÍGUEZ HURTADO.

Unidad: Calle Poniente entre 43 y 45, 6°, Avda Sur, Casa 2326, Col. Flor Blanca, San Salvador; tel. 2298-9638; e-mail info@unidad.org.sv; internet www.unidad.org.sv; f. 2013; electoral coalition; Leader ELÍAS ANTONIO (TONY) SACA GONZÁLEZ; comprises the following parties.

Concertación Nacional (CN): 15 Avda Norte y 3a Calle Poniente 244, San Salvador; tel. 2221-3752; fax 2281-9272; f. 2011 as successor party to the Partido de Conciliación Nacional (f. 1961); right-wing; Sec.-Gen. MANUEL RODRÍGUEZ.

Gran Alianza por la Unidad Nacional (GANA): 41 Avda Sur y 16 Calle Poniente 2143, Col. Flor Blanca, San Salvador; tel. 2279-0254; internet www.gana.org.sv; f. 2009 by fmr mems of ARENA (q.v.); Pres. JOSÉ ANDRÉS ROVIRA CANALES.

Partido de la Esperanza (PES): Centro de Gobierno, Alameda Juan Pablo II y 11 Avda Norte bis 507, San Salvador; tel. 2281-5498; fax 7998-1526; e-mail pdcsal@navegante.com.sv; f. 2011; successor to the disbanded Partido Demócrata Cristiano (f. 1960); 150,000 mems; advocates self-determination and Latin American integration; Sec.-Gen. RODOLFO ANTONIO PARKER SOTO.

Diplomatic Representation

EMBASSIES IN EL SALVADOR

Argentina: Calle La Sierra 3-I-B, Col. Escalón, San Salvador; tel. 2521-9400; fax 2521-9410; e-mail esalv@mrecic.gov.ar; Ambassador BETINA ALEJANDRA PASQUALI DE FONSECA.

Belize: Calle y Col. La Mascota, Residencial La Mascota 456, San Salvador; tel. and fax 2264-8024; e-mail embsalbel@yahoo.com; Ambassador CELIE PAZ MARIN.

Brazil: Blvd Sérgio Vieira de Mello 132, Col. San Benito, San Salvador; tel. 2298-3286; fax 2279-3934; e-mail embajada@brasil.org.sv; internet www.brasil.org.sv; Ambassador JOSÉ FIUZA NETO.

Canada: Centro Financiero Gigante, Torre A, Lobby 2, Alameda Roosevelt y 63 Avda Sur, Col. Escalón, San Salvador; tel. 2279-4655; fax 2279-0765; e-mail ssal@international.gc.ca; internet www.canadainternational.gc.ca/el_salvador-salvador; Ambassador PIERRE GIROUX.

Chile: Paseo Gen. Escalón 5355, Contiguo a Club Campestre, Col. Escalón, San Salvador; tel. 2263-4285; fax 2263-4308; e-mail embajadadechile@amnetsal.com; internet chileabroad.gov.cl/el-salvador; Ambassador JOSÉ RENATO SEPÚLVEDA NEBEL.

Colombia: Calle El Mirador 5120, Col. Escalón, San Salvador; tel. 2263-1936; fax 2263-1942; e-mail elsalvador@minrelext.gov.co; internet elsalvador.embajada.gov.co; Ambassador JULIO ANÍBAL RIAÑO VELANDIA.

Costa Rica: 5453 Calle Arturo Ambrogi, Col. Escalón, San Salvador; tel. 2264-3863; fax 2264-3866; e-mail embajada@embajadacostarica.org.sv; internet www.embajadacostarica.org.sv; Ambassador ADRIANA PRADO CASTRO.

Cuba: Calle Arturo Ambrogui 530, esq. Avda el Mirador, Col. Escalón, San Salvador; tel. 2508-0446; fax 2508-0455; e-mail embajada@sv.embacuba.cu; internet www.cubadiplomatica.cu/elsalvador; Ambassador ILIANA TERESA FONSECA LORENTE.

Dominican Republic: Edif. Colinas, 1°, Blvd El Hipódromo 253, Zona Rosa, Col. San Benito, San Salvador; tel. 2223-4036; fax 2223-3109; e-mail endosal@saltel.net; Ambassador VÍCTOR SÁNCHEZ PEÑA.

Ecuador: Pasaje Los Pinos 241, entre 77 y 79 Avda Norte, Col. Escalón, San Salvador; tel. 2263-5258; fax 2264-2973; e-mail ecuador@integra.com.sv; Ambassador SEGUNDO ANDRANGO.

France: 1a Calle Poniente 3718, Col. Escalón, Apdo 474, San Salvador; tel. 2521-9090; fax 2521-9092; e-mail info@ambafrance-sv.org; internet www.ambafrance-sv.org; Ambassador PHILIPPE VINOGRADOFF.

Germany: 7a Calle Poniente 3972, esq. 77a Avda Norte, Col. Escalón, Apdo 693, San Salvador; tel. 2247-0000; fax 2247-0099; e-mail info@san-salvador.diplo.de; internet www.san-salvador.diplo.de; Ambassador HEINRICH HAUPT.

Guatemala: 15 Avda Norte 135, entre Calle Arce y 1a Calle Poniente, San Salvador; tel. 2271-2225; fax 2221-3019; e-mail embelsalvador@minex.gob.gt; Ambassador LUIS ROLANDO TORRES CASANOVA.

Holy See: 87 Avda Norte y 7a Calle Poniente, Col. Escalón, Apdo 01-95, San Salvador (Apostolic Nunciature); tel. 2263-2931; fax 2263-3010; e-mail nunels@telesal.net; Apostolic Nuncio Most Rev. LUIGI PEZZUTO (Titular Archbishop of Torre di Proconsolare).

Honduras: 89 Avda Norte 561, entre 7a y 9a Calle Poniente, Col. Escalón, San Salvador; tel. 2263-2808; fax 2263-2296; e-mail embhon@integra.com.sv; internet www.sre.hn/elsalvador.html; Ambassador CÉSAR PINTO.

Israel: Centro Financiero Gigante, Torre B, 11°, Alameda Roosevelt y Avda Sur 63, San Salvador; tel. 2211-3434; fax 2211-3443; e-mail info@sansalvador.mfa.gov.il; internet sansalvador.mfa.gov.il; Ambassador SHMULIK ARIE BASS.

Italy: Calle la Reforma 158, Col. San Benito, Apdo 0199, San Salvador; tel. 2223-5184; fax 2298-3050; e-mail ambasciatore.sansalvador@esteri.it; internet www.ambsansalvador.esteri.it; Ambassador TOSCA BARUCCO.

Japan: World Trade Center, Torre 1, 6°, 89 Avda Norte y Calle El Mirador, Col. Escalón, Apdo 115, San Salvador; tel. 2528-1111; fax 2528-1110; internet www.sv.emb-japan.go.jp; Ambassador MASATAKA TARAHARA.

Korea, Republic: Edif. Torre Futura, 14°, Calle El Mirador y 87 Avda Norte, Local 5, Col. Escalón, San Salvador; tel. 2263-9145; fax 2263-0783; e-mail embcorea@mofat.go.kr; internet slv.mofat.go.kr; Ambassador MAENG DAL-YOUNG.

Mexico: Calle Circunvalación y Pasaje 12, Col. San Benito, Apdo 432, San Salvador; tel. 2248-9900; fax 2248-9906; e-mail embamex@intercom.com.sv; internet portal.sre.gob.mx/elsalvador; Ambassador RAÚL LÓPEZ LIRA NAVA.

Nicaragua: 7 Calle Poniente Bis, No 5135, Col. Escalón, San Salvador; tel. 2263-8770; fax 2263-8849; e-mail embanicsv@cancilleria.gob.ni; Ambassador GILDA MARÍA BOLT GONZÁLEZ.

Panama: Calle los Bambúes, Avda las Bugambilías 21, Col. San Francisco, San Salvador; tel. 2536-0601; fax 2536-0602; e-mail embpan@telesat.net; Ambassador ENRIQUE BERMÚDEZ MARTINELLI.

Peru: Avda Masferrer Norte 17P, Cumbres de la Escalafón, Col. Escalón, San Salvador; tel. 2523-9400; fax 2523-9401; e-mail embperu@telesal.net; internet www.embajadaperu.com.sv; Ambassador ERIC EDGARDO ANDERSON.

Qatar: Avda Boquerón, Lote 21, Poligono L, Urb. Cumbre de la Escalón, San Salvador; tel. 2562-1480; fax 2562-1883; e-mail eqatar.salvador@gmail.com; Ambassador ABDULRAHMAN MOHAMED HAMDAN AL-DOUSSARI.

Spain: Calle La Reforma 164 bis, Col. San Benito, San Salvador; tel. 2257-5700; fax 2257-5712; e-mail emb.sansalvador@maec.es; internet www.maec.es/embajadas/sansalvador; Ambassador FRANCISCO RABENA BARRACHINA.

Taiwan (Republic of China): Avda La Capilla 716, Blvd. del Hipódromo, Col. San Benito, Apdo 956, San Salvador; tel. 2263-1330; fax 2263-1329; e-mail sinoemb3@gmail.com; internet www.taiwanembassy.org/sv; Ambassador ANDREA SING YING LEE.

United Kingdom: Torre Futura, 14°, Plaza Futura, Calle El Mirador, Col. Escalón, San Salvador; tel. 2511-5757; e-mail britishembassy.elsalvador@fco.gov.uk; internet ukinelsalvador.fco.gov.uk; Ambassador LINDA MARY CROSS.

USA: Blvd Santa Elena Sur, Antiguo Cuscatlán, San Salvador; tel. 2501-2999; fax 2501-2150; internet sansalvador.usembassy.gov; Ambassador MARI CARMEN APONTE.

Uruguay: Edif. Gran Plaza 405, Blvd del Hipódromo 111, Col. San Benito, San Salvador; tel. 2279-1626; fax 2279-1627; e-mail urusalva@telesal.net; Ambassador MARÍA CRISTINA FIGUEROA URSI.

Venezuela: 7a Calle Poniente 3921, entre 75 y 77 Avda Norte, Col. Escalón, San Salvador; tel. 2263-3977; fax 2211-0027; e-mail embajadadevenezuela@telesal.net; internet embavenez-elsalvador .com.sv; Ambassador NORA MARGARITA URIBE TRUJILLO.

Judicial System

The Supreme Court of Justice comprises 15 Justices. There are the Courts of Second Instance, Courts of Appeal and other trial courts (Courts of Peace). The National Judiciary Council, an independent institution, is in charge of proposing candidates to serve as justices on the Supreme Court and judges for the courts of appeal and the trial courts.

Corte Suprema de Justicia: Frente a Plaza José Simeón Cañas, Centro de Gobierno, San Salvador; tel. 2271-8888; fax 2271-3767; internet www.csj.gob.sv; f. 1824; 15 magistrates, one of whom is its President; the Court is divided into 4 chambers: Constitutional Law, Civil Law, Criminal Law and Litigation; Pres. FLORENTÍN MELÉNDEZ (acting).

Attorney-General: LUIS ANTONIO MARTÍNEZ GONZÁLEZ.

Procurator-General for the Defence of Human Rights: OSCAR HUMBERTO LUNA.

Religion

Roman Catholicism is the dominant religion, but other denominations are also permitted. The Baptist Church, Seventh-day Adventists and Jehovah's Witnesses are represented.

CHRISTIANITY

The Roman Catholic Church

El Salvador comprises one archdiocese and seven dioceses. Roman Catholics represent some 76% of the total population.

Bishops' Conference: Conferencia Episcopal de El Salvador, 15 Avda Norte 1420, Col. Layco, Apdo 1310, San Salvador; tel. 2225-8997; fax 2226-5330; e-mail cedes.casa@telesal.net; internet iglesia .org.sv; f. 1974; Pres. Most Rev. JOSÉ LUIS ESCOBAR ALAS (Archbishop of San Salvador).

Archbishop of San Salvador: Most Rev. JOSÉ LUIS ESCOBAR ALAS, Arzobispado, Col. Médica, Avda Dr Emilio Alvarez y Avda Dr Max Bloch, Apdo 2253, San Salvador; tel. 2226-0501; fax 2226-4979; e-mail info@arzobispadosansalvador.org; internet www .arzobispadosansalvador.org.

The Anglican Communion

El Salvador comprises one of the five dioceses of the Iglesia Anglicana de la Región Central de América. The Iglesia Anglicana has some 5,000 members.

Bishop of El Salvador: Rt Rev. MARTÍN DE JESÚS BARAHONA PASCACIO, 47 Avda Sur, 723 Col. Flor Blanca, Apdo 01-274, San Salvador; tel. 2223-2252; fax 2223-7952; e-mail anglican.sal@integra .com.sv.

The Baptist Church

Baptist Association of El Salvador: Avda Sierra Nevada 922, Col. Miramonte, Apdo 347, San Salvador; tel. 2260-2070; e-mail abes1911_2011@hotmail.com; internet ubla.net/paises/elsalvador .htm; f. 1933; Pres. MAURICIO SALINAS SANDOVAL; 4,427 mems.

Other Churches

Church of Jesus Christ of Latter-day Saints (Mormons): San Salvador Temple, Avda El Espino, Col. San Benito frente al Redondel Roberto D'Abuisson, Antiguo Cuscatlan, San Salvador; tel. 2520-2631; internet www.lds.org; 114,674 mems.

Sínodo Luterano Salvadoreño (Iglesia Luterana Salvadoreña) (Salvadorean Lutheran Synod): Final 49 Avda Sur, Calle Paralela al Bulevar de los Próceres, San Salvador; tel. 2225-2843; fax 2248-3451; e-mail lutomg@sls.org.sv; internet sls.org.sv; Pres. Bishop MEDARDO E. GÓMEZ SOTO; 20,000 mems.

The Press

DAILY NEWSPAPERS

Co Latino: 23 Avda Sur 225, Apdo 96, San Salvador; tel. 2222-1009; fax 2271-0822; e-mail info@diariocolatino.com; internet nuevaweb .diariocolatino.com; f. 1890; evening; Dir FRANCISCO ELÍAS VALENCIA SORIANO; Editor PATRICIA MEZA; circ. 15,000.

El Diario de Hoy: 11 Calle Oriente 271 y Avda Cuscatancingo 271, Apdo 495, San Salvador; tel. 2231-7777; fax 2231-7869; e-mail redaccion@elsalvador.com; internet www.elsalvador.com; f. 1936; morning; ind; also publishes Diario de Occidente and Diario de Oriente (f. 1910); Dir ENRIQUE ALTAMIRANO MADRIZ; Editor RICARDO CHACÓN; circ. 115,000.

Diario Oficial: 4 Calle Poniente y 15 Avda Sur 829, San Salvador; tel. 2555-7829; fax 2222-4936; e-mail info@imprentanacional.gob.sv; internet www.imprentanacional.gob.sv; f. 1875; govt publ; Dir EDGAR ANTONIO MENDOZA CASTRO; circ. 1,000.

El Mundo: 15 Calle Poniente y 7a Avda Norte 521, San Salvador; tel. 2234-8000; fax 2222-8190; e-mail redaccion@elmundo.com.sv; internet www.elmundo.com.sv; f. 1967; morning; Exec. Dir ONNO WUELFERS; Editor ALVARO CRUZ ROJAS; circ. 40,215.

La Página: Avda La Capilla 319, Col. San Benito, San Salvador; tel. 2243-8969; fax 2521-5718; e-mail redaccion@lapagina.com.sv; internet www.lapagina.com.sv.

La Prensa Gráfica: Final Blvd Santa Elena, frente Embajada de EUA, Antiguo Cuscatlán, La Libertad, San Salvador; tel. 2241-2000; fax 2271-4242; e-mail opinion@laprensagrafica.com; internet www .laprensagrafica.com; f. 1915; general information; conservative, independent; Dir JOSÉ DUTRIZ; Editor RODOLFO DUTRIZ; circ. 97,312 (weekdays), 115,564 (Sundays).

PERIODICALS

Boletín Cultural Informativo: Universidad 'Dr José Matías Delgado', Km 8.5, Carretera Santa Tecla; tel. 2278-1011; fax 2289-5314; e-mail boculin@yahoo.es; internet www.ujmd.edu.sv; f. 2001; published by the Universidad 'Dr José Matías Delgado'; Dir CLAUDIA HÉRODIER.

Cultura: Dirección de Publicaciones e Impresos, 17 Avda Sur 430, San Salvador; tel. 2510-5318; fax 2221-4415; e-mail revistacultura .sv@gmail.com; internet revista-cultura.com; f. 1955; 3 a year; publ. by the National Council for Culture and the Arts; Dir MAURICIO ORELLANA SUÁREZ; circ. 1,000.

El Economista: Grupo Dutriz, Blvd Santa Elena, Antiguo Cuscatlán, La Libertad; tel. 2241-2677; e-mail eleconomista@eleconomista .net; internet www.eleconomista.net; f. 2005; owned by Grupo Dutriz; monthly; business and economics; Editor ALFREDO HERNÁNDEZ.

Ella: Final blvd Santa Elena, frente a embajada de EUA, Antiguo Cuscatlán, La Libertad; tel. 2241-2000; e-mail ella@laprensa.com.sv; internet ella.laprensagrafica.com; f. 1987; publ. by La Prensa Gráfica.

El Gráfico: Urb. y Blvd Santa Elena, Antiguo Cuscatlán, La Libertad; e-mail grafico@laprensa.com.sv; internet www.elgrafico .com; publ. by Grupo Dutriz; sports; fortnightly; Editor DANIEL HERRERA.

El Salvador Investiga: Proyección de Investigaciones, Edif. A5, 2°, Centro de Gobierno, San Salvador; tel. 2221-4439; e-mail direccion .investigaciones@concultura.gob.sv; internet www.concultura.gob .sv/revistainvestiga.htm; f. 2005; 2 a year; publ. by the National Council for Culture and the Arts; historical and cultural research; Editor MARIO COLORADO.

Motor City: Final blvd Santa Elena, frente a embajada de EUA, Antiguo Cuscatlán, La Libertad; tel. 2241-2000; e-mail motor@ laprensa.com.sv; internet www.laprensagrafica.com; publ. by La Prensa Gráfica; Editor ROBERTO FLORES PINTO.

PRESS ASSOCIATION

Asociación de Periodistas de El Salvador (Press Association of El Salvador): Edif. Casa del Periodista, Paseo Gen. Escalón 4130, San Salvador; tel. 2263-5335; e-mail info@apes.org.sv; internet www .apes.org.sv; Pres. JOSÉ LUIS BENITEZ; Sec.-Gen. RAQUEL MORÁN.

Publishers

Clásicos Roxsil, SA de CV: 4a Avda Sur 2–3, Nueva San Salvador; tel. 2228-1832; fax 2228-1212; e-mail roxanabe@navegante.com.sv; f. 1976; textbooks, literature; Dir ROSA VICTORIA SERRANO DE LÓPEZ; Editorial Dir ROXANA BEATRIZ LÓPEZ.

Dirección de Publicaciones e Impresos (DPI): 17a Avda Sur 430, San Salvador; tel. 2271-1071; e-mail direcciondepublicaciones@ cultura.gob.sv; internet www.dpi.gob.sv; f. 1953; literary, history and culture; Dir RÓGER LINDO.

Editorial Universidad Don Bosco: Calle Plan del Pino, Ciudadela Don Bosco, Soyapango, San Salvador; tel. 2251-8212; e-mail hflores@ udb.edu.sv; internet www.udb.edu.sv/editorial; f. 2005; academic periodicals and texts; Pres. Dr JOSÉ HUMBERTO FLORES.

UCA Editores: Blvd Los Próceres, Apdo 01-575, San Salvador; tel. 2210-6600; fax 2210-6650; e-mail ucaeditores@gmail.com; internet www.ucaeditores.com.sv/uca; f. 1975; social science, religion, economy, literature and textbooks; Dir ANDREU OLIVA.

PUBLISHERS' ASSOCIATION

Cámara Salvadoreña del Libro: Edif. Forty Seven, Local 4, Col. Flor Blanca, 47 Avda Norte y 1a Calle Poniente, Apdo 3384, San Salvador; tel. 2275-0293; fax 2261-2231; e-mail camsalibro@terra.com.sv; internet www.camsalibro.com; f. 1974; Pres. ANA DOLORES MOLINA DE FAUVET; Exec. Dir AMÉRICA DOMÍNGUEZ.

Broadcasting and Communications

TELECOMMUNICATIONS

Claro: Edif. F, 1°, Complejo Telecom Roma, Calle Liverpool y Final Calle El Progreso, Col. Roma, San Salvador; tel. 2250-5555; fax 2221-4849; e-mail clientes@claro.com.sv; internet www.claro.com.sv; telecommunications network, fmrly part of Administración Nacional de Telecomunicaciones (ANTEL), which was divested in 1998; changed name from CTE Antel Telecom in 1999; acquired by América Móvil, SA de CV (Mexico) in 2003; fixed line and mobile cellular operations; Exec. Pres. ERIC BEHNER.

Digicel: Edif. Palic, 5°, Alameda Dr Manuel Enrique Araujo y Calle Nueva No 1, Col. Escalón, San Salvador; tel. 2285-5100; fax 2285-5585; e-mail servicioalcliente.sv@digicelgroup.com; internet www.digicel.com.sv; owned by Digicel (USA); mobile telecommunications; CEO JOSÉ ANTONIO RODRÍGUEZ.

Intelfon, SA de CV (RED): Centro Financiero Gigante, Torre A, 12°, Of. 503, Alameda Roosevelt y 63 Avda Sur, San Salvador; tel. 2515-0000; e-mail rtrujillo@red.com.sv; internet www.red.com.sv; f. 2005; cellular and internet services; Dir JUAN JOSÉ BORJA PAPINI.

Telefónica Móviles El Salvador, SA de CV (Movistar): Torre Telefónica (Torre B de Centro Financiero Gigante), Alameda Roosevelt y 63 Avda Sur, Col. Escalón, San Salvador; tel. 2244-0144; e-mail telefonica.empresas@telefonica.com.sv; internet www.movistar.com.sv; mobile telecommunications; 92% owned by Telefónica Móviles, SA (Spain); Exec. Dir HERNÁN OZÓN.

Tigo El Salvador: Centro Financiero, Gigante Torre D, 9°, Avda Roosevelt, San Salvador; tel. 2246-9977; fax 2246-9999; e-mail servicioalcliente@tigo.com.sv; internet www.tigo.com.sv; mobile telecommunications and internet services; subsidiary of Millicom International Cellular (Luxembourg); CEO MARCELO JULIO ALEMÁN.

Regulatory Authority

Superintendencia General de Electricidad y Telecomunicaciones (SIGET): 16 Calle Poniente y 37 Avda Sur 2001, Col. Flor Blanca, San Salvador; tel. 2257-4438; fax 2257-4498; e-mail info@siget.gob.sv; internet www.siget.gob.sv; f. 1996; Supt LUIS EDUARDO MÉNDEZ MENÉNDEZ.

BROADCASTING

Radio

Radio Corporación FM: 69 Avda Norte, No 213, Col Escalón, San Salvador; tel. 2283-2222; fax 2224-1212; e-mail mercadeo@radiocorporacionfm.com.sv; internet www.radiocorporacionfm.com.sv; f. 1988; owns and operates 6 radio stations; Pres. JOSÉ LUIS SACA MELÉNDEZ.

Radio Nacional de El Salvador: Edif. Ministerio de Gobernación, Cto. de Gobierno, 10°, Alameda Juan Pablo II, San Salvador; tel. 2527-7272; e-mail info@turadioelsalvador.com; internet www.turadioelsalvador.com; f. 1926; non-commercial cultural station; Dir-Gen. RICARDO ALBERTO MARTÍNEZ BARRERA.

Radio Paz: 1 Calle Poniente 3412, Col. Escalón, Contiguo al Seminario San José de la Montaña, San Salvador; tel. 2245-2941; fax 2245-1069; e-mail director@radiopaz.com.sv; internet www.radiopaz.com.sv; f. 1998; operated by the Archdiocese of El Salvador; Gen. Man. MARITZA VILLA.

Television

Canal 8 (Agape TV): Centro Comunicaciones AGAPE, 1511 Calle Gerardo Barrios, Col. Cucumacuyán, San Salvador; tel. 2281-2828; fax 2211-0799; e-mail info@agapetv8.com; internet www.agapetv8.com; Catholic, family channel; Pres. FLAVIÁN MUCCI.

Canal 12: Blvd Santa Elena Sur 12, Antiguo Cuscatlán, La Libertad; tel. 2560-1212; fax 2278-0722; e-mail mercadotecnia@canal12.com.sv; internet www.canal12.com.sv; f. 1984; Dir ALEJANDRO GONZÁLEZ.

Grupo Megavisión: Calle Poniente entre 85 y 86 Avda Norte, Apdo 2789, San Salvador; tel. 2283-2121; e-mail serviciosmegavision@salnet.net; internet www.megavision.com.sv; operates Canal 21; Dir-Gen. FREDDY UNGO.

Grupo Televisivo Cuscatleco: 6a–10a Calle Poniente 2323, Col. Flor Blanca, San Salvador; tel. 2559-8326; fax 2245-6142; e-mail info.sv@tecoloco.com; internet www.tecoloco.com.sv; operates Canal 23, 25, 67 and 69 (in the west only).

Tecnovisión Canal 33: entre 75 y 77 Avda Nte, Istmania No 262, San Salvador; tel. 2559-3333; e-mail info@canal33.tv; internet www.canal33.tv; Pres. ENRIQUE RIBOBÓ.

Association

Asociación Salvadoreña de Radiodifusores (ASDER): Calle Las Jacarandas, Pasaje 3 No 7K, Urb. Maquilishuat, San Salvador; tel. 2563-5302; fax 2563-5304; e-mail informacionam@asder.com.sv; internet www.asder.com.sv; f. 1964; Pres. PEDRO LEONEL MORENO MONGE; Exec. Dir ANA MARÍA URRUTIA DE LARA.

Finance

(cap. = capital; res = reserves; dep. = deposits; m. = million; brs = branches; amounts in US dollars)

BANKING

Supervisory Bodies

Superintendencia del Sistema Financiero: 7a Avda Norte 240, Apdo 2942, San Salvador; tel. 2281-2444; fax 2281-1621; e-mail internacional@ssf.gob.sv; internet www.ssf.gob.sv; Supt VÍCTOR ANTONIO RAMÍREZ NAJARRO.

Superintendencia de Valores: Antiguo Edif. BCR, 2°, 1a Calle Poniente y 7a Avda Norte, San Salvador; tel. 2281-8900; fax 2221-3404; e-mail info@superval.gob.sv; internet www.superval.gob.sv; Supt RENÉ MAURICIO GUARDADO RODRÍGUEZ.

Central Bank

Banco Central de Reserva de El Salvador: Alameda Juan Pablo II, entre 15 y 17 Avda Norte, Apdo 01-106, San Salvador; tel. 2281-8000; fax 2281-8011; e-mail info@bcr.gob.sv; internet www.bcr.gob.sv; f. 1934; nationalized Dec. 1961; entered monetary integration process 2001; cap. 115.0m., res 171.2m., dep. 2,017.3m. (Dec. 2009); Pres. CARLOS GERARDO ACEVEDO; Vice-Pres. MARTA EVELYN DE RIVERA.

Commercial and Mortgage Banks

Banco Agrícola: Blvd Constitución 100, San Salvador; tel. 2267-5000; fax 2267-5930; e-mail info@bancoagricola.com; internet www.bancoagricola.com; f. 1955; merged with Banco Desarrollo in 2000; acquired Banco Capital in 2001; bought by Bancolombia in 2012; cap. 297.5m., res 250.3m., dep. 2,551m. (Dec. 2011); Chair. CARLOS ALBERTO RODRÍGUEZ LÓPEZ; Exec. Pres. RAFAEL BARRAZA DOMÍNGUEZ; 8 brs.

Banco Citibank de El Salvador, SA: Edif. Pirámide Cuscatlán, Km 10, Carretera a Santa Tecla, Apdo 626, San Salvador; tel. 2212-2000; fax 2228-5700; e-mail info@bancocuscatlan.com; internet www.citi.com.sv; f. 1972; acquired by Citi (USA) in 2008; cap. 155.7m., res 168.9m., dep. 2,011.3m. (Dec. 2008); Exec. Pres. JUAN ANTONIO MIRÓ LLORT; 31 brs.

Banco Davivienda Salvadoreño, SA (Bancosal): Edif. Centro Financiero, Avda Manuel E. Araujo y Avda Olímpica 3550, Apdo 0673, San Salvador; tel. 2214-2000; fax 2214-2755; internet www.davivienda.com.sv; f. 1885 as Banco Salvadoreño, SA; became Banco HSBC Salvadoreño in 2007; bought by Banco Davivienda (Colombia) in 2012 and present name adopted; cap. 150m., res 86m., dep. 1,418.5m. (Dec. 2011); Exec. Pres. (El Salvador) GERARDO JOSÉ SIMÁN SIRI; 74 brs.

Banco Hipotecario de El Salvador: Pasaje Senda Florida Sur, Col. Escalón, Apdo 999, San Salvador; tel. 2223-7713; fax 2298-2071; e-mail servicio.cliente@hipotecario.com.sv; internet www.bancohipotecario.com.sv; f. 1935; cap. 38.3m., res 10.8m., dep. 429m. (Dec. 2011); Pres. MANUEL RIVERA CASTRO; 16 brs.

Banco Promérica: Edif. Promérica, Centro Comercial La Gran Vía, Antiguo Cuscatlán; tel. 2513-5000; e-mail soluciones@promerica.com.sv; internet www.promerica.com.sv; f. 1996; privately owned; cap. 23.2m., res 3.7m., dep. 469.8m. (Dec. 2011); Chair. RAMIRO NORBERTO ORTIZ GUDÍAN; Exec. Pres. EDUARDO ALBERTO QUEVEDO MORENO.

Scotiabank El Slavador, SA (Canada): Centro Financiero, 25 Avda Norte, No 1230, San Salvador; tel. 2250-1111; fax 2234-4577; e-mail atencion.cliente@scotiabank.com.sv; internet www.scotiabank.com.sv; f. 1997; cap. 114.1m., res 67.5m., dep. 1,280.4m. (Dec. 2011); Pres. JEAN LUC RICH; Exec. Dir JUAN CARLOS GARCÍA VIZCAÍNO.

Public Institutions

Banco de Desarrollo de El Salvador (BANDESAL): Edif. World Trade Center II, 4°, San Salvador; tel. 2267-0000; fax 2267-0011; e-mail karla.martinez@bandesal.gob.sv; internet www.bandesal.gob

.sv; f. 1994 as Banco Multisectorial de Inversiones; adopted present name in 2011; Pres. OSCAR LINDO.

Banco de Fomento Agropecuario: Km 10.5, Carretera al Puerto de la Libertad, Santa Tecla, La Libertad, Nueva San Salvador; tel. 2241-0966; fax 2241-0800; internet www.bfa.gob.sv; f. 1973; state-owned; cap. 17.8m., dep. 174.8m. (Dec. 2010); Pres. NORA MERCEDES MIRANDA DE LÓPEZ; Gen. Man. JOSÉ ANTONIO PEÑATE; 27 brs.

Federación de Cajas de Crédito y Bancos de los Trabajadores (FEDECREDITO): 25 Avda Norte y 23 Calle Poniente, San Salvador; tel. 2209-9696; fax 2226-7161; e-mail informacion@fedecredito.com.sv; internet www.fedecredito.com.sv; f. 1943; Pres. MACARIO ARMANDO ROSALES ROSA.

Fondo Social para la Vivienda (FSV): Calle Rubén Darío 901, entre 15 y 17 Avda Sur, Apdo 2179, San Salvador; tel. 2231-2000; fax 2271-4011; e-mail comunicaciones@fsv.gob.sv; internet www.fsv.gob.sv; f. 1973; provides loans to workers for house purchases; Pres. FRANCISCO ANTONIO GUEVARA; Gen. Man. MARIANO ARÍSTIDES BONILLA.

Banking Association

Asociación Bancaria Salvadoreña (ABANSA): Pasaje Senda, Florida Norte 140, Col. Escalón, San Salvador; tel. 2298-6959; fax 2223-1079; e-mail info@abansa.net; internet www.abansa.org.sv; f. 1965; Pres. ARMANDO ARIAS; Exec. Dir MARCELA DE JIMÉNEZ.

STOCK EXCHANGE

Bolsa de Valores de El Salvador, SA de CV: Blvd Merliot y Avda Las Carretas, Urb. Jardines de la Hacienda, Antiguo Cuscatlán, La Libertad, San Salvador; tel. 2212-6400; fax 2278-4377; e-mail info@bolsadevalores.com.sv; internet www.bolsadevalores.com.sv; f. 1992; Pres. ROLANDO ARTURO DUARTE SCHLAGETER.

INSURANCE

Aseguradora Agrícola Comercial, SA: Alameda Roosevelt 3104, Apdo 1855, San Salvador; tel. 2261-8200; fax 2260-5592; e-mail informacion@acsasal.com.sv; internet www.acsasal.com.sv; f. 1973; Pres. LUIS ALFREDO ESCALANTE SOL; Gen. Man. RAÚL ANTONIO GUEVARA.

Aseguradora Popular, SA: Paseo Gen. Escalón 5338, Col. Escalón, San Salvador; tel. 2263-0700; fax 2263-1246; e-mail info@aseguradorapopular.com; internet aseguradorapopular.com; f. 1975; Pres. Dr CARLOS ARMANDO LAHÚD; Gen. Man. HERIBERTO PÉREZ AGUIRRE.

Aseguradora Suiza Salvadoreña, SA (ASESUISA): Alameda Dr Manuel Enrique Araujo, Plaza Suiza, Apdo 1490, Col. San Benito, San Salvador; tel. 2209-5000; fax 2209-5001; e-mail info@asesuisa.com; internet www.asesuisa.com; f. 1969; acquired in 2001 by Inversiones Financieras Banco Agrícola (Panama); Pres. Dr SERGIO RESTREPO ISAZA; Exec. Dir RICARDO COHEN.

La Central de Seguros y Fianzas, SA: Avda Olímpica 3333, Apdo 01-255, San Salvador; tel. 2268-6000; fax 2223-7647; e-mail gerenciaseguros@lacentral.com.sv; internet www.lacentral.com.sv; f. 1983; Pres. EDUARDO ENRIQUE CHACÓN BORJA; Man. (Insurance) MAURICIO E. ULLOA MORAZÁN.

Chartis Seguros El Salvador, SA: Calle Loma Linda 265, Col. San Benito, Apdo 92, San Salvador; tel. 2250-3200; fax 2250-3201; e-mail chartis.elsalvador@chartisinsurance.com; internet www.chartisinsurance.com; f. 1998 as AIG Unión y Desarrollo, SA; following merger of Unión y Desarrollo, SA and AIG; changed name as above in 2009; Gen. Man. PEDRO ARTANA.

Internacional de Seguros, SA (Interseguros): Edif. Plaza Credicorp Bank, Calle 50, 19º, 20º y 21º, San Salvador; tel. 2206-4000; fax 2210-1900; e-mail interseguros@interseguros.com.sv; internet isweb.iseguros.com/iseguros; f. 1910; merged with Seguros Universales in 2004; Pres. ROY ICAZA JIMÉNEZ; Exec. Vice-Pres. MAURICIO DE LA GUARDIA.

Mapfre La Centro Americana, SA: Alameda Roosevelt 3107, Apdo 527, San Salvador; tel. 2257-6666; fax 2223-2687; e-mail lacentro@lacentro.com; internet www.lacentro.com; f. 1915; acquired by Mapfre, SA in 2000; Pres. ANTONIO PENEDO CASMARTIÑO; Gen. Man. GILMAR NAVARRETE CASTAÑEDA.

Pan-American Life Insurance Co: Edif. PALIC, Alameda Dr Manuel Enrique Araujo y Calle Nueva 1, Col. Escalón, Apdo 255, San Salvador; tel. 2209-2700; fax 2245-2792; e-mail servicioalclientesv@panamericanlife.com; internet www.palig.com/regions/el_salvador.aspx; f. 1928; Country Man. JEAN CARLO CALDERÓN.

Scotia Seguros, SA: Calle Loma Linda 223, Col. San Benito, Apdo 1004, San Salvador; tel. 2209-7000; fax 2223-0734; e-mail contactenos@scotiaseguros.com.sv; internet www.scotiaseguros.com.sv; f. 1955; fmrly Compañía General de Seguros, SA; changed name as above in 2005; Pres. JUAN CARLOS GARCÍA VIZCAÍNO; Gen. Man. PEDRO GEOFFROY.

Seguros e Inversiones, SA (SISA): Carretera Panamericana, 10.5 Km, Santa Tecla, La Libertad; tel. 2241-0000; fax 2241-1213; e-mail servicioalcliente@sisa.com.sv; internet www.sisa.com.sv; f. 1962; Pres. JOSÉ EDUARDO MONTENEGRO PALOMO.

Association

Asociación Salvadoreña de Empresas de Seguros (ASES): Calle Los Castaños 120, Col. San Francisco, San Salvador; tel. 2223-7169; fax 2223-8901; e-mail asesgeneral@ases.com.sv; internet www.ases.com.sv; f. 1970; Pres. GILMAR NAVARRETE CASTAÑEDA; Exec. Dir Dr RAÚL BETANCOURT MENÉNDEZ.

Trade and Industry

GOVERNMENT AGENCIES AND DEVELOPMENT ORGANIZATIONS

Comisión Nacional de la Micro y Pequeña Empresa (CONAMYPE): Of. 41, 1°, Avda Norte y Avda Scout de El Salvador, No 115, San Salvador; tel. 2521-2200; fax 2521-2274; e-mail conamype@conamype.gob.sv; internet www.conamype.gob.sv; f. 1996; micro and small industrial devt; Pres. ARMANDO FLORES (Minister of the Economy); Exec. Dir ILEANA ROGEL.

Consejo Nacional de Ciencia y Tecnología (CONACYT): Avda Dr Emilio Alvarez, Pasaje Dr Guillermo Rodríguez Pacas 51, Col. Médica, San Salvador; tel. 2234-8400; fax 2225-6255; e-mail info@conacyt.gob.sv; internet www.conacyt.gob.sv; f. 1992; formulation and guidance of national policy on science and technology; Pres. ARMANDO FLORES; Exec. Dir CARLOS ROBERTO OCHOA CÓRDOBA.

Corporación de Exportadores de El Salvador (COEXPORT): Avda La Capilla 359A, Col. San Benito, San Salvador; tel. 2212-0200; fax 2243-3159; e-mail info@coexport.com.sv; internet www.coexport.com.sv; f. 1973 to promote Salvadorean exports; Pres. FRANCISCO BOLAÑOS; Exec. Dir SILVIA M. CUÉLLAR DE PAREDES.

Corporación Salvadoreña de Inversiones (CORSAIN): Avda Bunganbilias, Casa 14, Col. San Francisco, San Salvador; tel. 2224-6070; fax 2224-6877; e-mail info@corsain.gob.sv; internet www.corsain.gob.sv; Pres. EMILIO EDDY HENRÍQUEZ CERRITOS.

Fondo de Inversión Social para el Desarrollo Local (FISDL): Blvd Orden de Malta 470, Urb. Santa Elena, Antiguo Cuscatlán, La Libertad, San Salvador; tel. 2133-1200; fax 2133-1370; e-mail webmaster@fisdl.gob.sv; internet www.fisdl.gob.sv; f. 1990; poverty alleviation and development; Pres. CAROLINA AVALOS.

Instituto Salvadoreño de Fomento Cooperativo (INSAFOCOOP): Edif. Urrutia Abrego 2, Frente a INPEP, 15 Calle Poniente, No 402, San Salvador; tel. 2222-2563; fax 2222-4119; e-mail insafocoop@insafocoop.gob.sv; internet www.insafocoop.gob.sv; f. 1971; devt of co-operatives; Pres. FÉLIX CÁRCAMO.

Instituto Salvadoreño de Transformación Agraria (ISTA): Final Col. Las Mercedes, Km 5.5, Carretera a Santa Tecla, San Salvador; tel. 2527-2600; fax 2224-0259; e-mail info@ista.gob.sv; internet www.ista.gob.sv; f. 1976 to promote rural devt; empowered to buy inefficiently cultivated land; Pres. FEDERICO LÓPEZ BELTRÁN.

CHAMBER OF COMMERCE

Cámara de Comercio e Industria de El Salvador: 9a Avda Norte y 5a Calle Poniente, Apdo 1640, San Salvador; tel. 2231-3000; fax 2271-4461; e-mail camara@camarasal.com; internet www.camarasal.com; f. 1915; 2,000 mems; Pres. LUIS CARDENAL; brs in San Miguel, Santa Ana, Sonsonate and La Unión.

INDUSTRIAL AND TRADE ASSOCIATIONS

Asociación Azúcarera de El Salvador (AAES): 103 Avda Norte y Calle Arturo Ambrogi 145, Col. Escalón, San Salvador; tel. 2264-1226; fax 2263-0361; e-mail asosugar@sal.gbm.net; internet www.asociacionazucarera.com; national sugar asscn, fmrly Instituto Nacional del Azúcar; Pres. MARIO SALAVERRÍA; Dir JULIO ARROYO.

Asociación Cafetalera de El Salvador (ACES): 67 Avda Norte 116, Col. Escalón, San Salvador; tel. 2223-3024; fax 2298-6261; e-mail ascafes@telesal.net; f. 1930; coffee growers' asscn; Pres. JOSÉ ROBERTO INCLÁN ROBREDO; Exec. Dir AMIR SALVADOR ALABÍ.

Asociación Salvadoreña de Beneficiadores y Exportadores de Café (ABECAFE): 87 Avda Norte, Condominio Fountainblue 4, Col. Escalón, San Salvador; tel. 2263-2834; fax 2263-2833; e-mail abecafe@telesal.net; coffee producers' and exporters' asscn; Pres. CARLOS BORGONOVO.

Asociación Salvadoreña de Industriales: Calles Roma y Liverpool, Col. Roma, Apdo 48, San Salvador; tel. 2279-2488; fax 2267-9253; e-mail medios@asi.com.sv; internet www.industriaelsalvador

.com; f. 1958; 400 mems; manufacturers' asscn; Pres. JAVIER ERNESTO SIMAN; Exec. Dir JORGE ARRIAZA.

Cámara Agropecuaria y Agroindustrial de El Salvador (CAMAGRO): Calle El Lirio 19, Col. Maquilishuat, San Salvador; tel. 2264-4622; fax 2263-9448; e-mail contactenos@camagro.com; internet www.camagro.com; Pres. AGUSTÍN MARTÍNEZ.

Consejo Salvadoreño del Café (CSC) (Salvadorean Coffee Council): 1 Avda Norte y 13 Calle Poniente, Nueva San Salvador, La Libertad; tel. 2505-6600; fax 2505-6691; e-mail csc@consejocafe.org.sv; internet www.consejocafe.org; f. 1989 as successor to the Instituto Nacional del Café; formulates policy and oversees the coffee industry; Exec. Dir JOSÉ HUGO HERNÁNDEZ.

Unión de Cooperativas de Cafetaleras de El Salvador de RL (UCAFES): Avda Río Lempa, Calle Adriático 44, Jardines de Guadalupe, San Salvador; tel. 2243-2238; fax 2298-1504; union of coffee-growing co-operatives; Pres. ERNESTO LIMA.

EMPLOYERS' ORGANIZATION

Asociación Nacional de Empresa Privada (ANEP) (National Private Enterprise Association): 1 Calle Poniente y 71 Avda Norte 204, Col. Escalón, Apdo 1204, San Salvador; tel. 2209-8300; fax 2209-8317; e-mail communicaciones@anep.org.sv; internet www.anep.org.sv; national private enterprise asscn; Pres. JORGE DABOUB; Exec. Dir ARNOLDO JIMÉNEZ.

UTILITIES

Regulatory Authority

Superintendencia General de Electricidad y Telecomunicaciones (SIGET): see Broadcasting and Communications—Regulatory Authority.

Electricity

AES El Salvador: e-mail consultas@aes.com; internet www.aeselsalvador.com; Exec. Pres. ABRAHAM BICHARA; operates 4 distribution cos in El Salvador:

CLESA: 23 Avda Sur y 5a Calle Oriente, Barrio San Rafael, Santa Ana; tel. 2429-4000; f. 1892.

Compañía de Alumbrado Electric (CAESS): Calle El Bambú, Col. San Antonio, Ayutuxtepeque, San Salvador; tel. 2529-9999; f. 1890.

Distribuidora Eléctrica de Usulután (DEUSEM): Centro Comercial Puerta de Oriente Local 2, Usulután; tel. 2622-4000; f. 1957.

EEO: Final 8, Calle Poniente, Calle a Ciudad Pacífico, Plantel Jalacatal, San Miguel; tel. 2606-8000; f. 1995.

Comisión Ejecutiva Hidroeléctrica del Río Lempa (CEL): 9 Calle Poniente 950, entre 15 y 17 Avda Norte, Centro de Gobierno, San Salvador; tel. 2211-6000; fax 2207-1302; e-mail naguilar@cel.gob.sv; internet www.cel.gob.sv; f. 1948; hydroelectric electricity generation; Pres. IRVING PABEL TÓCHEZ MARAVILLA; Exec. Dir JAIME CONTRERAS.

Distribuidora de Electricidad del Sur (DELSUR): Edif. Corporativo DELSUR, Unidad de Comunicaciones, Final 17 Avda Norte y Calle El Boquerón, Santa Tecla, La Libertad; tel. 2233-5700; fax 2243-8662; e-mail comunicaciones@delsur.com.sv; internet www.delsur.com.sv; Pres. IVÁN DÍAZ MOLINA; Gen. Man. ALEXIS BUTTO.

LaGeo SA de CV: Final 15, Avda Sur y Blvd Sur, Col. Utila, Santa Tecla, La Libertad; tel. 2211-6700; fax 2211-6746; e-mail info@lageo.com.sv; internet www.lageo.com.sv; f. 1999; owned by INE-ENEL; 25% share market; operates Ahuachapán and Berlin geothermal fields; Pres. JULIO E. VALDIVIESO.

Water

Administración Nacional de Acueductos y Alcantarillados (ANDA): Edif. ANDA, Final Avda Don Bosco, Col. Libertad, San Salvador; tel. 2247-2700; fax 2225-3152; e-mail sugerencias@anda.gob.sv; internet www.anda.gob.sv; f. 1961; maintenance of water supply and sewerage systems; Pres. MARCO ANTONIO FORTÍN; Exec. Dir CARLOS MANUEL DERAS BARILLAS.

TRADE UNIONS

Central Autónoma de Trabajadores Salvadoreños (CATS): Calle Los Pinares 17, Col. Centroamérica, San Salvador; tel. 2211-2570; e-mail cats@catselsalvador.org; internet www.catselsalvador.org; Sec.-Gen. FRANCISCO QUIJANO; 30,000 mems (2010).

Central de Trabajadores Democráticos de El Salvador (CTD) (Democratic Workers' Confederation): Avda Norte 19 y Calle Poniente 17, No 135, Barrio San Miguelito, San Salvador; tel. and fax 2235-8043; e-mail ctdelsalv_orit@navegante.com.sv; Sec.-Gen. JOSÉ MARÍA AMAYA; 50,000 mems (2007).

Central de Trabajadores Salvadoreños (CTS) (Salvadorean Workers' Confederation): Calle Darío González 616, San Jacinto, San Salvador; tel. 2237-2315; fax 2270-1703; e-mail felixblancocts@hotmail.com; f. 1966; Christian Democratic; Pres. MIGUEL ÁNGEL VÁSQUEZ; 30,000 mems (2007).

Confederación General de Sindicatos (CGS) (General Confederation of Unions): Edif. Kury, 3a Calle Oriente 226, San Salvador; tel. and fax 2222-3527; f. 1958; admitted to ITUC/ORIT; Sec.-Gen. JOSÉ ISRAEL HUIZA CISNEROS; 27,000 mems.

Confederación Sindical de Trabajadoras y Trabajadores Salvadoreños (CSTS) (Salvadorean Workers' Union Federation): Blvd Universitario 2226, Col. San José, San Salvador; tel. 2225-2315; fax 2225-5936; e-mail confederacioncsts@gmail.com; internet www.cstsconfederacion.org; f. 2005; conglomerate of independent left-wing trade unions; Sec.-Gen. JULIO CESAR FLORES.

Confederación Unitaria de Trabajadores Salvadoreños (CUTS) (United Salvadorean Workers' Federation): 141 Avda A, Col. San José, San Salvador; tel. and fax 2226-2100; e-mail proyectocuts@salnet.net; internet www.cutselsalvador.org; left-wing; Sec.-Gen. BÁRBARA FIGUEROA.

Federación Nacional Sindical de Trabajadores Salvadoreños (FENASTRAS) (Salvadorean Workers' National Union Federation): 4 Calle Poniente, No 2438A, Col. Flor Blanca, San Salvador; tel. 2298-2954; fax 2298-2953; e-mail fenastras@hotmail.com; internet www.fenastras.org; f. 1972; left-wing; 35,000 mems in 16 affiliates; Sec.-Gen. JUAN JOSÉ HUEZO.

Transport

Comisión Ejecutiva Portuaria Autónoma (CEPA): Edif. Torre Roble, Blvd de Los Héroes, Col. Miramonte, Centro Comercial Metrocentro, San Salvador; tel. 2218-1300; fax 2121-1212; e-mail info@cepa.gob.sv; internet www.cepa.gob.sv; f. 1952; operates and administers the ports of Acajutla and Cutuco and the El Salvador International Airport, as well as Ferrocarriles Nacionales de El Salvador; Pres. ALBERTO ARENE; Gen. Man. SALVADOR VILLALOBOS.

RAILWAYS

In 2005 there were 554.8 km of railway track in the country. The main track linked San Salvador with the ports of Acajutla and Cutuco (also known as La Unión) and with Santa Ana. Operation of the railway network was suspended in 2005; however, a passenger service between San Salvador and Apopa (a distance of 12.5 km) resumed in 2007, and the rehabilitation of further sections of track was planned.

Ferrocarriles Nacionales de El Salvador (FENADESAL): Final Avda Peralta 903, Apdo 2292, San Salvador; tel. 2530-1700; e-mail salvador.sanabria@cepa.gob.sv; internet www.fenadesal.gob.sv; 555 km of track; administered by CEPA (q.v.); Gen. Man. SALVADOR SANABRIA.

ROADS

There were some 10,886 km of roads in 2000, including the Pan-American Highway (306 km). In 2012 the 216-km Carretera Longitudinal del Norte, connecting the north of El Salvador with the rest of the country, was opened.

Fondo de Conservación Vial (FOVIAL): Carretera a La Libertad, Km 10.5, Antiguo Cuscatlán, San Salvador; tel. 2257-8300; e-mail info@fovial.com; internet www.fovial.com; f. 2000; responsible for maintaining the road network; Exec. Dir ELIUD ULISES AYALA.

SHIPPING

The port of Acajutla is administered by CEPA (see above). Services are also provided by foreign lines. An expansion of the port of Cutuco (Puerto La Unión Centroamericana) was completed in 2009. In December 2013 El Salvador's flag registered fleet comprised six vessels, with an aggregate displacement of some 9,643 grt.

Autoridad Portuaria de La Unión: Depto de La Unión; tel. 2623-6100; e-mail info@launion.gob.sv; internet www.puertolaunion.gob.sv; Gen. Man. MILTON LACAYO.

CIVIL AVIATION

The El Salvador International Airport is located 40 km (25 miles) from San Salvador in Comalapa. The former international airport at Ilopango is used for military and private civilian aircraft; there are an additional 88 private airports.

TACA International Airlines: Santa Elena, Antiguo Cuscatlán, San Salvador; tel. 2267-8888; internet www.taca.com; f. 1931; allied with Avianca of Colombia in 2009; passenger and cargo services to Central America and the USA; Exec. Pres. FABIO VILLEGAS RAMÍREZ.

Tourism

In 2012 a total of 1,255,000 tourists visited the country. Tourism receipts, excluding passenger transport, stood at a provisional US $544m. in the same year.

Asociación Salvadoreña de Hoteles: Hotel Suites Las Palmas, Blvd del Hipódromo, Col. San Benito, San Salvador; tel. 2298-5383; fax 2298-5382; e-mail info@hoteles-elsalvador.com; internet www .hoteles-elsalvador.com; f. 1996; Pres. ALBERTO ASCENCIO; Exec. Dir MORENA TORRES; 33 mems.

Cámara Salvadoreña de Turismo (CASATUR): 63 Avda Sur, Pasaje y Urb., Santa Mónica 12- A, Col. Escalón, San Salvador; tel. 2298-6011; fax 2279-2156; e-mail info@casatur.org; internet www .casatur.org; f. 1978; non-profit org. concerned with promotion of tourism in El Salvador; Pres. RAFAEL LARET CASTILLO; Gen. Man. DALILA URRITIA.

Corporación Salvadoreña de Turismo (CORSATUR): Edif. Carbonel 1, Pasaje Carbonel, Alameda Doctor Manuel Enrique Araujo, Col. Roma, San Salvador; tel. 2243-7835; fax 2223-6120; e-mail info@corsatur.gob.sv; internet www.elsalvador.travel; f. 1996; Dir-Gen. ROBERTO VIERA.

Instituto Salvadoreño de Turismo (ISTU) (National Tourism Institute): 41 Avda Norte y Alameda Roosvelt 115, San Salvador; tel. 2260-9249; fax 2260-9254; e-mail informacion@istu.gob.sv; internet www.istu.gob.sv; f. 1950; Pres. MANUEL AVILÉS; Exec. Dir DOLORES EDUVIGES HENRÍQUEZ DE FUNES.

Defence

As assessed at November 2013, the armed forces totalled 15,300, of whom an estimated 13,850 (including 4,000 conscripts) were in the army, 700 were in the navy and 750 (including some 200 conscripts) were in the air force. There were also some 9,900 joint reserves. The Policía Nacional Civil numbered some 17,000. Military service is by compulsory selective conscription of males aged between 18 and 30 and lasts for one year.

Defence Budget: an estimated US $154m. in 2013.

Chief of the Joint Command of the Armed Forces: Maj.-Gen. JAIME LEONARDO PARADA GONZÁLEZ.

Chief of Staff of the Army: Brig.-Gen. FRANCISCO EUGENIO DEL CID DÍAZ.

Chief of Staff of the Navy: Capt. GUILLERMO JIMÉNEZ VÁSQUEZ.

Chief of Staff of the Air Force: Col CARLOS JAIME MENA TORRES.

Education

Education in El Salvador is provided free of charge in state schools and there are also numerous private schools. Pre-primary education—beginning at four years of age and lasting for three years—and primary education—beginning at the age of seven years and lasting for nine years—are officially compulsory. In 2012 enrolment at primary schools included 93% of children in the relevant age-group. Secondary education, from the age of 16, lasts two years for an academic diploma or three years for a vocational one. In 2012 enrolment at secondary schools included 62% of students in the relevant age group. Budget allocation for education was US $827m. in 2012.

EQUATORIAL GUINEA

Introductory Survey

LOCATION, CLIMATE, LANGUAGE, RELIGION, FLAG, CAPITAL

The Republic of Equatorial Guinea consists of the islands of Bioko (formerly Fernando Póo and subsequently renamed Macías Nguema Biyogo under the regime of President Francisco Macías Nguema), Corisco, Great Elobey, Little Elobey and Annobón (previously known also as Pagalu), and the mainland region of Río Muni (previously known also as Mbini) on the west coast of Africa. Cameroon lies to the north and Gabon to the east and south of Río Muni, while Bioko lies off shore from Cameroon and Nigeria. The small island of Annobón lies far to the south, beyond the islands of São Tomé and Príncipe. The climate is hot and humid, with average temperatures higher than 26°C (80°F). The official languages are Spanish, French and Portuguese. In Río Muni the Fang language is spoken, as well as those of coastal tribes such as the Combe, Balemke and Bujeba. Bubi is the indigenous language on Bioko, although Fang is also widely used, and Ibo is spoken by the resident Nigerian population. An estimated 90% of the population are adherents of the Roman Catholic Church, although traditional forms of worship are also followed. The national flag (proportions 2 by 3) has three equal horizontal stripes, of green, white and red, with a blue triangle at the hoist and the national coat of arms (a silver shield, containing a tree, with six yellow stars above and a scroll beneath) in the centre of the white stripe. The capital is Malabo (formerly Santa Isabel).

CONTEMPORARY POLITICAL HISTORY

Historical Context

In December 1963 the two provinces of Spanish Guinea (Río Muni, on the African mainland, and Fernando Póo—now Bioko—with other nearby islands) were merged to form Equatorial Guinea, with a limited measure of self-government. After 190 years of Spanish rule, independence was declared on 12 October 1968. Francisco Macías Nguema, Equatorial Guinea's first President, formed a coalition Government. In February 1970 Macías outlawed all existing political parties and formed the Partido Unico Nacional (PUN), which later became the Partido Unico Nacional de los Trabajadores (PUNT). A new Constitution, giving absolute powers to the President, was adopted in July 1973.

In August 1979 President Macías was overthrown in a coup led by his nephew, Lt-Col (later Gen.) Teodoro Obiang Nguema Mbasogo, hitherto the Deputy Minister of Defence. (Obiang Nguema subsequently ceased to use his forename.) Macías was found guilty of treason, genocide, embezzlement and violation of human rights, and was executed in September. The Spanish Government, which admitted prior knowledge of the coup, was the first to recognize the new regime, and remained a major supplier of financial and technical aid. In August 1982 Obiang Nguema was reappointed President for a further seven years, and later that month a new Constitution, which provided for an eventual return to civilian government, was approved by 95% of voters in a referendum.

The imposition, from 1979 to 1991, of a ban on organized political activity within Equatorial Guinea, and persistent allegations against the Obiang Nguema regime of human rights abuses and corruption, resulted in the development of a substantial opposition-in-exile. A series of attempted coups were reported during the 1980s, and in January 1986 the President reinforced his control by assuming the post of Minister of Defence. In August 1987 Obiang Nguema announced the establishment of a 'governmental party', the Partido Democrático de Guinea Ecuatorial (PDGE), while continuing to reject demands for the legalization of opposition parties. At legislative elections held in July 1988 some 99.2% of voters endorsed a single list of candidates who had been nominated by the President.

Domestic Political Affairs

In June 1989, at the first presidential election to be held since independence, Obiang Nguema, the sole candidate, reportedly received the support of more than 99% of the electorate. Opposition groupings criticized the conduct of the election and declared the result invalid. Following his success, the President appealed to dissidents to return to Equatorial Guinea and declared an amnesty for political prisoners. A new Constitution, containing provisions for a multi-party political system, was approved by an overwhelming majority of voters at a national referendum in November 1991. However, opposition movements rejected the Constitution, owing to the inclusion of clauses exempting the President from any judicial procedures arising from his tenure of office and prohibiting citizens who had not been continuously resident in Equatorial Guinea for 10 years from standing as election candidates, while requiring all political parties to submit a large deposit (which could not be provided by funds from abroad) as a condition of registration. In January 1992 a transitional Government (comprising only members of the PDGE) was formed, and a general amnesty was extended to all political exiles.

Multi-party legislative elections held in November 1993 were boycotted by most of the opposition parties in protest at Obiang Nguema's refusal to review contentious clauses of the electoral law promulgated in January 1993 or to permit impartial international observers to inspect the electoral register. The UN declined a request by the Equato-Guinean authorities to monitor the elections, contending that correct electoral procedures were evidently being infringed. Representatives of the Organization of African Unity (OAU—now the African Union—AU, see p. 186) were present and estimated that 50% of the electorate participated. The PDGE won 68 of the 80 seats in the House of Representatives, while, of the six opposition parties that presented candidates, the Convención Socialdemocrática Popular obtained six seats, the Unión Democrática y Social de Guinea Ecuatorial (UDS) won five seats and the Convención Liberal Democrática (CLD) secured one. Widespread electoral irregularities were alleged to have occurred. In December Silvestre Siale Bileka, hitherto Prime Minister of the interim Government, was appointed Prime Minister of the new administration, which included no opposition representatives.

In April 1994 Severo Moto Nsa, the founding leader of one of the most influential exiled opposition parties, the Partido del Progreso de Guinea Ecuatorial (PPGE), based in Spain, returned to Equatorial Guinea. In early 1995 the Constitution and electoral law were amended to reduce from 10 to five the minimum number of years required for candidates to have been resident in Equatorial Guinea.

At a presidential election held in February 1996 Obiang Nguema was returned to office, reportedly securing more than 90% of the votes cast. However, influential opposition leaders boycotted the contest, in protest at alleged electoral irregularities and official intimidation. In March Obiang Nguema appointed a new Prime Minister, Angel Serafin Seriche Dougan (hitherto a Deputy Minister).

In May 1997 Moto Nsa was arrested by the Angolan authorities with a consignment of arms, which were reportedly intended for use in a planned coup. Following his release in June, Moto Nsa was granted refuge in Spain. Meanwhile, the PPGE was banned and the party subsequently divided into two factions. In August Moto Nsa and 11 others were convicted *in absentia* of treason; Moto Nsa was sentenced to 101 years' imprisonment. In September the Government protested strongly to Spain for granting political asylum to Moto Nsa.

The 1999 legislative elections

Equatorial Guinea's second multi-party legislative elections took place in March 1999, amid allegations of electoral malpractice and of the systematic intimidation of opposition candidates by the security forces. The elections were contested by 13 parties, and some 99% of the electorate was estimated to have voted. According to the official results, the ruling PDGE obtained more than 90% of the votes, increasing its representation from 68 to 75 of the 80 seats in the House of Representatives. Two opposition parties, the Unión Popular (UP) and the Convergencia para la Democracia Social (CPDS), secured four seats and one seat, respectively. Both parties, however, refused to participate in the new administration, in protest at alleged violations of the electoral law. Following the election, Seriche Dougan was reappointed to the premiership, and in late July a new Council of Ministers was announced.

The new administration dismissed hundreds of civil servants, including a number of high-ranking officials, during its first three months in office, as part of efforts to eradicate corruption. Furthermore, in January 2000 a number of judicial officials, including the President of the Supreme Tribunal and the President of the Constitutional Court, were dismissed. Former Prime Minister Silvestre Siale Bileka was appointed to the presidency of the Supreme Tribunal. Nevertheless, in March the new Special Representative for Equatorial Guinea at the UN Human Rights Commission condemned the Equato-Guinean authorities for systematic and serious human rights violations and accused the Government of refusing to authorize the formation of human rights non-governmental organizations. Following intense lobbying by several African countries, the mandate of the Special Representative was terminated in April 2002. However, in December a new UN Human Rights Rapporteur arrived in Equatorial Guinea, with a mandate to investigate claims of human rights violations.

In late February 2001 Seriche Dougan announced the resignation of his Government, in response to further pressure from the President and the legislature. Cándido Muatetema Rivas, formerly Deputy Secretary-General of the PDGE, was subsequently appointed as Prime Minister and formed a new Council of Ministers. Five opposition members were appointed to the new Government, including Jeremías Ondo Ngomo, the President of the UP, as Minister-delegate for Communications and Transport.

In late 2002 a National Electoral Council was created, although international bodies remained unwilling to monitor the forthcoming presidential election in view of the perceived weakness of the country's electoral institutions. Nevertheless, several leading members of both the exiled and resident opposition—including Celestino Bonifacio Bacale Obiang of the CPDS and Tomás Mecheba Fernández of the Partido Socialista de Guinea Ecuatorial—declared their intention to oppose Obiang Nguema in the election. On the day of polling, 15 December, Bacale Obiang and other opposition candidates announced their withdrawal from the election, alleging widespread irregularities in voting procedures. According to the official results, Obiang Nguema was re-elected to the presidency, with 97.1% of the votes cast. The conduct of the election was condemned by the European Union (EU, see p. 273). Despite the newly re-elected President's appeal for opposition leaders to join the PDGE in a government of national unity, 'radical' opposition parties continued to refuse to participate in Obiang Nguema's administration. In February 2003 a new Government was formed, again headed by Prime Minister Rivas.

Attempted coup

In March 2004 the Government announced that a group of 15 suspected mercenaries had been arrested on suspicion of planning a coup, which President Obiang Nguema subsequently claimed had been funded by multinational companies and organized by Moto Nsa with the collusion of the Spanish Government. Following the death in custody of one of the accused, in November the remaining 14 defendants were found guilty of involvement in the coup attempt and received lengthy custodial sentences. Although Moto Nsa denied any involvement in the affair, he was sentenced *in absentia* by the court in Malabo to 63 years' imprisonment, while Nick du Toit, a former South African special forces officer alleged to have been the operational leader of the group in Equatorial Guinea, was sentenced to 34 years' imprisonment. Human rights organizations condemned the trial for grave abuses of procedure. Simon Mann, a South African-based British security consultant and the alleged leader of the coup plot, had been convicted in September of attempting illegally to procure weapons and was sentenced to seven years' imprisonment (subsequently reduced to four) in Zimbabwe, where he had been arrested. At the completion of that sentence in 2007, the Equato-Guinean authorities requested that Mann be extradited in order to undergo further legal proceedings, and in February 2008 Mann was transported to custody in Equatorial Guinea. His trial began in June, along with that of the Lebanese business executive Mohamed Salaam and six Equato-Guinean nationals (all former members of the proscribed PPGE), who faced charges relating to the arrest of Moto Nsa in Spain in April, when weapons were discovered in a vehicle that was being exported to Equatorial Guinea, in a separate apparent coup plot. In July Mann was sentenced to 34 years in prison, while Salaam received an 18-year sentence and four of the Equato-Guineans were imprisoned for six-year terms. Of the remaining two defendants one was given a one-year sentence and the other was acquitted.

In August 2004 Sir Mark Thatcher (a businessman and son of the former British Prime Minister Baroness Thatcher) had been arrested in Cape Town, South Africa, on suspicion of having provided financial support for the alleged coup attempt. Thatcher initially denied any involvement in the affair; however, in January 2005 he admitted contravening South African anti-mercenary legislation, and was fined R3m. and given a four-year suspended sentence. None the less, in March 2008 it was reported that the Government of Equatorial Guinea had issued an arrest warrant for Thatcher, after the Attorney-General, José Olo Obono, claimed that Mann had provided new evidence regarding Thatcher's involvement in the coup plot. Subsequently, at his trial in June, Mann told the court that Thatcher had been part of the 'management team' for the attempted coup, and that Ely Calil, a Lebanese businessman, had organized the plot; Mann also claimed that both the Spanish and South African Governments were involved. In September 2005, following investigations into another alleged coup plot in October 2004, 23 members of the armed forces were convicted of treason and received lengthy prison sentences. A further six senior members of the armed forces were sentenced to terms of imprisonment in the following month. Human rights groups claimed that confessions had been extracted under torture from those convicted.

Meanwhile, legislative and municipal elections were held concurrently on 25 April 2004. The PDGE won 68 of the 100 seats in an expanded House of Representatives, while a coalition of eight parties allied to Obiang Nguema secured a further 30 seats. International observers and the CPDS (which took the remaining two seats) denounced the results as fraudulent. The rate of participation by eligible voters was estimated at 97%. In June Prime Minister Rivas announced the resignation of his Government and Obiang Nguema subsequently appointed a new PDGE-dominated Council of Ministers, headed by Miguel Abia Biteo Boricó, hitherto Minister of State for Parliamentary Relations and Judicial Affairs.

In August 2006 the Government resigned, following accusations of corruption and ineptitude from President Obiang Nguema. None the less, many previous members of the Council of Ministers were reappointed to the new administration, including the President's son, Teodoro (Teodorín) Nguema Obiang Mangue, as Minister of Agriculture and Forestry. Ricardo Mangué Obama Nfubea succeeded Miguel Abia Biteo Borico as Prime Minister.

In February 2008 Obiang Nguema dissolved the House of Representatives and announced that legislative elections, scheduled for May 2009, would be brought forward by one year, and held with municipal elections on 4 May 2008. On that day the ruling PDGE won 99 of the 100 seats in the legislature, while the one remaining seat was obtained by the opposition CPDS. In the concurrent municipal elections, the PDGE and its allies won 319 seats and the CPDS 13. The CPDS condemned the conduct of the poll, citing irregularities at many polling stations, and alleging harassment of CPDS representatives. Nevertheless, the Constitutional Court confirmed the PDGE's overwhelming victory later in May. Obama Nfubea resigned from his position as Prime Minister in July. A new Government was subsequently named by Obiang Nguema and was headed by Ignacio Milam Tang, hitherto the country's ambassador to Spain.

In February 2009 it was reported that there had been an attack on the presidential palace in Malabo, for which the authorities initially held the Nigerian armed group Movement for the Emancipation of the Niger Delta (MEND) responsible. MEND denied any involvement in the incident and the Government subsequently accused Equato-Guinean opposition members of organizing and participating in the attack. Some 10 members of the UP were detained, while a number of foreign nationals were also arrested and later expelled from the country. Following the attack, several members of the Government, including the Minister of National Security, were dismissed. In November Mann, du Toit and three others who had been sentenced to terms of imprisonment for their roles in the 2004 coup attempt (see above) were pardoned by President Obiang Nguema and released. A government spokesperson stated that the decision to release Mann had been made on humanitarian and medical grounds.

Obiang Nguema's fourth term

At the presidential election held on 29 November 2009 Obiang Nguema secured a further term of office with 95.4% of the votes cast. The CPDS candidate Plácido Micó Abogo, Obiang Nguema's closest rival with just 3.6% of the vote, announced that the ballot had not been conducted fairly and that he would not accept the results of the election; with allies of the President occupying senior roles at the electoral authority, human rights organizations concurred that the ballot was unlikely to have been free and fair. Nevertheless, Obiang Nguema was inaugurated as President on 8 December. In January 2010 Milam Tang was reappointed to the premiership and he subsequently named a new Government. Ebiaca Moheete was promoted to the position of First Deputy Prime Minister, in charge of the Economic and Financial Sector, while Obiang Mangue retained responsibility for the agriculture and forestry portfolio, but also became a Minister of State. The following month Lucas Nguema Esono was appointed Secretary-General of the PDGE, replacing Filiberto Ntutumu Nguema, who had been awarded the position of Minister of State, in charge of Education, Science and Sports in the new Government.

In April 2010 seven Nigerians were sentenced to 12 years' imprisonment for their roles in the attack on the presidential palace in February 2009, although a number of Equato-Guinean citizens were acquitted of any involvement in the incident. However, in August 2010 four former military and government officials, including a former member of the President's personal security force, were convicted by a military court in Malabo of terrorism, treason and of carrying out an assault against the head of state, and were sentenced to death. The execution of the four men, which was confirmed by the Government later in August, was widely criticized by human rights organizations.

Constitutional amendments

In June 2010 President Obiang Nguema announced his intention to carry out a series of wide-ranging reforms, pledging to ensure peace, political stability and transparency in the country. Addressing criticism of his Government, he unveiled a five-point programme, which would be carried out over 10 years in close co-operation with international institutions, and which he hoped would encourage foreign investment in Equatorial Guinea. He also pledged to promote human and civil rights (the International Committee of the Red Cross would be invited to establish an office in Equatorial Guinea and to assist in reviewing all allegations of human rights violations in the country), and to improve the criminal justice system. Opponents of the Obiang Nguema regime rejected the reform package and claimed that it lacked credibility.

Obiang Nguema effected a reorganization of the Government in January 2011; most notably Bacale Obiang of the CPDS was appointed Minister-delegate to the Minister of the Economy, Trade and Business Development, while Francisco Mbá Olú Bahamonde, the President of the opposition Alianza Democrática Progresista, also joined the Council of Ministers. Further minor changes were made in April, primarily among the Secretaries of State, bringing more members of Obiang Nguema's family into the Government and raising concerns over the dynastic nature of his control of power.

In May 2011 Obiang Nguema announced the establishment of the Comisión Nacional para el Estudio de la Reforma de la Ley Fundamental de Guinea Ecuatorial (National Commission for the Study of the Reform of the Equatorial Guinean Constitution). Its members comprised primarily PDGE representatives, although other parties were also included. The CPDS, the UP and the Acción Popular de Guinea Ecuatorial (APGE) objected to Obiang Nguema's control of the allocation of the membership and his failure to consider their proposals, therefore declining the invitation to participate. They also raised concerns that the proposed schedule for implementing the reforms did not allow for sufficient open discussions. The Commission's report was submitted to parliament on 15 July and included proposals on the creation of a new Council of the Republic, a new Economic and Social Council, and the post of Ombudsman. On 13 November the public voted in a referendum on constitutional reform that provided for the creation of the post of Vice-President, the establishment of a bicameral legislature, and would limit the presidential term of office to two seven-year terms. Concerns were raised, however, that the text did not clarify whether Obiang Nguema would be required to step down at the end of his current term in 2016. According to official results, 97.7% of votes cast were in favour of the new Constitution; voter turnout was estimated at 91.8%. The constitutional amendments were promulgated on 16 February 2012.

In April 2012 a congress of the PDGE designated Obiang Nguema President for life and confirmed his son, Obiang Mangue, as leader of the party's youth movement, while his wife, Constancia Mangue, was appointed honorary President of the PDGE's women's organization. Obiang Nguema dissolved the Government on 18 May, prior to forming a new administration in accordance with the constitutional amendments. On 21 May the hitherto Prime Minister, Milam Tang, was appointed to the newly created post of Vice-President, in charge of Presidential Affairs, while Obiang Mangue became Second Vice-President, in charge of Defence and State Security. The post of Prime Minister was awarded to the hitherto Minister and Secretary-General of the Government, in charge of Administrative Co-ordination, Vicente Ehate Tomi (who retained the administrative co-ordination portfolio). A new, enlarged Council of Ministers, which included an even greater number of Obiang Nguema's close relatives, was established on 22 May. A series of arbitrary arrests of prominent opposition members during 2012 included that of UP leader Daniel Darío Martínez Ayacaba (who had been preparing to attend an opposition conference in Madrid, Spain) in December. In January 2013 press freedom groups expressed concerns at the death in suspicious circumstances of independent journalist Manuel Nze Nsongo. Later that month the Government scheduled legislative and local elections for 26 May, when voting would be held for 55 of the 70 seats in the new upper chamber, the Senate, established under the constitutional reforms (the remaining 15 senators were to be nominated by Obiang Nguema).

Recent developments: the 2013 legislative elections

According to an official government statement, at the elections on 26 May 2013 the PDGE secured 99 of the 100 seats in the House of Representatives and 54 of the 55 elective seats in the Senate, while the CPDS received the remaining legislative seat in both chambers. The PDGE also took 329 of the 334 municipalities in the local elections. Although AU observers reported no major violations, the CPDS strenuously rejected the results as fraudulent. The US Administration also severely criticized the conduct of the election campaign, citing arbitrary detentions, limits on the freedom of assembly and restrictions on opposition access to the media, and urged the creation of an independent electoral commission. A new Government, which was again headed by Tomi and included three Deputy Prime Ministers, was appointed in early September.

Allegations of Corruption

Equatorial Guinea enjoyed exceptionally high revenues from petroleum exports from the late 1990s; allegations emerged, however, that members of the Obiang Nguema regime were accruing private profits from national petroleum exports. In May 2003 controversy arose when the US-based Riggs Bank acknowledged that some US $500m. released by the US Senate had been paid into an account to which President Obiang Nguema was the sole signatory; the funds were 'frozen' by the US Senate in July 2004 pending further investigations. Also in July a US Senate report concluded that petroleum companies had made substantial payments to government officials, their families or entities owned by them in order to secure contracts. In January 2005 Riggs Bank admitted criminal liability in assisting Obiang Nguema in illicit financial transactions. Controversy arose in November 2006, following reports that the President's son Teodorín had purchased a property for $35m. in the USA (in addition to two luxury homes in South Africa). In October 2011 the US Department of Justice began legal proceedings to seize Obiang Mangue's US assets, valued at $71m., on the grounds that these had been obtained through corruption and money-laundering. The Equato-Guinean Government rejected the allegations and requested that the US courts dismiss the case. In April 2012 a US federal judge concluded that the complaint filed by the Department of Justice lacked sufficient evidence to support the allegations; in June, however, US prosecutors presented further charges with regard to the seizure of Obiang Mangue's assets.

In late 2010 a French court ruled that an investigation could proceed into corruption charges brought by Transparency International, which related to alleged irregularities with major purchases made in France by the Presidents of Equatorial Guinea, the Republic of the Congo and Gabon. In February 2012 French police searched Obiang Mangue's mansion in central Paris, and seized luxury goods and art objects. In April the

French Public Prosecutor approved a request made by magistrates for the issue of an international warrant for the arrest of Obiang Mangue on suspicion of using public funds to buy property in France. The Equato-Guinean Government accused France of attempting to destabilize the country and threatened to retaliate against French interests in Equatorial Guinea. The ruling PDGE organized demonstrations throughout the country in support of Obiang Mangue, and in Malabo over 2,000 people demonstrated outside the French embassy. The international arrest warrant for Obiang Mangue (who, meanwhile, had become Vice-President in the Equato-Guinean Government—see above) was formally issued in July. The mansion was seized by the French authorities in August, after which Equatorial Guinea filed a complaint at the International Court of Justice (ICJ, see p. 24) in September, accusing France of violating diplomatic immunity laws. In June 2013 a French appeals court upheld the arrest warrant issued against Obiang Mangue.

Foreign Affairs

Regional relations

In March 2003 relations between Equatorial Guinea and Gabon were strained following the occupation of the small island of Mbagne (Mbañé, Mbanie) by a contingent of Gabonese troops. Both countries had long claimed ownership of Mbagne and two smaller islands, which lie in potentially oil-rich waters in Corisco Bay, north of the Gabonese capital, Libreville, and south-west of the Equato-Guinean mainland. In June Equatorial Guinea rejected a Gabonese proposal to share any petroleum revenues from the island, and discussions between the two sides ended without agreement in December. However, in January 2004 Equatorial Guinea and Gabon issued a joint communiqué, accepting the appointment of a UN mediator in the dispute. In July a provisional agreement was reached to explore jointly for petroleum in the disputed territories, but in late 2006 negotiations were suspended indefinitely, potentially to be pursued at the ICJ. In 2008, following UN mediation, progress was made towards the referral of the case to the ICJ: in September the UN Secretary-General, Ban Ki-Moon, appointed Nicolas Michel, a Swiss legal expert, as a special adviser to assist in resolving the dispute. At a meeting of the two countries' leaders, convened by the UN Secretary-General in February 2011, Gabon and Equatorial Guinea reiterated their commitment to submitting their border dispute for ruling at the ICJ.

President Jacob Zuma of South Africa visited Equatorial Guinea in November 2009 to promote stronger economic relations between the two countries. Immediately prior to Zuma's visit four South Africans were pardoned and released from prison where they had been detained for their alleged involvement in the attempted coup in 2004. Representatives of the two countries met in November 2011 to discuss closer co-operation in a number of sectors.

Equatorial Guinea has assumed a greater role at a regional level in recent years. In February 2010 Equatorial Guinea was elected to the AU's 15-member Peace and Security Council, to serve a three-year term and in April the Parlement of the Communauté Economique et Monétaire de l'Afrique Centrale (CEMAC, see p. 330) was inaugurated in Malabo. In January 2011 Obiang Nguema was elected Chairperson of the Assembly of the AU for a one-year term. Visa requirements for member states of the CEMAC were officially abolished at the beginning of 2014; however, the Equato-Guinean authorities had expressed reservations about the free movement agreement and in January it was reported that the border with Cameroon and Gabon had been temporarily closed, apparently owing to concerns that an influx of migrant workers from those countries would affect employment. In the same month the expulsion of a number of Cameroonian nationals prompted tensions with that country.

Other external relations

While Spain (the former colonial power) has traditionally been a major trading partner and aid donor, Equatorial Guinea's entry in 1983 into the Customs and Economic Union of Central Africa (replaced in 1999 by the CEMAC) represented a significant move towards a greater integration with neighbouring francophone countries. In 1985 Equatorial Guinea joined the Franc Zone (see p. 329), with financial assistance from France. From mid-1993 Equato-Guinean-Spanish relations deteriorated, and in January 1994 the Spanish Government withdrew one-half of its aid to Equatorial Guinea in retaliation for the expulsion in December 1993 of a Spanish diplomat whom the Equato-Guinean authorities had accused of interfering in the country's internal affairs. In October 1999 the Spanish Government agreed to resume full assistance to its former colony, and during a visit to Madrid in March 2001 President Obiang Nguema held talks with Spanish Prime Minister José María Aznar, who agreed to normalize relations with Equatorial Guinea in the economic field. In 2003 relations improved further following Spain's support for Equatorial Guinea's territorial claims to the island of Mbagne (Mbañé, Mbanie). In April 2004 the Spanish Government cancelled 50% of Equatorial Guinea's debt, estimated at some €70m.

In February 2005 Obiang Nguema held talks in Bata with the Spanish Minister of Foreign Affairs and Co-operation, Miguel Angel Moratinos Cuyaubé, during which both parties expressed their desire to maintain cordial relations and high levels of co-operation between the two countries. In December the Spanish Government announced that the asylum granted to opposition leader Severo Moto Nsa was to be revoked in view of evidence that he had conspired to overthrow the Obiang Nguema regime. Moto Nsa announced his intention to return to Equatorial Guinea to demand the immediate holding of fair elections. Meanwhile, in June Moto Nsa had participated in a demonstration by exiled opposition groups at the Equato-Guinean embassy in Spain, which resulted in damage to embassy property and minor injuries to some of its staff. None the less, in March 2008 the Spanish Supreme Court accepted an appeal from Moto Nsa and ruled to uphold his asylum status, declaring that he did not pose a threat to Spain. In April Moto Nsa was arrested for arms-trafficking, after weapons were discovered at a Spanish port in a car bound for Equatorial Guinea, although he was released in August. Relations with Spain improved in July 2009 when Obiang Nguema approved the re-entry of Spanish firms to the Equato-Guinean market and the ministers responsible for foreign affairs from Spain and Equatorial Guinea signed an agreement pledging the mutual protection of investments.

Since 2006 Equatorial Guinea has held observer status within, but not full membership of, the Comunidade de Países de Língua Oficial Portuguesa (CPLP). President Obiang Nguema announced in 2008 that Portuguese was to be adopted as Equatorial Guinea's third official language and in 2009 strong ties were formed with CPLP member states, particularly Brazil and Portugal. In March 2010 a Portuguese delegation of government officials and businessmen visited Equatorial Guinea, and several trade agreements were signed. Following a request by Equatorial Guinea, in July the CPLP began formal negotiations with the authorities on full membership; however, the Equato-Guinean Government was required to demonstrate progress in the area of human rights before the country's admission to the CPLP.

CONSTITUTION AND GOVERNMENT

The present Constitution was approved by a national referendum on 16 November 1991 and amended in January 1995, providing for the introduction of multi-party democracy. Further amendments were adopted in February 2012. Executive power is vested in the President, who is directly elected for a seven-year term of office and is limited to two terms. The President is immune from prosecution for offences committed before, during or after his tenure of the post. Legislative power is held by a directly elected, 100-member House of Representatives and by a 70-member Senate, comprising 55 directly elected members and an additional 15 senators nominated by the President, which serve for a term of five years. The President appoints a Council of Ministers, headed by a Prime Minister, from among the members of the House of Representatives.

REGIONAL AND INTERNATIONAL CO-OPERATION

Equatorial Guinea is a member of the African Union (see p. 186) and of the Central African organs of the Franc Zone (see p. 329), including the Communauté Economique et Monétaire de l'Afrique Centrale (CEMAC, see p. 330).

Equatorial Guinea became a member of the UN in 1976.

ECONOMIC AFFAIRS

In 2012, according to estimates by the World Bank, Equatorial Guinea's gross national income (GNI), measured at average 2010–12 prices, was US $9,983m., equivalent to $13,560 per head (or $18,880 per head on an international purchasing-power parity basis). During 2003–12, it was estimated, the population increased at an average annual rate of 2.9%, while gross domestic product (GDP) per head increased, in real terms, by an average of 4.5% per year. Overall GDP increased, in real terms, at an average annual rate of 7.6% in 2003–12. Real GDP increased by 2.5% in 2012.

Agriculture (including hunting, forestry and fishing) contributed a provisional 1.3% of GDP in 2012, according to African Development Bank (AfDB) figures. The sector employed an estimated 62.1% of the labour force in mid-2014, according to FAO estimates. The principal cash crop is cocoa, which, according to the Banque de France, provided an estimated 1.2% of total export earnings in 2007. The Government is encouraging the production of bananas, spices (vanilla, black pepper and coriander) and medicinal plants for export. The main subsistence crops are sweet potatoes and cassava. Exploitation of the country's vast, but rapidly diminishing, forest resources (principally of okoumé and akoga timber) provided an estimated 0.7% (or 34,000m. francs CFA) of export revenue in 2007, according to the Banque de France. In 2011 some 57.5% of the country's land area was covered by forest, compared with 66.3% in 1990. Almost all industrial fishing activity is practised by foreign fleets, notably by those of countries of the European Union. During 2002–09, according to the World Bank, the real GDP of the agricultural sector increased at an average annual rate of 5.3%. According to the AfDB, the sector declined by 3.4% in 2011 and by 8.0% in 2012.

According to the AfDB, industry (including mining, manufacturing, construction and power) contributed a provisional 95.9% of GDP in 2012. During 2002–09, according to the World Bank, industrial GDP increased at an average annual rate of 14.3%; industrial GDP increased by 4.9% in 2009.

Extractive activities were minimal during the 1980s, and the mining sector employed less than 0.2% of the working population in 1983. However, the exploitation of onshore and offshore reserves of petroleum and of offshore deposits of natural gas led to unprecedented economic growth during the 1990s. Exports of petroleum commenced in 1992 and provided an estimated 82.5% of total export earnings in 2008, according to the IMF. According to the AfDB, the value of exports of crude petroleum totalled US $10,391m. in 2012. Mining contributed 89.4% of GDP in 2012, according to the provisional figures from the AfDB. Petroleum production increased from 91,000 barrels per day (b/d) in 2000 to an estimated 283,000 b/d in 2012, according to the BP Statistical Review of World Energy published in June 2013. Proven reserves of petroleum were some 1,700m. barrels at the end of 2012. Natural gas extraction also increased rapidly from the 1990s. Proven reserves at the country's largest gas field, Alba, were some 1,300,000m. cu ft in early 2006, although in 2010 the Equato-Guinean Government announced that it had raised the figure of its estimated reserves to around 4,500,000m. cu ft. Proven reserves of natural gas were 1,300,000m. cu ft at the end of 2013. The existence of deposits of gold, uranium, iron ore, titanium, tantalum and manganese has also been confirmed. During 2001–06 the GDP of the petroleum sector increased at an average annual rate of 32.3%, according to the IMF. Growth in 2012 was 4.3%, according to the AfDB.

The manufacturing sector contributed 0.1% of GDP in 2012, according to the AfDB. Wood-processing constitutes the main commercial manufacturing activity. During 2002–09, according to the World Bank, manufacturing GDP increased at an average annual rate of 28.3%. According to the AfDB, the sector contracted by 18.8% in 2011, but expanded by 20.6% in 2012.

According to the AfDB, construction contributed an estimated 5.7% of GDP in 2012. Construction GDP increased rapidly during the 2000s, and by 47.8% in 2009, mainly due to government investment in major infrastructures made possible by the rapidly increasing oil revenues. The sector expanded by 14.4% in 2011, and by 7.3% in 2012.

An estimated total of 31m. kWh of electric energy was generated in 2007. According to the EIA, in 2004 Equatorial Guinea had 15.4 MW of proven installed capacity and 5 MW–30 MW of estimated additional capacity, and in 2010 its proven installed capacity increased to 38.0 MW. There was about 4 MW of oil-fired thermal capacity and 1 MW of hydroelectric capacity on the mainland. Bioko was supplied by one hydroelectric plant (on the Riaba river) with an estimated capacity of 3.6 MW and two thermal plants, including the 10.4-MW Punta Europa gas-fired plant located at the northern end of the island. In 2004 there was a further 4 MW–6 MW of generation capacity at the AMPCO complex on Bioko. Imports of fuel products comprised 25.2% of the value of total imports in 2008.

According to the AfDB, the services sector contributed only 2.8% of GDP in 2012. The dominant services are public administration and defence, and trade, restaurants and hotels. During 2002–09, according to the World Bank, the GDP of the services sector increased at an average annual rate of 14.8%; it grew by 19.9% in 2009.

In 2008, according to IMF estimates, there was a visible merchandise trade surplus of US $10,555.2m., while the surplus on the current account of the balance of payments was $1,673m. In 2011 the USA was the principal source of imports (16.3%), and the People's Republic of China was the principal source of exports (16.4%). In the same year, other major importers were France and China, while the other principal destinations for exports were Japan, the USA and Taiwan. In 2011 crude petroleum constituted the principal source of export revenue followed by methanol and other gases, while the principal imports were metal goods, specialized machinery, petroleum, petroleum products and related materials, and other industrial machinery and parts.

In 2012 there was a budget surplus of 739.7m. francs CFA (equivalent to 7.4% of GDP). The country's general government gross debt was 707,383. francs CFA in 2012, equivalent to 7.8% of GDP. Equatorial Guinea's external debt was US $278.1m. at the end of 2006, of which $224.6m. was long-term public debt. According to AfDB estimates, the rate of inflation averaged 4.4% per year in 2003–12: the annual average rate of inflation was 4.5% in 2012.

The production and export of petroleum led to exceptional economic growth from the late 1990s and economic relations with the USA strengthened as a result of major investments in the development of Equato-Guinean oilfields by US energy companies. Furthermore, in 2005 an agreement on co-operation in hydrocarbon development was signed with the People's Republic of China; Equatorial Guinea subsequently benefited from the competition between the USA and China for stakes in the hydrocarbons sector. Petroleum revenue has financed significant infrastructure development; however, the continuing high level of poverty (with some 60% of Equato-Guineans estimated to subsist below the poverty threshold in 2013) has been variously attributed to corruption, the disadvantageous terms of many contracts negotiated by the state petroleum company, and reduced international aid. President Obiang Nguema's mass project for the construction of a new administrative capital, Oyala, in the interior of mainland Equatorial Guinea, with international tenders, also attracted widespread criticism. There were continuing concerns over senior level corruption, despite an announcement by Obiang Nguema, in 2010, of a 10-year plan that was designed, *inter alia*, to improve transparency with regard to oil revenues; Transparency International ranked Equatorial Guinea only 163rd out of 175 countries in its 2013 Corruptions Perceptions Index. The Government demonstrated concerns that the entry into force, in January 2014, of a free movement agreement between member states of the Communauté Economique et Monétaire de l'Afrique Centrale (see p. 330) (see Regional relations) would affect employment in the country. A decline in GDP growth after 2011, with a possible contraction predicted for 2014, was attributed by analysts to a fall in production at the country's main oil complex (where reserves were becoming depleted), although in mid-2013 production commenced at the offshore Alen gas field, operated by US company Noble Energy. In February 2014 the Equato-Guinean authorities organized a conference on economic diversification in the capital, Malabo, which was attended by international business and investment groups; on that occasion the Government announced that it would allocate US $1,000m. over three years, to be placed in a new state entity, with the aim of attracting foreign investment in non-energy sectors.

PUBLIC HOLIDAYS

2015: 1 January (New Year's Day), 3 April (Good Friday), 1 May (Labour Day), 25 May (President's Day), 4 June (Corpus Christi), 3 August (Liberty Day), 15 August (Constitution Day), 12 October (Independence Day), 8 December (Feast of the Immaculate Conception), 25 December (Christmas).

Statistical Survey

Source (unless otherwise stated): Dirección General de Estadística y Cuentas Nacionales, Ministerio de Planificacón, Desarrollo Económico e Inversiones Públicas, Malabo; tel. 333093352; internet www.dgecnstat-ge.org.

AREA AND POPULATION

Area: 28,051 sq km (10,831 sq miles): Río Muni 26,017 sq km, Bioko 2,017 sq km, Annobón 17 sq km.

Population: 300,000 (Río Muni 240,804, Bioko 57,190, Annobón 2,006), comprising 144,268 males and 155,732 females, at census of 4–17 July 1983 (Source: Ministerio de Asuntos Exteriores, Madrid, Spain); 406,151 at census of 4 July 1994 (provisional). *Mid-2014* (UN estimate): 778,062 (Source: UN, *World Population Prospects: The 2012 Revision*).

Density (mid-2014): 27.7 per sq km.

Population by Age and Sex (UN estimates at mid-2014): *0–14:* 300,668 (males 151,102, females 149,566); *15–64:* 455,884 (males 236,152, females 219,732); *65 and over:* 21,510 (males 11,077, females 10,433); *Total* 778,062 (males 398,331, females 379,731) (Source: UN, *World Population Prospects: The 2012 Revision*).

Provinces (population, census of July 1994): Annobón 2,820; Bioko Norte 75,137; Bioko Sur 12,569; Centro-Sur 60,341; Kié-Ntem 92,779; Litoral 100,047; Wele-Nzas 62,458.

Principal Town (incl. suburbs, UN estimate): Malabo 136,971 (Source: UN, *World Urbanization Prospects: The 2011 Revision*).

Births and Deaths (UN estimates, annual averages): Birth rate 37.5 per 1,000 in 2005–10; Death rate 15.2 per 1,000 in 2005–10. Source: UN, *World Population Prospects: The 2012 Revision*.

Life Expectancy (years at birth): 52.1 (males 50.7; females 53.6) in 2011. Source: World Bank, World Development Indicators database.

Economically Active Population (persons aged 6 years and over, 1983 census): Agriculture, hunting, forestry and fishing 59,390; Mining and quarrying 126; Manufacturing 1,490; Electricity, gas and water 224; Construction 1,929; Trade, restaurants and hotels 3,059; Transport, storage and communications 1,752; Financing, insurance, real estate and business services 409; Community, social and personal services 8,377; *Sub-total* 76,756; Activities not adequately defined 984; *Total employed* 77,740 (males 47,893, females 29,847); Unemployed 24,825 (males 18,040, females 6,785); *Total labour force* 102,565 (males 65,933, females 36,632). Note: Figures are based on unadjusted census data, indicating a total population of 261,779. The adjusted total is 300,000 (Source: ILO, *Yearbook of Labour Statistics*). *Mid-2014* ('000 persons, official estimates): Agriculture, etc. 192; Total labour force 309 (Source: FAO).

HEALTH AND WELFARE

Key Indicators

Total Fertility Rate (children per woman, 2011): 5.1.

Under-5 Mortality Rate (per 1,000 live births, 2011): 118.

HIV/AIDS (% of persons aged 15–49, 2011): 4.7.

Physicians (per 1,000 head, 2004): 0.3.

Hospital Beds (per 1,000 head, 2010): 2.1.

Health Expenditure (2010): US $ per head (PPP): 1,395.

Health Expenditure (2010): % of GDP: 4.2.

Health Expenditure (2010): public (% of total): 57.4.

Access to Water (% of persons, 2006): 43.

Access to Sanitation (% of persons, 2006): 51.

Total Carbon Dioxide Emissions ('000 metric tons, 2010): 4,679.1.

Carbon Dioxide Emissions Per Head (metric tons, 2010): 6.7.

Human Development Index (2012): ranking: 136.

Human Development Index (2012): value: 0.554.

For sources and definitions, see explanatory note on p. vi.

AGRICULTURE, ETC.

Principal Crops ('000 metric tons, 2012, FAO estimates): Sweet potatoes 95; Cassava 68; Coconuts 7; Oil palm fruit 36; Bananas 29; Plantains 43; Cocoa beans 1; Coffee, green 5. *Aggregate Production* ('000 metric tons, may include official, semi-official or estimated data): Total roots and tubers 199; Total fruits (excl. melons) 72.

Livestock ('000 head, year ending September 2012, FAO estimates): Cattle 5; Pigs 7; Sheep 40; Goats 9; Chickens 355; Ducks 31.

Livestock Products (metric tons, 2012, FAO estimates): Meat 587; Hen eggs 450.

Forestry ('000 cubic metres, 2012, FAO estimates): *Roundwood Removals:* Fuel wood 447; Sawlogs, veneer logs and logs for sleepers 525; Total 972. *Sawnwood:* 4 (all broadleaved).

Fishing (metric tons, live weight, 2011): Freshwater fishes 1,000 (FAO estimate); Clupeoids 3,030; Sharks, rays, skates, etc. 156; Marine fishes 855; Total catch (incl. others) 7,130 (FAO estimate).

Source: FAO.

MINING

Production: Crude petroleum ('000 metric tons, 2012): 13,241; Natural gas (million cu m, 2012): 7,800 (Sources: BP, *Statistical Review of World Energy*; US Geological Survey).

INDUSTRY

Palm Oil ('000 metric tons, FAO estimate): 5.5 in 2012. Source: FAO.

Veneer Sheets ('000 cubic metres, FAO estimate): 27.6 in 2012. Source: FAO.

Electric Energy (million kWh): 100 in 2007; 100 in 2008; 100 in 2009. Source: UN Industrial Commodity Statistics Database.

FINANCE

Currency and Exchange Rates: 100 centimes = 1 franc de la Coopération Financière en Afrique Centrale (CFA). *Sterling, Dollar and Euro Equivalents* (31 December 2013): £1 sterling = 783.286 francs CFA; US $1 = 475.641 francs CFA; €1 = 655.957 francs CFA; 10,000 francs CFA = £12.77 = $21.02 = €15.24. *Average Exchange Rate* (francs CFA per US dollar): 471.866 in 2011; 510.527 in 2012; 494.040 in 2013. *Note:* An exchange rate of 1 French franc = 50 francs CFA, established in 1948, remained in force until January 1994, when the CFA franc was devalued by 50%, with the exchange rate adjusted to 1 French franc = 100 francs CFA. This relationship to French currency remained in effect with the introduction of the euro on 1 January 1999. From that date, accordingly, a fixed exchange rate of €1 = 655.957 francs CFA has been in operation.

Budget ('000 million francs CFA, 2012): *Revenue:* Tax revenue 3,805.2; Non-tax revenue 80.0; Total revenue 3,885.2. *Expenditure:* Current expenditure 610.2 (Wages and salaries 90.4); Capital expenditure 2,535.3; Total expenditure 3,145.5. Source: African Development Bank.

International Reserves (excl. gold, US $ million at 31 December 2012): IMF special drawing rights 32.52; Reserve position in IMF 7.57; Foreign exchange 4,356.89; Total 4,396.98 Source: IMF, *International Financial Statistics*.

Money Supply ('000 million francs CFA at 31 December 2012): Currency outside depository corporations 251.11; Transferable deposits 1,228.99; Other deposits 208.52; *Broad money* 1,688.62 Source: IMF, *International Financial Statistics*.

Cost of Living (Consumer Price Index; base: 2000 = 100): All items 168.4 in 2010; 176.5 in 2011; 184.5 in 2012. Source: African Development Bank.

Expenditure on the Gross Domestic Product ('000 million francs CFA in current prices, 2012, provisional): Government final consumption expenditure 388.6; Private final consumption expenditure 1,010.9; Gross fixed capital formation 3,453.7; Change in inventories 0.2; *Total domestic expenditure* 4,853.4; Exports of goods and non-factor services 9,198.4; *Less* Imports of goods and services 4,044.5; *GDP at purchasers' values* 10,007.3. Source: African Development Bank.

Gross Domestic Product by Economic Activity ('000 million francs CFA in current prices, 2012, provisional): Agriculture, hunting, forestry and fishing 124.0; Mining and quarrying 8,830.3; Manufacturing 11.6; Electricity, gas and water 73.6; Construction 562.8; Trade, restaurants and hotels 70.0; Finance, insurance and real estate 74.9; Transport and communications 13.4; Public administration and defence 88.2; Other services 32.4; *GDP at factor cost* 9,881.1; Indirect taxes 126.1; *GDP at purchasers' values* 10,007.3. Note: Deduction for imputed bank service charge assumed to be distributed at origin. Source: African Development Bank.

Balance of Payments (US $ million, 2008): Exports of goods f.o.b. 14,465; Imports of goods c.i.f. –3,909; *Trade balance* 10,555; Services (net) –1,849; Net other income –6,953; *Balance on goods, services* *and income* 1,753; Current transfers (net) –81; *Current balance* 1,673; Direct investment (net) –570; Other investment (net) –693; Errors and omissions 424; *Overall balance* 834 (Source: IMF, *Republic of Equatorial Guinea: 2010 Article IV Consultation*—May 2010). *2012* ('000 million francs CFA): Trade balance 3,732.8; Services (net) –1.397.3; Other income (net) –3,077.0; Current transfers (net) –79.1; *Current balance* –820.6 (Source: African Development Bank).

EXTERNAL TRADE

Principal Commodities (distribution by SITC, US $ '000, 1990): *Imports c.i.f.:* Food and live animals 4,340; Beverages and tobacco 3,198 (Alcoholic beverages 2,393); Crude materials (inedible) except fuels 2,589 (Crude fertilizers and crude minerals 2,102); Petroleum and petroleum products 4,738; Chemicals and related products 2,378; Basic manufactures 3,931; Machinery and transport equipment 35,880 (Road vehicles and parts 3,764, Ships, boats and floating structures 24,715); Miscellaneous manufactured articles 2,725; Total (incl. others) 61,601. *Exports f.o.b.:* Food and live animals 6,742 (Cocoa 6,372); Beverages and tobacco 3,217 (Tobacco and tobacco manufactures 2,321); Crude materials (inedible) except fuels 20,017 (Sawlogs and veneer logs 12,839, Textile fibres and waste 7,078); Machinery and transport equipment 24,574 (Ships, boats and floating structures 23,852); Total (incl. others) 61,705 (Source: UN, *International Trade Statistics Yearbook*). *2011* (US $ million, estimates): Total imports f.o.b. 6,972.1 (Public sector equipment 3,914.6, Petroleum sector 1,925.9, Petroleum products 485.2, Other 646.4); Total exports f.o.b. 14,306.1 (Crude petroleum 10,233.9; Petroleum derivatives 3,367.3) (Source: IMF, *Republic of Equatorial Guinea: Statistical Appendix*—March 2012).

Principal Trading Partners (US $ million, 2011): *Imports c.i.f.:* China, People's Repub. 906.7; France 922.5; USA 975.2; Total (incl. others) 6,000.0. *Exports f.o.b.:* China, People's Repub. 2,300.9; Japan 1,819.5; Taiwan 1,101.8; USA 1,682.8; Total (incl. others) 14,042.0. Source: African Development Bank.

TRANSPORT

Road Traffic (estimates, motor vehicles in use at 31 December 2002): Passenger cars 1,811; Lorries and vans 727; Buses 302; Motorcycles 17.

Shipping: *Flag Registered Fleet* (at 31 December 2013): Vessels 36; Total displacement 24,785 grt (Source: Lloyd's List Intelligence—www.lloydslistintelligence.com). *International Sea-borne Freight Traffic* ('000 metric tons, 1990): Goods loaded 110; Goods unloaded 64 (Source: UN, *Monthly Bulletin of Statistics*).

Civil Aviation (traffic on scheduled services, 1998): Passengers carried ('000) 21; Passenger-km (million) 4 (Source: UN, *Statistical Yearbook*). *2004:* (traffic at Malabo and Bata airports): Total passengers movements 324,999 (arrivals 159,815, departures 165,184); Freight and mail carried 5,029.5 metric tons.

COMMUNICATIONS MEDIA

Telephones: 14,900 main lines in use in 2012.

Mobile Cellular Telephones: 501,100 subscribers in 2012.

Internet Users: 116,800 in 2011.

Broadband Subscribers: 1,500 in 2012.

Source: International Telecommunication Union.

EDUCATION

Pre-primary (2011/12 unless otherwise indicated): Schools 180*; Teachers 2,428 (males 277, females 2,151); Students 42,431 (males 21,258, females 21,173).

Primary (2011/12 unless otherwise indicated): Schools 483*; Teachers 3,517 (males 2,148, females 1,369); Students 92,029 (males 46,725, females 45,304).

Secondary (2001/02, estimates, unless otherwise indicated): Schools 59; Teachers 894 (males 855, females 39)†; Students 21,173 (males 13,463, females 7,710).

Higher (1999/2000): Teachers 206 (males 174, females 32); Students 1,003 (males 699, females 304).

* 1998 figure.

† 1999/2000 figure.

Pupil-teacher Ratio (primary education, UNESCO estimate): 26.2 in 2011/12.

Adult Literacy Rate: 94.2% (males 97.1%; females 91.1%) in 2011.

Source: UNESCO Institute for Statistics.

Directory

The Government

HEAD OF STATE

President and Supreme Commander of the Armed Forces: Gen. (retd) OBIANG NGUEMA MBASOGO (assumed office 25 August 1979; elected President 25 June 1989; re-elected 25 February 1996, 15 December 2002 and 29 November 2009).

COUNCIL OF MINISTERS
(April 2014)

President: Gen. (retd) OBIANG NGUEMA MBASOGO.

Vice-President, in charge of Presidential Affairs: IGNACIO MILAM TANG.

Second Vice-President, in charge of Defence and State Security: TEODORO (TEODORÍN) NGUEMA OBIANG MANGUE.

Prime Minister, in charge of Administrative Co-ordination: VICENTE EHATE TOMI.

First Deputy Prime Minister, in charge of the Political Sector and Democracy, and Minister of the Interior and Local Government: CLEMENTE ENGOGA NGUEMA ONGUENE.

Second Deputy Prime Minister, in charge of the Social Sector and Minister of Education and Science: LUCAS NGUEMA ESONO MBANG.

Third Deputy Prime Minister, in charge of Human Rights: ALFONSO NSUY MOKUY.

Minister of State at the Presidency of the Republic, in charge of Missions: ALEJANDRO EVUNA OWONO ASANGONO.

Minister of State at the Presidency of the Republic, in charge of Cabinet Affairs: BRAULIO NCOGO ABEGUE.

Minister of State at the Presidency of the Republic, in charge of Relations with Parliament and Legal Affairs: ÁNGEL MASIE MIBUY.

Minister of State at the Presidency of the Republic, in charge of Regional Integration: BALTASAR ENGOGA EDJO.

Minister of State at the Presidency of the Republic, in charge of the Prevention and Fight Against HIV/AIDS and Sexually Transmitted Diseases: TOMAS MECHEBA FERNANDEZ GALILEA.

Minister of State of National Defence: ANTONIO MBA NGUEMA MIKUE.

Minister and Secretary-General of the Government: FAUSTINO NDONG ESONO EYANG.

Minister Justice, Religion and Penitentiary Institutions: EVANGELINA-FILOMENA OYÓ EBULE.

Minister of Foreign Affairs and Co-operation: AGAPITO MBA MOKUY.

Minister of Trade and Business Development: CELESTINO-BONIFACIO BAKALE OBIANG.

Minister of Finance and the Budget: MARCELINO OWONO EDU.

Minister of the Economy, Planning and Public Investment: CONRADO OKENVE NDOHO.

Minister of Transport, Technology, Post and Telecommunications: FRANCISCO MBA OLO BAHAMONDE.

Minister of National Security: NICOLÁS OBAMA NCHAMA.

Minister of Health and Social Welfare: DIOSDADO VICENTE NSUE MILANG.

Minister of Public Works and Infrastructure: JUAN NKO MBULA.

Minister of Mines, Industry and Energy: GABRIEL MBEGA OBIANG LIMA.

Minister of Labour and Social Security: HERIBERTO MIKO MBENGONO.

Minister of Agriculture and Forestry: ALFREDO MITOGO MITOGO.

Minister of Information, the Press and Radio: TEOBALDO NCHASO MATOMBA.

Minister of Social Affairs and Gender Equality: MARI CARMEN ECORO.

Minister of Fisheries and the Environment: CRESCENCIO TAMARITE CASTAÑO.

Minister of the Civil Service and Administrative Reform: PURIFICACIÓN BUARI LASAQUERO.

Minister of Youth and Sport: FRANCISCO PASCUAL OBAMA ASUE.

Minister-delegate at the Presidency of the Republic, in charge of External Security: JUAN ANTONIO BIBANG NCHUCHUMA.

Minister-delegate at the Department of Culture and Tourism: GUILLERMINA MEKUY MBA OBONO.

Minister-delegate of Foreign Affairs and Co-operation: PEDRO ELA NGUEMA BUNA.

Minister-delegate of Justice, Religion and Penitentiary Institutions: JUAN OLO MBA NSENG.

Minister-delegate of National Defence: VICENTE EYA OLOMO.

Minister-delegate of the Interior and Local Government: LEOCADIO NDONG MOÑUNG.

Minister-delegate of Trade and Business Development: FORTUNATO OFA MBO NCHAMA.

Minister-delegate of Finance and the Budget, in charge of Duties and Taxes: EUCARIO BAKALE ANGUE.

Minister-delegate of the Economy, Planning and Public Investment: HERMES ELA MIFUMU.

Minister-delegate of Transport, Technology, Post and Telecommunications: JOAQUÍN ELEMA BORENGUE.

Minister-delegate of Civil Aviation: FAUSTO ABESO FUMA.

Minister-delegate of Education and Science: JESUS ENGONGA NDONG.

Minister-delegate of Health and Social Welfare: MIGUEL OBIANG ABESO.

Minister-delegate of Energy: FIDEL-MARCOS MEÑE NCOGO.

Minister-delegate of Labour and Social Security: JOSE ANGEL BORICO MOISES.

Minister-delegate of Public Works and Infrastructure: REGINALDO ASU MANGUE.

Minister-delegate of Agriculture and Forestry: SALOMON NFA NDONG.

Minister-delegate of Information, the Press and Radio: FEDERICO ABAGA ONDO.

Minister-delegate of the Civil Service and Administrative Reform: BALTASAR ESONO OWORO NFONO.

In addition there were 19 Vice-Ministers.

MINISTRIES

Office of the President: Malabo.

Ministry of Agriculture and Forestry: Apdo 504, Malabo.

Ministry of the Civil Service and Administrative Reform: Malabo.

Ministry of the Economy, Planning and Public Investment: Malabo.

Ministry of Education and Science: Malabo.

Ministry of Finance and the Budget: Malabo; internet www.ceiba-guinea-ecuatorial.org/guineees/indexbienv1.htm.

Ministry of Fisheries and the Environment: Malabo.

Ministry of Foreign Affairs and Co-operation: Malabo.

Ministry of Health and Social Welfare: Malabo.

Ministry of Information, the Press and Radio: Malabo.

Ministry of the Interior and Local Government: Malabo; fax 333092683.

Ministry of Justice, Religion and Penitentiary Institutions: Apdo 459, Malabo; fax 333092115.

Ministry of Labour and Social Security: Malabo.

Ministry of Mines, Industry and Energy: Calle 12 de Octubre s/n, Malabo; tel. 333093567; fax 333093353; internet www.equatorialoil.com.

Ministry of National Defence: Malabo; tel. 333092794.

Ministry of National Security: Malabo; tel. 333093469.

Ministry of Public Works and Infrastructure: Malabo.

Ministry of Social Affairs and Gender Equality: Malabo; tel. 333093469.

Ministry of the Social Sector and Human Rights: Malabo.

Ministry of Trade and Business Development: Apdo 404, Malabo; tel. 333093105; fax 333092043.

Ministry of Transport, Technology, Post and Telecommunications: Malabo; internet www.ceiba-guinea-ecuatorial.org/guineees/transport.htm.

Ministry of Youth and Sport: Malabo.

President

Presidential Election, 29 November 2009

Candidate	Votes	% of votes
Obiang Nguema Mbasogo (PDGE)	260,462	95.76
Plácido Micó Abogo (CPDS)	9,700	3.57
Archivaldo Montero (UP)	931	0.34
Bonaventura Monsuy Asumu (PCSD)	462	0.17
Carmelo Mba Bacale (APGE)	437	0.16
Total	271,992*	100.00

* The total number of votes officially attributed to candidates by the Constitutional Court amounted to 271,992. However, that body declared the total number of valid votes cast to be 271,964, and the percentage of votes awarded to Obiang Nguema Mbasogo to be 95.37%. According to the Constitutional Court, there were 1,167 invalid votes.

Legislature

HOUSE OF REPRESENTATIVES

House of Representatives (Cámara de Representantes del Pueblo): Malabo.

Speaker: Dr ÁNGEL SERAFÍN SERICHE.

General Election, 26 May 2013

Party	Seats
Partido Democrático de Guinea Ecuatorial (PDGE)	99
Convergencia para la Democracia Social (CPDS)	1
Total	100

SENATE

Senate (Senado): Malabo.

General Election, 26 May 2013

Party	Seats
Partido Democrático de Guinea Ecuatorial (PDGE)	54
Convergencia para la Democracia Social (CPDS)	1
Total	55*

* An additional 15 senators are nominated by the President of the Republic.

Election Commission

Constitutional Court: Malabo; Pres. SALVADOR ONDO NKUMU.

Political Organizations

Acción Popular de Guinea Ecuatorial (APGE): pro-Govt party; Pres. CARMELO MBA BACALE; Sec.-Gen. MIGUEL ESONO.

Alianza Nacional para la Restauración Democrática de Guinea Ecuatorial (ANRD): 95 Ruperto Chapi, 28100 Madrid, Spain; tel. (91) 623-88-64; f. 1974; Sec.-Gen. LUIS ONDO AYANG.

Convención Liberal Democrática (CLD): pro-Govt party; Pres. ALFONSO NSUE MOKUY.

Convención Socialdemocrática Popular (CSDP): pro-Govt party; Leader SECUNDINO OYONO.

Convergencia para la Democracia Social (CPDS): Calle Tres de Agosto 72, 2º, 1 Malabo; tel. 333092013; e-mail cpds@intnet.gq; internet www.cpds-gq.org; Pres. SANTIAGO OBAMA NDONG; Sec.-Gen. PLÁCIDO MICÓ ABOGO.

Demócratas por el Cambio (DECAM): coalition based in Madrid, Spain; e-mail press@guinea-ecuatorial.org; internet www.guinea-ecuatorial.org; f. 2005; 16 mem. orgs; Gen. Co-ordinator DANIEL OYONO.

Fuerza Demócrata Republicana (FDR): f. 1995; Pres. FELIPE ONDO OBIANG; Sec.-Gen. GUILLERMO NGUEMA ELA.

Movimiento para la Autodeterminación de la Isla de Bioko (MAIB): f. 1993 by Bubi interests seeking independence of Bioko; clandestine; Gen. Co-ordinator WEJA CHICAMPO.

Partido de la Convergencia Social Demócrata (PCSD): pro-Govt party; Pres. BUENAVENTURA MONSUY ASUMU.

Partido Democrático de Guinea Ecuatorial (PDGE): Malabo; internet www.pdge-ge.org; f. 1987; sole legal party 1987–92; Chair. Gen. (TEODORO) OBIANG NGUEMA MBASOGO; Sec.-Gen. LUCAS NGUEMA ESONO.

Partido del Progreso de Guinea Ecuatorial (PPGE): Madrid, Spain; e-mail ppge@telepolis.com; internet www.guinea-ecuatorial.org; f. 1983; Christian Democrat faction led by SEVERO MOTO NSA.

Partido Socialista de Guinea Ecuatorial (PSGE): pro-Govt party; Sec.-Gen. TOMÁS MECHEBA FERNÁNDEZ-GALILEA.

Unión para la Democracia y el Desarrollo Social (UDDS): f. 1990; Sec.-Gen. AQUILINO NGUEMA ONA NCHAMA; in Cameroon.

Unión Democrática Nacional (UDENA): Pres. PEDRO CRISTINO BUERIBERI BOKESA.

Unión Democrática y Social de Guinea Ecuatorial (UDS): pro-Govt party; Sec.-Gen. MIGUEL MBA NSANG.

Unión Popular (UP): internet up-ge.com; f. 1992; conservative; divided into two factions, one led by DANIEL DARÍO MARTÍNEZ AYACABA and another led by FAUSTINO ONDO in Madrid; Pres. ALFREDO MITOGO MITOGO ADA; Sec.-Gen. RICARDO ELA ONDO.

Diplomatic Representation

EMBASSIES IN EQUATORIAL GUINEA

Angola: Malabo; Ambassador ARMANDO MATEUS CADETE.

Brazil: Avda Parques de África, Carocolas, Apdo 119, Malabo; tel. 333099986; fax 333099987; Ambassador ELIANA DA COSTA Y SILVA.

Cameroon: 37 Calle Rey Boncoro, Apdo 292, Malabo; tel. and fax 333092263; Ambassador JOHN MPOUEL BALA LAZARE.

China, People's Republic: Carretera del Aeropuerto, Apdo 44, Malabo; tel. 333093505; fax 333092381; internet gq.chineseembassy.org/chn; Ambassador ZHAO HONGSHENG.

Congo, Republic: Malabo; Ambassador CÉLESTINE KOUAKOUA.

Cuba: Carretera de Luba y Cruce de Dragas s/n, Malabo; tel. and fax 333094793; e-mail embajada@gq.embacuba.cu; internet www.cubadiplomatica.cu/guineaecuatorial/ES/Inicio.aspx; Ambassador PEDRO FÉLIX DOÑA SANTANA.

France: Carretera del Aeropuerto, Apdo 326, Malabo; tel. 333092005; fax 333092305; e-mail chancellerie.malabo-amba@diplomatie.gouv.fr; internet www.ambafrance-gq.org; Ambassador FRANÇOIS BARATEAU.

Gabon: Calle de Argelia, Apdo 18, Malabo; Ambassador JANVIER OBIANG ALLOGHO.

Germany: Edificio Venus, 4º.Piso, Carretera del Aeropuerto, Km 4, Malabo; e-mail embajada.alemana.malabo@diplo.de; Ambassador MICHAEL OTTO KLEPSCH.

Guinea: Malabo.

Korea, Democratic People's Republic: Malabo; tel. 333092047; Ambassador KWAK JI HWAN.

Morocco: Avda Enrique Nvo, Apdo 329, Malabo; tel. 333092650; fax 333092655; Ambassador JILALI HILAL.

Nigeria: 4 Paseo de los Cocoteros, Apdo 78, Malabo; tel. and fax 333093385; Ambassador ADADU ECHI.

South Africa: Parque de las Avenidas de Africa s/n, Apdo 5, Malabo; tel. 333207737; fax 333092746; e-mail malabo@foreign.gov.za; Ambassador PAKAMISA AUGUSTINE SIFUBA.

Spain: Parque de las Avenidas de África s/n, Malabo; tel. 333092020; fax 333092611; e-mail emb.malabo@maec.es; Ambassador ARTURO SPIEGELBERG DE ORTUETA.

USA: K-3, Carretera de Aeropuerto, Malabo; tel. 333098895; fax 333098894; e-mail usembassymalabo@yahoo.com; internet malabo.usembassy.gov; Ambassador MARK L. ASQUINO.

Judicial System

The Supreme Court of Justice and the Constitutional Court sit in Malabo. The Supreme Court has four chambers (Civil and Social, Penal, Administrative and Common) and consists of a President and 12 magistrates, from whom the President of each chamber is selected. Provincial courts have been created in all provinces to replace the former courts of appeal. At present they are only functional in Malabo and Bata. Courts of first instance sit in Malabo and Bata, and may be convened in the other provincial capitals. Local courts may be convened when necessary.

Supreme Court of Justice (Corte Suprema de Justicia): Malabo; Pres. MARTIN NDONG NSUE.

Constitutional Court (Tribunal Constitucional): Malabo; Pres. SALVADOR ONDO NKUMU.

Attorney-General: DAVID NGUEMA OBIANG.

Religion

More than 90% of the population are adherents of the Roman Catholic Church. Traditional forms of worship are also followed.

CHRISTIANITY

The Roman Catholic Church

Equatorial Guinea comprises one archdiocese and two dioceses.

Bishops' Conference: Arzobispado, Apdo 106, Malabo; tel. 333092909; fax 333092176; e-mail arzobispadomalabo@hotmail.com; f. 1984; Pres. Most Rev. ILDEFONSO OBAMA OBONO (Archbishop of Malabo).

Archbishop of Malabo: Most Rev. ILDEFONSO OBAMA OBONO, Arzobispado, Apdo 106, Malabo; tel. 333092909; fax 333092176; e-mail arzobispadomalabo@hotmail.com.

Protestant Church

Iglesia Reformada Evangélica de Guinea Ecuatorial (Evangelical Reformed Church of Equatorial Guinea): Apdo 195, Malabo; f. 1960; c. 8,000 mems; Sec.-Gen. Pastor JUAN EBANG ELA.

The Press

Ebano: Malabo; f. 1940; weekly; govt-controlled.

El Árbol del Centro: Apdo 180, Malabo; tel. 333092186; fax 333093275; Spanish; cultural review; 6 a year; publ. by Centro Cultural Español de Malabo; Dir GLORIA NISTAL.

El Correo Deportivo: Malabo; tel. 222259223 (mobile); e-mail lagacetademalabo@gmail.com; monthly; Dir ROBERTO MARTIN PRIETO.

La Gaceta: Malabo; tel. 222259223 (mobile); e-mail lagacetademalabo@gmail.com; f. 1996; monthly; Dir ROBERTO MARTÍN PRIETO; circ. 3,000.

El Lector: Malabo; f. 2011; fortnightly; Dir ANTONIO NSUE ADÁ.

La Verdad: Talleres Gráficos de Convergencia para la Democracia Social, Calle Tres de Agosto 72, Apdo 441, Malabo; publ. by the Convergencia para la Democracia Social; 5 annually; Editor PLÁCIDO MICÓ ABOGO.

Poto-poto: Bata; f. 1940; weekly; govt-controlled.

Voz del Pueblo: Malabo; publ. by the Partido Democrático de Guinea Ecuatorial.

PRESS ASSOCIATIONS

Asociación para la Libertad de Prensa y de Expresión en Guinea Ecuatorial (ASOLPEGE Libre): Calle Isla Cabrera 3, 5°, 46026 Valencia, Spain; tel. (660) 930629; e-mail asopge_ngo@hotmail.com; f. 2006; Pres. PEDRO NOLASCO NDONG OBAMA.

Asociación de Periodistas Profesionales de Guinea Ecuatorial: Malabo; f. 2007 by former Secretary of State for Information, Santiago Ngua.

Publisher

Centro Cultural Español de Malabo: Apdo 180, Malabo; tel. 333092186; fax 333092722; e-mail ccem@orange.gq.

Broadcasting and Communications

TELECOMMUNICATIONS

Dirección General de Correos y de Telecomunicaciones: Malabo; tel. 333092857; fax 333092515; Man. Dir M. DAUCHAT.

Guinea Ecuatorial de Comunicación Sociedad Anónima (GECOMSA): Malabo.

Guinea Ecuatorial de Telecomunicaciones, SA (GETESA): Calle Rey Boncoro 27, Apdo 494, Malabo; tel. 333092815; fax 333093313; e-mail info@getesa.gq; internet www.getesa.gq; f. 1987; 60% state-owned, 40% owned by France Telecom; Man. FRANCISCO NVE NSOGO.

Hits Guinea Equatorial SA: Malabo; tel. 550002999; fax 550002998; e-mail info@hits-ge.com.

Regulatory Authority

Regulador de las Telecomunicaciones de Guinea Ecuatorial: Malabo.

RADIO

Radio Africa and Radio East Africa: Apdo 851, Malabo; e-mail pabcomain@aol.com; commercial station; owned by Pan American Broadcasting; music and religious programmes in English.

Radio Nacional de Guinea Ecuatorial: Apdo 749, Barrio Comandachina, Bata; Apdo 195, Avda 30 de Agosto 90, Malabo; tel. 333092260; fax 333092097; govt-controlled; commercial station; programmes in Spanish, French and vernacular languages; Dir (Bata) SEBASTIÁN ELÓ ASEKO; Dir (Malabo) JUAN EYENE OPKUA NGUEMA.

Radio Santa Isabel: Malabo; Spanish and French programmes.

Radio Televisión Asonga: Bata and Malabo; private; owned by Teodorín Ngumea Obiang.

TELEVISION

Televisión Nacional: Malabo; broadcasts in Spanish and French; Dir ERNESTO MFUMU MIKO.

Finance

(cap. = capital; res = reserves; dep. = deposits; m. = million; brs = branches; amounts in francs CFA)

BANKING

Central Bank

Banque des Etats de l'Afrique Centrale (BEAC): POB 501, Malabo; tel. 333092010; fax 333092006; e-mail beacmal@beac.int; internet www.beac.int; HQ in Yaoundé, Cameroon; agency also in Bata; f. 1973; bank of issue for mem. states of the Communauté Economique et Monétaire de l'Afrique Centrale (CEMAC, fmrly Union Douanière et Economique de l'Afrique Centrale), comprising Cameroon, the Central African Repub., Chad, the Repub. of the Congo, Equatorial Guinea and Gabon; cap. 88,000m., res 227,843m., dep. 4,110,966m. (Dec. 2009); Equatorial Guinea's deposits in 2010 totalled 776,000m; Gov. LUCAS ABAGA NCHAMA; Dir in Equatorial Guinea IVAN BACALE EBE MOLINA; 2 brs in Equatorial Guinea.

Commercial Banks

In 2008 there were four commercial banks in Equatorial Guinea.

Banco Nacional de Guinea Ecuatorial (BANGE): C/Naciones Unidas No 28, Apdo 430, Malabo; tel. 333099571; internet www.banco-nge.com; f. 2005; Dir-Gen. ROWELITO TANALIGA CAHILIG.

BGFIBANK Guinea Ecuatorial: Calle de Bata s/n, Apdo 749, Malabo; tel. 333096352; fax 333096373; e-mail agence_malabo@bgfi.com; internet www.bgfi.com/site/sp/bgfibank-guinea-ecuatorial.461.html; 55% owned by BGFIBANK, 35% owned by private shareholders, 10% state-owned; incorporated June 2001; cap. 5,000m., total assets 43,211m. (Dec. 2007); Chair. MELCHOR ESSONO EDJO; Dir-Gen. SERGE MICKOTO.

Caisse Commune d'Epargne et d'Investissement Bank Guinea Ecuatorial (CCEI-GE): Calle del Presidente Nasser, Apdo 428, Malabo; tel. 333092203; fax 333093311; e-mail geccei@hotmail.com; internet www.cceibankge.com; 51% owned by Afriland First Bank (Cameroon); f. 1995; cap. and res 5,172m., total assets 81,191m. (Dec. 2003); Pres. BÁLTASAR ENGONGA EDJO'O; Dir-Gen. JOSEPH CÉLESTIN TINDJOU DJAMENI.

Société Générale des Banques en Guinée Equatoriale (SGBGE): Avda de la Independencia, Apdo 686, Malabo; tel. 333093337; fax 333093366; e-mail particuliers.sgbge@socgen.com; internet www.sgbge.gq; f. 1986; present name adopted 1998; 45.79% owned by Société Générale SA (France), 31.79% state-owned, 11.45% owned by Société Générale de Banques au Cameroun, 11.13% owned by local investors; cap. and res 2,780m., total assets 48,624m. (Dec. 2001); Chair. MARCELINO OWONO EDU; Man. Dir CHRISTIAN DELMAS; 5 brs in Bata, Ebebeyin, Luba and Malabo.

Development Banks

Banco de Fomento y Desarrollo (BFD): Malabo; f. 1998; 30% state-owned; cap. 50m.

Banque de Développement des Etats de l'Afrique Centrale: see Franc Zone.

Financial Institution

Caja Autónoma de Amortización de la Deuda Pública: Ministry of the Economy, Trade and Business Devt, Apdo 404, Malabo; tel. 333093105; fax 333092043; management of state funds; Dir-Gen. RAFAEL TUN.

INSURANCE

Equatorial Guinean Insurance Company, SA (EGICO): Avda de la Libertad, Malabo; state-owned.

Trade and Industry

GOVERNMENT AGENCIES

Cámaras Oficiales Agrícolas de Guinea: Bioko and Bata; purchase of cocoa and coffee from indigenous planters, who are partially grouped in co-operatives.

Empresa General de Industria y Comercio (EGISCA): Malabo; f. 1986; parastatal body jtly operated with the French Société pour l'Organisation, l'Aménagement et le Développement des Industries Alimentaires et Agricoles (SOMDIA); import-export agency.

Oficina para la Cooperación con Guinea Ecuatorial (OCGE): Malabo; f. 1981; administers bilateral aid from Spain.

DEVELOPMENT ORGANIZATIONS

Agencia Española de Cooperación Internacional para el Desarrollo (AECID): Carretera del Aeropuerto, Malabo; tel. 333091621; fax 333092932; e-mail ucemalabo@guineanet.net; internet www.aecid.es.

Asociación Bienestar Familiar de Guinea Ecuatorial: Apdo 984, Malabo; tel. and fax (09) 33-13; e-mail abifage1@hotmail.com; family welfare org.

Asociación Hijos de Lommbe (A Vonna va Lommbe): Malabo; f. 2000; agricultural devt org.

Camasa: Finca Sampaka, Km 7 Camino a Luba, Malabo; tel. 333098692; e-mail casamallo@hotmail.com; internet www.camasa.net; f. 1906; agricultural devt on Bioko island; operates projects for the cultivation and export of cocoa, pineapple, coffee, vanilla, nutmeg, peppers and tropical flowers.

Centro de Estudios e Iniciativas para el Desarrollo de Guinea Ecuatorial (CEIDIGE): Malabo; internet www.eurosur.org/CEIDGE; umbrella group of devt NGOs; Pres. JOSÉ ANTONIO NSANG ANDEME.

Family Care Guinea Ecuatorial (FGCE): Malabo; f. 2000; health and education devt; Dir LAUREN TAYLOR STEVENSON.

Instituto Nacional de Promoción Agropecuaria (INPAGE): Malabo; govt agricultural devt agency; reorg. 2000.

Sociedad Anónima de Desarrollo del Comercio (SOADECO-Guinée): Malabo; f. 1986; parastatal body jtly operated with the French Société pour l'Organisation, l'Aménagement et le Développement des Industries Alimentaires et Agricoles (SOMDIA); devt of commerce.

CHAMBERS OF COMMERCE

Cámara de Comercio de Bioko: Avda de la Independencia 43, Apdo 51, Malabo; tel. and fax 333094576; e-mail camara@orange.gq; Pres. GREGORIO BOHO CAMO.

INDUSTRIAL AND TRADE ASSOCIATIONS

INPROCAO: Malabo; production, marketing and distribution of cocoa.

Unión General de Empresas Privadas de la República de Guinea Ecuatorial (UGEPRIGE): Apdo 138, Malabo; tel. 222278326 (mobile); fax 333090559.

UTILITIES

Electricity

Sociedad de Electricidad de Guinea Ecuatorial (SEGESA): Carretera de Luba, Apdo 139, Malabo; tel. 333093466; fax 333093329; state-owned electricity distributor; Man. Dir BENITO ONDO.

Major Companies

Abayak: Malabo; owned by President Obiang's family.

Efusilia: Malabo; owned by Armengol Ondo, President Obiang's brother.

ExxonMobil: Complejo Residencial Abajak, Malabo.

Guinea Ecuatorial de Petróleo (GEPetrol): Calle Acacio Mane 39, BP 965, Malabo; tel. 333096769; fax 333096692; e-mail laamaye@hotmail.com; internet www.equatorialoil.com/html/gepetrol.html; f. 2001; state-owned petroleum company; National Dir CÁNDIDO NSUE OKOMO.

Shimmer International: Bata; controls 90% of wood production in Rio Muni.

Sociedad Equatoguineana de Bebidas: Bata; production and bottling of various brands of beer, water and soft drinks; Dir-Gen. CYRIL BRUNEL.

Sociedad Nacional de Gas de Guinea Ecuatorial (SONAGAS, G.E.): Malabo; e-mail j.ndong@sonagas-ge.com; internet www.sonagas-ge.com; f. 2005; oversees gas exploration and devt; Dir-Gen. JUAN ANTONIO NDONG.

Sociedad Nacional de Vigilancia (SONAVI): Malabo; owned by Armengol Ondo.

Total Ecuatoguineana de Gestión (GE—Total): Malabo; f. 1984; 50% state-owned, 50% owned by Total (France); petroleum marketing and distribution.

TRADE UNIONS

A law permitting the establishment of trade unions was introduced in 1992. However, trade unions have not been granted authorization to operate.

Transport

RAILWAYS

There are no railways in Equatorial Guinea.

ROADS

In 2000 there were an estimated 2,880 km of roads and tracks. In 2006 a project commenced to build a further 2,000 km of roads.

Bioko: a semi-circular tarred road serves the northern part of the island from Malabo down to Batete in the west and from Malabo to Basacato Grande in the east, with a feeder road from Luba to Moka and Bahía de la Concepción. Since 2010 a six-lane motorway has linked Malabo and the international airport to the new city of Sipopo, 16 km from the capital.

Río Muni: a tarred road links Bata with the nearby town of Mbini in the south; another tarred road links Bata with the frontier post of Ebebiyín in the east and then continues into Gabon; previously earth roads joining Acurenam, Mongomo and Anisok are now tarred. A new road links Bata to Mongomo.

SHIPPING

The main ports are Bata (general cargo and most of the country's export timber), Malabo (general), Luba (bananas, timber and petroleum), Mbini and Cogo (timber). There are regular shipping services to Europe from Bata and Malabo; however, communications between Bata, Malabo and Annobón remain erratic. At 31 December 2013 Equatorial Guinea's flag registered fleet comprised 36 vessels, totalling 24,785 grt.

CIVIL AVIATION

There are three international airports; those in Malabo and Bata have both been expanded in recent years (including the construction of a new, asphalt-surfaced runway at Bata). A third international airport, in Mongomo, in eastern Río Muni (the tribal stronghold of the Obiang clan), was opened in October 2012. There are also five domestic airports. All flights operated by carriers based in Equatorial Guinea are prohibited from flying in European Union airspace. SONAGESA, jointly operated by GEPetrol and SONAIR of Angola, offers direct connections between Malabo and Houston, USA. Other international carriers regularly link Malabo to Madrid (Spain), Paris (France), Doula (Cameroon), Zürich (Switzerland), Amsterdam (Netherlands) and Frankfurt (Germany).

Air Consul: Apdo 77, Malabo; tel. and fax 333093291; Man. FERNANDEZ ARMESTO.

EGA—Ecuato Guineana de Aviación: Apdo 665, Malabo; tel. 333092325; fax 333093313; internet www.ecuatoguineana.com/ega/ega.htm; regional and domestic passenger and cargo services; Pres. MELCHOR ESONO EDJO.

Tourism

Tourism remains undeveloped. Future interest in this sector would be likely to focus on the unspoilt beaches of Río Muni and Bioko's scenic mountain terrain.

Defence

As assessed at November 2012, there were 1,100 men in the army, 120 in the navy and 100 in the air force. There was also a paramilitary force, referred to both as 'Antorchas' and 'Ninjas', which was trained by French military personnel. Military service is voluntary. Military training and aid has been provided by Morocco, Spain and Israel.

Defence Expenditure: Estimated at 3,800m. francs CFA in 2011.

Supreme Commander of the Armed Forces: Gen. (retd) OBIANG NGUEMA MBASOGO.

Inspector-Gen. of the Armed Forces and the Security Forces: Rear Adm. JOAQUÍN NDONG NVÉ.

Education

Education is officially compulsory and free for five years between the ages of six and 11. Primary education starts at six years of age and normally lasts for five years. Secondary education, beginning at the age of 12, spans a seven-year period, comprising a first cycle of four years and a second cycle of three years. According to UNESCO estimates, in 2012 total enrolment at primary schools included 61% of children in the relevant age-group (males 61%; females 61%), while secondary enrolment in 2005 was 22% of children in the relevant age-group (males 25%; females 19%). In 1999/2000 there were 1,003 pupils in higher education. Since 1979 assistance in the development of the educational system has been provided by Spain. Two higher education centres, at Bata and Malabo, are administered by the Spanish Universidad Nacional de Educación a Distancia. There is also a university, Universidad Nacional de Guinea Ecuatorial, founded in 1995, at Malabo and Bata, as well as the Escuela Nacional de Agricultura, a vocational college in Malabo. The French Government also provides considerable financial assistance. In September 2002 a new National Plan for Education was ratified. Its aims were to improve basic literacy and to introduce education on health-related topics. In 2003 spending on education represented 4.0% of total budgetary expenditure. According to UNESCO estimates, in 2011 the adult literacy rate was 94%, the highest in sub-Saharan Africa.

ERITREA

Introductory Survey

LOCATION, CLIMATE, LANGUAGE, RELIGION, FLAG, CAPITAL

The State of Eritrea, which has a coastline on the Red Sea extending for almost 1,000 km, is bounded to the north-west by Sudan, to the south and west by Ethiopia, and to the south-east by Djibouti. Its territory includes the Dahlak Islands, a low-lying coralline archipelago off shore from Massawa. Rainfall is less than 500 mm per year in lowland areas, increasing to 1,000 mm in the highlands. The temperature gradient is similarly steep: annual average temperatures range from 17°C (63°F) in the highlands to 30°C (86°F) in Massawa. The Danakil depression in the south-east, which is more than 130 m below sea-level in places, experiences some of the highest temperatures recorded, frequently exceeding 50°C (122°F). The major language groups in Eritrea are Afar, Bilien, Hedareb, Kunama, Nara, Rashaida, Saho, Tigre and Tigrinya. English is increasingly becoming the language of business and is the medium of instruction at secondary schools and at university. Arabic is also widely spoken. The population is fairly evenly divided between Tigrinya-speaking Christians (mainly Orthodox), the traditional inhabitants of the highlands, and the Muslim communities of the western lowlands, northern highlands and east coast; there are also systems of traditional belief adhered to by a small number of the population. The national flag (proportions 1 by 2) consists of a red triangle with its base corresponding to the hoist and its apex at the centre of the fly, in which is situated, towards the hoist, an upright gold olive branch with six clusters of three leaves each, framed by a wreath of two gold olive branches; the remainder of the field is green at the top and light blue at the base. The capital is Asmara.

CONTEMPORARY POLITICAL HISTORY

Historical Context

The Treaty of Ucciali, which was signed in 1889 between Italy and Ethiopia, gave the Italian Government control over what is today the State of Eritrea. Italian exploitation of the colony continued until the defeat of the Axis powers by the Allied forces in East Africa during the Second World War. The Eritrean national identity, which was established during the Italian colonial period, was further subjugated under British administration during 1941–52. As the Allied powers and the UN discussed the future of the former Italian colony, Ethiopian territorial claims helped to foment a more militant nationalism among the Eritrean population. In 1952 a federation was formed between Eritrea and Ethiopia; however, the absence of adequate provisions for the creation of federal structures allowed Ethiopia to reduce Eritrea's status to that of an Ethiopian province by 1962.

Resistance to the Ethiopian annexation was first organized in the late 1950s, and in 1961 the Eritrean Liberation Front (ELF) launched an armed struggle. In the mid-1970s a reformist group broke away from the ELF and formed the Popular Liberation Forces (renamed the Eritrean People's Liberation Front, EPLF, in 1977), and the military confrontation with the Ethiopian Government began in earnest. A major consequence of the split between the two Eritrean groups was the civil war of 1972–74. After two phases of desertion from the ELF to the EPLF, in 1977–78 and in 1985 (following a second civil war), the ELF was left without a coherent military apparatus.

Following the 1974 revolution in Ethiopia and the assumption of power by Mengistu Haile Mariam in 1977, thousands of new recruits joined the EPLF, and the armed struggle transformed into full-scale warfare. The numerically and materially superior Ethiopian forces achieved significant victories over the EPLF, which was forced to retreat to its stronghold in the north of Eritrea. The EPLF launched counter-attacks throughout the late 1980s and slowly drove back the Ethiopian forces on all fronts. In May 1991 units of the EPLF entered Asmara, after the Ethiopian troops had fled the capital, and immediately established an interim administration.

Following the liberation of Asmara by the EPLF, and of Addis Ababa, Ethiopia, by the Ethiopian People's Revolutionary Democratic Front (EPRDF), a conference was convened in London, United Kingdom, in August 1991. Both the USA and the Ethiopian delegation accepted the EPLF administration as the legitimate provisional Government of Eritrea, and the EPLF agreed to hold a referendum on independence in 1993. The provisional Government, which was to administer Eritrea during the two years prior to the referendum, drew most of its members from the EPLF. The Government struggled to rehabilitate and develop Eritrea's war-torn economy and infrastructure, and to feed a population largely dependent on food aid. The agricultural sector had been severely disrupted by the war, and urban economic activity was almost non-existent.

At the UN-supervised referendum held in April 1993, 99.8% of Eritreans who voted endorsed national independence. The anniversary of the liberation of Asmara, 24 May, was proclaimed Independence Day, and on 28 May Eritrea formally attained international recognition. In June Eritrea was admitted to the Organization of African Unity (OAU, now the African Union—AU, see p. 186). Following Eritrea's accession to independence, a four-year transitional period was declared, during which preparations were to proceed for establishing a constitutional and pluralist political system. At the apex of the transitional Government were three state institutions: the Consultative Council (the executive authority formed from the ministers, provincial administrators and heads of government authorities and commissions); the National Assembly (the legislative authority formed from the Central Committee of the EPLF, together with 30 members from the Provincial Assemblies and 30 individuals selected by the Central Committee); and the judiciary. One of the National Assembly's first acts was the election as Head of State of Issaias Afewerki, the Secretary-General of the EPLF, by a margin of 99 votes to five.

Domestic Political Affairs

In February 1994 the EPLF transformed itself into a political party, the People's Front for Democracy and Justice (PFDJ). An 18-member Executive Committee and a 75-member Central Committee were elected; President Afewerki was elected Chairman of the latter. In March the National Assembly adopted a series of resolutions whereby the former executive body, the Consultative Council, was formally superseded by a State Council. Other measures adopted included the creation of a 50-member Constitutional Commission and the establishment of a committee charged with the reorganization of the country's administrative divisions. It was decided that the National Assembly would henceforth comprise the 75 members of the PFDJ Central Committee and 75 directly elected members. However, no mechanism was announced for their election. All but eight of the 50 members of the Constitutional Commission were government appointees, and there was no provision for any opposition participation in the interim system.

A draft constitution was discussed at international conventions held by the Constitutional Commission in July 1994 and January 1995. In May the National Assembly approved proposals to create six administrative regions to replace the 10 regional divisions that had been in place since colonial rule. In November the Assembly approved new names for the regions and finalized details of their exact boundaries and sub-divisions; the new Constitution came into force in 1997.

It was initially announced that Eritrea's first post-independence elections, which were scheduled to have been held in 1998, but were postponed indefinitely following the outbreak of hostilities with Ethiopia (see below), would take place in December 2001. However, during 2001 the likelihood of elections taking place in that year diminished, as President Afewerki assumed an increasingly authoritarian position. In February he dismissed the Minister of Local Government, Mahmoud Ahmed Sherifo, and dissolved the electoral commission, which Sherifo had been appointed to head. In June Afewerki replaced the Ministers of Trade and Industry and of Maritime Resources. They were among a group of 15 senior PFDJ officials, including 11 former government ministers, who, in May, had signed a letter publicly accusing Afewerki of working in an 'illegal and unconstitutional manner'. In August the Chief Justice of the Supreme Court was dismissed after he openly expressed his disapproval of Afewerki's continued interference in court operations. In mid-September six of the G15, as the signatories of the letter criticizing Afewerki had become known, were arrested, and the Government announced the 'temporary suspension' of the independent press. A few days later a further five members of the G15 were detained.

Although no formal postponement of the legislative elections was announced, the failure of the National Assembly to convene to ratify legislation on the electoral system and on political pluralism by December 2001 made further delay inevitable. In late January 2002 the National Assembly ratified the electoral law, but failed to set an election date. Meanwhile, dissident members of the ruling PFDJ, including several members of the G15, announced the formation, in exile, of a new political party, the Eritrean People's Liberation Front—Democratic Party (EPLF—DP).

During 2004 several parties took steps to form a viable opposition movement to the PFDJ. In February, following talks in Germany, the EPLF—DP announced that it would reconstitute as the Eritrean Democratic Party (EDP), under the continued leadership of Mesfin Hagos. In May numerous former members of the ELF and the PFDJ combined to establish the Eritrean Popular Movement (EPM). In August two new coalitions were formed; the first united the EPM and four smaller parties under the umbrella of the Eritrean National Alliance (ENA), while the second brought the EDP, the ELF and the Eritrean Liberation Front—Revolutionary Council together. In 2004 the ENA was reorganized as the Eritrean Democratic Alliance (EDA) and in January 2005 Hiruy Tedla Bairu was elected leader of the coalition. In January 2008 the 11 opposition parties comprising the EDA met in Addis Ababa to consolidate the alliance after divisions had emerged in the previous year. Two additional parties were admitted to the coalition: the Eritrean Islamic Congress and the Eritrean People's Movement.

Despite the continued failure of the Government to announce a date for legislative elections, in 2009 political parties began to prepare for an eventual poll with three main opposition blocs emerging. In May 2009 four opposition parties (the ELF, Islah, al-Khalas and the Eritrean Federal Democratic Movement) joined forces as the Eritrean Solidarity Front. Later that month the Eritrean People's Party announced it was to merge with the Democratic Movement of Gash-Setit and was continuing discussions with the EDP regarding a merger. In June the Red Sea Afar Democratic Organization and the Democratic Movement for the Liberation of Eritrean Kunama signed an agreement establishing the Democratic Front of Eritrean Nationalities, while confirming their intention to continue to work under the umbrella of the EDA. However, Afewerki repeatedly stated his reluctance to implement a democratic framework. In August 2010 the EDA's 11 member organizations, together with other groups and civil society representatives, held a National Conference for Democratic Change in Addis Ababa during which plans were reportedly discussed to overthrow the Eritrean Government. The EDA claimed to have staged co-ordinated military attacks against government troops inside Eritrea in February, April and May, but the Eritrean Government refused to confirm such reports of attacks on its forces. Another National Conference for Democratic Change was convened in Ethiopia, in Hawassa, in November 2011.

Recent developments: army mutiny

At some point in 2012 (it being not evident from reports exactly when) Berhane Abrehe, who had been Minister of Finance since 2001, was removed from the post following a dispute over opacity in the distribution of mining revenues from the Bisha copper mine; he was succeeded by Berhane Habtemariam, a former manager of the Eritrean National Mining Corporation (ENAMCO). In October 2012 it was reported that two senior members of the armed forces had fled to Saudi Arabia and requested asylum; this was followed in November by the defection of Minister of Information Ali Abdu, formerly a close associate of President Afewerki, who was rumoured to have sought asylum in Canada. In early 2013 reports emerged that some 200 dissident members of the armed forces had briefly seized the Ministry of Information building on 21 January, and had forced the Director-General of the state radio and television agency to broadcast an appeal for the release of all political prisoners, and for the immediate implementation of the 1997 Constitution. Troops loyal to President Afewerki had rapidly regained control of the building. On 1 February the Ministry of Information issued a decree, which was strongly criticized by the international non-governmental organization Reporters without Borders, prohibiting the broadcasts of Qatar-based television news network Al Jazeera; transmissions on Al Jazeera's English-language channels were blocked by the authorities. The ban was apparently imposed in response to the network's reports of the insurrection, and of subsequent demonstrations by Eritrean exiles outside Eritrean diplomatic missions in Cairo, Egypt, and a number of Western European capitals in support of the soldiers and in opposition to the Government. The Eritrean authorities were also accused by Reporters without Borders of responsibility for a series of transmission- and cyber-attacks on an independent radio station, Radio Erena, which had been established by Eritrean journalists in Paris, France, in 2009.

Internally Displaced Persons and Refugees

According to estimates by the Internal Displacement Monitoring Centre (IDMC), in 2006 there remained some 40,000–45,000 internally displaced persons (IDPs) in Eritrea. In an effort to promote 'self-sufficiency', in September 2005 the Eritrean Government imposed severe restrictions on the distribution of food aid, and reduced from 1.3m. to 72,000 the number of people entitled to receive free food. The move was widely criticized, especially by the UN, and prompted fears of acute food shortages among the one-third of the population who were estimated to be dependent on humanitarian assistance. Government resettlement programmes reduced the number of IDPs to an estimated 32,000 by mid-2007. In October 2009 there were contradictory reports on the number of IDPs remaining in Eritrea; the Office for the Coordination of Humanitarian Affairs reported that all IDPs had been resettled or returned to their existing communities, while the IDMC claimed an estimated 10,000 remained in Eritrea. According to figures published by the UN High Commissioner for Refugees (UNHCR), in 2013 there were some 4,000 refugees—mainly from Somalia—in Eritrea who had been resident in the country for around 20 years. However, a concurrent trend has been the departure of Eritrean refugees, primarily to Sudan and Ethiopia. According to UNHCR estimates, there was a combined total of around 204,000 Eritrean refugees residing in Sudan and Ethiopia at the end of 2013. In October of that year the UN Special Rapporteur on Eritrea estimated that 2,000–3,000 Eritreans sought to flee the country every month as a result of the oppressive regime and indefinite military conscription. Over the last few years many Eritrean refugees have lost their lives while attempting to cross the Mediterranean Sea in crowded, unseaworthy vessels to seek asylum in Europe.

Foreign Affairs

Relations with Sudan

Relations between the transitional Government and Sudan, which had supported the EPLF during the war, deteriorated in December 1993, following an incursion by members of an Islamist group, the Eritrean Islamic Jihad (EIJ), into Eritrea from Sudan, during which all the members of the group, and an Eritrean army commander, were killed. In response, President Afewerki stressed the links between the EIJ and the Sudanese National Islamic Front, led by Dr Hassan al-Turabi, implying that the latter had prior knowledge of the incursion. However, following a swift denial by the Sudanese Government that it would interfere in the affairs of neighbouring states, Afewerki reaffirmed his support for the Sudanese authorities and his commitment to improving bilateral relations.

Relations between Eritrea and Sudan worsened in November 1994, when the Eritrean authorities accused Sudan of training 400 terrorists since August. In response, Sudan accused Eritrea of training some 3,000 Sudanese rebels in camps within Eritrea. In December Eritrea severed diplomatic relations with Sudan. Further destabilization was provoked in early 1995 by attacks and infiltration in Gash-Barka Province by the EIJ. The Eritrean authorities subsequently claimed to have identified six training camps on the Sudanese side of the border and also alleged that large numbers of Eritrean refugees in Sudan had been arrested by Sudanese security forces. Sudan responded by proposing Eritrea's suspension from the Intergovernmental Authority on Drought and Development (IGADD, now the Intergovernmental Authority on Development—IGAD, see p. 335), which had been attempting to mediate in Sudan's civil war. The Sudanese Government protested strongly against Eritrea's growing support for the Sudanese opposition grouping, the National Democratic Alliance (NDA), which held a number of conferences in Asmara in the mid-1990s.

In early 1999 Sudan took steps to resolve its differences with Ethiopia, thus increasing the tension between Eritrea and Sudan. In April, however, Sudan indicated its willingness also to improve relations with Eritrea, and in May a reconciliatory agreement was signed in Qatar, which, *inter alia*, restored diplomatic relations between the two countries. Following the renewed outbreak of hostilities between Eritrea and Ethiopia in May (see below), some 94,000 Eritreans crossed the border into Sudan. After the cessation of fighting in June, many Eritrean refugees were repatriated with the assistance of the UNHCR, and by January 2002 some 36,500 Eritreans had returned home. In January 2003 refugee status was withdrawn from more than 320,000 Eritreans in Sudan, although UNHCR maintained that its repatriation programme would continue until all those registered had been returned home. In October UNHCR condemned the deportation of more than 300 Eritrean refugees from Sudan after they had been detained for several weeks and despite an agreement between the UN agency and the Sudanese Commissioner for Refugees to transfer Eritreans to Khartoum, Sudan, where their asylum claims could be assessed.

In July 2001 Eritrea and Sudan signed an agreement on border security, which aimed to eradicate smuggling and illegal infiltration, as well as ensure the safe passage of people and goods across the common border. In December 2003 Sudanese President Lt-Gen. Omar Hassan Ahmad al-Bashir accused Eritrea of arming and training rebels in the Darfur region of Sudan and maintained that Eritrea was a destabilizing force in the region. Eritrea refuted the allegations. Relations improved in 2006, following two separate rounds of peace talks in Asmara between the Sudanese Government and the rebel coalition Eastern Front during June–July. Meanwhile, in mid-June President Afewerki met al-Bashir in Khartoum, and later that month the two countries agreed to restore diplomatic relations to ambassadorial level. However, in September al-Bashir accused Eritrea of interference in the Darfur region and urged Eritrea to expel the leaders of the National Redemption Front, which had launched attacks on Sudanese Government forces in Darfur, from Eritrean territory. Nevertheless, al-Bashir and the Eastern Front leadership returned to Asmara in mid-October to sign a peace agreement. In early November the common border between Eritrea and Sudan was officially re-opened. In June 2008 the Sudanese authorities banned all activity of Eritrean opposition groups that had been operating from Sudan, demonstrating a marked improvement in relations between the two countries. Al-Bashir visited Asmara in March 2009 and reiterated his commitment to the June 2008 agreement. In March 2010 talks were held in Tripoli, Libya, between Eritrea, Libya and Sudan. The respective presidential delegations met to discuss means of improving both regional and wider African security. Bilateral agreements on trade and economic co-operation were signed in July and the Sudanese and Eritrean Governments continued to display commitment to their agreement to suspend their backing of opposition groups. During President al-Bashir's two visits to Asmara in 2013, the two sides reached agreement on a number of joint infrastructure projects, including the construction of a coastal road and proposals for a 340-km electricity transmission line. In addition, Sudan subsequently committed to deport undocumented foreign nationals to support the Eritrean authorities' efforts to deter emigration and, ostensibly, people trafficking. (According to UNHCR figures, there was a total of more than 118,000 Eritrean refugees in Sudan at December 2013.) Moreover, Presidents Afewerki and al-Bashir adopted a joint position in supporting President Salva Kiir Mayardit of South Sudan during an outbreak of unrest in that country in early 2014.

Conflict with Ethiopia

In September 1993 the first meeting of the Ethiopian-Eritrean joint ministerial commission was held in Asmara, during which agreement was reached on measures to allow the free movement of nationals between each country, and on co-operation regarding foreign affairs and economic policy. Meetings held between President Afewerki and the Ethiopian President, Meles Zenawi, in December underlined the good relations prevailing between the two Governments.

However, relations deteriorated in late 1997 following Eritrea's adoption of a new currency (the nakfa) to replace the Ethiopian birr and the subsequent disruption of cross-border trade. In May 1998 fighting erupted between Eritrean and Ethiopian troops in the border region after both countries accused the other of having invaded their territory. Hostilities escalated in June around Badme, Zalambessa and Assab, resulting in numerous casualties for both sides. Eritrea and Ethiopia agreed to an aerial ceasefire later that month, following US and Italian mediation. In November President Afewerki and Prime Minister Meles of Ethiopia were present at different sessions of a special meeting of the OAU mediation committee in Ouagadougou, Burkina Faso, which was also attended by the Heads of State of that country, Zimbabwe and Djibouti. The committee's peace proposals were accepted by Ethiopia, but rejected by Eritrea, and in February 1999 the aerial ceasefire was broken and fighting resumed in the border region. In July both sides finally confirmed their commitment to the OAU's Framework Agreement. Afewerki announced that Eritrean troops would be withdrawn from all territory captured from Ethiopia since 6 May 1998. Under the agreement, Ethiopia was also required to withdraw from all Eritrean territory captured since 6 February 1999. After requesting clarification of technical arrangements to end the war, Ethiopia informed the OAU in September that it had rejected the peace agreement, owing to inconsistencies contained therein. Eritrea accused Ethiopia of deliberately stalling proceedings, while secretly preparing for a fresh offensive.

By late May 2000 Ethiopian forces had seized Zalambessa and Eritrean troops were withdrawn from the disputed areas, although Afewerki maintained that this was merely a 'gesture of goodwill' designed to revive the peace talks, which resumed in Algiers, Algeria, on 29 May. Two days later Meles stated that the war was over and that his troops had withdrawn from most of the territory it had captured from Eritrea. Following negotiations in early June both sides expressed their readiness, in principle, to accept the OAU's ceasefire agreement, and on 18 June the Ethiopian and Eritrean Ministers of Foreign Affairs signed an agreement, which provided for an immediate ceasefire and the deployment of a UN peacekeeping force in a 25-km temporary security zone (TSZ) inside Eritrea until the issue of the demarcation of the border had been settled. In September the UN Security Council approved the deployment of the UN Mission in Ethiopia and Eritrea (UNMEE), a 4,200-strong peacekeeping force, which was placed under the command of the Special Representative of the UN Secretary-General, Legwaila Joseph Legwaila. On 12 December Eritrea and Ethiopia signed an agreement in Algiers, which formally ended the conflict between the two countries. The agreement provided for a permanent cessation of all hostilities, the immediate return of all prisoners of war, the demarcation of the common border by an independent commission, and the establishment of a Claims Commission to assess the issues of compensation and reparations. Furthermore, both countries pledged to co-operate with an independent investigation, which aimed to determine the origins of the conflict.

By late January 2001 the UNMEE force had been fully deployed and on 18 April, after all troops had been withdrawn from the border area, UNMEE declared the establishment of the TSZ, marking the formal separation of the Eritrean and Ethiopian forces. In late June UNMEE presented the final map of the TSZ to Eritrea and Ethiopia, although it emphasized that it would not influence the work of the neutral boundary commission charged with determining the border between the two countries. Despite this announcement, the Ethiopian Government expressed its dissatisfaction with the map. At the eighth meeting of the Military Co-ordination Commission (MCC) in August both countries reiterated their objections to the existing boundaries of the TSZ. In mid-September UNMEE's mandate was extended for a further six months (and at six-monthly intervals thereafter until May 2006). In December Eritrea and Ethiopia began presenting their cases for border demarcation to the five-member Boundary Commission at the International Court of Justice (see p. 24) in The Hague, Netherlands.

In March 2003 the Boundary Commission categorically ruled Badme to be Eritrean territory. Meles subsequently complained that the decision was 'wrong and unjust' and vowed to continue to contest the ruling. The demarcation of the border was delayed until October; both the MCC and the UN expressed their frustration at the slow progress being made. The UN Security Council stated that Ethiopia had committed itself under the 2000 Algiers agreement to accept the Boundary Commission's decision as 'final and binding' and urged it to accept and implement the ruling. Both Legwaila and the Chairman of the Boundary Commission, Elihu Lauterpacht, were critical of Ethiopia's lack of compliance with its obligations under the terms of the peace accord, and the ongoing impasse was further compounded by the Commission's announcement in late October that border demarcation had been delayed indefinitely. Ethiopia maintained that it had agreed to allow demarcation to take place in the eastern sector of the border region, but that it refused to accept the ruling in other areas and had expressed grave concerns about the competency of the Boundary Commission. Eritrea continued, however, to insist that the ruling be fully implemented.

UN concerns over the lack of progress on the part of both Eritrea and Ethiopia in implementing the border ruling continued during 2004. Following accusations by Eritrean officials in May of serious malpractice on the part of the UN forces, Legwaila issued an ultimatum to Eritrea that it should either co-operate with the UN peacekeeping forces or ask its troops to leave. In September UNMEE's mandate was again extended, until March 2005, but it was announced that the peacekeeping mission would be reduced in size. Meanwhile, in November 2004 Ethiopia stated that it had, in principle, accepted the Boundary Commission's ruling of April 2002 and was prepared to re-enter into talks with Eritrea regarding the demarcation of the border. However, Eritrea dismissed this announcement as little more than a further attempt by Ethiopia to stall the process.

Relations deteriorated further in early 2005 as the UN Security Council and the European Union (EU, see p. 273) expressed concern over troop redeployments on both sides of the border. In March the Security Council appealed to both countries to reduce troop numbers to December 2004 levels. In October 2005 Ethiopia reaffirmed its acceptance of the Boundary Commission's ruling, and signalled its willingness to recommence talks with Eritrea. Despite protests from Legwaila and the UN Secretary-General, Kofi Annan, later that month Eritrea imposed restrictions upon the movements of UN vehicles, including a ban upon all UNMEE helicopter flights on its side of the border. In late November the UN Security Council unanimously adopted Resolution 1640, which demanded an end to all restrictions on UNMEE activities and the full implementation of the Boundary Commission's ruling, while also evoking the possibility of sanctions against Eritrea and Ethiopia, should the two countries not comply. In December Eritrea requested that all UNMEE peacekeepers and staff from Canada, Russia, the USA and EU member states leave the country. Some 180 UN staff were subsequently moved into Ethiopia, along with peacekeeping troops, within the 10-day deadline set by Eritrean officials.

In March 2006 Legwaila ended his term as Special Representative to the UN Secretary-General and expressed his disappointment at the continued impasse in the peace process. On 31 May the UN Security Council adopted Resolution 1681, which extended UNMEE's mandate for four months, while reducing the number of military personnel by 1,000 to 2,300. The Security Council called upon Eritrea to lift all restrictions placed upon UNMEE activities; however, the request was later rejected by the Eritrean authorities. In late September UNMEE's mandate was extended until 31 January 2007.

In mid-October 2006 UN officials urged Eritrea to withdraw 1,500 of its troops and 14 armoured vehicles from the TSZ; the Eritrean Government claimed that the soldiers were harvesting crops from state-run farms in the area. In mid-November both countries declined to attend a meeting of the Boundary Commission in The Hague to discuss border demarcation and subsequently rejected its recommendations. Following the meeting, the Boundary Commission issued a statement, which expressed frustration at both countries' refusal to co-operate with the Commission and insisted that, should no agreement be in place by November 2007, the Commission would unilaterally begin the physical demarcation of the border. Ethiopia later condemned the decision as 'illegal'. On 31 January 2007 the UN Security Council approved Resolution 1741, which extended UNMEE's mandate by six months, while further reducing the size of the mission, to 1,700 military personnel. UNMEE's mandate was subsequently further extended until the end of July 2008.

With Eritrea and Ethiopia continuing to dispute the demarcation of the common border, concerns that conflict could resume were heightened in September 2007 when both Governments deployed troops to the border region. In a letter to his Eritrean counterpart, the Ethiopian Minister of Foreign Affairs, Seyoum Mesfin, stated that the Ethiopian Government considered Eritrea to be in material breach of the Algiers agreement as its troops had occupied the TSZ and had restricted the movement of the UNMEE force. Both parties again insisted that they were committed to a peaceful resolution of the border dispute; however, neither side complied with the Boundary Commission's request of November 2006 physically to demarcate the border by the end of November 2007. In early December, prior to announcing its own dissolution, the Commission stated that the boundary that it had determined in November 2006 represented the official border between the two countries.

As a result of restrictions imposed by Eritrea, in early February 2008 UNMEE began preparations to withdraw its peacekeepers from that country and to relocate them across the border into Ethiopia. In previous months the UN had repeatedly urged the Eritrean Government to lift restrictions on the delivery of fuel supplies; however, these requests were not met and in mid-February UN personnel were forced to leave the area. It was subsequently reported that a number of peacekeepers had been prevented from leaving Eritrea, and the UN Security Council expressed its concern at the 'impediments and logistical constraints' placed upon the force. Eritrea continued to restrict UNMEE operations and Ethiopia also placed constraints on UN peacekeeping units that had withdrawn from Eritrea; on 30 July the UN Security Council voted to adopt Resolution 1827, terminating the mandate of UNMEE. In August 2009 the Claims Commission awarded Ethiopia a total of US $174m. in compensation for war damages, while Eritrea received $164m., resulting in a net payment to Ethiopia of $10m. Eritrea, stated that it would honour the ruling; however, Ethiopia declared that the compensation awarded was insufficient.

During 2010 Ethiopia continued to accuse Eritrea of sponsoring its opposition movements, most notably the Ogaden National Liberation Front and the Oromo Liberation Front. In March 2011, following a visit to New York, USA, during which, it was reported, he urged the international community to take action to prevent Eritrea from destabilizing the Horn of Africa region, Ethiopian Deputy Prime Minister and Minister of Foreign Affairs Hailemariam Desalegn announced a change of policy towards Eritrea from a defensive to a more belligerent stance. This new approach appeared to be confirmed the following month by Prime Minister Meles' offer of determined support to Eritrean opposition groups and his reiteration of claims that Eritrea was a conduit for foreign financing of terrorist groups in the region and had assisted in a foiled terrorist attack against the AU summit in Addis Ababa in January. The exiled Eritrean opposition in Ethiopia praised this active policy to bring about regime change. However, despite the fact that reports of the planned attack were also corroborated by the UN Monitoring Group on Somalia and Eritrea, the Eritrean ambassador to the AU denounced all the accusations as part of a campaign of disinformation by the Ethiopian authorities.

In March 2012 Ethiopian troops, for the first time since the end of the 1998–2000 border conflict, made an incursion into south-eastern Eritrea, attacking military camps at Ramid, Gelahbe and Gimbi, on the grounds that rebel groups based there had staged a series of raids in Ethiopian territory. The Ethiopian Government further accused the Eritrean authorities of involvement in an attack in Ethiopia's north-eastern Afar region in January in which five Western tourists were killed.

According to UNHCR figures, in December 2013 the number of Eritrean refugees in Ethiopia totalled more than 86,000. At early 2014 the border dispute between the two countries remained at an impasse, with the Ethiopian Prime Minister, Hailemariam Desalegn, continuing to seek preconditions to the implementation of a binding ruling and the Eritrean Government refusing to accept such a procedure.

Relations with Djibouti

Relations with neighbouring Djibouti have also been problematic, mainly due to territorial disputes. In April 1996 tensions mounted when Eritrea was accused of attacking positions in the disputed region of Ras Doumeira, on the border between the two countries. Later that month Djibouti formally rejected a map submitted by Eritrean officials, claiming it included territory belonging to Djibouti. In 1998 diplomatic relations were suspended following Afewerki's accusation that Djibouti was lending support to Ethiopia in the Ethiopia–Eritrea border dispute, although relations were restored in March 2000. Tensions resurfaced, in April 2008, after it was reported that Eritrean forces had mobilized near Ras Doumeira and crossed into Djiboutian territory, although Afewerki strongly denied the allegations. Djibouti responded by increasing troop numbers in the region and recalled all police and soldiers demobilized in the previous five years. Despite diplomatic attempts to settle the dispute, including appeals for restraint from the AU, hostilities broke out in June and numerous casualties were reported on both sides. The fighting drew strong international condemnation: the UN launched an investigation but Eritrea refused to co-operate, denying any wrongdoing, and President Ismaïl Omar Guelleh of Djibouti demanded joint demilitarization in the border region, appealing to the UN Security Council for mediation. Eritrea refused to comply with a request made by the UN Security Council in January 2009 ordering Eritrea to withdraw its forces from the area, and issued a strongly worded statement to the Security Council in May denying any involvement in the destabilization of either Djibouti or Somalia. In October the Djibouti Minister of Foreign Affairs and Co-operation accused Eritrea of arming and training militias to carry out acts of sabotage in Djibouti, and of fomenting chaos in the region. Following increasing pressure for the imposition of sanctions from numerous East African governments, in December the UN Security Council placed an arms embargo on Eritrea, imposed travel restrictions on political and military leaders and also froze the overseas funds and financial assets of those individuals. In March 2010 the EU imposed similar sanctions. In June Afewerki and Guelleh signed an agreement to end the border dispute between Eritrea and Djibouti, entrusting responsibility for establishing a method of resolving the demarcation issue and normalizing relations to a commission of Qatari advisers.

Relations with other countries

In August 2011 Afewerki agreed to hold talks with Ugandan President Yoweri Kaguta Museveni, whose country provides the majority of troops to the AU peacekeeping mission in Somalia. The meeting was viewed by analysts as a conciliatory move on the part of Afewerki, who was becoming increasingly isolated in the region and had continued to be accused of supporting extremist groups in Somalia (notably the militant Islamist group al-Shabaab). However, Eritrea's application to rejoin IGAD (from which it had suspended itself in 2007) was postponed by IGAD's Council of Ministers later that month, who instead demanded the imposition of further UN sanctions against Eritrea. In November 2011 the Kenyan Minister of Foreign Affairs announced a review of diplomatic ties with Eritrea in the wake of a report that arms had been flown to the Somali town of Baidoa from Eritrea. Afewerki denied the allegations and appealed for an independent investigation to be carried out.

CONSTITUTION AND GOVERNMENT

On 23 May 1997 the Eritrean Constitution was adopted, authorizing 'conditional' political pluralism and instituting a presidential regime, with a President elected for a maximum of two five-year terms. The President, as Head of State, would appoint a Prime Minister and judges of the Supreme Court; his or her mandate could be revoked should two-thirds of the members of the National Assembly so demand. A Transitional National Assembly (consisting of the 75 members of the PFDJ Central Committee, 60 members of the Constituent Assembly and 15 representatives of Eritreans residing abroad) was empowered to act as the legislature until the holding of elections to a new National Assembly. At March 2014 these had yet to take place.

REGIONAL AND INTERNATIONAL CO-OPERATION

Eritrea is a member of the African Union (AU, see p. 186), but did not participate actively in the AU for more than seven years following the recall of its AU ambassador in 2003. However, in January 2011 Eritrea reopened its AU mission in Addis Ababa and presented a new ambassador to the international organization. Eritrea is also a member of the Common Market for Eastern and Southern Africa (see p. 233) and of the Intergovernmental Authority on Development (IGAD, see p. 335), although the country unilaterally announced its suspension from IGAD in 2007. In July 2011 Eritrea requested that it be permitted formally to reactivate its membership of IGAD.

Eritrea became a member of the UN in 1993. Also in 1993 Eritrea was admitted to the group of African, Caribbean and Pacific (ACP) countries party to the Lomé Convention; in September 2001 Eritrea ratified the Cotonou Agreement (see p. 324), the successor of the Lomé Convention.

ECONOMIC AFFAIRS

In 2012, according to estimates by the World Bank, Eritrea's gross national income (GNI), measured at average 2010–12 prices, was US $2,771m., equivalent to $450 per head (or $560 per head on an international purchasing-power parity basis). During 2003–12, it was estimated, the population increased at an average annual rate of 3.6%. Gross domestic product (GDP) per head decreased, in real terms, by an average of 1.8% per year during 2003–12, while overall GDP increased at an average annual rate of 1.7% in 2003–12; growth in 2012 was 7.0%.

By far the most important sector of the economy is agriculture, which sustains 80% of the population. In 2011, according to the African Development Bank (AfDB), agriculture (including forestry and fishing) accounted for an estimated 17.0% of GDP; the sector engaged an estimated 72.4% of the labour force at mid-2014, according to FAO. Most sedentary agriculture is practised in the highlands, where rainfall is sufficient to cultivate the main crops: sorghum, barley, wheat, maize, millet and chick-peas. As a result of serious environmental degradation (caused directly and indirectly by the war of independence), water scarcity and unreliable rainfall, projects have been undertaken to build water reservoirs and small dams, while badly eroded hillsides have been terraced and new trees planted in order to prevent further soil erosion. Fishing activity is on a very small scale—the total catch amounted to just 2,639 metric tons in 2011—although, according to the UN, sustainable yields of as much as 70,000 tons per year may be possible. In real terms, according to the World Bank, the GDP of the agricultural sector decreased at an average annual rate of 1.0% in 2003–09; according to the AfDB, agricultural GDP increased by 33.1% in 2010, but decreased by 2.9% in 2011.

In 2011 industrial production (comprising mining, manufacturing, construction and utilities) accounted for an estimated 24.1% of GDP, according to the AfDB. Some 5.0% of the labour force were employed in the industrial sector in 1990. According to the World Bank, industrial GDP decreased, in real terms, at an average annual rate of 1.7% in 2003–09; the GDP of the sector grew by 1.4% in 2008, but declined by 0.2% in 2009. In August 2011 the launch of production at a new cement factory, at Gedem, which was supported by funding from the People's Republic of China and was considered the national strategic project by the Government, made a notable contribution to strong economic growth in that year.

Eritrea's mineral resources are believed to be of significant potential value, although in 2011 mining and quarrying accounted for only 1.8% of GDP, according to the AfDB. Of particular importance, in view of Eritrea's acute energy shortage, is the possibility of the existence of large reserves of petroleum and natural gas beneath the Red Sea. New legislation on mining, adopted in 1995, declared all mineral resources to be state assets, but recognized an extensive role for private investors in their exploitation. In 2008 the Government assigned two offshore blocks for hydrocarbon exploration and development to a Chinese joint-venture company, Defba Oil Share Co, and in 2010 assigned another block to Canada's Centric Energy Corpn (now Africa Oil Corpn). The Government amended the Mining Law in 2011 setting its share in each of the country's mining ventures to a non-participatory 10%, and increasing its option to buy into projects from the existing maximum of 20% to 30%. Other mineral resources include potash, zinc, magnesium, copper, nickel, iron ore, chromite, marble and gold. A joint venture between the Eritrean National Mining Corpn and South Boulder Mines Ltd of Australia is currently developing the world's first open-pit potash mine, at Colluli, which is due to go into production by 2016. According to the AfDB, the mining sector's GDP increased by 3.1% in 2010 and further by 14.8% in 2011.

The manufacturing sector provided an estimated 6.2% of GDP in 2011, according to the AfDB. Until mid-1997 imported petroleum was processed at the Assab refinery, the entire output of petroleum products of which was delivered to Ethiopia. In 1997 the Eritrean authorities announced that they would shut down the refinery (owing to high costs) and import refined petroleum for the immediate future. According to the World Bank, the GDP of the manufacturing sector declined, in real terms, at an average annual rate of 9.9% in 2003–09; manufacturing GDP increased by 8.4% in 2011, according to the AfDB.

According to the AfDB, the construction sector provided 16.2% of GDP in 2011; construction GDP increased by 3.2% in 2010 and further by 14.8% in 2011.

Most electric energy is provided by four thermal power stations, which are largely dependent on imported fuel. Imports of fuel and energy comprised an estimated 0.8% of the total cost of imports in 2003. However, electricity is provided to only around 10% of the population, the remainder relying on fuel wood and animal products. The Chinese-funded extension of capacity at the Hirgigo thermal power plant near Massawa was expected to be completed in 2014; the increase in output was expected to help to rectify power-supply problems in the capital, as well as to supply mining operations.

According to the AfDB, the services sector contributed 58.9% of GDP in 2011. The dominant services are trade, public administration and transport. According to the World Bank, the GDP of the services sector increased, in real terms, at an average annual rate of 0.4% in 2003–09; the GDP of the sector remained constant in 2008, but expanded by 4.2% in 2009.

In 2012, according to the AfDB, Eritrea recorded a visible merchandise trade deficit of 2,240m. nakfa, while there was a surplus of 1,021m. nakfa on the current account of the balance of payments. In 2003 the principal sources of non-petroleum imports were the USA (accounting for an estimated 15.9% of the total), the United Arab Emirates, Italy and Saudi Arabia. Exports in that year were mostly to Sudan (which took 19.7% of the total, compared with 83.8% in 2002), Italy, Netherlands and India. Eritrea's principal exports in 2003 were food and live animals, crude materials, basic manufactures, and miscellaneous manufactured articles. The main non-petroleum imports in that year were food and live animals, machinery and transport equipment, and basic manufactures.

In 2009 it was estimated by the AfDB that Eritrea's budget deficit reached 4,585m. nakfa. Eritrea's general government gross debt was 38,872m. nakfa in 2009, equivalent to 135.0% of GDP. Eritrea's external debt at the end of 2011 totalled US $1,055m., of which $1,014m. was public and publicly guaranteed debt. The annual rate of inflation averaged 18.3% in 2003–12. Consumer prices increased by an estimated average of 12.3% in 2012. In 2003 unemployment and underemployment were estimated to affect as many as 50% of the labour force.

Since independence the Eritrean Government has experienced severe difficulties: vast expenditure on the war with Ethiopia, coupled with the failure of successive harvests, increased Eritrea's already considerable reliance on donations from aid organizations, and the need to resettle the huge numbers of people displaced during the war placed a further strain on government finances. The economy remains, to a considerable extent, dependent on remittances from abroad, particularly given its limited holdings of foreign exchange reserves; some of these funds are raised as part of an illicit tax system imposed on the diaspora, even extending to human trafficking activities. The UN Somalia and Eritrea Monitoring Group has recommended sanctions on such taxes in countries with large populations of Eritrean migrants. Since 2008 the Government has allowed some controlled reforms, including the establishment of a free-trade zone in Massawa and the implementation of an automated customs data management system (drawn up by the United Nations Conference on Trade and Development), as well as the pursuit of a privatization programme. The authorities have also invested in infrastructure, including upgrading the ports of Massawa and Assab and the national railway. However, no IMF financial stability assessments have taken place and aid inflow has dwindled. As in various other African countries, Eritrea has been able to draw instead on financing from China and a number of Gulf states. The persistence of hostile relations with two of its neighbouring countries ensures that Eritrea remains an unfavourable investment environment for many other investors; this situation also serves to legitimize the continued diversion of labour and resources to the military. Nevertheless, in recent years economic hopes have centred on the development of large mineral deposits around Bisha and Asmara, as well as on strengthening interdependence with Sudan. Eritrea's first operational mine, at Bisha, entered into production in 2011. The mine produced low-cost gold-silver doré until mid-2013, when it switched to production of copper concentrate; the deposit was also expected to yield zinc. To date, the Bisha mine's operations have been successful overall, although a decline in production in 2012, accompanied by a decrease in international gold prices, was believed adversely to have affected the country's economic growth rate in that year. The Asmara mining project (involving deposits of copper, gold and zinc), undertaken by the Canadian Sunridge Gold Corpn, was scheduled to become operational in 2015, giving the economy further positive prospects. In early 2014 another gold mine was under construction, at Koka, as part of the Zara Gold Project, although its estimated completion date had been deferred to 2015. In 2013 the Government permitted an easing of the restrictions on foreign currency in a bid to counter the country's shortage of foreign exchange. A five-year National Development Plan, which was presented by President Issaias Afewerki in June 2011, focused on expanding the agricultural sector, and measures to develop new and existing infrastructure facilities. The Plan also emphasized the need to promote tourism as a source of revenue. To this end, the first phase of development on one of the Dahlak Islands was completed in 2012, with Qatari funding. Eritrea's economy demonstrated high growth of 7.0% in 2012, although according to World Bank estimates, the rate of growth of GDP was expected to decelerate to 6.0% in 2013, and further, to 3.5%, in 2014.

PUBLIC HOLIDAYS

2015: 1 January (New Year's Day), 2 January*† (Mouloud, Birth of the Prophet), 7 January (Coptic Christmas), 19 January (Coptic Epiphany), 8 March (Women's Day), 1 May (Workers' Day), 24 May (Independence Day), 20 June (Martyrs' Day), 17 July* (Id al-Fitr, end of Ramadan), 1 September (anniversary of the start of the armed struggle), 12 September (Coptic New Year's Day), 23 September* (Id al-Adha/Arafat), 28 September (Feast of the True Cross), 23 December*† (Mouloud, Birth of the Prophet), 25 December (Christmas).

* These holidays are dependent on the Islamic lunar calendar and may vary by one or two days from the dates given.

† This festival occurs twice (in the Islamic years AH 1436 and 1437) within the same Gregorian year.

Statistical Survey

Source (unless otherwise stated): Ministry of Trade and Industry, POB 1844, Asmara; tel. (1) 126155; fax (1) 120586.

Area and Population

AREA, POPULATION AND DENSITY*

Area (sq km)	121,144†
Population (census results)	
9 May 1984	
Males	1,374,452
Females	1,373,852
Total	2,748,304
Population (UN estimates at mid-year)‡	
2012	6,130,922
2013	6,333,139
2014	6,536,172
Density (per sq km) at mid-2014	54.0

* Including the Assab district.

† 46,774 sq miles.

‡ Source: UN, *World Population Prospects: The 2012 Revision*.

POPULATION BY AGE AND SEX

(UN estimates at mid-2014)

	Males	Females	Total
0–14	1,438,706	1,378,758	2,817,464
15–64	1,765,400	1,803,595	3,568,995
65 and over	59,020	90,693	149,713
Total	3,263,126	3,273,046	6,536,172

Source: UN, *World Population Prospects: The 2012 Revision*.

PRINCIPAL TOWNS

(estimated population at January 2013)

Asmara (capital)	712,882	Keren	84,512
Assab	104,075	Mitsiwa (Massawa)	54,715

BIRTHS AND DEATHS
(averages per year, UN estimates)

	1995–2000	2000–05	2005–10
Birth rate (per 1,000)	40.0	40.1	39.4
Death rate (per 1,000)	10.5	8.9	8.0

Source: UN, *World Population Prospects: The 2012 Revision*.

Life expectancy (years at birth): 61.7 (males 59.4; females 64.1) in 2011 (Source: World Bank, World Development Indicators database).

ECONOMICALLY ACTIVE POPULATION
('000, FAO estimates at mid-year)

	2012	2013	2014
Agriculture, etc.	1,634	1,680	1,726
Total labour force (incl. others)	2,236	2,310	2,385

Source: FAO.

Health and Welfare

KEY INDICATORS

Total fertility rate (children per woman, 2011)	4.4
Under-5 mortality rate (per 1,000 live births, 2011)	68
HIV/AIDS (% of persons aged 15–49, 2012)	0.7
Hospital beds (per 1,000 head, 2006)	1.2
Physicians (per 1,000 head, 2004)	0.05
Health expenditure (2010): US $ per head (PPP)	17
Health expenditure (2010): % of GDP	2.9
Health expenditure (2010): public (% of total)	45.2
Access to water (% of persons, 2008)	61
Access to sanitation (% of persons, 2008)	14
Total carbon dioxide emissions ('000 metric tons, 2010)	513.4
Carbon dioxide emissions per head (metric tons, 2010)	0.1
Human Development Index (2012): ranking	181
Human Development Index (2012): value	0.351

For sources and definitions, see explanatory note on p. vi.

Agriculture

PRINCIPAL CROPS
('000 metric tons, FAO estimates)

	2010	2011	2012
Wheat	32.7	28.8	33.0
Barley	67.0	65.3	70.0
Maize	18.0	20.0	22.0
Millet	17.2	19.7	20.0
Sorghum	63.7	75.0	80.0
Potatoes	0.2	0.1	0.2
Broad beans, horse beans, dry	0.1	0.1	0.1
Peas, dry	2.0	2.0	2.0
Chick-peas	6.3	7.2	7.2
Lentils	0.8	0.5	0.5
Vetches	2.4	2.3	2.3
Groundnuts, with shell	1.6	1.7	1.8
Sesame seed	0.2	0.2	0.2

Aggregate production ('000 metric tons, may include official, semi-official or estimated data): Total cereals 243.6 in 2010, 258.1 in 2011, 275.0 in 2012; Total roots and tubers 65.2 in 2010, 64.1 in 2011, 62.2 in 2012; Total vegetables (incl. melons) 55.8 in 2010, 52.5 in 2011, 55.0 in 2012.

Source: FAO.

LIVESTOCK
('000 head, year ending September, FAO estimates)

	2010	2011	2012
Cattle	2,057	2,065	2,070
Sheep	2,272	2,281	2,285
Goats	1,750	1,760	1,770
Camels	345	350	360
Chickens	1,250	1,300	1,350

Source: FAO.

LIVESTOCK PRODUCTS
('000 metric tons, FAO estimates)

	2010	2011	2012
Cattle meat	23.3	23.8	24.0
Sheep meat	6.4	6.4	6.5
Goat meat	6.0	6.0	6.0
Chicken meat	1.7	1.7	1.7
Camels' milk	23.1	23.5	23.8
Cows' milk	105.3	106.5	108.0
Goats' milk	9.1	9.2	9.2
Sheep's milk	5.7	5.7	5.8
Hen eggs	2.2	2.2	2.3
Wool, greasy	1.2	1.2	1.2

Source: FAO.

Fishing

(metric tons, live weight of capture)

	2009	2010	2011
Requiem sharks	165	307	281
Sea catfishes	42	128	106
Threadfin breams	62	165	159
Snappers and jobfishes	75	58	51
Narrow-barred Spanish mackerel	573	414	480
Tuna-like fishes	640	423	301
Barracudas	78	69	65
Carangids	79	109	100
Queenfishes	185	176	65
Penaeus shrimps	219	323	119
Total catch (incl. others)	3,030	3,286	2,639

Source: FAO.

Mining

('000 metric tons unless otherwise indicated)

	2009	2010	2011
Gold (kilograms)	30.0*	50.0	11,800
Marble ('000 sq m)*	32.0	36.0	36.0
Limestone*	3.0	3.0	3.0
Salt*	7.5	7.8	7.8
Granite*	25.0	25.0	25.0

* Estimate(s).

Source: US Geological Survey.

Industry

SELECTED PRODUCTS
('000 metric tons, unless otherwise indicated, estimates)

	2009	2010	2011
Cement	45.0	45.0	230.0
Basalt	45.0	50.0	50.0
Gravel	78.0	80.0	80.0
Coral	60.0	58.0	58.0
Electric energy (million kWh)	295	311	n.a.

Sources: US Geological Survey; UN Industrial Commodity Statistics Database.

Finance

CURRENCY AND EXCHANGE RATES

Monetary Units
100 cents = 1 nakfa.

Sterling, Dollar and Euro Equivalents (31 December 2013)
£1 sterling = 25.320 nakfa;
US $1 = 15.375 nakfa;
€1 = 21.204 nakfa;
1,000 nakfa = £39.50 = $65.04 = €47.16.

Note: Following its secession from Ethiopia in May 1993, Eritrea retained the Ethiopian currency, the birr. An exchange rate of US $1 = 5.000 birr was introduced in October 1992 and remained in force until April 1994, when it was adjusted to $1 = 5.130 birr. Further adjustments were made subsequently. In November 1997 the Government introduced a separate national currency, the nakfa, replacing (and initially at par with) the Ethiopian birr. The exchange rate in relation to the US dollar was initially set at the prevailing unified rate, but from 1 May 1998 a mechanism to provide a market-related exchange rate was established.

Average Exchange Rate (nakfa per US $)
2011 15.3750
2012 15.3750
2013 15.3750

BUDGET
(million nakfa)

Revenue*	2007	2008†	2009‡
Tax revenue	2,405	2,459	2,374
Direct taxes	1,512	1,719	1,580
Indirect domestic taxes	487	395	435
Import duties and taxes	406	345	360
Non-tax revenue	1,888	1,393	1,401
Total	4,293	3,853	3,775

Expenditure§	2007	2008†	2009‡
Current expenditure	5,900	6,905	6,824
Wages, salaries and allowances	2,234	2,275	2,430
Materials and services	2,316	2,531	2,398
Subsidies and transfers	706	1,311	931
Interest	644	788	1,065
Domestic	571	648	853
External	73	140	212
Capital expenditure	2,224	2,331	2,134
Central treasury	1,012	704	681
Externally financed	1,203	1,627	1,453
Total	8,124	9,236	8,958

* Excluding grants received (million nakfa): 628 in 2007; 604 in 2008 (estimate); 737 in 2009 (projected).
† Estimates.
‡ Projections.
§ Excluding net lending (million nakfa): –95 in 2007; 608 in 2008 (estimate); 139 in 2009 (projected).

Source: African Development Bank, *Interim Country Strategy Paper for Eritrea* (2009–11).

INTERNATIONAL RESERVES
(US $ million at 31 December)

	1999	2000	2001
Gold (national valuation)	19.7	10.4	10.5
Reserve position in IMF	0.0	0.0	0.0
Foreign exchange	34.2	25.5	39.7
Total	53.9	35.9	50.3

Foreign exchange: 84.3 in 2009; 108.6 in 2010; 109.3 in 2011.

IMF special drawing rights: 5.6 in 2010; 5.5 in 2011; 5.5 in 2012.

Source: IMF, *International Financial Statistics*.

MONEY SUPPLY
(million nakfa at 31 December)

	2009	2010	2011
Currency outside depository corporations	6,637	8,155	9,959
Transferable deposits	10,655	11,554	12,398
Other deposits	17,397	20,388	23,635
Broad money	34,689	40,097	45,992

Source: IMF, *International Financial Statistics*.

COST OF LIVING
(Consumer Price Index; base: 2000 = 100)

	2010	2011	2012
All items	523.1	592.9	665.5

Source: African Development Bank.

NATIONAL ACCOUNTS
(million nakfa at current prices)

Expenditure on the Gross Domestic Product

	2009	2010	2011
Private final consumption expenditure	25,561	27,790	31,169
Government final consumption expenditure	5,741	7,773	8,451
Gross capital formation	2,645	3,027	4,009
Total domestic expenditure	33,947	38,590	43,629
Exports of goods and services	1,293	1,559	5,764
Less Imports of goods and services	6,692	7,599	9,283
GDP in purchasers' values	28,547	32,549	40,109

Gross Domestic Product by Economic Activity

	2009	2010	2011
Agriculture, forestry and fishing	4,032	5,985	6,590
Mining and quarrying	471	541	704
Manufacturing	1,568	1,897	2,386
Construction	4,190	4,824	6,275
Wholesale and retail trade	5,667	5,880	7,402
Transport and communications	3,629	3,766	4,741
Public administration and defence	8,195	8,498	10,698
Sub-total	27,752	31,391	38,795
Indirect taxes (net)	795	1,158	1,314
GDP in purchasers' values	28,547	32,549	40,109

Source: African Development Bank.

BALANCE OF PAYMENTS
(US $ million)

	2000	2001*	2002†
Exports of goods f.o.b.	36.7	19.9	51.8
Imports of goods c.i.f.	−470.3	−536.7	−533.4
Trade balance	−433.5	−516.7	−481.7
Exports of services	60.7	127.5	132.6
Imports of services	−28.3	−33.4	−30.3
Balance on goods and services	−401.1	−422.6	−379.4
Other income (net)	−1.4	−4.6	−6.1
Balance on goods, services and income	−402.5	−427.2	−385.5
Private unrequited transfers (net)	195.7	175.0	205.6
Official unrequited transfers (net)	102.4	120.8	80.3
Current balance	−104.5	−131.4	−99.6
Capital account (net)	—	7.3	3.6
Financial account	98.7	94.8	64.6
Short-term capital (net)	−14.7	18.7	15.9
Net errors and omissions	−9.5	36.5	−7.6
Overall balance	−15.2	7.2	−39.0

* Preliminary figures.
† Estimates.

Source: IMF, *Eritrea: Selected Issues and Statistical Appendix* (June 2003).

2012 (Nakfa million): Trade balance –2,240; Services (net) 431; Income (net) –622; Current transfers (net) 3,451; *Current account*1,021 (Source: African Development Bank).

External Trade

PRINCIPAL COMMODITIES
(distribution by SITC, US $ '000)

Imports c.i.f. (excl. petroleum)	2001	2002	2003
Food and live animals	110.9	153.0	175.2
Animal and vegetable oils, fats and waxes	13.6	7.4	19.3
Chemicals and related products	45.5	36.4	26.2
Basic manufactures	101.5	115.6	63.3
Machinery and transport equipment	107.4	155.9	97.2
Miscellaneous manufactured articles	34.0	46.9	40.7
Total (incl. others)	422.9	537.9	432.8

Exports f.o.b.	2001	2002	2003
Food and live animals	8.8	37.7	2.4
Crude materials (inedible) except fuels	3.0	6.0	2.1
Chemicals and related products	0.7	0.6	0.1
Basic manufactures	5.6	4.8	1.1
Miscellaneous manufactured articles	0.5	1.5	0.7
Total (incl. others)	19.0	51.8	6.6

Source: UN, *International Trade Statistics Yearbook*.

PRINCIPAL TRADING PARTNERS
(US $ million)

Imports c.i.f.	2001	2002	2003
Belgium	11.9	13.7	8.6
Germany	11.8	16.4	6.7
Italy	79.0	70.4	50.1
Netherlands	13.9	17.4	10.4
Saudi Arabia	70.0	70.0	45.4
United Arab Emirates	64.6	90.7	52.9
United Kingdom	9.6	10.0	11.7
USA	20.4	38.5	68.9
Total (incl. others)	422.9	537.9	432.8

Exports f.o.b.	2001	2002	2003
Djibouti	—	0.8	—
Germany	0.7	0.5	0.1
India	3.2	0.5	0.5
Italy	2.1	1.8	0.8
Netherlands	0.4	0.3	0.7
Saudi Arabia	0.3	0.1	—
Sudan	9.7	43.4	1.3
Total (incl. others)	19.0	51.8	6.6

Source: UN, *International Trade Statistics Yearbook*.

Transport

ROAD TRAFFIC
(motor vehicles in use)

	1996	1997	1998
Number of registered vehicles	27,013	31,276	35,942

2007 (vehicles registered at 31 December): Passenger cars 31,033; Buses and coaches 1,825; Vans and lorries 22,514; Motorcycles and mopeds 3,042 (Source: IRF, *World Road Statistics*).

SHIPPING

Flag Registered Fleet
(at 31 December)

	2011	2012	2013
Number of vessels	17	17	17
Total displacement ('000 grt)	14	14	14

Source: Lloyd's List Intelligence (www.lloydslistintelligence.com).

CIVIL AVIATION

	1996	1997	1998
Passengers ('000)	168.1	173.8	105.2

Tourism

ARRIVALS BY COUNTRY OF ORIGIN

	2009	2010	2011
Germany	775	880	1,004
India	718	730	577
Italy	1,944	1,754	1,694
Japan	151	60	78
Kenya	234	247	343
Sudan	5,866	6,220	19,653
United Kingdom	843	703	968
USA	511	738	831
Total (incl. others)	79,334	83,947	107,090

Tourism receipts (US $ million, excl. passenger transport): 26 in 2009.

Source: World Tourism Organization.

Communications Media

	2010	2011	2012
Telephones ('000 main lines in use)	54.2	58.0	60.1
Mobile cellular telephones ('000 subscribers)	185.3	241.9	305.3
Internet subscribers ('000)	7.1	7.3	n.a.
Broadband subscribers	118	141	125

Source: International Telecommunication Union.

Education

(2011/12 unless otherwise indicated)

	Institutions*	Teachers	Pupils
Pre-primary	95	1,296	45,973
Primary	695	8,166	334,245
Secondary: General	44	6,721	263,080
Secondary: Teacher-training	2	47*	922*
Secondary: Vocational	n.a.	289	2,520
University and equivalent level†	n.a.	634	10,198

* 2001/02 figure(s).
† 2009/10 figures.

Sources: UNESCO Institute for Statistics; Ministry of Education, Asmara.

Pupil-teacher ratio (primary education, UNESCO estimate): 40.9 in 2011/12 (Source: UNESCO Institute for Statistics).

Adult literacy rate (UNESCO estimates): 68.9% (males 79.5%; females 59.0%) in 2011 (Source: UNESCO Institute for Statistics).

Directory

The Government

HEAD OF STATE

President: ISSAIAS AFEWERKI (assumed power May 1991; elected President by the National Assembly 8 June 1993).

CABINET
(April 2014)

The Government is formed by the People's Front for Democracy and Justice.

President: ISSAIAS AFEWERKI.

Minister of Defence: Gen. SEBHAT EPHREM.

Minister of Justice: FAWZIA HASHIM.

Minister of Foreign Affairs: OSMAN SALIH MUHAMMAD.

Minister of Information: (vacant).

Minister of Finance: BERHANE ABREHE.

Minister of Trade and Industry: ESTIFANOS HABTE.

Minister of Agriculture: AREFAINE BERHE.

Minister of Labour and Human Welfare: SALMA HASSEN.

Minister of Marine Resources: TEWOLDE KELATI.

Minister of Public Works: ABRAHA ASFAHA.

Minister of Energy and Mines: AHMED HAJJ ALI.

Minister of Education: SEMERE RUSOM.

Minister of Health: AMINA NURHUSSEIN.

Minister of Transport and Communications: WOLDEMIKAEL ABRAHA.

Minister of Tourism: ASKALU MENKERIOS.

Minister of Land, Water and the Environment: TESFAI GHEBRESELASSIE SEBHATU.

Minister of Local Government: (vacant).

MINISTRIES

Office of the President: POB 257, Asmara; tel. (1) 122132; fax (1) 125123.

Ministry of Agriculture: POB 1048, Asmara; tel. (1) 181499; fax (1) 181415.

Ministry of Defence: POB 629, Asmara; tel. (1) 165952; fax (1) 124990.

Ministry of Education: POB 5610, Asmara; tel. (1) 113044; fax (1) 113866; internet www.erimoe.gov.er.

Ministry of Energy and Mines: POB 5285, Asmara; tel. (1) 116872; fax (1) 127652; internet www.moem.gov.er.

Ministry of Finance: POB 896, Asmara; tel. (1) 118131; fax (1) 127947.

Ministry of Foreign Affairs: POB 190, Asmara; tel. (1) 127838; fax (1) 123788; e-mail tesfai@wg.eol.

Ministry of Health: POB 212, Asmara; tel. (1) 117549; fax (1) 112899.

Ministry of Information: POB 872, Asmara; tel. (1) 120478; fax (1) 126747; internet www.shabait.com.

Ministry of Justice: POB 241, Asmara; tel. (1) 127739; fax (1) 126422.

Ministry of Labour and Human Welfare: POB 5252, Asmara; tel. (1) 181846; fax (1) 181760; e-mail mlhw@eol.com.er.

Ministry of Land, Water and the Environment: POB 976, Asmara; tel. (1) 118021; fax (1) 123285.

Ministry of Local Government: POB 225, Asmara; tel. (1) 114254; fax (1) 120014.

Ministry of Marine Resources: POB 923, Asmara; tel. (1) 120400; fax (1) 122185; e-mail mofisha@eol.com.er; f. 1994.

Ministry of Public Works: POB 841, Asmara; tel. (1) 120302; fax (1) 120661.

Ministry of Tourism: POB 1010, Warsay Ave, Dembe Sembel (Green Building), Asmara; tel. (1) 154100; fax (1) 154081; e-mail eritreantourism@tse.com.er.

Ministry of Trade and Industry: POB 1844, Asmara; tel. (1) 120080; fax (1) 120586; e-mail berhanem69@yahoo.co.uk.

Ministry of Transport and Communications: POB 1840, Asmara; tel. (1) 114222; fax (1) 127048; e-mail motc.rez@eol.com.er.

Provincial Administrators

There are six administrative regions in Eritrea, each with regional, sub-regional and village administrations.

Anseba Province: GEGRGIS GHIRMAI.

Debub Province: MUSTAFA NUR HUSSEIN.

Debubawi Keyih Bahri Province: OSMAN MOHAMED OMAR.

Gash-Barka Province: KAHSAI GHEBREHIWOT.

Maakel Province: TEWELDE KELATI.

Semenawi Keyih Bahri Province: TSIGEREDA WOLDEGERGISH.

Legislature

NATIONAL ASSEMBLY

The National Assembly comprises the 75 members of the Central Committee of the People's Front for Democracy and Justice (PFDJ) and 75 directly elected members. In May 1997, following the adoption of the Constitution, the Constituent Assembly empowered a Transitional National Assembly (comprising the 75 members of the PFDJ, 60 members of the former Constituent Assembly and 15 representatives of Eritreans residing abroad) to act as the legislature until elections were held for a new National Assembly. As at March 2014, no such elections had taken place. In his role as Head of the Government and Commander-in-Chief of the Army, the President nominates individuals to head the various government departments. These nominations are ratified by the legislative body.

Chairman of the Transitional National Assembly: ISSAIAS AFEWERKI.

Election Commission

Election Commission: Asmara; f. 2002; five mems appointed by the President; Commissioner RAMADAN MOHAMMED NUR.

Political Organizations

Afar Federal Alliance: e-mail afa_f@hotmail.com; f. 2003.

Democratic Movement for the Liberation of Eritrean Kunama: Postfach 620 124, 50694, Köln, Germany; e-mail kcs@baden-kunama.com; internet www.baden-kunama.com; based in Germany; represents the Kunama minority ethnic group.

Eritrean Democratic Alliance (EDA): internet www.erit-alliance.com; f. 1999 as the Alliance of Eritrean National Forces, became Eritrean National Alliance in 2002, adopted present name in 2004; broad alliance of 13 parties opposed to PFDJ regime; Chair. BERHANE YEMANE 'HANJEMA'; Sec.-Gen. HUSAYN KHALIFA.

Eritrean Democratic Party (EDP): e-mail info@selfi-democracy.com; internet www.selfi-democracy.com; f. 2001 as the Eritrean People's Liberation Front—Democratic Party (EPLF—DP); breakaway group from the PFDJ; name changed to above in 2004; Chair. MESFIN HAGOS.

Eritrean Islamic Jihad (EIJ): radical opposition group; in Aug. 1993 split into a military wing and a political wing.

Eritrean Islamic Party for Justice and Development (EIPJD) (Al-Hizb Al-Islami Al-Eritree Liladalah Wetenmiya): internet www.alkhalas.org; f. 1988 as Eritrean Islamic Jihad Movement; changed name to al-Khalas in 1998; political wing of EIJ; Leader KHALIL MUHAMMAD AMER.

Eritrean Liberation Front (ELF): f. 1958; commenced armed struggle against Ethiopia in 1961; subsequently split into numerous factions (see below); mainly Muslim support; opposes the PFDJ; principal factions:

Eritrean Liberation Front—Central Command (ELF—CC): f. 1982; Chair. ABDALLAH IDRISS.

Eritrean Liberation Front—National Council (ELF—NC): Leader Dr BEYENE KIDANE.

Eritrean Liberation Front—Revolutionary Council (ELF—RC): Chair. AHMED WOLDEYESUS AMMAR.

Eritrean People's Democratic Front (EPDF): internet www.democrasia.org; f. 2004 by merger of People's Democratic Front for the Liberation of Eritrea and a faction of ERDF; Leader TEWOLDE GEBRESELASSIE.

Eritrean Popular Movement (EPM): f. 2004; Leader ABDALLAH ADEM.

Eritrean Revolutionary Democratic Front (ERDF): e-mail webmaster@eritreana.com; internet www.eritreana.com; f. 1997 following merger of Democratic Movement for the Liberation of Eritrea and a faction of People's Democratic Front for the Liberation of Eritrea; Leader BERHANE YEMANE 'HANJEMA'.

Gash Setit Organization: Leader ISMAIL NADA.

People's Front for Democracy and Justice (PFDJ): POB 1081, Asmara; tel. (1) 121399; fax (1) 120848; e-mail webmaster@shaebia.org; internet www.shaebia.org; f. 1970 as the Eritrean Popular Liberation Forces, following a split in the Eritrean Liberation Front; renamed the Eritrean People's Liberation Front in 1977; adopted present name in Feb. 1994; Christian and Muslim support; in May 1991 took control of Eritrea and formed provisional Govt; formed transitional Govt in May 1993; Chair. ISSAIAS AFEWERKI; Sec.-Gen. ALAMIN MOHAMED SAID.

Red Sea Afar Democratic Organization: Afar opposition group; Sec.-Gen. IBRAHIM HAROUN.

Diplomatic Representation

EMBASSIES IN ERITREA

China, People's Republic: 16 Ogaden St, POB 204, Asmara; tel. and fax (1) 185271; fax (1) 189361; e-mail chinaemb_er@mfa.gov.cn; internet er.china-embassy.org/chn; Ambassador NIU QIANG.

Djibouti: POB 5589, Asmara; tel. (1) 354961; fax (1) 351831; Ambassador AHMAD ISSA (recalled in June 2008).

Egypt: 5 Marsa Fatma St, POB 5570, Asmara; tel. and fax (1) 124935; fax (1) 123294; e-mail amb.egy.asmara@gmail.com; Ambassador MAHMOUD NAYEL.

France: 25 Nakfa St, POB 209, Asmara; tel. (1) 125196; fax (1) 123288; e-mail cad.asmara@diplomatie.gouv.fr; internet www.ambafrance-er.org; Ambassador STÉPHANE GRUENBERG.

Germany: SABA Building, 8th Floor, Warsay St, POB 4974, Asmara; tel. (1) 186670; fax (1) 186900; e-mail info@asmara.diplo.de; internet www.asmara.diplo.de; Ambassador VIKTOR RICHTER.

Iran: Asmara; Ambassador REZA AMERI.

Israel: 32 Abo St, POB 5600, Asmara; tel. (1) 188521; fax (1) 188550; e-mail info@asmara.mfa.gov.il; Ambassador ELIE ANTEBI.

Italy: 11 171–1 St, POB 220, Asmara; tel. (1) 120160; fax (1) 121115; e-mail ambasciata.asmara@esteri.it; internet www.ambasmara.esteri.it; Ambassador MARCELLO FONDI.

Libya: 9 Shelalo St, POB 2153, Asmara; tel. (1) 127514; fax (1) 127989; Chargé d'affaires a. i. Dr AL-HASAN ALI.

Russia: 21 Zobel St, POB 5667, Asmara; tel. (1) 127162; fax (1) 127164; e-mail rusemb@eol.com.er; Ambassador IGOR NIKOLAVIC CHUBAROV.

Saudi Arabia: 748 Ras Demaira St, Asmara; tel. (1) 154318; fax (1) 154321; e-mail eremb@mofa.gov.sa; Ambassador NASSER ALI AL-HOTI.

South Africa: 51–53 Hitseito St 245, Tiravalo, POB 11447, Asmara; tel. (1) 152521; fax (1) 153072; e-mail saemb_asma@yahoo.com; Ambassador MAHOMED IQBAL DAWOOD JHAZBHAY.

Sudan: 246 Hitseito St, Asmara; tel. (1) 202072; fax (1) 200760; e-mail sudanemb@eol.com.er; Ambassador SALAH MOHAMED AL-HASSAN.

United Kingdom: 66–68 Mariam Ghimbi St, POB 5584, Asmara; tel. (1) 120145; fax (1) 120104; e-mail asmara.enquiries@fco.gov.uk; internet www.ukineritrea.fco.gov.uk; Ambassador AMANDA SUSANNAH TANFIELD.

USA: 179 Ala St, POB 211, Asmara; tel. (1) 120004; fax (1) 127584; e-mail usembassyasmara@state.gov; internet eritrea.usembassy.gov; Chargé d'affaires a.i. SUE BREMNER.

Yemen: POB 5566, Asmara; tel. (1) 114434; fax (1) 117921; Ambassador Dr ABDELKADIR MOHAMMED HADI.

Judicial System

The judicial system operates on the basis of transitional laws, which incorporate pre-independence laws of the Eritrean People's Liberation Front, revised Ethiopian laws, customary laws and post-independence enacted laws. The independence of the judiciary in the discharge of its functions is unequivocally stated in Decree No. 37, which defines the powers and duties of the Government. It is subject only to the law and to no other authority. The court structure is composed of first instance sub-zonal courts, appellate and first instance zonal courts, appellate and first instance high courts, a panel of high court judges, presided over by the President of the High Court, and a Supreme Court presided over by the Chief Justice, as a court of last resort. The judges of the Supreme Court are appointed by the President of the State, subject to confirmation by the National Assembly.

Supreme Court: Asmara.

High Court: POB 241, Asmara; tel. (1) 127739; fax (1) 201828; e-mail prshict@eol.com.er; Pres. MENKERIOS BERAKI.

Attorney-General: ALEMSEGED HABTESELLASIE.

Religion

Eritrea is almost equally divided between Muslims and Christians. Most Christians are adherents of the Orthodox Church, although there are Protestant and Roman Catholic communities. A small number of the population follow traditional beliefs.

CHRISTIANITY

The Eritrean Orthodox Church

In September 1993 the separation of the Eritrean Orthodox Church from the Ethiopian Orthodox Church was agreed by the respective church leaderships. The Eritrean Orthodox Church announced that it was to create a diocese of each of the country's then 10 provinces. The first five bishops of the Eritrean Orthodox Church were consecrated in Cairo, Egypt, in September 1994. In May 1998 Eritrea's first Patriarch (Abune) was consecrated in Alexandria, Egypt. In January 2006 Eritrea's third Patriarch, Abune Antonios I (who had been under house arrest since August 2005), was deposed by the Holy Synod.

Patriarch (Abune): DIOSKOROS.

The Roman Catholic Church

An estimated 3% of the total population are Roman Catholics.

Bishop of Asmara: Rt Rev. ABBA MENGHISTEAB TESFAMARIAM, 19 Gonder St, POB 244, Asmara; tel. (1) 120206; fax (1) 126519; e-mail kimehret@gemel.com.er.

Bishop of Barentu: Rt Rev. THOMAS OSMAN, POB 9, Barentu; tel. and fax (1) 127283.

Bishop of Keren: Rt Rev. KIDANE YEBIO, POB 460, Keren; tel. (1) 401907; fax (1) 401604; e-mail cek@tse.com.er.

The Anglican Communion

Within the Episcopal Church in Jerusalem and the Middle East, Eritrea lies within the jurisdiction of the Bishop in Egypt.

Leader: ASFAHA MAHARY.

ISLAM

Eritrea's main Muslim communities are concentrated in the western lowlands, the northern highlands and the eastern coastal region.

Leader: Sheikh AL-AMIN OSMAN AL-AMIN.

The Press

There is no independent press in Eritrea.

Chamber News: POB 856, Asmara; tel. (1) 120045; fax (1) 120138; monthly; Tigrinya, Arabic and English; publ. by Asmara Chamber of Commerce.

Eritrea Alhaditha: Asmara; tel. (1) 127099; e-mail alhadisa@zena.gov.er; Arabic; publ. by the Ministry of Information; Editor-in-Chief MOHAMMEDNUR YAHYA.

Eritrea Haddas: Asmara; tel. (1) 201820; Tigrinya; govt publ; Editor-in-Chief MOHAMMED IDRIS MOHAMMED.

Eritrea Profile: POB 247, Asmara; tel. (1) 114114; fax (1) 127749; e-mail eritreaprofile@yahoo.com; internet www.shabait.com; f. 1994; twice-weekly; English; publ. by the Ministry of Information; Man. Dir AZZAZI ZEREMARIAM; Editor AMANUEL MESFUN (acting).

Haddas Ertra (New Eritrea): Asmara; tel. (1) 116266; fax (1) 127749; f. 1991; six times a week; Tigrinya; govt publ; Editor SAMSOM HAILE; circ. 49,200.

Newsletter: POB 856, Asmara; tel. (1) 121589; fax (1) 120138; e-mail encc@aol.com.er; monthly; Tigrinya, Arabic and English; publ. by Eritrean National Chamber of Commerce; Editor MOHAMMED-SFAF HAMMED.

Broadcasting and Communications

TELECOMMUNICATIONS

Eritrea Telecommunication Services Corpn (EriTel): 11 Semaetat St, POB 234, Asmara; tel. (1) 124655; fax (1) 120938; e-mail eritel@tse.com.er; internet www.eritel.com.er; f. 1991; public enterprise; operates fixed-line and mobile cellular networks and internet services; Gen. Man. TESFASELASSIE BERHANE.

TFanus: 46 Daniel Comboni Street, POB 724, Asmara; tel. (1) 202590; fax (1) 126457; e-mail support@tfanus.com.er; internet www.tfanus.com.er; f. 1996; internet service provider.

Regulatory Authority

Ministry of Transport and Communications (Communications Department): POB 4918, Asmara; tel. (1) 115847; fax (1) 126966; e-mail motc.rez@eol.com.er; Dir-Gen. MEKONNEN FISSEHAZION.

BROADCASTING

Radio

Voice of the Broad Masses of Eritrea (Dimtsi Hafash): POB 242, Asmara; tel. (1) 120426; fax (1) 126747; govt-controlled; programmes in Arabic, Tigrinya, Tigre, Saho, Oromo, Amharic, Afar, Bilien, Nara, Hedareb and Kunama; Dir-Gen. GHIRMAY BERHE; Technical Dir BERHANE GEREZGIHER.

Voice of Liberty: Asmara; e-mail VoL@selfi-democracy.com; internet selfi-democracy.com; radio programme of the EDP; broadcasts for one hour twice a week.

Television

ERI-TV: Asmara; tel. (1) 116033; e-mail aslmelashe@yahoo.com; internet www.eri.tv; f. 1992; govt station providing educational, tech., entertainment and information services through three channels; broadcasting began in 1993; programming in Arabic, English, Tigre and Tigrinya; broadcasts for eight hours daily; Dir-Gen. ASMELASH ABRAHA.

Finance

(cap. = capital; res = reserves; dep. = deposits; m. = million; brs = branches; amounts in nakfa)

In November 1997 Eritrea adopted the nakfa as its unit of currency, replacing the Ethiopian birr, which had been Eritrea's monetary unit since independence.

BANKING

Central Bank

Bank of Eritrea: 21 Nakfa St 175, POB 849, Asmara; tel. (1) 123033; fax (1) 122091; e-mail kibreabw@boe.gov.er; f. 1993; bank of issue; Gov. KIBREAB W. MARIAM (acting).

Other Banks

Commercial Bank of Eritrea: 208 Liberty Ave, POB 219, Asmara; tel. (1) 121844; fax (1) 124887; e-mail gm.cber@gemel.com.er; f. 1991; cap. 400.0m., res 344.5m., dep. 13,791.6m. (Dec. 2004); Chair. BERHANE ABREHE; Gen. Man. YEMANE TESFAY; 15 brs.

Eritrean Development and Investment Bank: 29 Bedho St, POB 1266, Asmara; tel. (1) 126777; fax (1) 201976; f. 1996; cap. 45m., total assets 194.2m. (Dec. 2003); provides medium- to long-term credit; Chair. HABTEAB TESFATSION; Gen. Man. Dr GOITOM W. MARIAM; 4 brs.

Housing and Commerce Bank of Eritrea: POB 235, Bahti Meskerem Sq., Asmara; tel. (1) 120350; fax (1) 202209; e-mail hcbgm@hcbe.com.er; internet erhcb.com; f. 1994; cap. 293m. (Dec. 2006); finances residential and commercial construction projects and commercial loans; Chair. HAGOS GHEBREHIWET; Gen. Man. BERHANE GHEBREHIWET; 10 brs.

INSURANCE

National Insurance Corporation of Eritrea Share Co (NICE): NICE Bldg, 171 Bidho Ave, POB 881, Asmara; tel. (1) 123000; fax (1) 123240; e-mail nice@nice-eritrea.com; internet www.nice-eritrea.com; f. 1992; partially privatized in 2004; 60% govt-owned; general and life; Chair. GIRMAI ABRAHA; Gen. Man. ZERU WOLDEMICHAEL.

Trade and Industry

DEVELOPMENT ORGANIZATION

Eritrea Free Zones Authority: Asmara; f. 2001; CEO ARAIA TSEGGAI.

CHAMBER OF COMMERCE

Eritrean National Chamber of Commerce: POB 856, Asmara; tel. (1) 121589; fax (1) 120138; e-mail encc@gemel.com.er.

TRADE ASSOCIATION

Red Sea Trading Corporation: 29/31 Ras Alula St, POB 332, Asmara; tel. (1) 127846; fax (1) 124353; f. 1983; import and export services; operated by the PFDJ; Gen. Man. NEGASH AFWORKI.

UTILITIES

Electricity

Eritrean Electricity Corporation (EEC): POB 911, Asmara; fax (1) 121468; e-mail eeahrg@eol.com.er; Gen. Man. ABRAHAM WOLDEMICHAEL.

Water

Dept of Water Resources: POB 1488, Asmara; tel. (1) 119636; fax (1) 124625; e-mail wrdmlwe@eol.com.er; f. 1992; Dir-Gen. MEBRAHTU EYASSU.

MAJOR COMPANIES

Exploration activities have identified reserves of base and precious metals. About 20 mining companies were involved in mineral exploration in different areas in the early 2010s.

Assab Salt Works: Assab; salt.

Bisha Mining Co.: 1 Mariam Gimby, POB 4276, Asmara; tel. (1) 124941; internet www.bishamining.com; gold and silver; Gen. Man. KEVIN MOXHAM.

Gedem Cement Factory: Massawa; cement.

Margran PLC: POB 1105, Bahti Meskerem; tel. (1) 125004; fax (1) 122395; e-mail margran@eol.com.er; granite.

TRADE UNION

National Confederation of Eritrean Workers (NCEW): Asmara; f. 1979; Sec.-Gen. TEKESTE BAIRE.

Transport

Eritrea's transport infrastructure was severely damaged during the three decades of war prior to independence. International creditors have since provided loans for the repair and reconstruction of the road network and for the improvement of port facilities.

RAILWAYS

The 306-km railway connection between Agordat, Asmara and the port of Massawa was severely damaged during the war of independence and ceased operations in 1975. However, in 1999 an 81-km section of the Asmara–Massawa line (between Massawa and Embatkala) became operational, and in 2001 a further 18-km section, connecting Embatkala and Ghinda, was added. In February 2003 the reconstruction of the entire Asmara–Massawa line was completed. In 2007 work started on the reconstruction of the 124-km railway line west of Asmara to Akordat and Bisha, with the aim of eventually constructing a new international link from Bisha to Kassala, Sudan.

Eritrean Railway: POB 6081, Asmara; tel. (1) 123365; fax (1) 201785; Co-ordinator, Railways Rehabilitation Project AMANUEL GEBRESELLASIE.

ROADS

Eritrea has a long road network for its land base, totalling 18,540 km. Roads that are paved require considerable repair, as do many of the bridges across seasonal water courses destroyed in the war. The programme to rehabilitate the road between Asmara and the port of Massawa was completed in 2000.

SHIPPING

Eritrea has two major seaports: Massawa, which sustained heavy war damage in 1990, and Assab, which has principally served Addis Ababa, in Ethiopia. Under an accord signed between the Ethiopian and Eritrean Governments in 1993, the two countries agreed to share the facilities of both ports. Since independence, activity in Massawa has increased substantially; however, activity at Assab declined following the outbreak of hostilities with Ethiopia in May 1998. At 31 December 2013 Eritrea's flag registered fleet numbered 17 vessels, with a total displacement of 14,009 grt.

Dept of Maritime Transport: POB 679, Asmara; tel. (1) 189156; fax (1) 186541; e-mail maritime@motc-gov.er; Dir-Gen. GHEBREMEDHIN HABTE KIDANE.

BC Marine Services: 189 Warsay St, POB 5638, Asmara; tel. (1) 202672; fax (1) 127477; e-mail info@bc-marine.com; internet www.bc-marine.com; f. 2000; services include marine consultancy, marine survey and ship management; brs in Assab and Massawa; Dir Capt. NAOD GEBREAMLAK HAILE.

Eritrean Shipping Lines: 80 Semaetat Ave, POB 1110, Asmara; tel. (1) 120359; fax (1) 120331; e-mail ersl@eol.com.er; f. 1992; provides shipping services in Red Sea and Persian (Arabian) Gulf areas and owns and operates four cargo ships; Gen. Man. TEWELDE TEKESTE.

Maritime Shipping Services Corpn (MSASC): POB 99, Massawa; tel. (1) 552729; fax (1) 552438; e-mail mssegm@tse.com.er; f. 1991 as Maritime Ship Services Enterprise; est. as a corpn 2006; shipping agents, stevedoring and shorehandling; Gen. Man. SIMON GHEBREGZIABHIER.

CIVIL AVIATION

There are three international airports: at Asmara, Assab and Massawa. There are also eight domestic airports.

Civil Aviation Department: POB 252, Asmara; tel. (1) 124335; fax (1) 124334; e-mail motc.rez@eol.com.er; handles freight and passenger traffic for eight scheduled carriers which use Asmara airport; Dir-Gen. PAULOS KAHSAY.

Eritrean Airlines: 89 Harnet Ave, POB 222, Asmara; tel. (1) 125500; fax (1) 125465; e-mail customer-rel@eritreanairlines.com.er; internet www.flyeritrea.com; CEO KUBROM DAFLA.

Nasair Eritrea: POB 11915, Asmara; tel. (1) 200700; fax (1) 117622; e-mail nasreddin@nasaireritrea.com; internet www.nasaireritrea.com; f. 2006; CEO NASREDDIN IBRAHIM.

Tourism

The Ministry of Tourism is overseeing the development of this sector, although its advance since independence has been inhibited by the country's war-damaged transport infrastructure, and by subsequent conflicts with Ethiopia and other regional tensions. Eritrea possesses many areas of scenic and scientific interest, including the Dahlak Islands (a coralline archipelago rich in marine life), off shore from Massawa, and the massive escarpment rising up from the coastal plain and supporting a unique ecosystem. In 2011 107,090 tourists visited Eritrea, representing an increase of 27.5% on the previous year. Tourism receipts in 2009 amounted to US $26m. Since May 2006 it has been necessary for foreign nationals to obtain a permit 10 days in advance in order to travel outside of the capital.

Eritrean Tourism Service Corpn: Asmara; operates govt-owned hotels.

Defence

As assessed at November 2013, Eritrea's active armed forces included an army of about 200,000, a navy of 1,400 and an air force of some 350; reserve forces numbered around 120,000. National service is compulsory for all Eritreans between 18 and 40 years of age (with certain exceptions), for a 16-month period, including four months of military training.

Defence Expenditure: Budgeted at US $78m. in 2012.

Education

Education is provided free of charge in government schools and at the six government technical institutes. There are also some fee-paying private schools. Education is officially compulsory for children between seven and 13 years of age. Primary education begins at the age of seven and lasts for five years. Secondary education, beginning at 12 years of age, lasts for as much as six years, comprising a first cycle of two years and a second of four years. According to UNESCO estimates, in 2012 primary enrolment included 33% of children in the relevant age-group (boys 35%; girls 31%), while the comparable ratio for secondary enrolment was 26% (boys 28%; girls 23%). Total government expenditure on education and training in 2006 was estimated at the equivalent of 2.0% of GDP. In 2004/05 there were some 5,500 students enrolled on Bachelors degree courses at the University of Asmara; however, the University of Asmara was officially closed in September 2006. Higher education was henceforth to be provided by six newly established technical institutes, each associated with a relevant government ministry. The institutes provide education in the fields of science, technology, business and economics, social sciences, agriculture and marine training. In 2009/10 there was a total of 10,198 tertiary-level students in Eritrea.

ESTONIA

Introductory Survey

LOCATION, CLIMATE, LANGUAGE, RELIGION, FLAG, CAPITAL

The Republic of Estonia is situated in north-eastern Europe. The country is bordered to the south by Latvia, and to the east by Russia. Estonia's northern coastline is on the Gulf of Finland, and its territory includes more than 1,520 islands, mainly off its western coastline in the Gulf of Rīga and the Baltic Sea. The largest of the islands are Saaremaa and Hiiumaa, in the Gulf of Rīga. The climate is influenced by Estonia's position between the Eurasian land mass and the Baltic Sea and the North Atlantic Ocean. The mean January temperature in Tallinn is −0.6°C (30.9°F); in July the mean temperature is 17.1°C (62.8°F). Average annual precipitation is 568 mm. The official language is Estonian, which is a member of the Baltic-Finnic group of the Finno-Ugric languages. Many of the Russian residents, who comprise around one-quarter of the total population, do not speak Estonian. Most of the population profess Christianity. By tradition, Estonians belong to the Evangelical Lutheran Church. Smaller Protestant sects and the Eastern Orthodox Church are also represented. The national flag (proportions 7 by 11) consists of three equal horizontal stripes, of blue, black and white. The capital is Tallinn.

CONTEMPORARY POLITICAL HISTORY

Historical Context

The Russian annexation of Estonia, formerly under Swedish rule, was formalized in 1721. In the late 19th century, as the powers of the dominant Baltic German nobility declined, Estonians experienced a national cultural revival, which culminated in political demands for autonomy during the 1905 Russian Revolution, and for full independence after the beginning of the First World War. In March 1917 the Provisional Government in Petrograd (St Petersburg), which had taken power after the abdication of Tsar Nicholas II, approved autonomy for Estonia. A Maapäev (Provisional Council) was elected as the country's representative body. However, in October the Bolsheviks staged a coup in Tallinn. As German forces advanced towards Estonia in early 1918, the Bolshevik troops were forced to leave. Major political parties united to form the Estonian Salvation Committee, and on 24 February an independent Republic of Estonia was proclaimed. A Provisional Government, headed by Konstantin Päts, was formed, but Germany refused to recognize Estonia's independence, and its troops occupied Estonia. Following Germany's capitulation in November, a Provisional Government assumed power. After a period of armed conflict, Estonia and Soviet Russia signed the Treaty of Tartu on 2 February 1920, under the terms of which the Soviet Government recognized Estonia's independence and renounced any rights to its territory. The major Western powers recognized Estonian independence in January 1921, and Estonia was admitted to the League of Nations.

Independence lasted until 1940. During most of this time the country had a liberal democratic political system, in which the Riigikogu (State Assembly) was dominant. However, the economic depression of the 1930s caused public dissatisfaction. In March 1934 Prime Minister Päts seized power in a bloodless coup. The State Assembly and political parties were disbanded, but in 1938 a new Constitution was adopted, providing for a presidential system of government, with a bicameral legislature. In April 1938 Päts was elected President.

In August 1939 the USSR and Germany signed a non-aggression treaty (the Nazi-Soviet or Molotov-Ribbentrop Pact). The 'Secret Protocols' to the treaty provided for the occupation of Estonia (along with various other territories) by the USSR. In September Estonia was forced to sign an agreement permitting the USSR to base troops there. In June 1940 the Government resigned, and the Soviet authorities appointed a new administration. In July elections were held, in which only candidates approved by the Soviet authorities were permitted to participate. On 21 July the new legislature proclaimed an Estonian Soviet Socialist Republic, and on 6 August the Republic was formally incorporated into the USSR. Soviet rule in Estonia lasted less than one year. In that short period mass deportations of Estonians, the expropriation of property and severe restrictions on cultural life ensued.

German forces entered Estonia in July 1941 and remained in occupation until September 1944. Thereafter, Soviet troops occupied the whole of the country, and the process of 'sovietization', including industrialization and the collectivization of agriculture, was resumed. Structural change in the economy was accompanied by increased political repression, and deportations of Estonians continued until the death of the Soviet leader Stalin (Iosif Dzhugashvili) in 1953. The most overt form of opposition to Soviet rule was provided by the 'forest brethren' (*metsavennad*) guerrilla movement, which conducted armed operations against Soviet personnel and institutions until the mid-1950s.

During the late 1970s and the 1980s the questions of 'russification' and environmental degradation became subjects of intense debate in Estonia. The policy of glasnost (openness), introduced by the Soviet leader, Mikhail Gorbachev, in 1986, allowed such discussion to spread beyond dissident groups. In August 1987 a demonstration attended by some 2,000 people commemorated the anniversary of the signing of the Nazi-Soviet Pact, and an Estonian Group for the Publication of the Molotov-Ribbentrop Pact (MRP-AEG) was subsequently formed. During 1988 the Nazi-Soviet Pact was duly published, and the MRP-AEG re-formed as the Estonian National Independence Party (ERSP), which sought the restoration of Estonian independence. Another opposition group, the Estonian Popular Front (Rahvarinne), which included many members of the ruling Communist Party of Estonia (EKP), and which advocated the transformation of the USSR into a confederal system, held its first congress in October. On 16 November the Estonian Supreme Soviet (Supreme Council—legislature) adopted a declaration of sovereignty, which included the right to annul all-Union (USSR) legislation. The Presidium of the USSR Supreme Soviet declared the declaration unconstitutional, but the Estonian Supreme Soviet affirmed its decision in December.

The adoption of Estonian as the state language was accepted by the Supreme Soviet in January 1989, and the tricolour of independent Estonia was reinstated as the official flag. Meanwhile, the ERSP refused to nominate candidates for elections to the all-Union Congress of People's Deputies in March, instead announcing plans for the registration by citizens' committees of all citizens of the 1918–40 Republic of Estonia and their descendants. Voters on an electoral register, thus compiled, would elect an Eesti Kongress (Congress of Estonia) as the legal successor to the pre-1940 Estonian legislature. Rahvarinne, however, participated in the elections to the Congress of People's Deputies and won 27 of the 36 contested seats. Five seats were won by the International Movement (Intermovement), a political group composed predominantly of ethnic Russians opposed to the growing influence of Estonian opposition movements. In October 1989 delegates at the second congress of Rahvarinne voted to adopt the restoration of Estonian independence as official policy. In November the Estonian Supreme Soviet voted to annul the 1940 decision to enter the USSR, declaring that the decision had been reached under coercion from Soviet armed forces.

On 2 February 1990 a mass rally was held to commemorate the anniversary of the 1920 Treaty of Tartu. Deputies attending the rally later met to approve a declaration urging the USSR Supreme Soviet to begin negotiations on restoring Estonia's independence. On 22 February the Estonian Supreme Soviet approved the declaration, and one day later voted to abolish the constitutional guarantee of power enjoyed by the EKP, thereby permitting largely free elections to take place to the Estonian Supreme Soviet in March. Rahvarinne won 43 of the 105 seats, and 35 were won by the Association for a Free Estonia and other pro-independence groups. The remainder were won by members of the Intermovement. Candidates belonging to the EKP, which was represented in all these groups, won 55 seats. At the first session of the new legislature, Arnold Rüütel, previously Chairman of the Presidium of the Supreme Soviet, was elected to the new post of Chairman of the Supreme Soviet, in which was vested those state powers that had been the preserve of the First Secretary of the EKP. On 30 March the Supreme Soviet adopted a declaration that proclaimed the beginning of a transitional period towards independence and denied the validity of Soviet power in the Republic.

In late February and early March 1990 some 580,000 people (excluding those who had migrated to Estonia after the Soviet occupation of 1940 and their descendants) took part in elections to the rival parliament to the Supreme Soviet, the Congress of Estonia. The Congress convened on 11–12 March 1990 and declared itself the constitutional representative of the Estonian people. The participants adopted resolutions demanding the restoration of Estonian independence and the withdrawal of Soviet troops from Estonia.

Domestic Political Affairs

In April 1990 the Supreme Soviet elected Edgar Savisaar, a leader of Rahvarinne, Prime Minister, and on 8 May it voted to restore the first five articles of the 1938 Constitution, which described Estonia's independent status. The formal name of pre-1940 Estonia, the Republic of Estonia, was also restored, as were the state emblems, flag and anthem. Although the Soviet authorities did not impose formal economic sanctions on Estonia (as they did with Lithuania), relations were severely strained. In mid-May Gorbachev (recently appointed as the first President of the USSR) annulled Estonia's declaration of independence, declaring that it violated the USSR Constitution. He also refused requests for negotiations on the status of the Republic prior to the rescission of the declaration of independence.

When troops of the USSR's Ministry of the Interior attempted military intervention in the other Baltic republics (Latvia and Lithuania) in January 1991, the Estonian leadership anticipated similar confrontation. Barricades and makeshift defences were erected, but no military action was taken. However, events in Latvia and Lithuania intensified popular distrust of Estonian involvement in a new union, which was being negotiated by other Soviet republics, and Estonia refused to participate in a referendum on the future of the USSR, which took place in nine of the republics in March. The Estonian authorities had conducted a poll on the issue of independence earlier in the same month. According to the official results, 82.9% of the registered electorate took part, of whom 77.8% voted in favour of Estonian independence.

When the conservative communist 'State Committee for the State of Emergency' announced that it had seized power in the USSR on 19 August 1991, Estonia, together with the other Baltic republics, expected military intervention to overthrow the pro-independence Governments. Gen. Fedor Kuzmin, the Soviet commander of the Baltic military district, informed Rüütel that he was taking full control of Estonia. Military vehicles entered Tallinn on 20 August, and troops occupied the city's television station, although the military command did not prevent a session of the Estonian Supreme Council from convening. Deputies adopted a resolution declaring the full and immediate independence of Estonia. After it became evident, on 22 August 1991, that the Soviet coup had collapsed, the Government began to take measures against persons who had supported the coup, while the Intermovement, the Communist Party of the Soviet Union and other anti-Government movements were banned in Estonia.

Consolidation of statehood

As the Estonian Government moved to assert its authority over former Soviet institutions, other countries quickly began to recognize its independence. On 6 September 1991 the recently formed USSR State Council finally recognized the re-establishment of Estonian independence. Later in the month Estonia, together with the other Baltic states, was admitted to the UN, as well as to the Conference on Security and Co-operation in Europe (CSCE), later the Organization for Security and Co-operation in Europe (OSCE, see p. 387). During the remainder of 1991 Estonia established diplomatic relations with most major states and was offered membership of leading international organizations. In internal politics, there was hope for a cessation of conflict between the Congress of Estonia and the Supreme Council, with the establishment of a Constitutional Assembly, comprising equal numbers of delegates from each body. In January 1992, following a series of disputes with the Supreme Council, Savisaar resigned as Prime Minister and was replaced by the erstwhile Minister of Transport, Tiit Vähi. The Supreme Council approved a new Council of Ministers at the end of the month.

The draft Constitution was approved by some 91% of the electorate in a referendum held in June 1992. Under the recently adopted Citizenship Law, only citizens of pre-1940 Estonia and their descendants, or those who had successfully applied for citizenship, were entitled to vote. This ruling drew strong criticism from Russian leaders, who were concerned that the rights of Estonia's large Russian minority were being violated. The new Constitution, which entered into force in July 1992, provided for a parliamentary system of government, with a strong presidency. Elections to the new legislature, the State Assembly, were to be held in September, concurrently with a direct presidential election, although subsequent presidents were to be elected by the State Assembly.

Legislative and presidential elections were duly held on 20 September 1992, with the participation of some 67% of the electorate. The country's Russian and other ethnic minorities, who represented 42% of the total population at that time, were again barred from voting (with the exception of those whose applications for citizenship had been granted). The elections to the 101-seat State Assembly were contested by some 40 parties and movements, largely grouped into eight coalitions. The nationalist Pro Patria alliance (Isamaa) emerged with the largest number of seats (29). The Secure Home alliance (KK), comprising some former communists, obtained 17 seats. The centrist Popular Front alliance (led by Rahvarinne) won 15 seats. The Moderates electoral alliance (Mõõdukad) obtained 12 seats, and the ERSP won 10 seats. None of the four candidates in the presidential election won an overall majority of the votes. The State Assembly was thus required to choose from the two most successful candidates: Rüütel, now a leading member of KK, and Lennart Meri, a former Minister of Foreign Affairs, who was supported by Isamaa. In early October the State Assembly elected Meri as Estonia's President.

A new coalition Government, comprising members of Isamaa, Mõõdukad and the ERSP and headed by Mart Laar, the leader of Isamaa, was announced in October 1992. Laar indicated that the principal objectives of his administration would be to negotiate the withdrawal of all Russian troops remaining in Estonia, as well as to accelerate a programme of privatization. In November four of the five constituent parties of the Isamaa alliance united to form the National Pro Patria Party (RKI), under Laar's leadership.

In November 1993 Laar survived a vote of no confidence in the State Assembly. Also in November, Rahvarinne was disbanded. In May–June 1994 four ministers resigned. Defections from the Isamaa faction within the State Assembly resulted in Laar's supporters retaining control of only 19 seats in the legislature by September. Following the revelation in that month that Laar had secretly contravened an agreement with the IMF, the State Assembly endorsed a vote of no confidence in the Prime Minister. In October Andres Tarand, hitherto Minister of the Environment, was appointed to replace Laar. A new Council of Ministers, which included representatives of the RKI, Mõõdukad, the ERSP and liberal and right-wing parties, was announced in November.

The results of the legislative elections, held on 5 March 1995, reflected widespread popular dissatisfaction with the parties of the governing coalition. The largest number of seats in the State Assembly (41 of the total of 101) was won by an alliance of the centrist Estonian Coalition Party (Eesti Koonderakond, led by Vähi) and the Estonian Rural Union (EME, in which Rüütel was a prominent figure). A coalition of the newly established Estonian Reform Party (ER, led by Siim Kallas, the President of the Bank of Estonia) and liberal groups obtained 19 seats, followed by Savisaar's Estonian Centre Party (EK, with 16). The RKI (in coalition with the ERSP) won only eight seats, while the Mõõdukad alliance obtained six seats. The Estonia is Our Home alliance (representing the Russian-speaking minority) won six seats. The participation rate was almost 70% of the registered electorate.

Vähi was confirmed as Prime Minister by the legislature in early April 1995, and the new Government—a coalition of the Eesti Koonderakond, the EME and the EK—was appointed later in the month. However, the Government survived only until early October, when it was revealed that Savisaar, the Minister of the Interior, had made clandestine recordings of conversations with other politicians concerning the formation of a new coalition government. The EK subsequently refused to accept his dismissal by Vähi. As a result of the effective collapse of the coalition, Vähi and the remaining members of the Council of Ministers tendered their resignations. In mid-October President Meri reappointed Vähi as Prime Minister, and a coalition Government, comprising members of the Eesti Koonderakond, the EME and the ER, was formed in late October. In December the RKI and the ERSP, which had campaigned jointly for the legislative elections in March, merged to form the Pro Patria Union (Isamaaliit).

A presidential election was held in the State Assembly on 26 August 1996, contested by the incumbent, Meri, and Rüütel. Following two further inconclusive rounds of voting, a larger electoral college, comprising the 101 deputies of the legislature and 273 representatives of local government, was convened on 20 September. As none of the five candidates contesting the election secured an overall majority, a further round of voting was held to choose between the leading candidates, Meri and Rüütel. The election was won by Meri, with 52% of the votes cast, and in October he was duly sworn in as President for a second term.

In October 1996 local government elections were held, in which the ER gained control of the Tallinn city Government. In November the Eesti Koonderakond concluded a co-operation agreement with the EK. Disagreements among the coalition partners led to the collapse of the Tallinn city leadership, and Savisaar was appointed as the new Chairman of the city Government, replacing the newly elected ER candidate. The ER threatened to leave the Government unless the co-operation agreement with the EK was cancelled, and in late November 1996 six ministers, including Kallas (hitherto the Minister for Foreign Affairs), resigned, causing the collapse of the ruling coalition. A minority Government, comprising the Eesti Koonderakond, the EME and independent members, was appointed in December. In early 1997 a series of allegations of abuse of office was made against Vähi. Although a legislative motion of no confidence, presented by the leaders of four opposition parties, was defeated by a narrow margin, Vähi tendered his resignation in February. Mart Siimann, the leader of the Eesti Koonderakond parliamentary faction, was appointed Prime Minister. In March a new minority Government, again comprising the Eesti Koonderakond, the EME and independent members, was appointed. In September Vähi announced his resignation from the Eesti Koonderakond and his retirement from political life; Siimann became the new party Chairman.

The 1999 legislative elections

At legislative elections held on 7 March 1999, the EK won 28 of the 101 seats; the ER and Isamaaliit each secured 18 seats, Mõõdukad (in alliance with the People's Party) 17, the EME seven and the United People's Party of Estonia six. Just 57.4% of the electorate participated in the polls. Although the EK obtained the largest number of seats, it was unable to assemble a majority. A centre-right coalition Government was thus formed by the ER, Isamaaliit and Mõõdukad; Laar, by that time leader of Isamaaliit, was appointed Prime Minister.

In May 1999 it was announced that some 300,000 non-citizens permanently resident in Estonia (principally ethnic Russians) were to be allowed to participate in local elections to be held in October. At the elections, the governing ER-Isamaaliit-Mõõdukad alliance obtained control of 13 of Estonia's 15 county governments, and, in alliance with representatives of the Russian population, of Tallinn City Council, where Jüri Mõis was appointed Mayor of Tallinn, after resigning as Minister of the Interior. In November the Moderates' Party and the People's Party merged to form the People's Party Moderates (RM). In June 2000 a new party, the Estonian People's Union (Eestimaa Rahvaliit), was formed by the merger of the Estonian Rural People's Party, the EME and the Pensioners' and Families' Party. Mõis resigned in May 2001, after being threatened with a fifth confidence vote. A member of Isamaaliit, Tõnis Palts, was elected as his successor.

Inconclusive rounds of voting in the presidential election took place in the State Assembly on 27–28 August 2001. The first round of the election was contested by Tarand of the RM and Peeter Kreitzberg of the opposition EK. Tarand was replaced as the candidate of the ruling coalition by Peeter Tulviste of Isamaaliit in the second and third rounds of voting, but neither candidate emerged as the victor. An electoral college, composed of the 101 parliamentary deputies and 266 representatives of local government, was therefore convened on 21 September. Toomas Savi of the governing ER (members of which had, hitherto, abstained from voting), and Rüütel, now the Honorary Chairman of Eestimaa Rahvaliit, participated at this stage, progressing to a second round, as the candidates with the greatest number of votes. Rüütel eventually emerged as the victor in the 'run-off' election, in which he secured 186 votes. He was sworn in as President on 8 October.

In December 2001 the ER announced that it was to leave the Tallinn city Government. It subsequently signed a coalition agreement with the EK, in what was widely regarded as an attempt to distance itself from the increasingly unpopular national Government, of which it remained a part. Palts was forced to resign as Mayor, when a censure motion, brought by members of the EK, was approved by a significant majority. His Isamaaliit left the city Government, and Savisaar was elected as Mayor of Tallinn in mid-December. These developments prompted Prime Minister Laar's Government to resign on 8 January 2002.

In mid-January 2002 the EK and the ER signed an agreement on the formation of an interim, coalition government, despite their contrasting political ideals; eight ministers were to be appointed from the EK and six from the ER. The parties of the coalition held fewer than one-half of the seats in the State Assembly and, therefore, required the support of Eestimaa Rahvaliit. On 22 January Kallas of the ER was approved as Prime Minister.

Following a ruling by the Supreme Court prohibiting the formation of electoral blocs, in July 2002 the State Assembly voted to permit their existence until 2005, in order to avoid a delay in holding the forthcoming local elections. The elections duly took place in October 2002. Parties represented in the national Government won the majority of the votes cast. In November Savisaar was re-elected as Mayor of Tallinn. Meanwhile, in response to their parties' poor performance, in late October Toomas Hendrik Ilves resigned as Chairman of the RM, and Laar resigned the chairmanship of Isamaaliit. In February 2003 the State Assembly approved an extension of the terms of local councils, from three years to four.

Eleven parties participated in the parliamentary elections held on 2 March 2003, in which the EK received 25.4% of the votes cast and 28 seats in the 101-member State Assembly. The right-wing Res Publica party (founded in 2001) obtained 24.6% and 28 seats, and the ER took 17.7% and 19 seats; Eestimaa Rahvaliit, Isamaaliit and the RM also secured representation in the State Assembly. The level of participation by the electorate was 58.2%. Although the EK secured the largest number of votes cast, Res Publica, the ER and Eestimaa Rahvaliit reached agreement on the formation of a three-party government. After Savisaar declined the President's offer to form a government, on 2 April Juhan Parts, the leader of Res Publica, was nominated as Prime Minister, and the new coalition Government was approved on 9 April. In September the Minister of Finance, Palts, resigned, after an investigation was initiated into allegations of tax evasion. In February 2004 the RM changed its name to the Estonian Social Democratic Party (SDE).

Accession to the European Union

Following Estonia's accession to the European Union (EU, see p. 273) in May 2004 (see Regional relations), in the following month the country took part in its first elections to the European Parliament. In October Savisaar resigned as Mayor of Tallinn, following a vote of no confidence by the City Council. He was replaced by Palts. In November Margus Hanson resigned as Minister of Defence, following the theft from his home of classified documents. (His immunity from prosecution was removed in March 2005, and in November, after a criminal investigation, Hanson was fined for negligence.) Also in November 2004 Andrus Ansip, the new Minister of the Economy and Communications, was elected Chairman of the ER, replacing Kallas, who had been appointed as the country's representative to the European Commission. In December the EK apparently sought to increase its support among the ethnic Russian population of Estonia, controversially signing a co-operation agreement with the de facto ruling party of Russia, United Russia. As a consequence, a number of EK members who supported closer co-operation and integration with the EU left the party; by the end of January 2005 the party's faction in the State Assembly had diminished from 28 to 19 members.

The Minister of Foreign Affairs, Kristiina Ojuland, was dismissed in February 2005, after a security audit revealed the disappearance of 91 classified documents. On 21 March the State Assembly adopted a motion of no confidence in Minister of Justice Ken-Marti Vaher. Three days later Parts announced the resignation of his Government. On 31 March the EK, the ER and Eestimaa Rahvaliit agreed to form a coalition. Ansip was nominated to lead a new Government, which was sworn into office on 13 April. Municipal elections took place on 16 October (in which, for the first time, voting was permitted by way of the internet). The EK won 25.5% of the votes cast nationwide, followed by the ER, Eestimaa Rahvaliit and Isamaaliit; Res Publica won just 8.5% of the ballot, compared with 15.2% in 2002. In the elections to the mayoralty of Tallinn, the EK won some 41% of the votes cast, but the party's Chairman, Savisaar, chose to retain his post as Minister of Economic Affairs and Communications, rather than be reappointed Mayor; in November another member of the party, Juri Ratas, was elected Mayor.

In August 2006 the EK and Eestimaa Rahvaliit signed an agreement pledging their support for the candidacy of Rüütel in the forthcoming presidential election, scheduled to take place in the State Assembly later that month. However, in the following week the two parties announced that they were to boycott the ballot after Rüütel announced that he would seek re-election only if the vote was decided by the electoral college system. In the initial ballot, held on 28 August, former Speaker of the legislature Ene Ergma, the sole candidate, attracted 65 votes, narrowly failing to secure the required two-thirds' majority (68 votes). Two further rounds of voting proved similarly inconclusive, with Ergma's sole competitor, the former Minister of Foreign Affairs, Ilves, securing 64 votes in each round. Responsibility for electing the President thus passed to the electoral college, which duly convened on 23 September and voted for Ilves over Rüütel by a margin of 174 to 162; Ilves was inaugurated on 9 October. Also in October Isamaaliit and Res Publica formally merged to form the Union of Pro Patria and Res Publica (IRL). It was subsequently agreed that Tõnis Lukas, hitherto Chairman of Isamaaliit, and Taavi Veskimägi, hitherto Chairman of Res Publica, would co-chair the IRL.

Legislative elections were held on 4 March 2007, with the participation of 61.9% of the electorate. Estonia was the first country to introduce internet voting at a national legislative election, although only a small proportion of the electorate chose to vote on-line. The ER was the most successful party, winning 31 seats and 27.8% of the votes cast, narrowly followed by the EK, with 29 seats and 26.1% of the votes. The IRL secured 19 seats and 17.9% of the votes, the SDE 10 seats and 10.6% of the votes. The Estonian Greens and Eestimaa Rahvaliit each obtained six seats and 7.1% of the votes. As in 2003, the EK, despite its strong performance in the polls, was excluded from the new Government. In late March 2007 the ER, the IRL, and the SDE announced that they had agreed to form a centre-right coalition commanding 60 of the 101 seats in the State Assembly. A new Government, again under the premiership of Ansip, was installed on 4 April. Urmas Paet of the ER was retained as Minister of Foreign Affairs; Jüri Pihl of the SDE was awarded the interior portfolio, while Jaak Aaviksoo of the IRL assumed responsibility for defence. On the following day Savisaar was elected as Mayor of Tallinn, replacing Ratas, who had been elected as a Vice-President of the State Assembly.

Divisions within the Government were evident in September 2008, as the coalition parties disagreed over measures to increase revenue and reduce expenditure in the 2009 budget, although a compromise was finally reached. In February the Government secured the approval of the State Assembly for a supplementary budget further curtailing expenditure for the year; the adoption of the austerity measures, which included a 10% reduction in public sector salaries, was linked to a vote of confidence in Ansip's administration.

Ansip dismissed the three SDE ministers from the governing coalition in May 2009, after disagreements over unemployment benefits and further proposals aimed at improving the country's fiscal position. Following the failure of talks to bring Eestimaa Rahvaliit into the ruling coalition to replace the SDE, the ER and the IRL continued in office as a minority administration. In early June Jürgen Ligi of the ER and Marko Pomerants of the IRL were appointed Minister of Finance and Minister of the Interior, respectively.

At elections to the European Parliament held on 7 June 2009, the EK obtained two of the country's six seats, winning 26.1% of the votes cast. An independent candidate, Indrek Tarand, secured a seat, having received 25.8% of the votes cast, while the ER, the IRL and the SDE also each took one seat. The elections were notable for the poor performance of the SDE, which had been the most successful party in the 2004 European polls, when it had won three seats. The voter turn-out, at 43.9%, was markedly higher than in 2004 (26.8%). The EK was also victorious in municipal elections conducted on 18 October 2009, securing 31.2% of the votes cast nationwide. The ER won 16.8% of the votes and the IRL obtained 14.1%. In Tallinn, the EK won 53.3% of the votes cast and 44 of the 79 seats on the City Council, with Savisaar re-elected as Mayor.

In early 2011 the campaign for the parliamentary elections, due to be held in March, was largely dominated by economic concerns; the ruling coalition pledged to reduce taxes if re-elected. However, from mid-December 2010 Savisaar, as both Mayor of Tallinn and Chairman of the EK, became the focus of a political scandal, after he was accused of receiving illegal donations for his party, notably from the President of Russian Railways, Vladimir Yakunin, a close ally of the Russian premier (and former, and subsequent, President), Vladimir Putin.

Recent developments: Ansip's final term as Prime Minister

On 23 March 2011 the ER and the IRL reached a preliminary agreement to continue their governing coalition. Ansip subsequently appointed a new Government, in which several of the senior positions remained unchanged, including Jürgen Ligi of the ER as Minister of Finance, Paet as Minister of Foreign Affairs and Marko Pomerants of the IRL as Minister of the Interior. Laar was appointed Minister of Defence.

In August 2011 a member of the Estonian United Left Party—which sought to represent the rights of the Russian minority—attempted to take hostage staff members in the offices of the Ministry of Defence in Tallinn. The gunman opened fire inside the building before he was shot and killed by police. No one else was injured during the incident. In December it emerged that two elected officials of the IRL—a parliamentary deputy and a member of Tallinn City Council—had engaged in the illicit sale of Estonian residence permits to entrepreneurs from Russia and other countries of the Commonwealth of Independent States. In an attempt to protect its reputation, the two officials were expelled from the party, while two IRL ministers—Vaher (Minister of the Interior) and Parts (Minister of Economic Affairs and Communications)—who were also allegedly implicated in the case, were to be subject to a vote of confidence from the party's ruling council. (The retention of both ministers was endorsed later in the month.)

At the end of January 2012 Urmas Reinsalu was elected leader of the IRL, replacing Laar, who, having announced his intention to resign several months earlier, was given the title of Honorary Chairman. In mid-February Laar was hospitalized, having suffered a stroke. Consequently Aaviksoo assumed Laar's ministerial responsibilities in addition to his own, although it was anticipated that Laar would return to his post following his recovery. However, in May Reinsalu also assumed responsibility for the defence portfolio from Laar, and stood in as Prime Minister during Ansip's absences from the country. Meanwhile, in March the Eestimaa Rahvaliit renamed itself the Estonian Conservative People's Party.

In early March 2012 some 16,000 teachers participated in three days of strike action in support of an increase in salaries. The action followed a year of rapid economic growth (the fastest in the EU), while Estonia was for the second year running the only euro area country to record a budgetary surplus, in part as a result of public sector pay freezes. The Government proposed an increase in teaching salaries of 15% with effect from 2013, but this was deemed unacceptable by the principal education union. In October doctors and nurses across Estonia went on strike over poor working conditions and salaries, arguing that many healthcare staff had already left the country as a result. The strike ended later in the month, after wage increases had been agreed. In November the Government submitted a proposal to the State Assembly to reduce the proposed increase to unemployment benefits in order to make available resources to pay for the wage increases in the healthcare sector.

In early December 2012 Kristen Michal of the ER resigned as Minister of Justice; in the previous year his alleged involvement in an apparent scheme of illicit party funding had resulted in a criminal investigation being opened against him. Although the charges were subsequently dropped, the ensuing damage to Michal's reputation was considered to have weakened his position. He was succeeded as Minister of Justice by the hitherto Minister of Social Affairs, Hanno Pevkur, who was, in turn, replaced by Taavi Rõivas. Public outrage over the party financing allegations resulted in the establishment, at the initiative of President Ilves, of a People's Assembly (Rahvakogu) website, through which citizens could make suggestions regarding the electoral system, political parties and the role of civil society. In April 2013 Ilves presented 16 of the People's Assembly's legislative proposals to the State Assembly for consideration, including a proposed reduction of the threshold required for parties to obtain representation in legislative elections from 5% to 3% of the votes cast, and for reducing the minimum membership required of registered political parties from 1,000 to 200. Among numerous other proposals presented by the People's Assembly that Ilves did not present for legislative consideration was one providing for direct popular election of the country's President.

On 23 February 2014 Ansip announced his intention of resigning as Prime Minister, stating that he wished the ER, in its campaign at legislative elections due to be held in March 2015, to offer a continuity of leadership and policy that he, after serving as premier since 2005, could no longer offer. On 4 March Ansip duly tendered his resignation; the members of his Government were to remain in place in an acting capacity pending the nomination by President Ilves, within a period of 14 days, of a new premier and the subsequent approval of a new Council of Ministers. On 14 March Ilves nominated Taavi Rõivas of the ER, hitherto the Minister of Social Affairs as Prime Minister. After Rõivas negotiated a new coalition between the ER and the SDE, the State Assembly voted in favour of his appointment on 24 March, and a new Council of Ministers assumed office two days later.

Foreign Affairs

Regional relations

Estonia pursues close relations with its Baltic neighbours, Latvia and Lithuania. In late 1991 the three states established a consultative interparliamentary body, the Baltic Assembly, with the aim of developing political and economic co-operation. The Baltic Assembly has maintained close links with the Nordic Council, and Estonia is also a member of the Council of the Baltic Sea States (see p. 250), established in March 1992. In January 2007 the Baltic states agreed to establish a joint Baltic battalion (under Lithuanian command), which would participate in the NATO Response Force from January 2010 (a joint Baltic battalion had previously operated in 1994–2003); another such battalion, under Estonian command, was planned to operate within the NATO Response Force by 2016. Meanwhile, meeting in Vilnius, Lithuania, in 2009, the three Baltic Prime Ministers signed a declaration on the implementation of joint energy infrastructure projects. As part of this strategy, and of wider European integration goals, the three countries established a common Nordic-Baltic energy market, which became fully functional in June 2013. Moreover, in February 2014, the combined region entered into a single energy trading market encompassing 15 countries, as part of the European Commission's North-Western Europe market coupling initiative. The infrastructural links to support this initiative were set out in 2009, under the complementary Baltic Energy Market Interconnection Plan, to be completed by 2015. One of the earliest elements to reach completion, in February 2014, was the 650 MW Estlink II undersea interconnector cable between Estonia and Finland. In addition, in 2014 Estonia and Latvia were in the preparatory phase of installing a third electrical cable to connect the two countries, with a projected completion date of 2020. The cable would increase capacity in the two countries by between 500 MW and 600 MW. Meanwhile, despite a joint commitment between Estonia, Lithuania, Latvia and Poland to construction a 1,300-MW nuclear power plant at Visaginas in Lithuania, development subsequently stalled. EU funding for a fast inter-Baltic passenger railway, Rail Baltica, was budgeted to become available in 2014, although political will to support the project, which would necessitate the conversion of existing railway lines from the broader, Russian, gauge to standard European gauge, appeared uncertain early in that year.

Since the restoration of Estonian independence in 1991, the republic's relations with Russia have been strained by a number of questions, most notably the presence of former Soviet troops and the rights of the large Russian minority in Estonia (equivalent to 25.2% of the population at January 2013, according to official estimates). Under the Citizenship Law of 1992—a modified version of that adopted in 1938—non-ethnic Estonians who settled in the republic after its annexation by the USSR in 1940, and their descendants, were obliged to apply for naturalization. Many of the requirements for naturalization—including an examination in the Estonian language—were criticized by the Russian Government. A new citizenship law, adopted in January 1995, gave non-citizens until July to apply for residence and work permits, by which time almost 330,000 people (more than 80% of the total number of non-citizens) had submitted applications. The deadline was extended until November 1996, and by October of that year some 110,000 people had taken Russian citizenship, while continuing to reside in Estonia. In May 1997 the Ministry of the Interior announced that Soviet passports were no longer valid in Estonia. In December 1998 the State Assembly approved legislation requiring elected officials to demonstrate sufficient command of Estonian to participate in the basic bureaucratic procedures of office. The legislation became effective in May 1999, and on 1 July a further amendment to the Language Law, pertaining to those employed in the services sector, came into force. In April 2000, following a statement by the OSCE High Commissioner on National Minorities that the language legislation contradicted international standards on freedom of expression, the law was amended, to make knowledge of Estonian compulsory only where it was deemed necessary for the sake of public interest. In November 2001 the requirement that electoral candidates be able to speak Estonian was abolished, although legislation adopted in the same month made Estonian the official language of parliament.

With the dissolution of the USSR in 1991, several thousand former Soviet troops remained stationed (under Russian command) on Estonian territory. Their withdrawal commenced in 1992, but the Russian leadership increasingly linked the progress of the troop withdrawals with the question of the citizenship, and other rights, of the Russian-speaking minority in Estonia. In July 1994 a bilateral agreement was reached, awarding civil and social guarantees to all Russian military pensioners in Estonia. The withdrawal of former Soviet troops was completed in August.

A further cause of tension in Estonian–Russian relations concerned Estonia's demand for the return of some 2,000 sq km (770 sq miles) of territory that had been ceded to Russia in 1944. In June 1994 Russian President Boris Yeltsin ordered the unilateral demarcation of Russia's border with Estonia according to the post-1944 boundary, although no agreement with Estonia had been concluded. During 1995 Estonia abandoned its demand for the return of the disputed territories. Instead, Estonia appealed only for minor amendments to be made to the existing line of demarcation, to improve border security; more importantly, it insisted that Russia recognize the 1920 Treaty of Tartu (in which Russia recognized Estonia's independence) as the basis of future relations between the two countries. However, the Russian Government maintained that the Treaty had lost its legal force, having been superseded by the declaration on bilateral relations signed by Russia and Estonia in 1991. In November 1996 the Estonian authorities announced that they were prepared to omit references to the Treaty of Tartu from the border agreement, which, however, Russia continued to refuse to sign.

Despite Russian misgivings, in September 2000 Estonia decreed that from 2001 a full visa regime would come into effect between the two countries (as part of Estonia's preparations for EU membership). Further tensions arose in December 2003, when the State Assembly approved amendments to legislation on foreign nationals, which prevented Russian military pensioners from obtaining permanent residency in Estonia.

President Rüütel refused an invitation from Russian President Vladimir Putin to attend celebrations in Moscow, the Russian capital, on 9 May 2005, commemorating the 60th anniversary of the end of the Second World War in Europe, on the grounds that, for Estonia, it marked the beginning of almost 50 years of Soviet occupation. However, on 18 May the Ministers of Foreign Affairs of Estonia and Russia signed a border agreement. The treaty was ratified by the State Assembly two days later, but the addition of a preamble making reference to the Soviet occupation of Estonia prompted Russia to revoke the agreement and demand renewed negotiations.

The approval, in February 2007, of legislation by the State Assembly providing for the relocation of a Soviet war monument in Tallinn, together with draft legislation proposing a ban on politically motivated public displays of Soviet and Nazi symbols in Estonia, provoked intense indignation from the Russian Government. When the monument was dismantled, in April, pending its relocation, several days of rioting ensued in Tallinn, as a result of which at least one person was killed and several hundred injured; at least 800 people were arrested. The Russian state-sponsored youth organization Nashi (Our Own) blockaded the Estonian embassy. In May Russia's state railway monopoly announced the suspension of deliveries of petroleum products to Estonia, purportedly on the grounds that it planned to carry out maintenance of the rail link to Estonia. The Estonian Minister of Foreign Affairs also claimed that elements in the Russian administration were responsible for a series of 'cyber-attacks' against the internet sites of Estonian government ministries, agencies and companies. (In March 2009 an activist with Nashi claimed that he and other members of the organization had organized these attacks.) Along with its fellow Baltic states, Estonia adopted a stance supportive of Georgia during that country's conflict with Russia in August 2008.

As Russia's relations with the USA and the EU began to improve in 2010, the tension with Estonia also gradually began to ease. President Ilves made a strongly symbolic gesture by attending Russia's Victory Day parade (commemorating the end of the Second World War) in the capital Moscow on 9 May—the first occasion an Estonian President had done so. In 2012 the foreign affairs committees of the Estonian State Assembly and the Russian State Duma resumed contact for the first time in several years. The first visit of an Estonian Prime Minister to Russia in over a decade took place in April 2013, and in June Kirill (Gundyayev), the Patriarch of Moscow and all Rus, visited Estonia.

Meanwhile, in September 2012 Russian Minister of Foreign Affairs Sergei Lavrov expressed his country's wish to resume border treaty negotiations. In the following month the State Assembly proposed—and all factions agreed—to re-open border talks, although Estonian Minister of Foreign Affairs Urmas Paet said that there was no reason to replace the existing treaty. On 18 February 2014 Paet and Lavrov met in Moscow, when a revised border agreement between Russia and Estonia was finally signed; before it could enter into effect, the treaty was to be ratified by the legislature of both countries. In what was interpreted as a further warming of relations with Russia, it was announced that Lavrov was to visit Estonia later in the year, in what would constitute the first visit by a Russian Minister of Foreign Affairs to the country.

In 2012 the Estonian Government denied permission to Nord Stream—a consortium of, inter alia, Gazprom of Russia and Wintershall AG of Germany—to conduct studies in the Baltic Sea (including within Estonian territorial waters) for the eventual construction of a possible two further natural gas pipelines to run between Russia and Germany. (The second of the two existing pipelines was inaugurated in October.) Estonian Minister of Defence Reinsalu had argued that the pipelines could pose further strategic and security threats, despite assurances that Nord Stream's request was not motivated by Russian intentions to use the pipelines to influence Estonia's politics.

In June 2007 President Ilves made an official visit to the USA, during which US President George W. Bush endorsed the Estonian Government's proposal for the establishment of a North Atlantic Treaty Organization (NATO, see p. 370) 'cyber-defence' research centre in Tallinn, with US participation. In May 2008 the defence force commanders of Estonia, Latvia, Lithuania, Italy, Germany, Spain and Slovakia signed a memorandum of understanding on the establishment of the NATO Cooperative Cyber Defence Centre of Excellence in Tallinn; the Centre received full NATO accreditation in October. In early February 2012 NATO extended its Baltic air policing mission (initiated in 2004) over Lithuania, Latvia and Estonia until 2018. Meanwhile, in June 2008 the Estonian delegation, headed by President Ilves, withdrew from the fifth World Congress of Finno-Ugric Peoples, which was being held in the Russian town of Khanty-Mansiisk, in protest at a speech by the chairman of the foreign affairs committee of the Russian State Duma criticizing Estonia's treatment of its ethnic Russian minority. In February 2009 the head of the security department at the Estonian Ministry of Defence during 2000–06, Herman Simm, pleaded guilty to treason and was sentenced to 12.5 years' imprisonment for having reportedly passed classified Estonian, and later NATO, military documents to the Russian Foreign Intelligence Service over a period of more than 10 years.

An important focus of Estonia's foreign policy was the attainment of full membership of the EU. In July 1995 Estonia became an associate member, and in October 2002 the European Commission approved a report, which identified 10 countries, including Estonia, as ready to join the EU on 1 May 2004. A national referendum was held on 14 September 2003, in which voters were asked whether they supported Estonia's proposed accession to the EU and the adoption of legislation amending the country's Constitution; 66.8% of the votes cast by 64.1% of the electorate were in favour of Estonia's accession, which duly took effect on 1 May 2004. In June Estonia was one of three new EU member states (alongside Lithuania and Slovenia) to be admitted to the exchange rate mechanism (ERM II) as a precursor to adopting the common European currency, the euro; the Estonian Government subsequently announced that it intended to adopt the euro by January 2007. However, in April 2006 the Government acknowledged that it would not be in a position to meet this deadline. In March 2009 the Government approved a new deadline of January 2011 for euro adoption. As a result of the Government's successful fiscal programme, the European Commission announced in May 2010 that Estonia had met the necessary economic criteria to adopt the euro; on 13 July EU ministers of finance endorsed Estonia's membership of the euro area. Estonia thus formally adopted the common European currency on 1 January 2011, becoming the first Baltic state to do so. Estonia voted to join the European Financial Stability Facility (EFSF) at the end of September 2011. The treaty establishing the European Stability Mechanism (ESM), which the Government signed in February 2012, was ratified by the State Assembly on 30 August after the Supreme Court ruled in favour of its constitutionality following a legal challenge.

Estonia ratified the draft European constitutional treaty in May 2006, but this was subsequently abandoned, after being rejected at referendums in France and the Netherlands. In December 2007 EU leaders signed a replacement treaty aimed at institutional reform, the Treaty of Lisbon, which was duly ratified by Estonia in June 2008, having been approved by 91 members of the State Assembly; it entered into force in December 2009, following its ratification by all EU member states. Meanwhile, in December 2007 Estonia, together with eight other nations, implemented the EU's Schengen Agreement, enabling its citizens to travel to and from other signatory states without border controls. In September 2012 the State Assembly voted to ratify the European Stability Mechanism (ESM) treaty—the last of the EU members states' parliaments to do so—thus supporting the idea of euro area governance and the provision of financial assistance to euro area members that found themselves in financial difficulty. Meanwhile, in late March 2012 the State Assembly amended Estonia's penal code so as to make trafficking in human beings a specific criminal offence. Estonia was the last of the EU countries to pass legislation relating to the criminalization of forced labour and sexual exploitation.

Estonia has become a leader in the information and communications technology sector within the Union, as demonstrated by the basing of the new EU Agency for Large-Scale Information Technology (IT) Systems in Tallinn in 2012.

Other external relations

In November 2006 US President George W. Bush became the first US Head of State to visit Estonia, accompanied by US Secretary of State Condoleezza Rice. Speaking at a joint press conference, Bush thanked Ilves for the Estonian Government's support in the US-led 'war on terror' and expressed his appreciation for Estonian co-operation 'in the name of common aims and values'. In November 2008 Estonia joined the USA's programme for visa-free travel. At a meeting held in Washington, DC, USA, in January 2011 between Estonia's Minister of Foreign Affairs, Urmas Paet, and US Secretary of State Hillary Clinton, the latter commended the Estonian authorities for the 'commitment to good governance, the rule of law, and fiscal responsibility' demonstrated since independence in 1991.

Estonia joined NATO's 'Partnership for Peace' programme of military co-operation in March 1994. In November 2002, at a NATO summit meeting held in Prague, Czech Republic, Estonia was one of seven countries to be invited formally to accede to the Alliance, and became a full member on 29 March 2004. In May 2008 the NATO Cooperative Cyber Defence Centre of Excellence was established in Tallinn.

CONSTITUTION AND GOVERNMENT

A new Constitution, based on that of 1938, was adopted by a referendum held on 28 June 1992 and took effect on 3 July. Legislative authority resides with the Riigikogu (State Assembly), which has 101 members, elected by universal adult suffrage for a four-year term. The State Assembly elects the President (Head of State) for a term of five years. The President is also Supreme Commander of Estonia's armed forces. Executive power is held by the Council of Ministers, which is headed by the Prime Minister, who is nominated by the President. Judicial power is exercised by the Supreme Court, district courts and rural and city, as well as administrative, courts. For administrative purposes, Estonia is divided into 15 counties (*maakonds*), which in turn are subdivided into cities, rural municipalities and towns.

REGIONAL AND INTERNATIONAL CO-OPERATION

Estonia is a member of the Council of the Baltic Sea States (see p. 250), of the Baltic Council (see p. 464), of the Council of Europe (see p. 252), and of the Organization for Security and Co-operation in Europe (see p. 387). In 2004 it acceded to the European Union (see p. 273).

Estonia joined the UN in 1991, and was admitted to the World Trade Organization (see p. 434) in 1999 and to the Organisation for Economic Co-operation and Development (see p. 379) in 2010. The country is a member of the North Atlantic Treaty Organization (NATO, see p. 370) and hosts the NATO Cooperative Cyber Defence Centre of Excellence, which was established in 2008.

ECONOMIC AFFAIRS

In 2012, according to World Bank estimates, Estonia's gross national income (GNI), measured at average 2010–12 prices, was US $21,200m., equivalent to $15,830 per head (or $22,030 per head on an international purchasing-power parity basis). During 2003–12, according to World Bank estimates, the population declined at an average annual rate of 0.1%, while gross domestic product (GDP) per head increased, in real terms, by an average of 3.1% per year. According to World Bank estimates, overall GDP increased, in real terms, at an average annual rate of 3.0% during 2003–12. According to chain-linked methodologies, real GDP increased by 9.6% in 2011 and by 3.9% in 2012.

Agriculture (including hunting, forestry and fishing) contributed 4.1% of GDP in 2012, when the sector provided 4.7% of employment. Animal husbandry is the main activity in the agricultural sector. Some 27.4% of Estonia's land is cultivable. The principal crops are wheat, barley, potatoes, rapeseed and fruit and vegetables. Forestry products are also important. During 2003–10, according to World Bank estimates, agricultural GDP grew, in real terms, at an average annual rate of 0.5%. According to chain-linked methodologies, the GDP of the sector increased by 12.4% in 2012.

Industry (including mining and quarrying, manufacturing, construction, and power) contributed 28.9% of GDP in 2012, when the sector provided 31.1% of employment. During 2003–10, according to World Bank estimates, industrial GDP increased, in real terms, at an average annual rate of 2.4%; industrial GDP decreased by 23.8% in 2009, but increased by 11.1% in 2010.

Mining and quarrying contributed 1.3% of GDP in 2012, when the sector provided 0.8% of employment. Estonia's principal mineral resource is oil shale, and there are also deposits of peat, phosphorite ore, limestone and granite. There are total estimated reserves of oil shale of some 4,000m. metric tons. Annual extraction of oil shale was 18.8m. tons in 2012, compared with some 31m. tons in 1980. Phosphorite ore is processed to produce phosphates for use in agriculture, but development of the industry has been accompanied by increasing environmental problems. In 2000–07 the GDP of the mining and quarrying sector increased, in real terms, at an average annual rate of 6.3%. According to chain-linked methodologies, the GDP of the mining and quarrying sector increased by 4.7% in 2011, but decreased by 2.3% in 2012.

In 2012 the manufacturing sector accounted for 15.4% of GDP and engaged 18.8% of the employed labour force. The sector is based on products of food- and beverage-processing (especially dairy products), textiles and clothing, fertilizers and other chemical products, and wood and timber products (particularly furniture). According to World Bank estimates, in 2003–10 the GDP of the manufacturing sector increased, in real terms, at an average annual rate of 3.2%. Real manufacturing GDP increased by 17.8% in 2011, but decreased by 1.9% in 2012, according to chain-linked methodologies.

The construction sector contributed 7.8% of GDP and engaged 9.4% of the employed labour force in 2012. According to chain-linked methodologies, sectoral GDP increased by 31.8% in 2011 and by 12.5% in 2012.

The country relies on oil shale for over 90% of its energy requirements, meaning that it is self-sufficient in terms of electricity generation and is a net exporter of electrical energy. Estlink, an under-sea electrical cable connecting the electricity networks of Estonia and Finland, became operational in January 2007 and has provided an additional source of revenue through the export of excess power; a second under-sea cable between Estonia and Finland, Estlink II, entered into operation in early 2014. Nevertheless, Estonia is dependent on Russian gas for its other energy needs, such as heating, and on Russian oil, for both domestic use and export. In 2011 the Government announced that Estonia would participate jointly (taking a 20% share) with the Governments of Lithuania, Latvia and Poland in the construction of a 1,300-MW nuclear power plant at Visaginas, Lithuania; however, development plans for the plant still had not been finalised in early 2014. In 2012 imports of mineral fuels accounted for 15.0% of total imports.

The services sector accounted for 66.9% of GDP and engaged 64.2% of the employed population in 2012. According to World Bank estimates, during 2003–10 the GDP of the services sector increased, in real terms, by an annual average rate of 2.0%; the GDP of the sector declined by 0.9% in 2010.

In 2012 Estonia recorded a visible merchandise trade deficit of US $1,201.4m., while there was a deficit of $404.8m. on the current account of the balance of payments. After 1991 trade with the West, particularly the Nordic countries, increased considerably. In 2012 Finland was Estonia's principal source of imports, accounting for 14.3% of the total. Other important sources of imports were Germany, Sweden, Latvia, Lithuania, Russia and Poland. In 2012 Sweden was the principal export trading partner, accounting for 15.9% of exports. Finland, Russia, Latvia and Lithuania were other important purchasers of exports. In 2012 the principal exports were machinery, mechanical and electrical appliances, mineral products, base metals and articles of base metal, wood, articles of wood, miscellaneous manufactured articles, and chemical products. The principal imports in that year were machinery, mechanical and electrical appliances, mineral products, vehicles, chemical products, base metals and articles of base metal, prepared foodstuffs and beverages, and plastics, rubber and articles thereof.

Official forecasts provided for a budgetary deficit of €62.2m. in 2014. Estonia's general government gross debt was €1,695m. euros in 2012, equivalent to 9.7% of GDP. According to ILO, during 2003–12 the annual rate of inflation averaged 4.5%. Consumer prices increased by 3.9% in 2012. In 2012 some 10.1% of the labour force were officially registered as unemployed.

Estonia was admitted to the Organisation for Economic Co-operation and Development in December 2010 and adopted the euro as the national currency in 2011, following disciplined efforts to maintain the fiscal deficit at less than 3% of GDP. This policy also enabled the country to emerge from the global financial and economic downturn without a burdensome level of debt. Moreover, the adoption of the euro made trade with other EU countries (which between them typically purchase around three-quarters of Estonian exports) more attractive and helped to encourage foreign investment. By 2010 positive growth had resumed, and the IMF assessed in 2013 that exports, which had come to substantially exceed the levels recorded before the economic crisis of 2008–09, had been the main driver of the recovery; domestic investment also played a significant role. Estonia has had the lowest rate of national debt as a percentage of GDP in the EU since joining in 2004; in 2012 this had risen slightly to 9.8%, but the EU average in that year was 85.1%. Moreover, Eurostat recorded that the rate of unemployment in Estonia had fallen from 16.9% in 2010 to 10.2% in 2012. Meanwhile, youth unemployment (of those aged 15–24 years), which reached a peak of 32.9% in 2010, declined to 20.9% by 2012. The economy's strong performance, particularly in 2011 and 2012, was attributed to the manufacturing, construction, and information and communications sectors, though the country had not yet reached its pre-crisis level of economic output. None the less, in 2011 Estonia recorded the strongest growth in the EU. Consecutive governments have sustained the course of conservative fiscal policy and macroeconomic reforms that has allowed the domestic economy to remain stable relative to others in the eurozone and elsewhere. The IMF forecast real GDP growth of 1.5% in 2013 and 2.5% in 2014, though Statistics Estonia estimated economic growth at 0.7% in 2013, after a slowdown in the final quarter of the year resulting from a downturn in the export of manufactured products and in transport revenue (related to trade relations with Russia), as well as in the agriculture and construction sectors (following a decline in government expenditure).

PUBLIC HOLIDAYS

2015: 1 January (New Year's Day), 24 February (Independence Day), 3 April (Good Friday), 1 May (Spring Day), 23 June (Victory Day, anniversary of the Battle of Võnnu in 1919), 24 June (Midsummer Day, Jaanipäev), 20 August (Restoration of Independence Day), 25–26 December (Christmas—Gregorian Calendar).

Statistical Survey

Source (unless otherwise stated): Statistical Office of Estonia (Statiskaamet), Endla 15, Tallinn 0100; tel. 625-9202; fax 625-9370; e-mail stat@stat.ee; internet www.stat.ee.

Area and Population

AREA, POPULATION AND DENSITY

Area (sq km)	45,227*
Population (census results)†	
31 March 2000	1,370,052
31 December 2011	
Males	600,526
Females	693,929
Total	1,294,455
Population (official estimates at 1 January)	
2012	1,294,486
2013	1,286,479
Density (per sq km) at 1 January 2013	28.4

* 17,462 sq miles.

† Figures refer to permanent inhabitants.

POPULATION BY AGE AND SEX

(official estimates at 1 January 2013)

	Males	Females	Total
0–14	103,476	97,694	201,170
15–64	416,781	435,987	852,768
65 and over	77,253	155,288	232,541
Total	597,510	688,969	1,286,479

POPULATION BY ETHNIC GROUP

(official estimates at 1 January 2013)

	Number	% of total population
Estonian	898,845	69.9
Russian	324,431	25.2
Ukrainian	22,368	1.7
Belorussian	12,327	1.0
Other	28,508	2.2
Total	1,286,479	100.0

POPULATION BY COUNTY

(official estimates at 1 January 2013)

County	Area (sq km)*	Population	Density (per sq km)	County town (with population)
Harju	4,333	555,566	128.2	Tallinn (395,392)
Hiiu	1,023	8,394	8.2	Kärdla (3,000)
Ida-Viru	3,364	146,283	43.5	Jõhvi (12,550)†
Järva	2,460	29,940	12.2	Paide (8,053)
Jõgeva	2,604	30,671	11.8	Jõgeva (5,406)
Lääne	2,383	23,810	10.0	Haapsalu (10,146)
Lääne-Viru	3,628	58,806	16.2	Rakvere (15,102)
Pärnu	4,807	81,428	16.9	Pärnu (39,276)
Põlva	2,165	27,028	12.5	Põlva (5,678)
Rapla	2,980	34,442	11.6	Rapla (9,006)†
Saare	2,922	30,966	10.6	Kuressaare (12,968)
Tartu	2,993	150,139	50.2	Tartu (97,117)
Valga	2,044	29,498	14.4	Valga (12,030)
Viljandi	3,423	46,702	13.6	Viljandi (17,215)
Võru	2,305	32,806	14.2	Võru (12,379)
Total	43,432	1,286,479	29.6	

* Excluding that part of Lake Peipsi that belongs to Estonia, and the area of Lake Võrtsjärv.

† Rural municipality.

PRINCIPAL TOWNS

(official population estimates at 1 January 2013)

Tallinn (capital)	395,392	Pärnu	39,276
Tartu	97,117	Kohtla-Järve	36,377
Narva	57,650		

BIRTHS, MARRIAGES AND DEATHS*

	Registered live births		Registered marriages		Registered deaths	
	Number	Rate (per 1,000)	Number	Rate (per 1,000)	Number	Rate (per 1,000)
2005	14,350	10.7	6,121	4.6	17,316	12.9
2006	14,877	11.1	6,954	5.2	17,316	12.9
2007	15,775	11.8	7,022	5.2	17,409	13.0
2008	16,028	12.0	6,127	4.6	16,675	12.4
2009	15,763	11.8	5,362	4.0	16,081	12.0
2010	15,825	11.8	5,066	3.8	15,790	11.8
2011	14,679	11.0	5,499	4.1	15,244	11.4
2012	14,056	10.9	5,888	4.6	15,450	12.0

* Revised figures, based on the results of the 1989 and 2000 population censuses.

Life expectancy (years at birth, official estimates): 76.2 (males 71.1; females 81.1) in 2012.

ECONOMICALLY ACTIVE POPULATION

(annual averages, '000 persons aged 15–74 years)

	2010	2011	2012
Agriculture, hunting, forestry and fishing	24.1	26.9	29.1
Mining and quarrying	6.9	6.1	5.2
Manufacturing	108.4	121.0	117.5
Electricity, gas and water supply	11.0	12.1	12.8
Construction	47.9	59.0	58.7
Wholesale and retail trade	80.0	81.3	80.7
Hotels and restaurants	19.4	19.2	19.3
Transport, storage and communications	56.0	65.0	69.1
Financial intermediation	9.4	10.2	10.5
Real estate, renting and business activities	50.2	50.8	54.9
Public administration and defence; compulsory social security	40.4	40.3	41.1
Education	56.1	57.2	62.7
Health and social work	34.6	35.5	35.7
Other services	26.6	24.6	27.1
Total employed	570.9	609.1	624.4
Unemployed	115.9	86.8	70.5
Total labour force	686.8	695.9	694.9

Health and Welfare

KEY INDICATORS

Total fertility rate (children per woman, 2011)	1.7
Under-5 mortality rate (per 1,000 live births, 2011)	4
HIV/AIDS (% of persons aged 15–49, 2011)	1.3
Physicians (per 1,000 head, 2011)	3.3
Hospital beds (per 1,000 head, 2011)	5.4
Health expenditure (2010): US $ per head (PPP)	1,294
Health expenditure (2010): % of GDP	6.3
Health expenditure (2010): public (% of total)	78.9
Access to water (% of persons, 2011)	99
Access to sanitation (% of persons, 2011)	98
Total carbon dioxide emissions ('000 metric tons, 2010)	18,338.7
Carbon dioxide emissions per head (metric tons, 2010)	13.7
Human Development Index (2012): ranking	33
Human Development Index (2012): value	0.846

For sources and definitions, see explanatory note on p. vi.

Agriculture

PRINCIPAL CROPS
('000 metric tons)

	2010	2011	2012
Wheat	327.6	360.4	485.0
Barley	254.8	294.4	340.5
Rye	25.1	30.9	57.3
Oats	54.5	62.4	79.1
Triticale (wheat-rye hybrid)	9.0	13.6	24.8
Potatoes	163.4	164.7	138.9
Peas, dry	12.1	15.4	12.9
Rapeseed	131.0	144.2	157.8
Cabbages and other brassicas	16.3	20.6	16.8
Cucumbers and gherkins	12.1	11.1	9.8
Tomatoes	5.2	6.4	4.8
Carrots and turnips	22.8	24.5	17.1
Apples	2.0	2.7	1.9

Aggregate production ('000 metric tons, may include official, semi-official or estimated data): Total cereals 678.5 in 2010, 770.7 in 2011, 991.6 in 2012; Total roots and tubers 163.7 in 2010, 165.2 in 2011, 139.4 in 2012; Total vegetables (incl. melons) 74.0 in 2010, 88.3 in 2011, 66.2 in 2012; Total fruits (excl. melons) 5.1 in 2010, 5.8 in 2011, 5.1 in 2012.

Source: FAO.

LIVESTOCK
('000 head, year ending September)

	2010	2011	2012
Cattle	235	236	238
Pigs	365	372	366
Sheep	77	79	84
Chickens*	1,769	2,020	2,010

* Unofficial figures.

Source: FAO.

LIVESTOCK PRODUCTS
('000 metric tons unless otherwise indicated)

	2010	2011	2012
Cattle meat	12.9	12.2	12.3
Pig meat	45.8	50.2	48.8
Chicken meat	16.0	17.5	16.5
Cows' milk	675.3	692.4	720.7
Hen eggs	11.4	11.4	11.1
Honey (metric tons)	681	694	957
Butter	6.0	6.5	4.0
Cheese	38.4	40.6	42.6

Source: FAO.

Forestry

ROUNDWOOD REMOVALS
('000 cubic metres, excl. bark)

	2010	2011	2012
Sawlogs, veneer logs and logs for sleepers	3,312	3,330	3,330
Pulpwood	1,872	1,845	1,980
Other industrial wood	72	54	54
Fuel wood	1,944	1,881	1,926
Total	7,200	7,110	7,290

Source: FAO.

SAWNWOOD PRODUCTION
('000 cubic metres, incl. railway sleepers)

	2010	2011	2012
Coniferous (softwood)	1,641	1,369	1,350
Broadleaved (hardwood)	130	134	150
Total	1,771	1,503	1,500

Source: FAO.

Fishing

('000 metric tons, live weight)

	2009	2010	2011
Capture	97.4	95.4	80.7
Atlantic herring	33.2	28.9	25.3
European sprat	47.3	47.9	35.0
Northern prawn	8.6	9.0	9.9
Aquaculture	0.7	0.6	0.4
Total catch	98.1	96.0	81.0

Source: FAO.

Mining

('000 metric tons)

	2010	2011	2012
Oil shale	17,900	18,700	18,800
Peat	965	927	671

Industry

SELECTED PRODUCTS

('000 metric tons unless otherwise indicated)

	2010	2011	2012
Distilled spirits ('000 hectolitres)	150.7	169.2	182.0
Wine ('000 hectolitres)	64.7	73.3	96.3
Beer ('000 hectolitres)	1,293.0	1,358.8	1,460.0
Soft drinks ('000 hectolitres)	505.6	315.2	483.7
Woven cotton fabric ('000 sq metres)	10,427	476	67
Carpets ('000 sq metres)	2,411	3,065	3,276
Footwear ('000 pairs)	1,462	1,553	952
Plywood ('000 cubic metres)	39.1	42.5	46.0
Particle board ('000 cubic metres)	204.3	206.9	157.1
Fibreboard (million sq metres)	3.6	8.1	7.8
Chemical wood pulp	72.8	70.6	74.4
Paper	69.5	67.6	72.1
Nitrogenous fertilizers*	0.3	0.1	4.1
Building bricks (million)	21.2	31.7	40.2
Cement	375.0	451.0	481.5
Electric energy (million kWh)	12,964	12,893	11,966

* In terms of nitrogen (N).

Finance

CURRENCY AND EXCHANGE RATES

Monetary Units

100 cents = 1 euro (€).

Sterling, Dollar and Euro Equivalents (31 December 2013)

£1 sterling = 1.194 euros;
US $1 = 0.725 euros;
€10 = £8.37 = $13.79.

Average Exchange Rate (euros per US $)

2011	0.7194
2012	0.7783
2013	0.7532

Note: In June 1992 the kroon replaced the rouble of the former USSR in Estonia, initially at a rate of one kroon per 10 roubles. The kroon was included in the second European exchange rate mechanism (ERM II) from June 2004, with a central parity of 1 euro = 15.6466 kroons. On 1 January 2011 the euro was introduced to circulate alongside the kroon until 14 January, after which period the euro was formally adopted as the sole official currency of Estonia.

STATE BUDGET

(€ million, budget forecasts)

Revenue	2013	2014
Tax revenue	5,109.3	5,457.5
Personal income tax	299.0	331.1
Corporate income tax	320.8	316.0
Social tax	2,065.0	2,245.7
Value added tax	1,575.0	1,672.9
Excise duties	795.6	836.9
Other taxes	53.9	54.9
Non tax revenue	1,488.3	1,365.8
Sales of goods and services	164.4	130.3
Subsidies	1,027.0	902.9
Other revenue	296.8	332.6
Transfers of revenues	1,051.7	1,175.0
Total	7,649.2	7,998.3

Expenditure by function	2013	2014
General public services	1,403.2	1,372.9
Defence	337.1	358.1
Public order and safety	379.2	421.5
Economic affairs	906.8	976.8
Environment protection	317.9	320.2
Housing and community amenities	10.0	—
Health	948.2	1,017.9
Recreation, culture and religion	180.0	206.9
Education	734.2	760.6
Social protection	2,482.6	2,667.1
Statistical discrepancy	–15.4	–41.4
Total	7,683.8	8,060.5

Source: Ministry of Finance, Tallinn.

INTERNATIONAL RESERVES

(US $ million at 31 December)

	2010	2011	2012
Gold (national valuation)	11.63	12.60	13.31
IMF special drawing rights	95.52	95.23	95.33
Reserve position in IMF	0.01	0.01	12.58
Foreign exchange	2,460.36	99.63	179.44
Total	2,567.52	207.47	300.66

Source: IMF, *International Financial Statistics*.

MONEY SUPPLY

(incl. shares, depository corporations, national residency criteria, € million at 31 December)

	2011	2012
Currency issued	2,173	2,180
Demand deposits	5,028	6,039
Other deposits	3,926	3,511
Securities other than shares	19	4
Shares and other equity	2,657	2,931
Other items (net)	462	456
Total	14,265	15,121

Source: IMF, *International Financial Statistics*.

COST OF LIVING

(Consumer Price Index; base: 2000 = 100)

	2010	2011	2012
Food (incl. beverages)	153.4	168.1	174.6
All items (incl. others)	150.5	158.1	164.3

Source: ILO.

NATIONAL ACCOUNTS

(€ million at current prices)

Expenditure on the Gross Domestic Product

	2010	2011	2012
Final consumption expenditure	10,511.8	11,315.2	12,259.1
Households	7,310.3	7,964.3	8,661.9
Non-profit institutions serving households	215.7	233.1	251.7
General government	2,985.7	3,117.8	3,345.4
Gross capital formation	2,837.3	4,341.3	4,907.9
Gross fixed capital formation	2,726.6	3,832.6	4,395.8
Changes in inventories Acquisitions, less disposals, of valuables	110.7	508.7	512.1
Total domestic expenditure	13,349.1	15,656.5	17,167.0
Exports of goods and services	11,387.7	14,677.8	15,771.7
Less Imports of goods and services	10,385.5	14,080.0	15,732.0
Statistical discrepancy	19.9	–37.9	208.4
GDP in market prices	14,371.1	16,216.4	17,415.1

Gross Domestic Product by Economic Activity

	2010	2011	2012
Agriculture, forestry and fishing	413.2	566.9	627.4
Mining and quarrying	173.9	187.9	203.1
Manufacturing	1,995.4	2,325.1	2,328.9
Electricity, gas and water supply	650.3	630.0	675.7
Construction	739.0	984.2	1,180.9
Wholesale and retail trade; repair of motor vehicles, motorcycles and personal and household goods	1,490.7	1,726.1	1,871.2
Hotels and restaurants	175.7	220.0	255.9
Transport, storage and communications	1,685.8	1,832.0	1,957.8
Financial intermediation	485.1	545.0	479.3
Real estate, renting and business activities	1,924.1	2,236.8	2,463.9
Public administration and defence; compulsory social security	1,421.0	1,469.4	1,582.6
Education	630.3	646.5	666.0
Health and social work	468.8	495.2	522.4
Other community, social and personal service activities	281.7	300.0	345.1
Gross value added in basic prices	12,535.1	14,165.0	15,160.2
Taxes on products *Less* Subsidies on products	1,836.0	2,051.4	2,254.9
GDP in market prices	14,371.1	16,216.4	17,415.1

BALANCE OF PAYMENTS
(US $ million)

	2010	2011	2012
Exports of goods	10,242.9	14,596.1	14,479.5
Imports of goods	−10,730.5	−15,340.5	−15,680.9
Balance on goods	−487.5	−744.4	−1,201.4
Exports of services	4,672.0	5,810.6	5,663.3
Imports of services	−2,777.4	−3,677.0	−3,906.7
Balance on goods and services	1,407.0	1,389.1	555.3
Primary income received	930.5	1,214.1	994.9
Primary income paid	−2,112.9	−2,545.8	−2,260.9
Balance on goods, services and primary income	224.6	57.4	−710.6
Secondary income received	735.4	847.0	789.1
Secondary income paid	−425.0	−493.8	−483.2
Current balance	535.0	410.6	−404.8
Capital account (net)	675.3	928.8	776.9
Direct investment assets	−590.1	1,311.1	−1,091.2
Direct investment liabilities	2,051.9	521.0	1,648.5
Portfolio investment assets	−397.3	1,411.4	−337.5
Portfolio investment liabilities	−189.2	167.7	214.7
Financial derivatives and employee stock options (net)	43.0	−54.6	87.9
Other investment assets	−1,726.3	−3,039.4	−2,146.4
Other investment liabilities	−1,442.1	−1,740.0	1,335.4
Net errors and omissions	−72.0	100.5	7.5
Reserves and related items	−1,111.8	17.1	90.8

Source: IMF, *International Financial Statistics*.

External Trade

PRINCIPAL COMMODITIES
(distribution by HS, € million)

Imports c.i.f.	2010	2011	2012
Prepared foodstuffs; beverages, spirits and vinegar; tobacco and manufactured substitutes	581.8	707.9	779.9
Mineral products	1,614.5	2,276.3	2,137.8
Mineral fuels, mineral oils and products of their distillation; bituminous substances, etc.	1,580.6	2,231.2	2,080.9
Petroleum oils and oils obtained from bituminous minerals, other than crude	1,291.9	1,854.0	1,629.8
Products of chemical or allied industries	734.9	963.9	1,134.3
Plastics, rubber and articles thereof	521.0	612.1	670.1
Plastics and articles thereof	423.2	487.4	522.0
Textiles and textile articles	461.7	536.1	564.9
Base metals and articles of base metal	825.0	1,111.3	1,071.6
Iron and steel	321.6	484.3	408.3
Machinery and mechanical appliances; electrical equipment; sound and television apparatus	2,199.2	3,505.4	3,944.9
Boilers, machinery and mechanical appliances; parts thereof	725.4	1,209.5	1,414.8
Electrical machinery equipment and parts; sound and television apparatus parts and accessories	1,473.8	2,295.9	2,530.1
Telephone sets (incl. telephones for cellular networks and other wireless networks)	425.5	838.7	780.0
Vehicles, aircraft, vessels and associated transport equipment	656.1	1,032.0	1,279.4
Vehicles other than railway or tramway rolling-stock, and parts and accessories	549.0	884.5	996.7
Motor cars and other motor vehicles mainly designed for personal transport	256.2	443.7	490.9
Total (incl. others)	9,268.3	12,726.8	13,847.6

Exports f.o.b.	2010	2011	2012
Live animals and animal products	318.9	388.7	424.5
Prepared foodstuffs; beverages, spirits and vinegar; tobacco and manufactured substitutes	349.1	409.9	507.9
Mineral products	1,376.0	2,061.6	1,874.5
Mineral fuels, mineral oils and products of their distillation	1,350.2	2,018.9	1,828.3
Petroleum oils and oils obtained from bituminous minerals, other than crude	1,051.4	1,671.3	1,474.4
Products of chemical or allied industries	395.3	564.8	645.0
Plastics, rubber and articles thereof	279.6	349.5	382.1
Wood and articles thereof; wood charcoal; cork and articles thereof	792.7	925.3	922.6
Wood and articles thereof; wood charcoal	791.7	923.8	921.5
Pulp of wood or of other fibrous cellulosic material; waste and scrap of paper or paperboard	277.7	314.4	316.0
Textiles and textile articles	300.1	349.7	361.8

Exports f.o.b.—*continued*	2010	2011	2012
Base metals and articles of base metal	793.9	1,032.6	1,029.9
Iron and steel	315.4	428.3	399.1
Machinery and mechanical appliances; electrical equipment; sound and television apparatus	1,978.1	3,291.5	3,579.7
Boilers, machinery and mechanical appliances; parts thereof	529.0	874.6	1,085.4
Electrical machinery equipment and parts; sound and television apparatus parts and accessories	1,449.1	2,416.8	2,494.3
Telephone sets (incl. telephones for cellular networks and other wireless networks)	607.8	1,301.6	1,316.6
Vehicles, aircraft, vessels and associated transport equipment	570.9	591.4	604.2
Vehicles other than railway or tramway rolling-stock, and parts and accessories	406.1	503.6	514.8
Miscellaneous manufactured articles	667.1	787.3	827.2
Furniture; bedding, mattresses, cushions, etc.; lamps and lighting fittings; prefabricated buildings	591.4	702.9	740.1
Total (incl. others)	8,743.0	12,003.4	12,517.9

PRINCIPAL TRADING PARTNERS
(€ million)

Imports c.i.f.	2010	2011	2012
Belarus	118.4	147.2	210.9
Belgium	155.0	234.7	269.9
China, People's Republic	281.6	455.7	480.6
Czech Republic	104.3	161.2	183.7
Denmark	174.9	200.0	221.3
Finland	1,378.1	1,604.5	1,985.7
France	164.4	210.1	246.8
Germany	1,046.3	1,304.3	1,421.0
Hungary	54.9	156.7	163.6
Italy	221.5	277.6	309.1
Latvia	1,012.2	1,137.8	1,266.8
Lithuania	725.0	1,041.0	1,182.9
Netherlands	308.5	465.2	527.2
Norway	128.5	141.9	182.5
Poland	586.7	852.2	878.7
Russia	762.8	1,264.6	1,003.7
Sweden	1,007.5	1,331.1	1,402.6
Ukraine	71.7	108.4	197.0
United Kingdom	199.2	438.7	531.3
USA	92.8	141.1	116.9
Total (incl. others)	9,268.3	12,726.8	13,847.6

Exports f.o.b.	2010	2011	2012
Belgium	112.3	144.2	230.9
China, People's Republic	112.2	203.1	101.2
Denmark	217.7	308.1	297.5
Finland	1,487.6	1,807.8	1,819.7
France	214.7	315.5	168.6
Germany	454.6	550.1	564.5
Italy	80.7	193.3	179.3
Latvia	776.8	954.1	1,098.0
Lithuania	437.1	553.1	662.1
Netherlands	203.1	319.4	306.3
Nigeria	165.0	391.4	177.0
Norway	299.8	360.8	419.7
Poland	142.6	182.2	175.8
Russia	844.4	1,312.3	1,511.5
Spain	64.7	163.5	137.6
Sweden	1,364.8	1,875.2	1,995.4
Turkey	99.8	148.2	160.7
Ukraine	88.4	105.6	118.5
United Kingdom	171.9	241.2	262.5
USA	330.9	749.8	584.0
Total (incl. others)	8,743.0	12,003.4	12,517.9

Transport

RAILWAYS
(traffic)

	2010	2011	2012
Passengers carried ('000)	4,803	4,736	4,416
Passenger-kilometres (million)	247.9	241.3	235.8
Freight carried ('000 metric tons)	46,726	48,262	44,684
Freight ton-kilometres (million)	6,642.3	6,260.6	5,126.4

ROAD TRAFFIC
('000 motor vehicles in use at 31 December)

	2010	2011	2012
Passenger cars	552.7	574.0	602.1
Buses and coaches	4.2	4.2	4.3
Lorries and vans	81.2	84.3	88.0
Motorcycles	19.7	21.1	22.8
Trailers	65.5	69.9	75.2

SHIPPING

Flag Registered Fleet
(at 31 December)

	2011	2012	2013
Number of vessels	147	147	146
Total displacement ('000 grt)	339.4	326.0	334.3

Source: Lloyd's List Intelligence (www.lloydslistintelligence.com).

International Sea-borne Freight Traffic
('000 metric tons)

	2010	2011	2012
Goods loaded	34,540	35,110	31,488
Goods unloaded	11,305	13,153	11,853

CIVIL AVIATION
(traffic on scheduled services)

	2010	2011	2012
Passengers carried ('000)	663.5	791.1	1,020.3
Passenger-km (million)	874.1	1,051.5	1,143.5

2012: Freight carried ('000 metric tons) 0.7; Total ton-km (million) 0.6.

Tourism

FOREIGN TOURIST ARRIVALS BY COUNTRY OF ORIGIN*

	2010	2011	2012
Finland	832,874	840,714	829,225
Germany	84,454	103,559	111,251
Latvia	72,684	85,229	100,638
Lithuania	34,107	47,003	47,397
Norway	40,414	51,510	48,479
Russia	141,964	203,204	266,192
Sweden	81,196	86,287	78,412
United Kingdom and Ireland	35,692	69,912	54,305
Total (incl. others)	1,563,952	1,807,919	1,873,519

* Figures refer to arrivals at registered accommodation establishments.

Tourism receipts (US $ million, excl. passenger transport, unless otherwise indicated): 1,073 in 2010; 1,249 in 2011; 1,226 in 2012 (provisional) (Source: World Tourism Organization).

Communications Media

	2010	2011	2012
Telephones ('000 main lines in use)	482.2	471.9	448.2
Mobile cellular telephones ('000 subscribers)	1,652.8	1,863.1	2,070.5
Internet subscribers ('000)	337.6	348.9	n.a.
Broadband subscribers ('000)	312.0	332.1	343.9
Book production: titles	3,760	3,716	3,971
Book production: copies (million)	5.5	4.4	4.6
Daily newspapers: titles	13	13	13
Other periodicals: titles	1,153	1,159	1,149
Other periodicals: average annual circulation (million copies)	25.8	25.3	28.2

Non-daily newspapers: 118 titles in 2010.

Source: partly International Telecommunication Union.

Education

(2011/12 unless otherwise indicated)

	Institutions	Teachers	Students
Pre-primary	644	6,754*	67,000
Primary	323†	6,141*	76,026‡
General secondary	221	12,259§	94,935‡
Special	43	n.a.	3,500
Vocational and professional	48	783	26,172
Universities, etc.	29	6,842‖	64,806¶

* 2007/08.
† 2004/05.
‡ 2006/07.
§ 2001/02.
‖ 2005/06.
¶ Including students enrolled in evening and correspondence courses.

Pupil-teacher ratio (primary education, UNESCO estimate): 11.7 in 2009/10 (Source: UNESCO Institute for Statistics).

Adult literacy rate (UNESCO estimates): 99.8% (males 99.8%; females 99.8%) in 2011 (Source: UNESCO Institute for Statistics).

Directory

The Government

HEAD OF STATE

President: TOOMAS HENDRIK ILVES (elected by vote of the Riigikogu 23 September 2006; inaugurated 9 October 2006; re-elected 29 August 2011; inaugurated 10 October 2011).

COUNCIL OF MINISTERS
(April 2014)

A coalition Government, comprising members of the Estonian Reform Party (ER) and the Social Democratic Party (SDE).

Prime Minister: TAAVI RÕIVAS (ER).

Minister of Education and Research: JEVGENI OSSINOVSKI (SDE).

Minister of Justice: ANDRES ANVELT (SDE).

Minister of Defence: SVEN MIKSER (SDE).

Minister of the Environment: KEIT PENTUS-ROSIMANNUS (ER).

Minister of Culture: URVE TIIDUS (ER).

Minister of Economic Affairs and Communications: URVE PALO (SDE).

Minister, responsible for Foreign Trade and Entrepreneurship: ANNE SULLING (ER).

Minister of Agriculture: IVARI PADAR (SDE).

Minister of Finance: JÜRGEN LIGI (ER).

Minister of the Interior: HANNO PEVKUR (ER).

Minister of Social Affairs: HELMEN KÜTT (SDE).

Minister, responsible for Health and Labour: URMAS KRUUSE (ER).

Minister of Foreign Affairs: URMAS PAET (ER).

MINISTRIES

Office of the President: A. Weizenbergi 39, Tallinn 15050; tel. 631-6202; fax 631-6250; e-mail vpinfo@vpk.ee; internet www.president.ee.

Office of the Prime Minister: Stenbocki maja, Rahukohtu 3, Tallinn 15161; tel. 693-5555; fax 693-5554; e-mail riigikantselei@riigikantselei.ee; internet www.valitsus.ee.

Ministry of Agriculture: Lai 39/41, Tallinn 15056; tel. 625-6101; fax 625-6200; e-mail pm@agri.ee; internet www.agri.ee.

Ministry of Culture: Suur Karja 23, Tallinn 15076; tel. 628-2250; fax 628-2200; e-mail min@kul.ee; internet www.kul.ee.

Ministry of Defence: Sakala 1, Tallinn 15094; tel. 717-0022; fax 717-0001; e-mail info@kaitseministeerium.ee; internet www.kaitseministeerium.ee.

Ministry of Economic Affairs and Communications: Harju 11, Tallinn 15072; tel. 625-6342; fax 631-3660; e-mail info@mkm.ee; internet www.mkm.ee.

Ministry of Education and Research: Munga 18, Tartu 50088; tel. 735-0222; fax 730-1080; e-mail hm@hm.ee; internet www.hm.ee.

Ministry of the Environment: Narva mnt. 7A, Tallinn 15172; tel. 626-2802; fax 626-2801; e-mail keskkonnaministeerium@envir.ee; internet www.envir.ee.

Ministry of Finance: Suur-Ameerika 1, Tallinn 15006; tel. 611-3558; fax 611-3664; e-mail info@fin.ee; internet www.fin.ee.

Ministry of Foreign Affairs: Islandi Väljak 1, Tallinn 15049; tel. 637-7000; fax 637-7099; e-mail vminfo@vm.ee; internet www.vm.ee.

Ministry of the Interior: Pikk 61, Tallinn 15065; tel. 612-5008; e-mail info@siseministeerium.ee; internet www.siseministeerium.ee; Note: The Office of the Minister of Regional Affairs forms part of the Ministry of the Interior.

Ministry of Justice: Tõnismägi 5A, Tallinn 15191; tel. 620-8100; fax 620-8109; e-mail info@just.ee; internet www.just.ee.

Ministry of Social Affairs: Gonsiori 29, Tallinn 15027; tel. 626-9301; fax 699-2209; e-mail info@sm.ee; internet www.sm.ee.

President

On 29 August 2011 a presidential election was conducted in the 101-member Riigikogu (State Assembly). TOOMAS HENDRIK ILVES, the incumbent, was elected to a second term of office in the first round of voting, securing 73 votes, more than the requisite two-thirds' majority (68 votes). The only other candidate, INDREK TARAND, received 25 votes. ILVES assumed office on 10 October.

Legislature

State Assembly
(Riigikogu)

Lossi plats 1A, Tallinn 15165; tel. 631-6331; fax 631-6334; e-mail riigikogu@riigikogu.ee; internet www.riigikogu.ee.

Speaker: ENE ERGMA.

General Election, 6 March 2011

Parties	Votes	%	Seats
Estonian Reform Party	164,255	28.56	33
Estonian Centre Party	134,124	23.32	26
Union of Pro Patria and Res Publica	118,023	20.52	23
Estonian Social Democratic Party	98,307	17.09	19
Other parties	44,542	7.74	—
Individual candidates	15,882	2.76	—
Total	575,133	100.00	101

Election Commission

Estonian National Electoral Committee (Vabariigi Valimiskomisjon): Lossi plats 1A, Tallinn 15165; tel. 631-6540; fax 631-6541; e-mail info@vvk.ee; internet www.vvk.ee; Chair. HEIKI SIBUL.

Political Organizations

Estonian Centre Party (Eesti Keskerakond): Toom-Rüütli 3/5, Tallinn 10130; tel. 627-3460; fax 627-3461; e-mail keskerakond@keskerakond.ee; internet www.keskerakond.ee; f. 1991; absorbed the Estonian Green Party in 1998 and the Estonian Pensioners' Party in 2005; Chair. EDGAR SAVISAAR; Sec.-Gen. PRIIT TOOBAL; 9,000 mems.

Estonian Christian Democrats (EKD) (Eesti Kristlikud Demokraadid): Jaama 2, 3rd Floor, Tallinn 11621; tel. 659-2357; fax 626-1431; e-mail ekd@erakond.eu; internet www.ekd.ee; f. 1998; fmrly Estonian Christian People's Party; present name adopted 2006; Chair. PEETER VÕSU.

Estonian Conservative People's Party (Eesti Konservatiivseks Rahvaerakonnaks): Pärnu mnt. 30–5, Tallinn 10141; tel. 616-1790; fax 616-1791; e-mail erl@erl.ee; f. 2000 as Estonian People's Union; present name adopted March 2012; right-wing; Chair. MARGO MILJAND; 10,000 mems (2009).

Estonian Greens (Erakond Eestimaa Rohelised): Haabersti kandekeskus, POB 4740, Tallinn 13503; tel. 502-6816; e-mail info@erakond.ee; internet roheline.erakond.ee; f. 2006; Chair. ALEKSANDER LAANE.

Estonian Reform Party (ER) (Eesti Reformierakond): Tõnismagi 9, Tallinn 10119; tel. 680-8080; fax 680-8081; e-mail info@reform.ee; internet www.reform.ee; f. 1994; liberal; Chair. TAAVI RÕIVAS; 11,151 mems (2012).

Estonian Social Democratic Party (SDE) (Sotsiaaldemokraatlik Erakond): Ahtri 10A, Tallinn 10151; tel. 611-6040; fax 611-6050; e-mail kantselei@sotsdem.ee; internet www.sotsdem.ee; f. 1999 as the People's Party Moderates, by merger of the People's Party and the Moderates' Party; name changed in 2004; Chair. SVEN MIKSER; Sec.-Gen. INDREK SAAR; 6,195 mems (2014).

Estonian United Left Party (Eestimaa Ühendatud Vasakpartei): Estonia pst. 7, Tallinn 10143; tel. 645-5335; fax 645-5336; e-mail info@vasak.ee; internet vasakpartei.ee; f. 2008 by merger of the Constitution Party (representing the Russian-speaking minority in Estonia) and the Estonian Left Party; extreme left-wing; Co-Chair. SERGEI JÜRGENS, HEINO RÜÜTEL; 2,500 mems (2008).

Union of Pro Patria and Res Publica (IRL) (Isamaa ja Res Publica Liit): Paldiski mnt. 13, Tallinn 10137; tel. 624-0400; e-mail info@irl.ee; internet www.irl.ee; f. 2006 by merger of the Pro Patria Union (f. 1995) and the Union for the Republic Res Publica (f. 2001); conservative, centre-right; Chair. URMAS REINSALU; 9,900 mems (2012).

Diplomatic Representation

EMBASSIES IN ESTONIA

Austria: Vambola 6, Tallinn 10114; tel. 627-8740; fax 631-4365; e-mail tallinn-ob@bmeia.gv.at; internet www.bmeia.gv.at/botschaft/tallinn; Ambassador RENATE KOBLER.

Azerbaijan: Pirita tee 20T, Tallinn 10127; tel. 640-5050; fax 640-5051; e-mail tallinn@mission.mfa.gov.az; internet www.azembassy.ee; Ambassador TOFIQ ZÜLFÜQAROV.

Belarus: Magdaleena 3B, Tallinn 11312; tel. 651-5500; fax 655-8001; e-mail estonia@mfa.gov.by; internet estonia.mfa.gov.by; Chargé d'affaires a.i. VADIM LAZERKO.

Belgium: Rataskaevu 2–9, Tallinn 10123; tel. 627-4100; fax 627-4101; e-mail tallinn@diplobel.fed.be; internet www.diplomatie.be/tallinn; Ambassador MARC THUNUS.

Brazil: Lauteri 5, 4th Floor, Tallinn 10114; tel. 633-7070; fax 633-7871; e-mail brasemb.talin@itamaraty.gov.br; Ambassador VERGNIAUD ELYSEU FILHO.

Bulgaria: Lauteri 5, Tallinn 10114; tel. 648-0388; fax 648-1110; e-mail heiki@kranich.ee; Chargé d'affaires a.i. RALITSA DYUBRAILOVA.

China, People's Republic: Narva mnt. 98, Tallinn 15009; tel. 601-5830; fax 601-5833; e-mail chinaemb@online.ee; internet www.chinaembassy.ee; Ambassador QU ZHE.

Czech Republic: Lahe 4, Tallinn 10150; tel. 627-4400; fax 631-4716; e-mail tallinn@embassy.mzv.cz; internet www.mzv.cz/tallinn; Ambassador RICHARD KADLČÁK.

Denmark: Wismari 5, Tallinn 15047; tel. 630-6400; fax 630-6421; e-mail tllamb@um.dk; internet estland.um.dk; Ambassador SØREN KELSTRUP.

Finland: Kohtu 4, Tallinn 15180; tel. 610-3200; fax 610-3281; e-mail sanomat.tal@formin.fi; internet www.finland.ee; Ambassador ALEKSI HÄRKÖNEN.

France: Toom-Kuninga 20, Tallinn 15185; tel. 616-1600; fax 616-1608; e-mail info@ambafrance-ee.org; internet www.ambafrance-ee.org; Ambassador MICHEL RAINERI.

Georgia: Viru väljak 2, Tallinn 10111; tel. 698-8590; fax 641-3000; e-mail tallinn.emb@mfa.gov.ge; internet www.estonia.mfa.gov.ge; Chargé d'affaires a.i. TAMAR MIKABERIDZE.

Germany: Toom-Kuninga 11, Tallinn 15048; tel. 627-5300; fax 627-5304; e-mail info@tallinn.diplo.de; internet www.tallinn.diplo.de; Ambassador CHRISTIAN MATTHIAS SCHLAGA.

Greece: Pärnu mnt. 12, 2nd Floor, Tallinn 10148; tel. 640-3560; fax 640-3561; e-mail gremb.tal@mfa.gr; internet www.mfa.gr/tallinn; Ambassador KONSTANTINOS KATSAMBIS.

Hungary: Narva mnt. 122, Tallinn 15025; tel. 605-1880; fax 605-4088; e-mail mission.tal@mfa.gov.hu; internet www.mfa.gov.hu/kulkepviselet/ee/ee; Ambassador ERIK HAUPT.

Ireland: Vene 2, 2nd Floor, Tallinn 10123; tel. 681-1888; fax 681-1889; e-mail tallinnembassy@dfa.ie; internet www.embassyofireland.ee; Ambassador PETER MCIVOR.

Italy: Vene 2, 3rd Floor, Tallinn 15075; tel. 627-6160; fax 631-1370; e-mail ambasciata.tallinn@esteri.it; internet www.ambtallinn.esteri.it; Ambassador MARCO CLEMENTE.

Japan: Harju 6, Tallinn 15069; tel. 631-0531; fax 631-0533; e-mail info@ti.mofa.go.jp; internet www.ee.emb-japan.go.jp; Ambassador TETSURO KAI.

Latvia: Tõnismägi 10, Tallinn 10119; tel. 627-7850; fax 627-7855; e-mail embassy.estonia@mfa.gov.lv; Ambassador JURIS BONE.

Lithuania: Uus 15, Tallinn 15070; tel. 616-4991; fax 641-2013; e-mail amb.ee@urm.lt; internet ee.mfa.lt; Ambassador NEILAS TANKEVIČIUS.

Macedonia, former Yugoslav republic: Suurtüki 4 A/13, Tallinn 10133; tel. and fax 644-0479; e-mail talin@mfa.gov.mk; internet www.missions.gov.mk/tallinn; Ambassador SAŠO VELJANOVSKI.

Moldova: Tatari 20/9–10, Tallinn 10116; tel. 642-0203; fax 642-0204; e-mail tallinn@mfa.md; internet www.estonia.mfa.md; Ambassador VICTOR GUZUN.

Netherlands: Rahukohtu 4-I, Tallinn 10130; tel. 680-5500; fax 680-5501; e-mail info@netherlandsembassy.ee; internet www.netherlandsembassy.ee; Ambassador JOS SCHELLAARS.

Norway: Harju 6, Tallinn 15054; tel. 627-1000; fax 627-1001; e-mail emb.tallinn@mfa.no; internet www.norra.ee; Ambassador LISE KLEVEN GREVSTAD.

Poland: Suur-Karja 1, Tallinn 10140; tel. 627-8201; fax 644-5221; e-mail eetalamb@msz.gov.pl; internet www.tallinn.polemb.net; Ambassador GRZEGORZ M. POZNAŃSKI.

Russia: Pikk 19, Tallinn 10133; tel. 646-4175; fax 646-4178; e-mail vensaat@online.ee; internet www.rusemb.ee; Ambassador YURII N. MERZLYAKOV.

Spain: Liivalaia 13–15, 6th Floor, Tallinn 10118; tel. 667-6651; fax 631-3767; e-mail emb.tallinn@mae.es; internet www.mae.es/embajadas/tallin; Ambassador ÁLVARO DE LA RIVA GUZMÁN DE FRUTOS.

Sweden: Pikk 28, Tallinn 15055; tel. 640-5600; fax 640-5695; e-mail ambassaden.tallinn@gov.se; internet www.sweden.ee; Ambassador ANDERS LJUNGGREN.

Turkey: Narva mnt. 30, Tallinn 10152; tel. 627-2880; fax 627-2885; e-mail embassy.tallinn@mfa.gov.tr; internet tallinn.emb.mfa.gov.tr; Ambassador AYŞENUR ALPASLAN.

Ukraine: Lahe 6, Tallinn 15170; tel. 601-5815; fax 601-5816; e-mail embassyofukraine@gmail.com; internet www.mfa.gov.ua/estonia; Ambassador VIKTOR V. KRYSHANIVSKY.

United Kingdom: Wismari 6, Tallinn 10136; tel. 667-4700; fax 667-4755; e-mail infotallinn@fco.gov.uk; internet www.ukinestonia.fco.gov.uk; Ambassador CHRISTOPHER B. HOLTBY.

USA: Kentmanni 20, Tallinn 15099; tel. 668-8100; fax 668-8265; e-mail usasaatkond@state.gov; internet estonia.usembassy.gov; Ambassador JEFFREY D. LEVINE.

Judicial System

Supreme Court
(Riigikohus)

Lossi 17, Tartu 50093; tel. 730-9002; fax 730-9003; e-mail info@riigikohus.ee; internet www.nc.ee.

Chief Justice and Chairman of the Constitutional Review Chamber: Märt Rask.

Chairman of the Civil Chamber: Ants Kull.

Chairman of the Criminal Chamber: Priit Pikamäe.

Chairman of the Administrative Law Chamber: Tõnu Anton.

Office of the Chancellor of Justice (Õiguskantsleri Kantselei): Kohtu 8, Tallinn 15193; tel. 693-8404; fax 693-8401; e-mail info@oiguskantsler.ee; internet www.oiguskantsler.ee; f. 1993; reviews general application of legislative and executive powers and of local governments for conformity with the Constitution, supervises activities of state agencies in guaranteeing constitutional rights and freedoms; Chancellor of Justice Indrek Teder.

Public Prosecutor's Office (Riigiprokuratuur): Wismari 7, Tallinn 15188; tel. 613-9400; fax 613-9402; e-mail info@prokuratuur.ee; internet www.prokuratuur.ee; State Prosecutor-Gen. Norman Aas.

Religion

CHRISTIANITY

Protestant Churches

Estonian Conference of Seventh-day Adventists (Seitsmenda Päeva Adventistide Kogudus Eesti Liit): Lille 18, Tartu 51010; tel. and fax 734-3211; e-mail info@advent.ee; internet www.advent.ee; f. 1917; Pres. David Nõmmik.

Estonian Evangelical Lutheran Church (Eesti Evangeelne Luterlik Kirik): Kiriku plats 3, Tallinn 10130; tel. 627-7350; fax 627-7352; e-mail konsistoorium@eelk.ee; internet www.eelk.ee; 172,000 mems; Archbishop Most Rev. Andres Põder.

Union of Free Evangelical Christian and Baptist Churches of Estonia (Eesti Evangeeliumi Kristlaste ja Baptistide Koguduste Liit): Koskla 18, Tallinn 10615; tel. 670-0698; fax 650-6008; e-mail liit@ekklesia.ee; internet www.ekklesia.ee; f. 1884; Pres. Meego Remmel.

United Methodist Church in Estonia (Eesti Metodisti Kirik): EMK Kirikuvalitsus, Narva mnt. 51, Tallinn 10152; tel. 668-8497; fax 668-8498; e-mail keskus@metodistikirik.ee; internet www.metodistikirik.ee; f. 1907; forms part of the Northern European Area of the United Methodist Church; Superintendent Taavi Hollman.

The Eastern Orthodox Church

Since February 1996 the Estonian Apostolic Orthodox Church has been under the jurisdiction of the Ecumenical Patriarchate of Constantinople (based in İstanbul, Turkey), as it had been between 1923 and 1940. The Estonian Orthodox Church of the Moscow Patriarchate was officially registered in April 2002.

Estonian Apostolic Orthodox Church (Eesti Apostlik Õigeusu Kirik): Wismari 32, Tallinn 10136; tel. and fax 660-0780; e-mail eoc@eoc.ee; internet www.eoc.ee; Metropolitan of Tallinn and All Estonia Stephanos; 64 congregations.

Estonian Orthodox Church (Moscow Patriarchate) (Moskva Patriarhaadi Eesti Õigeusu Kirik/Estonskaya Pravoslavnaya Tserkov Moskovskogo Patriarkhata): Pikk 64/4, Tallinn 10133; tel. 641-1301; fax 641-1302; e-mail mpeok@orthodox.ee; internet www.orthodox.ee; Metropolitan of Tallinn and All Estonia Kornelius; 32 congregations.

The Roman Catholic Church

There were an estimated 5,745 Roman Catholic adherents (of both the Latin and Byzantine rites) in Estonia.

Office of the Apostolic Administrator: Jaan Poska 47a, Tallinn 10150; tel. 601-3079; fax 601-3190; e-mail admapost@online.ee; internet katoliku.ee; Apostolic Administrator Most Rev. Philippe Jean-Charles Jourdan (Titular Bishop of Pertusa).

ISLAM

Estonian Islamic Congregation: Sütiste 52–76, Tallinn 13420; tel. 652-2403; f. 1928; Chair. of Bd Timur Seifullen.

JUDAISM

In the early 2000s there were an estimated 3,000 Jews resident in Estonia, principally in Tallinn.

Jewish Community of Estonia (Eesti Juudi Kogukond/Yevreiskaya Obshchina Estonii): Karu 16, Tallinn; POB 3576, Tallinn 10120; tel. 662-3034643-8566; fax 699-0568; e-mail community@jewish.ee; internet www.jewish.ee; Chair. Alla Jakobson.

The Press

In 2012 there were 13 officially registered daily newspapers and 118 non-daily newspapers published in Estonia. In 2012 some 1,149 periodicals were published.

PRINCIPAL NEWSPAPERS

In Estonian except where otherwise stated.

Äripäev (Business Daily): Pärnu mnt. 105, Tallinn 19094; tel. 667-0111; fax 667-0165; e-mail aripaev@aripaev.ee; internet www.ap3.ee; f. 1989; five days a week; business and finance; Editor-in-Chief Meelis Mandel; circ. 11,200 (June 2013).

Baltic Business News (BBN): Tallinn; tel. 667-0016; e-mail bbn@aripaev.ee; internet www.balticbusinessnews.com; daily; English; online; business and politics; affiliated with *Äripäev*; Editor Toomas Hõbemägi.

Eesti Päevaleht (Estonian Daily): Narva mnt. 13, Tallinn 10151; tel. 680-4400; fax 680-4401; e-mail mail@epl.ee; internet www.epl.ee; f. 1905; 6 a week; 50% owned by Ekspress Grupp; Editor-in-Chief Urmo Soonvald; circ. 22,300 (June 2013).

Postimees (Postman): Maakri 23a, Tallinn 10145; tel. 666-2202; fax 666-2201; e-mail online@postimees.ee; internet www.postimees.ee; f. 1857; 6 a week; Editor-in-Chief Merit Kopli; circ. 54,100 (June 2013).

SL Õhtuleht (Evening Gazette): Narva mnt. 13, POB 106, Tallinn 10151; tel. 614-4000; fax 614-4001; e-mail leht@ohtuleht.ee; internet www.ohtuleht.ee; f. 2000; 6 a week; 50% owned by Ekspress Grupp; popular; Editor-in-Chief Väino Koorberg; circ. 51,100 (June 2013).

Vesti dnya (News of the Day): Peterburi tee 53, Tallinn 11415; tel. 602-6865; fax 602-6867; e-mail vesti@vesti.ee; internet www.vesti.ee; five days a week; in Russian; also *Vesti nedeli* (News of the Week), Fridays; Chief Editor Aleksandr Chaplygin; circ. 8,300 (2008).

PRINCIPAL PERIODICALS

Akadeemia: Ülikooli 21, Tartu 51007; tel. 742-3050; e-mail akadeemia@akad.ee; internet www.akad.ee; f. 1989; monthly; journal of the Union of Writers; Editor-in-Chief Toomas Kiho; circ. 2,090.

Eesti Arst (Estonian Physician): Pepleri 32, Tartu 51010; tel. 742-7825; fax 742-7825; e-mail eestiarst@eestiarst.ee; internet www.eestiarst.ee; f. 1922; monthly; Editor-in-Chief Andres Soosaar; circ. 4,000.

Delovoye Vedomosti (Business Gazette): Pärnu mnt. 105, Tallinn 19094; tel. 667-0080; fax 667-0465; e-mail delo@mbp.ee; internet www.dv.ee; weekly; Russian; affiliated with business daily *Äripäev* (q.v.); Editor-in-Chief Oksana Kabrits; circ. 3,800 (June 2013).

Den za Dnem (Day to Day): Maakri 23a, Tallinn 10145; tel. 666-2511; fax 666-2395; e-mail tellimus@dzd.ee; internet www.dzd.ee; f. 1993; owned by Eesti Meedia (Schibsted Group); weekly; Russian; Editor-in-Chief Yevgeniya Garanzha; circ. 15,900 (June 2013).

Eesti Ekspress (Estonian Express): Narva mnt. 11e, Tallinn 10151; tel. 669-8080; fax 669-8154; e-mail ekspress@ekspress.ee; internet www.ekspress.ee; f. 1923; published regularly till 1940; resumed publication in 1990; weekly; owned by Ekspress Grupp; Publr Hans H. Luik; Editor-in-Chief Janek Luts; circ. 29,800 (June 2013).

Eesti Kirik (Estonian Church): Ülikooli 1, Tartu 51003; tel. 733-7790; fax 733-7792; e-mail ek@eelk.ee; internet www.eestikirik.ee; f. 1923; weekly; organ of the Estonian Evangelical Lutheran Church; Editor-in-Chief Sirje Semm; circ. 2,100 (June 2013).

Eesti Loodus (Estonian Nature): Baeri maja, Veski 4, Tartu 51005; tel. 742-1143; e-mail toimetus@el.loodus.ee; internet www.loodusajakiri.ee/eesti_loodus; f. 1933; monthly; popular science; illustrated; Editor-in-Chief Toomas Kukk; circ. 5,200.

Eesti Naine (Estonian Woman): Niine 11, Tallinn 10414; tel. 666-2638; fax 666-2557; e-mail info@naistemaailm.ee; internet www.naistemaailm.ee; f. 1924; monthly; Editor Aita Kivi; circ. 24,000.

Hea Laps (Good Kid): Harju 1, Tallinn 10146; tel. 631-4428; e-mail toimetus@healaps.ee; internet www.healaps.ee; f. 1994; monthly; for children; Editor-in-Chief Leelo Tungal.

Horisont (Horizon): Endla 3, Tallinn 10122; tel. 610-4105; fax 610-4109; e-mail horisont@horisont.ee; internet www.horisont.ee; f. 1967; 6 a year; popular science; Editor-in-Chief Kärt Jänes-Kapp; circ. 3,000.

Keel ja Kirjandus (Language and Literature): Roosikrantsi 6, Tallinn 10119; tel. 644-9228; e-mail kk@eki.ee; internet www.eki.ee/keeljakirjandus; f. 1958; monthly; publ. by Academy of Sciences and Union of Writers; Editor-in-Chief Joel Sang; circ. 900.

Kodukiri (Your Home): Maakri 23a, Tallinn 10145; tel. 666-2633; fax 666-2557; e-mail malle.pajula@kirjastus.ee; internet www.naistemaailm.ee; f. 1992; monthly; Editor-in-Chief Malle Pajula; circ. 50,000.

Komsomolskaya Pravda—Baltiya (Young Communist League Truth—Baltics): Lembitu tn. 8-2, Tallinn 10114; tel. 668-8900; fax 668-8902; e-mail info@kompravda.eu; internet www.kompravda.eu; f. 2007; weekly; in Russian; 'Northern European' edition of Komsomolskaya Pravda (Russia); Editor-in-Chief V. N. SUNGORKIN; circ. 10,000 (June 2013).

Maaleht (Country News): Narva mnt. 11E, Tallinn 10151; tel. 661-3300; fax 661-3344; e-mail ml@maaleht.ee; internet www.maaleht.ee; f. 1987; weekly; politics, culture, agriculture and country life; Editor-in-Chief AIVAR VIIDIK; circ. 42,700 (June 2013).

Oil Shale: Ehitajate tee 5, Tallinn 19086; tel. 501-1827; fax 620-3011; e-mail meelika@kirj.ee; internet www.kirj.ee/oilshale; f. 1984; quarterly; geology, chemistry, mining, oil shale industry, power engineering; Editor-in-Chief ANTO RAUKAS; circ. 200.

Sirp (Sickle): Voorimehe 9, Tallinn 10146; tel. 682-9070; fax 682-9071; e-mail sirp@sirp.ee; internet www.sirp.ee; f. 1940; weekly; the arts; Editor-in-Chief KAAREL TARAND; circ. 4,900 (2008).

Teater, Muusika, Kino (Theatre, Music, Cinema): Voorimehe 9, Tallinn 10146; tel. 683-3132; e-mail pille@temuki.ee; internet www.temuki.ee; f. 1982; monthly; Editor-in-Chief MADIS KOLK; circ. 1,500.

Vikerkaar (Rainbow): Voorimehe 9, Tallinn 10146; tel. 683-3140; fax 683-3101; e-mail vikerkaar@vikerkaar.ee; internet www.vikerkaar.ee; f. 1986; monthly; fiction, poetry, critical works; Editor-in-Chief MÄRT VÄLJATAGA; circ. 1,500.

NEWS AGENCY

BNS (Baltic News Service): Toompuiestee 35, Tallinn 15043; tel. 610-8800; fax 610-8811; e-mail bns@bns.ee; internet www.bns.ee; f. 1991; daily news bulletins in English, Estonian, Latvian, Lithuanian and Russian; Editor-in-Chief ARTŪRAS RAČAS.

PRESS ORGANIZATIONS

Estonian Newspaper Association (Eesti Ajalehtede Liit): Pärnu mnt. 67A, Tallinn 10134; tel. 646-1005; fax 631-1210; e-mail eall@eall.ee; internet www.eall.ee; f. 1990; 40 mem. newspapers; Man. Dir MART RAUDSAAR.

Estonian Press Council (Avaliku Sõna Nõukogu): Äriklienditeenindus, POB 1228, Tallinn 11402; tel. and fax 5300-5847; e-mail asn@asn.org.ee; internet www.asn.org.ee; f. 1991; non-governmental org.; Chair. Prof. EPP LAUK.

Union of Estonian Journalists (Eesti Ajakirjanike Liit): Gonsiori 21, Tallinn 10147; tel. 646-3699; e-mail eal@eal.ee; internet www.eal.ee; f. 1919; Dir PEETER ERNITS.

Publishers

Eesti Raamat (Estonian Book): Laki 26, Tallinn 12915; tel. and fax 658-7889; e-mail rein.poder.001@mail.ee; internet www.eestiraamat.ee; f. 1940; fiction for children and adults; Dir ANNE-ASTRI KASK.

Estonian Academy Publishers (EAP): Kohtu 6, Tallinn 10130; tel. 645-4504; fax 646-6026; e-mail niine@kirj.ee; internet www.kirj.ee; f. 1994; publishes nine academic journals incl. *Proceedings of the Estonian Academy of Sciences*, *Linguistica Uralica*, etc.; Dir ÜLO NIINE.

Ilmamaa: Vanemuise 19, Tartu 51014; tel. 742-7290; fax 742-7320; e-mail ilmamaa@ilmamaa.ee; internet www.ilmamaa.ee; f. 1993; general fiction, philosophy, cultural history; Dir MART JAGOMÄGI.

Ilo Publishing House: Tammsaare tee 47, Tallinn 11316; tel. 667-7855; fax 680-2230; e-mail ilo@ilo.ee; f. 1990; dictionaries, reference books, textbooks, history, management, psychology, law and children's books; Dir SIRJE-MAI PIHLAK.

Koolibri: POB 1793, Tallinn 11615; tel. 651-5300; fax 651-5301; e-mail koolibri@koolibri.ee; internet www.koolibri.ee; f. 1991; textbooks, dictionaries, children's books; Man. Dir KALLE KALJURAND.

Kunst (Fine Art): Lai 34, Tallinn 10133; POB 105, Tallinn 10502; tel. 641-1766; fax 641-1762; e-mail kunst.myyk@mail.ee; f. 1957; fine arts, fiction, tourism, history, biographies; Dir SIRJE HELME.

Logos: Narma mnt. 51, Tallinn 10152; tel. and fax 668-8499; e-mail logos@logos.ee; internet www.logos.ee; f. 1991; Christian; Chair. TIINA NÕLVAK.

Monokkel: POB 311, Tallinn 10503; tel. 501-6307; fax 656-9176; e-mail monokkel@hot.ee; internet www.hot.ee/monokkel; f. 1988; history, fiction; Dir ANTS ÕÕBIK.

Olion: Laki 26, Tallinn 12915; tel. 655-0175; fax 655-0173; e-mail kirjastus@olion.ee; internet www.olion.ee; f. 1989; politics, reference, history, biographies, children's books; Dir HÜLLE UNT.

Tartu Ülikool Kirjastus—University of Tartu Press: W. Struve 1, Tartu 50091; tel. 737-5961; fax 737-5944; e-mail tyk@ut.ee; internet www.tyk.ee; f. 1632; academic books and journals, textbooks, etc.; Man. Dir ÜLLE ERGMA.

Tiritamm: Endla 3, Tallinn 10122; tel. and fax 656-3570; e-mail tiritamm@tiritamm.ee; internet www.tiritamm.ee; f. 1991; children's books; Dir SIRJE SAIMRE.

Valgus: Tõnismägi 3A, Tallinn 10119; tel. 617-7010; fax 617-7016; e-mail info@kirjastusvalgus.ee; internet www.kirjastusvalgus.ee; f. 1965; scientific literature, resource materials and textbooks; Editor-in-Chief MADLI VALLIKIVI-PÄTS.

Varrak: Pärnu mnt. 67A, Tallinn 10134; tel. 616-1038; fax 616-1030; e-mail varrak@varrak.ee; internet www.varrak.ee; f. 1991; history, philosophy and sociology, literary fiction, science fiction, popular fiction and children's literature; Man. Dir PRIIT MAIDE.

PUBLISHERS' ASSOCIATION

Estonian Publishers' Association (Eesti Kirjastuste Liit): Roosikrantsi 6/207, Tallinn 10119; tel. 644-9866; fax 617-7550; e-mail kirjastusteliit@eki.ee; internet www.estbook.com; f. 1991; Chair. MART JAGOMÄGI; 29 mems (Jan. 2013).

Broadcasting and Communications

TELECOMMUNICATIONS

Eesti Telekom AS (Estonian Telecom Ltd): Valge 16, Tallinn 19095; tel. 611-1470; fax 631-1224; e-mail mailbox@telekom.ee; internet www.telekom.ee; f. 1992; privatized in 1999; subsidiaries include Eesti Mobiltelefon AS (EMT) and Elion Enterprises; CEO VALDO KALM.

Elisa Eesti: Sõpruse pst. 145, Tallinn 13417; tel. 681-1963; fax 681-1961; e-mail ariklient@elisa.ee; internet www.elisa.ee; mobile cellular telecommunications and internet service provider; Exec. Dir SAMI SEPPÄNEN.

EMT: Valge 16, Tallinn 19095; tel. 639-7130; fax 639-7132; e-mail info@emt.ee; internet www.emt.ee; f. 1991; wholly owned subsidiary of Eesti Telekom; mobile telecommunications and internet service provider; CEO VALDO KALM.

Tele2 Eesti: Jõe 2A, Tallinn 10151; tel. 686-6866; fax 686-6877; e-mail tele2@tele2.ee; internet www.tele2.ee; f. 1997; as AS Ritabell; present name adopted in 2001; mobile cellular telecommunications and internet service provider.

BROADCASTING

Supervisory Authority

Broadcasting Council: Gonsiori 21, Tallinn 15029; tel. 611-4305; fax 611-4457; e-mail rhn@er.ee; internet www.rhn.ee; mems appointed by Riigikogu (State Assembly); Chair. of Television AINAR RUUSSAAR; Chair. of Radio MARGUS ALLIKMAA.

Radio

The public broadcaster, Eesti Rahvusringhääling, was formed in 2007 by the merger of the public television and radio broadcasters. In 2005 there were additionally 28 private radio broadcasters operating in Estonia.

Eesti Rahvusringhääling (ERR) (Estonian Public Broadcasting): Gonsiori 27, Tallinn 15029; tel. 628-4100; fax 628-4155; e-mail err@err.ee; internet www.err.ee; f. 2007; radio broadcasts comprise five domestic channels (three in Estonian, one in Russian and one in English, French and German) and an external service in English; television broadcasts comprise one channel with programmes in Estonian and Russian; Chair. and Dir-Gen. AGU UUDELEPP.

Raadio Elmar: Õpetaja 9A, Tartu 51003; tel. 742-7520; e-mail elmar@elmar.ee; internet www.elmar.ee; one of six radio stations owned by Trio Grupp.

Raadio Kuku: Veerenni 58A, Tallinn 11314; tel. 630-7031; fax 630-7004; e-mail kuku@kuku.ee; internet www.kuku.ee; Editor-in-Chief HINDREK RIIKOJA.

Raadio Sky Plus: Pärnu mnt. 139F, Tallinn 11317; tel. 678-8777; e-mail info@skyplus.fm; internet www.skyplus.fm; owned by Sky Media.

Raadio Uuno: Veerenni 58A, Tallinn 11314; tel. 630-7080; e-mail uuno@uuno.ee; internet www.uuno.ee; f. 1994; Programme Man. ANDRES PANKSEPP.

Tartu Pereraadio (Tartu Family Radio): Annemõisa 8, Tartu 50708; tel. and fax 748-8458; e-mail pereraadio@pereraadio.ee; internet www.pereraadio.ee; f. 1994; Christian; Chief Exec. PAAVO PIHLAK.

Television

There are three national commercial television stations and one public broadcaster in Estonia. In addition, five cable television licences have been issued.

Eesti Rahvusringhääling (ERR) (Estonian Public Broadcasting): Gonsiori 27, Tallinn 15029; tel. 628-4100; fax 628-4155; e-mail err@err.ee; internet www.err.ee; f. 2007; radio broadcasts comprise five domestic channels (three in Estonian, one in Russian and one in English, French and German) and an external service in English; television broadcasts comprise one channel with programmes in Estonian and Russian; Chair. and Dir-Gen. AGU UUDELEPP.

Kanal 2 (Channel 2): Maakri 23A, Tallinn 10145; tel. 666-2450; fax 666-2451; e-mail info@kanal2.ee; internet www.kanal2.ee; f. 1993; commercial; Chief Exec. URMAS ORU.

TV3: Peterburgi tee 81, Tallinn 11415; tel. 622-0200; fax 622-0201; e-mail tv3@tv3.ee; internet www.tv3.ee; f. 1996; owned by Modern Times Group (Sweden); CEO PRIIT LEITO.

Broadcasting Association

Association of Estonian Broadcasters (AEB) (Eesti Ringhäälingute Liit): Ülemiste tee 3A, Tallinn 11415; tel. and fax 633-3235; e-mail erl@online.ee; internet www.ringhliit.ee; f. 1992; 19 mems; Man. Dir URMAS LOIT.

Finance

(cap. = capital; res = reserves; dep. = deposits; m. = million; brs = branches; amounts in euros, unless otherwise specified)

BANKING

Supervisory Authority

Finantsinspektsioon: Sakala 4, Tallinn 15030; tel. 668-0500; fax 668-0501; e-mail info@fi.ee; internet www.fi.ee; f. 2002; joining the functions of banking and insurance supervisory authority and securities inspectorate; Chair. of Supervisory Bd JÜRGEN LIGI; Chair. of Management Bd KILVAR KESSLER.

Central Bank

Bank of Estonia (Eesti Pank): Estonia pst. 13, Tallinn 15095; tel. 668-0719; fax 668-0836; e-mail info@eestipank.ee; internet www.eestipank.info; f. 1919; closed 1940; re-established 1990; bank of issue; cap. 600.0m. kroons, res 4,253.5m. kroons, dep. 27,027.5m. kroons (Dec. 2009); Gov. ARDO HANSSON.

Commercial Banks

Estonian Credit Bank (Eesti Krediidipank): Narva mnt. 4, Tallinn 15014; tel. 669-0900; fax 661-6037; e-mail info@krediidipank.ee; internet www.krediidipank.ee; f. 1992; cap. 25.0.m., res 1.9m., dep. 256.4m. (Dec. 2012); Pres. PAVEL GORBATSEVICH; Chair. of Bd ANDRUS KLUGE; 11 brs.

SEB Pank (SEB Bank): Tornimäe 2, Tallinn 15010; tel. 665-5100; fax 665-5103; e-mail info@seb.ee; internet www.seb.ee; f. 1992; 100% owned by Scandinaviska Enskilda Banken (SEB—Sweden); cap. 42.5m., res 106.6m., dep. 3,358.9m. (Dec. 2012); Chair. of Bd RIHO UNT; 90 brs.

Swedbank AS: Liivalaia 8, Tallinn 15040; tel. 631-0310; fax 631-0410; e-mail info@swedbank.ee; internet www.swedbank.ee; f. 1991; 100% owned by Swedbank (Sweden); fmrly AS Hansapank; present name adopted 2009; cap. 85m., res 75m., dep. 6,315m. (Dec. 2012); Chair. of Council MICHAEL WOLF; Chair. of Bd HÅKAN BERG; 50 brs.

Tallinn Business Bank (Tallinna Äripank): Vana-Viru 7, Tallinn 15097; tel. 668-8000; fax 668-8001; e-mail info@tbb.ee; internet www.tbb.ee; f. 1991; cap. 14.7m., res 0.6m., dep. 106.0m. (Dec. 2012); Chair. of Bd VALERI HARITONOV.

Banking Association

Estonian Banking Association (Eesti Pangaliit): Ahtri 12, Tallinn 10151; tel. 611-6567; fax 611-6568; e-mail pangaliit@pangaliit.ee; internet www.pangaliit.ee; f. 1992; Chair. of Bd PRIIT PERENS.

STOCK EXCHANGE

Tallinn Stock Exchange (Tallinna Börs): Tartu mnt. 2, Tallinn 10145; tel. 640-8800; fax 640-8801; e-mail tallinn@nasdaqomx.com; f. 1995; 62% owned by the NASDAQ OMX Group (USA); Chair. of Man. Bd ANDRUS ALBER.

INSURANCE

In 2013 there were five insurance organizations providing life insurance and nine providing non-life insurance in Estonia.

Estonian Insurance Association (Eesti Kindlustusseltside Liit): Mustamäe tee 46, Tallinn 10621; tel. 667-1800; e-mail info@eksl.ee; internet www.eksl.ee; f. 1993; Chair. of Bd MART JESSE; 17 mem. cos.

Insurance Companies

Compensa Life Vienna Insurance Group SE: Roosikrantsi 11, Tallinn 10119; tel. 610-3000; fax 610-3010; e-mail info@compensalife.ee; internet www.compensalife.eu/ee; f. 1993; Chair. OLGA REZNIK; 20 brs.

ERGO: Tammsaare 47, Tallinn 11316; tel. 610-6500; fax 610-6501; e-mail info@ergo.ee; internet www3.ergo.ee; f. 1990; provides non-life insurance (as ERGO Kindlustuse) and life insurance (ERGO Elukindlustus); Chair. of Supervisory Bd THOMAS HANS SCHIRMER.

If P&C Insurance: Lõõtsa 8A, Tallinn 11415; tel. 669-6684; fax 667-1101; e-mail info@if.ee; internet www.if.ee; f. 1991 as Eesti Kindlustus; subsidiary of Sampo Group; renamed AS Eesti Kindlustus 1996, AS Sampo Eesti Varakindlustus 1999, AS If Kindlustus 2002, and as above 2009; non-life; Chair. TORBJÖRN MAGNUSSON; Chief Exec. TIMO VUORINEN.

Mandatum Life Insurance Baltic SE: Viru väljak 2, Tallinn 10111; tel. 681-2300; fax 681-2399; e-mail info@mandatumlife.ee; internet www.mandatumlife.ee; f. 1997 as Sampo Life; present name adopted 2010; Chair. TIMO LAITINEN; CEO IMRE MADISON.

SEB Elu- ja Pensionikindlustus (SEB Life Insurance & Pensions Estonia): Tornimäe 2, Tallinn 15010; tel. 665-5100; fax 665-5103; e-mail info@seb.ee; internet www.seb.ee; f. 1998; fmrly Ühispanga Elukindlustuse; wholly owned by SEB Eesti; life insurance, pensions; Chair. of Management Bd RIHO UNT.

Seesam Insurance AS: Vambola 6, Tallinn 10114; tel. 628-1800; fax 628-1802; e-mail seesam@seesam.ee; internet www.seesam.ee; f. 1991; owned by the OP-Pohjola Group; non-life; Chair. of Management Bd TOOMAS ABNER; Chair. of Supervisory Bd JOUKO PÖLÖNEN.

Swedbank Insurance: Liivalaia 12, Tallinn 15039; tel. 888-2100; fax 888-2221; e-mail info@swedbank.ee; internet www.swedbank.ee; wholly owned by Swedbank AS (Sweden); life and non-life; Chair. PRIIT PERENS.

Trade and Industry

GOVERNMENT AGENCIES

Enterprise Estonia (Ettevõtluse Arendamise Sihtasutus): Lasnamäe 2, Tallinn 11412; tel. 627-9700; fax 627-9701; e-mail eas@eas.ee; internet www.eas.ee; f. 2000; Chair. ÜLARI ALAMETS.

Estonian Competition Authority (Kohkurentsiamet): Auna 6, Tallinn 10317; tel. 667-2400; fax 667-2401; e-mail info@konkurentsiamet.ee; internet www.konkurentsiamet.ee; f. 2008; supervises competition, with specific powers in the sectors of fuel and energy, and electronic and postal communications; Dir-Gen. MÄRT OTS.

Estonian Investment and Trade Agency (EITA): Lasnamäe 2, Tallinn 11412; tel. 627-9700; fax 627-9701; e-mail invest@eas.ee; internet www.investinestonia.com; Dir KRISTI TIIVAS.

Estonian Regional and Local Development Agency (Eesti Regionaalse ja Kohaliku Arengu Sihtasutus—ERKAS): Ahtri 8, 3rd Floor, Tallinn 10151; tel. 694-3431; fax 694-3425; e-mail erkas@erkas.ee; internet www.erkas.ee; f. 2002; Chair. JÜRI ROOS.

Estonian Technical Surveillance Authority (Tehnilise Järelevalve Amet): Sõle 23A, 10614 Tallinn; tel. 667-2011; fax 667-2001; e-mail info@tja.ee; internet www.tja.ee; f. 2008; co-ordinates management of the use of radio frequencies (incl. broadcasting), manages numbering plan for telecommunications services, various responsibilities in the field of communications, incl. railways; Dir-Gen. RAIGO UUKKIVI.

CHAMBERS OF COMMERCE

Estonian Chamber of Agriculture and Commerce (Eesti Põllumajandus-Kaubanduskoda—EPKK): Vilmsi 53G, Tallinn 10147; tel. 600-9349; fax 600-9350; e-mail info@epkk.ee; internet www.epkk.ee; f. 1996; Chair. of Bd AAVO MÖLDER.

Estonian Chamber of Commerce and Industry (ECCI) (Eesti Kaubandus-Tööstuskoda): Toom-Kooli 17, Tallinn 10130; tel. 604-0060; fax 604-0061; e-mail koda@koda.ee; internet www.koda.ee; f. 1925; brs in Tartu, Jõhvi, Pärnu and Kuressaare; Pres. TOOMAS LUMAN.

INDUSTRIAL AND TRADE ASSOCIATIONS

Asscn of Construction Material Producers of Estonia (Eesti Ehitusmaterjalide Tootjate Liit—EETL): Pärnu mnt. 141, Tallinn 11314; tel. 648-1918; fax 648-9062; e-mail eetl@hot.ee; internet www.hot.ee/eetl; Man. Dir ENNO RABANE.

Asscn of Estonian Food Industry (Eesti Toiduainetööstuse Liit): Saku 15/105, Tallinn 11314; tel. 648-4978; fax 631-2718; e-mail info@toiduliit.ee; internet www.toiduliit.ee; f. 1993; Dir SIRJE POTISEPP.

Central Union of Estonian Farmers (Eestimaa Põllumeeste Keskliit): J. Vilmsi 53G, Tallinn 10147; tel. and fax 600-8616; e-mail info@eptk.ee; internet www.eptk.ee; f. 1990; Chair. of Bd ÜLLAS HUNT.

Estonian Asscn of Fisheries (Eesti Kalaliit): Peterburi tee 2F, Tallinn 11415; tel. 622-1300; fax 622-1302; e-mail kalaliit@online.ee; internet www.kalaliit.ee; f. 1995; 28 mems; Chair. TOOMAS KÕUHKNA; Man. Dir VALDUR NOORMÄGI.

Estonian Asscn of Information Technology and Telecommunication Companies (Eesti Infotehnoloogia ja Telekommunikatsiooni Liit): Lõõtsa 6, Tallinn 11415; tel. 617-7145; fax 617-7146; e-mail info@itl.ee; internet www.itl.ee; f. 2000; 36 mems; Pres. TAAVI KOTKA; Chair. URMAS KÕLLI.

Estonian Asscn of Small and Medium-sized Enterprises (EVEA) (Eesti Väike-Ja Keskmiste Ettevõtjate Assotsiatsioon): Liivalaia 9, Tallinn 10118; tel. 641-0920; fax 641-0916; e-mail evea@evea.ee; internet www.evea.ee; f. 1988; Pres. MARINA KAAS; CEO KERSTI KRAAS.

Estonian Forest Industries Asscn (Eesti Metsatööstuse Liit—EMTL): Viljandi mnt. 18A, Tallinn 11216; tel. 656-7643; fax 656-7644; e-mail info@emtl.ee; internet www.emtl.ee; f. 1996; Man. Dir OTT OTSMANN.

Estonian Meat Asscn (Eesti Lihaliit): Lai 39/41, Tallinn 10133; tel. 641-1179; fax 641-1035; e-mail lihaliit@hot.ee; f. 1989; Chair. of Bd AIGAR PINDMAA; Man. Dir PEETER GRIGORJEV.

Estonian Oil Asscn (Eesti Õliühing): Kiriku 6, Tallinn 10130; tel. 664-1247; fax 641-8471; e-mail toomas@oilunion.ee; internet www.oilunion.ee; f. 1993; Chair. RAIVO VARE; 12 mem. orgs.

Estonian Trade Council (Eesti Väliskaubanduse Liit): Tammsaare tee 47, Tallinn 11316; tel. 684-1252; fax 659-7017; e-mail icc@icc-estonia.ee; internet www.icc-estonia.ee; f. 1991; 110 mems; non-profit org.; promotes export trade; Chair. of Bd TIIT TAMMEMÄGI.

Federation of the Estonian Chemical Industry (Eesti Keemiatööstuse Liit): Peterburi tee 46, Tallinn 11415; tel. and fax 613-9775; e-mail info@keemia.ee; internet www.keemia.ee; f. 1991; Man. Dir HALLAR MEYBAUM.

Federation of the Estonian Engineering Industry (Eesti Masinatööstuse Liit—EML): Mäealuse 4, Tallinn 12618; tel. 651-5578; e-mail emliit@emliit.ee; internet www.emliit.ee; f. 1991; represents over 50 metalworking, machine-building, electrotechnics and electronics enterprises; Chair. of Bd TÕNU LELUMEES.

Union of Estonian Automobile Enterprises (Eesti Autoettevõtete Liit): Akadeemia tee 20, Tallinn 12611; tel. 641-2511; fax 641-2523; e-mail al@autoettevoteliit.ee; internet www.autoettevoteteliit.ee; f. 1990; Chair. REIN SIIM; 77 mem. cos.

EMPLOYERS' ORGANIZATION

Estonian Employers' Confederation (Eesti Tööandjate Kesliit): Kiriku 6, Tallinn 10130; tel. 699-9301; fax 699-9310; e-mail ettk@ettk.ee; internet ettk.tooandjad.ee; f. 1991 as Confederation of Estonian Industry; Chair. of Bd MEELIS VIRKEBAU; Pres. ENN VESKIMÄGI; 24 brs.

UTILITIES

Electricity

Under terms agreed with the European Union, Estonia was permitted to postpone the liberalization of its electricity market until 2013, in order to allow the requisite investment to be made in the oil shale power plants that generate most of the country's electricity supply.

Operations of the Estlink submarine cable, connecting the electricity networks of Estonia and Finland, commenced in January 2007.

Eesti Energia (Estonian Energy Co): Laki 24, Tallinn 12915; tel. 715-2222; fax 715-2200; e-mail info@energia.ee; internet www.energia.ee; f. 1939; producer, transmitter and distributor of thermal and electric energy; manufacture of electric motors; electrical engineering; Chair. SANDOR LIIVE; 7,600 employees.

Gas

Eesti Gaas (Estonian Gas Co): Liivalaia 9, Tallinn 10118; tel. 630-3003; fax 631-3884; e-mail info@gaas.ee; internet www.gaas.ee; f. 1993; purchases and distributes natural gas; constructs pipelines; calibrates gas meters; Chair. TIIT KULLERKUPP; 255 employees.

Water

Tallinna Vesi (Tallinn Water Co): Ädala 10, Tallinn 10614; tel. 626-2200; fax 626-2300; e-mail tvesi@tvesi.ee; internet www.tallinnavesi.ee; f. 1997; supply and treatment of water; collection and treatment of waste water; 35.30% owned by United Utilities Tallinna (a subsidiary of United Utilities International, United Kingdom), 34.70% by Tallinn City Govt; CEO IAN PLENDERLEITH; 302 employees (April 2011).

TRADE UNIONS

Asscn of Estonian Energy Workers' Trade Unions (Eesti Energeetikatöötajate Ametiühingute Liit—EEAÜL): Gonsiori 3A, Tallinn 10117; tel. 715-5527; fax 715-5528; e-mail sander.vaikma@energia.ee; internet www.energeetik.ee; Chair. SANDER VAIKMA.

Confederation of Estonian Employee Unions (Teenistujate Ametiliitude Keskorganisatsioon—TALO): Gonsiori 21, Tallinn 10147; tel. 641-9800; fax 641-9805; e-mail talo@talo.ee; internet www.talo.ee; f. 1992; comprises nine mem. unions from the broadcasting, cultural, customs, education, engineering, journalism, radiology and scientific sectors; Chair. AGO TUULING.

Estonian Trade Union Confederation (Eesti Ametiühingute Keskliit—EAKL): Pärnu mnt. 41A, Tallinn 10119; tel. 641-2800; fax 641-2801; e-mail eakl@eakl.ee; internet www.eakl.ee; f. 1990; 19 professional mem. orgs; Chair. HARRI TALIGA; estimated 40,000 individual mems (2008).

Transport

RAILWAYS

In 2009 there were 792 km of railway track in use, of which 132 km were electrified.

Edelaraudtee: Kaare 25, Türi 72212; tel. 385-7123; fax 385-7121; e-mail info@edel.ee; internet www.edel.ee; f. 1997; owned by GB Railways (United Kingdom); operates freight services; former passenger inter-city services transferred to Elron (q.v.) in 2014; Dir KALVI PUKKA.

Eesti Raudtee (Estonian Railways): Toompuiestee 35, Tallinn 15073; tel. 615-8610; fax 615-8710; e-mail raudtee@evr.ee; internet www.evr.ee; f. 1918; privatized in 2001; renationalization completed in 2007; rail infrastructure operator and freight carrier; Chair. of Management Bd AHTI ASMANN; Chair of Supervisory Bd TAAVI MADIBERK; 860 employees (2012).

Elron: Vabaduse pst. 176, Tallinn 10917; tel. 673-7400; e-mail info@elron.ee; internet elron.ee; f. 1998 as Elektriraudtee; present name adopted October 2013; state-owned; suburban passenger services in and around Tallinn, and from 2014 commenced operating inter-city diesel passenger services formerly operated by Edelaraudtee (q.v., see p. 1719); Chair. TOIVO PROMM.

GoRail: Toompuiestee 37, Tallinn 10133; tel. 631-0043; fax 615-6720; e-mail info@gorail.ee; internet www.gorail.ee; f. 1998; owned by AS Go Group; operate direct, express, passenger rail services between Tallinn and St Petersburg and Moscow, both in Russia; CEO ALAR PINSEL.

ROADS

In 2010 Estonia had a total road network of 58,412 km, of which 1,603 km were main roads.

Estonian Road Administration (Maanteeamet): Pärnu mnt. 463A, Tallinn 10916; tel. 611-9300; fax 611-9360; e-mail info@mnt.ee; internet www.mnt.ee; f. 1990; state-owned; Dir-Gen. AIVO ADAMSON.

INLAND WATERWAYS

In 2012 there were 335 km of navigable inland waterways.

SHIPPING

Tallinn is the main port for freight transportation. There are regular passenger services between Tallinn and Helsinki, Finland. At December 2013 the flag registered fleet comprised 146 vessels, totalling 334,312 grt.

Estonian Maritime Administration (EMA) (Veeteede Amet): Valge 4, Tallinn 11413; tel. 620-5500; fax 620-5506; e-mail eva@vta.ee; internet www.vta.ee; f. 1990; state-owned; administers and implements state maritime safety policies, ship-control, pilot, lighthouse and hydrography services; Gen. Dir ANDRUS MAIDE; 375 employees.

Principal Shipping Companies

Eesti Merelaevandus (ESCO) (Estonian Shipping Co): Sadama 4, Tallinn 15096; tel. 640-9500; fax 640-9595; e-mail online@eml.ee; internet www.eml.ee; f. 1940; owned by Tschudi Shipping Co (Norway); liner services, ship-chartering and cargo-shipping; Chair of Supervisory Bd JON EDVARD SUNDNES; Man. Dir SOEREN ANDERSEN; 500 employees.

Saaremaa Laevakompanii (Saaremaa Shipping Co): Kohtu 1, Kuressaare 93819; tel. 452-4444; fax 452-4355; e-mail info@tuulelaevad.ee; internet www.tuulelaevad.ee; f. 1992; passenger and cargo services between mainland Estonia and Saaremaa, Hiiumaa and Vormsi islands; Dir-Gen. TÕNIS RIHVK.

Tallink Grupp: Sadama 5/7, Tallinn 10111; tel. 640-9800; fax 640-9810; e-mail info@tallink.ee; internet www.tallink.ee; f. 1989 as a joint-venture Estonian-Finnish co; in 1996–2002 known as Hansatee Grupp, reverted to previous name in 2002; passenger and cargo transport; operates high-speed ferries between Tallinn and Helsinki, Finland; also operates routes to St Petersburg, Russia, and Stockholm, Sweden; Chair. of Management Bd ENN PANT.

Shipowners' Association

Estonian Shipowners' Association (Eesti Laevaomanike Liit): Kopli 101, Tallinn 11712; tel. and fax 613-5528; e-mail reederid@hot.ee; Pres. Capt. TOIVO NINNAS.

Port Authorities

Port of Sillamäe (Sillamäe Sadam—Silport): Suur-Karja 5, Tallinn 10140; tel. 640-5271; fax 640-5279; e-mail silport@silport.ee; internet www.silport.ee; operations commenced Oct. 2005; deep sea port; navigable year-round; railway facilities; free trade zone; four terminals; privately owned; Chair. VITALY IVANOV.

Port of Tallinn (Tallinna Sadam): Sadama 25, Tallinn 15051; tel. 631-8555; fax 631-8166; e-mail ts@ts.ee; internet www.ts.ee; f. 1991; the Port of Tallinn consists of five constituent harbours: Old City, Muuga, Paljassaare, Paldiski South and Saaremaa; Chair. of Bd AIN KALJURAND; Harbour Master Y. KIKAS; 550 employees (2007).

CIVIL AVIATION

There is an international airport at Tallinn.

Civil Aviation Administration (Lennuamat): Rävala pst. 8, Tallinn 10143; tel. 610-3500; fax 610-3501; e-mail ecaa@ecaa.ee; internet www.ecaa.ee; f. 1990; Dir-Gen. KRISTJAN TELVE (acting).

Avies: Sepise 1, Tallinn 11101; tel. 630-1370; fax 630-1371; e-mail info@avies.ee; internet www.flyavies.ee; f. 1991; domestic passenger services between Tallinn and Saaremaa and Hiiumaa islands, international scheduled and charter passenger and cargo services; Man. Dir VLADIMIR PISARKOV.

Estonian Air: Lennujaama 13, Tallinn 11101; tel. 640-1160; fax 650-8748; e-mail info@estonian-air.ee; internet www.estonian-air.com; f. 1991; 49% owned by Scandinavian Airlines (Denmark/Norway/Sweden), 34% state-owned; passenger and cargo flights to destinations across Europe; CEO JAN PALMÉR.

Tourism

Estonia has a wide range of attractions for tourists, including the historic towns of Tallinn and Tartu, extensive nature reserves and coastal resorts. In 2012 there were 1,873,519 foreign visitors to Estonia (as measured by arrivals at registered accommodation establishments). In 2012 receipts from tourism (excluding passenger transport) totalled US $1,226m., according to provisional figures

Estonian Tourist Board (Turismiarenduskeskus): Lasnamäe 2, Tallinn 11412; tel. 627-9770; fax 627-9701; e-mail tourism@eas.ee; internet www.visitestonia.com; f. 1990; Dir TARMO MUTSO.

Defence

As assessed at November 2013, Estonia's total armed forces numbered 5,750, comprising an army of 5,300 (including conscripts), a navy of 200, and an air force of 250. There was also a reserve militia of 30,000. The duration of military service is eight months, or 11 months for officers and some specialists. In 1994 Estonia joined the 'Partnership for Peace' programme of military co-operation of the North Atlantic Treaty Organization (NATO, see p. 373), and became a full member of the Organization in March 2004.

Defence Expenditure: Budgeted at €387m. in 2014.

Commander of the Defence Forces: Brig.-Gen. RIHO TERRAS.

Chief of the General Staff: Col PEETER HOPPE.

Commander of the Army: Col INDREK SIREL.

Commander of the Navy: Capt. IGOR SCHVEDE.

Commander of the Air Force: Brig.-Gen. VALERI SAAR.

Education

Compulsory education begins at the age of seven and lasts for nine years. Students may then attend either general secondary school or vocational school. In 2011/12 there were 29 higher education institutions, at which 64,806 students were enrolled (including those undertaking evening and correspondence courses). In 2007/08 some 20% of students at primary and secondary schools received tuition in a language other than Estonian (mainly Russian). In 2009/10 enrolment at pre-primary schools included 88% of children in the corresponding age-group. In the same year enrolment in primary education included 95% of children in the relevant age-group, while secondary education enrolment included 94% of children in the relevant age-group. In 2006 enrolment in tertiary education was equivalent to 65% of those in the relevant age-group (males 49%; females 82%). Forecast government expenditure on education amounted to €760.6m. in 2014 (9.4% of total expenditure in that year).

ETHIOPIA

Introductory Survey

LOCATION, CLIMATE, LANGUAGE, RELIGION, FLAG, CAPITAL

The Federal Democratic Republic of Ethiopia is a landlocked country in eastern Africa; it has a long frontier with Somalia near the Horn of Africa. South Sudan and Sudan lie to the west, Eritrea to the north, Djibouti to the north-east and Kenya to the south. The climate is mainly temperate because of the high plateau terrain, with an annual average temperature of 13°C (55°F), abundant rainfall in some years and low humidity. The lower country and valley gorges are very hot and subject to recurrent drought. The official language is Amharic, but many other local languages are also spoken. English is widely used in official and commercial circles. The Ethiopian Orthodox (Tewahido) Church, an ancient Christian sect, has a wide following in the north and on the southern plateau. In much of the south and east the inhabitants include Muslims and followers of animist beliefs. The national flag (proportions 1 by 2) has three equal horizontal stripes, of green, yellow and red, superimposed in the centre of which is a blue disk bearing a yellow pentagram, resembling a star, with single yellow rays extending outwards from the inner angles of the star. The capital is Addis Ababa.

CONTEMPORARY POLITICAL HISTORY

Historical Context

In September 1974 Emperor Haile Selassie was deposed by the armed forces and his imperial regime was replaced by the Provisional Military Administrative Council (PMAC), known popularly as the Dergue (Committee), led by Brig.-Gen. Teferi Benti. In December Ethiopia was declared a socialist state; however, a radical programme of social and economic reforms led to widespread unrest, and in February 1977 Lt-Col Mengistu Haile Mariam executed Teferi and his closest associates, and replaced him as Chairman of the PMAC and as Head of State.

During 1977–78, in an attempt to end opposition to the regime, the Government imprisoned or killed thousands of its opponents. Political power was consolidated in a Commission for Organizing the Party of the Working People of Ethiopia (COPWE), largely dominated by military personnel. In September 1984, at the COPWE's third congress, the Workers' Party of Ethiopia (WPE) was formally inaugurated. Mengistu was unanimously elected Secretary-General of the party, which modelled itself on the Communist Party of the Soviet Union. In February 1987, at a referendum, some 81% of the electorate endorsed a new Constitution and in June national elections were held to an 835-seat legislature, the National Shengo (Assembly). In September, at the inaugural meeting of the new legislature, the PMAC was abolished, and the People's Democratic Republic of Ethiopia was declared. The National Shengo unanimously elected Mengistu as President of the Republic, and a 24-member Council of State was also elected, to act as the Shengo's permanent organ.

Numerous groups, encouraged by the confusion resulting from the 1974 revolution, launched armed insurgencies against the Government. Of these, the most effective were based in the Ogaden, Eritrea and Tigrai regions. Somalia laid claim to the Ogaden, which is populated mainly by ethnic Somalis. Somali troops supported incursions by forces of the Western Somali Liberation Front, and in 1977 the Somalis made major advances in the Ogaden. In 1978, however, they were forced to retreat, and by the end of 1980 Ethiopian forces had gained control of virtually the whole of the Ogaden region.

The former Italian colony of Eritrea was merged with Ethiopia, in a federal arrangement, in September 1952, and annexed to Ethiopia as a province in November 1962. A secessionist movement, the Eritrean Liberation Front (ELF), was founded in Egypt in 1958. The ELF eventually split into several rival factions, the largest of which was the Eritrean People's Liberation Front (EPLF). In 1978 government troops re-established control in much of Eritrea, and the EPLF retreated to the northern town of Nakfa. In 1982 an offensive by government troops failed to capture Nakfa, and in 1984 the EPLF made several successful counter-attacks. In mid-1986 government forces abandoned the north-east coast to the rebels.

An insurgent movement also emerged in Tigrai province in the late 1970s. The Tigrai People's Liberation Front (TPLF) was armed and trained by the EPLF, but relations between the two groups deteriorated sharply in the mid-1980s. The TPLF was weakened by conflict with other anti-Government groups, and in 1985 and 1986 government forces had considerable success against the TPLF.

In September 1987 the newly elected National Shengo announced that five areas, including Eritrea and Tigrai, were to become 'autonomous regions' under the new Constitution. Eritrea was granted a considerable degree of self-government, but both the EPLF and the TPLF rejected the proposals. In March 1988 EPLF forces captured the town of Afabet, after which the TPLF seized all the garrisons in north-western and north-eastern Tigrai. In early 1989, following major defeats in north-western Tigrai, government forces abandoned virtually the whole region to the TPLF.

Following the capture of Massawa port by the EPLF in February 1990 (presenting a direct threat to the continued survival of the Ethiopian army in Eritrea), President Mengistu was obliged to make a number of concessions. In March Ethiopian socialism was virtually abandoned, when the WPE was renamed the Ethiopian Democratic Unity Party, and membership was opened to non-Marxists. Mengistu began introducing elements of a market economy and dismantling many of the economic structures that had been established after the 1974 revolution.

By late April 1991, troops of the Ethiopian People's Revolutionary Democratic Front (EPRDF)—an alliance of the TPLF and the Ethiopian People's Democratic Movement (EPDM)—had captured Ambo, a town 130 km west of Addis Ababa, while EPLF forces were 50 km north of Assab, Ethiopia's principal port. On 21 May, faced with the prospect of the imminent defeat of his army, Mengistu fled the country. On 28 May, following the failure of negotiations in the United Kingdom, and with the public support of the USA, units of the EPRDF entered Addis Ababa. They encountered little resistance, and the EPRDF established an interim Government, pending the convening of a multi-party conference in July, which was to elect a transitional government. Meanwhile, the EPLF had gained control of the Eritrean capital, Asmara, and announced the establishment of a provisional Government to administer Eritrea, pending a referendum on the issue of independence.

In July 1991 a national conference adopted amendments to a national charter, presented by the EPRDF, and elected an 87-member Council of Representatives, which was to govern for a transitional period of two years, after which free national elections were to be held. The national charter provided guarantees for freedom of association and expression, and for self-determination for Ethiopia's various ethnic groups. The EPLF was not officially represented at the conference, but came to an agreement with the EPRDF, whereby the EPRDF accepted the formation of the EPLF's provisional Government of Eritrea and the determination by referendum of the future of the region. In late July the Council of Representatives established a commission to draft a new constitution and elected Meles Zenawi, the leader of the EPRDF (and of the TPLF), as Chairman of the Council, a position that made him President of the transitional Government and Head of State; in August it appointed a Council of Ministers. Following a referendum in April 1993 Eritrean independence was proclaimed on 24 May.

Domestic Political Affairs

Elections to a Constituent Assembly were conducted in Ethiopia in June 1994, in which the EPRDF won 484 of the 547 seats. The Constituent Assembly ratified a new Constitution in December, which provided for the establishment of a federal government and the division of the country (renamed the Federal Democratic Republic of Ethiopia) into nine states and two chartered cities. A new legislature, the Federal Parliamentary Assembly, was to be established, comprising two chambers: the House of People's Representatives (consisting of no more than 550 directly elected members) and the House of the Federation (composed of 117 deputies, elected by the new state assemblies). The EPRDF and its allies won an overwhelming victory in elections to the House of People's Representatives and state assemblies in May 1995. Most opposition parties boycotted the poll, although international observers accepted that the elections were conducted in a largely free and fair manner.

On 22 August 1995 the country's new Constitution and designation as the Federal Democratic Republic of Ethiopia were formally instituted. Later that day Dr Negasso Gidada, the EPRDF nominee, and a member of the Oromo People's Democratic Organization (OPDO, which was in alliance with the EPRDF), was elected President of the Federal Republic. A new Prime Minister, Meles Zenawi, was elected from among the members of the House of People's Representatives.

The trial of 69 former government officials, including ex-President Mengistu, opened in Addis Ababa in December 1994. The defendants, 23 of whom were being tried *in absentia* (including Mengistu, who was in exile in Zimbabwe), were accused of crimes against humanity and of genocide, perpetrated during 1974–91. In February 1997 the office of the Special Prosecutor announced that an additional 5,198 people would be indicted for war crimes and genocide, of whom nearly 3,000 would be tried *in absentia*. In April the Ethiopian High Court found 37 people (13 *in absentia*) guilty of crimes against humanity and genocide; they were sentenced to up to 20 years' 'rigorous' imprisonment. In December 2006 Mengistu, along with 71 others, was found guilty of genocide, and in January 2007 he was sentenced *in absentia* to life imprisonment. In May 2008 the life sentence was overturned by the Federal Supreme Court and Mengistu was sentenced to death, along with a number of his former political associates.

Legislative elections were held on 14 May 2000: the OPDO won the largest number of seats in the House of People's Representatives, taking 178 of the 546 available. The OPDO's major partners in the EPRDF, the Amhara National Democratic Movement (ANDM—as the EPDM had been renamed in 1994) and the TPLF, gained 134 and 38 seats, respectively, securing the coalition a majority in the lower chamber. In October the new legislature was sworn in, and Meles was re-elected as Prime Minister.

In late June 2001 President Gidada was dismissed from the executive committee of the OPDO, after it was alleged that he had refused to accept the party's programme of reform and was providing support to dissidents opposed to Meles. Gidada, in turn, accused the Government of embarking on a campaign of propaganda against him. Gidada was also expelled from the EPRDF; however, he remained insistent that he would complete his presidential term, which was scheduled to end in October. By September Meles had succeeded in re-establishing control over the TPLF, and therefore the EPRDF, following his re-election as Chairman of the party. On 8 October 2001 Lt Girma Wolde Giorgis was elected by the legislature to replace Gidada as President. Later that month Prime Minister Meles effected a major reorganization of the Council of Ministers. In 2003 a number of new political parties and coalition organizations were formed, the most significant of which were the United Ethiopian Democratic Party, which was created by the merger of the Ethiopian Democratic Unity Party and the Ethiopian Democratic Party, and the United Ethiopian Democratic Forces (UEDF), under the leadership of Dr Beyene Petros.

From December 2003 clashes between the Anuak and Nuer communities over disputed land in the Gambela region of the country escalated. The increase in violence was precipitated by the killing of eight officials from the office of the UN High Commissioner for Refugees (UNHCR) and the Federal Agency for Refugee and Returnee Affairs, reportedly committed by the Anuak, who had been angered by the proposed construction on their land of a camp to house Nuer refugees. The Anuak community was the target of a number of revenge attacks, which resulted in the death of some 100 people (although opposition sources indicated that the actual casualty figures were much higher), and it was alleged that the Government had actively encouraged reprisals against the Anuak community. As the violence escalated some 15,000 Anuak, including the President of the region, Okelo Akuai, sought refuge in Sudan. In late January 2004 some 200 people were killed after Anuak militants attacked a gold mine where many new settlers to the region were working. By mid-2004 the situation had calmed significantly and about 8,000 of those who had fled in January had returned to Gambela. In December UNHCR resumed operations in the region. An attack on a bus en route from Addis Ababa to Gambela in June 2006, in which at least 14 people died, was attributed to Anuak rebels.

The 2005 legislative elections

Legislative elections were held on 15 May 2005, although voting in the Somali regional state was postponed until 21 August. Provisional results for the House of People's Representatives, published by the National Electoral Board of Ethiopia (NEBE) in late May, awarded the EPRDF 302 seats, the Coalition for Unity and Democracy (CUD) 122 and the UEDF 57; the rate of voter participation was recorded at more than 90%. The results in some 300 constituencies were, however, disputed by both the EPRDF and opposition parties amid allegations of electoral fraud, while concerns over voting irregularities were also raised by observers from the European Union (EU, see p. 273). The NEBE agreed to undertake investigations in 143 of the contested constituencies and in June the EU brokered an agreement between the EPRDF and the CUD and the UEDF, according to which both sides pledged to accept the findings of the NEBE's investigations. The NEBE announced the official results of the legislative elections in early September, including results from the Somali regional state and from 31 constituencies where voting had been reheld, according to which the EPRDF took 327 seats, the CUD 109 seats and the UEDF 52 seats. A number of smaller parties secured the remaining seats. Despite agreeing to accept the NEBE's decision, the CUD renewed its allegations of electoral fraud and in early October some 100 CUD deputies boycotted the opening of the House of People's Representatives.

In November 2005 there were further violent clashes in Addis Ababa between police and demonstrators protesting against alleged voting irregularities in the legislative elections. It was reported that some 46 people were killed and around 150 people were injured during the confrontations. A number of senior members of the CUD were among some 130 people arrested later in November and subsequently charged with treason and attempted genocide. Proceedings against those accused, 25 of whom were being tried *in absentia*, commenced in the Federal High Court in February 2006. In March charges against 18 defendants were dropped. In June 2007 38 of the defendants were found guilty of violating the Constitution and 30 of those convicted were sentenced to life imprisonment, with the remainder handed lesser terms; however, in July all 38 were pardoned and freed from prison.

Meanwhile, in January 2006 the British Government announced that it was to suspend indefinitely its direct budgetary support to Ethiopia, owing to concerns over the political situation in the country. In May a new opposition coalition, the Alliance for Freedom and Democracy (AFD), was formed by the CUD and four rebel factions: the Ethiopian People's Patriotic Front; the Ogaden National Liberation Front (ONLF); the Oromo Liberation Front (OLF) and the Sidama Liberation Front. In August Meles announced that thousands of troops had been deployed against ONLF rebels, who were allegedly receiving support from Eritrea and Somali Islamists, in the Ogaden region. In the same month it was reported that around 150 members of the Ethiopian army had defected to Eritrea, including a senior commander who intended to join the OLF; two other key military figures allegedly followed in mid-September. In October it emerged that an official inquiry into the violent dispersal of demonstrations after the May 2005 elections had been suppressed by the Government; 193 protesters were reported to have been killed by Ethiopian security forces. Renewed violence in November 2009 resulted in the deaths of a number of Ethiopian troops as ONLF rebels launched an offensive in the Ogaden region. In January 2010 the Ethiopian Government announced that it had detained some 100 OLF rebels following clashes near Moyale in which the OLF claimed to have killed at least three Ethiopian soldiers. Meanwhile, in June 2007 the CUD was renamed the Unity for Democracy and Justice Party (Andinet) under the leadership of Birtukan Mideksa, hitherto Vice-President of the CUD.

In April 2009 the Ethiopian Government arrested 40 suspected members of a new opposition party, the Movement for Justice, Freedom and Democracy (Ginbot 7), which had adopted a platform sanctioning any means to effect political change. After being found guilty of plotting to overthrow the Government, in December five of the defendants were sentenced to death, while terms of life imprisonment were imposed on 33 others.

The 2010 general election

In October 2009 eight opposition organizations formed the Ethiopia Federal Democratic Unity Forum (FORUM) chaired by Dr Merara Gudina, leader of the Oromo People's Congress (OPC). Tensions increased in the period leading up to the May 2010 legislative elections, with the FORUM and the US-based international non-governmental organization Human Rights Watch (HRW) accusing the Government of orchestrating a campaign to suppress opposition activity. The FORUM alleged that its supporters had been subjected to harassment, intimidation and beatings. The situation deteriorated in March 2010, when a FORUM candidate was stabbed to death, which was followed by the murders of two FORUM activists in April and May, respectively. The Government denied any involvement in the killings and countered by blaming the opposition for the murder of one of its candidates in May. According to official sources, in the same month two people were also killed in a grenade attack at a meeting organized by the pro-Government OPDO. Meanwhile, in March Meles admitted that radio programming transmitted by the Voice of America (VOA), a worldwide broadcasting operation funded by the US Government, was being blocked within Ethiopia. Meles accused VOA of transmitting 'destabilizing propaganda' and likened its content to 1990s Rwandan broadcasts encouraging genocide, prompting condemnation by the US Administration.

The general election was held peacefully on 23 May 2010 and resulted in an emphatic victory for the EPRDF, which won 499 of the 547 seats contested. Pro-Government parties secured an additional 46 seats, while the FORUM (which had been weakened by internal divisions) only managed to gain control of a single seat; an independent candidate won the remaining seat. The rate of participation by the electorate was recorded at 93.4%. EU monitors announced that the election had not met international standards and criticized the Government's monopolization of state resources during campaigning, a stance reiterated by US officials, although African Union (AU, see p. 186) observers defended the results. The EPRDF claimed that the outcome reflected voter satisfaction with the Government's economic policies. Opposition leaders denounced the results, citing electoral irregularities and accusing the authorities of fraud. An appeal by Merara for the election to be held afresh was rejected by the NEBE and the Supreme Court in June.

Meles was unanimously re-elected as Prime Minister by the House of People's Representatives on 4 October 2010, and he appointed 10 new members to the Council of Ministers on the following day. Most notable among the changes was the appointment of Hailemariam Desalegn as Deputy Prime Minister and Minister of Foreign Affairs. Birtukan Mideksa, a prominent opposition leader who had been sentenced to life imprisonment for treason after the post-election unrest in 2005, was pardoned and released from gaol shortly afterwards. (Birtukan had been freed in 2007 but was rearrested the following year.) Her release was viewed by some commentators as an attempt by the Government to appease its international partners in the wake of the election controversy. However, the EPRDF's victory came under further scrutiny later that month, when a HRW report claimed that the Government had systematically refused to allocate food aid to supporters of the opposition; the authorities denied this accusation.

Following their overwhelming defeat in the legislative elections, a number of opposition parties underwent a process of restructuring. The remaining members of the FORUM announced in July 2010 that they had disbanded their loose coalition and formed a six-party front, committing themselves to a permanent alliance and a common policy platform. A new opposition grouping, the Alliance for Liberty, Equality and Justice in Ethiopia, was founded in August by Ginbot 7, the Afar People's Party and the Ethiopian Movement for Unity and Justice.

ONLF rebels attacked a military base in Malqaqa in May 2010 and claimed that they had gained control of the town, although the Government denied this and stated that the attack had been repelled. The leader of the United Western Somali Liberation Front, an Ogaden-based Islamist group, signed a peace deal with the Government in July, agreeing to disarm in exchange for an amnesty for its members. A similar peace agreement was signed by a faction of the ONLF, led by Salahdin Abdurahman Maow, in October. Both groups announced that they intended to regroup as political parties.

In March 2011 it was announced that nearly 250 members of the FORUM, principally of the Oromo Federalist Democratic Movement (OFDM), had been arrested in an apparent attempt to pre-empt anti-Government protests akin to those of the 'Arab Spring' in the Middle East and North Africa. In the same month it was reported that Meles had replaced some 150 officials belonging to the OPDO, after ordering their arrest on charges of corruption. In June Moga Firisa of the OFDM was elected as the new Chairman of the FORUM. In September five people, including opposition leader Andualem Arage and journalist Eskinder Nega, were arrested on the grounds that they were supporters of Ginbot 7 and involved in organizing acts of terrorism in the country; the detention earlier that month, on similar charges, of political activist Debebe Eshetu was also denounced by opposition groups. In August 2012 the OPC and the OFDM merged to form a new party, the Oromo Federal Congress (OFC), led by former OPC leader Gudina. In September two Swedish reporters, who, in December 2011, had been sentenced to 11 years' imprisonment for entering Ethiopia illegally and supporting terrorism (after entering the Ogaden region, in co-operation with the ONLF, in order to investigate human rights there), were released from prison in Addis Ababa, under an amnesty for 1,950 prisoners.

Recent developments: new Prime Minister

On 20 August 2012 Meles died in a hospital in Belgium; on the following day Hailemariam was appointed acting Prime Minister. On 15 September Hailemariam was elected to succeed Meles as Chairman of the EPRDF, and on 21 September the House of People's Representatives approved his nomination as premier in the country's first peaceful and constitutional transition of power. Also in September, Abay Weldu, the governor of Tigrai state, was elected as the new Chairman of the TPLF. In November the legislature approved a government reorganization effected by Hailemariam: the Minister of Communication and Information Technology, Debretsion Gebremikael, was also appointed Deputy Prime Minister, Co-ordinator of Finance and the Economy, while senior EPRDF official Muktar Kedir became Deputy Prime Minister, Co-ordinator of Good Governance and Minister of the Civil Service; Dr Tewedros Adhanom, hitherto Minister of Health, received the foreign affairs portfolio.

In December 2012 the Ethiopian High Federal Court sentenced two opposition leaders, Olbana Lelisa and Bekele Gerba, to 13 and eight years' imprisonment, respectively, for having links with the OLF; a further seven defendants received prison terms of between three and 12 years for rebel activities. In the same month charges of terrorism were upheld against 29 Muslims who had been arrested in July for planning protests (as part of an ongoing campaign) against government interference in the religious affairs of the Muslim community; their trial commenced in early 2013. In separate proceedings in January, nine Ethiopians and one Kenyan national were convicted (six *in absentia*) of planning terrorist attacks in the country in collaboration with Somali Islamist group al-Shabaab (see Regional relations), and were sentenced to prison terms of between three and 20 years.

On 2 June 2013 the holding of a peaceful demonstration, organized by the new Semayawi (Blue) Party, was permitted in Addis Ababa for the first time since 2005. The protesters appealed for the release of political prisoners, journalists and the organizers of Muslim protests staged in 2012. However, the authorities subsequently discouraged further such gatherings by Semayawi and Andinet.

In early July 2013 Prime Minister Hailemariam Desalegn carried out an extensive cabinet reorganization, including 10 new appointments; the post of justice minister, which was assigned to Getachew Ambaye, had been vacant since May, when Berhan Hailu had been dismissed from office. Following the expiry of President Wolde Giorgis' term in office, on 7 October both houses of the legislature unanimously elected former ambassador Dr Mulatu Teshome Wirtu as his replacement.

Foreign Affairs

Regional relations

Relations with Somalia have been problematic since the Ogaden War of 1977–78. However, in April 1988 Ethiopia and Somalia agreed to re-establish diplomatic relations, to withdraw troops from their common border and to exchange prisoners of war. In November 2000 the President of Somalia, Abdulkassim Salad Hasan, visited Ethiopia and held talks with senior Ethiopian officials; however, the Ethiopian authorities continued to refuse to recognize officially the Hasan administration and urged it to reach agreements with its opponents. In January 2001 relations between the countries deteriorated, after the Somali Prime Minister accused Ethiopia of continuing to assist the Somali-based Rahawin Resistance Army, which had taken control of a number of towns in south-west Somalia, and of involvement in an assassination attempt on the Speaker of Somalia's transitional legislature. Relations between Somalia and Ethiopia were further strained by Meles' claim that a number of members of al-Ittihad al-Islam (Islamic Union Party—which sought independence for Ethiopia's Ogaden province) were represented in the Somali Transitional National Government (TNG); the accusation was, however, forcefully denied by Hasan. Relations between Ethiopia and Somalia improved in early 2005 and Ethiopia signalled its support for the new Somali President, Col Abdullahi Yussuf Ahmed, following his election in January. In 2006, however, repeated accusations of incursions by Ethiopian troops in support of the TNG in Baidoa (where it had been relocated) caused relations to deteriorate once more. In October Meles admitted the presence of military trainers in Baidoa and described his country as being 'technically at war' with its neighbour and prepared for conflict. In December the Somali Supreme Islamic Courts Council (SSICC, as the Union of Islamic Courts had been restyled) issued a deadline for Ethiopian troops to leave Somalia within one week or face a major attack; the following week, amid reports of heavy fighting between Ethiopian troops and Islamist militias near Baidoa, the SSICC urged all Somalis to join the 'war' against Ethiopia. At the end of the month Meles admitted for the first time to active military involvement by his country in Somalia, claiming that his troops were defending Ethiopia's sovereignty against what he termed terrorists and anti-Ethiopian elements. Ethiopia was supported in its actions by the AU, which conceded that the presence of Islamist militias so close to its borders might be perceived as a threat. In June 2007 Meles pledged to withdraw Ethiopian forces from Somalia upon the arrival of an AU peacekeeping force, the AU Mission in Somalia (AMISOM); however, the pervading instability in Somalia meant that only a small number of the proposed 8,000 troops were deployed by mid-2007; in August the UN Security Council extended AMISOM's mandate by six months. Ethiopian forces were still present in February 2008—when the AMISOM mandate was extended by a further six months—as the number of peacekeepers deployed was still limited. In August the AMISOM mandate was extended again, and in November it was announced that all Ethiopian troops would leave Somalia by the end of the year. However, reports emerged during 2009 and 2010 of Ethiopian troops crossing into Somalia to pursue insurgents belonging to the Somali Islamist group al-Shabaab. In November 2011 the Ethiopian Government officially denied reports that its forces were participating in a large-scale military operation against al-Shabaab in Somalia. In early 2013, however, Ethiopian troops continued to support Somali government forces and AMISOM in efforts to regain control of south-central regions of Somalia from al-Shabaab. In July the Ethiopian Government announced that it had begun to pull its troops out of Baidoa, citing the return of relative stability to the former rebel stronghold; it denied, however, that a complete withdrawal of Ethiopian troops from Somalia was being planned. Two Somali suicide bombers planning to target an association football match in Addis Ababa accidentally blew themselves up on 13 October 2013 before they could carry out the action, which was perceived to be a revenge attack for the continuing presence of Ethiopian troops in Somalia. In February 2014 the 4,400 Ethiopian troops who remained in the country officially came under international command.

Following the military coup in Sudan in April 1985, full diplomatic relations were restored between Ethiopia and Sudan. Relations between the two countries were strained in the late 1980s, however, by the influx into Ethiopia of thousands of Sudanese refugees, fleeing from famine and civil war in southern Sudan. The vast majority of an estimated 380,000 refugees were reported to have returned to Sudan by early 1991, as a result of the civil war in Ethiopia. The change of government in Ethiopia in May 1991 led to a considerable improvement in relations, and in October President Meles and Sudan's leader, Lt-Gen. al-Bashir, signed an agreement on friendship and co-operation. Relations deteriorated sharply in 1995, following apparent Sudanese complicity in the attempted assassination of President Muhammad Hosni Mubarak of Egypt in Addis Ababa in June, but steadily improved after 1998, following Ethiopia's conflict with Eritrea; Eritrea had been supporting Sudanese opposition movements since 1994. A protocol concerning Ethiopian access to Port Sudan was signed between the two countries in March 2000 and ratified by the Ethiopian legislature in July 2003. In November 2004 Ethiopia and Sudan finalized an agreement on the demarcation of their common border, and requested financial assistance from international organizations in order to demarcate the border on the ground. In May 2008 it was announced that an agreement would soon be concluded. Despite Meles' insistence that no citizens would be displaced, in the following month there were reports that Ethiopians living in the border regions had been forced from their homes by Sudanese troops; there were also concerns that the demarcation would transfer holy and historic areas of Ethiopia to Sudan. By November 2009 preparations had been finalized in Ethiopia for the deployment of a 200-strong air force unit to Darfur in western Sudan (where civil conflict had broken out in 2003), in addition to the 1,600 ground troops already stationed in the region as part of the AU-UN peacekeeping mission, UNAMID. The Ethiopian Government has been keen to maintain good relations with Sudan, owing to its dependence on Sudanese petroleum and fears of closer Sudan-Eritrea ties. Following South Sudan's secession from Sudan in 2011, Ethiopia agreed to deploy more than 4,200 peacekeeping forces, with the backing of the UN Security Council, in the contested border region of Abyei.

Relations with Djibouti, which varied a little in the 2000s in relation to each country's stance on the situation in Somalia, have settled into a pragmatic focus on consolidating shared infrastructure to support Ethiopia's dependence on Djibouti port. Electricity exports from Ethiopia to Djibouti commenced in June 2011 and a memorandum of understanding was signed in February 2012 to construct a new road and oil pipeline from South Sudan linking Ethiopia to Djibouti.

Ethiopia and the newly independent Eritrea signed a treaty of co-operation during a visit by the Eritrean President, Issaias Afewerki, to Addis Ababa in July 1993. A further agreement, signed in late 1994, provided for the free movement of goods between the two countries without payment of customs dues. In late 1997, however, relations with Eritrea deteriorated, following that country's adoption of a new currency (to replace the Ethiopian birr) and the subsequent disruption of cross-border trade. Fighting between Ethiopian and Eritrean troops erupted in May 1998, with both countries accusing the other of having invaded their territory. Proposals by the UN Security Council and the Organization of African Unity (OAU), now the AU, to resolve the conflict were rejected by Eritrea, necessitating the convening of a special meeting of an OAU mediation committee in Ouagadougou, Burkina Faso, in November. Ethiopia welcomed the committee's proposals, which stressed the need to demilitarize and demarcate the disputed region, but Eritrea rejected the plans. Further mediation attempts to impose a ceasefire also failed.

In mid-May 2000 Ethiopian troops launched a major offensive near the disputed towns of Badme and Zalambessa, repelling Eritrean forces. Despite demands from the UN, hostilities continued, and on 18 May the UN Security Council unanimously approved the imposition of a 12-month arms embargo on Ethiopia and Eritrea. Shortly afterwards Zalambessa fell to the Ethiopian forces, and on 25 May the Eritrean Government announced the withdrawal of its troops from all disputed areas. On 31 May Prime Minister Meles stated that Ethiopia had no territorial claims over Eritrea and that the war between the two countries was over; nevertheless, sporadic fighting continued to take place. In early June both sides expressed their willingness, in principle, to accept the OAU's peace proposals and on 18 June the Ethiopian and Eritrean Ministers of Foreign Affairs signed an agreement, which provided for an immediate ceasefire and the establishment of a 25-km temporary security zone (TSZ) on the Eritrean side of the common border until the issue of the final demarcation of the border had been settled. In mid-September the UN Security Council approved the deployment of a 4,200-strong UN Mission in Ethiopia and Eritrea (UNMEE).

In December 2000 Ethiopia and Eritrea signed an agreement in Algiers, Algeria, which formally brought an end to the conflict. The agreement provided for a permanent cessation of all hostilities, the return of all prisoners of war, the demarcation of the common border by an independent commission, and the establishment of a Claims Commission to assess the issues of compensation and reparations. By late January 2001 the UNMEE force had arrived in the region and Ethiopian troops commenced their withdrawal from the territory they had captured from Eritrea. In March UNMEE's mandate was extended until September (and at six-monthly or four-monthly intervals thereafter) and on 16 April it was announced that the withdrawal of its forces was complete. In mid-May the arms embargo imposed on the two countries by the UN in May 2000 was lifted. In late June 2001 UNMEE presented the final map of the TSZ to Ethiopia and

Eritrea, although it emphasized that it would not influence the work of the neutral Boundary Commission charged with determining the border between the two countries. Despite this announcement, the Ethiopian Government expressed its dissatisfaction with the map, and at the eighth Military Co-ordination Committee (MCC) meeting in August both countries again stated their objections to the current boundaries of the TSZ.

In December 2001 Ethiopia and Eritrea began presenting their cases for border demarcation to the five-member Boundary Commission at the International Court of Justice (see p. 24) in The Hague, Netherlands. The Commission delivered its findings in April 2002. Both Ethiopia and Eritrea had committed themselves in advance to the acceptance of the report, which was carefully balanced, thus allowing both sides to claim success. However, the Commission did not identify on which side of the boundary line Badme lay, stating that delineation had been delayed, as extensive de-mining was required prior to placing boundary markers. In the absence of any decision, both countries immediately claimed to have been awarded Badme.

In early March 2003 the Boundary Commission reported to the UN Security Council that requests by Ethiopia for changes to the border ruling, in order to 'take better account of human and physical geography', threatened to undermine the peace process as a whole. Despite Ethiopia's claims that it had been promised that demarcations could be refined, later in March the Boundary Commission categorically ruled Badme to be Eritrean territory, thus rejecting Ethiopia's territorial claim over the town. Meles subsequently vowed to continue to contest the ruling. The demarcation of the border, which had originally been scheduled to take place in May, was postponed until July, and then further delayed until October. In a letter to the UN Security Council in October, Prime Minister Meles requested the establishment of a new body to resolve the crisis and again denounced the Boundary Commission's ruling as 'unacceptable'. However, the Security Council stated that Ethiopia had, under the 2000 Algiers accord, committed itself to accept the Boundary Commission's decision as 'final and binding' and urged it to accept and implement the border ruling. With no resolution to the ongoing impasse in sight, in late October the Boundary Commission announced that the demarcation of the border had been delayed indefinitely.

In November 2004 Ethiopia indicated that it would co-operate with UNMEE when Meles announced a five-point plan aimed at resolving the disputed border issue and declared that Ethiopia had, in principle, accepted the Boundary Commission's ruling. Meles' statement was dismissed by the Eritrean authorities as an attempt by Ethiopia to further stall the process. In mid-December the UN withdrew some 550 Kenyan troops from the TSZ in an attempt to reduce the costs of its military presence in the area.

Ethiopia and Eritrea continued to increase troop numbers in the border area in 2005, raising fears of a return to conflict. However, Ethiopia sought to reassure the international community that troop movements and the construction of trenches on its side of the TSZ were for defensive purposes only. In November the UN Security Council adopted Resolution 1640, which demanded full acceptance by Ethiopia of the Boundary Commission's ruling regarding border demarcation, that Eritrea lift restrictions on UNMEE operations, and that troop numbers on both sides of the border be reduced with immediate effect.

In early March 2006 at a Boundary Commission meeting in London, United Kingdom, agreement was reached between Ethiopia and Eritrea to hold further talks the following month, but these were subsequently postponed. In May the number of UNMEE military personnel in the region was reduced by 1,000 to 2,300. In November both Ethiopia and Eritrea failed to attend a meeting of the Boundary Commission in The Hague and rejected its proposals; the Commission, in response, issued a statement informing them that in the event of no agreement having been reached by November 2007 it would begin the physical demarcation of the border. In January 2007 UNMEE's strength was further reduced, to 1,700. By late 2007 neither side had complied with the Boundary Commission's request of November 2006 physically to demarcate the border. In early December 2007, prior to announcing its own dissolution, the Commission stated that the boundary that it had determined in November 2006 represented the official border between the two countries.

Eritrean-imposed restrictions on the movements of UN peacekeeping personnel and the delivery of fuel led the UN to relocate its peacekeepers in Eritrea to Ethiopia in mid-February 2008. It was subsequently reported that a number of peacekeepers had been prevented from leaving Eritrea and the UN Security Council expressed its concern at the 'impediments and logistical constraints' placed upon the force. UN Secretary-General Ban Ki-Moon warned of a possible return to hostilities if the peacekeeping force was withdrawn, but Eritrea continued to impede UN operations, eventually forcing UNMEE to abandon its mission in the region. On 30 July the UN Security Council adopted Resolution 1827, terminating the mandate of UNMEE; the last troops were withdrawn in October. In August 2009 the Claims Commission awarded Ethiopia a total of US $174m. in compensation for war damages, while Eritrea received $164m., resulting in a net payment to Ethiopia of $10m.

Arbitration efforts continued during 2008 and 2009, and an uneasy truce persisted, punctuated by occasional minor military clashes. However, in early January 2010 the Eritrean Government claimed that its troops had killed 10 Ethiopian soldiers after they attacked Eritrean positions near Zalambessa. The Ethiopian authorities denied that the incident had occurred and maintained that the Eritrean authorities were attempting to cover up an attack by a rebel Eritrean movement in which 25 Eritrean government soldiers were killed. Successive bomb attacks in Tigrai Region, bordering Eritrea, in April and May 2010 resulted in the deaths of five people. The Ethiopian Government blamed Eritrea for the explosions, claiming that they were an attempt by its neighbour to disrupt the legislative elections. In March 2011 Ethiopia warned that it would take all measures necessary against Eritrea, accusing it of planning attacks during the February AU summit in Addis Ababa; furthermore, the Ethiopian Government openly declared its support for Eritrea's opposition groups and appealed for regime change. Ethiopia also maintained that al-Shabaab continued to receive weapons and assistance from Eritrea. In December the UN Security Council imposed additional sanctions on Eritrea for supporting armed groups in Somalia. Nevertheless, Ethiopia—in an attempt to alleviate tensions in the wake of its incursion into Eritrean territory in March 2012, when Ethiopian troops killed at least 50 alleged members of the Afar Revolutionary Democratic Unity Front—offered peace talks on two occasions in 2013; Eritrea, however, did not respond positively to these propositions. In January 2013 the new Ethiopian Prime Minister, Hailemariam Desalegn, was elected to the annually rotating chairmanship of the AU.

Other external relations

In 1984 some 13,000 Falashas, a Jewish group in Ethiopia, reached Sudan, from where they were flown to Israel in a secret airlift. In May 1991 Israel evacuated a further 14,000 Falashas from Addis Ababa; some 10,000 Falashmura (Ethiopian Christians whose forefathers had converted from Judaism) were subsequently granted Israeli citizenship on humanitarian grounds. In March 1999 Israel pledged to examine the possibility of bringing the estimated 19,000 Jews remaining in Ethiopia to Israel, and in April 2000 the Israeli Minister of the Interior visited Ethiopia to investigate the claims of some 26,000 Ethiopians who maintained that they belonged to the Falashmura community and were thus eligible to settle in Israel under Israeli law. In February 2003 the Israeli Government ruled that the Falashmura had been forced to convert to Christianity to avoid religious persecution and that they had the right to settle in Israel. In January 2004 Ethiopia and Israel agreed to allow the Falashmura to be flown to Israel; some 17,000 Falashmura and a further 3,000 Falashas arrived in Israel by May 2008. Israel resumed the transportation of Falashmura in January 2010, following a suspension of the airlift process in August 2008. The Israeli Government announced in November 2010 that the remaining Falashmura in Ethiopia, some 8,000 people, would be granted the right to immigrate to Israel. In August 2013 the Israeli Government completed what was reported to be the final airlift of Ethiopian Jews to Israel.

In recent years the People's Republic of China has developed closer ties with Ethiopia and has made significant economic investment in the country. However, in April 2007 members of the ONLF killed more than 70 people, including nine Chinese oil workers, in an attack on a petroleum installation in the Somali region; seven Chinese citizens were kidnapped, although they were later released unharmed.

In November 2012 Ethiopia was elected to the UN Human Rights Council, despite protests by human rights groups, which cited continued violations by the Ethiopian authorities, including a series of arrests of Muslim protesters earlier that year (see Domestic Political Affairs).

CONSTITUTION AND GOVERNMENT

Under the provisions of the Constitution, adopted in December 1994, the country became a federation, consisting of nine states and two chartered cities, the capital, Addis Ababa, and Dire Dawa. The states have their own parliamentary assemblies, which also elect representatives to the House of the Federation, the upper chamber of the Federal Parliamentary Assembly. The lower chamber, the House of People's Representatives, consists of no more than 550 directly elected deputies, who each serve terms of five years. The Federal Parliamentary Assembly elects a President as Head of State with a six-year term of office. However, the President fulfils mainly ceremonial functions, executive power being the preserve of the Prime Minister. The Prime Minister, who is elected by the House of People's Representatives, appoints the Council of Ministers (subject to approval by the legislature), and acts as Commander-in-Chief of the armed forces. Unless otherwise provided in the Constitution, the term of office of the Prime Minister is the duration of the mandate of the House of People's Representatives.

REGIONAL AND INTERNATIONAL CO-OPERATION

Ethiopia is a member of the African Union (see p. 186), and the headquarters of that organization are based in Addis Ababa. It is also a member of the Common Market for Eastern and Southern Africa (see p. 233) and of the Intergovernmental Authority on Development (see p. 335). In July 2001 Ethiopia ratified the Cotonou Agreement (see p. 324), the successor of the Lomé Convention of the EU.

Ethiopia was one of the 51 founding member states of the UN, established in 1945. Ethiopia submitted a request for accession to the World Trade Organization (see p. 434) in January 2003.

ECONOMIC AFFAIRS

In 2012, according to estimates by the World Bank, Ethiopia's gross national income (GNI), measured at average 2010–12 prices, was US $37,391m., equivalent to $410 per head (or $1,140 per head on an international purchasing-power parity basis). During 2003–12, it was estimated, the population increased at an average annual rate of 2.7%, while gross domestic product (GDP) per head grew, in real terms, by an average of 7.4% per year. Overall GDP increased, in real terms, at an average annual rate of 10.3% during 2003–12; it rose by 8.5% in 2012.

Agriculture (including forestry and fishing) contributed an estimated 48.4% of GDP in 2012, according to the African Development Bank (AfDB). The sector employed 75.1% of the labour force at mid-2014, according to FAO estimates, reflecting the fact that Ethiopia has the lowest level of urbanization among African countries. The principal cash crop is coffee (which accounted for 29.2% of export earnings in 2012). The principal subsistence crops are cereals (maize, sorghum, wheat and barley) and sugar cane. According to the World Bank, during 2003–11 agricultural GDP increased at an average annual rate of 9.3%; it grew by 5.2% in 2011, despite the fact that in that year Ethiopia was affected by the worst regional drought in 60 years, according to the UN.

Industry (including mining, manufacturing, construction and power) employed 6.6% of the labour force in March 2005, and provided an estimated 10.0% of GDP in 2012, according to the AfDB. During 2003–11, according to the World Bank, industrial GDP increased by an average of 9.4% per year. Sectoral growth was 11.0% in 2011.

According to the AfDB, mining contributed only an estimated 1.4% of GDP in 2012, and employed less than 0.3% of the labour force in March 2005. Ethiopia has deposits of copper and potash. Gold, tantalite, soda ash, kaolin, dimension stones, precious metals and gemstones, salt, and industrial and construction materials are mined. In April 2000 a US company discovered large petroleum and natural gas deposits in the west of the country, and in June 2003 the Ethiopian Government granted a one-year exploration licence to Petronas of Malaysia. The licence was renewed in early 2004 to allow exploration over a larger area. However, Petronas ceased operations in Ethiopia in 2010 and at early 2014, despite continuing exploration projects being undertaken by local and foreign hydrocarbons companies, no commercial production of petroleum or gas had yet commenced. During 2002/03–2006/07 mining GDP increased by an estimated average of 3.9% per year; growth in 2006/07 was an estimated 6.0%. According to the AfDB, the sector's GDP increased by 57.7% in 2011 and by 12.7% in 2012.

Manufacturing employed only 4.9% of the labour force in March 2005, and contributed an estimated 3.6% of GDP in 2012, according to the AfDB. During 2003–11, according to the World Bank, manufacturing GDP increased at an average annual rate of 9.4%. Sectoral growth was 8.2% in 2011.

Construction employed only 1.4% of the labour force in March 2005, and contributed an estimated 4.0% of GDP in 2012, according to the AfDB. The GDP of the sector increased by 12.5% in 2012.

In years of normal rainfall, energy is derived principally from Ethiopia's massive hydroelectric power resources. In 2011 99.0% of Ethiopia's electricity was produced by hydroelectric power schemes. Moreover, the Government launched an ambitious 25-year plan in 2013 to transform the country into a renewable energy hub and a significant regional power supplier. The largest wind farm in sub-Saharan Africa, located in Tigrai province, commenced operations in October 2013. The wind farm, which comprised 84 turbines and had a capacity of 120 MW, was expected to produce about 400m. kWh per year. As part of its energy plans, the Government also signed an agreement with an Icelandic company in 2013 to construct a 1,000-MW geothermal power plant in the volcanically active Rift Valley. Imports of mineral fuels accounted for 19.7% of the cost of total imports in 2012. By 2013 Ethiopia's electricity generating capacity had reached some 2,200 MW.

Services, which consisted mainly of wholesale and retail trade, public administration and defence, and transport and communications, employed 13.1% of the labour force in March 2005, and contributed an estimated 41.6% of GDP in 2012, according to the AfDB. The combined GDP of the service sectors increased, in real terms, at an average rate of 12.0% per year during 2003–12, according to the World Bank. The sector grew by 8.6% in 2011.

According to IMF figures, in 2012 Ethiopia recorded a visible merchandise trade deficit of US $7,289.3m., and there was a deficit of $2,985.3m. on the current account of the balance of payments. In 2012 the principal source of imports (providing 21.3% of the total) was the People's Republic of China; other major suppliers were Saudi Arabia, India and Kuwait. The principal market for exports in that year were Somalia (taking 12.9% of the total), the Netherlands, Germany, China and Saudi Arabia. The principal exports in 2012 were coffee, edible vegetables and roots and tubers, cut flowers, oil seeds and live animals. The principal imports in that year were refined petroleum, boilers, machinery, etc., motor vehicles, electrical and electronic equipment, iron and steel, and cereals.

In the fiscal year 2013/14 Ethiopia's budgetary deficit was projected to reach 30,899m. birr. Ethiopia's general government gross debt was 156,466m. birr. in 2012, equivalent to 21.2% of GDP. Ethiopia is the principal African recipient of concessionary funding, and one of the largest recipients of European Union (EU) aid. In 2011 Ethiopia's total external debt was US $8,597m., of which $7,938m. was public and publicly guaranteed debt. In that year the cost of servicing long-term public and publicly guaranteed debt and repayments to the IMF was equivalent to 3.0% of the value of exports of goods, services and income (excluding workers' remittances). The annual rate of inflation averaged 30.3% in 2007/08–2011/12, according to the official estimates. Consumer prices increased by 33.7% in 2011/12. In March 2005, according to the International Labour Organization, 1,653,700 people were registered as unemployed, representing 5.0% of the total labour force.

Ethiopia remains one of the poorest countries in the world, and its economy continues to suffer from the effects of recurrent drought, which severely disrupts agricultural production. The Ethiopian economy is also heavily dependent on assistance and grants from abroad, while regional instability presents further obstacles to development. However, in recent years considerable investment in the country's infrastructure has been made to facilitate the distribution of aid supplies. The third phase of the AfDB-funded Mombasa–Nairobi–Addis Ababa Road Corridor Project, under way in 2012–17, as part of the Trans-Africa Highway network, was expected significantly to increase trade between Ethiopia and Kenya. In addition, in September 2010 construction began, with Chinese financing, of a 5,000-km railway system, which was to include a 781-km line between Addis Ababa and Djibouti that would provide the capital with its shortest route to a seaport. Meanwhile, building work began in late 2011 (again with Chinese funding) on a Light Rail Transit network in Addis Ababa—the country's first mass transit system. Despite its shortcomings, from 2004 the economy maintained consistent and broad-based growth, largely as a result of the expansion of the services and agricultural sectors, while domestic demand was fuelled by private consumption and public investment. The Government devised a Growth and Transformation Plan (GTP) for 2010–15, emphasizing the development of public sector agriculture, industry and infrastructure, while simultaneously attracting greater investment from China and India and encouraging more remittances from Ethiopians working abroad. Projects initiated under the GTP included the construction of the Grand Ethiopian Renaissance Dam, which, with a planned capacity of 6,000 MW, would be the largest hydroelectric power plant in Africa. However, the project, which was scheduled to be completed in mid-2017, proved controversial owing to the concerns of some countries over water-sharing. Although there were reports in early 2014 that the Ethiopian authorities had raised only a small proportion of its share of the funds (Ethiopia's contribution was to total US $3,000m., while the remaining $1,800m. was to be provided by Chinese banks), the Government claimed in February that construction work was progressing as scheduled and that the dam was around 30% complete. Following a dramatic rise in inflation to around 40% at mid-2011, the implementation of stringent government monetary policy coupled with a deceleration in global food and fuel prices reduced the rate to about 7.0% by mid-2013. Meanwhile, economic growth was sustained, with the IMF estimating a rise in real GDP of about 7.0% in 2012/13 and 7.5% in 2013/14, despite a decline in international coffee prices.

PUBLIC HOLIDAYS

2015: 3 January† (Mouloud, Birth of the Prophet), 7 January* (Christmas), 19 January* (Epiphany), 2 March (Battle of Adowa), 10 April* (Good Friday), 13 April* (Easter Monday), 1 May (May Day), 5 May (Patriots' Victory Day), 28 May (Downfall of the Dergue), 17 July† (Id al-Fitr, end of Ramadan), 12 September (New Year's Day), 23 September† (Id al-Adha/Arafat), 28 September* (Feast of the True Cross).

* Coptic holidays.

† These holidays are dependent on the Islamic lunar calendar and may vary by one or two days from the dates given.

Note: Ethiopia uses its own solar calendar; the Ethiopian year 2005 began on 11 September 2012.

Statistical Survey

Source (unless otherwise stated): Central Statistical Authority, POB 1143, Addis Ababa; tel. (11) 553010; fax (11) 550334; internet www.csa.gov.et.

Area and Population

AREA, POPULATION AND DENSITY

Area (sq km)	1,133,380*
Population (census results)	
11 October 1994	53,477,265
28 May 2007	
Males	37,217,130
Females	36,533,802
Total	73,750,932
Population (official estimates at July)	
2011	82,101,998
2012	84,320,987
2013	86,613,986
Density (per sq km) at July 2013	76.4

* 437,600 sq miles.

POPULATION BY AGE AND SEX

(UN estimates at mid-2014)

	Males	Females	Total
0–14	20,522,939	20,051,305	40,574,244
15–64	26,188,148	26,409,098	52,597,246
65 and over	1,564,951	1,769,587	3,334,538
Total	48,276,038	48,229,990	96,506,028

Source: UN, *World Population Prospects: The 2012 Revision*.

ADMINISTRATIVE DIVISIONS

(official population estimates at July 2013)

	Population		
	Males	Females	Total
Regional States			
1 Tigrai	2,489,994	2,571,997	5,061,991
2 Afar	917,999	732,000	1,649,999
3 Amhara	9,633,991	9,578,003	19,211,994
4 Oromia	16,227,993	15,992,008	32,220,001
5 Somali	2,957,999	2,360,001	5,318,000
6 Benishangul-Gumuz	522,997	504,997	1,027,994
7 Southern Nations, Nationalities and Peoples	8,903,996	8,983,009	17,887,005
8 Gambela	212,003	194,001	406,004
9 Harari	108,000	107,000	215,000
—*continued*			
Chartered Cities			
1 Dire Dawa	198,000	197,000	395,000
2 Addis Ababa	1,479,000	1,624,999	3,103,999
Total*	43,715,971	42,898,015	86,613,986

* Including 116,999 (males 63,999, females 53,000) persons, detailed as 'special enumeration', not allocated to administrative divisions.

Note: Totals may not be equal to the sum of components, owing to rounding of some data.

PRINCIPAL TOWNS

(official population estimates at July 2013)

Addis Ababa (capital)	3,103,673	Awasa	225,686
Mekele	286,624	Bahir Dar	198,909
Nazret	282,974	Jimma	155,434
Dire Dawa	269,134	Dessie	153,691
Gondar	264,964	Jijiga	152,674

BIRTHS AND DEATHS

(annual averages, UN estimates)

	1995–2000	2000–05	2005–10
Birth rate (per 1,000)	45.4	41.3	36.4
Death rate (per 1,000)	15.1	12.5	9.5

Source: UN, *World Population Prospects: The 2012 Revision*.

Life expectancy (years at birth): 62.3 (males 60.8; females 63.8) in 2011 (Source: World Bank, World Development Indicators database).

ECONOMICALLY ACTIVE POPULATION

('000 persons aged 10 years and over, March 2005)*

	Males	Females	Total
Agriculture, hunting, forestry and fishing	14,209.4	10,998.8	25,208.2
Mining and quarrying	51.4	30.6	82.1
Manufacturing	444.0	1,085.3	1,529.4
Electricity, gas and water	25.2	7.7	32.9
Construction	349.9	95.7	445.6
Wholesale and retail trade; repair of motor vehicles, motorcycles and personal and household goods	652.2	984.9	1,637.1

—continued	Males	Females	Total
Hotels and restaurants	96.8	672.3	769.1
Transport, storage and communications	132.0	14.5	146.4
Financial intermediation	21.6	16.3	37.9
Real estate, renting and business services	36.1	16.2	52.3
Public administration and defence; compulsory social security	242.0	125.9	367.9
Education	178.2	104.5	282.7
Social work	45.6	32.5	78.1
Community, social and personal services	303.5	135.2	438.7
Households with employed persons	23.1	225.5	248.6
Extra-territorial organizations and bodies	42.7	25.1	67.9
Sub-total	16,853.7	14,571.0	31,424.9
Not classifiable by economic activity	6.5	3.8	10.3
Total employed	16,860.3	14,574.8	31,435.1
Unemployed	427.9	1,225.8	1,653.7
Total labour force	17,288.2	15,800.6	33,088.8

* Excluding armed forces.

Source: ILO.

Mid-2014 (FAO estimates in '000): Agriculture, etc. 34,582; Total labour force 46,038 (Source: FAO).

Health and Welfare

KEY INDICATORS

Total fertility rate (children per woman, 2011)	4.0
Under-5 mortality rate (per 1,000 live births, 2011)	77
HIV/AIDS (% of persons aged 15–49, 2012)	1.3
Physicians (per 1,000 head, 2009)	0.03
Hospital beds (per 1,000 head, 2011)	6.3
Health expenditure (2010): US $ per head (PPP)	50
Health expenditure (2010): % of GDP	4.8
Health expenditure (2010): public (% of total)	52.9
Access to water (% of persons, 2011)	49
Access to sanitation (% of persons, 2011)	21
Total carbon dioxide emissions ('000 metric tons, 2010)	6,494.3
Carbon dioxide emissions per head (metric tons, 2010)	0.1
Human Development Index (2012): ranking	173
Human Development Index (2012): value	0.396

For sources and definitions, see explanatory note on p. vi.

Agriculture

PRINCIPAL CROPS
('000 metric tons)

	2010	2011	2012
Wheat	2,856	2,916	3,435
Barley	1,703	1,585	1,782
Maize	4,986	6,069	6,158
Oats	48	49	44
Millet (Dagusa)	635	652	742
Sorghum	3,960	3,951	3,604
Potatoes	447	475	863
Sweet potatoes	736	390	1,185
Yams	340	315	350*
Sugar cane*	2,400	2,500	2,700
Beans, dry	340	388	463
Broad beans, horse beans, dry	698	715	944
Peas, dry	257	263	327
Chick peas	323	400	410
Lentils	81	128	152
Vetches	201	306	326
Groundnuts, with shell	72	103	124
Castor beans†	7	7	7
Rapeseed	23*	75	73
Safflower seed	5	9	13
Sesame seed	328	245	181

—continued	2010	2011	2012
Linseed	65	113	122
Cabbages and other brassicas	351	367	394
Tomatoes	56	82	56
Onions and shallots, green*	26	33	34
Onions, dry	237	328	219
Garlic	128	124	223
Bananas	271	291	303
Oranges	44	49	36
Mangoes, mangosteens and guavas	66	73	70
Avocados	57	73	26
Papayas	40	43	39
Coffee, green	371	377	276

* FAO estimate(s).

† Unofficial figures.

Aggregate production ('000 metric tons, may include official, semi-official or estimated data): Total cereals 17,761 in 2010, 18,810 in 2011, 19,386 in 2012; Total roots and tubers 6,223 in 2010, 6,275 in 2011, 7,598 in 2012; Total vegetables (incl. melons) 1,803 in 2010, 1,787 in 2011, 1,930 in 2012; Total fruits (excl. melons) 681 in 2010, 729 in 2011, 672 in 2012.

Source: FAO.

LIVESTOCK
('000 head, year ending September)

	2010	2011	2012
Cattle	53,382	52,129	53,990
Sheep	25,509	24,221	25,489
Goats	22,787	22,613	24,061
Asses	6,210	6,438	6,748
Mules	385	369	350
Horses	2,028	1,962	1,907
Camels	1,102	979	916
Pigs*	31	32	32
Poultry	49,287	44,893	50,377

* FAO estimates.

Source: FAO.

LIVESTOCK PRODUCTS
('000 metric tons)

	2010	2011	2012
Cattle meat*	420.0	410.0	338.2
Sheep meat*	86.0	85.0	86.0
Goat meat*	66.3	68.0	68.0
Pig meat*	1.8	1.8	1.9
Chicken meat*	59.2	53.9	60.5
Game meat*	84.7	85.0	85.0
Cows' milk	4,058.0	3,329.9	3,805.0
Goats' milk*	52.5	55.0	57.5
Sheep's milk*	57.5	56.3	57.5
Hen eggs*	39.0	39.6	40.0
Honey	53.7	39.9	45.9
Wool, greasy*	8.0	8.0	8.0

* FAO estimates.

Source: FAO.

Forestry

ROUNDWOOD REMOVALS
('000 cubic metres, excl. bark, FAO estimates)

	2010	2011	2012
Sawlogs, veneer logs and logs for sleepers	11	11	11
Pulpwood	7	7	7
Other industrial wood	2,917	2,917	2,917
Fuel wood	101,274	102,609	103,966
Total	104,209	105,544	106,901

Source: FAO.

SAWNWOOD PRODUCTION
('000 cubic metres, incl. railway sleepers)

	2001	2002	2003
Coniferous (softwood)	25*	1	1
Broadleaved (hardwood)	35*	13	17
Total	60	14	18

* FAO estimate.

2004–12: Figures assumed to be unchanged from 2003 (FAO estimates).

Source: FAO.

Fishing

(metric tons, live weight of capture)

	2009	2010	2011
Common carp	293	182	929
Other cyprinids	1,936	1,971	1,900
Tilapias	7,554	12,110	16,279
North African catfish	3,143	2,050	3,279
Nile perch	2,740	1,017	844
Total catch (incl. others)	17,047	18,058	24,041

Source: FAO.

Mining

('000 metric tons, unless otherwise indicated, year ending 7 July)

	2007/08	2008/09	2009/10
Gold (kilograms)	3,465	6,251	5,936
Limestone	1,900	2,000*	2,000*
Gypsum and anhydrite	33	36*	36*
Pumice	35	250*	350*
Sandstone*	1,400	1,500	1,500

* Estimate(s).

Source: US Geological Survey.

Industry

SELECTED PRODUCTS
('000 metric tons, year ending 7 July, unless otherwise indicated)

	2000/01	2001/02	2002/03
Wheat flour	165	143	137
Macaroni and pasta	26	23	30*
Raw sugar	251	248*	295*
Wine ('000 hectolitres)	25	27*	32*
Beer ('000 hectolitres)	1,605	1,812*	2,123*
Mineral waters ('000 hectolitres)	395	395*	433*
Soft drinks ('000 hectolitres)	677	995	845*
Cigarettes (million)	1,904	1,511*	1,511*
Cotton yarn	5.7	7.7*	5.5*
Woven cotton fabrics ('000 sq m)	45,000	45,000*	41,000*
Nylon fabrics ('000 sq m)	1,300	1,000*	1,400*
Footwear (including rubber, '000 pairs)	n.a.	6,677	7,138
Soap	14.8	19.2*	11.6*
Tyres ('000)*	209	198	191
Clay building bricks ('000)*	20	22	21
Quicklime*	11	8	11
Cement*	819	919	890

* Year ending 31 December of later year.

Source: UN, *Industrial Commodity Statistics Yearbook*.

Raw sugar ('000 metric tons): 325.0 in 2004; 345.0 in 2005; 360.0 in 2006; 340.0 in 2007; 340 in 2008; 320 in 2009 (Source: UN Industrial Commodity Statistics Database).

Cement (hydraulic, '000 metric tons, year ending 7 July): 1,130.1 in 2003; 1,315.9 in 2004; 1,568.6 in 2005; 1,731 in 2006; 1,626 in 2007; 1,834 in 2008; 2,100 in 2009 (estimate); 2,200 in 2010 (estimate); 2,300 in 2011 (estimate) (Source: US Geological Survey).

Beer of millet ('000 metric tons): 220.7 in 2001; 208.0 in 2002; 244.1 in 2003 (Source: FAO).

Beer of barley ('000 metric tons, estimates): 350.9 in 2010; 356.6 in 2011; 815.7 in 2012 (Source: FAO).

Finance

CURRENCY AND EXCHANGE RATES

Monetary Units
100 cents = 1 birr.

Sterling, Dollar and Euro Equivalents (30 August 2013)
£1 sterling = 20.306 birr;
US $1 = 18.770 birr;
€1 = 18.066 birr;
100 birr = £4.92 = $5.33 = €5.54.

Average Exchange Rate (birr per US $)

2010	14.410
2011	16.899
2012	17.705

GENERAL BUDGET
(million birr, year ending 7 July)

Revenue	2011/12	2012/13*	2013/14†
Taxation	85,740	99,838	118,092
Taxes on income and profits	28,858	34,653	40,592
Domestic indirect taxes	23,326	27,964	33,396
Import duties	33,556	37,220	44,103
Other revenue	17,124	15,970	11,712
Total‡	102,864	115,808	129,804

Expenditure	2011/12	2012/13*	2013/14†
Current expenditure	51,445	60,555	70,251
Defence spending	6,486	6,500	7,500
Poverty-reduction expenditure§	24,994	29,775	34,224
Interest and charges	2,230	3,153	4,242
Domestic	1,388	1,784	2,589
External	842	1,369	1,653
Other current expenditure	17,735	21,128	24,285
Capital expenditure	72,971	97,432	106,261
Central treasury	57,439	76,578	83,438
External assistance (grants)	8,089	12,880	11,786
External loans	7,443	7,973	11,037
Total	124,417	157,987	176,511

* Estimates.

† Projections.

‡ Excluding grants received from abroad (million birr): 12,795 in 2011/12; 17,488 in 2012/13 (estimate); 15,808 in 2013/14 (projection).

§ Includes total spending on health, education, agriculture, roads and food security.

Source: IMF, *The Federal Democratic Republic of Ethiopia: Staff Report for the 2013 Article IV Consultation* (October 2013).

INTERNATIONAL RESERVES
(US $ million at 31 December, excluding gold)

	2007	2008	2009
IMF special drawing rights	0.1	—	27.4
Reserve position in IMF	11.6	11.5	11.8
Foreign exchange	1,278.1	859.0	1,741.7
Total	1,289.8	870.5	1,780.9

2010: IMF special drawing rights 150.0; Reserve position in IMF 11.6.

2011: IMF special drawing rights 149.3; Reserve position in IMF 11.5.

2012: IMF special drawing rights 149.4; Reserve position in IMF 11.5.

Source: IMF, *International Financial Statistics*.

MONEY SUPPLY
(million birr at 31 December)

	2006	2007	2008
Currency outside banks	11,606.4	14,445.8	17,432.9
Demand deposits at commercial banks	20,207.0	24,175.9	31,391.6
Total money (incl. others)	32,056.2	38,903.5	49,105.8

Source: IMF, *International Financial Statistics*.

COST OF LIVING
(Consumer Price Index; base: December 2006 = 100)

	2009/10	2010/11	2011/12
Food	187.2	216.6	307.0
Beverages	187.1	207.9	278.1
Clothing and footwear	188.5	242.2	323.4
Housing, water, electricity, gas and other fuels	159.1	191.1	219.4
Health	149.2	167.2	186.1
Transport and communication	134.9	171.0	202.9
Recreation and education	144.6	179.6	218.5
All items	177.9	210.2	281.0

NATIONAL ACCOUNTS
(million birr at current prices)

Expenditure on the Gross Domestic Product

	2010	2011	2012*
Government final consumption expenditure	32,888	43,638	51,808
Private final consumption expenditure	329,705	397,595	563,595
Gross fixed capital formation	94,497	141,382	254,708
Total domestic expenditure	457,090	582,615	870,111
Exports of goods and services	52,168	85,955	102,887
Less Imports of goods and services	126,319	162,490	236,385
GDP in purchasers' values	382,939	506,079	736,612

Gross Domestic Product by Economic Activity

	2010	2011	2012*
Agriculture, hunting, forestry and fishing	165,668	212,578	331,444
Mining and quarrying	2,475	6,810	9,301
Manufacturing	13,821	18,037	24,328
Electricity and water	4,393	5,488	7,746
Construction	15,882	19,100	27,221
Trade, hotels and restaurants	66,781	87,937	127,364
Finance, insurance and real estate	42,137	55,992	71,591
Transport and communications	15,982	19,891	29,154
Public administration and defence	12,199	17,447	22,323
Other services	18,001	26,587	34,248
Sub-total	357,339	469,867	684,720
Indirect taxes	28,412	39,431	56,882
Less imputed bank service charge	2,813	3,219	4,988
GDP in purchasers' values	382,939	506,079	736,612

* Provisional figures.

Source: African Development Bank.

BALANCE OF PAYMENTS
(US $ million)

	2010	2011	2012
Exports of goods	2,479.5	3,029.0	3,258.0
Imports of goods	−7,364.5	−8,328.9	−10,547.3
Balance on goods	−4,885.0	−5,299.8	−7,289.3
Exports of services	2,164.7	2,785.8	2,735.9
Imports of services	−2,546.3	−3,321.8	−3,582.6
Balance on goods and services	−5,266.6	−5,835.8	−8,136.0
Primary income received	8.1	8.8	8.7
Primary income paid	−71.7	−85.6	−105.5
Balance on goods, services and primary income	−5,330.1	−5,912.7	−8,232.9
Secondary income received	4,987.9	5,172.9	5,326.8
Secondary income paid	−83.2	−43.3	−79.3
Current balance	−425.4	−783.1	−2,985.3
Direct investment liabilities	288.3	626.5	278.6
Other investment assets	1,084.6	171.3	−142.7
Other investment liabilities	995.6	1,072.1	530.8
Net errors and omissions	−2,929.9	−1,795.8	2,648.6
Reserves and related items	−986.8	−708.9	330.0

Source: IMF, *International Financial Statistics*.

External Trade

PRINCIPAL COMMODITIES
(distribution by HS, US $ million)

Imports c.i.f.	2010	2011	2012
Vegetables and vegetable products	462.1	606.3	568.6
Cereals	374.4	471.4	453.2
Wheat and meslin	304.3	402.6	349.0
Animal, vegetable fats and oils, cleavage products, etc.	260.2	391.7	439.6
Palm oil and its fraction	222.7	330.9	391.5
Mineral products	1,687.0	1,715.3	2,554.5
Mineral fuels, oils, distillation products, etc.	1,642.1	1,632.0	2,504.7
Refined petroleum oils	1,544.4	1,484.3	2,383.0
Chemicals and related products	832.1	830.7	1,521.5
Pharmaceutical products	250.4	120.7	434.5
Fertilizers	246.0	341.0	629.7
Mixtures of nitrogen, phosphorous and potassium fertilizers	169.0	250.2	449.2
Plastics, rubber, and articles thereof	390.3	445.2	596.3
Textiles and textile articles	349.3	361.7	487.1
Iron and steel, other base metals and articles of base metal	788.3	830.1	1,378.5
Iron and steel	318.9	453.2	742.7
Articles of iron and steel	340.6	210.8	416.6
Machinery and mechanical appliances; electrical equipment; parts thereof	2,244.9	1,776.6	2,644.8
Boilers, machinery, etc.	1,115.7	1,150.3	1,669.0
Electrical and electronic equipment	1,129.2	626.3	975.8
Electric appliances for line telephony	529.3	107.0	168.8
Vehicles, aircraft, vessels and associated transport equipment	845.1	1,003.6	1,455.4
Vehicles other than railway, tramway	836.3	893.8	1,410.6
Trucks, motor vehicles for the transport of goods	382.2	357.6	660.2
Total (incl. others)	8,601.8	8,896.3	12,744.5

Exports f.o.b.	2010	2011	2012
Live animals and animal products	2,515.2	2,515.2	4,469.3
Live animals	132.4	190.4	324.3
Live bovine animals	77.6	137.8	172.1
Vegetables and vegetable products	1,685.2	1,906.4	3,193.2
Live trees, plants, bulbs, roots, cut flowers, etc.	165.1	191.4	604.5
Cut flowers and flower buds for bouquets, fresh or dried	143.8	168.9	526.3
Edible vegetables and roots and tubers	408.8	416.7	770.4
Vegetables, fresh or chilled	245.1	238.1	488.3
Dried vegetables, shelled	136.5	139.3	215.4
Coffee, tea, mate and spices	727.6	887.1	1,221.0
Coffee	699.1	846.9	1,188.0
Oil seed, oleagic fruits, grain, seed, fruit, etc.	345.4	368.7	534.0
Oil seeds	338.8	363.8	497.1
Raw hides and skins, leather, furskins, etc., and articles thereof	67.9	123.4	88.5
Raw hides, skins (except furskins) and leather	67.2	122.7	85.5
Pearls, precious or semi-precious stones, precious metals, and articles thereof	183.9	132.5	186.6
Gold	182.3	124.6	176.6
Machinery and mechanical appliances; electrical equipment; parts thereof	76.6	12.2	18.9
Total (incl. others)	2,329.8	2,614.9	4,066.8

Source: Trade Map-Trade Competitiveness Map, International Trade Centre, www.intracen.org/marketanalysis.

PRINCIPAL TRADING PARTNERS
(US $ million)

Imports c.i.f.	2010	2011	2012
Belgium	89.0	52.6	160.3
Brazil	124.4	81.5	142.8
China, People's Republic	2,062.1	1,718.1	2,718.2
Egypt	99.5	82.9	108.9
France (incl. Monaco)	106.4	142.9	228.2
Germany	206.7	189.6	216.2
India	619.7	749.3	1,115.5
Indonesia	87.3	188.4	352.1
Italy	391.0	386.7	634.7
Japan	473.5	443.4	531.2
Jordan	100.1	129.2	37.2
Korea, Republic	94.5	134.9	228.2
Kuwait	3.1	222.1	735.0
Malaysia	229.1	274.1	189.3
Morocco	102.2	30.5	183.3
Pakistan	53.9	108.9	51.0
Russia	91.4	270.9	135.0
Saudi Arabia	1,023.3	896.8	1,689.7
South Africa	58.6	93.1	140.0
Spain	92.2	91.7	150.8
Sudan	109.3	145.6	70.6
Thailand	126.6	131.5	174.1
Turkey	238.7	359.7	522.6
Ukraine	85.0	140.8	337.8
United Arab Emirates	485.7	482.5	288.4
United Kingdom	89.1	109.8	107.7
USA	483.6	489.0	471.8
Total (incl. others)	8,601.8	8,896.3	12,744.5

Exports f.o.b.	2010	2011	2012
Belgium	56.6	69.5	103.6
China, People's Republic	241.8	283.4	347.6
Djibouti	67.1	75.6	171.9
Egypt	46.3	46.1	79.4
France (incl. Monaco)	37.8	50.2	69.5
Germany	265.3	318.8	458.9
India	29.9	33.8	46.8
Israel	51.9	67.2	78.4
Italy	69.2	111.2	90.0
Japan	38.7	35.9	106.7
Jordan	16.8	26.6	47.0
Netherlands	173.4	181.2	502.2
Pakistan	24.4	13.4	46.8
Saudi Arabia	146.5	167.3	261.0
Somalia	224.1	243.3	524.1
South Africa	73.7	6.5	17.1
Sudan	151.3	178.4	189.1
Sweden	23.7	39.0	36.6
Switzerland-Liechtenstein	126.9	129.4	178.0
Turkey	33.3	45.2	51.4
United Arab Emirates	111.3	82.5	95.0
United Kingdom	57.8	67.5	62.9
USA	102.3	98.0	126.4
Total (incl. others)	2,329.8	2,614.9	4,066.8

Source: Trade Map-Trade Competitiveness Map, International Trade Centre, www.intracen.org/marketanalysis.

Transport

RAILWAYS
(traffic on the Addis Ababa–Djibouti line, year ending 7 July)*

	2008/09	2009/10
Passengers carried ('000)	55	35
Passenger-km (million)	14	5
Freight carried ('000 tons)	20	2
Freight (million net ton-km)	7	1

* Including traffic on the section of the line that runs through the Republic of Djibouti; data pertaining to freight include service traffic.

ROAD TRAFFIC
(motor vehicles in use, year ending 7 July)

	2001	2002	2003
Passenger cars	59,737	67,614	71,311
Buses and coaches	11,387	18,067	20,713
Lorries and vans	43,375	34,102	51,690
Motorcycles and mopeds	2,198	2,575	1,268
Road tractors	1,275	1,396	—
Total	117,972	123,754	144,982

2007: Passenger cars 70,834; Buses and coaches 17,098; Lorries and vans 148,997; Motorcycles and mopeds 7,328.

Source: IRF, *World Road Statistics*.

SHIPPING

Flag Registered Fleet
(at 31 December)

	2011	2012	2013
Number of vessels	8	9	17
Displacement (grt)	112,197	139,017	313,105

Source: Lloyd's List Intelligence (www.lloydslistintelligence.com).

International Sea-borne Shipping
(freight traffic, '000 metric tons, year ending 7 July)

	1996/97	1997/98	1998/99
Goods loaded	242	201	313
Goods unloaded	777	1,155	947

Source: former Ministry of Transport and Communications, Addis Ababa.

CIVIL AVIATION
(traffic on scheduled services)

	2011	2012
Kilometres flown (million)	100	119
Passengers carried ('000)	3,347	4,441
Passenger-km (million)	11,652	15,330
Total ton-km (million)	1,864	2,382

Source: UN, *Statistical Yearbook*.

2011/12 (traffic at Addis Ababa international airport, year ending 7 July): Aircraft movements 51,318; Passengers carried ('000) 5,183; Freight carried ('000 metric tons) 154,138; Mail carried ('000 metric tons) 530.

Tourism

TOURIST ARRIVALS BY COUNTRY OF ORIGIN

	2009	2010	2011
Canada	9,490	11,871	12,889
China, People's Republic	18,968	22,722	20,197
Djibouti	7,276	8,140	5,962
France	12,000	12,635	16,517
Germany	16,695	18,777	24,780
India	11,525	14,607	19,667
Italy	14,468	16,528	19,164
Kenya	15,532	15,322	19,904
Netherlands	7,864	8,863	9,052
Nigeria	11,905	10,434	16,437
Saudi Arabia	10,456	14,019	18,891
Somalia	4,020	4,543	1,842
South Africa	8,427	10,541	13,433
Sudan	12,515	12,979	17,922
United Arab Emirates	9,271	11,077	8,255
United Kingdom	23,154	25,090	28,945
USA	67,157	76,730	81,044
Total (incl. others)*	427,286	468,305	523,438

* Including Ethiopian nationals residing abroad.

Receipts from tourism (US $ million, excl. passenger transport): 329 in 2009; 522 in 2010; 763 in 2011.

Source: World Tourism Organization.

Communications Media

	2010	2011	2012
Telephones ('000 main lines in use)	908.9	829.0	797.5
Mobile cellular telephones ('000 subscribers)	6,854.0	14,126.7	20,523.9
Internet users ('000)	72.4	n.a.	n.a.
Broadband subscribers	4,107	4,592	37,754

Source: International Telecommunication Union.

Education

(2012/13)

	Institutions	Teachers	Students
Pre-primary	3,688	12,639	2,013,214
Primary	30,534	335,109	17,430,294
Secondary: grades 9–12	1,912	65,116	1,900,022
Secondary: teacher training	34	2,052	173,628
Secondary: technical and vocational	437	12,779	237,877
Higher education	99	23,905	585,152
Government	34	21,899	502,466
Non-government	65	2,006	82,686

Source: Ministry of Education, Addis Ababa.

Pupil-teacher ratio (primary education, UNESCO estimate): 53.7 in 2011/12 (Source: UNESCO Institute for Statistics).

Adult literacy rate (UNESCO estimates): 35.9% (males 50.0%; females 22.8%) in 2008 (Source: UNESCO Institute for Statistics).

Directory

The Government

HEAD OF STATE

President: Dr MULATU TESHOME WIRTU (took office 7 October 2013).

COUNCIL OF MINISTERS

(April 2014)

The Government is formed by members of the Amhara National Democratic Movement (ANDM), the South Ethiopian People's Democratic Movement (SEPDM), the Oromo People's Democratic Organization (OPDO), the Tigrai People's Liberation Front (TPLF) and the Somali People's Democratic Party (SPDP).

Prime Minister: HAILEMARIAM DESALEGN (SEPDM).

Deputy Prime Minister, Co-ordinator of Good Governance and Minister of the Civil Service: MUKTAR KEDIR (OPDO).

Deputy Prime Minister, Co-ordinator of Finance and the Economy and Minister of Communication and Information Technology: DEBRETSION GEBREMIKAEL (TPLF).

Deputy Prime Minister: DEMEKE MEKONNEN (ANDM).

Minister of Foreign Affairs: Dr TEWEDROS ADHANOM (TPLF).

Minister of Defence: SIRAJ FERGESA (SEPDM).

Minister of Federal Affairs: Dr SHIFERAW TEKELEMARIAM (SEPDM).

Minister of Justice: GETACHEW AMBAYE (ANDM).

Minister of Finance and Economic Development: SUFYAN AHMED (OPDO).

Minister of Agriculture: TEFERA DERIBEW (ANDM).

Minister of Industry: AHMED ABETEW (ANDM).

Minister of Trade: KEBEDE CHANE (ANDM).

Minister of Science and Technology: DEMITU HAMBESSA (OPDO).

Minister of Transport: WORKNEH GEBEYEHU (OPDO).

Minister of Urban Development, Housing and Construction: MEKURIA HAILE (SEPDM).

Minister of Water and Energy: ALEMAYEHU TEGENU (OPDO).

Minister of Mines: TOLLOSA SHAGI (ANDM).

Minister of Health: Dr KESETEBERHAN ADMASU (SEPDM).

Minister of Labour and Social Affairs: ABDULFETAH ABDULAHI HASSEN (SPDP).

Minister of Culture and Tourism: AMIN ABDULKADIR (ANDM).

Minister of Women, Youth and Children's Affairs: ZENEBU TADESSE (ANDM).

Minister of Education: SHIFERAW SHIGUTE (SEPDM).

Minister of Environment Protection and Forestry: BELETE TAFESE (TPLF).

Ministers and Policy Study and Research Advisers to the Prime Minister: BEREKET SIMON (ANDM), KUMA DEMEKSA (OPDO).

Minister, Head of the Government Communication Office: REDWAN HUSSEIN (SEPDM).

Minister, Government Chief Whip: ROMAN GEBRESILASIE (TPLF).

Minister, Director-General of the Ethiopian Revenues and Customs Authority: BEKIR SHALE (OPDO).

MINISTRIES

Office of the President: POB 1031, Addis Ababa; tel. (11) 1551000; fax (11) 1552030.

Office of the Prime Minister: POB 1013, Addis Ababa; tel. (11) 1552044; fax (11) 1552020.

Office for Government Communication Affairs: Addis Ababa; tel. (11) 5540486; fax (11) 5540473; e-mail shekemal@yahoo.com.

Ministry of Agriculture: POB 62347, Addis Ababa; tel. (11) 5538134; fax (11) 5530776; internet www.moa.gov.et.

Ministry of the Civil Service: Addis Ababa.

Ministry of Communication and Information Technology: Alta Bldg, 6th Floor, Mexico Sq., POB 1028, Addis Ababa; tel. (11) 5500191; fax (11) 5515894; internet www.mcit.gov.et.

Ministry of Culture and Tourism: POB 2183, Addis Ababa; tel. (11) 5512310; fax (11) 5512889; e-mail info@tourismethiopia.org; internet www.tourismethiopia.org.

Ministry of Defence: POB 1373, Addis Ababa; tel. (11) 5511777; fax (11) 5516053.

Ministry of Education: POB 1367, Addis Ababa; tel. (11) 1553133; fax (11) 1550877; internet www.moe.gov.et.

Ministry of Environment Protection and Forestry: Addis Ababa.

Ministry of Federal Affairs: POB 1031, Addis Ababa; tel. (11) 5512766; fax (11) 1552030.

Ministry of Finance and Economic Development: POB 1037, Addis Ababa; tel. (11) 1552400; fax (11) 1551355; e-mail infopr@mofed.gov.et; internet www.mofed.gov.et.

Ministry of Foreign Affairs: POB 393, Addis Ababa; tel. (11) 5517345; fax (11) 5514300; e-mail mfa.addis@telecom.net.et; internet www.mfa.gov.et.

Ministry of Health: POB 1234, Addis Ababa; tel. (11) 5517011; fax (11) 5519366; e-mail moh@telecom.net.et; internet www.moh.gov.et.

Ministry of Industry: Addis Ababa; tel. (11) 534942; fax (11) 5534932; internet www.moi.gov.et.

Ministry of Justice: POB 1370, Addis Ababa; tel. (11) 512288; fax (11) 517775; internet www.mojet.gov.et.

Ministry of Labour and Social Affairs: POB 2056, Addis Ababa; tel. (11) 5517080; fax (11) 5518396; e-mail molsa.comp@ethionet.et; internet www.molsa.gov.et.

Ministry of Mines: POB 486, Addis Ababa; tel. (11) 5153689; fax (11) 5517874.

Ministry of Science and Technology: Addis Ababa.

Ministry of Trade: POB 704, Addis Ababa; tel. (11) 5518025; fax (11) 5514288; e-mail henok_fekadu@yahoo.com.

Ministry of Transport: Addis Ababa; tel. (11) 5516166; fax (11) 5515665; e-mail nigusmen@yahoo.com; internet www.motr.gov.et.

Ministry of Urban Development, Housing and Construction: opp. National Bank of Ethiopia, POB 24134/1000, Addis Ababa; tel. (11) 5531688; fax (11) 5541268; internet www.mwud.gov.et.

Ministry of Water and Energy: Haile G/Silassie Rd, POB 5744 and 5673, Addis Ababa; tel. (11) 6611111; fax (11) 6610710; e-mail info@mowr.gov.et; internet www.mowr.gov.et.

Ministry of Women, Youth and Children's Affairs: POB 1364, Addis Ababa; tel. (11) 5517020.

Regional Governments

Ethiopia comprises nine regional governments and two chartered cities (Addis Ababa and Dire Dawa), all of which are vested with the authority for self-administration. The executive bodies are respectively headed by Presidents (regional states) and Chairmen (Addis Ababa and Dire Dawa).

PRESIDENTS
(April 2014)

Tigrai: ABAY WOLDU.

Afar: ISMAIL ALI SERRO.

Amhara: GEDU ANDARGATCHEW.

Oromia: MUKTAR KEDIR.

Somali: ABDI MOHAMED OMAR.

Benishangul-Gumuz: AHMED NASIR AHMED.

Southern Nations, Nationalities and Peoples: DESSIE DALKE.

Gambela: UMED UBONG.

Harari: MURAD ABDULHADIN.

CHAIRMEN
(April 2014)

Dire Dawa: ASAD ZIAD.

Addis Ababa: DIRIBA KUMA.

Legislature

FEDERAL PARLIAMENTARY ASSEMBLY

The legislature comprises an upper house, the House of the Federation (Yefedereshn Mekir Bet), with 108 seats (members are selected by state assemblies and are drawn one each from 22 minority nationalities and one from each professional sector of the remaining nationalities, and serve for a period of five years), and a lower house, the House of People's Representatives (Yehizbtewekayoch Mekir Bet), of no more than 550 directly elected members, who are also elected for a five-year term.

House of the Federation

Speaker: KASSA TEKLEBERHAN.

Deputy Speaker: MOHAMMED SIREE.

House of People's Representatives

Speaker: ABADULA GEMEDA.

Deputy Speaker: SHITAYE MINALE.

General Election, 23 May 2010

Party	Seats
Ethiopian People's Revolutionary Democratic Front (EPRDF)	499
Somali People's Democratic Party (SPDP)	24
Benishangul Gumuz People's Democratic Party (BGPDP)	9
Afar National Democratic Party (ANDP)	8
Gambela People's Unity Democratic Movement (GPUDM)	3
Amhara National Democratic Movement (ANDM)	1
Ethiopia Federal Democratic Unity Forum (FORUM/ Medrek)	1
Harari National League (HNL)	1
Independent	1
Total	547

Election Commission

National Electoral Board of Ethiopia (NEB): POB 40812, Addis Ababa; tel. (11) 5153416; e-mail info@electionethiopia.org; internet www.electionethiopia.org; f. 1993; independent board of seven politically non-affiliated mems appointed, on the Prime Minister's recommendation, by the House of People's Representatives; Chair. Dr MERGA BEKANA.

Political Organizations

A total of 79 political parties contested the 2010 legislative elections.

Afar National Democratic Party (ANDP): f. 1999; Leader ISMAIL ALI SERRO.

Benishangul Gumuz People's Democratic Party (BGPDP): f. 2009; Chair. HABTAMU HIKA.

Ethiopia Federal Democratic Unity Forum (FORUM/ Medrek): f. 2009; the Ethiopia Democratic Union Movement (EDUM) and the Somali Democratic Alliance Forces (SDAF) withdrew from the coalition in March 2010; Chair. MOGA FIRISA.

Ethiopian Social Democratic Party (ESDP): f. 1993 as the Council of Alternative Forces for Peace and Democracy in Ethiopia; opposes the EPRDF; Chair. Dr BEYENE PETROS.

Oromo Federalist Democratic Movement (OFDM): formed part of the Oromo Federalist Congress (OFC) for the 2010 elections; reportedly merged with the OPC (q.v.) in Feb. 2013 to form Oromo Federal Congress; Chair. BULCHA DEMEKSA; Sec.-Gen. BEKELE JIRATA.

Oromo People's Congress (OPC): Addis Ababa; e-mail oromopeoplescongress@yahoo.com; internet www.oromopeoplescongress.org; f. 2007 by fmr mems of the ONC; formed part of the Oromo Federalist Congress (OFC) for the 2010 elections; reportedly merged with OFDM (q.v.) in Feb. 2013 to form Oromo Federal Congress; Chair. Prof. MERERA GUDINA.

Southern Ethiopia People's Democratic Union (SEPDU): f. 1994; Chair. TILAHUN EADESHAW.

Union of Tigrians For Democracy and Sovereignty (ARENA): f. 2007; Chair. GEBRU ASTRAT.

Unity for Democracy and Justice Party (Andinet): f. 2008; Chair. Eng. GIZACHEW SHIFERAW.

Ethiopian Justice and Democratic Forces Front (EJDFF): f. 2008; Chair. GIRMAY HADERA.

Ethiopian Democratic Union (EDU): f. 2004; Chair. Dr KEBEDE HAILEMARIAM.

Ethiopian National Unity Party (ENUP): f. 2005; Chair. ZERIHUN GEBREGZIABER.

Oromia Liberation National Party (OLNP): Chair. Dr FARIS ISAYAS.

Unity of Southern Ethiopian Democratic Forces (USEDF): f. 2005; comprises Wolaita People's Democratic Front (WPDF), Gamo Democratic Union (GDU) and Gomogofa People's Democratic Union (GPDU); Chair. TEKLE BORENA.

Ethiopian National Democratic Party (ENDP): f. 1994 by merger of five pro-Govt orgs with mems in the Council of Representatives; comprises: the Ethiopian Democratic Organization, the Ethiopian Democratic Organization Coalition (EDC), the Gurage People's Democratic Front (GPDF), the Kembata People's Congress (KPC), and the Wolaita People's Democratic Front (WPDF); Chair. FEKADU GEDAMU; Gen. Sec. ZEMENE MOLLA.

Ethiopian People's Revolutionary Democratic Front (EPRDF): Addis Ababa; internet www.eprdf.org.et; f. 1989 by the TPLF as an alliance of insurgent groups seeking regional autonomy and engaged in armed struggle against the EDUP Govt; Chair. HAILEMARIAM DESALEGN; Vice-Chair. DEMEKE MEKONNEN; in May 1991, with other orgs, formed transitional Govt.

Amhara National Democratic Movement (ANDM): based in Tigrai; represents interests of the Amhara people; fmrly the Ethiopian People's Democratic Movement (EPDM); adopted present name in 1994; Chair. ADDISO LEGGESE.

Oromo People's Democratic Organization (OPDO): f. 1990 by the TPLF to promote its cause in Oromo areas; based among the Oromo people in the Shoa region; Leader MUKTAR KEDIR.

South Ethiopian People's Democratic Movement (SEPDM): f. 1992; Chair. HAILEMARIAM DESALEGN.

Tigrai People's Liberation Front (TPLF): f. 1975; the dominant org. within the EPRDF; Chair. ABAY WOLDU; Vice-Chair. DEBRETSION GEBREMIKAEL.

Gambela People's Unity Democratic Movement (GPUDM): f. 2008; Chair. OMOD OBANG ALUM.

Harari National League (HNL): f. 1994; Chair. YASIN HUSEIN.

Movement for Justice, Freedom and Democracy (Ginbot 7): 8647 Richmond Highway, Alexandria, VA 22309, USA; e-mail org@ginbot7.org; internet www.ginbot7.org; f. 2008; Leader BERHANU NEGA.

Ogaden National Liberation Front (ONLF): e-mail foreign@onlf.org; internet www.onlf.org; f. 1984; seeks self-determination for the Ogaden region; Chair. MOHAMED OMAR OSMAN.

Oromo Liberation Front (OLF): POB 73247, Washington, DC 20056, USA; tel. (202) 462-5477; fax (202) 332-7011; e-mail info@oromoliberationfront.org; internet www.oromoliberationfront.org; f. 1973; seeks self-determination for the Oromo people; participated in the Ethiopian transitional Govt until June 1992; Chair. DAWUD IBSA AYANA; Vice-Chair. ABDULFATTAH A. MOUSSA BIYYO.

Semayawi Party (Blue Party): e-mail info@semayawiparty.org; internet www.semayawiparty.org; Pres. Eng. YILKAL GETNET.

Sidama Liberation Front (SLF): e-mail info@sidamaliberation-front.org; internet www.sidamaliberation-front.org; campaigns for self-determination for Sidama people.

Somali People's Democratic Party (SPDP): St Jijiga Somali Regional 365; internet www.spdp.org.et; f. 1998 by merger of Ogaden National Liberation Front (ONLF) and the Ethiopian Somali Democratic League (ESDL—an alliance comprising the Somali Democratic Union Party, the Issa and Gurgura Liberation Front, the Gurgura Independence Front, the Eastern Gabooye Democratic Organization, the Eastern Ethiopian Somali League, the Horyal Democratic Front, the Social Alliance Democratic Organization, the Somali Abo Democratic Union, the Shekhash People's Democratic Movement, the Ethiopian Somalis' Democratic Movement and the Per Barreh Party); Chair. ABDIFETAH SHECK ABDULAHI; Sec.-Gen. AHMED ARAB ADEN.

Unity of Ethiopians for Democratic Change (UEDC): f. 2007 as replacement for the Alliance for Freedom and Democracy; coalition of political parties and rebel groups opposed to the Govt.

Benishangul People's Liberation Movement (BPLM): f. 1995; rebel group operating in western Ethiopia.

Ethiopian People's Front for Justice and Equality (EPFJE): armed anti-Govt group operating in southern Ethiopia; f. as Southern Ethiopian People's Front for Justice and Equality.

Ethiopian People's Patriotic Front: CP 182, 1211 Geneva 13, Switzerland; tel. 223406025; e-mail info@eppf.net; internet www.eppf.net; armed anti-Govt group operating mainly in north-western Ethiopia; Leader Prof. ALEBACHEW TEGEGNE.

Tigrai People's Democratic Movement (TPDM): f. 1979; rebel group operating in northern Tigrai region of Ethiopia.

Diplomatic Representation

EMBASSIES IN ETHIOPIA

Algeria: Woreda 23, Kebele 13, House No. 1819, POB 5740, Addis Ababa; tel. (11) 3719666; fax (11) 3719669; Ambassador ABDEL NACEUR BELAID.

Angola: Woreda 18, Kebele 26, House No. 6, POB 2962, Addis Ababa; tel. (11) 5510085; fax (11) 5514922; Ambassador ARCANJO MARIA DO NASCIMENTO.

Australia: Apt 383/384, Hilton Hotel, Menelik II Ave, POB 3715, Addis Ababa; tel. (11) 5523320; fax (11) 5523344; e-mail addisababa.info@dfat.gov.au; internet www.embassy.gov.au/ethiopia; Ambassador LISA FILIPETTO.

Austria: POB 1219, Addis Ababa; tel. (11) 3712144; fax (11) 3712140; e-mail addis-abeba-ob@bmeia.gv.at; internet www.bmeia.gv.at/botschaft/addis-abeba.html; Ambassador Dr ANDREAS MELÁN.

Belgium: Comoros St, Kebele 8, POB 1239, Addis Ababa; tel. (11) 6611813; fax (11) 6613646; e-mail addisababa@diplobel.fed.be; internet www.diplomatie.be/addisababa; Ambassador HUGUES CHANTRY.

Benin: Nifas Silk Sub-City, Kebele 04, House No. 990, POB 200084, Addis Ababa; tel. (11) 3722605; fax (11) 3722793; e-mail ambaben_addis@yahoo.fr; Ambassador FERDINAND MONTCHO.

Botswana: POB 22282, Addis Ababa; tel. (11) 715422; fax (11) 714099; Ambassador MMAMOSADINYANA P. J. MOLEFE.

Brazil: Bole Sub-City, Kebele 2, House No. 2830, POB 2458, Addis Ababa; tel. (11) 6620401; fax (11) 6620412; e-mail embradisadm@ethionet.et; Ambassador IZABEL CRISTINA DE AZEVEDO.

Bulgaria: Bole Kifle Ketema, Kebele 06, Haile Gabreselassie Rd, POB 987, Addis Ababa; tel. (11) 6610032; fax (11) 6613373; e-mail bulemba@ethionet.et; internet www.mfa.bg/embassies/ethiopia; Chargé d'affaires a.i. DRAGOVEST GORANOV.

Burkina Faso: Kebele 19, House No. 281, POB 19685, Addis Ababa; tel. (11) 6615863; fax (11) 6625857; e-mail ambfet@telecom.net.et; Ambassador MINATA SAMATÉ.

Burundi: Kirkos Cub-City, Kebele 03, House No. 047, POB 3641, Addis Ababa; tel. (11) 4651300; fax (11) 4650299; e-mail burundi.emb@ethionet.et; Ambassador ALAIN-AIME NYAMITWE.

Cameroon: Bole Rd, Woreda 18, Kebele 26, House No. 168, POB 1026, Addis Ababa; tel. (11) 5504488; fax (11) 5518434; Ambassador JACQUES-ALFRED NDOUMBÉ EBOULÉ.

Canada: Nefas Silk Lafto Kifle Ketema 3, Kebele 4, House No. 122, POB 1130, Addis Ababa; tel. (11) 3713022; fax (11) 3713033; e-mail addis@international.gc.ca; internet www.canadainternational.gc.ca/ethiopia-ethiopie/index.aspx; Ambassador DAVID USHER.

Cape Verde: Bole Rd, Higher 17, Kebele 19, House No. 107, POB 200093, Addis Ababa; tel. (11) 6610665; fax (11) 5516655; e-mail embcv@telecom.net.et; Chargé d'affaires a.i. CUSTODIA LIMA.

Chad: Bole Rd, Woreda 17, Kebele 20, House No. 2583, POB 5119, Addis Ababa; tel. (11) 6613819; fax (11) 6612050; e-mail amtchad@ethionet.et; Ambassador AHMAT AWAD SAKINE.

China, People's Republic: Jimma Rd, Woreda 24, Kebele 13, House No. 792, POB 5643, Addis Ababa; tel. (11) 3711960; fax (11) 3712457; e-mail chinaemb_et@mfa.gov.cn; internet et.china-embassy.org; Ambassador XIE XIAOYAN.

Congo, Democratic Republic: Makanisa Rd, Woreda 23, Kebele 13, House No. 1779, POB 2723, Addis Ababa; tel. (11) 3710111; fax (11) 3713485; Ambassador GÉRARD MAPANGO KEMISHANGA.

Congo, Republic: Woreda 3, Kebele 51, House No. 378, POB 5639, Addis Ababa; tel. (11) 5514188; fax (11) 5514331; Ambassador PIERRE-JUSTE MOUNZIKA-NTSIKA.

Côte d'Ivoire: Woreda 23, Kebele 13, House No. 1308, POB 3668, Addis Ababa; tel. (11) 3711213; fax (11) 3712178; Ambassador EUGÈNE ALLOU-ALLOU.

Cuba: Woreda 17, Kebele 19, House No. 197, POB 5623, Addis Ababa; tel. (11) 620459; fax (11) 620460; e-mail embacuba@ethiopia.cubaminrex.cu; Ambassador JUAN MANUEL RODRÍGUEZ VÁZQUEZ.

Czech Republic: Kebele 15, House No. 289, POB 3108, Addis Ababa; tel. (11) 5516132; fax (11) 5513471; e-mail addisabeba@embassy.mzv.cz; internet www.mzv.cz/addisababa; Ambassador MAREK LIBŘICKÝ.

Denmark: Bole Kifle Ketema, Kebele 3, House No. 'New', POB 12955, Addis Ababa; tel. (11) 6187075; fax (11) 6187057; e-mail addamb@um.dk; internet www.etiopien.um.dk; Ambassador STEPHAN SCHÖNEMANN.

Djibouti: Bole Sub-City, Kebele 03, House No. 003, POB 1022, Addis Ababa; tel. (11) 6613200; fax (11) 6612786; Ambassador MOHAMMED IDRISS FARAH.

Egypt: Gullele Sub-City, Kebele 02, Madgascar St, POB 1611, Addis Ababa; tel. (11) 1226422; fax (11) 1226432; e-mail embassy.addisababa@mfa.gov.eg; Ambassador MOHAMED FATHI AHMED EDREES.

Equatorial Guinea: Bole Rd, Woreda 17, Kebele 23, House No. 162, POB 246, Addis Ababa; tel. (11) 6626278; Ambassador Dr RUBÉN MAYE NSUE MANGUE.

Finland: Mauritania St, Kebele 12, House No. 1431, POB 1017, Addis Ababa; tel. (11) 3205920; fax (11) 3205923; e-mail sanomat.add@formin.fi; internet www.finland.org.et; Ambassador SIRPA MAENPAA.

France: Kabana, POB 1464, Addis Ababa; tel. (11) 1236022; fax (11) 1236029; e-mail scacamb@ethionet.et; internet www.ambafrance-et.org; Ambassador BRIGITTE COLLET.

Gabon: Woreda 17, Kebele 18, House No. 1026, POB 1256, Addis Ababa; tel. (11) 6611075; fax (11) 6613700; Ambassador ANDRÉ WILLIAM ANGUILE.

The Gambia: Kebele 3, House No. 79, POB 60083, Addis Ababa; tel. (11) 6624647; fax (11) 6627895; e-mail gambia@ethionet.et; Ambassador MOMODOU SAJO JALLOW.

Germany: Yeka Kifle Ketema (Khebena), Woreda 03, POB 660, Addis Ababa; tel. (11) 1235139; fax (11) 1235152; e-mail info@addis-abeba.diplo.de; internet www.addis-abeba.diplo.de; Ambassador LIESELORE CYRUS.

Ghana: Jimma Rd, Woreda 24, Kebele 13, House No. 108, POB 3173, Addis Ababa; tel. (11) 3711402; fax (11) 3712511; Ambassador ALBERT FRANCIS YANKEY.

Greece: off Debre Zeit Rd, POB 1168, Addis Ababa; tel. (11) 4654911; fax (11) 4654883; internet www.telecom.net.et/~greekemb; Ambassador NIKOLAOS PROTONOTARIOS.

Guinea: Debre Zeit Rd, Woreda 18, Kebele 14, House No. 58, POB 1190, Addis Ababa; tel. 912200181 (mobile); internet guineaaddisembassy@gmail.com; Ambassador SIDIBÉ FATOUMATA KABA.

Holy See: Makanissa Rd, POB 588, Addis Ababa (Apostolic Nunciature); tel. (11) 3712100; fax (11) 3711499; e-mail vatican.embassy@ethionet.et; Apostolic Nuncio Most Rev. GEORGE PANIKULAM (Titular Archbishop of Caudium).

India: Arada District, Kebele 13/14, House No. 224, POB 528, Addis Ababa; tel. (11) 1552100; fax (11) 1552521; e-mail amb.addisababa@mea.gov.in; internet www.indembassyeth.in; Ambassador SANJAY VERMA.

Indonesia: Mekanisa Rd, Higher 23, Kebele 13, House No. 1816, POB 1004, Addis Ababa; tel. (11) 3712104; fax (11) 3710873; e-mail kbriadis@ethionet.et; internet www.indonesia-addis.org.et; Ambassador RAMLI SA'UD.

Iran: 317–318 Jimma Rd, POB 1144, Addis Ababa; tel. (11) 3710037; fax (11) 3712299; internet www.iranembassy-addis.net; Ambassador MOHAMMED ALI BAHRAINI.

Ireland: Kazanches, Guinea Conakry St, POB 9585, Addis Ababa; tel. (11) 5180500; fax (11) 5523032; e-mail addisababaembassy@dfa.ie; internet www.embassyofireland.org.et; Ambassador AIDAN O'HARA.

Israel: Woreda 16, Kebele 22, House No. 283, POB 1266, Addis Ababa; tel. (11) 6460999; fax (11) 64619619; e-mail embassy@addisababa.mfa.gov.il; internet addisababa.mfa.gov.il; Ambassador BELAYNESH ZEVADIA.

Italy: Villa Italia, POB 1105, Addis Ababa; tel. (11) 1235717; fax (11) 1235689; e-mail ambasciata.addisabeba@esteri.it; internet www.ambaddisabeba.esteri.it; Ambassador RENZO MARIO ROSSO.

Japan: Woreda 18, Kebele 7, House No. 653, POB 5650, Addis Ababa; tel. (11) 5511088; fax (11) 5511350; e-mail japan-embassy@telecom.net.et; internet www.et.emb-japan.go.jp; Ambassador KAZUHIRO SUZUKI.

Kenya: Woreda 16, Kebele 1, POB 3301, Addis Ababa; tel. (11) 610033; fax (11) 611433; internet kenyaembassyaddis.org; Ambassador MONICA KATHINA JUMA.

Korea, Democratic People's Republic: Woreda 20, Kebele 40, House No. 892, POB 2378, Addis Ababa; tel. (11) 6182828; Ambassador KIM HYOK CHOL.

Korea, Republic: Jimma Rd, Old Airport Area, POB 2047, Addis Ababa; tel. (11) 3728111; fax 3728115; e-mail skorea.emb@ethionet.et; internet eth.mofat.go.kr; Ambassador KIM JONG-GEUN.

Kuwait: Woreda 17, Kebele 20, House No. 128, POB 19898, Addis Ababa; tel. (11) 6615411; fax (11) 6612621; Ambassador RASHED FALEH AL-HAJERY.

Lesotho: Bole Sub-City, Kebele 03, House No. 2118, Addis Ababa; tel. (11) 6614368; fax (11) 6612837; internet lesothoaddis.org; Ambassador NYOLOSI MPHALE.

Liberia: Roosevelt St, Woreda 21, Kebele 4, House No. 237, POB 3116, Addis Ababa; tel. (11) 5513655; e-mail liberianembassyethiopia@yahoo.com; Ambassador VIVIENNE TITI WREH.

Libya: Ras Tessema Sefer, Woreda 3, Kebele 53, House No. 585, POB 5728, Addis Ababa; tel. (11) 5511077; fax (11) 5511383; e-mail libyanembassy@ethionet.et; Chargé d'affaires a.i. MOHAMED B. S. ENWIES.

Madagascar: Woreda 17, Kebele 19, House No. 629, POB 60004, Addis Ababa; tel. (11) 612555; fax (11) 610127; e-mail emb.mad@ethionet.et; Chargé d'affaires a.i LUDOVICH RICHARD SETILAHY.

Malawi: Bole Rd, Woreda 23, Kebele 13, House No. 1021, POB 2316, Addis Ababa; tel. (11) 3711280; fax (11) 3719742; e-mail malemb@telecom.net.et; Ambassador Dr ISAAC GENESIS MUNLO.

Mali: Kebele 03, House No. 418, POB 4561, Addis Ababa; tel. (11) 168990; fax (11) 162838; e-mail ambamaliaddis@yahoo.com; Ambassador BOUBACAR GOURO DIALL.

Mauritania: Lidete Kifle Ketema, Kebele 2, House No. 431A, POB 200015, Addis Ababa; tel. (11) 3729165; fax (11) 3729166; Ambassador HAMADY OULD MEIMOU.

Mauritius: Kebele 03, House No. 750, POB 200222, Kifle Ketema, Addis Ababa; tel. (11) 6615997; fax (11) 6614704; e-mail addisemb@mail.gov.mu; internet www.addisababa.mail.gov.mu; Ambassador MAHENDR DOSIEAH.

Mexico: Shola Axion (Jacros Compound), Bole Sub-City, Kebele 14, House No. 050, POB 21021, Addis Ababa; tel. (11) 6479555; fax (11) 6479333; e-mail embetiopia@sre.gob.mx; internet embamex.sre.gob.mx/etiopia; Ambassador JUAN ALFREDO MIRANDA ORTIZ.

Morocco: 210 Bole Rd, POB 60033, Addis Ababa; tel. (11) 5508440; fax (11) 5511828; e-mail morocco.emb@ethionet.et; Ambassador ABDELJEBBAR BRAHIME.

Mozambique: Woreda 17, Kebele 23, House No. 2116, POB 5671, Addis Ababa; tel. (11) 3729199; fax (11) 3729197; Ambassador MANUEL JOSÉ GONÇALVES.

Namibia: Bole Sub-City, Kebele 19, House No. 575, POB 1443, Addis Ababa; tel. (11) 6611966; fax (11) 6612677; e-mail nam.emb@ethionet.et; Ambassador KAKENA S. K. NANGULA.

Netherlands: Old Airport Zone, Kifle Ketema, Lideta, Kebele 02/03, POB 1241, Addis Ababa; tel. (11) 3711100; fax (11) 3711577; e-mail add@minbuza.nl; internet ethiopia.nlembassy.org; Ambassador ALIDA PETRONELLA REMMELZWAAL.

Niger: Woreda 9, Kebele 23, POB 5791, Addis Ababa; tel. (11) 4651305; fax (11) 4651296; e-mail ambnigeraddis@yahoo.fr; Ambassador DIALLO AMINA DJIBO.

Nigeria: Gulele KK, Kebele 06, House No. 001, POB 1019, Addis Ababa; tel. (11) 1550644; Ambassador BULUS ZOM LOLO.

Norway: POB 8383, Addis Ababa; tel. (11) 3710799; fax (11) 3711255; e-mail emb.addisabeba@mfa.no; internet www.norway.org.et; Ambassador ODD INGE KVALHEIM.

Pakistan: Bole Kifle Ketema, Kebele 03, House No. 2038, POB 19795, Addis Ababa; tel. (11) 6188392; fax (11) 6188394; e-mail parepadisababa@mofa.gov.pk; internet www.mofa.gov.pk/ethiopia; Ambassador IMRAN YAWAR (designate).

Poland: House No. 583, Dej Belay Zeleke Rd, Guelele Sub-City, Kebele 08, POB 27207/1000, Addis Ababa; tel. (11) 1574189; fax (11) 1574222; e-mail addisabeba.amb.sekretariat@msz.gov.pl; internet www.addisabeba.msz.gov.pl; Ambassador JACEK JANKOWSKI.

Portugal: Sheraton Addis, Taitu St, POB 6002, Addis Ababa; tel. (11) 171717; fax (11) 173403; e-mail embportadis@hotmail.com; Ambassador Dr ANTÓNIO LUÍS PEIXOTO COTRIM.

Qatar: Mekanissa St, House No. 0646, Addis Ababa; tel. (11) 8966244; fax (11) 3722623; e-mail addisababa@mofa.gov.qa; Ambassador ABDULAZIZ SULTAN JASSIM AL-RUMEIHI.

Romania: Houses No. 9–10, Bole Kifle Ketema, Kebele 03, POB 2478, Addis Ababa; tel. (11) 6610156; fax (11) 6611191; e-mail roembaddis@ethionet.et; Ambassador GABRIEL CONSTANTINE.

Russia: POB 1500, Addis Ababa; tel. (11) 6612060; fax (11) 6613795; e-mail russemb@ethionet.et; Ambassador VALERY I. UTKIN.

Rwanda: POB 5618, Addis Ababa; tel. (11) 6610300; fax (11) 6610411; e-mail ambaddis@minaffet.gov.rw; internet www.ethiopia.embassy.gov.rw; High Commissioner JOSEPH NSENGIMANA.

Saudi Arabia: Kirkos Sub-City, Kebele 4, House No. 179B, POB 1104, Addis Ababa; tel. (11) 4425643; fax (11) 4425646; e-mail etemb@mofa.gov.sa; internet embassies.mofa.gov.sa/sites/ethiopia; Ambassador ABDULBAQI BIN AHMAD AJLAN.

Senegal: Africa Ave, POB 2581, Addis Ababa; tel. (11) 6611376; fax (11) 6610020; e-mail ambassene-addis@ethionet.et; Ambassador BASSIROU SÉNÉ.

Serbia: Woreda 15, Kebele 26, House No. 923, POB 1341, Addis Ababa; tel. (11) 5517804; fax (11) 5514192; e-mail serbembaddis@ethionet.et; internet www.addisababa.mfa.gov.rs; Ambassador (vacant).

Sierra Leone: Kefle Ketema-Nefas Silk Lafto, Kebele 05, House No. 2629, POB 5619, Addis Ababa; tel. (11) 3710033; fax (11) 3711911; e-mail salonembadd@yahoo.co.uk; Ambassador OSMAN KAMARA.

Slovakia: Kebele 2, Woreda 7, Yeka Sub-City, POB 6627, Addis Ababa; tel. (11) 6450849; fax (11) 6474656; e-mail slovakiaembassy@ethionet.et; internet www.mzv.sk/addisabeba; Ambassador JOZEF CIBULA.

Somalia: Bole Kifle Ketema, Kebele 20, House No. 588, POB 1643, Addis Ababa; tel. (11) 6180673; fax (11) 6180680; internet www.ethiopia.somaligov.net; Ambassador AHMED ABDISALAM ADAN.

South Africa: Alexander Pushkin St, Higher 23, Kebele 10, House No. 1885, Old Airport Area, POB 1091, Addis Ababa; tel. (11) 3713034; fax (11) 3711330; e-mail sa.embassy.addis@telecom.net.et; Ambassador NDUMISO NDIMA NTSHINGA.

South Sudan: Bole Olympia, Addis Ababa; tel. (11) 5522636; e-mail embassysouthsudan@yahoo.com; Ambassador ARAP DENG KUOL.

Spain: Botswana St, POB 2312, Addis Ababa; tel. (11) 1222544; fax (11) 1222542; e-mail emb.addisabeba@maec.es; Ambassador MIGUEL ÁNGEL FERNÁNDEZ-PALACIOS MARTÍNEZ.

Sudan: Kirkos, Kebele, POB 1110, Addis Ababa; tel. (11) 5516477; fax (11) 5519989; e-mail sudan.embassy@telecom.net.et; Ambassador Gen. ABDELRAHMAN SIRELKHATIM.

Swaziland: Bole Kifle Ketema, Kebele 13, House No. 1185, POB 416, Addis Ababa; tel. (11) 6263703; fax (11) 6262152; e-mail swaziaddis@ethionet.et; Ambassador PROMISE MSIBI.

Sweden: Lideta KK, Kebele 07/14, House No. 891, POB 1142, Addis Ababa; tel. (11) 5180000; fax (11) 5180030; e-mail ambassaden.addis-abeba@foreign.ministry.se; internet www.swedenabroad.se/addisabeba; Ambassador JAN SADEK.

Switzerland: Jimma Rd, Old Airport Area, POB 1106, Addis Ababa; tel. (11) 3711107; fax (11) 3712177; e-mail add.vertretung@eda.admin.ch; Ambassador ANDREA SEMADENI.

Tanzania: POB 1077, Addis Ababa; tel. (11) 5511063; fax (11) 5517358; Ambassador Prof. JORAM MUKAMA BISWARO.

Togo: Nifas Silk Lafto KK, Kebele 13, House No. 2234, POB 25523, Addis Ababa; tel. (11) 3206515; fax (11) 3729722; e-mail togo.emb@ethionet.et; Ambassador AMOKO HOLADEM KOUVAHE.

Tunisia: Wereda 17, Kebele 19, Bole Rd, POB 100069, Addis Ababa; tel. (11) 6612063; fax (11) 6614568; Ambassador SAHBI KHALFALLAH.

Turkey: POB 1506, Addis Ababa; tel. (11) 6612321; fax (11) 6611688; e-mail turk.emb@ethionet.et; Ambassador OSMAN YAVUZALP.

Uganda: Kirkos Kifle Ketema, Kebele 35, House No. 31, POB 5644, Addis Ababa; tel. (11) 5513088; fax (11) 5514355; e-mail uganda.emb@ethionet.et; Ambassador MULL KATENDE.

Ukraine: Woreda 17, Kebele 3, House No. 2116, POB 2358, Addis Ababa; tel. (11) 6611698; fax (11) 6621288; e-mail emb_et@mfa.gov.ua; Chargé d'affaires a.i. OLEKSANDER BURAVCHENKOV.

United Arab Emirates: Nifas Silk Lafto, Kebele 13, House No. 1826, POB 22055, Addis Ababa; tel. (11) 3203680; fax (11) 3203684; e-mail addis.ababa@mofa.gov.ae; Ambassador Dr YOUSEF EISA HASSAN AL-SABRI.

United Kingdom: POB 858, Addis Ababa; tel. (11) 6612354; fax (11) 6610588; e-mail britishembassy.addisababa@fco.gov.uk; internet www.ukinethiopia.gov.uk; Ambassador GREGORY DOREY.

USA: Entoto St, POB 1014, Addis Ababa; tel. (11) 5174000; fax (11) 5174001; e-mail pasaddis@state.gov; internet addisababa.usembassy.gov; Ambassador PATRICIA MARIE HASLACH.

Venezuela: Bole Kifle Ketema, Kebele 21, House No. 314–16, POB 1909, Addis Ababa; tel. (11) 6460601; fax (11) 5154162; Ambassador LUIS MARIANO JOUBERTT MATA.

Yemen: Old Airport Rd, Kebele 12, POB 664, Addis Ababa; tel. (11) 3712204; fax (11) 3711724; e-mail yemaa@ethionet.et; Ambassador DIRHIM ABDO NOMAN.

Zambia: Nifas Silk Kifle Ketema, Kebele 04, POB 1909, Addis Ababa; tel. (11) 3711302; fax (11) 3711566; e-mail zam.emb@ethionet.et; Ambassador SUSAN SIKANETA.

Zimbabwe: POB 5624, Addis Ababa; tel. (11) 6613877; fax (11) 6613476; e-mail zimbabwe.embassy@telecom.net.et; Ambassador Dr ANDREW HAMA MTETWA.

Judicial System

The 1994 Constitution stipulates the establishment of an independent judiciary in Ethiopia. Judicial powers are vested in the courts, both at federal and regional state level. The supreme federal judicial authority is the Federal Supreme Court. This court has the highest and final power of jurisdiction over federal matters. The regional states of the Federal Democratic Republic of Ethiopia can establish Supreme, High and First-Instance Courts. The Supreme Courts of the regional states have the highest and the final power of jurisdiction over state matters. They also exercise the jurisdiction of the Federal High Court. According to the Constitution, courts of any level are free from any interference or influence from government bodies, government officials or any other source. In addition, judges exercise their duties independently and are directed solely by the law.

Federal Supreme Court: POB 6166, Addis Ababa; tel. (11) 1553400; fax (11) 1550278; e-mail webadmin@federalsupremecourt.gov.et; f. 1995; comprises civil, criminal and military sections; its jurisdiction extends to the supervision of all judicial proceedings throughout the country; the Supreme Court is also empowered to review cases upon which final rulings have been made by the courts (including the Supreme Court) where judicial errors have occurred; Pres. TEGNE GETANEH.

Federal High Court: POB 3483, Addis Ababa; tel. (11) 2751911; fax (11) 2755399; e-mail fedhc@telecom.net.et; hears appeals from the state courts; has original jurisdiction; Pres. WUBESHET SHIFERAW.

Awraja Courts: regional courts composed of three judges, criminal and civil.

Warada Courts: sub-regional; one judge sits alone with very limited jurisdiction, criminal only.

Religion

About 45% of the population are Muslims and about 40% belong to the Ethiopian Orthodox (Tewahido) Church. There are also significant Evangelical Protestant and Roman Catholic communities. The Pentecostal Church and the Society of International Missionaries carry out mission work in Ethiopia. There are also Hindu and Sikh religious institutions. It has been estimated that 5%–15% of the population follow animist rites and beliefs.

CHRISTIANITY

Ethiopian Orthodox (Tewahido) Church

The Ethiopian Orthodox (Tewahido) Church is one of the five oriental orthodox churches. It was founded in AD 328, and in 1989 had more than 22m. members, 20,000 parishes and 290,000 clergy. The Supreme Body is the Holy Synod and the National Council, under the chairmanship of the Patriarch (Abune). The Church comprises 25 archdioceses and dioceses (including those in Jerusalem, Sudan, Djibouti and the Western Hemisphere). There are 32 Archbishops and Bishops. The Church administers 1,139 schools and 12 relief and rehabilitation centres throughout Ethiopia.

Patriarchate Head Office: POB 1283, Addis Ababa; tel. (11) 1116507; internet webmaster@ethiopianorthodox.org; internet www.ethiopianorthodox.org; Patriarch (Abune) Archbishop MATIAS; Gen. Sec. L. M. DEMTSE GEBRE MEDHIN.

The Roman Catholic Church

At 31 December 2006 there were in Ethiopia an estimated 68,138 adherents of the Alexandrian-Ethiopian Rite and 513,286 adherents of the Latin Rite.

Bishops' Conference: Ethiopian and Eritrean Episcopal Conference, POB 2454, Addis Ababa; tel. (11) 1550300; fax (11) 1553113; e-mail ecs@ethionet.et; internet www.ecs.org.et; f. 1966; Pres. Most Rev. BERHANEYESUS DEMEREW SOURAPHIEL (Metropolitan Archbishop of Addis Ababa).

Alexandrian-Ethiopian Rite

Adherents are served by one archdiocese (Addis Ababa) and two dioceses (Adigrat and Emdeber).

Archbishop of Addis Ababa: Most Rev. BERHANEYESUS DEMEREW SOURAPHIEL, Catholic Archbishop's House, POB 21903, Addis Ababa; tel. (11) 1111667; fax (11) 1551348; e-mail ecs@telecom.net.et.

Latin Rite

Adherents are served by the eight Apostolic Vicariates of Awasa, Gambela, Harar, Hosanna, Jimma-Bonga, Meki, Nekemte and Soddo.

Other Christian Churches

The Anglican Communion: Within the Episcopal Church in Jerusalem and the Middle East, the Bishop in Egypt has jurisdiction over seven African countries, including Ethiopia.

Armenian Orthodox Church: St George's Armenian Church, POB 116, Addis Ababa; f. 1923; Deacon VARTKES NALBANDIAN.

Ethiopian Evangelical Church (Mekane Yesus): POB 2087, Jomo Kenyatta Rd, Addis Ababa; tel. (11) 5533293; fax (11) 5534148; e-mail eecmyco@eecmy.org; internet www.eecmy.org; Pres. Rev. Dr WAKSEYOUM IDOSA; f. 1959; affiliated to Lutheran World Fed., All Africa Confed. of Churches and World Council of Churches; c. 5.57m. mems (2010).

Greek Orthodox Church: POB 571, Addis Ababa; tel. and fax (11) 1226459; Metropolitan of Axum Most Rev. PETROS YIAKOUMELOS.

Seventh-day Adventist Church: POB 145, Addis Ababa; tel. (11) 5511319; e-mail info@ecd.adventist.org; internet www.ecd.adventist.org; f. 1907; Pres. ALEMU HAILE; 130,000 mems.

ISLAM

Leader: Haji MOHAMMED AHMAD.

JUDAISM

A phased emigration to Israel of about 27,000 Falashas (Ethiopian Jews) took place during 1984–91. In February 2003 the Israeli Government ruled that the Falashmura (Ethiopian Christians whose forefathers had converted from Judaism) had been forced to convert to Christianity to avoid religious persecution and that they had the right to settle in Israel. In January 2004 Ethiopia and Israel agreed to allow the Falashmura to be flown to Israel; some 17,000 Falashmura and a further 3,000 Falashas had arrived in Israel by May 2008. However, a further 8,700 Falashmura remained in a transit camp in Gondar and the Israeli Government halted the transfer process in June. Israel resumed the transportation of Falashmura in January 2010, and in November the Israeli Government announced that the remaining Falashmura in Ethiopia—some 8,000 people—would be granted the right to emigrate to Israel. The final group (comprising some 450 Falashmura) was repatriated in August 2013, concluding the programme.

The Press

DAILIES

Addis Zemen: POB 30145, Addis Ababa; internet www.addiszemen.com; f. 1941; Amharic; circ. 40,000.

The Daily Monitor: POB 22588, Addis Ababa; tel. (11) 1560788; e-mail themonitor@telecom.net.et; f. 1993; English; Editor-in-Chief NAMRUD BERHANE TSAHAY; circ. 6,000.

Ethiopian Herald: POB 30701, Addis Ababa; tel. (11) 5156690; f. 1943; English; Editor-in-Chief TSEGIE GEBRE-AMLAK; circ. 37,000.

PERIODICALS

Abyotawit Ethiopia: POB 2549, Addis Ababa; fortnightly; Amharic.

Addis Fortune: Tegene Bldg, 7th Floor, House No. 542, Ginbot Haya Ave, Kebele 03, POB 259, Addis Ababa; tel. (11) 4163020; fax (11) 4163039; internet www.addisfortune.com; weekly; English; Man. Editor TAMRAT G. GIORGIS.

Addis Tribune: Tambek International, POB 2395, Addis Ababa; tel. (11) 6615228; fax (11) 6615227; e-mail tambek@telecom.net.et; internet www.addistribune.com; f. 1992; weekly; English; Editor-in-Chief YOHANNES RUPHAEL; circ. 6,000.

Al-Alem: POB 30232, Addis Ababa; tel. (11) 6625936; fax (11) 6625777; f. 1941; publ. by the Ethiopian Press Agency; weekly; Arabic; Editor-in-Chief EYOB GIDEY; circ. 2,500.

Birritu: National Bank of Ethiopia, POB 5550, Addis Ababa; tel. (11) 5530040; fax (11) 5514588; e-mail mulget17@yahoo.com; internet www.nbe.gov.et; f. 1982; quarterly; Amharic and English; banking, insurance and macroeconomic news; owned by National Bank of Ethiopia; circ. 2,500; Editor-in-Chief DEREJE ASEGEDEW; Dep. Editors-in-Chief MULUGETA AYALEW, BEKALU AYALEW.

Capital: POB 95, Addis Ababa; tel. (11) 5531759; fax (11) 5533323; e-mail syscom@telecom.net.et; internet www.capitalethiopia.com; f. 1998; weekly; Sunday; business and economics; Editor-in-Chief BEHAILU DESALEGN.

Ethiopian Reporter: Woreda 19, Kebele 56, House No. 221, POB 7023, Addis Ababa; tel. and fax (11) 4421517; e-mail mcc@telecom.net.et; internet www.ethiopianreporter.com; weekly; English and Amharic; Editor-in-Chief AMARE AREGAWI.

Maebel: Addis Ababa; weekly; Amharic; Editor-in-Chief ABERA WOGI.

Menilik: Editor-in-Chief ZELALEM GEBRE.

Negarit Gazeta: POB 1031, Addis Ababa; irreg.; Amharic and English; official gazette.

Nigdina Limat: POB 2458, Addis Ababa; tel. (11) 5513882; fax (11) 5511479; e-mail aachamber1@telecom.net.et; monthly; Amharic; publ. by the Addis Ababa (Ethiopia) Chamber of Commerce; circ. 6,000.

Press Digest: POB 12719, Addis Ababa; tel. (11) 5504200; fax (11) 5513523; e-mail phoenix.universal@telecom.net.et; f. 1993; weekly.

Satenaw: Editor-in-Chief TAMRAT SERBESA.

Tobia Magazine: POB 22373, Addis Ababa; tel. (11) 1556177; fax (11) 1552654; monthly; Amharic; Man. GOSHU MOGES; circ. 30,000.

Tobia Newspaper: POB 22373, Addis Ababa; tel. (11) 1556177; fax (11) 1552654; e-mail akpac@telecom.net.et; weekly; Amharic; Man. GOSHU MOGES; circ. 25,000.

Tomar: Benishangul; weekly; Amharic; Editor-in-Chief BEFEKADU MOREDA.

Yezareitu Ethiopia (Ethiopia Today): POB 30232, Addis Ababa; weekly; Amharic and English; Editor-in-Chief IMIRU WORKU; circ. 30,000.

NEWS AGENCY

Ethiopian News Agency (ENA): Patriot St, POB 530, Addis Ababa; tel. (11) 1550011; fax (11) 1551609; e-mail feedback@ena.gov.et; internet www.ena.gov.et; f. 1942; Chair. NETSANET ASFAW.

PRESS ASSOCIATIONS

Ethiopian Free Press Journalists' Association (EFJA): POB 31317, Addis Ababa; tel. and fax (11) 1555021; e-mail efja@telecom.net.et; f. 1993; granted legal recognition in 2000; activities suspended in late 2003; Pres. KIFLE MULAT.

Ethiopian Journalists' Association: POB 30288, Addis Ababa; tel. (11) 1117852; fax (11) 5513365; Pres. KEFALE MAMMO.

Publishers

Addis Ababa University Press: POB 1176, Addis Ababa; tel. (11) 1119148; fax (11) 1550655; f. 1968; educational and reference works in English, general books in English and Amharic; Editor MESSELECH HABTE.

Berhanena Selam Printing Enterprise: POB 980, Addis Ababa; tel. (11) 1553233; fax (11) 1553939; f. 1921; fmrly Govt Printing Press; publishes and prints newspapers, periodicals, books, security prints and other miscellaneous commercial prints; Gen. Man. MULUWORK G. HIWOT.

Educational Materials Production and Distribution Enterprise (EMPDE): POB 5549, Addis Ababa; tel. (11) 6463555; fax (11) 6461295; f. 1999; textbook publishers.

Ethiopia Book Centre: POB 1024, Addis Ababa; tel. (11) 1123336; f. 1977; privately owned; publr, importer, wholesaler and retailer of educational books.

Mega Publishing: POB 423, Addis Ababa; tel. (11) 1571714; fax (11) 1571715; general publishers.

Broadcasting and Communications

TELECOMMUNICATIONS

Ethiopian Telecommunication Agency (ETA): Bekelobet, Tegene Bldg, Kirkos District, Kebele 02/03, House No. 542, POB 9991, Addis Ababa; tel. (11) 4668282; fax (11) 4655763; e-mail tele.agency@ethionet.et; internet www.eta.gov.et; aims to promote the devt of high quality, efficient, reliable and affordable telecommunication services in Ethiopia; Dir-Gen. BALCHA REBA (acting).

Ethio Telecom (ETC): POB 1047, Addis Ababa; tel. (11) 6632597; fax (11) 6632674; e-mail etcweb@ethionet.et; internet www.ethionet.et; f. 1894; under the management of France Telecom since December 2010; Chair. DEBRE TSION GEBRE MICHAEL; CEO ANDUALEM ADMASSIE (acting).

BROADCASTING

Radio

Afro FM: Addis Ababa; tel. (11) 1552200; e-mail hasiet@afro105fm.com; internet www.afro105fm.com; f. 2009; broadcasts in English and other foreign languages.

Radio Ethiopia: POB 654, Addis Ababa; tel. (11) 1551011; internet www.angelfire.com/biz/radioethiopia; f. 1941; Amharic, English, French, Arabic, Afar, Oromifa, Tigre, Tigrinya and Somali; Gen. Man. KASA MILOKO.

Radio Fana: POB 30702, Addis Ababa; internet www.radiofana.com; f. 1994; Amharic; operated by the EPRDF; Gen. Man. WOLDU YEMESSEL.

Radio Voice of One Free Ethiopia: broadcasts twice a week; Amharic; opposes current Govts of Ethiopia and Eritrea.

Voice of the Revolution of Tigrai: POB 450, Mekele; tel. (34) 4410545; fax (34) 4405485; e-mail vort@telecom.net.et; f. 1985; Tigrinya and Afargna; broadcasts 57 hours per week; supports Tigrai People's Liberation Front.

There are also 16 community radio stations in Ethiopia.

Television

Ethiopian Radio and Television Agency (ERTA): POB 5544, Addis Ababa; tel. (11) 5155326; fax (11) 5512685; e-mail gd1@erat.gov.et; internet www.erta.gov.et; f. 1964; semi-autonomous station; accepts commercial advertising; programmes transmitted from Addis Ababa to 26 regional stations; Chair. BEREKET SIMON; Dir-Gen. ZERAY ASSGEDOM.

Regulatory Authority

Ethiopia Broadcasting Authority (EBA): Haile-Alem Bldg, nr Urael Church, Haile Gebreslase Rd, Kazanchiz, POB 43142, Addis Ababa; tel. (11) 5538759; fax (11) 5536750; internet www.eba.gov.et; Dir-Gen. DESTA TESFAW.

Finance

(cap. = capital; res = reserves; dep. = deposits; m. = million; br(s). = branch(es); amounts in birr)

BANKING

Central Bank

In early 2013 there were 19 banks and 19 microfinance institutions in Ethiopia.

National Bank of Ethiopia: Sudan Ave, POB 5550, Addis Ababa; tel. (11) 5517438; fax (11) 5514588; e-mail nbe.gov@ethionet.et; internet www.nbe.gov.et; f. 1964; bank of issue; cap. 500.0m., res 1,814.8m., dep. 35,781.3m. (June 2009); Chair. NEWAYE-KIRSTOS GEBREAB; Gov. TEKLEWOLD ATNAFU; 1 br.

Other Banks

Abay Bank SC: Jomo Kenyatta St, City-Kirkos Kebele-17/18, POB 5887, Addis Ababa; tel. (11) 5158782; fax (11) 5528882; internet www.abaybank.com.et; f. 2010; Chair. TADESSE KASSA KETEMA.

Addis International Bank SC (AdIB): Zequla Complex, Haile G/Selliassie St, POB 2455, Addis Ababa; tel. (11) 5549800; fax (11) 5540530; e-mail info@addisbanksc.com; internet www.addisbanksc.com; f. 2011; Chair. HAILE MELEKOT TEKLE GIORGIS; Pres. HAILU ALEMU; 5 brs.

Awash International Bank SC: Africa Ave, Bole Rd, POB 12638, Addis Ababa; tel. (11) 6614482; fax (11) 6639159; e-mail info@awashbank.com; internet www.awash-international-bank.com; f. 1994; cap. 540.0m., res 750.0m., dep. 5,700m. (Dec. 2009); Chair. GURMU GURMU; Pres. TSEHAY SHIFERAW; 64 brs.

Bank of Abyssinia SC: Red Cross Bldg, Ras Desta Damtew Ave, POB 12947, Addis Ababa; tel. (11) 5514130; fax (11) 5510409; e-mail info@bankofabyssinia.com; internet www.bankofabyssinia.com; f. 1905; closed 1935 and reopened 1996; commercial banking services; cap. 313.1m., res 132.6m., dep. 4,583.5m., total assets 5,476.6m. (June 2009); Chair. MAHARI ALEMAYEHU; Pres. ADDISU HABBA; 61 brs.

Bunna International Bank SC: Kebele 17 Daber Bldg, Arada Kifle Ketema, Addis Ababa; tel. (11) 1580825; fax (11) 1580832; internet www.bunnabanksc.com; f. 2009; Chair. MARSHAL FIKREMARKOS; Pres. ESHETU FANTAYE; 21 brs.

Commercial Bank of Ethiopia: Gambia St, POB 255, Addis Ababa; tel. (11) 5511271; fax (11) 5514522; e-mail cbe_cc@combanketh.com; internet www.combanketh.com; f. 1943; reorg. 1996; state-owned; cap. 4,000.0m., res 1,037.5m., dep. 43,480.3m. (June 2009); Chair. BEREKET SEMON; Pres. BEKALU ZELEKE; 331 brs.

Construction and Business Bank: Higher 21, Kebele 04, POB 3480, Addis Ababa; tel. (11) 5512300; fax (11) 5515103; e-mail cbbsics@ethionet.et; internet www.cbb.com.et; f. 1975 as Housing and Savings Bank; provides credit for construction projects and a range of commercial banking services; state-owned; cap. and res 80.8m., total assets 1,019.1m. (June 2003); Chair. DEMEKE MEKONEN; Pres. HAILEYESUS BEKELE; 20 brs.

Dashen Bank: Beklobet, Garad Bldg, Debre Zeit Rd, POB 12752, Addis Ababa; tel. (11) 4671803; fax (11) 4653037; e-mail dashen.bank@ethionet.et; internet www.dashenbanksc.com; f. 1995; cap. 591.8m., res 340.2m., dep. 10,375.9m. (June 2012); Pres. BERHANU W. SELASSIE; Chair. TEKLU HAILE; 122 brs.

Debub Global Bank SC: Mujib Tower, Woreda 04, Kirkos Sub-City, POB 100743, Addis Ababa; tel. (11) 4674087; fax (11) 8605196; e-mail info@debubglobalbank.com; internet www.debubglobalbank.com; f. 2012; Pres. WORKU LEMMA; 19 brs.

Development Bank of Ethiopia: Zosip Broz Tito St, POB 1900, Addis Ababa; tel. (11) 5511188; fax (11) 5511606; e-mail dbe@ethionet.et; internet www.dbe.com.et; f. 1909; provides devt finance for industry and agriculture, technical advice and assistance in project evaluation; state-owned; cap. and res 418.8m., total assets 3,163.2m. (June 2002); Chair. MELAKU FANTA; Pres. ESAYAS BAHRE; 32 brs.

Lion International Bank SC (LIB): Addis Ababa; tel. (11) 6626000; fax (11) 6625999; e-mail lionbank@ethionet.et; internet www.anbesabank.com; f. 2006; Chair. BERHANU G. MEDHIN; Pres. NEGUSU GEBREGZIABHER; 24 brs.

Enat Bank: POB 18401, Addis Ababa; tel. (11) 5504948; e-mail info@enatbanksc.com; internet www.enatbanksc.com; f. 2012; Chair. MEAZA ASHENAFI; Pres. FASIKA KEBEDE TEMESELEW.

NIB International Bank SC: Africa Avenue, Dembel City Centre, 6th Floor, POB 2439, Addis Ababa; tel. (11) 5503304; fax (11) 5527213; e-mail nibbank@ethionet.et; internet www.nibbank-et.com; f. 1999; cap. 487.1m., res 132.0m., dep. 3,497.0m. (June 2009); Chair. TAFESSE BOGALE; Pres. KIBRU FONDJA; 45 brs.

Oromia International Bank SC: POB 27530, Addis Ababa; tel. (11) 5572113; fax (11) 5572110; e-mail oib@orointbank.com; internet www.orointbank.com; f. 2008; cap. 197.2m., res 13.8m., dep. 820.9m. (June 2010); Chair. ABERA TOLA; Pres. ABIE SANO; 30 brs.

United Bank SC: Beklobet, Mekwor Plaza Bldg, Debe Zeit Rd, Kirkos District, Kebele 06, POB 19963, Addis Ababa; tel. (11) 4655222; fax (11) 4655243; e-mail hibretbank@ethionet.et; internet www.unitedbank.com.et; f. 1998; commercial banking services; cap. 355.2m., res 93.9m., dep. 3,615.7m. (June 2009); Chair. GETACHEW AYELE; Pres. BERHANU GETANEH; 72brs.

Wegagen Bank: Dembel Bldg, 6th–7th Floor, Africa Ave, POB 1018, Addis Ababa; tel. (11) 5523800; fax (11) 5523521; e-mail wegagen@ethionet.et; internet www.wegagenbanksc.com; f. 1997; commercial banking services; cap. 517.6m., res 183.3m., dep. 3,942.7m. (June 2009); Chair. SEBHAT NEGGA; Pres. and CEO ARAYA GEBRE EGIZHABER; 49 brs.

Zemen Bank: Josef Tito St, POB 1212, Addis Ababa; tel. (11) 5501111; fax (11) 5539042; e-mail customerservice@zemenbank.com; internet www.zemenbank.com; f. 2008; Chair. Dr BERHANE GHEBRAY; Pres. and CEO TSEGAY TETEMKE.

Bankers' Association

Ethiopian Bankers' Association: POB 23850, Addis Ababa; tel. and fax (11) 5533874; e-mail ethbankers@ethionet.et; internet ethiopianbankers.com; f. 2001; Sec.-Gen. DEREJE DEGEFU.

INSURANCE

In early 2013 there were 15 insurance companies operating in Ethiopia.

Africa Insurance Co: Bole Sub-City, Worda 02, House 3170, POB 12941, Addis Ababa; tel. (11) 6637716; fax (11) 6638253; e-mail africains@ethionet.et; internet www.africainsurancesc.com; f. 1994; Man. Dir and CEO KIROS JIRANIE.

Awash Insurance Co: Awash Tower, Sengatera, Ras Abebe Aregay St, POB 12637, Addis Ababa; tel. (11) 5570001; fax (11) 5570208; e-mail aic@ethionet.et; internet www.awashinsurance.com; f. 1994; cap. 32.7m.; Chair. KANAA DABA; Gen. Man. TSEGAYE KEMSI; 33 brs.

Ethiopian Insurance Corpn: POB 2545, Addis Ababa; tel. (11) 5512400; fax (11) 5517499; e-mail eic.md@ethionet.et; internet www.eic.com.et; f. 1976; life, property and legal liabilities insurance cover; Man. Dir YEWONDWOSEN ETEFA.

Global Insurance Co SC: Gobena Aba Tigu St, Somale Tera, POB 180112, Addis Ababa; tel. (11) 1567400; fax (11) 1566200; e-mail globalinsu@ethionet.et; internet www.globalinsurancesc.com; f. 1997; cap. 41.5m. (paid); Chair. AHMED A. SHERIEF; CEO YAHYA MOHAMMED AFFAN; 12 brs; 100 employees.

National Insurance Co of Ethiopia: ZEFCO Bldg, Debre Zeit Rd, Kirkos Sub-City, K05/06/07, House No. 894, POB 12645, Addis Ababa; tel. (11) 4661129; fax (11) 4650660; e-mail nice@telecom.net.et; internet www.niceinsurance-et.com; Chair. ALEMAYEHU HAILE; Man. Dir and CEO HABTEMATIAM SHUMGIZAW.

Nile Insurance Co: POB 12836, Addis Ababa; tel. (11) 5537709; fax (11) 5514592; e-mail nileinsu@mail.telecom.net.et; f. 1995; Gen. Man. DAWIT G. AMANUEL.

Nyala Insurance SC: Mickey Leland St, POB 12753, Addis Ababa; tel. (11) 6626667; fax (11) 6626706; internet www.nyalainsurance.com; Chair. MARDOUF S. BAZAHAM; CEO EYOB MEHERETTE.

Oromia Insurance Co SC (OIC): Biftu Bldg, 6th Floor, Ras Desta St, POB 10090, Addis Ababa; tel. (11) 8959580; fax (11) 5572116; e-mail oromiainsurance@ethionet.et; internet www.oromiainsurancecompany.com.et; f. 2009; Chair. ELIAS GENETI; CEO TESFAYE DESTA.

United Insurance Co SC: Alpaulo Bldg, Debrezeit Rd, Kirkos Sub-City, Woreda 06, POB 1156, Addis Ababa; tel. (11) 5515656; fax (11) 5513258; e-mail united.insurance@telecom.net.et; internet www.unitedinsurancesc.com; Chair. ZAFU EYESUS; Man. Dir MESERET BEZABEH.

Trade and Industry

GOVERNMENT AGENCIES

Ethiopian Investment Agency: POB 2313, Addis Ababa; tel. (11) 5510033; fax (11) 5514396; e-mail ethiopian.invest@ethionet.et; internet www.ethioinvest.org; f. 1992; Dir-Gen. FITSUM AREGA.

Privatization and Public Enterprises Supervising Agency: POB 11835, Addis Ababa; tel. (11) 5530343; fax (11) 5513955; e-mail epa.etio@ethionet.et; internet www.ppesa.gov.et; Dir-Gen. BEYENE GEBREMESKEL.

DEVELOPMENT ORGANIZATIONS

Entrepreneurship Development Center: Addis Ababa; f. 2013 by the Ministry of Urban Development, Housing and Construction in partnership with the United Nations Development Programme; CEO ETALEM ENGEDA.

Ethiopian Institute of Agricultural Research (EIAR): POB 2003, Addis Ababa; tel. (11) 6462633; fax (11) 6461294; internet www.eiar.gov.et; f. 1966; Dir-Gen. Dr SOLOMON ASSEFA.

CHAMBERS OF COMMERCE

Ethiopian Chamber of Commerce and Sectorial Associations: Mexico Sq., POB 517, Addis Ababa; tel. (11) 5514005; fax (11) 5517699; e-mail ethchamb@ethionet.et; internet www.ethiopianchamber.com; f. 1947; regional chambers in 11 localities; Pres. MULU SOLOMON; Sec.-Gen. GASHAW DEBEBE.

Addis Ababa Chamber of Commerce: POB 2458, Addis Ababa; tel. (11) 5513882; fax (11) 5511479; e-mail getachew@addischamber.com; internet www.addischamber.com; Pres. AYALEW ZEGEYE; Sec.-Gen. GETACHEW REGASSA.

INDUSTRIAL AND TRADE ASSOCIATIONS

Arsi Agricultural Development Enterprise: POB 115, Assela; tel. 223311261; fax 223311208; e-mail arsiagri@ethionet.et; internet www.arsiagri-enterprise.gov.et; f. 1980; privatization pending; CEO ASSEFA HAGOS.

Bale Agricultural Development Enterprise: Robe.

Coffee Plantation Development Enterprise (CPDE): Deber Zeit Rd, POB 4363, Addis Ababa; tel. (11) 4670688; fax (11) 4168788; f. 1993; Dir-Gen. EPHREM MERSIHEHAZEN.

Ethiopian Association of Basic Metal and Engineering Industries: Bole Sub-City, House Number 0377, Addis Ababa; tel. and fax (11) 6293429; e-mail eabmei@ethionet.et; internet www.eabmei.org; Pres. ASEGED MAMMO; Gen. Man. SOLOMON MULUGETA.

Ethiopian Cement Corpn: POB 5782, Addis Ababa; tel. (11) 1552222; fax (11) 1551572; Gen. Man. REDI GEMAL.

Ethiopian Chemical Corpn: POB 5747, Addis Ababa; tel. (11) 6184305; Gen. Man. ASNAKE SAHLU.

Ethiopian Coffee Export Enterprise: POB 2591, Addis Ababa; tel. (11) 5515330; fax (11) 5510762; f. 1977; Chair. SUFIAN AHMED; Gen. Man. DERGA GURMESSA.

Ethiopian Food Corpn: POB 2345, Addis Ababa; tel. (11) 5518522; fax (11) 5513173; f. 1975; produces and distributes food items, incl. edible oil, ghee substitute, pasta, bread, maize, wheat flour, etc.; Gen. Man. BEKELE HAILE.

Ethiopian Fruit and Vegetable Marketing Enterprise: POB 2374, Addis Ababa; tel. (11) 5519192; fax (11) 5516483; f. 1980; sole wholesale domestic distributor and exporter of fresh and processed fruit and vegetables, and floricultural products; Gen. Man. KAKNU PEWONDE.

Ethiopian Grain Trade Enterprise: POB 3321, Addis Ababa; tel. (11) 4652436; fax (11) 4652792; e-mail egte@ethionet.et; internet www.egtemis.com; Gen. Man. BERHANE HAILU.

Ethiopian Horticulture Producers and Exporters Association (EHPEA): NB Bldg, 6th Floor, Mickililand Rd, POB 22241, Addis Ababa; tel. (11) 6636750; fax (11) 6636753; e-mail ehpea@ethionet.et; internet www.ehpea.org.et; f. 2002; 70 mems; Pres. ZELALEM MESELE.

Ethiopian Import and Export Corpn (ETIMEX): Addis Ababa; tel. (11) 5511112; fax (11) 5515411; f. 1975; state trading corpn; import of building materials, foodstuffs, stationery and office equipment, textiles, clothing, chemicals, general merchandise, capital goods; Gen. Man. ASCHENAKI G. HIWOT.

Ethiopia Peasants' Association (EPA): f. 1978 to promote improved agricultural techniques, home industries, education, public health and self-reliance; comprises 30,000 peasant asscns with c. 7m. mems; Chair. (vacant).

Ethiopian Petroleum Enterprise: POB 3375, Addis Ababa; tel. and fax (11) 5512938; f. 1976; Gen. Man. YIGZAW MEKONNEN.

Ethiopian Pulses, Oilseeds and Spices Processors Exporters' Association: POB 5719, Addis Ababa; tel. (11) 1550597; fax (11) 1553299; f. 1975; Gen. Man. ABDOURUHMAN MOHAMMED.

Ethiopian Sugar Corpn: POB 20034, Addis Ababa; tel. (11) 5526653; fax (11) 5150927; e-mail info@etsugar.gov.et; internet www.etsugar.gov.et; f. 2010 to replace Ethiopian Sugar Development Agency; Dir-Gen. ABAY TSEHAYE.

Green Star Food Co LLC: POB 5579, Addis Ababa; tel. (11) 5526588; fax (11) 5526599; e-mail greenstar@telecom.net.et; f. 1984; fmrly the Ethiopian Livestock and Meat Corpn; production and marketing of canned and frozen foods; Gen. Man. DAWIT BEKELE.

Metals and Engineering Corpn (METEC): POB 21431, 1000 Addis Ababa; tel. (11) 5541572; fax (11) 1521141; internet www.metec.gov.et; comprises 15 semi-autonomous cos; Man. Dir Brig.-Gen. KINFE DAGNEW.

Natural Gum Processing and Marketing Enterprise: POB 62322, Addis Ababa; tel. (11) 5527082; fax (11) 5518110; e-mail natgum@ethionet.et; internet www.naturalgum.ebigchina.com; f. 1976; state-owned; Gen. Man. TEKLEHAIMANOT NIGATU BEYENE.

Pharmaceuticals Fund and Supply Agency (PFSA): POB 976, Addis Ababa; tel. (11) 2763266; fax (11) 2751770; e-mail pfsa@ethionet.et; Dir-Gen. HAILESELASSIE BIHON.

UTILITIES

Electricity

Ethiopian Electric Power Corpn (EEPCo): De Gaulle Sq., POB 1233, Addis Ababa; tel. (11) 1559567; fax (11) 1571860; e-mail eepcocommunication@yahoo.com; internet www.eepco.gov.et; Chair. DEBRETSION G/MICHAEL; Gen. Man. MIHRET DEBEBE.

Water

Addis Ababa Water and Sewerage Authority: POB 1505; Addis Ababa; tel. (11) 6623902; fax (11) 6623924; e-mail aawsa.ha@ethionet.et; f. 1971; Gen. Man. ASEGID GETACHEW.

TRADE UNION

Confederation of Ethiopian Trade Unions (CETU): POB 3653, Addis Ababa; tel. (11) 5155473; fax (11) 5514532; e-mail cetu@telecom.net.et; f. 1975; comprises nine industrial unions and 22 regional unions with a total membership of 320,000 (1987); Pres. KASSAHUN FOLLO; Sec.-Gen. MESFIN SILESHI.

Transport

RAILWAYS

Railway construction is a central component of Ethiopia's current five-year plan (2010–15) to boost economic growth. In 2010 construction of a 5,000-km railway network to link Addis Ababa with various parts of the country was started. Phase one of the five-year project included the construction of a new 2,000-km line to the border with Djibouti. Under phase two, work commenced in late 2011 on a 30-km light railway network in Addis Ababa. In 2012 agreement was reached with Turkey's Yapi Merkezi and China Communications Construction Company regarding the construction of 715-km of track connecting Ethiopia to the port of Tadjoura in northern Djibouti.

Chemin de Fer Djibouti-Ethiopien (CDE): POB 1051, Addis Ababa; tel. (11) 5517250; fax (11) 5513997; f. 1909; adopted present name in 1981; jtly owned by Govts of Ethiopia and Djibouti; 781 km of track (660 km in Ethiopia), linking Addis Ababa with Djibouti; Pres. ISMAIL IBRAHIM HOUMED.

Ethiopian Railways Corporation (ERC): POB 27558/1000, Addis Ababa; tel. (11) 6189060; fax (11) 6189065; internet www.erc.gov.et; f. 2007; CEO Dr GETACHEW BETRE.

ROADS

In 2007 the total road network comprised an estimated 44,359 km of primary, secondary and feeder roads, of which 13.7% were paved, the remainder being gravel roads. In addition, there are some 30,000 km of unclassified tracks and trails. A highway links Addis Ababa with Nairobi in Kenya, forming part of the Trans-East Africa Highway. In mid-2003 work commenced on the second phase of the Road Sector Development Programme, which upgraded 80% and 63% of paved and gravel roads, respectively, to an acceptable condition by 2007.

Comet Transport SC: POB 2402, Addis Ababa; tel. (11) 4423962; fax (11) 4426024; e-mail cometrans@ethionet.et; f. 1994; Gen. Man. ALEMU ASHENGO.

Ethiopian Road Transport Authority: POB 2504, Addis Ababa; tel. (11) 5510244; fax (11) 5510715; e-mail kasahun_khmariam@yahoo.com; internet www.rta.gov.et; enforces road transport regulations, promotes road safety, registers vehicles and issues driving licences; Gen. Man. KASAHUN H. MARIAM.

Ethiopian Roads Authority: POB 1770, Addis Ababa; tel. (11) 5517170; fax (11) 5514866; e-mail era2@ethionet.et; internet www.era.gov.et; f. 1951; construction and maintenance of roads, bridges and airports; Dir-Gen. ZAID WOLDE GEBREAL.

Public Transport Corpn: POB 5780, Addis Ababa; tel. (11) 5153117; fax (11) 5510720; f. 1977; urban bus services in Addis Ababa and Jimma, and services between towns; restructured into three autonomous enterprises in 1994 and scheduled for privatization; Man. Dir AHMED NURU.

SHIPPING

The formerly Ethiopian-controlled ports of Massawa and Assab now lie within the boundaries of the State of Eritrea. Although an agreement exists between the two Governments allowing Ethiopian access to the two ports, which can handle more than 1m. metric tons of merchandise annually, in mid-1998 Ethiopia ceased using the ports, owing to the outbreak of hostilities. Ethiopia's maritime trade currently passes through Djibouti (in the Republic of Djibouti), and also through the Kenyan port of Mombasa. An agreement was also signed in July 2003 to allow Ethiopia to use Port Sudan (in Sudan). At 31 December 2013 Ethiopia's flag registered fleet numbered 17 vessels, with a total displacement of 313,105 grt.

Ethiopian Shipping and Logistics Services Enterprise (ESLSE): Kirkos District, Kebele 15 (La Gare), POB 2572, Addis Ababa; tel. (11) 5518280; fax (11) 5519525; e-mail esl@ethionet.et; internet www.ethiopianshippinglines.com.et; f. 2011 following merger of the Ethiopian Shipping Lines Corpn, the Maritime and Transit Services Enterprise and the Dry Port Services Enterprise; serves Red Sea, Europe, Mediterranean, Gulf and Far East with its own fleet and chartered vessels; CEO AHMED TUSSA.

Maritime Affairs Authority: Tadesse Tefera Bldg, 5th Floor, opp. Hotel d'Afrique, POB 1861, Addis Ababa; tel. (11) 5503638; fax (11) 5503960; e-mail maritime@ethionet.et; internet www.maritime.gov.et; f. 2007; regulates maritime transport services; Dir-Gen. MEKONNEN ABERA.

CIVIL AVIATION

Ethiopia has two international airports (at Addis Ababa and Dire Dawa) and around 40 smaller airports and airfields. Bole International Airport in the capital handles 95% of the country's international air traffic and 85% of domestic flights.

Ethiopian Airlines: Bole International Airport, POB 1755, Addis Ababa; tel. (11) 6652222; fax (11) 6611474; e-mail publicrelations@ethiopianairlines.com; internet www.flyethiopian.com; f. 1945; operates regular domestic services and flights to some 80 destinations in Africa, Europe, the Middle East, Asia, South America and the USA; CEO TEWOLDE GEBREMARIAM.

Ethiopian Civil Aviation Authority (ECAA): POB 978, Addis Ababa; tel. (11) 6650200; fax (11) 6650281; e-mail civilaviation@ethionet.et; internet www.ecaa.gov.et; regulatory authority; provides air navigational facilities; Dir-Gen. Col WOSENYELEH HUNEGNAW.

Tourism

Ethiopia's tourist attractions include early Christian monuments and churches, the ancient capitals of Gondar and Axum, the Blue Nile (or Tississat) Falls and the National Parks of the Simien and Bale Mountains. Tourist arrivals in 2011 totalled 523,438. In that year receipts from tourism (excluding passenger transport) amounted to US $763m.

Ministry of Culture and Tourism: POB 2183, Addis Ababa; tel. (11) 5512310; fax (11) 5512889; e-mail tourismethiopia@ethionet.et; internet www.tourismethiopia.gov.et.

Defence

As assessed at November 2013, Ethiopia's active armed forces numbered an estimated 138,000, including an air force of some 3,000. A total of 6,560 soldiers were stationed abroad, of whom 105 were observers.

Defence Expenditure: Budgeted at 7,500m. birr for the fiscal year 2013/14.

Chief of Staff of the Armed Forces: Gen. SAMORA YUNIS.

Education

Education in Ethiopia is available free of charge, and, after a rapid growth in the number of schools, it became compulsory between the ages of seven and 13 years. Since 1976 most primary and secondary schools have been controlled by local peasant associations and urban dwellers' associations. Primary education begins at seven years of age and lasts for eight years. Secondary education, beginning at 15 years of age, lasts for a further four years, comprising two cycles of two years, the second of which provides preparatory education for entry to the tertiary level. According to UNESCO estimates, in 2009/10 total enrolment at primary schools included 81% of children in the appropriate age-group (84% of boys; 79% of girls), while secondary enrolment was equivalent to 36% of children in the appropriate age-group (39% of boys; 32% of girls). According to the Ministry of Education, in 2012/13 there were 99 institutions of higher education in Ethiopia, including universities in Addis Ababa, Bahir Dar, Alemanya, Jimma, Awassa and Makele. A total of 585,152 students were enrolled in higher education in 2012/13. In 2010 spending on education represented 25.4% of total government expenditure.

FIJI

Introductory Survey

LOCATION, CLIMATE, LANGUAGE, RELIGION, FLAG, CAPITAL

The Republic of Fiji comprises more than 300 islands, of which around 100 are inhabited, situated about 1,930 km (1,200 miles) south of the equator in the Pacific Ocean. The four main islands are Viti Levu (where some 70% of the country's population lives), Vanua Levu, Taveuni and Kadavu. The climate is tropical, with temperatures ranging from 16°C to 32°C (60°F–90°F). Rainfall is heavy on the windward side. Fijian and Hindi are the principal languages, but English is also widely spoken. In 2007 about 64% of the population were Christians (mainly Methodists), 28% Hindus and 6% Muslims. The national flag (proportions 1 by 2) is light blue, with the United Kingdom flag as a canton in the upper hoist. In the fly is the main part of Fiji's national coat of arms: a white field quartered by a red upright cross, the quarters containing sugar canes, a coconut palm, a stem of bananas and a dove bearing an olive branch; in chief is a red panel with a yellow crowned lion holding a white cocoa pod. The capital is Suva, on Viti Levu.

CONTEMPORARY POLITICAL HISTORY

Historical Context

The first Europeans to settle on the islands were sandalwood traders, missionaries and shipwrecked sailors, and in October 1874 Fiji was proclaimed a British possession. In September 1966 the British Government introduced a new Constitution for Fiji. It provided for a ministerial form of government, an almost wholly elected Legislative Council and the introduction of universal adult suffrage. Rather than using a common roll of voters, the Constitution introduced an electoral system that combined communal (Fijian and Indian) rolls with cross-voting. In September 1967 the Executive Council became the Council of Ministers, with Ratu Kamisese Mara, leader of the multiracial (but predominantly Fijian) Alliance Party (AP), as Fiji's first Chief Minister. Following a constitutional conference in April–May 1970, Fiji achieved independence, within the Commonwealth, on 10 October 1970. The Legislative Council was renamed the House of Representatives, and a second parliamentary chamber, the nominated Senate, was established. The British-appointed Governor became the first Governor-General of Fiji, while Ratu Sir Kamisese Mara (as he had become in 1969) took office as Prime Minister.

However, Fiji was troubled by racial tensions. Although the descendants of indentured Indian workers who were brought to Fiji in the late 19th century had grown to outnumber the native inhabitants, they were discriminated against in political representation and land ownership rights (see Land Ownership Issues for subsequent developments). A new electoral system was adopted in 1970 to ensure a racial balance in the legislature.

Domestic Political Affairs

At the legislative elections held in March 1972 the AP secured 33 of the 52 seats in the House of Representatives, while the National Federation Party (NFP), traditionally supported by the Indian population, took 19 seats. At elections in March–April 1977 the NFP won 26 seats, but was unable to form a government, subsequently splitting into two factions. The AP governed in an interim capacity until the holding of further elections in September, when it was returned with its largest-ever majority. While the two main parties professed multiracial ideologies, the Fijian Nationalist Party campaigned in support of its 'Fiji for the Fijians' programme in order to foster nationalist sentiment.

In 1980 Ratu Sir Kamisese Mara's suggestion that a government of national unity be formed was overshadowed by renewed disagreement between the AP and the NFP over land ownership. Fijians owned 83% of the land and strongly defended their traditional rights, while the Indian population pressed for greater security of land tenure. The AP retained power at the legislative elections held in July 1982, but its majority was reduced from 20 seats to four.

A new party, the Fiji Labour Party (FLP), was inaugurated in July 1985. Sponsored by the Fiji Trades Union Congress (FTUC), and under the presidency of Dr Timoci Bavadra, the FLP advocated the provision of free education and a national medical scheme, and hoped to work through farmers' organizations to win votes among rural electorates, which traditionally supported the NFP. During 1985–86 disagreements between the Government and the FTUC over economic policies led to labour unrest and the withdrawal, in June 1986, of government recognition of the FTUC as the unions' representative organization.

At legislative elections in April 1987 an alliance of the FLP and NFP won 28 seats (19 of which were secured by ethnic Indian candidates) in the House of Representatives, thus defeating the ruling AP, which took only 24 seats. The new Government, led by Bavadra, was therefore the first in Fijian history to contain a majority of ministers of Indian, rather than Melanesian, origin, although Bavadra himself was of Melanesian descent.

The coups of 1987 and subsequent events

On 14 May 1987 the Government was overthrown by a military coup, led by Lt-Col (later Maj.-Gen.) Sitiveni Rabuka. The Governor-General, Ratu Sir Penaia Ganilau, declared a state of emergency and appointed a 19-member advisory council, including Bavadra and Rabuka. Bavadra refused to participate in the council, denouncing it as unconstitutional and biased in its composition.

Widespread racial violence ensued, and there were several public demands for Bavadra's reinstatement as Prime Minister. In July 1987 the Great Council of Fijian Chiefs, comprising the country's 70 hereditary Melanesian leaders, approved plans for constitutional reform. In September negotiations began, on the initiative of Ganilau, between delegations led by the two former Prime Ministers, Bavadra and Mara, and it was subsequently announced that the two factions had agreed to establish an interim bipartisan Government.

On 25 September 1987, however, Rabuka staged a second coup and announced his intention to declare Fiji a republic. Despite Ganilau's refusal to recognize the seizure of power, Rabuka revoked the Constitution on 1 October and proclaimed himself head of state, thus deposing Queen Elizabeth II. Ganilau conceded defeat and resigned as Governor-General. At a meeting in Canada, Commonwealth heads of government formally declared that Fiji's membership of the Commonwealth had lapsed. Rabuka installed an interim Cabinet comprising mainly ethnic Fijians. Several cases of violations of human rights by the Fijian army were reported, as the regime assumed powers of detention without trial and suspended all political activity. In December Rabuka resigned as head of state. Although he had previously refused to accept the post, Ganilau became the first President of the Fijian Republic. Mara was reappointed Prime Minister, and Rabuka became Minister for Home Affairs. The new interim Cabinet included 11 members of Rabuka's outgoing administration, but no former minister of Bavadra's deposed Government.

In February 1988 Rotuma (the only Polynesian island in the country), which lies 386 km (240 miles) to the north-west of Vanua Levu, declared itself politically independent of Fiji, the newly acquired republican status of which it refused to recognize. Fijian troops were dispatched to the island and swiftly quelled the dissent.

A new draft Constitution, approved by the interim Government in September 1988, was rejected by a multiracial constitutional committee, which disputed the specific reservation of the principal offices of state for ethnic Fijians. In September 1989 the committee published a revised draft, which was again condemned by Bavadra and the FLP-NFP alliance. In November Bavadra died and was replaced as leader of the FLP-NFP alliance by his widow, Adi Kuini Bavadra.

In January 1990 Rabuka resigned from the Cabinet and returned to his military duties. Mara agreed to remain as Prime Minister until the restoration of constitutional government. In June the Great Council of Chiefs approved the draft Constitution, while also stating its intention to form a new party, the Soqosoqo ni Vakavulewa ni Taukei (SVT) or Fijian Political Party, to advocate the cause of ethnic Fijians. The new Constitution was finally promulgated on 25 July by President Ganilau.

The document was immediately condemned by the FLP-NFP alliance. Angered by the fact that a legislative majority was guaranteed to ethnic Fijians (who were allocated 37 of the 70 elective seats, compared with 27 Indian seats), and that the Great Council of Chiefs was to nominate ethnic Fijians to 24 of the 34 seats in the Senate and to appoint the President of the Republic, the opposition organized anti-Constitution demonstrations. In May 1991 the Commonwealth stated that Fiji would not be readmitted until it changed its racially biased Constitution. In July Rabuka resigned as Commander of the Armed Forces in order to rejoin the Cabinet as Deputy Prime Minister and Minister for Home Affairs, although later that year he relinquished these posts and assumed the leadership of the SVT.

Disagreements between the Government and the FTUC re-emerged in 1991. In May the Government announced a series of reforms to the labour laws, including the abolition of the minimum wage, restrictions on strike action and derecognition of unions that did not represent at least two-thirds of the workforce. However, in late 1992 the Government officially recognized the FTUC as the sole representative of workers in Fiji.

At the legislative elections of May 1992 the SVT secured 30 of the 37 seats reserved for ethnic Fijians, while the NFP won 14 and the FLP 13 of the seats reserved for Indian representatives. The FLP agreed to participate in Parliament and to support Rabuka in his bid for the premiership, in return for a guarantee from the SVT of a full review of the Constitution and of trade union and land laws. Rabuka was, therefore, appointed Prime Minister and formed a coalition Government (comprising 14 SVT ministers and five others).

In December 1992 Rabuka formally invited the opposition leaders, Jai Ram Reddy of the NFP and Mahendra Chaudhry of the FLP (formerly the National Secretary of the FTUC), to form a government of national unity. The initiative was largely welcomed, but Indian politicians expressed reluctance to participate in a government in which political control remained fundamentally vested with ethnic Fijians; conversely, nationalist extremists of the Taukei Solidarity Movement accused Rabuka of conceding too much political power to Fijian Indians. Following the appointment of a new Cabinet in June 1993, all 13 of the FLP legislators began an indefinite boycott of Parliament, in protest against Rabuka's failure to implement the reforms that he had agreed to introduce in return for their support for his election to the premiership in June 1992.

In December 1993 President Ganilau died. He was replaced by Ratu Sir Kamisese Mara, who took office on 18 January 1994 (and was re-elected on 18 January 1999).

At the legislative elections held in February 1994 the SVT won 31 of the 37 seats reserved for ethnic Fijians, while the Fijian Association Party (FAP, established in January by former members of the SVT) secured five. Of the 27 seats reserved for ethnic Indian representatives, 20 were won by the NFP. The SVT subsequently formed a governing coalition with the General Voters' Party (GVP, which represented the interests of the General Electors—i.e. the minority Chinese and European communities and people from elsewhere in the Pacific region resident in Fiji) and an independent member, under the premiership of Rabuka, who announced the formation of a new Cabinet composed entirely of ethnic Fijians. In response to international concern regarding the continued existence of Fiji's racially biased Constitution, Rabuka announced in June the establishment of a Constitutional Review Commission.

The issue of independence for the island of Rotuma was revived in September 1995 with the return of the King of Rotuma from exile. King Gagaj Sa Lagfatmaro, who had fled to New Zealand after receiving death threats during the military coups of 1987, appeared before the Constitutional Review Commission to petition for the island's independence within the Commonwealth, reiterating his view that Rotuma remained a British colony rather than a part of Fiji.

Racial tension intensified in October 1995, following the publication of the SVT's submission to the Constitutional Review Commission. In its report, the party detailed plans to abandon the present multiracial form of government, recommending instead the adoption of an electoral system based on racial representation, in which each ethnic group would select its own representatives. The expression of numerous extreme anti-Indian sentiments in the document was widely condemned (by both ethnic Fijians and ethnic Indians) as offensive.

Two of the four GVP members of the House of Representatives withdrew their support for the Government in early 1996, prompting an (unsuccessful) attempt by Rabuka to seek alternative coalition partners from among the opposition. The SVT was defeated in virtually every municipality at local elections in September.

Existing divisions within the Government were further exacerbated by the presentation to the House of Representatives, in September 1996, of the Constitutional Review Commission's report. The report included recommendations to enlarge the House of Representatives to 75 seats, with 25 seats reserved on a racial basis (12 for ethnic Fijians, 10 for Fijian Indians, two for General Electors and one for Rotuma Islanders), and also proposed that the size of the Senate should be reduced from 34 to 32 members (and the number of nominated ethnic Fijian senators be reduced from 24 to 15). In addition, it was proposed that the Prime Minister should be a Fijian of any race, while the President should continue to be an indigenous Fijian. Rabuka and Mara both endorsed the report, while several nationalist parties and a number of SVT legislators expressed strong opposition to the proposals and formed a parliamentary coalition. The parliamentary committee reviewing the report agreed on the majority of its recommendations, but proposed that the House of Representatives be enlarged to only 71 seats, with 46 seats reserved on a racial basis (23 for ethnic Fijians, 19 for Indians, three for General Electors and one for Rotuma Islanders) and 25 seats open to all races. A modified Constitution Amendment Bill was subsequently approved by both the House of Representatives and the Senate. Rabuka was anxious to reassure extremist nationalist Fijians that their interests would be protected under the amended Constitution and that indigenous Fijians would continue to play a pre-eminent role in government.

Despite opposition from both the FLP and the nationalist parties, Fiji was readmitted to the Commonwealth in October 1997. Rabuka was granted an audience with Queen Elizabeth II in London, United Kingdom, at which he formally apologized for the military coups of 1987. The new Constitution took effect on 27 July 1998.

In late 1998 Adi Kuini Vuikaba Speed (widow of former Prime Minister Bavadra) replaced Ratu Alifereti Finau Mara as leader of the FAP. Meanwhile, the GVP and the General Electors' Association merged to form the United General Party (UGP), and Rabuka was re-elected leader of the SVT. A new party, the Veitokani ni Lewenivanua Vakarisito (VLV, Christian Democratic Alliance), formed by several senior church and military leaders and former members of the nationalist Taukei Solidarity Movement, was widely criticized for its extremist stance.

At the legislative elections of May 1999, the first to be held under the new Constitution, Rabuka's coalition Government was defeated by the FLP, led by Mahendra Chaudhry, who became Fiji's first ethnic Indian Prime Minister. Chaudhry's broadly based Government (a coalition of the FLP, FAP, VLV and the Party of National Unity—PANU) initially seemed threatened by the reluctance of FAP members to serve under an Indian Prime Minister. The leaders were persuaded to remain in the coalition in the interests of national unity, after the intervention of President Mara. Political stability was further marred by demands for Chaudhry's resignation by the Fijian Nationalist Vanua Takolavo Party (NVTLP), and by a number of arson attacks, allegedly linked to the SVT. Following the SVT's decisive election defeat, Rabuka resigned as party leader. Rabuka was later appointed the first independent Chairman of the newly autonomous Great Council of Chiefs. The NVTLP was widely suspected to have been responsible for three bomb explosions in Suva in August. In the same month a parliamentary vote of no confidence against Prime Minister Chaudhry was overwhelmingly defeated. In the latter half of 1999 there were persistent demands by various nationalist groups (including the SVT) that Chaudhry be replaced by a leader of indigenous Fijian descent, and a number of demonstrations were organized, expressing disillusionment with the Government.

The Government's decision to disband the Fiji Intelligence Services from December 1999 was criticized by the opposition as 'foolish' and racially motivated. Plans to amend a number of laws that did not comply with the terms of the new Constitution and proposals to alter the distribution of power between the President and the Prime Minister, along with reports that the Government was planning to withdraw state funds previously provided to assist indigenous Fijian business interests, prompted further criticism from the opposition, and in February 2000 a faction of the FAP announced its withdrawal from the governing coalition. Furthermore, it was announced in April that the extremist nationalist Taukei movement (which had been inactive for several years) had been revived with the sole intention of removing the Prime Minister from office. The movement's campaign attracted considerable public support, which culminated in a march through Suva by some 5,000 people in early May, despite the army's reiteration of its support for Chaudhry.

The coup of 2000 and its repercussions

On 19 May 2000 a group of armed men, led by businessman George Speight, invaded the parliament building and ousted the Government, taking hostage Chaudhry and 30 other members of the governing coalition. President Mara condemned the coup and declared a state of emergency as Speight's supporters rampaged through the streets of Suva, looting and setting fire to Indian businesses. Speight declared that he had reclaimed Fiji for indigenous Fijians and had dissolved the Constitution. Moreover, he threatened to kill the hostages if the military intervened. Convening at Mara's invitation, the Great Council of Chiefs proposed the replacement of Chaudhry's Government with an interim administration, an amnesty for Speight and the rebels, and the amendment of the Constitution. Speight rejected the proposals, demanding that Mara also be removed from office. At the end of May Mara resigned and the Commander of the Armed Forces, Frank (Voreqe) Bainimarama, announced the imposition of martial law and a curfew to restore stability to the country.

Negotiations between the newly installed Military Executive Council and the Great Council of Chiefs continued throughout June 2000. Following the release of the four female captives from the parliament building, the Military Executive Council demanded the release of all hostages. The Military Executive Council appointed an interim administration of 19 indigenous Fijians led by Laisenia Qarase (the former managing director of the Merchant Bank of Fiji), which was sworn in on 4 July. Speight announced that he would not recognize the interim authority, and most of Fiji's mainstream political parties similarly denounced it. By mid-July Chaudhry and the remaining hostages had been released by the rebels. In accordance with Speight's wishes, Ratu Josefa Iloilovatu Uluivuda (or Josefa Iloilo), hitherto the First Vice-President, was then installed as President.

Incidents of civil unrest continued, as Speight sought to manipulate existing grievances, particularly disputes over land ownership, in order to mobilize greater support. At the end of July 2000, however, Speight was finally arrested, along with dozens of his supporters, for breaking the terms of his amnesty by refusing to relinquish weapons. In early August more than 300 rebels appeared in court, charged with a variety of firearms and public order offences. On 11 August Speight and 14 of his supporters were formally charged with treason. Meanwhile, a police investigation into a commercial deal involving the Fijian mahogany trade began; Speight had been chairman of both Fiji Pine Corporation and Fiji Hardwood Corporation before being dismissed in 1999. Chaudhry subsequently stated his belief that the coup had been motivated by commercial vested interests.

In early November 2000 about 40 soldiers staged an unsuccessful mutiny at army headquarters in Suva. Troops loyal to Bainimarama retook the barracks following an eight-hour assault in which five rebels and four loyal soldiers were killed. It was later revealed that a number of the rebel soldiers had been involved in the coup in May. The Chairman of the Great Council of Chiefs, Rabuka, denied New Zealand's allegations that he had been involved in the mutiny. In November 2002 Capt. Shane Stevens was sentenced to life imprisonment after having been found guilty of leading the mutiny two years earlier; 14 other soldiers received lesser sentences for their part in the uprising.

Later in November 2000 the High Court ruled that the existing Constitution was still valid and that the elected Parliament, ousted in the coup, remained Fiji's legitimate governing authority. In response, Qarase lodged an appeal against the ruling and declared that the interim authority, of which he was leader, would continue as the country's national government until new elections could be organized and a new constitution drafted within 18 months.

In February 2001 an international panel of judges at the Court of Appeal began the hearing against the November 2000 ruling, which found the abrogation of the 1997 Constitution to be illegal. In its final judgment the court ruled that the 1997 Constitution remained the supreme law of Fiji, that the interim civilian government could not prove that it had the support of a majority of Fijian people and was therefore illegal, and that, following Mara's resignation, the office of President remained vacant. The ruling was welcomed by many countries in the region, including Australia and New Zealand, and appeared to be accepted by Qarase's interim authority, which announced that it would organize elections as soon as possible. However, in March 2001 Iloilo informed Chaudhry by letter that he had been dismissed as Prime Minister, claiming that by advising Iloilo to dissolve the legislature in preparation for elections he had accepted that he no longer had the mandate of Parliament. Chaudhry rejected the decision as unconstitutional and unlawful. Ratu Tevita Momoedonu, a minister in Qarase's Government, was appointed Prime Minister. However, Iloilo dismissed Momoedonu, on the advice of the Great Council of Chiefs, and reinstated Qarase as head of the interim authority. It was subsequently announced that legislative elections would be held in August–September 2001.

There followed a period of factionalism and fragmentation among Fiji's political parties. Speight had already been appointed President of the new Matanitu Vanua (MV—Conservative Alliance Party), despite having been charged with treason for his part in the 2000 coup. In May 2001 Qarase formed the Soqosoqo Duavata ni Lewenivanua (SDL—Fiji United Party), a new contender for the indigenous Melanesian vote, thus rivalling the established SVT. Tupeni Baba, former Deputy Prime Minister in Chaudhry's Government, left the FLP and formed the New Labour United Party (NLUP). Qarase's SDL was victorious in the elections, but failed to obtain an overall majority, securing 31 of the 71 seats in the House of Representatives (rising to 32 following a by-election in late September). The FLP won 27 seats, the MV six seats and the NLUP two seats.

Refusing to allow the FLP any representation in his new Cabinet, Qarase was accused of contravening a provision of the Constitution whereby a party winning more than 10% of the seats in the House of Representatives was entitled to a ministerial post. Two members of the MV were included in the Cabinet. Qarase claimed that Chaudhry had not accepted that the Government should be based fundamentally on nationalist Fijian principles. In October 2001 Chaudhry refused to accept the position of Leader of the Opposition, a role that consequently fell to Prem Singh of the NFP. In December Parliament approved the Social Justice Bill, a programme of affirmative action favouring Fijians and Rotumans in education, land rights and business-funding policies.

Prime Minister Qarase defended himself against demands for his resignation in January 2002 following allegations that he had contravened the Electoral Act by pledging government funds to pro-indigenous Fijian businesses during the 2001 election campaign. In February 2002, furthermore, an appeal court ruled that the Prime Minister had violated the Constitution by failing to incorporate any member of the FLP in his Cabinet. Qarase had previously declared that he would resign if the legal challenge against him proved successful. In September the High Court ruled that Prem Singh was not entitled to retain his parliamentary seat (the validity of certain votes cast at the 2001 election having been questioned). The disputed seat was therefore allocated to a member of the FLP. The Supreme Court finally delivered its ruling on the issue of the inclusion of the FLP in the Cabinet in July 2003, finding in favour of Chaudhry and declaring that, in order to uphold the Constitution, Qarase should form a new cabinet that included eight members of the FLP. Qarase responded by proposing to retain the incumbent 22-member Cabinet and to add 14 FLP members. Both the opposition and the SVT leader, Rabuka, criticized the proposal, which would entail more than one-half of all members of the House of Representatives serving as government ministers. Chaudhry claimed that the positions offered to his party were too junior. However, Qarase remained intransigent, and at the end of August he formally nominated a Cabinet that included 14 FLP members (although Chaudhry was not among those named).

Although in June 2002 Prime Minister Qarase and Chaudhry had co-operated briefly in addressing the long-standing issue of the expiry of land leases, in August the FLP abandoned a second round of discussions on this matter and announced that it would boycott most of the proceedings in the current parliamentary session. Chaudhry accused the Government of attempting to accelerate the passage of legislation through Parliament without regard for the mandatory 30 days' notice of a bill being tabled. In September Qarase effected a reorganization of cabinet portfolios in which he assumed direct responsibility for the reform of the sugar industry.

The trial of Speight and his accomplices on charges of treason opened in May 2001. (Speight was refused bail to enable him to occupy the seat that he won in the legislative elections later in the year.) All the accused pleaded guilty to their involvement in the coup of May 2000, and at the conclusion of the trial in February 2002 Speight received the death sentence. However, within hours of the verdict President Iloilo signed a decree commuting the sentence to life imprisonment. Prison sentences of between 18 months and three years were imposed on 10 of Speight's accomplices, the charges of treason having been replaced by lesser charges of abduction. Between July 2002 and July 2004 a total of 86 people were arrested on charges relating to the coup, with the majority being found guilty of mutiny. Speight made a further court appearance in May on charges of hostage-taking during the 2000 coup. Chaudhry and another member of Parliament were claiming US $3.6m. in compensation for the 56 days that they had been held hostage in the government buildings by Speight and his accomplices. In August 2004 Vice-President Ratu Jope Seniloli was found guilty of treason and sentenced to four years' imprisonment. In November, however, he was unexpectedly released from prison on medical grounds, which were widely disputed. Upon his release, Seniloli resigned as Vice-President at the insistence of the military. In December the Great Council of Chiefs approved President Iloilo's nomination of Ratu Joni Madraiwiwi as the country's next Vice-President. In November 2004 Paramount Chief Ratu Inoke Takiveikata was sentenced to life imprisonment after being found guilty on several charges relating to the mutiny. (In June 2007, following questions about the impartiality of the presiding judge, a retrial of Takiveikata was ordered; however, in November 2007 he was again arrested, on separate charges of conspiracy to assassinate Bainimarama—see The coup of 2006 and abrogation of the Constitution.)

Meanwhile, in June 2003, during a public reconciliation ceremony, the High Chief of a district of Vanua Levu publicly apologized for his involvement in the coup and announced a ban, in his locality, on words that differentiated ethnic Fijians from their Indian Fijian neighbours. In May 2004 the Great Council of Chiefs issued an historic public apology to all Indian Fijians for injustices committed against them during the coups of 1987 and 2000.

In May 2005 the Government announced plans for a Reconciliation, Tolerance and Unity Bill, which would allow the review of convictions relating to involvement in the 2000 coup and the pardoning of prisoners. However, the proposals provoked considerable opposition, particularly from the FLP and from Hindu organizations. In the same month the Minister for Transport, Simione Kaitani, and four other individuals appeared in court on coup-related charges.

The reappointment in March 2006, by the Great Council of Chiefs, of Iloilo as President and Madraiwiwi as Vice-President was welcomed by Chaudhry and by the military as contributing to national stability. Although 25 political parties contested the legislative elections in May, only three of these won seats in the House of Representatives. The ruling SDL, which had joined forces with a number of smaller, conservative-leaning parties, secured 36 seats, while the FLP won 31 and the United People's Party (UPP—formerly the UGP—representing General Electors) two. The two successful independent candidates agreed to support the SDL.

Following his reappointment as Prime Minister in May 2006, Qarase offered seven of the 17 cabinet positions to the FLP, as required by the Constitution, although he restated his opposition to multi-party coalition government and expressed his hope that Chaudhry would not accept the proposal. Chaudhry, in turn, argued that his party was entitled to more posts and disputed the portfolios offered. The FLP was subsequently assigned nine positions in a 24-member Cabinet, although Chaudhry himself declined to accept a ministerial role.

The coup of 2006 and abrogation of the Constitution

Tensions between the Government and the military were exacerbated by repeated accusations made throughout 2006 by the Commander of the Armed Forces, Cdre Frank Bainimarama, of racism and corruption within Qarase's administration. In February Bainimarama issued a statement declaring that he would prevent the enactment of the Reconciliation, Tolerance and Unity Bill, and in October he demanded the resignation of the Government if it failed to reject the bill within three weeks. At the end of that month, while Bainimarama was absent from Fiji, visiting peacekeeping troops in the Middle East, an attempt was made to replace him. However, the Government's chosen replacement declined to accept the role, expressing support for Bainimarama. On 30 November Bainimarama issued a further ultimatum, giving Qarase 24 hours to comply with a list of demands. These demands included the removal of all government members who had supported or benefited from the armed coup of 2000 and the suspension of three controversial pieces of legislation condemned by Bainimarama as furthering the racist agenda of the Government: the Reconciliation, Tolerance and Unity Bill, providing amnesties for those convicted of involvement in the 2000 coup; the Qoliqoli Bill, giving ethnic Fijians control of fishing rights and development of the coast; and the Indigenous Claims Tribunal Bill. In a public address on Fijian television, Qarase agreed to suspend the bills.

On 5 December 2006 soldiers took up positions outside the Prime Minister's official residence, seized strategic installations and erected road blocks around Suva. Bainimarama met President Iloilo, who authorized the dissolution of Parliament and the establishment of an interim administration. Bainimarama declared that he had assumed executive control of the country, appointing Dr Jona Senilagakali as interim Prime Minister and urging all cabinet ministers to resign within a month. The coup was condemned by New Zealand, the United Kingdom and Australia; Qarase's request for military intervention was refused by Australia, but various sanctions against the country were announced. A state of emergency was subsequently declared. The suspension of Fiji's participation in meetings of the Commonwealth was announced on 9 December. Despite widespread international condemnation, there was considerable support for the coup within Fiji. Organizations representing Indian Fijians expressed support for Bainimarama, as did the Fiji Human Rights Commission, which had questioned the legitimacy of Qarase's Government.

On 4 January 2007 Bainimarama restored executive power to President Iloilo, and on the following day, upon the resignation of Senilagakali, Bainimarama was sworn in as interim Prime Minister. Bainimarama's appointment was swiftly approved by the Great Council of Chiefs. An interim Government was subsequently sworn in; notable appointments included that of Chaudhry as Minister for Finance, National Planning, Public Enterprise and the Sugar Industry, and Ratu Epeli Nailatikau as Minister for Foreign Affairs and External Trade. In mid-January, amid reports of intimidation on the part of the military in the aftermath of the coup, President Iloilo issued a decree granting immunity to Bainimarama, Senilagakali and members of the military and police force in the event of disciplinary action or prosecution. In February Bainimarama announced plans to hold elections in 2010, following an assessment of electoral procedures and the completion of a census. These proposals appeared to have been revised in April 2007, when it was reported that the Fijian Government had agreed to the holding of legislative elections within two years, during discussions with the European Union (EU) on the issue of the release of development aid, suspended as a result of the coup.

In April 2007 the Great Council of Chiefs rejected the government minister Ratu Epeli Nailatikau as a nominee for the post of Vice-President. The Council was suspended, and the Government announced a review of its procedures. Although its suspension was apparently rescinded in August, it was later reported that the official composition of the Council had been reduced from 55 to 52 members (following the dismissal of several chiefs, including the Chairman). At the end of May Bainimarama declared an end to the state of emergency. However, in September a state of emergency was temporarily reimposed in response to the arrival in Suva of Qarase, whose presence was regarded by the Government as a potential threat to stability; the order was rescinded in the following month. In early November some 16 arrests were made after plans for an apparent counter-coup, allegedly to include the assassination of Bainimarama, were reported to have been discovered. Several alleged conspirators, including a former senator, an intelligence official and Paramount Chief Ratu Inoke Takiveikata, who had been previously charged with mutiny, were subsequently indicted on charges such as treason and inciting mutiny.

A reorganization of the interim Cabinet was announced in January 2008, in which Bainimarama relinquished the home affairs and immigration portfolios, but assumed responsibility for others, including provincial development and indigenous and multi-ethnic affairs. Ratu Epeli Ganilau became Minister for Defence, National Security and Immigration. Bainimarama took charge of the 'People's Charter for Change, Peace and Progress', a directive proposed in September 2007 to establish new regulations for government procedures. Bainimarama expected the Charter to result in amendments to the Constitution. The draft Charter, which was released in August 2008 and was undergoing a consultation process, advocated the forging of a 'common national identity', the introduction of an Anti-discrimination Act, and a programme of reform in areas including governance and reconciliation. In anticipation of the forthcoming elections, Chaudhry resigned from the interim Cabinet, along with two other members of the FLP, in mid-August. However, shortly afterwards, Bainimarama announced that the election schedule was dependent upon the implementation of electoral reform and would therefore be subject to further delays. Following Chaudhry's departure, Bainimarama assumed personal responsibility for finance and national planning, while other portfolios were distributed among existing ministers. In a further reorganization announced in September, Bainimarama took control of the foreign affairs portfolio, transferring Ratu Epeli Nailatikau to the Ministry for Provincial Development and Indigenous and Multi-ethnic Affairs.

Meanwhile, in February 2008 it emerged that Bainimarama had assumed the role of Chairman of the Great Council of Chiefs. At the end of that month it was announced that the National Security Council, which had been dissolved in 1999, and the Fiji Intelligence Services were to be reconstituted. Also in February 2008, Qarase was charged with corruption and abuse of office by the Fiji Independent Commission Against Corruption; the allegations against the former premier pertained to his tenure as director of Fijian Holdings Ltd in 1999–2000. In March 2008 Qarase himself challenged the legality of the December 2006 coup and installation of an interim Government, but his case was dismissed by the High Court in October 2008.

In April 2009 the Court of Appeal overruled the High Court's decision, declaring that the Government installed by Bainimarama following the 2006 coup was illegal. However, the court rejected Qarase's appeal to be reinstated to the premiership, instead ordering President Iloilo to dissolve Parliament and to appoint an interim Prime Minister. Bainimarama resigned in response to the ruling. President Iloilo annulled the 1997 Constitution, reappointed himself as head of state and dismissed the entire judiciary; he then reappointed Bainimarama as Prime Minister and reinstated the Government, with modifications to some ministerial portfolios. The position of Vice-President was restored, Ratu Epeli Nailatikau being appointed to the post. President Iloilo also announced that elections would be held no later than 2014. Meanwhile, the building of the Reserve Bank of Fiji was occupied by the military, and the central bank's Governor was removed from office and reportedly detained. His replacement immediately announced that the Fijian currency had been devalued by 20%.

Once returned to power, Bainimarama enacted a Public Emergency Decree, outlawing gatherings of more than 100 people and imposing strict censorship laws whereby an authorized government official was to examine all news copy prior to publication. A number of international journalists were expelled from the country, and the Australian Broadcasting Corporation's radio transmitters were shut down. During subsequent weeks Bainimarama reinstated the Chief Magistrate, the Chief Justice and judges of the High Court and reopened the Magistrates' Court. Widespread international condemnation of the actions of President Iloilo and Prime Minister Bainimarama ensued, with the UN, Australia and New Zealand offering to mediate in political dialogue to restore democracy. Bainimarama's refusal to set a date for democratic elections before 2014 resulted in Fiji's suspension from the Pacific Islands Forum (see p. 416) in May 2009 and the country's full suspension from the Commonwealth in September.

In July 2009 Bainimarama announced plans for a new Constitution, to be enacted in 2013; the proposed Constitution, it was reported, would amend current land tenure arrangements under which indigenous Fijians owned 90% of land, and would lower the minimum voting age from 21 to 18 years. In late July 2009 President Iloilo, who was 88 years old and reportedly in ill health, announced his retirement, with effect from the beginning of August. (Iloilo died in February 2011.) Vice-President Nailatikau assumed the role in an acting capacity until October, when his position as President, for a term of three years, was confirmed. Bainimarama announced that the newly recreated post of Vice-President would not be filled.

The Public Emergency Decree, first enacted by Bainimarama in April 2009, was subsequently extended. A senior minister of the Fiji Methodist Church, Rev. Manasa Lasaro, was briefly detained in May for breaching the decree in a sermon that criticized the Government. In July a number of senior Church members were arrested on charges of organizing a meeting in contravention of the emergency decree. An additional decree, enacted in December, further reinforced the Government's control over public meetings and over the media.

Increasing suppression of dissent

In February 2010 Bainimarama was reported to have stated that he would relinquish his role as Prime Minister in advance of the proposed 2014 elections; however, he planned to continue as Commander of the Armed Forces. In March 2010 the interim Prime Minister announced that all politicians who had served since 1987 were to be banned from contesting the 2014 elections. Although the objective was apparently to change the political culture of Fiji, the decision was criticized by observers, who viewed the action as an attempt to influence the composition of the next Government.

In late February 2010 the High Court returned a verdict of guilty in the trial of eight men, including Paramount Chief Ratu Inoke Takiveikata, charged with conspiring to assassinate Bainimarama in 2007; the men were sentenced to terms of imprisonment ranging from three to seven years. In September 2010 the retrial of Takiveikata on charges of inciting the 2000 mutiny began (his original conviction having been declared invalid by the Court of Appeal in 2007—see The coup of 2000 and its repercussions); he was convicted in March 2011 and sentenced to life imprisonment.

Meanwhile, in early 2010 the human rights organization Amnesty International reiterated its concerns regarding the situation in Fiji, drawing attention to the continued use of intimidation and discrimination in the suppression of freedom of expression and to the constraints placed on the independence of the judiciary. In April, furthermore, proposals for the permanent imposition of stringent restrictions on the media provoked widespread criticism. The Media Industry Development Decree, which was to replace the emergency regulations implemented 12 months previously, would permit the authorities to enter news premises and seize any documentation, materials or equipment. The draft decree provided for hefty fines on media outlets found to have breached the regulations, while individual journalists, editors and publishers risked prison sentences in addition to substantial fines. Restrictions were also imposed on foreign ownership of the media. The decree was enacted in June, whereupon it was announced that within three months all media organizations should have at least 90% Fijian ownership or risk closure. It was feared that the country's principal daily newspaper, the Australian-owned *Fiji Times*, would therefore be forced to close. In September, however, ownership of the newspaper was sold to a Suva-based company.

The interim Deputy Prime Minister and Minister for Defence, National Security and Immigration, Ratu Epeli Ganilau, resigned from his post in November 2010, after disagreeing with a decision to deport an executive of the US-owned company Fiji Water (see Foreign Affairs).

In early March 2011, despite a renewed appeal by Amnesty International that the Government respect the right to protest, plans for an anti-Government demonstration were cancelled owing to the presence of large numbers of security personnel at the proposed venue for the rally. Amnesty International claimed that in the previous fortnight at least 10 politicians, trade unionists, critics of the Government and others had been arbitrarily arrested and subjected to severe physical assaults and other mistreatment by the Fiji military.

In May 2011 former army Chief of Staff Lt-Col Ratu Tevita Mara, son of the late former Prime Minister Ratu Sir Kamisese Mara, and former Commander of the Land Force Brig.-Gen. Pita Driti were charged with sedition and inciting mutiny after allegedly plotting to overthrow Bainimarama. Both men adamantly refuted the claims against them, insisting that the charges had been fabricated by the regime. Lt-Col Mara fled to Tonga a few days later, precipitating a diplomatic dispute between the Fijian and Tongan Governments (see Foreign Affairs). In February 2012 Brig.-Gen. Driti pleaded not guilty to the charges against him at the High Court in Suva.

In June 2011 it was announced that a dedicated Ministry of Sugar was to be established in Lautoka, on the west coast of Viti Levu, as part of government efforts to reform and revitalize the industry. Bainimarama was to retain responsibility for the portfolio, while Manasa Vaniqi was appointed to the newly created role of Permanent Secretary for Sugar.

In October 2011 Daniel Urai Manufolau, the President of the FTUC, was arrested on his return to Fiji from Australia, where he had met with a number of officials, including Prime Minister Julia Gillard, to discuss his concerns about the Bainimarama regime; he was subsequently charged with inciting political violence, having allegedly plotted to overthrow the interim Government. Urai, who staunchly denied the charges against him as a politically motivated fabrication, was released on bail in November. Urai appeared in court in July 2013 when the Director of Public Prosecutions applied to have the charges against him consolidated with those against the New Zealand businessman Jagnath Karunaratne, who was accused of writing anti-Government graffiti in Suva in August 2012. The cases against both defendants remained pending in early 2014. New charges against Urai and five other trade union members, of taking part in a strike at the Sheraton Hotel on 31 January 2013, were withdrawn in February 2014, following protests by international trade unionists. In November 2011 the interim Government implemented the Essential National Industries Employment Decree, which prohibited trade unions from operating in selected industries, including the national airline, four major banks, broadcasting and telecommunications, and utilities.

In September 2011 Bainimarama offered assurances that a new constitution would be drafted between September 2012 and September 2013, and pledged that the charter would establish a fully representative government based on an electoral system guaranteeing equal suffrage. The interim Prime Minister also announced that preparatory work was to commence in January 2012 on compiling an electronic register of voters for legislative elections scheduled to take place in 2014.

In July 2012 former Prime Minister Qarase was found guilty of abuse of office and discharge of duty—charges first brought against him in 2008 (see The coup of 2006 and abrogation of the Constitution)—and was sentenced to one year in prison in August; he was released in April 2013, having served eight months of his sentence.

Recent developments: the Public Order Act and new Constitution

The Public Emergency Decree in place since 2009 was rescinded in January 2012, in a development that was widely welcomed both within Fiji and further afield. However, hopes that the announcement might constitute an important development towards the restoration of democracy and augur an improvement in basic freedoms and human rights were dashed shortly afterwards, when the details of a new Public Order Act that had been introduced in place of the emergency regulations were revealed. The highly controversial new legislation stipulated, *inter alia*, that actions taken by the Prime Minister or senior police officers could not be legally challenged; afforded the police new, wide-ranging powers, including the right to use force to disperse gatherings deemed to constitute a threat to public safety; and imposed tighter controls on individuals suspected of breaking the law, as well as on the staging of meetings and other public gatherings. Widely regarded as being more repressive than the emergency decree that it replaced, the Public Order Act provoked expressions of concern and disappointment from prominent figures within Fiji and the international community.

In early March 2012 Bainimarama outlined plans for the preparation of the new constitution: following a civic education programme and public consultations, a five-member Constitutional Commission would submit a draft charter for the consideration of a Constituent Assembly, consisting of representatives of civil society groups, faith-based organizations, national institutions, political parties and the Government. Bainimarama announced in mid-March that President Nailatikau had approved a decree formally abolishing the Great Council of Chiefs (established by the British in 1876 as the Native Council) on the grounds that it had become highly politicized and 'perpetuated élitism'. However, the FLP criticized the move, asserting that the dissolution of the Council was a matter for indigenous Fijians to decide, while others accused the interim Government of seeking to curb potential dissent prior to negotiations on the new constitution. Nailatikau was reappointed to serve a further three-year presidential term on 12 November under an executive decree issued by the interim Government. Also in November Kenyan constitutional expert Prof. Yash Ghai, the Chairman of the Constitutional Commission, which had been established in April and sworn in by the Chief Justice in July, claimed that the body had suffered harassment at the hands of the Government. The following month a draft constitution was submitted to President Nailatikau; however, the Constituent Assembly, which was to review the document in January–February 2013, had not yet been established and no public consultations had taken place (as originally planned) prior to the submission of the draft. Furthermore, in a worrying development, Prof. Ghai alleged that the day after the draft constitution had been presented to Nailatikau the police confiscated all 600 printed copies of the document that were due to be distributed to the public, claiming that their production was illegal; the Constitutional Commission subsequently published the draft charter on the internet.

In January 2013 Bainimarama announced that the draft constitution was to be amended by the Office of the Attorney-General prior to being submitted to the Constituent Assembly. In the same month the Government approved a decree requiring all 17 existing political parties to re-register by 14 February to contest the next legislative elections. An increase in the membership threshold to become registered as a political party from 180 members to 5,000 was regarded as a significant bar both to existing and new parties, notably prompting the dissolution of the UPP in late January, while the SDL was renamed the Social Democratic Liberal Party (SODELPA) to conform with another new stipulation, that political parties have English rather than Fijian names. A further condition of registration was a ban on membership for civil servants, the armed forces and trade union officials. In mid-March the interim Prime Minister declared that the revised draft constitution had been completed, but that the formation of the Constituent Assembly had been delayed owing to difficulties in the registration of political parties (which were to be represented in the Assembly). On 21 March Bainimarama announced that the plan to form a Constituent Assembly had been abandoned. Instead, the draft constitution produced by the Office of the Attorney-General was released immediately for public consultation. In early May Registrar Mohammed Saneem announced that three political parties had been successful in applying for re-registration—the NFP, the FLP and SODELPA. In addition, at the end of the month a new party, the People's Democratic Party, which was supported by the FTUC and headed by former cabinet minister Adi Sivia Qoro, was officially registered and recognized. In June an appeals court confirmed that Qarase was disqualified from leading SODELPA as a result of his former conviction.

The final version of the new Constitution, which stipulated that the next parliamentary elections be held by 30 September 2014, was published on 23 August 2013. The charter provided for a unicameral Parliament, composed of 50 members elected by proportional representation for a four-year term, and a President appointed by Parliament for a three-year term (renewable only once). It also granted immunity from criminal prosecution to all those who since the 2006 coup had either held office as President, Prime Minister or government minister or who had served in the military forces, the police, the corrections service, the judiciary or the public service. On 23 August Bainimarama announced his intention to establish a new political party to contest the 2014 legislative elections. Having been approved by President Nailatikau, the new Constitution entered into force on 6 September 2013. The new charter was criticized by the international non-governmental organization Human Rights Watch for the restrictions that it placed on basic human rights, including freedom of expression, workers' rights, and freedom of assembly and association. It also attracted widespread opprobrium for its provision of full and irrevocable immunity to those who had been involved in the 2006 coup. In early March 2014 Bainimarama resigned from his post as Commander of the Armed Forces in order, as a civilian, to be able to contest the forthcoming legislative elections. Later that month the Government announced that the elections were to be held on 17 September.

Land Ownership Issues

In September 1995 the Government decided to transfer all state land (comprising some 10% of Fiji's total land area), hitherto administered by the Government Lands Department, to the Native Land Trust Board (NLTB) in order to allow the allocation of land to indigenous Fijians on the basis of native custom. However, concern among Fijian Indians increased following reports in early 1996 that many would not be able to renew their land leases (most of which were due to expire between 1997 and 2024) under the 1976 Agricultural Landlord and Tenant Act (ALTA). The reports were strongly denied by the Government, despite statements by several Fijian land-owning clans that Indians' leases would not be renewed. Moreover, a recently formed sugar-cane growers' association solely for ethnic Fijians, the Taukei Cane Growers' Association, announced its intention to campaign for ethnic Fijian control of the sugar industry, largely by refusing to renew land leases to ethnic Indians (who held some 85% of sugar farm leases). By the end of 2000 almost 2,000 land leases had expired, leaving many tenant farmers and their families homeless. Some 70 farmers, who had expressed a wish not to be resettled, received rehabilitation grants of $F28,000 in December 2000, although the authorities were criticized for their apparent slowness in processing the applications. In January 2001 the Government proposed that the administration of native land leases be transferred from the ALTA to the Native Land Trust Act (NLTA), prompting fears of increased bias in favour of ethnic Fijian landowners and further instability in the sugar industry. A further 1,500 leases expired during 2001.

A dispute between tribal landowners and the Government over compensation payments for land flooded by the Monosavu hydroelectric power station led to violence in July 1998. Landowners, who had been demanding compensation since the plant's construction in 1983, seized control of the station and carried out a series of arson attacks. The dispute finally ended in October 2005 when landowners were paid a total of $A40m. in compensation for the use of their land by the Fiji Electricity Authority.

Meanwhile, the issue of the expiry of land leases continued to threaten Fiji's vital sugar industry. A committee, comprising members of both the SDL and FLP, was established to try to negotiate land leases that would satisfy both Indian Fijian tenants and their predominantly ethnic Fijian landowners. Most of the 30-year leases drawn up under the ALTA were expiring, and both tenants and the FLP were opposed to its replacement by the NLTA, which they saw as disproportionately favouring landowners. Two parliamentary bills had been approved by the Senate in April 2002, reducing the land under state control to around 1% of the total and increasing the amount under the NLTB to over 90%. In August, however, the FLP withdrew from a second session of discussions on the issue of land leases. During 2003 more than 1,100 tenants on Vanua Levu were evicted following the expiry of their land leases. By late 2005 more than 3,500 farmers had received a total of $F26m. in assistance under the ALTA. In May 2009 the Fiji Independent Commission Against Corruption began an investigation into the NLTB's lease renewal procedures. In July 2010 the Government approved a new land reform programme; under the Land Use Decree, the ALTA was to be revoked and all leases of native land would thenceforth come under the legal framework of the NLTA. In addition, the tenure of indigenous land was to be extended from 30 years to up to 99 years.

Foreign Affairs

Relations between Fiji and India deteriorated as a result of the coup of May 1987, following which many ethnic Indians emigrated. In November 1989 the Fijian Government expelled the Indian ambassador for allegedly interfering in Fiji's internal affairs, and the status of the Indian embassy was downgraded to that of a consulate. Meanwhile, in January of that year statistical information, released by the interim Government, indicated that the islands' ethnic Fijians were in a majority for the first time since 1946. Following the adoption of significant constitutional reforms in 1997, diplomatic relations between Fiji and India improved considerably, and in October the Indian Government invited Fiji to open a High Commission in New Delhi. In February 1999 India removed its trade embargo against Fiji (which had been in force for 10 years), and in May India reopened its High Commission in Suva.

However, Fiji's relations with the international community suffered a major reversal following the coup of May 2000, which was condemned by the UN, the Commonwealth, India, the United Kingdom, Australia, New Zealand and several other nations in the region. In June Fiji was partially suspended from the Commonwealth (having been readmitted in October 1997 following its expulsion as a result of the coups of 1987) and a delegation from the organization visited the islands to demand the reinstatement of the 1997 Constitution. Australia, New Zealand and the Commonwealth withheld formal recognition of Qarase's Government when Parliament opened in October 2001, but in December the Commonwealth Ministerial Action Group recommended that Fiji be readmitted to meetings of the Commonwealth. In November 2002 Qarase's Government confirmed its intention to reopen the Fijian High Commission in India, claiming that it was needed to cater for the new business and diplomatic links being fostered by the administration. (The mission was reopened in April 2004.) Sanctions imposed by the EU remained in place until early 2002. In late 2003 the EU announced the resumption of development aid to Fiji (in abeyance since 2000). The EU suspended non-humanitarian aid after the coup of December 2006, which, once again, provoked widespread condemnation from the international community. Australia and New Zealand imposed a number of diplomatic sanctions against Fiji, placed travel restrictions on key military and government officials, and reduced aid, whereas India adopted the policy of engaging with the interim Government rather than isolating it. Fiji was once again partially suspended from the Commonwealth in December 2006, and, as a result of the Government's lack of progress in restoring democracy, fully suspended in September 2009, a decision that entailed the severance of all Commonwealth aid. In December 2010, nevertheless, the EU concluded an Interim Economic Partnership Agreement with Fiji.

In 1975 Fiji was the first Pacific island state to establish diplomatic relations with the People's Republic of China. In April 2006 Premier Wen Jiabao of China made an official visit to Fiji in order to promote greater co-operation between the two countries. China's financial support to Fiji, in the form of aid and infrastructure development, was reported to have increased substantially between 2006 and 2009, and China was one of the few nations to maintain such support following the abrogation of Fiji's Constitution in April 2009. Relations between Fiji and China continued to strengthen, with both countries pledging further to bolster bilateral dialogue and co-operation in a wide range of fields, including political and economic engagement. In July–August 2010 Bainimarama visited China, declaring his preference for close relations with that country, rather than with Australia and New Zealand. In September President Nailatikau paid an official visit to China, and in November Bainimarama returned there, at the head of a trade mission. In September 2012, during a visit to Fiji by Wu Bangguo, the Chairman of the Standing Committee of the Chinese National People's Congress, the two countries signed a further three economic agreements, including a US $114m. loan from China towards road construction in Fiji. Military ties between Fiji and China were further strengthened in November 2013 following a five-day visit to China by a high-ranking Fijian defence delegation headed by the Minister for Defence, National Security and Immigration, Joketani Cokanasiga, who held talks with his Chinese counterpart.

In March 2007 the Pacific Islands Forum Foreign Ministers convened to consider the conclusions of an 'eminent persons' group', which had travelled to Fiji to assess the situation following the coup of December 2006. In addition to its criticism of alleged breaches of human rights, the group had decided that a swift return to democracy was desirable; as a consequence, the Pacific Islands Forum stressed the need for a revised timetable for elections. In August 2008 the interim Prime Minister asserted that the existing schedule for elections in March 2009 was not attainable in view of the need for electoral reforms; Bainimarama subsequently failed to attend a summit meeting of Pacific Islands Forum leaders. Following President Iloilo's abrogation of the Constitution in April 2009 (see Domestic Political Affairs), the Pacific Islands Forum set Bainimarama a deadline of 1 May to announce a date for the holding of democratic elections later that year; failure to comply led to Fiji's indefinite suspension from the Forum. In February 2011 the Pacific Islands Forum Foreign Ministers met in Vanuatu, to discuss the situation in Fiji: the Fijian Minister for Foreign Affairs attended the meeting, which concluded that there had not been enough progress towards the restoration of democracy in Fiji for the contact group to recommend that the Forum change its policy on Fiji's membership. In August 2012, despite acknowledging that some advances had been made in the democratic process in Fiji, the Forum again decided to uphold the country's suspension from the organization. Claiming that the Pacific Islands Forum failed adequately to address the needs of the island peoples, Bainimarama established an alternative body (notably excluding Australia and New Zealand), the Pacific Islands Development Forum, which held its inaugural summit meeting in Nadi, Fiji, in early August 2013. The meeting, which focused on the environment and sustainable economic development, was attended by the political heads of 14 Pacific island states.

Fiji's formerly amicable relations with Australia and New Zealand have been rather turbulent since the coup of December 2006, with the latter two countries being among the harshest critics of Bainimarama's regime (particularly following the abrogation of the Constitution in April 2009). Between 2007 and 2010 a series of reciprocal diplomatic expulsions took place, usually precipitated by Fijian accusations of Australian or New Zealand interference in the country's internal affairs. Nevertheless, in January 2009, and again in January 2012, after heavy rains resulted in widespread flooding and a number of deaths in Fiji,

New Zealand and Australia were among several nations to offer immediate aid to the emergency relief effort, via non-governmental agencies. Following talks held in Sydney, Australia, in July 2012 between the Fijian Minister for Foreign Affairs, Ratu Inoke Kubuabola, and his Australian and New Zealand counterparts, during which the Fijian official reported on the progress being made towards the holding of democratic elections in 2014 and the drawing up of a new constitution, Australia and New Zealand agreed to restore full diplomatic relations with Fiji (including the exchange of high commissioners) and to be more flexible with travel sanctions.

In July 2010 a regional organization, the Melanesian Spearhead Group, cancelled a planned meeting at which Bainimarama had been due to assume the rotating chairmanship of the Group: the previous chairman, Edward Natapei, the Prime Minister of Vanuatu, stated that allowing Bainimarama to take the chair would not be in accordance with the organization's democratic ideals. In December, after Natapei had been replaced as Prime Minister of Vanuatu, Bainimarama was permitted to assume the chair of the Melanesian Spearhead Group; the Group's annual summit meeting was convened in Suva in April 2011. In January of that year Fiji held discussions with Kiribati aimed at improving the two countries' economic co-operation, in accordance with an agreement signed in September 2010. A similar agreement had been signed with Tuvalu earlier in 2010. In early 2013 there were reports that, in order to ensure food security for the country, the authorities of Kiribati were considering the purchase of land on the Fijian island of Vanua Levu, which could also potentially be settled by I-Kiribati in the event that rising sea levels forced them to leave their homeland. During a visit to Kiribati in February 2014, President Nailatikau stated that residents of Kiribati would be welcome to relocate to Fiji in the event of their islands being permanently flooded as a result of climate change

In November 2005 Fiji lodged a complaint with the International Seabed Authority concerning Tonga's sovereignty claims over the uninhabited Teleki (Minerva) Reefs. (Tonga's sovereignty proclamation was made by the Tongan King in June 1972 and was recognized by the South Pacific Forum in September.) Fiji submitted its complaint to UN officials for mediation in February 2011, claiming that the reefs (which lie within the Fijian exclusive economic zone) cannot be recognized by the UN's Convention on the Law of the Sea since they do not represent permanent terrestrial islands. In June the navies of the two countries came close to direct confrontation when the Fijian military dismantled Tonga's navigational equipment on the reefs. Bilateral tensions were also exacerbated by claims made by Bainimarama in May that the Tongan navy had breached Fiji's sovereignty by assisting former army Chief of Staff Lt-Col Tevita Mara to flee from Fiji, where he had been charged with sedition and mutiny (see Domestic Political Affairs). Later in May the Tongan Government rejected a Fijian request for Lt-Col Mara's extradition. It was reported in June that Lt-Col Mara had initiated a campaign in Australia to oust the Bainimarama regime. An extradition request subsequently submitted to the Australian Government by Fiji was rejected in July.

Meanwhile, in March 2009 the US ambassador's exhortations to the interim Government to restore democratic rule led to Bainimarama accusing the diplomat of interfering in Fiji's domestic affairs. Although the US authorities continued to refuse officially to recognize Bainimarama's administration, in November 2010 the Fiji Government welcomed a decision by the USA to choose Fiji to host the office of the expanded US aid programme in the Pacific. However, in June 2011 the US Assistant Secretary of State for East Asia and Pacific Affairs, Kurt Campbell, expressed mounting unease about alleged human rights violations committed by the Bainimarama regime, stating that the US Administration was 'concerned' by the ongoing situation in Fiji.

In May 2013 Fiji hosted a summit meeting of the Group of 77 (G-77) developing countries, which was chaired by interim Prime Minister Bainimarama.

Fiji currently maintains diplomatic relations with more than 80 countries. During 2011 Bainimarama presided over the formal opening of three new diplomatic missions, in Indonesia, South Africa and Brazil. In mid-2012 the Fijian Government further expanded its diplomatic representation abroad by opening two more diplomatic missions, in the Republic of Korea (South Korea) and the United Arab Emirates, thereby bringing the total number of such missions to 17. Fiji was admitted as a member of the Non-aligned Movement (see p. 467) in May 2011.

CONSTITUTION AND GOVERNMENT

Prior to the coup of December 2006, Fiji had a parliamentary form of government with a bicameral legislature, comprising an elected 71-seat House of Representatives and an appointed Senate, with 32 members. The Constitution, which remained in place following the coup of 2006 but was revoked in April 2009, stated that 46 seats in the House were reserved on a racial basis (23 for ethnic Fijians, 19 for Indians, three for other races—General Electors—and one for Rotuma Islanders) and 25 seats were open to all races. The Senate was appointed by the President of the Republic, 14 members on the advice of the Great Council of Chiefs (a 52-member traditional body comprising every hereditary chief—Ratu—of a Fijian clan), nine on the advice of the Prime Minister, eight on the advice of the Leader of the Opposition and one on the advice of the Rotuma Island Council. In March 2012 the Great Council of Chiefs was abolished. A new Constitution, produced by the Office of the Attorney-General, which provided for a unicameral Parliament, composed of 50 members elected by proportional representation for a four-year term, and a President appointed by Parliament for a three-year term (renewable only once), entered into force on 6 September 2013, following approval by President Frank Bainimarama. The new Constitution stipulated that parliamentary elections be held by 30 September 2014; in March of that year the Government announced that the elections were to be conducted on 17 September.

REGIONAL AND INTERNATIONAL CO-OPERATION

Fiji is a member of the Asian Development Bank (ADB, see p. 207), the Pacific Community (see p. 412) and the Colombo Plan (see p. 449). The country was suspended from the Pacific Islands Forum (see p. 416) in 2009; Fiji hosted the inaugural summit meeting of a new regional organization, the Pacific Islands Development Forum, in August 2013. Fiji is a signatory of the South Pacific Regional Trade and Economic Co-operation Agreement (SPARTECA, see p. 417) and of the Lomé Conventions and successor Cotonou Agreement (see p. 324) with the European Union (EU). Fiji participates in the Melanesian Spearhead Group, which among other benefits provides for free trade among member countries (the others being Papua New Guinea, Solomon Islands and Vanuatu). The country is also a member of the UN's Economic and Social Commission for Asia and the Pacific (ESCAP, see p. 28).

Fiji became a member of the UN in 1970 and joined the World Trade Organization (WTO, see p. 434) in 1996. Fiji is also a member of the International Sugar Organization (see p. 447) and was admitted to the Non-aligned Movement (see p. 467) in May 2011.

ECONOMIC AFFAIRS

In 2012, according to estimates by the World Bank, Fiji's gross national income (GNI), measured at average 2010–12 prices, was US $3,675m., equivalent to $4,200 per head (or $4,880 on an international purchasing-power parity basis). During 2003–12, it was estimated, the population increased at an average annual rate of 0.8%, while gross domestic product (GDP) per head increased, in real terms, by an average of 0.4% per year. Overall GDP rose at an average annual rate of 1.2% over the same period. According to the Asian Development Bank (ADB), GDP increased by 1.7% in 2012 and by 3.6% in 2013.

In 2011 agriculture (including forestry and fishing) contributed an estimated 11.7% of GDP. According to figures from the ADB, at mid-2008 the sector engaged 1.3% of those in paid employment (excluding subsistence workers). The principal cash crop is sugar cane. According to FAO estimates, production of sugar cane increased by 2.7% in 2012, compared with the previous year. In 2012 sugar and molasses together accounted for an estimated 16.7% of domestic export earnings (excluding re-exports), compared with 40.0% in 1994. Other significant export crops are coconuts and ginger, while the most important subsistence crop is paddy rice, production of which was estimated at 10,000 metric tons in 2012. Since the mid-2000s honey production has become an increasingly significant activity. The most important livestock products are beef and poultry meat. Fiji has significant timber reserves. Lumber accounted for 6.6% of domestic exports in 2012, earning an estimated $F69.0m. Fishing is an important activity, and in 2012 fish earned an estimated $F57.8m. in export revenue (5.5% of domestic export receipts). The entire agricultural sector was disrupted by unusually severe flooding in January 2009, which resulted in major losses of crops and livestock; further severe flooding was experienced in northern and western Fiji in early 2012. Meanwhile, losses also resulted from the impact of cyclones in December 2009, March 2010 and December 2012. According to the World Bank, during 2003–11 growth in agricultural GDP was negligible. The GDP of the agricultural sector increased by 8.1% in 2011 and by 2.6% in 2012, according to the ADB.

Industry (including mining, manufacturing, construction and utilities) engaged 30.3% of the employed population at mid-2008. In 2011 the sector provided an estimated 21.5% of GDP. According to the World Bank, the GDP of the industrial sector was estimated to have increased at an average rate of 0.4% per year during 2003–11. Industrial GDP increased by 1.4% in 2011, according to the ADB.

Mining contributed an estimated 1.4% of GDP in 2011. The sector engaged only 1.0% of the employed population in 2004. Following the resumption of gold-mining operations in October 2007, the sector recorded a good recovery in 2008–10. Gold production decreased from 1,856 kg in 2010 to 1,622 kg in 2011, but totalled 1,653 kg in 2012. Silver and copper are also mined. Operations at the country's first bauxite mine, in Nawailevu, commenced in November 2011. According to the ADB, during 2005–11 the mining sector's GDP declined at an average rate of 5.3% per year. According to official figures, mining GDP increased by 22.0% in 2010 and by 8.5% in 2011.

Manufacturing contributed an estimated 15.0% of GDP in 2011, and engaged 13.6% of paid employees in 2004. The most important branch of the sector is food-processing, in particular sugar, molasses and coconut oil. The bottling of mineral water for export became increasingly important from the early 2000s, with production more than doubling between 2001 and 2005, and by 2010 exports of bottled water contributed 11.1% of domestic export earnings. The loss of preferential access to the US market for Fijian garments at the beginning of 2005 substantially reduced export receipts from this source. The contribution of garments to domestic export earnings decreased from 23.8% of total revenue in 2004 to an estimated 8.5% in 2012. According to figures from the World Bank, manufacturing GDP decreased at an estimated average annual rate of 0.2% during 2003–11. According to official figures, sectoral GDP increased by 2.3% in 2011.

Construction contributed an estimated 2.8% of GDP in 2011, and engaged 5.4% of paid employees in 2004. According to figures from the ADB, the sector's GDP decreased at an estimated average annual rate of 1.6% during 2005–11. According to official figures, construction GDP increased by 7.2% in 2010, but declined by an estimated 1.7% in 2011.

Energy is derived principally from hydroelectric power. Imports of mineral fuels represented an estimated 30.6% of the total cost of imports in 2012. A new wind farm was opened in 2007, as part of a plan for the country to become completely reliant on renewable energy sources.

The services sector engaged 68.4% of the employed population at mid-2008, and contributed an estimated 66.8% of GDP in 2011. Although intermittently affected by political unrest, tourism is a major source of foreign exchange. Although revenue from tourism increased from $F1,074.0m. in 2011 to an estimated $F1,303.4m. in 2012, over the same period visitor arrivals (excluding cruise-ship passengers) decreased from 675,050 to 660,590. Australia and New Zealand are the most important sources of visitors. According to figures from the World Bank, during 2003–11 the GDP of the services sector rose at an average annual rate of 1.5%. Sectoral GDP expanded by 1.6% in 2012, according to the ADB.

Fiji consistently records a visible merchandise trade deficit; it amounted to US $762.9m. in 2012, when the country also recorded a deficit, of US $55.9m., on the current account of the balance of payments. The principal source of imports in 2012 was Singapore (31.8%). Other important suppliers were Australia, New Zealand, the People's Republic of China and the USA. The principal market for exports in 2012 was Australia (15.1%). Other important markets included the USA, the United Kingdom, Japan and New Zealand. The principal imports in 2012 were mineral fuels, followed by machinery and transport equipment, food products, manufactured goods and chemicals. Fiji's principal domestic exports were gold, sugar, fish, garments and lumber. Fiji also re-exports mineral fuels (including bunkers for ships and aircraft).

The overall budget deficit was estimated by the ADB at $F136.3m. in 2012, equivalent to 3.5% of GDP. In 2013/14 official development assistance from Australia was projected at $A58.2m. Aid from New Zealand in 2012/13 was budgeted at $NZ4.0m. Fiji's general government gross debt was $F3,567m. in 2011, equivalent to 53.0% of GDP. Fiji's outstanding external debt totalled an estimated US $1,026m. at the end of 2013. In that year the cost of debt-servicing was equivalent to 1.0% of the revenue from exports of goods and services. The average annual rate of inflation, according to ILO figures, was 4.7% in 2003–12. According to the ADB, consumer prices rose by 2.9% in 2013. An estimated 8.6% of the total labour force were unemployed at mid-2008, according to the ADB. From the late 1980s remittances from Fijians working overseas assumed increasing importance, although in 2007–08 a substantial reduction in this source of income was recorded, partly owing to the decrease in the number of Fijian security personnel employed in the Middle East. Remittances from Fijian personnel serving in the British Army have become a significant source of income. The total value of remittances from overseas workers was US $305.8m. in 2012.

The impact on Fiji's economy of the removal of the elected Government in the military coup of December 2006 was subsequently compounded by the sharp deterioration in global economic conditions in 2008/09 and by the political instability of 2009. The Fiji dollar was devalued by 20% in April 2009. The European Union suspended financial aid to the sugar cane industry following the events of April 2009, and in August interim Prime Minister Frank (Voreqe) Bainimarama dissolved the Sugar Cane Growers' Council, reportedly claiming that it was attempting to influence national politics. As the country's sugar industry continued to contract in 2010–11, there were substantial job losses in the sector. However, tourism recorded a strong recovery in 2010 and 2011, when visitor numbers increased by 16.5% and 6.8%, respectively. Fiji suffered severe flooding in January and March–April 2012; the floods in January were reported to have killed 11 people, destroyed around 55% of export crops (mainly sugar cane) and caused some $F30.6m. worth of damage. In December the country was hit by another natural disaster when the most powerful cyclone to strike Fiji in 20 years, Cyclone Evan, resulted in damage costing around $F75m. The 2013 budget provided for an increase in the personal tax threshold in a bid to increase consumer spending, the establishment of a tax-free zone (from Korovou to Tavua) to boost investment in the agricultural sector, and the lowering of corporate taxes for foreign companies operating in Fiji. Expenditure focused on infrastructural development (particularly roads and bridges), the maintenance of law and order, poverty alleviation and social welfare, and the development of pre-school education. A total of $F11m. was also allocated to the Fiji Electoral Commission to help preparations for the 2014 legislative elections. Owing to the considerable increase in expenditure and the negative impact of Cyclone Evan, according to the ADB, the budget deficit in 2013 reached the equivalent of 2.8% of GDP, compared with 1.6% in 2012. The education sector was allocated the largest share of total expenditure (nearly 19%) in the 2014 budget, which was announced in November 2013 and which envisaged a decrease in the fiscal deficit to 1.9% of GDP. GDP rose by 1.9% in 2011, driven by robust post-cyclone recoveries in the agriculture and tourism sectors. Despite the adverse impact on the economy of the flooding and Cyclone Evan, particularly on agriculture and tourism (with visitor numbers falling by 2.1%), overall GDP growth was 1.7% in 2012. The rate of growth accelerated to 3.6% in 2013, partly as a result of increased public expenditure on infrastructure and higher levels of consumption and investment demand (buoyed by rising investor confidence as the plans to hold elections progressed). The ADB forecast that GDP growth would moderate to 2.8% in 2014. Economic prospects for that year were expected to be largely influenced by the outcome of the general election in September; the installation of a democratically elected government would act as a major boost for renewed business confidence (both domestic and international).

PUBLIC HOLIDAYS

2015: 1 January (New Year's Day), 2 January*† (Birth of the Prophet Muhammad), 3–6 April (Easter), 10 October (Fiji Day), 11 November (Deepavali), 23 December*† (Birth of the Prophet Muhammad), 25–26 December (Christmas).

* This Islamic holiday is dependent on the lunar calendar and may vary by one or two days from the date given.

† This holiday occurs twice in 2015.

Statistical Survey

Sources (unless otherwise stated): Bureau of Statistics, POB 2221, Government Bldgs, Suva; tel. 3315144; fax 3303656; internet www.statsfiji.gov.fj; Reserve Bank of Fiji, POB 1220, Suva; tel. 3313611; fax 3301688; e-mail info@rbf.gov.fj; internet www.reservebank.gov.fj.

AREA AND POPULATION

Area (incl. the Rotuma group): 18,376 sq km (7,095 sq miles). Land area of 18,333 sq km (7,078 sq miles) consists mainly of the islands of Viti Levu (10,429 sq km—4,027 sq miles) and Vanua Levu (5,556 sq km—2,145 sq miles).

Population: 775,077 at census of 25 August 1996; 837,271 (males 427,176, females 410,095) at census of 16 September 2007; *Mid-2014* (Secretariat of the Pacific Community estimate): 863,966 (Source: Pacific Regional Information System).

Density (at mid-2014): 47.0 per sq km.

Population by Age and Sex (Secretariat of the Pacific Community estimates at mid-2014): *0–14:* 242,272 (males 125,223, females 117,049); *15–64:* 576,603 (males 294,974, females 281,629); *65 and over:* 45,091 (males 20,260, females 24,831); *Total* 863,966 (males 440,457, females 423,509). Source: Pacific Regional Information System.

Principal Towns (population at 2007 census): Suva (capital) 74,481; Lautoka 43,473; Nadi 11,685; Lami 10,752; Labasa 7,706; Ba 6,826.

Ethnic Groups (2007 census): Fijians 475,739; Indians 313,798; Rotuman 10,771; Chinese 4,704; European 2,953; Others 29,306; Total 837,271.

Births, Marriages and Deaths (registrations, 2009 unless otherwise indicated): Live births 18,854 (birth rate 21.4 per 1,000); Marriages 7,443 in 2005 (marriage rate 8.8 per 1,000); Deaths 3,921 (death rate 4.8 per 1,000). *2011:* Live births 20,425 (birth rate 22.7 per 1,000). Source: partly UN, *Population and Vital Statistics Report*.

Life Expectancy (years at birth): 69.6 (males 66.7; females 72.6) in 2011. Source: World Bank, World Development Indicators database.

Economically Active Population (paid employment, persons aged 15 years and over, 2004): Agriculture, hunting, forestry and fishing 89,523; Mining and quarrying 3,222; Manufacturing 43,088; Electricity, gas and water 2,508; Construction 16,950; Trade, restaurants and hotels 66,043; Transport, storage and communications 22,551; Financing, insurance, real estate and business services 10,220; Community, social and personal services 61,936; *Total employed* 316,041. *Mid-2008* (paid employment, '000 persons, unless otherwise indicated): Agriculture 1.7; Industry 39.5; Services 89.1; Total employed 130.3; Unemployed 28.3; Total labour force (incl. subsistence workers) 329.8. Source: partly Asian Development Bank.

HEALTH AND WELFARE

Key Indicators

Total Fertility Rate (children per woman, 2011): 2.6.

Under-5 Mortality Rate (per 1,000 live births, 2011): 16.

HIV/AIDS (% of persons aged 15–49, 2012): 0.2.

Physicians (per 1,000 head, 2009): 0.4.

Hospital Beds (per 1,000 head, 2009): 2.1.

Health Expenditure (2010): US $ per head (PPP): 194.

Health Expenditure (2010): % of GDP: 4.2.

Health Expenditure (2010): public (% of total): 70.2.

Access to Water (% of persons, 2011): 96.

Access to Sanitation (% of persons, 2011): 87.

Total Carbon Dioxide Emissions ('000 metric tons, 2010): 1,290.8.

Carbon Dioxide Emissions Per Head (metric tons, 2010): 1.5.

Human Development Index (2012): ranking: 96.

Human Development Index (2012): value: 0.702.

For sources and definitions, see explanatory note on p. vi.

AGRICULTURE, ETC.

Principal Crops ('000 metric tons, 2012, FAO estimates): Sugar cane 1,620; Coconuts 210.0; Rice, paddy 8.0 Cassava 70.0; Sweet potatoes 8.8; Yams 2.5; Taro 67.5; Aubergines (Eggplants) 3.4; Bananas 3.2; Pineapples 3.3; Ginger 2.4.

Livestock ('000 head, year ending 2012, FAO estimates): Cattle 310; Pigs 146; Sheep 6; Goats 251; Horses 46; Chickens 4,850; Ducks 90; Turkeys 75.

Livestock Products (metric tons, 2012, FAO estimates): Poultry meat 16,057; Cattle meat 7,600; Goat meat 205; Pig meat 4,005; Hen eggs 6,000; Cows' milk 62,000; Honey 335.

Forestry ('000 cu m, 2012, FAO estimates): *Roundwood Removals* (excl. bark): Sawlogs and veneer logs 233; Pulpwood 206; Other industrial wood 6; Fuel wood 37; Total 482. *Sawnwood Production* (incl. sleepers): 90.

Fishing ('000 metric tons, live weight, 2011): Capture 41.2 (FAO estimate) (Albacore 8.1; Yellowfin tuna 2.5; Other marine fishes 20.0 (FAO estimate); Crustaceans 0.3; Molluscs 2.5); Aquaculture 0.2; *Total catch* 41.4 (FAO estimate).

Source: FAO.

MINING

Production (kg, 2012): Gold 1,653; Silver 300 (Source: US Geological Survey).

INDUSTRY

Production (metric tons, 2011, unless otherwise indicated): Sugar 166,000; Molasses 107,000; Coconut oil 4,765; Flour 98,471; Soap 2,594; Cement 170,000; Paint ('000 litres) 4,014; Beer ('000 litres) 23,000; Soft drinks ('000 litres) 152,688; Cigarettes 457; Matches ('000 gross boxes) 99; Electric energy (million kWh) 872; Ice cream ('000 litres) 2,590; Toilet paper ('000 rolls) 18,650.

FINANCE

Currency and Exchange Rates: 100 cents = 1 Fiji dollar ($F). *Sterling, US Dollar and Euro Equivalents* (31 December 2013): £1 sterling = $F3.125; US $1 = $F1.898; €1 = $F2.617; $F100 = £32.00 = US $52.69 = €38.21. *Average Exchange Rate* ($F per US $): 1.7932 in 2011; 1.7899 in 2012; 1.9183 in 2013.

General Budget ($F million, 2012): *Revenue:* Current revenue 1,846.0 (Taxes 1,682.6, Non-taxes 163.4); Capital revenue 36.4; Grants 18.0; Total 1,900.4. *Expenditure:* General public services 247.9; Defence 100.1; Education 214.9; Health 130.3; Social security and welfare 6.1; Housing and community amenities 13.0; Economic services 124.7 (Agriculture 24.0; Industry 28.0; Transport, communications and other services 72.7); Total (incl. others) 2,018.3 (Current 1,463.9, Capital 553.3, Net lending 1.0). Source: Asian Development Bank.

International Reserves (US $ million at 31 December 2012): Gold (valued at market-related prices) 1.39; IMF special drawing rights 78.51; Reserve position in IMF 25.30; Foreign exchange 816.16; *Total* 921.36. Source: IMF, *International Financial Statistics*.

Money Supply ($F million at 31 December 2012): Currency outside depository corporations 436.9; Transferable deposits 1,660.9; Other deposits 2,529.1; Securities other than shares 182.9; *Broad money* 4,809.8. Source: IMF, *International Financial Statistics*.

Cost of Living (Consumer Price Index; base: January 2008 = 100): All items 107.0 in 2010; 114.8 in 2011; 118.7 in 2012.

Expenditure on the Gross Domestic Product ($F million at current prices, 2011, preliminary): Government final consumption expenditure 908.1; Private final consumption expenditure 4,492.0; Increase in stocks 206.0; Gross fixed capital formation 1,324.0; *Total domestic expenditure* 6,930.1; Exports of goods and services 3,994.0; *Less* Imports of goods and services 4,193.0; *GDP in purchasers' values* 6,731.0. Source: Asian Development Bank.

Gross Domestic Product by Economic Activity ($F million at current prices, 2011): Agriculture, forestry and fishing 631.9; Mining and quarrying 77.9; Manufacturing 806.6; Electricity, gas and water 121.2; Construction 151.4; Wholesale and retail trade, hotels and restaurants 1,028.4; Transport and communications 683.8; Finance, real estate, etc. 881.1; Public administration and defence 304.3; Education 239.6; Health and social work 94.3; Other community, social and personal service activities 364.8; *Sub-total* 5,385.3; Indirect taxes, less subsidies 1,153.5; *GDP in purchasers' values* 6,538.8.

Balance of Payments (US $ million, 2012): Exports of goods f.o.b. 1,213.3; Imports of goods f.o.b. –1,976.2; *Balance on goods* –762.9; Exports of services 1,221.7; Imports of services –574.8; *Balance on goods and services* –115.9; Primary income received 75.4; Primary income paid –226.9; *Balance on goods, services and income* –267.5; Current transfers received 277.3; Current transfers paid –65.7; *Current balance* –55.9; Capital account (net) 4.0; Direct investment assets –1.6; Direct investment liabilities 267.1; Other investment assets −82.5; Other investment liabilities 92.7; Net errors and omissions −122.7; *Reserves and related items* 101.1 (Source: IMF, *International Financial Statistics*).

EXTERNAL TRADE

Principal Commodities ($F million, 2012, provisional): *Imports c.i.f.* Food products 738.3; Mineral fuels 1,232.4; Chemicals 330.2; Manufactured goods 508.0; Machinery and transport equipment 764.2; Miscellaneous manufactured articles 306.3; Total (incl. others) 4,034.0. *Exports f.o.b.:* Fish 57.8; Sugar 174.6; Garments 88.8; Lumber 69.0; Gold 136.9; Total (incl. others) 1,045.1 (excl. re-exports 1,146.3).

Principal Trading Partners ($F million, 2012, provisional): *Imports c.i.f.:* Australia 738.1; China, People's Republic 355.5; Hong Kong 82.9; India 70.3; Japan 89.8; New Zealand 559.0; Singapore 1,284.0; Taiwan 54.9; USA 122.4; Total (incl. others) 4,034.0. *Exports (incl. re-exports):* Australia 330.6; China, People's Republic 29.0; Hong Kong 29.9; Japan 129.3; New Zealand 99.3; Taiwan 31.4; United Kingdom 182.1; USA 267.0; Total (incl. others) 2,191.4.

TRANSPORT

Road Traffic (motor vehicles registered at 31 December 2011): Private cars 89,756; Goods vehicles 45,556; Buses 2,388; Taxis 6,066; Rental vehicles 7,603; Motorcycles 5,165; Tractors 6,157; Total (incl. others) 171,157.

Shipping: *Flag Registered Fleet* (at 31 December 2013): Vessels 30; Total displacement (grt) 28,417 (Source: Lloyd's List Intelligence—www.lloydslistintelligence.com). *International Freight Traffic* ('000 metric tons, 1990): Goods loaded 568; Goods unloaded 625 (Source: UN, *Monthly Bulletin of Statistics*).

Civil Aviation (traffic on scheduled services, 2011): Kilometres flown 21 million; Passengers carried 1,276,205; Passenger-km 3,895 million; Total ton-km 404.0 million. Source: UN, *Statistical Yearbook*.

TOURISM

Foreign Visitors by Country of Residence (excluding cruise-ship passengers, 2012): Australia 337,291; Canada 13,426; New Zealand 106,122; Pacific Islands 38,886; United Kingdom 17,076; USA 56,478; Total (incl. others) 660,590.

Tourism Receipts ($F million): 976.7 in 2010; 1,074.0 in 2011; 1,303.4 in 2012 (provisional).

COMMUNICATIONS MEDIA

Telephones (2012): 88,417 main lines in use.

Mobile Cellular Telephones (2012): 858,809 subscribers.

Internet Subscribers (2011): 39,900.

Broadband Subscribers (at 30 December 2012): 13,516.

Source: International Telecommunication Union.

EDUCATION

(at 31 May 2009 unless otherwise indicated)

Pre-Primary: 451 schools (2003); 264 teachers (2002); 7,076 pupils (2002).

Primary: 721 schools; 5,173 teachers; 129,444 pupils.

General Secondary: 172 schools; 4,273 teachers; 67,072 pupils.

Vocational and Technical: 69 institutions; 391 teachers; 2,387 students.

Teacher Training: 4 institutions; 88 teachers; 633 students.

Medical (1989): 2 institutions; 493 students.

University (2004): 1 institution; 289 teachers; 16,444 students.

Pupil-teacher Ratio (primary education, UNESCO estimate): 30.8 in 2010/11.

Adult Literacy Rate (UN estimates, 1995–99): 92.9% (males 94.5%; females 91.4%). Source: UN Development Programme, *Human Development Report*.

Directory

The Government

HEAD OF STATE

President: Ratu EPELI NAILATIKAU (appointed Acting President 30 July 2009; inaugurated as President 5 Nov. 2009; reappointed 12 Nov. 2012).

CABINET

(April 2014)

Prime Minister, Minister for Finance, Strategic Planning and National Development and Statistics, Public Service, People's Charter for Change and Progress, Information, Provincial Development, iTaukei, Multi-Ethnic Affairs, Sugar, and Lands and Mineral Resources: Cdre FRANK (VOREQE) BAINIMARAMA.

Attorney-General, Minister for Justice, Anti-Corruption, Public Enterprises, Communications, Civil Aviation, Tourism, Industry and Trade and Acting Minister for Local Government, Urban Development, Housing and Environment: AIYAZ SAYED-KHAIYUM.

Minister for Foreign Affairs and International Co-operation: Ratu INOKE KUBUABOLA.

Minister for Health: Dr NEIL SHARMA.

Minister for Women, Social Welfare and Poverty Alleviation: Dr JIKO LUVENI.

Minister for Education, National Heritage, Culture and Arts: FILIPE BOLE.

Minister for Labour, Industrial Relations and Employment: JONE USUMATE.

Minister for Agriculture, Fisheries and Forests and Minister for Rural and Maritime Development and National Disaster Management: Lt-Col INIA BATITOKO SERUIRATU.

Minister for Public Utilities (Water and Energy), Works and Transport: TIMOCI LESI NATUVA.

Minister for Defence, National Security and Immigration: JOKETANI COKANASIGA.

Minister for Youth and Sports: Commdr VILIAME NAUPOTO.

MINISTRIES

Office of the President: Government House, Berkley Cres., Government Bldgs, POB 2513, Suva; tel. 3314244; fax 3301645.

Office of the Prime Minister: Government Bldgs, POB 2353, Suva; tel. 3211201; fax 3306034; e-mail pmsoffice@connect.com.fj; internet www.pmoffice.gov.fj.

Office of the Attorney-General: Government Bldgs, Victoria Parade, POB 2213, Suva; tel. 3309866; fax 3305421; internet www.ag.gov.fj.

Ministry of Defence, National Security and Immigration: Government Bldgs, POB 2349, Suva; tel. 3211401; fax 3300346; e-mail infohomaff@govnet.gov.fj.

Ministry of Education, National Heritage, Culture and Arts: Marela House, Thurston St, PMB, Suva; tel. 3314477; fax 3303511; internet www.education.gov.fj.

Ministry of Finance, Strategic Planning and National Development and Statistics: Government Bldgs, POB 2212, Suva; tel. 3307011; fax 3300834; e-mail psfinance@govnet.gov.fj.

Ministry of Foreign Affairs and International Co-operation: Government Bldgs, POB 2220, Suva; tel. 3309631; fax 3301741; e-mail info@foreignaffairs.gov.fj; internet www.foreignaffairs.gov.fj.

Ministry of Health: Government Bldgs, POB 2223, Suva; tel. 3306177; fax 3306163; e-mail info@health.gov.fj; internet www.health.gov.fj.

Ministry of Industry and Trade: Government Bldgs, POB 2118, Suva; tel. 3305411; fax 3302617; internet www.commerce.gov.fj.

Ministry of Information, National Archives and Library Services: Government Bldgs, POB 2225, Suva; tel. 3301806; fax 3305139; e-mail info@fiji.gov.fj; internet www.info.gov.fj.

Ministry of Lands and Mineral Resources: Government Bldgs, POB 2222, Suva; tel. 3313555; fax 3302730; e-mail lis@lands.gov.fj; internet www.lands.gov.fj.

Ministry of Local Government, Urban Development, Housing and Environment: Government Bldgs, POB 2131, Suva; tel. 3304364; fax 3303515; e-mail msovaki@govnet.gov.fj.

Ministry of Primary Industries: Government Bldgs, POB 2218, Suva; tel. 3301611; fax 3301595.

Ministry of Provincial Development, iTaukei Affairs and Multi-Ethnic Affairs: Government Bldgs, POB 2100, Suva; tel. 3311774; fax 3314717; e-mail tvolau@govnet.gov.fj.

Ministry of Public Enterprises: Government Bldgs, POB 2278, Suva; tel. 3315577; fax 3315035; internet www.fiji.gov.fj.

Ministry of Public Utilities (Water and Energy), Works and Transport: Government Bldgs, POB 2493, Suva; tel. 3384111; fax 3383198.

Ministry of Rural and Maritime Development and National Disaster Management: Government Bldgs, POB 2219, Suva; tel. 3313400; fax 3313035.

Ministry of Tourism: Suva; tel. 3315577; fax 3315035; e-mail joyce.qaqalailai@govnet.gov.fj.

Ministry of Women, Social Welfare and Poverty Alleviation: POB 14068, Suva; tel. 3312681; fax 3312357.

Legislature

Note: Parliament was dissolved on 6 December 2006, following the military coup of the previous day. The 2013 Constitution provided for a single-chamber Parliament, comprising 50 members elected by proportional representation for a four-year term. In March 2014 the Government announced that legislative elections were to take place on 17 September.

PARLIAMENT

Senate

The Senate was also known as the House of Review. The upper chamber comprised 32 appointed members.

House of Representatives

The lower chamber comprised 71 elected members: 23 representing ethnic Fijians, 19 representing ethnic Indians, three representing other races (General Electors), one for Rotuma Islanders and 25 seats open to all races.

General Election, 6–13 May 2006

	Communal Seats				
	Fijian	Indian	Other*	Open Seats	Total Seats
Fiji United Party (SDL)†	23	—	—	13	36
Fiji Labour Party (FLP)	—	19	—	12	31
United People's Party (UPP)‡	—	—	2	—	2
Independents	—	—	2	—	2
Total	23	19	4	25	71

* One Rotuman and three General Electors' seats.
† Renamed the Social Democratic Liberal Party in Jan. 2013.
‡ Dissolved in Jan. 2013.

Election Commission

Fiji Electoral Commission: 59–63 Upper High St, Toorak, Suva; tel. 3316225; fax 3302436; internet www.electionsfiji.org; Chair. CHEN BUNN YOUNG; Supervisor of Elections MOHAMMED SANEEM.

Political Organizations

Existing political organizations were required to reregister to contest the general election in 2014; the membership threshold required to achieve registration was notably increased from 180 members to 5,000. The following four parties successfully registered for the elections:

Fiji Labour Party (FLP): Government Bldgs, POB 2162, Suva; tel. 3373317; fax 3373173; e-mail flp@connect.com.fj; internet www.flp.org.fj; f. 1985; Pres. LAVENIA PADARATH; Sec.-Gen. MAHENDRA PAL CHAUDHRY.

National Federation Party (NFP): 124 Princes Rd, Tamavua, POB 4399, Samabula; tel. 3305811; fax 3305317; f. 1960; est. by merger of the multiracial (but mainly Indian) Fed. Party and Nat. Democratic Party; Pres. TUPOU DRAUNIDALO; Leader BIMAN PRASAD; Gen. Sec. KAMAL IYER.

People's Democratic Party (PDP): 103 Gordon St, POB 16076, Suva; f. 2013; backed by the Fiji Trades Union Congress; Pres. ADI SIVIA QORO; Sec. POSECI BUNE.

Social Democratic Liberal Party (SODELPA): 66 McGregor St, POB 17889, Suva; f. 2013 from fmr Soqosoqo Duavata ni Lewenivanua (Fiji United Party, f. 2001); Pres. RO TEIMUMU KEPA; Leader LAISENIA QARASE; Gen. Sec. PIO TABAIWALU; Spokesperson Ratu TUPENI BABA.

The Fiji Democracy and Freedom Movement (Pres. USAIA WAQATAIREWA) was established in Australia in 2009. Based in New Zealand, the Coalition for Democracy in Fiji was formed in 1987. Supporters of secession are concentrated in Rotuma.

Diplomatic Representation

EMBASSIES AND HIGH COMMISSIONS IN FIJI

Australia: 37 Princes Rd, POB 214, Suva; tel. 3382211; fax 3382065; e-mail public-affairs-suva@dfat.gov.au; internet www.fiji.embassy.gov.au; High Commissioner GLENN MILES (acting).

China, People's Republic: 183 Queen Elizabeth Dr., PMB, Nasese, Suva; tel. 3300215; fax 3300950; e-mail chinaemb_fj@mfa.gov.cn; internet fj.china-embassy.org/chn; Ambassador HUANG YONG.

France: Dominion House, 7th Floor, Thomson St, Suva; tel. 3310526; fax 3323901; e-mail presse@ambafrance-fj.org; internet www.ambafrance-fj.org; Ambassador GILLES MONTAGNIER.

India: LICI Bldg, Butt St, POB 471, Suva; tel. 3301125; fax 3301032; e-mail hc.suva@mea.gov.in; internet www.indianhighcommission.org.fj; High Commissioner VINOD KUMAR.

Indonesia: Ra Marama Bldg, 6th Floor, 91 Gordon St, POB 878, Suva; tel. 3316697; fax 3316696; e-mail kbrisuva@connect.com; internet www.kemlu.go.id/suva; Ambassador GARY RACHMAN MAKMUN JUSUF.

Japan: Dominion House, 2nd Floor, POB 13045, Suva; tel. 3304633; fax 3302984; e-mail eojfiji@connect.com.fj; internet www.fj.emb-japan.go.jp; Ambassador TAKUJI HANATANI.

Kiribati: 36 MacGregor Rd, POB 17937, Suva; tel. 3302512; fax 3315335; e-mail kiribatihighcom@connect.com.fj; High Commissioner RETETA RIMON.

Korea, Republic: Vanua House, 8th Floor, PMB, Suva; tel. 3300977; fax 3308059; e-mail korembfj@mofat.go.kr; internet fji.mofat.go.kr; Ambassador KIM SEONG-IN.

Malaysia: Pacific House, 5th Floor, POB 356, Suva; tel. 3312166; fax 3303350; e-mail malsuva@kln.gov.my; internet www.kln.gov.my/web/fji_suva; High Commissioner NOR AZAM MOHD IDRUS (acting).

Marshall Islands: Government Bldgs, 41 Borron Rd, POB 2038, Suva; tel. 3387821; fax 3387115; e-mail rmisuva@gmail.com; Ambassador AMATLAIN KABUA.

Micronesia, Federated States: 37 Loftus St, POB 15493, Suva; tel. 3304566; fax 3300842; e-mail fsmsuva@sopacsun.sopac.org.fj; Ambassador GERSON JACKSON.

Nauru: Ratu Sukuna House, 7th Floor, MacArthur St, POB 2420, Suva; tel. 3313566; fax 3302861; e-mail naurulands@connect.com.fj; High Commissioner JARDEN KEPHAS.

New Zealand: Reserve Bank of Fiji Bldg, 10th Floor, Pratt St, POB 1378, Suva; tel. 3311422; fax 3300842; e-mail nzhc@unwired.com.fj; internet www.nzembassy.com/fiji; Acting Head of Mission MARK RAMSDEN.

Papua New Guinea: 18 Rakua St, off Nailuva Rd, Government Bldgs, POB 2447, Suva; tel. 3304244; fax 3300178; e-mail kundufj@is.com.fj; High Commissioner PETER EAFEARE.

Solomon Islands: 34 Reki St, Government Bldgs, POB 2647, Suva; tel. 3100355; fax 3100356; e-mail solohicom@gmail.com; High Commissioner JOHN PATTESON OTI.

South Africa: Kimberly St, Suva; tel. 3311087; fax 3311086; e-mail freestate@connect.com.fj; Chargé d'affaires ABBEY MATOTO PINDELO.

Tuvalu: 16 Gorrie St, POB 14449, Suva; tel. 3301355; fax 3308479; e-mail s.laloniu@yahoo.com; High Commissioner AUNESE MAKOI SIMATI.

United Kingdom: Victoria House, 47 Gladstone Rd, POB 1355, Suva; tel. 3229100; fax 3229132; e-mail publicdiplomacysuva@fco.gov.uk; internet ukinfiji.fco.gov.uk; High Commissioner RODERICK DRUMMOND.

USA: 158 Princess Rd, Tamavua, Suva; tel. 3314466; fax 3308685; e-mail usembsuva@gmail.com; internet suva.usembassy.gov; Ambassador FRANKIE A. REED.

Vanuatu: 17 Mariko St, PMB 19249, Suva; High Commissioner NIKENIKE VUROBARAVU.

Judicial System

Justice is administered by the Supreme Court, the Fiji Court of Appeal, the High Court and the Magistrates' Courts. The Supreme Court of Fiji is the superior court of record, presided over by the Chief Justice. The 1990 Constitution provided for the establishment of Fijian customary courts and declared as final decisions of the Native Lands Commission in cases involving Fijian custom, etc. In April 2009, following the Court of Appeal's finding that the interim Government in place since the 2006 coup was illegal, the President of Fiji dismissed the entire judiciary.

Supreme Court: Suva; tel. 3211881; fax 3300674; e-mail enquiries@judicial.gov.fj; internet www.judiciary.gov.fj; Chief Justice ANTHONY GATES.

Court of Appeal: Victoria Parade, Suva; tel. 3211307; fax 3316284; Pres. WILLIAM CALANCHINI (acting).

High Court: Suva; Chief Registrar IRANI WAKISHTA ARACHCHI.

Magistrates' Courts: there are 15 Magistrates' Courts, which allow for 22 sitting resident magistrates; Chief Magistrate USAIA RATUVILI.

Office of the Attorney-General: Government Bldgs, POB 2213, Suva; tel. 3309866; fax 3305421; internet www.ag.gov.fj; Attorney-General AIYAZ SAYED-KHAIYUM (Minister for Justice); Solicitor-General SHARVADA SHARAMA.

Religion

CHRISTIANITY

Most ethnic Fijians are Christians. Methodists are the largest Christian group, followed by Roman Catholics. At the census of 2007 about 64.4% of the population were Christian (mainly Methodists, who comprised 34.6% of the total population).

Fiji Council of Churches: Government Bldgs, POB 2300, Suva; tel. and fax 3313798; e-mail fijichurches@connect.com.fj; f. 1964; nine mem. churches; Pres. Rev. APIMELEKI QILIHO; Gen. Sec. Rev. ISIRELI LEDUA KACIMAIWAI.

The Anglican Communion

In April 1990 Polynesia, formerly a missionary diocese of the Church of the Province of New Zealand, became a full and integral diocese. The diocese of Polynesia is based in Fiji but also includes Wallis and Futuna, Tuvalu, Kiribati, French Polynesia, Cook Islands, Tonga, Samoa and Tokelau. There were an estimated 6,319 adherents in 2007.

Bishop of Polynesia: Archbishop Dr WINSTON HALAPUA, Bishop's Office, 8 Desvoeux Rd, POB 35, Suva; tel. 3304716; fax 3302687; e-mail episcopus@connect.com.fj.

The Roman Catholic Church

Fiji comprises a single archdiocese. At 31 December 2007 there were an estimated 97,692 adherents in the country.

Bishops' Conference: Episcopal Conference of the Pacific Secretariat (CEPAC), 14 Williamson Rd, POB 289, Suva; tel. 3300340; fax 3303143; e-mail cepac@connect.com.fj; f. 1968; 17 mems; Pres. Most Rev. ANTHONY SABLAN APURON (Archbishop of Agaña, Guam); Sec.-Gen. Fr ROGER MCCARRICK.

Archbishop of Suva: Mgr PETERO MATACA, Archdiocesan Office, Nicolas House, 35 Pratt St, POB 109, Suva; tel. 3301955; fax 3301565.

Other Christian Churches

Methodist Church in Fiji & Rotuma (Lotu Wesele e Viti): Epworth Arcade, Nina St, POB 357, Suva; tel. 3311477; fax 3303771; e-mail methodistchhq@connect.com.fj; f. 1835; autonomous since 1964; 212,831 mems (2007); Pres. Rev. AME TUGAUE (acting); Gen. Sec. TEVITA NAWADRA.

Other denominations active in the country include the Assembly of God (with c. 7,000 mems), the Baptist Mission, the Congregational Christian Church and the Presbyterian Church.

HINDUISM

Most of the Indian community are Hindus. According to the census of 2007, 27.9% of the population were Hindus.

ISLAM

In 2007 some 6.3% of the population were Muslim. There are several Islamic organizations.

Fiji Muslim League: Samabula, POB 3990, Suva; tel. 3384566; fax 3370204; e-mail fijimuslim@connect.com.fj; f. 1926; Nat. Pres. HAFIZUD DEAN KHAN; Gen. Sec. MOHAMMAD TAABISH AKBAR; 26 brs and 3 subsidiary orgs.

SIKHISM

There were an estimated 2,540 Sikhs in Fiji in 2007.

Sikh Association of Fiji: Suva; Pres. MEJA SINGH.

BAHÁ'Í FAITH

National Spiritual Assembly: National Office, POB 639, Suva; tel. 3387574; fax 3387772; e-mail nsafiji@connect.com.fj; mems resident in 490 localities; national headquarters for consultancy and co-ordination.

The Press

NEWSPAPERS AND PERIODICALS

Coconut Telegraph: POB 249, Savusavu, Vanua Levu; f. 1975; monthly; serves rural communities; Editor LEMA LOW.

Fiji Calling: POB 12095, Suva; tel. 3305916; fax 3301930; publ. by Associated Media Ltd; every 6 months; English; Publr YASHWANT GAUNDER.

Fiji Cane Grower: POB 12095, Suva; tel. 3305916; fax 3305256.

Fiji Daily Post: 19 Ackland St, Viria East Industrial Subdivision, Vatuwaqa, Suva; tel. 3275176; fax 3275179; e-mail info@fijidailypost.com; internet www.fijidailypost.com; f. 1987 as *Fiji Post*; daily from 1989; English; 100% govt-owned since Sept. 2003; Chair. MALAKAI NAIYAGA; Editor-in-Chief ROBERT WOLFGRAMM.

Fiji Magic: POB 12095, Suva; tel. 3305916; fax 3302852; e-mail fijimagic@fijilive.com; internet www.fijilive.com/fijimagic; publ. by Associated Media Ltd; monthly; English; Publr YASHWANT GAUNDER; circ. 15,000.

Fiji Republic Gazette: Printing Dept, POB 98, Suva; tel. 3385999; fax 3370203; f. 1874; weekly; English.

Fiji Sun: 12 Amra St, Walubay, Suva; tel. 3307555; fax 3311455; e-mail peterl@fijisun.com.fj; internet www.fijisun.com.fj; re-est. 1999; daily; Publr and CEO PETER LOMAS; Editor EPINERI VULA.

Fiji Times: 177 Victoria Parade, Suva; tel. 3304209; fax 3301521; e-mail timesnews@fijitimes.com.fj; internet www.fijitimes.com; f. 1869; fmrly owned by News Ltd (Australia); acquired by Motibhai Group in Sept. 2010 following introduction of legislation limiting foreign ownership of media organizations; daily; English; Publr HANK ARTS; Editor-in-Chief FRED WESLEY; circ. 34,000.

Fiji Trade Review: The Rubine Group, POB 12511, Suva; tel. 3313944; monthly; English; Publr GEORGE RUBINE; Editor MABEL HOWARD.

Islands Business: 46 Gordon St, POB 12718, Suva; tel. 3303108; fax 3301423; e-mail editor@ibi.com.fj; internet www.islandsbusiness.com; regional monthly news and business magazine featuring the Fiji Islands Business supplement; English; Editor-in-Chief LAISA TAGA; circ. 3,500.

Na Tui: Government Bldgs, 422 Fletcher Rd, POB 2071, Suva; f. 1988; weekly; Fijian; Publr TANIELA BOLEA; Editor SAMISONI BOLATAGICI; circ. 7,000.

Nai Lalakai: 20 Gordon St, POB 1167, Suva; tel. 3304111; fax 3301521; e-mail fijitimes@is.com.fj; f. 1962; publ. by Fiji Times Ltd; weekly; Fijian; Editor SAMISONI KAKAIVALU; circ. 18,000.

Pacific Business: POB 12095, Suva; tel. 3305916; fax 3301930; publ. by Associated Media Ltd; monthly; English; Publr YASHWANT GAUNDER.

Pacific Telecom: POB 12095, Suva; tel. 3300591; fax 3302852; e-mail review@is.com.fj; publ. by Associated Media Ltd; monthly; English; Publr YASHWANT GAUNDER.

PACNEWS: Level 2, Damodar Centre, Gordon St, Suva; tel. 3315732; fax 3317055; e-mail pacnews1@connect.com.fj; internet www.pina.com.fj; daily news service for the Pacific region; Pres. MOSES STEVENS; Editor MAKERETA KOMAI.

Pactrainer: PMB, Suva; tel. 3303623; fax 3303943; e-mail pina@is.com.fj; monthly; newsletter of Pacific Journalism Development Centre; Editor PETER LOMAS.

The Review: POB 12095, Suva; tel. 3305916; fax 3301930; e-mail review@is.com.fj; publ. by Associated Media Ltd; monthly; English.

Sartaj: John Beater Enterprises Ltd, Raiwaqa, POB 5141, Suva; f. 1988; weekly; Hindi; Editor S. DASO; circ. 15,000.

Shanti Dut: 20 Gordon St, POB 1167, Suva; f. 1935; publ. by Fiji Times Ltd; weekly; Hindi; Editor NILAM KUMAR; circ. 12,000.

Top Shot: Suva; f. 1995; golf magazine; monthly.

The Weekender: 2 Denison Rd, POB 15652, Suva; tel. 3315477; fax 3305346; publ. by Media Resources Ltd; weekly; English; Publr JOSEFATA NATA.

PRESS ASSOCIATION

Fiji Islands Media Association: c/o Vasiti Ivaqa, POB 12718, Suva; tel. 3303108; fax 3301423; national press assen; operates Fiji Press Club and Fiji Journalism Training Institute; Sec. NINA RATULELE.

Publishers

Fiji Times Ltd: POB 1167, Suva; tel. 3304111; fax 3301521; e-mail timesnews@fijitimes.com.fj; f. 1869; Propr News Corpn Ltd; largest newspaper publr; also publrs of books and magazines; Man. Dir ANNE FESSELL.

University of the South Pacific: Laucala Campus, Suva; tel. 3231000; fax 3231551; e-mail webmaster@usp.ac.fj; internet www.usp.ac.fj; f. 1986; education, natural history, regional interests; Pres. Prof. RAJESH CHANDRA.

GOVERNMENT PUBLISHING HOUSE

Printing and Stationery Department: POB 98, Suva; tel. 3385999; fax 3370203.

Broadcasting and Communications

TELECOMMUNICATIONS

Digicel Fiji: Ground Floor, Kadavu House, Victoria Parade, POB 13811, Suva; tel. 3310200; fax 3310201; e-mail customercarefiji@digicelgroup.com; internet www.digicelfiji.com; f. 2008; CEO DAVID BUTLER.

Fiji International Telecommunications Ltd (FINTEL): 158 Victoria Parade, POB 59, Suva; tel. 3312933; fax 3305606; e-mail inquiries@fintelfiji.com; internet www.fintel.com.fj; f. 1976; 51% govt-owned; 49% owned by Amalgamated Telecoms Holding (ATH); Group CEO SAKARAIA TUILAKEPA; CEO IOANE KOROIVUKI.

KIDANET: 158 Victoria Parade, POB 51, Suva; tel. 3315749; fax 3310332; e-mail info@kidanet.com.fj; internet www.kidanet.com.fj; internet service provider; CEO JONE WESELE.

Telecom Fiji Ltd (TFL): Ganilau House, Edward St, PMB, Suva; tel. 3304019; fax 3305595; e-mail contact@tfl.com.fj; internet www.tfl.com.fj; provides internet services through its subsidiary Connect Fiji Ltd; owned by Amalgamated Telecom Holdings; Chair. TOM RICKETTS; CEO IVAN FONG (acting).

Vodafone Fiji Ltd: 168 Princes Rd, Tamavua, Suva; tel. 3312000; fax 3312007; e-mail aslam.khan@vodafone.com; internet www.vodafone.com.fj; 51% owned by Amalgamated Telecom Holdings Ltd, 49% by Vodafone International Holdings BV; GSM operator; CEO ASLAM KHAN.

BROADCASTING

All broadcasting licences were revoked by the interim Government in November 2009. Radio and television stations were issued with temporary licences.

Radio

Fiji Broadcasting Corporation Ltd—FBCL (Radio Fiji): 69 Gladstone Rd, POB 334, Suva; tel. 3314333; fax 3301643; internet www.fbc.com.fj; f. 1954; statutory body; jointly funded by govt grant and advertising revenue; Radio Fiji 1 broadcasts nationally on AM in English and Fijian; Radio Fiji 2 broadcasts nationally on AM in English and Hindi; Gold FM broadcasts nationally on AM and FM in English; Mirchi FM and 2Day FM broadcast, mainly musical programmes, in Hindi and English, respectively; Bula FM broadcasts musical programmes in Fijian; CEO RIYAZ SAYED KHAIYUM.

Communications Fiji Ltd: 231 Waimanu Rd, PMB, Suva; tel. 3314766; fax 3303748; e-mail info@fm96.com.fj; internet www.cfl.com.fj; f. 1985; operates 5 commercial stations; FM 96, f. 1985, broadcasts 24 hours per day, on FM, in English; Navtarang, f. 1989, broadcasts 24 hours per day, on FM, in Hindi; Viti FM, f. 1996, broadcasts 24 hours per day, on FM, in Fijian; Legend FM, f. 2002, and Radio Sargam, f. 2004, broadcast musical programmes; Man. Dir WILLIAM PARKINSON; Gen. Man. IAN JACKSON.

Radio Light/Radio Naya Jiwan/Nai Talai: Government Bldgs, 15 Tower St, POB 2525, Suva; tel. and fax 3319956; e-mail radiolight@connect.com.fj; internet www.radiolight.org; f. 1990; owned by Evangelical Bible Mission Trust Board; non-profit organization; broadcasts in English (Radio Light FM 104, FM 104.2), Hindi (Radio Naya Jiwan FM 94.6) and Fijian (Nai Talai); Gen. Man. DOUGLAS ROSE.

Radio Pasifik: The University of the South Pacific, Suva; tel. 3232131; fax 3312591; e-mail blumel_d@usp.ac.fj; f. 1996; educational, operated by CFDL Multimedia Unit; broadcasts in English, Fijian, French, Bislama, Tongan, Hindi and other Pacific island languages.

Television

Fiji Television Ltd: 20 Gorrie St, Government Bldgs, POB 2442, Suva; tel. 3305100; fax 3304630; e-mail info@fijitv.com.fj; internet www.fijione.tv; f. 1994; operates 2 services, Fiji 1, a free channel, and Sky Fiji, a 25-channel subscription service; Chair. PADAM LALA; Group CEO TEVITA GONELEVU.

Film and Television Unit (FTU): c/o Department of Information, Government Bldgs, Suva; video library; production unit established by Govt and Hanns Seidel Foundation (Germany); a weekly news magazine and local documentary programmes.

Finance

BANKING

(cap. = capital; res = reserves; dep. = deposits; m. = million; brs = branches; amounts in Fiji dollars)

Central Bank

Reserve Bank of Fiji: Pratt St, PMB, Suva; tel. 3313611; fax 3302094; e-mail info@rbf.gov.fj; internet www.rbf.gov.fj; f. 1984; replaced Central Monetary Authority of Fiji (f. 1973); bank of issue; administers Insurance Act, Banking Act and Exchange Control Act; cap. 2.0m., res 39.1m. (Dec. 2011); Gov. BARRY WHITESIDE.

Commercial Bank

Bank South Pacific: cnr of Renwick Rd and Pratt St, PMB, Suva; tel. 3314400; fax 3318393; internet www.bsp.com.fj; f. 1974; est. as National Bank of Fiji; 51% acquired from Fiji Govt by Colonial Ltd in 1999 and renamed Colonial National Bank; above name adopted after acquisition of the Colonial Group by BSP in 2009; cap. 15.0m., res 3.8m., dep. 605.1m. (Dec. 2010); Country Man. KEVIN MCCARTHY; 15 brs; 45 agencies.

Development Bank

Fiji Development Bank: 360 Victoria Parade, GPOB 104, Suva; tel. 3314866; fax 3314886; e-mail info@fdb.com.fj; internet www.fdb.com.fj; f. 1967; finances devt of natural resources, agriculture, transport, and other industries and enterprises; statutory body; applied for a commercial banking licence in Nov. 2004; cap. 56.1m., res 11.1m. (June 2010); Chair. ROBERT GORDON LYON; CEO DEVE TOGANIVALU; 9 brs.

Merchant Banks

Merchant Finance and Investment Company Ltd: Level 1, Ra Marama, 91 Gordon St, Suva; tel. 3314955; fax 3300026; e-mail info@mfl.com.fj; internet www.mfl.com.fj; f. 1986; fmrly Merchant Bank of Fiji Ltd; owned by Fijian Holdings Ltd (80%), South Pacific Trustees (20%); Gen. Man NAPOLIONI BATIMALA; 3 brs.

STOCK EXCHANGE

South Pacific Stock Exchange: Level 2, Plaza One, Provident Plaza, 33 Ellery St, POB 11689, Suva; tel. 3304130; fax 3304145; e-mail info@spse.com.fj; internet www.spse.com.fj; f. 1979; fmrly Suva Stock Exchange; name changed as above in 2000; Chair. Dr NUR BANO ALI; CEO JINITA PRASAD.

INSURANCE

Colonial Fiji Life Ltd: cnr of Renwick Rd and Pratt St, PMB, Suva; tel. 3314400; fax 3318393; internet www.colonial.com.fj; life and health; fmrly Blue Shield (Pacific) Ltd; owned by BSP Group, Australia; Man. Dir Ratu MALAKAI NAIYAG.

Dominion Insurance Ltd: 231 Waimanu Rd, POB 14468, Suva; tel. 3311055; fax 3303475; e-mail enquiries@dominioninsurance.com.fj; internet www.dominioninsurance.com.fj; general insurance; Chair. HARI PUNJA; Exec. Dir GARY S. CALLAGHAN.

FijiCare Insurance Ltd: 9th Floor, 343–359 FNPF Place, Victoria Parade, Suva; tel. 3302717; fax 3302119; e-mail inquiries@fijicare.com.fj; internet www.fijicare.com.fj; life and health; Chair. ROSS PORTER; Man. Dir PETER MCPHERSON.

New India Assurance Co Ltd: Harifam Centre, GPOB 71, Suva; tel. 3313488; fax 3302679; e-mail newindiasuva@connect.com.fj; internet www.niafiji.com; Chief Man. K. VENUKUMAR.

QBE Insurance (Fiji) Ltd: Queensland Insurance Center, 18 Victoria Parade, GPOB 101, Suva; tel. 3315455; fax 3300285; e-mail info.fiji@qbe.com; internet www.qbepacific.com/Insurance.html; owned by Australian interests; fmrly known as Queensland

Insurance (Fiji) Ltd, name changed as above 2004; Gen. Man. MATTHEW KEARNS.

SUN Insurance: Ground Floor, Kaunikuila House, Laucala Bay Rd, Suva; tel. 3313822; fax 3313882; e-mail info@suninsurance.com.fj; internet www.suninsurance.com.fj; f. 1999; general; Chair. PADAM RAJ LALA; CEO LOLESH K. SHARMA.

Tower Insurance Fiji Ltd: Tower House, Thomson St, GPOB 950, Suva; tel. 3315955; fax 3301376; internet www.towerinsurance.com .fj; owned by New Zealand interests; Gen. Man. PAUL ABSELL.

Trade and Industry

GOVERNMENT AGENCIES

Fiji Islands Trade and Investment Bureau: Civic House, 6th Floor, Victoria Parade, POB 2303, Suva; tel. 3315988; fax 3301783; e-mail info@ftib.org.fj; internet www.ftib.org.fj; f. 1980; restyled 1988, to promote and stimulate foreign and local economic devt investment; Chair. ADRIAN SOFIELD; CEO JITOKO TIKOLEVU.

Training and Productivity Authority of Fiji (TPAF): Beaumont Rd, POB 6890, Nasinu; tel. 3392000; fax 3340184; e-mail info@tpaf.ac.fj; internet www.tpaf.ac.fj; fmrly Fiji National Training Council; present name assumed in 2002; Dir-Gen. JONE USAMATE.

DEVELOPMENT ORGANIZATIONS

Fiji Development Company Ltd: FNPF Place, 350 Victoria Parade, POB 161, Suva; tel. 3304611; fax 3304171; e-mail hfc@is.com.fj; f. 1960; subsidiary of the Commonwealth Development Corpn; Man. F. KHAN.

Fijian Development Fund Board: POB 122, Suva; tel. 3312601; fax 3302585; f. 1951; funds derived from payments from sales of copra by indigenous Fijians; funds used only for Fijian devt schemes; CEO VINCENT TOVATA.

Land Development Authority: POB 5442, Raiwaqa; tel. 3383155; fax 3387157; e-mail rsingh010@govnet.gov.fj; internet www .agriculture.org.fj; f. 1961; co-ordinates devt plans for land and marine resources; Chair. RITESHNI LATA SINGH.

CHAMBERS OF COMMERCE

Ba Chamber of Commerce: POB 99, Ba; tel. 6670134; fax 6670132; Pres. DINESH PATEL.

Fiji Chamber of Commerce and Industry: POB 14803, Suva; tel. 314040; fax 302641; Pres. PETER MASEY.

Labasa Chamber of Commerce: POB 992, Labasa; tel. 8811467; fax 8813009; Pres. ASHOK KARAN.

Lautoka Chamber of Commerce and Industry: POB 366, Lautoka; tel. 6661834; fax 6662379; e-mail vaghco@connect.com.fj; Pres. NATWARLAL VAGH.

Levuka Chamber of Commerce: POB 85, Levuka; tel. 3440248; fax 3440252; Pres. ISHRAR ALI.

Nadi Chamber of Commerce and Industry: POB 2735, Nadi; tel. 6700240; fax 6702406; e-mail rraju@connect.com.fj; internet www .nadichamber.com; f. 1947; Pres. RAM RAJU.

Nausori Chamber of Commerce: POB 228, Nausori; tel. 3478235; fax 3400134; Pres. MOTI LAL.

Sigatoka Chamber of Commerce: POB 882, Sigatoka; tel. 6500064; fax 6520006; Pres. TOM WAQA.

Suva Chamber of Commerce and Industry: 8 Dominion House, POB 337, Suva; tel. 3314044; fax 3302188; e-mail scci@unwired.com .fj; internet www.suvachamber.org; f. 1902; Pres. Dr NUR BANO ALI; 150 mems.

Tavua-Vatukoula Chamber of Commerce: POB 698, Tavua; tel. and fax 6680390; Pres. SOHAN SINGH.

INDUSTRIAL AND TRADE ASSOCIATIONS

Fiji Kava Council: POB 17724, Suva; tel. 3386576; fax 3371844; Chair. Ratu JOSATEKI NAWALOWALO.

Fiji Sawmillers' Association: Yalalevu; e-mail jayd@islandchill .com; Pres. JAY DAYAL.

Fiji Sugar Corporation Ltd: 3rd Floor, Western House, cnr of Bila and Vidilo St, PMB, Lautoka; tel. 6662655; fax 6664685; nationalized 1974; buyer of sugar cane and raw sugar mfrs; Exec. Chair. ABDUL KHAN.

Mining and Quarrying Council: 42 Gorrie St, Suva; tel. 33313188; fax 3302183; e-mail employer@is.com.fj; Chief Exec. K. A. J. ROBERTS.

National Trading Corporation Ltd: POB 13673, Suva; tel. 3315211; fax 3315584; f. 1992; govt-owned body; develops markets for agricultural and marine produce locally and overseas; processes and markets fresh fruit, vegetables and ginger products; CEO APIAMA CEGUMALINA.

Native Lands Trust Board: GPOB 116, Suva; tel. 3312733; fax 3312014; e-mail info@nltb.com.fj; internet www.nltb.com.fj; manages holdings of ethnic Fijian landowners; Gen. Man. ALIPATE QETAKI.

Sustainable Forest Industries LTD (SFI): POB 1119, Nabua, Suva; tel. 3384999; fax 3370029; e-mail info@fijimahogany.com; internet www.fijimahogany.com; Man. Dir CHRISTOPHER DONLON.

EMPLOYERS' ORGANIZATIONS

Fiji Commerce and Employers Federation (FCEF): 42 Gorrie St, GPOB 575, Suva; tel. 3313188; fax 3302183; e-mail employer@fcef .com.fj; internet www.fcef.com.fj; f. 1960; represents 525 major employers with approx. 80,000 employees; fmrly Fiji Employers' Fed; Pres. HOWARD POLITINI (acting); CEO NESBITT HAZELMAN.

Fiji Manufacturers' Association: POB 1308, Suva; tel. and fax 3318811; e-mail fma@connect.com.fj; internet fijimanufacturers.org; f. 1971; CEO DESMOND WHITESIDE; 68 mems.

Local Inter-Island Shipowners' Association: POB 152, Suva; fax 3303389; e-mail consortship@connect.com.fj; Pres. DURGA PRASAD; Sec. LEO B. SMITH.

Textile, Clothing and Footwear Council: POB 10015, Nabua; tel. 3384777; fax 3370446; Pres. KALPESH SOLANKI.

UTILITIES

Electricity

Fiji Electricity Authority (FEA): PMB, Suva; tel. 3313333; fax 3311882; e-mail ceo@fea.com.fj; internet www.fea.com.fj; f. 1966; govt-owned; responsible for the generation, transmission and distribution of electricity throughout Fiji; CEO HASMUKH PATEL.

Water

Water Authority of Fiji: Kings Rd, 4 Miles, Nasinu, Suva; tel. 3346777; e-mail contact@waf.com.fj; internet www.waterauthority .com.fj; Chair. P. L. MUNASINGHE; CEO OPETAIA RAVAI.

TRADE UNIONS

Fiji Trades Union Congress (FTUC): 32 Des Voeux Rd, POB 1418, Suva; tel. 3315377; fax 3300306; e-mail ftucl@connect.com.fj; f. 1952; affiliated to ITUC; 35 affiliated unions; 33,000 mems; Pres. DANIEL URAI MANUFOLAU; Gen. Sec. FELIX ANTHONY.

Transport

RAILWAYS

Fiji Sugar Corporation Railway: Rarawai Mill, POB 155, Ba; tel. 6674044; fax 6670505; internet www.fsc.com.fj; for use in cane-harvesting season, May–Dec.; 595 km of permanent track and 225 km of temporary track (gauge of 600 mm), serving cane-growing areas at Ba, Lautoka and Penang on Viti Levu and Labasa on Vanua Levu; Exec. Chair. ABDUL KHAN.

ROADS

At the end of 2010 there were some 3,440 km of roads in Fiji, of which 49.2% were paved. A 500-km highway circles the main island of Viti Levu.

Land Transport Authority of Fiji: Lot 1, Daniva Rd, Valelevu, Nasinu; tel. 3392166; fax 3390026; e-mail infor@lta.com.fj; internet www.ltafiji.com; f. 1998; responsible for public transport services, vehicle registration, traffic management and road safety; Chair. GREG LAWLOR; CEO NAISA TUINACEVA.

SHIPPING

The principal ports of call are Suva, Lautoka, Levuka, Malau and Wairiki. On 31 December 2013 the flag registered fleet comprised 30 vessels, with a total displacement of 28,417 grt.

Maritime Safety Authority of Fiji (MSAF): POB 3259, Nadi; tel. 6750241; fax 6750242; e-mail jbilitaki@msaf.com.fj; internet www .msaf.com.fj; regulatory body for maritime sector; fmrly known as Fiji Islands Maritime Safety Administration (FIMSA); Chair. NIGEL SKEGGS; CEO NEALE JAMES SLACK.

Fiji Ports Corporation Ltd: POB 780, Suva; tel. 3312700; fax 3300064; e-mail fpcl@connect.com.fj; internet www.fijiports.com.fj; f. 2005; management and devt of Fiji's ports; CEO VAJIRA PIYASENA; Gen. Man. EMINONI KURUSIGA.

Ports Terminals Ltd: POB 780, Suva; f. 1998; subsidiary of Fiji Ports Corporation Ltd; stevedoring, pilotage and cargo handling at Suva and Lautoka ports; Gen. Man. EMINONI KURUSIGA.

Consort Shipping Line Ltd: Lot 4, Matua St, Suva; tel. 3313344; fax 3303389; e-mail consortshipping@connect.com.fj; internet www.consortshipping.com.fj; f. 1986; est. following merger of Interport Shipping and Wong's Shipping Co; CEO HECTOR SMITH; Man. Dir JUSTIN SMIT.

Fiji Maritime Services Ltd: c/o Fiji Ports Workers and Seafarers Union, 36 Edinburgh Drive, Suva; f. 1989 by PAF and the Ports Workers' Union; services between Lautoka and Vanua Levu ports.

Pacific Agencies (Fiji) Ltd: Lot 1 Foster Rd Walubay Suva; tel. 3315444; fax 3301127; e-mail info@pacshipfiji.com.fj; internet www.pacificagenciesfiji.com; f. 2000 after merger of Burns Philp and Forum Shipping; shipping agents, customs agents and international forwarding agents, crew handling; Gen. Man. CRAIG WILLIAM STRONG.

Transcargo Express Fiji Ltd: POB 936, Suva; tel. 3313266; fax 3303389; e-mail consortship@connect.com.fj; f. 1974; Man. Dir LEO B. SMITH.

CIVIL AVIATION

There is an international airport at Nadi (about 210 km from Suva), a smaller international airport at Nausori (Suva) and numerous other airfields. Nadi is an important transit airport in the Pacific.

Airports Fiji Ltd: Nadi International Airport, Nadi; tel. 6725777; fax 6725161; e-mail info@afl.com.fj; internet www.airportsfiji.com; f. 1999; owns and operates 15 public airports in Fiji, incl. 2 international airports, Nadi International Airport and Nausori Airport; Chair. ADRIAN SOFIELD; CEO TONY GOLLIN.

Fiji Airways: Air Pacific Centre, Nadi International Airport, POB 9266, Nadi; tel. 6720777; fax 6720512; e-mail service@airpacific.com.fj; internet www.fijiairways.com; f. 1951; est. as Air Pacific Ltd, name changed in 2012; domestic and international services from Nausori Airport (serving Suva) to Nadi, and international services to Tonga, Solomon Islands, Cook Islands, Vanuatu, Samoa, Kiribati, Tuvalu, Hawaii, Japan, Hong Kong, Australia, New Zealand and the USA; 51% govt-owned, 46% owned by Qantas (Australia); Chair. NALIN PATEL; CEO and Man. Dir STEFAN PICHLER.

Pacific Sun: Nadi International Airport, POB 9270, Nadi; tel. 6723555; fax 6723611; e-mail enquiries@pacificsun.com.fj; internet www.pacificsun.com.fj; f. 1980; wholly owned subsidiary of Air Pacific Ltd; acquired Sun Air 2007; scheduled flights to domestic and regional destinations; Gen. Man. SHAENAZ VOSS.

Tourism

Scenery, climate, fishing and diving attract visitors to Fiji, where tourism is an important industry. However, the sector has been intermittently affected by political unrest. The number of visitor arrivals totalled 660,590 in 2012. Most visitors are from Australia, New Zealand, the USA and the United Kingdom. Receipts from tourism totalled a provisional $F1,303.4m. in 2012.

Fiji Islands Hotels and Tourism Association (FIHTA): 42 Gorrie St, GPOB 13560, Suva; tel. 3302980; fax 3300331; e-mail info@fihta.com.fj; internet www.fihta.com.fj; fmrly Fiji Hotel Association; name changed as above in 2005; 90 active mems, over 300 assoc. mems; Pres. DIXON SEETO; Exec. Officer MICHAEL WONG.

Tourism Fiji: Nadi International Airport, POB 9217, Nadi; tel. 6722433; fax 6720141; e-mail marketing@tourismfiji.com.fj; internet www.fijime.com; Chair. ELIZABETH POWELL (acting); CEO RICK HAMILTON.

Defence

As assessed at November 2013, Fiji's total armed forces numbered 3,500 (3,200 in the army and 300 in the navy). Reserves numbered approximately 6,000. The country's membership of the Commonwealth has entitled Fijians to work in the British armed forces. In November 2013 a total of 168 Fijian soldiers were serving in Iraq under the auspices of the UN Assistance Mission for Iraq (UNAMI). The country's defence budget for 2014 was an estimated $F101m.

Commander-in-Chief: President of the Republic.

Commander of the Armed Forces: Brig. MOSESE TIKOITOGA.

Commander of the Land Force: Lt-Col JONE KALOUNIWAI.

Commander of the Navy: JOHN FOX.

Chief of Staff, Strategic Headquarters: Brig.-Gen. MOHAMMED AZIZ.

Education

Education in Fiji is compulsory and free at primary level. Primary education begins at six years of age and lasts for eight years. Secondary education, beginning at the age of 14, lasts for a further three years. State subsidies are available for secondary and tertiary education in cases of hardship. In May 2009 there were 721 state primary schools (with a total enrolment of 129,444 pupils) and 172 state secondary schools (with an enrolment of 67,072 pupils). There were 69 vocational and technical institutions (with 2,387 enrolled students). In the same year Fiji had four teacher-training colleges (with 633 students). According to UNESCO estimates, in 2010/11 enrolment at primary schools included 97% of children in the relevant age-group, while enrolment at secondary schools included 84% of children in the relevant age-group. The University of the South Pacific is based in Fiji. In 2004 university students (both on campus and at extension centres) totalled 16,444. The University of Fiji, a privately owned institution, was established in that year. In January 2010 six government colleges merged to form the Fiji National University. The budget for 2012 allocated $F258m. to education.

FINLAND

Introductory Survey

LOCATION, CLIMATE, LANGUAGE, RELIGION, FLAG, CAPITAL

The Republic of Finland lies in northern Europe, bordered to the far north by Norway and to the north-west by Sweden. Russia adjoins the whole of the eastern frontier. Finland's western and southern shores are washed by the Baltic Sea. The climate varies sharply, with warm summers and cold winters. The mean annual temperature is 5°C (41°F) in Helsinki and −0.4°C (31°F) in the far north. There are two official languages: more than 93% of the population speak Finnish and 6% speak Swedish. There is a small Sámi (Lapp) population in the north. The majority of the inhabitants profess Christianity; about 76% belong to the Evangelical Lutheran Church. The national flag (proportions 11 by 18) displays an azure blue cross (the upright to the left of centre) on a white background. The state flag has, at the centre of the cross, the national coat of arms (a yellow-edged red shield containing a golden lion and nine white roses). The capital is Helsinki.

CONTEMPORARY POLITICAL HISTORY

Historical Context

Finland formed part of the Kingdom of Sweden until 1809, when it became an autonomous Grand Duchy under the Russian Empire. During the Russian Revolution of 1917 the territory proclaimed its independence. Following a brief civil war, a democratic Constitution was adopted in 1919. The Soviet regime that came to power in Russia attempted to regain control of Finland, but acknowledged the country's independence in 1920.

Demands by the USSR for military bases in Finland and for the cession of part of the Karelian isthmus, in south-eastern Finland, were rejected by the Finnish Government in November 1939. As a result, the USSR attacked Finland, and the two countries fought the Winter War, a fiercely contested conflict lasting 15 weeks, before Finnish forces were defeated. Following its surrender, Finland ceded an area of 41,880 sq km (16,170 sq miles) to the USSR in March 1940. In the hope of recovering the lost territory, Finland joined Nazi Germany in attacking the USSR in 1941. However, a separate armistice between Finland and the USSR was concluded in 1944.

In accordance with a peace treaty signed in February 1947, Finland agreed to the transfer of about 12% of its pre-war territory (including the Karelian isthmus and the Petsamo area on the Arctic coast) to the USSR, and to the payment of reparations, which totalled about US $570m. when completed in 1952. Meanwhile, in April 1948 Finland and the USSR signed the Finno-Soviet Treaty of Friendship, Co-operation and Mutual Assistance (the YYA Treaty), which was extended for periods of 20 years in 1955, 1970 and again in 1983. A major requirement of the treaty was that Finland repel any attack made on the USSR by Germany, or its allies, through Finnish territory. (The treaty was replaced by a non-military agreement in 1992.)

Domestic Political Affairs

Since independence in 1917, the politics of Finland have been characterized by coalition governments (including numerous minority coalitions) and the development of consensus between parties. The Social Democratic Party (SDP) and the Centre Party have traditionally been the dominant participants in government. The conservative opposition gained significant support at a general election in March 1979, following several years of economic crises. However, a new centre-left coalition Government, comprising the Centre Party, the SDP, the Swedish People's Party (SPP) and the Finnish People's Democratic League (an electoral alliance that included the communists), was formed in May by a former Prime Minister, Dr Mauno Koivisto, a Social Democrat.

Dr Urho Kekkonen, who had been President since 1956, resigned in October 1981. Koivisto was elected President in January 1982. He was succeeded as head of the coalition by a former Prime Minister, Kalevi Sorsa, a Social Democrat. The coalition was re-formed in December 1982, without the Finnish People's Democratic League, which had refused to support austerity measures.

At the general election of March 1983, the SDP won 57 of the 200 seats in the Parliament (Eduskunta), compared with 52 in the 1979 election. In May Sorsa formed another centre-left coalition, comprising the SDP, the SPP, the Centre Party and the Finnish Rural Party.

The rise of conservative politics: 1987–1994

At a general election held in March 1987, the combined non-socialist parties gained a majority in the Eduskunta for the first time since the election of 1945. Although the SDP remained the largest single party, with 56 seats, the system of modified proportional representation enabled the conservative opposition National Coalition Party (NCP) to gain an additional nine seats, winning a total of 53, while increasing its share of the votes cast by only 1%. President Koivisto eventually invited Harri Holkeri, a former Chairman of the NCP, to form a coalition Government comprising the NCP, the SDP, the SPP and the Finnish Rural Party, thus avoiding a polarization of the political parties within the Eduskunta. Holkeri became the first conservative Prime Minister since 1946.

In February 1988 Koivisto retained office after the first presidential election by direct popular vote. He did not win the required absolute majority, however, and an electoral college was convened. Koivisto was re-elected after an endorsement by Holkeri, who had also contested the presidency and who had received the third highest number of direct votes (behind Paavo Väyrynen, the leader of the Centre Party).

At a general election held in March 1991, the Centre Party won 55 seats, the SDP 48 seats and the NCP 40. In April a coalition Government, comprising the Centre Party, the NCP, the SPP and the Finnish Christian Union, took office. The new coalition constituted the country's first wholly non-socialist Government for 25 years. The Chairman of the Centre Party, Esko Aho, was appointed Prime Minister. In the first stage of a presidential election, which took place in January 1994, the two most successful candidates were Martti Ahtisaari (the SDP candidate and a senior UN official) and Elisabeth Rehn (the SPP candidate and Minister of Defence), both of whom were supporters of Finland's application for membership of the European Union (EU, see p. 273), as the European Community had been restyled in late 1993. In accordance with constitutional changes adopted since the previous election (stipulating that, if no candidate gained more than 50% of the votes cast, the electorate should choose between the two candidates with the most votes), a second stage of the election took place in February 1994. Ahtisaari secured victory, with 53.9% of the votes cast, and took office in March.

The return of the SDP

At a general election held in March 1995, the SDP won 63 seats in the Eduskunta, the Centre Party 44, the NCP 39 and the Left Alliance (formed in 1990 by a merger of the communist parties and the Finnish People's Democratic League) 22. A new coalition Government was formed in April, comprising the SDP, the NCP, the SPP, the Left Alliance and the Green League. Paavo Lipponen, the leader of the SDP, replaced Aho as Prime Minister. Sauli Niinistö, the Chairman of the NCP, became Deputy Prime Minister.

Following a general election held in March 1999, the SDP remained the largest party in the Eduskunta, with 51 seats. The Centre Party won 48 seats and the NCP 46. In April the five parties of the outgoing Government agreed to form a new coalition. Lipponen remained Prime Minister, while Niinistö was reappointed as Minister of Finance.

A presidential election was held in January and February 2000. The first round of the ballot was won by Tarja Halonen (the SDP candidate and Minister of Foreign Affairs), who received 40% of the votes cast; the second largest share of the vote (34.4%) was obtained by Aho. Having won a second round of voting on 6 February (with 51.6% of the votes cast), Halonen took office as the first female President of Finland on 1 March.

A new Constitution entered into force on 1 March 2000, under the provisions of which the executive power of the President was significantly reduced while the real authority of the Eduskunta was increased, with the power of decision-making being divided more equally between the Eduskunta, the Cabinet (Valtioneuvosto) and the President. In addition, the President was to co-operate more closely with the Cabinet on issues of foreign policy.

Aho took leave from domestic politics for one year from August 2000, during which time Anneli Jäätteenmäki, a former Minister of Justice, replaced Aho as Chairman of the Centre Party. Popular support for Jäätteenmäki's leadership prompted Aho's resignation in mid-2002 and the election of Jäätteenmäki as Chairperson.

The construction of Finland's fifth nuclear reactor was approved by the Cabinet in January 2002 and by the Eduskunta in May, prompting the resignation of the Green League from the coalition Government. It was originally envisaged that the reactor would become operational in 2009. However, there were numerous delays, and in February 2013 it was announced that commercial production at the reactor was not expected to commence before 2016.

The 2003 and 2007 general elections

A general election was held on 16 March 2003; 69.7% of the electorate participated in the poll. The Centre Party gained the largest representation in the Eduskunta, winning 55 seats, while the SDP won 53. The NCP suffered a significant reverse, with the loss of six seats (winning 40 seats). In April the Centre Party formed a coalition Government with the SDP and the SPP, with Jäätteenmäki as Finland's first female Prime Minister.

Jäätteenmäki's premiership was, however, short-lived. On 18 June 2003 she resigned following allegations that she had improperly used classified foreign ministry information to discredit the outgoing Prime Minister, Lipponen, and secure victory for the Centre Party in the general election. One of the documents, which were leaked by a presidential aide, Martti Manninen, recorded exchanges between Lipponen and the US President, George W. Bush, in December 2002, and was reportedly used by Jäätteenmäki to portray Lipponen as being overly supportive of US policy regarding Iraq; the majority of Finns were opposed to the US-led military action launched in Iraq in March 2003 to remove the regime of Saddam Hussain. The Deputy Chairman of the Centre Party, Matti Vanhanen, who had been assigned the post of Minister of Defence in the new Government, replaced Jäätteenmäki as Prime Minister. Jäätteenmäki also stood down as Chairperson of the Centre Party; Vanhanen was elected to replace her in October. In March 2004 Jäätteenmäki was acquitted of inciting or assisting Manninen to divulge official secrets, but Manninen was found guilty of violating official secrecy and fined 80 days' salary.

Lipponen resigned as leader of the SDP in June 2005; Eero Heinäluoma, hitherto General Secretary of the party, was elected to succeed him. In September Heinäluoma entered the Cabinet as Deputy Prime Minister and Minister of Finance.

A presidential election was held on 15 and 29 January 2006. Nine candidates contested the first round of voting, at which the incumbent, Halonen, received the largest share of the votes cast, with 46.3%, followed by Niinistö, representing the NCP, who secured 24.1%, and the Prime Minister, Vanhanen, the Centre Party candidate, with 18.6%. Halonen narrowly defeated Niinistö in a second round of voting, in which 77.2% of the electorate participated, receiving 51.8% of the votes cast.

At the general election held on 18 March 2007, the Centre Party narrowly retained its position as the largest party in the Eduskunta, securing 51 seats. The largest gains were made by the NCP, which won 50 seats. By contrast, the SDP suffered a significant loss, taking only 45 seats. The election was characterized by the lowest rate of voter participation since 1939, at just 67.9%. In April 2007 the Centre Party, the NCP, the SPP and the Green League formed a new, centre-right coalition, with Vanhanen remaining as Prime Minister. Jyrki Katainen of the NCP was appointed as Deputy Prime Minister and Minister of Finance.

Jutta Urpilainen was elected SDP Chairperson in June 2008, succeeding Heinäluoma. At municipal elections held in October the NCP overtook the SDP to become the largest party, winning 23.5% of the votes cast, compared with 21.2% for the SDP and 20.1% for the Centre Party. The nationalist True Finns increased its share of the vote to 5.4%.

Election campaign funding controversies

The admission in May 2008 by the Chairman of the Centre Party's parliamentary group, Timo Kalli, that he had failed to disclose election campaign donations, owing to a lack of penalties in place for such a violation, prompted a series of similar revelations by other members of the Eduskunta, including several ministers. At the same time, it emerged that a significant proportion of candidates in the 2007 elections, principally from the Centre Party and including Prime Minister Vanhanen, had received contributions from an association called Kehittyvien Maakuntien Suomi (KMS—Finland's Developing Regions). The head of development of the Centre Party, Lasse Kontiola, subsequently admitted that he had helped to establish the organization, which was funded by business executives, without the knowledge of senior party members. New rules covering party financing were agreed by all the principal parties prior to the local elections in October 2008.

The issue of irregularities in election campaign funding arose again in mid-2009, when the Prime Minister was accused by the opposition SDP of lying in 2008 about a campaign funding meeting, and by a current affairs television programme of having accepted a bribe in the 1990s linked to an organization, Nuorisosäätiö (Youth Foundation), a housing organization with links to the Centre Party, which had made a large donation to his 2006 election campaign. Vanhanen vehemently denied the accusations and resisted calls for his resignation. Further revelations of funding irregularities subsequently emerged, principally with regard to the Centre Party, but also involving other parties.

In December 2009 Vanhanen unexpectedly announced that he would not stand for re-election as Chairman of the Centre Party at the party conference in June 2010, owing to health reasons. In June party members elected Mari Kiviniemi, the Minister of Public Administration and Local Government, to succeed Vanhanen. One week later, as expected, Vanhanen submitted his resignation as Prime Minister, and on 22 June Kiviniemi was sworn in as Prime Minister at the head of a renewed Cabinet.

The issue of Vanhanen's campaign funding caused renewed controversy in September 2010 when the Chancellor of Justice, Jaakko Jonkka, concluded an investigation into the former Prime Minister's connection with Nuorisosäätiö. Jonkka stated that he believed that Vanhanen had acted unlawfully when, as premier, he had authorized a grant from the state-administered Raha-automaattiyhdistys (RAY—Finland's Slot Machine Association) to the housing charity, despite the latter's contribution to his campaign fund. In February 2011 the Eduskunta's constitutional law committee decided that Vanhanen was guilty of dereliction of duty by not declaring his conflict of interest, but concluded that the charge was not serious enough to warrant Vanhanen's trial by the High Court of Impeachment. Later in February the committee's decision was ratified by a plenary session of the Eduskunta.

None the less, several people were tried during 2012 in connection with the political funding irregularities that emerged in 2008. In April 2012 Ilkka Kanerva, who was Minister of Foreign Affairs in 2007–08, and three businessmen were convicted of charges including accepting and offering bribes in a case linked to the Nova Group. Kanerva received a suspended prison sentence of one year and three months, while one of the businessmen was sentenced to six years' imprisonment, the others being given lesser terms. Antti Kaikkonen, a Centre Party deputy and Chairman of Nuorisosäätiö in 2003–09, was sentenced to a five-month suspended prison term in January 2013, having been found guilty of abusing his position by raising funds for Centre Party election candidates. At the same time Jukka Vihriälä, a former Centre Party deputy and Chairman of RAY in 1991–2009, received an 18-month suspended prison sentence for aggravated bribe-taking, while Jorma Heikkinen, a former attorney for Nuorisosäätiö, received a one-year suspended sentence for aggravated bribery.

The 2011 general election and 2012 presidential election

The general election held on 17 April 2011 was characterized by a massive increase in support for the True Finns, which took 19.1% of the votes cast and won 39 seats in the Eduskunta (34 more than at the 2007 election), thus becoming the third largest party. The NCP narrowly emerged as the largest grouping in the legislature for the first time in its history, with 20.4% of the vote and 44 seats (a loss of six), while the SDP came second with 42 seats. While all of the parliamentary parties apart from the True Finns suffered losses, the greatest decline in support was for the Centre Party, which took 35 seats (a loss of 16) and fell from first to fourth place. The participation rate, at 70.4%, was the highest since 1995. The True Finns, while maintaining its traditional anti-immigration stance, had focused its campaign on opposition to financial support for debt-stricken countries in the eurozone; the party had benefited from growing popular resentment that Finland, whose public finances were among the soundest in the European Union (EU), was being expected to rescue countries perceived as imprudent. The Chairman of the NCP, Jyrki Katainen, began negotiations to form a government in early May. In mid-May the True Finns withdrew from these talks, refusing to comply with Katainen's demand that prospective coalition partners support EU policy, notably regarding financial assistance for eurozone countries at risk of default.

In June 2011 Katainen announced the formation of a six-party coalition, comprising the NCP, the SDP, the Left Alliance, the Green League, the SPP and the Christian Democrats. The broad-based coalition held a comfortable majority in the Eduskunta, leaving just the True Finns and the Centre Party in opposition. The Eduskunta subsequently formally elected Katainen as Prime Minister and a new Cabinet was appointed. The NCP and the SDP were each allocated six of the 19 ministerial portfolios, the Left Alliance, the Green League and the SPP two apiece and the Christian Democrats one. Jutta Urpilainen, the Chairperson of the SDP, became Deputy Prime Minister and Minister of Finance, while her party colleague, Erkki Tuomioja, returned to the post of Minister of Foreign Affairs (which he had previously held in 2000–07), succeeding Alexander Stubb of the NCP, who was named Minister of European Affairs and Foreign Trade. Katainen pledged to balance the budget by 2015 through a combination of reductions in public expenditure and tax rises. At the behest of the SDP, the Government was also to insist that any future EU financial assistance for heavily indebted members of the eurozone be subject to strict conditions (see Regional relations). A motion of no confidence in the Government, tabled by The Finns (the new English name adopted by the True Finns in August, although not a direct translation of its name in Finnish) in protest against the response to the sovereign debt crisis in the eurozone, was defeated in December by 116 votes to 73.

The Eduskunta adopted various revisions to the Constitution in October 2011. The changes included the stipulation that the Prime Minister would formally represent Finland within the EU, rather than the President, the explicit recognition of Finland's membership of the EU, and provision for citizens to propose new laws to parliament if they could collect the signatures of 50,000 supporters. The amendments took effect in March 2012.

A presidential election was held on 22 January and 5 February 2012. The incumbent Halonen was ineligible for re-election, having served the maximum two terms permitted by the Constitution. At the first round of voting, contested by eight candidates, Niinistö, who had been narrowly defeated in the 2006 poll and had served as Speaker of the Eduskunta during the 2007–11 legislative term, received the largest share of the votes cast, with 37.0%, followed by Pekka Haavisto, the Green candidate, who secured 18.8%, Paavo Väyrynen, representing the Centre Party, with 17.5%, and Timo Soini, the Chairman of The Finns, with 9.4%. Niinistö easily defeated Haavisto in the second round of voting, at which a turnout of 66.0% was recorded, with 62.6% of the votes cast. He took office on 1 March 2012, becoming the first President from the NCP since 1956. The fact that both candidates in the second round were pro-European was notable, the economic difficulties in the eurozone having been a major theme of the electoral campaign, although the Eurosceptic Väyrynen and Soini together garnered more than one-quarter of the vote.

Recent developments: new party leaders and a cabinet reorganization

At a party congress in June, the Centre Party chose as its Chairman businessman Juha Sipilä, a relative political novice who had only been elected to the Eduskunta at the 2011 poll, with Väyrynen coming only third of the four candidates. The SPP also held a leadership election at a party congress in June 2012: Carl Haglund, a member of the European Parliament, defeated the Minister of Justice, Anna-Maja Henriksson, to succeed Stefan Wallin as SPP Chairman. Haglund also replaced Wallin as Minister of Defence in July.

The governing coalition parties consolidated their position at municipal elections held on 28 October 2012, together securing 66.4% of the votes cast nationwide. The NCP and the SDP remained the two strongest parties, with 21.9% and 19.6% of the vote, respectively, followed by the opposition Centre Party (18.7%) and The Finns (12.3%). Although the share of the vote won by The Finns represented a substantial improvement on that recorded at the 2008 municipal polls (5.4%), it was markedly lower than the 19.1% achieved by the party in the general election, prompting speculation that the Government's firm stance on the provision of emergency EU funding to struggling eurozone members had, to some extent, contained the rise in support for The Finns. Turnout was low, at 58.3%.

Ongoing plans for municipal reform were inevitably a major focus of discussion during the local election campaign. Following a series of voluntary mergers of municipalities in recent years, the Government claimed that, in view of increasing rural–urban migration and the ageing of the population, further consolidation was required in order to ensure the financial viability of the provision of public services. Earlier in October 2012 a motion of no confidence in the Government on the issue—the third to be tabled on the issue within a year—was defeated in the Eduskunta by a margin of 95 votes to 62. The Government's proposals, which entailed a significant reduction in the number of municipalities, were opposed by the Centre Party and The Finns. In November government ministers reached agreement on draft legislation on municipal reform, and a restructuring scheme was agreed in August 2013. Following a period of consultation, councils were to inform the Government which municipalities they intended to join by the end of 2013 and to compile reports on planned mergers by April 2014 in order to qualify for additional financial assistance to implement the restructuring process. Mergers were to be completed by 2017. Ten further municipalities merged in the course of 2013, but the scheme appeared to have stalled in 2014, ahead of the general election scheduled to be held in 2015.

Jan Vapaavuori of the NCP, who had served as Minister of Housing in 2007–11, was appointed as Minister of Economic Affairs in November 2012, replacing his party colleague, Jyri Häkämies, who was to assume the post of Director-General of Elinkeinoelämän Keskusliitto (the Confederation of Finnish Industries). Petteri Orpo succeeded Vapaavuori as Chairman of the NCP parliamentary group.

A parliamentary motion of no confidence in the Government was defeated in February 2013 by 103 votes to 67. The motion had been filed by The Finns in protest against the Government's economic policies, notably the rejection of a request for a €50m. loan from a shipyard in Turku that had been seeking (and subsequently failed) to secure a contract to build a new cruise liner. The SDP continued to lose electoral support and on 17 May effected a reorganization of its cabinet ministers. Economic concerns continued to dominate the Government's agenda and affect its popularity, with intra-cabinet disagreements in 2014 over planned austerity measures. In March the Government survived a further vote of no confidence on the matter of municipal structural reforms. In April Prime Minister Katainen announced that he intended to resign as chairman of the NCP (and thus also as premier) in June.

Foreign Affairs

Regional relations

Finland has traditionally maintained a neutral stance in foreign affairs. It joined the UN and the Nordic Council (see p. 467) in 1955, but became a full member of the European Free Trade Association (EFTA) only in 1986, although a free trade agreement between Finland and the European Community (EC) took effect in 1974. In 1989 Finland joined the Council of Europe. In 1991, following the collapse of the USSR, Finland unilaterally abrogated the 1948 Finno-Soviet Treaty of Friendship, Co-operation and Mutual Assistance, which had bound Finland to a military defence alliance with the USSR and prevented the country from joining any international organization (including the EC) whose members posed a military threat to the USSR. In March 1992 the Finnish Government formally applied to join the EC. Following a referendum in which 56.9% of votes cast were in favour of membership, Finland left EFTA and joined the European Union (EU, see p. 273), as the EC had been restyled, in 1995.

Finland consolidated its commitment to European integration, joining the Economic and Monetary Union (EMU), which commenced on 1 January 1999, and the Schengen Agreement on the freedom of movement in 1996. Finland regards its role in the EU as one of advocacy for the so-called 'Northern Dimension'—the Nordic and Baltic countries and Russia. In 2008 the Eduskunta ratified the Treaty of Lisbon, which was designed to reform the institutions of the EU to improve decision-making following its enlargement. The treaty entered into effect across the EU on 1 December 2009. Finland has also participated in the EU drive to strengthen regional infrastructure links, jointly establishing two underwater cable connections with Estonia as part of a wider EU plan to integrate regional power markets; Estlink I became operational in 2006 and Estlink II in 2014.

Although the coalition Government that took office in Finland in June 2011 did not include the Eurosceptic True Finns, which had made large gains at the April general election, the new administration insisted that it would impose strict conditions on its support for future emergency financial assistance from the EU's European Financial Stability Facility (EFSF) to debt-stricken members of the eurozone, including the involvement of the private sector and the provision of collateral to Finland by recipient countries. In August the Governments of Finland and Greece, which was seeking a second financial rescue package in addition to assistance agreed in May 2010, reached a provisional agreement under which Greece would place a sum of money equal to Finland's contribution to its emergency funding plan into a Finnish escrow account as collateral. However, this bilateral accord prompted several other eurozone members to demand similar arrangements, leading to a delay in the implementation of a second bailout for Greece. The dispute was resolved in October, when eurozone ministers responsible for finance concluded a new, more complex, collateral agreement; notably, any country requesting collateral would itself have to fulfil certain conditions in exchange, including the payment of its share of the capital of the European Stability Mechanism (ESM, a permanent rescue fund that was expected to come into force in July 2012) at the time of its establishment rather than over a five-year period. Although this new arrangement was available in principle to all countries contributing to the rescue plan for Greece, only Finland opted to pursue it. The Greek and Finnish Governments duly signed a new agreement on collateral in February 2012, following which the Eduskunta approved Finland's participation in a further EFSF funding plan for Greece. In June 2012 the Eduskunta approved the ratification of the treaty establishing the ESM, which entered into force in September (slightly later than anticipated). The Finnish Government concluded a collateral agreement with Spain in July, in return for its support for emergency EU funding to recapitalize the Spanish banking sector; as with the rescue plan for Greece, Finland was the only country to seek collateral. In November Finland opted not to join a group of 11 other EU member states undertaking preparatory work on the proposed introduction of a financial transactions tax; the Finnish Government was deeply divided over the issue, with the SDP, the Left Alliance and the Green League in favour of involvement and the NCP, the Christian Democrats and the SPP opposing participation. In December Finland became the 12th eurozone member to ratify an intergovernmental treaty on new, stricter fiscal arrangements (the so-called fiscal compact), which had been signed by 25 of the 27 EU member states in March, thus triggering its entry into force on 1 January 2013.

Meanwhile, at a meeting of EU ministers of internal affairs in September 2011 and again in March 2013, Finland, together with the Netherlands, vetoed the admission of Bulgaria and Romania to the EU's Schengen area (which would allow the removal of border controls between these states and existing members of the area), owing to concerns regarding corruption and organized crime. In November Finland agreed to a proposal on the removal of air and sea border controls with Bulgaria and Romania in March 2012, followed by that of land borders in July, but continued Dutch opposition prevented this occurring.

The pursuance of friendly relations with the USSR, and latterly Russia, has generally been regarded as a priority in Finnish foreign affairs. In October 1989 Mikhail Gorbachev became the first Soviet head of state to visit Finland since 1975, and recognized Finland's neutral status. The Finno-Soviet Treaty of Friendship was replaced in January 1992 by a 10-year agreement, signed by Finland and Russia, which involved no military commitment. The agreement was to be automatically renewed for five-year periods unless annulled by either signatory. The new treaty also included undertakings by the two countries not to use force against each other and to respect the inviolability of their common border and each other's territorial integrity. Finnish foreign policy towards Russia in the late 2000s included advocacy for a closer strategic relationship between the EU and Russia. In February 2010 Finland gave its final approval for the construction of a Russian-owned gas pipeline, Nord Stream, under the Baltic Sea, amid concerns from countries bordering the sea over the pipeline's potential environmental impact. The pipeline, which would carry gas directly from Russia to Germany, thus bypassing Russia's neighbours, commenced operations in September 2011.

Other external relations

Although Finland did not become a member of the North Atlantic Treaty Organization (NATO, see p. 370), owing to its policy of military neutrality, it did join NATO's Partnership for Peace framework in 1994 and participates in certain NATO-led operations. Finland contributed troops to the International Security Assistance Force (ISAF) in Afghanistan from 2002 and the Kosovo Force (KFOR) operation responsible for establishing and maintaining security in Kosovo from 1999, and also participated in the peacekeeping force in Bosnia and Herzegovina, from which it withdrew its troops in 2009. The debate surrounding membership of NATO was reinvigorated following the Russian action in Georgia in 2008. Despite support for an application for full NATO membership from senior figures of the NCP, the President and a majority of the public remained averse to such a measure. In its January 2009 security and defence policy report, however, the Government stated that it would continue to uphold the possibility of seeking full membership of NATO in the future. Meanwhile, in January 1997 Finland began participation in two of the then 13 EU 'battlegroups', to be deployed in rotation in crisis areas. Finland also contributed troops to an EU Force (EUFOR) mission in Bosnia and Herzegovina and to the UN Mission in the Central African Republic and Chad (MINURCAT) until the end of its mandate in December 2010.

Relations between Finland and the USA are cordial. US policy before the dissolution of the USSR was to support Finnish neutrality and, thereafter, was to engage actively in trade and economic relations. Following the terrorist attacks of 11 September 2001 in the USA, Finland did not participate in the US-led retaliatory military action against the Taliban regime in Afghanistan. Finnish military personnel did, however, take part in the subsequent peacekeeping operation in Afghanistan. Finland was opposed to military action against the regime of Saddam Hussain in Iraq in early 2003 without a UN Security Council resolution, but indicated that it would be prepared to take part in military action under UN auspices and in possible humanitarian and peacekeeping operations. In the event, Finland pledged US $5.1m. for reconstruction in Iraq, but did not send any troops.

CONSTITUTION AND GOVERNMENT

The Constitution of Finland entered into force on 1 March 2000, amending the Constitution of July 1919. Finland has a republican Constitution, under the provisions of which executive power is divided between the Eduskunta (Parliament), the Valtioneuvosto (Cabinet) and the President. The unicameral Eduskunta has 200 members, elected by universal adult suffrage for four years on the basis of proportional representation. The President is elected for six years by direct popular vote. Legislative power is exercised by the Eduskunta. The Eduskunta elects the Prime Minister, who is then appointed by the President. The other government ministers are appointed by the President on the basis of nominations by the Prime Minister. At February 2013, following many municipal mergers, Finland was divided into 320 municipalities, which are guaranteed self-government and are entitled to levy taxes. The Åland Islands are guaranteed self-government. In their native region the Sámi have linguistic and cultural autonomy.

REGIONAL AND INTERNATIONAL CO-OPERATION

Finland joined the European Union (EU, see p. 273) in 1995, and participated in the introduction of the single European currency, the euro, in January 1999. Finland is a member of the Nordic Council (see p. 467), the Arctic Council, the Council of Europe (see p. 252), the Council of the Baltic Sea States (see p. 250) and the Organization for Security and Co-operation in Europe (OSCE, see p. 387).

Finland joined the UN in 1955. As a contracting party to the General Agreement on Tariffs and Trade, Finland joined the World Trade Organization (WTO, see p. 434) on its establishment in 1995. Finland is a member of the Organisation for Economic Co-operation and Development (OECD, see p. 379) and participates in the Partnership for Peace framework of the North Atlantic Treaty Organization (NATO, see p. 370).

ECONOMIC AFFAIRS

In 2012, according to estimates by the World Bank, Finland's gross national income (GNI), measured at average 2010–12 prices, was US $254,148m., equivalent to $46,940 per head (or $38,630 per head on an international purchasing-power parity basis). During 2003–12, it was estimated, the population increased at an average annual rate of 0.4%, while gross domestic product (GDP) per head increased, in real terms, by an average of 1.1% per year. Overall GDP increased, in real terms, at an average annual rate of 1.5% in 2003–12; GDP grew by 2.8% in 2011, but declined by 0.2% in 2012.

Agriculture (including hunting, forestry and fishing) contributed an estimated 2.8% of GDP in 2012 and together with mining and quarrying employed 4.4% of the working population in 2012. Forestry is the most important branch of the sector. Animal husbandry is the predominant form of farming. The major crops are barley, oats, wheat and potatoes. During 2003–12 agricultural GDP increased, in real terms, by an average of 2.0% per year; agricultural GDP increased by 4.2% in 2011, but decreased by 4.3% in 2012.

Industry (including mining, manufacturing, construction and power) provided 26.0% of GDP in 2012 and employed 25.4% of the working population in 2008. Industrial GDP increased, in real terms, by an average of 0.2% per year during 2003–12; industrial GDP decreased by 0.6% in 2011 and by 6.6% in 2012.

Mining and quarrying contributed 0.4% of GDP in 2012 and employed 0.2% of the working population in 2008. Gold is the major mineral export, and zinc ore, copper ore and lead ore are also mined in small quantities. The GDP of the mining sector increased, in real terms, at an average rate of 2.9% per year during 2003–12; mining GDP decreased by 6.8% in 2011, but increased by 0.3% in 2012.

Manufacturing provided 15.4% of GDP in 2012 and together with utilities employed 15.5% of the working population in 2012. The most important branches of manufacturing measured by value of output in 2006 were electrical and optical equipment, including the electronics industry (particularly mobile telephones), pulp, paper and paper products, metal products, chemical products and non-electrical machinery and equipment. The GDP of the manufacturing sector decreased, in real terms, at an average rate of 0.2% per year during 2003–12; the sector's GDP decreased by 1.1% in 2011 and by 8.4% in 2012.

Construction provided 6.9% of GDP in 2012 and employed 7.1% of the working population in 2012. Construction GDP increased, in real terms, by an average of 1.5% per year during 2003–12; the sector's GDP increased by 3.1% in 2011, but decreased by 4.8% in 2012.

Of total energy generated in 2012, 32.7% was derived from nuclear energy, 23.9% from hydroelectric power, 10.5% from coal and 9.4% from natural gas. In late 2012 there were four nuclear reactors in operation. Construction of a 1,600-MW fifth nuclear reactor, in Olkiluoto in south-west Finland, was subject to delays and it was not expected to commence commercial production before 2016, several years later than originally planned and hugely over budget. Despite these difficulties, the construction of a further reactor at Olkiluoto, as well as a new nuclear plant in northern Finland, Hanhikivi 1, were under consideration in 2014. Meanwhile, preparatory moves towards the construction of a liquefied natural gas terminal in Tornio were under way in 2014. Imports of mineral fuels comprised 21.8% of the total cost of imports in 2012.

Services provided 71.2% of GDP in 2012 and engaged 73.1% of the employed labour force in 2012. In real terms, the combined GDP of the services sector increased at an average rate of 1.8% per year during 2003–12; the sector's GDP increased by 1.1% in 2012.

In 2012 Finland recorded a visible merchandise trade surplus of US $3,611m., but there was a deficit of $3,698m. on the current account of the balance of payments. In 2012 the principal source of imports was Russia (providing 17.8% of total imports); other major sources were Germany, Sweden, the People's Republic of China and the Netherlands. Sweden was the principal market for exports in the same year (accounting for 11.1% of total exports); other major purchasers were Russia, Germany, the USA, the Netherlands and the United Kingdom. The European Union (EU, see p. 273) accounted for 53.3% of exports and 53.6% of imports in 2012. The principal exports in 2012 were basic manufactures (mainly paper and paperboard), machinery and transport equipment (mainly electronic products, notably mobile telephones), chemicals and related products, mineral fuels and lubricants, crude materials and miscellaneous manufactured articles. The principal imports were machinery and transport equipment, mineral fuels and lubricants, chemicals and related products, basic manufactures, miscellaneous manufactured articles, crude materials, and food and live animals.

In 2012, according to official figures, there was a general government deficit of €3,009m., equivalent to 1.6% of GDP. Finland's general government gross debt was €103.131m. in 2012, equivalent to 53.6% of GDP. According to the ILO, the average annual rate of inflation was 1.8% during 2003–12. Consumer prices increased by 2.7% in 2012. The average rate of unemployment was 7.7% in 2012.

Finland's economy depends chiefly on exports, notably metal products, paper and high-technology products. However, trade was severely affected by the global economic downturn that began in late 2008, with exports and GDP decreasing by 21.3% and 8.5%, respectively, in 2009. The general government balance moved into deficit in 2009 for the first time in 10 years. By mid-2010 strong growth in the world economy, particularly in Finland's principal trading partners (Russia, Germany and Sweden), had brought about a recovery in the country's exports and GDP, which increased by 7.5% and 3.3%, respectively, in 2010. However, GDP growth decelerated to 2.8% in 2011 and declined by 0.2% in 2012; preliminary figures for 2013 showed a continued contraction, of 1.4%, as the result of a decline in private consumption and of weak investment. Export competitiveness was also undermined by rising labour costs, unemployment and difficulties in key industrial sectors, exemplified by downsizing and redundancies at Nokia Corporation, hitherto a significant tax contributor and employer. Consequently, public expenditure was the main driver of growth. The Government that took office in June 2011 aimed to balance the budget by 2015 by implementing rigorous austerity measures. The general and central government deficits narrowed to 0.7% and 3.1% of GDP, respectively, in 2011, but increased again in 2012, and reached an estimated 2.0% and 3.4%, respectively, in 2013. Moreover, the high costs associated with the demographic pressures of a rapidly ageing population, in conjunction with generous welfare benefits, were expected to put further pressure on public finances in the medium term. However, signs of continued economic slowdown led the Government to consider spreading planned spending cuts of some €3,000m. over three years from 2015, instead of the previous plan for 2014/15 implementation. In early 2014 the Organisation for Economic Co-operation and Development reiterated that Finland should take determined action to implement structural reforms to revive economic growth, restore competitiveness and preserve high standards of living. Meanwhile, in January 2014 the IMF added Finland to the countries required to undergo mandatory assessment of the stability of its financial sector, although the country was not scheduled for assessment in 2014. Nevertheless, government debt remained relatively low in eurozone terms at an estimated 56.9% of GDP in 2013, and in early 2014 Finland was one of only three eurozone countries to retain an AAA credit rating.

PUBLIC HOLIDAYS

2015: 1 January (New Year's Day), 6 January (Epiphany), 3 April (Good Friday), 6 April (Easter Monday), 1 May (May Day), 14 May (Ascension Day), 24 May (Whit Sunday), 19–20 June (Midsummer), 1 November (All Saints' Day), 6 December (Independence Day), 24–26 December (Christmas).

Statistical Survey

Source (unless otherwise stated): Statistics Finland, 00022 Helsinki; tel. (9) 17342220; fax (9) 17342279; e-mail library@stat.fi; internet www.stat.fi.

Note: Figures in this survey include data for the autonomous Åland Islands, unless otherwise stated.

Area and Population

AREA, POPULATION AND DENSITY

Area (sq km)	
Land	303,893
Inland water	34,539
Total	338,432*
Population (census results)†	
31 December 2000	5,181,115
31 December 2010	
Males	2,638,416
Females	2,736,860
Total	5,375,276
Population (at 31 December)	
2011	5,401,267
2012	5,426,674
Density (per sq km) at 31 December 2012	17.9‡

* 130,669 sq miles; including Åland Islands (1,552 sq km—599 sq miles).
† From 2010 Finland abandoned data collection and enumeration through traditional census methodologies in favour of an annual register based system of population reporting.
‡ Land area only.

POPULATION BY AGE AND SEX
(population at 31 December 2012)

	Males	Females	Total
0–14	455,556	435,836	891,392
15–64	1,779,297	1,737,792	3,517,089
65 and over	431,769	586,424	1,018,193
Total	2,666,622	2,760,052	5,426,674

REGIONS
(population at 31 December 2012)

	Land area (sq km)*	Population	Density (per sq km)*
Uusimaa (Nyland)†	9,096	1,566,835	172.3
Varsinais-Suomi (Egentliga Finland)	10,661	468,936	44.0
Satakunta	7,957	224,934	28.3
Kanta-Häme (Egentliga Tavastland)	5,200	175,472	33.7
Pirkanmaa (Birkaland)	12,446	496,568	39.9
Päijät-Häme (Päijänne-Tavastland)	5,125	202,548	39.5
Kymenlaakso (Kymmenedalen)	5,148	181,421	35.2
Etelä-Karjala (Södra Karelen)	5,613	132,355	23.6
Etelä-Savo (Södra Savolax)	13,977	153,426	11.0
Pohjois-Savo (Norra Savolax)	16,768	248,233	14.8
Pohjois-Karjala (Norra Karelen)	17,763	165,754	9.3
Keski-Suomi (Mellersta Finland)	16,704	275,161	16.5
Etelä-Pohjanmaa (Södra Österbotten)	13,444	194,058	14.4
Pohjanmaa (Österbotten)	7,750	179,663	23.2
Keski-Pohjanmaa (Mellersta Österbotten)	5,019	68,610	13.7
Pohjois-Pohjanmaa (Norra Österbotten)	35,507	400,670	11.3
Kainuu (Kajanaland)	21,501	80,685	3.8
Lappi (Lappland)	92,662	182,844	2.0
Ahvenanmaa (Åland)	1,552	28,501	18.4
Total	303,893	5,426,674	17.9

* According to regional divisions at 1 January 2012; excluding inland waters, totalling 34,539 sq km.
† Including the former Itä-Uusimaa (Östra Nyland) region, which was consolidated with Uusimaa from 1 January 2011.

PRINCIPAL TOWNS
(population at 31 December 2012)*

Helsinki (Helsingfors) (capital)	603,968	Lahti	103,016
Espoo (Esbo)	256,824	Kouvola	87,296
Tampere (Tammerfors)	217,421	Pori (Björneborg)	83,285
Vantaa (Vanda)	205,312	Joensuu	74,168
Oulu (Uleåborg)	190,847	Lappeenranta (Villmanstrand)	72,424
Turku (Åbo)	180,225	Hämeenlinna	67,497
Jyväskylä	133,482	Vaasa	65,674
Kuopio	105,136	Rovaniemi	60,877

* According to regional divisions at 1 January 2012.

BIRTHS, MARRIAGES AND DEATHS

	Registered live births*		Registered marriages†		Registered deaths*	
	Number	Rate (per 1,000)	Number	Rate (per 1,000)	Number	Rate (per 1,000)
2005	57,745	11.0	29,283	5.6	47,928	9.1
2006	58,840	11.2	28,236	5.4	48,065	9.1
2007	58,729	11.1	29,497	5.6	49,077	9.3
2008	59,530	11.2	31,014	5.8	49,094	9.2
2009	60,430	11.3	29,836	5.6	49,883	9.3
2010	60,980	11.3	29,952	5.6	50,887	9.5
2011	59,961	11.1	28,408	5.3	50,585	9.4
2012	59,493	11.0	28,878	5.3	51,707	9.5

* Including Finnish nationals temporarily outside the country.
† Data relate only to marriages in which the bride was domiciled in Finland.

Life expectancy (years at birth): 80.5 (males 77.3; females 83.8) in 2011 (Source: World Bank, World Development Indicators database).

ECONOMICALLY ACTIVE POPULATION
('000 persons aged 15 to 74 years)

	2010	2011	2012
Agriculture, forestry and fishing; mining and quarrying	115	110	109
Manufacturing; electricity, gas and water	388	384	382
Construction	172	176	175
Wholesale and retail trade; repair of motor vehicles, and household goods	298	303	300
Hotels and restaurants	83	83	86
Transport, storage and communications	251	246	245
Financial intermediation; insurance and real estate activities	321	328	336
Public administration and defence; compulsory social security	117	116	113
Education	174	179	175
Health and social work	379	396	409
Other community, social and personal service activities	139	141	142
Sub-total	2,437	2,462	2,472
Not classifiable by economic activity	12	11	11
Total employed	2,447	2,474	2,483
Unemployed	224	209	207
Total labour force	2,672	2,682	2,690

Health and Welfare

KEY INDICATORS

Total fertility rate (children per woman, 2011)	1.9
Under-5 mortality rate (per 1,000 live births, 2011)	3
HIV/AIDS (% of persons aged 15–49, 2011)	0.1
Physicians (per 1,000 head, 2009)	2.9
Hospital beds (per 1,000 head, 2009)	6.2
Health expenditure (2010): US $ per head (PPP)	3,252
Health expenditure (2010): % of GDP	9.0
Health expenditure (2010): public (% of total)	74.5
Total carbon dioxide emissions ('000 metric tons, 2010)	61,844.0
Carbon dioxide emissions per head (metric tons, 2010)	11.5
Human Development Index (2012): ranking	21
Human Development Index (2012): value	0.892

For sources and definitions, see explanatory note on p. vi.

Agriculture

PRINCIPAL CROPS

('000 metric tons; farms with arable land of 1 ha or more)

	2010	2011	2012
Wheat	724.4	974.8	887.1
Barley	1,340.2	1,514.3	1,581.1
Rye	68.5	78.4	64.1
Oats	809.7	1,043.1	1,073.1
Mixed grain	46.5	57.2	53.2
Potatoes	659.1	673.3	489.6
Rapeseed	178.5	115.1	73.2
Sugar beet	542.1	675.7	410.0
Cucumbers and gherkins	42.6	47.8	43.1
Carrots and turnips	67.5	72.8	55.8

Aggregate production ('000 metric tons, may include official, semi-official or estimated data): Total cereals 2,992 in 2010, 3,670 in 2011, 3,661 in 2012; Total roots and tubers 659 in 2010, 673 in 2011, 490 in 2012; Total vegetables (incl. melons) 251 in 2010, 277 in 2011, 247 in 2012; Total fruits (excl. melons) 17 in 2010, 21 in 2011–12.

Source: FAO.

LIVESTOCK

('000 head at 1 May; farms with arable land of 1 ha or more)

	2010	2011	2012
Horses	74	76	74
Cattle	926	914	912
Sheep	126	129	130
Pigs*	1,367	1,335	1,290
Poultry	4,896	5,729	6,333

* Including piggeries of dairies.

Source: FAO.

LIVESTOCK PRODUCTS

('000 metric tons)

	2010	2011	2012
Cattle meat	83.0	83.5	81.1
Pig meat	203.2	201.9	192.9
Chicken meat	87.7	93.6	99.3
Cows' milk*	2,336.3	2,300.7	2,296.7
Hen eggs	61.5	62.8	62.2

* Millions of litres.

Source: FAO.

Forestry

ROUNDWOOD REMOVALS

('000 cubic metres, excl. bark)

	2010	2011	2012
Sawlogs, veneer logs and logs for sleepers	19,993.3	19,641.6	19,322.3
Pulpwood	25,983.4	25,884.6	25,291.9
Fuel wood	4,974.8	5,240.6	5,352.8
Total	50,951.5	50,766.8	49,966.9

Source: FAO.

SAWNWOOD PRODUCTION

('000 cu m, incl. railway sleepers)

	2010	2011	2012
Coniferous (softwood)	9,400.0	9,700.0	9,300.0
Broadleaved (hardwood)	73.0	50.0	50.0*
Total	9,473.0	9,750.0	9,350.0*

* FAO estimate.

Source: FAO.

Fishing

('000 metric tons, live weight)

	2009	2010	2011
Capture	154.6	156.2	153.8
Roaches	3.6	4.1	4.3
Northern pike	8.8	8.2	8.2
European perch	10.6	8.9	9.1
Vendace	4.2	4.6	4.6
Atlantic herring	90.8	92.8	98.0
European sprat	23.2	24.6	15.8
Aquaculture	13.6	11.8	11.3
Rainbow trout	12.7	11.0	9.9
Total catch	168.2	167.9	165.1

Note: Figures exclude aquatic mammals, recorded by number rather than by weight. The catch of grey seals was: 475 in 2009; 349 in 2010; 261 in 2011.

Source: FAO.

Mining

('000 metric tons unless otherwise indicated)

	2009	2010	2011
Copper ore*	14.6	14.7†	16.0
Nickel ore*	40.8	41.0†	48.5
Zinc ore*	56.4	55.6	64.1
Chromium ore‡	247	250	250†
Cobalt (metric tons)§	4,665	9,413	10,441
Mercury (metric tons)	6	6	5
Silver (metric tons)§	60.0	64.6	73.1
Gold (kg)§	1,785	1,800†	6,417
Platinum (kg)§	265	275†	275†
Phosphate rock (incl. apatite, metric tons)‖	660	700†	800
Peat: for fuel	5,576	4,032	4,000†
Peat: for horticulture	876	768†	760†

* Figures refer to the metal content of ores.

† Estimated production.

‡ Figures refer to the gross weight of chromite. The estimated chromic oxide content (in '000 metric tons) was: 85 in 2009; 85 in 2010 (estimate); 85 in 2011 (estimate).

§ Figures refer to production of metal and (for cobalt) powder and salts.

‖ Figures refer to gross weight. The phosphorus oxide content (in metric tons) was: 234 in 2009; 265 in 2010 (estimate); 280 in 2011 (estimate).

Source: US Geological Survey.

Industry

SELECTED PRODUCTS

('000 metric tons unless otherwise indicated)

	2002	2003	2004*
Cellulose	7,503	7,446	7,852
Newsprint	1,190	1,238	1,217
Other paper, boards and cardboards	11,362	12,113	13,218
Plywoods and veneers ('000 cu m)	1,135	1,168	1,388
Cement	1,198	1,493	1,270
Pig iron and ferro-alloys	2,829	3,091	3,037
Electricity (net, million kWh)	71,618	80,377	82,171
Sugar	161	202	193
Rolled steel products (metric tons)	3,975	4,090	4,157
Cigarettes (million)	4,130	3,946	n.a.

* Preliminary data.

2009: Cement 1,052,000 metric tons (Source: US Geological Survey); Electricity (net) 69,207m. kWh.

2010: Cement 1,200,000 metric tons (estimate) (Source: US Geological Survey); Electricity (net) 77,203m. kWh.

2011: Cement 1,514,000 metric tons (Source: US Geological Survey); Electricity (net) 70,390m. kWh.

2012: Electricity (net) 67,710m. kWh.

Finance

CURRENCY AND EXCHANGE RATES

Monetary Units

100 cent = 1 euro (€).

Sterling and Dollar Equivalents (31 December 2013)

£1 sterling = 1.194 euros;
US $1 = 0.725 euros;
€10 = £8.37 = $13.79.

Average Exchange Rate (euros per US $)

2011 0.7194
2012 0.7783
2013 0.7532

Note: The national currency was formerly the markka (Finnmark). From the introduction of the euro, with Finnish participation, on 1 January 1999, a fixed exchange rate of €1 = 5.94573 markkaa was in operation. Euro notes and coins were introduced on 1 January 2002. The euro and local currency circulated alongside each other until 28 February, after which the euro became the sole legal tender.

BUDGET

(€ million)

Revenue	2012	2013*	2014†
Taxes and other levies	37,321	39,923	40,057
Taxes on income and property	11,521	12,610	12,328
Taxes on turnover	16,619	17,657	17,880
Excise duties	6,448	6,711	6,975
Other taxes	2,609	2,793	2,715
Other levies	124	152	160
Miscellaneous revenues	6,065	4,936	4,742
Sub-total	43,386	44,859	44,799
Interest on investments and profits received	1,925	1,922	1,995
Loans receivable	5,126	7,754	7,126
Total	50,437	54,536	53,920

Expenditure	2012	2013*	2014†
President of the Republic	16	40	38
Parliament	146	158	158
Council of State	83	84	85
Ministry of Foreign Affairs	1,284	1,303	1,294
Ministry of Justice	887	870	896
Ministry of the Interior	1,293	1,317	1,264
Ministry of Defence	2,804	2,876	2,751
Ministry of Finance	17,415	16,982	16,947
Ministry of Education and Culture	6,541	6,656	6,597
Ministry of Agriculture and Forestry	2,678	2,723	2,657
Ministry of Transport and Communications	2,401	2,964	2,968
Ministry of Employment and the Economy	3,765	3,842	3,376
Ministry of Social Affairs and Health	11,990	12,593	12,810
Ministry of the Environment	279	261	267
Public debt	1,864	1,866	1,814
Total	53,446	54,536	53,920

* Preliminary, excluding supplementary budget.

† Budget proposals.

INTERNATIONAL RESERVES

(US $ million at 31 December)

	2010	2011	2012
Gold (Eurosystem valuation)	2,228.2	2,487.7	2,629.1
IMF special drawing rights	1,841.0	1,717.6	1,729.4
Reserve position in IMF	565.9	831.9	1,026.6
Foreign exchange	4,919.9	5,307.6	5,697.2
Total	9,555.0	10,344.8	11,082.3

Source: IMF, *International Financial Statistics*.

MONEY SUPPLY

(incl. shares, depository corporations, national residency criteria, € million at 31 December)

	2010	2011	2012
Currency issued	14,392	15,184	15,598
Bank of Finland	10,978	11,688	12,350
Demand deposits	69,958	74,084	80,986
Other deposits	44,733	47,182	42,685
Securities other than shares	68,547	80,206	87,680
Money market fund shares	8,039	9,062	3,168
Shares and other equity	31,614	33,151	32,680
Other items (net)	7,302	7,191	7,501
Total	244,586	266,060	270,297

Source: IMF, *International Financial Statistics*.

COST OF LIVING

(Consumer Price Index; base: 2010 = 100)

	2011	2012
Food and non-alcoholic beverages	106.3	111.8
Alcoholic beverages and tobacco	100.8	107.9
Clothing and footwear	101.2	103.9
Housing, water, electricity, gas and other fuels	106.3	108.1
Furniture, household equipment	102.3	103.9
Health	100.7	101.1
Transport	103.9	108.6
Communication	98.0	91.7
Recreation and culture	99.7	100.2
Education	103.2	105.0
Restaurants and hotels	102.5	106.4
Miscellaneous goods and services	103.6	107.8
All items	103.4	106.3

NATIONAL ACCOUNTS
(€ million at current prices)

National Income and Product

	2010	2011	2012
Compensation of employees	74,923	78,457	80,933
Employers' social contributions	17,169	18,144	18,866
Operating surplus	36,801	38,242	36,678
Domestic factor incomes	128,893	134,843	136,477
Consumption of fixed capital	28,959	30,012	31,388
Gross domestic product at factor cost	157,852	164,855	167,865
Indirect taxes, less subsidies	20,872	23,824	24,676
GDP in purchasers' values	178,724	188,679	192,541
Factor income received from abroad *Less* Factor income paid abroad	2,660	491	–238
Gross national product	181,384	189,170	192,303
Less Consumption of fixed capital	28,959	30,012	31,388
National income in market prices	152,425	159,158	160,915
Other current transfers from abroad *Less* Other current transfers from abroad	–2,056	–1,872	–1,671
National disposable income	150,369	157,286	159,244

Expenditure on the Gross Domestic Product

	2010	2011	2012
Government final consumption expenditure	44,224	46,182	48,306
Private final consumption expenditure	99,084	105,182	108,546
Changes in inventories	–729	2,070	311
Acquisitions, less disposals, of valuables	66	69	69
Gross fixed capital formation	33,698	36,632	37,724
Total domestic expenditure	176,343	190,135	194,956
Exports of goods and services	72,117	77,313	78,118
Less Imports of goods and services	69,736	78,671	79,762
Statistical discrepancy	0	–98	–771
GDP in purchasers' values	178,724	188,679	192,541
GDP at constant 2000 prices	156,965	161,244	159,911

Gross Domestic Product by Economic Activity

	2010	2011	2012
Agriculture, hunting, forestry and fishing	4,486	4,711	4,683
Mining and quarrying; manufacturing; electricity, gas and water	33,351	32,993	31,533
Construction	10,460	11,018	11,492
Wholesale and retail trade; hotels and restaurants; transportation and storage	26,250	28,168	28,872
Information and communication	7,783	8,236	8,341
Financial intermediation and insurance	4,407	4,680	4,661
Real estate activities	18,440	19,767	20,598
Business, administrative and support service activities	12,153	13,152	13,834
Public administration; defence; education; health and social work	33,241	34,644	36,182
Other community, social and personal services	4,989	5,231	5,351
Sub-total	155,560	162,600	165,547
Taxes, less subsidies, on products	23,164	26,079	26,994
GDP in purchasers' values	178,724	188,679	192,541

BALANCE OF PAYMENTS
(US $ million)

	2010	2011	2012
Exports of goods	75,065	82,756	76,453
Imports of goods	–64,675	–79,265	–72,841
Balance on goods	10,390	3,491	3,611
Exports of services	22,159	26,193	24,769
Imports of services	–26,523	–28,955	–29,994
Balance on goods and services	6,026	730	–1,613
Primary income received	17,747	18,672	17,279
Primary income paid	–15,631	–18,897	–17,641
Balance on goods, services and primary income	8,142	504	–1,975
Secondary income received	2,258	2,950	3,132
Secondary income paid	–4,455	–5,143	–4,855
Current balance	5,944	–1,689	–3,698
Capital account (net)	234	264	265
Direct investment assets	–14,993	3,552	–8,378
Direct investment liabilities	12,226	–6,008	4,332
Portfolio investment assets	–28,543	–6,233	–20,365
Portfolio investment liabilities	15,009	17,118	32,368
Financial derivatives and employee stock options (net)	–114	1,660	1,382
Other investment assets	–38,811	–116,025	–2,327
Other investment liabilities	47,993	117,861	15,175
Net errors and omissions	–1,121	–10,066	–18,114
Reserves and related items	–2,173	435	640

Source: IMF, *International Financial Statistics*.

External Trade

PRINCIPAL COMMODITIES
(€ million)

Imports c.i.f.	2010	2011	2012
Food and live animals	2,851	3,248	3,467
Beverages and tobacco	495	546	496
Crude materials (inedible) except fuels	4,716	5,203	4,844
Mineral fuels, lubricants, etc.	9,497	13,137	12,997
Animal and vegetable oils and fats	299	240	301
Chemicals and related products	5,943	6,643	6,980
Basic manufactures	6,353	7,127	6,658
Machinery and transport equipment	14,911	16,793	16,118
Miscellaneous manufactured articles	5,115	5,615	5,658
Total (incl. others)	51,899	60,535	59,517

Exports f.o.b.	2010	2011	2012
Food and live animals	1,141	1,368	1,367
Beverages and tobacco	135	152	160
Crude materials (inedible) except fuels	3,533	4,059	4,273
Mineral fuels, lubricants, etc.	4,162	5,481	6,202
Animal and vegetable oils and fats	50	36	50
Chemicals and related products	5,539	6,350	6,350
Basic manufactures	16,805	18,055	16,843
Machinery and transport equipment	17,118	16,654	16,612
Miscellaneous manufactured articles	3,003	3,225	3,399
Total (incl. others)	52,439	56,855	56,878

PRINCIPAL TRADING PARTNERS
(€ million)*

Imports c.i.f.	2010	2011	2012
Belgium	1,228	1,268	1,259
Brazil	641	839	811
China, People's Republic	3,797	4,398	4,602
Czech Republic	607	706	611
Denmark	1,240	1,342	1,390
Estonia	1,264	1,554	1,547
France	2,028	1,980	1,820
Germany	6,878	7,528	7,335
India	350	673	350
Italy	1,450	1,583	1,592
Japan	912	930	740
Korea, Republic	465	601	871
Netherlands	2,804	3,151	3,370
Norway	1,198	1,950	2,166
Poland	954	1,184	1,192
Russia	9,217	11,319	10,583
Spain	679	801	752
Sweden	5,249	6,029	6,369
Switzerland	594	647	673
United Kingdom	1,622	1,777	1,760
USA	1,790	2,226	1,995
Total (incl. others)	51,899	60,535	59,517

Exports f.o.b.	2010	2011	2012
Austria	426	634	619
Belgium	1,423	1,584	1,731
Brazil	546	544	727
Canada	639	902	596
China, People's Republic	2,733	2,667	2,607
Denmark	1,007	1,163	1,031
Estonia	1,130	1,339	1,710
France	1,780	1,762	1,692
Germany	5,274	5,625	5,253
India	610	625	483
Italy	1,350	1,347	1,341
Japan	880	975	1,068
Korea, Republic	666	568	694
Netherlands	3,335	3,852	3,557
Norway	1,406	1,596	1,804
Poland	1,351	1,576	1,409
Russia	4,716	5,337	5,688
Spain	1,060	988	829
Sweden	6,026	6,739	6,291
Switzerland	627	733	841
Turkey	775	790	699
United Kingdom	2,435	2,913	2,889
USA	3,681	2,919	3,605
Total (incl. others)	52,439	56,855	56,878

* Imports by country of production; exports by country of consumption.

Transport

RAILWAYS
(traffic)

	2010	2011	2012
Passengers ('000 journeys)	68,950	68,376	69,300
Passenger-km (million)	3,959	3,882	4,035
Freight carried ('000 metric tons)	35,795	34,827	n.a.
Freight ton-km (million)	9,750	9,395	9,275

ROAD TRAFFIC
(registered motor vehicles at 31 December)

	2010	2011	2012
Passenger cars	2,877,484	2,978,729	3,057,484
Lorries and vans	464,408	488,939	508,011
Motorcycles	226,877	236,661	244,968
Tractors	376,807	383,951	391,335
Snowmobiles*	121,976	125,937	130,581

* Excluding Åland Islands.

SHIPPING

Flag Registered Fleet
(at 31 December)

	2011	2012	2013
Number of vessels	275	290	292
Total displacement ('000 grt)	1,220.6	1,488.6	1,464.7

Source: Lloyd's List Intelligence (www.lloydslistintelligence.com).

International Sea-borne Freight Traffic

	2010	2011	2012
Number of vessels entered	25,373	n.a.	n.a.
Goods ('000 metric tons):			
loaded	41,786	44,208	44,220
unloaded	51,488	54,168	49,836

Source: partly UN, *Monthly Bulletin of Statistics*.

CANAL TRAFFIC

	2008	2009	2010
Vessels in transit	34,255	42,199	47,778
Goods carried ('000 metric tons)	2,116	1,083	1,660

CIVIL AVIATION
(traffic on scheduled services)

	2010	2011
Kilometres flown (million)	148	172
Passengers carried ('000)	8,436	9,235
Passenger-km (million)	17,786	20,386
Total ton-km (million)	2,352	2,568

Source: UN, *Statistical Yearbook*.

Passengers carried ('000): 8,362 in 2012 (Source: World Bank, World Development Indicators database).

Tourism

FOREIGN TOURIST ARRIVALS
(overnight stays at accommodation establishments)

Country of residence	2010	2011	2012
Estonia	205,429	228,187	235,301
France	213,414	213,588	217,850
Germany	510,280	541,031	534,276
Italy	142,389	156,509	130,915
Japan	136,804	146,433	176,936
Netherlands	165,779	164,593	164,903
Norway	159,377	173,254	182,629
Russia	1,056,424	1,286,598	1,506,678
Spain	113,804	130,046	96,836
Sweden	517,849	552,129	536,992
Switzerland	107,859	118,009	132,933
United Kingdom	406,272	389,037	405,415
USA	178,482	201,854	198,691
Total (incl. others)	5,005,068	5,507,468	5,803,956

Tourism receipts (US $ million, excl. passenger transport): 3,051 in 2010; 3,820 in 2011; 4,139 in 2012 (provisional) (Source: World Tourism Organization).

Communications Media

	2010	2011	2012
Newspapers:			
number	194	188	183
total circulation ('000 copies)	2,886	2,745	2,547
Other periodicals: number	3,056	2,933	2,814
Book production: titles	12,017	11,404	11,513
Telephones ('000 main lines in use)*	1,250	1,080	890
Mobile cellular telephones ('000 subscribers)*	8,390	8,940	9,320
Broadband subscribers ('000)*	1,572.7	1,588.7	1,645.0

* Source: International Telecommunication Union.

2009: Internet users ('000 aged 15 years and over) 4,393.1 (Source: International Telecommunication Union).

Education

(2011 unless otherwise indicated)

	Institutions*	Teachers†	Students
Comprehensive schools‡	2,952	44,313	541,931
Senior secondary schools	395	7,295	109,046
Vocational and professional institutions	275	14,058	279 266
Polytechnics	31	6,034	139,857
Universities	20	7,755	168,983

* 2010 figures.
† 2003 figures.
‡ Comprising six-year primary stage and three-year lower secondary stage.

Pupil-teacher ratio (primary education, UNESCO estimate): 13.7 in 2010/11 (Source: UNESCO Institute for Statistics).

Directory

The Government

HEAD OF STATE

President: SAULI NIINISTÖ (took office 1 March 2012).

CABINET

(Valtioneuvosto)
(April 2014)

A coalition comprising the National Coalition Party (NCP), the Social Democratic Party (SDP), the Swedish People's Party (SPP), the Green League (Green) and the Christian Democrats (CD).

Prime Minister: JYRKI KATAINEN (NCP).

Minister of Finance: JUTTA URPILAINEN (SDP).

Minister of Foreign Affairs: ERKKI TUOMIOJA (SDP).

Minister of European Affairs and Foreign Trade: ALEXANDER STUBB (NCP).

Minister of International Development: PEKKA HAAVISTO (Green).

Minister of Justice: ANNA-MAJA HENRIKSSON (SPP).

Minister of the Interior: PÄIVI RÄSÄNEN (CD).

Minister of Defence: CARL HAGLUND (SPP).

Minister of Education and Communications: KRISTA KIURU (SDP).

Minister of Agriculture and Forestry: JARI KOSKINEN (NCP).

Minister of Transport and Local Government: HENNA VIRKKUNEN (NCP).

Minister of Economic Affairs: JAN VAPAAVUORI (NCP).

Minister of Labour: LAURI IHALAINEN (SDP).

Minister of Social Affairs and Health: PAULA RISIKKO (NCP).

Minister of Health and Social Services: SUSANNA HUOVINEN (SDP).

Minister of the Environment: VILLE NIINISTÖ (Green).

Minister of Culture and Housing: PIA VIITANEN (SDP).

MINISTRIES

Office of the President: Mariankatu 2, 00170 Helsinki; tel. (9) 661133; fax (9) 638247; e-mail presidentti@tpk.fi; internet www.presidentti.fi.

Prime Minister's Office: Snellmaninkatu 1A, Helsinki; POB 23, 00023 Government; tel. (9) 16001; fax (9) 16022165; e-mail info@vnk.fi; internet www.vnk.fi.

Ministry of Agriculture and Forestry: Hallituskatu 3A, Helsinki; POB 30, 00023 Government; tel. (9) 16001; fax (9) 16054202; e-mail kirjaamo.mmm@mmm.fi; internet www.mmm.fi.

Ministry of Defence: Eteläinen Makasiinikatu 8, POB 31, 00131 Helsinki; tel. (9) 16001; fax (9) 653254; e-mail tiedotus@defmin.fi; internet www.defmin.fi.

Ministry of Education and Culture: Meritullinkatu 10, Helsinki; POB 29, 00023 Government; tel. (2953) 30004; fax (9) 1359335; e-mail kirjaamo@minedu.fi; internet www.minedu.fi.

Ministry of Employment and the Economy: Aleksanterinkatu 4, 00170 Helsinki; POB 32, 00023 Government; tel. (10) 606000; fax (9) 16062166; e-mail kirjaamo@tem.fi; internet www.tem.fi.

Ministry of the Environment: Kasarmikatu 25, Helsinki; POB 35, 00023 Government; tel. (2952) 50000; fax (9) 16039320; e-mail kirjaamo.ym@ymparisto.fi; internet www.ymparisto.fi.

Ministry of Finance: Snellmaninkatu 1A, Helsinki; POB 28, 00023 Government; tel. (295) 16001; fax (9) 16033123; e-mail valtiovarainministerio@vm.fi; internet www.vm.fi.

Ministry of Foreign Affairs: Merikasarmi, Laivastokatu 22, POB 176, 00023 Helsinki; tel. (9) 5350000; fax (9) 629840; e-mail kirjaamo.um@formin.fi; internet formin.finland.fi.

Ministry of the Interior: Kirkkokatu 12, Helsinki; POB 26, 00023 Government; tel. (71) 8780171; fax (71) 8788555; e-mail kirjaamo@intermin.fi; internet www.intermin.fi.

Ministry of Justice: Eteläesplanadi 10, Helsinki; POB 25, 00023 Government; tel. (9) 16003; fax (9) 16067730; e-mail oikeusministerio@om.fi; internet www.oikeusministerio.fi.

Ministry of Social Affairs and Health: Meritullinkatu 8, 00170 Helsinki; POB 33, 00023 Government; tel. (295) 16001; fax (9) 6980709; e-mail kirjaamo@stm.fi; internet www.stm.fi.

Ministry of Transport and Communications: Eteläesplanadi 16, Helsinki; POB 31, 00023 Government; tel. (9) 16001; fax (9) 16028596; e-mail info@lvm.fi; internet www.lvm.fi.

President and Legislature

PRESIDENT

Presidential Election, 22 January and 5 February 2012

	First round votes (%)	Second round votes (%)
Sauli Niinistö (NCP)	37.0	62.6
Pekka Haavisto (Green)	18.8	37.4
Paavo Väyrynen (Centre)	17.5	—
Timo Soini (True Finns)	9.4	—
Paavo Lipponen (SDP)	6.7	—
Paavo Arhinmäki (Left Alliance)	5.5	—
Eva Biaudet (SPP)	2.7	—
Sari Essayah (CD)	2.5	—
Total	100.0	100.0

PARLIAMENT

Suomen Eduskunta

Mannerheimintie 30, 00102 Helsinki; tel. (9) 4321; fax (9) 4322274; e-mail parliament@parliament.fi; internet www.eduskunta.fi.

Speaker: EERO HEINÄLUOMA (SDP).

Secretary-General: SEPPO TIITINEN.

General Election, 17 April 2011

Party	Votes	% of votes	Seats
Kansallinen Kokoomus (National Coalition Party)	599,138	20.38	44
Suomen Sosialidemokraattinen Puolue (Finnish Social Democratic Party)	561,558	19.10	42
Perussuomalaiset/ Sannfinländarna (True Finns)	560,075	19.05	39
Suomen Keskusta (Finnish Centre Party)	463,266	15.76	35
Vasemmistoliitto (Left Alliance)	239,039	8.13	14
Vihreä Liitto (Green League)	213,172	7.25	10
Svenska Folkpartiet (Swedish People's Party)	125,785	4.28	9
Suomen Kristillisdemokraatit (Finnish Christian Democrats)	118,453	4.03	6
Others	59,085	2.01	1*
Total	2,939,571	100.00	200

* Including a representative of the Åland Islands.

Election Commission

Unit for Democracy, Language Affairs and Fundamental Rights: POB 25, 00023 Government; internet www.om.fi/en/etusivu/ministerio/organisaatio/demokratiakielijaperusoikeusasioidenyksikko; dept of the Ministry of Justice; Dir KIRSI PIMIÄ.

Political Organizations

In February 2014 there were 16 registered political parties in Finland.

Itsenäisyyspuolue (IP) (Independence Party): Nikinsaarentie 31, 62900 Alajärvi; tel. (40) 565366; fax (06) 5574728; e-mail info@ipu.fi; internet www.itsenaisyyspuolue.fi; promotes national independence and social equality; Chair. ANTTI PESONEN.

Kansallinen Kokoomus (National Coalition Party—NCP): Kansakoulukuja 3A, 2nd Floor, 00100 Helsinki; tel. (20) 7488488; fax (20) 7488505; e-mail info@kokoomus.fi; internet www.kokoomus.fi; f. 1918; moderate conservative political ideology; Chair. JYRKI KATAINEN; Party Sec. TARU TUJUNEN; Chair., Parliamentary Group PETTERI ORPO; 41,000 mems.

Kommunistinen Työväenpuolue—Rauhan ja Sosialismin Puolesta (Communist Workers' Party): Tikkuraitti 11A, POB 93, 01301 Vantaa; tel. (9) 8571022; fax (9) 8573097; e-mail ktp@ktpkom.fi; internet www.ktpkom.fi; f. 1988; Sec.-Gen. Hannu TUOMINEN.

Köyhien Asialla (For The Poor): Elsankuja 2B 9, 02230 Espoo; tel. (50) 5291171; e-mail info@koyhienasialla.fi; internet www.koyhienasialla.fi; f. 2002; Chair. TERTTU SAVOLA.

Muutos 2011 (M11) (Change 2011): POB 5, 37801 Akaa; tel. (44) 5857435; e-mail oula.lintula@muutos2011.fi; internet www.muutos2011.fi; f. 2010; Chair. JARI LEINO; Sec. MARKO PARKKOLA; 403 mems.

Perussuomalaiset (True Finns—The Finns): Yrjönkatu 8–10B 25, 00120 Helsinki; tel. (9) 0207430800; fax (9) 0207430801; e-mail puoluetoimisto@perussuomalaiset.fi; internet www.perussuomalaiset.fi; f. 1995 by mems of defunct Suomen Maaseudun Puolue (Finnish Rural Party); changed the English version of its name from True Finns to The Finns in 2011, although not a direct translation; Swedish name, Sannfinländarna; Chair. TIMO SOINI; Sec.-Gen. RIIKKA SLUNGA-POUTSALO.

Piraattipuolue (Pirate Party of Finland): Franzéninkatu 5E 1, 00500 Helsinki; tel. (9) 453102344; e-mail info@piraattipuolue.fi; internet piraattipuolue.fi; f. 2009; campaigns for freedom of speech and reform of copyright and intellectual property laws; Chair. HARRI KIVISTÖ.

Sinivalkoinen Rintama (Blue and White Front r.p.): c/o Olavi Mäenpää, Turunmaankatu 2A1, 20740 Turku; tel. (50) 5590119; e-mail olavi.maenpaa@turku.fi; f. 2009; fmrly Vapauspuolue-Suomen tulevaisuus (Liberty Party-Future of Finland); name changed 2013; Chair. OLAVI MÄENPÄÄ.

Suomen Keskusta (Finnish Centre Party): Apollonkatu 11A, 00100 Helsinki; tel. (10) 2897000; fax (10) 2897240; e-mail puoluetoimisto@keskusta.fi; internet www.keskusta.fi; f. 1906; radical centre party founded to promote the interests of the rural population, now reformist movement favouring individual enterprise, equality and decentralization; Chair. JUHA SIPILÄ; Party Sec. TIMO LAANINEN; Chair., Parliamentary Group KIMMO TIILIKAINEN; over 200,000 mems.

Suomen Kommunistinen Puolue (SKP) (Communist Party of Finland): Hitsaajankatu 9A, 6th Floor, 00810 Helsinki; tel. (9) 77438150; fax (9) 77438160; e-mail skp@skp.fi; internet www.skp.fi; f. 1918; incorporated into Vasemmistoliitto (Left Alliance) in 1990; refounded 1997 following disputes in the latter party; Chair. JUHA-PEKKA VÄISÄNEN; Sec.-Gen. HEIKKI KETOHARJU; 3,000 mems.

Suomen Kristillisdemokraatit (Finnish Christian Democrats—CD): Karjalankatu 2C, 7th Floor, 00520 Helsinki; tel. (9) 34882200; fax (9) 34882228; e-mail kd@kd.fi; internet www.kd.fi; f. 1958 as Suomen Kristillinen Liitto (Finnish Christian Union); present name adopted 2001; Chair. PÄIVI RÄSÄNEN; Sec.-Gen. ASMO MAANSELKÄ; Chair., Parliamentary Group PETER ÖSTMAN; 12,000 mems.

Suomen Sosialidemokraattinen Puolue (Finnish Social Democratic Party—SDP): Saariniemenkatu 6, 00530 Helsinki; tel. (9) 478988; fax (9) 712752; e-mail palaute@sdp.fi; internet www.sdp.fi; f. 1899; constitutional socialist programme; mainly supported by the urban working and middle classes; Chair. JUTTA URPILAINEN; Gen. Sec. REIJO PAANANEN; Chair., Parliamentary Group JOUNI BACKMAN; 50,000 mems.

Suomen Työväenpuolue (Finnish Workers' Party): POB 780, 00101 Helsinki; tel. (40) 7641163; e-mail tyovaenpuolue@suomi24.fi; internet www.tyovaenpuolue.org; f. 1999; Chair. JUHANI TANSKI; Sec.-Gen. HEIKKI MÄNNIKKÖ.

Svenska Folkpartiet (Swedish People's Party—SPP): Simonkatu 8A, 00100 Helsinki; POB 430, 00101 Helsinki; tel. (9) 693070; fax (9) 6931968; e-mail info@sfp.fi; internet www.sfp.fi; f. 1906; liberal party representing the interests of the Swedish-speaking minority; Chair. CARL HAGLUND; Sec.-Gen. JOHAN JOHANSSON; 37,000 mems.

Vasemmistoliitto (Vas) (Left Alliance): Lintulahdenkatu 10, 3rd Floor, 00500 Helsinki; tel. (9) 7737700; e-mail vas@vasemmistoliitto.fi; internet www.vasemmisto.fi; f. 1990 by merger of the Finnish People's Democratic League (f. 1944), the Communist Party of Finland (f. 1918), the Democratic League of Finnish Women, and left-wing groups; Chair. PAAVO ARHINMÄKI; Sec.-Gen. MARKO VARAJÄRVI; Chair., Parliamentary Group ANNIKA LAPINTIE; 10,000 mems.

Vihreä Liitto (Green League): Fredrikinkatu 33A, 3rd Floor, 00120 Helsinki; tel. (9) 58604160; fax (9) 58604161; e-mail vihreat@vihreat.fi; internet www.vihreat.fi; f. 1987; Chair. and Leader VILLE NIINISTÖ; c. 4,400 mems.

Diplomatic Representation

EMBASSIES IN FINLAND

Argentina: Bulevardi 5A 11, 00120 Helsinki; tel. (9) 42428700; fax (9) 42428701; Ambassador ROBERTO DANIEL PIERINI.

Austria: Unioninkatu 22, 00130 Helsinki; tel. (9) 6818600; fax (9) 665084; e-mail helsinki-ob@bmeia.gv.at; internet www.bmeia.gv.at/botschaft/helsinki.html; Ambassador Dr ELISABETH KEHRER.

Belarus: Unioninkatu 18, 00130 Helsinki; tel. (9) 42472056; fax (9) 42472057; e-mail finland@mfa.gov.by; internet www.finland.new.mfa.gov.by; Ambassador ALEXANDER P. OSTROVSKY.

Belgium: Kalliolinnantie 5, 00140 Helsinki; tel. (9) 170412; fax (9) 628842; e-mail helsinki@diplobel.fed.be; internet www.diplomatie.be/helsinki; Ambassador IVO GOEMANS.

Brazil: Itäinen puistotie 4B 1, 00140 Helsinki; tel. (9) 6841500; fax (9) 650084; e-mail brasemb@brazil.fi; internet www.brazil.fi; Ambassador NORTON DE ANDRADE MELLO RAPESTA.

Bulgaria: Kuusisaarentie 2B, 00340 Helsinki; tel. (9) 4584055; fax (9) 4584550; e-mail embassy.helsinki@mfa.bg; internet www.mfa.bg/embassies/finland; Ambassador LYUBOMIR TODOROV.

Canada: Pohjoisesplanadi 25B, POB 779, 00101 Helsinki; tel. (9) 228530; fax (9) 22853385; e-mail hsnki@international.gc.ca; internet www.canadainternational.gc.ca/finland-finlande; Ambassador ANDRÉE N. COOLIGAN.

Chile: Erottajankatu 11, 2nd Floor, 00130 Helsinki; tel. (9) 6126780; fax (9) 61267825; e-mail info@embachile.fi; internet www.embachile.fi; Ambassador EDUARDO PABLO TAPIA RIEPEL.

China, People's Republic: Vanha Kelkkamäki 11, 00570 Helsinki; tel. (9) 22890110; fax (9) 22890168; e-mail chinaemb_fi@mfa.gov.cn; internet fi.chineseembassy.org; Ambassador YU QINGTAI.

Croatia: Kruunuvuorenkatu 5, 4th Floor, 00160 Helsinki; tel. (9) 6850170; fax (9) 6222221; e-mail croemb.helsinki@mvpei.hr; Ambassador KRESIMIR KOPCIC.

Cuba: Frederikinkatu 61, 3rd Floor, 00100 Helsinki; tel. (9) 6802022; fax (9) 643163; e-mail embahelsinki@cuba.fi; internet www.cubadiplomatica.cu/finlandia; Ambassador ENRIQUE ORTA GONZÁLEZ.

Cyprus: Bulevardi 5A 19, 00120 Helsinki; tel. (9) 6962820; fax (9) 677428; e-mail mail@cyprusembassy.fi; internet www.cyprusembassy.fi; Ambassador FILIPPOS KRITIOTIS.

Czech Republic: Armfeltintie 14, 00150 Helsinki; tel. (9) 6120880; fax (9) 630655; e-mail helsinki@embassy.mzv.cz; internet www.mfa.cz/helsinki; Ambassador MARTIN TOMČO.

Denmark: Mannerheimintie 8, 6th Floor, POB 1042, 00100 Helsinki; tel. (9) 6841050; fax (9) 6985156; e-mail helamb@um.dk; internet www.ambhelsingfors.um.dk; Ambassador JETTE NORDAM.

Egypt: Kasarmikatu 44, 3rd Floor, 00130 Helsinki; tel. (9) 4777470; fax (9) 47774721; e-mail secretaryofembassy@hotmail.com; Ambassador MAHMOUD GAMIL AHMED ELDIEB.

Estonia: Itäinen puistotie 10, 00140 Helsinki; tel. (9) 6220260; fax (9) 62202610; e-mail embassy.helsinki@mfa.ee; internet www.estemb.fi; Ambassador MART TARMAK.

France: Itäinen puistotie 13, 00140 Helsinki; tel. (9) 618780; fax (9) 61878342; e-mail ambassade.france@welho.com; Ambassador ERIC LEBÉDEL.

Germany: Krogiuksentie 4B, 00340 Helsinki; POB 5, 00331 Helsinki; tel. (9) 458580; fax (9) 45858258; e-mail info@helsinki.diplo.de; internet www.helsinki.diplo.de; Ambassador Dr THOMAS GÖTZ.

Greece: Maneesikatu 2A 4, 00170 Helsinki; tel. (9) 6229790; fax (9) 2781200; e-mail gremb.hel@mfa.gr; internet www.mfa.gr/helsinki; Ambassador CHRISTOS KONTOVOUNISIOS.

Hungary: Kuusisaarenkuja 6, 00340 Helsinki; tel. (9) 484144; fax (9) 480497; e-mail mission.hel@kum.hu; internet www.mfa.gov.hu/emb/helsinki; Ambassador KRISTÓF FORRAI.

Iceland: Pohjoisesplanadi 27C, 2nd Floor, 00100 Helsinki; tel. (9) 6122460; fax (9) 61224620; e-mail emb.helsinki@mfa.is; internet www.iceland.org/fi; Ambassador KRISTIN ARNADOTTIR.

India: Kulosaarentie 32, 00570 Helsinki; tel. (9) 2289910; fax (9) 6221208; e-mail amb.helsinki@mea.gov.in; internet www.indianembassy.fi; Ambassador ALADIYAN MANICKAM.

Indonesia: Kuusisaarentie 3, 00340 Helsinki; tel. (9) 4470370; fax (9) 4582882; e-mail info@indonesian-embassy.fi; internet www.indonesian-embassy.fi; Ambassador ELIAS GINTING.

Iran: Kulosaarentie 9, 00570 Helsinki; tel. (9) 6869240; fax (9) 68692410; e-mail embassy@iran.fi; Ambassador SAEED RASOUL MOUSSAVI.

Iraq: Lars Sonckintie 2, 00570 Helsinki; tel. (9) 68188727; fax (9) 6848977; e-mail info@iraqiembassy.fi; internet www.iraqiembassy.fi; Ambassador SAAD ABDULWAHAB JAWAD KINDEEL.

Ireland: Erottajankatu 7A, 00130 Helsinki; POB 33, 00131 Helsinki; tel. (9) 6824240; fax (9) 646022; e-mail helsinkiembassy@dfa.ie; internet www.embassyofireland.fi; Ambassador DÓNAL DENHAM.

Israel: Yrjönkatu 36A, 00100 Helsinki; tel. (9) 6812020; fax (9) 1356959; e-mail info@helsinki.mfa.gov.il; internet helsinki.mfa.gov.il; Ambassador DAN ASHBEL.

Italy: Itäinen puistotie 4A, 00140 Helsinki; tel. (9) 6811280; fax (9) 6987829; e-mail ambasciata.helsinki@esteri.it; internet www.ambhelsinki.esteri.it; Ambassador GIORGIO VISETTI.

Japan: Unioninkatu 20–22, 00130 Helsinki; tel. (9) 6860200; fax (9) 633012; e-mail inquiry@hk.mofa.go.jp; internet www.fi.emb-japan.go.jp; Ambassador KENJI SHINODA.

Korea, Republic: Erottajankatu 7A, 00130 Helsinki; tel. (9) 2515000; fax (9) 25150055; e-mail korembfi@mofat.go.kr; internet fin.mofat.go.kr; Ambassador DONGHEE CHANG.

Latvia: Armfeltintie 10, 00150 Helsinki; tel. (9) 47647244; fax (9) 47647288; e-mail embassy.finland@mfa.gov.lv; internet www.mfa.gov.lv/fi/helsinki; Ambassador UGIS BAMBE.

Lithuania: Rauhankatu 13A, 00170 Helsinki; tel. (9) 6844880; fax (9) 68448820; e-mail info@lithuania.fi; internet fi.mfa.lt; Ambassador ARŪNAS JIEVALTAS.

Malaysia: Aleksanterinkatu 17, 00100 Helsinki; tel. (10) 3202030; fax (10) 3202041; e-mail malhsinki@kln.gov.my; internet www.kln.gov.my/perwakilan/helsinki; Ambassador Datin SERI BLANCHE OLBERY.

Mexico: Simonkatu 12A 12, 7th Floor, 00100 Helsinki; tel. (9) 5860430; fax (9) 6949411; e-mail mexican.embassy@welho.com; Ambassador NORMA PENSADO MORENO.

Morocco: Unioninkatu 15A, 00300 Helsinki; tel. (9) 6122480; fax (9) 635160; e-mail embassy.of.morocco@co.inet.fi; Ambassador MOHAMMED ARIAD.

Netherlands: Erottajankatu 19B, 00130 Helsinki; tel. (9) 228920; fax (9) 22892228; e-mail hel@minbuza.nl; internet finland.nlambassade.org; Ambassador HENK SWARTTOUW.

Norway: Rehbinderintie 17, 00150 Helsinki; POB 116, 00151 Helsinki; tel. (9) 6860180; fax (9) 657807; e-mail emb.helsinki@mfa.no; internet www.norja.fi; Ambassador JØRG WILLY BRONEBAKK.

Peru: Lönnrotinkatu 7B 11, 00120 Helsinki; tel. (9) 7599400; fax (9) 75994040; e-mail secretary@embassyofperu.fi; internet www.peruembassy.fi; Ambassador Dr PABLO PORTUGAL.

Poland: Armas Lindgrenintie 21, 00570 Helsinki; tel. (9) 618280; fax (9) 6847477; e-mail helsinki.amb.info@msz.gov.pl; internet www.helsinki.polemb.net; Ambassador JANUSZ NIESYTO.

Portugal: Unioninkatu 22, 00130 Helsinki; tel. (9) 6824370; fax (9) 663550; e-mail emb.port@portugal.fi; Ambassador MARIA DE FÁTIMA DE PINA PERESTRELLO.

Romania: Stenbäckinkatu 24, 00250 Helsinki; tel. (9) 2414414; fax (9) 2413272; e-mail romania@romania.fi; internet helsinki.mae.ro; Ambassador MARIAN CĂTĂLIN AVRAMESCU.

Russia: Tehtaankatu 1B, 00140 Helsinki; tel. (9) 661876; fax (9) 661006; e-mail rusembassy@co.inet.fi; internet www.rusembassy.fi; Ambassador ALEKSANDR Y. RUMYANTSEV.

Saudi Arabia: Stenbäckinkatu 26, 00250 Helsinki; tel. (9) 4778870; fax (9) 4543060; e-mail secretary@saudiembassy.fi; internet embassies.mofa.gov.sa; Ambassador NAIF AL ABOUD.

Serbia: Kulosaarentie 36, 00570 Helsinki; tel. (9) 6848522; fax (9) 6848783; e-mail info.ambascghki@kolumbus.fi; internet www.helsinki.mfa.rs; Ambassador SLAVKO KRULJEVIĆ.

Slovakia: Vähäniityntie 5, 00570 Helsinki; tel. (9) 68117810; fax (9) 68117820; e-mail emb.helsinki@mzv.sk; internet www.mzv.sk/helsinki; Ambassador JURAJ PODHORSKÝ.

South Africa: Pohjoinen Makasiinikatu 4, 00160 Helsinki; tel. (9) 68603100; fax (9) 68603160; e-mail saembfin@dirco.gov.za; internet www.southafricanembassy.fi; Ambassador SELLO MOLOTO.

Spain: Kalliolinnantie 6, 00140 Helsinki; tel. (9) 6877080; fax (9) 170923; e-mail emb.helsinki@maec.es; internet www.maec.es/embajadas/helsinki/es/home; Ambassador MARÍA JESÚS FIGA LÓPEZ-PALOP.

Sweden: Pohjoisesplanadi 7B, 00170 Helsinki; POB 329, 00171 Helsinki; tel. (9) 6877660; fax (9) 655285; e-mail ambassaden.helsingfors@foreign.ministry.se; internet www.sverige.fi; Ambassador ANDERS LIDÉN.

Switzerland: Kalliolinnantie 16A 2a, 00140 Helsinki; tel. (9) 6229500; fax (9) 62295050; e-mail hel.vertretung@eda.admin.ch; internet www.eda.admin.ch/helsinki; Ambassador MAURICE DARIER.

Thailand: Bulevardi 12, 2nd Floor, 00120 Helsinki; tel. (9) 61226415; fax (9) 61226466; e-mail chancery@thaiembassy.fi; internet www.thaiembassy.org; Ambassador RACHANANT THANANANT.

Tunisia: Liisankatu 14B 31, 00170 Helsinki; tel. (9) 68039614; fax (9) 68039610; e-mail at.helsinki@kolumbus.fi; Chargé d'affaires a.i. MUSTAPHA WASSIM ABID.

Turkey: Puistokatu 1B A 3, 00140 Helsinki; tel. (9) 61226100; fax (9) 61226150; e-mail embassy.helsinki@mfa.gov.tr; internet helsinki.be.mfa.gov.tr; Ambassador ADNAN BASAGA.

Ukraine: Vähäniityntie 9, 00570 Helsinki; tel. (9) 2289000; fax (9) 2289001; e-mail embassy@ukraine.fi; internet www.ukraine.fi; Chargé d'affaires a.i. OLEKSII SELIN.

United Kingdom: Itäinen puistotie 17, 00140 Helsinki; tel. (9) 22865100; fax (9) 22865284; e-mail info.helsinki@fco.gov.uk; internet www.ukinfinland.fco.gov.uk; Ambassador SARAH PRICE.

USA: Itäinen puistotie 14B, 00140 Helsinki; tel. (9) 616250; fax (9) 61625800; e-mail arc@usembassy.fi; internet finland.usembassy.gov; Ambassador BRUCE J. ORECK.

Venezuela: Bulevardi 1A 62, POB 285, 00100 Helsinki; tel. (9) 6860440; fax (9) 640971; e-mail embavenefin@embavene.fi; internet www.embavene.fi; Chargé d'affaires a.i. ERNESTO NAVAZIO MOSSUCCA.

Viet Nam: Kulosaarentie 12, 00570 Helsinki; tel. (9) 6229900; fax (9) 62299022; e-mail vietnamfinland@gmail.com; internet www.vietnamembassy-finland.org; Ambassador VAN KHOA BUI.

Judicial System

The administration of justice is independent of the Government and judges can be removed only by judicial sentence. The compulsory retirement age for judges is 67.

SUPREME COURT

Korkein oikeus/Högsta domstolen: Pohjoisesplanadi 3, POB 301, 00171 Helsinki; tel. (9) 95640000; fax (9) 95640154; e-mail korkein.oikeus@oikeus.fi; internet www.kko.fi; consists of a President and at least 15 Justices appointed by the President of the Republic; it is the final court of appeal in civil and criminal cases, and supervises judges and executive authorities; President PAULIINE KOSKELO.

SUPREME ADMINISTRATIVE COURT

Korkein hallinto-oikeus/Högsta förvaltningsdomstolen: Fabianinkatu 15, POB 180, 00131 Helsinki; tel. (10) 3640200; fax (10) 3640382; e-mail korkein.hallinto-oikeus@oikeus.fi; internet www.kho.fi; consists of a President and 20 Justices appointed by the President of the Republic; it is the highest tribunal for appeals in administrative cases; President PEKKA VIHERVUORI.

COURTS OF APPEAL

There are Courts of Appeal at Turku, Vaasa, Kuopio, Helsinki, Kouvola, and Rovaniemi, consisting of a President and an appropriate number of members.

ADMINISTRATIVE COURTS

There are eight Administrative Courts, which hear the appeals of private individuals and corporate bodies against the authorities in tax cases, municipal cases, construction cases, social welfare and health care cases and other administrative cases. In certain of these, the appeal must be preceded by a complaint to a separate lower appellate body. The state and municipal authorities also have a right of appeal in certain cases.

DISTRICT COURTS

Courts of first instance for almost all suits. Appeals lie to the Court of Appeal, and then to the Supreme Court. The composition of the District Court is determined by the type of case to be heard. Civil cases and 'ordinary' criminal cases can be considered by one judge. Other criminal cases and family law cases are heard by a judge and a panel of three lay judges (jurors). Other civil cases are heard by three legally qualified judges. There are 27 District Courts.

SPECIAL COURTS

In addition there are a number of special courts with more restricted jurisdictions. These are the High Court of Impeachment; the Insurance Court; the Labour Court; and the Market Court. There is no constitutional court in Finland, but the Constitutional Committee of Parliament has been entrusted with the process of verifying the compatibility of new legislation with the Constitution.

CHANCELLOR OF JUSTICE

The Chancellor of Justice (Oikeuskansleri) is responsible for ensuring that authorities and officials comply with the law. He is the chief public prosecutor, and acts as counsel for the Government.

Office of the Chancellor of Justice: Snellmaninkatu 1, Helsinki; POB 20, 00023 Government; tel. (9) 16001; fax (9) 16023975; e-mail kirjaamo@okv.fi; internet www.okv.fi; Chancellor of Justice JAAKKO JONKKA.

PARLIAMENTARY OMBUDSMAN

The Eduskunnan Oikeusasiamies is the Finnish Ombudsman appointed by the Eduskunta to supervise the observance of the law.

Office of the Parliamentary Ombudsman: Arkadiankatu 3, 00102 Helsinki; tel. (9) 4321; fax (9) 4322268; e-mail oikeusasiamies@eduskunta.fi; internet www.oikeusasiamies.fi; f. 1919; Parliamentary Ombudsman PETRI JÄÄSKELÄINEN.

In addition to the Chancellor of Justice and the Parliamentary Ombudsman, there are also specialized authorities that have similar duties in more limited fields. These include the Consumer Ombudsman, the Ombudsman for Equality, the Data Protection Ombudsman, the Ombudsman for Aliens and the Bankruptcy Ombudsman.

Religion

In 2012 76.4% of the population were members of the Evangelical Lutheran Church and around 1.1% belonged to the Orthodox Church. Some 21.0% of the population professed no religious affiliation.

CHRISTIANITY

Suomen ekumeeninen neuvosto/Ekumeniska rådet i Finland (Finnish Ecumenical Council): Katajanokankatu 7A, POB 185, 00161 Helsinki; tel. (9) 1802369; fax (9) 174313; e-mail heikki.huttunen@ekumenia.fi; internet www.ekumenia.fi; f. 1917; 11 mem. churches; Pres. Rt Rev. TEEMU SIPPO; Gen. Sec. Rev. HEIKKI HUTTUNEN.

National Churches

Suomen evankelis-luterilainen kirkko (Evangelical Lutheran Church of Finland): Council for International Relations, Satamakatu 11, POB 185, 00161 Helsinki; tel. (9) 18021; fax (9) 1802350; e-mail kirkkohallitus@evl.fi; internet www.evl.fi; 4.3m. mems (2010); Leader Archbishop Dr KARI MÄKINEN.

Suomen Ortodoksinen Kirkko (Orthodox Church of Finland): Karjalankatu 1, 70110 Kuopio; tel. (206) 100210; fax (206) 100211; e-mail kirkollishallitus@ort.fi; internet www.ort.fi; 60,000 mems; Leader Archbishop LEO of Karelia and All Finland.

The Roman Catholic Church

Finland comprises the single diocese of Helsinki, directly responsible to the Holy See. There were 11,530 adherents in the country (0.2% of the population) in 2012. The Bishop participates in the Scandinavian Episcopal Conference (based in Sweden).

Bishop of Helsinki: Rt Rev. TEEMU SIPPO, Rehbinderintie 21, 00150 Helsinki; tel. (9) 6877460; fax (9) 639820; e-mail curia@catholic.fi; internet www.katolinen.net.

Other Churches

Finlands svenska baptistsamfund (Finland Swedish Baptist Union): Rådhusgatan 44, 65100 Vasa; POB 54, 65101 Vasa; tel. (6) 3464500; fax (6) 3464510; e-mail fsb@baptist.fi; internet www.baptist.fi; f. 1856; publishes *Missionsstandaret* (12 a year); Gen. Sec. PETER SJÖBLOM; 1,300 mems.

Finlands svenska metodistkyrka (United Methodist Church in Finland—Swedish-speaking): Apollogatan 5, 00100 Helsinki; e-mail kyrkostyrelsen@metodistkyrkan.fi; internet www.metodistkyrkan.fi; f. 1881; District Superintendent Rev. MAYVOR WÄRN-RANCKEN; 1,000 mems.

Jehovan Todistajat (Jehovah's Witnesses): Puutarhatie 60, 01300 Vantaa; POB 68, 01301 Vantaa; tel. (9) 825885; fax (9) 82588285; internet www.watchtower.org; 19,094 mems.

Myöhempien Aikojen Pyhien Jeesuksen Kristuksen Kirkko (The Church of Jesus Christ of Latter-day Saints—Mormon): Mäkipellonaukio 2, 00320 Helsinki; tel. (9) 6962750; fax (9) 69627510; e-mail 2015803@ldschurch.org; internet www.mormonit.fi; 4,604 mems; Mission Pres. D. M. RAWLINGS.

Suomen Adventtikirkko (Seventh-day Adventist Church in Finland): Ketarantie 4E, 33680 Tampere; POB 94, 33101 Tampere; tel. (3) 3611111; fax (3) 3600454; e-mail mervi.tukiainen@adventtikirkko.fi; internet www.adventtikirkko.fi; f. 1894; 5,469 mems; Pres. KALERVO AROMÄKI; Sec. ANNE VRCELJ.

Suomen Baptistikirkko (Finnish Baptist Union): Kissanmaankatu 19, 33530 Tampere; tel. (44) 3881112; e-mail jari.portaankorva@baptisti.fi; internet www.baptisti.fi; Dir JARI PORTAANKORVA; 692 mems.

Suomen Metodistikirkko (United Methodist Church—Finnish-speaking): Punavuorenkatu 2B 17, 00120 Helsinki; tel. (9) 628135; e-mail suomen@metodistikirkko.fi; internet www.metodistikirkko.fi; District Superintendent Rev. PASI RUNONEN; 849 mems.

Suomen Vapaakirkko (Evangelical Free Church of Finland): Lukiokatu 15, POB 198, 13101 Hämeenlinna; tel. (3) 6445150; fax (3) 6122153; e-mail svk@svk.fi; internet www.svk.fi; f. 1923; Pres. Rev. HANNU VUORINEN; 15,280 mems.

The Anglican Church and the Salvation Army are also active in the country.

BAHÁ'Í FAITH

Suomen Bahá'í-yhteisö (Bahá'í Community of Finland): POB 423, 00101 Helsinki; tel. (9) 790875; fax (9) 790058; e-mail info@bahai.fitiedotus@bahai.fi; internet www.bahai.fi; f. 1953; 700 mems.

JUDAISM

Helsingin Juutalainen Seurakunta (Jewish Community of Helsinki): Synagogue and Community Centre, Malminkatu 26, 00100 Helsinki; tel. (9) 6854584; fax (9) 6948916; e-mail srk@jchelsinki.fi; internet www.jchelsinki.fi; Pres. GIDEON BOLOTOWSKY; Exec. Dir DAN KANTOR; 1,200 mems.

ISLAM

In 2012 there were 10,596 members of Islamic congregations. There are around 20 registered mosques or religious communities.

Suomen Islamilainen Yhdyskunta (Islamic Society of Finland): Lonnrotinkatu 22A 5, POB 87, 00101 Helsinki; tel. (9) 2782551; fax (9) 6121156; e-mail yhdyskunta@rabita.fi; internet www.rabita.fi; f. 1987; Imam ANAS HAJJAR.

The Press

In 2012 there were 183 newspapers in Finland; the total circulation for all types of newspaper was some 2.5m. A number of dailies are printed in Swedish. The most popular daily papers are *Helsingin Sanomat*, *Ilta-Sanomat*, *Aamulehti* and *Iltalehti*.

PRINCIPAL DAILIES

(average net circulation figures, for the year 2010, unless otherwise indicated)

Helsinki

Helsingin Sanomat: Töölönlahdenkatu 2, POB 18, 00089 Sanomat; tel. (9) 1221; fax (9) 1222366; e-mail janne.virkkunen@sanomat.fi; internet www.hs.fi; f. 1889; independent; Publr and Senior Editor-in-Chief MIKAEL PENTIKÄINEN; circ. 374,503 (weekdays), 447,682 (weekend).

Hufvudstadsbladet: Mannerheimvägen 18, POB 217, 00101 Helsinki; tel. (9) 12531; fax (9) 642930; e-mail nyheter@hbl.fi; internet www.hbl.fi; f. 1864; Swedish-language; independent; Editor-in-Chief JENS BERG; circ. 47,702 (weekdays), 50,030 (weekend).

Iltalehti: Aleksanterinkatu 9, POB 372, 00100 Helsinki; tel. (10) 665100; fax (9) 177313; e-mail il.toimitus@iltalehti.fi; internet www.iltalehti.fi; f. 1981; afternoon; independent; Man. Dir KARI KIVELÄ; Editor-in-Chief PANU POKKINEN; circ. 107,052 (weekdays), 136,245 (weekend).

Ilta-Sanomat: Töölönlahdenkatu 2, POB 45, 00089 Sanomat; tel. (9) 1221; fax (9) 1223419; e-mail uutiset@sanoma.fi; internet www.iltasanomat.fi; f. 1932; afternoon; 6 a week; independent; Publr and Editor-in-Chief TAPIO SADEOJA; circ. 150,351 (weekdays), 189,524 (weekend).

Kauppalehti (Finnish Business Daily): Eteläesplanadi 20, POB 189, 00101 Helsinki; tel. (10) 665101; fax (10) 6652423; internet www.kauppalehti.fi; f. 1898; weekdays; Man. Dir JUHA-PETRI LOIMOVUORI; Editor-in-Chief HANNU LEINONEN; circ. 70,118.

Uutispäivä Demari: Haapaniemenkatu 7–9B, 17th and 18th Floors, 00530 Helsinki; POB 338, 00531 Helsinki; tel. (9) 701041; fax (9) 7010567; e-mail toimitus@demari.fi; internet www.demari.fi; f. 1895; chief organ of the Social Democratic Party; Man. Dir HEIKKI NYKANEN; Editor-in-Chief JUHA PELTONEN; circ. 14,119.

Hämeenlinna

Hämeen Sanomat: Vanajantie 7, POB 530, 13111 Hämeenlinna; tel. (3) 61511; fax (3) 6151492; e-mail toimitus@hameensanomat.fi; internet www.hameensanomat.fi; f. 1879; independent; Man. Dir PAULI UUSI-KILPONEN; Editor-in-Chief PAULI UUSI-KILPONEN; circ. 28,296.

Joensuu

Karjalainen: Kosti Aaltosentie 9, 80140, Joensuu; POB 99, 80141 Joensuu; tel. (13) 2551; fax (13) 2552363; e-mail toimitus@karjalainen.fi; internet www.karjalainen.fi; f. 1874; independent; Man. Dir RAIMO PUUSTINEN; Editor PASI KOIVUMAA; circ. 45,584.

Jyväskylä

Sanomalehti Keskisuomalainen Oy: Aholaidantie 3, POB 159, 40101 Jyväskylä; tel. (14) 622000; fax (14) 622272; internet www.ksml.fi; f. 1871; Editor-in-Chief PEKKA MERVOLA; circ. 73,559.

Kemi

Pohjolan Sanomat: Sairaalakatu 2, 94100 Kemi; tel. (10) 6656555; fax (10) 6656322; e-mail ps.toimitus@pohjolansanomat.fi; internet www.pohjolansanomat.fi; f. 1915; Man. Dir MARTTI NIKKANEN; Editor-in-Chief HEIKKI LÄÄKKÖLÄ; circ. 20,070 (weekdays), 20,221 (Sat.).

Kokkola

Keskipohjanmaa: Eteläväylä, POB 45, 67101 Kokkola; tel. (20) 7504400; fax (20) 7504488; e-mail toimitus@kpk.fi; internet www.keskipohjanmaa.net; f. 1917; independent; Man. Dir EINO LAUKKA; Editor-in-Chief LASSI JAAKKOLA; circ. 25,479.

Kotka

Kymen Sanomat: Tornatorintie 3, 48100 Kotka; POB 27, 48101 Kotka; tel. (5) 210015; fax (5) 21005206; e-mail uutiset@kymensanomat.fi; internet www.kymensanomat.fi; f. 1902; independent; Man. Dir JARMO KOSKINEN; Editor PEKKA LAKKA; circ. 23,208.

Kouvola

Kouvolan Sanomat: Lehtikaari 1, POB 40, 45101 Kouvola; tel. (5) 280014; fax (5) 28004706; e-mail toimitus@kouvolansanomat.fi; internet www.kouvolansanomat.fi; f. 1909; independent; Man. Dir JUHA OKSANEN; Editor-in-Chief PEKKA LAKKA; circ. 27,273 (weekdays), 27,610 (Sat.).

Kuopio

Savon Sanomat: Vuorikatu 21, POB 68, 70101 Kuopio; tel. (17) 303111; fax (17) 303375; e-mail lukijansanomat@iwn.fi; internet www.savonsanomat.fi; f. 1907; independent; Man. Dir HEIKKI AURASMAA; Editor-in-Chief JARI TOURUNEN; circ. 61,546.

Lahti

Etelä-Suomen Sanomat: Ilmarisentie 7, POB 80, 15101 Lahti; tel. (3) 75751; fax (3) 7575466; e-mail heikki.hakala@ess.fi; internet www.ess.fi; f. 1914; independent; Man. Dir JUKKA OTTELA; Editor-in-Chief HEIKKI HAKALA; circ. 58,400.

Lappeenranta

Etelä-Saimaa: Lauritsalantie 1, POB 3, 53501 Lappeenranta; tel. (5) 538813; fax (5) 53883206; e-mail lukijat@esaimaa.fi; internet www.esaimaa.fi; f. 1885; independent; Editor PEKKA LAKKA; circ. 30,288 (weekdays), 30,816 (Sat.).

Mikkeli

Länsi-Savo: Teollisuuskatu 2–6, 50130 Mikkeli; POB 6, 50101 Mikkeli; tel. (15) 3501; fax (15) 3503337; e-mail asiakaspalvelu@lansi-savo.fi; internet www.lansi-savo.fi; independent; Man. Dir JUKKA TIKKA; Editor-in-Chief TAPIO HONKAMAA; circ. 25,018.

Oulu

Kaleva: Lekatie 1, 90140 Oulu; POB 170, 90401 Oulu; tel. (8) 5377111; fax (8) 5377206; e-mail kaleva@kaleva.fi; internet www.kaleva.fi; f. 1899; independent; Man. Dir TAISTO RISKI; Editor-in-Chief MARKKU MANTILA; circ. 78,216 (weekdays), 80,324 (weekend).

Pori

Satakunnan Kansa: Pohjoisranta 11E, POB 58, 28100 Pori; tel. (10) 665132; fax (10) 6658330; e-mail sk.toimitus@satakunnankansa.fi; internet www.satakunnankansa.fi; f. 1873; independent; Editor-in-Chief PETRI HAKALA; circ. 49,989.

Rovaniemi

Lapin Kansa: Veitikantie 2–8, 96100 Rovaniemi; tel. (10) 665022; fax (10) 6657720; e-mail lktoimitus@lapinkansa.fi; internet www.lapinkansa.fi; f. 1928; independent; Man. Dir JUHA RUOTSALAINEN; Editor-in-Chief ANTTI KOKKONEN; circ. 32,691 (weekdays), 32,887 (Sat.).

Salo

Salon Seudun Sanomat: Örninkatu 14, POB 117, 24101 Salo; tel. (2) 77021; fax (2) 7702200; e-mail jarmo.vahasilta@sss.fi; internet www.sss.fi; independent; Man. Dir KIRSTI KIRJONEN; Editor-in-Chief JUKKA HOLMBERG; circ. 21,828.

Savonlinna

Itä-Savo: Olavinkatu 60, POB 101, 57101 Savonlinna; tel. (15) 3503400; fax (15) 3503444; e-mail asiakaspalvelu@ita-savo.fi; internet www.ita-savo.fi; Man. Dir JUHA PELKONEN; Editor-in-Chief TUOMO YLI-HUTTALA; circ. 16,674.

Seinäjoki

Ilkka: Koulukatu 10, 60100 Seinäjoki; POB 60, 60101 Seinäjoki; tel. (6) 2477830; fax (6) 4186500; e-mail ilkka.toimitus@ilkka.fi; internet www.ilkka.fi; f. 1906; independent; Man. Dir MATTI KORKIATUPA; Editor-in-Chief MATTI KALLIOKOSKI; circ. 53,768.

Tampere

Aamulehti: Itäinenkatu 11, 33210 Tampere; tel. (10) 665111; fax (10) 6653140; e-mail matti.apunen@aamulehti.fi; internet www.aamulehti.fi; f. 1881; Editor JOUKO JOKINEN; circ. 131,539.

Turku

Turun Sanomat: Länsikaari 15, POB 95, 20101 Turku; tel. (2) 2693297; fax (2) 2693274; e-mail ts.toimitus@ts-group.fi; internet www.turunsanomat.fi; f. 1904; independent; Man. Dir MIKKO KETONEN; Editors-in-Chief KARI VAINIO, RIITTA MONTO; circ. 107,119.

Tuusula

Keski-Uusimaa: Klaavolantie 5, POB 52, 04301 Tuusula; tel. (9) 273000; fax (9) 27300205; e-mail toimitus@keskiuusimaa.fi; internet www.keskiuusimaa.fi; independent; Man. Dir JORMA HÄMÄLÄINEN; Editor-in-Chief PENTTI KIISKI; circ. 20,444.

Vaasa

Pohjalainen: Hietasaarenkatu 19, 65100 Vaasa; POB 37, 65101 Vaasa; tel. (6) 3249111; fax (6) 3249355; e-mail toimitus@pohjalainen.fi; internet www.pohjalainen.fi; f. 1903; independent; Man. Dir MATTI KORKIATUPA; Editor KALLE HEISKANEN; circ. 25,517.

Vasabladet: Hietasaarenkatu 20, POB 52, 65101 Vaasa; tel. (6) 3260211; fax (6) 3129003; e-mail nyheter@vasabladet.fi; internet www.vasabladet.fi; f. 1856; Swedish-language; liberal independent; Man. Dir JENS LILLSUNDE; Editor-in-Chief CAMILLA BERGGREN; circ. 21,529.

PRINCIPAL PERIODICALS

(average net circulation figures, for the year 2012, unless otherwise indicated)

7 päivää: Pursimiehenkatu 29–31A, 00150 Helsinki; POB 124, 00151 Helsinki; tel. (9) 86217000; fax (9) 86217230; e-mail asiakaspalvelu@seiskalive.fi; internet www.seiska.fi; f. 1992; weekly; publ. by Aller Media AS; television and radio; Editor-in-Chief EEVA-HELENA JOKITAIPALE; circ. 170,867.

Ahjo: Hakaniemenranta 1, POB 107, 00531 Helsinki; tel. (20) 774001; fax (20) 7741240; e-mail ahjo@metalliliitto.fi; internet www.ahjo.fi; 16 a year; for metal industry employees; Editor-in-Chief HEIKKI PISKONEN; circ. 160,000.

Aku Ankka (Donald Duck): Lapinmäentie 1, 00350 Helsinki; POB 100, 00040 Helsinki; tel. (9) 1201; fax (9) 1205569; e-mail asiakaspalvelu@sanomamagazines.fi; internet www.akuankka.fi; f. 1951; weekly; children's; Editor-in-Chief JUKKA HEISKANEN; circ. 282,794.

Apu: Risto Rytintie 33, 00081 A-lehdet, Helsinki; tel. (9) 75961; fax (9) 75983101; e-mail marja.aarnipuro@apu.fi; internet www.apu.fi; f. 1933; weekly; family journal; Editor-in-Chief MARJA AARNIPURO; circ. 149,050.

Avotakka: Risto Rytintie 33, 00081 A-lehdet, Helsinki; tel. (9) 75961; fax (9) 75983110; e-mail johanna.falck@a-lehdet.fi; internet www.avotakka.fi; f. 1967; monthly; interior decoration; Editor-in-Chief JOHANNA FALCK; circ. 82,245.

Diabetes: Kirjoniementie 15, 33680 Tampere; tel. (3) 2860111; fax (3) 2860422; e-mail diabetesliitto@diabetes.fi; internet www.diabetes.fi; f. 1949; 9 a year; health; publ. by Finnish Diabetes Asscn; Editor-in-Chief TARJA SAMPO; circ. 61,607.

Eeva: Risto Rytintie 33, 00081 A-lehdet, Helsinki; tel. (9) 75961; fax (9) 786858; e-mail riitta.nykanen@a-lehdet.fi; internet www.eeva.fi; f. 1934; monthly; women's; Editor-in-Chief RIITTA NYKÄNEN; circ. 98,5436.

Erä: Maistraatinportti 1, 00015 Helsinki; tel. (9) 15661; fax (9) 145650; e-mail sepp.suuronen@kuvalehdet.fi; internet www.eralehti.fi; 13 a year; fishing and outdoor leisure; Editor JARI KAALIKOSKI; circ. 41,710.

ET-lehti: Lapinmäentie 1, 00350 Helsinki; POB 100, 00040 Sanoma Magazines; tel. (9) 1201; fax (9) 1205428; e-mail et-lehti@sanomamagazines.fi; internet www.et-lehti.fi; monthly; over-50s magazine; Editor-in-Chief RIITTA KORHONEN; circ. 226,853.

Gloria: Lapinmäentie 1, 00350 Helsinki; POB 100, 00040 Sanoma Magazines; tel. (9) 1201; fax (9) 1205427; e-mail gloria@sanomamagazines.fi; internet www.gloria.fi; monthly; women's; Editor-in-Chief MINNA JUTI; circ. 46,277.

Hevosurheilu: Tulkinkuja 3, 02650 Espoo; tel. (20) 7605300; fax (20) 7605390; e-mail hevosurheilu@hevosurheilu.fi; internet www.hevosurheilu.fi; independent; horse-racing; Editor-in-Chief JUSSI LÄHDE; circ. 23,588.

Hymy: Maistraatinportti 1, 00015 Kuvalehdet, Helsinki; tel. (9) 156665; fax (9) 1566511; e-mail esko.tulusto@kuvalehdet.fi; internet www.hymy.fi; monthly; family journal; Editor KARI KALLONEN; circ. 73,788.

Hyvä Terveys: Lapinmäentie 1, 00350 Helsinki; POB 100, 00040 Sanoma Magazines; tel. (9) 1201; fax (9) 1205456; e-mail hyva.terveys@sanomamagazines.fi; internet www.hyvaterveys.fi; 15 a year; health; Editor-in-Chief TAINA RISTO; circ. 127,385.

IT-Invalidityö: Mannerheimintie 107, 00280 Helsinki; tel. (9) 613191; fax (9) 1461443; e-mail fpd@invalidiliitto.fi; internet www.invalidiliitto.fi/portal/fi; 10 a year; for disabled people; Editor-in-Chief SINIKKA RANTALA; circ. 29,340.

Kaksplus: Maistraatinportti 1, 00015 Otavamedia; tel. (9) 1566591; e-mail kaksplus@otavamedia.fi; internet kaksplus.fi; f. 1969; monthly; for families with young children; Editor-in-Chief EMMA KOIVULA; circ. 17,794.

Kansan Uutiset: Vilhonvuorenkatu 11C 7, 00500 Helsinki; POB 64, 00501 Helsinki; tel. (9) 759601; fax (9) 75960319; e-mail ku@kansanuutiset.fi; internet www.kansanuutiset.fi; f. 1957; organ of the Left Alliance; Editor-in-Chief JOUKO JOENTAUSTA.

Katso: Pursimiehenkatu 29–31A, 00150 Helsinki; POB 124, 00151 Helsinki; tel. (9) 86217000; fax (9) 86217177; e-mail katso@katso.fi; internet www.katso.fi; f. 1960; 49 issues a year; TV, radio, film and video; Editor-in-Chief KIRSI LINDH-MANSIKKA; circ. 26,460.

Kauneus ja terveys: Risto Rytintie 33, 00081 A-lehdet, Helsinki; tel. (9) 75961; fax (9) 75983106; e-mail asiakaspalvelu@a-lehdet.fi; internet www.kauneusjaterveys.fi; 16 a year; health and beauty; Editor TITTA KIURU; circ. 72,764.

Kirkko ja kaupunki: Kasarmikatu 23, 15A, 00130 Helsinki; tel. (9) 0207542255; fax (9) 0207542343; e-mail toimitus@kirkkojakaupunki.fi; internet www.kirkkojakaupunki.fi; weekly; church and community; Editor-in-Chief SEPPO SIMOLA; circ. 203,279 (2011).

Kodin Kuvalehti: Lapinmäentie 1, 00350 Helsinki; POB 100, 00040 Helsinki; tel. (9) 1201; fax (9) 1205468; e-mail kodin.kuvalehti@sanomamagazines.fi; internet www.kodinkuvalehti.fi; fortnightly; family magazine; Editor MINNA MCGILL; circ. 158,375.

Kotilääkäri: Maistraatinportti 1, 00015 Otavamedia, Helsinki; tel. (9) 15661; e-mail kotilaakari@otavamedia.fi; internet www.kotilaakari.fi; f. 1889; monthly; health, well-being and beauty; Editor-in-Chief MARJATTA LEINO; circ. 28,841.

Kotiliesi: Maistraatinportti 1, 00015 Otavamedia, Helsinki; tel. (9) 15661; e-mail kotiliesi@otavamedia.fi; internet www.kotiliesi.fi; f. 1922; 26 a year; women's; Editor-in-Chief LEENI PELTONEN; circ. 119,105.

Kotivinkki: Risto Rytintie 33, 00081 A-lehdet, Helsinki; tel. (9) 75961; e-mail outi.gylden@a-lehdet.fi; internet www.kotivinkki.fi; 23 a year; women's; Editor-in-Chief OUTI GYLDÉN; circ. 90,734.

Maaseudun Tulevaisuus (The Rural Future): Simonkatu 6, POB 440, 00100 Helsinki; tel. (9) 204132100; e-mail ilmoitus@maaseuduntulevaisuus.fi; internet www.maaseuduntulevaisuus.fi; f. 1916; independent; Man. Dir HEIKKI LAURINEN; Editor-in-Chief LAURI KONTRO; circ. 81,774).

Me Naiset: Lapinmäentie 1, 00350 Helsinki; POB 100, 00040 Helsinki; tel. (9) 1201; fax (9) 1205414; e-mail menaiset@sanomamagazines.fi; internet www.menaiset.fi; f. 1952; weekly; women's; Editor JOHANNA LAHTI; circ. 138,594.

Metsälehti: Pohjoinen Rautatiekatu 21B, 00100 Helsinki; tel. (9) 31549800; fax (9) 31549879; e-mail eliisa.kallioniemi@metsalehti.fi; internet www.metsakustannus.fi; f. 1933; fortnightly; forestry; owned by the Forestry Development Centre Tapio; Editor-in-Chief ELIISA KALLIONIEMI; circ. 34,403.

MikroBitti: Lapinmäentie 1, 00350 Helsinki; POB 100, 00040 Sanoma Magazine; tel. (9) 1201; fax (9) 1205456; e-mail otto@mikrobitti.fi; internet www.mbnet.fi; f. 1984; monthly; Editor-in-Chief PASI ANDREJEFF; circ. 58,957.

MikroPC: Annankatu 34–36B, 00100 Helsinki; POB 920, 00101 Helsinki; tel. (20) 44240; e-mail asiakaspalvelu@talentum.com; internet mikropc.net; 12 a year; computers; Editor-in-Chief MIKKO TORIKKA; circ. 12,285 (2011).

Partio: Töölönkatu 55, 00250 Helsinki; tel. (9) 88651100; fax (9) 88651199; e-mail info@partio.fi; internet www.partio.fi; 4 a year; the Scout movement; Editor MINNA HELLE; circ. 39,256.

Pellervo: Simonkatu 6, POB 77, 00101 Helsinki; tel. (9) 4767501; fax (9) 6948845; e-mail toimisto@pellervo.fi; internet www.pellervo.fi; f. 1899; monthly; agricultural and co-operative, home and country life journal; organ of the Confederation of Finnish Co-operatives; Editor-in-Chief TEEMU PAKARINEN; circ. 31,961 (2011).

PerusSuomalainen: Mannerheimintie 40B 56, 00100 Helsinki; tel. (20) 7430800; fax (20) 7430801; e-mail peruss@perussuomalaiset.fi; internet www.perussuomalaiset.fi; f. 1996; 12 a year; organ of the Perussuomalaiset/Sannfinländarna (PS—The Finns); Editor MATIAS TURKKILA; circ. 100,000 (2011).

Pirkka: POB 410, 00811 Helsinki; tel. (9) 42427330; internet www.pirkka.fi; 10 a year; Swedish; Editor-in-Chief MINNA JÄRVENPÄÄ; circ. 1,720,139.

Reserviläinen: Döbelninkatu 2, 00260 Helsinki; tel. (9) 40562016; fax (9) 499875; e-mail toimitus@reservilainen.fi; internet www.reservilainen.fi; 8 a year; military; Editor MIRVA BROLA; circ. 69,000 (2011).

Sähköviesti/Elbladet: Fredrikinkatu 51–53B, POB 100, 00101 Helsinki; tel. (9) 530520; fax (9) 53052900; e-mail pekka.tiusanen@energia.fi; internet www.energiaviesti.fi; f. 1939; quarterly; publ. by Finnish Energy Industries; Editor-in-Chief PEKKA TIUSANEN; circ. 601,387 (2011).

Seura: Maistraatinportti 1, 00015 Kuvalehdet; tel. (9) 15661; fax (9) 145650; e-mail seura@kuvalehdet.fi; internet www.seura.fi; f. 1934; 49 a year; family journal; Editor-in-Chief SAIJA HAKONIEMI; circ. 143,485.

STTK—lehti: Mikonkatu 8A, 6th Floor, 00100 Helsinki; POB 421, 00101 Helsinki; tel. (9) 131521; fax (9) 652367; e-mail marja-liisa.rajakangas@sttk.fi; internet www.sttk.fi; 8 a year; organ of STTK

(Finnish Confed. of Professionals); Editor-in-Chief MARJA-LIISA RAJAKANGAS; circ. 30,000 (2011).

Suomen Kuvalehti: Maistraatinportti 1, 00240 Helsinki; tel. (9) 15661; fax (9) 1566212; e-mail suomen.kuvalehti@kuvalehdet.fi; internet www.suomenkuvalehti.fi; f. 1916; 49 a year; illustrated news; Editor-in-Chief TAPANI RUOKANEN; circ. 86,786.

Suuri Käsityö: Lapinmäentie 1, 00350 Helsinki; POB 100, 00040 Helsinki; tel. (9) 1201; fax (9) 1205352; e-mail suuri.kasityolehti@sanomamagazines.fi; internet www.suurikasityo.fi; f. 1974; monthly; needlework, knitting and dress-making magazine; Editor-in-Chief HEIDI LAAKSONEN; circ. 60,185.

Talouselämä: Annankatu 34–36B, 00100 Helsinki; POB 920, 00101 Helsinki; tel. (9) 204424390; fax (9) 204424108; e-mail te@talentum.fi; internet www.talouselama.fi; f. 1938; 46 a year; economy, business; Man. Dir AARNE AKTAN; Editor-in-Chief REIJO RUOKANEN; circ. 80,868.

Taloustaito: Kalevankatu 4, 00100 Helsinki; tel. (9) 618871; fax (9) 604435; e-mail antti.marttinen@veronmaksajat.fi; internet www.taloustaito.fi; economics and taxation; Editor-in-Chief ANTTI MARTTINEN; circ. 242,250.

Tieteen Kuvalehti: Siltasaarenkatu 18–20A, 00530 Helsinki; tel. (20) 7608590; internet tieku.fi; f. 1986; 18 a year; science, nature, technology; publ. by Bonnier Publications Int; Editor JENS HENNEBERG; circ. 36,785.

Tekniikan Maailma: Maistraatinportti 1, 00240 Helsinki; tel. (9) 15661; fax (9) 1566511; e-mail tekniikan.maailma@kuvalehdet.fi; internet www.tekniikanmaailma.fi; f. 1953; 23 a year; motoring, technology, aviation, photography; Editor-in-Chief VELIMATTI HONKANEN; circ. 120,298.

Tekniikka & Talous: Annankatu 34–36B, 00100 Helsinki; POB 920, 00101 Helsinki; tel. (20) 4424100; fax (20) 4424101; e-mail tilpal@talentum.fi; internet www.tekniikkatalous.fi; Editor-in-Chief TERHO PUUSTINEN; circ. 60,018.

Tiede: Lapinmäentie 1, 00350 Helsinki; POB 100, 00040 Sanoma Magazines; tel. (9) 1201; e-mail tiede@sanomamagazines.fi; internet www.tiede.fi; f. 1980; popular science; Editor-in-Chief JUKKA RUUKKI; circ. 60,951.

Trendi: Risto Rytintie 33, 00081 A-lehdet, Helsinki; tel. (9) 75961; e-mail jenni.lieto@a-lehdet.fi; internet www.trendi.fi; 12 a year; women's lifestyle; Editor-in-Chief JENNI LIETO; circ. 44,395.

Tuulilasi: Risto Rytintie 33, 00081 A-lehdet, Helsinki; tel. (9) 75961; fax (9) 75983103; e-mail tuulilasi@a-lehdet.fi; internet www.tuulilasi.fi; f. 1963; 16 a year; motoring; Editor-in-Chief LAURI LARMELA; circ. 68,748.

Työ Terveys Turvallisuus: Topeliuksenkatu 41A, 00250 Helsinki; tel. (30) 4741; fax (30) 4742478; e-mail info-ttt@ttl.fi; internet www.ttl.fi; f. 1971; 6 a year; occupational safety and health; Editor-in-Chief HARRI VAINIO; circ. 55,928.

Valitut Palat: Pitäjänmäentie 14, 00380 Helsinki; POB 106, 00381 Helsinki; tel. (9) 503441; fax (9) 5034499; e-mail asiakaspalvelu@valitutpalat.fi; internet www.valitutpalat.fi; monthly; Finnish Reader's Digest; Editor-in-Chief ILKKA VIRTANEN; circ. 157,979.

Veikkaaja: Töölönlahdenkatu 2, POB 45, 00089 Helsinki; tel. (9) 1221; fax (9) 1223419; e-mail tilaajapalvelu@urheilusanomat.fi; internet www.veikkaaja.fi; 51 a year; sports; Editor-in-Chief TAPIO SADEOJA; circ. 40,017.

Voi hyvin: Risto Rytintie 33, 00081 A-lehdet, Helsinki; tel. (9) 75961; fax (9) 75983109; e-mail voihyvin@a-lehdet.fi; internet www.voihyvin.fi; f. 1986; 10 a year; health, well-being; Editor-in-Chief KRISTA LAUNONEN; circ. 43,378.

Yhteishyvä: Fleminginkatu 34, 00510 Helsinki; tel. (9) 1882621; fax (9) 1882626; e-mail kirsi.ervola@sok.fi; internet www.yhteishyva.fi; f. 1905; monthly; free to members of co-operative group; Editor-in-Chief KIRSI ERVOLA; circ. 1,815,893.

NEWS AGENCY

Oy Suomen Tietotoimisto—Lehtikuva (STT—Lehtikuva): Malminkatu 16A, 00100 Helsinki; POB 550, 00101 Helsinki; tel. (9) 695811; fax (9) 69581335; e-mail toimitus@stt.fi; internet www.stt.fi; f. 1887; 8 regional bureaux; independent national agency distributing domestic and international news in Finnish and Swedish; formed by the merger of Suomen Tietotoimisto and Lehtikuva; CEO and Editor-in-Chief MIKA PETTERSSON.

PRESS ASSOCIATIONS

Aikakauslehtien Liitto (Finnish Periodical Publishers' Association): Lönnrotinkatu 11A, POB 267, 00121 Helsinki; tel. (9) 22877280; fax (9) 603478; e-mail toimisto@aikakauslehdet.fi; internet www.aikakauslehdet.fi; f. 1946; aims to further the interests of publishers of magazines and periodicals, to encourage co-operation between publishers, and to improve standards; Chair. RAILI MÄKINEN.

Sanomalehtien Liitto—Tidningarnas Förbund (Finnish Newspapers Association): Lönnrotinkatu 11, POB 415, 2nd Floor, 00121 Helsinki; tel. (9) 22877300; fax (9) 22877335; e-mail info@sanomalehdet.fi; internet www.sanomalehdet.fi; f. 1908; represents newspapers' interests; 184 mem. newspapers; Exec. Dir JUKKA HOLMBERG.

Suomen Journalistiliitto—Finlands Journalistförbund r.y. (Union of Journalists): Siltasaarenkatu 16, 00530 Helsinki; tel. (9) 6122330; fax (9) 605396; e-mail info@journalistiliitto.fi; internet www.journalistiliitto.fi; f. 1921; 15,000 mems; Pres. ARTO NIEMINEN.

Publishers

Alfamer/Karisto Oy: Kaisaniemenkatu 13, 00100 Helsinki; tel. (9) 7742810; fax (9) 77428111; e-mail alfamer@alfamer.fi; internet www.alfamer.fi; motor sports, militaria; Man. Dir EIJA SAHLBERG.

Oy Amanita Ltd: Salkolantie 25, 31470 Somerniemi; tel. (2) 7489500; fax (2) 7489510; e-mail info@amanita.fi; internet www.amanita.fi; f. 1982; non-fiction; Man. Dir LAURI LINNILÄ.

Art House Oy: Bulevardi 19C, 00120 Helsinki; tel. (9) 6940752; fax (9) 6933762; e-mail myynti@arthouse.fi; internet www.arthouse.fi; f. 1975; Finnish and foreign fiction, non-fiction, popular science, horror, fantasy, science fiction, detective fiction; Publr PAAVO HAAVIKKO.

Atena Kustannus Oy: Asemakatu 6, POB 436, 40101 Jyväskylä; tel. (10) 4214200; e-mail atena@atena.fi; internet www.atena.fi; f. 1986; cultural history, popular science, current affairs, biography; Pres. PEKKA MÄKELÄ.

Basam Books Oy: Hämeentie 155A 6, POB 42, 00561 Helsinki; tel. and fax (9) 75793839; e-mail info@basambooks.fi; internet www.basambooks.fi; f. 1993; independent; literary fiction, poetry, non-fiction; Publr BATU SAMALETDIN.

Gummerus Kustannus Oy: Lapinlahdenkatu 1C, POB 749, 00100 Helsinki; tel. (10) 6836200; fax (9) 58430200; e-mail info@gummerus.fi; internet www.gummerus.fi; f. 1872; fiction, non-fiction, reference, dictionaries, languages; independent; Man. Dirs JUHANI PEKKALA, LIISA SUVIKUMPU.

Hogrefe Psykologien Kustannus Oy: Kaisaniemenkatu 10, 00100 Helsinki; tel. (9) 6126060; fax (9) 6123005; e-mail myynti@psykologienkustannus.fi; internet www.psykologienkustannus.fi; f. 1965; literature on psychology; Man. Dir ALEKSI LEVO.

Karisto Oy: Paroistentie 2, POB 102, 13101 Hämeenlinna; tel. (3) 63151; fax (3) 6161565; e-mail kustannusliike@karisto.fi; internet www.karisto.fi; f. 1900; non-fiction and fiction, printing; Man. Dir MIKA KOTILAINEN.

Kirjapaja: Itälahdenkatu 27A, 00210 Helsinki; tel. (9) 6877450; fax (9) 68774545; e-mail mira.pitkanen@kirjapaja.fi; internet www.kirjapaja.fi; f. 1942; Christian literature, general fiction, non-fiction, reference, juvenile; Vice-Pres. ANNE-MARIA LANTTA.

Kustannus-Mäkelä Oy: POB 14, 03601 Karkkila; tel. (9) 2257995; fax (9) 2257660; e-mail makela@kustannusmakela.fi; internet www.kustannusmakela.fi; f. 1971; juvenile, fiction; Man. Dir ORVO MÄKELÄ.

Oy Like Kustannus Ltd: POB 37, 00521 Helsinki; tel. (9) 6229970; fax (9) 1351372; e-mail like@like.fi; internet www.like.fi; f. 1987; film literature, fiction, non-fiction, comics; Man. Dir PÄIVI PAAPPANEN.

Maahenki Oy: Eerikinkatu 28, 00180 Helsinki; tel. (9) 7512020; fax (9) 75120211; e-mail maahenki@msl.fi; internet www.maahenki.fi; art, nature; Man. Dir ULLA SARVIALA.

Otava Publishing Co Ltd: Uudenmaankatu 10, 00120 Helsinki; tel. (9) 19961; fax (9) 1996560; e-mail pasi.vainio@otava.fi; internet www.otava.fi; f. 1890; part of Otava-United Magazines Group Ltd; non-fiction, fiction, children's and textbooks; Man. Dir PASI VAINIO.

Schildts & Söderströms: Bulevarden 7, POB 870, 00120 Helsinki; tel. (9) 6841860; fax (9) 68418610; e-mail info@sets.fi; internet www.sets.fi; f. 2012 following the merger of Schildts Förlags Ab (f. 1913) and Söderströms Förlag (f. 1891); subjects mainly in Swedish; Man. Dir BARBRO TEIR.

Suomalaisen Kirjallisuuden Seura, SKS (Finnish Literature Society): Mariankatu 7A, 4th Floor, 00170 Helsinki; tel. (20) 1131231; fax (9) 13123220; e-mail sks@finlit.fi; internet www.finlit.fi/books; f. 1834; Finnish language and literature, linguistics, folklore, cultural studies and history; Publishing Dir TERO NORKOLA.

Tammi Publishers: Korkeavuorenkatu 37, POB 410, 00101 Helsinki; tel. (10) 5060300; fax (10) 5060399; e-mail tammi@tammi.fi; internet www.tammi.fi; f. 1943; fiction, general, non-fiction, children's, juvenile, textbooks, educational materials, audio books; owned by Bonnier AB; Pres. JACOB DALBORG.

Weilin & Göös Oy: Bulevardi 12, 00120 Helsinki; tel. (9) 43771; fax (9) 4377270; e-mail asiakaspalvelu@wg.fi; internet www.wg.fi; f. 1872; non-fiction, encyclopedias; Dir JAANA KORPI.

Werner Söderström Corpn (WSOY): POB 222, 00121 Helsinki; Korkeavuorenkatu 37, POB 314, 00101 Helsinki; tel. (10) 5060200; internet www.wsoy.fi; f. 1878; fiction and non-fiction, science, juvenile, textbooks, reference, comics, the printing industry; Pres. JACOB DAHLBORG.

PUBLISHERS' ASSOCIATION

Suomen Kustannusyhdistys (Finnish Book Publishers' Association): Lönnrotinkatu 11A, POB 177, 00121 Helsinki; tel. (9) 22877252; fax (9) 6121226; e-mail sirkku.palomaki@kustantajat.fi; internet www.kustantajat.fi; f. 1858; Pres. PASI VAINIO; Dir SAKARI LAIHO; 100 mems.

Broadcasting and Communications

REGULATORY AUTHORITY

Finnish Communications Regulatory Authority (FICORA): Itämerenkatu 3A, POB 313, 00181 Helsinki; tel. (9) 69661; fax (9) 6966410; internet www.ficora.fi; f. 1988; affiliated to Ministry of Transport and Communications; CEO ASTA SIHVONEN-PUNKKA.

TELECOMMUNICATIONS

DNA Ltd: Ansatie 6A B, POB 41, 01741 Vantaa; tel. (44) 0440; internet www.dna.fi; f. 2007; offers mobile communications services through DNA Finland Ltd and fixed-network broadband and television services through DNA Services Ltd; Chair. LEINO JARMO; CEO JUKKA LEINONEN.

Elisa Corpn: Ratavartijankatu 5, Helsinki; POB 1, 00061 Elisa; tel. (10) 26000; fax (10) 26060; internet www.elisa.com; Chair. RISTO SIILASMAA; CEO VELI-MATTI MATTILA.

Finnet International Ltd: Sinebrychoffinkatu 11, POB 949, 00101 Helsinki; tel. (9) 315315; fax (9) 605531; e-mail fl@finnet.fi; internet www.finnet.fi; Chair. RISTO LINTURI.

Telecon Ltd: POB 55, 02231 Espoo; tel. (40) 9526900; e-mail info@telecon.fi; internet www.telecon.fi; f. 1980; Man. Dir JOUKO JOKINEN.

TeliaSonera Finland Oyj: Teollisuuskatu 15, Helsinki; POB 220, 00051 Sonera; tel. (20) 401; fax (20) 4069100; e-mail yritysasiakaspalvelu@sonera.com; internet www.teliasonera.fi; f. 2002 by merger of Telia AB (Sweden) and Sonera Ltd; Chair. ANDERS NARVINGER; Pres. and CEO JOHAN DENNELIND.

BROADCASTING

Radio

The first commercial radio stations were introduced in 1985 and there were 59 stations by 1990. The economic recession of the early 1990s led to the collapse of many commercial stations. However, the industry began to recover in the late 1990s, and the first national commercial radio station, Radio Nova, was launched in May 1997. In 1999 RAB Finland was established to promote and develop the Finnish private radio industry by providing information services. By 2008 the number of commercial radio stations reached 57.

In May 1999 the first part of the national Digital Audio Broadcast (DAB) network was launched by Yleisradio (YLE—Finnish Broadcasting Company). The Finnish DAB transmitter network was closed down in 2005; YLE continued its digital transmissions through the Digital Video Broadcasting (DVB) television network.

Yleisradio Oy (YLE) (Finnish Broadcasting Company): YLE Centre, Radiokatu 5, 00024 Helsinki; tel. (9) 14801; fax (9) 14803216; e-mail fbc@yle.fi; internet www.yle.fi; f. 1926; 99.9% state-owned, with management appointed by the Administrative Council; Chair. KARI NEILIMO; Dir-Gen. LAURI KIVINEN.

YLE Radio 1 (Radio Ylen Ykkönen): POB 6, 00024 Helsinki; 24-hour arts and culture in Finnish; Dir HEIKKI PELTONEN.

YLE R2 (YleX): POB 17, 00024 Helsinki; tel. (9) 14801; fax (9) 1482650; e-mail jyri.kataja-rahko@yle.fi; internet ylex.fi; f. 2003; 24-hour popular culture for young people in Finnish; Dir JYRI KATAJA-RAHKO.

YLE R3 (Radio Suomi): 24-hour news, current affairs, sport, regional programmes in Finnish; Dir MARJA KESKITALO.

YLE R4 (Radio Extrem): Swedish-language channel for young people.

YLE R5 (Radio Vega): POB 62, 00024 Rundradion; tel. (9) 14801; e-mail mika.kosunen@yle.fi; internet www.yle.fi/vega; news, current affairs, art, culture and regional programmes in Swedish; Dir MIKA KOSUNEN.

YLE Radio Finland: POB 78, 00024 Yleisradio; tel. (9) 14804320; fax (9) 14801169; e-mail rfinland@yle.fi; internet www.yle.fi/rfinland; broadcasts in Finnish, Swedish, English, German, French, Russian and Classical Latin.

YLE Sámi Radio: POB 38, 99871 Inari; tel. (16) 6757500; fax (16) 6757501; e-mail sami.radio@yle.fi; internet www.yle.fi/samiradio; Sámi-language network covering northern Lapland.

Digita Oy: Jämsänkatu 2, 00520 Helsinki; POB 135, 00521 Helsinki; tel. (20) 411711; fax (20) 4117234; e-mail info@digita.fi; internet www.digita.fi; f. 1999; operates the radio and television broadcasting network covering the whole of Finland; 36 main broadcasting stations and 151 substations; Man. Dir SIRPA OJALA.

Groove FM: Pursimiehenkatu 29–31C, 00150 Helsinki; tel. (20) 7768360; e-mail juha.kakkuri@groovefm.fi; internet www.groovefm.fi; Station Dir JUHA KAKKURI.

Iskelmä: Tallberginkatu 1C, 00180 Helsinki; tel. (20) 7474000; e-mail erkka.jaakkola@sbs.fi; internet www.iskelma.fi; Media Dir JUHA OURILA.

NRJ: Kiviaidankatu 2I, 00210 Helsinki; tel. (9) 681900; fax (9) 68190102; e-mail marko.lintussari@nrj.fi; internet www.nrj.fi; Man. Dir ANTTI PAKKALA.

RadioMedia: Lönnrotinkatu 11A, POB 312, 00121 Helsinki; tel. (9) 22877340; fax (9) 648221; e-mail info@radiomedia.fi; internet www.radiomedia.fi; f. 1999; promotes Finnish private radio industry by providing extensive information services free of charge; Man. Dir STEFAN MÖLLER.

Radio Nova: Ilmalankatu 2C, POB 123, 00241 Helsinki; tel. (9) 88488700; fax (9) 88488720; e-mail toimitus@radionova.fi; internet www.radionova.fi; largest commercial radio station; 74% owned by Alma Media; Marketing Dir PÄIVI NURMESNIEMI.

Radio SuomiPOP: Pursimiehenkatu 29–31C, 00150 Helsinki; tel. (20) 7768360; e-mail studio@radiosuomipop.fi; internet www.radiosuomipop.fi; Station Dir JUHA KAKKURI.

The Voice: Tallberginkatu 1C, 00180 Helsinki; tel. (20) 7474000; e-mail toimitus@voice.fi; internet www.voice.fi; Commercial Dir OUTI REKOLA.

Television

Digital Video Broadcasting (DVB) began in Finland in 2001. Analogue transmission networks were closed down from 1 September 2007.

Yleisradio (YLE): operates 5 national channels: TV 1, TV 2, YLE FST (in Swedish), TV Finland (digital satellite channel broadcast in Nordic countries and elsewhere in Europe) and YLE Teema (a specialized channel for culture, education and science)

YLE/TV 1: POB 97, 00024 Yleisradio; tel. (9) 14801; fax (9) 14803424; e-mail riitta.pihlajamaki@yle.fi; internet www.yle.fi/tv1; f. 1957; programmes in Finnish; Channel Controller RIITTA PIHLAJAMÄKI.

YLE TV2: POB 196, 33101 Tampere; tel. (3) 3456111; fax (3) 3456892; e-mail ilkka.saari@yle.fi; internet www.yle.fi/tv2; f. 1964; programmes in Finnish and Swedish; Channel Controller ILKKA SAARI.

Canal Digital Finland Oy: POB 866, 33101 Tampere; tel. (20) 7699000; fax (20) 7699006; e-mail asiakaspalvelu@canaldigital.fi; internet www.canaldigital.fi; f. 1998; subsidiary of Telenor ASA (Norway).

MTV Finland: Ilmalantori 2, Helsinki; tel. (9) 6224176; e-mail palaute@mtv3.fi; internet www.mtv3.fi; f. 1957; independent nationwide commercial television company comprising 9 channels: MTV3 and Subtv, as well as 7 subscription channels (MTV3 MAX, MTV3 Fakta, MTV Ava, MTV3 Sarja, MTV3 Scifi, Sub Juniori and Sub Leffa); became part of Alma Media Corpn in 1998; acquired by Bonnier (Sweden) in 2005; Pres. and CEO PEKKA KARHUVAARA.

Nelonen Media (Sanoma Entertainment Finland Oy): POB 350, 00151 Helsinki; Tehtaankatu 27–29D, 00150 Helsinki; tel. (9) 45451; fax (9) 4545400; e-mail hans.edin@nelonen.fi; internet www.nelonenmedia.fi; f. 1997; fmrly Oy Ruutunelonen Ab; independent commercial television co; part of Sanoma Group; Pres. HANS EDIN.

Finance

The Bank of Finland is the country's central bank and the centre of Finland's monetary and banking system. It functions 'under guarantee and supervision of the Eduskunta (Parliament) and the Bank supervisors delegated by the Eduskunta'.

At the end of 2011 there were a total of 313 banks operating in Finland.

BANKING

(cap. = capital; res = reserves; dep. = deposits; m. = million; brs = branches; amounts in euros)

Supervisory Authority

Financial Supervisory Authority (FIN-FSA): Snellmaninkatu 6, POB 103, 00101 Helsinki; tel. (10) 8315339; fax (10) 8315328; e-mail finanssivalvonta@finanssivalvonta.fi; internet www.finanssivalvonta.fi; f. 2009 to replace the Financial Supervision Authority and the Insurance Supervisory Authority; maintains confidence in the financial markets by supervising the markets and the bodies working within them; Chair. PENTTI HAKKARAINEN; Dir-Gen. ANNELI TUOMINEN.

Central Bank

Suomen Pankki/Finlands Bank (Bank of Finland): Snellmaninaukio, POB 160, 00101 Helsinki; tel. (10) 8311; fax (9) 174872; e-mail info@bof.fi; internet www.bof.fi; f. 1811; Bank of Issue under the guarantee and supervision of the Eduskunta; cap. 841m., res 1,334m., dep. 14,402m. (Dec. 2010); Gov. ERKKI LIIKANEN; 4 brs.

Commercial Banks

Danske Bank PLC: Hiililaiturinkuja 2, Helsinki; POB 1568, 00075 Sampo; tel. (10) 5460000; fax (10) 5462533; internet www.danskebank.fi; f. 1886 as Postisäästöpankki; name changed as above 2012; owned by Danske Bank (Denmark) (q.v.); cap. 106m., res 271.2m., dep. 19,592.8m. (Dec. 2012); CEO RISTO TORNIVAARA; 63 brs.

Nordea Bank Finland PLC (Nordea Pankki Suomi Oyj): Aleksanterinkatu 36B, 00100 Helsinki; tel. (9) 1651; fax (9) 16554500; internet www.nordea.fi; f. 1995; cap. 2,319m., res 3,474m., dep. 156,939m. (Dec. 2013); Group CEO CHRISTIAN CLAUSEN; 416 brs.

Co-operative Banks

Pohjola Bank PLC: Teollisuuskatu 1B, 00510 Helsinki; POB 308, 00013 Helsinki; tel. (10) 252011; fax (10) 2522002; internet www.pohjola.fi; f. 1902 as Osuuspankkien Keskuspankki Oyj; current name adopted 2008; cap. 428m., res 1,257m., dep. 21,746m. (Dec. 2013); part of OP–Pohjola Group Central Co-operative; Chair. REIJO KARHINEN; Pres. and CEO ERKKI MIKAEL SILVENNOINEN; 677 brs.

POP Bank: Hevosenkenkä 3, 02600 Espoo; tel. (9) 6811700; fax (9) 68117070; internet www.poppankki.fi; f. 1997; group comprising co-operative banks; cap. 200m., dep. 1,600m., total assets 2,062m. (Dec. 2000); Pres. HEIKKI SUUTALA; 111 brs.

Savings Bank

Aktia Bank Plc (Aktia Savings Bank PLC): Mannerheimintie 14, POB 207, 00100 Helsinki; tel. (10) 2475000; fax (10) 2476356; e-mail aktia@aktia.fi; internet www.aktia.fi; f. 1852 as Helsingfors Sparbank; current name adopted 2008; cap. 163m., res 136.4m., dep. 5,102.4m. (Dec. 2012); Chair. DAG WALLGREN; Man. Dir JUSSI LAITINEN; approx. 55 brs.

Mortgage Banks

OP-Asuntoluottopankki (OP Mortgage Bank): POB 308, 00101 Helsinki; tel. (9) 4041; fax (9) 4042620; e-mail iloniemi@pohjola.com; f. 2000; part of OP–Pohjola Group Central Co-operative; Man. Dir LAURI ILONIEMI.

Investment Bank

Nordiska Investeringsbanken (Nordic Investment Bank): Fabianinkatu 34, POB 249, 00171 Helsinki; tel. (10) 618001; fax (10) 6180723; e-mail info@nib.int; internet www.nib.int; f. 1975; owned by Govts of Denmark, Estonia, Finland, Iceland, Latvia, Lithuania, Norway and Sweden; all member countries are represented on the Bd of Dirs by their ministers responsible for finance and the economy; cap. 418.6m., res 2,195.1m., dep. 4,193m. (Dec. 2013); Pres. and CEO HENRIK NORMANN.

Banking Associations

Finanssialan Keskusliitto r.y. (Federation of Finnish Financial Services): Bulevardi 28, 00120 Helsinki; tel. (20) 7934200; fax (20) 7934202; e-mail fk@fkl.fi; internet www.fkl.fi; f. 2007 by merger of the Finnish Bankers' Association, the Federation of Finnish Insurance Companies, the Employers' Association of Finnish Financial Institutions and the Finnish Finance Houses' Association; Chair. ARI KAPERI; Man. Dir PIIA-NOORA KAUPPI.

Säästöpankkiliitto (Finnish Savings Banks Association): Linnoitustie 9, POB 68, 02601 Espoo; tel. (9) 548051; fax (20) 6029108; e-mail pasi.kamari@saastopankki.fi; internet www.saastopankki.fi; f. 1906; 33 mems; Chair. JUSSI HAKALA; Man. Dir PASI KÄMÄRI; 256 brs.

Suomen Hypoteekkiyhdistys (Mortgage Society of Finland): Yrjönkatu 9A, 2nd Floor, 00101 Helsinki; POB 509, 00101 Helsinki; tel. (9) 228361; fax (9) 647443; e-mail hypo@hypo.fi; internet www.hypo.fi; f. 1860; Pres. ARI PAUNA.

STOCK EXCHANGE

NASDAQ OMX Helsinki: Fabianinkatu 14, POB 361, 00131 Helsinki; tel. (9) 616671; fax (9) 61667368; e-mail nordicexchange.helsinki@nasdaqomx.com; internet www.nasdaqomx.com; f. 1912 as Helsingin Pörssi; merged with OMX AB (Sweden) in 2003; became part of OMX Nordic Exchange with Copenhagen (Denmark), Reykjavík (Iceland) and Stockholm (Sweden) exchanges in 2006; acquired by NASDAQ Stock Market, Inc (USA) in 2008; Group CEO ROBERT GREIFELD.

INSURANCE

In January 2011 there were 63 insurance companies operating in Finland, 24 of which were branches of foreign insurance companies.

A-Vakuutus Oy (A-Vakuutus Mutual Insurance Co): Lapinmäentie 1, 00350 Helsinki; tel. (10) 253000; fax (10) 2532908; e-mail a-vakuutus@a-vakuutus.fi; internet www.a-vakuutus.fi; non-life; Man. Dir JOUKO PÖLÖNEN.

Eurooppalainen Insurance Co Ltd: Lapinmäentie 1, 00013 Pohjola; tel. (10) 253000; internet www.eurooppalainen.fi; f. 1922; non-life; part of Pohjola Bank plc; Man. Dir MIKAEL SILVENNOINEN.

Garantia Insurance Co Ltd: Salomonkatu 17A, 9th Floor, POB 600, 00101 Helsinki; tel. (20) 7479800; fax (20) 7479801; e-mail garantia@garantia.fi; internet www.garantia.fi; f. 1993; non-life; Man. Dir MIKAEL ENGLUND.

If Vahinkovakuutusyhtiö Oy (If P & C Insurance Ltd): Niittyportti 4, 02200 Espoo; tel. 10191515; fax 105144028; internet www.if.fi; f. 1999; subsidiary of Sampo plc; Chair. KARI STADIGH; Pres. and CEO TORBJÖRN MAGNUSSON.

Keskinäinen Eläkevakuutusyhtiö Ilmarinen (Ilmarinen Mutual Pension Insurance Co): Porkkalankatu 1, 00018 Ilmarinen; tel. (10) 28411; fax (10) 2843445; e-mail info@ilmarinen.fi; internet www.ilmarinen.fi; f. 1961; statutory employment pensions; Man. Dir HARRI SAILAS.

Keskinäinen Henkivakuutusosakeyhtiö Suomi (Suomi Mutual Life Assurance Co): Aleksanterinkatu 15B, 00100 Helsinki; POB 1068, 00101 Helsinki; tel. (10) 2530066; fax (10) 2527806; e-mail hvpalvelukeskus@suomi-yhtio.fi; internet www.suomi-yhtio.fi; f. 1890; life insurance; Pres. and CEO JARI SOKKA.

Keskinäinen työeläkevakuutusyhtiö Varma (Varma Mutual Pension Insurance Co): Salmisaarenranta 11, POB 1, 00098 Varma; tel. (10) 2440; fax (10) 2444752; e-mail info@varma.fi; internet www.varma.fi; f. 1998; fmrly Varma-Sampo; CEO RISTO MURTO.

Keskinäinen Vakuutusyhtiö Fennia (Fennia Mutual Insurance Co): Televisiokatu 1, 00017 Helsinki; tel. (10) 5031; fax (10) 5037680; e-mail info@fennia.fi; internet www.fennia.fi; f. 1882; non-life; Man. Dir ANTTI KULJUKKA.

Keskinäinen Vakuutusyhtiö Kaleva (Kaleva Mutual Insurance Co): Bulevardi 56, 00100 Helsinki; POB 347, 00101 Helsinki; tel. (10) 515225; internet www.kalevavakuutus.fi; f. 1874; Man. Dir MATTI RANTANEN.

LähiTapiola Keskinäinen Eläkevakuutusyhtiö (LähiTapiola Mutual Pension Insurance Co): Revontulentie 7, POB 9, 02010 Tapiola; tel. (9) 4531; fax (20) 6051084; internet www.lahitapiola.fi; Chair. and Pres. ERKKI MOISANDER; Man. Dir SATU HUBER.

LähiTapiola Keskinäinen Henkivakuutusyhtiö (LähiTapiola Mutual Life Insurance Co): 02010 Tapiola; tel. (9) 4531; fax (9) 4532146; internet www.lahitapiola.fi; Chair. and Pres. ERKKI MOISANDER; Man. Dir MINNA KOHMO.

LähiTapiola Keskinäinen Vakuutusyhtiö (LähiTapiola General Mutual Insurance Co): 02010 Tapiola; tel. (9) 4531; fax (9) 4532146; internet www.lahitapiola.fi; non-life; Chair. and Pres. ERKKI MOISANDER; Man. Dir JUKKA KINNUNEN.

LähiTapiola Vakuutus Keskinäinen Yhtiö (Local Insurance Mutual Co): Revontulenkuja 1, POB 50, 02601 Espoo; tel. (20) 5222111; fax (20) 5222332; e-mail myynti@lahivakuutus.fi; internet www.lahivakuutus.fi; f. 1917; non-life; name changed as above following merger with Tapiola Group in 2012; Chair. and Pres. ERKKI MOISANDER.

Mandatum Life Insurance Co ltd: Bulevardi 56, 00120 Helsinki; tel. (10) 515225; e-mail asiakaspalvelu@mandatumlife.fi; internet www.mandatumlife.fi; f. 1997; subsidiary of Sampo plc; Chair. KARI STADIGH; CEO PETRI NIEMISVIRTA.

Nordea Life Assurance Finland: Aleksis Kiven Katu 9, 00020 Helsinki; tel. (9) 16527601; fax (9) 16527666; internet www.nordea.fi/selekta; Man. Dir PEKKA LUUKKANEN.

Palonvara Mutual Insurance Co: Oksasenkatu 1, 53100 Lappeenranta; tel. (20) 5222004; fax (20) 5223100; e-mail palvelu@

palonvara.fi; internet www.palonvara.fi; f. 1912; non-life; Man. Dir JUKKA HERTTI.

Pohjantähti Keskinäinen Vakuutusyhtiö (Pohjantähti Mutual Insurance Co): Keinusaarentie 2, POB 164, 13101 Hämeenlinna; tel. (20) 7634000; fax (3) 5899890; internet www.pohjantahti.fi; f. 1895; non-life; Pres. and CEO EERO YLÄ-SOININMÄKI.

Vahinkovakuutusosakeyhtiö Pohjola (Pohjola Non-Life Insurance Co Ltd): Lapinmäentie 1, 00013 Pohjola; tel. (10) 253000; internet www.pohjola.fi; f. 1891; non-life; Chair. REIJO KARHINEN; Pres. MIKAEL SILVENNOINEN.

Veritas Eläkevakuutus (Veritas Pension Insurance Co Ltd): Olavintie 2, POB 133, 20101 Turku; tel. (10) 55010; fax (10) 5501690; e-mail veritas@veritas.fi; internet www.veritas.fi; f. 1905; Pres. PETER BOSTRÖM; Man. Dir JAN-ERIK STENMAN.

Insurance Associations

Federation of Accident Insurance Institutions: Bulevardi 28, POB 275, 00121 Helsinki; tel. (40) 4504208; internet www.tvl.fi; f. 1920; publishes *Tapaturmavakuutuslehti* quarterly (circ. 3,300); Man. Dir JUSSI KAUMA.

Finnish Motor Insurers' Centre: Bulevardi 28, 00120 Helsinki; tel. (40) 4504750; fax (40) 4504696; internet www.lvk.fi; f. 1938; Man. Dir ULLA NIKU-KOSKINEN.

Finnish Pension Alliance TELA: Lastenkodinkuja 1, 00180 Helsinki; tel. (10) 6806700; fax (10) 6806706; e-mail tela@tela.fi; internet www.tela.fi; f. 1964; Pres. and CEO HARRI SAILAS.

Nordic Nuclear Insurers: Kalevankatu 18A, 00100 Helsinki; tel. (9) 6803410; fax (9) 68034115; internet www.atompool.com; f. 2002; Man. Dir EERO HOLMA.

Trade and Industry

GOVERNMENT AGENCIES

Finpro: Porkkalankatu 1, POB 358, 00181 Helsinki; tel. (20) 46951; fax (20) 4695200; e-mail info@finpro.fi; internet www.finpro.fi; f. 1919 as Finnish Export Association; Chair. HARRI KERMINEN; Pres. and CEO KARI HÄYRINEN.

Invest in Finland: Porkkalankatu 1, 00180 Helsinki; tel. (20) 46951; fax (20) 4695201; e-mail info@investinfinland.fi; internet www.investinfinland.fi; promoting foreign investments to Finland; merged with Finpro in 2011; Chair., Bd of Dirs PAUL PAUKKU; CEO TUOMO AIRAKSINEN.

CHAMBERS OF COMMERCE

Helsingin Seudun Kauppakamari (Helsinki Region Chamber of Commerce): Kalevankatu 12, 00100 Helsinki; tel. (9) 228601; fax (9) 22860228; e-mail kauppakamari@helsinki.chamber.fi; internet www.helsinki.chamber.fi; f. 1917; Chair. JUKKA HIENONEN; Man. Dir HEIKKI J. PERÄLÄ; 6,500 mems.

Keskuskauppakamari (Finland Chamber of Commerce): Aleksanterinkatu 17, POB 1000, 00101 Helsinki; tel. (9) 42426200; fax (9) 650303; e-mail keskuskauppakamari@chamber.fi; internet www.keskuskauppakamari.fi; f. 1918; CEO RISTO E. J. PENTTILÄ; 17,200 mems; represents 19 regional chambers of commerce.

INDUSTRIAL AND TRADE ASSOCIATIONS

Betoniteollisuus r.y. (Finnish Concrete Industry Asscn): Unioninkatu 14, POB 11, 00131 Helsinki; tel. (9) 12991; fax (9) 1299291; e-mail jussi.mattila@betoni.com; internet www.betoni.com; f. 1929; Chair. LAURI KIVEKÄS; Man. Dir JUSSI MATTILA; 48 mems.

Centralförbundet för lant- och skogsbruksproducenter (Central Union of Agricultural Producers and Forest Owners): Simonkatu 6, POB 510, 00100 Helsinki; tel. (20) 4131; fax (20) 4132409; e-mail michael.hornborg@mtk.fi; internet www.mtk.fi; f. 1917; Pres. JUHA MARTTILA; Sec.-Gen. ANTTI SAHI; 152,500 mems.

Kalatalouden Keskusliitto (Federation of Finnish Fisheries Associations): Malmin kauppatie 26, 00700 Helsinki; tel. (9) 6844590; fax (9) 68445959; e-mail kalastus@ahven.net; internet www.ahven.net; f. 1891; Dir MARKKU MYLLYLÄ; 616,000 mems.

Metsäteollisuus r.y. (Finnish Forest Industries' Federation): Snellmaninkatu 13, 00170 Helsinki; POB 336, 00171 Helsinki; tel. (9) 13261; fax (9) 1324445; e-mail forest@forestindustries.fi; internet www.forestindustries.fi; f. 1918; Chair. JUSSI PESONEN; mems: 120 cos in the forestry industry and sales or trade asscns.

Sähköenergialiitto r.y. (Finnish Electricity Association): c/o Oy Turku Energia, POB 105, 20101 Turku; tel. 447422706 (mobile); e-mail sener.energia@gmail.com; internet www.sener.fi; f. 1926; research on electricity networks and electrical applications; Man. JARKKO LEHTONEN; 74 mems.

Suomalaisen Työn Liitto (Association for Finnish Work): Mikonkatu 17A, 00100 Helsinki; POB 429, 00101 Helsinki; tel. (9) 6962430; fax (9) 69624333; e-mail stl@avainlippu.fi; internet www.avainlippu.fi; f. 1978; public relations for Finnish products and for Finnish work; Chair. of Council JYRI HÄKÄMIES; Chair., Bd of Dirs PEKKA SAIRANEN; Man. Dir PEKKA TSUPARI; c. 1,200 mems.

Suomen Kaupan Liitto (Federation of Finnish Commerce): Eteläranta 10, POB 340, 00130 Helsinki; tel. (9) 172850; fax (9) 17285120; e-mail kauppa@kauppa.fi; internet www.kauppa.fi; f. 2005 by merger of the Federation of Finnish Commerce and Trade and the Commercial Employers' Association; Man. Dir JUHANI PEKKALA; 36 mem. asscns with more than 10,000 firms.

Svenska lantbruksproducenternas centralförbund (Central Union of Swedish-speaking Agricultural Producers): Fredriksgatan 61A 34, 00100 Helsinki; tel. (9) 5860460; fax (9) 6941358; e-mail holger.falck@slc.fi; internet www.slc.fi; f. 1945; Chair. HOLGER FALCK; 13,000 mems.

Teknisen Kaupan (Association of Finnish Technical Traders): Sarkiniementie 3, 4th Floor, 00210 Helsinki; tel. (9) 6824130; fax (9) 68241310; e-mail tekninen.kauppa@tekninen.fi; internet www.tekninen.fi; f. 1918; organization of the main importers dealing in steel and metals, machines and equipment, heavy chemicals and raw materials; Chair. TUOMO VÄÄNÄNEN; Man. Dir MARKKU UITTO; 400 mems.

EMPLOYERS' ORGANIZATIONS

Elinkeinoelämän Keskusliitto (EK) (Confederation of Finnish Industries): Eteläranta 10, 00130 Helsinki; POB 30, 00131 Helsinki; tel. (9) 42020; fax (9) 42022299; e-mail netti@ek.fi; internet www.ek.fi; f. 1907; aims to promote co-operation between cos and mem. organizations and to protect the interests of mems in employment issues; 27 asscns consisting of about 16,000 enterprises with 950,000 employees; Chair. OLE JOHANSSON; Dir-Gen. JYRI HÄKÄMIES.

Autoliikenteen Työnantajaliitto r.y. (Employers' Federation of Road Transport): Nuijamiestentie 7, 00400 Helsinki; tel. (9) 47899480; fax (9) 5883995; e-mail mari.vasarainen@alt.fi; internet www.alt.fi; f. 1945; Chair. ANTTI NORRLIN; c. 1,000 mems.

Elintarviketeollisuusliitto r.y. (Finnish Food and Drink Industries' Federation): Pasilankatu 2, POB 115, 00240 Helsinki; tel. (9) 148871; fax (9) 14887201; e-mail info@etl.fi; internet www.etl.fi; Chair. JUHA GRÖHN; Dir-Gen. HEIKKI JUUTINEN.

Kemianteollisuus (KT) r.y. (Chemical Industry Federation): Eteläranta 10, POB 4, 00131 Helsinki; tel. (9) 172841; fax (9) 630225; internet www.chemind.fi; Chair. HARRI KERMINEN; Dir-Gen. TIMO LEPPÄ.

Kenkä- ja Nahkateollisuus r.y. (Association of Finnish Shoe and Leather Industries): Eteläranta 10, 00130 Helsinki; tel. (9) 172841; fax (9) 179588; e-mail olavi.viljanmaa@jalas.com; Chair. OLAVI VILJANMAA.

Kumiteollisuus r.y. (Rubber Manufacturers' Association of Finland): Eteläranta 10, 7th Floor, 00130 Helsinki; POB 4, 00131 Helsinki; tel. (9) 172841; fax (9) 630225; e-mail sami.nikander@kemianteollisuus.fi; internet www.kumiteollisuus.fi; f. 1961; Chair. KIM GRAN; Man. Dir SAMI NIKANDER; 17 mems.

Lääketeollisuus r.y. (Pharma Industry Finland—PIF): Porkkalankatu 1, 00180 Helsinki; POB 206, 00181 Helsinki; tel. (9) 61504900; fax (9) 61504941; e-mail pif@pif.fi; internet www.pif.fi; Chair. ILPO TOLONEN; Gen. Man. JUSSI MERIKALLIO.

Muoviteollisuus r.y. (Finnish Plastics Industries Federation): Eteläranta 10, POB 4, 00131 Helsinki; tel. (9) 172841; fax (9) 171164; e-mail vesa.karha@plastics.fi; internet www.plastics.fi; Chair. KIMMO KEDONPÄÄ.

Palvelualojen Työnantajat (Service Sector Employers—PALTA): Eteläranta 10, POB 62, 00131 Helsinki; tel. (20) 5955000; fax (20) 5955001; e-mail info@palta.fi; internet www.palta.fi; f. 2011 following the merger of Tieto- ja tekniikka-alojen työnantajaliitto (TIKLI) with three other service sector orgs; Chair. RÖNKKÖ TUOMO; 1,700 mems.

Rakennusteollisuus RT r.y. (Confederation of Finnish Construction Industries): Unioninkatu 14, POB 381, 00130 Helsinki; tel. (9) 12991; fax (9) 628264; e-mail rt@rakennusteollisuus.fi; internet www.rakennusteollisuus.fi; f. 2001; Chair. LAURI KIVEKÄS; Dir-Gen. TARMO PIPATTI; 2,600 mem. cos.

Satamaoperaattorit r.y. (Finnish Port Operators' Asscn): Köydenpunojankatu 8, 00180 Helsinki; tel. (9) 6859530; fax (9) 68595353; e-mail juha.mutru@satamaoperaattorit.fi; internet www.satamaoperaattorit.fi; f. 1906; fmrly Suomen Lastauttajain Liitto (SLL) r.y; Chair. MATTI ESKO; Man. Dir JUHA MUTRU.

Suunnittelu- ja konsulttitoimistojen liitto (SKOL) r.y. (Finnish Association of Consulting Firms—SKOL): Eteläranta 10, POB 10, 00131 Helsinki; tel. (9) 19231; fax (9) 624462; e-mail skolry@teknologiateollisuus.fi; internet www.skolry.fi; f. 1951; Man. Dir MATTI MANNONEN; 205 mems.

Teknokemian Yhdistys r.y. (Finnish Cosmetic, Toiletry and Detergent Association): Eteläranta 10, 00130 Helsinki; POB 311, 00131 Helsinki; tel. (9) 172841; e-mail info@teknokemia.fi; internet www.teknokemia.fi; Dir-Gen. SARI KARJOMAA; 52 mems.

Teknologiateollisuus r.y. (Technology Industries of Finland): Eteläranta 10, POB 10, 00131 Helsinki; tel. (9) 19231; fax (9) 624462; e-mail martti.maenpaa@teknologiateollisuus.fi; internet www.teknologiateollisuus.fi; f. 1903 as Metalliteollisuuden Keskusliitto r.y.; Chair. PEKKA LUNDMARK; Man. Dir MARTTI MÄENPÄÄ.

Viestinnän Keskusliitto (Federation of the Finnish Media Industry): Lönnrotinkatu 11A, POB 291, 00121 Helsinki; tel. (9) 22877200; fax (9) 603527; e-mail hakan.gabrielsson@vkl.fi; internet www.vkl.fi; Man. Dir VALTTERI NIIRANEN.

Yleinen Teollisuusliitto r.y. (General Industry Association): Eteläranta 10, 7th Floor, POB 325, 00130 Helsinki; tel. (9) 6220410; fax (9) 176135; internet www.ytl.fi; Chair. MARKKU TALONEN; Man. Dir MARKKU KÄPPI.

Kultaseppien Työnantajaliitto r.y. (Employers' Association of Goldsmiths): Eteläranta 10, 00130 Helsinki; tel. (9) 172841; fax (9) 630225; Chair. ILKKA RUOHOLA.

Suomen Kiinteistöliitto r.y. (Finnish Real Estate Federation): Annankatu 24, 3rd Floor, 00100 Helsinki; tel. (9) 16676761; fax (9) 16676400; e-mail info@kiinteistoliitto.fi; internet www.kiinteistoliitto.fi; f. 1907; Pres. MATTI INHA; Man. Dir HARRI HILTUNEN; 26 mem asscns.

Suomen Varustamot r.y. (Finnish Shipowners' Association): see under Shipping.

Tupakkateollisuusliitto r.y. (Finnish Tobacco Industries' Federation): Eteläranta 10, POB 325, 00131 Helsinki; tel. (45) 3186650; e-mail paavo.heiskanen@ytl.fi; Chair. KIMMO SAVINAINEN.

UTILITIES

Electricity

Fortum Oyj: Keilaniementie 1, 02150 Espoo; POB 1, 00048 Fortum; tel. (10) 4511; fax (10) 4524777; e-mail asiakapavelu@fortum.com; internet www.fortum.fi; f. 1998 following merger of the Imatran Voima Group and the Neste Group; 50.76% state-owned; generation, distribution and sale of electricity and heat, as well as the operation and maintenance of power plants; listed on the Helsinki exchange in Dec. 1998; Chair. SARI BALDAUF; Pres. and CEO TAPIO KUULA.

Kemijoki Oy: Valtakatu 11, POB 8131, 96101 Rovaniemi; tel. (20) 7034400; fax (16) 7402380; e-mail info@kemijoki.fi; internet www.kemijoki.fi; f. 1954; electric power; 50.1% state-owned; Chair. of Supervisory Bd MATTI RUOTSALA; Pres. and CEO TUOMAS TIMONEN; 266 employees.

Pohjolan Voima Oy (PVO): Töölönkatu 4, POB 40, 00101 Helsinki; tel. (9) 693061; fax (9) 69306335; e-mail info@pvo.fi; internet www.pohjolanvoima.fi; Pres. and CEO LAURI VIRKKUNEN.

Regional electricity providers operate, of which the largest is Helsingin Energia.

Helsingin Energia (Helsinki Energy): Kampinkuja 2, 00090 Helen; tel. (9) 6171; fax (9) 6172360; e-mail helsingin.energia@helen.fi; internet www.helen.fi; f. 1909; municipal undertaking; generates and distributes electrical power and district heating; distributes natural gas; Man. Dir SEPPO RUOHONEN.

Gas

Gasum Oy: Miestentie 1, POB 21, 02151 Espoo; tel. (20) 4471; fax (20) 4478619; e-mail minna.ojala@gasum.fi; internet www.gasum.fi; f. 1994; imports and sells natural gas, owns and operates natural gas transmission system; operates 4 subsidiaries, Gasum Energiapalvelut Oy, Gasum Paikallisjakelu Oy, Gasum Eesti AG and Kaasupörssi Oy; 31% owned by Fortum, 25% owned by OAO Gazprom (Russia), 24% state-owned and 20% owned by E.ON Ruhrgas International AG (Germany); Pres. and CEO ANTERO JÄNNES.

Water

Helsingin seudun ympäristöpalvelut (Helsinki Region Environmental Services Authority): Opastinsilta 6A, 00520 Helsinki; POB 100, 00520 Helsinki; tel. (9) 15611; fax (9) 15612011; e-mail hsy@hsy.fi; internet www.hsy.fi; responsible for water supply and sewerage of the greater Helsinki area; Man. Dir RAIMO INKINEN.

CO-OPERATIVES

Pellervo (Confederation of Finnish Co-operatives): Simonkatu 6, POB 77, 00101 Helsinki; tel. (9) 4767501; fax (9) 6948845; e-mail toimisto@pellervo.fi; internet www.pellervo.fi; f. 1899; central organization of co-operatives; Man. Dir SAMI KARHU; 340 mem. societies (incl. 11 central co-operative societies).

Munakunta (Co-operative Egg Producers' Association): Piispanristintie 8, POB 6, 20761 Piispanristi; tel. (2) 214420; fax (2) 2144222; e-mail info@munakunta.fi; internet www.kultamuna.fi; f. 1922; Man. Dir JAN LÄHDE; 500 mems.

Valio Ltd (Finnish Co-operative Dairies' Association): Meijeritie 6, 00370 Helsinki; POB 10, 00039 Valio; tel. (10) 381121; fax (9) 5625068; e-mail pekka.laaksonen@valio.fi; internet www.valio.fi; f. 1905; production and marketing of dairy products; Pres. and CEO PEKKA LAAKSONEN.

TRADE UNIONS

Akava (Confederation of Unions for Professional and Managerial Staff): Rautatieläisenkatu 6, 00520 Helsinki; tel. (20) 7489400; fax (9) 142595; internet www.akava.fi; f. 1950; 30 affiliates, incl. asscns of doctors, engineers, social workers and teachers; Pres. STURE FJÄDER; total membership 552,800.

Suomen Ammattiliittojen Keskusjärjestö (SAK) r.y. (Central Organization of Finnish Trade Unions): Hakaniemenranta 1A, 00530 Helsinki; POB 157, 00531 Helsinki; tel. (20) 774000; fax (20) 7740225; e-mail sak@sak.fi; internet www.sak.fi; f. 1907; 20 affiliated unions comprising over 1m. mems; Pres. LAURI LYLY.

STTK (Finnish Confederation of Professionals): Mikonkatu 8A, 6th Floor, POB 421, 00101 Helsinki; tel. (9) 131521; fax (9) 652367; e-mail sttk@sttk.fi; internet www.sttk.fi; f. 1946; Pres. MIKKO MÄENPÄÄ; 18 affiliated unions; 608,000 mems.

Transport

ADMINISTRATIVE BODIES

Liikennevirasto (Finnish Transport Agency): Opastinsilta 12A, POB 33, 00521 Helsinki; tel. (20) 637373; fax (20) 6373700; e-mail viestinta@liikennevirasto.fi; internet www.fta.fi; f. 2010 by merger of waterways section of Finnish Maritime Administration, Finnish Rail Administration and Finnish Road Administration; attached to the Ministry of Transport and Communications; responsible for maintenance and development of transport infrastructure; Dir-Gen. ANTTI VEHVILÄINEN.

TraFi (Transport Safety Agency): Kumpulantie 9, POB 320, 00101 Helsinki; tel. (29) 5345000; fax (20) 5345095; e-mail kirjaamo@trafi.fi; internet www.trafi.fi; f. 2010 by merger of 4 sectoral bodies; attached to Ministry of Transport and Communications; responsible for safety and supervision of maritime, rail and road traffic and civil aviation; Dir-Gen. KARI WIHLMAN.

RAILWAYS

Finland had 5,944 km of wide-gauge (1,524 mm Russian gauge) railways in 2012, providing internal services and connections with Sweden and Russia. The state rail network is owned by the Finnish Transport Agency which oversees the maintenance and development of the country's rail network (see Administrative Bodies), while VR Group operates train services on the network. A high-speed rail link between Helsinki and St Petersburg, Russia became operational in December 2010. An underground railway service has been provided by Helsinki City Transport since 1982. In 2010 it was proposed to build a 312-km cross-border railway line linking Finland's main railway hub of Kolari to Skibotn in Norway. An 18-km railway route connecting the Helsinki-Vantaa airport and the adjacent Aviapolis business and commercial district to the Helsinki commuter rail network was under construction in 2012. The line, known as the Ring Rail Line Kehärata, was expected to open in 2015.

Karhula-Sunila Railway: Ratakatu 8, 48600 Karhula; tel. (5) 298221; fax (5) 298225; f. 1937; goods transport; privately owned; operates 10 km of railway (1,524 mm gauge); Man. PERTTI HONKALA.

VR Group: Vilhonkatu 13, POB 488, 00101 Helsinki; tel. (307) 10; fax (307) 21700; e-mail contactcenter@vr.fi; internet www.vr.fi; began operating 1862; joint-stock co since 1995; operates 5,784 km of railways; Pres. and CEO MIKAEL ARO; Chief Financial Officer OUTI HENRIKSSON.

ROADS

Finland had 78,161 km of highways in 2010, of which 13,328 km were main roads (including 779 km of motorway). Some 65% of the road network was paved in that year. In 2010 €823m. was spent on road infrastructure, including private roads.

Destia: Heidehofintie 2, POB 206, 01301 Helsinki; tel. (20) 44411; fax (20) 4442297; e-mail destia@destia.fi; internet www.destia.fi; f. 2008 to assume activities of fmr Tieliikelaitos (Finnish Road Enterprise); state-owned enterprise; provides transport infrastructure and transport environment services; Pres. and CEO HANNU LEINONEN.

INLAND WATERWAYS

Finland has a total of 19,500 km (approx.) of public, charted fairways. Lakes cover 33,672 sq km. The inland waterway system comprises 7,842 km of buoyed-out channels, 40 open canals and 37 lock canals. Merchant shipping routes include about 4,000 km. The total length of canals is 116 km. The most economically significant canal is the Saimaa Canal, which is 43 km long and connects Lake Saima to the Gulf of Finland. In 2006 cargo vessel traffic on inland waterways (including on the Saimaa Canal) amounted to 2.4m. metric tons, timber floating amounted to 0.9m. tons and passenger traffic to 479,709 passengers. The Finnish Transport Agency (see Administrative Bodies) is responsible for maintaining the inland waterways.

SHIPPING

The chief port of export is Kotka. Reclamation of land was carried out to build a second container port in Kotka. It opened in 2001 and has the capacity to handle 500,000 20-ft equivalent units (TEUs) of cargo per year. The main port of import is Helsinki, which has three specialized harbours. The West Harbour handles most of the container traffic, the North Harbour cargo ferry traffic and the South Harbour passenger traffic. Other important international ports are Turku (Åbo), Rauma and Hamina. The Transport Safety Agency (see Administrative Bodies) is responsible for maritime administration. At 31 December 2013 the flag registered fleet numbered 292 registered vessels, with a combined displacement of 1.47m. grt, of which 40 were general cargo and 23 were passenger ships.

Port Authority Association

Suomen Satamaliitto (Finnish Port Association): Toinen Linja 14, 00530 Helsinki; tel. (9) 7711; fax (9) 7530474; e-mail info@satamaliitto.fi; internet www.finnports.com; f. 1923; 31 mems; Exec. Dir ANNALEENA MÄKILÄ.

Port Authorities

HaminaKotka: Merituulentie 424, POB 196, 48310 Kotka; tel. (20) 7908800; fax (20) 7908891; e-mail marketing@haminakotka.fi; internet www.haminakotka.fi; Man. Dir KIMMO NASKI.

Helsinki: Port of Helsinki, Olympiaranta 3, POB 800, 00099 Helsinki; tel. (9) 3101621; fax (9) 31033802; e-mail port.helsinki@hel.fi; internet www.portofhelsinki.fi; Man. Dir KIMMO MÄKI.

Rauma: Port of Rauma, Hakunintie 19, 26100 Rauma; tel. (2) 8344712; fax (2) 8226369; e-mail harbour.office@portofrauma.com; internet www.portofrauma.com; Port Dir HANNU ASUMALAHTI; Harbour Master and Port Security Officer TANJA ROBERTS.

Turku: Turku Port Authority, Linnankatu 90, 20100 Turku; tel. (2) 2674111; fax (2) 2674125; e-mail turkport@port.turku.fi; internet www.port.turku.fi; Man. Dir CHRISTIAN RAMBERG; Harbour Master KARI RIUTTA.

Shipowners' Association

Suomen Varustamot r.y. (Finnish Shipowners' Association): Hämeentie 19, 00500 Helsinki; tel. (10) 8410500; e-mail info@shipowners.fi; internet www.shipowners.fi; f. 1932 as Suomen Varustamoyhdistys r.y; adopted current name in June 2008 following a merger with the Cargo Ship Association and the Åland Shipowners' Association; 27 mems; Man. Dir OLOF WIDÉN.

Principal Companies

ESL Shipping Oy: Lintulahdenkuja 10, POB 91, 00500 Helsinki; tel. (9) 5211; fax (9) 5219999; e-mail operations@eslshipping.fi; internet www.eslshipping.fi; worldwide tramp services; subsidiary of Aspo Oyj; Pres. MARKUS KARJALAINEN.

Finnlines PLC: Porkkalainkatu 20A, POB 197, 00180 Helsinki; tel. (10) 34350; fax (10) 3435200; e-mail info.fi@finnlines.com; internet www.finnlines.com; f. 1949; liner and contract services between Finland and other European countries; overland and inland services combined with direct sea links; Pres. and CEO UWE BAKOSCH; 85 cargo ferries.

Alfons Håkans Oy Ab: Linnankatu 36C, 20100 Turku; tel. (2) 515500; fax (2) 2515873; e-mail office.turku@alfonshakans.fi; internet www.alfonshakans.fi; Man. Dir and Chair. STEFAN HÅKANS; 32 tugs and 4 barges.

Rettig Oy Ab Bore: Bulevardi 46, POB 115, 00121 Helsinki; tel. (9) 61883300; fax (9) 61883398; e-mail info@bore.eu; internet www.bore.eu; f. 1897; acquired Bror Husell Chartering Ab in 2005 and Rederi Ab Engship in 2006; Man. Dir THOMAS FRANCK; 17 cargo ships, 3 car carriers and 1 bulk vessel.

RG Line Oy Ab: Satamaterminaali, 65170 Vaasa; tel. (20) 7716810; fax (20) 7716820; e-mail info@rgline.com; internet www.rgline.com; operates ferry services across the Gulf of Bothnia from Vaasa to Umeå, Sweden.

Tallink Silja Oy: Keilaranta 9, POB 43, 02151 Espoo; tel. (9) 18041; fax (9) 1804402; internet www.tallinksilja.com; f. 2006 by merger of Tallink Finland Oy and Silja Oy; part of the AS Tallink Group; passenger and cargo services in the Baltic; CEO ENN PANT; 19 vessels.

CIVIL AVIATION

An international airport is situated at Helsinki-Vantaa, 19 km from Helsinki. International and domestic services also operate to and from airports at Ivalo, Joensuu, Jyväskylä, Kajaani, Kemi-Tornio, Kokkola-Pietarsaari (formerly Kruunupyy), Kuopio, Lappeenranta, Mariehamn, Oulu, Pori, Rovaniemi, Savonlinna, Tampere-Pirkkala, Turku, Vaasa and Varkaus. Domestic services are available at airports at Enontekiö, Kittilä, Kuusamo and Mikkeli. The Transport Safety Agency (see Administrative Bodies) is the regulatory authority for civil aviation.

Finavia Corporation: Lentäjäntie 3, POB 50, 01531 Vantaa; tel. (20) 708000; fax (20) 7082099; e-mail info@finavia.fi; internet www.finavia.fi; state-owned commercial enterprise; provides air navigation services and maintains state-owned airports; Pres. and CEO KARI SAVOLAINEN.

Principal Airlines

Blue1: POB 168, 01531 Vantaa; tel. (20) 5856000; fax (20) 5856001; e-mail blue1@blue1.com; internet www.blue1.com; f. 1988 as Air Botnia; name changed in 2004; domestic and international services; member of SAS Group since 1998 and of Star Alliance since 2004; Pres. and CEO STEFAN WENTJÄRVI.

Finnair Oyj: Tietotie 11A, POB 15, 01053 Vantaa; tel. (9) 81881; fax (9) 8184979; e-mail maria.mroue@finnair.fi; internet www.finnair.com; f. 1923; 55.8% state-owned; 12 domestic services, 39 European services and 12 international services (to Asia and North America); Pres. and CEO PEKKA VAURAMO.

Tourism

Europe's largest inland water system, vast forests, wildlife, magnificent scenery and the possibility of holiday seclusion are Finland's main attractions. Most visitors come from Sweden, Germany, Russia, the United Kingdom, the Netherlands and Norway. Overnight stays by foreign tourists at registered accommodation establishments totalled some 5.8m. in 2012, compared with 4.9m. in 2009. Receipts from tourism (excluding passenger traffic) amounted to an estimated US $4,139m. in 2012.

Matkailun edistämiskeskus (Finnish Tourist Board): Töölönkatu 11, POB 625, 00101 Helsinki; tel. (29) 5058000; fax (29) 5058999; e-mail mek@mek.fi; internet www.mek.fi; f. 1973; Dir-Gen. JAAKKO LEHTONEN.

Defence

As assessed at November 2013, the armed forces of Finland numbered 22,200 comprising an army of 16,000 (including 11,000 conscripts), a navy of 3,500 (including 1,900 conscripts) and an air force of 2,700 (including 750 conscripts). There were also some 354,000 reserves and a 2,800-strong border guard (under the Ministry of the Interior). In November 2004 the European Union (EU) defence ministers agreed to create a number of 'battlegroups' (each comprising about 1,500 men), which could be deployed at short notice to carry out peacekeeping activities at crisis points around the world. The EU battlegroups, two of which were to be ready for deployment at any one time, following a rotational schedule, reached full operational capacity from 1 January 2007. In November 2012 Denmark, Finland, Iceland, Sweden and Norway agreed to the joint operation of military transport aircraft. In 2013 Finnish troops contributed to operations in countries including Afghanistan and Lebanon.

Defence Expenditure: Budget estimated at €2,751m. in 2014.

Chief of Defence: Gen. ARI PUHELOINEN.

Education

The Ministry of Education and Culture is the central body responsible for providing education. Tuition is free and the core curriculum is the same for all students. All children are entitled to receive one year of voluntary pre-primary education, usually at the age of six years. Compulsory schooling is provided in comprehensive schools and lasts for nine years, divided into a six-year lower stage, beginning at the age of seven, and a three-year upper stage (or lower secondary stage), beginning at the age of 13. Some comprehensive schools offer a voluntary 10th year in which additional basic education is provided. After comprehensive school, pupils may continue their studies, either at a general upper secondary school or a vocational upper secondary school. The upper secondary school curriculum is designed for three years but may be completed in two or four years. Courses leading to basic vocational qualifications take three years to complete. The matriculation examination taken at the end of three years of general upper secondary school gives eligibility for higher education, as do a Finnish polytechnic degree, a post-secondary level vocational qualification or a three-year vocational diploma. In 2011/12 enrolment at pre-primary level included 69% of children in the relevant age-group. Enrolment at primary schools in that year included 98% of those in the relevant age-group, while the comparable rate for secondary enrolment was 93%. Higher education is provided by 20 universities and 31 polytechnics. In 2005 enrolment at tertiary level was equivalent to 92% of those in the relevant age-group. Of total proposed budgetary expenditure by the central Government in 2014, €6,597m. (equivalent to 12.2% of total proposed expenditure) was allocated to the Ministry of Education and Culture.

FINNISH EXTERNAL TERRITORY

THE ÅLAND ISLANDS

Introductory Survey

LOCATION, LANGUAGE, RELIGION, FLAG, CAPITAL

The Åland Islands are a group of more than 6,500 islands (of which some 80 are inhabited) in the Gulf of Bothnia, between Finland and Sweden. Swedish is the official language, spoken by 89.1% of the inhabitants at the end of 2012; of the remaining population, 4.8% were Finnish-speaking. The majority profess Christianity: in 2012 81% were adherents of the Evangelical Lutheran Church of Finland (compared with 95% in 1990). The flag displays a red cross, bordered with yellow, on a blue background, the upright of the cross being to the left of centre. The capital is Mariehamn, which is situated on Åland, the largest island in the group.

CONTEMPORARY POLITICAL HISTORY

For geographical and economic reasons, the Åland Islands were traditionally associated closely with Sweden. In 1809, when Sweden was forced to cede Finland to Russia, the islands were incorporated into the Finnish Grand Duchy. However, following Finland's declaration of independence from the Russian Empire in 1917, the Ålanders demanded the right to self-determination and sought to be reunited with Sweden, with support from the Swedish Government. In 1920 Finland granted the islands autonomy but refused to acknowledge their secession, and in 1921 the Åland question was referred to the League of Nations. In June the League granted Finland sovereignty over the islands, while directing that certain conditions pertaining to national identity be included in the autonomy legislation offered by Finland and that the islands should be a neutral and non-fortified region. Elections were held in accordance with the new legislation, and the new provincial parliament (Landsting) held its first plenary session on 9 June 1922. The revised Autonomy Act of 1951 provided for independent rights of legislation in internal affairs and for autonomous control over the islands' economy. This Act could not be amended or repealed by the Finnish legislature without the consent of the Landsting.

In 1988 constitutional reform introduced the principle of a majority parliamentary government, to be formed by the Lantrådskandidat, the member of the Landsting nominated to conduct negotiations between the parties. These negotiations may yield two alternative outcomes: either the nominee will submit a proposal to create a new government or the nominee will fail to reach agreement on a new government (in which case renewed negotiations will ensue). The first formal parliamentary government and opposition were duly established. The governing coalition consisted of the three largest parties that had been elected to the Landsting in October 1987 (the Centre Party, the Liberals and the Moderates), which together held 22 seats in the 30-member legislature.

At a general election held in October 1991 the Centre Party increased its representation in the Landsting to 10, while the Liberal Party won seven seats, and the Moderates and Social Democrats won six and four seats, respectively. The Centre and Moderate Parties formed a new coalition Government, in which the Liberal Party was replaced by the Social Democratic Party.

A revised Autonomy Act, providing Åland with a greater degree of autonomous control, took effect on 1 January 1993. The rules regarding legislative authority were modernized, and the right of the Åland legislature (henceforth known as the Lagting) to enact laws was extended. Åland was given greater discretion with respect to its budget, and the revised Act also introduced changes in matters such as right of domicile, land-ownership regulations and administrative authority. The Autonomy Act contains a provision that, in any treaty which Finland may conclude with a foreign state and to which Åland is a party, the Lagting must consent to the statute implementing the treaty in order for the provision to enter into force in Åland. A referendum on the issue of Åland's proposed accession to membership of the European Union (EU, see p. 273) in 1995 was held in November 1994, immediately after similar referendums in Finland and Sweden had shown a majority in favour of membership. (A small majority of Åland citizens had supported Finland's membership.) Despite low participation in the referendum, 73.7% of the votes cast supported membership and Åland duly joined the EU, together with Finland and Sweden, on 1 January 1995. Under the terms of the treaty of accession, Åland was accorded special exemption from tax union with the EU in order to stimulate the ferry and tourism industries. (In 1998 two of Europe's largest ferry operators, Silja and Viking—both Finnish, re-routed their major services via Åland in order to continue to conduct duty-free sales, which were later abolished within the rest of the EU.)

A general election was held in October 1995. The Centre Party secured nine seats and the Liberal Party won eight, while the Moderates and Social Democrats maintained the representation that they had achieved in the previous parliament. The new coalition Government was composed of members of the Centre and Moderate Parties and one independent.

At a general election held in October 1999 the Centre Party and the Liberal Party each won nine seats. The Moderate Party secured only four seats, while the Social Democrats maintained their level of representation. The Obunden Samling (Non-aligned Coalition) won four seats. A coalition Government was formed comprising the Centre Party, the Moderate Party and the Independents. In March 2001, following a motion of no confidence in the Lagting, the Chairman (Lantråd) of the Government, Roger Nordlund of the Centre Party, dissolved the coalition and formed a new administration comprising members of the Centre Party and the Liberal Party.

A general election was held on 19 October 2003, at which the Centre Party and the Liberal Party each won seven seats. The two parties formed a new Government in coalition with the Social Democrats (who had won six seats) and the Moderate Party (with four seats), under Nordlund.

In August 2004 the Finnish Government agreed new, more stringent regulations securing the islands' demilitarized status, following reports that this had been violated by troop movements over the past two decades.

In January 2005, following a motion of no confidence in the Lagting, the governing coalition was dissolved and Nordlund formed a new administration comprising members of the Centre Party, the Social Democrats and the Moderate Party.

In May 2006 the European Court of Justice (ECJ) ruled that Finland was in breach of EU regulations on tobacco products by allowing the continued sale of snus (Swedish oral tobacco) in the Åland Islands. (The sale of oral tobacco was prohibited in the EU in 1992, but Sweden was granted an exemption from the ban when it joined the Union in 1995.) Trade in snus, particularly on ferries registered in the Islands, had been worth several million euros annually. As Finland had no powers to legislate in health matters in the Islands, the matter was referred to the Lagting, which in January 2007 adopted legislation with the aim of complying with the Court's judgment; however, this was deemed insufficient by the European Commission, as it only prohibited snus (rather than oral tobacco in general) from entering the market, and did not apply to the sale of snus on vessels registered in the Åland Islands once they had left Finnish territorial waters. In October the European Commission referred the case to the Court of Justice for a second time. Consequently, the Lagting adopted further legislation, which was enacted in January 2008, introducing an outright ban on snus sales on Åland-registered ships, including in Swedish territorial waters; as a result, the European Commission withdrew its case against Finland later in 2008.

The opposition Liberal Party became the largest party in the Lagting following a general election held on 21 October 2007, at which it won 10 seats. The Centre Party won eight seats, while the Independents took four. The representation of the Moderate Party and the Social Democrats declined to three seats each. A turnout of 67.8% was recorded. The Liberal Party and the Centre Party subsequently formed a coalition Government, under Viveka Eriksson, the Liberal leader.

In September 2008 Finland ratified the Lisbon Treaty, which aimed to improve decision-making in the enlarged EU. However, the Åland Islands, which under the amended Act of Autonomy was also required to ratify the treaty, demanded concessions from the Finnish Government prior to ratification. The Åland Government's demands included a seat in the European Parliament, the right to appear before the European Court of Justice (where Åland had been represented by Finland in the case regarding snus sales), participation in the meetings of the Council and shared control over the principle of subsidiarity (that the EU should only act when an objective can be better achieved at the supranational level). By November 2009 no formal concessions appeared to have been granted by the Finnish Government; none the less, on 25 November the Lagting voted to ratify the treaty, six days before it was scheduled to enter into effect across the EU. Earlier in November the Lagting's legal affairs committee had recommended that the legislature approve the treaty, but urged the Åland Government to continue to seek greater participation for the islands in EU affairs.

At a general election held on 16 October 2011, the ruling coalition partners, the Liberal Party and the Centre Party, lost their majority, their respective representation declining to six and seven seats. The

Social Democrats increased their number of seats, to six, while the Moderates and the Independents each secured four seats and the separatist Åland's Future three. A turnout of 66.6% was recorded. Later that month a new coalition Government, comprising the Social Democrats, the Centre Party, the Independents and the Moderates, was formed under Camilla Gunell of the Social Democrats.

GOVERNMENT

The Åland Islands are governed according to the Autonomy Act, which was introduced in 1920, revised in 1951 and further revised with effect from January 1993. The Islands' demilitarized status and autonomy are guaranteed by international treaties. The legislative body is the Lagting, comprising 30 members, elected every four years on a basis of proportional representation. All Ålanders over the age of 18 years, possessing Åland regional citizenship, have the right to vote and to seek election. An Executive Council (Landskapsregeringen), consisting of five to seven members, is elected by the Lagting, and its Chairman (Lantråd) is the highest-ranking politician in Åland after the Speaker (Talman) of the Lagting. The President has the right to veto Lagting decisions only when the Lagting exceeds its legislative competence, or when there is a threat to the security of the country. The Governor of Åland represents the Government of Finland and is appointed by the Finnish President (with the agreement of the Speaker of the Åland legislature). The Åland Islands elects one representative to the Finnish Parliament, the Eduskunta. There are 16 municipalities in the Åland Islands.

REGIONAL CO-OPERATION

The Åland Islands joined the European Union (EU, see p. 273) in 1995, together with Finland, following a referendum in November 1994. The islands have had their own representation in the Nordic Council since 1970.

ECONOMIC AFFAIRS

In 2010 the gross domestic product (GDP) of the Åland Islands, measured at current prices, was €1,172.2m. In 2011 4.3% of the working population were employed in agriculture (including hunting, forestry and fishing), which contributed 2.6% of GDP in 2010. Forests covered 60% of the islands in 2012, and only 9.0% of the total land area was arable. The principal crops are potatoes, onions, sugar beet, apples and wheat. Dairy farming and sheep rearing are also important.

Industry (including mining, manufacturing, construction and power) provided 12.0% of GDP in 2010 and employed 15.3% of the working population in 2011. Manufacturing contributed 5.5% of GDP in 2010 and engaged 6.9% of the working population in 2011.

Since 1960 the economy of the islands has expanded and diversified. Fishing has declined as a source of income, and shipping (particularly the operation of ferry services between Finland and Sweden), trade and tourism have become the dominant economic sectors. In 2010 services accounted for 87.4% of GDP and engaged 80.5% of the employed labour force. The transport sector, including shipping, employed 12.4% in 2011, and, together with storage and communications, contributed 29.3% of GDP in 2010. The political autonomy of the islands and their strategic location between Sweden and Finland have contributed to expanding banking and trade sectors; financial services engaged 3.3% of the employed labour force in 2011, while trade and hotels employed 14.2%. Tourist arrivals totalled 422,322 in 2012.

The Finnish state collects taxes, duties and fees from the Åland Islands, which receives 0.45% of total Finnish government income in return. If the taxes raised in the Åland Islands exceed 0.5% of corresponding Finnish tax revenues, the islands receive the excess amount in the form of a tax redemption. Consumer prices increased at an average annual rate of 1.7% in 2002–12; prices rose by 2.3% in 2012 and by 1.2% in 2013. The unemployment rate stood at 3.9% in 2013. Finland participated in Economic and Monetary Union (EMU), introducing the single European currency, the euro, in January 1999. The Finnish currency, the markka, was used by the islands until the end of 2001. Euro notes and coins were introduced on 1 January 2002, and, as in Finland as a whole, the euro became the sole legal tender from 1 March 2002. As part of a €6,250,000 operational programme for 2007–13 focusing on competitiveness and employment, the EU assessed the main challenges to the region to stem from its ageing population, lack of higher education opportunities, dependence on the marine and shipping sector and structural problems relating to the decline of agricultural jobs, as well as regional development disparities between the main city of Mariehamn and the rest of the archipelago. The islands' location between southern Finland and the Stockholm region of Sweden provides a strategic advantage, but also makes the region sensitive to economic fluctuations in these neighbouring markets.

Statistical Survey

Source: Statistics Åland, POB 1187, 22111 Mariehamn; tel. (18) 25490; fax (18) 19495; e-mail info@asub.ax; internet www.asub.ax.

AREA AND POPULATION

Area: 13,324 sq km (5,144 sq miles), of which 1,553 sq km (600 sq miles) is land and 11,772 sq km (4,545 sq miles) is water.

Population (official figures at 31 December 2012): 28,502 (males 14,207, females 14,295).

Density (land area only, 31 December 2012): 18.4 per sq km.

Population by Age and Sex (official figures at 31 December 2012): *0–14:* 4,665 (males 2,419, females 2,246); *15–64:* 18,310 (males 9,208, females 9,102); *65 and over:* 5,527 (males 2,580, females 2,947); *Total* 28,502 (males 14,207, females 14,295).

Principal Towns (official figures at 31 December 2012): Mariehamn (capital) 11,346; Godby 906; Storby 518; Prästgården 419; Ödkarby 366; Söderby 352.

Births, Marriages and Deaths (2012): Registered live births 292 (birth rate 10.2 per 1,000); Marriages 141 (marriage rate 4.9 per 1,000); Deaths 323 (death rate 11.3 per 1,000).

Life Expectancy (years at birth, 2008–12): 81.5 (males 79.7; females 83.2).

Immigration and Emigration (2012): Immigrants 885 (Finland 353; Sweden 348); Emigrants 708 (Finland 252; Sweden 366).

Employment (2011): Agriculture, fishing and aquaculture 592; Mining and quarrying 14; Manufacturing 964; Electricity, gas, steam and air conditioning supply 73; Water supply, sewerage, waste management and remediation activities 100; Construction 954; Wholesale and retail trade, and repair of motor vehicles 1,367; Transportation and storage 1,706; Accommodation and food services 588; Information and communication 533; Finance and insurance activities 449; Real estate 80; Professional, scientific and technical activities 476; Administrative and support services 345; Public administration and defence 1,091; Education 994; Health and social work 2,630; Arts, entertainment and recreation 374; Other service activities 469; *Sub-total* 13,799; Activities not classified 201; *Total employed* 14,000; Unemployed 422; *Total labour force* 14,422. *2012* (preliminary): Total employed 13,928; Unemployed 546; Total labour force 14,474.

HEALTH AND WELFARE

Physicians (2003): 59.

Hospital Beds (2012): 201.

AGRICULTURE, ETC.

Agricultural Production (metric tons, 2012, unless otherwise indicated): Milk ('000 litres) 14,440; Beef 510; Pork 6; Mutton 73; Poultry 1,497 (2002); Eggs 276; Wheat 3,104; Rye 769; Triticale (wheat-rye hybrid) 81 (2003); Barley and oats 2,453; Peas 45; Turnip rape 40 (2006); Sugar beet 4,760 (2011); Potatoes 14,878; Onions 5,372; Cucumbers 73; Leeks 127; Chinese cabbage and lettuce 679; Apples 2,603; Strawberries ('000 litres) 15; Tomatoes 178; Parsley ('000 bunches) 23; Dill ('000 bunches) 9; Celery 16; Carrots 71.

Livestock (2012 unless otherwise indicated): Cattle 7,902; Pigs 294 (2009); Hens 16,198; Sheep 12,531; Horses 176.

Forestry Production (cu m, roundwood, 2012): Logs 71,758; Pulp 146,664.

Fishing (metric tons, live weight, 2012): Capture 2,443 (Baltic herring and sprat 1,124; Cod 1,033; Whitefish 50; Perch 95; Pike-perch 13; Pike 13); Aquaculture 4,314; *Total catch* 6,757.

INDUSTRY

Selected Indicators (2012): Electric energy 64m. kWh (incl. 61m. kWh from wind power); Dwellings completed 229.

FINANCE

Currency: Finnish currency was used until the end of 2001. Euro notes and coins were introduced on 1 January 2002, and the euro became the sole legal tender from 1 March. For details of exchange rates, see Finland.

Budget (€ '000, 2012): Revenue 314,386; Expenditure 344,122.

Cost of Living (Consumer Price Index; base: 2000 = 100): All items 116.8 in 2010; 121.1 in 2011; 123.9 in 2012.

Expenditure on the Gross Domestic Product (€ million at current prices, 2010): Wages and salaries 510; Employers' contribution to social security 115; Operating surplus 254; Fixed capital depreciation 201; *Total domestic expenditure* 1,080; Indirect taxes 141; *Less* Subsidies 49; *GDP in market prices* 1,172.

Gross Domestic Product by Economic Activity (€ million at current prices, 2010): Agriculture, hunting, forestry and fishing 28.2; Mining and quarrying 1.0; Manufacturing 59.1; Construction 48.1; Energy supply and water 21.2; Trade, restaurants and hotels 100.7; Transport, storage and communications 316.2; Financing, insurance, real estate and business services 182.0; Government services 228.7; Other community, social and personal services 80.9; Non-profit institutions 14.4; *GDP at factor cost* 1,080.4; Indirect taxes 140.6; *Less* Subsidies 48.8; *GDP in purchasers' values* 1,172.2.

EXTERNAL TRADE

2012 (€ '000): *Imports:* Total 427,574 (Live animals and products thereof 39,657; Vegetable products 9,201; Edible preparations, beverages, liquors and tobacco 32,472; Mineral products 9,058; Articles of plastics and rubber 18,318; Pulp and paper 28,467; Textiles and textile articles 28,150; Machinery, equipment and appliances 46,798; Miscellaneous manufactured articles 13,668); *Exports:* Total 154,515 (Live animals and products thereof 4,860; Products of the chemicals or allied industries 6,449; Articles of plastics and rubber 21,855; Wood and cork and products thereof 7,997; Textiles and textile articles 6,353; Base metals and articles of base metals 2,798; Optical appliances 5,214). Note: Figures exclude trade with mainland Finland.

TRANSPORT

Road Traffic (registered motor vehicles, 31 December 2012): Private motor cars 20,866; Vans 4,156; Lorries 716; Buses 45; Motorcycles 1,561; Tractors 3,741.

Shipping: *Flag Registered Fleet* (2013): Vessels 29; Total displacement 226,270 grt (Source: Lloyd's List Intelligence—www.lloydslist intelligence.com). *Traffic:* 8,062 vessels entered (2012); 2,224,692 passenger arrivals (incl. ferry services, 2008).

Civil Aviation (traffic, Mariehamn airport, 2012): Passengers 54,087; Freight 12 metric tons; Post 203 metric tons.

TOURISM

Tourist Arrivals (2012): 422,322 (162,751 from Finland; 203,492 from Sweden).

EDUCATION

Primary and Secondary Schools (2012): Institutions 23 (Comprehensive schools 23, of which 9 also offer upper-stage education); Pupils 2,813 (Comprehensive schools 1,810, Upper-stage schools 1,003).

Pupils Enrolled in Post-Comprehensive Education (2012): General programme 459 (males 191, females 268); Vocational 771 (males 438, females 333); Other 48 (males 20, females 28); Åland University of Applied Sciences 525 (males 351, females 174).

Directory

Government and Legislature

The legislative body is the Lagting, comprising 30 members, elected every four years on a basis of proportional representation. All Ålanders over the age of 18 years, possessing Åland regional citizenship, have the right to vote and to seek election. An Executive Council (Landskapsregeringen), consisting of five to seven members, is elected by the Lagting, and its Chairman (Lantråd) is the highest-ranking politician in Åland after the Speaker (Talman) of the Lagting. The Finnish President has the right to veto Lagting decisions only when the Lagting exceeds its legislative competence, or when there is a threat to the security of the country. The Governor of Åland represents the Government of Finland and is appointed by the Finnish President (with the agreement of the Speaker of the Åland legislature).

Governor: PETER LINDBÄCK.

EXECUTIVE COUNCIL
(Landskapsregeringen)

Självstyrelsegården, POB 1060, 22111 Mariehamn; tel. (18) 25000; fax (18) 19155; e-mail marina.sundstrom@regeringen.ax; internet www.regeringen.ax.

The governing coalition comprises members of the Social Democrats, the Centre Party, the Independents and the Moderates. Its composition in April 2014 was as follows:

Chairman (Lantråd): CAMILLA GUNELL (Social Democrats).

Deputy Chairman (Vicelantråd) and Minister of Finance: ROGER NORDLUND (Centre Party).

Minister for Infrastructure: VERONICA THÖRNROOS (Centre Party).

Minister for Social and Environmental Affairs: CARINA AALTONEN (Social Democrats).

Minister for Enterprise: FREDRIK KARLSTRÖM (Independents).

Minister for Education and Culture: JOHAN EHN (Moderates).

Minister for Administrative Affairs: WILLE VALVE (Moderates).

PARLIAMENT
(Lagting)

Självstyrelsegården, POB 69, 22101 Mariehamn; tel. (18) 25000; fax (18) 13302; e-mail susanne.eriksson@regeringen.ax; internet www.lagtinget.ax.

Speaker (Talman): BRITT LUNDBERG (Centre Party).

Election, 16 October 2011

	Votes	% of votes	Seats
Åländsk Center (Centre Party)	3,068	23.65	7
Liberalerna på Åland (Liberal Party)	2,630	20.27	6
Ålands Socialdemokrater (Social Democrats)	2,404	18.53	6
Moderaterna på Åland (Moderates of Åland)	1,810	13.95	4
Obunden Samling (Independents)	1,639	12.63	4
Ålands Framtid (Åland's Future)	1,286	9.91	3
Valmansf. för Henrik Appelqvist	138	1.06	—
Total	12,975	100.00	30

Political Organizations

Unless otherwise indicated, the address of each of the following organizations is: Ålands Lagting, 6th Floor, POB 69, 22101 Mariehamn; tel. (18) 25000; fax (18) 13302.

Åländsk Center (Centre Party): tel. (18) 25360; fax (18) 16630; e-mail centern@lagtinget.ax; internet www.centern.ax; f. 1976; Chair. HARRY JANSSON.

Ålands Framtid (Åland's Future): tel. (18) 25366; e-mail info@alandsframtid.ax; internet www.alandsframtid.ax; f. 2003; separatist; Leader AXEL JONSSON.

Ålands Socialdemokrater (Social Democrats): Ekonomiegatan 1, POB 69, 22101 Mariehamn; tel. (18) 25461; e-mail socialdemokraterna@lagtinget.ax; internet www.socialdemokraterna.ax; Chair. CAMILLA GUNELL; Sec. HELENA FLÖJT-JOSEFSSON.

Liberalerna på Åland (Liberal Party): tel. (18) 25362; fax (18) 16075; e-mail liberalerna@lagtinget.ax; internet www.liberalerna.ax; Chair. KATRIN SJÖGREN.

Moderaterna Åland (Moderates of Åland): tel. (18) 25357; e-mail moderat@lagtinget.ax; internet www.moderaterna.ax; Chair. JOHAN EHN.

Obunden Samling (Independents): tel. (18) 25368; fax (18) 16370; e-mail danne.sundman@lagtinget.ax; internet www.obs.ax; f. 1987; Chair. GUN-MARI LINDHOLM.

Religion

The majority of the islands' population is Christian. In 2012 some 81.0% of inhabitants were adherents of the Evangelical Lutheran Church of Finland. In 2006 there were small numbers of Jehovah's Witnesses (49), Roman Catholics (39), Greek Orthodox Christians (24) and Adventists (12); 58 people practised other religions.

The Press

Ålandstidningen: Strandgatan 16, POB 50, 22101 Mariehamn; tel. (18) 26026; fax (18) 15755; e-mail niklas.lampi@alandstidningen.ax; internet www.tidningen.ax; f. 1891; 6 a week; Man. Dir DAN-JOHAN DAHLBLOM; Editor-in-Chief NIKLAS LAMPI; circ. 10,355 (2007).

Nya Åland: Uppgårdsvägen 6, POB 21, 22100 Mariehamn; tel. (18) 23444; fax (18) 23450; e-mail redaktion@nyan.ax; internet www

.nyan.ax; f. 1981; 5 a week; Man. Dir STEFAN NORRGRANN; Editor-in-Chief JONAS BLADH; circ. 7,256 (2005).

Broadcasting and Communications

TELECOMMUNICATIONS

Ålands Mobiltelefon Ab: POB 1230, 22101 Mariehamn; tel. (18) 291464; e-mail info@amt.ax; internet www.gsm.aland.fi; f. 1989; licensed to operate both GSM and UMTS networks on the islands.

Ålands Telefonandelslag: Hantverkargränd 1, 22150 Jomala; tel. (18) 41053; fax (18) 41299; e-mail jomala@altel.ax; internet www.altel.ax; f. 1910.

Mariehamns Telefon Ab: Ålandsvägen 52, POB 1228, 22111 Mariehamn; tel. (18) 27044; fax (18) 15900; e-mail anders@mtel.ax; internet www.mtel.ax; f. 1892; Dir ANDERS JOHNSSON.

RADIO AND TELEVISION

Ålands Radio och TV Ab: Ålandsvägen 24, POB 140, 22101 Mariehamn; tel. (18) 26060; fax (18) 26520; e-mail info@radiotv.ax; internet www.radiotv.ax; f. 1996; broadcasts radio programmes in Swedish, 115.5 hours a week; operates 3 analogue and 5 digital television channels; Man. Dir PIA ROTHBERG-OLOFSSON; Editor-in-Chief ASTRID OLHAGEN.

Steel FM: Strandgränd 2, 22100 Mariehamn; tel. (18) 16200; fax (18) 22079; e-mail mail@steelfm.net; internet www.steelfm.net; commercial radio broadcaster; Dir FREDRIK KARLSTRÖM.

TV Åland: Elverksgatan 1, 22100 Mariehamn; tel. (18) 14035; fax (18) 14037; e-mail redaktion@tv.ax; internet www.tv.ax; f. 1984; television producer and broadcaster; broadcasts by cable to 75% of islands; Dir KAJ GRUNDSTRÖM.

Finance

BANKS

(cap. = capital; res = reserves; dep. = deposits; m. = million; amounts in euros; brs = branches)

Ålandsbanken Abp (Bank of Åland): Nygatan 2, POB 3, 22100 Mariehamn; tel. (204) 29011; fax (204) 29228; e-mail aland@alandsbanken.fi; internet www.alandsbanken.fi; f. 1919 as Ålands Aktiebank; name changed to Bank of Åland Ltd 1980, changed as above in 1998; merged with Ålands Hypoteksbank Ab in November 1995; cap. 29.1m., res 85.2m., dep. 2,690.1m. (Dec. 2012); Chair. KAJ-GUSTAF BERGH; Man. Dir PETER WIKLÖF; 16 brs.

Andelsbanken för Åland: Köpmansgatan 2, POB 34, 22101 Mariehamn; tel. (18) 6330; e-mail andelsbanken.for.aland@op.fi; co-operative; mem. of OP–Pohjola Group; Man. Dir HÅKAN CLEMES.

Nordea Bank Finland PLC and Pohjola Bank PLC are also represented.

INSURANCE

Alandia Group: Ålandsvägen 31, POB 121, 22101 Mariehamn; tel. (18) 29000; fax (18) 13290; e-mail mhamn@alandia.com; internet www.alandia.com; f. 1938; life, non-life and marine; comprises 3 subsidiaries; Man. Dir LEIF NORDLUND.

Ålands Ömsesidiga Försäkringsbolag (Åland Mutual Insurance Co): Köpmansgatan 6, POB 64, 22101 Mariehamn; tel. (18) 27600; fax (18) 27610; e-mail info@omsen.ax; internet www.omsen.ax; f. 1866; life and non-life; Chair. STURE CARLSON; Man. Dir GÖRAN LINDHOLM.

Trade and Industry

TRADE ASSOCIATIONS

Ålands Företagareförening (Åland Business Asscn): Skarpansvägen 17, 22100 Mariehamn; tel. (18) 23277; fax (457) 5267141; e-mail ombudsman@foretagare.ax; internet www.foretagare.ax; f. 1957; c. 250 mem. cos; Chair. DICK JANSSON.

Ålands Näringsliv (Invest in Åland): Nygatan 6, 22100 Mariehamn; tel. (18) 29029; fax (18) 21129; e-mail info@naringsliv.ax; internet www.naringsliv.ax; f. 2011 by the merger of Åland Chamber of Commerce, the Åland Employers' Confederation and Åland Businesmen's Asscn; Chair. PETER WIKLÖF; Man. Dir DANIEL DAHLÉN.

EMPLOYERS' ORGANIZATIONS

Ålands Fiskodlarförening (Åland Fish Farmers' Asscn): Tingsvägen 3, 22710 Föglö; tel. (18) 17834; fax (18) 17833; e-mail info@fiskodlarna.aland.fi; internet www.fiskodlarna.aland.fi; Chair. MARCUS ERIKSSON.

Ålands Producentförbund (Åland Agricultural Producers' Asscn): Ålands Landsbygdscentrum, Jomalagårdsväg 17, 22150 Jomala; tel. (18) 329840; fax (18) 329801; e-mail birgitta.eriksson@landsbygd.aland.fi; f. 1946; Chair. ANDERS ENGLUND; Man. Dir HENRY LINDSTRÖM.

UTILITIES

Electricity

Ålands Elandelslag: Godbyvägen 193, 22100 Mariehamn; tel. (18) 39250; fax (18) 31562; e-mail info@el.ax; internet www.el.ax; f. 1957; distribution; Man. Dir JAN WENNSTRÖM.

Ålands Vindenergi Andelslag: Hamngatan 8, 22100 Mariehamn; tel. (18) 526300; fax (18) 12090; e-mail postmaster@allwinds.ax; internet www.alandsvindenergi.ax; there are 21 wind power farms on the Åland islands, 8 of which it owns; owns 20% of shares in Leovind Ab, which owns 6 turbines; Chair. ANNETTE LARSON; Man. Dir HENRIK LINDQVIST.

Kraftnät Åland: Elverksgatan 10, POB 71, 22101 Mariehamn; tel. (18) 5395; fax (18) 539250; e-mail info@kraftnat.ax; internet www.kraftnat.ax; f. 1996; production, transmission; fully owned by Åland government; Man. Dir JAN KAHLROTH.

Water

Ålands Vatten Ab: Vattenverksvägen 34, 22150 Jomala; tel. (18) 32860; fax (18) 31471; e-mail alandsvatten@vatten.ax; internet www.vatten.ax; f. 1970; supplies water to 70% of population; Man. Dir CHRISTIAN NORDAS.

VA-verket: Torggatan 17, POB 5, 22101 Mariehamn; tel. (18) 5310; fax (18) 531206; e-mail info@mariehamn.ax; internet www.mariehamn.ax; Dir JOUNI HUHTALA.

TRADE UNIONS

FFC-facken på Åland: POB 108, 22101 Mariehamn; tel. (18) 16207; fax (18) 17207; internet www.facket.ax; Chair. PER-ÅKE ASPBÄCK; Gen. Sec. CHRISTINA HENRIKSSON.

Tjänstemannaorganisationerna på Åland, TCÅ r.f. (Union of Salaried Employees in Åland): Norragatan 1B5, 22100 Mariehamn; tel. (18) 16210; e-mail facket@tca.ax; Chair. YVONNE ASPHOLM; Dir MARIE-SUSANNE STENWALL.

Transport

The islands are linked to the Swedish and Finnish mainlands by ferry services and by air services from Mariehamn airport. There are no railways, but local bus services are available, along with inter-island ferries.

Ålandstrafiken: Strandgatan 25, 22100 Mariehamn; tel. (18) 525100; fax (18) 17815; e-mail info@alandstrafiken.ax; internet www.alandstrafiken.ax; operates buses on the islands and ferry services between the islands.

ROADS

In 2008 there was a road network of 918.6 km, of which 757.6 km were paved. There is also a bicycle route network, covering some 61.2 km in 2008.

SHIPPING

Ferry services operate from the Åland Islands to Sweden, the Finnish mainland and Estonia.

Principal Companies

Birka Line Abp: Torggatan 2, POB 158, 22101 Mariehamn; tel. (18) 28050; fax (18) 15118; e-mail brage.jansson@birkaline.com; internet www.birkaline.com; f. 1971; shipping service; Man. Dir BRAGE JANSSON.

Birka Cargo Ab Ltd: Torggatan 2B, POB 175, 22101 Mariehamn; tel. (18) 28050; fax (18) 23223; e-mail info@birkacargo.com; internet www.birkacargo.com; f. 1990 as United Shipping Ltd Ab; 7 ro-ro vessels; Man. Dir JARI SORVETTULA.

Lundqvist Rederierna: Norra Esplanadgatan 9B, 22100 Mariehamn; tel. (18) 26050; fax (18) 26428; e-mail info@lundqvist.aland.fi; internet www.lundqvist.aland.fi; f. 1927; tanker services; Man. Dir BEN LUNDQVIST; total tonnage c. 820,000 dwt.

Rederiaktiebolaget Eckerö (Eckerö Linjen): Torggatan 2, POB 158, 22101 Mariehamn; tel. (18) 28030; fax (18) 12011; e-mail info@eckerolinjen.fi; internet www.eckerolinjen.fi; f. 1960; operates ferry routes between the Åland Islands and Sweden, and between Finland and Estonia; Man. Dir BJÖRN BLOMQVIST.

Rederiaktiebolaget Gustaf Erikson: Norra Esplanadgatan 4B, 22100 Mariehamn; tel. (18) 27070; fax (18) 12670; e-mail info@geson.aland.fi; internet www.geson.ax; f. 1913; manages dry cargo and refrigerated vessels; Man. Dir GUN ERIKSON-HJERLING.

Rederi Ab Lillgaard: Köpmansgatan 9, POB 136, 22101 Mariehamn; tel. (18) 13120; fax (18) 17220; e-mail info@lillgaard.aland.fi; internet www.lillgaard.aland.fi; f. 1966; operates services from the Åland Islands to the Finnish mainland and Sweden; Man. Dir ANDERS NORDLUND.

Viking Line Abp: Norragatan 4, POB 166, 22101 Mariehamn; tel. (18) 27000; fax (18) 16944; e-mail nn@vikingline.fi; internet www.vikingline.fi; f. 1963; operates cruise and ferry services between Finland and Sweden and throughout the Baltic Sea; 7 car/passenger vessels; total tonnage 212,474 grt; Chair. BEN LUNDQVIST; Man. Dir and Chief Exec. MIKAEL BACKMAN.

CIVIL AVIATION

The islands' airport is at Mariehamn. In 2012 the airport handled 54,087 passengers, 12 metric tons of freight and 203 tons of post. It is served by Finnair and AirÅland Ab.

AirÅland Ab: Mariehamns Airport, Flygfältsvägen 67, 22120 Mariehamn; tel. (18) 17110; fax (18) 23730; e-mail info@airaland.com; internet www.airaland.com; f. 2005; routes from Mariehamn to Helsinki and Stockholm; the Swedish company NextJet operates all AirÅland Ab flights; CEO CARIN HOLMQVIST.

Tourism

The Åland archipelago has numerous bays, inlets, islands and open stretches of water, and is an area of great natural beauty. Cycling, canoeing, kayaking and hiking attract tourists to the islands. Major tourist attractions include the Maritime Museum, the museum ship Pommern and the Maritime Quarter. Most visitors are from the Nordic countries, particularly from mainland Finland and Sweden. In 2012 tourist arrivals totalled 422,322 (including 162,751 from Finland and 203,492 from Sweden).

Ålands Turist Förbund (Åland Tourism Board): Storagatan 8, 22100 Mariehamn; tel. (18) 24000; fax (18) 24265; e-mail info@visitaland.com; internet www.visitaland.com; f. 1989; CEO LOTTA BERNER-SJÖLUND.

Ålands Turist och Konferens Ab: Hotell Arkipelag, Strandgatan 35, 22100 Mariehamn; tel. (18) 15349; fax (18) 21077; e-mail info@turist-konferens.aland.fi; internet www.turist-konferens.aland.fi; Man. Dir HENRIK NORDSTRÖM.

Defence

By law, the archipelago is demilitarized. For general details, see Finland.

Education

The education system is similar to that of Finland, except that Swedish is the language of instruction and Finnish an optional subject. There is one university: Åland University of Applied Sciences. In 2012 a total of 1,278 people were undertaking post-secondary general or vocational education in the Åland Islands. In 2012 there were 525 students at the Åland University of Applied Sciences.

FRANCE

Introductory Survey

LOCATION, CLIMATE, LANGUAGE, RELIGION, FLAG, CAPITAL

The French Republic is situated in Western Europe. It is bounded to the north by the English Channel (la Manche), to the east by Belgium, Luxembourg, Germany, Switzerland and Italy, to the south by the Mediterranean Sea, Andorra, Monaco, and Spain, and to the west by the Atlantic Ocean. The Mediterranean island of Corsica is part of metropolitan France, while 12 overseas possessions (French Guiana, Guadeloupe, Martinique, Réunion, French Polynesia, Mayotte, Saint-Barthélemy, Saint-Martin, Saint Pierre and Miquelon, the Wallis and Futuna Islands, the French Southern and Antarctic Territories, and New Caledonia) also form an integral part of the Republic. The climate is temperate throughout most of the country, but in the south it is of the Mediterranean type, with warm summers and mild winters. The principal language is French; additionally, small minorities speak Alsatian, Basque, Breton, Corsican and Provençal, among other regional languages and dialects. A majority of French citizens profess Christianity, and about 74% of the population are adherents of the Roman Catholic Church. Other Christian denominations are represented, and there are also Muslim and Jewish communities. The national flag (proportions 2 by 3) has three equal vertical stripes, of blue, white and red. The capital is Paris.

CONTEMPORARY POLITICAL HISTORY

Historical Context

In September 1939, following Nazi Germany's invasion of Poland, France and the United Kingdom declared war on Germany, thus entering the Second World War. In June 1940 France was forced to sign an armistice, following a swift invasion and occupation of French territory by German forces. After the liberation of France from German occupation in 1944, a provisional Government took office under Gen. Charles de Gaulle, leader of the Free French forces during the wartime resistance. The war in Europe ended in May 1945, when German forces surrendered at Reims. In 1946, following a referendum, the Fourth Republic was established and de Gaulle announced his intention to retire from public life.

France had 26 different Governments from 1946 until the Fourth Republic came to an end in 1958 with an insurrection in Algeria (then an overseas department) and the threat of civil war. In May 1958 the President, René Coty, invited Gen. de Gaulle to form a government. In June the Assemblée Nationale (National Assembly) invested de Gaulle as Prime Minister, with the power to rule by decree for six months. A new Constitution, approved by referendum in September, was promulgated in October; thus the Fifth Republic came into being, with de Gaulle taking office as President in January 1959. The new system provided for a strong presidency, the authority of which would be strengthened by national referendums and a stable executive.

The early years of the Fifth Republic were overshadowed by the Algerian crisis. De Gaulle granted Algeria independence in 1962, withdrew troops and repatriated French settlers. In May 1968 students and workers joined in a revolt against the Government's authoritarian education and information policies, low wage rates and lack of social reform. For a time the Republic appeared threatened, but the student movement collapsed and the general strike was settled by large wage rises. In April 1969 President de Gaulle resigned following his defeat in a referendum on regional reform.

Domestic Political Affairs

Georges Pompidou, who had been Prime Minister from 1962–68, was elected President in June 1969. The Gaullist government coalition was returned at a general election in March 1973. Pompidou died in April 1974. In the presidential election held in May, Valéry Giscard d'Estaing, formerly leader of the centre-right Républicains Indépendants (RI), narrowly defeated François Mitterrand, the First Secretary of the Parti Socialiste (PS). A coalition Government was formed from members of the RI, the Gaullist Union des Démocrates pour la République (UDR) and the centrist parties. In August 1976 Jacques Chirac resigned as Prime Minister and subsequently undertook to transform the UDR into a new party, the Rassemblement pour la République (RPR). In February 1978 the governing non-Gaullist parties formed the Union pour la Démocratie Française (UDF) to compete against RPR candidates in the legislative elections held in March, when the governing coalition retained a working majority.

In the April/May 1981 presidential election Mitterrand defeated Giscard d'Estaing. At elections for a new National Assembly, held in June, the PS and associated groups, principally the Mouvement des Radicaux de Gauche (MRG), won an overall majority of seats, following which four members of the Parti Communiste Français (PCF) were appointed to the Council of Ministers. The new Government introduced a programme of social and labour reforms, including the nationalization of several major industrial enterprises and financial institutions.

Legislative elections took place in March 1986, using for the first time a system of proportional representation based on party lists. Although the PS remained the largest single party in the new National Assembly, the centre-right parties, led by an RPR-UDF alliance, commanded a majority of seats. The PCF suffered a severe decline in support, while the far-right Front National (FN) won legislative representation for the first time. A period of political 'cohabitation' ensued when Mitterrand invited the RPR leader, Chirac, to form a new Council of Ministers.

In April 1986 Chirac introduced legislation allowing his Government to legislate by decree on economic and social issues and on the proposed reversion to a voting system comprising single-member constituencies for legislative elections. However, Mitterrand insisted on exercising the presidential right to withhold approval of decrees that reversed the previous Government's social reforms. Accordingly, in July Chirac resorted to the 'guillotine' procedure (setting a time-limit for consideration of legislative proposals) to gain parliamentary consent for legislation providing for the privatization of 65 state-owned companies, which, since it had been approved by the predominantly right-wing Sénat (Senate) and the Constitutional Council, the President was legally bound to approve.

Mitterrand was re-elected as President in May 1988, defeating Chirac. A general election took place in June, with a reintroduced single-seat majority voting system, at which an alliance of the PS and the MRG secured the largest number of seats. Michel Rocard of the PS, who had been appointed as Prime Minister following the presidential election, resumed that role. Rocard resigned in May 1991 and was succeeded by Edith Cresson, France's first female Prime Minister. However, after the poor performance of the PS in regional elections in March 1992, Cresson was replaced in April by Pierre Bérégovoy. In June the National Assembly approved constitutional changes allowing the ratification of the Treaty on European Union (the Maastricht Treaty), subject to approval by referendum. In the referendum, held in September, 51.1% of voters supported ratification.

At elections to the National Assembly held in March 1993, the RPR won 247 of the 577 seats, the UDF 213 and the PS 54. Chirac had indicated that he was not available for the post of Prime Minister as he intended to concentrate on his candidacy in the 1995 presidential election. Another RPR member, Edouard Balladur, was therefore appointed premier.

In the first round of voting in the presidential election in April 1995, Lionel Jospin, the PS candidate, obtained 23% of the votes, while Chirac and Balladur, both representing the RPR, took 21% and 19%, respectively. Jean-Marie Le Pen, the leader of the FN, won 15%. In the second round, in May, Chirac defeated Jospin, taking 53% of the votes. Chirac appointed Alain Juppé (Minister of Foreign Affairs in the previous Government) as Prime Minister at the head of an RPR/UDF coalition.

At legislative elections held in May–June 1997, the PS secured 241 seats, the RPR 134 and the UDF 108. The unexpected victory of the PS, which began a further period of 'cohabitation', was widely attributed to public dissatisfaction with Juppé's administration and the imposition of economic austerity measures necessitated under the terms of Economic and Monetary Union

(EMU) within the European Union (EU, see p. 273). Jospin became Prime Minister at the head of a 'plural left' coalition.

In March 1999 a Paris public prosecutor upheld a ruling of the Constitutional Council that the President of the Republic enjoyed immunity from prosecution for all crimes, other than high treason, for the duration of his presidential term. This decision followed the disclosure of documentation purporting to show that Chirac had been aware of the existence of at least 300 fictitious employees, reputedly including RPR members or supporters, on the payroll of the Paris city council during his tenure as Mayor in 1977–95. In September 2000 a transcript of a videotape made by Jean-Claude Méry, a former RPR official who had been imprisoned on charges of embezzlement in the mid-1990s, was published posthumously in the French daily newspaper *Le Monde*. In the recording Méry stated that Chirac had personally ordered him to arrange for municipal funds to be diverted to political parties. In December Michel Roussin, who had been Chirac's principal private secretary from 1989–93, was arrested, while the former unofficial treasurer for the RPR was questioned. Their testimony, which was leaked to the press, included details of the systematic levying of an illegal commission on public works contracts awarded by the council.

In April 2001 the investigating judge in the case, Eric Halphen, announced the existence of evidence implicating Chirac in the alleged illegal use of funds in the Paris city council, but stated that the doctrine of presidential immunity prevented Chirac from being brought to trial. New revelations concerning Chirac's purported involvement in financial malpractice emerged in June: the President was alleged to have spent up to 3.1m. francs of state 'secret funds'—issued annually by the Office of the Prime Minister for the security services, to pay bonuses to staff, and as a contingency fund—on luxury holidays for himself and his family in 1992–95, although suspicions were voiced that the finance for these trips might have originated from the alleged illicit commission payments made by building firms to the Paris city council. Chirac declared himself innocent of all charges made against him, and confirmed that he would not participate in any court case. In September 2001 the Appeal Court dismissed Halphen as the leading investigator into the case regarding the use of illicit funds in the Paris city council; Halphen was ruled to have exceeded his powers by calling the President as a witness, and by introducing certain items of evidence, including Méry's videotape. Although the case could be tried again, this decision effectively ruled out any development in the case so long as Chirac remained President. In October the Court of Cassation confirmed the Constitutional Council's directive that an incumbent President could not be prosecuted, additionally ruling that a head of state could not undergo formal investigation while in power, even for offences allegedly committed prior to taking office.

Meanwhile, the tensions caused by the prolonged period of 'cohabitation' from 1997 prompted moves towards constitutional change. In June 2000 the National Assembly approved a reduction in the presidential term from seven to five years, in order to bring it into line with the life of a parliament. Amid concerns that the Senate might not support the bill by the two-thirds' majority required, Chirac called a referendum. Held in September, the referendum attracted only a 30.6% turnout; 73.2% of voters were in favour of the change, which would take effect from the 2002 presidential election. In May 2001 the Constitutional Council approved a proposal, aimed at preventing a further period of 'cohabitation', to hold the presidential election in advance of the parliamentary elections due in May 2002.

The 2002 presidential election

Prior to the first round of the presidential election, which was held in April 2002, Chirac and Jospin had been widely expected to progress to a second round. However, partly as a result of the wide choice of candidates (16), a relatively low turnout, and a campaign focus on issues related to 'insecurity' and law and order, Jospin polled only 16.2% of the valid votes cast, while Chirac won 19.9% and Le Pen 16.9%. The splintering of the governmental 'plural left' coalition proved detrimental for Jospin and the PS, as four of the coalition partners presented individual candidates for the presidency, together securing 16.3% of votes cast. The qualification of Le Pen for the second-round poll precipitated widespread demonstrations, and the majority of the defeated candidates rallied around Chirac as the preferred candidate. In the second round, in May, Chirac's victory, with 82.2% of the vote, was widely interpreted as a resounding defeat for the far right. Chirac appointed Jean-Pierre Raffarin, of Démocratie Libérale (DL), as Prime Minister. Raffarin appointed an interim Government, including Nicolas Sarkozy as Minister of the Interior, Interior Security and Local Freedoms, Michèle Alliot-Marie as Minister of Defence and Dominique de Villepin as Minister of Foreign Affairs. Chirac was subsequently instrumental in the organization of a new centre-right electoral alliance, which was initially titled the Union pour la Majorité Présidentielle.

At the legislative elections in June 2002 the Union pour la Majorité Présidentielle, which incorporated the greater part of the RPR and DL, and significant elements of the UDF, secured 355 of the 577 seats in the National Assembly, while a further 43 representatives of other parties of the centre-right and right were elected, thus ensuring a clear working majority for the pro-presidential grouping. Of the 176 seats awarded to parties of the broad left, the PS was the most successful, with 140 deputies. The new Government was largely unchanged from the interim administration and cited law and order, a programme of decentralization, and further privatizations among its priorities. In November the Union pour la Majorité Présidentielle formally constituted itself as the Union pour un Mouvement Populaire (UMP), absorbing the RPR and DL, in addition to factions of the UDF and the Rassemblement pour la France; Juppé was elected as President of the new party.

Further concerns at the extent of corrupt practices in public life were raised during the trial in late 2003 of Juppé and 26 other defendants on charges that the Paris city council and private companies had illegally paid staff of the RPR during Juppé's tenure as Secretary-General of the party (in 1988–95) and as Deputy Mayor of Paris (1983–95). In January 2004 Juppé was found guilty and given an 18 months' suspended prison sentence; 13 business executives also received suspended terms of imprisonment. In addition, Juppé was banned from holding public office for a period of 10 years, but was permitted to remain in office as Mayor of Bordeaux, and as a parliamentary deputy, pending an appeal. Although the constitutional immunity from prosecution and investigation of the President of the Republic prevented any inquiry into Chirac's behaviour, the judges ruled that Juppé had been directly subordinate to Chirac in the latter's capacity as President of the RPR. (Moreover, Chirac was the Mayor of Paris for the entire duration of Juppé's service as the Deputy Mayor.) Following Juppé's conviction, Chirac and other leading figures in the UMP rallied to his support. (In December 2004 the appeal court upheld the conviction, but reduced the length of the ban on holding public office from 10 years to one; Juppé subsequently resigned as Mayor of Bordeaux, having relinquished the UMP presidency in July.)

In March 2003 the two houses of Parliament, meeting in congress, approved several constitutional changes relating to the proposed decentralization programme, which provided for the eventual possibility of territorial units receiving varying degrees of autonomy and powers, for the institution of deliberative assemblies and for the holding of local referendums in such territories. Moreover, the amendments permitted the introduction of legislation pertaining to decentralization on a temporary, or experimental, basis. Notably, the first article of the Constitution was amended to assert that the organization of the Republic was decentralized. However, attempts to implement policies that utilized the new constitutional provisions initially proved unsuccessful—in a local referendum in Corsica in July voters rejected proposals to reorganize the administration of the island, and in December voters in the Overseas Departments of Guadeloupe and Martinique rejected proposals to restructure and simplify their territorial administration.

A major topic of political debate in 2003 and early 2004 concerned the wearing of the Islamic headscarf by female Muslim pupils at state schools. Although a 1989 ruling of the Council of State declared that the wearing of religious symbols in state schools did not violate the principle of the secularity of the state, formalized in 1905, so long as they were deemed to be of a 'non-ostentatious' nature, the ruling had subsequently been used to exclude a number of Muslim students from educational establishments. Legislation explicitly forbidding the wearing of conspicuous religious symbols, including the Muslim headscarf/veil, Jewish skullcaps and large Christian crosses, in state-operated primary and secondary schools came into effect in September 2004.

Widespread public discontent with the Government was reflected in the outcome of regional and cantonal elections held in March 2004, as a result of which the parties of the centre-right lost control of 13 regions to parties of the left and centre-left, which thereby controlled all of the regions of metropolitan France excluding Alsace and Corsica. Raffarin tendered his resignation as Prime Minister on 30 March, but was immediately reappointed to that position by President Chirac. Sarkozy was appointed as Minister of State, Minister of the Economy, Finance and Industry in a new Government formed the following day, and was replaced as Minister of the Interior, Internal Security and Local Freedoms by de Villepin. In November Sarkozy was elected President of the UMP, following the resignation of Juppé in July. At the insistence of President Chirac that the head of the ruling party should not be permitted simultaneously to hold ministerial office, Sarkozy resigned from the Government.

De Villepin appointed Prime Minister

In May 2005 a national referendum took place on the ratification of the Treaty establishing a Constitution for Europe. Following an intense campaign, in which Chirac and leading members of the UMP and the PS had demonstrated their support for the EU constitutional treaty, 54.9% of those voting rejected its ratification. Raffarin subsequently resigned as Prime Minister. He was succeeded by de Villepin, while Sarkozy returned to the Government as Minister of State, Minister of the Interior and Land Management (while continuing to head the UMP).

In October 2005 violence broke out in Clichy-sous-Bois, a suburb of Paris largely populated by immigrant communities and suffering from high unemployment and poor social housing, following the deaths of two youths (both of whom were of African extraction) who had allegedly been fleeing a police identity check. The rioting subsequently spread to several suburbs to the north-east of the capital. By early November some 300 towns and cities across France were experiencing unrest, mainly led by young males of African origin, while some 9,500 riot police had been deployed in an attempt to curb the violence. As the violence claimed a fatality, de Villepin announced a series of enhanced security measures and a programme aimed at improving education, employment and housing in deprived suburban areas. None the less, rioting continued, and on 8 November de Villepin imposed a state of emergency. Adopting an uncompromising stance, Sarkozy announced that all convicted rioters who were not of French nationality would be deported, including those holding residence permits. By mid-November, as the violence subsided, nearly 300 schools and public buildings had been burned down and 4,770 people had been arrested. In December the Prime Minister launched a national campaign against discrimination, with measures including the imposition of fines on businesses found to have practised discrimination and incentives for companies to locate in deprived areas and to employ young people. The state of emergency was lifted in January 2006.

In April 2006, following a series of mass demonstrations and strike action in Paris and other cities, the Government abandoned plans for a new employment contract that would have allowed small companies to dismiss workers aged under 26 years more easily during their first two years of employment. De Villepin's popularity suffered a further reverse in May, following the disclosure of an apparent attempt by the Prime Minister to discredit his political rivals (including Sarkozy) in an investigation into secret 'offshore' accounts with the Luxembourg bank Clearstream.

At a PS congress in November 2006, Ségolène Royal, a regional councillor, was elected as the party's presidential candidate. In January 2007 the UMP elected Sarkozy unopposed as the party's candidate for the presidency, in accordance with a change to the party's statutes allowing members to select the presidential candidate; he resigned from the Government in March. The first round of the presidential election, held on 22 April, was contested by 12 candidates. Sarkozy and Royal progressed to the second round of voting, winning 31.2% and 25.9% of the valid votes cast, respectively. The UDF candidate, François Bayrou, won 18.6% of the vote, while Le Pen's support declined to only 10.4%. The rate of participation in the election was high, at 83.8% of eligible voters. At the second round of the election, held on 6 May, Sarkozy was elected as President, securing 53.1% of the vote.

The Sarkozy presidency

Sarkozy formally acceded to the presidency on 16 May 2007. François Fillon, a close adviser of the President and former Minister of National Education, Higher Education and Research, was appointed Prime Minister, while Juppé returned to government office as Minister of State, Minister of Ecology and Sustainable Development. The new Council of Ministers included prominent figures from across the political divide, in an attempt to accord the Government greater political legitimacy in its implementation of radical reforms. Bernard Kouchner, a member of Royal's presidential campaign team and former minister under Jospin, was appointed Minister of Foreign and European Affairs, while Hervé Morin, a member of the UDF, was allocated the defence portfolio.

At elections to the National Assembly, held on 10 and 17 June 2007, the UMP remained the largest party in the lower house, but with a reduced majority, winning 313 of 577 seats. Despite losing the presidential election and suffering the subsequent defection of Kouchner, the PS secured 186 seats. Prior to the elections the UDF was restyled the Mouvement Démocrate (MoDem) by its leader, Bayrou, while former members of the UDF allied to the President established a new party, the Nouveau Centre. In the event the Nouveau Centre won 22 seats, while MoDem took just three. Following the elections Sarkozy reappointed Fillon as Prime Minister and effected a government reorganization. The erstwhile Minister of the Economy, Finance and Employment, Jean-Louis Borloo, assumed the post vacated by Juppé, who failed to win re-election to the National Assembly, and Borloo was, in turn, replaced by Christine Lagarde (hitherto Minister of Agriculture and Fisheries).

Investigations into allegations of wrongdoing on the part of members of the previous administration continued. In November 2007 Chirac (having lost his right to immunity from prosecution following the end of his presidency) was placed under formal investigation regarding misuse of public funds in relation to the alleged existence of fictitious city council employees during his tenure as Mayor of Paris. Furthermore, in December 2009 Chirac was placed under formal investigation regarding his alleged involvement in the payment of wages to RPR supporters under false pretences during his mayoralty. Chirac's trial in both cases, on charges of embezzlement and breach of trust, commenced in March 2011. In December Chirac was convicted of the charges against him and received a two-year suspended prison sentence (six of his co-defendants were also given suspended prison terms); although he continued to plead his innocence, he announced that he lacked the strength to appeal against the verdict. Meanwhile, de Villepin was placed under formal investigation by magistrates leading inquiries into the Clearstream affair in July 2007. In late 2008 it was announced that de Villepin was to stand trial for complicity in false accusation and using forgeries, among other charges, in relation to this case. De Villepin claimed that the charges were politically motivated, owing to his rivalry with Sarkozy. The trial of de Villepin and four other defendants commenced in September 2009. In January 2010 de Villepin was cleared of the charges against him, but three of the remaining defendants were convicted for their roles in the affair. De Villepin established a new political movement, République Solidaire, in June, and relinquished his membership of the UMP in February 2011.

In October 2007 new legislation increasing restrictions on immigration was approved by Parliament. The legislation included provisions for the evaluation of individual immigrants' knowledge of French language and culture, and the compilation of population statistics based on ethnicity. Opposition to the legislation, however, focused on the provision for voluntary DNA testing of immigrants from non-EU countries who were suspected of falsely claiming to have a relative resident in France. The measure prompted the PS to refer the proposed bill to the Constitutional Council. In November the Constitutional Council approved the provision on DNA testing, but declared the compilation of population statistics by ethnicity to be unconstitutional.

In February 2008 the FN leader, Le Pen, was convicted of conspiring to justify war crimes and denying crimes against humanity, following comments he had made regarding the occupation of France by German forces in 1940–44 in an interview in a far-right periodical in 2005. He received a three-month suspended prison sentence and a fine of €10,000.

In July 2008 significant constitutional changes were narrowly approved by the National Assembly and the Senate. Parliament was awarded new powers to oversee certain presidential appointments and to set its own agenda for one-half of its sessions (formerly, the entire agenda was decided by the Prime Minister and the Council of Ministers). The use of motions of confidence to force legislation through the National Assembly was restricted, Parliament had to be notified of any deployment of troops within three days, and parliamentary approval was required for military action extending beyond four months. The President was limited to two terms of office and curbs were imposed on the President's emergency powers. However, the

President was now permitted to address Parliament in a joint session, a right that had been denied to the holder of that office since 1875.

In January 2009 large numbers of public and private sector workers took part in a one-day nationwide strike organized by trade unions in protest at a government economic stimulus plan, which the unions criticized for its perceived failure to offer adequate protection for workers and wages. The strike, which represented the most serious challenge to Sarkozy's authority since his election to the presidency, resulted in widespread disruption. Rejecting concessions, including new welfare measures and tax reductions for the low-paid, as inadequate, union and opposition leaders called a further one-day nationwide strike in March, which attracted even greater support than the previous day of action.

Debate on national identity

In June 2009 Sarkozy exercised his new-found right under the recent constitutional amendments to outline government policy for the forthcoming year before a joint session of Parliament, an event viewed by many commentators as a manifestation of the President's increasing assumption of political and executive control at the expense of the Prime Minister. Sarkozy provoked controversy during his speech by expressing support for a proposed parliamentary inquiry on the wearing of all-enveloping female Islamic dress. His declaration that the *burqa* was 'not welcome' in France helped to revive political debate on Islamic clothing, some five years after the wearing of conspicuous religious symbols had been outlawed in state schools. In November Eric Besson, the Minister of Immigration, Integration, National Identity and Shared Development, announced the launch of a debate on French national identity, which would include public consultations organized by local authorities, with the aim of addressing tensions in community relations exemplified by the controversy over the *burqa*. In February 2010 Fillon announced a series of government proposals arising from the debate: these included measures to strengthen the teaching of 'republican values' in schools and a requirement that candidates for French citizenship sign a charter of rights and responsibilities. New legislation, which outlawed the covering of the face in public and prescribed penalties of one year's imprisonment and a sizeable fine for anyone forcing a woman to wear a full-face veil (*niqab*), was approved by the National Assembly in July and by the Senate in September; the law entered into force in April 2011. In the same month, a week before the legislation took effect, the UMP hosted a debate on the compatibility of religious practices with France's secular laws. Islamic leaders declined to participate in the debate, as did the Prime Minister, who warned that it risked stigmatizing Muslims. Issues discussed in the debate included the Muslim practice of holding prayer meetings in the street when mosques were too crowded, the refusal of Muslim women to be treated by male doctors, and the withdrawal of Muslim schoolchildren from lessons in mandatory subjects such as physical education and biology. In September the Government announced a ban with immediate effect on praying outdoors in Paris, prompting criticism from some Muslim groups, which accused the Government of bowing to pressure from the FN.

The Government suffered a heavy defeat at regional elections held on 14 and 21 March 2010. The PS, led by Martine Aubry, who had narrowly defeated Ségolène Royal in a controversial leadership contest in November 2008, achieved its best result for 30 years. In the second round of voting, the PS in alliance with Europe Ecologie (an electoral coalition led by Les Verts) and other parties of the left, won 54.1% of the votes cast, emerging with control of all but one of metropolitan France's 22 regions (having added the Territorial Collectivity of Corsica to the 20 regions hitherto controlled by the left). The UMP and its right-wing allies won 35.4% of the vote, while the FN performed strongly, securing 9.4%; many commentators believed that the recent debate on national identity and Islamic dress contributed to the FN's resurgence by encouraging anti-immigrant sentiment. Sarkozy's standing had been adversely affected by his attempts to introduce a number of unpopular reforms, notably a planned increase in the retirement age.

Pension reforms and the deportation of Roma

In June 2010 Eric Woerth, the Minister of Labour, Solidarity and the Civil Service, announced details of the Government's plans for reform of the state pension system, which constituted part of wider efforts to reduce the burgeoning budget deficit. Notably, the proposals envisaged raising the minimum retirement age from 60 to 62 years by 2018 and the qualifying age for a full pension from 65 to 67 years. Trade unions organized a one-day strike and rallies later that month in protest against the planned reforms, having already staged nationwide demonstrations in May in anticipation of Woerth's announcement. In July the reputations of both President and Woerth were tarnished by accusations that they had accepted allegedly illegal donations to the UMP and to Sarkozy's 2007 presidential election campaign from Liliane Bettencourt, the principal shareholder of the L'Oréal cosmetics business, whose financial affairs were undergoing a police investigation. Sarkozy and Woerth strongly rejected the allegations, but, on the President's advice, Woerth resigned as treasurer of the UMP; he left the Government in a reorganization in November. As Parliament began to consider the pension legislation in early September, trade unions renewed their protests against the planned reforms. Several days of action, involving strikes and demonstrations across the country, were organized in September and October, attended by up to 1.2m. people according to official figures (or 3.5m. according to the unions) and causing severe disruption within the public sector. None the less, the legislation secured parliamentary approval in October, following some minor concessions by the Government, and was promulgated in November. (In November 2011 the Government brought forward the increase in the minimum retirement age from 2018 to 2017.)

A government decision in July 2010 to expel illegal Roma migrants provoked condemnation from opposition parties, human rights groups and the European Commission and European Parliament. The policy was introduced in response to an attack on a police station in central France by a group of Roma, following an incident in which a young traveller who had driven through a checkpoint without stopping had been shot dead by a gendarme. President Sarkozy ordered the dismantlement of 300 unauthorized Roma camps within three months and the immediate return of Roma who had committed public order offences or were living in France illegally to their countries of origin, mainly Romania and Bulgaria (citizens of which required work or residency permits if they wished to remain in France longer than three months). The President also pledged to withdraw French citizenship from foreign-born persons convicted of serious offences. With opinion polls indicating significant public support for such stringent measures, critics claimed that Sarkozy's principal motivation was to improve his personal standing and to attract voters away from the FN. As the deportation of Roma continued, in September the European Commission threatened to initiate legal proceedings against France unless the French Government demonstrated that it would incorporate a directive on the free movement of EU citizens within the Union into French law. The Government subsequently provided the assurances demanded by the Commission, promising to include the necessary measures in a new immigration bill recently presented to Parliament. In accordance with earlier pledges, this proposed legislation required candidates for French citizenship to sign a charter of rights and responsibilities and, most controversially, provided for the removal of citizenship from anyone who had acquired it within the previous 10 years if they were sentenced to at least five years' imprisonment by a French or foreign court. The immigration bill was approved by the National Assembly in October, despite opposition from some UMP deputies, but was rejected by the Senate in February 2011. A revised version of the bill, which did not include the provision relating to the removal of citizenship, was adopted by Parliament in May. Meanwhile, in February it was announced that more than 3,700 Roma had been returned to their countries of origin since July 2010, and that 70% of unauthorized Roma camps had been dismantled.

Towards the 2012 elections

Sarkozy effected a government reorganization in November 2010, retaining Fillon as Prime Minister and appointing Alain Juppé as Minister of State, Minister of Defence and Veterans. Notable departures included those of Woerth and of Kouchner, who had publicly expressed reservations about the expulsion of Roma; Minister of State Michèle Alliot-Marie replaced Kouchner as Minister of Foreign and European Affairs. A further reorganization in February 2011 was occasioned by the resignation of Alliot-Marie, who had sustained harsh criticism for her close links to the regime of the recently deposed Tunisian President, Zine al-Abidine Ben Ali (see Foreign Affairs). She was replaced as Minister of Foreign and European Affairs by Juppé, whose defence portfolio was assumed by Gérard Longuet.

Jean-Marie Le Pen retired as President of the FN in January 2011; his daughter, Marine Le Pen, was elected as his successor, subsequently declaring her intention to contest the presidency in 2012. Also in January, the PS confirmed that it would hold a primary election in October, in which any registered French voter who supported left-wing values could take part, in order to select the party's candidate for the state presidency. Royal had surprised other members of the party in November 2010 with her early announcement that she intended to seek the PS presidential nomination; François Hollande, Aubry's predecessor as First Secretary of the party, declared his candidacy in March 2011, followed by Aubry herself in June. Dominique Strauss-Kahn, a former finance minister and Managing Director of the IMF since 2007, had also been considered a likely contender. However, his arrest in New York, USA, in May 2011, on charges of sexual assault, led to his resignation from the IMF and effectively ended his presidential ambitions, at least for 2012, despite the criminal charges against him being withdrawn in August 2011.

Meanwhile, the PS and the FN both performed strongly in local elections in March 2011, with the UMP barely surpassing the FN in terms of its share of the vote in the first round. At indirect partial elections to the Senate held on 25 September, the centre-right parties, dominated by the UMP, lost their majority in the upper chamber for the first time since the establishment of the Fifth Republic in 1958. Jean-Pierre Bel of the PS was duly elected President of the Senate on 1 October, defeating the incumbent, Gérard Larcher of the UMP.

The appointment of Christine Lagarde as Strauss-Kahn's replacement at the IMF necessitated a ministerial reorganization in June 2011. Among the changes, François Baroin, hitherto Minister of the Budget, Public Finances, the Civil Service and State Reform, and Government Spokesman, succeeded Lagarde as Minister of the Economy, Finance and Industry.

Hollande was selected as the presidential candidate of the PS at the party's primary election, defeating Aubry with 56.6% of the votes cast in a second round held on 16 October 2011, in which almost 2.9m. people voted. Six candidates had contested the first round in October, at which Hollande had won 39.2% of the vote and Aubry 30.4%; Arnaud Montebourg, who advocated far-ranging political and constitutional reforms, was notably placed third, with 17.2% of the vote, while Royal secured only 6.9%. With a solid lead in opinion polls, Hollande presented his election manifesto in January 2012, pledging to create 60,000 jobs in the education sector and 150,000 jobs for young people, and to introduce a 15% increase in tax on bank profits and a new, higher rate of income tax of 45% for those earning more than €150,000 per year; he later additionally proposed a 75% rate of tax on annual incomes exceeding €1m. and stated that the EU's 'fiscal compact' would not be ratified by France without some renegotiation. The decision by the credit rating agency Standard & Poor's to downgrade France's long-term sovereign debt rating to AA+ that month represented a significant reverse for Sarkozy's Government, which had emphasized the importance of retaining the country's AAA rating when announcing austerity measures in November 2011. Sarkozy did not confirm his intention to seek re-election until February 2012, when he defended his economic policies, including raising the retirement age and lowering the number of state employees, insisting that France's economic position would have deteriorated further without such action. In March, in an apparent attempt to court right-wing voters, the President proposed reducing the number of immigrants to France from 180,000 to 100,000 per year.

During the run-up to the presidential election the Government's campaign against Islamist extremism was heightened in the wake of the murder of seven people (including three Jewish children) in the Toulouse area by an Islamist gunman in March 2012. A series of raids and arrests of suspected Islamist militants was carried out at a number of locations throughout France; 13 of the detainees were subsequently charged with terrorism offences. In addition, the Government proposed new anti-terrorism legislation aimed at preventing the recruitment and training of potential terrorists. Following France's military intervention in Mali in January 2013 (see Other external relations), the Government warned of possible Islamist retaliatory attacks in France and increased its domestic terrorism threat level accordingly.

The Hollande presidency

The first round of the presidential election was held on 22 April 2012 and was contested by 10 candidates. Hollande narrowly defeated Sarkozy, with 28.6% of the valid votes cast against the latter's 27.2%. Marine Le Pen came third with 17.9% of the vote (a record share for an FN presidential candidate), her pledge to give French citizens priority over foreigners for jobs, housing and social welfare proving popular amid rising unemployment. At the second round of the election, held on 6 May, Hollande again defeated Sarkozy, winning 51.6% of the votes against his opponent's 48.4%. On 15 May Hollande was sworn in as the first Socialist French President for 17 years and on the following day he appointed Jean-Marc Ayrault, the long-standing leader of the PS in the National Assembly, as the new Prime Minister. Other notable appointments included Hollande's chief campaign manager, Pierre Moscovici, as Minister of the Economy and Finance, and former Prime Minister Laurent Fabius as Minister of Foreign Affairs.

At elections to the National Assembly held on 10 and 17 June 2012, the PS secured 280 seats—compared with 186 in 2007—and, with the support of its left-wing allies, commanded a very narrow overall majority in the lower house (as well as controlling a majority in the Senate). The UMP's tally of seats decreased from an absolute majority of 313 to 194, while the FN, reflecting its strong performance in the presidential election, obtained seats in the legislature (albeit only two) for the first time since 1997. Despite the apparent strength of the left-wing in both Parliament and in local and regional government, the new administration's popularity soon began to founder as it was forced to adopt a number of harsh measures in an attempt to address the numerous problems caused by the ailing economy (notably the high levels of public debt and rising unemployment). The increasing marginalization and discontent felt by many of the country's unemployed youth was vividly illustrated by the riots that erupted in the northern city of Amiens in mid-August. Sixteen police officers were injured in clashes with the rioters (many of whom were from immigrant backgrounds) and police forces throughout France were placed on high alert.

The new Government's controversial plans to legalize same-sex marriage and to introduce legislation to allow gay couples to adopt children provoked a series of public protests and counter-protests throughout France attended by tens of thousands of people. Despite the scale of the opposition, supported by the Catholic Church and the conservative opposition, the proposed bill was approved by Parliament in April 2013 and was promulgated in May.

Meanwhile, following his failure to retain the presidency and the UMP's subsequent defeat in the legislative elections, Sarkozy withdrew from front-line politics (although it was widely rumoured that he intended to stand for re-election in the 2017 presidential elections). In July 2012 the former President's home and offices in Paris were searched by the police as part of an investigation into allegations of the illicit funding of Sarkozy's 2007 presidential election campaign by the heiress Liliane Bettencourt (in the wake of his loss of office, Sarkozy no longer enjoyed presidential immunity). Sarkozy was placed under formal investigation over the claims in March 2013 and in the following month French prosecutors launched an investigation into allegations that he had also received illegal campaign funds from the former Libyan leader Col Muammar al-Qaddafi. In October the case against Sarkozy regarding Bettencourt was dropped.

The UMP was severely weakened in the latter half of 2012 as a result of an acrimonious leadership struggle between former Prime Minister Fillon and the more right-wing Jean-François Copé, who had held the position of Secretary-General of the party since 2010. The UMP was thrown into turmoil in November 2012 when both candidates claimed victory in the vote to elect the new leader of the party amid mutual accusations of electoral fraud. Although the final official result awarded a narrow victory to Copé (who won by just 98 votes), Fillon demanded a recount on the grounds that 1,300 votes from three overseas territories had been omitted. Fillon claimed that, if these votes were included in the final tally, he would win the leadership contest by 26 votes. Ultimately, however, following a fresh ballot count by an internal party commission, Copé was confirmed as the new leader of the UMP, with an increased majority, at the end of November. Fillon, who refused to recognize the legality of the recount, established a breakaway faction of the UMP, the Rassemblement-UMP (R-UMP), comprising more than 70 parliamentary deputies, and demanded another leadership vote within three months. A compromise was reached between Copé and Fillon in December when they agreed to hold a new leadership contest (under the auspices of an independent body) before October 2013; the R-UMP was dissolved in January of that year.

In March 2013 Jérôme Cahuzac, Minister-delegate to the Minister of Economy and Finance, in charge of the Budget, resigned from his post after he was alleged to have used an undeclared Swiss bank account for about 20 years in order to avoid tax. Having initially adamantly denied the allegations, Cahuzac admitted after his resignation that the reports were in fact correct. This was seen as a highly embarrassing scandal for Hollande, owing to the fact that it took place against a background of increasing government demands that the public make ever greater sacrifices in an attempt to revive the economy and to the fact that the President had sought to distance his administration from the financial scandals and perceived lack of integrity of the Sarkozy presidency. Cahuzac, who was charged with tax fraud, was officially excluded from the PS in early April and all ministers were required to publish full details of their personal wealth on an official website by the middle of that month. Also in April, in a further bid for greater transparency within government and in an attempt to regain public trust, Hollande drew up draft legislation to appoint a special prosecutor charged with handling cases of fraud and corruption and to create a central agency to combat such misdeeds among the ranks of officialdom. Despite these attempts at re-establishing his credibility, the President's popularity ratings continued to plummet as the economy showed no signs of any real recovery. Hollande's administration suffered a further setback in July when the Minister of Ecology, Sustainable Development and Energy, Delphine Batho, was dismissed from office for publicly criticizing planned cuts in government expenditure. As support for the PS declined, the popularity of the FN, under the 'modernizing' leadership of Marine Le Pen, appeared to be gaining strength—as indicated by its victory over the UMP in a regional by-election in October, and an increased share of votes in municipal elections held in March 2014, when the FN won control of some 14 towns. Following heavy losses for the PS in the municipal elections, at which the party lost control of some 150 towns and cities, President Hollande appointed Manuel Valls, hitherto Minister of the Interior, as the new Prime Minister, replacing Ayrault. On 2 April a new Council of Ministers took office, in which Europe Ecologie Les Verts (as the Greens had been restyled in November 2010), which had previously run two ministries, refused to participate.

Corsica

Demands for the independence of Corsica increased markedly during the 1960s and 1970s, with particular discontent being expressed at the resettlement on the island of French citizens displaced from Algeria following its independence in 1962. In 1972 the status of Corsica was upgraded to that of a region, administered by a centrally appointed préfet. (It had hitherto formed an administrative department within the region of Provence-Alpes-Côte d'Azur.) The assassination of two gendarmes at Aléria, in eastern Corsica, in August 1975, marked a significant escalation in the campaign for Corsican independence; from 1976 the clandestine Fronte di Liberazione Naziunale di a Corsica (FLNC) was regarded as the leading pro-independence organization. Also in 1976, Corsica was subdivided into two departments, Corse-du-Sud and Haute-Corse. Demands for greater autonomy or independence persisted, with intermittent bombing campaigns conducted by separatists both in Corsica and in continental France. As a result of decentralization legislation of 1982, the status of Corsica was elevated to that of a Territorial Collectivity, with its own directly elected 61-seat assembly, and an administration with augmented executive powers. In April 1991 the National Assembly adopted legislation granting greater autonomy to Corsica; a seven-member Executive Council was to be formed, chosen from a 51-member Corsican Assembly, which would be elected in 1992.

In February 1998, in the most serious act of violence committed by separatist militants to date, the Préfet of Corsica, Claude Erignac, was assassinated. The killing was condemned by the FLNC and the primary suspect in the case, Yvan Colonna, was convicted of murder in December 2007 and sentenced to life imprisonment. Meanwhile, peace negotiations involving the Government and representatives of Corsica commenced in Paris in December 1999. Four Corsican militant groups called an unconditional ceasefire, and pledged to disarm should their aims, including the recognition of the Corsican people as a nation, and the granting of official status to the Corsican language on the island, be achieved. The peace process resulted in agreement on a number of proposals known as the Matignon Accords, which were approved in the Corsican Assembly in July 2000. Under the proposals, subject to the maintenance of peace on Corsica, and the approval of the National Assembly, a referendum would be held on eventual revisions to the Constitution in 2004, prior to the introduction of a single political and administrative body for the island with formal, but limited, legislative powers, replacing the two existing administrative departments. The proposals also provided for instruction in the Corsican language to take place in all primary schools. Although most militant groups maintained a ceasefire following the signature of the accords, increasing concern was expressed at the prevalence of organized crime in Corsica, while sporadic, low-level attacks by militants continued. In May 2001 the National Assembly approved a more moderate version of the bill to amend the status of Corsica, with a view to presenting a text that would be acceptable to the Constitutional Council; consequently, Corsican language instruction at primary schools was to be optional, rather than compulsory, and the French Parliament would be required to pass enabling legislation before local bills approved by the Corsican Assembly could take effect. By September the process envisaged by the accords appeared to be stalling; the moderate nationalist leader Jean-Guy Talamoni, who had been involved in negotiating the accords, announced that the moderate separatist Corsica Nazione had decided to withdraw from the provisions of the accords. The final bill on greater autonomy, which had been subject to further amendments had received the approval of both the National Assembly and the Senate by December. In January 2002 the Constitutional Council ruled that the section of the bill that permitted the Corsican Assembly to amend national legislation on the island was illegitimate, although the section of the law that permitted the optional use of Corsican language in primary schools was approved.

In April 2002, following the defeat of Lionel Jospin in the first round of the presidential election and a statement by Jacques Chirac to the effect that Corsican aspirations for greater autonomy were insignificant, nationalists on the island announced their withdrawal from the Matignon process. In May the FLNC-Union des Combatants (FLNC-UDC—as the main faction of the organization was now known) announced that it was to resume its dissident campaign, while stating its preference for a negotiated settlement. In June the new centre-right Government unexpectedly announced that it was to seek several constitutional amendments that would permit the eventual decentralization of a number of powers, and that Corsica could be expected to be affected by these measures. In July Nicolas Sarkozy, the Minister of the Interior, visited Corsica, where he announced efforts to relaunch a dialogue with nationalists. However, amid scepticism regarding the Government's intentions, the number of small-scale bomb attacks on the island increased sharply in 2002, to reach the highest annual total recorded (in excess of 220) since 1997. In February 2003 the Corsican Assembly voted in favour of a proposal, supported by Sarkozy, whereby the two administrative departments in Corsica were to be replaced by a single collectivity, subject to approval by a referendum in Corsica. Following the endorsement in March by the National Assembly of constitutional changes that permitted local referendums, it was announced that such a plebiscite was to be held in July. Although several separatist groups, including the FLNC-UDC, Corsica Nazione, and the political wing of the FLNC-UDC, Indipendenza, announced their support for the proposal, other more radical groups expressed concern that plans to devolve to the new collectivity limited legislative and additional tax-raising powers that had been included in the Matignon Accords had not been revived. At the referendum, which was held on 6 July and attracted a relatively high turnout of 60.5%, the proposal was defeated, with 51.0% of the votes against the restructuring.

Following the defeat of the Government's proposal in the referendum, there was an escalation of violence by Corsican separatist groups, both in Corsica and in mainland France. The FLNC-UDC, which announced in July 2003 that it was to end its ceasefire, claimed responsibility for two bomb attacks in Nice and a series of bombings in Corsica later in the month. In October Sarkozy announced that measures to combat widespread violence, terrorism and organized crime on Corsica would now be a government priority. However, the incidence of bombings and other attacks accelerated in 2004, despite the FLNC-UDC's reiteration in May of its commitment to the unconditional ceasefire that it had announced in November 2003. Many of these attacks, the majority of which were claimed by the Clandestini Corsi group, were on North African Muslims. In March 2005 the FLNC-UDC ended its ceasefire to coincide with the start of the trial in Paris of its alleged leader, Charles Pieri, who was accused of extortion, misappropriation of funds, financing terrorism and associating with criminals for a terrorist enterprise. Pieri, who had been imprisoned since December 2003, was convicted and sentenced to a 10-year custodial sentence; he was released in December 2009.

Militant activity in Corsica continued throughout 2006, with the FLNC-UDC claiming responsibility for a series of attacks. In May 2007 13 members of a militant separatist organization, FLNC des Anonymes, were convicted by a court in Paris of perpetrating a succession of bombings in Corsica during 2001–02 and received sentences of between one and 11 years' imprisonment, while the group's alleged leader, Antoine Marchini, was sentenced to 12 years' imprisonment for his role in the attacks. In December 2007 militants carried out a number of bombings on the island, following the conviction of Colonna and the arrest of 13 members of Corsica Nazione suspected of involvement in bomb attacks carried out in 2006–07.

The political situation in Corsica remained tense in 2008. In January around 500 protesters occupied the Corsican Assembly in Ajaccio after a demonstration led by nationalist groups and trade unions. During the occupation, offices within the Assembly building were set on fire. Five people were arrested in connection with the arson attack and placed under judicial investigation. The initial judicial hearing at a court in Ajaccio was marked by violent clashes between separatist protesters and police in the regional capital and in Bastia. Four of the defendants were acquitted later in 2008; all four were members of U Rinnovu, a nationalist movement founded in 1998. Meanwhile, in May 2008 a hitherto unrecognized organization, FLNC 1976, claimed responsibility for 26 recent attacks in Corsica, including the destruction of public buildings, police stations and holiday homes. The newly established movement sought to reunite the factions of the FLNC—the FLNC-UDC and the FLNC du 22 Octobre (founded in October 2002). In February 2009 Corsica Nazione, U Rinnovu and two other nationalist movements merged to form a new pro-independence political party, Corsica Libera, led by Talamoni.

In January 2010 the FLNC-UDC claimed responsibility for 14 bomb attacks, which had taken place over the preceding months, and renewed its threats against the authorities, in protest at a controversial 20-year development plan supported by the mainland French Government and the Corsican executive. The Construction and Sustainable Development Plan of Corsica (Plan d'Aménagement et de Développement Durable de la Corse—PADDUC), which envisaged sanctioning development on previously protected land, also attracted criticism from environmental groups and moderate pro-independence parties. At the regional elections in March a left-wing grouping led by Paul Giacobbi of the Parti Radical de Gauche won 24 of the 51 seats in the Corsican Assembly, following 26 years of political dominance by the right; Giacobbi was elected President of the Executive Council.

In response to the murder of a prominent Corsican lawyer in October 2012 and the fatal shooting of the President of the Chamber of Commerce and Industry of South Corsica the following month, the French Government pledged to restore order on the island by rigorously tackling the escalating organized crime (particularly money laundering and racketeering).

Developments in the Overseas Territories

In November 1998, following a lengthy campaign for the independence of the Pacific overseas territory of New Caledonia by indigenous Melanesian (Kanak) separatists, a referendum on self-determination was held in the territory. At the referendum a gradual transfer of powers to local institutions was approved, and the Republican Constitution was amended accordingly. Further enabling legislation was approved by Parliament in February 1999, and certain powers were transferred to local institutions in subsequent years. Notably, the constitutional amendments approved in March 2003 that sought to permit other communities eventually to gain increased autonomy were not to apply to New Caledonia.

Proposals to restructure the administration of France's Caribbean overseas territories, Guadeloupe and Martinique, were rejected in referendums held in July 2003. However, in concurrent referendums held in Saint-Barthélemy and Saint-Martin, the electorate voted in favour of seceding from Guadeloupe to assume the status of Overseas Collectivities. The administrative process was completed in February 2007, when it was approved by the Constitutional Council.

In January 2004 the National Assembly approved an organic law and an ordinary law, the combined effect of which was to grant the status of Overseas Collectivity to French Polynesia; this legislation was finally approved, with minor amendments, in February, by the Constitutional Council and came into effect the following month. At a referendum held in the Overseas Collectivity of Mayotte in March 2009, the electorate voted overwhelmingly in favour of becoming an Overseas Department with the same political status as Metropolitan Departments. The result was welcomed by the French Government, but the African Union—AU (see p. 186) and the Government of the Comoros, which claims sovereignty over Mayotte, rejected the referendum. Despite these objections, Mayotte's change of status took effect at the end of March 2011.

Foreign Affairs

Regional relations

France was a founder member of the European Community, which became the European Union (EU, see p. 273) in 1992 under the Treaty on European Union (the Maastricht Treaty). The French Government was an enthusiastic proponent of efforts to strengthen integration within the EU, most notably the Treaty establishing a Constitution for Europe. Following the rejection of the constitutional treaty at referendums in France and the Netherlands in 2005, in December 2007 a new treaty was signed in Lisbon, Portugal, by the heads of state or of government of the then 27 EU member countries. The so-called Lisbon Treaty was ratified by the French Parliament in February 2008, and entered into force across the EU in December 2009.

In May 1992 France and Germany announced that they would establish a joint defence force, the Eurocorps, which would be based on the Franco-German Brigade (established in 1987) and would provide the foundation for the formation of a European army under the aegis of Western European Union. In January 1993 an agreement was signed between NATO and the French and German Governments, establishing formal links between the Eurocorps and NATO's military structure (although the former was to remain an independent entity). Between 1993 and 1996 Belgium, Spain and Luxembourg also agreed to participate in the Eurocorps, which became operational in November 1995. The force maintains its headquarters in Strasbourg and currently consists of some 60,000 troops (12,000 of which are contributed by France) from the five so-called 'framework' nations; the troops are pledged for deployment, when requested, in EU, UN, Organization for Security and Co-operation in Europe (OSCE) or NATO rapid response peacekeeping missions. Eurocorps troops were deployed in Bosnia and Herzegovina and in Kosovo in 2000 and in Afghanistan in 2004–05 and again in 2012. To meet the need to improve Europe's rapid response capabilities, from early 2007 a series of EU 'battlegroups' (each consisting of 1,500–2,500 troops) became operational for deployment to crisis areas. In March 2009 President Sarkozy won a vote of confidence in the National Assembly over his decision to bring France back into NATO's integrated military command structure, despite criticism from opponents that such a move would weaken French independence from the USA. Sarkozy insisted that the country would benefit from being able to take part in strategic decision-making and emphasized the fact that France would retain its independent nuclear capability and autonomy in defence decisions. In May 2011 the foreign ministers of the so-called 'Weimar Triangle' grouping, comprising France, Germany and Poland, agreed to pursue a trilateral initiative for the establishment of an EU civil and military planning headquarters independent of NATO.

Relations deteriorated between France and Germany following the election of Sarkozy as President in May 2007. The German Government expressed its opposition to several of Sarkozy's foreign affairs initiatives, notably the negotiation of accords on nuclear energy with Libya and French plans to form a so-called Mediterranean Union, comprising the seven EU member states in the Mediterranean region (Cyprus, France, Greece, Italy, Malta, Portugal and Spain) and certain littoral Middle Eastern and North African states. Germany feared that such an organization would undermine the ongoing Euro-Mediterranean Partnership (the Barcelona Process—a framework launched in 1995 for co-operation between all EU member states and 10 other Mediterranean states). However, in March 2008 Sarkozy and the German Chancellor, Angela Merkel, announced that an agreement had been reached, under which all EU member states would be involved in the formation of the new union, which was restyled the Union for the Mediterranean and inaugurated in July. The Union also included the 10 Mediterranean partners in the Barcelona Process, including Turkey, which agreed in March to participate, following reassurances from France that the Union would not, as originally envisaged, function as an alternative to Turkey's membership of the EU.

Tensions arose between Sarkozy and Merkel in May 2010, at an emergency summit of leaders of eurozone member states in Brussels, over the proposed establishment of the European Financial Stability Facility (EFSF), a temporary fund to support member countries suffering severe financial difficulties with the aim of preserving the stability of the currency. Sarkozy reportedly threatened to withdraw France from economic and monetary union if Germany did not support the €440,000m. fund, before agreement on its creation was finally reached. Relations between the two leaders subsequently improved, however, and they jointly advocated the establishment of a permanent crisis mechanism, the European Stability Mechanism (ESM), on which EU heads of government reached agreement in October. At bilateral talks in December, Sarkozy and Merkel affirmed their commitment to the single currency and also welcomed the stationing of a battalion of German troops in the French town of Illkirch-Graffenstaden, near Strasbourg, the first time German troops had been based in France since the Second World War. In December 2011, prior to a summit meeting of EU heads of state and of government, Sarkozy and Merkel jointly proposed a series of measures aimed at strengthening economic and fiscal policy co-ordination and surveillance within the eurozone, including a commitment to balanced budgets and automatically triggered sanctions for any country recording a fiscal deficit exceeding 3% of gross domestic product. Amid mounting concern regarding the sovereign debt crisis in the eurozone, the majority of EU member states agreed, in principle, to the proposals at the summit meeting, with the exception of the United Kingdom, which vetoed their incorporation into an existing treaty owing to its opposition to a tax on financial transactions. In March 2012 the heads of state and of government of 25 of the 27 EU member states signed the so-called 'fiscal compact' (the Treaty on Stability, Co-ordination and Governance in the Economic and Monetary Union), with the Czech Republic joining the United Kingdom in withholding its assent; the compact came into force on 1 January 2013 (having been ratified by more than the 12 eurozone member countries required for the compact to take effect).

Despite having openly supported Sarkozy in the 2012 presidential election, Chancellor Merkel pledged to work with the new French President, François Hollande, in attempting to resolve the eurozone economic crisis. However, the two leaders held rather different opinions as to the optimum mode of approach: Hollande stressed that he wished to focus on stimulating new growth through fresh expenditure and job creation, while Merkel insisted that emphasis should continue to be placed on fiscal austerity and debt reduction (as laid out in the fiscal compact). In the latter half of the year, however, Hollande was criticized for apparently abandoning his electoral promise to seek a renegotiation of the fiscal compact.

A dispute with Italy arose in April 2011 after the Italian Government granted temporary residence permits to some 20,000 recent immigrants (mostly Tunisians fleeing the civil unrest in their home country), thereby allowing them to travel freely within the EU. Large numbers of Tunisian migrants tried to cross the border into France in the preceding weeks, many of whom were returned by the French authorities. Italy contended that this denial of entry was in breach of the EU's Schengen Agreement on internal borders. (The European Commission later stated that France had acted within its rights in turning back the migrants.) In September the French, German and Spanish ministers responsible for home affairs rejected as inadequate the European Commission's proposals to extend the existing safeguard mechanism to Schengen area procedures, which allowed extraordinary national border controls to be imposed for a limited time in response to exceptional circumstances (involving terrorist, safety or security threats); the ministers objected to a five-day limit on the restoration of border controls, after which time the authorization of the Commission would be required. Despite the opposition of the Commission and the European Parliament, in June 2012 the home affairs ministers of the EU member states drew up a draft proposal to introduce an emergency mechanism whereby internal border controls could be unilaterally reimposed for up to two years by an individual state if another member state did not reliably control its border. Also included in the proposed amendments to the Schengen Agreement was a significant expansion of the grounds on which the closure of intra-European borders could be justified. These proposals were prompted by the notable increase in uncontrolled refugee movements in southern Europe as a result of the 'Arab Spring' and the ongoing economic crisis. The European Parliament approved a compromise package of amendments to the Schengen Agreement in June 2013, but stressed that the reimposition of border controls should be used only as a last resort.

Other external relations

France has been active in promoting the establishment of regional peacekeeping forces in Africa. In the early 1990s French troops were dispatched to Rwanda to train government forces and to supply military equipment, following the outbreak of armed conflict between the Government and the opposition Front Patriotique Rwandais. In April 1994 French troops re-entered Rwanda to establish a 'safe humanitarian zone' for refugees fleeing the civil war. Evidence emerged in early 1998 that appeared to support allegations that France had sold arms to Rwanda during the massacres in 1994 (after the imposition of a UN embargo on the delivery of military equipment to any party in the conflict). The Rwandan Government rejected the findings of a commission of inquiry, subsequently established to investigate the affair, which effectively exonerated France. Bilateral relations further deteriorated following the decision in November 2006 by a French magistrate to issue arrest warrants for nine senior Rwandan military and government officials on suspicion of involvement in the killing in 1994 of the former Rwandan President, Juvénal Habyarimana. The magistrate also alleged that the incumbent Rwandan President, Paul Kagame, had ordered the missile attack in which Habyarimana was killed (which had been the catalyst for the massacres); however, under French law, as a head of state, Kagame was immune from prosecution. The Rwandan Government, which denied the allegations, subsequently severed relations with France. Despite a further deterioration in relations occasioned by the publication by the Rwandan Government in August 2008 of a report alleging the involvement of several senior French military and political figures (among them, Mitterrand and de Villepin) in the 1994 massacres, full diplomatic relations were restored in November 2009. In February 2010 Sarkozy became the first French President to visit Rwanda since 1984; during his visit he admitted that France and the international community had made 'mistakes' in their failure to prevent the massacres, but did not issue a formal apology. In March 2010 Agathe Habyarimana, the widow of the former President, who was the subject of an extradition request by Rwandan prosecutors for her alleged role in the genocide, was arrested at her home near Paris; however, in September 2011 a Parisian court rejected the Rwandan request for her extradition. Also in September 2011, Kagame visited France in an attempt to strengthen bilateral relations, holding talks with Sarkozy. Meanwhile, in December 2010 a French judge, Marc Trévidic, placed six senior Rwandan military officials—including the Minister of Defence and the Chief of Defence Staff—under judicial investigation in connection with the killing of Juvénal Habyarimana after questioning them in Burundi for several days (with the agreement of the Rwandan authorities); the warrants for their arrest that were issued in 2006 were subsequently revoked. In January 2012 Trévidic announced that a team of technical experts charged with re-examining the attack in which Habyarimana was killed had concluded that the evidence indicated that the missiles involved could not have been fired from a base occupied by forces loyal to Kagame; however, by early 2014 the investigation under Trévidic appeared to have reached no clear conclusion. In a significant development in the quest for justice, in February 2014 the trial opened in Paris of a former Rwanda army and intelligence chief, Pascal Simbikangwa, on charges of complicity in the 1994 genocide; Simbikangwa had been arrested by the French authorities in 2008 while living under an alias on the island of Mayotte. Simbikangwa was found guilty in March and sentenced to 25 years' imprisonment. Relations worsened in April 2014, however, when the French Government cancelled its participation in the commemorations in Kigali, Rwanda, of the 20th anniversary of the genocide, following comments made in the press by Kagame accusing France of direct involvement in the 1994 massacres.

From late 2002 more than 3,000 French troops were dispatched to Côte d'Ivoire to assist the 550 French troops already based there, initially to protect French citizens resident in the country from civil unrest and subsequently to monitor a ceasefire between Ivorian government troops and rebel forces in the north of the country. Following the recommencement of military operations by Ivorian government forces against the rebel-controlled north, nine French troops were killed during an air strike in November 2004. The French military, acting on the direct orders of President Chirac, responded by disabling the Ivorian air force on the ground. France's perceived intervention in the conflict provoked riots in the principal city, Abidjan, and elsewhere in the country, and numerous attacks were carried out against French civilians and targets. French troops entered Abidjan to secure the international airport and protect French and other foreign citizens, airlifting an estimated 9,000 people out of the city. (The French Government subsequently admitted that its forces had killed some 20 Ivorian civilians during clashes with rioters; the Ivorian authorities claimed the number was significantly higher.) Around 600 troops were subsequently flown in to reinforce the French military presence in Côte d'Ivoire, while diplomatic relations between the two countries remained tense. France reduced its military presence in Côte d'Ivoire from 2,400 troops at early 2008 to 900 by mid-2009. In December 2010 the French Government advised the 15,000 French nationals in Côte d'Ivoire to leave the country temporarily, amid security concerns following a disputed presidential election in the previous month. In April 2011 French troops stationed in the country assisted forces loyal to Alassane Ouattara, the winner of the presidential election, to oust outgoing President Laurent Gbagbo, who had refused to cede office. President Sarkozy attended Ouattara's formal inauguration as Ivorian President in May. Sarkozy and Ouattara signed a joint security agreement in January 2012, during a state visit by the Ivorian President to France. By this time the number of French troops in Côte d'Ivoire, which had been increased to some 1,600 during the first half of 2011, had again been reduced, to 450, with a further reduction, to 300, envisaged; according to the security agreement, their main role was to train local forces.

Relations between France and Angola were adversely affected in 2008 by the opening of a trial of 42 people charged with involvement in illegal arms transactions with Angola in 1993–98. The Angolan President, José Eduardo dos Santos, was implicated in allegations of corruption in connection with the arms deals, while senior French political figures, including Jean-Christophe Mitterrand, the son of the former President, who had acted as adviser to his father on African affairs, and Charles Pasqua, who had been the Minister of the Interior in 1986–88, were among the defendants. In October 2009 all but six of the defendants were convicted; Pasqua was sentenced to one year's imprisonment (subsequently overturned on appeal), while Mitterrand received a two-year suspended sentence and a substantial fine.

In January 2013 some 4,000 French troops were dispatched to Mali, in response to a request by the Malian interim President, Dioncounda Traoré, to help the government troops launch a counter-offensive against Islamist forces that had seized control of much of northern Mali and were advancing south towards the capital, Bamako. By the end of the month the air strikes conducted by the French military (which were unanimously backed by the UN Security Council) had proved effective and most of the major towns that had been captured by the jihadists (including Timbuktu and Gao) had been retaken. In early February President Hollande visited Timbuktu, where he pledged that French troops would remain in Mali as long as required and would not leave until they had handed over operations to the UN-supported African-led International Support Mission to Mali (AFISMA), which was under the organization of the Economic Community of West African States (ECOWAS). Hollande also stated that his Government would help to rebuild Mali and promised to donate more aid to this end. A phased withdrawal of French troops from Mali commenced in April, although the French Government announced that some 1,000 troops would remain in the country indefinitely to counter the ongoing threat from Islamist militants. Responsibility for security in Mali was transferred to a new UN peacekeeping force—the UN Multidimensional Integrated Stabilization Mission in Mali (MINUSMA)—in July.

Following an escalation in communal violence in the Central African Republic (CAR), in November 2013 the French Government pledged to dispatch additional troops to assist the AU peacekeeping force operating there in a bid to restore order; around 400 French troops were already stationed in the country's capital, Bangui. The first French reinforcements arrived in the CAR in early December; by the middle of the month, amid escalating violence, a total of about 1,600 French troops were stationed in the country. Following the passage of a UN resolution in early December, the AU peacekeeping mission transferred responsibility for operations to the newly established African-led International Support Mission to the Central African Republic (Mission internationale de soutien à la Centrafrique sous conduite africaine—MISCA).

France's relations with the USA have frequently been characterized by a desire to establish French independence of action, particularly with regard to military concerns and international relations. In the aftermath of the terrorist attacks in New York and Washington, DC, attributed to the militant Islamist al-Qa'ida organization, on 11 September 2001, France offered full military and logistical support to the USA in its campaign against al-Qa'ida. However, France criticized several aspects of the foreign policy of the Administration of US President George W. Bush. Although France supported UN Security Council Resolution 1441 (presented by the USA and the United Kingdom) in November 2002, which demanded the expedited admittance of UN weapons inspectors to Iraq, it opposed any UN Security Council resolution authorizing any automatic resort to force against Iraq, and was a prominent opponent of the US-led military action that commenced in March 2003. However, following the conclusion of large-scale hostilities in Iraq, France gave full support to UN Security Council Resolution 1483, approved in May, which recognized the Coalition Provisional Authority as the legal occupying power in Iraq.

The election of Sarkozy as President in May 2007 precipitated a significant improvement in relations between France and the USA. Following US pleas for members of NATO to increase the deployment of forces in Afghanistan, Sarkozy announced in April 2008 that he would send an additional 700 troops to the country. The despatch of a further 250 French troops to join NATO's International Security Assistance Force (ISAF) in Afghanistan was announced in July 2010, bringing the total number of French forces deployed in that country to 4,000 (the fifth largest contingent after the USA, the United Kingdom, Germany and Italy). A phased withdrawal of French troops from Afghanistan commenced in October 2011, as part of NATO's plan to end its combat mission in that country by the end of 2014. Following the killing of four French soldiers by a member of the Afghan National Army in January 2012, President Sarkozy announced that France would complete its withdrawal of combat troops from Afghanistan by the end of 2013, a year ahead of the NATO deadline. However, in fulfilment of one of his electoral pledges, the new French President, François Hollande, brought the completion date of the withdrawal forward to the end of 2012 (while promising to increase non-military aid to Afghanistan). In early 2013 around 1,500 non-combat, logistical French troops remained in Afghanistan, some 500 of whom were involved in the training of the Afghan military. Franco-US relations soured somewhat in October, following leaked reports that the US National Security Agency had secretly tapped millions of telephone calls and text messages in France between December 2012 and January 2013. In February 2014 Hollande undertook a state visit to the USA, during which he held discussions with US President Barack Obama on a number of issues including Iran, the global economic recovery and measures to combat climate change.

One of the priorities of French foreign policy under the presidency of Sarkozy was to secure an increased role for France in the Middle East. In early 2012 France was a strong proponent of enforcing stricter sanctions against Iran, amid ongoing concerns regarding its nuclear enrichment programme; in July the EU imposed an embargo on Iranian petroleum exports and a freeze on the assets of the Iranian central bank in the EU. However, following a landmark interim agreement on the Iranian nuclear programme reached between Iran and the so-called P5+1 (the five permanent members of the UN Security Council—including France—and Germany) in Geneva in November 2013, the EU eased some of its sanctions against Iran in January 2014.

During a visit to the Persian (Arabian) Gulf area in January 2008, Sarkozy announced that France was to establish a permanent military base in Abu Dhabi, the United Arab Emirates (UAE). The President also signed an agreement with the UAE, under which France was to assist the development of a programme to produce nuclear energy in that country. The French base in Abu Dhabi was officially inaugurated by Sarkozy in May 2009. A visit to Iraq by Sarkozy in February 2009—the first by a French head of state since 2003—signalled the President's willingness to renew bilateral ties with the country. Following a resurgence in sectarian violence in Iraq, in November 2013 France offered to provide the beleaguered country with arms, training and intelligence co-operation.

Initiatives by President Sarkozy to establish closer diplomatic and economic relations with Libya provoked widespread criticism. In July 2007 Sarkozy travelled to Libya for an official state visit, during which he signed an agreement on defence co-operation and a memorandum of understanding on the development of civil nuclear technology in Libya. During a state visit to France in December by the Libyan leader, Col Muammar al-Qaddafi, several bilateral agreements were signed, including, most controversially, contracts for the sale of military equipment to Libya and a further agreement on nuclear energy.

The French Government was criticized for its slow response to large-scale pro-democracy demonstrations in Tunisia that eventually led to the flight from that country of its President, Zine al-Abidine Ben Ali, in January 2011. Criticism was particularly focused on the Minister of State, Minister of Foreign and European Affairs, Michèle Alliot-Marie, who had responded to the anti-Government demonstrations by offering French assistance in training the regime's internal security forces; Alliot-Marie resigned in February. During a visit to Tunis by President Hollande in July 2013, the French leader pledged €500m. to support Tunisia's democratic transition. In contrast to its initial response to the situation in Tunisia, France was swift to show its support for the popular movement against Qaddafi's regime in Libya that emerged in mid-February. As the situation in Libya descended into civil war, on 10 March France became the first country to recognize the National Transitional Council, based in the rebel-held city of Benghazi, as the legitimate representative of the Libyan people. Later in March France led international efforts to secure a UN Security Council resolution authorizing an air exclusion zone over Libya. Following the adoption on 17 March of Resolution 1973, which permitted UN member states to take 'all necessary measures' (short of military occupation) to protect civilians in Libya, French and British air and naval forces played a particularly prominent role in the international coalition against Qaddafi's forces, which came under NATO command at the end of March. France also supplied arms to rebel forces, despite concerns that this could be regarded as a breach of Resolution 1973. After Qaddafi and his forces had been ejected from the Libyan capital, Tripoli, in August, Sarkozy, together with British Prime Minister David Cameron, visited the city in September. The NATO operation in Libya ended in October, following the capture by opposition forces of the last remaining government-controlled city and the death of Qaddafi at the hands of the rebels.

In April 2011 Sarkozy was one of several foreign leaders to urge the Syrian authorities to halt the violent suppression of anti-Government protests that had commenced in mid-March. In August, by which time it was estimated that more than 2,000 people had been killed since the uprising began, Sarkozy called for the Syrian President, Bashar al-Assad, to relinquish office. France was also a strong advocate of exerting greater international pressure on Assad's administration to end the violence in Syria, supporting two draft UN Security Council resolutions condemning government repression in that country in October 2011 and February 2012; however, the resolutions were vetoed by both the People's Republic of China and Russia. In March 2013, by which time some 70,000 people had been killed in the Syrian conflict, President Hollande urged the EU to lift its arms embargo on Syria so that it could supply arms to the rebel forces in their struggle against Assad's regime. In August the death of around 1,400 people in Damascus in a chemical weapons attack, allegedly carried out by Syrian government troops, heightened the French Government's resolve that some retaliatory action should be taken.

France's relations with Turkey were severely strained in 2011 by the introduction to the French Parliament of draft legislation outlawing the denial of killings deemed by French law to constitute genocide, including the massacre of Armenians under the Ottoman Empire during the First World War, which Parliament had voted to recognize as genocide in 2001. President Sarkozy, who supported the proposed law, insisted that it applied to all acts of genocide and was not aimed at any state in particular. Following the bill's approval by the National Assembly in December 2011, the Turkish Prime Minister recalled the Turkish ambassador to France (which is home to an estimated 500,000 ethnic Armenians) and suspended bilateral political and military co-operation. The legislation was approved by the Senate in January 2012, but a group of legislators subsequently referred it to the Constitutional Council, which ruled in February that the law was unconstitutional on the grounds that it infringed on freedom of expression.

CONSTITUTION AND GOVERNMENT

The Constitution of the Fifth Republic was promulgated in 1958 following its approval at a referendum. Under its terms, legislative power is held by the bicameral Parliament (Parlement), comprising a Senate (Sénat) and a National Assembly (Assemblée Nationale). Members of the Senate are elected by an electoral college (326 senators represent departments in Metropolitan France and the Overseas Departments, 10 represent Overseas Territories and 12 represent French nationals abroad). A law approved by Parliament in July 2003 introduced a number of reforms to senatorial elections; henceforth, senators were to be elected for a term of six years, with one-half of the seats renewable every three years (compared with a term of nine years and one-third of the seats renewable every three years previously). With effect from 2011, the number of senators was increased to 348, and the minimum age for eligible candidates to the Senate was reduced from 35 to 30 years. (The first stage of reform, whereby the number of senators increased from 321 to 331, took place at the partial senatorial elections held in September 2004; this number was subsequently increased to 343 at the partial senatorial elections held in September 2008.) The National Assembly has 577 members, with 555 for metropolitan France and 22 for the overseas possessions. Members of the National Assembly are elected by universal adult suffrage, under a single-member constituency system of direct election, using a second ballot if the first ballot failed to produce an absolute majority for any one candidate. The term of the National Assembly is five years, subject to dissolution. Executive power is held by the President. Since 1962 the President has been directly elected by popular vote (using two ballots if necessary). A constitutional amendment passed in October 2000 shortened the term of office from seven to five years, and a further amendment enacted in July 2008 limited the President to a maximum of two consecutive terms in office. The President appoints a Council of Ministers, headed by the Prime Minister, which administers the country and is responsible to Parliament.

Metropolitan France comprises 22 administrative regions containing 96 departments. Under the decentralization law of March 1982, administrative and financial power in metropolitan France was transferred from the préfets, who became Commissaires de la République, to locally elected departmental assemblies (Conseils Généraux) and regional assemblies (Conseils Régionaux). Corsica has its own directly elected legislative assembly (the Assemblée de Corse). The 12 overseas possessions comprise five Overseas Regions and Departments (Régions et Départements d'Outre Mer—French Guiana, Guadeloupe, Martinique, Mayotte and Réunion); five Overseas Collectivities (Collectivités d'Outre Mer—French Polynesia, Saint-Barthélemy, Saint-Martin, Saint Pierre and Miquelon and the Wallis and Futuna Islands); and two other territories (the French Southern and Antarctic Territories, and New Caledonia—which has a unique status as a *sui generis* Collectivity); all of which are integral parts of the French Republic. At a referendum held in the Overseas Collectivity of Mayotte in March 2009, the electorate voted overwhelmingly in favour of becoming an Overseas Department of France; the change took effect at the end of March 2011.

REGIONAL AND INTERNATIONAL CO-OPERATION

France was a founder member of the European Community, now the European Union (EU, see p. 273), and uses the single currency, the euro. France is also a member of the Council of Europe (see p. 252), which is based in Strasbourg, and the Organization for Security and Co-operation in Europe (OSCE, see p. 387). France is the host nation for the European Space Agency (see p. 270).

France was a founder member of the UN in 1945, and is a permanent member of the Security Council. As a contracting party to the General Agreement on Tariffs and Trade, France joined the World Trade Organization (WTO, see p. 434) on its establishment in 1995. France participates in the Group of Eight major industrialized nations (G8, see p. 465) and the Group of 20 major industrialized and systemically important emerging market nations (G20, see p. 456). France is also a member of the North Atlantic Treaty Organization (NATO, see p. 370) and the Organisation for Economic Co-operation and Development (OECD, see p. 379), which has its headquarters in Paris. It presides over the Franc Zone (see p. 329).

ECONOMIC AFFAIRS

In 2012, according to estimates by the World Bank, France's gross national income (GNI), measured at average 2010–12 prices, was US $2,742,891m., equivalent to $41,750 per head (or $36,720 on an international purchasing-power parity basis). During 2003–12, it was estimated, the population grew by an average of 0.6% per year, while gross domestic product (GDP) per head increased, in real terms, by an average of 0.5% per year. Overall GDP increased, in real terms, at an average rate of 1.1% per year in 2003–12; real GDP rose by 2.0% in 2011 and neither increased nor decreased in 2012, measured both at constant prices and according to chain-linked methodologies.

In 2012 agriculture (including forestry and fishing) contributed 2.0% of GDP and engaged 2.9% of the economically active population. The principal crops are wheat, sugar beet, maize and barley. Livestock, dairy products and wine are also important. According to World Bank figures, agricultural GDP increased, in real terms, by an average of 3.0% per year in 2003–09. According to chain-linked methodologies, the sector's GDP grew by 6.3% in 2011, but declined by 5.8% in 2012.

Industry (including mining, manufacturing, construction and power) provided 18.8% of GDP and employed 20.7% of the working population in 2012. Industrial GDP decreased, in real terms, by an average of 0.7% per year during 2003–09, according to World Bank figures.

In 2012 mining and quarrying, along with utilities, contributed 2.6% of GDP and employed 0.1% of the working population. Petroleum and natural gas are extracted and metallic minerals, including iron ore, copper and zinc, are mined. The production of coal, an industry which used to dominate the sector, came to an end in 2004 with the closure of France's last operating coal mine. According to chain-linked methodologies, the mining and quarrying sector declined by 6.4% in 2012.

Manufacturing provided 10.1% of GDP and employed 12.2% of the working population in 2012. Manufacturing GDP decreased, in real terms, at an average annual rate of 1.5% in 2003–09, according to World Bank figures. According to chain-linked methodologies, the sector expanded by 2.1% in 2011, but declined by 1.9% in 2012.

In 2012 the construction sector provided 6.3% of GDP and employed 6.9% of the working population. According to chain-linked methodologies, sectoral GDP declined by 0.7% in 2012.

France has only limited fossil fuel resources and in the early 2000s was the world's largest producer of nuclear power per head of population. In 2012 nuclear power provided 76.6% of total electricity production and hydroelectric power 10.2%. In that year France had 58 nuclear power stations, many of which would need to be replaced in around 2020. Construction work on a new nuclear reactor, the European Pressurized Reactor (EPR), began at Flamanville in Normandy in 2007 and the much delayed reactor was scheduled to be operational in 2016. Construction of a second EPR, at Penly in Normandy, which was due to begin in 2012, was shelved indefinitely. Imports of energy products comprised 17.9% of the value of total merchandise imports in 2012; in the early 2000s the major sources of petroleum imported to France were Saudi Arabia and Norway.

Services accounted for 79.2% of GDP and employed 76.4% of the working population in 2012. France is consistently the country with the largest number of tourist visitors in the world; there were an estimated 83.0m. tourist arrivals in 2012 and tourism receipts in that year totalled US $53,697m., according to provisional figures by the World Tourism Organization. The GDP of the services sector increased, in real terms, at an average rate of 1.5% per year in 2003–09, according to World Bank figures. According to chain-linked methodologies, GDP for market services rose by 2.9% in 2011 and by 0.5% in 2012, while GDP for non-market services rose by 1.1% in 2011 and by 0.6% in 2012.

In 2012 France recorded a visible merchandise trade deficit of US $76,070m., and there was a deficit of $57,250m. on the current account of the balance of payments. In 2012 the principal source of imports (providing 17.3% of the total) was Germany; other major sources were the People's Republic of China, Belgium, Italy, the USA and Spain. Germany was also the principal market for exports in that year (accounting for 16.4% of the total); other major trading partners were Italy, Belgium, Spain, the United Kingdom and the USA. The European Union (EU) as a whole provided 57.3% of imports in 2012 and took 59.2% of exports. The principal exports in 2012 were nuclear reactors and machinery, aircraft and spacecraft, motor vehicles, electrical and electronic equipment, iron and steel, other base metals and articles of base metal, prepared foodstuffs beverages, spirits, vinegar, tobacco, and articles thereof, pharmaceutical products, and plastics and rubber articles. The principal imports in that year were mineral fuels and lubricants, nuclear reactors and machinery, motor vehicles, electrical and electronic equipment, and iron and steel, other base metals and articles of base metal.

The general government deficit for 2012 was €98,800m., equivalent to 4.9% of GDP. France's general government gross debt was €1,833,800m. in 2012, equivalent to 90.2% of GDP. The average annual rate of inflation in 2003–12 was 1.7%. Consumer prices increased by 1.4% in 2012, according to official figures. The rate of unemployment rose from 9.8% in 2012 to 10.7% in early 2013.

The French economy, which is currently the second largest in Europe after Germany, was less severely affected than most advanced economies by the global financial crisis and downturn that began in late 2008, partly owing to the country's high levels of government spending and generous social security provisions, which helped to maintain consumer demand. The economy emerged from recession in mid-2009 after four quarters of negative growth, and GDP contracted by just 2.7% in 2009 (compared with 4.3% in the eurozone as a whole), before returning to positive growth, of 1.5% in 2010 and 2.0% in 2011. However, the unemployment rate remained high in 2011, particularly among youth. Moreover, stimulus measures introduced to counter the economic crisis had exacerbated the fiscal deficit, which amounted to 7.1% of GDP in 2010. Following the introduction of austerity measures by the Government of Nicolas Sarkozy, the deficit decreased to 5.2% of GDP in 2011; this was, nevertheless, still considerably higher than the EU-mandated limit of 3%. In January 2012 the credit rating agency Standard & Poor's lowered France's long-term sovereign debt rating from AAA to AA+. Amid a deteriorating economic outlook and the ongoing debt crisis in the eurozone, the new Socialist Government of François Hollande came to power in mid-2012. The new President vowed to focus on growth rather than austerity and favoured tax increases (particularly for those on high incomes) rather than expenditure cuts. In 2012 government gross debt rose to more than 90% of GDP and the fiscal deficit remained above 3% of GDP (at 4.9%). Furthermore, unemployment continued to grow (exceeding 3m. in September 2012, for the first time since 1999), partly as a result of a downturn in the manufacturing sector. According to official figures, overall GDP remained constant in 2012 and was predicted to increase by only around 0.1% in 2013. In November 2012, in an apparent shift in policy direction, the Government announced that it planned to increase value-added tax, reduce payroll taxes and implement some cuts in public spending in order to provide funds for the country's ailing corporate sector (in an attempt to make it more competitive). In 2013 government gross debt increased to 93.4% of GDP and was forecast to rise to a record 95.1% in 2014. However, the fiscal deficit narrowed further in 2013, to an estimated 4.3% of GDP; in May the EU Commission agreed to defer to 2015 the deadline for France to reach or go below the 3% threshold. Unemployment continued to rise in 2013, from 10.7% early in the year to 11.1% in December (more than 3.3m.). With the French economy showing little sign of any real recovery, in November Standard & Poor's further downgraded the country's credit rating to AA. Following its initial rejection in December 2012 by the Constitutional Court on technical grounds, Hollande's plan to introduce a 75% rate of tax on annual incomes exceeding €1m. was approved by the Court in December 2013 following the introduction of a number of amendments. The controversial levy was to be in force for only two years (2013–14).

PUBLIC HOLIDAYS

2015: 1 January (New Year's Day), 6 April (Easter Monday), 1 May (Labour Day), 8 May (Liberation Day), 14 May (Ascension Day), 25 May (Whit Monday), 14 July (National Day, Fall of the Bastille), 15 August (Assumption), 1 November (All Saints' Day), 11 November (Armistice Day), 25 December (Christmas Day).

Statistical Survey

Source (unless otherwise stated): Institut national de la statistique et des études économiques, 18 blvd Adolphe Pinard, 75675 Paris Cedex 14; tel. 1-45-17-50-50; internet www.insee.fr.

Note: Unless otherwise indicated, figures in this survey refer to metropolitan France, excluding the Overseas Possessions.

Area and Population

AREA, POPULATION AND DENSITY

Area (sq km)	543,965*
Population (census results)†	
8 March 1999	58,518,395
1 January 2011‡	63,070,344
Population (official estimates at 1 January)§	
2012	63,409,191
2013	63,703,191
Density (per sq km) at 1 January 2013	117.1

* 210,026 sq miles.

† Excluding professional soldiers and military personnel outside the country with no personal residence in France.

‡ New annual census methodology. Data refer to median figures based on the collection of raw data over a five-year period (2009–13).

§ Provisional figures.

POPULATION BY AGE AND SEX

(official estimates at 1 January 2013, provisional)

	Males	Females	Total
0–14	6,000,263	5,740,656	11,740,919
15–64	20,129,195	20,551,307	40,680,502
65 and over	4,743,580	6,538,190	11,281,770
Total	30,873,038	32,830,153	63,703,191

NATIONALITY OF THE POPULATION

(numbers resident in France at 1999 census, revised figures)

Country of citizenship	Population	%
France	55,257,502	94.42
Portugal	553,663	0.95
Morocco	504,096	0.86
Algeria	477,482	0.82
Turkey	208,049	0.36
Italy	201,670	0.34
Spain	161,762	0.28
Tunisia	154,356	0.26
Germany	78,381	0.31
Belgium	66,666	0.11
Yugoslavia*	50,543	0.09
Poland	33,758	0.06
Others	772,760	1.32
Total	58,520,688	100.00

* The successor states of the former Socialist Federal Republic of Yugoslavia, comprising Bosnia and Herzegovina, Croatia, the former Yugoslav republic of Macedonia, Slovenia and the Federal Republic of Yugoslavia (now Montenegro and Serbia).

REGIONS

(official population estimates at 1 January 2012, preliminary)

	Area (sq km)	Population	Density (per sq km)	Principal city
Alsace	8,280.2	1,857,477	224.3	Strasbourg
Aquitaine	41,308.4	3,286,605	79.6	Bordeaux
Auvergne	26,012.9	1,352,619	52.0	Clermont-Ferrand
Basse-Normandie	17,589.3	1,480,171	84.2	Caen
Bourgogne (Burgundy)	31,582.0	1,646,600	52.1	Dijon
Bretagne (Brittany)	27,207.9	3,249,815	119.4	Rennes
Centre	39,150.9	2,562,227	65.4	Orléans
Champagne–Ardenne	25,605.8	1,333,163	52.1	Châlons-en-Champagne
Corse (Corsica)	8,679.8	316,578	36.5	Ajaccio
Franche-Comté	16,202.3	1,179,374	72.8	Besançon
Haute-Normandie	12,317.4	1,850,685	150.2	Rouen
Ile-de-France	12,012.3	11,914,812	991.9	Paris
Languedoc-Roussillon	27,375.8	2,686,054	98.1	Montpellier
Limousin	16,942.3	746,230	44.0	Limoges
Lorraine	23,547.4	2,356,585	100.1	Nancy
Midi-Pyrénées	45,347.9	2,929,285	64.6	Toulouse
Nord-Pas-de-Calais	12,414.1	4,049,685	326.2	Lille
Pays de la Loire	32,081.8	3,630,139	113.2	Nantes
Picardie (Picardy)	19,399.5	1,924,607	99.2	Amiens
Poitou-Charentes	25,809.5	1,789,711	69.3	Poitiers
Provence-Alpes-Côte d'Azur	31,399.6	4,924,439	156.8	Marseille
Rhône-Alpes	43,698.2	6,342,330	145.1	Lyon
Total	543,965.4	63,409,191	116.6	—

PRINCIPAL TOWNS*

(incl. suburbs, estimated population at 1 January 2007)

Paris (capital)	10,197,678	Metz	322,459
Marseille–Aix-en-Provence	1,433,462	Montpellier	320,760
Lyon	1,422,331	Tours	307,146
Lille	1,014,586	Saint-Etienne	283,996
Nice	946,630	Rennes	281,734
Toulouse	858,233	Avignon	275,613
Bordeaux	809,224	Orléans	268,470
Nantes	569,961	Clermont-Ferrand	261,239
Toulon	546,801	Béthune	258,967
Douai-Lens	512,029	Mulhouse	239,859
Strasbourg	440,704	Dijon	237,925
Grenoble	427,739	Le Havre	235,818
Rouen	389,876	Angers	226,809
Valenciennes	355,709	Reims	211,966
Nancy	330,232	Brest	205,195

* Data refer to contiguous urban agglomerations (*unités urbaines*).

Mid-2011 ('000, incl. suburbs, UN estimate): Paris 10,620 (Source: UN, *World Urbanization Prospects: The 2011 Revision*).

BIRTHS, MARRIAGES AND DEATHS*

	Registered live births		Registered marriages		Registered deaths	
	Number	Rate (per 1,000)	Number	Rate (per 1,000)	Number	Rate (per 1,000)
2005	774,355	12.7	276,303	4.5	527,533	8.7
2006	796,896	13.0	267,260	4.4	516,416	8.4
2007	785,985	12.7	267,194	4.3	521,016	8.4
2008	796,044	12.8	258,739	4.2	532,131	8.6
2009	793,420	12.7	245,151	3.9	538,116	8.6
2010†	802,224	12.7	245,334	3.9	540,469	8.6
2011†	792,996	12.5	231,100	3.7	534,795	8.5
2012†	790,290	12.4	235,000	3.7	559,227	8.8

* Including data for national armed forces outside the country.

† Provisional figures.

Life expectancy (years at birth): 81.7 (males 78.4; females 85.1) in 2011 (Source: World Bank, World Development Indicators database).

ECONOMICALLY ACTIVE POPULATION

(labour force survey, annual averages, '000 persons aged 15 years and over)

	2010	2011	2012
Agriculture, forestry and fishing	747.9	750.0	750.4
Mining and quarrying	25.5	23.4	27.5
Manufacturing	3,177.8	3,201.3	3,130.9
Electricity, gas and water supply	392.4	368.4	379.5
Construction	1,819.7	1,795.8	1,769.4
Wholesale and retail trade; repair of motor vehicles, motorcycles and personal and household goods	3,313.1	3,197.9	3,214.2
Hotels and restaurants	959.2	975.9	966.6
Transport, storage and communications	2,043.2	2,044.6	2,040.0
Financial intermediation	854.8	859.6	840.5
Real estate, renting and business activities (incl. scientific and technical)	2,899.5	3,108.0	3,116.8
Public administration and defence; compulsory social security	2,574.6	2,508.8	2,440.1
Education	1,747.1	1,729.6	1,845.9
Health and social work	3,357.4	3,398.9	3,462.6
Other community, social and personal service activities	1,053.6	1,096.5	1,060.1
Households with employed persons	588.2	598.1	585.0
Extra-territorial organizations and bodies	19.6	28.7	22.8
Sub-total	25,573.6	25,685.9	25,652.3
Not classifiable by economic activity	118.8	92.1	102.0
Total employed	25,692.5	25,778.0	25,754.3
Unemployed	2,652.7	2,612.1	2,811.2
Total labour force	28,345.1	28,390.1	28,565.5
Males	14,836.1	14,837.9	14,926.6
Females	13,509.1	13,552.2	13,638.9

Note: Totals may not be equal to the sum of components, owing to rounding.

Health and Welfare

KEY INDICATORS

Total fertility rate (children per woman, 2011)	2.0
Under-5 mortality rate (per 1,000 live births, 2011)	4
HIV/AIDS (% of persons aged 15–49, 2011)	0.4
Physicians (per 1,000 head, 2011)	3.4
Hospital beds (per 1,000 head, 2009)	6.9
Health expenditure (2010): US $ per head (PPP)	3,997
Health expenditure (2010): % of GDP	11.7
Health expenditure (2010): public (% of total)	76.9
Total carbon dioxide emissions ('000 metric tons, 2010)	361,272.8
Carbon dioxide emissions per head (metric tons, 2010)	5.6
Human Development Index (2012): ranking	20
Human Development Index (2012): value	0.893

For sources and definitions, see explanatory note on p. vi.

Agriculture

PRINCIPAL CROPS

('000 metric tons)

	2010	2011	2012
Wheat	38,207.0	35,994.0	40,300.8
Rice, paddy	113.6	128.3	123.2
Barley	10,102.0	8,775.0	11,347.0
Maize	13,974.6	15,913.3	15,614.1
Rye	150.8	124.4	160.3
Oats	392.0	318.5	400.8
Sorghum (excl. sorghum for forage and silage)	285.9	281.6	239.2
Buckwheat	125.9	91.4	105.0
Triticale (wheat-rye hybrid)	2,060.7	1,987.3	2,300.8
Potatoes	6,622.0	7,440.2	6,340.8
Sugar beet	31,874.8	38,106.1	33,688.4
Broad beans, horse beans, dry	483.3	344.8	273.5
Peas, dry	1,073.3	670.1	565.3
Soybeans (soya beans)	136.7	122.5	104.3
Sunflower seed	1,635.6	1,880.7	1,573.0
Rapeseed	4,811.1	5,369.0	5,463.1
Linseed	40.8	30.4	49.4
Cabbages and other brassicas	100.0	113.1	108.9
Artichokes	48.0	50.6	42.5
Lettuce and chicory	327.0	314.0	328.3
Spinach	80.1	110.5	106.6
Tomatoes	645.2	597.5	588.7
Cauliflowers and broccoli	356.5	364.6	344.4
Pumpkins, squash and gourds	104.1	123.5	109.0
Cucumbers and gherkins	141.1	134.9	135.5
Onions and shallots, green	60.2	60.7	60.1
Onions, dry	329.2	420.5	385.9
Beans, green	49.4	37.0*	70.7
Peas, green	570.5	635.3	591.1
String beans	250.0	207.4	229.2
Carrots and turnips	388.8	624.5	545.0
Maize, green	351.2	415.0	264.0
Mushrooms and truffles	119.3	115.7	116.6
Chicory roots	113.6	100.9	92.7
Cantaloupes and other melons	290.1	276.7	291.8
Apples	1,788.4	1,857.3	1,382.9
Pears	148.5	170.8	124.0
Apricots	144.9	155.1	189.7
Sweet cherries	44.9	48.1	30.4
Peaches and nectarines	311.0	301.8	275.5
Plums and sloes	247.6	176.8	209.3
Strawberries	50.4	50.8	55.2
Grapes	5,794.4	6,588.9	5,338.5
Kiwi fruit	70.7	73.5	65.2
Tobacco, unmanufactured	18.4	14.0	12.6

* FAO estimate.

Aggregate production ('000 metric tons, may include official, semi-official or estimated data): Total cereals 65,628.9 in 2010, 63,864.5 in 2011, 70,981.6 in 2012; Total roots and tubers 6,622.0 in 2010, 7,440.2 in 2011, 6,340.8 in 2012; Total vegetables (incl. melons) 5,593.0 in 2010, 5,926.3 in 2011, 5,637.0 in 2012; Total fruits (excl. melons) 8,683.1 in 2010, 9,511.5 in 2011, 7,754.2 in 2012.

Source: FAO.

LIVESTOCK

('000 head, year ending 30 September)

	2010	2011	2012
Cattle	19,545.8	19,085.6	19,009.0
Pigs	14,283.9	13,984.9	13,764.9
Sheep	7,922	7,618	7,464
Goats	1,435	1,381	1,310
Horses	423	425	415
Asses*	15	15	15
Mules	33	33	31
Chickens	143,973	150,825	154,169
Ducks	26,141	26,786	26,270
Turkeys	24,260	23,743	22,144

* FAO estimates.

Source: FAO.

LIVESTOCK PRODUCTS
('000 metric tons)

	2010	2011	2012
Cattle meat	1,530.3	1,566.5	1,491.7
Sheep meat	118.7	115.0	113.8
Pig meat	2,254.7	2,218.0	2,179.9
Chicken meat	1,023.8	1,046.4	1,056.5
Duck meat	282.3	290.9	279.7
Turkey meat	404.6	398.0	378.5
Cows' milk	23,331.8	24,361.1	23,983.2
Sheep's milk	265.3	273.6	274.7
Goats' milk	648.4	655.3	624.0
Honey	13.8	13.8	11.8
Hen eggs*	905.6	839.5	853.6
Wool, greasy†	14	14	15

* Unofficial figures.
† FAO estimates.

Source: FAO.

Forestry

ROUNDWOOD REMOVALS
('000 cubic metres, excluding bark)

	2010	2011*	2012*
Sawlogs, veneer logs and logs for sleepers	18,099	18,035	18,670
Pulpwood	11,215	9,844	10,691
Other industrial wood	321	508	445
Fuel wood	26,174	26,653	26,291
Total	55,808	55,041	56,097

* FAO estimates.

Source: FAO.

SAWNWOOD PRODUCTION
('000 cubic metres, including railway sleepers)

	2010	2011*	2012*
Coniferous (softwood)	6,894	7,213	6,852
Broadleaved (hardwood)	1,422	1,462	1,389
Total	8,316	8,675	8,241

* FAO estimates.

Source: FAO.

Fishing

('000 metric tons, live weight)

	2009	2010	2011
Capture*	419.9	425.9	419.2
Saithe (Pollock)	10.0	3.3	11.4
Atlantic herring	3.8	4.4	10.8
European pilchard (Sardine)	39.8	26.2	23.0
Skipjack tuna	37.1	35.7	30.8
Yellowfin tuna	41.5	42.8	43.2
Atlantic mackerel	12.4	13.7	15.4
Blue whiting (Poutassou)	7.0	7.9	4.4
Monkfishes (Angler)	17.6	17.3	15.7
Aquaculture*	233.9	224.4	225.9
Rainbow trout	32.8	32.0*	33.0*
Pacific cupped oyster	103.5	95.0*	95.0*
Blue mussel	61.6	61.8	61.8
Total catch*	653.8	650.3	645.1

* FAO estimate(s).

Note: Figures exclude aquatic plants ('000 metric tons, all capture): 18.9 in 2009; 22.6 in 2010; 9.2 in 2011. Figures also exclude coral (metric tons): 9.0 in 2009; 9.0 in 2010; 10.0 in 2011 and sponges (metric tons, FAO estimates): 0.3 in 2009; 0.2 in 2010; 0.2 in 2011.

Source: FAO.

Mining

('000 metric tons unless otherwise indicated)

	2009	2010	2011
Crude petroleum ('000 barrels)	6,624	6,606	6,508
Natural gas (marketed production, million cu m)	1,444	1,245	1,132
Gold (kg)*†	1,500	1,500	
Kaolin and kaolinitic clay‡	519	315	315
Salt*	6,200	5,867	5,430
Gypsum and anhydrite (crude)	3,351	3,440	4,231
Mica*	20	20	20
Talc (crude)*	420	420	420

* Estimates.
† Figures refer to the metal content of ores and concentrates.
‡ Figures refer to marketable production.

Source: US Geological Survey.

Industry

SELECTED PRODUCTS
('000 metric tons unless otherwise indicated)

	2009	2010	2011
Wine*	6,114	5,846	6,591
Chemical wood pulp*	1,025	1,073	1,103
Newsprint*	873	984	942
Liquefied petroleum gas ('000 barrels)†	29,236	24,346	24,300
Motor gasoline (petrol—'000 barrels)†	133,225	115,596	115,000
Jet fuels and kerosene ('000 barrels)†	39,274	35,113	35,100
Distillate fuel oil ('000 barrels)†	246,959	224,950	224,900
Residual fuel oil ('000 barrels)†	61,137	59,313	59,300
Coke-oven coke	3,291	3,219	n.a.
Pig iron†	8,104	10,137	9,698
Crude steel†	12,840	15,414	15,780
Aluminium (unwrought—primary)†	345	356	334
Lead (unwrought)†	82.0‡	82.0‡	53.9
Zinc (incl. slab and secondary)†	161.0	163.0	164.0
Electric energy (incl. Monaco, million kWh)	542,184	n.a.	n.a.

* Source: FAO.
† Source: US Geological Survey.
‡ Estimate.

2009: Wheat flour ('000 metric tons) 4,537.

2012 ('000 metric tons): Chemical wood pulp 1,058; Newsprint 878.

Source (unless otherwise indicated): UN Industrial Commodities Statistics Database.

Finance

CURRENCY AND EXCHANGE RATES

Monetary Units
100 cent = 1 euro (€).

Sterling and Dollar Equivalents (31 December 2013)
£1 sterling = 1.194 euros;
US $1 = 0.725 euros;
€10 = £8.37 = $13.79.

Average Exchange Rate (euros per US $)

2011	0.7194
2012	0.7783
2013	0.7532

Note: The national currency was formerly the French franc. From the introduction of the euro, with French participation, on 1 January 1999, a fixed exchange rate of €1 = 6.5596 French francs was in operation. Euro notes and coins were introduced on 1 January 2002. The euro and local currency circulated alongside each other until 17 February, after which the euro became the sole legal tender.

GOVERNMENT FINANCE

(general government transactions, € '000 million)

Revenue	2010	2011	2012
Taxes	496.1	534.0	562.2
Taxes on income and inheritance	204.7	224.6	243.4
Taxes on capital	7.7	10.3	9.6
Taxes on production and imports	288.4	305.2	314.0
Social contributions	361.0	375.6	387.0
Other revenue	101.1	103.0	103.1
Total	958.3	1,012.7	1,052.4

Expenditure	2010	2011	2012
Compensation of employees	259.4	262.7	267.7
Use of goods and services	112.0	109.6	114.0
Interest	47.0	52.6	52.1
Subsidies	32.3	29.5	30.5
Grants	377.7	388.7	403.5
Other social benefits	117.9	122.0	125.1
Other expenses	86.9	89.1	93.9
Net acquisition of non-financial assets	62.4	64.3	64.2
Total	1,095.6	1,118.5	1,151.2

INTERNATIONAL RESERVES

(US $ million at 31 December)

	2010	2011	2012
Gold*	110,424	123,285	130,291
IMF special drawing rights	15,000	14,675	14,586
Reserve position in IMF	4,589	7,789	8,474
Foreign exchange	36,211	26,147	30,350
Total	166,224	171,896	183,701

* Valued at market-related prices.

Source: IMF, *International Financial Statistics*.

MONEY SUPPLY

(incl. shares, depository corporations, national residency criteria, € million at 31 December)

	2010	2011	2012
Currency issued	160,097	168,950	173,530
Banque de France	83,781	91,628	98,826
Demand deposits	502,493	527,854	543,348
Other deposits	1,081,448	1,234,267	1,276,583
Securities other than shares	1,164,674	1,241,945	1,213,706
Money market fund shares	391,301	348,332	363,743
Shares and other equity	574,224	610,750	635,188
Other items (net)	–449,953	–644,879	–682,323
Total	3,424,284	3,487,219	3,523,775

Source: IMF, *International Financial Statistics*.

COST OF LIVING

(Consumer Price Index, December of each year; base: January 1998 = 100)

	2010	2011	2012
Food (incl. non-alcoholic beverages)	125.2	129.5	132.3
Alcoholic beverages and tobacco	165.0	171.8	180.9
Clothing and footwear	107.7	110.9	112.2
Housing, water, gas, electricity, etc.	138.0	143.3	147.5
Furniture and household items	114.2	117.0	118.3
Health care and pharmaceuticals	102.6	102.6	101.9
Transport	135.3	140.9	143.2
Post and telecommunications	82.1	79.8	70.0
Leisure and culture (goods and services)	90.9	90.4	90.4
Education	136.7	139.2	141.4
Hotels, cafés and restaurants	131.8	135.1	138.5
All items (incl. others)	122.1	125.1	126.8

NATIONAL ACCOUNTS

(€ '000 million at current prices)

Expenditure on the Gross Domestic Product

	2010	2011	2012
Final consumption expenditure	1,606.9	1,645.2	1,675.0
Households	1,085.3	1,113.9	1,129.8
Non-profit institutions serving households	39.8	41.4	42.5
General government	481.8	490.0	502.7
Gross capital formation	373.7	415.5	402.4
Gross fixed capital formation	377.2	400.0	401.8
Changes in inventories	–4.2	14.8	–0.1
Acquisitions, less disposals, of valuables	0.7	0.7	0.7
Total domestic expenditure	1,980.6	2,060.7	2,077.4
Exports of goods and services	494.5	538.3	557.6
Less Imports of goods and services	538.3	597.6	602.6
GDP in market prices	1,936.7	2,001.4	2,032.3

Gross Domestic Product by Economic Activity

	2010	2011	2012
Agriculture, forestry and fishing	31.8	34.2	35.8
Industry (incl. energy)	222.7	227.6	228.3
Food products, beverages and tobacco	30.4	31.8	34.3
Mining, energy and water supply	43.4	44.1	46.8
Automobile, electronic and intermediate goods industries	148.9	151.7	147.1
Coke and refined petroleum	2.3	2.1	1.9
Construction	106.2	111.0	114.1
Mainly market services	987.0	1,017.8	1,030.6
Trade, transport, hotels and restaurants	320.2	329.4	332.7
Information and communications	86.7	84.8	82.5
Financial activities	84.0	85.5	87.5
Real estate and renting activities	229.0	236.7	239.9
Business services	208.0	220.9	226.0
Other services	59.1	60.5	61.9
Mainly non-market services	393.3	403.2	412.1
Public administration and defence; compulsory social security	136.1	139.2	142.0
Education, health and social work	257.2	264.0	270.1
Gross value added at basic prices	1,741.0	1,793.8	1,820.9
Taxes, less subsidies, on products	195.8	207.6	211.4
GDP in market prices	1,936.7	2,001.4	2,032.3

BALANCE OF PAYMENTS
(US $ '000 million)*

	2010	2011	2012
Exports of goods	515.84	592.92	567.35
Imports of goods	−579.17	−686.44	−643.43
Balance on goods	−63.33	−93.52	−76.07
Exports of services	188.19	222.84	201.26
Imports of services	−168.00	−191.92	−174.21
Balance on goods and services	−43.14	−62.60	−49.03
Primary income received	196.42	217.62	184.13
Primary income paid	−145.01	−155.26	−145.93
Balance on goods, services and primary income	8.27	−0.24	−10.83
Secondary income received	32.10	33.57	31.20
Secondary income paid	−74.10	−82.54	−77.62
Current balance	−33.73	−49.22	−57.25
Capital account (net)	0.06	0.01	−0.49
Direct investment assets	−69.37	−62.92	−39.81
Direct investment liabilities	39.04	40.83	28.12
Portfolio investment assets	39.39	228.85	8.05
Portfolio investment liabilities	115.86	89.20	44.31
Financial derivatives and employee stock options liabilities	34.05	19.56	18.49
Other investment assets	−167.98	−118.63	85.30
Other investment liabilities	51.87	−128.12	−44.00
Net errors and omissions	−1.39	−27.94	−37.22
Reserves and related items	7.79	−8.38	5.50

* Figures refer to transactions of metropolitan France, French Guiana, Guadeloupe, Martinique, Mayotte, Monaco and Réunion with the rest of the world.

Source: IMF, *International Financial Statistics*.

External Trade

PRINCIPAL COMMODITIES
(distribution by HS, US $ million)

Imports*	2010	2011	2012
Prepared foodstuffs; beverages, spirits, vinegar; tobacco and articles thereof	23,306.8	26,746.6	25,821.2
Mineral products	86,630.1	119,332.7	118,901.6
Mineral fuels, oils, distillation products, etc.	82,758.9	114,781.2	114,935.8
Crude petroleum oils	35,319.2	52,125.9	47,566.4
Petroleum oils, not crude	23,518.0	32,993.4	37,159.8
Petroleum gases	18,163.8	23,755.7	24,258.3
Chemicals and related products	71,155.9	81,293.1	79,284.1
Organic chemicals	16,952.9	19,999.4	20,526.3
Pharmaceutical products	25,010.5	26,486.0	26,379.6
Medicament mixtures put in dosage	19,237.5	19,654.6	19,340.6
Plastics, rubber, and articles thereof	30,447.9	35,219.1	32,332.4
Plastics and articles thereof	23,082.3	25,834.7	24,084.4
Textiles and textile articles	28,042.5	31,366.2	28,121.8
Iron and steel, other base metals and articles of base metal	43,673.2	52,707.9	45,056.0
Iron and steel	14,462.1	18,111.5	14,342.1
Machinery and mechanical appliances; electrical equipment; parts thereof	123,342.3	137,393.0	127,140.9
Boilers, machinery, etc.	67,218.7	77,464.0	72,693.3
Electrical and electronic equipment	56,123.6	59,929.0	54,447.6
Vehicles, aircraft, vessels and associated transport equipment	82,376.1	93,885.7	89,242.4
Vehicles other than railway, tramway	55,954.1	64,219.1	55,168.0
Cars (incl. station wagons)	31,166.6	35,698.9	30,297.5
Aircraft, spacecraft, and parts thereof	24,444.8	27,269.8	31,148.7
Optical, medical apparatus, etc.; clocks and watches; musical instruments; parts thereof	20,576.6	22,194.7	21,851.6
Optical, photo, technical, medical apparatus	18,281.8	19,289.3	18,644.3
Total (incl. others)	599,171.5	700,851.6	663,268.6

Exports	2010	2011	2012
Vegetables and vegetable products	16,089.5	20,640.6	18,307.0
Prepared foodstuffs; beverages, spirits, vinegar; tobacco and articles thereof	32,223.9	37,489.6	37,434.4
Mineral products	20,148.6	28,117.3	26,452.1
Mineral fuels, oils, distillation products, etc.	18,719.1	26,552.3	24,952.2
Chemicals and related products	85,381.4	92,548.5	90,961.2
Pharmaceutical products	33,536.7	32,911.1	34,745.9
Medicament mixtures put in dosage	27,170.7	26,428.1	27,282.3
Plastics, rubber and articles thereof	27,369.3	31,967.9	29,683.9
Plastics and articles thereof	19,403.7	22,367.0	20,895.0
Iron and steel, other base metals and articles of base metal	40,281.1	46,640.6	41,023.9
Iron and steel	16,615.8	19,329.2	17,064.8
Machinery and mechanical appliances; electrical equipment; parts thereof	102,289.9	113,978.6	108,707.0
Boilers, machinery, etc.	58,802.0	66,389.1	64,238.1
Electrical and electronic equipment	43,487.9	47,589.6	44,468.8
Vehicles, aircraft, vessels and associated transport equipment	97,616.5	105,219.4	104,535.2
Vehicles other than railway, tramway	47,147.8	53,103.3	46,806.8
Cars (incl. station wagons)	21,089.0	23,163.1	20,176.9
Parts and access of motor vehicles	16,978.6	18,816.9	16,415.5
Aircraft, spacecraft, and parts thereof	46,404.1	49,813.5	54,507.0
Aircraft, (helicopter, aeroplanes) and spacecraft (satellites)	40,818.5	43,346.6	47,278.9
Optical, medical apparatus, etc.; clocks and watches; musical instruments; parts thereof	18,954.6	20,665.8	19,727.4
Optical, photo, technical, medical apparatus	17,252.2	18,462.8	17,317.0
Total (incl. others)	511,651.0	581,541.9	556,575.7

* Including re-imports.

Source: Trade Map-Trade Competitiveness Map, International Trade Centre, www.intracen.org/marketanalysis.

PRINCIPAL TRADING PARTNERS
(US $ million)

Imports*	2010	2011	2012
Austria	5,876.3	6,460.8	6,634.5
Belgium	46,993.3	54,401.7	50,091.9
China, People's Republic	48,872.7	56,189.4	53,037.0
Czech Republic	6,640.4	8,130.8	7,141.4
France	7,110.5	8,204.3	6,306.2
Germany	103,433.8	118,607.8	114,581.6
Ireland	7,745.4	9,001.0	8,956.1
Italy	44,971.0	50,752.1	47,128.6
Japan	11,719.3	12,995.9	11,757.4
Kazakhstan	4,246.1	7,170.2	6,749.3
Libya	6,263.2	2,779.3	5,520.7
Netherlands	25,188.4	30,107.8	28,818.7
Norway	6,490.6	9,451.8	7,187.1
Poland	9,124.2	10,684.6	10,156.3
Russia	16,136.1	19,348.5	15,366.4
Saudi Arabia	3,531.7	6,340.5	7,085.7
Spain	37,184.8	41,946.5	39,666.5
Sweden	7,474.2	8,369.0	7,449.2
Switzerland	14,600.1	16,081.5	15,563.1
Turkey	7,159.7	8,173.1	7,288.8
United Kingdom	25,974.0	30,586.2	29,304.4
USA	35,234.6	39,589.9	42,364.1
Total (incl. others)	599,171.5	700,851.6	663,268.6

Exports	2010	2011	2012
Algeria	6,933.3	8,004.7	8,178.2
Belgium	38,471.5	41,857.9	40,758.3
Brazil	4,731.1	5,551.1	5,951.1
China, People's Republic	14,551.3	18,716.1	19,387.8
Germany	82,988.7	96,159.8	91,548.5
Hong Kong	5,578.6	6,107.9	7,678.4
Italy	41,337.6	47,480.2	41,070.3
Japan	7,793.3	9,065.2	9,491.7
Korea, Republic	4,252.8	5,823.2	4,725.1
Morocco	5,281.2	5,965.0	5,179.2
Netherlands	21,333.8	24,888.3	23,573.7
Poland	7,849.8	9,229.1	8,506.1
Portugal	5,547.5	5,486.9	4,619.3
Russia	8,319.0	10,352.9	11,726.3
Saudi Arabia	5,190.5	4,366.1	4,137.3
Singapore	6,663.0	7,146.3	7,539.6
Spain	37,979.6	42,281.3	37,564.9
Sweden	6,694.3	7,792.7	6,514.8
Switzerland	15,054.3	18,229.4	17,649.7
Turkey	8,303.3	9,320.1	8,875.0
United Kingdom	34,343.8	38,470.7	37,531.4
USA	29,230.6	32,468.2	34,113.8
Total (incl. others)	511,651.0	581,541.9	556,575.7

* Including re-imports.

Source: Trade Map-Trade Competitiveness Map, International Trade Centre, www.intracen.org/marketanalysis.

Transport

RAILWAYS
(traffic)

	2006	2007	2008
Paying passengers ('000 journeys)	1,013,000	1,042,860	1,085,540
Passenger-km (million)	n.a.	80,370	85,030
Freight carried ('000 metric tons)	107,710	105,710	97,440
Freight ton-km (million)	n.a.	40,630	37,270

Source: Société Nationale des Chemins de fer Français, Paris.

ROAD TRAFFIC
('000 motor vehicles in use at 31 December)

	2008	2009	2010
Passenger cars	30,850	31,050	31,300
Lorries and vans	6,280	6,300	6,359
Buses and coaches	84	85	86
Motorcycles and mopeds	2,710	3,532	3,000

Source: IRF, *World Road Statistics*.

INLAND WATERWAYS

	2003	2004	2005
Freight carried ('000 metric tons)	54,661	57,994	59,510
Freight ton-km (million)	6,890	7,316	7,856

Source: Voies navigables de France.

SHIPPING

Flag Registered Fleet
(all registers, at 31 December)

	2011	2012	2013
Number of vessels	1,004	1,016	1,022
Total displacement ('000 grt)	6,896.8	6,377.9	5,816.8

Source: Lloyd's List Intelligence (www.lloydslistintelligence.com).

Sea-borne Freight Traffic
('000 metric tons)

	2003	2004	2005
Goods loaded	93,010	96,100	100,660
Goods unloaded	220,610	223,580	227,100

2010: Goods loaded 99,864; Goods unloaded 199,308.

2012: Goods loaded 96,924; Goods unloaded 193,212.

Source: UN, *Monthly Bulletin of Statistics*.

CIVIL AVIATION
(revenue traffic on scheduled services)*

	2010	2011	2012
Passengers carried ('000)	60,759	69,754	72,352
Passenger-km (million)	167,959	136,357	140,791
Total ton-km (million)	4,955	4,228	4,246

* Including data for airlines based in French overseas possessions.

Source: Direction Générale de l'Aviation Civile.

Tourism

FOREIGN TOURIST ARRIVALS BY COUNTRY OF ORIGIN
('000, estimates)

	2009	2010	2011
Belgium and Luxembourg	10,900	10,742	10,734
Germany	10,692	11,410	11,648
Italy	7,250	7,178	7,987
Netherlands	7,224	7,002	6,497
Spain	4,874	4,939	5,467
Switzerland (incl. Liechtenstein)	5,438	5,450	5,667
United Kingdom and Ireland	12,881	12,897	12,823
USA	3,061	2,909	3,325
Total (incl. others)	76,766	77,648	81,411

Total tourist arrivals ('000): 83,018 in 2012 (provisional).

Receipts from tourism (US $ million, excl. passenger transport): 46,915 in 2010; 54,512 in 2011; 53,697 in 2012 (provisional).

Source: World Tourism Organization.

Communications Media

	2010	2011	2012
Telephones ('000 main lines in use)	40,622	40,043	39,290
Mobile cellular telephones ('000 subscribers)	57,785	59,816	62,280
Internet subscribers ('000)	21,800	n.a.	n.a.
Broadband subscribers ('000)	21,337	22,749	23,960

Source: International Telecommunication Union.

Education

(2004/05, public and private, metropolitan France, French Guiana, Guadeloupe, Martinique and Réunion)

	Students ('000)		
	Males	Females	Total
Pre-primary	1,335.7	1,273.8	2,609.5
Primary	2,011.2	1,913.4	3,924.6
Integration and adaptation schooling	30.9	20.5	51.4
Secondary:			
Lower	1,626.2	1,568.1	3,194.3
Upper—Professional	389.0	324.8	713.8
Upper—General/Technical	681.0	834.6	1,515.5
Higher	n.a.	n.a.	2,268.4

Source: Ministry of National Education, Higher Education and Research, Paris.

Students ('000, 2011/12, public and private, metropolitan France, French Guiana, Guadeloupe, Martinique and Réunion): Pre-primary 2,539.1; Primary 4,067,6; Integration and adaptation schooling 45.1; Secondary (Lower) 3,165,9; Secondary (Upper—Professional) 691.1; Secondary (Upper—General/Technical) 1,433.1; Higher 2,347.5.

Institutions (2012/13, public and private, metropolitan France, French Guiana, Guadeloupe, Martinique and Réunion): Pre-primary 15,558, Primary and Integration and adaptation schooling 37,379, Secondary (Lower) 7,051, Secondary (Upper—Professional) 1,602, Secondary (Upper—General/Technical) 2,652, Higher (Universities) 80, Higher (Other) 3,974.

Teachers (2004/05, public and private, metropolitan France, French Guiana, Guadeloupe, Martinique and Réunion, excl. trainee teachers): Pre-primary, Primary and Integration and adaptation schooling 364,315, Secondary (Lower) 237,277, Secondary (Upper) 250,367, Higher 87,724.

Directory

The Government

HEAD OF STATE

President: FRANÇOIS HOLLANDE (took office 15 May 2012).

COUNCIL OF MINISTERS
(April 2014)

Prime Minister: MANUEL VALLS.

Minister of Foreign Affairs and International Development: LAURENT FABIUS.

Minister of Ecology, Sustainable Development and Energy: SÉGOLÈNE ROYAL.

Minister of National Education, Higher Education and Research: BENOÎT HAMON.

Keeper of the Seals, Minister of Justice: CHRISTIANE TAUBIRA.

Minister of Finance and Public Accounts: MICHEL SAPIN.

Minister of Economy, Industrial Recovery and Digital Economy: ARNAUD MONTEBOURG.

Minister of Social Affairs and Health: MARISOL TOURAINE.

Minister of Labour, Employment and Social Dialogue: FRANÇOIS REBSAMEN.

Minister of Defence: JEAN-YVES LE DRIAN.

Minister of the Interior: BERNARD CAZENEUVE.

Minister of Women's Rights, Cities, Youth and Sports: NAJAT VALLAUD-BELKACEM.

Minister of Decentralization, State Reform and Public Service: MARYLISE LEBRANCHU.

Minister of Culture and Communication: AURÉLIE FILIPPETTI.

Minister of Agriculture, Food and Forestry, Government Spokesperson: STÉPHANE LE FOLL.

Minister of Housing and Territorial Equality: SYLVIA PINEL.

Minister of Overseas Territories: GEORGE PAU-LANGEVIN.

Secretary of State for Relations with Parliament: JEAN-MARIE LE GUEN.

Secretary of State to the Minister of Foreign Affairs and International Development, in charge of European Affairs: HARLEM DÉSIR.

Secretary of State to the Minister of Foreign Affairs and International Development, in charge of Foreign Trade, Tourism Development and French Nationals Abroad: FLEUR PELLERIN.

Secretary of State to the Minister of Foreign Affairs and International Development, in charge of Development and Francophonie: ANNICK GIRARDIN.

Secretary of State to the Minister of Ecology, Sustainable Development and Energy, in charge of Transport, Maritime Economy and Fisheries: FRÉDÉRIC CUVILLIER.

Secretary of State to the Minister of National Education, Higher Education and Research, in charge of Higher Education and Research: GENEVIÈVE FIORASO.

Secretary of State to the Minister of Finance and Public Accounts, in charge of the Budget: CHRISTIAN ECKERT.

Secretary of State to the Minister of Economy, Industrial Recovery and Digital Economy, in charge of Trade, Crafts, Social Economy, Solidarity and Consumer Affairs: VALÉRIE FOURNEYRON.

Secretary of State to the Minister of Economy, Industrial Recovery and Digital Economy, in charge of Digital Economy: AXELLE LEMAIRE.

Secretary of State to the Minister of Defence, in charge of Veterans and Memory: KADER ARIF.

Secretary of State to the Minister of Decentralization, State Reform and Public Service, in charge of Territorial Reform: ANDRÉ VALLINI.

Secretary of State to the Minister of Social Affairs and Health, in charge of the Elderly, Family and Autonomy: LAURENCE ROSSIGNOL.

Secretary of State to the Minister of Social Affairs and Health, in charge of Disabled People and Combating Exclusion: SÉGOLÈNE NEUVILLE.

Secretary of State to the Minister of Women's Rights, Cities, Youth and Sports, in charge of Sports: THIERRY BRAILLARD.

MINISTRIES

Office of the President: Palais de l'Elysée, 55–57 rue du Faubourg Saint Honoré, 75008 Paris; tel. 1-42-92-81-00; fax 1-47-42-24-65; internet www.elysee.fr.

Office of the Prime Minister: Hôtel de Matignon, 57 rue de Varenne, 75007 Paris; tel. 1-42-75-80-00; fax 1-42-75-78-31; e-mail premier-ministre@premier-ministre.gouv.fr; internet www.premier-ministre.gouv.fr.

Ministry of Agriculture, Food and Forestry: 78 rue de Varenne, 75349 Paris Cedex 07; tel. 1-49-55-49-55; fax 1-49-55-40-39; e-mail infodoc@agriculture.gouv.fr; internet www.agriculture.gouv.fr.

Ministry of Culture and Communication: 3 rue de Valois, 75001 Paris; tel. 1-40-15-80-00; fax 1-40-15-85-30; e-mail point.culture@culture.fr; internet www.culture.gouv.fr.

Ministry of Decentralization, State Reform and Public Service: 80 rue de Lille, 75007 Paris; tel. 1-40-04-04-04; internet www.fonction-publique.gouv.fr.

Ministry of Defence: 14 rue Saint Dominique, 75007 Paris; tel. 1-80-50-14-00; fax 1-47-05-40-91; e-mail sdbc.courrier-ministre.fct@intradef.gouv.fr; internet www.defense.gouv.fr.

Ministry of Ecology, Sustainable Development and Energy: 92055 La Défense Cedex; tel. 1-40-81-21-22; internet www.developpement-durable.gouv.fr.

Ministry of the Economy and Finance: 139 rue de Bercy, 75572 Paris Cedex 12; tel. 1-40-04-04-04; internet www.economie.gouv.fr.

Ministry of Foreign Affairs and International Development: 37 quai d'Orsay, 75351 Paris Cedex 07; tel. 1-43-17-53-53; fax 1-43-17-52-03; internet www.diplomatie.gouv.fr.

Ministry of Housing and Territorial Equality: 92055 La Défense Cedex; tel. 01-40-81-21-22; internet www.territoires.gouv.fr.

Ministry of the Interior: place Beauvau, 75008 Paris; tel. 1-49-27-49-27; fax 1-43-59-89-50; e-mail sirp@interieur.gouv.fr; internet www.interieur.gouv.fr.

Ministry of Justice: 13 place Vendôme, 75042 Paris Cedex 01; tel. 1-44-77-60-60; fax 1-44-77-60-02; e-mail cyberjustice@justice.gouv.fr; internet www.justice.gouv.fr.

Ministry of Labour, Employment and Social Dialogue: 101 rue de Grenelle, 75700 Paris; tel. 1-40-56-60-00; fax 1-44-38-20-20; internet www.travail-solidarite.gouv.fr.

Ministry of National Education, Higher Education and Research: 1 rue Descartes, 75231 Paris Cedex 05; tel. 1-55-55-90-01; e-mail sup-info@education.gouv.fr; internet www.enseignementsup-recherche.gouv.fr.

Ministry of Overseas Territories: 27 rue Oudinot, 75007 Paris; tel. 1-53-69-20-00; internet www.outre-mer.gouv.fr.

Ministry of Social Affairs: 14 ave Duquesne, 75007 Paris; tel. 1-40-56-60-00; internet www.social-sante.gouv.fr.

Ministry of Women's Rights, Cities, Youth and Sports: 110 rue de Grenelle, 75357 Paris Cedex 07; tel. 1-40-45-90-00; internet www.sports.gouv.fr.

President and Legislature

PRESIDENT

Presidential Election, First Ballot, 22 April 2012

Candidates	Votes	% of votes
François Hollande (Parti Socialiste)	10,272,705	28.63
Nicolas Sarkozy (Union pour un Mouvement Populaire)	9,753,629	27.18
Marine Le Pen (Front National)	6,421,426	17.90
Jean-Luc Mélenchon (Front de Gauche)*	3,984,822	11.10
François Bayrou (Mouvement Démocrate)	3,275,122	9.13
Eva Joly (Europe Ecologie Les Verts)	828,345	2.31
Nicolas Dupont-Aignan (Debout la République)	643,907	1.79
Philippe Poutou (Nouveau Parti Anticapitaliste)	411,160	1.15
Nathalie Arthaud (Lutte Ouvrière)	202,548	0.56
Jacques Cheminade (Solidarité et Progrès)	89,545	0.25
Total	35,883,209	100.00

* A coalition of left-wing parties, including the Parti de Gauche and the Parti Communiste.

Presidential Election, Second Ballot, 6 May 2012

Candidate	Votes	% of votes
François Hollande (Parti Socialiste)	18,000,668	51.64
Nicolas Sarkozy (Union pour un Mouvement Populaire)	16,860,685	48.36
Total	34,861,353	100.00

PARLIAMENT
(Parlement)

**National Assembly
(Assemblée Nationale)**

126 rue de l'Université, 75355 Paris Cedex 07; tel. 1-40-63-60-00; fax 1-45-55-75-23; e-mail infos@assemblee-nationale.fr; internet www.assemblee-nationale.fr.

President: CLAUDE BARTOLONE (PS).

General Election, 10 June and 17 June 2012

Party	% of votes cast in first ballot	% of votes cast in second ballot*	Seats
Parti Socialiste (PS)	29.35	40.91	280
Union pour un Mouvement Populaire (UMP)	27.12	37.95	194
Various left-wing candidates	3.40	1.82	22
Europe Ecologie Les Verts	5.46	3.60	17
Various right-wing candidates	3.51	3.08	15
Parti Radical de Gauche	1.65	2.34	12
Le Nouveau Centre	2.20	2.47	12
Front de Gauche†	6.91	1.08	10
Parti Radical	1.24	1.35	6
Front National (FN)	13.60	3.66	2
Alliance Centriste (AC)	0.60	0.54	2
Le Centre pour la France (CEN)‡	1.77	0.49	2
Regionalist candidates	0.56	0.59	2
Various far-right candidates	0.19	0.13	1
Various far-left candidates	0.98	—	—
Various ecologist candidates	0.96	—	—
Others	0.52	—	—
Total	100.00	100.00	577

* Held where no candidate had won the requisite overall majority in the first ballot, between candidates who had received at least 12.5% of the votes in that round. The total number of valid votes cast was 25,952,859 in the first round, and 23,029,183 in the second round.

† Alliance of Parti Communiste Français and Parti de Gauche.

‡ Alliance led by Mouvement Démocrate (MoDem).

**Senate
(Sénat)**

15 rue de Vaugirard, 75291 Paris Cedex 06; tel. 1-42-34-20-00; fax 1-42-34-26-77; e-mail communication@senat.fr; internet www.senat.fr.

President: JEAN-PIERRE BEL (PS).

Senators are elected for a term of six years, with one-half of the seats renewable every three years; seats are allocated through a combination of majority voting and proportional representation. The minimum age for eligible candidates to the Sénat is 30 years.

A partial election to the Sénat took place on 25 September 2011, when the number of senators was increased to 348. The strength of the parties at 11 October 2011 was as follows:

Grouping	Seats
Groupe Socialiste, Apparentés et Groupe Europe Écologie Les Verts Rattaché	140
Groupe Union pour un Mouvement Populaire	132
Groupe de l'Union Centriste et Républicaine	31
Groupe Communiste Républicain et Citoyen	21
Groupe du Rassemblement Démocratique et Social Européen	16
Non-attached	8
Total	348

Territorial Collectivity of Corsica

In 1992 Corsica officially assumed the status of a Collectivité Territoriale (Territorial Collectivity), in accordance with legislation approved by Parliament in the previous year, gaining a degree of political and administrative autonomy. The island of Corsica is generally considered as one of the 22 régions of metropolitan France.

The 51-member Assemblée de Corse (Corsican Assembly) was constituted following elections held in March 1992. Members of the Assembly are elected by universal suffrage for a term of six years, according to a system of proportional representation. Three additional seats are allocated to the list receiving the largest number of votes. The nine-member Conseil Exécutif (Executive Council) is elected by the Assembly from among the members of the largest parliamentary group.

President of the Executive Council: PAUL GIACOBBI (PRG—L'Alternance).

Members: PAUL MARIE BARTOLI, EMMANUELLE DE GENTILI, PIERRE GHIONGA, MARIA GUIDICELLI, JEAN-LOUIS LUCIANI, MARIE-THÉRÈSE OLIVESI, VANINA PIERI, JEAN ZUCCARELLI.

President of the Corsican Assembly: DOMINIQUE BUCCHINI (PCF—L'Alternance).

Corsican Assembly (Assemblée de Corse): 22 cours Grandval, 20187 Ajaccio Cedex 1; tel. 4-95-51-64-64; fax 4-95-51-67-75; e-mail contact@corse.fr; internet www.corse.fr; f. 1982.

Election, 14 and 21 March 2010

	Seats
L'Alternance*	24
Rassembler pour la Corse†	12
Femu a Corsica‡	11
Corsica Libera	4
Total	51

* Electoral list comprising the Parti Radical de Gauche (PRG), the Parti Communiste Français (PCF), the Parti de Gauche (PG), the Parti Socialiste (PS) and allies.

† Electoral list comprising the Union pour un Mouvement Populaire (UMP) and allies.

‡ Moderate nationalist electoral list.

Political Organizations

Alliance Centriste (AC): 31 rue de Tournon, 75006 Paris; tel. 1-46-33-77-60; fax 1-46-33-77-91; internet www.alliancecentriste.fr; f. 2009; centrist; part of the Union des Démocrates et Indépendants; Pres. JEAN ARTHUIS; Sec.-Gen. THIERRY BENOIT.

Les Alternatifs: 40 rue de Malte, 75011 Paris; tel. 1-43-57-44-80; fax 1-43-57-64-50; e-mail contact@alternatifs.org; internet www.alternatifs.org; f. 1997; socialist, ecologist, feminist; Spokesperson JEAN-JACQUES BOISLAROUSSIE.

Centre National des Indépendants et Paysans (CNIP): 6 rue Quentin Bauchart, 75008 Paris; tel. 1-47-23-47-00; fax 1-47-23-47-03; e-mail contact@cni.asso.fr; internet www.cni.asso.fr; f. 1949; right-wing; works with the Union pour un Mouvement Populaire; Pres. GILLES BOURDOULEIX; Sec.-Gen. BRUNO NORTH.

Chasse Pêche Nature Traditions (CPNT): 245 blvd de la Paix, BP 87546, 64075 Pau Cedex; tel. 5-59-14-71-71; fax 5-59-14-71-72; internet www.cpnt.fr; f. 1989 as Chasse-Pêche-Traditions; emphasizes defence of rural traditions and the sovereignty of the state within Europe; Pres. FRÉDÉRIC NIHOUS; Sec.-Gen. ERICK MAROLLEAU.

Corsica Libera: 1 rue Miot, BP 304, 20297 Bastia Cedex; tel. 4-95-31-66-96; fax 4-95-31-78-91; e-mail corsicalibera@corsicalibera.com; internet www.corsicalibera.com; f. 2009 by merger of 4 Corsican separatist parties, incl. Corsica Nazione (f. 1992); Pres. ERIC SIMONI; Leader JEAN-GUY TALAMONI.

Debout la République (DLR): 17 rue des Rossignols, BP 18, 91330 Yerres; tel. 1-69-49-17-37; e-mail courrier@debout-la-republique.fr; internet www.debout-la-republique.fr; f. 2008; Gaullist, republican; Pres. NICOLAS DUPONT-AIGNAN; Sec.-Gen. JEAN-PIERRE ANTONI.

Europe Ecologie Les Verts: 247 rue du Faubourg Saint-Martin, 75010 Paris; tel. 1-53-19-53-19; fax 1-53-19-03-93; e-mail verts@lesverts.fr; internet www.lesverts.fr; f. 1984; ecologist; fmrly called Les Verts; name changed to above following merger with Europe Ecologie in Nov. 2010; Nat. Sec. EMMANUELLE DURAND.

Force Européenne Démocrate: 176 ave Jean Jaurès, 93000 Bobigny; internet www.forceeuropeennedemocrate.fr; f. 2012; centrist; part of the Union des Démocrates et Indépendants; Pres. JEAN-CHRISTOPHE LAGARDE.

Front National (FN): 76–78 rue des Suisses, 92000 Nanterre; tel. 1-41-20-20-00; fax 1-41-12-10-86; e-mail contact@frontnational.com; internet www.frontnational.com; f. 1972; extreme right-wing nationalist; Pres. MARINE LE PEN; Sec.-Gen. STEEVE BRIOIS.

Génération Ecologie: 35 ave du Pont Juvenal, 34000 Montepellier; tel. and fax 9-52-47-48-40; e-mail gen.ecologie@gmail.com; internet www.generationecologie.org; f. 1991; ecologist; Pres. YVES PIETRASANTA; Sec.-Gen. FRÉDÉRIC BŒUF-SALOR.

La Gauche Moderne: 7 rue Boutard, 92200 Neuilly-sur-Seine; e-mail contact.lagauchemoderne@gmail.com; internet www.lagauchemoderne.org; f. 2007; moderate, left-wing; part of the Union des Démocrates et Indépendants; Pres. JEAN-MARIE BOCKEL; Sec.-Gen. CHRISTIAN DEBÈVE.

Lutte Ouvrière (LO): BP 233, 75865 Paris Cedex 18; tel. 1-48-10-86-20; fax 1-48-10-86-26; e-mail contact@lutte-ouvriere.org; internet www.lutte-ouvriere.org; f. 1968; Trotskyist; Spokesperson NATHALIE ARTHAUD.

Mouvement Démocrate (MoDem): 133 bis rue de l'Université, 75007 Paris; tel. 1-53-59-20-00; fax 1-53-59-20-59; internet www.mouvementdemocrate.fr; f. 1978 as the Union pour la Démocratie Française (UDF) to unite for electoral purposes non-Gaullist 'majority' candidates; reconstituted as a unified party in 1998; reconstituted in November 2007 to oppose the UMP; elements of the UDF allied to fmr President, Nicolas Sarkozy, left the party and formed the Nouveau Centre in May 2007; contested the 2012 legislative elections as the main part of the Le Centre pour la France (CEN) coalition; Pres. FRANÇOIS BAYROU; Sec.-Gen. MARC FESNEAU.

Mouvement Ecologiste Indépendant (MEI): 26 ter rue Nicolaï, 75012 Paris; tel. 3-84-47-48-80; e-mail jacques.lancon@orange.fr; internet m-e-i.fr; f. 1994; ecologist; 1,000 mems; Pres. ANTOINE WAECHTER; Nat. Sec. JACQUES MAUHOURAT.

Mouvement National Républicain (MNR): BP 10008, 93161 Noisy-le-Grand Cedex; tel. 9-51-45-84-93; fax 9-51-45-84-93; e-mail presse@m-n-r.fr; internet www.m-n-r.fr; f. 1999 by breakaway faction of FN; extreme right-wing nationalist; Sec.-Gen. HUBERT SAVON.

Mouvement pour la France (MPF): 33 ave de Ségur, 75007 Paris; e-mail contact@pourlafrance.fr; internet www.pourlafrance.fr; f. 1994; far-right, nationalist; Pres. PHILIPPE DE VILLIERS; Sec.-Gen. PATRICK LOUIS.

Mouvement Républicain et Citoyen (MRC): 3 ave de Corbéra, 75012 Paris; tel. 1-55-78-05-40; fax 1-44-83-83-10; e-mail contact@mrc-france.org; internet www.mrc-france.org; f. 2002 as Pôle Républicain on the basis of the Mouvement des Citoyens; present name adopted 2003; socialist; sceptical of increased European integration or devolution of powers from the nation-state; Pres. JEAN-LUC LAURENT.

Le Nouveau Centre: 84 rue de Grenelle, 75007 Paris; tel. 1-44-39-28-00; fax 1-44-39-28-09; e-mail contact@le-nouveaucentre.org; internet www.le-nouveaucentre.org; f. 2007 by mems of the UDF allied to the then President, Nicolas Sarkozy, and his UMP party; part of the Union des Démocrates et Indépendants; Pres. HERVÉ MORIN; Sec.-Gen. PHILIPPE VIGIER; Parliamentary Leader FRANÇOIS SAUVADET.

Nouveau Parti Anticapitaliste (NPA): 2 rue Richard Lenoir, 93100 Montreuil; tel. 1-48-70-42-30; fax 1-48-59-39-59; e-mail ecrire@npa2009.org; internet www.npa2009.org; f. Feb. 2009 to replace the dissolved Ligue Communiste Révolutionnaire (LCR); socialist, democratic, ecologist; seeks to break with traditional hierarchical party structures; 9,123 mems; Principal Speaker CHRISTINE POUPIN.

Parti Communiste Français (PCF): 2 place du Colonel Fabien, 75019 Paris; tel. 1-40-40-12-12; fax 1-40-40-13-56; e-mail pcf@pcf.fr; internet www.pcf.fr; advocates independent foreign policy; formed the Front de Gauche with the Parti de Gauche in 2008; Nat. Sec PIERRE LAURENT.

Parti de Gauche (PG): 63 ave de la République, 75011 Paris; e-mail contact@lepartidegauche.fr; internet www.lepartidegauche.fr; f. 2008 by fmr mems of PS and MARS-Gauche Républicaine; left-wing, republican; formed the Front de Gauche with the Parti Communiste Français in 2008; Co-Pres JEAN-LUC MÉLENCHON, MARTINE BILLARD.

Parti Radical: 1 place de Valois, 75001 Paris; tel. 1-42-61-02-02; fax 1-42-61-02-04; e-mail contact@laurenthenart.com; internet www.partiradical.net; f. 1901; fmrly affiliated to the UMP; part of the Union des Démocrates et Indépendants; Sec.-Gen. and acting Pres. LAURENT HÉNART.

Parti Radical de Gauche (PRG): 13 rue Duroc, 75007 Paris; tel. 1-45-66-67-68; fax 1-45-66-47-93; e-mail prg@prg.com.fr; internet www.planeteradicale.org; f. 1972 as the Mouvement des Radicaux de Gauche; left-wing; Pres. JEAN-MICHEL BAYLET; Sec.-Gen. JEAN-BERNARD BROS.

Parti Socialiste (PS): 10 rue de Solférino, 75333 Paris Cedex 07; tel. 1-45-56-77-00; fax 1-47-05-15-78; e-mail interps@parti-socialiste.fr; internet www.parti-socialiste.fr; f. 1971; First Sec. JEAN-CHRISTOPHE CAMBADÉLIS.

Rassemblement pour l'Indépendance et la Souveraineté de la France (RIF): BP 10014, 75362 Paris Cedex 08; tel. and fax 1-46-44-94-16; e-mail secretariat.rif@tele2.fr; f. 2003; nationalist, opposed to the transfer of powers from nation-states to the European Union; Pres. ALAIN BOURNAZEL; Sec.-Gen. ROBERT CHARPENTIER.

République Solidaire: 91 bis rue du Cherche-Midi, 75006 Paris; tel. 1-84-16-10-47; internet www.republiquesolidaire.fr; f. 2010; republican; Pres. JEAN-PIERRE GRAND; Sec.-Gen. MARC BERNIER.

Solidarité et Progrès (S&P): BP 27, 92114 Clichy Cedex; tel. 1-76-69-14-50; fax 1-47-39-05-80; internet www.solidariteetprogres.org; f. 1996; associated with the LaRouche movement; Pres. JACQUES CHEMINADE.

Union des Démocrates et Indépendants (UDI): 22 bis rue des Volontaires, 75015 Paris; tel. 1-53-71-20-17; e-mail contact@parti-udi.fr; internet www.parti-udi.fr; f. 2012; centrist; comprises several ind. parties, incl. Alliance Centriste, Force Européenne Démocrate, La Gauche Moderne, Nouveau Centre, Parti Radical, Parti Libéral Démocrate; Pres. YVES JÉGO (acting).

Union pour un Mouvement Populaire (UMP): 238 rue de Vaugirard, 75015 Paris; tel. 1-40-76-60-00; e-mail webmaster@u-m-p.org; internet www.u-m-p.org; f. 2002; founded as Union pour la Majorité Présidentielle by mems of the fmr Rassemblement pour la République and Démocratie Liberale parties, in conjunction with elements of the UDF, now MoDem (q.v.); centre-right grouping formed to ensure that President Jacques Chirac had a majority grouping in the Assemblée Nationale; 317,771 mems. (Jan. 2007); Pres. JEAN-FRANÇOIS COPÉ; First Vice-Pres. JEAN-PIERRE RAFFARIN.

Diplomatic Representation

EMBASSIES IN FRANCE

Afghanistan: 32 ave Raphaël, 75016 Paris; tel. 1-45-25-05-29; fax 1-42-24-47-14; e-mail contact@ambafghanistan-fr.com; internet www.ambafghanistan-fr.com; Ambassador Dr ASSAD OMER.

Albania: 57 ave Marceau, 75116 Paris; tel. 1-47-23-31-00; fax 1-47-23-59-85; e-mail contact@amb-albanie.fr; internet www.amb-albanie.fr; Ambassador DRITAN TOLA.

Algeria: 50 rue de Lisbonne, 75008 Paris; tel. 1-53-93-20-20; fax 1-53-93-20-69; e-mail chancellerie@amb-algerie.fr; internet www.amb-algerie.fr; Ambassador AMAR BENDJAMA.

Andorra: 1 place d'Andorre, 75016 Paris; tel. 1-40-06-03-30; fax 1-40-06-03-64; e-mail ambaixada@andorra.ad; Ambassador MARIA UBACH FONT.

Angola: 19 ave Foch, 75116 Paris; tel. 1-45-01-58-20; fax 1-45-00-33-71; e-mail sg@emb-ang.fr; internet www.emb-ang.fr; Ambassador MIGUEL DA COSTA.

Argentina: 6 rue Cimarosa, 75116 Paris; tel. 1-44-05-27-00; fax 1-45-53-46-33; e-mail efran@mrecic.gov.ar; internet www.efran.mrecic.gov.ar; Ambassador MARIA DEL CARMEN SQUEFF.

Armenia: 9 rue Viète, 75017 Paris; tel. 1-42-12-98-00; fax 1-42-12-98-03; e-mail ambarmen@wanadoo.fr; internet www.france.mfa.am; Ambassador VIGUEN TCHITETCHIAN.

Australia: 4 rue Jean Rey, 75724 Paris; tel. 1-40-59-33-00; fax 1-40-59-33-10; e-mail info.paris@dfat.gov.au; internet www.france.embassy.gov.au; Ambassador RIC WELLS.

Austria: 6 rue Fabert, 75007 Paris; tel. 1-40-63-30-63; fax 1-45-55-63-65; e-mail paris-ob@bmeia.gv.at; internet www.amb-autriche.fr; Ambassador Dr URSULA PLASSNIK.

Azerbaijan: 78 ave d'Iéna, 75016 Paris; tel. 1-44-18-60-20; fax 1-44-18-60-25; e-mail paris@mission.mfa.gov.az; internet www.azambassade.fr; Ambassador ELCHIN AMIRBAYOV.

Bahrain: 3 bis place des Etats-Unis, 75116 Paris; tel. 1-47-23-48-68; fax 1-47-20-55-75; e-mail ambassade@ambahrein-france.com; internet www.ambahrein-france.com; Ambassador Dr NASSER AL-BELOOSHI.

Bangladesh: 9 ave Henry Martin, 75016 Paris; tel. 1-46-51-90-33; fax 1-46-51-90-35; e-mail bangembpar@yahoo.com; Ambassador MOHAMMED ENAMUL KABIR.

Belarus: 38 blvd Suchet, 75016 Paris; tel. 1-44-14-69-79; fax 1-44-14-69-70; e-mail france@mfa.gov.by; internet france.mfa.gov.by; Ambassador PAVEL LATUSHKA.

Belgium: 9 rue de Tilsitt, 75840 Paris Cedex 17; tel. 1-44-09-39-39; fax 1-47-54-07-64; e-mail paris@diplobel.fed.be; internet www.diplomatie.be/paris; Ambassador PATRICK VERCAUTEREN DRUBBEL.

Benin: 87 ave Victor Hugo, 75116 Paris; tel. 1-45-00-98-82; fax 1-45-01-82-02; e-mail contact@ambassade-benin.fr; internet www.ambassade-benin.fr; Ambassador JULES-ARMAND ANIAMBOSSOU.

Bolivia: 12 ave du Président Kennedy, 75016 Paris; tel. 1-42-24-93-44; fax 1-45-25-86-23; e-mail embolivia.paris@wanadoo.fr; Ambassador JEAN-PAUL GUEVARA ÁVILA.

Bosnia and Herzegovina: 174 rue de Courcelles, 75017 Paris; tel. 1-42-67-34-22; fax 1-40-53-85-22; e-mail amb.pariz@mvp.gov.ba; Ambassador NINA SAJIĆ.

Brazil: 34 cours Albert 1er, 75008 Paris; tel. 1-45-61-63-00; fax 1-42-89-03-45; e-mail ambassade@bresil.org; internet www.bresil.org; Ambassador JOSÉ MAURICIO BUSTANI.

Brunei: 7 rue de Presbourg, 75116 Paris; tel. 1-53-64-67-60; fax 1-53-64-67-83; e-mail ambassade.brunei@wanadoo.fr; Ambassador Dato' Paduka ZAINIDI Haji SIDUP.

Bulgaria: 1 ave Rapp, 75007 Paris; tel. 1-45-51-85-90; fax 1-45-51-18-68; e-mail bulgamb@wanadoo.fr; internet www.amb-bulgarie.fr; Ambassador ANGUEL TCHOLAKOV.

Burkina Faso: 159 blvd Haussmann, 75008 Paris; tel. 1-43-59-90-63; fax 1-42-56-50-07; e-mail contact@ambaburkina-fr.org; internet ambaburkina-fr.org; Ambassador ERIC Y. TIARÉ.

Burundi: 10–12 rue de l'Orme, 75019 Paris; tel. 1-45-20-60-61; fax 1-45-20-02-54; e-mail ambabu.paris@wanadoo.fr; Ambassador DIEUDONNÉ NDABARUSHIMANA.

Cambodia: 4 rue Adolphe Yvon, 75116 Paris; tel. 1-45-03-47-20; fax 1-45-03-47-40; e-mail arc@ambcambodgeparis.info; internet www.ambcambodgeparis.info; Ambassador NARANG NOUTH.

Cameroon: 73 rue d'Auteuil, 75016 Paris; tel. 1-47-43-98-33; fax 1-46-51-24-52; Ambassador LEJEUNE MBELLA MBELLA.

Canada: 35 ave Montaigne, 75008 Paris; tel. 1-44-43-29-00; fax 1-44-43-29-99; e-mail paris_webmaster@international.gc.ca; internet www.canadainternational.gc.ca/france; Ambassador LAWRENCE CANNON.

Cape Verde: 3 rue de Rigny, 75008 Paris; tel. 1-42-12-73-50; fax 1-40-53-04-36; e-mail ambassade-cap-vert2@wanadoo.fr; internet www.ambassadecapvert.fr; Ambassador MARIA FÁTIMA DA VEIGA.

Central African Republic: 30 rue des Perchamps, 75116 Paris; tel. 1-45-25-39-74; fax 1-55-74-40-25; e-mail accueil@amb-rcaparis.org; internet www.amb-rcaparis.org; Ambassador EMMANUEL BONGO PASSI.

Chad: 65 rue des Belles Feuilles, 75116 Paris; tel. 1-45-53-36-75; fax 1-45-53-16-09; e-mail ambassadedutchadparis@wanadoo.fr; internet ambatchad-paris.org; Ambassador HISSÈNE BRAHIM TAHA.

Chile: 2 ave de la Motte-Picquet, 75007 Paris; tel. 1-44-18-59-60; fax 1-44-18-59-61; e-mail echile.francia@minrel.gov.cl; internet chileabroad.gov.cl/francia; Ambassador JORGE EDWARDS VALDÉS.

China, People's Republic: 11 ave George V, 75008 Paris; tel. 1-49-52-19-50; fax 1-47-20-24-22; e-mail chinaemb_fr@mfa.gov.cn; internet www.amb-chine.fr; Ambassador ZHAI JUN.

Colombia: 22 rue de l'Elysée, 75008 Paris; tel. 1-42-65-46-08; fax 1-42-66-18-60; e-mail eparis@cancilleria.gov.co; internet www.embcolfrancia.com; Ambassador FEDERICO RENJIFO.

Comoros: 20 rue Marbeau, 75116 Paris; tel. 1-40-67-90-54; fax 1-40-67-72-96; Ambassador AHMED BOURHANE.

Congo, Democratic Republic: 32 cours Albert 1er, 75008 Paris; tel. 1-42-25-57-50; fax 1-45-62-16-52; e-mail contact@ambardcparis.com; internet www.ambardcparis.com; Ambassador CHRISTIAN ILEKA ATOKI.

Congo, Republic: 37 bis rue Paul Valéry, 75116 Paris; tel. 1-45-00-60-57; fax 1-40-67-17-33; e-mail ambacongo_france@yahoo.fr; Ambassador HENRI LOPES.

Costa Rica: 4, Square Rapp, 4ème étage, 75007 Paris; tel. 1-45-78-96-96; fax 1-45-78-99-66; e-mail embcr@wanadoo.fr; internet www.ambassade-costarica.org; Ambassador CARLOS BONILLA SANDOVAL.

Côte d'Ivoire: 102 ave Raymond Poincaré, 75116 Paris; tel. 1-53-64-62-62; fax 1-45-00-47-97; e-mail rciparis@ambassadecotedivoire.fr; internet www.ambassadecotedivoire.fr; Ambassador CHARLES PROVIDENCE GOMIS.

Croatia: 7 sq. Thiers, 75116 Paris; tel. 1-53-70-02-80; fax 1-53-70-02-90; e-mail vrh.pariz@mvep.hr; internet fr.mvp.hr; Ambassador IVO GOLDSTEIN.

Cuba: 16 rue de Presles, 75015 Paris; tel. 1-45-67-55-35; fax 1-45-66-80-92; e-mail embacu@ambacuba.fr; internet www.cubadiplomatica.cu/francia; Ambassador HÉCTOR IGARZA.

Cyprus: 23 rue Galilée, 75116 Paris; tel. 1-47-20-86-28; fax 1-40-70-13-44; e-mail paris@mfa.gov.cy; Ambassador MARIOS LYSSIOTIS.

Czech Republic: 15 ave Charles Floquet, 75007 Paris; tel. 1-40-65-13-00; fax 1-40-65-13-13; e-mail paris@embassy.mzv.cz; internet www.mzv.cz/paris; Ambassador MARIE CHATARDOVÁ.

Denmark: 77 ave Marceau, 75116 Paris; tel. 1-44-31-21-21; fax 1-44-31-21-88; e-mail paramb@um.dk; internet www.ambparis.um.dk; Ambassador ANNA DORTE RIGGELSEN.

Djibouti: 26 rue Emile Ménier, 75116 Paris; tel. 1-47-27-49-22; fax 1-45-53-50-53; e-mail ambassadeur@ambdjibouti.org; Ambassador RACHAD FARAH.

Dominican Republic: 45 rue de Courcelles, 75008 Paris; tel. 1-53-63-95-95; fax 1-45-63-35-63; e-mail embajadom@wanadoo.fr; internet www.embajadadominicana.fr; Ambassador ROSA MARGARITA HERNANDEZ.

Ecuador: 34 ave de Messine, 75008 Paris; tel. 1-45-61-10-21; fax 1-42-56-06-64; e-mail embajadaenfrancia@ambassade-equateur.fr; internet www.ambassade-equateur.fr; Ambassador CARLOS JÁTIVA NARANJO.

Egypt: 56 ave d'Iéna, 75116 Paris; tel. 1-53-67-88-30; fax 1-47-23-06-43; e-mail paris_emb@mfa.gov.eg; Ambassador NASSER KAMEL.

El Salvador: 12 rue Galilée, 75116 Paris; tel. 1-47-20-42-02; fax 1-40-70-01-95; e-mail embparis@wanadoo.fr; Ambassador FRANCISCO GALINDO-VELEZ.

Equatorial Guinea: 29 blvd de Courcelles, 75008 Paris; tel. 1-45-61-98-20; fax 1-45-61-98-25; e-mail embarege_paris@hotmail.com; Ambassador MARIOLA BINDANG OBIANG.

Eritrea: 1 rue de Staël, 75015 Paris; tel. 1-43-06-15-56; fax 1-43-06-07-51; Ambassador FASSIL GEBRESELASSIE TEKLE.

Estonia: 17 rue de la Baume, 75008 Paris; tel. 1-56-62-22-00; fax 1-49-52-05-65; e-mail estonie@mfa.ee; internet www.est-emb.fr; Ambassador SVEN JÜRGENSON.

Ethiopia: 35 ave Charles Floquet, 75007 Paris; tel. 1-47-83-83-95; fax 1-43-06-52-14; e-mail embeth@free.fr; Ambassador NEGA TSEGAYE TESSEMA.

Finland: 1 place de Finlande, 75007 Paris; tel. 1-44-18-19-20; fax 1-45-55-51-57; e-mail sanomat.par@formin.fi; internet www.amb-finlande.fr; Ambassador RISTO PIIPPONEN.

Gabon: 41 rue de la Bienfaisance, 75008 Paris; tel. 1-42-99-68-68; fax 1-72-81-05-89; e-mail cab.ambassadegabonfrance@yahoo.fr; internet www.affaires-etrangeres.gouv.ga/ambassade/france; Ambassador GERMAIN NGOYO MOUSSAVOU.

The Gambia: 117 rue St Lazare, 75008 Paris; tel. 1-73-18-00-60; fax 1-53-04-05-99; e-mail ambgambia_france117@hotmail.com; Ambassador OUSMAN BADJIE.

Georgia: 104 ave Raymond Poincaré, 75116 Paris; tel. 1-45-02-16-16; fax 1-45-02-16-01; e-mail ambassade.georgie@mfa.gov.ge; internet www.france.mfa.gov.ge; Ambassador ECATERINE SIRADZE-DELAUNAY.

Germany: 13–15 ave Franklin D. Roosevelt, 75008 Paris; tel. 1-53-83-45-00; fax 1-53-83-45-02; e-mail ambassade@amb-allemagne.fr; internet www.paris.diplo.de; Ambassador SUSANNE MARIANNE WASUM-RAINER.

Ghana: 8 Villa Saïd, 75116 Paris; tel. 1-45-00-09-50; fax 1-45-00-81-95; e-mail ambghanaparis@yahoo.fr; Ambassador GENEVIÈVE DELALI TSEGAH.

Greece: 17 rue Auguste Vacquerie, 75116 Paris; tel. 1-47-23-72-28; fax 1-47-23-73-85; e-mail mfapar@wanadoo.fr; internet www.amb-grece.fr; Ambassador THÉODORE M. PASSAS.

Guatemala: 2 rue Villebois-Marueil, 75017 Paris; tel. 1-42-27-78-63; fax 1-47-54-02-06; Ambassador MARCO TULIO CHICAS SOSA.

Guinea: 51 rue de la Faisanderie, 75116 Paris; tel. 1-47-04-81-48; fax 1-47-04-57-65; e-mail accueil@ambaguinee-paris.org; Ambassador AMARA CAMARA.

Guinea-Bissau: 94 rue Saint Lazare, 75009 Paris; tel. 1-48-74-36-39; fax 1-48-78-36-39; e-mail ambaguineebxo@wanadoo.fr; Ambassador (vacant).

Haiti: 10 rue Théodule Ribot, BP 275, 75017 Paris; tel. 1-47-63-47-78; fax 1-42-27-02-05; e-mail ambhaitiparis@orange.fr; Chargé d'affaires a.i. FRITZNER GASPARD.

Holy See: 10 ave du Président Wilson, 75116 Paris (Apostolic Nunciature); tel. 1-53-23-01-50; fax 1-47-23-65-44; e-mail noncapfr@wanadoo.fr; Apostolic Nuncio Most Rev. LUIGI VENTURA.

Honduras: 8 rue Crevaux, 75116 Paris; tel. 1-47-55-86-45; fax 1-47-55-86-48; e-mail ambassade.honduras@yahoo.com; Ambassador GUSTAVO ADOLFO CARVAJAL SINISTERRA.

Hungary: 5 bis sq. de l'ave Foch, 75116 Paris; tel. 1-45-00-94-97; fax 1-56-36-02-68; e-mail mission.par@mfa.gov.hu; internet www.mfa.gov.hu/emb/paris; Ambassador Dr LÁSZLÓ TRÓCSÁNYI.

Iceland: 52 ave Victor Hugo, 75116 Paris; tel. 1-44-17-32-85; fax 1-40-67-99-96; e-mail paris@mfa.is; internet www.iceland.is/fr; Ambassador BERGLIND ÁSGEIRSDÓTTIR.

India: 15 rue Alfred Dehodencq, 75016 Paris; tel. 1-40-50-70-70; fax 1-40-50-09-96; e-mail pic.2@wanadoo.fr; internet www.amb-inde.fr; Ambassador ARUN K. SINGH.

Indonesia: 47–49 rue Cortambert, 75016 Paris; tel. 1-45-03-07-60; fax 1-45-04-50-32; e-mail komparis@online.fr; internet www.amb-indonesie.fr; Ambassador REZLAN ISHAR JENIE.

Iran: 4 ave d'Iéna, 75116 Paris; tel. 1-40-69-79-00; fax 1-40-70-01-57; e-mail cabinet@amb-iran.fr; internet www.amb-iran.fr; Ambassador ALI AHANI.

Iraq: 53 rue de la Faisanderie, 75016 Paris; tel. 1-45-53-33-70; fax 1-45-53-33-80; e-mail paremb@iraqmfamail.com; internet www.amb-iraq.fr; Ambassador FARID MUSTAFA KAMIL YASSEIN.

Ireland: 12 ave Foch, 75116 Paris; tel. 1-44-17-67-00; fax 1-44-17-67-50; e-mail paris@dfa.ie; internet www.embassyofireland.fr; Ambassador RORY MONTGOMERY.

Israel: 3 rue Rabelais, 75008 Paris; tel. 1-40-76-55-00; fax 1-40-76-55-55; e-mail information@paris.mfa.gov.il; internet paris1.mfa.gov.il; Ambassador YOSSI GAL.

Italy: 51 rue de Varenne, 75343 Paris Cedex 07; tel. 1-49-54-03-00; fax 1-45-54-04-10; e-mail ambasciata.parigi@esteri.it; internet www.ambparigi.esteri.it; Ambassador GIANDOMENICO MAGLIANO.

Japan: 7 ave Hoche, 75008 Paris; tel. 1-48-88-62-00; fax 1-42-27-50-81; e-mail info-fr@ps.mofa.go.jp; internet www.fr.emb-japan.go.jp; Ambassador YOICHI SUZUKI.

Jordan: 80 blvd Maurice Barrès, 92200 Neuilly-sur-Seine; tel. 1-55-62-00-00; fax 1-55-62-00-06; e-mail amjo.paris@wanadoo.fr; Ambassador MAKRAM MUSTAFA QUEISI.

Kazakhstan: 59 rue Pierre Charron, 75008 Paris; tel. 1-45-61-52-00; fax 1-45-61-52-01; e-mail info@amb-kazakhstan.fr; internet www.amb-kazakhstan.fr; Ambassador NURLAN DANENOV.

Kenya: 3 rue Freycinet, 75116 Paris; tel. 1-56-62-25-25; fax 1-47-20-44-41; e-mail info@ambassade-kenya.fr; internet www.kenyaembassyparis.org; Ambassador SALMA AHMED.

Korea, Republic: 125 rue de Grenelle, 75007 Paris; tel. 1-47-53-01-01; fax 1-47-53-00-41; e-mail koremb-fr@mofat.go.kr; internet fra.mofat.go.kr; Ambassador LEE HYE-MIN.

Kuwait: 2 rue de Lübeck, 75116 Paris; tel. 1-47-23-54-25; fax 1-47-20-33-59; Ambassador ALI SULAIMAN AL-SAEID.

Laos: 74 ave Raymond Poincaré, 75116 Paris; tel. 1-45-53-02-98; fax 1-47-57-27-89; e-mail ambalaoparis@wanadoo.fr; internet www.laoparis.com; Ambassador KHOUANTA PHALIVONG.

Latvia: 6 villa Saïd, 75116 Paris; tel. 1-53-64-58-10; fax 1-53-64-58-19; e-mail embassy.france@mfa.gov.lv; internet www.am.gov.lv/paris; Ambassador SANITA PAVLUTA-DESLANDES.

Lebanon: 3 villa Copernic, 75116 Paris; tel. 1-40-67-75-75; fax 1-40-67-16-42; e-mail na@ambliban.fr; internet www.ambassadeliban.fr; Chargé d'affaires a.i. GHADY EL KHOURY.

Liberia: 12 place du Général Catroux, 75017 Paris; tel. 1-47-63-58-55; fax 1-42-12-76-14; e-mail libem.paris@wanadoo.fr; Ambassador DUDLEY MCKINLEY THOMAS.

Libya: 6–8 rue Chasseloup-Laubat, 75015 Paris; tel. 1-47-04-71-60; fax 1-47-55-96-25; Sec. of the People's Bureau MANSOUR SAYF AL-NASR.

Lithuania: 22 blvd de Courcelles, 75017 Paris; tel. 1-40-54-50-50; fax 1-40-54-50-75; e-mail amb.fr@urm.lt; internet fr.mfa.lt; Ambassador JOLANTA BALČIŪNIENĖ.

Luxembourg: 33 ave Rapp, 75007 Paris; tel. 1-45-55-13-37; fax 1-45-51-72-29; e-mail paris.amb@mae.etat.lu; internet paris.mae.lu; Ambassador PAUL DÜHR.

Macedonia, former Yugoslav republic: 5 rue de la Faisanderie, 75116 Paris; tel. 1-45-77-10-50; fax 1-45-77-14-84; e-mail paris@mfa.gov.mk; internet www.missions.gov.mk/paris; Ambassador AGRON BUDJAKU.

Madagascar: 4 ave Raphaël, 75016 Paris; tel. 1-45-04-62-11; fax 1-45-03-58-70; e-mail accueil@ambassade-madagascar.fr; Ambassador NARISOA RAJAONARIVONY.

Malaysia: 2 bis rue Bénouville, 75116 Paris; tel. 1-45-53-11-85; fax 1-47-27-34-60; e-mail malparis@kln.gov.my; internet www.kln.gov.my/web/fra_paris; Ambassador TAN SRI ISMAIL OMAN.

Mali: 89 rue du Cherche-Midi, BP 175, 75263 Paris Cedex 06; tel. 1-45-48-58-43; fax 1-45-48-55-34; e-mail ambamali.paris@wanadoo.fr; Ambassador BOUBACAR SIDIKI TOURE.

Malta: 23 rue d'Artois, 75008 Paris; tel. 1-56-59-75-90; fax 1-45-62-00-36; e-mail maltaembassy.paris@gov.mt; internet www.mfa.gov.mt/france; Ambassador VINCENT CAMILLERI.

Mauritania: 5 rue de Montévidéo, 75116 Paris; tel. 1-45-04-88-54; fax 1-40-72-82-96; e-mail ambassade.mauritanie@wanadoo.fr; Ambassador CHEYAKH OULD ELY.

Mauritius: 127 rue de Tocqueville, 75017 Paris; tel. 1-42-27-30-19; fax 1-40-53-02-91; e-mail paris@amb-maurice.fr; Ambassador MOHAMED OULD KHALIL.

Mexico: 9 rue de Longchamp, 75116 Paris; tel. 1-53-70-27-70; fax 1-47-55-65-29; e-mail embfrancia@sre.gob.mx; internet www.sre.gob.mx/francia; Ambassador AGUSTÍN GARCÍA-LÓPEZ.

Moldova: 22 rue Berlioz, 75116 Paris; tel. 1-40-67-11-20; fax 1-40-67-11-23; e-mail ambassade.moldavie@wanadoo.fr; Ambassador OLEG SEREBRIAN.

Monaco: 22 blvd Suchet, 75116 Paris; tel. 1-45-04-74-54; fax 1-45-04-45-16; e-mail ambassade.en.france@gouv.mc; Ambassador SOPHIE THÉVENOUX.

Mongolia: 5 ave Robert Schuman, 92100 Boulogne-Billancourt; tel. 1-46-05-28-12; fax 1-46-05-30-16; e-mail info@ambassadedemongolie.fr; internet www.ambassademongolie.fr; Ambassador MUNDAGBAATAR BATSAIKHAN.

Montenegro: 216 blvd Saint-Germain, 75007 Paris; tel. 1-53-63-80-30; fax 1-42-22-83-90; e-mail ambasadacg@orange.fr; Ambassador IRENA RADOVIC.

Morocco: 5 rue Le Tasse, 75016 Paris; tel. 1-45-20-69-35; fax 1-45-20-22-58; e-mail info@amb-maroc.fr; internet www.amb-maroc.fr; Ambassador CHAKIB BENMOUSSA.

Mozambique: 82 rue Laugier, 75017 Paris; tel. 1-47-64-91-32; fax 1-44-15-90-13; e-mail embamocparis@wanadoo.fr; Ambassador ALEXANDRE DA CONCEIÇÃO ZANDAMELA.

Myanmar: 60 rue de Courcelles, 75008 Paris; tel. 1-56-88-15-90; fax 1-45-62-13-30; e-mail me-paris@wanadoo.fr; Ambassador HAN THU.

Namibia: 80 ave Foch, 75016 Paris; tel. 1-44-17-32-65; fax 1-44-17-32-73; e-mail info@embassyofnamibia.fr; internet www.embassyofnamibia.fr; Ambassador FRIEDA NANGULA ITHETE.

Nepal: 45 bis rue des Acacias, 75017 Paris; tel. 1-46-22-48-67; fax 1-42-27-08-65; e-mail nepalinparis@noos.fr; Ambassador MOHAN KRISHNA SHRESTHA.

Netherlands: 7–9 rue Eblé, 75007 Paris; tel. 1-40-62-33-00; fax 1-40-62-34-56; e-mail ambassade@amb-pays-bas.fr; internet www.amb-pays-bas.fr; Ambassador ED KRONENBURG.

New Zealand: 7 rue Léonard de Vinci, 75116 Paris; tel. 1-45-01-43-43; fax 1-45-01-43-44; e-mail embassy.nz.fr@gmail.com; internet www.nzembassy.com/france; Ambassador ROSEMARY BANKS.

Niger: 154 rue de Longchamp, 75116 Paris; tel. 1-45-04-80-60; fax 1-45-04-79-73; e-mail ambassadeniger@wanadoo.fr; Ambassador ABDERAHAMANE MAYAKI ASSANE.

Nigeria: 173 ave Victor Hugo, 75116 Paris; tel. 1-47-04-68-65; fax 1-47-04-47-54; e-mail embassy@nigeriafrance.com; internet www.nigeriafrance.com; Ambassador HAKEEM O. SULAIMAN.

Norway: 28 rue Bayard, 4e étage, 75008 Paris; tel. 1-53-67-04-00; fax 1-53-67-04-40; e-mail emb.paris@mfa.no; internet www.norvege.no; Ambassador TARALD O. BRAUTASET.

Oman: 50 ave d'Iéna, 75116 Paris; tel. 1-47-23-01-63; fax 1-47-23-77-10; Ambassador AHMED BIN NASSER BIN HAMAD AL-MAHERZI.

Pakistan: 18 rue Lord Byron, 75008 Paris; tel. 1-45-62-23-32; fax 1-45-62-89-15; e-mail pakemb_paris@yahoo.com; internet www.pakembparis.com; Ambassador GHALIB IQBAL.

Panama: 145 ave de Suffren, 75015 Paris; tel. 1-45-66-42-44; fax 1-45-67-99-43; e-mail panaemba.francia@wanadoo.fr; Ambassador HENRY J. FAARUP.

Paraguay: 1 rue St Dominique, 75007 Paris; tel. 1-42-22-85-05; fax 1-42-22-83-57; e-mail paraguay.ambassade@wanadoo.fr; Ambassador EMILIO GIMÉNEZ FRANCO.

Peru: 50 ave Kléber, 75116 Paris; tel. 1-53-70-42-03; fax 1-47-04-32-55; e-mail perou.ambassade@amb-perou.fr; internet www.amb-perou.fr; Ambassador CRISTINA VELITA DE LABOUREIX.

Philippines: 4 Hameau de Boulainvilliers/45 rue du Ranelagh, 75016 Paris; tel. 1-44-14-57-00; fax 1-46-47-56-00; e-mail ambaphilparis@wanadoo.fr; internet www.parispe.dfa.gov.ph; Chargé d'affaires a.i. DEENA JOY D. AMATONG.

Poland: 1 rue de Talleyrand, 75343 Paris Cedex 07; tel. 1-43-17-34-05; fax 1-43-17-35-07; e-mail paris.amb.info@msz.gov.pl; internet www.paryz.msz.gov.pl; Ambassador TOMASZ ORŁOWSKI.

Portugal: 3 rue de Noisiel, 75116 Paris; tel. 1-47-27-35-29; fax 1-44-05-94-02; e-mail mailto@embaixada-portugal-fr.org; internet www.embaixada-portugal-fr.org; Ambassador JOSÉ FILIPE MORAES CABRAL.

Qatar: 1 rue de Tilsitt, 75008 Paris; tel. 1-45-51-90-71; fax 1-45-51-77-07; e-mail paris@mofa.gov.qa; internet www.qatarambassade.com; Ambassador MESHAL BIN HAMAD MOHAMED JABR AL-THANI.

Romania: 5 rue de l'Exposition, 75007 Paris; tel. 1-47-05-10-46; fax 1-45-56-97-47; e-mail secretariat@amb-roumanie.fr; internet paris.mae.ro; Ambassador BOGDAN MAZURU.

Russia: 40–50 blvd Lannes, 75116 Paris; tel. 1-45-04-05-50; fax 1-45-04-17-65; e-mail ambrus@wanadoo.fr; internet www.france.mid.ru; Ambassador ALEKSANDRE ORLOV.

Rwanda: 12 rue Jadin, 75017 Paris; tel. 1-71-19-91-91; fax 1-71-19-99-95; e-mail ambarwanda.paris@gmail.com; Ambassador JACQUES KABALE NYANGEZI.

San Marino: 22 rue d'Artois, 75008 Paris; tel. and fax 1-47-23-04-75; e-mail saint-marin@wanadoo.fr; Ambassador GIANPIERO SAMORI.

Saudi Arabia: 5 ave Hoche, 75008 Paris; tel. 1-56-79-40-00; fax 1-56-79-40-01; e-mail amb.arabiesaoudite@gmail.com; Ambassador Dr MUHAMMAD BIN ISMAIL AL AL-SHEIKH.

Senegal: 14 ave Robert Schuman, 75007 Paris; tel. 1-47-05-39-45; fax 1-45-56-04-30; e-mail repsen@wanadoo.fr; internet www.ambasseneparis.com; Ambassador PAUL BADJI.

Serbia: 5 rue Léonard de Vinci, 75116 Paris; tel. 1-40-72-24-24; fax 1-40-72-24-11; e-mail ambasadapariz@wanadoo.fr; internet www.paris.mfa.gov.rs; Ambassador RAJKO RISTIĆ.

Seychelles: 51 ave Mozart, 75016 Paris; tel. 1-42-30-57-47; fax 1-42-30-57-40; e-mail ambsey@aol.com; Ambassador BERNARD SHAMLAYE.

Singapore: 16 rue Murillo, 75008 Paris; tel. 1-45-00-33-61; fax 1-45-00-61-79; e-mail singemb_par@sgmfa.gov.sg; internet www.mfa.gov.sg/paris; Ambassador TAN YORK CHOR.

Slovakia: 125 rue du Ranelagh, 75016 Paris; tel. 1-77-93-73-33; fax 1-42-88-76-53; e-mail emb.paris@mzv.sk; internet www.mzv.sk/paris; Ambassador MAREK EŠTOK.

Slovenia: 28 rue Bois-le-Vent, 75016 Paris; tel. 1-44-96-50-71; fax 1-45-24-67-05; e-mail vpa@gov.si; internet paris.embassy.si; Ambassador VERONIKA STABEJ.

Somalia: 26 rue Dumont d'Urville, 75116 Paris; tel. 1-39-52-73-08; e-mail webmaster@somaligov.net; internet www.france.somaligov.net; Ambassador (vacant).

South Africa: 59 quai d'Orsay, 75343 Paris Cedex 07; tel. 1-53-59-23-23; fax 1-53-59-23-68; e-mail info@afriquesud.net; internet www.afriquesud.net; Ambassador DOLANA MSIMANG.

Spain: 22 ave Marceau, 75008 Paris Cedex 08; tel. 1-44-43-18-00; fax 1-47-23-59-55; e-mail emb.paris@mae.es; internet www.maec.es/subwebs/embajadas/paris; Ambassador CARLOS BASTARRECHE SAGÜES.

Sri Lanka: 16 rue Spontini, 75016 Paris; tel. 1-55-73-31-31; fax 1-55-73-18-49; e-mail sl.france@wanadoo.fr; internet www.srilankaembassy.fr; Ambassador Prof. KARUNARATNE HANGAWATT.

Sudan: 11 rue Alfred Dehodencq, 75016 Paris; tel. 1-42-25-55-71; fax 1-54-63-66-73; e-mail ambassade-du-soudan@wanadoo.fr; Ambassador NASRELDIN AHMED WALI.

Suriname: 94 rue du Ranelagh, 75016 Paris; tel. 1-45-25-93-00; fax 1-56-43-76-96; e-mail amb.frankrijk@foreignaffairs.gov.sr; internet www.ambassadesurinamefr.org; Ambassador HARVEY H. NAARENDORP.

Sweden: 17 rue Barbet-de-Jouy, 75007 Paris; tel. 1-44-18-88-00; fax 1-44-18-88-40; e-mail info@amb-suede.fr; internet www.swedenabroad.com/paris; Ambassador GUNNAR LUND.

Switzerland: 142 rue de Grenelle, 75007 Paris; tel. 1-49-55-67-00; fax 1-49-55-67-67; e-mail vertretung@par.rep.admin.ch; internet www.eda.admin.ch/paris; Ambassador JEAN-JACQUES DE DARDEL.

Syria: 20 rue Vaneau, 75007 Paris; tel. 1-40-62-61-00; fax 1-47-05-92-73; e-mail info@ambassadesyrie.fr; internet www.ambassadesyrie.fr; Ambassador MOUNZIR MAKHOUS.

Tajikistan: 40 ave de Saxe, 75007 Paris; tel. 1-43-06-45-20; Ambassador HOMIDJON T. NAZAROV.

Tanzania: 13 ave Raymond Poincaré, 75116 Paris; tel. 1-53-70-63-66; fax 1-47-55-05-46; e-mail ambtanzanie@wanadoo.fr; Ambassador BEGUM KARIM-TAJ.

Thailand: 8 rue Greuze, 75116 Paris; tel. 1-56-26-50-50; fax 1-56-26-04-45; e-mail thaipar@wanadoo.fr; internet www.thaiembassy.fr; Ambassador APICHART CHINWANNO.

Togo: 8 rue Alfred Roll, 75017 Paris; tel. 1-43-80-12-13; fax 1-43-80-06-05; e-mail france@ambassadetogo.org; internet france.ambassadetogo.org; Ambassador CALIXTE BATOSSIE MADJOULBA.

Tunisia: 25 rue Barbet-de-Jouy, 75007 Paris; tel. 1-45-55-95-98; fax 1-45-56-02-64; e-mail atn.paris@wanadoo.fr; internet ambassade-tunisie.fr; Ambassador ADEL FEKIH.

Turkey: 16 ave de Lamballe, 75016 Paris; tel. 1-53-92-71-11; fax 1-45-20-41-91; e-mail ambassade.paris@mfa.gov.tr; internet paris.emb.mfa.gov.tr; Ambassador HAKKI AKIL.

Turkmenistan: 13 rue Picot, 75116 Paris; tel. 1-47-55-05-36; fax 1-47-55-05-68; e-mail turkmenamb@free.fr; Ambassador TCHARY G. NIYAZOV.

Uganda: 13 ave Raymond Poincaré, 75116 Paris; tel. 1-56-90-12-20; fax 1-45-05-21-22; e-mail uganda.embassy@club-internet.fr; Ambassador NISHIMA JAYANT MADHVANI.

Ukraine: 21 ave de Saxe, 75007 Paris; tel. 1-43-06-07-37; fax 1-43-06-02-94; e-mail ambassade-ukraine@wanadoo.fr; internet www.mfa.gov.ua/france; Ambassador OLEXANDR KUPCHYSHYN.

United Arab Emirates: 2 blvd de la Tour Maubourg, 75007 Paris; tel. 1-44-34-02-00; fax 1-47-55-61-04; e-mail ambassade.emirats@wanadoo.fr; Ambassador MUHAMMAD ABDULLAH AL-MEER RAEESI.

United Kingdom: 35 rue du Faubourg St Honoré, 75383 Paris Cedex 08; tel. 1-44-51-31-00; fax 1-44-51-32-34; e-mail public.paris@

fco.gov.uk; internet ukinfrance.fco.gov.uk; Ambassador Sir PETER RICKETTS.

USA: 2 ave Gabriel, 75382 Paris Cedex 08; tel. 1-43-12-22-22; fax 1-42-66-97-83; internet france.usembassy.gov; Chargé d'affaires a.i. MARK TAPLIN.

Uruguay: 15 rue Le Sueur, 75116 Paris; tel. 1-45-00-81-37; fax 1-45-01-25-17; e-mail amburuguay.urugalia@fr.oleane.com; Ambassador Dr OMAR GONZÁLEZ MESA.

Uzbekistan: 22 rue d'Aguesseau, 75008 Paris; tel. 1-53-30-03-53; fax 1-53-30-03-54; e-mail contact@ouzbekistan.fr; internet www.ouzbekistan.fr; Ambassador RAVSHAN USMANOV.

Venezuela: 11 rue Copernic, 75116 Paris; tel. 1-45-53-29-98; fax 1-47-55-64-56; e-mail info@amb-venezuela.fr; internet www.embavenez-paris.fr; Ambassador HÉCTOR MICHEL MUJICA RICARDO.

Viet Nam: 62–66 rue Boileau, 75016 Paris; tel. 1-44-14-64-00; e-mail vnparis@club-internet.fr; Ambassador DUONG CHI DUNG.

Yemen: 25 rue Georges Bizet, 75116 Paris; tel. 1-53-23-87-87; fax 1-47-23-69-41; e-mail ambyemenparis@easynet.fr; Ambassador KHALED ISMAIL AL-AKWA'A.

Zambia: 18 ave de Tourville, 75007 Paris; tel. 1-56-88-12-70; fax 1-56-88-03-50; e-mail zambiansparis@wanadoo.fr; Chargé d'affaires PHILOMENA KACHESA.

Zimbabwe: 10 rue Jacques Bingen, 75017 Paris; tel. 1-56-88-16-00; fax 1-56-88-16-09; e-mail zimparisweb@wanadoo.fr; internet www.ambassade-zimbabwe.com; Ambassador DAVID HAMADZIRIPI.

Judicial System

The judiciary is independent of the Government. Judges of the Court of Cassation (Cour de Cassation) and the First President of the Court of Appeal (Cour d'Appel) are appointed by the executive from nominations of the High Council of the Judiciary.

Subordinate cases are heard by Tribunaux d'Instance and more serious cases by Tribunaux de Grande Instance. Parallel to these Tribunals are the Tribunaux de Commerce, for commercial cases, composed of judges elected by traders and manufacturers among themselves. These do not exist in every district. Where there is no Tribunal de Commerce, commercial disputes are judged by Tribunaux de Grande Instance.

The Boards of Arbitration (Conseils des Prud'hommes) consist of an equal number of workers or employees and employers ruling on the differences that arise over Contracts of Work.

The Correctional Courts (Tribunaux Correctionnnels) for criminal cases correspond to the Tribunaux de Grande Instance for civil cases. They pronounce on all graver offences (délits), including those involving imprisonment. Offences committed by juveniles of under 18 years go before specialized tribunals.

From all these Tribunals appeal lies to the Court of Appeal (Cours d'Appel).

The Courts of Assize (Cours d'Assises) have no regular sittings, but are called when necessary to try every important case, such as murder. They are presided over by judges who are members of the Courts of Appeal, and are composed of elected judges (jury). Their decision is final, except where shown to be wrong in law, and then recourse is to the Court of Cassation. The Court of Cassation is not a supreme court of appeal but a higher authority for the proper application of the law. Its duty is to see that judgments are not contrary either to the letter or the spirit of the law; any judgment annulled by the Court involves the trying of the case anew by a court of the same category as that which made the original decision.

A programme of extensive reforms in the judicial system, which aimed to reduce political control of the judiciary and to increase citizens' rights, was introduced in stages between 1997 and 2001. A notable innovation introduced by these reforms was the introduction of the convention that a person accused of a crime is presumed innocent unless otherwise proven.

In 2011 reforms to reduce the number of judicial districts from 1,190 to 862 were completed.

Court of Cassation (Cour de Cassation): 5 quai de l'Horloge, 75055 Paris Cedex 01; tel. 1-44-32-95-95; fax 1-44-32-78-29; e-mail webmstre@courdecassation.fr; internet www.courdecassation.fr; seven First Attorneys-General, 29 Attorneys-General, 88 Counsellors and 65 Junior Counsellors; First Pres. VINCENT LAMANDA; Attorney-General JEAN-CLAUDE MARIN.

Paris Court of Appeal (Cour d'Appel de Paris): 34 quai des Orfèvres, 75055 Paris Cedex 01; tel. 1-44-32-52-52; internet www.ca-paris.justice.fr; there are 61 Presidents of Chambers, 124 Counsellors, 22 Attorneys-General and 36 Deputies; First Pres. JACQUES DEGRANDI; Solicitor-Gen. FRANÇOIS FALLETTI.

Tribunal de Grande Instance de Paris: 4 blvd du Palais, 75055 Paris RP; tel. 1-44-32-51-51; fax 1-43-29-12-55; internet www.ca-paris.justice.fr; Pres. CHANTAL ARENS; Solicitor of the Republic of Paris FRANÇOIS MOLINS.

Tribunal de Commerce de Paris: 1 quai de Corse, 75181 Paris Cedex 04; tel. 1-44-32-83-83; fax 1-40-46-07-28; e-mail sandrine.carret@greffe-tc-paris.fr; internet www.greffe-tc-paris.fr; Pres. FRANK GENTIN.

Tribunal des Conflits: Conseil d'Etat, 1 place du Palais Royal, 75100 Paris Cedex 01; tel. 1-40-20-80-87; internet www.tribunal-conflits.fr; decides whether cases shall be submitted to the ordinary or administrative courts; Pres. THE KEEPER OF THE SEALS, MINISTER OF JUSTICE; Vice-Pres. JEAN-LOUIS GALLET.

Audit Court (Cour des Comptes): 13 rue Cambon, 75001 Paris Cedex 01; tel. 1-42-98-95-00; fax 1-42-60-01-59; e-mail courdescomptes@ccomptes.fr; internet www.ccomptes.fr; an administrative tribunal competent to judge the correctness of public accounts. It is the arbiter of common law of all public accounts laid before it. The judgments of the Court may be annulled by the Council of State (Conseil d'Etat); First Pres. DIDIER MIGAUD; Solicitor-Gen. GILLES JOHANET.

Chambres Régionales et Territoriales des Comptes: In 1983 jurisdiction over the accounts of local administrations (régions, départements and communes) and public institutions (hospitals, council housing, etc.) was transferred from the Audit Court (Cour des Comptes) to local Chambres Régionales. Chambres Territoriales were subsequently created in New Caledonia (in 1988), French Polynesia (in 1990), and Mayotte, Saint-Barthélémy, Saint-Martin and Saint Pierre and Miquelon (in 2007). The 32 courts (26 Chambres Régionales and six Chambres Territoriales) are autonomous, but under the jurisdiction of the state. Appeals may be brought before the Audit Court.

Council of State (Conseil d'Etat): 1 place du Palais-Royal, 75100 Paris 01 SP; tel. 1-40-20-80-00; fax 1-40-20-80-08; e-mail chantal.leveque@conseil-etat.fr; internet www.conseil-etat.fr; the Council of State (Conseil d'Etat) is the consultative organ of the Government and the supreme administrative court. It gives opinions to the Government in the legislative and administrative domain (interior, finance, public works and social sections) and has three functions in administrative jurisdiction: to judge in the first and last resort such cases as appeals against excess of power laid against official decrees or individuals; to judge appeals against judgments made by Tribunaux Administratifs, Cours Administratives d'Appel and resolutions of courts of litigation; and to annul decisions made by various specialized administrative authorities that adjudicate without appeal, such as the Audit Court (Cour des Comptes); Pres. THE PRIME MINISTER; Vice-Pres. JEAN-MARC SAUVÉ; Gen. Sec. FRANÇOISE SENERS.

Administrative Tribunals (Tribunaux Administratifs): Certain cases arising between civil servants (when on duty) and the Government, or between any citizen and the Government are judged by special administrative courts. The Administrative Tribunals (Tribunaux Administratifs), of which there are 29 in metropolitan France and nine in the overseas possessions, are situated in the capital of each area.

Constitutional Council (Conseil Constitutionnel): 2 rue de Montpensier, 75001 Paris; tel. 1-40-15-30-00; fax 1-40-20-93-27; e-mail informatique@conseil-constitutionnel.fr; internet www.conseil-constitutionnel.fr; Pres. JEAN-LOUIS DEBRÉ.

Religion

CHRISTIANITY

Conseil d'Eglises Chrétiennes en France: 58 ave de Breteuil, 75007 Paris; tel. 1-72-36-69-60; fax 1-73-72-96-67; e-mail anne.jan@cef.fr; f. 1987; ecumenical organization comprising representatives from all Christian denominations to express opinions on social issues; 21 mems; Pres. Pastor CLAUDE BATY, Cardinal ANDRÉ VINGT-TROIS, Most Rev. EMMANUEL (ADAMAKIS); Secs Pastor JANE STRANZ, Fr FRANCK LEMAÎTRE.

The Roman Catholic Church

For ecclesiastical purposes, France comprises nine Apostolic Regions, together forming 24 archdioceses (of which one, Strasbourg, is directly responsible to the Holy See), 72 dioceses (including one, Metz, directly responsible to the Holy See) and one Territorial Prelature. The Archbishop of Paris is also the Ordinary for Catholics of Oriental Rites. At 31 December 2006 an estimated 74.4% of the population were adherents of the Roman Catholic Church.

Bishops' Conference: Conférence des Evêques de France, 58 ave de Breteuil, 75007 Paris; tel. 1-72-36-68-00; fax 1-73-72-97-22; e-mail cef@cef.fr; internet www.cef.fr; Pres. Cardinal ANDRÉ VINGT-TROIS (Archbishop of Paris); Sec.-Gen. Fr ANTOINE HÉROUARD.

Archbishop of Lyon and Primate of Gaul: Cardinal PHILIPPE BARBARIN, 6 ave Adolphe Max, 69321 Lyon Cedex 05; tel. 4-78-81-48-15; fax 4-78-81-47-70; e-mail petre@lyon.catholique.fr; internet lyon .catholique.fr.

Archbishop of Albi: Most Rev. JEAN MARIE HENRI LEGREZ.

Archbishop of Auch: Most Rev. MAURICE GARDÈS.

Archbishop of Avignon: Most Rev. JEAN-PIERRE MARIE CATTENOZ.

Archbishop of Besançon: JEAN-LUC MARIE MAURICE LOUIS BOUILLERET.

Archbishop of Bordeaux: Cardinal JEAN-PIERRE RICARD.

Archbishop of Bourges: Most Rev. ARMAND MAILLARD.

Archbishop of Cambrai: Most Rev. FRANÇOIS GARNIER.

Archbishop of Chambéry: Most Rev. PHILIPPE BALLOT.

Archbishop of Clermont: Most Rev. HIPPOLYTE SIMON.

Archbishop of Dijon: Most Rev. ROLAND MINNERATH.

Archbishop of Marseille: Most Rev. GEORGES PAUL PONTIER.

Archbishop of Montpellier: Most Rev. PIERRE-MARIE CARRÉ.

Archbishop of Paris: Cardinal ANDRÉ VINGT-TROIS.

Archbishop of Poitiers: Most Rev. PASCAL JEAN MARCEL WINTZER.

Archbishop of Reims: Most Rev. THIERRY JORDAN.

Archbishop of Rennes: Most Rev. PIERRE D'ORNELLAS.

Archbishop of Rouen: Most Rev. JEAN-CHARLES DESCUBES.

Archbishop of Sens-Auxerre: Most Rev. YVES PATENÔTRE.

Archbishop of Strasbourg: Most Rev. JEAN-PIERRE GRALLET.

Archbishop of Toulouse: Most Rev. ROBERT JEAN-LOUIS LE GALL.

Archbishop of Tours: Most Rev. BERNARD-NICOLAS JEAN-MARIE AUBERTIN.

Protestant Churches

There are some 950,000 Protestants in France.

Eglise Méthodiste: 3 rue Paul Verlaine, 30100 Alès; tel. 4-66-86-20-72; the total Methodist community was estimated at 1,000 mems in 2001.

Fédération Protestante de France: 47 rue de Clichy, 75311 Paris Cedex 09; tel. 1-44-53-47-00; fax 1-42-81-40-01; e-mail fpf@protestants.org; internet www.protestants.org; f. 1905; Pres. Pastor FRANÇOIS CLAVAIROLY; Gen. Sec. Pastor YVES PARREND.

The Federation includes:

Armée du Salut (Foundation and Congregation): 60 rue des Frères Flavien, 75976 Paris Cedex 20; tel. 1-43-62-25-00; fax 1-43-62-25-57; e-mail info@armeedusalut.fr; internet www .armeedusalut.fr; f. 1881; Pres. Lt-Col MASSIMO PAONE.

Communauté Protestante Evangélique de Vannes: 18 blvd Edouard Herriot, 56000 Vannes; tel. and fax 2-97-47-16-75; e-mail communauteprotestante.vannes@wanadoo.fr; Pres. of the Council of the Church MARK PLUNIER.

Eglise Evangélique Luthérienne de France: 16 rue Chauchat, 75009 Paris; tel. 1-44-79-04-73; fax 3-81-94-20-70; e-mail eelfparis@orange.fr; internet www.eelf.org; 10,400 mems (2010); f. 1872; Pres. Pastor JOËL DAUTHEVILLE; Sec. JEANNIE FAVRE.

Eglise Protestante de la Confession d'Augsbourg d'Alsace et de Lorraine: 1 quai St Thomas, BP 80022, 67081 Strasbourg Cedex; tel. 3-8825-90-00; fax 3-88-25-90-99; e-mail contact@uepal .fr; internet www.uepal.fr; 250,000 mems; mem. of Union des Eglises Protestantes d'Alsace et de Lorraine; Pres. Prof. JEAN-FRANÇOIS COLLANGE.

Eglise Protestante Evangélique de Rochefort: 42 Quéreux de la Laiterie, 17300 Rochefort; tel. 5-46-87-10-82.

Eglise Protestante Réformée d'Alsace et de Lorraine: 1 quai St Thomas, BP 80022, 67081 Strasbourg Cedex; tel. 3-88-25-90-00; fax 3-88-25-90-99; e-mail contact@uepal.fr; mem. of Union des Eglises Protestantes d'Alsace et de Lorraine; 33,000 mems; Pres. Pastor GEOFFROY GOETZ.

Eglise Réformée de France: 47 rue de Clichy, 75311 Paris Cedex 09; tel. 1-48-74-90-92; fax 1-42-81-52-40; e-mail contact@unacerf .org; internet www.eglise-reformee-fr.org; 350,000 mems; Pres. Nat. Council Pastor LAURENT SCHLUMBERGER; Gen. Sec. Pastor ESTHER WIELAND-MARET.

Fédération des Eglises Evangéliques Baptistes de France: 47 rue de Clichy, 75311 Paris Cedex 09; tel. 1-53-20-15-40; fax 1-53-20-15-41; e-mail secretariat@feebf.com; internet www.feebf.com; 6,000 mems; f. 1910; Pres. JEAN DUPUPET.

Mission Populaire Evangélique de France: 47 rue de Clichy, 75009 Paris Cedex 09; tel. 1-48-74-98-58; fax 1-48-78-52-37; e-mail mpef@free.fr; internet www.missionpopulaire.org; 4,000 mems; f. 1871; Pres. Pastor BERTRAND VERGNIOL.

Union des Eglises Evangéliques Libres de France: 12 rue Claude-Perrault, 31500 Toulouse; tel. 5-61-26-06-18; fax 5-61-99-92-82; e-mail pierre.lacoste@protstants.org; internet www.ueel .org; 2,500 mems; Pres. Pastor PIERRE LACOSTE; Sec. RAYMOND CHAMARD.

Union Nationale des Eglises Protestantes Réformées Evangéliques de France: 74 rue Henri Revoil, 30900 Nîmes; tel. 4-66-23-95-05; e-mail uneprefcompta@orange.fr; internet www.unepref .com; f. 1938; 3,500 mems; Pres. JEAN-RAYMOND STAUFFACHER; Sec. MONIQUE BRUGUIÈRE.

Scots Kirk Paris (Church of Scotland): 17 rue Bayard, 75008 Paris; tel. and fax 1-48-78-47-94; e-mail scotskirk@wanadoo.fr; internet www.scotskirkparis.com; Minister Rev. JIM COWIE.

The Orthodox Church

There are about 200,000 Orthodox believers in France, of whom 100,000 are Russian Orthodox and 50,000 Greek Orthodox. There are 85 parishes and eight monasteries.

Administration of Russian Orthodox Churches in Western Europe (Jurisdiction of the Ecumenical Patriarchate): Cathédrale St Alexandre-Nevski, 12 rue Daru, 75008 Paris; tel. and fax 1-46-22-38-91; e-mail administration.diocesaine@exarchat.eu; internet www.exarchat.eu; Pres. Most Rev. JOB (Archbishop of Russian Orthodox Churches in Western Europe and Exarch of the Ecumenical Patriarch).

Assembly of the Orthodox Churches of France (Greek Orthodox Church): Cathédrale St Stéphane, 7 rue Georges Bizet, 75116 Paris; tel. 1-47-20-82-35; fax 1-47-20-83-15; e-mail eglise.orthodoxe .grecque@wanadoo.fr; f. 1997; Metropolitan of France Most Rev. EMMANUEL (ADAMAKIS).

Russian Orthodox Church (Moscow Patriarchate): 26 rue Péclet, 75015 Paris; tel. 1-48-28-99-90; fax 1-48-28-74-54; e-mail presse@egliserusse.eu; internet www.egliserusse.eu; the diocese of Chersonesus covers France, Portugal, Spain and Switzerland; Bishop of Chersonesus NESTOR SIROTENKO.

The Anglican Communion

Within the Church of England, France forms part of the diocese of Gibraltar in Europe. The Bishop is resident in London (United Kingdom).

Archdeacon of France: Ven. IAN NAYLOR, Presbytère Anglican, 11 rue de la Buffa, 06000 Nice; tel. 4-93-87-19-83; fax 4-93-82-25-09; e-mail anglican@free.fr.

Other Christian Denominations

Société Religieuse des Amis (Quakers, Assemblée de France)/ Centre Quaker International: 114 rue de Vaugirard, 75006 Paris; tel. 1-45-48-74-23; e-mail assembleedefrance@gmail.com; internet quaker.chez-alice.fr; f. 1920; 10 meetings nationwide; Clerk SYLVETTE THOMPSON.

ISLAM

In numerical terms, Islam is the second most important religion in France; in 2006 there were about 5m. adherents, of whom some 35% resided in the Ile-de-France region.

Conseil Français du Culte Musulman (CFCM): 270 rue Lecourbe, 75015 Paris; tel. 1-45-58-05-73; fax 1-45-58-24-06; internet www.lecfcm.fr; f. 2003 to represent Islamic interests to the public authorities; Pres. DALIL BOUBAKEUR; Sec.-Gen. ANOUAR KBIBECH.

Fédération Nationale des Musulmans de France (FNMF): 33 rue Polonceau, 75018 Paris; e-mail fnmf1@aol.com; f. 1985; 20 asscns; Pres. MOHAMED BECHARI.

Institut Musulman de la Grande Mosquée de Paris: 2 bis place du Puits de l'Ermite, 75005 Paris; tel. 1-45-35-97-33; fax 1-45-35-16-23; e-mail rectorat@mosquee-de-paris.net; internet www .mosquee-de-paris.net; f. 1926; cultural, diplomatic, social, judicial and religious sections; research and information and commercial annexes; Rector Dr DALIL BOUBAKEUR.

JUDAISM

There are about 650,000 Jews in France.

Conseil Représentatif des Institutions Juives de France (CRIF): 39 rue Broca, 75005 Paris; tel. 1-42-17-11-11; fax 1-42-17-11-50; e-mail infocrif@crif.org; internet www.crif.org; 63 asscns; Pres. ROGER CUKIERMAN.

Consistoire Central—Union des Communautés Juives de France: 19 rue Saint Georges, 75009 Paris; tel. 1-49-70-88-00; fax 1-42-81-03-66; e-mail administration@consistoirecentral.fr; internet www.consistoiredefrance.fr; f. 1808; 230 asscns; Chief Rabbi of France (vacant); Pres. JOËL MERGUI; Dir-Gen. FRÉDÉRIC ATTALI.

Consistoire Israélite de Paris: 17 rue Saint Georges, 75009 Paris; tel. 1-40-82-26-26; internet www.consistoire.org; f. 1808; 40,000 mems; Pres. JOËL MERGUI; Chief Rabbi of Paris MICHEL GUGENHEIM; Chief Rabbi of the Consistoire Israélite de Paris ALAIN GOLDMANN.

Fonds Social Juif Unifié (FSJU): Espace Rachi, 39 rue Broca, 75005 Paris; tel. 1-42-17-10-47; fax 1-42-17-10-82; e-mail info@fsju.org; internet www.fsju.org; f. 1950; unites the principal organizations supporting Jewish cultural, educational and social activity in France, and seeks to establish closer links between French Jewry and Israel; Pres. PIERRE BESNAINOU.

BAHÁ'Í FAITH

Centre National Bahá'í: 45 rue Pergolèse, 75116 Paris; tel. 1-45-00-90-26; e-mail info@bahai.fr; internet www.bahai-fr.org.

The Press

Most major daily newspapers are owned by individual publishers or by the powerful groups that have developed round either a company or a single personality. The major groups are as follows:

Amaury Group: 25 ave Michelet, 93408 Saint Ouen Cedex; tel. 1-40-10-30-30; fax 1-40-11-15-26; owns *Le Parisien*, *Aujourd'hui en France*, the sports daily *L'Equipe*, the bi-weekly magazine *France Football*, the weekly *L'Equipe Magazine* and the monthly *Vélo Magazine*; Pres. MARIANNE SIPROUDHIS; Man. Dir MARIE-ODILE AMAURY.

Bayard Presse: 18 rue Barbès, 92128 Montrouge Cedex; tel. 1-74-31-60-60; e-mail communication@bayard-presse.com; internet www.bayardpresse.fr; f. 1873; Roman Catholic press group; owns 143 publs worldwide, incl. the national daily *La Croix*, the magazines *Pèlerin*, *Panorama*, *Notre Temps* and several specialized religious publications; Pres. GEORGES SANEROT.

Lagardère Active: 121 ave de Malakoff, 75216 Paris Cedex 16; tel. 1-40-69-16-00; fax 1-40-69-18-54; e-mail contactpresse@hfp.fr; internet www.lagardere.com; f. 2006 by merger of Hachette Filipacchi Médias (f. 1999) and Lagardère Active; controls magazines in France incl. *Paris-Match*, *Pariscope*, *Jeune et Jolie*, *Photo*, *France-Dimanche*, *Elle*, *Télé 7 Jours*; owns 220 magazines worldwide; CEO DENIS OLIVENNES.

Mondadori France: 8 rue François Ory, 92543 Montrouge Cedex; tel. 1-41-33-50-01; e-mail contact@mondadori.fr; internet www.mondadori.fr; fmrly Editions Mondiales, and subsequently Emap France; present name adopted 2006; owned by Arnoldo Mondadori Editore, SpA (Italy); controls more than 40 magazines in France, incl. *Nous Deux*, *FHM*, *Science et Vie*, *Télé-Star*, *Top Santé*, *Télépoche*, *Auto Plus* and also specialized magazines; Man. Dir ERNESTO MAURI.

DAILY NEWSPAPERS (PARIS)

La Croix: 18 rue Barbès, 92128 Montrouge Cedex; tel. 1-74-31-60-60; fax 1-74-31-60-69; e-mail lecteurs.lacroix@bayard-presse.com; internet www.la-croix.com; f. 1883; Roman Catholic; Editor JEAN-BAPTISTE DE FOMBELLE; Dir DOMINIQUE QUINIO; circ. in France 98,918 (2012).

Les Echos: 16 rue du Quatre Septembre, 75112 Paris Cedex 02; tel. 1-49-53-65-65; fax 1-45-61-48-92; e-mail redassist@lesechos.fr; internet www.lesechos.fr; f. 1908; acquired by Groupe LVMH in 2007; economic and financial; Editor-in-Chief HENRI GIBIER; circ. in France 119,613 (2012).

L'Equipe: 4 rue Rouget-de-l'Isle, 92130 Issy-les-Moulineaux Cedex; tel. 1-40-93-20-20; fax 1-40-93-20-08; e-mail courrierdeslecteurs@lequipe.presse.fr; internet www.lequipe.fr; f. 1946; sport; owned by Groupe Amaury; Chair. LOUIS GILLET; Editorial Dir FABRICE JOUHAUD; circ. in France 279,615 (2011).

Le Figaro: 14 blvd Haussmann, 75009 Paris; tel. 1-42-21-62-00; fax 1-42-21-64-05; internet www.lefigaro.fr; f. 1828; owned by Groupe Dassault; morning; news and literary; magazine on Sat; 3 weekly supplements; Pres. SERGE DASSAULT; Dir-Gen. OLIVIER COSTA DE BEAUREGARD; Editorial Dir FRANZ-OLIVIER GIESBERT; circ. in France 329,367 (2011).

France-Soir: 13 rue Camille Desmoulins, 92130 Issy-les-Moulineaux; tel. 1-56-21-00-00; internet www.francesoir.fr; f. 1941 as *Défense de la France*; present title adopted 1944; Editor RÉMY DESSARTS; circ. in France 23,934 (2008).

L'Humanité: 32 rue Jean Jaurès, 93528 Saint-Denis Cedex; tel. 1-49-22-72-72; fax 1-49-22-74-00; internet www.humanite.presse.fr; f. 1904; communist; morning; Pres. PATRICK LE HYARIC; Editorial Dir PATRICK APEL-MULLER; circ. 49,061 (2008).

International Herald Tribune: 6 bis rue des Graviers, 92521 Neuilly-sur-Seine Cedex; tel. 1-41-43-93-00; fax 1-41-43-93-38; e-mail iht@iht.com; internet www.iht.com; f. 1887; present name adopted 1966; owned by The New York Times Co (USA); English language; Publr STEPHEN DUNBAR-JOHNSON; Man. Editor ALISON SMALE; worldwide circ. 240,322 (2008).

Le Journal Officiel de la République Française: 26 rue Desaix, 75727 Paris Cedex 15; tel. 1-40-58-75-00; fax 1-45-79-17-84; e-mail info@journal-officiel.gouv.fr; internet www.legifrance.gouv.fr; f. 1870; official journal of the Govt; publishes laws, decrees, parliamentary proceedings, and economic bulletins; Dir XAVIER PATIER.

Libération: 11 rue Béranger, 75154 Paris Cedex 03; tel. 1-42-76-17-89; fax 1-42-72-94-93; internet www.liberation.com; f. 1973; 37.8% owned by Edouard de Rothschild; Pres. and Editorial Dir FRANÇOIS MOULIAS, (vacant); circ. in France 119,165 (2011).

Metro: 35 rue Greneta, 75002 Paris; tel. 1-55-34-45-00; fax 1-55-34-45-03; e-mail courrier@publications-metro.fr; internet www.metrofrance.com; f. 2002; distributed free of charge in Paris, Marseille, Lyon, Toulouse, Lille, Bordeaux, Nice, Nantes, Rennes, Strasbourg and Cannes; Propr Metro International (Sweden); Dir-Gen. SOPHIE SACHNINE; Editor CHRISTOPHE JOLY; circ. 490,382 (2011).

Le Monde: 80 blvd Auguste Blanqui, 75707 Paris Cedex 13; tel. 1-42-17-20-00; fax 1-42-17-21-21; e-mail lemonde@lemonde.fr; internet www.lemonde.fr; f. 1944; independent; Chair., Supervisory Bd PIERRE BERGÉ; Dir of Publication LOUIS DREYFUS; Editorial Dir NATALIE NOUGAYRÈDE; circ. in France 292,062 (2011).

Paris-Turf: Société des Editions France Libre, Bâtiment 270, 45 ave Victor Hugo, BP 60279 Aubervilliers, 93534 La Plaine Saint-Denis Cedex; e-mail info@paris-turf.com; internet www.paris-turf.com; horse racing; Editorial Dir FRANÇOIS HALLOPÉ; circ. 55,894 (2011).

Le Parisien: 25 ave Michelet, 93405 Saint-Ouen Cedex; tel. 1-40-10-30-30; fax 1-40-10-35-16; e-mail courriers@leparisien.com; internet www.leparisien.fr; f. 1944; morning; sold in Paris and surrounding areas; Dir-Gen. JEAN HORNAIN; Editorial Dir THIERRY BORSA; circ. in France (incl. *Aujourd'hui en France*) 454,298 (2011).

Le Quotidien du Médecin: 21 rue Camille Desmoulins, 92789 Issy-les-Moulineaux Cedex; tel. 1-73-28-13-11; fax 1-73-28-13-10; e-mail redaction@quotimed.com; internet www.quotimed.com; medical journal; Pres. and Dir-Gen. Dr GÉRARD KOUCHNER; Editorial Dir RICHARD LISCIA; circ. 179,949 (Dec. 2011).

La Tribune: 26 rue d'Oradour-sur-Glane, 75725 Paris Cedex 15; tel. 1-44-82-16-16; fax 1-44-82-17-92; e-mail directiondelaredaction@latribune.fr; internet www.latribune.fr; economic and financial; Pres., Dir of Publication VALÉRIE DECAMP; Editorial Dir JACQUES ROSSELIN; circ. in France 77,122 (2008).

20 Minutes: 50–52 blvd Hausmann, 75427 Paris Cedex 09; tel. 1-53-26-65-65; fax 1-53-26-65-68; e-mail redac-chef@20minutes.fr; internet www.20minutes.fr; f. 2002; distributed free of charge; Propr Schibsted (Norway); Pres. PIERRE-JEAN BOZO; circ. (2008) 475,287 (Paris), 782,091 (total France).

SUNDAY NEWSPAPERS (PARIS)

Le Journal du Dimanche: 121 ave de Malakoff, 75216 Paris Cedex 16; tel. 1-40-69-16-00; fax 1-40-69-18-54; internet www.lejdd.fr; owned by Groupe Lagardère; Editorial Dir DENIS OLIVENNES; circ. 257,257 (2011).

Le Parisien Dimanche: 25 ave Michelet, 93405 Saint Ouen Cedex; tel. 1-40-10-30-30; fax 1-40-10-35-16; e-mail infoat@leparisien.fr; internet www.leparisien.fr; circ. 199,204 (2011).

PRINCIPAL PROVINCIAL DAILY NEWSPAPERS

Amiens

Le Courrier Picard: 29 rue de la République, BP 1021, 80010 Amiens Cedex 01; tel. 3-22-82-60-00; fax 3-22-82-60-11; e-mail courrier@courrier-picard.fr; internet www.courrier-picard.fr; f. 1944; Chair./Man. MICHEL COLLET; Editor-in-Chief DIDIER LOUIS; circ. 58,239 (2011).

Angers

Le Courrier de l'Ouest: 4 blvd Albert Blanchoin, BP 10728, 49007 Angers Cedex 01; tel. 2-41-68-86-88; fax 2-41-44-31-43; e-mail redac.angers@courrier-ouest.com; internet www.courrierdelouest.fr; f. 1944; acquired in 2005 by Ouest-France group; Pres. and Man. Dir MATTHIEU FUCHS; Editor-in-Chief PATRICE GULLIER; circ. 99,253 (2008).

Angoulême

La Charente Libre: 16903 Angoulême Cedex 09; tel. 5-45-94-16-00; fax 5-45-94-16-19; e-mail charente@charentelibre.fr; internet www.charentelibre.com; Publishing Dir JEAN-PIERRE BARJOU; Editorial Dir JACQUES GUYON; Editor-in-Chief JEAN-LOUIS HERVOIS; circ. 34,929 (2011).

Auxerre

L'Yonne Républicaine: 8–12 ave Jean Moulin, 89000 Auxerre; tel. 3-86-49-52-00; fax 3-86-46-52-35; e-mail direction@lyonne

-republicaine.fr; internet www.lyonne-republicaine.fr; f. 1944; Pres. and Dir-Gen. JEAN-PIERRE CAILLARD; Editor-in-Chief DIDIER LAGEDAMON; circ. 36,134 (2008).

Bordeaux

Sud-Ouest: 23 quai de Queyries, 33094 Bordeaux Cedex; tel. 5-35-31-31-31; fax 5-56-00-32-17; e-mail contact@sudouest.com; internet www.sudouest.com; f. 1944; independent; Pres. and Dir of Publication BRUNO FRANCESCHI; Editor-in-Chief PATRICK VENRIES; circ. 288,524 (2011).

Bourges

Le Berry Républicain: 1–3 place Berry, 18023 Bourges Cedex; tel. 2-48-27-63-63; fax 2-48-48-17-19; e-mail redaction.berry@centrefrance.com; internet www.leberry.fr; Editor-in-Chief BERNARD STEPHAN; circ. 34,915 (weekdays), 11,350 (Sun.) (2011).

Chalon-sur-Saône

Le Journal de Saône-et-Loire: 9 rue des Tonneliers, BP 134, 71100 Chalon-sur-Saône; tel. 3-85-44-68-68; fax 3-85-93-02-96; e-mail infos@lejsl.com; internet www.lejsl.com; f. 1826; Editor-in-Chief MICHEL MEKKI; circ. 58,831 (2008).

Chartres

L'Echo Républicain: 21 rue Vincent Chevard, 28000 Chartres; tel. 2-37-88-88-88; fax 2-37-91-17-42; internet www.lechorepublicain.fr; f. 1929; Pres. and Dir-Gen. RICHARD METZGER; Editor-in-Chief HUGUES DE LESTAPIS; circ. 31,575 (2011).

Clermont-Ferrand

La Montagne: 245 rue du Clos Four, 63056 Clermont-Ferrand Cedex 2; tel. 4-73-17-17-17; fax 4-73-17-18-19; e-mail lamontagne@centrefrance.com; internet www.lamontagne.fr; f. 1919; independent; Pres. and Dir-Gen. JEAN-PIERRE CAILLARD; Editors-in-Chief PHILIPPE ROUSSEAU, PHILIPPE VAZEILLE; circ. 183,982 (2011).

Dijon

Le Bien Public-Les Dépêches: 7 blvd du Chanoîne Kir, BP 550, 21015 Dijon Cedex; tel. 3-80-42-42-42; fax 3-80-42-44-35; e-mail bienpublic@lebienpublic.fr; internet www.bienpublic.com; f. 1850 as Le Bien Public; merged with *Les Dépêches* in 2001; Pres. JEAN VIANSSON PONTÉ; Editor-in-Chief JEAN-LOUIS PIERRE; circ. 43,378 (2011).

Epinal

Vosges Matin: 40 quai des Bons Enfants, 88000 Epinal Cedex; tel. 3-29-82-98-00; fax 3-29-82-99-29; e-mail vomredacweb@vosgesmatin.fr; internet www.vosgesmatin.fr; f. 1945; Editor-in-Chief GÉRARD NOËL; circ. 26,232 (2008).

Grenoble

Le Dauphiné Libéré: Isles des Cordées, 38913 Veurey-Voroize Cedex; tel. 4-76-88-71-00; fax 4-76-88-70-96; e-mail redaction@ledauphine.com; internet www.ledauphine.com; f. 1945; Pres., Dir-Gen. and Editor-in-Chief HENRI-PIERRE GUILBERT; circ. 227,187 (2011).

Lille

La Voix du Nord: 8 place du Général de Gaulle, BP 549, 59023 Lille Cedex; tel. 3-20-78-40-40; fax 3-20-78-42-44; e-mail contact@lavoixdunord.fr; internet www.lavoixdunord.fr; f. 1944; Dir-Gen. JACQUES HARDOIN; Editor-in-Chief JEAN-MICHEL BRETONNIER; circ. 259,912 (2011).

Limoges

L'Echo du Centre: 29 rue Claude-Henri Gorceix, 87022 Limoges Cedex 09; tel. 5-55-04-49-99; fax 5-55-04-49-78; internet www.l-echo.info; f. 1943; five edns; communist; Dir of Publication GUY DUMIGNARD; Editor-in-Chief BERNARD CUNY.

Le Populaire du Centre: 15 rue du Général-Catroux, BP 541, 87011 Limoges Cedex 1; tel. 5-55-58-59-00; fax 5-55-58-59-77; e-mail lepopulaire@centrefrance.com; internet www.lepopulaire.fr; f. 1905; Chair. and Dir of Publication ALAIN VÉDRINE; Editor-in-Chief OLIVIER BONNICHON; circ. 40,884 (2011).

Lyon

Le Progrès: 4 rue Montrochet, 69002 Lyon; tel. 4-72-22-23-23; fax 4-78-90-52-40; internet www.leprogres.fr; f. 1859; Dir of Publication PIERRE FANNEAU; circ. 202,794 (2011).

Tribune de Lyon: 9 rue de l'Arbre sec, 69001 Lyon; tel. 4-72-69-15-15; fax 4-72-44-92-04; e-mail fsapy@tribunedelyon.fr; internet www.tribunedelyon.fr; f. 2005; daily; Dir of Publication FRANÇOIS SAPY; circ. 2,543 (2010).

Le Mans

Le Maine Libre: 28–30 place de l'Eperon, BP 299, 72013 Le Mans Cedex 2; tel. 2-43-83-72-50; fax 2-43-28-28-19; e-mail redaction@maine-libre.com; internet www.lemainelibre.fr; acquired in 2005 by the Ouest-France group; Pres. and Dir-Gen. MATTHIEU FUCHS; Editor-in-Chief JÉRÔME GLAIZE; circ. 44,973 (2011).

Marseille

La Marseillaise: 19 cours d'Estienne d'Orves, BP 1862, 13001 Marseille Cedex 01; tel. 4-91-57-75-00; fax 4-91-57-75-25; internet www.journal-lamarseillaise.com; f. 1944; communist; Man. Dir PAUL BIAGGINI; Editor-in-Chief ROLLAND MARTINEZ.

MarseillePlus: 248 ave Roger-Salengro, 13015 Marseille; tel. 4-91-84-00-00; fax 4-91-84-80-07; e-mail redaction@marseilleplus.com; internet www.marseilleplus.com; f. 2002; Mon.–Fri. mornings; distributed free of charge; Editorial Dir GUILHEM RICAVY; circ. 60,718 (2011).

La Provence: 248 ave Roger-Salengro, 13015 Marseille; tel. 4-91-84-45-45; fax 4-91-84-49-95; e-mail contact@laprovence.com; internet www.laprovence.com; f. 1996 by merger of *Le Provençal* with *Le Méridional*; Dir of Publication STÉPHANE DUHAMEL; Editorial Dir HEDI DAHMANI; circ. 130,388 (2011).

Metz

Le Républicain Lorrain: 3 ave des Deux Fontaines, 57140 Woippy; tel. 3-87-34-17-89; fax 3-87-34-17-90; e-mail pm.pernet@republicain-lorrain.fr; internet www.republicain-lorrain.fr; f. 1919; independent; Dir-Gen. and Dir of Publication PIERRE WICKER; Editor-in-Chief JACQUES VIRON; circ. 123,592 (2011).

Montpellier

Midi Libre: Mas de Grille, 34923 Montpellier Cedex 09; tel. 4-67-07-67-07; fax 4-67-07-68-13; internet www.midilibre.com; f. 1944; Pres. and Dir of Publication ALAIN PLOMBAT; Editorial Dir PHILIPPE PALAT; circ. 140,375 (2011).

Direct Montpellier Plus: Les portes d'Antigone, Bldg A, 43 place Vauban, 2nd Floor, 340000 Montpellier; internet www.direct-montpellier-plus.com; f. 2005 by *Midi Libre*; daily; distributed free of charge; Editorial Dir ALAIN PLOMBAT.

Morlaix

Le Télégramme: 7 voie d'accès au Port, BP 243, 29672 Morlaix; tel. 2-98-62-11-33; fax 2-98-63-45-45; e-mail telegramme@bretagne-online.com; internet www.letelegramme.com; f. 1944; fmrly *Le Télégramme de Brest et de l'Ouest*; Pres. and Man. Dir EDOUARD COUDURIER; Editor-in-Chief MARCEL QUIVIGER; circ. 204,785 (2011).

Mulhouse

L'Alsace: 18 rue de Thann, 68945 Mulhouse Cedex 09; tel. 3-89-32-70-00; fax 3-89-32-11-26; e-mail redaction@alsapresse.com; internet www.alsapresse.com; f. 1944; Chair. JACQUES ROMANN; Editor-in-Chief FRANCIS LAFFON; circ. 97,244 (2008).

Nancy

L'Est Républicain: rue Théophraste-Renaudot, Nancy Houdemont, 54185 Heillecourt Cedex; tel. 3-83-59-80-26; fax 3-83-59-80-13; e-mail secretariat.general@estrepublicain.fr; internet www.estrepublicain.fr; f. 1889; Dir of Publication PIERRE WICKER; Editor-in-Chief RÉMI GODEAU; circ. 149,172 (2011).

Nantes

Presse Océan: 15 rue Deshoulières, BP 22418, 44024 Nantes Cedex 01; tel. 2-40-44-24-00; fax 2-40-44-24-40; e-mail redac.locale.nantes@presse-ocean.com; internet www.presseocean.fr; f. 1944; acquired in 2005 by the Ouest-France group; Dir of Publication MATTHIEU FUCHS; Editor-in-Chief DOMINIQUE LUNEAU; circ. 32,684 (2011).

Nevers

Le Journal du Centre: 3 rue du Chemin de Fer, BP 106, 58001 Nevers; tel. 3-86-71-45-27; fax 3-86-71-45-20; e-mail redaction.jdc@centrefrance.com; internet www.lejdc.fr; f. 1943; Dir of Publication JEAN-PIERRE CAILLARD; Editor-in-Chief JEAN-YVES VIF; circ.27,940 (2011).

Nice

Nice-Matin: 214 route de Grenoble, BP 4, 06290 Nice Cedex 03; tel. 4-93-18-28-38; fax 4-93-83-93-97; internet www.nicematin.fr;

f. 1945; Dir of Publication DOMINIQUE BERNARD; Editor-in-Chief OLIVIER BISCAYE; circ. 101,882 (2011).

Orléans

La République du Centre: rue de la Halte, 45770 Saran; tel. 2-38-78-79-80; fax 2-38-78-79-79; e-mail dleger@larep.com; internet www.larep.com; f. 1944; Dir of Publication JEAN-PIERRE CAILLARD; Editor-in-Chief CHRISTINE BROUDIC; circ. 39,905 (2011).

Perpignan

L'Indépendant: 'Le Mas de la Garrigue', 2 ave Alfred Sauvy, 66605 Rivesaltes Cedex; tel. 4-68-64-88-88; fax 4-68-64-88-38; internet www.lindependant.com; f. 1846; daily; also *Indépendant-Dimanche* (Sun.); Pres. OLIVIER GEROLAMI; Editorial Dir JOSÉ LOZANO; circ. 60,119 (2011).

Reims

L'Union: 5 rue de Talleyrand, 51083 Reims Cedex; tel. 3-26-50-50-50; fax 3-26-50-51-69; e-mail dirgen@journal-lunion.fr; internet www.lunion.presse.fr; f. 1944; Chair. JACQUES TILLIER; Editor-in-Chief SÉBASTIEN LACROIX; circ. 106,381 (2008).

Rennes

Ouest-France: 10 rue du Breil, 35051 Rennes Cedex 09; tel. 2-99-32-60-00; fax 2-99-32-60-25; internet www.ouest-france.fr; f. 1944; publ. by non-profit-making Association pour le soutien des principes de la démocratie humaniste; 40 local editions (weekdays), 9 editions (Sun.); the largest circulation of any daily newspaper in France; Chair. and Man. Dir FRANÇOIS RÉGIS HUTIN; Editor-in-Chief JEAN-LUC ÉVIN; circ. Mon.–Fri. 748,223; Sun. 359,174 (2011).

Roubaix

Nord-Eclair: 42 rue du Général Sarrail, 59100 Roubaix Cedex 1; tel. 3-20-25-02-50; fax 3-20-25-62-98; e-mail contact@nordeclair.fr; internet www.nordeclair.fr; f. 1944; Pres. JACQUES HARDOIN; Dir-Gen. and Editorial Dir JEAN-RENÉ LORE; circ. 24,267 (2011).

Rouen

Paris-Normandie: 33 rue des Grosses Pierres, BP 40047, 76250 Deville-lès-Rouen; tel. 2-35-14-56-56; fax 2-35-14-56-15; e-mail redaction.web@paris-normandie.fr; internet www.paris-normandie.com; f. 1944; Pres. and Dir-Gen. PHILIPPE HERSANT; Editor-in-Chief SOPHIE BLOCH; circ. 52,606 (2011).

Strasbourg

Les Dernières Nouvelles d'Alsace: 17–21 rue de la Nuée Bleue, BP 406/R1, 67077 Strasbourg Cedex; tel. 3-88-21-55-00; fax 3-88-21-56-41; e-mail dnasug@sdv.fr; internet www.dna.fr; f. 1877; non-party; Dir-Gen. FRANCIS HIRN; Editor-in-Chief DOMINIQUE JUNG; circ. 168,238 (2011).

Toulon

Var Matin: 214 route de Grenoble, BP 4, 06290 Nice Cedex 3; tel. 4-93-18-28-38; fax 4-94-63-49-98; internet www.varmatin.com; f. 1975; Dir of Publication Dominique BERNARD; Editor-in-Chief OLIVIER BISCAYE; circ. 70,209 (2011).

Toulouse

La Dépêche du Midi: ave Jean Baylet, 31095 Toulouse Cedex; tel. 5-62-11-33-00; fax 5-61-44-74-74; internet www.ladepeche.com; f. 1870; Dir of Publication BRUNO PACHENT; Editor-in-Chief JEAN-CLAUDE SOULERY; circ. 177,863 (2011).

Tours

La Nouvelle République du Centre-Ouest: 232 ave de Grammont, 37048 Tours Cedex 1; tel. 2-47-31-70-00; fax 2-47-31-70-70; e-mail nr.redactionenchef@nrco.fr; internet www.lanouvellerepublique.fr; f. 1944; non-party; Pres. OLIVIER SAINT-CRICQ; Editor-in-Chief BRUNO BÉCARD; circ. 183,482 (2011).

Troyes

L'Est-Eclair: 71 ave du Maréchal Leclerc, 10120 St André les Vergers; tel. 3-25-71-75-75; fax 3-25-79-58-54; e-mail redaction@lest-eclair.fr; internet www.lest-eclair.fr; f. 1945; Pres. and Dir of Publication JACQUES TILLIER; Editor-in-Chief PATRICK PLANCHENAULT; circ. 25,852 (2011).

SELECTED PERIODICALS

(average net circulation figures for 2012, unless otherwise stated)

Current Affairs and Politics

Annales—Histoire, Sciences sociales: 190–198 ave de France, 75013 Paris; tel. 1-49-54-24-75; fax 1-49-54-26-88; e-mail annales@ehess.fr; internet www.editions.ehess.fr/revues/annales-histoire-sciences-sociales; f. 1929; 4 a year; Editorial Dir ETIENNE ANHEIM.

Armées d'Aujourd'hui: Délégation à l'Information et à la Communication de la Défense, 14 rue Saint-Dominique, 75700 Paris; tel. 1-56-77-23-03; fax 1-56-77-23-04; e-mail journalistes@dicod.defense.gouv.fr; monthly; military and technical; produced by the Délégation à l'Information et à la Communication de la Défense; Editor-in-Chief Lt Col PHILIPPE DUPAS; circ. 100,000 (2008).

Le Canard Enchaîné: 173 rue Saint Honoré, 75051 Paris Cedex 01; tel. 1-42-60-31-36; fax 1-42-27-97-87; e-mail redaction@lecanardenchaine.fr; internet lecanardenchaine.fr; f. 1915; weekly; satirical; Dir MICHEL GAILLARD; Editors-in-Chief LOUIS-MARIE HOREAU, ERIK EMPTAZ; circ. 537,000 (2010).

Charlie Hebdo: 26 rue Serpollet, 75020 Paris; tel. 1-76-21-53-00; fax 1-76-21-53-01; e-mail redaction@charliehebdo.fr; internet www.charliehebdo.fr; f. 1992 (as revival of 1969–81 publication); left-wing, satirical; Editor and Dir of Publication STÉPHANE CHARBONNIER; Editor-in-Chief GÉRARD BIARD.

Commentaire: 116 rue du Bac, 75007 Paris; tel. 1-45-49-37-82; fax 1-45-44-32-18; e-mail infos@commentaire.fr; internet www.commentaire.fr; f. 1978; quarterly; Dir JEAN-CLAUDE CASANOVA.

Courrier International: 6–8 rue Jean-Antoine de Baïf, 75212 Paris Cedex 13; tel. 1-46-46-16-00; fax 1-46-46-16-01; e-mail communication@courrierinternational.com; internet www.courrierinternational.com; f. 1990; weekly; current affairs and political; Editorial Dir ERIC CHOL; circ. 199,422.

L'Express: 29 rue de Châteaudun, 75308 Paris Cedex 09; tel. 1-75-55-10-00; fax 1-75-55-12-05; internet www.lexpress.fr; f. 1953; weekly, Thur.; Editorial Dir CHRISTOPHE BARBIER; circ. 521,989.

L'Humanité Dimanche (HD): 5 rue Pleyel, Immeuble Calliope, 93528 Saint-Denis Cedex; tel. 1-49-22-72-72; fax 1-49-22-73-37; internet www.humanite.presse.fr; f. 2006 to replace *L'Humanité Hebdo*; current affairs; weekly (Sun.); Editor PATRICK APEL-MULLER.

Marianne: 32 rue René Boulanger, 75484 Paris Cedex 10; tel. 1-53-72-29-00; fax 1-53-72-29-72; internet www.marianne.net; f. 1997; weekly, Sat.; current affairs; Dir MAURICE SZAFRAN; Editorial Dir ERIC CONAN; circ. 246,715.

Le Monde Diplomatique: 1–3 ave Stephen Pichon, 75013 Paris Cedex; tel. 1-53-94-96-01; fax 1-53-94-96-26; e-mail secretariat@monde-diplomatique.fr; internet www.monde-diplomatique.fr; f. 1954; monthly; international affairs; Pres. and Dir of Publication SERGE HALIMI; circ. 144,000.

Le Nouvel Observateur: 12 place de la Bourse, 75002 Paris; tel. 1-44-88-34-34; e-mail ljoffrin@nouvelobs.com; internet hebdo.nouvelobs.com; f. 1964; weekly, Thur.; left-wing political and literary; Dir of Publication LAURENT JOFFRIN; circ. 526,732.

Paris-Match: 149 rue Anatole France, 92534 Levallois-Perret Cedex; tel. 1-41-34-60-00; fax 1-41-34-79-59; e-mail parismatch@hfp.fr; internet www.parismatch.com; f. 1949; weekly, Thur.; magazine of French and world affairs; Editorial Dir OLIVIER ROYANT; Editor-in-Chief GILLES MARTIN-CHAUFFIER; circ. 670,913.

Passages: 10 rue Clément, 75006 Paris; tel. 1-43-25-23-57; fax 1-43-25-62-59; e-mail passages4@wanadoo.fr; internet www.passages-adapes.fr; f. 1987; quarterly; multidisciplinary discussions of geostrategic issues, seeking to present major contemporary events in an ethical and historical perspective; Dir EMILE H. MALET.

Le Peuple: 263 rue de Paris, Case 432, 93514 Montreuil Cedex; tel. 1-48-18-83-05; fax 1-48-59-28-31; e-mail lepeuplecgt@free.fr; internet www.lepeuple-cgt.com; f. 1921; fortnightly; official organ of the Confédération Générale du Travail (trade union confederation); Dir DANIEL PRADA; Editor-in-Chief FRANÇOISE DUCHESNE.

Le Point: 74 ave du Maine, 75014 Paris; tel. 1-44-10-10-10; fax 1-44-10-12-19; e-mail support@lepoint.fr; internet www.lepoint.fr; f. 1972; weekly, Thur.; politics and current affairs; Pres. and Dir-Gen. CYRILLE DUVAL; Editor-in-Chief JÉRÔME BÉGLÉ; circ. 432,813.

Politique Internationale: 11 rue du Bois de Boulogne, 75116 Paris; tel. 1-45-00-15-26; fax 1-45-00-16-87; internet www.politiqueinternationale.com; f. 1978; quarterly; Dir-Gen. PATRICK WAJSMAN; Editor-in-Chief ANNE LE FUR.

Regards: 5 villa des Pyrénées, 75020 Paris; e-mail remi.douat@regards.fr; internet www.regards.fr; monthly; communist; politics, current affairs, culture; Dir of Publication CLÉMENTINE AUTAIN; Editor-in-Chief CATHERINE TRICOT.

Revue Défense Nationale: Ecole Militaire, 1 place Joffre, BP 8607, 75325 Paris Cedex 07; tel. 1-44-42-31-90; fax 1-44-42-31-89; e-mail contact@defnat.com; internet www.defnat.com; f. 1939; monthly; publ. by Cttee for Study of National Defence; strategic debate, military, economic, political and scientific problems; Dir Adm. ALAIN COLDEFY; Editor-in-Chief JEAN DUFOURCQ.

Revue des Deux Mondes: 97 rue de Lille, 75007 Paris; tel. 1-47-53-61-94; fax 1-47-53-61-99; e-mail presse@revuedesdeuxmondes.fr; internet www.revuedesdeuxmondes.fr; f. 1829; monthly; current affairs; Pres. MARC LADREIT DE LACHARRIÈRE; Editor-in-Chief MICHEL CRÉPU.

Rivarol: 82 blvd Masséna, 75013 Paris; tel. 1-53-34-97-97; fax 1-53-34-97-98; e-mail contact@rivarol.com; internet www.rivarol.com; f. 1951; weekly; conservative; political, literary and satirical; Dir FABRICE JÉRÔME BOURBON.

Technikart: Passage du Cheval-Blanc, 2 rue de la Roquette, 75011 Paris; tel. 1-43-14-33-44; fax 1-43-14-33-40; e-mail rturcat@technikart.com; internet www.technikart.com; monthly; cultural review; Editor-in-Chief RAPHAËL TURCAT; circ. 38,500 (2008).

La Vie: 80 blvd Auguste-Blanqui, 75013 Paris; tel. 1-48-88-46-00; fax 1-48-88-46-01; e-mail courrier@lavie.fr; internet www.lavie.fr; f. 1945; acquired by Le Monde SA in 2000; weekly; general, Christian; Dir of Publication BÉATRICE GARRETTE; circ. 116,215.

VSD: 13 rue Henri Barbusse, 92624 Gennevilliers Cedex; tel. 1-73-05-45-45; fax 1-56-99-51-28; e-mail lecteurs@vsd.fr; internet www.vsd.fr; f. 1977; weekly, Wed.; current affairs, leisure; Dir of Publication ROLF HEINZ; Editor-in-Chief PHILIPPE BOURBEILLON; circ. 137,098.

The Arts

L'Architecture d'Aujourd'hui: 19 rue Martel, 75010 Paris; tel. 1-58-05-17-49; fax 1-58-05-16-98; e-mail redaction@larchitecturedaujourdhui.fr; internet www.larchitecturedaujourdhui.fr; f. 1930; relaunched in 2009; 6 a year; Dir of Publication ANTOINE VERNHOLES.

Beaux Arts Magazine: 3 carrefour de Weiden, 92130 Issy-les-Moulineaux; tel. 1-41-08-38-00; e-mail beauxarts@dipinfo.fr; internet www.beauxartsmagazine.com; f. 1983; monthly; review of art, architecture, cinema, design; Dir of Publication THIERRY TAITTINGER; Editor-in-Chief FABRICE BOUSTEAU; circ. 61,246.

Critique: 7 rue Bernard Palissy, 75006 Paris; tel. 1-44-39-39-20; fax 1-44-39-39-23; e-mail critique@wanadoo.fr; f. 1946; 9 a year; publ. by Les Éditions de Minuit; general review of French and foreign literature, philosophy, art, social sciences and history; Dir PHILIPPE ROGER.

Diapason: 8 rue François Ory, 92543 Montrouge Cedex; tel. 1-41-33-50-01; internet www.diapasonmag.fr; f. 1956; monthly; classical music; Editor-in-Chief EMMANUEL DUPUY; circ. 37,016.

Esprit: 212 rue Saint Martin, 75003 Paris; tel. 1-48-04-92-90; fax 1-48-04-50-53; e-mail redaction@esprit.presse.fr; internet www.esprit.presse.fr; f. 1932; 10 a year; philosophy, history, sociology; Dir OLIVIER MONGIN; Editor-in-Chief MARC-OLIVIER PADIS.

Les Inrockuptibles: 24 rue Saint Sabin, 75011 Paris; tel. 1-42-44-16-16; fax 1-42-44-16-00; e-mail christian.fevret@inrocks.com; internet www.lesinrocks.com; f. 1986; weekly, Tue.; music, cinema, literature and television; Editorial Dir BERNARD ZEKRI; circ. 60,318.

Lire: 29 rue de Châteaudun, 75308 Paris Cedex 09; tel. 1-75-55-10-00; fax 1-75-55-17-04; e-mail redaction@lire.fr; internet www.lire.fr; f. 1975; monthly; literary review; Editorial Dir FRANÇOIS BUSNEL; circ. 67,110.

Livres-Hebdo: 35 rue Grégoire-de-Tours, 75006 Paris; tel. 1-44-41-28-00; fax 1-43-29-77-85; internet www.livreshebdo.fr; f. 1979; weekly; book publishing; Editor-in-Chief CHRISTINE FERRAND; circ. 163,320.

Le Magazine Littéraire: 717 route des Boulangers, 78926 Yvelines Cedex 9; tel. 1-55-56-71-25; e-mail courrier@magazine-litteraire.com; internet www.magazine-litteraire.com; f. 1966; monthly; literature; Editorial Dir JOSEPH MACÉ-SCARON; circ. 31,712.

Le Matricule des Anges: BP 20225, 34004 Montpellier Cedex 1; tel. and fax 4-67-92-29-33; e-mail lmda@lmda.net; internet www.lmda.net; f. 1992; monthly; literary criticism; Dir of Publication THIERRY GUICHARD.

La Quinzaine Littéraire: 135 rue Saint-Martin, 75194 Paris Cedex 04; tel. 1-48-87-48-58; fax 1-48-87-13-01; e-mail nadeau.maurice@orange.fr; internet www.quinzaine-litteraire.net; f. 1966; fortnightly; Dir MAURICE NADEAU; Editor-in-Chief ERIC PHALIPPOU.

Rock & Folk: 12 rue Mozart, 92587 Clichy Cedex; tel. 1-41-40-32-32; internet www.rocknfolk.com; f. 1966; monthly; music; publ. by Éditions Larivière; Editor-in-Chief PHILIPPE MANŒUVRE; circ. 36,399.

Les Temps Modernes: 26 rue de Condé, 75006 Paris; tel. 1-43-29-08-47; fax 1-40-51-83-38; e-mail les.temps.modernes@free.fr; f. 1945 by J.-P. Sartre; 6 a year; literary review; publ. by Gallimard; Dir CLAUDE LANZMANN.

Economic and Financial

Capital: 13 rue Henri Barbusse, 92624 Gennevilliers Cedex; tel. 1-73-05-48-53; fax 1-47-92-65-90; e-mail capital@prismamedia.com; internet www.capital.fr; f. 1991; monthly; business, finance; Editor-in-Chief FRANÇOIS GENTHIAL; circ. 305,379.

Challenges: 33 rue Vivienne, 75002 Paris; tel. 1-44-88-34-34; e-mail pf@challenges.fr; internet www.challenges.fr; weekly; economics and politics; Editor-in-Chief VINCENT BEAUFILS; circ. 231,209.

L'Expansion: 29 rue de Châteaudun, 75308 Paris Cedex 09; tel. 1-75-55-10-00; internet www.lexpansion.com; f. 1967; monthly; economics and business; Editorial Dir CHRISTINE KERDELLANT; circ. 142,630.

Mieux Vivre Votre Argent: 29 rue de Châteaudun, 75308 Paris Cedex 09; tel. 1-75-55-10-00; fax 1-75-55-11-40; e-mail jpviallon@mieuxvivre.fr; internet www.votreargent.fr; monthly; f. 1918; investment, economics; Dir of Publication RIK DE NOLF; Editor-in-Chief JEAN-FRANÇOIS FILLIATRE; circ. 221,876.

Le Monde-Initiatives: 1–3 ave Stephen Pichon, 75013 Paris; tel. 1-53-94-96-26; fax 1-53-94-96-01; e-mail initiatives@lemonde.fr; f. 2002; monthly; circ. 50,000 (2002).

Le Nouvel Economiste: 38 bis rue du Fer à Moulin, 75005 Paris; tel. 1-75-44-41-00; e-mail patrick.arnoux@nouveleconomiste.fr; internet www.nouveleconomiste.fr; f. 1976; weekly, Fri.; Pres. and Editorial Dir HENRI J. NIJDAM; circ. 16,929.

L'Usine Nouvelle: Antony Parc II–10, place du Général de Gaulle, 92160 Antony Cedex; tel. 1-77-92-92-92; fax 1-56-79-42-34; internet www.usinenouvelle.com; f. 1945; weekly, Thur; technical and industrial journal; Editorial Dir LAURENT GUEZ; Editor-in-Chief THIBAUT DE JAEGHER; circ. 48,094.

Valeurs Actuelles: 1 rue Lulli, 75002 Paris; tel. 1-40-54-11-00; fax 1-40-54-12-85; internet www.valeursactuelles.com; f. 1966; weekly; politics, economics, international affairs; Dir-Gen. YVES DE KERDREL; circ. 88,241.

History and Geography

Annales de Géographie: 21 rue de Montparnasse, 75006 Paris; tel. 1-44-39-54-47; fax 1-40-46-49-93; e-mail infos@armand-colin.com; f. 1891; every 2 months.

Cahiers de Civilisation Médiévale: 24 rue de la Chaine, 86022 Poitiers Cedex 9; tel. 5-49-45-45-63; fax 5-49-45-45-73; e-mail blaise.royer@univ-poitiers.fr; internet cescm.labo.univ-poitiers.fr/spip.php?rubrique58; f. 1958; Centre d'études Supérieures de Civilisation Médiévale; quarterly; pluri-disciplinary medieval studies, concentrating on the 10th–12th centuries; Dir MARTIN AURELL; circ. 1,000 (2013).

GEO: 413 rue Henri Barbusse, 92624 Gennevilliers Cedex; tel. 1-73-05-45-45; internet www.geomagazine.fr; f. 1979; monthly; architecture, culture, people, photo-journalism, travel; Editor-in-Chief ERIC MEYER; circ. 249,248.

La Géographie: 184 blvd Saint Germain, 75006 Paris; tel. 1-45-48-54-62; fax 1-42-22-40-93; e-mail socgeo@socgeo.org; internet www.socgeo.org; f. 1821; quarterly of the Société de Géographie; Chair. Prof. JEAN-ROBERT PITTE; Editor-in-Chief GILLES FUMEY.

L'Histoire: 74 ave du Maine, 75014 Paris; tel. 1-44-10-10-10; fax 1-44-10-54-47; e-mail courrier@histoire.presse.fr; internet www.histoire.presse.fr; f. 1978; monthly; Dir-Gen. PHILIPPE CLERGET; Editor-in-Chief VALÉRIE HANNIN; circ. 55,915.

Historia: 74 ave du Maine, 75014 Paris; tel. 1-44-10-10-10; fax 1-44-10-54-30; e-mail pczete@tallandier.fr; internet www.historia.fr; f. 1909; monthly; Editor-in-Chief PIERRE BARON; circ. 75,464.

National Geographic France: 13 rue Henri Barbusse, 92230 Gennevilliers; tel. 1-73-05-45-45; e-mail publication@nationalgeographic.fr; internet www.nationalgeographic.fr; f. 1999; monthly; geography, people, science, travel; Dir MARTIN TRAUTMANN; Editor-in-Chief JEAN-PIERRE VRIGNAUD; circ. 92,647.

Revue d'Histoire Diplomatique: 13 rue Soufflot, 75005 Paris; tel. 1-43-54-05-97; fax 1-46-34-07-60; e-mail librairie@pedone.info; internet www.pedone.info; f. 1837; quarterly; Editors BÉNÉDICTE PEDONE-RIBOT, MARC PEDONE.

Revue Historique: 56 rue Jacob, 75006 Paris; tel. 1-58-71-71-35; e-mail revuehistorique@puf.com; f. 1876; quarterly; Dirs CLAUDE GAUVARD, JEAN-FRANÇOIS SIRINELLI.

Revue de Synthèse: Centre International de Synthèse, 45 rue d'Ulm, 75005 Paris; tel. 1-44-32-26-54; fax 1-44-32-26-56; e-mail revuedesynthese@ens.fr; internet www.revue-de-synthese.eu; f. 1900; 4 a year; history, philosophy, social sciences; Editor-in-Chief ERIC BRIAN.

Home, Fashion and General

Art & Décoration: 149 rue Anatole France, 92534 Levallois-Perret Cedex; tel. 1-45-65-48-48; e-mail artdeco@lagardere-active.com;

internet www.maison-deco.com/magazine-art-decoration; f. 1897; 6 a year; Dir of Publication JEAN MASSIN; Editor-in-Chief CLÉMENCE BLANCHARD; circ. 303,003.

Be: 149 rue Anatole France, 92534 Levallois-Perret Cedex; tel. 1-41-34-60-00; e-mail anne.bianchi@lagardere-active.com; internet www.be.com; f. 2010; monthly; women's magazine; publ. by Lagardère Active; Editor-in-Chief ANNE BIANCHI; circ. 151,424.

Closer: 8 rue François Ory, 92543 Montrouge Cedex; tel. 1-46-48-48-14; internet www.closermag.fr; f. 2005; weekly; publ. by Mondadori France; celebrity news, TV, radio, films; Editor-in-Chief LAURENCE PIEAU; circ. 393,009.

Cosmopolitan: 10 blvd des Frères Voisin, 92792 Issy-les-Moulineaux Cedex 9; tel. 1-41-46-88-88; fax 1-41-48-84-93; e-mail cosmopub@gmc.tm.fr; internet www.cosmopolitan.fr; f. 1973; monthly; Editor-in-Chief SYLVIE OVERNOY; circ. 420,152.

Elle: 149 rue Anatole France, 92300 Levallois-Perret; tel. 1-41-34-60-00; fax 1-41-34-67-97; e-mail ellemagazine@hfp.fr; internet www.elle.fr; f. 1945; monthly; Dirs-Gen. ARNAUD LAGARDÈRE, ARJIL COMMANDITÉE-ARCO; Editor-in-Chief VALÉRIE TORANIAN; circ. 409,162.

Femme Actuelle: 13 rue Henri Barbusse, 92624 Gennevilliers; tel. 1-73-05-45-45; e-mail lectrices@femmeactuelle.fr; internet www.femmeactuelle.fr; f. 1984; weekly, Mon.; Editor-in-Chief ISABELLE CATÉLAN; circ. 843,416.

Ici-Paris: 149 rue Anatole France, 92534 Levallois-Perret; tel. 1-41-34-60-00; fax 1-41-34-89-34; f. 1945; weekly; celebrity gossip, news; publ. by Lagadère Active; Editors-in-Chief GIANNI LORENZON, JOËL LAFFAY; circ. 331,720.

Le Journal de la Maison: 149–151 rue Anatole France, 92534 Levallois-Perret Cedex; tel. 1-41-34-60-00; internet www.maison-deco.com/magazine-le-journal-de-la-maison; monthly; home; Editor-in-Chief ANNE GASTINEAU; circ. 178,625.

Marie-Claire: 10 blvd des Frères Voisin, 92792 Issy-les-Moulineaux Cedex 9; tel. 1-41-46-88-88; fax 1-41-46-86-86; e-mail mcredac@gmc.tm.fr; internet www.marieclaire.fr; f. 1954; monthly; Editor-in-Chief CHRISTINE LEIRITZ; circ. 494,382.

Marie-France: 10 blvd des Frères Voisin, 92792 Issy-Les-Moulineaux; tel. 1-41-46-83-77; e-mail contact@mariefrance.fr; f. 1944; monthly; Dir of Publication PASCAL CHEVALIER; circ. 186,353.

Maxi: 30–32 rue de Chabrol, 75010 Paris; tel. 1-40-22-75-00; fax 1-48-24-08-40; e-mail courrier@maxi.presse.fr; internet www.maxi-mag.fr; f. 1986; weekly; 100% subsidiary of Bauer Media Group; Editor-in-Chief KATHARINA HORBATSCH; circ. 429,897.

Modes et Travaux: 8 rue François Ory, 92543 Montrouge Cedex; tel. 1-46-48-48-48; fax 1-46-48-19-00; e-mail redaction.modesettravaux@mondadori.fr; internet www.modesettravaux.fr; f. 1919; monthly; publ. by Mondadori France; Editor PATRICIA WAGNER; circ. 461,919.

Notre Temps: 18 rue Barbès, 92128 Montrouge; tel. 1-74-31-60-60; fax 1-74-31-60-90; e-mail redaction@notretemps.com; internet www.notretemps.com; f. 1968; monthly; for retired people; Editor-in-Chief CAROLE RENUCCI; circ.880,960.

Nous Deux: 8 rue François Ory, 92543 Montrouge Cedex; tel. 1-46-48-43-40; fax 1-46-48-43-20; e-mail contact@mondadori.fr; f. 1947; weekly; Editor MARION MINUIT; circ. 296,405.

Parents: 149–151 rue Anatole France, 92534 Levallois-Perret Cedex; tel. 1-41-34-60-00; fax 1-41-34-70-79; e-mail catherine.lelievre@lagardere-active; internet www.parents.fr; f. 1969; monthly; magazine for parents; Editorial Dir CATHERINE LELIÈVRE; circ.272,729.

Pleine Vie: 8 rue François Ory, 92543 Montrouge Cedex; tel. 1-41-33-10-31; e-mail jeanne.thiriet@mondadori.fr; internet www.pleinevie.fr; f. 1997; monthly; intended for women aged 50 and over; Editor JEANNE THIRIET; circ. 730,000.

Point de Vue: 23 rue du Châteaudun, 75308 Paris Cedex 09; tel. 1-75-55-10-00; e-mail info@pointdevue.fr; internet www.pointdevue.fr; f. 1945; weekly, Mon.; general illustrated; publ. by Roularta Media; Editorial Dir COLOMBE PRINGLE; circ. 239,240.

Prima: 13 rue Henri Barbusse, 92624 Gennevilliers Cedex; tel. 1-73-05-45-45; internet www.prima.fr; f. 1982; monthly; intended for women of 40 years and over; also *Prima Maison* and *Prima Cuisine Gourmande*; Editor-in-Chief GWENDOLINE MICHAELIS; circ. 396,548.

Psychologies Magazine: 149–151 rue Anatole France, 92534 Levallois–Perret Cedex; tel. 1-41-34-60-00; e-mail laurence.r@psychologies.com; internet www.psychologies.com; monthly; Dir-Gen. ARNAUD DE SAINT SIMON; Editor-in-Chief ISABELLE MAURY; circ. 353,496.

Public: 149 rue Anatole France, 92534 Levallois-Perret Cedex; tel. 1-41-34-60-00; fax 1-41-34-90-98; internet www.public.fr; f. 2003; weekly, Mon.; celebrity news, TV, radio, films; Editorial Dir NICOLAS PIGASSE; Editor-in-Chief ANAÏS JOUVANCY; circ. 339,848.

Questions de Femmes: 117 rue de la Tour, 75116 Paris; tel. 1-45-03-80-00; e-mail fazire@groupe-ayache.com; internet www.questionsdefemmes.com; f. 1996; monthly; Editor-in-Chief FABIENNE AZIRE; circ. 85,557.

Santé Magazine: 22 rue Letellier, 75015 Paris; tel. 1-43-23-45-72; e-mail direction@santemagazine.fr; internet www.santemagazine.fr; f. 1976; monthly; health; Editor-in-Chief ALINE PERRAUDIN; circ. 349,841.

Top Santé: 8 rue François Ory, 92543 Montrouge Cedex; tel. 1-46-48-43-66; internet www.topsante.com; f. 1990; monthly; health; Editor SOPHIE DELAUGÈRE; circ. 404,385.

Vivre Plus: 18 rue Barbès, 92128 Montrouge Cedex; tel. 1-74-31-60 60; fax 1-74-31-60-69; internet www.vivreplus.fr; f. 2004 as *Côté Femme*; restyled as above 2006; monthly; aimed at women aged 40 years and above; Editor-in-Chief ODILE AMBLARD.

Vogue Paris: 26 rue Cambacérès, 75008 Paris; tel. 1-53-43-60-00; fax 1-53-43-61-61; e-mail info@condenast.fr; internet www.vogue.fr; monthly; Editor-in-Chief EMMANUELLE ALT; Publr DELPHINE ROYANT; circ. 160,050.

Voici: 13 rue Henri Barbusse, 92624 Gennevilliers Cedex; tel. 1-73-05-45-45; e-mail voici@prisma-presse.com; internet www.voici.fr; f. 1987; weekly, Mon.; celebrity news, TV, radio, films; Editor-in-Chief MARION ALOMBERT; circ. 426,238.

Leisure Interests and Sport

Cahiers du Cinéma: 65 rue Montmartre, 75002 Paris; tel. 1-53-44-75-75; fax 1-43-43-95-04; e-mail sdelorme@cahiersducinema.com; internet www.cahiersducinema.com; f. 1951; monthly; film reviews; Dir of Publication JÉRÔME CUZOL; Editor-in-Chief STÉPHANE DELORME; circ. 21,900.

Le Chasseur Français: 8 rue François Ory, 92543 Montrouge Cedex; tel. 1-41-33-50-01; f. 1885; monthly; hunting, shooting, fishing; Dir of Publication ERNESTO MAURI; Editor-in-Chief ANTOINE BERTON; circ. 308,533.

France-Football: 4 cours de l'Ile Seguin, BP 10302, 92102 Boulogne-Billancourt Cedex; tel. 1-40-93-20-20; fax 1-40-93-20-17; internet www.francefootball.fr; f. 1947; weekly; owned by Amaury Group; Editorial Dir DENIS CHAUMIER; circ. 101,240.

Le Journal de Mickey: 10 rue Thierry Le Luron, 92592 Levallois-Perret; tel. 1-41-34-88-73; fax 1-41-34-93-90; e-mail journaldemickey@lagardere-active.com; internet www.journaldemickey.com; f. 1934; weekly; cartoon magazine; publ. by Disney Hachette Presse; circ. 135,322.

Pariscope: 149–151 rue Anatole France, 92534 Levallois-Perret Cedex; tel. 1-41-34-60-60; fax 1-41-34-78-30; f. 1965; listings and reviews of events in Paris and Ile-de-France; weekly; Dir of Publication THOMAS KOUCK; Editorial Dir NATHALIE PESICIC; circ. 50,057.

Photo: 21 ave Gaston Monmousseau, 93240 Stains; tel. 1-48-22-11-66; e-mail photo@photo.fr; internet www.photo.fr; f. 1967; monthly; specialist photography magazine; Editorial Dir ERIC COLMET-DAÂGE; circ. 26,380.

Positif: 38 rue Milton, 75009 Paris; tel. 1-43-26-17-80; fax 1-43-26-29-77; e-mail posed@wanadoo.fr; internet www.revue-positif.net; f. 1952; monthly; film reviews; publ. by Editions Scope; Editor-in-Chief MICHEL CIMENT.

Première: 149 rue Anatole France, 92534 Levallois-Perret Cedex; tel. 1-41-34-60-00; fax 1-41-34-89-92; internet www.premiere.fr; monthly; film reviews; Dir of Publication THOMAS KOUCK; Editor-in-Chief MATHIEU CARRATIER; circ. 139,078.

Télé 7 Jours: 149 rue Anatole France, 92534 Levallois-Perret Cedex; tel. 1-41-34-60-00; fax 1-41-34-79-70; e-mail claire.leost@lagardere-active.com; internet www.tele7.fr; weekly; television; Dir of Publication CLAIRE LEOST; Editorial Dir THIERRY MOREAU; circ. 1,357,506.

Télé Poche: 8 rue François Ory, 92543 Montrouge Cedex; tel. 1-41-33-50-00; fax 1-41-33-57-48; e-mail pierreyves.simon@emapfrance.com; internet www.telepoche.fr; f. 1966; weekly; publ. by Mondadori France; television; Editor-in-Chief ERIC PAVON; circ. 493,606.

Télérama: 8 rue Jean-Antoine de Baïf, Paris 75212 Cedex 13; tel. 1-55-30-55-30; fax 1-47-64-02-04; internet www.telerama.fr; f. 1972; weekly, Wed.; radio, TV, film, literature and music; Editorial Dir FABIENNE PASCAUD; circ. 621,417.

Télé Star: 8 rue François Ory, 92543 Montrouge Cedex; tel. 1-41-33-53-50; e-mail lecteurs.telestar@mondadori.fr; internet www.telestar.fr; f. 1976; weekly; television; Editorial Dir ERIC PAVON; circ. 1,093,507.

Télé Z: 10 ave de Messine, 75008 Paris; tel. 1-53-83-93-40; internet www.telez.fr; weekly; television; Editor-in-Chief LUCIE DUKAT; circ. 1,400,083.

Vélo Magazine: cours de l'Ile Seguin, BP 10302, 92102 Boulogne-Billancourt Cedex; tel. 1-40-93-20-20; fax 1-40-93-20-09; e-mail redac@velomagazine.fr; internet www.velomagazine.fr; monthly; cycling; Editor-in-Chief GILLES COMTE; circ. 49,539.

Voiles et Voiliers: 21 rue du Faubourg Saint-Antoine, 75550 Paris Cedex 11; tel. 1-44-87-87-87; fax 1-44-87-87-09; e-mail accueil@voilesetvoiliers.com; internet www.voilesetvoiliers.com; monthly; sailing and nautical sports; Dir of Publication FRANÇOIS RÉGIS HUTIN; circ. 51,025.

Religion and Philosophy

Actualité Juive: 14 rue Raymonde Salez, 93260 Les Lilas; tel. 1-43-60-20-20; fax 1-43-60-20-21; e-mail a-j-presse@actuj.com; internet www.actuj.com; weekly; Dir LYDIA BENATTAR; circ. 17,000 (2004).

Etudes: 14 rue d'Assas, 75006 Paris; tel. 1-44-39-48-48; fax 1-44-39-48-17; e-mail etudes@free.fr; internet www.revue-etudes.com; f. 1856; monthly; general interest; Editor-in-Chief FRANÇOIS EUVÉ.

France Catholique: 60 rue de Fontenay, 92350 Le Plessis-Robinson; tel. 1-46-30-79-01; fax 1-46-30-04-64; e-mail france-catholique@wanadoo.fr; internet www.france-catholique.fr; weekly; Dir FRÉDÉRIC AIMARD; Editor-in-Chief GÉRARD LECLERC; circ. 16,000 (2004).

Le Monde des Religions: 80 blvd Auguste-Blanqui, 75707 Paris Cedex 13; tel. 1-48-88-46-00; fax 1-42-27-04-19; e-mail contact@lemondedesreligions.fr; internet www.lemondedesreligions.fr; f. 2003 to replace *Actualité des Religions*; 6 a year; Editorial Dir VIRGINIE LAROUSSE; circ. 43,306.

Pèlerin: 18 rue Barbès, 92128 Montrouge; tel. 1-74-31-60-60; fax 1-74-31-60-21; e-mail pelerin@bayard-presse.com; internet www.pelerin.info; f. 1873; weekly; Dir GEORGES SANEROT; Editor-in-Chief ANTOINE D'ABBUNDO; circ. 211,091.

Philosophie Magazine: 10 rue Ballu, 75009 Paris; tel. 1-43-80-46-10; internet www.philomag.com; f. 2006; monthly; Dir FABRICE GERSCHEL; Editor CÉDRIC ENJALBERT; circ. 53,489.

Prier: 80 blvd Auguste-Blanqui, 75707 Paris Cedex 13; tel. 1-48-88-46-00; fax 1-42-27-29-03; e-mail contacts-prier@mp.com.fr; internet www.prier.presse.fr; f. 1978; monthly; review of modern prayer and contemplation; Editor XAVIER ACCART.

Réforme: 53–55 ave du Maine, 75014 Paris; tel. 1-43-20-32-67; fax 1-43-21-42-86; e-mail reforme@reforme.net; internet www.reforme.net; f. 1945; weekly; considers current affairs from a Protestant Christian perspective; Dir ANTOINE NOUIS; Editor-in-Chief NATHALIE DE SENNVILLE-LEENHARDT; circ. 6,000 (2003).

Revue des Sciences Philosophiques et Théologiques: Le Saulchoir, 45 rue de la Glacière, 75013 Paris; tel. 1-42-17-45-60; internet rspt.fr; f. 1907; quarterly; Dir GILLES BERCEVILLE.

Silence: Ecologie, Alternatives, Non-violence: 9 rue Dumenge, 69317 Lyon Cedex 04; tel. 4-78-39-55-33; fax 4-78-28-85-12; internet www.revuesilence.net; f. 1982; monthly.

Témoignage Chrétien: 3–5 rue de Metz, 75010 Paris; tel. 1-44-83-82-82; fax 1-44-83-82-88; e-mail initialeduprenom.nom@temoignagechretien.fr; internet www.temoignagechretien.fr; f. 1941; weekly; Christianity and politics; Editor-in-Chief CHRISTINE PEDOTTI.

La Voix Protestante: 14 rue de Trévise, 75009 Paris; tel. 1-47-70-23-53; fax 1-48-01-09-13; e-mail direction@lavoixprotestante.org; internet www.erf-rp.org; monthly review of Protestant churches in Paris and Eastern regions; Dir DANIEL CASSOU.

Science and Technology

Air et Cosmos: 1 bis ave de la République, 75011 Paris; tel. 1-49-29-30-00; fax 1-49-29-32-01; e-mail air-cosmos@air-cosmos.com; internet www.aerospacemedia.com; f. 1963; weekly; aerospace; Dir-Gen. and Editorial Dir ROBERT MONTEUX; Editor-in-Chief GUILLAUME LECOMPTE-BOINET; circ. 20,290.

Annales de Chimie—Science des Matériaux: Lavoisier SAS, 14 rue de Provigny, 94236 Cachan Cedex; tel. 1-47-40-67-00; fax 1-47-40-67-02; e-mail acsm@lavoisier.fr; internet acsm.revuesonline.com; f. 1789; 6 a year; chemistry and material science.

L'argus: 11–13 rue des Petits Hotels, 75010 Paris; tel. 1-53-29-11-00; internet www.largus.fr; f. 1927; motoring weekly; Editorial Dir DIDIER LAURENT; circ. 29,946.

Astérisque: Société Mathématique de France, Institut Henri Poincaré, 11 rue Pierre et Marie Curie, 75231 Paris Cedex 05; tel. 1-44-27-67-99; fax 1-40-46-90-96; e-mail revues@smf.ens.fr; internet smf.emath.fr/publications/asterisque; f. 1973; 6–8 a year; mathematics; Editor-in-Chief ERIC VASSEROT; Sec. NATHALIE CHRISTIAËN.

L'Astronomie: 3 rue Beethoven, 75016 Paris; tel. 1-42-24-13-74; fax 1-42-30-75-47; e-mail redac.saf@wanadoo.fr; internet www.saf-lastronomie.com; f. 1887; monthly; publ. by Société Astronomique de France; Editor-in-Chief MARIE-CLAUDE PASKOFF.

Auto-Moto: 149 rue Anatole France, 92534 Levallois-Perret Cedex; tel. 1-41-34-60-00; fax 1-41-34-95-26; e-mail redaction@autonews.fr; internet www.autonews.fr; monthly; cars; Dir BRUNO LESOUËF; Editor-in-Chief CHRISTOPHE BOULAIN; circ. 241,075.

Auto Plus: 8 rue François Ory, 92543 Montrouge Cedex; tel. 1-41-33-51-16; fax 1-41-33-57-06; e-mail olivier.bernis@mondadori.fr; internet www.autoplus.fr; fortnightly; cars; Editor-in-Chief OLIVIER BERNIS; circ. 305,359.

Biochimie: Centre universitaire des Saints Pères, 45 rue des Saints Pères, 75270 Paris Cedex 06; tel. 1-42-86-33-77; fax 1-42-86-33-73; e-mail redaction.biochemie@ibpc.fr; internet www.elsevier.com/locate/biochi; f. 1914; monthly; biochemistry; Editor-in-Chief RICHARD BUCKINGHAM.

Electronique Pratique: 3 blvd Ney, 75018 Paris; tel. 1-44-65-80-80; fax 1-44-65-80-90; e-mail publicite@electroniquepratique.com; internet www.electroniquepratique.com; monthly; electronics; Editorial Dir PATRICK VERCHER.

Industries et Technologies: Antony Parc II–10, place du Général de Gaulle, 92160 Antony Cedex; tel. 1-77-92-92-92; fax 1-77-92-98-51; e-mail p.wagner@industries-technologies.com; internet www.industries-technologies.com; f. 1958 as Industries et Techniques; present name adopted 2002; monthly; Editor-in-Chief MURIEL DE VERICOURT.

Ingénieurs de l'Automobile: Editions VB, 7 rue Jean Mermoz, 78000 Versailles; tel. 1-39-20-88-05; fax 1-39-20-88-06; e-mail vblcda@lcda.fr; internet www.lcda.fr/site/ingenieurs_de_l_automobile-gb.php; f. 1927; 6 a year; technical automobile review, in French and English; Editor-in-Chief ERIC BIGOURDAN; circ. 9,000 (2012).

Matériaux et Techniques: EDP Sciences, 17 ave du Hoggar, Parc d'Activités de Courtaboeuf, BP 112, 91944 Les Ulis Cedex A; tel. 1-69-18-75-75; fax 1-69-28-84-91; e-mail contact@edpsciences.org; internet www.mattech-journal.org; f. 1913; 7 a year; review of engineering research and progress on industrial materials; publ. by EDP Sciences; Editors-in-Chief RENÉ GRAS, VINCENT VERNEY.

Le Monde Informatique: 40 blvd Henri Sellier, 92150 Suresnes; tel. 1-41-97-02-02; fax 1-41-97-02-01; e-mail redac_weblmi@it-news-info.com; internet www.lemondeinformatique.fr; f. 1981; weekly; information science; Editor-in-Chief SERGE LEBLAL; circ. 29,236 (2006).

Le Moniteur des Travaux Publics et du Bâtiment: 17 rue d'Uzès, 75108 Paris Cedex 02; tel. 1-40-13-30-30; fax 1-40-13-50-21; e-mail contact.groupemoniteur@groupemoniteur.fr; internet www.lemoniteur.fr; f. 1903; weekly; construction; Dir-Gen. OLIVIER DE LA CHAISE; Dir of Publication GUILLAUME PROT; circ. 48,257.

Psychologie Française: 71 ave Edouard-Vaillant, 92774 Boulogne Cedex; tel. 1-55-20-58-32; fax 1-55-20-58-34; e-mail a.dore@elsevier.com; f. 1956; quarterly; review of the Société Française de Psychologie, publ. by Elsevier France; Editor ALINE CHEVALIER.

La Recherche: 74 ave du Maine, 75014 Paris; tel. 1-40-10-10-10; fax 1-40-10-54-30; e-mail courrier@larecherche.fr; internet www.larecherche.fr; monthly; science; Dir of Publication PHILIPPE CLERGET; Editor-in-Chief ALINE RICHARD; circ. 38,422.

Science et Vie: 8 rue François Ory, 92543 Montrouge Cedex; tel. 1-41-33-50-01; fax 1-46-48-48-67; e-mail svmens@mondadori.fr; internet www.science-et-vie.com; f. 1913; monthly; Dir of Publication CARMINE PERNA; Editorial Dir MATTHIEU VILLIERS; circ. 338,218.

Sciences et Avenir: 12 place de la Bourse, 75002 Paris; tel. 1-44-88-34-34; e-mail redaction@sciences-et-avenir.com; internet sciencesetavenirmensuel.nouvelobs.com; monthly; Dir of Publication LAURENT JOFFRIN; circ. 270,576.

NEWS AGENCIES

Agence France-Presse (AFP): 13 place de la Bourse, 75002 Paris; tel. 1-40-41-46-46; fax 1-40-41-46-32; e-mail contact@afp.com; internet www.afp.fr; f. 1944; 24-hour service of world political, financial, entertainment, science and technology, sporting news, and photographs; 200 bureaux, and 2,260 correspondents worldwide; Pres. and Dir-Gen. EMMANUEL HOOG; Editor-in-Chief MARIELLE EUDES.

Agence Parisienne de Presse: 16 rue Saint Fiacre, 75002 Paris; tel. 1-42-36-51-02; fax 1-42-36-04-62; f. 1949; Man. Dir MICHEL BURTON.

Infomédia SAS: 58 rue de Châteaudun, 75009 Paris; tel. 1-48-01-87-34; e-mail redaction@infomedia-sas.com; internet www.infomedia-sas.com; f. 1988; economic and financial news; Pres. JEAN-DAMIEN CHÂTELAIN.

PRESS ASSOCIATIONS

Comité de Liaison de la Presse: 13 rue Lafayette, 75009 Paris; tel. 1-44-06-42-57; e-mail comite-liaison-presse@orange.fr; liaison organization for press, radio and cinema.

Fédération Française des Agences de Presse (FFAP): 24 rue du Faubourg Poissonnière, 75010 Paris; tel. 1-42-47-01-00; e-mail contact@ffap.fr; internet www.ffap.fr; comprises 5 syndicates (news, photographs, television, general information and multimedia) with a total membership of 109 agencies; Pres. and Dir of Publication KATHLEEN GROSSET.

Fédération Nationale de la Presse Française (FNPF): 13 rue La Fayette, 75009 Paris; tel. 1-53-20-90-50; fax 1-44-90-43-72; f. 1944; mems: Syndicat de la Presse Quotidienne Nationale, Syndicat Professionnel de la Presse Magazine et d'Opinion, Syndicat de la Presse Quotidienne Départementale, Fédération de la Presse Périodique Régionale, Fédération Nationale de la Presse d'Information Spécialisée.

Fédération Nationale de la Presse d'Information Spécialisée: 17 rue Castagnary, 75015 Paris; tel. 1-44-90-43-60; fax 1-44-90-43-72; e-mail contact@fnps.fr; internet www.fnps.fr; comprises Syndicat National de la Presse Agricole et Rurale (SNPAR), Syndicat de la Presse et de l'Edition des Professions de Santé (SPEPS), Syndicat de la Presse Culturelle et Scientifique (SPCS), Syndicat de la Presse Economique, Juridique et Politique (SPEJP), Syndicat de la Presse Professionnelle (SP—PRO), Syndicat de la Presse Magazine et Spécialisée (SPMS) and Syndicat de la Presse Sociale (SPS), representing some 1,350 specialized or professional publications; Pres. CHRISTIAN BRUNEAU.

Fédération de la Presse Périodique Régionale: 72 rue d'Hauteville, 75010 Paris; tel. 1-45-23-98-00; fax 1-45-23-98-01; e-mail sphr@sphr.fr; internet www.sphr.fr; f. 1970; present name adopted 1992; mems: Syndicat de la Presse Hebdomadaire Régionale, Syndicat National des Publications Régionales, Syndicat de la Presse Judiciaire de Province, Syndicat National de la Presse Judiciaire; represents 250 regional periodical publications; Pres. ERIC LEJEUNE; Sec.-Gen. WILLIAMS CAPTIER.

Syndicat de la Presse Quotidienne Régionale: 17 place des Etats-Unis, 75116 Paris; tel. 1-40-73-80-20; fax 1-47-20-48-94; internet www.spqr.fr; f. 1986; regional dailies; Pres. JEAN VIANSSON PONTÉ; Sec.-Gen. JACQUES HARDOIN.

PRESS INSTITUTE

Institut Français de Presse: 83 bis rue Notre Dame des Champs, 75006 Paris; tel. 1-53-63-53-20; e-mail ifp@u-paris2.fr; internet ifp.u-paris2.fr; f. 1937; university training programme in mass communication and journalism; maintains research and documentation centre; open to research workers, students, journalists; Dir NATHALIE SONNAC.

Publishers

Actes Sud: Le Méjan, place Nina-Berberova, BP 90038, 13633 Arles; tel. 4-90-49-86-91; fax 4-90-96-95-25; e-mail contact@actes-sud.fr; internet www.actes-sud.fr; f. 1978; French and translated literature, music, theatre, studies of Arabic and Islamic civilizations; Pres. FRANÇOISE NYSSEN; Editorial Dir BERTRAND PY.

Editions Albin Michel: 22 rue Huyghens, 75014 Paris Cedex 14; tel. 1-42-79-10-00; fax 1-43-27-21-58; e-mail virginie.caminade@albin-michel.fr; internet www.albin-michel.fr; f. 1901; general, fiction, history, classics; Pres. FRANCIS ESMÉNARD; Man. Dir RICHARD DUCOUSSET.

Armand Colin Editeur: 21 rue du Montparnasse, 75006 Paris Cedex 06; tel. 1-44-39-54-47; fax 1-40-46-49-93; e-mail infos@armand-colin.com; internet www.armand-colin.com; f. 1870; imprint of Hachette Livre; literature, history, human and social sciences, university textbooks; Dir-Gen. PHILIPPE CLÉMENÇOT.

Assouline: 26 place Vendome, 75001 Paris; tel. 1-42-60-76 09; fax 1-42-60-33-85; e-mail production@assouline.com; internet www.assouline.com; f. 1994; art, fashion, design, lifestyle; Dir PROSPER ASSOULINE.

Editions de l'Atelier: 51-55 rue Hoche, 94200 Ivry-sur-Seine; tel. 1-45-15-20-20; fax 1-45-15-20-22; e-mail contact@editionsatelier.com; internet www.editionsatelier.com; f. 1929; religious, educational, political and social, including labour movement; Dir-Gen. BERNARD STÉPHAN.

Groupe Bayard: 18 rue Barbès, 92128 Montrouge Cedex; tel. 1-74-31-60-60; fax 1-74-31-61-61; e-mail communication@bayardpresse.com; internet www.groupebayard.com; f. 1870; children's books, religion, human sciences; Pres. GEORGES SANEROT; Man. Dir HUBERT CHICOU.

Beauchesne Editeur: 7 Cité du Cardinal Lemoine, 75005 Paris; tel. 1-53-10-08-18; fax 1-53-10-85-19; e-mail contact@editions-beauchesne.com; internet www.editions-beauchesne.com; f. 1850; scripture, religion and theology, philosophy, religious history, politics, encyclopaedias; Man. Dir JEAN-ETIENNE MITTELMANN.

Editions Belfond: 12 ave d'Italie, 75627 Paris Cedex 13; tel. 1-44-16-05-00; fax 1-44-16-05-06; e-mail belfond@placedesediteurs.com; internet www.belfond.fr; f. 1963; fiction, poetry, documents, history, arts; Chair. JÉRÔME TALAMON; Editorial Dir JULIETTE JOSTE.

Berger-Levrault: 104 ave du Président Kennedy, 75016 Paris; tel. 1-40-64-42-32; fax 1-40-64-42-30; e-mail ble@berger-levrault.fr; internet www.berger-levrault.fr; f. 1676; fine arts, health, social and economic sciences, law; Pres. and Dir-Gen. ALAIN SOURISSEAU; Man. Dir PIERRE-MARIE LEHUCHER.

Bordas: 31 ave Pierre de Coubertin, 75013 Paris; tel. 1-72-36-40-00; fax 1-72-36-40-10; e-mail cjacqueson@bordas.tm.fr; internet www.editions-bordas.com; f. 1946; imprint of Editis (q.v.); encyclopaedias, dictionaries, history, geography, arts, children's and educational; Pres. OLIVIER QUERENET DE BREVILLE; Dir of Publication CATHERINE LUCET.

Buchet-Chastel: 7 rue des Canettes, 75006 Paris; tel. 1-44-32-05-60; fax 1-44-32-05-61; e-mail informations@libella.fr; internet www.buchetchastel.fr; f. 1929; literature, music, crafts, religion, practical guides; part of the Libella publishing group; Chair. VERA MICHALSKI.

Editions Calmann-Lévy: 31 rue de Fleurus, 75006 Paris; tel. 1-49-54-36-00; e-mail editions@calmann-levy.com; internet www.editions-calmann-levy.com; f. 1836; French and foreign literature, history, social sciences, economics, sport, leisure; Dir-Gen. FLORENCE SULTAN.

Editions Casterman: 87 quai Panhard et Levassor, 75647 Paris Cedex 13; tel. 1-55-28-12-00; fax 1-55-28-12-60; e-mail info@casterman.com; internet www.casterman.com; f. 1780; juvenile, comics, fiction, education, leisure, art; since 1999 subsidiary of Flammarion; Editorial Dir BENOÎT MOUCHARD.

Editions du Cerf: 24 rue des Tanneries, 75013 Paris; tel. 1-80-05-36-36; fax 1-80-05-36-10; internet www.editionsducerf.fr; f. 1929; religion, history, philosophy; Chair. MICHEL BON; Man. Dir JEAN-FRANÇOIS COLOSIMO.

Editions Champ Vallon: rue Gérin, 01420 Seyssel; tel. and fax 4-50-56-15-51; e-mail info@champ-vallon.com; internet www.champ-vallon.com; f. 1980; social sciences, literary history, literary criticism; Dirs MYRIAM MONTEIRO-BRAZ, PATRICK BEAUNE.

Editions Chiron: 1155 rue de Fontenay, 94300 Vincennes; tel. 1-30-48-74-50; fax 1-34-98-02-44; e-mail info@editionschiron.com; internet www.editionschiron.com; f. 1907; sport, education, fitness, health, dance, games; Dir THIERRY HEUNINCK.

Editions Dalloz: 31–35 rue Froidevaux, 75685 Paris Cedex 14; tel. 1-40-64-54-54; fax 1-40-64-54-97; e-mail ventes@dalloz.fr; internet www.dalloz.fr; f. 1824; law, philosophy, political science, business and economics; imprint of Hachette Livre; Pres. and Dir-Gen. SYLVIE FAYE.

Dargaud: 15–27 rue Moussorgski, 75895 Paris Cedex 18; tel. 1-53-26-32-32; fax 1-53-26-32-00; e-mail contact@dargaud.fr; internet www.dargaud.fr; f. 1943; juvenile, cartoons, comics, video, graphic novels; Dir-Gen. JEAN-CHRISTOPHE DELPIERRE.

Editions de Boccard: 11 rue de Médicis, 75006 Paris; tel. 1-43-26-00-37; fax 1-43-54-85-83; e-mail info@deboccard.com; internet www.deboccard.com; f. 1866; history, archaeology, religion, orientalism, medievalism; Dir ISABELLE MALAISE.

La Découverte: 9 bis rue Abel Hovelacque, 75013 Paris; tel. 1-44-08-84-01; fax 1-44-08-84-39; e-mail ladecouverte@editionsladecouverte.com; internet www.editionsladecouverte.fr; f. 1959; imprint of Editis (q.v.); economic, social and political science, literature, history; Man. Dir FRANÇOIS GÈZE.

Editions Denoël: 33 rue Saint-André des Arts, 75006 Paris; tel. 1-44-39-73-73; fax 1-44-39-73-90; e-mail denoel@denoel.fr; internet www.denoel.fr; f. 1930; imprint of Editions Gallimard; general literature, science fiction, crime, history; Dir-Gen. BÉATRICE DUVAL.

La Documentation Française: 29 quai Voltaire, 75344 Paris Cedex 07; tel. 1-40-15-70-00; fax 1-40-15-72-30; e-mail depcom@ladocumentationfrancaise.fr; internet www.ladocumentationfrancaise.fr; f. 1945; govt publs; politics, law, economics, culture, science; Dir of Publication XAVIER PATIER.

Dunod: 5 rue Laromiguière, 75005 Paris Cedex; tel. 1-40-46-35-00; fax 1-40-46-49-95; e-mail infos@dunod.com; internet www.dunod.com; f. 1800; science, computer science, electronics, economics, accountancy, management, psychology and humanities; imprint of Hachette Livre; Dir-Gen. NATHALIE DE BAUDRY D'ASSON.

Edilarge Editions Ouest-France: 13 rue du Breil, 35063 Rennes Cedex; tel. 2-99-32-58-27; fax 2-99-32-58-30; e-mail editorial@edilarge.fr; internet www.edilarge.fr; history, guides; subsidiary of Ouest-France group; fmrly Editions Ouest-France; Chair. FRANÇOIS-XAVIER HUTIN; Dir-Gen. SERVANE BIGUAIS.

Edisud: Les Joncades Basses 13210 Saint-Rémy-de-Provence; tel. 4-90-90-21-10; fax 4-42-21-56-20; e-mail info@edisud.com; internet www.edisud.com; f. 1971; health, wellness; Dir CHARLY-YVES CHAUDOREILLE.

Editis: 30 pl. d'Italie, 75702 Paris Cedex 13; tel. 1-53-53-30-00; fax 1-72-36-47-10; e-mail benoit.liva@vupublishing.net; internet www

.editis.com; f. 1835 as Havas; renamed Vivendi Universal Publishing 2001, then VUP-Investima 10 in 2003; present name adopted Oct. 2003; wholly owned subsidiary of Grupo Planeta since May 2008; education, literature, reference; imprints include Bordas, La Découverte, Editions First, Fleuve Noir, Editions Nathan, Editions Robert Laffont, Le Robert; Dir of Publishing ALAIN KOUCK.

Editions Eyrolles: 61 blvd Saint Germain, 75240 Paris Cedex 05; tel. 1-44-41-11-11; fax 1-44-41-11-44; e-mail editeurs@editions-eyrolles.com; internet www.editions-eyrolles.com; f. 1918; science, computing, technology, electronics, management, law; Pres. and Dir-Gen. SERGE EYROLLES.

Fayard: 13 rue du Montparnasse, 75006 Paris; tel. 1-45-49-82-00; fax 1-45-49-82-54; e-mail rights@editions-fayard.fr; internet www.editions-fayard.fr; f. 1857; literature, biography, history, religion, essays, music; CEO SOPHIE DE CLOSETS.

Editions des Femmes Antoinette Fouque: 35 rue Jacob, 75006 Paris; tel. 1-42-22-60-74; fax 1-42-22-62-73; e-mail contact@desfemmes.fr; internet www.desfemmes.fr; f. 1973; mainly women authors; fiction, essays, art, history, politics, psychoanalysis, talking books; Dir ANTOINETTE FOUQUE.

Editions First: 12 ave d'Italie, 75013 Paris; tel. 1-45-49-60-00; fax 1-45-49-60-01; e-mail firstinfo@efirst.com; internet www.efirst.com; f. 1992; imprint of Editis (q.v.); general non-fiction; Pres. VINCENT BARBARE.

Editions Flammarion: 87 quai Panhard et Levassor, 75647 Paris Cedex 13; tel. 1-40-51-31-00; fax 1-43-29-21-48; internet editions.flammarion.com; f. 1876; general literature, art, human sciences, sport, children's books, medicine; subsidiary of Flammarion Group; Pres. and Dir-Gen. TERESA CREMISI.

Editions Fleurus: 15–27 rue Moussorgski, 75018 Paris; tel. 1-53-26-33-35; fax 1-53-26-33-36; e-mail fleuruseditions@fleuruseditions.com; internet www.editionsfleurus.com; f. 1944; arts, education, leisure, religion; also Mame, Mango, Rustica, Tardy, Critérion, Desclée, Droguet et Ardant; Chair. VINCENT MONTAGNE; Man. Dir HILAIRE DE LAAGE.

Fleuve Noir: 12 ave d'Italie, 75627 Paris Cedex 13; tel. 1-44-16-05-00; fax 1-44-16-05-07; e-mail deborah.druba@universpoche.com; internet www.fleuvenoir.fr; f. 1949; imprint of Editis (q.v.); general fiction, crime, thrillers, fantasy and science fiction; Pres. and Dir-Gen. MARIE-CHRISTINE CONCHON; Editorial Dir DEBORAH DRUBA.

Editions Foucher: 11 rue Paul Bert, 92247 Malakoff Cedex; tel. 1-41-23-65-65; e-mail cfages@editions-foucher.fr; internet www.editions-foucher.fr; f. 1936; science, economics, law, medicine textbooks; Dir of Publication OLIVIER JAOUI.

Editions Gallimard: 5 rue Gaston-Gallimard, 75328 Paris Cedex 07; tel. 1-49-54-42-00; fax 1-45-44-94-03; e-mail pub@gallimard.fr; internet www.gallimard.fr; f. 1911; general fiction, literature, history, poetry, children's, philosophy; Dir ANTOINE GALLIMARD; Editorial Dir TERESA CREMISI.

Editions Grasset et Fasquelle: 61 rue des Saints Pères, 75006 Paris; tel. 1-44-39-22-00; fax 1-42-22-64-18; e-mail dfanelli@grasset.fr; internet www.grasset.fr; f. 1907; contemporary literature, criticism, general fiction and children's books; Pres. OLIVIER NORA.

Librairie Gründ: 60 rue Mazarine, 75006 Paris; tel. 1-44-16-09-00; fax 1-45-49-60-01; e-mail grund@grund.fr; internet www.grund.fr; f. 1880; art, natural history, children's books, guides; Chair. ALAIN GRÜND.

Hachette Livre: 43 quai de Grenelle, 75905 Paris Cedex 15; tel. and fax 1-43-92-30-00; internet www.hachette.com; f. 1826; group comprises over 40 publishing houses in France and abroad, particularly in the United Kingdom and Spain; Pres. and Dir-Gen. ARNAUD NOURRY.

L'Harmattan Edition: 7 rue de l'Ecole Polytechnique, 75005 Paris; tel. 1-40-46-79-20; fax 1-43-25-82-03; e-mail harmat@worldnet.fr; internet www.editions-harmattan.fr; f. 1975; politics, human sciences, developing countries; Dir DENIS PRYEN.

Editions Hatier: 8 rue d'Assas, 75278 Paris Cedex 06; tel. 1-49-54-49-54; fax 1-40-49-00-45; e-mail informationspedagogiques@editions-hatier.fr; internet www.editions-hatier.fr; f. 1880; children's books, fiction, history, science, nature guides; Chair. BERNARD FOULON; Dir-Gen. CÉLIA ROSENTRAUB.

Hermann: 6 rue Labrouste, 75015 Paris; tel. 1-45-57-45-40; fax 1-40-60-12-93; e-mail hermann.sa@wanadoo.fr; internet www.editions-hermann.fr; f. 1876; sciences and art, humanities; Editorial Dir ARTHUR COHEN.

J'ai Lu: 87 quai Panhard et Levassor, 75647 Paris Cedex 13; tel. 1-40-51-31-00; fax 1-43-29-21-48; e-mail ajasmin@jailu.com; internet www.jailu.com; f. 1958; fiction, paperbacks; subsidiary of Flammarion Group; Chair. CHARLES-HENRI FLAMMARION; Man. Dir BERTRAND LOBRY.

Editions Julliard: 24 ave Marceau, 75008 Paris; tel. 1-53-67-14-00; fax 1-53-67-14-14; internet www.julliard.fr; f. 1942; general literature, biography, essays; imprint of Editions Robert Laffont/Editis (qq.v.); Dirs BETTY MIALET, BERNARD BARRAULT.

Editions du JurisClasseur: 141 rue de Javel, 75747 Paris Cedex 15; tel. 1-45-58-93-76; fax 1-45-58-94-00; e-mail editorial@juris-classeur.com; internet www.juris-classeur.com; mem. of Groupe Lexis-Nexis (ReedElsevier); imprints include Litec and Légisoft; law, economics, taxation; Dir of Publication PHILIPPE CARILLON.

Karthala Editions: 22–24 blvd Arago, 75013 Paris; tel. 1-43-31-15-59; fax 1-45-35-27-05; e-mail karthala@orange.fr; internet www.karthala.com; f. 1980; politics, history, geography, anthropology, religious studies, Christianity, Islam, the Arabic-speaking world; Exec. Dir XAVIER AUDRAIN; Dir of Publication ROBERT AGENEAU.

Editions Jeanne Laffitte: 25 Cours d'Estienne d'Orves, BP 1903, 13225 Marseille Cedex 01; tel. 4-91-59-80-43; fax 4-91-54-25-64; e-mail editions@jeanne-laffitte.com; internet www.jeanne-laffitte.com; f. 1978; art, geography, culture, medicine, history; Chair. and Man. Dir JEANNE LAFFITTE.

Editions Robert Laffont: 24 ave Marceau, 75381 Paris Cedex 08; tel. 1-53-67-14-00; fax 1-53-67-14-14; e-mail gmessina@robert-laffont.fr; internet www.laffont.fr; f. 1941; imprint of Editis (q.v.); Pres. and Dir-Gen. ALAIN KOUCK.

Larousse: 21 rue du Montparnasse, 75006 Paris Cedex 06; tel. 1-44-39-44-00; fax 1-44-39-43-43; e-mail livres-larousse@larousse.fr; internet www.larousse.com; f. 1852; general, specializing in dictionaries, illustrated books on scientific subjects, encyclopaedias, classics; imprint of Hachette Livre (q.v.); Dir of Publication ISABELLE JEUGE-MAYNART.

Editions J.-C. Lattès: 17 rue Jacob, 75006 Paris; tel. 1-44-41-74-00; fax 1-43-25-30-47; e-mail mpageix@editions-jclattes.fr; internet www.editions-jclattes.fr; f. 1968; imprint of Hachette Livre (q.v.); general fiction and non-fiction, biography; Man. Dir ISABELLE LAFFONT.

Letouzey et Ané: 87 blvd Raspail, 75006 Paris; tel. 1-45-48-80-14; fax 1-45-49-03-43; e-mail letouzey@free.fr; internet www.letouzey.com; f. 1885; theology, religion, archaeology, history, ecclesiastical encyclopaedias and dictionaries, biography; Man. Dir FLORENCE LETOUZEY.

Le Livre de Poche: 31 rue de Fleurus, 75006 Paris Cedex 06; tel. 1-49-54-37-00; fax 1-49-54-37-01; internet www.livredepoche.com; f. 1953; general literature, dictionaries, encyclopaedias; Man. Editor LAURA BEHN.

Editions Magnard: 5 allée de la 2ème Division Blindée, 75015 Paris; fax 1-42-79-46-80; e-mail contact@magnard.fr; internet www.magnard.fr; f. 1933; children's and educational books; subsidiary of Editions Albin Michel; Dir of Publication GUILLAUME DERVIEUX.

Elsevier Masson: 62 rue Camille Desmoulins, 92442 Issy les Moulineaux Cedex; tel. 1-71-16-55-99; e-mail infos@elsevier-masson.fr; internet www.elsevier-masson.fr; f. 2005; medicine and science, books and periodicals; publrs for various academies and societies; subsidiary of Elsevier; Pres. DANIEL RODRIGUEZ.

Mercure de France: 26 rue de Condé, 75006 Paris; tel. 1-55-42-61-90; e-mail mercure@mercure.fr; internet www.mercuredefrance.fr; f. 1893; general fiction, history, biography, sociology; Pres. and Man. Dir ISABELLE GALLIMARD.

Editions de Minuit: 7 rue Bernard Palissy, 75006 Paris; tel. 1-44-39-39-20; fax 1-44-39-39-23; e-mail contact@leseditionsdeminuit.fr; internet www.leseditionsdeminuit.fr; f. 1945; general literature; Man. Dir IRÈNE LINDON.

Editions Nathan: 25 ave Pierre de Coubertin, 75211 Paris Cedex 13; tel. 1-45-87-50-00; fax 1-47-07-57-57; e-mail frubert@nathan.fr; internet www.nathan.fr; f. 1881; educational books for all levels; Man. Dir CATHERINE LUCET.

Editions Payot & Rivages: 106 blvd Saint Germain, 75006 Paris; tel. 1-44-41-39-90; fax 1-44-41-39-69; e-mail editions@payotrivages.com; internet www.payot-rivages.fr; f. 1917; literature, human sciences, philosophy; Pres. FRANÇOISE NYSSEN; Dir-Gen. BENOÎTE MOUROT.

Editions Picard: 82 rue Bonaparte, 75006 Paris; tel. 1-43-26-97-78; fax 1-43-26-42-64; e-mail livres@librairie-picard.com; internet www.editions-picard.com; f. 1869; archaeology, architecture, history of art, history, pre-history, auxiliary sciences, linguistics, musicological works, antiquarian books; Chair. and Man. Dir CHANTAL PASINI-PICARD.

Editions Plon: 12 ave d'Italie, 75013 Paris; tel. 1-44-16-09-00; fax 1-44-41-30-53; e-mail stephane.billerey@editions-plon.com; internet www.plon.fr; f. 1852; imprint of Editis (q.v.); fiction, history, anthropology, human sciences, biography; Pres. and Dir-Gen. VINCENT BARBARE.

Editions P.O.L.: 33 rue Saint André des Arts, 75006 Paris; tel. 1-43-54-21-20; fax 1-43-54-11-31; e-mail pol@pol-editeur.fr; internet www

.pol-editeur.fr; literature; arts; Dir-Gen. PAUL OTCHAKOVSKI-LAURENS.

Presses de la Cité: 12 ave d'Italie, 75625 Paris Cedex 13; tel. 1-44-16-05-00; e-mail pressesdelacite@placedesediteurs.com; internet www.pressesdelacite.com; f. 1944; subsidiary of Editis (q.v.); fiction and factual literature for general audience; Dir JEAN ARCACHE.

Presses de Sciences Po: 117 blvd Saint-Germain, 75006 Paris; tel. 1-45-49-83-64; fax 1-45-49-83-34; e-mail info.presses@sciences-po.fr; internet www.pressesdesciencespo.fr; f. 1975; history, politics, linguistics, economics, sociology, health, sustainable development; Dir MARIE-GENEVIÈVE VANDESANDE.

Presses Universitaires de France: 6 ave Reille, 75014 Paris Cedex 14; tel. 1-58-10-31-00; fax 1-58-10-31-82; e-mail info-ventes@puf.com; internet www.puf.com; f. 1921; philosophy, psychology, psychoanalysis, psychiatry, education, sociology, theology, history, geography, economics, law, linguistics, literature, science; Editorial Dir MONIQUE LABRUNE.

Presses Universitaires de Grenoble: 5 place Robert-Schuman, BP 1549, 38025 Grenoble Cedex 1; tel. 4-76-29-43-09; fax 4-76-44-64-31; e-mail editorial@pug.fr; internet www.pug.fr; f. 1972; psychology, law, economics, management, history, statistics, literature, medicine, science, politics; Man. Dir SYLVIE BIGOT.

Presses Universitaires de Nancy—Editions Universitaires de Lorraine: 42–44 ave de la Libération, BP 3347, 54014 Nancy Cedex; tel. 3-54-50-46-90; fax 3-54-50-46-94; e-mail edulor-edition@univ-lorraine.fr; internet www.univ-lorraine.fr/content/presses-universitaires-de-nancy-editions-universitaires-de-lorraine; f. 1976; literature, history, law, social sciences, politics; Dir FERRI BRIQUET.

Editions Privat: 10 rue des Arts, BP 38028, 31080 Toulouse Cedex 06; tel. 5-61-33-77-00; fax 5-34-31-64-44; e-mail info@editions-privat.com; internet www.editions-privat.com; f. 1839; regional, national and international history, heritage, health; Pres. OLIVIER LAMARQUE.

Editions du Seuil: 25 blvd Romain Rolland, 75993 Paris Cedex 14; tel. 1-40-46-50-50; fax 1-40-46-43-00; e-mail contact@seuil.com; internet www.seuil.com; f. 1935; acquired by La Martinière in 2003; modern literature, fiction, illustrated books, non-fiction; Pres. and Dir-Gen. OLIVIER BÉTOURNÉ.

Editions du Signe: 1 rue Alfred Kastler, BP 10094, Eckbolsheim, 67038 Strasbourg Cedex 02; tel. 3-88-78-91-91; fax 3-88-78-91-99; e-mail info@editionsdusigne.fr; internet www.editionsdusigne.fr; f. 1987; Christianity; Chair. and Man. Dir CHRISTIAN RIEHL.

Editions Stock: 31 rue de Fleurus, 75006 Paris Cedex 06; tel. 1-49-54-36-55; fax 1-49-54-36-62; e-mail hamalric@editions-stock.fr; internet www.editions-stock.fr; f. 1708; literature, translations, biography, human sciences, guides; Dir of Publication MANUEL CARCASSONNE; Man. Editor MARIE-CHARLOTTE BROSSIER.

Succès du Livre: 60 rue St André des Arts, 75006 Paris; tel. 1-44-41-65-00; fax 1-44-41-65-36; internet www.succesdulivre.com; f. 1987; fiction, biography; Pres. ALEXANDRE FALCO.

Editions de la Table Ronde: 3326 rue de Condé, 75006 Paris; tel. 1-40-46-70-70; fax 1-40-46-71-01; e-mail editionslatableronde@editionslatableronde.fr; internet www.editionslatableronde.fr; f. 1944; fiction, essays, religion, travel, theatre, youth; Dir-Gen. ALICE DÉON.

Editions Tallandier: 2 rue Rotrou, 75006 Paris; tel. 1-40-46-43-88; fax 1-40-46-43-98; e-mail info@tallandier.com; internet www.tallandier.com; f. 1865; history, reference; Dir XAVIER DE BARTILLAT.

Editions Tawhid: 6 impasse Victor Hugo, 69003 Lyon 3; tel. 4-72-74-19-39; fax 4-78-24-01-56; e-mail info@edition-tawhid.com; internet www.islam-france.com; Islamic interest; Man. Dir YAMIN MAKRI.

Editions Vigot: 23–27 rue de l'Ecole de Médecine, 75006 Paris; tel. 1-43-29-54-50; fax 1-46-34-56-12; e-mail ventelibraires@vigot.fr; internet www.vigot.fr; f. 1890; medicine, pharmacology, nature, veterinary science, sport, fitness, tourism, cookery; Chair. CHRISTIAN VIGOT; Man. Dir DANIEL VIGOT.

Librairie Philosophique J. Vrin: 6 place de la Sorbonne, 75005 Paris; tel. 1-43-54-03-47; fax 1-43-54-48-18; e-mail contact@vrin.fr; internet www.vrin.fr; f. 1911; university textbooks, philosophy, education, science, law, religion; Dir of Publication DENIS ARNAUD.

Librairie Vuibert: 5 allée de la 2ème Division Blindée, 75015 Paris; tel. 1-42-79-44-00; fax 1-42-79-46-80; e-mail valerie.devillers@vuibert.fr; internet www.vuibert.com; f. 1877; school and university textbooks, psychology, law; subsidiary of Editions Albin Michel; Dir of Publication GUILLAUME DERVIEUX.

XO Editions: 33 ave du Maine, BP 142, 75755 Paris Cedex 15; tel. 1-56-80-26-80; fax 1-56-80-26-72; e-mail edito@xoeditions.com; internet www.xoeditions.com; f. 2000; general fiction, biography, current affairs, politics; Dir BERNARD FIXOT.

PUBLISHERS' AND BOOKSELLERS' ASSOCIATIONS

Cercle de la Librairie (Syndicat des Industries et Commerces du Livre): 35 rue Grégoire de Tours, 75006 Paris Cedex; tel. 1-44-41-28-00; fax 1-44-41-28-19; e-mail librairie@electre.com; internet www.cercledelalibrairie.org; f. 1847; a syndicate of the book trade, grouping the principal asscns of publrs, booksellers and printers; Chair. DENIS MOLLAT; Man. Dir PHILIPPE BEAUVILLARD.

Chambre Syndicale de l'Edition Musicale: 74 rue de la Fédération, 75015 Paris; tel. 1-48-74-09-29; e-mail csdem@csdem.org; internet www.csdem.org; f. 1925; music publrs' asscn; Pres. NELLY QUEROL.

Fédération Française Syndicale de la Librairie: 24 place de la République, 14100 Lisieux; tel. 2-31-62-16-87; fax 2-31-63-97-37; f. 1892; booksellers' asscn; Chair. COLETTE HEDOUX.

Syndicat National de l'Edition: 115 blvd Saint-Germain, 75006 Paris; tel. 1-44-41-40-50; fax 1-44-41-40-77; internet www.sne.fr; f. 1892; publrs' asscn; 670 mems; Chair. VINCENT MONTAGNE.

Syndicat National de la Librairie Ancienne et Moderne: 4 rue Gît-le-Cœur, 75006 Paris; tel. 1-43-29-46-38; fax 1-43-25-41-63; e-mail slam-livre@wanadoo.fr; internet www.slam-livre.fr; f. 1914; booksellers' asscn; 250 mems; Pres. ANNE LAMORT.

Broadcasting and Communications

TELECOMMUNICATIONS

Alcatel-Lucent: 3 ave Octave Gréard, 75007 Paris; tel. 1-40-76-10-10; fax 1-40-76-14-00; e-mail execoffice@alcatel-lucent.com; internet www.alcatel-lucent.com; f. 2006 by merger of Alcatel (f. 1898) and Lucent (USA, f. 1996); telecommunications and business systems, broadband access, terrestrial and submarine optical networks; Chair. PHILIPPE CAMUS; CEO MICHEL COMBES.

Bouygues Télécom: 32 ave Hoche, 75008 Paris; tel. 1-44-20-10-00; internet www.bouygtel.com; f. 1994; mobile cellular telecommunications; Pres. and Dir-Gen. PHILIPPE MARIEN.

Groupe Iliad (Free): 8 rue de la Ville l'Evêque, 75008 Paris; tel. (1) 73-50-20-00; fax (1) 73-50-20-01; e-mail presse@iliad.fr; internet www.iliad.fr; f. 1991; provides fixed-line telecommunications, broadband internet and television through subsidiaries Free, One.Tel and Iliad Télécom; subsidiary Free Mobile awarded licence to operate mobile cellular telecommunications in 2009; Pres. CYRIL POIDATZ; Dir-Gen. MAXIME LOMBARDINI.

Numericable: 10 rue Albert Einstein, 77420 Champs-sur-Marne; tel. 1-55-92-46-00; fax 1-55-92-46-90; e-mail communication@ncnumericable.com; internet www.numericable.fr; f. 2006 by merger of NC Numéricâble (f. 1997) and Noos (f. 1986); fixed-line operator, consumer internet access, cable television; Dir-Gen. PIERRE DANON.

Orange: 78 rue Olivier de Serres, Paris 75015; tel. 1-44-44-22-22; fax 1-44-44-80-34; e-mail infos.groupe@orange.com; internet www.orange.com; 33.1% state-owned, following privatization in 2004; fmrly France Télécom; name changed to present 2013; Chair. and CEO STÉPHANE RICHARD.

SFR: 1 place Carpeaux, Tour Séquoia, 92915 Paris La Défense Cedex; tel. 8-05-77-66-66; internet www.sfr.fr; f. 1993; mobile cellular telecommunications; 100% owned by Vivendi SA; merged with Neuf Cegetel in 2008; 15m. subscribers (March 2010); Pres. and Dir-Gen. JEAN-YVES CHARLIER.

REGULATORY AUTHORITIES

Agence Nationale des Fréquences (ANFR): 78 ave du Général de Gaulle, BP 400, 94704 Maisons-Alfort Cedex; tel. 1-45-18-72-73; fax 1-45-18-72-00; e-mail rtte@anfr.fr; internet www.anfr.fr; Pres. ARNAUD MIQUEL; Dir-Gen. GILLES BRÉGANT.

Autorité de Régulation des Communications Electroniques et des Postes (ARCEP): 7 sq. Max Hymans, 75730 Paris Cedex 15; tel. 1-40-47-70-00; fax 1-40-47-71-98; e-mail courrier@arcep.fr; internet www.arcep.fr; f. 2005; fmrly Autorité de Régulation des Télécommunications; Chair. JEAN-LUDOVIC SILICANI; Dir-Gen. PHILIPPE DISTLER.

BROADCASTING

Conseil Supérieur de l'Audiovisuel (CSA): Tour Mirabeau, 39–43 quai André Citroën, 75739 Paris Cedex 15; tel. 1-40-58-38-00; fax 1-45-79-00-06; internet www.csa.fr; f. 1989 as replacement for the Commission Nationale de la Communication et des Libertés (CNCL); supervises all French broadcasting; awards licences to private radio (including digital radio) and television stations, allocates frequencies, has a co-decisional power to appoint chairs of public broadcasting companies, monitors programme standards; consists of 9 mems, appointed for 6 years: 3 nominated by the Pres. of the Republic; 3 by the Pres. of the Assemblée Nationale; and 3 by the Pres. of the Sénat; Pres. MICHEL BOYON; Gen. Man. OLIVIER JAPIOT.

Institut National de l'Audiovisuel: 4 ave de l'Europe, 94360 Bry-sur-Marne Cedex; tel. 1-49-83-26-74; fax 1-49-83-23-89; e-mail assistance@ina.fr; internet www.ina.fr; f. 1975; research and professional training in the field of broadcasting; radio and TV archives, TV production; Publ. *Les Nouveaux Dossiers de l'Audiovisuel*; (6 a year); Pres. and Dir-Gen. MATHIEU GALLET.

Télédiffusion de France (TDF): 106 ave Marx Dormoy, 92120 Montrouge; tel. 1-55-95-10-00; e-mail e-tdf@tdf.fr; internet www.tdf.fr; f. 1975; partly privatized 1987; restructured in 2007; comprises 3 sections: TDF France, TDF Multimedia and TDF International; responsible for broadcasting programmes produced by the production companies, for the organization and maintenance of the networks, for study and research into radio and television equipment; broadcasts digital terrestial television; Dir-Gen. OLIVIER HUART.

Radio

State-controlled Radio

Public radio services are provided by three entities: Radio France for the domestic audience; Réseau France Outre-mer for the French overseas departments and territories; and Radio France Internationale for foreign countries (and those of foreign origin in France).

Société Nationale de Radiodiffusion (Radio France): 116 ave du Président Kennedy, 75786 Paris Cedex 16; tel. 1-56-40-22-22; fax 1-56-40-35-87; internet www.radio-france.fr; f. 1975; planning and production of radio programmes; provides 7 national services, 43 local stations and 2 European services; Pres. and Dir-Gen. JEAN-LUC HAAS.

France Bleu: Maison de Radio France, 75220 Paris Cedex 16; tel. 1-56-40-37-86; e-mail brigitte.tauzin@radiofrance.com; internet www.francebleu.com; f. 1980, restructured 2000; network of domestic services; Dir ANNE BRUCY.

France Culture: tel. 1-56-40-27-91; e-mail caroline.cesbron@radiofrance.com; internet franceculture.com; domestic, nationwide service; Dir OLIVIER POIVRE D'ARVOR.

France-Info: tel. 1-56-40-20-43; e-mail romain.beignon@radiofrance.com; internet www.france-info.com; domestic, nationwide service; continuous news and information; f. 1987; Dir PHILIPPE CHAFFANJON.

France Inter: tel. 1-56-40-37-57; e-mail emmanuel.perreau@radiofrance.com; internet www.franceinter.com; domestic, nationwide service; general programmes, for entertainment and information; Dir PHILIPPE VAL.

France Musique: tel. 1-56-40-36-12; e-mail christophe.sillieres@radiofrance.com; internet www.francemusique.com; domestic, nationwide service; Dir OLIVIER MOREL-MAROGER.

Le Mouv': tel. 5-62-30-70-16; internet www.lemouv.com; domestic, nationwide service; music and general interest for people aged 18–35; f. 1997; Dir PATRICE BLANC FRANCARD.

Réseau FIP: tel. 1-56-40-16-15; internet www.fipradio.fr; f. 1971; comprises 10 local stations; continuous music; Dir JULIEN DELLI FIORI.

Radio France Internationale (RFI): 116 ave du Président Kennedy, BP 9516, 75786 Paris Cedex 16; tel. 1-56-40-12-12; fax 1-56-40-47-59; internet www.rfi.fr; f. 1975; broadcasts on MW and FM transmitters, mainly to Africa, Eastern Europe, North America, the Caribbean, South-East Asia and the Middle East, in French; also broadcasts in 19 other languages: Albanian, Arabic, Bulgarian, Cambodian, Créole, Croatian, English, Farsi, German, Laotian, Mandarin, Polish, Portuguese, Romanian, Russian, Serbian, Spanish, Turkish, Vietnamese; Pres. and Dir-Gen. (vacant).

Réseau France Outre-mer (RFO): 35–37 rue Danton, 92240 Malakoff; tel. 1-55-22-71-00; fax 1-55-22-74-76; e-mail rfo@rfo.fr; internet www.rfo.fr; f. 1983; fmrly FR3 DOM-TOM; controls broadcasting in the French overseas territories; 10 local stations providing 2 radio networks, 2 television channels, the latter broadcasting material from various state and private channels as well as local programmes, and 1 satellite television channel; Dir CLAUDE ESCLATINE.

Independent Radio

BFM: 12 rue d'Oradour sur Glane, 75015 Paris; tel. 1-71-19-11-81; fax 1-71-19-11-80; e-mail stemplet@radiobfm.com; internet www.radiobfm.com; f. 1992; broadcasts on cable and 14 FM frequencies; politics, economics; Pres. ALAIN WEILL; Dir-Gen. NICOLAS LESPAULE.

Chérie FM: 22 rue Boileau, 75203 Paris Cedex 16; tel. 1-40-71-40-00; e-mail vgrandclaude@nrj.fr; internet www.cheriefm.fr; broadcasts popular music and entertainment programming on FM nationwide; mem. of Groupe NRJ.

Europe 1: 26 bis rue François, 75008 Paris; tel. 1-53-35-72-60; fax 1-47-23-19-00; e-mail courrier@europe1.fr; internet www.europe1.fr; owned by Groupe Lagardère, which also owns Europe 2 (for younger listeners) and RFM; broadcasting on long wave and 99 FM frequencies; Pres. DENIS OLIVENNES.

Nostalgie: 22 rue Boileau, 75203 Paris Cedex 16; tel. 1-40-71-40-00; e-mail sbosc@nrj.fr; internet www.nostalgie.fr; mem. of Groupe NRJ; broadcasts popular music and entertainment programming on FM nationwide; Dir STÉPHANE BOSC.

NRJ: 22 rue Boileau, 75203 Paris Cedex 16; tel. 1-40-71-40-00; e-mail vgrandclaude@nrj.fr; internet www.nrj.fr; broadcasts contemporary popular music and entertainment programming on FM nationwide; Pres. and Dir-Gen. JEAN-PAUL BAUDECROUX.

Radio Classique: 12 bis place Henri Bergson, 75382 Paris Cedex 08; tel. 1-40-08-50-00; fax 1-40-08-50-80; internet www.radioclassique.fr; f. 1983; classical music; Pres. FRANCIS MOREL.

Radio Monte-Carlo (RMC): 12 rue d'Oradour sur Glane, 75740 Paris Cedex 15; tel. 1-71-19-11-91; fax 1-71-19-11-90; internet www.rmcinfo.fr; broadcasting on long wave and 148 FM frequencies; information, talk and sports programmes.

RTL: 22 rue Bayard, 75008 Paris; tel. 1-41-86-21-49; fax 1-40-70-42-72; e-mail contact@rtl.fr; internet www.rtl.fr; broadcasting on long wave and 150 FM frequencies; CEO CHRISTOPHER BALDELLI.

Skyrock: 37 bis rue Grenéta, 75002 Paris; tel. 1-44-88-82-00; fax 1-44-88-89-57; internet www.skyrock.com; f. 1986; contemporary rap and hip-hop music; Pres. PIERRE BELLANGER; Dir-Gen. FRANK CHENEAU.

Television

In November 2011 France completed the transfer from analogue to digital television.

State-controlled Television

France Télévisions: 7 esplanade Henri-de-France, 75907 Paris; tel. 1-56-22-60-00; fax 1-56-22-60-21; internet www.francetelevisions.fr; f. 1992; supervisory authority for the national public television networks (France 2, France 3 and France 5: see below); Pres. RÉMY PFLIMLIN; Sec.-Gen. YVES ROLLAND.

France 2: 7 esplanade Henri-de-France, 75907 Paris Cedex 15; tel. 1-56-22-42-42; fax 1-56-22-55-87; e-mail contact@france2.fr; internet www.france2.fr; f. 1975; general programmes for a nationwide audience; Dir-Gen. BERTRAND MOSCA.

France 3 (F3): 7 esplanade Henri-de-France, 75907 Paris Cedex 15; tel. 1-56-22-30-30; internet www.france3.fr; f. 1975 as France Régions 3 (FR3); general programmes for a nationwide audience (with a larger proportion of cultural and educational programmes than France 2), and regional programmes transmitted from 13 regional stations; Dir-Gen. FRANÇOIS GUILBEAU.

France 4: 7 esplanade Henri-de-France, 75907 Paris Cedex 15; tel. 1-56-22-68-68; fax 1-56-22-68-69; e-mail yann.renoard@francetv.fr; internet www.france4.fr; f. 2005; 100% owned by France Télévisions; digital TV station; creative and cultural programming; Dir-Gen. EMMANUELLE GUILBART.

France 5: 2–4 rue Horace Vernet, 92785 Issy-les-Moulineaux Cedex 09; tel. 1-56-22-91-91; e-mail telespectateurs@france5.fr; internet www.france5.fr; f. 1994 as La Cinquième; present name adopted 2002; educational programmes and documentaries; Dir-Gen. BRUNO PATINO.

France 24: 5 rue des Nations Unies, 92445 Issy-les-Moulineaux; tel. 1-73-01-24-24; fax 1-73-01-24-56; e-mail webdesk@france24.com; internet www.france24.com; f. 2006; jointly owned by TF1 and France Télévisions; cable, satellite and internet broadcasts; 24-hour news broadcasts in Arabic, English and French; aims to present international news from a French perspective; CEO (vacant).

ARTE France: 8 rue Marceau, 92785 Issy-les-Moulineaux Cedex 09; tel. 1-55-00-77-77; fax 1-55-00-77-00; internet www.arte.tv; f. 1992 to replace La Sept; arts, cultural programmes, in French and German; Pres. VÉRONIQUE CAYLA; Dir-Gen. ANNE DURUPTY.

TV5 Monde: 131 ave de Wagram, 75017 Paris; tel. 1-44-18-55-55; internet www.tv5.org; f. 1984; broadcasts French-language programmes via satellite and cable to 203 countries worldwide; 49% owned by Audiovisuel Extérieur de la France, 12.58% by France Télévisions and 3.29% by ARTE France; Dir-Gen. MARIE-CHRISTINE SARAGOSSE; Dir of Programmes FREDERICK-LOUIS BOULAY.

Television programmes for France's overseas departments and territories are provided by Réseau France Outre-mer (see under Radio).

Independent Television

Canal Plus: 1 place du Spectacle, 92863 Issy-Les-Moulineaux Cedex 9; tel. 1-71-35-35-35; fax 1-44-25-12-34; internet www.canalplus.fr; f. 1984; 80% owned by Vivendi, 20% by Groupe Lagadère; coded programmes financed by audience subscription; uncoded programmes financed by advertising sold by Canal Plus; specializes in drama (including films) and sport; launched a 'pay-per-view' service for sports events in 1996; produces 21 theme channels in 6 countries; Pres. and Dir-Gen. BERTRAND MÉHEUT.

demain.tv: 1 rue Patry, 92220 Bagneux; tel. 1-45-36-89-00; fax 1-45-36-89-01; e-mail contact@demain.fr; internet www.demain.fr; f. 1997; information about employment for job-seekers; Dir-Gen. EMMANUEL DES MOUTIS.

Direct8: Tour Bolloré, 31-32 quai de Dion-Bouton, 92811 Puteaux; tel. 1-46-96-48-88; fax 1-46-96-40-28; e-mail emissions@direct8.net; internet www.direct8.fr; f. 2005; free-to-air digital television channel; 60% owned by Groupe Canal Plus and 40% owned by Bolloré Média; Pres. VINCENT BOLLORÉ; Dir of Programmes GUY LAGACHE.

Gulli: 12 rue d'Oradour-sur-Glane, 75015 Paris; tel. 1-56-36-55-55; fax 1-56-36-55-59; e-mail tachaine@gullitv.fr; internet www.gullitv.fr; f. 2005; free-to-air digital television channel for children; Dir-Gen. ANTOINE VILLENEUVE.

i>TELE: 6 allée de la 2ème DB, 75015 Paris; tel. 1-53-91-50-00; fax 1-53-91-51-45; e-mail communication.itele@canal-plus.com; internet www.itele.fr; f. 1999; free-to-air digital television channel; 24-hr news broadcasts; part of Groupe Canal Plus; Dir-Gen. CÉCILIA RAGUENEAU.

LCI (La Chaîne Info): 1 quai du Point du Jour, 92656 Boulogne-Billancourt Cedex; tel. 1-41-41-12-34; e-mail ccomfi@tf1.fr; internet lci.tf1.fr; f. 1994; news, information; part of Groupe TF1; Pres. NONCE PAOLINI; Dir-Gen. ERIC REVEL.

M6: 89 ave Charles de Gaulle, 92575 Neuilly-sur-Seine Cedex; tel. 1-41-92-61-61; fax 1-41-92-66-10; e-mail pholl@m6.fr; internet www.m6.fr; f. 1986 as TV6; re-formed as M6 1987; 48.43% owned by RTL Group; subsidiaries include W9 (a free-to-air digital television channel); specializes in drama, music and magazines; Chair., Man. Bd NICOLAS DE TAVERNOST.

NT1: 132 ave du Président Wilson, 93213 La Plaine-Saint-Denis; tel. 1-49-22-20-01; fax 1-49-22-20-71; e-mail contact@nt1.fr; internet www.nt1.tv; free-to-air digital television channel; owned by AB Groupe; Pres. CLAUDE BERDA.

Télévision Française 1 (TF1): 1 quai du Point du Jour, 92656 Boulogne-Billancourt Cedex; tel. 1-41-41-12-34; fax 1-41-41-28-40; internet www.tf1.fr; f. 1975 as a state-owned channel, privatized 1987; 43.1% owned by Bouygues SA; general programmes; Pres. and Dir-Gen. NONCE PAOLINI.

Finance

(cap. = capital; res = reserves; dep. = deposits; m. = million; br(s) = branch(es); amounts in euros)

BANKING

Central Bank

Banque de France: 39 rue Croix des Petits Champs, BP 140-01, 75001 Paris; tel. 1-42-92-42-92; fax 1-42-92-45-00; e-mail infos@banque-france.fr; internet www.banque-france.fr; f. 1800; nationalized 1946; became independent 1994; acts as banker to the Treasury, issues bank notes, controls credit and money supply and administers France's gold and currency assets; in 1993 the Assemblée Nationale approved legislation to make the Banque de France an independent central bank, with a General Council to supervise activities and appoint the principal officials, and a 9-mem. monetary policy committee, independent of govt control, to be in charge of French monetary policy; a mem. of the European System of Central Banks since June 1998; cap. and res 25,870m., dep. 118,397m., total assets 506,050m. (Dec. 2009); Gov. CHRISTIAN NOYER; 96 brs.

Financing Institution

Société de Financement de l'Economie Française (SFEF): Paris; f. Oct. 2008 to assist the banking sector in the financial crisis; 66% owned by a group of 7 banks, 34% state-owned; provider of govt-guaranteed loans to banks; Chair. FRANÇOISE MALRIEU; Dir-Gen. HENRY RAYMOND.

State Savings Bank

Caisse des Dépôts et Consignations: 56 rue de Lille, 75356 Paris Cedex 07; tel. 1-58-50-00-00; fax 1-58-50-02-46; internet www.caissedesdepots.fr; f. 1816; manages state savings system, holds widespread investments in industrial cos; res 4,284m., dep. 93,910m., total assets 286,648m. (Dec. 2012); Dir-Gen. JEAN-PIERRE JOUYET; 1 br.

Commercial Banks

Allianz Banque: Tour Neptune, 20 place de Seine, La Défense, 92400 Courbevoie; tel. 1-53-24-48-48; fax 1-53-24-48-41; e-mail serviceclient@banqueagf.fr; internet www.allianzbanque.fr; f. 2000; affiliated to Group Allianz; Pres. PASCAL THÉBÉ; Dir-Gen. FABIEN WATHLÉ.

Arkea Banque Enterprises et Institutionnels: allée Louis Lichou, 29480 Le Relecq-Kerhuon Cedex; tel. 2-99-29-92-00; fax 2-98-43-83-03; e-mail banque-ei@arkea.com; internet www.arkea-banque-ei.com; f. 1985; present name adopted 2000; subsidiary of Crédit Mutuel Arkéa; cap. 530m., res 54.2m., dep. 5,058.2m. (Dec. 2012); Chair. MARCEL GARNIER; Pres., Executive Bd GÉRARD BAYOL.

Banque BIA: 67 ave Franklin D. Roosevelt, 75008 Paris; tel. 1-53-76-62-62; fax 1-42-89-09-59; e-mail contact@bia-paris.fr; internet www.bia-paris.fr; f. 1975 as Banque Intercontinentale Arabe; present name adopted 2006; 50% owned by Banque Extérieure d'Algérie, 50% by Libyan Arab Foreign Bank; cap. 158.1m., res 1.8m., dep. 1,142.4m. (Dec. 2012); Chair. MUHAMMAD LOUKAL.

Banque CIC Est: 31 rue Jean Wenger-Valentin, 67958 Strasbourg Cedex 9; tel. 3-88-37-61-23; fax 3-88-37-61-81; internet www.cic.fr; f. 2008 from merger of CIC Banque SNVB and CIC Banque CIAL; 100% owned by Crédit Industriel et Commercial; cap. 225.0m., res 886.3m., dep. 44,740m. (Dec. 2009); Chair. and Dir-Gen. NICOLAS THÉRY; Gen. Mans LUC DYMARSKI, PIERRE JACHEZ.

Banque CIC Sud Ouest: 42 cours du Chapeau Rouge, 33000 Bordeaux; tel. 5-56-00-59-50; fax 5-57-85-55-74; internet www.cic.fr/sb; f. 1880 as Société Bordelaise de Crédit Industriel et Commercial et de Dépôts; present name adopted in 2010; 100% owned by Crédit Industriel et Commercial; cap. 155.3m., res 86.3m., dep. 9,239.3m. (Dec. 2012); Chair. and Dir-Gen. PASCALE RIBAULT; 265 brs.

Banque CIO-BRO: BP 84001, 2 ave Jean-Claude Bonduelle, 44040 Nantes Cedex 1; tel. 0-83-97-89-37; fax 2-40-12-93-80; e-mail cio-international@cio.cic.fr; internet www.cic.fr/cio-bro; f. 2006 by merger of Crédit Industriel de l'Ouest (f. 1957) and Banque Régionale de l'Ouest (f. 1913); 100% owned by Crédit Industriel et Commercial; Chair. MICHEL MICHENKO; Man. Dir JEAN-PIERRE BICHON.

Banque Degroof France SA: 1 rond-point des Champs-Élysées, 75008 Paris; tel. 1-45-61-55-55; fax 1-45-61-96-25; internet www.degroof.fr; f. 2011; 100% owned by Banque Degroof SA (Belgium); Chair. REGNIER HAEGELSTEEN; Man. Dir LIONEL GIOT.

Banque Espírito Santo et de la Vénétie: 45 ave Georges Mandel, 75116 Paris; tel. 1-44-34-48-00; fax 1-44-34-48-48; e-mail besv@besv.fr; internet www.besv.fr; f. 1945; present name adopted 1998; absorbed Via Banque in 2002; 42% owned by Espirito Santo Financial Group SA (Luxembourg); cap. 75.1m., res 77.8m., dep. 476.6m. (Dec. 2012); Pres. PHILLIPE GUIRAL; 1 br.

Banque Européenne du Crédit Mutuel (BECM): 34 rue du Wacken, 67000 Strasbourg Cedex 9; tel. 3-88-14-74-74; fax 3-88-14-75-10; e-mail becm@becm.fr; internet www.creditmutuel.fr/becm/fr; f. 1992 as Banque de l'Economie—Crédit Mutuel; name changed as above in June 2012; cap. 378.3m., dep. 1,546.7m., total assets 8,320.4m. (Dec. 2006); Chief Exec. RENÉ DANGEL; 27 brs.

Banque Fédérative du Crédit Mutuel: 34 rue du Wacken, 67000 Strasbourg; tel. 3-88-14-88-14; fax 3-88-14-67-00; internet www.bfcm.creditmutuel.fr; f. 1895; cap. 1,327m., res 10,455m., dep. 145,830m. (Dec. 2012); Pres. and Chair. ETIENNE PFLIMLIN; Dir-Gen. MICHEL LUCAS; 16 brs.

Banque Nationale de Paris Intercontinentale: 12 rue Chauchat, 75009 Paris; tel. 1-40-14-22-11; fax 1-40-14-69-34; internet www.bnpgroup.com; f. 1940; present name adopted 1972; 100% owned by BNP Paribas; cap. 30.5m., res 5.0m., dep. 8.9m. (Dec. 2008); Chair. and Dir-Gen. BAUDOUIN PROT.

Banque Neuflize OBC: 3 ave Hoche, 75008 Paris; tel. 1-56-21-70-00; fax 1-56-21-84-60; internet www.neuflizeobc.fr; f. 1966 as De Neuflize, Schlumberger, Mallet & Cie; acquired clients of fmr Banque OBC—Odier Bungener Courvoisier and adopted present name 2006; 100% owned by ABN AMRO France; private banking; cap. 383.5m., res 168.2m., dep. 6,410.7m. (Dec. 2012); Chair., Supervisory Bd JEROEN RIJPKEMA; Pres. and Chair., Management Bd PHILLIPE VAYSSETTES; 12 brs.

Banque Palatine: 42 rue d'Anjou, 75382 Paris Cedex 08; tel. 1-55-27-94-94; e-mail contact@palatine.fr; internet www.palatine.fr; f. 1971; fmrly Banque Sanpaolo; present name adopted 2005; 100% owned by Caisse Nationale des Caisses d'Epargne; cap. 538.8m., res 234.8m., dep. 9,834m. (Dec. 2012); Chair., Supervisory Bd PIERRE-YVES DRÉAN; Chair., Management Bd JEAN-YVES FOREL; 60 brs.

BNP Paribas: 16 blvd des Italiens, 75009 Paris; tel. 1-40-14-45-46; fax 1-40-14-69-40; internet www.bnpparibas.com; f. 2000 by merger of Banque Nationale de Paris and Paribas; cap. 26,812m., res 1,935m., dep. 741,689m. (Dec. 2013); Pres. BAUDOUIN PROT; CEO JEAN-LAURENT BONNAFÉ.

Cetelem: 14 bis blvd de l'Hôpital, 75221 Paris Cedex 05; tel. 1-55-43-55-43; fax 1-55-43-55-30; e-mail frederic.tardy@cetelem.fr; internet www.cetelem.fr; f. 1953; owned by BNP Paribas; cap. 848.8m., res

1,423.3m., dep. 32,906.8m. (Dec. 2006); Chair. and CEO FRANÇOIS VILLEROY DE GALHAU.

CIC Nord Ouest: 33 ave le Corbusier, BP 567, 59800 Lille; tel. 3-20-12-64-64; fax 3-20-12-64-05; e-mail brouchbr@cmcic.fr; internet www.cic.fr; f. 2006 by merger of Banque Scalbert-Dupont (f. 1977) and Crédit Industriel de Normandie (f. 1932); 100% owned by Crédit Industriel et Commercial; cap. 230m., res 92m., dep. 16,906m. (Dec. 2012); Chair. and Dir-Gen. STELLI PRÉMAOR.

Compagnie Financière Edmond de Rothschild Banque: 47 rue du Faubourg St Honoré, 75401 Paris Cedex 08; tel. 1-40-17-25-25; fax 1-40-17-24-02; e-mail info@lcfr.fr; internet www.lcf-rothschild.fr; f. 1971; present name adopted 1986; cap. 83.1m., res 209.2m., dep. 1,586.4m. (Dec. 2012); Chair., Supervisory Bd BENJAMIN DE ROTHSCHILD; Dir-Gen. MARC LÉVY.

Crédit Agricole Corporate and Investment Bank (Calyon): 9 quai Paul Doumer, 92920 Paris La Défense Cedex; tel. 1-41-89-00-00; fax 1-41-89-36-33; internet www.ca-cib.com; f. 1975 as Banque Indosuez, subsequently Crédit Agricole Indosuez and Calyon Corporate and Investment Bank; present name adopted 2010; 100% owned by Crédit Agricole; merchant and 'offshore' banking; cap. 7,255m., res 8,265m., dep. 185,161m. (Dec. 2012); Pres. JEAN-PAUL CHIFFLET; Chief Exec. JEAN YVES HOCHER; 15 brs in France, 44 outside France.

Crédit Foncier de France: 19 rue des Capucines, 75001 Paris Cedex 01; tel. 1-42-44-80-00; fax 1-42-44-86-99; e-mail cbuying-france@creditfoncier.fr; internet www.creditfoncier.fr; f. 1852; 100% owned by Caisses d'Epargne et de Prévoyance; mortgage banking; cap. 1,731m., res 1,848m., dep. 44,365m. (Dec. 2012); Chair., Bd of Dirs FRANÇOIS DROUIN; Chief Exec. BRUNO DELETRÉ; 162 brs.

Crédit Industriel et Commercial (CIC): 6 ave de Provence, 75009 Paris Cedex 09; tel. 1-45-96-96-96; fax 1-45-96-96-66; internet www.cic.fr; f. 1990 by merger; present name adopted 1999; 70.81% owned by Banque Fédérative du Crédit Mutuel; cap. 608m., res 9,056m., dep. 109,327m. (Dec. 2012); Chair. and Dir-Gen. MICHEL LUCAS; Gen. Man. ALAIN FRADIN.

Crédit du Nord: 59 blvd Haussmann, 75008 Paris; tel. 1-40-22-40-22; fax 3-20-57-74-05; internet www.credit-du-nord.fr; f. 1974 by merger; name changed as above in 1976; 80% owned by Société Générale; cap. 890.3m., res 228.5m., dep. 34,786.5m. (Dec. 2012); Chair. JEAN-FRANÇOIS SAMMARCELLI; 675 brs.

HSBC France: 103 ave des Champs-Elysées, 75419 Paris Cedex 08; tel. 1-40-70-70-40; fax 1-40-70-70-09; e-mail contact@hsbc.fr; internet www.hsbc.fr; 100% owned by HSBC Bank PLC (United Kingdom); f. 2005 by merger of CCF (fmrly Crédit Commercial de France) with 3 other banks; cap. 337.0m., res 237m., dep. 64,081m. (Dec. 2012); CEO JEAN BEUNARDEAU; 223 brs in France.

HSBC Private Bank France: 103 ave des Champs-Elysées, 75008 Paris Cedex 08; tel. 1-49-52-20-00; fax 1-49-52-20-99; internet www.hsbcprivatebankfrance.com; f. 2003 by merger; 100% owned by HSBC Holdings plc; cap. 43m., res 138.5m., dep. 869m. (Dec. 2009); Chief Exec. EDWARD ARCHER.

LCL—Le Crédit Lyonnais: 19 blvd des Italiens, 75002 Paris; tel. 1-42-95-70-00; fax 1-42-68-37-19; internet www.lcl.com; f. 1863 as Crédit Lyonnais; present name adopted 2005; privatized 1999; acquired by Crédit Agricole in June 2003; cap. 1,848m., res 2,328m., dep. 86,139m. (Dec. 2012); Gen. Dir YVES NANQUETTE; Chief Exec. LAURENT PAILLASSOT; 2,064 brs.

Lyonnaise de Banque: 8 rue de la République, 69001 Lyon; tel. 4-78-92-02-12; fax 4-78-92-03-00; e-mail ddi@lb.cicomore.fr; internet www.cic.fr/lb; f. 1865 as Société Lyonnaise de Dépôts et de Crédit Industriel; name changed as above in 1988; 100% owned by Crédit Industriel et Commercial; cap. 260.8m., res 145.5m., dep. 13,324.5m. (Dec. 2012); Chair. and Chief Exec. RÉMY WEBER; 368 brs.

Natixis: 45 rue Saint Dominique, 75007 Paris Cedex 02; tel. 1-58-32-30-00; internet www.natixis.com; f. 1999 as Natexis Banques Populaires; present name adopted 2006; 71.54% owned by BPCE (France); cap. 4,938m., res 5,410m., dep. 254,930m. (Dec. 2012); Chair. FRANÇOIS PEROL; CEO LAURENT MIGNON.

Société Générale: Tour Société Générale, 17 cours Valmy, 92972 Paris La Défense; tel. 1-42-14-20-00; fax 1-53-43-87-69; internet www.socgen.com; f. 1864; name changed as above in 1983; cap. 975m., res 25,602m., dep. 592,219m. (Dec. 2012); Chair. and CEO FRÉDÉRIC OUDÉA; 2,000 brs in France.

Société Marseillaise de Crédit (SMC): 75 rue Paradis, 13006 Marseille; tel. 4-91-13-33-00; fax 4-91-13-33-16; e-mail infos@smc.fr; internet www.smc.fr; f. 1865; owned by Crédit du Nord (France); cap. 24.5m., res 278.2m., dep. 5,800.3m. (Dec. 2012); Chair. and Chief Exec. EMMANUEL BARTHÉLÉMY; Gen. Man. and Pres. OLIVIER DELAPORTE; 174 brs.

Union de Banques Arabes et Françaises (UBAF): 190 ave Charles de Gaulle, 92523 Neuilly-sur-Seine Cedex; tel. 1-46-40-61-01; fax 1-47-38-13-88; e-mail ubaf.paris@ubaf.fr; internet www.ubaf.fr; f. 1970; 47.01% owned by Crédit Agricole CIB, 52.99% by Arab banks and institutions; cap. 250.7m., res 35.5m., dep. 1,339.4m. (Dec. 2012); Chair., Management Bd FAROUK EL-OKDAH; CEO SERGE DE BEAUFORT.

VTB Bank (France) SA (BCEN—Eurobank): 79–81 blvd Haussmann, 75382 Paris Cedex 08; tel. 1-40-06-43-21; fax 1-40-06-48-48; internet www.vtb.fr; f. 1921 as Comptoir Parisien de Banque et de Change; changed name to Banque Commerciale pour l'Europe du Nord in 1972; present name adopted 2006; 87.04% owned by VTB Bank (Austria); cap. 185.3m., res 57.4m., dep. 524.8m. (Dec. 2012); Chair., Supervisory Council MIKHAIL YAKUNIN; Chair., Executive Bd RICHARD VORNBERG.

Co-operative and Savings Banks

BPCE: 50 ave Pierre Mendès, Paris Cedex 13; tel. 1-58-40-41-42; internet www.bpce.fr; f. 2009 by merger of Banque Fédérale des Banques Populaires (BFBP) with Caisse Nationale des Caisses d'Epargne (CNCE); controls and co-ordinates 20 co-operative Banques Populaires (including those listed below) and 17 Caisses d'Epargne; cap. 17,502m., res 10,042m., dep. 582,334m. (Dec. 2012); Chair. FRANÇOIS PÉROL.

Banque Populaire d'Alsace: 4 quai Kléber, 67000 Strasbourg; tel. 3-88-62-77-11; fax 3-88-62-70-35; e-mail contact@alsace.banquepopulaire.fr; internet www.alsace.banquepopulaire.fr; f. 2003 by merger of Banque Populaire de la Région Economique de Strasbourg and Banque Populaire du Haut Rhin; cap. 402.6m., res 525.9m., dep. 4,860.2m. (Dec. 2012); Pres. THIERRY CAHN; Dir-Gen. CHRISTINE JACGLIN; 96 brs.

Banque Populaire Aquitaine Centre Atlantique: 10 quai des Queyries, 33072 Bordeaux Cedex; tel. 5-49-08-65-20; e-mail contact@bpaca.banquepopulaire.fr; internet www.bpaca.banquepopulaire.fr; formed by merger of Banque Populaire du Sud-Ouest and Banque Populaire Centre-Atlantique; cap. 523.1m., res 771.9m., dep. 8,059.4m. (Dec. 2012); Chair. JACQUES RAYNAUD; Gen. Man. DOMINIQUE GARNIER.

Banque Populaire Bourgogne Franche-Comté: 14 blvd de la Trémouille, BP 20810, 21008 Dijon Cedex; tel. 8-20-33-75-00; fax 8-20-20-36-20; internet www.bpbfc.banquepopulaire.fr; f. 2002 by merger of Banque Populaire de Bourgogne and Banque Populaire de Franche-Comté, du Mâconnais et de l'Ain; cap. 530.9m., res 379.8m., dep. 7,126.5m. (Dec. 2012); Pres. MICHAEL GRASS; Dir-Gen. BRUNO DUCHESNE; 151 brs.

Banque Populaire Côte d'Azur (BPCA): BP 241, 457 promenade des Anglais, 06024 Nice; tel. 4-93-21-52-00; fax 4-93-21-54-45; e-mail contact@cotedazur.banquepopulaire.fr; internet www.cotedazur.banquepopulaire.fr; f. 1986; present name adopted 2002; cap. 197m., res 323.3m., dep. 2,940.7m. (Dec. 2012); Pres. BERNARD FLEURY; Gen. Man. JEAN-FRANÇOIS COMAS; 100 brs.

Banque Populaire Loire et Lyonnais: 141 rue Garibaldi, BP 3152, 69003 Lyon; tel. 4-89-95-55-55; fax 4-78-71-03-99; e-mail contact@bp2l.banquepopulaire.fr; internet www.loirelyonnais.banquepopulaire.fr; f. 2000 by merger of Banque Populaire de Lyon and Banque Populaire de la Loire; cap. 425.4m., res 334.2m., dep. 5,024.9m. (Dec. 2012); Chair. JEAN BRUNET-LECOMTE; Gen. Man. JEAN-PIERRE LEVAYER.

Banque Populaire du Massif Central: BP 53, 18 blvd Jean Moulin, 63002 Clermont-Ferrand; tel. 4-73-23-46-23; fax 4-73-23-47-99; internet www.massifcentral.banquepopulaire.fr; f. 1920; cap. 196m., res 373.1m., dep. 3,463.4m. (Dec. 2012); Pres. DOMINIQUE MARTINIE; Gen. Man. CATHERINE HALBERSTADT.

Banque Populaire Rives de Paris: 76–78 ave de France, 75024 Paris Cedex 13; tel. 1-40-92-61-00; fax 1-46-57-61-53; internet www.rivesparis.banquepopulaire.fr; f. 2004 by merger of BICS-Banque Populaire and Banque Populaire Nord de Paris; cap. 705.7m., res 1,253.2m., dep. 13,528.7m. (Dec. 2012); Chair. MARC JARDIN; Gen. Man. YVES GEVIN.

BRED Banque Populaire: 18 quai de la Rapée, 75604 Paris Cedex 12; tel. 1-48-98-60-00; fax 1-40-04-71-57; e-mail webmaster@bred.fr; internet www.bred.fr; f. 1919; present name adopted 1994; cap. 520.3m., res 453.9m., dep. 19,318.7m. (Dec. 2012); Chair. STEVE GENTILI; Gen. Man. OLIVIER KLEIN; 339 brs (including 70 in the French Overseas Departments).

Crédit Coopératif: BP 211, Parc de la Défense, 33 rue des Trois Fontanot, 92002 Nanterre; tel. 1-47-24-85-00; fax 1-47-24-89-25; e-mail din@coopanet.com; internet www.credit-cooperatif.coop; f. 1893; present name adopted 2001; joined the Banque Fédérale des Banques Populaires group in 2002; merged with Caisse Centrale de Crédit Coopératif in 2003; cap. 780m., res 504.2m., dep. 9,698.9m. (Dec. 2012); Pres. JEAN-LOUIS BANCEL.

Caisse Centrale du Crédit Mutuel: 88–90 rue Cardinet, 75847 Paris Cedex 17; tel. 1-44-01-10-10; fax 1-44-01-12-30; internet www.creditmutuel.com; f. 1963; central organization of 10 autonomous banks (Caisses Fédérales); cap. 126.9m., res 294m., dep. 5,205.6m. (Dec. 2012); Chair. BERNARD FLOURIOT; Gen. Man. ALAIN FRADIN.

Crédit Agricole: 91–93 blvd Pasteur, 75015 Paris; tel. 1-43-23-52-02; fax 1-43-23-20-28; internet www.credit-agricole.fr; f. 1920; central institution for co-operative banking group comprising 39 Caisses Regionales and a central bank (CNCA); emphasis on agribusiness; cap. 7,494m., res 38,704m., dep. 701,916m. (Dec. 2012); Pres. RENÉ CARRON; Chief Exec. JEAN LAURENT; 9,130 brs.

Crédit Mutuel Arkéa: 1 rue Louis Lichou, 29480 Le Relecq-Kerhoun; tel. 2-98-00-22-22; fax 2-98-00-27-24; internet www.arkea.com; f. 2002; co-operative and mutual savings bank; cap. 2,018.9m., res 2,461.5m., dep. 30,824.2m. (Dec. 2012); Chair. JEAN-PIERRE DENIS; Gen. Man. RONAN LE MOAL.

Supervisory Body

Association Française des Etablissements de Crédit et des Entreprises d'Investissement (AFECEI): 36 rue Taitbout, 75009 Paris; tel. 1-48-01-88-88; fax 1-48-24-13-31; e-mail atassi@afecei.asso.fr; internet www.afecei.asso.fr; f. 1984; advises the Govt on monetary and credit policy and supervises the banking system; 14 mems; Pres. JEAN-PAUL CHIFFLET; Dir-Gen. ARIANE OBOLENSKY.

Banking Association

Fédération Bancaire Française: 18 rue La Fayette, 75009 Paris Cedex 09; tel. 1-48-00-52-52; fax 1-42-46-76-40; e-mail fbf@fbf.fr; internet www.fbf.fr; f. 1941; 390 mems; Pres. JEAN-PAUL CHIFFLET; Dir-Gen. ARIANE OBOLENSKY.

STOCK EXCHANGE

Euronext Paris: 39 rue Cambon, 75039 Paris Cedex 01; tel. 1-49-27-10-00; fax 1-49-27-11-71; e-mail info@euronext.com; internet www.euronext.fr; formed in 2000 by merger of Amsterdam, Paris and Brussels exchanges, and joined in 2002 by the Lisbon stock exchange and the London futures exchange LIFFE; merged with the New York Stock Exchange in 2007 to form NYSE Euronext; Chair. JAN-MICHIEL HESSELS.

Stock Exchange Associations

Autorité des Marchés Financiers (AMF): 17 place de la Bourse, 75082 Paris Cedex 2; tel. 1-53-45-60-00; fax 1-53-45-61-00; e-mail centrededoc@amf-france.org; internet www.amf-france.org; f. 2003 by merger of Commission des Opérations de Bourse and Conseil des Marchés Financiers; 350 mems (2007); Pres. GÉRARD RAMEIX; Sec.-Gen. BENOÎT DE JUVIGNY.

Fédération des Investisseurs Individuels et des Clubs d'Investissement (F2iC): 39 rue Cambon, 75001 Paris; tel. 1-42-60-12-47; fax 1-42-60-10-14; e-mail info@f2ic.fr; internet www.f2ic.fr; f. 1968; fmrly Fédération Française des Clubs d'Investissement (FFCI); represents shareholders and investment clubs in matters concerning public and political institutions; Pres. CHARLES-HENRI D'AUVIGNY; Sec.-Gen. ALDO SICURANI.

INSURANCE

AG2R La Mondiale: 32 ave Emile Zola, Mons en Baroeul, 59370 Lille Cedex 9; tel. 3-20-67-37-00; internet www.ag2rlamondiale.fr; f. 1905; renamed as above in 2010 following merger of La Mondiale and AG2R; life insurance; Dir-Gen. ANDRÉ RENAUDIN.

Allianz (AGF): 87 rue de Richelieu, 75002 Paris; tel. 1-44-86-20-00; fax 1-44-86-42-42; e-mail ecrire@allianz.fr; internet www.allianz.fr; f. 1968 by merger; affiliated to Allianz (Germany); name changed as above 2009; insurance and reinsurance; Pres. and Dir-Gen. JACQUES RICHIER.

Assurances du Crédit Mutuel IARD, SA: BP 373 R 10, 34 rue du Wacken, 67010 Strasbourg Cedex; tel. 3-88-14-90-90; fax 3-88-14-90-00; internet www.creditmutuel.fr; Pres. MICHEL LUCAS; Dir ALAIN FRADIN.

Aviva: 580 ave de l'Europe, 92270 Bois Colombes Cedex; tel. 1-76-62-50-00; e-mail veronique_eriaud@aviva.fr; internet www.aviva.fr; f. 1998 as CGU France by merger to incorporate fmr Abeille Assurances; present name adopted 2002; affiliated to CGNU Group (United Kingdom); CEO NICOLAS SCHIMEL.

AXA Assurances IARD: 313 Terrasses de l'Arche, 92727 Nanterre Cedex; tel. 1-47-74-10-01; fax 1-47-74-10-01; internet www.axa.fr; CEO NICOLAS MOREAU; Chair., Management Bd HENRI DE CASTRIES.

Caisse Centrale des Assurances Mutuelles Agricoles: 8–10 rue d'Astorg, 75008 Paris; tel. 1-44-56-77-77; fax 1-44-56-79-46; e-mail relations.exterieures@groupama.com; internet www.groupama.com; affiliated to Groupama; CEO THIERRY MARTEL.

Caisse Nationale de Prévoyance-Assurances (CNP): 4 place Raoul Dautry, 75716 Paris Cedex 15; tel. 1-42-18-88-88; fax 1-42-34-70-14; internet www.cnp.fr; f. 1945; general insurance; Pres EDMOND ALPHANDÉRY; CEO GILLES BENOIST.

Cardif: 8 rue du Port, 92728 Nanterre Cedex; tel. 1-41-42-83-00; internet www.cardif.fr; general insurance; Dir-Gen. ERIC LOMBARD.

GAN Assurances: 8–10 rue d'Astorg, 75383 Paris Cedex 08; tel. 1-70-94-20-00; fax 1-42-47-67-66; e-mail gan.rimbault.philippe@wanadoo.fr; internet www.ganassurances.fr; f. 1820, fire; f. 1830, life; f. 1865, accident; affiliated to Groupama; Pres. JEAN-FRANÇOIS LEMOUX; Dir ERIC GELPE.

Garantie Mutuelle des Fonctionnaires: 76 rue de Prony, 75857 Paris Cedex 17; tel. 1-47-54-10-10; fax 1-47-54-18-97; e-mail webgmf@gmf.fr; internet www.gmf.fr; f. 1934; Pres. and CEO THIERRY DEREZ; Man. Dir PATRICE FORGET.

Generali France: 11 blvd Haussmann, 75311 Paris Cedex 09; tel. 1-58-38-74-00; fax 1-58–38–74–01; e-mail dep-agence-web-interne@generali.fr; internet www.generali-patrimoine.fr; f. 1832; subsidiary of Generali (Italy); Pres. and CEO CLAUDE TENDIL.

Groupama SA: 8–10 rue d'Astorg, 75008 Paris; tel. 1-49-31-31-311-44-56-77-77; e-mail relations.exterieures@groupama.com; internet www.groupama.com; life insurance; CEO THIERRY MARTEL.

Mutuelles du Mans Assurances (MMA): 14 blvd Alexandre Oyon, 72030 Le Mans Cedex 09; tel. 2-43-41-72-72; fax 2-43-41-72-26; internet www.mma.fr; f. 1828; life and general insurance; comprises 3 companies: MMA-IARD, DAS and MMA-VIE; Pres. and Dir-Gen. JEAN-CLAUDE SEYS; Dir-Gen. JACQUES LENORMAND.

Predica: 50 rue de la Procession, 75724 Paris Cedex 15; tel. 1-43-23-03-33; fax 1-43-23-03-47; e-mail communication-pole-assurances@ca-predica.fr; internet www.ca-predica.fr; affiliated to Crédit Agricole; general insurance; Pres. PIERRE DERAJINSKI; Dir-Gen. JÉRÔME GRIVET.

Suravenir: BP 103, 232 rue Général Paulet, 29802 Brest Cedex 09; tel. 2-98-34-65-00; fax 2-98-34-65-11; internet www.suravenir.fr; f. 1984; subsidiary of Crédit Mutuel Arkéa; general insurance; Pres., Supervisory Bd JEAN-PIERRE CORLAY; Pres., Management Bd BERNARD LE BRAS.

UAF Patrimoine: 50–56 rue de la Procession, 75015 Paris; tel. 1-43-23-60-13; e-mail brigitte.le-morvan@ca-predica.fr; internet www.uafpatrimoine.fr; life insurance; part of Predica; Dir ERIC MORVAN.

Insurance Associations

Chambre Syndicale des Courtiers d'Assurances (CSCA): 91 rue Saint Lazare, 75009 Paris; tel. 1-48-74-19-12; fax 1-42-82-91-10; e-mail csca@csca.fr; internet www.csca.fr; f. 2006; formed by merger of the Fédération Française des Courtiers d'Assurances and the Syndicat Français des Assureurs Conseils; c. 1,000 mems; Chair. DOMINIQUE SIZES.

Syndicat Français des Assureurs-Conseils: 14 rue de la Grange Batelière, 75009 Paris; tel. 1-55-33-51-51; fax 1-48-00-93-01; e-mail sfac@sfac-assurance.fr; internet www.sfac-assurance.fr; Pres. ALAIN MORICHON.

Fédération des Agents Généraux d'Assurances (AGEA): 30 rue Olivier Noyer, 75014 Paris; tel. 1-70-98-48-00; e-mail regis.devaux@agea.fr; internet www.agea.fr; Pres. HERVÉ DE VEYRAC.

Fédération Française des Sociétés d'Assurances (FFSA): 26 blvd Haussmann, 75311 Paris; tel. 1-42-47-90-00; fax 1-42-47-93-11; internet www.ffsa.fr; f. 1937; Pres. BERNARD SPITZ; Sec.-Gen. GILLES WOLKOWITSCH.

Trade and Industry

GOVERNMENT AGENCIES

Agence Française pour les Investissements Internationaux (AFII) (Invest In France Agency—IFA): 77 blvd Saint-Jacques, 75680 Paris Cedex 14; tel. 1-44-87-17-17; fax 1-40-74-73-29; e-mail info@afii.fr; internet www.invest-in-france.org; f. 2001; promotes and assists foreign investment in France; Pres. DAVID APPIA; Man. Dir SERGE BOSCHER.

Conseil du Commerce de France: 40 blvd Malesherbes, 75008 Paris; tel. 1-40-15-03-03; fax 1-40-15-97-22; e-mail conseilducommerce@cdcf.com; internet www.cdcf.com; Pres. GÉRARD ATLAN; Sec.-Gen. FANNY FAVOREL-PIGE.

UBIFRANCE—l'Agence Française pour le Développement International des Entreprises: 77 blvd Saint-Jacques, 75998 Paris Cedex 14; tel. 1-40-73-30-00; fax 1-40-73-39-79; e-mail Claire.rocheteau@ubifrance.fr; internet www.ubifrance.fr; f. 2004 by merger of the Centre Français du Commerce Extérieur and the association UBIFrance; Dir-Gen. CHRISTOPHE LECOURTIER.

DEVELOPMENT ORGANIZATIONS

Agence pour la Création d'Entreprises (APCE): 14 rue Delambre, 75682 Paris Cedex 14; tel. 1-42-18-58-58; fax 1-42-18-58-00;

e-mail info@apce.com; internet www.apce.com; Pres. JEAN-CLAUDE VOLOT; Dir-Gen. ALAIN BELAIS.

Groupe IDI: 18 ave Matignon, 75008 Paris; tel. 1-55-27-80-00; fax 1-40-17-04-44; e-mail idi@idi.fr; internet www.idi.fr; f. 1970 as Institut de Développement Industriel; provides venture capital, takes equity shares in small and medium-sized businesses; Chair. LUCE GENDRY.

CHAMBERS OF COMMERCE

There are Chambers of Commerce in all the larger towns for all the more important commodities produced or manufactured.

Assemblée des Chambres Françaises de Commerce et d'Industrie: 46 ave de la Grande Armée, 75858 Paris Cedex 17; tel. 1-40-69-37-00; fax 1-47-20-61-28; e-mail contactsweb@acfci.cci.fr; internet www.acfci.cci.fr; f. 1964; unites 154 local and 21 regional Chambers of Commerce and Industry; Pres. ANDRÉ MARCON.

Chambre de Commerce et d'Industrie de Paris: 27 ave de Friedland, 75382 Paris Cedex 08; tel. 1-55-65-55-65; fax 1-55-65-78-68; e-mail cpdp@ccip.fr; internet www.ccip.fr; f. 1803; Pres. PIERRE-ANTOINE GAILLY; Dir-Gen. PIERRE TROUILLET; 307,000 mems in Paris and surrounding regions (Hauts de Seine, Seine-Saint-Denis and Val de Marne).

INDUSTRIAL AND TRADE ASSOCIATIONS

Armateurs de France: 47 rue de Monceau, 75008 Paris; tel. 1-53-89-52-52; fax 1-53-89-52-53; e-mail info@armateursdefrance.org; internet www.armateursdefrance.org; f. 1903; fmrly Comité Central des Armateurs de France; shipping; Pres. RAYMOND VIDIL; Delegate-Gen. ERIC BANEL; 57 mems.

Assemblée Permanente des Chambres d'Agriculture (APCA): 9 ave George V, 75008 Paris; tel. 1-53-57-10-10; fax 1-53-57-10-05; e-mail accueil@apca.chambagri.fr; internet www.chambres-agriculture.fr; f. 1929; agriculture; Pres. GREY VASSEUR.

Association Nationale des Industries Alimentaires (ANIA): 21 rue Leblanc, 75015 Paris; tel. 1-53-83-86-00; fax 1-53-83-92-37; e-mail infos@ania.net; internet www.ania.net; f. 1971; food produce; Pres. JEAN-RENÉ BUISSON; 22 nat. feds and 20 regional asscns.

Chambre Syndicale de l'Ameublement, Négoce de Paris et de l'Ile de France: 15 rue de la Cerisaie, 75004 Paris; tel. 1-42-72-13-79; fax 1-42-72-02-36; e-mail info@meubleparis.net; internet www.franceameublement.fr; f. 1860; furnishing; Chair. NICOLE PHILIBERT; 350 mems.

Chambre Syndicale des Céramistes et Ateliers d'Art de France: 6 rue Jadin, 75017 Paris; tel. 1-44-01-08-30; fax 1-44-01-08-35; e-mail info@ateliersdart.com; internet www.ateliersdart.com; f. 1886; craft and design trades; Chair. SERGE NICOLE; Sec.-Gen. NICOLE CRESTOU; 5,400 mems.

Comité des Constructeurs Français d'Automobiles: 2 rue de Presbourg, 75008 Paris; tel. 1-49-52-51-00; fax 1-49-52-51-88; e-mail ccfa@ccfa.fr; internet www.ccfa.fr; f. 1909; motor manufacturing; Chair. PATRICK BLAIN; 6 mems.

Comité National des Pêches Maritimes et des Elevages Marins (CNPMEM): 134 ave de Malakoff, 75116 Paris; tel. 1-72-71-18-00; fax 1-72-71-18-50; e-mail cnpmem@comite-peches.fr; internet www.comite-peches.fr; marine fisheries; Pres. GÉRARD ROMITI; 136 mems.

Comité Professionnel du Pétrole (CPDP): 212 ave Paul Doumer, 92508 Rueil-Malmaison Cedex; tel. 1-47-16-94-60; fax 1-47-08-10-57; e-mail contact@cpdp.org; internet www.cpdp.org; f. 1950; petroleum industry; Pres. OLIVIER GANTOIS; 80 mems.

Commissariat à l'Energie Atomique (CEA) (Atomic Energy Commission): Bâtiment le ponant D, 25 rue Leblanc, 75015 Paris; tel. 1-64-50-10-00; fax 1-40-56-29-70; e-mail dcom@aramis.cea.fr; internet www.cea.fr; f. 1945; promotes the uses of nuclear energy in science, industry and national defence; involved in research on nuclear materials; reactor development; fundamental research; innovation and transfer of technologies; military applications; biotechnologies; robotics; electronics; new materials; radiological protection and nuclear safety; Gen. Administrator and High Commissioner BERNARD BIGOT.

Confédération des Industries Céramiques de France (CICF): 114 rue La Boétie, 75008 Paris; tel. 1-58-18-30-40; fax 1-42-66-09-00; e-mail cicf@ceramique.org; internet www.ceramique.org; f. 1937; ceramic industry; Chair. PHILIPPE MAURISSET; Sec.-Gen. DELPHINE PALOUX-HUSSON; 85 mems, 5 affiliates.

Les Entreprises du Médicament (LEEM): 88 rue de la Faisanderie, 75782 Paris Cedex 16; tel. 1-45-03-88-88; fax 1-45-04-47-71; e-mail dcre@leem.org; internet www.leem.org; fmrly Syndicat National de l'Industrie Pharmaceutique; pharmaceuticals; Chair. CHRISTIAN LAJOUX; 326 mem. cos.

FEBEA (France) (Fédération des Enterprises de la Beauté): 137 rue de l'Université, 75007 Paris; tel. 1-56-69-67-89; fax 1-56-69-67-90; e-mail febea@febea.fr; internet www.febea.fr; makers of perfume, cosmetics and toiletries; Pres. ALAIN GRANGÉ CABANE; 300 mems.

Fédération des Chambres Syndicales de l'Industrie du Verre: 114 rue la Boétie, 75008 Paris; tel. 1-42-65-60-02; fax 1-42-66-23-88; e-mail contact@fedeverre.fr; internet www.fedeverre.fr; f. 1938; glass industry; Pres. MICHEL GARDES.

Fédération des Chambres Syndicales des Minerais, Minéraux Industriels et Métaux non-Ferreux (FEDEM): 17 rue de l'Amiral Hamelin, 75783 Paris Cedex 16; tel. 1-40-76-44-50; fax 1-45-63-61-54; e-mail contact@fedem.fr; internet www.fedem.fr; f. 1945; minerals and non-ferrous metals; Chair. CATHERINE TISSOT-COLLE; Delegate-Gen. CLAIRE DE LANGERON; 16 affiliated syndicates.

Fédération des Exportateurs de Vins et Spiritueux de France: 7 rue de Madrid, 75008 Paris; tel. 1-45-22-75-73; fax 1-45-22-94-16; e-mail contact@fevs.com; internet www.fevs.com; f. 1922 as Commission d'Exportation des Vins de France; exporters of wines and spirits; Pres. CLAUDE DE JOUVENCEL; 450 mems.

Fédération Française de l'Acier (FFA): 5 rue Luigi Cherubini, 93212 La Plaine Saint-Denis Cedex; tel. 1-71-92-20-18; fax 1-71-92-25-00; e-mail svp.clients@ffa.fr; internet www.ffa.fr; f. 1945; steel-making; Pres. PHILIPPE DARMAYAN.

Fédération Française du Bâtiment (FFB): 33 ave Kléber, 75784 Paris Cedex 16; tel. 1-40-69-51-00; fax 1-45-53-58-77; e-mail ffbbox@ffb.fr; internet www.ffbatiment.fr; f. 1906; building trade; Pres. DIDIER RIDORET; 57,000 mems.

Fédération Française des Industries Lainière et Cotonnière (FFILC): BP 121, 37–39 rue de Neuilly, 92582 Clichy Cedex; tel. 1-47-56-31-48; fax 1-47-37-06-20; e-mail uitcotonlaine@textile.fr; internet www.textile.fr; f. 1902; manufacturing of wool, cotton and associated textiles; Pres. BENOÎT HACOT; 400 mems.

Fédération Française de la Tannerie-Mégisserie (FFTM): 122 rue de Provence, 78087 Paris; tel. 1-45-22-96-45; fax 1-42-93-37-44; e-mail fftm@leatherfrance.com; internet www.leatherfrance.com; f. 1885; leather industry; 100 mems.

Fédération des Industries Electriques, Electroniques et de Communication (FIEEC): 17 rue de l'Amiral Hamelin, 75783 Paris Cedex 16; tel. 1-45-05-70-53; fax 1-45-05-16-79; e-mail comm@fieec.fr; internet www.fieec.fr; f. 1925; electrical and electronics industries; Delegate-Gen. ERIC JOURDE; c. 1,000 mems.

Fédération des Industries Mécaniques: 39–41 rue Louis Blanc, 92400 Courbevoie; tel. 1-47-17-60-00; fax 1-47-17-64-37; e-mail webmaster@mail.fimeca.com; internet www.fim.net; f. 1840; mechanical and metal-working; Pres. JÉRÔME FRANTZ; Dir-Gen. MICHEL ATHIMON.

Fédération des Industries Nautiques: 200 Port de Javel Haut, 75015 Paris; tel. 1-44-37-04-00; fax 1-45-77-21-88; e-mail info@fin.fr; internet www.fin.fr; f. 1964; nautical industries; Pres. JEAN-FRANÇOIS FOUNTAINE; Vice-Pres YVES LYON-CAEN, COLETTE CERTOUX; 750 mems.

Fédération Nationale du Bois (FNB): 6 rue François 1er, 75008 Paris; tel. 1-56-69-52-00; fax 1-56-69-52-09; e-mail infos@fnbois.com; internet www.fnbois.com; f. 1884; timber and wood products; Chair. LAURENT DENORMANDIE; 1,850 mems.

Fédération du Négoce de Bois et des Matériaux (FFNB): 215 bis blvd St Germain, 75007 Paris; tel. 1-45-48-28-44; fax 1-45-48-42-89; e-mail contact@fnbm.fr; internet www.fnbm.fr; timber trade; Pres. GÉRAUD SPIRE; Delegate-Gen. LAURENT MARTIN SAINT LÉON; 1,100 mems.

Fédération Nationale des Chambres Syndicales des Horlogers, Bijoutiers, Joailliers et Orfèvres (HBJO): 249 rue Saint Martin, 75003 Paris; tel. 1-44-54-34-00; fax 1-44-54-34-07; e-mail fedhbjo@wanadoo.fr; internet www.fedehbjo.com; jewellery, watch- and clock-making; Pres. GÉRARD ATLAN; Delegate-Gen. CAROLE GROUESY; 1,300 mems.

Fédération Nationale de l'Industrie Laitière: 42 rue de Châteaudun, 75314 Paris Cedex 09; tel. 1-49-70-72-85; fax 1-42-80-63-94; e-mail fnil@atla.asso.fr; internet www.maison-du-lait.com; f. 1946; dairy products; Pres. OLIVIER PICOT.

Les Fondeurs de France: 45 rue Louis Blanc, 92038 Paris La Défense Cedex; tel. 1-43-34-76-30; fax 1-43-34-76-31; e-mail contact@fondeursdefrance.org; internet www.fondeursdefrance.org; f. 1897; metal casting; Pres. LAURENT LAJOYE; Dir-Gen. JEAN-LUC BRILLANCEAU; 300 mems.

Groupe Intersyndical de l'Industrie Nucléaire (GIIN): 39–41 rue Louis Blanc, 92400 Courbevoie; tel. 1-47-17-62-78; fax 1-43-34-76-25; e-mail contact@giin.fr; internet www.giin.fr; f. 1959; aims to promote the interests of the French nuclear industry; 200 mem. firms.

Groupement des Industries de Construction et d'Activités Navales: 19–21 rue du Colonel Pierre Avia, 75015 Paris; tel. 1-47-36-80-80; fax 1-40-93-57-72; e-mail contact@gican.asso.fr; internet www.gican.asso.fr; f. 1992; owned by the French marine industry; Chair.

JEAN-MARIE POIMBOEUF; Delegate-Gen. JEAN-MARIE CARNET; 160 mems.

Groupement des Industries Françaises Aéronautiques et Spatiales (GIFAS): 8 rue Galilée, 75116 Paris; tel. 1-44-43-17-00; fax 1-40-70-91-41; e-mail infogifas@gifas.asso.fr; internet www.gifas.asso.fr; f. 1910; aerospace industry; Pres. JEAN-PAUL HERTEMAN; 300 mems.

Syndicat Général des Cuirs et Peaux: 18 blvd Montmartre, 75009 Paris; tel. 1-45-08-08-54; fax 1-40-39-97-31; e-mail cuirsetpeaux@wanadoo.fr; internet www.sgcp.net; f. 1977; present name adopted 1996; untreated leather and hides; Chair. DENIS GEISSMANN; 26 mems.

Union des Armateurs à la Pêche de France: 59 rue des Mathurins, 75008 Paris; tel. 1-42-66-32-60; fax 1-47-42-91-12; e-mail uapf@uapf.org; f. 1945; fishing vessels; Chair. JEAN-MARIE ZARZA; Delegate-Gen. MARC GHIGLIA.

Union des Fabricants de Porcelaine de Limoges: 7 bis rue du Général Cérez, 87000 Limoges; tel. 5-55-77-29-18; fax 5-55-77-36-81; e-mail ufpl@porcelainelimoges.org; porcelain manufacturing; Chair. BERTRAND RAYNAUD.

Union des Industries Chimiques (UIC): Le Diamant A, 14 rue de la République, 92800 Paris La Défense Cedex 10; tel. 1-46-53-11-00; fax 1-46-96-00-59; e-mail uicgeneral@uic.fr; internet www.uic.fr; f. 1860; chemical industry; Pres. OLIVIER HOMOLLE; Dir-Gen. JEAN PELIN; 25 affiliated unions.

Union des Industries Métallurgiques et Minières (UIMM): 56 ave de Wagram, 75017 Paris; tel. 1-40-54-20-20; fax 1-47-66-22-74; e-mail uimm@uimm.fr; internet www.uimm.fr; metallurgy and mining; Chair. FRÉDÉRIC SAINT-GEOURS; 223 mems.

Union des Industries Papetières pour les Affaires Sociales (UNIPAS): 23–25 rue d'Aumale, 75009 Paris; tel. 1-53-89-25-27; fax 1-53-89-25-26; e-mail contact@unipas.org; internet www.unipas.org; f. 1864; paper, cardboard and cellulose; Chair. JEAN-PIERRE QUÉRÉ; Sec.-Gen. ARNAUD COUVREUR.

Union des Industries Textiles: 37–39 rue de Neuilly, BP 121, 92113 Clichy Cedex; tel. 1-47-56-31-00; fax 1-47-30-25-28; e-mail uit@textile.fr; internet www.textile.fr; f. 1900; textiles; Chair. YVES DUBIEF; 570 mem. cos (2012).

Union des Métiers et des Industries de l'Hôtellerie (UMIH): 22 rue d'Anjou, 75008 Paris; tel. 1-44-94-19-94; fax 1-47-42-15-20; e-mail fnih@imagenet.fr; internet www.umih.fr; hospitality; Chair. ROLAND HÉGUY.

Union Nationale de l'Imprimerie et de la Communication (UNIC): 68 blvd Saint Marcel, 75005 Paris; tel. 1-44-08-64-46; fax 1-43-36-09-51; e-mail unic@com-unic.fr; internet www.com-unic.fr; f. 2008 by merger of Fédération de l'Imprimerie et de la Communication Graphique (FICG) and Syndicat National des Industries de la Communication Graphique et de l'Imprimerie Françaises (SICOGIF); printing, communication and design; Pres. JACQUES CHIRAT; 1,300 mems.

Union Professionnelle Artisanale (UPA): 53 rue Ampère, 75017 Paris; tel. 1-47-63-31-31; fax 1-47-63-31-10; e-mail upa@upa.fr; internet www.upa.fr; f. 1975; unites crafts and other manual workers in 3 trade bodies and more than 100 regional organizations; Chair. JEAN-PIERRE CROUZET.

EMPLOYERS' ORGANIZATIONS

Association Française des Entreprises Privées (AGREF): Paris; represents the interests of 81 of the largest enterprises in France; Chair. PIERRE PRINGUET.

Centre des Jeunes Dirigeants d'Entreprise (CJD): 19 ave Georges V, 75008 Paris; tel. 1-53-23-92-50; fax 1-53-23-92-30; e-mail cjd@cjd.net; internet www.cjd.net; f. 1938; asscn for young entrepreneurs (under 45 years of age); Pres. MICHEL MEUNIER; 3,000 mems.

Confédération Générale des Petites et Moyennes Entreprises (CGPME): 10 terrasse Bellini, 92806 Puteaux Cedex; tel. 1-47-62-73-73; fax 1-47-73-08-86; internet www.cgpme.fr; small and medium-sized cos; Chair. JEAN-FRANÇOIS ROUBAUD.

Les Entrepreneurs et Dirigeants Chrétiens (Les EDC): 24 rue Hamelin, 75116 Paris; tel. 1-45-53-09-01; fax 1-47-27-43-32; e-mail lesedc@lesedc.org; internet www.lesedc.org; fmrly Centre Français du Patronat Chrétien; asscn of Christian employers; Nat. Pres. ROBERT LEBLANC.

Entreprise et Progrès: 41 blvd Malesherbes, 75008 Paris; tel. 1-45-74-52-62; fax 1-45-74-52-63; e-mail contact@entreprise-progres.com; internet www.entreprise-progres.net; f. 1970; represents 110 enterprises; Pres. DENIS TERRIEN; Sec.-Gen. BEATRICE BOURGES.

Entreprises de Taille Humaine Indépendantes et de Croissance (ETHIC): 260 blvd Saint Germain, 75007 Paris; tel. 1-71-18-33-68; fax 1-71-18-33-76; e-mail btorjman@ethic.fr; internet www.ethic.fr; f. 1976; represents small enterprises and promotes ethical values in business; Pres. SOPHIE DE MENTHON.

Mouvement des Entreprises de France (MEDEF): 55 ave Bosquet, 75007 Paris Cedex 07; tel. 1-53-59-19-19; fax 1-45-51-20-44; internet www.medef.fr; f. 1998 to replace Conseil National du Patronat Français; employers' asscn grouping 700,000 cos from all sectors of activity in 85 professional feds and 152 regional orgs; Pres. PIERRE GATTAZ; Dir-Gen. MICHEL GUILBAUD.

UTILITIES

Electricity

EDF: 22–30 ave de Wagram, 75382 Paris Cedex 8; tel. and fax 1-40-42-22-22; e-mail masteredf@edfgdf.fr; internet www.edf.fr; established under the Electricity and Gas Industry Nationalization Act of 1946 as Electricité de France; responsible for generating and supplying electricity for distribution to consumers in metropolitan France; 15% of the company was sold to the private sector in November 2005; Chair. and CEO HENRI PROGLIO.

Gas

GDF SUEZ: 23 rue Philibert Delorme, 75840 Paris Cedex 17; tel. 1-47-54-24-35; fax 1-47-54-74-42; internet www.gdfsuez.com; established as Gaz de France under the Electricity and Gas Industry Nationalization Act of 1946; responsible for distribution of gas in metropolitan France; partially privatized in 2005; present name adopted in July 2008 following merger with Suez; merged with International Power (United Kingdom) in 2011; Chair. and CEO GÉRARD MESTRALLET.

Water

Lyonnaise des Eaux: 1 rue d'Astorg, 75008 Paris; e-mail sophie.le.scaon@lyonnaise-des-eaux.fr; internet www.lyonnaise-des-eaux.fr; f. 1858; fmrly Suez-Lyonnaise des Eaux; present name adopted 2001; Pres. and CEO JEAN-LOUIS CHAUSSADE.

Veolia Eau (Veolia Water): 52 rue d'Anjou, 75384 Paris Cedex 8; tel. 1-49-24-49-24; fax 1-49-24-69-59; e-mail webmaster@veoliawater.com; internet www.veoliawater.com; f. 1853 as the Compagnie Générale des Eaux; subsidiary of Veolia Environnement; provides drinking water and manages waste water; CEO JEAN-MICHEL HERREWYN.

TRADE UNIONS

There are three major trade union organizations: the Confédération Française Démocratique du Travail (CFDT), the Confédération Générale du Travail (CGT) and Force Ouvrière (FO).

Confédération Française Démocratique du Travail (CFDT): 4 blvd de la Villette, 75955 Paris Cedex 19; tel. 1-42-03-80-00; fax 1-53-72-85-67; e-mail international@cfdt.fr; internet www.cfdt.fr; f. 1919 as Confédération Française des Travailleurs Chrétiens—CFTC; present title and constitution adopted 1964; moderate; co-ordinates 1,100 trade unions, 95 departmental and overseas unions, 3 confederal unions and 14 affiliated professional federations, all of which are autonomous. There are also 22 regional orgs; affiliated to European Trade Union Confederation and to ITUC; Sec.-Gen. LAURENT BERGER; 868,600 mems.

Confédération Générale du Travail (CGT) (Labour): 263 rue de Paris, 93516 Montreuil Cedex; tel. 1-48-18-80-00; fax 1-49-88-18-57; e-mail info@cgt.fr; internet www.cgt.fr; f. 1895; National Congress is held every 3 years; Sec.-Gen. THIERRY LEPAON; 700,000 mems.

Force Ouvrière (FO): 141 ave du Maine, 75680 Paris Cedex 14; tel. 1-40-52-82-00; fax 1-40-52-82-02; internet www.force-ouvriere.fr; f. 1948 by breakaway from the more left-wing CGT; mem. of ITUC and of the European Trade Union Confederation; Sec.-Gen. JEAN-CLAUDE MAILLY; c. 1m. mems.

Other federations:

Confédération Française de l'Encadrement (CFE—CGC): 59 rue du Rocher, 75008 Paris; tel. 1-55-30-12-12; fax 1—55-30-13-13; e-mail presse@cfecgc.fr; internet www.cfecgc.fr; f. 1944; organizes managerial staff, professional staff and technicians; co-ordinates unions in every industry and sector; Nat. Pres. BERNARD VAN CRAEYNEST; Sec.-Gen. CAROLE COUVERT; 160,000 mems (2006).

Confédération Française des Travailleurs Chrétiens (CFTC): 128 ave Jean Jaurès, 93697 Pantin Cedex; tel. 1-73-30-49-00; fax 1-73-30-49-18; e-mail eurint@cftc.fr; internet www.cftc.fr; f. 1919; present form in 1964 after majority CFTC became CFDT; mem. European Trade Union Confederation, World Confederation of Labour; Chair. PHILIPPE LOUIS; Sec.-Gen. PASCALE COTON; 142,000 mems.

Fédération Nationale des Syndicats Autonomes de l'Enseignement Supérieur et de la Recherche: 48 rue Vitruve, 75020 Paris; tel. 1-46-59-01-01; fax 1-46-59-01-23; e-mail supautonome@free.fr; internet autonomesup.com; f. 1948; higher education and research; Pres. JEAN-LOUIS CHARLET; Sec.-Gen. MICHEL GAY.

Fédération Nationale des Syndicats d'Exploitants Agricoles (FNSEA) (National Federation of Farmers' Unions): 11 rue de la Baume, 75008 Paris; tel. 1-53-83-47-47; fax 1-53-83-48-48; e-mail fnsea@fnsea.fr; internet www.fnsea.fr; f. 1946; comprises 92 departmental federations and 32,000 local unions; Pres. XAVIER BEULIN; 600,000 mems.

Fédération Syndicale Unitaire (FSU): 104 rue Romain Rolland, 93260 Les lilas; tel. 1-41-63-27-30; fax 1-41-63-15-48; e-mail fsu.nationale@fsu.fr; internet www.fsu.fr; f. 1993; federation of civil service and education workers' unions; Sec.-Gen. BERNADETTE GROISON; 163,000 mems.

UNSA Education: 87 bis ave Georges Gosnat, 94853 Ivry-sur-Seine Cedex; tel. 1-56-20-29-50; fax 1-56-20-29-89; e-mail national@unsa-education.org; internet www.unsa-education.org; f. 1948; federation of teachers' unions; comprises 24 mem. unions; fmrly Fédération de l'Education Nationale; Sec.-Gen. LAURENT ESCURE.

Transport

RAILWAYS

Most of the French railways are controlled by the Société Nationale des Chemins de fer Français (SNCF), established in 1937, while the Réseau Ferré de France (RFF, f. 1997) manages track and infrastructure. The SNCF is divided into 22 régions (areas). In 2011 the RFF operated 30,884 km of track, of which 16,321 km were electrified. A high-speed service (train à grande vitesse—TGV) operates between Paris and various other destinations: Lyon (TGV Sud-Est), extending to Marseille or Nîmes (TGV Méditerranée), Bordeaux or Nantes (TGV Atlantique), Lille (TGV Nord Europe) and Strasbourg and destinations in Germany, Luxembourg and Switzerland (TGV Est Européen). The Rhine–Rhône high-speed line opened in 2011, linking central and eastern France with Germany and Switzerland. A high-speed line to Barcelona began direct services in late 2013. Further high-speed lines, between Nîmes and Montpellier and Brittany and the Loire Valley, were expected to be completed by 2017. The Parisian transport system is controlled by a separate authority, the Régie Autonome des Transports Parisiens (RATP). A number of small railways in the provinces are run by independent organizations.

Réseau Ferré de France (RFF): 92 ave de France, 75648 Paris Cedex 13; tel. 1-53-94-30-00; fax 1-53-94-38-00; internet www.rff.fr; f. 1997 to assume ownership and financial control of national rail infrastructure; state-owned; Pres. and Dir-Gen. JACQUES RAPOPORT; Asst Gen. Dir ALAIN QUINET.

Société Nationale des Chemins de fer Français (SNCF): 34 rue du Commandant Mouchotte, 75014 Paris; tel. 1-53-25-32-30; fax 1-53-25-61-08; e-mail webcom@sncf.fr; internet www.sncf.fr; f. 1937; Pres. GUILLAUME PÉPY.

Channel Tunnel (Le Tunnel sous la Manche)

Groupe Eurotunnel: BP 69, 62904 Coquelles Cedex; tel. 3-21-00-65-43; internet www.eurotunnel.fr; Anglo-French consortium contracted to design, finance and construct the Channel Tunnel under a concession granted for a period up to 2052 (later extended to 2086); receives finance exclusively from the private sector, including international commercial banks; the Channel Tunnel was formally opened in May 1994; operates a series of road vehicle 'shuttle' trains and passenger and freight trains through the Channel Tunnel; Chair. and Chief Exec. JACQUES GOUNON.

ROADS

At 31 December 2010 there were 11,466 km of motorways (*autoroutes*), 8,980 km of highways, 378,000 km of secondary roads and 630,000 km of other roads.

Fédération Nationale des Transports Routiers (FNTR): 6 rue Ampère, 75017 Paris; tel. 1-44-29-04-29; fax 1-44-29-04-01; e-mail contact@fntr.fr; internet www.fntr.fr; f. 1933; road transport; Chair. JEAN-CHRISTOPHE PIC; 12,500 mem. cos.

METROPOLITAN TRANSPORT

Régie Autonome des Transports Parisiens (RATP): 54 quai de la Rapée, 75599 Paris Cedex 12; tel. 1-58-78-20-20; internet www.ratp.fr; f. 1949; state-owned; operates the Paris underground (comprising 16 lines totalling 200 km, and 381 stations), Réseau Express Régional (RER) suburban railways (totalling 115 km in 2007), 3 suburban tramlines, and 345 bus routes; Chair. and CEO PIERRE MONGIN.

Five provincial cities also have underground railway systems: Marseille, Lyon, Lille, Rennes and Toulouse. Tram networks have been constructed in several provincial cities since the 1980s.

INLAND WATERWAYS

In 2011 there were 5,019 km of navigable waterways.

Voies navigables de France: 175 rue Ludovic Boutleux, BP 30820, 62408 Béthune Cedex; tel. 3-21-63-24-24; fax 3-21-63-24-42; e-mail direction-generale@vnf.fr; internet www.vnf.fr; f. 1991; management and development of France's inland waterways; responsible for 3,800 km of navigable canals and 2,900 km of navigable rivers; Pres. ALAIN GEST; Dir-Gen. MARC PAPINUTTI.

SHIPPING

Seven of the major ports, Marseille, Le Havre, Dunkerque, Nantes Saint-Nazaire, Rouen, Bordeaux and La Rochelle, are operated by autonomous authorities (Grands Ports Maritimes), although the state retains supervisory powers. At 31 December 2013 the flag registered fleet numbered 1,022 vessels, with a combined displacement of 5.8m. grt., of which 37 were general cargo ships and 234 were fishing vessels.

Conseil Supérieur de la Marine Marchande (CSMM): 3 pl. de Fontenoy, 75007 Paris; tel. 1-44-49-81-84; fax 1-44-49-80-81; e-mail jean-marie.berthet@developpement-durable.gouv.fr; internet www.csmm.equipement.gouv.fr; f. 1896; merged with the Conseil National des Communautés Portuaires (f. 1987) in 2002; govt consultative and co-ordinating body for maritime transport, ports and port authorities; 39 mems, including 12 trade union mems; Pres. MICHEL QUIMBERT; Sec.-Gen. JEAN-MARIE BERTHET.

Grand Port Maritime de Bordeaux: 182 quai de Bacalan, CS 41320, 33082 Bordeaux Cedex; tel. 5-56-90-58-00; fax 5-56-90-58-77; e-mail postoffice@bordeaux-port.fr; internet www.bordeaux-port.fr; Dir-Gen. CHRISTOPHE MASSON.

Grand Port Maritime de Dunkerque: 2505 route de l'Ecluse Trystram, BP 46534, 59386 Dunkerque Cedex 01; tel. 3-28-28-78-78; fax 3-28-28-78-77; internet www.dunkerque-port.fr; CEO CHRISTINE CABAU WOEHREL.

Grand Port Maritime du Havre: Terre-Plein de la Barre, BP 1413, 76067 Le Havre Cedex; tel. 2-32-74-74-00; fax 2-32-74-74-29; e-mail internetpah@havre-port.fr; internet www.havre-port.fr; f. 2008; Exec. Dir HERVÉ MARTEL.

Grand Port Maritime de La Rochelle: BP 70394, 17001 La Rochelle Cedex 1; tel. (5) 46-00-53-60; fax (5) 46-43-12-54; internet www.larochelle.port.fr; Dir-Gen. MICHEL PUYRAZAT.

Grand Port Maritime de Marseille: 23 pl. de la Joliette, BP 81965, 13226 Marseille Cedex 02; tel. 4-91-39-40-00; fax 4-91-39-57-00; e-mail gpmm@marseille-port.fr; internet www.marseille-port.fr; Dir-Gen. JEAN-CLAUDE TERRIER.

Grand Port Maritime de Nantes Saint Nazaire: 18 quai Ernest Renaud, BP 18609, 44186 Nantes Cedex 4; tel. 2-40-44-20-20; fax 2-40-44-21-81; internet www.nantes.port.fr; f. 1966; Dir-Gen. JEAN-PIERRE CHALUS.

Grand Port Maritime de Rouen: 34 blvd de Boisguilbert, BP 4075, 76022 Rouen Cedex 03; tel. 2-35-52-54-56; fax 2-35-52-54-13; e-mail dg@rouen.port.fr; internet www.rouen.port.fr; Dir-Gen. PHILIPPE DEISS.

Port de Calais: 54 rue du quai de la Loire, CS 90283, 62105 Calais Cedex; tel. 3-21-46-29-00; fax 3-21-46-29-99; e-mail webmaster@calais-port.fr; internet www.calais-port.com; Pres. JEAN-MARC PUISSESSEAU.

Principal Shipping Companies

Note: Not all the vessels belonging to the companies listed below are registered under the French flag.

Brittany Ferries: Port du Bloscon, BP 72, 29680 Roscoff Cedex; tel. 2-98-29-28-13; fax 2-98-29-27-00; e-mail service.client@brittany-ferries.fr; internet www.brittany-ferries.fr; f. 1972 as Bretagne-Angleterre-Irlande (BAI); transport between France, Ireland, Spain and the United Kingdom; Chair. JEAN MARC ROUÉ; Man. Dir MARTINE JOURDREN.

Compagnie Maritime Marfret: 13 quai de la Joliette, 13002 Marseille; tel. 4-91-56-91-00; fax 4-91-56-91-01; e-mail bvidil@marfret.fr; internet www.marfret.fr; f. 1951 as Marseille-Fret; name changed to present in 1987; freight services to the Mediterranean, South America, the Caribbean, Canada and northern Europe; Chair RAYMOND VIDIL; Dir-Gen. BERNARD VIDIL.

Consortium Européen de Transports Maritimes (CETRAMAR): 87 ave de la Grande Armée, 75782 Paris Cedex 16; tel. 1-40-66-11-11; fax 1-45-00-77-35; f. 1964; Chair. PHILIPPE POIRIER D'ANGÉ D'ORSAY; Man. Dir ANDRÉ MAIRE; displacement 564,291 grt.

Corsica Ferries: 5 bis rue Chanoîne Leschi, BP 275, 20296 Bastia; tel. 4-95-32-95-95; fax 4-95-32-14-71; e-mail infos@corsicaferries.com; internet www.corsica-ferries.fr; f. 1968; affiliated to Groupe Lota Maritime; passenger and freight ferry services between Corsica, Sardinia, mainland France, and mainland Italy; Pres. PASCAL LOTA; CEO PIERRE MATTEI.

Esso France: 2 rue des Martinets, 92569 Rueil-Malmaison Cedex; tel. 1-47-10-60-00; fax 1-47-10-60-03; internet www.esso.com/europe-french/fr_homepage.asp; f. 1952; merged with Mobil Oil Française in 2003; Chair. and Man. Dir PATRICK HEINZLE.

Groupe CMA—CGM: 4 quai d'Arenc, 13235 Marseille Cedex 02; tel. 4-88-91-90-00; fax 4-88-91-90-95; internet www.cma-cgm.com; f. 1996 by merger of Compagnie Générale Maritime and Compagnie Maritime d'Affrètement; freight services to USA, Canada, the Caribbean, Central and South America, the Mediterranean, the Middle East, the Far East, India, Australia, New Zealand, Indonesia, East Africa, and other Pacific and Indian Ocean areas; 25 ships owned; Chair. and CEO JACQUES R. SAADÉ; displacement 1,900,000 grt (2001).

Louis Dreyfus Armateurs (LDA): 28 quai Gallieni, 92158 Suresnes Cedex; tel. 1-70-38-60-00; fax 1-70-79-15-02; e-mail gehannep@lda.fr; internet www.lda.fr; gas and bulk carriers; Pres. PHILIPPE LOUIS-DREYFUS; CEO PIERRE GEHANNE.

Maersk Tankers France SAS: 35 ter ave André Morizet, 92100 Boulogne Billancourt; tel. 1-46-99-60-15; fax 1-72-70-34-90; e-mail managementmtpar@maersk.com; internet www.maersktankers.com; subsidiary of A.P. Møller-Mærsk AS (Denmark); fmrly Broström Tankers, SAS; name changed to present in June 2010; oil product and chemical coastal tankers and tramping; CEO HANNE B. SØRENSEN.

Société d'Armement et de Transport (Socatra): 9 allées de Tourny, 33000 Bordeaux; tel. 5-56-00-00-56; fax 5-40-16-02-31; e-mail management@socatra.com; internet www.socatra.com; f. 1977; Chair. F. BOZZONI; Man. Dir M. DUBOURG.

Société Nationale Maritime Corse-Méditerranée (SNCM): 61 blvd des Dames, BP 61963, 13226 Marseille Cedex 02; tel. 4-91-56-32-00; fax 4-91-56-36-36; e-mail info@sncm.fr; internet www.sncm.fr; passenger and roll-on/roll-off ferry services between France and Corsica, Sardinia, North Africa; 25% state-owned, managed by Veolia Transport (owners of a 28% share) from 2006; Chair. GÉRARD COUTURIER; displacement 141,454 grt.

Société Services et Transports: route du Hoc Gonfreville-L'Orcher, 76700 Harfleur; tel. 2-35-24-72-00; fax 2-35-53-36-25; petroleum and gas transport, passenger transport; Chair. YVES ROUSIER; Man. Dir JACQUES CHARVET; displacement 118,274 grt.

CIVIL AVIATION

The principal international airports are at Orly and Roissy-Charles de Gaulle (Paris), Bordeaux, Lille, Lyon, Marseille, Nice, Strasbourg and Toulouse.

Aéroports de Paris: 291 blvd de Raspail, 75675 Paris Cedex 14; tel. 1-43-35-70-00; fax 1-43-35-72-00; e-mail webmaster@adp.fr; internet www.adp.fr; f. 1945; majority state-controlled authority in charge of Paris airports at Orly and Roissy-Charles de Gaulle, 11 other airports for light aircraft, including Le Bourget, and a heliport at Issy-les-Moulineaux; Chair. and CEO. AUGUSTIN DE ROMANET; Man. Dir FRANÇOIS RUBICHON.

Airlines

Air France–KLM: 45 rue de Paris, 95747 Roissy Cedex; tel. 1-41-56-78-00; fax 1-41-56-70-29; internet www.airfranceklm.com; f. 2004 by the merger of Air France (France) and KLM (Netherlands); Chair. and CEO ALEXANDRE DE JUNIAC.

Air France: 45 rue de Paris, 95747 Roissy Cedex; tel. 1-41-56-78-00; fax 1-41-56-70-29; internet www.airfrance.fr; f. 1933; 18.6% state-owned; merged with KLM (Netherlands) in 2004; internal, international, European and intercontinental services; 240 destinations in 105 countries worldwide; Chair. and CEO FRÉDÉRIC GAGEY.

Brit Air: Aéroport, CS 27925-29679 Morlaix; tel. 2-98-63-63-63; fax 2-98-62-77-66; internet www.britair.com; f. 1973; domestic and European flights; wholly owned by Air France; Pres. and Dir-Gen. MARC LAMIDEY.

Corsairfly: 2 ave Charles Lindbergh, 94636 Rungis Cedex; tel. 1-49-79-49-59; tel. www.corsairfly.com; f. 1981; scheduled flights between metropolitan France and Italy, Madagascar, Morocco, Kenya, and the French overseas possessions, and chartered flights to other medium- and long-range destinations; owned by TUI AG Group (Germany); Pres. PIERRE CHESNEAU; Man. Dir HERVÉ PIERRET.

Hex'Air: La Relhiade, 43320 Chaspuzac; tel. 4-71-08-62-28; fax 4-71-08-04-10; e-mail contact@hexair.com; internet www.hexair.com; f. 1991; domestic services; Pres. and Dir-Gen. ALEXANDRE ROUCHON.

Régional—Compagnie Aérienne Européenne: Aéroport Nantes Atlantique, 44345 Bouguenais Cedex; tel. 2-40-13-53-00; fax 2-40-13-53-08; e-mail contact@regional.com; internet www.regional.com; f. 2001 by merger of Flandre Air, Proteus and Regional Airlines; operates European and domestic flights; subsidiary of Air France; Pres. and Dir-Gen. JEAN-YVES GROSSE.

XL Airways France: BP 13760, 95727 Roissy Cedex; tel. 9-69-32-09-12; e-mail relationsclientele@xlairways.fr; internet www.xlairways.fr; f. 1995 as Star Airlines; acquired by XL Leisure Group (United Kingdom) in 2006; charter and scheduled flights between France and Corsica, Cuba, the Dominican Republic, Egypt, Italy, the Maldives, Mexico, Morocco, Senegal and Tunisia; Dir-Gen. LAURENT MAGNIN.

Airline Associations

Fédération Nationale de l'Aviation Marchande (FNAM): 28 rue de Châteaudun, 75009 Paris; tel. 1-45-26-23-24; fax 1-45-26-23-95; e-mail info@fnam.fr; internet www.fnam.fr; f. 1990; Pres. LIONEL GUÉRIN; Delegate-Gen. GUY TARDIEU.

Chambre Syndicale du Transport Aérien (CSTA): 28 rue de Châteaudun, 75009 Paris; tel. 1-45-26-23-24; fax 1-45-26-23-95; e-mail info@fnam.fr; f. 1947; represents French airlines at national level; Pres. LIONEL GUÉRIN.

Tourism

France is the world's most popular tourist destination. Paris is famous for its boulevards, historic buildings, theatres, art treasures, fashion houses, restaurants and night clubs. The Mediterranean and Atlantic coasts and the French Alps are the most popular tourist resorts. Among other attractions are the many ancient towns, the châteaux of the Loire, the fishing villages of Brittany and Normandy, and spas and places of pilgrimage, such as Vichy and Lourdes. The theme park, Disneyland Resort Paris, also attracts large numbers of tourists. There were some 81.4m. tourist arrivals in 2011; tourism receipts totalled US $53,697m. in 2012, according to provisional figures. Most visitors are from the United Kingdom and Ireland, Germany, Belgium and Luxembourg, and Italy.

Atout France: 79–81 rue de Clichy, 75009 Paris; tel. 1-42-96-70-00; e-mail editorial@atout-france.fr; internet www.atout-france.fr; f. 2009 following merger of Maison de la France and ODIT France; Pres. FRANÇOIS HUWART; Dir-Gen. CHRISTIAN MANTEI.

Direction Générale de la Compétitivité, de l'Industrie et des Services (DGCIS): 67 rue Barbès, 94200 Ivry-sur-Seine; internet www.dgcis.gouv.fr; f. 2009; Dir PASCAL FAURE.

There are Regional Tourism Committees in the 22 metropolitan regions. There are more than 3,600 Offices de Tourisme and Syndicats d'Initiative (tourist offices operated by the local authorities) throughout France.

Defence

French military policy is decided by the Supreme Defence Council. Military service was compulsory until November 2001, when legislation to create fully professional armed forces took effect. As assessed at November 2013, the total active armed forces numbered 222,200, comprising an army of 119,050, a navy of 37,850, an air force of 47,550, and other staff numbering 17,750. In addition, there was a paramilitary gendarmerie of 103,400. Reserves stood at 29,650 (army 16,000; navy 5,500; air force 4,750; other staff 3,400); there were also 40,000 paramilitary reserves. In November 2011 civilian forces stood at 70,976 (army 20,600; navy 7,091; air force 7,517; paramilitary gendarmerie 1,925; other staff 35,768). France is a member of the North Atlantic Treaty Organization (NATO) and possesses its own nuclear weapons. France withdrew from the integrated military command of NATO in 1966, but re-entered it in April 2009. In November 2004 the European Union (EU) ministers responsible for defence agreed to create a number of 'battlegroups' (each comprising about 1,500 troops), which could be deployed at short notice to crisis areas around the world. The EU battlegroups, two of which were to be ready for deployment at any one time, following a rotational schedule, reached full operational capacity from 1 January 2007.

Defence Expenditure: Budgeted at €39,4000m. in 2013.

Chief of Staff of the Armed Forces: Gen. PIERRE DE VILLIERS.

Chief of Staff of the Ground Forces: Gen. BERTRAND RACT MADOUX.

Chief of Staff of the Navy: Adm. BERNARD ROGEL.

Chief of Staff of the Air Forces: Gen. DENIS MERCIER.

Director-General of the National Gendarmerie: DENIS FAVIER.

Education

Responsibility for education in France rests with the Ministry of National Education, Youth and Community Life, which defines the curriculum to be followed in schools. Administrative control of the education system, from primary to higher levels, is delegated to 30 educational districts (académies). Education is compulsory and free for children aged six to 16 years. In 2012/13 enrolment at primary level included 98% of children in the relevant age-group, while enrolment at secondary level included 97% of children in the relevant age-group. Primary education begins at six years of age and lasts for five years. At the age of 11 all pupils enter the first cycle of secondary education (enseignement secondaire), with a four-year general course at a collège. At the age of 15 pupils may enter the second cycle at a lycée d'enseignement général et technologique, choosing a course leading to the general or technological baccalauréat examination after three years. Alongside these lycées, vocational education is provided in the lycées professionnels, where pupils prepare for the professional baccalauréat over three years or a vocational qualification (certificat d'aptitude professionnelle—CAP) over two years. In 2009/10 16.9% of pupils attended France's 8,780 private schools (including écoles élémentaires, collèges and lycées), most of which are administered by the Roman Catholic Church.

The minimum qualification for entry to university is the baccalauréat and anyone possessing that qualification is entitled to receive a university education. There are three levels of university education. The first degree, the licence, is obtained after three years of study. The master recherche and master professionnel are obtained after five years of study; the master recherche is required for progress to the doctorat, while the master professionnel provides vocational education. The doctorat requires eight years' study and the submission of a thesis. Universities are complemented by the prestigious grandes écoles, entry to which is by competitive examination; these institutions have traditionally supplied France's administrative élite. In 2012/13 there were 80 universities under the Ministries of Education (including universities in the French Overseas Regions and Departments); in the same year there was a total of 3,974 other higher education institutions.

Total expenditure on education (including the overseas departments, excluding Mayotte) was estimated at €139.4m. in 2012.

FRENCH OVERSEAS POSSESSIONS

Ministry of Overseas Territories: 27 rue Oudinot, 75007 Paris, France; tel. 1-53-69-20-00; internet www.outre-mer.gouv.fr.
Minister of Overseas Territories: GEORGE PAU-LANGEVIN.
The national flag of France, proportions two by three, with three equal vertical stripes, of blue, white and red, is used in the Overseas Possessions

French Overseas Regions and Departments

As amended in March 2003, the Constitution defines French Guiana, Guadeloupe, Martinique and Réunion as being simultaneously Régions d'Outre-mer (Overseas Regions) and Départements d'Outre-mer (Overseas Departments) within the French Republic. National legislation is fully applicable, although, other than in the areas of justice, the police, the armed forces and public freedoms, some provision is made for local adaptation within the framework of the law. At a referendum held in the Collectivité d'Outre-mer (Overseas Collectivity) of Mayotte in March 2009, the electorate voted in favour of becoming an Overseas Department of France. The change took effect at the end of March 2011.

FRENCH GUIANA

Introductory Survey

LOCATION, CLIMATE, LANGUAGE, RELIGION, CAPITAL

French Guiana (Guyane) lies on the north coast of South America, with Suriname to the west and Brazil to the south and east. The climate is humid, with a season of heavy rains from April to July and another short rainy season in December and January. Average temperature at sealevel is 27°C (85°F), with little seasonal variation. French is the official language, but a Creole patois is also spoken. The majority of the population belongs to the Roman Catholic Church, although other Christian churches are represented. The capital is Cayenne.

CONTEMPORARY POLITICAL HISTORY

Historical Context

French occupation commenced in the early 17th century. After brief periods of Dutch, English and Portuguese rule, the territory was finally confirmed as French in 1817. The colony steadily declined, after a short period of prosperity in the 1850s as a result of the discovery of gold in the basin of the Approuague river. French Guiana, including the notorious Devil's Island, was used as a penal colony and as a place of exile for convicts and political prisoners before the practice was halted in 1937. The colony became a Department of France in 1946.

Domestic Political Affairs

French Guiana's reputation as an area of political and economic stagnation was dispelled by the growth of pro-independence sentiments, and the use of violence by a small minority, compounded by tensions between the Guyanais and large numbers of immigrant workers. In 1974 French Guiana was granted regional status, as part of France's governmental reorganization, thus acquiring greater economic autonomy. In that year, none the less, demonstrations against unemployment, the worsening economic situation and French government policy with regard to the Department led to the detention of leading trade unionists and pro-independence politicians. Further industrial and political unrest in the late 1970s prompted the Parti Socialiste Guyanais (PSG), then the strongest political organization, to demand greater autonomy for the Department. In 1980 there were several bomb attacks against 'colonialist' targets by an extremist group, Fo nou Libéré la Guyane. Reforms introduced by the French Socialist Government in 1982–83 devolved some power over local affairs to the new Conseil Régional (Regional Council). In the 1983 election to the Regional Council the left-wing parties gained a majority of votes, but not of seats, and the balance of power was held by the separatist Union des Travailleurs Guyanais (UTG), the political wing of which became the Parti National Populaire Guyanais (PNPG) in 1985. At the election to the Conseil Général (General Council) held in 1985, the PSG and left-wing independents secured a majority of seats.

The PSG increased its strength on the Regional Council following an election in 1986, and Georges Othily of the PSG was re-elected President of the Council. Left-wing parties again won a majority of seats at the election to the General Council in 1988. In September 1989 Othily was elected to take French Guiana's seat in the French Sénat (Senate). Othily had been expelled from the PSG for having worked too closely with the opposition parties. However, he attracted support from those who regarded the party's domination of French Guiana as corrupt. In December Othily formed his own party, the Forces Démocratiques Guyanaises (FDG), which included other dissident members of the PSG.

The PSG dominated in elections to both the General Council and the Regional Council in 1992: party leader Elie Castor retained the presidency of the General Council while PSG Secretary-General Antoine Karam was elected as President of the Regional Council. In a referendum in September, 67% of voters in French Guiana approved ratification of the Treaty on European Union (see p. 273), although a high abstention rate was recorded.

At the 1993 elections to the Assemblée Nationale (National Assembly) Léon Bertrand of the Gaullist Rassemblement pour la République (RPR) was re-elected, along with Christiane Taubira-Delannon, the founder of the independent left-wing Walwari movement. The PSG's representation in the General Council fell following the 1994 cantonal elections; none the less, one of its members, Stéphan Phinéra-Horth, was subsequently elected President of the Council.

A boycott of classes by secondary school pupils, who were demanding improved conditions of study, escalated in November 1996 into a crisis that was regarded as exemplifying wider social tensions between the Department and metropolitan France. The refusal of the Prefect, Pierre Dartout, to receive schools' representatives prompted protests in Cayenne, which swiftly degenerated into rioting and looting. The central Government dispatched anti-riot police to assist the local security forces. However, the conviction of several people implicated in the rioting provoked further protests and clashes with security forces, and a one-day general strike in Cayenne, organized by the UTG, was widely observed. The extent of the security forces' actions in suppressing the demonstrations was criticized, as was the approach of the Department's administrators. An agreement on the students' material demands was reached, but, to considerable local acclaim, the ministers announced the establishment of separate Academies for French Guiana, Guadeloupe and Martinique, as well as additional primary educational facilities, and a programme was declared to improve academic standards in secondary schools.

In April 1997 violent incidents followed the arrest of five pro-independence activists suspected of setting fire to the home of the public prosecutor during the disturbances of November 1996. Five others, including leading members of the UTG and the PNPG, were subsequently detained in connection with the arson incident. The transfer of all 10 detainees to Martinique prompted further violent protests in Cayenne: police reinforcements were dispatched by the central Government to help suppress the violence.

In 1997 Léon Bertrand and Christiane Taubira-Delannon were both re-elected to the National Assembly. Elections to the Regional and General Councils were held in 1998. The PSG lost seats on both bodies. Karam was re-elected to the presidency of the Regional Council. André Lecante, an independent left-wing councillor, was elected as President of the General Council. In September Georges Othily was re-elected to the Senate.

Demands for further autonomy

In January 1999 representatives of 10 separatist organizations from French Guiana, Guadeloupe and Martinique, including the Mouvement de la Décolonisation et d'Emancipation Sociale (MDES) and the PNPG, signed a joint declaration denouncing 'French colonialism', in which they stated their intention to campaign for the reinstatement of the three Caribbean Overseas Departments on a UN list of territories to be decolonized. Following a series of meetings, in December the Presidents of the Regional Councils of French Guiana, Guadeloupe and Martinique signed a joint declaration in Basse-Terre, Guadeloupe, affirming their intention to propose, to the President and the Government, a legislative amendment aimed at creating a new status of overseas region. However, the Secretary of State for Overseas Departments and Territories, Jean-Jack Queyranne, in early 2000 dismissed the declaration as unconstitutional and exceeding the mandate of politicians responsible. In March, during a visit to the Department by Queyranne, rioting broke out following his refusal to meet a delegation of separatist organizations. Later that month the Regional Council overwhelmingly rejected reforms proposed by Queyranne, which included the creation of a Congress in French Guiana, as well as the extension of the Departments' powers in areas such as regional co-operation. Nevertheless, the proposals were approved by the National Assembly in November, and ratified by the Constitutional Council in the following month.

In November 2000 several people were injured following riots in Cayenne. The riots followed a pro-autonomy march, organized by the UTG. Protesters claimed they had been excluded from talks on French Guiana's status. Nevertheless, discussions were held in December in Paris attended by Queyranne's successor, Christian Paul, various senior politicians from French Guiana and representatives from the PSG, the RPR, Walwari, and the FDG. In 2001, following further consultations, it was agreed that a document detailing proposals for increased autonomy for French Guiana was to be drawn up by local officials and was to be presented to the French Government for approval. These proposals included: the division of the territory into four districts; the creation of a Collectivité Territoriale (Territorial Collectivity), governed by a 41-member Assembly elected for a five-year term; and the establishment of an independent executive council. There was also a request that the territory be given control over legislative and administrative affairs, as well as legislative authority on matters concerning French Guiana alone. In November the French Government announced itself to be in favour of the suggested constitutional developments; in March 2003 a constitutional amendment conferred the status of Région d'Outre-mer (Overseas Region) on French Guiana.

At elections to the presidency of the General Council in 2001, the left-wing independent candidate Joseph Ho-Ten-You defeated André Lecante. At the legislative elections held in 2002, Taubira-Delannon was re-elected to the National Assembly.

In 2002 the gendarmerie, in co-operation with the national police, began a series of operations in the south of the Department aimed at stopping the illegal gold trade. As well as causing extensive environmental damage, unlicensed gold-mining operations were a chief cause of illegal immigration, and a focus for other criminal activities, such as drugs-smuggling and gun-running.

In elections to the Regional Council in March 2004 the PSG won a majority of seats. Antoine Karam was duly re-elected as President of the Council. In May 2005 a national referendum was held on ratification of the European Union constitutional treaty: in the Department 60.1% of participating voters were in favour of adopting the treaty; however, voter turnout was just 23.1%. The treaty was ultimately rejected by a majority of voters in metropolitan France.

At the first round of the national presidential election in April 2007, the Union pour un Mouvement Populaire (UMP) candidate, Nicolas Sarkozy, won 41% of the votes cast in the Department, ahead of Ségolène Royal of the PS, who attracted 33% of ballot. At the second round, held on 6 May, Sarkozy secured the presidency, winning 53% of the votes cast in the Department. Meanwhile, at elections to the National Assembly, held in June, Taubira-Delannon, representing Walwari, and Chantal Berthelot of the PSG secured the Department's two seats. Following municipal elections in March 2008, Alain Tien-Long replaced Pierre Désert as President of the General Council. At an election held on 21 September Georges Patient and Jean-Etienne Antoinette were elected as the Department's senate representatives.

Efforts to halt illegal gold-mining were intensified in 2008. In February, during a visit to French Guiana, President Sarkozy announced a four-month deployment of gendarmes and military personnel in Operation Harpie, which aimed to disrupt unlicensed mining activities and combat illegal immigration, especially from Brazil. As part of his visit, Sarkozy met Brazilian President Lula da Silva and agreed to increase border co-operation between the two countries. Operation Harpie was expanded and renewed for a further six months in 2009. However, with the problem of illegal gold-mining persisting, Operation Harpie became a permanent mission from March 2010. According to official data, there were 771 unauthorized mining sites in French Guiana in 2013, up from 392 in 2011. A visit to the region by French President François Hollande in December 2013 apparently prompted the Brazilian legislature to approve a 2008 co-operation agreement with France concerning the prevention of illegal mining activity in the border region.

Referendum on autonomy

President Sarkozy, during a visit to the region in June 2009, proposed a series of referendums on the issue of increased autonomy for the French Overseas Regions in the Caribbean. French Guiana's plebiscite was duly held on 10 January 2010. The electorate, fearful of losing economic support from mainland France and unwilling to confer greater power upon the local political élite, voted overwhelmingly to reject any increase in autonomy, with 69.8% voting against the proposal. The rate of participation by the electorate was 48.2%. A further referendum on institutional reform was held on 24 January, and 57.5% of participants voted in favour of changing the status of French Guiana to a Collectivité Unique (Single Collectivity), replacing the existing two-tier departmental and regional administrative structure. Only 27.4% of the electorate took part in the plebiscite. The authorities hoped that the merger of the departmental and regional levels of government would increase efficiency and reduce operating costs. In mid-2011 the National Assembly approved legislation to facilitate this transition to a Collectivity. Polls were scheduled for 2015 to elect the 51 members of a new, consolidated legislative body, which would replace the Regional Council and the General Council.

Regional and national elections

At elections to the Regional Council held on 14 and 21 March 2010, the UMP list secured 21 of the 31 council seats, with 56.1% of the ballot. The left-wing list, led by Walwari and the MDES, obtained the remaining 10 seats and won 43.9% of the votes cast. Rodolphe Alexandre was elected as President of the Regional Council. The rate of participation by the electorate was 50.5%. Municipal elections were conducted on 20 and 27 March 2011, following which Alain Tien-Long was re-elected as President of the General Council. In April Denis Labbé was appointed as Prefect, replacing Daniel Férey.

The first round of the French presidential election was conducted on 21 April 2012 (one day earlier than in mainland France): François Hollande, representing the PS, attracted 42.6% of the territory's votes, compared with 27.2% for Sarkozy. A second round run-off election was held two weeks later, at which Hollande secured 62.1% of the ballot, defeating Sarkozy, who attracted 37.95%. Hollande also triumphed nationally and was sworn in as President in mid-May. Christiane Taubira-Delannon of French Guiana was notably appointed as Keeper of the Seals, Minister of Justice in Hollande's new cabinet. In legislative elections, which took place in June, Berthelot was re-elected to the National Assembly, while the territory's remaining mandate was won by Gabriel Serville of the PSG. Eric Spitz replaced Labbé as Prefect in June 2013.

Recent developments: economic unrest

The French Minister of Overseas Territories, Victorin Lurel, visited French Guiana in September 2012 to hold discussions with the local authorities regarding the high cost of living in the territory. A bill to address the problem of inflated prices in French Guiana and other French Overseas Possessions, drafted by Lurel, was approved by Parliament in November. The legislation provided for the imposition of price controls on a range of staple goods and the introduction of measures to encourage competition. In December 2013 the French Government extended the price controls to cover petrol purchases in the French Overseas Regions and Departments. However, on multiple occasions between mid-2013 and early 2014 owners of petrol stations in French Guiana and other French Overseas Departments, fearing that the move would disrupt their business model and undermine profit margins, closed their establishments in a co-ordinated act of protest. The closures ended in February 2014 after a compromise was agreed with the French authorities.

Municipal polls took place on 23 and 30 March 2014, after which an election to the presidency of the General Council was scheduled to be held.

CONSTITUTION AND GOVERNMENT

France is represented in French Guiana by an appointed Prefect. There are two councils with local powers: the General Council, with 19 members, and the Regional Council, with 31 members. Both are elected by universal adult suffrage for a period of six years. French Guiana elects two representatives to the National Assembly in Paris, and sends two elected representatives to the Senate. French Guiana is also represented at the European Parliament.

ECONOMIC AFFAIRS

In 2012, according to official estimates, French Guiana's gross domestic product (GDP), measured at current prices, was €3,600m., equivalent to €15,294 per head; growth in 2012 was 4.0%. Between 1999 and 2007 GDP increased, in real terms, at an average rate of 4.3% per year. Between the censuses of 2006 and 2012 the population increased at an average annual rate of 2.5%.

Agriculture (including fishing) engaged an estimated 0.6% of the economically active population in 2012. In 2003 the sector contributed 4.6% of GDP. In 2012 agricultural products accounted for some 5.2% of total export earnings, at €11.6m. The dominant activities are fisheries and forestry, although the contribution of the latter to export earnings has declined in recent years. In 2011 shrimp production was recorded at 944 metric tons. The aquaculture industry faced competition from shrimp producers in Latin America and Asia and rising fuel prices and in 2005 the Compagnie Française de Pêche Nouvelle went into liquidation. The principal crops for local consumption are cassava, vegetables and rice, and sugar cane is grown for making rum; rum production in 2012 was 2,626 hl. Livestock rearing was also largely for subsistence. In 2012 Guianese abattoirs produced an estimated 1,141 tons of meat, mostly pork, poultry and beef. Rice, pineapples and citrus fruit are cultivated for export. According to UN estimates, agricultural GDP decreased at an average annual rate of 0.8% in 1990–98; in 1998 agricultural GDP increased by an estimated 0.3%.

Industry, including construction and agrarian and food industries, contributed an estimated 20.3% to GDP in 2003, while in 2012 it engaged 16.0% of the employed labour force. The mining sector is dominated by the extraction of gold, which involves small-scale alluvial operations as well as larger local and multinational mining concerns. The first new concession in 70 years was awarded to Cambior in 2004 for a 25-year period. The US Geological Survey estimated gold production in 2012 at a 1,300 kg. Gold exports in 2012 were put at €70.6m. Crushed rock for the construction industry is the only other mineral extracted in significant quantities. Deposits of bauxite, columbo-tantalite and kaolin are also present. There is little manufacturing activity, except for the processing of fisheries products (mainly shrimp-freezing) and the distillation of rum. The manufacturing sector engaged 5.5% of the employed labour force in 2012. In 1990–98 industrial GDP (excluding construction) increased at an average annual rate of 7.8%. The construction sector engaged 7.5% of the employed labour force in 2012. It expanded at an average of 2.0% per year in 1990–98.

French Guiana's Petit-Saut 116-MW hydroelectric dam, on the Sinnamary river, provided most of the territory's electrical energy requirements. Imports of fuels and combustibles accounted for 14.6% of total imports in 2012.

The services sector engaged an estimated 83.5% of the employed labour force in 2012 and, according to official sources, contributed 75.2% of GDP in 2003. The European Space Agency's satellite-launching centre at Kourou has provided a considerable stimulus to the economy, most notably the construction sector (which engaged an estimated 7.5% of the employed labour force in 2012). The space centre was estimated to contribute approximately one-quarter of French Guiana's GDP and approximately one-half of its tax revenues. In 2013 there were three rocket launches. The tourism sector expanded in the last two decades of the 20th century, although its potential is limited by the lack of infrastructure away from the coast. In 2009 some 83,000 visitor arrivals were recorded, while receipts from tourism totalled US $49m. in 2007. In 2003 it was estimated that tourism contributed 3% of GDP.

French Guiana recorded a merchandise trade deficit of some €1,263.1m in 2012. In that year the principal source of imports was metropolitan France (which supplied 43.0% of total imports); the Department's other major suppliers were Trinidad and Tobago, Martinique and Germany. Metropolitan France was also the principal market for exports in that year (49.8%); other important purchasers were Trinidad and Tobago, Switzerland, Germany and Italy. The principal imports in 2012 were capital industry products, chemicals, petroleum products, products of agriculture and food industries, consumer industry products, and metals and metal products; the principal exports were capital industry products, mineral products, and products of agriculture and food industries.

According to preliminary figures, the 2013 regional budget was balanced at €147.8m. The departmental budget for that year put revenue at €354.3m., while expenditure was €388.4m. The annual rate of inflation averaged 1.8% in 2003–12; the average rate of inflation in 2012 was 1.5%. Unemployment in mid-2012 was estimated at 22.3% of the total labour force. However, there is a shortage of skilled labour, offset partly by immigration.

Economic development in French Guiana has been hindered by the Department's location, poor infrastructure and unskilled labour force, although there is considerable potential for further growth in the fishing, forestry, mining and tourism sectors. A particular concern was the high rate of unemployment. French Guiana's geographical characteristics—large parts of the territory are accessible only by river—have resulted in difficulties in regulating key areas of the economy, such as gold-mining and forestry. Despite registering GDP growth of 3.6% in 2009, French Guiana did not escape the negative effects of the global financial crisis in that year, with the country experiencing declining levels of investment and a reduction in gold output. The economy remained sluggish in 2010, although a recovery in gold exports was a positive development, and strong internal demand resulted in GDP expanding by 2.5% in that year. Increased activity in the construction and space sectors supported economic growth of 4.0% in 2011. Rising gold exports and buoyant levels of investment and domestic consumption also contributed to this recovery, while the tourism industry registered modest growth. A significant offshore petroleum discovery was announced in September, potentially containing up to 700m. barrels of oil, although further exploratory drilling conducted in 2012–13 yielded disappointing results. In spite of a deceleration in domestic demand, GDP rose by 3.3% in 2012, again primarily driven by increased gold shipments and robust growth in the construction and space sectors.

PUBLIC HOLIDAYS

2015: 1 January (New Year's Day), 16–17 February (Lenten Carnival), 18 February (Ash Wednesday), 6 April (Easter Monday), 1 May (Labour Day), 8 May (Liberation Day), 14 May (Ascension Day), 25 May (Whit Monday), 10 June (Abolition of Slavery), 14 July (National Day, Fall of the Bastille), 15 August (Assumption), 1 November (All Saints' Day), 11 November (Armistice Day), 25 December (Christmas Day).

Statistical Survey

Sources (unless otherwise indicated): Institut National de la Statistique et des Etudes Economiques (INSEE), Service Régional de Guyane, ave Pasteur, BP 6017, 97306 Cayenne Cédex; tel. 5-94-29-73-00; fax 5-94-29-73-01; internet www.insee.fr/fr/insee_regions/guyane; Chambre de Commerce et d'Industrie de la Guyane (CCIG), Hôtel Consulaire, pl. de l'Esplanade, BP 49, 97321 Cayenne Cédex; tel. 5-94-29-96-00; fax 5-94-29-96-34; internet www.guyane.cci.fr.

AREA AND POPULATION

Area: 83,534 sq km (32,253 sq miles).

Population: 157,213 at census of 8 March 1999; 237,549 at census of 1 January 2011. Note: According to new census methodology, data in 2011 refer to median figures based on the collection of raw data over a five-year period (2009–13). *Mid-2014* (UN estimate): 255,455 (Source: UN, *World Population Prospects: The 2012 Revision*.

Density (at mid-2014): 3.1 per sq km.

Population by Age and Sex (UN estimates at mid-2014): *0–14:* 81,462 (males 41,506, females 39,956); *15–64:* 161,422 (males 80,121, females 81,301); *65 and over:* 12,571 (males 6,115, females 6,456); *Total* 255,455 (males 127,742, females 127,713) (Source: UN, *World Population Prospects: The 2012 Revision*.

Principal Towns (population at 2010 census): Cayenne (capital) 55,753; Saint-Laurent-du-Maroni 38,367; Matoury 28,110; Kourou 25,189; Rémire-Montjoly 19,279.

Births, Marriages and Deaths (2011): Registered live births 6,259 (birth rate 26.4 per 1,000); Registered marriages 634 (marriage rate 2.7 per 1,000); Registered deaths 714 (death rate 3.0 per 1,000).

Life Expectancy (years at birth): 76.7 (males 73.4; females 80.5) in 2012. Source: Pan American Health Organization.

Employment (persons aged 15 years and over, provisional estimates at 31 December 2012): Agriculture, forestry and fishing 277; Mining, electricity, gas and water supply 1,470; Manufacturing 2,682; Construction 3,680; Wholesale and retail trade; repair of motor vehicles, motorcycles, etc. 4,704; Transport 2,421; Hotels and restaurants 1,622; Information and communication 634; Financial intermediation 573; Real estate, renting and business activities 4,845; Public administration and defence; education, health and social work 24,068; Other community, social and personal service activities 2,060; *Total employed* 49,036. Note: Data exclude 3,339 persons employed without salary.

HEALTH AND WELFARE

Key Indicators

Total Fertility Rate (children per woman, 2012): 3.1.

Under-5 Mortality Rate (per 1,000 live births, 2011): 15.0.

Physicians (per 1,000 head, c. 2010): 1.8.

Hospital Beds (per 1,000 head, 2011): 2.8.

Access to Water (% of persons, 2004): 84.

Access to Sanitation (% of persons, 2004): 78.

Source: mostly Pan American Health Organization.

For other sources and definitions, see explanatory note on p. vi.

AGRICULTURE, ETC.

Principal Crops ('000 metric tons, 2012, FAO estimates): Rice, paddy 2.0; Cassava 23.9; Sugar cane 3.6; Cabbages and other brassicas 5.3; Tomatoes 4.4; Cucumbers and gherkins 2.0; Beans, green 1.0; Bananas 9.0; Plantains 3.5. *Aggregate Production* ('000 metric tons, may include official, semi-official or estimated data): Total vegetables (incl. melons) 21.2; Total fruits (excl. melons) 23.9.

Livestock ('000 head, 2012, FAO estimates): Cattle 14.5; Pigs 8.9; Sheep 1.4.

Livestock Products (metric tons, 2012): Cattle meat 312; Pig meat 359; Chicken meat 470 (FAO estimates); Cows' milk 260 (FAO estimates); Hen eggs 1,036 (FAO estimates).

Forestry ('000 cubic metres, 2012, FAO estimates unless otherwise indicated): *Roundwood Removals* (excl. bark): Sawlogs, veneer logs and logs for sleepers 74.9 (unofficial figure); Other industrial wood 9.0; Fuel wood 137.3; Total 221.2. *Sawnwood Production* (incl. railway sleepers): Total 31.5.

Fishing (metric tons, live weight, 2011, FAO estimates): Capture 3,950 (Marine fishes 3,077; Shrimps 944); Aquaculture 35; *Total catch* 3,985.

Source: FAO.

MINING

Production ('000 metric tons unless otherwise indicated, 2011, estimates): Cement 62,000; Gold (metal content of ore, kilograms, reported figure) 1,300; Sand 500. Source: US Geological Survey.

INDUSTRY

Production (2012): Rum 2,626 hl; Electric energy 870 million kWh (Source: l'Institut d'Emission des Départements d'Outre-mer, *Rapport Annuel 2012*).

FINANCE

Currency and Exchange Rates: 100 cent = 1 euro (€). *Sterling and Dollar Equivalents* (31 December 2013): £1 sterling = €1.194; US $1 = €0.725; €10 = £8.37 = $13.79. *Average Exchange Rate* (euros per US dollar): 0.719 in 2011; 0.778 in 2012; 0.753 in 2013. Note: The national currency was formerly the French franc. From the introduction of the euro, with French participation, on 1 January 1999, a fixed exchange rate of €1 = 6.55957 French francs was in operation. Euro notes and coins were introduced on 1 January 2002. The euro and French currency circulated alongside each other until 17 February, after which the euro became the sole legal tender. Some of the figures in this Survey are still in terms of francs.

Budgets (excl. debt rescheduling, € million, 2013, preliminary): *Regional Government:* Current revenue 101.6 (Taxes 67.9, Grants 33.7); Capital revenue 46.2; Total 147.8. Current expenditure 85.6; Capital expenditure 62.2; Total 147.8. *Departmental Government:* Revenue 354.3 (Current revenue 312.7, Capital revenue 41.6); Expenditure 388.4 (Current expenditure 323.9, Capital expenditure 64.5). Source: Département des Etudes et des Statistiques Locales.

Money Supply (million French francs at 31 December 1996): Currency outside banks 3,000; Demand deposits at banks 1,621; *Total money* 4,621.

Cost of Living (Consumer Price Index; base: 2000 = 100): All items 119.2 in 2010; 121.6 in 2011; 123.4 in 2012. Source: ILO.

Gross Domestic Product (US $ million at constant 1990 prices): 1,668 in 2001; 1,695 in 2002; 1,722 in 2003. Source: UN, *Statistical Yearbook*.

Expenditure on the Gross Domestic Product (€ million at current prices, 2011, estimates): Total final consumption expenditure 3,550 (General government and non-profit institutions serving households 1,752, Households 1,798); Gross capital formation 1,008; *Total domestic expenditure* 4,558; Exports of goods and services 1,167; *Less* Imports of goods and services 2,627; Statistical discrepancy 524; *GDP in purchasers' values* 3,622. Source: Institut d'Emission des Départements d'Outre-mer, *Guyane: Rapport Annuel 2012*.

Gross Domestic Product by Economic Activity (€ million at current prices, 2003): Agriculture, hunting, forestry and fishing 95; Food industries 39; Manufacturing 180; Energy 40; Construction 163; Services 1,564 (Restaurants and hotels 42, Transport –85, Commerce 223, Other market services 560; Non-market services 824); *Sub-total* 2,081; Financial intermediation services indirectly measured –42; Import duties, less subsidies 169; *GDP in purchasers' values* 2,207.

EXTERNAL TRADE

Principal Commodities (€ million, 2012): *Imports c.i.f.:* Agriculture, forestry and fishing 15.2; Products of agriculture and food industries 215.7; Consumer industry products 153.0 (Pharmaceuticals 55.7); Capital industry products 446.0 (Industrial and agricultural machinery 125.9; Transport equipment 164.9); Mineral products, rubber and plastic 63.0; Chemicals 258.3; Metal and metal products 92.9; Petroleum products 217.2; Total (incl. others) 1,486.5. *Exports f.o.b.:* Agriculture, forestry and fishing 0.6; Products of agriculture and food industries 11.0; Consumer industry products 1.2; Capital industry products 118.8 (Electronic goods and computer equipment 26.6; Industrial and agricultural machinery 18.6; Transport equipment 69.6); Mineral products, rubber and plastic 70.6; Metals and products thereof 9.4; Petroleum products 1.4; Total (incl. others) 223.4 (Source: Institut d'Emission des Départements d'Outre-mer, *Guyane: Rapport Annuel 2012*).

Principal Trading Partners (€ million, 2008): *Imports c.i.f.:* France (metropolitan) 485.4; Germany 31.9; Italy 17.6; Martinique 38.4; Netherlands 21.2; Spain 17.0; Trinidad and Tobago 51.4; Total (incl. others) 1,065.0. *Exports f.o.b.:* France (metropolitan) 37.3; Germany 11.4; Guadeloupe 7.7; Italy 9.5; Martinique 8.3; Spain 2.5; Switzerland 15.0; Total (incl. others) 96.3. *2010* (€ million): Total imports 1,081.8; Total exports 158.3. *2011* (€ million): Total imports 1,333.1; Total exports 154.4 (Source: Institut d'Emission des Départements d'Outre-mer, *Guyane: Rapport Annuel 2011*). *2012* (€ million): Total imports 1,486.5; Total exports 223.4 (Source: Institut d'Emission des Départements d'Outre-mer, *Guyane: Rapport Annuel 2012*).

TRANSPORT

Road Traffic ('000 motor vehicles in use, 2001): Passenger cars 32.9; Commercial vehicles 11.9 (Source: UN, *Statistical Yearbook*). *2002:* 50,000 motor vehicles in use. *1 January 2010:* ('000 motor vehicles in use): Buses 0.4; Vans and trucks 17.3.

Shipping: *Flag Registered Fleet* (at 31 December 2013): Vessels registered 2; Total displacement: 3,881 grt. Source: Lloyd's List Intelligence (www.lloydslistintelligence.com).

International Sea-borne Shipping (traffic, 2005 unless otherwise indicated): International vessels entered 115; Goods loaded 25,103 metric tons; Goods unloaded 472,567 metric tons (Source: CCIG); Passengers carried 275,300 (1998). *2012* (metric tons): Goods carried 642,950 in 2011; 662,772 in 2012 (Source: Institut d'Emission des Départements d'Outre-mer, *Guyane: Rapport Annuel 2012*).

Civil Aviation (2012): Aircraft movements 9,334; Freight carried (incl. post) 6,064 metric tons; Passengers carried 428,865. Source: Institut d'Emission des Départements d'Outre-mer, *Guyane: Rapport Annuel 2012*.

TOURISM

Tourist Arrivals by Country (2007): France 62,016; Guadeloupe 14,362; Martinique 22,739; Total (incl. others) 108,801. *2009:* 83,000 tourist arrivals.

Receipts from Tourism (US $ million, incl. passenger transport): 49 in 2007.

Source: World Tourism Organization.

COMMUNICATIONS MEDIA

Telephones ('000 main lines in use): 45.5 in 2010.

Mobile Cellular Telephones ('000 subscribers): 217.7 in 2009.

Personal Computers ('000 in use): 33 in 2004.

Internet Users ('000): 58.0 in 2009.

Broadband Subscribers ('000): 30.2 in 2009.

Source: International Telecommunication Union.

EDUCATION

Pre-primary (2012/13): 43 institutions; 15,419 students (14,526 state, 893 private).

Primary (2012/13): 119 institutions (111 state, 8 private); 27,702 students (25,852 state, 1,850 private).

Specialized Pre-primary and Primary (2012/13): 435 students (435 state only).

Secondary (2012/13): 47 institutions (42 state, 5 private); 32,371 students (0,104 state, 2,267 private).

Higher (2011/12): 2,720 students.

Teachers (2008/09 unless otherwise indicated): *Primary:* 2,243 teachers (2,121 state, 122 private); *Secondary:* 2,433 teachers (2,285 state, 148 private); *Higher* (2004/05): 63 teachers. Source: Ministère de l'Education Nationale, *Repères et références statistiques. 2011/12* (state schools): 2,306 in primary; 2,573 in secondary; 90 in higher.

Adult Literacy Rate: 83.0% (males 83.6%, females 82.3%) in 1998. Source: Pan American Health Organization.

Directory

The Government

(April 2014)

HEAD OF STATE

President: FRANÇOIS HOLLANDE.

Prefect: ERIC SPITZ, Préfecture, 1 rue Fiedmont, BP 7008, 97307 Cayenne Cédex; tel. 5-94-39-45-00; fax 5-94-30-02-77; e-mail courrier@guyane.pref.gouv.fr; internet www.guyane.pref.gouv.fr.

DEPARTMENTAL ADMINISTRATION

President of the General Council: ALAIN TIEN-LIONG, Hôtel du Département, pl. Léopold Héder, BP 5021, 97397 Cayenne Cédex; tel. 5-94-29-55-00; fax 5-94-29-55-25; e-mail atienliong@cg973.fr; internet www.cg973.fr.

President of the Economic, Social and Environmental Regional Committee: JEAN-PIERRE CONSTANTIN, 66 ave du Général de Gaulle, 97300 Cayenne; tel. 5-94-28-96-01; fax 5-94-30-73-65; e-mail info@cesr-guyane.fr; internet www.cesr-guyane.fr.

President of the Regional Council: RODOLPHE ALEXANDRE (UMP), Cité Administrative Régionale, 4179 route de Montabo, Carrefour de Suzini, BP 7025, 97307 Cayenne Cédex; tel. 5-94-29-20-20; fax 5-94-31-95-22; e-mail cabcrg@cr-guyane.fr; internet www.cr-guyane.fr.

Elections, 14 and 21 March 2010

	Seats
Guyane 73*	21
Deux Ans: Un Marathon pour Bâtir†	10
Total	31

* Electoral list comprising the Union pour un Mouvement Populaire (UMP) and allies.

† Electoral list comprising various left-wing parties led by Walwari and the Mouvement de Décolinisation et d'Emancipation Sociale (MDES).

REPRESENTATIVES TO THE FRENCH PARLIAMENT

Deputies to the French National Assembly: GABRIEL SERVILLE (Gauche Démocrate et Républicaine), CHANTAL BERTHELOT (Socialiste, Républicain et Citoyen).

Representatives to the French Senate: GEORGES PATIENT (Groupe Socialiste), JEAN-ETIENNE ANTOINETTE (Groupe Socialiste).

Political Organizations

Forces Démocratiques de Guyane (FDG): 41 rue du 14 Juillet, BP 403, 97300 Cayenne; tel. 5-94-28-96-79; fax 5-94-30-80-66; e-mail g.othily@senat.fr; f. 1989 by a split in the PSG; Sec.-Gen. GIL HORTH.

Mouvement de Décolonisation et d'Emancipation Sociale (MDES): 21 rue Maissin, 97300 Cayenne; tel. 5-94-30-55-97; fax 5-94-30-97-73; e-mail mdes.parti@wanadoo.org; f. 1991; pro-independence; Sec.-Gen. MAURICE PINDARD.

Parti Progressiste Guyanais (PPG): 1994 Route de Montabo, 97300 Cayenne; e-mail jmj_taubira@yahoo.fr; internet www.partiprogressisteguyanais.fr; f. 2013; Sec.-Gen. JEAN-MARIE TAUBIRA.

Parti Socialiste (PS): 7 rue de l'Adjudant Pindard, 97300 Cayenne Cédex; tel. 5-94-37-81-33; fax 5-94-37-81-56; e-mail fede973.partisocialiste@wanadoo.fr; internet guyane.parti-socialiste.fr; departmental br. of the metropolitan party; Leader LÉON JEAN BAPTISTE EDOUARD; Sec. PAUL DEBRIETTE.

Parti Socialiste Guyanais (PSG): 1 Cité Césaire, BP 46, 97300 Cayenne; tel. 5-94-28-11-44; fax 5-94-28-46-92; e-mail partisocialisteguyanais@orange.fr; f. 1956; left-wing; Sec.-Gen. MARIE JOSÉ LALSIE.

Union pour un Mouvement Populaire (UMP): 42 rue du Docteur Barrat, 97300 Cayenne; tel. 5-94-28-80-74; fax 5-94-28-80-75; internet www.u-m-p.org; f. 2002 as Union pour la Majorité Presidentielle by mems of the fmr Rassemblement pour la République and Union pour la Démocratie Française; centre-right; departmental br. of the metropolitan party; Pres., Departmental Cttee RÉMY-LOUIS BUDOC.

Les Verts Guyane: 64 rue Madame Payé, 97300 Cayenne; tel. 5-94-40-97-27; e-mail tamanoir.guyane@wanadoo.fr; internet guyane.lesverts.fr; ecologist; departmental br. of the metropolitan party; Regional Sec. JOSÉ GAILLOU.

Walwari: 35 rue Schoelcher, BP 803, 97300 Cayenne Cédex; tel. 5-94-30-31-00; fax 5-94-31-84-95; e-mail info@walwari.org; internet www.walwari.org; f. 1993; left-wing; Leader CHRISTIANE TAUBIRA-DELANNON; Sec.-Gen. JOËL PIED.

Judicial System

Court of Appeal: 1 rue Louis Blanc, 97300 Cayenne; tel. 5-94-27-48-48; fax 5-94-27-48-72; Pres. PIERRE GOUZENNE.

There is also a Tribunal de Grande Instance and a Tribunal d'Instance.

Religion

CHRISTIANITY

The Roman Catholic Church

French Guiana comprises the single diocese of Cayenne, suffragan to the archdiocese of Fort-de-France, Martinique. Some 80% of the population are Roman Catholics. French Guiana participates in the Antilles Episcopal Conference, currently based in Port of Spain, Trinidad and Tobago.

Bishop of Cayenne: Rt Rev. EMMANUEL M. P. L. LAFONT, Evêché, 24 rue Madame Payé, BP 378, 97328 Cayenne Cédex; tel. 5-94-28-98-48; fax 5-94-30-20-33; e-mail emmanuel.lafont@wanadoo.fr; internet www.guyane.catholique.fr.

The Anglican Communion

Within the Church in the Province of the West Indies, French Guiana forms part of the diocese of Guyana. The Bishop is resident in Georgetown, Guyana. There were fewer than 100 adherents in 2000.

Other Churches

In 2000 there were an estimated 7,000 Protestants and 7,200 adherents professing other forms of Christianity.

Assembly of God: 1051 route de Raban, 97300 Cayenne; tel. 5-94-35-23-04; fax 5-94-35-23-05; e-mail jacques.rhino@wanadoo.fr; internet www.addguyane.fr; Pres. JACQUES RHINO; c. 500 mems.

Church of Jesus Christ of Latter-day Saints (Mormons): Route de la Rocade, 97305 Cayenne; c. 362 mems.

Seventh-day Adventist Church: Mission Adventiste de la Guyane, 39 rue Schoëlcher, BP 169, 97324 Cayenne Cédex; tel. 5-94-25-64-26; fax 5-94-37-93-02; e-mail adventiste.mission@wanadoo.fr; f. 1949; Pres. and Chair. ALAIN LIBER; Sec.-Treas. DANIEL CARBIN; 2,299 mems.

The Jehovah's Witnesses are also represented.

The Press

France-Guyane: 17 rue Lallouette, BP 428, 97329 Cayenne; tel. 5-94-29-70-00; fax 5-94-29-70-02; e-mail infos@franceguyane.fr; internet www.franceguyane.fr; daily; Publishing Dir DENIS BERRIAT; Editor-in-Chief JÉRÔME RIGOLAGE; circ. 9,000.

Le Marron—Petit Journal de Kourou: BP 53, 97372 Kourou; tel. 5-94-32-49-54; fax 5-94-32-10-70; e-mail pjk@blada.com; internet www.blada.com; f. 2001; Dir ODILE FARJAT.

La Semaine Guyanaise: 6 ave Louis Pasteur, 97300 Cayenne; tel. 5-94-31-09-83; fax 5-94-31-95-20; e-mail semaineguyanaise@nplus.gf; internet www.semaineguyanaise.com; weekly (Thur.); Dir ALAIN CHAUMET; Editor-in-Chief JÉRÔME VALLETTE.

Ròt Kozé: 11 rue Maissin, 97300 Cayenne; tel. 5-94-30-55-97; fax 5-94-30-97-73; e-mail redacteur@rotkoze.com; internet www.rotkoze.com; f. 1990; left-wing organ of the MDES party; monthly; Dir MAURICE PINDARD.

Publishers

Editions Anne C.: 8 Lot Mapaou, route de Baduel, BP 212, 97325 Cayenne; tel. and fax 5-94-35-20-10; e-mail canne@nplus.gf; internet www.redris.pagesperso-orange.fr/HTML/Livres.htm; f. 1998; French-Creole children's and youth literature; Dir NICOLE PARFAIT-CHAUMET.

Ibis Rouge Editions: chemin de la Levée, BP 267, 97357 Matoury Cédex; tel. 5-94-35-95-66; fax 5-94-35-95-68; e-mail jlm@ibisrouge.fr; internet www.ibisrouge.fr; f. 1995; general literature, French-Creole, and academic; Publr JEAN-LOUIS MALHERBE; agencies in Guadeloupe and Martinique.

PUBLISHERS' ASSOCIATION

Promolivres Guyane: BP 96, 97394 Rémire-Montjoly Cédex; tel. 5-94-29-55-56; fax 5-94-38-52-82; e-mail promolivreguyane@wanadoo.fr; f. 1996; asscn mems incl. editors, booksellers, journalists and librarians; promotes French Guianese literature; Pres. TCHISSÉKA LOBELT.

Broadcasting and Communications

TELECOMMUNICATIONS

Digicel Antilles Françaises et Guyane: see Martinique—Telecommunications; Dir-Gen. FRANCK ROGIER.

France Telecom: 76 ave Voltaire, BP 8080, 97300 Cayenne; tel. 5-94-39-91-15; fax 5-94-39-91-00; e-mail eline.miranda@francetelecom.com.

Orange Caraïbe: see Guadeloupe—Telecommunications.

Outremer Telecom: 112 ave du Général de Gaulle, 97300 Cayenne; tel. 5-94-28-71-15; fax 5-94-23-93-59; e-mail communication@outremer-telecom.fr; internet www.outremer-telecom.fr; f. 1998; mobile telecommunications provider; Group CEO JEAN-MICHEL HEGESIPPE.

ONLY: 112 ave du Général de Gaulle, 97300 Cayenne; tel. 5-94-28-71-15; fax 5-94-23-93-59; e-mail contact@outremer-telecom.fr; internet www.only.fr; f. 2004 as Outremer Telecom Guyane; subsidiary of Outremer Telecom, France; present name adopted following merger of Volubis, ONLY and OOL in 2006; mobile and fixed telecommunications provider.

BROADCASTING

Guyane 1ère (Outre-mer Première): ave le Grand Boulevard, Z.A.D. Moulin à Vent, 97354 Rémire-Montjoly; tel. 5-94-25-67-00; fax 5-94-25-67-64; internet guyane.la1ere.fr; acquired by Groupe France Télévisions in 2004; fmrly Société Nationale de Radio-Télévision Française d'Outre-mer; name changed to Réseau France Outre-mer (RFO) in 1998; present name adopted in 2010; Radio-Guyane Inter accounts for 46.6% of listeners (2003); Télé Guyane/RFO1 and RFO (Tempo) account for 52.3% and 7.5% of viewers, respectively (2003); Dir-Gen. GENEVIÈVE GIARD; Regional Dir FRED AYANGMA.

Radio

KFM Guyane: 6 rue François Arago, 97300 Cayenne; tel. 5-94-31-30-38; fax 5-94-37-84-20; internet www.kfmguyane.skyrock.com; f. 1993 as Radio Kikiwi; present name adopted 2003.

Métis FM: Cayenne; internet www.metis.fm; popular music station.

Mig FM Guyane: 100 ave du Général de Gaulle, 97300 Cayenne; tel. 5-94-30-77-67; fax 5-94-31-86-81; f. 1995; Creole.

NRJ Guyane: 2 blvd de la République, 97300 Cayenne; tel. 5-94-39-54-88; fax 5-94-39-54-79; e-mail wladimir@nrjguyane.com; internet www.nrjguyane.com; f. 2006; commercial radio station; Man MARC HO-A-CHUCK.

Ouest FM Guyane: Cayenne; tel. 5-94-38-29-19; e-mail contact@ouestfm.net; internet www.ouestfm.net; commercial music station.

Radio Joie de Vivre: 39 rue Schoëlcher, 97324 Cayenne Cédex; BP 169, 97300 Cayenne; tel. 5-94-31-29-00; fax 5-94-29-47-26; f. 1993; operated by the Seventh-day Adventist church; Gen. Man. ESAÏE AUGUSTE.

Radio Littoméga (RLM): 24 blvd Malouet, BP 108, 97320 Saint-Laurent-du-Maroni; tel. 5-94-34-22-09; e-mail centre.cl@wanadoo.fr; internet www.rlm100.com; f. 1994; Dir ARIELLE BERTRAND.

Radio Mosaïque: 11 rue Sainte-Catherine, cité Brutus, 97300 Cayenne; tel. 5-94-30-94-76; e-mail guyanes@free.fr; commercial radio station; Man. BÉRIL BELVU.

Radio Ouassailles: rue Maurice Mongeot, 97360 Mana; tel. 5-94-34-80-96; fax 5-94-34-13-89; e-mail radio.ouassailles@wanadoo.fr; f. 1994; French and Creole; Man. RÉMY AUBERT.

Radio Saint-Gabriel: Salle Paul VI, Cité Mirza, 97300 Cayenne; tel. 5-94-31-17-11; fax 5-94-28-17-51; e-mail radiosaintgabriel@wanadoo.fr; f. 2001; Roman Catholic; Man. HENRI-CLAUDE ASSÉLOS.

Radio Toucan Fréquence International (TFI): 1 pl. du Vidé, BP 68, 97300 Kourou; tel. 5-94-32-96-11; fax 5-94-39-71-61; e-mail direction@tfifm.com; internet www.tfifm.com; f. 1983; part of Groupe I-Medias Antilles-Guyane; commercial radio station.

Radio UDL (Union Défense des Libertés): 7 rue Félix Eboué, BP 5, 97393 Saint-Laurent-du-Maroni; tel. 5-94-34-10-61; fax 5-94-34-04-78; e-mail radio.udl@wanadoo.fr; internet www.udlguyane.com; f. 1982; Man. JEAN GONTRAND.

Radio Voix dans le Désert: 5 chemin du Château, 97300 Cayenne; tel. 5-94-31-73-95; fax 01-73-76-88-00; e-mail president@rvld.fr; internet www.rvld.fr; f. 1993; operated by the Assembly of God church; Pres. EDDY LAUTRIC.

Television

Antenne Créole Guyane: 31 ave Louis Pasteur, 97300 Cayenne; tel. 5-94-28-82-88; fax 5-94-29-13-08; e-mail acg@acg.gf; internet www.acg.gf; f. 1994; sole local private TV station; gen. interest with focus on music and sports; produces 30% of own programmes; received by 95% of the population, accounting for 25% of viewers (2003); Pres. MARC HO-A-CHUCK; Gen. Man. WLADIMIR MANGACHOFF.

Canal+ Guyane: 14 Lotissement Marengo, Z. I. de Collery, 97300 Cayenne; tel. 8-10-50-15-02; fax 5-94-30-53-35; internet www.canalplus-caraibes.com/guyane; f. 1996; subsidiary of Groupe Canal+, France; satellite TV station; Dir OLEG BACCOVICH.

Finance

(cap. = capital; res = reserves; dep. = deposits; m. = million; brs = branches)

BANKING

Central Bank

Institut d'Emission des Départements d'Outre-mer (IEDOM): 8 rue Christophe Colomb, BP 6016, 97306 Cayenne Cédex; tel. 5-94-29-36-50; fax 5-94-30-02-76; e-mail direction@iedom-guyane.fr; internet www.iedom.fr; f. 1959; Dir FABRICE DUFRESNE.

Commercial Banks

Banque Française Commerciale Antilles-Guyane (BFC Antilles-Guyane): 8 pl. des Palmistes, BP 111, 97345 Cayenne; tel. 5-94-29-11-11; fax 5-94-30-13-12; e-mail service-client@bfc-ag.com; internet www.bfc-ag.com; f. 1985; Regional Dir JOCELYN MATHIAS.

BNP Paribas Guyane SA: 2 pl. Victor Schoëlcher, BP 35, 97300 Cayenne; tel. 5-94-39-63-00; fax 5-94-30-23-08; e-mail bnpg@bnpparibas.com; internet www.bnpparibas.com; f. 1964 following purchase of BNP Guyane (f. 1855); name changed 2000; 94% owned by BNP Paribas SA, 3% by BNP Paribas Martinique and 3% by BNP Paribas Guadeloupe; Dir and CEO ANTOINE GARCIA; Gen. Sec. JACQUES SALGE; 2 brs.

Crédit Agricole: see Martinique—Finance.

Development Bank

Société Financière pour le Développement Economique de la Guyane (SOFIDEG): PK 3, 700 route de Baduel, BP 860, 97339 Cayenne Cédex; tel. 5-94-29-94-29; fax 5-94-30-60-44; e-mail sofideg@nplus.gf; f. 1982; bought from the Agence Française de Développement (AFD—q.v.) by BRED-BP in 2003; Dir FRANÇOIS CHEVILLOTTE.

Insurance

Allianz IARD: 34 rue Léopold Heder, BP 462, 97300 Cayenne Cédex; tel. 5-94-30-27-66; fax 5-94-30-69-09; e-mail agfguyana@wanadoo.fr; internet www.allianz.fr; life and short-term insurance; Dir (Latin America) Dr HELGA JUNG.

Groupama Antilles Guyane: see Martinique—Insurance.

Trade and Industry

GOVERNMENT AGENCIES

Direction de l'Agriculture et de la Forêt (DAF): Parc Rebard, BP 5002, 97305 Cayenne Cédex; tel. 5-94-29-63-74; fax 5-94-29-63-63; e-mail daf.guyane@agriculture.gouv.fr; internet daf.guyane.agriculture.gouv.fr; Dir FRANÇOIS CAZOTTES.

Direction Régionale et Départementale des Affaires Maritimes (DRAM): 2 bis, rue Mentel, BP 6008, 97306 Cayenne Cédex; tel. 5-94-29-36-15; fax 5-94-29-36-16; e-mail Dram-Guyane@developpement-durable.gouv.fr; responsible for shipping, fishing and other maritime issues at nat. and community level; Dir STÉPHANE GATTO.

Direction Régionale de l'Industrie, de la Recherche et de l'Environnement (DRIRE): Pointe Buzaré, BP 7001, 97307 Cayenne Cédex; tel. 5-94-29-75-30; fax 5-94-29-07-34; e-mail drire-antilles-guyane@industrie.gouv.fr; internet www.ggm.drire.gouv.fr; active in industry, business services, transport, public works, tourism and distribution; Regional Dir JOEL DURANTON.

DEVELOPMENT ORGANIZATIONS

Agence de l'Environnement et de la Maîtrise de l'Energie (ADEME): 28 ave Léopold Heder, 97300 Cayenne Cédex; tel. 5-94-31-73-60; fax 5-94-30-76-69; e-mail ademe.guyane@ademe.fr; internet www.ademe-guyane.fr; Dir SUZANNE PONS.

Agence Française de Développement (AFD): Lotissement les Héliconias, route de Baduel, BP 1122, 97345 Cayenne Cédex; tel. 5-94-29-90-90; fax 5-94-30-63-32; e-mail afdcayenne@afd.fr; internet www.afd-guyane.org; fmrly Caisse Française de Développement; Dir ROBERT SATGE.

Agence Régionale de Développement Économique de la Guyane (ARD): 1 pl. Schoëlcher, BP 325, 97325 Cayenne Cédex; tel. 5-94-25-66-66; fax 5-94-25-43-19; e-mail ard .guyane-developpement@wanadoo.fr; f. 2009 to replace Agence pour la Création et le Développement des Entreprises en Guyane; Pres. CAROL OSTORERO; Dir PASCAL VELINORE.

Fédération des Organisations Amérindiennes de Guyane (FOAG): Centre des Cultures, rue Capt. Charles Claude, 97319 Awala Yalirnapo; tel. 6-94-42-27-76; fax 5-94-33-50-06; e-mail foag@ nplus.gf; f. 1993; civil liberties org. representing the rights of the indigenous peoples of French Guiana; Pres. Chief JEAN AUBÉRIC CHARLES.

CHAMBERS OF COMMERCE

Chambre d'Agriculture: 8 ave du Général de Gaulle, BP 544, 97333 Cayenne Cédex; tel. 5-94-29-61-95; fax 5-94-31-00-01; e-mail chambre.agriculture.973@wanadoo.fr; internet www .chambres-agriculture.fr; Pres. CHRISTIAN EPAILLY; Dir THIERRY BASSO.

Chambre de Commerce et d'Industrie de la Guyane (CCIG): Hôtel Consulaire, pl. de l'Esplanade, BP 49, 97321 Cayenne Cédex; tel. 5-94-29-96-00; fax 5-94-29-96-34; e-mail contact@guyane.cci.fr; internet www.guyane.cci.fr; Pres. JEAN-PAUL LE PELLETIER.

Chambre de Métiers: 41 Lotissement, Artisanal Zone Galmot, 97300 Cayenne Cédex; tel. 5-94-25-24-70; fax 5-94-30-54-22; e-mail m.toulemonde@cm-guyane.fr; internet www.cm-guyane.fr; Pres. HARRY CONTOUT; Sec.-Gen. FRANCELINE MATHIAS-DANIEL.

Jeune Chambre Economique de Cayenne: 1 Cité A. Horth, route de Montabo, BP 1094, Cayenne; tel. 5-94-31-62-99; fax 5-94-31-76-13; internet www.jcicayenne.com; f. 1960; Pres. YÂSIMÎN VAUTOR; Gen. Sec. ANGÉLIQUE BOURGEOIS.

EMPLOYERS' ORGANIZATIONS

Groupement Régional des Agriculteurs de Guyane (GRAGE): PK 15 route nationale 1, Domaine de Soula, 97355 Macouria; tel. 5-94-38-71-26; e-mail 973@confederationpaysanne.fr; internet www .grage.gf; affiliated to the Confédération Paysanne; Pres. SYLVIE HORTH.

MEDEF Guyane: 27A Résidence Gustave Stanislas, Source de Baduel, BP 820, 97338 Cayenne Cédex; tel. 5-94-31-17-71; fax 5-94-30-32-13; e-mail updg@nplus.gf; internet medefguyane.fr; f. 2005; fmrly Union des Entreprises de Guyane; Pres. ALAIN CHAUMET.

Ordre des Pharmaciens du Département Guyane: 7 Avenue du Général de Gaulle, 97300 Cayenne; tel. 5-94-32-17-62; fax 5-94-32-17-66; e-mail delegation_guyane@ordre.pharmacien.fr; internet www.ordre.pharmacien.fr; Pres. ALINE ABAUL-BALUSTRE.

Syndicat des Transformateurs du Bois de Guyane (STBG): Menuiserie Cabassou, PK 4.5, route de Cabassou, 97354 Remire-Montjoly; tel. 5-94-31-34-49; fax 5-94-35-10-51; f. 2002; represents artisans using wood; Pres. YVES ELISE; Sec. FRANÇOIS AUGER.

UTILITIES

Electricity

EDF Guyane: blvd Jubelin, BP 6002, 97306 Cayenne; tel. 5-94-39-64-00; fax 5-94-30-10-81; internet guyane.edf.com; electricity producer; Dir JEAN-PHILIPPE BLAVA.

Water

Société Guyanaise des Eaux: 2738 route de Montabo, BP 5027, 97306 Cayenne Cédex; tel. 5-94-25-59-26; fax 5-94-30-59-60; internet www.suez-environnement.fr; f. 1978; CEO JEAN-LOUIS CHAUSSADE; Gen. Man. RODOLPHE LELIEVRE.

TRADE UNIONS

Centrale Démocratique des Travailleurs Guyanais (CDTG): 99–100 Cité Césaire, BP 383, 97328 Cayenne Cédex; tel. 5-94-31-02-32; fax 5-94-31-81-05; e-mail sg.cdtg@wanadoo.fr; internet cdtg-guyane.com; affiliated to the Confédération Française Démocratique du Travail; Sec.-Gen. GÉRARD FAUBERT.

Fédération Syndicale Unitaire Guyane (FSU): Mont Lucas, Bât G, No C37, 97300 Cayenne; tel. 5-94-30-05-69; fax 5-94-38-36-58; e-mail fsu973@fsu.fr; f. 1993; departmental br. of the Fédération Syndicale Unitaire; represents public sector employees in teaching, research and training, and also agriculture, justice, youth and sports, and culture; Sec. ALAIN BRAVO.

Union Départementale Confédération Française des Travailleurs Chrétiens Guyane (UD CFTC): 19 lot Gibelin 1, BP 763, 97351 Matoury Cédex; tel. 5-94-35-63-14; fax 5-94-90-59-05; e-mail lydie.leneveu@wanadoo.fr; Sec. LYDIE LENEVEU.

Transport

RAILWAYS

There are no railways in French Guiana.

ROADS

In 2004 there were 1,300 km (808 miles) of roads in French Guiana, of which 397 km were main roads. Much of the network is concentrated along the coast, although proposals for a major new road into the interior of the Department were under consideration.

SHIPPING

Grand Port Maritime de Guyane at Dégrad-des-Cannes, on the estuary of the river Mahury, is the principal port, handling the majority of maritime traffic. There are other ports at Le Larivot, Saint-Laurent-du-Maroni and Kourou. Saint-Laurent is used primarily for the export of timber, and Le Larivot for fishing vessels. There are river ports on the Oiapoque and on the Approuague. There is a ferry service across the Maroni river between Saint-Laurent and Albina, Suriname. The rivers provide the best means of access to the interior, although numerous rapids prevent navigation by large vessels. A bridge across the Oyapock river, linking the cities of Oiapoque in Brazil and Saint-Georges de l'Oyapock in French Guiana and funded by the Governments of France and Brazil, was completed in 2011. In December 2013 French Guiana's flag registered fleet comprised two vessels, with an aggregate displacement of some 3,881 grt.

Compagnie Maritime Marfret: Immeuble Face Scierie Patoz, Z. I. Degrad-des-Cannes, 97354 Rémire-Montjoly; tel. 5-94-31-04-04; fax 5-94-35-18-44; e-mail jccelse@marfret.fr; internet www .marfret.fr; Gen. Man. JEAN-CHRISTIAN CELSE-L'HOSTE.

Grand Port Maritime de Guyane: Z. I. de Dégrad-des-Cannes, Rémire-Montjoly, 97354 Cayenne Cédex; tel. 5-94-35–44–90; f. 1974 as Port International Dégrad-des-Cannes; under management of Chambre de Commerce et de l'Industrie de la Guyane 1988–2012; publicly owned entity with a supervisory board from 2013.

SOMARIG (Société Maritime et Industrielle de la Guyane): Z. I. de Dégrad-des-Cannes, Rémire-Montjoly, BP 81, 97354 Cayenne Cédex; tel. 5-94-35-42-00; fax 5-94-35-53-44; e-mail cay.genmbox@ cma-cgm.com; internet www.cma-cgm.com; f. 1960; owned by Groupe CMA—GGM (France); Man. Dir HERVÉ ROUCHON.

CIVIL AVIATION

Rochambeau International Airport, situated 17.5 km (11 miles) from Cayenne, is equipped to handle the largest jet aircraft. There are also airports at Maripasoula, Saul and Saint Georges. Access to remote inland areas is frequently by helicopter.

Air Guyane: Aéroport de Rochambeau, 97300 Matoury; tel. 5-94-29-36-30; fax 5-94-30-54-37; e-mail reservations@airguyane.com; internet www.airguyane.com; f. 1980; 46% owned by Guyane Aéro Invest, 20% owned by Sodetraguy; operates domestic services; Pres. CHRISTIAN MARCHAND.

Tourism

The main attractions are the natural beauty of the tropical scenery and the Amerindian villages of the interior. In 2005 there were 27 hotels with some 1,184 rooms. Receipts from tourism in 2007 were US $49m. while in 2009 tourist arrivals totalled an estimated 83,000.

Comité du Tourisme de la Guyane: 12 rue Lallouette, BP 801, 97338 Cayenne Cédex; tel. 5-94-29-65-00; fax 5-94-29-65-01; e-mail ctginfo@tourisme-guyane.com; internet www.tourisme-guyane .com; Pres. SYLVIE DESERT; Dir-Gen. ERIC MADELEINE.

Délégation Régionale au Tourisme, au Commerce et à l'Artisanat pour la Guyane: 9 rue Louis Blanc, BP 7008, 97300 Cayenne Cédex; tel. 5-94-28-92-90; fax 5-94-31-01-04; e-mail 973.pole3e@ dieccte.gouv.fr; Delegate DIDIER BIRONNEAU (acting).

L'Ensemble Culturel Régional (ENCRE): 82 ave du Général de Gaulle, BP 6007, 97306 Cayenne Cédex; tel. 5-94-28-94-00; fax 5-94-28-94-04; e-mail encre.crg@wanadoo.fr; f. 2004 by merger of Ecole Nationale de Musique et de Danse and Office Culturel de la Région Guyane; fmrly Asscn Régionale de Développement Culturel; Pres. ANTOINE KARAM.

Fédération des Offices du Tourisme et Syndicat d'Initiative de la Guyane (FOTSIG): 12 rue Lallouette, BP 702, 97301 Cayenne; tel. 5-94-30-96-29; fax 5-94-31-23-41; e-mail frguyane@fnotsi.net; Pres. JULIETTE GOUSSET.

Defence

As assessed at November 2013, France maintained a military force of 2,200 in French Guiana, including a gendarmerie. The headquarters is in Cayenne.

Education

Education is modelled on the French system and is compulsory and free for children between six and 16 years of age. Primary education begins at six years of age and lasts for five years. Secondary education, beginning at 11 years of age, lasts for up to seven years, comprising a first cycle of four years and a second of three years. In 2012/13 there were 43 pre-primary schools, 119 primary schools and 47 secondary schools. In the same period there were 43,121 students in pre-primary and primary education, while in secondary education there were 32,371 students, of whom some 93% were educated in the state sector. Higher education in law, administration, French language and literature and teacher training is provided by a branch of the Université des Antilles et de la Guyane in Cayenne; there is also a technical institute at Kourou and an agricultural college. In 2011/12 some 2,720 students were enrolled in higher education in French Guiana.

GUADELOUPE

Introductory Survey

LOCATION, CLIMATE, LANGUAGE, RELIGION, CAPITAL

Guadeloupe is the most northerly of the Windward Islands group in the West Indies. Dominica lies to the south, and Antigua and Montserrat to the north-west. Guadeloupe is formed by two large islands, Grande-Terre and Basse-Terre, separated by a narrow sea channel (but linked by a bridge), with a smaller island, Marie-Galante, to the south-east, and another, La Désirade, to the east. The climate is tropical, with an average temperature of 26°C (79°F), and a more humid and wet season between June and November. French is the official language, but a Creole patois is widely spoken. The majority of the population profess Christianity, and belong to the Roman Catholic Church. The capital is the town of Basse-Terre; the other main town and the principal commercial centre is Pointe-à-Pitre, on Grande-Terre.

CONTEMPORARY POLITICAL HISTORY

Historical Context

Guadeloupe was first occupied by the French in 1635, and has remained French territory, apart from a number of brief occupations by the British in the 18th and early 19th centuries. It gained departmental status in 1946.

Domestic Political Affairs

The deterioration of the economy and an increase in unemployment provoked industrial and political unrest during the 1960s and 1970s, including outbreaks of serious rioting in 1967. Pro-independence parties (which had rarely won more than 5% of the total vote at elections in Guadeloupe) resorted, in some cases, to violence as a means of expressing their opposition to the economic and political dominance of white, pro-French landowners and government officials. In 1980 and 1981 there was a series of bomb attacks on hotels, government offices and other targets by a group called the Groupe de Libération Armée, and in 1983 and 1984 there were further bombings by a group styling itself the Alliance Révolutionnaire Caraïbe (ARC). Further sporadic acts of violence continued in 1985–88.

In 1974 Guadeloupe was granted the status of a Region, and an indirectly elected Conseil Régional (Regional Council) was formed. In direct elections to a new Regional Council in 1983 the centre-right coalition succeeded in gaining a majority of the seats and control of the administration. In 1984 Lucette Michaux-Chevry, the President of the Conseil Général (General Council), formed a new conservative centre party, Le Parti de la Guadeloupe, which remained in alliance with the right-wing Rassemblement pour la République (RPR). However, at the election for the General Council held in 1985, the left-wing combination of the Parti Socialiste (PS) and the Parti Communiste Guadeloupéen (PCG) gained a majority of seats on the enlarged Council, and the PS leader, Dominique Larifla, was elected its President. In July demonstrations and a general strike, organized by pro-separatist activists in order to obtain the release of a leading member of the Mouvement Populaire pour une Guadeloupe Indépendante, quickly intensified into civil disorder and rioting in the main commercial centre, Pointe-à-Pitre.

In elections to the Regional Council in 1986, the two left-wing parties together won a majority of seats. As a result, José Moustache of the RPR was replaced as President of the Council by Félix Proto of the PS. The left-wing parties also won a majority of seats at the election to the General Council in the same year, and Larifla was re-elected President of the Council.

In April 1989 the separatist Union Populaire pour la Libération de la Guadeloupe (UPLG) organized protests in Port Louis to demand the release of 'political prisoners', which led to violent clashes with the police. A number of activists of the now disbanded ARC staged a hunger strike while awaiting trial in Paris, accused in connection with politically motivated offences. Anti-Government demonstrations took place in the following month. Demands included the release of the prisoners held in France, a rejection of the Single European Act and the granting of a series of social measures. In June the Assemblée Nationale (National Assembly) approved legislation granting an amnesty for crimes that had taken place before July 1988, and that were intended to undermine the authority of the French Republic in the Overseas Departments. The agreement of those seeking greater independence in Guadeloupe to work within the democratic framework had gained parliamentary support for the amnesty. In March 1990 the UPLG declared that it would henceforth participate in elections, and would seek associated status (rather than full independence) for Guadeloupe.

In March 1992 concurrent elections were held to the General Council and the Regional Council. Larifla was re-elected as President of the former, despite his refusal to contest as part of the local official PS list of candidates. In the election to the Regional Council the official PS list (headed by Frédéric Jalton) secured nine seats and the dissident PS members seven. Former members of the PCG, who had formed a new organization, the Parti Progressiste Démocratique Guadeloupéen (PPDG), won five seats. The RPR, the centre-right Union pour la Démocratie Française (UDF) and other right-wing candidates formed an electoral alliance, Objectif Guadeloupe, to contest the elections, together securing 15 of the 41 seats in the Regional Council. Jalton's refusal to reach an agreement with the dissident PS members prompted Larifla's list to support the presidential candidacy of Michaux-Chevry. Thus, despite an overall left-wing majority in the Regional Council, the right-wing Michaux-Chevry was elected as President. In December, however, the French Council of State declared the election to the Regional Council invalid, owing to the failure of Larifla's list to pay a registration deposit. Other heads of lists were subsequently found to have submitted incomplete documents to the election commission. Fresh elections took place in January 1994, at which Objectif Guadeloupe took 22 seats, while the PS and dissident PS retained a total of only 10 seats.

In a referendum in September 1992 68% of voters in Guadeloupe endorsed ratification of the Treaty on European Union (see p. 273), although a high abstention rate was recorded.

The persistence of divisions between the socialists was evident at the 1993 election to the National Assembly. Michaux-Chevry was re-elected, as were Eric Moutoussamy (for the PPDG) and Jalton. Larifla, meanwhile, was defeated by Edouard Chammougon, a candidate of the independent right. The left retained control of the General Council following cantonal elections in 1994. Larifla was subsequently re-elected President of the Council.

Michaux-Chevry and Larifla were elected to the French Sénat (Senate) in September 1995; Philippe Chaulet of the RPR was subsequently elected to take Michaux-Chevry's seat in the National Assembly.

The RPR performed strongly in the election to the Regional Council in March 1998; Michaux-Chevry was re-elected President of the Council. The composition of the General Council remained largely unchanged following concurrent cantonal elections, although the RPR doubled its representation; Marcellin Lubeth, of the PPDG, was elected to the presidency, defeating Larifla.

Social and industrial unrest intensified in Guadeloupe in October 1999, prior to a two-day visit by Prime Minister Lionel Jospin. Demonstrations escalated into rioting in Pointe-à-Pitre, following the sentencing of Armand Toto—a leading member of the Union

Générale des Travailleurs de la Guadeloupe (UGTG)—to four months' imprisonment for assaulting two policemen and threatening to kill another while occupying the premises of a motor vehicle company in support of a dismissed worker. Moreover, banana producers demonstrated around the port of Basse-Terre, demanding aid for the restructuring of their businesses as compensation for a significant decline in banana prices on the European market. Jospin announced an emergency plan for the banana sector.

Demands for further autonomy

In December 1999 the Presidents of the Regional Councils of French Guiana, Guadeloupe and Martinique signed a joint declaration in Basse-Terre, affirming their intention to propose a legislative amendment aimed at creating a new status of overseas region. The declaration, however, was dismissed by the Secretary of State for Overseas Departments and Territories, Jean-Jack Queyranne, in February 2000 as unconstitutional. Amended proposals regarding the institutional evolution of Guadeloupe were approved by the National Assembly in November, and in December they were ratified by the Constitutional Council.

Jacques Gillot of Guadeloupe Unie, Socialisme et Réalité (GUSR) secured the presidency of the General Council in the wake of the March 2001 municipal elections.

Following a meeting of members of the Regional Council and the General Council in June 2001, a series of administrative restructuring proposals was agreed upon. These included: the division of the territory into four districts; the creation of a Collectivité Territoriale (Territorial Collectivity), governed by a 41-member Assembly elected for a five-year term; and the establishment of an independent executive council. Furthermore, the proposals included a request that the territory be given control over legislative and administrative affairs, as well as legislative authority on matters concerning Guadeloupe alone. In March 2003 the French parliament approved constitutional changes that, *inter alia*, allowed for local referendums to be held on proposals for greater decentralization in overseas possessions. Under the changes, the Department of Guadeloupe was also designated an Région d'Outre-mer (Overseas Region). In the referendum, held in December, some 73% of participating voters rejected legislative reforms that envisaged the replacement of the General Council and the Regional Council with a single assembly, owing to fears that restructuring would lead to autonomy for the Department and the consequent loss of central government funding. However, at the referendums concurrently held in the dependencies of Saint-Barthélemy and Saint-Martin, a clear majority of voters in each commune (95.5% and 76.2%, respectively) were in favour of seceding from Guadeloupe to form separate Collectivités d'Outremer (Overseas Collectivities—q.v.). The reorganization was subsequently approved by the French on 6 February 2007 and by the National Assembly the following day. On 21 February Saint-Barthélemy and the French part of Saint-Martin were formally designated Overseas Collectivities. Following elections to their respective Conseils Territoriaux (Territorial Councils), held in July 2007, the two Overseas Collectivities acceded to administrative independence. Each Overseas Collectivity was to elect one representative to the (in 2008) and one deputy to the National Assembly (in 2012); in the interim, they were to continue to be represented by Guadeloupean parliamentarians.

In June 2002 all four incumbent deputies were defeated in an election to the National Assembly; they were replaced by Gabrielle Louis-Carabin and Joël Beaugendre, both representing the Union pour la Majorité Présidentielle (UMP), a right-wing alliance that included the Objectif Guadeloupe, Eric Jalton, also of a right-wing coalition, and Victorin Lurel of the PS. The RPR subsequently merged into the successor party to the UMP, Union pour un Mouvement Populaire (also known as the UMP).

At an election to the Regional Council in March 2004 the UMP alliance, led by Michaux-Chevry, was resoundingly defeated by the Guadeloupe pour Tous list, a coalition comprising the PS, the PPDG, the GUSR and other left-wing candidates. Lurel subsequently became President of the Regional Council.

In May 2005 a national referendum was held on ratification of the European Union constitutional treaty: some 58.6% of participating voters in the Department were in favour of adopting the treaty; however, only 22% of the electorate exercised their right to vote. The treaty was ultimately rejected by a majority of voters in metropolitan France.

Nicolas Sarkozy of the UMP won 43% of the votes cast in Guadeloupe in the first round of the 2007 national presidential election, ahead of PS candidate Ségolène Royal, who attracted 38% of the vote. Sarkozy emerged victorious in the second round, winning 49% of the vote in the Department. At elections to the National Assembly, held on 10 and 17 June, Gabrielle Louis-Carabin of the UMP, Lurel of the PS and Eric Jalton of the PCG were reelected, while Jeanny Marc-Matthiasin of the GUSR was also successful. At municipal elections held in March 2008 the PS and GUSR retained control of the General Council, and Gillot was subsequently re-elected as its President.

Internal unrest

From January 2009 the island suffered overwhelming disruption as a result of a general strike organized by Lyannaj Kont Pwofitasyon (LKP—League against Profiteering), an alliance of 47 trade unions, political parties and other associations, over the rising cost of living. Violent protests continued throughout February, and military police from metropolitan France were deployed in order to restore order. The 44-day strike ended in March and businesses began to reopen after a deal was agreed between the unions, the local authorities and employers' representatives, involving widespread measures to improve living standards. However, a further LKP-led demonstration, attended by over 1,000 protesters, was organized to coincide with the visit of President Sarkozy to the archipelago in June. During his visit Sarkozy proposed a referendum on the issue of increased autonomy for Guadeloupe, but this option was subsequently rejected by the Guadeloupean authorities. Nevertheless, in accordance with legislation approved by the National Assembly in late 2010, the territory's institutions were to be restructured. The exact nature of this reform was under debate in early 2014, although the number of elected representatives was expected to be reduced from 81 to 45.

Local and national elections

In an election to the Regional Council held in March 2010, the PS-led list, Tous pour la Guadeloupe, secured an overwhelming victory in the first round of voting, with 56.5% of the ballot, gaining 31 of the 41 council seats. The UMP alliance, Ensemble pour la Guadeloupe, and the left-wing Région Autrement obtained four seats each, with 14.0% and 12.4% of the votes cast, respectively, while the Pou Gwadloup an nou ay list took the remaining two seats with 7.0% of the ballot. Lurel was re-elected as President of the Regional Council. The rate of participation by the electorate was 49.8%. Left-wing candidates performed strongly in the municipal polls conducted on 20 and 27 March 2011, and Gillot was subsequently re-elected as President of the General Council. Gillot was also re-elected to the on 25 September, while Felix Desplan of the PS and Jacques Cornano, a left-wing independent, secured the territory's other two seats. Meanwhile, in August Amaury de Saint-Quentin was appointed as Prefect.

The first round of the French presidential election was conducted on 21 April 2012 (one day earlier than in mainland France): François Hollande, representing the PS, attracted 57.0% of the territory's votes, compared with 23.4% for Sarkozy. A second round run-off election was held two weeks later, at which Hollande secured 71.9% of the ballot in the region, defeating Sarkozy, who attracted 28.1%. Hollande also triumphed nationally and was sworn in as President in mid-May. Lurel was notably appointed as Minister of Overseas Territories in Hollande's new cabinet; another Guadeloupean, George Pau-Langevin, was named as Minister-delegate to the Minister of National Education. In legislative elections, which took place in June, Lurel, Jalton and Louis-Carabin were re-elected to the National Assembly, while the territory's remaining mandate was won by Ary Chalus, an independent left-wing candidate. Since Lurel had accepted a position in the Council of Ministers, he was replaced in the legislature by his alternate, Hélène Vainqueur-Christophe of the PS, and in August he was succeeded as President of the Regional Council by Josette Borel-Lincertin (also a member of the PS). Marcelle Pierrot became the islands' new Prefect in January 2013.

Recent developments: economic unrest

Lurel returned to Guadeloupe in September 2012 to hold discussions with business and labour organizations regarding the high cost of living in the territory. Proposed legislation to address the problem of inflated prices (and consequent social unrest) in Guadeloupe and other French Overseas Possessions, drafted by Lurel, was approved by the French Parliament in November. Most notably, the legislation provided for the imposition of price controls on a range of staple goods and the introduction of measures to encourage competition. In December 2013 the French Government extended the price controls to cover petrol purchases in the French Overseas Regions and Departments. However, on multiple occasions between mid-2013 and early 2014, owners of petrol stations in Guadeloupe, French Guiana, Martinique, Mayotte and Réunion, fearing that the move would disrupt their business model and undermine profit margins, closed their establishments in a co-ordinated act of protest. The closures ended in February 2014 after a compromise was agreed with the French authorities.

Municipal polls took place on 23 and 30 March 2014, after which an election for the presidency of the General Council was scheduled to be held. Meanwhile, Guadeloupe (along with Martinique) was formally admitted to the Association of Caribbean States (see p. 449) as an associate member in April.

CONSTITUTION AND GOVERNMENT

France is represented in Guadeloupe by an appointed prefect. There are two councils with local powers: the 42-member Conseil Général (General Council) and the 41-member Conseil Régional (Regional Council). Both are elected by universal adult suffrage for a period of up to six years. Guadeloupe elects four deputies to the National Assembly in Paris, and sends three indirectly elected representatives to the Senate. The Department is also represented at the European Parliament.

ECONOMIC AFFAIRS

In 2011, according to official estimates, Guadeloupe's gross domestic product (GDP), measured at current prices, was €7,900m., equivalent to €19,589 per head. During 1993–2008 GDP increased, in real terms, at an average annual rate of 3.1%. Between the censuses of 2000 and 2011, according to provisional figures, the population increased at an average annual rate of 0.3%. GDP grew by 2.7% in 2010.

Agriculture, hunting, forestry and fishing contributed an estimated 2.8% of GDP in 2010 and engaged an estimated 1.5% of the employed population in 2012. In 2012, according to provisional official figures, agricultural produce (including that related to agrarian production and food industries) accounted for 45.0% of exports. The principal cash crops are bananas and sugar cane. Yams, sweet potatoes and plantains are the chief subsistence crops. Fishing, mostly at an artisanal level, fulfils about two-thirds of domestic requirements, and there is some shrimp-farming. According to UN estimates, agricultural GDP decreased at an average annual rate of 0.3% in 1990–98; the sector increased by 4.1% in 1998.

The industrial sector (including mining, manufacturing, construction, power and food industries) contributed an estimated 12.5% of GDP in 2010 and engaged an estimated 12.4% of the employed population in 2012. Construction contributed 7.7% of GDP in 2010 and engaged an estimated 5.4% of the working population in 2012. The main manufacturing activity is food processing, particularly sugar production, rum distillation, and flour-milling. The sugar industry declined in recent years, owing to deteriorating equipment and a reduction in the area planted with sugar cane (from 20,000 ha in 1980 to 11,184 ha in 2010, although this figure recovered to an estimated 15,000 ha by 2012). Industrial GDP (excluding construction) increased at an average annual rate of 5.2% in 1990–98. Construction expanded at an average rate of 2.2% per year in the same period.

Of some 700,000 tons of petroleum imported annually, about one-third is used for the production of electricity. Efforts are currently being concentrated on the use of renewable energy resources—notably solar, geothermal and wind power—for energy production; there is also thought to be considerable potential for the use of bagasse (a by-product of sugar cane) as a means of generating energy in Guadeloupe. The 64 MW power plant at Le Moule produces some 400m. kWh of electricity annually—almost one-third of Guadeloupe's requirements—using a mixture of coal (75%) and bagasse (25%). Imports of fuels and combustibles accounted for a provisional 19.7% of total expenditure on imports in 2012. In 2012 Guadeloupe's total electricity consumption was 1,792m. kWh.

The services sector engaged an estimated 86.1% of the employed population in 2012 and provided an estimated 84.7% of GDP in 2010. Tourism is the Department's principal source of income, and there is significant potential for the further development of the sector, particularly eco-tourism. In 2011 tourist arrivals totalled some 418,000 and receipts from tourism amounted to US $582m. In 2008 93.9% of arrivals came from metropolitan France or dependent territories.

In 2012 Guadeloupe recorded a merchandise trade deficit of some €2,456.3m., according to provisional figures. In that year the value of exports was €216.1m., less than one-10th of the total value of imports, which were worth €2,672.4m. The principal source of imports was metropolitan France (52.1% in 2008), which was also the principal market for exports (38.5%). The USA, Germany, and Trinidad and Tobago are also important trading partners. According to provisional official figures, the principal exports in 2012 were agricultural, fishing and food products, transport equipment, mechanical and electrical equipment, petroleum products, and metals and metallic products. The principal imports were petroleum products, agricultural, fishing and food products, mechanical and electrical equipment, transport equipment, and pharmaceutical products.

Guadeloupe's departmental budget was balanced at a preliminary €676.9m in 2013. The regional budget registered a surplus of €54.7m. in 2011. The annual rate of inflation averaged 2.0% in 2003–12. In 2012 the annual inflation rate was 1.9%. Some 22.9% of the labour force was unemployed in 2012.

Guadeloupe's location, small domestic market, and inflated labour and service costs have restricted economic growth. The banana sector was adversely affected by the end of the EU's quota system from 2006 and the gradual elimination of tariffs on non-European bananas from 2010 led to a further contraction in the sector. The sugar industry was also adversely affected by modernization. The global financial crisis had a severe impact upon the territory, and GDP contracted by 4.8% in 2009. Nevertheless, the economy recovered in 2010, with higher levels of investment and domestic consumption supporting GDP growth of 2.7%. There was also a revival in the tourism sector, owing in part to the holding of the 'Route du Rhum' yacht race. Agricultural performance was undermined by adverse weather conditions, while ash from a volcanic eruption on the neighbouring island of Montserrat in February also caused significant damage to crops. In spite of strong export growth (particularly in the banana sector), an upturn in tourist spending and robust levels of domestic consumption, overall economic expansion slowed to 1.3% in 2011, owing mainly to a sharp deceleration in investment inflows. GDP growth maintained its downward trajectory in 2012 as the economy expanded by just 0.6%. The construction industry continued to struggle in that year, while a slowdown in domestic demand and the high unemployment rate were further concerns. Stop-over tourist arrivals registered a modest decline in 2012, although this was offset to some extent by a concomitant rise in cruise ship visitors.

PUBLIC HOLIDAYS

2015: 1 January (New Year's Day), 15–16 February (Lenten Carnival), 17 February (Ash Wednesday), 3–6 April (Easter), 1 May (Labour Day), 8 May (Victory Day), 14 May (Ascension Day), 25 May (Whit Monday), 10 June (Abolition of Slavery), 14 July (National Day), 15 August (Assumption), 1 November (All Saints' Day), 11 November (Armistice Day), 25 December (Christmas Day).

Statistical Survey

Sources (unless otherwise indicated): Institut National de la Statistique et des Etudes Economiques (INSEE), Service Régional de la Guadeloupe, ave Paul Lacavé, BP 96, 97102 Basse-Terre; tel. 5-90-99-02-50; internet www.insee.fr/fr/regions/guadeloupe; Service de Presse et d'Information, Ministère des Départements et Territoires d'Outre-mer, 27 rue Oudinot, 75700 Paris 07 SP, France; tel. 1-53-69-20-00; fax 1-43-06-60-30; internet www.outre-mer.gouv.fr.

AREA AND POPULATION

(Note: In July 2007 Saint-Barthélemy and Saint-Martin seceded from Guadeloupe to become Overseas Collectivities.)

Area: 1,630 sq km (629.3 sq miles), comprising continental Guadeloupe 1,438 sq km (Basse-Terre à l'Ouest 848 sq km, Grande-Terre à l'Est 590 sq km) and dependencies 194 sq km (La Désirade 22 sq km, Iles des Saintes 14 sq km, Marie-Galante 158 sq km).

Population: 422,496 at census of 8 March 1999; 404,635 at census of 1 January 2011. Note: According to new census methodology, data in 2011 refer to median figures based on the collection of raw data over a five-year period (2009–13). *Mid-2014* (UN estimate): 468,017 (Source: UN, *World Population Prospects: The 2012 Revision*).

Density (at mid-2014): 287.1 per sq km.

Population by Age and Sex (UN estimates at mid-2014): *0–14:* 99,172 (males 50,572, females 48,600); *15–64:* 304,533 (males 142,436, females 162,097); *65 and over:* 64,312 (males 27,347, females 36,965); *Total* 468,017 (males 220,355, females 247,662). Source: UN, *World Population Prospects: The 2012 Revision*.

Principal Towns (population at 2010 census): Les Abymes 68,534; Baie-Mahault 30,251; Le Gosier 26,311; Sainte-Anne 24,192; Petit Bourg 23,199; Le Moule 22,381; Sainte-Rose 20,155; Capesterre-Belle-Eau 19,321; Pointe-à-Pitre 16,427; Basse-Terre (capital) 11,915.

Births, Marriages and Deaths (2011): Registered live births 5,384 (birth rate 13.3 per 1,000); Registered marriages 1,259 (marriage rate 3.1 per 1,000); Registered deaths 2,835 (death rate 7.0 per 1,000).

Life Expectancy (years at birth): 79.9 (males 76.1, females 83.6) in 2012. Source: Pan American Health Organization.

Employment (persons aged 15 years and over, provisional estimates at 31 December 2012): Agriculture, forestry and fishing 1,752; Mining and water supply 2,039; Manufacturing 6,253; Construction 6,389; Wholesale and retail trade; repair of motor vehicles, motorcycles, etc. 14,924; Transport, storage and communication 8,045; Hotels and restaurants 4,717; Financial intermediation 3,216; Real estate, renting and business activities 11,706; Public administration, health and social work 51,591; Other community, social and personal service activities 7,800; *Total employed* 118,432. Note: Data exclude 7,784 persons employed without salary.

HEALTH AND WELFARE

Key Indicators

Total Fertility Rate (children per woman, 2012): 2.1.

Under-5 Mortality Rate (per 1,000 live births, 2011): 7.6.

Physicians (per 1,000 head, c. 2010): 2.6.

Hospital Beds (per 1,000 head, 2009): 5.8.

Access to Water (% of persons, 2004): 98.

Access to Sanitation (% of persons, 2004): 64.

Source: mainly Pan American Health Organization.

For other sources and definitions, see explanatory note on p. vi.

AGRICULTURE, ETC.

Principal Crops ('000 metric tons, 2012, FAO estimates): Sweet potatoes 1.7; Sugar cane 1,000.0; Cabbages and other brassicas 2.5; Lettuce and chicory 3.9; Tomatoes 4.7; Cucumbers and gherkins 5.6; Bananas 60.0; Plantains 8.0. *Aggregate Production* ('000 metric tons, may include official, semi-official or estimated data): Total roots and tubers 15.2; Total vegetables (incl. melons) 50.5; Total fruits (excl. melons) 85.2.

Livestock ('000 head, year ending September 2012, FAO estimates): Cattle 75.0; Chickens 300.

Livestock Products ('000 metric tons, 2012, FAO estimates): Cattle meat 3.0; Pig meat 1.5; Chicken meat 1.4; Hen eggs 2.0.

Forestry ('000 cu m, 2012, FAO estimates): *Roundwood Removals* (excl. bark): Sawlogs, veneer logs and logs for sleepers 0.3; Fuel wood 15.0; Total 15.3. *Sawnwood Production* (incl. railway sleepers): Total 1.0.

Fishing (metric tons, live weight, 2011, FAO estimates): Capture 9,750 (Common dolphinfish 700; Other mackerel-like fishes 1,600; Marine fishes 7,075; Stromboid conchs 150); Aquaculture 12; *Total catch* 9,762.

Source: FAO.

MINING

Production ('000 metric tons, 2010, estimates): Cement 230; Pumice 210; Salt 49. Source: US Geological Survey.

INDUSTRY

Production (2012): Sugar 46,731 metric tons; Rum 81,950 hl; Electric energy 1,898 million kWh. Source: Institut d'Emission des Départements d'Outre-mer, *Guadeloupe: Rapport Annuel 2012*.

FINANCE

Currency and Exchange Rates: The French franc was used until the end of February 2002. Euro notes and coins were introduced on 1 January 2002, and the euro became the sole legal tender from 18 February. Some of the figures in this Survey are still in terms of francs. For details of exchange rates, see French Guiana.

Budget: *French Government* (€ million, 2005): Revenue 1,132; Expenditure 1,040. *Regional Budget* (€ million, 2011): Current revenue 256.2 (Taxes 178.5, Other current revenue 77.7); Capital revenues 191.3; Total 447.5. Current expenditure 236.7; Capital expenditure 156.1; Total 392.8 (Source: Institut d'Emission des Départements d'Outre-mer, *Guadeloupe: Rapport Annuel 2012*). *Departmental Budget* (excl. debt rescheduling, € million, 2013, preliminary): Revenue 676.9 (Current revenue 604.6, Capital revenue 72.4); Expenditure 676.9 (Current expenditure 583.9, Capital expenditure 93.0) (Source: Département des Etudes et des Statistiques Locales).

Money Supply (million French francs at 31 December 1996): Currency outside banks 1,148; Demand deposits at banks 6,187; Total money 7,335.

Cost of Living (Consumer Price Index; base: 2000 = 100): All items 122.0 in 2010; 125.1 in 2011; 127.5 in 2012. Source: ILO.

Gross Domestic Product (US $ million at constant 1990 prices): 3,543 in 2001; 3,707 in 2002; 3,844 in 2003. Source: UN, *Statistical Yearbook*.

Expenditure on the Gross Domestic Product (€ million at current prices, 2011, estimates): Total final consumption expenditure 8,488 (General government and non-profit institutions serving households 3,362, Households 5,126); Gross fixed capital formation 1,476; *Total domestic expenditure* 9,964; Exports of goods and services 889; *Less* Imports of goods and services 2,664; Statistical discrepancy –279; *GDP in purchasers' values* 7,910. Source: Institut d'Emission des Départements d'Outre-mer, *Guadeloupe: Rapport Annuel 2012*.

Gross Domestic Product by Economic Activity (€ million at current prices, 2006): Agriculture, hunting, forestry and fishing 197; Food industries 87; Other manufacturing 265; Energy 37; Construction 713; Services 6,094 (Restaurants and hotels 253, Transport 249, Commerce 948, Other market services 2,269, Non-market services 2,375); *Sub-total* 7,393; Financial intermediation services indirectly measured (FISIM) –325; Import duties, less subsidies 690; *GDP in purchasers' values* 7,758.

EXTERNAL TRADE

Principal Commodities (€ million, 2012, provisional): *Imports c.i.f.:* Products of agriculture, fishing and food industries 474.5; Textiles, clothing, leather and footwear 126.4; Chemicals 116.6; Pharmaceutical products 148.7; Mineral products, rubber and plastic 127.9; Metal and metal products 146.7; Mechanical and electrical equipment 468.6; Transport equipment 268.3; Petroleum products 527.5; Miscellaneous manufactured goods 116.6; Total (incl. others) 2,672.4. *Exports f.o.b.:* Products of agriculture, fishing and food industries 97.3; Petroleum products 11.8; Chemicals 9.0; Mechanical and electrical equipment 22.4; Transport equipment 25.6; Metals and metallic products 9.0; Total (incl. others) 216.1. (Source: Institut d'Emission des Départements d'Outre-mer, *Guadeloupe: Rapport Annuel 2012*).

Principal Trading Partners (€ million, 2008): *Imports c.i.f.:* Aruba 98; China, People's Repub. 87; France (metropolitan) 1,355; Germany 110; Italy 65; Martinique 210; Spain 40; USA 146; Total (incl. others) 2,601. *Exports f.o.b.:* France (metropolitan) 79; French Guiana 40; Germany 3; Martinique 44; Poland 5; Portugal 4; USA 4; Total (incl. others) 205. *2010* (€ million): Total imports 2,232.6; Total exports 178.4. *2011* (€ million): Total imports 2,642.4; Total exports 234.8 (Source: Institut d'Emission des Départements d'Outre-mer, *Guadeloupe: Rapport Annuel 2011*). *2012* (€ million, provisional): Total imports 2,672.4; Total exports 216.1 (Source: Institut d'Emission des Départements d'Outre-mer, *Guadeloupe: Rapport Annuel 2012*.

TRANSPORT

Road Traffic ('000 motor vehicles in use, 2002): Passenger cars 117.7; Commercial vehicles 31.4 (Source: UN, *Statistical Yearbook*). *1 January 2010* ('000 motor vehicles in use): Buses 0.8; Vans and trucks 39.6.

Shipping: *Flag Registered Fleet* (at 31 December 2013): Vessels 13; Total displacement 4,224 grt (Source: Lloyd's List Intelligence—www.lloydslistintelligence.com). *International Sea-borne Traffic* (2010 unless otherwise indicated): Freight vessels entered 1,257 (1995); Freight vessels departed 1,253 (1995); Gross freight handled 3,156,160 metric tons; Containers handled 150,534 TEUs; Passengers carried 924,446 (2004).

Civil Aviation (2012): Aircraft movements 26,931; Freight carried (incl. post) 14,004 metric tons; Passengers carried 1,994,575. Source: Institut d'Emission des Départements d'Outre-mer, *Guadeloupe: Rapport Annuel 2012*.

TOURISM

Tourist Arrivals by Country (2000): Canada 10,431; France 440,779; Italy 15,670; Switzerland 9,766; USA 92,474; Total (incl. others) 623,134. *2007:* France 391,910; Total (incl. others) 423,172. *2008:* France 406,871; Total (incl. others) 433,358. *2009:* Total 347,000. *2010:* Total 392,000. *2011:* Total 418,000.

Receipts from Tourism (US $ million, incl. passenger transport): 293 in 2009; 510 in 2010; 582 in 2011.

Source: partly World Tourism Organization.

COMMUNICATIONS MEDIA

Telephones ('000 main lines in use): 255.7 in 2010.

Mobile Cellular Telephones ('000 subscribers): 314.7 in 2004.

Internet Users ('000): 109.0 in 2009.

Source: International Telecommunication Union.

EDUCATION

Pre-primary (2012/13): 134 institutions; 19,614 students (17,554 state, 2,060 private).

Primary (2012/13): 206 institutions; 35,584 students (31,648 state, 3,936 private).

Specialized Pre-primary and Primary (2012/13): 540 students (521 state, 19 private).

Secondary (2012/13): 94 institutions; 50,019 students (44,705 state, 5,314 private).

Higher (2011/12): 9,113 students.

Teachers (2007/08 unless otherwise indicated): *Primary:* 3,382 (3,139 state, 243 private); *Secondary:* 4,675 (4,223 state, 452 private); *Higher* (2004/05): 203. Source: Ministère de l'Education Nationale, *Repères et références statistiques. 2011/12* (state schools): 3,050 in primary; 4,074 in secondary; 244 in higher.

Adult Literacy Rate: 90.1 (males 89.7; females 90.5) in 1998. Source: Pan American Health Organization.

Directory

The Government

(April 2014)

HEAD OF STATE

President: FRANÇOIS HOLLANDE.

Prefect: MARCELLE PIERROT, Préfecture, Palais d'Orléans, rue Lardenoy, 97109 Basse-Terre Cédex; tel. 5-90-99-39-00; fax 5-90-81-58-32; e-mail webmestre@guadeloupe.pref.gouv.fr; internet www.guadeloupe.pref.gouv.fr.

DEPARTMENTAL ADMINISTRATION

President of the General Council: Dr JACQUES GILLOT (Divers Gauche), Hôtel du Département, blvd Félix Eboué, 97109 Basse-Terre; tel. 5-90-99-77-77; fax 5-90-99-76-00; e-mail info@cg971.fr; internet www.cg971.fr.

President of the Economic and Social Committee: GÉRARD LUREL, 16 rue Peynier, 97100 Basse-Terre; tel. 5-90-41-05-15; fax 5-90-41-05-23; e-mail cr-cesr-guadeloupe@wanadoo.fr; internet www.cr-guadeloupe.fr.

President of the Culture, Education and Environment Committee: CAMILLUS RABIN, 16 rue Peynier, 97100 Basse-Terre; tel. 5-90-41-05-15; fax 5-90-41-05-23; e-mail cr-cesr-guadeloupe@wanadoo.fr; internet www.cr-guadeloupe.fr.

President of the Regional Council: JOSETTE BOREL-LINCERTIN (PS), 1 rue Paul Lacavé, Petit-Paris, 97109 Basse-Terre; tel. 5-90-80-40-40; fax 5-90-81-34-19; internet www.cr-guadeloupe.fr.

Elections, 14 and 21 March 2010

	Seats
Tous pour la Guadeloupe*	31
Ensemble pour la Guadeloupe†	4
Région Autrement‡	4
Pou Gwadloup an nou ay	2
Total	41

* Comprising the Parti Socialiste (PS) and other left-wing candidates.
† Comprising the Union pour un Mouvement Populaire (UMP) and other right-wing candidates.
‡ Comprising smaller left-wing parties and dissident socialists.

REPRESENTATIVES TO THE FRENCH PARLIAMENT

Deputies to the French National Assembly: ERIC JALTON (Socialiste, Républicain et Citoyen), GABRIELLE LOUIS-CARABIN (Socialiste, Républicain et Citoyen), ARY CHALUS (Radical, Républicain, Démocrate et Progressiste), HÉLÈNE VAINQUEUR-CHRISTOPHE (Socialiste, Républicain et Citoyen).

Representatives to the French Senate: JACQUES CORNANO (Groupe Socialiste), FÉLIX DESPLAN (Groupe Socialiste), JACQUES GILLOT (Groupe Socialiste).

Political Organizations

Combat Ouvrier: BP 213, 97156 Pointe-à-Pitre Cédex; tel. 5-90-26-23-58; e-mail menendez@wanadoo.fr; internet www.combat-ouvrier.net; Trotskyist; associated with national party Lutte Ouvrière; mem. of the Internationalist Communist Union; Leader JEAN-MARIE NOMERTIN.

Guadeloupe Unie, Socialisme et Réalité (GUSR): Pointe-à-Pitre; e-mail gusr@ais.gp; internet perso.mediaserv.net/gusr; 'dissident' faction of the Parti Socialiste; Pres. GUY LOSBAR.

Konvwa pou Liberasyon Nasyon Gwadloup (KLNG): Pointe-à-Pitre; f. 1997; pro-independence; Leader LUC REINETTE.

Parti Communiste Guadeloupéen (PCG): 119 rue Vatable, 97110 Pointe-à-Pitre; tel. 5-90-88-23-07; f. 1944; Sec.-Gen. FÉLIX FLÉMIN.

Parti Socialiste (PS): 8 Résidence Légitimus, blvd Légitimus, 97110 Pointe-à-Pitre; tel. and fax 5-90-21-65-72; fax 5-90-83-20-51; e-mail fede971@parti-socialiste.fr; internet www.parti-socialiste.fr; Regional Sec. MAX MATHIASIN.

Pou Gwadloup an nou ay: Pointe-à-Pitre; youth party; Leader CÉDRIC CORNET.

Union pour un Mouvement Populaire (UMP): Les Portes de Saint Martin Bellevue, 97150 Saint Martin; tel. and fax 5-90-87-50-01; fax 5-90-87-75-72; e-mail ump-sxm@laposte.net; internet www.u-m-p.org; f. 2002; centre-right; local br. of the metropolitan party; Pres., Departmental Cttee LAURENT BERNIER.

Les Verts Guadeloupe: 5 rue François Arago, 97110 Pointe-à-Pitre; tel. 5-90-35-41-90; fax 5-90-25-02-62; internet guadeloupe.lesverts.fr; ecologist; departmental br. of the metropolitan party; Regional spokespersons HARRY DURIMEL, JOCELYNE HATCHI.

Other political organizations included Mouvement pour la Démocratie et le Développement (MDDP), Union Populaire pour la Libération de la Guadeloupe (UPLG), Mouvman Gwadloupéyen (MG), Parti Progressiste Démocratique Guadeloupéen (PPDG), Renouveau Socialiste; and the coalitions Priorité à l'Education et à l'Environnement and Union pour une Guadeloupe Responsable.

Judicial System

Court of Appeal: Palais de Justice, 4 blvd Félix Eboué, 97100 Basse-Terre; tel. 5-90-80-63-36; fax 5-90-80-63-19; e-mail ca-basse-terre@justice.fr; First Pres. HENRY ROBERT; Procurator-Gen. CATHERINE CHAMPRENAULT.

There are two Tribunaux de Grande Instance and four Tribunaux d'Instance.

Religion

The majority of the population belong to the Roman Catholic Church.

CHRISTIANITY

The Roman Catholic Church

Guadeloupe comprises the single diocese of Basse-Terre, suffragan to the archdiocese of Fort-de-France, Martinique. Some 76% of the population are Roman Catholics. The Bishop participates in the Antilles Episcopal Conference, based in Port of Spain, Trinidad and Tobago.

Bishop of Basse-Terre: Mgr JEAN-YVES RIOCREUX, Evêché, pl. Saint-Françoise, BP 369, 97100 Basse-Terre Cédex; tel. 5-90-81-36-69; fax 5-90-81-98-23; e-mail eveche@catholique-guadeloupe.info; internet www.catholique-guadeloupe.info.

OTHER CHURCHES

Seventh-day Adventist Church: Eglise Adventiste de la Guadeloupe, BP 5, 97181 Les Abymes Cédex; tel. 5-90-82-79-76; fax 5-90-83-44-24; e-mail adventiste.federation@wanadoo.fr; internet www.adventiste-gp.org; f. 1931; Pres. ALAIN ANGERVILLE; Sec. JACQUES BIBRAC; 12,007 members (2011).

Other denominations active in Guadeloupe include the Baptist Church and Jehovah's Witnesses.

The Press

Destination Guadeloupe: Pointe-à-Pitre; tel. 4-66-77-62-37; e-mail virginie@destination-guadeloupe.com; internet www.destination-guadeloupe.com; tourism; monthly; Dir VIRGINIE LARNAC.

France Antilles: ZAC Moudong Sud, 97122 Baie-Mahault; tel. 5-90-90-25-25; fax 5-90-91-78-31; e-mail f.breland@media-antilles.fr; internet www.guadeloupe.franceantilles.fr; f. 1964; subsidiary of Groupe France Antilles; daily; Dir ALEXANDRE THEVENET; circ. 50,000.

Match: 35 rue Peynier, 97110 Pointe-à-Pitre; tel. 5-90-82-18-68; fax 5-90-82-01-87; f. 1943; fortnightly; Dir (vacant); circ. 6,000.

Nouvelles Etincelles: 119 rue Vatable, 97110 Pointe-à-Pitre; tel. 5-90-91-00-85; fax 5-90-91-06-53; e-mail nouvelles-etincelles@wanadoo.fr; internet nouvellesetincelles.com; f. 1944 as l'Etincelle, organ of the Parti Communiste Guadeloupéen (q.v.); present name adopted 2005; weekly; Dir CHRISTIAN CÉLESTE; circ. 5,000.

Publishers

Editions Exbrayat: 12 Allée des Marguerites, Les Jardins d'Arnouville, 97170 Petit-Bourg; tel. 5-90-26-32-33; fax 5-90-26-32-66; e-mail andre.exbrayat@exbrayat.com; internet commerce.ciel.com/exbrayat; Dir PAQUITA EXBRAYAT-SANCHEZ.

Editions Jasor: 46 rue Schoëlcher, 97110 Pointe-à-Pitre; tel. 5-90-91-18-48; fax 5-90-21-07-01; e-mail editionsjasor@wanadoo.fr; f. 1989; French-Creole culture, biography and language, and youth fiction; Dir RÉGINE JASOR.

PLB Editions: route de Mathurin, 97190 Gosier; tel. 5-90-89-91-17; fax 5-90-89-91-05; e-mail plbeditions@wanadoo.fr; internet www.plbeditions.com; f. 1997; regional natural history and French-Creole youth fiction; Dirs CHANTAL MATTET, THIERRY PETIT LE BRUN.

Broadcasting and Communications

TELECOMMUNICATIONS

CaribSat: 1406 rue Henri Becquerel, BP 2287, 97122 Baie-Mahault; internet www.caribsat.fr; internet service provider, providing satellite broadband services from late 2013; Man. MARYSE COPPET.

Digicel Antilles Françaises et Guyane: see Martinique—Telecommunications; Dir-Gen. (Guadeloupe) VINCENT VIENNET.

Orange Caraïbe: BP 2203, 97196 Jarry Cédex; tel. 5-90-38-45-55; fax 8-10-50-05-59; e-mail webmaster@orange.gp; internet www.orangecaraibe.com; f. 1996; subsidiary of Orange France; fixed lines, mobile telecommunications and internet services provider; network coverage incl. Martinique and French Guiana; Dir-Gen. JEAN-PHILIPPE GAY.

Outremer Telecom: SCI, Brand, voie Verte, Z. I. de Jarry, 97122 Baie-Mahault; e-mail communication@outremer-telecom.fr; internet www.outremer-telecom.fr; f. 1998; mobile telecommunications provider; Group CEO JEAN-MICHEL HEGESIPPE.

ONLY: SCI, Brand, voie Verte, Z. I. de Jarry, 97122 Baie-Mahault; e-mail communication@outremer-telecom.fr; internet www.outremer-telecom.fr; f. 1998 as Outremer Telecom Guadeloupe; present name adopted following merger of Volubis, ONLY and OOL in 2006; subsidiary of Outremer Telecom, France; fixed and mobile telecommunications provider.

BROADCASTING

Guadeloupe 1ère (Outre-mer Première): Morne Bernard Destrellan, BP 180, 97122 Baie-Mahault Cédex; tel. 5-90-60-96-96; fax 5-90-60-96-82; e-mail rfo@rfo.fr; internet guadeloupe.la1ere.fr; f. 1964; acquired by Groupe France Télévisions in 2004; fmrly Société Nationale de Radio-Télévision Française d'Outre-mer; name changed as Réseau France Outre-mer (RFO) in 1998; present name adopted in 2010; radio and TV; Dir-Gen. GENEVIÈVE GIARD; Regional Dir ROGER CESSY.

Radio

Kilti FM: Immeuble 573 rue de la Chapelle, Z. I. de Jarry, 97122 Baie-Mahault; tel. 5-90-32-52-61; fax 5-90-25-66-03; e-mail kiltifm@wanadoo.fr; f. 2006; French and Creole; Man. ORTEZ SONGO.

NRJ Guadeloupe: 2 blvd de la Marne, 97200 Fort-de-France; tel. 5-96-63-63-63; fax 5-96-73-73-15; e-mail webmaster@nrjantilles.com; internet www.nrjantilles.com; Dir FRANCK FÉRANDIER-SICARD; Dir JEAN-CHRISTOPHE MARTINEZ.

Ouest FM: Immeuble Vivies, rue Thomas Edyson, Z. I. Jarry, 97122 Baie-Mahault; tel. 5-94-38-29-19; fax 5-90-26-02-97; e-mail contact@ouestfm.com; internet www.ouestfm.net; f. 2008; commercial radio station; French.

Radio Caraïbes International (RCI Guadeloupe): Carrefour Grand Camp, BP 40, 97151 Pointe-à-Pitre Cédex; tel. 5-90-83-96-96; fax 5-90-83-96-97; internet gp.rci.fm; f. 1962; Man. THIERRY FUNDÉRÉ.

Radio Contact: 40 bis, rue Lamartine, 97110 Pointe-à-Pitre; tel. 5-90-82-25-41; fax 5-96-91-56-77; internet www.radio-contact.net; operated by l'Asscn Citoyenne de Sauvegarde et de Défense des Intérêts des Guadeloupéens; Pres. OCTAVIE LOSIO; Man. HENRI YOYOTTE.

Radio Inter S'Cool (RIS): Lycée Ducharmoy, 97120 Saint-Claude; tel. and fax 5-90-80-38-40; e-mail contact@gupilvision.com; internet www.radiointerscool.net; educational and school-focused programmes; French and Creole; Pres. JAQUES REMUS.

Radio Tanbou: 153 résidence Espace, 97110 Pointe-à-Pitre; tel. 5-90-21-66-45; fax 5-90-21-66-48; e-mail kontak@radyotanbou.com; internet www.radyotanbou.com; French and Creole; operated by the l'Asscn pour le Développement de l'Information et de la Culture Guadeloupéenne.

RHT Guadeloupe (Radio Haute Tension): route de Petit Marquisat, Routhiers, 97130 Capesterre Belle Eau; tel. 5-90-99-08-12; e-mail ruddycornelie@radiohautetension.fr; internet www.radiohautetension.fr; f. 1986; Dir RUDDY CORNELIE.

Zouk Radio: Immeuble Général Bricolage, Petit Pérou, 97139 Les Abymes; tel. 5-90-89-25-80; fax 5-90-89-26-22; internet www.zoukradio.fr; commercial music station; French and Creole.

Television

Antilles Télévision (ATV): see Martinique—Television.

Archipel 4: Immeuble Debs-Montauban, 97190 Gosier; tel. 5-93-21-05-20; f. 2002; Chair. JEAN-CLAUDE THOMASEAU.

Canal Plus Antilles: Immeuble Canal Media, Moudong Centre Jarry, 97122 Baie-Mahault; tel. 5-90-38-09-00; fax 5-90-38-09-04; e-mail mrichol@canalantilles.gp; internet www.canalantilles.com; f. 1993; subsidiary of Groupe Canal Plus, France; satellite TV station; Pres. JEAN-NOËL TRONC.

Canal 10: Immeuble CCL, blvd de Houelbourg, ZI de Jarry, BP 2271, 97122 Baie-Mahault; tel. 5-90-26-73-03; fax 5-90-26-61-25; e-mail contact@canal10-tv.com; internet www.canal10-tv.com; f. 1990; focus on social, economic and cultural issues in Guadeloupe; produces 100% of its programmes; Dir MICHEL RODRIGUEZ.

Eclair TV (ETV): Basse-Terre Télévision, Pintade, 97100 Basse-Terre; tel. 5-90-60-15-30; fax 5-90-60-15-33; e-mail eclairfm.com@orange.fr; f. 1998; community station local to Basse-Terre; Pres. (vacant).

La Une Guadeloupe (L'A1): 20 rue Henri Becquerel, Z. I. de Jarry, 97122 Baie-Mahault; tel. 5-90-38-06-06; fax 5-90-38-06-07; f. 1998; fmrly TCI; gen. interest; purchases 65% of programmes from TF1, France (2003); Pres. JOSÉ GADDARKHAN.

Finance

(cap. = capital; res = reserves; dep. = deposits; m. = million; brs = branches; amounts in euros unless otherwise indicated)

BANKING

Central Bank

Institut d'Emission des Départments d'Outre-mer (IEDOM): Parc d'activité la Providence, ZAC de Dothémare, BP 196, 97139 Les Abymes; tel. 5-90-93-74-00; fax 5-90-93-74-25; e-mail iedom-pap-etudes@iedom-guadeloupe.fr; internet www.iedom.fr; Dir CHARLES APANON.

Commercial Banks

Banque des Antilles Françaises: Parc d'Activités de la Jaille, BP 46, Bâtiments 5 et 6, 97122 Baie-Mahault; tel. 5-90-60-42-00; fax 5-90-60-99-33; internet www.bdaf.fr; f. 1967 by merger of Banque de la Martinique and Banque de la Guadeloupe; subsidiary of Financière Océor, France; cap. 83.7m., res –7.7m., dep. 1,244.4m. (Dec. 2010); Pres. and Chair. CHRISTIAN CAMUS; Gen. Man. DIDIER LOING; 19 brs.

Banque Française Commerciale Antilles-Guyane (BFC Antilles-Guyane): Immeuble BFC, Grand Camp-La Rocade, 97139 Pointe-à-Pitre; tel. 5-90-21-56-52; fax 5-90-21-56-62; e-mail f.aujoulat@bfc-ag.com; internet www.bfc-ag.com; f. 1976 as br. of Banque Française Commerciale, SA, separated 1984; cap. 51.1m., res 6.1m., dep. 667.5m. (Dec. 2011); Chair. CHRISTIAN DUVILLET; Dir-Gen. ALAIN STASSINET.

BNP Paribas Guadeloupe: pl. de la Rénovation, BP 161, 97155 Pointe-à-Pitre; tel. 5-90-90-58-58; fax 5-90-90-04-07; e-mail dg@bnp.gp; internet guadeloupe.bnpparibas.net; f. 1941; subsidiary of BNP Paribas, France; Gen. Man. DANIEL DELANIS; Gen. Sec. FRANCOIS PASETTI; 12 brs.

BRED Banque Populaire (BRED-BP): Immeuble Simcar, blvd Marquisat de Houelbourg, Z. I. Jarry, 97122 Baie-Mahault; tel. 5-90-82-65-46; internet www.bred.banquepopulaire.fr; cap. 242m. (Oct. 2005); Group Chair. STÈVE GENTILI.

Crédit Agricole de la Guadeloupe: Petit Pérou, 97176 Abymes Cédex; tel. 5-90-90-65-65; fax 5-90-90-65-89; e-mail catelnet@ca-guadeloupe.fr; internet www.ca-guadeloupe.fr; total assets 1,228.1m. (Dec. 2003); Pres. CHRISTIAN FLÉREAU; Gen. Man. ROGER WUNSCHEL; 30 brs.

Crédit Maritime de la Guadeloupe: 36 rue Achille René-Boisneuf, BP 292, 97175 Pointe-à-Pitre; tel. 5-90-21-08-40; fax 5-90-89-52-42; e-mail pointe-a-pitre-agence-cmm@creditmaritime.com; internet www.creditmaritime-outremer.com; Dir GÉRARD CADIC; 4 agencies.

Société Générale de Banque aux Antilles (SGBA): 30 rue Frébault, BP 55, 97152 Pointe-à-Pitre; tel. 5-90-25-49-77; fax 5-90-25-49-78; e-mail sgba@wanadoo.fr; internet www.sgba.fr; f. 1979; cap. 32.6m., res –15.3m., dep. 360.5m. (Dec. 2009); Pres. JEAN-LOUIS MATTEI; Gen. Man. MICHEL PECHEUR; 5 brs in Guadeloupe, 3 brs in Martinique.

Development Bank

Société de Crédit pour le Développement de Guadeloupe (SODEGA): Carrefour Raizet Baimbridge, BP 54, 97152 Pointe-à-Pitre; tel. 5-90-82-65-00; fax 5-90-90-17-91; e-mail credit@sodega.fr; internet www.sodega.fr; f. 1970; bought from the Agence Française de Développement (q.v.) by BRED Banque Populaire (q.v.) in 2003.

INSURANCE

Allianz Vie France: Le Patio de Grand Camp, BP 212, 97156 Pointe-à-Pitre Cédex; tel. 5-90-21-38-88; fax 5-90-82-78-25; e-mail agf.guavie@wanadoo.fr; internet www.allianz.fr; life insurance.

GAN Guadeloupe: 59–61 rue Achille René Boisneuf, BP 152, 97171 Pointe-à-Pitre Cédex; tel. 5-90-89-32-00; fax 5-90-04-43; internet www.groupama.es; subsidiary of Groupama, France; Dir-Gen. ALEXANDRE PASCAL; Man. GILLES CANO.

Mutuelle d'Assurance de Guadeloupe (MAG): Immeuble Capma & Capmi, blvd Légitimus, (face à Air France), 97110 Pointe-à-Pitre Cédex; tel. 5-90-82-22-71; fax 5-90-91-19-40; internet www.monceauassurances.com; fmrly Capma & Capmi; Chair. and Dir Gen. GILLES DUPIN.

Optimum Assurances: 3 bis rue Henri Bequerel, Jarry, 97122 Baie-Mahault; tel. 5-90-26-96-47; fax 5-90-26-81-27; internet www.assurances-guadeloupe.info; Dir-Gen. URBALD REINE.

WAB Assurances: Immeuble Stratégie, Moudong Sud, 97122 Baie-Mahault Cédex; tel. 5-90-32-66-66; fax 5-90-32-66-74; e-mail philippe.bech@wab-assu.com; internet www.wabassu.fr; f. 2005; Dir-Gen. PHILIPPE BECH.

Trade and Industry

GOVERNMENT AGENCIES

Direction de l'Alimentation, de l'Agriculture et de la Forêt (DAAF): Jardin Botanique, 97100 Basse-Terre; tel. 5-90-99-09-09; fax 5-90-99-09-10; e-mail daaf971@agriculture.gouv.fr; internet daaf971@agriculture.gouv.fr; Dir VINCENT FAUCHER.

Direction Régionale des Affaires Maritimes (DRAM): 20 rue Henri Becquerel, BP 2466, 97085 Jarry; tel. 5-90-41-95-50; fax 5-90-90-07-33; e-mail Dram-Guadeloupe@developpement-durable.gouv.fr; responsible for shipping, fishing and other maritime issues at a national and community level; Dir FRÉDÉRIC BLUA.

Direction Régionale du Commerce Extérieur Antilles-Guyane (DRCE): see Martinique—Trade and Industry.

Direction Régionale de l'Industrie, de la Recherche et de l'Environnement (DRIRE): 552 rue de la Chapelle, Z. I. Jarry, 97122 Baie-Mahault; tel. 5-90-38-03-47; fax 5-90-38-03-50; e-mail pierre.juan@industrie.gouv.fr; internet www.ggm.drire.gouv.fr; active in industry, business services, transport, public works, tourism and distribution; Departmental Co-ordinator MICHEL MASSON.

DEVELOPMENT ORGANIZATIONS

Agence de l'Environnement et de la Maîtrise de l'Energie (ADEME): Immeuble Café Center, rue Ferdinand Forest, Z. I. Jarry, 97122 Baie-Mahault; tel. 5-90-26-78-05; fax 5-90-26-87-15; e-mail ademe.guadeloupe@ademe.fr; internet www.ademe.fr; developing energy and waste management; Man. CLAUDE COROSINE.

Agence Française de Développement (AFD): Parc d'activités de la Jaille, Bâtiment 7, BP 110, 97122 Baie-Mahault; tel. 5-90-89-65-65; fax 5-90-83-03-73; e-mail afdpointeaPitre@afd.fr; internet www.afd-guadeloupe.org; fmrly Caisse Française de Développement; Man. BERTRAND BOISSELET.

CHAMBERS OF COMMERCE

Chambre d'Agriculture de la Guadeloupe: Espace régional Agricole, Convenance BP 35, 97122 Baie-Mahault; tel. 5-90-25-17-17; fax 5-90-26-07-22; e-mail cda_direction@guadeloupe.chambagri.fr; Pres. ERIC NELSON; Dir JOËL PEDURAND.

Chambre de Commerce et d'Industrie de Région des Iles de Guadeloupe: Hôtel Consulaire, rue Félix Eboué, 97110 Pointe-à-Pitre Cédex; tel. 5-90-93-76-00; fax 5-90-90-21-87; e-mail contact@pointe-a-pitre.cci.fr; internet www.pointe-a-pitre.cci.fr; f. 1832; Pres. COLETTE KOURY; Sec. HENRI NAGAPIN; 34 full mems and 17 assoc. mems.

Chambre de Métiers et de l'Artisanat de la Guadeloupe (CMA): route Choisy, BP 61, 97120 Saint-Claude; tel. 5-90-80-23-33; fax 5-90-80-08-93; e-mail sgstc@cmguadeloupe.org; internet www.cmguadeloupe.org; Pres. JOËL LOBEAU; 11,630 mems (2005).

EMPLOYERS' ORGANIZATIONS

Association des Moyennes et Petites Industries (AMPI): rue Pierre et Marie Curie, Z.I. Jarry, BP 2325, 97187 Jarry Cédex; tel. 5-90-26-38-27; fax 5-90-95-52-57; e-mail mpi.guadeloupe@wanadoo.fr; internet www.industrieguadeloupe.com; f. 1974; Pres. FRANK DESALMA; Gen. Sec CHRISTOPHE WACHTER; 117 mem. cos.

Interprofession Guadeloupéenne pour la Canne à Sucre (IGUACANNE): Espace Régional Agricole de Convenance, 97122 Baie-Mahault; f. 2005; represents sugar cane growers, sugar producers and professional bodies; Pres. ATHANASE COQUIN.

Ordre des Pharmaciens du Département Guadeloupe: Immeuble Capital 16, 1°, ZAC de Houelbourg, SUD 2, 97122 Baie-Mahault; tel. 5-90-21-66-05; fax 5-90-21-66-07; e-mail delegation_guadeloupe@ordre.pharmacien.fr; Pres. MAGGY CHEVRY-NOL.

Syndicat des Producteurs-Exportateurs de Sucre et de Rhum de la Guadeloupe et Dépendances: Z. I. Jarry, 97122 Baie-Mahault; BP 2015, 97191 Pointe-à-Pitre; tel. 5-90-23-53-15; fax 5-90-23-52-34; f. 1937; Pres. M. VIGNERON; 4 mems.

Union des Entreprises-Mouvement des Entreprises de France (UDE-MEDEF): Immeuble SCI BTB, voie Principale de Jarry, Baie-Mahault; tel. 5-90-26-83-58; fax 5-90-26-83-67; e-mail ude.medef@medef-guadeloupe.com; Pres. WILLY ANGÈLE.

UTILITIES

Electricity

EDF Guadeloupe: BP 85, 97153 Pointe-à-Pitre; tel. 5-90-82-40-34; fax 5-90-83-30-02; e-mail marie-therese.fournier@edfgdf.fr; internet guadeloupe.edf.fr; electricity producer; Dir YVAN DELMAS; Man. MAX BORDELAIS.

Water

Veolia Water—Compagnie Générale des Eaux Guadeloupe: 18 ZAC de Houelbourg III, Voie verte de Jarry, 97122 Baie-Mahault; tel. 5-90-89-76-76; fax 5-90-91-39-10; e-mail mail-elise@gde-guadeloupe.com; internet www.generaledeseaux.gp; fmrly SOGEA; Dir (Americas) AUGUSTE LAURENT.

TRADE UNIONS

Confédération Générale du Travail de la Guadeloupe (CGTG): 4 Cité Artisanale de Bergevin, BP 779, 97110 Pointe-à-Pitre Cédex; tel. 5-90-82-34-61; fax 5-90-91-04-00; f. 1961; Sec.-Gen. JEAN-MARIE NOMERTIN; 5,000 mems.

Fédération Syndicale Unitaire Guadeloupe (FSU): BP 82, 97005 Pointe-à-Pitre Cedéx; tel. 5-90-23-13-66; fax 5-90-23-19-83; e-mail fsu971@fsu.fr; internet sd971.fsu.fr; f. 1993; departmental br. of the Fédération Syndicale Unitaire; represents public sector employees in teaching, research and training, and also agriculture, justice, youth and sports, and culture; Sec. GUY-LUC BELROSE.

Union Générale des Travailleurs de la Guadeloupe (UGTG): rue Paul Lacavé, 97110 Pointe-à-Pitre; tel. 5-90-83-10-07; fax 5-90-89-08-70; e-mail ugtg@ugtg.org; internet www.ugtg.org; f. 1973; confederation of pro-independence trade unions incl. Union des Agents de la Sécurité Sociale (UNASS), l'Union des Employés du Commerce (UEC), Union des Travailleurs de l'Etat et du Département (UTED), l'Union des Travailleurs des Collectivités (UTC), l'Union des Travailleurs de l'Hôtellerie, du Tourisme et de la Restauration (UTHTR), l'Union des Travailleurs des Produits Pétroliers (UTPP), l'Union des Travailleurs de la Santé (UTS), and l'Union des Travailleurs des Télécommunications (UTT); Gen. Sec. ELIE DOMOTA; 4,000 mems.

Transport

RAILWAYS

There are no railways in Guadeloupe.

ROADS

There were 2,069 km (1,286 miles) of roads in Guadeloupe, of which 323 km were Routes Nationales.

SHIPPING

The Guadeloupe Port Caraïbes (formerly Port Autonome de la Guadeloupe) comprises five sites. The two principal seaports are at Pointe-à-Pitre, which offers both cargo-handling and passenger facilities, and the container terminal at Jarry (Baie-Mahault); the smaller port of Basse-Terre caters to freight and inter-island passenger traffic. There is also a sugar terminal at Folle-Anse (Saint-Louis); and a marina at Bas-du-Fort with 1,000 berths for pleasure craft. In December 2013 Guadeloupe's flag registered fleet comprised 13 vessels, with an aggregate displacement of some 4,224 grt.

Agence Petrelluzzi Transit et Maritime: 17 rue de la Chapelle, 97122 Baie Mahault; tel. 5-90-38-12-12; fax 5-90-26-69-26; e-mail info@transitpetrelluzzi.com; internet transitpetrelluzzi.com; f. 1896; Dir PATRICK PETRELLUZZI.

Compagnie Générale Maritime Antilles-Guyane: Route du WTC, Zone Portuaire, BP 92, 97122 Baie-Mahault; tel. 5-90-25-57-00; fax 5-90-25-57-81; e-mail ptp.mbellemare@cma-cgm.com; internet www.cma-cgm.com; subsidiary of CMA-CGM, France; shipping agents, stevedoring; Gen. Man. MARLÈNE BELLEMARE.

Guadeloupe Port Caraïbes: Quai Ferdinand de Lesseps, BP 485, 97165 Pointe-à-Pitre Cédex; tel. 5-90-68-61-70; fax 5-90-68-61-71; e-mail contact@port-guadeloupe.com; internet guadeloupe-portcaraibes.com; port authority; fmrly Port Autonome de la Guadeloupe; became a Grand Port Maritime, a publicly owned entity administered by a supervisory board, following adoption of legislation in 2013; Dir-Gen. LAURENT MARTENS.

Compagnie Générale Portuaire: Marina Bas-du-Fort, 97110 Pointe-à-Pitre; tel. 5-90-93-66-20; fax 5-90-90-81-53; e-mail marina@marina-pap.com; internet www.marina-pap.com; port authority; Man. PHILIPPE CHEVALLIER; Harbour Master TONY BRESLAU; 1,000 berths for non-commercial traffic.

Société Guadeloupéenne de Consignation et Manutention (SGCM): 8 rue de la Chapelle, BP 2360, 97001 Jarry Cédex; tel. 5-90-38-05-55; fax 5-90-26-95-39; e-mail gerard.petrelluzzi@sgcm.fr; f. 1994; shipping agents, stevedoring; also operates Navimar Cruises inter-island tour co; Gen. Man. GERARD PETRELLUZZI; 17 berths.

Transcaraïbes S.A.: BP 2453, 97085 Pointe-à-Pitre; tel. 5-90-26-63-27; fax 5-90-26-67-49; e-mail transcaraibes.gpe@wanadoo.fr; f. 1976; shipping agents, stevedoring; office in Martinique; Gen. Man. ERIK URGIN.

CIVIL AVIATION

Raizet International Airport is situated 3 km (2 miles) from Pointe-à-Pitre and is equipped to handle jet-engined aircraft. There are smaller airports on the islands of Marie-Galante, La Désirade and Saint-Barthélémy. The island is served by a number of regional airlines, including LIAT (see Antigua and Barbuda). In 2013 American Airlines began a direct service from Miami, FL, to Pointe-à-Pitre.

Air Antilles Express: Aeroport Pôle Caraibes, Point-à-Pitre; tel. 5-90-21-14-47; e-mail ar@media-caraibes.com; internet www.airantilles.com; f. 2002; subsidiary of Compagnie Aerienne Inter Regionale Express, France; serves Guadeloupe, Martinique, St-Barthélemy, St-Martin, Sint Maarten and the Dominican Republic; seasonal flights to San Juan, La Romana, Antigua and St Lucia; Dir CHRISTIAN MARCHAND.

Air Caraïbes (CAT): Aéroport International Guadeloupe, Pôle Caraïbes, 97139 Abymes; tel. 5-90-82-47-41; fax 5-90-82-47-49; e-mail drh@aircaraibes.com; internet www.aircaraibes.com; f. 2000 following merger of Air St Martin, Air St Barts, Air Guadeloupe and Air Martinique; owned by Groupe Dubreuil; operates daily inter-island, regional and international services within the Caribbean, and flights to Brazil, French Guiana and Paris; CEO SERGE TSYGALNITZKY; 16 aircraft; 800,000 passengers (2006).

Air Caraïbes Atlantique: Aéroport, 97232 Le Lamentin; f. 2003; subsidiary of Air Caraïbes; services between Pointe-à-Pitre, Fort-de-France (Martinique) and Paris; Pres. FRANÇOIS HERSEN.

Tourism

Guadeloupe is a popular tourist destination, especially for visitors from metropolitan France (who account for some 89% of tourists) and the USA. The main attractions are the beaches, the mountainous scenery and the unspoilt beauty of the island dependencies. In 2011 some 418,000 tourists visited Guadeloupe. Receipts from tourism totalled US $582m. in the same year.

Comité du Tourisme: 5 sq. de la Banque, BP 555, 97166 Pointe-à-Pitre Cédex; tel. 5-90-82-09-30; fax 5-90-83-89-22; e-mail info@lesilesdeguadeloupe.com; internet www.lesilesdeguadeloupe.com; Pres. JOSETTE BOREL-LINCERTIN; Dir THIERRY GARGAR.

Délégation Régionale au Tourisme, au Commerce et l'Artisanat: 5 rue Victor Hugues, 97100 Basse-Terre; tel. 5-90-81-10-44; fax 5-90-81-94-82; e-mail drtourisme.guadeloupe@wanadoo.fr; Dir CHRISTIAN FOURCRIER.

Syndicat d'Initiative de Pointe-à-Pitre: Centre Commercial de la Marina, 97110 Pointe-à-Pitre; tel. 5-90-90-70-02; fax 5-90-90-74-70; e-mail syndicatinitiativedepap@wanadoo.fr; internet www.sivap.gp; Pres. DENYS FORTUNE; Man. NADIA DEGLAS.

Defence

As assessed at November 2013, France maintained a military force of about 1,250 in Fort-de-France (Martinique).

Education

The education system is similar to that of metropolitan France (see the chapter on French Guiana). In 2012/13 there were 134 pre-primary and 206 primary schools. Secondary education was provided at 94 institutions in 2012/13. In 2012/13 there were 19,614 students in pre-primary and 35,584 in primary education (a further 540 pupils attended specialized pre-primary and primary schools), while in secondary education there were 50,019 students, of whom some 89% attended state schools. A branch of the Université des Antilles et de la Guyane, at Pointe-à-Pitre, has faculties of law and economics, sciences, medicine, teacher training, sports science and humanities. In addition, there are colleges of agriculture, fisheries, hotel management, nursing, midwifery and child care. In 2011/12 there was a total of 9,113 students in higher education.

MARTINIQUE

Introductory Survey

LOCATION, CLIMATE, LANGUAGE, RELIGION, CAPITAL

Martinique is one of the Windward Islands in the West Indies, with Dominica to the north and Saint Lucia to the south. The island is dominated by the volcanic peak of Mont Pelée. The climate is tropical, but tempered by easterly and north-easterly breezes. The more humid and wet season runs from July to November, and the average temperature is 26°C (79°F). French is the official language, but a Creole patois is widely spoken. The majority of the population professes Christianity and belongs to the Roman Catholic Church. The capital is Fort-de-France.

CONTEMPORARY POLITICAL HISTORY

Historical Context

Martinique has been a French possession since 1635. The prosperity of the island was based on the sugar industry, which was devastated by the volcanic eruption of Mont Pelée in 1902. Martinique became a Department of France in 1946, when the Governor was replaced by a Prefect, and an elected Conseil Général (General Council) was created.

During the 1950s there was a growth of nationalist feeling, as expressed by Aimé Césaire's Parti Progressiste Martiniquais (PPM) and the Parti Communiste Martiniquais (PCM). However, economic power remained concentrated in the hands of the *békés* (descendants of white colonial settlers), who owned most of the agricultural land and controlled the lucrative import-export market. This provided little incentive for innovation or self-sufficiency, and fostered resentment against lingering colonial attitudes.

Domestic Political Affairs

In 1974 Martinique, together with Guadeloupe and French Guiana, was given regional status as part of France's governmental reorganization. An indirectly elected Conseil Régional (Regional Council) was created, with some control over the local economy. In 1982 and 1983 the socialist Government of President François Mitterrand made further concessions towards autonomy by giving the local councils greater control over taxation, local police and the economy. At the first direct elections to the new Regional Council, held in February 1983, left-wing parties (the PPM, the PCM and the Fédération Socialiste de la Martinique—FSM) won a majority of seats. This success, and the election of Césaire as President of the Regional Council, strengthened his influence against the pro-independence elements in his own party. (Full independence for Martinique attracted support from only a small minority of the population; the majority sought reforms that would bring greater autonomy, while retaining French control.) The Mouvement Indépendantiste Martiniquais (MIM), the most vocal of the separatist parties, fared badly in the elections, obtaining less than 3% of the total vote. At an election to the enlarged General Council in 1985, the left-wing parties increased their representation, but the centre-right coalition of the Union pour la Démocratie Française (UDF) and the Rassemblement pour la République (RPR) maintained their control of the administration.

At the general election to the Assemblée Nationale (National Assembly) in 1986, Césaire and a member of the FSM were elected from a unified list of left-wing candidates, while the RPR and the UDF (which had also presented a joint list) each won one seat. In the concurrent election to the Regional Council the left-wing parties (including the PPM, the FSM and the PCM) won a narrow majority of seats. Césaire retained the presidency of the Council until 1988, when he relinquished the post to Camille Darsières (the Secretary-General of the PPM). Indirect elections were also held in 1986 for Martinique's two seats in the Sénat (Senate). The left-wing parties again united, and Martinique acquired a left-wing senator for the first time since 1958, a PPM member, while the other successful candidate belonged to the UDF.

Left-wing candidates secured all four seats at elections to the National Assembly in 1988 and the parties of the left also achieved a majority at elections to the General Council. Emile Maurice of the

RPR was, none the less, elected President of the Council for a seventh term.

In 1990 the results of the 1986 election to the Regional Council were annulled because of a technicality, and another election was held. Pro-independence candidates secured nine seats (of which seven were won by the MIM). The PPM-FSM-PCM coalition lost its absolute majority on the Regional Council; Camille Darsières was, however, re-elected to the presidency of the Regional Council. At an election to the General Council in 1992, left-wing parties secured a narrow majority. Claude Lise, a PPM deputy to the National Assembly, was elected President of the Council. In concurrent elections to the Regional Council the RPR and the UDF, contesting the election as the Union pour la France (UPF), won the most seats. Emile Capgras of the PCM was elected President of the Regional Council.

In September 1992 72% of voters in Martinique approved ratification of the Treaty on European Union (see p. 273), although the abstention rate was high.

In the 1993 elections to the National Assembly André Lesueur and Pierre Petit of the RPR were elected, as was a third right-wing candidate, Anicet Turinay of the UPF. In September 1995 Lise was elected to the Senate, while the incumbent PPM representative, Rodolphe Désiré, was returned to office.

At elections to the National Assembly in 1997, Turinay and Petit, representing the RPR, were re-elected, together with Camille Darsières of the PPM and Alfred Marie-Jeanne of the MIM. At elections to the Regional Council in the following year, the left retained its majority. Marie-Jeanne was elected President of the Regional Council. In a concurrent election to the General Council the left again increased its majority; Lise was re-elected to the presidency of the General Council.

A two-month strike by workers in the banana sector, which had severely disrupted economic activity around the port of Fort-de-France, was ended in January 1999, when a pay agreement was reached. However, in October, prior to a two-day visit to Martinique by Prime Minister Lionel Jospin, banana producers occupied the headquarters of the French naval forces for several days, demanding the disbursement of exceptional aid to compensate for a dramatic decline in prices on the European market. The Prime Minister announced an emergency plan for the banana sector and agreed, in principle, to a proposal for greater autonomy for the local authorities in conducting relations with neighbouring countries and territories.

In December 1999 the Presidents of the Regional Councils of French Guiana, Guadeloupe and Martinique signed a joint declaration in Basse-Terre, Guadeloupe, affirming their intention to propose, to the Government, a legislative amendment aimed at creating a new status of overseas region, despite an earlier statement to the contrary by Jospin. Modified proposals regarding the institutional future and socio-economic development of the Departments were approved by the National Assembly and in December were ratified by the Constitutional Council. Following a meeting of members of the Regional Council and the General Council in June 2001, a series of proposals on greater autonomy was agreed upon. These included: the division of the territory into four districts; the creation of a Collectivité Territoriale (Territorial Collectivity), governed by a 41-member Assembly elected for a five-year term; and the establishment of an independent executive council. Furthermore, the proposals included a request that the territory be given control over legislative and administrative affairs, as well as legislative authority on matters concerning Martinique alone. In March 2003 the two houses of the French parliament approved constitutional changes that, *inter alia*, allowed for local referendums to be held on proposals for greater decentralization in overseas possessions. The status of Région d'Outre-mer (Overseas Region) was also conferred on Martinique. In the referendum, held on 7 December, some 51% of participating voters rejected legislative reforms that envisaged the replacement of the General Council and the Regional Council with a single assembly.

In municipal elections held in March 2001 the PPM retained control of the majority of municipalities. In the concurrently held election to the General Council, Lise was re-elected President. At elections to the National Assembly in June 2002, Marie-Jeanne was re-elected, while Turinay lost his seat to Louis-Joseph Manscour of the PS, and Darsières lost his to Pierre-Jean Samot of the left-wing Bâtir le Pays Martinique (BPM); Alfred Almont, representing the right-wing alliance of the Union pour la Majorité Présidentielle (UMP) and the RPR, secured the remaining seat. The RPR subsequently merged into the successor party to the UMP, the Union pour un Mouvement Populaire (also known as the UMP). In March 2003 the French Constitutional Council ordered Samot to resign for having broken campaign funding rules. A by-election was held in May 2003, which was won by Philippe Edmond-Mariette, also of BPM.

At an election to the Regional Council in March 2004 the Patriotes Martiniquais, a pro-independence alliance, comprising the MIM, the Conseil National des Comités Populaires and the Alliance pour le Pays Martinique (which was absorbed by the two larger groupings after the first round of voting), won an overwhelming majority, obtaining 28 of the 41 council seats. A joint list comprising the PPM and other left-wing candidates obtained nine seats, while the right-wing Forces Martiniquaises de Progrès secured the remaining four seats.

In May 2005 a national referendum was held on ratification of the European Union constitutional treaty: 69% of voters in the Department were in favour of adopting the treaty, although turnout was low. The treaty was ultimately rejected by a majority of voters in metropolitan France. In December more than 1,000 protesters took part in demonstrations in Fort-de-France against a law, approved in the previous February, that proposed changing the school syllabus to reflect the 'positive' role of French colonialism. In January 2006 the relevant article of law was removed in accordance with a ruling by the Constitutional Council that it lay outside the competence of the legislature.

In the first round of the 2007 national presidential election Ségolène Royal of the PS won 49% of the votes cast on the island, ahead of Nicolas Sarkozy, the UMP candidate, who attracted 34% of the ballot. Royal won 61% of the second round vote in the Department, however, nationally, Sarkozy emerged victorious. At elections to the National Assembly in June, Marie-Jeanne, Manscour and Almont were all re-elected, while Serge Letchimy of the PPM was also successful. Following elections to the General Council in March 2008, Lise was again re-elected as the Council's President.

A general strike began in early February 2009 in protest against the increasingly high cost of living, following similar unrest in Guadeloupe. Riot police were sent from metropolitan France in an effort to control the demonstrations, and violent confrontations between police and protesters ensued. The strike, which had caused significant economic disruption, ended on 11 March.

Regional and national elections

A referendum on the issue of increased autonomy for the island was held on 10 January 2010. The electorate, fearful of losing economic support from mainland France and unwilling to confer greater power upon the local political élite, voted overwhelmingly to reject any increase in autonomy, with 78.9% voting against the proposal. The rate of participation by the electorate was 55.4%.

In elections to the Regional Council on 14 and 21 March 2010, the PPM won a decisive victory, with 48.4% of the ballot, gaining 26 of the Council's 41 seats. The MIM secured 12 seats and the UMP-led list obtained the remaining three, with 41.0% and 10.6% of the votes cast, respectively. Letchimy was duly elected as President of the Regional Council. The rate of participation by the electorate was 55.1%. Following the UMP's poor electoral performance, in May a group of disaffected members formed a new right-wing party, the Parti Régionaliste Martiniquais. Left-wing candidates performed strongly in the municipal polls conducted on 20 and 27 March 2011, following which the BPM's Josette Manin (representing a PPM-led coalition) was elected as Martinique's first female President of the General Council. Also in that month, Laurent Prévost was appointed as Prefect. In September Serge Larcher of the PPM was re-elected to the Senate, while another left-wing candidate, Maurice Antiste, won control of the island's second Senate seat.

The first round of the French presidential election was conducted on 21 April 2012 (one day earlier than in mainland France): François Hollande, representing the PS, attracted 52.0% of the territory's votes, compared with 26.3% for Sarkozy. A second round run-off election was held two weeks later, at which Hollande secured 68.4% of the ballot, defeating Sarkozy, who attracted 31.6%. Hollande also triumphed nationally and was sworn in as President in mid-May. In legislative elections, which took place in June, Marie-Jeanne and Letchimy were re-elected to the National Assembly, while the island's two remaining mandates were won by Jean-Philippe Nilor (of the MIM) and Bruno Nestor Azerot (an independent left-wing candidate).

The French Minister of Overseas Territories, Victorin Lurel, visited Martinique in September 2012 to hold discussions with the local authorities regarding the high cost of living on the island. A bill to address the problem of inflated prices (and consequent social unrest) in Martinique and other French Overseas Possessions, drafted by Lurel, was approved by the French Parliament in November. Most notably, the legislation provided for the imposition of price controls on a range of staple goods and the introduction of measures to encourage competition. In December 2013 the French Government extended the price controls to cover petrol purchases in the French Overseas Regions and Departments. However, on multiple occasions between mid-2013 and early 2014, owners of petrol stations in Martinique, French Guiana, Guadeloupe, Mayotte and Réunion, fearing that the move would disrupt their business model and undermine profit margins, closed their establishments in a co-ordinated act of protest. The closures ended in February 2014 after a compromise was agreed with the French authorities.

Recent developments: institutional reform

A further referendum on institutional reform was held on 24 January 2010, and 68.3% of participants voted in favour of changing the status of Martinique to a Collectivité Unique (Single Collectivity), replacing the existing two-tier departmental and regional administrative structure. Only 35.8% of the electorate took part in the plebiscite. The authorities hoped that the merger of the departmental and regional levels of government would increase efficiency and reduce operating costs. A joint committee to examine the institutional transition, comprising members of the Regional Council and the General Council, agreed in mid-2010 that the Collectivity would be officially designated the Collectivité de la Martinique. In mid-2011 the National Assembly approved legislation to facilitate this transition. Polls were scheduled for 2015 to elect the 51 members of a new, consolidated legislative body, which would replace the Regional Council and the General Council. In turn, the new assembly would then elect a nine-member executive council. These arrangements were endorsed by the Constitutional Council in April 2013.

Municipal polls took place on 23 and 30 March 2014, after which an election for the presidency of the General Council was scheduled to be held. Meanwhile, Martinique (along with Guadeloupe) was formally admitted to the Association of Caribbean States (see p. 449) as an associate member in April.

CONSTITUTION AND GOVERNMENT

France is represented in Martinique by an appointed Prefect. There are two councils with local powers: the 45-member Conseil Général (General Council) and the 41-member Conseil Régional (Regional Council). Both are elected by universal adult suffrage for a period of up to six years. Martinique elects four deputies to the National Assembly in Paris, and sends two indirectly elected representatives to the Senate. The Department is also represented at the European Parliament.

ECONOMIC AFFAIRS

In 2011, according to official estimates, Martinique's gross domestic product (GDP), measured at current prices, was estimated at €8,300.0m., equivalent to €21,131 per head. During 2000–10 GDP increased, in real terms, at an average rate of 4.0% per year; growth in 2010 was 4.6%. According to provisional figures, in 2002–11 the population increased at an average annual rate of 0.1%.

Agriculture, hunting, forestry and fishing contributed 2.4% of GDP in 2008, and according to provisional figures engaged an estimated 3.6% of the active labour force in 2012. The principal cash crops are bananas, sugar cane (primarily for the production of rum), limes, melons and pineapples. The cultivation of cut flowers is also of some significance. Roots and tubers and vegetables are grown for local consumption. Agricultural production increased at an average rate of 1.3% per year during 1990–98; the sector declined by 0.2% in 1999.

According to provisional figures, the industrial sector (including construction and public works) engaged 12.1% of the employed population in 2012 and contributed 14.1% of GDP in 2008. The most important manufacturing activities are petroleum refining (exports of fuels and combustibles accounted for 51.0% of the value of total exports in 2012) and the production of agricultural products (21.5% of exports in 2012), the production of rum being of particular significance. Other areas of activity include metals, cement, chemicals, plastics, wood, printing and textiles.

In 2012 construction engaged a preliminary 5.2% of the employed labour force and in 2008 the sector contributed 5.9% to GDP.

Energy is derived principally from mineral fuels. In 2012 imports of fuels and combustibles (including crude petroleum destined for the island's refinery) accounted for 13.5% of the value of total imports.

The services sector engaged a provisional 84.3% of the employed population in 2012 and provided 83.5% of GDP in 2008. Tourism is a major activity on the island and one of the most important sources of foreign exchange: in 2012 478,359 visitor arrivals were recorded while earnings from the tourism industry totalled an estimated €516m. in 2011; the vast majority of visitors were from metropolitan France (80.3% in 2009).

>In 2012 Martinique's merchandise trade deficit totalled €2,351.3m. In that year Martinique's export earnings were worth only approximately 14.7% of the total value of imports. Metropolitan France was the principal source of imports (54.9% in 2008); Guadeloupe was the principal market for exports (57.2%) in that year. French Guiana, member countries of the European Union (EU, see p. 273) and the USA were also significant trading partners. The principal exports in 2012 were fuels and combustibles, agricultural products and products of food industries. The principal imports in 2012 included natural hydrocarbons, mechanical, electrical and electronic equipment, food industry products, fuels and combustibles, transport equipment and pharmaceutical products.

In 2011 the regional budget showed a deficit of €17.7m., while in 2013 the departmental budget was balanced at €644.5m., according to preliminary figures. The annual rate of inflation averaged 1.5% in 2003–12; consumer prices increased by 1.4% in 2012. Some 21.3% of the labour force was unemployed in 2012.

Martinique's economic development has created a society that combines a relatively high standard of living with a weak economic base in agricultural and industrial production. The linking of wage levels to those of metropolitan France, despite the island's lower level of productivity, has increased labour costs and restricted development. Martinique's economy was badly affected by the global financial crisis of 2008–09, mainly owing to a dramatic decline in investment. Nevertheless, the economy recovered in 2010, with increasing internal demand and a resurgent tourism industry driving GDP growth of 4.6%. Exports also rose sharply during the year, although activity in the construction and agricultural sectors was subdued. Real GDP expanded by just 1.0% in 2011, owing to lower agricultural productivity, a decline in exports and a deceleration in domestic consumption. The cruise ship sector suffered a slowdown in that year, although the broader tourism industry continued to recover, while the inauguration of several large-scale construction projects ensured that investment levels remained steady. In spite of an increase in exports and cruise ship arrivals during 2012, the economy registered zero growth in that year as a result of lower domestic demand, a fall in stop-over tourists and a downturn in construction activity. Moreover, the unemployment rate (21.3% in 2012) was still very high, while sporadic outbreaks of industrial unrest were a further source of concern.

PUBLIC HOLIDAYS

2015: 1 January (New Year's Day), 16–17 February (Lenten Carnival), 18 February (Ash Wednesday), 3–6 April (Easter), 1 May (Labour Day), 8 May (Victory Day), 14 May (Ascension Day), 25 May (Whit Monday), 10 June (Abolition of Slavery), 14 July (National Day), 15 August (Assumption), 1 November (All Saints' Day), 11 November (Armistice Day), 25 December (Christmas Day).

Statistical Survey

Sources (unless otherwise indicated): Institut National de la Statistique et des Etudes Economiques (INSEE), Service Régional de Martinique, Centre Administratif Delgrès, blvd de la Pointe des Sables, Hauts de Dillon, BP 641, 97262 Fort-de-France Cédex; tel. 5-96-60-73-73; fax 5-96-60-73-50; e-mail antilles-guyane@insee.fr; internet www.insee.fr/fr/regions/martinique; Ministère des Départements et Territoires d'Outre-mer, 27 rue Oudinot, 75700 Paris 07 SP; tel. 1-53-69-20-00; fax 1-43-06-60-30; internet www.outre-mer.gouv.fr.

AREA AND POPULATION

Area: 1,100 sq km (424.7 sq miles).

Population: 381,427 at census of 8 March 1999; 392,291 at census of 1 January 2011. Note: According to new census methodology, data in 2011 refer to median figures based on the collection of raw data over a five-year period (2009–13). *Mid-2014* (UN estimate): 404,705 (Source: UN, *World Population Prospects: The 2012 Revision*).

Density (at mid-2014): 367.9 per sq km.

Population by Age and Sex (UN estimates at mid-2014): *0–14:* 73,529 (36,661 males, 36,868 females); *15–64:* 263,669 (120,459 males, 143,210 females); *65 and over:* 67,507 (28,975 males, 38,532 females); *Total:* 404,705 (186,095 males, 218,610 females).

Principal Towns (at 2010 census): Fort-de-France (capital) 87,216; Le Lamentin 39,360; Le Robert 23,918; Schoelcher 20,814.

Births, Marriages and Deaths (2011): Registered births 4,475 (birth rate 11.4 per 1,000); Registered marriages 1,095 (marriage rate 2.8 per 1,000); Registered deaths 2,741 (death rate 7.0 per 1000).

Life Expectancy (years at birth): 80.6 (males 77.3; females 83.7) in 2012. Source: Pan American Health Organization.

Employment (persons aged 15 years and over at 31 December 2012, provisional): Agriculture, hunting, forestry and fishing 4,492; Mining, quarrying and utilities 2,415; Manufacturing 6,205; Construction 6,447; Trade 14,419; Hotels and restaurants 5,021; Transportation and storage 5,633; Communication 2,087; Finance and insurance 3,650; Real estate activities 800; Professional services 12,678; Public administration, education, health and other social services 50,908; Other services 9,634; *Total* 124,389. Note: Figures for employment exclude 8,794 persons employed without salary.

HEALTH AND WELFARE

Key Indicators

Total Fertility Rate (children per woman, 2012): 1.8.

Under-5 Mortality Rate (per 1,000 live births, 2011): 8.5.

Physicians (per 1,000 head, 2010): 26.2.

Hospital Beds (per 1,000 head, 2009): 4.1.

Source: mainly Pan American Health Organization.

For definitions and other sources, see explanatory note on p. vi.

AGRICULTURE, ETC.

Principal Crops ('000 metric tons, 2012, FAO estimates): Yams 1.4; Sugar cane 325.0; Lettuce and chicory 7.8; Tomatoes 6.5; Cucumbers and gherkins 6.2; Bananas 260.0; Plantains 14.0; Pineapples 2.2. *Aggregate Production* ('000 metric tons, may include official, semi-official or estimated data): Total vegetables (incl. melons) 34.8; Total fruits (excl. melons) 277.9.

Livestock ('000 head, year ending September 2012, FAO estimates): Cattle 18; Sheep 12; Pigs 12; Goats 6.

Livestock Products ('000 metric tons, 2012, FAO estimates): Cattle meat 1.1; Pig meat 1.1; Chicken meat 1.3; Cows' milk 2.8; Hen eggs 2.7.

Forestry ('000 cubic metres, 2012, FAO estimates): *Roundwood Removals* (excl. bark): Sawlogs, veneer logs and logs for sleepers 2.4; Fuel wood 10.0; Total 12.4. *Sawnwood Production* (incl. railway sleepers): 1.0.

Fishing (metric tons, live weight, 2011, FAO estimates): Capture 5,000 (Clupeoids 3,300; Common dolphinfish 100; Other marine fishes 850; Caribbean spiny lobster 100; Clams, etc. 345); Aquaculture 92; *Total catch* 5,092.

Source: FAO.

MINING

Production ('000 metric tons, 2010, estimates): Cement 221; Pumice 130; Salt 200. Source: US Geological Survey.

INDUSTRY

Production ('000 metric tons, 2010 unless otherwise indicated): Motor spirit (petrol) 139 (estimate); Kerosene 116 (estimate); Gas-diesel (distillate fuel) oils 191 (2009); Residual fuel oils 371 (2009); Liquefied petroleum gas 19 (estimate); Electric energy (million kWh) 1,778 (estimate) (Source: UN Industrial Commodity Statistics Database). *2011:* Raw sugar 3,781 metric tons; Rum (hl) 83.0. *2012:* Raw sugar 2,920 metric tons; Rum (hl) 85.4. (Source: Institut d'Emission des Départements d'Outre-mer, *Martinique: Rapport Annuel 2012*).

FINANCE

Currency and Exchange Rates: The French franc was used until the end of 2001. Euro notes and coins were introduced on 1 January 2002, and the euro became the sole legal tender from 18 February. Some of the figures in this Survey are still in terms of francs. For details of exchange rates, see French Guiana.

Budget: *French Government* (million French francs, 1998): Revenue 4,757; Expenditure 8,309. *Regional Budget* (€ million, 2011): Current revenue 256.0 (Taxes 163.6, Grants 81.3; Other current revenue 11.1); Capital revenue 135.6; Total 391.6. Current expenditure 191.5 (Wages and salaries 44.1; Goods and services 18.5; Subsidies 106.8); Capital expenditure 217.8; Total 409.3. *Departmental Budget* (forecasts, million French francs, 2001): Tax revenue 836.9 (Departmental taxes 332.0, Fuel tax 295.0, Transfer taxes, etc. 58.0, Motor vehicle tax 68.0, Fiscal subsidy 53.0); Other current revenue 886.6 (Refunds of social assistance 65.0, Operational allowance 315.0, Decentralization allowance 477.0); Capital revenue 499.5 (EU development funds 71.0, Capital allowances 59.0, Other receipts 101.4, Borrowing 270.0); Total 2,223.0. Current expenditure 1,482.2 (Finance service 57.1, Permanent staff 394.7, General administration 65.1, Other indirect services 69.0, Administrative services 108.4, Public health 49.9, Social assistance 503.6, Support costs of minimum wage 99.8, Economic services 114.7); Capital expenditure 740.8 (Road system 139.5, Networks 47.9, Education and culture 111.5, Other departmental programmes 101.6, Other public bodies 83.7, Other programmes 96.3, Non-programme expenditure 162.3); Total 2,223.0. *2013* (€ million, excl. debt rescheduling, preliminary): Total revenue 644.5 (Current revenue 593.0, Capital revenue 51.4); Total expenditure 644.5 (Current expenditure 555.3, Capital expenditure 89.1) (Sources: partly Département des Etudes et des Statistiques Locales, Institut d'Emission des Départements d'Outre-mer, *Martinique: Rapport Annuel 2012*).

Money Supply (million French francs at 31 December 1998): Currency outside banks 924; Demand deposits at banks 6,330; Total money 7,254.

Cost of Living (Consumer Price Index; base: 2000 = 100): All items 121.4 in 2010; 124.5 in 2011; 126.3 in 2012. Source: ILO.

Gross Domestic Product (€ million at current prices, estimates): 7,702 in 2009; 8,128 in 2010 (estimate); 8,271 in 2011 (estimate). Source: Institut d'Emission des Départements d'Outre-mer, *Martinique: Rapport Annuel 2012*.

Expenditure on the Gross Domestic Product (€ million at current prices, 2011, estimates): Total final consumption expenditure 8,867 (General government and non-profit institutions serving households 3,600, Households 5,267); Changes in stocks 12; Gross fixed capital formation 1,616; *Total domestic expenditure* 10,495; Exports of goods and services 701; *Less* Imports of goods and services 2,925; *GDP in purchasers' values* 8,271. Source: Institut d'Emission des Départements d'Outre-mer, *Martinique: Rapport Annuel 2012*.

Gross Domestic Product by Economic Activity (€ million at current prices, 2006): Agriculture 160; Food industries 122; Other manufacturing 282; Energy 164; Construction 453; Services 6,088 (Restaurants and hotels 232, Transport 222, Commerce 852, Other market services 2,387, Non-market services 2,395); *Sub-total* 7,269; *Less* Financial intermediation services indirectly measured 298; Taxes, less subsidies 667; *GDP in purchasers' values* 7,638.

EXTERNAL TRADE

Principal Commodities (€ million, 2012): *Imports c.i.f.:* Agriculture, forestry and fishing 48.7; Natural hydrocarbons, etc. 480.4; Products of food industries 390.2; Textiles, clothing, leather and footwear 103.9; Petroleum products 371.6; Chemicals 119.7; Pharmaceutical products 140.5; Rubber, plastic and mineral products 136.4; Metal and metal products 122.2; Mechanical, electronics and electrical equipment 392.1; Transport equipment 248.4; Miscellaneous manufactured products 103.8; Total (incl. others) 2,755.2. *Exports f.o.b.:* Agriculture, forestry and fishing 86.8; Products of food industries 50.1; Petroleum products 206.2; Metal and metal products 10.8; Mechanical, electronics and electrical equipment 9.4; Transport equipment 13.3; Total (incl. others) 403.9. (Source: Institut d'Emission des Départements d'Outre-mer, *Martinique: Rapport Annuel 2012*).

Principal Trading Partners (€ million, 2008): *Imports c.i.f.:* Aruba 78; France (metropolitan) 1,519; Germany 72; Guadeloupe 44; Italy 45; Japan 36; Netherlands 54; Spain 26; United Kingdom 326; USA 199; Total (incl. others) 2,766. *Exports f.o.b.:* Antigua 4; France (metropolitan) 90; French Guiana 38; Guadeloupe 210; Netherlands Antilles 3; USA 9; Total (incl. others) 367. *2011* (€ million): Total imports 2,709.4; Total exports 308.3. (Source: Institut d'Emission des Départements d'Outre-mer, *Martinique: Rapport Annuel 2011*). *2012* (€ million): Total imports 2,755.2; Total exports 403.9. (Source: Institut d'Emission des Départements d'Outre-mer, *Martinique: Rapport Annuel 2012*).

TRANSPORT

Road Traffic ('000 motor vehicles in use, 1995): Passenger cars 95.0; Commercial vehicles 21.5 (Source: UN, *Statistical Yearbook*). *1 January 2010* ('000 motor vehicles in use): Buses 1.2; Vans and tractors 34.3.

Shipping: *Flag Registered Fleet* (at 31 December, 2013): Vessels 3; Total displacement 510 grt (Source: Lloyd's List Intelligence—www.lloydslistintelligence.com). *International Sea-borne Traffic* (2006, provisional figures): Goods loaded 950,000 metric tons (petroleum products 359,000 metric tons); Goods unloaded 2,302,000 metric tons (petroleum products 1,109,000 metric tons).

Civil Aviation (2012 unless otherwise indicated): Freight (incl. 2,667 metric tons of post) carried 13,914 metric tons (2009); Passengers carried 1,565,981. Source: partly Institut d'Emission des Départements d'Outre-mer, *Martinique: Rapport Annuel 2012*.

TOURISM

Tourist Arrivals by Country (excl. same-day visitors and cruise ship arrivals, 2003): France (metropolitan) 357,726; Guadeloupe 40,668; French Guiana 10,619; Total (incl. others) 453,159. *2009* (excl. same-day visitors and cruise ship arrivals): Total 441,648 (France 354,846; French Guiana 7,141; Guadeloupe 38,094; USA 6,290). *Total Arrivals* (excl. same-day visitors and cruise ship arrivals): 478,060 in 2010; 498,578 in 2011; 478,359 in 2012 (Source: partly Institut d'Emission des Départements d'Outre-mer, *Martinique: Rapport Annuel 2012*).

Receipts from Tourism (€ million, excl. passenger transport): 420 in 2009; 472 in 2010; 516 in 2011. Source: World Tourism Organization.

COMMUNICATIONS MEDIA

Telephones ('000 main lines in use): 172.0 in 2010.

Mobile Cellular Telephones ('000 subscribers): 295.4 in 2004.

Personal Computers: 82,000 in 2004.

Internet Users ('000): 170.0 in 2009.

Broadband Subscribers: 6,000 in 2010.

Source: International Telecommunication Union.

EDUCATION

Pre-primary (2012/13): 15,798 students (14,751 state, 1,047 private).

Primary (2012/13): 26,107 students (23,779 state, 2,328 private).

Specialized Pre-primary and Primary (2012/13): 334 students (334 state).

Secondary (2012/13): 39,362 students (35,483 state, 3,879 private).

Higher (2011/12): 7,941 students.

Teachers (2004/05): *Primary:* 3,031 (2,787 state, 244 private); *Secondary:* 4,553 (4,177 state, 376 private); *Higher:* 186. Source: Ministère de l'Education Nationale, *Repères et références statistiques—édition 2005. 2011/12* (state schools): 2,695 in primary; 3,696 in secondary; 202 in higher.

Institutions (2003/04): 258 primary schools; 41 lower secondary schools; 22 state upper secondary schools; 24 private institutions. Source: Préfecture de Martinique, *Livret d'accueil des services de l'Etat en Martinique. 2012/13:* 72 pre-primary schools; 180 elementary and special schools; 80 secondary schools.

Adult Literacy Rate: 98.0% (males 97.6%, females 98.3%) in 2005. Source: Pan American Health Organization.

Directory

The Government

(April 2014)

HEAD OF STATE

President: FRANÇOIS HOLLANDE.

Prefect: LAURENT PRÉVOST, Préfecture, 82 rue Victor Sévère, BP 647–648, 97262 Fort-de-France Cédex; tel. 5-96-39-36-00; fax 5-96-71-40-29; e-mail contact.prefecture@martinique.pref.gouv.fr; internet www.martinique.pref.gouv.fr.

DEPARTMENTAL ADMINISTRATION

President of the General Council: JOSETTE MANIN (PPM), Conseil général de la Martinique, blvd Chevalier Sainte-Marthe, 97200 Fort-de-France Cédex; tel. 5-96-55-26-00; fax 5-96-73-59-32; internet www.cg972.fr.

President of the Economic, Social and Environmental Regional Committee: MICHEL CRISPIN, Hôtel de la Région, ave Gaston Deferre, Plateau Roy Cluny, BP 601, 97200 Fort-de-France; tel. 5-96-59-63-00; fax 5-96-59-64-31; e-mail cesr-s@region-martinique.com; internet www.cr-martinique.fr.

President of the Culture, Education and Environment Committee: GÉRARD LACOM, Hôtel de la Région, ave Gaston Deferre, Plateau Roy Cluny, BP 601, 97200 Fort-de-France; tel. 5-96-59-64-43; fax 5-96-59-63-21; e-mail ccee@cr-martinique.fr; internet www.cr-martinique.fr.

President of the Regional Council: SERGE LETCHIMY, Hôtel de la Région, ave Gaston Deferre, BP 601, 97200 Fort-de-France Cédex; tel. 5-96-59-63-00; fax 5-96-72-68-10; e-mail service.communication@cr-martinique.fr; internet www.cr-martinique.fr.

Elections, 14 and 21 March 2010

	Seats
Parti Progressiste Martiniquais (PPM)	26
Mouvement Indépendantiste Martiniquais (MIM)	12
Rassembler la Martinique*	3
Total	41

* Electoral list comprising the Union pour un Mouvement Populaire (UMP) and allies.

REPRESENTATIVES TO THE FRENCH PARLIAMENT

Deputies to the French National Assembly: ALFRED MARIE-JEANNE (Gauche, Démocrate et Républicaine), SERGE LETCHIMY (Socialiste, Républicain et Ritoyen), BRUNO NESTOR AZEROT (Gauche, Démocrate et Républicaine), JEAN-PHILIPPE NILOR (Gauche, Démocrate et Républicaine).

Representatives to the French Senate: SERGE LARCHER (Groupe Socialiste), MAURICE ANTISTE (Groupe Socialiste).

Political Organizations

Bâtir le Pays Martinique: Fort-de-France; f. 1998; left-wing; split from the Parti Communiste Martiniquais; Leader PIERRE-JEAN SAMOT; Nat. Sec. DAVID ZOBDA.

Combat Ouvrier: BP 821, 97258 Fort-de-France Cédex; e-mail l.maugee972@orange.fr; internet www.combat-ouvrier.net; Trotskyist; mem. of the Communist Internationalist Union; Leader GHISLAINE JOACHIM-ARNAUD.

Conseil National des Comités Populaires (CNCP): 8 rue Pierre et Marie Curie, Terres Sainville, 97200 Fort-de-France; tel. 5-96-63-75-23; e-mail cncp@netcaraibes.com; internet www.m-apal.com; f. 1983; pro-independence party affiliated to the Union Général des Travailleurs de Martinique; contested the 2004 regional elections in alliance with the MIM; Pres. JOSETTE MASSOLIN; Spokesperson ROBERT SAÉ.

Fédération Socialiste de la Martinique (FSM): 52 rue du Capitaine Pierre-Rose, 97200 Fort-de-France; tel. 5-96-60-14-88; fax 5-96-63-81-06; e-mail federation.socialiste-martinique@wanadoo.fr; internet martinique.parti-socialiste.fr; local br. of the Parti Socialiste (PS); Fed. Sec. LOUIS JOSEPH MANSCOUR; Spokesperson FRÉDÉRIC BUVAL.

Forces Martiniquaises de Progrès (FMP): 12 rue Ernest Deproge, 97200 Fort-de-France; tel. 5-96-57-74-10; fax 5-96-63-36-19; e-mail miguel.laventure@fmp-regionales.org; internet www.jrdmedias.com/laventure/index.html; f. 1998 to replace the local br. of the Union pour la Démocratie Française; Pres. MIGUEL LAVENTURE.

Mouvement des Démocrates et Écologistes pour une Martinique Souveraine (MODEMAS): Fort-de-France; f. 1992; left-wing, pro-independence; Pres. GARCIN MALSA.

Mouvement Indépendantiste Martiniquais (MIM): Fort-de-France; internet www.mim-matinik.org; f. 1978; pro-independence party; First Sec. ALFRED MARIE-JEANNE.

Mouvement Populaire Franciscain: angle des rues Couturier et Holo, 97240 Le François; tel. 5-96-54-20-40; e-mail direction@pont-abel.fr; left-wing; Leader MAURICE ANTISTE.

Osons Oser: Fort-de-France; f. 1998; right-wing; affiliated with the metropolitan Union pour un Mouvement Populaire (UMP); Pres. PIERRE PETIT; Vice-Pres. JENNY DULYS-PETIT.

Parti Communiste Martiniquais (PCM): angle des rues A. Aliker et E. Zola, Terres-Sainville, 97200 Fort-de-France; tel. 5-96-71-86-83; fax 5-96-63-13-20; e-mail ed.justice@wanadoo.fr; internet journal-justice-martinique.com; f. 1957; Sec.-Gen. GEORGES ERICHOT.

Parti Progressiste Martiniquais (PPM): Ancien Réservoir de Trénelle, 97200 Fort-de-France; tel. 5-96-71-88-01; fax 5-96-72-68-56; e-mail contact@ppm-martinique.fr; internet www.ppm-martinique.fr; f. 1958; left-wing; Leader SERGE LETCHIMY; Sec.-Gen. DIDIER LAGUERRE.

Parti Régionaliste Martiniquais: Fort-de-France; f. 2010 by fmr mems of UMP (q.v.); right-wing; Pres. CHANTAL MAIGNAN; Sec.-Gen. CHRISTIAN RAPHA.

Rassemblement Démocratique pour la Martinique (RDM): Résidence Pichevin 2, Bâtiment Hildevert, Les Hauts du Port, 97200 Fort-de-France; tel. 5-96-71-89-97; internet rfdm.e-monsite.com; f. 2006; Sec.-Gen. CLAUDE LISE.

Union pour un Mouvement Populaire (UMP): angle des rues de la République et Vincent Allègre, 97212 Saint Joseph; tel. 5-96-57-96-68; fax 5-96-57-32-68; internet www.u-m-p.org; centre-right; local br. of the metropolitan party; Pres., Departmental Cttee MARC SEFIL.

Les Verts Martinique: Lotissement Donatien, 54 rue Madinina, Cluny, 97200 Fort-de-France; tel. and fax 5-96-71-58-21; e-mail louisleonce@wanadoo.fr; ecologist; departmental br. of the metropolitan party; Leader LOUIS-LÉONCE LECURIEUX-LAFFERONNAY.

Judicial System

Court of Appeal: ave St John Perse, Morne Tartenson, BP 634, 97262 Fort-de-France Cédex; tel. 5-96-70-62-62; fax 5-96-63-52-13; e-mail ca-fort-de-france@justice.fr; highest court of appeal for Martinique and French Guiana; First Pres. BRUNO STEINMANN; Procurator-Gen. JEAN JACQUES BOSC.

There are two Tribunaux de Grande Instance, at Fort-de-France and Cayenne (French Guiana), and three Tribunaux d'Instance (two in Fort-de-France and one in Cayenne).

Religion

The majority of the population belong to the Roman Catholic Church.

CHRISTIANITY

The Roman Catholic Church

Some 80% of the population are Roman Catholics. Martinique comprises the single archdiocese of Fort-de-France. The Archbishop participates in the Antilles Episcopal Conference, based in Port of Spain, Trinidad and Tobago.

Archbishop of Fort-de-France and Saint-Pierre: Most Rev. GILBERT MARIE MICHEL MÉRANVILLE, Archevêché, 5–7 rue du Révérend Père Pinchon, BP 586, 97207 Fort-de-France Cédex; tel. 5-96-63-70-70; fax 5-96-63-75-21; e-mail archeveche-martinique@wanadoo.fr; internet martinique.catholique.fr.

Other Churches

Among the denominations active in Martinique are the Assembly of God, the Evangelical Church of the Nazarene and the Seventh-day Adventist Church.

The Press

Antilla: Le Lamentin, BP 46, 97281 Fort-de-France, Cédex 1; tel. 5-96-75-48-68; fax 5-96-75-58-46; e-mail antilla@orange.fr; internet www.antilla-blog.com; f. 1981; weekly; politics and economics; Publ. Dir ALFRED FORTUNE; Editor-in-Chief TONY DELSHAM.

France Antilles: pl. François Mitterrand, 97207 Fort-de-France; tel. 5-96-59-08-83; fax 5-96-60-29-96; e-mail redaction.fa@media-antilles.fr; internet www.martinique.franceantilles.fr; f. 1964; subsidiary of Groupe France Antilles; daily; Editor PAUL-HENRI COSTE; circ. 30,000 (Martinique edn).

Journal Asé Pléré Annou Lité (Journal APAL): 8 rue Pierre et Marie Curie, Terres Sainville, 97200 Fort-de-France; tel. 5-96-63-75-23; fax 5-96-70-30-82; e-mail journ.apal@orange.fr; internet www.m-apal.com; f. 1983; monthly; organ of the Conseil Nat. des Comités Populaires (q.v.) and the Union Général des Travailleurs de Martinique (q.v.); Dir ROBERT SAÉ.

Journal Combat Ouvriére: 1111 Rés Matéliane, L'Aiguille, 97128 Goyave; e-mail l.maugee972@orange.fr; internet www.combat-ouvrier.net; f. 1970; fortnightly; communist; Publ. Dir PHILIPPE ANAIS; circ. 14,000.

Justice: angle rue André Aliker et E. Zola, 97200 Fort-de-France; tel. 5-96-71-86-83; fax 5-96-63-13-20; e-mail ed.justice@wanadoo.fr; internet journal-justice-martinique.com; f. 1920; weekly; organ of the Parti Communiste Martinique (q.v.); Dir FERNAND PAPAYA; circ. 8,000.

Le NAIF-Magazine: Résidence K, Pointe des Nègres, route Phare, 97200 Fort-de-France; tel. 5-96-61-62-55; fax 5-96-61-85-76; e-mail docedouard@yahoo.fr; internet www.lenaif.net; weekly; publ. by CIC; Owner CAMILLE CHAUVET.

Le Progressiste: c/o Parti Progressiste Martiniquais, Ancien Réservoir de Trénelle, 97200 Fort-de-France; tel. 5-96-71-88-01; e-mail d.compere@ool.fr; internet www.ppm-martinique.fr; weekly; organ of the PPM; Publ. Dir DANIEL COMPERE; circ. 13,000.

TV Magazine: pl. François Mitterand, 97232 Lamentin; tel. 5-96-42-51-28; fax 5-96-42-98-94; e-mail tv.mag@media-antilles.fr; f. 1989; weekly; Editor-in-Chief LUCIENNE CHÉNARD.

Publishers

Editions Exbrayat: 5 rue des Oisillons, route de Balata, 97234 Fort-de-France; tel. 5-96-64-60-58; fax 5-96-64-70-42; e-mail editions.exbrayat@exbrayat.com; internet commerce.ciel.com/exbrayat; regional art, history, natural history, culinaria, maps and general fiction; 2 brs in Guadeloupe; Commercial Dir PAQUITA EXBRAYAT-SANCHEZ; Sec. HERMINIE MARIE-CLAIRE.

Editions Lafontaine: Bâtiment 12, Maniba, 97222 Case Pilote; tel. and fax 5-96-78-87-98; e-mail info@editions-lafontaine.com; internet www.editions-lafontaine.com; f. 1994; Creole, French and English literature, general fiction, culture, history, youth and educational; Dir JEANNINE 'JALA' LAFONTAINE.

Broadcasting and Communications

TELECOMMUNICATIONS

Digicel Antilles Françaises Guyane: Oasis, Quartier Bois Rouge, 97224 Ducos; tel. 8-10-63-56-35; fax 5-96-42-09-01; e-mail contact@digicelgroup.fr; internet www.digicel.fr; f. 2000 as Bouygues Telecom Caraïbe; acquired from Bouygues Telecom, France, in 2006; mobile cellular telephone operator; network coverage incl. Guadeloupe and French Guiana; CEO (French Caribbean) YANN KEREBEL; Dir-Gen. (Martinique) SÉBASTIEN AUBÉ.

Orange Caraïbe: see Guadeloupe—Telecommunications.

Outremer Telecom: Z. I. la Jambette, BP 280, 97285 Lamentin Cédex 2; e-mail communication@outremer-telecom.fr; internet www.outremer-telecom.fr; f. 1998; mobile telecommunications provider; CEO JEAN-MICHEL HEGESIPPE.

ONLY: Z. I. la Jambette, BP 280, 97285 Lamentin Cédex 2; e-mail communication@outremer-telecom.fr; internet www.outremer-telecom.fr; f. 1998 as Outremer Telecom Martinique; present name adopted following merger of Volubis, ONLY and OOL in 2006; telecommunications provider; subsidiary of Outremer Telecom, France; Head of Operations (French West Indies and French Guiana) FRÉDÉRIC HAYOT.

BROADCASTING

Atlantic FM Martinique: Lorrain; tel. 5-96-71-33-38; e-mail radio.atlanticfm@yahoo.fr; internet www.atlanticfm.fr.

Martinique 1ère (Outre-mer Première): La Clairière, BP 662, 97263 Fort-de-France; tel. 5-96-59-52-00; fax 5-96-59-52-26; internet martinique.la1ere.fr; acquired by Groupe France Télévisions in 2004; fmrly Société Nationale de Radio-Télévision Française d'Outre-mer; name changed to Réseau France Outre-mer (RFO) in 1998; present name adopted in 2010; Dir-Gen. GENEVIÈVE GIARD; Regional Dir STÉPHANIE GAUMONT.

Radio

Radio Asé Pléré Annou Lité (Radio APAL) (Radio Pèp-la): 8 rue Pierre et Marie Curie, Terres Sainville, 97200 Fort-de-France; tel. 5-96-63-75-23; fax 5-96-70-30-82; e-mail radio.apal@orange.fr; internet www.m-apal.com; f. 1989; affiliated to the Conseil Nat. des Comités Populaires (q.v.) and the Union Général des Travailleurs de Martinique (q.v.); French and Creole; Dir MICHEL NE'DAN; Station Man. JEAN-CLAUDE LOUIS-SYDNEY.

Radio Banlieue Relax (RBR): 107 ave Léona Gabriel, Cité Dillon, 97200 Fort-de-France; tel. 5-96-60-00-90; fax 5-96-73-06-53; e-mail radio.br@orange.fr; internet www.rbrfm.com; f. 1981; regional social and cultural programmes; Pres. FRANTZ CLÉORON; Dir JOCELYN HERTÉ.

Radio Canal Antilles (RCA): plateau Fofo, 97233 Schoelcher; tel. 5-96-61-74-19; fax 5-96-61-23-58; internet membres.multimania.fr/canalantilles; f. 1980; fmrly Radio 105; regional social and cultural programmes; Radio France Internationale relay; Pres. SERGE POGNON.

Radio Caraïbes International (RCI Martinique): 2 blvd de la Marne, 97200 Fort-de-France Cédex; tel. 5-96-63-98-70; fax 5-96-63-26-59; internet www.rcimartinique.fm; commercial radio station; Dir JOSÉ ANELKA; Station Man. VINCENT CHRÉTIEN; Editor-in-Chief JEAN-PHILIPPE LUDON.

Radio Evangile Martinique (REM): 54 Route des Religieuses, 97200 Fort-de-France; tel. 5-96-70-68-48; fax 5-96-70-17-51; e-mail rem@evgi.net; internet rem.evgi.net; f. 1993; Pres. RAYMOND SORMAIN; Dir LUCIEN COIQUE.

Radio Fréquence Atlantique (RFA): 10 rue du Docteur Laveran, 97232 Le Lamentin; tel. 5-96-42-35-51; fax 5-96-51-04-26; e-mail r.f.a@wanadoo.fr; internet www.radiorfa.fr; operated by Société Martiniquaise de Communication; Dir JOSEPH LEVI.

Other radio stations include: Chérie FM (formerly Campêche FM); Difé Radio; Fun Radio (formerly Maxxi FM); Radio 22; Radio Actif Martinique; Radio Alizés; Radio Archipel; Radio Espérance; Radio Espoir; Radio Inter Tropicale; Radio Solidarité Rurale—La Voix des Mornes; and West Indies Radio.

Television

Antilles Télévision (ATV): 28 ave des Arawacks, Chateauboeuf, 97200 Fort-de-France; tel. 5-96-75-44-44; fax 5-96-75-55-65; e-mail contact@atvweb.fr; internet www.antillestelevision.com; f. 1993; general interest; accounts for 22% of viewers; also broadcasts to French Guiana and Guadeloupe; Chair. FABRICE JEAN-JEAN; Dir-Gen. DANIEL ROBIN; Editor-in-Chief KARL SIVATTE.

Canal Plus Antilles: see Guadeloupe—Television.

Kanal Martinique Télévision (KMT) (Kanal Matinik Télévision): voie 7, Renéville, 97200 Fort-de-France; tel. 5-96-63-64-85; e-mail webmaster@kmttelevision.com; internet kmttelevision.com; f. 2004; operated by l'Asscn pour le Développement des Techniques Modernes de Communication; Pres. ROLAND LAOUCHEZ.

Finance

(cap. = capital; res = reserves; dep. = deposits; m. = million; brs = branches; amounts in euros)

BANKING

Central Bank

Institut d'Emission des Départements d'Outre-mer (IEDOM): 1 blvd du Général de Gaulle, BP 512, 97206 Fort-de-France Cédex; tel. 5-96-59-44-00; fax 5-96-59-44-04; e-mail agence@iedom-martinique.fr; internet www.iedom.fr; Dir VICTOR-ROBERT NUGENT.

Commercial Banks

Banque des Antilles Françaises: see Guadeloupe—Finance.

BNP Paribas Martinique: 72 ave des Caraïbes, BP 588, 97200 Fort-de-France; tel. 5-96-59-46-00; fax 5-96-63-71-42; e-mail bnpm@bnp.mq; internet martinique.bnpparibas.net; f. 1941; subsidiary of BNP Paribas, France; 12 brs; Gen. Man. ALAIN THOLLIEZ.

BRED Banque Populaire: Z. I. la Jambette, 97232 Le Lamentin; tel. 5-96-63-77-63; e-mail courrier-direct@bred.fr; internet www.bred.banquepopulaire.fr; cap. 242m. (Oct. 2005); Regional Man. BRUNO DUVAL; brs in Martinique and French Guiana.

Crédit Agricole: rue Case Nègre, pl. d'Armes, BP 370, 97232 Le Lamentin Cédex 2; tel. 8-20-39-93-10; fax 5-96-51-37-12; internet www.ca-martinique.fr; f. 1950; total assets 1,263m. (Dec. 2004); Pres. XAVIER DELIN; Gen. Man. JEAN-MARIE CARLI; 30 brs in Martinique and French Guiana.

Société Générale de Banque aux Antilles (SGBA): see Guadeloupe—Finance.

INSURANCE

AGF Allianz Vie France: ZAC de l'Etang Z'Abricots, Bâtiment C, 97200 Fort-de-France; tel. 5-96-50-55-61; fax 5-96-50-55-71; e-mail marvie1@agfmar.com; internet www.allianz.fr; life insurance; subsidiary of Allianz Group.

Assurance Outre-mer: Hauts Dillon Delgres, Fort-de-France; tel. 5-96-73-09-70; fax 5-96-70-09-25; e-mail contact@assurance-outremer.fr; internet www.assurance-outremer.com; Dir-Gen. THIERRY COAT.

DPA Assurance: 126 route des Religieuses 97200 Fort de France; tel. 5-96-63-84-49; fax 5-96-63-09-52; e-mail dp.a@wanadoo.fr; internet www.dpa-assurances.com.

Groupama Antilles Guyane: 10 Lotissement Bardinet Dillon, BP 559, 97242 Fort-de-France Cédex; tel. 5-96-75-33-33; fax 5-96-75-06-78; internet www.groupama.fr; f. 1978; Group CEO THIERRY MARTEL; Dir-Gen. DIDIER COURIER; 6 brs in Martinique, 7 brs in Guadeloupe, 3 brs in French Guiana.

Groupement Français d'Assurances Caraïbes (GFA Caraïbes): 46–48 rue Ernest Desproges, 97205 Fort-de-France; tel. 5-96-59-04-04; fax 5-96-72-49-94; e-mail contact@gfa-caraibes.fr; internet www.gfacaraibes.fr; subsidiary of Gruppo Generali, Italy; Chair. JEAN-CLAUDE WULLENS; Man. Dir STÉPHANE COUDOUR.

Trade and Industry

GOVERNMENT AGENCIES

Direction Régionale du Commerce Extérieur Antilles-Guyane (DRCE): Bureaux 406 et 408, BP 647, 97262 Fort-de-France Cédex; tel. 5-96-39-49-90; fax 5-96-60-08-14; e-mail drceantilles@missioneco.org; internet www.tresor.economie.gouv.fr/region/antilles-guyane; Regional Dir MICHEL ROUSSELLIER; Regional Asst (Martinique) XAVIER BUCHOUX.

Direction Régionale de l'Industrie, de la Recherche et de l'Environnement (DRIRE): see French Guiana—Trade and Industry.

Direction de la Santé et du Développement Social (DSDS): Centre d'Affaires AGORA, l'Etang Z'abricots, Pointe des Grives, BP 658, 97263 Fort-de-France Cédex; tel. 5-96-39-42-43; fax 5-96-60-60-12; e-mail josiane.pinville@sante.gouv.fr; internet www.martinique.sante.gouv.fr; Dir CHRISTIAN URSULET.

DEVELOPMENT ORGANIZATIONS

Agence Française de Développement (AFD): 1 blvd du Général de Gaulle, BP 804, 97244 Fort-de-France Cédex; tel. 5-96-59-44-73; fax 5-96-59-44-88; e-mail afdfortdefrance@groupe-afd.org; internet www.afd.fr; fmrly Caisse Française de Développement; Man. ERIC BORDES.

Secrétariat Général pour les Affaires Régionales (SGAR)—Bureau de la Coopération Régionale: Préfecture, 97262 Fort-de-France; tel. 5-96-39-49-78; fax 5-96-39-49-59; e-mail jean-charles.barrus@martinique.pref.gouv.fr; successor to the Direction de l'Action Economique Régionale (DAER); research, documentation, and technical and administrative advice on investment in industry and commerce; Chief JEAN-CHARLES BARRUS.

CHAMBERS OF COMMERCE

Chambre d'Agriculture: pl. d'Armes, BP 312, 97286 Le Lamentin Cédex 2; tel. 5-96-51-75-75; fax 5-96-51-93-42; e-mail ca972@martinique.chambagri.fr; internet www.martinique.chambagri.fr; Pres. LOUIS-DANIEL BERTOME; Dir NICAISE MONROSE.

Chambre de Commerce et d'Industrie de la Martinique: 50 rue Ernest Desproge, BP 478, 97200 Fort-de-France Cédex; tel. 5-96-55-28-00; fax 5-96-60-66-68; e-mail dic@martinique.cci.fr; internet www.martinique.cci.fr; f. 1907; Pres. MANUEL BAUDOUIN; Dir-Gen. FRANTZ SABIN.

Chambre des Métiers et de l'Artesanat de la Martinique: 2 rue du Temple, Morne Tartenson, BP 1194, 97200 Fort-de-France; tel. 5-96-71-32-22; fax 5-96-70-47-30; e-mail cmm972@wanadoo.fr; internet www.cma-martinique.com; f. 1970; Pres. HERVÉ LAUREOTE; Sec.-Gen. HERVÉ ETILÉ; 8,000 mems.

INDUSTRIAL ORGANIZATION

Association Martiniquaise pour la Promotion de l'Industrie (AMPI): Centre d'Affaires de la Martinique, Bâtiment Pierre, 1er étage, Californie, BP 1042, 97232 Le Lamentin; tel. 5-96-50-74-00; fax 5-96-50-74-37; e-mail industrie@ampi.mq; internet www.industriemartinique.com; f. 1972 as Asscn des Moyennes et Petites Industries; 119 mem. cos; Pres. PIERRE MARIE-JOSEPH; Sec.-Gen. RICHARD CRESTOR.

EMPLOYERS' ORGANIZATIONS

Banalliance: Centre d'Affaires le Baobab, rue Léon Gontran Damas, 97232 Le Lamentin; tel. 5-96-57-42-42; fax 5-96-57-35-18; f. 1996; banana growers' alliance; Pres. DANIEL DISER; Dir-Gen. SANDRA ALEXIA; 220 mems.

Banamart: Quartier Bois Rouge, 97224 Ducos; tel. 5-96-42-43-44; fax 5-96-51-47-70; internet www.banamart.com; f. 2005 by merger of SICABAM and GIPAM; represents banana producers; Pres. NICOLAS MARRAUD DES GROTTES; Dir-Gen. PIERRE MONTEUX.

IMALFLHOR (Interprofession Martiniquaise des Fruits, Legumes et Produits Horticoles): Immeuble La Chapelle, Route du stade, Place d'Armes; tel. 5-96-59-70-56; fax 5-96-51-06-63; e-mail contact.imaflhor@gmail.com; internet sites.google.com/site/imaflhor/home; f. 2010; supports and develops agricultural production; Chair. FRANÇOIS DE MEILLAC.

Ordre des Médecins de la Martinique: 80 rue de la République, 97200 Fort-de-France; tel. 5-96-63-27-01; fax 5-96-60-58-00; e-mail martinique@972.medecin.fr; Pres. HELENON RAYMOND; Sec.-Gen. ELANA EMILE.

Ordre des Pharmaciens de la Martinique: Apt G-01, Immeuble Gaëlle, Résidence Studiotel-Grand Village, BP 587, 97233 Schoelcher; tel. 5-96-52-23-67; fax 5-96-52-20-92; e-mail delegation_martinique@ordre.pharmacien.fr; internet www.ordre.pharmacien.fr; Pres. JEAN BIGON.

UTILITIES

Electricity

EDF Martinique (Electricité de France Martinique): Pointe des Carrières, BP 573, 97242 Fort-de-France Cédex 01; tel. 5-96-59-20-00; fax 5-96-60-29-76; e-mail edf-services-martinique@edfgdf.fr; internet www.edf.fr/martinique; f. 1975; electricity supplier; successor to Société de Production et de Distribution d'Electricité de la Martinique (SPDEM); Chair. and CEO HENRI PROGLIO; 174,753 customers (2006).

Water

Veolia Water-Société Martiniquaise des Eaux (SME): pl. d'Armes, BP 213, 97284 Le Lamentin Cédex 02; tel. 5-96-51-80-51; fax 5-96-51-80-55; e-mail sme@sme.mq; internet www.smeaux.fr; f. 1977 as Société Martiniquaise des Eaux; Dir-Gen. JEAN-PIERRE PIERRE.

TRADE UNIONS

Confédération Générale du Travail de la Martinique (CGTM): Maison des Syndicats, blvd Général de Gaulle, 97200 Fort-de-France; tel. 5-96-70-25-89; fax 5-96-63-80-10; e-mail contact@

cgt-martinique.fr; internet www.cgt-martinique.fr; f. 1961; affiliated to World Fed. of Trade Unions; Sec.-Gen. GHISLAINE JOACHIM-ARNAUD.

Fédération Syndicale Unitaire Martinique (FSU): route des Religieuses, Bâtiment B, Cité Bon Air, 97200 Fort-de-France; tel. 5-96-63-63-27; fax 5-96-71-89-43; e-mail fsu@fsu-martinique.fr; internet www.fsu-martinique.fr; f. 1993; departmental br. of the Fédération Syndicale Unitaire; represents public sector employees in teaching, research and training, and also agriculture, justice, youth and sports, and culture; Sec.-Gen. BERNADETTE GROISON.

Union Générale des Travailleurs de Martinique (UGTM): 8 rue Pierre et Marie Curie, Terres Sainville, 97200 Fort-de-France; tel. 5-96-63-75-23; fax 5-96-70-30-82; e-mail ugtm.centrale@wanadoo.fr; f. 1999; Pres. LÉON BERTIDE; Sec.-Gen. PATRICK DORÉ.

UNSA Education Martinique (UE): Maison des Syndicats, Salles 4–5, Jardin Desclieux, 97200 Fort-de-France; tel. 5-96-72-64-74; fax 5-96-70-16-80; e-mail unsa-education972@orange.fr; internet www.unsa-education.org; 22-mem. fed; Sec.-Gen. MIREILLE JACQUES.

Transport

RAILWAYS

There are no railways in Martinique.

ROADS

There were 2,077 km (1,291 miles) of roads in 1998, of which 261 km were motorways and first-class roads.

SHIPPING

CMA-CGM CGM Antilles-Guyane: ZIP de la Pointe des Grives, BP 574, 97242 Fort-de-France Cédex; tel. 5-96-55-32-00; fax 5-96-63-08-87; e-mail fdf.jgourdin@cma-cgm.com; internet www.cma-cgm.com; subsidiary of CMA-CGM, France; also represents other passenger and freight lines; Pres. RODOLPHE SAADÉ; Man. Dir JACQUES GOURDIN.

Direction Régionale des Affaires Maritimes (DRAM): Centre de Sécurité des Navires, Fort-de-France Cédex; tel. 5-96-60-42-44; fax 5-96-63-67-30; e-mail affaires.maritimes.martinique@wanadoo.fr; Dir LUC NOSLIER.

Grand Port Maritime de la Martinique: quai de l'Hydro Base, BP 782, 97244 Fort-de-France Cédex; tel. 5-96-59-00-00; fax 5-96-71-35-73; e-mail contact@martinique.port.fr; internet www.martinique.port.fr; f. 1953 under management of Chambre de Commerce et de l'Industrie de la Martinique; present name adopted 2013 when port became publicly owned entity under supervisory body; Dir JEAN-RÉMY VILLAGEOIS.

CIVIL AVIATION

Aimé Césaire International Airport is located at Le Lamentin, 12 km from Fort-de-France and is equipped to handle jet-engined aircraft. Three scheduled airlines operate flights to Paris: Air France, Corsair and Air Caraïbes. Regional services are provided primarily by Air Caraïbes: to Guadeloupe, St-Martin, St-Barthélemy, St Lucia and Guyana. Air France also provides a regular service to French Guiana. The regional airline LIAT (based in Antigua and Barbuda) provides scheduled services to all islands of the Eastern Caribbean. In 2013 American Airlines began a direct service from Miami, USA, to Fort-de-France. Seaborne Airlines also was expected to launch a weekly service from San Juan to Martinique in 2013. Plans to upgrade the airport at Le Lamentin were agreed in June of that year.

Direction des Services Aéroportuaires: BP 279, 97285 Le Lamentin; tel. 5-96-42-16-00; fax 5-96-42-18-77; e-mail aeroport@martinique.cci.fr; internet www.martinique.aeroport.fr; Dir FRANTZ THODIARD.

Air Caraïbes: see Guadeloupe—Transport.

Tourism

Martinique's tourist attractions are its beaches and coastal scenery, its mountainous interior, and the historic towns of Fort-de-France and Saint-Pierre. In 2005 there were 97 hotels, with some 4,676 rooms. In 2012 the number of tourists who stayed on the island totalled 478,359. Receipts from tourism were €516m. in 2011.

Comité Martiniquais du Tourisme: Immeuble Beaupré, Pointe de Jaham, 97233 Schoelcher; tel. 5-96-61-61-77; fax 5-96-61-22-72; e-mail infos.cmt@martiniquetourisme.com; internet www.martiniquetourisme.com; Pres. KARINE ROY-CAMILLE.

Délégation Régionale au Tourisme: 41 rue Gabriel Périé, 97200 Fort-de-France; tel. 5-96-71-42-68; fax 5-96-73-00-96; e-mail drtmartinique.ndl@wanadoo.fr; Delegate VALÉRIE LEOTURE.

Fédération Martiniquaise des Offices de Tourisme et Syndicats d'Initiative (FMOTSI): Maison du Tourisme Vert, 9 blvd du Général de Gaulle, BP 491, 97207 Fort-de-France Cédex; tel. 5-96-63-18-54; fax 5-96-70-17-61; e-mail contact@fmotsi.net; internet www.fmotsi.net; f. 1984; Pres. JOSÉ REINETTE; Sec.-Gen. JEAN-MARC LUSBEC.

Defence

As assessed at November 2013, France maintained a military force of about 1,250. There was also a naval base, headquartered in Fort-de-France, and a gendarmerie.

Education

The educational system is similar to that of metropolitan France (see chapter on French Guiana). In 2011/12 there were 75 pre-primary schools, 183 primary schools and 80 secondary schools. In 2011/12 there were 43,503 pupils in pre-primary and primary education, while in secondary education there were 40,673 students, of whom some 90% attended state schools. Higher education is provided by a branch of the Université des Antilles et de la Guyane. There are also colleges of agriculture, fisheries, hotel management, nursing, midwifery and childcare. In 2011/12 there were 7,941 students enrolled in higher education on the island, of which 4,629 were enrolled at the university. Departmental expenditure on education and culture was estimated at €44.1m. in 2006.

MAYOTTE

Introductory Survey

LOCATION, CLIMATE, LANGUAGE, RELIGION, CAPITAL

Mayotte forms part of the Comoros archipelago, which lies between the island of Madagascar and the east coast of the African mainland. The territory comprises a main island, Mayotte (Mahoré), and a number of smaller islands. The climate is tropical, with temperatures averaging between 24°C and 27°C (75°F to 81°F) throughout the year. The official language is French, but Shimaore (Maorese) and Shibushi are also spoken. Islam is the main religion. The capital is Dzaoudzi, which is connected to the island of Pamandzi by a causeway.

CONTEMPORARY POLITICAL HISTORY

Historical Context

Since the Comoros unilaterally declared independence in July 1975, Mayotte has been administered separately by France. The independent Comoran state claims sovereignty of Mayotte, and officially represents it in international organizations, including the UN. In December 1976 France introduced the special status of Collectivité Territoriale (Territorial Collectivity) for the island. Following a coup in the Comoros in May 1978, Mayotte rejected the new Government's proposal that it should rejoin the other islands under a federal system, and reaffirmed its intention of remaining linked to France. In December 1979 the Assemblée Nationale (National Assembly) approved legislation that extended Mayotte's special status for another five years, during which the islanders were to be consulted. In October 1984, however, the National Assembly further prolonged Mayotte's status, and the referendum on the island's future was postponed indefinitely.

Domestic Political Affairs

Relations between the main political party on Mayotte, the Mouvement Populaire Mahorais (MPM) and the French Government rapidly deteriorated after the Franco-African summit in November 1987, when the French Prime Minister, Jacques Chirac, expressed reservations concerning the elevation of Mayotte to the status of a Département d'Outre-mer (Overseas Department), despite his announcement, in early 1986, that he shared the MPM's aim to upgrade Mayotte's status. In the second round of the French presidential election, which took place in May 1988, François Mitterrand, the incumbent President and the candidate of the Parti Socialiste (PS), received 50.3% of the votes cast on Mayotte, defeating Chirac, the candidate of the Rassemblement pour la République (RPR). At elections to the French National Assembly, which took place in June, Henry Jean-Baptiste was re-elected as Mayotte's representative to that body. (Later that month, he joined the newly formed centrist group in the National Assembly, the Union du Centre.) In elections to the Conseil Général (General Council) of Mayotte in September and October, the MPM retained the majority of seats.

In 1989–90 concern about the number of Comoran immigrants seeking employment on the island resulted in an increase in racial tension. A paramilitary organization, known as Caiman, was subsequently formed in support of the expulsion of illegal immigrants, but was refused legal recognition by the authorities. In June 1992 growing resentment resulted in further attacks against Comoran immigrants resident in Mayotte. In September representatives of the MPM met the French Prime Minister, Pierre Bérégovoy, to request the reintroduction of entry visas to restrict immigration from the Comoros. Later that month the MPM organized a boycott of Mayotte's participation in the French referendum on the Treaty on European Union (see p. 273), in support of the provision of entry visas.

At elections to the National Assembly, which took place in March 1993, Jean-Baptiste was returned, securing 53.4% of the votes cast, while the Secretary-General of the RPR, Mansour Kamardine, received 44.3% of the votes.

Elections to the General Council (which was enlarged from 17 to 19 members) took place in March 1994: the MPM retained 12 seats, while the RPR secured four seats, and independent candidates three seats. During an official visit to Mayotte in November, the French Prime Minister, Edouard Balladur, announced the reintroduction of entry visas as a requirement for Comoran nationals, and the adoption of a number of security measures, in an effort to reduce illegal immigration to the island.

In elections to the French Sénat (Senate) in September 1995, the incumbent MPM representative, Marcel Henry, was returned by a large majority; Mayotte's representation in the Senate was later increased to two seats. During a visit to Mayotte in October, the French Secretary of State for Overseas Departments and Territories pledged that a referendum on the future status of the island would be conducted by 1999. In October 1996 he confirmed that two commissions, one based in Paris and the other in Mayotte, were preparing a consultation document and announced that the resulting referendum would take place before the end of the decade.

Partial elections to fill nine seats in the General Council were held in March 1997; the MPM secured three seats (losing two that it had previously held), the RPR won three seats, the local PS one seat, and independent right-wing candidates two seats. In elections to the National Assembly Jean-Baptiste, representing the alliance of the Union pour la Démocratie Française (UDF) and the Force Démocrate, defeated Kamardine, securing 51.7% of the votes cast in the second round of voting, which took place in June.

In April 1998 one of the commissions charged with examining the future status of Mayotte submitted its report, which concluded that the present status of Territorial Collectivity was no longer appropriate, but did not advocate an alternative. In May the MPM declared its support for an adapted form of departmental administration. In May 1999 Jean-Baptiste introduced draft legislation to the National Assembly, which proposed the holding of a referendum regarding the island's future before the end of the year. In August, following negotiations between the French Secretary of State for Overseas Departments and Territories, Jean-Jack Queyranne, and island representatives, Mayotte members of the RPR and the PS and Younoussa Bamana, the leader of the MPM, signed a draft document providing for the transformation of Mayotte into a Collectivité Départementale (Departmental Collectivity), if approved at a referendum. However, both Henry and Jean-Baptiste rejected the document. The two politicians subsequently announced their departure from the MPM and formed a new political party, the Mouvement Départementaliste Mahorais (MDM), while reiterating their demands that Mayotte be granted full overseas departmental status.

Mayotte becomes a Departmental Collectivity

Following the approval of Mayotte's proposed new status by the General Council (by 14 votes to five) and the municipal councils, an accord to this effect was signed by Queyranne and political representatives of Mayotte on 27 January 2000. On 2 July a referendum was held, in which the population of Mayotte voted overwhelmingly in favour of the January accord, granting Mayotte the status of Departmental Collectivity for a period of 10 years. In November the commission established to define the terms of Mayotte's new status published a report, which envisaged the transfer of executive power from the Prefect to the General Council by 2004, the dissolution of the position of Prefect by 2007 and the concession of greater powers to the island's Government, notably in the area of regional co-operation.

At elections to the General Council, held in March 2001, no party established a majority. The MPM experienced significant losses, with only four of its candidates being elected, while the RPR won five seats, the Mouvement des Citoyens (MDC) two, the MDM one, the PS one, and various right-wing independent candidates six seats. Bamana was re-elected as President of the General Council. The French parliament approved Mayotte's status as a Departmental Collectivity in July. In September Philippe de Mester succeeded Pierre Bayle as Prefect.

In the first round of the French presidential election, which was held on 21 April 2002, Chirac received the highest number of votes on Mayotte, winning 43.0% of the valid votes cast; the second round, held on 5 May, was also won resoundingly by Chirac, who secured 88.3% of votes cast on the island, defeating the candidate of the extreme right-wing Front National, Jean-Marie Le Pen. At elections to the National Assembly, held in June, Kamardine, representing the recently formed Union pour la Majorité Présidentielle (UMP, which incorporated the RPR, the Démocratie Libérale and significant elements of the UDF), defeated the MDM-UDF candidate, Siadi Vita. Jean-Jacques Brot replaced de Mester as Prefect in July. In November the UMP was renamed the Union pour un Mouvement Populaire (retaining the same acronym).

At elections to the General Council in March 2004, the UMP won eight seats in alliance with the MPM, which secured one seat, while the MDM and the MDC, also in alliance, obtained five and two seats, respectively; independent candidates were elected to the remaining three seats. With the election of Saïd Omar Oili, an independent, as President of the General Council on 2 April, executive power was transferred from the Prefect to the Council. In January 2005 Jean-Paul Kihl replaced Brot as Prefect. In May a national referendum on ratification of the European Union (EU) constitutional treaty was held: 86.5% of Mayotte's electorate voted in favour of adopting the treaty; however, it was ultimately rejected by a majority of French voters. In November more than 500 trade union members protested in Mamoudzou as part of a general strike for greater social equality with metropolitan France. There was a further two-day strike in December.

In November 2005 a French parliamentary commission was convened to report on the state of illegal immigration in Mayotte. The commission's first report, which was published in February 2006, found that there were between 45,000 and 60,000 illegal immigrants living in Mayotte, of whom 90% were Comoran. (According to the census of 2002 the official French population numbered 160,265.) The number of births on the island had risen by more than 50% over a 10-year period, reaching 7,676 in 2004, of which some two-thirds were to women lacking official documentation. The report proposed closer co-operation with the Comoran authorities. Recommendations to stem the flow of immigrants included the introduction of biometric identity cards in Mayotte and the Comoros, and an increase in the number of border police.

Nicolas Sarkozy of the UMP secured 30.5% of the votes cast on Mayotte in the first round of the French presidential election, held on 22 April 2007. However, in the second round, which took place on 6 May, Ségolène Royal of the PS won 60.0% of the votes cast, although Sarkozy was elected to the presidency. At elections to the National Assembly, held on 10 and 17 June, Kamardine was defeated by Abdoulatifou Aly, who was affiliated to the Mouvement Démocrate (MoDem), which had been formed following the presidential election by François Bayrou, the leader of the UDF, to oppose Sarkozy's UMP.

Meanwhile, in February 2007 Vincent Bouvier replaced Kihl as Prefect and, although that position was scheduled to be abolished in 2007, Bouvier remained in the post until July 2008, when Denis Robin assumed the position. Also in February 2007 new legislation approved by the French National Assembly introduced statutory and institutional measures granting Mayotte many of the powers afforded to territories with full overseas departmental status, with the exception of certain fiscal, financial and social welfare powers. This followed a constitutional amendment in 2003 whereby Mayotte acquired the status of Collectivité d'Outre-mer (Overseas Collectivity) and expedited the process towards becoming an Overseas Department. The 2007 legislation provided a framework for measures to be implemented to facilitate the transfer of full fiscal control to Mayotte by January 2014.

Elections for 10 of the 19 seats in the General Council took place over two rounds held on 9 and 16 March 2008. The UMP, the MDM and the Nouvel Élan pour Mayotte (founded in 2007 by Omar Oili) all secured two seats, the PS won one seat and three seats were taken by independent candidates. On 20 March Ahamed Attoumani Douchina was elected to replace Omar Oili as President of the Council.

Mayotte becomes an Overseas Department

The question of Mayotte's status once again became prevalent in April 2008 when the General Council adopted a resolution providing for the transfer of Mayotte's status from that of Overseas Collectivity to an Overseas Department. The resolution required that a public consultation on the matter be held within 12 months. In January 2009 the text of the question to be put to the Mayotte electorate was approved and Sarkozy declared that the consultation would take place on 29 March. At the referendum, which was held as scheduled, 95.2% of voters approved of Mayotte attaining the status of an Overseas Department within the French Republic (despite the recognition of the island by the African Union and the Comoran Government as an inseparable part of the Comoran state). Some 61% of those eligible to vote participated in the ballot. In October 2010 the French Senate adopted the departmentalization of Mayotte and the following month the National Assembly approved the appropriate legislation.

Meanwhile, in August 2009 Hubert Derache replaced Robin as Prefect. In early December protests on Pamandzi against the rise in the cost of living resulted in some 15 people being injured during clashes with the security forces. In January 2010 President Sarkozy made a brief visit to Mayotte during which he discussed the issue of immigration with local officials. In November trade unions on Mayotte organized a day of strike action to demand better working conditions and pay.

On 31 March 2011 Mayotte officially became the 101st Department of France and the fifth Overseas Department. On 3 April Daniel Zaïdani was elected President of the General Council and in July Thomas Degos replaced Derache as Prefect. In October the authorities of Mayotte made an official request to the EU to recognize Mayotte as a Région Ultrapériphérique (Outermost Region) of France. Recognition as an RUP would allow Mayotte to draw upon EU funds to aid its economic development.

Persistent unrest on the island caused by the continued high cost of living led to a 44-day general strike in October and early November 2011, followed by a further two days' shutdown in December. The French Prime Minister, François Fillon, dispatched Denis Robin, a former Prefect of Mayotte, to attempt to mediate an agreement between trade unions, employers and the Government to end the strike action. In late December an agreement was signed, imposing until March 2012 a reduction in the price of 11 staple goods; in addition, families with modest incomes were to receive food tokens.

The 2012 elections

The first round of the French presidential election was conducted on 22 April 2012: Sarkozy attracted 48.7% of Mayotte's votes, compared with 36.6% for François Hollande of the PS. A second round election was held two weeks later, at which Sarkozy secured 51.0% of the ballot, defeating Hollande, who obtained 49.1%. Nevertheless, Hollande triumphed nationally and was sworn in as President in mid-May. In the French legislative elections held on 10 and 17 June, Mayotte's representation in the National Assembly was increased to two seats; the seats were won by Ibrahim Aboubacar, representing the PS, and Boinali Saïd, an independent left-wing candidate. In July the EU approved Mayotte's petition to be recognized as an Outermost Region; this new status was to come into effect on 1 January 2014.

The French Minister of Overseas Territories, Victorin Lurel, visited Mayotte in July 2012 to hold discussions with the local authorities regarding the high cost of living on the island. A bill to address the problem of inflated prices (and consequent social unrest) in the French Overseas Possessions, was promulgated by President Hollande in November.

In January 2013 Jacques Witkowski was appointed to replace Degos as Prefect. In response to a further series of public sector strikes, Lurel, during a visit to Mayotte in October, signed a decree approving price indexation for public officials of up to 5%, with retroactive effect from 1 January; nevertheless, industrial unrest continued. In November Lurel announced a further decree, which was to enter into force on 1 January 2014, to regulate fuel prices in the Overseas Departments, thereby reducing the profits of oil companies. The new legislation was met with opposition by French oil and gas company Total, and in early 2014 petrol service stations owned by Total were closed on Mayotte in protest at its introduction.

Recent developments: Mayotte receives Outermost Region status

Meanwhile, in June 2013 it was announced that Witkowski would request the French Government to dissolve Mayotte's police Groupement d'Intervention Régional (Regional Intervention Force—GIR), after five of its members were taken into custody in connection with a drugs-trafficking network on the island. A former head of the GIR, Gérard Gautier, was arrested in France in November and subsequently extradited to Mayotte, where he was charged with involvement in drugs-trafficking operations. Also in November the French Minister of the Interior, Manuel Valls, responding to demands by the UMP representative in the Senate regarding increased insecurity and crime on Mayotte, pledged to visit the island in early 2014. Mayotte officially became an Outermost Region on 1 January.

(For further details of the recent history of the island, see the Comoros.)

CONSTITUTION AND GOVERNMENT

The Constitution of the Fifth Republic of France, adopted by referendum on 28 September 1958 and promulgated on 6 October 1958 applies on Mayotte. The French Government is represented in Mayotte by an appointed Prefect. There is a Conseil Général (General Council), with 19 members, elected by universal adult suffrage for a term of three years; the members of the Council elect a President who acts as head of government. In April 2004 the executive powers of the Prefect were transferred to the General Council. Mayotte elects two deputies to the Assemblée Nationale (National Assembly) and two representatives to the Sénat (Senate). Mayotte is also represented at the European Parliament. Mayotte became an Overseas Department in March 2011 and received the status of Région Ultrapériphérique (Outermost Region) on 1 January 2014.

ECONOMIC AFFAIRS

Mayotte's gross domestic product (GDP) per head in 2009 was €6,575, according to official figures. Total GDP in that year amounted to €1,396m. Between the censuses of 2002 and 2007 the population of Mayotte increased at an average annual rate of 3.1%.

The economy is based mainly on agriculture. In 2007 8.5% of the employed labour force were engaged in this sector. The principal export crops are ylang ylang (an ingredient of perfume) and vanilla. Mayotte imports large quantities of foodstuffs, which comprised 23.4% of the value of total imports in 2012. In 2003 it was estimated that some 44% of the population was dependent on *gratte* (subsistence) farming. Cassava, maize and pigeon peas are cultivated for domestic consumption; while rice is widely eaten there is little domestic production. More than 90% of farms grow bananas, often mixed with coconuts (grown for their milk and oil, both of which are used in cooking); together banana and coconut plantations occupy some 45% of agricultural land (approximately 20,000 ha in total, some 55% of the surface area of Mayotte). Mangoes are also widespread, and around one-third of mango trees grow wild. Livestock-rearing (of cattle, goats—for meat—and chickens) and fishing are also important activities. Aquaculture was first introduced in 1998 and in 2005 there were five producers catering mainly to the export market.

Industry (which is dominated by the construction sector) engaged 12.7% of the employed population in 2007. There are no mineral resources on the island. Imports of mineral products comprised 2.6% of the value of total imports in 2012 and base metals and metal products comprised 6.0%. Mayotte also imports considerable quantities of machinery (4.1% of the value of total imports) and transport equipment (8.4%).

Services engaged 78.8% of the employed population in 2007. The annual number of tourist arrivals (excluding cruise-ship passengers) totalled 45,800 in 2012; receipts from tourism in 2006 amounted to €16.3m.

In 2012 Mayotte recorded a trade deficit of €319.5m. The principal export in 2012 was fish; exports of ylang ylang were also significant. The principal imports in that year were foodstuffs, petroleum products, transport equipment, plastic materials and rubber, and base metals and metal products. The main source of imports in 2009 was France (50.8%); the People's Republic of China was another major supplier. France was also the principal market for exports (taking 40.0% of exports in that year); the other significant purchasers were the Comoros and Réunion.

In 2012 Mayotte's total budgetary revenue was €310.4m., while total expenditure was €269.5m. The annual rate of inflation recorded by Mayotte averaged 2.7% in 2006–12; consumer prices increased by 2.8% in the year to December 2012. Some 17.6% of the labour force was unemployed in 2009.

Mayotte suffers from a persistently high trade deficit, owing to its reliance on imports, and is largely dependent on French aid. As Mayotte's labour force has continued to increase (mostly owing to a high birth rate and the continued arrival of immigrants, many of them entering the territory illegally—see Recent History, above), youth unemployment has caused particular concern. The French Government agreed a new, six-year development contract with Mayotte for 2008–14 valued at €551m., which was designed to ensure the archipelago's economic and social autonomy. With Mayotte's new status as a French Overseas Department, measures were adopted in 2011 to align, by increments, the island's minimum wage with that of France. However, Mayotte's short-term economic prospects remained hampered by high levels of public debt, an uncompetitive agricultural industry and undeveloped tourism infrastructure. From late 2011 public sector strikes disrupted trade and deterred visitors; despite measures undertaken by the French Government to address social discontent by reducing inequalities with mainland France, including a decree approving price indexation for public officials in October 2013, industrial unrest persisted. Nevertheless, after the European Union (EU) officially granted Mayotte the status of a Région Ultrapériphérique (Outermost Region) of France on 1 January 2014, the island was expected to benefit from increased development funding. Shortly beforehand, in December 2013 the EU approved a grant of €60m. for 2014–20 towards the development of the island's rural agricultural sector. In early 2014 petrol stations owned by French oil and gas company Total were closed in Mayotte, in protest against the introduction of French legislation to regulate fuel prices in the Overseas Departments (thereby reducing the profits of oil companies).

PUBLIC HOLIDAYS

The principal holidays of metropolitan France are observed.

Statistical Survey

Source (unless otherwise indicated): Institut National de la Statistique et des Études Économiques (INSEE) de Mayotte; Z.I. Kawéni, BP 1362, 97600 Mamoudzou; tel. 269-61-36-35; fax 269-61-39-56; e-mail antenne-mayotte@insee.fr; internet www.insee.fr/fr/regions/mayotte/default.asp.

AREA AND POPULATION

Area: 374 sq km (144 sq miles).

Population: 186,452 at census of 31 July 2007; 212,645 at census of 21 August 2012. *Mid-2014* (UN estimate): 228,071 (Source: UN, *World Population Prospects: The 2012 Revision*).

Density (at mid-2014): 609.8 per sq km.

Population by Age and Sex (UN estimates at mid-2014): *0–14:* 101,748 (males 51,935, females 49,813); *15–64:* 120,916 (males 59,200, females 61,716); *65 and over:* 5,407 (males 2,837, females 2,570); *Total* 228,071 (males 113,972, females 114,099) (Source: UN, *World Population Prospects: The 2012 Revision*).

Population by Country of Origin (2002, before adjustment for double counting): Mayotte 103,705; France 6,323; Comoros 45,057; Madagascar-Mauritius-Seychelles 4,601; Total (incl. others) 160,301.

Principal Towns (population of communes at 2012 census): Mamoudzou 57,281; Koungou 26,488; Dzaoudzi (capital) 14,311; Dembeni 10,923; Tsingoni 10,454; Sada 10,195; Bandraboua 10,132.

Births and Deaths (2007): Registered live births 7,658 (birth rate 41.1 per 1,000); Registered deaths 587 (death rate 3.1 per 1,000). *2009:* Birth rate 39.0 per 1,000; Death rate 3.0 per 1,000.

Life expectancy (years at birth): 77.6 (males 74.0; females 81.3) in 2010 (Source: World Bank, World Development Indicators database).

Economically Active Population (persons aged 14 years and over, census of 31 July 2007): Agriculture and fishing 3,204; Construction 3,024; Other industry 1,805; Wholesale and retail trade 3,154; Hotels and restaurants 609; Transport, telecommunications and real estate 5,043; Public administration 6,535; Education, health and social care 7,247; Other services 7,289; *Total employed* 37,910 (males 24,157, females 13,753); Unemployed 13,614 (males 5,922, females 7,692); *Total labour force* 51,524 (males 30,079, females 21,445). *2009* (labour force survey March–June, persons aged 15 years and over): Total employed 35,600; Unemployed 7,600; Total labour force 43,200.

HEALTH AND WELFARE

Key Indicators

Total Fertility Rate (children per woman, 2004): 4.5.

Physicians (per 1,000 head, 1997): 0.4.

Hospital Beds (per 1,000 head, 2007): 1.5.

For definitions see explanatory note on p. vi.

AGRICULTURE, ETC.

Livestock (2003): Cattle 17,235; Goats 22,811; Chickens 80,565.

Fishing (metric tons, live weight, 2011): Capture 29,185 (Skipjack tuna 11,305; Yellowfin tuna 13,478); Aquaculture 70 (FAO estimate); *Total catch* 29,255 (FAO estimate). Source: FAO.

INDUSTRY

Electric Energy (million kWh, consumption): 271 in 2012 (Source: Institut d'Emission des Départements d'Outre-mer, *Rapport Annuel 2012*).

FINANCE

Currency and Exchange Rates: 100 cent = 1 euro. *Sterling and Dollar Equivalents* (31 December 2013): £1 sterling = €1.194; US $1 = €0.725; €10 = £8.37 = US $13.79. *Average Exchange Rate* (euros per US dollar): 0.7194 in 2011; 0.7782 in 2012; 0.7532 in 2013. The French franc was used until the end of February 2002. Euro notes and coins were introduced on 1 January 2002, and the euro became the sole legal tender from 18 February. Some of the figures in this Survey are still in terms of French francs.

Budget of the Collectivity (€ million, 2012): Total revenue 310.4; Total expenditure 269.5 (Source: Institut d'Emission des Départements d'Outre-mer, *Rapport Annuel 2012*).

French State Expenditure (€ million, 2012): Direct expenditure 436.5; Indirect expenditure 82.8; *Total expenditure* 519.3 (Source: Institut d'Emission des Départements d'Outre-mer, *Rapport Annuel 2012*).

Money Supply (million French francs at 31 December 1997): Currency outside banks 789; Demand deposits 266; Total money 1,055.

Cost of Living (Consumer Price Index for December; base: December 2006 = 100): 112.4 in 2010; 113.8 in 2011; 117.0 in 2012.

Expenditure on the Gross Domestic Product (€ million, 2009, INSEE estimates): Government final consumption expenditure 726; Private final consumption expenditure 799; Gross fixed capital formation 372; *Total domestic expenditure* 1,897; Exports of goods and services 31; *Less* Imports of goods and services 532; *GDP in purchasers' values* 1,396.

EXTERNAL TRADE

Principal Commodities (€ million, 2012): *Imports c.i.f.:* Foodstuffs 76.4; Petroleum products 72.7; Chemical products 16.1; Pharmaceutical products 16.2; Textiles 10.2; Plastic materials and rubber 20.5; Base metals and metal products 19.6; Machinery and appliances 13.4; Electrical and optical equipment 18.6; Transport equipment 27.5; Total (incl. others) 326.8. *Exports f.o.b.:* Agricultural products 0.5; Foodstuffs 0.2; Base metals and metal products 1.3; Machinery and appliances 0.9; Transport equipment 2.3; Total (incl. others) 7.3 (Source: Institut d'Emission des Départements d'Outre-mer, *Rapport Annuel 2012*).

Principal Trading Partners (€ million, 2009): *Imports:* Brazil 7.5; China, People's Republic 28.8; France (Metropolitan) 185.0; Mauritius 4.5; South Africa 5.8; United Arab Emirates 8.2; Total (incl. others) 364.3. *Exports* (incl. re-exports): Total 5.1. Note: The principal markets for exports are France (Metropolitan—some 40% of exports in 2009), Comoros (15% in 2009) and Réunion.

TRANSPORT

Road Traffic (2008): Motor vehicles in use 7,781.

Shipping (2012, unless otherwise indicated): *Maritime Traffic:* Vessel movements 530 (2005); Goods unloaded 289,620 metric tons; Goods loaded 44,763 metric tons; Passengers 35,150 (arrivals 9,149, departures 26,001). *Barges* (2002): Passengers 11,845; Light vehicles 532. *Cruise Ships* (2005): Vessel movements 36; Passengers 6,857.

Civil Aviation (2012): *Passengers Carried:* 305,219. *Freight Carried:* 1,424 metric tons. *Post Carried:* 708 metric tons (Source: Institut d'Emission des Départements d'Outre-mer, *Rapport Annuel 2012*).

TOURISM

Foreign Tourist Arrivals (excl. cruise-ship passengers): 52,800 in 2010; 48,200 in 2011; 45,800 in 2012.

Foreign Tourist Arrivals by Country of Residence (2012): France (metropolitan) 24,700; Réunion 19,000; Total (incl. others) 45,800.

Tourism Receipts (€ million): 13.7 in 2004; 14.5 in 2005; 16.3 in 2006.

COMMUNICATIONS MEDIA

Telephones ('000 main lines in use, 2012): 10.0.

Mobile Cellular Telephones ('000 subscribers, 2008): 48.1.

Internet Users ('000, 2000): 1.8.

Source: International Telecommunication Union.

EDUCATION

Pre-primary (2012/13): 71 schools; 17,366 pupils.

Primary (2012/13): 135 schools (including special schools); 33,997 pupils.

General Secondary (2012/13 unless otherwise indicated): 19 schools (2009); 20,227 pupils.

Vocational and Technical (2012/13 unless otherwise indicated): 9 institutions (2009); 11,338 students.

Students Studying in France or Réunion (2009): Secondary 1,452; Higher 2,253; *Total* 3,705.

Teaching Staff (2012, state schools): Primary 2,680; Secondary 2,019; Higher 16.

Directory

The Government

(April 2014)

HEAD OF STATE

President: FRANÇOIS HOLLANDE.

Prefect: JACQUES WITKOWSKI.

DEPARTMENTAL ADMINISTRATION

President of the General Council: DANIEL ZAÏDANI, 108 rue de l'Hôpital, BP 101, 97600 Mamoudzou; tel. 269-61-12-33; fax 269-61-10-18; internet www.cg976.fr.

REPRESENTATIVES TO THE FRENCH PARLIAMENT

Deputies to the French National Assembly: BOINALI SAÏD (Divers Gauche), IBRAHIM ABOUBACAR (PS).

Representatives to the French Senate: THANI MOHAMED SOILIHI (Divers Gauche), ABDOURAHAMANE SOILIHI (UMP).

GOVERNMENT DEPARTMENTS

Office of the Prefect: BP 676, Kawéni, 97600 Mamoudzou; tel. 269-63-50-00; fax 269-60-18-89; e-mail communication@mayotte.pref.gouv.fr; internet www.mayotte.pref.gouv.fr.

Department of Agriculture and Forestry: 15 rue Mariazé, BP 103, 97600 Mamoudzou; tel. 269-61-12-13; fax 269-61-10-31; e-mail daf976@agriculture.gouv.fr; internet daf.mayotte.agriculture.gouv.fr.

Department of Education: rue Sarahangué, BP 76, 97600 Mamoudzou; tel. 269-61-10-24; fax 269-61-09-87; e-mail vice-rectorat@ac-mayotte.fr; internet www.ac-mayotte.fr.

Department of Health and Social Security: rue de l'Hôpital, BP 104, 97600 Mamoudzou; tel. 269-61-12-25; fax 269-61-19-56.

Department of Public Works: rue Mariazé, BP 109, 97600 Mamoudzou; tel. 269-61-12-54; fax 269-61-07-11; e-mail de-mayotte@equipement.gouv.fr.

Department of Work, Employment and Training: 3 bis, rue Mahabou, BP 174, 97600 Mamoudzou; tel. 269-61-16-57; fax 269-61-03-37; internet www.dtefp-mayotte.travail.gouv.fr.

Department of Youth and Sports: 14 rue Mariazé, BP 94, 97600 Mamoudzou; tel. 269-61-60-50; fax 269-61-82-10; e-mail dd976@jeunesse-sports.gouv.fr.

Political Organizations

Fédération du Front National (FN): route nationale 1, M'tsahara, 97630 M'tzamboro; BP 1331, 97600 Mamoudzou Cédex; tel. and fax 269-60-50-24; Regional Sec. ALI-MANSOIB SOIHIBOU.

Fédération de Mayotte de l'Union pour un Mouvement Populaire (UMP): route nationale, Immeuble 'Jardin Créole', 97600 Mamoudzou; tel. 269-61-64-64; fax 269-60-87-89; e-mail alisouf@ump976.org; centre-right; local branch of the metropolitan party; Departmental Pres. ASSANI HAMISSI; Departmental Sec. ALI SOUF.

Fédération du Mouvement National Républicain (MNR) de Mayotte: 15 rue des Réfugiers, 97615 Pamandzi; tel. and fax 269-60-33-21; Departmental Sec. ABDOU MIHIDJAY.

Mouvement des Citoyens (MDC): Chirongui; Leader ALI HALIFA.

Mouvement Départementaliste Mahorais (MDM): 97610 Dzaoudzi; f. 2001 by fmr mems of the MPM; Pres. ZOUBERT ADINANI; Sec.-Gen. MOHAMED ALI BEN ALI.

Mouvement de la Gauche Ecologiste de Mayotte: 6 avenue Mamanne, Quartier Artisanal, Localité de Pamandzi, 97600 Pamandzi; tel. and fax 269-61-09-70; internet mayotte.lesverts.fr; fmrly Les Verts Mayotte; affiliated to Mouvement de la Gauche Réunionnaise; Gen. Sec. AHAMADA SALIME.

Mouvement Populaire Mahorais (MPM): route de Vahibé, Passamainti, 97600 Mamoudzou; Leader YOUNOUSSA BAMANA.

Parti Socialiste (PS): BP 314, 97600 Mamoudzou; local branch of the metropolitan party; Fed. Sec. IBRAHIM ABUBACAR.

Judicial System

Palais de Justice: Immeuble Espace, BP 106 (Kawéni), 97600 Mamoudzou; tel. 269-61-11-15; fax 269-61-19-63.

Tribunal de Grande Instance: 16 rue de l'hôpital, BP 106, 97600 Mamoudzou; tel. 269-61-11-15; fax 269-61-19-63; Pres. JEAN-BAPTISTE FLORI.

Tribunal d'Instance: Mamoudzou; Pres. ALAIN CHATEAUNEUF.

Procureur de la République: PHILIPPE FAISANDIER.

Religion

Muslims comprise about 98% of the population. Most of the remainder are Christians, mainly Roman Catholics.

CHRISTIANITY

The Roman Catholic Church

Mayotte is within the jurisdiction of the Apostolic Administrator of the Comoros.

Office of the Apostolic Administrator: 7 rue de l'Hôpital, BP 1012, 97600 Mamoudzou; tel. and fax 269-61-11-53; fax 269-61-48-25.

The Press

Albalad: Immeuble Mega, 97600 Kawéni, Mamoudzou; tel. 269-60-66-15; e-mail halda.halidi@awicompany.fr; internet www.albaladmayotte.com; f. 2010; owned by Al Waseet International; daily; French; Dir of Publication PASCAL ABLA; Editor-in-Chief HALDA HALIDI; circ. 1,000.

Flash Infos Mayotte: Société Mahoraise de Presse, 7 rue Salamani Cavani/M'Tsapéré, BP 60, 97600 Mamoudzou; tel. 269-61-20-04; fax 269-60-35-90; e-mail flash-infos@wanadoo.fr; internet www.mayottehebdo.com; f. 1999; owned by Somapresse; daily e-mail bulletin; Dir LAURENT CANAVATE.

Horizon Austral: Société Mahoraise de Presse, 7 rue Salamani Cavani/M'Tsapéré, BP 60, 97600 Mamoudzou; tel. 269-61-20-04; fax 269-60-35-90; e-mail contact@mayottehebdo.com; internet www.mayottehebdo.com; f. 2007; owned by Somapresse; Dir of Publication LAURENT CANAVATE.

Le Mahorais: 11 centre commercial, Lukida, 97600 Mamoudzou; tel. 269-61-66-75; fax 269-61-66-72; internet www.lemahorais.com; weekly; French; Publ. Dir SAMUEL BOSCHER; Editor-in-Chief LUCIE TOUZÉ.

Mayotte Hebdo: Société Mahoraise de Presse, 7 rue Salamani Cavani/M'Tsapéré, BP 60, 97600 Mamoudzou; tel. 269-61-20-04; fax 269-60-35-90; e-mail contact@mayottehebdo.com; internet www.mayottehebdo.com; f. 2000; weekly; French; incl. the economic supplement *Mayotte Eco* and cultural supplement *Tounda* (weekly); owned by Somapresse; Dir LAURENT CANAVATE; circ. 2,300.

Mayotte Magazine: BP 268, Z.I. Kawéni, 97600 Mamoudzou; tel. 06-39-09-03-29; e-mail contact@mayottemagazine.com; internet www.mayottemagazine.fr; f. 2007; 4 a year; Dir STÉPHANIE LÉGERON.

Zan'Goma: Impasse du Jardin Fleuri, Cavani, 97600 Mamoudzou; f. 2005; monthly; French; Publ. Dir MONCEF MOUHOUDHOIRE.

Broadcasting and Communications

TELECOMMUNICATIONS

Mayotte Télécom Mobile: 27, pl. Mariaźe, 97600 Mamoudzou; mobile cellular telephone operator; local operation of Société Réunionnaise du Radiotéléphone based in Réunion.

RADIO AND TELEVISION

Mayotte 1ère: BP 103, 97610 Dzaoudzi; tel. 269-60-10-17; fax 269-60-18-52; e-mail annick.henry@rfo.fr; internet mayotte.la1ere.fr; f. 1977; acquired by Groupe France Télévisions in 2004; fmrly Réseau France Outre-mer, name changed as above in 2010; radio broadcasts in French and more than 70% in Mahorian; television transmissions began in 1986; a satellite service was launched in 2000; Dir-Gen. GENEVIÈVE GIARD; Regional Dir GERALD PRUFER.

Finance

(br(s). = branch(es))

BANKS

In 2010 there were three commercial banks, two mutual banks and two other financial institutions in Mayotte.

Issuing Authority

Institut d'Emission des Départements d'Outre-mer: ave de la Préfecture, BP 500, 97600 Mamoudzou; tel. 269-61-05-05; fax 269-61-05-02; internet agence@iedom-mayotte.fr; internet www.iedom.fr; Dir VICTOR-ROBERT NUGENT.

Commercial Banks

Banque Française Commerciale Océan Indien: route de l'Agriculture, BP 222, 97600 Mamoudzou; tel. 269-61-10-91; fax 269-61-17-40; e-mail pleclerc@bfcoi.com; internet www.bfcoi.com; f. 1976; jtly owned by Société Générale and Mauritius Commercial Bank Ltd; Pres. GÉRALD LACAZE; brs at Dzaoudzi and Sada.

Banque de la Réunion: 30 pl. Mariage, 97600 Mamoudzou; tel. 269-61-20-30; fax 269-61-20-28; internet www.banquedelareunion.fr; owned by Groupe Banque Populaire et Caisse d'Epargne (France); 2 brs.

BRED Banque Populaire: Centre d'Affaires Mayotte, pl. Mariage, Z.I. 3, 97600 Mamoudzou; tel. 269-64-80-86; fax 269-60-51-10; internet www.bred.fr; owned by Groupe Banque Populaire et Caisse d'Epargne (France).

INSURANCE

AGF: pl. Mariage, BP 184, 97600 Mamoudzou; tel. 269-61-44-33; fax 269-61-14-89; e-mail jl.henry@wanadoo.fr; Gen. Man. JEAN-LUC HENRY.

Groupama: BP 665, Z.I. Nel, Lot 7, 97600 Mamoudzou; tel. 269-62-59-92; fax 269-60-76-08.

Prudence Créole: Centre Commercial et Médical de l'Ylang, BP 480, 97600 Mamoudzou; tel. 269-61-11-10; fax 269-61-11-21; e-mail prudencecreolemayotte@wanadoo.fr; 87% owned by Groupe Générali; 2 brs.

Vectra Paic Océan Indien: BP 65, 55 champs des Ylangs, 97680 Combani; tel. 269-62-44-54; fax 269-62-46-97; e-mail cfonteneau@wanadoo.fr.

Trade and Industry

DEVELOPMENT ORGANIZATION

Agence Française de Développement (AFD): Résidence Sarah, pl. du Marché, BP 610, Kawéni, 97600 Mamoudzou; tel. 269-64-35-00; fax 269-62-66-53; e-mail afdmamoudzou@groupe-afd.org; internet www.afd.fr; Dir PATRICK SALLES.

EMPLOYERS' ORGANIZATIONS

Mouvement des Entreprises de France Mayotte (MEDEF): Z.I. Kawéni, Immeuble GMOI, BP 570, 97600 Mamoudzou; tel. 269-61-44-22; fax 269-61-46-10; e-mail contact@medef-mayotte.com; internet www.medef-mayotte.com; Pres. LAURENT HAVET; Sec.-Gen. VINCENT SCHUBLIN.

Ordre National des Médecins: BP 675 Kawéni, 97600 Mamoudzou; tel. 269-61-02-47; fax 269-61-36-61.

UTILITIES

Electricity

Electricité de Mayotte (EDM): BP 333, Z.I. Kawéni, 97600 Kawéni; tel. 269-62-96-80; internet www.electricitedemayotte.com; f. 1997; subsidiary of SAUR; Dir-Gen. AUGUSTO SOARES DOS REIS.

Water

Syndicat Intercommunal de l'Eau et de l'Assainissement de Mayotte (SIEAM): BP 289, 97600 Mamoudzou; tel. 269-62-11-11; fax 269-61-55-00; e-mail sieam@sieam.fr; internet www.sieam.fr; Pres. MAOULIDA SOULA.

TRADE UNIONS

Confédération Inter-Syndicale de Mayotte (CISMA-CFDT): 18 rue Mahabou, BP 1038, 97600 Mamoudzou; tel. 269-61-12-38; fax 269-61-36-16; f. 1993; Gen. Sec. SAÏD BOINALI.

Fédération Départementale des Syndicats d'Exploitants Agricoles de Mayotte (FDSEAM): 150 rue Mbalamanga-Mtsapéré, 97600 Mamoudzou; tel. and fax 269-61-34-83; e-mail fdsea.mayotte@wanadoo.fr; f. 1982; Pres. LAÏNA MOGNÉ-MALI; Dir ALI BACAR.

Union Départementale Force Ouvrière de Mayotte (FO): Z. I. de Kaweni, Rond Point El-Farouk, BP 1109, 97600 Mamoudzou; tel. 269-61-18-39; fax 269-61-22-45; Sec.-Gen. HAMIDOU MADI MCOLO.

Transport

ROADS

In 2011 the road network totalled approximately 230 km, of which 90 km were main roads.

SHIPPING

Coastal shipping is provided by locally owned small craft. There is a deep-water port at Longoni. Construction of a second quay at Longoni was proposed under the 2006 budget; in December 2008 the Agence Française de Développement approved the allocation of a €10m. loan towards the extension of Longoni port.

Service des Affaires Maritimes: BP 37, 97615 Pamandzi; tel. 269-60-31-38; fax 269-60-31-39; e-mail c.mait.sam-mayotte@developpment-durable.gouv.fr; Head of Service OLIVIER BISSON.

Service des Transports Maritimes (STM): BP 186, 97600 Dzaoudzi; tel. 269-64-39-72; fax 269-60-80-25; e-mail denys.cormy@cg976.fr; internet www.mayotte-stm.com; Dir DENYS CORMY; 8 vessels.

CIVIL AVIATION

There is an airport at Dzaoudzi, serving daily commercial flights to the Comoros; four-times weekly flights to Réunion; twice-weekly services to Madagascar; twice-weekly direct flights to Paris, France; and weekly services to Kenya and Mozambique. In January 2004 plans were approved for the construction of a new runway to allow the commencement of direct flights to Paris, France; the runway was scheduled to be completed by 2015. Plans for a new terminal at the airport in Dzaoudzi were announced in late 2010 as a result of which the number of visitors passing through the airport each year was expected to increase to 615,000 by 2025; the new terminal was expected to become operational in 2014.

Air Austral: pl. Mariage, BP 1429, 97600 Mamoudzou; tel. 269-60-90-90; fax 269-61-61-94; e-mail mayotte@air-austral.com; internet www.air-austral.com; Pres. GÉRARD ETHÈVE.

Tourism

Tropical scenery provides the main tourist attraction. Excluding cruise-ship passengers, Mayotte received 45,800 visitors in 2012; tourism receipts totalled €16.3m. in 2006. In 2007 there were nine hotels, with a total of some 366 rooms.

Comité Départemental du Tourisme de Mayotte (CDTM): rue Amiral Lacaze 5, 97400 Saint-Denis, Réunion; tel. 269-61-09-09; fax 269-61-03-46; e-mail mayottetourisme.lareunion@orange.fr; internet www.mayotte-tourisme.com; Dir GEORGE MECS.

RÉUNION

Introductory Survey

LOCATION, CLIMATE, LANGUAGE, RELIGION, CAPITAL

Réunion is an island in the Indian Ocean, lying about 800 km (500 miles) east of Madagascar. The climate varies greatly according to altitude: at sea level it is tropical, with average temperatures between 20°C (68°F) and 28°C (82°F), but in the uplands it is much cooler, with average temperatures between 8°C (46°F) and 19°C (66°F). Rainfall is abundant, averaging 4,714 mm annually in the uplands, and 686 mm at sea level. The population is of mixed origin, including people of European, African, Indian and Chinese descent. The official language is French. A large majority of the population are Christians belonging to the Roman Catholic Church. The capital is Saint-Denis.

CONTEMPORARY POLITICAL HISTORY

Historical Context

Réunion was first occupied by France in 1642, and was ruled as a colony until 1946, when it received full departmental status. In 1974 it became an Département d'Outre-mer (Overseas Department) with the status of a region.

In 1978 the Organization of African Unity (OAU, now the African Union, see p. 186) adopted a report recommending measures to hasten the independence of the island, and condemned its occupation by a 'colonial power'. However, while the left-wing political parties on the island advocated increased autonomy (amounting to virtual self-government), there was little popular support for complete independence.

Domestic Political Affairs

In June 1992 a delegation from the Conseil Régional (Regional Council) met French President François Mitterrand to submit proposals for economic reforms, in accordance with the aim of establishing parity between Réunion and metropolitan France. In July, however, the French Government announced increases in social security benefits that were substantially less than had been expected, resulting in widespread discontent on the island. In September the Parti Communiste Réunionnais (PCR), which in alliance with the Free-DOM list of independent candidates controlled 26 of the 45 seats in the Regional Council, demanded that the electorate refuse to participate in the forthcoming French referendum on ratification of the Treaty on European Union (see p. 273), in protest at the alleged failure of the French Government to recognize the requirements of the Overseas Departments. At the referendum, which took place later that month, the ratification of the treaty was approved by the voters of Réunion, although only 26.3% of the registered electorate voted.

Elections to the French National Assembly were held in March 1993; two incumbent right-wing deputies retained their seats, while the PCR, the Parti Socialiste (PS) and the Rassemblement pour la République (RPR) each secured one of the remaining seats. At elections to the 47-seat Conseil Général (General Council), which took place in March 1994, the PCR retained 12 seats, while the number of PS deputies increased to 12. The number of seats held by the RPR and the Union pour la Démocratie Française (UDF) declined to five and 11, respectively. The PCR and PS subsequently established a coalition (despite the long-standing differences between the two parties), thereby securing the support of 24 of the 47 seats in the General Council. In April a member of the PS, Christophe Payet, was elected President of the General Council; the right-wing parties (which had held the presidency of the General Council for more than 40 years) boycotted the poll. The PS and PCR signed an agreement whereby the two parties were to control the administration of the General Council jointly.

In the second round of the French presidential election, which took place in May 1995, the socialist candidate, Lionel Jospin, secured 56% of the votes cast on Réunion, while Jacques Chirac, the official candidate of the RPR, won 44% of the votes (although Chirac obtained the highest number of votes overall).

Equality with metropolitan France

With effect from the beginning of 1996 the social security systems of the Overseas Departments were aligned with those of metropolitan France. In February Alain Juppé, the French Prime Minister, invited representatives from the Overseas Departments to Paris to participate in discussions on social equality and development. Paul Vergès, joint candidate of the PCR and the PS, was elected to the French Sénat (Senate) in April, securing 51.9% of the votes cast. In the by-election to replace Vergès, which took place in September, Claude Hoarau, the PCR candidate, was elected as a deputy to the National Assembly with 56.0% of the votes cast. A new majority alliance between Free-DOM, the RPR and the UDF was subsequently formed in the Regional Council, with the re-election of its 19-member permanent commission in October.

Four left-wing candidates were successful in elections to the National Assembly held in May and June 1997. Claude Hoarau (PCR) retained his seat and was joined by Huguette Bello and Elie Hoarau, also both from the PCR, and Michel Tamaya (PS), while André Thien Ah Koon, representing the RPR-UDF coalition, was re-elected.

In February 1998 the PCR (led by Vergès), the PS and several right-wing mayors presented a joint list of candidates, known as the Rassemblement, to contest forthcoming elections. In the elections to the Regional Council, which took place on 15 March, the Rassemblement secured 19 seats, while the UDF obtained nine seats and the RPR eight, with various left-wing candidates representing Free-DOM winning five. Vergès was elected President of the Regional Council on 23 March, with the support of the deputies belonging to the Rassemblement and Free-DOM groups. In concurrent elections to an expanded 49-member General Council, right-wing candidates (including those on the Rassemblement's list) secured 27 seats, while left-wing candidates obtained 22 seats, with the PCR and the PS each winning 10 seats. At the end of the month Jean-Luc Poudroux, of the UDF, was elected President of the General Council, owing to the support of two left-wing deputies.

At municipal elections, held in March 2001, the left-wing parties experienced significant losses. Notably, the PS mayor of Saint-Denis, Michel Tamaya, was defeated by the RPR candidate, René-Paul Victoria. At elections to the General Council, held concurrently, the right-wing parties also made substantial gains, obtaining 38 of the 49 seats; the UDF retained its majority, and Poudroux was re-elected as President. In July Elie Hoarau was obliged to resign from the National Assembly, following his conviction on charges of electoral fraud, as a result of which he received a one-year prison sentence and was barred from holding public office for a period of three years.

In the first round of the French presidential election, which was held on 21 April 2002, Jospin secured 39.0% of the valid votes cast in the Department (although he was eliminated nationally), followed by Chirac, who received 37.1%. In the second round, on 5 May, Chirac overwhelmingly defeated the candidate of the extreme right-wing Front National, Jean-Marie Le Pen, with 91.9% of the vote. At elections to the National Assembly in June, Thien Ah Koon, allied to the new Union pour la Majorité Présidentielle (UMP, which had recently been formed by the merger of the RPR, the Démocratie Libérale and elements of the UDF), and Bello were re-elected. Tamaya lost his seat to Victoria of the UMP, Claude Hourau lost to Bertho Audifax of the UMP, while Elie Hourau, who was declared ineligible to stand for re-election, was replaced by Christophe Payet of the PS. (In November the UMP was renamed the Union pour un Mouvement Populaire.)

In elections to the Regional Council, which took place on 21 and 28 March 2004, the Alliance, a joint list of candidates led by the PCR, secured 27 seats. The UMP won 11 seats, and an alliance of the PS and Les Verts Réunion obtained seven seats. Following concurrent elections to the General Council, to renew 25 of the 49 seats, right-wing candidates held 30 seats, while left-wing candidates held 19. On 1 April Nassimah Dindar of the UMP was elected to succeed Poudroux as President of the General Council. Paul Vergès was re-elected as President of the Regional Council on the following day. In February 2005 Gélite Hoarau replaced Vergès as the PCR's representative to the Sénat.

In May 2005 a national referendum on ratification of the proposed constitutional treaty of the European Union (EU) was held: 59.9% of Réunion's electorate joined with a majority of French voters in rejecting the treaty; voter turnout on the island was around 53%.

Presidential and local elections

In the first round of the French presidential election, held on 22 April 2007, Ségolène Royal of the PS secured 46.2% of the votes cast in Réunion, while Nicolas Sarkozy of the UMP received 25.1%. Sarkozy was elected to the presidency in the second round of voting on 6 May; however, voting on Réunion again favoured Royal, who received 63.6% of the island vote. At legislative elections in June, Victoria and Bello both retained their seats in the National Assembly, but Audifax lost his seat to Jean-Claude Fruteau of the PS. Didier Robert of the UMP defeated Paul Vergès, while Patrick Lebreton of the PS was also elected. In March 2008 Dindar was re-elected to the presidency of the General Council.

In January 2009 workers in Guadeloupe, a French overseas territory in the Caribbean, commenced industrial action in protest against rising fuel and food prices. The unrest rapidly spread to other Departments, including Réunion, where unemployment and living costs had increased significantly. In March protests staged in Saint-Denis to demand price reductions and a wage increase for low-paid workers degenerated into violence; police responded by firing tear gas to disperse the crowds.

In January 2010 President Sarkozy visited Réunion for the first time since his election to the presidency. Also in that month Michel Lalande replaced Pierre-Henry Maccioni as Prefect. Elections to the Regional Council took place on 14 and 21 March 2010 at which the La Réunion en Confiance alliance led by Robert won 27 seats. The Liste de l'Alliance, headed by Vergès' PCR, took 12 seats, while the PS-led Pour une Réunion plus Juste avec l'Union des Socialistes alliance secured six seats. On 26 March Robert was elected to succeed Vergès as President of the Regional Council.

In early 2012 further social unrest erupted, initially directed at the high cost of fuel prices with transporters blocking fuel outlets; subsequently protests at the generally high cost of living spread across the island and security forces were brought in from France to quell the violence. Some 233 arrests were made and nine police officers were injured, according to the Prefecture. Following negotiations between local politicians, civil society representatives, transporters and petrol companies, an agreement was reached to lower prices of fuel and electricity for households on modest income and to freeze prices for 60 staple products from March.

Recent developments: the 2012 elections

The first round of the French presidential election was conducted on 22 April 2012: François Hollande, representing the PS, attracted 53.3% of the island's votes, compared with 18.0% for Sarkozy. A second round election was held two weeks later, at which Hollande secured 71.5% of the ballot, comprehensively defeating Sarkozy, who won only 28.5%. Hollande also triumphed nationally and was sworn in as President in mid-May. In the legislative elections, which took place on 10 and 17 June, Réunion's representation in the National Assembly was increased from five to seven seats. The PS secured five of the seats, with the two remaining mandates won, respectively, by an independent left-wing candidate and a representative of Le Centre pour la France (a coalition led by the Mouvement Démocrate).

Jean-Luc Marx was inaugurated as the island's new Prefect on 27 August, replacing Lalande.

The French Minister of Overseas Territories, Victorin Lurel, visited Réunion in July 2012 to hold discussions with the local authorities regarding the high cost of living on the island. A bill to address the issue of inflated prices (and consequent social unrest) in Réunion and other French Overseas Possessions, drafted by Lurel, was promulgated by President Hollande in November.

In October 2013 EU Regional Policy Commissioner Johannes Hahn attended the annual conference of the Presidents of Europes's Outermost Regions on Réunion, which was hosted by Robert (as chair of the Outermost Regions); Hahn also visited EU-financed ecological research projects undertaken on the island. In November the French Minister of Labour, Employment, Vocational Training and Social Dialogue, Michel Sapin, visited Réunion, where he announced further measures to address the continued high rate of unemployment and to promote vocational training. In the same month Lurel announced a decree, which was to enter into force on 1 January 2014, to regulate fuel prices in the Overseas Departments. The French Government declared a state of natural disaster on Réunion in early January, following a severe cyclone in which one person was killed, and Lurel made a further visit to the island.

CONSTITUTION AND GOVERNMENT

The Constitution of the Fifth Republic of France, adopted by referendum on 28 September 1958 and promulgated on 6 October 1958 applies on Réunion. France is represented in Réunion by an appointed Prefect. There are two councils with local powers: the 49-member Conseil Général (General Council) and the 45-member Conseil Régional (Regional Council). Both are elected for up to six years by direct universal suffrage. Réunion has seven directly elected deputies in the French Assemblée Nationale (National Assembly) and four indirectly elected representatives in the Sénat (Senate). The Department is also represented at the European Parliament.

REGIONAL AND INTERNATIONAL CO-OPERATION

Réunion is represented by France in the Indian Ocean Commission (IOC, see p. 451) which it joined in 1986. Réunion was given the right to host ministerial meetings of the IOC, but would not be allowed to occupy the presidency, owing to its status as a non-sovereign state. As an integral part of France, Réunion belongs to the European Union (see p. 273).

ECONOMIC AFFAIRS

Réunion's gross national income (GNI) in 1995 was estimated at 29,200m. French francs, equivalent to about 44,300 francs per head. Between the censuses of 1999 and 2008, Réunion's population increased at an average annual rate of 1.6%. In 2010, according to official figures, Réunion's gross domestic product (GDP), measured at current prices, was €14,900m.; in that year GDP per head totalled €17,730. GDP increased, in real terms, at an average annual rate of 5.4% in 2001–10; it declined by 1.2% in 2012.

Agriculture (including hunting, forestry and fishing) contributed 1.3% of GDP in 2007, and engaged an estimated 1.4% of the salaried working population in 2012. The principal cash crops are sugar cane (sugar accounted for 37.9% of export earnings in 2007), maize, tobacco, vanilla, and geraniums and vetiver root, which are cultivated for the production of essential oils. Other major crops are tomatoes, cauliflowers, potatoes, cabbages, and lettuce and chicory. Fishing and livestock production are also important to the economy. According to the UN, agricultural GDP increased at an average annual rate of 3.9% during 1990–2000; growth in 2001 was 3.1%.

Industry (including mining, manufacturing, construction and power) contributed 16.6% of GDP in 2007, and employed an estimated 13.3% of the working salaried population in 2012. The principal branch of manufacturing is food-processing, particularly the production of sugar and rum. Other significant sectors include the fabrication of construction materials, mechanics, printing, metalwork, textiles and garments, and electronics. According to the UN, industrial GDP (excluding construction) increased at an average annual rate of 4.3% during 1990–99; growth in 2001 was 3.7%.

There are no mineral resources on the island. Energy is derived principally from thermal and hydroelectric power. Power plants at Bois-Rouge and Le Gol produce around 45% of the island's total energy requirements; almost one-third of the electricity generated is produced using bagasse, a by-product of sugar cane. Imports of petroleum fuel comprised 13.8% of the value of total imports in 2012.

Services (including transport, communications, trade and finance) contributed 82.0% of GDP in 2007, and employed an estimated 85.4% of the salaried working population in 2012. The public sector accounts for more than two-thirds of employment in the services sector. Tourism is also significant; in 2011, 446,500 tourists visited Réunion. According to the World Tourism Organisation, tourism revenue totalled €434m. in 2011.

Réunion's economy is overwhelmingly dependent on imports and as a result the island recorded a merchandise trade deficit of € 4,393m. in 2012. The principal sources of imports in 2010 were France (54.2%), Singapore and the People's Republic of China. The principal market for exports in 2010, were France (31.6%), Mayotte, Spain, Madagascar and Hong Kong. The principal exports in 2012 were prepared foodstuffs, industrial products, industrial and household waste, transport equipment, and electrical and electronic equipment and components. The principal imports in 2012 were prepared foodstuffs, electrical and electronic equipment and components, refined petroleum products, transport equipment, pharmaceutical products, metal products, miscellaneous manufactured products, textiles and footwear, plastic products, and chemicals and perfumes.

In 2009 the budget balanced at €750m. The departmental budget for that year amounted to €1,415.0m.; some 62.5% of revenue was to be provided by the State. The annual rate of inflation averaged 1.9% in 2000–12; consumer prices increased by 1.0% in 2012. According to ILO, an estimated 28.5% of the labour force were unemployed in 2012.

Réunion has a relatively developed economy, but is dependent on financial aid from France. The economy has traditionally been based on agriculture, and is, therefore, vulnerable to poor climatic conditions. From the 1990s the production of sugar cane (the principal agricultural activity) was adversely affected by increasing urbanization, which resulted in a decline in agricultural land. Economic progress has been largely sustained by tourism. According to the French Institut National de la Statistique et des Etudes Economiques, GDP contracted by 1.2% in 2012, largely owing to the ongoing crisis in the eurozone. Early that year violent protests were precipitated by high fuel prices; the French Government subsequently adopted legislation in an effort to mitigate social discontent in the Overseas Departments, notably imposing price controls on a range of staple goods in November. In October 2013 the French Government announced measures to address the continued high rate of unemployment, including the provision of an additional 5,000 subsidized contracts (90%–95% state-financed), although local officials were urged to implement the existing 20,000 subsidized contracts. Réunion's Action Plan for growth in 2014–20, submitted to the European Commission in mid-2013, cited a focus on youth and employment as its main priority; the Plan also emphasized the authorities' commitment to the development of renewable energy sources and reduction in energy dependence (a major solar power plant had been established at Bois-Rouge), and the need to improve the island's accessibility, with the rehabilitation of transport links and establishment of information technology infrastructure, in order to expand external trade, and to strengthen growth in the tourism sector towards a long-term objective of 1m. tourist arrivals by 2020. The European Union co-financed ongoing research projects in Réunion on the impact of global change on plant health, biodiversity conservation and related issues in the agricultural sector.

PUBLIC HOLIDAYS

2015: 1 January (New Year's Day), 6 April (Easter Monday), 1 May (Labour Day), 8 May (Liberation Day), 14 May (Ascension Day), 25 May (Whit Monday), 14 July (National Day, Fall of the Bastille), 15 August (Assumption), 1 November (All Saints' Day), 11 November (Armistice Day), 20 December (Abolition of Slavery Day), 25 December (Christmas Day).

Statistical Survey

Source (unless otherwise indicated): Institut National de la Statistique et des Études Économiques, Service Régional de la Réunion, 15 rue de l'Ecole, 97490 Sainte-Clotilde; tel. 262-48-81-00; fax 262-41-09-81; internet www.insee.fr/fr/insee_regions/reunion.

AREA AND POPULATION

Area: 2,507 sq km (968 sq miles).

Population: 706,180 (males 347,076, females 359,104) at census of 8 March 1999; 828,581 at census of 1 January 2011. Note: According to new census methodology, data in 2011 refer to median figures based on the collection of raw data over a five-year period (2009–13). *Mid-2014* (UN estimate): 885,329 (Source: UN, *World Population Prospects: The 2012 Revision*).

Density (at mid-2014): 353.1 per sq km.

Population by Age and Sex (UN estimates at mid-2014): *0–14:* 220,697 (males 111,902, females 108,795); *15–64:* 587,355 (males 288,819, females 298,536); *65 and over:* 77,277 (males 33,397, females 43,880); *Total* 885,329 (males 434,118, females 451,211) (Source: UN, *World Population Prospects: The 2012 Revision*).

Principal Localities (population at 1 January 2010): Saint-Denis (capital) 145,022; Saint-Paul 103,346; Saint-Pierre 79,228; Le Tampon 73,365; Saint-André 53,955; Saint-Louis 52,038.

Births, Marriages and Deaths (2011): Registered live births 14,124 (birth rate 16.9 per 1,000); Registered marriages 2,738 (marriage rate 3.3 per 1,000); Registered deaths 4,002 (death rate 4.8 per 1,000).

Life Expectancy (years at birth, 2011): Males 76.5; females 82.9.

Economically Active Population (persons aged 15 years and over, 1999 census): Agriculture, hunting, forestry and fishing 9,562; Mining, manufacturing, electricity, gas and water 13,424; Construction 11,003; Wholesale and retail trade 24,658; Transport, storage and communications 5,494; Financing, insurance and real estate 4,851; Business services 11,225; Public administration 39,052; Education 23,325; Health and social work 17,376; Other services 13,707; *Total employed* 173,677 (males 100,634, females 73,043); Unemployed 124,203 (males 63,519, females 60,684); *Total labour force* 297,880 (males 164,153, females 133,727). Figures exclude 967 persons on compulsory military service (males 945, females 22). *2011* (salaried workers at 1 January, provisional): Agriculture 2,766; Mining and utilities 3,391; Manufacturing 13,181; Construction 14,179; Trade 31,616; Transport 11,204; Hotels and restaurants 6,895; Information and communication 3,963; Financial activities and real estate 7,106; Private services 21,272; Public administration, education, human health and social action 93,762; Other service activities 21,945; Total employed 231,280; Unemployed 24,394; Total labour force 255,674. *2012* (persons aged 15 years and over, provisional estimates at 31 December): Agriculture, forestry and fishing 3,132; Mining and utilities 3,468; Manufacturing 13,136; Construction 13,452; Wholesale and retail trade; repair of motor vehicles, motorcycles, etc. 31,480; Transport 11,123; Hotels and restaurants 7,039; Information and communication 4,179; Financial activities and real estate 7,199; Private services 21,560; Public administration and defence; education, health and social work 89,924; Other community, social and personal service activities 21,110; *Total employed* 226,802. Note: Data exclude 23,325 persons employed without salary.

HEALTH AND WELFARE

Key Indicators

Total Fertility Rate (children per woman, 2008): 2.5.

Physicians (per 1,000 head, 2011): 2.1.

Hospital Beds (per 1,000 head, 2000): 3.7.

For definitions, see explanatory note on p. vi.

AGRICULTURE, ETC.

Principal Crops ('000 metric tons, 2012, FAO estimates): Maize 16.0; Potatoes 6.0; Sugar cane 1,900.0; Cabbages and other brassicas 3.4; Lettuce and chicory 3.5; Tomatoes 9.5; Cauliflowers and broccoli 6.5; Pumpkins, squash and gourds 1.0; Eggplants (Aubergines) 1.0; Onions and shallots, green 5.3; Beans, green 3.7; Carrots and turnips 2.2; Bananas 7.5; Tangerines, mandarins, clementines and satsumas 4.0; Mangoes, mangosteens and guavas 2.6; Pineapples 22.0. *Aggregate Production* ('000 metric tons, may include official, semi-official or estimated data): Total vegetables (incl. melons) 50.0; Total fruits (excl. melons) 70.6.

Livestock ('000 head, 2012, FAO estimates): Cattle 27.0; Pigs 68.5; Sheep 1.0; Goats 42.0; Chickens 15,000.

Livestock Products ('000 metric tons, 2012, FAO estimates): Cattle meat 1.7; Pig meat 14.9; Chicken meat 17.2; Rabbit meat 1.9; Cow's milk 33.0; Hen eggs 7.0.

Forestry ('000 cu m, 1991): *Roundwood Removals:* Sawlogs, veneer logs and logs for sleepers 4.2; Other industrial wood 0.9 (FAO estimate); Fuel wood 31.0 (FAO estimate); Total 36.1. *Sawnwood Production:* 2.2. *1992–2012:* Annual production assumed to be unchanged from 1991 (FAO estimates).

Fishing (metric tons, live weight, 2011, FAO estimates): Capture 2,550 (Albacore 425; Yellowfin tuna 350; Bigeye tuna 320; Swordfish 1,031; Common dolphinfish 79); Aquaculture 115 (FAO estimate); *Total catch* (incl. others) 2,665 (FAO estimate).

Source: FAO.

INDUSTRY

Selected Products (metric tons, 2012, unless otherwise indicated): Sugar 208,700; Oil of geranium 2 (2007); Oil of vetiver root 0.4 (2002); Rum (hl) 97,500; Electric energy (million kWh) 2,811 (Source: partly Institut d'Emission des Départements d'Outre-mer, *Rapport Annuel 2012*).

FINANCE

Currency and Exchange Rates: The French franc was used until the end of February 2002. Euro notes and coins were introduced on 1 January 2002, and the euro became the sole legal tender from 18 February. Some of the figures in this Survey are still in terms of francs. For details of exchange rates, see Mayotte.

Budgets (€ million, 2011): *Departmental Budget* Current revenue 1,342.2 (Tax revenue 823.8, Grants 480.4, Other 38.0); Capital revenue 107.2; Total revenue 1,449.4. Current expenditure 1,235.2 (Wages 187.9, Other goods and services 41.9, Interest payments 15.1, Other 990.3); Capital expenditure 230.9; Total expenditure 1,466.1. *Regional Budget:* Revenue 662.4 (Current 443.7, Capital 218.7); Expenditure 678.6 (Current 297.1, Capital 381.4).

Money Supply (million francs at 31 December 1996): Currency outside banks 4,050; Demand deposits at banks 7,469; Total money 11,519.

Cost of Living (Consumer Price Index; base: 2000 = 100): All items 120.6 in 2010; 123.5 in 2011; 124.7 in 2012. Source: ILO.

Expenditure on the Gross Domestic Product (€ million at current prices, 2010): Private final consumption expenditure 9,590; Government final consumption expenditure 5,720; Gross capital formation 3,150; *Total domestic expenditure* 18,460; Exports of goods 280; *Less* Imports of goods 4,260; Tourist expenditure 300; Statistical discrepancy 120; *GDP in market prices* 14,900.

Gross Domestic Product by Economic Activity (€ million at current prices, 2007): Agriculture, forestry and fishing 177; Mining, manufacturing, electricity, gas and water 917; Construction 1,274; Wholesale and retail trade 1,182; Transport and communications 820; Finance and insurance 704; Public administration 1,521; Education, health and social work 3,128; Other services (incl. hotels and restaurants) 3,472; *Sub-total* 13,196; *Less* Financial intermediation services indirectly measured 462; *Gross value-added at basic prices* 12,734; Taxes on products, *less* subsidies on products 1,235; *GDP in market prices* 13,969.

EXTERNAL TRADE

Principal Commodities (€ million, 2012): *Imports:* Animals and animal products 106.6; Prepared foodstuffs 762.0; Refined petroleum products 640.0; Electrical and electronic equipment and components 747.3 (Information products and electronics 277.7, Electronic equipment and household electrical goods 203.0, Industrial and agricultural machinery 266.6); Transport equipment 596.6; Other industrial products 1,668.7 (Textiles and footwear 250.2, Paper and paperboard 141.2, Chemicals and perfumes 238.8, Pharmaceutical products 275.8, Plastic products 245.0, Metal products 253.5, Miscellaneous manufactured products 264.1); Total (incl. others) 4,654.5. *Exports:* Prepared foodstuffs 183.4; Refined petroleum products 13.0; Industrial and household waste 28.3; Electrical and electronic equipment and components 19.3 (Information products and electronics 8.1); Transport equipment 23.3; Other industrial products 33.7 (Chemicals and perfumes 10.1; Metal products 14.1); Total (incl. others) 306.8 (Source: Source: Institut d'Emission des Départements d'Outre-mer, *Rapport Annuel 2012*).

Principal Trading Partners (€ million, 2010): *Imports:* Belgium 52.1; China, People's Republic 287.5; France 2,312.8; Germany 200.6; Italy 89.8; Singapore 389.8; South Africa 100.0; Spain 62.0; Total (incl. others) 4,265.2. *Exports f.o.b.:* France 88.9; Hong Kong 13.4; Italy 6.7; Japan 10.5; Madagascar 15.1; Mauritius 7.4; Mayotte 26.5; Spain 18.0; USA 8.4; Total (incl. others) 281.5.

TRANSPORT

Road Traffic (1 January 2005): Motor vehicles in use 338,500.

Shipping: *Flag Registered Fleet* (at 31 December 2013): Vessels 15; Total displacement 12,351 grt (Source: Lloyd's List Intelligence—www.lloydslistintelligence.com); *Traffic* (2012 unless otherwise indicated): Passengers carried 48,918; Vessels entered 709 (2007); Freight unloaded 3,478,400 metric tons; Freight loaded 620,500 metric tons; Containers unloaded 111,952 TEUs (2007); Containers loaded 112,921 TEUs (2007).

Civil Aviation (2012): Passenger arrivals 1,044,000; Passenger departures 1,049,000; Freight unloaded 41,069 metric tons; Freight loaded 7,400 metric tons (Source: Institut d'Emission des Départements d'Outre-mer, *Rapport Annuel 2012*).

TOURISM

Tourist Arrivals: 420,300 in 2010; 471,300 in 2011; 446,500 in 2012 (Source: Institut d'Emission des Départements d'Outre-mer, *Rapport Annuel 2012*).

Arrivals by Country of Residence (2012): France (metropolitan) 355,900; Other EU 16,800; Mauritius 17,600; Total (incl. others)

446,500 (Source: Institut d'Emission des Départements d'Outre-mer, *La Réunion: Rapport Annuel 2012*).

Tourism Receipts (US $ million, excl. passenger transport): 425 in 2009; 392 in 2010; 434 in 2011 (Source: World Tourism Organisation).

COMMUNICATIONS MEDIA

Telephones ('000 main lines in use, 2010): 480.9.

Mobile Cellular Telephones ('000 subscribers, 2008): 579.2.

Internet Users ('000, 2009): 300.

Broadband Subscribers ('000, 2009): 185.

Source: International Telecommunication Union.

EDUCATION

Pre-primary and Primary (2012/13): Schools 522 (pre-primary 158, primary 364); public sector pupils 109,179 (pre-primary 40,544, primary 68,635); private pupils 9,409 (pre-primary 3,353, primary 6,056).

Secondary (2012/13): Schools 129 (118 public sector, 11 private); pupils 100,611 (public sector 93,212, private 7,399).

University (2011/12): Institution 3; students 11,593.

Other Higher (2011/12): Students 5,879.

Teaching Staff (2011/12, state schools): Pre-primary and primary 6,150; Secondary 8,429; University 481.

Directory

The Government

(April 2014)

HEAD OF STATE

President: FRANÇOIS HOLLANDE.

Prefect: JEAN-LUC MARX, Préfecture, pl. du Barachois, 97405 Saint-Denis Cédex; tel. 262-40-77-77; fax 262-41-73-74; e-mail courrier@reunion.pref.gouv.fr; internet www.reunion.pref.gouv.fr.

DEPARTMENTAL ADMINISTRATION

President of the General Council: NASSIMAH DINDAR (UMP), Hôtel du Département, 2 rue de la Source, 97488 Saint-Denis Cédex; tel. 262-90-30-30; fax 262-90-39-99; internet www.cg974.fr.

President of the Regional Council: DIDIER ROBERT (UMP), Hôtel de Région Pierre Lagourgue, ave René Cassin, Moufia, BP 7190, 97719 Saint-Denis Cédex 9; tel. 262-48-70-00; fax 262-48-70-71; e-mail region.reunion@cr-reunion.fr; internet www.regionreunion.com.

Election, Regional Council, 14 and 21 March 2010

Party	Seats
La Réunion en Confiance*	27
Liste de l'Alliance†	12
Pour une Réunion Plus Juste avec l'Union des Socialistes‡	6
Total	45

* An alliance led by the UMP.
† An alliance led by the PCR.
‡ An alliance led by the PS.

REPRESENTATIVES TO THE FRENCH PARLIAMENT

Deputies to the French National Assembly: ERICKA BAREIGTS (PS), HUGUETTE BELLO (Divers Gauche), JEAN JACQUES VLODY (PS), PATRICK LEBRETON (PS), JEAN-CLAUDE FRUTEAU (PS), MONIQUE ORPHÉ (PS), THIERRY ROBERT (Le Centre pour la France/MoDem).

Representatives to the French Senate: JACQUELINE FARREYROL (UMP), MICHEL FONTAINE (UMP), PAUL VERGÈS (PCR), MICHEL VERGOZ (PS).

GOVERNMENT OFFICES

Direction de l'Alimentation, de l'Agriculture et de la Forêt (DAAF): blvd de la Providence, 97489 Saint-Denis Cédex; tel. 262-30-89-89; fax 262-30-89-99; e-mail daaf974@agriculture.gouv.fr; internet www.daaf974.agriculture.gouv.fr.

Direction des Affaires Culturelles—Océan Indien (DAC OI): 23, rue Labourdonnais, BP 224, 97464 Saint-Denis Céedex; tel. 262-210-91-71; fax 262-41-61-93; e-mail la-reunion@culture.gouv.fr; internet www.la-reunion.culture.gouv.fr.

Direction de l'Environnement, de l'Aménagement et du Logement (DEAL): 2 rue Juliette Dodu, 97706 Saint-Denis Cédex; tel. 262-40-26-26; fax 262-40-27-27; e-mail deal-reunion@developpement-durable.gouv.fr; internet www.reunion.developpement-durable.gouv.fr.

Direction des Entreprises, de la Concurrence, de la Consommation, du Travail et de l'Emploi (DIECCTE): 112 rue de la République, 97488, Saint-Denis Cédex; tel. 262-94-07-07; fax 262-94-08-30; e-mail dd-974.direction@direccte.gouv.fr.

Direction de la Jeunesse, des Sports et de la Cohésion Sociale (DJSCS): 14 allée des Saphirs, 97487 Saint-Denis Cédex; tel. 262-20-96-40; fax 262-20-96-41; internet www.reunion.drjscs.gouv.fr.

Direction de la Mer Sud Océan Indien (DM SOI): 11 rue de la Compagnie, 97487 Saint-Denis Cédex; tel. 262-90-19-60; fax 262-21-70-57; e-mail DM-SOI@developpement-durable.gouv.fr; internet www.dm.sud-ocean-indien.developpement-durable.gouv.fr.

Direction Départementale de la Sécurité Publique (Police Nationale) (DDSP): 5 rue Malartic, Saint-Denis Cédex; tel. 262-90-74-74; fax 262-21-35-17.

Political Organizations

Mouvement Démocrate (MoDem): Saint-Denis; internet www.mouvementdemocrate.fr; f. 2007; fmrly Union pour la Démocratie Française (UDF); centrist.

Mouvement pour l'Indépendance de la Réunion (MIR): f. 1981 to succeed the fmr Mouvement pour la Libération de la Réunion; grouping of parties favouring autonomy; Leader ANSELME PAYET.

Parti Communiste Réunionnais (PCR): Saint-Denis; f. 1959; Pres. PAUL VERGÈS; Sec.-Gen. ELIE HOARAU.

Mouvement pour l'Egalité, la Démocratie, le Développement et la Nature: affiliated to the PCR; advocates political unity; Leader RENÉ PAYET.

Parti Socialiste (PS)—Fédération de la Réunion (PS): 190 route des Deux Canons Immeuble, Futura, 97490 Saint-Clotilde; tel. 262-29-32-06; fax 262-28-53-03; e-mail psreunion@wanadoo.fr; internet www.parti-socialiste.fr; left-wing; Sec. ANNETTE GILBERT.

Union pour un Mouvement Populaire (UMP)—Fédération de la Réunion: 6 bis blvd Vauban, BP 11, 97461 Saint-Denis Cédex; tel. 262-20-21-18; fax 262-41-73-55; f. 2002; centre-right; local branch of the metropolitan party; Departmental Sec. DIDIER ROBERT.

Les Verts Réunion: Apt 30, Res ARIAL, 132 rue Général de Gaulle, 97400 Saint-Denis; tel. 262-55-73-52; fax 262-25-03-03; e-mail sr-verts-reunion@laposte.net; internet lesverts.fr; ecologist; Regional Sec. JEAN ERPELDINGER.

Judicial System

Court of Appeal: Palais de Justice, 166 rue Juliette Dodu, 97488 Saint-Denis; tel. 262-40-58-58; fax 262-20-16-37; Pres. DOMINIQUE FERRIÈRE.

Religion

A substantial majority of the population are adherents of the Roman Catholic Church. There is a small Muslim community.

CHRISTIANITY

The Roman Catholic Church

Réunion comprises a single diocese, directly responsible to the Holy See. The number of adherents is equivalent to around 80% of the population.

Bishop of Saint-Denis de la Réunion: Mgr GILBERT GUILLAUME MARIE-JEAN AUBRY, Evêché, 36 rue de Paris, BP 55, 97461 Saint-Denis Cédex; tel. 262-94-85-70; fax 262-94-85-73; e-mail eveche.lareunion@wanadoo.fr; internet www.diocese-reunion.org.

The Press

DAILIES

Journal de l'Ile de la Réunion: Centre d'affaires Cadjee, 62 blvd du Chaudron, BP 40019, 97491 Sainte-Clotilde Cédex; tel. 262-48-66-00; fax 262-48-66-50; internet www.clicanoo.re; f. 1951; CEO and Dir of Publication JEAN-BAPTISTE MARIOTTI; Editor-in-Chief YVES MONT-ROUGE; circ. 35,000.

Quotidien de la Réunion et de l'Océan Indien: BP 303, 97712 Saint-Denis Cédex 9; tel. 262-92-15-10; fax 262-28-25-28; e-mail laredaction@lequotidien.re; internet www.lequotidien.re; f. 1976; Dir MAXIMIN CHANE KI CHUNE; circ. 38,900.

Témoignages: 6 rue du Général Emile Rolland, BP 1016, 97828 Le Port Cédex; tel. 262-55-21-21; e-mail temoignages@wanadoo.fr; internet www.temoignages.re; f. 1944; affiliated to the Parti Communiste Réunionnais; daily; Dir JEAN-MAX HOARAU; Editor-in-Chief ALAIN ILAN CHOJNOW; circ. 6,000.

PERIODICALS

Al-Islam: Centre Islamique de la Réunion, BP 437, 97459 Saint-Pierre Cédex; tel. 262-25-45-43; fax 262-35-58-23; e-mail centre-islamique-reunion@wanadoo.fr; internet www.islam-reunion.com; f. 1975; 4 a year; Dir ISSAC GANGAT.

L'Eco Austral: Technopole de la Réunion 2, rue Emile Hugot, BP 10003, 97801 Saint-Denis Cédex 9; tel. 262-41-51-41; fax 262-41-31-14; internet www.ecoaustral.com; f. 1993; monthly; regional economic issues; Editor ALAIN FOULON; circ. 50,000.

L'Economie de la Réunion: c/o INSEE, Parc Technologique, 10 rue Demarne, BP 13, 97408 Saint-Denis Messag Cédex 9; tel. 262-48-89-00; fax 262-48-89-89; e-mail bureau-de-presse@insee.fr; internet www.insee.fr/reunion; 4 a year; Dir of Publication VALERIE ROUX; Editor-in-Chief CLAIRE GRANGE.

Lutte Ouvrière—Ile de la Réunion: BP 184, 97470 Saint-Benoît; fax 262-48-00-98; e-mail contact@lutte-ouvriere-ile-de-la-reunion.org; internet www.lutte-ouvriere.org/en-regions/la-reunion; monthly; Communist; digital.

Le Mémento Industriel et Commercial Réunionnais: 80 rue Pasteur, BP 397, 97468 Saint-Denis; tel. 262-21-94-12; fax 262-41-10-85; e-mail memento@memento.fr; internet www.memento.fr; f. 1970; monthly; Editor-in-Chief GEORGES-GUILLAUME LOUAPRE-POTTIER; circ. 20,000.

La Réunion Agricole: Chambre d'Agriculture, 24 rue de la Source, BP 134, 97463 Saint-Denis Cédex; tel. 262-94-25-94; fax 262-21-06-17; e-mail herve.cailleaux@reunion.chambagri.fr; internet www.reunion.chambagri.fr; f. 2007; monthly; Dir JEAN BERNARD GONTHIER; Chief Editor HERVÉ CAILLEAUX; circ. 8,000.

Leader Réunion: 14 rue de la Guadeloupe, ZA Foucherolles, 97490 Sainte-Clotilde; tel. 262-92-10-60; Dir of Publication CAROLE MANOTE.

Visu: 97712 Saint-Denis Cédex 9; tel. 262-90-20-60; fax 262-90-20-61; weekly; Editor-in-Chief PHILIPPE PEYRE; circ. 53,000.

NEWS AGENCY

Imaz Press Réunion: 12 rue Victor MacAuliffe, 97400 Saint-Denis; tel. 262-20-05-65; fax 262-20-05-49; e-mail ipr@ipreunion.com; internet www.ipreunion.com; f. 2000; photojournalism and news agency; Dir RICHARD BOUHET.

Broadcasting and Communications

TELECOMMUNICATIONS

Orange Réunion: 35 blvd du Chaudron, BP 7431, 97743 Saint-Denis Cédex 9; tel. 262-20-02-00; fax 262-20-67-79; internet reunion.orange.fr; f. 2000; subsidiary of Orange France; mobile cellular telephone operator.

Outremer Telecom Réunion: 12 et 14 rue Henri Cornu, Technopole de la Réunion, BP 150, 97801 Saint-Denis, Cedex 9; tel. 262-20-023-00; fax 262-97-53-99; internet www.outremer-telecom.fr; telecommunications provider.

Société Réunionnaise du Radiotéléphone (SRR): 21 rue Pierre Aubert, 97490 Sainte-Clotide; BP 17, 97408 Saint-Denis, Messag Cédex 9; tel. 262-48-19-70; fax 262-48-19-80; internet www.srr.fr; f. 1995; subsidiary of SFR Cegetel, France; mobile cellular telephone operator; CEO JEAN-PIERRE HAGGAÏ; 431,719 subscribers in Réunion, 46,341 in Mayotte (as Mayotte Télécom Mobile) in 2003.

BROADCASTING

Réunion 1ère: 1 rue Jean Chatel, 97716 Saint-Denis Cédex; tel. 262-40-67-67; fax 262-21-64-84; internet reunion.la1ere.fr; acquired by Groupe France Télévisions in 2004; fmrly Réseau France Outremer, present name adopted in 2010; radio and television relay services in French; broadcasts two television channels (Télé-Réunion and Tempo) and three radio channels (Radio-Réunion, France-Inter and France-Culture); Dir-Gen. GENEVIÈVE GIARD; Regional Dir ROBERT MOY.

Radio

In 2005 there were 46 licensed private radio stations. These included:

Antenne Réunion Radio: Saint-Denis; e-mail direction@antennereunion.fr; internet www.antennereunion.fr; f. 2011.

Cherie FM Réunion: 3 rue de Kerveguen, 97400 Sainte-Clotilde; tel. 262-97-32-00; fax 262-97-32-32; Editor-in-Chief LEA BERTHAULT.

NRJ Réunion: 3 rue de Kerveguen, 97490 Sainte-Clotilde; tel. 262-97-32-00; fax 262-97-51-10; e-mail c.duboc@h2r.re; commercial radio station; Station Man. SYLVAIN PEGUILLAN.

Radio Festival: 3 rue de Kerveguen, 97490 Sainte-Clotilde; tel. 262-97-32-00; fax 262-97-32-32; e-mail redaction@radiofestival.fr; internet www.radiofestival.re; f. 1995; commercial radio station; Pres. MARIO LECHAT; Editor-in-Chief JEAN-PIERRE GERMAIN.

Radio Free-DOM: 131 rue Jules Auber, BP 666, 97400 Saint-Denis Cédex; tel. 262-41-51-51; fax 262-21-68-64; e-mail freedom@freedom.fr; internet www.freedom.fr; f. 1981; commercial radio station; Dir Dr CAMILLE SUDRE.

Television

Antenne Réunion: rue Emile Hugot, BP 80001, 97801 Saint-Denis Cédex 9; tel. 262-48-28-28; fax 262-48-28-26; e-mail direction@antennereunion.fr; internet www.antennereunion.fr; f. 1991; broadcasts 10 hours daily; Pres. CHRISTOPHE DUCASSE; Dir-Gen. PHILIPPE ROUSSEL.

Canal Réunion: 6 rue René Demarne, Technopole de la Réunion, 97490 Sainte-Clotilde; tel. 262-97-98-99; fax 262-97-98-90; e-mail contact@canalreunion.net; internet www.canalreunion.com; subscription television channel; broadcasts a minimum of 19 hours daily; Chair. JEAN-NOEL TRONC; Dir JEAN-BERNARD MOURIER.

TV-4: 8 chemin Fontbrune, 97400 Saint-Denis; tel. 262-52-73-73; broadcasts 19 hours daily.

Other privately owned television services include TVB, TVE, RTV, Télé-Réunion and TV-Run.

Finance

(cap. = capital; res = reserves; dep. = deposits; m. = million; brs = branches)

BANKING

Central Bank

Institut d'Emission des Départements d'Outre-mer: 4 rue de la Compagnie des Indes, 97487 Saint-Denis Cédex; tel. 262-90-71-00; fax 262-21-41-32; e-mail agence@iedom-reunion.fr; internet www.iedom.fr/reunion; Dir ARNAUD BELLAMY-BROWN.

Commercial Banks

Banque Française Commerciale Océan Indien (BFCOI): 60 rue Alexis de Villeneuve, BP 323, 97466 Saint-Denis Cédex; tel. 262-40-55-55; fax 262-25-21-47; e-mail webmaster@bfcoi.com; internet www.bfcoi.com; f. 1976; cap. €16.7m., res €65.9m., dep. €1,302.4m. (Dec. 2008); Pres. PIERRE GUY-NOEL; Gen. Man. ROGER MUNOZ; 8 brs.

Banque Nationale de Paris Intercontinentale: 67 rue Juliette Dodu, BP 113, 97463 Saint-Denis; tel. 262-40-30-02; fax 262-41-39-09; e-mail contactreunion@bnpparibas.com; internet www.bnpgroup.com; f. 1927; 100% owned by BNP Paribas; Chair. MICHEL PEBEREAU; Man. Dir DANIEL DEGUIN; 16 brs.

Banque de la Réunion (BR), SA: 27 rue Jean Chatel, 97711 Saint-Denis Cédex; tel. 262-40-01-23; fax 262-40-00-61; internet www.banquedelareunion.fr; f. 1853; owned by Groupe Banque Populaire et Caisse d'Epargne (France); cap. €65.4m., res €112.0m., dep. €2,010.8m. (Dec. 2008); Pres. BRUNO DELETRE; Gen. Man. BENOÎT CATEL; 20 brs.

BRED-Banque Populaire: 33 rue Victor MacAuliffe, 97461 Saint-Denis; tel. 262-90-15-60; fax 262-90-15-99.

Crédit Agricole de la Réunion: Parc Jean de Cambiaire, Cité des Lauriers, BP 84, 97462 Saint-Denis Cédex; tel. 262-40-81-81; fax 262-40-81-40; internet www.ca-reunion.fr; f. 1949; total assets €2,564m. (Dec. 2004); Chair. CHRISTIAN DE LA GIRODAY; Gen. Man. PIERRE MARTIN.

Development Bank

Société Financière pour le Développement Economique de la Réunion (SOFIDER): 3 rue Labourdonnais, BP 867, 97477 Saint-Denis Cédex; tel. 262-40-32-32; fax 262-40-32-00; internet www.sofider.re; part of the Agence Française de Développement; Dir-Gen. CLAUDE PÉRIOU.

INSURANCE

More than 20 major European insurance companies are represented in Saint-Denis.

AGF Vie La Réunion: 185 ave du Général de Gaulle, BP 797, 97476 Saint-Denis Cédex; tel. 262-94-72-23; fax 262-94-72-26; e-mail agfoi-vie@agfoi.com.

Capma & Capmi: 18 rue de la Cie des Indes, 97499 Saint-Denis; tel. 262-21-10-56; fax 262-20-32-67.

Groupama Océan Indien et Pacifique: 13 rue Fénelon, BP 626, 97473 Saint-Denis Cédex; tel. 262-26-12-61; fax 262-41-50-79; Chair. DIDIER FOUCQUE; Gen. Man. MAURICE FAURE (acting).

Trade and Industry

GOVERNMENT AGENCIES

Agence de Gestion des Initiatives Locales en Matière Européenne (AGILE)—Cellule Europe Réunion: 3 rue Felix Guyon, 97400 Saint-Denis; tel. 262-90-10-80; fax 262-21-90-72; e-mail celleurope@agile-reunion.org; internet www.agile-reunion.org; responsible for local application of EU structural funds; Dir SERGE JOSEPH.

Agence Régionale de Santé Océan Indien (ARS-OI): 2 bis ave Georges Brassens, CS 60050, 97408 Saint-Denis Messag Cédex 9; tel. 262-97-90-00; e-mail ars-oi-delegation-reunion@ars.sante.fr; internet www.ars.ocean-indien.sante.fr; f. 2010; responsible for implementation of health policies in Réunion and Mayotte; Dir-Gen. CHANTAL DE SINGLY.

Conseil Economique Social et Environnemental Régional (CESER): 10 rue du Béarn, BP 17191, 97804 Saint-Denis Messag Cédex 9; tel. 262-97-96-30; fax 262-97-96-31; e-mail ceser-reunion@ceser-reunion.fr; internet www.ceser-reunion.fr; f. 1984; Pres. JEAN-RAYMOND MONDON.

Direction Régionale du Commerce Extérieur (DRCE): 3 rue Serge Ycard, 97490 Sainte-Clotilde; tel. 262-92-24-70; fax 262-92-24-76; e-mail reunion@missioneco.org; internet www.missioneco.org/reunion; Dir PHILIPPE GENIER.

DEVELOPMENT ORGANIZATIONS

Agence de Développement de la Réunion (AD): rue Serge Ycart, BP 33, 97490 Sainte-Clotilde Cedex; tel. 262-92-24-92; fax 262-92-24-88; e-mail info@adreunion.com; internet www.adreunion.com; Chair. JISMY SOUPRAYENMESTRY.

Agence Française de Développement (AFD): 44 rue Jean Cocteau, BP 2013, 97488 Saint-Denis Cédex; tel. 262-90-00-90; fax 262-21-74-58; e-mail afdstdenis@re.groupe-afd.org; internet www.afd.fr; Dir MARC DUBERNET.

Association pour le Développement Industriel de la Réunion: 8 rue Philibert, BP 327, 97466 Saint-Denis Cédex; tel. 262-94-43-00; fax 262-94-43-09; e-mail adir@adir.info; internet www.adir.info; f. 1975; Pres. MAURICE CERISOLA; Sec.-Gen. FRANÇOISE DELMONT DE PALMAS; 190 mems.

Chambre d'Agriculture de la Réunion: 24 rue de la Source, BP 134, 97463 Saint-Denis Cédex; tel. 262-94-25-94; fax 262-21-06-17; e-mail president@reunion.chambagri.fr; internet www.reunion.chambagri.fr; Pres. JEAN-YVES MINATCHY; Gen. Man. JEAN-FRANÇOIS APAYA.

Jeune Chambre Economique de Saint-Denis de la Réunion: 25 rue de Paris, BP 1151, 97483 Saint-Denis; internet saintdenis.jcer.fr; f. 1963; Chair. SYLVIE CRESPO; 30 mems.

CHAMBERS OF COMMERCE

Chambre de Commerce et d'Industrie de la Réunion (CCIR): 5 bis rue de Paris, BP 120, 97463 Saint-Denis Cédex; tel. 262-94-20-00; fax 262-94-22-90; e-mail sg.dir@reunion.cci.fr; internet www.reunion.cci.fr; f. 1830; Pres. ERIC MAGAMOOTOO; Dir MOHAMED AHMED.

Chambre de Métiers et de l'Artisanat: 42 rue Jean Cocteau, BP 261, 97465 Saint-Denis Cédex; tel. 262-21-04-35; fax 262-21-68-33; e-mail cdm@cm-reunion.fr; internet www.cm-reunion.fr; f. 1968; Pres. BERNARD PICARDO; Sec. BENJAMINE DE OLIVEIRA; 14 mem. orgs.

EMPLOYERS' ASSOCIATIONS

Conseil de l'Ordre des Pharmaciens: 1 bis rue Sainte Anne, Immeuble le Concorde, Appt. 26, 1er étage, 97400 Saint-Denis; tel. 262-41-85-51; fax 262-21-94-86; e-mail delegation_reunion@ordre.pharmacien.fr; Pres. CHRISTIANE VAN DE WALLE.

Fédération Régionale des Coopératives Agricoles de la Réunion (FRCA): 8 bis, route de la Z. I. No. 2 97410, Saint-Pierre; tel. 262-96-24-40; fax 262-96-24-41; internet www.frca-reunion.coop; f. 1979; Pres. JEAN-FLORE BARRET; Sec.-Gen. RITO FERRERE; 27 mem. orgs.

Coopérative Agricole des Huiles Essentielles de Bourbon (CAHEB): 83 rue de Kerveguen, 97430 Le Tampon; BP 43, 97831 Le Tampon; tel. 262-27-02-27; fax 262-27-35-54; e-mail caheb@geranium-bourbon.com; f. 1963; represents producers of essential oils; Pres. MARIE ROSE SEVERIN; Sec.-Gen. LAURENT JANCI.

Société Coopérative Agricole Fruits de la Réunion: 18 Bellevue Pâturage, 97450 Saint-Louis; fax 262-91-41-04; f. 2002; Pres. CHRISTIAN BARRET.

Union Réunionnaise des Coopératives Agricoles (URCOOPA): Z. I. Cambaie, BP 90, 97862 Saint-Paul Cedex; tel. 262-45-37-10; fax 262-45-37-05; e-mail urcoopa@urcoopa.fr; internet www.urcoopa.fr; f. 1982; represents farmers; comprises Coop Avirons (f. 1967), Société Coopérative Agricole Nord-Est (CANE), SICA Lait (f. 1961), and CPPR; Pres. ARY MONDON; Dir-Gen. OLIVIER RONIN.

Mouvement des Entreprises de France Réunion (MEDEF): 14 rampes Ozoux, BP 354, 97467 Saint-Denis; tel. 262-20-01-30; fax 262-41-68-56; e-mail medef.reunion@wanadoo.fr; Pres. FRANÇOIS CAILLÉ.

Ordre National de Médecins: 3 résidence Laura, 4 rue Milius, 97400 Saint-Denis; tel. 262-20-11-58; fax 262-21-08-02; e-mail reunion@974.medecin.fr; internet www.odmreunion.net; Pres. Dr YVAN TCHENG.

Syndicat des Pharmaciens de la Réunion: 1 ave Marcel Hoarau, 97490 Sainte-Clotilde; tel. 262-28-53-60; fax 262-28-79-67; e-mail synd974@resopharma.fr; Pres. FRÉDE SAUTRON.

Syndicat des Producteurs de Rhum de la Réunion: chemin Frédéline, BP 354, 97453 Saint-Pierre Cédex; tel. 262-25-84-27; fax 262-35-60-92; Chair. OLIVIER THIEBLIN.

Syndicat du Sucre de la Réunion: BP 50109, 40 route Gabriel Macé, 97492 Sainte-Clotilde, Cedex; tel. 262-47-76-76; fax 262-21-87-35; internet www.sucre.re; f. 1908; Pres. PHILIPPE LABRO.

TRADE UNIONS

CFE-CGC de la Réunion: 1 Rampes Ozoux, Résidence de la Rivière, Appt 2A, BP 873, 97477 Saint-Denis Cédex; tel. 262-90-11-95; fax 262-90-11-99; e-mail union@cfecgcreunion.com; internet www.cfecgcreunion.com; departmental br. of the Confédération Française de l'Encadrement-Confédération Générale des Cadres; represents engineers, teaching, managerial and professional staff and technicians; Pres. ALAIN IGLICKI; Sec.-Gen. DANIEL THIAW-WING-KAI.

Fédération Départementale des Syndicats d'Exploitants Agricoles de la Réunion (FDSEA): 105 rue Amiral Lacaze, Terre Sainte, 97410 Saint-Pierre; tel. 262-96-33-53; fax 262-96-33-90; e-mail fdsea-reunion@wanadoo.fr; affiliated to the Fédération Nationale des Syndicats d'Exploitants; Sec.-Gen. JEAN-BERNARD HOARAU.

Fédération Syndicale Unitaire Réunion (FSU): 4 rue de la Cure, BP 279, 97494 Sainte-Clotilde Cédex; tel. 262-86-29-46; fax 262-22-35-28; e-mail fsu974@fsu.fr; internet sd974.fsu.fr; f. 1993; departmental br. of the Fédération Syndicale Unitaire; represents public sector employees in sectors incl. teaching, research, and training, and also agriculture, justice, youth and sports, and culture; Sec. CHRISTIAN PICARD.

Union Départementale Confédération Française Démocratique du Travail (UD CFDT): Résidence Pointe des Jardins, 1 rue de l'Atillerie, 97400 Saint-Denis; tel. 262-41-22-85; fax 262-41-26-85; e-mail usctr@wanadoo.fr.

Union Départementale Force Ouvrière de la Réunion (FO): 81 rue Labourdonnais, BP 853, 97477 Saint-Denis Cédex; tel. 262-21-31-35; fax 262-41-33-23; e-mail eric.marguerite@laposte.net; Sec.-Gen. ERIC MARGUERITE.

Union Régionale UNSA-Education: BP 169, 97464 Saint-Denis Cédex; tel. 262-20-02-25; fax 262-21-58-65; e-mail urreunio@unsa.org; represents teaching staff; Sec.-Gen. ERIC CHAVRIACOUTY.

Transport

ROADS

A route nationale circles the island, generally following the coast and linking the main towns. Another route nationale crosses the island from south-west to north-east linking Saint-Pierre and Saint-Benoît. In 1994 there were 370 km of routes nationales, 754 km of departmental roads and 1,630 km of other roads; 1,300 km of the roads were bituminized.

Société d'Economie Mixte des Transports, Tourisme, Equipements et Loisirs (SEMITTEL): 24 chemin Benoite-Boulard, 97410 Saint-Pierre; tel. 262-55-40-60; fax 262-55-49-56; e-mail contact@semittel.re; f. 1984; bus service operator; Pres. MARRIE PERIANAYAGOM.

Société des Transports Départementaux de la Réunion (SOTRADER): 2 allée Bonnier, 97400 Saint-Denis; tel. 262-94-89-40; fax 262-94-89-50; f. 1995; bus service operator; Dir-Gen. FRÉDÉRIC DELOUYE.

SHIPPING

In 1986 work was completed on the expansion of the Port de la Pointe des Galets, which was divided into the former port in the west and a new port in the east (the port Ouest and the port Est), known together as Port-Réunion. In 2009 some 3.3m. metric tons of freight were unloaded and 594,700 tons loaded at the two ports. In 2012 legislation was adopted in France which transformed Port-Réunion into the Grand Port Maritime de La Réunion, a publicly-owned entity administered by a supervisory board.

Port Authority (Concession Portuaire): rue Evariste de Parny, BP 18, 97821 Le Port Cédex; tel. 262-42-90-00; fax 262-42-47-90; internet www.reunion.port.fr; Dir BRUNO DAVIDSEN.

CMA CGM Réunion: 85 rue Jules Verne, Z.I. No. 2, BP 2007, 97822 Le Port Cédex; tel. 262-55-10-10; fax 262-43-23-04; e-mail lar.genmbox@cma-cgm.com; internet www.cmacgm.com; f. 1996 by merger of Cie Générale Maritime and Cie Maritime d'Affrètement; shipping agents; Man. Dir JÉRÔME DELHOUME.

Mediterranean Shipping Co France (Réunion), S.A. (MSC): 1 bis, Gustave Eiffel, Z.A.C. 2000, BP 221, 97825 Le Port Cédex; tel. 262-42-78-00; fax 262-42-78-10; e-mail msclareunion@mscfr.mscgva.ch; internet www.mscreunion.com.

Réunion Ships Agency (RSA): 17 rue R. Hoareau, BP 10186, 97825 Le Port Cédex; tel. 262-43-33-33; fax 262-42-03-10; e-mail rsa@indoceanic.com; internet www.indoceanic.com; f. 1975; subsidiary of Indoceanic Services; Man. Dir HAROLD JOSÉ THOMSON.

Société d'Acconage et de Manutention de la Réunionnaise (SAMR): 3 ave Théodore Drouhet, Z.A.C. 2000, BP 40, 97821 Le Port Cédex; tel. 262-55-17-55; fax 262-55-17-62; stevedoring; Pres. DOMINIQUE LAFONT; Man. MICHEL ANTONELLI.

Société de Manutention et de Consignation Maritime (SOMACOM): 3 rue Gustave Eiffel, Zac 2000, BP 97420, Le Port; tel. 262-42-60-00; fax 262-42-60-10; stevedoring and shipping agents; Gen. Man. DANIEL RIGAT.

Société Réunionnaise de Services Maritimes (SRSM): 3 ave Théodore Drouhet, Z.A.C. 2000, BP 2006, 97822 Le Port Cédex; tel. 262-55-17-55; fax 262-55-17-62; e-mail n.hoarau@dri-reunion.com; freight only; Man. MICHEL ANTONELLI.

CIVIL AVIATION

Réunion's international airport, Roland Garros-Gillot, is situated 8 km from Saint-Denis. The Pierrefonds airfield, 5 km from Saint-Pierre, commenced operating as an international airport in 1998 following its development at an estimated cost of nearly 50m. French francs. Air France, Corsair and Air Austral operate international services. In 2009 Roland Garros-Gillot handled some 1.75m. passengers, while Pierrefonds airport handled 126,651 passengers.

Air Austral: 4 rue de Nice, 97400 Saint-Denis; tel. 262-90-90-91; fax 262-29-28-95; e-mail reservation@air-austral.com; internet www.airaustral.com; f. 1975; subsidiary of Air France; CEO MARIE-JOSEPH MALÉ.

Tourism

Réunion's attractions include spectacular scenery and a pleasant climate. In January 2010 the island had around 2,090 hotel rooms. In 2012 some 446,500 tourists visited Réunion. According to the World Tourism Organisation, receipts from tourism (excluding passenger transport) totalled US $392m. in 2010.

Délégation Régionale au Commerce, à l'Artisanat et au Tourisme: Préfecture de la Réunion, 97400 Saint-Denis; tel. 262-40-77-58; fax 262-50-77-15; Dir PHILIPPE JEAN LEGLISE.

L'Île de la Réunion Tourisme (IRT): pl. du 20 décembre 1848, BP 615, 97472 Saint-Denis Cédex; tel. 262-21-00-41; fax 262-21-00-21; e-mail ctr@la-reunion-tourisme.com; internet www.reunion.fr; fmrly Comité du Tourisme de la Réunion; name changed as above in 2009; Pres. JACQUELINE FARREYROL.

Office du Tourisme Intercommunal du Nord: 2 pl. Etienne Regnault, 97400 Saint-Denis; tel. 262-41-83-00; fax 262-21-37-76; e-mail info@ot-nordreunion.com; Pres. FRÉDÉRIC FOUCQUE; Dir CATHERINE GLAVNIK.

Defence

Réunion is the headquarters of French military forces in the Indian Ocean and French Southern and Antarctic Territories. As assessed at November 2009, there were 1,000 French troops stationed on Réunion and Mayotte, including a gendarmerie.

Education

Education is modelled on the French system, and is compulsory for 10 years between the ages of six and 16 years. Primary education begins at six years of age and lasts for five years. Secondary education, which begins at 11 years of age, lasts for up to seven years, comprising a first cycle of four years and a second of three years. In the academic year 2012/13 there were 43,897 pupils enrolled at pre-primary schools and 74,691 at primary schools. In 2011/12 there were 100,611 pupils enrolled at secondary schools. There is a university, with several faculties, providing higher education in law, economics, politics, and French language and literature, and a teacher-training college. In 2011/12 11,593 students were enrolled at the university.

French Overseas Collectivities

As amended in March 2003, the Constitution defines French Polynesia, Saint Pierre and Miquelon, and the Wallis and Futuna Islands as having the status of Collectivités d'Outre-mer (Overseas Collectivities) within the French Republic. Under an organic law of February 2007, Saint-Barthélemy and Saint-Martin were, additionally, each accorded the status of Overseas Collectivity. The territories within this category have a greater degree of independence than do the Overseas Departments and Territories, with the particular status of each being defined by an individual organic law. Local assemblies may establish internal legislation. An organic law of February 2004 accords to French Polynesia the unique designation of Pays d'Outre-mer (Overseas Country), while it retains the legal status of an Overseas Collectivity. Mayotte, which was previously an Overseas Collectivity became an Overseas Department of France at the end of March 2011.

FRENCH POLYNESIA

Introductory Survey

LOCATION, CLIMATE, LANGUAGE, RELIGION, FLAG, CAPITAL

French Polynesia comprises several scattered groups of islands in the South Pacific Ocean, lying about two-thirds of the way between the Panama Canal and New Zealand. Its nearest neighbours are the Cook Islands, to the west, and the Line Islands (part of Kiribati), to the north-west. French Polynesia consists of the following island groups: the Windward Islands (Iles du Vent—including the islands of Tahiti and Moorea) and the Leeward Islands (Iles Sous le Vent—located about 160 km north-west of Tahiti) which, together, constitute the Society Archipelago; the Tuamotu Archipelago, which comprises some 80 atolls scattered east of the Society Archipelago in a line stretching north-west to south-east for about 1,500 km; the Gambier Islands, located 1,600 km south-east of Tahiti; the Austral Islands, lying 640 km south of Tahiti; and the Marquesas Islands, which lie 1,450 km north-east of Tahiti. There are 35 islands and 83 atolls in all, of which 76 are populated. The average monthly temperature throughout the year varies between 20°C (68°F) and 29°C (84°F), and most rainfall occurs between November and April, the average annual precipitation being 1,625 mm (64 in). The official languages are French and Tahitian. Seven Polynesian languages and their dialects are spoken by the indigenous population. The principal religion is Christianity; about 54% of the population is Protestant and some 38% Roman Catholic. The official flag is the French tricolour. Subordinate to this, the French Polynesian flag (proportions 2 by 3), comprises three horizontal stripes, of red, white (half the depth) and red, with, in the centre, the arms of French Polynesia, consisting of a representation in red of a native canoe, bearing a platform supporting five stylized persons, on a circular background (five wavy horizontal dark blue bands, surmounted by 10 golden sunrays). The capital is Papeete, on the island of Tahiti.

CONTEMPORARY POLITICAL HISTORY

Historical Context

Tahiti, the largest of the Society Islands, and the other island groups were annexed by France in the late 19th century. The islands were governed from France under a decree of 1885 until 1946, when French Polynesia became an Overseas Territory (Territoire d'Outre-Mer), administered by a Governor in Papeete. A Territorial Assembly and a Council of Government were established to advise the Governor.

Between May 1975 and May 1982 a majority in the Territorial Assembly sought independence for French Polynesia. Following pressure by Francis Sanford, leader of the largest autonomist party in the Assembly, a new Constitution for the territory was negotiated with the French Government and approved by a newly elected Assembly in 1977. Under the provisions of the new statute, France retained responsibility for foreign affairs, defence, monetary matters and justice, but the powers of the territorial Council of Government were increased, especially in the field of commerce. The French Governor was replaced by a High Commissioner, who was to preside over the Council of Government and was head of the administration, but had no vote. The Council's elected Vice-President, responsible for domestic affairs, was granted greater powers. An Economic, Social and Cultural Council, responsible for all development matters, was also created, and French Polynesia's economic zone was extended to 200 nautical miles (370 km) from the islands' coastline.

Domestic Political Affairs

Following elections to the Territorial Assembly in May 1982, the Gaullist Tahoera'a Huiraatira (People's Rally), led by Gaston Flosse, which secured 13 of the 30 seats, formed successive ruling coalitions, first with the Ai'a Api (New Land) party and in September with the Te Pupu Here Ai'a Te Nuna'a Ia Ora (Patriotic Party for an Autonomous Polity). Seeking self-government, especially in economic matters, elected representatives of the Assembly held discussions with the French Government in Paris in 1983, and in September 1984 a new statute was approved by the French Assemblée Nationale (National Assembly). This allowed the territorial Government greater powers, mainly in the sphere of commerce and development; the Council of Government was replaced by a Council of Ministers, whose President was to be elected from among the members of the Territorial Assembly. Flosse became the first President of the Council of Ministers.

At elections held in March 1986 the Tahoera'a Huiraatira gained the first outright majority to be achieved in the territory, winning 24 of the 41 seats in the Territorial Assembly. Leaders of opposition parties expressed dissatisfaction with the election result, claiming that the Tahoera'a Huiraatira victory had been secured only as a result of the disproportionate allocation of seats to one of the five constituencies. The constituency at the centre of the dispute comprised the Mangareva and Tuamotu islands, where the two French army bases at Hao and Mururoa constituted a powerful body of support for Flosse and the Tahoera'a Huiraatira. At concurrent elections for French Polynesia's two seats in the National Assembly in Paris, Flosse and Alexandre Léontieff, the candidates of the Rassemblement pour la République (RPR—to which the Tahoera'a Huiraatira was affiliated, latterly the Union pour un Mouvement Populaire), were elected. Later in March the French Prime Minister, Jacques Chirac, appointed Flosse as Secretary of State for South Pacific Affairs in the French Council of Ministers. Flosse ceded his seat in the National Assembly to Edouard Fritch.

In April 1986 Flosse was re-elected President of the Council of Ministers. However, he was severely criticized by leaders of the opposition for his allegedly inefficient and extravagant use of public funds, and was accused of corrupt electoral practice. Flosse resigned as President in February 1987, and was replaced by Jacques Teuira.

In December 1987, amid growing discontent over his policies, Teuira and the entire Council of Ministers resigned and were replaced by a coalition of opposition parties and the Te Tiaraama party (a breakaway faction of the Tahoera'a Huiraatira) under the presidency of Alexandre Léontieff. Amendments to the Polynesian Constitution, which were approved by the French legislature and enacted by July 1990, augmented the powers of the President of the Council of Ministers and increased the competence of the Territorial Assembly.

At territorial elections in March 1991 the Tahoera'a Huiraatira won 18 of the 41 seats. Flosse then formed a coalition with the Ai'a Api to secure a majority of 23 seats in the Territorial Assembly. Emile Vernaudon, leader of the Ai'a Api, was elected President of the Assembly and Flosse was elected President of the Council of Ministers. In September Flosse announced the end of the coalition between his party and the Ai'a Api, accusing Vernaudon of disloyalty, and signed a new alliance with the Te Pupu Here Ai'a Te Nuna'a Ia Ora, led by Jean Juventin.

In April 1992 Flosse was found guilty of fraud (relating to an illegal sale of government land to a member of his family) and there were widespread demands for his resignation. In November Juventin and Léontieff were charged with 'passive' corruption, relating to the construction of a golf course by a Japanese company. In the following month the French Court of Appeal upheld the judgment against Flosse, who received a six-month suspended prison sentence. The case provoked a demonstration by more than 3,000 people in January 1993, demanding the resignation of Flosse and Juventin. In September 1994 Flosse succeeded in having the conviction rescinded, on a procedural issue, in a second court of appeal. In October 1997, however, Léontieff was found guilty of accepting substantial bribes in order to facilitate a business venture and was sentenced to three years' imprisonment (one-half of which was to be suspended). In May

1998 Léontieff was sentenced to a further three years' imprisonment (two of which were to be suspended) for corruption.

When the French authorities resumed nuclear testing in September 1995 (see Nuclear Testing and Relations with Metropolitan France), peaceful protests in Tahiti rapidly developed into full-scale riots, as several thousand demonstrators rampaged through Papeete, demanding an end to French rule.

In November 1995 the Territorial Assembly adopted a draft statute of autonomy, which proposed the extension of the territory's powers to areas such as fishing, mining and shipping rights, international transport and communications, broadcasting and the offshore economic zone. However, France would retain full responsibility for defence, justice and security in the islands. Advocates of independence for French Polynesia criticized the statute for promising only relatively superficial changes. The statute was approved by the French National Assembly in December and entered into force in April 1996.

At territorial elections in May 1996 the Tahoera'a Huiraatira achieved an outright majority, securing 22 of the 41 seats, although the principal pro-independence party, Tavini Huiraatira/Front de Libération de la Polynésie (FLP), won 10 seats, making considerable gains throughout the territory (largely owing to increased popular hostility towards France since the resumption of nuclear-weapons tests at Mururoa Atoll—see Nuclear Testing and Relations with Metropolitan France). Flosse defeated the pro-independence leader, Oscar Temaru, to remain as President of the Council of Ministers, and Justin Arapari was elected President of the Territorial Assembly. Allegations of voting irregularities led to the annulment of the results in 11 constituencies; following by-elections in May 1998, the Tahoera'a Huiraatira increased its representation by one seat.

At elections for French Polynesia's two seats in the French National Assembly in May 1997 Michel Buillard and Emile Vernaudon, both supporters of the RPR, were elected. Flosse was re-elected as the territory's representative to the French Sénat (Senate) in September 1998.

In 1999 a constitutional amendment designating French Polynesia as an Overseas Country (Pays d'Outre-Mer) and creating a new Polynesian citizenship was approved by the French legislature. Although France was to retain control over areas such as foreign affairs, defence, justice and electoral laws, French Polynesia would have the power to negotiate with other Pacific countries and sign its own international treaties. The constitutional amendment was presented to a joint session of the French Senate and National Assembly for final ratification in January 2000, although no decision on the matter was taken.

In November 1999 Flosse was found guilty of corruption, on charges of accepting more than 2.7m. French francs in bribes from the owner of an illegal casino, allegedly to help fund his party. Flosse was sentenced to a two-year suspended prison term, a large fine and a one-year ban on seeking office. Flosse's refusal to resign as President of the Council of Ministers prompted demonstrations in Tahiti. In late 2000 Flosse lodged an appeal with the High Court, which reversed the ruling in May 2001, and in November of the following year the Court of Appeal in Paris announced that Flosse should be pardoned.

In December 2000 provision was made for the number of seats in the Territorial Assembly to be increased from 41 to 49, in an attempt to reflect demographic changes more accurately. At elections in May 2001, the Tahoera'a Huiraatira secured 28 seats and a fifth successive term in office. The pro-independence Tavini Huiraatira took 13 seats. Flosse was subsequently re-elected President of the Council of Ministers. In June 2002 elections for the territory's two seats in the National Assembly were won by Tahoera'a Huiraatira candidates Michel Buillard and Béatrice Vernaudon. In May 2003 it was announced that French Polynesia was to be allocated one additional seat in the French Senate.

In July 2003 about 2,000 islanders, led by Oscar Temaru, demonstrated in favour of self-determination during an official visit to French Polynesia by President Jacques Chirac. Also in that month, the Territorial Assembly followed the French legislature in ratifying the constitutional amendment that would allow French Polynesia to be designated as an Overseas Country of France. The final text of the autonomy statute was approved by the National Assembly in January 2004, and a decree of formal designation was signed by President Chirac in March. French Polynesia was thus granted greater authority over matters such as labour law, civil aviation and regional relations, with France retaining control of law and order, defence and money supply.

At elections to the newly expanded Assembly in May 2004, the Tahoera'a Huiraatira won 28 of the 57 seats. An opposition coalition, the Union pour la Démocratie (UPD), comprising the pro-independence Tavini Huiraatira and various minor parties, secured 27 seats and the remaining two seats were taken by opposition parties favouring autonomy. The Tahoera'a Huiraatira thus lost its overall majority in the Assembly for the first time in 20 years. Antony Géros of Tavini Huiraatira was elected President of the Assembly and Oscar Temaru, leader of Tavini Huiraatira, was elected President of the Council of Ministers.

In September 2004 disagreement over the appropriation bill brought the legislative process to a halt. Three members of the Assembly resigned from the UPD coalition, two of them to sit as independents, with the third joining the opposition Tahoera'a Huiraatira. In October separate motions of no confidence were filed against the Government by the Tahoera'a Huiraatira and the newly formed Te' Avei'a (Te Ara) party, which included six former members of the ruling UPD coalition. Oscar Temaru's appeals to the French Government to dissolve the Assembly and to hold new elections were supported by 22,000 people in the largest demonstration ever witnessed in French Polynesia. The French Minister for Overseas Territories, Brigitte Girardin, refused to accept that such demands were justified. The motions of no confidence were endorsed by 29 of the 57 legislators (the members of the UPD refusing to vote), thus requiring the Assembly to choose a new President of the Council of Ministers. The 23 Tahoera'a Huiraatira and six Te' Avei'a members elected Gaston Flosse as President. However, the UPD members boycotted the vote and refused to recognize Flosse's authority. Temaru and his ministers refused to vacate the presidential building, forcing Flosse's newly appointed 17-member Council of Ministers to operate in adjacent buildings.

The validity of Oscar Temaru's removal and the subsequent vote to elect Gaston Flosse as President of the Council of Ministers were both upheld by the French Conseil d'Etat (Council of State). Under the new autonomy statute, the Assembly could vote to dissolve itself if it received a petition from 10% of the electorate, roughly equivalent to 15,000 people; by 19 November 2004 the UPD claimed to have collected 42,890 signatures, representing some 28% of the electorate. Both Temaru and Flosse sent delegations to Paris, to make representations to the French Government, led respectively by Nicole Bouteau (leader of the No Oe e Te Nunaa party) and Edouard Fritch. Following an investigation into the conduct of the legislative elections, the French Council of State in mid-November declared the results in the Windward Islands null and void, thus requiring the holding of by-elections within three months. The decision also meant that the 37 legislators affected automatically lost their seats, among them Flosse, Temaru and the President of the Assembly, Antony Géros, who was replaced by Hiro Tefaarere. At the end of November leading representatives from all parties, including Flosse, Temaru, Bouteau, Philip Schyle (of the Fe'tia Api party) and Jacky Briant (of the Heuira-Greens party), were summoned to Paris for discussions. Despite an initial agreement in principle to hold fresh legislative elections, the talks broke down in early December. In mid-December the French Council of State validated Flosse's appointment as President.

By-elections were held in the Windward Islands constituency in February 2005. The parties of Bouteau and Schyle stood on a joint platform (the Alliance pour une Démocratie Nouvelle—ADN) offering a 'third way'. The Tahoera'a Huiraatira won 10 of the 37 seats, and the seven-party UPD coalition won 25 seats. The ADN took the constituency's remaining two seats. Overall, therefore, the Tahoera'a Huiraatira and the UPD now held 27 seats each in the Assembly. The ADN held three seats, but refused to co-operate with either the Tahoera'a Huiraatira or the UPD, as a result of which neither of the two groupings was able to form a majority. Temaru introduced a motion of no confidence against Flosse, which was endorsed by 30 of the 57 members. Temaru was subsequently elected President of the Council of Ministers by 29 votes to 26 and Antony Géros was returned as President of the Assembly.

In July 2005 the former Secretary-General of the Tahoera'a Huiraatira and minister under Flosse, Jean-Christophe Bouissou, left the party to form the Rautahi Party. He was joined by two other former ministers, Temauri Foster and Emma Algan, leaving the Tahoera'a Huiraatira with 23 seats in the Assembly and the UPD 29 seats. In November the Government presented an economic reform programme that included a proposed increase in the minimum wage to be financed through a 'solidarity' tax on personal income. However, a series of public protests culminating in a four-day general strike led the Temaru Government to seek alternative sources of revenue, principally by increasing the duty on alcohol and tobacco. In December two more members of the Tahoera'a Huiraatira left the party, to sit as independent members of the Assembly, reducing the party's representation to 21 seats.

In February 2006 Temaru signed a new agreement with French High Commissioner Anne Boquet, on behalf of the French Government, regarding the proportion of the economic development grant (dotation générale de développement économique—DGDE—see Economic Affairs) that could be used towards the Government's operating costs: the proportion would be reduced gradually from 50% in 2005 to 20% from 2008. Meanwhile, in January 2006 the Minister for Post and Telecommunications and Sports, Emile Vernaudon, was convicted of having used public property for personal benefit while serving as Mayor of Mahina (a district of Papeete) between 1992 and 1999; he received a one-year suspended prison sentence and substantial fine. In April 2006 Antony Géros was replaced as President of the Assembly by Philip Schyle, of the Fe'tia Api party.

In June 2006 a criminal court in Tahiti found former President Gaston Flosse guilty of corruption in relation to his son's purchase of a hotel. Flosse was given a three-month suspended prison sentence, but was not disqualified from his positions as member of the Territorial Assembly and representative to the Senate in Paris. In October members of the O Oe To Oe Rima trade union protesting against rises in the cost of living erected road blockades in Papeete and subsequently gained access to the presidential palace. The protesters demanded that Oscar Temaru, who was attending a meeting of the Pacific Islands Forum (see p. 416) in Fiji, return to Papeete for negotiations. In November reports emerged of dissent within the ruling coalition and in the following month the Assembly approved a motion of no confidence in the Government, resulting in Temaru's removal from office. In late December 31 of the 57 members of the legislature voted in favour of installing Gaston Tong Sang, a member of the Tahoera'a Huiraatira party and Mayor of Bora Bora, as President.

In February 2007 hundreds of opposition supporters took to the streets of Papeete to demand the holding of new elections. In March Emile Vernaudon was convicted of corruption and therefore barred from public office. He was given a suspended 18-month prison sentence (in December he was arrested on further charges). In April Edouard Fritch was narrowly elected President of the Assembly. In the same month the formation of the Te Niu Hau Manahune (Principle of Democracy) party, under the leadership of Teina Maraeura, was announced. The group advocated the establishment of a federal system for French Polynesian archipelagos and declared its support for the candidate of the Union pour un Mouvement Populaire (UMP), Nicolas Sarkozy, in the forthcoming French presidential election. At the second round of this election, in May, 51.9% of French Polynesian voters chose Sarkozy over the candidate of the Parti Socialiste, Ségolène Royal (a slightly narrower margin than in metropolitan France). In June, at French legislative elections, the two Tahoera'a Huiraatira candidates were elected as deputies to the National Assembly: Buillard, an incumbent deputy, defeated Temaru to regain one of the seats, while Bruno Sandras was newly elected to the second seat.

Political instability within French Polynesia continued to pose a threat during 2007. Gaston Tong Sang's Government survived a second unsuccessful motion of no confidence in June (the first having taken place in January), but it suffered a serious setback in July with the withdrawal of the Tahoera'a Huiraatira, Tong Sang's own party, from the majority grouping in the Assembly. The decision signalled a major shift in local politics, which had perhaps been foreshadowed by the intensification of criticism of Tong Sang by the Tahoera'a Huiraatira leader, Gaston Flosse. Five members of the Tahoera'a Huiraatira resigned from the Council of Ministers. The precarious situation had already prompted the French Government to hold talks with Tong Sang, Flosse, Temaru and other politicians in an attempt to resolve the continuing instability. Tong Sang was finally removed from office at the end of August, when a third no-confidence motion in his leadership was approved by 35 assembly members. In mid-September Temaru was elected President, defeating Fritch in a second round of voting, Tong Sang having been eliminated in the first. A new Council of Ministers was duly announced, in which Temaru assumed responsibility for international relations and other portfolios, while Antony Géros was appointed Vice-President and Minister of Finance, Housing and Land Issues.

At a parliamentary session later in September 2007, Temaru stated that a 'pact' had been negotiated between the two major political parties, thus ensuring a clear majority in the Assembly, which, it was hoped, would lead to greater political stability. In October Temaru attended discussions in France with President Sarkozy while reform legislation was being prepared for submission to the French National Assembly. Proposals for reform, including the introduction of two election rounds and the setting of a maximum of 15 appointees to the Council of Ministers, were approved by the French Senate in November. Meanwhile, following his defeat, Tong Sang announced the creation of the O Porinetia To Tatou Ai'a (Polynesia, Our Homeland) party, which elected him as its President in December.

At the first round of legislative elections, held on 27 January 2008, the To Tatou Ai'a coalition, of which Tong Sang's O Porinetia To Tatou Ai'a was a leading member, secured more votes in important constituencies than Temaru's political alliance, the Union pour la Démocratie (UPLD), and the Tahoera'a Huiraatira. At the second round of elections, on 10 February, To Tatou Ai'a won a total of 27 seats, while the UPLD secured 20 and the Tahoera'a Huiraatira only 10. Owing to the lack of an overall majority, discussions on the establishment of a coalition ensued, and the election of Edouard Fritch of the Tahoera'a Huiraatira as President of the Assembly suggested that the two pro-autonomy parties had reached an agreement. The Assembly then conducted a vote to select the next President of French Polynesia. Gaston Flosse unexpectedly declared his candidacy and was able to defeat Tong Sang after Temaru, the third candidate, withdrew from the contest, and Flosse gained the support of members of the UPLD. A new parliamentary alliance, between the Tahoera'a Huiraatira and the UPLD, had been established: the Union pour le Développement, la Stabilité et la Paix (Union for Development, Stability and Peace—UDSP). Temaru was elected President of the Assembly in late February, following Fritch's resignation from the post.

Increasing political instability

The installation of a new Government did not bring the expected political stability. In April 2008 the establishment of Te Mana o Te May Motu (The Power of the Islands), a new parliamentary grouping reported to be allied with To Tatou Ai'a, was announced. Later in that month a no-confidence motion submitted by Tong Sang against the Flosse Government resulted in Flosse's removal from office; two members of Flosse's coalition group had reportedly defected to Te Mana o Te May Motu. Tong Sang was elected President. In August a former Minister for Industry and Small and Medium Businesses and President of the Assembly, Hiro Tefaarere, established a new political party, A rohi (Let's Act). Tefaarere expressed frustration with the prevailing political situation, which was perceived to be dominated by the pro- and anti-independence movements. Gaston Flosse was re-elected as a representative to the French Senate in September, while Richard Tuheiava, a member of the UPLD, secured the newly created second seat for French Polynesia. Flosse resigned from the UMP, and was subsequently charged with misuse of public funds relating to his time in office (see below). In December the Government lost its majority in the Assembly when one member of the coalition withdrew. In February 2009 Tong Sang resigned as President, prompted by an impending motion of no confidence. Within days, Oscar Temaru was elected as President. Edouard Fritch was subsequently elected to replace Temaru as President of the Assembly.

Meanwhile, in February 2009 Gaston Flosse received a further criminal conviction, having been found guilty of misappropriating some 2.4m. francs CFP of public funds in 2004. He received a suspended one-year prison sentence and a fine of 2m. francs CFP, in addition to being barred from holding public office for one year. Flosse appealed against the conviction, and in November 2011 his suspension from public office was overturned—thus enabling him to retain his French parliamentary seat. In a further prosecution, in May 2010, Flosse was convicted of obstructing an investigation into a former intelligence unit that had operated during his presidency, by destroying the records of its activities, and in October the French Polynesian Court of Appeal upheld his conviction (as did the Court of Cassation in France in September 2011).

In the mean time, in April 2009 Philip Schyle, of Gaston Tong Sang's To Tatou Ai'a coalition, replaced Fritch as President of the Assembly, following a parliamentary vote. Shortly afterwards President Temaru presented a new Council of Ministers, incorporating several supporters of Gaston Tong Sang in the coalition Government.

In October 2009 six legislators representing the outer islands withdrew from the coalition Government, claiming that their views had been disregarded, and consequently Temaru's support in the Assembly was seriously reduced. Mounting public concern at the ongoing political instability led to a demonstration protesting against a forthcoming parliamentary motion of no confidence in Papeete. Nevertheless, the motion was successful and the Government was duly removed from office. Gaston Tong Sang was appointed to replace Temaru, becoming President for the third time since 2006.

In January 2010 President Sarkozy referred to the political situation in French Polynesia as a 'comedy', and announced that he would initiate further reforms of the electoral system and institutions there, in order to provide greater political stability. While Tong Sang was visiting France for discussions (which encompassed the nuclear compensation issue—see Nuclear Testing and Relations with Metropolitan France) in that month, he submitted a proposal that the French Polynesian President be directly chosen by the local electorate, rather than elected by the members of the French Polynesian Assembly, with the objective of increasing political stability.

In February 2010 thousands of islanders were forced to evacuate their homes when the most severe cyclone for decades struck French Polynesia; the Tuamotu Archipelago was the worst affected area. Hundreds of houses were seriously damaged or completely destroyed by Cyclone Oli. The cost of repairs to housing and infrastructure was unofficially estimated to be 2,000m. francs CFP.

In April 2010, Oscar Temaru was elected President of the Assembly following Philip Schyle's unexpected resignation. The result indicated that the coalition between Flosse's party, the Tahoera'a Huiraatira, and Tong Sang's To Tatou Ai'a had been seriously undermined. Tong Sang immediately asked President Sarkozy to dissolve the Assembly and call early legislative elections. Sarkozy replied that electoral reform was necessary before any elections could take place. In discussions on electoral reform in late 2010 the French Government suggested that any motion of no confidence (the instrument that had frequently been used to defeat recent administrations) should require the support of at least 60% of members of the Assembly. It also suggested that the Society Archipelago adopt an electoral system separate from that of the other islands, and that the number of seats in the Assembly be reduced. Members of all the principal political groupings criticized the proposals.

In January 2011 Emile Vernaudon was found guilty of misusing funds amounting to 114m. francs CFP belonging to the Office des Postes et Télécommunications (OPT—the state-owned post and telecommunications company) during 2005–06. Vernaudon was sentenced to five years in prison and barred from holding public office for five years. Furthermore, 11 other officials were convicted of similar offences in connection with the OPT, including Gaston Flosse, who, in January 2013, was sentenced to five years' imprisonment for his role in the affair.

In February 2011 the proposed budget, which included reductions in expenditure, was approved by the Assembly, but President Tong Sang refused to accept the vote, publishing his own version of the budget. The matter of which budget was valid was referred to the French Supreme Court. Tong Sang dismissed Vice-President Edouard Fritch and five cabinet ministers in March for failing to support his proposed budget. A motion to annul Tong Sang's budget was approved by 44 of the 57 members of the Assembly, and at the beginning of April he was removed from office following his defeat in a parliamentary motion of no confidence. Oscar Temaru, leader of the pro-independence Tavini Huiraatira, thus returned to the position of President. In April Jacqui Drollet secured election to the post of President of the Assembly.

In the largest trial to date in French Polynesian history, a total of 87 people appeared in court in April 2011 in connection with payments made to individuals during the presidency of Gaston Flosse in 1990s. In what became known as the 'phantom jobs case', it was alleged that Flosse had secured the support of numerous politicians, journalists, trade unionists and clergymen by paying them a salary for jobs that did not exist. In October Flosse was found guilty of making corrupt payments and was sentenced to four years' imprisonment. A total of 56 people were convicted in the case. In February 2013 the Court of Appeal amended Flosse's sentence to a four-year suspended prison term and a fine of €125,000. He was additionally to be deprived of his civic rights for a three-year period. However, he subsequently lodged an appeal with the Court of Cassation in Paris, thus allowing him to contest the territorial elections due in April and May.

Meanwhile, the deteriorating economic situation in French Polynesia continued to cause concern, and in April 2011 more than 3,000 people demonstrated outside the parliament buildings to protest against a perceived lack of action by politicians to address issues such as rising unemployment. In May the French Government agreed to provide a loan of €41.9m. from the Agence Française de Développement to ease the economic crisis. In the following month the Territorial Assembly approved an economic reform plan that envisaged a number of controversial measures, including salary reductions of up to 50% for public sector workers and the closure of the news agency Agence Tahitienne de Presse.

Further electoral reforms and the 2013 elections

In August 2011 President Sarkozy promulgated legislation approved by the French Government amending the islands' electoral system. The reforms, which were all aimed at increasing political stability, included a new system of proportional representation (whereby the winning list in the second round of polling would receive one-third of the 57 seats in the Assembly, with the remainder distributed according to the lists' relative strength); a reduction in the number of members of the Council of Ministers from up to 15 to between seven and 10; and a requirement of 60% of votes, rather than a simple majority, for a motion of no confidence to succeed. In addition, the President of the Council of Ministers of French Polynesia would be limited to serving a maximum of two consecutive terms. Contrary to earlier proposals, the number of seats in the Assembly was maintained at 57. However, having hitherto comprised six electoral constituencies, the islands would henceforth constitute one, albeit composed of eight sections: three for the Windward Islands (Iles du Vent—Society Islands) and one each for the Leeward Islands (Iles Sous le Vent—Society Islands), the Gambier Islands-East Tuamotu Archipelago, the West Tuamotu Archipelago, the Austral Islands and the Marquesas Islands.

In September 2011 Oscar Temaru caused controversy and risked jeopardizing relations with France when he lobbied leaders at a Pacific Islands Forum meeting to support French Polynesia's bid to be reinscribed on the UN's list of Non-Self-Governing Territories. (Former French President Charles de Gaulle had removed French Polynesia from the list in 1946.) The Pacific Islands Forum declined to endorse the decolonization campaign, although the leaders of Vanuatu and Solomon Islands spoke in favour of French Polynesia's reinscription on the list at the UN General Assembly in New York, USA, in that month. Following Temaru's continued lobbying of the UN, a draft resolution to re-inscribe the territory was lodged with the General Assembly's secretariat in early 2013. The public declaration of support for reinscription by the Maohi Protestant Church—the dominant Christian denomination in French Polynesia—was a significant development in mid-2012. In a statement the Church argued that reinscription would be an effective way to protect the islands' heritage and to hold the French Government accountable for its actions at the nuclear test sites of Mururoa and Fangataufa.

At the French presidential election of 2012, Sarkozy secured the largest share of the vote in French Polynesia in the second round, in May, winning 53.3%, but was defeated nationwide by François Hollande of the Parti Socialiste. At elections to the French National Assembly in June, contested by a total of 47 candidates, the Tahoera'a Huiraatira secured all three of French Polynesia's seats (the territory having been allocated an additional seat), with Edouard Fritch, Jonas Tahuaitu and Jean-Paul Tuaiva elected as deputies.

In January 2013 a new political grouping, the A Ti'a Porinetia (Rally of Polynesians), incorporating members of the To Tatou Ai'a and a number of smaller organizations, was launched under the leadership of former economy minister Teva Rohfritsch. The new electoral rules required party lists to secure a minimum of 12.5% of the votes to proceed to a second round, which appeared to encourage the formation of larger groupings.

Following the first round of elections, on 21 April 2013, three parties were eligible to contest the second round on 5 May: Flosse's Tahoera'a Huiraatira, Temaru's UPLD and Rohfritsch's A Ti'a Porinetia. In the event, the Tahoera'a Huiraatira won a decisive victory, securing 19 seats, with the additional 19 seats allocated to the leading party under the new electoral system (bringing its total to 38), while the UPLD took 11 seats and A Ti'a Porinetia eight. Temaru attributed his party's loss to the effects of the severe economic crisis. Later in the month the Assembly elected Flosse to his fifth term of office as President. However, Flosse risked losing his position should his appeal against a conviction for corruption be rejected by the French Court of Cassation.

Recent developments: a fifth term for Flosse

Despite attempts by Gaston Flosse to withdraw the resolution from the agenda, on 17 May 2013, the day that Flosse took office as President, the UN General Assembly voted to reinscribe French Polynesia on its list of Non-Self-Governing Territories. In the following month, in accordance with a resolution approved by the Assembly, Flosse wrote to President Hollande requesting that the French Government organize a referendum on self-determination in the territory. Flosse stated that he would not recognize any future referendum organized under the auspices of the UN and that he would urge his supporters to boycott any such poll. By early 2014 the French authorities had not formally responded to the request.

Meanwhile, Flosse's reputation as a controversial figure continued to affect his new administration. In July 2013 two former members of the disbanded Groupement d'Intervention de La Polynésie (GIP)a militia-like unit created by Flosse in the late 1990s, initially to assist with emergency relief efforts, but which subsequently became associated with alleged political operations against Flosse's opponents-were charged with the murder of a journalist in December 1997. Jean-Pascal Couraud, editor-in-chief of *Les Nouvelles* newspaper and a staunch critic of Flosse, was alleged to have been drowned following interrogation by the GIP members.

The threat posed to Flosse's presidency in the event of the French Court of Cassation upholding his conviction on corruption charges was deferred in October 2013, when the date for the appeal hearing was postponed from January 2014 to late June. Temaru condemned the decision to delay the hearing. His earlier description of the Government as 'a gang of criminals with a convict as a President' had prompted Flosse to launch a defamation case in August 2013.

In April 2014 the French Senate lifted the parliamentary immunity of Flosse with regard to further corruption charges, brought against him in February, of abusing public funds by arranging for a free water supply to a neighbourhood containing his residence. His son-in-law Edouard Fritch had also been charged with the same offence. Despite the charges, Fritch won the mayoral election in Pirae in March and thus had to relinquish his seat in the National Assembly because of the limit on the number of mandates a French politician can hold. Tahoera'a Huiraatira nominated one of its Territorial Assembly members, Maina Sage, to contest the seat in the French National Assembly vacated by Fritch.

The small anti-independence Rautahi Party, which had split from Tahoera'a Huiraatira in 2005, was dissolved in April 2014; its members were expected to rejoin Tahoera'a Huiraatira.

Nuclear Testing and Relations with Metropolitan France

France's use of French Polynesia for the purposes of nuclear testing was highly controversial. In July 1962 the French Government transferred its nuclear-testing facilities to Mururoa and Fangataufa atolls, in the Tuamotu Archipelago, establishing the Centre d'Expérimentation du Pacifique (CEP). The first nuclear device was tested at Fangataufa four years later in July 1966. In July 1985 the *Rainbow*

Warrior, the flagship of the anti-nuclear environmentalist group Greenpeace, which was to have led a protest flotilla to Mururoa, was sunk in Auckland Harbour, New Zealand, in an explosion that killed one crew member. Two agents of the French secret service, the Direction Générale de Sécurité Extérieure (DGSE), were subsequently convicted of manslaughter and imprisoned in New Zealand. According to official reports, between 1966 and 1974 France conducted 46 atmospheric tests in the territory; 147 underground tests were carried out between 1975 and 1991. In April 1992 the French Government announced that nuclear tests would be suspended until the end of the year. In January 1993 French Polynesia accepted assistance worth 7,000m. francs CFP in compensation for lost revenue and in aid for development projects.

Shortly after his election in May 1995, President Jacques Chirac announced that France would resume nuclear testing, with a programme of eight tests between September 1995 and May 1996. The decision provoked almost universal outrage in the international community, and was condemned for its apparent disregard for regional opinion, as well as for undermining the considerable progress made towards a worldwide ban on nuclear testing. Scientists also expressed concern at the announcement; some believed that further explosions at Mururoa might lead to the collapse of the atoll, which had already been weakened considerably. Large-scale demonstrations and protest marches throughout the region were accompanied by boycotts of French products and the suspension of several trade and defence co-operation agreements. Opposition to the French Government intensified in July 1995, when French commandos violently seized *Rainbow Warrior II*, the flagship of Greenpeace, and its crew, which had been protesting peacefully near the test site. Chirac continued to defy mounting international pressure to reverse the decision to carry out the tests.

French Polynesia became the focus of world attention when the first test of this series took place in September 1995. In defiance of international opinion, a further five tests were carried out, the sixth and final one being conducted in January 1996. In early 1996 the French Government confirmed reports by a team of independent scientists that radioactive isotopes had leaked into the waters surrounding the atoll, but denied that they represented a threat to the environment. Work to dismantle facilities at the test site began in 1997 and was completed in July 1998. Some 1,800 French military personnel were present at the CEP site in 1998.

In early 1999 a study by the Commission de Recherche et d'Information Indépendantes sur la Radioactivité (CRIIRAD), a French non-governmental organization, reported that there was serious radioactive leakage into underground water, lagoons and the ocean at Mururoa and Fangataufa atolls, and a French government official admitted that fractures had been found in the coral cone at the Mururoa and Fangataufa nuclear testing sites. During President Chirac's visit to Papeete in July 2003 some 200 members of an association of those formerly employed at Mururoa and Fangataufa—Moruroa e Tatou—staged a demonstration to demand that France recognize the connection between nuclear testing and the subsequent health problems of those involved. The Nuclear Veterans' Association continued to seek compensation from the French Government: according to the group around 30% of some 15,000 former nuclear workers were either suffering—or had died—from cancers or related diseases.

In May 2005 CRIIRAD published declassified secret reports from 1966 on nuclear testing in the Gambier Islands, which suggested that the French military had deliberately suppressed information about the extent of contamination from radioactive fallout. In October a French Polynesian commission of inquiry visited Mangareva, Tureia and Hao with officials from CRIIRAD. The commission reported that, contrary to the information given to the public, each of the 46 atmospheric tests between 1966 and 1974 had caused radioactive fallout on the islands around the test sites.

In January 2009 France agreed to finance the rehabilitation of its former military base on the atoll of Hao. The 'clean-up' operation, which was expected to take seven years, was projected to cost the equivalent of US $80m. In March it was announced that the French Government was to establish an independent commission to examine individual compensation claims from civilian and military workers affected by the nuclear tests, and in December the French legislature voted in favour of compensation payments; 18 illnesses, including leukaemia and thyroid cancer, were to be formally recognized by the French Government. Prior to the adoption of the legislation, an estimated 2,000 demonstrators attended a peaceful march in Papeete, claiming that the scope of the new law was inadequate. In October 2013 the organization Moruroa e Tatou wrote an open letter to the French President, François Hollande, criticizing his Government's reluctance to accept its obligations to the test victims and his failure to carry out promised amendments to the compensation law. By December 2013 of almost 900 compensation claims lodged with the French authorities, only 12 had been upheld.

In February 2010 French Polynesia concluded a new agreement with France, under which the DGDE, which had been introduced to offset the loss of revenue resulting from the closure of the nuclear testing facilities, would be replaced at the end of the year by three new financial instruments, as part of an arrangement that would continue to take into consideration the economic legacy of the nuclear testing programme. However, the annual sum provided would remain unchanged, at some 18,000m. francs CFP (nearly €151m.). About 60% of this funding was to be disbursed by the French Polynesian Government, while more than 30% was to be allocated to approved infrastructure projects.

In March 2011, amid increasing fears for the stability of Mururoa Atoll, the local Government urged the French President to dispatch experts to the area to assess the risks to the population if the atoll were to collapse and release radiation, and possibly trigger a tsunami. The French authorities sought to dispel such concerns, stating that ongoing monitoring of the atoll would provide sufficient warning of a potential collapse. Further declassified documents, released in mid-2013, provided evidence that the entire territory had been affected by radioactive fallout, and that Tahiti had been exposed to levels of plutonium some 500 times higher than the maximum accepted safe level of the material, contrary to official public information communicated subsequent to the tests.

CONSTITUTION AND GOVERNMENT

French Polynesia was designated as an Overseas Country (Pays d'Outre-Mer) within the French Republic in 2004. Its status is that of an Overseas Collectivity (Collectivité d'Outre-Mer). The French Government is represented in French Polynesia by its High Commissioner, and controls various important spheres of government, including defence, foreign diplomacy and justice. A local Assembly, with 57 members (increased from 49 at the May 2004 election), is elected for a five-year term by universal adult suffrage. The Assembly may elect a President of an executive body, the Council of Ministers, who in turn submits a list of between seven and 10 members of the Assembly to serve as ministers (decreased from 15 in legislation promulgated by the French President in August 2011), for approval by the Assembly.

In addition, French Polynesia elects three deputies to the French Assemblée Nationale (National Assembly) in Paris and two representatives to the French Sénat (Senate), all chosen on the basis of universal adult suffrage. French Polynesia is also represented at the European Parliament.

REGIONAL AND INTERNATIONAL CO-OPERATION

French Polynesia forms part of the Franc Zone (see p. 329), and is an associate member of the UN's Economic and Social Commission for Asia and the Pacific (ESCAP, see p. 28). Although France is also a member of the organization, French Polynesia has membership in its own right of the Pacific Community (see p. 412), which is based in New Caledonia and provides technical advice, training and assistance in economic, cultural and social development to the region. In October 2006 French Polynesia became an associate member of the Pacific Islands Forum (see p. 416). In November 2011 leaders from French Polynesia, American Samoa, the Cook Islands, Niue, Samoa, Tokelau, Tonga and Tuvalu formed the Polynesian Leaders' Group. The group was to hold annual summit meetings with the aim of sharing knowledge in the areas of the economy, education and the environment, and of promoting Polynesian culture, tradition and languages.

ECONOMIC AFFAIRS

In 2000, according to World Bank estimates, French Polynesia's gross national income (GNI), measured at average 1998–2000 prices, was US $3,795m., equivalent to $16,150 per head (or $24,680 per head on an international purchasing-power parity basis). During 2003–12, it was estimated, the population rose at an average annual rate of 1.1%. According to the UN's Economic and Social Commission for Asia and the Pacific (ESCAP), gross domestic product (GDP) per head increased at an average annual rate of 0.7% in 2000–05 and of 0.4% in 2005–10. Overall GDP increased at an average annual rate of 2.1% in 2000–05 and of 1.6% in 2005–10. According to UN estimates, real GDP increased by 2.1% in 2009.

According to UN estimates, agriculture, forestry and fishing contributed only 2.5% of GDP in 2009. The sector engaged 9.2% of the employed labour force at the 2007 census, and 2.9% of salaried workers at the end of 2012. Coconuts are the principal cash crop, and in 2012, according to FAO, the estimated harvest was 90,000 metric tons. The quantity of copra exported increased from 5,365.6 tons in 2004 to 5,703.1 tons in 2005; however, the value of copra exports decreased from 297.6m. francs CFP to 291.9m. over the same period. Monoï oil is produced by macerating tiaré flowers in coconut oil, and in 2007 355 tons of the commodity (representing an increase of 36% over the previous year) were exported. Vegetables, fruit (including pineapples, citrus fruit and noni fruit), vanilla and coffee are also cultivated. In 2007 vanilla exports reached 10.9 tons and provided revenue of 230m. francs CFP. Most commercial fishing, principally for tuna, is conducted, under licence, by Japanese and Korean fleets. The total fish catch in 2011 was 12,913 tons. In addition, production by the aquaculture sector, mainly shrimps, reached 54 tons. Another important activity is the production of cultured black pearls. The quantity of cultured pearls totalled 9,131 kg in 2008, providing export earnings of 8,316m. francs CFP (compared with 20,173.2m. in 2000). According to UN figures, the GDP of the agricultural sector contracted at an average annual rate of 2.9% in 2000–09. Agricultural GDP was estimated to have increased by 0.9% in 2009.

According to UN estimates, industry (comprising mining, manufacturing, construction and utilities) provided 12.9% of GDP in 2009. In 2007 17.3% of the employed labour force were engaged in the industrial sector. The sector engaged 14.8% of salaried workers at the end of 2012. According to the UN, industrial GDP increased at an average annual rate of 0.8% in 2000–09. The GDP of the industrial sector was estimated to have expanded by 1.6% in 2009. There is a small manufacturing sector, which is heavily dependent on agriculture. Coconut oil and copra are produced, as are beer, dairy products and vanilla essence.

According to UN estimates, mining, manufacturing and utilities provided 7.3% of GDP in 2009 (with manufacturing alone accounting for 5.6%). Mining and manufacturing engaged 6.4% of the employed labour force in 2007, and utilities a further 0.6%. Mining, manufacturing and utilities engaged 0.2%, 6.2% and 1.5% of salaried workers, respectively, at the end of 2011. The sectoral GDP decreased at an average annual rate of 0.3% in 2000–09, according to figures from the UN. The GDP of the sector was estimated to have expanded by 1.6% in 2009. Deposits of cobalt were discovered during the 1980s, and in early 2014 the Government was considering reviving phosphate mining on Makatea Atoll.

Construction is an important industrial activity, contributing 5.6% of GDP in 2009. The sector engaged 10.3% of the employed labour force in 2007, and 7.1% of salaried workers at the end of 2012. According to the UN, the GDP of the construction sector decreased at an average annual rate of 1.5% in 2000–09. The GDP of the sector was estimated to have expanded by 1.5% in 2009.

Hydrocarbon fuels are the main source of energy in French Polynesia, with the Papeete thermal power station providing about three-quarters of the total electricity produced. Mineral fuels accounted for 16.0% of the total value of merchandise imports in 2012. Hydroelectric power dams, with the capacity to generate more than one-third of the electricity requirements of Tahiti's population, have been constructed. Solar energy is also increasingly important, especially on the less-populated islands. Electricity production on Tahiti reached 587,2m. kWh in 2012.

The services sector provided 84.6% of GDP in 2009. Services engaged 73.4% of the employed labour force in 2007, and 82.3% of salaried workers at the end of 2012. The GDP of the services sector expanded at an average annual rate of 2.5% in 2000–09, according to UN estimates. The sector's GDP was estimated to have increased by 2.2% in 2009. Tourism is a major source of revenue. In 2012 168,978 tourists visited French Polynesia, compared with 162,776 in the previous year. In 2012 31.1% of visitor arrivals were from the USA, 21.2% from France and 7.7% from Japan. Receipts from tourism in 2011 totalled an estimated US $385m.

In 2012, according to the Institut d'Émission d'Outre-Mer (IEOM—the French overseas reserve bank), French Polynesia recorded a visible merchandise trade deficit of 145,798m. francs CFP. On the current account of the balance of payments there was a surplus of 23,698m. francs CFP. In 2012 the principal sources of imports were France (which provided 24.1% of total imports), the People's Republic of China, the Republic of Korea, the USA, New Zealand and Singapore. The principal markets for exports in that year were Hong Kong (accounting for 27.5% of the total), Japan, France and the USA. The principal imports included mineral products; machinery and mechanical appliances, electrical equipment, and sound and television apparatus; prepared foodstuffs, beverages, spirits and vinegar, and tobacco and manufactured substitutes; live animals and animal products; products of chemical or allied industries; and vehicles, aircraft, vessels and associated transport equipment. The principal exports were cultured pearls, precious and semi-precious stones and related items; and live animals and animal products.

The 2009 budget was expected to be balanced, with revenue equalling expenditure at 140,567m. francs CFP. In the 2012 budget, spending amounted to 147,891m. francs CFP, of which operational expenditure accounted for 113,350m. and investments 34,541m. In 2003 an economic development grant (DGDE) from metropolitan France, amounting to some 18,000m. francs CFP (almost €151m.) annually and to be paid in perpetuity, was introduced to offset the loss of revenue resulting from the closure of the nuclear testing facilities. The DGDE was replaced by three new financial instruments at the end of 2010, but the annual sum provided remained unchanged. About 60% of the funding was to be disbursed by the French Polynesian Government, while about 30% was to be allocated to approved infrastructure projects. In 2011 state expenditure by France in French Polynesia totalled 172,482m. francs CFP.

The annual rate of inflation averaged 1.5% during 2000–12. Consumer prices rose by 1.2% in 2012. A high unemployment rate (11.7% of the labour force in 2007) has been exacerbated by the predominance of young people in the population.

The financial crisis in the islands resulted in a reported contraction in the economy of some 6.7% in both 2011 and 2012. During this period investor confidence remained weak, and international credit monitoring agencies continued to cite political instability as a major factor in the successive downgrading of their ratings for French Polynesia. The crisis also caused increasing hardship for the local population and exacerbated an unemployment rate that by the end of 2012 had risen to an estimated 30% of young people. In late 2012, following a series of discussions in Paris, the French Government agreed to release €34m. of €50m. in financial assistance that had been withheld by the previous administration. The territorial Government proposed a devaluation of the Pacific franc, as part of its draft budget for 2013, claiming that the measure would boost the competitiveness of the islands' exports and reduce inflation. However, fears that it would greatly increase the cost of imported goods meant that a devaluation was not included in the final budget. The new Government elected in mid-2013 announced plans to raise some US $100m. by increasing taxes on higher earners, as well as on sales of alcohol and tobacco, and in its budget for 2014 proposed reducing the public sector by some 300 employees, in an attempt to tackle the estimated $300m. of public debt. Attracting foreign investment was a principal strategy of the new administration's economic policy. Following an official visit to China in late 2013, President Flosse announced that Chinese investment of some $2,000m. would finance a major tourism development in Tahiti, as well as a fisheries project. Moreover, additional plans to construct a new port in the south of Tahiti and to rebuild the island's international airport—both with Chinese co-operation—were envisaged. Another potential source of revenue emerged in early 2014, following the granting to an Australian company of a licence to investigate the possibility of resuming phosphate mining on Makatea Atoll in the Tuamotu Archipelago, which had been heavily mined from the late 1800s until 1966.

PUBLIC HOLIDAYS

2015: 1 January (New Year's Day), 5 March (Arrival of the Gospel), 3 April (Good Friday), 6 April (Easter Monday), 1 May (Labour Day), 8 May (Victory Day), 14 May (Ascension Day), 25 May (Whit Monday), 29 June (Internal Autonomy Day), 14 July (Fall of the Bastille), 15 August (Assumption), 1 November (All Saints' Day), 11 November (Armistice Day), 25 December (Christmas Day).

Statistical Survey

Source (unless otherwise indicated): Institut Statistique de la Polynésie Française, Immeuble Uupa, 1er étage, rue Edouard Ahne, BP 395, 98713 Papeete; tel. 473434; fax 427252; e-mail ispf@ispf.pf; internet www.ispf.pf.

AREA AND POPULATION

Area: Total 4,167 sq km (1,609 sq miles); Land area 3,521 sq km (1,359 sq miles).

Population: 259,596 at census of 20 August 2007; 268,270 at census of 22 August 2012. *By Island Group* (2012 census, preliminary): Society Archipelago 235,503 (Windward Islands 200,881, Leeward Islands 34,622); Marquesas Archipelago 9,264; Austral Islands 6,839; Tuamotu-Gambier Islands 16,664; Total 268,270.

Density (land area only, 2012 census): 76.2 per sq km.

Population by Age and Sex (UN estimates at mid-2014): *0–14:* 62,682 (males 31,986, females 30,696); *15–64:* 196,534 (males 100,804, females 95,730); *65 and over:* 20,617 (males 10,121, females 10,496); *Total* 279,833 (males 142,911, females 136,922) (Source: UN, *World Population Prospects: The 2012 Revision*.

Ethnic Groups (census of 15 October 1983): Polynesian 114,280; 'Demis' 23,625 (Polynesian-European 15,851, Polynesian-Chinese 6,356, Polynesian-Other races 1,418); European 19,320; Chinese 7,424; European-Chinese 494; Others 1,610; Total 166,753. *1988 Census* ('000 persons): Polynesians and 'Demis' 156.3; Others 32.5.

Principal Towns (population at 2012 census): Faa'a 29,687; Papeete (capital) 25,769; Punaauía 27,613; Moorea-Maiao 17,236; Pirae 14,129; Mahina 14,351; Paea 12,541; Taiarapu-Est 12,253; Papara 11,143.

Births, Marriages and Deaths (2010): Registered live births 4,579 (birth rate 17.0 per 1,000); Marriages 1,330 (marriage rate 5.0 per 1,000); Registered deaths 1,261 (death rate 4.7 per 1,000).

Life Expectancy (years at birth, 2011): 75.9 (males 73.7; females 78.2) (Source: World Bank, World Development Indicators database).

Economically Active Population (persons aged 14 years and over, 2007 census, excluding persons in military service): Agriculture, hunting, forestry and fishing 8,809; Mining and manufacturing 6,081; Electricity, gas and water 585; Construction 9,825; Trade, restaurants and hotels 21,064; Transport, storage and communications 7,049; Financial services 1,666; Real estate, housing and services to business 4,391; Other private services 5,326; Education, health and social welfare 15,115; Public administration 15,347; *Total employed* 95,258 (males 56,674, females 38,584); Unemployed 12,668 (males 7,006, females 5,662); *Total labour force* 107,926 (males 63,680, females 44,246). *2011* (salaried workers at 31 December): Agriculture, hunting, forestry and fishing 1,755; Mining and quarrying 151; Manufacturing 3,909; Electricity, gas and water 964; Construction 4,740; Trade, restaurants and hotels 16,212; Transport, storage and communications 6,824; Financial services 1,658; Real estate, housing and services to business 4,971; Public administration 14,037; Education 413; Health and social welfare 3,637; Other community, social and personal services 2,203; Persons employed in private households 1,549; Total 63,023.*2012* (salaried workers at 31 December): Agriculture 1,764; Construction 4,345; Other industry 4,712; Services 50,382 Total 61,203.

HEALTH AND WELFARE

Key Indicators

Total Fertility Rate (children per woman, 2010): 2.1.

Physicians (per 1,000 head, 2012): 1.9.

Total Carbon Dioxide Emissions ('000 metric tons, 2010): 883.7.

Carbon Dioxide Emissions Per Head (metric tons, 2010): 3.3.

For definitions, see explanatory note on p. vi.

AGRICULTURE, ETC.

Principal Crops (metric tons, 2012, FAO estimates): Cassava 4,100; Other roots and tubers 6,000; Sugar cane 3,500; Vegetables and melons 6,527; Pineapples 4,350; Coconuts 90,000; Vanilla 60; Coffee, green 20.

Livestock (year ending September 2012, FAO estimates): Cattle 7,400; Horses 2,200; Pigs 30,000; Goats 16,800; Sheep 440; Chickens 305,000; Ducks 30,000.

Livestock Products (metric tons, 2012, FAO estimates): Cattle meat 135; Pig meat 1,624; Goat meat 75; Chicken meat 630; Cows' milk 1,200; Hen eggs 2,800; Other poultry eggs 88; Honey 50.

Fishing (metric tons, live weight, 2011): Capture 12,852 (Skipjack tuna 893; Albacore 3,479; Yellowfin tuna 1,049; Bigeye tuna 607; Blue marlin 459; Wahoo 326; Common dolphinfish 489; Other marine fishes 4,198); Aquaculture 61; *Total catch* 12,913. Note: Figures exclude pearl oyster shells: 2,843.

Source: FAO.

INDUSTRY

Selected Products (metric tons, 2012, unless otherwise indicated): Copra 12,140; Coconut oil 6,879 (2010); Oilcake 6,992; Electric energy (Tahiti only) 527m. kWh. Source: partly Institut d'Emission d'Outre-Mer.

FINANCE

Currency and Exchange Rates: 100 centimes = 1 franc de la Communauté française du Pacifique (franc CFP or Pacific franc). *Sterling, Dollar and Euro Equivalents* (31 December 2013): £1 sterling = 142.495 francs CFP; US $1 = 86.529 francs CFP; €1 = 119.332 francs CFP; 1,000 francs CFP = £7.02 = $11.56 = €8.38. *Average Exchange Rate* (francs CFP per US $): 85.84 in 2011; 92.88 in 2012; 89.88 in 2013. Note: Until 31 December 1998 the value of the franc CFP was fixed at 5.5 French centimes (1 French franc = 18.1818 francs CFP). Since the introduction of the euro, on 1 January 1999, an official exchange rate of 1,000 francs CFP = €8.38 (€1 = 119.332 francs CFP) has been in operation. Accordingly, the value of the franc CFP has been adjusted to 5.4969 French centimes (1 French franc = 18.1920 francs CFP), representing a 'devaluation' of 0.056%.

Territorial Budget (million francs CFP, 2012): Current revenue 123,217 (Direct taxes 24,154; Indirect taxes 57,148); Expenditure 147,891 (Current 113,350, Capital 34,541).

French State Expenditure (million francs CFP): 175,558 (incl. military budget 21,005) in 2009; 178,995 in 2010; 172,482 in 2011.

Money Supply (million francs CFP at 31 December 2012): Currency in circulation 15,527; Demand deposits 159,874; *Total money* 175,401. Source: Institut d'Emission d'Outre-Mer.

Cost of Living (Consumer Price Index, annual averages; base: 2000 = 100): All items 116.1 in 2010; 118.2 in 2011; 119.6 in 2012. Source: UN, *Monthly Bulletin of Statistics*.

Gross Domestic Product (million francs CFP at constant 2005 prices): 367,556.1 in 2007; 376,575.8 in 2008; 384,320.4 in 2009. Source: UN Statistics Division, National Accounts Main Aggregates Database.

Expenditure on the Gross Domestic Product (million francs CFP at current prices, 2009): Government final consumption expenditure 41,878.4; Private final consumption expenditure 398,672.3; Increase in stocks 852.2; Gross fixed capital formation 98,433.9; *Total domestic expenditure* 539,836.8; Exports of goods and services 70,012.2; *Less* Imports of goods and services 220,176.9; *GDP in purchasers' values* 389,672.1. Source: UN National Accounts Main Aggregates Database.

Gross Domestic Product by Economic Activity (million francs CFP at current prices, 2009): Agriculture, hunting, forestry and fishing 9,967.4; Mining, electricity, gas and water 6,451.8; Manufacturing 22,364.2; Construction 22,377.9; Trade, restaurants and hotels 96,303.7; Transport, storage and communications 29,627.9; Other activities 209,691.5; *Sub-total* 396,784.4; Net of indirect taxes –7,112.3 (obtained as a residual); *GDP in purchasers' values* 389,672.1. Source: UN National Accounts Main Aggregates Database.

Balance of Payments (million francs CFP, 2012): Exports of goods 12,502; Imports of goods –158,300; *Trade balance* –145,798; Exports of services 105,218; Imports of services –48,033; *Balance on goods and services* –88,613; Other income (net) 58,485; *Balance on goods, services and income* –30,128; Current transfers (net) 53,825; *Current balance* 23,698; Capital account (net) –57; Direct investment (net) 9,952; Portfolio investment (net) 1,990; Other investment (net) –15,661; *Overall balance* 19,922. Source: Institut d'Emission d'Outre-Mer.

EXTERNAL TRADE

Principal Commodities (million francs CFP, 2012, excl. military transactions): *Imports c.i.f.:* Live animals and animal products 14,364.8 (Meat and edible meat offal 8,901.5); Vegetable products 5,398.9; Prepared foodstuffs; beverages, spirits and vinegar; tobacco and manufactured substitutes 19,679.8 (Preparations of cereals, flour, starch or milk 4,788.7); Mineral products 29,039.1 (Mineral fuels, mineral oils and products of their distillation; bituminous substances; mineral waxes 27,606.0); Products of chemical or allied industries 13,612.9 (Pharmaceutical products 7,148.2); Plastics, rubber and articles thereof 6,066.0; Base metals and articles thereof 8,273.2; Machinery and mechanical appliances; electrical equipment; sound and television apparatus 24,663.7 (Boilers, machinery, mechanical appliances and parts 14,031.8; Electrical machinery, equipment, etc. 10,632.0); Vehicles, aircraft, vessels and associated transport equipment 13,049.3 (Road vehicles, parts and accessories 9,032.4); Miscellaneous manufactured articles 5,997.4; Total (incl. others) 158,537.9. *Exports f.o.b.:* Live animals and animal products 1,854.8 (Fish and crustaceans, molluscs and other aquatic invertebrates 1,583.2); Animal or vegetable fats and oils, and products thereof 719.0; Prepared foodstuffs; beverages, spirits and vinegars; tobacco and manufactured substitutes 756.7 (Preparations of vegetables, fruit, nuts or other parts of plants 650.6); Natural or cultured pearls, precious or semi-precious stones, precious metals and articles thereof; imitation jewellery; coin 7,793.4; Total (incl. others) 12,918.8.

Principal Trading Partners (million francs CFP, 2012, excl. military transactions): *Imports:* Australia 6,385.4; Belgium 2,518.0; China, People's Republic 15,573.3; France 38,147.9; Germany 4,597.9 Italy 3,922.2; Japan 2,932.1; Korea, Republic of 15,431.4; Netherlands 1,862.9; New Zealand 13,338.0; Singapore 13,073.3; Spain 2,213.0; Thailand 4,353.9; United Kingdom 1,677.0; USA 15,328.2; Total (incl. others) 158,537.9. *Exports:* China, People's Republic 295.8; France 1,997.2; Hong Kong 3,555.1; Japan 3,593.4; New Caledonia 280.1; New Zealand 157.3; Singapore 133.4; USA 2,190.0; Total (incl. others) 12,918.8.

TRANSPORT

Road Traffic (1987): Total vehicles registered 54,979. *2007 Census:* Private cars 4,602; Vans 3,108; Trucks 80; Special vehicles 19; Two wheelers 3,463; Trailers 20; Total 11,292. *2009:* Four-wheelers 15,909; Two-wheelers 2,432; Total 18,341.

Shipping (2012, unless otherwise indicated): *International Traffic:* Passengers carried 27,852 (2003); Freight handled 848,489 (loaded 40,895, unloaded 807,594) metric tons. *Domestic Traffic:* Passengers carried 1,585,858; Total freight handled 411,901 metric tons. Source: Institut d'Emission d'Outre-Mer.

Civil Aviation (2012): *International Traffic:* Passengers carried 520,756; Freight handled 9,543 metric tons. *Domestic Traffic:* Passengers carried 628,049; Freight handled 2,205 metric tons.

TOURISM

Visitors: 153,919 in 2010; 162,776 in 2011; 168,978 in 2012.

Tourist Arrivals by Country of Residence (2012): Australia 10,224; Canada 7,034; France 35,898; Germany 3,552; Italy 9,409; Japan 12,989; New Caledonia 4,022; New Zealand 7,166; USA 52,527; Total (incl. others) 168,978. Source: Institut d'Emission d'Outre-Mer.

Tourism Receipts (US $ million, excl. passenger transport): 440 in 2009; 403 in 2010; 385 in 2011. Source: World Tourism Organization.

COMMUNICATIONS MEDIA

Telephones (2012): 55,000 main lines in use.

Mobile Cellular Telephones (subscribers, 2012): 226,000.

Internet Subscribers (2009): 30,500.

Broadband Subscribers (2012): 40,200.

Source: International Telecommunication Union.

EDUCATION

Pre-primary (2008/09, unless otherwise indicated): 40 schools (2006/07); 408 teachers (1996/97); 14,306 pupils.

Primary (incl. special schools and young adolescents' centres, 2012/13, unless otherwise indicated): 231 schools (incl. pre-primary, 2010/11); 2,811 teachers (1996/97); 38,149 pupils.

Secondary (2012/13 unless otherwise indicated): 51 schools (first and second cycles, 2008/09); 2,035 teachers (general secondary only, 1998/99); 31,166 pupils.

Tertiary (2006/07, unless otherwise indicated): 50 teachers (1999); 681 students.

Source: partly Institut d'Emission d'Outre-Mer.

Directory

The Government

High Commissioner: LIONEL BEFFRE.

Secretary-General: GILLES CANTAL.

COUNCIL OF MINISTERS
(April 2014)

The Government is formed by Tahoera'a Huiraatira.

President and Minister of Employment, International and European Affairs, with responsibility for the Fight against Poverty and Exclusion, for the Elderly and People with Disabilities, and Relations with Municipalities: GASTON FLOSSE.

Vice-President and Minister of the Economy, Finance and the Budget, and Public Service, with responsibility for Enterprise and Industry, the Promotion of Exports and the Fight against Inflation: NUIHAU LAUREY.

Minister for Public Works, Urban Development and Energy, and Land and Sea Transport: ALBERT SOLIA.

Minister for Marine Resources, Mines and Research, with responsibility for Fisheries, Aquaculture and Relations with French Polynesia's Institutions: TEARII ALPHA.

Minister for Education, Higher Education, Youth and Sports, with responsibility for Community Life: MICHEL LEBOUCHER.

Minister for Housing, Land Affairs, the Digital Economy, Communication and Handicrafts, and Government Spokesman: MARCEL TUIHANI.

Minister for Tourism, Ecology, Culture, Spatial Planning and Air Transport: JEFFREY SALMON.

Minister for Health and Labour, with responsibility for Social Welfare, Professional Training, Social Dialogue, the Rights of Women and the Fight against Addiction: BÉATRICE CHANSIN.

Minister for Agriculture, Food Production and Livestock Rearing, Equality and the Development of Archipelagos: TOMAS MOUTAME.

Minister for Solidarity and Family: MANOLITA LY.

GOVERNMENT OFFICES

Office of the High Commissioner of the Republic: ave Pouvanaa a Oopa, Nouveau Bâtiment, BP 115, 98713 Papeete; tel. 468700; fax 468769; e-mail courrier@polynesie-francaise.pref.gouv.fr; internet www.polynesie-francaise.pref.gouv.fr.

Office of the President of the Government: Quartier Broche, ave Pouvana'a A Opa, BP 2551, 98713 Papeete; tel. 472000; fax 472210; internet www.presidence.pf.

Ministry of Agriculture, Food Production and Livestock Rearing, Equality and the Development of Archipelagos: route de l'Hippodrome, Tuterai Tane, Pirae; tel. 544900; fax 478302.

Ministry of the Economy, Finance and the Budget, and Public Service: Bâtiment de la Culture, 1er étage, rue des Poilus Tahitiens, Papeete; tel. 803000; fax 453355; e-mail charles.garnier@europe.gov.pf; internet web.presidence.pf.

Ministry of Education, Higher Education, Youth and Sports: Immeuble Papineau, 6ème étage, Papeete; tel. 478383; fax 472290; e-mail secretariat@education.min.gov.pf; internet web.presidence.pf.

Ministry of Health and Labour: 24 ave Du Petit-Thouars, Face au parking Tarahoi, Papeete; tel. 472500; fax 433942.

Ministry of Housing, Land Affairs, the Digital Economy, Communication and Handicrafts: Immeuble Tefenua, 5ème étage, rue Dumont d'Urville, BP 2551, 98713 Papeete; tel. 549575; fax 454343; internet web.presidence.pf.

Ministry of Marine Resources, Mines and Research: Bâtiment de l'Ancien Gouvernement, ave Pouvanaa a Oopa, Papeete; tel. 504455; fax 478302; e-mail secretariat@maritime.min.gov.pf; internet web.presidence.pf.

Ministry of Public Works, Urban Development and Energy, and Land and Sea Transport: Bâtiment Administratif A2, 5ème étage, rue du Commandant Destremeau, BP 2551, 98713 Papeete; tel. 468019; fax 483792; e-mail secretariat@equipement.min.gov.pf; internet www.equipement.gov.pf.

Ministry of Solidarity and Employment, International and European Affairs: Quartier Broche, avenue Pouvanaa a Oopa, Papeete; tel. 472000; fax 478331; e-mail secretariat@solidarite.min.gov.pf; internet web.presidence.pf.

Ministry of Tourism, Ecology, Culture, Spatial Planning and Air Transport: Bâtiment du GIE Tahiti Tourisme, Quai des paquebots, Papeete; tel. 508860; e-mail contact@tourisme.min.gov.pf; internet web.presidence.pf.

Economic, Social and Cultural Council (CESC): Immeuble Te Raumaire, ave Bruat, BP 1657, 98714 Papeete; tel. 416500; fax 419242; e-mail cesc@cesc.pf; internet www.cesc.pf; f. 1977; est. as Economic and Social Council; present name adopted in 1990; Pres. JEAN TAMA; Sec.-Gen. ALEXA BONNETTE.

Legislature

ASSEMBLY

Elections to the Assembly took place over two rounds, in accordance with the modified electoral process, on 21 April and 5 May 2013.

President: EDOUARD FRITCH.

Assembly: Assemblée de la Polynésie Française, rue du Docteur Cassiau, BP 28, 98713 Papeete; tel. 416300; fax 416372; e-mail administratif@assemblee.pf; internet www.assemblee.pf.

Election (second round), 5 May 2013

Party	Seats
Tahoera'a Huiraatira*	38
Union pour la Démocratie (UPLD)†	11
A Ti'a Porinetia	8
Total	57

* The Tahoera'a Huiraatira's total includes the 19 seats allocated to the winning list in the second round under the new electoral system.

† Coalition led by Tavini Huiraatira.

PARLIAMENT

Deputies to the French National Assembly: JONAS TAHUAITU (DVD), JEAN-PAUL TUAIVA (DVD); a by-election to replace EDOUARD FRITCH (Divers droite—DVD) was expected to take place in June 2014.

Representatives to the French Senate: GASTON FLOSSE (Tahoera'a Huiraatira), RICHARD TUHEIAVA (Union pour la Démocratie—UPLD).

Political Organizations

A Ti'a Porinetia (Rally of Polynesians): e-mail contact@atiaporinetia.org; internet www.atiaporinetia.org; f. 2013; coalition of parties fmrly belonging to the To Tatou Ai'a coalition and a number of smaller groups; Pres. TEVA ROHFRITSCH.

Fe'tia Api (New Star): c/o Assemblée de la Polynésie Française, rue du Docteur Cassiau, BP 28, 98713 Papeete; tel. 416131; fax 416136; f. 1996; part of Alliance pour une Démocratie Nouvelle coalition; pro-autonomy; Leader PHILIP SCHYLE.

Heiura-Les Verts Polynésiens: BP 44, Bora Bora; tel. and fax 677174; e-mail heiura@heiura-lesverts.pf; ecologist; Leader JACKY BRYANT.

Ia Mana Te Nunaa (Power to the People): BP 140 114, Arue, Tahiti 98701; tel. 426699; e-mail iamanatenunaa@mail.pf; internet www.iamanatenunaa.com; f. 1976; advocates 'socialist independence'; Pres. JACQUI DROLLET.

No Oe E Te Nunaa (This Country is Yours): Immeuble Fara, rue Nansouty, BP 40205, Fare Tony, 98713 Papeete; tel. 423718; e-mail contact@noetn.com; internet www.noetn.com; favours autonomy; part of Alliance pour une Démocratie Nouvelle coalition; Leader NICOLE MOEA BOUTEAU; Sec.-Gen. ROSALIE TIRIANA ZAVAN.

O Porinetia To Tatou Ai'a (Polynesia, Our Homeland): BP 4061, 98713 Papeete; tel. and fax 584848; e-mail contact@oporinetia.pf; internet www.oporinetia.pf; f. 2007; est. by fmr mems of Tahoera'a Huiraatira; leading mem. of A Ti'a Porinetia (fmrly To Tatou Ai'a) coalition; Pres. GASTON TONG SANG.

Taatiraa No Te Hau: POB 41636, Papeete; tel. 437494; fax 422546; f. 1977; Pres. CHARLES FONG LOI.

Tahoera'a Huiraatira (People's Rally): rue du Commandant Destremeau, BP 471, Papeete; tel. 429898; fax 450004; e-mail tahitinui@tahoeraa.pf; internet tahoeraahuiraatira.pf; f. 1977; fmrly l'Union Tahitienne; supports links with France, with internal autonomy; affiliated to the metropolitan Union pour un Mouvement Populaire (UMP); Pres. GASTON FLOSSE; Pres.-Delegate EDOUARD FRITCH; Sec.-Gen. BRUNO SANDRAS.

Tapura Amui No Te Faatereraa Manahune-Tuhaa Pae: c/o Assemblée de la Polynésie Française, rue du Docteur Cassiau, BP 28, 98713 Papeete; represents the Austral Islands; Leader CHANTAL FLORES.

Tavini Huiraatira No Te Ao Ma'ohi/Front de Libération de la Polynésie (Polynesian People's Servant): rue des Remparts, Papeete; tel. 424902; fax 434209; e-mail contact@tavinihuiraatira.com; internet www.tavinihuiraatira.com; f. 1977; leading mem. of Union pour la Démocratie (Union for Democracy—UPLD) coalition; independence movement; anti-nuclear; Leader OSCAR TEMARU; Sec.-Gen. LÉON TEFAU.

Te' Avei'a (Te Ara): BP 11 362, 98709 Mahina, Tahiti; tel. and fax 851385; e-mail mail@teaveia.pf; internet www.teaveia.pf; f. 2004; est. by fmr mems of Fe'tia Api and Tavini Huiraatira; Pres. ANTONIO PEREZ.

Te Henua Enana Kotoa: Nuku Hiva, BP 56 Taiohae; tel. and fax 920422; Leader LOUIS TAATA.

Te Niu Hau Manahune (Principle of Democracy): Rangiroa; f. 2007; Pres. TEINA MARAEURA; Vice-Pres BENOÎT KAUTAI, TEMAURI FOSTER.

Te Pupu Here Ai'a Te Nuna'a Ia Ora (Patriotic Party for an Autonomous Polity): BP 3195, Papeete; tel. 420766; f. 1965; advocates autonomy.

Judicial System

Audit Office: Chambre Territoriale des Comptes, rue Edouard Ahnne, BP 331, 98713 Papeete; tel. 509710; fax 509719; e-mail ctcpf@pf.ccomptes.fr; Pres. JEAN LACHKAR; Clerk of the Court MARIE-HÉLÈNE ANDRIOT.

Court of Administrative Law: rue Pouvana'a A Opa, BP 4522, 98713 Papeete; tel. 509025; fax 451724; e-mail tadelapolynesiefrancaise@mail.pf; internet polynesie-francaise.tribunal-administratif.fr; Pres. JEAN-YVES TALLEC; Clerk of the Court DONA GERMAIN.

Court of Appeal: Cour d'Appel de Papeete, 42 ave Pouvana'a A Opa, BP 101, 98713 Papeete; tel. 415500; fax 424416; e-mail sec.pp.ca-papeete@justice.fr; internet www.ca-papeete.justice.fr; Pres. OLIVIER AIMOT; Attorney-Gen. SERGE SAMUEL; Clerk of the Court RENE ARLANDA.

Court of the First Instance: Tribunal de Première Instance de Papeete, ave Bruat, BP 4633, 78718 Papeete; tel. 415500; fax 454012; e-mail sec.pr.tpi-papeete@justice.fr; internet www.ca-papeete.justice.fr; Pres. Sir FRANCIS JULLEMIER MILLASSEAU; Procurator JOSÉ THOREL; Clerk of the Court KARL LEQUEUX.

Religion

About 54% of the population are Protestants and 38% are Roman Catholics.

CHRISTIANITY

Protestant Church

Maohi Protestant Church: BP 113, Papeete; tel. 460600; fax 419357; e-mail eepf@mail.pf; f. 1884; autonomous since 1963; fmrly l'Eglise Evangélique en Polynésie Française (Etaretia Evaneria I Porinetia Farani); Pres. of Council Rev. TAAROANUI MARAEA; c. 95,000 mems.

The Roman Catholic Church

French Polynesia comprises the archdiocese of Papeete and the suffragan diocese of Taiohae o Tefenuaenata (based in Nuku Hiva, Marquesas Is). At 31 December 2007 there were an estimated 101,090 adherents in French Polynesia. The Archbishop and the Bishop participate in the Episcopal Conference of the Pacific, based in Fiji.

Archbishop of Papeete: (vacant), Archevêché, BP 94, Vallée de la Mission, 98713 Papeete; tel. 420251; fax 424032; e-mail catholic@mail.pf.

Other Churches

Other denominations active in French Polynesia include the Assemblies of God, Church of Jesus Christ of Latter-day Saints (Mormon), Sanito and Seventh-day Adventist missions. At mid-2000 there were an estimated 30,000 adherents to other forms of Christianity.

The Press

La Dépêche de Tahiti: Ave George Clémenceau, BP 50, 98713 Papeete; tel. 475283; fax 475260; e-mail journal@ladepeche.pf; internet www.ladepeche.pf; f. 1964; acquired by Groupe France Antilles in 1988; daily; French; Man. Dir ALEXANDRE THÉVENET; Editor LARA DUPUY; circ. 20,500.

Fenua'Orama: BP 629, 98713 Papeete; tel. 475293; fax 475297; e-mail fenuaorama@hersantmedia.pf; publ. by Groupe France Antilles; monthly; women's lifestyle; Editor-in-Chief DANIEL PARDON; circ. 13,700.

L'Hebdo Maohi: Papeete; tel. and fax 4581827; e-mail journal@hebdo.pf; internet www.hebdo.pf; weekly; Man. and Publ. Dir TERII PAQUIER; circ. 3,000.

Journal Officiel de la Polynésie Française: c/o Imprimerie Officielle, 43 rue des Poilus Tahitiens, BP 117, 98713 Papeete; tel. 500580; fax 425261; e-mail imprimerie.officielle@imprimerie.gov.pf; f. 2004 as *Compte Rendu Intégral des Débats de l'Assemblée de la Polynésie Française*; bi-weekly; publ. by the Imprimerie Officielle; circ. 100.

Les Nouvelles de Tahiti: Immeuble Sarateva, Carrefour de la Fautaua, BP 629, Papeete; tel. 475200; fax 475209; e-mail redac@lesnouvelles.pf; internet www.lesnouvelles.pf; f. 1957; daily; French; Gen. Man. ALEXANDRE THÉVENET; Editor-in-Chief MURIEL PONTAROLLO; circ. 6,500.

Le Semeur Tahitien: BP 94, 98713 Papeete; tel. 502351; fax 424032; e-mail catholic@mail.pf; f. 1909; 22 a year; French; publ. by the Roman Catholic Church; Editor ROSA TAUHIRO.

Tahiti Beach Press: BP 887, 98713 Papeete; tel. 426850; fax 423356; e-mail tahitibeachpres@mail.pf; internet www.tahitibeachpress.com; f. 1980; monthly; English; Publr G. WARTI; circ. 10,000.

Tahiti Pacifique Magazine: BP 368, Maharepa, Moorea; tel. 562894; fax 563007; e-mail tahitipm@mail.pf; internet tahiti-pacifique.com; monthly; French; Dir and Editor ALEX W. DU PREL; circ. 6,500.

Ve'a Katorika: BP 94, 98713 Papeete; tel. 502351; fax 424032; e-mail archeveche@catholic.pf; internet www.diocesedepapeete.com; f. 1909; monthly; publ. by the Roman Catholic Church; Administrator MICHEL COPPENRATH.

Ve'a Porotetani: BP 113, Papeete; tel. 460623; fax 419357; e-mail eepf@mail.pf; f. 1921; monthly; French and Tahitian; publ. by the Maohi Protestant Church; Dir TAARII MARAEA; Editor-in-Chief EVA RAAPOTO; circ. 5,000.

Other publications include *Le To'ere*, weekly; *Conso + Info Plus*, *Tahiti Business* and *Ve'a Ora Magazine*, monthly; and *Dixit* and *Fenua Economie*, annually.

NEWS AGENCY

Agence France-Presse (AFP): BP 629, Papeete; tel. 508100; fax 508109; Group Chair. and CEO EMMANUEL HOOG; Group Man. Dir RÉMI TOMASZEWSKI.

Publishers

Editions Haere Pō: BP 1958, Papeete 98713; tel. and fax 480401; e-mail haerepotahiti@mail.pf; internet www.haerepo.org; f. 1981; travel, history, linguistics, literature, culture, anthropology, religion, land tenure and local interest.

Au Vent des Iles: BP 5670, 98716 Pirae; tel. 509595; fax 509597; e-mail mail@auventdesiles.pf; internet www.auventdesiles.pf; f. 1992; South Pacific interest, fiction and trade; Gen. Man. CHRISTIAN ROBERT.

GOVERNMENT PRINTER

Imprimerie Officielle: 43 rue des Poilus Tahitiens, BP 117, 98713 Papeete; tel. 500580; fax 425261; e-mail imprimerie.officielle@imprimerie.gov.pf; f. 1843; printers, publrs; Dir CLAUDINO LAURENT.

Broadcasting and Communications

TELECOMMUNICATIONS

Office des Postes et Télécommunications (OPT): Hôtel des Postes, 8 rue de la Reine Pomare IV, 98714 Papeete; tel. 414242; fax 436767; e-mail contact@opt.pf; internet www.opt.pf; state-owned telecommunications co; subsidiaries incl. Tahiti Nui Telecom (international voice services), Tikiphone (mobile network), Mana (internet service), Tahiti Nui Satellite (satellite broadcaster), ISS (software and network solutions); Chair. FRANÇOIS VOIRIN; Dir-Gen. BENJAMIN TEIHOTU (acting).

Tahiti Nui Telecommunications (TNT): BP 11843, 98709 Mahina; tel. 415400; fax 437553; e-mail admin.tnt@tahitinui-telecom.com; internet www.tahitinui-telecom.com; f. 2001; owned by OPT; provides international telephone services; Chair. JEAN-CLAUDE TERIIEROOITERAI.

Tikiphone SAS (Vini): POB 440, 98713 Papeete; tel. 481313; fax 482300; internet www.tikiphone.pf; f. 1994; subsidiary of OPT; operates Vini, French Polynesia's first mobile telephone network; more than 208,000 subscribers; Gen. Man. YANNICK TERIIEROOITERAI.

Regulatory Authority

Agence de Réglementation du Numérique: Immeuble Toriki, rue Dumont d'Urville, Quartier Orovini, BP 5019, 98716 Pirae; tel. 544535; fax 532801; e-mail direction@arn.gov.pf; internet www.arn.pf; fmrly Services des Postes et Télécommunications; name changed as above 2011; Dir TAMATOA POMMIER.

BROADCASTING

Radio

RFO Polynésie: Centre Pamatai, Faa'a, BP 60125, 98702 Papeete; tel. 861616; fax 861611; e-mail rfopfr@mail.pf; internet polynesie.la1ere.fr; f. 1934; public service radio and television station operated by Réseau France Outre-Mer (RFO), Paris; daily programmes in French and Tahitian; Dir-Gen. GENEVIÈVE GIARD; Regional Dir MICHEL KOPS.

Private Stations

Since 2004 some 17 stations have been licensed. There are currently around 25 commercial radio stations in French Polynesia.

NRJ Tahiti: BP 50, 98718 Papeete; tel. and fax 421042; fax 464346; internet www.nrj.pf; affiliated to NRJ France; French; entertainment; broadcasts 14 hrs daily; Station Man. NADINE RICHARDSON.

Radio Maohi: Maison des Jeunes, Pirae; tel. 819797; fax 825493; e-mail tereo@mail.pf; French and Tahitian; owned by the political party Tahoera'a Huiraatira.

Radio One: Fare Ute, BP 3601, 98713 Papeete; tel. 434100; fax 422421; e-mail contact@radio1.pf; internet www.radio1.pf; French; relays Europe 1 news bulletins from Paris; CEO SONIA ALINE.

Radio (Te Reo O) Tefana (La Voix de Tefana): BP 6295, 98702 Faa'a; tel. 819797; fax 825493; e-mail tereo@mail.pf; f. 1987; French and Tahitian; affiliated to the Tavini Huiraatira party; Pres. VITO MAAMAATUAIAHUTAPU; Dir and Station Man. TERIIMATEATA MANA; Editor-in-Chief MICAËL TAPUTU.

Radio Te Vevo O Te Tiaturiraa: 51 rue Dumont d'Urville, BP 1817, 98713 Papeete; tel. 412341; fax 412322; e-mail contacts@mail.pf; religious; affiliated with the Assemblies of God church; Treas. THIERRY ALBERT.

Other radio stations include Pacific FM, Radio Fara, Radio la Voix de l'Espérance (LVDL), Radio Ma'ohi-RTL, Radio Maria No Te Hau, Radio Paofai, Radio Te Vevo No Papara, Star FM and Tiare FM.

Television

RFO Polynésie: see Radio**TNS** (Tahiti Nui Satellite): 8 rue de la Reine Pomare IV, 98714 Papeete; tel. 414370; fax 432707; e-mail tns@opt.pf; internet www.tns.pf; f. 2000; 100% owned by the Office des Postes et Télécommunications; news and entertainment; relays 25 television channels and 6 radio channels, in French, Tahitian and English, incl. TNTV; also relays ABC Asia Pacific Television, Australia, and Canal Plus, France; Man. VETEA TROUCHE-BONNO; over 10,000 subscribers.

TNTV (Tahiti Nui Television): Quartier Mission, BP 348, 98713 Papeete; tel. 473636; fax 532721; e-mail tntv@tntv.pf; internet www.tntv.pf; f. 2000; broadcasts in French and Tahitian 19 hours daily; Chair. MEDERIC BERNARDINO; Dir-Gen. PHILIPPE ROUSSEL.

Finance

(cap. = capital; res = reserves; dep. = deposits; m. = million; brs = branches; amounts in francs CFP)

BANKING

Commercial Banks

Banque de Polynésie SA: 355 blvd Pomare, BP 530, 98713 Papeete; tel. 466666; fax 466664; e-mail bdp@sg-bdp.pf; internet www.sg-bdp.pf; f. 1973; 80% owned by Société Générale, France; cap. 1,380m., res 3,352m., dep. 136,408.2m. (Dec. 2011); Chair. JEAN-LOUIS MATTEI; Gen. Man. OLIVIER RAUCH; 25 brs.

Banque de Tahiti SA: 38 rue François Cardella, BP 1602, 98713 Papeete; tel. 417000; fax 423376; e-mail contact@bt.pf; internet www.banque-tahiti.pf; f. 1969; owned by Financière Océor (95.4%); merged with Banque Paribas de Polynésie in 1998; cap. 1,814.8m., res 5,271.2m., dep. 180,703.7m. (Dec. 2008); Chair. PHILIPPE GARSUAULT; Dir-Gen. PATRICE TEPELIAN; 18 brs.

Banque SOCREDO—Société de Crédit et de Développement de l'Océanie: 115 rue Dumont d'Urville, BP 130, 98713 Papeete; tel. 415123; fax 433661; e-mail socres@bank-socredo.pf; internet www.socredo.pf; f. 1959; public body; in partnership with French cos BNP Paribas, Cardif Assurance and Crédit Agricole, which provide technical assistance; cap. 22,000m., res 8,950.7m., dep. 160,838.6m. (Dec. 2011); Chair. CLAUDE PERIOU; Gen. Man. JAMES ESTALL; 26 brs.

Insurance

AGF Vie & AGF IART Polynésie Française: Immeuble Sienne, rue Dumont d'Urville, BP 4452, 98713 Papeete; tel. 549100; fax 549101; e-mail gestion-vie@agf.pf; internet www.allianz.fr; life and general non-life insurance.

GAN Pacifique: 9 ave Bruat, BP 339, 98713 Papeete; tel. 503150; fax 431918; subsidiary of Groupama, France; general non-life insurance; Chair. JEAN-FRANÇOIS LEMOUX; CEO PASCAL ALEXANDRE.

Poe-ma Insurances: Marina Fare Ute, BP 4652, 98713 Papeete; tel. 502650; fax 450097; e-mail info@poema.pf; internet www.poema.pf; f. 1991; general non-life insurance; Man. Dir VINCENT GEORGE.

Trade and Industry

GOVERNMENT AGENCIES

Direction Générale des Affaires Economiques (DGAE): Fare Ute, Bâtiment des Affaires Economiques, BP 82, 98713 Papeete; tel. 509797; fax 434477; e-mail dgae@economie.gov.pf; internet www.dgae.gov.pf; Man. Dir HERVÉ DUQUESNAY.

Etablissement Public des Grands Travaux (EGT): 51 rue du Commandant Destremeau, BP 9030, Motu Uta, 98715 Papeete; tel. 508100; fax 508102; e-mail contact@egt.pf; internet www.egt.pf; responsible for public works; Pres. JONAS TAHUAITU; Dir ERIC NOBLE-DEMAY.

Service de l'Artisanat Traditionnel (ART): Immeuble Lejeune, 1er étage, 82 rue du Général de Gaulle, BP 4451, 98713 Papeete; tel. 545400; fax 532321; e-mail secretariat@artisanat.gov.pf; f. 1984; Dir LAETITIA GALENON.

Service de l'Emploi, de la Formation et de la Insertion Professionnelles (SEFI): Immeuble Papineau, rue Tepano Jaussen, 2ème étage, BP 540, 98713 Papeete; tel. 461212; fax 450280; internet www.sefi.pf; Dir PAUL NATIER.

Service du Commerce Extérieur: 53 rue Nansouty, Immeuble Teissier au 1er étage, BP 20727, 98713 Papeete; tel. 506464; fax 436420; e-mail commerceexterieur@economie.gov.pf; internet www.tahiti-export.pf; Dir WILLIAM VANIZETTE.

Service du Développement de l'Industrie et des Métiers (SDIM): BP 9055, Motu Uta, 98715 Papeete; tel. 502880; fax 412645; e-mail infos@sdim.pf; internet www.sdim.pf; f. 1988; industry and small business devt administration; Dir DENIS GRELLIER.

Société de Financement du Développement de la Polynésie Française (SOFIDEP): Centre Paofai, Bâtiment BC, 1er étage, blvd Pomare, BP 345, 98713 Papeete; tel. 509330; fax 509333; e-mail sem.sofidep@mail.pf; Dir PIERRE FONTAINE.

DEVELOPMENT ORGANIZATIONS

Agence Française de Développement (AFD): Immeuble Hokule'a, 2 rue Cook Paofai, BP 578, 98713 Papeete; tel. 544600; fax 544601; e-mail afdpapeete@pf.groupe-afd.org; internet www.afd.fr; public body; devt finance institute; Dir FRANÇOIS GIOVALUCCHI.

Moruroa e Tatou (Moruroa et Nous): 403 blvd Pomare, BP 5456, 98716 Pirae, Papeete; tel. 460666; e-mail moruroaetatou@mail.pf; internet www.moruroaetatou.com; f. 2001; represents fmr employees of the Centre d'Expérimentation du Pacifique (CEP) and their families; Pres. ROLAND POUIRA OLDHAM; c. 4,500 mems.

SODEP (Société pour le Développement et l'Expansion du Pacifique): BP 4441, Papeete; tel. 429449; f. 1961; est. by a consortium of banks and private interests; regional devt and finance co.

CHAMBERS OF COMMERCE

Chambre de Commerce, d'Industrie, des Services et des Métiers de Polynésie Française (CCISM): 41 rue du Docteur Cassiau, BP 118, 98713 Papeete; tel. 472700; fax 540701; e-mail info@cci.pf; internet www.ccism.pf; f. 1880; Pres. GILLES YAU; Gen. Man. ABNER GILLOUX; 34 mems.

Chambre d'Agriculture et de la Pêche Lagonaire: route de l'Hippodrome, BP 5383, Pirae; tel. 425393; fax 438754; e-mail courrier@vanille.pf; f. 1886; Pres. HENRI TAURAA; Sec.-Gen. JACQUES ROOMATAAROA; 10 mems.

Jeune Chambre Economique de Tahiti: BP 20669, Papeete; tel. 810114; fax 702703; e-mail contact@jcitahiti.com; internet www.jcitahiti.com; Pres. THIERRY LEOU.

EMPLOYERS' ORGANIZATIONS

Confédération Générale des Petites et Moyennes Entreprises de Polynésie Française Te Rima Rohi (CGPME): BP 1733, 98713 Papeete; tel. 426333; fax 835608; e-mail courrier@cgpme.pf; internet www.cgpme.pf; Pres. CHRISTOPHE PLÉE; c. 1,000 mems.

Affiliated organizations include:

Chambre Syndicale des Fleuristes de Polynésie Française: tel. 800505; fax 573649; e-mail tahitifleurs@mail.pf; f. 2007; Pres. ALAIN MENARD.

Syndicat des Gérants de Stations Services (SGSS): tel. 455479; fax 427314; Pres. CHRISTIAN BASTIEN.

Syndicat des Restaurants, Bars et Snacks Bars de Polynésie Française (SRBSBPF): Le Mandarin, BP 302, 98713 Papeete; tel. 503350; fax 421632; e-mail charl.beaumont@mail.pf; Pres. CHARLES BEAUMONT.

Syndicat Polynésien des Entreprises et Prestataires de Service (SPEPS): tel. 584629; fax 545641; e-mail rdp@mail.pf; Pres. SÉBASTIEN BOUZARD.

Union Polynésienne de l'Hôtellerie (UPHO): 76 rue Wallis, BP 1733 Motu Uta, Papeete; tel. 426333; fax 429553; e-mail chris.beaumont@mail.pf; Pres. CHRISTOPHE BEAUMONT.

Union Polynésienne des Professions Libérales (UPPL): BP 4554, Papeete; e-mail gibeaux.tahiti@mail.pf; Pres. CHARLIE GIBEAUX.

MEDEF Polynésie Française (MEDEF PF): Immeuble Farnham, rue Clappier, BP 972, 98713 Papeete; tel. 541040; fax 423237; e-mail medef@medef.pf; internet www.medef.pf; f. 1983; fmrly Conseil des Employeurs; affiliated to Mouvement des Entreprises de France (MEDEF); comprises 15 professional and interprofessional orgs, representing 500 cos; Pres. LUC TAPETA-SERVONNAT; Sec.-Gen. JEAN-CLAUDE LECUELLE.

Affiliated organizations include:

Association des Transporteurs Aériens Locaux de Polynésie Française (ATAL): BP 314, 98713 Papeete; tel. 864004; fax 864009; Pres. MARCEL GALENON.

Association Tahitienne des Professionnels de l'Audiovisuel (ATPA): Papeete; internet www.atpa.tv; f. 2004; 17 mems.

Chambre Syndicale des Commissionnaires en Douane, Agents de Fret et Déménageurs de Polynésie Française: BP 972, 98713 Papeete; tel. 541044; fax 423237; e-mail cscdafd@medef.pf; Pres. TITAINA SANNE-BOURNE.

Comité de Polynésie de l'Association Française des Banques: c/o Banque de Tahiti, BP 1602, 98713 Papeete; tel. 417030; fax 423376; e-mail ptepelian@bt.pf; Pres. PATRICE TEPELIAN.

Fédération Générale du Commerce: BP 1607, 98713 Papeete; tel. 541042; fax 422359; e-mail fgc@mail.pf; internet www.fgc.pf; Pres. JACQUES BILLON-TYRARD; Sec. PATRICIA LO MONACO.

Professionnels du Conseil et de la Formation (PCF): Immeuble Farnham, 1er étage, rue Clappier, Papeete; tel. 541040; fax 423237; e-mail mcdc@mail.pf; f. 2004; established as Organisation Professionnelle du Conseil, de l'Intérim et de la Formation; name changed as above 2012; represents workers in consultancy, training, audit and research, communication and expertise; 10 mem. cos; Pres. FANNY GOSSE; Sec. LAURENT DEVEMY.

Syndicat des Agences Maritimes au Long Cours: BP 274, 98713 Papeete; tel. 428972; fax 432184; e-mail amitahiti@amitahiti.pf; Pres. MAEVA SIU.

Syndicat des Employeurs du Secteur de l'Assurance (SESA): BP 358, 98713 Papeete; tel. 506262; fax 506263; Pres. ALAIN LEBRIS.

Syndicat des Industriels de Polynésie Française (SIPOF): Immeuble Farnham, BP 3521, 98713 Papeete; tel. 541040; fax 423237; e-mail sipof@medef.pf; internet www.sipof.pf; f. 1974; represents workers in industry, engineering, manufacturing and printing; 2,222 mems in 61 cos; Co-Pres FRANCIS GUEBEL, YOANN LAMISSE; Sec. SÉBASTIEN MOLLARD.

Syndicat Professionnel des Concessionnaires Automobiles: BP 916, 98713 Papeete; tel. 454545; fax 431260; Pres. PAUL YEO CHICHONG.

Union des Industriels de la Manutention Portuaire (UNIM): BP 570, 98713 Papeete; tel. 545700; fax 426262; Pres. JULES CHANGUES.

Groupement Interprofessionnel du Monoï de Tahiti (GIMT): BP 14 165, Arue, Tahiti; tel. 414851; fax 431849; internet www.monoidetahiti.pf; f. 1992; asscn of monoï manufacturers.

UTILITIES

Electricity

Electricité de Tahiti (EDT): route de Puurai, BP 8021, Faa'a-Puurai; tel. 867777; fax 834439; e-mail ressourceshumaines@edt.pf; internet www.edt.pf; subsidiary of Groupe Suez, France; Pres. HERVÉ DUBOST-MARTIN; Gen. Man. DOMINIQUE BAYEN; c. 103,920 customers (2012).

Water

Polynésienne des Eaux: BP 20795, 98713 Papeete; tel. 505800; fax 421548; e-mail contact@polynesienne-des-eaux.pf.

TRADE UNIONS

Under French Polynesian legislation, to be officially recognized, trade unions must receive the vote of at least 5% of the workforce at professional elections.

Chambre Syndicale des Métiers du Génie Civil et des Travaux Publics (CSMGCTP): BP 51120, 98716 Pirae; tel. 502100; fax 436922; Pres. DANIEL PALACZ.

Confédération des Syndicats des Travailleurs de Polynésie/Force Ouvrière (CSTP/FO): Immeuble Farnham, 1er étage, BP 1201, 98713 Papeete; tel. 426049; fax 450635; e-mail pfrebault@cstp-fo.pf; Pres. COCO TERAIEFA CHANG; Sec.-Gen. PATRICK GALENON.

Confédération des Syndicats Indépendants de la Polynésie Française (CSIP): Immeuble Allegret, 1er étage, ave du Prince Hinoï, BP 468, 98713 Papeete; tel. 532274; fax 532275; Sec.-Gen. CYRIL LE GAYIC.

Confédération Syndicale A Tia I Mua (CFDT): Fare Ia Ora, Mamao, BP 4523, Papeete; tel. 544010; fax 450245; e-mail atiaimua@ifrance.com; affiliated to the Confédération Française Démocratique du Travail; Gen. Sec. JEAN-MARIE YAN TU.

Conseil Fédéral des Syndicats Libres de Polynésie O Oe To Oe Rima: Immeuble Brown, 1er étage, BP 52866, 98716 Pirae; tel. 483445; fax 483445; Gen. Sec. RONALD TEROROTUA.

Union Fédérale des Syndicats Autonomes/Confédération OTAHI (OTAHI UFSA): ancien Immeuble SETIL, 1er étage, ave du Prince Hinoi, BP 148, 98713 Papeete; tel. 450654; fax 451327; Sec.-Gen. LUCIE TIFFENAT.

Transport

ROADS

French Polynesia has 792 km of roads, of which about one-third are bitumen-surfaced and two-thirds stone-surfaced.

Direction des Transports Terrestres: 93 ave Pomare V, Fariipiti, BP 4586, 98713 Papeete; tel. 502060; fax 436021; e-mail dtt@transport.gov.pf; internet www.transports-terrestres.pf; f. 1988; Dir ROLAND TSU.

SHIPPING

The principal port is at Papeete, on Tahiti.

Port Authority: Port Autonome de Papeete, BP 9164, Motu Uta, 98715 Papeete; tel. 474800; fax 421950; e-mail portppt@portppt.pf; internet www.portdepapeete.pf; Harbour Master MARCEL PELLETIER; Port Dir PATRICK BORDET.

Agence Maritime Internationale de Tahiti: BP 274, 98713 Papeete; tel. 428972; fax 432184; e-mail amitahiti@amitahiti.pf; f. 1978; services from Asia, the USA, Australia, New Zealand and Europe; Gen. Mans JEAN SIU, MAEVA SIU.

CMA CGM Papeete: 2 rue Wallis, BP 96, Papeete; tel. 545252; fax 436806; e-mail ppt.genmbox@cma-cgm.com; internet www.cma-cgm.com; fmrly CGM Tour du Monde SA; shipowners and agents; international freight services; Group Chair. and CEO JACQUES R. SAADÉ; Dir RODOLPHE SAADÉ.

Compagnie Polynésienne de Transport Maritime: BP 220, 98713 Papeete; tel. 426242; fax 434889; e-mail aranui@mail.pf; internet www.aranui.com; shipping co; Dir JULES WONG; Gen. Man. PHILIPPE WONG.

EURL Transport Maritime des Tuamotu Ouest: BP 1816, 98713 Papeete; tel. 422553; fax 422557; inter-island passenger service; Dir SIMÉON RICHMOND.

SA Compagnie Française Maritime de Tahiti: Immeuble Importex, No. 45, Fare Ute, POB 368, 98713 Papeete; tel. 426393; fax 420617; e-mail taporo@mail.pf; Pres. and Man. MORTON GARBUTT.

SARL Société de Transport Insulaire Maritime (STIM): BP 635, 98713 Papeete; tel. 549954; fax 452444; Dir ROLAND PAQUIER.

Société de Navigation des Australes: BP 1890, Papeete; tel. 509609; fax 420609; e-mail snathp@mail.pf; inter-island passenger service; Dir HERVÉ DANTON.

CIVIL AVIATION

There is one international airport, Faa'a airport, 6 km from Papeete, on Tahiti, and there are numerous smaller airports and aerodromes throughout French Polynesia. Since October 2004 the Government has commissioned studies into the possible siting of a new international airport on Tubai in the Austral Islands, or in the Marquesas at either Nuku Hiva or Hiva Oa. International services are operated by Air France, Air Tahiti Nui, Air New Zealand, LAN-Chile, Hawaiian Airlines (USA) and Air Calédonie International.

Service d'Etat de l'Aviation Civile: BP 6404, 98702, Faa'a, Papeete; tel. 861000; fax 861009; e-mail webmaster@seac.pf; internet www.seac.pf; Dir PATRICK MOUYSSET.

Aéroport de Tahiti (ADT): BP 60161, 98702, Faa'a Centre; tel. 866060; fax 837391; e-mail secretariat@tahiti-aeroport.pf; internet www.tahiti-aeroport.pf; f. 2010; 50% govt-owned; management and devt of airports at Faa'a, Bora Bora, Raiatea and Rangiroa; Dir-Gen. FRÉDÉRIC MOR.

Air Moorea: BP 6019, 98702 Faa'a; tel. 864262; fax 864269; e-mail direction@airmoorea.pf; internet www.airmoorea.pf; f. 1968; operates internal services between Tahiti and Moorea Island and domestic charter flights; Pres. MARCEL GALENON; CEO FREDDY CHANSEAU.

Air Tahiti: BP 314, 98713 Papeete; tel. 864012; fax 864069; e-mail direction.generale@airtahiti.pf; internet www.airtahiti.aero; f. 1953; Air Polynésie 1970–87; operates domestic services to 46 islands; Chair. CHRISTIAN VERNAUDON; CEO MARCEL GALENON.

Air Tahiti Nui: Immeuble Dexter, Pont de l'Est, BP 1673, 98713 Papeete; tel. 460303; fax 460290; e-mail fly@airtahitinui.pf; internet www.airtahitinui.com; f. 1996; commenced operations 1998; scheduled services to the USA, France, Japan, New Zealand and Australia; CEO ETIENNE HOWAN.

Tourism

Tourism is an important and developed industry in French Polynesia, particularly on Tahiti. Tourist arrivals increased from 162,776 in 2011 to 168,978 in 2012. Most visitors are from the USA, France and Japan. In 2011 earnings from tourism totalled an estimated US $385m.

GIE Tahiti Tourisme: Fare Manihini, blvd Pomare, BP 65, 98713 Papeete; tel. 504030; fax 436619; e-mail hvaxelaire@tahiti-tourisme.pf; internet www.tahiti-tourisme.pf; f. 1966 as autonomous public body; transformed into private corpn in 1993; relaunched Dec. 2005 following merger between GIE Tahiti Tourisme and Tahiti Manava Visitors' Bureau; Chair. HIRIA OTTINO; CEO ANNE-SOPHIE LESUR.

Service du Tourisme (SDT): Paofai Bldg (Entry D), blvd Pomare, Papeete; tel. 476200; fax 476202; e-mail service.tourisme@tourisme.gov.pf; govt dept; manages Special Fund for Tourist Development; Dir ROLAND BOPP.

Defence

As assessed at November 2013, France maintained a combined force of 1,000 army and navy personnel in French Polynesia. France began testing nuclear weapons at Mururoa and Fangataufa atolls, in the Tuamotu Archipelago, in 1966. The military presence has been largely connected with the Centre d'Expérimentation du Pacifique (CEP) and the Commission d'Energie Atomique (CEA). An indefinite suspension of tests was announced in mid-1993. In June 1995, however, the French Government announced its decision to resume nuclear testing at Mururoa Atoll. The final test was conducted in January 1996. The defence budget for 2006 was 24,000m. francs CFP.

Commander of the French Armed Forces in French Polynesia, of the Pacific Maritime Area and of the Centre d'Expérimentation du Pacifique: Rear-Adm. ANNE CULLERE.

Education

Education is compulsory for eight years between six and 14 years of age. It is free of charge for day pupils in government schools. Primary education, lasting six years, is financed by the territorial budget, while secondary and technical education are supported by state funds. A total of 14,306 children were enrolled in kindergarten in 2008/09. In 2012/13 38,149 pupils attended primary school. Secondary education is provided by public lycées, public high schools and private or church schools. A total of 31,166 pupils attended secondary school in 2012/13. The French Polynesian Government assumed responsibility for secondary education in 1988. Technical and professional education includes eight technical institutions, a tourism training programme, preparation for entrance to the metropolitan Grandes Ecoles, a National Conservatory for Arts and Crafts and training centres for those in the construction industry, health services, traditional handicrafts, primary school teaching and social work. The French University of the Pacific was established in French Polynesia in 1987. In 1999 it was divided into two separate branches, of which the University of French Polynesia is now based in Papeete. In 2012 a total of 3,051 students were enrolled at the Papeete branch. In 2004 French state spending on education, higher education and research amounted to 50,500m. francs CFP.

SAINT-BARTHÉLEMY

Saint-Barthélemy is one of the Leeward Islands in the Lesser Antilles. The volcanic island lies in the Caribbean Sea, 230 km north-west of Guadeloupe and 20 km south-east of Saint-Martin. Saint-Barthélemy occupies only 21 sq km, but has green-clad volcanic hillsides, as well as white beaches and surrounding reefs and islets. The climate is tropical, moderated by the sea, with an annual average temperature of 27.5°C (81°F) and a more humid and wet season between May and November. The island normally receives about 1,100 mm (43 ins) of rain annually. According to official estimates, at 1 January 2011 Saint-Barthélemy had a permanent population of 9,035 predominantly white inhabitants of Breton, Norman and Poitevin descent. There are fewer descendants of the Swedish inhabitants, who ruled Saint-Barthélemy for almost one century (until a referendum in 1878). French is the official language, but English and two Creole patois are widely spoken. A Norman dialect of French is also still sometimes in use. The majority of the population professes Christianity and belongs to the Roman Catholic Church. The principal town is Gustavia, its main port, in the south-west.

On 7 December 2003 the Guadeloupean dependency of Saint-Barthélemy participated in a department-wide referendum on Guadeloupe's future constitutional relationship with France. Although the proposal to streamline administrative and political processes was defeated, an overwhelming majority of those participating in Saint-Barthélemy, 95.5%, voted in favour of secession from Guadeloupe to form a separate Collectivité d'Outre-mer (Overseas Collectivity). The reorganization was subsequently approved by the French Sénat (Senate) on 6 February 2007 and by the Assemblée Nationale (National Assembly) the following day. On 21 February the island was formally designated an Overseas Collectivity.

Legislative elections to form a 19-member legislative assembly, the Conseil Territorial (Territorial Council), were held in July 2007. At the first round of elections the Saint-Barth d'abord/Union pour un Mouvement Populaire (UMP) list, headed by Bruno Magras, won a clear majority of 72.2% of the total votes cast, thereby obviating the need for a second round. The election was also contested by three other groupings: the Tous unis pour St-Barthélemy list, lead by Karine Miot-Richard, the Action Equilibre et Transparence list headed by Maxime Desouches—each of which secured 9.9% of the ballot—and Benoît Chauvin's Ensemble pour St-Barthélemy, which attracted the remaining 7.9% of the votes cast. Some 70.6% of the electorate participated in the election. The Saint-Barth d'abord/UMP list obtained 16 of the 19 legislative seats, while the three other contenders were allocated one seat each. On 15 July Magras assumed the presidency of the Territorial Council and Saint-Barthélemy was officially installed as an Overseas Collectivity.

At an election held on 21 September 2008 Michel Magras of the UMP was elected as the territory's representative to the French Senate. In December 2011 Philippe Chopin replaced Jacques Simonnet as Prefect-Delegate. In elections to the Territorial Council on 18 March 2012, Magras's party, Saint-Barth d'abord, won 73.8% of the ballot and retained its 16 seats. The list led by Tous pour Saint Barth increased its representation to two seats while the remaining seat was secured by Saint Barth en Mouvement.

The first round of the French presidential election was conducted on 21 April 2012 (one day earlier than in mainland France). Nicolas Sarkozy, representing the UMP, attracted 43.6% of the votes in Saint-Barthélemy and Saint-Martin, compared with 26.8% for François Hollande of the Parti socialiste. A second round run-off election was held two weeks later, at which Sarkozy secured 59.4% of the ballot, defeating Hollande, who won 40.6%. Nevertheless, Hollande triumphed nationally and was sworn in as President in mid-May. In an election to the National Assembly in June Daniel Gibbes of the UMP was chosen to represent the territory (and Saint-Martin).

Legislation to address the problem of inflated prices in Saint-Barthélemy and other French Overseas Possessions was approved by the French Parliament in November 2012. Most notably, the legislation provided for the imposition of price controls on a range of staple goods and the introduction of measures to encourage competition.

Prefect-Delegate: PHILIPPE CHOPIN.

Territorial Council

Hôtel de la Collectivité, BP 133, Gustavia; e-mail contact@comstbarth.fr; internet www.comstbarth.fr.

President: BRUNO MAGRAS (Saint-Barth d'abord/UMP).

Election, 18 March 2012

	Seats
Saint-Barth d'abord	16
Tous pour Saint Barth	2
Saint Barth en Mouvement	1
Total	19

Deputy to the French National Assembly: DANIEL GIBBES (UMP).

Representative to the French Senate: MICHEL MAGRAS (UMP).

SAINT-MARTIN

The Collectivité d'Outre-mer (French Overseas Collectivity) of Saint-Martin forms the northern half of the island of Saint Martin (the remainder, Sint Maarten, being part of the Kingdom of the Netherlands). The small volcanic island lies among the Leeward group of the Lesser Antilles in the Caribbean Sea, 8 km south of the British Overseas Territory of Anguilla and 265 km north-west of the French Overseas Department of Guadeloupe, of which Saint-Martin was formerly a dependency. The 10.2-km border between the French and the Dutch territories of the island is the only land frontier in the Lesser Antilles. Saint-Martin occupies about 60% of the island (51 sq km or 20 sq miles). The climate is tropical and moderated by the sea. Saint-Martin normally receives about 1,000 mm (43 ins) of rain annually. According to official estimates, at 1 January 2011 Saint-Martin had a population of 36,286. French is the official language, but a Creole patois is widely spoken, as well as English, Dutch and Spanish. The majority of the population professes Christianity and belongs to the Roman Catholic Church. The principal town is Marigot, in the south-west of the territory, on the north coast of the island, between the sea and the Simpson Bay Lagoon.

On 7 December 2003 the Guadeloupean dependency of Saint-Martin participated in a department-wide referendum on Guadeloupe's future constitutional relationship with France. Although the proposal to streamline administrative and political processes was defeated, a majority of those participating in Saint-Martin, 76.2%, elected to secede from Guadeloupe to form a separate Overseas Collectivity. The reorganization was subsequently approved by the French Sénat (Senate) on 6 February 2007 and by the Assemblée Nationale (National Assembly) the following day. On 21 February the territory of Saint-Martin was formally designated an Overseas Collectivity.

Legislative elections to form a 23-member legislative assembly to be known as the Conseil Territorial (Territorial Council) were held in July 2007. At the first round ballot, held on 1 July, the Union pour le Progrès/Union pour un Mouvement Populaire (UPP/UMP) list, headed by Louis-Constant Fleming, won 40.4% of the total votes cast, while the Rassemblement, responsabilité et réussite (RRR) list, led by Alain Richardson, secured 31.9%, and Jean-Luc Hamlet's Réussir Saint-Martin obtained 10.9%. As no list emerged with an absolute majority, a further round of voting was contested by the three parties that had secured more than 10% of the vote. At this second round, held on 8 July, the UPP/UMP list won 49.0% of the vote and obtained 16 of the 23 legislative seats, the RRR received 42.2% of the vote (six seats), and Réussir Saint-Martin 8.9% (one seat). Voter participation was slightly higher, at 50.8%. Fleming assumed the presidency of the Territorial Council on 15 July, and Saint-Martin was officially installed as an Overseas Collectivity. However, in July 2008 Fleming was forced to resign the presidency after the French Council of State disqualified him from his seat on the Territorial Council for one year, owing to irregularities in his financial accounts for the 2007 election campaign. In August the Territorial Council elected Frantz Gumbs as its new President; however, in April 2009 the Council of State annulled the election of Gumbs due to voting irregularities. First Vice-President Daniel Gibbes was installed as interim President pending a re-run of the election, which was to be held within 30 days. On 5 May Gumbs was re-elected as President with 16 votes, defeating Alain Richardson, who received six votes, and Marthe Ogoundélé, who gained one vote.

Meanwhile, at an election held on 21 September 2008 Fleming, representing the UMP, was elected as Saint-Martin's representative to the French Senate. In December 2011 Philippe Chopin replaced Jacques Simonnet as Prefect-Delegate. First round elections to the 16-member Territorial Council took place on 18 March 2012. The RRR won the largest percentage of valid votes (34.1%, or 3,077 votes), just ahead of the list headed by Daniel Gibbes (Team Daniel Gibbes 2012), which secured 32.0% (2,889 votes). The UPP attracted 13.3% of the ballot. The RRR consolidated its success at a second round of voting, held on 25 March; the party secured 56.9% of the ballot (5,451 votes), compared to Team Daniel Gibbes 2012, which attracted 43.1% (4,134 votes). Alain Richardson was sworn in as President of the Territorial Council on 1 April. However, Gibbes was chosen to represent the territory (and Saint-Barthélemy) in elections to the National Assembly in June.

The first round of the French presidential election was conducted on 21 April 2012 (one day earlier than in mainland France). Nicolas Sarkozy of the UMP attracted 43.6% of the votes in Saint-Martin and Saint-Barthélemy, compared with 26.8% for François Hollande of the Parti socialiste. A second round run-off election was held two weeks later, at which Sarkozy secured 59.4% of the ballot, defeating Hollande, who won 40.6%. Nevertheless, Hollande triumphed nationally and was sworn in as President in mid-May.

Legislation to address the problem of inflated prices in Saint-Martin and other French Overseas Possessions was approved by the French Parliament in November 2012. Most notably, the bill provided for the imposition of price controls on a range of staple goods and the introduction of measures to encourage competition.

The Council of State ordered Richardson to relinquish the presidency of the Territorial Council in April 2013 after it was determined that he had breached campaign finance regulations. Aline Hanson was installed as his replacement later that month. Meanwhile, in December Fleming resigned as the territory's senator. An election to determine his successor was not due to be conducted until September 2014, however, leaving Saint-Martin without senatorial representation in the interim.

Prefect-Delegate: PHILIPPE CHOPIN.

Territorial Council

rue de l'Hôtel de la Collectivité, BP 374, Marigot; tel. 5-90-87-50-04; fax 5-90-87-88-53; internet www.com-saint-martin.fr.

President: ALINE HANSON.

Election, 18 and 25 March 2012

	% of first round votes	% of second round votes
Rassemblement, responsabilité et réussite (RRR)	34.1	56.9
Team Daniel Gibbes 2012	32.0	43.1
Union pour le Progrès (UPP)	13.3	—
Saint Martin pour Tous	9.4	—
Movement for the Advancement of the People (MAP)	7.4	—
Génération Solidaire	3.7	—
Total	100.0	100.0

Deputy to the French National Assembly: DANIEL GIBBES (UMP).

Representative to the French Senate: (vacant).

SAINT PIERRE AND MIQUELON

Introductory Survey

LOCATION, CLIMATE, LANGUAGE, RELIGION, CAPITAL

The territory of Saint Pierre and Miquelon (Iles Saint-Pierre-et-Miquelon) consists of a number of small islands which lie about 25 km (16 miles) from the southern coast of Newfoundland and Labrador, Canada, in the North Atlantic Ocean. The principal islands are Saint Pierre, Miquelon (Grande Miquelon) and Langlade (Petite Miquelon)—the last two being linked by an isthmus of sand. Winters are cold, with temperatures falling to −20°C (−4°F), and summers are mild, with temperatures averaging between 10° and 20°C (50° and 68°F). The islands are particularly affected by fog in June and July. The language is French, and the majority of the population profess Christianity and belong to the Roman Catholic Church. The capital is Saint-Pierre, on the island of Saint Pierre.

CONTEMPORARY POLITICAL HISTORY

Historical Context

The islands of Saint Pierre and Miquelon are the remnants of the once extensive French possessions in North America. They were confirmed as French territory in 1815.

Domestic Political Affairs

Saint Pierre and Miquelon gained departmental status in July 1976. The departmentalization proved unpopular with many of the islanders, since it incorporated the territory's economy into that of the European Community (EC, now European Union, see p. 273—EU), and was regarded as failing to take into account the islands' isolation and dependence on Canada for supplies and transport links. In 1982 socialist and other left-wing candidates, campaigning for a change in the islands' status, were elected unopposed to all seats in the territory's General Council (Conseil général). Saint Pierre and Miquelon was excluded from the Mitterrand administration's decentralization reforms, undertaken in 1982.

In 1976 Canada imposed an economic interest zone extending to 200 nautical miles (370 km) around its shores. Fearing the loss of traditional fishing areas and thus the loss of the livelihood of the fishermen of Saint Pierre, the French Government claimed a similar zone around the islands. Hopes of discovering valuable reserves of petroleum and natural gas in the area heightened the tension between France and Canada.

In December 1984 legislation was approved giving the islands the status of a Territorial Collectivity (Collectivité territoriale) with effect from 11 June 1985. This was intended to allow Saint Pierre and Miquelon to receive the investment and development aid suitable for its position, while allaying Canada's fears of EC exploitation of its offshore waters. France continued to claim a 200-mile fishing and economic zone around Saint Pierre and Miquelon, while Canada wanted the islands to have only a 12-mile zone. The dispute was submitted to international arbitration. Discussions began in March 1987, and negotiations to determine quotas for France's catch of Atlantic cod over the period 1988–91 were to take place simultaneously. In the meantime, Canada and France agreed on an interim fishing accord, which would allow France to increase its cod quota. The discussions collapsed in October, however, and French trawlers were prohibited from fishing in Canadian waters. In February 1988 Albert Pen and Gérard Grignon, Saint Pierre's elected representatives to the French legislature, together with two members of the Saint Pierre administration and 17 sailors, were arrested for fishing in Canadian waters. This episode, and the arrest of a Canadian trawler captain in May for fishing in Saint Pierre's waters, led to an unsuccessful resumption of negotiations in September. An agreement was reached on fishing rights in March 1989, whereby France's annual quotas for Atlantic cod and other species were determined for the period until the end of 1991. At the same time the Governments agreed upon the composition of an international arbitration tribunal which would delineate the disputed maritime boundaries and exclusive economic zones.

The international arbitration tribunal's ruling, issued in June 1992, was generally deemed to be favourable to Canada. France was allocated an exclusive economic zone around the territory totalling 2,537 square nautical miles (8,700 sq km), compared with its demand for more than 13,000 square nautical miles. The French authorities claimed that the sea area granted would be insufficient to sustain the islands' fishing community. Talks on new fishing quotas for the area off Newfoundland (known as Newfoundland and Labrador from 2001) failed, and, in the absence of a new agreement, industrial fishing in the area was effectively halted until November 1994, when the Governments of the two countries signed an accord specifying new quotas for a period of at least 10 years. In the following month deputies in the French National Assembly (Assemblée nationale) expressed concern that the terms of the agreement would be detrimental to Saint Pierre and Miquelon's interests, although the Government asserted that the accord recognized the islanders' historic fishing rights in Canadian waters.

In September 1992 some 64% of voters approved ratification of the Treaty on European Union (see p. 273), although only a small percentage of the electorate participated in the referendum.

A number of government proposals regarding the socio-economic and institutional development of the Overseas Departments, certain provisions of which were also to be applied to Saint Pierre and Miquelon, were definitively approved by the French National Assembly in November 2000. Measures included provisions for improving and supporting the economic development of the islands, as well as the introduction of proportional representation in elections to the General Council. In the June 2002 general election Gérard Grignon, representing an alliance of the Union pour la Majorité Présidentielle and the Union pour la Démocratie Française (UDF), was re-elected to the National Assembly, with 69% of the second round votes.

In March 2003, as part of a wider constitutional reform, the islands were given the status of an Overseas Collectivity (Collectivité d'outre-mer). At elections to the Senate in September 2004 the mayor of Miquelon, Denis Detcheverry, narrowly defeated the mayor of Saint Pierre, Karine Claireaux. In May 2005 a national referendum was held on ratification of the EU constitutional treaty: 62.7% of the local electorate voted in favour of adopting the treaty; however, voter turnout was only 37.1%. The treaty was ultimately rejected by a majority of voters in metropolitan France. At elections to the General Council in March 2006 Archipel Demain won 13 of Saint Pierre's 15 seats; the left-wing Cap sur l'Avenir (CSA) took the remaining two seats. Archipel Demain also won three of the four available seats allocated to Miquelon; SPM Ensemble took the remaining seat. Stéphane Artano of Archipel Demain was elected President of the General Council.

Further provisions of the 2003 constitutional reform were effected in February 2007, following the approval by the French Parliament of an organic law that amended the statutes and institutions of

French Overseas Possessions. The legislation redesignated the General Council as a Territorial Council (Conseil territorial) and granted local government wider fiscal powers and greater control over the operation of the exclusive economic zone. In the second round of the elections to the National Assembly in June, Grignon was narrowly defeated by Annick Girardin, representing the Parti Radical de Gauche in association with CSA. In October 2009 Jean-Régis Borius succeeded Jean-Pierre Berçot as Prefect of the territory. In 2011 Artano remained as President of the Territorial Council despite having been convicted, in November 2009, of misappropriation of public funds and fined €7,500 by the territory's Higher Court of Appeal. Artano had approved expense claims deemed excessive from his predecessor, Marc Plantegenest. Plantegenest was fined €60,000 and given a four-month suspended prison sentence. Both men appealed the convictions, but in November 2010 the original decision was upheld.

In September 2011 the mayor of Saint Pierre, Karine Claireaux, representing the Parti Socialiste (PS), was elected to the French Senate. Claireaux secured a majority in the first round of voting, defeating Grignon, who was representing the Union pour un Mouvement Populaire (UMP), and Detcheverry, the outgoing senator. In November Patrice Latron succeeded Jean-Régis Borius as Prefect of the territory. The elections to the Territorial Council in March 2012 were contested by Archipel Demain and the left-wing, CSA-led Ensemble pour l'Avenir electoral list: Archipel Demain secured 15 seats; CSA candidates won the remaining four seats. At the end of March Artano was re-elected as President of the Council. In the first round of the French presidential election, held on 22 April, François Hollande of the PS won 33.8% of the votes cast on the islands, ahead of the incumbent, Nicolas Sarkozy of the UMP, who received 18.6%. Hollande, who secured 65.3% of the islands' votes in the second round, on 6 May, was elected President nationally. Annick Girardin was re-elected to the National Assembly at the first round of elections, held on 10 June.

In mid-2012 a strategic action plan (2012–14), published under the auspices of the Office of the Prefect, established a new framework for French state support for the islands. The document identified five strategic priorities that were to guide French central policy on the territory: economic diversification; sustainable development of the fisheries, ports and agriculture; enhanced social cohesion; increased regional trade and integration (especially with regard to Canada); and greater efficiency in public services. The French Minister of Overseas Territories, Victorin Lurel, completed an official visit to the islands in February 2013, during which he reiterated the central Government's support for efforts to diversify the economy of Saint Pierre and Miquelon, in particular through the promotion of aquaculture and the development of port and tourism infrastructure.

In June 2013 the governments of Canada and France reached agreement on an Enhanced Co-operation Agenda, aiming to boost bilateral trade and economic co-operation. As part of the initiative, regional co-operation between Saint Pierre and Miquelon and Canada's Atlantic provinces was to be developed. However, in the context of growing international competition for control of the potentially enormous energy resources in the North Atlantic and Arctic regions, the long-standing Canadian–French dispute over coastal limits was rekindled in 2013. In July, during a meeting with St Pierre and Miquelon's representatives to the French Parliament, President Hollande pledged to 'defend the interests of the archipelago' and confirmed France's intention to submit a claim with the UN for the extension of the continental shelf of Saint-Pierre and Miquelon. In December Canada lodged a submission with the UN Commission on the Limits of the Continental Shelf providing information (albeit incomplete) in support of a substantial expansion of the limits of its continental shelf in the Atlantic Ocean, which, if accepted, would permit Canada to expand its territorial waters beyond 200 nautical miles. In response, in February 2014 the French National Assembly adopted a resolution, co-sponsored by Annick Girardin, affirming the legislature's support for the extension of the continental shelf of Saint Pierre and Miquelon. Moreover, in a development that appeared to indicate the growing importance of the territorial issue for the French authorities, in early April Annick Girardin became the first elected representative from Saint Pierre and Miquelon to serve in the French Government. Girardin was appointed Secretary of State to the Minister of Foreign Affairs and International Development, with responsibility for Development and the Francophonie, following a cabinet reorganization effected by newly elected French Prime Minister Manuel Valls.

Meanwhile, at municipal elections in March 2014, Karine Claireaux was re-elected as mayor of Saint Pierre; representatives of Claireaux's Ensemble pour Construire electoral list became the largest group in the Saint Pierre municipal council, with 22 members, ahead of the CSA list (seven members) led by Yannick Cambray. In Miquelon-Langlade, 15 members were elected to the municipal council on a non-party basis.

In early 2014 President of the Council Artano called for a debate on the possible institutional evolution of Saint Pierre and Miquelon to a 'collectivité unique' (single collectivity), in order to streamline administrative and political processes by replacing the existing structure (consisting of two municipalities and the Territorial Council) with a single administrative unit. This topic was discussed in March during a visit to the Islands by the French Minister-delegate for Decentralization, Anne-Marie Escoffier.

CONSTITUTION AND GOVERNMENT

Since 2003 St Pierre and Miquelon has had the status of an Overseas Collectivity (Collectivité d'outre-mer). The French Government is represented in the territory by an appointed Prefect. There is a Territorial Council (Conseil territorial, known as the General Council—Conseil général—until February 2007), with 19 members (15 for Saint Pierre and four for Miquelon), elected by adult universal suffrage for a period of six years. The Council holds powers that are broadly similar to those exercised by the regional and departmental assemblies in mainland France. The President of the Council is the head of the local government. Saint Pierre and Miquelon elects one deputy to the National Assembly (Assemblée nationale) and one representative to the Senate (Sénat) in Paris. In addition, there are two municipal councils, each headed by a mayor, responsible for local services in St Pierre (29 members) and Miquelon-Langlade (15 members).

ECONOMIC AFFAIRS

In 2008 the GDP of Saint Pierre and Miquelon was estimated at €172m. in current prices, equivalent to €28,327 per head. GDP per head increased by an estimated average of 1.6% per year during 2004–08.

In 2008 the primary sector accounted for less than 1% of GDP, and employed less than 5% of the economically active population. The soil and climatic conditions of Saint Pierre and Miquelon do not favour agricultural production, which is mainly confined to smallholdings, except for market-gardening and the production of eggs and chickens.

The principal economic activity of the islands is traditionally fishing and related industries. However, the sector has been severely affected by disputes with Canada regarding territorial waters and fishing quotas, and a five-year moratorium, from 1992, led to the near-collapse of the important cod fishery. By 2005 the fishing fleet had been reduced to some 26 vessels, of which only 15 were considered to be active. New arrangements have been to the detriment of Saint Pierre and Miquelon, although there is some optimism regarding the potential for the exploitation of shellfish, notably mussels and scallops. The total fish catch increased from 747 metric tons in 1996 to 6,485 tons in 2000. However, thereafter the trend has been one of steady decline: the industrial fishing catch decreased from more than 2,000 tons in 2001 to less than 500 tons in 2012. By 2012 the total fish catch had fallen to 2,666 tons, some 83% of which came from traditional or small-scale fishing.

Fish-processing—producing frozen and salted fish, and fish meal for fodder—provided the basis for industrial activity, employing around 100 people in 2006. Much of the fish processed was imported. Electricity is generated by two thermal power stations, with a combined capacity of 26.2 MW, and a wind power station (on Miquelon) with a capacity of 0.6 MW. In 2011 the French state-owned energy company EDF confirmed plans to construct a new 20 MW thermal power plant in St Pierre; the plant was scheduled to replace the existing facilities by 2015. The islands' energy needs are almost entirely dependent on imports of petroleum products from the USA and Canada. Although wind power contributed just 2.0% of total energy generated in 2012, it is expected to be an increasingly significant component in the islands' future energy strategy.

The construction sector provided 8.0% of GDP in 2008, and employed 5.8% of the working population in 2007. Services accounted for some 84% of GDP in 2008, and employed almost 85% of the working population in 2007.

The resolution of a boundary dispute between the Canadian provinces of Nova Scotia and Newfoundland and Labrador in 2002 accorded the islands about 500 sq miles of waters over the Gulf of Saint Lawrence basin, believed to contain substantial reserves of petroleum and gas. In May 2005, following four years of negotiations, the Governments of France and Canada signed an agreement on the exploration and exploitation of 'transboundary' hydrocarbon fields. Two Canadian oil companies were given exclusive licences to explore the area until April 2006. In 2009 ConocoPhillips Canada and Bardoil Energy SPM, a locally registered company, filed applications for two exploration licences within the French exclusive economic zone. However, in mid-2010 it was reported that ConocoPhillips had withdrawn its application.

The replenishment of ships' (mainly trawlers') supplies was formerly an important economic activity, but has now also been adversely affected by the downturn in the industrial fishing sector. Efforts were made to promote tourism, and the opening of the Saint Pierre–Montréal air route in 1987 led to an increase in air traffic in the 1990s. In 1999 the completion of a new airport capable of accommodating larger aircraft further improved transport links.

Tourist arrivals in 2012, at 17,210, were some 50% higher than figures for 2011 (11,450). This was attributed in large part to the growing number of visits by cruise ships to the archipelago.

In 2012 Saint Pierre and Miquelon recorded a merchandise trade deficit of €77.9m. Most trade is with Canada and France and other countries of the EU (see p. 273). The only significant exports are fresh, frozen and prepared fish, which provided 82.9% of the total value of non-entrepôt exports in 2011. The principal imports are mineral fuels and food and beverages. Items such as clothing and other consumer goods are generally imported from France.

The annual rate of inflation averaged 6.0% in 1997–2005; consumer prices increased by 3.3% in 2012. The rate of unemployment in 2012 was estimated at 6.7%.

Given the decline of Saint Pierre and Miquelon's fishing industry, the development of port services and aquaculture, and the expansion of tourism (particularly from Canada and the USA) are regarded as the principal means of maintaining economic progress. Hydrocarbon exploration has also been identified as a potential future source of revenue, if not from direct exploitation of resources within Saint Pierre and Miquelon's own territory, then by providing services to companies operating in Canadian waters. In mid-2013 the French authorities reiterated the country's intention to submit a claim before the UN Commission on the Limits of the Continental Shelf to thousands of square miles of sea bed around Saint Pierre and Miquelon, thought to be rich with petroleum deposits. The announcement was in anticipation of Canada's completion of a project to map the Atlantic sea bed off its eastern coast (see Domestic Political Affairs). It is expected that Canada will take all measures to contest the claim. Greater economic co-operation with Canada's Atlantic provinces has been identified as a requisite for long-term growth and stability in Saint Pierre and Miquelon, although this was likely to be dependent on a satisfactory resolution of the French–Canadian territorial dispute. The economy is dominated by public services and consumer spending, while construction (mainly public works) has also become an important economic activity. The islands remain highly dependent on budgetary assistance from the French central Government, and face potential problems in the future due to their ageing population, with increasing numbers of young people leaving the islands to study and work in mainland France and Canada. In 2011 the islands' largest fish-processing company and a major local employer, SPM Seafoods International, was placed in receivership. The development contributed to the ongoing decline in the fish catch.

PUBLIC HOLIDAYS

2015: 1 January (New Year's Day), 6 April (Easter Monday), 1 May (Labour Day), 8 May (Liberation Day), 14 May (Ascension Day), 25 May (Whit Monday), 14 July (National Day, Fall of the Bastille), 15 August (Assumption), 1 November (All Saints' Day), 11 November (Armistice Day), 25 December (Christmas Day).

Statistical Survey

Source: Préfecture, pl. du Lieutenant-Colonel Pigeaud, BP 4200, 97500 Saint-Pierre; tel. 41-10-10; fax 41-47-38.

AREA AND POPULATION

Area: 242 sq km (93.4 sq miles): Saint Pierre 26 sq km, Miquelon-Langlade 216 sq km.

Population: 6,125 at census of March 2006; 6,080 (Saint Pierre 5,456, Miquelon Langlade 624) at census of 1 January 2011. Note: According to new census methodology, data in 2011 refer to median figures based on the collection of raw data over a five-year period (2009–13). *2013* (estimate at 1 January): 6,312 (Saint Pierre 5,687, Miquelon Langlade 625).

Density (at 1 January 2013): 26.1 per sq km.

Births, Marriages and Deaths (1997): Live births 92; Marriages 36; Deaths 51. *2012:* Live births 54; Deaths 39.

Economically Active Population (1999): Fish and fish-processing 76; Other manufacturing 194; Construction 261; Transport 150; Trade 418; Financial services 79; Real estate services 7; Business services 383; Education 490; Government employees 732; *Total employed* 2,790; Unemployed 408; *Total labour force* 3,198. *2006 Census* (preliminary): Total employed 2,876; Registered unemployed 318; Total labour force 3,194 (males 1,751, females 1,443). *2007:* Total employed 2,876 (Agriculture 137, Construction 167, Other industry 133, Administration, teaching, health and welfare 1,265, Trade, transport and other services 1,174). *Unemployment* (at 31 December 2012): 221 (males 123, females 98).

AGRICULTURE

Principal Crops (metric tons unless otherwise indicated, 2012 unless otherwise indicated): Lettuce ('000 units) 9.1 (2011); Potatoes 8.2 (2011); Tomatoes 6 (FAO estimate); Strawberries 1 (FAO estimate) (Source: partly FAO).

Livestock ('000 head, 2012, FAO estimates): Sheep 0.3; Chickens 40; Ducks 1 (Source: FAO).

FISHING

Total Catch (all capture, metric tons, live weight, 2010): Atlantic cod 459; Yellowtail flounder 580; Queen crab 250; Total (incl. others) 2,043.

Source: FAO.

FINANCE

Currency and Exchange Rates: French currency was used until the end of 2001. Euro notes and coins were introduced on 1 January 2002, and the euro became the sole legal tender from 18 February. Some of the figures in this Survey are still in terms of French francs. For details of exchange rates, see French Guiana.

Expenditure by Metropolitan France (million francs, 1997): 280.

Budget (€ 'million, 2011): *Revenue:* Current 29.3 (Direct taxes 11.6; Indirect taxes 10.4; Grants and subsidies 4.9); Capital 6.2; Total 35.4. *Expenditure:* Current 26.1; Capital 10.5; Total 36.7. Source: Institut d'Emission des Départements d'Outre-mer.

Money Supply (million francs at 31 December 1997): Currency outside banks 281; Demand deposits at banks 897; Total money 1,178.

Cost of Living (Consumer Price Index at December; base: December 1998 = 100): 146.3 in 2010; 152.9 in 2011; 157.9 in 2012.

Expenditure on the Gross Domestic Product (€ million at current prices, 2007): Government final consumption expenditure 82.7; Private final consumption expenditure 110.4; Gross fixed capital formation 40.2; Change in stocks –1.2; *Total domestic expenditure* 232.1; Exports of goods and services 8.3; *Less* Imports of goods and services 79.2; *GDP in purchasers' values* 161.1. Source: Institut d'Emission des Départements d'Outre-mer.

Gross Domestic Product by Economic Activity (€ million, 2008): Agriculture, forestry and fishing 1.1; Construction 12.5; Other industry 4.6; Trade 14.6; Hotels and restaurants 3.2; Information and communication 3.7; Transport and storage 3.7; Scientific and technical professional services 4.1; Financial services 8.0; Public administration 77.6; Other services (incl. private households) 23.9; *Sub-total* 157.0; Taxes, less subsidies, on products and imports 15.0; *GDP in purchasers' values* 172.0. Source: Institut d'Emission des Départements d'Outre-mer.

EXTERNAL TRADE

Principal Commodities (€ million, 2012): *Imports:* 79.1 (Food and beverages 16.3, Mineral fuels 21.5, Other—largely raw materials 41.4); *Exports:* 1.2 (Fresh or frozen fish 0.4; Other fish preparations 0.7; Molluscs, fresh frozen 0.1). Note: Totals for imports and exports exclude entrepôt movements (€0.5m. of imports–mostly fish for food manufacturing, and €0.2m. of exports) (Source: Institut d'Emission des Départements d'Outre-mer).

Note: Most trade is with Canada, France (imports), other countries of the European Union (exports) and the USA.

TRANSPORT

Road Traffic (2011): 6,342 motor vehicles in use.

Shipping (2007): Ships entered 867 (Source: Service des Douanes). *Flag Registered Fleet* (at 31 December 2013): Vessels 3; Total displacement 638 grt (Source: Lloyd's List Intelligence—www.lloydslistintelligence.com).

Civil Aviation (2012): Passengers carried 35,471; Freight carried 74.0 metric tons (Source: Service de l'Aviation Civile de Saint Pierre et Miquelon).

TOURISM

Tourist Arrivals: 12,323 in 2010; 11,450 in 2011; 17,210 in 2012.

Tourist Arrivals by Country of Residence (2012): France 1,830; Other (mostly Canada and USA) 15,380; *Total* 17,210.

Source: Institut d'Emission des Départements d'Outre-mer.

COMMUNICATIONS MEDIA

Radio Receivers (estimate, '000 in use): 5.0 in 1997.

Television Receivers (estimate, '000 in use): 3.5 in 1997.

EDUCATION

Primary (2002 unless otherwise indicated): 8 institutions; 73 teachers; 674 students (2011).

Secondary (2002 unless otherwise indicated): 2 institutions; 56 teachers; 364 students (2011).

Technical (2002 unless otherwise indicated): 1 institution; 25 teachers; 139 students (2011).

Source: Service de l'Education Nationale de Saint Pierre et Miquelon.

Note: At the time of the 2006 census, 211 students of higher education were studying outside of Saint Pierre and Miquelon.

Directory

The Government

(April 2014)

HEAD OF STATE

President: FRANÇOIS HOLLANDE.

Prefect: PATRICE LATRON, pl. du Lieutenant-Colonel Pigeaud, BP 4200, 97500 Saint-Pierre; tel. 41-10-10; fax 41-47-38; e-mail courrier@saint-pierre-et-miquelon.pref.gouv.fr; internet www.saint-pierre-et-miquelon.pref.gouv.fr.

TERRITORIAL COUNCIL

Conseil Territorial: 2 pl. de Monseigneur François Maurer, BP 4208, 97500 Saint-Pierre; tel. 41-01-02; fax 41-22-97; e-mail accueil@ct975.fr; internet www.cg975.fr; the Conseil territorial (fmrly the Conseil général) has 19 mems: Saint Pierre 15, Miquelon four. Following the last election to the Conseil territorial, held in March 2012, the composition of the Conseil by party was as follows: Archipel Demain 15, Cap sur l'Avenir 4.

President: STÉPHANE ARTANO.

Economic, Social and Cultural Committee: rue Bordas, BP 4313, 97500 Saint-Pierre; tel. 41-45-50; fax 41-42-45; e-mail comite.ec.soc.spm@cheznoo.net; advisory body; 20 appointed members; Pres. XAVIER LANDRY.

GOVERNMENT OFFICES

Directorate of Land, Food and the Sea: blvd Constant Colmay, BP 4217, 97500 Saint-Pierre; tel. 41-12-00; fax 41-39-50; e-mail dtam-975@equipement-agriculture.gouv.fr; internet www.saint-pierre-et-miquelon.developpement-durable.gouv.fr; Dir JEAN-FRANÇOIS PLAUT.

Directorate of Social Cohesion, Labour, Employment and Population: 8 rue des Petits Pêcheurs, BP 4212, 97500 Saint-Pierre; tel. 41-19-60; fax 41-19-61; e-mail stefp.975.administration@travail.gouv.fr; Dir ALAIN FRANCES.

Directorate of Tax Services: 27 blvd Constant Colmay, BP 4236, 97500 Saint-Pierre; tel. 41-10-80; fax 41-32-51; e-mail dsf.saint-pierre-et-miquelon@dgfip.finances.gouv.fr; internet services-fiscaux.spmnet.com; Dir PASCALE BOYER.

National Education Service: place du Général de Gaulle, BP 4239, 97500 Saint-Pierre; tel. 41-04-60; fax 41-26-04; e-mail ia@ac-spm.fr; internet www.ac-spm.fr; Man. PHILIPPE ANDRE.

Territorial Health Administration: blvd Port en Bessin, BP 4333, 97500 Saint-Pierre; tel. 41-16-90; fax 41-16-91; e-mail dd975-direction@sante.gouv.fr; Man. RAYMOND DELVIN.

REPRESENTATIVES TO THE FRENCH PARLIAMENT

Deputy to the French National Assembly: ANNICK GIRARDIN (PRG-SPM).

Representative to the French Senate: KARINE CLAIREAUX (PS).

Political Organizations

Archipel Demain: 7 rue des Français Libres, BP 1179, 97500 Saint-Pierre; tel. 41-42-19; fax 41-48-06; e-mail contact@archipeldemain.fr; internet www.archipeldemain.fr; f. 1985; Pres. GÉRARD GRIGNON; Sec.-Gen. BERNARD BRIAND; incl. Archipel Demain Miquelon (Leader CÉLINE GASPARD).

Cap sur l'Avenir (CSA): 7 rue René Autin, BP 4477, 97500 Saint-Pierre; tel. 41-99-98; fax 41-99-97; e-mail agirardin@assemblee-nationale.fr; internet capsurlavenir975.unblog.fr; f. 2000; left-wing and green coalition; associated with the PRG-SPM; Pres. ANNICK GIRARDIN.

Ensemble pour Construire: BP 305, 97500 Saint-Pierre; e-mail ensemblepourconstruire@cheznoo.net; internet www.ensemblepourconstruire.com; affiliated with the metropolitan Parti Socialiste; supported the Ensemble pour l'Avenir electoral list during the 2012 elections to the Conseil territorial; Pres. KARINE CLAIREAUX.

Parti Radical de Gauche SPM (PRG-SPM): 7 rue René Autin, BP 4477, 97500 Saint-Pierre; tel. 41-99-08; fax 41-99-97; internet www.planeteradicale.org/-St-Pierre-et-Miquelon; local br. of the metropolitan party; associated with CSA; Pres. YANNICK CAMBRAY; Sec. TATIANA VIGNEAU.

SPM Ensemble: c/o Mairie de Miquelon, 2 rue du Baron de l'espérance, Miquelon, 97500 Saint-Pierre; internet spmensemble.oldiblog.com; f. 2006; left-wing, independent; advocates parity between the islands of Saint-Pierre and Miquelon; STÉPHANE COSTE.

Union pour un Mouvement Populaire (UMP): 15 rue Ange Gautier, BP 113, 97500 Saint-Pierre; tel. 41-35-73; fax 41-29-97; e-mail francoiszimmermann@ump975.org; internet www.ump975.net; centre-right; local br. of the metropolitan party; Pres., Departmental Cttee FRANÇOIS ZIMMERMANN.

Judicial System

Tribunal Supérieur d'Appel: 14 rue Emile Sasco, BP 4215, 97500 Saint-Pierre; tel. 41-03-20; fax 41-03-23; e-mail francois.billon@justice.fr; Presiding Magistrate JEAN-YVES GOUEFFON; Procurator HERVÉ LEROY.

Tribunal de Première Instance: 4 rue Borda, BP 4215, 97500 Saint-Pierre; tel. 41-03-20; fax 41-41-03-22; Presiding Magistrate VÉRONIQUE VEILLARD.

Religion

Almost all of the inhabitants are adherents of the Roman Catholic Church.

CHRISTIANITY

The Roman Catholic Church

The islands form the Apostolic Vicariate of the Iles Saint-Pierre et Miquelon. At 31 December 2006 there were an estimated 6,076 adherents.

Vicar Apostolic: MARIE PIERRE FRANÇOIS AUGUSTE GASCHY (Titular Bishop of Usinaza), Vicariat Apostolique, BP 4245, 97500 Saint-Pierre; tel. 41-02-40; fax 41-47-09; e-mail mission-catho.spm@wanadoo.fr.

Other Churches

Eglise Evangélique de Saint-Pierre et Miquelon: 5 bis rue Paul Lebailly, BP 4325, 97500 Saint-Pierre; tel. 41-92-39; fax 41-59-75; e-mail pasteurspm@cheznoo.net; internet www.cheznoo.net/eglise_evangelique.spm; f. 1995; affiliated to the Fédération Nationale des Assemblées de Dieu de France and Commission des Eglises Evangéliques d'Expression Française à l'Extérieure; Pastor FRANCIS NOVERT.

The Press

L'Echo des Caps Hebdo: rue Georges Daguerre, BP 4213, 97500 Saint-Pierre; tel. 41-10-90; fax 41-49-33; e-mail echohebd@cheznoo.net; internet www.mairie-stpierre.fr/fr/32-l-echo-des-caps.html; f. 1982; weekly; Dir KARINE CLAIREAUX; Editor-in-Chief JEAN-LOUIS MAHÉ; circ. 3,300.

Recueil des Actes Administratifs: 4 rue du Général Leclerc, BP 4233, 97500 Saint-Pierre; tel. 41-24-50; fax 41-20-85; e-mail imprimeriepref@cheznoo.net; f. 1866; monthly; Dir DANIEL KOELSCH.

Le Vent de la Liberté: 1 rue Amiral Muselier, BP 1179, 97500 Saint-Pierre; tel. 41-42-19; fax 41-48-06; e-mail archipel@cheznoo.net; f. 1986; monthly; Dir GÉRARD GRIGNON; circ. 550.

Broadcasting and Communications

TELECOMMUNICATIONS

SPM Telecom: 6 pl. du Général de Gaulle, BP 4253, 97500 Saint Pierre; tel. 41-00-15; fax 41-00-19; e-mail accueil@spmtelecom.com; internet www.spmtelecom.com; Dir XAVIER BOWRING.

RADIO AND TELEVISION

Réseau Outre-mer 1ère: BP 4227, 97500 Saint-Pierre; tel. 41-11-11; fax 41-11-80; internet saintpierremiquelon.la1ere.fr; acquired by Groupe France Télévisions in 2004; fmrly Société Nationale de

Radio-Télévision Française d'Outre-mer, became Réseau France Outre-mer (RFO) in 1998, present name adopted in 2010; broadcasts 24 hours of radio programmes daily on three stations and 195 hours of television programmes weekly on two channels, Télé St Pierre et Miquelon and Tempo; Gen. Man. YVES GARNIER; Regional Dir MOZARIO GABBANI.

Radio Atlantique: 1er étage du Centre Culturel et Sportif, BP 1282, 97500 Saint-Pierre; tel. 41-24-93; fax 41-56-33; e-mail contact@radioatlantique.com; internet www.cheznoo.net/radioatlantique; f. 1982; private; broadcasts 24 hours of radio programmes daily; Pres. ANDRÉ URTIZBÉRÉA; Sec. MYLÈNE BOUROULT.

Finance

(cap. = capital, res = reserves, dep. = deposits; m. = million; amounts in euros)

BANKING

Central Bank

Institut d'Emission des Départements d'Outre-mer (IEDOM): 22 pl. du Général de Gaulle, BP 4202, 97500 Saint-Pierre; tel. 41-06-00; fax 41-25-98; e-mail agence@iedom-spm.fr; internet www.iedom.fr; f. 1978; Dir YANN CARON.

Commercial Bank

Banque de Saint-Pierre et Miquelon (BDSPM): 2 rue Jacques Cartier, BP 4223, 97500 Saint-Pierre; tel. 41-07-00; fax 41-07-42; internet www.bdspm.fr; f. 1889; name changed as above in 2009, following merger with Crédit Saint Pierrais; subsidiary of Groupe BPCE, France; cap. 15.5m., res 0.2m., dep. 113.2m. (Dec. 2010); Pres. PHILIPPE GARSUAULT; Dir-Gen. PIERRE BALSAN; 2 brs.

In addition, two metropolitan banks—la Banque Postale and la Caisse d'épargne Ile-de-France—have branches in St Pierre and Miquelon.

Co-operative Bank

Coopérative immobilière des îles Saint-Pierre-et-Miquelon (CISPM): 29 rue du Maréchal de Lattre de Tassigny, BP 1025, 97500 Saint-Pierre; tel. 41-03-40; fax 41-44-77; e-mail cispm@cheznoo.net; internet www.cispm.unblog.fr; f. 1950; Dir SABINE ROS.

INSURANCE

Cabinet Paturel Assurances, Allianz: 29 bis rue Boursaint, BP 4288, 97500 Saint-Pierre; tel. 41-04-40; fax 41-51-65; e-mail npaturel@allianz-spm.fr; internet www.allianz-spm.fr; Dir NATHALIE PATUREL.

Mutuelle des Iles: 52 rue Maréchal Foch, BP 1112, 97500 Saint-Pierre; tel. 41-28-69; fax 41-51-13; e-mail mispm@cheznoo.net.

Trade and Industry

DEVELOPMENT AGENCIES

Agence Française de Développement (AFD): 22 place du Général de Gaulle, BP 4202, 97500 Saint-Pierre; tel. 41-06-00; fax 41-25-98; e-mail ledom-spm@iedom-spm.fr; internet saintpierreetmiquelon.afd.fr; fmrly Caisse Française de Développement; Man. BRUNO CLAVREUL.

Société de Développement et de Promotion de l'Archipel (SODEPAR): Palais Royal, rue Borda, BP 4365, 97500 Saint-Pierre; tel. 41-15-15; fax 41-15-16; e-mail sodepar.spm@sodepar.com; internet www.sodepar.com; f. 1989; economic devt agency; Chair. STÉPHANE ARTANO; Dir FRANÇOISE LETOURNEL.

CHAMBER OF COMMERCE

Chambre d'Agriculture, de Commerce, d'Industrie, de Métiers et de l'Artisanat (CACIMA): 4 rue Constant-Colmay, BP 4207, 97500 Saint-Pierre; tel. 41-45-12; fax 41-32-09; e-mail cacim@ccimspm.org; internet www.cacimaspm.fr; Pres. XAVIER BOWRING; Sec. ROMUALD DERRIBLE.

TRADE UNIONS

Syndicat des Armateurs à la Pêche Côtière: BP 937, 97500 Saint-Pierre; tel. 41-30-13; fax 41-73-89; e-mail kenavo@cheznoo.net; Pres. JEAN BEAUPERTUIS.

Syndicat CFDT (Union Interprofessionnelle SPM): 15 rue du Docteur Dunan, BP 4352, 97500 Saint-Pierre; tel. 41-23-20; fax 41-27-99; e-mail cfdt.spm@cheznoo.net; internet www.cfdtspm.com; affiliated to the Confédération Française Démocratique du Travail; Sec.-Gen. VÉRONIQUE PERRIN.

Union Départementale Force Ouvrière: 15 rue du Docteur Dunan, BP 4241, 97500 Saint-Pierre; tel. 41-25-22; fax 41-46-55; e-mail udfospm975@cheznoo.net; affiliated to the Confédération Générale du Travail-Force Ouvrière; Sec.-Gen. ALAIN TANGUY.

Union Intersyndicale CGT de Saint-Pierre et Miquelon: rue du 11 Novembre, 97500 Saint-Pierre; tel. 41-41-86; fax 41-30-21; e-mail cgtsp@cheznoo.net; affiliated to the Confédération Générale du Travail; Sec.-Gen. RONALD MANET.

UNSA-Education: rue du Docteur Dunan, 97500 Saint-Pierre; tel. 41-38-05; fax 41-34-08; e-mail 975@se-unsa.org; represents teaching staff; Sec.-Gen. ANDRÉ URTIZBEREA.

Transport

SHIPPING

Packet boats and container services operate between Saint-Pierre and Halifax, Nova Scotia (Canada), Boston, MA (USA), and France. There is a ferry service between Saint-Pierre, Miquelon and Newfoundland and Labrador. The seaport at Saint-Pierre has three jetties and 1,200 metres of quays.

Alliance Europe Le Havre: 1 rue Abbé Pierre Gervain, 97500 Saint-Pierre; tel. 20-53-53; fax 20-53-86; e-mail corinne.spm@alliance-europe.fr; internet alliance-europe.fr; f. 2004 as successor to Compagnie Maritime des Transports Frigorifiques (f. 1980); operates weekly container and ro-ro shipping services between Saint Pierre and Miquelon and ports in northern Europe; also operates air freight service; Gen. Man. JEAN-MARC ROUX.

Régie de Transports Maritimes: pl. du Général de Gaulle, BP 4468, 97500 Saint-Pierre; tel. 41-08-75; fax 41-98-95; e-mail rtm@cg975.fr; internet www.cg975.fr; govt-operated; operates inter-island passenger ferry services and services between Saint-Pierre and Newfoundland, Canada; Dir CAROLINE CECCHETTI.

CIVIL AVIATION

There is an airport on Saint Pierre, served by airlines linking the territory with five destinations in Canada.

Service de l'Aviation Civile de Saint-Pierre et Miquelon: Aérodrome Saint-Pierre Pointe Blanche, BP 4265, 97500 Saint-Pierre; tel. 41-18-00; fax 41-18-18; e-mail sacspm@aviation-civile.gouv.fr; internet www.cheznoo.net/sacspm; Dir LUC COLLET.

Air Saint-Pierre: 18 rue Albert Briand, Saint-Pierre, BP 4225, 97500 Saint-Pierre; tel. 41-00-00; fax 41-00-02; e-mail contact@airsaintpierre.com; internet www.airsaintpierre.com; f. 1964; connects the territory directly with Newfoundland and Labrador, Nova Scotia and Québec, Canada; Pres. BENOIT OLANO; Man. THIERRY BRIAND.

Tourism

There were an estimated 17,210 tourist arrivals in 2012, an increase of 50.3% compared with figures for the previous year (11,450). In 2010 there were 18 establishments offering tourist accommodation.

Comité Régional du Tourisme: pl. du Général de Gaulle, BP 4274, 97500 Saint-Pierre; tel. 41-02-00; fax 41-33-55; e-mail info@tourismespm.com; internet www.st-pierre-et-miquelon.info; f. 1989; fmrly Service Loisirs Accueil; Pres. FRANÇOIS RIVOLLET; Dir PIERRE-YVES CASTAING.

Defence

France is responsible for the islands' defence.

Education

The education system is modelled on the French system, and education is compulsory for children aged between six and 16 years. In 2002 there were eight primary schools, two secondary schools (one of which is private and has a technical school annex) and one technical school. At the time of the 2006 census, 211 students of higher education were studying outside Saint Pierre and Miquelon. Agreements with universities in New Brunswick, Newfoundland and Labrador and Nova Scotia allow students from Saint Pierre and Miquelon to enjoy the same rights as Canadian students.

THE WALLIS AND FUTUNA ISLANDS

Introductory Survey

LOCATION, CLIMATE, LANGUAGE, RELIGION, CAPITAL

Wallis and Futuna comprises two groups of islands: the Wallis Islands, including Wallis Island (also known as Uvea) and 10 islets *(motu)* on the surrounding reef, and Futuna (or Hooru) to the south-west, comprising the two small islands of Futuna and Alofi. The islands are located north-east of Fiji and west of Samoa. Temperatures are generally between about 23°C (73°F) and 30°C (86°F), and there is a cyclone season between December and March. French and the indigenous Polynesian languages Wallisian (Uvean) and Futunian are spoken throughout the islands. Nearly all of the population is nominally Roman Catholic. The capital is Mata'Utu, on Wallis Island.

CONTEMPORARY POLITICAL HISTORY

Historical Context

French protectorate status was formalized for Wallis and for the two kingdoms of Futuna in the 19th century. The islands were subsequently treated as a dependency of New Caledonia. During the Second World War (1939–45), Wallis was used as an air force base by the USA. In 1959 the traditional Kings and chiefs requested integration into the French Republic. The islands formally became a Territoire d'Outre-Mer (Overseas Territory) in July 1961, following a referendum in December 1959, in which 94.4% of the electorate requested this status (almost all the opposition was in Futuna, which itself recorded dissent from only 22.2% of the voters; Wallis was unanimous in its acceptance).

Although there was no movement in Wallis and Futuna seeking secession of the territory from France (in contrast with the situation in the other French Pacific Territories, French Polynesia and New Caledonia), the two Kings whose kingdoms share the island of Futuna requested in November 1983, through the Territorial Assembly, that the island groups of Wallis and Futuna become separate Overseas Territories of France, arguing that the administration and affairs of the territory had become excessively concentrated on the island of Wallis.

Domestic Political Affairs

At elections to the 20-member Territorial Assembly in March 1982, the Rassemblement pour la République (RPR) and its allies won 11 seats, while the remaining nine were secured by candidates belonging to, or associated with, the Union pour la Démocratie Française (UDF). Later that year one member of the Lua Kae Tahi, a group affiliated to the metropolitan UDF, defected to the RPR group. In November 1983, however, three of the 12 RPR members joined the Lua Kae Tahi, forming a new majority. In the subsequent election for President of the Territorial Assembly, this 11-strong bloc of UDF-associated members supported the ultimately successful candidate, Falakiko Gata, even though he had been elected to the Territorial Assembly in 1982 as a member of the RPR.

In April 1985 Falakiko Gata formed a new political party, the Union Populaire Locale (UPL), which was committed to giving priority to local, rather than metropolitan, issues.

In 1987 a dispute broke out between two families both laying claim to the throne of Sigave, the northern kingdom on the island of Futuna. The conflict arose following the deposition of the former King, Sagato Keletaona, and his succession by Sosefo Vanaï. The intervention of the island's administrative authorities, who attempted to ratify Vanaï's accession to the throne, was condemned by the Keletaona family as an interference in the normal course of local custom, according to which such disputes are traditionally settled by a fight between the protagonists.

At elections to the Territorial Assembly in March 1987, the UDF (together with affiliated parties) and the RPR each won seven seats. However, by forming an alliance with the UPL, the RPR maintained its majority, and Falakiko Gata was subsequently re-elected President. At elections to the French Assemblée Nationale (National Assembly) in June 1988, Benjamin Brial was re-elected deputy. However, the result was challenged by an unsuccessful candidate, Kamilo Gata, and, following an investigation by the French Constitutional Council, was declared invalid, owing to electoral irregularities. At a rescheduled poll in January 1989, Kamilo Gata was again elected, with 57.4% of the total votes.

Statistical information, gathered in 1990, showed that the emigration rate of Wallis and Futuna islanders had risen to over 50%. In October of that year 13,705 people (of whom 97% were Wallisians and Futunians) lived in the territory, while 14,186 were resident in New Caledonia. At the 1996 census the number of Wallisians and Futunians resident in New Caledonia had increased to 17,563. According to the results, a proportion of the islanders had chosen to emigrate to other French Overseas Possessions or to metropolitan France, mainly owing to the lack of employment opportunities in the islands.

At elections to the Territorial Assembly in March 1992, the newly founded Taumu'a Lelei (Bright Future) secured 11 seats, while the RPR won nine. The new Assembly was remarkable for being the first since 1964 in which the RPR did not hold a majority. At elections to the French National Assembly in March 1993, Kamilo Gata was re-elected deputy, obtaining 52.4% of the total votes cast to defeat Clovis Logologofolau. In June 1994 the Union Locale Force Ouvrière organized a general strike in protest at the increasing cost of living in the territory and the allegedly inadequate education system. It was reported that demonstrations continued for several days, during which the Territorial Assembly building was damaged in an arson attack.

In October 1994 it was reported that the King of Sigave (or Keletaona), Lafaele Malau, had been deposed by a unanimous decision of the kingdom's chiefs. The action followed the appointment of two customary leaders to represent the Futunian community in New Caledonia, which had led to unrest among the inhabitants of Sigave.

At elections to the Territorial Assembly in December 1994, the RPR secured 10 seats, while a coalition group, Union Populaire pour Wallis et Futuna (UPWF), won seven, and independent candidates three. Mikaele Tauhavili was subsequently elected President of the Assembly.

Elections to the Territorial Assembly took place in March 1997. A participation rate of 87.2% was recorded at the poll, in which RPR candidates secured 14 seats and left-wing candidates (including independents and members of various political groupings) won six seats. Victor Brial, a representative of the RPR, was elected President. At the second round of elections to the French National Assembly, in June, Brial defeated Kamilo Gata, obtaining 3,241 votes (51.3% of the total).

Allegations that irregularities had occurred in the elections of March 1997 were investigated and upheld for 11 of the seats. As a result, new elections were organized for the 11 seats in September 1998, following which the RPR's representation in the Assembly was reduced from 14 to 11 seats, while left-wing and independent members increased their share of seats from six to nine. Also in September 1998, in a second round of voting, Fr Robert Laufoaulu was elected to the French Sénat (Senate), defeating Kamilo Gata in a vote by the Territorial Assembly. Laufoaulu, a priest and director of Catholic education in the islands, stood as a left-wing candidate, but was nominated by RPR members elected with the support of right-wing politicians.

In March 1999 festivities were held to commemorate the 40th anniversary of the accession of the King of Wallis Island (or Lavelua) Tomasi Kulimoetoke.

In January 2001 two candidates of the RPR contested the presidency of the Territorial Assembly. Patalione Kanimoa was elected by the majority of the RPR (eight votes) and of the UPWF (four votes). Soane Muni Uhila, the previous President of the Territorial Assembly, then formed a new party, La Voix des Peuples Wallisiens et Futuniens, along with five other RPR dissidents. The new majority RPR-UPWF grouping elected Albert Likuvalu (of the UPWF) president of the permanent commission.

In June 2001 senior officials from Wallis and Futuna and from New Caledonia agreed on a project to redefine their bilateral relationship under the Nouméa Accord (see New Caledonia) on greater autonomy, signed in 1998. The Accord gave the New Caledonian authorities the power to control immigration from Wallis and Futuna; following decades of migration, the population of Wallis and Futuna was 15,000, while the number of migrants and descendants from the islands in New Caledonia had risen to 20,000. In exchange for controlling immigration, New Caledonia stated that it would make a financial contribution to economic development in Wallis and Futuna. The Nouméa Accord also envisaged a separate arrangement allowing for open access to New Caledonia for residents of Wallis and Futuna.

In January 2002 a delegation from Wallis and Futuna met French President Jacques Chirac in Paris to discuss the situation of members of their community living in New Caledonia. Under the Nouméa Accord, New Caledonia was to have signed a separate agreement with Wallis and Futuna better to define the islanders' status, with particular regard to the job market.

At elections in March 2002 for the Territorial Assembly, the RPR won 12 of the 20 seats, while socialist candidates, or affiliated independents, won eight. Of some 9,500 registered voters, 83% participated in the poll. The election campaign was the first to give parties coverage on television and radio, provided by the national broadcasting company. The territory's only newspaper, *Te-Fenua Fo'ou*, ceased publication in April, following a dispute over the King of Wallis's alleged support for an electoral candidate, Make Pilioko. The newspaper contested that Pilioko, a former member of the Territorial Assembly, was unfit for office, having been convicted in 1999 of misuse of public funds. The publisher and editor of *Te-Fenua Fo'ou*, respectively Michel Boudineau and Laurent Gourlez (both of whom were French), were summoned before the King and ordered not to publish any further articles on the matter. However, the newspaper asserted its right to freedom of expression and, in defiance of the King, printed and distributed its next edition from New Caledonia. The police subsequently removed computers and other equipment from the newspaper's office in Mata'Utu. Boudineau filed a complaint with the French authorities for theft and obstruction of press freedom but, none the less, was forced to close the publication.

At elections to the National Assembly in June 2002, Victor Brial, representing a coalition of the Union pour la Majorité Présidentielle (subsequently Union pour un Mouvement Populaire—UMP) and the RPR, was re-elected as the Wallis and Futuna deputy, winning 50.4% of the votes cast in the first round. (The RPR was fully absorbed into the UMP structure that year.) However, in December the French Constitutional Council ruled that the result was invalid as certain ballot papers had been improperly marked; Brial (now representing the UMP) subsequently won the by-election in March 2003. Meanwhile, in November 2002 Soane Patita Maituka was enthroned as King of Alo (known as the Tu'i Agaifo) following the deposition of Sagato Alofi in the previous month. In December the French Senate approved a bill providing for a constitutional amendment that would allow Wallis and Futuna (along with French Polynesia) to be designated as a Pays d'Outre-Mer (Overseas Country); both houses of the French legislature in Paris ratified the amendments to the Constitution in March 2003. Wallis and Futuna was given the status of a Collectivité d'Outre-Mer (Overseas Collectivity).

In October 2003 Pasilio Keletaona was deposed as King of Sigave by members of his own clan. He was succeeded in March 2004 by Visesio Moeliku. In December 2003 the President of New Caledonia signed an accord governing relations between France, New Caledonia, and Wallis and Futuna. The conclusion of the agreement, which had been negotiated two years previously in an attempt to address the situation of the 20,000 Wallis and Futuna islanders permanently resident in New Caledonia, had been delayed by the continuing ethnic tensions there. Under the agreement, Wallis and Futuna and New Caledonia were henceforth to deliver separate public services. Concerns had been raised by the former's increasing debt (estimated to total 2,500m. francs CFP) to the Government of New Caledonia, a major creditor being the New Caledonian hospital. It was therefore hoped that Wallis and Futuna would become more self-sufficient in the areas of health and secondary education and that the islanders would be encouraged to remain on Wallis and Futuna, while those already settled in New Caledonia would become more integrated.

In February 2005 Albert Likuvalu, representing the newly formed Alliance grouping, a coalition of UDF members and left-wing independents, was elected President of the Territorial Assembly by 11 votes to nine, replacing Patalione Kanimoa of the UMP grouping. The Alliance comprised three members of the UDF and two left-wing ministers, including Likuvalu himself; they were supported by the UPWF grouping.

In January 2005 the local court found the Lavelua's grandson, Tomasi Tuugahala, guilty of unintentional homicide while driving under the influence of alcohol. Tuugahala took refuge in the Lavelua's palace and refused to surrender himself to the police. The King of Wallis and his chiefs claimed that the matter had been settled in accordance with traditional custom, but the incident brought them into confrontation with the French authorities and with pro-reform groups in Wallis and Futuna who wished to depose the Lavelua. In May the King's Prime Minister, Kapeliele Faupala, criticized the Chief Administrator of the islands, Xavier de Fürst, for interfering in traditional affairs and urged him to leave the territory. Later in the month Tuugahala gave himself up to the authorities and was flown to New Caledonia to begin an 18-month prison sentence. However, in June de Fürst suspended allowances and salaries to the Lavelua and his Council of Ministers, while officially recognizing an alternative council composed of members of rival royal families from Futuna, headed by Clovis Logologofolau.

In August 2005 the King of Wallis reiterated a pledge of allegiance to France but maintained that the crisis was the result of de Fürst's interference. In September the alternative council of ministers announced its intention to install Chief Sosefo Mautamakia as King of Wallis, prompting protests by supporters of the incumbent Lavelua, who mounted blockades and occupied the international airport. Meanwhile, in the New Caledonian capital of Nouméa, a group of some 500 supporters marched to the French High Commission to present a petition demanding the intervention of France. The Secretary-General of the French High Commission in New Caledonia, Louis Lefranc, was dispatched to undertake negotiations; he reaffirmed France's recognition of Tomasi Kulimoetoke as Lavelua and overruled de Fürst's earlier decisions. As a result of negotiations among the royal clans themselves, no attempt was made to install a new King. In November Emeni Simete of the UMP replaced Albert Likuvalu as President of the Territorial Assembly.

In March 2006 the two Kings of Futuna, accompanied by ministers of the kingdoms and members of the local assembly, travelled to France to meet President Jacques Chirac, Prime Minister Dominique de Villepin and other senior government officials. The delegation emphasized the need for improved transport links between Futuna and Wallis, citing disruption caused on Futuna by recent severe weather conditions and the temporary cessation of flights between the two islands because of a faulty aircraft. In August Xavier de Fürst was replaced by Richard Didier as Chief Administrator.

In January 2007 a delegation from Wallis visited Futuna, amid reported tensions between the islands, to present a Memorandum of Understanding encompassing the three kingdoms, the details of which were not immediately publicized. At the legislative elections in April 2007, in which some 74% of registered voters participated, three new members were elected to the Territorial Assembly, with many votes, as usual, cast according to clan loyalties. Pesamino Taputai was elected as the Assembly's President, receiving the support of 12 of the 20 members. In his inaugural speech Taputai urged the islands' leaders to address the various issues that continued to impede good relations between Wallis and Futuna.

The results of Wallis and Futuna's participation in the second round of the French presidential election, in May 2007, showed similar levels of support for the two candidates: Nicolas Sarkozy of the UMP, who secured a majority overall, received 50.2% of the votes cast locally, while the Parti Socialiste (PS) candidate, Ségolène Royal, received 49.8%. Elections to the French National Assembly were held in the following month, with the incumbent UMP deputy, Victor Brial, defeated in the second round by the PS-affiliated candidate, Albert Likuvalu, who received 51.8% of the votes. In December 2007 the islands' former deputy to the National Assembly, Victor Brial, was elected President of the Territorial Assembly. Brial received 13 out of 20 votes, including those of members affiliated with the UMP and the Mouvement Démocrate (MoDem—formerly known as the UDF), while his only opponent, Siliako Lauhéa, received six.

In May 2007 the King of Wallis, Lavelua Tomasi Kulimoetoke, died after 48 years in office. Following his death, the subject of his successor was declared taboo for six months. The Council of Ministers of Wallis temporarily exercised royal duties and was charged with choosing a new king. In July 2008 the Council announced its decision to nominate Kapiliele Faupala, who had presided over the local Council of Ministers since 2004. Despite some vocal opposition by certain other royal clans on the island of Wallis to Faupala's nomination, his coronation took place later that month at a ceremony in Mata'Utu. Meanwhile, it had emerged in August 2007 that Soane Patita Maituka, the King of Alo, was in hospital in New Caledonia with a serious illness. In February 2008, following criticism of the style of leadership of the Tu'i Agaifo and the reaching of a unanimous decision by the four chiefly clans of Alo, the King was removed from office. Petelo Vikena, a former public servant, was subsequently chosen to replace him, and his coronation took place in November 2008. However, the choice of Vikena was not supported by some chiefly clans, which criticized the unilateral appointment by the chiefly council and the lack of consensus.

In July 2008 the French Government appointed Philippe Paolantoni as the new Chief Administrator of Wallis and Futuna, to succeed Richard Didier. In the French senatorial elections of September Fr Robert Laufoaulu was re-elected to represent Wallis and Futuna for a second six-year term.

Recent Developments

In January 2010, amid reports of acts of vandalism against royal property, Petelo Vikena abdicated as King of Alo. Meanwhile, the King of Sigave, Visesio Moeliku, was reported to have relinquished his position several months previously. The kingdom of Futuna was thus placed in an unusual situation, being required to function without either of its two Kings. In July Polikalepo Kolivai was crowned King of Sigave, although two rival clans refused to recognize his accession.

In March 2010 a cyclone was reported to have destroyed 90% of traditional houses on Futuna, as well as most of the island's crops and many public amenities. French military aircraft based in New Caledonia, followed by a warship, brought emergency supplies of food and other necessities, and in June the French Minister in charge of the Overseas Possessions, Marie-Luce Penchard, undertook to provide financial and technical assistance for rebuilding Futuna's infrastructure. In the same month Penchard, while visiting New Caledonia, signed an agreement on the status of migrants from Wallis and Futuna in New Caledonia, who were more numerous than those remaining in Wallis and Futuna itself (see above).

From April 2010 the supply of electricity and water on Wallis was intermittently disrupted when employees of the utility company Electricité et Eau de Wallis et Futuna (EEWF, a subsidiary of the French Groupe Suez) staged a strike, reportedly in support of an executive who had been dismissed for misconduct. In July the King of Wallis announced that the contract with EEWF had been terminated (although such an action was not legally within his powers), and the company's offices were taken over by a small group of employees, who stated that they were establishing a new company with the support of the King. Hundreds of people participated in protests, urging the restoration of power and water supplies. Later that month the new Chief Administrator, Michel Jeanjean, authorized the police to intervene to allow access to the power plant, after which normal supplies were resumed.

In December 2010 Victor Brial was replaced as President of the Territorial Assembly by Siliaki Lauhéa, the leader of the UPWF. Lauhéa was himself succeeded in October by Pesamino Taputai.

In July 2011 the Australian Parliamentary Secretary for Pacific Island Affairs, Richard Marles, became the first Australian member of Parliament to visit Wallis and Futuna. Along with France's Minister in charge of the Overseas Possessions, Marie-Luce Penchard, he had travelled to Wallis and Futuna to join celebrations marking the 50th anniversary of the islands' status as a French Overseas Territory. During their visits the two ministers discussed regional co-operation in the Pacific, and Marles stated his country's commitment to continue to provide support in times of humanitarian crisis and to assist in the protection of the islands' vital fisheries resources.

Ongoing concern about the rising cost of living culminated in demonstrations throughout the islands attended by some 1,500 people in November 2011. Protesters demanding lower fuel prices and air fares marched to the government buildings in Mata'Utu. The demonstrations coincided with widespread strike action by public sector employees demanding the same system of pay indexation as their French state counterparts.

Elections to the Territorial Assembly were conducted on 25 March 2012, attracting a turnout of 86%. Notably, the incumbent President of the Territorial Assembly, Pesamino Taputai, and his two predecessors, Siliaki Lauhéa and Victor Brial, all failed to secure re-election to the legislature. Vetelino Nau of the UPWF was elected as President of the Territorial Assembly, receiving 11 out of 20 votes, including those of six unaffiliated members. Sosefo Suve of Taumu'a Lelei was elected to replace Nau in November.

At the French presidential election of 2012 the successful PS candidate, François Hollande, received 56.1% of the votes cast in Wallis and Futuna in the second round of voting, in May, in contrast to the other French Pacific Territories, which returned majorities for the incumbent Nicolas Sarkozy. The territory also distinguished itself by registering the highest voter participation rate of any part of the Republic, at some 82% of the electorate. In the closely contested second round of the French legislative elections, in June, the UMP's candidate, David Vergé, defeated his closest rival, Mikaele Kulimoetoke, by just 42 votes; Likuvalu of the PS had been eliminated in the first round. A number of Vergé's opponents filed a challenge against the result, and in January 2013 the French Constitutional Council annulled his election, citing irregularities in his campaign accounts. Vergé was dismissed from his seat and barred from seeking public office for 12 months. An election to select a new deputy took place on 17 March, concurrently with polls to fill four seats in the Territorial Assembly, which had become vacant in December 2012, after the French Conseil d'Etat (Council of State) annulled the election in March of the four members representing the constituency of Alo. In a run-off poll held on 24 March 2013, Napoli Polutele, an independent who was supported by the UMP, was elected to the French National Assembly with 37.5% of the votes cast, defeating Kulimoetoke, who received 32.3% and Lauriane Vergé (the wife of David Vergé), who secured 30.2%. Nivaleta Iloai became the first female President of the Territorial Assembly upon her election to the position on 1 April. Polutele's decision in June to join the Socialist group in the French National Assembly led to persistent criticism by members of the UMP in Wallis and Futuna, who had supported Polutele and funded his electoral campaign.

In December 2012 Cyclone Evan caused substantial damage to property and roads on Wallis, including the destruction of 300 homes. Supplies were dispatched from New Caledonia in the aftermath of the storm, and, in a significant demonstration of French solidarity with the territory, the Minister of Overseas Territories, Victorin Lurel, made an official visit to the island to assess the damage. Some US $400,000 in emergency assistance was subsequently made available for rehabilitation works.

Michel Aubouin replaced Michel Jeanjean as Chief Administrator at the end of March 2013.

In August 2013 Wallis and Futuna held a ceremony to mark a two-year partnership with the European Union (EU, see p. 273) and the Pacific Community (see p. 412), which had resulted in an integrated programme intended to respond effectively to natural disasters in the islands, particularly tsunamis. In the following month the territory successfully hosted the South Pacific Mini Games, in which athletes from 20 countries and territories competed.

Following four years of negotiations between the chiefly clans of Alo to select a successor to Petelo Vikena (who had abdicated the throne in January 2010), in mid-January 2014 Petelo Sea was nominated to be the new King of Alo; his enthronement took place later that month.

CONSTITUTION AND GOVERNMENT

The Collectivité d'Outre-Mer (Overseas Collectivity) of Wallis and Futuna is administered by a representative of the French Government, the Chief Administrator, who is assisted by the Territorial Assembly. The Assembly has 20 members and is elected for a five-year term. The three traditional kingdoms, one on Wallis and two sharing Futuna, have equal rights, although the Kings' powers are limited. In addition, Wallis and Futuna elects one deputy to the French Assemblée Nationale (National Assembly) in Paris and one representative to the French Sénat (Senate). The islands may also be represented at the European Parliament.

REGIONAL AND INTERNATIONAL CO-OPERATION

Wallis and Futuna forms part of the Franc Zone (see p. 329). Although France is also a member of the organization, Wallis and Futuna has membership in its own right of the Pacific Community (see p. 412), which is based in New Caledonia and provides technical advice, training and assistance in economic, cultural and social development to the region. Wallis and Futuna was granted observer status at the Pacific Islands Forum (see p. 416) in 2006 and submitted an application for associate membership in 2008.

ECONOMIC AFFAIRS

In 1995 it was estimated that Wallis and Futuna's gross domestic product (GDP) was US $28.7m., equivalent to some $2,000 per head. Most monetary income in the islands is derived from government employment and from remittances sent home by islanders employed in New Caledonia and metropolitan France.

Agricultural activity is of a subsistence nature. Yams, taro, bananas, cassava and other food crops are also cultivated. Tobacco is grown for local consumption. Pigs, goats and chickens are reared on the islands. Apiculture was revived in 1996, and in 2000 honey production was sufficient to meet the demands of the local market. Fishing activity in the exclusive economic zone of Wallis and Futuna increased during the 1990s; the total catch was estimated at 833 metric tons in 2011, compared with 70 tons in 1991.

Mineral fuels are the main source of electrical energy, although it is hoped that hydroelectric power can be further developed, especially on Futuna. There is a 4,000-kW thermal power station on Wallis, and a 2,600-kW thermal power station on Futuna. The hydroelectric power station on the Vainifao river, on Futuna, provides around 10% of the production needed. Total electricity output in 2012 amounted to 19.0m. kWh.

There were 291 businesses operating in Wallis and Futuna in 2000, of which 24 were in the industrial and artisanal sector, 68 in construction and 199 in the service and commercial sectors; 47 of those businesses were located on Futuna. A new commercial centre opened in Wallis in 2002. The tourism sector is very limited. In 2008 Wallis had four hotels and Futuna two establishments. In November 2005 the French Government agreed to provide some €8m. towards expanding the domestic airport at Vele, on Futuna, to receive international traffic. Foreign visitor arrivals, mainly from New Caledonia and France, totalled 2,456 in 2006.

In 2012 the value of the islands' imports reached 6,125m. francs CFP. In that year the major imports were prepared foodstuffs, followed by pharmaceutical and cosmetic products, transport equipment, mechanical equipment, household equipment, and chemicals, rubber and plastic products. Exports of Trochus shells provided revenue of 11.6m. francs CFP in 2006. However, total exports declined to 1.0m. francs CFP in 2009. Traditional food products, mother of pearl (from the Trochus shell) and handicrafts are the only significant export commodities. Exports of copra from Wallis ceased in 1950, and from Futuna in the early 1970s. The principal sources of imports in 2007 were France, which supplied 27.8% of the total, Singapore and Australia. In 2004 most of the islands' exports were purchased by Italy. In August 2001 the frequency of supplies to Wallis and Futuna was significantly improved when the Sofrana shipping company, based in Auckland, began operating a new route linking New Zealand, Tonga and the Samoas to Wallis and Futuna.

There was a deficit of 380m. francs CFP on the territorial budget in 2012. French aid to Wallis and Futuna increased from a total of 7,048m. francs CFP in 1999 to 12,064.2m. francs CFP in 2008. In December 2002 France proposed a broad 15-year sustainable development strategy for Wallis and Futuna.

The annual rate of inflation in 2008–12 averaged 2.8%. The annual rate of inflation at December 2012 was 4.8%. The high level of unemployment has remained a major economic and social issue; 12.8% of the total labour force was classified as unemployed and seeking work at the time of the 2008 census. More than 50% of those in formal employment are engaged in the public sector.

Wallis and Futuna is heavily dependent upon metropolitan France and on remittances from islanders working overseas, particularly in New Caledonia. In 2003 the National Assembly in Paris approved the Overseas Territories Development Bill, providing support for economic and social development in its Pacific Territories by attracting foreign investment. In early 2007 France concluded an agreement with Wallis and Futuna to provide US $50m. over the period 2007–11 for the purposes of infrastructural development. Priority was also to be given to the areas of health, education and vocational training. Funding from the European Union (EU, see p. 273) of €16.5m. for the period 2008–13 was to focus on renewable energy, improved management of the islands' natural resources and sustainable development; EU funding, under the 11th European Development Fund (2014–20), increased to €19.6m. Of the estimated 20% of the population in salaried employment, some 70% work in the public sector. The islands suffer from problems associated with an ageing population, as a large proportion of younger people seek employment opportunities overseas. The territory is also vulnerable to the effects of severe climatic events, such as cyclones and tidal surges, which are expected to increase in frequency with changing weather patterns. Construction projects associated with the islands' hosting of the South Pacific Mini Games in September 2013 led to increased economic activity during 2012 and 2013. Exploratory investigations during 2013 revealed the presence of cobalt deposits in the seabed near the islands, and it seemed likely that this resource could be exploited to provide a potential alternative source of revenue for Wallis and Futuna.

PUBLIC HOLIDAYS

2015: 1 January (New Year's Day), 6 April (Easter Monday), 28 April (Saint Pierre-Chanel Day), 1 May (Labour Day), 8 May (Victory Day), 14 May (Ascension Day), 25 May (Whit Monday), 29 June (Saints Peter and Paul Day), 14 July (Fall of the Bastille), 29 July (Territory Day), 15 August (Assumption), 1 November (All Saints' Day), 11 November (Armistice Day), 25 December (Christmas Day).

Statistical Survey

Source (unless otherwise indicated): Service Territorial de la Statistique et des Etudes Economiques, Immeuble Pukavila, RT1, BP 638, Mata'Utu, Falaleu, 98600 Wallis; tel. 722403; fax 722487; e-mail stats@wallis.co.nc; internet www.spc.int/prism/Country/WF/WFindex.html.

AREA AND POPULATION

Area (sq km): 142. *By Island:* Uvea (Wallis Island) 78; Futuna Island 46; Alofi Island 18. The collectivity also includes a group of uninhabited volcanic and coralline islets (18 sq km).

Population: 13,445 (males 6,669, females 6,776) at census of 21 July 2008; 12,197 at census of 22 July 2013: Wallis Island—Uvea 8,584; Futuna Island 3,613 (Alo 2,156, Sigave 1,457).

Density (at 2013 census): 85.9 per sq km.

Population by Age and Sex (at 2008 census): *0–14:* 4,081 (2,181 males, 1,900 females); *15–64:* 8,387 (4,047 males, 4,340 females); *65 and over:* 977 (441 males, 536 females); *Total:* 13,445 (6,669 males, 6,776 females).

Principal Villages (population at 2013 census): Mata'Utu (capital) 1,075; Utufua 615; Liku 589; Falaleu 586; Alele 551; Ono 537; Taoa 531.

Births, Marriages and Deaths (2009 unless otherwise indicated): Registered live births 230 (birth rate 17.2 per 1,000); Registered marriages 53 (marriage rate 3.9 per 1,000, 2008); Registered deaths 90 (death rate 6.7 per 1,000, 2008). *2012* Registered live births 176 (birth rate 14.2 per 1,000); Registered deaths 78 (death rate 6.3 per 1,000).

Life Expectancy (years at birth): 74.3 (males 73.1; females 75.5) in 2003.

Economically Active Population (2008 census): Total employed 3,373 (males 1,867, females 1,506); Unemployed persons seeking work 496 (males 296, females 200); Total labour force 3,869 (males 2,163, females 1,706). *2012:* Total employed 2,062.

HEALTH AND WELFARE

Key Indicators

Total Fertility Rate (children per woman, census of 2008): 2.0.

Under-5 Mortality Rate (per 1,000 live births, average of 2005–2008): 5.2.

Physicians (per 1,000 head, 2003): 0.7.

Access to Sanitation (% of persons, census of July 2003): 80.9.

Access to Water (% of persons, census of July 2003): 68.5.

For definitions, see explanatory note on p. vi.

AGRICULTURE, ETC.

Principal Crops ('000 metric tons, 2012, FAO estimates): Cassava 2.0; Taro (coco yam) 1.5; Yams 0.5; Other roots and tubers 1.0; Coconuts 3.2; Vegetables and melons 0.7; Bananas 6.5. *Aggregate Production* ('000 metric tons, may include official, semi-official or estimated data): Total fruits (excl. melons) 12.0; Total roots and tubers 5.0.

Livestock ('000 head, year ending September 2012, FAO estimates): Pigs 25; Goats 7; Chickens 65.

Livestock Products (metric tons, 2012, FAO estimates): Pig meat 315; Goat meat 15; Chicken meat 48; Cows' milk 48; Hen eggs 50; Honey 10.

Fishing (metric tons, live weight, 2011, FAO estimates): Total catch 833 (Marine fishes 793). Figures exclude Trochus shells (metric tons) 29.

Source: FAO.

INDUSTRY

Selected Products (metric tons, 2012, unless otherwise indicated): Coconut oil 164 (FAO estimate); Copra 252.5 (2006, FAO estimate); Electric energy 19.0m. kWh (Wallis Island 15.6; Futuna Island 3.4). Sources: FAO; Institut d'Emission d'Outre-Mer.

FINANCE

Currency and Exchange Rates: see French Polynesia.

Territorial Budget (million francs CFP, 2012): *Revenue:* Current 2,864; Capital 187; Total 3,051. *Expenditure:* Current 2,994; Capital 437; Total 3,431.

Aid from France ('000 million francs CFP, 2008): Total expenditure 12.1 (Education 5.7, Health 3.1, Other expenditure by Ministère de l'Outre-Mer 3.3). Source: Institut d'Emission d'Outre-Mer.

Money Supply (million francs CFP at 31 December 2012): Currency in circulation 2,140; Demand deposits 3,663; *Total money* 5,803. Source: Institut d'Emission d'Outre-Mer.

Cost of Living (Consumer Price Index at December; base: June 2008 = 100): All items 105.2 in 2010; 109.4 in 2011; 114.6 in 2012.

EXTERNAL TRADE

Principal Commodities (million francs CFP): *Imports c.i.f.* (2012): Prepared foodstuff 1,697; Pharmaceutical and cosmetic products 438; Household equipment 332; Transport equipment 391; Mechanical equipment 347; Electrical and electronic equipment 263; Chemicals, rubber and plastic products 321; Metals and metal products 285; Fuels 1,153; Total (incl. others) 6,125. *Exports f.o.b.* (2001): Preparations of molluscs and other aquatic invertebrates 0.3; Coral and shells 5.5; Braids and mats of vegetable material 0.9; Total 5.6. *2009:* Total exports 1.0. Source: mainly Institut d'Emission d'Outre-Mer.

Principal Trading Partners: *Imports c.i.f.* ('000 million francs CFP, 2007): Australia 0.7; Fiji 0.3; France (incl. Monaco) 1.5; New Caledonia 0.3; New Zealand 0.5; Singapore 0.8; Total (incl. others) 5.4. *Exports f.o.b.* (million francs CFP, 2004): Italy 4.6; Total 4.6. Source: mainly Institut d'Emission d'Outre-Mer.

TRANSPORT

Road Traffic (vehicles in use, 2001): Scooters 1,093; Cars 1,293. Source: Ministère de l'Agriculture, de l'Alimentation, de la Pêche et des Affaires Rurales, *Recensement agricole du territoire 2001*.

Shipping: *Flag Registered Fleet* (at 31 December 2013): Vessels registered 3; Total displacement: 32,880 grt. Source: Lloyd's List Intelligence (www.lloydslistintelligence.com).

Civil Aviation (2012): *Domestic Traffic:* Aircraft movements 1,472; Passenger movements 14,066; Freight handled 36.2 metric tons; Mail handled 12.0 metric tons. *International Traffic:* Aircraft movements 342; Passenger movements 29,477; Freight handled 137.7 metric tons; Mail handled 73.0 metric tons. Source: Institut d'Emission d'Outre-Mer.

TOURISM

Foreign Visitors (2006): *Total Arrivals:* 2,456. *Overnight Stays in Hotel Establishments:* 607.

Foreign Visitor Arrivals by Nationality (2006): Australia 37; Fiji 45; France 674; French Polynesia 62; New Caledonia 1,310; Total (incl. others) 2,456.

COMMUNICATIONS MEDIA

Telephones (2012): 3,130 main lines installed.

Internet Users (2009): 1,300.

Broadband Subscribers (2012): 1,177.

Source: International Telecommunication Union.

EDUCATION

Pre-primary (2005): 3 institutions; 260 pupils.

Primary (2012, unless otherwise indicated): 18 institutions (2008); 1,972 pupils (incl. pre-primary). Source: Institut d'Emission d'Outre-Mer.

Secondary (2012, unless otherwise indicated): 7 institutions (2 vocational) (2006); 1,929 students. Source: Institut d'Emission d'Outre-Mer.

Higher (students, 2005/06): 14 in New Caledonia; 60 in metropolitan France; 6 in French Polynesia. Source: Institut d'Emission d'Outre-Mer.

Teachers (2003): Pre-primary and primary 168; Secondary 209.

Adult Literacy Rate (census of July 2003): 78.8% (males 78.2%; females 79.3%).

Directory

The Government

(April 2014)

Chief Administrator (Administrateur Supérieur): MICHEL AUBOUIN.

COUNCIL OF THE TERRITORY

The Council is chaired by the Chief Administrator and comprises the members by right (the Kings of Wallis, Sigave and Alo) and three appointed members.

GOVERNMENT OFFICES

Government Headquarters: Bureau de l'Administrateur Supérieur, BP 16, Mata'Utu, Havelu, Hahake, 98600 Uvea, Wallis Islands; tel. 722727; fax 722300; e-mail webmestre@wallis-et-futuna.pref.gouv.fr; internet www.wallis-et-futuna.pref.gouv.fr.

Department of Catholic Schools: Direction Diocésaine de l'Enseignement Catholique, BP 80, Mata'Utu, 98600 Uvea, Wallis Islands; tel. 722766; fax 722815; e-mail decwf.wallis@wallis.co.nc; responsible for pre-primary and primary education since 1969.

Department of Cultural Affairs: BP 131, Mata'Utu, Aka'aka, 98600 Uvea, Wallis Islands; tel. 722563; fax 722667; e-mail culture.wf@mail.wf.

Department of the Environment: BP 294, Mata'Utu, Havelu, Hahake, 98600 Uvea, Wallis Islands; tel. 720351; fax 720597; e-mail senv@mail.wf.

Department of Justice: BP 12, Mata'Utu, Havelu, Hahake, 98600 Uvea, Wallis Islands; tel. 722715; fax 722531; e-mail tpi@wallis.co.nc.

Department of Labour and Social Affairs Inspection (SITAS): BP 385, Mata'Utu, Hahake, 98600 Uvea; tel. 722288; fax 722384; e-mail sitas.wf@mail.wf.

Department of Public Works and Rural Engineering: BP 13, Mata'Utu, Kafika, Hahake, 98600 Uvea, Wallis Islands; tel. 722626; fax 722115; e-mail tpwallis@mail.wf.

Department of Rural Affairs and Fisheries: BP 19, Mata'Utu, Aka'aka, 98600 Uvea, Wallis Islands; tel. 722606; fax 720404; e-mail ecoru@mail.wf; internet www.wallis-et-futuna.pref.gouv.fr.

Department of Youth and Sports: BP 51, Mata'Utu, Kafika, Hahake, 98600 Uvea; tel. 722188; fax 722322; e-mail mjs-986@jeunesse-sports.gouv.fr; internet www.bafa-bafd.jeunes.gouv.fr.

Health Agency: Agence de Santé, BP 4G, 98600 Uvea, Wallis Islands; tel. 720700; fax 723399; e-mail sante@adswf.org; operates 2 hospitals at Sia on Uvea and Kaleveleve on Futuna, respectively.

Legislature

TERRITORIAL ASSEMBLY

The Territorial Assembly has 20 members and is elected for a five-year term. Within the Assembly, ministers may form political groupings of five members or more. These groupings are not necessarily formed along party lines, and alliances may be made in support of a common cause. The most recent general election took place on 25 March 2012.

President: NIVALETA ILOAI (Union Populaire pour Wallis et Futuna).

Territorial Assembly: Assemblée Territoriale, BP 31, Mata'Utu, Havelu, Hahake, 98600 Uvea, Wallis Islands; tel. 722004; fax 721807; e-mail cab-pres.at@wallis.co.nc.

PARLIAMENT

Deputy to the French National Assembly: NAPOLI POLUTELE (Ind.).

Representative to the French Senate: Fr ROBERT LAUFOAULU (UMP).

The Kingdoms

WALLIS

(Capital: Mata'Utu on Uvea)

Lavelua, King of Wallis: KAPILIELE FAUPALA.

Council of Ministers (Aliki Fau): The Council is composed of six ministers who assist the King:

Kivalu: the Prime Minister and King's spokesman at official meetings.

Mahe: the second Prime Minister and King's counsel.

Kulitea: responsible for cultural and customary matters.

Uluimonoa: responsible for the sea.

Fotuatamai: responsible for health and hygiene.

Mukoifenua: responsible for land and agriculture.

In addition, the Puliuvea is responsible for the King's security and the maintenance of public order.

The Kingdom of Wallis is divided into three administrative districts (Hihifo, Hahake, Mua), and its traditional hierarchy includes three district chiefs (Faipule), 20 village chiefs (Pule) and numerous hamlet chiefs (Lagiaki).

SIGAVE

(Capital: Leava on Futuna)

Keletaona, King of Sigave: POLIKALEPO KOLIVAI.

Council of Ministers: six ministers, chaired by the King.

The Kingdom of Sigave is located in the north of the island of Futuna; there are five village chiefs.

ALO

(Capital: Ono on Futuna)

Tu'i Agaifo, King of Alo: PETELO SEA.

Council of Ministers: five ministers, chaired by the King.

The Kingdom of Alo comprises the southern part of the island of Futuna and the entire island of Alofi. There are nine village chiefs.

Political Organizations

Alliance: c/o Assemblée Territoriale; f. 2005; coalition of UDF mems and left-wing independents; Pres. APITONE MUNIKIHAAFATA.

Mouvement Démocrate (MoDem): c/o Assemblée Territoriale; fmrly known as Union pour la Démocratie Française; name changed as above in 2007; centrist; based on Uvean (Wallisian) support.

Taumu'a Lelei (Bright Future): c/o Assemblée Territoriale; f. 1992; Leader SOANE MUNI UHILA.

Union pour un Mouvement Populaire (UMP): c/o Assemblée Territoriale; f. 2002; est. as Union pour la Majorité Présidentielle; includes fmr mems of Rassemblement pour la République; centre-right; local br. of the metropolitan party; Territorial Leader ROBERT LAUFOAULU; Territorial Sec. VICTOR BRIAL.

Union pour Wallis et Futuna (UPWF): c/o Assemblée Territoriale; f. 1994; est. as Union Populaire pour Wallis et Futuna; affiliated to Parti Socialiste of France since 1998; Leader SILIAKO LAUHÉA.

Judicial System

The Statute provided for two parallel judicial systems: customary law, which applied to the indigenous population; and French state law. The competencies of the respective systems are not always clearly defined, which has been a cause of tensions between the indigenous monarchy and the French authorities. On Uvea, under customary law there are separate courts for civil matters (Fono Puleaga) and village matters (Fono Fenua). Disputes over land are dealt with by the Council of the Territory, presided over by the King. A similar system exists on Futuna. Judgments may be referred to a Chambre d'Annulation at the Court of Appeal at Nouméa, New Caledonia.

Court of the First Instance: Tribunal de Première Instance, BP 12, Havelu, Mata'Utu, Hahake, 98600 Uvea, Wallis Islands; tel. 722715; fax 722531; e-mail pr.tpi@wallis.co.nc; f. 1983; Pres. FRANCIS ALARY.

Religion

Almost all of the inhabitants profess Christianity and are adherents of the Roman Catholic Church.

CHRISTIANITY

The Roman Catholic Church

The Territory comprises a single diocese, suffragan to the archdiocese of Nouméa (New Caledonia). The diocese estimated that there were 14,400 adherents at 31 December 2007. The Bishop participates in the Catholic Bishops' Conference of the Pacific, currently based in Fiji.

Bishop of Wallis and Futuna: GHISLAIN MARIE RAOUL SUZANNE DE RASILLY, Evêché Lano, BP G6, Mata'Utu, 98600 Uvea, Wallis Islands; tel. 722932; fax 722783; e-mail eveche.wallis@wallis.co.nc.

The Press

'Uvea Mo Futuna: Tuku'atu Ha'afuasia, Uvea, Wallis Islands; e-mail filihau@uvea-mo-futuna.com; f. 2002; daily; electronic; Editor FILIHAU ASI TALATINI.

The Territory's only newspaper, *Te-Fenua Fo'ou*, was forced to close in April 2002, following a dispute with the King of Wallis. *Fenua Magazine* was launched by a group of local business people in September 2002 but closed in September 2003 owing to a lack of advertising revenue. There is currently no printed press in Wallis and Futuna.

Broadcasting and Communications

TELECOMMUNICATIONS

France Câbles et Radio Wallis et Futuna (FCR WF): Télécommunications Extérieures de Wallis et Futuna, BP 54, Mata'Utu, 98600 Uvea, Wallis Islands; tel. 722436; fax 722255; e-mail fcr@mail.wf; owned by FCR–SA–Orange Group; Man. JACQUES PAMBRUN.

Service des Postes et Télécommunications: BP 00, Mata'Utu, 98600 Uvea, Hahake, Wallis Islands; tel. 720809; fax 722662; e-mail pio.tui@wallis.co.nc; internet www.spt.wf; Dir MANUELE TAOFIFENUA; Head of Postage Stamp Section PIO TUI.

BROADCASTING

Radio and Television

France Télévisions Pôle Wallis et Futuna: BP 102, Pointe Matala, Mata'Utu, 98600 Uvea, Wallis Islands; tel. 721300; fax 722446; e-mail rfo.wallis@wallis.co.nc; internet wallisfutuna.rfo.fr; f. 1979; acquired by Groupe France Télévisions in 2004; fmrly Radiodiffusion Française d'Outre-Mer, present name adopted in 1998; transmitters at Mata'Utu (Uvea) and Alo (Futuna); programmes broadcast 24 hours daily in Uvean (Wallisian), Futunian and French; a television service on Uvea, transmitting for 12 hours daily in French, began operations in 1986; a television service on Futuna was inaugurated in 1994; satellite television began operations in 2000; Regional Dir JEAN-JACQUES AGOSTINI; Station Man. LOUIS AUGUSTE; Editor-in-Chief NORBERT TAOFIFENUA.

Finance

BANKING

Bank of Issue

Institut d'Emission d'Outre-Mer: BP G5, Mata'Utu, 98600 Uvea, Wallis Islands; tel. 722505; fax 722003; e-mail direction@ieomwf.fr; internet www.ieom.fr/wallis-et-futuna; f. 1998; Dir GUY DELAMAIRE.

Other Banks

Agence Française de Développement: Route territoriale n°1, Aka'aka, Hahake, BP 976, Wallis Islands; tel. 720107; fax 722551; e-mail afdmatautu@afd.fr; internet wallisetfutuna.afd.fr; fmrly Caisse Française de Développement; devt bank; Man. JEAN-YVES CLAVEL.

Banque de Wallis et Futuna: BP 59, Mata'Utu, 98600 Uvea, Wallis Islands; tel. 722124; fax 722156; e-mail bertrand.creuze@bnpparibas.com; internet www.bnpparibas.com/en/bnp-paribas-wallis-futuna; f. 1991; 51% owned by BNP Paribas (New Caledonia); CEO BERTRAND CREUZE.

Paierie de Wallis et Futuna: BP 29, Mata'Utu, 98600 Uvea, Wallis Islands; tel. 721250; fax 722120; Man. LOUIS WAESELYNCK.

Insurance

GAN Assurances: BP 52, Mata'Utu, Hahake, 98600 Uvea, Wallis Islands; subsidiary of GAN Assurances, France; general non-life insurance.

Poe-ma Insurances: Matala'a, Utufua, Mua, BP 728, Vaitupu, 98600 Uvea, Wallis Islands; tel. 450096; fax 450097; e-mail poema@mail.pf.

Trade and Industry

UTILITIES

Electricité et Eau de Wallis et Futuna (EEWF): BP 28, Mata'Utu, 98600 Uvea, Wallis Islands; tel. 721500; fax 721196; e-mail eewf@wallis.co.nc; 32.4% owned by the territory and 66.6% owned by Electricité et Eau de Calédonie (Groupe Suez, France); production and distribution of electricity on Wallis and Futuna; production and distribution of potable water on Wallis since 1986; Dir JEAN-MARC PETIT.

TRADE UNIONS

Union Interprofessionnelle CFDT Wallis et Futuna (UI CFDT): BP 178, Mata'Utu, 98600 Uvea, Wallis Islands; tel. 721880; Sec.-Gen. KALOLO HANISI.

Union Territoriale Force Ouvrière: BP 325, Mata'Utu, 98600 Uvea, Wallis Islands; tel. 721732; fax 721732; Sec.-Gen. CHRISTIAN VAAMEI.

Transport

ROADS

Uvea has a few kilometres of road, one route circling the island, and there is also a partially surfaced road circling the island of Futuna; the only fully surfaced roads are in Mata'Utu.

SHIPPING

There are two wharves on Uvea for bulk goods, at Mata'Utu, and liquid fuels, at Halalo, respectively. There is one wharf at Leava on Futuna. Wallis and Futuna is served by two container ships: the *Southern Moana*, operated jointly by Moana Services of New Caledonia and Pacific Direct Line of New Zealand between Auckland (New Zealand), Nouméa (New Caledonia) and the islands; and the *Sofrana Bligh*, operated by SOFRANA between Auckland and the islands. Plans to expand the harbour facilities at Mata'Utu and to make improvements to the fishing port of Halalo have been subject to delay.

Société Française Navigation (SOFRANA): BP 24, Mata'Utu, 98600 Uvea, Wallis Islands; tel. 720511; fax 720568; f. 1986; subsidiary of Sofrana Unilines, New Zealand; 1 vessel.

CIVIL AVIATION

There is an international airport in Hihifo district on Uvea, about 5 km from Mata'Utu. Air Calédonie International (Aircalin—New Caledonia) is the only airline to serve Wallis and Futuna. The company operates five flights a week from Wallis to Futuna, one flight a week from Wallis to Tahiti (French Polynesia) and two flights a week from Wallis to Nouméa (New Caledonia). The airport on Futuna is at Pointe Vele, in the south-east, in the Kingdom of Alo.

Service d'Etat de l'Aviation Civile de Wallis et Futuna: BP 01, Mata'Utu, Malae, Hihifo, 98600 Uvea, Wallis Islands; tel. 721201; fax 722954; e-mail seac-wf.encadrement@mail.wf; Dir VALERIE PUCCI.

Tourism

Tourism remains undeveloped. There are four small hotels on Uvea, Wallis Islands. In 2006 foreign visitors to the islands totalled 2,456. In 2008 Wallis had four hotels and Futuna two establishments. The 2013 Pacific Mini Games were held on Wallis and Futuna in September that year.

Defence

Defence is the responsibility of France. The French naval command for the Pacific area is based in French Polynesia.

Education

Education is compulsory for children aged between six and 16 years. Primary education lasts for five years. Each village has a primary school run by the state. The main education medium in village schools is French. In 2008 there were 18 primary schools and seven secondary schools (including two vocational schools) in Wallis and Futuna. Primary and pre-primary pupils totalled 1,972 and secondary students 1,929 in 2012. In 2005/06 a total of 80 students were attending various universities overseas. A two-year post-secondary programme was established in the islands in 1990.

Other French Overseas Territories

The other French territories are the French Southern and Antarctic Territories, and New Caledonia. The latter has a unique status as a Collectivité *sui generis* within the framework of the French Republic. Powers are devolved to New Caledonia under the terms of the 1998 Nouméa Accord.

THE FRENCH SOUTHERN AND ANTARCTIC TERRITORIES

Introduction

The Terres australes et antarctiques françaises (French Southern and Antarctic Territories) are administered under a special statute. The territory comprises Adélie Land, a narrow segment of the mainland of Antarctica together with a number of offshore islets, three groups of sub-Antarctic islands (the Kerguelen and Crozet Archipelagos, and Saint-Paul and Amsterdam Islands) in the southern Indian Ocean, and the Iles Eparses, in the Indian Ocean, comprising Bassas da India, Juan da Nova, Europa and Les Glorieuses, which are also claimed by Madagascar, and Tromelin, also claimed by Madagascar and Mauritius.

Under the terms of legislation approved by the French Government in 1955, the French Southern and Antarctic Territories were placed under the authority of a chief administrator, responsible to the government member for the overseas possessions. The Prefect and Chief Administrator is assisted by a Consultative Council, which meets at least twice annually. The Council is composed of seven members who are appointed for five years by the government member for the overseas possessions (from among members of the Office of Scientific Research and from those who have participated in scientific missions in the sub-Antarctic islands and Adélie Land). Under the terms of a decree promulgated in 1997, administration of the French Southern and Antarctic Territories was formally transferred from Paris to Saint-Pierre, Réunion, in April 2000. The Iles Eparses, administrative control of which was transferred from the Prefect of Réunion to the Prefect and Chief Administrator of the French Southern and Antarctic Territories in January 2005, became an integral part of the French Southern and Antarctic Territories under an organic law promulgated in February 2007.

From 1987 certain categories of vessels were allowed to register under the flag of the Kerguelen Archipelago, provided that 25% of their crew (including the captain and at least two officers) were French. These specifications were amended to 35% of the crew and at least four officers in April 1990. Under new legislation enacted in May 2005 this 'Kerguelen Register' was replaced with a new French International Register, whereby, *inter alia*, the captain, one officer and at least 25% of the crew would be required to be nationals of a European Union (EU) member state, or of a country in the European Economic Area. In 2013 21 vessels were registered to the French Southern Territories, of which seven were fishing vessels.

A permanent French base was established in 1950 at Martin de Viviès, on Amsterdam Island, followed by a second at Port-aux-Français, in the Kerguelen Archipelago, in 1951. The first permanent French base on the mainland was built in 1952 at Port Martin. Having been destroyed by fire, it was replaced in 1956 by a new permanent base at Dumont d'Urville. A fourth base was opened in 1964 at Alfred Faure on Ile de la Possession, in the Crozet Archipelago. In 1992 the French Government created a Public Interest Group, the Institut Français pour la Recherche et la Technologie Polaires (IFRTP—renamed the Institut Polaire Français Paul Emile Victor—IPEV—in 2002), to assume responsibility for the organization of scientific and research programmes in the French Southern and Antarctic Territories. Under an agreement between the IFRTP and Italy's Programma Nazionale di Ricerche in Antartide in 1993, work began on a joint project, Concordia, with a permanent base to be established at Dome C. Concordia was officially opened for winter operation in 2005. France is a signatory to the Antarctic Treaty (see p. 462).

Fishing for crayfish, Patagonian toothfish and tuna in the territories' Exclusive Economic Zones is strictly regulated by quotas (see Statistical Survey). During 2012 38 vessels were licensed to fish in the Iles Eparses zone, and eight in the Southern territories. Following the implementation of a new satellite surveillance system in February 2004, illegal fishing incursions were believed to have been reduced by some 90% by November 2005. An agreement to increase co-operation between France and Australia in combating illegal fishing in the southern Antarctic was signed in 2007 and was ratified by Australia in 2011 (it had previously been ratified by the French Government).

Limited numbers of tourists have since 1994 been permitted to visit Crozet, Kerguelen and Amsterdam: about 60 tourists travel to the territories each year aboard the supply and oceanographic vessel *Marion Dufresne II*. In 2006 Crozet, Kerguelen, Amsterdam and Saint Paul were designated as nature and marine reserves.

Statistical Survey

Area (sq km): Kerguelen Archipelago 7,215, Crozet Archipelago 340, Amsterdam Island 58, Saint-Paul Island 8, Adélie Land (Antarctica) 432,000, Iles Eparses 39 (Bassas da India 1, Europa 28, Juan de Nova 4, Les Glorieuses 5, Tromelin 1).

Population (the population, comprising members of scientific missions, fluctuates according to season, being higher in the summer, but the average is around 225; the figures given are approximate): Kerguelen Archipelago, Port-aux-Français 80; Amsterdam Island at Martin de Viviès 30; Adélie Land at Base Dumont d'Urville 27; the Crozet Archipelago at Alfred Faure (on Ile de la Possession) 35; Saint-Paul Island is uninhabited; Total population (April 2000): 172. *2003/04:* Adélie Land at Base Concordia 41 (joint French-Italian team).

Fishing (catch quotas in metric tons): *2008/9:* Crayfish (spiny lobsters) in Amsterdam and Saint-Paul: 400. *2012/13:* Patagonian toothfish (caught by French and foreign fleets) in the Kerguelen and Crozet Archipelagos: 5,800.

Currency: French currency was used until the end of 2001. Euro notes and coins were introduced on 1 January 2002, and the euro became the sole legal tender from 18 February. For details of exchange rates, see French Guiana.

Budget: Around €26m. in domestic revenues per year (revenues derived from duties levied on the catch of 46 licensed fishing vessels was estimated at €5.6m. in 2012), supplemented with subsidies from the French overseas ministry and grants from the French environment ministry.

External Trade: Exports consist mainly of crayfish and other fish to France and Réunion. The Territories also derive revenue from the sale of postage stamps and other philatelic items.

Directory

Government: rue Gabriel Dejean, 97410 Saint Pierre, Réunion; tel. 262-96-78-78; fax 262-96-78-06; e-mail amandine.george@taaf.fr; internet www.taaf.fr; Prefect, Chief Administrator PASCAL BOLOT.

Consultative Council: Pres. JEAN-PIERRE CHARPENTIER.

Publications: The central administration in Réunion produces two quarterly publications relating to the French Southern and Antarctic Territories: the legal bulletin *Journal officiel des Terres australes et antarctiques françaises* and a newsletter, *Terres Extrêmes*.

Institut Polaire Français Paul Emile Victor (IPEV): Technopôle de Brest-Iroise, BP 75, 29280 Plouzané, France; tel. 2-98-05-65-00; fax 2-98-05-65-55; e-mail communication-ipev@ipev.fr; internet www.institut-polaire.fr; f. 1992 as Institut Français pour la Recherche et la Technologie Polaires, name changed 2002; Dir YVES FRENOT; 5 permanent bases.

Research Stations: There are meteorological stations and geophysical research stations on Kerguelen, Amsterdam, Adélie Land and Crozet. Research in marine microbiology is conducted from the

Crozet and Kerguelen Archipelagos, and studies of atmospheric pollution are carried out on Amsterdam Island. Additionally, a joint French-Italian research station, Concordia, operates at Dome C. The French atomic energy authority, the Commissariat à l'Energie Atomique, also maintains a presence on Crozet, Kerguelen and Adélie Land.

Transport: An oceanographic and supply vessel, the *Marion Dufresne II*, operated by the French Government, provides regular links between Réunion and the sub-Antarctic islands. A polar research vessel, *Astrolabe*, operated by P&O Maritime Services, France and operating from Hobart, Tasmania, calls five times a year at the Antarctic mainland.

NEW CALEDONIA

Introductory Survey

LOCATION, CLIMATE, LANGUAGE, RELIGION, CAPITAL

New Caledonia comprises one large island and several smaller ones, lying in the South Pacific Ocean, about 1,500 km (930 miles) east of Queensland, Australia. The main island, New Caledonia (Grande Terre), is long and narrow, and has a total area of 16,372 sq km. Rugged mountains divide the west of the island from the east, and there is little flat land. The nearby Loyalty Islands, which are administratively part of New Caledonia, are 1,981 sq km in area, and a third group of islands, the uninhabited Chesterfield Islands, lies about 400 km north-west of the main island. The islands are surrounded by the world's largest continuous coral barrier reef, encompassing some 40,000 sq km. The climate is generally mild, with an annual average temperature of about 24°C (75°F) and a rainy season between December and March. The average rainfall in the east of the main island is about 2,000 mm (80 in) per year, and in the west about 1,000 mm (40 in). French is the official language and the mother tongue of the Caldoches (French settlers). The indigenous Kanaks (Melanesians) also speak Melanesian languages: 29 languages were taken into account at the census of 1996, when it was recorded that 38% of the total indigenous Kanak population spoke a Melanesian language. Other immigrants speak Polynesian and Asian languages. New Caledonians almost all profess Christianity, the majority of whom are Roman Catholics. There is a substantial Protestant minority. The capital is Nouméa, on the main island.

CONTEMPORARY POLITICAL HISTORY

Historical Context

New Caledonia became a French possession in the 19th century, when the island was annexed as a dependency of Tahiti. A separate administration was subsequently established, and a Conseil Général (General Council) was elected to defend local interests. France took possession of Melanesian land and began mining nickel and copper. This displacement of the indigenous Kanak population provoked a number of rebellions. New Caledonia became a Territoire d'Outre-Mer (Overseas Territory) of the French Republic in 1946. In 1956 the first Territorial Assembly, with 30 members, was elected by universal adult suffrage, although the French Governor effectively retained control of the functions of government. New Caledonian demands for a measure of self-government were answered in 1976 by a new statute, which gave the Council of Government, elected from the Territorial Assembly, responsibility for certain internal affairs. The post of Governor was replaced by that of French High Commissioner to the territory. In 1978 the Kanak-supported, pro-independence parties obtained a majority of the posts in the Council of Government. In early 1979, however, the French Government dismissed the Council, following its failure to support a proposal for a 10-year 'contract' between France and New Caledonia on the grounds that the plan did not acknowledge the possibility of New Caledonian independence. The territory was then placed under the direct authority of the High Commissioner.

Domestic Political Affairs

A general election was held in July 1979, but new electoral legislation, which affected mainly the pro-independence parties, ensured that minor parties failed to gain representation in the Assembly. Two parties loyal to France—Rassemblement pour la Calédonie dans la République (RPCR) and Fédération pour une Nouvelle Société Calédonienne (FNSC)—together won 22 of the 36 seats.

Political tension increased in September 1981, following the assassination of Pierre Declercq, the Secretary-General of the pro-independence Union Calédonienne (UC). In December the French Government proposed reforms that included equal access for all New Caledonians to positions of authority, land reforms and the fostering of Kanak cultural institutions. To assist in effecting these changes, the French Government announced that it would rule by decree for a period of at least one year. In 1982 the FNSC joined with the opposition Front Indépendantiste (FI) to form a government that was more in favour of the proposed reforms.

In November 1983 the French Government proposed a five-year period of increased autonomy from July 1984 and a referendum in 1989 to determine New Caledonia's future. The statute was rejected by the Territorial Assembly in April 1984, but approved none the less by the French Assemblée Nationale (National Assembly) in September. Under the provisions of the statute, the Territorial Council of Ministers was given responsibility for many internal matters of government, its President henceforth being an elected member instead of the French High Commissioner; a second legislative chamber, with the right to be consulted on development planning and budgetary issues, was created at the same time. All of the main parties seeking independence (except the Libération Kanak Socialiste—LKS—party, which left the FI) boycotted elections for the new, enlarged Territorial Assembly in November 1984. Only 50.1% of the electorate participated in the polls, at which the anti-independence RPCR won 34 of the 42 seats. Following the dissolution of the FI, a new pro-independence movement, the Front de Libération Nationale Kanak Socialiste (FLNKS), was formed. On 1 December the FLNKS Congress established a 'provisional' Government, headed by Jean-Marie Tjibaou. Amid escalating violence, three settlers were murdered that month by pro-independence activists and 10 Kanaks were killed by *métis* (mixed race) settlers.

In January 1985 Edgard Pisani, the new High Commissioner, announced a plan under which the territory might become independent 'in association with' France on 1 January 1986, subject to the result of a referendum in July 1985. Kanak groups opposed the plan, insisting that the indigenous population be allowed to determine its own fate. At the same time, the majority of the population, which supported the RPCR, demonstrated against the plan and in favour of remaining within the French Republic. A resurgence of violence followed the announcement of Pisani's plan, and a state of emergency was declared after two incidents in which a leading member of the FLNKS was killed by security forces and the son of a French settler was killed by Kanak activists.

In April 1985 the French Prime Minister, Laurent Fabius, proposed the deferral of the referendum on independence until an unspecified date not later than the end of 1987 and the division of the territory into four regions, each to be governed by its own elected autonomous council, which would have extensive powers in the spheres of planning and development, education, health and social services, land rights, transport and housing. The elected members of all four councils together would serve as regional representatives in a Territorial Congress (to replace the Territorial Assembly). The 'Fabius plan' was generally well received by the FLNKS, but condemned by the RPCR, and the proposals were rejected by the predominantly anti-independence Territorial Assembly in May. Nevertheless, the necessary legislation was approved by the French National Assembly in July, and the Fabius plan entered into force. Elections were held in September: as expected, only in the region around Nouméa, where the bulk of the population was non-Kanak, was an anti-independence majority recorded. However, the pro-independence Melanesians, despite their majorities in the three non-urban regions, would be in a minority in the Territorial Congress.

The FLNKS boycotted elections to the French National Assembly in March 1986, in which only about 50% of the electorate in New Caledonia participated. In May the French Council of Ministers approved a draft law providing for a referendum to be held in New Caledonia within 12 months, at which voters would choose between independence and a further extension of regional autonomy. In December, despite strong French diplomatic opposition, the UN General Assembly voted to re-inscribe New Caledonia on the UN list of non-self-governing territories, thereby affirming the population's right to self-determination. The FLNKS boycotted the referendum on 13 September 1987, at which 98.3% of the votes cast were in favour of New Caledonia's continuation as part of the French Republic. At 59%, the turnout was higher than expected, although 90% of the electorate abstained in constituencies inhabited by a majority of Kanaks.

In October 1987 seven pro-French loyalists were acquitted of murdering 10 Kanak separatists in 1984. Jean-Marie Tjibaou, who reacted to the ruling by declaring that his supporters would have to abandon their stance of pacifism, and his deputy, Yeiwéné Yeiwéné, were indicted for 'incitement to violence'. In April 1988 four gendarmes were killed, and 27 held hostage in a cave on the island of Uvéa (the neighbouring Wallis Island), by supporters of the FLNKS. Although 12 of the hostages were subsequently released, six members of a French anti-terrorist squad were captured. French security forces laid siege to the cave, and made an assault upon it in May, leaving 19 Kanaks and two gendarmes dead. Following the siege, allegations that three Kanaks had been executed or left to die, after being arrested, led to an announcement by the new French Socialist Government that a judicial inquiry into the incident was to be opened.

At elections to the French National Assembly in June 1988, both New Caledonian seats were retained by the RPCR. Michel Rocard, the new French Prime Minister, chaired negotiations in Paris between Jacques Lafleur (leader of the RPCR) and Jean-Marie Tjibaou, both of whom agreed to transfer the administration of the territory to Paris for 12 months. Under the provisions of the agreement (known as the Matignon Accord), the territory was to be divided into three administrative provinces prior to a territorial plebiscite on independence to be held in 1998. Only people resident in the territory in 1988, and their direct descendants, would be allowed to vote in the plebiscite. The agreement also provided for a programme of economic development, training in public administration for Kanaks and institutional reforms. The Matignon Accord was presented to the French electorate in a referendum, held on 6 November 1988, and approved by 80% of those voting (although an abstention rate of 63% of the electorate was recorded). The programme was approved by a 57% majority in New Caledonia, where the rate of abstention was 37%. In November, under the terms of the agreement, 51 separatists were released from prison, including 26 Kanaks implicated in the incident on Uvéa.

In May 1989 Tjibaou and Yeiwéné were murdered by separatist extremists, alleged to be associated with the Front Uni de Libération Kanak (FULK), which had hitherto formed part of the FLNKS but opposed the Matignon Accord. Elections to the three Provincial Assemblies were nevertheless held, as scheduled, in June: the FLNKS won a majority of seats in the North Province and the Loyalty Islands Province, while the RPCR obtained a majority in the South Province. The RPCR also emerged as the dominant party in the Territorial Congress, with 27 of the 54 seats; the FLNKS secured 19 seats.

The year of direct rule by France ended on 14 July 1989, when the Territorial Congress and Provincial Assemblies assumed the administrative functions allocated to them in the Matignon Accord. In November the French National Assembly approved an amnesty (as stipulated in the Matignon Accord) for all who had been involved in politically motivated violence in New Caledonia before August 1988, despite strong opposition from the right-wing French parties. In April 1991 the LKS announced its intention to withdraw from the Matignon Accord, accusing the French Government, as well as several Kanak political leaders, of seeking to undermine Kanak culture and tradition. At elections for the New Caledonian representative to the French Sénat (Senate) in September 1992, the RPCR's candidate, Simon Loueckhote, narrowly defeated Roch Wamytan, the Vice-President of the FLNKS.

At provincial elections in July 1995 the RPCR retained an overall majority in the Territorial Congress, while the FLNKS remained the second largest party. Considerable gains were made by a newly formed party led by Nouméa businessman Didier Leroux, Une Nouvelle-Calédonie pour Tous (UNCT). However, a political crisis subsequently arose as a result of the UNCT's decision to align itself with the FLNKS, leaving the RPCR with a minority of official positions in the congressional committees. Lafleur would not accept a situation in which the UNCT appeared to be the dominant party in the chamber, and Pierre Frogier, the RPCR President of the Congress, refused to convene a congressional sitting under such circumstances. The deadlock was broken when the FLNKS proposed the allocation of congressional positions on a proportional basis.

Elections to the French National Assembly in May–June 1997 were boycotted by the pro-independence FLNKS and LKS, resulting in a relatively low turnout. Lafleur and Frogier, both RPCR candidates, were elected to represent New Caledonia. Intensive negotiations involving the RPCR, the FLNKS and the French Government took place in late 1995 and early 1996. France's refusal to grant final approval for a large-scale nickel smelter project in the North Province until the achievement of consensus in the discussions on autonomy prompted accusations of blackmail from several sources within the territory and resulted in the virtual cessation of negotiations during the remainder of 1996. The FLNKS argued that the smelter project should be administered by local interests, consistent with the process of reallocating responsibility for the economy from metropolitan France to the territory as advocated in the Matignon Accord.

In February 1997 the French Minister for Overseas Territories, Jean-Jacques de Peretti, visited New Caledonia in a failed attempt to achieve an exchange agreement on nickel between the Société Minière du Sud Pacifique (SMSP), controlled by the North Province, and a subsidiary of the French mining conglomerate Eramet, Société Le Nickel (SLN). However, at the end of the month, in a complete reversal of policy, the French Government announced its decision not to compensate SLN for any losses incurred, provoking strong criticism from SLN and Eramet and protests from shareholders and employees of the company. During March large-scale demonstrations were held by the UC and the pro-independence trade union, the Union Syndicale des Travailleurs Kanak et des Exploités (USTKE), in support of SMSP's acquisition of the smelter. Meanwhile, another trade union, the Union des Syndicates des Ouvriers et Employés de Nouvelle Caledonie (USOENC, which represented a high proportion of SLN employees), organized a protest rally against the unequal exchange of mining sites. Frustrated at SLN's seemingly intransigent position during the negotiations, the FLNKS organized protests and blockades at all the company's major mining installations and restricted shipments of ore around New Caledonia, forcing the closure of four mines. In January 1998 Roch Wamytan (now President of the FLNKS) urged the French Prime Minister, Lionel Jospin, to settle the dispute in order that official negotiations on the political future of New Caledonia, in preparation for the referendum, might begin. The position of the FLNKS had been somewhat undermined by the decision, in the previous month, of a breakaway group of pro-independence politicians—including prominent members of the UC, the Parti de Libération Kanak (PALIKA), and the LKS—to begin negotiations with the RPCR concerning the dispute. These moderate supporters of independence formed the Fédération des Comités de Coordination des Indépendantistes (FCCI) in 1998.

In February 1998, in response to the demands of Kanak political leaders, the French Government, Eramet, SMSP and others signed the Bercy Accord, whereby Eramet was to relinquish control of its site at Koniambo, located in the North Province, in exchange for the Poum mine, operated by SMSP, in the South Province. (The Bercy Accord was the foundation for the 'rebalancing' of New Caledonia's economy under the Nouméa Accord—see below—by creating wealth beyond the South Province.) In April SMSP formed a joint venture with the Canadian mining company Falconbridge to develop the Koniambo nickel deposits. If construction of a nickel smelter had not begun by the end of 2005, control of the nickel deposits was to revert from SMSP to SLN. Meanwhile, the French Government agreed to pay compensation of some 1,000m. French francs to Eramet for the reduction in the company's reserves. An agreement was concluded in February 1999 to enable the transfer of 30% of SLN's share capital (and 8% of Eramet's capital) to a newly created company representing local interests, the Société Territoriale Calédonienne de Participation Industrielle (STCPI), to be owned by the development companies of the three New Caledonian provinces. In July 2000, following two years of negotiations, New Caledonia's political leaders signed an agreement on the formation of the STCPI, the new company to be owned equally by PROMOSUD (representing the South Province) and NORDIL (combining the interests of the North Province and the Loyalty Islands). In September shares in SLN and Eramet were transferred to the STCPI, reducing Eramet's interest in SLN from 90% to 60%.

The Nouméa Accord

Tripartite negotiations on the constitutional future of New Caledonia resumed in Paris in February 1998 between representatives of the French Government, the FLNKS and the RPCR. In April, following a final round of talks in Nouméa, an agreement was concluded by the three sides. The agreement, which became known as the Nouméa Accord, postponed the referendum on independence for a period of 15–20 years but provided for a gradual transfer of powers to local institutions, with the exception of defence, foreign policy, law and order, justice and monetary affairs, which were to remain the responsibility of the French Government until after the referendum. The document also acknowledged the negative impact of many aspects of French colonization on New Caledonia and emphasized the need for greater recognition of the importance of the Kanak cultural identity in the political development of the islands. The Nouméa Accord was signed on 5 May.

In July 1998 the French legislature adopted the proposed changes regarding the administration of New Caledonia, which were to be incorporated in an annex to the French Constitution. In the following month the French Minister for Overseas Territories, Jean-Jack Queyranne, returned to New Caledonia for discussion on draft legislation for the devolution process. The Nouméa Accord, which designated New Caledonia as a Pays d'Outre-Mer (Overseas Country) of France, was presented to the electorate in a referendum on 8 November, when it was decisively approved, with 71.9% of votes cast in favour of the agreement. The North Province registered the strongest vote in favour of the agreement (95.5%), while the South Province recorded the most moderate level of approval (62.9%). In December the French National Assembly unanimously approved draft legislation regarding the definitive adoption of the accord. The Senate similarly approved the legislation, in February 1999. However, in March the French Constitutional Council declared its intention to allow any French person who had resided in New Caledonia for 10 years or more to vote in provincial elections. This decision was criticized by Roch Wamytan, leader of the FLNKS, as well as by French legislators, who claimed that it breached the Nouméa Accord, whereby only those residing in New Caledonia in 1998 would be permitted to vote in provincial elections. Pro-independence groups threatened to boycott the elections (to be held in May). In response, the French Government announced that the Accord would be honoured, claiming that the Constitutional Council had breached the Nouméa Accord, and stating that this contravention would be rectified. In June the French Council of Ministers announced that it had drafted legislation restricting eligibility for voting in provincial elections and in any future referendums on sovereignty to those who had been eligible to vote in the November 1998 referendum on the Nouméa Accord and to their children upon reaching the age of majority. This decision was condemned by the right-wing Front National, and by Lafleur, leader of the RPCR.

At the general election held on 9 May 1999, no party gained an absolute majority. However, the RPCR won 24 of the 54 seats in the Congress and formed a coalition with the recently established FCCI and, on an informal level, with the Front National, thus creating an anti-independence block of 31 seats in the chamber. The pro-independence FLNKS won 18 seats. Simon Loueckhote was re-elected President of the Congress. On 28 May the Congress elected Jean Lèques as the first President of the Government (Council of Ministers) of New Caledonia, under the increased autonomy terms of the Nouméa Accord. The new Government was elected on the basis of proportional representation and replaced the French High Commissioner as New Caledonia's executive authority. Meanwhile, results of the elections in the Loyalty Islands Province were challenged by the LKS, the FCCI and the RPCR, following the issue by the electoral commissioner for the province of a report claiming that a large number of irregularities had occurred. Fresh elections were held in the province in June 2000, at which a coalition of the RPCR, FCCI, LKS and FULK obtained six seats, the FLNKS six seats, and PALIKA two seats. The composition of the Congress therefore remained unchanged.

Municipal elections confirmed the predominance of the RPCR in the south in March 2001, when it won 39 of the 49 seats in Nouméa. However, overall, the RPCR controlled only 14 of the 33 municipalities in New Caledonia, while pro-independence parties, principally the UC, PALIKA, LKS and FLNKS, held 19. The FLNKS won a majority in the north and took all three communes in the Loyalty Islands. Jean Lèques resigned as President and was replaced by fellow RPCR politician Frogier in April. Déwé Gorodey of the FLNKS was elected Vice-President. The election to the two most senior posts took place after the Congress had elected an 11-member Government consisting of seven RPCR-FCCI coalition members, three from the FLNKS and one from the UC. In October the French Conseil d'Etat (State Council) ruled that the 11th seat in the New Caledonian Government had been incorrectly allocated to the FLNKS. As a result, FCCI leader Raphaël Mapou replaced Aukusitino Manuohalalo of the FLNKS as Minister for Social Security and Health. Roch Wamytan was replaced as President of the UC by his deputy, Pascal Naouna. In November Wamytan lost the presidency of the FLNKS, following a leadership struggle between its two main factions, the UC and PALIKA. The political bureau of the FLNKS was to lead the party until its internal disputes were settled.

Prior to the French legislative elections of June 2002, the RPCR became affiliated to the metropolitan Union pour la Majorité Presidentielle—latterly Union pour un Mouvement Populaire—to form Le Rassemblement-UMP. The UC and PALIKA could not agree upon their choice of President for the FLNKS. The UC therefore refused to take part in the elections and urged its supporters to abstain from the poll, thereby depriving the President of PALIKA, Paul Néaoutyine, of any chance of re-election to the National Assembly in Paris. Lafleur, now representing Le Rassemblement-UMP, was thus re-elected as a deputy, as was Frogier, also for Le Rassemblement-UMP.

In November 2002 the sole UC member of the Government, Gerald Cortot, resigned, prompting the immediate dissolution of the Government, as stipulated in the Nouméa Accord. The Council of Ministers was reduced to 10 members, and the Congress appointed a new administration, with Frogier reappointed as President; the incoming Government contained seven members of the Rassemblement-UMP-FCCI coalition, two from the FLNKS and one from the UC.

In May 2003, at a congress of the FLNKS, officials of the party reportedly claimed that the terms of the Nouméa Accord were not being fully observed by the French Government. In July USTKE called a general strike to coincide with a visit to New Caledonia by the French President, Jacques Chirac, and organized a rally attended by 2,000 protesters. Chirac's four-day visit also provoked demonstrations by several hundred members of the UC. Kanak representatives, meanwhile, expressed dismay at their exclusion from meetings with the French President.

At the legislative elections in May 2004 Le Rassemblement-UMP lost its majority in the South Province, where it won only 16 of the 40 seats, and thus in the Congress of New Caledonia, occupying only 16 of the 54 seats. The recently formed, anti-independence Avenir Ensemble secured 19 seats in the South Province and proceeded to take 16 seats in the Congress. Each Provincial Assembly in turn elected its President: Philippe Gomès of Avenir Ensemble became President of the South Province, replacing Lafleur; Néaoutyine of the Union Nationale pour l'Indépendance (UNI) was re-elected in the North Province; and Néko Hnépeune, also of the UNI-FLNKS alliance, was elected President in the Loyalty Islands. In late May the incoming Congress elected Harold Martin of Avenir Ensemble as its President and began the process of appointing a new Government. In early June Marie-Noëlle Thémereau of Avenir Ensemble and Gorodey of the UNI-FLNKS were respectively nominated President and Vice-President. However, the Government disintegrated within hours, following the resignation of the three Rassemblement-UMP ministers, who claimed that their party was entitled to four posts under power-sharing terms set out in the Nouméa Accord. The Congress granted Le Rassemblement-UMP the seats, but with the result that the decision of the Council of Ministers on its leadership reached a stalemate. In late June a new vote returned Thémereau and Gorodey to their elected posts. The incoming Government endorsed a code of conduct that emphasized the importance of consensus-building among the parties. In January 2005 representatives of Avenir Ensemble for the first time took part in discussions with the French Government in Paris.

In October 2004 an operating licence was granted to Canadian mining company Inco for the development of a proposed nickel-cobalt plant at Goro in the South Province. Concerns about the disposal of industrial waste into the sea had been raised in a public inquiry in the previous August, and in February 2005 protesters from a Kanak environmental organization, Réébhù Nùù, blockaded the Goro site. In December Goro was again blockaded, this time by protesters from another Kanak organization, the Conseil Autochtone pour la Gestion des Ressources Naturelles en Kanaky Nouvelle-Calédonie (CAUGERN), which had been formed in July. CAUGERN received the support of USTKE and the local Customary Senate in raising concerns relating to the socio-economic and political impact of nickel-mining activities, as well as with regard to the environmental repercussions.

Control of the Koniambo mine was transferred to the Canadian company Falconbridge and SMSP in December 2005. In 2006 plans for a merger between Inco and Falconbridge were cancelled; Falconbridge was subsequently acquired by a Swiss-based company, Xstrata PLC. (Under the terms of a 2007 agreement, Xstrata Nickel has a 49% stake and SMSP a 51% stake in the Koniambo joint venture.) Inco became a wholly owned subsidiary of the Brazilian enterprise, Companhia Vale do Rio Doce (CVRD). In April 2006 the development of the Goro Nickel mine again became a major issue when members of Réébhù Nùù blockaded access routes to the site and caused damage to equipment estimated at US $10m. Construction work at the nickel plant was halted. The FLNKS assumed the role of mediator on behalf of Réébhù Nùù, Goro Nickel, the New Caledonian Government and community leaders, while USTKE announced its support for the Réébhù Nùù campaign. Following reassurances about the security of the site, Goro Nickel announced that it would restart construction work. However, opposition to the project persisted, and demonstrations continued. In June a New Caledonian court ruled that the possible environmental consequences of the scheme had not been comprehensively investigated, and cancelled its licence to operate; however, the company's construction licence remained intact. In July Réébhù Nùù, joined by CAUGERN, warned of further action if Goro Nickel failed to halt construction by a deadline of 24 September. On 25 September the CSTNC began a general strike to demand the expulsion of several hundred Filipino employees of Goro Nickel and the resignations of local government officials. In November Réébhù Nùù succeeded in gaining an injunction from a French court on Goro Nickel's construction of a waste facility. This ruling was rescinded in February 2007. Mounting costs, continuing local opposition and technical problems further delayed the project, which was not expected to reach full production until 2014.

In April 2006 Lafleur founded a new political party with Simon Loueckhote, the Rassemblement pour la Calédonie (RPC). In early 2007 the French legislature approved a constitutional amendment that limited voting rights to those who had been resident in New Caledonia prior to 1998. Due to enter into force in 2009, the legislation did not cover the French presidential and legislative elections of 2007. Nicolas Sarkozy of the UMP defeated Ségolène Royal of the Parti Socialiste in the second round of the presidential election, in May, garnering 62.9% of the votes in New Caledonia. Sarkozy's margin of victory was significantly smaller within metropolitan France. Elections to the National Assembly were held in June. Although the Rassemblement-UMP candidates, incumbent deputy Frogier and Gaël Yanno, received the largest number of votes in their respective constituencies, their failure to secure an absolute majority resulted in the scheduling of a second round. Avenir Ensemble candidates, along with former Rassemblement-UMP member Lafleur, did not receive enough votes to proceed to the next stage. In the second round, Yanno secured a decisive victory over FLNKS candidate Charles Washetine, the Minister for Education and Research, while Frogier was re-elected, defeating Charles Pidjot of the FLNKS by a smaller margin.

As had been widely anticipated, Thémereau of Avenir Ensemble resigned from the position of President in July 2007, although the Council of Ministers was to remain in place until the appointment of a new Government. Frogier was elected President of the Congress of New Caledonia in late July, following reports that Avenir Ensemble and Le Rassemblement-UMP had signed an agreement, a so-called 'majority accord', into which the President of the RPC, Loueckhote, had also entered. The Congress elected a new Council of Ministers in August, meeting an FLNKS demand for four of the 11 cabinet positions. Martin was subsequently elected President and Gorodey returned to the position of Vice-President.

In October 2007 the French High Commissioner in New Caledonia, Michel Mathieu, resigned amid reports of a disagreement with the French Minister-Delegate for the Overseas Possessions, Christian Estrosi, who had signalled a new approach to the issue of strike action in New Caledonia. Yves Dassonville replaced Mathieu in November. In January 2008 a USTKE strike in Nouméa escalated into violence following police intervention; several people were injured, and in April 23 members of USTKE, including the union's leader, were given prison sentences for their involvement in the clashes. In November Louis Kotra Uregei was elected President of the Parti Travailliste, which had been formed in the previous year in conjunction with USTKE. Meanwhile, Frogier was re-elected as President of the Congress in July.

Recent developments: the elections of 2009 and beyond

In March 2009, as required by the Nouméa Accord, the New Caledonian Congress unanimously approved new legislation governing the operations of the nickel industry (see Economic Affairs). Legislative elections were held in the territory's three provinces on 10 May, whereupon each Provincial Assembly elected its President. Pierre Frogier of Le Rassemblement-UMP replaced Philippe Gomès as President of the South Province. Paul Néaoutyine, leader of the UNI, was re-elected in the North Province. In the Loyalty Islands Néko Hnépeune, also of the UNI-FLNKS, was re-elected as President. Members of anti-independence parties occupied 31 of the 54 seats in the New Caledonian Congress (of which Le Rassemblement-UMP took 13). Calédonie Ensemble, established in 2008 by former members of Avenir Ensemble and led by Gomès, was allocated 10 seats. The pro-independence groups made some gains and took 23 seats, eight of which were occupied by the UC and eight by the UNI.

At its inaugural session, the Congress chose Gomès as the territory's President. Disagreements delayed the election of the Vice-President until mid-June 2009, when Pierre Ngaihoni of the UC was appointed to the position. Other appointments to the Council of Ministers included that of Philippe Germain, whose responsibilities included economic affairs. Martin replaced Frogier as President of the New Caledonian Congress. However, the Parti Travailliste lodged a formal complaint with regard to the conduct of the elections and in October 2009, following the confirmation of irregularities relating mainly to the extensive use of proxy votes, the results of the Loyalty Islands were declared invalid by the State Council in France. At new polls, on 6 December, the UC-FLNKS alliance retained six seats in the Provincial Assembly, while the Parti Travailliste increased its representation from two to four seats, the LKS won two seats and two seats were taken by another pro-independence grouping.

Industrial unrest continued intermittently. A dispute at the local airline, arising from the dismissal of an employee, escalated into rioting in May 2009, when the police used tear gas and grenades to quell the disturbance. In June the USTKE called a general strike following the refusal by Air Calédonie to pay striking workers during several weeks of industrial action and the sentencing of union leader Gérard Jodar to one year's imprisonment. A further confrontation between USTKE demonstrators and the police occurred in July, during a visit by the new French Minister for Overseas Possessions, Marie-Luce Penchard. Businesses in Nouméa were similarly disrupted by USTKE action. An estimated 20,000 demonstrators, including business leaders and politicians, joined a march in Nouméa to protest against the disruption. In October three USTKE members were found guilty of involvement in the violence during the protests and each defendant was sentenced to one year's imprisonment, eight months of which were suspended.

The gradual process of transferring powers from metropolitan France continued, as stipulated in the Nouméa Accord (with the exception of certain areas such as defence and foreign policy, which were to remain the responsibility of the French Government until after the referendum on independence that was to take place between 2014 and 2018). With responsibility for primary education, post and telecommunications, training in public administration, labour, external trade and mining having already been granted to the New Caledonian authorities, in November 2009 the local Congress unanimously approved three laws providing for the transfer of responsibility for various other areas from the French authorities: secondary and private primary education; the policing and security of domestic maritime transport; and the policing and security of internal air transport. In September 2010 Dassonville and Gomès signed a formal agreement on the transfer of powers from the metropolitan Government. The policing and security of domestic maritime transport duly became the responsibility of New Caledonia in two stages, in January and July 2011, followed by secondary and private primary education in January 2012 (although the French Government was to continue to pay the salaries of teaching staff), and by the policing and security of internal air transport in January 2013. In accordance with legislation adopted by the Congress in December 2011, the transfer of responsibility for civil and commercial law and for civil security were effected in July 2013 and January 2014, respectively.

In June 2010, meanwhile, Penchard again visited New Caledonia and held discussions with the various party leaders in order to establish the agenda for a meeting on the further implementation of the Nouméa Accord, which took place in Paris later that month. It was resolved at a subsequent meeting that a committee of experts would be established to study the options for the future political status of New Caledonia. At the same time the French Government undertook to provide 45,000m. francs CFP in development assistance for New Caledonia during the period 2011–15. In July 2010 the French Prime Minister, François Fillon, paid a visit to New Caledonia, during which the 'Kanak' flag (which had formed a symbol of the pro-independence movement over the past 20 years) was, with the approval of the Congress, officially raised for the first time, concurrently with the French national flag. However, the display of two flags was regarded by some as symbolizing disunity, and President Gomès, among others, argued that a new single flag should be designed to represent New Caledonia following decolonization. A new French High Commissioner, Albert Dupuy, replaced Dassonville in October 2010.

In February 2011 members of the pro-independence UC withdrew from the Council of Ministers, on the grounds that Gomès was opposed to the use of two flags. As this resignation automatically resulted in the removal from office of the entire Government (in accordance with the Nouméa Accord), Gomès protested that the flag dispute was a ploy to remove him from office. He accused Le Rassemblement-UMP of allying itself with the UC to this end and pledged to disrupt future governments until a fresh general election was called. In early March the Congress elected a new 11-member collegial Government, in proportion to the parties' representation in the legislature. However, the new administration collapsed within minutes after one of the incoming ministers of Calédonie Ensemble submitted his resignation. Martin of Avenir Ensemble, who had replaced Gomès of Calédonie Ensemble as President, continued in office in an interim capacity, with Guy Tuyienon of the UC as his Vice-President. The crisis intensified a fortnight later when another Government was appointed, only to disintegrate immediately when Calédonie Ensemble withdrew. In April, following a further unsuccessful attempt to establish a government, Penchard travelled to New Caledonia in an attempt to resolve the crisis.

In May 2011, following three days of negotiations in Paris between political leaders from New Caledonia and members of the French Government, the French Prime Minister François Fillon announced that the Congress would elect a new collegial government on 10 June, rather than proceed with an early general election as initially requested by Gomès. At the election to the Government in June, Martin was re-elected as President and Tuyienon as Vice-President. Despite initial threats to withdraw once again, Calédonie Ensemble agreed to remain in the collegial Government following the election. Meanwhile, the French Senate approved changes to the electoral law of New Caledonia that were designed to promote greater political stability. Henceforth, an incoming government was be given a grace period of 18 months, thus permitting the exercise of a definite mandate. In July the French Prime Minister hosted further talks in Paris between the signatories to the Nouméa Accord to review the agreement in advance of its entering its final phase (2014–18) when, under the terms of the Accord, a referendum on independence could be held in the territory.

In August 2011 Nicolas Sarkozy made his first presidential visit to the Pacific islands. During his visit he endorsed the Government's recent decision to use the indigenous 'Kanak' flag alongside the French tricolour in all official settings. He also appealed for restraint between different political groups and condemned the violence on Maré Island earlier that month when, during a blockade of the island's airport in a dispute over high local air fares and land ownership, four people had been killed and more than 20 injured in clashes between armed groups.

At elections to the French Senate in September 2011, New Caledonia contested two seats, having been allocated an additional seat. Pierre Frogier and Hilarion Vendégou, both representing the UMP group, were successful, ending Frogier's long-standing mandate as a deputy of the French National Assembly. At the French presidential election of 2012, Sarkozy secured the largest share of the vote in New Caledonia in the second round in May, winning 63.0%, but was defeated nationwide by François Hollande of the Parti Socialiste. Sarkozy had reaffirmed his desire for New Caledonia to remain within the French Republic during his electoral campaign, while pro-independence groups had urged voters to support Hollande. Elections to the National Assembly were conducted in June. Philippe Gomès and Sonia Lagarde, both representing Calédonie Ensemble, were narrowly elected as New Caledonia's deputies in a second round of voting, after coming in second place in the first round. Gomès defeated Jean-Pierre Djaïwé of the FLNKS in the constituency previously held by Frogier (where the Rassemblement-UMP candidate, Éric Gay, had come only third in the first round), while Lagarde's victory was over incumbent Rassemblement-UMP deputy Gaël Yanno. Both Gomès and Lagarde subsequently joined a new centre-right parliamentary group in the National Assembly, the Union des Démocrates et Indépendants, which became a political party in September; while affiliating themselves to this new party, they affirmed the political autonomy of Calédonie Ensemble and its members.

Meanwhile, Calédonie Ensemble also secured the presidency of the Congress in August 2012, when Gérard Poadja defeated the incumbent, Roch Wamytan, the FLNKS-UC candidate, in a third round of voting. Senator Frogier resigned as President of the South Province in September in order to devote himself to revitalizing Le Rassemblement-UMP, following its poor performance in the legislative elections in June. Cynthia Ligeard, also of Le Rassemblement-UMP and hitherto Vice-President of the province, was elected as his successor.

The new French Minister for Overseas Territories, Victorin Lurel, made his first official visit to New Caledonia in late November 2012 in preparation for the 10th round of talks between the signatories to the Nouméa Accord, which was hosted by French Prime Minister Jean-Marc Ayrault in Paris in early December. During the discussions the French Government provided assurances regarding the fulfilment of existing commitments, including the provision of general development assistance and long-promised funding for the construction of two new schools. As regards the ongoing process of transferring responsibility for certain areas to New Caledonia, the Prime Minister announced the establishment of an inter-ministerial structure charged with assisting the New Caledonian authorities to exercise their new powers. The signatories welcomed the recent decision of the Congress to create a commission to consider the contentious issue of designing a new single flag (pending which the 'Kanak' flag and the French national flag would continue to be displayed together), and decided that a 'conference of Presidents', involving those of the Provincial Assemblies, the local Council of Ministers and the Congress, should be formed to consider changes to the division of fiscal resources between the three provinces, the current system being unfavourable to the South Province.

Gomès resigned from his post in the collegial Government in mid-December 2012, being replaced by Frédéric de Greslan, also of Calédonie Ensemble. At the same time the party lodged a motion of censure against the Government with the Congress, claiming that insufficient progress was being made in implementing political, economic and social reforms and that the principles of collegiality and solidarity were not being respected. However, this was convincingly defeated three days later, by 36 votes to 18.

Jean-Jaques Brot took office as the French High Commissioner in New Caledonia on 27 February 2013, following the retirement of the incumbent Dupuy. French Prime Minister Jean-Marc Ayrault visited New Caledonia in July, underlining France's commitment to the final phase of the Nouméa Accord, providing for the organization of a self-determination referendum between 2014 and 2018. In August Wamytan of the FLNKS-UC reassumed the presidency of the Congress following his victory (in three rounds of voting) over two anti-independence candidates, the incumbent Poadja, of Calédonie Ensemble, and Loueckhote of the RPC.

In February 2014, in the run-up to the legislative elections scheduled to be held in May, Wamytan claimed that there were major discrepancies in the two electoral rolls of New Caledonia (the Special Roll for those eligible to vote and the Annex Table for those not eligible). The congressional President asserted that, in contravention of the Nouméa Accord, around 6,700 of those registered on the Special Roll had taken up residency in New Caledonia after 1998, and that furthermore some 2,000 young indigenous Kanak voters who should have been listed on the Special Roll were instead on the Annex Table, which allowed them to vote only in elections to the French Parliament. Conversely, a number of anti-independence politicians claimed that some 4,000 Kanaks had wrongly been included on the Special Roll. The French Government sent a group of senior magistrates to New Caledonia to investigate the various allegations.

Regional Affairs

During a visit to Nouméa in September 2008, the French Minister of Defence, Hervé Morin, stated that the number of French military personnel stationed in New Caledonia was to be reduced by 10%–15%, partly owing to the islands' proximity to the regional power of Australia. New Caledonia was to be designated as a regional hub for marine defence. Closer co-operation with the armed forces of both Australia and New Zealand was envisaged following visits to Nouméa by senior delegations from these two countries in April 2009. A new defence co-operation agreement between France and Australia entered into force in July 2009, and in March 2010 a senior delegation, which included the French High Commissioner in New Caledonia, the President of the local Government and the Presidents of the three provinces, was invited to visit Australia, where the leadership hoped to enlist support for New Caledonia's objective of becoming a full (rather than an associate) member of the Pacific Islands Forum (see p. 416). Other matters under discussion included bilateral trade relations. In November the first annual bilateral consultation between New Caledonia and Australia took place. New Caledonia's application for full membership of the Pacific Islands Forum was rejected at a meeting of the organization in September 2011.

In February 2010 a bilateral co-operation agreement with Vanuatu, first signed in June 2006, was renewed for a period of five years. The accord provided for greater collaboration in the areas of education, health, culture, trade, law and order, and good governance. In June 2010 a mission of the Melanesian Spearhead Group (MSG), led by the Prime Minister of Vanuatu, Edward Natapei, and including senior ministers from Fiji, Papua New Guinea and Solomon Islands, visited New Caledonia and expressed concern at the slow progress being made in implementing the Nouméa Accord, and in particular at the persistent economic and social imbalance between the provinces of New Caledonia. The pro-independence organization FLNKS, which is a member of the MSG, hosted the Group's summit meeting which took place in Nouméa in June 2013, under the chairmanship of party spokesman Victor Tutugoro.

CONSTITUTION AND GOVERNMENT

New Caledonia was designated as an Overseas Country (Pays d'Outre-Mer) in 1999. Its status of Collectivité *sui generis*, conferred following a constitutional revision of 2003, is unique within the French Republic in that the local assembly is permitted to pass its own laws and a local citizenship may be bestowed upon permanent residents. The French Government is represented in New Caledonia by its High Commissioner, and controls a number of important spheres, including external relations and defence. In July 1989 administrative reforms were introduced, as stipulated in the Matignon Accord (which had been approved by national referendum in November 1988). New Caledonia was divided into three Provinces (North, South and Loyalty Islands), each governed by an assembly, which is elected on a proportional basis. The members of the three Provincial Assemblies together form the Congress. Members are subject to re-election every five years. The responsibilities of the Congress include New Caledonia's budget and fiscal affairs, infrastructure and primary education, while the responsibilities of the Provincial Assemblies include local economic development, land reform and cultural affairs. The Government of New Caledonia is elected by the Congress, and comprises between seven and 11 members. Under the terms of the Nouméa Accord (which was approved by a referendum in November 1998), the Government replaces the French High Commissioner as New Caledonia's executive authority. A gradual transfer of power from metropolitan France to local institutions was to be effected over a period of between 15 and 20 years under the terms of the Nouméa Accord.

In addition, New Caledonia elects two deputies to the French National Assembly in Paris and two representatives to the French Senate on the basis of universal adult suffrage; one Economic and Social Councillor is also nominated. New Caledonia may also be represented at the European Parliament.

REGIONAL AND INTERNATIONAL CO-OPERATION

New Caledonia forms part of the Franc Zone (see p. 329). It is an associate member of the UN's Economic and Social Commission for Asia and the Pacific (ESCAP, see p. 28) and a member, in its own right, of the Pacific Community (see p. 412). New Caledonia became an associate member of the Pacific Islands Forum (see p. 416) in 2006. New Caledonia's application for full membership of the Pacific Islands Forum was rejected at a meeting of the organization in September 2011. The Front de Libération Nationale Kanak Socialiste (FLNKS) was admitted to the Melanesian Spearhead Group in 1990.

ECONOMIC AFFAIRS

In 2000, according to World Bank estimates, New Caledonia's gross national income (GNI) at average 1998–2000 prices totalled US $2,989.6m., equivalent to $14,060 per head (or $22,210 per head on an international purchasing-power parity basis). During 2003–12, it was estimated, the population rose by an average of 1.5% per year. According to the UN Economic and Social Commission for Asia and the Pacific (ESCAP), gross domestic product (GDP) per head increased, in real terms, at an average annual rate of 1.9% in 2001–11. Overall GDP increased at an average annual rate of 3.5% over the same period. According to UN estimates, GDP expanded by 2.9% in 2012.

Agriculture, forestry and fishing contributed only an estimated 1.3% of GDP in 2010. In 2012 1.8% of the employed labour force were engaged in the sector. Maize, yams, sweet potatoes and coconuts have traditionally been the principal crops, and pumpkins (squash) became an important export crop for the Japanese market from the 1990s. Livestock consists mainly of cattle, pigs and poultry. The main fisheries products are albacore, tuna and prawns (most of which are exported to Japan). The aquaculture industry has expanded steadily, with production of blue shrimp reaching 1,561 metric tons in 2011, in comparison with 691 tons in 1994. In 2012 exports of marine products were worth 1,942m. francs CFP, thus accounting for 1.6% of total exports. According to UN estimates, the GDP of the agricultural sector was estimated to have decreased at an average rate of 0.1% per year in 2003–12; agricultural GDP rose by 9.8% in 2011, but by only 0.8% in 2012.

Industry (comprising mining, manufacturing, construction and utilities) provided an estimated 26.6% of GDP in 2010. The industrial sector employed 23.7% of the working population in 2012. According to UN estimates, the GDP of the industrial sector expanded at an average rate of 2.9% per year in 2003–12; industrial GDP increased by 1.3% in 2012.

Although mining employed only 1.8% of New Caledonia's working population in 2012, it constitutes the most important industrial activity. In 2010 the mining and processing of nickel contributed an estimated 8.4% of GDP. New Caledonia is a major producer of ferro-nickel and is believed to possess about one-quarter of the world's known nickel reserves. After Russia and Canada, New Caledonia is currently the world's third largest producer of nickel. Output of nickel ore totalled 9.7m wet tons in 2012. In that year the export revenue from nickel ore, ferro-nickel and nickel matte amounted to a total of 106,876m. francs CFP, accounting for 87.2% of total export revenue. Following various delays, the Goro Nickel plant, one of the largest such construction projects in the world, was not expected to reach full production capacity until some point in 2014, after which it was anticipated that 60,000 metric tons of nickel and at least 4,300 tons of cobalt would be produced annually. The similarly controversial Koniambo facility, with an annual production capacity of 60,000 tons, entered into production in April 2013, and was expected to reach full production levels at the end of 2014. In 1999 a joint French and Australian research mission made an offshore discovery of what was believed to be the world's largest gas deposit, measuring an estimated 18,000 sq km. It was hoped that this might indicate the presence of considerable petroleum reserves. According to UN estimates, the GDP of the mining sector (including utilities) expanded at an average annual rate of 1.2% in 2003–12; sectoral GDP increased by 23.1% in 2011, but by only 1.4% in 2012.

The manufacturing sector, which engaged 10.5% of the employed labour force in 2012, consists mainly of small and medium-sized enterprises, most of which are situated around the capital, Nouméa, producing building materials, furniture, salted fish, fruit juices and perishable foods. Food-processing and other manufacturing activities accounted for an estimated 6.5% of GDP in 2010.

The construction sector provided an estimated 10.3% of GDP in 2010, and engaged 9.8% of the employed labour force in 2012. According to UN estimates, the GDP of the construction sector expanded at an average annual rate of 5.3% in 2003–12; sectoral GDP increased by 11.7% in 2011, but by only 1.1% in 2012.

Electrical energy is provided mainly by thermal power stations (some 80% in 2004), by hydroelectric plants, and more recently by wind power. Mineral products accounted for 23.9% of total imports in 2012. As part of the Government's plans to reduce expensive imports of diesel fuel, six 5-MW wind farms have been established at two different sites, with a combined total of more than 100 hurricane-proof turbines producing electricity for about 50,000 people. Plans for the nickel plant at Koniambo envisaged the construction of a 390-MW power station. In 2012 production of electric energy reached an estimated 2,264m. kWh.

Service industries contributed an estimated 72.1% of GDP in 2010, and engaged 74.5% of the employed labour force in 2012. According to UN estimates, the GDP of the services sector increased at an average annual rate of 3.5% in 2003–12. The GDP of the services sector increased by 3.3% in 2012. Although service industries, notably tourism, continue to make the largest contribution to the New Caledonian economy, the tourism sector has failed to witness an expansion similar to that experienced in many other Pacific islands, and tourist arrivals have been intermittently affected by political unrest. The majority of tourists come from France, Australia and Japan. The number of visitor arrivals by air increased slightly from 111,875 in 2011 to 112,204 in 2012. Over the same period the number of visiting cruise-ship passengers rose from 235,684 to 277,941. Receipts from tourism amounted to €133.3m. in 2010.

In 2012 New Caledonia's merchandise trade deficit was 161,764m. francs CFP, and there was a deficit of 175,396m. francs CFP on the current account of the balance of payments in that year. The principal imports in 2012 were mineral products, machinery and electrical equipment, food products, beverages and tobacco, transport equipment, chemical products, and base metals and articles. The principal exports in that year remained nickel products, prawns and fish. France was the main supplier of imports in 2012, accounting for 22.2% of the total. Other important suppliers of imports were Singapore and Australia. The principal markets for New Caledonia's exports in 2012 were France, representing 17.8% of the total, Japan, the Republic of Korea, Taiwan, the People's Republic of China and Australia.

The 2011 territorial budget projected expenditure of 30,558m. francs CFP. Over the period 2011–15 France was to provide development assistance of 45,000m. francs CFP for New Caledonia. The annual rate of inflation in Nouméa averaged 1.9% in 2003–12. Consumer prices rose by 1.8% in 2012. In 2011 the total of those registered as unemployed averaged 6,873, equivalent to 7.3% of the total labour force.

The economy of New Caledonia has been dominated by the nickel industry. The Koniambo mining project, which became operational in April 2013, was expected to achieve production capacity of 60,000 metric tons of nickel metal per year by the end of 2014 (equivalent to 5% of global production). The Goro plant was scheduled to generate a similar output by that date, but production in 2012–13 was substantially lower than expected, owing to significant technical problems that halted production for several months, casting doubt on the future profitability of the facility. Both operations were to continue to receive substantial tax concessions from the French Government. A nickel stabilization fund was also established: with an initial allocation of 1,500m. francs CFP, the fund was intended to counter substantial fluctuations in international nickel prices, which decreased by two-thirds during 2009, but rose by nearly 40% in 2010 (largely owing to Chinese demand for stainless steel). However, prices were weak in 2011 and 2012, declining by 23.4% on average during the latter year, with world supply exceeding demand—the same situation, of oversupply and declining prices on the global market, prevailed during 2013. Despite the fall in revenue from nickel exports, the rest of the economy performed quite well, with the rate of growth of GDP decelerating only slightly, from 3.3% in 2011 to 2.9% in 2012, according to UN figures. The number of tourist arrivals declined to its lowest level for 15 years in 2009, largely as a result of the global economic downturn. Nevertheless, a continued decrease in arrivals by air in 2010 was offset by a substantial increase in cruise-ship visitors. There was a further strong expansion, of 26.8%, in the number of cruise-ship visitors in 2011, while the holding of the Pacific Games in New Caledonia in August–September that year contributed to a 13.8% increase in arrivals by air. More modest rises in cruise-ship visitors and air arrivals, of 17.9% and 0.3%, respectively, were recorded in 2012. The rising cost of living, particularly of food, energy and transport, resulted in demonstrations and industrial action throughout 2011. In November 2012 legislation adopted by the French legislature aimed at addressing the high cost of living in its overseas territories included provisions on curbing bank fees in New Caledonia, which were of particular concern; overall, prices in New Caledonia were some 34% higher on average than in metropolitan France, while food prices were up to 90% higher. Nevertheless, large-scale protests against high consumer prices continued in 2013, with a 12-day general strike being organized in May. To end the strike, the authorities agreed to lower by 10% the prices of around 500 products deemed essential to consumer requirements, to freeze prices of other goods (with the exception of alcohol and tobacco), to introduce subsidies for domestic air travel, and to reduce telecommunications costs and bank and health care fees. These measures were to remain in place until the end of 2014.

PUBLIC HOLIDAYS

2015: 1 January (New Year's Day), 6 April (Easter Monday), 1 May (Labour Day), 8 May (Liberation Day), 14 May (Ascension Day), 25 May (Whit Monday), 14 July (Fall of the Bastille), 15 August (Assumption), 24 September (Anniversary of possession by France), 1 November (All Saints' Day), 11 November (Armistice Day), 25 December (Christmas Day).

Statistical Survey

Source (unless otherwise stated): Institut de la Statistique et des Etudes Economiques, BP 823, 98845 Nouméa; tel. 275481; fax 288148; internet www.isee.nc.

AREA AND POPULATION

Area (sq km): New Caledonia island (Grande Terre) 16,372; Loyalty Islands 1,981 (Lifou 1,207, Maré 642, Ouvéa 132); Isle of Pines 152; Belep Archipelago 70; Total 18,575 (7,172 sq miles).

Population: 230,789 at census of 31 August 2004; 245,580 at census of 27 July 2009. *Population by Province* (2009 census): Loyalty Islands 17,436; North Province 45,137; South Province 183,007. *2014* (UN estimate at mid-year): 259,823 (Source: UN, *World Population Prospects: The 2012 Revision*).

Density (mid-2014): 14.0 per sq km.

Population by Age and Sex (UN estimates at mid-2014): *0–14:* 58,206 (males 29,906, females 28,300); *15–64:* 175,439 (males 88,668, females 86,771); *65 and over:* 26,178 (males 12,669, females 13,509); *Total* 259,823 (males 131,243, females 128,580) (Source: UN, *World Population Prospects: The 2012 Revision*.

Ethnic Groups (2009 census): Indigenous Kanaks (Melanesians) 99,078; French and other Europeans 71,721; Wallisians and Futunians (Polynesian) 21,262; Tahitians (Polynesian) 4,985; Indonesians 3,985; Others 44,549.

Principal Towns (population of communes at 2009 census): Nouméa (capital) 97,579; Le Mont-Dore 25,683; Dumbéa 24,103; Païta 16,358.

Births, Marriages and Deaths (2010): Registered live births 4,178 (birth rate 16.7 per 1,000); Registered marriages 908 (marriage rate 3.6 per 1,000); Registered deaths 1,191 (death rate 4.8 per 1,000).

Life Expectancy (years at birth, 2011): 76.0 (males 73.2; females 79.0). Source: World Bank, World Development Indicators database.

Economically Active Population (salaried workers, annual averages, 2011): Agriculture, hunting, forestry and fishing 1,528; Mining and quarrying 1,534; Manufacturing 8,958; Electricity, gas and water 1,390; Construction 8,518; Trade, and repairs of vehicles and domestic goods 9,883; Hotels and restaurants 4,886; Transport and communications 5,298; Financing activities 2,182; Real estate and business services 7,687; Public administration 802; Education 2,716; Health and welfare 2,206; Other private sector services 5,175; Non-market services 24,034; *Total employed* 86,797; Unemployed 6,873; *Total labour force* 93,670. *2012:* Agriculture, hunting, forestry and fishing 1,640; Mining and quarrying 1,590; Manufacturing 9,317; Electricity, gas and water 1,452; Construction 8,669; Trade, and repairs of vehicles and domestic goods 9,990; Hotels and restaurants 4,887; Transport and communications 5,215; Financing activities 2,147; Real estate and business services 8,262; Public administration 807; Education 2,786; Health and welfare 2,417; Other private sector services 5,179; Non-market services 24,550; Total employed 88,908.

HEALTH AND WELFARE

Key Indicators

Total Fertility Rate (children per woman, 2007): 2.2.

Physicians (per 1,000 head, 2008): 2.2.

Hospital Beds (per 1,000 head, 2003): 3.7.

Total Carbon Dioxide Emissions ('000 metric tons, 2010): 3,920.0.

Carbon Dioxide Emissions Per Head (metric tons, 2010): 15.7.

For definitions, see explanatory note on p. vi.

AGRICULTURE, ETC.

Principal Crops ('000 metric tons, 2012, FAO estimates): Maize 3.0; Potatoes 1.7; Sweet potatoes 1.7; Cassava 1.5; Yams 6.0; Coconuts 19.0; Vegetables (incl. melons) 5.3; Bananas 0.8.

Livestock ('000 head, year ending September 2012, FAO estimates): Horses 12.0; Cattle 92.0; Pigs 37.5; Sheep 2.4; Goats 8.2; Poultry 600.

Livestock Products (metric tons, 2012): Cattle meat 3,408; Pig meat 2,550; Chicken meat 848; Cows' milk 265 (FAO estimate); Hen eggs 3,050 (FAO estimate).

Forestry ('000 cu m, 2012, FAO estimates): *Roundwood Removals:* Sawlogs and veneer logs 12.7; Fuel wood 12.2; Other industrial wood 2.0; Total 26.9. *Sawnwood Production:* 3.3 (all broadleaved) in 1994. *1995–2012:* Sawnwood production assumed to be unchanged from 1995 (FAO estimates).

Fishing (metric tons, live weight, 2011): Capture 3,737 (Albacore 1,736; Yellowfin tuna 585; Other marine fishes 282; Sea cucumbers 339); Aquaculture 1,561 (Blue shrimp 1,539); *Total catch* 5,298 (excl. trochus shells 144).

Source: FAO.

MINING

Production (2012, provisional): Nickel ore (metal content, '000 metric tons) 62.2; Nickel ore ('000 wet tons) 9,659.

INDUSTRY

Production (2012 unless otherwise indicated, provisional): Ferro-nickel 43,030 metric tons (nickel content); Nickel matte 13,417 metric tons (nickel content); Electric energy 2,264 million kWh; Cement 138,000 metric tons (2011, estimate, Source: US Geological Survey).

FINANCE

Currency and Exchange Rates: see French Polynesia.

French Government Budget Expenditure ('000 million francs CFP, incl. military expenditure, preliminary): 137.0 in 2009; 147.2 in 2010; 147.3 in 2011.

Territorial Budget (million francs CFP, 2011): *Revenue:* Current 28,236 (Direct taxes 11,403, Indirect taxes 10,537, Other 6,296); Capital 2,095; Total 30,331. *Expenditure:* Current 27,149 (Transfers to provinces 7,430); Capital 3,410; Total 30,558.

Money Supply (million francs CFP at 31 December 2012): Currency in circulation 17,351; Demand deposits 255,688; *Total money* 273,039. Source: Institut d'Emission d'Outre-Mer.

Cost of Living (Consumer Price Index for Nouméa, December each year; base: December 2010 = 100): All items 102.6 in 2011; 104.3 in 2012.

Gross Domestic Product (US $ million at constant 2005 prices): 7,343.7 in 2010; 7,588.8 in 2011; 7,806.2 in 2012. Source: UN Statistics Division, National Accounts Main Aggregates Database.

Expenditure on the Gross Domestic Product (million francs CFP at current prices, 2011, estimates): Government final consumption expenditure 209,114; Private final consumption expenditure 540,670; Gross fixed capital formation 378,301; Change in inventories –13,660; *Total domestic expenditure* 1,114,426; Exports of goods and services 180,793; *Less* Imports of goods and services 447,373; *GDP in purchasers' values* 847,847.

Gross Domestic Product by Economic Activity (€ million at current prices, 2010, estimates): Agriculture, hunting, forestry and fishing 9,760; Nickel mining and processing 62,304; Food processing 15,038; Miscellaneous manufacturing 33,616; Electricity, gas and water 9,596; Construction 76,552; Trade 97,944; Transport and telecommunications 54,559; Banks and insurance 27,734; Business services 57,276; Services to households 161,595; Public administration 134,104; *Sub-total* 740,079; *Less* Financial intermediation services indirectly measured 19,488; *Gross value added in basic prices* 720,591; Taxes and subsidies on products (net) 91,507; *GDP in market prices* 812,098.

Balance of Payments (million francs CFP, 2012): Exports of goods 122,579; Imports of goods –284,343; *Trade balance* –161,764; Exports of services 50,970; Imports of services –127,607; *Balance on goods and services* –238,401; Other income received 54,432; Other income paid –51,359; *Balance on goods, services and income* –235,328; Current transfers received 86,699; Current transfers paid –26,768; *Current balance* –175,396; Capital account (net) 645; Direct investment (net) 221,892; Portfolio investment (net) 7,677; Other investment (net) –36,025; *Overall balance* 18,792. Source: Institut d'Emission d'Outre-Mer.

EXTERNAL TRADE

Principal Commodities (million francs CFP, 2012): *Imports:* Food products, beverages and tobacco 40,266; Mineral products 71,983; Chemical products 21,345; Plastic and rubber articles 11,683; Paper and paper articles 4,903; Textiles and textile articles 7,043; Base metals and articles thereof 17,385; Machinery and mechanical appliances, and electrical equipment 47,810; Transport equipment 35,858; Total (incl. others) 301,352. *Exports:* Nickel ore 22,799; Ferro-nickel 64,002; Nickel matte 20,075; Marine products 1,942 (Prawns 1,145); Total (incl. others) 122,557.

Principal Trading Partners (million francs CFP, 2012): *Imports:* Australia 32,771; France 66,941; Japan 5,789; New Zealand 13,224; Singapore 56,097; USA 12,100; Total (incl. others) 301,352. *Exports:* Australia 11,378; China, People's Republic 12,664; France 21,864; Japan 18,852; Korea, Republic 14,559; South Africa 3,617; Taiwan 14,264; USA 5,789; Total (incl. others) 122,557.

TRANSPORT

Road Traffic (motor vehicles in use, 2001): Total 85,499.

Shipping (2012 unless otherwise indicated): *Domestic Traffic* ('000 metric tons): Freight unloaded 3,280; Freight loaded 94. *International Traffic:* ('000 metric tons, 2010): Freight unloaded 109,006; Freight loaded 496,113. *Flag Registered Fleet* (at 31 December 2013): Vessels 1; Total displacement 821 grt (Source: Lloyd's List Intelligence—www.lloydslistintelligence.com).

Civil Aviation (La Tontouta international airport, Nouméa, 2012): *Aircraft Movements:* Aircraft arriving 1,906; Aircraft departing 1,906. *Passenger Traffic:* Passengers arriving 243,693; Passengers departing 242,866. *Freight Traffic:* Freight unloaded 4,378 metric tons; Freight loaded 1,254 metric tons. *Mail:* Mail arriving 807 metric tons; Mail departing 189 metric tons. (Source: Department of Civil Aviation).

TOURISM

Foreign Arrivals: *Arrivals by Air:* 98,562 in 2010; 111,875 in 2011; 112,204 in 2012. *Cruise-ship Passenger Arrivals:* 183,245 in 2010; 235,684 in 2011; 277,941 in 2012.

Tourist Arrivals by Country of Residence (arrivals by air, 2012): Australia 17,729; France 38,746; Japan 17,430; New Zealand 6,242; Total (incl. others) 112,204 (Source: Institut d'Emission d'Outre-Mer).

Tourism Receipts (€ million): 137.8 in 2008; 133.8 in 2009; 133.3 in 2010.

COMMUNICATIONS MEDIA

Telephones (2012): 80,000 main lines in use.

Mobile Cellular Telephones (2012): 231,000 subscribers.

Internet Subscribers (2009): 33,100.

Broadband Subscribers (2012): 47,900.

Source: International Telecommunication Union.

EDUCATION

Pre-primary (2012 unless otherwise indicated): 83 schools (2004); 12,732 pupils.

Primary (2012): 269 schools (incl. pre-primary); 1,960 teachers (incl. pre-primary); 22,603 pupils (incl. special education).

Secondary (2012): 77 schools; 2,770 teachers (incl. higher); 32,486 pupils.

Higher (2005): 4 institutions; 111 teaching staff.

Adult Literacy Rate (1989): Males 94.0%; Females 92.1%.

Directory

The Government

(April 2014)

STATE GOVERNMENT

High Commissioner: JEAN-JACQUES BROT (took office 27 February 2013).

Secretary-General: THIERRY SUQUET.

LOCAL GOVERNMENT

Secretary-General: ALAIN SWETSCHKIN.

COUNCIL OF MINISTERS

The coalition Government is led by L'Avenir Ensemble and includes Calédonie Ensemble (EC), the Union Calédonienne (UC), Le Rassemblement-UMP, Union Nationale pour l'Indépendance (UNI) and the Parti Travailliste.

President, responsible for Regional Co-operation, External Relations, Customs, Agriculture Fisheries and Animal Rearing, and International Air Transport: HAROLD MARTIN (L'Avenir Ensemble).

Vice-President and Minister for Mines, Infrastructure, Development Plan NC 2025, Domestic Air Travel and Transport (Surface and Marine): GILBERT TYUIENON (UC).

Minister for the Budget, Financial Affairs, Taxation, the Digital Economy, and Energy: SONIA BACKES (Le Rassemblement-UMP).

Minister for the Civil Service: FRÉDÉRIC DE GRESLAN (CE).

Minister for Economy, External Trade, Land Management, Sustainable Development, Conservation of Natural Resources and the Exclusive Economic Zone: ANTHONY LECREN (UC).

Minister for Culture and Citizenship, Women Affairs and Relations with the Communes: DÉWÉ GORODEY (UNI).

Minister for Youth and Sports, Primary and Secondary Education and Social Dialogue: JEAN-CLAUDE BRIAULT (Le Rassemblement-UMP).

Minister for Traffic and Road Safety: PHILIPPE DUNOYER (CE).

Minister for Human Resources, Professional Integration, Revenue Affairs, and Labour and Employment: GEORGES MANDAOUE (Parti Travailliste).

Minister for Health, Social Protection, Solidarity, the Disabled, and Vocational Training: SYLVIE ROBINEAU (L'Avenir Ensemble).

Minister for Ecology and Sustainable Development: HÉLÈNE IEKAWE (CE).

GOVERNMENT OFFICES

Office of the High Commissioner: Haut-commissariat de la République en Nouvelle-Calédonie, 1 ave du Maréchal Foch, BP C5, 98844 Nouméa Cedex; tel. 266300; fax 272828; e-mail haussariat@nouvelle-caledonie.gouv.fr; internet www.nouvelle-caledonie.gouv.fr.

Secretariat-General of the High Commissioner: 9 bis rue de la République, BP C5, 98844 Nouméa Cedex; tel. 246711; fax 246740; internet www.nouvelle-caledonie.gouv.fr.

New Caledonian Government: Présidence du Gouvernement, 8 route des Artifices, Artillerie, BP M2, 98849 Nouméa Cedex; tel. 246565; fax 246580; e-mail presidence@gouv.nc; internet www.gouv.nc.

Office of the Secretary-General of the Government of New Caledonia: 8 route des Artifices, BP M2, 98849 Nouméa Cedex; tel. 246532; fax 246620; e-mail alain.swetschkin@gouv.nc; internet www.gouv.nc.

GOVERNMENT DEPARTMENTS

Department of the Budget and Financial Affairs (DBAF): 18 ave Paul Doumer, BP M2, 98849 Nouméa Cedex; tel. 256083; fax 283133; e-mail dbaf@gouv.nc.

Department of Civil Aviation: 179 rue Gervolino, BP H01, 98849 Nouméa Cedex; tel. 265200; fax 265202; e-mail dac-nc@aviation-civile.gouv.fr; internet www.dac.nc.

Department of Computer Technology (DTSI): 127 rue Arnold Daly, Magenta Ouemo, BP 15101, 98804 Nouméa Cedex; tel. 275888; fax 281919; e-mail dtsi@gouv.nc.

Department of Cultural and Customary Affairs (DACC): 8 rue de Sébastopol, BP T5, 98852 Nouméa Cedex; tel. 269766; fax 269767; e-mail secretariat.dacc@gouv.nc.

Department of Economic Affairs (DAE): 7 rue du Général Galliéni, BP 2672, 98846 Nouméa Cedex; tel. 232250; fax 232251; e-mail dae@gouv.nc; internet www.dae.gouv.nc.

Department of Education (DENC): Immeuble Foch, 19 ave du Maréchal Foch, BP 8244, 98807 Nouméa Cedex; tel. 239600; fax 272921; e-mail denc@gouv.nc; internet www.denc.gouv.nc.

Department of Fiscal Affairs (DSF): Hôtel des Impôts, 13 rue de la Somme, BP D2, 98848 Nouméa Cedex; tel. 257500; fax 251166; e-mail dsf@gouv.nc; internet www.dsf.gouv.nc.

Department of Health and Social Services (DASS): 5 rue Général Galliéni, BP N4, 98851 Nouméa Cedex; tel. 243700; fax 243702; e-mail dass@gouv.nc; internet www.dass.gouv.nc.

Department of Human Resources and Civil Service (DRHFPT): 18 ave Paul Doumer, BP M2, 98849 Nouméa Cedex; tel. 256000; fax 274700; e-mail drhfpt@gouv.nc; internet www.drhfpt.gouv.nc.

Department of Industry, Mines and Energy (DIMENC): 1 ter rue Edouard Unger, 1ère, Vallée du Tir, BP 465, 98845 Nouméa Cedex; tel. 270230; fax 272345; e-mail dimenc@gouv.nc; internet www.dimenc.gouv.nc.

Department of Infrastructure, Topography and Land Transport (DITTT): 1 bis rue Edouard Unger, 1ère, Vallée du Tir, BP A2, 98848 Nouméa Cedex; tel. 032800; fax 281760; e-mail dittt@gouv.nc; internet www.dittt.gouv.nc.

Department of Labour and Employment (DTE): 12 rue de Verdun, BP 141, 98845 Nouméa Cedex; tel. 275572; fax 270494; e-mail dte@gouv.nc; internet www.dtnc.gouv.nc.

Department of Veterinary, Food and Rural Affairs (DAVAR): 209 rue Auguste Bénébig, Haut Magenta, BP 256, 98845 Nouméa Cedex; tel. 255100; fax 255129; e-mail davar@gouv.nc; internet www.davar.gouv.nc.

Department of Vocational Training (DFPC): 19 ave du Maréchal Foch, BP 110, 98845 Nouméa Cedex; tel. 246622; fax 281661; e-mail dfpc@gouv.nc; internet www.dfpc.gouv.nc.

Department of Youth and Sports (DJS): 23 rue Jean Jaurès, BP 810, 98845 Nouméa Cedex; tel. 252384; fax 254585; e-mail djsnc@gouv.nc; internet www.djs.gouv.nc.

Legislature

PROVINCIAL ASSEMBLIES

Members of the Provincial Assemblies are elected on a proportional basis for a five-year term. Each Provincial Assembly elects its President. A number of the members of the Provincial Assemblies sit together to make up the Congress of New Caledonia. The Assembly of the North Province has 22 members (including 15 sitting for the Congress), the Loyalty Islands 14 members (including seven for the Congress) and the South Province has 40 members (including 32 for the Congress).

North Province: BP 41, 98860 Koné; tel. 417100; fax 472475; e-mail presidence@province-nord.nc; internet www.province-nord.nc; Pres. PAUL NÉAOUTYINE (UNI-FLNKS).

South Province: Hôtel de la Province Sud, route des Artifices, Port Moselle, BP L1, 98849 Nouméa Cedex; tel. 258000; fax 274900; e-mail cabinet@province-sud.nc; internet www.province-sud.nc; Pres. CYNTHIA LIGEARD (Le Rassemblement-UMP).

Loyalty Islands Province: BP 50, Wé, 98820 Lifou; tel. 455100; fax 451440; e-mail presidence@loyalty.nc; internet www.province-iles.nc; Pres. NÉKO HNÉPEUNE (UNI-FLNKS).

Election, 10 May 2009 (provisional results by province)

Party	North	South	Loyalty Islands
Le Rassemblement-UMP	1	15	—
Union Calédonienne-Front de Libération Nationale Kanak Socialiste (UC-FLNKS)	8	—	6
Calédonie Ensemble (CE)	—	11	—
Union Nationale pour l'Indépendance (UNI)	9	—	—
L'Avenir Ensemble	—	8	—
Front de Libération Nationale Kanak Socialiste (FLNKS)	—	4	—
Union Nationale pour l'Indépendance-Front de Libération Nationale Kanak Socialiste (UNI-FLNKS)	—	—	4
Parti Travailliste	3	—	2
Dynamique Autochtone (Le Mouvement de la Diversité)	—	—	2
Rassemblement pour la Calédonie (RPC)	—	2	—
Une Province Pour Tous	1	—	—
Total	22	40	14

Note: In October 2009, following the confirmation of irregularities in the conduct of the election, notably with regard to the use of proxy votes, the results of the Loyalty Islands were declared invalid by the Council of State in France. The province thus returned to the polls on 6 December: the UC-FLNKS alliance was reported to have retained six seats, the Parti Travailliste increased its representation to four seats, the Libération Kanak Socialiste (LKS) won two seats and two seats were taken by another pro-independence grouping

CONGRESS

A proportion of the members of the three Provincial Assemblies sit together, in Nouméa, as the Congress of New Caledonia. There are 54 members (32 from the South Province, 15 from the North Province and seven from the Loyalty Islands Province) of a total of 76 sitting in the Provincial Assemblies.

President: ROCH WAMYTAN, Congrès de la Nouvelle-Calédonie, 1 blvd Vauban, BP P3, 98851 Nouméa Cedex; tel. 273129; fax 270219; e-mail courrier@congres.nc; internet www.congres.nc.

Election, 10 May 2009 (provisional results for New Caledonia as a whole)

Party	Votes	%	Seats
Le Rassemblement-UMP	19,888	20.60	13
Calédonie Ensemble (CE)	16,253	16.83	10
Union Calédonienne (UC)	11,247	11.65	8
Union Nationale pour l'Indépendance (UNI)	10,162	10.52	8
L'Avenir Ensemble-Le Mouvement de la Diversité	11,308	11.71	6
Parti Travailliste	7,692	7.97	3
Front de Libération Nationale Kanak Socialiste (FLNKS)	5,342	5.53	3
Rassemblement pour la Calédonie (RPC)	4,304	4.46	2
Libération Kanak Socialiste (LKS)	1,852	1.92	1
Others	8,510	8.81	—
Total	96,558	100.00	54

PARLIAMENT

Deputies to the French National Assembly: PHILIPPE GOMÈS (Divers droite—DVD-CE), SONIA LAGARDE (DVD-CE).

Representatives to the French Senate: (elected in September 2011) PIERRE FROGIER (UMP), HILARION VENDÉGOU (UMP).

Political Organizations

L'Avenir Ensemble (AE): 2 bis blvd Vauban, 98800 Nouméa; tel. 281179; fax 281011; e-mail avenirensemble@lagoon.nc; internet www.avenirensemble.nc; f. 2004; combined list incl. fmr mems of Rassemblement pour la Calédonie dans la République and Alliance pour la Calédonie; anti-independence party; supports unification of all ethnic groups; Leader HAROLD MARTIN.

Calédonie Ensemble (CE): 13 route de Vélodrome, 98800 Nouméa; tel. 288905; fax 288906; internet www.caledonieensemble.nc; f. 2008; anti-independence party est. by fmr mems of L'Avenir Ensemble; Leader PHILIPPE GOMÈS.

Fédération des Comités de Coordination des Indépendantistes (FCCI): 42 ter rue de Verdun, Nouméa; internet www.fcci-nc.org; f. 1998; est. by breakaway group of FLNKS; includes Front du Développement des Iles Loyauté and Front Uni de Libération Kanak; Leaders RAPHAËL MAPOU, FRANÇOIS BURCK.

Front Calédonien (FC): extreme right-wing; Leader M. SARRAN.

Front de Libération Nationale Kanak Socialiste (FLNKS): 9 rue Austerlitz, Immeuble SAM3, 98800 Nouméa Cedex; tel. 265880; fax 265887; f. 1984; est. following dissolution of Front Indépendantiste; pro-independence; Spokesman VICTOR TUTUGORO; a grouping of the following parties:

Parti de Libération Kanak (PALIKA): f. 1975; Leader PAUL NÉAOUTYINE.

Rassemblement Démocratique Océanien (RDO): Nouméa; f. 1994; est. by breakaway faction of Union Océanienne (f. 1989); supports Kanak sovereignty; Chair. ALOISIO SAKO.

Union Calédonienne (UC): 4 rue de la Gazelle, Aérodrome de Magenta, Nouméa; tel. 272599; fax 276257; internet union-caledonienne.com; f. 1952; pro-independence; left FLNKS coalition prior to elections of 2004 but subsequently returned; 11,000 mems; Pres. DANIEL GOA; Sec.-Gen. GÉRARD REIGNIER.

Union Progressiste Mélanésienne (UPM): f. 1974; est. as Union Progressiste Multiraciale; Pres. VICTOR TUTUGORO; Sec.-Gen. RENÉ POROU.

Front National (FN): 12 bis rue du Général Mangin, 98800 Nouméa; tel. 258068; fax 258064; e-mail george@province-sud.nc; internet www.frontnational.com; right-wing; Leader GUY GEORGE.

Génération Calédonienne: f. 1995; youth-based; aims to combat corruption in public life; Pres. JEAN-RAYMOND POSTIC.

Le Groupe MUR: BP 1211, 98845 Nouméa Cedex; tel. and fax 419385; coalition of Mouvement des Citoyens Calédoniens, Union Océanienne (f. 1989) and Rassemblement des Océaniens dans la Calédonie; Jt Pres TINO MANUOHALALO (MCC), MICHEL HEMA (UO), MIKAELE TUIFUA (ROC).

Libération Kanak Socialiste (LKS): Maré, Loyalty Islands; moderate, pro-independence; contested the 2009 elections in the Loyalty Islands as Dynamique Autochtone; Leader NIDOÏSH NAISSELINE.

Le Mouvement de la Diversité (LMD): 98802 Nouméa; tel. 997700; fax 240620; f. 2009; allied to L'Avenir Ensemble; Pres. SIMON LOUECKHOTE.

Mouvement Populaire Calédonien (MPC): Nouméa; f. 2013; est. following a split in Le Rassemblement—UMP; Leader GAËL YANNO.

Parti Travailliste: Nouméa; f. 2007; pro-independence; Pres. LOUIS KOTRA UREGEI.

Le Rassemblement-UMP: 13 rue de Sébastopol, BP 306, 98845 Nouméa; tel. 282620; fax 284033; e-mail contact@rassemblement.nc; internet www.rassemblement.nc; f. 1976; est. as Rassemblement pour la Calédonie dans la République; affiliated to the metropolitan

Union pour un Mouvement Populaire; in favour of retaining the status quo in New Caledonia; Leader PIERRE FROGIER; Sec.-Gen. THIERRY SANTA.

A coalition of the following parties:

Centre des Démocrates Sociaux (CDS): f. 1971; Leader JEAN LÈQUES.

Parti Républicain (PR): Leader PIERRE MARESCA.

Rassemblement pour la Calédonie (RPC): 5 rue, Lamartine, Orphanage, 98800 Nouméa; internet rpc1.e-monsite.com; f. 2006; Pres. ISABELLE LAFLEUR.

Union Calédonienne Renouveau (UC Renouveau): Hôtel de la province des îles Loyauté, BP 50, Wé Lifou; tel. 455100; fax 451440; Leader JACQUES LALIE.

Union Nationale pour l'Indépendance (UNI): c/o Le Congrès de la Nouvelle Calédonie, Nouméa ; electoral coalition comprising all the constituents of the FLNK except the UC; Leader PAUL NÉAOUTYINE.

Minor political organizations that participated in the elections of May 2009 included: Avance, Calédonie Mon Pays, Génération Destin Commun, Ouverture Citoyenne, and Patrimoine et Environnement avec les Verts.

Judicial System

Court of Administrative Law: 85 ave du Général de Gaulle, Immeuble Carcopino 3000, 4ème étage, BP 63, 98851 Nouméa Cedex; tel. 250630; fax 250631; e-mail greffe.ta-noumea@juradm.fr; internet www.ta-noumea.juradm.fr; f. 1984; Pres. RÉGIS FRAISSE.

Court of Appeal: Palais de Justice, BP F4, 98848 Nouméa; tel. 279356; fax 269185; e-mail pp.ca-noumea@justice.fr; internet www.ca-noumea.justice.fr; First Pres. THIERRY DRACK; Procurator-Gen. ANNIE BRUNET-FURSTER.

Court of the First Instance: 2 blvd Extérieur, BP F4, 98848 Nouméa; tel. 279372; fax 276531; e-mail p.tpi-noumea@justice.fr; Pres. JEAN PRADAL; Procurator of the Republic CLAIRE LANET; there are 2 subsidiary courts, with resident magistrates, at Koné (North Province) and Wé (Loyalty Islands Province).

Customary Senate of New Caledonia: Sénat Coutumier, 68 ave J. Cook, BP 1059, Nouville; tel. 242000; fax 249320; e-mail senat-coutumier@gouv.nc; f. 1990; consulted by Local Assembly and French Govt on matters affecting land, Kanak tradition and identity; composed of 16 elected mems (2 from the regional council of each of the 8 custom areas) for a 5-year period; Pres. PAUL VAKIÉ.

Religion

The majority of the population is Christian, with Roman Catholics comprising about 55% of the total in 2002. About 3% of the inhabitants, mainly Indonesians, are Muslims.

CHRISTIANITY

The Roman Catholic Church

The Territory comprises a single archdiocese, with an estimated 131,000 adherents in December 2007. The Archbishop participates in the Catholic Bishops' Conference of the Pacific, based in Fiji.

Archbishop of Nouméa: Most Rev. MICHEL-MARIE-BERNARD CALVET, Archevêché, 4 rue Mgr-Fraysse, BP 3, 98845 Nouméa; tel. 265353; fax 265352; e-mail archeveche@ddec.nc; internet www.ddec.nc/diocese.

The Anglican Communion

Within the Church of the Province of Melanesia, New Caledonia forms part of the diocese of Vanuatu. The Archbishop of the Province is the Bishop of Central Melanesia (resident in Honiara, Solomon Islands). At mid-2000 there were an estimated 160 adherents.

Protestant Churches

At mid-2000 there were an estimated 30,000 adherents.

Eglise évangélique en Nouvelle-Calédonie et aux Iles Loyauté: BP 277, Nouméa; f. 1960; Pres. Rev. SAILALI PASSA; Gen. Sec. Rev. TELL KASARHEROU.

Other churches active in the Territory include the Assembly of God, the Free Evangelical Church, the New Apostolic Church, the Pentecostal Evangelical Church, the Presbyterian Church and the Tahitian Evangelical Church. At mid-2000 there were an estimated 15,500 adherents professing other forms of Christianity.

The Press

L'Avenir Calédonien: 10 rue Gambetta, Nouméa; organ of the Union Calédonienne; Dir GABRIEL PAÏTA.

La Calédonie Agricole: BP 111, 98845 Nouméa Cedex; tel. 243160; fax 284587; internet www.chambres-agriculture.fr; quarterly; official publ. of the Chambre d'Agriculture; Pres. GÉRARD PASCO; Man. YANNICK COUETE; Chief Editors PIERRE ARDORINO, SOPHIE GOLFIER; circ. 4,000.

Le Chien Bleu: BP 16018, Nouméa; tel. 288505; fax 261819; e-mail courrier@lechienbleu.nc; internet www.lechienbleu.nc; monthly; satirical; Man. Editor ETIENNE DUTAILLY.

Eglise de Nouvelle-Calédonie: BP 3, 98845 Nouméa; fax 265352; f. 1976; monthly; official publ. of the Roman Catholic Church; circ. 450.

Les Infos: 42 route de l'Anse-Vata, BP 8134, 98807 Nouméa; tel. 251808; fax 251882; e-mail lesinfos@lagoon.nc; weekly; Editor-in-Chief THIERRY SQUILLARIO.

Journal Officiel de la Nouvelle-Calédonie: Imprimerie Administrative, BP M2, 98849, Nouméa Cedex; tel. 256001; fax 256021; e-mail webmestre.juridoc@gouv.nc; internet www.juridoc.gouv.nc; f. 1853; est. as *Bulletin Officiel de la Nouvelle-Calédonie*; present name adopted in 1988; only the paper version is official; twice a week; publ. by Govt of New Caledonia; record of state legislative devts in New Caledonia.

Mwà Vée: Centre Tjibaou, BP 378, 98845 Nouméa; tel. 414555; fax 414556; e-mail adck@adck.nc; f. 1993; quarterly; French; publ. by l'Agence de Développement de la Culture Kanak; Kanak history, culture and heritage; Publr EMMANUEL KASARHE'ROU; Editor GÉRARD DEL RIO.

Les Nouvelles Calédoniennes: 41–43 rue de Sébastopol, BP G5, 98848 Nouméa; tel. 272584; fax 281627; e-mail xserre@canl.nc; internet www.lnc.nc; f. 1971; daily; Publr FRÉDÉRIC AURAND; Gen. Man. FRANÇOIS LEVASSOR; Editor-in-Chief XAVIER SERRE; circ. 20,000.

Tazar: Immeuble Gallieni II, 12 rue de Verdun, 98800 Nouméa; tel. 282277; fax 283443; monthly; publ. by Mission d'Insertion des Jeunes de la Province Sud; youth.

Télé 7 Jours: Route de Vélodrome, BP 2080, 98846 Nouméa Cedex; tel. 284598; weekly.

NEWS AGENCY

Agence France-Presse (AFP): 15 rue Docteur Guégan, 98800 Nouméa; tel. 263033; fax 278699; Correspondent FRANCK MADOEUF.

Publishers

Editions d'Art Calédoniennes: 3 rue Guynemer, BP 1626, Nouméa; tel. 277633; fax 281526; art, reprints, travel.

Editions du Santal: 5 bis rue Emile-Trianon, 98846 Nouméa; tel. and fax 262533; history, art, travel, birth and wedding cards; Dir PAUL-JEAN STAHL.

Grain de Sable: BP 577, 98845 Nouméa; tel. and fax 273057; e-mail graindesable@canl.nc; internet www.pacific-bookin.com; literature, travel; Publr LAURENCE VIALLARD.

Ile de Lumière: BP 8401, Nouméa Sud; tel. 289858; history, politics.

Savannah Editeur SNP: Yacht Marianne, BP 3086, 98846 Nouméa; tel. 784711; e-mail savannahmarc@hotmail.com; f. 1994; est. as Savannah Edns; present name adopted in 2006; sports, travel, leisure; Publr JOËL MARC.

Société d'Etudes Historiques de la Nouvelle-Calédonie: BP 63, 98845 Nouméa; tel. 767155; e-mail seh-nc@lagoon.nc; f. 1969; Pres. VALET GABRIEL.

Broadcasting and Communications

TELECOMMUNICATIONS

Citius: Immeuble Administratif, 1 rue du Contre Amiral Joseph Bouzet, Route de Nouville, 98800 Nouméa; tel. 266604; fax 266642; e-mail visio@citius.nc; internet www.citius.nc; f. 2008; Man. PASCAL BOUTTIER.

Offices des Postes et Télécommunications (OPT): Le Waruna, 2 rue Monchovet, Port Plaisance, 98841 Nouméa Cedex; tel. 268217; fax 262927; e-mail direction@opt.nc; internet www.opt.nc; provides postal and fixed-line tel. services, and operates Mobilis mobile cellular tel. network (f. 2003); Dir-Gen. JEAN-YVES OLLIVAUD.

BROADCASTING

Radio

Nouvelle-Calédonie 1ère: Nouvelle-Calédonie 1ère, 1 rue Maréchal Leclerc, Mont Coffyn, BP G3, 98848 Nouméa Cedex; tel. 239999; fax 239975; e-mail comrfonc@francetv.fr; internet nouvellecaledonie.la1ere.fr; f. 1942; fmrly Radiodiffusion Française d'Outre-mer (RFO); French; relays Radio Australia's French service; Dir-Gen. MICHEL KOPS; Regional Dir WALLES KOTRA.

NRJ Nouvelle-Calédonie: 41–43 rue Sébastopol, BP G5, 98848 Nouméa; tel. 263434; fax 279447; e-mail nrj@nrj.nc; internet www.nrj.nc; f. 1984; Dir RICARDO GREMY.

Radio Djiido (Kanal K): Résidence La Caravelle, 3 rue Sainte Cécile, Vallée du Tir, BP 10459, 98805 Nouméa Cedex; tel. 778768; fax 272187; e-mail radiodjiido@radiodjiido.nc; internet www.radiodjiido.nc; f. 1985; pro-independence community station; broadcasts in French; socio-cultural programmes; 60% local news, 30% regional, 10% international; Station Man. THIERRY KAMÉRÉMOIN; Editor-in-Chief CÉDRICK WAKAHUGNEME.

Radio Océane: 1 ave d'Auteuil, Lotissement FSH, Koutio, 98835 Dumbéa; tel. 410095; fax 410099; e-mail oceane.fm@lagoon.nc; Dir YANN DUVAL.

Radio Rythme Bleu: 8 ave Foch, BP 578, 98845 Nouméa Cedex; tel. 254646; fax 284928; e-mail rrb@lagoon.nc; internet www.rrb.nc; f. 1984; music and local, nat. and int. news; Pres. JEAN-YVES PELTIER; Dir ELIZABETH NOUAR.

Television

RFO-Télé Nouvelle-Calédonie: Réseau France Outre-mer (RFO), 1 rue Maréchal Leclerc, Mont Coffyn, BP G3, 98848 Nouméa Cedex; tel. 239999; fax 239975; internet www.rfo.fr; f. 1965; part of the France Télévisions group, France; 3 channels; Gen. Man. BERNARD JOYEUX; Editor-in-Chief GONZAGUE DE LA BOURDONNAYE.

Canal+ Calédonie: 30 rue de la Somme, BP 1797, 98845 Nouméa; tel. 265343; fax 265338; e-mail abonnement@canal-caledonie.com; internet www.canalcaledonie.com; subsidiary of Canal Plus, France; subscription service; broadcasts 24 hours daily; CEO SERGE LAMAGNÈRE.

Canal Outre-mer (Canal+): Nouméa; f. 1995; cable service.

NCTV: Immeuble Koné-La Grange, rue de la Caférie, 98860 KONÉ; tel. 475880; internet www.nctv.nc; f. 2013; first indigenous television station; Head JEAN PIERRE DJAIWE.

Finance

(cap. = capital; res = reserves; dep. = deposits; m. = million; brs = branches; amounts in francs CFP unless otherwise stated)

BANKING

Agence Française de Développement: 1 rue Barleux, BP J1, 98849 Nouméa Cedex; tel. 242600; fax 282413; e-mail afdnoumea@afd.fr; internet nc.afd.fr; Gen. Man. JEAN-MICHEL SEVERINO; Pres. LAURENCE TUBIANA.

Banque Calédonienne d'Investissement (BCI): 54 ave de la Victoire, BP K5, 98849 Nouméa; tel. 256565; fax 274035; e-mail bci@bci.nc; internet www.bci.nc; f. 1988; cap. 7,500m.; Chair. DIDIER LEROUX; Dir-Gen. JEAN-PIERRE GIANOTTI.

Banque de Nouvelle-Calédonie: 10 ave Foch, BP L3, 98849 Nouméa Cedex; tel. 257402; fax 275619; e-mail contact@bnc.nc; internet www.bnc.nc; f. 1974; adopted present name in 2002; 95.8% owned by Financière Océor, France; cap. 7,999m., dep. 96,878m. (Dec. 2009); Pres. PHILIPPE GARSUAULT; Gen. Man. OLIVIER GUEDSON; 7 brs.

BNP Paribas Nouvelle-Calédonie (France): 37 ave Henri Lafleur, BP K3, 98849 Nouméa Cedex; tel. 258400; fax 258469; e-mail bnp.nc@bnpparibas.com; internet www.bnpparibas.nc; f. 1969 as Banque Nationale de Paris; present name adopted in 2001; cap. €28.0m. (Dec. 2011); CEO PATRICK SOULAGES; 10 brs.

Société Générale Calédonienne de Banque: 44 rue de l'Alma, Siège et Agence Principale, BP G2, 98848 Nouméa Cedex; tel. 256300; fax 256322; e-mail svp.sgcb@sgcb.nc; internet www.sgcb.com; f. 1981; cap. 1,068.3m., res 8,900m., dep. 135,024.3m. (Dec. 2010); Gen. Man. JEAN-PIERRE DUFOUR; Chair. JEAN-LOUIS MATTEI; 21 brs.

INSURANCE

AGF Vie & AGF IART Nouvelle-Calédonie: 99 ave du Générale de Gaulle, BP 152, 98845 Nouméa; tel. 283838; fax 281628; e-mail agfvienc@agfvie.nc; life and general non-life insurance.

GAN Pacifique: 30 route de la Baie des Dames, Immeuble Le Centre-Ducos, BP 7953, 98800 Nouméa Cedex; tel. 243070; fax 278884; e-mail ganoumea@canl.nc; subsidiary of GAN Assurances, France; general non-life insurance; Chair. JEAN-FRANÇOIS LEMOUX; Dir-Gen. PATRICK REYNAUD.

Poe-ma Insurances: 3 rue Sébastopol, BP 8069, 98807 Nouméa; tel. 274263; fax 274267; e-mail info@poema.nc; Bureau Man. FREDERIC DUCOS.

Trade and Industry

DEVELOPMENT ORGANIZATIONS

Agence de Développement de la Culture Kanak (ADCK): Centre Culturel Tjibaou, rue des Accords de Matignon, BP 378, 98845 Nouméa Cedex; tel. 414555; fax 414546; e-mail adck@adck.nc; internet www.adck.nc; Pres. MARIE-CLAUDE TJIBAOU; Dir EMMANUEL KASARHEROU.

Agence de Développement Economique de la Nouvelle-Calédonie (ADECAL): 15 rue Guynemer, BP 2384, 98846 Nouméa Cedex; tel. 249077; fax 249087; e-mail adecal@offratel.nc; internet www.adecal.nc; f. 1995; promotes investment within New Caledonia; Gen. Man. JEAN-MICHEL ARLIE.

Agence de Développement Rural et d'Aménagement Foncier (ADRAF): 1 rue de la Somme, BP 4228, 98847 Nouméa Cedex; tel. 258600; fax 258604; e-mail adraf@adraf.nc; internet www.adraf.nc; f. 1986, reorg. 1989; acquisition and redistribution of land; Chair. MICHEL MATHIEU; Dir-Gen. JULES HMALOKO.

Conseil Economique et Social: 30 route Baie des Dames, Immeuble Le Centre, Ducos, BP 4766, 98847 Nouméa Cedex; tel. 278517; fax 278509; e-mail ces@gouv.nc; internet www.ces.gouv.nc; represents trade unions and other orgs involved in economic, social and cultural life; Pres. YVES TISSANDIER; Sec.-Gen. FRANÇOIS-PAUL BUFNOIR.

Institut Calédonien de Participation (ICAP): 1 rue Barleux, BP J1, 98849 Nouméa; tel. 276218; fax 282280; e-mail icap@icap.nc; internet www.icap.nc; f. 1989; est. to finance devt projects and encourage the Kanak population to participate in the market economy; Pres. PAUL NÉAOUTYINE; Man. YVES GOYETCHE.

Institut pour le Développement des Compétences en Nouvelle-Calédonie: 1 rue de la Somme, BP 497, 98845 Nouméa Cedex; tel. 281082; fax 272079; e-mail idc.nc@idcnc.nc; internet www.idcnc.nc; f. 2006; Dir PHILIPPE MARTIN.

Société de Développement et d'Investissement des Iles Loyauté (SODIL SA): 12 rue du Général Mangin, Immeuble Richelieu, BP 2217, 98846 Nouméa Cedex; tel. 276663; fax 276709; e-mail sodil@lagoon.nc; f. 1991; financing, promotion and sustainable devt of industry, tourism and artisanal cos; priority areas are transport, food-processing, aquaculture, and regional and int. tourism; Pres. HNAEJË HAMU; Man. SAMUEL HNEPEUNE.

Société d'Equipement de Nouvelle-Calédonie (SECAL): 28 rue du Général Mangin, BP 2517, 98846 Nouméa Cedex; tel. 232666; fax 232676; e-mail contact@secal.nc; internet www.secal.nc; f. 1971; urban management and devt, public sector construction and civil engineering; Pres. SIMONE MIGNARD.

Société de Financement et de Développement de la Province Sud (PROMOSUD): BP 295, 98845 Nouméa Cedex; tel. 241972; fax 271326; e-mail info@promosud.nc; internet www.promosud.nc; f. 1991; financing, promotion and economic devt of cos in priority sectors, incl. tourism, fishing and aquaculture, and processing industries; Pres. PIERRE BRETEGNIER; Man. THIERRY PAYEN.

Société de Financement et d'Investissement de la Province Nord (SOFINOR): 85 ave du Général de Gaulle, BP 66, 98800 Nouméa; tel. 281353; fax 281567; e-mail dirgen@smsp.nc; internet www.sofinor.nc; f. 1990; economic devt, management and financing; priority areas include mining and metal production, aquaculture and fishing, tourism, transport, real estate and engineering; Pres. GUIGUI DOUNEHOTE; Man. LOUIS MAPOU.

CHAMBERS OF COMMERCE

Chambre d'Agriculture: 3 rue A. Desmazures, BP 111, 98845 Nouméa Cedex; tel. 243160; fax 284587; e-mail direction@canc.nc; f. 1909; Pres. GÉRARD PASCO; Dir YANNICK COUETTE; 33 mems.

Chambre de Commerce et d'Industrie: 15 rue de Verdun, BP M3, 98849 Nouméa Cedex; tel. 243100; fax 243131; e-mail cci@cci.nc; internet www.cci.nc; f. 1879; Pres. ANDRÉ DESPLAT; Gen. Man. MICHEL MERZEAU; 12,000 mems.

Chambre de Métiers et de l'Artisanat: 10 ave James Cook, BP 4186, 98846 Nouméa Cedex; tel. 282337; fax 282729; e-mail cma@cma.nc; internet www.cma.nc; Pres. JEAN-CLAUDE MERLET; Sec.-Gen. PAUL SANCHEZ.

EMPLOYERS' ORGANIZATION

MEDEF de Nouvelle-Calédonie (Fédération Patronale des Chefs d'Entreprise en Nouvelle-Calédonie): 6 rue Jean Jaurès, 98800 Nouméa Cedex; tel. 273525; fax 274037; e-mail medefnc@medef.nc; internet www.medef.nc; f. 1936; represents leading cos of New Caledonia in defence of professional interests, co-ordination, documentation and research in socio-economic fields; affiliated to Mouvement des Entreprises de France; Pres. JEAN-FRANÇOIS BOUILLAGUET.

UTILITIES

Electricity

Electricité et Eau de Nouvelle-Calédonie (EEC): 15 rue Jean Chalier, PK 4, 98800 Nouméa Cedex; tel. 463636; fax 463510; e-mail clientele@eec.nc; internet www.eec.nc; f. 1929; est. as UNLECO; present name adopted in 1984; subsidiary of GDF SUEZ, France; producers and distributors of electricity; Pres. and Dir-Gen. FRANÇOIS GUICHARD; Gen. Man. YVES MORAULT.

Société Néo-Calédonienne d'Energie (ENERCAL): 87 ave du Général de Gaulle, BP C1, 98848 Nouméa Cedex; tel. 250250; fax 250253; e-mail dg@enercal.nc; internet www.enercal.nc; f. 1955; 16% owned by EDEV, France; production and distribution of electricity; Chair. JEAN-PIERRE AIFA; CEO JEAN-MICHEL DEVÉZA.

Water

Société Calédonienne des Eaux (CDE): 13 rue Edmond Harbulot, PK 6, BP 812, 98845 Nouméa Cedex; tel. 413737; fax 433796; e-mail clientele@cde.nc; water distribution; Gen. Man. ALAIN CARBONEL.

TRADE UNIONS

Confédération Générale des Travailleurs de Nouvelle-Calédonie (COGETRA): Vallée du Tir.

.

Confédération Générale du Travail-Force Ouvrière de Nouvelle-Calédonie (CGT-FO NC): 13 rue Jules Ferry, BP R2, 98851 Nouméa Cedex; tel. 274950; fax 278202; e-mail cgtfonc@lagoon.nc; f. 1984; Sec.-Gen. JACQUES BERNALEAU.

Confédération Syndicale des Travailleurs de Nouvelle-Calédonie (CSTNC): 49 rue Auer Ducos, 98800 Nouméa; tel. and fax 269648; e-mail cst-nc@laposte.net; Sec.-Gen. SYLVAIN NÉA.

Union Territoriale de la Confédération Française de l'Encadrement-Confédération Générale des Cadres (UT-CFE-CGC): Centre Commercial La Belle Vie, 224 rue Jacques Ikékawé, PK 6, BP 30536, 98895 Nouméa Cedex; tel. and fax 410300; fax 410310; e-mail utcfecgc@utcfecgc.nc; internet www.utcfecgc.nc; f. 1996; territorial br. of the Confédération Française de l'Encadrement-Confédération Générale des Cadres; Pres. CHRISTOPHE COULSON; Sec.-Gen. JEAN MARIE ARMAND.

Transport

ROADS

In 2006 there was a total of 5,622 km of roads in New Caledonia. In 2005 there were some 2,559 km of unsealed roads, some 410,680 km of urban roads and 890,450 km of rural tracks. There was a further estimated 350 km of unrecorded urban roads within Nouméa.

Société Anonyme des Voies Express à Péage (SAVEXPRESS): 15 rue de Verdun, BP M3, 98849 Nouméa Cedex; tel. 411930; fax 412899; e-mail savexpress@savexpress.nc; f. 1979; highway management and devt; Chair. CYNTHIA LIGEARD; Man. MAXIME CHASSOT.

SHIPPING

Most traffic is through the port of Nouméa. Passenger and cargo services, linking Nouméa to other towns and islands, are regular and frequent. There is also a harbour for yachts and pleasure craft at Nouméa.

Port Autonome de la Nouvelle-Calédonie: 34 ave James Cook, BP 14, 98845 Nouméa Cedex; tel. 255000; fax 275490; e-mail noumeaportnc@canl.nc; Port Man. PHILIPPE LAFLEUR; Harbour Master JEAN LEDEN.

Moana Services: 2 bis rue Berthelot, BP 2099, 98846 Nouméa; tel. 273898; fax 259315; e-mail moana@canl.nc; internet www.moana.nc; f. 2000; shipping and logistics agency; representatives for Moana Shipping (Wallis), Maersk Line (Denmark) and PFL Cargo (New Zealand); Gen. Man. LUCIEN BOURGADE.

SEM de la Baie de la Moselle (SODEMO): 6 rue de la Frégate-Nivôse, BP 2960, 98846 Nouméa; tel. 277197; fax 277129; e-mail contact@sodemo.nc; internet www.sodemo.nc; f. 1987; operates Port Moselle for pleasure craft and boatyard; Pres. JEAN WASMAN; Man. FRANÇOIS LE BRUN.

Sofrana NC: 14 ave James Cook, BP 1602, 98845 Nouméa; tel. 275191; fax 272611; e-mail info@sofrana.nc; internet www.sofrana.nc; f. 1968; subsidiary of Sofrana Holding; shipping agents and stevedores; barge operators; Chair. JEAN-BAPTISTE LEROUX; Gen. Man. FRANÇOIS BURNOUF.

CIVIL AVIATION

There is an international airport, La Tontouta, 47 km from Nouméa, and an internal network, centred on Magenta airport, which provides air services linking Nouméa to other towns and islands. A major expansion of the airport at La Tontouta was effected in 2008–12. Air Calédonie International (Aircalin) operates flights to various Asia-Pacific destinations. Other airlines providing services to the island include Air New Zealand, Air Vanuatu and Qantas.

Air Calédonie: Aérodrome, 100 rue Roger Gervolino, BP 212, 98845 Nouméa Cedex; tel. 250302; fax 281340; e-mail direction@air-caledonie.nc; internet www.air-caledonie.nc; f. 1954; services throughout mainland New Caledonia and its islands; operates 4 aircraft; Pres. NIDOÏSH NAISSELINE; CEO WILLIAM IHAGE.

Air Calédonie International (Aircalin): 47 rue de Sébastopol, BP 3736, 98846 Nouméa Cedex; tel. 265500; fax 265561; internet www.aircalin.com; f. 1983; 27% owned by Agence pour la Desserte Aérienne de la Nouvelle-Calédonie (NC Air Transport Agency), 72% by Caisse Nationale des Caisses d'Epargne et de Prévoyance, 1% by others; services to Sydney and Brisbane (Australia), Auckland (New Zealand), Nadi (Fiji), Papeete (French Polynesia), Wallis and Futuna Islands, Port Vila (Vanuatu), Osaka and Tokyo (Japan) and Seoul (Republic of Korea); Chair. and Dir BERNARD DELADRIÈRE; Pres. and CEO JEAN-MICHEL MASSON.

Cofely Airport Pacific: La Tontouta International Airport, BP 5, 98840 La Tontouta; tel. 352600; fax 352601; e-mail secretariat@cofely-airport-pacific.nc; f. 1995; fmrly Tontouta Air Service; renamed as above 2011; owned by Endel Group; operates Tontouta airport and freight management services; Gen. Man. ELVIR PEROCEVIC.

Tourism

The number of visitors arriving by air in New Caledonia increased from 111,875 in 2011 to 112,204 in 2012; in the latter year 34.5% came from France, 15.8% from Australia and 15.5% from Japan. The number of visiting cruise-ship passengers rose from 183,245 in 2010 to 235,684 in 2011. A total of 2,643 hotel rooms were available in 2004. In 2010 receipts from tourism amounted to €133.3m. New Caledonia hosted the Pacific Games in August–September 2011.

GIE Nouvelle-Calédonie Tourisme Point Sud: Galerie Nouméa Centre, 20 rue Anatole France, BP 688, 98845 Nouméa Cedex; tel. 242080; fax 242070; e-mail info@nctps.com; internet www.nouvellecaledonietourisme-sud.com; f. 2001; Dir-Gen. JEAN-MICHEL FOUTREIN.

GIE Nouvelle-Calédonie Tourisme Province Nord: Centre Commercial Le Village, 35 ave du Maréchal Foch, BP 115, 98845 Nouméa Cedex; tel. 277805; fax 274887; e-mail info@tourismeprovincenord.nc; internet www.tourismeprovincenord.nc; f. 2003; Dir JACQUELINE RIAHI.

Defence

As assessed at November 2013, France maintained a 1,500-strong force, including army and navy personnel, as well as a gendarmerie, in New Caledonia. The French naval command for the Pacific area is based in French Polynesia.

Commander of the French Armed Forces in New Caledonia: Brig.-Gen. JEAN-FRANÇOIS PARLANTI.

Education

Education is compulsory for 10 years between six and 16 years of age. Schools are operated by both the state and churches, under the supervision of three Departments of Education: the Provincial department responsible for primary level education, the New Caledonian department responsible for primary level inspection, and the state department responsible for secondary level education. Primary education begins at six years of age, and lasts for five years; secondary education, beginning at 11 years of age, comprises a first cycle of four years and a second, three-year cycle. Overall, in 2006 73.7% of pre-primary and primary pupils, and 67.6% of secondary pupils, were enrolled at public institutions. In 2012 there were 12,732 pupils enrolled in pre-primary education, 22,603 in primary education (including special education) and 32,486 in secondary education. Four institutions provide higher education. Students may also attend universities in France. In 1987 the French University of the Pacific (based in French Polynesia) was established, with a centre in Nouméa, and divided into two universities in 1999. Several other vocational tertiary education centres exist in New Caledonia, including a teacher-training college and two agricultural colleges. In 2003 total public expenditure on education was 66,914m. francs CFP, of which some 42,362m. francs CFP was provided by the French state.

GABON

Introductory Survey

LOCATION, CLIMATE, LANGUAGE, RELIGION, FLAG, CAPITAL

The Gabonese Republic is an equatorial country on the west coast of Africa, with Equatorial Guinea and Cameroon to the north and the Republic of the Congo to the south and east. The climate is tropical, with an average annual temperature of 26°C (79°F) and an average annual rainfall of 2,490 mm (98 ins). The official language is French, but Fang (in the north) and Bantu dialects (in the south) are also widely spoken. About 60% of the population are Christians, mainly Roman Catholics. Most of the remainder follow animist beliefs. The national flag (proportions 3 by 4) has three equal horizontal stripes, of green, yellow and blue. The capital is Libreville.

CONTEMPORARY POLITICAL HISTORY

Historical Context

Formerly a province of French Equatorial Africa, Gabon was granted internal autonomy in November 1958, and proceeded to full independence on 17 August 1960. Léon M'Ba, the new Republic's President, established Gabon as a one-party state. Following his death in November 1967, M'Ba was succeeded by the Vice-President, Albert-Bernard (later Omar) Bongo, who organized a new ruling party, the Parti Démocratique Gabonais (PDG). Gabon enjoyed political stability and rapid economic growth in the 1970s, underpinned by substantial foreign investment in the development and exploitation of its petroleum reserves. However, the social and economic problems that accompanied the subsequent decline in world petroleum prices led to the emergence in 1981 of a moderate opposition group, the Mouvement de Redressement National (MORENA), which demanded the restoration of a multi-party system and formed a government-in-exile in Paris, France, from where it unsuccessfully sought to put forward a candidate to challenge Bongo in the presidential election held in November 1986.

Domestic Political Affairs

In May 1989 the Chairman of MORENA, Fr Paul M'Ba Abessole, visited Gabon and, after a meeting with Bongo, announced that he and many of his supporters would return to Gabon. In January 1990 representatives of MORENA announced that M'Ba Abessole had been dismissed from the leadership of the movement, following his declaration of support for the Government. M'Ba Abessole subsequently formed a breakaway faction, known as MORENA des Bûcherons (renamed Rassemblement National des Bûcherons—RNB—in 1991 to avoid confusion with the rival MORENA—Originels).

A number of arrests took place in October 1989, following an alleged conspiracy to overthrow the Government. It was claimed that the plot had been initiated by Pierre Mamboundou, the leader of the Union du Peuple Gabonais (UPG, an opposition movement based in Paris). In early 1990 Bongo announced that extensive political reforms, including a multi-party system, were to be introduced at the end of a five-year transitional period. In March a national conference, attended by representatives of more than 70 political organizations, rejected these proposals and demanded the immediate establishment of a multi-party system and the formation of a new government, which would hold office only until legislative elections could take place. Bongo acceded to the decisions of the conference, and in late April Casimir Oyé Mba, the Governor of the Banque des Etats de l'Afrique Centrale, was appointed Prime Minister of a transitional administration, which included several opposition members. In May constitutional changes were approved that would facilitate the transition to a multi-party political system. Future elections to the presidency would be contested by more than one candidate, and the tenure of office would be reduced to five years, renewable only once.

Legislative elections were scheduled for 16 and 23 September 1990. The first round of the elections was disrupted by violent protests by voters who claimed that the PDG was engaging in electoral fraud. Following further allegations of widespread electoral malpractices, results in 32 constituencies were declared invalid, although the election of 58 candidates (of whom 36 were members of the PDG) was confirmed. The interim Government subsequently conceded that electoral irregularities had taken place, and further voting was postponed until 21 and 28 October. At the elections the PDG won an overall majority in the 120-member Assemblée Nationale (National Assembly), with 62 seats, while opposition candidates secured 55 seats.

In November 1990 a Government of National Unity, under Oyé Mba, was formed. Sixteen posts were allocated to members of the PDG, while the remaining eight portfolios were distributed among members of five opposition parties. A new draft Constitution, which was promulgated on 22 December, endorsed reforms that had been included in the transitional Constitution, introduced in May. Further measures included the proposed establishment of an upper house, the Sénat (Senate). A Constitutional Council was to replace the administrative chamber of the Supreme Court, and a National Communications Council was to be created.

The final composition of the National Assembly was determined in March 1991, when elections took place in five constituencies, where the results had been annulled, owing to alleged malpractice. Following the completion of the elections, the PDG held a total of 66 seats in the National Assembly, while various opposition groups held 54 seats. The two most prominent opposition movements, the Parti Gabonais du Progrès (PGP) and the RNB, held 19 and 17 seats, respectively.

In May 1991 six opposition parties formed an alliance, the Coordination de l'Opposition Démocratique (COD), in protest against the delay in the implementation of the new Constitution. The COD also demanded the appointment of a new Prime Minister, the abolition of certain institutions under the terms of the Constitution, and the liberalization of the state-controlled media. Following a general strike, organized by the COD, Bongo announced the resignation of the Council of Ministers, and declared that he was prepared to implement fully the new Constitution. He also claimed that, in accordance with the Constitution, several institutions, including the High Court of Justice, had been dissolved, and that a Constitutional Court and a National Communications Council had been established. However, opposition parties within the COD refused to be represented in a new Government of National Unity, of which Oyé Mba was appointed as Prime Minister. In June Oyé Mba appointed a new coalition Government, in which 14 members of the previous Council of Ministers retained their portfolios. Members of MORENA—Originels, the Union Socialiste Gabonaise (USG) and the Association pour le Socialisme au Gabon were also represented in the Government.

Bongo re-elected

Bongo was re-elected to the presidency on 5 December 1993, winning 51.2% of the votes cast, while M'Ba Abessole secured 26.5% of the votes. The official announcement of the results prompted rioting by opposition supporters. Five deaths were reported after security forces suppressed the unrest, and a national curfew and state of alert were subsequently imposed. M'Ba Abessole, however, claimed victory and formed a Haut Conseil de la République, later redesignated as the Haut Conseil de la Résistance (HCR), which included the majority of opposition presidential candidates, and a parallel government. Despite reports by international observers that the elections had been conducted fairly, the opposition appealed to the Constitutional Court to annul the results, on the grounds that the Government had perpetrated electoral malpractice.

The Constitutional Court ruled against the appeal by the opposition and endorsed the election results, and on 22 January 1994 Bongo was officially inaugurated as President. In mid-February the national curfew and the state of alert were repealed, but later that month were reimposed, after a general strike, in support of demands for an increase in salaries to compensate for a devaluation of the CFA franc in January, degenerated into violence. Strike action was suspended after four days, following negotiations between the Government and trade unions; nine people had been killed during that period, according to official figures (although the opposition claimed that a total of 38 had died).

In March 1994 the National Assembly approved a constitutional amendment that provided for the establishment of a Senate (which the opposition had resisted). In August the opposition parties announced that they were prepared to participate in a coalition government, on condition that it was installed as a transitional organ pending legislative elections. In September negotiations between the Government and opposition took place in Paris, under the auspices of the Organization of African Unity (OAU, now the African Union—AU, see p. 186), in order to resolve remaining differences concerning the results of the presidential election and the proposed formation of a government of national unity.

At the end of September 1994 an agreement was reached whereby a transitional coalition government was to be installed, with local government elections scheduled to take place after a period of one year, followed by legislative elections six months later; the electoral code was to be revised and an independent electoral commission established, in an effort to ensure that the elections be conducted fairly. In early October Oyé Mba resigned from office and dissolved the Council of Ministers. Shortly afterwards Bongo appointed Dr Paulin Obame-Nguema of the PDG as Prime Minister. Obame-Nguema subsequently formed a 27-member Council of Ministers, which included six opposition members. The composition of the new Government was, however, immediately criticized by the opposition, on the grounds that it was entitled to one-third of ministerial portfolios in proportion to the number of opposition deputies in the National Assembly; the HCR announced that the opposition would boycott the new administration, which, it claimed, was in violation of the Paris accord. Four opposition members consequently refused to accept the portfolios allocated to them, although two of these finally agreed to join the Government. (The portfolios that remained vacant were later assigned to a further two opposition members.)

At a national referendum held on 24 July 1995 the constitutional provisions adopted under the terms of the Paris accord were approved by 96.5% of votes cast, with 63% of the electorate participating. In May 1996 Bongo agreed to establish a Commission Nationale Electorale (National Election Commission—CNE) to formulate an electoral timetable, in consultation with all the official parties. Access to state-controlled media and election funding was to be equitably divided. On 20 May the National Assembly's mandate expired, and Obame-Nguema's Government resigned at the beginning of June, in accordance with the Paris accord. Bongo, however, rejected the resignation on the grounds that the Government should, before leaving office, organize the elections and finalize pending agreements with the IMF and the World Bank.

Legislative elections were rescheduled on several occasions, owing to the delay in the release of the local election results and the failure to revise electoral registers in time. The PDG obtained 47 of the 55 seats that were decided in the first round of voting on 15 December 1996. The opposition disputed the results and urged a boycott of the second round of voting. The PDG secured a substantial majority of the seats decided in the second round, which was held on 29 December, winning 84 seats, while the RNB obtained seven, the PGP six and independent candidates four, with a further 14 seats shared by the Cercle des Libéraux Réformateurs (CLR), the UPG, the USG and others. Polling was unable to proceed for the five remaining seats, and results in a number of other constituencies were later annulled, owing to irregularities. (Following by-elections held in August 1997, during which five people were reportedly killed in violent incidents in north-east Gabon, the PDG held 88 seats, the PGP nine and the RNB five.) Obame-Nguema was reappointed Prime Minister on 27 January, and a new Council of Ministers, dominated by members of the PDG, was announced on the following day. The PGP, the main opposition party represented in the National Assembly, had refused to participate in the new Government.

Elections to the new Senate took place on 26 January and 9 February 1997, with senators to be elected by members of municipal councils and departmental assemblies. The PDG won 53 of the Senate's 91 seats, while the RNB secured 20 seats, the PGP four, the Alliance Démocratique et Républicaine (ADERE) three, the CLR one, and the Rassemblement pour la Démocratie et le Progrès (RDP) one, with independent candidates obtaining nine seats. The results for a number of seats were annulled, however, and in subsequent by-elections, held later that year, the PDG increased its representation to 58 seats, while the RNB held 20 seats and the PGP four.

Constitutional amendments

In April 1997 a congress of deputies and senators adopted constitutional amendments which extended the presidential term to seven years and provided for the creation of the post of Vice-President (who was not to have any power of succession). In late May Didjob Divungui-di-N'Dingue of the ADERE was appointed to the new post.

In September 1998 opposition parties withdrew their members from the CNE in protest against alleged irregularities in the voter registration process for the forthcoming presidential poll. At the election, which was held on 6 December, Bongo was re-elected with 66.6% of votes cast, while Mamboundou received 16.5% of the votes and M'Ba Abessole secured 13.4%. The reported rate of participation was 53.8%. Opposition parties rejected the results, again alleging electoral malpractice, and called for fresh elections to be held. None the less, Bongo was inaugurated as President on 21 January 1999, and a new 42-member Council of Ministers, headed by Jean-François Ntoutoume Emane, was subsequently appointed.

Elections to the National Assembly took place on 9 and 23 December 2001. Three opposition parties accused the Government of falsely inflating voter registration lists and boycotted the elections, while others called for the first round to be annulled, as a result of reputed irregularities and high abstention rates. In the event, the elections were postponed in three districts until 6 January 2002, owing to violent incidents, and voting was repeated on 20 January in a further two constituencies where candidates had received the same number of votes and in a third district where violence had marred the initial ballot. An outbreak of the Ebola virus resulted in the indefinite postponement of voting in the north-eastern district of Zadie. The PDG won 86 seats in the Assembly, which were supplemented by 19 seats secured by independents with links to the PDG and other parties affiliated to the ruling party. Opposition parties obtained a total of 14 seats (the Rassemblement pour le Gabon—RPG—as the RNB had been restyled, eight, the Parti Social-Démocrate—PSD—two and the UPG one). A new, enlarged 39-member Council of Ministers, which included four opposition representatives, was appointed in late January. Ntoutoume Emane was reappointed as Prime Minister, while M'Ba Abessole was named Minister of State for Human Rights and Missions.

During March and April 2002 the Constitutional Court annulled the results of voting in the December 2001 elections to the National Assembly in 12 constituencies owing to irregularities. On 26 May and 9 June by-elections took place in these 12 constituencies and in Zadie; the PDG won 10 of the 13 seats contested, increasing its representation to 88 seats. Elections to the Senate took place on 9 February 2003; the PDG won more than 60 of the upper chamber's 91 seats, followed by the RPG, which secured eight seats.

In July 2003 the National Assembly voted to revoke the Constitution's limit on the number of terms of office for which the President was eligible to seek re-election. Opposition politicians claimed that Bongo thus intended to become 'President-for-Life' by means of continuous fraud in future presidential elections. In September, in response to a series of strikes and protests, the Government and representatives of labour groups announced the signing of a so-called 'social truce', which included commitments to lower the prices of essential items and reduce the extent of political patronage over the following three years. However, renewed protests over reductions in state expenditure were staged in early 2004.

In early September 2004 President Bongo Ondimba (who had added his father's name to his own in November 2003) carried out a minor cabinet reorganization, in which several leading opposition figures were awarded ministerial portfolios. It was widely believed that the inclusion of opposition leaders in the Government was intended to reduce the number of candidates opposing Bongo Ondimba and the PDG in the upcoming presidential and legislative elections. In October 2005 disquiet arose among opposition groups, following the decision of the CNE to exclude nine presidential candidates, two of whom subsequently appealed successfully against their exclusion, from contesting the election.

At the presidential election held on 27 November 2005 Bongo Ondimba was re-elected, receiving 79.2% of votes cast. Mamboundou, the candidate of the UPG, received 13.6%, while Zacharie Myboto, a former government minister representing the Union Gabonaise pour la Démocratie et le Développement

(UGDD), received 6.6%. The rate of voter participation was recorded at 63.5%. Mamboundou and Myboto disputed the validity of the results, alleging electoral malpractice, and each claimed victory for himself. However, international election observers declared the elections to have been largely free and transparent. The ensuing unrest caused by supporters of the defeated candidates was broadly quelled following the deployment of security forces throughout the country in January 2006. On 20 January President Bongo Ondimba appointed Jean Eyéghé Ndong of the PDG as Prime Minister, who later that month formed an expanded Council of Ministers composed overwhelmingly of PDG members.

The PDG consolidates power

Legislative elections took place on 17 December 2006, although voting in seven constituencies was postponed until 24 December for logistical reasons. The PDG retained control of the National Assembly, winning 82 of the 120 seats, while parties allied to the PDG secured a further 17 seats; the opposition won 17 seats (the UPG secured the largest number of opposition seats with eight) and independents won four. Electoral observers endorsed the results, but the opposition complained that it had not been given adequate access to state media during the election campaign. In late January 2007 Ndong, who had been reappointed to the premiership, announced a largely unchanged 50-member Council of Ministers, which was again dominated by members of the PDG. Results in 20 constituencies were subsequently annulled owing to allegations of procedural irregularities and fraud. By-elections were held on 10 June at which the PDG won 11 of the 20 seats available. Parties allied to the PDG won six seats, while the opposition took two; the remaining seat was secured by an independent candidate.

In December 2007 President Bongo Ondimba appointed a new Government, retaining Ndong as Prime Minister; further governmental reorganizations were effected in February 2008 and January 2009. At elections to the Senate held on 18 January 2009 the ruling PDG retained its majority, winning 75 of the 102 seats in the upper house.

The presidency of Ali Bongo Ondimba

On 8 June 2009 the death was announced of President Bongo Ondimba. It was reported that he had died of a heart attack while receiving medical treatment in Spain; he had 'temporarily' withdrawn from public duties the previous month following the death of his wife in March. Under the terms of the Constitution, interim power was transferred to Rose Francine Rogombé, the President of the Senate, who was charged with responsibility for organizing a presidential election within 45 days. Despite requests by the political opposition for a delay to the timetable to allow an extensive revision of the electoral register, the Constitutional Court declared that the ballot would take place on 30 August. The PDG's selection of Ali Bongo Ondimba, the son of the former President and Minister of National Defence, as its presidential candidate resulted in serious divisions within the party and in mid-June Prime Minister Ndong announced the resignation of his Government and his intention to contest the election as an independent candidate. Interim President Rogombé named Paul Biyoghé Mba as Ndong's successor and the outgoing Government was reappointed virtually unchanged.

At the presidential election, which was held as scheduled on 30 August 2009, Bongo Ondimba secured 41.7% of the valid votes cast, and independent candidate André Mba Obame (the Minister of the Interior) was placed second with 25.9%, while Mamboundou, again representing the UPG, secured 25.2% of the votes. Violent protests ensued, most notably in Libreville and Port-Gentil, resulting in the deaths of at least three people and French business interests and diplomatic offices in Gabon were attacked. It was subsequently announced that a recount of the votes would take place; finally on 12 October the Constitutional Court announced that Bongo Ondimba had secured 41.8% of the valid votes cast, while the share of votes attributed to Mamboundou and Mba Obame was amended to 25.6% and 25.3%, respectively, thus reversing their placings in the election.

Ali Bongo Ondimba was sworn in as President on 16 October 2009 and a new Government, reduced in size from 44 to 30 members, was appointed the following day. Biyoghé Mba retained the premiership and Angélique Ngoma was named Minister of National Defence, while Anicette Nang Ovika became Minister of Justice, Keeper of the Seals. No opposition party members were accorded ministerial positions.

In February 2010 three political movements representing the Fang ethnic group (the UGDD, the Mouvement Africain de Développement and the Rassemblement National des Républicains) united under the leadership of Mba Obame to form the Union Nationale. However, in January 2011 the Ministry of the Interior announced the dissolution of the Union Nationale and accused Mba Obame of treason after he declared himself the victor of the 2009 presidential election and appointed a 19-member parallel government. Rallies held in support of Mba Obame degenerated into violent clashes between demonstrators and the security forces. Mba Obame and his associates fled to the Libreville premises of the UN Development Programme, refusing to leave until late February 2011 due to safety concerns. The operations of numerous media outlets that had provided coverage of Mba Obame and other opposition figures were suspended by the government-controlled Conseil National de la Communication throughout 2011 and early 2012.

Meanwhile, in January 2011 President Bongo Ondimba effected a reorganization of the Council of Ministers, appointing 10 new ministers. Most notable among the changes announced were the respective appointments of Emmanuel Issozet Ngondet as Minister of the Budget, Public Accounts and the Civil Service, responsible for State Reform, and of Pacôme Rufin Ondzounga as Minister of National Defence. In March three military officials were sentenced to prison terms of up to seven years, after being found guilty of planning to stage a coup against President Bongo Ondimba in 2009.

Legislative elections were conducted on 17 December 2011. According to the official results, the ruling PDG secured an overwhelming victory, winning 114 seats in the National Assembly. Of the remaining six seats, the RPG secured three, while the CLR, the PSD and the Union pour la Nouvelle République each obtained a single seat. AU observers endorsed the results, although they reported some 'shortcomings'. The rate of participation by the electorate was only 34.3%. Numerous opposition parties had urged a boycott, arguing that the elections would lack transparency since biometric voting cards had not been issued. In February 2012 the Constitutional Court annulled the results in six PDG-controlled constituencies because of voting irregularities. By-elections in those constituencies were conducted in May, when the PDG again won all six seats.

Biyoghé Mba resigned as Prime Minister in February 2012; Raymond Ndong Sima, hitherto the minister responsible for agriculture, was appointed as his successor. Ndong Sima announced a new Government later that month. Notably, Issozet Ngondet was named as the new Minister of Foreign Affairs, International Co-operation and Francophone Affairs, although the other key portfolios were left largely unaltered.

Mba Obame, who had been receiving medical treatment abroad since mid-2011, returned to Gabon on 11 August 2012. An unsanctioned demonstration was held in Libreville on 15 August in support of his demands for a national reconciliation conference and fresh legislative elections. Violent confrontations ensued between Mba Obame's supporters and the security forces, resulting in approximately 60 arrests and the death of one demonstrator. On the following day the premises of TV+, a television station owned by Mba Obame, came under attack by heavily armed assailants, who destroyed the station's broadcasting equipment. (The TV+ building was attacked again in early September.) In September 33 of the detained protesters received one-year prison terms for their involvement in the unrest. Also in that month 20 opposition parties, including Mba Obame's Union Nationale (still officially dissolved), established a coalition, the Union des Forces de Changement. This new opposition grouping signed an accord appealing for a national conference to be convened to discuss 'democratic political change' within the country. (Mba Obame subsequently left the country again to seek medical treatment.)

Recent developments: new Government

Local elections were conducted on 14 December 2013; later that month the CNE announced provisional results according to which the PDG had won 1,517 of the 2,404 municipal seats and secured control of the majority of departmental assemblies overall. Subsequently, a PDG candidate, Rose Christiane Ossouka Raponda, previously the Minister of the Budget, was elected Mayor of Libreville on 26 January 2014 (replacing former premier Ntoutoume Emane). Meanwhile, on 24 January President Bongo Ondimba appointed Daniel Ona Ondo (hitherto First Vice-President of the National Assembly) as Prime Minister. A new Government, in which Issozet Ngondet and other principal ministers were retained, was formed at the end of

January; among the newly appointed members, Minister of the Interior, Public Security, Immigration and Decentralization Guy Bertrand Mapangou and Minister of National Defence Ernest Mpouho were regarded as particularly close associates of Bongo Ondimba.

Foreign Affairs

Regional relations

In March 2003 relations with Equatorial Guinea became tense, following Gabon's occupation of the uninhabited island of Mbagne (Mbañé, Mbanie), situated in Corisco Bay, north of Libreville. Both countries claimed sovereignty over the island. Equatorial Guinea rejected Bongo's proposal for joint exploitation of any petroleum reserves found in the vicinity of the island, despite an official visit to Libreville in early May by the Equato-Guinean President, Gen. (Theodoro) Obiang Nguema Mbasogo. Attempts to reach a negotiated settlement failed in December, although the two countries agreed to the appointment of a UN mediator in the dispute in January 2004 and in July a provisional agreement was reached to explore jointly for petroleum in the disputed territories. However, in late 2006 negotiations were suspended indefinitely. In February 2011 Obiang Nguema and Ali Bongo Ondimba, attending a meeting hosted by UN Secretary-General Ban Ki-Moon in New York, USA, confirmed that they would seek the intervention of the International Court of Justice in settling the dispute.

Gabon is a member of the Communauté Economique et Monétaire de l'Afrique Centrale (CEMAC, see p. 330), which was officially established in 1999. The Gabonese Government contributed troops to regional peacekeeping operations, including a contingent in the Central African Republic (CAR) that was created by CEMAC in late 2002, and a successor Communauté Economique des Etats de l'Afrique Centrale (see p. 450) mission from 2008. Visa requirements for member states of the CEMAC were officially abolished at the beginning of 2014; however, the Government of Equatorial Guinea, which had expressed reservations about the free movement agreement, in January temporarily closed the border with Gabon and Cameroon, apparently owing to concerns over a possible influx of migrant workers from those countries.

Other external relations

President Omar Bongo Ondimba pursued a policy of close co-operation with France in the fields of economic and foreign affairs. Relations became strained in March 1997, however, when allegations that Bongo had been a beneficiary in an international fraud emerged during a French judicial investigation into the affairs of the petroleum company Elf Aquitaine (now part of Total). In October 1999 a further judicial investigation into the affairs of Elf Aquitaine, carried out by Swiss authorities, revealed that André Tarallo (a senior Elf Aquitaine executive) had used bank accounts in that country secretly to transfer large sums of money to several African heads of state, among them Bongo. Bongo denied personally receiving direct payments from Elf and maintained that such 'bonus' payments were made only to the Gabonese Government. However, a report released in November, following a separate investigation by the US Congress into money-laundering and corruption among political figures, alleged further improper financial dealing between Bongo and Elf. In March 2003 the trial commenced in Paris of 37 defendants accused of permitting the embezzlement of the equivalent of some €300m. of funds from Elf Aquitaine. In November Tarallo was sentenced to four years' imprisonment and fined €2m., while 29 others also received prison terms. Tarallo was released on the grounds of ill-health in January 2004; however, his sentence was increased to seven years' imprisonment, following appeals by the prosecution in March 2005. Following the election to the French presidency of Nicolas Sarkozy (who had pledged to implement stricter immigration policies) in May 2007, further tensions ensued between France and Gabon. In early 2008 two Gabonese students were deported, although a visit to Gabon by a delegation of French officials in April signalled an improvement in relations. Nevertheless, in February 2009 the French authorities announced that they had frozen a number of Bongo Ondimba's bank accounts, following a ruling by a court in Bordeaux, France, in October 2008 that he return a payment of some €450,000 made to him in order to secure the release of a French businessman who had been imprisoned in Libreville in 1996.

In November 2009, on his first visit abroad since acceding to the presidency, Ali Bongo Ondimba met President Sarkozy in Paris and in February 2010 Sarkozy made a reciprocal visit to Gabon. A visit to Gabon by French Prime Minister François Fillon in July 2011 was censured by opposition groups critical of France's support of President Bongo Ondimba. Nevertheless, Fillon announced that the French garrison in Gabon would be upgraded to the status of France's main military base in the region. Reports emerged in September alleging that former French President Jacques Chirac and other prominent French politicians had received clandestine payments totalling US $20m. from the leaders of several ex-French colonies in Africa, including Omar Bongo Ondimba, in exchange for French support for their respective regimes. Despite denials by the French and Gabonese authorities, in November a former government official in Omar Bongo Ondimba's administration corroborated these allegations. President Bongo Ondimba met the new French President, François Hollande, in Paris in July 2012, amid further criticism from Gabonese opposition groups, which accused Hollande of reneging on electoral pledges to end the 'Françafrique' policy perceived to maintain France's influence in Africa while upholding corrupt regimes.

Following a visit to Gabon in February 2004 by the Chinese President, Hu Jintao, agreements were signed providing for greater economic co-operation between the two countries; most notably, the French oil corporation Total concluded an agreement to export Gabonese oil to the People's Republic of China. Relations were further strengthened following Bongo Ondimba's visit to China in September, during which he secured some US $5m. in aid from the Jintao administration. However, in 2013 the Gabonese Government withdrew exploitation rights of onshore oil assets from Addax Petroleum of China, owing to alleged breaches of contract; following a legal dispute at an international tribunal, in January 2014 Addax Petroleum paid US $400m. to continue exploitation in the country.

CONSTITUTION AND GOVERNMENT

The Constitution of March 1991 provides for a multi-party system, and vests executive power in the President, who is directly elected by universal suffrage for a period of seven years. The President appoints the Prime Minister, who is Head of Government and who (in consultation with the President) appoints the Council of Ministers. Legislative power is vested in the Assemblée Nationale, comprising 120 members, who are elected by direct universal suffrage for a term of five years, and the 102-member Sénat (Senate), which is elected by members of municipal councils and departmental assemblies for a term of six years. The independence of the judiciary is guaranteed by the Constitution. Gabon is divided into nine provinces, each under an appointed governor, and 37 prefectures.

REGIONAL AND INTERNATIONAL CO-OPERATION

Gabon is a member of the African Union (see p. 186), of the Central African organs of the Franc Zone (see p. 329) and of the Communauté Economique des Etats de l'Afrique Centrale (CEEAC, see p. 450).

Gabon became a member of the UN in 1960. As a contracting party to the General Agreement on Tariffs and Trade, Gabon joined the World Trade Organization (see p. 434) on its establishment in 1995.

ECONOMIC AFFAIRS

In 2012, according to estimates by the World Bank, Gabon's gross national income (GNI), measured at average 2010–12 prices, was US $16,438m., equivalent to $10,070 per head (or $14,290 per head on an international purchasing-power parity basis). During 2003–12, it was estimated, the population increased at an average annual rate of 2.4%, while gross domestic product (GDP) per head increased, in real terms, by an average of 0.7% per year. Overall GDP increased, in real terms, at an average annual rate of 3.2% in 2003–12. GDP increased by 6.1% in 2012.

Agriculture (including forestry and fishing) contributed a provisional 4.3% of GDP in 2012, according to the African Development Bank (AfDB). About 23.8% of the labour force was estimated to be employed in the agricultural sector in mid-2014, according to FAO estimates. Cocoa, coffee, oil palm and rubber are cultivated for export. Gabon has yet to achieve self-sufficiency in staple crops: imports of food, live animals and prepared foodstuffs accounted for 15.0% of the value of total imports in 2010. The principal subsistence crops are plantains, cassava and yams. The exploitation of Gabon's forests (which cover about 85% of the land area) is a principal economic activity. In 2010 wood and wood products accounted for an estimated 3.0%

of total exports. Although Gabon's territorial waters contain important fishing resources, their commercial exploitation is minimal. According to World Bank estimates, agricultural GDP increased at an average annual rate of 1.4% in 2002–11. According to the AfDB, the sector grew by 5.5% in 2012.

Industry (including mining, manufacturing, construction and power) contributed a provisional 64.7% of GDP in 2012, according to the AfDB. About 14.1% of the working population were employed in the sector in 1991. According to World Bank estimates, industrial GDP increased at an average annual rate of 1.8% in 2002–11; industrial GDP expanded by 7.3% in 2011.

Mining accounted for a provisional 56.5% of GDP in 2012 (with the majority of that contributed by the petroleum sector alone), according to the AfDB. In 2010 sales of petroleum and petroleum products provided an estimated 87.1% of export revenue. Production of crude petroleum was estimated at 245,000 barrels per day (b/d) in 2012, down from some 364,000 b/d in 1997. However, recent explorations have doubled oil reserves compared with 1996 levels. At the end of 2013 Gabon had proven petroleum reserves of 2,000m. barrels, sufficient to sustain production at current levels for some 22 years. Proven natural gas reserves totalled 1,000,000m. cu ft at the end of 2013. Gabon is among the world's foremost producers and exporters of manganese (which contributed an estimated 2.4% of export earnings in 2010). In 2011 4,100 metric tons of manganese was mined. Major reserves of iron ore remain undeveloped, and there are also substantial niobium (columbium) reserves at Mabounie. Small amounts of gold are extracted, and the existence of many mineral deposits, including talc, barytes, phosphates, rare earths, titanium and cadmium, has also been confirmed. In 1996–2002, according to the IMF, mining GDP declined at an estimated average annual rate of 6.5%. According to the AfDB, the mining sector grew by 2.4% in 2012.

According to the AfDB, the manufacturing sector contributed a provisional 4.1% of GDP in 2012. The principal activities are the refining of petroleum and the processing of other minerals, the preparation of timber and other agro-industrial processes. The chemicals industry is also significant. According to World Bank estimates, manufacturing GDP increased at an average annual rate of 2.2% in 2002–11; it increased by 5.3% in 2011. According to the AfDB the sector grew by 4.4% in 2012.

The construction sector contributed a provisional 2.3% of GDP in 2012, according to AfDB figures. The sector grew by 7.7% in that year.

In 2011 some 45.7% of electrical energy was provided by hydroelectric power, with the remainder provided by natural gas (33.0%) and petroleum (20.7%). Imports of mineral products comprised an estimated 12.2% of the total value of merchandise imports in 2010. Construction began of a new hydroelectric dam in Mitzic in December 2010 by French company Bouygues SA; the project was expected to cost US $108m. with a projected capacity of 40 MW.

Services engaged 18.8% of the economically active population in 1991 and, according to the AfDB, provided a provisional 31.0% of GDP in 2012. According to World Bank estimates, the GDP of the services sector increased at an average annual rate of 3.9% in 2002–11; services GDP increased by 3.1% in 2011.

According to IMF estimates, in 2011 Gabon recorded a merchandise trade surplus of 7,084,000m. francs CFA, and there was a surplus of 2,655,000m. francs CFA on the current account of the balance of payments. In 2010 the principal source of imports (30.7%) was France; other major sources were Belgium, the USA and the People's Republic of China. The principal market for exports in that year was the USA (58.3%); the Netherlands, Malaysia and China were also important purchasers. The principal exports in 2010 were mineral fuels and lubricants and wood and wood products. The principal imports in that year were machinery, mechanical and electrical equipment and parts thereof, mineral products, base metals and their articles, vehicles and associated transport equipment, chemicals and related products, live animals and animal products, and prepared foodstuffs.

In 2012 there was an estimated budgetary deficit of 38,000m. francs CFA. Gabon's general government gross debt was 1,532,090m. francs CFA in 2011, equivalent to 17.3% of GDP. Gabon's external debt totalled US $2,879m. at the end of 2011, of which $2,464m. was public and publicly guaranteed debt. In 2005 the cost of servicing long-term public and publicly guaranteed debt and repayments to the IMF was equivalent to 3.4% of the value of exports of goods, services and income (excluding workers' remittances). According to the ILO, in 2003–12 the average annual rate of inflation was 2.2%. Consumer prices increased by 2.7% in 2012. The Government estimated about 20% of the labour force to be unemployed in 1996.

Gabon's potential for economic growth is based on its considerable mineral and forestry resources. Petroleum provides the country's principal source of income; however, reserves in existing fields are in decline. Following his accession to the presidency, in October 2009 Ali Bongo Ondimba announced the adoption of an extensive public investment programme (totalling US $12,000m. over seven years), which was intended to transform Gabon into an emerging economy by 2025. The export of unprocessed timber was banned in January 2010 to encourage the creation of a domestic processing industry. As part of government efforts to stimulate growth and economic diversification, a Special Economic Zone was established near Libreville in September 2011, while the Central African Stock Exchange, serving the member states of the Communauté Economique et Monétaire de l'Afrique Centrale (see p. 330), has been operational in the capital, Libreville, since 2008. Loans totalling US $439m. were secured from the AfDB in late 2011 to fund various infrastructural development projects. Capital spending further increased during preparations for the African Cup of Nations football tournament, which Gabon co-hosted in early 2012. By 2013 the Government's public investment programme had proved successful in increasing revenue from non-oil sectors, particularly mining (the construction of new manganese plants having stimulated production and exports of the mineral), wood-processing and construction. Meanwhile, early that year the Government withdrew exploitation rights of an onshore oil field from Addax Petroleum of China, owing to alleged breaches of contract, and transferred control of the assets to the Gabon Oil Co., which had been established in 2011 in order to increase government participation in the oil sector. According to official figures, GDP growth increased to 6.3% in 2013 and a further slight rise was projected for 2014. However, higher public expenditure had resulted in the overall budget balance moving into deficit in 2012, with rising deficits projected by the IMF over the following five years. IMF reports additionally noted the country's continuing high rate of unemployment (estimated at 20% overall) and widespread poverty. The new Government that was formed in January 2014 was instructed by President Bongo Ondimba to focus on social objectives.

PUBLIC HOLIDAYS

2015: 1 January (New Year's Day), 6 April (Easter Monday), 17 April (Women's Day), 1 May (Labour Day), 14 May (Ascension Day), 25 May (Whit Monday), 17 July* (Id al-Fitr, end of Ramadan), 15 August (Assumption), 17 August (Anniversary of Independence), 23 September* (Id al-Adha, Feast of the Sacrifice), 1 November (All Saints' Day), 25 December (Christmas).

* These holidays are dependent on the Islamic lunar calendar and may vary by one or two days from the dates given.

Statistical Survey

Source (unless otherwise stated): Direction Générale de la Statistique et des Etudes Economiques, Ministère de la Planification et de la Programmation du Développement, BP 2119, Libreville; tel. 01-72-13-69; fax 01-72-04-57; e-mail plan@dgsee.yahoo.fr; internet www.stat-gabon.org.

Area and Population

AREA, POPULATION AND DENSITY

Area (sq km)	267,667*
Population (census results)	
31 July 1993	
Males	501,784
Females	513,192
Total	1,014,976
1 December 2003	1,269,000†
Population (UN estimates at mid-year)‡	
2012	1,632,572
2013	1,671,715
2014	1,711,295
Density (per sq km) at mid-2014	6.4

* 103,347 sq miles.

† Provisional (Source: UN, *Population and Vital Statistics Report*).

‡ Source: UN, *World Population Prospects: The 2012 Revision*.

POPULATION BY AGE AND SEX

(UN estimates at mid-2014)

	Males	Females	Total
0–14	331,569	325,204	656,773
15–64	489,929	477,366	967,295
65 and over	38,910	48,317	87,227
Total	860,408	850,887	1,711,295

Source: UN, *World Population Prospects: The 2012 Revision*.

REGIONS

(1993 census)

Region	Area (sq km)	Population	Density (per sq km)	Chief town
Estuaire	20,740	463,187	22.3	Libreville
Haut-Ogooué	36,547	104,301	2.9	Franceville
Moyen-Ogooué	18,535	42,316	2.3	Lambaréné
N'Gounié	37,750	77,781	2.1	Mouila
Nyanga	21,285	39,430	1.9	Tchibanga
Ogooué-Ivindo	46,075	48,862	1.1	Makokou
Ogooué-Lolo	25,380	43,915	1.7	Koulamoutou
Ogooué-Maritime	22,890	97,913	4.3	Port-Gentil
Woleu-N'Tem	38,465	97,271	2.5	Oyem
Total	267,667	1,014,976	3.8	

PRINCIPAL TOWNS

(population at 1993 census)

Libreville (capital)	419,596	Mouila	16,307
Port-Gentil	79,225	Lambaréné	15,033
Franceville	31,183	Tchibanga	14,054
Oyem	22,404	Koulamoutou	11,773
Moanda	21,882	Makokou	9,849

Mid-2011 (incl. suburbs, UN estimate): Libreville (capital) 686,356 (Source: UN, *World Urbanization Prospects: The 2011 Revision*).

BIRTHS AND DEATHS

(annual averages, UN estimates)

	1995–2000	2000–05	2005–10
Birth rate (per 1,000)	34.3	33.4	32.9
Death rate (per 1,000)	10.8	11.2	10.2

Source: UN, *World Population Prospects: The 2012 Revision*.

Life expectancy (years at birth): 62.7 (males 61.7; females 63.8) in 2011 (Source: World Bank, World Development Indicators database).

ECONOMICALLY ACTIVE POPULATION

('000 persons, 1991, estimates)

	Males	Females	Total
Agriculture, etc.	187	151	338
Industry	62	9	71
Services	69	26	95
Total labour force	318	186	504

Source: UN Economic Commission for Africa, *African Statistical Yearbook*.

2005 (persons aged 15 years and over): Total employed 639,180; Unemployed 115,499; Total labour force 664,117.

Mid-2014 (estimates in '000): Agriculture, etc. 188; Total 789 (Source: FAO).

Health and Welfare

KEY INDICATORS

Total fertility rate (children per woman, 2011)	3.2
Under-5 mortality rate (per 1,000 live births, 2011)	66
HIV/AIDS (% of persons aged 15–49, 2012)	4.0
Physicians (per 1,000 head, 2004)	0.3
Hospital beds (per 1,000 head, 2010)	6.3
Health expenditure (2010): US $ per head (PPP)	532
Health expenditure (2010): % of GDP	3.5
Health expenditure (2010): public (% of total)	51.8
Access to water (% of persons, 2011)	88
Access to sanitation (% of persons, 2011)	33
Total carbon dioxide emissions ('000 metric tons, 2010)	2,574.2
Carbon dioxide emissions per head (metric tons, 2010)	1.7
Human Development Index (2012): ranking	106
Human Development Index (2012): value	0.683

For sources and definitions, see explanatory note on p. vi.

Agriculture

PRINCIPAL CROPS

('000 metric tons, FAO estimates)

	2010	2011	2012
Maize	41	44	44
Cassava (Manioc)	250	255	300
Taro (Cocoyam)	58	60	63
Yams	190	195	200
Sugar cane	245	265	260
Groundnuts, with shell	18	23	24
Oil palm fruit	20	20	20
Bananas	17	17	17
Plantains	325	295	285
Natural rubber	20	21	21

Aggregate production ('000 metric tons, may include official, semi-official or estimated data): Total cereals 43 in 2010, 45 in 2011, 46 in 2012; Total roots and tubers 501 in 2010, 514 in 2011, 567 in 2012; Total vegetables (incl. melons) 48 in 2010, 50 in 2011, 51 in 2012; Total fruits (excl. melons) 359 in 2010, 333 in 2011, 325 in 2012.

Source: FAO.

LIVESTOCK
('000 head, year ending September, FAO estimates)

	2010	2011	2012
Cattle	37	38	38
Pigs	215	215	218
Sheep	197	198	200
Goats	95	96	100
Chickens	3,100	3,100	3,100

Source: FAO.

LIVESTOCK PRODUCTS
('000 metric tons, FAO estimates)

	2010	2011	2012
Cattle meat	1.1	1.1	1.2
Pig meat	3.2	3.2	3.2
Chicken meat	3.8	3.8	3.8
Rabbit meat	1.9	1.9	1.9
Game meat	25.1	25.5	26.2
Cows' milk	2.4	2.4	2.5
Hen eggs	2.4	2.4	2.5

Source: FAO.

Forestry

ROUNDWOOD REMOVALS
('000 cubic metres)

	2005	2006	2007
Sawlogs, veneer logs and logs for sleepers	3,200	3,500	3,400
Fuel wood*	1,070	1,070	1,070
Total*	4,270	4,570	4,470

* FAO estimates.

2008–12: Production assumed to be unchanged from 2007 (FAO estimates).

Source: FAO.

SAWNWOOD PRODUCTION
('000 cubic metres, incl. railway sleepers, unofficial figures)

	2009	2010	2011
Total	250	338	500

2012: Production assumed to be unchanged from 2009 (FAO estimates).

Source: FAO.

Fishing

('000 metric tons, live weight)

	2008	2009*	2010*
Capture	42.5*	32.0	32.0
Tilapias	4.7*	4.4	4.4
Other freshwater fishes	5.0*	5.0	5.0
Barracudas	0.4	0.3	0.3
Bobo croakers	1.4	1.0	1.0
West African croakers	1.1	0.8	0.8
Lesser African threadfin	0.8	5.0	5.0
Bonga shad	8.3	5.6	5.6
Penaeus shrimp	0.1	—	—
Aquaculture	0.1	0.1	0.2
Total catch	42.6*	32.1	32.2

* FAO estimate(s).

2011: Figures assumed to be unchanged from 2010 (FAO estimates).

Source: FAO.

Mining

	2009	2010	2011
Crude petroleum ('000 barrels)	83,950	91,250	89,425
Natural gas (million cu m)*	200	200	200
Diamonds (carats)*	500	500	500
Manganese ore ('000 metric tons): gross weight†	1,992	3,201	4,070
Manganese ore ('000 metric tons): metal content‡	881	1,416	1,872
Gold (kg)*†§	300	300	300

* Estimated production.

† Figures refer to the metal content of ore.

‡ Figures refer to the weight of chemical-grade pellets.

§ Excluding production smuggled out of the country (estimated at more than 400 kg annually).

Source: US Geological Survey.

Industry

PETROLEUM PRODUCTS
('000 metric tons)

	2008	2009	2010
Motor spirit (petrol)	84	90	96
Kerosene	25	27	29
Distillate fuel oils	258	176	n.a.
Residual fuel oils and asphalt	364	392	420
Butane	13.5	n.a.	n.a.

Source: mostly UN Industrial Commodity Statistics Database.

SELECTED OTHER PRODUCTS
(metric tons unless otherwise indicated)

	2007	2008	2009
Flour	55,917	60,137	61,877
Refined palm oil	3,612	4,100	6,546
Timber production ('000 cu m)	287.4	244.6	196.4
Veneer sheets ('000 cu m)	264.6	263.0	264.1
Raw sugar	25,935	25,808	26,239
Beer ('000 hl)	1,000.0	1,068.1	1,126.2
Wine ('000 hl)	n.a.	43.3	38.3
Soft drinks ('000 hl)	800.4	848.7	917.4
Hydraulic cement	228,601	230,000*	250,000*
Electric energy (million kWh)	1,736	1,837	1,860

* Estimate.

Electric energy (million kWh): 1,847 in 2010.

Hydraulic cement (metric tons, estimates): 250,000 in 2010; 200,000 in 2011.

Sources: partly US Geological Survey; UN Industrial Commodity Statistics database.

Finance

CURRENCY AND EXCHANGE RATES

Monetary Units
100 centimes = 1 franc de la Coopération Financière en Afrique Centrale (CFA).

Sterling, Dollar and Euro Equivalents (31 December 2013)
£1 sterling = 783.286 francs CFA;
US $1 = 475.641 francs CFA;
€1 = 655.957 francs CFA;
10,000 francs CFA = £12.77 = $21.02 = €15.24.

Average Exchange Rate (francs CFA per US $)
2011 471.87
2012 510.53
2013 494.04

Note: An exchange rate of 1 French franc = 50 francs CFA, established in 1948, remained in force until January 1994, when the CFA franc was devalued by 50%, with the exchange rate adjusted to 1 French franc = 100 francs CFA. This relationship to French currency remained in effect with the introduction of the euro on 1 January 1999. From that date, accordingly, a fixed exchange rate of €1 = 655.957 francs CFA has been in operation.

BUDGET
('000 million francs CFA)

Revenue	2011	2012*	2013†
Taxes	1,309	1,140	1,280
Taxes on income, profits and capital gains	686	444	560
Individual	200	72	71
Corporations and other enterprises	486	372	489
Taxes on goods and services	198	253	261
Taxes on international trade and transactions	375	390	398
Other taxes	51	53	61
Other revenue	1,160	1,406	1,267
Non-oil tax revenue	1,082	1,230	1,201
Other non-oil revenue	78	176	66
Total	2,469	2,546	2,547

Expenditure‡	2011	2012*	2013†
Current expenditure	1,172	1,466	1,530
Wages and salaries	450	529	551
Goods and services	299	333	360
Interest payments	79	88	147
Capital expenditure	1,000	1,044	1,217
Domestically financed investment	750	796	848
Externally financed investment	250	248	369
Total	2,172	2,510	2,747

* Estimates.
† Projections.
‡ Excluding net lending ('000 million francs CFA): 19 in 2011; 74 in 2012 (estimate); 40 in 2013 (projection).

Source: IMF, *Gabon: 2012 Article IV Consultation* (March 2013).

INTERNATIONAL RESERVES
(US $ million at 31 December)

	2010	2011	2012
Gold*	9.64	19.62	21.61
IMF special drawing rights	204.53	203.89	204.11
Reserve position in IMF	0.83	0.93	1.02
Foreign exchange	1,530.53	1,952.49	2,146.44
Total	1,745.53	2,176.93	2,373.18

* Valued at market-related prices.

Source: IMF, *International Financial Statistics*.

MONEY SUPPLY
('000 million francs CFA at 31 December)

	2010	2011	2012
Currency outside depository corporations	287.80	351.22	357.85
Transferable deposits	645.31	885.35	863.95
Other deposits	465.07	540.01	731.99
Total money	1,398.17	1,776.59	1,953.79

Source: IMF, *International Financial Statistics*.

COST OF LIVING
(Consumer Price Index; base: 2000 = 100)

	2007	2008	2009
Clothing	109.8	109.5	107.2
Rent, water, electricity, gas and other fuels	113.1	123.4	128.5
All items (incl. others)	112.7	118.5	120.8

All items: 122.6 in 2010; 124.1 in 2011; 127.4 in 2012.

Food (Consumer Price Index; base: 2007 = 100): 111.8 in 2009; 116.7 in 2010; 121.4 in 2011.

Source: ILO.

NATIONAL ACCOUNTS
('000 million francs CFA at current prices)

Expenditure on the Gross Domestic Product

	2010	2011	2012*
Government final consumption expenditure	853	912	993
Private final consumption expenditure	2,179	2,338	2,548
Gross fixed capital formation	1,664	1,968	2,033
Changes in inventories	58	—	—
Total domestic expenditure	4,754	5,218	5,574
Exports of goods and services	4,020	4,895	4,884
Less Imports of goods and services	2,209	2,503	2,645
GDP at purchasers' values	6,565	7,610	7,813

Gross Domestic Product by Economic Activity

	2010	2011	2012*
Agriculture, livestock, hunting, forestry and fishing	269	293	315
Mining and quarrying	3,438	4,229	4,138
Manufacturing	261	281	303
Electricity, gas and water	100	112	126
Construction	140	153	170
Trade, restaurants and hotels	374	399	437
Finance, insurance and real estate	711	764	834
Transport and communications	274	290	321
Public administration and defence	549	607	674
GDP at factor cost	6,117	7,128	7,318
Indirect taxes	449	482	495
GDP at purchasers' values	6,565	7,610	7,813

* Provisional figures.

Note: Deduction for imputed bank service charge assumed to be distributed at origin.

Source: African Development Bank.

BALANCE OF PAYMENTS
('000 million francs CFA)

	2010	2011*	2012†
Exports of goods f.o.b.	7,464	10,463	9,927
Petroleum	6,512	9,382	8,760
Imports of goods f.o.b.	–2,718	–3,378	–3,502
Trade balance	4,747	7,084	6,425
Services and other income (net)	–3,221	–4,116	–3,839
Balance on goods, services and income	1,525	2,969	2,586
Current transfers (net)	–237	–313	–301
Current balance	1,289	2,655	2,285
Direct investment (net)	499	696	696
Other investment assets and liabilities (net)	–1,098	–1,829	–2,294
Errors and omissions	–1,012	–1,011	–575
Overall balance	–321	511	112

* Estimates.
† Projections.

Source: IMF, *Gabon: 2012 Article IV Consultation* (March 2013).

External Trade

PRINCIPAL COMMODITIES
(distribution by SITC, US $ million)

Imports	2007	2008	2009
Food and live animals	308.8	359.3	352.9
Meat and meat preparations	98.8	117.8	104.6
Cereal and cereal preparations	89.6	105.0	111.1
Beverages and tobacco	49.8	54.4	54.1
Mineral fuels, lubricants, etc.	103.1	121.2	182.2
Petroleum, petroleum products and related materials	90.4	117.7	168.3
Chemicals and related products	192.8	332.7	243.7
Medicinal and pharmaceutical products	67.7	178.3	73.7
Basic manufactures	432.2	425.1	562.9
Iron and steel	190.3	150.3	217.5
Machinery and transport equipment	796.5	996.5	884.5
General industrial machinery and equipment	179.3	304.9	224.5
Electrical machinery, apparatus and appliances	93.4	109.0	119.6
Road vehicles	199.7	226.5	187.6
Miscellaneous manufactured articles	171.4	195.5	170.7
Total (incl. others)	2,110.2	2,563.1	2,500.9

Exports	2007	2008	2009
Crude materials (inedible), except fuels	754.3	744.1	637.9
Cork and wood	499.8	477.2	447.4
Metalliferous ore and metal scrap	226.4	211.3	161.5
Manganese ores and concentrates	223.0	206.9	157.5
Mineral fuels, lubricants, etc.	5,256.7	8,530.2	4,452.7
Basic manufactures	170.2	170.3	121.6
Cork and wood manufactures	164.8	156.4	111.0
Veneers, plywood, particle board and other wood	164.8	156.4	111.0
Total (incl. others)	6,302.0	9,565.9	5,356.0

Source: UN, *International Trade Statistics Yearbook*.

2010 ('000 million francs CFA): *Imports:* Live animals and animal products 82.1 (Meat and edible offal 55.3); Vegetable products 59.1; Prepared foodstuffs 79.8; Mineral products 179.4 (Petroleum and petroleum products 156.1); Chemical products 115.6; Plastics and articles 53.2; Base metals and articles of base metal 164.4 (Iron or steel 103.3); Machinery, mechanical and electrical equipment and parts thereof 424.9 (Mechanical equipment 323.7; Electrical equipment 101.1); Vehicles and associated transport equipment 155.4 (Road vehicles 102.9); Total imports (incl. others) 1,475.4. *Exports:* Petroleum 3,715.8; Manganese ores and concentrates 103.2; Wood and wood products 128.6; Total exports (incl. others) 4,262.1.

PRINCIPAL TRADING PARTNERS
(US $ million)

Imports c.i.f.	2007	2008	2009
Belgium	276.9	352.1	392.6
Brazil	43.7	58.9	45.3
Cameroon	65.4	60.3	52.1
China, People's Republic	82.7	101.0	122.2
Congo, Republic	15.3	56.4	19.5
France (incl. Monaco)	760.0	907.8	823.7
Germany	50.2	44.0	37.0
Greece	32.4	6.2	0.1
India	22.2	20.7	31.7
Italy	57.2	56.6	128.8
Japan	56.3	52.5	52.6
Netherlands	67.5	87.6	103.3
South Africa	44.8	42.1	44.8
Spain	58.2	48.0	46.0
Sweden	30.1	13.2	6.5
Thailand	43.6	72.7	42.5
Togo	11.0	29.8	3.5
United Arab Emirates	25.7	27.3	28.7
United Kingdom	33.7	64.1	72.1
USA	126.0	190.7	178.4
Total (incl. others)	2,110.2	2,563.1	2,500.9

Exports f.o.b.	2007	2008	2009
Bermuda	0.0	124.3	0.0
China, People's Republic	599.7	1,260.0	427.9
Congo, Republic	17.3	29.2	82.4
France (incl. Monaco)	711.7	574.3	244.9
India	57.6	613.1	43.3
Italy	75.4	266.7	36.2
Japan	349.0	66.1	5.4
Korea, Republic	8.2	2.1	86.1
Malaysia	155.1	133.0	215.3
Netherlands	31.3	346.9	159.3
South Africa	20.3	26.3	60.1
Spain	95.3	314.8	282.1
Thailand	198.4	0.3	1.1
Trinidad and Tobago	22.1	163.2	0.0
United Kingdom	97.2	2.0	112.4
USA	3,366.6	4,966.2	3,160.4
Total (incl. others)	6,302.0	9,565.9	5,356.0

Source: UN, *International Trade Statistics Yearbook*.

2010 ('000 million francs CFA): *Imports:* Belgium 199.2; Benin 31.8; Cameroon 24.1; China, People's republic 103.7; France 452.3; Germany 23.4; Italy 39.0; Japan 27.1; Netherlands 60.0; South Africa 24.0; Spain 25.1; Thailand 28.9; United Kingdom 56.3; USA 159.7; Total (incl. others) 1,475.4. *Exports:* Australia 96.5; China, People's Republic 218.2; France 161.9; India 86.7; Indonesia 61.8; Malaysia 219.9; Netherlands 236.1; Spain 130.3; Switzerland 80.6; Trinidad and Tobago 186.5; USA 2,485.2; Total (incl. others) 4,262.1.

Transport

RAILWAYS
(traffic)

	2007	2008	2009
Passengers carried ('000)	215.3	220.2	211.9
Freight carried ('000 metric tons)	4,382	n.a.	2,878

ROAD TRAFFIC
(estimates, motor vehicles in use)

	1994	1995	1996
Passenger cars	22,310	24,000	24,750
Lorries and vans	14,850	15,840	16,490

Source: IRF, *World Road Statistics*.

SHIPPING

Flag Registered Fleet
(at 31 December)

	2011	2012	2013
Number of vessels	55	57	59
Total displacement ('000 grt)	169.9	170.3	170.6

Source: Lloyd's List Intelligence (www.lloydslistintelligence.com).

International Sea-borne Freight Traffic
(million metric tons, Port-Gentil and Owendo)

	2007	2008	2009
Goods loaded	5,593	5,270	3,977
Goods unloaded	1,488	1,611	1,579

CIVIL AVIATION
(traffic on scheduled services)

	2007	2008	2009
Kilometres flown (million)	10	10	10
Passengers carried ('000)	535	546	525
Passenger-kilometres (million)	947	966	931
Total ton-kilometres (million)	161	157	148

Source: UN, *Statistical Yearbook*.

Passengers carried: 226,388 in 2010; 112,651 in 2011; 8,298 in 2012 (Source: World Bank, World Development Indicators database).

Tourism

	2001	2002	2003
Tourist arrivals	169,191	208,348	222,257
Tourism receipts (US $ million, incl. passenger transport)	46	77	84

Receipts from tourism (US $ million, incl. passenger transport): 74 in 2004; 13 in 2005.

Source: World Tourism Organization.

Communications Media

	2010	2011	2012
Telephones ('000 main lines in use)	30.4	22.5	17.0
Mobile cellular telephones ('000 subscribers)	1,610.0	2,370.2	2,930.0
Internet subscribers ('000)	22.2	n.a.	n.a.
Broadband subscribers ('000)	4.1	4.5	5.0

Source: International Telecommunication Union.

Education

(2010/11 unless otherwise indicated, estimates)

	Institutions	Teachers	Pupils		
			Males	Females	Total
Pre-primary	9*	517†	22,416	22,809	45,225
Primary	1,175*	12,961	162,708	155,238	317,946
Secondary:					
General	88‡	5,062	70,623	75,457	146,080
Technical and vocational	11‡	394†	5,025‖	2,562‖	7,587‖
Tertiary	2*	585¶	4,806¶	2,667¶	7,473¶

* 1991/92 figure.
† 2000/01 figure.
‡ 1996 figure.
§ 1999/2000 figure.
‖ 2001/02 figure.
¶ 1998/99 figure.

Source: UNESCO Institute for Statistics.

Pupil-teacher ratio (primary education, UNESCO estimate): 24.5 in 2010/11 (Source: UNESCO Institute for Statistics).

Adult literacy rate (UNESCO estimates): 89.0% (males 92.3%; females 85.6%) in 2011 (Source: UNESCO Institute for Statistics).

Directory

Note: The telephone numbers listed in this Directory are those used when dialling from within Gabon. In order successfully to dial from abroad, it is necessary to omit the initial 0.

The Government

HEAD OF STATE

President: ALI BONGO ONDIMBA (inaugurated 16 October 2009).

Vice-President: DIDJOB DIVUNGUI-DI-N'DINGUE.

COUNCIL OF MINISTERS
(April 2014)

The Government is formed by members of the Parti Démocratique Gabonais.

Prime Minister and Head of Government: Prof. DANIEL ONA ONDO.

Minister of Foreign Affairs, the Francophonie and Regional Integration: EMMANUEL ISSOZET NGONDET.

Minister of Social Security and National Solidarity: BRIGITTE MBA ANGUILLET.

Minister of Higher Education and Scientific Research: PACÔME MOUBELET BOUBEYA.

Minister of National Education and Technical and Professional Training: Prof. LÉON NZOUBA.

Minister of Agriculture, Stockbreeding, Fisheries and Food Security: LUC OYOUBI.

Minister of Relations with the Constitutional Institutions, Government Spokesperson: DENISE MEKAM'NE.

Minister of Trade, Small and Medium-sized Enterprises, Handicrafts and the Development of Services: GABRIEL TCHANGO.

Minister of Justice, Keeper of the Seals: SÉRAPHIN MOUNDOUNGA.

Minister of Health: FIDÈLE MENGUE M'ENGOUANG.

Minister of Youth and Sport: BLAISE LOUEMBÉ.

Minister of the Promotion of Investment, Infrastructure, Housing and Territorial Management: MAGLOIRE NGAMBIA.

Minister of Forests, the Environment and the Protection of Natural Resources: NOËL NELSON MESSONE.

Minister of the Economy and Planning: CHRISTOPHE AKAGHA MBA.

Minister of Culture, the Arts and Civic Education: IDA RÉTÉNO ASSONOUET.

Minister of the Digital Economy, Communication and Posts: PASTOR NGOUA NEME.

Minister of Mines, Industry and Tourism: RÉGIS IMMONGAULT TATAGANI.

Minister of the Interior, Public Security, Immigration and Decentralization: GUY BERTRAND MAPANGOU.

Minister of the Budget and Public Accounts: CHRISTIAN MAGNAGNA.

Minister of Petroleum and Hydrocarbons: ETIENNE NGOUBOU.

Minister of National Defence: ERNEST MPOUHO.

Minister of Energy and Water Resources: DÉSIRÉ GUEDON.

Minister of the Civil Service, Administrative Reform and the Modernization of Judicial and Institutional Frameworks: SERGE MAURICE MABIALA.

Minister of Labour, Employment and Professional Training: EMANE SIMON NTOUTOUME.

Minister of Transport: PAULETTE MENGUÉ M'OWONO.

Minister of Human Rights, Equal Opportunities and Gabonese Nationals Abroad: ALEXANDRE TAPOYO.

Minister-delegate to the Minister of the Interior, Public Security, Immigration and Decentralization: JEAN PIERRE OYIBA.

Minister-delegate to the Minister of Foreign Affairs, the Francophonie and Regional Integration: DIEUDONNÉ NZENGUÉ.

Minister-delegate to the Minister of Social Security and National Solidarity: MARIE FRANÇOISE DIKOUMBA.

Minister-delegate to the Minister of the Economy and Planning: MARCELLIN AGAYA.

Minister-delegate to the Minister of Transport: RAPHAËL NGAZOUZE.

Minister-delegate to the Minister of National Education and Technical and Professional Training: SERGE ENAME NSOLET.

Minister-delegate to the Minister of Forests, the Environment and the Protection of Natural Resources: LOUIS PHILIPPE MVÉ NKOGHÉ.

MINISTRIES

Office of the Prime Minister: BP 546, Libreville; tel. 01-74-70-90; fax 01-77-20-04; internet www.primature.gouv.ga.

Ministry of Agriculture, Stockbreeding, Fisheries and Food Security: BP 551, Libreville; tel. 01-72-15-79; fax 01-77-37-44; internet www.agriculture.gouv.ga.

Ministry of the Budget and Public Accounts: BP 165, Libreville; tel. 01-79-50-00; fax 01-79-57-37; internet www.budget.gouv.ga.

Ministry of the Civil Service, Administrative Reform and the Modernization of Judicial and Institutional Frameworks: Libreville.

Ministry of Culture, the Arts and Civic Education: Libreville.

Ministry of the Digital Economy, Communication and Posts: Libreville.

Ministry of the Economy and Planning: BP 747, Immeuble Arambo, Libreville; tel. 01-79-55-27; fax 01-72-18-18; internet www.economie.gouv.ga.

Ministry of Energy and Water Resources: Libreville.

Ministry of Foreign Affairs, the Francophonie and Regional Integration: BP 2245, Libreville; tel. 01-74-23-71; fax 01-74-23-74; e-mail mae@diplomatie.gouv.ga; internet www.affaires-etrangeres.gouv.ga.

Ministry of Forests, the Environment and the Protection of Natural Resources: blvd Triomphal Omar Bongo Ondimba, BP 199, Libreville; tel. 01-76-13-81; internet www.eaux-forets.gouv.ga.

Ministry of Health: BP 50, Libreville; tel. 01-76-36-11; internet www.sante.gouv.ga.

Ministry of Higher Education and Scientific Research: Libreville.

Ministry of Human Rights, Equal Opportunities and Gabonese Nationals Abroad: Libreville.

Ministry of Mines, Industry and Tourism: BP 874, Libreville; tel. 01-77-86-54; e-mail sg@mines.gouv.ga; internet www.mines.gouv.ga.

Ministry of the Interior, Public Security, Immigration and Decentralization: BP 2110, Libreville; tel. 01-74-35-06; fax 01-72-13-89; internet www.interieur.gouv.ga.

Ministry of Justice: BP 547, Libreville; tel. 01-74-66-28; fax 01-72-33-84; internet www.justice.gouv.ga.

Ministry of Labour, Employment and Professional Training: Libreville.

Ministry of National Defence: BP 13493, Libreville; tel. and fax 01-77-86-96; internet www.defense-nationale.gouv.ga.

Ministry of National Education and Technical and Professional Training: BP 6, Libreville; tel. 01-72-44-61; fax 01-72-19-74.

Ministry of Petroleum and Hydrocarbons: BP 1172, Libreville; internet www.petrole.gouv.ga.

Ministry of the Promotion of Investment, Infrastructure, Housing and Territorial Management: BP 803, Libreville; tel. 01-74-71-96; fax 01-77-33-31; internet www.equipement.gouv.ga.

Ministry of Relations with the Constitutional Institutions: Libreville.

Ministry of Social Security and National Solidarity: BP 5684, Libreville; tel. 01-72-26-61; internet www.affaires-sociales.gouv.ga.

Ministry of Trade, Small and Medium-sized Enterprises, Handicrafts and the Development of Services: BP 4120, Libreville; tel. 01-72-49-75; internet www.pme.gouv.ga.

Ministry of Transport: BP 803, Libreville; tel. 01-74-71-96; fax 01-77-33-31.

Ministry of Youth and Sport: BP 2150, Libreville; tel. 01-74-00-19; fax 01-74-65-89.

President

Presidential Election, 30 August 2009

Candidate	Valid votes	% of valid votes
Ali Bongo Ondimba (PDG)	141,952	41.73
André Mba Obame (Ind.)	88,028	25.88
Pierre Mamboundou (UPG)	85,797	25.22
Zacharie Myboto (UGDD)	13,418	3.94
Casimir Oyé Mba (Ind.)	3,118	0.92
Pierre-Claver Maganga Moussavou (PSD)	2,576	0.76
Bruno Ben Moubamba (Ind.)	963	0.28
Georges Bruno Ngoussi (Ind.)	915	0.27
Jules Artides Bourdès Ogouliguende (CDJ)	695	0.20
Albert Ondo Ossa (Ind.)	674	0.20
Others	2,028	0.60
Total	340,178*	100.00

* The total number of votes officially attributed to candidates by the Constitutional Court amounted to 340,164. However, that body declared the total number of valid votes cast to be 340,178. Additionally, there were 17,443 spoiled ballots. Several of the defeated candidates formally protested against the results and a recount of the votes was subsequently held. On 12 October the Constitutional Court announced that Bongo Ondimba had secured 141,665 valid votes, equating to 41.79%, while the number of votes attributed to Mamboundou and Mba Obame was amended to 86,875 (25.64%) and 85,814 (25.33%), respectively, thus reversing their placings in the election. No figures for the remaining candidates or the total number of votes cast were made available.

Legislature

NATIONAL ASSEMBLY

National Assembly: Libreville; internet www.assemblee.ga.

President: Guy Ndzouba Ndama.

General Election, 17 December 2011

Party	Seats
Parti Démocratique Gabonais (PDG)	114*
Rassemblement pour le Gabon (RPG)	3
Cercle des Libéraux Réformateurs (CLR)	1
Parti Social-Démocrate (PSD)	1
Union pour la Nouvelle République (UPNR)	1
Total	120†

* One seat was won in alliance with the Parti Gabonais du Centre Indépendant (PGCI).

† The results of voting in six constituencies were subsequently annulled by the Constitutional Court owing to irregularities. On 5 May 2012 by-elections were held for the six seats, all of which were won by the PDG, leaving party representations unchanged.

SENATE

Senate: Libreville; internet www.senat.ga.

President: Rose Francine Rogombé.

Election, 18 January 2009

Party	Seats
Parti Démocratique Gabonais (PDG)	75
Rassemblement pour le Gabon (RPG)	6
Parti Gabonais du Centre Indépendent (PGCI)	3
Union du Peuple Gabonais (UPG)	3
Cercle des Libéraux Réformateurs (CLR)	2
Parti Social-Démocrate (PSD)	2
Union Gabonaise pour la Démocratie et le Développement (UGDD)	2
Alliance Démocratique et Républicaine (ADERE)	1
Independents	8
Total	102

Following the appointment of a PDG senator as ambassador to France, a by-election was held on 5 May 2012 for the vacated seat. This was won by the PDG

Election Commission

Commission Electorale Nationale Autonome et Permanente (CENAP): Libreville; f. 2006 to replace the Commission Nationale Electorale; Pres. appointed by the Constitutional Court; Pres. René Aboghé Ella.

Political Organizations

Alliance Démocratique et Républicaine (ADERE): Pres. (vacant); Sec.-Gen. Didjob Divungui-di-N'Dingue.

Cercle des Libéraux Réformateurs (CLR): f. 1993 by breakaway faction of the PDG; Leader Jean-Boniface Assele.

Congrès pour la Démocratie et la Justice (CDJ): tel. 01-70-00-00; e-mail contact@bourdes-gabon.com; internet www.bourdes-gabon.com; Pres. Jules Bourdès Ogouliguende.

Front National (FN): f. 1991; Leader Martin Efayong.

Mouvement d'Emancipation Socialiste du Peuple: Leader Mouanga Mbadinga.

Parti Démocratique Gabonais (PDG): Immeuble PETROGAB, BP 75384, Libreville; tel. 01-70-31-21; fax 01-70-31-46; internet www.pdg-gabon.org; f. 1968; sole legal party 1968–90; Leader Ali Bongo Ondimba; Sec.-Gen. Faustin Boukoubi.

Parti Gabonais du Centre Indépendant (PGCI): allied to the PDG; Leader Jérôme Okinda.

Parti Gabonais du Progrès (PGP): f. 1990; Pres. (vacant); Vice-Pres. Joseph-Benoît Mouity.

Parti Social-Démocrate (PSD): f. 1991; Leader Pierre-Claver Maganga Moussavou.

Rassemblement des Démocrates Républicains (RDR): Leader Max Mebale M'Obame.

Rassemblement pour la Démocratie et le Progrès (RDP): Pres. Alain Claude Bilie Bi Nze.

Rassemblement pour le Gabon (RPG): f. 1990 as MORENA des Bûcherons; renamed Rassemblement National des Bûcherons in 1991, name changed as above in 2000; allied to the PDG; Leader Fr Paul M'Ba Abessole; Vice-Pres. Prof. Vincent Moulengui Boukosso.

Rassemblement National des Bûcherons—Démocratique (RNB): Libreville; f. 1991; Leader Pierre André Kombila.

Union Démocratique et Sociale (UDS): f. 1996; Leader Hervé Assamanet.

Union pour la Nouvelle République (UPNR): Immeuble Score, 657 ave du Col Parant, BP 4049, Libreville; tel. 01-77-40-13; fax 01-77-40-17; e-mail info@louisgastonmayila.com; internet www.louisgastonmayila.com; f. 2007 following the merger of the Front pour l'Unité Nationale (FUNDU) and the Rassemblement des Républicains Indépendants (RRI); Leader Louis-Gaston Mayila.

Union du Peuple Gabonais (UPG): BP 6048, Awendjé, Libreville; tel. 07-14-61-61 (mobile); internet www.upg-gabon.org; f. 1989 in Paris, France; Leader (vacant); Sec.-Gen. David Badinga.

Union pour le Progrès National (UPN): Leader Daniel Tengue Nzoundo.

Diplomatic Representation

EMBASSIES IN GABON

Algeria: Bord de mer, BP 4008, Libreville; tel. 01-44-38-02; fax 01-73-14-03; e-mail algerie@ambassade-lbv-algerie.com; Ambassador Djihed-Eddine Belkas.

Angola: BP 4884, Libreville; tel. 01-73-04-26; fax 01-73-76-24; Chargé d'affaires Emílio José de Carvahlo Guerra.

Benin: BP 3851, Akebe, Libreville; tel. 01-73-76-82; fax 01-73-77-75; e-mail ambassade.benin@inet.ga; internet www.maebenin.bj/Libreville.htm; Ambassador Symphorien Codjo Achodé.

Brazil: blvd de l'Indépendance, BP 3899, Libreville; tel. 01-76-05-35; fax 01-74-03-43; e-mail emblibreville@inet.ga; internet libreville.itamaraty.gov.br; Ambassador Bruno Luiz dos Santos Cobuccio.

Cameroon: blvd Léon Mba, BP 14001, Libreville; tel. 01-73-28-00; Ambassador Samuel Mvondo Ayolo.

China, People's Republic: blvd Triomphale Omar Bongo, BP 3914, Libreville; tel. 01-74-32-07; fax 01-74-75-96; e-mail gzy@internetgabon.com; Ambassador Sun Jiwen.

Congo, Democratic Republic: BP 2257, Libreville; tel. 01-73-11-61; fax 01-73-81-41; Ambassador Kabangi Kaumbu Bula.

Congo, Republic: BP 269, Libreville; tel. 01-73-29-06; e-mail ambacobrazzalibreville@yahoo.fr; Ambassador Pierre Nzila.

Côte d'Ivoire: Charbonnages, BP 3861, Libreville; tel. 01-73-82-70; fax 01-73-82-87; e-mail ambacigabon@yahoo.fr; Ambassador PHILIPPE MANGOU.

Egypt: Immeuble Floria, 1 blvd de la Mer, Quartier Batterie IV, BP 4240, Libreville; tel. 01-73-25-38; fax 01-73-25-19; Ambassador HISHAM FATHY MOHAMED.

Equatorial Guinea: BP 1462, Libreville; tel. 01-73-25-23; fax 01-73-25-22; Ambassador JOSÉ ESONO BACALE.

France: 1 rue du pont Pirah, BP 2125, Libreville; tel. 01-79-70-00; fax 01-79-70-09; e-mail scac@ambafrance-ga.org; internet www.ambafrance-ga.org; Ambassador JEAN-FRANÇOIS DESMAZIERES.

Germany: blvd de l'Indépendance, Immeuble les Frangipaniers, BP 299, Libreville; tel. 01-76-01-88; fax 01-72-40-12; e-mail amb-allegmagne@inet.ga; internet www.libreville.diplo.de; Ambassador STEFAN GRAF.

Guinea: BP 4046, Libreville; tel. 01-73-85-09; fax 01-73-85-11; Ambassador MOHAMED SAMPIL.

Italy: Immeuble Personnaz et Gardin, 321 rue de la Mairie, BP 2251, Libreville; tel. 01-74-28-92; fax 01-74-80-35; e-mail ambasciata.libreville@esteri.it; internet www.amblibreville.esteri.it; Ambassador UMBERTO MALNATI.

Japan: blvd du Bord de Mer, BP 2259, Libreville; tel. 01-73-22-97; fax 01-73-60-60; e-mail amb.japon@lv.mofa.go.jp; internet www.ga.emb-japan.go.jp; Ambassador MASAO KOBAYASHI.

Korea, Republic: BP 2620, Libreville; tel. 01-73-40-00; fax 01-73-99-05; e-mail gabon-ambcoree@mofa.go.kr; internet gab.mofa.go.kr; Ambassador CHEOLKYU CHOE.

Lebanon: BP 3341, Libreville; tel. and fax 01-73-68-77; e-mail amb.lib.gab@inet.ga; Ambassador KENJ EL HAJAL.

Mali: BP 4007, Quartier Batterie IV, Libreville; tel. 01-73-82-73; fax 01-73-82-80; e-mail ambamaga@yahoo.fr; Ambassador DADIE YACOUBA DAGNAKO.

Mauritania: BP 3917, Libreville; tel. 01-74-31-65; fax 01-74-01-62; Ambassador El Hadj THIAM.

Morocco: blvd de l'Indépendance, Immeuble CK 2, BP 3983, Libreville; tel. 01-77-41-51; fax 01-77-41-50; e-mail sifamalbv@inet.ga; Ambassador ALI BOJI.

Nigeria: ave du Président Léon-M'Ba, Quartier blvd Léon-M'Ba, BP 1191, Libreville; tel. 01-73-22-03; fax 01-73-29-14; e-mail nigeriamission@internetgabon.com; Ambassador BASSEY ARCHIBONG.

Russia: BP 3963, Libreville; tel. 01-72-48-68; fax 01-72-48-70; e-mail ambrusga@mail.ru; internet www.gabon.mid.ru; Ambassador DMITRY V. KOURAKOV.

São Tomé and Príncipe: BP 489, Libreville; tel. 01-72-09-94; Ambassador URBINO JOSÉ GONHALVES BOTELÇO.

Saudi Arabia: Haut de Gue-Gue, derrière l'Hotel Intercontinental, Libreville; tel. 01-73-84-44; fax 01-73-58-37; e-mail gaemb@mofa.gov.sa; internet embassies.mofa.gov.sa/sites/gabon; Ambassador ADNAN ABDULRAHMAN ABDUL ALMANDEEL.

Senegal: Quartier Sobraga, BP 3856, Libreville; tel. 01-77-42-67; fax 01-77-42-68; e-mail ambasengab@yahoo.fr; Ambassador SAOUDATOU NDIAYE SECK.

South Africa: Immeuble les Arcades, 142 rue des Chavannes, BP 4063, Libreville; tel. 01-77-45-30; fax 01-77-45-36; e-mail libreville.consular@foreign.gov.za; Ambassador PEARL NOMVUME MAGAQA.

Spain: Immeuble Diamant, 2ème étage, blvd de l'Indépendance, BP 1157, Libreville; tel. 01-72-12-64; fax 01-74-88-73; e-mail ambespga@mail.mae.es; Ambassador ANTONIO ALVAREZ BARTHE.

Togo: BP 14160, Libreville; tel. 01-73-29-04; fax 01-73-32-61; Ambassador ESSOHOHANAM ADEWI.

Ukraine: BP 23746, Libreville; tel. 01-44-51-03; e-mail emb_ga@mfa.gov.ua; Ambassador SERGIY MISHUSTIN.

USA: Avorbam, La Sablière, BP 4000, Libreville; tel. 01-45-71-00; fax 01-74-55-07; e-mail usembassylibreville@state.gov; internet libreville.usembassy.gov; Chargé d'affaires, a.i. DANTE PARADISO.

Judicial System

Justice is dispensed on behalf of the Gabonese people by the three autonomous chambers of the Supreme Court (judicial, administrative and accounting), the Constitutional Court, the Council of State, the Courts of Appeal, the Audit Court, the Provincial Courts, the High Court and the other special courts of law.

Supreme Court (Cour de Cassation): BP 1043, Libreville; tel. 01-72-17-00; fax 01-76-66-18; three chambers: judicial, administrative and accounting; Pres. HONORÉ MOUNDOUNGA.

Constitutional Court: BP 547, Libreville; tel. 01-76-62-88; fax 01-76-10-17; has jurisdiction on: the control of the constitutionality of laws before promulgation; all electoral litigations; all matters concerning individual fundamental rights and public liberties; the interpretation of the Constitution; and arbitration of conflicts of jurisdiction arising among the state's institutions; Pres. MARIE MADELEINE MBORANTSUO.

Council of State: BP 547, Libreville; tel. 01-72-17-00; Pres. MARTIN AKENDENGUE.

Courts of Appeal: Libreville and Franceville.

Court of State Security: Libreville; 13 mems; Pres. FLORENTIN ANGO.

Audit Court (Cour des Comptes): BP 752, Libreville; tel. 01-70-54-15; fax 01-70-40-81; e-mail cour_des_comptes_gabon@yahoo.fr; Pres. GILBERT NGOULAKIA.

Religion

About 60% of Gabon's population are Christians, mainly adherents of the Roman Catholic Church. About 40% are animists and fewer than 1% are Muslims.

CHRISTIANITY

The Roman Catholic Church

Gabon comprises one archdiocese, four dioceses and one apostolic prefecture. Some 50% of the population are Roman Catholics.

Bishops' Conference: Conférence Episcopale du Gabon, BP 2146, Libreville; tel. 01-72-20-73; f. 1989; Pres. Most Rev. TIMOTHÉE MODIBO-NZOCKENA (Bishop of Franceville).

Archbishop of Libreville: Most Rev. BASILE MVÉ ENGONE, Archevêché, Sainte-Marie, BP 2146, Libreville; tel. and fax 01-72-20-73; e-mail basilemve@yahoo.fr.

Protestant Churches

Christian and Missionary Alliance: BP 13021, Libreville; tel. 01-73-24-39; e-mail fdgabon@gmail.com; active in the south of the country; Dir Dr DAVID THOMPSON; 115 org. mem. churches, 11,226 baptized mems.

Eglise Evangélique du Gabon: BP 10080, Libreville; tel. 01-72-41-92; f. 1842; independent since 1961; 205,000 mems; Pres. Pastor JEAN-JACQUES NDONG EKOUAGHÉ; Sec. Rev. BASILE NGUEMA OLLOGHO.

The Evangelical Church of South Gabon and the Evangelical Pentecostal Church are also active in Gabon.

The Press

La Concorde: Libreville; f. 2005; owned by TV+ group; daily; Dir FRANÇOIS ONDO EDOU; circ. 10,000.

Economie Gabon +: Immeuble BICP, BP 4562, Libreville; tel. 04-79-49-05 (mobile); e-mail contact@economie-gabon.com; internet www.economie-gabon.com; quarterly; Editor-in-Chief PHILIPPE CHANDEZON.

Gabon Libre: BP 6439, Libreville; tel. 01-72-42-22; weekly; Dir DZIME EKANG; Editor RENÉ NZOVI.

Gabon-Matin: BP 168, Libreville; daily; publ. by Agence Gabonaise de Presse; Man. HILARION VENDANY; circ. 18,000.

Gabon Show: Libreville; f. 2004; independent; satirical; printed in Cameroon; Man. Editor FULBERT WORA; weekly; circ. 3,000.

Journal Officiel de la République Gabonaise: BP 563, Libreville; f. 1959; fortnightly; Man. EMMANUEL OBAMÉ.

Ngondo: BP 168, Libreville; monthly; publ. by Agence Gabonaise de Presse.

Le Peuple: BP 2170, Libreville; tel. 06-03-09-94 (mobile); e-mail lepeuple@lepeuple.info; internet www.lepeuple.info; f. 2002; weekly; Dir of Publication and Editor-in-Chief AUGUSTIN MVEME OBIANG.

Le Progressiste: blvd Léon-M'Ba, BP 7000, Libreville; tel. 01-74-54-01; f. 1990; Dir BENOÎT MOUITY NZAMBA; Editor JACQUES MOURENDE-TSIOBA.

La Relance: BP 268, Libreville; tel. 01-72-93-08; weekly; publ. of the Parti Démocratique Gabonais; Pres. JACQUES ADIAHÉNOT; Dir RENÉ NDEMEZO'O OBIANG.

Le Réveil: BP 20386, Libreville; tel. and fax 01-73-17-21; weekly; Man. ALBERT YANGARI; Editor RENÉ NZOVI; circ. 8,000.

L'Union: Sonapresse, BP 3849, Libreville; tel. 01-73-58-61; fax 01-73-58-62; e-mail mpg@inet.ga; f. 1974; 75% state-owned; daily; official govt publ; Dir-Gen. ALBERT YANAGRI; circ. 20,000.

Zoom Hebdo: Carrefour London, BP 352, Libreville; tel. 01-76-44-54; fax 01-74-67-50; e-mail zoomhebdo@assala.net; internet www

.zoomhebdo.com; Friday; f. 1991; Dir-Gen. HANS RAYMOND KWAAITAAL; circ. 12,000–20,000.

NEWS AGENCIES

Agence Gabonaise de Presse (AGP): BP 168, Libreville; tel. 01-44-35-07; fax 01-44-35-09; internet www.agpgabon.ga; f. 1960; Pres. LIN JOËL NDEMBET; Dir OLIVIER MOUKETOU.

Association Professionnelle de la Presse Ecrite Gabonaise (APPEG): BP 3849, Libreville; internet www.gabon-presse.org.

BERP International: BP 8483, Libreville; tel. 06-06-62-91 (mobile); fax 01-77-58-81; e-mail berp8483@hotmail.com; internet www.infosplusgabon.com/berp.php3; f. 1995; Dir ANTOINE LAWSON.

Publishers

Gabonaise d'Imprimerie (GABIMP): BP 154, Libreville; tel. 01-70-20-88; fax 01-70-31-85; e-mail gabimp@inet.ga; f. 1973; Dir CLAIRE VIAL.

Multipress Gabon: blvd Léon-M'Ba, BP 3875, Libreville; tel. 01-73-22-33; fax 01-73-63-72; e-mail secretariat@multipress-gabon.com; internet multipress-gabon.com; monopoly distributors of magazines and newspapers; f. 1973; Dir-Gen. JEAN-LUC PHALEMPIN.

Société Imprimerie de Gabon: BP 9626, Libreville; f. 1977; Man. Dir AKWANG REX.

Société Nationale de Presse et d'Edition (SONAPRESSE): BP 3849, Libreville; tel. and fax 01-73-58-60; e-mail unionplus@intergabon.com; internet union.sonapresse.com; f. 1975; Man. Dir ALBERT YANGARI.

Broadcasting and Communications

TELECOMMUNICATIONS

At the end of 2013 there were four providers of mobile cellular telephone services in Gabon, while Gabon Télécom was the sole provider of fixed-line services.

Airtel Gabon SA: 124 ave Bouët, Montagne Sainte, BP 9259, Libreville; tel. 07-28-01-11 (mobile); e-mail info.africa@airtel.com; internet africa.airtel.com/gabon; f. 2000; fmrly Zain Gabon, present name adopted 2010; Dir-Gen. ANTOINE PAMBORO.

Gabon Télécom: Immeuble du Delta Postal, BP 20000, Libreville; tel. 01-78-70-00; fax 01-78-67-70; e-mail gabontelecom@gabontelecom.ga; internet www.gabontelecom.ga; f. 2001; provider of telecommunications, incl. satellite, internet and cellular systems; 51% owned by Maroc Telecom; Dir-Gen. OUSSALAH LHOUSSAINE.

Moov Gabon: Immeuble Rénovation, bvld du Bord de Mer, BP 12470, Libreville; tel. 01-76-83-83; fax 01-76-83-88; internet www.moov.ga; f. 2000; Dir-Gen. ABDOULAYE CISSÉ.

USAN Gabon: Libreville; e-mail info@azur-gabon.com; internet www.azur-gabon.com; f. 2009; provides mobile cellular services under Azur network; Dir-Gen. GEORGE AKOURY.

Regulatory Authorities

Agence de Régulation des Communications Electroniques et des Postes (ARCEP): Quartier Haut de Gué-Gué, face Bureau de la Francophonie, BP 50000, Libreville; tel. 01-44-68-11; fax 01-44-68-06; e-mail artel@inet.ga; internet www.artel.ga; f. 2012 following merger of the Agence de Régulation des Télécommunications (f. 2001) and the Agence de Régulation des Postes (f. 2001); Pres. LIN MOMBO; Dir-Gen. SERGE ESSONGUÉ EWAMPONGO.

Agence Nationale des Infrastructures Numériques et des Fréquences: Cours Pasteur, Immeuble de la Solde, BP 798, Libreville; tel. 01-79-52-77; e-mail info@aninf.ga; internet www.aninf.ga; f. 2011; Dir-Gen. ALEX BERNARD BONGO ONDIMBA.

BROADCASTING

Conseil National de la Communication: BP 6437, Libreville; tel. 01-72-82-60; fax 01-72-82-71; e-mail infos@cnc.ga; f. 1991; Pres. GUY BERTRAND MAPANGOU.

Radio

The national network, 'La Voix de la Rénovation', and a provincial network broadcast for 24 hours each day in French and local languages.

Africa No. 1: BP 1, Libreville; tel. 01-74-07-34; fax 01-74-21-33; e-mail africaradio1@yahoo.fr; internet www.africa1.com; f. 1981; 35% state-controlled; int. commercial radio station; daily programmes in French and English; Pres. ELMAHJOUR AMMAR GOMAA; Sec.-Gen. LOUIS BARTHÉLEMY MAPANGOU.

Radiodiffusion-Télévision Gabonaise (RTG): BP 150, Libreville; tel. 01-73-20-25; fax 01-73-21-53; internet www.rtg1.ga; f. 1959; state-controlled; broadcasts two channels RTG1 and RTG2; Dir-Gen. (RTG1) DAVID ELLA MINTSA; Dir-Gen. (RTG2) FLORENCE MBANI; Dir of Radio GILLES TERENCE NZOGHE.

Radio Génération Nouvelle: tel. 07-42-72-83; e-mail contact@generation-nouvelle.org; internet generation-nouvelle.org; f. 1996; Dir JEAN-BONIFACE ASSELE.

Television

Radiodiffusion-Télévision Gabonaise (RTG): see Radio.

Radio Télévision Nazareth (RTN): Okala Carrière, BP 9563, Libreville; tel. 01-76-82-58; fax 01-72-20-44; e-mail rtntv@yahoo.fr; internet www.rtngabon.info; Pres. and Dir-Gen. GEORGES BRUNO NGOUSSI.

Télé-Africa: BP 4269, Libreville; tel. 01-72-49-22; fax 01-76-16-83; f. 1985; daily broadcasts in French.

TV Sat (Société de Télécommunications Audio-Visuelles): Immeuble TV SAT BP 184, Libreville; tel. 01-72-49-22; fax 01-76-16-83; f. 1994.

TV+: Immeuble Dumez, Bord de mer, BP 8344, Libreville; operation suspended in Jan. 2012; Owner ANDRÉ MBA OBAME.

Finance

(cap. = capital; res = reserves; dep. = deposits; m. = million; brs = branches; amounts in francs CFA)

BANKING

In early 2013 there were nine banks and three other financial institutions in Gabon.

Central Bank

Banque des Etats de l'Afrique Centrale (BEAC): BP 112, Libreville; tel. 01-76-13-52; fax 01-74-45-63; e-mail beaclbv@beac.int; internet www.beac.int; HQ in Yaoundé, Cameroon; f. 1973; bank of issue for mem. states of the Communauté Economique et Monétaire de l'Afrique Centrale (CEMAC, fmrly Union Douanière et Economique de l'Afrique Centrale), comprising Cameroon, the Central African Repub., Chad, the Repub. of the Congo, Equatorial Guinea and Gabon; cap. 88,000m., res 227,843m., dep. 4,110,966m. (Dec. 2007); Gov. LUCAS ABAGA NCHAMA; Dir in Gabon DENIS MEPOREWA; 4 brs in Gabon.

Commercial Banks

Banque Internationale pour le Commerce et l'Industrie du Gabon, SA (BICIG): ave du Colonel Parant, BP 2241, Libreville; tel. 01-76-26-13; fax 01-74-40-34; e-mail bicignet@bnpparibas.com; internet bicig-gabon.com; f. 1973; 26.30% state-owned, 46.67% owned by BNP Paribas SA; cap. 18,000.0m., res 1,612.8m., dep. 316,272.6m., (Dec. 2010); Pres. ETIENNE GUY MOUVAGHA TCHIOBA; Dir-Gen. CLAUDE AYO-IGUENDHA; 9 brs.

BGFI Bank: blvd de l'Indépendence, BP 2253, Libreville; tel. 01-74-32-40; fax 01-79-62-19; e-mail agence_libreville@bgfi.com; internet www.bgfi.com; f. 1972 as Banque Gabonaise et Française Internationale (BGFI); name changed as above in March 2000; cap. 73,853.3m., res 11,848.9m., dep. 423,141.7m. (Dec. 2009); Pres. and Dir-Gen. HENRI-CLAUDE OYIMA; 9 brs.

Citibank: 810 blvd Quaben, rue Kringer, BP 3940, Libreville; tel. 01-73-19-16; fax 01-73-37-86; total assets 1,000m. (Dec. 2004); Dir-Gen. GORDON ACHA.

Ecobank Gabon: 214 ave Bouet, 9e étage, Montagne Sainte, BP 12111, Libreville; tel. 01-76-20-71; fax 01-76-20-75; e-mail ecobankga@ecobank.com; internet www.ecobank.com; Chair. JOSEPH BERRE OWONDAULT; Dir-Gen. JEAN-BAPTISTE SIATÉ.

Orabank Gabon: Immeuble des Frangipaniers, blvd de l'Indépendance, BP 20333, Libreville; tel. 01-77-50-78; fax 01-72-41-97; e-mail info-ga@orabank.net; internet www.orabank.net; f. 2002; cap. 1,250m., res –394.3m., dep. 21,594.9m. (Dec. 2006); 85.47% owned by Oragroup SA (Togo); Pres. RENÉ-HILAIRE ADIAHENO; Dir-Gen. MAMOUDOU KANE; 3 brs.

Union Gabonaise de Banque, SA (UGB): ave du Colonel Parant, BP 315, Libreville; tel. 01-77-70-00; fax 01-76-46-16; e-mail ugbdio@internetgabon.com; internet www.ugb-banque.com; f. 1962; a subsidiary of Groupe Attijariwafa Bank; cap. 7,400.0m., res 6,471.8m., dep. 301,704.8m. (Dec. 2011); Dir-Gen. ABDELAZIZ YAAQOUBI; 4 brs.

Development Banks

Banque Gabonaise de Développement (BGD): rue Alfred Marche, BP 5, Libreville; tel. 01-76-24-29; fax 01-74-26-99; e-mail infos@bgd-gabon.com; internet www.bgd-gabon.com; f. 1960; 69.01%

state-owned; cap. 25,200m., res 7,677m. (Dec. 2006); Dir-Gen. ROGER OWONO MBA.

Banque de l'Habitat du Gabon (BHG): BP 574, Libreville; tel. 01-76-99-75; fax 01-76-99-77; Dir-Gen. MAGLOIRE NGAMBIA.

Financial Institutions

Alios Finance Gabon (AFG): Immeuble SOGACA, BP 63, Libreville; tel. 01-76-08-46; fax 01-76-01-03; internet www.alios-finance.com; car finance; 43% owned by CFAO Gabon, 10% state-owned; cap. and res 2,828.0m., total assets 18,583.0m. (Dec. 2003); Dir-Gen. FAISSAL CHAHROUR.

BICI-Bail Gabon: Immeuble BICIG, 5ème étage, ave du Colonel Parant, BP 2241, Libreville; tel. 01-77-75-52; fax 01-77-48-15; internet www.bicig.ga/bicibail.htm; BNP Paribas-owned.

Société Financière Transafricaine (FINATRA): blvd de l'Indépendance, BP 8645, Libreville; tel. and fax 01-77-40-87; e-mail finatra@bgfi.com; internet www.bgfi.com; f. 1997; 50% owned by BGFI Bank; cap. 2,000m., total assets 14,613m. (Dec. 2003); Dir-Gen. MARIE CÉLINE NTSAME-MEZUI.

INSURANCE

In 2010 there were eight insurance companies in Gabon, of which three provided life insurance and five provided non-life insurance.

Assinco: BP 7812, Libreville; tel. 01-72-19-25; fax 01-72-19-29; e-mail assinco@assinco-sa.com; internet assinco-sa.com; Dir EUGÉNIE DENDÉ.

Assureurs Conseils Gabonais (ACG): Immeuble Shell-Gabon, rue de la Mairie, BP 2138, Libreville; tel. 01-74-32-90; fax 01-76-04-39; e-mail acg@ascoma.com; represents foreign insurance cos; Dir MICHELLE VALETTE.

Axa Gabon: 1935 blvd de l'Indépendance, BP 4047, Libreville; tel. 01-79-80-80; fax 01-74-18-46; e-mail axa-assurances@axa-gabon.ga; internet www.axa-gabon.com; f. 1985; Dir JOËL MULLER.

Colina Assurances Gabon: Immeuble Rénovation, ave du Colonel Parant, BP 6239, Libreville; tel. 01-76-06-51; fax 01-76-06-52; e-mail gabon@groupecolina.com; non-life insurance; Dir-Gen. ERARD NONYU MOUTASSIE.

Gras Savoye Gabon: ave du Colonel Parant, BP 2148, Libreville; tel. 01-74-31-53; fax 01-74-68-38; e-mail contact@ga.grassavoye.com; internet www.ga.grassavoye.com; Dir CHRISTOPHE ROUDAUT.

NSIA Gabon: Résidence les Frangipaniers, Blvd de l'Indépendance, BP 2221–2225, Libreville; tel. 01-72-13-90; fax 01-74-17-02; e-mail nsiagabon@groupensia.com; internet www.nsiagabon.com; f. 2000 by acquisition of Assurances Mutuelles du Gabon; name changed as above in 2006; non-life insurance; owned by NSIA Participations S.A. Holding (Côte d'Ivoire); Dir-Gen. CÉSAR EKOMIE-AFENE.

NSIA Vie Gabon: BP 2221, Libreville; tel. 01-72-13-90; fax 01-74-17-02; e-mail nsiaviegabon@groupensia.com; Dir-Gen. FIDÈLE MBANA.

OGAR Gabon: 1881 blvd de l'Indépendance, BP 201, Libreville; tel. 01-76-15-96; fax 01-76-58-16; e-mail ogar@inet.ga; non-life insurance; Pres. BERNARD BARTOSZEK; also OGAR Vie for life insurance.

Union des Assurances du Gabon-Vie (UAG-Vie): ave du Colonel Parant, BP 2137, Libreville; tel. 01-74-34-34; fax 01-72-48-57; e-mail uagvie@uagvie.com; internet www.sunu-group.com; life insurance; 80.65% owned by Groupe SUNU; Pres. ALBERT ALEWINA CHAVIHOT; Dir-Gen. APOLLINAIRE EVA ESSANGONE.

Insurance Association

Fédération Gabonaise des Sociétés d'Assurances (FEGASA): BP 4005, Libreville; tel. 01-74-45-29; fax 01-77-58-23; Pres. FIDÈLE MBANA.

Trade and Industry

GOVERNMENT AGENCIES

Agence Gabonaise de Sécurité Alimentaire: Libreville; Pres. ANDRE JULES NDJAMBE; Dir-Gen. DR SYLVAIN PATRICK ENKORO.

Centre de Développement des Entreprises (CDE): Quartier Okala, BP 13740, Libreville; tel. 01-76-87-65; fax 01-76-87-64; internet www.cdegabon.com; f. 2010 to replace the Agence pour la Promotion des Investissements Privés du Gabon (APIP); promotes private investment; Pres. ANICETTE NANDA OVIGA; Dir-Gen. ALFRED NGUIA BANDA.

Comité de Privatisation: Libreville; Sec.-Gen. FÉLIX ONKEYA.

Conseil Economique et Social du Gabon: BP 1075, Libreville; tel. 01-73-19-46; fax 01-73-19-44; comprises representatives from salaried workers, employers and Govt; commissions on economic, financial and social affairs, and forestry and agriculture; Pres. ANTOINE DE PADOUE MBOUMBOU MIYAKOU.

Fonds Gabonais d'Investissement Stratégique: Libreville; f. 2010; Pres. CLAUDE AYO INGUENDA; Dir SERGE THIERRY MICKOTO CHAVAGNE.

DEVELOPMENT ORGANIZATIONS

Agence de Collecte et Commercialisation des Produits Agricoles (ACCOPA): Libreville; Pres. CHRISTIAN MENVIE M'OBAME; Dir-Gen. CHRIS MOMBO NZASSI.

Agence Française de Développement (AFD): blvd de l'Indépendance, BP 64, Libreville; tel. 01-74-33-74; fax 01-74-51-25; e-mail afdlibreville@groupe-afd.org; internet www.afd.fr; Dir YVES PICARD.

Agence Nationale des Grands Travaux (ANGT): Immeuble du bord de mer, 1er étage, à côté de l'ancien gouvernorat, BP 23765, Libreville; tel. 07-04-62-77 (mobile); e-mail info@angtmedia.com; internet www.angt-gabon.com; f. 2010; Dir-Gen. JIM DUTTON.

Agence Nationale de Promotion de la Petite et Moyenne Entreprise (PromoGabon): BP 2111, Libreville; tel. 06-26-79-19 (mobile); fax 01-74-89-59; internet www.promogabon.ga; f. 1964; state-controlled; promotes and assists small and medium-sized industries; Pres. SIMON BOULAMATARI; Man. Dir GEORGETTE ONGALA.

Agence de Régulation du Marché des Produits Forestiers: Libreville; Dir-Gen. PIERRE NGAVOURA.

Conservation et Utilisation Rationelle des Ecosystèmes Forestiers en Afrique Centrale (ECOFAC): Bas de Gué-Gué, BP 14533, Libreville; tel. and fax 01-73-23-43.

Fonds de Garantie pour le Logement (FGL): Libreville; f. 2011.

Groupes d'Etudes et de Recherches sur la Démocratie et le Développement Economique et Social au Gabon (GERDDES-Gabon): BP 13114, Libreville; tel. 06-25-14-38 (mobile); fax 07-38-04-20 (mobile); e-mail gerddesgabon@yahoo.fr; internet gerddes-gabon.asso-web.com; f. 1991; Pres. MARYVONNE C. NTSAME NDONG.

Institut Gabonais d'Appui au Développement (IGAD): BP 20423, Libreville; tel. and fax 01-74-52-47; e-mail igad@inet.ga; internet www.igadgabon.com; f. 1992; Dir-Gen. CHRISTIAN RENARDET.

Office National du Développement Rural (ONADER): Libreville; Pres. PAUL STEEVE FLAVIEN ONDZOUNGA; Dir BLAISE ESSIELE.

Office National de Laboratoires Agricoles: Libreville; Pres. JEAN FIRMIN KOUMAZOCK; Dir-Gen. PATRICK MBA BEKOUNG.

Office des Recherches, d'Introduction, d'Adaptation et de Multiplication du Matériel Végétal (ORIAM): Libreville; Pres. CHARLES MBA BISSIGUÉ; Dir-Gen. HENRI-GRÉGOIRE NGOUA ASSOUMÉ.

Programme Régionale de Gestion de l'Information Environnementale en Afrique Centrale (PRGIE): BP 932, Libreville; tel. 01-44-12-40; fax 01-77-42-61; e-mail urge@adie-prgie.org.

Société d'Investissement pour l'Agriculture Tropicale: BP 3928, Libreville; tel. 01-72-22-16; fax 01-72-22-17; e-mail gabon@siat-group.com; internet www.siatgabon.com; f. 2004; Pres. PIERRE VANDEBEECK; DirG-en. GERT VANDERSMISSEN.

CHAMBER OF COMMERCE

Chambre de Commerce, d'Agriculture, d'Industrie et des Mines du Gabon: BP 2234, Libreville; tel. 01-72-20-64; fax 01-74-12-20; f. 1935; regional offices at Port-Gentil and Franceville; Pres. JEAN BAPTISTE BIKALOU; Dir-Gen. ALAIN REMPANOT MEPIAT.

EMPLOYERS' ORGANIZATIONS

Confédération Patronale Gabonaise: Immeuble les Frangipaniers, blvd de l'Indépendence, BP 410, Libreville; tel. 01-76-02-43; fax 01-74-86-52; e-mail infocpg@patronatgabonais.ga; internet www.lacpg.org; f. 1959; represents industrial, mining, petroleum, public works, forestry, banking, insurance, commercial and shipping interests; Pres. HENRI-CLAUDE OYIMA; Sec.-Gen. CHRISTIANE QUINIO.

Syndicat des Industries du Gabon: BP 2175, Libreville; tel. 01-72-02-29; fax 01-74-52-13; e-mail sociga@ga.imptob.com; Pres. JACQUES-YVES LAUGE.

Union Nationale du Patronat Syndical des Transports Urbains, Routiers et Fluviaux du Gabon (UNAPASYTRUFGA): BP 1025, Libreville; f. 1977; represents manufacturers of vehicle and construction parts; Pres. LAURENT BELLAL BIBANG-BI-EDZO; Sec.-Gen. AUGUSTIN KASSA-NZIGOU.

UTILITIES

In 2011 the Government announced the formation of the state-owned Société d'Electricité, de Téléphone, et d'Eau du Gabon, which was to cover the provision of basic services.

Société d'Energie et d'Eau du Gabon (SEEG): BP 2187, Libreville; tel. 01-76-78-07; fax 01-76-11-34; e-mail laroche.lbv@inet.ga;

internet www.seeg-gabon.com; f. 1950; 51% owned by Veolia (France); controls 35 electricity generation and distribution centres and 32 water production and distribution centres; Pres. and Dir-Gen. CHRISTIAN LEFAIX.

TRADE UNIONS

Confédération Gabonaise des Syndicats Libres (CGSL): BP 8067, Libreville; tel. 06-03-97-73 (mobile); e-mail cgsl_2012@yahoo.fr; f. 1991; Sec.-Gen. JEAN CLAUDE BEKALÉ; 19,000 mems (2007).

Confédération Syndicale Gabonaise (COSYGA): BP 14017, Libreville; tel. 06-68-07-26 (mobile); fax 01-74-21-70; e-mail mintsacosyga@yahoo.fr; f. 1969 by the Govt, as a specialized organ of the PDG, to organize and educate workers, to contribute to social peace and economic devt, and to protect the rights of trade unions; Gen. Sec. MARTIN ALLINI; 14,610 mems (2007).

Organisation Nationale des Employés du Pétrole (ONEP): Libreville; Sec.-Gen. PAUL AIMÉ BAGAFOU.

Transport

RAILWAYS

The construction of the Transgabonais railway, which comprises a section running from Owendo (the port of Libreville) to Booué (340 km) and a second section from Booué to Franceville (357 km), was completed in 1986. By 1989 regular services were operating between Libreville and Franceville. Some 3.6m. metric tons of freight and 226,079 passengers were carried on the network in 2010, which in that year totalled 814 km. In 1998 the railways were transferred to private management.

Agence des Régulation des Transports Ferroviaires (ARTF): Libreville; advisor, controller and arbiter in the devt of the railways; Pres. CÉLESTIN NDOLIA-NHAUD.

Société d'Exploration du Chemin de Fer Transgabonais (SETRAG): BP 578, Libreville; tel. 01-70-24-78; fax 01-70-20-38; operates Transgabonais railway; 84% owned by COMILOG; Chair. HENRI JOBIN.

ROADS

In 2007 there were an estimated 9,170 km of roads, including 2,793 km of main roads and 6,377 km of secondary roads; about 11.9% of the road network was paved.

AGS Frasers: BP 9161, Libreville; tel. 01-70-23-16; fax 01-70-41-56; e-mail direction-gabon@ags-demenagement.com; internet www.agsfrasers.com; Man. BERNARD DURET.

APRETRAC: BP 4542, Libreville; tel. 01-72-84-93; fax 01-74-40-45; e-mail apretrac@assala.net; Dir CHRISTOPHE DISSOU.

Action Rapide Transit (ART): BP 9391, Libreville; tel. 01-73-79-40; fax 01-73-79-51; e-mail contactlbv@artgabon.com; internet artgabon.com; f. 1993; freight; Dir-Gen. PHILIPPE BERGON.

Fonds Routier (FR): Galerie des Jardins d'Ambre, BP 16201, Libreville; tel. 01-76-93-90; fax 01-76-93-96; e-mail info@fer-gabon.org; internet www.frgabon.org; f. 1993; Pres. RAPHAËL MAMIAKA; Dir-Gen. LANDRY PATRICK OYAYA.

GETMA Gabon: BP 7510, Libreville; tel. 01-70-28-14; fax 01-70-40-20; Dir BERTRAND ROSE.

Trans form: BP 7538, Libreville; tel. 01-70-43-95; fax 01-70-21-91; e-mail transformgab@yahoo.fr; f. 1995; Dir JEAN-PIERRE POULAIN.

INLAND WATERWAYS

The principal river is the Ogooué, navigable from Port-Gentil to Ndjolé (310 km) and serving the towns of Lambaréné, Ndjolé and Sindara.

Compagnie de Navigation Intérieure (CNI): BP 3982, Libreville; tel. 01-72-39-28; fax 01-74-04-11; f. 1978; scheduled for privatization; responsible for inland waterway transport; agencies at Port-Gentil, Mayumba and Lambaréné; Chair. JEAN-PIERRE MENGWANG ME NGYEMA; Dir-Gen. FRANÇOIS OYABI.

SHIPPING

The principal deep-water ports are Port-Gentil, which handles mainly petroleum exports, Owendo, 15 km from Libreville, which services mainly barge traffic, and Mayumba. The main ports for timber are at Owendo, Mayumba and Nyanga, and there is a fishing port at Libreville. A new terminal for the export of minerals, at Owendo, was opened in 1988. At 31 December 2013 Gabon's flag registered fleet numbered 59 vessels and had a total displacement of 170,602 grt.

Compagnie de Manutention et de Chalandage d'Owendo (COMACO): BP 2131, Libreville; tel. 01-70-26-35; f. 1974; Pres. GEORGES RAWIRI; Dir in Libreville M. RAYMOND.

Compagnie Nationale de Navigation Intérieure et Internationale: Libreville.

Conseil Gabonais des Chargeurs (CGC): Libreville; internet www.cgcworld.com; f. 1971; Pres. LUCCHERIE NGAYILA; Dir-Gen. LILIANE NADÈGE NGARI.

Office des Ports et Rades du Gabon (OPRAG): Owendo, BP 1051, Libreville; tel. 01-70-00-48; fax 01-70-37-35; e-mail info@ports-gabon.com; internet ports-gabon.com; f. 1974; 25-year management concession acquired in April 2004 by the Spanish PIP group; national port authority; Pres. ALI BONGO ONDIMBA; Dir-Gen. RIGOBERT IKAMBOUAYAT NDÉKA.

SAGA Gabon: Zone OPRAG, BP 518, Port-Gentil; tel. 01-55-58-19; fax 01-55-21-71; e-mail sagalbv@internetgabon.com; internet www.saga.fr; Chair. G. COGNON; Man. Dir DANIEL FERNÁNDEZ.

SDV Gabon: Zone Portuaire d'Owendo, BP 77, Libreville; tel. 01-70-26-36; fax 01-70-23-34; e-mail shipping.lbv@ga.dti.bollore.com; internet www.sdv.com; freight by land, sea and air.

Société Nationale d'Acconage et de Transit (SNAT): BP 3897, Libreville; tel. 01-70-04-04; fax 01-70-13-11; e-mail snat.direction@ga.dti.bollore.com; freight transport and stevedoring; Dir-Gen. MARC GÉRARD.

CIVIL AVIATION

There are international airports at Libreville, Port-Gentil and Franceville, and 65 other public and 50 private airfields, linked mostly with the forestry and petroleum industries.

Agence Nationale de l'Aviation Civile (ANAC): BP 2212, Libreville; tel. 01-44-54-00; fax 01-44-54-01; e-mail anac@anac-gabon.com; internet www.anacgabon.org; f. 2008; Pres. EMMANUEL NZÉ-BÉKALÉ; Dir-Gen. DOMINIQUE OYINAMONO.

Gabon Fret: BP 20384, Libreville; tel. 01-73-20-69; fax 01-73-44-44; e-mail gabonfret.gf@gabonfret.com; internet www.gabonfret.com; f. 1995; air freight handlers; Dir DOMINIQUE OYINAMONO.

Nouvelle Air Affaires Gabon: BP 3962, Libreville; tel. 01-73-25-13; fax 01-73-49-98; e-mail online@sn2ag.com; internet www.sn2ag.com; f. 1975; domestic passenger chartered and scheduled flights, and medical evacuation; Chair. HERMINE BONGO ONDIMBA.

Société de Gestion de l'Aéroport de Libreville (ADL): BP 363, Libreville; tel. 01-73-62-44; fax 01-73-61-28; e-mail dg@adlgabon.com; internet www.adlgabon.com; f. 1988; 26.5% state-owned; management of airport at Libreville; Pres. CHANTAL LIDJI BADINGA; Dir-Gen. JEAN-MARC SANSOVINI.

Tourism

Tourist arrivals were estimated at 186,000 in 2009, and receipts from tourism totalled US $13m. in 2005. The tourism sector is being extensively developed, with new hotels and associated projects and the promotion of national parks.

Centre Gabonais de Promotion Touristique (GABONTOUR): 622 ave du Colonel Parant, BP 2085, Libreville; tel. 01-72-85-04; fax 01-72-85-03; e-mail accueil@gabontour.ga; internet www.gabontour.ga; f. 1988; Dir-Gen. ALBERT ENGONGA BIKORO.

Office National Gabonais du Tourisme: BP 161, Libreville; tel. 01-72-21-82.

Defence

As assessed at November 2013, the army consisted of 3,200 men, the air force of 1,000 men and the navy of an estimated 500 men. Paramilitary forces (gendarmerie) numbered 2,000. Military service is voluntary. France maintains a detachment of 900 troops in Gabon.

Defence Expenditure: Budgeted at an estimated 139,000m. francs CFA for 2013.

Commander-in-Chief of the Armed Forces: Gen. JEAN-CLAUDE ELLA EKOGHA.

Education

Education is officially compulsory and free of charge for 10 years between six and 16 years of age. According to UNESCO estimates, in 2000/01 80% of children in the relevant age-group (81% of boys; 80% of girls) attended primary schools, while in 2001/02 enrolment at secondary schools was equivalent to 53% of children in the relevant age-group. Primary and secondary education is provided by the State and mission schools. Primary education begins at the age of six and lasts for five years. Secondary education, beginning at 12 years of age, lasts for up to seven years, comprising a first cycle of four years and a second of three years. The Université Omar Bongo is based at Libreville and the Université des Sciences et des Techniques de Masuku at Franceville. Many students go to France for university and technical training. In 2000 spending on education represented 3.8% of total budgetary expenditure.

THE GAMBIA

Introductory Survey

LOCATION, CLIMATE, LANGUAGE, RELIGION, FLAG, CAPITAL

The Republic of The Gambia is a narrow territory around the River Gambia on the west coast of Africa. Apart from a short coastline on the Atlantic Ocean, the country is a semi-enclave in Senegal. The climate is tropical, with a rainy season from July to September. Away from the river swamps most of the terrain is covered by savannah bush. Average temperatures in Banjul range from 23°C (73°F) in January to 27°C (81°F) in July, while temperatures inland can exceed 40°C (104°F). English is the official language, while the principal vernacular languages are Mandinka, Fula and Wolof. About 85% of the inhabitants are Muslims; most of the remainder are Christians, and there are a small number of animists. The national flag (proportions 2 by 3) has red, blue and green horizontal stripes, with two narrow white stripes bordering the central blue band. The capital is Banjul.

CONTEMPORARY POLITICAL HISTORY

Historical Context

Formerly administered with Sierra Leone, The Gambia became a separate British colony in 1888. A universal adult franchise was established in 1960. Following legislative elections in May 1962, the leader of the People's Progressive Party (PPP), Dr (later Sir) Dawda Kairaba Jawara, became Premier. Full internal self-government followed in October 1963. On 18 February 1965 The Gambia became an independent country within the Commonwealth, with Jawara as Prime Minister. The country became a republic on 24 April 1970, whereupon Jawara took office as President. He was re-elected in 1972 and again in 1977.

The first direct presidential election was held in May 1982. Jawara, who was opposed by the leader of the National Convention Party (NCP), Sheriff Mustapha Dibba, was re-elected, with 72% of the votes cast. In the concurrent legislative elections the PPP won 27 of the 35 elective seats in the House of Representatives. At legislative elections in March 1987 the PPP took 31 of the 36 directly elected seats in the House of Representatives. In the presidential election Jawara was re-elected with 59% of the votes cast; Dibba received 27% of the votes, and Assan Musa Camara, a former Vice-President who had recently formed the Gambian People's Party (GPP), won 14%. Rumours of corruption and the abuse of power at ministerial level persisted throughout the decade.

Plans were announced in August 1981 for a confederation of The Gambia and Senegal, to be called Senegambia. The confederal agreement came into effect in February 1982; a Confederal Council of Ministers, headed by President Abdou Diouf of Senegal (with President Jawara as his deputy), held its inaugural meeting in January 1983, as did a 60-member Confederal Assembly. However, the confederation was dissolved in September, and a period of tension between the two countries followed: Senegal accused The Gambia of harbouring rebels of the Mouvement des Forces Démocratiques de la Casamance (MFDC), an organization seeking independence for the Casamance region—which is virtually separated from the northern segment of Senegal by the enclave of The Gambia. In January 1991 the two countries signed an agreement of friendship and co-operation.

Jawara was elected for a sixth time in April 1992, receiving 58% of the votes cast, while Dibba took 22%. In elections to the House of Representatives the PPP retained a clear majority, with 25 elected members. The NCP secured six seats, the GPP two and independent candidates the remaining three.

Domestic Political Affairs

On 22 July 1994 Jawara was deposed by a self-styled Armed Forces Provisional Ruling Council (AFPRC), a group of five young army officers led by Lt (later Col) Yahya Jammeh, in a bloodless coup. The AFPRC suspended the Constitution and banned all political activity. Jammeh pronounced himself Head of State and appointed a mixed civilian and military Government. Purges of the armed forces and public institutions were implemented, and in November it was announced that 10 of Jawara's former ministers would be tried on charges of corruption.

The AFPRC's timetable for a transition to civilian rule, published in October 1994, envisaged a programme of reform culminating in the inauguration of new elected institutions in December 1998. The length of the transition period prompted criticism both internationally and domestically. In November 1994 Jammeh commissioned a National Consultative Committee (NCC) to make recommendations regarding a possible shortening of the period of transition to civilian rule; the NCC proposed a return to civilian government in 1996.

The draft of a report by a Constitutional Review Commission (established in April 1995) was published in March 1996. Opponents of the AFPRC criticized provisions of the Constitution that, they alleged, had been formulated with the specific intention of facilitating Jammeh's election to the presidency (although the Head of State had frequently asserted that he would not seek election).

A constitutional referendum took place on 8 August 1996, at which 70.4% of voters endorsed the new document. A presidential decree was issued in the following week reauthorizing party political activity. Shortly afterwards, however, a further decree (Decree 89) was promulgated, according to which all holders of executive office in the 30 years prior to July 1994 were to be prohibited from seeking public office, with the PPP, the NCP and the GPP barred from contesting the forthcoming presidential and parliamentary elections; the measure was strongly criticized by the Commonwealth Ministerial Action Group on the Harare Declaration (CMAG, see p. 237). Thus, the only parties from the Jawara era authorized to contest the elections were the People's Democratic Organization for Independence and Socialism (PDOIS) and the People's Democratic Party.

In August 1996 a political party supporting Jammeh, the Alliance for Patriotic Reorientation and Construction (APRC) was established. In early September Jammeh resigned from the army, in order to contest the presidency as a civilian, as required by the Constitution. According to official results of the presidential election held on 26 September, Jammeh secured the presidency with 55.8% of the votes cast, ahead of Ousainou Darboe, the leader of the United Democratic Party (UDP), who received 35.8%. The rate of participation by voters was again high, although observers, including CMAG, expressed doubts as to the credibility of the election results. The dissolution of the AFPRC was announced the same day. Jammeh was inaugurated as President on 18 October.

At legislative elections, which took place on 2 January 1997, the APRC won an overwhelming majority in the National Assembly, securing 33 elective seats. The UDP obtained seven elective seats, the National Reconciliation Party (NRP) two, the PDOIS one and independent candidates two. As Head of State, Jammeh was empowered by the Constitution to nominate four additional members of parliament, from whom the Speaker and Deputy Speaker would be chosen. The opening session of the National Assembly, on 16 January, denoted the full entry into force of the Constitution and thus the inauguration of the Second Republic. Under the new Constitution, ministers of cabinet rank were designated Secretaries of State, and the Government was reorganized accordingly in March.

In May 2001 the National Assembly and the President approved a number of constitutional amendments, which were to be submitted to a referendum. The opposition protested against the proposed changes, which included the extension of the presidential term from five to seven years, the introduction of a presidential prerogative to appoint local chiefs, and the replacement of the permanent Independent Election Commission (IEC) with an ad hoc body.

The 2001 presidential election

In July 2001 Jammeh announced the abrogation of Decree 89, although several prominent individuals who had participated in pre-1994 administrations, including Jawara, remained prohibited from seeking public office. None the less, the PPP, the

NCP and the GPP were subsequently re-established. In August the UDP, the PPP and the GPP formed a coalition and announced that Darboe would be its presidential candidate in an election scheduled for October.

A number of violent incidents were reported during the week before the presidential election. Nevertheless, the presidential election was held, as scheduled, on 18 October 2001. Jammeh was re-elected to the presidency, with 52.8% of the votes cast, according to official results, ahead of Darboe, who won 32.6%. Although Darboe conceded defeat, members of the opposition subsequently disputed the legitimacy of the results, reiterating claims of violations in voting procedures. None the less, international observers described the poll as being largely free and fair. In December, at his inauguration, President Jammeh granted an unconditional amnesty to Jawara, guaranteeing the former President's security should he decide to return to The Gambia.

In December 2001 the UDP-PPP-GPP coalition announced that it would boycott legislative elections scheduled for January 2002, as a result of the alleged addition of some 50,000 foreign citizens to electoral lists and the reputed transfer of voters between the electoral lists of different constituencies. Having denied these accusations, the IEC announced that the APRC had secured 33 of the 48 elective seats in the enlarged National Assembly, in constituencies where the party was unopposed owing to the boycott. At the elections, which took place on 17 January, the APRC won 12 of the 15 contested seats, giving the party an overall total of 45 elective seats; the PDOIS obtained two seats, and the NRP one. An additional five members of parliament were appointed by President Jammeh, in accordance with the Constitution. Dibba, whose NCP had formed an alliance with the APRC prior to the elections, was appointed Speaker of the new National Assembly.

In May 2002 the National Assembly approved legislation that imposed stricter regulations over the print media, in accordance with which all journalists not working for the state-controlled media would be required to register with a National Media Commission (NMC). The law was condemned by the Gambia Press Union. In June Jawara returned to The Gambia from exile; at the end of the month he was officially received by Jammeh and later tendered his resignation as leader of the PPP.

In June 2003 the NMC was created, despite continuing opposition from journalists, and was given far-reaching powers, including the authority to imprison journalists for terms of up to six months. In December legislation providing for terms of imprisonment of up to three years for journalists found guilty of libel or sedition, and obliging members of the media to re-register with the state, was approved by the National Assembly, despite protests by members of the Gambian and international media. In December 2004 Deyda Hydara, the editor of the independent newspaper *The Point*, who had been severely critical of the new legislation, was murdered in Banjul. The incident precipitated a demonstration in the capital, reportedly attended by several hundred journalists, and later that month a one-week media strike was observed.

The National Alliance for Democracy and Development (NADD), a coalition of five opposition parties, including the NRP, the PDOIS and the UDP, was formed in January 2005 with the aim of presenting a single candidate to contest the presidential election scheduled to take place in late 2006. In June 2005 four deputies, among them three opposition leaders—Hamat Bah of the NRP and Sidia Jatta and Halifa Sallah of the PDOIS—were expelled from the National Assembly following their registration as members of the NADD. (According to Gambian law, deputies were not permitted to switch allegiance between political parties during the term of a parliament.) By-elections to the vacant seats were held in September at which the NADD retained three of the contested constituencies, while the APRC took the remaining seat. In November Bah and Sallah, along with another senior member of the NADD, Omar Jallow, were arrested and charged with sedition. They were released on bail in mid-December and in February 2006 all charges against them were dropped. However, in the same month a rift in the NADD became apparent, with the NRP and the UDP withdrawing and forming a new coalition.

A presidential election was held on 22 September 2006, at which Jammeh won 67.3% of the votes cast. His nearest rival was Darboe (candidate for the UDP, the NRP and the Gambia Party for Democracy and Progress) with 26.7%, while Halifa Sallah of the NADD was placed third with some 6.0%. Some 59% of the eligible electorate participated in the ballot.

Jammeh's third elective term

The ruling APRC won 42 seats at legislative elections held on 25 January 2007, while the UDP took four seats, the NADD one seat and an independent candidate one seat. Sallah and Bah failed to be re-elected to the National Assembly. The rate of voter participation was officially recorded at 41.7%.

A cabinet reorganization was effected in September 2007 in which Crispin Grey-Johnson was appointed Secretary of State for Foreign Affairs and National Assembly Matters. Further governmental changes were implemented in November when Secretary of State for Health and Social Welfare Dr Tamsir Mbowe was dismissed. Although no official reason was given, Mbowe was earlier reported to have made controversial claims that President Jammeh had succeeded in finding a cure for HIV/AIDS. The following month Maj. Dr Malick Njie was named as Mbowe's successor.

In March 2008 the Cabinet came under further scrutiny when allegations of fraud and inefficiency were reported; two ministers were subsequently dismissed. Dr Omar Touray assumed responsibility for the foreign affairs portfolio in a further cabinet change later that month, while another two minor governmental reorganizations were effected in February 2009. Constitutional amendments, which were adopted by the National Assembly in April, provided for a change in the title of members of the Government from Secretary of State to Minister.

Halifa Sallah was arrested and detained in June 2009 along with a number of other journalists and editors, reportedly accused of being disrespectful to President Jammeh with regard to the murder of Hydara in 2004 in articles published in Sallah's newspaper *Foroyaa*. In July 2009 six journalists were imprisoned on charges of sedition; they were pardoned and released in September, although President Jammeh reiterated that those who were disrespectful towards him would be subjected to punishment.

The army Chief of Defence Staff, Gen. Lang Tombong Tamba, was dismissed in October 2009 and replaced by his hitherto deputy, Brig.-Gen. Massaneh Kinteh. A further four senior military officials were also dismissed. In February 2010 President Jammeh implemented a major reorganization of the Government, appointing four new ministers and creating a new Ministry of Economic Planning and Industrial Development; two additional reorganizations followed in March. Also in March six senior members of the security forces, most notably the Commander of the Navy, Sarjo Fofona, were removed from their posts and placed under arrest. Later that month Fofona, Tamba and Lt-Col Ndure Cham (another former Chief of Defence Staff), *inter alios*, were accused of planning a coup against the Jammeh regime during the previous year and were charged with treason. Eight of the accused, including Tamba and other high-ranking military officers, were found guilty in July and received death sentences, a decision that was condemned by the European Union (EU, see p. 273). The Court of Appeal and the Supreme Court upheld these sentences in April 2011 and October 2012, respectively. (In June 2010 prosecutors also accused Tamba and Fofona of taking part in a plot to overthrow the President in 2006. Both received prison sentences of 20 years on this charge in May 2011.) Critics of the regime claimed that the coup plot was a fabrication devised by Jammeh to remove potential political rivals.

Senior UDP official Femi Peters was fined and imprisoned for one year in April 2010, after being convicted of orchestrating an illegal public meeting, prompting expressions of concern from the EU, the United Kingdom and the USA. An appeal against Peters' sentence was rejected in August, although he was released in December. The President carried out another cabinet reorganization in June, most notably replacing Ousman Jammeh with Dr Mamadou Tangara as Minister of Foreign Affairs, International Co-operation and Gambians Abroad. The Office of the President assumed responsibility for the energy and higher education portfolios in the same month. Abdou Kolley, after being replaced as Minister of Finance and Economic Affairs in March, was restored to his former position in a further government reorganization in July. Additional changes were made to the Government in early 2011, following the death of the Minister of Health and Social Welfare, Dr Abu Bakarr Gaye. Fatim Badjie, who had been dismissed as Minister of Information and Communication Infrastructure in 2009, returned to the Cabinet as Gaye's replacement in February 2011, while in January Mambury Njie, hitherto the Minister of Economic Planning and Industrial Development, had assumed responsibility for the finance and economic affairs portfolio.

Jammeh retains the presidency

In March 2011 the head of the IEC announced that a presidential election would take place on 24 November, to be followed by legislative elections in early 2012 and local government elections in 2013. President Jammeh stated that his party, the APRC, would not campaign, as he was confident of being re-elected. Several opposition politicians publicly stated that the shortening of the election campaign period to 11 days placed them at a significant electoral disadvantage, given the President's permanent access to national media. A report published in July by the Observatory for the Protection of Human Rights Defenders expressed concern at the repression of journalists and civil society in The Gambia, and voiced fears that such instances could increase as the election approached.

In June 2011 the former Minister of Communications and Information Technology, Amadou Scatred Janneh, was one of four people arrested on suspicion of conspiracy to commit treason and sedition. The four were allegedly members of a civil society organization named Coalition for Change—The Gambia, which claimed to challenge dictatorship and promote basic freedoms through non-violent action. Janneh was sentenced to life imprisonment in January 2012 (his three co-accused received six-year prison terms), although he was granted a presidential pardon in September.

In October 2011 the main opposition parties announced that they had failed to agree on a single joint candidate to oppose Jammeh in the forthcoming presidential election. On 24 November Jammeh was re-elected to the office of the President for a fourth term, receiving 71.5% of votes cast. His nearest opponent, Darboe of the UDP, won 17.4% of the votes, while Hamat Bah, representing a United Front of four opposition parties—the Gambia Party for Democracy and Progress (GPDP), the NADD, the NRP, and the PDOIS—took 11.1%. The rate of voter participation was 83%. Two days prior to the polling date, the Economic Community of West African States (see p. 260) had announced that it would not be observing the elections, stating that conditions within the country—including domination of mass media by the ruling party, a lack of neutrality in state institutions, and widespread intimidation of the opposition and electorate—were not conducive to the holding of free and fair elections. Nevertheless, the elections were observed by missions from the African Union (AU), the Commonwealth, and the Organization of Islamic Co-operation. These bodies broadly agreed that the elections had been conducted in a fair and transparent manner, although the AU mission observed in its report that the APRC had benefited from superior media access and financial resources.

In December 2011 former justice minister and maritime law expert Fatou Bensouda was elected Chief Prosecutor to the International Criminal Court in the Hague, Netherlands (thus becoming the first African to assume that post). In February 2012 Jammeh effected a major reorganization of his Cabinet; only eight members of the outgoing Government were retained, although Tangara and Njie were again respectively appointed to head the foreign affairs and finance ministries.

Legislative elections, which were held on 29 March 2012, were boycotted by all opposition parties with the exception of the NRP, which took one seat. The APRC was unopposed in 25 constituencies and won 43 of the 48 elective seats available. The remaining four seats were secured by independent candidates. An official voter turnout of 50% was recorded.

In April 2012 Jammeh announced that Njie had replaced Tangara as Minister of Foreign Affairs, International Co-operation and Gambians Abroad. Tangara became Minister of Fisheries, Water Resources and National Assembly Matters, while Kolley was again appointed to head the finance ministry. Later in April, in a further reorganization of the Government, Tangara was moved to head the higher education ministry, with President Jammeh assuming responsibility for Tangara's former portfolio. Ousman Sonko was reappointed as Minister of the Interior in May. Chief of Defence Staff Lt-Gen. Masanneh Kinteh, along with another high-ranking officer in the armed forces, was dismissed in July. Tangara was again given control of the foreign affairs portfolio in August, while Njie briefly assumed responsibility for higher education until his dismissal later that month. In November Susan Waffa-Ogoo became the minister responsible for foreign affairs, with Tangara resuming his former role at the higher education ministry. Also in that month Jammeh appointed new heads of the fisheries, health, lands, and information ministries. Jammeh again made changes to the composition of the Government in January and March 2013 (his frequent reorganizations of the Cabinet and the military regarded by analysts as an effort to preclude any serious threat to his authority).

Meanwhile, in August 2012 Jammeh attracted international censure when he announced his intention to expedite the executions of all prisoners who had been sentenced to death, many of whom had been convicted of political offences such as treason. Amid allegations of due process violations, nine of the 47 detainees on death row were executed later that month (the first official enactment of capital punishment in the country since 1985); however, ostensibly due to international pressure, Jammeh suspended the remaining executions in September. The authorities closed two newspapers that had provided coverage of the executions, while a new opposition group, the National Transitional Council of The Gambia, was formed in Senegal. In November Njie, who had reportedly criticized Jammeh for authorizing the executions, was arrested, and in the following month was charged with committing an unspecified economic crime. Baba Leigh, a prominent imam who had also condemned the executions, was detained in December, and former Minister of Justice Amie Bensouda was arrested and released on bail in the same month, although no formal charges were announced. (Leigh was finally released from detention in May 2013, following expressions of concern from the EU and the USA.)

Local government elections, which were held on 4 April 2013, were boycotted by all opposition parties, except for the NRP, on the grounds that the IEC had not provided a fair electoral system. The APRC secured 104 of the 114 council seats, while independents won the remaining 10 seats, the NRP failed to obtain any of the seats that it contested. An independent candidate, Abdoulie Bah, notably defeated the APRC incumbent to secure the mayoralty of Banjul. In May the Minister of Justice and Attorney-General, Lamin Jorbarteh, was removed from his post and arrested on several charges, including abuse of office. On 5 July the National Assembly approved legislation that introduced new penalties for the publication of material deemed anti-Government on the internet. In August Amie Joof, who had replaced Jorbateh as Minister of Justice and Attorney-General, was dismissed while in the USA; she was succeeded in the post by Mama Fatima Singhateh. In December Jorbarteh and two other former senior officials, who were accused of conspiring to remove a former Chief Justice, Joseph Wowo, were sentenced to two years' imprisonment by a Special Criminal Court in Banjul. In January 2014 the Court also sentenced Wowo to two years' imprisonment, while imposing a further one-year term on Jorbarteh, for abuse of office. In early March the Chief Justice was again replaced.

Recent developments: The Gambia's withdrawal from the Commonwealth

Meanwhile, at the end of September 2013 human rights activists staged protests in New York to coincide with a visit by Jammeh, who delivered a speech highly critical of perceived Western interference in The Gambia's affairs at the UN General Assembly. On 2 October Jammeh announced the decision to withdraw The Gambia from the Commonwealth, which he referred to as a neo-colonial institution, and later issued a statement that the Governments of the USA and the United Kingdom had waged a concerted campaign to destabilize the country. Two books authored by Jammeh, which denounced British rule of The Gambia and alleged looting of its resources, and detailed perceived ways in which the country had been disadvantaged by membership of the Commonwealth, were promoted nationwide from February 2014.

Foreign Affairs

Regional relations

After the 1994 coup The Gambia's traditional aid donors and trading partners suspended much co-operation. The Jammeh administration therefore sought new links: diplomatic relations with Libya, severed in 1980, were restored in November 1994, and numerous co-operation agreements ensued. Links with the Republic of China (Taiwan) were re-established in July 1995, whereupon Taiwan became one of The Gambia's major sources of funding. In November 2013, however, The Gambia terminated diplomatic relations with Taiwan, citing 'national strategic interest', and the ambassadors of both countries were withdrawn.

Despite the presence in Senegal of prominent opponents of his Government, Jammeh also sought to improve relations with that country. In June 1997 the two countries agreed to take joint measures to combat insecurity, illegal immigration, arms-trafficking and drugs-smuggling. In January 1998 the Government of Senegal welcomed an offer by Jammeh to mediate in the conflict in the southern province of Casamance: the separatist MFDC is chiefly composed of the Diola ethnic group, of which Jammeh is a member. In December 2000 the Gambian Government sent a delegation to participate in talks between the MFDC and the Senegalese Government. A dispute between the two countries arose in August 2005 when Gambian authorities increased the price of the ferry across the Gambia river at Banjul and in retaliation Senegalese lorry drivers commenced a blockade of the common border. The conflict was resolved in October, under the mediation of the Nigerian President, Olusegun Obasanjo, and an agreement was reached to build a bridge over the Gambia river. However, renewed fighting in Senegal's Casamance province from March 2006 resulted in further inflows of refugees into The Gambia, including a number of rebel leaders sought by the Senegalese authorities.

The Government severed diplomatic relations with Iran in November 2010. Although no formal explanation for this action was provided, Gambian officials intimated that it was related to the interception by Nigerian authorities, the previous month, of a consignment of illegal weapons from Iran that was allegedly en route to The Gambia. The final destination of the arms shipment was reportedly a property in The Gambia belonging to President Jammeh (although the Gambian Government dismissed this claim), and there was speculation in Senegal that the weapons would have been smuggled across the border to the MFDC to aid the separatist insurgency, raising tensions between the two West African nations. Nevertheless, bilateral relations improved, following discussions in January 2011 between Tangara and high-ranking Senegalese officials (including President Abdoulaye Wade) in Senegal. In February Senegal and The Gambia agreed to establish a Boundary Management Commission to address matters relating to their common border. In August, in an official state visit to The Gambia, Wade reiterated the hope that President Jammeh would assist in enabling a peaceful resolution to the situation in Casamance, a sentiment that was echoed by the new Senegalese President, Macky Sall, in April 2012. However, relations were strained following the controversial prisoner executions that took place in The Gambia in August (see Domestic Political Affairs), as two Senegalese citizens were among those executed. Meanwhile, Jammeh travelled to Mauritania in May 2012 for talks with the Mauritanian leadership; six co-operation accords, mainly concerning economic matters, were concluded during his visit.

Other external relations

Relations with the United Kingdom were strained in 2001, following the expulsion of the British Deputy High Commissioner, Bharat Joshi, from The Gambia in August. The Gambian authorities alleged that the diplomat had interfered in the country's internal affairs, following his attendance at an opposition meeting. In September the Gambian Deputy High Commissioner in London was expelled from the United Kingdom, and further retaliatory measures were implemented against The Gambia. Relations were restored during 2002, although in January of that year the EU representative, George Marc-André, was declared *persona non grata* by the Gambian authorities and requested to leave the country. The Gambian Government suspended political dialogue with the EU in January 2013, having rejected demands for improved governance and respect for human rights (which included the free operation of independent media, the removal of restrictions on accessing and sharing information electronically, and a moratorium on the death penalty). The Gambia's withdrawal from the Commonwealth in October was widely regarded as a response to continued criticism of the country's human rights situation.

CONSTITUTION AND GOVERNMENT

The Constitution of the Second Republic of The Gambia, which was approved in a national referendum on 8 August 1996, entered into full effect on 16 January 1997. The Constitution provides for the separation of the powers of the executive, legislative and judicial organs of state. Under its terms, the Head of State is the President of the Republic, who is directly elected by universal adult suffrage. No restriction is placed on the number of times a President may seek re-election. Legislative authority is vested in the National Assembly, elected for a five-year term and comprising 48 members elected by direct suffrage and five members nominated by the President of the Republic. The President appoints government members, who are responsible both to the Head of State and to the National Assembly. Tribalism and other forms of sectarianism in politics are forbidden. The Gambia is divided into eight local government areas.

REGIONAL AND INTERNATIONAL CO-OPERATION

The Gambia is a member of the African Union (see p. 186), of the Economic Community of West African States (ECOWAS, see p. 260), of the Community of Sahel-Saharan States—CEN-SAD (see p. 450) and of the Gambia River Basin Development Organization (OMVG, see p. 451).

The Gambia became a member of the UN in 1965, was admitted to the World Trade Organization (WTO, see p. 434) in 1996.

ECONOMIC AFFAIRS

In 2012, according to estimates by the World Bank, The Gambia's gross national income (GNI), measured at average 2010–12 prices, was US $912m., equivalent to $510 per head (or $1,860 on an international purchasing-power parity basis). During 2003–12, it was estimated, the population increased at an average annual rate of 3.2%, while gross domestic product (GDP) per head increased by 0.2%. Overall GDP increased, in real terms, at an average annual rate of 3.4% in 20023–12; GDP declined by 4.3% in 2011, but increased by 6.0% in 2012.

Agriculture (including forestry and fishing) contributed 30.7% of GDP in 2011, according to the African Development Bank (AfDB). According to FAO, 74.7% of the labour force were estimated to be employed in the sector in mid-2014. The dominant agricultural activity has traditionally been the cultivation of groundnuts, and exports of that commodity accounted for an estimated 68.2% of domestic export earnings in 1999. However, in 2011 groundnuts accounted for just 2.0% of total exports, although production volumes had increased throughout the late 2000s. A significant proportion of the groundnut crop is frequently smuggled for sale in Senegal. Cotton, citrus fruits, mangoes, avocados and sesame seed are also cultivated for export. The principal staple crops are millet, rice, maize and sorghum, although The Gambia remains heavily dependent on imports of rice and other basic foodstuffs. Fishing makes an important contribution to the domestic food supply. According to the World Bank, agricultural GDP decreased at an average annual rate of 1.7% in 2003–11. Growth of 11.2% was recorded in 2010; however, agricultural GDP decreased by 36.6% in 2011.

Industry (including manufacturing, construction, mining and power) contributed 12.0% of GDP in 2011, according to the AfDB. About 10.3% of the labour force were employed in the sector at the time of the 1993 census. According to the World Bank, industrial GDP increased at an average annual rate of 2.7% in 2003–11; growth in 2011 was 4.7%.

The Gambia has few viable mineral resources, although seismic surveys have indicated the existence of petroleum deposits off shore. Deposits of kaolin and salt are currently unexploited. In early 2008 the discovery of commercially exploitable quantities of uranium was announced. Mining contributed 2.6% of GDP in 2011, according to the AfDB, and the GDP of the sector grew by 7.6% in 2011.

Manufacturing contributed 4.7% of GDP in 2011, according to the AfDB, and employed 6.6% of the labour force in 1993. The sector is dominated by agro-industrial activities, most importantly the processing of groundnuts and fish. Beverages and construction materials are also produced for the domestic market. According to the World Bank, manufacturing GDP increased at an average annual rate of 2.6% in 2003–11; growth in the sector 2011 was 3.9%.

According to the AfDB, construction contributed 3.4% of GDP in 2011, while the construction sector alone employed 3.0% of the total labour force in 1993. The sector grew by 9.2% in 2011.

The Gambia is highly reliant on imported energy. According to estimates by the World Bank, imports of mineral fuels and lubricants comprised an estimated 22.0% of the value of total merchandise imports in 2011.

The services sector contributed 57.4% of GDP in 2011, according to the AfDB, and employed about 34.3% of the labour force in 1993. The tourism industry is of particular significance as a generator of foreign exchange. Tourism contributed about 16% of annual GDP in the late 2000s, and employed some 10,000 workers at that time. The Jammeh administration has expressed its intention further to exploit the country's potential as a transit point for regional trade and also as a centre for regional finance and telecommunications. According to World Bank estimates, the GDP of the services sector increased at an average annual rate of 4.9% in 2003–11; growth in 2011 was 8.8%.

In 2012 The Gambia recorded an estimated visible merchandise trade deficit of US $176.4m., while there was a deficit of $15.8m. on the current account of the balance of payments. In 2011 the principal source of imports was Côte d'Ivoire, which supplied an estimated 21.1% of total imports; other major sources were Denmark, Brazil and the People's Republic of China. The largest market for exports in that year was Senegal (an estimated 35.3% of total exports). Other major purchasers were Mali, Guinea and Guinea-Bissau. The Gambia's principal exports in 2009 were food and live animals (which contributed 35.3% of total exports). The principal exports in 2011 were textile and textile articles, prepared foodstuffs beverages and spirits tobacco, vegetable products, and live animals and animal products. The principal imports in 2011 were mineral products (largely mineral fuels and oils), vegetable products, machinery and mechanical appliances, electrical and electronic equipment, vehicles, aircraft and transport equipment, and animal and vegetable fats and oils.

In 2012, according to the IMF, the budget was balanced, with revenue equalling expenditure at 7,397m. dalasi. The Gambia's general government gross debt was 23,057m. dalasi in 2012, equivalent to 79.2% of GDP. The Gambia's total external debt was US $466m. at the end of 2011, of which $385m. was public and publicly guaranteed debt. In that year, the cost of servicing long-term public and publicly guaranteed debt and repayments to the IMF was equivalent to 7.5% of the value of exports of goods, services and income (excluding workers' remittances). According to ILO the average annual rate of inflation was 5.3% in 2003–12; consumer prices increased by an average of 4.3% in 2012. The rate of unemployment was estimated at some 26% of the labour force in mid-1994.

Relations between The Gambia and the international financial community have often been strained, particularly owing to concerns over alleged inaccuracies in economic data provided by the Gambian authorities. Nevertheless, the IMF, which had resumed assistance in 2007, approved credit of US $9m. in February 2009 to reduce the detrimental effects of the global financial crisis on the country's key sectors, and further funding was authorized in February 2010 and January 2011. To support the Government's Programme for Accelerated Growth and Employment 2012–15, the Fund approved a $28m. Extended Credit Facility (ECF) in May 2012. According to the IMF, real GDP contracted significantly in 2011 as a result of a devastating drought, which caused widespread crop failure during the 2011/12 growing season. By late 2012, however, the economy had staged a recovery, driven by a resurgence in crop production and a robust tourism sector, and growth had strengthened to more than 6% by 2013. A 15% valued-added tax entered into force in January 2013, as part of an effort by the Government to boost revenues and modernize the tax regime. In May the IMF completed the first performance review under the ECF arrangement and released a disbursement of $2.3m. Official figures projected GDP growth to increase to 7.5% in 2014. However, the IMF expressed concern at the country's high budget deficit (estimated at 8% of GDP in 2013), which necessitated increased domestic borrowing, and its potentially unsustainable public debt, urging restraint in extra-budgetary expenditure and the adoption of additional adjustment measures. The Government's budget for 2014 was designed to restrain domestic borrowing to 2.5% of GDP in that year (from about 6% in 2013), and thereby reduce the strain on government finances. Meanwhile, the Government, having withdrawn from the Commonwealth in October and ended relations with the Republic of China (Taiwan), previously a major source of funding, in November, sought new economic partners; in February 2014 a memorandum of understanding was signed with a Turkish company for the construction of a solar energy complex in The Gambia, while in March plans for a new trade agreement with Spain were announced.

PUBLIC HOLIDAYS

2015: 1 January (New Year's Day), 2 January*† (Eid al-Moulid, Birth of the Prophet), 18 February (Independence Day), 3 April (Good Friday), 6 April (Easter Monday), 1 May (Workers' Day), 25 May (African Liberation Day), 22 July (Anniversary of the Second Republic), 13 July* (Laylat al-Qadr, Night of Power), 17 July* (Eid al-Fitr, end of Ramadan), 15 August (Assumption/St Mary's Day), 23 September* (Eid al-Kebir, Feast of the Sacrifice), 14 October* (Islamic New Year), 23 October* (Ashoura), 23 December*† (Eid al-Moulid, Birth of the Prophet), 25 December (Christmas).

* These holidays are dependent on the Islamic lunar calendar and may vary by one or two days from the dates given.

† These holidays are dependent on the Islamic lunar calendar and may vary by one or two days from the dates given. This festival occurs twice (in the Islamic years AH 1436 and 1437) within the same Gregorian year.

Statistical Survey

Sources (unless otherwise stated): Department of Information Services, 14 Daniel Goddard St, Banjul; tel. 4225060; fax 4227230; Central Statistics Department, Central Bank Building, 1/2 Ecowas Ave, Banjul; tel. 4228364; fax 4228903; e-mail director@csd.gm; internet www.gambia.gm/Statistics/statistics.html.

Area and Population

AREA, POPULATION AND DENSITY

Area (sq km)	11,295*
Population (census results)	
15 April 2003	1,360,681
8 April 2013†	
Males	930,699
Females	951,751
Total	1,882,450
Population (UN estimate at mid-year)‡	
2014	1,908,953
Density (per sq km) at mid-2014	169.0

* 4,361 sq miles.

† Provisional.

‡ Source: UN, *World Population Prospects: The 2012 Revision*; estimate not adjusted to take account of results of 2013 census.

ETHNIC GROUPS

1993 census (percentages): Mandinka 39.60; Fula 18.83; Wolof 14.61; Jola 10.66; Serahule 8.92; Serere 2.77; Manjago 1.85; Bambara 0.84; Creole/Aku 0.69; Others 1.23.

POPULATION BY AGE AND SEX

(UN estimates at mid-2014)

	Males	Females	Total
0–14	440,609	433,088	873,697
15–64	480,336	509,945	990,281
65 and over	23,285	21,690	44,975
Total	944,230	964,723	1,908,953

Note: Estimates not adjusted to take account of results of 2013 census.

Source: UN, *World Population Prospects: The 2012 Revision*.

ADMINISTRATIVE DIVISIONS
(population at 2013 census, provisional)

Banjul	31,301	Kerewan	221,054
Basse	239,916	Kuntaur	99,108
Brikama	699,704	Mansakonko	82,361
Georgetown	126,910		
Kanifing	382,096	**Total**	1,882,450

PRINCIPAL TOWNS
(population at 1993 census)

Serrekunda	151,450	Lamin	10,668
Brikama	42,480	Gunjur	9,983
Banjul (capital)	42,407	Basse	9,265
Bakau	38,062	Soma	7,925
Farafenni	21,142	Bansang	5,405
Sukuta	16,667		

Mid-2011 (incl. suburbs, UN estimate): Banjul 506,277 (Source: UN, *World Urbanization Prospects: The 2011 Revision*).

BIRTHS AND DEATHS
(annual averages, UN estimates)

	1995–2000	2000–05	2005–10
Birth rate (per 1,000)	45.8	44.8	43.6
Death rate (per 1,000)	12.7	11.6	10.5

Source: UN, *World Population Prospects: The 2012 Revision*.

Life expectancy (years at birth): 58.4 (males 57.1; females 59.7) in 2011 (Source: World Bank, World Development Indicators database).

ECONOMICALLY ACTIVE POPULATION*
(persons aged 10 years and over, 1993 census)

	Males	Females	Total
Agriculture, hunting and forestry	82,886	92,806	175,692
Fishing	5,610	450	6,060
Mining and quarrying	354	44	398
Manufacturing	18,729	2,953	21,682
Electricity, gas and water supply	1,774	84	1,858
Construction	9,530	149	9,679
Wholesale and retail trade; repair of motor vehicles, motorcycles and personal and household goods	33,281	15,460	48,741
Hotels and restaurants	3,814	2,173	5,987
Transport, storage and communications	13,421	782	14,203
Financial intermediation	1,843	572	2,415
Other community, social and personal service activities	25,647	15,607	41,254
Sub-total	196,889	131,080	327,969
Activities not adequately defined	10,421	6,991	17,412
Total labour force	207,310	138,071	345,381

* Figures exclude persons seeking work for the first time, but include other unemployed persons.

Mid-2014 (estimates in '000): Agriculture, etc. 677; Total labour force 906 (Source: FAO).

Health and Welfare

KEY INDICATORS

Total fertility rate (children per woman, 2011)	4.8
Under-5 mortality rate (per 1,000 live births, 2011)	101
HIV/AIDS (% of persons aged 15–49, 2012)	1.3
Physicians (per 1,000 head, 2008)	0.1
Hospital beds (per 1,000 head, 2011)	1.1
Health expenditure (2010): US $ per head (PPP)	90
Health expenditure (2010): % of GDP	4.4
Health expenditure (2010): public (% of total)	56.1
Access to water (% of persons, 2011)	89
Access to sanitation (% of persons, 2011)	68
Total carbon dioxide emissions ('000 metric tons, 2010)	473.0
Carbon dioxide emissions per head (metric tons, 2010)	0.3
Human Development Index (2012): ranking	165
Human Development Index (2012): value	0.439

For sources and definitions, see explanatory note on p. vi.

Agriculture

PRINCIPAL CROPS
('000 metric tons)

	2010	2011	2012
Rice, paddy	99.9	51.1	54.2
Maize	66.0	23.6	30.1
Millet	158.0	87.2	116.1
Sorghum	39.0	20.6	23.1
Cassava (Manioc)*	8.9	9.7	10.5
Groundnuts, with shell	137.6	83.9	119.6
Oil palm fruit*	35.0	35.0	35.0
Guavas, mangoes and mangosteens*	1.2	1.3	1.3

* FAO estimates.

Aggregate production ('000 metric tons, may include official, semi-official or estimated data): Total cereals 363.5 in 2010, 183.2 in 2011, 224.3 in 2012; Total pulses 2.1 in 2010, 2.2 in 2011, 2.5 in 2012; Total vegetables (incl. melons) 12.2 in 2010, 12.0 in 2011, 12.5 in 2012; Total fruits (excl. melons) 8.6 in 2010, 8.8 in 2011, 9.0 in 2012.

Source: FAO.

LIVESTOCK
('000 head, year ending September)

	2010	2011	2012
Cattle	425	398	373
Goats	352	304	312
Sheep	251	180*	112
Pigs	29	15*	6
Asses	42	56	58*
Horses	38	28*	19
Chickens	850	1,000*	1,274

* FAO estimate.

Source: FAO.

LIVESTOCK PRODUCTS
('000 metric tons, FAO estimates)

	2010	2011	2012
Cattle meat	4.1	3.8	3.8
Goat meat	0.9	0.8	0.8
Sheep meat	0.7	0.5	0.3
Chicken meat	1.2	1.3	1.5
Game meat	1.2	1.3	1.3
Cows' milk	9.3	9.4	9.5
Hen eggs	0.9	0.9	1.0

Source: FAO.

Forestry

ROUNDWOOD REMOVALS
('000 cubic metres, excluding bark, FAO estimates)

	2010	2011	2012
Sawlogs, veneer logs and logs for sleepers*	106	106	106
Other industrial wood†	7	7	7
Fuel wood	694	703	712
Total	807	816	825

* Assumed to be unchanged since 1994.
† Assumed to be unchanged since 1993.

Source: FAO.

Fishing

('000 metric tons, live weight of capture)

	2009	2010	2011
Tilapias	1.2	1.2	1.1
Sea catfishes	3.8	3.8	3.7
Bonga shad	12.6	12.6	12.2
Sardinellas	7.6	7.6	7.3
Sharks, rays, skates	0.5	0.5	0.5
Total catch (incl. others)	45.9	46.4*	45.0*

* FAO estimate.

Source: FAO.

Mining

	2009	2010	2011
Laterites ('000 metric tons)	103	226	1,035
Silica sand ('000 metric tons)	1,062	1,121	n.a.

2007 (metric tons): Clay 6,713; Zircon 355.

Source: US Geological Survey.

Industry

SELECTED PRODUCTS
('000 metric tons unless otherwise stated)

	2009	2010	2011
Beer of barley*	3.5	3.4	3.0
Palm oil—unrefined*	2.1	3.0	3.0
Groundnut oil†	18.8	20.0	12.0
Electric energy (million kWh)‡	242.0	245.2	n.a.

* FAO estimates.
† Unofficial figures.
‡ Source: UN Industrial Commodity Statistics Database.

Beer of millet ('000 metric tons, FAO estimates): 50.4 in 2003, 55.4 in 2004–05.

2012 ('000 metric tons): Palm oil—unrefined 3.2 (FAO estimate); Groundnut oil 12.0 (unofficial figure).

Source: mainly FAO.

Finance

CURRENCY AND EXCHANGE RATES

Monetary Units
100 butut = 1 dalasi (D).

Sterling, Dollar and Euro Equivalents (30 August 2013)
£1 sterling = 53.7110 dalasi;
US $1 = 34.6700 dalasi;
€1 = 45.8857 dalasi;
1,000 dalasi = £18.62 = $28.84 = €21.79.

Average Exchange Rate (dalasi per US $)
2010 28.012
2011 29.462
2012 32.077

BUDGET
(million dalasi)

Revenue*	2011	2012†	2013‡
Tax revenue	3,780	4,221	5,001
Direct taxes	1,225	1,520	1,629
Domestic taxes on goods and services	1,683	1,833	2,049
Taxes on international trade	830	856	1,310
Other taxes	42	12	13
Non-tax revenue	484	565	610
Total	4,264	4,786	5,611

Expenditure§	2011	2012†	2013‡
Current expenditure	4,579	5,068	5,882
Wages and salaries	1,693	1,804	1,875
Other goods and services	1,273	1,540	2,320
Interest payments	967	1,079	1,160
Internal	785	877	940
External	183	202	220
Subsidies	646	645	527
Capital expenditure	2,292	3,607	2,267
Gambia Local Fund	307	299	409
Foreign financed	1,985	3,308	1,857
Total	6,871	8,675	8,149

* Excluding grants received (million dalasi): 1,355 in 2011; 2,611 in 2012 (preliminary); 1,659 in 2013 (projection).
† Preliminary figures.
‡ Projections.
§ Excluding lending minus repayments (million dalasi): –1,252 in 2011; –1,278 in 2012 (preliminary); –878 in 2013 (projection).

Source: IMF, *The Gambia: Staff Report for the 2013 Article IV Consultation; Informational Annex; Press Release on the Executive Board Discussion; and Statement by the Executive Director for The Gambia* (September 2013).

INTERNATIONAL RESERVES
(US $ million at 31 December)

	2010	2011	2012
IMF special drawing rights	37.88	37.73	37.45
Reserve position in IMF	2.37	2.37	2.37
Foreign exchange	161.37	183.15	196.42
Total	201.63	223.24	236.24

Source: IMF, *International Financial Statistics*.

MONEY SUPPLY
(million dalasi at 31 December)

	2009	2010	2011
Currency outside banks	2,004.81	2,064.62	2,376.33
Demand deposits at commercial banks	3,594.96	3,957.34	4,290.49
Total money	5,599.77	6,021.96	6,666.82

2012: Currency outside depository corporations 2,818.59; Transferable deposits 4,524.47; Other deposits 8,254.87; *Broad money*15,597.92.

Source: IMF, *International Financial Statistics*.

COST OF LIVING
(Consumer Price Index for Banjul and Kombo St Mary's; base: 1974 = 100)

	1997	1998	1999
Food	1,511.8	1,565.8	1,628.8
Fuel and light	2,145.8	1,854.9	2,076.0
Clothing*	937.5	981.8	999.9
Rent	1,409.6	1,431.3	1,428.6
All items (incl. others)	1,441.5	1,457.3	1,512.8

* Including household linen.

All items (Consumer Price Index for Banjul and Kombo St Mary's; base: 2005 = 100): 117.4 in 2009; 123.4 in 2010; 129.3 in 2011 (Source: IMF, International Financial Statistics).

NATIONAL ACCOUNTS
(million dalasi at current prices)

Expenditure on the Gross Domestic Product

	2009	2010	2011
Government final consumption expenditure	2,511	2,674	2,839
Private final consumption expenditure	20,147	24,791	21,834
Gross capital formation	6,421	4,903	8,122
Total domestic expenditure	29,079	32,368	32,795
Exports of goods and services	1,847	1,185	2,789
Less Imports of goods and services	6,929	6,890	8,988
GDP in purchasers' values	23,997	26,663	26,596

Gross Domestic Product by Economic Activity

	2009	2010	2011
Agriculture, hunting, forestry and fishing	6,292	7,719	5,715
Mining and quarrying	603	705	790
Manufacturing	1,195	1,260	1,460
Electricity, gas and water	299	331	349
Construction	910	992	1,131
Wholesale and retail trade; restaurants and hotels	6,460	6,659	7,275
Finance, insurance and real estate	3,034	3,193	3,670
Transport and communications	2,653	3,114	3,464
Public administration and defence	440	526	565
Other services	602	663	699
Sub-total	22,488	25,162	25,118
Less Imputed bank service charge	1,017	848	1,014
GDP at factor cost	21,470	24,314	24,103
Indirect taxes, *less* subsidies	2,527	2,349	2,494
GDP in market prices	23,997	26,663	26,596

Source: African Development Bank.

BALANCE OF PAYMENTS
(US $ million, year ending 30 June)

	2010	2011	2012
Exports of goods	139.92	162.14	182.46
Imports of goods	–245.76	–295.60	–358.84
Balance on goods	–105.84	–133.46	–176.38
Exports of services	130.64	143.73	151.46
Imports of services	–73.17	–68.41	–80.67
Balance on goods and services	–48.37	–58.14	–105.59
Primary income received	14.35	13.05	9.83
Primary income paid	–22.40	–28.79	–28.47
Balance on goods, services and primary income	–56.42	–73.88	–124.23
Secondary income received	212.75	181.59	163.10
Secondary income paid	–135.28	–60.37	–54.68
Current balance	21.05	47.34	–15.80
Capital account (net)	—	4.15	—
Direct investment liabilities	37.37	36.18	33.52
Other investment assets	20.30	–0.32	24.92
Other investment liabilities	–82.24	–34.85	–82.47
Net errors and omissions	–89.75	–101.86	–24.93
Reserves and related items	–93.27	–49.36	–64.77

Source: IMF, *International Financial Statistics*.

External Trade

PRINCIPAL COMMODITIES
(distribution by HS, US $ million)

Imports c.i.f.	2009	2010	2011
Live animals and animal products	7.6	8.8	10.4
Vegetable products	45.3	42.4	49.8
Cereals	30.5	21.4	30.6
Rice	30.5	21.4	30.6
Wheat or meslin flour	6.8	11.9	11.0
Milling products; malt, starches, insulin; wheat gluten	8.2	12.6	11.6
Animal, vegetable fats and oils	22.6	12.2	18.2
Fixed vegetable fats, oils and their fractions	21.6	11.1	17.3
Prepared foodstuffs; beverages and spirits; tobacco, etc.	29.0	37.0	32.4
Sugars and sugar confectionery	13.0	22.8	14.5
Cane or beet sugar and chemically pure sucrose, in solid form	12.4	22.4	13.7
Mineral products	61.9	68.0	87.2
Salt, sulphur, earth, stone, plaster, lime and cement	14.6	9.7	11.5
Cements, portland, aluminous, slag, and similar hydraulic materials	14.2	9.1	10.7
Mineral fuels, oils, etc.	47.3	58.3	75.7
Petroleum oils, not crude	47.0	57.9	75.5
Chemicals and related products	24.8	9.6	22.4
Pharmaceutical products	13.3	3.3	10.4
Textiles and textile articles	16.1	15.8	16.5
Iron and steel, and base metals	8.6	5.8	14.9
Machinery and mechanical appliances	31.2	37.6	36.0
Machinery, boilers, etc.	16.3	14.6	12.2
Electrical and electronic equipment	14.9	23.1	23.8
Vehicles, aircraft and transport equipment	31.0	24.6	23.2
Vehicles other than railway, tramway	30.9	23.8	22.6
Total (incl. others)	303.9	285.0	343.7

Exports f.o.b.	2009	2010	2011
Live animals and animal products	7.9	6.2	7.0
Fish, crustaceans, molluscs and preparations thereof	4.1	5.9	2.9
Fish, fresh, whole	0.1	1.3	0.3
Fish, frozen, whole	3.3	3.6	1.7
Dairy products	3.9	0.3	4.1
Milk and cream, concentrated or sweetened	3.7	0.1	1.6
Vegetable products	12.3	10.8	8.7
Edible fruit, nuts, peel of citrus fruit, melons	5.2	3.4	2.2
Brazil nuts, cashew nuts and coconuts	3.3	3.3	2.1
Coffee, tea, maté and spices	3.4	0.1	3.1
Tea	3.2	0.1	1.6
Oil seed, oleagic fruits, grain, seed, fruit, etc.	3.2	7.2	1.9
Groundnuts, not roasted	3.1	7.1	1.9
Animal, vegetable fats and oils, cleavage products, etc.	7.4	7.0	3.6
Groundnut oil and fractions	6.6	6.7	—
Prepared foodstuffs; beverages and spirits; tobacco, etc.	7.4	3.3	12.1
Sugars and sugar confectionery	0.8	0.8	3.5
Cane or beet sugar and chemically pure sucrose, in solid form	0.7	0.7	3.0
Meat, fish and seafood food preparations	1.2	0.9	3.8
Vegetable, fruit, nuts, etc. and food preparations	3.6	0.1	1.6
Fruit and vegetable juices, unfermented	3.5	—	0.3
Residues, wastes of food industry, animal fodder	1.1	1.2	0.1
Groundnut oil-cake and other solid residues	1.1	1.2	0.0
Mineral products	3.5	2.9	1.6
Salt, sulphur, earth, stone, plaster, lime and cement	3.5	2.7	0.8
Natural sands of all kinds, except metal-bearing	3.5	2.7	0.8
Plastics and plastic articles	1.4	1.3	4.3
Plastics and articles thereof	1.4	1.3	4.0
Plastic packing goods or closures, stoppers, lids, caps, etc.	1.4	1.2	3.9
Textiles and textile articles	17.2	0.5	46.81
Man made filaments	16.4	—	41.4
Woven fabrics of synthetic filament yarn	15.9	—	41.3
Other made textile articles, sets, worn clothing, etc.	0.6	0.5	5.2
Worn clothing and articles	0.6	0.5	5.2
Machinery and mechanical appliances; electrical equipment; parts thereof	3.2	1.1	2.3
Electrical and electronic equipment	2.9	0.5	1.8
Primary cells and primary batteries	2.4	0.2	0.7
Vehicles, aircraft, vessels and associated transport equipment	2.0	0.3	1.2
Vehicles other than railway, tramway	2.0	0.3	1.2
Total (incl. others)	66.0	35.0	94.7

Source: Trade Map-Trade Competitiveness Map, International Trade Centre, www.intracen.org/marketanalysis.

PRINCIPAL TRADING PARTNERS
(US $ million)

Imports c.i.f.	2009	2010	2011
Belgium	11.4	8.1	15.3
Brazil	17.3	37.1	33.3
China, People's Repub.	34.9	21.3	30.1
Côte d'Ivoire	43.5	56.2	72.5
Denmark	49.1	20.9	49.1
France (incl. Monaco)	10.2	5.4	8.0
Germany	17.2	9.1	11.8
Hong Kong	3.9	1.4	2.5
India	10.8	9.1	9.5
Japan	4.5	2.5	3.8
Netherlands	17.2	16.7	13.9
Senegal	5.6	6.1	16.5
Singapore	5.6	1.5	7.9
Spain	6.5	11.5	4.6
Thailand	10.8	7.0	2.6
Turkey	8.5	6.6	13.2
United Arab Emirates	8.6	6.1	7.5
United Kingdom	23.7	11.1	16.2
USA	7.1	5.1	5.7
Total (incl. others)	303.9	285.0	343.7

Exports f.o.b.	2009	2010	2011
France (incl. Monaco)	4.9	5.6	1.5
Guinea	15.8	2.0	21.9
Guinea-Bissau	9.2	0.8	10.7
Mali	.09	0.2	15.8
Netherlands	0.9	0.8	0.7
Senegal	17.7	5.6	33.4
United Kingdom	4.9	8.9	2.2
Total (incl. others)	66.0	35.0	94.7

Source: Trade Map-Trade Competitiveness Map, International Trade Centre, www.intracen.org/marketanalysis.

Transport

ROAD TRAFFIC
(motor vehicles in use, estimates)

	2002	2003	2004
Passenger cars	7,919	8,168	8,109
Buses	2,261	1,300	1,200
Lorries and vans	1,531	1,862	1,761

2007: Passenger cars 8,815; Buses and coaches 1,012; Vans and lorries 2,601.

2010: Passenger cars 9,107; Buses and coaches 1,389.

Source: IRF, *World Road Statistics*.

SHIPPING

Flag Registered Fleet
(at 31 December)

	2011	2012	2013
Number of vessels	9	8	8
Total displacement (grt)	33,372	29,396	29,396

Source: Lloyd's List Intelligence (www.lloydslistintelligence.com).

International Sea-borne Freight Traffic
('000 metric tons)

	1996	1997	1998
Goods loaded	55.9	38.1	47.0
Goods unloaded	482.7	503.7	493.2

CIVIL AVIATION
(traffic on scheduled services)

	1992	1993	1994
Kilometres flown (million)	1	1	1
Passengers carried ('000)	19	19	19
Passenger-km (million)	50	50	50
Total ton-km (million)	5	5	5

Source: UN, *Statistical Yearbook*.

Tourism

FOREIGN VISITORS BY COUNTRY OF ORIGIN*

	2009	2010	2011
Belgium	3,118	1,983	2,234
Denmark	4,547	2,627	1,316
Germany	3,539	2,290	3,020
Netherlands	14,246	8,870	12,906
Norway	4,123	1,370	1,253
Sweden	8,302	6,493	6,387
United Kingdom	63,937	40,250	46,982
USA	1,930	1,263	2,036
Total (incl. others)	141,569	91,099	106,393

* Air charter tourist arrivals.

Receipts from tourism (US $ million, excl. passenger transport): 63 in 2009; 32 in 2010; 96 in 2011.

Source: World Tourism Organization.

Communications Media

	2010	2011	2012
Telephones ('000 main lines in use)	48.8	50.4	64.2
Mobile cellular telephones ('000 subscribers)	1,478.3	1,401.2	1,526.2
Broadband subscribers	400	400	500

Internet users ('000): 130.1 in 2009.

Sources: International Telecommunication Union.

Education

(2006/07)

	Institutions	Teachers	Students		
			Males	Females	Total
Primary	491	4,428	108,540	111,883	220,423
Junior secondary	186	2,385	34,432	32,047	66,479
Senior secondary	66	845	19,024	14,697	33,721

Source: Department of State for Education, Banjul.

2011/12 (UNESCO estimates): *Pupils:* Pre-primary 64,677 (2009/10); Primary 244,033; Secondary 124,397 (2009/10) (Source: UNESCO Institute for Statistics).

Pupil-teacher ratio (primary education, UNESCO estimate): 33.9 in 2011/12 (Source: UNESCO Institute for Statistics).

Adult literacy rate (UNESCO estimates): 51.1% (males 60.9%; females 41.9%) in 2010 (Source: UNESCO Institute for Statistics).

Directory

The Government

HEAD OF STATE

President: Col (retd) Alhaji YAHYA A. J. J. JAMMEH (proclaimed Head of State 26 July 1994; elected President 26 September 1996, re-elected 18 October 2001, 22 September 2006 and 24 November 2011).

Vice-President: Dr ISATOU NJIE-SAIDY.

THE CABINET
(April 2014)

President and Minister of Defence: Col (retd) Alhaji YAHYA A. J. J. JAMMEH.

Vice-President and Minister of Women's Affairs: Dr ISATOU NJIE-SAIDY.

Minister of Presidential Affairs and Secretary-General and Head of the Civil Service: MOMODOU SABALLY.

Minister of Finance and Economic Affairs: KEBBA S. TOURAY.

Minister of Tourism and Culture: FATOU MASS JOBE-NJIE.

Minister of Foreign Affairs, International Co-operation and Gambians Abroad: MAMOUR ALIEU JAGNE.

Minister of Basic and Secondary Education: FATOU LAMIN FAYE.

Minister of Health and Social Welfare: OMAR SEY.

Minister of Trade, Industry, Regional Integration and Employment: ABDOU KOLLEY.

Minister of Forestry and the Environment: FATOU NDEYE GAYE.

Minister of Fisheries and Water Resources: MASS AXI GAI.

Minister of Higher Education, Research, Science and Technology: Dr ABOUBACAR SENGHORE.

Minister of Lands and Regional Government: MOMODOU F. K. KOLLEY.

Minister of Justice and Attorney-General: MAMA FATIMA SINGHATEH.

Minister of Information and Communication Infrastructure: NANA GREY-JOHNSON.

Minister of the Interior: OUSMAN SONKO.

Minister of Youth and Sports: ALIEU K. JAMMEH.

Minister of Agriculture: SOLOMON OWENS.

Minister of Transport, Works and Infrastructure, and National Assembly Matters: BALA GARBA JAHUMPA.

MINISTRIES

Office of the President: PMB, State House, Banjul; tel. 4223811; e-mail info@statehouse.gm; internet www.statehouse.gm.

Office of the Vice-President: State House, Banjul; tel. 4227605; fax 4224401; e-mail info@ovp.gov.gm; internet www.ovp.gov.gm.

Ministry of Agriculture: The Quadrangle, Banjul; tel. 4228270; fax 4229325; e-mail info@moa.gov.gm; internet www.moa.gov.gm.

Ministry of Basic and Secondary Education: Willy Thorpe Bldg, Banjul; tel. 4228232; fax 4224180; e-mail info@mobse.gov.gm; internet www.mobse.gov.gm.

Ministry of Finance and Economic Affairs: The Quadrangle, POB 9686, Banjul; tel. 4227221; fax 4227954; e-mail info@mof.gov.gm; internet www.mof.gov.gm.

Ministry of Fisheries and Water Resources: Marina Parade, Banjul; tel. 4227773; fax 4225009; e-mail info@mofwrnam.gov.gm; internet www.mofwrnam.gov.gm.

Ministry of Foreign Affairs, International Co-operation and Gambians Abroad: 4 Marina Parade, Banjul; tel. 4223577; fax 4227917; e-mail info@mofa.gov.gm; internet www.mofa.gov.gm.

Ministry of Forestry and the Environment: Kairaba Ave, Serekunda; tel. 4399447; fax 4399518; e-mail info@mofen.gov.gm; internet www.mofen.gov.gm.

Ministry of Health, Social Welfare and National Assembly Matters: The Quadrangle, Banjul; tel. 4228624; fax 4229325; e-mail info@moh.gov.gm; internet www.moh.gov.gm.

Ministry of Information and Communication Infrastructure: GRTS Bldg, MDI Rd, Kanifing, Banjul; tel. 4378028; fax 4378029; e-mail info@moici.gov.gm; internet www.moici.gov.gm.

Ministry of the Interior: 5 J. R. Forster St, Banjul; tel. 4223277; fax 4201320; e-mail info@moi.gov.gm; internet www.moi.gov.gm.

Ministry of Justice and Attorney-General's Chambers: Marina Parade, Banjul; tel. 4225352; fax 4229908; e-mail info@moj.gov.gm; internet www.moj.gov.gm.

Ministry of Petroleum: Bertil Harding Highway, Kotu, Banjul; tel. 8806317; fax 8200896; e-mail info@mop.gov.gm; internet www.mop.gov.gm.

Ministry of Regional Administrations, Lands and Traditional Rulers: The Quadrangle, Banjul; tel. 4222022; fax 4225261; e-mail info@molgl.gov.gm; internet www.molgl.gov.gm.

Ministry of Tourism and Culture: New Administrative Bldg, The Quadrangle, Banjul; tel. 4229844; fax 4227753; e-mail info@motc.gov.gm; internet www.motc.gov.gm.

Ministry of Trade, Regional Integration and Employment: Central Bank Bldg, Independence Dr., Banjul; tel. 4228868; fax 4227756; e-mail info@motie.gov.gm; internet www.motie.gov.gm.

Ministry of Works, Construction and Infrastructure: MDI Rd, Kanifing, Banjul; tel. 4375761; fax 4375765; e-mail info@mowci.gov.gm; internet www.mowci.gov.gm.

Ministry of Youth and Sports: The Quadrangle, Banjul; tel. 4225264; fax 4225267; e-mail info@moys.gov.gm; internet www.moys.gov.gm.

President

Presidential Election, 24 November 2011

Candidate	Valid votes	% of valid votes
Yahya A. J. J. Jammeh (APRC)	470,550	71.54
Ousainou N. Darboe (UDP)	114,177	17.36
Hamat Bah (Independent)	73,060	11.11
Total*	657,787	100.00

* In addition, there were 264 invalid votes.

Legislature

National Assembly: Parliament Buildings, Independence Dr., Banjul; tel. 4227241; fax 4225123; e-mail assemblyclerk@yahoo.com; internet www.nationalassembly.gm.

Speaker: ABDOULIE BOJANG.

General Election, 29 March 2012*

Party	Votes	% of votes	Seats
Alliance for Patriotic Reorientation and Construction (APRC)	80,289	51.82	43
National Reconciliation Party (NRP)	14,606	9.43	1
Independents	60,055	38.76	4
Total	154,950	100.00	48†

* The election was boycotted by six of the seven main opposition parties, including the United Democratic Party and the National Alliance for Democracy and Development.

† The President of the Republic is empowered by the Constitution to nominate five additional members of parliament. The total number of members of parliament is thus 53.

Election Commission

Independent Electoral Commission (IEC): Election House, Bertil Harding Highway, Kanifing East Layout, POB 793 Banjul; tel. 4373804; fax 4373803; e-mail info@iec.gm; internet www.iec.gm; f. 1997; Chair. Alhaji MUSTAPHA CARAYOL.

Political Organizations

Alliance for Patriotic Reorientation and Construction (APRC): Sankung Sillah Bldg, Kairaba Ave, Banjul; tel. 9745687; f. 1996; governing party; Chair. President YAHYA A. J. J. JAMMEH.

Gambia Moral Congress (GMC): 78 Bertil Harding Highway, Kotu, Banjul; e-mail info@Gambia-Congress.org; internet www.gambia-congress.org; f. 2008; Exec. Chair. MAI N. K. FATTY.

The Gambia Party for Democracy and Progress (GPDP): POB 4014, Kombo St Mary, Serrekunda; tel. 9955226; f. 2004; Sec.-Gen. HENRY GOMEZ.

National Alliance for Democracy and Development (NADD): 30 Papa Sarr St, Churchill, Serrekunda; f. Jan. 2005 to contest 2006 elections; Co-ordinator HALIFA SALLAH; comprises parties listed below.

People's Democratic Organization for Independence and Socialism (PDOIS): POB 2306, 1 Sambou St, Churchill, Serrekunda; tel. and fax 4393177; e-mail foroyaa@qanet.gm; f. 1986; socialist; Leaders HALIFA SALLAH, SAM SARR, SIDIA JATTA.

People's Progressive Party (PPP): c/o Omar Jallow, Ninth St East, Fajara M Section, Banjul; tel. and fax 4392674; f. 1959; fmr ruling party in 1962–94; centrist; Chair. OMAR JALLOW.

National Convention Party (NCP): 38 Sayerr Jobe Ave, Banjul; tel. 6408128 (mobile); f. 1977; left-wing; Leader EBRIMA JANKO SANYANG.

National Democratic Action Movement (NDAM): 1 Box Bar Rd, Nema, Brikama Town, Western Division, Banjul; tel. 7788882; e-mail ndam_gambia@hotmail.com; f. 2002; reformist; Leader and Sec.-Gen. LAMIN WAA JUWARA.

National Reconciliation Party (NRP): 69 Daniel Goddard St, Banjul; tel. 4201371; fax 4201732; f. 1996; formed an alliance with the UDP in 2006; Leader HAMAT N. K. BAH.

United Democratic Party (UDP): 1 Rene Blain St, Banjul; tel. 4221730; fax 4224601; e-mail info@udpgambia.com; f. 1996; formed an alliance with the NRP in 2006 and with the GMC in 2011; reformist; Sec.-Gen. and Leader OUSAINOU N. DARBOE; Nat. Pres. DEMBO BOJANG.

Diplomatic Representation

EMBASSIES IN THE GAMBIA

Cuba: C/801, POB 4627, Banjul; tel. and fax 4495382; e-mail embacuba@ganet.gm; Ambassador (vacant).

Guinea-Bissau: 78 Atlantic Rd, Fajara (Bakau), Banjul; tel. 4226862; Ambassador FRANCISCA MARIA MONTEIRA SILVA VAZ TURPIN.

Libya: Independence Dr., Banjul; tel. 4223213; fax 4223214; Ambassador Dr ALI MUHAMMAD DUKALY.

Nigeria: 52 Garba Jalumpa Ave, Bakau, POB 630, Banjul; tel. 4495803; fax 4496456; e-mail nighcgambia@yahoo.com; Ambassador ESTHER JOHN AUDU.

Qatar: Banjul; tel. 4410889; fax 4410700; e-mail banjul@mofa.gov.qa; Ambassador MUHAMMAD NASSER ESSA AL-KAABI.

Senegal: 159 Kairaba Ave, POB 385, Banjul; tel. 4373752; fax 4373750; Ambassador BABACAR DIAGNE.

Sierra Leone: 67 Daniel Goddard St, Banjul; tel. 4228206; fax 4229819; e-mail mfodayyumkella@yahoo.co.uk; Ambassador SOULAY DARAMY.

Turkey: 29 Kaira Ave, 4th St, Brufut Gardens, Banjul; e-mail embassy.banjul@mfa.gov.tr; Ambassador ENGIN SONER.

United Kingdom: 48 Atlantic Rd, Fajara, POB 507, Banjul; tel. 4495133; fax 4496134; e-mail bhcbanjul@fco.gov.uk; internet ukingambia.fco.gov.uk/en; Ambassador DAVID MORELY.

USA: The White House, Kairaba Ave, Fajara, PMB 19, Banjul; tel. 4392856; fax 4392475; e-mail consularbanjul@state.gov; internet banjul.usembassy.gov; Chargé d'affaires a.i. MICHAEL ARIETTI.

Venezuela: Banjul; Ambassador EDUARDO MEDINA RUBIO.

Judicial System

The judicial system of The Gambia is based on English Common Law and legislative enactments of the Republic's parliament, which include an Islamic Law Recognition Ordinance whereby an Islamic Court exercises jurisdiction in certain cases between, or exclusively affecting, Muslims.

The Constitution of the Second Republic guarantees the independence of the judiciary. The Supreme Court is defined as the final court of appeal. Provision is made for a special criminal court to hear and determine all cases relating to theft and misappropriation of public funds.

Supreme Court of The Gambia: Law Courts, Independence Dr., Banjul; tel. 4227383; fax 4228380; consists of the Chief Justice and up to six other judges; Chief Justice ELI NAWAZ CHOWHAN.

Court of Appeal: Banjul; Pres. ESTHER AWO OTA.

High Court: Banjul; consists of the Chief Justice and up to seven other judges.

The **Banjul Magistrates Court**, the **Kanifing Magistrates Court** and the **Divisional Courts** are courts of summary jurisdiction presided over by a magistrate or in his absence by two or more lay justices of the peace. There are resident magistrates in all divisions. The magistrates have limited civil and criminal jurisdiction, and appeal from these courts lies with the Supreme Court. **Islamic Courts** have jurisdiction in matters between, or exclusively affecting, Muslim Gambians and relating to civil status, marriage, succession, donations, testaments and guardianship. The Courts administer Islamic *Shari'a* law. A cadi, or a cadi and two assessors, preside over and constitute an Islamic Court. Assessors of the Islamic Courts are Justices of the Peace of Islamic faith. **District Tribunals** have appellate jurisdiction in cases involving customs and traditions. Each court consists of three district tribunal members, one of whom is selected as president, and other court members from the area over which it has jurisdiction.

Attorney-General: MAMA FATIMA SINGHATEH.

Solicitor-General: PA HARRY JAMMEH.

Religion

More than 90% of the population are Muslims. The remainder are mainly Christians, and there are small numbers of animists, mostly of the Diola and Karoninka ethnic groups.

ISLAM

Banjul Central Mosque: King Fahd Bin Abdul Aziz Mosque, Box Bar Rd, POB 562, Banjul; tel. 4228094; Imam Ratib Alhaji CHERNO KAH.

The Gambia Supreme Islamic Council: MDI Rd, Kanifing South, POB 804, Banjul; tel. 4484740; fax 4371977; f. 1962; Pres. Alhaji MOMODOU LAMIN TOURAY.

CHRISTIANITY

The Gambia Christian Council: MDI Rd, Kanifing, POB 27, Banjul; tel. 4392092; f. 1966; seven mems (churches and other Christian bodies); Chair. Rt Rev. ROBERT P. ELLISON (Roman Catholic Bishop of Banjul); Sec.-Gen. Rev. PRISCILLA JOHNSON.

The Anglican Communion

The diocese of The Gambia, which includes Senegal and Cape Verde, forms part of the Church of the Province of West Africa (CPWA). In September 2012 the CPWA was subdivided into two internal provinces: the Internal Province of Ghana, comprising the 10 dioceses in Ghana, and the Internal Province of West Africa, comprising the remaining five dioceses. The Primate and Metropolitan of the Province of West Africa and the Archbishop of the Internal Province of West Africa is the Bishop of The Gambia. There are about 1,500 adherents in The Gambia.

Primate and Metropolitan of the Province of West Africa, Archbishop of the Internal Province of West Africa and Bishop of The Gambia: Rt Rev. Dr SOLOMON TILEWA JOHNSON, Bishopscourt, POB 51, Banjul; tel. 4228405; fax 4229495; e-mail anglican@qanet.gm.

The Roman Catholic Church

The Gambia comprises a single diocese (Banjul), directly responsible to the Holy See. Some 3% of the population are Roman Catholics. The diocese administers a development organization (Caritas, The Gambia), and runs a number of schools and training centres. The Gambia participates in the Inter-territorial Catholic Bishops' Conference of The Gambia and Sierra Leone (based in Freetown, Sierra Leone).

Bishop of Banjul: Rt Rev. ROBERT PATRICK ELLISON, Bishop's House, POB 165, Banjul; tel. 4391957; fax 4390998; e-mail rpel202@yahoo.co.uk.

Protestant Churches

Abiding Word Ministries (AWM): 156 Mosque Rd, PMB 207, Serrekunda Post Office, Serrekunda; tel. 7640126; fax 4374069; e-mail info@awmgambia.com; internet www.awmgambia.com; f. 1988; Senior Pastor Rev. FRANCIS FORBES.

Evangelical Lutheran Church in The Gambia: POB 5275, Brikama West Coast Region; tel. 9083755; fax 7043336; e-mail leadership@elctg.org; internet www.elctg.org.

Methodist Church: 1 Macoumba Jallow St, POB 288, Banjul; tel. 4227506; fax 4228510; f. 1821; Chair. and Gen. Supt Rev. WILLIAM PETER STEPHENS.

BAHÁ'Í FAITH

National Spiritual Assembly: POB 2532, Serrekunda; tel. 4229015; e-mail nsagambia@gamtel.gm; internet bci.org/bahaigambia.

The Press

All independent publications are required to register annually with the Government and to pay a registration fee.

The Daily News: 65 Kombo Sillah Dr., Churchill's Town, POB 2849, Serrekunda; tel. 8905629; e-mail dailynews34@yahoo.com; internet dailynews.gm; f. 2009; 3 a week; Dir MADI M. K. CEESAY; Editor-in-Chief SAIKOU JAMMEH.

The Daily Observer: Gacem Rd, Kanifing Industrial Area, Bakau, POB 131, Banjul; tel. 4399801; fax 4496878; e-mail webmaster@observer.gm; internet www.observer.gm; f. 1992; daily; pro-Govt; Dep. Editor-in-Chief ALHAGIE JOBE; circ. 5,000.

Foroyaa (Freedom): 1 Sambou St, Churchill's Town, POB 2306, Serrekunda; tel. and fax 4393177; e-mail online@foroyaa.gm; internet www.foroyaa.gm; f. 1987; daily; publ. by the PDOIS; Editors HALIFA SALLAH, SAM SARR, SIDIA JATTA.

The Gambia Daily: Dept of Information, 14 Daniel Goddard St, Banjul; tel. 4225060; fax 4227230; e-mail gamna@gamtel.gm; f. 1994; govt organ; Dir of Information EBRUMA COLE; circ. 500.

The Point: 2 Garba Jahumpa Rd, Fajara, POB 66, Bakau, New Town, Banjul; tel. 4497441; fax 4497442; e-mail thepoint13@yahoo.com; internet www.thepoint.gm; f. 1991; 3 a week; Man. Dir PAP SAINE; Editor-in-Chief BABOUCARR SENGHORE; circ. 3,000.

The Standard: Sait Matty Rd, POB 4566, Bakau; tel. 4496466; fax 4496481; e-mail info@standard.gm; internet www.standard.gm; f. 2010; daily; Publr SHERIFF BOJANG.

NEWS AGENCY

The Gambia News Agency (GAMNA): Dept of Information, 14 Daniel Goddard St, Banjul; tel. 4225060; fax 4227230; e-mail gamna@gamtel.gm; Dir EBRIMA COLE.

PRESS ASSOCIATION

The Gambia Press Union (GPU): 78 Mosque Rd, Serrekunda, POB 1440, Banjul; tel. and fax 4377020; e-mail gpu@qanet.gm; internet www.gambiapressunion.org; f. 1978; affiliated to West African Journalists' Association; Pres. EMIL TOURAY; Sec.-Gen. GIBAIRU JANNEH.

Publishers

National Printing and Stationery Corpn: Sankung Sillah St, Kanifing; tel. 4374403; fax 4395759; f. 1998; state-owned.

Baroueli: 73 Mosque Rd, Serrekunda, POB 976, Banjul; tel. 4392480; e-mail baroueli@qanet.gm; f. 1986; educational.

Observer Company: Bakau New Town Rd, Kanifing, PMB 131, Banjul; tel. 4496087; fax 4496878; e-mail webmaster@observer.gm; internet www.observer.gm; f. 1995; indigenous languages and non-fiction.

Sunrise Publishers: POB 955, Banjul; tel. 4393538; e-mail sunrise@qanet.gm; internet www.sunrisepublishers.net; f. 1985; regional history, politics and culture; Man. PATIENCE SONKO-GODWIN.

Broadcasting and Communications

TELECOMMUNICATIONS

In 2013 the Gambia telecommunications sector comprised four mobile cellular telephone operators and one fixed-line operator. A fifth mobile licence was issued to Nigeria-owned Globacom in 2010.

Africell (Gambia): 43 Kairaba Ave, POB 2140, Banjul; tel. 4376022; fax 4376066; e-mail mmakkaoui@africell.gm; internet www.africell.gm; f. 2001; provider of mobile cellular telecommunications; CEO ALIEU BADARA MBYE.

Comium Gambia: 27 Kairaba Ave, Pipeline, KSMD, Banjul; tel. 6601601; fax 6601602; e-mail info@comium.gm; internet www.comium.gm; f. 2007; operates mobile cellular telephone network under the Nakam brand; Man. Dir AMER ATWI.

The Gambia Telecommunications Co Ltd (GAMTEL): Gamtel House, 3 Nelson Mandela St, POB 387, Banjul; tel. 4229999; fax 4228004; e-mail gen-info@gamtel.gm; internet www.gamtel.gm; f. 1984; state-owned; Man. Dir BABOUCARR SANYANG.

Gamcel: 59 Mamadi Maniyang Highway, Kanifing; tel. 4398169; fax 4372932; internet www.gamcel.gm; f. 2000; wholly owned subsidiary of GAMTEL providing mobile cellular telephone services.

QCell Gambia: QCell House, Kairaba Ave, Serrekunda; tel. 3333111; fax 4376311; e-mail support@qcell.gm; internet www.qcell.gm; f. 2008; mobile cellular services; CEO MUHAMMED JAH.

BROADCASTING

Radio

The Gambia Radio and Television Services (GRTS): GRTV Headquarters, MDI Rd, Kanifing, POB 158, Banjul; tel. 4373913; fax 4374242; e-mail bora@gamtel.gm; internet www.grts.gm; f. 1962; state-funded, non-commercial broadcaster; radio broadcasts in English, Mandinka, Wolof, Fula, Diola, Serer and Serahuli; Dir-Gen. LAMIN MANGA.

Capital FM 100.4: 2 Kairaba Ave; tel. 7979359; e-mail saul@capitalfm.gm.

Farafenni Community Radio: Farafenni; tel. 9931964; Gen. Man. SAINEY DIBBA.

Brikama Community Radio Station: Brikama; tel. 4483000; fax 4484100; e-mail brikamacommunityradio@yahoo.co.uk; f. 1998; FM broadcaster; Admin. Man. BAKARY K. TOURAY.

Kora FM: 10 Kanifing, Banjul; internet 4399756; e-mail info@korafm.gm; internet korafm.gm; independent commercial broadcaster.

Paradise FM: Banjul; internet www.paradisefm.gm; operates from 3 stations: 105.7 Mhz in Kololi, 105.5 Mhz in Farafenni and 105.8 Mhz in Basse.

Radio 1 FM: 44 Kairaba Ave, POB 2700, Serrekunda; tel. 4396076; fax 4394911; e-mail george.radio1@qanet.gm; f. 1990; private station broadcasting FM music programmes to the Greater Banjul area; Dir GEORGE CHRISTENSEN.

Teranga FM: Sinchu Alhagie Village, Kombo North, West Coast Region; f. 2009; Man. ISMAILA SISAY.

West Coast Radio: Manjai Kunda, POB 2687, Serrekunda; tel. 4460911; fax 4461193; e-mail info@westcoast.gm; internet www.westcoast.gm; FM broadcaster; Man. Dir PETER GOMEZ.

Unique FM: Garba Jahumpa Rd, Bakau; tel. 7555777; internet www.uniquefm.gm; f. 2007; Man. LAMIN MANGA.

The Gambia also receives broadcasts from Radio Democracy for Africa (f. 1998), a division of the Voice of America, and the British Broadcasting Corpn.

Television

The Gambia Radio and Television Services (GRTS): see Radio; television broadcasts commenced 1995.

There is also a private satellite channel, Premium TV.

Finance

(cap. = capital; res = reserves; dep. = deposits; m. = million; br(s). = branch(es); amounts in dalasi)

BANKING

At the end of 2011 there were 13 banks operating in the country, of which one was an Islamic bank and 13 were conventional commercial banks.

Central Bank

Central Bank of The Gambia: 1–2 ECOWAS Ave, Banjul; tel. 4228103; fax 4226969; e-mail info@cbg.gm; internet www.cbg.gm; f. 1971; bank of issue; monetary authority; cap. 81.0m., res 4.3m., dep. 1,702.7m. (Dec. 2009); Gov. AMADOU COLLEY.

Other Banks

Access Bank (Gambia) Ltd: 47 Kairaba Ave, Fajara, POB 3177, Serrekunda; tel. 4396679; fax 4396640; e-mail jammehm@accessbankgambia.com; internet www.accessbankplc.com/gm; f. 2007; Man. Dir OLEKA OJIOGO.

Arab-Gambian Islamic Bank: 7 ECOWAS Ave, POB 1415, Banjul; tel. 4222222; fax 4223770; e-mail info@agib.gm; internet www.agib.gm; f. 1996; 21.1% owned by The Gambia National Insurance Co Ltd, 20.0% owned by Islamic Development Bank (Saudi Arabia); cap. and res 9.0m., total assets 116.9m. (Dec. 2001); Chair. ADAM NURU; Man. Dir SALISU SIRAJO; 1 br.

Bank PHB: 11A Liberation Ave, POB 211, Banjul; tel. 4227944; fax 4229312; e-mail mgcisse@ibc.gm; internet gambia.bankphb.com; f. 1968; fmrly International Bank for Commerce (Gambia) Ltd, name changed as above August 2008 following acquisition by Bank PHB Nigeria; cap. 60m., res 59.9m., dep. 434.6m. (Dec. 2006); Man. Dir CHUKS CHIBUNDU; 2 brs.

Banque Sahelo-Saherienne pour l'Investissement et Commerce Gambie Ltd: 52 Kairaba Ave, PMB 204, KMC; tel. 4498078; fax 4498080; e-mail bsic@bsicgambia.gm; internet www.bsicgambia.gm; f. 2008; Gen. Man. YOUSEF SGHAYER AHMED TURKMAN.

Ecobank Gambia Ltd: 42 Kairaba Ave, POB 3466, Serrekunda; tel. 4399030; fax 4399034; e-mail egacustomercare@ecobank.com; internet www.ecobank.com; cap. 79.5m., dep. 629m. (Dec. 2009); Man. Dir MAREME MBAYE NDIAYE.

First International Bank Ltd: 2 Kairaba Ave, Serrekunda; tel. and fax 4396580; e-mail info@fibgm.com; internet www.fibankgm.com; f. 1999; 61.9% owned by Slok Ltd (Nigeria); cap. 150.7m., res 6.8m., dep. 570.3m. (Dec. 2010); Chair. EDRISSA JOBE; Man. Dir YASSIN BAYO; 8 brs.

Guaranty Trust Bank (Gambia): 56 Kairaba Ave, Fajara, POB 1958, Banjul; tel. 4376371; fax 4376398; e-mail corpaffgm@gtbank.com; internet www.gambia.gtbplc.com; f. 2002; subsidiary of Guaranty Trust Bank PLC (Nigeria); Chair. AMADOU SAMBA; Man. Dir OLUFEMI OMOTOSO.

International Commercial Bank (Gambia) Ltd: GIPFZA House, Ground Floor, 48 Kairaba Ave, Serrekunda, KMC, POB 1600, Banjul; tel. 4377878; fax 4377880; e-mail icbank@icbank-gambia.com; internet www.icbank-gambia.com; f. 2005; CEO LALIT MOHAN TEWARI; 3 brs.

Skye Bank Gambia: 70 Kairaba Ave, Fajara, KSMD; tel. 4414370; e-mail info@skyebankgm.com; subsidiary of Skye Bank PLC (Nigeria); Man. Dir AKIM YUSUF.

Standard Chartered Bank (Gambia) Ltd: 8/10 ECOWAS Ave, POB 259, Banjul; tel. 4202929; fax 4202692; e-mail Humphrey.Mukwereza@gm.standardchartered.com; internet www.standardchartered.com/gm; f. 1894; 75% owned by Standard Chartered Holdings BV, The Netherlands; cap. 60m., res 157.6m., dep. 2,183.7m. (Dec. 2009); Chair. MOMODOU B. A. SENGHORE; CEO HUMPHREY MUKWEREZA; 5 brs.

Trust Bank Ltd (TBL): 3–4 ECOWAS Ave, POB 1018, Banjul; tel. 4225777; fax 4225781; e-mail info@trustbank.gm; internet www.tblgambia.com; f. 1997; fmrly Meridien BIAO Bank Gambia Ltd; 22.12% owned by Data Bank, 36.97% by Social Security and Housing Finance Corpn; cap. 200.0m., res 121.1m., dep. 3,477.4m. (Dec. 2011); Chair. KEN OFORI ATTA; Man. Dir PA MACOUMBA NJIE; 17 brs.

Zenith Bank (Gambia) Ltd: 49 Kairaba Ave, Fajara, POB 2823, Serrekunda; tel. 4399471; e-mail enquiry@zenithbank.gm; internet www.tblgambia.com; f. 2008; subsidiary of Zenith Bank PLC; Man. Dir EMEKA ANYAEGBUNA.

INSURANCE

At the end of 2011 there were 11 insurance companies operating in the country, of which nine provided non-life insurance, one life insurance and one both non-life and life insurance.

Capital Express Assurance (Gambia) Ltd: 22 Anglesea St, POB 268, Banjul; tel. 4227480; fax 4229219; e-mail capinsur@gamtel.gm; f. 1985; subsidiary of Capital Express Assurance Limited (Nigeria); CEO KUNLE ADEGBOYE.

The Gambia National Insurance Co Ltd (GNIC): 19 Kairaba Ave, Fajara, KSMD, POB 750, Banjul; tel. 4395725; fax 4395716; e-mail info@gnic.gm; internet www.gnic.gm; f. 1974; privately owned; Chair. MATARR O. DRAMMEH; Man. Dir FYE K. CEESAY; 3 brs.

Global Security Insurance Co Ltd: 73A Independence Dr., POB 1400, Banjul; tel. 4223716; fax 4223715; e-mail global@gamtel.gm; f. 1996; Man. Dir EBOU L. BITTAYE.

Great Alliance Insurance Co: 10 Nelson Mandela St, POB 1160, Banjul; tel. 4227839; fax 4229444; f. 1989; Pres. BAI MATARR DRAMMEH; Man. Dir DEBORAH H. FORSTER.

IGI Gamstar Insurance Co Ltd: 79 Daniel Goddard St, POB 1276, Banjul; tel. 4228610; fax 4229755; e-mail gamstarinsurance@hotmail.com; f. 1991; Man. Dir FRANK UCHE.

International Insurance Co. Ltd: Duwa Jabbi Bldg, 5 OAU Blvd, POB 1254, Banjul; tel. 4202761; fax 4202763; e-mail iic@gamtel.gm; Man. Dir SENOR THOMAS-SOWE.

Londongate (Gambia) Insurance Co: 1–3 Liberation Ave, POB 602, Banjul; tel. 4201740; fax 4201742; e-mail izadi@londongate.gm; internet www.londongate.co.uk/gambia_profile.htm; f. 1999; owned by Boule & Co Ltd; Man. Dir ISHA JANNEH.

New Vision Insurance Co Ltd: 3–4 ECOWAS Ave, POB 239, Banjul; tel. 4223045; fax 4223040; Dir BIRAN BAH.

Prime Insurance Co Ltd: 10C Nelson Mandela St, POB 277, Banjul; tel. 4222476; fax 4222475; e-mail info@primeinsurance.gm; internet www.primeinsurance.gm; f. 1997; Gen. Man. DAWDA SARGE.

Sunshine Insurance Company Ltd: 7/8 Nelson Mandela St, Banjul; tel. 4202645; fax 4202648; e-mail sunshine.insurance@qanet.gm; Man. Dir ALMAMY B. JOBARTEH.

Takaful Gambia Ltd: 22 Serign Modou Sillah St, Banjul; tel. 4227480; fax 4229219; e-mail info@takaful.gm; Man. Dir MAMODOU M. JOOF.

Insurance Association

Insurance Association of The Gambia (IAG): IAG Secretariat, 10C Nelson Mandela St, POB 277, Banjul; tel. 4229952; fax 4201637; e-mail info@iag.gm; internet www.iag.gm; f. 1987; Pres. DAWDA SARGE; Sec.-Gen. HENRY M. JAWO.

Trade and Industry

GOVERNMENT AGENCIES

The Gambia Investment and Export Promotion Agency (GIEPA): GIEPA House, 48A Kairaba Ave, Serrekunda, KMC, POB 757, Banjul; tel. 4377377; fax 4377379; e-mail info.info@giepa.gm; internet www.giepa.gm; f. 2001; fmrly The Gambia Investment Promotion and Free Zones Agency (f. 2001), the implementing agency of the Gateway Project, funded by the World Bank and the Gambian Government, responsible for fostering local and foreign direct investment; name changed as above in 2010; Chair. FATOU SINYAN MERGAN; CEO FATOU M. JALLOW.

Indigenous Business Advisory Services (IBAS): POB 2502, Bakau; tel. 4496098; e-mail payibas@gamtel.gm; Man. Dir MANGA SANYANG.

DEVELOPMENT AGENCY

The Gambia Rural Development Agency (GARDA): Soma Village, Jarra West, PMB 452, Serrekunda; tel. 4496676; fax 4390095; f. 1990; Exec. Dir KEBBA BAH.

CHAMBER OF COMMERCE

The Gambia Chamber of Commerce and Industry (GCCI): 55 Kairaba Ave, KSMD, POB 3382, Serrekunda; tel. 8807445; fax 4378936; e-mail info@gcci.gm; internet gcci.gm; f. 1967; Pres. BAI MATARR DRAMMEH; CEO ALIEU SECKA.

INDUSTRIAL AND TRADE ASSOCIATION

The Gambia Cotton Growers Association: Banjul; Pres. ALPHA BAH; Sec.-Gen. OMAR SUMPO CEESAY.

UTILITIES

Public Utilities Regulatory Authority (PURA): 94 Kairaba Ave, POB 4230, Bakau; tel. 4399601; fax 4399905; e-mail info@pura.gm; internet www.pura.gm; f. 2001; monitors and enforces standards of performance by public utilities; Chair. DODOU BAMMY JAGNE; Dir-Gen. ABDOULIE JOBE.

National Water and Electricity Co Ltd (NAWEC): 53 Mamady Manjang Highway, Kanifing, POB 609, Banjul; tel. 4376607; fax 4375990; e-mail nawecmd@qanet.gm; internet www.nawec.gm; f. 1996; in 1999 control was transferred to the Bassau Development Corpn, Côte d'Ivoire, under a 15-year contract; electricity and water supply, sewerage services; Chair. MUSTAPHA COLLEY; Man. Dir EBRIMA SANYANG.

TRADE UNIONS

The Gambia National Trades Union Congress (GNTUC): Trade Union House, 31 OAU Blvd, POB 698, Banjul; Pres. MUSTAPHA WADA; Sec.-Gen. EBRIMA GARBA CHAM.

The Gambia Workers' Confederation: Trade Union House, 72 OAU Blvd, POB 698, Banjul; tel. and fax 4222754; e-mail gambiawc@hotmail.com; f. 1958 as The Gambia Workers' Union; present name adopted in 1985; Sec.-Gen. PA MOMODOU FAAL; 52,000 mems (2007).

Transport

Gambia Public Transport Service Co: Factory St, Kanifing Housing Estate, POB 801, Kanifing; tel. 4392230; fax 4392454; f. 2013 to replace The Gambia Public Transport Corpn; operates road transport and ferry services; Man. Dir BAKARY HUMA.

RAILWAYS

There are no railways in The Gambia.

ROADS

In 2004 there were an estimated 3,742 km of roads in The Gambia, of which 1,652 km were main roads, and 1,300 km were secondary roads. In that year only 19.3% of the road network was paved. Some roads are impassable in the rainy season. The expansion and upgrading of the road network is planned, as part of the Jammeh administration's programme to improve The Gambia's transport infrastructure. Among intended schemes is the construction of a motorway along the coast, with the aid of a loan of US $8.5m. from Kuwait.

SHIPPING

The River Gambia is well suited to navigation. A weekly river service is maintained between Banjul and Basse, 390 km above Banjul, and a ferry connects Banjul with Barra. Small ocean-going vessels can reach Kaur, 190 km above Banjul, throughout the year. The Gambia's flag registered fleet consisted of eight vessels, totalling 29,396 grt, at 31 December 2013.

The Gambia Ports Authority: 34 Liberation Ave, POB 617, Banjul; tel. 4227266; fax 4227268; e-mail info@gamport.gm; internet www.gamports.com; f. 1972; Man. Dir MOHAMMED LAMIN GIBBA.

The Gambia Shipping Agency Ltd: 1A Cotton St, POB 257, Banjul; tel. 4227518; fax 4227929; e-mail thomas.nielsen@bollore.com; f. 1984; shipping agents and forwarders; Gen. Man. THOMAS NIELSEN; 30 employees.

Interstate Shipping Co (Gambia) Ltd: 43 Buckle St, POB 220, Banjul; tel. 4229388; fax 4229347; e-mail interstate@gamtel.gm; transport and storage; Man. Dir B. F. SAGNIA.

Maersk Gambia Ltd: 80 OAU Blvd, POB 1399, Banjul; tel. 4224450; fax 4224025; e-mail gamsalimp@maersk.com; f. 1993; owned by Maersk Line.

CIVIL AVIATION

Banjul International Airport is situated at Yundum, 27 km from the capital.

The Gambia Civil Aviation Authority (GCAA): Banjul International Airport, Yundum; tel. 4472831; fax 4472190; e-mail dggcaa@qanet.gm; internet www.gcaa.aero/portal; f. 1991; Chair. SALIFU MBOGE; Dir-Gen. ABDOULIE JAMMEH.

The Gambia International Airlines: PMB 353, Banjul; tel. 4472770; fax 4223700; internet www.gia.gm; f. 1996; state-owned; sole handling agent at Banjul, sales agent; Chair. MUHAMMED M. O. KAH; Man. Dir BAKARY NYASSI.

Tourism

Tourists are attracted by The Gambia's beaches and also by its abundant birdlife. A major expansion of tourism facilities was carried out in the early 1990s. Although there was a dramatic decline in tourist arrivals in the mid-1990s (owing to the political instability), the tourism sector recovered well. An annual 'Roots Festival' was inaugurated in 1996, with the aim of attracting African-American visitors to The Gambia. In 2011 some 106,393 tourists visited The Gambia, while earnings from tourism totalled US $96m. in that year.

The Gambia Hotel Association: c/o Golden Beach Hotel, Coastal Rd, POB 2345, Bijilo; tel. 4465111; fax 4463722; e-mail gambiahotels@gamtel.gm; internet www.gambiahotels.gm; Chair. ALIEU SECKA.

The Gambia Tourist Authority: Kololi, POB 4085, Bakau; tel. 4462491; fax 4462487; e-mail info@gta.gm; internet www.visitthegambia.gm; f. 2001; Chair. and Dir-Gen. ALIEU MBOGE.

Defence

As assessed at November 2013, the Gambian National Army comprised 800 men (including a marine unit of about 70 and the National Guards) in active service. The Armed Forces comprise the Army, the Navy and the National Guards. Military service has been mainly voluntary; however, the Constitution of the Second Republic, which entered into full effect in January 1997, makes provision for conscription.

Defence Expenditure: Estimated at D189m. in 2012.

Chief of Defence Staff: Maj.-Gen. OUSMAN BADJIE.

Commander of the Gambian National Army: Brig.-Gen. SERIGN MODOU NJIE.
Commander of the Navy: Commodore SILLAH KUJABBIE.

Education

Primary education, beginning at seven years of age, is free but not compulsory and lasts for nine years. It is divided into two cycles of six and three years. Secondary education, from 16 years of age, lasts for a further three years. According to UNESCO estimates, in 2012 total enrolment at primary schools included 71% of children in the relevant age-group (boys 69%; girls 73%), while secondary enrolment in 2010 was equivalent to 57% of the appropriate age-group (boys 59%; girls 56%). The Jammeh administration has, since 1994, embarked on an ambitious project to improve educational facilities and levels of attendance and attainment. A particular aim has been to improve access to schools for pupils in rural areas. Post-secondary education is available in teacher training, agriculture, health and technical subjects. The University of The Gambia, at Banjul, was officially opened in 2000. Some 2,842 students were enrolled at the university in 2009/10. In 2010 spending on education represented 22.8% of total budgetary expenditure.

GEORGIA

Introductory Survey

LOCATION, CLIMATE, LANGUAGE, RELIGION, FLAG, CAPITAL

Georgia is situated in the west and central South Caucasus, on the southern foothills of the Greater Caucasus mountain range. There is a frontier with Turkey to the south-west and a western coastline on the Black Sea. The northern frontier with Russia follows the axis of the Greater Caucasus. Armenia lies to the south, and Azerbaijan to the south-east. Two territories within Georgia remained outside the control of the central Government: Abkhazia (with the formal status of an autonomous republic), in the north-west, and the former autonomous oblast of South Ossetia, in the north. The autonomous republic of Ajara, is located in south-west Georgia. The Black Sea coast and the Rion plains have a warm, humid, subtropical climate, with annual rainfall of more than 2,000 mm and average temperatures of 6°C (42°F) in January and 23°C (73° F) in July. Eastern Georgia has a more continental climate, with cold winters and hot, dry summers. The official language is Georgian, a member of the South Caucasian (Kartavelian) language group, which is written in the Georgian script. Most of the population are adherents of Christianity; the principal denomination is the Georgian Orthodox Church. Islam is professed by Ajars, Azeris, Kurds and some others. The national flag (proportions 100 by 147) consists of a white field, with a centred red cross and a smaller red cross in each quarter. The capital is Tbilisi.

CONTEMPORARY POLITICAL HISTORY

Historical Context

A powerful kingdom in medieval times, Georgia subsequently came under periods of foreign domination, and was annexed by the Russian Empire from the 19th century. An independent Georgian state was established on 26 May 1918, ruled by a Menshevik Socialist Government. Although it received recognition from the Bolshevik Government of Soviet Russia in May 1920, Bolshevik troops invaded Georgia and proclaimed a Georgian Soviet Socialist Republic (SSR) on 25 February 1921. In December 1922 it was absorbed into the Transcaucasian Soviet Federative Socialist Republic (TSFSR), which, on 22 December, became a founder member of the USSR. In 1936 the TSFSR was disbanded and Georgia reverted to the status of an SSR.

During the 1930s Georgians suffered persecution under the Soviet leader, Stalin (Iosif V. Dzhugashvili), himself a Georgian. Most members of the Georgian leadership were dismissed after Stalin's death in 1953, and demonstrations in support of Stalin in the Georgian capital, Tbilisi, in 1956 were violently dispersed. In 1972 the First Secretary of the Communist Party of Georgia (SKP), Eduard Shevardnadze, attempted to remove officials who had been accused of corruption. Shevardnadze remained leader of the SKP until 1985, when he became Minister of Foreign Affairs of the USSR.

The increased freedom of expression that followed the election of Mikhail Gorbachev as Soviet leader in 1985 allowed the formation of 'unofficial groups', which were prominent in organizing demonstrations in November 1988 against russification in Georgia. In February 1989 Abkhazians renewed a campaign for secession from Georgia (see Abkhazia). On the night of 8–9 April Soviet security forces attacked demonstrators who were advocating Georgian independence in the Georgian capital, Tbilisi, killing 16 people. Despite the resignation of state and party officials, anti-Soviet sentiment increased sharply. In November the Georgian Supreme Soviet (Supreme Council—legislature), which was dominated by SKP members, declared the supremacy of Georgian laws over all-Union (USSR) laws. In February 1990 the same body declared Georgia 'an annexed and occupied country', and in March abolished the SKP's monopoly on power. Legislation permitting full multi-party elections was adopted in August.

In the elections to the Supreme Soviet, held on 28 October and 11 November 1990, the pro-independence Round Table–Free Georgia coalition, founded earlier in the year and led by Zviad Gamsakhurdia, a former dissident, won 155 seats in the 250-seat chamber, and 64% of the votes cast, while the SKP won 64 seats. All associations involved in the election campaign had declared support for Georgia's independence. The elections were boycotted by many non-ethnic Georgians.The new Supreme Soviet convened on 14 November and elected Gamsakhurdia as its Chairman. It renamed the territory the Republic of Georgia and adopted the flag of the 1918–21 state. Tengiz Sigua was appointed Chairman of the Council of Ministers. The new Supreme Soviet declared illegal the conscription of Georgians into the Soviet armed forces. Many young men were reported to have joined nationalist paramilitary groups or the National Guard (a de facto republican army), which the Supreme Soviet established in January 1991.

The Georgian authorities boycotted the all-Union referendum on the future of the USSR, held in March 1991, but voting took place in Abkhazia and in the former autonomous oblast of South Ossetia (which had been abolished in December 1990). It was reported that in both territories there was overwhelming support for the preservation of the USSR. On 31 March 1991 the Government conducted a referendum on the restoration of Georgian independence. Of those eligible to vote, 95% participated in the referendum, 93% of whom voted for independence, according to official figures. On 9 April the Georgian Supreme Council approved a decree formally restoring the independence of Georgia, which thus became the first republic to secede from the USSR. Gamsakhurdia won direct elections to the new post of executive President, held in May, receiving 86.5% of the votes cast. Voting did not take place in Abkhazia or South Ossetia.

Domestic Political Affairs

Gamsakhurdia was strongly criticized, after he initially refrained from publicly condemning the attempted coup by conservative communists in Moscow, the Russian and Soviet capital, in August 1991 (the SKP was subsequently disbanded). After the coup collapsed, Tengiz Kitovani, the former leader of the National Guard (who had been dismissed by Gamsakhurdia in August), announced that 15,000 of his men were no longer subordinate to the President. Sigua resigned as Chairman of the Council of Ministers in mid-August, joining Kitovani in opposition to Gamsakhurdia. In September opposition parties organized a series of demonstrations to demand Gamsakhurdia's resignation. Several people were killed in clashes. Gamsakhurdia ordered the arrest of prominent opposition leaders, imposing a state of emergency in Tbilisi.

In December 1991 armed conflict broke out in Tbilisi, as the opposition, led by Kitovani and by Jaba Ioseliani, the leader of the paramilitary *Mkhedrioni* (Horsemen), attempted to oust the President. More than 100 people were killed. On 2 January 1992 the opposition declared Gamsakhurdia deposed and formed a Military Council, which appointed Sigua as acting Chairman of the Council of Ministers. Gamsakhurdia and some of his supporters ('Zviadists') fled Georgia four days later. The office of President was abolished, and the functions of Head of State were, instead, to be exercised by the Chairman of the Supreme Council. Sigua subsequently formed a new Government.

The return of Eduard Shevardnadze

In March 1992 Shevardnadze returned to Georgia, and a State Council, comprising 50 members, drawn from all the major political organizations, including Sigua, Ioseliani and Kitovani, and led by Shevardnadze. By April government troops had re-established control in the rebellious areas. In July, however, Zviadists took hostage a deputy premier was taken hostage in western Georgia. This was followed by the kidnapping of the Minister of Internal Affairs, and several other officials. In response, the State Council dispatched more than 3,000 National Guardsmen to Abkhazia, where the hostages were believed to be held, prompting armed resistance by Abkhazian militia. By August several of the hostages had been released.

An estimated 75% of the electorate participated in elections to the Supreme Council held on 11 October 1992, contested by more than 30 parties and alliances. Voting did not take place in South Ossetia, Mingrelia (south-east of Abkhazia) and parts of Abkhazia. The centrist Peace bloc won 29 seats, more than any other grouping, in the 235-member legislature. Shevardnadze was the sole candidate at the concurrent direct election of the legislature's Chairman (Head of State), winning more than 95% of the votes cast. The new Supreme Council convened in November.

Opposition towards Shevardnadze from within his own administration prompted the dismissal, in May 1993, of Kitovani as Minister of Defence. In August the Council of Ministers tendered its resignation. In September Shevardnadze appointed a new Council of Ministers, headed by Otar Patsatsia, a former SKP official, and offered his own resignation, which the Supreme Council rejected. By late September Shevardnadze's position was made more precarious by a Zviadist resurgence in western Georgia. As the rebel forces advanced eastwards, Shevardnadze persuaded the Supreme Council to agree to Georgia's membership of the Commonwealth of Independent States (CIS, see p. 243), established in December 1991 by 11 former Soviet republics. In October 1993 Russian troops were dispatched to Georgia, and by November the Zviadists had been entirely routed from the country. In January 1994 it was reported that Gamsakhurdia had committed suicide.

Following the restoration of a degree of stability in Georgia (outside Abkhazia), Shevardnadze created his own party, the Citizens' Union of Georgia (SMK). Sigua and Kitovani established a National Liberation Front with the declared aim of regaining control of Abkhazia, although the organization was subsequently banned. In August 1995 the Supreme Council adopted a new Constitution, which provided for a strong executive presidency. The post of Prime Minister was to be abolished and the most senior position in the Government to be the Minister of State. The territorial status of Abkhazia and Ajara was not defined, while the incorporation of the former South Ossetian territories into various other regions was confirmed. The official signing of the Constitution was postponed until 17 October following an assassination attempt against Shevardnadze. After Igor Giorgadze, the Minister of State Security, was subsequently named by state prosecutors as the chief instigator of the plot, he fled abroad, along with two other alleged plotters.

A presidential election was held on 5 November 1995, in which Shevardnadze won almost 75% of the votes cast. Elections to the new 235-member unicameral Sakartvelos Parlamenti (Georgian Parliament) were held concurrently, under a mixed system of voting. Only three parties contesting the 150 seats to be filled by proportional representation succeeded in obtaining the 5% of the votes required. Of these, Shevardnadze's SMK won 90 seats, the National Democratic Party of Georgia 31, and the All-Georgian Union of Revival, chaired by Aslan Abashidze, the leader of the Autonomous Republic of Ajara, 25. A further two rounds of voting were conducted before all remaining 85 single-mandate seats were filled. The SMK held a total of 107 seats. Parliament convened in late November, electing as its Chairman Zurab Zhvania, the General Secretary of the SMK. In December Shevardnadze formed a new Government, led by Minister of State Nikoloz Lekishvili.

Meanwhile, in late 1995 criminal proceedings commenced in Tbilisi against Kitovani, in connection with the NLF attempted raid on Abkhazia. In September 1996 Kitovani was convicted on charges of establishing an illegal armed formation and was sentenced to eight years' imprisonment. (He was released in May 1999.) In May 1996 Ioseliani was convicted of complicity in the August 1995 assassination attempt on Shevardnadze and imprisoned. In June 1996 supporters of Gamsakhurdia received lengthy prison sentences for their roles in the civil conflict of 1993.

In February 1998 Shevardnadze survived a further attempt on his life. In March Guram Absandze, a former Minister of Finance, was arrested in Moscow and returned to Georgia to stand trial on charges of organizing the assassination attempt. Absandze was sentenced to 17 years' imprisonment in 2001 (he was later pardoned). Further arrests were made in May 1999, in connection with a new plot to overthrow Shevardnadze. All of those arrested were reported to have links with Giorgadze; one of the accused died in detention, and 10 others were sentenced to terms of imprisonment in November 2001. In August 1998 the hitherto ambassador to Russia, Vazha Lortkipanidze, was appointed Minister of State. In October Zviadists staged an armed insurrection in western Georgia. Following the escape of the captured rebel leaders, the Minister of State Security, Jemal Gakhokidze, resigned later in the month.

In July 1999 Parliament approved a constitutional amendment, increasing from 5% to 7% the quorum for parliamentary representation in those seats elected by proportional representation. Some 32 parties and blocs contested legislative elections, held in two rounds, on 31 October and 14 November, in which 68% of the electorate participated. The SMK obtained 130 seats. The Union for the Revival of Georgia bloc, led by Abashidze, and the Industry Will Save Georgia (MGS) bloc secured 58 seats and 15 seats, respectively. Despite opposition allegations of irregularities, Organization for Security and Co-operation in Europe (OSCE, see p. 387) observers declared the elections lawful.

In the presidential election of 9 April 2000, Shevardnadze secured 79.8% of the votes cast. Electoral violations were noted by the OSCE, but the Parliamentary Assembly of the Council of Europe (PACE, see p. 252) reported no major infringements. On 11 May Parliament endorsed the appointment of Giorgi Arsenishvili as Minister of State.

In September 2001 the Minister of Justice, Mikheil Saakashvili, resigned, apparently in response to a perceived lack of support for his anti-corruption campaign. Shortly afterwards, he founded a new political party, the National Movement (NM). In the same month Shevardnadze resigned as Chairman of the SMK. In October public discontent culminated in large-scale protests in Tbilisi, after security officials raided Rustavi 2, an independent television station that had been critical of the Government. Zhvania urged the Minister of State Security and the Minister of Internal Affairs to resign, to avert further protests. However, the latter refused to comply with this request, and popular protests intensified. On 1 November Shevardnadze dismissed the Government. The Prosecutor-General subsequently resigned, as did Zhvania, who was replaced as parliamentary Chairman by Nino Burjanadze. Later in the month, a new Government was formed, with Avtandil Jorbenadze as Minister of State. Zhvania founded a new political party, the United Democrats (ED), in June 2002. At municipal elections, held in that month, the SMK suffered a serious reverse, and the breakaway New Conservative Party (AKP) won the largest number of seats nationwide. Jorbenadze was subsequently elected as Chairman of the SMK.

The 'rose revolution' and the Saakashvili presidency

On 2 November 2003 elections were held to Parliament. Preliminary results indicated that the pro-Shevardnadze For a New Georgia bloc had obtained the majority of the votes cast. However, international monitors from the Council of Europe and the OSCE noted electoral irregularities, and there were widespread allegations of falsification. On 4 November a large protest was staged in Tbilisi against the conduct of the elections; Saakashvili (who claimed that his NM had attracted the most support) led demands for Shevardnadze's resignation. Further large-scale protest demonstrations subsequently took place.

On 20 November 2003 the Central Electoral Commission (CEC) announced the final results of the elections (five members of the Commission refused to endorse the results). The For a New Georgia bloc received 57 legislative seats (including 38 of the 150 seats allocated by proportional representation), followed by Abashidze's renamed Democratic Union of Revival (DAP), with 39 seats (33 on a proportional basis), and the NM, with 36 seats (32 on a proportional basis). The Georgian Labour Party (SLP) obtained 21 seats, the Burjanadze-Democrats (B-D) bloc, formed by Zhvania and Burjanadze, 16, the New Right bloc 15 and the MGS bloc two; 16 seats were won by independents, and elections were scheduled to be repeated in other constituencies. The NM and the B-D bloc reiterated claims that the results were invalid, while Western governments also criticized the conduct of the elections. A referendum, held concurrently with the parliamentary elections, approved an eventual reduction in the number of parliamentary deputies to a maximum of 150. Saakashvili announced that a protest march would be staged on 22 November, with the intent of preventing the new legislature from convening. On that day some 30,000 demonstrators proceeded to the parliament building, precipitating what became known as the 'rose revolution'. Troops attached to the Ministry of Internal Affairs failed to prevent protesters from besieging the main parliamentary chamber, and Shevardnadze was evacuated from the building. He subsequently declared a nationwide state of emergency. On 23 November Shevardnadze and Saakashvili attended a meeting, mediated by the Russian Minister of Foreign Affairs, Igor Ivanov, at which Shevardnadze agreed to tender his resignation, in return for guarantees of immunity from prosecution. Burjanadze assumed the presidency in an interim capacity, pending an election, and the state of emergency was lifted. Jorbenadze and several other ministers resigned on 25 November, when the Supreme Court annulled the results of the legislative elections for the 150 mandates allocated by proportional representation. On 27 November Zhvania was approved as

Minister of State, and new government appointments were made.

In the presidential election, held on 4 January 2004, Saakashvili obtained 96.3% of the votes cast, with an electoral turnout of 88.0%. Saakashvili was inaugurated as President on 25 January. In early February Parliament adopted several constitutional amendments proposed by Saakashvili, providing, *inter alia*, for the reintroduction of the post of Prime Minister. On 17 February Parliament approved the composition of a new Government, headed by Zhvania as Prime Minister, comprising predominantly young, Western-educated ministers, none of whom had served in the Shevardnadze administration. In March Saakashvili announced the appointment of Salomé Zurabishvili, hitherto the French ambassador to Georgia, as Minister of Foreign Affairs.

Elections to fill the 150 proportional seats in Parliament were held on 28 March 2004. A coalition of the NM and the ED won 67.3% of the votes cast and 135 seats (giving them a total of 152 seats of the 235 in Parliament, including the single-mandate seats elected in November 2003). Although international observers commended the conduct of the elections, some violations were reported. The Rightist Opposition—an alliance of MGS and the AKP—was the only other grouping to secure seats in the legislature on a party-list basis (with 7.5% of the votes and 15 seats—giving them 23 seats overall). Abashidze, whose DAP obtained 6.0% of the proportional votes, claimed that the results had been falsified. In April 2004 Parliament re-elected Burjanadze as Chairman. As part of a ministerial reorganization in June, Irakli Okruashvili became Minister of Internal Affairs, while Kakha Bendukidze, a prominent industrialist, was appointed Minister of the Economy. In the same month the Republican Party of Georgia (SRP) announced that it would no longer co-operate with the NM-ED bloc. In November the NM and the ED merged to form the United National Movement (ENM), headed by Saakashvili. In December Okruashvili was appointed Minister of Defence; the Ministry of State Security was merged with the Ministry of Internal Affairs, and Bendukidze became State Minister, responsible for Economic Reform.

On 3 February 2005 Prime Minister Zhvania was discovered dead, apparently from poisoning attributed to a domestic gas leak. On 17 February Parliament approved a reorganized Government, headed by the hitherto Minister of Finance, Zurab Noghaideli; Konstantine Kemularia, hitherto Chairman of the Supreme Court, became Deputy Prime Minister and Minister of Justice. On 23 February Parliament endorsed the constitutional amendments providing for a reduction in the number of parliamentary deputies, with effect from the scheduled 2008 legislative elections. In July 2005 Parliament approved legislation providing for the election of the mayor of Tbilisi by the Tbilisi City Council, rather than directly by the electorate.

On 13 October 2005 Parliament ratified the Framework Convention for the Protection of National Minorities, honouring one of Georgia's commitments on joining the Council of Europe in 1999. However, delays in the preparation of the document prompted a number of deputies to demand the dismissal of Zurabishvili as Minister of Foreign Affairs; her removal on 19 October prompted protest rallies.

In late March 2006 three opposition factions—the Democratic Front (comprising the Conservative Party of Georgia and the SRP), the AKP, and MGS—launched a boycott of parliamentary proceedings, in protest at Parliament's decision to remove the mandate of an SRP deputy. Also in March a protest against the reportedly routine use of violence by police officers was staged outside the parliament building in Tbilisi. Four officers belonging to the interior ministry's special police force were arrested on suspicion of the killing of a bank employee, Sandro Girgvliani, and in July they were convicted and issued custodial sentences. On 21 July Giorgi Khaindrava was dismissed as State Minister, responsible for Conflict Resolution, following his outspoken criticism of the response of the Minister of Internal Affairs, Vano Merabishvili, to Girgvliani's killing.

In September 2006 some 29 people were arrested on suspicion of plotting a coup, 13 of whom were subsequently charged. At municipal elections on 5 October, the ENM secured a decisive victory, attracting 66.5% of the total votes cast. On 10 November Okruashvili was dismissed as Minister of Defence, after he made controversial comments regarding South Ossetia; he was replaced by Davit Kezerashvili.

In January 2007 President Saakashvili signed into force a series of constitutional amendments, as a result of which the President would no longer dismiss or appoint judges. Additionally, presidential and legislative elections were henceforth to be conducted simultaneously; thus the next presidential election was brought forward by several months. In September 2007 Parliament approved a government reorganization. Later in the month Okruashvili, who had established a new opposition party, the Movement for a United Georgia (MES), publicly accused Saakashvili of corruption and of conspiring to kill a prominent Georgian businessman resident in the United Kingdom, Arkadi (Badri) Patarkatsishvili, who owned several media organizations in Georgia. Okruashvili was subsequently arrested on charges of financial malpractice, prompting a large rally to demand his release and the holding of early legislative elections. In October Okruashvili withdrew the accusations of criminal behaviour he had made against Saakashvili, and also confessed to criminal charges against him; he was released on bail. In November he stated that he had been forced to retract the accusations while in detention, and left Georgia. Later that month he was detained in Germany in response to a request of the Georgian authorities, but was subsequently transferred to France, where he was released on bail in January 2008. In March a Georgian court found Okruashvili guilty of embezzlement, and sentenced him *in absentia* to 11 years' imprisonment. In April it was announced that France had granted Okruashvili political asylum.

Meanwhile, in October 2007 a 10-party opposition alliance presented a joint manifesto to the authorities, demanding early legislative elections, electoral reform, and the release of political prisoners. In November Patarkatsishvili declared that he would fund organized opposition protests. In early November the opposition led a campaign of rallies outside the parliamentary building demanding Saakashvili's resignation. On 7 November special forces violently dispersed opposition supporters; later that day the Government declared a national state of emergency, under which broadcasts of the Imedi television channel (partially owned by Patarkatsishvili) were suspended. On the following day Saakashvili announced that a presidential election would be held on 5 January 2008, to be followed by a referendum on early legislative elections. The authorities announced that two opposition leaders had been charged with espionage and conspiring to overthrow the Government with Russian support, and that Patarkatsishvili was suspected of complicity. On 16 November the state of emergency was ended by parliamentary decree; on the same day Saakashvili dismissed Noghaideli and nominated Vladimer Gurgenidze, hitherto the Chairman of the (privately owned) Bank of Georgia, to the premiership. Parliament subsequently approved a reorganized Government. On 25 November Saakashvili resigned the presidency, in order to campaign for the forthcoming election; Burjanadze replaced him in an interim capacity. In early December Imedi resumed broadcasts.

President Saakashvili re-elected

The alliance of nine opposition parties nominated Levan Gachechiladze, a non-partisan parliamentary deputy, as their presidential candidate. In December 2007 Patarkatsishvili announced his withdrawal from the poll and returned to the United Kingdom, claiming that the Georgian authorities planned his assassination. At the presidential election, held on 5 January 2008, Saakashvili was re-elected with 53.5% of votes cast; Gachechiladze secured 25.7% of the votes. At the concurrent referendum on the scheduling of early legislative elections, some 79.9% of votes cast were in favour of the proposal. The CEC officially recognized the election results on 13 January and Saakashvili was inaugurated on 20 January. Parliament approved a reorganized administration in late January (opposition deputies boycotted the session). In February the death of Patarkatsishvili at his British residence prompted speculation that he had been assassinated, but medical investigations concluded that he had died from natural causes. In March, prior to legislative elections, which it had brought forward to May, Parliament adopted further constitutional amendments, reducing the number of legislative deputies from 235 to 150, of whom 75 were to be elected by proportional representation and 75 in single-member constituencies.

In early May 2008 Saakashvili appointed Ekaterine Tkeshelashvili (Prosecutor-General since January) as Minister of Foreign Affairs, replacing Davit Bakradze, after the latter resigned to head the ENM list of candidates in the forthcoming parliamentary elections. In the elections, held on 21 May, the ENM secured 59.2% of votes cast on a party-list basis and 119 seats overall in the legislative elections, while the Joint Opposition (National Council, New Rights) alliance—comprising eight parties, among them MES, Georgia's Way (led by Zurabishvili), the

Conservative Party of Georgia and the New Rights (AM), as well as four individual deputies—won 17.7% of votes and 17 seats. Although an international observer mission issued a generally positive assessment of the elections, the Joint Opposition accused the authorities of extensive electoral malpractice, and announced a boycott of the new Parliament. Bakradze was elected parliamentary Chairman in June.

On 9 August 2008, two days after military conflict with Russia broke out in South Ossetia (see Regional relations and South Ossetia), and which subsequently spread to other regions of Georgia, Parliament approved a presidential decree declaring a state of war with Russia, and martial law within Georgia. In October, in the aftermath of the conflict, Saakashvili dismissed Gurgenidze as Prime Minister. Grigol Mgaloblishvili, hitherto Ambassador to Turkey, was nominated to replace him. Parliament approved the appointment of Mgaloblishvili and four new ministers on 1 November. An opposition demonstration was staged in early November to demand Saakashvili's resignation, after political leaders accused him of responsibility for Georgia's defeat in the military conflict with Russia. Meanwhile, several former prominent supporters of Saakashvili expressed increasing dissatisfaction with his leadership. In November Burjanadze established a new opposition party, the Democratic Movement—United Georgia (DM—ES), and in early December Noghaideli also announced the creation of a political association, the Movement for a Fair Georgia (MSS). In November, a group of opposition deputies that did not support the parliamentary boycott formed a new party, the Democratic Party of Georgia, headed by Gia Tortladze. In December Saakashvili reorganized the Government; Vasil (Davit) Sikharulidze, hitherto Ambassador to the USA, became Minister of Defence, and Grigol Vashadze was appointed Minister of Foreign Affairs. Shortly beforehand, it was announced that Irakli Alasania, the Permanent Representative of Georgia to the UN, had submitted his resignation; after returning to Georgia, he criticized the Government and demanded that Saakashvili step down. Burjanadze also demanded that an early presidential election be conducted. On 30 January 2009 Mgaloblishvili tendered his resignation as Prime Minister on grounds of ill health. On the same day Saakashvili nominated First Deputy Prime Minister and Minister of Finance Nika Gilauri as his successor.

Approval of new Constitution

In early 2009, following disagreements within the main opposition, Alasania established a new opposition grouping, the Alliance for Georgia, comprising the SRP and the AM. In March the Ministry of Internal Affairs announced that its forces had arrested 10 suspects, of whom nine were members of the DM—ES, on charges of the illegal purchase of armaments; Burjanadze dismissed broadcast video evidence as part of a campaign by the authorities against her party. In April demonstrations demanding the resignation of Saakashvili commenced in Tbilisi and other major cities; these protests, which were attended by as many as 50,000 people, continued daily until July.

Meanwhile, on 5 May 2009, the authorities announced that they had acted to forestall an army mutiny at a military base east of Tbilisi. In July a commission empowered to draft a new Constitution was convened, although representatives of the main opposition declined invitations to participate. Also in May Alasania established a new opposition party, Our Georgia—Free Democrats (ChS—DD). In August Saakashvili transferred Sikharulidze to the position of foreign affairs adviser to the President; he was succeeded as Minister of Defence by Bachana Akhalaia. This appointment was criticized by numerous human rights groups and opposition figures, on the grounds that Akhalaia had been responsible for the maltreatment of prisoners when he had headed Georgia's penitential department.

In December 2009 a mother and child were killed in Kutaisi, during the controversial destruction of a memorial to Georgian soldiers who had died fighting for the Soviet Army in the Second World War. (A new parliament building was to be built on the site.) In response, President Saakashvili dismissed the local regional governor, and in February 2010 three directors of the company that had undertaken the demolition were imprisoned on charges of contravening safety regulations. In the same month Noghaideli signed a co-operation agreement on behalf of the MSS with Boris Gryzlov, the Chairman of the Supreme Council of the de facto ruling party of Russia, United Russia. This development was strongly criticized by senior members of the ruling ENM, but obtained the support of some opposition parties. In early March Burjanadze also made a visit to Russia, where she met Russian premier Vladimir Putin and Minister of Foreign Affairs Sergei Lavrov. Also in March the Imedi television channel (the Director-General of which was a close ally of President Saakashvili) broadcast a fabricated news bulletin that purported to show an ongoing invasion of Georgia by Russia, and announced that Saakashvili had been assassinated and that several prominent opposition figures, among them Burjanadze and Noghaideli, had expressed support for the invasion. The Georgian National Communications Commission ordered Imedi to apologize to the public for the broadcast, which had provoked mass panic domestically.

The ENM secured a decisive victory in nationwide local elections on 30 May 2010, receiving more than 65% of votes cast. In the first direct mayoral election in Tbilisi, the incumbent, Giorgi Ugulava of the ENM, retained the office with about 55% of the votes, defeating Alasania. OSCE and Council of Europe observers issued a report stating that the conduct of the elections had demonstrated progress towards meeting democratic commitments but noted incidences of malpractice. In July Saakashvili reorganized the Government.

On 19 July 2010 the state commission submitted proposed constitutional amendments to Parliament; the main opposition parties and prominent civil society organizations urged further discussion, and complained of a lack of media coverage and public debate. On 15 October Parliament approved a new Constitution, providing for the transfer of many executive powers from the President to the Prime Minister and the Government. The new text was to take effect after the next presidential election, scheduled for October 2013. Observers suggested that the changes were designed to allow Saakashvili, who was constitutionally prohibited from seeking re-election as President, to retain substantial powers as a future premier. Meanwhile, in October 2010 several prominent opposition leaders, including Gachechiladze and Okruashvili, established a new political movement, the Georgian Party. In November Tkeshelashvili was appointed Deputy Prime Minister, State Minister, responsible for Reintegration. Later that month one person was killed in a bomb attack near the SLP offices in central Tbilisi (following similar explosions near the US embassy in September, and near the city's principal railway station in October). In November Zurabishvili resigned as leader of Georgia's Way. In January 2011 members of the MSS voted to remove Noghaideli from the chairmanship of the party, replacing him with Sergo Javkhidzre; Noghaideli subsequently established a new party, Fair Georgia. On 28 June a court in Tbilisi convicted 15 people (three *in absentia*) of acts of terrorism in connection with the bomb attacks in Tbilisi in late 2010.

Anti-Government protests

On 21 May 2011 several days of anti-Government protests, led by Burjanadze, began in Tbilisi and Batumi. On 26 May (Independence Day) police forces violently dispersed the crowd of demonstrators, resulting in the death of at least four people. More than 100 protesters were arrested. (A number of policemen were subsequently dismissed for excessive use of force.) At the end of May Parliament approved controversial new legislation prohibiting the public display of Nazi and Soviet symbols, and placing restrictions on former Soviet officials from holding office. In June Gachechiladze and other senior members of the Georgian Party announced their resignation from the party, effectively leaving it without leadership in the country. Later in June Okruashvili (who remained in France) was charged *in absentia* with forming an armed group, in connection with an alleged conspiracy to organize a Russian-supported insurrection in Georgia. In June the ENM submitted proposed changes to the electoral law, and subsequently signed an agreement with several other parties, including the Christian Democratic Movement (KDM) and the AM (previously members of the Joint Opposition); however, the remaining six parties of the coalition rejected the agreement. On 1 July a constitutional amendment was approved, providing for the relocation of Parliament from Tbilisi to Kutaisi after the 2012 elections. In July 2011 large demonstrations, led by Georgian Orthodox Church priests, were staged in Tbilisi in protest at the introduction of legislation extending new rights to minority religious groups. In September a Tbilisi court imposed terms of imprisonment on 15 opposition members who had been charged with supporting Okruashvili's alleged conspiracy.

In December 2011 a wealthy businessman, Bidzina Ivanishvili, who had announced his intention to oppose Saakashvili in the next presidential election, formed a movement known as Georgian Dream (QO), with the aim of also contesting the 2012 parliamentary elections. Later in the month Parliament adopted legislation that imposed restrictions on financing political parties. Meanwhile, Ivanishvili's Georgian citizenship was abrogated by a presidential order, on the grounds that he had contravened regulations by obtaining French, as well as Georgian and Russian citizenship, and in January 2012 he appointed his wife, Ekaterina Khvedelidze, to head QO. In February Ivanishvili formally established QO as a coalition incorporating his own party (which became known as Georgian Dream—Democratic Georgia) and other main opposition groups, including ChS—DD and the SRP. Although Ivanishvili subsequently announced his willingness to rescind his French citizenship, in April the authorities rejected his request that his Georgian citizenship be reinstated. The founding congress of QO as a political party was held later in the month.

On 22 May 2012 Parliament adopted constitutional amendments permitting citizens of European Union (EU, see p. 273) member states to seek election in Georgia. Although this measure permitted Ivanishvili to stand as a candidate, he dismissed the measure as 'absurd'. Later in the month supporters of Ivanishvili staged a large anti-Government protest in central Tbilisi. Smaller similar demonstrations in took place in other towns. In early June Tbilisi City Court fined Ivanishvili some US $90.9m., after he was found guilty of violating party funding rules, including the free distribution of satellite dishes to allow people to view a television channel owned by Khvedelidze. (On appeal, the sum was reduced by around one-half.) Earlier in the year Ivanishvili had been fined $1.7m. for making illegal donations to political parties. On 29 June Parliament adopted amendments to the electoral code, notably obligating providers of cable television to transmit channels broadcasting news programming for a period of 60 days prior to the holding of national elections (thereby increasing public access to a number of opposition television channels). Parliament approved Saakashvili's appointment of Merabishvili as Prime Minister on 4 July. Most of the members of the outgoing Government remained in office, while Merabishvili was succeeded in his former position of Minister of Internal Affairs by the hitherto Minister of Defence, Akhalaia, whose former portfolio was allocated to the hitherto Minister of Education and Science, Dimitri Shashkin. On 1 August Saakashvili announced that elections to Parliament would be held on 1 October. Ivanishvili subsequently accused Saakashvili of misusing his authority to impose measures against opposition leaders.

In September 2012 the broadcast of a video documenting torture and abuse in a prison in Tbilisi prompted outrage and large demonstrations in the capital. Khatuna Kalmakhelidze resigned as Minister of Prisons and Probation. Akhalaia subsequently also resigned as Minister of Internal Affairs.

The 2012 legislative elections and defeat of the ENM

In elections to Parliament, conducted on 1 October 2012, Ivanishvili's QO coalition was the most successful grouping, obtaining 55.0% of the votes cast to those seats allocated on the basis of proportional representation, and 85 of the 150 electoral seats overall. The ENM was the only other party to obtain representation, with 40.3% of the votes cast and 65 seats. Shortly after preliminary figures showed that the ENM had been defeated, Saakashvili announced that he accepted the election results, and that he would endorse the appointment of ministerial nominees proposed by Ivanishvili (as Prime Minister-designate). Later in the month Saakashvili announced the restoration of Ivanishvili's Georgian citizenship. On 25 October Parliament approved the appointment of a Government led by Ivanishvili. The new administration included two Deputy Prime Ministers: former international footballer Kakha Kaladze, who also became Minister of Energy and Natural Resources; and ChS—DD leader Alasania, who concurrently held the defence portfolio.

In November 2012 the new authorities arrested a number of senior members of Saakashvili's administration, including Akhalaia, who, together with the hitherto Chief of Joint Staff of the Armed Forces and a former army commander, was subsequently charged with abuse of power. The ENM criticized the detentions as having been politically motivated. In the same month Okruashvili was arrested upon his return from exile in France. In January 2013 he was acquitted of the corruption charges for which he had received the 11-year prison sentence, and released on bail (with other charges pending against him, including those relating to the formation of an armed group). On 12 January Parliament enacted an amnesty providing for the release of some 3,000 people in detention and the reduction of sentences for others, having overturned a veto of the legislation by President Saakashvili. The struggle between the ruling coalition and the President was also reflected in a demand by the new Minister of Foreign Affairs later in January that Saakashvili replace all the country's principal ambassadors. Meanwhile, divisions emerged within the QO coalition, on 21 January Alasania was dismissed as deputy premier, while remaining Minister of Defence. Following an attempt by Ivanishvili to postpone Saakashvili's annual address to Parliament, the President decided to make the speech at the National Library on the scheduled day, 8 February; however, proceedings were disrupted by anti-Government protesters, including released prisoners, some of whom assaulted ENM deputies. Saakashvili, who accused QO of orchestrating the protests, finally conducted the address at the presidential palace. On the same day Ivanishvili appointed the Minister of Education and Science, Giorgi Margvelashvili, additionally to the post of Deputy Prime Minister.

Continuing antagonism between Ivanishvili and Saakashvili focused on constitutional amendments proposed by QO, which notably removed the President's power to dismiss or appoint a government without parliamentary approval. The ENM subsequently agreed to support the constitutional amendments, which were adopted by Parliament on 25 March and signed into effect by Saakashvili two days later.

Riots, in which at least 17 of people were injured, broke out in central Tbilisi in May 2013, after several thousand protesters, whose leaders included Orthodox Church priests, attempted to disrupt a small demonstration by homosexual activists. Both Ivanishvili and Patriarch Ilia II of the Georgian Orthodox Church (who had demanded that the demonstration be prohibited) condemned the violence. Later in May the Secretary-General of the ENM and former Prime Minister, Merabishvili, and the Governor of Kakheti Mhkare (region) a former minister and incumbent regional Governor, Zurab Tchiaberashvili, were arrested on corruption charges, including the misuse of public funds to finance the ENM's 2012 election campaign. Rallies were subsequently staged nationwide in support of Merabishvili.

On 26 July 2013 Giorgi Kvirikashvili, the hitherto Minister of Economic and Sustainable Development was appointed additionally as First Deputy Prime Minister; Margvelashvili had resigned from his government position, after being selected as the candidate of QO in the presidential election scheduled for 27 October. Following a series of primary votes, on 27 July Bakradze was confirmed as the presidential candidate of the ENM. In August Akhalaia was acquitted on charges of having exceeded his powers, although he remained in detention, pending trial on further charges. Akhalaia was sentenced to three years' and nine months' imprisonment in October, having been convicted of using excessive force to suppress a prison uprising in 2006.

Recent developments: the 2013 presidential election

On 27 October 2013 Margvelashvili was decisively elected President, obtaining 62.1% of the votes cast in an election contested by 23 candidates. Bakradze was placed second, with 21.7%, and Burjanadze was third, with 10.2%. On 17 November Margvelashvili was inaugurated as President; on the same day the Constitution adopted in 2010 officially entered into effect. (In early October Parliament had approved a further constitutional amendment, proposed by QO, which reduced some powers vested in the Prime Minister.) Meanwhile, Ivanishvili confirmed that he was to resign as Prime Minister. Parliament confirmed the appointment of the hitherto Minister of Internal Affairs, Irakli Garibashvili, as Prime Minister on 20 November. Garibashvili also succeeded Ivanishvili as the Chairman of QO on 24 November. A senior police official, Aleksandre Tchikaidze, received the internal affairs portfolio.

In December 2013 disagreements between parliamentary deputies on the occasion of the adoption of the state budget for 2014 escalated into a violent altercation. Later that month a court in Tbilisi ordered the removal from office of Ugulava of the capital's mayor, pending his trial on charges of misappropriating public funds. At the end of the month the Government appointed a constitutional review commission, which was to revise the Constitution by September 2014, and also indicated its intention to reverse the recent relocation of Parliament to Kutaisi. A new Prosecutor-General, Giorgi Badashvili, was appointed in January 2014, following the resignation of his recently appointed predecessor, Otar Partskhaladze, in response to the revelation that he had a previous criminal conviction in Germany. In February Merabishvili was sentenced to five years' imprisonment on charges including abuse of office and bribing voters, while Tchiaberashvili received a fine of 52,000 lari. In the same month the trial *in absentia* of Davit Kezerashvili, the Minister of Defence under President Saakashvili, began; Kezerashvili had been detained in France the previous October after various criminal charges had been brought against him by the Georgian Government, but a French court refused a request for his extradition on the grounds that the case was politically motivated. In March the Office of the Prosecutor-General summoned former President Saakashvili (who had taken up a position at a lecturer at a university in the USA and who stated that he had been advised to leave Georgia because of the risk that he would be arrested) for questioning in connection with 10 cases under investigation, including the death of former premier Zhvania in 2005 and government action against the Imedi television channel in 2007–08. Elguja Khokrishvili was appointed Minister of Regional Development and Infrastructure in mid-April, replacing Davit Narmania, who had resigned to contest direct elections, scheduled for May, as the QO candidate to the post of mayor of Tbilisi.

Ajara

The Autonomous Republic of Ajara, in south-west Georgia, proved to be the least troubled of the country's three autonomous territories (for information on the other two territories, which claim secession from Georgia, see Abkhazia and South Ossetia). Despite being of ethnic Georgian origin, the Adjars retained a sense of separate identity, owing to their adherence to Islam. In April 1991 there were prolonged demonstrations against proposals to abolish Ajaran autonomy. Elections to the Supreme Council (legislature) of Ajara were held in September 1996, and Aslan Abashidze, Chairman of the Supreme Council since 1991, was re-elected to that position.

In November 2001 Abashidze contested unopposed a direct election to the new post of Head of the Republic, which replaced that of Chairman of the Ajaran Supreme Council, following the approval of several amendments to the region's Constitution in July. In the same month he was appointed as President Shevardnadze's personal representative for conflict resolution in Abkhazia. In early December Ajara's new bicameral legislature (composed of the Council of the Republic and the Senate) held its inaugural session.

In response to the resignation of President Shevardnadze on 23 November 2003, Abashidze declared a state of emergency in Ajara. In March 2004, after the new President, Mikheil Saakashvili, was prevented from entering Ajara, he issued an ultimatum, demanding that Abashidze recognize the authority of the central Government and ensure that forthcoming national parliamentary elections were conducted in the region. Economic sanctions were imposed on Ajara, and Abashidze declared a renewed state of emergency and a curfew. Following Russian mediation, Abashidze agreed to allow the organization of elections in Ajara, in exchange for the removal of the economic blockade and the withdrawal of Georgian troops from neighbouring areas. The state of emergency was suspended, and legislative elections duly proceeded on 28 March.

Tensions escalated further on 2 May 2004, when Abashidze ordered the destruction of bridges linking Ajara with neighbouring regions of Georgia, following military manoeuvres by government troops close to the boundary. Saakashvili immediately threatened to dismiss Abashidze, unless the Ajaran leader agreed to comply with the 'Georgian constitutional framework' within 10 days. Large public demonstrations against Abashidze ensued. Following discussions with Igor Ivanov, now the Chairman of the Security Council of the Russian Federation, on 5 May Abashidze resigned and departed for Russia. Saakashvili imposed presidential rule on Ajara, and on 6 May Parliament voted to approve the President's authority to dismiss the legislature and the Government of Ajara, and to schedule new elections there, thereby substantially reducing the territory's autonomy. The Ajaran Supreme Council also voted to abolish the post of Head of the Republic, scheduled new parliamentary elections, and dissolved itself. Levan Varshalomidze was appointed as the head of an interim council to rule the region. On 20 June elections to the new unicameral legislature, the Supreme Council, took place. The pro-presidential Saakashvili—Victorious Ajara party received 75% of the votes cast and 28 of the 30 seats in the Council. On 1 July Parliament approved legislation granting the President of Georgia the authority to dismiss the Ajaran Government, dissolve the Ajaran parliament and annul its legislation. Mikheil Makharadze was elected Chairman of the newly elected Supreme Council; Varshalomidze was the sole candidate for Chairman of the Government. Abashidze's personal assets were confiscated by the authorities on the grounds that they had been acquired illegally. In December, moreover, a warrant was issued for his arrest on charges of abuse of office, terrorist offences, and embezzlement. The relocation of the Constitutional Court of Georgia from Tbilisi to Abashidze's former residence in Batumi took effect from September 2006. In January 2007 the Batumi city court convicted Abashidze *in absentia* of abuse of office and the embezzlement of state funds, and sentenced him to 15 years' imprisonment.

On 30 July 2008 the Supreme Council adopted amendments to Adjara's electoral code, prior to forthcoming legislative elections, scheduled for 4 October: the Council was to be reduced from 30 to 18 deputies; the minimum requisite share of the votes cast for parties to obtain representation from party list was reduced from 7% to 5%; and the composition of the local Central Election Commission (CEC) was reformed to include opposition representatives. In September, following the conflict in South Ossetia and other parts of Georgia, the CEC rescheduled the elections to the Supreme Council for 3 November. A number of opposition parties consequently declared a boycott of the poll, and a voter turnout of only 44.9% was recorded. Saakashvili's ENM secured about 78.8% of votes cast, while the KDM (established by a former associate of Abashidze, Giorgi Targamadze) was the only other party to gain representation, with 14.7% of votes.

In March 2009 the head of the republican branch of the DM—ES, Zurab Avaliani, was detained, along with nine others, pending trial on charges of illegal arms-smuggling and plotting politically motivated violence. (Avaliani was subsequently sentenced to 18 months' imprisonment on charges of illegal possession of firearms.) In April 2010, despite his membership of the ruling ENM, Varshalomidze openly criticized the centralization of powers in Georgia and demanded the restoration of greater autonomy to Ajara. In May the head of the Ministry of Internal Affairs emergency situations service in Ajara was killed in an explosion near Batumi; in early 2011, following the arrest of two suspects, the Georgian authorities claimed that the killing had been ordered by Russian military intelligence agents based in Abkhazia.

In May 2012 several amendments to Ajara's Constitution were approved, including an increase in the number of deputies in the Supreme Council, with effect from the elections due to be held in October, from 18 to 21. At the elections, held concurrently with those to the Georgian Parliament on 1 October, the QO coalition of Bidzina Ivanishvili was the most successful group in Ajara, obtaining 57.6% of the votes cast to those seats elected on the basis of party lists; the ENM was the only other party to obtain representation, with 37.4% of the vote. On 28 October Avtandil Beridze became Chairman of the Supreme Council. Ivanishvili's nomination of Archil Khabadze, hitherto director of Cartu Bank's Batumi branch office, as Chairman of the Government was approved by the Supreme Council on 30 October, and a new Government headed by him was subsequently formed. Meanwhile, Ivanishvili's new Georgian Government issued pledges to increase the autonomous powers of Ajara. In March 2013 Davit Baladze was appointed as the new Minister of Finance and the Economy of Ajara.

Foreign Affairs

Regional relations

Georgia was one of only four republics of those that had constituted the USSR not to join the CIS at its formation in December 1991. However, as civil and separatist conflicts threatened to destroy Georgia, Shevardnadze was forced to reverse policy on the CIS, and in late 1993 the republic was admitted to that body. Relations with Russia were strained by developments in Abkhazia from 1992, although in February 1994 Georgia and Russia signed a 10-year treaty of friendship and co-operation, which provided, *inter alia*, for the establishment of Russian military bases in Georgia. In May 1999 Georgia failed to renew its adherence to the CIS Collective Security Treaty. (In March 2006 Georgia and Russia signed an agreement providing for Russia's withdrawal from the military bases that it maintained at Akhalkalaki and Batumi and from its Tbilisi headquarters; the withdrawal of Russian forces from the military bases was completed ahead of schedule, in November 2007.)

The lifting of customs and travel restrictions on the Russian–Abkhazian border in September 1999 angered Georgia, and further tension occurred later in the year, owing to the renewed conflict in Russia's Chechen Republic (Chechnya). Georgia denied allegations that it was harbouring Chechen soldiers and selling arms to Chechen separatists. During 2000 there were violent disturbances and kidnappings in the Pankisi Gorge, close to the Chechen border. Russia's decision to implement a full visa regime for Georgian citizens entering its territory from January 2001 caused further antagonism, particularly since citizens of Abkhazia and South Ossetia were to be exempt from the requirement. In January 2002 Georgian security forces launched a campaign to restore order to Pankisi. Later that month the Georgian Deputy Minister of State Security was shot dead in the Pankisi Gorge, and in February four police officers were held hostage for three days there. In May a US-led military-training programme commenced in Georgia, to equip the armed forces for operations in Pankisi, where international Islamist militants were reported to have established bases. In August Georgia accused Russia of perpetrating an act of aggression, when the aerial bombardment of Pankisi by unmarked aircraft led to at least one death; Russia denied responsibility. In October President Shevardnadze and his Russian counterpart, Vladimir Putin, reached an agreement, according to which the two countries were to resume joint patrols of their common border.

Relations with Russia deteriorated after the accession to power in Georgia of President Mikheil Saakashvili. The decision of the Georgian Parliament, in February 2006, to request the replacement of Russian peacekeepers in South Ossetia with international forces threatened to aggravate tensions in relations. In March Russia banned the import of wine from Georgia, ostensibly owing to suspected contamination with pesticides (Russia having hitherto been the main market of Georgian wine exports). In October President Saakashvili announced that four Russian military officers, who had been detained in September on suspicion of espionage, had been transferred to the authority of the OSCE, which arranged for their return to Russia. In response to the detention of the officers, Russia withdrew its ambassador from Georgia, suspended all transport and postal links between the two countries, and expelled several hundred ethnic Georgians (who the Russian authorities stated were illegal immigrants) from Russia. (Russia's ambassador returned to Tbilisi in January 2007.) In August the Georgian authorities urged the international community to condemn the alleged violation of Georgian airspace by two military aircraft originating from Russia, and the apparent launch of a missile near South Ossetia. Georgia expelled three Russian embassy staff in November, on the grounds that they were engaged in subversive activities against the Government, prompting Russia to expel three Georgian diplomats in retaliation.

In July 2008 Russia acknowledged that four Russian aircraft had entered airspace over South Ossetia, claiming that the mission was intended to deter Georgia from flying military reconnaissance drones over the region. On 7–8 August Georgian troops launched an attack against Tskhinvali and other regions of South Ossetia; shortly afterwards, Russian troops entered the territory through the Roki tunnel, and rapidly obtained control over the region. In a statement subsequently shown to be greatly exaggerated, Russian President Dmitrii Medvedev accused Georgia of perpetrating 'genocide', claiming that up to 2,000 people had been killed as a result of the Georgian attack. Russian aircraft commenced bombardment of Georgian targets, including the town of Gori, the port of Poti and the military base at Senaki. On 9 August Parliament approved a presidential decree declaring a state of war with Russia, and martial law within Georgia. On 12 August Russian President Dmitrii Medvedev ordered an end to Russia's military operations. Georgia and Russia agreed to a peace plan, mediated by French President Nicolas Sarkozy on behalf of the EU, providing for an immediate ceasefire and the withdrawal of Russian troops to pre-conflict positions. However, Russia failed to implement fully the withdrawal of troops as stipulated. On 14 August Parliament voted unanimously in favour of Georgia's withdrawal from the CIS (to take full effect from the following year). On 26 August Medvedev endorsed legislation by which Russia officially recognized South Ossetia and Abkhazia as independent, sovereign states. Georgia, the USA and EU condemned the decision, and only a small number of states subsequently extended recognition. On 29 August Georgia formally suspended diplomatic relations with Russia.

Following an EU-mediated peace agreement, reached on 8 September 2008, Russia announced that 3,800 of its troops were to remain in each of South Ossetia and Abkhazia, although all remaining forces would be withdrawn from all other Georgian territories within 10 days of the deployment of EU monitors. On 17 September Russia signed friendship, economic and military co-operation treaties with South Ossetia and Abkhazia. Following the deployment of the European Union Monitoring Mission in Georgia (EUMM) on 1 October, the withdrawal of the remaining Russian troops from areas adjacent to the two secessionist territories was verified by the deadline of 10 October. However, Georgia claimed that Russia was in violation of the ceasefire agreement, on the grounds that it retained troops in areas previously held by Georgian forces, and that the number of troops in South Ossetia and Abkhazia exceeded the pre-conflict levels. Meanwhile, on 9 October the Council of CIS Foreign Ministers officially suspended Georgia's membership. (Full withdrawal from the organization was finalized in August 2009.) In November discussions between Russian, US and Georgian representatives, also attended by South Ossetian and Abkhazian officials, were reconvened in Geneva, Switzerland, under the aegis of the UN, the EU and the OSCE (and subsequently continued to be held at intervals). At the end of December the mandate of the OSCE mission in Georgia (deployed in South Ossetia since 1992) expired, owing to Russia's refusal to approve a further extension.

A report by Human Rights Watch, issued in January 2009, cited 'indiscriminate and disproportionate attacks' by both Russia and Georgia; following investigations by both Governments, Russia (despite its earlier claims) had only been able to attribute 162 fatalities to Georgian forces. An independent report supported by the EU into the conflict, which was published in September, concluded that Georgia had instigated the conflict, and that its initial attack upon Tshkhinvali was not warranted by international law, while Russia's military response was described as disproportionate, and its recognition of South Ossetia and Abkhazia as independent states a violation of international law.

In March 2009 Russia confirmed that military bases were to be established in Abkhazia and South Ossetia. On 30 April President Medvedev signed border treaties with Abkhazia and South Ossetia, under which Russia was to guard the state borders of Abkhazia prior to the establishment of Abkhazian border forces. The EU expressed 'deep concern' at both agreements, which it stated violated the terms of the peace agreement. The mandate of UNOMIG expired on 15 June, after its extension had been vetoed by Russia.

Contacts between Russia and Georgia remained 'frozen' during 2009, although the only road crossing between Russia and those regions of Georgia controlled by the Georgian authorities, closed since 2006, reopened in March 2010. In October the Russian Ministry of Foreign Affairs denounced as an attempt to destabilize the region a decision by the Georgian authorities to abolish visa requirements for the residents of Russia's seven North Caucasus republics. In November Georgia announced the arrest of 13 people suspected of being members of a Russian espionage network, including four Russian citizens. In early December six people were arrested in connection with a series of explosions in Tbilisi. In June 2011 a Russian military officer who had been based in Abkhazia, Yevgenii Borisov, was sentenced to 30 years' imprisonment *in absentia* for organizing the bomb attacks; Borisov's deputy received a life sentence *in absentia* and a further four defendants were sentenced to terms of 30 years (one *in absentia*), while lesser sentences were imposed on the remaining eight.

Following an appeal brought by Georgia against Russia, which accused Russian forces of ethnically motivated abuses in both South Ossetia and Abkhazia during the 2008 conflict, in April 2011 the International Court of Justice dismissed the case, on the grounds that Georgia had made no attempt to resolve the dispute with Russia beforehand. In November, after lengthy discussions between Georgian and Russian representatives in Bern, Switzerland, it was announced that the negotiators had finally reached an agreement that would allow Russia to join the World Trade Organization (WTO, see p. 434); trade between Russia and Abkhazia and South Ossetia was to be controlled by Swiss monitors. A presidential decree, announced by Saakashvili in February 2012 in a perceived gesture of reconciliation, ended visa restrictions on Russian citizens, who were henceforth permitted to remain in Georgia for 90 days without a visa.

A new Government headed by Bidzina Ivanishvili, who had pledged to improve bilateral relations with Russia, was installed following elections in October 2012; nevertheless, it was subsequently confirmed that Georgia would not restore diplomatic relations until Russia ended its presence in South Ossetia and Abkhazia. On 1 November Ivanishvili appointed Zurab Abashidze, the Georgian ambassador to Russia in 2000–04, to the new post of the Prime Minister's Special Representative for

Relations with Russia. In December 2012 the first direct discussions between Georgian and Russian officials since the 2008 conflict were conducted in Geneva, when a plan for a partial normalization in bilateral relations was agreed. The head of the Georgian Orthodox Church, Catholicos-Patriarch of All Georgia Ilia II, made an official visit to Russia, at the invitation of his Russian counterpart, in January 2013.

Georgia's relations with Russia deteriorated during 2013. Measures unilaterally implemented by the Russian military in May to amend the South Ossetian administrative border with Georgia, slightly expanding the area under separatist control, and the subsequent erection of fencing along the new border, were met with strong protests from the Georgian Government and international community. A monument to former Soviet leader Stalin, which had been erected, without official authorization, in September in the eastern town of Telavi, was removed by members of a pro-Western foundation in December. In January 2014 Parliament adopted a resolution expressing 'extreme concern' over developments in Ukraine (where the Government's withdrawal from the signature of an EU Association Agreement had precipitated an escalating political crisis), and emphasizing that Georgia's decision to sign an Agreement with the EU was irreversible. Tensions over administrative boundaries with the separatist regions continued: President Margvelashvili protested that the Russian authorities' unilateral extension of its border zone with Abkhazia 11 km further into the separatist territory, purportedly to maintain security during the organization of the Sochi Winter Olympics in February (in territories that immediately neighboured Abkhazia), constituted a violation of Georgian sovereignty. Russia's military seizure of the Crimea region of Ukraine at the end of February and formal annexation of the territory in March (see the chapter on Ukraine) prompted considerable concern in Georgia. On 7 March, shortly after a further resolution adopted by Parliament condemned Russia's intervention in Crimea, Russian military aircraft entered Georgia's airspace in contravention of the 2008 peace agreement. Bilateral discussions on the normalization of relations were suspended, and later in March the Georgian Government denounced the annexation as a considerable threat to regional stability.

Other external relations

Relations with the USA became increasingly cordial in the mid-2000s. Following his inauguration as President, in February 2004 Saakashvili visited Washington, DC, USA, where he attended talks with US President George W. Bush. In May 2005 President Bush made a state visit to Georgia, during which he endorsed the Government's efforts to bring about reform. In July 2006 Saakashvili again visited Washington, DC, on which occasion President Bush affirmed his support for Georgian aspirations to North Atlantic Treaty Organization (NATO, see p. 370) membership. In September 2008, following the military conflict with Russia (see Regional relations), US Vice-President Dick Cheney announced that the USA would pledge US $1,000m. in reconstruction aid to Georgia. In January 2009 Georgia and the USA signed a bilateral charter on strategic partnership in areas that included defence, trade and energy. Although the new Administration of President Barack Obama, which came to power in that month, sought to achieve a rapprochement with Russia, in July Vice-President Joe Biden visited Tbilisi and reaffirmed US support for the Saakashvili administration. In August 2011 the US Senate adopted a resolution condemning the continuing presence of Russian troops in Abkhazia and South Ossetia. Following discussions with Obama in Washington, DC, in January 2012, Saakashvili announced plans for significantly increased defence co-operation between Georgia and the USA. Amid an escalating political crisis in Ukraine (see above), in late February 2014 Prime Minister Garibashvili visited Washington, DC, to meet Obama and other US officials, who pledged assistance for Georgia's EU integration process.

In November 2002 Georgia formally applied for membership of NATO. In October 2004 NATO approved a two-year Individual Partnership Action Plan with Georgia. At a NATO summit meeting, conducted in Bucharest, Romania in April 2008, the Alliance failed to extend offers of a Membership Action Plan (MAP) to Georgia. Following a summit meeting in Lisbon, Portugal, in November 2010, NATO issued a final declaration reiterating support for Georgia's eventual full membership of the Alliance. In December 2011 the Georgian Government welcomed a statement by NATO that officially named Georgia (among others) as an 'aspirant' state. Following premier Garibashvili's visit to Washington, DC, in February 2014, the US Administration expressed support for the extension of a NATO MAP to Georgia.

In 1996 Georgia signed an agreement on partnership and co-operation with the EU, and in 1999 it joined the Council of Europe. In March 2005 the European Commission recommended strengthening relations with Georgia under its European Neighbourhood Policy, in which Georgia had been included in June 2004. In December 2008 the European Commission presented an Eastern Partnership programme, offering further economic integration, and enhanced trade and visa arrangements, for Georgia, Armenia, Azerbaijan, Ukraine, Moldova and Belarus. In July 2010 the EU began negotiations with Georgia on the establishment of an Association Agreement, which was to entail the creation of a free trade area. The Georgia-EU Co-operation Council was convened in Brussels in December 2012, when an objective for negotiations on the Association Agreement to be concluded by November 2013 was announced. At an EU summit meeting in Vilnius, Lithuania, on 28–29 November, President Margvelashvili duly initialled the Association Agreement, which included free trade area provisions, and also signed a framework agreement for Georgian participation in EU-led crisis management operations. Negotiations with the EU on the removal of visa restrictions for Georgian citizens proceeded, and, amid increasing tensions with Russia, EU officials brought forward the planned signature of the Agreement to mid-2014.

CONSTITUTION AND GOVERNMENT

Under the Constitution of August 1995, as subsequently revised, the President of Georgia is Head of State and the head of the executive, and also Commander-in-Chief of the Armed Forces. The President is directly elected for a five-year term (and may not hold office for more than two consecutive terms). The Government is accountable to the President, to whom it acts as an advisory body. The Government is headed by the Prime Minister. The supreme legislative body is the unicameral Sakartvelos Parlamenti (Georgian Parliament), which is directly elected for four years. Of the 150 parliamentary deputies, 75 are elected on the basis of proportional representation and 75 in single-member constituencies. A new Constitution, approved by Parliament in October 2010, which transferred many powers from the President to the Prime Minister and the Government, took effect on 17 November 2013. Judicial power is exercised by the Supreme Court, the members of which are elected by Georgian Parliament, on the recommendation of the President, and by general courts. Georgia contains two nominally autonomous territories: the Autonomous Republic of Ajara; and Abkhazia. The status of Abkhazia and South Ossetia were both disputed; following conflict in August 2008, both territories became entirely under the control of their respective separatist authorities, with Russian military support. Those parts of the country under central government control are divided into nine mkharebi (regions—singular mkhare) headed by trustees (governors) appointed by the President, and the city of Tbilisi, headed by a mayor. A second tier of local government comprises seven cities of special status and 60 districts (raions), and a third tier comprises a total of 966 villages and settlements.

REGIONAL AND INTERNATIONAL CO-OPERATION

Georgia is a member of the Organization of the Black Sea Economic Co-operation (see p. 401), the Council of Europe (see p. 252) and the Organization for Democracy and Economic Development (GUAM, see p. 467).

Georgia joined the UN in 1992 and became a full member of the World Trade Organization (WTO, see p. 434) in 2000.

ECONOMIC AFFAIRS

In 2012, according to estimates by the World Bank, Georgia's gross national income (GNI), measured at average 2010–12 prices, was US $14,786m., equivalent to $3,280 per head (or $5,860 per head on an international purchasing-power parity basis). During 2003–12, it was estimated, the population decreased by an average of 0.5% per year, while gross domestic product (GDP) per head increased, in real terms, at an average annual rate of 5.5%. According to official estimates, overall GDP increased, in real terms, by an average of 6.1% annually during 2003–12. Real GDP increased by 3.2% in 2013, according to the Asian Development Bank (ADB).

Agriculture contributed 8.5% of GDP in 2012, and the sector engaged 53.4% of the total employed labour force in 2007. Georgia's favourable climate allows the cultivation of subtropical crops, such as tea and oranges. Other fruits (including wine grapes), flowers, tobacco and grain are also cultivated, and hazelnuts have increased in importance in recent years. The mountain pastures are used for sheep- and goat-farming. In 2002 private farms accounted for 94% of the agricultural crop harvest. During 2003–12, according to official figures, agricultural GDP declined, in real terms, by an average of 2.1% per year. Real GDP of the sector decreased by 3.7% in 2012, but increased by 9.6% in 2013, according to the ADB.

Industry contributed 24.2% of GDP in 2012, and the sector engaged 10.4% of the total employed labour force in 2007. According to official figures, industrial GDP increased, in real terms, at an average annual rate of 7.9% in 2003–12. Real industrial GDP increased by 9.5% in 2012 and by a further 0.9% in 2013, according to the ADB.

Mining and quarrying accounted for just 1.0% of GDP in 2012, and the sector engaged 0.3% of the total employed labour force in 2007. The principal minerals extracted are manganese ore, petroleum and coal. There are also deposits of copper, gold, silver and natural gas. During 2003–12, according to the official figures, mining GDP increased, in real terms, by an average of 3.6% per year; real GDP of the sector decreased by 8.4% in 2011, but increased by 6.6% in 2012.

The manufacturing sector (including household processing) contributed 12.7% of GDP in 2012; the sector engaged 4.9% of the total employed labour force in 2007. During 2003–12, according to official figures, manufacturing GDP increased, in real terms, by an average of 10.4% per year; real GDP of the sector increased by 13.6% in 2012.

The construction sector contributed 7.7% of GDP in 2012; the sector engaged 4.2% of the employed labour force in 2007. According to official figures, during 2003–12 construction GDP increased, in real terms, by an average of 8.9% per year; the sector's GDP increased, in real terms, by 13.6% in 2012.

Hydroelectric power provided 77.4% of the country's electricity in 2011. However, Georgia's largest hydroelectric power station was located in the secessionist region of Abkhazia, and the IMF estimated that more than one-third of the power it produced was consumed without payment. Imports of mineral fuels and lubricants comprised 18.8% of total imports in 2012. After 1999 Georgia was involved in a number of regional development projects to deliver both petroleum and gas through international pipelines. Georgia also hoped to develop its own energy resources. New gas-turbine electricity generators commenced operations in 2006, and the reconstruction of several hydroelectric power plants was proposed, as part of measures intended to make Georgia self-sufficient in electricity.

The services sector contributed 67.3% of GDP in 2012; the sector engaged 36.2% of the employed labour force in 2007. Trade and transport and communications are the sector's most significant areas of activity, with telecommunications and hotels and restaurants demonstrating the greatest growth in the early 2000s. During 2003–12, according to official figures, the GDP of the services sector increased, in real terms, at an average annual rate of 7.6%. According to the ADB, real sectoral GDP increased by 3.3% in 2013.

In 2012 Georgia recorded a visible merchandise trade deficit of US $4,226.1m., and there was a deficit of $1,912.0m. on the current account of the balance of payments. In 2012 Turkey was the principal source of imports (accounting for 17.8% of the total); other major sources were Azerbaijan, Ukraine, the People's Republic of China, Germany and Russia. The principal market for exports in that year was Azerbaijan (accounting for 26.4% of the total); other important purchasers were Armenia, the USA, Ukraine and Turkey. The principal imports in 2012 were mineral products (especially petroleum and petroleum oils), machinery and electrical equipment, vehicles, vessels, aircraft and other transport equipment (especially motor cars), base metals and articles thereof, chemicals, prepared foodstuffs, beverages, spirits and tobacco, and vegetable products. The principal exports in that year were vehicles, vessels, aircraft and other transport equipment (especially motor cars), base metals and articles thereof, prepared foodstuffs, beverages, spirits and tobacco, chemicals, vegetable products, and mineral products.

In 2012 there was a budgetary deficit of 104.3m. lari (equivalent to 0.4% of GDP). Georgia's general government gross debt was 8,442m. lari in 2012, equivalent to 32.3% of GDP. At the end of 2011 Georgia's total external debt was US $11,124m., of which $4,343m. was public and publicly guaranteed debt; in that year, the cost of servicing long-term public and publicly guaranteed debt and repayments to the IMF was equivalent to 26.9% of the value of exports of goods, services and income (excluding workers' remittances). The annual rate of inflation averaged 5.8% during 2004–13; consumer prices in five major cities decreased by 1.4% in 2012. In 2012 the average rate of unemployment was 15.0%.

In 1992 Georgia became a member of the IMF and the World Bank, and also joined the European Bank for Reconstruction and Development (EBRD, see p. 267).

The administration of President Mikheil Saakashvili, which came to power in 2004, introduced wide-ranging reforms, and implemented anti-corruption measures, and foreign direct investment increased substantially. A Russian embargo on the import of various Georgian foodstuffs and beverages, implemented in 2005, forced the country to seek new markets. A continued government priority was the promotion of Georgia as a regional trade and logistic centre, following the establishment of free industrial zones at the port of Poti and in Kutaisi.In December 2011 the European Union (EU, see p. 273) declared that Georgia had made satisfactory progress in implementing reforms preparatory to EU integration, and that negotiations would begin on the establishment of a free trade area under the Eastern Partnership framework (see Other external relations). Eurobond issues by the Government, the Bank of Georgia, Georgian Railways and Georgian Oil and Gas Corporation were undertaken in 2011–12. At the request of the Georgian authorities, in April the IMF approved a precautionary stand-by credit facility, totalling US $386m., for a period of two years. Following the establishment of a new Government in Georgia later that year, it was announced that Russia had agreed, in principle, to resume imports of Georgia wine. However, Georgia's initialling of an EU Association Agreement, which included free trade area provisions, in November 2013 and the subsequent political crisis in Ukraine (see Regional relations) resulted in a further severe deterioration in relations with Russia. The planned signature of the Association Agreement was subsequently brought forward to mid-2014, and the US Administration also pledged additional financial assistance. Meanwhile, in March 2014 the Government granted permission to Russian-owned RMG Gold to resume mining operations at the south-eastern Sakdrisi site, despite opposition on environmental and cultural heritage grounds. A slowdown in Georgia's strong GDP growth levels to a projected 3.1% in 2013 (according to official figures) was principally attributed to a fall in investment levels, amid post-election uncertainty. The IMF predicted a return to growth of about 6% in 2014; however, there were increasing concerns that the continued regional crisis involving Russia and Ukraine would have a negative impact on Georgia's trade, remittance flows and tourism industry.

PUBLIC HOLIDAYS

2015: 1–2 January (New Year), 7 January (Christmas), 19 January (Theophany), 3 March (Mothers' Day), 8 March (International Women's Day), 21 March (Nowruz, Spring Holiday), 9 April (Restoration of Independence Day), 10–13 April (Easter and Commemoration of the Deceased), 9 May (Victory Day), 12 May (St Andrew's Day), 26 May (Independence Day), 28 August (Assumption), 14 October (Mtskhetoba), 23 November (St George's Day).

Statistical Survey

Source (unless otherwise indicated): National Statistics Office of Georgia, 0181 Tbilisi, Guramishvili 39, Tskneti; tel. (32) 36-72-10; fax (32) 36-72-13; e-mail info@geostat.ge; internet www.geostat.ge.

Area and Population

AREA, POPULATION AND DENSITY

Area (sq km)	69,700*
Population (census results)†	
12 January 1989	5,400,841
17 January 2002‡	
Males	2,061,753
Females	2,309,782
Total	4,371,535
Population (official estimates at 1 January)§	
2011	4,469,200
2012	4,497,600
2013	4,483,800
Density (per sq km) at 1 January 2013‖	64.3

* 26,911 sq miles, including a significant amount of territory outside of Georgian government control.

† Population is *de jure*. The de facto total at the 2002 census was 4,355,700.

‡ Those territories of the former Autonomous Oblast (region) of South Ossetia that remained outside Georgian government control, as well as those of the separatist 'Republic of Abkhazia', were not included in the census of 2002; it was estimated that around 230,000 people lived in these territories at that time. An Abkhazian census, conducted in that territory in February 2011, reported a population of 240,705.

§ Excluding the population of those territories not under the control of the central Government.

‖ Area figure includes, whereas population figure excludes, territories not under Georgian government control, therefore actual density can be assumed to be significantly lower.

POPULATION BY AGE AND SEX

('000, official estimates at 1 January 2013)

	Males	Females	Total
0–14	402.1	360.8	762.9
15–64	1,501.8	1,598.4	3,100.2
65 and over	234.9	385.8	620.7
Total	2,138.8	2,345.0	4,483.8

POPULATION BY ETHNIC GROUP

(2002 census result, excl. areas outside Georgian government control)

	Number ('000)	% of total population
Georgian	3,661.2	83.8
Azeri	284.8	6.5
Armenian	248.9	5.7
Russian	67.7	1.5
Ossetian	38.0	0.9
Kurdish	20.8	0.5
Others	50.1	1.1
Total (incl. others)	4,371.5	100.0

ADMINISTRATIVE DIVISIONS

('000, official population estimates at 1 January 2013*)

Territory	Population	Principal city
Autonomous Republic		
Ajara	394.2	Batumi (160.0)
Mkharebi (Regions)		
Guria	139.2	Ozurgeti (77.9)
Imereti	703.9	Kutaisi (196.5)
Kakheti	405.1	Telavi (70.9)
Kvemo Kartli	511.1	Rustavi (122.5)
Mtskheta-Mtianeti	108.9	Mtskheta (57.3)
Racha-Lechkumi and Kvemo-Svaneti	46.3	Ambrolauri (13.8)
Samegrelo-Zemo Svaneti	476.9	Zugdidi (177.2)
Samstkhe-Javakheti	213.5	Akhaltsikhe (48.4)
Shida Kartli†	313.5	Gori (145.7)
Capital City		
Tbilisi	1,171.2	—
Total	4,483.8	—

* These figures exclude the population of the 'Republic of Abkhazia', which declared an enumerated population of 240,705 at February 2011.

† Most of the territories of South Ossetia are included in Shida Kartli Mkhare.

PRINCIPAL TOWNS

(estimates at 1 January 2013)

Tbilisi (capital)	1,171,200	Gori*	145,700
Kutaisi	196,500	Marneuli*	129,800
Zugdidi*	177,200	Rustavi	122,500
Batumi	160,000	Gardabani*	99,700

* Figure refers to the population of the municipality.

BIRTHS, MARRIAGES AND DEATHS

	Registered live births		Registered marriages		Registered deaths	
	Number	Rate (per 1,000)	Number	Rate (per 1,000)	Number	Rate (per 1,000)
2005	46,512	10.7	18,012	4.1	42,984	9.9
2006	47,795	10.9	21,845	5.0	42,255	9.6
2007	49,287	11.2	24,891	5.7	41,178	9.4
2008	56,565	12.9	31,414	7.2	43,011	9.8
2009	63,377	14.4	31,752	7.2	46,625	10.6
2010	62,585	14.1	34,675	7.8	47,864	10.7
2011	58,014	12.9	30,863	6.9	49,818	11.1
2012	57,031	12.7	30,412	6.8	49,348	11.0

Life expectancy (years at birth, official estimates): 74.7 (males 70.2; females 79.0) in 2012.

ECONOMICALLY ACTIVE POPULATION

(annual averages, '000 persons)*

	2005	2006	2007
Agriculture, hunting and forestry	947.8	966.4	910.5
Mining and quarrying	5.8	3.4	4.7
Manufacturing	89.8	81.5	82.7
Electricity, gas and water supply	23.4	18.4	18.2
Construction	43.1	54.8	71.2
Wholesale and retail trade; repair of motor vehicles and personal and household goods	188.2	168.1	168.8
Hotels and restaurants	16.3	16.9	18.0
Transport, storage and communications	69.3	77.8	71.7
Financial intermediation	13.3	14.3	17.3
Real estate, renting and business activities	25.9	26.9	34.7
Public administration and defence; compulsory social security	81.8	78.5	64.3
Education	130.9	132.2	124.2
Health and social work	58.0	52.2	59.9

—continued	2005	2006	2007
Other community, social and personal service activities	38.2	41.9	43.9
Private households with employed persons	9.2	11.7	11.1
Extra-territorial organizations and bodies	3.3	2.3	2.9
Sub-total	1,744.3	1,747.3	1,704.3
Activities not adequately defined	0.3	—	—
Total employed	1,744.6	1,747.3	1,704.3
Unemployed	279.3	274.5	261.0
Total labour force	2,023.9	2,021.8	1,965.3
Males	1,074.4	1,085.9	1,031.8
Females	949.5	935.9	933.5

* Figures exclude employment in the informal sector, estimated to total about 750,000 persons at the end of 1997, and those employed in the armed forces.

2012: Total employed 1,724.0; Unemployed 305.1; Total labour force 2,029.1.

Source: mainly ILO.

Health and Welfare

KEY INDICATORS

Total fertility rate (children per woman, 2011)	1.5
Under-5 mortality rate (per 1,000 live births, 2011)	21
HIV/AIDS (% of persons aged 15–49, 2012)	0.3
Physicians (per 1,000 head, 2011)	4.2
Hospital beds (per 1,000 head, 2009)	3.1
Health expenditure (2010): US $ per head (PPP)	524
Health expenditure (2010): % of GDP	10.2
Health expenditure (2010): public (% of total)	23.6
Access to water (% of persons, 2011)	98
Access to sanitation (% of persons, 2011)	93
Total carbon dioxide emissions ('000 metric tons, 2010)	6,241.2
Carbon dioxide emissions per head (metric tons, 2010)	1.4
Human Development Index (2012): ranking	72
Human Development Index (2012): value	0.745

For sources and definitions, see explanatory note on p. vi.

Agriculture

PRINCIPAL CROPS
('000 metric tons)

	2010	2011	2012
Wheat	48.4	96.8	80.7
Barley	23.3	30.3	18.9
Maize	141.1	269.6	267.0
Potatoes	228.8	273.9	249.7
Sunflower seed	2.6	8.0*	9.0†
Cabbages and other brassicas	27.1	35.2	34.5
Tomatoes	56.0	61.6	63.9
Cucumbers and gherkins	28.6	25.5	38.7
Onions, dry	19.0	14.6	17.8
Watermelons	40.9	42.8	36.7
Oranges	1.4	0.6	3.5
Apples	21.1	64.3	45.0
Pears	13.7	17.6	16.1
Sour (Morello) cherries	3.0	2.7	5.1
Peaches and nectarines	6.9	19.1	7.1
Plums and sloes	6.7	7.2	10.7

—continued	2010	2011	2012
Grapes	120.7	159.6	144.0
Hazelnuts (with shell)	28.8	31.1	24.7
Tea	3.5	2.9	2.6
Tobacco, unmanufactured†	0.1	0.1	0.1

* Unofficial figure.
† FAO estimate(s).

Aggregate production ('000 metric tons, may include official, semi-official or estimated data): Total cereals 220.2 in 2010, 404.7 in 2011, 374.7 in 2012; Total treenuts 36.1 in 2010, 38.1 in 2011, 30.8 in 2012; Total roots and tubers 228.8 in 2010, 273.9 in 2011, 249.7 in 2012; Total vegetables (incl. melons) 216.6 in 2010, 228.6 in 2011, 235.2 in 2012; Total fruits (excl. melons) 260.6 in 2010, 363.4 in 2011, 347.7 in 2012.

Source: FAO.

LIVESTOCK
('000 head at 1 January)

	2010	2011	2012
Horses*	40.0	40.0	40.0
Cattle	1,014.7	1,049.4	1,087.6
Buffaloes†	17.5	17.8	18.0
Pigs	135.2	110.1	105.1
Sheep	602.3	596.8	576.8
Goats	71.5	57.1	53.6
Chickens†	6,190	6,050	5,900
Turkeys†	485	471	460

* FAO estimates.
† Unofficial figures.

Source: FAO.

LIVESTOCK PRODUCTS
('000 metric tons)

	2010	2011	2012
Cattle meat	26.7	21.3	6.2
Sheep meat*	4.9	3.8	2.5
Pig meat	12.8	11.6	11.8
Chicken meat	11.6	12.0	11.7
Cows' milk	581.0	575.5	594.6*
Hen eggs*	24.6	26.8	26.3

* Unofficial figure(s).

Source: FAO.

Forestry

ROUNDWOOD REMOVALS
('000 cu m, excl. bark, unofficial figures)

	2005	2006	2007
Sawlogs, veneer logs and logs for sleepers	81.0	168.2	105.0
Other industrial wood	81.0	—	—
Fuel wood	453.9	473.0	733.0
Total	615.9	641.2	838.0

2008–12: Production assumed to be unchanged from 2007 (FAO estimates).

Source: FAO.

SAWNWOOD PRODUCTION
('000 cu m, incl. railway sleepers)

	2005	2006	2007
Coniferous (softwood)	6.9*	55.0	30.0
Broadleaved (hardwood)	215.0†	45.0	40.0
Total	221.9*	100.0	70.0

* FAO estimate.
† Unofficial figure.

2008–12: Production assumed to be unchanged from 2007 (FAO estimates).

Source: FAO.

Fishing

(metric tons, live weight)

	2009	2010	2011
Capture*	50,002	46,023	26,497
Mullets	1	11	1
European anchovy	34,752	40,819	25,919
Sea snails*	476	476	450
Aquaculture*	470	470	650
Total catch*	50,472	46,493	27,147

* FAO estimate(s).

Source: FAO.

Mining

('000 metric tons unless otherwise indicated)

	2009	2010	2011*
Coal	168.5	240.6	250.0
Crude petroleum	53.9	51.1	50.0
Natural gas (million cu m)	12.2	7.9	7.9
Manganese ore*	400.0	400.0	400.0
Cement	870.4	856.9	860.0

* Estimated production.

Source: US Geological Survey.

Industry*

SELECTED PRODUCTS

('000 metric tons unless otherwise indicated)

	2007	2008	2009
Refined sugar	133.9	n.a.	n.a.
Wine ('000 hl)	160.0	182.9	152.2
Beer ('000 hl)	709	625	685
Vodka and liqueurs ('000 hl)	75	98	138
Soft drinks ('000 hl)	1,828	1,462	1,247
Mineral water ('000 hl)	n.a.	1,132	1,046
Cigarettes (million)	4,874	5,156	5,218
Residual fuel oils	13	17	5
Building bricks (million)	12.4	10.2	6.4
Electric energy (million kWh)	8,580	8,440	8,165

2010 (million kWh): Electric energy 9,992.

Source: mainly UN Industrial Commodity Statistics Database.

Wine ('000 metric tons, unofficial figures): 104.3 in 2009; 103.4 in 2010; 110.8 in 2011 (Source: FAO).

* Data for those areas of South Ossetia outside central government control and for the separatist 'Republic of Abkhazia' are not included.

Finance

CURRENCY AND EXCHANGE RATES

Monetary Units

100 tetri = 1 lari.

Sterling, Dollar and Euro Equivalents (31 December 2013)

£1 sterling = 2.859 lari;
US $1 = 1.736 lari;
€1 = 2.395 lari;
100 lari = £34.97 = $57.59 = €41.76.

Average Exchange Rate (lari per US $)

2011 1.686
2012 1.651
2013 1.663

BUDGET

(million lari)*

Revenue†	2010	2011	2012
Tax revenue	4,867.5	6,134.8	6,671.0
Taxes on income	1,202.1	1,551.1	1,764.8
Taxes on profits	575.9	832.3	851.0
Value-added tax	2,203.1	2,784.4	3,040.3
Excise	560.8	615.0	659.6
Customs duties	70.4	93.3	90.1
Other taxes	255.2	258.7	265.2
Other current revenue	526.2	515.4	618.2
Capital revenue	286.1	449.2	329.9
Total	5,679.8	7,099.4	7,619.1

Expenditure‡	2010	2011	2012
Wages and salaries	1,120.2	1,136.2	1,202.6
Use of goods and services	1,138.6	1,211.0	1,297.8
Interest	206.1	288.0	253.5
Subsidies	380.0	426.0	514.1
Social benefits	1,623.6	1,655.5	1,857.6
Grants	10.5	13.0	16.7
Other current expenditure	1,001.3	1,056.9	1,353.4
Capital expenditure	1,540.8	1,675.3	1,498.5
Total	7,021.1	7,461.9	7,994.2

* Figures represent a consolidation of the state budget (covering the central Government and local administrations) and extra-budgetary funds.

† Excluding grants received (million lari): 472.1 in 2010; 223.5 in 2011; 270.8 in 2012.

‡ Including net lending.

INTERNATIONAL RESERVES

(excl. gold, US $ million at 31 December)

	2010	2011	2012
IMF special drawing rights	222.41	223.27	221.29
Reserve position in the IMF	0.02	0.01	0.02
Foreign exchange	2,041.36	2,594.91	2,651.65
Total	2,263.79	2,818.19	2,872.95

Source: IMF, *International Financial Statistics*.

MONEY SUPPLY

(million lari at 31 December)

	2010	2011	2012
Currency outside depository corporations	1,372.99	1,438.99	1,550.03
Transferable deposits	2,321.82	2,629.58	2,711.79
Other deposits	2,504.20	3,029.20	3,641.92
Broad money	6,199.01	7,097.78	7,903.74

Source: IMF, *International Financial Statistics*.

COST OF LIVING

(Consumer Price Index for five cities*; base: December 2003 = 100)

	2010	2011	2012
Food and non-alcoholic beverages	201.0	202.7	195.4
Alcoholic beverages and tobacco	170.7	173.2	176.1
Clothing and footwear	88.8	84.1	81.4
Housing, utilities and other fuels	169.7	175.3	171.0
Household furnishings and maintenance	128.0	127.2	126.2
Health	162.9	164.7	169.3
Transport	153.6	176.0	175.8
Education	151.5	151.6	149.1
Recreation and culture	111.5	112.5	108.5
All items (incl. others)	166.6	170.0	167.7

* Tbilisi, Kutaisi, Batumi, Gori and Telavi.

NATIONAL ACCOUNTS

(million lari at current prices)

National Income and Product

	2010	2011	2012
Compensation of employees	6,010.3	7,755.2	8,823.8
Net operating surplus	5,974.2	5,979.1	5,825.2
Net mixed income	3,647.9	4,321.5	4,794.1
Domestic primary incomes	15,632.4	18,055.8	19,443.1
Consumption of fixed capital	2,126.8	2,660.8	2,797.0
Gross domestic product (GDP) at factor cost	17,759.2	20,716.6	22,240.1
Taxes on production and imports	3,089.5	3,751.5	4,055.2
Less Subsidies	105.3	124.1	128.0
GDP in market prices	20,743.4	24,344.0	26,167.3
Primary incomes received from abroad	742.8	1,273.7	1,778.8
Less Primary incomes paid abroad	1,383.4	1,986.0	2,020.5
Gross national income (GNI)	20,102.8	23,631.7	25,925.6
Less Consumption of fixed capital	2,126.8	2,660.8	2,797.0
Net national income	17,976.0	20,970.9	23,128.6
Current transfers from abroad	2,108.3	2,431.5	2,504.7
Less Current transfers paid abroad	151.7	217.6	178.9
Net disposable income	19,932.6	23,184.8	25,454.4

Expenditure on the Gross Domestic Product

	2010	2011	2012
Government final consumption expenditure	4,371.0	4,430.5	4,632.5
Private final consumption expenditure	15,527.2	18,017.8	18,875.4
Increase in stocks	468.7	893.7	1,078.6
Gross fixed capital formation	4,009.0	5,474.3	6,496.8
Total domestic expenditure	24,375.9	28,816.3	31,083.3
Exports of goods and services	7,250.0	8,822.9	9,983.0
Less Imports of goods and services	10,945.1	13,334.2	15,124.3
Statistical discrepancy	62.6	39.0	225.3
GDP in market prices	20,743.4	24,344.0	26,167.3
GDP at constant 2003 prices	12,771.3	13,687.5	14,533.6

Gross Domestic Product by Economic Activity

	2010	2011	2012
Agriculture, forestry and fishing	1,509.9	1,854.9	1,933.3
Mining and quarrying	181.0	208.8	230.8
Manufacturing	1,654.8	2,085.6	2,288.5
Electricity, gas and water supply	534.2	634.8	637.0
Processing of products by households	536.9	655.8	601.0
Construction	1,100.0	1,407.9	1,756.9
Wholesale and retail trade; repair of motor vehicles, motorcycles and personal and household goods	3,024.9	3,552.7	3,769.5
Hotels and restaurants	411.7	466.3	510.6
Transport, storage and communications	2,076.9	2,212.0	2,395.5
Financial intermediation	476.7	536.1	633.5
Real estate, renting and business activities*	1,478.1	1,804.6	1,963.0
Public administration and defence; compulsory social security	2,343.1	2,443.0	2,526.3
Education	874.0	1,050.0	1,092.3
Health and social services	1,202.0	1,275.5	1,362.2
Other community, social and personal services	825.5	1,021.7	1,066.2
Private households with employed persons	20.1	25.2	29.3

—continued	2010	2011	2012
Sub-total	18,249.9	21,234.9	22,795.9
Less Financial intermediation services indirectly measured	235.5	259.5	290.8
Gross value added in basic prices	18,014.4	20,975.4	22,505.3
Taxes on products	2,834.3	3,492.7	3,790.0
Less Subsidies on products	105.3	124.1	128.0
GDP in market prices	20,743.4	24,344.0	26,167.3

* Including imputed rent of owner-occupied dwellings.

BALANCE OF PAYMENTS

(US $ million)

	2010	2011	2012
Exports of goods	2,393.3	3,223.0	3,459.1
Imports of goods	−5,021.3	−6,722.6	−7,685.2
Balance on goods	−2,628.1	−3,499.6	−4,226.1
Exports of services	1,640.8	2,018.9	2,562.3
Imports of services	−1,092.5	−1,265.2	−1,447.5
Balance on goods and services	−2,079.8	−2,745.9	−3,111.3
Primary income received	556.6	758.0	1,077.5
Primary income paid	−771.2	−1,180.6	−1,224.0
Balance on goods, services and primary income	−2,294.3	−3,168.5	−3,257.8
Secondary income received	1,051.7	1,339.0	1,454.1
Secondary income paid	−85.0	−129.9	−108.3
Current balance	−1,327.6	−1,959.3	−1,912.0
Capital account (net)	198.3	145.8	131.6
Direct investment assets	−190.4	−182.7	−216.9
Direct investment liabilities	869.1	1,084.3	831.3
Portfolio investment assets	−0.6	—	−33.1
Portfolio investment liabilities	239.5	64.1	859.7
Financial derivatives and employee stock options assets	1.8	12.1	10.7
Financial derivatives and employee stock options liabilities	−1.0	−7.0	−5.2
Other investment assets	−411.0	205.2	−349.0
Other investment liabilities	472.5	985.9	856.4
Net errors and omissions	−23.5	14.6	−22.6
Reserves and related items	−173.0	363.1	150.7

Source: IMF, *International Financial Statistics*.

External Trade

PRINCIPAL COMMODITIES

(distribution by HS, US $ million)

Imports	2010	2011	2012
Vegetable products	289.2	363.3	414.6
Cereals	186.9	206.4	255.8
Wheat and meslin	174.2	184.2	240.0
Prepared foodstuffs; beverages, spirits and vinegar and tobacco	464.8	543.7	552.0
Mineral products	1,071.5	1,369.0	1,473.1
Mineral fuels, oils, distillation products, etc.	958.6	1,264.9	1,337.4
Petroleum and petroleum oils	696.9	911.0	951.0
Petroleum gases	160.5	236.6	252.7
Chemicals and related products	440.0	510.0	582.5
Pharmaceutical products	221.0	228.4	264.2

Imports—*continued*	2010	2011	2012
Medicaments	191.9	201.4	232.5
Plastics, rubber and articles thereof	230.6	294.9	346.9
Textiles and textile articles	215.3	285.7	228.3
Base metals and articles thereof	396.1	594.1	655.0
Machinery and electrical equipment	772.1	1,220.3	1,380.5
Vehicles, vessels, aircraft and other transport equipment	549.0	783.7	998.5
Vehicles other than railway, tramway	524.9	705.0	920.1
Motor cars	401.7	510.5	662.8
Miscellaneous manufactured articles	164.7	207.8	247.4
Total (incl. others)	5,257.1	7,057.8	7,842.1

Exports	2010	2011	2012
Vegetable products	122.8	165.9	178.6
Edible fruit, nuts, peel of citrus fruit, melons	93.4	140.0	97.7
Fresh or dried nuts	75.1	130.1	83.7
Prepared foodstuffs; beverages, spirits and vinegar and tobacco	182.3	216.9	266.5
Beverages, spirits and vinegar	152.1	192.2	233.1
Undenatured ethyl alcohol, spirits, liqueurs and other spirituous beverages	55.7	67.9	80.0
Mineral products	163.5	189.2	142.2
Ores, slag and ash	85.8	95.8	57.4
Copper ores and concentrates	74.5	85.1	53.5
Mineral fuels, oils, distillation products, etc.	70.6	72.5	49.1
Chemicals and related products	142.8	228.5	261.1
Fertilizers	84.2	144.1	137.3
Nitrogenous minerals or chemical fertilizers	84.2	144.1	137.2
Natural or cultured pearls, precious or semi-precious stones	125.9	118.6	96.8
Pearls, precious stones, metals, coins, etc.	125.9	118.6	96.8
Unwrought, semi-manufactured or powdered gold	117.6	109.9	88.0
Base metals and articles thereof	488.1	527.2	454.9
Iron and steel	418.3	439.9	372.6
Ferro alloys	264.0	254.9	260.5
Ferrous waste and scrap	109.4	116.8	43.9
Vehicles, vessels, aircraft and other transport equipment	301.9	546.5	670.7
Vehicles other than railway, tramway	246.8	489.0	637.3
Motor cars	227.4	450.3	587.3
Total (incl. others)	1,677.5	2,189.1	2,377.5

PRINCIPAL TRADING PARTNERS
(US $ million)

Imports c.i.f.	2010	2011	2012
Austria	51.5	78.0	82.7
Azerbaijan	484.6	610.8	633.5
Brazil	80.6	110.2	120.1
Bulgaria	131.7	255.6	271.5
China, People's Republic	335.2	524.8	566.0
Czech Republic	57.8	91.9	82.9
France	75.0	97.3	106.1
Germany	333.4	480.6	541.9
Greece	72.6	61.9	50.9
Iran	55.1	64.8	99.4
Italy	136.9	184.8	271.0
Japan	170.4	174.1	312.6

Imports c.i.f.—*continued*	2010	2011	2012
Kazakhstan	94.5	70.6	131.8
Netherlands	105.2	133.2	142.7
Poland	55.7	63.1	85.8
Romania	140.8	188.3	259.0
Russia	290.5	389.7	473.8
Spain	34.1	82.2	88.3
Turkey	886.7	1,272.4	1,392.9
Turkmenistan	59.2	55.5	30.7
Ukraine	560.9	705.6	597.1
United Arab Emirates	159.2	226.4	161.7
United Kingdom	66.3	88.5	115.1
USA	177.8	245.8	213.2
Total (incl. others)	5,257.1	7,057.8	7,842.1

Exports f.o.b.	2010	2011	2012
Armenia	166.8	223.0	261.0
Azerbaijan	256.2	425.9	626.9
Belarus	23.8	28.3	33.5
Belgium	22.0	33.6	60.4
Bulgaria	66.8	93.7	69.7
Canada	118.7	114.8	104.6
China, People's Republic	26.8	28.9	25.6
Germany	35.0	49.1	38.6
Italy	26.0	75.5	53.3
Kazakhstan	50.1	156.9	62.3
Mexico	4.1	28.6	7.3
Netherlands	17.8	17.7	11.8
Romania	29.7	19.8	3.5
Russia	34.7	36.6	45.8
Spain	32.7	23.7	15.9
Turkey	216.8	227.6	142.8
Ukraine	110.4	141.2	167.0
United Arab Emirates	28.3	40.0	38.9
USA	187.2	143.5	226.2
Total (incl. others)	1,677.5	2,189.1	2,377.5

Transport

RAILWAYS
(traffic)

	2010	2011	2012
Passengers carried (million)	3.2	3.3	3.1
Passenger-km (million)	654.4	641.4	625.4
Freight ('000 tons)	19,930.1	20,123.4	20,076.0
Freight net ton-km (million)	6,227.5	6,054.8	5,976.6

ROAD TRAFFIC
('000 motor vehicles in use)

	2011	2012	2013
Passenger cars	577.2	620.9	672.7
Buses	47.6	49.2	51.2
Lorries and vans	65.6	73.0	78.5
Total (incl. others)	702.7	762.2	831.6

SHIPPING

Flag Registered Fleet
(at 31 December)

	2011	2012	2013
Number of vessels	247	196	173
Total displacement ('000 grt)	362.0	185.7	136.3

Source: Lloyd's List Intelligence (www.lloydslistintelligence.com).

CIVIL AVIATION
(traffic on scheduled services)

	2010	2011	2012
Passengers carried ('000)*	200	200	200
Passenger-km (million)	368.9	413.5	360.1
Freight ('000 metric tons)	0.5	1.2	0.4
Total ton-km (million)	0.9	1.5	0.5

* Figures are rounded.

Tourism

FOREIGN TOURIST ARRIVALS

Country of residence	2009	2010	2011
Armenia	351,049	547,510	699,382
Azerbaijan	418,992	497,969	714,418
Germany	15,351	17,619	22,204
Greece	14,300	16,424	17,664
Israel	16,757	19,447	25,438
Russia	127,937	170,584	278,458
Turkey	384,482	535,593	738,085
Ukraine	39,339	47,596	58,966
United Kingdom	10,633	10,985	12,613
USA	16,934	20,0181	24,236
Total (incl. others)	1,500,049	2,031,717	2,822,363

Total foreign tourist arrivals ('000): 1,790 in 2012 (provisional).

Tourism receipts (US $ million, excl. passenger transport): 659 in 2010; 955 in 2011; 1,411 in 2012 (provisional).

Source: World Tourism Organization.

Communications Media

	2010	2011	2012
Telephones ('000 main lines in use)	1,105.9	1,340.4	1,276.1
Mobile cellular telephones ('000 subscribers)	3,980.0	4,430.3	4,698.6
Internet subscribers ('000)	254.1	n.a.	n.a.
Broadband subscribers ('000)	253.9	324.5	392.1
Newspapers: titles	225	284	301
Newspapers: circulation ('000)	800	100	100

Source: International Telecommunication Union.

Education

(2008/09 unless otherwise indicated)

	Institutions	Students*
Pre-primary schools†	1,197	77,922
General education: schools (primary)‡§ General education: schools (secondary)§	2,320	559,415
General education: evening schools†	14	100
State secondary professional schools	30	2,177
Private secondary professional schools	4	434
State higher schools (incl. universities)§	19	80,009
Private higher schools (incl. universities)§	38	29,524

* Some figures are rounded.
† Data for 2005/06.
‡ Including primary schools covering part of the secondary syllabus.
§ Data for 2012/13.

Teachers (2007/08, unless otherwise indicated): Pre-primary 7,783 (2004/05); Total in general day schools 68,670 (60,506 in public schools, 8,164 in private schools—2012/13); Total in secondary professional schools 873 (803 public, 70 private—2008/09); Total full- and part-time professors in institutes of higher education 11,424 in 2008 (7,142 in public institutions, 4,282 in non-state institutions).

Pupil-teacher ratio (primary education, UNESCO estimate): 6.3 in 2011/12 (Source: UNESCO Institute for Statistics).

Adult literacy rate (UNESCO estimates): 99.7% (males 99.8%; females 99.7%) in 2011 (Source: UNESCO Institute for Statistics).

Directory

The Government

HEAD OF STATE

President: GIORGI MARGVELASHVILI (elected 27 October 2013; inaugurated 17 November 2013).

GOVERNMENT
(April 2014)

The Government principally comprises members of Georgian Dream-Democratic Georgia and Our Georgia—Free Democrats, and also includes representatives of the National Forum, the Republican Party of Georgia, and independents.

Prime Minister: IRAKLI GARIBASHVILI.

First Deputy Prime Minister, Minister of Economic and Sustainable Development: GIORGI KVIRIKASHVILI.

Deputy Prime Minister, Minister of Energy: KAKHA KALADZE.

State Minister, responsible for European and Euro-Atlantic Integration: ALEKSI PETRIASHVILI.

State Minister, responsible for Reconciliation and Civic Equality: PAATA ZAKAREISHVILI.

State Minister, responsible for Diaspora Affairs: KONSTANTIN SURGULADZE.

Minister of Education and Science: TAMAR SANIKIDZE.

Minister of Regional Development and Infrastructure: ELGUJA KHOKRISHVILI.

Minister of Finance: NODAR KHADURI.

Minister of Sport and Youth Affairs: LEVAN KIPIANI.

Minister of Environmental Protection and Natural Resources: KHATUNA GOGALADZE.

Minister of Defence: IRAKLI ALASANIA.

Minister of Justice: TEA TSULUKIANI.

Minister of Culture and the Protection of Monuments: GURAM ODISHARIA.

Minister of Internally Displaced Persons from the Occupied Territories, Accommodation, and Refugees: DAVIT DARAKHVELIDZE.

Minister of Foreign Affairs: MAIA PANJIKIDZE.

Minister of Agriculture: SHALVA PIPIA.

Minister of Internal Affairs: ALEKSANDRE TCHIKAIDZE.

Minister of Labour, Health and Social Affairs: DAVIT SERGEENKO.

Minister of Prisons and Probation: SOZAR SUBARI.

MINISTRIES

Office of the President: 0103 Tbilisi, M. Abdushelishvili 1; tel. (32) 228-27-36; fax (32) 228-27-14; e-mail secretariat@admin.gov.ge; internet www.president.gov.ge.

Chancellery of the Government: 0134 Tbilisi, P. Ingorovka 7; tel. (32) 299-09-00; fax (32) 292-10-69; e-mail primeminister@geo.gov.ge; internet www.government.gov.ge.

Office of the State Minister, responsible for European and Euro-Atlantic Integration: 0134 Tbilisi, P. Ingorovka 7; tel. and fax (32) 293-28-67; e-mail office@eu-nato.gov.ge; internet www.eu-nato.gov.ge.

Office of the State Minister, responsible for Diaspora Affairs: 0134 Tbilisi, P. Ingorovka 7; tel. (32) 293-17-42; fax (32) 293-17-05; e-mail info@diaspora.gov.ge; internet www.diaspora.gov.ge.

Office of the State Minister, responsible for Reconciliation and Civic Equality: 0134 Tbilisi, P. Ingorovka 7; tel. (32) 298-92-56; fax (32) 292-16-50; e-mail press@smr.gov.ge; internet www.smr.gov.ge.

Ministry of Agriculture: 0159 Tbilisi, Gelovani 6; tel. (32) 237-66-89; fax (32) 237-80-13; e-mail infomoa@moa.gov.ge; internet moa.gov.ge.

Ministry of Culture and the Protection of Monuments: 0105 Tbilisi, Sanapiro 4; tel. (32) 293-22-55; fax (32) 299-99-66; e-mail pr@culture.gov.ge; internet www.mcs.gov.ge.

Ministry of Defence: 0112 Tbilisi, Gen. Kvinitadze 20; tel. and fax (32) 272-35-35; e-mail pr@mod.gov.ge; internet www.mod.gov.ge.

Ministry of Economic and Sustainable Development: 0108 Tbilisi, Chanturia 12; tel. (32) 299-11-11; fax (32) 292-15-34; e-mail ministry@economy.ge; internet www.economy.ge.

Ministry of Education and Science: 0102 Tbilisi, D. Uznadze 52; tel. (32) 220-02-20; fax (32) 243-88-12; e-mail pr@mes.gov.ge; internet www.mes.gov.ge.

Ministry of Energy and Natural Resources: 0105 Tbilisi, Sanapiro 2; tel. (32) 235-78-04; fax (32) 235-78-28; e-mail mail@energy.gov.ge; internet www.energy.gov.ge.

Ministry of Environmental Protection and Natural Resources: 0114 Tbilisi, G. Gulua 6; tel. (32) 272-72-34; e-mail pr@moe.gov.ge; internet www.moe.gov.ge.

Ministry of Finance: 0114 Tbilisi, V. Gorgasali 16; tel. (32) 226-14-44; fax (32) 245-74-55; e-mail minister@mof.ge; internet www.mof.ge.

Ministry of Foreign Affairs: 0108 Tbilisi, Sh. Chitadze 4; tel. (32) 294-50-00; fax (32) 294-50-01; e-mail inform@mfa.gov.ge; internet www.mfa.gov.ge.

Ministry of Labour, Health and Social Affairs: 0119 Tbilisi, A. Tsereteli 144; tel. (32) 251-00-12; fax (32) 251-00-19; e-mail info@moh.gov.ge; internet www.moh.gov.ge.

Ministry of Internal Affairs: 0190 Tbilisi, Kakheti 38; tel. (32) 241-84-44; fax (32) 241-10-17; e-mail monitoringi@mia.gov.ge; internet www.police.ge.

Ministry of Internally Displaced Persons from the Occupied Territories, Accommodation, and Refugees: 0177 Tbilisi, Tamarashvili 15 A; tel. (32) 231-15-98; fax (32) 231-15-96; e-mail info@mra.gov.ge; internet www.mra.gov.ge.

Ministry of Justice: 0146 Tbilisi, Gorgasali 24A; tel. (32) 240-52-02; fax (32) 275-82-37; e-mail press-center@justice.gov.ge; internet www.justice.gov.ge.

Ministry of Labour, Health and Social Affairs: 0119 Tbilisi, A. Tsereteli 144; tel. (32) 251-00-12; fax (32) 251-00-19; e-mail info@moh.gov.ge; internet www.moh.gov.ge.

Ministry of Prisons and Probation: 0177 Tbilisi, Al. Qazbegi 42; tel. (32) 231-27-34; fax (32) 231-19-01; e-mail info@mcla.gov.ge; internet www.mcla.gov.ge.

Ministry of Regional Development and Infrastructure: 0177 Tbilisi, Al. Qazbegi 12; tel. (32) 251-07-12; e-mail press@mrdi.gov.ge; internet www.mrdi.gov.ge.

Ministry of Sport and Youth Affairs: 0162 Tbilisi, Cholokashvili 9; tel. (32) 223-54-33; fax (32) 229-20-49; e-mail sport@msy.gov.ge; internet msy.gov.ge.

President

Presidential Election, 27 October 2013

Candidates	Votes	%
Giorgi Margvelashvili (QO—DS)	1,012,569	62.12
Davit Bakradze (ENM)	354,103	21.72
Nino Burjanadze (DM—ES)	166,061	10.19
Shalva Natelashvili (SLP)	46,984	2.88
Giorgi Targamadze (KDM)	17,354	1.06
Others	32,917	2.02
Total	1,629,988	100.00

Legislature

Georgian Parliament (Sakartvelos Parlamenti)

Kutaisi, Abashidze 26; tel. (32) 228-90-06; fax (32) 299-93-86; e-mail contact@parliament.ge; internet www.parliament.ge.

Chairman: DAVIT USUPASHVILI.

General Election, 1 October 2012

Parties and blocs	%*	Seats A†	Seats B†	Seats Total
Bidzina Ivanishvili—Georgian Dream‡	54.97	44	41	85
United National Movement—More Benefits To The People	40.34	33	32	65
Others	4.70	—	—	—
Total	100.00	77	73	150

* Percentage refers to the share of the vote cast for seats awarded on the basis of party lists.

† Of the 150 seats in the Sakartvelos Parlamenti, 77 (A) are awarded according to proportional representation on the basis of party lists, and 73 (B) are elected in single-mandate constituencies.

‡ An electoral alliance of Georgian Dream-Democratic Georgia; the Conservative Party of Georgia; Industry Will Save Georgia; the National Forum; Our Georgia—Free Democrats; and the Republican Party of Georgia.

Election Commission

Central Electoral Commission of Georgia (CEC): 0108 Tbilisi, Aghmashenebeli 13-km; tel. (32) 251-00-51; e-mail correspondence@cec.gov.ge; internet www.cec.gov.ge; Chair. TAMAR ZHVANIA.

Political Organizations

In early 2008 some 190 political parties and alliances were registered with the Central Electoral Commission. The following were among the most prominent parties in mid-2013:

Christian Democratic Movement (KDM) (Kristianul-demokratiuli modzraoba): 0162 Tbilisi, Tsagareli 59; tel. (32) 214-10-33; fax (32) 214-10-38; e-mail info@cdm.ge; internet www.cdm.ge; f. 2008; joined the Alliance of European Conservatives and Reformists in 2012; Chair. GIORGI TARGAMADZE.

Conservative Party of Georgia (SKP) (Sakartvelos konservatiuli partia): 0179 Tbilisi, Krtsanisis II shesakhvevi 15-17; tel. (32) 225-27-90; fax (32) 222-61-23; e-mail office@conservatives.ge; internet www.conservatives.ge; f. 2001; joined the Georgian Dream coalition in advance of legislative elections in 2012, led by the Georgian Dream-Democratic Georgia party (q.v.); Chair. ZVIAD DZIDZIGURI (acting); 12,000 mems.

Democratic Movement—United Georgia (DM—ES) (Demokratiuli modzraoba—ertiani sakartvelo): 0160 Tbilisi, Abuladze 8; tel. (32) 255-03-77; e-mail mail@democrats.ge; internet www.democrats.ge; f. 2008; opposed to regime of Pres. Saakashvili; Chair. NINO BURJANADZE; 35,000 mems (2012).

Democratic Party of Georgia: c/o Sakartvelos Parlamenti, 0118 Tbilisi, Rustaveli 8; f. 2008; right-of-centre; Chair. GIA TORTLADZE.

European Democrats of Georgia: Tbilisi, Kvinitadze 4; tel. (32) 230-78-71; e-mail europeandemocrats@gmail.com; internet www.ged.ge; f. 2011; Chair. PAATA DAVITAIA.

Freedom (Tavisupleba): Tbilisi, Rustaveli 37; tel. (32) 299-52-28; f. 2004 by a son of former President Zviad Gamsakhurdia; nationalist; Leader KONSTANTINE GAMSAKHURDIA.

Georgian Dream—Democratic Georgia (QO—DS) (Qartuli Ocneba—Demokratiuli Sakartvelo): 0105 Tbilisi, Erekle II Moedani 3; tel. (32) 219-77-11; internet www.gd.ge; f. 2012; founded by prominent businessman Bidzina Ivanishvili; Chair. MANANA KOBAKHIDZE.

Georgian Labour Party (SLP) (Sakartvelos leiboristuli partia): 0112 Tbilisi, Javakhishvili 88; tel. (32) 291-16-17; fax (32) 294-29-22; e-mail georgianlabourparty@gmail.com; internet www.labour.ge; f. 1996; Chair. SHALVA NATELASHVILI.

Georgian Party: Tbilisi; f. 2010; opposed to administration of Pres. Saakashvili; Chair. IRAKLI OKRUASHVILI (in exile).

Georgia's Way (Sakartvelos gza): 0108 Tbilisi, Barnovi 60; tel. and fax (32) 291-45-46; e-mail info@twg.ge; internet www.twg.ge; f. 2006; Chair. TEIMURAZ MURVANIDZE.

Industry Will Save Georgia (MGS) (Mretsveloba Gadaarchens Sakartvelos): 0105 Tbilisi, Marjvena Sanapiro 7; tel. (32) 294-09-81; f. 1999; Leader GIORGI TOPHADZE.

Movement for a Fair Georgia (MSS) (Modzraoba samartliani sakartvelostvis): 0160 Tbilisi, Lvovi 56; tel. (32) 291-92-22; f. 2008; opposes regime of Pres. Saakashvili; signed co-operation agreement with de facto ruling party of Russia, United Russia, in Feb. 2010; Chair. SERGO JAVKHIDZE.

National Forum: Tbilisi; f. 2006; joined the Georgian Dream coalition in advance of legislative elections in 2012, led by the Georgian Dream-Democratic Georgia party (q.v.); Leader KAKHABER SHARTAVA.

New Rights (AM) (Axali Memarjveneebi—Axlebi): 0179 Tbilisi, I. Abashidze 18; tel. (32) 272-35-58; fax (32) 222-23-47; e-mail info@nrp.ge; internet www.nrp.ge; f. 2001 as New Conservative Party; Chair. PIKRIA CHIKHRADZE; Gen. Sec. MAMUKA KATSITADZE.

Our Georgia—Free Democrats (ChS—DD) (Chveni Sakartvelo—Davisuphali demokratebi): 0194 Tbilisi, E. Cherkezishvili 4; tel. (32) 210-48-83; f. 2009; right-of-centre; opposed to administration of Pres. Saakashvili; joined the Georgian Dream coalition in advance of legislative elections in 2012, led by the Georgian Dream-Democratic Georgia party (q.v.); Leader IRAKLI ALASANIA.

Republican Party of Georgia (SRP) (Sakartvelos respublikuri partia): 0108 Tbilisi, Phanaskerteli 20/81; tel. (32) 292-00-58; fax (32) 292-06-34; e-mail respublikelebi@gmail.com; internet www.republicans.ge; f. 1995; absorbed Georgian Popular Front (f. 1989); politically, economically and socially liberal; joined the Georgian Dream coalition in advance of legislative elections in 2012, led by the Georgian Dream-Democratic Georgia party (q.v.); Chair. KHATUNA SAMNIDZE.

United National Movement (ENM) (Ertiani natsionaluri modzraoba): 0118 Tbilisi, Kakheti 45A; tel. (32) 292-30-84; fax (32) 292-30-91; e-mail info@unm.ge; internet www.unm.ge; f. Nov. 2004 by merger of National Movement and United Democrats; liberal conservative; Chair. MIKHEIL SAAKASHVILI; Sec.-Gen. IVANE MERABISHVILI.

Diplomatic Representation

EMBASSIES IN GEORGIA

Armenia: 0102 Tbilisi, Tetelashvili 4; tel. (32) 295-94-43; fax (32) 296-42-87; e-mail armgeorgiaembassy@mfa.am; Ambassador HOVHANNES MANUKIAN.

Azerbaijan: Tbilisi, Kipshidzse 2/1; tel. (32) 224-22-20; fax (32) 224-22-33; e-mail tbilisi@mission.mfa.gov.az; internet www.azembassy.ge; Ambassador AZER TOFIG HUSEYN.

Brazil: Tbilisi, Chanturia 6/2; tel. (32) 293-24-19; fax (32) 293-24-16; e-mail brasemb.tbilisi@itamaraty.gov.br; Ambassador CARLOS ALBERTO LOPES ASFORA.

Bulgaria: 0102 Tbilisi, V. Gorgasali 15; tel. (32) 291-01-94; fax (32) 291-02-70; e-mail embassy.tbilisi@mfa.bg; internet www.mfa.bg/embassies/georgia; Ambassador PLAMEN BONCHEV.

China, People's Republic: 0179 Tbilisi, Barnov 52, POB 224; tel. (32) 225-90-00; fax (32) 225-09-96; e-mail chinaemb_ge@mfa.gov.cn; Ambassador YUE BI.

Czech Republic: 0162 Tbilisi, Chavchavadze 37/6; tel. (32) 291-69-40; fax (32) 291-67-44; e-mail tbilisi@embassy.mzv.cz; internet www.mzv.cz/tbilisi; Ambassador TOMÁŠ PERNICKÝ.

Estonia: 0171 Tbilisi, Saburtalo, Likhauri 4; tel. (32) 236-51-22; fax (32) 236-51-38; e-mail tbilisisaatkond@mfa.ee; internet www.tbilisi.vm.ee; Ambassador PRIIT TURK.

France: 0114 Tbilisi, Krtsanisi 49; tel. (32) 272-14-90; fax (32) 272-13-55; e-mail ambafrance@access.sanet.ge; internet www.ambafrance-ge.org; Ambassador RENAUD SALINS.

Germany: 0103 Tbilisi, Telavi 20, Sheraton Metekhi Palace Hotel; tel. (32) 244-73-00; fax (32) 244-73-64; e-mail info@tiflis.diplo.de; internet www.tiflis.diplo.de; Ambassador Dr ORTWIN HENNIG.

Greece: 0179 Tbilisi, T. Tabidze 37D; tel. (32) 291-49-70; fax (32) 291-49-80; e-mail gremb.tbi@mfa.gr; internet www.greekembassy.ge; Ambassador ELEFTHERIOS PROIOS.

Holy See: 0108 Tbilisi, Jgenti 40, Nutsubidze Plateau; tel. (32) 253-76-01; fax (32) 253-67-04; e-mail nuntius@vatican.ge; Apostolic Nuncio MAREK SOLCZYŃSKI (Titular Archbishop of Caesarea in Mauretania).

Hungary: 0160 Tbilisi, Lvovi 83; tel. (32) 239-90-08; fax (32) 239-90-04; e-mail mission.tbs@mfa.gov.hu; internet www.mfa.gov.hu/kulkepviselet/ge/hu; Ambassador SÁNDOR SZABÓ.

Iran: 0160 Tbilisi, Chavchavadze 80; tel. (32) 291-36-56; fax (32) 291-36-28; e-mail embassy@iran.ge; Ambassador ABBAS TALEBIFAR.

Iraq: 0179 Tbilisi, Kobuleti 16; tel. (32) 223-45-01; fax (32) 229-45-03; e-mail iraqiageoemb@yahoo.com; Ambassador BAKIR AHMAD AZIZ ALJAF.

Israel: 0102 Tbilisi, D. Agmashenebeli 61; tel. (32) 255-65-00; fax (32) 255-65-33; e-mail press@tbilisi.mfa.gov.il; internet tbilisi.mfa.gov.il; Ambassador YUVAL FUCHS.

Italy: 0108 Tbilisi, Chitadze 3A; tel. (32) 299-64-18; fax (32) 299-64-15; e-mail embassy.tbilisi@esteri.it; internet www.ambtbilisi.esteri.it; Ambassador FEDERICA FAVI.

Japan: Tbilisi, Krtsanisi 7D; tel. (32) 275-21-11; fax (32) 275-21-12; e-mail protocol@tb.mofa.go.jp; internet www.ge.emb-japan.go.jp; Ambassador TOSHIO KAITANI.

Kazakhstan: 0179 Tbilisi, Shatberashvili 23; tel. (32) 299-76-84; fax (32) 229-24-89; e-mail tbilisi@mfa.kz; Ambassador ERMUHAMED ERTYSBAEV.

Latvia: 0160 Tbilisi, Odessa 4; tel. (32) 224-48-58; fax (32) 238-14-06; e-mail embassy.georgia@mfa.gov.lv; Ambassador ELITA GAVELE.

Lithuania: 0162 Tbilisi, T. Abuladze 25; tel. (32) 291-29-33; fax (32) 222-17-93; e-mail amb.ge@urm.lt; internet ge.mfa.lt; Ambassador JONAS PASLAUSKAS.

Netherlands: 0103 Tbilisi, Telavi 20, Sheraton Metekhi Palace Hotel; tel. (32) 227-62-00; fax (32) 227-62-32; e-mail tbi@minbuza.nl; internet www.dutchembassy.ge; Ambassador HANS PETER PAUL MARIA HORBACH.

Poland: 0108 Tbilisi, Zubalashvili 19; tel. (32) 292-03-98; fax (32) 292-03-97; e-mail tbilisi.amb.sekretariat@msz.gov.pl; internet www.tbilisi.msz.gov.pl; Ambassador ANDRZEJ CIESZKOWSKI.

Romania: Tbilisi, Lvov Kushitashvili 7; tel. (32) 238-53-10; fax (32) 238-52-10; e-mail ambasada@caucasus.net; Ambassador DUMITRU BADEA.

Sweden: 0162 Tbilisi, Kipshidze 15; tel. (32) 255-03-20; fax (32) 222-48-90; e-mail ambassaden.tbilisi@gov.se; Ambassador DIANA JANSE.

Switzerland: 0114 Tbilisi, Krtsanisi 11; tel. (32) 275-30-01; fax (32) 275-30-06; e-mail tif.vertretung@eda.admin.ch; internet www.eda.admin.ch/tbilisi; Ambassador Dr GUENTHER BAECHLER.

Turkey: 0162 Tbilisi, Chavchavadze 35; tel. (32) 225-20-72; fax (32) 222-06-66; e-mail tiblisbe@dsl.ge; internet tbilisi.emb.mfa.gov.tr; Ambassador LEVENT GÜMRÜKÇÜ.

Ukraine: 0162 Tbilisi, Chavchavadze 76; tel. (32) 231-11-61; fax (32) 231-11-81; e-mail emb_ge@mfa.gov.ua; internet www.mfa.gov.ua/georgia; Ambassador VASYL H. TSYBENKO.

United Kingdom: 0114 Tbilisi, Krtsanisi 51; tel. (32) 227-47-47; fax (32) 227-47-92; e-mail british.embassy.tbilisi@fco.gov.uk; internet www.gov.uk/government/world/georgia; Ambassador ALEXANDRA HALL.

USA: 0131 Tbilisi, Balanchivadze 11; tel. (32) 227-70-00; fax (32) 253-23-10; e-mail tbilisivisa@state.gov; internet georgia.usembassy.gov; Ambassador RICHARD NORLAND.

Judicial System

Constitutional Court: 6010 Ajara, Batumi, M. Abashidze 16-18; tel. (422) 27-00-99; fax (422) 27-01-44; e-mail const@constcourt.ge; internet www.constcourt.ge; f. 1996; consists of 9 members; Pres. GIORGI PAPUASHVILI.

Supreme Court: 0110 Tbilisi, Zubalashvili 32; tel. (32) 299-01-64; fax (32) 299-70-01; e-mail info@supremecourt.ge; internet www.supremecourt.ge; Chair. KONSTANTIN KUBLASHVILI.

High Council of Justice: 0144 Tbilisi, Bochorma 12; tel. (32) 227-31-00; fax (32) 227-31-01; e-mail council@hcoj.gov.ge; internet www.hcoj.gov.ge; f. 1997; 15-member council that co-ordinates the appointment of judges and their activities; Chair. KONSTANTIN KUBLASHVILI (Chair. of the Supreme Court); Exec. Sec. LEVAN MURUSIDZE.

Prosecutor-General: GIORGI BADASHVILI, 0114 Tbilisi, Gorgasali 24; tel. (32) 240-52-22; e-mail presscenter@pog.gov.ge; internet pog.gov.ge.

Religion

CHRISTIANITY

The Orthodox Church

The Georgian Orthodox Church is divided into 27 dioceses.

Georgian Patriarchate: 0105 Tbilisi, Erekle II Moedani 1; tel. (32) 299-03-78; fax (32) 298-71-14; e-mail info@patriachate.ge; internet www.patriarchate.ge; Catholicos-Patriarch of All Georgia ILIA II.

The Roman Catholic Church

The Apostolic Administrator of Latin Rite Catholics of the Caucasus (Armenia and Georgia) is resident in Tbilisi.

Apostolic Administrator of Latin Rite Catholics of the Caucasus: Most Rev. GIUSEPPE PASOTTO (Titular Bishop of Musti), 0105 Tbilisi, G. Abesadze 6; tel. and fax (32) 99-60-50; e-mail ammapost@geo.net.ge.

The Armenian Apostolic Church

Primate of the Armenian Apostolic Church in Georgia: Rt Rev. Bishop VAZGEN MIRZAKHANIAN, 0105 Tbilisi, Krasilnaya 5, St Gevork Church; tel. (32) 272-17-50.

ISLAM

The principal Islamic communities in Georgia are those among the Adjars and Abkhaz (who are Sunni Muslims) and Azeris (who are Shi'ite). There is only one mosque in Tbilisi, which is shared by Sunni and Shi'ite communities. A new Muslim Affairs Department was established in 2011, to assume the jurisdiction over Georgia hitherto held by the Spiritual Board of Muslims of the Caucasus, based in Azerbaijan.

Muslim Affairs Department of Georgia: 0105 Tbilisi, Botankuri 32; f. 2011; non-governmental organization; Chair. Mufti JAMAL BAGSHADZE.

JUDAISM

A large part of the country's long-established Jewish population emigrated, particularly to Israel, after the collapse of the USSR. In 2009 there were an estimated 30,000 Jews in Georgia, with the largest communities in Tbilisi and Kutaisi.

The Press

PRINCIPAL NEWSPAPERS

In 2005 some 88 newspaper titles were printed. Those listed below appear in Georgian, except where otherwise stated.

Asaval-Dasavali: 0160 Tbilisi, Abladzis 39; tel. (32) 215-25-25; e-mail mail@asavali.ge; internet www.asavali.ge; weekly; Editor-in-Chief LASHA NADAREISHVILI.

Droni (The Times): 0108 Tbilisi, Kostava 14; tel. (32) 299-56-54; e-mail newspdroni@usa.net; internet www.droni.ge; 2 a week; Editor-in-Chief GIORGI CHOCHISHVILI.

Georgia Today: 0105 Tbilisi, Nato Vachnadze 9; tel. (32) 292-08-30; fax (32) 292-08-82; e-mail info@georgiatoday.ge; internet www.georgiatoday.ge; f. 2000; weekly; in English; Gen. Man. GEORGE SHARASHIDZE.

Georgian Times: 0107 Tbilisi, Kikodze 12; tel. (32) 293-44-05; fax (32) 293-49-63; e-mail editor@geotimes.ge; internet www.geotimes.ge; f. 1993; weekly, Mondays; in English, Georgian and Russian; Editors DALI BZHALAVA, NANA GAGUA.

The Messenger: 0108 Tbilisi, Belinski 43; tel. (32) 293-91-69; fax (32) 293-62-32; e-mail messenger@messenger.com.ge; internet www.messenger.com.ge; f. 1919, revived 1990 and 1993; daily; in English; Editor-in-Chief ZAZA GACHECHILADZE.

Resonance (Rezonansi): 0160 Tbilisi, Gotua 3; tel. (32) 237-79-69; fax (32) 238-79-69; e-mail resonancenewspaper@yahoo.com; internet www.resonancedaily.com; f. 1990; daily; Editor-in-Chief ZURAB MATCHARADZE; circ. 7,000.

PRINCIPAL PERIODICALS

Dila (The Morning): 0196 Tbilisi, Kostava 14; tel. (32) 293-41-30; e-mail dila1904@yahoo.com; internet www.dila.ge; f. 1904; present name adopted 1947; every two weeks; illustrated; for 5- to 12-year-olds; Editor-in-Chief DODO TSIVTSIVADZE; circ. 4,500.

Liberali: Tbilisi; internet www.liberali.ge; f. 2009; weekly; current affairs, politics; Editor-in-Chief SHORENA SHAVERDASHVILI; circ. 5,000 (2010).

Metsniereba da Tekhnologiebi (Science and Technologies): 0108 Tbilisi, Rustaveli 52, Georgian Academy of Sciences; e-mail tech@gw.acnet.ge; f. 1949; monthly; journal of the Georgian Academy of Sciences; English, Georgian and Russian; Editor VLADIMER CHAVCHANIDZE.

Sakartvelos Metsnierebata Erovnuli Akademiis Moambe/ Bulletin of Georgian National Academy of Sciences: 0108 Tbilisi, Rustaveli 52; tel. (32) 299-75-93; fax (32) 299-88-91; e-mail bulletin@science.org.ge; internet www.science.org.ge/bulletin; f. 1940; 3 a year; in Georgian and English; Editor-in-Chief THOMAS V. GAMKRELIDZE.

Tabula: Tbilisi; tel. (32) 242-03-00; fax (32) 291-61-21; e-mail info@tabula.ge; internet www.tabula.ge; f. 2010; politics and current affairs; supports administration of Pres. Saakashvili (2004–13) and free market economics; Chief Editor TAMAR CHERGOLEISHVILI.

NEWS AGENCIES

Civil.ge: 0171 Tbilisi, Dolidze 2; tel. (32) 233-25-16; e-mail civilgeorgia@una.ge; internet www.civil.ge; f. 2001; in Georgian, English and Russian; independent; Editor-in-Chief GIORGI SEPASHVILI.

Inter-Press: 0160 Tbilisi, Iosebidze 49; tel. (32) 238-78-00; fax (32) 245-07-80; e-mail interpress@ipn.ge; internet www.interpressnews.ge; f. 2000; in Georgian, Russian and English.

Prime News Agency (PNA): 0105 Tbilisi, Leselidze 28; tel. (32) 292-32-63; fax (32) 292-32-65; e-mail info@primenewsonline.com; f. 1997; news on Armenia, Azerbaijan and Georgia; Gen. Man. DEMNA CHAGELISHVILI.

Sarke Information Agency: 0102 Tbilisi, D. Agmashenebeli 54; tel. (32) 295-06-59; fax (32) 295-08-37; e-mail info@sarke.com; internet www.sarke.com; f. 1992; professional agency for economic and business news in Georgia; privately owned; Dir VALERIAN KHUKHUNASHVILI; Editor-in-Chief VICTORIA GUJELASHVILI.

JOURNALISTS' ASSOCIATIONS

Independent Association of Georgian Journalists: 0105 Tbilisi, Lermontov 10; tel. (599) 207-70-52; fax (32) 293-44-05; e-mail pochkhua@geotimes.ge; internet www.iagj.org.ge; f. 2000; Pres. ZVIAD POCHKHUA.

Journalists' Federation of Georgia: 0105 Tbilisi, Erekle II Moedani 6; tel. (32) 298-24-46; e-mail foraf@geotvr.ge.

Publishers

Ganatleba (Education): 0164 Tbilisi, Chubinashvili 50; tel. (32) 295-50-97; f. 1957; educational, literature; Dir L. KHUNDADZE.

Meridian Publishing Co (Sh. P. Kh. Gamomtsemloba 'Meridiani'): Tbilisi, A. Kazbegi 45; tel. (32) 239-15-22; fax (32) 295-56-35; e-mail info@meridianpub.com; f. 1994; academic and schools; Editor-in-Chief GIORGI GIGINEISHVILI.

Metsniereba (Sciences): 0160 Tbilisi, Gamrekeli 19; tel. and fax (32) 237-22-97; e-mail publicat@gw.acnet.ge; f. 1941; owned by Georgian Academy of Sciences; Dir DAVID KOLOTAURI; Editor CISANA KARTOZIA.

Nakaduli (Stream): 0194 Tbilisi, Pekini 28; tel. (32) 238-46-52; e-mail ngvineria@yahoo.com; f. 1938; books for children and youth.

Sakartvelo (Georgia): 0102 Tbilisi, Marjanishvili 5; tel. (32) 295-42-01; f. 1921; fmrly *Sabchota Sakartvelo* (Soviet Georgia); political, scientific and fiction; Dir JANSUL GVINJILIA.

Tbilisi State University Publishing House: 0128 Tbilisi, Chavchavadze 14; tel. (32) 225-14-32; e-mail publishing@tsu.ge; f. 1933; scientific and educational literature; Dir TAMAR EBRALIDZE.

Broadcasting and Communications

TELECOMMUNICATIONS

In 2012 there were 1.3m. fixed telephone lines and 4.7m. subscriptions to mobile telephone services in the country.

Georgian National Communications Commission (Sakartvelos Komunikatsiebis Erovnuli Komisia): 0144 Tbilisi, Ketevan Tsamebuli Ave/Bochorma 50/18; tel. (32) 292-16-67; fax (32) 292-16-25; e-mail post@gncc.ge; internet www.gncc.ge; f. 2000; Chair. KARLO KVITAISHVILI.

Geocell (Geoseli): 0160 Tbilisi, Gotua 3, POB 48; tel. (32) 277-01-77; fax (32) 277-01-01; e-mail social@geocell.ge; internet www.geocell.com.ge; f. 1996; mobile cellular communications.

Magti: 0186 Tbilisi, Politkovskaya 5; tel. (32) 217-17-17; fax (32) 217-11-71; e-mail office@magtigsm.ge; internet www.magticom.ge; f. 1997; mobile cellular communications; launched 3G mobile services July 2006; Gen. Dir LARS P. REICHELT.

Maximali: 0108 Tbilisi, Aghmashenebeli 147; tel. (32) 242-99-99; fax (32) 242-92-92; e-mail office@vtel.ge; internet www.maximali.ge; f. 2008; wireless internet service provider; covers six major cities including Tbilisi, Batumi, Rustavi and Poti, and 20 rural areas; owned by VTEL Georgia; Exec. Dir TEIMURAZ GOGOBERIDZE.

Silknet: 0112 Tbilisi, Tsinamdzgvrishvili 95; tel. (32) 210-00-00; fax (32) 210-00-01; internet www.silknet.com; fmrly United Telecommunications Co of Georgia, operating under the brand names Vaneks and Elektrosvyaz Ajarii, present name adopted March 2010; owned by Bank TuranAlem (Kazakhstan); mobile telecommunications and internet service provider; CEO LEVAN BUCHUKURI.

Telecom Georgia (Sakartvelos Telekomi): 0108 Tbilisi, Rustaveli 31; tel. (32) 244-18-00; fax (32) 244-18-29; f. 1994; provides international telecommunications services; 100% owned by Metromedia International Group Inc (USA); Gen. Dir OTAR ZUMBURIDZE.

BROADCASTING

Television

Georgian Public Broadcasting (SSM) (Sakartvelos Sazogadoebrivi Mautsqebeli): 0171 Tbilisi, Kostava 68; tel. (32) 240-93-77; e-mail info@gpb.ge; internet www.gpb.ge; f. 2005; comprises two television channels: Public TV (f. 1956) and Second Channel (f. 1971), and two radio stations: Public Radio (f. 1925) and Radio Two (f. 1995); Gen. Dir GIORGI BARATASHVILI.

Imedi TV: 0159 Tbilisi, Lubliana 5; tel. (32) 246-31-59; fax (32) 246-30-41; e-mail contact@imedi.ge; internet www.imedi.ge; f. 2001; Dir-Gen. GIORGI ARVELADZE.

Mze TV (Sun TV): 0171 Tbilisi, Kostava 75B; tel. (32) 233-55-98; e-mail reklama@mze.ge; internet www.mze.ge; f. 2003; Dir ZAZA TANANASHVILI.

Rustavi 2: 0177 Tbilisi, Vazha-Pshavela 45; tel. (32) 220-11-11; fax (32) 253-69-11; e-mail tv@rustavi2.com; internet www.rustavi2.com; f. 1994; independent; Gen. Dir GIORGI GEGESHIDZE.

Radio

Georgian Public Broadcasting (SSM): see Television.

Radio Imedi: 0159 Tbilisi, Lubliana 5; tel. (32) 292-11-88; fax (32) 292-11-99; e-mail news4@radioimedi.ge; internet www.radio-imedi.ge; f. 2001; national broadcasting, 24 hours; news; Dir IRAKLI KHETERELI.

Radio Sakartvelo (Radio Georgia): 0159 Tbilisi, Marshal Gelovani 2; tel. (32) 238-30-30; fax (32) 233-60-60; e-mail contact@fortuna.ge; internet www.fortuna.ge; f. 1999; owns and operates 4 stations, incl. Radio Fortuna and Radio Fortuna Plus; popular and classical music; Gen. Dir TAMAR CHIGOGIDZE.

Finance

(cap. = capital; res = reserves; dep. = deposits; m. = million; brs = branches; amounts in lari, unless otherwise indicated)

BANKING

Central Bank

National Bank of Georgia: 0105 Tbilisi, Leonidze 3–5; tel. (32) 240-64-06; fax (32) 244-25-77; e-mail info@nbg.gov.ge; internet www.nbg.gov.ge; f. 1991; cap. 15.0m., res 108.8m., dep. 2,750.9m. (Dec. 2009); Pres. and Chair. of Bd GIORGI KADAGIDZE.

Other Banks

In 2012 some 23 commercial banks were in operation in Georgia.

Bank of Georgia (Sakartvelos Banki): 0160 Tbilisi, Gagarin 29A; tel. (32) 244-44-44; fax (32) 244-42-47; e-mail ir@bog.ge; internet www.bankofgeorgia.ge; f. 1991; present name adopted 1994; cap. 37.0m., res 641.0m., dep. 2,814.2m. (Dec. 2012); 77.5% owned by BNY (Nominees) Ltd (United Kingdom); CEO IRAKLI GILAURI; 164 brs.

Bank Republic: 0179 Tbilisi, Gr. Abashidze 2; tel. (32) 292-55-55; fax (32) 292-55-44; e-mail info@republic.ge; internet www.republic.ge; f. 1991; 93.64% owned by Société Générale (France); cap. 76.0m., res 55.0m., dep. 490.3m. (Dec. 2012); Chair. of Bd LASHA PAPASHVILI; CEO CHRISTIAN CARMAGNOLLE.

Basisbank: 0103 Tbilisi, K. Tsamebuli 1; tel. (32) 292-29-22; fax (32) 298-65-48; e-mail info@basisbank.ge; internet www.basisbank.ge; f. 1993; cap. 9.1m., res 30.1m., dep. 121.4m. (Dec. 2012); Gen. Dir DAVID TSAAVA.

Cartu Bank: 0162 Tbilisi, Chavchavadze 39A; tel. (32) 292-55-92; fax (32) 291-22-79; e-mail info@cartubank.ge; internet www.cartubank.ge; f. 1996; cap. 93.1m., res 25.0m., dep. 67.0m. (Dec. 2012); Dir-Gen. NODAR JAVAKHISHVILI; 5 brs.

Kor Standard Bank (Standartbank): 0162 Tbilisi, Chavchavadze 43; tel. (32) 250-77-00; fax (32) 250-77-07; e-mail info@ksb.ge; internet www.ksb.ge; f. 2000 as Agro-Business Bank (ABG); name changed to Standard Bank in 2005; current name adopted after merger with Kor Bank Georgia in 2008; development bank; cap. 100m., dep. 265m., total assets 361m. (Dec. 2012); Gen. Dir GEORGE GLONTI; 61 brs.

Liberty Bank: 0162 Tbilisi, Chavchavadze 74; tel. (32) 255-55-00; fax (32) 291-22-69; e-mail info@libertybank.ge; internet www.libertybank.ge; f. 2002; fmrly People's Bank of Georgia; name changed as above after 91.2% stake acquired by Liberty Investments Holding in 2009; cap. 53.3m., res 64.2m., dep. 725.0m. (Dec. 2012); CEO LADO GURGENIDZE.

PrivatBank: 0119 Tbilisi, Tsereteli 114; tel. (32) 255-55-55; fax (32) 235-50-80; e-mail pbankgeorgia@privatbank.ge; internet www.privatbank.ge; f. 1992; present name adopted 2010; cap. 93m., res 16m., dep. 240m. (Dec. 2012); Chair. of Bd BOGDAN LESYUK.

ProCredit Bank, Georgia: 0160 Tbilisi, Kazbegi 21; tel. (32) 220-22-22; fax (32) 220-22-23; e-mail info@procreditbank.ge; internet www.procreditbank.ge; f. 1999; present name adopted 2003; owned by ProCredit Holding (Germany); cap. 80.0m., 28.3m., dep. 536.0m. (Dec. 2012); Gen. Dir SASCHA TERNES; 60 brs.

TBC Bank: 0102 Tbilisi, Marjanishvili 7; tel. (32) 227-27-27; fax (32) 277-27-74; e-mail info@tbcbank.com.ge; internet www.tbcbank.com.ge; f. 1992; owned by international financial institutions; cap. 16.5m., res 295.5m., dep. 2,939.0m. (Dec. 2012); Pres. of Bd of Dirs VAKHTANG BUTSKHRIKIDZE; 13 brs.

VTB Georgia (VneshTorgBank Georgia): 0114 Tbilisi, Chanturia 14; tel. (32) 250-55-05; fax (32) 293-32-91; e-mail info@vtb.ge; internet www.vtb.com.ge; f. 1995 as United Georgian Bank; name changed as above 2006; 96.3% owned by VTB OJSC (Russia); cap. 148.0m., res 1.0m., dep. 294.2m. (Dec. 2012); Dir-Gen. ARCHIL KONTSELIDZE; 19 brs.

STOCK EXCHANGE

Georgian Stock Exchange (Sakartvelos Saphondo Birsha): 0162 Tbilisi, Chavchavadze 74A; tel. (32) 222-07-18; fax (32) 225-18-76; e-mail info@gse.ge; internet www.gse.ge; f. 1999; Chair. of Supervisory Bd GEORGE LOLADZE; Gen. Dir VAKHTANG SVANADZE.

INSURANCE

Insurance State Supervision Service of Georgia (Sakartvelos Dazghvevis Sakhelmtsipho Zedamkhedvelobis Samsakhuri): 0164 Tbilisi, G. Chitaia 21; tel. (32) 295-64-89; fax (32) 295-71-42; e-mail isssg@inbox.ge; f. 1997; provides state regulation of insurance activity; Dir ARCHIL TSERTSVADZE.

Aldagi BCI Insurance Co (Aldagi Bisiai Sadazghvevo kompania): 0179 Tbilisi, Qazgegis 3-5, Melikishvili 10; tel. (32) 244-48-08; fax (32) 229-49-05; e-mail aldagi@aldagi.com.ge; internet www.bci.ge; formed by merger of Aldagi Insurance Co and British-Caucasian Insurance Co.

Alpha Insurance Co: 0100 Tbilisi, Vazha Phshavelas 27 B; tel. (32) 239-15-01; fax (32) 239-93-70; e-mail info@aversi.ge; f. 2009; subsidiary of Aversi Pharma; Dir PAATA KURTANIDZE.

Archimedes Global Georgia: 0177 Tbilisi, Otar Chkheidzis 10; tel. (32) 245-11-45; e-mail info@archimedes.ge; internet www.archimedes.ge; f. 2007; medical; owned by Archimedes Global (Israel); Dir TEA AKHALADZE.

GPI (Georgian Pension and Insurance) Holding Co (Jipiai Holdingi): 0171 Tbilisi, Kostava 67; tel. (32) 250-51-11; fax (32) 236-52-22; e-mail info@gpih.ge; internet www.gpih.ge; f. 2001; majority share owned by Vienna Insurance Group—VIG (Austria); merged with VIG-owned IRAO Insurance Co in 2011, retaining separate brands; Gen. Dir PAATA LOMADZE.

IC Group Insurance Co: 0162 Tbilisi, Mosashvili 24; tel. (32) 220-88-88; fax (32) 291-24-27; e-mail icgroup@icgroup.ge; internet www.icgroup.ge; f. 2005; acquired People's Insurance Co in 2009.

Unison Insurance Co: 0160 Tbilisi, Budapeshti 15; tel. (32) 299-19-91; fax (32) 295-22-40; e-mail unison@unison.ge; internet www.unison.ge; f. 2011; Gen. Dir VASIL AKHRAKHADZE.

Trade and Industry

GOVERNMENT AGENCY

National Investment Agency: Invest In Georgia: 0108 Tbilisi, Chanturia 12; tel. (32) 243-34-33; fax (32) 298-27-55; e-mail enquiry@investingeorgia.org; internet www.investingeorgia.org; f. 2002 to promote foreign direct investment; Dir KETI BOCHORISHVILI.

CHAMBERS OF COMMERCE

Georgian Chamber of Commerce and Industry (GCCI) (Sakartvelos Savachro-Samoetsvelo Palata): 0114 Tbilisi, Berdznis 29; tel. (32) 272-07-10; fax (32) 72-31-81; e-mail info@gcci.ge; internet www.gcci.ge; f. 1960; brs in Sukhumi and Batumi; Pres. KAKHA BAINDURASHVILI.

Chamber of Commerce and Industry of Ajara (Acharas Savachro-Samoetsvelo Palata): 6000 Ajara, Batumi, Melashvili 26; tel. (422) 27-28-41; fax (422) 27-28-43; e-mail acci@acci.ge; internet www.acci.ge; f. 2004; Pres. TAMAZ SHAVADZE; Exec. Dir IRAKLI SAMNIDZE.

TRADE ASSOCIATIONS

Agricultural Development Association of Georgia (ADA): 0102 Tbilisi, Doki 2; tel. (995) 958-86-28; e-mail ada@access.sanet.ge; Chair. ALEXANDER LAZASHVILI.

Association of Georgian Exporters: 0177 Tbilisi, Jikia 5; tel. (32) 224-43-02; fax (32) 224-43-03; e-mail gea@gepa.org.ge; Gen. Dir TAMAZ AGLADZE.

Georgian Employers' Association (GEA): 0177 Tbilisi, Gazapkhuli 14; tel. (32) 221-02-54; fax (32) 223-21-71; e-mail employer@employer.ge; internet www.employer.ge; f. 2000; Dir ELGUJA MELADZE.

UTILITIES

Regulatory Authorities

Georgian National Energy Regulation Committee (SEMEK) (Sakartvelos Energetikis Maregulirebeli Erovnuli Komisia): 4600 Kutaisi, Chechelashvili 26; tel. (431) 225-61-20; fax (431) 225-61-21; e-mail mail@gnerc.org; internet www.gnerc.org; f. 1997; Chair. IRINA MILORAVA.

State Agency for the Regulation of Oil and Gas Resources (SAROGR): 0177 Tbilisi, Al. Qazbegi 45; tel. and fax (32) 225-33-11; e-mail sarogr@access.sanet.ge; f. 1999; Pres. ANDRIA KOTETISHVILI.

Electricity

In February 2007 Energo-Pro (Czech Republic) completed its purchase of 62.5% of Georgia's electricity distribution market, including six hydroelectric power plants and two distribution companies.

Electricity System Commercial Operator (ESCO) (Elektroenergetikuli Sistamis Komertsiuli Operatori): 0105 Tbilisi, Tskneti, Baratashvili 2; tel. (32) 241-04-20; fax (32) 260-19-15; e-mail office@esco.ge; internet www.esco.ge; f. 2006; trades electricity and reserve capacity in order to maintain the balance of supply and demand; Gen. Dir IRINA MILORAVA.

Georgian State Electrosystem (GSE) (Sakartvelos Sakhelmtsipho Elektrosistema—SSE): 0105 Tbilisi, Baratashvilis 2; tel. (32) 251-02-02; fax (32) 298-37-04; e-mail info@gse.com.ge; internet www.gse.com.ge; f. 2002 by merger; operator of electricity transmission grid; Chair. of Managing Bd SULKHAN ZUMBURIDZE.

Gas

Georgian Oil and Gas Corpn (GOGC) (Sakartvelos Navtobisa da Gazis Korporatsia) (SNGK): 0152 Tbilisi, Kakhetis Gzatketsili 21; tel. (32) 224-40-40; fax (32) 224-40-41; e-mail public@gogc.ge; internet www.gogc.ge; f. 2006; state-owned; exclusive operator, owner, user, disposer and manager of natural and liquid gas imports and transit in Georgia; Gen. Dir DAVID TVALABEISHVILI.

KazTransGaz Tbilisi: 0194 Tbilisi, Mitskevich 18 A; tel. (32) 238-76-25; fax (32) 237-56-51; e-mail info@ktg-tbilisi.ge; internet www.tbilgazi.ge; fmrly Tbilgazi; gas distribution co for the Tbilisi region; privatized in 2006; 100% owned by KazTransGaz (Kazakhstan); Dir-Gen. GIORGI KOIAVA.

Water

Tbilisi Water Utility (Tbilisis Tskali): 0179 Tbilisi, M. Kostava 1st Alley 33; tel. (32) 248-71-10; scheduled for privatization; fmrly Tbiltskalkanali; water supply and sewerage system; Dir GIORGI GELBAKIANI.

TRADE UNION CONFEDERATION

Georgian Trade Union Confederation (GTUC) (Sakartvelos Prophesiuli Kavshirebis Gaertianeba): 0100 Tbilisi, Vazha Phshavelas 43; tel. and fax (32) 238-29-95; e-mail gtua@geo.net.ge; internet www.gtuc.ge; f. 1995; total membership approx. 259,172; in Feb. 2005 the association ceded 90% of its property to the state; Chair. IRAKLI PETRIASHVILI; 25 mem. unions.

Transport

RAILWAYS

In 2010 Georgia's rail network totalled approximately 1,566 km, of which 1,486 km were electrified. In December 2004 the construction of a railway between Kars, Turkey, and Azerbaijan via Akhalkalaki, Georgia, was agreed; the project was scheduled for completion in 2015.

In 2013 the Tbilisi Metro comprised two lines with 22 stations, totalling 26.4 km in length. A short extension was under construction.

Georgian Railways (Sakartvelos Rkinigza): 0112 Tbilisi, Tamar Mepis 15; tel. (32) 219-95-73; fax (32) 219-95-72; e-mail sag@railway.ge; internet www.railway.ge; f. 1872; Chair. and Dir-Gen. MAMUKA BAKHTADZE.

Tbilisi Metro: 0112 Tbilisi, Vagzlis Moedani 2; tel. (32) 235-77-77; fax (32) 293-41-41; e-mail info@metro.ge; internet www.ttc.com.ge; f. 1966; operated by Tbilisi Transport Co; Gen. Dir ZURAB KIKALISHVILI.

ROADS

In 2010 the total length of roads in use was an estimated 19,109 km (including 1,495 km of main roads and 5,446 km of secondary roads).

SHIPPING

There are international shipping services to and from Black Sea and Mediterranean ports. The main ports are at Batumi (in the Autonomous Republic of Ajara, q.v.) and Poti. At 31 December 2013 the Georgian flag registered fleet comprised 173 vessels, with a combined displacement of 136,324 grt.

Poti Sea Port (Photis Sazghvao Navsadguri): 4401 Samegrelo-Zemo Svaneti Mkhare, Poti, D. Agmashenebeli 52; tel. (393) 22-06-60; fax (393) 22-06-88; e-mail contact@potiseaport.com; f. 1858; commercial port; Gen. Dir JOSEPH CROWLEY.

CIVIL AVIATION

Georgia's primary airport is Tbilisi International Airport, Lochini. There are three other airports in operation, in Batumi, Kutaisi and Senaki.

Civil Aviation Authority: 0160 Tbilisi, Al. Qazbegi 12; tel. (32) 236-30-29; fax (32) 294-75-09; f. 2002; Dir GIORGI MZHAVANADZE.

Georgian Airways (Jorjian Airveisi): 0108 Tbilisi, Rustaveli 12; tel. (32) 299-97-30; fax (32) 299-96-60; e-mail info@georgian-airways.com; internet www.georgian-airways.com; f. 1993; fmrly Airzena, renamed as above in 2004; privately owned; flights to destinations in Europe and the Middle East; CEO IASE ZAUTASHVILI.

Tourism

Georgia's numerous sites of interest to tourists include the historic buildings of Tbilisi and the ancient Georgian capital of Mtskheta, the cave cities at Uplistsikhe and Vardzia, and the mountain landscapes of Svaneti and vineyards of Kazbegi. According to provisional data from the World Tourism Organization, there were 1.79m. tourist arrivals in 2012, when receipts from tourism (including passenger transport) totalled US $1,411m.

Georgian National Tourism Administration: 0105 Tbilisi, Sanapiro 4; tel. (32) 243-69-99; fax (32) 243-60-87; e-mail info@gnta.ge; internet www.gnta.ge; forms part of the Ministry of Economic and Sustainable Development; Chair. GIORGI SIGUA.

Defence

Following the dissolution of the USSR in December 1991, Georgia began to create a unified army from the various existing paramilitary and other groups. Compulsory military service lasts for 18 months. As assessed at November 2013, total armed forces numbered some 20,650: an army of 17,750, an air force of 1,300 and a National Guard of 1,600. There were also paramilitary forces of 11,700, comprising a border guard of 5,400 and 6,300 troops controlled by the Ministry of Internal Affairs. The navy was merged with the coastguard in 2009, also under the auspices of the Ministry of Internal Affairs.

In March 1994 Georgia joined the 'Partnership for Peace' programme of military co-operation of the North Atlantic Treaty Organization (NATO). In November 2004 Georgia became the first country to present an Individual Partnership Action Plan to NATO.

An Organization for Security and Co-operation in Europe (OSCE) Mission to Georgia was deployed from 1992 until 2008 to support the peace process in South Ossetia and Abkhazia. Following conflict in Georgia in August 2008 and subsequent peace agreements, the European Union Monitoring Mission in Georgia (EUMM) commenced deployment on 1 October; the EUMM comprised some 340 personnel, including 200 monitors contributed by 22 countries. Russia had announced its intention to maintain 3,800 troops each in South Ossetia and Abkhazia and to establish military bases there. At the end of August 2009, however, the Chief of the General Staff of the Russian armed forces stated that the number of Russian troops in Abkhazia and South Ossetia had been reduced to 1,700 in each. (As assessed at November 2012, there were 7,000 Russian troops within the internationally recognized boundaries of Georgia.)

Defence Expenditure: Budgeted at 711m. lari in 2014.

Chief of the General Staff: Maj.-Gen. VAKHTANG KAPANADZE.

Commander of the Land Forces: Col IVERI SUBELIANI (acting).

Commander of the Air Forces: Col GOCHA SHINGAZRDILOV.

Education

Education is compulsory for nine years, between the ages of six and 14. Primary education begins at six years of age. Secondary education, beginning at the age of 10, lasts for a maximum of seven years, comprising a compulsory cycle of five years and an optional second cycle of two years. In 2007/08 pre-primary enrolment was equivalent to 58% of children in the relevant age-group. In 2011/12 primary enrolment included 98% of the relevant age-group; the ratio for secondary enrolment was 79% of the relevant age-group in 2007/08.

In addition to state institutions, many private institutions of higher education were opened after 1991; there were 108 in 2009/10. In 2009/10 there were 102,710 students enrolled at institutions of higher education (including universities). In 2008 state expenditure on education amounted to 553.8m. lari (8.0% of total consolidated state budgetary expenditure.

GEORGIAN SECESSIONIST TERRITORIES

Two regions within the constitutional boundaries of Georgia—Abkhazia and South Ossetia—have declared independence from the Georgian state, and in practice exist separately from Georgia. In neither case has the independence of the proclaimed republics been widely recognized, with Russia being the principal supporter of the ensuing secessionist polities.

ABKHAZIA

Introductory Survey

STATUS

The self-styled 'Republic of Abkhazia', located in the north-west of Georgia, and neighbouring Russia to the north and the Black Sea to the west, declared its independence from Georgia in July 1992, precipitating military conflict. The conflict continued until 1994, following which Abkhazia enjoyed a de facto independence from Georgia, although the formal status of the territory remained unresolved, and ensuing peace talks were inconclusive. There was renewed conflict in 2008, with Russia intervening to support the Abkhazian separatists, and later that year Russia formally announced that it recognized the statehood of the 'Republic of Abkhazia'. A small number of other countries subsequently extended recognition to the separatist authorities.

LOCATION, CLIMATE, LANGUAGE, RELIGION, FLAG, CAPITAL

Abkhazia is situated in the north-west of Georgia, and covers an area of 8,665 sq km. Russia lies to the north, across the River Psou, while the remainder of Georgia lies to the east, across the River Ingur (Enguri). The south-western boundary is with the Black Sea. The climate is mild and mostly subtropical. Average temperatures in the principal city, Sukhumi, range from 7°C (44°F) in January to 23°C (73°F) in July, although the climate in the mountainous regions is substantially cooler. Precipitation averages around 1,390 mm per year in the lowlands, but in the highlands may exceed 3,000 mm. The population principally speak Abkhaz, a language of the North-western Caucasian family that is usually written in a form of the Cyrillic script, although Russian is also in general use. Although most Abkhaz outside Abkhazia are Muslims, a survey undertaken in the territory in 2003 found that a small majority of the population of the territory were adherents of Orthodox Christianity, with around one-sixth of the population adhering to Islam. The separatist authorities use a flag (proportions 1 by 2) with seven horizontal stripes, alternately green and white. A red canton contains a white hand surmounted by an arch of seven white stars. The principal city and capital of the self-proclaimed 'Republic' is Sukhumi (Sukhum, known as Aqwa in Abkhaz).

CONTEMPORARY POLITICAL HISTORY

Historical Context

Formerly a colony of the Eastern Roman or 'Byzantine' Empire, Abkhazia was an important power in the ninth and 10th centuries, but it was later dominated by Georgian, Turkish and Russian rulers. For much of the Soviet period it formed a nominally Autonomous Republic (ASSR) within the Georgian Soviet Socialist Republic (SSR). However, following the Bolshevik occupation of 1921, it was initially granted the status of an SSR, before the Soviet leader, Stalin (Iosif Dzhugashvili), absorbed it into Georgia in 1931 (which, itself, constituted part of the Transcaucasian Soviet Federative Socialist Republic until 1936). Tens of thousands of ethnic Georgians were subsequently resettled in Abkhazia. A movement for secession from Georgia was revived in 1989, by which time the predominantly Muslim Abkhaz comprised only 17.8% of the area's population, and Georgians constituted the largest ethnic group (45.7%). The Georgian Government repeatedly rejected Abkhazian secessionist demands, which were also fiercely resisted by the local Georgian population. In 1989 the total population was 537,000, of which 17.8% were Abkhazians, and 45.7% ethnic Georgians.

In August 1990 the Abkhazian Supreme Soviet voted to declare independence from Georgia. This declaration was pronounced invalid by the Georgian Supreme Soviet. Later in the month Georgian deputies in the Abkhazian legislature succeeded in reversing the declaration of independence, and inter-ethnic unrest (which had erupted in 1989) continued. Following the overthrow of Zviad Gamsakhurdia as President of Georgia in January 1992, there was renewed unrest in Abkhazia, as large numbers of ethnic Georgians demonstrated in support of Gamsakhurdia. In July the Abkhazian legislature declared the sovereignty of the 'Republic of Abkhazia'.

Domestic Political Affairs

A period of armed conflict began in August 1992, when the Georgian Government dispatched some 3,000 members of the National Guard to the republic, in order to release senior officials who had been taken hostage by supporters of Gamsakhurdia and who were being held in Abkhazia. The Chairman of the Abkhazian legislature and leader of the independence campaign, Vladislav Ardzinba, retreated north with his forces, while Russian paratroopers were dispatched to the region to protect Russian (former Soviet) military bases, amid reports that Russia was supplying military assistance to the separatists. In October separatist forces regained control of northern Abkhazia; hostilities intensified further in the first half of 1993. A provisional peace agreement was signed in July by Georgian and Abkhazian leaders. The ceasefire held until September, when, after intense fighting, Abkhazian forces recaptured Sukhumi, the republic's capital, on 30 September. Almost all Georgian forces were expelled from Abkhazia, and the Georgian Head of State, Eduard Shevardnadze, was forced to flee Sukhumi by air, under heavy bombardment, after the leader of the pro-Shevardnadze administration in Abkhazia, Zhiuli Shartava, was assassinated. Several hundred people were believed to have been killed during the fighting, and more than 200,000 people (mostly ethnic Georgians) fled Abkhazia. In December Georgian and Abkhazian officials signed an eight-point Memorandum of Understanding at UN-sponsored talks in Geneva, Switzerland. A small number of UN military personnel, part of the UN Observer Mission in Georgia (UNOMIG), were subsequently dispatched to Sukhumi in a peacekeeping capacity.

Peace talks were conducted throughout 1994, with the fundamental disagreement between the Georgian and Abkhazian delegations concerning the future status of Abkhazia: Ardzinba demanded full independence, while the Georgian Government insisted on the preservation of Georgia's territorial integrity. A full ceasefire was declared in May, in accordance with which 2,500 Commonwealth of Independent States (CIS)—mainly Russian—peacekeepers were deployed in June, joining an augmented UN observer force. Nevertheless, hostilities continued.

In November 1994 the Abkhazian legislature adopted a new Constitution, declaring the 'Republic of Abkhazia' to be a sovereign state. Ardzinba was elected as President. The Georgian Government condemned this declaration of sovereignty, and the peace negotiations were suspended. Protests were also expressed by the USA, Russia and the UN Security Council, all of which reaffirmed their recognition of Georgia's territorial integrity. Peace talks were resumed in 1995. In January 1996, at a summit meeting of CIS leaders in Moscow, Russia, it was agreed to implement Shevardnadze's request for economic sanctions to be imposed against Abkhazia until it consented to rejoin Georgia.

On 23 November 1996 elections to the secessionist Abkhazian 'legislature', the People's Assembly, were held. In March 1997 the Abkhazian faction in Parlamenti staged a hunger strike, demanding the withdrawal of the CIS peacekeeping forces from Abkhazia. However, the peacekeepers' mandate was repeatedly extended. The mandate of UNOMIG, which expired on 31 July, was subsequently granted successive six-monthly extensions. Russian proposals for a settlement of the conflict, which provided for substantial autonomy for Abkhazia within Georgia, were welcomed by Shevardnadze, but rejected by Ardzinba. In August, for the first time since 1992, Ardzinba visited Tbilisi, together with the Russian Minister of Foreign Affairs, Yevgenii Primakov, where they met Shevardnadze. In November 1997 it was agreed to establish a joint Co-ordinating Council, in which representatives of the parties to the conflict, as well as Russian, UN and European Union (EU, see p. 273) delegates, were to participate.

In May 1998 Abkhazian troops attempted to enter the neutral zone between Abkhazia and the remainder of Georgia, resulting in tens of thousands of ethnic Georgian refugees fleeing the region. Negotiations resumed in June. In January 1999 Ardzinba agreed to Georgia's principal demand for the repatriation to Gali of some 35,000 ethnic Georgians who had been forced to flee. On 3 October Ardzinba, the sole candidate, was re-elected President, in an internationally unrecognized poll. In a referendum held concurrently, 97% of the votes cast were reported to have upheld Abkhazian independence. In July 2000 a UN-sponsored protocol on stabilization measures was signed by Abkhazia and Georgia, although violent incidents continued.

In March 2001, at a summit meeting held in Yalta, Crimea, Ukraine, under UN auspices, Abkhazia and Georgia signed an accord renouncing the use of force. Hostilities resumed in October, when a UN helicopter was shot down over the Kodori Gorge, killing all nine passengers. The operations of UNOMIG were suspended, and violence in the region intensified. The Abkhazian authorities blamed Georgia for subsequent aerial attacks on villages in the Kodori Gorge. The Georgian Government, in turn, attributing responsibility for the attacks to Russia, dispatched troops to the region in October, in what the UN deemed a violation of the 1994 ceasefire agreement.

In October 2001 Parlamenti voted to request the immediate withdrawal of the CIS peacekeeping forces from Abkhazia; however, Shevardnadze argued against their removal, as no substitute force was forthcoming. UNOMIG resumed its activities in February 2002, following the extension of its mandate. At a CIS summit meeting held in March Shevardnadze and the Russian President, Vladimir Putin, agreed to amend the mandate of the CIS peacekeeping forces, to satisfy Georgian demands, among them the inclusion of forces from countries other than Russia. Abkhazian legislative elections, held on 2 March, were again deemed to be illegal by the Georgian Government. Following a protocol signed by the Georgian and Abkhazian authorities in April, the Georgian troops were withdrawn from the Kodori Gorge. In July the UN Security Council adopted Resolution 1427, which urged the resumption of negotiations on Abkhazia's status within Georgia.

In January 2003 the Georgian National Security Council ruled that the country would not approve a renewal of the CIS peacekeepers' mandate (which had recently expired) unless a number of conditions were met. In February the National Security Council finally removed all objections to the renewal of the peacekeepers' mandate, and in early March, following talks in Sochi, Russia, Shevardnadze and Russian President Vladimir Putin agreed to expedite the repatriation of displaced persons to Abkhazia, and to extend indefinitely the mandate of the CIS peacekeeping forces, until either Georgia or Abkhazia demanded their withdrawal.

The Presidency of Sergei Bagapsh, 2004–11

An internationally unrecognized presidential election took place on 3 October 2004, in which former Prime Minister of Abkhazia, Raul Khajimba, the candidate endorsed by Ardzinba and supported by Russia, was initially declared the winner. However, Khajimba's rival Sergei Bagapsh was ultimately judged to have received the most votes, by a narrow margin. Khajimba disputed this result, demanding the annulment of the ballot. An agreement was reached on 6 December, under the mediation of Russian officials, according to which the two candidates were to participate jointly in a new election. Bagapsh was to contest the presidency, with Khajimba as his Vice-President, and with the powers of the latter role to be augmented by an amendment to the separatist territory's 'constitution'. In the repeated election on 12 January 2005, Bagapsh was elected President with some 90% of the votes cast. Following his inauguration in February, Bagapsh nominated Aleksandr Ankvab, a close ally, as Prime Minister.

In October 2005 Parlamenti adopted a resolution establishing a deadline of 15 June 2006 for the Russian peacekeeping forces in the region to demonstrate compliance with their mandate. In February 2006 negotiations took place in Geneva, under the aegis of the UN, between representatives of the Georgian and Abkhazian authorities. In May the UN-sponsored Co-ordinating Council convened in Tbilisi to oversee talks between the two sides. In July Georgian forces launched an operation to disarm an armed militia group, Monadire (Hunter), in the upper Kodori Gorge, capture its leader, Emzar Kvitsiani, and 'restore constitutional order' to the region. On 27 July President Saakashvili announced that Georgian forces had, for the first time in 13 years, regained full control of the Kodori Gorge and surrounding regions; on the following day Saakashvili ordered the Abkhazian parliament-in-exile to relocate to Chkhalta, in the newly captured region, which was officially designated Upper Abkhazia. In an address at a session of the UN General Assembly in September, Saakashvili stated that Georgia would acquiesce to an agreement on the non-resumption of hostilities and the safe return of refugees only if Russian peacekeeping troops in Abkhazia were replaced by a multinational police force. In October the UN Security Council adopted a resolution that urged Georgia to refrain from 'provocative' actions in Abkhazia.

On 4 and 18 March 2007 some 108 candidates contested the (unrecognized) elections for Abkhazia's 35-member legislature. In mid-March three military helicopters made a series of aerial bombings in the Georgian-controlled Kodori Gorge. Both the Russian and separatist Abkhazian authorities denied any involvement in the attacks, although reports stated that the helicopters had entered the territory from Russian airspace. Following the announcement in July that Russia was to host the 2014 Winter Olympic Games in Sochi, near the border with Abkhazia, reports that Russian enterprises intended to import materials for the construction of sports facilities from Abkhazia (with considerable potential benefit to the local economy) prompted strong protests from Georgia. The widespread practice of granting Russian passports to residents of Abkhazia (and of South Ossetia) was a significant source of tension between Georgia and Russia from the mid-2000s, which intensified in early 2008; in March Russia announced its unilateral withdrawal from the CIS sanctions against the separatist Abkhazian regime imposed in 1996. Also in March 2008 the separatist Abkhazian authorities rejected a new proposal for a resolution of the status of the territory (granting it extensive autonomous powers within Georgia) presented by President Saakashvili.

In May 2008 Russia (which in April had announced that it was to establish closer relations with the separatist territories) dispatched 400 troops to Abkhazia, with the stated intention of repairing a railway line; Georgia formally protested against the measure. In June a bomb exploded in Sukhumi, prompting the Abkhazian authorities, which claimed that Georgian special forces had perpetrated that and other attacks with the aim of destabilizing the region, to close the border between Abkhazia and the remainder of Georgia. On 9 August, following the onset of hostilities in and around South Ossetia, the Abkhazian separatists forces commenced military action to expel Georgian troops from the Kodori Gorge. Two days later, Russia announced that some 9,000 Russian troops had been dispatched to Abkhazia; on 12 August Abkhazian forces, with Russian support, were reported to have regained control of the Kodori Gorge. Later in August a mass demonstration was staged in Abkhazia to urge Russia to recognize the region's independence. An EU-mediated peace agreement was reached on 8 September; Russia announced its intention of maintaining 3,800 troops in each of Abkhazia and South Ossetia. Following Russia's formal recognition, on 26 August, of Abkhazia and South Ossetia as independent states, on 24 September the Abkhazian People's Assembly ratified a friendship and co-operation treaty (signed by the leaders of the two separatist Republics and the Russian President on 17 September) committing Russia to military support. Bagapsh confirmed that two Russian military bases would be established in Abkhazia, and announced that the security of the border between Abkhazia and the remainder of Georgia would be strengthened. Meanwhile, on 6 September Nicaragua formally recognized the independence of both Abkhazia and South Ossetia, becoming the second state to do so. On 9 October the Council of CIS Foreign Ministers, officially confirming the suspension of Georgia's membership of the organization, also announced the suspension of the activities of the CIS peacekeeping forces in Abkhazia. Meanwhile, the Abkhazian (and South Ossetian) authorities refused an EU Monitoring Mission (EUMM) in Georgia, established under the September peace agreement, access to their territories.

In January 2009 the United Abkhazia movement, which was founded in 2004, and was closely associated with Bagapsh, was formally reconstituted as a political party. In March 2009 the Russian Government signed an agreement providing for the extension of some 2,360m. roubles in financial aid to Abkhazia. In the same month a military agreement allowing a Russian military base to remain in the territory for 49 years was signed. On 30 April Russian President Dmitrii Medvedev signed border treaties with Abkhazia (and South Ossetia), which provided for Russia to guard the state borders of Abkhazia prior to the establishment of Abkhazian border forces. Meanwhile, separatist officials had given residents a deadline of 20 March, by which time they would be required to renounce their Georgian citizenship and receive Abkhazian (or Russian) passports.

A joint statement, issued in May 2009, by the opposition Forum of National Unity of Abkhazia (FNEA) and a war veterans' union strongly criticized Bagapsh after he granted various economic concessions, including the transfer of control, for a period of 10 years, over Abkhazia's airport and railways, to Russia. In late May the authorities signed a five-year agreement giving Rosneft, the Russian state-owned oil company, the right to prospect for petroleum and natural gas off Abkhazia's Black Sea coast. At the end of the month Khajimba resigned as Vice-President, following a number of disagreements with Bagapsh (the position remained vacant until February 2010).

On 12 August 2009 Putin, as Russian premier, visited Abkhazia to reaffirm Russian support for the separatist regime, announcing that Russia would finance the reinforcement of Abkhazia's borders and further Russian military operations within the territory, in addition to providing budgetary aid. On the same day two explosions in Sukhumi and Gagra killed two people and injured three. The

Abkhazian authorities blamed Georgian security services for the blasts. At the end of the month the Russian Army's Chief of the General Staff, Gen. Nikolai Makarov, stated that troop levels had been reduced to 1,700 in both Abkhazia and South Ossetia. In September Venezuela became the third state to recognize the independence of both Abkhazia and South Ossetia. (An Abkhazian embassy opened in the Venezuelan capital, Caracas, in July 2010, and Bagapsh subsequently made an official visit to the country.)

In the (internationally unrecognized) presidential election held on 12 December 2009, contested by five candidates, Bagapsh was overwhelmingly elected to a further term of office, receiving, according to official figures, 61.2% of the votes cast; his nearest rival was Khajimba, with 15.3%. The official rate of participation was 73.5%. On 12 February 2010 Bagapsh was inaugurated to a new presidential term, and Ankvab was appointed Vice-President; one day later he was replaced as Prime Minister by Sergei Shamba, hitherto Minister of Foreign Affairs.

On 17 February 2010 Abkhazia signed an agreement with Russia allowing the construction of a land base at Gudauta, which would accommodate up to 3,000 Russian land troops for at least 49 years. In August, shortly after a visit to Abkhazia by President Medvedev, Russia announced that it had deployed anti-aircraft missiles in the territory; the EU expressed concern, stating that the deployment would be in contravention of the ceasefire agreement. On 7 September the UN General Assembly adopted a non-binding resolution (following similar resolutions in 2008 and 2009) reiterating the right of return of all displaced persons and refugees to breakaway Abkhazia and South Ossetia; in the same month Shamba stated that unless Georgia officially recognized Abkhazia's independence it would be impossible for ethnic Georgian refugees to return to the region. In a concession to demands by the Abkhaz and South Ossetian delegations in the ongoing negotiations in Geneva, President Saakashvili, addressing the European Parliament in November 2010, declared that Georgia would 'never use military force to restore its territorial integrity'; although the Presidents of Abkhazia and South Ossetia issued similar pledges, Russia welcomed the announcement without making a reciprocal affirmation.

The search for international recognition

On 29 May 2011 Bagapsh died, following a lung operation. In the ensuing election to the Abkhazian presidency, held on 26 August, Ankvab, who had been acting President since Bagapsh's death, was elected President, obtaining 54.9% of the votes cast in a poll contested by three candidates (including Shamba) and in which 71.9% of the electorate participated. On 26 September Ankvab was inaugurated as President, with Mikhail Logua serving as Vice-President. One day later Ankvab appointed Leonid Lakerbaya as Prime Minister, and a new Government was appointed during October.

Abkhazia has made only limited progress towards obtaining international recognition for the secessionist administration. In May 2011 the Pacific island state of Vanuatu announced that it had become the fifth state to recognize Abkhazian statehood (after Russia, Nicaragua, Venezuela and Nauru, while failing to extend such recognition to South Ossetia). Following the inauguration of a new Prime Minister in Vanuatu in June, recognition was rescinded, but it was reinstated in the following month. (However, in March 2013 the Vanuatu authorities announced that they had not extended formal recognition to Abkhazia, and instead announced the intention of entering into diplomatic relations with Georgia.) Tuvulu also recognized the statehood of Abkhazia in September (although in March 2014 it withdrew this recognition, instead establishing diplomatic relations with Georgia). Meanwhile, the Abkhazian authorities and Russia strongly opposed the Georgian Government's introduction in July of 'neutral' identity documents, which allowed residents of Abkhazia and South Ossetia to travel abroad without accepting Georgian citizenship.

On 22 February 2012 an assassination attempt against Ankvab was staged by unidentified assailants, who attacked the presidential convoy near Sukhumi, killing two of his bodyguards. The first round of elections to the Abkhazian secessionist legislature were held on 10 March, with a second round in 20 of the single-mandate constituencies on 24 March. It was announced by the regions's electoral commission that independent candidates nominated by civic 'initiative groups' had secured 26 of the 35 seats, while the opposition FNEA had received four seats and United Abkhazia, which supported Ankvab, three seats. (Polls were to be repeated in two constituencies at a later date, owing, respectively, to insufficient voter turnout and electoral irregularities in the first round.) The opening session of the new National Assembly took place on 3 April, when a deputy of long standing, Valerii Bganba, was elected Speaker. Meanwhile, on 16 March, Medvedev announced the creation of a new post, of Representative of the Russian President to Abkhazia (similar posts were also created later that month for South Ossetia and the Moldovan secessionist territory of Transnistria). Aleksandr Tkachev, who had been recently appointed to a fourth term as the Governor of the neighbouring Krasnodar Krai (province) of Russia, was appointed additionally to that role. By mid-April six suspects (of whom two were subsequently released) had been detained in the investigation into the assassination attempt against Ankvab. However, two of the suspects, including former Minister of Internal Affairs, Almasbei Kchach, were found dead during April, with both deaths being officially attributed to suicide.

In April 2012 the Abkhazian foreign ministry announced its withdrawal from meetings of the joint Incident Prevention and Response Mechanism (IPRM—undertaken between international security monitors and local security officials in the areas of tension since early 2009), accusing the head of the EUMM, Andrzej Tyszkiewicz, of bias and disrespect of Abkhazia's sovereignty, and demanding that he leave the region. Following postponement of IPRM meetings, the Abkhazian authorities declared that they were prepared to continue participation, on the condition that the EUMM would no longer be represented by Tyszkiewicz. In May 2012 the Russian Government announced that its security forces had discovered large caches of armaments in Abkhazia, and accused the Georgian authorities of supporting the terrorist activities of Chechen rebels. In June the Abkhazian authorities appealed to the UN, the USA and the Organization for Security and Co-operation in Europe (OSCE) to pressure the Georgian authorities to end what they termed as acts of terrorism in the border Gali district, claiming that they were responsible for the kidnapping of a number of civilians in the region. Georgia welcomed an OSCE resolution, adopted in June, which acknowledged Georgia's territorial integrity and referred to Abkhazia and South Ossetia as 'occupied territories'. Georgian Prime Minister Bidzina Ivanishvili, whose party coalition was elected to government in October, proposed the restoration of the railway link between Georgia and Russia via Abkhazia, while Ankvab indicated that he was willing to negotiate on the issue.

In late February 2013 anti-Government protests, led by Khajimba and his FNEA, and called in response to an increase in electricity costs and bread prices, were attended by around 1,500 people in Sukhumi. At further demonstrations, in early March, Khajimba demanded that Lakerbaya's administration resign. In early April Giorgi Baramia resigned as Chairman of the Government of the Autonomous Republic of Abkhazia, based in Tbilisi and recognized by the Georgian authorities. Later in the month President Saakashvili refused to confirm in post his acting successor, Vakhtang Kolbaya, on the grounds that Kolbaya, an associate of the former Chairman of the Georgian legislature, Nino Burjanadze (who had become increasingly closely linked with the ruling authorities in Russia), was purportedly connected to the 'occupying forces'. (Consequently, Kolbaya remained formally acting Chairman.) Meanwhile, the FNEA criticized the issuing of Abkhazian passports to ethnic Georgians residents in the Gali district of Eastern Abkhazia, on the grounds that the correct procedures for granting passports to non-ethnic Abkhaz were not being followed. In mid-June, a party congress of United Abkhazia announced the withdrawal of its support for President Ankvab, and that the party was, henceforth, to constitute part of the opposition. Although this decision was not without controversy (and resulted in the resignation of a proportion of the party's members), in the following month United Abkhazia was one of several political parties and groups, among them the FNEA, to form an opposition Co-ordination Council. In August Ankvab met Putin (who had returned to the Russian presidency in 2012) on two occasions, in Sochi, and in Abkhazia, in what appeared to be a demonstration of continued Russian support for his administration. On 9 September the First Secretary at the Russian Embassy in Sukhumi, Dmitrii Vishernev, was assassinated outside his home in the city; the killing was condemned by a joint statement of the members of the Abkhazian National Assembly as constituting not simply a crime, but also a determined attempt to undermine the territory's relations with Russia. It was announced that Ankvab would personally supervise the investigation into Vishernev's killing. In late September Putin appointed his close ally, Vladislav Surkov, as a presidential aide with special responsibilities for Russian socio-economic relations with Abkhazia and South Ossetia. Meanwhile, the participation of members of Russian Don Cossack organizations in commemorative parades held in Sukhumi on 30 September, to mark the 20th anniversary of Abkhazia's de facto independence, precipitated controversy, chiefly as a result of some of the imagery carried by members of these organizations, including references to the extreme Russian nationalist 'Black Hundreds' organizations of pre-Soviet Russia.

On 10 July 2013 a Co-ordination Council of opposition parties was formed in Abkhazia; notably it included the United Abkhazia party, which, until the previous month, had supported the separatist President, Ankvab. In September the First Secretary at the Russian Embassy in Sukhumi, Dmitrii Vishernev, was assassinated outside his home in the city; a statement issued by the Abkhazian National Assembly condemned the killing, describing it as an attempt to undermine the territory's relations with Russia. In November a National Assembly deputy was charged with the abduction and murder of Russian businessman Sergey Klemantovich and a female companion. In late December Logua announced his resignation as Vice-President, on the grounds of ill health. No replacement was appointed, and in early February 2014 Ankvab submitted draft constitutional legislation to the National Assembly providing for the abolition of the post of vice-president.

Recent developments: increased regional tensions

Meanwhile, under a decree issued in January 2014, the Russian Government was to provide financial aid of some 1,000m. roubles annually to Abkhazia during 2014–16. On 20 January 2014 the Russian authorities unilaterally extended their border zone with 11 km further into Abkhazia, purportedly to support increased security during the organization of the Sochi Winter Olympics in February (which were held in territories adjacent to Abkhazia), prompting strenuous protests from the new Georgian President, Giorgi Margvelashvili. Abkhazia also temporarily relaxed visa restrictions for foreign nationals seeking to enter the republic from Russia in an attempt to benefit economically from the event; however, the Georgian Government again protested that the decision constituted a violation of Georgian law and that such tourists would be liable for criminal prosecution. In the event, the intensified security measures imposed by Russia on the region, including the border zone, prior to the Games amid concerns of terrorist attacks, effectively suspended most cross-border traffic. Russia's annexation of the Crimean peninsula of Ukraine in February–March exacerbated tensions with the Georgian authorities; Ankhab declared recognition of the results of a referendum conducted in Crimea on 16 March (widely considered illegal by the international community), at which its population voted overwhelmingly in support of the territory joining Russia as a federal subject.

PUBLIC HOLIDAYS

2015: 1–2 January (New Year), 7 January (Christmas), 14 January (Azhurnyhua, Creation of the World and Renewal), 8 March (International Women's Day), 9 May (Victory Day), 23 September* (Kurbannykhua, Feast of the Sacrifice), 30 September (Liberation Day), 26 November (Constitution Day).

* This holiday is dependent on the Islamic lunar calendar and may vary by one or two days from the date given.

Directory: Abkhazia

The Government of the 'Republic of Abkhazia'

PRESIDENT AND VICE-PRESIDENT

President: ALEKSANDR ANKVAB.

Vice-President: (vacant).

CABINET OF MINISTERS

(April 2014)

Prime Minister: LEONID LAKERBAYA.

First Deputy Prime Minister: INDIRA VARDANIYA.

Deputy Prime Minister, Minister of Finance: VLADIMIR DELBA.

Deputy Prime Minister: ALEKSANDR STRANICHKIN.

Deputy Prime Minister: BESLAN ESHBA.

Minister of Defence: Gen.-Col MIRAB KISHMARIYA.

Minister of Internal Affairs: Gen.-Maj. OTAR KHETSIYA.

Minister of Foreign Affairs: VYACHESLAV CHIRIKBA.

Minister of Justice: YEKATERINA ONISHCHENKO.

Minister of the Economy: DAVID IRADYAN.

Minister of Taxes and Duties: RAUF TSIMTSBA .

Minister of Agriculture: BESLAN JOPUA.

Minister of Education: DAUR NACHKEBIYA.

Minister of Culture: BADRA GUNBA.

Minister of Health: ZURAB MARSHAN.

Minister of Labour and Social Development: OLGA KOLTUKOVA.

Note: The Chairmen of the State Customs Committee, and of the State Committees for The Management of State Property and Privatization, of Resorts and Tourism, of Youth Affairs and Sport, of Repatriation, and of Ecology and Nature are also members of the Cabinet of Ministers.

MINISTRIES

Office of the President: 384900 Sukhumi, nab. Makhajirov 32; tel. (840) 222-46-22; fax (840) 222-71-17; e-mail sukhum-krma@yandex .ru; internet www.abkhaziagov.org.

Office of the Cabinet of Ministers: 384900 Sukhumi, ul. nab. Makhajirov 32; tel. (840) 226-46-21; e-mail info@govabk.org.

Ministry of Agriculture: 384900 Sukhumi, ul. Lakoba 21; tel. (840) 226-19-05.

Ministry of Culture: 384900 Sukhumi, ul. Lakoba 21; tel. (840) 229-75-44; fax (840) 229-75-42; e-mail mc_ra@mail.ru; internet mkra .org.

Ministry of Defence: 384900 Sukhumi, Abjuiskoye shosse 57; tel. (840) 226-57-86.

Ministry of the Economy: 384900 Sukhumi, ul. Lakoba 21; tel. (840) 226-45-81.

Ministry of Education: 384900 Sukhumi, ul. Zvanba 9; tel. (840) 226-46-51; e-mail minobr-ra@yandex.ru.

Ministry of Finance: 384900 Sukhumi, ul. Lakoba 21; tel. (840) 226-30-05; e-mail minfinra@yandex.ru.

Ministry of Foreign Affairs: 384900 Sukhumi, ul. Lakoba 21; tel. (840) 226-70-69; fax (840) 226-34-45; e-mail info@mfaapsny.org; internet www.mfaapsny.org.

Ministry of Health: 384900 Sukhumi, ul. Zvanba 20; tel. and fax (840) 226-10-77; e-mail mz_apsny@rambler.ru.

Ministry of Internal Affairs: 384900 Sukhumi, ul. Akademika Marra 35; tel. (840) 229-72-73; e-mail minfinra@yandex.ru; internet mvdra.org.

Ministry of Justice: 384900 Sukhumi, ul. Lakoba 21; tel. (840) 226-67-66.

Ministry of Labour and Social Development: 384900 Sukhumi, ul. Zvanba 9; tel. and fax (840) 226-97-13; e-mail mintruda@mail.ru.

Ministry of Taxes and Duties: 384900 Sukhumi, ul. Lakoba 109; tel. (840) 226-97-03; fax (8402) 26-97-58; e-mail mns_ra@mail.ru.

THE AUTONOMOUS REPUBLIC OF ABKHAZIA

Note: A nominal officially recognized Government of the territory, listed below, and a legislature, the Supreme Council, continued to be based in Tbilisi, with additional representative offices in Kutaisi and Zugdidi, although in practice the separatist 'Republic of Abkhazia' controlled the entire territory that officially constitutes the Autonomous Republic.

Chairman of the Government: VAKHTANG KOLBAYA (acting).

Minister of Education and Culture: DIMITRI JAIANI.

Minister of Finance and the Economy: VASIL KHORAVA.

Minister of Regional Management: KONSTANTINE KUCHUKHIDZE.

Minister of Labour, Health and Social Welfare: KETEVAN BAKARADZE.

Minister of Civil Concord and Conflict Resolution: LELA GULEDANI.

Note: the Chairmen of the Departments for: Refugee Affairs; Justice; and Agriculture, Environmental Protection and Natural Resources are also members of the Government of the Autonomous Republic of Abkhazia.

Representative Office of the Government of the Autonomous Republic of Abkhazia: 0186 Tbilisi, Kazbegi 42; tel. (32) 237-61-44; fax (32) 37-46-22; e-mail info@abkhazia.gov.ge; internet www .abkhazia.gov.ge.

President

Presidential Election, 26 August 2011

Candidates	Votes	%
Aleksandr Ankvab	58,657	54.90
Sergei Shamba	22,456	21.02
Raul Khajimba	21,177	19.82
Against all candidates	2,023	1.89
Total*	106,845	100.00

* Including 2,532 invalid votes (2.37% of the total).

Legislature

The National Assembly of the 'Republic of Abkhazia'

384900 Sukhumi, ul. Zvanba 1; tel. (840) 226-65-39; e-mail mail@ parlamentra.org; internet www.parlamentra.org.

Speaker: VALERII BGANBA.

Election Commission

Central Election Commission: Sukhumi; Chair. BATAL TABAGUA.

General Election, 10 March and 24 March 2012*

Parties and blocs	Seats
Independents	27
Forum of National Unity of Abkhazia	4
United Abkhazia	3
Communist Party of Abkhazia	1
Total	35

* Including the result of repeat elections held in one constituency on 6 May, and in another constituency on 20 May and 3 June.

Political Organizations

The following are among the principal political parties to operate in Abkhazia.

Communist Party of Abkhazia: 384900 Sukhumi; f. 1921; reconstituted 1991; Pres. LEV SHAMBA.

Forum of National Unity of Abkhazia (FNEA): 384900 Sukhumi; f. 2005 as social organization, constituted as political party in 2008; mem. of opposition Co-ordination Council, established Jul. 2013; Chair. RAUL KHAJIMBA.

Party for the Economic Development of Abkhazia (Partiya ERA): 384900 Sukhumi, ul. Lakoba 34; tel. (8402) 26-04-44; e-mail info@era-abkhazia.org; internet www.era-abkhazia.org; f. 2007; economically reformist, supportive of business interests; mem. of opposition Co-ordination Council, established Jul. 2013; Chair. BESLAN BUTBA.

People's Party of Abkhazia (Kiaraz): 384900 Sukhumi, ul. Guliya 6; tel. (840) 226-19-57; fax (840) 226-17-77; internet www.kiaraz.org; f. 1992; democratic centralist; mem. of opposition Co-ordination Council, established Jul. 2013; Chair. YAKUB LAKOBA.

Republican Party of Abkhazia: 384900 Sukhumi; Chair. IVLIAN KHAINDRAVA.

Social Democratic Party of Abkhazia: 384900 Sukhumi; f. 2004; Chair. GENNADY ALAMIYA.

United Abkhazia: 384900 Sukhumi; f. 2004 as a socio-political movement, constituted as political party 2009; formerly supportive of administration of Pres. Ankvab, but joined opposition Co-ordination Council, established Jul. 2013; Chair. DAUR TARBA.

Diplomatic Representation

EMBASSY IN ABKHAZIA

At April 2014 the 'Republic of Abkhazia' was officially recognized by the four UN member states of Nauru, Nicaragua, Russia and Venezuela. Three other unrecognized secessionist territories in the post-Soviet space—Nagornyi Karabakh, South Ossetia and Transnistria—also stated their recognition of Abkhazia's statehood. By 2013 only Russia and the unrecognized 'Republic of South Ossetia' maintained embassies in Abkhazia. In practice, since March 2012, Russia's relations with Abkhazia have also been managed by a Presidential Representative to the territory, ALEKSANDR N. TKACHEV, the Governor of the neighbouring Krasnodar Krai.

Russia: 384900 Sukhumi, ul. Lakoba 103; tel. (840) 226-91-04; fax (840) 226-36-93; e-mail rusembsukhum@mail.ru; internet www.abkhazia.mid.ru; Ambassador SEMEN V. GRIGORIYEV.

The Press

In 2012, besides the newspaper *Respublika Abkhaziya* and the news agency Apsnypress, both of which were owned by the secessionist authorities, there were several private newspapers. Their circulation ranged from 1,000 to 5,000.

PRINCIPAL NEWSPAPERS

Chegemskaya Pravda (The Chegem Truth): 384900 Sukhumi, ul. Jonua 6; f. 2004; in Russian; weekly; Editor-in-Chief INAL KHASHIG; circ. 1,100 (2011).

Ekho Abkhazii (Echo of Abkhazia): 384900 Sukhumi, ul. Adigalar 34; f. 2001; weekly; in Russian; Editor VITALI SHARIA.

Novyi Den (New Day): 384900 Sukhumi; weekly; pro-opposition; Editor SERGEI ARUTINOV.

Nuzhnaya Gazeta (The Essential Newspaper): 384900 Sukhumi; tel. (940) 921-78-75; e-mail izika@mail.ru; internet www.abh-ng.ru; f. 1997; weekly; Russian; Editor-in-Chief IZIDA CHANIA; circ. 3,000 (2011).

Respublika Abkhaziya (The Republic of Abkhazia): 384900 Sukhumi; tel. (840) 226-89-89; internet www.gazeta-ra.info; owned by the authorities of the 'Republic of Abkhazia'; Russian; 3 a week; Chief Editor V. CHAMAGUA; weekly circ. 3,130 (2012).

NEWS AGENCY

Apsnypress: 384900 Sukhumi, Zvanba 9; tel. (840) 226-41-37; e-mail apsnypress@mail.ru; internet www.apsnypress.info; f. 1995; owned by the authorities of the 'Republic of Abkhazia'; Dir MANANA GURGULIA.

Finance

(cap. = capital; res = reserves; dep. = deposits; m. = million)

BANKING

Central Bank

National Bank of the 'Republic of Abkhazia': 384900 Sukhumi, ul. Leona 14; tel. (840) 229-76-23; fax (840) 229-76-22; e-mail info@a.nb-ra.org; internet www.nb-ra.org; f. 1991; cap. US $370.0m.; Chair. ILLARION ARGUN.

Trade and Industry

CHAMBER OF COMMERCE

Chamber of Commerce and Industry: Sukhumi, Konfederatov 37; tel. (840) 226-33-87; e-mail info@tppra.org; internet www.tppra.org; Pres. GENNADY GAGULIA.

SOUTH OSSETIA

Introductory Survey

STATUS

The self-styled 'Republic of South Ossetia' (formerly the 'South Ossetian Soviet Democratic Republic'), located in the north of Georgia, and neighbouring Russia (the Republic of North Osetiya—Alaniya) to the north, across the Greater Caucasus Range, declared its independence from the Georgian Soviet Socialist Republic in September 1990. In response, the Georgian authorities formally abolished the nominally autonomous status of the territory, and violent conflict broke out. This continued until 1992, following which many areas that had been included in the former South Ossetian Autonomous Oblast enjoyed a de facto independence from Georgia, although the formal status of the territory remained unresolved, and ensuing peace talks were inconclusive. There was renewed conflict in 2008, when Russia intervened to support the South Ossetian separatists, who succeeded in obtaining control of those sections of territory in the region that had remained under Georgian control. Later that year Russia formally announced that it recognized the statehood of the 'Republic of South Ossetia'. A small number of other countries subsequently extended recognition to the separatist authorities.

LOCATION, CLIMATE, LANGUAGE, RELIGION, FLAG, CAPITAL

South Ossetia is situated in the north of Georgia, and covers an area of 3,900 sq km. It borders Russia (principally the Republic of North Osetiya—Alaniya) to the north, the boundary comprising part of the Great Caucasus Range, while the remainder of Georgia lies to the west, south and east. The climate of South Ossetia is milder than that of the North Caucasus, although snowfall can occur in the highlands at any time of year. Average temperatures in Tshkhinvali range from 5°C (41°F) in January to 20°C (68°F) in July. Precipitation in southern lowland regions averages 350 mm–600 mm per year, but amounts to 1,000 mm–1,800 mm in the highlands. The population speak Ossetian, an Indo-European language of the Persian group commonly written in the Cyrillic script, while Russian and Georgian are also in use. Most Ossetians are adherents of Orthodox Christianity. The separatist authorities use a flag (proportions 1 by 2) with three equal horizontal stripes, of white, red and yellow. The principal city and capital of the self-proclaimed 'Republic' is Tshkhinvali.

CONTEMPORARY POLITICAL HISTORY

Historical Context

Ossetia (Osetiya), the original inhabitants of which are an Orthodox Christian East Iranian people, was divided into two territories under the Soviet leader (1924–54) Stalin (Iosif Dzhugashvili), with North Osetiya (later North Osetiya—Alaniya) falling under Russian jurisdiction as a nominally Autonomous Republic and South Ossetia assuming the lesser status of an Autonomous Oblast (region) within Georgia. At the census of 1979 ethnic Ossetians comprised 66% of the oblast's population. The long-standing Georgian animosity towards the Ossetians was exacerbated by the Ossetians' traditional pro-Russian stance. Tensions intensified in 1989, when Ossetian demands for greater autonomy and eventual reunification with North Osetiya (and thus integration into Russia) led to violent clashes between local Georgians and Ossetians. Troops of the Soviet Ministry of Internal Affairs were dispatched to South Ossetia in January 1990, but in September the South Ossetian Supreme Soviet (legislature) proclaimed South Ossetia's independence from Georgia (as the 'South Ossetian Soviet Democratic Republic') and its state sovereignty within the USSR. This decision was declared unconstitutional by the Georgian Supreme Soviet, which in December revoked the region's nominally autonomous status. Following renewed violence, the Georgian legislature declared a state of emergency in Tskhinvali, the principal city in South Ossetia.

Domestic Political Affairs

In January 1991 Soviet President Mikhail Gorbachev annulled both South Ossetia's declaration of independence and the Georgian Supreme Soviet's decision of December 1990. Violence continued throughout 1991, with the resulting displacement of many thousands of refugees. In December the South Ossetian Supreme Soviet declared a state of emergency and a general mobilization, in response to the Georgian Government's dispatch of troops to the region. In the same month the South Ossetian legislature adopted a second declaration of the region's independence, as well as a resolution in favour of its integration into Russia. The resolutions were endorsed at a referendum held in the region in January 1992. Hostilities continued, compounded by the intervention of Georgian government troops.

In June 1992 negotiations between Georgian leader Eduard Shevardnadze and President Boris Yeltsin of Russia led to an agreement to secure a resolution to the conflict (in which more than 400 Georgians and 1,000 Ossetians had been killed since 1989). Joint Peacekeeping Forces (JPKF), comprising Georgian, Ossetian and Russian troops, were deployed in July 1992, and the return of refugees began. An Organization for Security and Co-operation in Europe (OSCE) mission to Georgia was established in December. However, some parts of South Ossetia remained effectively a seceded territory; on 23 December 1993 the separatist authorities introduced a new 'Constitution', which referred to the 'Republic of South Ossetia'. (The region was characterized by the existence of areas controlled either by supporters of the central Government in Tbilisi, or of the separatist 'Republic', a state of affairs that continued until 2008.) In July 1995 representatives from Georgia, Russia, North Osetiya and South Ossetia reopened talks on a political settlement, under the aegis of the OSCE. Following a series of meetings between President Shevardnadze and Ludvig Chibirov, the Chairman of the South Ossetian legislature, to negotiate South Ossetia's political status, in September 1996 the separatist legislature approved an amendment to its Constitution to allow the introduction of a presidential system of government; Chibirov was elected 'President' on 10 November.

Quadripartite negotiations were held throughout 1997. Talks held in Moscow in March confirmed the principle of Georgia's territorial integrity, while allowing a measure of self-determination for South Ossetia. In September Shevardnadze and Chibirov signed an agreement on the return of refugees to South Ossetia. Legislative elections took place in the separatist-controlled regions of South Ossetia in May 1999; the local Communist Party (KP) secured about 39% of the votes cast. In April 2001 a referendum was held in South Ossetia, at which 69% of those who participated voted in favour of adopting amendments to the 1993 Constitution, including the designation of both Georgian and Russian as official languages, in addition to Ossetian.

Eduard Kokoyev (Kokoiti) elected President

In a presidential election held in November–December 2001 a Russian-based businessman, Eduard Kokoyev (Kokoiti), emerged as the victor, after a second round of voting, securing 55% of the votes cast. Kokoyev was inaugurated on 18 December. Kokoyev subsequently consolidated his power in the territory, and his Unity Party won a majority of seats in legislative elections held on 23 May 2004.

Proposals for the granting to South Ossetia of broad autonomy, presented by the Georgian Government of President Mikheil Saakashvili in 2004–05, were consistently rejected by the separatist leadership. In early 2006 the Georgian Parliament (Sakartvelos Parlamenti) adopted a resolution, urging the Government to replace Russian peacekeepers deployed in South Ossetia as part of the JPKF with an international force, following concern that Russian troops had been providing armaments to separatists. Amid rising tensions, in July Oleg Alborov, secretary of South Ossetia's 'National Security Council', was killed when a bomb exploded outside his residence in Tskhinvali. South Ossetian officials alleged that the attack had been staged at the orders of Georgia. In August South Ossetian officials began issuing Russian passports to residents of the territory, provoking outrage from Georgia; it was reported in 2007 that most of the citizens in those regions under separatist control had been issued with Russian passports.

On 12 November 2006 a presidential election was held in those areas of South Ossetia controlled by the separatist authorities. Kokoyev was overwhelmingly elected to a second term in office, reportedly attracting 98.1% of the votes cast. The poll coincided with a referendum on whether South Ossetia should preserve its de facto independent status. Results released by the 'South Ossetian Central Election Commission' indicated that 99% of those who voted had cast their ballots in favour of independence; voter turnout was reported to be 95.2% of the registered electorate. Concurrently, what was termed an 'alternative election' for a regional President was held in the Georgian-controlled South Ossetian territories; this poll was won by Dmitry Sanakoyev, a former rebel leader. A referendum held in these territories also overwhelmingly expressed approval for the commencement of negotiations with the central authorities in Tbilisi on the establishment of a federal Georgian state, of which South Ossetia would form a unit. Although these polls were not officially recognized, nationally or internationally, Sanakoyev adopted the title 'President of South Ossetia' and announced the formation of an alternative 'Government', based in the village of Kurta, in December. On 10 May 2007 Sanakoyev became head of the new Provisional Administration of South Ossetia, officially established under a resolution by Parlamenti on 8 May.

Renewed military conflict

From early 2008 peacekeeping officials reported an increasing number of ceasefire violations in South Ossetia. In July the Russian authorities acknowledged that four Russian aircraft had entered airspace over the region. The South Ossetian separatist authorities reported that six people were killed in a Georgian bombardment of Tskhinvali on 1 August, although Georgia claimed that South Ossetian forces had initiated the hostilities. Following further exchanges of fire and shelling, on 3 August the separatist South Ossetian authorities began to evacuate children to Russia.

On 7–8 August 2008 Georgian troops commenced a concerted offensive, including an aerial bombardment, against Tskhinvali; the Georgian Government announced that its troops had entered the city and had secured control of most of South Ossetia, stating that its purpose was to 'restore constitutional order'. In response, Russia deployed large numbers of troops into South Ossetia, purportedly to protect the security of Russian citizens resident there. After an intensive counter-offensive, the Russian military (supported by volunteer militias, particularly from Chechnya) rapidly claimed to have gained control of Tskhinvali and repulsed the Georgian troops; the separatists also gained control of neighbouring regions hitherto under Georgian control. Looting, retaliatory attacks against ethnic Georgians and burning of Georgian villages were subsequently reported by human rights organizations. In a statement subsequently shown to be greatly exaggerated, the Russian President, Dmitrii Medvedev, accused Georgia of perpetrating 'genocide' against the ethnic Ossetian population, and alleged that up to 2,000 people had been killed as a result of the Georgian attack on Tskhinvali. Russian aircraft commenced bombardment of Georgian targets, including the port of Poti and the military base at Senaki. On 26 August Russia recognized South Ossetia and Abkhazia as independent, sovereign states. Georgia, the USA and the European Union (EU) condemned the decision.

Following an EU-mediated peace agreement, reached on 8 September 2008, the deployment of an EU Monitoring Mission (EUMM) commenced in Georgia on 1 October (although the authorities of South Ossetia and Abkhazia refused monitors access to their territories); the Russian Government had announced that 3,800 Russian troops were to remain in each of South Ossetia and Abkhazia. On 17 September Russia signed friendship, economic and military co-operation treaties with the leaders of South Ossetia and Abkhazia. On 3 October a car bomb at a Russian military base near Tskhinvali killed nine Russian troops; Kokoyev attributed the attack to Georgian special forces. On 22 October Aslanbek Bulantsev, previously the head of the Russian Federal Security Service (FSB) directorate's financial department in Vladikavkaz, North Osetiya—Alaniya, was appointed Chairman of the Government (prime minister), replacing Yurii Morozov. A report by US-based Human Rights Watch, issued in January 2009, concluded that South Ossetian forces had perpetrated numerous abuses against ethnic Georgians in the territory, including abductions and killings. In March the Russian Government signed an agreement providing for the extension of some 2,800m.

roubles in financial aid to South Ossetia; the territory was also to receive 8,500m. roubles in post-conflict reconstruction aid. On 29 March a Georgian policeman died and six others were injured in an explosion while patrolling the borders of South Ossetia; 11 other police officers had been killed in the region since the imposition of the official ceasefire.

In April 2009 the electoral commission refused to register the opposition People's Party, led by Roland Kelekhsayev, to contest legislative elections in the following month; a few days previously it had permitted a newly established group, which the opposition claimed comprised allies of Kokoyev, to register under the same name. It also rejected the candidacy of Vyacheslav Gobozov, the Chairman of the opposition Fatherland Party. In the elections, held on 31 May, three parties, all of which were perceived as broadly supportive of Kokoyev, won seats in the legislature. Kokoyev's Unity Party received 46.3% of the votes cast and secured 17 seats; the People's Party won 22.6% of the votes cast and nine seats, while the KP obtained 22.2% of the vote and eight seats.

Following a series of reported disputes over the control of reconstruction funding, Kokoyev dismissed Bulantsev as Chairman of the Government on 3 August 2009. Vadim Brovtsev, the head of a firm producing construction materials in Chelyabinsk, Russia, was appointed to the post the following day. The anniversary of the declaration of independence—which was formally recognized only at that time by Russia and Nicaragua (although Venezuela and Nauru extended recognition later in the year)—was marked by the renewed affirmation of support from the Russian leadership. An official ceremony, staged in Tskhinvali in August, marked the inauguration of a gas pipeline, financed by the Russian state-controlled corporation, Gazprom, linking South Ossetia with North Osetiya—Alaniya, enabling the region to receive gas directly from Russia. In September Russia and South Ossetia signed a defence agreement permitting Russia to maintain military bases in the territory for a period of at least 49 years.

The publication of an independent fact-finding report in September 2009, supported by the EU, was a cause of contention in both Georgia and Russia. The report concluded that Georgia had instigated the conflict, and that its initial attack upon Tshkhinvali was not warranted by international law, while Russia's military response was described as disproportionate, and its recognition of South Ossetia and Abkhazia as independent states as in violation of international law.

In April 2010 Brovtsev attracted increasing government and media pressure, owing to allegations of official involvement by the separatist authorities in the embezzlement of Russian funds allocated for reconstruction. During the ongoing negotiations in Geneva, Switzerland, President Saakashvili, addressing the European Parliament in November, declared that Georgia would 'never use military force to restore its territorial integrity'; although the Presidents of Abkhazia and South Ossetia issued similar pledges, Russia made no reciprocal affirmation. In January 2011 Russian and South Ossetian troops conducted joint military exercises in the territory.

The 2011 and 2012 presidential elections

On 15 June 2011 the Supreme Court of South Ossetia ruled against proposals to hold a constitutional referendum, providing for the abolition of restrictions on the number of terms a president was permitted to serve, deciding that the legislature was permitted to authorize such a measure. On 5 October the South Ossetian legislature voted to remove Stanislav Kochiyev as its Chairman, in protest against his persistent opposition to the proposed constitutional changes. The presidential election, which was conducted on 13 and 27 November, appeared to have been won in the second round by the former Minister of Education, Alla Jioyeva, who defeated the Russian-supported candidate, Anatolii Bibilov, receiving around 59% of the votes cast. (Also on 13 November a referendum was held, at which 83.5% of votes cast, with a voter turnout of about 65%, were in favour of making Ossetian and Russian the territory's official languages.) On 29 November the Supreme Court upheld a challenge to the election result by Bibilov and ordered that a new poll be conducted, from which Jioyeva was to be barred from participating, owing to alleged irregularities in her campaign. Popular protests ensued and the arrest of a number of local activists was reported. Jioyeva denounced the planned repeated poll as illegitimate and announced her intention to stage her own 'inauguration' ceremony on 10 February 2012. On 9 February, however, she was hospitalized, during a raid on her offices by security forces. In the first round of the repeated election, held on 25 February and contested by four candidates, the head of the region's security service, Leonid Tibilov was placed first, with 42.5% of the votes cast, according to preliminary figures, and his nearest challenger was a special envoy for human rights issues, David Sanakoyev, with 24.6%. (Bibilov did not contest the election.) At the 'run-off' poll, held on 8 April, Tibilov was elected to the presidency, with 54.1% of the votes cast. Sanakoyev officially recognized the legitimacy of the election results, while urging that alleged incidents of irregularities be investigated. Tibilov was inaugurated as President on 19 April. On 25 April Tibilov signed a decree dismissing Brovtsev as acting premier, and appointed Rostik Khugayev, a businessman from Samara, Russia, as his successor. Tibilov announced that an investigation was to be opened into alleged widespread corruption and embezzlement (in particular, of funding supplied by Russia for post-war reconstruction) by the outgoing administration, and announced that he intended to form a 'government of national unity. At the end of May Sanakoyev was appointed as Minister of Foreign Affairs, replacing the long-standing incumbent, Murat Jioyev, who became Tibilov's special envoy for post-conflict resolution issues. Alla Jioyeva was appointed as a Deputy Chairman of the Government, while Bibilov became Minister of Civil Defence, Emergency Situations and Clean-up Operations.

Meanwhile, on 26 March 2012 Medvedev announced the creation of a new post, of Representative of the Russian President to South Ossetia (similar posts were also created in the same month for Abkhazia and the Moldovan secessionist territory of Transnistria). Taimuraz Mamsurov, the head of the neighbouring Republic (within the Russian Federation) of North Osetiya—Alaniya, was appointed additionally to that role. The Georgian authorities welcomed an OSCE resolution, adopted in June, that acknowledged Georgia's territorial integrity and referred to Abkhazia and South Ossetia as 'occupied territories'. (At that time the statehood of the 'Republic of South Ossetia' was still only recognized by five countries—Russia, Nicaragua, Venezuela, Nauru and Tuvalu—and of these Tuvalu subsequently, in March 2014, withdrew recognition.)

In August 2012 the Georgian Government condemned an official visit by President Medvedev to Tskhinvali as in contravention of the Law On Occupied Territories of Georgia, adopted in October 2008, which imposed restrictions on entry to the regions. In September 2012 an unsuccessful attempt was made to kill South Ossetia's Deputy Minister of Defence with an explosive device; later that month the South Ossetian authorities announced that their troops had arrested an official of the Georgian Ministry of Internal Affairs, following an attack on a border security post. In January 2013 Tibilov declared that the new Georgian Government headed by Bidzina Ivanishvili, which was installed in October 2012, had failed to resolve human rights issues in accordance with pre-election pledges: in particular, that the Law On Occupied Territories remained in force, and that South Ossetian citizens who had been convicted in Georgia remained in detention, despite the Georgian legislature's approval, in December 2012, of an amnesty for a large number of political prisoners. In the same month the South Ossetian Ministry of Justice registered three new political parties, among them one led by Sanakoyev, New Ossetia, and another led by Bibilov, United Ossetia.

As concerns about corruption (and, in particular, the associate failure to rehouse permanently some of those displaced by the 2008 conflict) in South Ossetia continued, the Prosecutor-General appointed by Tibilov, former Chairman of the Government Merab Chigoyev (a member of the KP) opened numerous criminal investigations into cases of corruption; by mid-2013 international arrest warrants had been requested against three former government officials. Meanwhile, Russia reduced the level of assistance funding allocated to South Ossetia, having conducted its own enquiry into the embezzlement of funding in the territory.

Tibilov met Russian President Vladimir Putin in Sochi for discussions in May 2013. A decision, implemented by the Russian military in that month, to unilaterally amend the South Ossetian administrative border with the remainder of Georgia, resulting in a slight expansion of the areas of the territory under separatist control, provoked considerable controversy, and also led to a number of arrests of Georgians deemed to have illicitly crossed the border. The subsequent construction of barbed wire fencing along the new de facto border (which resumed in early 2014) prompted further vehement protests from the Georgian Government and expressions of concern from the international community.

Recent developments: resignation of the Government

Meanwhile, controversy surrounded the future status of South Ossetia: while both Medvedev and Putin had described the recognition of South Ossetia as an independent state as irreversible, discussion continued on possible unification with North Osetiya, or on the eventual admission of South Ossetia to the Russian-led customs union. In September 2013 Putin, appointed a close ally, Vladislav Surkov, as a presidential aide with special responsibilities for Russian socio-economic relations with Abkhazia and South Ossetia. The South Ossetian authorities signed wide-ranging cooperation agreements with North Osetiya and another Russian territory in the North Caucasus, the Karachai-Cherkess Republic, in November. Under a decree issued in January 2014, the Russian Government was to provide financial aid of some 1,000m. roubles annually to South Ossetia during 2014–16. In early January Bibilov's United Ossetia requested that Tibilov schedule concurrently with forthcoming legislative elections a referendum on South Ossetia's proposed unification with North Osetiya within the Russian Federation. (Tibilov indicated that he considered organization of a referendum to be unnecessary.) On 20 January 2014 Tibilov dismissed Khugayev's Government, citing delays in post-war reconstruction, and increasing social and economic problems, and also acknowledging the previous misappropriation of Russian funds. Domenti Kulumbegov, First Deputy Chairman of the Government since June 2013, and who had also served as deputy premier under Kokoiti, was appointed acting Chairman, and the outgoing Cabinet of Ministers remained in office in an interim capacity.

Russia's annexation of the Crimea region of Ukraine in February–March 2014 exacerbated tensions with the Georgian authorities; the South Ossetian Ministry of Foreign Affairs expressed recognition of the results of a referendum conducted in Crimea on 16 March (widely considered illegal by the international community), at which its population voted overwhelmingly in support of the territory joining Russia as a federal subject. On 2 April Tibilov formally appointed Kulumbegov as Chairman of the Government, after Parliament had endorsed his nomination. Later in the month several of the incumbent ministers were formally confirmed in their existing positions, while other members of the outgoing administration further continued to remain in office in an acting capacity, pending the formation of a new Government. Meanwhile, in March Tibilov scheduled South Ossetian legislative elections for 8 June; by late April some nine parties had announced their intention of presenting candidates.

PUBLIC HOLIDAYS

2015: 1–2 January (New Year), 7 January (Christmas), 8 March (International Women's Day), 10–13 April (Easter), 1 May (Labour Day), 9 May (Victory Day), 26 August (Independence Day).

Directory: South Ossetia

The Government of the 'Republic of South Ossetia'

HEAD OF STATE

President: Leonid Tibilov (elected 8 April 2012, inaugurated 19 April).

CABINET OF MINISTERS

(April 2014)

Chairman: Domenti Kulumbegov.

Head of the Presidential Administration: Boris Chochiyev (acting).

Deputy Chairman: Alan Tekov.

Deputy Chairman: Erik Pukhayev.

Minister of Agriculture: Mairbeg Guchmazov (acting).

Minister of Foreign Affairs: David Sanakoyev (acting).

Minister of Defence: Valerii Yakhnovets.

Minister of Internal Affairs: Akhsar Lavoyev.

Minister of Civil Defence, Emergency Situations and Clean-up Operations: Anatolii Bibilov (acting).

Minister of Justice: Murat Vaneyev (acting).

Minister of Finance: Aza Khabalova.

Minister of Economic Development: Vilyam Dzagoyev.

Minister of Education and Science: Marina Chibirova.

Minister of Health and Social Development: Grigorii Kulijanov.

Minister of Culture: Makharbeg Kokoyev (acting).

Minister of Construction, Architecture, and Housing and Community Services: Eduard Dzagoyev.

MINISTRIES

Office of the Presidency and Government: 100001 Tskhinvali, Govt House, ul. Stalina 18; tel. and fax (9974) 45-25-52; e-mail ospress@mail.ru; internet presidentruo.org.

Ministry of Agriculture: 100001 Tskhinvali, ul. Khetgurova 1; tel. (1) 45-00–01; fax (44) 45–47–63.

Ministry of Construction, Architecture, and Housing and Community Services: 100001 Tskhinvali, ul. Khetgurova 1; tel. (9974) 45-00-01; fax (44) 45-47-63.

Ministry of Civil Defence, Emergency Situations and Clean-up Operations: 100001 Tskhinvali, ul. Khetgurova 1; tel. (9974) 45-00-01; fax (44) 45-47-63.

Ministry of Culture: 100001 Tskhinvali, ul. Stalina 12; tel. (9974) 45-34-81.

Ministry of Defence: 100001 Tskhinvali, ul. Khetgurova 1; tel. (9974) 45-00-01; fax (44) 45-47-63.

Ministry of Economic Development: 100001 Tskhinvali, ul. Khetgurova 1; tel. (9974) 45-00-01; fax (44) 45-47-63.

Ministry of Education and Science: 100001 Tskhinvali, ul. Khetgurova 1; tel. (9974) 45-00-01; fax (44) 45-47-63.

Ministry of Finance: 100001 Tskhinvali, ul. Stalina 18, 4th Floor; tel. (9974) 45-26-52; e-mail ospress@yandex.ru.

Ministry of Foreign Affairs: 100001 Tskhinvali, ul. Stalina 18, 4th Floor; tel. and fax (9974) 45-22-43; e-mail mfa-rso@mail.ru; internet mfa-rso.su.

Ministry of Health and Social Development: 100001 Tskhinvali, ul. Khetgurova 1; tel. (9974) 45-00-01; fax (44) 45-47-63.

Ministry of Internal Affairs: 100001 Tskhinvali, ul. Khetgurova 1; tel. (9974) 45-00-01; fax (44) 45-47-63.

Ministry of Justice: 100001 Tskhinvali, ul. Khetgurova 1; tel. (9974) 45-00-01; fax (44) 45-47-63.

President

Presidential Election, First Round, 25 March 2012, preliminary results

Candidates	%
Leonid Tibilov	42.48
David Sanakoyev	24.58
Dmitrii Medoyev	23.79
Stanislav Kochiyev	5.26
Against all candidates	0.80
Total*	100.00

* Including invalid votes (3.09% of the total).

Second Round, 8 April 2012, final results

Candidates	Votes	%
Leonid Tibilov	15,786	54.12
David Sanakoyev	12,439	42.65
Against all candidates	279	0.96
Total*	29,166	100.00

* Including 662 invalid votes (2.27% of the total).

Legislature

Parliament of the Republic of South Ossetia

100001 Tskhinvali, ul. Moskovskaya 5; internet www.parofrso.ru.

Chairman: Stanislav Kochiyev.

General Election, 31 May 2009, preliminary results

Parties and blocs	Votes	%	Seats
Unity South Ossetian Republican Political Party	21,246	46.38	17
People's Party of the Republic of South Ossetia	10,345	22.58	9
Communist Party of the Republic of South Ossetia	10,194	22.25	8
Fatherland Republican Socialist Party of South Ossetia	2,918	6.37	—
Total*	45,813	100.00	34

* Including 1,110 invalid votes (equivalent to 2.42% of the total).

Election Commission

Central Electoral Commission: Tskhinvali; internet www.cik.ruo.su; Chair. Bella Pliyeva.

Political Organizations

In mid-2014 the following political parties were among those registered in South Ossetia.

Communist Party of the Republic of South Ossetia (CP): c/o 100001 Tskhinvali, Parliament Bldg; internet kpruo.ru; f. 1993; supports the unification of South Ossetia and North Osetiya—Alaniya; Chair. Stanislav Kochiyev.

Fatherland Republican Socialist Party of South Ossetia (Fydybasta): Tshkinvali; supports the devt of an inclusive democratic state; Leader Stanislav Gobozov.

Iriston–Freedom Square (Ossetia–Freedom Square): 100001 Tshkinvali; f. 2012; Chair. ALLA JIOYEVA.

A Just Ossetia (Spravedlivaya Osetiya/Raestag Ir): 100001 Tskhinvali; f. 2009; Chair. KOSTA KOSHTE.

New Ossetia (Novaya Osetiya/Nauag Iryston): Tskhinvali; f. 2012; Chair. DAVID SANAKOYEV.

People's Party of the Republic of South Ossetia: 100001 Tskhinvali, ul. Geroev 3; e-mail npruo@km.ru; internet www.npruo.ru; supports an independent, democratic and socially liberal South Ossetia; Chair. KAZIMIR PLIYEV.

United Ossetia (Yedinaya Osetiya): Tskhinvali; f. 2012; supports continued self-determination of South Ossetia, whether as an independent state, in union with North Osetiya—Alaniya as part of the Russian Federation, as a member state of a proposed Eurasian Union, or in some other manner; Chair. ANATOLII BIBILOV.

Unity South Ossetian Republican Political Party: c/o 100001 Tskhinvali, Parliamentary Bldg; f. 2003; supports a strong state with an executive presidency, and the integration of South Ossetia with North Osetiya—Alaniya and a strengthening of links with the Russian Federation; Chair. ZURAB KOKOYEV.

Diplomatic Representation

EMBASSY IN SOUTH OSSETIA

At April 2014 the 'Republic of South Ossetia' was officially recognized by the four UN member states of Nauru, Nicaragua, Russia and Venezuela. Three other unrecognized secessionist territories in the post-Soviet space—Abkhazia, Nagornyi Karabakh and Transnistria—also stated their recognition of South Ossetia's statehood. By 2013 only Russia maintained an embassy in South Ossetia. In practice, since March 2012, Russia's relations with South Ossetia have also been managed by a Presidential Representative to the territory, TAIMURAZ D. MAMSUROV, the head of the neighbouring Republic of North Osetiya—Alaniya.

Russia: 100001 Tskhinvali, ul. Ostrovskogo 17; tel. (997) 4453960; fax (997) 4456863; e-mail rusembrso@yandex.ru; Ambassador ELBRUS K. KARGIYEV.

The Press

SELECTED PUBLICATIONS

XXI vek (The 21st Century): Tskhinvali; published sporadically; Editor TIMUR TSKHOVREBOV.

Khurzaerin (Sunrise): Tskhinvali; e-mail mail@xurzarin.ru; internet www.xurzarin.ru; f. 1924; fmrly *Soveton Iryston (Soviet Ossetia)*; 5 a week; social, political and economic affairs; in Ossetian; circ. 1,700 (2012).

Yuzhnaya Osetiya (South Ossetia): 383570 Tskhinvali, ul. Moskovskaya 7; tel. (9974) 45-26-42; e-mail southosetiya@yandex.ru; internet www.ugo-osetia.ru; f. 1983; owned by the Government and parliament of the 'Republic of South Ossetia'; in Russian; social and political affairs; publishes official documents of the 'Republic of South Ossetia'; 3 a week; Editor LUDVIG CHIBIROV.

NEWS AGENCIES

OSinform Information Agency (OSinform Informatsionnoye Agentstvo): Tskhinvali; tel. (929) 808-00-11; e-mail info@osinform.ru; internet www.osinform.ru; f. 2006; Dir LIRA TSKHOVREBOVA.

RES—Republic Information Agency (Informatsionnoye agenstvo 'RES'): 100001 Tskhinvali, ul. Stalina 16; tel. and fax (9997) 45-50-52; internet www.cominf.org; f. 1992; subsidiary of the State Committee of the 'Republic of South Ossetia' for Information, Communications and Mass Media; Dir ALLA JIOYEVA.

Finance

BANKING

Central Bank

National Bank of South Ossetia: Tskhinvali, ul. Stalina 20; tel. (34) 45-24-33; Chair. FELIX ZASSEYEV.

Trade and Industry

CHAMBER OF COMMERCE

Chamber of Commerce and Industry of the 'Republic of South Ossetia' (CCIRSO): 100001 Tskhinvali, ul. Kommunarov 124; tel. (9744) 45-18-59; e-mail tppuo@yandex.ru; internet www.cciirso.com; f. 2002; Chair. ROIN KOZAYEV.

GERMANY

Introductory Survey

LOCATION, CLIMATE, LANGUAGE, RELIGION, FLAG, CAPITAL

The Federal Republic of Germany, which was formally established in October 1990 upon the unification of the Federal Republic of Germany (FRG, West Germany) and the German Democratic Republic (GDR, East Germany), lies in the heart of Europe. It is bordered by nine countries: Denmark to the north, the Netherlands, Belgium, Luxembourg and France to the west, Switzerland and Austria to the south, and the Czech Republic and Poland to the east. The climate is temperate, with an annual average temperature of 9°C (48°F), although there are considerable variations between the North German lowlands and the Bavarian Alps. The language is German. There is a small Sorbian-speaking minority (numbering about 100,000 people). About 31% of the population are Roman Catholics and a further 31% are members of the Evangelical Lutheran (Protestant) church. The national flag (proportions 3 by 5) consists of three equal horizontal stripes, of black, red and gold. The capital is Berlin.

CONTEMPORARY POLITICAL HISTORY

Historical Context

Following the defeat of the Nazi regime and the ending of the Second World War in 1945, Germany was divided, according to the Berlin Agreement, into US, Soviet, British and French occupation zones. Berlin was similarly divided. The former German territories east of the Oder and Neisse rivers, with the city of Danzig (now Gdańsk), became part of Poland, while the northern part of East Prussia, around Königsberg (now Kaliningrad), was transferred to the USSR. After the failure of negotiations to establish a unified German administration, the US, French and British zones were integrated economically in 1948. In May 1949 a provisional Constitution, the Basic Law (Grundgesetz), came into effect in the three zones (except in Saarland), and federal elections were held in August. On 21 September 1949 a new German state, the Federal Republic of Germany (FRG), was established in the three western zones. The FRG was governed from Bonn in North Rhine-Westphalia (Nordrhein-Westfalen). (Saarland was not incorporated into the FRG until 1957.) In October 1949 Soviet-occupied Eastern Germany declared itself the German Democratic Republic (GDR), with the Soviet zone of Berlin as its capital. This left the remainder of Berlin (West Berlin) as an effective enclave of the FRG within the territory of the GDR, although it remained formally under British, French and US occupation.

The FRG and the GDR developed divergent political and economic systems. The leaders of the GDR created a socialist state, based on the Soviet model. As early as 1945 large agricultural estates in eastern Germany were nationalized, followed in 1946 by major industrial concerns. Exclusive political control was exercised by the Sozialistische Einheitspartei Deutschlands (SED, Socialist Unity Party of Germany), which had been formed in April 1946 by the merger of the Communist Party of Germany and the branch of the Sozialdemokratische Partei Deutschlands (SPD, Social Democratic Party of Germany) in the Soviet zone. Other political parties in eastern Germany were under the strict control of the SED; no independent political activity was permitted.

The transfer, as war reparations, of foodstuffs, livestock and industrial equipment to the USSR from eastern Germany had a devastating effect on the area's economy in the immediate post-war period. In June 1953 increasing political repression and severe food shortages led to uprisings and strikes, which were suppressed by Soviet troops. The continued failure of the GDR to match the remarkable economic recovery of the FRG prompted a growing number of refugees to cross from the GDR to the FRG (between 1949 and 1961 an estimated 2.5m. GDR citizens moved permanently to the FRG). Emigration was accelerated by the enforced collectivization of many farms in 1960, and in August 1961 the GDR authorities hastily constructed a guarded wall between East and West Berlin (the Berlin Wall).

Domestic Political Affairs

In May 1971 Walter Ulbricht was succeeded as First Secretary (later restyled General Secretary) of the SED by Erich Honecker. Ulbricht remained Chairman of the Council of State (Head of State), a post that he had held since 1960, until his death in August 1973. He was succeeded in this office by Willi Stoph, but in October 1976 Stoph returned to his previous post as Chairman of the Council of Ministers, and Honecker became Chairman of the Council of State. Under Honecker, despite some liberalization of relations with the FRG, there was little relaxation of repressive domestic policies. Honecker strongly opposed the political and economic reforms that began in the USSR and some other Eastern European countries in the mid-1980s.

The 1949 elections in the FRG resulted in victory for the conservative Christlich-Demokratische Union Deutschlands (CDU, Christian Democratic Union of Germany), together with its sister party in Bavaria, the Christlich-Soziale Union (CSU, Christian Social Union). The SPD was the largest opposition party. Dr Konrad Adenauer, the leader of the CDU, was elected Federal Chancellor by the Bundestag (Federal Assembly); Theodor Heuss became the first President of the Republic, the constitutional head of state (a largely ceremonial position). Under Adenauer's chancellorship (which lasted until 1963) and the direction of Dr Ludwig Erhard, his Minister of Economics (and successor as Chancellor), the FRG rebuilt itself rapidly to become one of the most affluent and economically dynamic states in Europe, as well as an important strategic ally of other Western European states and the USA. The Paris Agreement of 1954 gave full sovereign status to the FRG from 5 May 1955, and also granted it membership of the North Atlantic Treaty Organization (NATO, see p. 370).

The CDU/CSU held power in coalition with the SPD from 1966 to 1969, under the chancellorship of Dr Kurt Kiesinger, but lost support at the 1969 general election. The SPD formed a coalition Government with the Freie Demokratische Partei (FDP, Free Democratic Party), under the chancellorship of Willy Brandt, the SPD leader. Following elections in November 1972, the SPD became, for the first time, the largest party in the Bundestag. In May 1974, however, Brandt resigned as Chancellor after the discovery that his personal assistant had been a clandestine agent of the GDR. He was succeeded by Helmut Schmidt, also of the SPD. The SPD-FDP coalition retained a majority in the Bundestag at the elections of 1976 and 1980. In September 1982 the coalition collapsed when the two parties failed to agree on budgetary measures. In October the FDP formed a Government with the CDU/CSU, under the chancellorship of the CDU leader, Dr Helmut Kohl. This new partnership was consolidated by the results of the general election of March 1983, when the CDU/CSU substantially increased its share of the vote. The CDU/CSU-FDP coalition retained office after the general election of January 1987.

During 1949–69 the FRG, under the CDU/CSU, remained largely isolated from Eastern Europe, owing to the FRG Government's refusal to recognize the GDR as an independent state or to maintain diplomatic relations with any other states that recognized the GDR. When Brandt became Chancellor in 1969, he adopted a more conciliatory approach to relations with Eastern Europe and, in particular, towards the GDR, a policy which came to be known as Ostpolitik. In 1970 formal discussions were conducted between representatives of the GDR and the FRG for the first time, and there was a significant increase in diplomatic contacts between the FRG and the other countries of Eastern Europe. In 1970 treaties were signed with the USSR and Poland, in which the FRG formally renounced claims to the eastern territories of the Third Reich and recognized the 'Oder–Neisse line' as the border between Germany (actually the GDR) and Poland. Further negotiations between the GDR and the FRG, following a quadripartite agreement on West Berlin in September 1971, clarified access rights to West Berlin and also allowed West Berliners to visit the GDR. In December 1972 the two German states signed a Basic Treaty, agreeing to develop normal, neighbourly relations with each other, to settle all differences without resort to force, and to respect each other's independence. The treaty permitted both the FRG and the GDR to join the UN in September 1973, and allowed many western countries to establish diplomatic relations with the GDR, although both German states continued to deny each other formal diplomatic recognition.

In December 1981 the first official meeting for 11 years took place between the two countries' leaders, when Chancellor Schmidt travelled to the GDR for discussions with Honecker. Inter-German relations deteriorated following the deployment, in late 1983, of US nuclear missiles in the FRG, and the subsequent siting of additional Soviet missiles in the GDR. Nevertheless, official contacts were maintained, and Honecker made his first visit to the FRG in September 1987.

The fall of the Berlin Wall

Relations between the two German states were dramatically affected by political upheavals that occurred in the GDR in late 1989 and 1990. In the latter half of 1989 many thousands of disaffected GDR citizens emigrated illegally to the FRG, via Czechoslovakia, Poland and Hungary. The exodus was accelerated by the Hungarian Government's decision, in September 1989, to permit citizens of the GDR to leave Hungary without exit visas. Meanwhile, there was a growth in popular dissent within the GDR, led by Neues Forum (New Forum), an independent citizens' action group which had been established to encourage discussion of democratic reforms, justice and environmental issues.

In early October 1989, following official celebrations to commemorate the 40th anniversary of the foundation of the GDR, anti-Government demonstrations erupted in East Berlin and other large towns. In mid-October, as the political situation became more unsettled, Honecker resigned as General Secretary of the SED, Chairman of the Council of State and Chairman of the National Defence Council, citing reasons of ill health. He was replaced in all these posts by Egon Krenz, a senior member of the SED Politburo. Krenz immediately initiated a dialogue with Neues Forum (which was legalized in November) and with church leaders. There was also a liberalization of the media, and an amnesty was announced for all persons who had been detained during the recent demonstrations and for those imprisoned for attempting to leave the country illegally. However, large demonstrations, to demand further reforms, continued in many towns throughout the GDR.

On 7 November 1989, in a further attempt to placate the demonstrators, the entire membership of the GDR Council of Ministers resigned. On the following day the SED Politburo also resigned and was replaced. On 9 November restrictions on foreign travel for GDR citizens were ended, and all border crossings to the FRG were opened. During the weekend of 10–11 November an estimated 2m. GDR citizens crossed into West Berlin, and the GDR authorities began to dismantle sections of the Berlin Wall. Dr Hans Modrow, a leading member of the SED who was regarded as an advocate of greater reforms, was appointed Chairman of a new Council of Ministers. The new Government pledged to introduce comprehensive political and economic reforms and to hold free elections in 1990.

In early December 1989 the Volkskammer (the GDR's legislature) voted to remove provisions in the Constitution that protected the SED's status as the single ruling party. However, the mass demonstrations continued, prompted by revelations of corruption and personal enrichment by the former leadership and of abuses of power by the State Security Service (Staatssicherheitsdienst, known colloquially as the Stasi, which was subsequently disbanded). A special commission was established to investigate such charges, and former senior officials, including Honecker and Stoph, were expelled from the SED and placed under house arrest, pending legal proceedings. As the political situation became increasingly unstable, the SED Politburo and Central Committee, including Krenz, resigned, and both bodies, together with the post of General Secretary, were abolished. Shortly afterwards, Krenz also resigned as Chairman of the Council of State; he was replaced by Dr Manfred Gerlach, the Chairman of the Liberal-Demokratische Partei Deutschlands (LDPD, Liberal Democratic Party of Germany). Dr Gregor Gysi, a prominent defence lawyer who was sympathetic to the opposition, was elected to the new post of Chairman of the SED (restyled the Partei des Demokratischen Sozialismus—PDS, Party of Democratic Socialism, in February 1990).

In December 1989 and January 1990 all-party talks took place in the GDR, resulting in the formation, in February, of a new administration, designated the Government of National Responsibility (still led by Modrow), to remain in office until elections were held. The GDR's first free legislative elections took place on 18 March 1990, with the participation of 93% of those eligible to vote. The East German CDU obtained 40.8% of the total votes cast, while the newly re-established East German SPD and the PDS secured 21.8% and 16.4%, respectively. In April a coalition Government was formed, headed by Lothar de Maizière, leader of the Eastern CDU. Five parties were represented in the new Government: the CDU, the SPD, the Liga der Freien Demokraten (League of Free Democrats) and two smaller parties. The PDS was not invited to join the coalition.

The reunification of Germany

As a result of the changes within the GDR and the subsequent free contact between Germans of east and west, the reunification of the two German states became a realistic possibility. In November 1989 Chancellor Kohl proposed a plan for the eventual unification of the two countries by means of an interim confederal arrangement. In December Kohl made his first visit to the GDR, where he held discussions with the East German leadership. The two sides agreed to develop contacts at all levels and to establish joint economic, cultural and environmental commissions. The GDR Government initially insisted that the GDR remain a sovereign, independent state. However, in February 1990, in response to growing popular support among GDR citizens for unification, Modrow publicly advocated the establishment of a united Germany. Shortly afterwards, Kohl and Modrow met in Bonn, where they agreed to establish a joint commission to achieve full economic and monetary union between the GDR and the FRG. The new coalition Government of the GDR, formed in April, pledged its determination to achieve German unification in the near future. In May the legislatures of the GDR and the FRG approved the Treaty Between the FRG and the GDR Establishing a Monetary, Economic and Social Union, which came into effect on 1 July. Later in July the Volkskammer approved the re-establishment on GDR territory of the five Länder (states)—Brandenburg, Mecklenburg-Western Pomerania (Mecklenburg-Vorpommern), Saxony (Sachsen), Saxony-Anhalt (Sachsen-Anhalt) and Thuringia (Thüringen)—which had been abolished by the GDR Government in 1952. On 31 August 1990 the Treaty Between the FRG and the GDR on the Establishment of German Unity was signed in East Berlin by representatives of the two Governments. The treaty stipulated, *inter alia*, that the newly restored Länder would accede to the FRG on 3 October 1990, and that the 23 boroughs of East and West Berlin would jointly form the Land (state) of Berlin.

Owing to the complex international status of the FRG and the GDR and the two countries' membership of opposing military alliances (respectively, NATO and the Warsaw Pact), the process of German unification also included negotiations with other countries. In February 1990 representatives of 23 NATO and Warsaw Pact countries agreed to establish the so-called 'two-plus-four' talks (the FRG and the GDR, plus the four countries that had occupied Germany after the Second World War—France, the USSR, the United Kingdom and the USA) to discuss the external aspects of German unification. In June both German legislatures approved a resolution recognizing the inviolability of Poland's post-1945 borders, stressing that the eastern border of a future united Germany would remain along the Oder–Neisse line. In July, at bilateral talks in the USSR with Chancellor Kohl, the Soviet leader, Mikhail Gorbachev, agreed that a united Germany would be free to join whichever military alliance it wished, thus permitting Germany to remain a full member of NATO. The USSR also pledged to withdraw its armed forces (estimated at 370,000 in 1990) from GDR territory within four years, and it was agreed that a united Germany would reduce the strength of its armed forces to 370,000 within the same period. This agreement ensured a successful result to the 'two-plus-four' talks, which were concluded in September in the Soviet capital, Moscow, where the Treaty on the Final Settlement with Respect to Germany was signed. In late September the GDR withdrew from the Warsaw Pact.

On 1 October 1990 representatives of the four countries that had occupied Germany after the Second World War met in New York, USA, to sign a document in which Germany's full sovereignty was recognized. Finally, on 3 October, the two German states were formally unified. On the following day, at a session of the Bundestag (which had been expanded to permit the representation of former deputies of the GDR Volkskammer), five prominent politicians from the former GDR were sworn in as Ministers without Portfolio in the Federal Government. The

Federal President, Richard von Weizsäcker, became the first President of the reunified nation.

Prior to unification, the CDU, the SPD and the FDP of the GDR had merged with their respective counterparts in the FRG to form three single parties. At state elections in the newly acceded Länder, held in mid-October 1990, the CDU won control of four Land legislatures, while the SPD gained a majority only in Brandenburg. This surge of support for Chancellor Kohl and the CDU was confirmed by the results of elections to the Bundestag in early December (the first all-German elections since 1933), at which the CDU and CSU secured a total of 319 seats in the 662-member Bundestag. Kohl was formally re-elected to the post of Federal Chancellor in January 1991, immediately after the formation of the new Federal Government. This comprised 20 members, but included only three politicians from the former GDR. The FDP's representation was increased from four to five ministers, reflecting the party's increased representation in the legislature. In June 1991 the Bundestag voted in favour of Berlin as the future seat of the legislature and of government; the transfer of most organs of government from Bonn to Berlin took place in 1999.

Events following reunification: 1991–98

One of the most serious problems confronting the Government following unification was that of escalating unemployment in eastern Germany, as a result of the introduction of market-orientated reforms intended to integrate the economic system of the former GDR with that of the rest of the country. A substantial increase in the crime rate in eastern Germany was also recorded. A further disturbing issue, particularly in the eastern Länder, was the resurgence of extreme right-wing and neo-Nazi groups. Moreover, there were also fears of a resurgence of political violence, following a series of terrorist acts culminating in the assassination, in April 1991, of Detlev Rohwedder, the executive head of the Treuhandanstalt (the trustee agency that had been established in March 1990 to supervise the privatization of state-owned enterprises in the former GDR). Responsibility for this and other attacks was claimed by the Rote Armee Fraktion (Red Army Faction), an extreme left-wing terrorist organization that had been active in the FRG during the 1970s. (The Red Army Faction eventually disbanded in 1998.)

Investigations into the abuse of power by the former GDR administration, conducted during the early 1990s, prompted the dismissal or resignation from government posts of several former SED politicians. In January 1991 the authorities temporarily suspended efforts to arrest Honecker on charges of manslaughter (for complicity in the deaths of people who had been killed while attempting to escape from the GDR), owing to the severe ill health of the former GDR leader. In March it was announced that Honecker had been transferred, without the permission of the German authorities, to the USSR, and in December he took refuge in the Chilean embassy in Moscow. In January 1992 some 2m. Stasi files were opened to public scrutiny. In February Erich Mielke, the former head of the Stasi, was brought to trial on charges of murder, and in September Markus Wolf, the former head of East Germany's intelligence service, was charged with espionage, treason and corruption; both were subsequently found guilty and each was sentenced to six years' imprisonment. Meanwhile, Honecker returned to Germany from Russia in July 1992. He was brought to trial in November, together with five other defendants (among them Mielke and Stoph), on charges of manslaughter and embezzlement. In April 1993, however, the charges against Honecker were suspended. (The former East German leader, who was terminally ill, had been allowed to leave for Chile in January of that year; he died in May 1994.) Stoph was also released on grounds of ill health.

In May 1994 Roman Herzog, the candidate of the CDU (previously the President of the Federal Constitutional Court) was elected Federal President by the Bundesversammlung (Federal Convention, a body comprising the members of the Bundestag and delegates chosen by the regional legislatures); he took office in July. The CDU/CSU-FDP coalition was re-elected at a general election held in October; its majority in the Bundestag was, however, sharply reduced, from 134 to 10 seats. In November the ruling coalition negotiated a new political programme, which prioritized the creation of jobs. Shortly afterwards Kohl was formally re-elected as the Federal Chancellor.

In May 1995 the Federal Constitutional Court ruled that alleged former East German spies should not be prosecuted by federal courts regarding crimes that were committed against the Federal Republic on behalf of the former GDR prior to unification; consequently, in October the 1992 conviction of Markus Wolf was overturned. In November 1996 the Constitutional Court ruled that the legal principles of the FRG regarding human rights could be retroactively applied to actions carried out within the former GDR. Thus, in May 1997 Wolf was convicted on charges of abduction, coercion and assault, receiving a suspended sentence of two years' imprisonment. In August Egon Krenz and two other former senior SED members, Günther Schabowski and Günther Kleiber, were found guilty of the manslaughter and attempted manslaughter of people who had sought to flee the former GDR; all three were sentenced to terms of imprisonment. (Schabowski and Kleiber were pardoned in September 2000.)

The activities of extreme right-wing organizations increased significantly in 1997, and during the latter half of the year a series of incidents was reported that suggested the infiltration of some sections of the armed forces by neo-Nazi interests. In April 1998 the extreme right-wing and openly xenophobic Deutsche Volksunion (DVU, German People's Union) won unprecedented support at an election to the Land parliament for the economically depressed region of Saxony-Anhalt in eastern Germany, securing 12.9% of the votes cast.

Tensions within the CDU/CSU-FDP coalition became apparent in 1997, mainly concerning the desirability and means of meeting the 'convergence criteria' for participation in European Economic and Monetary Union (EMU) by 1999. Record levels of unemployment continued to cause concern, as well as an unexpectedly large deficit on the 1997 budget. In April 1998, despite evidence of widespread opposition to the new single European currency, the Bundestag voted in favour of Germany's participation in EMU.

The SPD-led coalition: 1998–2005

At the general election held in September 1998 the CDU/CSU-FDP coalition was decisively defeated by the SPD, which won 298 of the 669 seats in the Bundestag. Following the election, Kohl resigned as Chairman of the CDU; he was replaced by the party's parliamentary leader, Dr Wolfgang Schäuble. Meanwhile, the SPD and Bündnis 90/Die Grünen (Alliance 90/The Greens, which held 47 seats) negotiated a coalition pact. In October Gerhard Schröder of the SPD, formerly the Minister-President of Lower Saxony (Niedersachsen), was elected Federal Chancellor by a large majority of Bundestag members. The new Federal Government included three ministers representing Bündnis 90/Die Grünen, the most prominent of whom was the new Federal Vice-Chancellor and Minister of Foreign Affairs, Joschka Fischer. Oskar Lafontaine, the Chairman of the SPD, was appointed Minister of Finance.

Lafontaine resigned in March 1999, apparently in protest at an evident lack of support for his economic policies and management from within both the business community and the Government; he also vacated his seat in the Bundestag and the chairmanship of the SPD. Hans Eichel of the SPD was appointed as the new Minister of Finance. In the following month Schröder was elected to the post of Chairman of the SPD. In May Johannes Rau, the candidate of the SPD (hitherto Minister-President of North Rhine-Westphalia) was elected Federal President, taking office in July.

During November 1999 the opposition CDU became embroiled in a scandal concerning the discovery of a system of secret bank accounts, which had been used to deposit undisclosed donations to the party throughout the 1990s. (In accordance with the Basic Law, all substantial funding of political parties must be declared.) Allegations subsequently emerged that the CDU leadership had covertly accepted a large bribe from the then state-owned French oil company Elf Aquitaine, in connection with its purchase in 1992 of an eastern German oil refinery. It was also alleged that, in 1998, the CDU had granted an export licence to an arms exporting interest in return for an undeclared party donation. The former Chancellor, Kohl, admitted knowledge of some secret party funding, but repeatedly refused to name any sources; in January 2000 Kohl was forced to resign from his honorary chairmanship of the CDU after he became the subject of a criminal investigation. In that month Schäuble established an independent inquiry into the funding scandal, which subsequently revealed that irregularities had persisted for decades in German politics. In February Schäuble resigned as Chairman of the CDU, accepting responsibility for mishandling the funding scandal.

The CDU's Secretary-General, Angela Merkel, was elected Chairman at the party congress in April 2000. Merkel, who had secured significant support as a result of her determination to expose the CDU's financial irregularities, was considered more liberal than her predecessors. In May the state prosecutor concluded that there were sufficient grounds for the criminal prosecution of Kohl on charges of fraud and bribery (although, as an incumbent member of the legislature, Kohl was immune from prosecution). In his testimony in June to the parliamentary committee Kohl admitted accepting illegal secret contributions to party funds, but denied allegations that such donations had influenced government policy decisions. In February 2001 Kohl accepted the proposal of the state prosecutor that he should pay a fine of DM 300,000 in exchange for the abandonment of the criminal investigation into his acceptance of illegal contributions; this arrangement subsequently gained judicial approval. The parliamentary inquiry continued, however, as did Kohl's refusal to name the illegal contributors to his party.

In December 1999 the Government agreed to pay a substantial sum in compensation to people who had worked as forced labourers for German companies or been deprived of their assets under the Nazi regime; it was hoped that this would forestall a growing number of lawsuits taken out against German industrial interests and banks by survivors of the Holocaust. Chancellor Schröder announced that the Government would provide one-half of the proposed DM 10,000m. fund; the remainder was to be raised by Germany's largest banks and companies. The compensation agreement was signed in July 2000, and, following the resolution of legal difficulties, payments began in May 2001.

In June 2000, following negotiations between the Government and the nuclear industry, Schröder announced that an agreement had been concluded to decommission the country's 19 nuclear power plants (which accounted for almost one-third of power requirements) without compensation by 2021. Although a significant number of members of Bündnis 90/Die Grünen had favoured an immediate cessation of nuclear power generation, in September 2001 the Federal Government adopted a bill regulating the phasing out of nuclear power, which was subsequently approved by the Bundestag.

In August 2000, in response to growing fears concerning the escalation of neo-Nazi violence against immigrants, the Government announced a series of measures to combat racist attacks. An application to the Constitutional Court to ban the extremist right-wing Nationaldemokratische Partei Deutschlands (NPD, National Democratic Party of Germany) on the grounds that it was anti-Semitic, racist and supported violence was approved by the Bundesrat (Federal Council, the upper chamber of the legislature) in November and by the Bundestag in December. In January 2002, however, the Court postponed hearing the case when it emerged that one of the senior NPD activists whose statements were to be used in evidence against the party was an informant for the Bundesamt für Verfassungsschutz (BfV—Office for the Protection of the Constitution); the Court dismissed the case in March 2003.

In late September 2001, following attacks on New York and Washington, DC, USA by suspected Islamist extremists, the Government abolished the so-called 'religious privilege', thus removing legal protection for, and allowing the banning of, any religious organization suspected of promoting terrorism. In December police raided the premises of 20 militant Islamist groups throughout Germany, some of which were suspected of having links with the al-Qa'ida organization of the Saudi-born militant Islamist Osama bin Laden (which was widely believed to have organized the attacks in the USA in September). Evidence subsequently emerged that at least three of the presumed perpetrators of the US atrocities had recently lived in Hamburg and other German cities. Plans to introduce more liberal immigration laws were abandoned, and further new legislation was introduced to increase national security, including the extension of existing anti-terrorism legislation, which had hitherto only covered terrorist acts in Germany, to apply, in addition, to such acts committed in other countries. Measures to block funding channels for militant activists allowed the police access to bank account details of alleged terrorists. Further steps to control money-laundering were introduced, including the foundation of a centralized Financial Intelligence Unit.

At the general election held on 22 September 2002 the SPD-Bündnis 90/Die Grünen coalition was re-elected with a reduced majority. The SPD's position was severely weakened and the Government's popularity suffered as a result of financial austerity measures adopted in an attempt to ward off economic recession. At two Land elections in February 2003 the SPD suffered emphatic defeats by the CDU, which thus strengthened the CDU's majority in the Bundesrat to such an extent that it was able to block government legislation.

In August 2003 the Federal Government approved the 12 bills that comprised Schröder's Agenda 2010 package of economic reforms, the main aims of which were to reduce the rate of unemployment and to revive Germany's stagnant economy. The proposals were, however, deeply unpopular among the general public, trade unions (which had long been traditional allies of the SPD) and many members of the SPD. Bills to reform health provision and labour regulations were adopted by the Bundestag in September, as were welfare and tax reforms in October. The welfare legislation proposed the merging of unemployment benefit and social welfare payments (in effect reducing the level of benefits paid). Tax reductions were proposed to stimulate consumption and thereby reduce public indebtedness (which was at its highest level in Germany's post-war history). For the majority, however, most of the benefits accrued from these reductions were likely to be swiftly cancelled out by a lowering of tax concessions and subsidies. In November the CDU used its majority in the Bundesrat to block the legislation on debt-financed tax reductions, fearing that the debt burden would overwhelm the economy rather than revive it. The tax legislation was eventually approved in December, amended to incorporate smaller tax reductions than originally proposed.

At the SPD conference held in November 2003, Schröder was re-elected Chairman of the party; however, many SPD members felt that the Agenda 2010 reforms were a betrayal of the party's core values, and during 2003 the party lost some 5% of its membership. In December the various bills comprising Agenda 2010, including the amended tax reductions, were finally adopted by both legislative bodies. Bitterness and divisions remained within the SPD, and in February 2004 Schröder announced his resignation as Chairman of the SPD; he was, however, to remain in his post as Chancellor. The SPD elected Franz Müntefering as its new leader at a special party conference in March.

In May 2004 the Bundesversammlung elected Dr Horst Köhler (hitherto the Managing Director of the International Monetary Fund—IMF), the joint candidate of the CDU and the FDP, as the new Federal President; he was inaugurated on 1 July. (Köhler was elected Federal President for a second term in May 2009.)

In July 2004 the Bundesrat adopted legislation on the reform (and ultimately a reduction) of unemployment and social welfare benefits. Opposition, manifested in street protests, was strong throughout Germany, but particularly so in the Länder of the former GDR, where long-term unemployment was endemic. Lafontaine, the former Minister of Finance, demanded Schröder's resignation, openly incited revolt within the SPD and threatened to support a left-wing political movement composed of disaffected SPD members and trade unionists. None the less, the legislation on welfare reform took effect in January 2005. Declining support for the SPD was demonstrated in Land elections in 2004-05, reflecting not only the widespread anger at the reforms, but also the long-standing frustration of many east Germans at the failure to achieve economic integration of the east since reunification.

Following the SPD's defeat in North Rhine-Westphalia in May 2005, Schröder announced his intention to call an early general election, ostensibly because the CDU's increased majority in the Bundesrat rendered his Government unviable. As the Basic Law does not technically allow early elections, Schröder called and deliberately lost a vote of confidence in his administration in July, thereby enabling President Köhler to dissolve the Bundestag. Two legal challenges against this process were dismissed by the Federal Constitutional Court in August, and the election was confirmed for 18 September.

As the rift between Schröder and the left wing of the SPD deepened, Lafontaine left the party and, in July 2005, established a new party with the PDS and other defectors from the SPD, known as Linkspartei.PDS (Die Linke—Left Party.PDS). Die Linke formed an electoral alliance with another left-wing grouping, Wahlalternative Arbeit und soziale Gerechtigkeit (WASG—Electoral Alternative Jobs and Social Justice). Its manifesto included the repeal of social reforms, an increase in the minimum wage and the imposition of higher taxes on the rich. The party swiftly gained considerable support, particularly in the east. (In June 2007 the two parties completed a formal merger, as Die Linke, under the joint leadership of Lafontaine and Prof. Lothar Bisky.)

The 'grand coalition': 2005–09

At the election to the Bundestag, held on 18 September 2005, the CDU/CSU won a total of 225 of the 614 seats (later increased to 226 following a delayed ballot in one constituency), while the

SPD secured 222. Owing to the strong performance of Die Linke, which won 54 seats, neither the CDU/CSU nor the SPD could form a majority government with their preferred coalition partners (respectively the FDP, with 61 seats, and Bündnis 90/Die Grünen, with 51 seats). Neither party was willing to form a coalition with Die Linke. Following three weeks of negotiations among the parties, Merkel was designated Chancellor on 10 October at the head of a 'grand coalition' of the CDU/CSU and SPD. The coalition agreement focused on a programme of job creation, economic reform and reform of the federal system, abandoning the CDU's election campaign proposals for a reduction in income tax for those earning high salaries and the liberalization of employment legislation. Müntefering was designated Vice-Chancellor and Minister of Labour and Social Affairs, and the SPD retained control of a total of eight of the 14 ministries. Merkel was formally elected as Federal Chancellor by the Bundestag on 22 November, becoming both the first woman and the first former citizen of the GDR to lead the country.

Amendments to 25 articles of the Basic Law were approved by the Bundestag on 30 June 2006 and by the Bundesrat on 7 July. The amendments were intended to simplify relations between the two legislative houses, as well as between the Federal and Land Governments, and to define their respective responsibilities more clearly. The reforms were intended to expedite the legislative process, since the amendments substantially reduced the number of bills needing approval from the Bundesrat. Conversely, the Land Governments represented in the Bundesrat gained increased authority over services, including schools and prisons. In July the coalition partners reached an agreement on the reform of health care provision, which was intended to reduce rising costs and to limit reliance on employers' contributions to finance health insurance schemes: the proposals were formally approved by the Bundestag in February 2007, and implementation of the reforms was completed on 1 January 2009.In July 2006, meanwhile, anti-terrorism legislation, adopted following the 11 September 2001 attacks in the USA, was renewed for a five-year period by the Government. Under the renewed legislation, the Bundesnachrichtendienst (BND—the federal intelligence service) was given greater powers, including access to information regarding passengers on international flights.

At an SPD conference in October 2007, party members voted to approve a policy programme that appeared to move the party toward the left. Prior to the conference, some senior members of the party, including Müntefering, had criticized proposals to relax some of the measures included in the Schröder Government's Agenda 2010 programme. In November 2007 Müntefering announced his resignation from the Government, citing personal reasons. Olaf Scholz was appointed to replace him as Minister of Labour and Social Affairs, while the Minister of Foreign Affairs, Frank-Walter Steinmeier, assumed the additional role of Vice-Chancellor. In September 2008 continuing internal disagreements within the SPD culminated in the resignation of Kurt Beck as party Chairman. Müntefering was confirmed as his successor by a special party conference in October. Steinmeier had earlier been selected as the party's candidate for the chancellorship at the next federal election.

In June 2008 the Government approved a draft bill to provide extensive new powers for the Bundeskriminalamt (Federal Criminal Police Office—BKA) to combat terrorism, allowing the BKA to search computers via the internet, monitor telephone conversations and put an individual's home under surveillance, even if he or she was not suspected of a crime. Despite criticism from the opposition and from human rights groups, the legislation was passed by the Bundestag in November, and was approved by the Bundesrat in December, following the inclusion of several amendments, notably that prior permission by the judiciary would always be required for remote searches of computers.

During 2008 and 2009 the Government sought to mitigate the effects of worldwide recession on the German economy. In October 2008 it announced that it would guarantee private bank deposits, in order to maintain confidence in the banking system, and over the following three months it announced new spending totalling some €80,000m., to stimulate the economy. The CSU Federal Minister of Economics and Technology, Michael Glos, resigned from that post in early February 2009, expressing dissatisfaction with his role in the Government and a lack of support from Merkel; he was replaced by Karl-Theodor zu Guttenberg, hitherto Secretary-General of the CSU. Disagreements between the SPD and the CDU intensified in early 2009, leading to the postponement of policy initiatives, including environmental measures and labour market reforms.

Merkel retains power at the 2009 election

At the general election in September 2009 the CDU/CSU together won 239 of the 622 seats in the Bundestag, while the SPD sustained a severe loss of support, securing 146 seats (compared with 222 in 2005). The FDP increased its representation, winning 93 seats, while Die Linke and Bündnis 90/Die Grünen also increased their representation (to 76 and 68 seats, respectively). Prior to the election Merkel had strongly indicated that the FDP was the preferred coalition partner of the CDU/CSU. As the parties together held a clear majority of seats in the Bundestag, negotiations on forming a coalition proceeded swiftly. Following the conclusion of an agreement on policy, which included a commitment to the tax reductions demanded by the FDP, the new Government was sworn in on 28 October: it included the FDP Chairman, Guido Westerwelle, as Vice-Chancellor and Minister of Foreign Affairs, while Rainer Brüderle of the FDP became Minister of Economics and Technology. FDP members were also allocated the ministries in charge of justice, health and development. Wolfgang Schäuble, previously the Minister of the Interior, became Minister of Finance, and the defence portfolio was given to zu Guttenberg of the CSU, previously the Minister of Economics and Technology. After the election Müntefering resigned from the chairmanship of the SPD and was replaced by Sigmar Gabriel, a former Minister of the Environment.

In November 2009 the Chief of Staff of the Bundeswehr (armed forces), Gen. Wolfgang Schneiderhan, together with an official in the Federal Ministry of Defence, resigned in response to a controversy over an air attack by US forces in Afghanistan in September, which had been requested by a German commander in the area (see Foreign Affairs). It was alleged by a national newspaper, *Bild*, that the Ministry of Defence had withheld information on the number of civilians killed in the attack. The Minister of Labour and Social Affairs, Franz Josef Jung, who had been Minister of Defence at the time of the attack, also resigned. (He was replaced by Ursula von der Leyen, who had hitherto held responsibility for family affairs.) A parliamentary inquiry into the events began in December, and the affair reinforced widespread public disquiet over Germany's military involvement in Afghanistan, which had been presented by the Government as a mission to assist reconstruction rather than as participation in the conflict there. In December the Government gained parliamentary approval for measures intended to accelerate economic recovery, which included tax reductions (for individuals and businesses) that had been favoured by the FDP. Critics of the plan expected it to add to an already unprecedented level of public debt.

In January 2010 Lafontaine announced his retirement as joint Chairman of Die Linke and as a member of the Bundestag, owing to ill health. At a party conference in May Klaus Ernst and Gesine Lötzsch were elected to succeed him and Bisky, who had also retired as joint Chairman of the party. In February the Federal Constitutional Court ruled that the controversial reform of unemployment and social welfare benefits introduced by the Schröder Government in 2004 was unconstitutional, on the grounds that it failed to guarantee a 'dignified minimum' income for the recipients of benefits. The Court ordered the Government to implement a new system of welfare benefits by January 2011, requiring a significant increase in government expenditure.

Challenges for the CDU and the FDP

In early May 2010 the legislature approved loans to Greece amounting to €22,400m. over a three-year period, as part of the emergency assistance approved earlier in that month by the ministers responsible for finance of countries participating in the single European currency, the euro (see Regional relations). The unpopularity of this measure within Germany at a time of domestic economic austerity was believed to have led to a decline in support for the CDU at a regional election in North Rhine-Westphalia in May: the SPD also lost support, and Bündnis 90/Die Grünen and Die Linke made considerable gains. (In July the SPD and Bündnis 90/Die Grünen formed a minority government in North Rhine-Westphalia, reliant on the support of Die Linke.) As a result of the CDU's defeat in North Rhine-Westphalia, the Federal Government lost its majority in the Bundesrat. Later in May the Minister-President of Hesse, Roland Koch, a senior conservative member of the CDU, resigned from his post in what was perceived as a withdrawal of support for Merkel's leadership.

On 31 May 2010 President Köhler unexpectedly announced his resignation, following criticism of comments he had made about Germany's military involvement in Afghanistan, which were interpreted by some as implying that Germany's commercial interests justified military deployment abroad. At the election of a new Federal President on 30 June, Christian Wulff of the CDU (hitherto Minister-President of Lower Saxony) was the successful candidate, defeating Joachim Gauck, a pastor and respected former East German dissident: however, since as many as three rounds of voting in the Bundesversammlung had been necessary to ensure a sufficient majority in his support, the election was regarded as a humiliating rebuke for the Government. Meanwhile, earlier in June there were widespread protests following the Government's announcement of a four-year programme of economic austerity measures, with the aim of reducing the budgetary deficit.

In September 2010 the Government announced a delay in the planned closure of Germany's 17 remaining nuclear power stations: the operations of the most recently built nuclear plants were to continue for a further 14 years beyond 2021 (the deadline originally decided by the SPD-led Government in 2000), while older plants were to continue in use for eight years after 2021. It was stipulated that the companies operating the nuclear power stations should make substantial contributions to the development of renewable energy sources. Despite large anti-nuclear demonstrations, the plan was approved by the Bundestag in October 2010. In November the Minister of Defence, zu Guttenberg, announced that, controversially, conscription to the armed forces was to be suspended with effect from July 2011, and was to be replaced by voluntary military or community service.

During 2010 there were indications that Germany was making a rapid recovery from recession, and that unemployment was decreasing. In November Angela Merkel was re-elected unopposed to the leadership of the CDU. In March 2011 zu Guttenberg resigned from his ministerial post, after being accused of using unattributed material in the doctoral thesis that he had submitted in 2006: he denied the allegations, but the University of Bayreuth revoked his doctorate. He was replaced as Minister of Defence by Thomas de Maizière, hitherto Minister of the Interior, a position now allocated to Hans-Peter Friedrich (chairman of the CSU group in the Bundestag).

At an election in Hamburg in February 2011 the CDU (which had hitherto governed the city in coalition with Bündnis 90/Die Grünen) was defeated by the SPD, which secured an absolute majority in the city legislature. Following a severe earthquake in Japan in March 2011, which seriously damaged the Fukushima nuclear power station, large demonstrations opposing nuclear power took place in four German cities. The Government ordered safety reviews to be undertaken at all the country's nuclear power stations, and in May it announced the permanent closure of the seven oldest reactors (an eighth was already off-line), and the closure of the remainder by 2022. Critics of the revised policy expressed the fear that despite a proposed acceleration in the development of renewable sources of energy, there would be an increase in emissions of carbon dioxide from coal- and gas-fired power stations.

At regional elections held in March 2011 Bündnis 90/Die Grünen, which opposed nuclear power, attracted greatly increased support. In Saxony-Anhalt the CDU formed a coalition with the SPD, as before; Bündnis 90/Die Grünen almost doubled their share of the votes, but the FDP's share declined below 5%, and the party thus lost its representation in the Land legislature, since parties winning less than 5% of the votes were not allocated seats. In Baden-Württemberg, controlled by the CDU since the 1950s, Bündnis 90/Die Grünen received almost one-quarter of the votes, and was able to form a coalition with the SPD, led by Winfried Kretschmann, the first member of Bündnis 90/Die Grünen to become a Land premier. On the same day, at an election in Rhineland-Palatinate (previously controlled by the SPD), the share of the votes won by Bündnis 90/Die Grünen more than tripled, and here too the party formed a coalition with the SPD; although the CDU had slightly increased its share of the votes, the FDP again lost its representation in the Land legislature. In response Rainer Brüderle, the Federal Minister of Economics and Technology, resigned from the leadership of the FDP in Rhineland-Palatinate. In April 2011 Guido Westerwelle resigned as national Chairman of the FDP and as Federal Vice-Chancellor, but retained his post as Minister of Foreign Affairs. In May Philipp Rösler, hitherto the Minister of Health, replaced Westerwelle as Chairman of the FDP and Vice-Chancellor, also assuming Brüderle's post as Minister of Economics and Technology.

Further Land elections in 2011 continued to reveal a decline in the popularity of the CDU and of its federal coalition partner, the FDP, particularly the latter, whose advocacy of tax reductions and relatively sceptical attitude towards the European Union (EU) had failed to attract support; the share of the votes won by Bündnis 90/Die Grünen, on the other hand, consistently increased. In Bremen, in May, the governing coalition of the SPD and Bündnis 90/Die Grünen was returned to power: the FDP again lost all its seats. In September 2011, in Mecklenburg-Western Pomerania, the ruling 'grand coalition' of the SPD and the CDU was re-elected, while the FDP yet again lost its representation, and Bündnis 90/Die Grünen entered the legislature and was thus represented in all 16 Land legislatures for the first time. Also in September, at an election in Berlin, the CDU increased its support slightly, but the FDP again failed to attract enough votes to stay in the city's legislature. Bündnis 90/Die Grünen increased its support, and the Piratenpartei Deutschland (Pirate Party Germany, originally formed in 2006 to campaign for, among other things, freedom of information) unexpectedly entered the city legislature. In November 2011 the SPD formed a 'grand coalition' in Berlin with the CDU.

In late September 2011 a vote took place in the federal legislature on the proposed enhancement of the European Financial Stability Facility (EFSF) so as to assist Greece and other members of the eurozone that were experiencing severe economic difficulties. Despite dissent within the ruling coalition parties, and public resentment at the high cost of supporting other EU members, the Government won the vote, which had been regarded as a test of confidence in Chancellor Merkel's European policy (see Regional relations).

In November 2011 the existence of a violent neo-Nazi group, the Nationalsozialistischer Untergrund (NSU—National Socialist Underground), based in Zwickau, was revealed only after the suicide of two of its members: the group was believed to have been responsible for 10 murders, mostly of people of Turkish origin, since 2000, and for two bomb attacks and a number of bank robberies. There was widespread concern that the police and security services had not identified the group earlier, owing to an apparent lack of co-ordination, and to a false assumption that the murders were attributable to feuds between criminal gangs within the Turkish community. Suspected accomplices who were subsequently arrested included a former official of the extreme right-wing NPD. In November 2012 Beate Zschäpe, a member of the Zwickau group, was charged with complicity in the 10 murders. In December 2011, meanwhile, federal and state ministers responsible for internal affairs agreed to make a new attempt to ban the NPD, which, although unsuccessful in federal elections, currently had representation in two Land legislatures (Mecklenburg-Western Pomerania and Saxony); a previous attempt to ban the party had been rejected by the Constitutional Court in 2003. In January 2012 ministers approved the establishment of a national register of right-wing extremists. In December ministers for internal affairs from all 16 Länder again unanimously urged a ban on the NPD on the grounds that the party encouraged xenophobia, disregarded human rights and was anti-democratic, and in December 2013 the ministers submitted a formal request to the Constitutional Court for such a ban: the Federal Government, however, did not support the petition, on the grounds that the NPD would benefit from the publicity and should be opposed in other ways.

In February 2012 President Wulff resigned, after prosecutors had asked the Bundestag to remove his presidential immunity from prosecution, in order to allow possible legal proceedings against him for improper conduct: Wulff had received a low-interest home loan from the wife of a businessman in 2008, and subsequently denied (in the legislature of Lower Saxony, where he was then Minister-President) having financial dealings with the businessman, and in December 2011 he had allegedly attempted to prevent a prominent newspaper, *Bild*, from reporting the story. On resigning Wulff denied that he had done anything illegal, but acknowledged that he had lost public trust. (Wulff was subsequently acquitted by the Lower Saxony Land court in February 2014 of taking bribes.) Joachim Gauck, the unsuccessful candidate in the 2010 presidential election, was nominated for the post of Federal President by the SPD and Bündnis 90/Die Grünen, with the support of Merkel: Gauck was elected by the Bundesversammlung in March 2012.

An early regional election was held in Saarland in March 2012, following the breakdown of the 'experimental' governing coalition there comprising the CDU, the FDP and Bündnis 90/Die Grünen: support for the CDU increased slightly, but the FDP lost its representation. Support for the SPD increased, and the Piratenpartei won four seats. The CDU and the SPD formed a coalition administration in Saarland with effect from May. Two further Land elections took place in May. In Schleswig-Holstein the governing CDU-FDP coalition was defeated; Die Linke lost its representation, and the Piratenpartei entered the legislature. A new governing coalition was formed in June 2012 by the SPD, Bündnis 90/Die Grünen and the Südschleswigscher Wählerverband, a small party representing the Danish-speaking minority. In North Rhine-Westphalia, meanwhile, the May election (which took place after the minority SPD-Bündnis 90/Die Grünen administration lost a vote on the budget in March) revealed an increase in support for the SPD, while the CDU, whose electoral campaign had emphasized the importance of regional debt reduction, lost votes. The incumbent coalition, therefore, continued in office in North Rhine-Westphalia, this time with a secure majority. Once again the Piratenpartei won seats (thus achieving a place in four regional legislatures to date), but Die Linke lost its representation. At both the May Land elections the FDP performed better than in recent months, retaining its representation (albeit reduced) in Schleswig-Holstein and increasing its support in North Rhine-Westphalia. Later in May Norbert Röttgen, until the recent Land election the chairman of the CDU in North Rhine-Westphalia, and widely blamed for the party's defeat, was dismissed from his post as Federal Minister of the Environment, Nature Conservation and Nuclear Safety; his ministerial post was assumed by Peter Altmaier, also of the CDU.

In September 2012 Peer Steinbrück, who had been Federal Minister of Finance in 2005–09, was selected as the SPD's candidate for the post of Chancellor, should his party be successful in the federal election to be held in the following year. In December 2012 the CDU re-elected Merkel as party chairwoman and as its candidate for Chancellor. In January 2013 an election in Lower Saxony resulted in a defeat for the CDU-FDP administration: although it remained the largest party, the CDU lost support, while the SPD, Bündnis 90/Die Grünen and the FDP all increased their share of the votes. Die Linke did not receive sufficient votes to keep its representation in the Land legislature; the Piratenpartei also failed to win any seats. The SPD and Bündnis 90/Die Grünen formed a coalition administration for Lower Saxony, with a one-seat majority. This result gave SPD-led Länder a majority in the Bundesrat.

In March 2013 the German authorities banned three Islamist groups on the grounds that they were anti-democratic, and in June police raids were made on a suspected Islamist militant network in Baden-Württemberg, Bavaria and Saxony. Meanwhile, the trial of the neo-Nazi Zschäpe and four alleged accomplices began in May. In August a committee of members of the Bundestag issued a report on neo-Nazi activities, deploring failures on the part of the security services in investigating the murders allegedly committed by the NSU, and urging stricter and better co-ordinated surveillance of extreme right-wing groups; according to official figures, such groups had been responsible for more than 800 violent crimes during the previous year.

Recent developments: a new 'grand coalition'

In April 2013 a new political party, Alternative für Deutschland (AfD), held its inaugural conference: the party's principal objective was the dismantling of the single European currency, which it claimed had failed to solve the problems of the EU's poorer member states. The AfD aimed to attract support from Germans who objected to giving financial support to failing European economies (see Regional relations). In August campaigning for the next month's federal election began, with the ruling CDU/CSU citing its success in maintaining the country's economic stability as a reason for voters' support, while the campaign proposals of the principal opposition party, the SPD, included the introduction of a statutory minimum wage and an increase on taxes for the highest-paid. In September, shortly before the federal election, a regional election took place in Bavaria: the CSU regained the absolute majority which it had lost in 2009, while the FDP, with which it had been governing in coalition, received less than 5% of the votes and was therefore excluded from the Bavarian legislature. Another election followed, in Hesse (on the same day as the federal election) when the CDU won most seats, but not enough to form an administration on its own: eventually, in December 2013, a coalition was announced in Hesse between the CDU and Bündnis 90/Die Grünen.

At the federal election on 23 September 2013 the CDU/CSU narrowly failed to achieve an absolute majority, securing a combined total of 311 seats, while the SPD won 193, Die Linke 64 and Bündnis 90/Die Grünen 63. The FDP received slightly less than 5% of 'second' (party) votes (4.8%) and therefore lost its entire representation in the Bundestag (where it had previously held 93 seats); the party's Chairman, Philipp Rösler, immediately announced his resignation. The AfD received 4.7% of 'second' votes and thus likewise failed to gain any seats, but its performance was perceived as relatively successful for such a recently formed party. In October the SPD agreed to begin formal negotiations on entering a 'grand coalition' with the CDU/CSU, as had existed twice before (in 1966–69 and 2005–09). Discussions continued until late November 2013 (while the previous Government continued in office in a 'caretaker' capacity). The SPD succeeded in securing the introduction of a statutory minimum wage, a reduction of the retirement age and an increase in public spending, but the party's demand for higher taxes for the most wealthy was not met. On 17 December, following approval of the coalition agreement in a vote by SPD members, the Bundestag confirmed Merkel as Chancellor at the head of a CDU/CSU-SPD coalition Government. The new administration included Sigmar Gabriel, the Chairman of the SPD, as Vice-Chancellor and Minister of Economic Affairs and Energy, Frank-Walter Steinmeier (SPD) as Minister of Foreign Affairs (the post he had held under the 2005–09 'grand coalition'), and Thomas de Maizière (CDU) as Minister of the Interior, while Wolfgang Schäuble (CDU) remained in the post of Minister of Finance.

Foreign Affairs

Regional relations

The orientation of Germany's foreign policy after unification broadly followed that of the FRG. The united Germany remained committed to a leading role in the European Community (EC—now EU), of which the FRG was a founding member, and NATO, while placing greater emphasis on defence co-operation with France. Germany was also strongly committed to close relations with Eastern Europe, in particular with the USSR and, subsequently, its successor states.

In December 1992 the Bundestag ratified the Treaty on European Union (the Maastricht Treaty). At the same time the lower house approved an amendment to the Basic Law (negotiated in May 1992 with the Länder), whereby the state assemblies would be accorded greater involvement in the determination of German policy within the EC. The Bundesrat ratified the Maastricht Treaty later in December 1992. In April 1998 the Bundestag approved Germany's participation in Economic and Monetary Union (EMU), which took effect in January 1999. Following the eventual approval of the draft EU constitutional treaty on 18 June 2004 by the Heads of State and of Government of the member countries, German legislative ratification, which required a two-thirds' majority in both houses, was secured in May 2005. However, following the subsequent rejection of the proposed constitution at public referendums in France and the Netherlands, the process of ratification in other member countries halted. In June 2007 a preliminary agreement was reached for a reform treaty to replace the defunct constitutional treaty. The reform treaty was signed by EU leaders in Lisbon, Portugal, in December 2007, and was ratified by the Bundestag in May 2008. In June 2009 the Federal Constitutional Court rejected a legal challenge by members of the federal legislature (mostly belonging to Die Linke) who claimed that the so-called Treaty of Lisbon was incompatible with German law: the Court ruled, however, that new domestic legislation must be adopted to ensure greater participation by the Bundestag in EU decisions affecting Germany. The Treaty of Lisbon entered into effect across the EU in December 2009. In May 2010 the German Government, with other countries participating in the common European currency, the euro, undertook to provide assistance for the severely indebted Greek economy, and to establish a temporary emergency fund, the EFSF, in order to ensure financial stability within the eurozone. Merkel argued that the Treaty of Lisbon should be amended to provide a permanent mechanism for helping member states to avoid insolvency, and the establishment of the European Stability Mechanism (ESM), to replace the EFSF, was agreed by EU heads of state and government in December 2010. Following ratification by member states, the ESM was formally inaugurated in October 2012.

During 2011 the German Government undertook a leading role in maintaining the stability of the eurozone, by providing assistance for heavily indebted member states (although this was widely unpopular among German tax-payers), and by urging the adoption of more rigorous rules and closer EU integration to prevent future sovereign debt crises. In May the Bundestag approved Germany's contribution to an assistance programme for Portugal, but proposals for a second bailout for Greece, to prevent that country being obliged to default on its debts, proved more controversial, particularly among members of Merkel's own party, the CDU, and the FDP. In September the Bundestag voted in favour of enhancing the EFSF by increasing Germany's guarantee commitments. Merkel repeatedly urged the adoption of measures for closer fiscal and economic integration and enforceable budgetary discipline in the EU, but at a meeting of EU heads of state and government in December proposals for a 'fiscal compact' to be incorporated in amendments to the Treaty of Lisbon were defeated when the United Kingdom imposed its veto, after safeguards for British financial services were not forthcoming. The compact was to be adopted, instead, by a separate intergovernmental treaty (the Treaty on Stability, Co-ordination and Governance in the Economic and Monetary Union), according to which members would agree to adopt binding legislation on balancing their budgets; failure to adhere to this would incur penalties imposed by the European Court of Justice. At a further summit meeting in January 2012 it was announced that all EU members except the Czech Republic and the United Kingdom had agreed to support the pact (which was formally concluded in March, subject to ratification by member states, and which entered into force on 1 January 2013). In February EU ministers of finance finally agreed upon a second assistance programme for Greece, with the aim of reducing Greece's debt to 120% of gross domestic product by 2020. The programme, involving loans of more than €130,000m. and (as demanded by Germany) reductions in the value of bonds held by private creditors, was conditional upon extremely stringent reductions in public spending, under external supervision, and aroused considerable resentment of Germany in Greece. The assistance was approved by the Bundestag in February 2012. In June the Bundestag voted to ratify both the establishment of the ESM and the fiscal compact: objections were immediately submitted to the Constitutional Court by members of Die Linke and other opponents, who argued that the measures were unconstitutional and would therefore require a national referendum. The Court overruled the objections in September, but stated that the German legislature must approve any increase in Germany's contribution to the ESM.

During 2012 the German Government maintained its insistence on the imposition of austerity measures on indebted countries in the eurozone, despite disagreement with, among others, the newly elected French Government. Merkel expressed firm opposition to proposals for the introduction of 'eurobonds' (debt jointly guaranteed by all eurozone member governments, in order to reduce the cost of borrowing for the most indebted states), arguing that this would remove incentives for reform, and would violate EU treaties and the German constitution. At a meeting of EU heads of government in June, however, Merkel agreed to compromise on proposals that she had previously rejected, allowing the ESM to provide support for banks directly (instead of through governments), and permitting the ESM to buy government bonds in order to reduce a country's borrowing costs. At the same meeting she succeeded in securing agreement on establishing a system for the supervision of eurozone banks. In July the Bundestag voted by a large majority in favour of EU assistance for Spanish banks. Despite Greece's difficulties in reducing its debt levels, the German Government repeatedly affirmed that the stability of the eurozone depended on retaining Greek membership, and in November the Bundestag voted, again by a large majority, to approve the payment of the next instalment of assistance for Greece, which had been delayed during negotiations by the IMF and EU institutions on easing the terms of the bailout. At discussions begun by heads of government in November on the Multi-annual Financial Framework (MFF) for 2014–20, the basis for the EU's annual budgets, Germany, among others, rejected the European Commission's proposal for an increase of 5% in spending, compared with the previous seven-year period, and succeeded in gaining agreement in February 2013 on a reduction in the MFF.

In 2013, during negotiations on the creation of an EU banking union, the German Government urged that the role of the European Central Bank (ECB) as a banking supervisory authority should be limited, and that taxpayers' money should not be used to rescue failing banks. A complex agreement concluded in December envisaged a Single Resolution Mechanism, comprising a fund which would be used to assist or to close down failing banks; this fund would be created by an annual levy on eurozone banks, initially paid into national resolution funds, which after 10 years would be merged into a common resolution fund. In February 2014 the German Government conceded that the transition period could be reduced to five years, provided that the levy on banks was increased accordingly.

While close relations with France remained a priority following Merkel's election as Chancellor in November 2005, she expressed the belief that Germany had worked too exclusively with France in the past and announced her intention to strengthen relations with smaller EU states and the USA. Following the election in May 2007 of Nicolas Sarkozy as French President, the two leaders differed over agreements signed by Sarkozy during late 2007 for the sale of nuclear technology to countries in the Middle East, and French proposals for a grouping to link the seven EU member states in the Mediterranean region and Middle Eastern and African littoral countries; however, in March 2008, following negotiations between French and German representatives, Merkel and Sarkozy announced an agreement on the formation of the Union for the Mediterranean, which incorporated all EU member states. In February 2011 the German and French Governments initiated what later became known as the Euro-Plus Pact, an agreement among EU members to work towards raising the age at which workers qualified for pensions, abolishing wage indexation, harmonizing corporate taxes, and creating legally binding limits on budget deficits. During 2011, as the two governments co-operated in seeking a solution to the eurozone debt crisis, the French Government disagreed with Germany's insistence on the involvement of private investors in reducing Greece's debt (since several French banks held large amounts of Greek debt), but supported the fiscal compact on budgetary discipline. Following his election in May 2012 the socialist President of France, François Hollande, urged the adoption of measures to stimulate economic growth within the eurozone, rather than the austerity programmes favoured by the German Government; he initially refused to support the EU's fiscal pact, but agreed to do so after the adoption in June of an additional plan to stimulate growth. Hollande argued in favour of the introduction of 'eurobonds', which Merkel opposed. Although agreeing with the German Government on the necessity of eurozone banking supervision, the French favoured supervision of all eurozone banks by the ECB, while the Germans urged supervision only of the largest banks and questioned the suitability of the ECB for assuming this role.

In the course of the negotiations on EU enlargement during the 1990s, Germany strongly supported Poland's accession (which took place in May 2004), citing the need for reconciliation with its eastern neighbour. In August 2004 Chancellor Schröder attended a ceremony in Warsaw to mark the 60th anniversary of the failed uprising there, during which he acknowledged the 'immeasurable suffering' inflicted by Nazi troops on Poland. The Polish Government, as well those of Estonia, Latvia, Lithuania and Ukraine, opposed the construction of a pipeline to transport natural gas to Germany from Russia, fearing that it could be used to divert energy away from those countries for political reasons. The appointment in November 2007 of a new, largely pro-EU Government in Poland improved relations between the two countries: the new Polish Prime Minister, Donald Tusk, visited Berlin in mid-December for a meeting with Merkel, following which the two leaders affirmed the friendly nature of relations between Germany and Poland, and promised close co-operation over the planned gas pipeline.

In October 2005 preliminary negotiations for the possible accession of Turkey to the EU began. In February 2008, during a visit to Germany, the Turkish Prime Minister, Reçep Tayyip Erdoğan, urged the sizable Turkish population within Germany to retain their ethnic identity, and provoked an angry reaction from several German politicians, who expressed fears that such remarks could undermine efforts to integrate people of Turkish origin into German society. Merkel's Government continued to express concern over democratic standards in Turkey, and over the Turkish refusal to recognize Cyprus, and favoured offering Turkey a 'privileged partnership' with the EU, rather than full membership.

In the early 21st century Russia was the source of around one-third of Germany's natural gas requirements, and the security of this supply (about 80% of which arrived via Ukraine) was of major concern to the German Government. In September 2005 the two Governments concluded an agreement on the construction of a pipeline directly linking Russia and Germany under the

Baltic Sea. The 'Nord Stream' pipeline (actually twin pipelines) was intended to transport up to 27,500m. cu m of Russian natural gas per year to Western Europe. It was approved by neighbouring countries, despite environmental concerns; construction began in April 2010 and transport of gas through the first of the pipelines began in November 2011, and through the second in October 2012. In November 2010 Merkel expressed support for Russia's application to join the World Trade Organization (see p. 434) and for the eventual establishment of a free trade area between Russia and the EU. The German Government expressed concern at allegations of electoral fraud in the Russian legislative elections in December 2011 and the presidential election in May 2012. Following Vladimir Putin's re-election as President in May, the two leaders exchanged visits, but Merkel criticized the Russian Government's treatment of its political opponents, and in November the Bundestag approved a motion deploring deteriorating standards of human rights in Russia. The German Government also criticized Russia's continuing support for the administration of President Bashar al-Assad in Syria during the anti-government unrest that began in 2011 (see Other external relations), urging Russia not to provide the Syrian authorities with advanced weaponry. In February 2014 the German, French and Polish ministers responsible for foreign affairs attempted to mediate in the violent dispute between the Ukrainian Government and opposition, and in early March Merkel expressed to President Putin her view that Russia's intervention in the Crimea region of Ukraine was a breach of international law.

Other external relations

Following the Iraqi invasion and annexation of Kuwait in August 1990, the German Government expressed support for the deployment of US-led allied forces in the region of the Persian (Arabian) Gulf, and contributed substantial amounts of financial and technical aid to the effort to liberate Kuwait, although there were mass demonstrations against the allied action in many parts of Germany. Germany did not contribute troops to the allied force, in accordance with a provision in the Basic Law that was widely interpreted as prohibiting intervention outside the area of NATO operations. In July 1992, however, the Government announced that it was to send a naval destroyer and reconnaissance aircraft to the Adriatic Sea to participate in the UN force monitoring the observance of UN sanctions on the Federal Republic of Yugoslavia (FRY). This deployment was subsequently approved by the Bundestag. In April 1993 the Constitutional Court ruled that German forces could join the UN operation to enforce an air exclusion zone over Bosnia and Herzegovina. Germany dispatched troops to assist the UN relief effort in Somalia in mid-1993. In May 1994 the Constitutional Court declared the participation of German military units in collective international defence and security operations, with the approval of the Bundestag in each instance, to be compatible with the Basic Law. From March to early June 1999 Germany participated in the NATO military offensive against the FRY, despite misgivings from left-wing elements within the ruling SPD-Bündnis 90/Die Grünen coalition. From 2004 onwards Germany participated in the EU peacekeeping operation in Bosnia and Herzegovina.

In the aftermath of the terrorist attacks in the USA on 11 September 2001, Chancellor Schröder pledged 'unlimited solidarity' with the US Administration, and announced plans to send 3,900 troops to take part in the US-led military action in Afghanistan, although these plans were strongly opposed by the majority of members of the junior partner in the governing coalition, Bündnis 90/Die Grünen. In November Schröder narrowly won a parliamentary vote on the troop deployment, which was linked to a vote of confidence in his Government. In November 2002 the Bundestag voted to extend the deployment of troops in Afghanistan by a further year, and the mandate was thereafter renewed annually, with the size of the German contingent participating in the International Security Assistance Force (ISAF) increasing to almost 5,000 by 2011. In September 2009 an estimated 100 Afghan civilians were killed in an air attack by US forces: the attack had been requested by a local German commander. The incident led to the resignation in November of the Chief of Staff of the Bundeswehr. Although the mandate for maintaining German forces in Afghanistan was again renewed by the Bundestag in December, the events reinforced domestic opposition to their deployment in that country. From mid-2010 the German Government increased to 200 the number of German police officers involved in training and developing the Afghan police force. The number of German troops participating in ISAF was reduced in 2012, in accordance with the planned phasing-out of the ISAF mission by the end of 2014. Germany undertook to continue investing up to €430m. annually in Afghanistan in 2014–16, primarily for developing the rule of law and combating corruption. In March 2013 a German court began hearing a lawsuit brought by the families of the civilians killed in the 2009 air attack, demanding compensation, but the case was dismissed in December 2013.

Germany opposed US plans for the reconstruction of Iraq following the removal of Saddam Hussain in March–April 2003 and advocated instead greater UN involvement and the swifter transfer of governing powers to Iraqis. In September, however, Chancellor Schröder offered to provide resources for the training of Iraqi police, security staff and military personnel (while continuing to refuse to send German peacekeeping troops to Iraq). The continuing 'war on terror' precipitated further tensions in late 2005, following reports that the USA's Central Intelligence Agency (CIA) had routed over 400 flights through German airports, allegedly with the knowledge of the Minister of the Interior, as part of its programme of 'extraordinary rendition'. Under this programme, it was alleged, suspected Islamist militants were secretly transferred to third countries, some of which were suspected of practising torture, for interrogation. Germany's relations with the USA improved after Merkel took office, and the importance of bilateral co-operation was emphasized during her first official visit to the USA in January 2006, which was returned by the US President, George W. Bush, in July. In November 2009 Merkel visited the USA for discussions with President Barack Obama, during which she requested that US nuclear weapons should no longer be stationed in Germany. The USA is Germany's principal trading partner outside the EU, but has frequently voiced concern over Germany's consistently large export surplus, urging that Germany should stimulate domestic demand for the benefit of other exporters. In October 2013 Merkel described as 'completely unacceptable' revelations that the US intelligence services had monitored her mobile telephone conversations; further outrage was caused by reports that equipment in the US and British embassies in Germany had been used to intercept government communications.

From 2006 Germany participated, with the permanent members of the UN Security Council, in discussions on Iran's nuclear programme (the so-called P5 + 1 talks), with the aim of dissuading Iran from developing nuclear weapons; in November 2013 participants reached agreement on a reduction of economic sanctions against Iran in return for an undertaking to delay nuclear development over a six-month period. In February 2014 the P5 +1 group began negotiations with Iran on a longer-term agreement.

After a popular movement began in February 2011 against Col Muammar al-Qaddafi's regime in Libya, which by March had descended into civil war, Chancellor Merkel was criticized for abstaining from a vote on a UN Security Council resolution, proposed by the United Kingdom, France and Lebanon, authorizing an air exclusion zone over Libya. Germany was the only Western nation to abstain from the vote, which none the less resulted in the adoption of a resolution that permitted UN member states to take 'all necessary measures' (short of military occupation) to protect civilians in Libya. During 2011 and 2012 the German Government repeatedly demanded an end to violence against civilians by the Syrian Government, urged the Syrian President to resign, and supported economic sanctions against Syria. As the situation in Syria deteriorated during 2013 the German Government refused to support proposals for providing weapons to anti-government forces in Syria, or for military intervention in that country, although it approved the provision of humanitarian aid.

The People's Republic of China is one of Germany's principal trading partners. From 2002 China became Germany's second largest export market outside Europe (after the USA), and by 2010 China had become Germany's principal supplier of imports. Merkel made an official visit to China in July 2010, when the two Governments announced that intergovernmental consultations would take place annually, and in June 2011 the Chinese Premier, Wen Jiabao, visited Germany; during his visit, a number of agreements on economic and other co-operation were concluded. During a further visit in April 2012 Wen expressed the hope that bilateral trade would double over the next three years. While visiting China in August (her second visit there in that year) Merkel urged China to assist the eurozone by continuing to increase its investments in European sovereign bonds and companies. During a visit by the new Chinese

Premier, Li Keqiang, in May 2013, Merkel assured him that Germany would expedite negotiations between the EU and China on the pricing of the latter's exports, particularly in view of accusations that China was unfairly subsidizing exports of solar panels and telephone equipment.

CONSTITUTION AND GOVERNMENT

The Basic Law (Grundgesetz), which came into force in the British, French and US Zones of Occupation in Germany (excluding Saarland) on 23 May 1949, became the Constitution of the entire German nation with the accession of the five newly re-established eastern Länder (states) and East Berlin to the Federal Republic on 3 October 1990.

Germany is a federal republic with a bicameral legislature. The country's main legislative organ, is the Bundestag (Federal Assembly), with 631 deputies, who are elected for four years by universal adult suffrage (using a mixed system of proportional representation and direct voting). The upper chamber is the Bundesrat (Federal Council), which consists of 69 members representing the 16 Länder. Each Land has between three and six seats, depending on the size of its population. The term of office of Bundesrat members varies in accordance with Land election dates.

Executive authority rests with the Bundesregierung (Federal Government), led by the Bundeskanzler (Federal Chancellor), who is elected by an absolute majority of the Bundestag and appoints the other Ministers. The Bundespräsident (Federal President) is elected by a Bundesversammlung (Federal Convention), which meets only for this purpose and consists of the Bundestag and an equal number of members elected by Land parliaments. The President is a constitutional head of state with little influence on government.

Germany is composed of 16 Länder (states). Each Land has its own constitution, legislature and government, with the right to enact laws except on matters that are the exclusive right of the Federal Government, such as defence, foreign affairs and finance. Education, police, culture and environmental protection are in the control of the Länder. Local responsibility for the execution of Federal and Land laws is undertaken by the Gemeinden (communities).

REGIONAL AND INTERNATIONAL CO-OPERATION

Germany was a founding member of the European Community, now European Union (EU, see p. 273) and participated in the introduction of the single European currency, the euro, in January 1999. It is also a member of the Council of Europe (see p. 252), of the Organization for Security and Co-operation in Europe (OSCE, see p. 387), and of the Council of the Baltic Sea States (see p. 250).

Germany joined the UN in 1973; it was elected as a non-permanent member of the Security Council for the period 2011–12. As a contracting party to the General Agreement on Tariffs and Trade, Germany joined the World Trade Organization (WTO, see p. 434) on its establishment in 1995. Germany is a member of the Organisation for Economic Co-operation and Development (OECD, see p. 379) and the North Atlantic Treaty Organization (NATO, see p. 370). It participates in the Group of Eight major industrialized nations (G8, see p. 465) and the Group of 20 major industrialized and systemically important emerging market nations (G20, see p. 456).

ECONOMIC AFFAIRS

In 2012, according to estimates by the World Bank, Germany's gross national income (GNI), measured at average 2010–12 prices, was US $3,603,895m., equivalent to $44,010 per head (or $41,890 per head on an international purchasing-power parity basis). During 2003–12 Germany's population registered a decrease of 0.1%, while gross domestic product (GDP) per head grew, in real terms, by an average of 1.5% annually. According to the World Bank, overall GDP expanded, in real terms, at an average annual rate of 1.4% in 2003–12; GDP increased by 0.7% in 2012.

Agriculture (including hunting, forestry and fishing) engaged 1.5% of the employed labour force in 2013, and provided 0.8% of Germany's GDP in 2012. The principal crops are wheat, sugar beet, barley and potatoes. Wine production is also important in western Germany. According to the UN, agricultural GDP increased, in real terms, at an average annual rate of 1.7% in 2003–12; it declined by 22.5% in 2011, but increased by 1.6% in 2012.

Industry (including mining, power, manufacturing and construction) engaged 24.7% of the employed labour force in 2013 and contributed 30.5% of GDP in 2012. According to UN figures, industrial GDP increased at an average annual rate of 1.6% in 2003–12; it increased by 6.3% in 2011, but declined by 1.6% in 2012.

The mining sector (together with energy, gas and water supply) engaged 1.3% of the employed labour force in 2013 and contributed 3.5% of GDP in 2012. The principal mining activities are the extraction of lignite (low-grade brown coal), hard coal and salts. According to the UN, GDP of mining along with utilities decreased, in real terms, at an average annual rate of 0.7% in 2003–12; it decreased by 15.0% in 2011, but increased by 1.3 in 2012.

The manufacturing sector employed 17.4% of the employed labour force in 2013, and provided 22.4% of GDP in 2012. Measured by value of output, the principal branches of manufacturing in 2004 were motor vehicles and parts (accounting for 20.1% of the total), non-electric machinery (11.4%), chemical products (9.7%) and food products (9.0%). According to UN figures, real manufacturing GDP increased at an average annual rate of 2.3% in 2003–12; it expanded by 9.6% in 2011, but declined by 1.8% in 2012.

The construction sector employed 5.9% of the employed labour force in 2013, and provided 4.7% of GDP in 2012. According to the UN, the GDP of the sector declined by an average annual rate of 0.3% during 2003–12; construction GDP, increased by 4.6% 2011, but declined by 2.4% in 2012.

Of the total energy produced in 2012, coal accounted for 46.9%, nuclear power for 16.3%, natural gas for 11.5% and hydroelectric power for 3.5%. In 2010, in a reversal of a decision in 2000 to end the use of nuclear power by 2021, the Government announced plans to delay the closure of its 17 nuclear power plants. In March 2011, following radiation leaks from a nuclear plant in Japan that had been damaged in an earthquake, this decision was suspended and seven nuclear reactors were shut down. (An eighth was already off-line.) In August 2011 revisions to the Atomic Energy Act entered into force, whereby nuclear power use for commercial electricity generation was to be phased out by 2022. In 2012 imports of mineral fuels accounted for an estimated 14.8% of Germany's total imports.

Services engaged 73.8% of the employed labour force in 2013, and contributed 68.7% of GDP in 2012. According to the UN, the GDP of the services sector increased, in real terms, at an average annual rate of 1.5% in 2003–12. Financial services, real estate, renting and business activities accounted for 27.2% of GDP in 2012. Trade, transport and communications accounted for 18.6% of GDP in 2012. The real GDP of this sector grew at an average annual rate of 1.2% in 2002–11. Overall services GDP grew by 1.4% in 2012.

In 2012 Germany recorded a visible merchandise trade surplus of US $238,160m., and there was a surplus of $238,710m. on the current account of the balance of payments. Germany was the world's largest exporter of goods in the years 2004–08, although exports from the People's Republic of China exceeded those from Germany in 2009 by over $20,000m. Germany conducted more than one-half of its total trade with other countries of the European Union (EU, see p. 273) in 2008. The principal source of imports in 2012 was the Netherlands (providing 9.5% of the total imports) followed by the People's Republic of China, France, the USA, Italy and the United Kingdom. France was the principal export trading partner, purchasing 9.4% of exports in 2012; the other major purchasers of exports were the USA, the United Kingdom, the Netherlands, the People's Republic of China, Austria and Italy. The principal imports in 2012 were machinery and transport equipment, mineral fuels and lubricants, manufactured goods chiefly classified by material, and chemicals and related products. The principal exports were machinery and transport equipment, chemicals and related products, and manufactured goods chiefly classified by material.

The general government deficit for 2011 was €22,800m., equivalent to 0.9% of GDP. In 2012 general government gross debt was €2,183,782m., equivalent to 81.9% of GDP. Annual inflation averaged 1.7% during 2003–12. Consumer prices rose by an annual average of 2.0% in 2012. The unemployment rate was 6.5% in 2012.

Germany is the largest economy in Europe, although the area comprising the former German Democratic Republic (East Germany) remains less prosperous than the former Federal Republic of Germany (West Germany). Following the rapid deterioration in global financial conditions from the end of 2007, in 2008 the

German economy officially entered a recession. As a major exporter (particularly of machinery and vehicles), Germany was vulnerable to the global decline in demand, which was exacerbated by the rise in the value of the euro, and caused a sharp decline in industrial output. German banks demonstrated some resilience during the global financial crisis, owing to their comparatively low ratios of debt to capital, although the Government was forced to intervene to support several banks. Measures were adopted to stimulate the economy, requiring a substantial rise in borrowing: as a result, in 2009 the budgetary deficit amounted to 3.2% of GDP, thus exceeding the 3% upper limit stipulated by the EU's Stability and Growth Pact. During 2009 an increase in unemployment was prevented largely by a system of short-time working, whereby the Government subsidized companies that retained their employees while reducing working hours. Germany's GDP declined by 5.1% in 2009, the largest contraction in the country's post-war history. In 2010, however, GDP increased by 3.7%, reflecting an unexpectedly rapid growth in exports and investment. In June the Government announced a controversial programme of austerity measures, with the aim of reducing the budgetary deficit to below 3.0% of GDP by 2013 and achieving a balanced budget by 2016. The budgetary deficit decreased more quickly than anticipated, to 0.8% of GDP in 2011, reflecting an increase in tax revenues, and a surplus equivalent to 0.1% of GDP was recorded in 2012, followed by a balanced budget in 2013. GDP growth was maintained in 2011, at 3.0%, slowing to 0.7% in 2012, when there was a decline in exports to other eurozone members, although this was offset by strong growth in exports to countries outside the EU. Unemployment averaged 5.2% in 2013 (compared with an average of around 12% in the euro area as a whole). Germany's GDP increased by 0.4% in 2013, with export levels still affected by the economic problems of other members of the eurozone; although modest, growth was sustained by domestic demand, as employment levels remained high and relatively generous wage increases stimulated consumer spending. Low interest rates also served to stimulate consumption and support housing construction. A statutory minimum wage was introduced at the beginning of 2014. The Deutsche Bundesbank (the central bank) predicted GDP growth of 1.7% in 2014, reflecting an improvement in exports and corporate investment.

PUBLIC HOLIDAYS

2015: 1 January (New Year's Day), 6 January (Epiphany)*, 3 April (Good Friday), 6 April (Easter Monday), 1 May (Labour Day), 14 May (Ascension Day), 25 May (Whit Monday), 4 June (Corpus Christi)*, 15 August (Assumption)*, 3 October (Day of Unity), 31 October (Reformation Day)*, 1 November (All Saints' Day)*, 18 November (Day of Prayer and Repentance)*, 25–26 December (Christmas), 31 December (New Year's Eve).

* Religious holidays observed in certain Länder only.

Statistical Survey

Source (unless otherwise indicated): Statistisches Bundesamt, 65180 Wiesbaden; tel. (611) 752405; fax (611) 753330; e-mail info@destatis.de; internet www.destatis.de.

Area and Population

AREA, POPULATION AND DENSITY

Area (sq km)*	357,124
Population (census results)	
9 May 2011†	
Males	39,153,540
Females	41,066,140
Total	80,219,695
Population (official estimates at 31 December)	
2011	80,327,900
2012	80,523,746
Density (per sq km) at 31 December 2012	225.5

* 137,886 sq miles.

† Figures are rounded according to differing methodologies, as a result the total may not be equal to the sum of components.

POPULATION BY AGE AND SEX

('000 persons at 2011 census)

	Males	Females	Total
0–14	5,525.0	5,255.6	10,780.6
15–64	26,604.0	26,317.7	52,921.6
65 and over	7,024.6	9,492.9	16,517.5
Total	39,153.6	41,066.1	80,219.7

Note: Totals may not be equal to the sum of components, owing to rounding.

LÄNDER

(official population estimates at 31 December 2012)

	Area (sq km)	Population	Density (per sq km)	Capital
Baden-Württemberg	35,751	10,569,111	295.6	Stuttgart
Bayern (Bavaria)	70,550	12,519,571	177.5	München
Berlin	892	3,375,222	3,783.9	Berlin
Brandenburg	29,482	2,449,511	83.1	Potsdam
Bremen	404	654,774	1,620.7	Bremen
Hamburg	755	1,734,272	2,297.0	Hamburg
Hessen (Hesse)	21,115	6,016,481	284.9	Wiesbaden
Mecklenburg-Vorpommern (Mecklenburg-Western Pomerania)	23,189	1,600,327	69.0	Schwerin
Niedersachsen (Lower Saxony)	47,635	7,778,995	163.3	Hannover
Nordrhein-Westfalen (North Rhine-Westphalia)	34,088	17,554,329	515.0	Düsseldorf
Rheinland-Pfalz (Rhineland-Palatinate)	19,854	3,990,278	201.0	Mainz
Saarland	2,569	994,287	387.0	Saarbrücken
Sachsen (Saxony)	18,420	4,050,204	219.9	Dresden
Sachsen-Anhalt (Saxony-Anhalt)	20,449	2,259,393	110.5	Magdeburg
Schleswig-Holstein	15,799	2,806,531	177.6	Kiel
Thüringen (Thuringia)	16,172	2,170,460	134.2	Erfurt
Total	357,124	80,523,746	225.5	—

PRINCIPAL TOWNS
(official population estimates at 31 December 2012)

Berlin (capital)	3,375,222	Karlsruhe	296,033
Hamburg	1,734,272	Mannheim	294,627
München (Munich)	1,388,308	Augsburg	272,699
Köln (Cologne)	1,024,373	Wiesbaden	272,636
Frankfurt am Main	687,775	Gelsenkirchen	257,607
Stuttgart	597,939	Mönchengladbach	255,087
Düsseldorf	593,682	Braunschweig (Brunswick)	245,798
Dortmund	572,087	Chemnitz	241,210
Essen	566,862	Aachen (Aix-la-Chapelle)	240,086
Bremen	546,451	Kiel	239,866
Dresden	525,105	Halle an der Saale*	231,440
Leipzig	520,838	Magdeburg	229,924
Hannover (Hanover)	514,137	Krefeld	222,026
Nürnberg (Nuremberg)	495,121	Freiburg im Breisgau	218,043
Duisburg	486,816	Lübeck	211,713
Bochum	362,213	Oberhausen	210,005
Wuppertal	342,885	Erfurt	203,485
Bielefeld	328,314	Rostock	202,887
Bonn	309,869	Mainz	202,756
Münster	296,599		

* Including Halle-Neustadt.

BIRTHS, MARRIAGES AND DEATHS

	Registered live births		Registered marriages		Registered deaths	
	Number	Rate (per 1,000)	Number	Rate (per 1,000)	Number	Rate (per 1,000)
2005	685,795	8.3	388,451	4.7	830,270	10.1
2006	672,724	8.2	373,681	4.5	821,627	10.0
2007	684,862	8.3	368,922	4.5	827,155	10.1
2008	682,514	8.3	377,055	4.6	844,439	10.3
2009	665,126	8.1	378,439	4.6	854,544	10.4
2010	677,947	8.3	382,047	4.7	858,768	10.5
2011	662,685	8.1	377,816	4.6	852,328	10.4
2012	673,544	8.4	387,423	4.8	869,582	10.8

Life expectancy (years at birth): 80.7 (males 78.4; females 83.2) in 2011 (Source: World Bank, World Development Indicators database).

IMMIGRATION AND EMIGRATION
('000 persons)

	2010	2011	2012
Immigrant arrivals	798.3	958.3	1,080.9
Emigrant departures	670.6	679.0	712.0

ECONOMICALLY ACTIVE POPULATION
('000 persons aged 15 years and over, annual averages, preliminary)

	2011	2012	2013
Agriculture, forestry and fishing	674	668	637
Industry	7,724	7,838	7,855
Manufacturing	7,162	7,274	7,297
Construction	2,423	2,460	2,480
Trade, transport, accommodation and food services	9,503	9,579	9,591
Information and communication	1,213	1,245	1,258
Financial and insurance activities	1,202	1,198	1,189
Real estate, renting and business activities	5,816	5,898	6,023
Public services, education, health and other services	12,597	12,722	12,808
Total employed	41,152	41,608	41,841
Unemployed	2,976	2,897	n.a.
Total labour force	44,128	44,505	n.a.

Health and Welfare

KEY INDICATORS

Total fertility rate (children per woman, 2011)	1.4
Under-five mortality rate (per 1,000 live births, 2011)	4
HIV/AIDS (% of persons aged 15–49, 2011)	0.1
Physicians (per 1,000 head, 2009)	3.6
Hospital beds (per 1,000 head, 2009)	8.2
Health expenditure (2010): US $ per head (PPP)	4,342
Health expenditure (2010): % of GDP	11.5
Health expenditure (2010): public (% of total)	76.8
Total carbon dioxide emissions ('000 metric tons, 2010)	745,383.8
Carbon dioxide emissions per head (metric tons, 2010)	9.1
Human Development Index (2012): ranking	5
Human Development Index (2012): value	0.920

For sources and definitions, see explanatory note on p. vi.

Agriculture

PRINCIPAL CROPS
('000 metric tons)

	2010	2011	2012
Wheat	24,107	22,800	22,432
Barley	10,412	8,734	10,422
Maize	4,073	5,184	4,991
Rye	2,903	2,521	3,893
Oats	600	627	758
Triticale (wheat-rye hybrid)	2,157	2,004	2,295
Potatoes	10,202	11,800	10,666
Sugar beet	23,432	29,578	27,891
Broad beans, dry	56	61	61
Sunflower seed	47	53	63
Rapeseed	5,698	3,870	4,821
Cabbages and other brassicas	787	829	803
Cauliflowers and broccoli	152	144	177
Cucumbers and gherkins	243	250	244
Onions, dry	387	506	485
Beans, green	41	39	45
Carrots and turnips	554	534	593
Grapes*	953	1,250	1,226
Apples	835	898	972
Pears	39	47	34
Cherries	31	37	23
Plums and sloes	49	59	36
Strawberries	157	154	156
Currants	12	10	11

* Unofficial figures.

Aggregate production ('000 metric tons, may include official, semi-official or estimated data): Total cereals 44,314 in 2010, 41,938 in 2011, 44,942 in 2012; Total roots and tubers 10,202 in 2010, 11,800 in 2011, 10,666 in 2012; Total vegetables (incl. melons) 3,351 in 2010, 3,594 in 2011, 3,821 in 2012; Total fruits (excl. melons) 2,176 in 2010, 2,572 in 2011, 2,567 in 2012.

Source: FAO.

LIVESTOCK
('000 head at December)

	2010	2011	2012
Horses	461.8	490.0*	500.0*
Cattle	12,809.5	12,562.6	12,477.4
Pigs	26,509.0	26,758.1	28,131.7
Sheep	2,088.5	2,088.5	1,657.8
Goats	150	160	162
Chickens	114,113	118,640†	121,040†
Geese and guinea fowls	278	272†	268*
Ducks	3,164	2,930†	3,000*
Turkeys	11,344	11,196†	12,000*

* FAO estimate.
† Unofficial figure.

Source: FAO.

LIVESTOCK PRODUCTS
('000 metric tons)

	2010	2011	2012
Cattle meat	1,205.0	1,170.4	1,146.3
Sheep meat	38.3	39.9	36.5
Pig meat	5,488.4	5,616.1	5,474.0
Chicken meat	837.1	895.9	903.3
Cows' milk	29,616.3	30,323.5	30,506.9
Goats' milk	12.6	12.9	13.0
Hen eggs	662.4	782.3	832.0
Honey	23.2	25.8	15.7
Wool, greasy*	12.8	13.0	13.5

* FAO estimates.

Source: FAO.

Forestry

ROUNDWOOD REMOVALS
('000 cubic metres, excluding bark, FAO estimates)

	2010	2011	2012
Sawlogs, veneer logs and logs for sleepers	29,748	29,016	26,632
Pulpwood	12,659	13,249	13,211
Other industrial wood	2,980	3,093	3,020
Fuel wood	9,031	10,783	9,476
Total	54,418	56,141	52,338

Source: FAO.

SAWNWOOD PRODUCTION
('000 cubic metres, including railway sleepers)

	2010	2011	2012
Coniferous (softwood)	21,161	21,633	20,032
Broadleaved (hardwood)	898	996	999
Total	22,059	22,628	21,031

Source: FAO.

Fishing

('000 metric tons, live weight)

	2009	2010	2011
Capture	244.0	243.1	233.9
Freshwater fishes	12.5	12.0	13.0
Atlantic cod	18.6	19.5	16.4
Saithe (Pollock)	15.7	13.0	11.6
Blue whiting (Poutassou)	5.0	9.1	0.3
Atlantic herring	37.5	37.0	37.0
European sprat	29.2	21.1	14.7
Atlantic horse mackerel	16.5	21.4	24.6
Atlantic mackerel	22.4	18.9	24.1
Common shrimp	17.3	18.4	17.0
Aquaculture	38.9	40.7	39.1
Common carp	9.9	9.6	5.1
Rainbow trout	20.1	20.0	9.3
Blue mussel	3.6	4.9	20.8
Total catch	283.0	283.8	273.0

Note: Figures exclude aquatic mammals, recorded by number rather than by weight. The number of harbour porpoises caught was: 8 in 2009; 4 in 2010; 5 in 2011.

Source: FAO.

Mining

('000 metric tons unless otherwise indicated)

	2009	2010	2011
Coal, lignite	169,857	169,403	176,502
Coal, anthracite and bituminous	13,766	12,900	12,059
Crude petroleum ('000 42-gallon barrels)	20,500	18,400	19,600
Natural gas, marketable (million cu m)	14,380	12,571	11,900

Source: US Geological Survey.

Industry

SELECTED PRODUCTS
('000 metric tons unless otherwise indicated)

	2010	2011	2012
Margarine	407	409	395
Flour	5,365	5,408	5,531
Refined sugar	3,497	4,234	4,184
Beer ('000 hl)	86,738	87,084	86,083
Cigarettes (million)	217,593	220,060	206,175
Cotton yarn (pure and mixed)	21	n.a.	n.a.
Woven cotton fabrics ('000 sq m)	159,785	n.a.	n.a.
Newsprint	2,561	2,459	2,211
Motor spirit (petrol)	21,542	21,016	20,578
Diesel oil*	29,774	30,426	30,638
Cement	29,661	33,532	31,925
Sulphuric acid	1,690	1,761	2,071
Nitrogenous fertilizers	1,373	1,345	1,330
Artificial resins and plastics	17,747	17,471	16,682
Synthetic rubber	1,076	1,077	1,033
Soap	132	350	155
Aluminium (unwrought):			
primary	329	317	282
secondary	837	851	822
Refined lead (unwrought)	326	n.a.	n.a.
Passenger cars and minibuses ('000)	6,065	6,589	6,199
Bicycles ('000)	1,290	1,327	1,195
Footwear ('000 pairs)†	n.a.	22,471	18,547
Electricity (million kWh)	n.a.	554,304	512,718

* Including light heating oil.
† Excluding rubber and plastic footwear.

Finance

CURRENCY AND EXCHANGE RATES

Monetary Units
100 cent = 1 euro (€).

Sterling and Dollar Equivalents (31 December 2013)
£1 sterling = 1.194 euros;
US $1 = 0.725 euros;
€10 = £8.37 = $13.79.

Average Exchange Rate (euros per US $)

2011	0.7194
2012	0.7783
2013	0.7532

Note: The national currency was formerly the Deutsche Mark (DM). From the introduction of the euro, with German participation, on 1 January 1999, a fixed exchange rate of €1 = DM 1.95583 was in operation. Euro notes and coins were introduced on 1 January 2002. The euro and local currency circulated alongside each other until 28 February, after which the euro became the sole legal tender.

GOVERNMENT FINANCE

(general government transactions, non-cash basis, € '000 million)

Summary of Balances

	2009	2010	2011
Revenue	1,071.7	1,087.3	1,154.9
Less Expense	1,147.1	1,197.9	1,177.7
Net operating balance	–75.4	–110.5	–22.8
Less Net acquisition of non-financial assets	–2.4	–7.0	–3.2
Net lending/borrowing	–73.0	–103.6	–19.7

Revenue

	2009	2010	2011
Taxes	552.0	553.2	593.8
Taxes on income, profits and capital gains	265.4	264.5	289.3
Taxes on goods and services	267.6	269.0	283.0
Social contributions	410.8	421.1	436.9
Grants	4.0	5.3	4.6
Other revenue	105.0	107.8	119.6
Total	1,071.7	1,087.4	1,154.9

Expense/Outlays

Expense by economic type	2009	2010	2011
Compensation of employees	191.0	195.3	200.0
Use of goods and services	115.9	121.0	126.5
Consumption of fixed capital	42.6	43.1	44.5
Interest	63.6	63.4	65.9
Subsidies	27.9	27.9	26.9
Grants	21.2	25.8	25.6
Social benefits	622.9	633.0	633.3
Other expense	62.2	88.5	55.4
Total	1,147.1	1,197.9	1,177.7

Outlays by functions of government*	2009	2010	2011
General public services	149.2	155.2	159.8
Defence	26.1	26.2	27.6
Public order and safety	39.4	40.2	41.3
Economic affairs	92.4	118.9	91.6
Environmental protection	18.9	17.0	17.3
Housing and community amenities	16.5	15.7	14.5
Health	174.3	178.5	182.5
Recreation, culture and religion	19.7	20.4	21.3
Education	104.4	107.0	110.4
Social protection	504.1	511.8	508.3
Total	1,144.7	1,191.0	1,174.5

* Including net acquisition of non-financial assets.

Source: IMF, *Government Finance Statistics Yearbook*.

2012 (general government transactions, € '000 million, provisional): Total revenue 1,193.8 (Taxes 617.7, Social contributions 448.9, Other revenue 127.1); Total expenditure 1,191.5 (Social benefits 643.4, Compensation of employees 203.8, Interest 63.8, Gross capital formation 41.4, Other expenditure 239.1).

INTERNATIONAL RESERVES

(US $ million at 31 December)

	2010	2011	2012
Gold (Eurosystem valuation)	154,202	171,926	181,434
IMF special drawing rights	18,769	18,265	17,908
Reserve position in IMF	6,169	10,580	11,549
Foreign exchange	37,356	38,083	37,964
Total	216,496	238,854	248,855

Source: IMF, *International Financial Statistics*.

MONEY SUPPLY

(incl. shares, depository corporations, national residency criteria, € '000 million at 31 December)

	2010	2011	2012
Currency issued	217.2	229.2	235.6
Deutsche Bundesbank	374.3	399.7	435.9
Demand deposits	1,087.4	1,144.5	1,311.4
Other deposits	1,811.6	1,869.5	1,770.5
Securities other than shares	1,479.4	1,419.0	1,303.8
Money market fund shares	9.8	6.2	7.3
Shares and other equity	494.4	521.0	557.2
Other items (net)	–427.2	–385.0	–360.8
Total	4,672.6	4,804.4	4,824.9

Source: IMF, *International Financial Statistics*.

COST OF LIVING

(Consumer Price Index for all private households; base: 2005 = 100)

	2010	2011	2012
Food	112.5	115.7	119.4
Alcohol and tobacco	113.0	114.6	117.9
Clothes and shoes	103.7	105.6	108.5
Housing, energy and fuel	110.1	113.5	116.1
Furniture and household goods	104.6	105.1	106.1
Health	104.7	105.5	107.7
Transport	112.1	116.9	120.4
Communications	88.0	85.6	84.5
Recreation and culture	101.3	102.3	104.2
Education	131.8	128.8	113.0
Restaurants and hotels	109.9	111.5	113.9
Miscellaneous goods and services	108.4	110.2	110.2
All items	108.2	110.7	112.9

NATIONAL ACCOUNTS

(€ million at current prices, rounded to nearest €10m.)

National Income and Product

	2010	2011	2012
Compensation of employees	1,270,380	1,325,920	1,377,630
Net operating surplus/mixed income	651,830	686,120	676,630
Domestic primary incomes	1,922,210	2,012,040	2,054,260
Consumption of fixed capital	380,180	391,070	402,120
Gross domestic product (GDP) at factor cost	2,302,390	2,403,110	2,456,380
Net taxes on production and imports*	192,610	206,790	210,020
GDP in market prices	2,495,000	2,609,900	2,666,400
Balance of primary income from abroad	54,400	59,020	63,670
Gross national income (GNI)	2,549,400	2,668,920	2,730,070
Less Consumption of fixed capital	380,180	391,070	402,120
Net national income	2,169,220	2,277,850	2,327,950
Current transfers from abroad	13,620	15,120	14,670
Less Current transfers paid abroad	48,770	46,600	48,370
Net national disposable income	2,134,070	2,246,370	2,294,250

* Data obtained as residuals.

Expenditure on the Gross Domestic Product

	2010	2011	2012
Government final consumption expenditure	487,180	499,580	514,350
Private final consumption expenditure	1,435,090	1,498,350	1,533,870
Increase in stocks	–2,520	3,150	–10,280
Gross fixed capital formation	435,050	473,170	470,550
Total domestic expenditure	2,354,800	2,474,250	2,508,490
Exports of goods and services	1,188,590	1,321,430	1,381,030
Less Imports of goods and services	1,048,390	1,185,780	1,223,120
GDP in purchasers' values	2,495,000	2,609,900	2,666,400

Gross Domestic Product by Economic Activity

	2010	2011	2012
Agriculture, hunting, forestry and fishing	17,810	18,460	19,980
Mining and quarrying* Electricity, gas and water supply*	84,330	78,010	82,580
Manufacturing	489,300	529,790	534,360
Construction	102,100	109,180	111,320
Wholesale and retail trade; repair of motor vehicles, motorcycles and personal and household goods; and transport and accommodation	326,270	339,090	347,480
Information and communication	90,230	94,660	96,020
Financial intermediation and insurance	101,780	101,470	94,420
Real estate, renting and business activities†	511,020	537,090	553,800
Public administration and defence; compulsory social security Education Health and social work Other community, social and personal service activities, incl. hotels and restaurants Private households with employed persons	512,320	527,140	546,830
Gross value added in basic prices	2,235,160	2,334,890	2,386,790
Taxes, less subsidies, on products*	259,840	275,010	279,610
GDP in market prices	2,495,000	2,609,900	2,666,400

* Data obtained as residuals.

† Including deduction for financial intermediation services indirectly measured.

BALANCE OF PAYMENTS
(US $ '000 million)

	2010	2011	2012
Exports of goods	1,282.47	1,515.93	1,460.12
Imports of goods	−1,073.06	−1,294.68	−1,221.97
Balance on goods	209.41	221.25	238.16
Exports of services	253.56	274.11	268.50
Imports of services	−276.25	−306.73	−303.27
Balance on goods and services	186.72	188.63	203.39
Primary income received	252.32	275.71	253.87
Primary income paid	−180.22	−194.28	−171.11
Balance on goods, services and primary income	258.82	270.06	286.15
Secondary income received	23.10	27.76	24.17
Secondary income paid	−74.19	−74.50	−71.61
Current balance	207.73	223.32	238.71
Capital account (net)	−0.74	0.91	0.05
Direct investment assets	−93.01	−45.55	−87.67
Direct investment liabilities	27.99	42.79	27.22
Portfolio investment assets	−231.37	−31.02	−139.20
Portfolio investment liabilities	62.76	72.11	54.45
Financial derivatives and employee stock options (net)	−22.97	−38.23	−22.95
Other investment assets	−161.51	−197.30	−230.95
Other investment liabilities	233.96	−24.78	100.48
Net errors and omissions	−20.71	1.66	61.56
Reserves and related items	2.13	3.91	1.70

Source: IMF, *International Financial Statistics*.

OVERSEAS DEVELOPMENT AID
(€ million)

	2009	2010	2011
Bilateral	5,096	6,082	6,256
Multilateral	3,578	3,722	3,880
Total	8,674	9,804	10,136

External Trade

PRINCIPAL COMMODITIES
(distribution by SITC, € million)

Imports c.i.f.	2010	2011	2012
Food and live animals	47,772	52,639	54,190
Crude materials (inedible) except fuels	31,528	38,095	36,428
Mineral fuels, lubricants, etc.	92,604	121,686	135,294
Petroleum, petroleum products, etc.	60,813	78,844	87,866
Chemicals and related products	104,239	114,160	113,755
Organic chemicals	20,654	23,276	24,553
Medicinal and pharmaceutical products	35,989	37,027	35,973
Basic manufactures	105,157	124,255	116,620
Machinery and transport equipment	285,389	303,480	300,255
Power-generating machinery and equipment	24,326	28,552	28,406
General industrial machinery, equipment and parts	28,584	33,774	34,591
Office machines and automatic data-processing equipment	29,831	27,762	26,809
Telecommunications and sound equipment	26,338	26,486	29,362
Other electrical machinery, apparatus and appliances	65,022	66,422	62,024
Road vehicles (incl. air-cushion vehicles) and parts	60,638	71,174	72,674
Other transport equipment	34,238	28,411	26,228
Miscellaneous manufactured articles	90,872	101,072	101,684
Articles of apparel and clothing accessories (excl. footwear)	25,060	28,179	26,649
Total (incl. others)	797,097	902,523	905,925

Exports f.o.b.	2010	2011	2012
Food and live animals	41,244	45,878	48,735
Chemicals and related products	151,138	162,980	170,950
Medical and pharmaceutical products	49,832	50,818	56,031
Basic manufactures	127,984	145,602	142,635
Machinery and transport equipment	457,874	510,453	528,945
Power-generating machinery and equipment	35,898	39,785	42,197
Machinery specialized for particular industries	41,000	48,844	47,884
General industrial machinery and equipment	66,806	75,920	78,522
Office machines and automatic data-processing equipment	20,478	19,877	19,002
Telecommunications and sound equipment	16,901	17,342	18,691
Electrical machinery, apparatus and appliances	76,303	81,094	80,040
Road vehicles (incl. air-cushion vehicles) and parts	154,383	177,938	183,026
Other transport equipment	33,332	34,756	43,318
Miscellaneous manufactured articles	99,423	108,940	109,795
Total (incl. others)	951,960	1,061,225	1,095,766

PRINCIPAL TRADING PARTNERS
(€ million)

Imports c.i.f.	2010	2011	2012
Austria	33,012.8	37,028.4	36,419.4
Belgium	33,304.0	38,327.7	37,763.0
Brazil	9,444.8	11,259.9	10,614.7
China, People's Republic	77,270.2	79,528.2	78,529.3
Czech Republic	28,701.5	32,684.2	32,493.0
Denmark	10,629.7	12,178.1	11,346.2
France	60,672.6	65,948.3	64,035.5
Hungary	16,387.9	18,207.9	18,466.5
Ireland	13,555.7	12,334.0	10,093.2
Italy	41,977.3	47,843.5	47,957.2
Japan	22,475.3	23,595.1	21,910.3
Korea, Republic	11,270.6	9,622.7	8,457.0
Netherlands	67,205.1	81,804.3	85,737.9
Norway	17,166.9	20,634.0	26,273.1
Poland	27,637.0	32,305.4	33,027.3
Russia	31,840.2	40,886.2	42,765.1
Slovakia	9,174.4	10,726.1	12,015.1
Spain	21,954.7	22,490.7	23,206.5
Sweden	12,819.8	14,115.4	13,774.0
Switzerland-Liechtenstein	32,910.3	37,422.9	38,206.7
Turkey	10,016.8	11,790.5	12,071.1
United Kingdom	37,922.7	44,740.7	42,820.1
USA	45,241.1	48,531.5	51,070.5
Total (incl. others)	797,096.9	902,522.8	905,925.4

Exports f.o.b.	2010	2011	2012
Austria	52,156.3	57,670.9	56,591.2
Belgium	45,039.2	46,976.3	43,822.2
Brazil	10,385.9	11,163.1	11,727.5
China, People's Republic	53,790.9	64,863.1	66,746.1
Czech Republic	26,708.2	30,824.5	31,288.7
Denmark	14,053.6	14,769.3	14,893.9
France	89,581.8	101,444.3	102,910.7
Hungary	14,133.5	15,774.5	16,207.2
India	9,281.7	10,855.6	10,421.0
Italy	58,588.7	62,043.6	55,528.7
Japan	13,149.4	15,115.4	17,137.8
Korea, Republic	10,259.0	11,698.2	13,399.0
Netherlands	62,978.3	69,422.8	70,380.8
Poland	37,665.5	43,502.7	41,823.2
Russia	26,354.3	34,458.8	38,103.3
Spain	34,222.0	34,811.1	31,047.5
Sweden	19,376.6	22,034.3	21,092.1
Switzerland-Liechtenstein	42,155.6	48,446.7	49,472.5
Turkey	16,252.5	20,118.3	20,100.0
United Kingdom	58,665.8	65,569.7	73,282.5
USA	65,574.2	73,775.6	86,971.4
Total (incl. others)	951,959.5	1,061,225.3	1,095,766.4

Transport

FEDERAL RAILWAYS
(traffic)

	2010	2011	2012
Passengers (million)	2,431	2,474	2,571
Freight carried ('000 tons)	355,715	374,737	366,140
Freight net ton-km (million)	107,317	113,317	110,065

ROAD TRAFFIC
('000 licensed vehicles at 1 January)

	2011	2012	2013
Passenger cars	42,301.6	42,927.6	43,431.1
Lorries	2,441.4	2,528.7	25,785.7
Buses	76.5	76.0	76.0
Motorcycles	3,827.9	3,908.1	3,983.0
Trailers	6,057.3	6,213.9	6,358.6

SHIPPING
Inland Waterways

	2010	2011	2012
Freight ton-km (million)	62,278	55,027	58,487

Flag Registered Fleet
(at 31 December)

	2011	2012	2013
Number of vessels	1,287	1,211	1,195
Total displacement ('000 grt)	16,022.4	14,246.5	12,731.9

Source: Lloyd's List Intelligence (www.lloydslistintelligence.com).

International Sea-borne Traffic
(incl. transshipments, '000 metric tons)

	2010	2011	2012
Freight unloaded	166,786	177,085	179,126
Freight loaded	102,922	112,480	119,667

CIVIL AVIATION
(traffic on scheduled services)

	2010	2011
Kilometres flown (million)	1,331	1,418
Passengers carried ('000)	101,852	112,016
Passenger-km (million)	201,537	220,036
Total ton-km (million)	27,767	29,925

Source: UN, *Statistical Yearbook*.

Passengers carried ('000): 110,576 in 2012 (Source: World Bank, World Development Indicators database).

Tourism

FOREIGN TOURIST ARRIVALS
('000)*

Country of residence	2010	2011	2012
Austria	1,387.7	1,494.7	1,567.5
Belgium and Luxembourg	1,347.3	1,412.6	1,470.2
Denmark	1,214.3	1,242.8	1,356.7
France	1,366.2	1,462.1	1,535.1
Italy	1,524.1	1,538.4	1,581.0
Japan	605.2	642.5	734.5
Netherlands	3,917.6	4,035.8	4,169.4
Poland	604.3	684.2	737.3
Spain	842.8	889.5	889.7
Sweden	859.3	846.6	897.0
Switzerland	2,028.4	2,301.5	2,489.6
United Kingdom	1,986.9	2,054.8	2,162.5
USA	2,206.3	2,163.8	2,314.0
Total (incl. others)	26,875.3	28,099.8	30,410.5

* Figures refer to arrivals at all accommodation types.

Tourism receipts (€ million, excl. passenger transport): 34,679 in 2010; 38,869 in 2011; 38,114 in 2012 (provisional) (Source: World Tourism Organization).

Communications Media

	2010	2011	2012
Telephones ('000 main lines in use)	52,900	51,800	50,700
Mobile cellular telephones ('000 subscribers)	104,560	108,700	107,658
Broadband subscribers ('000)	26,090	27,186	27,907

Source: International Telecommunication Union.

Education

(2010/11 unless otherwise indicated)

	Teachers	Students
Pre-primary	231,698	2,362,441
Primary	252,845	2,989,678
Secondary:		
lower secondary	403,058	4,802,512
upper secondary:		
general	125,480	1,401,481
vocational	55,997	1,324,277
Post-secondary non-tertiary:		
general	13,422	520,872
vocational	16,911	
Higher:		
non-university institutions	353,690*	917,062†
universities and equivalent institutions		1,701,159†

* 2012.

† 2012/13, preliminary.

Source: mainly UNESCO Institute for Statistics.

Pupil-teacher ratio (primary education, UNESCO estimate): 11.8 in 2010/11 (Source: UNESCO Institute for Statistics).

Directory

The Government

HEAD OF STATE

Federal President: Joachim Gauck (assumed office 18 March 2012).

THE FEDERAL GOVERNMENT

(April 2014)

A coalition of the Christlich-Demokratische Union Deutschlands/ Christlich-Soziale Union (CDU/CSU) and the Sozialdemokratische Partei Deutschlands (SPD).

Federal Chancellor: Angela Merkel (CDU).

Federal Vice-Chancellor and Federal Minister of Economic Affairs and Energy: Sigmar Gabriel (SPD).

Federal Minister of Foreign Affairs: Frank-Walter Steinmeier (SPD).

Federal Minister of the Interior: Thomas de Maizière (CDU).

Federal Minister of Justice and Consumer Protection: Heiko Maas (SPD).

Federal Minister of Finance: Wolfgang Schäuble (CDU).

Federal Minister of Labour and Social Affairs: Andrea Nahles (SPD).

Federal Minister of Food and Agriculture: Christian Schmidt (CSU).

Federal Minister of Defence: Ursula von der Leyen (CDU).

Federal Minister of Family Affairs, Senior Citizens, Women and Youth: Manuela Schwesig (SPD).

Federal Minister of Health: Herrmann Gröhe (CDU).

Federal Minister of Transport and Digital Infrastructure: Alexander Dobrindt (CSU).

Federal Minister of the Environment, Nature Conservation, Building and Nuclear Safety: Barbara Hendricks (SPD).

Federal Minister of Education and Research: Johanna Wanka (CDU).

Federal Minister of Economic Co-operation and Development: Gerd Müller (CSU).

Head of the Federal Chancellery and Federal Minister for Special Tasks: Peter Altmaier (CDU).

MINISTRIES

Office of the Federal President: 11010 Berlin; Bundespräsidialamt, Spreeweg 1, 10557 Berlin; tel. (30) 20000; fax (30) 20001999; e-mail bundespraesidialamt@bpra.bund.de; internet www.bundespraesident.de.

Federal Chancellery: Bundeskanzler-Amt, Willy-Brandt Str. 1, 10557 Berlin; tel. (30) 40000; fax (30) 40002357; e-mail internetpost@bpa.bund.de; internet www.bundeskanzlerin.de.

Press and Information Office of the Federal Government: Dorotheenstr. 84, 10117 Berlin; 11044 Berlin; tel. (30) 182720; fax (30) 18102720; e-mail internetpost@bundesregierung.de; internet www.bundesregierung.de.

Federal Ministry of Defence: Stauffenbergstr. 18, 10785 Berlin; tel. (30) 1824000; fax (30) 18245357; e-mail poststelle@bmvg.bund.de; internet www.bmvg.de.

Federal Ministry of Economic Co-operation and Development: Dahlmannstr. 4, 53113 Bonn; Postfach 120322, 53045 Bonn; tel. (228) 995350; fax (228) 995353500; e-mail info@bmz.bund.de; internet www.bmz.de.

Federal Ministry of Economic Affairs and Energy: 11019 Berlin; Scharnhorststr. 34–37, 10115 Berlin; tel. (30) 186150; fax (30) 186157010; e-mail info@bmwi.bund.de; internet www.bmwi.de.

Federal Ministry of Education and Research: Heinemannstr. 2, 53175 Bonn; tel. (228) 99570; fax (228) 995783601; e-mail information@bmbf.bund.de; internet www.bmbf.de.

Federal Ministry of the Environment, Nature Conservation, Building and Nuclear Safety: Stresemannstr. 128–130, 10117 Berlin; tel. (30) 183050; fax (30) 183054375; e-mail service@bmu.bund.de; internet www.bmu.de.

Federal Ministry of Family Affairs, Senior Citizens, Women and Youth: Glinkastr. 24, 10117 Berlin; tel. (30) 185550; fax (30) 185551145; e-mail poststelle@bmfsfj.bund.de; internet www.bmfsfj.de.

Federal Ministry of Finance: 11016 Berlin; Wilhelmstr. 97, 10117 Berlin; tel. (30) 186820; fax (30) 186824248; e-mail poststelle@bmf.bund.de; internet www.bundesfinanzministerium.de.

Federal Ministry of Food and Agriculture: 11055 Berlin; Wilhelmstr. 54, 10117 Berlin; tel. (30) 185290; fax (30) 185294262; e-mail poststelle@bmelv.bund.de; internet www.bmelv.de.

Federal Ministry of Foreign Affairs: 11013 Berlin; Werderscher Markt 1, 10117 Berlin; tel. (30) 18170; fax (30) 18173402; e-mail poststelle@auswaertiges-amt.de; internet www.auswaertiges-amt.de.

Federal Ministry of Health: 53107 Bonn; Rochusstr. 1, 53123 Bonn; tel. (228) 994410; fax (228) 994411921; e-mail info@bmg.bund.de; internet www.bmg.bund.de.

Federal Ministry of the Interior: Alt-Moabit 101D, 10559 Berlin; tel. (30) 186810; fax (30) 186812926; e-mail poststelle@bmi.bund.de; internet www.bmi.bund.de.

Federal Ministry of Justice and Consumer Protection: Mohrenstr. 37, 10117 Berlin; tel. (30) 185800; fax (30) 185809525; e-mail poststelle@bmj.bund.de; internet www.bmj.de.

Federal Ministry of Labour and Social Affairs: Wilhelmstr. 49, 10117 Berlin; tel. (30) 185270; fax (30) 185271830; e-mail info@bmas.bund.de; internet www.bmas.de.

Federal Ministry of Transport and Digital Infrastructure: Invalidenstr. 44, 10115 Berlin; tel. (30) 183000; fax (30) 183001920; e-mail buergerinfo@bmvbs.bund.de; internet www.bmvbs.de.

Legislature

Federal Assembly (Bundestag)

Pl. der Republik 1, 11011 Berlin; tel. (30) 2270; fax (30) 22736979; e-mail mail@bundestag.de; internet www.bundestag.de.

President: Prof. Dr NORBERT LAMMERT (CDU).

Vice-Presidents: PETER HINTZE (CDU/CSU), Dr JOHANNES SINGHAMMER (CDU/CSU), EDELGARD BULMAHN (SPD), ULLA SCHMIDT (SPD), PETRA PAU (Die Linke), CLAUDIA ROTH (Bündnis 90/Die Grünen).

General Election, 22 September 2013

Parties and Groups	Votes*	% of votes*	Seats
Christlich-Demokratische Union Deutschlands/Christlich-Soziale Union (CDU/CSU)†	18,165,446	41.54	311
Sozialdemokratische Partei Deutschlands (SPD)	11,252,215	25.73	193
Die Linke	3,755,699	8.59	64
Bündnis 90/Die Grünen	3,694,057	8.45	63
Freie Demokratische Partei (FDP)	2,083,533	4.76	—
Alternative für Deutschland (AfD)	2,056,985	4.70	—
Others	2,718,921	6.22	—
Total	43,726,856	100.00	631

* Figures refer to valid second votes (i.e. for state party lists). The total number of valid first votes (for individual candidates) was 44,309,925. In addition, there were 684,883 invalid first votes and 583,069 invalid second votes.

† Of which the CDU received 14,921,877 votes (34.13%—255 seats) and the CSU received 3,243,569 votes (7.42%—56 seats).

Federal Council (Bundesrat)

Niederkirchnerstr. 1–4, 10117 Berlin; tel. (18) 91000; fax (30) 189100400; e-mail bundesrat@bundesrat.de; internet www.bundesrat.de.

The Bundesrat has 69 members. Each Land (state) has three, four, five or six votes, depending on the size of its population, and may send as many members to the sessions as it has votes. The head of government of each Land is automatically a member of the Bundesrat. Members of the Federal Government attend the sessions, which are held every two to three weeks.

President: STEPHAN WEIL (SPD) (1 Nov. 2013–31 Oct. 2014).

Länder	Seats
Nordrhein-Westfalen (North Rhine-Westphalia)	6
Bayern (Bavaria)	6
Baden-Württemberg	6
Niedersachsen (Lower Saxony)	6
Hessen (Hesse)	5
Sachsen (Saxony)	4
Rheinland-Pfalz (Rhineland-Palatinate)	4
Berlin	4
Schleswig-Holstein	4
Brandenburg	4
Sachsen-Anhalt (Saxony-Anhalt)	4
Thüringen (Thuringia)	4
Hamburg	3
Mecklenburg-Vorpommern (Mecklenburg-Western Pomerania)	3
Saarland	3
Bremen	3
Total	69

The Land Governments

The 16 Länder of Germany are autonomous but not sovereign states, enjoying a high degree of self-government and extensive legislative powers. Thirteen of the Länder have a Government (Landesregierung) and an Assembly (Landtag). The equivalent of the Landesregierung in Berlin, Bremen and Hamburg is the Senate (Senat). The equivalent of the Landtag is the House of Representatives (Abgeordnetenhaus) in Berlin and the City Council (Bürgerschaft) in Bremen and Hamburg.

BADEN-WÜRTTEMBERG

The Constitution was adopted by the Assembly in Stuttgart on 11 November 1953 and came into force on 19 November. The Minister-President, who is elected by the Assembly, appoints and dismisses Ministers. The Government is currently formed by a coalition of Bündnis 90/Die Grünen and the SPD.

Minister-President: WINFRIED KRETSCHMANN (Bündnis 90/Die Grünen).

Landtag von Baden-Württemberg

Haus des Landtags, Konrad-Adenauer-Str. 3, 70173 Stuttgart; tel. (711) 20630; fax (711) 2063299; e-mail post@landtag-bw.de; internet www.landtag-bw.de.

President of Assembly: GUIDO WOLF (CDU).

Election, 27 March 2011

Party	Seats
Christlich-Demokratische Union Deutschlands (CDU)	60
Bündnis 90/Die Grünen	36
Sozialdemokratische Partei Deutschlands (SPD)	35
Freie Demokratische Partei (FDP)	7
Total	138

The Land is divided into four administrative districts: Stuttgart, Karlsruhe, Tübingen and Freiburg.

BAYERN (BAVARIA)

The Constitution of Bavaria provides for a unicameral Assembly and a Constitutional Court. Provision is also made for referendums. The Minister-President, who is elected by the Assembly for five years, appoints the Ministers and Secretaries of State with the consent of the Assembly.

Minister-President: HORST SEEHOFER (CSU).

Bayerischer Landtag

Landtagsamt, Maximilaneum, 81627 München; tel. (89) 41260; fax (89) 41261392; e-mail landtag@bayern.landtag.de; internet www.bayern.landtag.de.

President of Assembly: BARBARA STAMM (CSU).

Election, 15 September 2013

Party	Seats
Christlich-Soziale Union (CSU)	101
Sozialdemokratische Partei Deutschlands (SPD)	42
Freie Wähler	19
Bündnis 90/Die Grünen	18
Total	180

Bayern is divided into seven districts: Mittelfranken, Oberfranken, Unterfranken, Schwaben, Niederbayern, Oberpfalz and Oberbayern.

BERLIN

The House of Representatives (Abgeordnetenhaus) is the legislative body. The executive agency is the Senate, which is composed of the Governing Mayor (Regierender Bürgermeister) and up to 10 Senators, from among whom the deputy mayor is elected. The Governing Mayor and the senators are elected by a majority of the House of Representatives. The Senate is responsible to the House of Representatives and dependent on its confidence.

Regierender Bürgermeister: KLAUS WOWEREIT (SPD).

Abgeordnetenhaus von Berlin (House of Representatives)

Niederkirchnerstr. 5, 10117 Berlin; tel. (30) 23250; e-mail verwaltung@parlament-berlin.de; internet www.parlament-berlin.de.

President of House of Representatives: RALF WIELAND (SPD).

Election, 18 September 2011

Party	Seats
Sozialdemokratische Partei Deutschlands (SPD)	48
Christlich-Demokratische Union Deutschlands (CDU)	39
Bündnis 90/Die Grünen	30
Die Linke	20
Piratenpartei Deutschland	15
Total	152

BRANDENBURG

The Constitution of Brandenburg was adopted on 14 June 1992 and came into force on 20 August. It was amended on 7 April 1999. The Assembly elects the Minister-President, who appoints Ministers. The Government is currently formed of a coalition of the SPD and Die Linke.

Minister-President: Dr DIETMAR WOIDKE (SPD).

Landtag Brandenburg

Postfach 601064, 14410 Potsdam; Am Havelblick 8, 14473 Potsdam; tel. (331) 9660; fax (331) 9661210; e-mail poststelle@landtag.brandenburg.de; internet www.landtag.brandenburg.de.

President of Assembly: GUNTER FRITSCH (SPD).

Election, 27 September 2009

Party	Seats
Sozialdemokratische Partei Deutschlands (SPD)	31
Die Linke	26
Christlich-Demokratische Union Deutschlands (CDU)	19
Freie Demokratische Partei (FDP)	7
Bündnis 90/Die Grünen	5
Total	88

BREMEN

The Constitution of the Free Hanseatic City of Bremen was approved by referendum on 12 October 1947. The main constitutional organs are the City Council (Bürgerschaft), the Senate and the Constitutional Court. The Senate is the executive organ elected by the Council for the duration of its own tenure of office. The Senate elects from its own ranks two Mayors (Bürgermeister), one of whom becomes President of the Senate. Decisions of the Council are subject to the delaying veto of the Senate. The Government is currently formed from a coalition of the SPD and Bündnis 90/Die Grünen.

First Bürgermeister and President of the Senate: JENS BÖHRNSEN (SPD).

Bremische Bürgerschaft (Bremen City Council)

Am Markt 20, 28195 Bremen; tel. (421) 3614555; fax (421) 36112492; e-mail geschaeftsstelle@buergerschaft.bremen.de; internet www.bremische-buergerschaft.de.

President of the City Council: CHRISTIAN WEBER (SPD).

Election, 22 May 2011

Party	Seats
Sozialdemokratische Partei Deutschlands (SPD)	36
Bündnis 90/Die Grünen	21
Christlich-Demokratische Union Deutschlands (CDU)	20
Die Linke	5
Bürger in Wut (BIW)	1
Total	83

HAMBURG

The Constitution of the Free and Hanseatic City of Hamburg was adopted in June 1952. The City Council (Bürgerschaft) elects the President of the Senate (government), who appoints and dismisses members of the Senate. The Senate is currently composed of members of the SPD.

President of Senate and First Bürgermeister: OLAF SCHOLZ (SPD).

Bürgerschaft der Freien und Hansestadt Hamburg (Hamburg City Council)

Rathaus, Rathausmarkt 1, 20095 Hamburg; tel. (40) 428312408; fax (40) 428312558; e-mail oeffentlichkeitsservice@bk.hamburg.de; internet www.hamburgische-buergerschaft.de.

President: CAROLA VEIT (SPD).

Election, 20 February 2011

Party	Seats
Sozialdemokratische Partei Deutschlands (SPD)	62
Christlich-Demokratische Union Deutschlands (CDU)	28
Bündnis 90/Die Grünen—Grüne Alternative Liste (GAL)	14
Freie Demokratische Partei (FDP)	9
Die Linke	8
Total	121

HESSEN (HESSE)

The Constitution of this Land dates from 1 December 1946. The Minister-President is elected by the Assembly, and appoints and dismisses Ministers with its consent. The Assembly can force the resignation of the Government by a vote of no confidence. The Government is currently formed by a coalition of the CDU and the FDP.

Minister-President: VOLKER BOUFFIER (CDU).

Hessischer Landtag

Schlosspl. 1–3, 65183 Wiesbaden; tel. (611) 3500; fax (611) 350434; e-mail oeffentlichkeit@ltg.hessen.de; internet www.hessischer-landtag.de.

President of Assembly: NORBERT KARTMANN (CDU).

Election, 22 September 2013

Party	Seats
Christlich-Demokratische Union Deutschlands (CDU)	47
Sozialdemokratische Partei Deutschlands (SPD)	37
Bündnis 90/Die Grünen	14
Die Linke	6
Freie Demokratische Partei (FDP)	6
Total	110

Hessen is divided into three governmental districts: Kassel, Giessen and Darmstadt.

MECKLENBURG-VORPOMMERN (MECKLENBURG-WESTERN POMERANIA)

The Constitution was adopted by the Assembly on 14 May 1993. The Assembly elects the Minister-President, who appoints and dismisses Ministers. The Government is currently formed by a coalition of the SPD and the CDU.

Minister-President: Dr ERWIN SELLERING (SPD).

Landtag Mecklenburg-Vorpommern

Schloss, Lennéstr. 1, 19053 Schwerin; tel. (385) 5250; fax (385) 5252141; e-mail poststelle@landtag-mv.de; internet www.landtag-mv.de.

President of Assembly: SYLVIA BRETSCHNEIDER (SPD).

Election, 4 September 2011

Party	Seats
Sozialdemokratische Partei Deutschlands (SPD)	27
Christlich-Demokratische Union Deutschlands (CDU)	18
Die Linke	14
Bündnis 90/Die Grünen	7
Nationaldemokratische Partei Deutschlands (NPD)	5
Total	71

NIEDERSACHSEN (LOWER SAXONY)

The Constitution was adopted by the Assembly on 19 May 1993 and came into force on 1 June. The Minister-President is elected by the Assembly, with whose consent he/she appoints and dismisses Ministers. The Government is currently formed of a coalition of the SPD and Bündnis 90/Die Grünen.

Minister-President: STEPHAN WEIL (SPD).

Landtag Niedersachsen

Hinrich-Wilhelm-Kopf-Pl. 1, 30159 Hannover; tel. (511) 30300; fax (511) 30302806; e-mail poststelle@lt.niedersachsen.de; internet www.landtag-niedersachsen.de.

President of Assembly: BERND BUSEMANN (CDU).

Election, 20 January 2013

Party	Seats
Christlich-Demokratische Union Deutschlands (CDU)	54
Sozialdemokratische Partei Deutschlands (SPD)	49
Bündnis 90/Die Grünen	20
Freie Demokratische Partei (FDP)	14
Total	137

NORDRHEIN-WESTFALEN (NORTH RHINE-WESTPHALIA)

The present Constitution was adopted by the Assembly on 6 June 1950, and was endorsed by the electorate in the elections held on 18 June. The Government is presided over by the Minister-President, who appoints Ministers. After an early election which was held on 13 May 2012 the SPD and Bündnis 90/Die Grünen formed a Government.

Minister-President: HANNELORE KRAFT (SPD).

Landtag von Nordrhein-Westfalen

Postfach 101143, 40002 Düsseldorf; Pl. des Landtags 1, 40221 Düsseldorf; tel. (211) 8840; fax (211) 8842258; e-mail email@landtag.nrw.de; internet www.landtag.nrw.de.

President of Assembly: CARINA GÖDECKE (SPD).

Election, 13 May 2012

Party	Seats
Sozialdemokratische Partei Deutschlands (SPD)	99
Christlich-Demokratische Union Deutschlands (CDU)	67
Bündnis 90/Die Grünen	29
Freie Demokratische Partei (FDP)	22
Piratenpartei Deutschland	20
Total	237

The Land is divided into five governmental districts: Düsseldorf, Münster, Arnsberg, Detmold and Köln.

RHEINLAND-PFALZ (RHINELAND-PALATINATE)

The three chief agencies of the Constitution of this Land are the Assembly, the Government and the Constitutional Court. The Minister-President is elected by the Assembly, with whose consent he or she appoints and dismisses Ministers. Following the election of 27 March 2011, the SPD formed a coalition with Bündnis 90/Die Grünen.

Minister-President: MALU DREYER (SPD).

Landtag Rheinland-Pfalz

Postfach 3040, 55020 Mainz; Deutschhauspl. 12, 55116 Mainz; tel. (6131) 2080; fax (6131) 2082447; e-mail poststelle@landtag.rlp.de; internet www.landtag.rlp.de.

President of Assembly: JOACHIM MERTES (SPD).

Election, 27 March 2011

Party	Seats
Sozialdemokratische Partei Deutschlands (SPD)	42
Christlich-Demokratische Union Deutschlands (CDU)	41
Bündnis 90/Die Grünen	18
Total	101

SAARLAND

Under the Constitution, which came into force on 1 January 1957, Saarland was politically integrated into the FRG as a Land. It was economically integrated into the FRG in July 1959. The Minister-President is elected by the Assembly. Following an early election on 25 March 2012, the CDU formed a coalition with the SPD.

Minister-President: ANNEGRET KRAMP-KARRENBAUER (CDU).

Landtag des Saarlandes

Postfach 101833, 66018 Saarbrücken; Franz-Josef-Röder Str. 7, 66119 Saarbrücken; tel. (681) 50020; fax (681) 5002546; e-mail r.riemann@landtag-saar.de; internet www.landtag-saar.de.

President of the Assembly: HANS LEY (CDU).

Election, 25 March 2012

Party	Seats
Christlich-Demokratische Union Deutschlands (CDU)	19
Sozialdemokratische Partei Deutschlands (SPD)	17
Die Linke	9
Piratenpartei Deutschland	4
Bündnis 90/Die Grünen	2
Total	51

SACHSEN (SAXONY)

The Constitution of Sachsen was adopted on 26 May 1992 and came into force on 6 June. The Assembly elects the Minister-President and can force the resignation of the Government by a vote of no confidence, if a majority of parliamentarians can agree on a replacement candidate. The Government is currently formed from a coalition of the CDU and FDP.

Minister-President: STANISLAW TILLICH (CDU).

Sächsischer Landtag

Postfach 120705, 01008 Dresden; Bernhard-von-Lindenau Pl. 1, 01067 Dresden; tel. (351) 49350; fax (351) 4935900; e-mail info@slt.sachsen.de; internet www.landtag.sachsen.de.

President of Assembly: Dr MATTHIAS RÖSSLER (CDU).

Election, 30 August 2009

Party	Seats
Christlich-Demokratische Union Deutschlands (CDU)	58
Die Linke	29
Sozialdemokratische Partei Deutschlands (SPD)	14
Freie Demokratische Partei (FDP)	14
Bündnis 90/Die Grünen	9
Nationaldemokratische Partei Deutschlands (NPD)	8
Total	132

Sachsen is divided into three districts: Chemnitz, Dresden and Leipzig.

SACHSEN-ANHALT (SAXONY-ANHALT)

The Constitution of Sachsen-Anhalt was adopted on 16 July 1992. The Assembly elects the Minister-President, who appoints and dismisses Ministers. The Government is formed by a coalition of the CDU and SPD.

Minister-President: Dr REINER HASELOFF (CDU).

Landtag von Sachsen-Anhalt

Dompl. 6–9, 39104 Magdeburg; tel. (391) 5600; fax (391) 5601123; e-mail kontakt@lt.sachsen-anhalt.de; internet www.landtag.sachsen-anhalt.de.

President of Assembly: DETLEF GÜRTH (CDU).

Election, 20 March 2011

Party	Seats
Christlich-Demokratische Union Deutschlands (CDU)	41
Die Linke	29
Sozialdemokratische Partei Deutschlands (SPD)	26
Bündnis 90/Die Grünen	9
Total	105

SCHLESWIG-HOLSTEIN

The Provisional Constitution was adopted by the Assembly on 13 December 1949. The Assembly elects the Minister-President, who appoints and dismisses Ministers. The Government is currently formed by a coalition of the SPD, Bündnis 90/Die Grünen and the SSW.

Minister-President: TORSTEN ALBIG (SPD).

Landtag Schleswig-Holstein

Düsternbrooker Weg 70, 24105 Kiel; tel. (431) 9880; fax (431) 9881119; e-mail annette.wiese-krukowska@landtag.ltsh.de; internet www.landtag.ltsh.de.

President of Assembly: KLAUS SCHLIE (CDU).

Election, 6 May 2012

Party	Seats
Christlich-Demokratische Union Deutschlands (CDU)	22
Sozialdemokratische Partei Deutschlands (SPD)	22
Bündnis 90/Die Grünen	10
Freie Demokratische Partei (FDP)	6
Piratenpartei Deutschland	6
Südschleswigscher Wählerverband (SSW)	3
Total	69

THÜRINGEN (THURINGIA)

The Constitution of Thüringen was adopted on 25 October 1993. The Assembly elects the Minister-President and can force the resignation of the Government by a vote of no confidence, if a majority of parliamentarians agree on a replacement candidate. The Government is currently formed of a coalition of the CDU and the SPD.

Minister-President: CHRISTINE LIEBERKNECHT (CDU).

Thüringer Landtag

Jürgen-Fuchs Str. 1, 99096 Erfurt; tel. (361) 3772006; fax (361) 3772004; e-mail pressestelle@landtag.thueringen.de; internet www.thueringen.de/tlt.

President of Assembly: BIRGIT DIEZEL (CDU).

Election, 30 August 2009

Party	Seats
Christlich-Demokratische Union Deutschlands (CDU)	30
Die Linke	27
Sozialdemokratische Partei Deutschlands (SPD)	18
Freie Demokratische Partei (FDP)	7
Bündnis 90/Die Grünen	6
Total	88

Election Commission

Bundeswahlleiter (Federal Returning Officer): Statistisches Bundesamt, 65180 Wiesbaden; tel. (611) 754863; fax (611) 724000; e-mail bundeswahlleiter@destatis.de; internet www.bundeswahlleiter.de; Federal Returning Officer RODERICH EGELER (Pres., Federal Office of Statistics); Deputy Federal Returning Officer DIETER SARREITHER.

Political Organizations

Alternative für Deutschland (AfD) (Alternative for Germany): Frankfurter Landstr. 153–155, 61231 Bad Nauheim; e-mail geschaeftsstelle@alternativefuer.de; internet www.alternativefuer.de; f. 2013; anti-euro; Spokespersons Dr KONRAD ADAM, Prof. Dr BERND LUCKE.

Bündnis 90/Die Grünen (Alliance 90/The Greens): Pl. vor dem Neuen Tor 1, 10115 Berlin; tel. (30) 284420; fax (30) 28442210; e-mail info@gruene.de; internet www.gruene.de; f. 1993; merger of Bündnis 90 (f. 1990 as an electoral political assen of citizens' movements of the former GDR) and Die Grünen (f. 1980, largely composed of the membership of the Grüne Aktion Zukunft, the Grüne Liste, Umweltschutz and the Aktionsgemeinschaft Unabhängiger Deutscher, also including groups of widely varying political views); essentially left-wing party programme includes ecological issues, democratization of society at all levels, social justice, comprehensive disarmament; Co-Chair. SIMONE PETER, CEM ÖZDEMIR; Sec.-Gen. MICHAEL KELLNER.

Bürger in Wut (BIW) (Citizens in Rage): Torstr. 195, 10115 Berlin; tel. (30) 208664660; fax (30) 208664661; e-mail info@buerger-in-wut.de; internet www.buerger-in-wut.de; f. 2004; supports free democracy; Chair. JAN TIMKE.

Christlich-Demokratische Union Deutschlands/Christlich-Soziale Union (CDU/CSU) (Christian Democratic and Christian Social Union): Pl. der Republik 1, 11011 Berlin; tel. (30) 22755550; fax (30) 22756061; e-mail fraktion@cducsu.de; internet www.cducsu.de; alliance of the CDU and its sister party in Bavaria, the CSU; forms a single group in the Bundestag; Parliamentary Leader VOLKER KAUDER.

CDU: Klingelhöferstr. 8, 10785 Berlin; tel. (30) 220700; fax (30) 22070111; e-mail info@cdu.de; internet www.cdu.de; f. 1945; became a federal party in 1950; advocates united action between Catholics and Protestants for rebuilding German life on a Christian-Democratic basis, while guaranteeing private property and the freedom of the individual, and for a 'free and equal Germany in a free, politically united and socially just Europe'; other objectives are to guarantee close ties with allies within NATO and the EU; c. 520,000 mems; Chair. Dr ANGELA MERKEL; Sec.-Gen. Dr PETER TAUBER.

CSU: Franz Josef Strauss-Haus, Nymphenburger Str. 64, 80335 München; tel. (89) 12430; fax (89) 1243299; e-mail landesleitung@csu-bayern.de; internet www.csu.de; f. 1945; Christian Social party, aiming for a free market economy 'in the service of man's economic and intellectual freedom'; also combines national consciousness with support for a united Europe; 181,000 mems; Chair. HORST SEEHOFER; Sec.-Gen. ANDREAS SCHEUER.

Deutsche Kommunistische Partei (DKP) (German Communist Party): Hoffnungstr. 18, 45127 Essen; tel. (201) 1778890; fax (201) 17788929; e-mail pv@dkp-online.de; internet www.dkp.de; Chair. PATRIK KÖBELE.

Freie Demokratische Partei (FDP) (Free Democratic Party): Reinhardtstr. 14, 10117 Berlin; tel. (30) 28495820; fax (30) 28495822; e-mail fdp-point@fdp.de; internet www.fdp-bundespartei.de; f. 1948; represents democratic liberalism and makes the individual the focal point of the state and its laws and economy; in Aug. 1990 incorporated the 3 liberal parties of the former GDR—the Association of Free Democrats, the German Forum Party and the FDP; publishes *Elde*; c. 70,000 mems; Chair. CHRISTIAN LINDNER; Parliamentary Leader RAINER BRÜDERLE; Sec.-Gen. NICOLA BEER.

Freie Wähler (FW) (Independent Voters): Mühlenstr. 1, 27777 Ganderkesee; tel. (4222) 2094925; fax (4222) 2094923; e-mail info@freiewaehler.eu; internet www.freiewaehler.eu; f. 1946; non-ideological, centrist; regional orgs in all 16 Länder; Chair. HUBERT AIWANGER; c. 280,000 mems.

Die Linke (Left Party): Karl-Liebknecht-Haus, Kleine Alexanderstr. 28, 10178 Berlin; tel. (30) 24009397; fax (30) 24009310; e-mail bundesgeschaeftsstelle@die-linke.de; internet www.die-linke.de; successor to the Sozialistische Einheitspartei Deutschlands (SED—Socialist Unity Party, f. 1946 as a result of the unification of the Social Democratic Party and the Communist Party in Eastern Germany), which had been the dominant political force in the GDR until late 1989; renamed Partei des Demokratischen Sozialismus 1990; restyled Linkspartei.PDS 2005; adopted present name 2007 following merger with Wahlalternative Arbeit und soziale Gerechtigkeit (WASG—Electoral Alternative Jobs and Social Justice); has renounced Stalinism, opposes fascism, right-wing extremism and xenophobia, advocates a socially and ecologically sustainable market economy with public, collective and private ownership of the means of production, opposes terrorism, supports international disarmament and peaceful solutions to international conflicts; Co-Chair. KATJA KIPPING, BERND RIEXINGER; Parliamentary Leader GREGOR GYSI; Sec.-Gen. MATTHIAS HÖHN.

Nationaldemokratische Partei Deutschlands (NPD) (National Democratic Party of Germany): Seelenbinderstr. 42, 12555 Berlin; Postfach 840157, 12531 Berlin; tel. (30) 650110; fax (30) 65011140; e-mail parteizentrale@npd.de; internet www.npd.de; f. 1964; right-wing; 7,000 mems; youth organization Junge Nationaldemokraten (JN), 6,000 mems; Chair. UDO PASTÖRS.

Neues Forum (New Forum): Winsstr. 60, 10405 Berlin; tel. (30) 2479404; fax (30) 24725605; e-mail info@neuesforum.de; internet www.neuesforum.de; f. 1989 as a citizens' action group; played prominent role in democratic movement in former GDR; campaigns for peace, social justice and protection of the environment; Leaders SABINE SCHAAF, REINHARD SCHULT, KLAUS TONNDORF.

Piratenpartei Deutschland (Pirate Party of Germany): Pflugstr. 9A, 10115 Berlin; tel. (30) 27572040; fax (30) 609897517; e-mail bgs_anfragen@piratenpartei.de; internet www.piratenpartei.de; f. 2006; advocates freedom of information, environmental protection, transparency of government; Chair. THORSTEN WIRTH.

Die Republikaner (REP) (Republican Party): Postfach 870210, 13162 Berlin; tel. (8233) 7950871; fax (8233) 7951138; e-mail bgst@rep.de; internet www.rep.de; f. 1983; conservative right-wing; publishes *Neue Republik*; c. 15,000 mems; Chair. Dr ROLF SCHLIERER.

Sozialdemokratische Partei Deutschlands (SPD) (Social Democratic Party of Germany): Willy-Brandt-Haus, Wilhelmstr. 141, 10963 Berlin; tel. (30) 25991500; fax (30) 25991507; e-mail parteivorstand@spd.de; internet www.spd.de; f. 1863; maintains that a vital democracy can be built only on the basis of social justice; advocates for the economy as much competition as possible, as much planning as necessary to protect the individual from uncontrolled economic interests; favours a positive attitude to national defence, while supporting controlled disarmament; rejects any political ties with communism; 548,491 mems (July 2007); Chair. SIGMAR GABRIEL; Parliamentary Leader THOMAS OPPERMANN; Sec.-Gen. YASMIN FAHIMI.

Südschleswigscher Wählerverband (SSW) (South Schleswig Voters' Committee): Schiffbrücke 42, 24939 Flensburg; tel. (461) 14408310; fax (461) 14408313; e-mail info@ssw.de; internet www

.ssw.de; f. 1948; represents the Danish minority in Schleswig-Holstein and Friesian community in northern Germany; Chair. FLEMMING MEYER; Gen. Sec. MARTIN LORENZEN.

There are also numerous other small parties, none of which is represented in the Bundestag, covering all shades of the political spectrum and various regional interests.

Diplomatic Representation

EMBASSIES IN GERMANY

Afghanistan: Taunusstr. 3, Ecke Kronbergerstr. 5, 14193 Berlin; tel. (30) 20673510; fax (30) 20673525; e-mail info@botschaft-afghanistan.de; internet www.botschaft-afghanistan.de; Chargé d'affaires ABED NADJIB.

Albania: Friedrichstr. 231, 10969 Berlin; tel. (30) 2593040; fax (30) 25931890; e-mail kanzlei@botschaft-albanien.de; internet www.botschaft-albanien.de; Ambassador VALTER IBRAHIMI.

Algeria: Görschstr. 45, 13187 Berlin; tel. (30) 437370; fax (30) 48098716; e-mail info@algerische-botschaft.de; internet www.algerische-botschaft.de; Ambassador EDDINE AOUAM.

Angola: Wallstr. 58, 10179 Berlin; tel. (30) 2408970; fax (30) 24089712; e-mail botschaft@botschaftangola.de; internet www.botschaftangola.de; Ambassador ALBERT CORREIA NETO.

Argentina: Kleiststr. 23–26, 4th Floor, 10787 Berlin; tel. (30) 2266890; fax (30) 2291400; e-mail info_ealem@mrecic.gov.ar; internet www.embargent.de; Ambassador DANIEL ADÁN DZIEWEZO POLSKI.

Armenia: Nussbaumallee 4, 14050 Berlin; tel. (30) 40509110; fax (30) 40509125; e-mail armgermanyembassy@mfa.am; internet www.botschaft-armenien.de; Ambassador VAHAN HOVANNESIAN.

Australia: Wallstr. 76–79, 10179 Berlin; tel. (30) 8800880; fax (30) 880088210; e-mail info.berlin@dfat.gov.au; internet www.germany.embassy.gov.au; Ambassador PETER MARTIN TESCH.

Austria: Stauffenbergstr. 1, 10785 Berlin; tel. (30) 202870; fax (30) 2290569; e-mail berlin-ob@bmeia.gv.at; internet www.oesterreichische-botschaft.de; Ambassador Dr RALPH SCHEIDE.

Azerbaijan: Hubertusallee 43, 14193 Berlin; tel. (30) 2191613; fax (30) 21916152; e-mail berlin@mission.mfa.gov.az; internet www.azembassy.de; Ambassador PARVIZ SHAHBAZOV.

Bahrain: Klingelhöferstr. 7, 10785 Berlin; tel. (30) 86877777; fax (30) 86877788; Ambassador IBRAHIM MAHMOUD AHMED ABDULLAH.

Bangladesh: Dovestr. 1, 5th Floor, 10587 Berlin; tel. (30) 3989750; fax (30) 39897510; e-mail info@bangladeshembassy.de; internet www.bangladeshembassy.de; Ambassador MUHAMMAD ALI SORCAR.

Belarus: Am Treptower Park 32, 12435 Berlin; tel. (30) 5363590; fax (30) 53635923; e-mail germany@mfa.gov.by; internet www.germany.mfa.gov.by; Ambassador ANDREI GIRO.

Belgium: Jägerstr. 52–53, 10117 Berlin; tel. (30) 206420; fax (30) 20642200; e-mail berlin@diplobel.fed.be; internet www.diplomatie.be/berlin; Ambassador RENIER WILLEM JOSEPH NIJSKENS.

Benin: Englerallee 23, 14195 Berlin; tel. (30) 23631470; fax (30) 236314740; Ambassador ISIDORE BIO.

Bolivia: Wichmannstr. 6, 10787 Berlin; tel. (30) 2639150; fax (30) 26391515; e-mail berlin@embajada-bolivia.de; internet www.bolivia.de; Ambassador ELIZABETH SALGUERO CARRILLO.

Bosnia and Herzegovina: Ibsenstr. 14, 10439 Berlin; tel. (30) 81471210; fax (30) 81471211; e-mail mail@botschaftbh.de; internet www.botschaftbh.de; Ambassador EDIN DILBEROVIĆ.

Brazil: Wallstr. 57, 10179 Berlin; tel. (30) 726280; fax (30) 72628320; e-mail brasemb.berlim@itamaraty.gov.br; internet berlim.itamaratay.gov.br/de; Ambassador MARIA LUIZA RIBEIRO VIOTTI.

Brunei: Kronenstr. 55–58, 10117 Berlin; tel. (30) 20607600; fax (30) 20607666; e-mail berlin@brunei-embassy.de; Ambassador Dato' Paduka HAJI ABDUL JALIL bin HAJI AHMAD.

Bulgaria: Mauerstr. 11, 10117 Berlin; tel. (30) 2010922; fax (30) 2086838; e-mail embassy.berlin@mfa.bg; internet www.mfa.bg/embassies/germany; Ambassador RADI DRAGNEV NAIDENOV.

Burkina Faso: Karolingerpl. 10–11, 14052 Berlin; tel. (30) 30105990; fax (30) 301059920; e-mail embassy_burkina_faso@t-online.de; internet www.embassy-bf.org; Ambassador MARIE ODILE BONKOUNGOU BALIMA.

Burundi: Berliner Str. 36, 10715 Berlin; tel. (30) 2345670; fax (30) 23456720; e-mail info@burundi-embassy-berlin.com; internet www.burundiembassy-germany.de; Ambassador EDOUARD BIZIMANA.

Cambodia: Benjamin-Vogelsdorff-Str., 13187 Berlin; tel. (30) 48637901; fax (30) 48637973; e-mail rec-berlin@t-online.de; internet www.kambodscha-botschaft.de; Ambassador THAI CHUN.

Cameroon: Ulmenallee 32, 14050 Berlin; tel. (30) 89068090; fax (30) 890680929; e-mail berlin@ambacam.de; internet www.ambacam.de; Ambassador JEAN-MARC MPAY.

Canada: Leipziger Pl. 17, 10117 Berlin; tel. (30) 203120; fax (30) 20312590; e-mail brlin@international.gc.ca; internet www.canadainternational.gc.ca/germany-allemagne; Ambassador MARIE GERVAIS-VIDRICAIRE.

Cape Verde: Stavanger Str. 16, 10439 Berlin; tel. (30) 20450955; fax (30) 20450966; e-mail info@embassy-capeverde.de; internet www.embassy-capeverde.de; Ambassador MARIA CRISTINA RODRIGUES DE ALMEIDA PEREIRA.

Chad: Lepsiusstr. 114, 12165 Berlin; tel. (30) 31991620; fax (30) 319916220; e-mail contact@ambatchadberlin.de; internet www.ambatchadberlin.de; Chargé d'affaires a.i. SOLALTA NGARMBATINAN.

Chile: Mohrenstr. 42, 10117 Berlin; tel. (30) 7262035; fax (30) 726203603; e-mail comunicaciones@echilealemania.de; internet www.embajadaconsuladoschile.de; Ambassador JORGE EDUARDO O'RYAN SCHÜTZ.

China, People's Republic: Märkisches Ufer 54, 10179 Berlin; tel. (30) 275880; fax (30) 27588221; internet www.china-botschaft.de; Ambassador SHI MINGDE.

Colombia: Kurfürstenstr. 84, 5th Floor, 10787 Berlin; tel. (30) 2639610; fax (30) 26396125; e-mail info@botschaft-kolumbien.de; internet www.botschaft-kolumbien.de; Ambassador JUAN MAYR MALDONADO.

Congo, Democratic Republic: Ulmenallee 42A, 14050 Berlin; tel. (30) 30111298; fax (30) 30111297; e-mail ambardc_berlin@yahoo.de; Ambassador KAMANGA CLEMENTINE SHAKEMBO.

Congo, Republic: Grabbeallee 47, 13156 Berlin; tel. (30) 49400753; fax (30) 48479897; e-mail botschaftkongobzv@hotmail.de; Ambassador JACQUES YVON NDOLOU.

Costa Rica: Dessauer Str. 28–29, 10963 Berlin; tel. (30) 26398990; fax (30) 26557210; e-mail emb@botschaft-costarica.de; internet www.botschaft-costarica.de; Ambassador JOSÉ JOAQUÍN CHAVERRI SIEVERT.

Côte d'Ivoire: Schinkelstr. 10, 14193 Berlin; tel. (30) 8906960; fax (30) 890696206; e-mail contact@ambaci.de; internet www.ambaci.de; Ambassador HOUADJA LÉON ADOM KACOU.

Croatia: Ahornstr. 4, 10787 Berlin; tel. (30) 21915514; fax (30) 23628965; e-mail berlin@mvpei.hr; internet de.mfa.hr; Ambassador Dr RANKO VILOVIĆ.

Cuba: Stavangerstr. 20, 10439 Berlin; tel. (30) 44717319; fax (30) 9164553; e-mail embacuba-berlin@t-online.de; internet www.cubadiplomatica.cu/alemania; Ambassador RENÉ JUAN MUJICA CANTELAR.

Cyprus: Wallstr. 27, 10179 Berlin; tel. (30) 3086830; fax (30) 27591454; e-mail info@botschaft-zypern.de; internet www.botschaft-zypern.de; Ambassador MINAS A. HADJIMICHAEL.

Czech Republic: Wilhelmstr. 44, 10117 Berlin; tel. (30) 226380; fax (30) 2294033; e-mail berlin@embassy.mzv.cz; internet www.mzv.cz/berlin; Ambassador RUDOLF JINDRÁK.

Denmark: Rauchstr. 1, 10787 Berlin; tel. (30) 50502000; fax (30) 50502050; e-mail beramb@um.dk; internet tyskland.um.dk; Ambassador PER POULSEN-HANSEN.

Dominican Republic: Dessauer Str. 28–29, 10963 Berlin; tel. (30) 25757760; fax (30) 25757761; e-mail info@embajadadominicana.de; Ambassador GABRIEL RAFAEL CALVENTI.

Ecuador: Joachimstaler Str. 10–12, 10719 Berlin; tel. (30) 8009695; fax (30) 800969699; e-mail alemania@embassy-ecuador.org; internet www.ecuadorembassy.de; Ambassador JORGE ENRIQUE JURADO MOSQUERA.

Egypt: Stauffenbergstr. 6–7, 10785 Berlin; tel. (30) 4775470; fax (30) 4771049; e-mail embassy@egyptian-embassy.de; internet www.egyptian-embassy.de; Ambassador MUHAMMAD ABD AL-HAMID IBRAHIM HIGAZY.

El Salvador: Joachim-Karnatz-Allee 47, 10557 Berlin; tel. (30) 2064660; fax (30) 20646629; e-mail embasalvarfa@googlemail.com; internet www.botschaft-elsalvador.de; Ambassador ANITA CRISTINA ESCHER ECHEVERRÍA.

Equatorial Guinea: Rohlfsstr. 17–19, 14195 Berlin; tel. (30) 88663877; fax (30) 88663879; e-mail botschaft@guinea-ecuatorial.de; internet www.botschaft-aequatorialguinea.de; Ambassador CÁNDIDO MUATETEMA RIVAS.

Eritrea: Stavangerstr. 18, 10439 Berlin; tel. (30) 4467460; fax (30) 44674621; e-mail embassyeritrea@t-online.de; internet www.botschaft-eritrea.de; Ambassador PETROS TSEGGAI ASGHEDOM.

Estonia: Hildebrandstr. 5, 10785 Berlin; tel. (30) 25460602; fax (30) 25460601; e-mail embassy.berlin@mfa.ee; internet www.estemb.de; Ambassador Dr KAJA TAEL.

Ethiopia: Boothstr. 20A, 12207 Berlin; tel. (30) 772060; fax (30) 7720626; e-mail emb.ethiopia@t-online.de; internet www.aethiopien-botschaft.de; Ambassador FESSEHA ASGHEDOM TESSEMA.

Finland: Rauchstr. 1, 10787 Berlin; tel. (30) 505030; fax (30) 50503333; e-mail sanomat.ber@formin.fi; internet www.finnland.de; Ambassador PÄIVI LUOSTARINEN.

France: Pariser Pl. 5, 10117 Berlin; tel. (30) 590039000; fax (30) 590039110; e-mail kanzlei@botschaft-frankreich.de; internet www.ambafrance-de.org; Ambassador MAURICE GOURDAULT-MONTAGNE.

Gabon: Hohensteiner Str. 16, 14197 Berlin; tel. (30) 89733440; fax (30) 89733444; e-mail botschaft@botschaft-gabun.de; internet www.botschaft-gabun.de; Ambassador JEAN-CLAUDE BOUYOBART.

Georgia: Rauchstr. 11, 10787 Berlin; tel. (30) 4849070; fax (30) 48490720; e-mail berlin.emb@mfa.gov.ge; internet germany.mfa.gov.ge; Ambassador LADO CHANTURIA.

Ghana: Stavanger Str. 17 und 19, 10439 Berlin; tel. (30) 5471490; fax (30) 44674063; e-mail chancery@ghanaemberlin.de; internet www.ghanaemberlin.de; Ambassador PAUL KING ARYENE.

Greece: Jägerstr. 54–55, 10117 Berlin; tel. (30) 206260; fax (30) 20626444; e-mail info@griechische-botschaft.de; internet www.mfa.gr/germany; Ambassador PANAYOTIS ZOGRAFOS.

Guatemala: Joachim-Karnatz-Allee 47, 10557 Berlin; tel. (30) 2064363; fax (30) 20643659; e-mail sekretariat@botschaft-guatemala.de; internet www.botschaft-guatemala.de; Ambassador CARLOS HUMBERTO JIMÉNEZ LICONA.

Guinea: Jägerstr. 67–69, 10117 Berlin; tel. (30) 20074330; fax (30) 200743333; e-mail berlin@ambaguinee.de; Ambassador Dr IBRAHIMA SORY SOW.

Haiti: Uhlandstr. 14, 10623 Berlin; tel. (30) 88555134; fax (30) 88624279; e-mail amb.allemagne@diplomatie.ht; Chargé d'affaires a.i. PIERRE LACARRIER.

Holy See: Lilienthalstr. 3A, 10965 Berlin; Postfach 610218, 10923 Berlin; tel. (30) 616240; fax (30) 61624300; e-mail apostolische@nuntiatur.de; internet www.nuntiatur.de; Apostolic Nuncio Most Rev. NIKOLA ETEROVIC (Titular Archbishop of Cibale).

Honduras: Cuxhavenerstr. 14, 10555 Berlin; tel. (30) 39749711; fax (30) 39749712; e-mail informacion.embahonduras.de@gmail.com; Ambassador RAMON CUSTODIO ESPINOZA.

Hungary: Unter den Linden 76, 10117 Berlin; tel. (30) 203100; fax (30) 2291314; e-mail infober@kum.hu; internet www.mfa.gov.hu/kulkepviselet/de; Ambassador Dr JÓZSEF CZUKOR.

Iceland: Rauchstr. 1, 10787 Berlin; tel. (30) 50504000; fax (30) 50504300; e-mail infoberlin@mfa.is; internet www.botschaft-island.de; Ambassador GUNNAR SNORRI GUNNARSSON.

India: Tiergartenstr. 17, 10785 Berlin; tel. (30) 257950; fax (30) 25795102; e-mail infowing@indianembassy.de; internet www.indianembassy.de; Ambassador VIJAY KESHAV GOKHALE.

Indonesia: Lehrter Str. 16–17, 10557 Berlin; tel. (30) 478070; fax (30) 44737142; internet www.botschaft-indonesien.de; Ambassador FAUZI BOWO.

Iran: Podbielskiallee 65–67, 14195 Berlin; tel. (30) 843530; fax (30) 84353534; e-mail info@iranbotschaft.de; internet berlin.mfa.gov.ir; Ambassador ALI REZA SHEIKH ATTAR.

Iraq: Pacelliallee 19–21, 14195 Berlin; tel. (30) 814880; fax (30) 81488222; e-mail info@iraqiembassy-berlin.de; internet www.iraqiembassy-berlin.de; Ambassador Dr HUSSAIN M. F. ALKHATEEB.

Ireland: Jägerstr. 51, 10117 Berlin; tel. (30) 220720; fax (30) 22072299; e-mail berlin@dfa.ie; internet www.embassyofireland.de; Ambassador MICHAEL COLLINS.

Israel: Auguste-Viktoria-Str. 74–76, 14193 Berlin; tel. (30) 89045500; fax (30) 89045309; e-mail botschaft@israel.de; internet www.israel.de; Ambassador YAKOV HADAS-HANDELSMAN.

Italy: Hiroshimastr. 1, 10785 Berlin; tel. (30) 254400; fax (30) 25440169; e-mail segreteria.berlino@esteri.it; internet www.ambberlino.esteri.it; Ambassador ELIO MENZIONE.

Jamaica: Schmargendorfer Str. 32, 12159 Berlin; tel. (30) 85994511; fax (30) 85994540; e-mail info@jamador.de; internet www.jamador.de; Ambassador ANN LOUISE JOBSON.

Japan: Hiroshimastr. 6, 10785 Berlin; tel. (30) 210940; fax (30) 21094228; e-mail info@botschaft-japan.de; internet www.de.emb-japan.go.jp; Ambassador TAKESHI NAKANE.

Jordan: Heerstr. 201, 13595 Berlin; tel. (30) 3699600; fax (30) 36996011; e-mail jordan@jordanembassy.de; internet www.jordanembassy.de; Ambassador MAZEN IZZEDDIN AL-TAL.

Kazakhstan: Nordendstr. 14–17, 13156 Berlin; tel. (30) 47007111; fax (30) 47007125; e-mail info@botschaft-kaz.de; internet www.botschaft-kasachstan.de; Ambassador NURLAN ONZHANOV.

Kenya: Markgrafenstr. 63, 10969 Berlin; tel. (30) 2592660; fax (30) 25926650; e-mail office@embassy-of-kenya.de; internet www.kenyaembassyberlin.de; Ambassador KENNEDY NYAUNCHO OSINDE.

Korea, Democratic People's Republic: Glinkastr. 5–7, 10117 Berlin; tel. (30) 20625990; fax (30) 22651929; e-mail info@dprkorea-emb.de; Ambassador RI SI-HONG.

Korea, Republic: Stülerstr. 8–10, 10787 Berlin; tel. (30) 260650; fax (30) 2606551; e-mail koremb-ge@mofat.go.kr; internet www.koreaemb.de; Ambassador JAE SHIN-KIM.

Kosovo: Wallstr. 65, 10179 Berlin; tel. (30) 24047690; fax (30) 240476929; e-mail embassy.germany@ks-gov.net; Ambassador SKENDER XHAKALIU.

Kuwait: Griegstr. 5–7, 14193 Berlin; tel. (30) 8973000; fax (30) 89730010; e-mail info@kuwait-botschaft.de; internet www.kuwait-botschaft.de; Ambassador MONTHER AL-EISSA.

Kyrgyzstan: Otto-Suhr-Allee 146, 10585 Berlin; tel. (30) 34781338; fax (30) 34781362; e-mail info@botschaft-kirgisien.de; internet www.botschaft-kirgisien.de; Ambassador Dr BOLOT OTUNBAEV.

Laos: Bismarckallee 2A, 14193 Berlin; tel. (30) 89060647; fax (30) 89060648; e-mail info@laos-botschaft.de; Ambassador KHAMVONE PHANOUVONG.

Latvia: Reinerzstr. 40–41, 14193 Berlin; tel. (30) 8260020; fax (30) 82600233; e-mail embassy.germany@mfa.gov.lv; internet www.mfa.gov.lv/berlin; Ambassador ELITA KUZMA.

Lebanon: Berliner Str. 127, 13187 Berlin; tel. (30) 47498610; fax (30) 47487858; e-mail lubnan@t-online.de; internet www.libanesische-botschaft.info; Ambassador Dr MUSTAPHA ADIB.

Lesotho: Kurfürstenstr. 84, 10787 Berlin; tel. (30) 2575720; fax (30) 25757222; e-mail info@lesothoembassy.de; internet www.lesothoembassy.de; Ambassador LINEO LYDIA NTOANE.

Liberia: Kurfürstenstr. 84, 10787 Berlin; tel. (30) 26391194; fax (30) 26394893; e-mail info@liberiaembassygermany.de; internet www.liberiaembassygermany.de; Ambassador ETHEL DAVIES.

Libya: Podbielskiallee 42, 14195 Berlin; tel. (30) 2005960; fax (30) 20059699; e-mail info@libysche-botschaft.de; internet www.libyschebotschaft.de; Sec. of the People's Bureau SENNUSSI ABDULKADER KWIDEER.

Liechtenstein: Mohrenstr. 42, 10117 Berlin; tel. (30) 52000630; fax (30) 52000631; e-mail vertretung@ber.llv.li; Ambassador Prince STEFAN OF LIECHTENSTEIN.

Lithuania: Charitéstr. 9, 10117 Berlin; tel. (30) 8906810; fax (30) 89068115; e-mail info-botschaft@mfa.lt; internet de.mfa.lt; Ambassador DEIVIDAS MATULIONIS.

Luxembourg: Klingelhöferstr. 7, 10785 Berlin; tel. (30) 2639570; fax (30) 26395727; e-mail berlin.amb@mae.etat.lu; internet berlin.mae.lu; Ambassador GEORGES JOSEPH NICOLAS SANTER.

Macedonia, former Yugoslav republic: Hubertusallee 5, 14193 Berlin; tel. (30) 8906950; fax (30) 89541194; e-mail makedonische.botschaft@t-online.de; Ambassador KORNELIJA UTEVSKA-GLIGOROVSKA.

Madagascar: Seepromenade 92, Postfach 100168, 14612 Falkensee (Brandenburg); tel. (3322) 23140; fax (3322) 231429; e-mail info@botschaft-madagaskar.de; internet www.botschaft-madagaskar.de; Chargé d'affaires a.i. RADAFIARISOA LÉA RAHOLINIRINA.

Malawi: Westfälische Str. 86, 10709 Berlin; tel. (30) 8431540; fax (30) 84315430; e-mail malawiberlin@aol.com; internet www.malawiembassy.de; Chargé d'affaires a.i. OLIVER M. C. KUMBAMBE.

Malaysia: Klingelhöferstr. 6, 10785 Berlin; tel. (30) 8857490; fax (30) 88574950; e-mail mwberlin@malemb.de; internet www.malemb.de; Ambassador Dato SALMAN BIN L. AHMAD.

Mali: Kurfürstendamm 72, 10709 Berlin; tel. (30) 3199883; fax (30) 31998848; e-mail ambmali@01019freenet.de; internet www.ambassade-repmali-berlin.de; Ambassador HAWA BA KEÏTA.

Malta: Klingelhöferstr. 7, 10785 Berlin; tel. (30) 2639110; fax (30) 26391123; e-mail maltaembassy.berlin@gov.mt; Ambassador ALBERT FRIGGIERI.

Mauritania: Kommandantenstr. 80, 10117 Berlin; tel. (30) 2065883; fax (30) 20674750; e-mail ambarim.berlin@gmx.de; Ambassador OULD MOHAMED M'BARECK BEBBE.

Mauritius: Kurfürstenstr. 84, 10787 Berlin; tel. (30) 2639360; fax (30) 26558323; e-mail berlin@mauritius-embassy.de; internet www.mauritius-embassy.de; Ambassador SAROJINI SEENEEVASSEN-FRERS.

Mexico: Klingelhöferstr. 3, 10785 Berlin; tel. (30) 2693230; fax (30) 269323700; e-mail mail@mexale.de; internet embamex.sre.gob.mx/alemania; Ambassador PATRICIA ESPINOSA CANTELLANO.

Moldova: Gotlandstr. 16, 10439 Berlin; tel. (30) 44652970; fax (30) 44652972; e-mail office@botschaft-moldau.de; internet www.germania.mfa.md; Ambassador AURELIU CIOCOI.

Monaco: Klingelhöferstr. 7, 10785 Berlin; tel. (30) 2639033; fax (30) 2690344; e-mail berlin@ambassade-monaco.de; Ambassador CLAUDE JOËL GIORDAN.

Mongolia: Dietzgenstr. 31, 13156 Berlin; tel. (30) 4748060; fax (30) 47480616; e-mail mongolbot@aol.com; internet www

.botschaft-mongolei.de; Chargé d'affaires a.i. BATTUR KHOSHUUD DAVAAKHUU.

Montenegro: Charlottenstr. 35–36, 10117 Berlin; tel. (30) 51651070; fax (30) 516510712; e-mail germany@mfa.gov.me; Ambassador VERA JOLIČIĆ-KULIŠ.

Morocco: Niederwallstr. 39, 10117 Berlin; tel. (30) 2061240; fax (30) 20612420; e-mail kontakt@botschaft-marokko.de; internet www.maec.gov.ma/berlin; Ambassador Dr OMAR ZNIBER.

Mozambique: Stromstr. 47, 10551 Berlin; tel. (30) 39876500; fax (30) 39876503; e-mail info@embassy-of-mozambique.de; Ambassador AMADEU PAULO SAMUEL DA CONCEIÇÃO.

Myanmar: Thielallee 19, 14195 Berlin; tel. (30) 2061570; fax (30) 20615720; e-mail info@botschaft-myanmar.de; internet www.botschaft-myanmar.de; Ambassador SOE NWE.

Namibia: Reichsstr. 17, 14052 Berlin; tel. (30) 2540950; fax (30) 25409555; e-mail namibiaberlin@aol.com; internet www.namibia-botschaft.de; Ambassador NEVILLE MELVIN GERTZE.

Nepal: Guerickestr. 27, 2nd Floor, 10587 Berlin; tel. (30) 34359920; fax (30) 34359906; e-mail berlin@nepalembassy.de; internet www.nepalembassy-germany.com; Ambassador SURESH PRASAD PRADHAN.

Netherlands: Klosterstr. 50, 10179 Berlin; tel. (30) 209560; fax (30) 20956441; e-mail bln@minbuza.nl; internet deutschland.nlbotschaft.org; Ambassador MONICA THEODORA VAN DAALEN.

New Zealand: Friedrichstr. 60, 10117 Berlin; tel. (30) 206210; fax (30) 20621114; e-mail nzembber@infoem.org; internet www.nzembassy.com/germany; Ambassador PETER HOWARD RIDER.

Nicaragua: Joachim-Karnatz-Allee 45, 10557 Berlin; tel. (30) 2064380; fax (30) 22487891; e-mail embajada.berlin@embanic.de; Chargé d'affaires a.i. KARLA LUZETTE BETETA BRENES.

Niger: Machnowerstr. 24, 14165 Berlin; tel. (30) 80589660; fax (30) 80589662; e-mail ambaniger@t-online.de; internet www.ambassade-niger.de; Ambassador AMINATOU GAOH.

Nigeria: Neue Jakobstr. 4, 10179 Berlin; tel. (30) 212300; fax (30) 21230212; e-mail info@nigeriaembassygermany.org; internet www.nigeriaembassygermany.org; Ambassador ABDU USMAN ABUBAKAR.

Norway: Rauchstr. 1, 10787 Berlin; tel. (30) 505058600; fax (30) 505058601; e-mail emb.berlin@mfa.no; internet www.norwegen.no; Ambassador SVEN ERIK SVEDMAN.

Oman: Clayallee 82, 14195 Berlin; tel. (30) 8100510; fax (30) 81005199; Ambassador Dr KHALID SULAIMAN ABD AL-RAHMAN BA OMAR.

Pakistan: Schaperstr. 29, 10719 Berlin; tel. (30) 212440; fax (30) 21244210; e-mail mail@pakemb.de; internet www.pakemb.de; Ambassador SYED HASAN JAVED.

Panama: Wichmannstr. 6, 10787 Berlin; tel. (30) 22605811; fax (30) 22605812; e-mail info@botschaft-panama.de; internet www.botschaft-panama.de; Ambassador JUAN RAMON PORRAS DE LA GUARDIA.

Paraguay: Hardenbergstr. 12, 10623 Berlin; tel. (30) 3199860; fax (30) 31998617; e-mail embapar@embapar.de; Ambassador RAÚL ALBERTO FLORENTIN ANTOLA.

Peru: Mohrenstr. 42, 10117 Berlin; tel. (30) 2064103; fax (30) 20641077; e-mail info@embaperu.de; internet www.botschaft-peru.de; Ambassador JOSÉ ANTONIO MEIER ESPINOSA.

Philippines: Uhlandstr. 97, 10715 Berlin; tel. (30) 8649500; fax (30) 8732551; e-mail info@philippine-embassy.de; internet www.philippine-embassy.de; Ambassador MARIA CLEOFE NATIVIDAD.

Poland: Lassenstr. 19–21, 14193 Berlin; tel. (30) 223130; fax (30) 2213155; e-mail berlin.amb.sekretariat@msz.gov.pl; internet berlin.msz.gov.pt; Ambassador Dr JERZY MARGAŃSKI.

Portugal: Zimmerstr. 56, 10117 Berlin; tel. (30) 590063500; fax (30) 590063600; e-mail mail@botschaftportugal.de; internet www.botschaftportugal.de; Ambassador LUÍS DE ALMEIDA SAMPAIO.

Qatar: Hagenstr. 56, 14193 Berlin; tel. (30) 862060; fax (30) 86206150; internet www.katar-botschaft.de; Ambassador ABD AL-RAHMAN MUHAMMAD AL-KHULAIFI.

Romania: Dorotheenstr. 62–66, 10117 Berlin; tel. (30) 21239202; fax (30) 21239399; e-mail office@rumaenische-botschaft.de; internet berlin.mae.ro; Ambassador Dr LAZĂR COMĂNESCU.

Russia: Unter den Linden 63–65, 10117 Berlin; tel. (30) 2291110; fax (30) 2299397; e-mail info@russische-botschaft.de; internet www.russische-botschaft.de; Ambassador VLADIMIR M. GRININ.

Rwanda: Jägerstr. 67–69, 10117 Berlin; tel. (30) 20916590; fax (30) 209165959; e-mail info@rwanda-botschaft.de; internet www.rwanda-botschaft.de; Ambassador CHRISTINE NKULIKIYINKA.

Saudi Arabia: Tiergartenstr. 33–34, 10785 Berlin; tel. (30) 8892500; fax (30) 88925179; Ambassador Prof. Dr OSSAMA ABD AL-MAJID ALI SHOBOKSHI.

Senegal: Dessauer Str. 28–29, 10963 Berlin; tel. (30) 8562190; fax (30) 85621921; internet www.botschaft-senegal.de; Ambassador ABDOUL AZIZ NDIAYE.

Serbia: Taubertstr. 18, 14193 Berlin; tel. (30) 8957700; fax (30) 8252206; e-mail info@botschaft-smg.de; internet berlin.mfa.rs; Chargé d'affaires a.i. MIODRAG MIŠIĆ.

Sierra Leone: Herwarthstr. 4, 12207 Berlin; tel. (30) 77205850; fax (30) 772058529; e-mail embassy@slembassy-germany.org; internet www.slembassy-germany.org; Ambassador JONGOPIE SIAKA STEVENS.

Singapore: Vossstr. 17, 10117 Berlin; tel. (30) 2263430; fax (30) 22634375; e-mail singemb_ber@sgmfa.gov.sg; internet www.singapore-embassy.de; Ambassador JAI S. SOHAN.

Slovakia: Hildebrandstr. 25, 10785 Berlin; tel. (30) 88926200; fax (30) 88926222; e-mail emb.berlin@mzv.sk; internet www.mzv.sk/berlin; Ambassador IGOR SLOBODNÍK.

Slovenia: Hausvogteipl. 3–4, 10117 Berlin; tel. (30) 2061450; fax (30) 20614570; e-mail vbn@gov.si; internet berlin.veleposlanistvo.si; Ambassador MARTA KOS MARKO.

Somalia: Heilmanring 10, 13627 Berlin; tel. (30) 80201438; Ambassador MOHAMUD MOHAMED TIFOW.

South Africa: Tiergartenstr. 18, 10785 Berlin; tel. (30) 220730; fax (30) 22073190; e-mail berlin.info@foreign.gov.za; internet www.suedafrika.org; Ambassador MAKHENKESI ARNOLD STOFILE.

South Sudan: Leipziger Pl. 8, 10117 Berlin; tel. (30) 20644590; fax (30) 206445919; e-mail info@embassy-southsudan.de; internet www.embassy-southsudan.de; Ambassador SITONA ABDALLA OSMAN.

Spain: Lichtensteinallee 1, 10787 Berlin; tel. (30) 2540070; fax (30) 25799557; e-mail emb.berlin.inf@maec.es; internet www.maec.es/subwebs/embajadas/berlin; Ambassador JUAN PABLO GARCÍA-BERDOY Y CEREZO.

Sri Lanka: Niklasstr. 19, 14163 Berlin; tel. (30) 80909749; fax (30) 80909757; e-mail info@srilanka-botschaft.de; internet www.srilanka-botschaft.de; Ambassador UPALI SARRATH KONGAHAGE.

Sudan: Kurfürstendamm 151, 10709 Berlin; tel. (30) 8906980; fax (30) 89409693; e-mail poststelle@sudan-embassy.de; internet www.sudan-embassy.de; Ambassador Dr BAHA AD-DIN HANAFI MANSOUR WAHEESH.

Sweden: Rauchstr. 1, 10787 Berlin; tel. (30) 505060; fax (30) 50506789; e-mail ambassaden.berlin@foreign.ministry.se; internet www.swedenabroad.com/berlin; Ambassador STAFFAN CARLSSON.

Switzerland: Otto-von-Bismarck-Allee 4A, 10557 Berlin; tel. (30) 3904000; fax (30) 3911030; e-mail ber.vertretung@eda.admin.ch; internet www.eda.admin.ch/berlin; Ambassador Dr URS CHRISTIAN TIMOTHEUS GULDIMANN.

Syria: Rauchstr. 25, 10787 Berlin; tel. (30) 501770; fax (30) 50177311; e-mail info@syrianembassy.de; internet www.syrianembassy.de; Ambassador (vacant).

Tajikistan: Perleberger Str. 43, 10559 Berlin; tel. (30) 3479300; fax (30) 34793029; e-mail info@botschaft-tadschikistan.de; Ambassador IMOMUDIN M. SATTOROV.

Tanzania: Eschenallee 11, 14050 Berlin; tel. (30) 3030800; fax (30) 30308020; e-mail info@tanzania-gov.de; internet www.tanzania-gov.de; Ambassador PHILIP S. MARMO.

Thailand: Lepsiusstr. 64–66, 12163 Berlin; tel. (30) 794810; fax (30) 79481511; e-mail general@thaiembassy.de; internet www.thaiembassy.de; Ambassador NONGNUTH PHETCHARATANA.

Togo: Grabbeallee 43, 13156 Berlin; tel. (30) 49908968; fax (30) 49908967; e-mail bbotschafttogo@web.de; internet www.botschaft-togo.de; Ambassador ESSOHANAM COMLA PAKA.

Tunisia: Lindenallee 16, 14050 Berlin; tel. (30) 3641070; fax (30) 30820683; e-mail at.berlin@tunesien.tn; Ambassador ELYES GHARIANI.

Turkey: Tiergartenstr. 19–21, 10179 Berlin; tel. (30) 275850; fax (30) 27590915; e-mail botschaft.berlin@mfa.gov.tr; Ambassador HÜSEYIN AVNI KARSLIOĞLU.

Turkmenistan: Langobardenallee 14, 14052 Berlin; tel. (30) 30102452; fax (30) 30102453; e-mail info@botschaft-turkmenistan.de; internet www.botschaft-turkmenistan.de; Ambassador KHALNAZAR A. AGAKHANOV.

Uganda: Axel-Springer-Str. 54A, 10117 Berlin; tel. (30) 2060990; fax (30) 24047557; e-mail info@ugandaembassyberlin.de; internet www.ugandaembassyberlin.de; Ambassador MARCEL R. TIBALEKA.

Ukraine: Albrechtstr. 26, 10117 Berlin; tel. (30) 28887214; fax (30) 28887163; e-mail ukremb@ukrainishe-botschaft.de; internet www.mfa.gov.ua/germany; Ambassador PAVLO KLIMKIN.

United Arab Emirates: Hiroshimastr. 18–20, 10787 Berlin; tel. (30) 516516; fax (30) 51651900; internet www.uae-embassy.de; Ambassador JUMAA MUBARAK AL-JUNAIBI.

United Kingdom: Wilhelmstr. 70, 10117 Berlin; tel. (30) 204570; e-mail ukingermany@fco.gov.uk; internet www.gov.uk/government/world/germany; Ambassador SIMON MCDONALD.

USA: Clayallee 170, 14191 Berlin; tel. (30) 83050; fax (30) 83051050; internet germany.usembassy.gov; Ambassador JOHN B. EMERSON.

Uruguay: Budapester Str. 39, 10787 Berlin; tel. (30) 2639016; fax (30) 26390170; e-mail urubrande@t-online.de; Ambassador ALBERTO ANTONIO GUANI AMARILLA.

Uzbekistan: Perleberger Str. 62, 10559 Berlin; tel. (30) 3940980; fax (30) 39409862; e-mail botschaft@uzbekistan.de; internet www.uzbekistan.de; Ambassador DURBEK AMANOV.

Venezuela: Schillstr. 10, 10785 Berlin; tel. (30) 8322400; fax (30) 83224020; e-mail embavenez.berlin@botschaft-venezuela.de; internet www.botschaft-venezuela.de; Ambassador RODRIGO OSWALDO CHAVES SAMUDIO.

Viet Nam: Elsenstr. 3, 12435 Berlin; tel. (30) 53630108; fax (30) 53630200; e-mail sqvnberlin@t-online.de; internet www.vietnambotschaft.org; Ambassador NGUYEN THI HOANG ANH.

Yemen: Budapester Str. 37, 10787 Berlin; tel. (30) 8973050; fax (30) 89730562; e-mail info@botschaft-jemen.de; internet www.botschaft-jemen.de; Ambassador Dr ABD AL-RAHMAN ABD-ALLA SALEM BAHABIB.

Zambia: Axel-Springer-Str. 54A, 10117 Berlin; tel. (30) 2062940; fax (30) 20629419; e-mail info@zambiaembassy.de; internet www.zambiaembassy.de; Ambassador BWALYA STANLEY KASONDE CHITI.

Zimbabwe: Kommandantenstr. 80, 10117 Berlin; tel. (30) 2062263; fax (30) 20455062; Ambassador HEBSON MAKUVISE.

Judicial System

Justice is administered in accordance with the federal structure through the courts of the Federation and the Länder, as well as the Federal Constitutional Court and the Constitutional Courts of the Länder. Judges are independent and responsible to the law. They are not removable except by the decision of a court. One-half of the judges of the Federal Constitutional Court are elected by the Bundestag and the other half by the Bundesrat. A committee for the selection of judges participates in the appointment of judges of the Superior Federal Courts.

FEDERAL CONSTITUTIONAL COURT

Bundesverfassungsgericht: Schlossbezirk 3, 76131 Karlsruhe; Postfach 1771, 76006 Karlsruhe; tel. (721) 91010; fax (721) 9101382; e-mail bverfg@bundesverfassungsgericht.de; internet www.bundesverfassungsgericht.de; Pres. Prof. Dr ANDREAS VOSSKUHLE; Vice-Pres. Prof. Dr FERDINAND KIRCHHOF.

SUPERIOR FEDERAL COURTS

Bundesarbeitsgericht (Federal Labour Court): Hugo-Preuss-Pl. 1, 99084 Erfurt; tel. (361) 26360; fax (361) 26362000; e-mail bag@bundesarbeitsgericht.de; internet www.bundesarbeitsgericht.de; Pres. INGRID SCHMIDT; Vice-Pres. Dr RUDI MÜLLER-GLÖGE.

Bundesgerichtshof (Federal Court of Justice): Herrenstr. 45A, 76133 Karlsruhe; tel. (721) 1590; fax (721) 1592512; e-mail poststelle@bgh.bund.de; internet www.bundesgerichtshof.de; Pres. (vacant); Vice-Pres. WOLFGANG SCHLICK; Federal Prosecutor-Gen. HARALD RANGE.

Bundessozialgericht (Federal Social Court): Graf-Bernadotte-Pl. 5, 34119 Kassel; tel. (561) 31071; fax (561) 3107475; e-mail bundessozialgericht@bsg.bund.de; internet www.bsg.bund.de; Pres. PETER MASUCH; Vice-Pres. Dr RUTH WETZEL-STEINWEDEL.

Bundesverwaltungsgericht (Federal Administrative Court): Simsonpl. 1, 04107 Leipzig; Postfach 100854, 04008 Leipzig; tel. (341) 20070; fax (341) 20071000; e-mail pressestelle@bverwg.bund.de; internet www.bverwg.de; Pres. (vacant); Vice-Pres. KLAUS RENNERT.

Bundesfinanzhof (Federal Financial Court): Ismaninger Str. 109, 81675 München; Postfach 860240, 81629 München; tel. (89) 92310; fax (89) 9231201; e-mail bundesfinanzhof@bfh.bund.de; internet www.bundesfinanzhof.de; Pres. Prof. Dr RUDOLF MELLINGHOFF; Vice-Pres. HERMANN-ULRICH VISKORF.

Religion

CHRISTIANITY

Arbeitsgemeinschaft Christlicher Kirchen in Deutschland (Council of Christian Churches in Germany): Ludolfusstr. 2–4, 60487 Frankfurt a.M.; Postfach 900617, 60446 Frankfurt a.M.; tel. (69) 2470270; fax (69) 24702730; e-mail info@ack-oec.de; internet www.oekumene-ack.de; 25 affiliated Churches, including the Roman Catholic Church and the Orthodox Church in Germany; Pres. Bishop Dr MARTIN HEIN.

The Roman Catholic Church

Germany comprises seven archdioceses and 20 dioceses. In 2011 there were some 24.5m. adherents (about 30.0% of the population).

Bishops' Conference: Deutsche Bischofskonferenz, Kaiserstr. 161, 53113 Bonn; tel. (228) 103214; fax (228) 103254; e-mail pressestelle@dbk.de; internet www.dbk.de; Pres. Dr ROBERT ZOLLITSCH; Sec. Dr HANS LANGENDÖRFER.

Archbishop of Bamberg: Prof. Dr LUDWIG SCHICK, Dompl. 3, 96049 Bamberg; tel. (951) 5020; fax (951) 502250.

Archbishop of Berlin: RAINER MARIA WOELKI, Niederwallstr. 8–9, 10117 Berlin; Postfach 040406, 10064 Berlin; tel. (30) 326840; fax (30) 32684276; e-mail info@erzbistumberlin.de; internet www.erzbistumberlin.de.

Archbishop of Freiburg im Breisgau: Dr ROBERT ZOLLITSCH, Schoferstr. 2, 79098 Freiburg i. Br.; tel. (761) 2188243; fax (761) 2188427; e-mail erzbischof@ordinariat-freiburg.de; internet www.erzbistum-freiburg.de.

Archbishop of Hamburg: (vacant), Postfach 101925, 20013 Hamburg; Danzigerstr. 52A, 20099 Hamburg; tel. (40) 24877100; fax (40) 24877233; e-mail pforte@egv-erzbistum-hh.de; internet www.erzbistum-hamburg.de.

Archbishop of Köln (Cologne): (vacant), Marzellenstr. 32, 50668 Köln; tel. (221) 16420; fax (221) 16421700; e-mail info@erzbistum-koeln.de; internet www.erzbistum-koeln.de.

Archbishop of München (Munich) and Freising: Cardinal Dr REINHARD MARX, Rochsusstr. 5–7, 80333 München; Postfach 100551, 80079 München; tel. (89) 21370; fax (89) 21371585; e-mail pressestelle@erzbistum-muenchen.de; internet www.erzbistum-muenchen.de.

Archbishop of Paderborn: HANS-JOSEF BECKER, Erzbischöfliches Generalvikariat, Dompl. 3, 33098 Paderborn; tel. (5251) 1251287; fax (5251) 1251470; e-mail info@erzbistum-paderborn.de; internet www.erzbistum-paderborn.de.

The Evangelical (Protestant) Church

In 2011 the Evangelische Kirche in Deutschland, which includes the Lutheran, Uniate and Reformed Protestant Churches, had some 23.6m. members, amounting to about 28.9% of the population.

Evangelische Kirche in Deutschland (EKD) (Evangelical Church in Germany): Herrenhäuser Str. 12, 30419 Hannover; tel. (511) 27960; fax (511) 2796707; e-mail presse@ekd.de; internet www.ekd.de; the governing bodies of the EKD are its Synod of 120 clergy and lay members, which meets at regular intervals, the Conference of member churches, and the Council, composed of 15 elected members; the EKD has an ecclesiastical secretariat of its own (the Evangelical Church Office), including a special office for foreign relations; Chair. of the Council NIKOLAUS SCHNEIDER.

Synod of the EKD: Herrenhäuser Str. 12, 30419 Hannover; tel. (511) 2796114; fax (511) 2796707; e-mail synode@ekd.de; Pres. Dr IRMGARD SCHWAETZER.

Deutscher Evangelischer Kirchentag (German Evangelical Church Convention): Magdeburger Str. 59, 36037 Fulda; Postfach 1555, 36005 Fulda; tel. (661) 969500; fax (661) 9695090; e-mail fulda@kirchentag.de; internet www.kirchentag.de; Pres. GERHARD ROBBERS; Gen. Sec. Dr ELLEN UEBERSCHÄR.

Churches and Federations within the EKD:

Reformierter Bund (Reformed Alliance): Knochenhauerstr. 33, 30159 Hannover; tel. (511) 47399374; fax (511) 47399428; e-mail info@reformierter-bund.de; internet www.reformierter-bund.de; f. 1884; unites the Reformed Territorial Churches and Congregations of Germany (with an estimated 2m. mems). The central body of the Reformed League is the 'Moderamen', the elected representation of the various Reformed Churches and Congregations; Moderator Rev. PETER BUKOWSKI; Gen. Sec. Rev. JÖRG SCHMIDT.

Union Evangelischer Kirchen in der EKD (UEK): Herrenhäuser Str. 12, 30419 Hannover; tel. (511) 2796529; fax (511) 2796717; e-mail postfach@uek-online.de; internet www.uek-online.de; f. 2003 by merger of Arnoldshainer Konferenz and Evangelische Kirche der Union; union of 13 regional churches (10 United, two Reformed and one Lutheran) with approx. 13.4m. mems; promotes unity among churches in the EKD; Chair. Bishop Dr ULRICH FISCHER (Evangelical Church in Baden); Vice-Chair. CHRISTIAN DRÄGERT (Evangelical Church in the Rhineland), BRIGITTE ANDRAE (Evangelical Church in Central Germany).

Bremen Evangelical Church: Franziuseck 2–4, 28199 Bremen; tel. (421) 55970; fax (421) 5597265; e-mail kirchenkanzlei@kirche-bremen.de; internet www.kirche-bremen.de; Pres. EDDA BOSSE.

Church of Lippe: Leopoldstr. 27, 32756 Detmold; Postfach 2153, 32711 Detmold; tel. (5231) 97660; fax (5231) 976850; e-mail lka@lippische-landeskirche.de; internet www.lippische-landeskirche.de; Supt Dr MARTIN DUTZMANN.

Evangelical Church in Baden: Blumenstr. 1, 76133 Karlsruhe; tel. (721) 91750; fax (721) 9175553; e-mail info@ekiba.de; internet www.ekiba.de; Bishop Dr ULRICH FISCHER.

Evangelical Church in Berlin-Brandenburg-schlesische Oberlausitz: Georgenkirchstr. 69, 10249 Berlin; tel. (30) 243440; fax (30) 24344500; e-mail info@ekbo.de; internet www.ekbo.de; Bishop Dr MARKUS DRÖGE.

Evangelical Church in Central Germany: Michaelisstr. 39, 99084 Erfurt; tel. (361) 518000; fax (361) 51800198; e-mail landeskirchenamt@ekmd.de; internet www.ekmd-online.de; 858,453 mems; Bishop ILSE JUNKERMANN.

Evangelical Church in Hessen and Nassau: Pauluspl. 1, 64285 Darmstadt; tel. (6151) 405289; fax (6151) 405441; e-mail info@ekhn.de; internet www.ekhn.de; Pres. Dr VOLKER JUNG.

Evangelical Church of Kurhessen-Waldeck: Wilhelmshöher Allee 330, 34131 Kassel; Postfach 410260, 34114 Kassel-Wilhelmshöhe; tel. (561) 93780; fax (561) 9378400; e-mail landeskirchenamt@ekkw.de; internet www.ekkw.de; Bishop Prof. Dr MARTIN HEIN.

Evangelical Church of the Palatinate: Dompl. 5, 67346 Speyer; tel. (6232) 6670; fax (6232) 667480; e-mail landeskirchenrat@evkirchepfalz.de; internet www.evpfalz.de; Pres. CHRISTIAN SCHAD.

Evangelical Church in the Rhineland: Hans-Böckler-Str. 7, 40476 Düsseldorf; Postfach 300339, 40403 Düsseldorf; tel. (211) 45620; fax (211) 4562444; e-mail lka@ekir.de; internet www.ekir.de; Pres. NIKOLAUS SCHNEIDER.

Evangelical Church of Westphalia: Altstädter Kirchpl. 5, 33602 Bielefeld; tel. (521) 5940; fax (521) 594466; e-mail landeskirchenamt@lka.ekvw.de; internet www.ekvw.de; Pres. ANNETTE KURSCHUS.

Vereinigte Evangelisch-Lutherische Kirche Deutschlands (VELKD) (The United Evangelical-Lutheran Church of Germany): Herrenhäuserstr. 12, 30419 Hannover; Postfach 210220, 30419 Hannover; tel. (511) 2796527; fax (511) 2796182; e-mail zentrale@velkd.de; internet www.velkd.de; f. 1948; unites all but 3 of the Lutheran territorial Churches within the Evangelical Church in Germany; Presiding Bishop Dr GERHARD ULRICH (Schleswig-Holstein); 9.7m. mems.

Evangelical-Lutheran Church in Bavaria: Katharina-von-Bora-Str. 11, 80333 München; tel. (89) 55950; fax (89) 5595484; e-mail landesbischof@elkb.de; internet www.bayern-evangelisch.de; Bishop Prof. Dr HEINRICH BEDFORD-STROHM; 2.5m. mems.

Evangelical-Lutheran Church in Brunswick: Dietrich-Bonhoeffer-Str. 1, 38300 Wolfenbüttel; tel. (5331) 8020; fax (5331) 802707; e-mail info@lk-bs.de; internet www.landeskirche-braunschweig.de; Bishop Prof. Dr FRIEDRICH WEBER.

Evangelical-Lutheran Church of Hannover: Haarstr. 6, 30169 Hannover; tel. (511) 5635830; fax (511) 56358311; e-mail landesbischoefin@evlka.de; internet www.evlka.de; Bishop RALF MEISTER; 2.9m. mems.

Evangelical-Lutheran Church in Northern Germany: Königstr. 54, 22767 Hamburg; tel. (306) 201100; fax (306) 201109; e-mail info@nordkirche.de; internet www.nordkirche.de; f. 2012 by the merger of Evangelical Lutheran Church of Mecklenburg, Evangelical-Lutheran Church of North Elbe and the Pomeranian Evangelical Church; Chair. Rt Rev. GERHARD ULRICH (Schleswig and Holstein).

Evangelical-Lutheran Church of Schaumburg-Lippe: Herderstr. 27, 31665 Bückeburg; tel. (5722) 9600; fax (5722) 96010; e-mail lka@lksl.de; internet www.landeskirche-schaumburg-lippe.de; Bishop Dr KARL-HINRICH MANZKE.

Also affiliated to the EKD:

Evangelical-Lutheran Church in Oldenburg: Philosophenweg 1, 26121 Oldenburg; tel. (441) 77010; fax (441) 77012199; e-mail info@kirche-oldenburg.de; internet www.kirche-oldenburg.de; Bishop JAN JANSSEN; 446,899 mems.

Evangelical-Lutheran Church in Württemberg: Augustenstr. 124, 70197 Stuttgart; Postfach 101342, 70012 Stuttgart; tel. (711) 2227658; fax (711) 2227681; e-mail kontakt@elk-wue.de; internet www.elk-wue.de; Bishop FRANK OTFRIED JULY.

Evangelical-Lutheran Church of Saxony: Lukasstr. 6, 01069 Dresden; Postfach 120552, 01006 Dresden; tel. (351) 46920; fax (351) 4692109; e-mail kirche@evlks.de; internet www.evlks.de; 784,706 mems; Bishop JOCHEN BOHL.

Evangelical-Reformed Church: Saarstr. 6, 26789 Leer; tel. (491) 91980; fax (491) 9198251; e-mail info@reformiert.de; internet www.reformiert.de; Pres. Rev. JANN SCHMIDT.

Herrnhuter Brüdergemeine/Europäisch-Festländische Brüder-Unität (European Continental Province of the Moravian Church): Badwasen 6, 73087 Bad Boll; tel. (7164) 94210; fax (7164) 942199; f. 1457; there are 25 congregations in Germany, Denmark, Estonia, Latvia, the Netherlands, Sweden, Albania and Switzerland, with approx. 18,000 mems; Chair. FRIEDER VOLLPRECHT.

Other Protestant Churches

Arbeitsgemeinschaft Mennonitischer Gemeinden in Deutschland (Association of Mennonite Congregations in Germany): Stauferstr. 43, 85051 Ingolstadt; tel. (841) 9008216; e-mail amg.frieder.boller@mennoniten.de; internet www.mennoniten.de; f. 1886; re-organized 1990; Chair. Pastor FRIEDER BOLLER.

Bund Evangelisch-Freikirchlicher Gemeinden in Deutschland K.d.ö.R. (Union of Evangelical Free Churches (Baptists) in Germany): Johann-Gerhard-Oncken-Str. 7, 14641 Wustermark; tel. (33234) 74105; fax (33234) 74199; e-mail info@baptisten.de; internet www.baptisten.de; f. 1942; Pres. HARTMUT RIEMENSCHNEIDER; Gen. Sec. CHRISTOPH STIBA.

Bund Freier evangelischer Gemeinden (Covenant of Free Evangelical Churches in Germany): Goltenkamp 4, 58452 Witten; Postfach 4005, 58426 Witten; tel. (2302) 9370; fax (2302) 93799; e-mail info@bund.feg.de; internet www.feg.de; f. 1854; Pres. ANSGAR HÖRSTING; Administrator KLAUS KANWISCHER; 40,000 mems.

Evangelisch-altreformierte Kirche von Niedersachsen (Evangelical Reformed Church of Lower Saxony): Hauptstr. 33 49824 Laar; tel. (5947) 242; e-mail beuke1@ewetel.net; f. 1838; Sec. Rev. Dr GERRIT JAN BEUKER.

Evangelisch-methodistische Kirche (United Methodist Church): Ludolfusstr. 2–4, 60487 Frankfurt a.M.; tel. (69) 2425210; fax (69) 242521129; e-mail bischoefin@emk.de; internet www.emk.de; f. 1968; Presiding Bishop ROSEMARIE WENNER.

Freikirche der Siebenten-Tags-Adventisten (Seventh-Day Adventist Church): Senefelderstr. 15, 73760 Ostfildern; Postfach 4260, 73745 Ostfildern; tel. (711) 4481914; fax (711) 4481960; e-mail info@adventisten.de; internet www.adventisten.de; f. 1863; Pres. JOHANNES NAETHER.

Die Heilsarmee in Deutschland (Salvation Army in Germany): Salierring 23–27, 50677 Köln; tel. (221) 208190; fax (221) 20819899; e-mail info@heilsarmee.de; internet www.heilsarmee.de; f. 1886; Leader Col HORST CHARLET.

Mülheimer Verband Freikirchlich-Evangelischer Gemeinden (Pentecostal Church): Habenhauser Dorfstr. 27, 28279 Bremen; tel. (421) 8399130; fax (421) 8399136; e-mail geschaeftsstelle@muelheimer-verband.de; internet www.muelheimer-verband.de; f. 1913.

Selbständige Evangelisch-Lutherische Kirche (Independent Evangelical-Lutheran Church): Schopenhauerstr. 7, 30625 Hannover; tel. (511) 557808; fax (511) 551588; e-mail selk@selk.de; internet www.selk.de; f. 1972; Pres. Bishop HANS JOERG VOIGT; Exec. Sec. Rev. MICHAEL SCHAETZEL; 34,934 mems.

Other Christian Churches

Other Christian churches had 4.5m.–5m. members in 2005, of whom 1.5m.–2m. persons were members of Orthodox churches.

Alt-Katholische Kirche (Old Catholic Church): Gregor-Mendel-Str. 28, 53115 Bonn; tel. (228) 232285; fax (228) 238314; e-mail konfig@alt-katholisch.de; internet www.alt-katholisch.de; seceded from the Roman Catholic Church as a protest against the declaration of Papal infallibility in 1870; belongs to the Utrecht Union of Old Catholic Churches; in full communion with the Anglican Communion; Bishop Dr MATTHIAS RING; 25,000 mems.

Apostelamt Jesu Christi: Madlower Hauptstr. 39, 03050 Cottbus; tel. (355) 541227; e-mail kha@kirche-apostelamt-jesu-christi.eu; internet www.kirche-ajc.de.

Armenisch-Apostolische Orthodoxe Kirche in Deutschland (Armenian Apostolic Orthodox Church in Germany): Allensteiner Str. 5, 50735 Köln; tel. (221) 7126223; fax (221) 7126267; e-mail armenische_dioezese@hotmail.com; Archbishop KAREKIN BEKDJIAN.

Griechisch-Orthodoxe Metropolie von Deutschland (Greek Orthodox Metropolitanate of Germany): Dietrich-Bonhoeffer-Str. 2, 53227 Bonn; Postfach 300555, 53185 Bonn; tel. (228) 9737840; fax (228) 97378424; e-mail sekretariat@orthodoxie.net; internet www.orthodoxie.net; f. 1963; Metropolitan of Germany and Exarch of Central Europe AUGOUSTINOS LABARDAKIS.

Religiöse Gesellschaft der Freunde (Quäker) (Religious Society of Friends—Quakers): Planckstr. 20, 10117 Berlin; tel. (30) 2082284;

fax (30) 20458142; e-mail berlin@quaeker.org; internet www.quaeker.org; f. 1925; 300 mems.

Russische Orthodoxe Kirche—Berliner Diözese (Russian Orthodox Church): Wildensteiner Str. 10, 10318 Berlin; tel. (30) 5099611; fax (30) 5098153; e-mail red.stimme@snafu.de; Archbishop of Berlin and Germany Archbishop FEOFAN.

ISLAM

Of those who answered the non-compulsory question on religion in the 2011 census, 1.9% designated themselves as Muslim.

Zentralrat der Muslime in Deutschland eV (ZMD) (Central Council of Muslims in Germany): Steinfelder Gasse 32, 50670 Köln; tel. (221) 1394450; fax (221) 1394681; e-mail sekretariat@zentralrat.de; internet www.zentralrat.de; f. 1994; 21 mem. asscns; Pres. Dr AIMAN A. MAZYEK.

JUDAISM

The membership of Jewish synagogues in Germany numbered some 105,000 in 2012.

Zentralrat der Juden in Deutschland (Central Council of Jews in Germany): Tucholskystr. 9, Leo-Baeck-Haus, 10117 Berlin; Postfach 040207, 10061 Berlin; tel. (30) 2844560; fax (30) 28445613; e-mail info@zentralratdjuden.de; internet www.zentralratdjuden.de; Pres. Dr DIETER GRAUMANN; Sec.-Gen. STEPHAN J. KRAMER; 105,000 mems (2012).

Jüdische Gemeinde zu Berlin (Jewish Community in Berlin): Oranienburger Str. 28–31, 10117 Berlin; tel. (30) 880280; fax (30) 88028103; e-mail service@jg-berlin.org; internet www.jg-berlin.org; Pres. Dr GIDEON JOFFE.

The Press

A significant feature of the German press is the large number of daily newspapers published in regional centres, of which the *Westdeutsche Allgemeine Zeitung* in Essen has the largest circulation. The most important national publications are *Bild* in Hamburg and *Süddeutsche Zeitung* in Munich, followed by the *Frankfurter Allgemeine Zeitung* in Frankfurt am Main and Berlin's *Die Welt*.

There are strict limits on press ownership. In 1968 a government commission stipulated various restrictions on the proportions of circulation that any one publishing group should be allowed to control: (1) 40% of the total circulation of newspapers or 40% of the total circulation of magazines; (2) 20% of the total circulation of newspapers and magazines together; (3) 15% of the circulation in one field if the proportion owned in the other field is 40%. However, many of the most important newspapers and magazines are controlled by large publishing groups.

Axel Springer Verlag AG: Axel-Springer-Str. 65, 10888 Berlin; and Axel-Springer-Pl. 1, 20350 Hamburg; tel. (30) 25910; fax (30) 251606; tel. (40) 34700; fax (40) 345811; internet www.asv.de; f. 1946; includes 5 major dailies *Berliner Morgenpost*, *Bild*, *BZ*, *Die Welt*, *Hamburger Abendblatt*, 3 Sunday papers *Bild am Sonntag*, *BZ am Sonntag*, *Welt am Sonntag*, and radio, television, women's and family magazines; Chair. Dr MATHIAS DÖPFNER.

Bauer Verlagsgruppe: Burchardstr. 11, 20077 Hamburg; and Charles-de-Gaulle-Str. 8, 81737 München; tel. (40) 30190; fax (40) 30191043; tel. (89) 67860; fax (89) 6374404; internet www.bauerverlag.de; f. 1875; publ. 42 magazines in Germany, incl. *Auf einen Blick*, *Bravo*, *Neue Post*, *Tina*, *tv14*, *tv Hören und Sehen*, *TV Movie*; Pres. HEINZ HEINRICH BAUER.

Gruner + Jahr AG & Co KG: Am Baumwall 11, 20459 Hamburg; tel. (40) 37030; fax (40) 37036000; e-mail unternehmenskommunikation@guj.de; internet www.guj.de; publ., among others, *Brigitte*, *Capital*, *Eltern*, *GEO*, *Schöner Wohnen* and *Stern*; Mems, Exec. Bd. JULIA JÄKEL, TORSTEN-JÖRN KLEIN, ACHIM TWARDY.

Hubert Burda Media Holding GmbH & Co KG: Arabellastr. 23, 81925 München; tel. (89) 9250-0; e-mail info@hubert-burda-media.com; internet www.burda.de; f. 1908; publs 74 magazine titles in Germany, incl. *Bild + Funk*, *Bunte*, *Burda Modemagazin*, *Elle*, *Focus*, *Freizeit Revue*, *Freundin*, *Meine Familie & Ich*; Chair. Dr HUBERT BURDA.

WAZ Mediengruppe: Friedrichstr. 34–38, 45128 Essen; tel. (201) 804-0; fax (201) 8041644; e-mail kontakt@waz-mediengruppe.de; internet www.waz-mediengruppe.de; f. 1976; publ. regional dailies, incl. *Westdeutsche Allgemeine Zeitung*, and magazines incl. *Frau Aktuell* and *Gong*; Man. Dirs BODO HOMBACH, CHRISTIAN NIENHAUS.

PRINCIPAL DAILIES

Aachen

Aachener Zeitung: Dresdner Str. 3, 52068 Aachen; Postfach 500110, 52085 Aachen; tel. (241) 5101310; fax (241) 5101360; e-mail redaktion@zeitungsverlag-aachen.de; internet www.az-web.de; f. 1946; Editor-in-Chief BERND MATHIEU; circ. 128,711 (Dec. 2011, with *Aachener Nachrichten*).

Augsburg

Augsburger Allgemeine: Curt-Frenzel-Str. 2, 86167 Augsburg; tel. (821) 7770; fax (821) 7772039; e-mail redaktion@augsburger-allgemeiner.de; internet www.augsburger-allgemeine.de; Editor-in-Chief WALTER ROLLER; circ. 331,637 (March 2012, with *Allgäuer Zeitung*).

Bautzen

Serbske Nowiny: Tuchmacherstr. 27, 02625 Bautzen; tel. (3591) 577232; fax (3591) 577202; e-mail redaktion@serbske-nowiny.de; internet www.serbske-nowiny.de; f. 1842; evening; Sorbian; Editor JANEK SCHÄFER.

Berlin

Berliner Kurier: Karl-Liebknecht-Str. 29, 10178 Berlin; tel. (30) 23279; fax (30) 23275533; e-mail post@berliner-kurier.de; internet www.berliner-kurier.de; f. 1990; evening; publ. by Berliner Verlag GmbH; Editor-in-Chief HANS-PETER BUSCHHEUER; circ. 117,456 (Dec. 2011).

Berliner Morgenpost: Axel-Springer-Str. 65, 10888 Berlin; tel. (30) 25910; fax (30) 2516071; e-mail redaktion@morgenpost.de; internet www.morgenpost.de; f. 1898; publ. by Ullstein GmbH; Editor-in-Chief CARSTEN ERDMANN; circ. 126,411 (Dec. 2011).

Berliner Zeitung: Karl-Liebknecht-Str. 29, 10178 Berlin; tel. (2) 23279; fax (30) 23275533; e-mail berliner-zeitung@berliner-zeitung.de; internet www.berliner-zeitung.de; f. 1945; morning (except Sun.); publ. by Berliner Verlag GmbH; Editor BRIGITTE FEHRLE; circ. 144,229 (Dec. 2011).

B.Z.: B.Z. Ullstein GmbH, Kurfürstendamm 21–22, 10719 Berlin; tel. (30) 25910; fax (30) 259173006; e-mail redaktion@bz-berlin.de; internet www.bz-berlin.de; f. 1877; Mon.–Sat.; Editor-in-Chief PETER HUTH; circ. 161,726 (Dec. 2011, with *B.Z. am Sonntag*).

Der Tagesspiegel: Askanischer Pl. 3, 10963 Berlin; tel. (30) 290210; fax (30) 26009332; e-mail redaktion@tagesspiegel.de; internet www.tagesspiegel.de; f. 1945; Editors-in-Chief STEPHAN-ANDREAS CASDORFF, LORENZ MAROLDT; circ. 131,178 (Dec. 2011).

Die Welt: Axel-Springer-Str. 65, 10888 Berlin; tel. (30) 25910; fax (30) 259171606; internet www.welt.de; f. 1946; publ. by Axel Springer Verlag AG; Editor-in-Chief JAN-ERIC PETERS; circ. 263,817 (Dec. 2011, Mon.–Fri. only).

Bielefeld

Neue Westfälische: Niedernstr. 21–27, 33602 Bielefeld; Postfach 100225, 33502 Bielefeld; tel. (521) 5550; fax (521) 555348; e-mail redaktion@neue-westfaelische.de; internet www.nw-news.de; f. 1967; publ. by Zeitungsgruppe Neue Westfälische; Editor-in-Chief THOMAS SEIM; circ. 253,082 (Dec. 2011).

Braunschweig
(Brunswick)

Braunschweiger Zeitung: Hamburger Str. 277, 38114 Braunschweig; Postfach 8052, 38130 Braunschweig; tel. (531) 39000; fax (531) 3900610; e-mail chefredaktion@bzv.de; internet www.braunschweiger-zeitung.de; Editor-in-Chief ARMIN MAUS; circ. 157,105 (Dec. 2011).

Bremen

Weser-Kurier: Martinistr. 43, 28195 Bremen; Postfach 107801, 28078 Bremen; tel. (421) 36710; fax (421) 36711000; e-mail chefredaktion@weser-kurier.de; internet www.weser-kurier.de; f. 1945; Editor-in-Chief SILKE HELLWIG; circ. 168,424 (Dec. 2011, with *Bremer Nachrichten*).

Chemnitz

Freie Presse: Brückenstr. 15, 09111 Chemnitz; Postfach 261, 09002 Chemnitz; tel. (371) 6560; fax (371) 65617070; e-mail die.tageszeitung@freiepresse.de; internet www.freiepresse.de; f. 1963; morning; Editor TORSTEN KLEDITZSCH; circ. 277,442 (Dec. 2011, incl. regional edns).

Cottbus

Lausitzer Rundschau: Str. der Jugend 54, 03050 Cottbus; Postfach 100279, 03002 Cottbus; tel. (355) 4810; fax (355) 481245; e-mail redaktion@lr-online.de; internet www.lr-online.de; independent; morning; Editor-in-Chief JOHANNES FISCHER; circ. 93,042 (Dec. 2011).

Darmstadt

Darmstädter Echo: Holzhofallee 25–31, 64295 Darmstadt; Postfach 100155, 64276 Darmstadt; tel. (6151) 387373; fax (6151) 387900; e-mail chefredaktion@darmstaedter-echo.de; internet www.echo-online.de; f. 1945; Editor-in-Chief Dr MICHAEL HORN; circ. 88,828 (Dec. 2011).

Dortmund

Westfälische Rundschau: Friedrichstr. 34–36, 45128 Essen; tel. (201) 8040; internet www.wr.de; publ. by WAZ Mediengruppe; Editor-in-Chief MALTE HINZ; circ. 210,000 (2008).

Dresden

Sächsische Zeitung: Haus der Presse, Ostra-Allee 20, 01067 Dresden; tel. (351) 48640; fax (351) 48642354; e-mail redaktion@sz-online.de; internet www.sz-online.de; f. 1946; morning; publ. by Gruner + Jahr AG; Editor-in-Chief THOMAS SCHULTZ-HOMBERG; circ. 285,000 (Dec. 2011).

Düsseldorf

Handelsblatt: Kasernenstr. 67, 40213 Düsseldorf; Postfach 102741, 40018 Düsseldorf; tel. (211) 8870; fax (211) 8872980; e-mail handelsblatt@vhb.de; internet www.handelsblatt.de; Mon.–Fri.; business and finance; publ. by Verlagsgruppe Handelsblatt GmbH; Editor-in-Chief BERND ZIESEMER; circ. 147,208 (Dec. 2011).

Rheinische Post: Zülpicherstr. 10, 40549 Düsseldorf; tel. (211) 5050; fax (211) 5051929; internet www.rp-online.de; f. 1946; Editor-in-Chief SVEN GÖSMANN; circ. 373,810 (Dec. 2011, incl. regional edns).

Westdeutsche Zeitung: Königsallee 27, 40212 Düsseldorf; tel. (211) 83820; fax (211) 83822225; e-mail westdeutsche.zeitung@wz-newsline.de; internet www.wz-newsline.de; Editor-in-Chief LOTHAR LEUSCHEN (acting); circ. 159,246 (Dec. 2011).

Erfurt

Thüringer Allgemeine: Gottstedter Landstr. 6, 99092 Erfurt; tel. (361) 2274; fax (361) 2275007; e-mail redaktion@thueringer-allgemeine.de; internet www.thueringer-allgemeine.de; f. 1946; morning; Editor-in-Chief PAUL-JOSEF RAUE; circ. 338,500 (Sept. 2011, with *Ostthüringer Zeitung* and *Thüringische Landeszeitung*).

Essen

Neue Ruhr Zeitung/Neue Rhein Zeitung: Friedrichstr. 34–38, 45128 Essen; tel. (201) 8040; fax (201) 8041070; e-mail redaktion@nrz.de; internet www.derwesten.de/nachrichten/nrz.html; f. 1946; Editor-in-Chief RÜDIGER OPPERS; circ. 180,000.

Westdeutsche Allgemeine Zeitung: Friedrichstr. 34–38, 45128 Essen; tel. (201) 8040; fax (201) 8042841; e-mail zentralredaktion@waz.de; internet www.derwesten.de/nachrichten/faz.html; f. 1948; Editor-in-Chief ULRICH REITZ; circ. 580,000.

Frankfurt am Main

Frankfurter Allgemeine Zeitung: Hellerhofstr. 2–4, 60327 Frankfurt a.M.; tel. (69) 75910; fax (69) 75912332; e-mail info@faz.net; internet www.faz.net; f. 1949; Editors WERNER D'INKA, BERTHOLD KOHLER, Dr GÜNTHER NONNENMACHER, Dr FRANK SCHIRRMACHER, HOLGER STELTZNER; circ. 380,427 (Dec. 2011).

Frankfurter Neue Presse: Frankenallee 71–81, 60327 Frankfurt a.M.; Postfach 100801, 60008 Frankfurt a.M.; tel. (69) 75010; fax (69) 75014846; e-mail fnp.redaktion@fsd.de; internet www.fnp.de; independent; Editor-in-Chief RAINER M. GEFELLER.

Frankfurter Rundschau: Karl-Gerold-Pl. 1, 60594 Frankfurt a.M.; tel. (69) 21991; fax (69) 21993720; e-mail politik@fr-online.de; internet www.fr-online.de; f. 1945; Editor-in-Chief Dr UWE VORKÖTTER; circ. 124,479 (Dec. 2011).

Freiburg im Breisgau

Badische Zeitung: Pressehaus, Basler Str. 88, 79115 Freiburg i. Br.; tel. (761) 4960; fax (761) 4965029; e-mail redaktion@badische-zeitung.de; internet www.badische-zeitung.de; f. 1946; Editor-in-Chief THOMAS HAUSER; circ. 148,061 (Dec. 2011).

Gera

Ostthüringer Zeitung: Alte Str. 3, 04626 Löbichau; tel. (3447) 525911; fax (3447) 525914; e-mail redaktion@otz.de; internet www.otz.de; morning; Editor-in-Chief JÖRG RIEBARTSCH.

Hagen

Westfalenpost: Schürmannstr. 4, 58097 Hagen; tel. (2331) 9170; fax (2331) 9174206; e-mail westfalenpost@westfalenpost.de; internet www.derwesten.de/nachrichten/wp.html; f. 1946; publ. by WAZ Mediengruppe; Editor-in-Chief STEFAN HANS KLÄSENER.

Halle an der Saale

Mitteldeutsche Zeitung: Delitzscher Str. 65, 06112 Halle (Saale); tel. (345) 5650; fax (345) 5654350; e-mail service@mz-web.de; internet www.mz-web.de; f. 1946 as *Freiheit* (organ of the ruling party in the GDR); refounded 1990 following unification; publ. by M. DuMont Schauberg Gruppe; Editors-in-Chief HANS-JÜRGEN GREYE, HARTMUT AUGUSTIN; circ. 221,404 (Dec. 2011).

Hamburg

Bild: Axel-Springer-Pl. 1, 10969 Hamburg; tel. (40) 34700; fax (40) 345811; internet www.bild.de; f. 1952; publ. by Axel Springer Verlag AG; Chief Editor KAI DIEKMANN; circ. 2,715,105 (Dec. 2011).

Hamburger Abendblatt: Axel-Springer-Pl. 1, 20350 Hamburg; tel. (40) 34700; fax (40) 34726110; internet www.abendblatt.de; publ. by Axel Springer Verlag AG; Editor-in-Chief LARS HAIDER; circ. 212,263 (Dec. 2011).

Hamburger Morgenpost: Griegstr. 75, 22763 Hamburg; tel. (40) 8090570; fax (40) 9057640; e-mail verlag@mopo.de; internet www.mopo.de; publ. by Morgenpost Verlag; Editor-in-Chief FRANK NIGGEMEIER; circ. 107,584 (Dec. 2011).

Hannover
(Hanover)

Hannoversche Allgemeine Zeitung: August-Madsack-Str. 1, 30559 Hannover; tel. (511) 5180; fax (511) 5182899; e-mail redaktion@haz.de; internet www.haz.de; Editors-in-Chief HENDRIK BRANDT, MATTHIAS KOCH; circ. 540,570 (Dec. 2011).

Heidelberg

Rhein-Neckar-Zeitung: Neugasse 2, 69117 Heidelberg; tel. (6221) 5190; fax (6221) 519217; e-mail rnz-kontakt@rnz.de; internet www.rnz.de; f. 1945; morning; Publrs JOACHIM KNORR, WINFRIED KNORR, INGE HOELTZCKE, DANIEL SCHULZE; circ. 92,754 (Dec. 2011).

Ingolstadt

Donaukurier: Stauffenbergstr. 2A, 85051 Ingolstadt; tel. (841) 96660; fax (841) 9666255; e-mail ingolstadt.redaktion@donaukurier.de; internet www.donaukurier.de; f. 1872; Editor-in-Chief GERD SCHNEIDER; circ. 88,772 (Dec. 2011).

Kassel

Hessische/Niedersächsische Allgemeine: Frankfurter Str. 168, 34121 Kassel; Postfach 101009, 34010 Kassel; tel. (561) 20300; fax (561) 2032406; e-mail info@hna.de; internet www.hna.de; f. 1959; independent; Editor-in-Chief HORST SEIDENFADEN; circ. 224,507 (Dec. 2011).

Kempten

Allgäuer Zeitung: Heisinger Str. 14, 87437 Kempten; Postfach 3155, 87440 Kempten; tel. (831) 2060; fax (831) 206123; e-mail redaktion@azv.de; internet www.all-in.de; f. 1945; Publrs GEORG FÜRST VON WALDBURG-ZEIL, GÜNTER HOLLAND, ELLINOR HOLLAND; circ. 102,874 (Dec. 2011).

Kiel

Kieler Nachrichten: Fleethörn 1–7, 24103 Kiel; Postfach 1111, 24100 Kiel; tel. (431) 9030; fax (431) 9032935; internet www.kn-online.de; publ. by Axel Springer Verlag; Editor-in-Chief JÜRGEN HEINEMANN; circ. 103,053 (Dec. 2011).

Koblenz

Rhein-Zeitung: August-Horch-Str. 28, 56070 Koblenz; tel. (261) 89200; fax (261) 892770; e-mail redaktion@rhein-zeitung.net; internet www.rhein-zeitung.de; Editor-in-Chief CHRISTIAN LINDNER; circ. 198,688 (Mon.–Fri.), 216,837 (Sat.) (2011).

Köln
(Cologne)

Express: Postfach 100410, 50450 Köln; Amsterdamer Str. 192, 50735 Köln; tel. (221) 2240; fax (211) 2242700; e-mail info@express.de; internet www.express.de; f. 1964; publ. by DuMont Schauberg Gruppe; Editor-in-Chief RUDOLF KREITZ; circ. 182,498 (Dec. 2011).

Kölner Stadt-Anzeiger: Amsterdamer Str. 192, 50735 Köln; tel. (221) 2240; fax (221) 2242524; internet www.ksta.de; f. 1876; Editor-in-Chief PETER PAULS; circ. 328,092 (Dec. 2011, with *Kölnische Rundschau*).

Kölnische Rundschau: Stolkgasse 25–45, 50667 Köln; Postfach 102145, 50461 Köln; tel. (221) 1632551; fax (221) 1632491; e-mail koeln@kr-redaktion.de; internet www.rundschau-online.de; f. 1946; Publr HELMUT HEINEN.

Konstanz

Südkurier: Max-Stromeyer-Str. 178, 78467 Konstanz; Postfach 102001, Presse- und Druckzentrum, 78420 Konstanz; tel. (7531) 9990; fax (7531) 991485; e-mail chefredaktion@suedkurier.de; internet www.suedkurier.de; f. 1945; Editor-in-Chief STEFAN LUTZ; circ. 131,191 (Dec. 2011).

Leipzig

Leipziger Volkszeitung: Peterssteinweg 19, 04107 Leipzig; tel. (341) 21810; fax (341) 21811640; e-mail post@lvz-online.de; internet www.lvz-online.de; f. 1894; morning; publ. by Verlagsgesellschaft Madsach and Axel Springer Verlag AG; Editor-in-Chief JAN EMENDÖRFER; circ. 217,014 (Dec. 2011).

Leutkirch im Allgäu

Schwäbische Zeitung: Rudolf-Roth-Str. 18, 88299 Leutkirch im Allgäu; Postfach 1145, 88291 Leutkirch im Allgäu; tel. (7561) 80100; fax (7561) 80378; e-mail redaktion@schwaebische-zeitung.de; internet www.schwaebische-zeitung.de; f. 1945; Editor-in-Chief HENDRIK GROTH; circ. 175,051 (Dec. 2011).

Lübeck

Lübecker Nachrichten: Herrenholz 10–12, 23556 Lübeck; tel. (451) 1440; fax (451) 1441022; e-mail redaktion@ln-luebeck.de; internet www.ln-online.de; f. 1945; Tue.–Sun.; publ. by Axel Springer Verlag AG; Editor-in-Chief GERALD GOETSCH; circ. 104,033 (Dec. 2011).

Ludwigshafen

Die Rheinpfalz: Amtsstr. 5–11, 67059 Ludwigshafen; Postfach 211147, 67011 Ludwigshafen; tel. (621) 590201; fax (621) 5902272; e-mail rheinpfalz@rheinpfalz.de; internet www.rheinpfalz.de; Editor-in-Chief MICHAEL GARTHE; circ. 243,572 (Dec. 2011).

Magdeburg

Volksstimme: Bahnhofstr. 17, 39104 Magdeburg; tel. (391) 59990; fax (391) 388400; e-mail chefredaktion@volksstimme.de; internet www.volksstimme.de; f. 1890; morning; 18 regional edns; publ. by Magdeburger Verlags- und Druckhaus GmbH; Editor-in-Chief ALOIS KÖSTER; circ. 193,615 (Dec. 2011, incl. regional edns).

Mainz

Allgemeine Zeitung: Erich-Dombrowski-Str. 2, 55127 Mainz; tel. (6131) 4830; fax (6131) 485868; e-mail az-mainz@vrm.de; internet www.main-rheiner.de; f. 1850; publ. by Verlagsgruppe Rhein-Main; Editor-in-Chief FRIEDRICH ROEINGH; circ. 95,494 (March 2008, incl. regional edns).

Mannheim

Mannheimer Morgen: Dudenstr. 12–26, 68167 Mannheim; Postfach 102164, 68021 Mannheim; tel. (621) 39201; fax (621) 3921376; e-mail redaktion@mamo.de; internet www.morgenweb.de; f. 1946; Editor-in-Chief HORST ROTH; circ. 125,634 (Dec. 2011).

München
(Munich)

Abendzeitung: Rundfunkpl. 4, 80335 München; tel. (89) 23770; fax (89) 2377409; e-mail info@abendzeitung.de; internet www.abendzeitung.de; f. 1948; evening; Editor-in-Chief ARNO MAKOWSKY; circ. 131,399 (Dec. 2011).

Münchner Merkur: Paul-Heyse-Str. 2–4, 80336 München; tel. (89) 53060; fax (89) 5306408; internet www.merkur-online.de; Editor-in-Chief KARL SCHERMANN; circ. 268,762 (Dec. 2011).

Süddeutsche Zeitung: Hultschiner Str. 8, 81677 München; tel. (89) 21830; fax (89) 21839715; e-mail wir@sueddeutsche.de; internet www.sueddeutsche.de; f. 1945; publ. by Süddeutscher-Verlag GmbH; Editor-in-Chief KURT KISTER; circ. 427,748 (Dec. 2011).

TZ: Paul-Heyse-Str. 2–4, 80336 München; tel. (89) 53060; fax (89) 5306552; e-mail sekretariat@tz-online.de; internet www.tz-online.de; f. 1968; Editor-in-Chief RUDOLF BÖGEL; circ. 141,250 (Dec. 2011).

Münster

Westfälische Nachrichten: An der Hansalinie 1, 48163 Münster; tel. (251) 6900; fax (251) 6904570; internet www.wn.de; Editor-in-Chief Dr NORBERT TIEMANN; circ. 210,030 (June 2008, incl. regional edns).

Neubrandenburg

Nordkurier: Friedrich-Engels-Ring 29, 17033 Neubrandenburg; tel. (395) 45750; fax (395) 4575694; e-mail chefredaktion@nordkurier.de; internet www.nordkurier.de; Editor-in-Chief Dr ANDRÉ UZULIS; circ. 88,841 (Dec. 2011).

Nürnberg
(Nuremberg)

Nürnberger Nachrichten: Marienstr. 9–11, Postfach 90327, 90402 Nürnberg; tel. (911) 2160; fax (911) 2162432; e-mail info@nordbayern.de; internet www.nn-online.de; f. 1945; Editor-in-Chief HEINZ-JOACHIM HAUCK; circ. 282,469 (Dec. 2011).

Oldenburg

Nordwest-Zeitung: Peterstr. 28–34, 26121 Oldenburg; Postfach 2527, 26015 Oldenburg; tel. (441) 998801; fax (441) 99882029; internet www.nwz-online.de; publ. by Nordwest-Zeitung Verlagsgesellschaft mbH & Co KG; Editor-in-Chief ROLF SEELHEIM; circ. 123,706 (Dec. 2011).

Osnabrück

Neue Osnabrücker Zeitung: Breiter Gang 10–16 and Grosse Str. 17–19, 49074 Osnabrück; Postfach 4260, 49032 Osnabrück; tel. (541) 3100; fax (541) 310485; e-mail redaktion@neue-oz.de; internet www.neue-oz.de; f. 1967; Editor-in-Chief RALF GEISENHANSLÜKE; circ. 282,238 (Dec. 2011).

Passau

Passauer Neue Presse: Medienstr. 5, 94036 Passau; tel. (851) 8020; fax (851) 802256; e-mail info@pnp.de; internet www.pnp.de; f. 1946; Editor-in-Chief ERNST FUCHS; circ. 166,010 (Dec. 2011).

Potsdam

Märkische Allgemeine: Friedrich-Engels-Str. 24, 14473 Potsdam; Postfach 601153, 14411 Potsdam; tel. (331) 28400; fax (331) 2840310; e-mail chefredaktion@mazonline.de; internet www.maerkischeallgemeine.de; f. 1990; morning; independent; Chief Editor Dr KLAUS ROST; circ. 138,092 (Dec. 2011).

Regensburg

Mittelbayerische Zeitung: Kumpfmühler Str. 9, 93047 Regensburg; tel. (941) 207270; fax (941) 207307; e-mail mittelbayerische@mittelbayerische.de; internet www.mittelbayerische.de; f. 1945; Editor-in-Chief MANFRED SAUERER; circ. 119,375 (Dec. 2011).

Rostock

Ostsee-Zeitung: Richard-Wagner-Str. 1A, 18055 Rostock; tel. (81) 3650; fax (81) 365244; e-mail redaktion@ostsee-zeitung.de; internet www.ostsee-zeitung.de; f. 1952; publ. by Axel Springer Verlag AG; Editor-in-Chief JAN EMENDÖRFER; circ. 149,553 (Dec. 2011, incl. regional edns).

Saarbrücken

Saarbrücker Zeitung: Gutenbergstr. 11–23, 66117 Saarbrücken; tel. (681) 5020; fax (681) 502501; internet www.saarbruecker-zeitung.de; f. 1761; Editor PETER STEFAN HERBST; circ. 149,308 (Dec. 2011).

Stuttgart

Stuttgarter Nachrichten: Plieninger Str. 150, 70567 Stuttgart; Postfach 104452, 70039 Stuttgart; tel. (711) 72050; fax (711) 72057138; e-mail cvd@stn.zgs.de; internet www.stuttgarter-nachrichten.de; f. 1946; Editor-in-Chief CHRISTOPH REISINGER; circ. 201,729 (Dec. 2011, with *Stuttgarter Zeitung*).

Stuttgarter Zeitung: Plieninger Str. 150, 70567 Stuttgart; Postfach 106032, 70049 Stuttgart; tel. (711) 72050; fax (711) 72051112; e-mail redaktion@stz.zgs.de; internet www.stuttgarter-zeitung.de; f. 1945; Editor-in-Chief JOACHIM DORFS.

Trier

Trierischer Volksfreund: Hanns-Martin-Schleyer-Str. 8, 54294 Trier; Postfach 3770, 54227 Trier; tel. (651) 71990; fax (651) 7199990; e-mail redaktion@volksfreund.de; internet www.volksfreund.de; Editor-in-Chief ISABELL FUNK; circ. 92,685 (Dec. 2011).

Würzburg

Main-Post: Berner Str. 2, 97084 Würzburg; tel. (931) 60010; fax (931) 6001242; e-mail redaktion@mainpost.de; internet www.mainpost.de; f. 1883; independent; Editor-in-Chief MICHAEL REINHARD; circ. 128,325 (Dec. 2011).

SUNDAY AND WEEKLY PAPERS

Bayernkurier: Nymphenburger Str. 64, 80636 München; tel. (89) 120040; fax (89) 12004133; e-mail redaktion@bayernkurier.de; internet www.bayernkurier.de; f. 1950; weekly; organ of the CSU; Editor-in-Chief PETER HAUSMANN; circ. 63,364 (Dec. 2011).

Bild am Sonntag: Axel-Springer-Pl. 1, 20350 Hamburg; tel. (40) 34700; fax (40) 34726110; internet www.bild-am-sonntag.de; f. 1956; Sunday; publ. by Axel Springer Verlag AG; Editor-in-Chief WALTER MAYER; circ. 1,394,173 (Dec. 2011).

B.Z. am Sonntag: Axel-Springer-Str. 65, 10888 Berlin; tel. (30) 25910; fax (30) 259173131; e-mail redaktion@bz-berlin.de; internet www.bz-berlin.de; f. 1992; publ. by Ullstein GmbH; Editor-in-Chief PETER HUTH; circ. 88,670 (Dec. 2011).

Frankfurter Allgemeine Sonntagszeitung: Hellerhofstr. 2–4, 60327 Frankfurt a.M.; tel. (69) 75910; fax (69) 75911773; e-mail sonntagszeitung@faz.de; internet www.faz.de; Sunday; Publrs WERNER D'INKA, BERTHOLD KOHLER, GÜNTHER NONNENMACHER, FRANK SCHIRRMACHER, HOLGER STELTZNER; circ. 401,337 (Dec. 2011).

Sonntag Aktuell: Plieninger Str. 150, 70567 Stuttgart; Postfach 104462, 70039 Stuttgart; tel. (711) 72050; fax (711) 72057138; e-mail redaktion@soak.zgs.de; internet www.sonntag-aktuell.de; Sunday; Editor-in-Chief ANDREAS BRAUN; circ. 643,139 (Dec. 2011).

Welt am Sonntag: Axel-Springer-Str. 65, 10888 Berlin; tel. (30) 25910; fax (30) 259171606; e-mail leserbriefe@wams.de; internet www.welt.de; f. 1948; Sunday; publ. by Axel Springer Verlag AG; Editor-in-Chief JAN-ERIC PETERS; circ. 402,287 (Dec. 2010).

Die Zeit: Buceriusstr., Eingang Speersort 1, Pressehaus, 20095 Hamburg; tel. (40) 32800; fax (40) 327111; e-mail diezeit@zeit.de; internet www.zeit.de; f. 1946; weekly; Editor-in-Chief GIOVANNI DI LORENZO; circ. 537,129 (Dec. 2011).

SELECTED PERIODICALS

Agriculture

Bauernzeitung: Wilhelmsaue 37, 10713 Berlin; Postfach 310448, 10634 Berlin; tel. (30) 464060; fax (30) 46406319; e-mail info@bauernverlag.de; internet www.bauernzeitung.de; f. 1960; weekly; covers agricultural news in Brandenburg, Mecklenburg-Western Pomerania, Saxony, Saxony-Anhalt and Thüringen; Editor-in-Chief Dr THOMAS TANNEBERGER; circ. 23,369 (Jan.–March 2013).

Bayerisches Landwirtschaftliches Wochenblatt: Bayerstr. 57, 80335 München; Postfach 200523, 80005 München; tel. (89) 53098901; fax (89) 5328537; e-mail ulrich.graf@dlv.de; internet www.wochenblatt-dlv.de; f. 1810; weekly; organ of the Bayerischer Bauernverband; Editor-in-Chief SEPP KELLERER; circ. 102,936 (Jan.–March 2013).

dlz agrarmagazin: Postfach 400580, 80705 München; Lothstr. 29, 80797 München; tel. (89) 127051; fax (89) 12705546; e-mail dlv.muenchen@dlv.de; internet www.dlz-agrarmagazin.de; monthly; publ. by Deutscher Landwirtschaftsverlag GmbH; Editor-in-Chief DETLEF STEINERT; circ. 70,279 (Jan.–March 2013).

Eisenbahn-Landwirt: Ostring 6, 76131 Karlsruhe; Postfach 2026, 76008 Karlsruhe; tel. (721) 62830; fax (721) 628310; e-mail info@druck-verlag-sw.de; internet www.druck-verlag-sw.de; f. 1918; monthly; gardening; organ of the Hauptverband der Bahn-Landwirtschaft; publ. by Druckhaus Karlsruhe, Druck + Verlagsgesellschaft Südwest mbH; Dir ROLF HAASE; circ. 72,647 (Jan.–March 2013).

Landpost: Wollgrasweg 31, 70599 Stuttgart; tel. (711) 167790; fax (711) 4586093; e-mail info@vdaw.de; internet www.vdaw.de; f. 1945; weekly; agriculture and gardening; Editor ERICH REICH; circ. 12,597 (Jan.–March 2013).

Top Agrar: Hülsebrockstr. 2–8, 48165 Münster; Postfach 7847, 48042 Münster; tel. (2501) 801640; fax (2501) 801654; e-mail redaktion@topagrar.com; internet www.topagrar.com; monthly; focusing on key agricultural issues; Editors BERTHOLD ACHLER, HEINZ-GÜNTER TOPÜTH, Dr LUDGER SCHULZE PALS; circ. 114,744 (Jan.–March 2013).

The Arts and Literature

Art. Das Kunstmagazin: Am Baumwall 11, 20459 Hamburg; tel. (40) 37030; fax (40) 37035618; e-mail kunst@art-magazin.de; internet www.art-magazin.de; f. 1979; monthly; publ. by Gruner + Jahr AG & Co KG; Editor-in-Chief TIM SOMMER; circ. 53,336 (2010).

Cinema: Christoph-Probst-Weg 1, 20251 Hamburg; tel. (40) 41310; e-mail info@milchstrasse.de; internet www.cinema.de; monthly; film reviews, interviews; publ. by Cinema Verlag GmbH; Editor-in-Chief ARTUR JUNG; circ. 77,221 (Jan.–March 2013).

Literarische Welt: Axel-Springer-Str. 65, 10888 Berlin; tel. (30) 25910; fax (30) 259171606; e-mail literaturwelt@welt.de; internet www.welt.de/kultur/literarischewelt; f. 1971; weekly; literary supplement of *Die Welt*; Editor THOMAS SCHMID.

Musikexpress: Mehringdamm 33, 10960 Berlin; tel. (30) 881880; fax (30) 88188223; e-mail redaktion@musikexpress.de; internet www.musikexpress.de; f. 1983; monthly; popular music; publ. by Axel Springer Mediahouse Berlin GmbH; Editor-in-Chief SEVERIN MEVISSEN; circ. 53,706 (Jan.–March 2013).

Praxis Deutsch: Im Brande 17, 30926 Seelze/Velber; tel. (511) 40004150; fax (511) 40004170; e-mail redaktion.pd@friedrich-verlag.de; internet www.friedrich-verlag.de; 6 a year; German language and literature; publ. by Erhard Friedrich Verlag GmbH; circ. 11,341 (Sept. 2008).

Theater der Zeit: Klosterstr. 68, 10179 Berlin; tel. (30) 24722414; fax (30) 24722415; e-mail redaktion@theaterderzeit.de; internet www.theaterderzeit.de; f. 1946; 10 a year; theatre, drama, opera, children's theatre, puppet theatre, dance; Editors HARALD MÜLLER, Dr FRANK RADDATZ, DORTE LENA EILERS, GUNNAR DECKER, DÖRING MIRKA; circ. 5,000.

Theater heute: Knesebeckstr. 59–61, 10719 Berlin; tel. (30) 25449510; fax (30) 25449512; e-mail redaktion@theaterheute.de; internet www.theaterheute.de; f. 1960; monthly, with a yearbook in August; Editors BARBARA BURCKHARDT, EVA BEHRENDT, Dr FRANZ WILLE; circ. 15,000.

xia intelligente architektur: Fasanenweg 18, 70771 Leinfelden-Echterdingen; tel. (711) 7591286; fax (711) 7591410; e-mail ait-red@ait-online.de; internet www.xia-online.de; f. 1890; quarterly; Editor Dr FRIEDRICH H. DASSLER; circ. 16,458 (Oct. 2010).

Economics, Finance and Industry

Absatzwirtschaft: Grafenberger Allee 293, 40237 Düsseldorf; Postfach 101102, 40002 Düsseldorf; tel. (211) 8870; fax (211) 8871420; e-mail absatzwirtschaft@fachverlag.de; internet www.absatzwirtschaft.de; f. 1958; monthly; marketing; Editor-in-Chief CHRISTOPH BERDI; circ. 25,139 (Jan.–March 2013).

Börse Online: Bayerstr. 71–73, 80335 München; tel. (89) 272640; fax (89) 27264199; e-mail verlag@finanzen.net; f. 1987; weekly; German and international stocks and stock-related investments; publ. by Finanzen Verlag GmbH; Editor-in-Chief FRANK BERNHARD WERNER; circ. 39,118 (Jan.–March 2013).

Capital: Am Baumwall 11, 20459 Hamburg; tel. (40) 37030; fax (40) 31990310; e-mail capital@capital.de; internet www.capital.de; f. 1962; monthly; business magazine; publ. by Gruner + Jahr AG & Co KG; Editor-in-Chief HORST VON BUTTLAR; circ. 163,186 (Jan.–March 2013).

Creditreform: Grafenberger Allee 293, 40237 Düsseldorf; Postfach 101102, 40002 Düsseldorf; tel. (211) 8870; fax (211) 8871410; e-mail creditreform-service@fachverlag.de; internet www.creditreform-magazin.de; f. 1879; Editor-in-Chief INGO SCHENK; circ. 129,870 (Jan.–March 2013).

H&V Journal Handelsvermittlung und Vertrieb: Springer-Verlag GmbH, Tiergartenstr. 17, 69121 Heidelberg; tel. (6221) 4870; f. 1949; monthly; Editor-in-Chief (vacant); circ. 10,132 (Jan.–March 2013).

Impulse: Hammerbrookstr. 93, 20097 Hamburg; tel. (40) 60945220; fax (40) 609452299; e-mail chefredaktion@impulse.de; internet www.impulse.de; f. 1980; monthly; business and entrepreneurship; publ. by Impulse Medien GmbH; Editor-in-Chief Dr NIKOLAUS FÖRSTER; circ. 63,606 (Jan.–March 2013).

Industrieanzeiger: Ernst-Mey-Str. 8, 70771 Leinfelden-Echterdingen; tel. (711) 7594451; fax (711) 7594398; e-mail werner.goetz@konradin.de; internet www.industrieanzeiger.de; f. 1879; 32 a year; Editor-in-Chief WERNER GÖTZ; circ. 40,028 (Jan.–March 2013).

Management International Review: University of Kiel, Westring 425, 24118 Kiel; tel. (431) 8801635; fax (431) 8803963; e-mail mir@bwl.uni-kiel.de; internet www.mir-online.de; f. 1960; 6 a year; English; publ. by Axel Springer Verlag AG; Editors Prof. Dr MICHAEL-JÖRG OESTERLE (Stuttgart), Prof. Dr JOACHIM WOLF (Kiel).

VDI Nachrichten: VDI-Pl. 1, 40468 Düsseldorf; Postfach 101054, 40001 Düsseldorf; tel. (211) 61880; fax (211) 6188316; e-mail redaktion@vdi-nachrichten.com; internet www.vdi-nachrichten.com; f. 1923; weekly, Fri.; technology and economics; Editor-in-Chief KEN FOUHY; circ. 162,718 (Jan.–March 2013).

WirtschaftsWoche: Kasernenstr. 67, 40213 Düsseldorf; tel. (211) 8870; fax (211) 8872980; e-mail roland.tichy@wiwo.de; internet www.wiwo.de; weekly; business; Editor-in-Chief ROLAND TICHY; circ. 173,251 (Jan.–March 2013).

Home, Fashion and General

Bild der Frau: Axel-Springer-Pl. 1, 20350 Hamburg; tel. (40) 34700; e-mail service@bildderfrau.de; internet www.bildderfrau.de; f. 1983; weekly; publ. by Axel Springer Verlag AG; Editor-in-Chief SANDRA IMMOOR; circ. 902,664 (Jan.–March 2013).

Bravo: Charles-de-Gaulle-Str. 8, 81737 München; tel. (89) 67860; e-mail post@bravo.de; internet www.bravo.de; weekly; publ. by Bauer Verlagsgruppe; for young people; Editor-in-Chief NADINE NORDMANN; circ. 248,221 (Jan.–March 2013).

Brigitte: Am Baumwall 11, 20459 Hamburg; tel. (40) 37030; fax (40) 37035845; e-mail infoline@brigitte.de; internet www.brigitte.de; f. 1954; fortnightly; women's magazine; also publishes *Brigitte Balance* (2 a year; circ. 130,000, Oct. 2010) and *Brigitte Woman* (monthly; circ. 237,815, Jan.–March 2013); publ. by Gruner + Jahr AG & Co KG; Editor-in-Chief STEPHAN SCHÄFER; circ. 574,096 (Jan.–March 2013).

Bunte: Arabellastr. 23, 81925 München; tel. (89) 92500; fax (89) 92502340; e-mail bunte@burda.com; internet www.bunte.de; f. 1948; weekly; celebrity gossip; publ. by Bunte Entertainment Verlag GmbH; Editor-in-Chief PATRICIA RIEKEL; circ. 564,747 (Jan.–March 2013).

Burda Style: Arabellastr. 23, 81925 München; tel. (89) 92500; fax (89) 92502340; e-mail service@burdastyle.de; internet www.burdastyle.de; f. 1949; monthly; fashion, patterns; publ. by Hubert Burda Media Holding GmbH & Co KG; Editor-in-Chief DAGMAR BILY; circ. 134,998 (Jan.–March 2013).

Cosmopolitan: Charles-de-Gaulle-Str. 8, 81737 München; tel. (89) 67860; fax (89) 67869719; e-mail info@cosmopolitan.de; internet www.cosmopolitan.de; f. 1980; monthly; lifestyle; Editor-in-Chief KERSTIN WENG; circ. 258,572 (Jan.–March 2013).

Elle: Arabellastr. 23, 81925 München; tel. (89) 92500; fax (89) 92502340; e-mail elleonline@elle.burda.com; internet www.elle.de; monthly; fashion; also publishes *Elle Decoration* (6 a year; circ. 109,887); publ. by Hubert Burda Media Holding GmbH & Co KG; Editor-in-Chief SABINE NEDELCHEV; circ. 206,264 (Jan.–March 2013).

Eltern: Weihenstephaner Str. 7, 81673 München; tel. (89) 415200; fax (89) 4152651; e-mail redaktion@eltern.de; internet www.eltern.de; f. 1966; monthly; for parents of young children; also publishes *Eltern Family* (monthly; for parents of older children; circ. 135,450); publ. by Gruner + Jahr AG & Co KG; Editor-in-Chief MARIE-LUISE LEWICKI; circ. 264,728 (Jan.–March 2013).

Essen & Trinken: Am Baumwall 11, 20459 Hamburg; tel. (40) 37034214; fax (40) 37034212; e-mail service@essen-und-trinken.de; internet www.essen-und-trinken.de; f. 1972; monthly; food and drink; also publishes *Essen & Trinken Für Jeden Tag* (monthly; recipes; circ. 191,800); publ. by Gruner + Jahr AG & Co KG; Editors-in-Chief CLEMENS VON LUCK, ELISABETH HERZEL; circ. 192,789 (Jan.–March 2013).

Familie & Co: Schnewlinstr. 6, 79098 Freiburg i. Br.; tel. (761) 70578559; fax (761) 70578656; e-mail redaktion@familymedia.de; internet www.familie.de; f. 1996; monthly; publ. by Family Media GmbH & Co; also publishes *Baby & Co* (circ. 96,085); Editor-in-Chief DIRK MÜLLER; circ. 176,612 (Jan.–March 2013).

Frau aktuell: Münchener Str. 101/09, 85737 Ismaning; tel. (89) 272700; fax (89) 272708990; e-mail fa@mzv-direkt.de; internet www.frau-aktuell.de; f. 1965; weekly; publ. by Westdeutsche Zeitschriftenverlag GmbH & Co KG; circ. 177,974 (Jan.–March 2013).

Frau und Mutter: Prinz Georg Str. 44, 40477 Düsseldorf; tel. (211) 4499240; fax (211) 4499289; e-mail redaktion@kfdfum.de; internet www.frauundmutter.de; monthly; women's magazine published by the Catholic Women's Community; Editors BARBARA LECKEL, NIKOLA HOLLMAN; circ. 506,500 (Jan.–March 2013).

Frau im Spiegel: Münchener Str. 101/09, 85737 Ismaning; tel. (89) 272700; fax (89) 272708990; e-mail fis@mzv-direkt.de; internet www.frau-im-spiegel.de; f. 1947; weekly; aimed at women over 35; also publishes *Frau im Spiegel Legenden* (quarterly; focusing on a particular celebrity); Editor-in-Chief CLAUDIA CIESLARCZYK; circ. 270,292 (Jan.–March 2013).

Frau im Trend: Burda Senator Verlag GmbH, Arabellastr. 23, 81925 Munich; tel. (89) 92500; fax (89) 92502340; e-mail freizeitfreunde@burda.com; women's magazine; Editor-in-Chief THOMAS OTTO; circ. 313,771 (Jan.–March 2013).

Freizeit Revue: Hubert-Burda-Pl. 1, 77652 Offenburg; tel. (781) 8401; fax (781) 842254; e-mail freizeitfreunde@burda.com; internet www.freizeitfreunde.de; weekly; celebrities, food, health and beauty; publ. by Hubert Burda Media Holding GmbH & Co KG; Editor-in-Chief ROBERT PÖLZER; circ. 843,047 (Jan.–March 2013).

Freundin: Arabellastr. 23, 81925 München; tel. (89) 92500; fax (89) 92502340; e-mail freundin@burda.com; internet www.freundin.com; f. 1948; fortnightly; for young women; publ. by Hubert Burda Media Holding GmbH & Co KG; Editor-in-Chief NIKOLAUS ALBRECHT; circ. 406,928 (Jan.–March 2013).

Für Sie: Jahreszeitenverlag GmbH, Possmoorweg 2, 22301 Hamburg; tel. (40) 27170; e-mail redaktion@fuer-sie.de; internet www.fuer-sie.de; fortnightly; women's magazine; Editor-in-Chief SABINE FÄTH; circ. 371,234 (Jan.–March 2013).

Gala: Schaarsteinweg 14, 20459 Hamburg; tel. (40) 37030; fax (40) 37034364; e-mail redaktion@gala.de; internet www.gala.de; f. 1994; weekly; celebrity gossip; publ. by Norddeutsche Verlagsgesellschaft mbH; Editor-in-Chief CHRISTIAN KRUG; circ. 326,050 (Jan.–March 2013).

GEO: Am Baumwall 11, 20459 Hamburg; tel. (40) 37030; fax (40) 37035648; e-mail info@geo.de; internet www.geo.de; f. 1976; monthly; reports on science, politics and religion; publ. by Gruner + Jahr AG & Co KG; also publishes *GEO Epoche* (quarterly; history; circ. 76,452), *GEO Saison* (monthly; travel; circ. 92,988), *GEO Special* (6 a year; travel; circ. 58,951), *Geolino* (monthly; general interest for children aged 8–14 years; circ. 197,200); Editor-in-Chief PETER-MATTHIAS GAEDE; circ. 289,552 (Jan.–March 2013).

Guter Rat: Superillu Verlag GmbH & Co KG, Zimmerstr. 28, 10969 Berlin; tel. (30) 23876600; fax (30) 23876395; e-mail redaktion@guter-rat.de; internet www.guter-rat.de; f. 1945; monthly; consumer magazine; Editor-in-Chief WERNER ZEDLER; circ. 230,623 (Jan.–March 2013).

Das Haus: Postfach 810164, 81901 München; Arabellastr. 23, 81925 München; tel. (89) 92500; fax (89) 92503055; e-mail userservice@haus.de; internet www.haus.de; 10 a year; home improvement; publ. by Hubert Burda Media Holding GmbH & Co KG; Editor-in-Chief GABY MIKETTA; circ. 1,890,456 (Oct.–Dec. 2010).

Living At Home: Am Baumwall 11, 20459 Hamburg; tel. (40) 37034267; fax (40) 37035838; e-mail info@livingathome.de; internet www.livingathome.de; f. 2000; monthly; lifestyle magazine covering furnishing, decorating, cooking, entertaining and gardening; publ. by Exclusive & Living digital GmbH; Editor-in-Chief BETTINA BILLERBECK; circ. 160,267 (Jan.–March 2013).

Meine Familie & Ich: Arabellastr. 23, 81925 München; tel. (89) 92500; fax (89) 92502340; e-mail redaktion@daskochrezept.de; internet www.daskochrezept.de; 13 a year; food and drink, health and beauty; publ. by MFI Verlag GmbH; Editor-in-Chief BIRGITT MICHA; circ. 396,290 (Jan.–March 2013).

Neue Post: Burchardstr. 11, 20067 Hamburg; tel. (40) 30194123; fax (40) 30194133; e-mail info@bauerdigital.de; internet neue-post.wunderweib.de; weekly; celebrity gossip, women's interest; publ. by Bauer Verlagsgruppe; Editor-in-Chief KATHRIN KELLERMANN; circ. 687,575 (Jan.–March 2013).

Petra: Jahreszeiten Verlag GmbH, Possmoorweg 2, 22301 Hamburg; tel. (40) 27170; fax (40) 27172056; e-mail redaktion@petra.de; internet www.petra.de; monthly; fashion and beauty; Editor-in-Chief NINA MAURISCHAT; circ. 242,149 (Jan.–March 2013).

Reader's Digest Deutschland: Verlag Das Beste GmbH, Vordernbergstr. 6, 70191 Stuttgart; Postfach 106020, 70049 Stuttgart; tel. (711) 66020; fax (711) 6602547; e-mail verlag@readersdigest.de; internet www.readersdigest.de; f. 1948; owned by Reader's Digest Assn Inc, Pleasantville, NY (USA); magazines, general, serialized and condensed books, music and video programmes; Man. Dir WERNER NEUNZIG; circ. 583,959 (Jan.–March 2013).

Schöner Wohnen: Am Baumwall 11, 20459 Hamburg; tel. (40) 37030; fax (40) 37035677; e-mail info@schoener-wohnen.de; internet www.schoener-wohnen.de; f. 1960; monthly; homes and gardens; publ. by Gruner + Jahr AG & Co KG; Editor-in-Chief STEPHAN SCHÄFER; circ. 274,745 (Jan.–March 2013).

7 Tage: Postfach 2071, 76490 Baden-Baden; Rotweg 8, 76532 Baden-Baden; tel. (7221) 35010; fax (7221) 3501204; e-mail kontakt@klambt.de; internet www.klambt.de; f. 1843; weekly, Mon.; celebrities, women's interest; Editor-in-Chief PETER VIKTOR KULIG; circ. 105,863 (Sept. 2008).

Law

Der Betrieb: Grafenberger Allee 293 40237, Düsseldorf; Postfach 101102, 40002 Düsseldorf; tel. (211) 8870; fax (211) 8871410; e-mail m.wieczorek@fachverlag.de; internet www.der-betrieb.de; weekly; business administration, revenue law, corporate law, labour and social legislation; Editor MARKO WIECZOREK; circ. 19,453 (Jan.–March 2013).

Deutsche Richterzeitung: Geschäftsstelle des Deutschen Richterbundes, Kronenstr. 73, 10117 Berlin; tel. (30) 20612520; fax (30) 20612525; e-mail redaktion@richterzeitung.de; internet www.driz.de; f. 1909; monthly; publ. by Carl Heymanns Verlag; Chair., Editorial Bd SVEN REBEHN; circ. 11,000 (2010).

Juristenzeitung: Wilhelmstr. 18, 72074 Tübingen; Postfach 2040, 72010 Tübingen; tel. (7071) 9230; fax (7071) 51104; e-mail info@mohr.de; internet www.mohr.de; f. 1951; fortnightly; Editors MATTHIAS JESTAEDT, HERBERT ROTH, ROLF STÜRNER, JOACHIM VOGEL; circ. 4,500 (2008).

Juristische Rundschau: Genthiner Str. 13, 10785 Berlin; tel. (30) 30260050; fax (30) 3026005251; e-mail info@degruyter.com; internet www.degruyter.de; f. 1925; monthly; publ. by De Gruyter Rechtswissenschaften Verlags GmbH; Editors-in-Chief Prof. Dr DIRK OLZEN, Dr GERHARD SCHÄFER.

Neue Juristische Wochenschrift: Beethovenstr. 7B, 60325 Frankfurt a.M.; Postfach 110241, 60037 Frankfurt a.M.; tel. (69)

7560910; fax (69) 75609149; e-mail redaktion@njw.de; internet www.njw.de; f. 1947; weekly, Fri.; Editor-in-Chief TOBIAS FREUDENBERG; circ. 33,030 (Jan.–March 2013).

Rabels Zeitschrift für ausländisches und internationales Privatrecht: Mittelweg 187, 20148 Hamburg; tel. (40) 41900234; fax (40) 41900288; e-mail rabelsz@mpipriv.de; internet www.mpipriv.de; f. 1927; quarterly; German, English and French contributions, English summaries; Editors JÜRGEN BASEDOW, KLAUS HOPT, REINHARD ZIMMERMANN.

Zeitschrift für die gesamte Strafrechtswissenschaft: Lützowstr. 33, 10785 Berlin; tel. (30) 30260050; fax (30) 3026005251; e-mail info@degruyter.com; internet www.degruyter.de; f. 1881; quarterly; publ. by De Gruyter Rechtswissenschaften Verlags GmbH; Editor-in-Chief Prof. Dr KRISTIAN KÜHL.

Leisure Interests and Sport

AUTO BILD: Axel-Springer-Pl. 1, 20350 Hamburg; tel. (40) 34700; fax (40) 345660; e-mail redaktion@autobild.de; internet www.autobild.de; f. 1986; weekly; publ. by Axel Springer Verlag AG; Editor-in-Chief BURKHARD KNOPKE; circ. 472,496 (Jan.–March 2013).

Auto Motor und Sport: Leuschnerstr. 1, 70174 Stuttgart; tel. (711) 1821416; fax (711) 1822220; e-mail redaktion_ams@motorpresse.de; internet www.auto-motor-und-sport.de; fortnightly; publ. by Motor Presse Stuttgart GmbH & Co KG; Editors-in-Chief RALPH ALEX, JENS KATEMANN; circ. 368,107 (Jan.–March 2013).

Bild + Funk: Münchener Str. 101/09, 85737 Ismaning; tel. (89) 272700; fax (89) 27270749; e-mail redaktion@bildundfunk.de; internet www.bildundfunk.de; weekly, Fri.; publ. by Gong Verlag GmbH & Co KG; radio and television; Editor-in-Chief CARSTEN PFEFFERKORN; circ. 145,125 (Jan.–March 2013).

Computer Bild Spiele: Axel-Springer-Pl. 1, 20350 Hamburg; tel. (40) 34729136; fax (40) 34726749; e-mail leserbriefe@computerbildspiele.de; internet www.computerbildspiele.de; f. 1999; monthly; computer gaming; publ. by Axel Springer Verlag AG; Editor-in-Chief CHRISTIAN BIGGE; circ. 145,482 (Jan.–March 2013).

FF Magazin: Meyer & Meyer Fachverlag & Buchhandel GmbH, Von-Coels-Str. 390, 52080 Aachen; tel. (241) 958100; fax (241) 9581010; e-mail verlag@m-m-sports.com; internet www.ff-magazin.com; f. 2004; 10 a year; women's football; Editor-in-Chief MARTINA VOSS; circ. 30,000.

Funk Uhr: Axel-Springer-Pl. 1, 20350 Hamburg; tel. (40) 34723824; fax (40) 34722601; e-mail funkuhrabo@axelspringer.de; f. 1952; weekly; television listings; publ. by Axel Springer Verlag AG; Editor-in-Chief CHRISTIAN HELLMANN; circ. 506,316 (Jan.–March 2013).

GameStar: Lyonel-Feininger-Str. 26, 80807 München; tel. (89) 360860; fax (89) 36086118; e-mail brief@gamestar.de; internet www.gamestar.de; f. 1996; monthly; computer gaming; publ. by IDG Entertainment Media GmbH; Editor-in-Chief MICHAEL TRIER; circ. 87,072 (Jan.–March 2013).

Garten Flora: Wilhelmsaue 37, 10713 Berlin; tel. (30) 464060; e-mail info@bauernverlag.de; internet www.gartenflora.de; f. 1985 as *Flora Garten*; name changed to present 2011; monthly; gardening; publ. by Deutscher Bauernverlag GmbH; Editor-in-Chief CHRISTIAN GEHLER; circ. 169,465 (Jan.–March 2013).

Gong: Gong Verlag GmbH & Co KG, Münchner Str. 101/09, 85737 Ismaning; Postfach 400748, 401809 München; tel. (89) 272700; fax (89) 272707490; e-mail redaktion@gong.de; internet www.gong.de; f. 1948; radio and TV weekly; Editor-in-Chief CARSTEN PFEFFERKORN; circ. 266,864 (Jan.–March 2013).

Hörzu: Axel-Springer-Pl. 1, Postfach 4110, 20350 Hamburg; tel. (40) 34700; fax (40) 34729629; e-mail leserbriefe@hoerzu.de; internet www.hoerzu.de; f. 1946; weekly; radio and television; publ. by Axel Springer Verlag AG; Editor-in-Chief CHRISTIAN HELLMANN; circ. 1,259,142 (Oct. 2010).

Kicker-Sportmagazin: Badstr. 4–6, 90402 Nürnberg; tel. (911) 2160; fax (911) 9922420; e-mail info@kicker.de; internet www.kicker.de; f. 1920; 2 a week; illustrated sports magazine; publ. by Olympia Verlag GmbH; Editor-in-Chief JEAN-JULIEN BEER; circ. (Jan.–March 2013) 186,852 (Mon.), 161,206 (Thur.).

Mein schöner Garten: Hubert-Burda-Pl. 1, 77652 Offenburg; tel. (781) 8401; fax (781) 842254; e-mail garten@burda.com; internet www.mein-schoener-garten.de; monthly; gardening; publ. by Hubert Burda Media GmbH & Co KG; Editor-in-Chief ANDREA KÖGEL; circ. 408,593 (Jan.–March 2013).

Sport Bild: Axel-Springer-Str. 65, 10888 Hamburg; tel. (40) 348830; fax (40) 34725435; e-mail sportbild@sportbild.de; internet www.sportbild.de; f. 1988; weekly; publ. by Axel Springer Verlag AG; Editor-in-Chief MANFRED HART; circ. 402,222 (Jan.–March 2013).

TV Digital: Axel-Springer-Pl. 1, 20350 Hamburg; tel. (40) 34700; fax (40) 34729629; e-mail leserservice@tvdigital.de; internet www.tvdigital.de; f. 2004; fortnightly; publ. by Axel Springer Verlag AG; Editor-in-Chief CHRISTIAN HELLMANN; circ. 1,955,750 (Jan.–March 2013).

TV Hören und Sehen: Burchardstr. 11, 20077 Hamburg; tel. (40) 30190; fax (40) 30191991; e-mail briefe@tv-hoeren-und-sehen.de; internet www.tvhus.de; f. 1962; weekly; television listings; publ. by Bauer Verlagsgruppe; Editor-in-Chief UWE BOKELMANN; circ. 730,034 (Jan.–March 2013).

Medicine, Science and Technology

Angewandte Chemie: Boschstr. 12, 69469 Weinheim; Postfach 101161, 69451 Weinheim; tel. (6201) 606315; fax (6201) 606331; e-mail angewandte@wiley-vch.de; internet www.angewandte.de; f. 1888; applied chemistry; weekly; also publishes international edn in English; publ. by Wiley-VCH Verlag GmbH & Co KGaA; Editor-in-Chief PETER GÖLITZ.

Ärztliche Praxis: Gabrielenstr. 9, 80636 München; tel. (89) 89817404; fax (89) 89817400; e-mail khp@rbi.de; internet www.aerztlichepraxis.de; weekly; publ. by Reed Business Information GmbH; Editor-in-Chief ANDREAS BORCHERT; circ. 56,243 (Sept. 2008).

Chemie Ingenieur Technik: Boschstr. 12, 69469 Weinheim; Postfach 101161, 69451 Weinheim; tel. (6201) 606520; fax (6201) 606203; e-mail cit@wiley.com; internet www.cit-journal.de; f. 1928; monthly; publ. by Wiley-VCH Verlag GmbH & Co KG; Editor Dr BARBARA BÖCK.

Der Chirurg: Tiergartenstr. 17, 69121 Heidelberg; tel. (6221) 4870; fax (6221) 48784210; e-mail christiane.jurek@springer.com; internet www.derchirurg.de; f. 1928; surgery; monthly; publ. by Springer Science + Business Media Deutschland GmbH; Editor-in-Chief HENNING DRALLE.

Computer Bild: Axel-Springer-Pl. 1, 20350 Hamburg; tel. (40) 34723933; fax (40) 34729377; e-mail redaktion@computerbild.de; internet www.computerbild.de; f. 1996; fortnightly; publ. by Axel Springer Verlag AG; Editor-in-Chief AXEL TELZEROW; circ. 498,908 (Jan.–March 2013).

Deutsche Apotheker Zeitung: Birkenwaldstr. 44, 70191 Stuttgart; Postfach 101061, 70009 Stuttgart; tel. (711) 25820; fax (711) 2582290; e-mail daz@deutscher-apotheker-verlag.de; internet www.deutscher-apotheker-verlag.de; f. 1861; weekly, Thur.; Editor-in-Chief PETER DITZEL; circ. 29,140 (Jan.–March 2013).

Deutsche Medizinische Wochenschrift: Rüdigerstr. 14, 70469 Stuttgart; Postfach 301120, 70469 Stuttgart; tel. (711) 8931232; fax (711) 8931235; e-mail martin.middeke@thieme.de; internet www.thieme.de/dmw; f. 1875; weekly; Editor-in-Chief Prof. Dr MARTIN MIDDEKE; circ. 7,610 (Jan.–March 2013).

Deutsche Zahnärztliche Zeitschrift: Deutscher Ärzte-Verlag, Dieselstr. 2, 50859 Köln; Postfach 400265, 50832 Köln; tel. (2234) 7011242; fax (2234) 701115; e-mail dey@aerzteverlag.de; internet www.online-dzz.de; f. 1945; monthly; dental medicine; Editors Prof. Dr WERNER GEURTSEN, Prof. Dr GUIDO HEYDECKE; circ. 18,000 (Jan. 2013).

Elektro Automation: Ernst-Mey-Str. 8, 70771 Leinfelden-Echterdingen; tel. (711) 7594417; fax (711) 7594221; e-mail ea.redaktion@konradin.de; internet www.ea-online.de; f. 1948; monthly; publ. by Konradin Verlag Robert Kohlhammer GmbH; Editor-in-Chief MICHAEL CORBAN; circ. 18,034 (Jan.–March 2013).

Erziehung und Wissenschaft: Stamm Verlag GmbH, Goldammerweg 16, 45134 Essen; tel. (201) 843000; fax (201) 472590; e-mail info@stamm.de; internet www.erziehungundwissenschaft.de; f. 1948; monthly; organ of the Gewerkschaft Erziehung und Wissenschaft; national edn, plus 5 regional edns; Editor-in-Chief ULF RÖDDE; circ. 260,719 (Jan.–March 2013).

Geographische Rundschau: Georg-Westermann-Allee 66, 38104 Braunschweig; tel. (531) 708385; fax (531) 708374; e-mail gr@westermann.de; internet www.geographischerundschau.de; f. 1949; 11 a year; Man. Editor REINER JUENGST; circ. 6,000 (2013).

Handchirurgie, Mikrochirurgie, Plastische Chirurgie: Rüdigerstr. 14, 70469 Stuttgart; Postfach 301120, 70451 Stuttgart; tel. (711) 89310; fax (711) 8931453; f. 1969; 6 a year; Editors KARL-JOSEF PROMMERSBERGER, RICCARDO E. GIUNTA; circ. 1,600.

International Journal of Earth Sciences (Geologische Rundschau): Geologische Vereinigung eV, Vulkanstr. 23, 56743 Mendig; tel. (02652) 989360; fax (02652) 989361; e-mail info@g-v.de; internet www.g-v.de; f. 1910; 8 a year; English; general, geological; publ. by Springer Science + Business Media Deutschland GmbH; Editor-in-Chief Prof. Dr WOLF-CHRISTIAN DULLO.

International Journal of Materials Research (Zeitschrift für Metallkunde): Max-Planck-Institut für Metallforschung, Heisenbergstr. 3, 70569 Stuttgart; tel. (711) 6893651; fax (711) 6893653; e-mail ijmr@is.mpg.de; internet www.ijmr.de; monthly; publ. by Carl Hanser Verlag; Editor-in-Chief Prof. Dr ERIC J. MITTEMEIJER.

Journal of Neurological Surgery: Georg Thieme Verlag, Rüdigerstr. 14, 70469 Stuttgart; Postfach 301120, 70469 Stuttgart; tel.

(711) 89310; fax (711) 8931298; e-mail zblneurochir@thieme.de; f. 1936; quarterly; German and English; neuro-surgery, spinal surgery, traumatology; Editor Prof. Dr V. ROHDE; circ. 1,650 (2008/09).

Journal of Neurology: Springer Verlag, Tiergartenstr. 17, 69121 Heidelberg; tel. (6221) 4878434; fax (6221) 48768434; e-mail christine.lodge@springer.com; internet www.jon.springer.de; f. 1891; official journal of the European Neurological Society; Editors-in-Chief Dr ROGER A. BARKER, Prof. Dr MICHAEL STRUPP, Prof. Dr MASSIMO FILIPPI.

Medizinische Klinik: Neumarkter Str. 43, 81673 München; tel. (89) 43721300; fax (89) 43721399; e-mail verlag@urban-vogel.de; internet www.urban-vogel.de; f. 1904; monthly; official organ of the Deutsche Gesellschaft für Innere Medizin; publ. by Verlag Urban & Vogel GmbH; Editor ANNA-MARIA WORSCH; circ. 20,118 (Oct. 2010).

Nachrichten aus der Chemie: Varrentrappstr. 40–42, 60486 Frankfurt a.M.; Postfach 900440, 60444 Frankfurt a.M.; tel. (69) 79170; fax (69) 7917232; e-mail gdch@gdch.de; internet www.gdch.de; f. 1953; monthly; journal of the German Chemical Society; Editor-in-Chief Dr ERNST GUGGOLZ; circ. 30,051 (Oct. 2010).

National Geographic Deutschland: Am Baumwall 11, 20459 Hamburg; tel. (40) 37035511; fax (40) 37035598; internet www.nationalgeographic.de; f. 1999; monthly; culture, history, nature, the Earth, the universe, people, animals, archaeology, paleontology, travel, research, expeditions; also publishes *NG World* (German and English; monthly; for children aged 7–13 years; circ. 91,021); Editor-in-Chief THOMAS SCHMIDT; circ. 166,844 (Jan.–March 2013).

natur: Konradin Medien GmbH, Bretonischer Ring 13, 85630 Grasbrunn; tel. (89) 45616220; fax (89) 45616300; e-mail redaktion-natur@konradin.de; internet www.natur.de; f. 1904; monthly; popular nature journal; Editor-in-Chief JAN BERNDORFF; circ. 54,276 (Jan.–March 2013).

Naturwissenschaftliche Rundschau: Birkenwaldstr. 44, 70191 Stuttgart; Postfach 101061, 70009 Stuttgart; tel. (711) 2582295; fax (711) 2582283; e-mail nr@wissenschaftliche-verlagsgesellschaft.de; internet www.naturwissenschaftliche-rundschau.de; f. 1948; publ. by Gesellschaft Deutscher Naturforscher und Ärzte; monthly; scientific; Editor Dr KLAUS REHFELD; circ. 2,500.

Planta Medica: Georg Thieme Verlag, Rüdigerstr. 14, 70469 Stuttgart; Postfach 301120, 70451 Stuttgart; tel. (711) 89310; fax (711) 8931298; e-mail plantamedica@thieme.de; internet www.thieme.de/fz/plantamedica; f. 1953; 18 a year; official organ of the Society of Medicinal Plant Research; Editor-in-Chief Prof. Dr LUC PIETERS.

P.M.: Weihenstephaner Str. 7, 81673 München; tel. (89) 415200; fax (89) 4152565; e-mail kontakt@pm-magazin.de; internet www.pm-magazin.de; f. 1978; monthly; technology, natural sciences, medicine, psychology, nature and the environment, history, philosophy, anthropology, culture, multimedia, the internet; publ. by Gruner + Jahr AG & Co KG; Editor-in-Chief HANS-HERMANN SPRADO; circ. 229,737 (Jan.–March 2013).

rfe-Electrohandler: Am Friedrichshain 22, 10407 Berlin; tel. (30) 421510; fax (30) 42151251; e-mail rfe.redaktion@hussberlin.de; internet www.rfe-eh.de; f. 1952; monthly; technology and marketing of consumer goods, electronics, digital imaging, multimedia, audio, video, broadcasting, TV; Man. Editor HORST WINKLER; circ. 15,310 (Jan.–March 2013).

Zeitschrift für Allgemeinmedizin: Dieselstr. 2, 50859 Köln; Postfach 400265, 50832 Köln; tel. (2234) 70110; fax (2234) 7011255; e-mail bluhme-rasmussen@aerzteverlag.de; internet www.online-zfa.de; f. 1924; monthly; general and family medicine; publ. by Deutscher Ärzte-Verlag; Editors Prof. Dr HEINZ-HARALD ABHOLZ, Prof. Dr MICHAEL M. KOCHEN, Dr SUSANNE RABADY, Prof. Dr WILHELM NIEBLING, Prof. Dr ANDREAS SÖNNICHSEN.

Zeitschrift für Zahnärztliche Implantologie: Deutscher Ärzte-Verlag, Dieselstr. 2, 50859 Köln; Postfach 400265, 50832 Köln; tel. (2234) 7011241; fax (2234) 70116241; e-mail schubert@aerzteverlag.de; internet www.online-zzi.de; f. 1984; quarterly; dental medicine, implantology; Editors Prof. Dr STEFAN SCHULTZE-MOSGAU, Dr PETER GEHRKE, Dr KARL-LUDWIG ACKERMANN, Prof. Dr MARTIN LORENZONI, Prof. Dr GERMÁN GÓMEZ-ROMÁN; circ. 9,100 (March 2013).

Politics, History and Current Affairs

akzente: Dag-Hammarskjöld-Weg 1–5, 65760 Eschborn; tel. (6196) 790; fax (6196) 791115; e-mail akzente@giz.de; internet www.giz.de; quarterly; politics, essays, photo-journalism, int. and devt co-operation; publ. by the Deutsche Gesellschaft für Internationale Zusammenarbeit (GIZ) GmbH; Editor WOLFGANG BARINA; circ. 8,000.

Deutschland: Frankfurter Societäts-Medien GmbH, Frankenallee 71–81, 60327 Frankfurt a.M.; tel. (69) 75014352; fax (69) 75014361; e-mail deutschland@fs-medien.de; internet www.deutschland.de; 2 in a month; edns in German, Arabic, Chinese, English, French, Hungarian, Japanese, Portuguese, Russian, Spanish, Turkish; Editor-in-Chief PETER HINTEREDER; circ. 378,123 (Sept. 2008).

Eulenspiegel: Gubener Str. 47, 10243 Berlin; tel. (30) 2934630; fax (30) 29346321; e-mail verlag@eulenspiegel-zeitschrift.de; internet www.eulenspiegel-zeitschrift.de; f. 1946; political, satirical and humorous monthly; Editor-in-Chief Dr MATHIAS WEDEL; circ. 100,000.

FOCUS: Arabellastr. 23, 81925 München; tel. (89) 92500; fax (89) 92502026; e-mail anzeigen@focus.de; internet www.focus.de; f. 1993; weekly; political, general; publ. by FOCUS Magazin Verlag GmbH; Editor-in-Chief JÖRG QUOOS; circ. 539,281 (Jan.–March 2013).

Gesellschaft-Wirtschaft-Politik (GWP): Sürderstr. 22A, 51375 Leverkusen; tel. (214) 4029097; fax (214) 5006147; e-mail redaktion@gwp-pb.de; internet www.budrich-journals.de; f. 1951; quarterly; economics, politics, sociology, education; publ. by Verlag Barbara Budrich; Editors Prof. Dr SIBYLLE REINHARDT, Prof. Dr STEFAN HRADIL, Prof. Dr ROLAND STURM, EDMUND BUDRICH.

Internationale Politik: Rauchstr. 17–18, 10787 Berlin; tel. (30) 25423145; fax (30) 25423167; e-mail tempel@dgap.org; internet www.internationalepolitik.de; f. 1945; 6 a year; journal of the German Council on Foreign Relations; edns in English (*IP International Edition*, quarterly) and Russian (bimonthly); Editor-in-Chief Dr SYLKE TEMPEL; circ. 5,500.

Merkur (Deutsche Zeitschrift für europäisches Denken): Mommsenstr. 27, 10629 Berlin; tel. (30) 32709414; fax (30) 32709415; e-mail merkur.zeitschrift@snafu.de; internet www.online-merkur.de; f. 1947; monthly, 12 a year; double issue in Oct./Nov; literary, political, aesthetic; Editor CHRISTIAN DEMAND; Man. Editor EKKEHARD KNÖRER; circ. 4,800.

Neue Gesellschaft/Frankfurter Hefte: c/o Friedrich-Ebert-Stiftung Berlin, Hiroshimastr. 17, 10785 Berlin; tel. (30) 269357151; fax (30) 269359238; e-mail ng-fh@fes.de; internet www.ng-fh.de; f. 1946; monthly; cultural, political; Editor-in-Chief THOMAS MEYER; circ. 6,000.

Der Spiegel: Ericusspitze 1, 20457 Hamburg; tel. (40) 30072687; fax (40) 30072247; e-mail spiegel@spiegel.de; internet www.spiegel.de; f. 1947; weekly; political, general; Editor-in-Chief WOLFGANG BÜCHNER; circ. 894,270 (Jan.–March 2013).

Stern: Am Baumwall 11, 20459 Hamburg; tel. (40) 37030; e-mail info@stern.de; internet www.stern.de; f. 1948; weekly; news, history, lifestyle; publ. by Gruner + Jahr AG & Co KG; also publishes *Stern Fotographie* (quarterly; circ. 10,000) and *Stern Gesund Leben* (6 a year; circ. 94,297); Editor-in-Chief FRANK THOMSEN; circ. 837,619 (Jan.–March 2013).

Universitas: Happelstr. 12, 69120 Heidelberg; tel. (6221) 6739800; e-mail universitas@heidelberger-lese-zeiten-verlag.de; internet www.heidelberger-lese-zeiten-verlag.de; f. 1946; monthly; scientific, literary and philosophical; Editor DIRK KATZSCHMANN; circ. 1,500.

VdK-Zeitung: Wurzerstr. 4A, 53175 Bonn; tel. (228) 820930; fax (228) 8209343; e-mail kontakt@vdk.de; internet www.vdk.de; f. 1950; monthly; publ. by Sozialverband VdK Deutschland eV; also maintains office in Munich; Editors JOSEF MÜSSENICH, ALBRECHT ENGEL, MICHAEL PAUSDER; circ. 1,469,655 (Jan.–March 2013).

vorwärts: Stresemannstr. 30, 10963 Berlin; Postfach 610322, 10925 Berlin; tel. (30) 25594100; fax (30) 25594192; e-mail verlag@vorwaerts.de; internet www.vorwaerts.de; f. 1994; affiliated to the Social Democratic Party (SPD); publ. by Berliner vorwärts Verlagsgesellschaft mbH; Editor-in-Chief KARIN NINK; circ. 405,937 (Jan.–March 2013).

Religion and Philosophy

chrismon plus rheinland: Kaiserswerther Str. 450, 40474 Düsseldorf; Postfach 302255, 40402 Düsseldorf; tel. (211) 43690150; fax (211) 43690100; e-mail redaktion@chrismon-rheinland.de; internet www.chrismon-rheinland.de; f. 2004; monthly; Protestant; Editor-in-Chief VOLKER GÖTTSCHE; circ. 16,596 (Oct. 2010).

Christ in der Gegenwart: Hermann-Herder-Str. 4, 79104 Freiburg i. Br.; tel. (761) 2717276; fax (761) 2717243; e-mail cig@herder.de; internet www.christ-in-der-gegenwart.de; f. 1948; weekly; Editor-in-Chief JOHANNES RÖSER; circ. 32,669 (Jan.–March 2013).

Christlicher Digest: Hauptstr. 108, 77652 Offenburg; tel. (781) 28948707; fax (781) 28948709; e-mail info@christlicherdigest.de; internet www.christlicherdigest.de; f. 2002 by merger of *Evangelischer Digest* (f. 1958), *Katholischer Digest* (f. 1949) and *Der Sonntagsbrief* (f. 1974); monthly, 10 a year; publ. by Verlag Christlicher Digest GmbH & Co KG; Editor FRED HEINE; circ. 40,000.

Der Dom: Karl-Schurz-Str. 26, 33100 Paderborn; tel. (5251) 153241; fax (5251) 153133; e-mail redaktion@derdom.de; internet www.derdom.org; f. 1946; weekly, Sun.; Catholic; publ. by Bonifatius GmbH, Druck-Buch-Verlag; Editor-in-Chief MATTHIAS NÜCKEL; circ. 33,500 (Dec. 2012).

Katholische Sonntagszeitung für Deutschland: Postfach 111920, 86044 Augsburg; Hafnerberg 2, 86152 Augsburg; tel. (821) 502420; fax (821) 5024241; e-mail redaktion@suv.de; internet www.katholische-sonntagszeitung.de; f. 1885; weekly; Publr Dr JOHANNES MÜLLER; circ. 57,719 (Jan.–March 2013).

Katholisches Sonntagsblatt: Senefelderstr. 12, 73760 Ostfildern; Postfach 4280, 73745 Ostfildern; tel. (711) 4406121; fax (711) 4406170; e-mail redaktion@kathsonntagsblatt.de; internet www.kathsonntagsblatt.de; f. 1848; weekly; publ. by Schwabenverlag AG; Editor-in-Chief REINER SCHLOTTHAUER; circ. 43,942 (Jan.–March 2013).

Kirche+Leben: Cheruskerring 19, 48147 Münster; tel. (2361) 5828833; fax (2361) 5828856; e-mail info@bmv-verlag.de; internet www.kirche-und-leben.de; f. 1945; weekly; Catholic; Editor-in-Chief Dr HANS-JOSEF JOEST; circ. 81,349 (Jan.–March 2013).

Kirchenzeitung für das Erzbistum Köln: Ursulapl. 1, 50668 Köln; Postfach 102041, 50460 Köln; tel. (221) 1619131; fax (221) 1619216; e-mail redaktion@kirchenzeitung-koeln.de; internet www.kirchenzeitung-koeln.de; weekly; Editor-in-Chief ROBERT BOECKER; circ. 32,449 (Jan.–March 2013).

Philosophisches Jahrbuch: Philosophie Department Lehrstuhl III, Geschwister-Scholl-Pl. 1, 80539 München; e-mail redaktion.phj@lrz.uni-muenchen.de; f. 1893; 2 a year; publ. by Verlag Karl Alber GmbH; Editor MARCELA GARCÍA.

PRESS ORGANIZATION

Deutscher Presserat (German Press Council): Fritschestr. 27/28, 10585 Berlin; Postfach 100549, 10565 Berlin; tel. (30) 3670070; fax (30) 36700720; e-mail info@presserat.de; internet www.presserat.de; f. 1956; self-regulatory body, composed of publishers and journalists; formulates guidelines and investigates complaints against the press; Dir LUTZ TILLMANNS.

NEWS AGENCIES

dpa (Deutsche Presse-Agentur GmbH): Mittelweg 38, 20148 Hamburg; Postfach 130282, 20102 Hamburg; tel. (40) 41130; fax (40) 411332305; e-mail info@dpa.com; internet www.dpa.de; f. 1949; supplies all the daily newspapers, broadcasting stations and more than 1,000 further subscribers throughout Germany with its international, national and regional text, photo, audio, graphics and online services; English, Spanish, Arabic and German language news is also transmitted via direct satellite and the internet to press agencies, newspapers, radio and television stations, online services and non-media clients in more than 100 countries; 1,200 employees worldwide; Dir-Gen. MICHAEL SEGBERS; Editor-in-Chief WOLFGANG BÜCHNER.

PRESS AND JOURNALISTS' ASSOCIATIONS

Bundesverband Deutscher Zeitungsverleger eV (German Newspaper Publishers' Association): Markgrafenstr. 15, 10969 Berlin; tel. (30) 7262980; fax (30) 726298299; e-mail bdzv@bdzv.de; internet www.bdzv.de; f. 1954; 11 affiliated Land asscns; Pres. HELMUT HEINEN; Dir-Gen. WOLFF DIETMAR.

Deutscher Journalisten-Verband (German Journalists' Association): Charlottenstr. 17, 10117 Berlin; tel. (30) 72627920; fax (30) 726279213; e-mail djv@djv.de; internet www.djv.de; f. 1949; 17 Land asscns; Chair. MICHAEL KONKEN; Man. Dir KAJO DÖHRING.

Verband Deutscher Zeitschriftenverleger eV (VDZ) (Association of German Magazine Publishers): Haus der Presse, Markgrafenstr. 15, 10969 Berlin; tel. (30) 7262980; fax (30) 7262898103; e-mail info@vdz.de; internet www.vdz.de; f. 1929; 5 affiliated Land asscns; Pres. Dr HUBERT BURDA; CEO STEPHAN SCHERZER.

Verein der Ausländischen Presse in Deutschland eV (VAP) (Foreign Press Association): Pressehaus 1306, Schiffbauerdamm 40, 10117 Berlin; tel. (30) 22489547; fax (30) 22489549; e-mail info@vap-deutschland.org; internet www.vap-deutschland.org; f. 1906; c. 400 mems; Chair. ROZALIA ROMANIEC.

Publishers

The following is a selection of the most prominent German publishing firms:

ADAC Verlag GmbH & Co KG: Hansastr. 19, 80686 München; tel. (89) 76760; fax (89) 6762925; e-mail verlag@adac.de; internet www.adac.de; f. 1958; guidebooks, legal brochures, maps, magazines; Pres. Dr PETER MEYER.

Apollo Medien GmbH: Emil-Hoffmann-Str. 1, 50996 Köln; tel. (2236) 3999200; fax (2236) 3999229; e-mail apollo@apollo-medien.de; internet www.apollo-medien.de; f. 1981 as SYBEX Verlags- und Vertriebs-GmbH; name changed to present in 2011; computer books and software; Man. Dirs HOLGER SCHNEIDER, ANJA SCHRIEVER.

Aufbau Verlag GmbH & Co KG: Prinzenstr. 85, 10969 Berlin; tel. (30) 283940; fax (30) 28394100; e-mail info@aufbau-verlag.de; internet aufbau-verlag.de; f. 1945; fiction, non-fiction, classical literature; Dirs RENÉ STRIEN, TOM ERBEN, MATTHIAS KOCH.

J. P. Bachem Verlag GmbH: Ursulapl. 1, 50668 Köln; tel. (221) 1619900; fax (221) 1619909; e-mail verlag@bachem.de; internet www.bachem-verlag.de; f. 1818; history, dialect, art history, architecture, sociology and walking/cycling tours of the Cologne, Ruhr and Rhine area; church and society; Dir CLAUS BACHEM.

Bauverlag BV GmbH: Avenwedderstr. 55, 33311 Gütersloh; tel. (1805) 5522533; fax (1805) 5522535; e-mail leserservice@bauverlag.de; internet www.bauverlag.de; f. 2002 following the merger of Fachzeitschriften GmbH (Gütersloh) and Bauverlag GmbH (Walluf); civil engineering, architecture, environment, energy, etc.; Dir KARL-HEINZ MÜLLER.

Verlag C. H. Beck oHg: Wilhelmstr. 9, 80801 München; Postfach 400340, 80703 München; tel. (89) 381890; fax (89) 38189398; e-mail info@beck.de; internet www.beck.de; f. 1763; law, science, theology, archaeology, philosophy, philology, history, politics, art, literature; Dirs Dr HANS DIETER BECK, Dr WOLFGANG BECK.

Bibliographisches Institut GmbH: Mecklenburgische Str. 53, 14197 Berlin; tel. (30) 897858230; fax (30) 89785978233; internet www.bi-media.de; f. 1805; encyclopaedias, dictionaries, atlases, textbooks, calendars; Chair. MARION WINKENBACH; Dirs TIMO BLÜMER, KLAUS KÄMPFE-BURGHARDT.

BLV Buchverlag GmbH & Co KG: Lothstr. 19, 80797 München; tel. (89) 1202120; fax (89) 120212120; e-mail blv.verlag@blv.de; internet www.blv.de; f. 1946; gardening, nature, sports, fitness, hunting, fishing, food and drink, health; Man. Dir ANTJE WOLF.

Breitkopf & Härtel KG: Walkmühlstr. 52, 65195 Wiesbaden; tel. (611) 450080; fax (611) 450085961; e-mail info@breitkopf.com; internet www.breitkopf.com; f. 1719; music and music books; Dir LIESELOTTE SIEVERS.

Bruckmann Verlag GmbH: Infanteriestr. 11A, 80797 München; tel. (89) 1306990; fax (89) 130699100; e-mail info@bruckmann.de; internet www.bruckmann.de; f. 1858; travel guides, illustrated travel books, video cassettes; Publishing Dir SABINE SCHULZ.

Bund-Verlag GmbH: Heddernheimer Landstr. 144, 60439 Frankfurt a.M.; Postfach, 60424 Frankfurt a.M.; tel. (69) 7950100; fax (69) 79501011; e-mail kontakt@bund-verlag.de; internet www.bund-verlag.de; f. 1947; labour and social law; Man. Dir RAINER JÖDE.

Verlag Georg D. W. Callwey GmbH & Co: Streitfeldstr. 35, 81673 München; tel. (89) 4360050; fax (89) 436005113; e-mail info@callwey.de; internet www.callwey.de; f. 1884; architecture, gardens, crafts; Man. Dirs Dr MARCELLA PRIOR-CALLWEY, DOMINIK BAUR-CALLWEY.

Carlsen Verlag GmbH: Völckersstr. 14–20, 22765 Hamburg; Postfach 500380, 22703 Hamburg; tel. (40) 398040; fax (40) 39804390; e-mail info@carlsen.de; internet www.carlsen.de; f. 1953; children's and comic books; Dirs RENATE HERRE, JOACHIM KAUFMANN.

Delius Klasing Verlag: Siekerwall 21, 33602 Bielefeld; tel. (521) 5590; fax (521) 55988114; e-mail info@delius-klasing.de; internet www.delius-klasing.de; f. 1911; yachting, motor boats, surfing, mountain biking, race biking, football, motor cars; Dir KONRAD DELIUS.

Deutsche Verlags-Anstalt (DVA): Neumarkter Str. 28, 81673 München; tel. (89) 41360; fax (89) 41363721; e-mail markus.desaga@dva.de; internet www.randomhouse.de/dva; f. 1831; general; owned by Random House Group Ltd (United Kingdom).

Deutscher Taschenbuch Verlag GmbH & Co KG (DTV): Friedrichstr. 1A, 80801 München; Postfach 750219, 80704 München; tel. (89) 381670; fax (89) 346428; e-mail verlag@dtv.de; internet www.dtv.de; f. 1961; general fiction, history, music, reference, children, natural and social sciences, medicine, textbooks; Man. Dirs WOLFGANG BALK, BERND BLÜM.

Egmont vgs Verlagsgesellschaft mbH: Gertrudenstr. 30–36, 50667 Köln; Postfach 101251, 50452 Köln; tel. (221) 208110; fax (221) 2081166; e-mail info@vgs.de; internet www.vgs.de; f. 1970; fiction, hobbies, natural sciences, culture, popular culture, cinema, television, history; Man. Dir KLAUS-THORSTEN FIRNIG.

Bildungsverlag EINS GmbH: Hansestr. 115, 51149 Köln; tel. (220) 38982101; fax (220) 38982190; e-mail sco@bildungsverlag1.de; internet www.bildungsverlag1.de; f. 2001 by merger of Gehlen, Kieser, Stam Verlag, Wolf, Dürr+Kessler and Konkordia; educational; Dir WILMAR DIEPGROND.

Elsevier GmbH: Hackerbrücke 6, 80335 München; Postfach 201930, 80019 München; tel. (89) 53830; fax (89) 5383939; e-mail info@elsevier.de; internet www.elsevier.de; f. 1878; biological science, medical science; Dirs OLAF LODBROK, MARTIN BECK.

S. Fischer Verlag GmbH: Postfach 700355, 60553 Frankfurt a.M.; Hedderichstr. 114, 60596 Frankfurt a.M.; tel. (69) 60620; fax (69)

6062214; e-mail kontakt@fischerverlage.de; internet www.fischerverlage.de; f. 1886; general, paperbacks; Pres. Dr JÖRG BONG; Man. Dirs MICHAEL JUSTUS, Dr UWE ROSENFELD.

Franz Cornelsen Bildungsgruppe: Mecklenburgische Str. 53, 14197 Berlin; tel. (30) 897850; fax (30) 89786299; e-mail mail@franz-cornelsen-bildungsholding.de; internet www.franz-cornelsen-bildungsholding.de; f. 1946 as Cornelsen Verlag GmbH & Co; name changed to present in 2010; school textbooks, educational software; Chair. Dr ALEXANDER BOB; Man. Dirs Dr HANS-ULRICH DANIEL, URBAN MEISTER.

Franzis Verlag GmbH: Richard-Reitzner-Allee 2, 85540 München; tel. (89) 255561000; fax (89) 255561679; e-mail info@franzis.de; internet www.franzis.de; f. 1924; Gen. Mans THOMAS KÄSBOHRER, WERNER MÜTZEL, WOLFGANG MATERNA.

GRÄFE UND UNZER Verlag GmbH: Grillparzerstr. 12, 81675 München; tel. (89) 419810; fax (89) 41981113; e-mail sarah.kirchner@graefe-und.unzer.de; internet www.graefe-und-unzer.de; f. 1990; cookery and wine, fitness, health and well-being, self-help, gardening, nature, pets; Dirs Dr CHRISTIAN KOPP, DOROTHEE SEELIGER, Dr TILL WAHNBAECK.

Walter de Gruyter GmbH: Genthiner Str. 13, 10785 Berlin; Postfach 303421, 10728 Berlin; tel. (30) 260050; fax (30) 26005251; e-mail info@degruyter.com; internet www.degruyter.com; f. 1919; humanities and theology, literary studies, linguistics, law, natural sciences, medicine, mathematics; imprints: Birkhäuser, Versita, De Gruyter Akademie, De Gruyter Mouton, De Gruyter Oldenbourg and De Gruyter Saur; Pres. ANKE BECK.

De Gruyter Saur: Rosenheimer Str. 143, 81671 München; Postfach 401649, 80716 München; tel. (89) 769020; fax (89) 76902150; e-mail info@degruyter.com; internet www.saur.de; f. 1949; library science, reference, dictionaries, encyclopaedias, books, journals, microfiches, CD-ROMs, DVDs, online databases; brs in Leipzig, Osnabrück and Zürich (Switzerland); an imprint of Walter de Gruyter GmbH & Co KG.

Carl Hanser Verlag GmbH & Co KG: Kolbergerstr. 22, 81679 München; Postfach 860420, 81631 München; tel. (89) 998300; fax (89) 984809; e-mail info@hanser.de; internet www.hanser.de; f. 1928; modern literature, plastics, technology, chemistry, science, economics, computers, children's books; Man. Dirs WOLFGANG BEISLER, STEPHAN D. JOSS, JO LENDLE.

Harenberg Kommunikation Verlags- und Mediengesellschaft mbH & Co KG: Postfach 101852, 44018 Dortmund; Königswall 21, 44137 Dortmund; tel. (231) 90560; fax (231) 9056110; e-mail post@harenberg.de; internet www.harenberg.de; f. 1973; almanacs, encyclopaedias, calendars, periodicals; Man. Dir CHRISTOPH HELLERUNG.

Haufe-Lexware GmbH & Co KG: Munzinger Str. 9, 79111 Freiburg i. Br.; tel. (761) 8980; fax (761) 8983990; e-mail info@haufe-lexware.com; internet haufe-lexware.com; f. 1934; business, law, taxation, information management, finance, social science; Man. Dirs MARTIN LAQUA, MARKUS REITHWIESNER.

Verlag Herder GmbH: Hermann-Herder-Str. 4, 79104 Freiburg i. Br.; tel. (761) 27170; fax (761) 2717520; e-mail info@herder.de; internet www.herder.de; f. 1801; Catholic literature; Publr MANUEL GREGOR HERDER.

Heyne Verlag: Neumarkter Str. 28, 81673 München; tel. (89) 41360; fax (89) 41363721; e-mail vertrieb.verlagsgruppe@randomhouse.de; internet www.heyne.de; f. 1934; fiction, biography, history, cinema, etc.; Publr ULRICH GENZLER.

Hoffmann und Campe Verlag: Harvestehuder Weg 42, 20149 Hamburg; tel. (40) 441880; fax (40) 44188202; e-mail email@hoca.de; internet www.hoffmann-und-campe.de; f. 1781; biography, fiction, history, economics, science; Man. Dir MARKUS KLOSE.

Hüthig GmbH: Im Weiher 10, 69121 Heidelberg; Postfach 102869, 69018 Heidelberg; tel. (6221) 4890; fax (6221) 489481; e-mail fachmedien@huethig.de; internet www.huethig.de; f. 1925; chemistry, chemical engineering, metallurgy, dentistry, etc.; Dir FABIAN MÜLLER.

Langenscheidt GmbH & Co KG: Mies-van-der-Rohe-Str. 1, 80807 München; tel. (89) 360960; fax (89) 36096222; e-mail presse@langenscheidt.de; internet www.langenscheidt.de; f. 1972; dictionaries, language courses, reference; Man. Dir CARSTEN KURREIK.

S. Karger GmbH: Wilhelmstr. 20A, 79098 Freiburg i. Br.; tel. (761) 452070; fax (761) 4520714; e-mail information@karger.de; internet www.karger.de; f. 1890; medicine, psychology, natural sciences; Dirs THOMAS KARGER, GABRIELLA KARGER TRAVELLA, SIBYLLE GROSS.

Verlag Kiepenheuer & Witsch GmbH & Co KG: Bahnhofsvorpl. 1, 50667 Köln; tel. (221) 376850; fax (221) 3768511; e-mail redaktion@kiwi-verlag.de; internet www.kiwi-verlag.de; f. 1947; general fiction, biography, history, sociology, politics; Man. Dir HELGE MALCHOW.

Ernst Klett Verlag GmbH: Rotebühlstr. 77, 70178 Stuttgart; Postfach 106016, 70049 Stuttgart; tel. (711) 66721333; fax (711) 6672000; e-mail pr@klett.de; internet www.klett.de; f. 1897; primary school and secondary school textbooks, atlases, teaching aids; Publr MICHAEL KLETT.

Verlag W. Kohlhammer GmbH: Hessbrühlstr. 69, 70565 Stuttgart; tel. (711) 78630; fax (711) 78638430; e-mail kohlhammer@kohlhammer.de; internet www.kohlhammer.de; f. 1866; periodicals, general textbooks; Man. Dirs Dr JÜRGEN GUTBROD, LEOPOLD FREIHERR VON UND ZU WEILER.

Kösel-Verlag: Flüggenstr. 2, 80639 München; tel. (89) 178010; fax (89) 17801111; e-mail info@koesel.de; internet www.koesel.de; f. 1593; philosophy, religion, psychology, spirituality, family and education; Head of Publishing MARTIN SCHERER.

Kreuz Verlag GmbH: Hermann-Herder-Str. 4, 79104 Freiburg i. Br.; tel. (761) 2717440; fax (761) 2717360; e-mail service@verlagkreuz.de; internet www.kreuzverlag.de; f. 1983; theology, psychology, pedagogics; Dirs OLAF CARSTENS, MANUEL HERDER, HANS DIETER VOGT.

Verlag für Kunst und Kunsttherapie GmbH: Neckarstr. 13, 72622 Nürtingen; tel. (70) 2256343; fax (70) 2253286; e-mail info@verlag-kunst-kunsttherapie.de; internet www.verlag-kunst-kunsttherapie.de; f. 1952; art books and reproductions; Man. Dir Prof. JÜRGEN THIES.

Peter Lang GmbH—Internationaler Verlag der Wissenschaften: Eschborner Landstr. 42–50, 60489 Frankfurt a.M.; Postfach 940225, 60460 Frankfurt a.M.; tel. (69) 7807050; fax (69) 78070550; e-mail zentrale.frankfurt@peterlang.com; internet www.peterlang.de; f. 1971; sociology, humanities, politics, communications, linguistics, science of law, literature, theology, economics, education, history; Dir Dr JÖRG MEIDENBAUER.

Langenscheidt GmbH & Co KG: Mies-van-der-Rohe-Str. 1, 80807 München; tel. (89) 360960; fax (89) 36096222; e-mail presse@langenscheidt.de; internet www.langenscheidt.de; f. 1972; dictionaries, language courses, reference; Man. Dir CARSTEN KURREIK.

Bastei Lübbe GmbH & Co KG: Schanzenstr. 6–20, 51063 Köln; tel. (221) 82000; internet www.luebbe.de; f. 1964; general fiction and non-fiction, biography, history, etc.; Publr STEFAN LÜBBE; Man. Dir THOMAS SCHIERACK.

Luchterhand-Fachverlag: Luxemburger Str. 449, 50939 Köln; tel. (2631) 8012000; fax (2631) 8012204; internet www.luchterhand-fachverlag.de; f. 1924; insurance, law, taxation, labour; imprint of Wolters Kluwer Deutschland GmbH; Man. Dir Dr ULRICH HERMANN.

Mairdumont GmbH & Co KG: Marco-Polo-Str. 1, 73760 Ostfildern; tel. (711) 45020; fax (711) 4502310; internet www.mairdumont.com; f. 1848; road maps, atlases, tourist guides; Man. Dirs Dr STEPHANIE MAIR-HUYDTS, Dr FRANK MAIR, Dr THOMAS BRINKMANN, UWE ZACHMANN.

J. B. Metzler Verlag: Werastr. 21–23, 70182 Stuttgart; Postfach 103241, 70028 Stuttgart; tel. (711) 21940; fax (711) 2194119; e-mail info@metzlerverlag.de; internet www.metzlerverlag.de; f. 1682; literature, music, linguistics, history, cultural studies, philosophy, textbooks; Dir VOLKER DABELSTEIN.

Verlag Moderne Industrie AG & Co KG: Justus-von-Liebig-Str. 1, 86899 Landsberg; tel. (8191) 1250; fax (8191) 125211; e-mail info@mi-verlag.de; internet www.mi-verlag.de; f. 1952; management, investment, technical; Man. Dir FABIAN MÜLLER.

Verlagsgesellschaft Rudolf Müller GmbH & Co KG: Stolberger Str. 84, 50933 Köln; Postfach 410949, 50869 Köln; tel. (221) 54970; fax (221) 5497326; e-mail info@rudolf-mueller.de; internet www.rudolf-mueller.de; f. 1840; architecture, construction, engineering, education; Publrs Dr CHRISTOPH MÜLLER, RUDOLF M. BLESER.

MVS Medizinverlage Stuttgart GmbH & Co KG: Rüdigerstr. 14, 70469 Stuttgart; Postfach 301120, 70451 Stuttgart; tel. (711) 89310; fax (711) 8931298; e-mail kundenservice@thieme.de; internet www.thieme.de/thieme-gruppe/mvs-medizinverlage-stuttgart17193.htm; imprints are Hippokrates, Sonntag, Enke, TRIAS, Haug Sachbuch; CEO Dr THOMAS SCHERB.

Verlag Friedrich Oetinger GmbH: Poppenbütteler Chaussee 53, 22397 Hamburg; Postfach 658220, 22374 Hamburg; tel. (40) 60790902; fax (40) 6072326; e-mail oetinger@verlagsgrupper-oetinger.de; internet www.oetinger.de; f. 1946; juvenile, illustrated books; Man. Dirs SILKE WEITENDORF, TILL WEITENDORF.

Pabel-Moewig Verlag KG: Karlsruher Str. 31, 76437 Rastatt; tel. (7222) 130; fax (7222) 13218; e-mail info@vpm.de; internet www.vpm.de; f. 1989; magazines; Gen. Man. WALTER A. FUCHS.

Piper Verlag GmbH: Georgenstr. 4, 80799 München; tel. (89) 3818010; fax (89) 338704; e-mail info@piper.de; internet www.piper.de; f. 1904; literature, philosophy, theology, psychology, natural sciences, political and social sciences, history, biographies, music; Dirs MARCEL HARTGES, HANS-JOACHIM HARTMANN.

Verlagsgruppe Random House GmbH: Neumarkter Str. 28, 81673 München; tel. (89) 41360; fax (89) 41363721; e-mail vertrieb .verlagsgruppe@randomhouse.de; internet www.randomhouse.de; f. 1994; part of Penguin Random House (est. 2013); general, reference; Man. Dirs Dr FRANK SAMBETH, KLAUS ECK, CLAUDIA REITTER.

Ravensburger Buchverlag Otto Maier GmbH: Robert-Bosch-Str. 1, 88214 Ravensburg; tel. (751) 860; fax (751) 861311; e-mail buchverlag@ravensburger.de; internet www.ravensburger.de; f. 1883; subsidiary of Ravensburger AG; Man. Dir KARSTEN SCHMIDT.

Philipp Reclam jun. Verlag GmbH: Siemensstr. 32, 71254 Ditzingen bei Stuttgart; tel. (7156) 1630; fax (7156) 163197; e-mail info@reclam.de; internet www.reclam.de; f. 1828; literature, literary criticism, fiction, history of culture and literature, philosophy and religion, biography, fine arts, music; Dirs FRANK R. MAX, FRANZ SCHÄFER.

Rowohlt Verlag GmbH: Hamburger Str. 17, 21465 Reinbek bei Hamburg; tel. (40) 72720; fax (40) 7272319; e-mail info@rowohlt.de; internet www.rowohlt.de; f. 1908/1953; politics, science, fiction, translations of international literature; Dirs PETER KRAUS VOM CLEFF, ALEXANDER FEST.

Schattauer GmbH: Hoelderlinstr. 3, 70174 Stuttgart; tel. (711) 229870; fax (711) 2298750; e-mail info@schattauer.de; internet www .schattauer.de; f. 1949; medicine and related sciences; Man. Dirs DIETER BERGEMANN, Dr WULF BERTRAM, JAN HAAF.

Verlag Dr Otto Schmidt KG: Postfach 511026, 50946 Köln; Gustav-Heinemann-Ufer 58, 50968 Köln; tel. (221) 9373801; fax (221) 93738900; e-mail info@otto-schmidt.de; internet www .otto-schmidt.de; f. 1905; university textbooks, jurisprudence, tax law; Man. Dir Dr FELIX HEY.

Egmont Franz Schneider Verlag GmbH: Gertrudenstr. 30–36, 50667 Köln; Postfach 101251, 50452 Köln; tel. (221) 208110; fax (221) 2081166; e-mail info@schneiderbuch.de; internet www .schneiderbuch.de; f. 1913; children's books; Man. Dir KLAUS THORSTEN FIRNIG.

Springer Science+Business Media Deutschland GmbH: Heidelberger Pl. 3, 14197 Berlin; tel. (30) 827870; fax (30) 8214091; internet www.springer.com; f. 1842; wholly owned subsidiary of Springer Science+Business Media Netherlands BV; CEO DERK HAANK.

Stollfuss Medien GmbH & Co KG: Dechenstr. 3–11, 53115 Bonn; tel. (228) 7240; fax (228) 72491181; e-mail info@stollfuss.de; internet www.stollfuss.de; reference, fiscal law, economics, investment, etc.; Man. Dir WOLFGANG STOLLFUSS.

Suhrkamp Verlag GmbH & Co KG: Pappelallee 78–79, 10437 Berlin; tel. (30) 7407440; fax (30) 740744199; e-mail info@suhrkamp .de; internet www.suhrkamp.de; f. 1950; modern German and foreign literature, philosophy, poetry; Chair. ULLA UNSELD-BERKÉWICZ.

Georg Thieme Verlag: Rüdigerstr. 14, 70469 Stuttgart; Postfach 301120, 70451 Stuttgart; tel. (711) 89310; fax (711) 8931298; e-mail info@thieme.com; internet www.thieme.de; f. 1886; medicine and natural sciences; Man. Dirs Dr ALBRECHT HAUFF, Dr WOLFGANG KNÜPPE.

Thienemann Verlag GmbH: Blumenstr. 36, 70182 Stuttgart; tel. (711) 210550; fax (711) 2105539; e-mail info@thienemann.de; internet www.thienemann.de; f. 1849; picture books, children's books, juveniles; Man. Dir CHRISTIAN SCHUMACHER-GEBLER.

Verlag Eugen Ulmer GmbH & Co: Wollgrasweg 41, 70599 Stuttgart; Postfach 700561, 70574 Stuttgart; tel. (711) 45070; fax (711) 4507120; e-mail info@ulmer.de; internet www.ulmer.de; f. 1868; agriculture, horticulture, science, periodicals; Dir MATTHIAS ULMER.

Verlag Ullstein GmbH: Charlottenstr. 13, 10969 Berlin; tel. (30) 25913570; fax (30) 25913523; f. 1894; literature, art, music, theatre, modern history, biography; Pres. Dr JÜRGEN RICHTER.

Ullstein Buchverlage GmbH: Friedrichstr. 126, 10117 Berlin; tel. (30) 23456300; fax (30) 23456303; e-mail info@ullstein-buchverlage .de; internet www.ullsteinbuchverlage.de; f. 1894; general fiction, history, art, philosophy, religion, psychology; Dirs Dr SIV BUBLITZ, Dr ALEXANDER LORBEER.

Wiley-VCH Verlag GmbH & Co KGaA: Boschstr. 12, 69469 Weinheim; Postfach 101161, 69451 Weinheim; tel. (6201) 6060; fax (6201) 606328; e-mail info@wiley-vch.de; internet www.wiley-vch .de; f. 1921; natural sciences, especially chemistry, chemical engineering, civil engineering, architecture, biotechnology, materials science, life sciences, information technology and physics, scientific software, business, management, computer science, finance and accounting; Man. Dirs BIJAN GHAWAMI, Dr JON WALMSLEY.

PRINCIPAL ASSOCIATION OF BOOK PUBLISHERS AND BOOKSELLERS

Börsenverein des Deutschen Buchhandels eV (German Publishers and Booksellers Association): Braubachstr. 16, 60311 Frankfurt a.M.; tel. (69) 1306325; fax (69) 1306399; e-mail verleger-ausschuss@boev.de; internet www.boersenverein.de; f. 1825; Chair. HEINRICH RIETHMÜLLER; Man. Dir ALEXANDER SKIPIS.

Broadcasting and Communications

REGULATORY AUTHORITIES

Bundesnetzagentur für Elektrizität, Gas, Telekommunikation, Post und Eisenbahnen (Bundesnetzagentur) (Federal Network Agency for Electricity, Gas, Telecommunications, Post and Railways): Tulpenfeld 4, 53113 Bonn; Postfach 8001, 53105 Bonn; tel. (228) 140; fax (228) 148872; e-mail poststelle@bnetza.de; internet www.bundesnetzagentur.de; f. 1997; fmrly Regulierungsbehörde für Telekommunikation und Post, renamed 2005; responsible for supervising the liberalization and deregulation of the post and telecommunications sector, as well as electricity, gas and railways; Pres. JOCHEN HOMANN.

die medienanstalten: Friedrichstr. 60, 10117 Berlin; tel. (30) 2064690; fax (30) 2064691; e-mail info@die-medienanstalten.de; internet www.die-medienanstalten.de; consortium of 14 Land commercial media authorities.

TELECOMMUNICATIONS

Deutsche Telekom AG: Postfach 2000, 53105 Bonn; Friedrich-Ebert-Allee 140, 53113 Bonn; tel. (228) 1810; fax (228) 18171915; e-mail info@telekom.de; internet www.telekom.de; f. 1989; partially privatized 1995 with further privatization pending; 14.8% state-owned, 16.9% owned by Kreditanstalt für Wiederaufbau, 68.3% owned by private shareholders; fmr monopoly over national telecommunications network removed 1998; Chair., Supervisory Bd Prof. Dr ULRICH LEHNER; Chair., Management Bd and CEO TIMOTHEUS HÖTTGES.

E-Plus Service GmbH & Co. KG: Edison-Allee 1, 14473 Potsdam; tel. (211) 4480; fax (211) 4482222; e-mail kundenservice@eplus.de; internet www.eplus.de; f. 1993; 13.6m. subscribers (June 2007); owned by KPN Mobile NV (Netherlands); Chair., Supervisory Bd EELCO BLOK; Chair., Management Bd and CEO THORSTEN DIRKS.

Kabel Deutschland Holding AG: Betastr. 6–8, 85774 Unterföhring; tel. (89) 96010187; fax (89) 96010888; e-mail elmar.baur@kabeldeutschland.de; internet www.kabeldeutschland.de; f. 2003; fixed-line telephone through cable, mobile services, broadband internet and cable TV services; 76.57% owned by Vodafone Group PLC (UK); Chair., Supervisory Bd PHILIPP HUMM; CEO ADRIAN V. HAMMERSTEIN.

Mobilcom debitel AG: Hollerstr. 126, 24782 Büdelsdorf; tel. (180) 5022240; e-mail info@mobilcom.de; internet www.mobilcom-debitel .de; f. 2009 following merger with mobilCom Communicationstecknik AG; mobile cellular telecommunications and internet service provider; Mans STEPHAN BRAUER, JOACHIM PREISIG, CHRISTOPH VILANEK.

Telefónica O_2 Germany GmbH & Co OHG: Georg-Brauchle-Ring 23–25, 80992 München; tel. (89) 24421201; fax (89) 24421209; internet www.de.o2.com; f. 1995 as VIAG Interkom; name changed to O_2 Germany in 2002; mobile cellular telecommunications; acquired by Telefónica SA (Spain) 2006; 18.3m. subscribers (March 2010); CEO RENÉ SCHUSTER.

T-Mobile Deutschland GmbH: POB 300463, 53184 Bonn; Landgrabenweg 151, 53227 Bonn; tel. (228) 93631717; fax (228) 93631719; e-mail info@telekom.de; internet www.t-mobile.de; f. 1993; 34.3m. subscribers (June 2007); subsidiary of Deutsche Telekom AG; Chair., Management Bd GEORG PÖLZL.

Vodafone D2 GmbH: Am Seestern 1, 40547 Düsseldorf; tel. (211) 5330; fax (211) 5332200; e-mail kontakt@vodafone.com; internet www.vodafone.de; f. 1992 as Mannesmann Mobilfunk GmbH; present name adopted 2000; 38m. subscribers (March 2010); subsidiary of Vodafone Group PLC (UK); acquired fixed-line services provider Arcor AG in 2008; Chair., Management Bd and CEO FRIEDRICH JOUSSEN.

BROADCASTING

Radio

Regional public radio stations are co-ordinated by the ARD (see Public Stations). There are also numerous regional commercial radio stations.

In early 2009 Digital Audio Broadcasting (DAB) services were available to approximately 80% of the population.

Public Stations

Arbeitsgemeinschaft der öffentlich-rechtlichen Rundfunkanstalten der Bundesrepublik Deutschland (ARD) (Association of Public Law Broadcasting Organizations): Bertramstr. 8, 60320 Frankfurt a.M.; tel. (69) 15687211; fax (69) 15687100; e-mail info@ard.de; internet www.ard.de; f. 1950; Chair. PETER BOUDGOUST; the co-ordinating body of Germany's public service radio and television organizations; each of the following organizations broadcasts radio and television channels:

Bayerischer Rundfunk (BR): Rundfunkpl. 1, 80355 München; tel. (89) 590001; fax (89) 59002375; e-mail info@br.de; internet www.bronline.de; Dir-Gen. Prof. Dr ULRICH WILHELM.

Deutsche Welle: Kurt-Schumacher-Str. 3, 53113 Bonn; tel. (228) 4290; fax (228) 4293000; e-mail info@dw-world.de; internet www.dw-world.de; f. 1953; German short-wave radio (DW-Radio), satellite television service (DW-TV) and online service; broadcasts daily in 30 languages for Europe and overseas; Dir-Gen. PETER LIMBOURG.

Hessischer Rundfunk (hr): Bertramstr. 8, 60320 Frankfurt a.M.; tel. (69) 1551; fax (69) 1552900; internet www.hr-online.de; Dir-Gen. Dr HELMUT REITZE.

Mitteldeutscher Rundfunk (mdr): Kanstr. 71–73, 04275 Leipzig; tel. (341) 3000; fax (341) 3006788; e-mail zuschauerservice@mdr.de; internet www.mdr.de; f. 1992; Dir-Gen. Prof. Dr KAROLA WILLE.

Norddeutscher Rundfunk (NDR): Rothenbaumchaussee 132–134, 20149 Hamburg; tel. (40) 41560; fax (40) 447602; e-mail info@ndr.de; internet www.ndr.de; f. 1956; Dir-Gen. LUTZ MARMOR.

Radio Bremen: Diepenau 10, 28195 Bremen; tel. (421) 2460; fax (421) 24641200; e-mail info@radiobremen.de; internet www.radiobremen.de; f. 1945; Dir-Gen. JAN METZGER.

Rundfunk Berlin-Brandenburg (rbb): Masurenallee 8–14, 14057 Berlin; tel. (30) 97993-0; fax (30) 97993-19; e-mail presse@rbb-online.de; internet www.rbb-online.de; f. 2003; Dir-Gen. DAGMAR REIM.

Saarländischer Rundfunk (SR): Funkhaus Halberg, 66100 Saarbrücken; tel. (681) 6020; fax (681) 6023874; e-mail info@sr-online.de; internet www.sr-online.de; f. 1952; Dir-Gen. THOMAS KLEIST.

Südwestrundfunk (SWR): Neckarstr. 230, 70150 Stuttgart; tel. (49) 9290; fax (49) 9292600; e-mail info@swr.de; internet www.swr.de; Dir-Gen. PETER BOUDGOUST.

Westdeutscher Rundfunk (WDR): Appellhofpl. 1, 50667 Köln; tel. (221) 2200; fax (221) 2204800; e-mail redaktion@wdr.de; internet www.wdr.de; Dir-Gen. MONIKA PIEL.

Deutschlandradio: Raderberggürtel 40, 50968 Köln; tel. (221) 3450; fax (221) 3454802; e-mail hoererservice@dradio.de; internet www.dradio.de; f. 1994 by merger of Deutschlandfunk, Deutschlandsender Kultur and RIAS Berlin; national public service radio broadcaster; 3 stations: Deutschlandfunk, Deutschlandradio Kultur and DRadio Wissen; jtly managed by ARD and ZDF; Dir-Gen. Dr WILLI STEUL.

Commercial Radio

Verband Privater Rundfunk und Telemedien eV (VPRT) (Asscn of Commercial Broadcasters and Audiovisual Cos): Stromstr. 1, 10555 Berlin; tel. (30) 398800; fax (30) 39880148; e-mail info@vprt.de; internet www.vprt.de; f. 1984; 140 mems (April 2011); Man. Dir CLAUS GREWENIG.

Television

There are three main public service television channels. The autonomous regional broadcasting organizations combine to provide material for the First Programme, which is produced by ARD. The Second Programme (Zweites Deutsches Fernsehen—ZDF) is completely separate and is controlled by a public corporation of all the Länder. It is partly financed by advertising. The Third Programme (ARTE Deutschland) provides a cultural and educational service, with contributions from both ARD and ZDF. There are also three other public service channels (KI.KA, Phoenix and 3Sat), which are jointly managed by ARD and ZDF. Commercial television channels also operate.

Analogue broadcasting was discontinued throughout Germany in early December 2008.

Public Stations

ARD: Programmdirektion Deutsches Fernsehen: Arnulfstr. 42, 80335 München; tel. (89) 59003344; fax (89) 59003249; e-mail info@daserste.de; internet www.daserste.de; co-ordinates the regional public service television organizations (see Radio); Chair. MONIKA PIEL; Dir of Programmes VOLKER HERRES.

ARTE Deutschland TV GmbH: Postfach 100213, 76483 Baden-Baden; tel. (7221) 9369-0; fax (7221) 9369-70; internet www.arte.tv; f. 1991; arts, cultural programmes, in French and German; Pres. Dr VÉRONIQUE CAYLA.

KI.KA—Der Kinderkanal ARD/ZDF: Gothaer Str. 36, 99094 Erfurt; tel. (361) 2181890; fax (361) 2181848; e-mail kika@kika.de; internet www.kika.de; f. 1997; children's programming; jtly managed by ARD and ZDF; Dir Prof. Dr KAROLA WILLE.

Phoenix: Langer Grabenweg 45–47, 53175 Bonn; tel. (1802) 8217; fax (1802) 8213; e-mail info@phoenix.de; internet www.phoenix.de; f. 1997; digital channel broadcasting news and current affairs programmes; jtly managed by ARD and ZDF; Dir of Programming CHRISTOPH MINHOFF.

Zweites Deutsches Fernsehen (ZDF): 55100 Mainz; tel. (6131) 700; fax (6131) 7012157; e-mail info@zdf.de; internet www.zdf.de; f. 1961 by the Land govts as a second television channel; Dir-Gen. MARKUS SCHÄCHTER; Dir of Programmes Dr THOMAS BELLUT.

3Sat: ZDF-Str. 1, 55127 Mainz; tel. (6131) 700; fax (6131) 702157; e-mail info@zdf.de; internet www.3sat.de; f. 1984; satellite channel broadcasting cultural programmes in Germany, Austria and German-speaking areas of Switzerland; 32.5% each owned by ARD and ZDF, 25.0% owned by ÖRF (Austria) and 10.0% owned by SRG SSR idée suisse (Switzerland); Dir-Gen. Dr MARKUS SCHÄCHTER.

Commercial Television

Kabel Deutschland Holding AG: see Telecommunications.

ProSiebenSat.1 Media AG: Medienallee 7, 85774 Unterföhring; tel. (89) 950710; fax (89) 95071122; e-mail info@prosiebensat1.com; internet www.prosiebensat1.com; f. 2000 by merger of ProSieben Media AG (f. 1989) and Sat.1 (f. 1984); operates Sat.1, ProSieben, Kabel eins and sixx; Chair., Management Bd THOMAS EBELING; Chair., Supervisory Bd GÖTZ MÄUSER.

RTL Television GmbH: Picassopl. 1, 50679 Köln; tel. (49) 2214560; fax (49) 2214561690; e-mail pressezentrum@rtl.de; internet www.rtl-television.de; f. 1984; subsidiary of RTL Group (Luxembourg); CEO ANKE SCHÄFERKORDT.

Sky Deutschland AG: Medienallee 26, 85774 Unterföhring; tel. (89) 995802; fax (89) 99586239; e-mail info@sky.de; internet www.sky.de; f. 1988; fmrly called Premiere Fernsehen GmbH & Co KG; name changed to present in 2009; subscriber service offering 53 television channels; 54.5% stake owned by News Corporation; CEO BRIAN SULLIVAN.

Verband Privater Rundfunk und Telemedien eV (VPRT): see under Radio; represents privately owned satellite, cable and digital television cos.

VOX Film- und Fernseh- GmbH: Picassopl. 1, 50679 Köln; tel. (221) 9534370; e-mail mail@vox.de; internet www.vox.de; f. 1991; cable, satellite and digital terrestrial channel broadcasting entertainment programmes; 99.7% owned by RTL Group (Luxembourg) and 0.3% owned by Development Company for Television Program; CEO FRANK HOFFMANN.

Association

Bundesverband Digitale Wirtschaft eV (BVDW): Berliner Allee 57, 40212 Düsseldorf; tel. (211) 6004560; fax (211) 60045633; e-mail info@bvdw.org; internet www.bvdw.org; 630 mems (July 2013); Pres. MATTHIAS EHRLICH; Man. Dir TANJA FELLER.

Finance

(cap. = capital; res = reserves; dep. = deposits; m. = million; brs = branches; amounts in euros)

The Deutsche Bundesbank, the central bank of Germany, consists of the central administration in Frankfurt am Main (considered to be the financial capital of the country), nine main regional offices (Hauptverwaltungen) and 47 smaller branches. In carrying out its functions as determined by law the Bundesbank is independent of the Federal Government, but is required to support the Government's general economic policy. As a member of the European System of Central Banks (ESCB), the Bundesbank implements the single monetary policy determined by the Governing Council of the European Central Bank (ECB).

All credit institutions other than the Bundesbank are subject to supervision through the Federal Financial Supervisory Authority (Bundesanstalt für Finanzdienstleistungsaufsicht) in Bonn. Banks outside the central banking system are divided into three groups: private commercial banks, credit institutions incorporated under public law and co-operative credit institutions. All these commercial banks are 'universal banks', conducting all kinds of customary banking business. There is no division of activities. As well as the commercial banks there are a number of specialist banks, such as private or public mortgage banks.

The group of private commercial banks includes all banks incorporated as a company limited by shares (Aktiengesellschaft—AG, Kommanditgesellschaft auf Aktien—KGaA) or as a private limited company (Gesellschaft mit beschränkter Haftung—GmbH) and those which are known as 'regional banks' because they do not usually function throughout Germany; and those banks which are established as sole proprietorships or partnerships and mostly have no branches outside their home town. The main business of all private commercial banks is short-term lending. The private bankers fulfil the most varied tasks within the banking system.

The public law credit institutions are the savings banks (Sparkassen) and the Landesbank-Girozentralen. The latter act as central banks and clearing houses on a national level for the savings banks. Laws governing the savings banks limit them to certain sectors—credits, investments and money transfers—and they concentrate on the areas of home financing, municipal investments and the trades. In 2011 there were 426 Sparkassen and 10 Landesbank-Girozentralen in Germany.

The head institution of the co-operative system is the DZ BANK (Deutsche Zentral-Genossenschaftsbank AG). In 2012 there were 1,102 credit co-operatives and two central institutions.

In 2012 there were 1,854 banks in Germany.

SUPERVISORY BODY

Bundesanstalt für Finanzdienstleistungsaufsicht (BaFin) (Federal Financial Supervisory Authority): Postfach 1253, 53002 Bonn; Graurheindorfer Str. 108, 53117 Bonn; tel. (228) 41080; fax (228) 41081550; e-mail poststelle@bafin.de; internet www.bafin.de; f. 2002; independent public-law institution; supervises banks, financial services providers, insurance cos and securities trading; Pres. Dr ELKE KÖNIG.

BANKS

Central Banking System

Germany participates in the ESCB, which consists of the ECB and the national central banks of all European Union (EU) member states.

Deutsche Bundesbank: Postfach 100602, 60006 Frankfurt a.M.; Wilhelm-Epstein-Str. 14, 60431 Frankfurt a.M.; tel. (69) 95660; fax (69) 95663077; e-mail presse-information@bundesbank.de; internet www.bundesbank.de; f. 1957; aims, in conjunction with the other members of the ESCB, to maintain price stability in the eurozone. The Bundesbank, *inter alia*, holds and maintains foreign reserves of the Federal Republic of Germany, arranges for the execution of domestic and cross-border payments and contributes to the stability of payment and clearing systems. The Bundesbank (which has nine regional offices—Hauptverwaltungen—and 47 smaller branches) is the principal bank of the Federal Land Govts, carrying accounts for public authorities, executing payments and assisting with borrowing on the capital market. The Bundesbank has reserve positions in, and claims on, the IMF and the ECB. The Executive Board determines the Bundesbank's business policy; members of the Federal Govt may take part in the deliberations of the Board; cap. 2,500m., res 2,500m., dep. 131,673m. (Dec. 2009); Pres. Prof. Dr JENS WEIDMANN; Vice-Pres. SABINE LAUTENSCHLÄGER.

Hauptverwaltung Bayern: Ludwigstr. 13, 80539 München; tel. (89) 28895; fax (89) 28893598; e-mail pressestelle.hv-muenchen@bundesbank.de; internet www.bundesbank.de/hv/hv_muenchen.php; Pres. ALOIS MÜLLER.

Hauptverwaltung Berlin: Postfach 120163, 10591 Berlin; Leibnizstr. 10, 10625 Berlin; tel. (30) 34750; fax (30) 34751990; e-mail pressestelle.hv-berlin@bundesbank.de; internet www.bundesbank.de/hv/hv_berlin.php; Pres. CLAUS TIGGES.

Hauptverwaltung Düsseldorf: Postfach 101148, 40002 Düsseldorf; Berliner Allee 14, 40212 Düsseldorf; tel. (211) 8740; fax (211) 8742424; e-mail stab.hv-duesseldorf@bundesbank.de; internet www.bundesbank.de/hv/hv_duesseldorf.php; Pres. NORBERT MATYSIK.

Hauptverwaltung Frankfurt: Postfach 111232, 60047 Frankfurt a.M.; Taunusanlage 5, 60329 Frankfurt a.M.; tel. (69) 23880; fax (69) 23881044; e-mail pressestelle.hv-frankfurt@bundesbank.de; internet www.bundesbank.de/hv/hv_frankfurt.php; Pres. HANS-JOACHIM KOHSE.

Hauptverwaltung Hamburg: Postfach 570348, 22772 Hamburg; Willy-Brandt-Str. 73, 20459 Hamburg; tel. (40) 37070; fax (40) 37073342; e-mail pressestelle.hv-hamburg@bundesbank.de; internet www.bundesbank.de/hv/hv_hamburg.php; Pres. ADELHEID SAILER-SCHUSTER.

Hauptverwaltung Hannover: Postfach 245, 30002 Hannover; Georgspl. 5, 30159 Hannover; tel. (511) 30330; fax (511) 30332500; e-mail pressestelle.hv-hannover@bundesbank.de; internet www.bundesbank.de/hv/hv_hannover.php; Pres. STEPHAN FREIHERR VON STENGLIN.

Hauptverwaltung Leipzig: Postfach 901121, 04358 Leipzig; Str. des 18. Oktober 48, 04103 Leipzig; tel. (341) 8600; fax (341) 8602389; e-mail pressestelle.hv-leipzig@bundesbank.de; internet www.bundesbank.de/hv/hv_leipzig.php; Pres. HANS CHRISTOPH POPPE.

Hauptverwaltung Rheinland-Pfalz und Saarland: Postfach 3009, 55020 Mainz; Hegelstr. 65, 52122 Mainz; tel. (6131) 3770; e-mail pressestelle.hv-mainz@bundesbank.de; internet www.bundesbank.de/hv/hv_mainz.php; Pres. STEFAN HARDT.

Hauptverwaltung Stuttgart: Postfach 106021, 70049 Stuttgart; Marstallstr. 3, 70173 Stuttgart; tel. (711) 9440; fax (711) 9441903; e-mail hv-stuttgart@bundesbank.de; internet www.bundesbank.de/hv/hv_stuttgart.php; Pres. BERNHARD SIBOLD.

Private Commercial Banks

In 2012 183 commercial banks were operating in Germany. The most prominent of these are listed below:

Berliner Volksbank eG: 10892 Berlin; Budapester Str. 35, 10787 Berlin; tel. (30) 30630; fax (30) 30631550; e-mail service@berliner-volksbank.de; internet www.berliner-volksbank.de; f. 1880; cap. 349.3m., res 325.3m., dep. 8,801.1m. (Dec. 2012); Chair., Management Bd Dr HOLGER HATJE; 170 brs.

BHF-Bank Aktiengesellschaft: Bockenheimer Landstr. 10, 60323 Frankfurt a.M.; tel. (69) 7180; fax (69) 7182296; e-mail corp-comm@bhf-bank.com; internet www.bhf-bank.com; f. 1970 by merger of Frankfurter Bank (f. 1854) and Berliner Handels-Gesellschaft (f. 1856); current name adopted 2005; cap. 200m., res 294.7m., dep. 5,200.7m. (Dec. 2012); Man. Dir MATTHIAS GRAF VON KROCKOW; 12 brs.

Commerzbank AG: Kaiserpl., 60311 Frankfurt a.M.; tel. (69) 13620; fax (69) 285389; e-mail info@commerzbank.com; internet www.commerzbank.de; f. 1870; acquired Dresdner Bank in Jan. 2009; 25.0% stake owned by Federal Govt; cap. 8,204m., res 9,328m., dep. 320,703m. (Dec. 2012); Chair., Supervisory Bd KLAUS-PETER MÜLLER; Chair., Management Bd MARTIN BLESSING.

Deutsche Bank AG: Theodor-Heuss-Allee 70, 60486 Frankfurt a.M.; tel. (69) 9100; fax (69) 91034225; e-mail deutsche.bank@db.com; internet www.deutsche-bank.de; f. 1870; cap. 2,380m., res 22,425m., dep. 646,262m. (Dec. 2012); Chair., Supervisory Bd PAUL ACHLEITNER; Co-Chair., Management Bd ANSHU JAIN, JÜRGEN FITSCHEN; 983 brs.

HSBC Trinkaus & Burkhardt AG: Königsallee 21–23, 40212 Düsseldorf; tel. (211) 9100; fax (211) 910616; internet www.hsbctrinkhaus.de; f. 1785; current name adopted 2006; cap. 75.4m., res 442.5m., dep. 12,947.2m. (Dec. 2012); Chair., Management Bd ANDREAS SCHMITZ; 7 brs.

Sal. Oppenheim Jr & Cie KGaA: Postfach 102743, 50467 Köln; Unter Sachsenhausen 4, 50667 Köln; tel. (221) 14501; fax (221) 1451512; e-mail info@oppenheim.de; internet www.oppenheim.de; f. 1789; name changed as above in 2010; cap. 700m., res 1,139m., dep. 5,034m. (Dec. 2012); Chair. MATTHIAS GRAF VON KROCKOW; 11 brs.

SEB AG: 60283 Frankfurt a.M.; Ulmenstr. 30, 60283 Frankfurt a.M.; tel. (69) 2580; fax (69) 2587578; e-mail info@seb.de; internet www.seb.de; f. 1958 as BfG Bank AG; adopted current name 2001; owned by Skandinaviska Enskilda Banken AB (Sweden); cap. 775.2m., res 522m., dep. 27,225.5m. (Dec. 2012); Chair., Management Bd JAN SINCLAIR; 175 brs.

Targobank AG & Co KGaA: Postfach 101818, 40009 Düsseldorf; Kasernenstr. 10, 40213 Düsseldorf; tel. (211) 89840; fax (211) 8984222; internet www.targobank.de; f. 1926 as KKB Bank KGaA; acquired by Crédit Mutuel Group (France) in 2008; present name adopted in 2010; cap. 133.1m., res 687.1m., dep. 10,675.1m. (Dec. 2012); Chair., Management Bd FRANZ JOSEF NICK; 286 brs.

UBS Deutschland AG: Landstr. 2–4, 60313 Frankfurt a.M.; tel. (69) 21790; fax (69) 21796511; internet www.ubs.com/deutschland; f. 1998 as Warburg Dillon Read AG by merger of Schweizerischer Bankverein (Deutschland) and Union Bank of Switzerland (Deutschland) AG; present name adopted 2005; cap. 176m., res 221.4m., dep. 4,709.6m. (Dec. 2012); Chair. and CEO STEPHAN ZIMMERMANN; 10 brs.

UniCredit Bank AG (HypoVereinsbank): Kardinal-Faulhaber-Str. 1, 80333 München; tel. (89) 3780; fax (89) 378113422; e-mail info@unicreditgroup.de; internet www.hypovereinsbank.de; f. 1998 by merger of Bayerische Hypotheken- und Wechsel Bank AG (f. 1835) and Bayerische Vereinsbank AG (f. 1869); 95.4% owned by UniCredito Italiano SpA; name changed as above in 2009; cap. 2,407m., res 17,606m., dep. 137,859m. (Dec. 2012); Chair., Supervisory Bd FEDERICO GHIZZONI; Chair., Bd of Management Dr THEODOR WEIMER; 618 brs.

Public-Law Credit Institutions

Together with the private banks, the banks incorporated under public law (savings banks—Sparkassen—and their central clearing houses—Landesbank-Girozentralen) play a major role within the

German banking system. In 2012 there were 423 savings banks and nine central clearing houses.

BayernLB: Brienner Str. 18, 80333 München; tel. (89) 217101; fax (89) 217123578; e-mail kontakt@bayernlb.de; internet www.bayernlb.de; f. 1972 as Bayerische Landesbank Girozentrale; present name adopted 2002; cap. 6,556m., res 4,735m., dep. 174,975m. (Dec. 2012); Chair., Management Bd GERD HÄUSLER.

Bremer Landesbank Kreditanstalt Oldenburg-Girozentrale (Bremer Landesbank): Domshof 26, 28195 Bremen; tel. (421) 3320; fax (421) 3322322; e-mail kontakt@bremerlandesbank.de; internet www.bremerlandesbank.de; f. 1983; 92.5% owned by Norddeutsche Landesbank and 7.5% owned by Bremen city council; cap. 245m., res 510m., dep. 22,432m. (Dec. 2012); Chair. Dr STEPHAN ANDREAS KAULVERS.

DekaBank Deutsche Girozentrale: Mainzer Landstr. 16, 60325 Frankfurt am Main; tel. (69) 71470; fax (69) 71471376; e-mail konzerninfo@deka.de; internet www.dekabank.de; f. 1999 by merger of Deutsche Girozentrale-Deutsche Kommunalbank and Dekabank GmbH; present name adopted 2002; central institution of Sparkassen org.; issues bonds (Pfandbriefe); cap. 191.7m., res 262m., dep. 61,024.2m. (Dec. 2012); Chair., Management Bd FRANZ S. WAAS.

HSH Nordbank AG: Gerhart-Hauptmann-Pl. 50, 20095 Hamburg; tel. (40) 33330; fax (40) 333334001; e-mail info@hsh-nordbank.com; internet www.hsh-nordbank.com; f. 2003 by merger of Hamburgische Landesbank-Girozentrale and Landesbank Schleswig-Holstein Girozentrale; 12.37% owned by Hamburg city council, 10.97% by Schleswig-Holstein Land Govt; cap. 3,018m., res 504m., dep. 71,242m. (Dec. 2012); Chair. HILMAR KOPPER; CEO Dr CONSTANTIN VON OESTERREICH.

Landesbank Baden-Württemberg (LBBW): Postfach 106049, 70049 Stuttgart; Am Hauptbahnhof 2, 70173 Stuttgart; tel. (711) 1270; fax (711) 12743544; e-mail kontakt@lbbw.de; internet www.lbbw.de; f. 1999 by merger of Landesgirokasse, L-Bank Landeskreditbank Baden-Württemberg and Südwestdeutsche Landesbank Girozentrale; 19.57% owned by Land Govt of Baden-Württemberg; cap. 2,584m., res 6,547m., dep. 64,069m. (Dec. 2012); Chair., Management Bd HANS-JÖRG VETTER.

Landesbank Berlin AG: Alexanderpl. 2, 10178 Berlin; tel. (30) 869801; fax (30) 86983074; e-mail information@lbb.de; internet www.lbb.de; f. 1818; name changed as above in 2006; cap. 1,200m., res 1,015m., dep. 50,048m. (Dec. 2012); Chair., Management Bd Dr JOHANNES EVERS; 150 brs.

Landesbank Hessen-Thüringen Girozentrale (Helaba): Main Tower, Neue Mainzer Str. 52–58, 60297 Frankfurt a.M.; tel. (69) 913201; fax (69) 291517; e-mail presse@helaba.de; internet www.helaba.de; f. 1953; 8.10% owned by Hesse Land Govt, 4.05% by Thuringia Land Govt, 68.85% by Sparkassen- und Giroverband Hessen-Thüringen, 4.75% each by Rheinischer Sparkassen- und Giroverband, Sparkassenverband Westfalen-Lippe, FIDES Beta GmbH and FIDES Alpha GmbH; cap. 2,509m., res 1,689m., dep. 53,082m. (Dec. 2012); Chair., Management Bd HANS-DIETER BRENNER.

Landesbank Saar (SaarLB): Ursulinenstr. 2, 66111 Saarbrücken; tel. (681) 38301; fax (681) 3831200; e-mail service@saarlb.de; internet www.saarlb.de; f. 1941; name changed as above in 2003; 49.9% owned by Bayerische Landesbank, 35.2% by Saarland Land Govt; cap. 260.6m., res 94.4m., dep. 12,284.5m. (Dec. 2012); Chair., Management Bd THOMAS-CHRISTIAN BUCHBINDER.

Norddeutsche Landesbank Girozentrale (NORD/LB): Friedrichswall 10, 30159 Hannover; tel. (511) 3610; fax (511) 3612502; e-mail info@nordlb.de; internet www.nordlb.de; f. 1970 by merger of several north German banks; cap. 1,607m., res 3,316m., dep. 89,654m. (Dec. 2012); Chair., Management Bd Dr GUNTER DUNKEL; 108 brs.

Portigon AG: Herzogstr. 15, 40217 Düsseldorf; tel. (211) 82601; fax (211) 8266119; e-mail presse@portigon.com; internet www.portigon.com; f. 2012; fmrly known as WestLB AG; cap. 499m., res –667m., dep. 12,702m. (Dec. 2012); Chair., Management Bd DIETRICH VOIGTLÄNDER; 3 brs.

Central Bank of Co-operative Banking System

DZ BANK AG (Deutsche Zentral-Genossenschaftsbank): Pl. der Republik, 60265 Frankfurt a.M.; tel. (69) 744701; fax (69) 74471685; e-mail mail@dzbank.de; internet www.dzbank.de; f. 1949; cap. 3,160m., res 1,303m., dep. 200,631m. (Dec. 2012); Chair., Management Bd WOLFGANG KIRSCH; 46 brs.

DZ BANK is a specialist wholesale bank and is the central institution in the German co-operative banking sector, which comprises local co-operative banks, three regional central banks and a number of specialist financial institutions. In 2012 there were 1,102 credit co-operatives and two central institutions.

Specialist Banks

Although Germany is considered the model country for universal banking, banks that specialize in certain types of business are also extremely important. A selection of the most prominent among these is given below:

Aareal Bank AG: Paulinenstr. 15, 65189 Wiesbaden; tel. (611) 3480; fax (611) 3482549; e-mail aareal@aareal-bank.com; internet www.aareal-bank.com; f. 1923; privatized 1989; fmrly DePfa Bank AG, present name adopted 2002; cap. 480m., res 613m., dep. 12,954m. (Dec. 2012); Chair. Dr WOLF SCHUMACHER.

Berlin-Hannoversche Hypothekenbank AG (Berlin Hyp): Budapester Str. 1, 10787 Berlin; tel. (30) 259990; fax (30) 25999131; e-mail kommunikation@berlinhyp.de; internet www.berlinhyp.de; f. 1996 by merger; cap. 753.4m., res 75.3m., dep. 21,536.7m. (Dec. 2012); Chair., Management Bd Dr JOHANNES EVERS; Chair., Supervisory Bd JAN BETTINK.

COREALCREDIT BANK AG: Postfach 170162, 60075 Frankfurt a.M.; Grüneburgweg 58–62, 60322 Frankfurt a.M.; tel. (69) 71790; fax (69) 7179100; e-mail info@corealcredit.de; internet www.corealcredit.com; f. 1962 as Allgemeine Hypotheken Bank AG; name changed to Allgemeine HypothekenBank Rheinboden in 2001; present name adopted 2007; specializes in commercial property market; cap. 100.3m., res 1,373.4m., dep. 4,074m. (Dec. 2012); Chair., Management Bd Dr CLAUS NOLTING; 6 brs.

Deutsche Hypothekenbank AG: Georgspl. 8, 30159 Hannover; tel. (511) 30450; fax (511) 3045459; e-mail mail@deutsche-hypo.de; internet www.deutsche-hypo.de; f. 1872; subsidiary of Norddeutsche Landesbank Girozentrale; cap. 230.6m., res 681.7m., dep. 9,713.5m. (Dec. 2012); Chair., Supervisory Bd Dr GUNTER DUNKEL; Chair., Management Bd Dr THOMAS STEPHAN BÜRKLE; 6 brs.

Deutsche Pfandbriefbank AG: Von-der-Tann-Str. 2, 80539 München; tel. (89) 28800; fax (89) 288010319; e-mail info@hyporealestate.de; internet www.hyporealestate.com; f. 2001 as HVB Real Estate Bank AG; adopted current name 2009 following merger with Depfa Deutsche Pfandbriefbank AF; part of Hypo Real Estate Group (under state control since 2009); cap. 1,379m., res 5,047m., dep. 19,692m. (Dec. 2012); Chair., Supervisory Bd Dr BERND THIEMANN; Chair., Management Bd MANUELA BETTER.

Deutsche Postbank AG: Friedrich-Ebert-Allee 114–126, 53113 Bonn; tel. (228) 9200; fax (228) 92035151; e-mail presse@postbank.de; internet www.postbank.de; f. 1990; 51.98% owned by Deutsche Bank AG; cap. 547m., res 1,944m., dep. 151,231m. (Dec. 2012); Chair., Management Bd STEFAN JÜTTE; 850 brs.

Hypothekenbank Frankfurt AG: Helfmann-Park 5, 65760 Eschborn; tel. (69) 25480; fax (69) 254871204; e-mail roland.fischer@hypothekenbankfrankfurt.com; internet www.hypothekenbankfrankfurt.com; f. 2012; fmrly known as Eurohypo AG; part of Commerzbank Group; cap. 914m., res 2,333m., dep. 64,822m. (Dec. 2012); CEO and Chair., Management Bd Dr THOMAS KÖNTGEN; 16 brs.

IKB Deutsche Industriebank AG: Postfach 101118, 40002 Düsseldorf; Wilhelm-Bötzkes-Str. 1, 40474 Düsseldorf; tel. (211) 82210; fax (211) 82213959; e-mail info@ikb.de; internet www.ikb.de; f. 1949; fmrly Industriekreditbank AG; name changed as above in 1991; cap. 1,621.3m., res 563.3m., dep. 25,400.3m. (March 2012); Chair., Management Bd HANS JÖRG SCHÜTTLER; 7 brs.

KfW Bankengruppe (Kreditanstalt für Wiederaufbau): Postfach 111141, 60046 Frankfurt a.M.; Palmengartenstr. 5–9, 60325 Frankfurt a.M.; tel. (69) 74310; fax (69) 74312944; e-mail info@kfw.de; internet www.kfw.de; f. 1948; 80% owned by Federal Govt and 20% by Land Govts; cap. 3,300m., res 9,609m., dep. 441,390m. (Dec. 2012); Chair., Management Bd Dr ULRICH SCHRÖDER.

Münchener Hypothekenbank eG (MünchenerHyp): Karl-Scharnagl-Ring 10, 80539 München; tel. (89) 538780; fax (89) 5387900; e-mail serviceteam800@muenchenerhyp.de; internet www.muenchenerhyp.de; f. 1896; cap. 503.2m., res 283.8m., dep. 7,982.5m. (Dec. 2012); Chair., Supervisory Bd KONRAD IRTEL; Chair., Management Bd Dr LOUIS HAGEN; 11 brs.

Bankers' Organizations

Bankenverband—Bundesverband deutscher Banken (Association of German Banks): Postfach 040307, 10062 Berlin; Burgstr. 28, 10178 Berlin; tel. (30) 16630; fax (30) 16631399; e-mail bankenverband@bdb.de; internet www.bdb.de; f. 1951; Gen. Man. MICHAEL KEMMER.

Bundesverband der Deutschen Volksbanken und Raiffeisenbanken eV (BVR) (National Association of German Co-operative Banks): Schellingstr. 4, 10785 Berlin; tel. (30) 20210; fax (30) 20211900; e-mail info@bvr.de; internet www.bvr.de; f. 1972; Pres. UWE FRÖHLICH; 1,121 mems (2011).

Bundesverband Öffentlicher Banken Deutschlands eV (VÖB) (Association of German Public Sector Banks): Lennéstr. 11, 10785 Berlin; tel. (30) 81920; fax (30) 8192222; e-mail presse@voeb.de;

internet www.voeb.de; 34 mems and 28 assoc. mems; Pres. GUNTER DUNKEL; Chair. Dr HANS RECKERS.

Deutscher Sparkassen- und Giroverband eV (German Savings Banks Asscn): Charlottenstr. 47, 10117 Berlin; tel. (30) 202250; fax (30) 20225250; e-mail info@dsgv.de; internet www.dsgv.de; Pres. HEINRICH HAASIS.

STOCK EXCHANGES

Bayerische Börse AG: Karolinenplatz 6, 80333 München; tel. (89) 5490450; fax (89) 54904531; e-mail info@boerse-muenchen.de; internet www.boerse-muenchen.de; f. 1830; 77 mems; Management Bd ANDREAS SCHMIDT, JOCHEN THIEL.

Berlin: Börse Berlin AG, Fasanenstr. 85, 10623 Berlin; tel. (30) 3110910; fax (30) 31109179; e-mail kundenbetreuung@boerse-berlin.de; internet www.boerse-berlin.de; f. 1685; 109 mems; Pres. Dr JÖRG WALTER.

Düsseldorf: Börse Düsseldorf AG, Ernst-Schneider-Pl. 1, 40212 Düsseldorf; tel. (211) 13890; fax (211) 133287; e-mail kontakt@boerse-duesseldorf.de; internet www.boerse-duesseldorf.de; f. 1935; 110 mem. firms; Chair. DIRK ELBERSKIRCH.

Frankfurt am Main: Deutsche Börse AG, Börsenpl. 4, 60313 Frankfurt a.M.; tel. (69) 2110; fax (69) 21111021; internet www.exchange.de; f. 1585 as Frankfurter Wertpapierbörse; 269 mems; CEO RETO FRANCIONI; Chair., Supervisory Bd KURT F. VIERMETZ.

North Germany (Hamburg): BÖAG Börsen AG, Kleine Johannisstr. 2–4, 20457 Hamburg; tel. (40) 3613020; fax (40) 36130223; internet www.boersenag.de; f. 1999 by merger of Hanseatische Wertpapierbörse Hamburg and Niedersächsische Börse zu Hannover; 109 mems; Pres. UDO BANDOW; Chair. Dr THOMAS LEDERMANN.

North Germany (Hannover): BÖAG Börsen AG, Rathenaustr. 2, 30159 Hannover; tel. (511) 327661; fax (511) 324915; e-mail s.lueth@boersenag.de; internet www.boersenag.de; f. 1999 by merger of Hanseatische Wertpapierbörse Hamburg and Niedersächsische Börse zu Hannover; 81 mems; Chair. Prof. Dr HANS HEINRICH PETERS.

Stuttgart: Boerse-Stuttgart AG, Börsenstr. 4, 70174 Stuttgart; tel. (711) 2229850; fax (711) 222985555; e-mail info@boerse-stuttgart.de; internet www.boerse-stuttgart.de; f. 1861; 121 mems; Pres. ROLF LIMBACH; Man. Dir Dr CHRISTOPH MURA.

INSURANCE

German law specifies that property and accident insurance may not be jointly underwritten with life, sickness, legal protection or credit insurance by the same company. Insurers are therefore obliged to establish separate companies to cover the different classes of insurance. In March 2010 there were 2,217 insurance companies operating in Germany.

Aachener und Münchener Lebensversicherung AG: Aachen-Münchener-Pl. 1, 52064 Aachen; tel. (241) 4560; fax (241) 4565678; e-mail service@amv.de; internet www.amv.de; f. 1868; subsidiary of Generali Deutschland Holding AG; Chair. MICHAEL WESTKAMP.

Allianz AG: Königinstr. 28, 80802 München; tel. (89) 38000; fax (89) 38003425; e-mail info@allianz.de; internet www.allianz.de; f. 1890; Chair., Supervisory Bd Dr WERNER ZEDELIUS; Chair., Management Bd Dr MARKUS RIEß.

Allianz Lebensversicherungs-AG: 10850 Berlin; tel. (89) 100104; fax (89) 400104; e-mail lebensversicherung@allianz.de; internet www.allianz.com; f. 1922; Chair., Supervisory Bd Dr HELMUT PERLET; Chair., Management Bd MICHAEL DIEKMANN.

Allianz Private Krankenversicherungs AG: Fritz-Schäffer-Str. 9, 81737 München; tel. (89) 67850; fax (89) 67856523; e-mail service.apkv@allianz.de; internet www.allianz.de; f. 1925; Chair, Supervisory Bd Dr MAXIMILIAN ZIMMERER; Chair, Management Bd Dr BIRGIT KÖNIG.

Allianz Versicherungs AG: Königinstr. 28, 80802 München; tel. (89) 38000; fax (89) 38003425; e-mail info@allianz.de; internet www.allianz.de; f. 1985; Chair. Dr WERNER ZEDELIUS.

AXA Krankenversicherung AG: Colonia-Allee 10–20, 50167 Köln; tel. (1803) 556622; fax (221) 14832602; internet www.axa.de; f. 1962; 100% owned by AXA Konzern AG; Chair., Supervisory Bd JACQUES DE VAUCLEROY; Chair., Management Bd Dr THOMAS BUBERL.

AXA Lebensversicherung AG: Colonia-Allee 10–20, 51067 Köln; tel. (1803) 556622; fax (221) 14822750; e-mail service@axa.de; internet www.axa.de; f. 1853; Chair., Supervisory Bd JACQUES DE VAUCLEROY; Chair., Management Bd Dr THOMAS BUBERL.

AXA Versicherung AG: Colonia-Allee 10–20, 51067 Köln; tel. (221) 14819727; fax (221) 14822740; e-mail service@axa.de; internet www.axa.de; f. 1839 as Colonia Kölnischer Freuer Versicherung AG; present name adopted 2001; non-life insurance; Chair., Supervisory Bd JACQUES DE VAUCLEROY; Chair., Management Bd Dr THOMAS BUBERL.

Continentale Krankenversicherung AG: Ruhrallee 92, 44139 Dortmund; tel. (231) 9190; fax (231) 9193255; e-mail info@continentale.de; internet www.continentale.de; f. 1926; Chair., Supervisory Bd Dr HORST HOFFMANN; Chair., Management Bd HELMUT POSCH.

DBV-Winterthur Lebensversicherung AG: Frankfurter Str. 50, 65189 Wiesbaden; tel. (1803) 328100; fax (1803) 328400; e-mail info@dbv.de; internet www.dbv.de; f. 1871; Chair. BERNHARD GERTZ.

Debeka Krankenversicherungsverein AG: Ferdinand-Sauerbruch-Str. 18, 56073 Koblenz; tel. (261) 4980; fax (261) 4985555; e-mail kundenservice@debeka.de; internet www.debeka.de; f. 1905; Chair. PETER GREISLER; Gen. Man. UWE LAUE.

Deutsche Krankenversicherung AG: Aachener Str. 300, 50933 Köln; tel. (221) 57894005; fax (1805) 786000; e-mail service@dkv.com; internet www.dkv.com; f. 1927; Chair. Dr CLEMENS MUTH.

ERGO Lebensversicherung AG: Überseering 45, 22297 Hamburg; tel. (211) 4777100; fax (40) 63763302; e-mail info@ergo.de-mail.de; internet www.ergo.de; subsidiary of ERGO Versicherungsgruppe AG, part of Munich Re; f. 1899; Chair. Dr DANIEL VON BORRIES.

ERGO Versicherungsgruppe AG: Victoriaplatz 2, 40477 Düsseldorf; tel. (211) 4770; fax (211) 4771500; e-mail kontakt@ergo.de; internet www.ergo.com; f. 1997; subsidiary of Munich Re; Chair., Supervisory Bd Dr NIKOLAUS VON BOMHARD; Chair., Management Bd Dr TORSTEN OLETZKY.

Gothaer Versicherungsbank Versicherungsverein AG: Arnoldipl. 1, 50969 Köln; tel. (221) 30907070; fax (221) 30907079; e-mail info@gothaer.de; internet www.gothaer.de; f. 1820; Chair., Supervisory Bd Dr WERNER GÖRG; Chair., Management Bd Dr ROLAND SCHULZ.

Haftpflicht-Unterstützungs-Kasse kraftfahrender Beamter Deutschlands AG in Coburg (HUK-COBURG): Bahnhofspl., 96450 Coburg; tel. (9561) 960; fax (9561) 963636; e-mail info@huk-coburg.de; internet www.huk.de; f. 1933; CEO Dr WOLFGANG WEILER.

HDI Versicherung AG: HDI Pl. 1, 30659 Hannover; tel. (511) 3031444; fax (511) 6451152916; e-mail sach.vertrag@hdi.de; internet www.hdi.de; f. 1903; name changed 2012.

HDI-Gerling Industrie Versicherung AG: HDI Pl. 1, 30659 Hannover; tel. (511) 6450; fax (511) 6454545; e-mail info@hdi-gerling.de; internet www.hdi-gerling.de; f. 2001; Chair. Dr CHRISTIAN HINSCH.

HDI-Gerling Lebensversicherung AG: Charles de Gaulle Platz 1, 50679 Köln; tel. (221) 1445599; fax (221) 1443833; e-mail leben.service@hdi-gerling.de; internet www.hdi-gerling.com; f. 1918; Chair. HEINZ-PETER ROß.

IDUNA Vereinigte Lebensversicherung AG für Handwerk, Handel und Gewerbe: Neue Rabenstr. 15–19, 20354 Hamburg; tel. (40) 41240; fax (40) 41242958; e-mail info@signal-iduna.de; internet www.signal-iduna.de; f. 1906; part of Signal Iduna Group; Chair., Supervisory Bd REINHOLD SCHULTE; Chair., Managing Bd ULRICH LEITERMANN.

LVM Versicherungen: Kolde-Ring 21, 48126 Münster; tel. (251) 7020; fax (251) 7021099; e-mail info@lvm.de; internet www.lvm.de; f. 1896; Chair. JOCHEN BORCHERT; Gen. Man. JOCHEN HERWIG.

R + V Versicherung-AG Reinsurance: Raiffeisenplatz 1, 65189 Wiesbaden; tel. (800) 5331112; fax (611) 5334500; e-mail ruv@ruv.de; internet www.ruv.de; f. 1935; all classes of reinsurance; Chair. Dr FRIEDRICH CASPERS.

SIGNAL Krankenversicherung AG: Joseph-Scherer-Str. 3, 44139 Dortmund; tel. (231) 1350; fax (231) 1354638; e-mail info@signal-iduna.de; internet www.signal-iduna.de; f. 1907; part of Signal Iduna Group; Chair., Supervisory Bd REINHOLD SCHULTE; Chair., Managing Bd ULRICH LEITERMANN.

Talanx AG: Riethorst 2, 30659 Hannover; tel. (511) 37470; fax (511) 37472525; e-mail info@talanx.com; internet www.talanx.com; f. 1996; owned by HDI; Chair., Supervisory Bd WOLF-DIETER BAUMGARTL; CEO HERBERT K. HAAS.

Volksfürsorge Deutsche Lebensversicherung AG: Raboisen 38-40, 20095 Hamburg; tel. (40) 28654477; fax (40) 28653369; e-mail service@volksfuersorge.de; internet www.volksfuersorge.de; f. 1913.

Württembergische AG Versicherungs-Beteiligungsgesellschaft: Gutenbergstr. 30, 70176 Stuttgart; tel. (711) 6620; fax (711) 662822520; e-mail keu@wuerttembergische.de; internet www.wuerttembergische.de; f. 1828; Chair., Supervisory Bd ALEXANDER ERDLAND; Chair., Management Bd NORBERT HEINEN.

Reinsurance

DARAG Deutsche Versicherungs- und Rückversicherungs-AG: Hafenstr. 32, 22880 Wedel; tel. (41) 370160; fax (41) 37016179; e-mail info@darag.de; internet www.darag.de; f. 1958; re-formed 1990; fire and non-life, technical, cargo transport, marine hull, liability, aviation insurance and reinsurance; Chair., Supervisory Bd GÜNTHER SKRZYPEK; Chair., Management Bd ARNDT GOSSMANN.

Deutsche Rückversicherung AG: Postfach 290110, 40528 Düsseldorf; Hansaallee 177, 40549 Düsseldorf; tel. (211) 455401; fax (211) 4554199; e-mail info@deutscherueck.de; internet www.deutscherueck.de; f. 1951; Chair., Supervisory Bd Dr FRANK WALTHES; Gen. Man. Dr ARNO JUNKE.

General Reinsurance AG: Theodor-Heuss-Ring 11, 50668 Köln; tel. (221) 97380; fax (221) 9738494; e-mail askgenre@genre.com; internet www.genre.com; f. 1846; acquired by General Re in 2009; name changed as above in 2010; Chair. FRANKLIN MONTROSS, IV.

Hamburger Internationale Rückversicherung AG: Postfach 1161, 25452 Rellingen; Halstenbeker Weg 96A, 25462 Rellingen; tel. (4101) 4710; fax (4101) 471298; f. 1965; Chair., Exec. Bd Dr WOLFGANG EILERS.

Hannover Rückversicherung AG: Postfach 610369, 30603 Hannover; Karl-Wiechert-Allee 50, 30625 Hannover; tel. (511) 56040; fax (511) 56041188; e-mail info@hannover-re.com; internet www.hannover-re.com; f. 1966; Chair., Supervisory Bd HERBERT K. HAAS; Chair., Management Bd ULRICH WALLIN.

Münchener Rückversicherungs-Gesellschaft AG (Munich RE): Königinstr. 107, 80802 München; tel. (89) 38910; fax (89) 399056; internet www.munichre.com; f. 1880; all classes of reinsurance; Chair. Dr NIKOLAUS VON BOMHARD.

Swiss Re Germany AG: Dieselstr. 11, 85774 Unterföhring bei München; tel. (89) 38440; fax (89) 38442279; e-mail info.srmuc@swissre.com; internet www.swissre.com; Chair. Dr WALTER B. KIELHOLZ; Gen. Man. MICHEL M. LIÈS.

Principal Insurance Association

Gesamtverband der Deutschen Versicherungswirtschaft eV (German Insurance Asscn): Wilhelmstr. 43/43G, 10117 Berlin; tel. (30) 20205000; fax (30) 20206000; e-mail berlin@gdv.de; internet www.gdv.de; f. 1948; affiliating 1 mem. asscn and 470 mem. cos; Pres. Dr ALEXANDER ERDLAND; CEO Dr JÖRG VON FÜRSTENWERTH.

Trade and Industry

GOVERNMENT AGENCIES

Bundesverband Grosshandel, Aussenhandel, Dienstleistungen eV (Federation of German Wholesale and Foreign Trade): Am Weidendamm 1A, 10117 Berlin; tel. (30) 59009950; fax (30) 590099519; e-mail info@bga.de; internet www.bga.de; f. 1949; wholesale, foreign trade and services sector; Man. Dir GERHARD HANDKE; 77 mem. asscns.

Finanzmarktstabilisierungsanstalt (Financial Market Stabilization Agency): Taunusanlage 6, 60329 Frankfurt a.M.; tel. (69) 23883000; fax (69) 9566509090; e-mail info@soffin.de; internet www.soffin.de; f. Oct. 2008 by Federal Govt to manage a stabilization fund; provides emergency funding for financial institutions; may grant up to €400m. to guarantee debt securities and liabilities, and up to €10m. for recapitalization; Chair., Management Cttee Dr CHRISTOPHER PLEISTER.

Germany Trade & Invest GmbH: Friedrichstr. 60, 10117 Berlin; tel. (30) 2000990; fax (30) 200099111; e-mail office@gtai.com; internet www.gtai.com; f. 2009 following merger of Bundesagentur für Aussenwirtschaft with Invest in Germany GmbH; promoted by Federal Ministry of Economics and Energy; Chair. and Co-CEO Dr BENNO BUNSE; Co-CEO Dr JÜRGEN FRIEDRICH.

Hauptverband des Deutschen Einzelhandels eV: Am Weidendamm 1A, 10117 Berlin; tel. (30) 7262500; fax (30) 72625099; e-mail hde@einzelhandel.de; internet www.einzelhandel.de; f. 1947; Chair. JOSEF SANKTJOHANSER; Exec. Dir STEFAN GENTH.

Der Mittelstandsverbund—ZGV eV: Am Weidendamm 1A, 10117 Berlin; tel. (30) 590099618; fax (30) 59099617; e-mail info@mittelstandsverbund.de; internet www.mittelstandsverbund.de; f. 1992; Pres. WILFRIED HOLLMANN; c. 320 mems.

CHAMBERS OF COMMERCE

Deutscher Industrie- und Handelkammerstag eV (DIHK) (Association of German Chambers of Commerce and Industry): Breite Str. 29, 10178 Berlin; tel. (30) 203080; fax (30) 203081000; e-mail info@dihk.de; internet www.dihk.de; Pres. ERIC SCHWEITZER; Chief Exec. Dr MARTIN WANSLEBEN; affiliates 80 Chambers of Commerce and Industry.

There are Chambers of Industry and Commerce in all the principal towns and also 13 regional associations including:

Arbeitsgemeinschaft Hessischer Industrie- und Handelskammern: Börsenpl. 4, 60313 Frankfurt a.M.; tel. (69) 21971384; fax (69) 21971448; e-mail info@ihk-hessen.de; internet www.ihk-hessen.de; Chair. MATHIAS MÜLLER; Man. Dir MATTHIAS GRÄSSLE; 10 mems.

Arbeitsgemeinschaft der Industrie- und Handelskammern in Mecklenburg-Vorpommern: Ludwig-Bölkow-Haus, Graf-Schack-Allee 12, 19053 Schwerin; tel. (385) 51030; fax (385) 5103999; e-mail info@schwerin.ihk.de; internet www.ihkzuschwerin.de; Pres. HANS THON; Man. Dir SIEGBERT EISENACH (acting).

Arbeitsgemeinschaft Norddeutscher Industrie- und Handelskammern (IHK Nord): Adolphspl. 1, 20457 Hamburg; tel. (40) 36138459; fax (40) 36138553; e-mail info@ihk-nord.de; internet www.ihk-nord.de; Chair. FRANK HORCH; Sec. Dr MAIKE BIELFELDT.

Baden-Württembergischer Industrie- und Handelskammertag: Jägerstr. 40, 70174 Stuttgart; tel. (711) 22550060; fax (711) 22550077; e-mail info@bw.ihk.de; internet www.bw.ihk.de; Pres. Dr PETER KULITZ; Man. Dir (vacant).

Bayerischer Industrie- und Handelskammertag eV (BIHK): Balanstr. 55–59, 81541 München; tel. (89) 51160; fax (89) 51161290; e-mail info@bihk.de; internet www.bihk.de; f. 1909; Pres. Prof. Dr ERICH GREIPL; Chief Exec. Dr MANFRED GÖẞL; 930,000 mems.

IHK-Arbeitsgemeinschaft Rheinland-Pfalz: Schlossstr. 2, 56068 Koblenz; tel. (261) 1060; fax (261) 106-234; e-mail info@koblenz.ihk.de; internet www.ihk-arbeitsgemeinschaft-rlp.de; Pres. PETER ADRIAN; four mems.

IHK Industrie- und Handelskammer Erfurt: Arnstädter Str. 34, 99096 Erfurt; tel. (361) 34840; fax (361) 3485950; e-mail info@erfurt.ihk.de; internet www.erfurt.ihk.de; f. 1991; Pres. DIETER BAUHAUS.

IHK Schleswig-Holstein: Bergstr. 2, 24103 Kiel; tel. (431) 51940; fax (431) 5194234; e-mail ihk@kiel.ihk.de; internet www.ihk-schleswig-holstein.de; Chair. CHRISTOPH ANDREAS LEICHT; Man. Dir PETER MICHAEL STEIN.

Industrie- und Handelskammer Chemnitz: Str. der Nationen 25, 09111 Chemnitz; Postfach 464, 09004 Chemnitz; tel. (371) 69000; fax (371) 6900191565; e-mail chemnitz@chemnitz.ihk.de; internet www.chemnitz.ihk24.de; Pres. GUNNAR BERTRAM.

Industrie- und Handelskammer Hannover: Schiffgraben 49, 30175 Hannover; tel. (511) 31070; fax (511) 3107333; e-mail info@hannover.ihk.de; internet www.hannover.ihk.de; f. 1899; Pres. Dr HANNES REHM; Man. Dir Dr WILFRIED PREWO.

Industrie- und Handelskammer Magdeburg: Alter Markt 8, Postfach 1840, 39104 Magdeburg; tel. (391) 56930; fax (391) 5693193; e-mail kammer@magdeburg.ihk.de; internet www.magdeburg.ihk.de; f. 1825; Pres. KLAUS OLBRICHT.

Industrie- und Handelskammer Potsdam: Breite Str. 2A–C, 14467 Potsdam; Postfach 600855, 14408 Potsdam; tel. (331) 2786251; fax (331) 2786190; e-mail info@potsdam.ihk.de; internet www.potsdam.ihk24.de; f. 1990; public; 72,000 mem. cos; Pres. Dr VICTOR STIMMING; CEO RENÉ KOHL.

Vereinigung der Industrie- und Handelskammern in Nordrhein-Westfalen: Marienstr. 8, 40212 Düsseldorf; tel. (211) 367020; fax (211) 3670221; e-mail info@ihk-nrw.de; internet www.ihk-nrw.de; Pres. PAUL BAUWENS-ADENAUER; Chief Exec. Dr RALF MITTELSTÄDT; 16 mems.

INDUSTRIAL AND TRADE ASSOCIATIONS

Bundesverband der Deutschen Industrie eV (Federation of German Industry): Breite Str. 29, 10178 Berlin; tel. (30) 20281566; fax (30) 20282566; e-mail presse@bdi.eu; internet www.bdi.eu; Pres. ULRICH GRILLO; Dir-Gen. Dr MARKUS KERBER; 83 mems.

Arbeitsgemeinschaft Keramische Industrie eV (Ceramics): Schillerstr. 17, 95100 Selb; Postfach 1624, 95090 Selb; tel. (9287) 8080; fax (9287) 70492; e-mail info@keramverband.de; internet www.keramverbaende.de; Pres. ROLF-MICHAEL MÜLLER.

Bundesverband Baustoffe—Steine und Erden eV (Building Materials): Kochstr. 6–7, 10969 Berlin; Postfach 610486, 10928 Berlin; tel. (30) 72619990; fax (30) 726199912; e-mail info@bvbaustoffe.de; internet www.baustoffindustrie.de; f. 1948; Pres. ANDREAS KERN.

Bundesverband der Deutschen Entsorgungswirtschaft (BDE) (Waste Disposal and Recycling): Behrenstr. 29, 10117 Berlin; tel. (30) 59003350; fax (30) 590033599; e-mail info@bde-berlin.de; internet www.bde-berlin.de; Pres. PETER KURTH; Dir-Gen. ANNE BAUM-RUDISCHHAUSER.

Bundesverband der Deutschen Gießerei-Industrie (BDG) (Foundries): Sohnstr. 70, 40237 Düsseldorf; Postfach 101961, 40010 Düsseldorf; tel. (211) 68710; fax (211) 6871333; e-mail info@bdguss.de; internet www.bdguss.de; f. 1865; Pres. GERHARD EDER; Man. Dir Dr ERWIN FLENDER.

Bundesverband der Deutschen Luft- und Raumfahrtindustrie eV (BDLI) (German Aerospace Industries Asscn): Friedrichstr. 60, 10117 Berlin; tel. (30) 2061400; fax (30) 20614090; e-mail kontakt@bdli.de; internet www.bdli.de; f. 1955; Pres. BERNHARD GERWERT; Man. Dir DIETMAR SCHRICK; 200 mems.

Bundesverband Glasindustrie eV (Glass): Am Bonneshof 5, 40474 Düsseldorf; Postfach 101753, 40008 Düsseldorf; tel. (211) 4796134; fax (211) 9513751; e-mail info@bvglas.de; internet www.bvglas.de; Chair. Prof. UDO UNGEHEUER; 4 mem. asscns.

Bundesverband Schmuck und Uhren eV (Jewellery, Clocks and Silverware): Poststr. 1, 75172 Pforzheim; tel. (7231) 1455510; fax (7231) 1455521; e-mail info@bv-schmuck-uhren.de; internet www.bv-schmuck-uhren.de; Pres. Dr PHILIPP REISERT; Man. Dir THILO BRÜCKNER.

Bundesvereinigung der Deutschen Ernährungsindustrie eV (BVE) (Food): Claire-Waldorf-Str. 7, 10117 Berlin; tel. (30) 2007860; fax (30) 200786299; e-mail bve@bve-online.de; internet www.bve-online.de; f. 1949; Chair. JÜRGEN ABRAHAM; Chief Gen. Man. Prof. Dr MATTHIAS HORST.

Centralvereinigung Deutscher Wirtschaftsverbände für Handelsvermittlung und Vertrieb (Trade and Marketing): Am Weidendamm 1A, 10117 Berlin; tel. (30) 72625600; fax (30) 72625699; e-mail centralvereinigung@cdh.de; internet www.cdh.de; f. 1902; Pres. HEINRICH SCHMIDT; 18,000 mems.

Deutscher Hotel- und Gaststättenverband eV (DEHOGA): Am Weidendamm 1A, 10117 Berlin; tel. (30) 7262520; fax (30) 72625242; e-mail info@dehoga.de; internet www.dehoga-bundesverband.de; f. 1949; Pres. ERNST FISCHER; CEO INGRID HARTGES; over 75,000 mems.

GermanFashion Modeverband Deutschland eV: An Lyskirchen 14, Postfach 101865, 50676 Köln; tel. (221) 77440; fax (221) 7744137; e-mail info@germanfashion.net; internet www.germanfashion.net; Pres. GERD OLIVER SEIDENSTICKER.

Gesamtverband der deutschen Textil- und Modeindustrie eV (Textiles and Clothing): Reinhardtstr. 12–14, 10117 Berlin; tel. (30) 7262200; fax (30) 72622044; e-mail info@textil-mode.de; internet www.textil-mode.de; f. 1948; Pres. PETER SCHWARTZE; Dir-Gen. Dr WOLF RÜDIGER BAUMANN.

Gesamtverband kunststoffverarbeitende Industrie eV (GKV) (Plastics): Kaiser-Friedrich-Promenade 43, 61348 Bad Homburg; tel. (6172) 926661; fax (6172) 926674; e-mail tinfo@gkv.de; internet www.gkv.de; f. 1950; Chair. BERND KRUSE; Man. Dir Dr OLIVER MÖLLENSTÄDT; 750 mems.

Hauptverband der Deutschen Bauindustrie eV (Building): Kurfürstenstr. 129, 10785 Berlin; tel. (30) 212860; fax (30) 21286240; e-mail info@bauindustrie.de; internet www.bauindustrie.de; f. 1948; Pres. Prof. THOMAS BAUER; Dir-Gen. MICHAEL KNIPPER; 23 mem. asscns.

Hauptverband der Deutschen Holz und Kunststoffe verarbeitenden Industrie und verwandter Inustriezweige eV (HDH) (Woodwork and Plastic): Flutgraben 2, 53604 Bad-Honnef; tel. (2224) 93770; fax (2224) 937777; e-mail info@hdh-ev.de; internet www.hdh-ev.de; f. 1948; Pres. HELMUT LÜBKE; Man. Dir DIRK-UWE KLAAS; 24 mem. asscns.

Hauptverband Papier- und Kunststoffverarbeitung eV (HPV) (Paper and Plastic): Chausseestr. 22, 10115 Berlin; tel. (30) 24781830; fax (30) 247818340; e-mail info@hpv-ev.org; internet www.hpv-ev.org; f. 1948; 10 regional groups, 20 production groups; Pres. Dr HEINRICH SPIES; Dir-Gen. HELGE MARTIN KROLLMANN; 1,300 mems.

Mineralölwirtschaftsverband eV (German Petroleum Association): Georgenstr. 25, 10117 Berlin; tel. (30) 20220530; fax (30) 20220555; e-mail info@mwv.de; internet www.mwv.de; f. 1946; Chair. Dr UWE FRANKE; Man. Dir Dr KLAUS PICARD.

SPECTARIS—Deutscher Industrieverband für optische, medizinische und mechatronische Technologien eV (Optical, Medical and Mechatronical Technologies): Werderscher Markt 15, 10117 Berlin; tel. (30) 4140210; fax (30) 41402133; e-mail info@spectaris.de; internet www.spectaris.de; f. 1949; CEO Dr TOBIAS WEILER.

Verband der Automobilindustrie eV (Motor Cars): Behrenstr. 35, 10117 Berlin; Postfach 80462, 10004 Berlin; tel. (30) 8978420; fax (30) 897842600; e-mail info@vda.de; internet www.vda.de; Pres. MATTHIAS WISSMANN.

Verband der Chemischen Industrie eV (VCI) (Chemical Industry): Mainzer Landstr. 55, 60329 Frankfurt a.M.; tel. (69) 25560; fax (69) 25561471; e-mail dialog@vci.de; internet www.vci.de; f. 1877; Pres. Dr KARL-LUDWIG KLEY; Dir-Gen. Dr UTZ TILLMANN; 1,650 mems.

Verband Deutscher Maschinen- und Anlagenbau eV (VDMA) (German Engineering Federation): Lyoner Str. 18, 60528 Frankfurt a.M.; Postfach 710864, 60498 Frankfurt a.M.; tel. (69) 66030; fax (69) 75608111; e-mail vdma@vdma.org; internet www.vdma.org; f. 1892; Pres. Dr THOMAS LINDNER; Gen. Man. Dr HANNES HESSE.

Verband Deutscher Papierfabriken eV (Paper): Adenauerallee 55, 53113 Bonn; tel. (228) 267050; fax (228) 2670562; internet www.vdp-online.de; Pres. Dr MORITZ J. WEIG; Dir-Gen. KLAUS WINDHAGEN.

Verband der Kali- und Salzindustrie eV (VKS) (Potash and Salt): Reinhardtstr. 18A, 10117 Berlin; Postfach 080651, 10006 Berlin; tel. (30) 84710690; fax (30) 847106921; e-mail info.berlin@vks-kalisalz.de; internet www.vks-kalisalz.de; f. 1905; Chair. NORBERT STEINER; Man. Dir HARTMUT BEHNSEN.

Verband für Schiffbau und Meerestechnik eV (German Shipbuilding and Ocean Industries Asscn): Steinhoeft 11, 20459 Hamburg; tel. (40) 2801520; fax (40) 28015230; e-mail info@vsm.de; internet www.vsm.de; f. 1884; Pres. HARALD FASSMER; Man. Dirs REINHARD LUEKEN, Dr RALF SOEREN MARQUARDT.

Verein der Zuckerindustrie (Sugar): Am Hofgarten 8, 53113 Bonn; tel. (228) 22850; fax (228) 2285100; e-mail wvz-vdz@zuckerverbaende.de; internet www.zuckerverbaende.de; f. 1850; Chair. AXEL AUMÜLLER; Dir-Gen. GÜNTER TISSEN.

Vereinigung Rohstoffe und Bergbau eV (German Mining Association): Postfach 120736, 10597 Berlin; Am Schillertheater 4, 10625 Berlin; tel. (30) 3151820; fax (30) 31518235; e-mail info@v-r-b.de; internet www.v-rohstoffe-bergbau.de; f. 1953; Pres. Dr JOACHIM GEISLER; Gen. Man. Dr THORSTEN DIERCKS; 12 mem. asscns.

Wirtschaftsverband der Deutschen Kautschukindustrie eV (WDK) (Rubber): Zeppelinallee 69, 60487 Frankfurt a.M.; Postfach 900360, 60443 Frankfurt a.M.; tel. (69) 79360; fax (69) 7936175; e-mail info@wdk.de; internet www.wdk.de; f. 1894; Pres. RAINER LANDWEHR; Man. Dir BORIS ENGELHARDT; 120 mems.

Wirtschaftsverband Erdöl- und Erdgasgewinnung eV (Oil and Gas Producers): Berliner Allee 26, 30175 Hannover; tel. (511) 121720; fax (511) 1217210; e-mail info@erdoel-erdgas.de; internet www.erdoel-erdgas.de; f. 1945; Pres. Dr GERNOT KALKOFFEN; Gen. Man. JOSEF SCHMID.

Wirtschaftsverband Stahlbau und Energietechnik (SET) (Steel and Energy): Sternstr. 36, 40479 Düsseldorf; tel. (211) 4987092; fax (211) 4987036; e-mail info@set-online.de; internet www.set-online.de; Chair. KLAUS DIETER RENNERT; Dir-Gen. R. MAASS.

WirtschaftsVereinigung Metalle (Metal): Wallstr. 58–59, 10179 Berlin; tel. (30) 726207100; fax (30) 726207198; e-mail info@wvmetalle.de; internet www.wvmetalle.de; Pres. OLIVER BELL; Dir-Gen. MARTIN KNEER.

Wirtschaftsvereinigung Stahl (Steel): Sohnstr. 65, 40237 Düsseldorf; Postfach 105464, 40045 Düsseldorf; tel. (211) 67070; fax (211) 6707310; e-mail info@stahl-online.de; internet www.stahl-online.de; f. 1998; Pres. HANS-JÜRGEN KERKHOFF.

WSM—Wirtschaftsverband Stahl- und Metallverarbeitung eV (Steel and Metal-processing Industry): Kaiserwerther Str. 137, 40474 Düsseldorf; tel. (211) 4564151; fax (211) 4564169; e-mail info@wsm-net.de; internet www.wsm-net.de; Pres. Dr GERHARD BRÜNINGHAUS; Dir-Gen. CHRISTIAN VIETMEYER.

Zentralverband des Deutschen Handwerks: Mohrenstr. 20–21, 10117 Berlin; tel. (30) 206190; fax (30) 20619460; e-mail info@zdh.de; internet www.zdh.de; f. 1949; Pres. OTTO KENTZLER; Gen. Sec. HOLGER SCHWANNECKE; 53 mem. chambers, 48 asscns.

Zentralverband Elektrotechnik- und Elektronikindustrie eV (ZVEI) (Electrical and Electronic Equipment): Lyoner Str. 9, 60528 Frankfurt a.M.; tel. (69) 63020; fax (69) 6302317; e-mail zvei@zvei.org; internet www.zvei.org; f. 1918; Pres. FRIEDHELM LOH; CEO Dr KLAUS MITTELBACH; 1,400 mems.

EMPLOYERS' ORGANIZATIONS

Bundesvereinigung der Deutschen Arbeitgeberverbände (BDA) (Confederation of German Employers' Associations): Breite Str. 29, 10178 Berlin; tel. (30) 20330; fax (30) 20331055; e-mail bda@arbeitgeber.de; internet www.bda-online.de; f. 1904; represents the professional and regional interests of German employers in the social policy field, affiliates 14 regional asscns and 52 branch asscns, of which some are listed under industrial asscns; Pres. Prof. Dr DIETER HUNDT; Man. Dir Dr REINHARD GÖHNER.

Affiliated associations:

Arbeitgeberverband der Cigarettenindustrie eV (Employers' Association of Cigarette Manufacturers): Kapstadtring 10, 22297 Hamburg; tel. (40) 63784840; fax (40) 63784842; e-mail md@adc-online.de; internet www.adc-online.de; f. 1950; Pres. MICHAEL WENZEL; Dir MICHAEL DREIER.

Arbeitgeberverband der Deutschen Binnenschiffahrt eV (Employers' Association of German Inland Waterway Transport): Dammstr. 15–17, 47119 Duisburg; Postfach 170428, 47184 Duisburg; tel. (203) 8000631; fax (203) 8000621; e-mail info@schulschiff-rhein.de; internet www.schulschiff-rhein.de; f. 1974; Pres. VOLKER SEEFELDT; Dir JÖRG RUSCHE.

Arbeitgeberverband der Deutschen Kautschukindustrie (ADK) eV (German Rubber Industry Employers' Association): Schiffgraben 36, 30175 Hannover; tel. (511) 85050; fax (511)

8505203; e-mail info@adk-verband.de; internet www.adk-ev.de; Pres. Dr SVEN VOGT; Gen. Man. Dr VOLKER SCHMIDT.

Arbeitgeberverband Deutscher Eisenbahnen eV (German Railway Employers' Association): Volksgartenstr. 54A, 50677 Köln; tel. (221) 9318450; fax (221) 93184588; e-mail info@agvde.de; internet www.agvde.de; Pres. DIETMAR SCHWEIZER; Dir Dr HANS-PETER ACKMANN.

Arbeitgeberverband des Privaten Bankgewerbes eV (Private Banking Employers' Association): Burgstr. 28, 10178 Berlin; tel. (30) 590011270; fax (30) 590011279; e-mail service@agvbanken.de; internet www.agvbanken.de; f. 1954; Pres. ULRICH SIEBER; Dir Dr GERD BENRATH; 140 mems.

Arbeitgeberverband der Versicherungsunternehmen in Deutschland (Employers' Association of Insurance Companies): Arabellastr. 29, 81925 München; tel. (89) 9220010; fax (89) 92200150; e-mail agvvers@agv-vers.de; internet www.agv-vers.de; f. 1950; Pres. and Dir-Gen. Dr JOSEF BEUTELMANN; Dir-Gen. Dr MICHAEL NIEBLER.

Bundesarbeitgeberverband Chemie eV (Federation of Employers' Associations in the Chemical Industry): Abraham-Lincoln-Str. 24, 65189 Wiesbaden; Postfach 1280, 65002 Wiesbaden; tel. (611) 778810; fax (611) 7788123; e-mail info@bavc.de; internet www.bavc.de; f. 1949; Pres. MARGRET SUCKALE; Dir-Gen. WOLFGANG GOOS; 10 mem. asscns.

Bundesarbeitgeberverband Glas und Solar eV: Max-Joseph-Str. 5, 80333 München; Postfach 200219, 80002 München; tel. (89) 41119430; fax (89) 411194344; e-mail info@bagv.de; internet www.bagv.de; f. 2010; fmrly Arbeitgeberverband der Deutschen Glasindustrie eV; Pres. THOMAS KIETSCHMANN; CEO MARC HELBIG.

Deutscher Bauernverband eV (DBV) (German Farmers' Association): Claire-Waldoff-Str. 7, 10117 Berlin; tel. (30) 31904407; fax (30) 31904431; e-mail presse@bauernverband.net; internet www.bauernverband.de; f. 1948; Pres. JOACHIM RUKWIED; Sec.-Gen. Dr HELMUT BORN.

Gesamtmetall—Die Arbeitgeberverbände der Metall- und Elektro-Industrie eV (Federation of the Metal Trades Employers' Associations): Vossstr. 16, 10117 Berlin; Postfach 060249, 10052 Berlin; tel. (30) 551500; e-mail info@gesamtmetall.de; internet www.gesamtmetall.de; f. 1890; Pres. RAINER DULGER; 22 mem. asscns.

Vereinigung der Arbeitgeberverbände der Deutschen Papierindustrie eV (Federation of Employers' Associations of the German Paper Industry): Scheffelstr. 29, 76593 Gernsbach; Postfach 1232, 76585 Gernsbach; tel. (228) 2672810; fax (228) 215270; e-mail vap@papierzentrum.org; internet www.vap-papier.de; Pres. EBERHARD POTEMPA; Dir STEPHAN MEISSNER; 8 mem. asscns.

Vereinigung der Arbeitgeberverbände energie- und versorgungswirtschaftlicher Unternehmungen (Employers' Federation of Energy and Power Supply Enterprises): Theaterstr. 3, 30159 Hannover; tel. (511) 911090; fax (511) 9110940; e-mail agv.energie@t-online.de; internet www.vaeu.de; f. 1962; Pres. HARTMUT GELDMACHER; Dir Dr BERNHARD BECK; 7 mem. asscns.

Regional employers' associations:

Arbeitgeber- und Wirtschaftsverbände Sachsen-Anhalt eV (AWSA) (Employers' and business associations of Saxony-Anhalt): Humboldtstr. 14, 39112 Magdeburg; Postfach 4152, 39106 Magdeburg; tel. (391) 6288819; fax (391) 6288810; e-mail info@aw-sa.de; internet www.wir-setzen-akzente.de; Pres. KLEMENS GUTMANN; Gen. Man. MATTHIAS MENGER; 31 mem. asscns.

Landesvereinigung Baden-Württembergischer Arbeitgeberverbände eV: Löffelstr. 22–24, 70597 Stuttgart; Postfach 700501, 70574 Stuttgart; tel. (711) 76820; fax (711) 7651675; e-mail info@agv-bw.de; internet www.agv-bw.de; f. 1951; Pres. Dr DIETER HUNDT; Dir PEER-MICHAEL DICK; 41 mem. asscns.

Landesvereinigung der Unternehmensverbände Nordrhein-Westfalen eV (North Rhine-Westphalia Federation of Employers' Associations): Uerdinger Str. 58–62, 40474 Düsseldorf; Postfach 300643, 40406 Düsseldorf; tel. (211) 45730; fax (211) 4573179; e-mail info@unternehmernrw.net; internet www.unternehmernrw.net; Pres. HORST-WERNER MAIER-HUNKE; Dir Dr LUITWIN MALLMANN; 92 mem. asscns.

Landesvereinigung Unternehmerverbände Rheinland-Pfalz eV (LVU) (Federation of Employers' Associations in the Rhineland Palatinate): Hindenburgstr. 32, 55118 Mainz; Postfach 2966, 55019 Mainz; tel. (6131) 55750; fax (6131) 557539; e-mail contact@lvu.de; internet www.lvu.de; f. 1963; Pres. Dr GERHARD F. BRAUN.

Die Unternehmensverbände im Lande Bremen eV (Federation of Employers' Associations in the Land of Bremen): Schiller Str. 10, 28195 Bremen; Postfach 100727, 28007 Bremen; tel. (421) 368020; fax (421) 3680249; e-mail info@uvhb.de; internet www.uvhb.de; Pres. INGO KRAMER; Dir CORNELIUS NEUMANN-REDLIN; 21 mem. asscns.

Unternehmerverbände Niedersachsen eV (UVN) (Federation of Employers' Associations in Lower Saxony): Schiffgraben 36, 30175 Hannover; tel. (511) 8505243; fax (511) 8505268; e-mail uvn@uvn-online.de; internet www.uvn-online.de; f. 1951; Pres. WERNER M. BAHLSEN; CEO Dr VOLKER MÜLLER; 65 mem. asscns.

UVNord—Vereinigung der Unternehmensverbände in Hamburg und Schleswig-Holstein eV (Federation of Employers' Associations in Hamburg and Schleswig-Holstein): Kapstadtring 10, 22297 Hamburg; Postfach 601969, 22219 Hamburg; tel. (40) 63785120; fax (40) 63785151; e-mail froehlich@uvnord.de; internet www.uvnord.de; f. 2000; Pres. Prof. Dr ULI WACHHOLTZ; Dir Dr MICHAEL THOMAS FRÖHLICH; 67 mem. asscns.

vbw—Vereinigung der Bayerischen Wirtschaft eV (Federation of Employers' Associations in Bavaria): Max-Joseph-Str. 5, 80333 München; Postfach 202026, 80020 München; tel. (89) 55178100; fax (89) 55178111; e-mail info@vbw-bayern.de; internet www.vbw-bayern.de; Pres. RANDOLF RODENSTOCK; Gen. Man. BERTRAM BROSSARDT; 100 mem. asscns.

Verband der Wirtschaft Thüringens eV (Association of Thuringian Management): Postfach 900353, 99007 Erfurt; Lossiusstr. 1, 99094 Erfurt; Postfach 900353, 99007 Erfurt; tel. (361) 67590; fax (361) 6759222; e-mail info@vwt.de; internet www.vwt.de; Pres. WOLGANG ZAHN; Dir STEPHAN FAUTH; 37 mem. asscns.

Vereinigung der Unternehmensverbände in Berlin und Brandenburg eV (Federation of Employers' Associations in Berlin and Brandenburg): Am Schillertheater 2, 10625 Berlin; tel. (30) 310050; fax (30) 31005166; e-mail uvb@uvb-online.de; internet www.uvb-online.de; Pres. BURKHARD ISCHLER; 60 mem. asscns.

Vereinigung der hessischen Unternehmerverbände eV (Hessian Federation of Enterprise Associations): Emil-von-Behring-Str. 4, 60439 Frankfurt a.M.; Postfach 500561, 60394 Frankfurt a.M.; tel. (69) 958080; fax (69) 95808126; e-mail info@vhu.de; internet www.vhu.de; f. 1947; Pres. Prof. DIETER WEIDEMANN; Dir and Sec. VOLKER FASBENDER; 64 mem. asscns.

Vereinigung der Saarländischen Unternehmensverbände eV (Federation of Employers' Associations in Saarland): Harthweg 15, 66119 Saarbrücken; Postfach 650433, 66143 Saarbrücken; tel. (681) 954340; fax (681) 9543474; e-mail kontakt@vsu.de; internet www.vsu.de; Pres. Dr OSWALD BUBEL; Dir Dr JOACHIM MALTER; 19 mem. asscns.

Vereinigung der Sächsischen Wirtschaft eV (VSW) (Federation of Employers' Associations in Saxony): Washingtonstr. 16/16A, 01139 Dresden; Postfach 300200, 01131 Dresden; tel. (351) 255930; fax (351) 2559378; e-mail vsw@hsw-mail.de; internet www.wirtschaftsverbaende-sachsen.de; f. 1998; Pres. BODO FINGER; Gen. Man. Dr ANDREAS WINKLER; 40 mem. asscns.

Vereinigung der Unternehmensverbände für Mecklenburg-Vorpommern eV (Federation of Employers' Associations of Mecklenburg-Western Pomerania): Graf-Schack-Allee 10, 19053 Schwerin; tel. (385) 6356100; fax (385) 6356151; e-mail info@vumv.de; internet www.vumv.de; Pres. HANS-DIETER BREMER; Dir Dr THOMAS KLISCHAN; 27 mem. asscns.

UTILITIES

Regulatory Authority

Bundesnetzagentur für Elektrizität, Gas, Telekommunikation, Post und Eisenbahnen: see Broadcasting and Communications.

Electricity and Gas

Supply of electricity and gas is dominated by four companies (RWE, E.ON, Vattenfall Europe and EnBW). A large number of regional utilities, many of which are part-owned by the four major companies, supply electricity and gas to towns and municipalities in one or more of the federal Länder.

Energie Baden-Württemberg AG (EnBW): Durlacher Allee 93, 76131 Karlsruhe; tel. (49) 7216300; e-mail kontakt@enbw.com; internet www.enbw.com; production, distribution and supply of electricity and gas; CEO HANS-PETER VILLIS.

E.ON AG: E.ON-Pl. 1, 40479 Düsseldorf; tel. (211) 45790; fax (211) 4579501; e-mail info@eon.com; internet www.eon.com; f. 2000 by merger of VEBA AG and VIAG AG; production, distribution and supply of electricity and gas; operates in 19 countries worldwide; Chair. and CEO Dr JOHANNES TEYSSEN.

E.ON Energie AG: Brienner Str. 40, 80333 München; tel. (89) 125401; fax (89) 12543906; e-mail info@eon-energie.com; internet www.eon-energie.com; f. 2000 by merger of Bayernwerk AG and Preussenelektra AG; production, transmission and supply of electricity; subsidiary of E.ON AG; Chair. INGO LUGE.

E.ON Ruhrgas AG: Brüsseler Pl. 1, 45131 Essen; tel. (201) 18400; fax (201) 1843766; e-mail info@eon-ruhrgas.com; internet www.eon-ruhrgas.com; f. 1926; distribution and supply of natural gas; subsidiary of E.ON AG; Chair., Management Bd KLAUS SCHÄFER.

EWE AG: Donnerschweer Str. 22–26, 26122 Oldenburg; tel. (441) 48050; fax (441) 48053999; e-mail info@ewe.de; internet www.ewe.de; f. 1943; supplier of electricity and natural gas; serves northern Germany; Chair., Management Bd Dr WERNER BRINKER.

GASAG Berliner Gaswerke AG: Henriette-Herz-Pl. 4, 10178 Berlin; tel. (30) 78720; fax (30) 78724794; e-mail service@gasag.de; internet www.gasag.de; f. 1992; regional gas supplier for Berlin; Man. Dirs ANDREAS PROHL, OLAF CZERNOMORIEZ.

GasVersorgung Süddeutschland GmbH (GVS): Am Wallgraben 135, 70565 Stuttgart; tel. (711) 78120; fax (711) 78121411; e-mail sunc@gvs-erdgas.de; internet www.gvs-erdgas.de; f. 1961; supplies gas to 750 towns and municipalities in Baden-Württemberg; CEO SCIPIONE CHIALÀ.

Mainova AG: Solmsstr. 38, 60623 Frankfurt a.M.; tel. (69) 21302; fax (69) 21381122; internet www.mainova.de; f. 1998 by merger of Stadtwerke Frankfurt and Maingas AG; supply of electricity, natural gas and water in Frankfurt am Main and surrounding area; 75.2% owned by Frankfurt a.M. city administration, 24.4% owned by Thüga AG; Chair. and CEO Dr CONSTANTIN H. ALSHEIMER.

MITGAS Mitteldeutsche Gasversorgung GmbH: Industriestr. 10, 06184 Halle (Saale); Postfach 300552, 06025 Halle (Saale); tel. (34605) 60; fax (34605) 61610; e-mail service@mitgas.de; internet www.mitgas.de; f. 2000; regional gas supplier with customers in Saxony, Saxony-Anhalt and Thuringia; 24.60% owned by VNG-Beteiligungs-GmbH; Man. Dirs CARL-ERNST GIESTING, Dr ANDREAS AUERBACH.

RWE AG: Opernpl. 1, 45128 Essen; Postfach 103061, 45030 Essen; tel. (201) 1200; internet www.rwe.de; f. 1898; production, distribution and supply of electricity, gas and water; subsidiaries in 6 European countries (Czech Republic, Hungary, the Netherlands, Poland, Slovakia, the UK) and the USA; Chair. Dr MANFRED SCHNEIDER; CEO PETER TERIUM.

swb AG: Theodor-Heuss-Allee 20, 28215 Bremen; tel. (421) 3590; fax (421) 3592499; e-mail info@swb-gruppe.de; internet www.swb-gruppe.de; f. 1854; supplies electricity, natural gas and water in Bremen and northern Germany; 100% owned by EWE AG; Co-Chair. Management Bd Dr THOMAS NEUBER, JÖRG BUDDE.

Vattenfall Europe AG: Chausseestr. 23, 10115 Berlin; tel. (30) 818222; fax (30) 81823950; e-mail info@vattenfall.de; internet www.vattenfall.de; f. 2002 by merger of Bewag, HEW, LAUBAG and VEAG; production, distribution and supply of electricity; Chair., Management Bd TUOMO J. HATAKKA.

WINGAS GmbH & Co KG: Friedrich-Ebert-Str. 160, 34119 Kassel; Postfach 104020, 34112 Kassel; tel. (561) 3010; fax (561) 3011702; e-mail info@wingas.de; internet www.wingas.de; f. 1993; distribution of natural gas; also supplies gas to public utilities, regional gas suppliers, industrial facilities and power plants; jt venture of Wintershall Holding AG and Gazprom (Russia); Chair. Dr GERHARD KÖNIG; Man. Dir ARTOUR CHAKHDINAROV.

Water

Responsibility for water supply lies with the municipalities. As a result, there are over 6,000 water supply utilities in Germany. The ownership structures of those utilities are diverse. Many municipalities have formed limited or joint-stock companies with private sector partners to manage water supply, such as the supplier for the capital (Berliner Wasserbetriebe), while others have contracted private companies to provide water services.

Berliner Wasserbetriebe: Neue Jüdenstr. 1, 10179 Berlin; tel. (800) 2927587; fax (30) 86442810; e-mail info@bwb.de; internet www.bwb.de; f. 1856; merger in 1988 of Berliner Wasserwerke and Berliner Entwässerungswerke; supplier of water and sanitation services to Berlin; subsidiary of Berlinerwasser Gruppe (50.1% owned by Berlin regional Govt, 24.95% each by RWE AG and Veolia Environment (France); Chair., Management Bd JÖRG SIMON.

Gelsenwasser AG: Willy-Brandt-Allee 26, 45891 Gelsenkirchen; tel. (209) 7080; fax (209) 708650; e-mail info@gelsenwasser.de; internet www.gelsenwasser.de; privately owned enterprise, supplying water and sanitation services by agreement with several municipalities in North Rhine-Westphalia and across Germany; also supplies electricity and gas; Chair., Management Bd HENNING R. DETERS.

Association

Bundesverband der Energie- und Wasserwirtschaft eV (BDEW) (German Association of Energy and Water Companies): Reinhardtstr. 32, 10117 Berlin; tel. (30) 3001990; fax (30) 3001993900; e-mail info@bdew.de; internet www.bdew.de; f. 2007; c. 1,800 mems; Pres. EWALD WOSTE; Chair., Management Bd HILDEGARD MÜLLER.

TRADE UNIONS

The main German trade union federations are the Deutscher Gewerkschaftsbund (DGB), the dbb beamtenbund und tarifunion and the Christlicher Gewerkschaftsbund Deutschlands (CGB). Following German unification in October 1990, the trade unions of the former GDR were absorbed into the member unions of the DGB.

National Federations

Christlicher Gewerkschaftsbund Deutschlands (Christian Workers' Union—CGB): Obentrautstr. 57, 10963 Berlin; tel. (30) 21021730; fax (30) 21021740; e-mail cgb.bund@cgb.info; internet www.cgb.info; f. 1899; 16 affiliated unions; Pres. MATTHÄUS STREBL; Gen. Sec. CHRISTIAN HERTZOG; c. 280,000 mems.

dbb beamtenbund und tarifunion (Civil Servants' Federation): Friedrichstr. 169–170, 10117 Berlin; tel. (30) 408140; fax (30) 40814999; e-mail post@dbb.de; internet www.dbb.de; f. 1918; 40 affiliated unions; Pres. PETER HEESEN; 1.3m. mems (2012).

Deutscher Gewerkschaftsbund (DGB): Henriette-Herz-Pl. 2, 10178 Berlin; tel. (30) 240600; fax (30) 24060324; e-mail info.bvv@dgb.de; internet www.dgb.de; f. 1949; 8 affiliated unions; Pres. MICHAEL SOMMER; Vice-Pres. ELKE HANNACK; 6,151,184 mems (2012).

Transport

RAILWAYS

At 2011 the length of railway lines in use in Germany was 33,576 km, of which 19,826 km were electrified. High-speed InterCity Express (ICE) trains operate between several German cities, and offer links to Austria (Vienna and Innsbruck), Belgium (Brussels and Liège), Denmark (Copenhagen and Arhus), France (Paris and Marseille), the Netherlands (Arnhem, Utrecht and Amsterdam) and Switzerland (Zürich and Interlaken); plans to offer a direct ICE service from London to Frankfurt were subject to delays and the service was not expected to operate before 2016.

Regulatory Bodies

Eisenbahn-Bundesamt (EBA) (Federal Railway Authority): Heinemannstr. 6, 53175 Bonn; tel. (228) 98260; fax (228) 9826199; e-mail poststelle@eba.bund.de; internet www.eba.bund.de; supervisory and authorizing body; ensures safety of railway passengers; supervises construction; inspects and approves rolling stock and monitors safe condition of railway infrastructure and signalling; Pres. GERALD HÖRSTER.

Bundeseisenbahnvermögen (BEV) (Federal Railroad Assets): Kurt-Georg-Kiesinger-Allee 2, 53175 Bonn; tel. (228) 30770; fax (228) 3077160; e-mail bonn@bev.bund.de; internet www.bev.bund.de; Pres. MARIE-THERES NONN.

Federal Railway

Deutsche Bahn AG (German Railways): Potsdamer Pl. 2, 10785 Berlin; tel. (1805) 996633; fax (30) 29761919; e-mail medienbetreuung@bku.db.de; internet www.deutschebahn.com; f. 1994 by merger of Deutsche Bundesbahn and Deutsche Reichsbahn; state-owned; CEO and Chair., Management Bd RÜDIGER GRUBE; Chair., Supervisory Bd Dr UTZ-HELLMUTH FELCHT.

Metropolitan Railways

Berliner Verkehrsbetriebe (BVG) (Berlin Transport Authority): Anstalt des öffentlichen Rechts, Holzmarktstr. 15–17, 10179 Berlin; tel. (30) 19449; fax (30) 25649256; e-mail info@bvg.de; internet www.bvg.de; f. 1929; operates 144.9 km of underground railway; also runs tram and bus services; Chair., Management Bd Dr SIGRID EVELYN NIKUTTA.

Hamburger Hochbahn AG: Steinstr. 20, 20095 Hamburg; tel. (40) 32880; fax (40) 326406; e-mail info@hochbahn.de; internet www.hochbahn.de; f. 1911; operates 104.7 km of underground railway on 4 lines; also operates 120 bus routes; Chair., Management Bd GÜNTER ELSTE; Chair., Supervisory Bd FRANK HORCH.

Münchner Verkehrsgesellschaft mbH (MVG): Emmy-Noether-Str. 2, 80287 München; tel. (89) 21910; fax (89) 21912378; e-mail lobundtadel@mvg.swm.de; internet www.mvg-mobil.de; subsidiary of Stadtwerke München GmbH; operates underground railway (6 lines totalling 91 km), tramway (10 lines totalling 71 km), 67 bus lines (452 km); Chair., Management Bd HERBERT KÖNIG.

VAG Verkehrs-Aktiengesellschaft: 90338 Nürnberg; Südliche Fürther Str. 5, 90429 Nürnberg; tel. (911) 2830; fax (911) 2834800; e-mail service@vag.de; internet www.vag.de; wholly owned subsidiary of Städtische Werke Nürnberg GmbH; operates underground railway (3 lines totalling 31 km), tramway (5 lines totalling 34 km) and bus services (53 routes); Chair., Management Bd JOSEF HASLER; Chair., Supervisory Bd Dr MICHAEL REINDL.

Association

Verband Deutscher Verkehrsunternehmen (VDV) (Association of German Transport Undertakings): Kamekestr. 37–39, 50672 Köln; tel. (221) 579790; fax (221) 57979-8000; e-mail info@vdv.de; internet www.vdv.de; f. 1895; public transport, freight transport by rail; publishes *Der Nahverkehr* (10 a year), *Bus + Bahn* (monthly) and *Güterbahnen* (quarterly); Pres. JÜRGEN FENSKE; Exec. Dir OLIVER WOLFF.

ROADS

In 2010 there were 12,819 km of motorway, 39,710 km of highways and 178,253 km of secondary roads in a total road network of 643,782 km.

INLAND WATERWAYS

The inland waterways network in Germany centres around the Rhine, Danube and Elbe rivers. The Main–Danube Canal linking the North Sea and the Black Sea was opened in 1992. There were around 7,675 km of navigable inland waterways in 2012. Inland shipping accounts for about 12.1% of total freight traffic.

Associations

Bundesverband der Deutschen Binnenschiffahrt eV (BDB): Dammstr. 15–17, 47119 Duisburg; tel. (203) 8000650; fax (203) 8000621; e-mail infobdb@binnenschiff.de; internet www.binnenschiff.de; f. 1978; central Inland Waterway Association to further the interests of operating firms; Pres. GEORG HÖTTE; Man. Dirs JENS SCHWANEN, JÖRG RUSCHE.

Bundesverband Öffentlicher Binnenhäfen eV: Leipziger Pl. 8, 10117 Berlin; tel. (30) 39881981; fax (30) 340608553; e-mail info-boeb@binnenhafen.de; internet www.binnenhafen.de; Pres. RAINER SCHÄFER; Man. Dir BORIS KLUGE.

Bundesverband der Selbstständigen Abteilung Binnenschiffahrt eV (BDS): August-Bier-Str. 18, 53129 Bonn; tel. (228) 746337; fax (228) 746569; e-mail zentrale@bds-binnenschiffahrt.de; internet www.bds-binnenschiffahrt.de; Man. Dir ANDREA BECKSCHÄFER.

Deutsche Binnenreederei AG: Revaler Str. 100, 10245 Berlin; tel. (30) 293760; fax (30) 29376201; e-mail dbr@binnenreederei.de; internet www.binnenreederei.de; f. 1949; Dir-Gen. PIOTR CHAJDEROWSKI.

Unternehmensverband Hafen Hamburg eV: Mattentwiete 2, 20457 Hamburg; tel. (40) 3789090; fax (40) 37890970; e-mail info@uvhh.de; internet www.uvhh.de; Pres. GUNTHER BONZ.

Verein für europäische Binnenschiffahrt und Wasserstraßen eV (VBW): Dammstr. 15–17, 47119 Duisburg; tel. (203) 8000627; fax (203) 8000628; e-mail info@vbw-ev.de; internet www.vbw-ev.de; f. 1877; represents all brs of the inland waterways; Pres. HEINZ-JOSEF JOERIS.

SHIPPING

The port of Hamburg is the largest in Germany and the fourth largest in Europe. Other principal ports are Bremerhaven, Rostock-Überseehafen and Wilhelmshaven. At 31 December 2013 the flag registered fleet totalled 1,195 vessels, with a combined displacement of 12.7m. grt, of which 129 were general cargo ships and 96 were fishing vessels. Some important shipping companies are:

Argo Shipping GmbH: Postfach 107529, 28075 Bremen; Am Wall 187–189, 28195 Bremen; tel. (421) 2575184; fax (421) 2575432; e-mail argoshipping@argo-adler.de; internet www.argo-adler.de; f. 1896; shipowners; Propr MAX ADLER.

Aug. Bolten, Wm. Miller's Nachfolger GmbH & Co KG: Postfach 112269; Mattentwiete 8, 20457 Hamburg; tel. (40) 36010; fax (40) 3601423; e-mail info@aug-bolten.de; internet www.aug-bolten.de; shipowner, manager and broker, port agent; Man. Dirs OLE KRAFT, MICHAEL SAY.

Bugsier- Reederei- und Bergungs-Gesellschaft mbH & Co: Johannisbollwerk 10, 20459 Hamburg; tel. (40) 311110; fax (40) 313693; e-mail info@bugsier.de; internet www.bugsier.de; salvage, towage, tugs, ocean-going heavy lift cranes, submersible pontoons, harbour tugs; Man. Dirs J. W. SCHUCHMANN, HAJO SCHUCHMANN.

Christian F. Ahrenkiel GmbH & Co KG: An der Alster 45, 20099 Hamburg; tel. (40) 248380; fax (40) 24838375; e-mail info@ahrenkiel.net; internet www.ahrenkiel.net; f. 1950; shipowners, operators and managers; Man. Dirs KLAUS G. WOLFF, OLAF STAATS.

DAL Deutsche Afrika-Linien/John T. Essberger GmbH & Co KG: Palmaille 45, 22767 Hamburg; tel. (40) 380160; fax (40) 38016629; e-mail info@rantzau.de; internet www.dal.biz; Europe and South Africa; Man. Dirs HARTMUT LÜHR, Dr E. VON RANTZAU, H. VON RANTZAU.

Deutsche Seereederei GmbH: Lange Str. 1A, 18055 Rostock; tel. (381) 4584043; fax (381) 4584001; e-mail info@deutsche-seereederei.de; internet www.deutsche-seereederei.de; shipping, tourism, real estate, industry and finance; Man. Dirs ARNO PÖKER, MICHAEL WESTENBERGER.

Ernst Russ GmbH: Alsterufer 10, 20354 Hamburg; tel. (40) 414070; fax (40) 41407111; e-mail info@ernst-russ.de; internet www.ernst-russ.de; f. 1893; worldwide.

F. Laeisz Schiffahrtsgesellschaft mbH & Co KG: Postfach 111111, 20411 Hamburg; Trostbrücke 1, 20457 Hamburg; tel. (40) 368080; fax (40) 364876; e-mail info@laeisz.de; internet www.laeisz.de; f. 1983; CEO NIKOLAUS H. SCHÜES.

Hamburg Südamerikanische Dampfschiffahrts-Gesellschaft KG: Postfach 111533, 20415 Hamburg; Willy-Brandt-Str. 59–61, 20457 Hamburg; tel. (40) 37050; fax (40) 37052400; e-mail central@ham.hamburgsud.com; internet www.hamburgsud.com; f. 1871; worldwide services; Chair. Dr OTTMAR GAST.

Hapag-Lloyd AG: Ballindamm 25, 20095 Hamburg; tel. (40) 30010; fax (40) 336432; e-mail info.de@hlag.com; internet www.hapag-lloyd.com; f. 1970; 61.6% stake owned by Albert Ballin consortium (comprising city of Hamburg, Kühne Holding AG, Signal Iduna, HSH Nordbank, M.M.Warburg Bank and HanseMerkur); 38.4% stake owned by TUI AG; Chair. MICHAEL BEHRENDT.

John T. Essberger GmbH & Co KG: Palmaille 45, 22767 Hamburg; tel. (40) 380160; fax (40) 38016629; e-mail info@rantzau.de; internet www.essberger.biz; f. 1924; Man. Dirs Dr E. VON RANTZAU, H. VON RANTZAU, HARTMUT LÜHR.

KG Fisser & v. Doornum GmbH & Co: Bernhard-Nocht-Str. 113, 20359 Hamburg; tel. (40) 441860; fax (40) 4108050; e-mail management@fissership.com; internet www.fissership.com; f. 1879; tramping services; Man. Dirs Dr MICHAEL FISSER, SVEN HEYMANN.

Oldenburg-Portugiesische Dampfschiffs-Rhederei GmbH & Co KG (OPDR): Kajen 10, 20459 Hamburg; tel. (40) 361580; fax (40) 364431; e-mail info@opdr.de; internet www.opdr.de; f. 1882; Gibraltar, Spain, Portugal, Madeira, North Africa, Canary Islands; Man. Dirs TILL OLE BARRELET, MARK WILKINSON.

Oldendorff Carriers GmbH & Co KG: Postfach 2135, 23509 Lübeck; Willy-Brandt-Allee 6, 235544 Lübeck; tel. (451) 15000; fax (451) 73522; internet www.oldendorff.com; fmrly Egon Oldendorff; Chair. HENNING OLDENDORFF; CEO PETER TWISS.

Peter Döhle Schiffahrts-KG: Elbchaussee 370, 22609 Hamburg; tel. (40) 381080; fax (40) 38108255; e-mail pd-info@doehle.de; internet www.doehle.de; f. 1956; shipbrokers, chartering agent, shipowners; Pres. JOCHEN DÖHLE.

Rhenus Maritime Services GmbH (RMS): Kraussstr. 1A, 47119 Duisburg; tel. (203) 8040; fax (203) 804330; e-mail info.rms@de.rhenus.com; internet www.rheinmaas.de; f. 1948; CEO THOMAS MAAßEN, THOMAS ULLRICH.

Sloman Neptun Schiffahrts-AG: Postfach 101469, 28014 Bremen; Langenstr. 44, 28195 Bremen; tel. (421) 17630; fax (421) 1763321; e-mail info@sloman-neptun.com; internet www.sloman-neptun.com; f. 1873; liner services from Northern Europe and Mediterranean to North Africa; gas carriers; agencies; Mans SVEN-MICHAEL EDYE, DIRK LOHMANN.

Walther Möller & Co: Gr. Elbstr. 14, 22767 Hamburg; tel. (40) 3803910; fax (40) 38039199; e-mail info@wmco.de; internet www.wmco.de; f. 1941; LARS PETZ.

Shipping Organizations

Verband Deutscher Reeder eV (German Shipowners' Association): Burchardstr. 24, 20095 Hamburg; Esplanade 6, 20354 Hamburg; tel. (40) 350970; fax (40) 35097211; e-mail vdr@reederverband.de; internet www.reederverband.de; f. 1907; Pres. MICHAEL BEHRENDT; CEO RALF NAGEL.

Zentralverband der Deutschen Seehafenbetriebe eV (Federal Association of German Seaport Operators): Am Sandtorkai 2, 20457 Hamburg; tel. (40) 3662034; fax (40) 366377; e-mail info@zds-seehaefen.de; internet www.zds-seehaefen.de; f. 1934; Chair. KLAUS DIETER PETERS; 199 mems.

CIVIL AVIATION

There are two international airports in the Berlin region (a third, Tempelhof airport, closed in October 2008) and further international airports at Dresden, Düsseldorf, Frankfurt, Hamburg, Hannover, Köln-Bonn, Leipzig, München and Stuttgart. Construction of a major new international airport at Schönefeld, south-east of Berlin, to be known as Berlin Brandenburg Willy Brandt Airport, commenced in 2007 but was subject to lengthy delays; the airport was scheduled to open in 2012, but at early 2014 no official opening date had yet been announced.

Air Berlin GmbH & Co Luftverkehrs KG: Saatwinkler Damm 42-43, 13627 Berlin; tel. (30) 34343434; fax (30) 41021003; e-mail serviceteam@airberlin.com; internet www.airberlin.com; f. 1979; offers flights to 170 destinations in Germany and some 40 other; CEO WOLFGANG PROCK-SCHAUER.

Condor Flugdienst GmbH: Condor Pl. 1, 60549 Frankfurt am Main; tel. (6107) 9390; fax (6107) 939440; internet www.condor.com; f. 1956; subsidiary of Thomas Cook AG; low-cost airline; Chair., Management Bd RALF TECKENTRUP; Chair., Supervisory Bd HEINER WILKENS.

Deutsche Lufthansa AG: Flughafen-Bereich West, 60546 Frankfurt a.M.; tel. (69) 6960; internet konzern.lufthansa.com; f. 1953; extensive worldwide network; Chair., Supervisory Bd WOLFGANG MAYRHUBER; Chair., Exec. Bd CHRISTOPH FRANZ.

Germania Fluggesellschaft: Riedemannweg 58, 13627 Berlin; tel. (30) 522808700; e-mail info@germania.aero; internet www.flygermania.de; f. 1979; operates as Germania; charter and scheduled flights.

Germanwings GmbH: Germanwings-Str. 2, 51147 Köln; tel. (900) 1919100; fax (220) 31027300; e-mail kontakt@germanwings.com; internet www.germanwings.com; f. 2002; low-cost airline, offers flights to 60 destinations within Europe; owned by Deutsche Lufthansa AG; CEO THOMAS WINKELMANN.

Lufthansa Cargo AG: Flughafen-Bereich West, Tor 25, Gebäude 451, 60546 Frankfurt a.M.; tel. (69) 6960; fax (69) 69691185; e-mail lhcargo@dlh.de; internet lufthansa-cargo.com; f. 1994; wholly owned subsidiary of Deutsche Lufthansa AG; freight-charter worldwide; Chair., Management Bd KARL ULRICH GARNADT; Chair., Supervisory Bd SIMONE MENNE.

Lufthansa CityLine GmbH: Flughafen Köln/Bonn, Waldstr. 247, 51147 Köln; tel. (2203) 5960; fax (2203) 596801; e-mail lh-cityline@dlh.de; internet www.lufthansacityline.com; scheduled services; subsidiary of Deutsche Lufthansa AG; Man. Dirs STEPHAN KLAR, KLAUS FROESE.

TUIfly GmbH: Flughafenstr. 10, Postfach 420240, 30855 Langenhagen; tel. (511) 97270; fax (511) 9727739; internet www.tuifly.com; f. 2007 following merger of Hapag-Lloyd Flug and Hapag-Lloyd Express; charter and scheduled passenger services; Exec. Chair. MICHAEL FRENZEL.

Tourism

Germany's tourist attractions include spas, summer and winter resorts, mountains, medieval towns and castles, and above all a variety of fascinating cities. The North and Baltic Sea coasts, the Rhine Valley, the Black Forest, the mountains of Thuringia, the Erzgebirge and Bavaria are the most popular areas. The total number of foreign visitors was 30.4m. in 2012; preliminary estimates for receipts from tourism in 2012 totalled €38,114m.

Deutsche Zentrale für Tourismus eV (DZT) (German National Tourist Board): Beethovenstr. 69, 60325 Frankfurt a.M.; tel. (69) 97464; fax (69) 97464233; e-mail info@germany.travel; internet www.germany.travel; f. 1948; CEO PETRA HEDORFER.

Defence

Germany is a member of the North Atlantic Treaty Organization (NATO). In October 2006 the Government endorsed a review of German defence policy, which contained proposals to redefine the primary role of the Bundeswehr from border defence to intervention in international conflicts. Under the proposals, the Bundeswehr would be expanded to allow for the deployment of up to 14,000 troops in five international missions simultaneously. As assessed at November 2013, Germany's armed forces totalled some 186,450. This included an army of 62,500, a navy of 16,000, an air force of 31,350, a joint support service of 44,900, a joint medical service of 19,650 and other staff of 12,050. There was also a reserve of 40,320 (army 15,350; navy 1,850; air force 4,900; joint support service 12,850; joint medical service 4,950; and MoD 420). In July 2011 conscription to the armed forces was suspended.

As assessed at November 2013, the USA had 50,500 troops stationed in Germany and the United Kingdom 16,500, while France maintained forces of 2,000 personnel. Canada had 226 troops stationed in Germany.

In November 2004 the European Union (EU) ministers responsible for defence agreed to create a number of 'battlegroups' (each comprising about 1,500 men), which could be deployed at short notice to crisis areas around the world. The EU battlegroups, two of which were to be ready for deployment at any one time, following a rotational schedule, reached full operational capacity from 1 January 2007.

Defence Expenditure: Budget estimated at €33,300m. for 2013.

Chief of Staff of the Bundeswehr: Lt-Gen. VOLKER WIEKER.

Education

The Basic Law (Grundgesetz) assigns control of the education system to the governments of the Länder and to the Schulamt (lower-level school supervisory authorities). There is, however, quite close co-operation to ensure a large degree of conformity in the system. Enrolment at pre-primary level included 91% of children in the relevant age-group in 2009. Compulsory schooling, which is free, begins at six years of age and continues for nine years (or 10 years in some Länder). Until the age of 18 years, all young people who do not continue to attend a full-time school must attend a part-time vocational school, the Berufsschule. Primary education lasts four years (six years in Berlin and Brandenburg). In 2011/12 enrolment at primary level included 98% of children in the relevant age-group. Attendance at elementary school (Grundschule) is obligatory for all children, after which their education continues at secondary school. Secondary education, which lasts for up to nine years, is divided into lower secondary, which is compulsory, between the ages of 10 and 15/16 years, and upper secondary, which lasts from 15/16 years of age to 18/19 years. At the end of the lower secondary cycle pupils who reach the required standard receive a leaving certificate, the Hauptabschluss or Mittlerer Schulabschluss. There are four principal types of secondary school: grammar school (Gymnasium), intermediate school (Realschule), high school (Hauptschule) and comprehensive school (Gesamtschule). At upper secondary, admission to the Gymnasiale Oberstuf (which has also been established in schools other than the Gymnasium) is dependent on high achievement in the lower secondary leaving certificate, and admission to vocational education at upper secondary level is also based on achievement at lower secondary level. The Abitur (grammar school leaving certificate) is a prerequisite for entry into university education. Post-secondary non-tertiary education takes place at vocational schools (Berufsfachschule), technical colleges (Fachoberschule), at evening classes or through a dual system of vocational school and training in a work placement. Tertiary education includes universities, technical colleges (Technische Hochschule), universities of applied sciences (Fachhochschule), teacher training colleges and colleges of art and music. According to preliminary official figures, 1,701,159 students were enrolled in universities and equivalent institutions in 2012/13, and a further 917,062 were enrolled in non-university higher education.

In 2011 government expenditure on education amounted to €110,400m. (equivalent to 9.4% of total government expenditure).

GHANA

Introductory Survey

LOCATION, CLIMATE, LANGUAGE, RELIGION, FLAG, CAPITAL

The Republic of Ghana lies on the west coast of Africa, with Côte d'Ivoire to the west and Togo to the east. It is bordered by Burkina Faso to the north. The climate is tropical, with temperatures generally between 21°C and 32°C (70°–90°F) and average annual rainfall of 2,000 mm (80 in) on the coast, decreasing inland. English is the official language, but there are 10 major national languages (each with more than 250,000 speakers), the most widely spoken being Akan, Ewe, Mole-Dagomba and Ga. Christians comprise an estimated 71.2% of the population, around 17.6% are Muslims and a sizeable minority follow traditional beliefs and customs. The national flag (proportions 2 by 3) has three equal horizontal stripes, of red, yellow and green, with a five-pointed black star in the centre of the yellow stripe. The capital is Accra.

CONTEMPORARY POLITICAL HISTORY

Historical Context

Ghana was formed as the result of a UN-supervised plebiscite in May 1956, when the British-administered section of Togoland, a UN Trust Territory, voted to join the Gold Coast, a British colony, in an independent state. Ghana was duly granted independence, within the Commonwealth, on 6 March 1957 and Dr Kwame Nkrumah, the Prime Minister of the former Gold Coast since 1952, became Prime Minister of the new state. Ghana became a republic on 1 July 1960, with Nkrumah as President. In 1964 the Convention People's Party, led by Nkrumah, was declared the sole authorized party.

In February 1966 Nkrumah was deposed in a military coup, the leaders of which established a governing National Liberation Council, led by Gen. Joseph Ankrah. In April 1969 Ankrah was replaced by Brig. (later Lt-Gen.) Akwasi Afrifa, and a new Constitution was introduced. Power was returned in October to an elected civilian Government, led by Dr Kofi Busia. However, in response to increasing economic and political difficulties, the army again seized power in January 1972, under the leadership of Lt-Col (later Gen.) Ignatius Acheampong. In July 1978 Acheampong was deposed by his deputy, Lt-Gen. Frederick Akuffo, who assumed power in a bloodless coup. Tensions within the army became evident in May 1979, when junior military officers staged an unsuccessful coup attempt. The alleged leader of the conspirators, Flight-Lt Jerry Rawlings, was imprisoned, but was subsequently released by other officers. On 4 June he and his associates successfully seized power, amid popular acclaim, established the Armed Forces Revolutionary Council, and introduced measures to eradicate corruption. Acheampong and Akuffo were among nine senior officers who were convicted on charges of corruption and executed.

Civilian rule was restored in September 1979; however, on 31 December 1981 Rawlings seized power for a second time, and established a governing Provisional National Defence Council (PNDC), with himself as Chairman. The PNDC's policies initially received strong support, but discontent with the regime and with the apparent ineffectiveness of its economic policies was reflected by a series of coup attempts.

Domestic Political Affairs

In July 1990, in response to pressure from Western aid donors to introduce further democratic reforms, the PNDC announced that a National Commission for Democracy (NCD) would organize a series of regional debates to consider Ghana's political and economic future. In December Rawlings announced proposals for the introduction of a constitution by the end of 1991; the PNDC was to consider recommendations presented by the NCD, and subsequently to convene a consultative body to determine constitutional reform.

In March 1991 the NCD presented a report on the democratic process, which recommended the election of an executive President for a fixed term, the establishment of a legislature and the creation of the post of Prime Minister. In May the PNDC endorsed the restoration of a multi-party system and approved the NCD's recommendations, although the formation of political associations remained prohibited. Later in May the Government announced the establishment of a 260-member Consultative Assembly, which was to present a draft constitution to the PNDC. The Government also appointed a nine-member committee of constitutional experts, who, in August, submitted a series of recommendations for constitutional reform, which included the establishment of a parliament and a council of state. It was proposed that the President, who would also be Commander-in-Chief of the Armed Forces, would be elected by universal suffrage for a four-year term of office, while the leader of the party that commanded a majority in the legislature would be appointed as Prime Minister. Later in August Rawlings announced that presidential and legislative elections were to take place in late 1992. In December 1991 the Government established an Interim National Electoral Commission (INEC), which was to be responsible for the demarcation of electoral regions and the supervision of elections and referendums. In March 1992 Rawlings announced a programme for transition to a multi-party system, which was to be completed on 7 January 1993.

At the end of March 1992 the Consultative Assembly approved the majority of the constitutional recommendations that had been submitted to the PNDC. However, the proposed creation of the post of Prime Minister was rejected by the Assembly; executive power was to be vested in the President, who would appoint a Vice-President. Opposition groups subsequently objected to a provision in the draft Constitution that members of the Government be exempt from prosecution for human rights violations allegedly committed during the PNDC's rule. At a national referendum on 28 April, however, the draft Constitution was approved by 92% of votes cast, with 43.7% of the electorate voting.

On 18 May 1992 the Government introduced legislation permitting the formation of political associations; political parties were henceforth required to apply to the INEC for legal recognition, although emergent parties were not permitted to use names or slogans associated with 21 former political organizations that remained proscribed. In June a number of political associations were established, many of which were identified with supporters of former President Nkrumah; six opposition movements, including the People's National Convention (PNC), were subsequently granted legal recognition. In the same month a coalition of pro-Government organizations, the National Democratic Congress (NDC), was formed to contest the forthcoming elections on behalf of the PNDC. However, an existing alliance of Rawlings' supporters, the Eagle Club, refused to join the NDC, and created its own political organization, the Eagle Party (later known as the EGLE—Every Ghanaian Living Everywhere—Party). In August the Government promulgated a new electoral code, which included a provision that in the event that no presidential candidate received more than 50% of votes cast the two candidates with the highest number of votes would contest a second round within 21 days. In September, in accordance with the new Constitution, Rawlings officially retired from the air force (while retaining the post of Commander-in-Chief of the Armed Forces in his capacity as Head of State) and accepted a nomination to contest the presidential election as a candidate of the NDC. The NDC, the EGLE Party and the National Convention Party (NCP) subsequently formed a pro-Government electoral coalition, the Progressive Alliance.

Rawlings was elected President on 3 November 1992, securing 58.3% of the votes cast. The four opposition parties that had presented candidates, the PNC, the New Patriotic Party (NPP), the National Independence Party (NIP) and the People's Heritage Party (PHP), claimed that there had been widespread electoral malpractice, although international observers maintained that, despite isolated irregularities, the election had been conducted fairly. Later in November these four parties withdrew from the forthcoming legislative elections (scheduled for 8 December), in protest at the Government's refusal to comply with their demands for the compilation of a new electoral register and the investigation of alleged misconduct during the presidential election. As a result, the legislative elections were postponed until late December and the nomination of new candidates permitted. In December the opposition claimed that many of its members had left Ghana, as a result of widespread intimidation by the Government. In the legislative elections, which took place on 29 December, the NDC secured 189 of the 200 seats in the Parliament, while the NCP obtained eight seats, the EGLE Party one seat and independent candidates the remaining two. According to official figures, however, only 29% of the electorate voted in the elections.

Establishment of the Fourth Republic

On 7 January 1993 Rawlings was sworn in as President of what was designated the Fourth Republic, the PNDC was dissolved and the new Parliament was inaugurated. In May a 17-member Council of Ministers was inaugurated. In December the PHP, the NIP and a faction of the PNC, all of which comprised supporters of ex-President Nkrumah, merged to form a new organization, the People's Convention Party (PCP).

Presidential and parliamentary elections were scheduled for December 1996. In May the Popular Party for Democracy and Development merged with the PCP, and in August the NPP and the PCP formed an electoral coalition, the Great Alliance; it was subsequently announced that John Kufuor, of the NPP, was to be the Great Alliance's presidential candidate. The NCP stated that it would support the NDC in the forthcoming elections, and in September the NDC nominated Rawlings as its presidential candidate. By 18 September, the official deadline for the nomination of candidates, only the Great Alliance, the Progressive Alliance (the NDC, the EGLE Party and the Democratic People's Party—DPP) and the PNC had succeeded in having their nomination papers accepted.

In the presidential election, which took place on 7 December 1996, Rawlings was re-elected, with 57.2% of the votes cast, while Kufuor secured 39.8%. In the parliamentary elections the NDC's representation was reduced to 133 seats, while the NPP won 60 seats, the PCP five and the PNC one seat. (The final seat was won by the NPP in a by-election in June 1997 following a legal dispute.) Despite opposition claims of malpractice, international observers declared that the elections had been conducted fairly, and an electoral turnout of 76.8% was reported. At the end of December the PCP announced that the Great Alliance had broken down. On 7 January 1997 Rawlings was sworn in as President.

In August 1998 the NCP and the PCP merged to form the Convention Party. An earlier attempt by the party to register as the Convention People's Party (CPP) had been rejected on the grounds that the use of the name of a proscribed party was unconstitutional. (This decision was reversed in 2000, however, when the Convention Party was permitted to adopt the name and logo of Nkrumah's former party.) In October 1998 the NPP nominated Kufuor to stand as its presidential candidate, in elections due to be held in 2000. At an NDC congress in December 1998 the position of 'Life Chairman' of the party was created for Rawlings, who confirmed that he would comply with the terms of the Constitution and not stand for a third term as President, and subsequently announced that the incumbent Vice-President, Prof. John Evans Atta Mills, was to contest the election on behalf of the NDC. In June 1999, owing to dissatisfaction within the NDC at the changes carried out at the party congress and at Rawlings' pronouncement regarding his successor, a group of party members broke away to form a new political organization, the National Reform Party (NRP). At the end of April Mills had been elected unopposed as the NDC presidential candidate.

An estimated 62% of the electorate voted in the elections, which took place on 7 December 2000. Observers from the Organization of African Unity (now the African Union, see p. 186) declared the polling to have been conducted in an orderly and fair manner. In the elections to the 200-seat Parliament the NPP won 100 seats, while the NDC obtained 92 seats, the PNC three, the CPP one, and independent candidates four. The NPP thus became the largest parliamentary party for the first time, gaining an unprecedented degree of support in rural areas. In the presidential election Kufuor won 48.2% of the valid votes cast, and Mills 44.5%, thus necessitating a second round, which proceeded on 28 December; Kufuor was elected to the presidency, with 56.9% of the valid votes cast.

The Kufuor presidency

On 7 January 2001 Kufuor was inaugurated as President and subsequently appointed a new Government, which notably included one member from each of the CPP, the NRP and the PNC. Kufuor ordered the suspension of the heads of six public sector financial institutions, to facilitate an investigation into allegations of embezzlement, while in February he announced that a National Reconciliation Commission (NRC) was to be established to investigate allegations of human rights abuses and other violations committed by state representatives. The NRC was officially launched in May and commenced public hearings in January 2003, by which time some 2,800 complaints had been received, mostly relating to events that took place under military regimes.

In March 2002 the Minister of the Interior and the Minister for the Northern Region both resigned, following the deaths of some 40 people during clashes between the Mamprusi and Kusasi ethnic groups in the north of Ghana, which had been prompted by the abduction and murder of Ya-na Yakuba Andani, king of the Dagomba, in Yendi. A commission of inquiry was established, headed by traditional leaders, and a state of emergency was declared. The state of emergency ended in the majority of districts in October 2003, but remained in place in Tamale municipality and Yendi district until August 2004. Unrest, however, continued during 2005. Renewed violence broke out in mid-2009, in which three people were killed. A curfew was established in an attempt to curtail the fighting.

Meanwhile, in April 2002 the election of Dr Obed Asamoah as the new Chairman of the NDC created divisions within the party between supporters of Asamoah and Rawlings. In September a number of accusations of financial impropriety were made against Rawlings and his former associates. In November, following the arrest of three NDC deputies on charges of fraud and the reckless loss of state revenues, the NDC boycotted the Parliament in protest; this followed an earlier boycott over a controversial US $1,000m. development loan. In February 2004 Rawlings appeared before the NRC to answer questions about the murders of three high court judges and a retired military officer in 1982, and about extrajudicial military killings in 1984. In July 2004 the NRC ended its hearings, prior to the submission of its report in October, which recommended that victims of state brutality receive compensation and that state institutions, including the security services, be reformed.

Parliamentary and presidential elections were held on 7 December 2004. Kufuor, representing the NPP, was declared the winner of the presidential election after securing 52.4% of the valid votes cast, while Mills (the NDC's candidate) won 44.6%. In the elections to the enlarged Parliament the NPP won 128 of the 230 seats, with 55.6% of the vote, while the NDC took 94 seats, the PNC four and the CPP three. The new Parliament was inaugurated on 7 January 2005. On the same day Kufuor was sworn in as President, following which he reorganized the Government. Kufuor effected a further cabinet reorganization in April 2006, while in October he alleged that former President Rawlings had been seeking foreign support in order to overthrow the Government.

The Mills presidency

With Kufuor ineligible for re-election to the presidency, Nana Addo Dankwa Akufo-Addo, who had held the foreign affairs portfolio until July 2007, was to represent the NPP, while Mills was again selected as the candidate of the NDC. As preparations for the presidential and legislative elections began in late August 2008 violence threatened to undermine the conduct of the ballot. Conflict at a political rally, believed to be a result of continued unrest over the murder of Andani in Dagomba in 2002, left at least three people dead and many more injured. The announcement by the Electoral Commission (EC) that the electoral register could contain as many as 1m. false names further heightened tensions. Nevertheless, voting proceeded in a largely peaceful atmosphere. In the first round of the presidential election, on 7 December 2008, Akufo-Addo won 49.1% of the votes cast while Mills secured 47.9%. As no candidate had secured more than 50% of the valid votes cast, Mills and Akufo-Addo contested a second round of voting, held on 28 December, at which Mills emerged the winner with some 50.2% of votes cast. He was inaugurated as President on 7 January 2009. Following legislative elections, held concurrently with the first round of the presidential election, the NDC became the largest party in the Parliament, with 113 of the 230 seats, while the NPP's representation was reduced to 109 seats; the PNC took two seats and the CPP one seat.

The Minister of Health, Dr George Sepa Yankey, and the Minister of State at the Presidency, Seidu Amadu, resigned in October 2009 following allegations that they had accepted bribes from a British construction company, which had in the previous month been ordered by a British court to pay fines of more than

US $7m. for offering illegal payments to officials in Ghana in the 1990s; five other senior Ghanaian officials were also implicated in the alleged corruption. (However, following a police investigation, all seven officials were exonerated in June 2011.) Mills carried out a reorganization of the Government in January 2010 and, again, in January 2011.

In January 2010 President Mills inaugurated a Constitution Review Commission (CRC), which was charged with recommending changes to the 1992 Constitution for approval at a referendum. Community and district constitutional review consultations, with the aim of soliciting public contributions to the work of the CRC, began in April. It was reported that public opinion strongly favoured restructuring of the principal state organs, and in particular a redistribution and separation of power between the presidential executive and the legislature. In December 2011 Mills received the CRC's final report, which recommended, *inter alia*, restricting the President's power of appointment, strengthening Parliament and the independence of the judiciary, and greater decentralization to local government. The report also advocated the creation of a National Development Planning Commission, the abrogation of the death penalty and, controversially, the preservation of the constitutional clauses granting former PNDC members immunity from prosecution. The Government established an Implementation Committee in October 2012 to move forward with the majority of the CRC's recommendations.

Mills' authority had been undermined throughout his presidency by the relentless, public criticism of his administration by former President Rawlings. The divisions within the NDC culminated in July 2011, when Rawlings' wife, Nana Konadu Agyeman Rawlings, stood against Mills in a primary election to select the ruling party's 2012 presidential candidate. In the event, Mills secured the NDC presidential nomination after winning 97% of the votes cast, reinforcing his control over the party. (Nana Rawlings resigned from the NDC in October 2012 and was promptly named as the presidential nominee of the recently formed National Democratic Party; however, she failed to meet the deadline for submission of the relevant paperwork and her candidature was consequently rejected by the EC.)

In accordance with a Supreme Court judgment, Mills declared in November 2011 that prisoners would be entitled to vote in the 2012 presidential and legislative elections and that special measures to facilitate this would be effected.

Mills reorganized the Cabinet in January 2012, notably appointing Benjamin Kunbuor (hitherto Minister of the Interior) as Attorney-General and Minister of Justice. Martin Amidu had been dismissed from these two posts earlier that month after making public remarks about alleged government corruption.

Recent developments: Mahama becomes President

President Mills died on 24 July 2012 after suffering a stroke. Vice-President John Dramani Mahama was duly sworn in as his successor later that day, while Kwesi Bekoe Amissah-Arthur subsequently assumed the vice-presidency. This constitutional transfer of power—still a relatively uncommon occurrence in West Africa—earned Ghana international plaudits and underlined the strength of the country's maturing democracy. In August Mahama was confirmed as the NDC's candidate in the approaching presidential poll.

Mahama secured a first round victory in the presidential election, held on 7 December 2012, winning 50.7% of the vote compared with 47.7% for Akufo-Addo of the NPP. In several constituencies, owing to technical problems with new biometric equipment, voting also took place on the following day. The rate of participation by the electorate was approximately 80%. Although international observers expressed satisfaction with the conduct of the election, the NPP denounced the results as fraudulent and submitted an appeal to the Supreme Court. NPP supporters organized protests in Accra and Kumasi, some of which turned violent. In the concurrent legislative elections, the NDC gained control of 148 parliamentary seats, while the NPP obtained 123, independent candidates three and the PNC one. (A bill had been adopted in October to increase the number of seats in Parliament from 230 to 275.) Mahama was sworn in as President on 7 January 2013; with the notable exception of former President Kufuor, the ceremony was boycotted by members of the NPP. Later that month Mahama announced his new Cabinet, which included Kwesi Ahwoi as Minister of the Interior, Seth Terpker as Minister of Finance and Economic Planning, Hannah Tetteh as Minister of Foreign Affairs and Regional Integration, and Marietta Brew Appiah-Oppong as Attorney-General and Minister of Justice. The NPP ended its boycott of parliamentary proceedings in March. After protracted consideration, the Supreme Court on 29 August rejected the NPP's legal challenge and upheld Mahama's victory in the 2012 presidential election.

Foreign Affairs

Ghana was in 2013 the fifth largest African contributing nation to UN peacekeeping operations and the 10th largest of all peacekeeping contributing nations. At February 2014 Ghana contributed 2,864 personnel to UN peacekeeping missions worldwide. At that time, Ghana notably deployed sizeable contingents in the Democratic Republic of the Congo (DRC), the Darfur region of Sudan, Liberia, Mali, South Sudan and Côte d'Ivoire, and outside Africa contributed 870 troops to the UN Interim Force in Lebanon.

In October 1992 Ghana denied claims that it was implicated in subversive activity by Togolese dissidents based in Ghana and in March 1993 the Rawlings administration further denied allegations, made by the Togolese Government, of Ghanaian complicity in an armed attack on the residence of Togo's President, Gen. Gnassingbé Eyadéma. In January 1994 relations with Togo deteriorated further, following an attempt to overthrow the Togolese Government, which the Togolese authorities claimed had been staged by armed dissidents based in Ghana. The Ghanaian chargé d'affaires in Togo was arrested, and Togolese forces killed 12 Ghanaians and attacked a customs post and several villages near the border. Ghana, however, denied any involvement in the coup attempt, and threatened to retaliate against further acts of aggression. Later that year, however, relations improved, and in November full diplomatic links were formally restored. In December Togo's border with Ghana (which had been closed in January 1994) was reopened. Following the death of Eyadéma in early 2005 and the subsequent unrest in Togo precipitated by the assumption of power by Eyadéma's son, Faure Gnassingbé, some 15,000 Togolese refugees were reported to have registered in Ghana. In August 2009 President Gnassingbé visited Ghana for meetings with President Mills and senior security officials to discuss improved border security and the control of cross-border crime and drugs- and people-trafficking. In May 2010 it was reported that some 3,500 refugees had fled from Ghana into northern Togo, as a result of renewed ethnic conflict and land disputes in the north of the country.

During the conflict in Liberia, which commenced in December 1989, Ghana contributed troops to the Monitoring Group (ECOMOG) of the Economic Community of West African States (ECOWAS, see p. 260). As Chairman of the ECOWAS Conference of Heads of State and Government, Rawlings mediated negotiations between the warring Liberian factions in the mid-1990s, and by mid-1997 some 17,000 Liberian refugees had arrived in Ghana. In 2003 Ghana also hosted peace negotiations concerning Liberia, and from September contributed troops to the ECOWAS Mission in Liberia (ECOMIL). In October the Ghanaian troops were transferred to a longer-term UN stabilization force, the UN Mission in Liberia (UNMIL, see p. 87), which replaced ECOMIL, with a mandate to support the implementation of a comprehensive peace agreement in that country. In late 2005 there were some 40,000 Liberian refugees registered in Ghana, a number of whom were in the process of repatriation, and by the end of 2010 the number of Liberian refugees remaining in Ghana was 11,585. Due to the improving security climate in Liberia, in June 2012 the Ghanaian Government revoked the refugee status that had been granted to Liberians who had fled the conflict in their country. Former refugees were required to return to Liberia or apply for residency in Ghana. Meanwhile, in February 2010 the Liberian President, Ellen Johnson Sirleaf, made a two-day visit to Ghana following which it was agreed to reactivate the Ghana-Liberia Permanent Joint Commission for Co-operation. Ghana contributed 745 personnel to UNMIL at February 2014.

In June 1997 Ghana, Côte d'Ivoire, Guinea and Nigeria formed the 'committee of four', which was established by ECOWAS to monitor the situation in Sierra Leone, following the staging of a military coup; troops were dispatched to participate in a peacekeeping force. Following the reinstatement of the democratically elected Government in March, ECOMOG units remained in the country and continued to launch attacks against rebel forces, which still retained control of a number of areas. In December 2005 the Ghanaian troops participating in the UN Mission in Sierra Leone (UNAMSIL) returned to Ghana on the termination of the peacekeeping mission.

In November 2001 some 400 Ghanaian troops were dispatched to participate in peacekeeping duties in the DRC, under the auspices of the UN Mission in the Democratic Republic of the Congo (MONUC, see p. 91). Ghana continued to participate in the UN peacekeeping contingent (which had been reconstituted as the UN Organization Stabilization Mission in the Democratic Republic of the Congo—MONUSCO), contributing 488 personnel at February 2014.

After the outbreak of an armed rebellion in Côte d'Ivoire in September 2002, Ghana denied accusations by the Ivorian rebels that it had intervened in support of President Laurent Gbagbo. In October Ghana pledged to provide troops to an ECOWAS military mission in Côte d'Ivoire (ECOMICI), and the first contingent of the 266 Ghanaian soldiers to be contributed was deployed in February 2003. Further ECOWAS summit meetings on Côte d'Ivoire took place in Accra in March and November 2003. Ghanaian troops in Côte d'Ivoire were to be transferred to a UN Operation in Côte d'Ivoire (UNOCI, see p. 90), which was deployed from April 2004. A conference held in Accra in August 2004 led to the signing of a peace accord between rival Ivorian factions, Accra III. At February 2014 194 Ghanaian personnel were deployed in Côte d'Ivoire as part of UNOCI. Political instability and factional violence in Côte d'Ivoire following a disputed presidential election in late 2010 precipitated the inflow of large numbers of Ivorian refugees into Ghana (estimated to total 18,000 by October 2011). Alassane Ouattara, who had been sworn in as the new Ivorian President in May 2011 after months of fighting, visited Ghana in October and pressured Mills to extradite Ivorian refugees accused of committing human rights abuses during the post-election turmoil. A repatriation accord was also signed by Ghana, Côte d'Ivoire and the office of the UN High Commissioner for Refugees (UNHCR), to facilitate the voluntary return of Ivorian refugees, while former fighters were to be resettled in other countries. Côte d'Ivoire closed its border with Ghana in September 2012 as a result of an apparent cross-border raid that had targeted Ivorian troops. The authorities in Côte d'Ivoire suspected that the attack had been perpetrated by pro-Gbagbo militants sheltering in Ghana. Indeed, a UN report, leaked in the following month, alleged that a regional network of Gbagbo-aligned combatants had established its headquarters in Ghana and was orchestrating destabilizing activities in Côte d'Ivoire. The Ivorian Government reopened the border to air traffic in late September, and the land and sea frontiers were normalized in October following the implementation of additional border security measures. A number of Gbagbo loyalists were arrested in Ghana during 2012, and the Ghanaian authorities extradited Charles Blé Goude, a former member of Gbagbo's Government who was accused of committing war crimes, to Côte d'Ivoire in January 2013. Bilateral relations eased following the death of former Ghanaian President John Atta Mills in 2012, who had been perceived to favour Gbagbo. In February 2014 representatives from Ghana and Côte d'Ivoire resumed talks aimed at resolving a long-standing dispute over the maritime boundary between the two countries. According to UNHCR estimates, 9,567 Ivorian refugees were present in Ghana at February 2014.

Although in March 2011 the United Kingdom pledged to increase annual aid to Ghana to £100m. by 2014/15 (up from £85m. in 2010/11), British Prime Minister David Cameron caused controversy in Ghana in late 2011 by indicating that aid would be reduced to nations that failed to reform discriminatory laws against homosexuals. President Mills firmly rejected any liberalization of Ghana's conservative laws regarding homosexuality and criticized Cameron for encroaching on domestic Ghanaian affairs.

CONSTITUTION AND GOVERNMENT

Under the terms of the Constitution, which was approved by national referendum on 28 April 1992, Ghana has a multi-party political system. Executive power is vested in the President, who is the Head of State and Commander-in-Chief of the Armed Forces. The President is elected by direct universal suffrage for a maximum of two four-year terms of office. Legislative power is vested in a 275-member unicameral Parliament, which is elected by direct universal suffrage for a four-year term. The President appoints a Vice-President, and nominates a Council of Ministers, subject to approval by the Parliament. The Constitution also provides for a 25-member Council of State, principally comprising regional representatives and presidential nominees, and a 20-member National Security Council, chaired by the Vice-President, which act as advisory bodies to the President.

Ghana has 10 regions, each headed by a Regional Minister, who is assisted by a regional co-ordinating council. The regions constitute 216 districts, each with an Assembly (either Metropolitan, Municipal or District), which is headed by a Chief Executive (either Metropolitan, Municipal or District). Regional colleges, which comprise representatives selected by the Metropolitan, Municipal and District Assemblies and by regional Houses of Chiefs, elect a number of representatives to the Council of State.

REGIONAL AND INTERNATIONAL CO-OPERATION

Ghana is a member of the African Union (see p. 186) and of the Economic Community of West African States (ECOWAS, see p. 260).

Ghana became a member of the UN in 1957 and was admitted to the World Trade Organization (WTO, see p. 434) in 1995. Ghana also participates in the Group of 77 (G77, see p. 451) developing countries. Ghana is also a member of the International Cocoa Organization (ICCO, see p. 446), and of the International Coffee Organization (ICO, see p. 446). In 2004 Ghana became a full member of the Community of Sahel-Saharan States (see p. 450).

ECONOMIC AFFAIRS

In 2012, according to estimates by the World Bank, Ghana's gross national income (GNI), measured at average 2010–12 prices, was US $39,423m., equivalent to $1,550 per head (or $1,940 on an international purchasing-power parity basis). During 2003–12, it was estimated, the population increased at an average annual rate of 2.5%, while gross domestic product (GDP) per head grew, in real terms, by an average of 4.9% per year. Overall GDP increased at an average annual rate of 7.5% in 2003–12; growth in 2012 was 7.9%.

Agriculture (including forestry and fishing) contributed 22.7% of GDP in 2012. An estimated 53.5% of the economically active population was employed in the sector at mid-2014, according to FAO. The principal cash crop is cocoa beans, contributing 10.5% of total exports in 2012. Ghana is the world's second largest producer after Côte d'Ivoire, and, according to FAO, 879,300 metric tons of cocoa beans were harvested in 2012. Coffee, bananas, cassava, oil palm, coconuts, limes, kola nuts and shea-nuts (karité nuts) are also produced. The development of the palm oil and cassava sectors is currently being undertaken. Timber production is also important, with the forestry sector accounting for 2.5% of GDP in 2012, and cork and wood, and manufactures thereof, contributing 2.0% of total export earnings in that year. In 2009 Ghana signed a Voluntary Partnership Agreement on Forest Law Enhancement, Governance and Trade with the European Union (EU, see p. 273), which commits each party to trade only in verified legal timber and timber products. Fishing satisfies more than three-quarters of domestic requirements, and contributed 1.6% of GDP in 2012. During 2007–12, according to official figures, agricultural GDP increased at an average annual rate of 4.4%; however, growth in 2012 was only 1.4%.

Industry (including mining, manufacturing, construction and power) contributed 27.3% of GDP in 2012. Industrial GDP increased at an average annual rate of 14.3% in 2007–12; growth in 2011 was an impressive 41.2%, moderating to 7.0% in 2012.

Mining contributed 8.8% of GDP in 2012. Gold and diamonds are the major minerals exported (in 2011 gold production was 82,993 kg), although Ghana also exploits large reserves of bauxite and manganese ore. The Government is attempting to increase exploitation of salt, bauxite and clay. The GDP of the mining sector increased by an average of 33.1% per year in 2007–12; mining GDP grew by a massive 206.7% in 2011, mostly owing to the commencement of crude petroleum production, before decelerating to 5.0% in 2012.

Manufacturing contributed 6.9% of GDP in 2012. The most important sectors are food processing, textiles, vehicles, cement, paper, chemicals and petroleum. Manufacturing GDP increased at an average annual rate of 6.2% in 2007–12; sectoral growth reached 17.0% in 2011 before slowing down to 5.0% in 2012.

The construction sector contributed 10.5% of GDP in 2012. The GDP of the sector increased at an average annual rate of 15.2% in 2007–12; growth was 11.2% in 2012.

According to figures published by the World Bank, some 67.5% of Ghana's production of electricity was from hydroelectric power in 2011, with the Akosombo and Kpong plants being the major sources, and 24.3% from natural gas. Electricity is exported to Benin and Togo. The Government is seeking to double the country's electricity generation capacity, primarily through thermal and renewable energy sources. In 2004 the World

Bank agreed to finance the construction of the West African Gas Pipeline, which was to supply natural gas from Nigeria to Ghana, Benin and Togo; the first gas was delivered in 2010. Imports of petroleum comprised 2.5% of the total value of merchandise imports in 2012.

The services sector contributed 50.0% of GDP in 2012. The GDP of the services sector increased at an average annual rate of 8.6% in 2007–12; growth in 2012 was 10.2%.

In 2012, according to IMF figures, Ghana recorded a visible merchandise trade deficit of US $4,219.8m, and there was a deficit of $4,777.5m. on the current account of the balance of payments. In 2012 the principal source of imports was the People's Republic of China (17.2%); other major sources were the USA, the United Kingdom and Belgium. South Africa was the principal market for exports (taking 24.2% of the total) in that year; other important purchasers were India, the UAE, France (including Monaco), Italy and Switzerland-Liechtenstein. The principal exports in 2012 were gold (which accounted for 37.9% of total export earnings), crude petroleum, and Brazil nuts, cashew nuts and coconuts. The principal imports in 2012 were machinery, mechanical appliances and electrical equipment; vehicles, aircraft, vessels and associated transport equipment; iron and steel, and articles thereof; and chemicals and related products.

Ghana's overall budget deficit for 2012 was 4,276.3m. Ghana cedis. General government gross debt was 26,169m. Ghana cedis in 2011, equivalent to 43.8% of GDP. Ghana's total external debt amounted to US $11,289m. at the end of 2011, of which $7,402m. was public and publicly guaranteed debt. In that year the cost of debt-servicing long-term public and publicly guaranteed debt and repayments to the IMF was equivalent to 2.4% of the value of exports of goods, services and income (excluding workers' remittances). In 2003–12 the average annual rate of inflation was 13.3%. Consumer prices increased by 9.2% in 2012. In 2010 around 5.8% of the total labour force was unemployed in Ghana.

Although Ghana's economy made steady progress following the transfer to civilian rule in 1992, it remained vulnerable to unfavourable weather conditions, while continued reliance on commodity exports increased the country's exposure to the vagaries of the global market. In September 2009 the Government announced a series of structural reforms to counter the adverse effects of the international economic downturn. Economic growth recovered, to 8.0%, in 2010, partly owing to rises both in volumes and prices of gold and cocoa. Real GDP expanded by 15.0% in 2011. This dramatic increase in growth, one of the highest rates worldwide, was driven predominantly by petroleum production, which had commenced in December 2010. GDP growth in 2011 was also fuelled by gold and cocoa exports, the international prices of which had remained consistently high, while the construction and service sectors registered renewed economic activity. In mid-2011 Ghana achieved the World Bank per head income threshold for classification as a lower middle income country, resulting in a decrease in funding commitments from many donors and a growing reliance on non-concessional financing. Structural factors relating to economic management began to complicate the country's development from 2012. The current account deficit reached 12.2% of GDP in that year as a result of pre-election expenditure, with the public sector wage bill rising by 47% and the provision of large-scale energy subsidies. In June 2013 the Government partially removed subsidies for petroleum products and from October implemented a regular price adjustment regime for utilities. Despite these measures, the current account deficit expanded to 13.0% of GDP in 2013, placing further pressure on international reserves. The consequent weakening of the domestic currency, together with large administered price increases, contributed to a rise in inflation to 13.5% by the end of the year. Meanwhile, the price of gold, Ghana's most valuable export, declined by 28% in 2013. Based on data for the first nine months of the year, the IMF predicted that GDP would expand by 5.5% in 2013. Furthermore, the Fund forecast that growth momentum would continue to weaken and that inflationary pressures would persist in 2014. The Government responded by freezing public sector wages and recruitment, coupled with additional tax increases, including raising value-added tax from 12.5% to 15.0%. The risk that such measures could restrict growth, meant that the economy would remain overly reliant on and vulnerable to international commodity prices in the mean time. In early 2014 President Mahama announced plans to focus on efforts to add value to the country's exports and to boost local food production. As in other emerging markets, Ghana experienced considerable currency depreciation in early 2014 as a result of adjustments to the US dollar, to which the central bank responded by imposing capital controls, restricting trade transactions to the national currency and raising the interest rate. Consequently, the cedi fell to its lowest value in 20 years against the dollar, which, in turn, negatively affected foreign direct investment.

PUBLIC HOLIDAYS

2015: 1 January (New Year's Day), 6 March (Independence Day), 3–6 April (Easter), 1 May (Labour Day), 25 May (African Union Day), 1 July (Republic Day), 17 July* (Eid-al-Fitr, end of Ramadan), 21 September (Founder's Day), 23 September* (Eid-al-Adha, Feast of the Sacrifice), 4 December (National Farmers' Day), 25–26 December (Christmas).

* These holidays are dependent on the Islamic lunar calendar and may vary by one or two days from the dates given.

Statistical Survey

Source (except where otherwise stated): Ghana Statistical Service, POB GP1098, Accra; tel. (30) 2671732; fax (30) 2671731; internet www.statsghana.gov.gh

Area and Population

AREA, POPULATION AND DENSITY

Area (sq km)	238,533*
Population (census results)	
26 March 2000	18,912,079
26 September 2010	
Males	12,024,845
Females	12,633,978
Total	24,658,823
Population (UN estimates at mid-year)†	
2012	25,366,464
2013	25,904,600
2014	26,442,176
Density (per sq km) at mid-2014	110.9

* 92,098 sq miles.

† Source: UN, *World Population Prospects: The 2012 Revision*; estimates not adjusted to take account of the results of the 2010 census.

POPULATION BY AGE AND SEX
(UN estimates at mid-2014)

	Males	Females	Total
0–14	5,163,396	4,948,138	10,111,534
15–64	7,553,185	7,863,823	15,417,008
65 and over	409,080	504,554	913,634
Total	13,125,661	13,316,515	26,442,176

Source: UN, *World Population Prospects: The 2012 Revision*.

REGIONS
(population at 2010 census)

Region	Area (sq km)	Population	Density (per sq km)	Capital
Ashanti	24,389	4,780,380	196.0	Kumasi
Brong Ahafo	39,557	2,310,983	58.4	Sunyani
Central	9,826	2,201,863	224.1	Cape Coast
Eastern	19,323	2,633,154	136.3	Koforidua
Greater Accra	3,245	4,010,054	1,235.8	Accra
Northern	70,384	2,479,461	35.2	Tamale
Upper East	8,842	1,046,545	118.4	Bolgatanga
Upper West	18,476	702,110	38.0	Wa
Volta	20,570	2,118,252	103.0	Ho
Western	23,921	2,376,021	99.3	Takoradi
Total	238,533	24,658,823	103.4	

PRINCIPAL TOWNS
(population at 2010 census)

Kumasi	2,035,064	Tema	402,637
Accra (capital)	1,848,614	Tamale	371,351
Sekondi-Takoradi	559,548	Cape Coast	169,894

Mid-2011 (incl. suburbs, UN estimate): Accra 2,573,220 (Source: UN, *World Urbanization Prospects: The 2011 Revision*).

BIRTHS AND DEATHS
(annual averages, UN estimates)

	1995–2000	2000–05	2005–10
Birth rate (per 1,000)	35.1	34.3	33.1
Death rate (per 1,000)	10.6	10.5	9.6

Source: UN, *World Population Prospects: The 2012 Revision*.

Life expectancy (years at birth): 60.8 (males 59.9; females 61.7) in 2011 (Source: World Bank, World Development Indicators database).

ECONOMICALLY ACTIVE POPULATION
(persons aged 15 years and over at 2010 census)

	Males	Females	Total
Agriculture, hunting, forestry and fishing	2,303,140	2,008,595	4,311,735
Mining and quarrying	92,353	21,852	114,205
Manufacturing	449,826	670,296	1,120,122
Electricity, gas and water	27,690	13,141	40,831
Construction	308,527	8,998	317,525
Trade, restaurants and hotels	687,439	1,836,662	2,524,101
Transport, storage and communications	380,946	29,672	410,618
Financing, insurance, real estate and business services	158,493	81,175	239,668
Public administration and defence	111,618	42,012	153,630
Education	228,400	177,800	406,200
Health and social services	54,835	69,556	124,391
Household activities	33,626	44,307	77,933
Activities of extra-territorial organizations	2,015	917	2,932
Other services	217,940	311,847	529,787
Total employed	5,056,848	5,316,830	10,373,678
Unemployed	283,346	349,648	632,994
Total labour force	5,340,194	5,666,478	11,006,672

Mid-2014 (estimates in '000): Agriculture, etc. 6,724; Total labour force 12,566 (Source: FAO).

Health and Welfare

KEY INDICATORS

Total fertility rate (children per woman, 2011)	4.1
Under-5 mortality rate (per 1,000 live births, 2011)	78
HIV/AIDS (% of persons aged 15–49, 2012)	1.4
Physicians (per 1,000 head, 2009)	0.1
Hospital beds (per 1,000 head, 2011)	0.9
Health expenditure (2010): US $ per head (PPP)	85
Health expenditure (2010): % of GDP	5.2
Health expenditure (2010): public (% of total)	58.2
Access to water (% of persons, 2011)	86
Access to sanitation (% of persons, 2011)	14
Total carbon dioxide emissions ('000 metric tons, 2010)	8,998.8
Carbon dioxide emissions per head (metric tons, 2010)	0.4
Human Development Index (2012): ranking	135
Human Development Index (2012): value	0.558

For sources and definitions, see explanatory note on p. vi.

Agriculture

PRINCIPAL CROPS
('000 metric tons)

	2010	2011	2012
Rice, paddy	491.6	464.0	481.1
Maize	1,871.7	1,684.0	1,949.9
Millet	219.0	183.9	179.7
Sorghum	324.4	287.1	280.0
Sweet potatoes*	120.0	130.0	135.0
Cassava (Manioc)	13,504.1	14,240.9	14,547.3
Taro (Cocoyam)	1,354.8	1,299.6	1,270.3
Yams	5,960.5	6,295.5	6,638.9
Sugar cane*	145.0	145.0	148.0
Groundnuts, with shell	530.9	465.1	475.1
Coconuts	292.0†	292.0†	305.0*
Oil palm fruit	2,004.3	2,004.3*	1,900.0*
Tomatoes	318.5	320.5	321.0
Chillies and peppers, green	90.0	95.0	110.0
Onions, dry	100.0	120.0	130.0
Beans, green*	27.6	28.0	30.0
Okra	50.0	55.0	60.0
Bananas	70.0	75.0	80.0
Plantains	3,537.7	3,619.8	3,556.5
Oranges	580.0	600.0	625.0
Lemons and limes*	46.0	45.0	46.0
Pineapples	50.0†	55.0†	56.0*
Cocoa beans	632.0	700.0	879.3
Natural rubber	20.2	20.2	20.2

* FAO estimate(s).
† Unofficial figure.

Aggregate production ('000 metric tons, may include official, semi-official or estimated data): Total cereals 2,907 in 2010, 2,619 in 2011, 2,891 in 2012; Total roots and tubers 20,940 in 2010, 21,966 in 2011, 22,592 in 2012; Total vegetables (incl. melons) 636 in 2010, 672 in 2011, 709 in 2012; Total fruits (excl. melons) 4,483 in 2010, 4,603 in 2011, 4,580 in 2012.

Source: FAO.

LIVESTOCK
('000 head, year ending September)

	2010	2011	2012
Horses	2.7	2.7*	2.7*
Asses*	14.3	14.3	14.4
Cattle	1,454	1,498	1,543
Pigs	536	568	602
Sheep	3,759	3,887	4,019
Goats	4,855	5,137	5,435
Chickens	47,752	52,575	57,885

* FAO estimate(s).

Source: FAO.

LIVESTOCK PRODUCTS
('000 metric tons)

	2010	2011	2012
Cattle meat	20.0	20.6	21.2
Sheep meat	16.9	17.5	18.1
Goat meat	19.2	20.3	21.2
Pig meat	18.0	19.1	20.2
Chicken meat	37.2	41.0	46.3
Game meat*	74.1	74.3	74.3
Cows' milk*	38.7	39.0	41.0
Hen eggs*	36.7	39.8	40.0

* FAO estimates.

Source: FAO.

Forestry

ROUNDWOOD REMOVALS
('000 cubic metres, excl. bark)

	2010	2011	2012
Sawlogs, veneer logs and logs for sleepers	1,250	1,289	1,282
Fuel wood*	37,791	38,985	40,203
Total	39,041	40,274	41,485

* FAO estimates.

Source: FAO.

SAWNWOOD PRODUCTION
('000 cubic metres, incl. railway sleepers)

	2010	2011	2012
Total (all broadleaved)*	513	515	519

* Unofficial figures.

Source: FAO.

Fishing

('000 metric tons, live weight)

	2009	2010	2011
Capture*	321.8	351.2	333.5
Freshwater fishes*	88.7	90.0	90.0
Bigeye grunt	17.4	13.7	8.1
Red pandora	3.9	4.8	4.3
Round sardinella	19.5	36.7	21.5
Madeiran sardinella	6.3	11.3	10.7
European anchovy	54.4	45.1	51.2
Skipjack tuna	36.1	53.8	50.4
Yellowfin tuna	18.4	12.5	10.8
Bigeye tuna	10.6	6.8	4.4
Atlantic bumper	2.6	7.5	10.9
Aquaculture*	7.2	10.2	19.0
Total catch*	329.0	361.4	352.6

* FAO estimates.

Source: FAO.

Mining

('000 metric tons unless otherwise indicated)

	2009	2010	2011
Bauxite	490	595	408
Manganese ore: gross weight	882	1,529	1,729
Manganese ore: metal content	248	426	484*
Silver (kg)†	3,928	3,313	3,088
Gold (kg)‡	79,883	76,332	82,993
Salt (unrefined)	250	85	100*
Diamonds ('000 carats)	376	334	302

* Estimated figure.

† Silver content of exported doré.

‡ Gold content of ores and concentrates, excluding smuggled or undocumented output.

Crude petroleum: 400,000 barrels in 2004.

Source: US Geological Survey.

Industry

SELECTED PRODUCTS
('000 metric tons unless otherwise indicated)

	2007	2008	2009
Groundnut oil*	32.4	63.4	65.5
Coconut oil†	7.0	7.0	7.0
Palm oil†	122.0	128.0	130.0
Palm kernel oil†	16.0	16.0	16.0
Beer of barley*	129.5	138.5	142.0
Gasoline (petrol)	493	391	135
Jet fuel	66	21	10
Kerosene	122	169	49
Distillate fuel oil	398.0	361.0	102.8
Residual fuel oil	49.0	225.0	25.3
Cement‡	1,800	1,800	1,800
Electric energy (million kWh)	6,978	8,324	8,958

* FAO estimates.

† Unofficial figures.

‡ Estimates.

2010: Groundnut oil 72.2 (FAO estimate); Coconut oil 9.8 (FAO estimate); Palm oil 120.0 (unofficial figure); Palm kernel oil 16.0 (unofficial figure); Beer of barley 86.4 (FAO estimate); Electric energy (million kWh) 10,167.

2011: Groundnut oil 62.7 (FAO estimate); Coconut oil 9.9 (FAO estimate); Palm oil 122.0 (unofficial figure); Palm kernel oil 21.0 (FAO estimate); Beer of barley 120.0 (FAO estimate); Cement 1,800 (estimated figure); Electric energy (million kWh) 11,200.

2012: Groundnut oil 64.2 (FAO estimate); Coconut oil 9.6 (FAO estimate); Palm oil 122.0 (unofficial figure); Palm kernel oil 14.1 (FAO estimate); Electric energy (million kWh) 12,164.

Sources: FAO; US Geological Survey; Energy Commission of Ghana, UN Industrial Commodity Statistics Database.

Finance

CURRENCY AND EXCHANGE RATES

Monetary Units
100 Ghana pesewas = 1 Ghana cedi.

Sterling, Dollar and Euro Equivalents (31 December 2013)
£1 sterling = 3.6230 Ghana cedis;
US $1 = 2.2000 Ghana cedis;
€1 = 3.0340 Ghana cedis;
10 Ghana cedis = £2.76 = $4.55 = €3.30.

Average Exchange Rate (Ghana cedis per US $)

2011	1.5119
2012	1.7958
2013	1.9540

Note: A new currency, the Ghana cedi, equivalent to 10,000 new cedis (the former legal tender), was introduced over a six-month period beginning in July 2007. Some statistical data in this survey are still presented in terms of the former currency, the new cedi.

GENERAL BUDGET
(million Ghana cedis)

Revenue*	2010	2011	2012
Tax revenue	6,504.5	9,854.6	12,655.2
Income and property	2,454.0	4,036.6	5,536.2
Personal (PAYE)	1,014.6	1,360.9	2,204.4
Company tax	987.7	1,568.0	2,361.5
Domestic goods and services	374.4	606.2	730.3
Petroleum tax	256.5	438.5	544.5
International trade	1,146.2	1,516.0	1,990.1
Import duties	1,136.2	1,511.0	1,886.9
Value added tax	1,618.3	2,376.1	2,777.3
Import exceptions	386.4	634.6	778.9
National health insurance levy	388.0	550.2	714.0
Other	137.3	135.0	128.4
Non-tax revenue	1,226.1	1,822.0	2,853.0
Total	7,730.6	11,676.6	15,508.2

Expenditure	2010	2011	2012
Recurrent expenditure	8,045.9	9,705.0	15,973.4
Wages and salaries	3,182.5	4,534.9	6,665.5
Goods and services	961.8	723.9	1,321.9
Transfers	1,991.4	2,504.6	4,477.8
National Health Fund (NHF)	351.3	377.0	587.2
Reserve fund	470.8	330.5	1,072.1
Interest payments	1,439.4	1,611.2	2,436.2
Domestic (accrual)	1,124.3	1,307.9	1,879.7
External (accrual)	315.0	303.3	556.4
Capital expenditure	3,168.6	3,675.0	4,971.3
Domestic	1,136.0	1,962.8	2,436.7
External	2,032.6	1,712.2	2,534.6
Total	11,214.5	13,380.0	20,944.7

* Excluding grants received (million Ghana cedis): 1,080.2 in 2010; 1,175.0 in 2011; 1,160.3 in 2012.

Source: Bank of Ghana, Accra.

INTERNATIONAL RESERVES
(US $ million at 31 December)

	2010	2011	2012
Gold (national valuation)	303.4	321.7	337.2
IMF special drawing rights	448.6	430.6	398.5
Foreign exchange	4,314.6	5,052.8	4,969.0
Total	5,066.6	5,805.1	5,704.7

Source: IMF, *International Financial Statistics*.

MONEY SUPPLY
(million Ghana cedis at 31 December)

	2010	2011	2012
Currency outside depository corporations	2,929.2	3,767.3	4,923.0
Transferable deposits	5,709.8	8,296.7	10,892.5
Other deposits	4,998.3	6,216.1	7,051.5
Broad money	13,637.3	18,280.0	22,867.1

Source: IMF, *International Financial Statistics*.

COST OF LIVING
(Consumer Price Index; annual averages; base: 2002 = 100)

	2009	2010	2011
Food and non-alcoholic beverages	275.0	291.8	303.6
Clothing and footwear	226.1	262.3	296.2
Housing, water, electricity and other fuels	385.2	424.7	469.7
Health	502.2	553.7	596.8
Transport	450.6	494.1	603.9
Communications	273.2	273.0	273.5
Recreation and culture	430.3	519.7	563.7
Education	277.9	281.0	288.1
All items (incl. others)	303.9	336.5	365.8

2012 (Consumer Price Index; annual averages; base: 2002 = 100): Food and non-alcoholic beverages 317.4; Clothing and footwear 337.0; Housing, water, electricity and other fuels 506.8; Health 649.8; *All items* (incl. others) 399.4. (Source: Bank of Ghana, Accra).

NATIONAL ACCOUNTS
(million Ghana cedis at current prices)

Expenditure on the Gross Domestic Product

	2010	2011	2012
Government final consumption expenditure	4,768	9,955	9,923
Private final consumption expenditure	35,860	36,757	44,536
Increase in stocks	480	2,405	1,361
Gross fixed capital formation	11,354	15,317	21,219
Total domestic expenditure	52,462	64,434	77,039
Exports of goods and services	13,572	26,390	33,522
Less Imports of goods and services	21,134	29,727	41,107
Statistical discrepancy	1,143	–1,280	3,655
GDP in purchasers' values	46,042	59,816	73,109
GDP in constant 2006 prices	24,252	27,891	30,099

Gross Domestic Product by Economic Activity

	2010	2011	2012
Agriculture and livestock	10,295	11,654	12,636
Forestry and logging	1,614	1,549	1,705
Fishing	1,001	952	1,057
Mining and quarrying	1,013	4,690	5,956
Manufacturing	2,941	3,842	4,680
Electricity and water	634	747	834
Construction	3,706	4,995	7,110
Transport, storage and communications	5,409	6,986	8,937
Wholesale and retail trade, restaurants and hotels	5,294	6,289	7,395
Finance, insurance, real estate and business services	4,185	5,057	6,664
Public administration and defence	3,024	3,897	4,871
Education	1,877	2,307	2,732
Health and social work	674	728	872
Other community, social and personal services	1,722	2,159	2,492
Sub-total	43,388	55,852	67,942
Indirect taxes, less subsidies	2,654	3,964	5,167
GDP at market prices	46,042	59,816	73,109

BALANCE OF PAYMENTS
(US $ million)

	2010	2011	2012
Exports of goods	7,960.1	12,785.4	13,543.4
Imports of goods	–10,922.1	–15,842.7	–17,763.2
Balance on goods	–2,962.0	–3,057.3	–4,219.8
Exports of services	1,477.3	1,871.1	3,259.4
Imports of services	–3,003.2	–3,666.6	–4,236.4
Balance on goods and services	–4,488.0	–4,852.7	–5,196.8
Primary income received	52.9	55.4	55.3
Primary income paid	–634.7	–1,304.0	–2,185.9
Balance on goods, services and primary income	–5,069.8	–6,101.4	–7,327.4
Secondary income (net)	2,322.4	2,597.4	2,549.9
Current balance	–2,747.3	–3,503.9	–4,777.5
Capital account (net)	337.5	445.1	283.0
Direct investment assets	—	–25.4	–1.1
Direct investment liabilities	2,527.4	3,222.2	3,294.5
Portfolio investment assets	–201.4	437.4	1,338.2
Portfolio investment liabilities	–84.4	–310.1	–216.3
Other investment liabilities	843.3	763.8	–871.6
Net errors and omissions	–251.4	–673.8	187.6
Reserves and related items	423.8	355.3	–763.2

Source: IMF, *International Financial Statistics*.

External Trade

PRINCIPAL COMMODITIES
(distribution by HS, US $ million)

Imports c.i.f.	2010	2011	2012
Live animals and animal products	343.0	586.0	554.9
Vegetables and vegetable products	381.1	647.8	578.2
Cereals	320.1	546.7	470.4
Prepared foodstuffs; beverages, spirits, vinegar; tobacco and articles thereof	459.7	652.6	606.1
Mineral products	345.8	488.3	775.0
Salt, sulphur, earth, stone, plaster, lime and cement	258.7	366.6	418.4
Chemicals and related products	858.9	1,337.2	1,393.1
Miscellaneous chemical products	317.7	464.5	432.4
Insecticides, fungicides, herbicides packaged for retail sale	255.4	370.9	337.2
Plastics, rubber, and articles thereof	532.8	625.6	682.2
Plastics and articles thereof	265.0	419.8	438.0
Rubber and articles thereof	267.7	205.9	244.2
Pulp of wood, paper and paperboard, and articles thereof	161.4	1,965.2	942.2
Printed books, newspapers, pictures, etc.	33.4	1,797.6	775.9
Stamps; cheque forms, banknotes, bond certificates, etc.	—	1,758.9	730.1
Iron and steel, other base metals and articles of base metal	978.1	1,181.9	1,440.5
Iron and steel	262.7	400.1	419.2
Articles of iron or steel	445.9	494.1	718.5
Machinery and mechanical appliances; electrical equipment; parts thereof	2,065.5	3,031.2	3,306.6
Machinery, nuclear reactors, boilers, etc.	1,212.7	1,835.4	2,093.2
Electrical, electronic equipment	852.8	1,195.9	1,213.4
Vehicles, aircraft, vessels and associated transport equipment	1,240.1	1,935.2	2,362.1
Vehicles other than railway, tramway	1,068.3	1,910.0	2,315.1
Cars (incl. station wagon)	525.1	860.4	1,064.5
Trucks, motor vehicles for the transport of goods	334.0	628.0	796.8
Total (incl. others)	8,057.1	13,573.3	14,011.9

Exports f.o.b.	2010	2011	2012
Vegetables and vegetable products	70.1	1,134.5	3,312.2
Edible fruit, nuts, peel of citrus fruit, melons	22.7	554.3	3,138.3
Brazil nuts, cashew nuts & coconuts	15.2	512.4	3,128.0
Prepared foodstuffs; beverages, spirits, vinegar; tobacco and articles thereof	1,027.3	2,442.0	2,118.0
Cocoa and cocoa preparations	975.9	2,294.4	2,040.9
Cocoa beans, raw, roasted	847.4	2,071.6	1,971.7
Mineral products	108.0	7,499.3	4,747.0
Mineral fuels, oils, distillation products, etc.	6.0	7,338.1	4,560.9
Crude petroleum oils	—	2,862.0	3,691.2
Petroleum gases	3.5	4,330.8	621.4
Wood, wood charcoal, cork, and articles thereof	196.8	484.6	378.3
Wood and articles of wood, wood charcoal	196.4	482.9	377.4
Pearls, precious stones, metals, coins, etc.	3,369.2	4,852.8	7,111.3
Gold, unwrought or in semi-manufactured forms	3,367.9	4,836.6	7,107.3
Total (incl. others)	5,233.4	18,400.6	18,761.2

Source: Trade Map-Trade Competitiveness Map, International Trade Centre, www.intracen.org/marketanalysis.

PRINCIPAL TRADING PARTNERS
(US $ million)

Imports c.i.f.	2010	2011	2012
Australia	109.1	160.3	212.0
Belgium	445.6	809.3	924.1
Brazil	213.3	282.5	191.2
Canada	184.9	253.0	216.1
China, People's Republic	1,060.9	2,062.1	2,405.3
Congo, Republic	8.7	5.5	2.7
France (incl. Monaco)	498.4	269.2	240.8
Germany	272.4	481.0	540.5
India	320.0	578.7	592.4
Indonesia	83.8	106.1	130.7
Italy (incl. San Marino)	190.9	276.2	289.4
Japan	148.9	181.5	269.3
Korea, Republic	344.2	336.9	315.8
Netherlands	278.8	415.6	414.3
Nigeria	34.6	54.0	285.6
South Africa	333.2	398.1	485.8
Spain	114.5	193.9	264.4
Sweden	126.3	249.5	201.2
Thailand	158.2	335.7	243.5
United Arab Emirates	143.7	307.1	357.2
United Kingdom	387.5	2,243.9	1,403.2
USA	1,101.3	1,307.3	1,563.8
Total (incl. others)	8,057.1	13,573.3	14,011.9

Exports f.o.b.	2010	2011	2012
Belgium	110.1	403.4	130.7
Benin	37.6	87.3	85.5
Burkina Faso	72.9	500.6	369.5
China, People's Republic	51.3	257.9	628.1
Côte d'Ivoire	26.5	717.4	81.8
Estonia	79.0	122.0	81.0
France (incl. Monaco)	65.0	1,722.4	1,412.4
Germany	67.4	169.7	198.0
India	48.6	722.2	1,876.7
Italy (incl. San Marino)	38.6	1,041.5	1,229.3
Japan	41.4	65.8	90.8
Malaysia	30.9	139.6	272.7
Mali	126.7	21.6	58.4
Netherlands	291.8	710.7	760.5
Nigeria	101.1	197.0	249.0
South Africa	2,798.7	3,146.8	4,544.2
Spain	66.8	132.6	268.9
Switzerland-Liechtenstein	215.5	865.9	1,214.8
Togo	70.1	4,594.0	879.8
Turkey	29.8	171.2	228.3
United Arab Emirates	353.4	993.9	1,637.6
United Kingdom	175.8	378.7	260.8
USA	102.8	444.9	297.3
Total (incl. others)	5,233.4	18,400.6	18,761.2

Source: Trade Map-Trade Competitiveness Map, International Trade Centre, www.intracen.org/marketanalysis.

Transport

RAILWAYS
(traffic)

	2002	2003	2004
Passenger-km (million)	61	86	80
Net ton-km (million)	244	242	216

Source: UN, *Statistical Yearbook*.

ROAD TRAFFIC
(motor vehicles in use at 31 December)

	2006	2007	2009*
Passenger cars	275,424	493,770	439,527
Buses and coaches	43,665	121,113	145,144
Lorries and vans	92,154	158,379	124,512
Motorcycles and mopeds	100,636	149,063	203,756

* Data for 2008 were not available.

Source: IRF, *World Road Statistics*.

SHIPPING

Flag Registered Fleet
(at 31 December)

	2011	2012	2013
Number of vessels	119	118	125
Total displacement ('000 grt)	92.5	93.0	112.9

Source: Lloyd's List Intelligence (www.lloydslistintelligence.com).

International Sea-borne Freight Traffic
(estimates, '000 metric tons)

	1991	1992	1993
Goods loaded	2,083	2,279	2,424
Goods unloaded	2,866	2,876	2,904

Source: UN Economic Commission for Africa, *African Statistical Yearbook*.

CIVIL AVIATION
(traffic on scheduled services)

	2002	2003	2004
Kilometres flown (million)	12	12	5
Passengers carried ('000)	256	241	96
Passenger-km (million)	912	906	363
Total ton-km (million)	107	101	41

Source: UN, *Statistical Yearbook*.

Passengers carried: 131,837 in 2010; 383,414 in 2011; 532,748 in 2012 (Source: World Bank, World Development Indicators database).

Tourism

ARRIVALS BY NATIONALITY

	2004	2005	2006
Côte d'Ivoire	28,069	25,155	25,921
France	21,096	10,089	11,915
Germany	28,168	14,094	17,132
Liberia	15,310	14,472	16,938
Netherlands	14,133	13,663	14,673
Nigeria	80,131	47,983	56,278
Togo	17,472	11,888	13,859
United Kingdom	50,547	36,747	36,795
USA	38,508	50,475	62,795
Total (incl. others)*	583,819	428,533	497,129

* Includes Ghanaian nationals resident abroad: 158,917 in 2004; 159,821 in 2005; 155,826 in 2006.

Total tourist arrivals ('000): 698 in 2008; 803 in 2009; 931 in 2010.

Receipts from tourism (US $ million, excl. passenger transport): 768 in 2009; 620 in 2010; 694 in 2011.

Source: World Tourism Organization.

Communications Media

	2010	2011	2012
Telephones ('000 main lines in use)	277.9	284.7	285.0
Mobile cellular telephones ('000 subscribers)	17,436.9	21,165.8	25,618.4
Internet subscribers ('000)	53.1	63.0	n.a.
Broadband subscribers ('000)	50.1	62.6	64.4

Source: International Telecommunication Union.

Education

(2012/13 unless otherwise indicated)

			Students ('000)		
	Institutions	Teachers	Males	Females	Total
Pre-primary	19,277	45,223	807,738	796,767	1,604,505
Primary	19,854	129,599	2,096,218	2,009,695	4,105,913
Junior secondary	12,436	93,797	759,884	692,701	1,452,585
Senior secondary	828	37,218	455,908	386,679	842,587
Tertiary*	n.a.	10,013	183.9	111.4	295.3

* 2011/12 figures.

2012/13 (unless otherwise indicated): *Teacher training* 39 institutions; *Technical and vocational institutes* 181 institutions; *Universities* 7 institutions (1998/99).

Source: UNESCO and Ministry of Education, Accra.

Pupil-teacher ratio (primary education, UNESCO estimate): 33.0 in 2011/12 (Source: UNESCO Institute for Statistics).

Adult literacy rate (UNESCO estimates): 67.3% (males 73.2%; females 61.2%) in 2010 (Source: UNESCO Institute for Statistics).

Directory

The Government

HEAD OF STATE

President and Commander-in-Chief of the Armed Forces: JOHN DRAMANI MAHAMA (took office 24 July 2012; re-elected 7 December).

Vice-President: KWESI BEKOE AMISSAH-ARTHUR.

CABINET
(April 2014)

Minister of Finance and Economic Planning: SETH TERPKER.

Minister of Foreign Affairs and Regional Integration: HANNAH TETTEH.

Minister of Local Government and Rural Development: AKWESI OPPONG FOSU.

Minister of Food and Agriculture: CLEMENT KOFI HUMADO.

Minister of Education: Prof. JANE OPOKU AGYEMANG.

Minister of the Environment, Science and Technology: Dr KWADWO OTENG AGYEI.

Minister of Lands and Natural Resources: Alhaji INUSAH FUSEINI.

Minister of Roads and Highways: Alhaji AMINA SULEMANA.

Minister of Water Resources, Works and Housing: COLLINS DAUDA.

Minister of Communications: Dr EDWARD OMANE BOAMAH.

Minister of Information: MAHAMA AYARIGA.

Minister of Gender, Children and Social Protection: NANA OYE LITHUR.

Minister in Charge of Government Business in Parliament: BENJAMIN BEWA-NYOG KUNBUOR.

Minister of Justice, Attorney-General: MARIETTA BREW APPIAH-OPPONG.

Minister of Energy and Petroleum: EMMANUEL ARMAH KOFI BUAH.

Minister of Transport: DZIFA ATTIVOR.

Minister of Employment and Labour Relations: NII ARMAH ASHIETEY.

Minister of Health: HANNY-SHERRY AYITTEY.

Minister of Youth and Sports: ELVIS AFRIYIE-ANKRAH.

Minister of Chieftaincy and Traditional Affairs: Dr HENRY SEIDU DAANNAA.

Minister of the Interior: KWESI AHWOI.

Minister of Defence: MARK WOYONGO.

Minister of Trade and Industry: HARUNA IDDRISU.

Minister of Tourism, Culture and Creative Arts: ELIZABETH OFOSU-AGYARE.

Ministry of Fisheries and Aquaculture Development: NAYON BILIJO.

Ministers of State at the Presidency: ALHASSAN AZONG, Dr MUSTAPHA AHMED, ABDUL RASHID HASSAN PELPUO, FIFI FIAVI FRANKLIN KWETEY, COMFORT DOYOE CUDJOE GHANSAH.

REGIONAL MINISTERS
(April 2014)

Ashanti: SAMUEL SARPONG.

Brong Ahafo: ERIC OPOKU.

Central: EBENEZER KWODWO TEYE ADDO.

Eastern: JULIUS DEBRAH.

Greater Accra: NII LARYEA AFOTEY AGBO.

Northern: Alhaji LIMUNA MOHAMMED-MUNIRU.

Upper East: Dr EPHRAIM AVEA NSOH.

Upper West: DEDE ANWATAAZUMO ZIEDENG.

Volta: HELEN ADLOA NTOSO.

Western: PAUL EVANS AIDOO.

MINISTRIES

Office of the President: Flagstaff House, Liberation Crescent, Accra; tel. (30) 2666997; e-mail contact@presidency.gov.gh; internet www.oop.gov.gh.

Ministry of Communications: POB M38, Accra; tel. (30) 2666465; fax (30) 2667114; e-mail info@moc.gov.gh; internet www.moc.gov.gh.

Ministry of Culture and Chieftaincy: POB 1627, State House, Accra; tel. (30) 2685012; fax (30) 2678361; e-mail chieftancycultur@yahoo.com.

Ministry of Defence: Burma Camp, Accra; tel. (30) 2775665; fax (30) 2772241; e-mail kaddok@internetghana.com.

Ministry of Education: POB M45, Accra; tel. (30) 2683627; fax (30) 2664067; e-mail pro@moe.gov.gh; internet www.moe.gov.gh.

Ministry of Employment and Social Welfare: POB 1627, State House, Accra; tel. (30) 2684532; fax (30) 2663615.

Ministry of Energy: FREMA House, Spintex Rd, POB T40 (Stadium Post Office), Stadium, Accra; tel. (30) 2683961; fax (30) 2668262; e-mail moen@energymin.gov.gh; internet www.energymin.gov.gh.

Ministry of the Environment, Science and Technology: POB M232, Accra; tel. (30) 2660005.

Ministry of Finance and Economic Planning: POB M40, Accra; tel. (30) 2665587; fax (30) 2666079; e-mail minister2009@mofep.gov.gh; internet www.mofep.gov.gh.

Ministry of Food and Agriculture: POB M37, Accra; tel. (30) 2663036; fax (30) 2668245; e-mail info@mofa.gov.gh; internet www.mofa.gov.gh.

Ministry of Foreign Affairs and Regional Integration: Treasury Rd, POB M53, Accra; tel. (30) 2664952; fax (30) 2665363; e-mail ghmaf00@ghana.com; internet www.mfa.gov.gh.

Ministry of Health: POB M44, Accra; tel. (30) 2684208; fax (30) 2663810; e-mail info@moh-ghana.org; internet www.moh-ghana.org.

Ministry of Information: POB M41, Accra; tel. and fax (30) 2229870; e-mail webmaster@mino.gov.gh; internet www.ghana.gov.gh.

Ministry of the Interior: POB M42, Accra; tel. (30) 2684400; fax (30) 2684408; e-mail mint@mint.gov.gh; internet www.mint.gov.gh.

Ministry of Justice and Attorney-General's Department: POB M60, Accra; tel. (30) 2665051; fax (30) 2667609; e-mail info@mjag.gov.gh.

Ministry of Lands and Natural Resources: POB M212, Accra; tel. (30) 2687314; fax (30) 2666801; e-mail motgov@hotmail.com; internet www.ghana-mining.org/ghweb/en/ma.html.

Ministry of Local Government and Rural Development: POB M50, Accra; tel. (30) 2664763; fax (30) 2682003; e-mail info@mlgrdghanagov.com; internet www.mlgrdghanagov.com.

Ministry of Roads and Highways: Accra; tel. (30) 2618668; fax (30) 2672676; internet www.mrt.gov.gh.

Ministry of Tourism: POB 4386, Accra; tel. (30) 2666314; fax (30) 2666182; e-mail humphrey.kuma@tourism.gov.gh; internet www.touringghana.com.

Ministry of Trade and Industry: POB M47, Accra; tel. (30) 2663327; fax (30) 2662428; e-mail info@moti.gov.gh; internet www.moti.gov.gh.

Ministry of Transport: POB M57, Accra; tel. (30) 2681780; fax (30) 2681781; e-mail info@mot.gov.gh; internet mot.gov.gh.

Ministry of Water Resources, Works and Housing: POB M43, Accra; tel. (30) 2665940; fax (30) 2685503; e-mail mwh@ighmail.com.

Ministry of Women's and Children's Affairs: POB M186, Accra; tel. (30) 2688187; fax (30) 2688182; e-mail info@mowacgov.com; internet www.mowacghana.net.

Ministry of Youth and Sports: POB M252, Accra; tel. (30) 2664716; fax (30) 2662794; e-mail moysgh@gmail.com; internet www.moys.gov.gh.

President

Presidential Election, 7 December 2012

Candidate	Valid votes	% of valid votes
John Dramani Mahama (NDC)	5,574,761	50.70
Nana Addo Dankwa Akufo-Addo (NPP)	5,248,898	47.74
Papa Kwesi Nduom (PPP)	64,362	0.59
Henry Herbert Lartey (GCPP)	38,223	0.35
Hassan Ayariga (PNC)	24,617	0.22
Abu Sakara Foster (CPP)	20,323	0.18
Jacob Osei Yeboah (Ind.)	15,201	0.14
Kwasi Addai Odike (UFP)	8,877	0.08
Total	10,995,262*	100.00

* Excluding 251,720 spoiled papers.

Legislature

PARLIAMENT

Parliament: Parliament House, Accra; tel. (30) 2664042; fax (30) 2665957; e-mail clerk@parliament.gh; internet www.parliament.gh.

Speaker: EDWARD DOE ADJAHO.

General Election, 7 December 2012

Party	Seats
National Democratic Congress (NDC)	148
New Patriotic Party (NPP)	123
People's National Convention (PNC)	1
Independents	3
Total	275

COUNCIL OF STATE

The Council of State is an advisory body of the President of the Republic. It consists of a former Chief Justice, a former Chief of Defence Staff of the Armed Forces, a former Inspector-General of Police, the President of the National House of Chiefs, 10 elected members (one from each of Ghana's regions) and 11 members appointed by the President. The Chairman is elected by members from among their number.

Chairman: JOHN HENRY MARTEY NEWMAN.

Election Commission

Electoral Commission (EC): POB M214, Accra; tel. (30) 2228421; internet www.ec.gov.gh; f. 1993; appointed by the President; Chair. Dr KWADWO AFARI-GYAN.

Political Organizations

Convention People's Party (CPP): 64 Mango Tree Ave, Asylum Down, POB 10939, Accra-North; tel. (30) 2227763; e-mail info@conventionpeoplesparty.org; internet conventionpeoplesparty.org; f. 1998 as Convention Party by merger of the National Convention Party (f. 1992) and the People's Convention Party (f. 1993); present name adopted in 2000; Nkrumahist; Chair. SAMIA YABA NKRUMAH; Gen. Sec. IVOR KOBINA GREENSTREET.

Democratic Freedom Party (DFP): POB 1040, Accra; tel. (30) 2237590; internet votedfp.org; f. 2006; Leader Dr OBED YAO ASAMOAH.

Democratic People's Party (DPP): 698/4 Star Ave, Kokomlemle, Accra; tel. (30) 2221671; f. 1992; Chair. THOMAS WARD-BREW; Gen. Sec. G. M. TETTEY.

EGLE (Every Ghanaian Living Everywhere) Party: POB TN 16132, Teshie Nungua, Accra; tel. (30) 2713994; fax (30) 2776894; f. 1992 as the Eagle Party.

Great Consolidated People's Party (GCPP): Citadel House, POB 3077, Accra; tel. (30) 2311498; f. 1996; Nkrumahist; Chair. Dr HENRY HERBERT LARTEY; Sec.-Gen. NICHOLAS MENSAH.

National Democratic Congress (NDC): 641/4 Ringway Close, POB 5825, Kokomlemle, Accra-North; tel. (30) 2223195; fax (30) 2220743; e-mail info@ndc.org.gh; internet www.ndc.org.gh; f. 1992; party of fmr Pres. Jerry Rawlings; Chair. Dr KWABENA ADJEI; Gen. Sec. JOHNSON ASIEDU NKETIAH.

National Democratic Party (NDP): Accra; f. 2012 by breakaway faction of NDC; Chair. Dr NII ARMAH JOSIAH ARYEH; Gen. Sec. Dr JOSPEH MAMBOA ROCKSON.

National Reform Party (NRP): 31 Mango Tree Ave, Asylum Down, POB 19403, Accra-North; tel. (30) 2228578; fax (30) 2227820; f. 1999 by a breakaway group from the NDC; Sec.-Gen. OPOKU KYERETWIE.

New Patriotic Party (NPP): C912/2 Duade St, Kokomlemle, POB 3456, Accra-North; tel. (30) 2227951; fax (30) 2224418; f. 1992; Gen. Sec. NANA OHENE NTOW.

People's National Convention (PNC): POB AC 120, Arts Centre, Accra; tel. (30) 2236389; f. 1992; Nkrumahist; Chair. Alhaji AHMED RAMADAN; Gen. Sec. BERNARD MORNAH.

Progressive People's Party (PPP): Asylum Down, Accra; tel. (30) 7020483; e-mail communications@pppghana.org; internet www.pppghana.org; f. 2011; Leader PAPA KWESI NDUOM.

Reformed Patriotic Democrats (RPD): POB 13274, Kumasi; tel. 243616660 (mobile); f. 2007 by former mems of the NPP; Founding Leader KWABENA AGYEI.

United Front Party (UFD): 14 Blohum St, Kumasi; tel. (540) 379242; f. 2012; Sec.-Gen. SAMUEL BEKOE OWUSU.

United Ghana Movement (UGM): 1 North Ridge Cres., POB C2611, Cantonments, Accra; tel. (30) 2225581; fax (30) 2223506; e-mail info@ugmghana.org; f. 1996 by a breakaway group from the NPP; Chair. WEREKO BROBBY.

United Renaissance Party (URP): Nima Hwy, POB 104, Accra-North; tel. (30) 28914411; f. 2006; Chair. KOFI WAYO.

Diplomatic Representation

EMBASSIES AND HIGH COMMISSIONS IN GHANA

Algeria: 22 Josif Broz Tito Ave, POB 2747, Cantonments, Accra; tel. (30) 2776719; fax (30) 2776828; e-mail embdzacc@africaonline.com.gh; Ambassador LARBI KATTI.

Angola: 5 Agbaamo St, Airport West Residential Area, Accra; tel. (30) 2766477; fax (30) 2775791; e-mail sec@angolaembassyghana.org; internet www.angolaembassyghana.org; Ambassador ANA MARIA TELES CARREIRA.

Australia: 2 Second Rangoon Close (cnr Josef B. Tito Ave), Cantonments, Accra; tel. (30) 2216400; fax (30) 2216410; e-mail Accrahc.Enquiries@dfat.gov.au; internet www.ghana.embassy.gov.au; High Commissioner JOANNA MARIE ADAMSON.

Benin: 129A North Airport Rd, Accra; tel. (30) 2774860; fax (30) 2774889; Ambassador PIERRE SADELER.

Brazil: Millennium Heights Bldg 2A, 14 Liberation Link, Airport Commercial Area, POB CT3859, Accra; tel. (30) 2774908; fax (30) 2778566; e-mail brasemb@africaonline.com.gh; internet www.embrazil.com.gh; Ambassador LUIS IRENE GALA.

Bulgaria: 3 Kakramadu Rd, POB 3193, East Cantonments, Accra; tel. (30) 2772404; fax (30) 2774231; e-mail bulemb2003@yahoo.com; internet www.mfa.bg/accra; Chargé d'affaires a.i. GEORGE MITEV.

Burkina Faso: 772 Asylum Down, off Farrar Ave, POB 65, Accra; tel. (30) 2221988; fax (30) 2221936; e-mail ambafaso@ghana.com; Ambassador SINI PIERRE SANOU.

Canada: 42 Independence Ave, Sankara Interchange, POB 1639, Accra; tel. (30) 2211521; fax (30) 2211523; e-mail accra@international.gc.ca; internet www.canadainternational.gc.ca/ghana; High Commissioner CHRISTOPHER THORNLEY.

China, People's Republic: 6 Agostino Neto Rd, Airport Residential Area, POB 3356, Accra; tel. (30) 2777073; fax (30) 2774527; e-mail chinaemb_gh@mfa.gov.cn; internet gh.chineseembassy.org; Ambassador GONG JIANZHONG.

Colombia: Plot 16, 1st Circular Road, Cantonments, Accra; tel. 233302797677; e-mail eghana@cancilleria.gov.co; Ambassador CLAUDIA DINORA TORBAY QUINTERO.

Côte d'Ivoire: 9 18th Lane, off Cantonments Rd, POB 3445, Christiansborg, Accra; tel. (30) 2774611; fax (30) 2773516; e-mail acigh@ambaci-ghana.org; internet www.ambaci-ghana.org; Ambassador BERNARD EHUI KOUTOUA.

Cuba: 22A Akosombo Rd, Airport Residential Area, POB 9163 Airport, Accra; tel. (30) 2775868; fax (30) 2774998; e-mail embghana@africaonline.com.gh; Ambassador JORGE FERNANDO LEFEBRE NICOLÁS.

Czech Republic: C260/5, 2 Kanda High Rd, POB 5226, Accra-North; tel. (30) 2223540; fax (30) 2225337; e-mail accra@embassy.mzv.cz; internet www.mzv.cz/accra; Ambassador MILOSLAV MACHÁLEK.

Denmark: 67 Dr Isert Rd, North Ridge, POB CT596, Accra; tel. (30) 2253473; fax (30) 2228061; e-mail accamb@um.dk; internet www.ambaccra.um.dk; Ambassador MARGIT THOMSEN.

Egypt: 38 Senchi St, Airport Residential Area, Accra; tel. (30) 2776854; fax (30) 2776795; e-mail boustaneaccra@hotmail.com; internet www.mfa.gov.eg/Accra_Emb; Ambassador OMAR AHMED ABDELWAHAB SELIM.

Ethiopia: 2 Milne Close, Airport Residential Area, POB 1646, Accra; tel. (30) 2775928; fax (30) 2776807; e-mail ethioemb@ghana.com; Ambassador GIFTY ABASIGA ABABULGU.

France: 12th Rd, off Liberation Ave, POB 187, Accra; tel. (30) 2214550; fax (30) 2214589; e-mail info@ambafrance-gh.org; internet www.ambafrance-gh.org; Ambassador FRÉDÉRIC CLAVIER.

Germany: 6 Ridge St, North Ridge, POB 1757, Accra; tel. (30) 2211000; fax (30) 2221347; e-mail info@accra.diplo.de; internet www.accra.diplo.de; Ambassador RÜDIGER JOHN.

Guinea: 11 Osu Badu St, Dzorwulu, POB 5497, Accra-North; tel. (30) 2777921; fax (30) 2760961; e-mail embagui@ghana.com; Ambassador KABA ARAFAN KABINET.

Holy See: 8 Drake Ave, Airport Residential Area, POB 9675, Accra; tel. (30) 2777759; fax (30) 2774019; e-mail nuncio@ghana.com;

Apostolic Nuncio Most Rev. JEAN-MARIE SPEICH (Titular Archbishop of Sulci).

India: 9 Ridge Rd, Roman Ridge, POB CT 5708, Cantonments, Accra; tel. (30) 2775601; fax (30) 2772176; e-mail indiahc@ncs.com.gh; internet www.indiahc-ghana.com; High Commissioner K. JEEVA SAGAR.

Iran: 12 Arkusah St, Airport Residential Area, POB 12673, Accra-North; tel. (30) 2774474; fax (30) 2777043; Ambassador MOHAMMED SULEYMANI.

Israel: 2 First Circular Rd, Unit 1, Josni Residence Cantonments, Accra; tel. (30) 2743838; fax (30) 2743857; Ambassador SHARON BAR-LI.

Italy: Jawaharlal Nehru Rd, POB 140, Accra; tel. (30) 2775621; fax (30) 2777301; e-mail ambasciata.accra@esteri.it; internet www.ambaccra.esteri.it; Ambassador LUCA FRATINI.

Japan: Fifth Ave, POB 1637, West Cantonments, Accra; tel. (30) 2765060; fax (30) 2762553; internet www.gh.emb-japan.go.jp; Ambassador NAOTO NIKAI.

Korea, Democratic People's Republic: 139 Nortei Ababio Loop, Ambassadorial Estate, Roman Ridge, POB 13874, Accra; tel. (30) 2777825; Ambassador KIM PYONG GI.

Korea, Republic: 3 Abokobi Rd, POB GP13700, East Cantonments, Accra-North; tel. (30) 2776157; fax (30) 2772313; e-mail ghana@mofat.go.kr; internet gha.mofat.go.kr; Ambassador KIM JEA-MIN.

Lebanon: F864/1, off Cantonments Rd, Osu, POB 562, Accra; tel. (30) 2776727; fax (30) 2764290; e-mail lebanon@its.com.gh; Ambassador ALI HASSAN HALABI.

Liberia: 10 Odoi Kwao St, Airport Residential Area, POB 895, Accra; tel. (30) 2775641; fax (30) 2775987; Ambassador (vacant).

Libya: 14 Sixth St, Airport Residential Area, POB 9665, Accra; tel. (30) 2774819; fax (30) 2774953; Ambassador Dr ALI AHMED GHUDBAN.

Malaysia: 18 Templesi Lane, Airport Residential Area, POB 16033, Accra; tel. (30) 2763691; fax (30) 2764910; e-mail mwaccra@africaonline.com.gh; High Commissioner Dato' HAJJAH RAZINAH GHAZALI.

Mali: 1st Bungalow, Liberia Rd, Airport Residential Area, POB 1121, Accra; tel. and fax (30) 2666942; e-mail ambamali@ighmail.com; Ambassador AÏSSATA KONANDJI COULIBALY.

Morocco: 1 Switchback Lane, PMB 117, Accra; tel. (30) 2775669; fax (30) 2785549; e-mail ambassade.maroc.ghana@gmail.com; Ambassador NOUZHA ALAOUI M'HAMDI.

Netherlands: 89 Liberation Rd, Ako Adjei Interchange, POB CT1647, Accra; tel. (30) 2214350; fax (30) 2773655; e-mail acc@minbuza.nl; internet ghana.nlembassy.org; Ambassador HANS DOCTER.

Niger: E104/3 Independence Ave, POB 2685, Accra; tel. (30) 2224962; fax (30) 2229011; Ambassador ABDOULMOUMINE HADJIO.

Nigeria: 20/21 Onyasia Cres., Roman Ridge Residential Area, Accra; tel. (30) 2776158; fax (30) 2776159; e-mail admin.hc@nigeriahighcommissionghana.org; internet www.nigeriahighcommissionghana.org; High Commissioner ADEMOLA OLUSEYI ONAFOWOKAN.

Russia: Jawaharlal Nehru Rd, Switchback Lane, POB 1634, Accra; tel. (30) 2775611; fax (30) 2772699; e-mail russia@4u.com.gh; internet www.ghana.mid.ru; Ambassador VLADIMIR V. BARBIN.

Saudi Arabia: 10 Noi Fetreke St, Roman Ridge Ambassadorial Estate Ext., Airport Residential Area, POB 670, Accra; tel. (30) 2774311; fax (30) 2774829; e-mail ghemb@mofa.gov.sa; internet embassies.mofa.gov.sa/sites/ghana; Ambassador HISHAM MISHAL AL-SUWAILEM.

Senegal: 8F Odoi Kwao St, Airport Residential Area, PMB CT 342, Cantonments, Accra; tel. (30) 2770285; fax (30) 2770286; e-mail senegalaccra@hotmail.fr; Ambassador CHÉRIF OUMAR DIAGNÉ.

Sierra Leone: 83A Senchi St, Airport Residential Area, POB 55, Cantonments, Accra; tel. (30) 2769190; fax (30) 2769189; e-mail slhc@ighmail.com; High Commissioner MOKOWA ADU- GYAMFI.

South Africa: Speed House 1, 3rd Soula St, Labone North POB 298, Accra; tel. (30) 2740450; fax (30) 2762381; e-mail sahcgh@africaonline.com.gh; High Commissioner JEANETTE T. NDLOVU.

Spain: Drake Ave Extension, Airport Residential Area, PMB KA44, Accra; tel. (30) 2774004; fax (30) 2776217; e-mail emb.accra@maec.es; internet www.spanish-embassy.com/accra.html; Ambassador (vacant).

Switzerland: Kanda Highway, North Ridge, POB 359, Accra; tel. (30) 2228125; fax (30) 2223583; e-mail acc.vertretung@eda.admin.ch; internet www.eda.admin.ch/accra; Ambassador GERHARD BRÜGGER.

Togo: Togo House, near Cantonments Circle, POB C120, Accra; tel. (30) 2777950; fax (30) 2765659; e-mail togamba@ighmail.com; Ambassador JEAN-PIERRE GBIKPI-BENISSAN.

United Kingdom: Osu Link, off Gamel Abdul Nasser Ave, POB 296, Accra; tel. and fax (30) 2213250; fax (30) 2213274; e-mail high.commission.accra@fco.gov.uk; internet ukinghana.fco.gov.uk; High Commissioner Dr PETER EDWARD JONES.

USA: 24 Fourth Circular Rd, POB GP 2288, Cantonments, Accra; tel. (30) 2741150; fax (30) 2741692; e-mail pressaccra@state.gov; internet ghana.usembassy.gov; Ambassador GENE A. CRETZ.

Zambia: 6 Agostino Neto Rd, Airport Residential Area, Accra; tel. (30) 2767689; e-mail info@zamhighghana.org; High Commissioner TIMOTHY MWABA WALAMBA.

Judicial System

The civil law in force in Ghana is based on the Common Law, doctrines of equity and general statutes that were in force in England in 1874, as modified by subsequent Ordinances. Ghanaian customary law is, however, the basis of most personal, domestic and contractual relationships. Criminal Law is based on the Criminal Procedure Code, 1960, derived from English Criminal Law, and since amended. The Superior Court of Judicature comprises a Supreme Court, a Court of Appeal, a High Court and a Regional Tribunal; Inferior Courts include Circuit Courts, Circuit Tribunals, Community Tribunals and such other Courts as may be designated by law. In 2001 'fast-track' court procedures were established to accelerate the delivery of justice.

Supreme Court: Accra; consists of the Chief Justice and not fewer than nine other Justices; is the final court of appeal in Ghana and has jurisdiction in matters relating to the enforcement or interpretation of the Constitution; Chief Justice GEORGINA THEODORA.

Court of Appeal: Consists of the Chief Justice and not fewer than five Judges of the Court of Appeal. It has jurisdiction to hear and determine appeals from any judgment, decree or order of the High Court.

High Court: Comprises the Chief Justice and not fewer than 12 Justices of the High Court. It exercises original jurisdiction in all matters, civil and criminal, other than those for offences involving treason. Trial by jury is practised in criminal cases in Ghana and the Criminal Procedure Code, 1960, provides that all trials on indictment shall be by a jury or with the aid of Assessors.

Circuit Courts: Exercise original jurisdiction in civil matters where the amount involved does not exceed 10 Ghana cedis. They also have jurisdiction with regard to the guardianship and custody of infants, and original jurisdiction in all criminal cases, except offences where the maximum punishment is death or the offence of treason. They have appellate jurisdiction from decisions of any District Court situated within their respective circuits.

District Courts: To each magisterial district is assigned at least one District Magistrate who has original jurisdiction to try civil suits in which the amount involved does not exceed 5 Ghana cedis. District Magistrates also have jurisdiction to deal with all criminal cases, except first-degree felonies, and commit cases of a more serious nature to either the Circuit Court or the High Court. A Grade I District Court can impose fines and sentences of imprisonment of up to two years and a Grade II District Court may impose fines and a sentence of imprisonment of up to 12 months. A District Court has no appellate jurisdiction, except in rent matters under the Rent Act.

Juvenile Courts: Jurisdiction in cases involving persons under 17 years of age, except where the juvenile is charged jointly with an adult. The Courts comprise a Chairman, who must be either the District Magistrate or a lawyer, and not fewer than two other members appointed by the Chief Justice in consultation with the Judicial Council. The Juvenile Courts can make orders as to the protection and supervision of a neglected child and can negotiate with parents to secure the good behaviour of a child.

National Public Tribunal: Considers appeals from the Regional Public Tribunals. Its decisions are final and are not subject to any further appeal. The Tribunal consists of at least three members and not more than five, one of whom acts as Chairman.

Regional Public Tribunals: Hears criminal cases relating to prices, rent or exchange control, theft, fraud, forgery, corruption or any offence which may be referred to them by the Provisional National Defence Council.

Special Military Tribunal: Hears criminal cases involving members of the armed forces. It consists of between five and seven members.

Attorney-General: MARIETTA BREW APPIAH-OPPONG.

Religion

According to the 2010 census, 71.2% of the population were Christians and 17.6% Muslims, while 5.2% followed indigenous beliefs. 5.3% of the population did not profess any religion.

CHRISTIANITY

Christian Council of Ghana: POB GP919, Accra; tel. (30) 2776678; fax (30) 2776725; e-mail info@christiancouncilofghana.org; internet www.christiancouncilofghana.org; f. 1929; advisory body comprising 16 mem. churches and 2 affiliate Christian orgs (2005); Chair. Most Rev. Prof. AMENU AMENU; Gen. Sec. Rev. Dr KWABENA OPUNI-FRIMPONG.

Ghana Pentecostal and Charismatic Council: Otenshie, East Legon, POB CT 483, Accra; tel. and fax (30) 2522226; e-mail info@gpccghana.org; internet gpccghana.org; f. 1969; Pres. Apostle Dr OPOKU ONYINAH; Gen. Sec. Apostle SAMUEL YAW ANTWI.

The Anglican Communion

Anglicans in Ghana are adherents of the Church of the Province of West Africa, comprising 15 dioceses and a missionary region, of which 10 are in Ghana. In 2012 two internal provinces were created out of the Province of West Africa, one for Ghana and the other for West Africa itself. The Archbishop of the Internal Province of West Africa is the Primate and Metropolitan of the Province of West Africa.

Archbishop of the Internal Province of Ghana and Bishop of Kumasi: Rt Rev. DANIEL YINKAH SAFO, Bishop's Office, St Cyprian's Ave, POB 144, Kumasi; tel. and fax (32) 2024117; e-mail anglicandioceseofkumasi@yahoo.com.

Bishop of Accra: Rt Rev. Dr DANIEL SYLVANUS MENSAH TORTO, Bishopscourt, POB 8, Accra; tel. (30) 2662292; fax (30) 2668822; e-mail adaccra@ghana.com.

Bishop of Cape Coast: Rt Rev. DANIEL ALLOTEY, Bishopscourt, POB A233, Adisadel Estates, Cape Coast; tel. (33) 2132502; fax (33) 2132637; e-mail danallotey@priest.com.

Bishop of Dunkwa-on-Offin: Rt Rev. EDMUND DAWSON AHMOAH, POB DW42, Dukwa-on-Offin; tel. (24) 4464764.

Bishop of Ho: Rt Rev. MATTHIAS MEDADUES-BADOHU, Bishopslodge, POB MA 300, Ho; e-mail matthiaskwab@googlemail.com.

Bishop of Koforidua: Rt Rev. FRANCIS QUASHIE, POB 980, Koforidua; tel. (34) 2022329; fax (34) 2022060; e-mail cpwa_gh@yahoo.com; internet koforidua.org.

Bishop of Sekondi: Rt Rev. JOHN KWAMINA OTOO, POB 85, Sekondi; tel. (31) 20669125; e-mail angdiosek@yahoo.co.uk.

Bishop of Sunyani: Rt Rev. Dr FESTUS YEBOAH-ASUAMAH, Bishop's House, POB 23, Sunyani, BA; tel. (35) 2027205; fax (35) 2027203; e-mail anglicandiocesesyi@yahoo.com.

Bishop of Tamale: Rt Rev. Dr JACOB AYEEBO, POB 110, Tamale NR; tel. (37) 2022639; fax (37) 2022906; e-mail bishopea2000@yahoo.com.

Bishop of Wiawso: Rt Rev. ABRAHAM KOBINA ACKAH, POB 4, Sefwi, Wiawso; e-mail bishopackah@yahoo.com.

The Roman Catholic Church

Ghana comprises four archdioceses, 15 dioceses and one apostolic vicariate. Some 13% of the total population are Roman Catholics.

Ghana Bishops' Conference: National Catholic Secretariat, POB 9712, Airport, Accra; tel. (30) 2500491; fax (30) 2500493; e-mail dscncs@africaonline.com.gh; internet www.ghanacbc.org; f. 1960; Pres. Rt Rev. LUCAS ABADAMLOORA (Bishop of Navrongo-Bolgatanga).

Archbishop of Accra: Most Rev. GABRIEL CHARLES PALMER-BUCKLE, Chancery Office, POB 247, Accra; tel. (30) 2222728; fax (30) 2231619; e-mail cpalmerbuckle@yahoo.com; internet www.accracatholic.org.

Archbishop of Cape Coast: Most Rev. MATTHIAS KOBENA NKETSIAH, Archbishop's House, POB 112, Cape Coast; tel. (33) 2133471; fax (33) 2133473; e-mail archcape@ghanacbc.com.

Archbishop of Kumasi: Most Rev. GABRIEL JUSTICE YAW ANOKYE, POB 99, Kumasi; tel. (32) 2024012; fax (32) 2029395; e-mail cadiokum@ghana.com.

Archbishop of Tamale: Most Rev. PHILIP NAAMEH, Archbishop's House, Gumbehini Rd, POB 42, Tamale; tel. and fax (37) 2022425; e-mail tamdio2@yahoo.co.uk.

Other Christian Churches

African Methodist Episcopal Zion Church: POB MP522, Mamprobi, Accra; tel. (30) 2669200; f. 1898; Pres. Rt Rev. SETH O. LARTEY.

Christian Methodist Episcopal Church: POB AN 7639, Accra; tel. 244630267 (mobile); internet www.cmetenth.org/Ghana%20Regional%20Conference.htm; Pres. KENNETH W. CARTER; Mission Supervisor Rev. ADJEI K. LAWSON.

Church of Pentecost: POB 2194 Accra; tel. (30) 2777611; fax (30) 2774721; e-mail info@thecophq.org; internet www.thecophq.org; Chair. Apostle Dr OPOKU ONYINAH; Gen. Sec. Apostle ALFRED KODUAH; 1,503,057 mems.

Evangelical-Lutheran Church of Ghana: POB KN197, Kaneshie, Accra; tel. 244314136 (mobile); e-mail elcga@africaonline.com.gh; Pres. Rt Rev. Dr PAUL KOFI FYNN; 27,521 mems (2010).

Evangelical-Presbyterian Church of Ghana: 19 Main St, Tesano, PMB, Accra-North; tel. (30) 2220381; fax (30) 2233173; e-mail epchurch@ghana.com; f. 1847; Moderator Rev. FRANCIS AMENU; 295,000 mems.

Ghana Baptist Convention: POB AN 19909, Accra-North; tel. (30) 2242316; fax (30) 2242319; e-mail ags@gbconvention.com; internet gbconvention.com; f. 1963; Pres. Rev. Dr STEPHEN K. ASANTE; Sec. Rev. DAVID NARTEH OCANSEY; 65,000 mems.

Ghana Mennonite Church: POB 5485, Accra; fax (30) 2220589; f. 1957; Moderator Rev. EMMANUEL GALBAH-NUSETOR; Sec. JOHN ADETA; 5,000 mems.

Ghana Union Conference of Seventh-day Adventists: POB GP1016, Accra; tel. (30) 2223720; fax (30) 2227024; e-mail info@adventistgh.org; internet www.adventistgh.org; f. 1943; Pres. Pastor SAMUEL A. LARMIE; Sec. Pastor KWAME KWANIN-BOAKYE; 368,171 mems.

Methodist Church of Ghana: Wesley House, E252/2, Liberia Rd, POB 403, Accra; tel. (30) 2670355; fax (30) 2679223; e-mail mcghqs@ucomgh.com; internet www.methodistchurch-gh.org; Presiding Bishop Most Rev. Dr EMMANUEL ASANTE; 584,969 mems (2007).

Presbyterian Church of Ghana: POB 1800, Accra; tel. (30) 2662511; fax (30) 2665594; e-mail info@pcgonline.org; internet www.pcgonline.org; f. 1828; Moderator Rev. Prof. EMMANUEL MARTEY; Clerk Rev. Dr SAMUEL AYETE-NYAMPONG; 422,500 mems.

The African Methodist Episcopal Church, the Christ Reformed Church, the F'Eden Church, the Gospel Revival Church of God, the Religious Society of Friends (Quakers) and the Society of the Divine Word are also active in Ghana.

ISLAM

According to the 2010 census, Muslims had a particularly large concentration in the Northern Region, comprising some 60% of its population. The majority are Malikees.

Coalition of Muslim Organizations (COMOG): Accra; Pres. Alhaji ADAM MAHAMA (acting).

Ghana Muslim Representative Council: Accra.

Chief Imam: Sheikh USMAN NUHU SHARABUTU.

BAHÁ'Í FAITH

National Spiritual Assembly: POB AN 7098, Accra-North; tel. (30) 2222127; e-mail bahaighana@yahoo.com; Sec. GLADYS QUARTEY-PAPAFIO.

The Press

DAILY NEWSPAPERS

The Daily Dispatch: 1 Dade Walk, North Labone, POB C1945, Cantonments, Accra; tel. (30) 2763339; e-mail ephson@usa.net; Editor BEN EPHSON.

Daily Graphic: Graphic Communications Group Ltd, 3 Graphic Rd, POB 742, Accra; tel. (30) 2684001; fax (30) 2234754; e-mail gpack@graphic.com.gh; internet www.graphic.com.gh; f. 1950; state-owned; Editor RANSFORD TETTEH; circ. 100,000.

Daily Guide: POB 115, Accra; tel. (30) 2229576; fax (30) 2231459; e-mail dailyguidenews@yahoo.com; internet dailyguideghana.com; owned by Western Publications Ltd; Editor FORTUNE ALIMI.

Ghanaian Chronicle: 37 Bobo St, Tesano, PMB, Accra-North; tel. (30) 2232713; fax (30) 2232608; e-mail chronicl@africaonline.com.gh; internet www.ghanaian-chronicle.com; Editor EMMANUEL AKLI; circ. 60,000.

The Ghanaian Times: New Times Corpn, Ring Rd West, POB 2638, Accra; tel. (30) 228282; fax (30) 220733; e-mail info@newtimes.com.gh; internet www.newtimes.com.gh; f. 1958; state-owned; Editor ENIMIL ASHON; circ. 45,000.

The Mail: POB CT4910, Cantonments, Accra; e-mail mike@accra-mail.com; internet www.accra-mail.com; Editor Alhaji ABDUL RAHMAN HARUNA ATTAH.

The Statesman: House No. 359/4, Faanofa Rd, Kokomlemle, Accra; tel. and fax 244217504 (mobile); fax (30) 2220043; e-mail statesman_gh@yahoo.com; internet www.thestatesmanonline.com; f. 1949; official publ. of the New Patriotic Party; Editor-in-Chief ASARE OTCHERE-DARKO; Editor KWABENA AMANKWAH.

The Telescope: Takoradi; f. 2005; Editor LOUIS HENRY DANSO.

PERIODICALS

Thrice-weekly

The Independent: Clear Type Press Bldg Complex, off Graphic Rd, POB 4031, Accra; tel. and fax (30) 2661091; f. 1989; Editor Andrew Arthur.

Network Herald: 34 Crescent Rd, Labone, Accra; tel. (30) 2701184; fax (30) 2762173; e-mail support@ghana.com; internet www.networkherald.gh; f. 2001; Editor Elvis Quarshie.

Bi-weekly

Ghana Palaver: Palaver Publications, POB WJ317, Wejia, Accra; tel. (30) 2850495; e-mail editor@ghana-palaver.com; internet www.ghana-palaver.com; f. 1994; Editor Jojo Bruce Quansah.

The Ghanaian Lens: Accra; internet www.ghanaianlens.com; Editor Kobby Fiagbe.

The Ghanaian Voice: Newstop Publications, POB 514, Mamprobi, Accra; tel. (30) 2324644; fax (30) 2314939; Editor Christiana Ansah; circ. 100,000.

Weekly

Business and Financial Times: POB CT16, Cantonments, Accra; tel. and fax (30) 2785366; fax (30) 2775449; e-mail info@thebftonline.com; internet www.thebftonline.com; f. 1989; 4 a week; Editor William Selassy Adjadogo; circ. 40,000.

The Crusading Guide: POB 8523, Accra-North; tel. (30) 2763339; fax (30) 2761541; internet www.ghanaweb.com/CrusadingGuide; Editor Kweku Baako, Jr.

Free Press: Tommy Thompson Books Ltd, POB 6492, Accra; tel. (30) 2225994; independent; Editor Frank Boahene.

Ghana Life: Ghana Life Publications, POB 11337, Accra; tel. (30) 2229835; Editor Nikki Boa-Amponsem.

Ghana Market Watch: Accra; internet www.ghanamarketwatch.com; f. 2006; financial; CEO Amos Dotse.

Graphic Showbiz: Graphic Communications Group Ltd, POB 742, Accra; tel. (30) 2684001; fax (30) 2684025; e-mail graphicshowbiz@gmail.com; internet www.graphicghana.info; f. 2000; state-owned; Editor Nanabanyin Dadson.

Graphic Sports: Graphic Communications Group Ltd, POB 742, Accra; tel. (30) 2228911; fax (30) 2234754; e-mail info@graphicghana.com; state-owned; Editor Felix Abayateye; circ. 60,000.

Gye Nyame Concord: Accra; e-mail gnconcord@yahoo.com; internet www.ghanaweb.com/concord.

The Heritage: POB AD676, Arts Center, Accra; tel. (30) 2236051; fax (30) 2237156; e-mail heritagenewspaper@yahoo.co.uk; internet www.theheritagenews.com; Chair. Stephen Owusu; Editor A. C. Ohene.

The Mirror: Graphic Communications Group Ltd, POB 742, Accra; tel. (30) 2228911; fax (30) 2234754; e-mail info@graphicghana.com; internet www.graphicghana.info; f. 1953; state-owned; Sat.; Editor E. N. O. Provencal; circ. 90,000.

The National Democrat: Democrat Publications, POB 13605, Accra; Editor Elliot Felix Ohene.

Public Agenda: Box MP2989, Accra-North; tel. (21) 2238820; e-mail pagenda@4u.com.gh; f. 1994; Editor Amos Safo; circ. 12,000.

The Standard: Standard Newspapers & Magazines Ltd, POB KA 9712, Accra; tel. (30) 2513537; fax (30) 2500493; e-mail snam.ncs@ghanacbc.org; internet www.ghanacbc.org; Roman Catholic; Editor Isaac Fritz Andoh; circ. 10,000.

The Vanguard: Accra; Editor Osbert Lartey.

The Weekend: Newstop Publications, POB 514, Mamprobi, Accra; tel. (30) 2324644; fax (30) 2314939; Editor Emmanuel Yartey; circ. 40,000.

Weekly Spectator: New Times Corpn, Ring Rd West, POB 2638, Accra; tel. (30) 2228282; fax (30) 2229398; internet spectator.newtimesonline.com/spectator; state-owned; f. 1963; Sun.; Editor Enimil Ashon; circ. 165,000.

Other

The African Woman Magazine: Ring Rd West, POB AN 15064, Accra; tel. and fax (30) 2241636; e-mail mail@theafricanwoman.com; internet www.theafricanwoman.com; f. 1957; monthly; Editor Nii Adumuah Orgle.

AGI Newsletter: c/o Asscn of Ghana Industries, POB 8624, Accra-North; tel. (30) 2779023; e-mail agi@agighana.org; internet www.agighana.org; f. 1974; monthly; Editor Carlo Hey; circ. 1,500.

AGOO: Newstop Publications, POB 514, Mamprobi, Accra; tel. (30) 2324644; fax (30) 2314939; monthly; lifestyle magazine; Publr Kojo Bonsu.

Armed Forces News: General Headquarters, Directorate of Public Relations, Burma Camp, Accra; tel. (30) 2776111; f. 1966; quarterly; Editor Adotey Ankrah-Hoffman; circ. 4,000.

Business Watch: Sulton Bridge Co Ltd, POB C3447, Cantonments, Accra; tel. (30) 2233293; monthly.

Christian Messenger: Presbyterian Book Depot Bldg, POB 3075, Accra; tel. and fax (30) 2663124; e-mail danbentil@yahoo.com; f. 1883; English-language; fortnightly; Editor George Martinson; circ. 40,000.

Ghana Journal of Science: National Science and Technology Press, Council for Scientific and Industrial Research, POB M32, Accra; tel. (30) 2500253; monthly; Editor Dr A. K. Ahafia.

Ghana Review International (GRi): POB GP14307, Accra; tel. (30) 2677437; fax (30) 2677438; e-mail accra@ghanareview.com; internet www.ghanareview.com; publishes in Accra, London and New York; CEO Nana Otuo Acheampong; print circ. 100,000.

Ghana Today: Information Services Dept, POB 745, Accra; tel. (30) 2228011; fax (30) 2228089; e-mail isd@mino.gov.gh; English; political, economic, investment and cultural affairs; Dir Elvis Adanyina.

Ideal Woman (Obaa Sima): POB 5737, Accra; tel. (30) 2221399; f. 1971; monthly; Editor Kate Abbam.

New Legon Observer: POB LG 490, Accra, Ghana; tel. (30) 2512503; fax (30) 2512504; e-mail newlegonobserver@ug.edu.gh; internet www.egnghana.org/publications/newLegonObserver.php; f. 2007; publ. by Ghana Society for Development Dialogue; fortnightly; Acting Editor Ernest Aryeetey.

The Post: Ghana Information Services, POB 745, Accra; tel. (30) 2228011; fax (30) 2228089; e-mail isd@mino.gov.gh; f. 1980; monthly; current affairs and analysis; Dir Alphonse Koblavie (acting); circ. 25,000.

Radio and TV Times: Ghana Broadcasting Corpn, Broadcasting House, POB 18167, Accra; tel. (30) 2508927; fax (30) 2773612; f. 1960; quarterly; Editor Sam Thompson; circ. 5,000.

Students World: POB M18, Accra; tel. (30) 2774248; fax (30) 2778715; e-mail afram@wwwplus.co.za; f. 1974; monthly; educational; Man. Editor Eric Ofei; circ. 10,000.

Uneek: POB 230, Achimota, Accra; tel. (30) 2543853; fax (30) 2231355; e-mail info@uneekmagazine.com; internet www.uneekmagazine.com; f. 1998; monthly; leisure, culture; CEO and Editor Francis Adams.

The Watchman: Watchman Gospel Ministry, POB GP4521, Accra; tel. (24) 3780716; e-mail watchmannewspaper@yahoo.com; f. 1986; Christian news; monthly; Pres. and CEO Divine P. Kumah; Chair. Dr E. K. Opuni; circ. 2,000.

Other newspapers include **The Catalyst**, **The Crystal Clear Lens**, **The Enquirer** and **Searchlight**. There are also internet-based news sites, including **Ghana Today**, at www.ghanatoday.com, and **ThisWeekGhana**, at www.thisweekghana.com.

NEWS AGENCY

Ghana News Agency: POB 2118, Accra; tel. (30) 2662381; fax (30) 2669841; e-mail ghnews@ghana.com; internet www.ghananewsagency.org; f. 1957; Gen. Man. Nana Appau Duah; 10 regional offices and 110 district offices.

PRESS ASSOCIATION

Ghana Journalists' Association: POB 4636, Accra; tel. and fax (30) 2234694; e-mail info@gjaghana.org; internet gjaghana.org; Pres. Ransford Tetteh.

Publishers

Advent Press: Osu La Rd, POB 0102, Osu, Accra; tel. (30) 2777861; fax (30) 2775327; e-mail eaokpoti@ghana.com; f. 1937; publishing arm of the Ghana Union Conference of Seventh-day Adventists; Gen. Man. Emmanuel C. Tetteh.

Adwinsa Publications (Ghana) Ltd: 17 Suncity Rd, Agbogba North Legon, POB 92, Legon, Accra; tel. and fax (24) 2366537; e-mail adwinsa@yahoo.com; internet www.adwinsa.com; f. 1977; general, educational; Man. Dir Kwaku Oppong Amponsah.

Afram Publications: C 184/22 Midway Lane, Abofu-Achimota, POB M18, Accra; tel. (24) 4314103; e-mail info@aframpubghana.com; internet aframpubghana.com; f. 1973; textbooks and general; Chair. Prof. Esi Sutherland Addy; Man. Dir Harriet Tagoe.

Africa Christian Press: POB 30, Achimota, Accra; tel. (30) 2244147; fax (30) 2220271; e-mail acpbooks@ghana.com; f. 1964; religious, fiction, theology, children's, leadership; Gen. Man. Richard A. B. Crabbe.

Allgoodbooks Ltd: POB AN10416, Accra-North; tel. (30) 2664294; fax (30) 2665629; e-mail allgoodbooks@hotmail.com; f. 1968; children's; Man. Dir MARY ASIRIFI.

Asempa Publishers: POB GP919, Accra; tel. 289672514; e-mail asempa@iburstgh.com; f. 1970; religion, social issues, African music, fiction, children's; Gen. Man. SARAH O. APRONTI.

Catholic Book Centre: North Liberia Rd, POB 3285, Accra; tel. (30) 2226651; fax (30) 2237727.

Educational Press and Manufacturers Ltd: POB 9184, Airport-Accra; tel. (30) 2220395; f. 1975; textbooks, children's; Man. G. K. KODUA.

Encyclopaedia Africana Project: POB 2797, Accra; tel. (30) 2776939; fax (30) 2779228; e-mail eap@africaonline.com.gh; internet encyclopaediaafricana.org; f. 1962; reference; Dir GRACE BANSA.

Frank Publishing Ltd: POB MB414, Accra; tel. (30) 2240711; f. 1976; secondary school textbooks; Man. Dir FRANCIS K. DZOKOTO.

Ghana Publishing Co Ltd (Assembly Press): Barnes Rd, POB 124, Accra; tel. (30) 2664338; fax (30) 2664330; e-mail info@ghanapublishingcompany.com; internet www.ghanapublishingcompany.com; f. 1965; state-owned; textbooks and general fiction and non-fiction; Chair. Rev. HELENA OPOKU-SARKODIE; Man. Dir DAVID K. DZREKE.

Ghana Universities Press: POB GP4219, Accra; tel. (30) 2513401; fax (30) 2513402; f. 1962; scholarly, academic and general and textbooks; CEO Dr JOHN K. BOSOMTWE (acting).

Sam-Woode Ltd: A979/15 1st Adoley Link, Sahara-Dansoma, POB 12719, Accra-North; tel. (30) 2305287; fax (30) 2310482; e-mail samwoode@ghana.com; internet samwoode.com; f. 1984; educational and children's; Chair. KWESI SAM-WOODE; CEO RICHARD K. OGUAA.

Sedco Publishing Ltd: Sedco House, 5 Tabon St, North Ridge, POB 2051, Accra; tel. (30) 2221332; fax (30) 2220107; e-mail info@sedcopublishing.com; internet www.sedcopublishing.com; f. 1975; educational; Chair. COURAGE K. SEGBAWU; Man. Dir FRANK SEGBAWU.

Smartline (Publishing) Ltd: C3 Coastal Estates, DTD Batsonaa, Spintex Rd, Accra; tel. (30) 2810555; fax (30) 2810426; e-mail info@smartlinepublishers.com; internet smartlinepublishers.com; f. 1997; CEO ELLIOT AGYARE.

Sub-Saharan Publishers: POB 358, Legon, Accra; tel. and fax (30) 2233371; e-mail sub-saharan@ighmail.com; Man. Dir AKOSS OFORI-MENSAH.

Unimax Macmillan Ltd: 42 Ring Rd South Industrial Area, POB 10722, Accra-North; tel. (30) 2227443; fax (30) 2225215; e-mail info@unimacmillan.com; internet www.unimacmillan.com; representative of Macmillan UK; atlases, educational and children's; Man. Dir EDWARD ADDO.

Waterville Publishing House: 101 Miamona Cl., South Industrial Area, POB 195, Accra; tel. (30) 2689973; fax (30) 2689974; e-mail e.amoh@a-riiscompany; internet a-riiscompany.com; f. 1963; general fiction and non-fiction, textbooks, paperbacks, Africana; Man. Dir EMMANUEL AMOH.

Woeli Publishing Services: 19 Agbogba Highway, POB NT601, Accra New Town; tel. and fax (30) 289535570; e-mail woeli@woelipublishing.com; internet www.woelipublishing.com; f. 1984; children's, fiction, academic; Dir WOELI A. DEKUTSEY.

PUBLISHERS' ASSOCIATIONS

Ghana Book Development Council: POB M430, Accra; tel. (30) 2229178; f. 1975; govt-financed agency; promotes and co-ordinates writing, production and distribution of books; Exec. Dir D. A. NIMAKO.

Ghana Book Publishers' Association (GBPA): POB LT471, Laterbiokorshie, Accra; tel. (30) 2912764; fax (30) 2810641; e-mail ghanabookpubs@yahoo.co.uk; internet www.ghanabookpublishers.org; f. 1976; Pres. ASARE KONADU YAMOAH.

Private Newspaper Publishers' Association of Ghana (PRINPAG): POB 125, Darkuman, Accra; Exec. Sec. KENTEMAN NII LARYEA SOWAH.

Broadcasting and Communications

REGULATORY AUTHORITY

National Communications Authority (NCA): 1 Rangoon Close, POB 1568, Cantonments, Accra; tel. (30) 2776621; fax (30) 2763449; e-mail info@nca.org.gh; internet www.nca.org.gh; f. 1996; regulatory body; Chair. KOFI TOTOBI QUAKYI; Dir-Gen. PAAROCK ASSUMAN VANPERCY.

TELECOMMUNICATIONS

In 2013 there were six companies operating in the telecommunications sector in Ghana. Airtel Ghana and Vodafone Ghana provided both mobile cellular and fixed-line telephone services, whereas the four other operators provided solely mobile cellular telephone services. At December 2012 there were 284,981 subscribers to fixed-line services and 25.6m. subscribers to mobile services.

Airtel Ghana: PMB, Accra; e-mail customercare.gh@gh.airtel.com; internet africa.airtel.com; f. 2008; name changed as above in 2010; provides both mobile cellular and fixed-line telephone services; Man. Dir PHILIP SOWAH; 10,320 fixed-line and 3.19m. mobile subscribers (Dec. 2012).

Expresso Telecoms Ghana: POB 10208, Accra; tel. 28282100 (mobile); fax 28210103 (mobile); internet www.expressotelecom.com; frmly Kasapa Telecom Ltd; present name adopted 2010; owned by Expresso Telecom Group (UAE); Man. Dir EL AMIR AHMED EL AMIR YOUSIF; 165,863 subscribers (Dec. 2012).

Glo Mobile Ghana: 4 Adjuma Cres., South Industrial Area, Kaneshie, Accra; e-mail info@glomobileghana.com; internet www.gloworld.com/Ghana; COO GEORGE ANDAH; 1.5m. subscribers (Dec. 2012).

Millicom Ghana Ltd: Millicom Place, Barnes Rd, PMB 100, Accra; tel. 277551000 (mobile); fax 277503999 (mobile); e-mail info@tigo.com.gh; internet www.tigo.com.gh; f. 1990; mobile cellular telephone services through the network Tigo; Man. Dir CARLOS CACERES; 3.69m. subscribers (Dec. 2012).

MTN Ghana: Auto Parts Bldg, 41A Graphic Rd, South Industrial Area, POB 281, International Trade Fair Lane, Accra; tel. 244300000 (mobile); fax (30) 2231974; e-mail customercare@mtn.com.gh; internet www.mtn.com.gh; f. 1994; Ghana's largest mobile cellular telephone provider, through the network MTN (fmrly Areeba); 100% owned by MTN (South Africa); CEO SERAME TAUKOBONG; 11.73m. subscribers (Dec. 2012).

Vodafone Ghana: Telecom House, nr Kwame Nkrumah Circle, PMB 221, Accra-North; tel. (30) 2200200; fax (30) 2221002; e-mail info.gh@vodafone.com; internet www.vodafone.com.gh; f. 1995; name changed as above in 2008, following acquisition of 70% shares in Ghana Telecommunications Company (GT) by Vodafone Group PLC (United Kingdom), 30% govt-owned; operates mobile cellular, fixed-line networks and data services; Chair. KOBINA QUANSAH; CEO HARIS BROUMIDIS; 274,661 fixed-line and 5.25m. mobile subscribers (Dec. 2012).

BROADCASTING

There are internal radio broadcasts in English, Akan, Dagbani, Ewe, Ga, Hausa and Nzema, and an external service in English and French. There are three transmitting stations, with a number of relay stations. The Ghana Broadcasting Corporation operates two national networks, Radio 1 and Radio 2, which broadcast from Accra, and four regional FM stations. In October 2013 there were 28 television and 328 radio stations licensed in Ghana. The Government intends to switch off the analogue television signal and replace it with digital broadcasting throughout the country by the end of 2014.

Ghana Broadcasting Corpn (GBC): Broadcasting House, Ring Rd Central, Kanda, POB 1633, Accra; tel. and fax (30) 2227779; e-mail radioghana@yahoo.com; internet www.gbcghana.com; f. 1935; Dir-Gen. Maj. ALBERT B. DON-CHEBE; Dir of TV (vacant); Dir of Radio YAW OWUSU ADDO.

CitiFM: 11 Tettey Loop, Adabraka, Accra; tel. (30) 2226171; fax (30) 2224043; e-mail info@citifmonline.com; internet www.citifmonline.com; f. 2004; Man. Dir SAMUEL ATTA MENSAH.

Joy FM: 355 Faanofa St, Kokomlemle, POB 17202, Accra; tel. (30) 2701199; fax (30) 2224405; e-mail info@myjoyonline.com; internet www.myjoyonline.com; f. 1995; news, information and music broadcasts; Dir KWESI TWUM.

Metro TV: POB C1609, Cantonments, Accra; tel. (30) 2765701; fax (30) 2765703; e-mail admin@metroworld.tv; internet www.metrotv.com.gh; Chair. KWADWO DABO FRIMPONG; CEO TALAL FATTAL.

Radio Ada: POB KA9482, Accra; tel. (30) 2500907; fax (30) 2516442; e-mail radioada@kalssinn.net; f. 1998; community broadcasts in Dangme; Dirs ALEX QUARMYNE, WILNA QUARMYNE.

Radio Gold FM: POB 17298, Accra; tel. (30) 3300281; fax (30) 3300284; e-mail radiogold@ucomgh.com; internet www.myradiogoldlive.com; Man. Dir BAFFOE BONNIE.

Sky Broadcasting Co Ltd: 45 Water Rd, Kanda Overpass, North Ridge, POB CT3850, Cantonments, Accra; tel. (30) 2225716; fax (30) 2221983; e-mail vayiku@yahoo.com; internet www.spirit.fm; f. 2000; Gen. Man. STEVE ESHUN.

TV3: 12th Rd, Kanda (opposite French embassy), Accra; tel. (30) 2763458; fax (30) 2763450; e-mail info@tv3.com.gh; internet www.tv3.com.gh; f. 1997; private television station; progamming in English and local languages; CEO SANTOKH SINGH.

Vibe FM: Pyramid House, 3rd Floor, Ring Rd Central, Accra; internet www.vibefm.com.gh; educational; CEO MIKE COOKE.

Finance

(cap. = capital; res = reserves; dep. = deposits; m. = million; brs = branches; amounts in Ghana cedis)

BANKING

At the end of 2012 there were 26 deposit money banks (of which 15 were foreign owned), 136 rural and community banks (RCBs) and 52 non-banking financial institutions in Ghana. There was also a mini central bank for the RCBs, ARB Apex Bank Ltd, financed mainly through the Rural Financial Services Project, which is a Government of Ghana project.

Central Bank

Bank of Ghana: 1 Thorpe Rd, POB 2674, Accra; tel. (30) 2666174; fax (30) 2662996; e-mail bogsecretary@bog.gov.gh; internet www.bog.gov.gh; f. 1957; bank of issue; cap. 10.0m., res 741.1m., dep. 3,685.9m. (Dec. 2009); Gov. Dr HENRY AKPENAMAWU KOFI WAMPAH.

Commercial Banks

Bank of Africa (Ghana) Ltd: 131–3 Farrar Ave, Cantonments, POB C1541, Accra; tel. (30) 2249690; fax (30) 2249697; e-mail enquiries@boaghana.com; internet www.boaghana.com; f. 1997; fmrly Amalgamated Bank Ltd, present name adopted 2011; cap. 77.4m., res 19.4m., dep. 476.8m. (Dec. 2012); Man. Dir KOBBY ANDAH; 18 brs.

Energy Bank Ghana Ltd: 30 Independence Ave (Gnat Height), Ridge Area, Accra; tel. (30) 2234033; fax (30) 2234337; internet www.energybankghana.com; f. 2009; commenced operations in 2011; cap. 60.0m., res 4.8m., dep. 115.7m. (Dec. 2012); Chair. Dr JIMOH IBRAHIM; Man. Dir and CEO SAM AYININUOLA.

Fidelity Bank: Ridge Towers, PMB 43, Cantonments, Accra; tel. (30) 2214490; fax (30) 2678868; e-mail info@myfidelitybank.net; internet www.fidelitybank.com.gh; f. 2006; cap. 83.0m., res 32.0m., dep. 1,134.2m. (Dec. 2012); Chair. WILLIAM PANFORD BRAY; CEO and Man. Dir EDWARD EFFAH; 8 brs.

Ghana Commercial Bank Ltd: Thorpe Rd, POB 134, Accra; tel. (30) 2663964; fax (30) 2662168; e-mail gcbmail@gcb.com.gh; internet www.gcb.com.gh; f. 1953; 21.4% state-owned; cap. 72.0m., res 110.0m., dep. 2,330.3m. (Dec. 2012); Chair. Dr FRITZ AUGUSTINE GOCKEL; Man. Dir SIMON DORNOO; 158 brs.

Prudential Bank Ltd: 8 Nima Ave, Ring Rd Central, PMB GPO, Accra; tel. (30) 2781201; fax (30) 2781210; e-mail headoffice@prudentialbank.com.gh; internet www.prudentialbank.com.gh; f. 1996; cap. 62.4m., res 21.9m., dep. 554.0m. (Dec. 2012); Exec. Chair. JOHN SACKAH ADDO; Man. Dir STEPHEN SEKYERE ABANKWA; 16 brs.

uniBank (Ghana) Ltd: Royal Castle Rd, POB AN15367, Kokomlemle, Accra; tel. (30) 2233328; fax (30) 2253695; e-mail info@unibankghana.com; internet www.unibankghana.com; f. 2001; cap. 60.1m., res 30.8m., dep. 765.8m. (Dec. 2012); Chair. OPOKU-GYAMFI BOATENG; Man. Dir FELIX NYARKO-PONG.

Development Banks

Agricultural Development Bank (ADB): ADB House, 37 Independence Ave, POB 4191, Accra; tel. (30) 2770403; fax (30) 2784893; e-mail info@agricbank.com; internet www.agricbank.com; f. 1965; 51.8% state-owned, 48.2% owned by Bank of Ghana; credit facilities for farmers and commercial banking; cap. 75.0m., res 104.6m., dep. 965.0m. (Dec. 2012); Chair. Alhaji IBRAHIM ADAM; Man. Dir STEPHEN KPORDZIH; 50 brs.

National Investment Bank Ltd (NIB): 37 Kwame Nkrumah Ave, POB 3726, Accra; tel. (30) 2661701; fax (30) 2661730; e-mail info@nib-ghana.com; internet www.nib-ghana.com; f. 1963; 86.4% state-owned; provides long-term investment capital, jt venture promotion, consortium finance man. and commercial banking services; cap. 70.0m., res –9.6m., dep. 336.7m. (Dec. 2009); Chair. TOGBE AFEDE; Man. Dir P. T. KWAPONG; 27 brs.

Merchant Banks

CAL Bank Ltd: 23 Independence Ave, POB 14596, Accra; tel. (30) 2680068; fax (30) 2680081; e-mail info@calbank.net; internet www.calbank.net; f. 1990; cap. 100.0m., res 129.6m., dep. 833.8m. (Dec. 2013); Chair. PAAROCK VANPERCY; Man. Dir FRANK BRAKO ADU, Jr.

Ecobank Ghana Ltd (EBG): 19 7th Ave, Ridge West, POB 16746, Accra; tel. (30) 2681146; fax (30) 2680428; e-mail ecobankgh@ecobank.com; internet www.ecobank.com; f. 1989; 92.2% owned by Ecobank Transnational Inc (Togo, operating under the auspices of the Economic Community of West African States); merged with The Trust Bank Ltd June 2012; cap. 226.6m., res 143.7m., dep. 2,740.9m. (Dec. 2012); Chair. LIONEL VAN LARE DOSOO; Man. Dir SAMUEL ASHITEY ADJEI; 7 brs.

First Atlantic Bank Ltd: Atlantic Pl., 1 Seventh Ave, Ridge West, POB C1620, Cantonments, Accra; tel. (30) 2682203; fax (30) 2479245; e-mail info@firstatlanticbank.com.gh; internet www.firstatlanticbank.com.gh; f. 1994; cap. 36.6m., res 16.3m., dep. 130.1m. (Dec. 2011); Chair. KAREN AKIWUMI-TANOH; Man. Dir GABRIEL EDGAL.

Merchant Bank (Ghana) Ltd: Merban House, 44 Kwame Nkrumah Ave, POB 401, Accra; tel. (30) 2666331; fax (30) 2667305; e-mail info@merchantbank.com.gh; internet www.merchantbank.com.gh; f. 1972; cap. 26.8m., res 27.2m., dep. 680.2m. (Dec. 2011); Chair. MARIAN ROSAMOND BARNOR; Man. Dir JOSEPH NII BUDU TETTEH; 21 brs.

Foreign Banks

Barclays Bank of Ghana Ltd (UK): Barclays House, John Evans Atta Mills High St, POB 2949, Accra; tel. (30) 2664901; fax (30) 2669254; e-mail barclays.ghana@barclays.com; internet www.barclays.com/africa/ghana; f. 1971; 90% owned by Barclays Bank Plc; 10% owned by Govt of Ghana; cap. 115.0m., res 152.0m., dep. 1,506.0m. (Dec. 2011); Man. Dir PATIENCE AKYIANU; 62 brs.

Guaranty Trust Bank (Ghana) Ltd: 25A Castle Rd, Ambassadorial Area Ridge, PMB CT416, Accra; tel. (30) 2676474; fax (30) 2662727; e-mail gh.corporateaffairs@gtbank.com; internet www.gtbghana.com; f. 2004; 70% owned by Guaranty Trust Bank Plc, 15% owned by Netherlands Development Finance Co (FMO), 15% owned by Alhaji Yusif Ibrahim; cap. 76.2m., res 22.9m., dep. 266.0m. (Dec. 2011); Man. Dir LEKAN SANUSI.

International Commercial Bank (Ghana) Ltd (Taiwan): Meridian House, Ring Rd Central, PMB 16, Accra; tel. (30) 2236136; fax (30) 2238228; e-mail icb@icbank-gh.com; internet www.icbank-gh.com; f. 1996; cap. and res 31,205m., total assets 218,318m. (Dec. 2003); CEO SANJEEV ANAND; 11 brs.

Societe Generale Ghana Ltd: Ring Rd Central, POB 13119, Accra; tel. (30) 2202001; fax (30) 2248920; internet www.societegenerale.com.gh; f. 1976 as Social Security Bank; 51.0% owned by Société Générale, France; cap. 62.3m., res 95.3m., dep. 926.1m. (Dec. 2013); Chair. KOFI AMPIM; Man. Dir GILBERT HIE; 45 brs.

Stanbic Bank Ghana: Valco Trust House, Castle Rd Ridge, POB CT2344, Cantonments, Accra; tel. (30) 2687670; fax (30) 2687669; e-mail customercare@stanbic.com.gh; internet www.stanbic.com.gh; f. 1999; subsidiary of the Standard Bank of South Africa Ltd; cap. and res 14,981m., total assets 97,253m. (Dec. 2001); Chair. DENNIS W. KENNEDY; Man. Dir ANDANI ALHASSAN; 2 brs.

Standard Chartered Bank Ghana Ltd (UK): 6 John Evans Atta Mills High St, POB 768, Accra; tel. (30) 2664591; fax (30) 2667751; internet www.standardchartered.com/gh; f. 1896 as Bank of British West Africa; cap. 61.6m., res 187.2m., dep. 1,708.9m. (Dec. 2012); Chair. ISHMAEL YAMSON; Country CEO KWEKU BEDU ADDO; 23 brs.

Zenith Bank Ghana (Nigeria): Premier Towers, Liberia Rd, PMB CT393, Accra; tel. (30) 2611500; fax (30) 2660760; e-mail info@zenithbank.com.gh; internet www.zenithbank.com.gh; cap. 61.2m., res 48.7m., dep. 791.5m. (Dec. 2012); Chair. MARY CHINERY-HESSE; CEO DANIEL ASIEDU; 19 brs.

Banking Association

Ghana Association of Bankers (GAB): POB 41, Accra; tel. (30) 2670629; fax 2667138; e-mail info@ghanaassociationofbankers.com; internet ghanaassociationofbankers.com; f. 1980; CEO DANIEL ATO KWAMINA MENSAH.

STOCK EXCHANGE

Ghana Stock Exchange (GSE): Cedi House, 5th Floor, Liberia Rd, POB 1849, Accra; tel. (30) 2669908; fax (30) 2669913; e-mail info@gse.com.gh; internet www.gse.com.gh; f. 1990; 35 listed cos in early 2009; Chair. NORBERT KUDJAWU; Man. Dir KOFI YAMOAH.

INSURANCE

At 1 January 2013 there were 25 non-life insurance companies, 18 life insurance companies and two reinsurance companies in Ghana.

Donewell Insurance Co Ltd: F333/1 Carl Quest St, Kuku Hill, Osu RE, POB 2136, Osu, Accra; tel. (30) 2760483; fax (30) 2760484; e-mail info@donewellinsurance.com; internet www.donewellinsurance.com; f. 1992; Chair. NKANSAH NKANSAH; Man. Dir NII OTINKORANG-ANKRAH.

Enterprise Insurance Co Ltd: Enterprise House, 11 John Evans Atta Mills High St, POB GP50, Accra; tel. (30) 2666847; fax (30) 2666186; e-mail info@enterprisegroup.com.gh; internet enterprisegroup.net.gh; f. 1972; Chair. TREVOR TREFGARNE; Group CEO GEORGE OTOO.

Ghana Life Insurance Co: House No 17, Aviation Rd, Airport Residential Area, POB 8168, Accra; e-mail info@ghanalifeinsurance.com; internet www.ghanalifeinsurance.net; f. 1980; Chair. Eng.

Chief Cyril U. O. Ajagu; Man. Dir and CEO Ivan Avereyireh Abubakar.

Ghana Union Assurance Co Ltd: F828/1 Ring Rd East, POB 1322, Accra; tel. (30) 2780627; fax (30) 2780647; e-mail gua@ghanaunionassurance.com; internet ghanaunionassurance.com; f. 1973; insurance underwriting; Man. Dir Nana Agyei Duku.

Metropolitan Insurance Co Ltd: Caledonian House, Kojo Thompson Rd, POB GP20084, Accra; tel. (30) 2220966; fax (30) 2237872; e-mail met@metinsurance.com; internet www.metinsurance.com; f. 1991; Chair. Sam E. Jonah; CEO Kwame-Gazo Agbenyadzie.

Phoenix Life Assurance Co: Phoenix House, Kanda Highway, Accra; internet www.phoenixlifegh.com; Chair. Emmanuel Adu-Sarkodee; Man. Dir Jemima Kissi.

SIC Insurance Co Ltd: 28/29 Ring Road East, Osu, POB 2363, Accra; tel. (30) 2780600; fax (30) 2662205; e-mail sicinfo@sic-gh.com; internet www.sic-gh.com; f. 1962; 60% state-owned; all classes of insurance; Chair. Max Cobbina; Man. Dir Doris Awo Nkani.

Social Security and National Insurance Trust (SSNIT): Pension House, POB MB 149, Accra; tel. (30) 266773; fax (30) 2686373; e-mail public@ssnit.org.gh; internet www.ssnit.org.gh; f. 1972; covers over 974,666 contributors (Feb. 2012); Chair. Kwame Pepra; Dir-Gen. Ernest Thompson.

Starlife Assurance Co Ltd: C653/3 5th Cres., Asylum Down, POB AN 5783, Accra; tel. (30) 2258946; fax (30) 2258947; e-mail info@starlifegh.com; internet www.starlife.com.gh; f. 2005; Chair. Opoku Gyamfi Boateng; Exec. Vice-Chair. Frank Oppong-Yeboah.

Vanguard Assurance Co Ltd: 21 Independence Ave, POB 1868, Accra; tel. (30) 2666485; fax (30) 2782921; e-mail vacmails@vanguardassurance.com; internet www.vanguardassurance.com; f. 1974; foreign travel, general accident, marine, motor and life insurance; Chair. Kwadwo Obuaobisa Keteku; CEO Gideon Amenyedor; 13 brs.

Regulatory Authority

National Insurance Commission: Insurance Pl., 67 Independence Ave, POB CT3456, Cantonments, Accra; tel. (30) 2238300; fax (30) 2237248; e-mail info@nicgh.org; internet www.nicgh.org; f. 2006; Chair. Frederick Quayenortey; Commr of Insurance Lydia Lariba Bawa.

Insurance Association

Ghana Insurers Association (GIA): 248/9 Kanda, Sunyani Ave, Accra; tel. (30) 2251092; e-mail info@ghanainsurers.org; Pres. Kwame-Gazo Agbenyadzie.

Trade and Industry

GOVERNMENT AGENCIES

Divestiture Implementation Committee: F35, 5 Ring Rd East, North Labone, POB CT102, Cantonments, Accra; tel. (30) 2772049; fax (30) 2773126; e-mail info@dic.com.gh; internet www.dic.com.gh; f. 1988; Chair. Seth Terpker; Exec. Sec. Benson Poku-Adjei.

Environmental Protection Agency (EPA): 91 Starlets Rd, POB M326, Accra; tel. (30) 2664697; fax (30) 2662690; e-mail epaed@africaonline.com.gh; internet www.epa.gov.gh; f. 1974; Chair. Emmanuel F. Siisi-Wilson; Exec. Dir Daniel S. Amlalo.

Export Development and Agricultural Investment Fund (EDAIF): Ghana Olympic Committee Bldg, 3rd Floor, Ridge, POB MB493, Accra; tel. (30) 2918968; fax (30) 2671573; e-mail info@edifghana.org; internet www.edifgh.org; f. 2000; established as Export Development and Investment Fund; named changed as above 2012; Chair. Prof. Francis Dodoo; Chief Exec. Dr Barfour Osei.

Forestry Commission of Ghana (FC): 4 3rd Ave Ridge, PMB 434, Accra; tel. (30) 2401210; fax (30) 2401197; e-mail info@hq.fcghana.com; internet www.fcghana.org; CEO Samuel Afari-Dartey.

Ghana Export Promotion Authority (GEPA): Republic House, Tudu Rd, POB M146, Accra; tel. (30) 2683153; fax (30) 2677256; e-mail gepa@gepaghana.org; internet www.gepaghana.com; f. 1974; Chair. Kobina Ade Coker; CEO Agyeman Kwadwo Owusu.

Ghana Free Zones Board: 5th Link Rd, East Cantonments, POB M626, Accra; tel. (30) 2780535; fax (30) 2785036; e-mail info@gfzb.com.gh; internet www.gfzb.gov.gh; f. 1995; approves establishment of cos in export-processing zones; Chair. Haruna Iddrisu; Exec. Sec. Kwadwo Twum Boafo.

Ghana Heavy Equipment Ltd (GHEL): Old Warehouse under the Bridge, Airport West, POB 1524, Accra; tel. (30) 2680118; fax (30) 2660276; e-mail info@ghelgh.com; internet www.ghelgh.com; fmrly subsidiary of Ghana National Trading Corpn; organizes exports, imports and production of heavy equipment; CEO Yidana Mahami.

Ghana Investment Promotion Centre (GIPC): Public Services Commission Bldg, Ministries, POB M193, Accra; tel. (30) 2665125; fax (30) 2663801; e-mail info@gipcghana.com; internet www.gipcghana.com; f. 1994; negotiates new investments, approves projects, registers foreign capital and decides extent of govt participation; Chair. Dr Michael Agyekum Addo; CEO Mawuena Dumor Trebah.

Ghana Minerals Commission (MINCOM): 12 Switchback Rd Residential Area, POB M248, Cantonments, Accra; tel. (30) 2771318; fax (30) 2773324; e-mail mincom@mc.ghanamining.org; internet www.ghanamining.org; f. 1986 to regulate and promote Ghana's mineral industry; CEO Benjamin Nii Ayi Aryee.

Ghana National Petroleum Authority (NPA): Centurion Bldg No. 11, 5 Circular Rd, PMB CT, Accra; tel. (30) 2766196; fax (30) 2766193; e-mail info@npa.gov.gh; internet www.npa.gov.gh; f. 2005; oversees petroleum sector; Chair. Kojo Fynn; Chief Exec. Alex Mould.

Ghana Standards Authority: POB MB245, Accra; tel. (30) 2500065; fax (30) 2500092; e-mail info@gsa.gov.gh; internet www.gsa.gov.gh; f. 1967; establishes and promulgates standards; promotes standardization, industrial efficiency and devt and industrial welfare, health and safety; operates certification mark scheme; 402 mems; Chair. Samuel Adu-Yeboah; Exec. Dir Dr George Ben Crentsil.

Ghana Trade Fair Co Ltd: Trade Fair Centre, POB 111, Accra; tel. (30) 2776611; fax (30) 2772012; e-mail info@tradefair.com.gh; internet www.tradefair.com.gh; f. 1989; Chair. Capt. (retd) Kojo Butah; CEO Ebenezer Erasmus Okpoti Koney (acting).

Ghana Trade and Investment Gateway Project (GHATIG): POB M47, Accra; tel. (30) 2663439; fax (30) 2773134; e-mail gateway1@ghana.com; promotes private investment and trade, infrastructural devt of free-trade zones and export-processing zones.

GNPA Ltd: POB 15331, Accra-North; tel. (30) 2228321; fax (30) 2221049; e-mail info@gnpa-ghana.com; internet www.gnpa-ghana.com; f. 1976 as Ghana National Procurement Agency; state-owned; part of Ministry of Trade and Industry; procures and markets a wide range of goods and services locally and abroad; CEO Douglas Y. Kumasi (acting).

National Board for Small-scale Industries (NBSSI): POB M85, Accra; tel. (30) 2668641; fax (30) 2661394; e-mail nbssided@ghana.com; f. 1985; part of Ministry of Trade and Industry; promotes small and medium-scale industrial and commercial enterprises by providing credit, advisory services and training; Exec. Dir Lukman Abdul-Rahim.

DEVELOPMENT ORGANIZATIONS

Agence Française de Développement (AFD): 8th Rangoon Close, Ring Rd Central, POB 9592, Airport, Accra; tel. (30) 2778755; fax (30) 2778757; e-mail afdaccra@afd.fr; internet www.afd.fr; f. 1985; fmrly Caisse Française de Développement; Resident Man. Amélie July.

Private Enterprise Foundation (PEF): POB CT1671, Cantonments, Accra; tel. (30) 2515603; fax (30) 2515600; e-mail info@pefghana.org; internet www.pefghana.org; f. 1994; promotes development of private sector; Pres. Asare Akuffo.

Social Investment Fund: off El-Wak Stadium Rd, nr Agricultural Engineering Dept, POB 3919, Cantonments, Accra; tel. (30)2778921; fax (30) 2778404; e-mail info@sifinghana.org; internet www.sifinghana.org; f. 1998; Chair. Jacob Benjamin Quartey-Papafio; Exec. Dir Joseph Acheampong.

CHAMBER OF COMMERCE

Ghana Chamber of Commerce and Industry (GCCI): World Trade Centre, 1st Floor, POB 2325, Accra; tel. (30) 2662860; fax (30) 2662866; e-mail info@ghanachamber.org; internet www.ghanachamber.org; f. 1961; promotes and protects industry and commerce, organizes trade fairs; 3,500 individual mems and 10 mem. chambers; Pres. Seth Adjei Baah; CEO Stephen Oteng.

INDUSTRIAL AND TRADE ORGANIZATIONS

Federation of Associations of Ghanaian Exporters (FAGE): POB M124, Accra; tel. (30) 2766176; fax (30) 2766253; e-mail fage-ghana@gmx.net; non-governmental, not-for-profit org. for exporters of non-traditional exports; Pres. Anthony Sikpa; over 2,500 mems.

Forestry Commission of Ghana, Timber Industry Development Division (TIDD): 4 Third Ave, Ridge, POB MB434, Accra; tel. (30) 2221315; fax (30) 2220818; e-mail info@hq.fcghana.com; internet www.ghanatimber.org; f. 1985; promotes the development of the timber industry and the sale and export of timber; Exec. Dir Dr Ben Donkor.

Ghana Cocoa Board (COCOBOD): Cocoa House, 41 Kwame Nkrumah Ave, POB 933, Accra; tel. (30) 2661872; fax (30) 2661681; e-mail cocobod@cocobod.gh; internet www.cocobod.gh; f. 1947; monopoly purchaser of cocoa until 1993; responsible for purchase, grading and export of cocoa, coffee and sheanuts; also encourages production and scientific research aimed at improving quality and yield of these crops; controls all exports of cocoa; subsidiaries include the Cocoa Marketing Co (Ghana) Ltd and the Cocoa Research Institute of Ghana; Chair. Dr PERCIVAL YAW KURANCHIE; CEO Dr STEPHEN K. OPUNI.

Grains and Legumes Development Board: POB 4000, Kumasi; tel. (32) 2024231; fax (32) 2024778; e-mail gldb@africaonline.com.gh; f. 1970; subsidiary of Ministry of Food and Agriculture; produces, processes and stores seeds and seedlings, and manages national seed security stocks; Chair. Dr GODFRIED ADJEI DIXON; Exec. Dir Dr ROBERT AGYEIBI ASUBOAH.

EMPLOYERS' ORGANIZATION

Ghana Employers' Association (GEA): State Enterprises Commission Bldg, POB GP2616, Accra; tel. (30) 2678455; fax (30) 2678405; e-mail gea@ghanaemployers.com; internet www.ghanaemployers.com; f. 1959; 600 mems (2006); Pres. TERENCE RONALD DARKO; First Vice-Pres. YAW ADU GYAMFI.

Affiliated Bodies

Association of Ghana Industries (AGI): Addison House, 2nd Floor, Trade Fair Centre, POB AN8624, Accra-North; tel. (30) 2779023; fax (30) 2763383; e-mail agi@agighana.org; internet www.agighana.org; f. 1957; Pres. JAMES ASARE-ADJEI; Exec. Dir SETH TWUM-AKWABOAH; c. 500 mems.

Ghana Booksellers' Association: POB 10367, Accra-North; tel. (30) 2773002; fax (30) 2773242; e-mail minerva@ghana.com; Pres. FRED J. REIMMER; Gen. Sec. ADAMS AHIMAH.

Ghana Chamber of Mines: 22 Sir Arku Korsah Rd, Airport Residential Area, POB 991, Accra; tel. (30) 2760652; fax (30) 2760653; e-mail chamber@ghanachamberofmines.org; internet www.ghanachamberofmines.org; f. 1928; Pres. DANIEL OWIREDU; CEO Dr TONI AUBYNN.

Ghana Timber Association (GTA): POB 1020, Kumasi; tel. and fax (32) 2025153; f. 1952; promotes, protects and develops timber industry; Pres. BOATENG OPOKU.

UTILITIES

Regulatory Bodies

Energy Commission (EC): Ghana Airways Ave, Airport Residential Area, Plot 40, Spintex Rd, PMB Ministries, Accra; tel. (30) 2813756; fax (30) 2813764; e-mail info@energycom.gov.gh; internet www.energycom.gov.gh; f. 2001; Chair. Dr FRANCIS DAKURAH; Exec. Sec. Dr ALFRED OFOSU AHENKORAH.

Public Utilities Regulatory Commission (PURC): 51 Liberation Rd, African Liberation Circle, POB CT3095, Cantonments, Accra; tel. (30) 2244181; fax (30) 2244188; e-mail purcsec@purc.com.gh; internet www.purc.com.gh; f. 1997; Chair. EMMANUEL KWAKU ANNAN.

Electricity

Electricity Co of Ghana (ECG): Electro-Volta House, POB 521, Accra; tel. (30) 2676727; fax (30) 2666262; e-mail ecgho@ghana.com; internet www.ecgonline.info; Chair. Dr TONY OTENG GYASI; Man. Dir WILLIAM HUTTON-MENSAH.

Ghana Grid Company Ltd (GRIDCo): POB CS 7979, Tema; tel. (30) 27011185; fax (30) 2676180; e-mail info@gridcogh.com; internet www.gridcogh.com; f. 2006; Chair. EMMANUEL APPIAH KORANG; CEO Dr THOMAS WOBIL ANSAH.

Volta River Authority (VRA): Electro-Volta House, 28th February Rd, POB MB77, Accra; tel. (30) 2664941; fax (30) 2662610; e-mail prunit@vra.com; internet www.vra.com; f. 1961; govt owned; controls the generation and distribution of electricity; Northern Electricity Department of VRA f. 1987 to distribute electricity in northern Ghana; Prof. AKILAGPA SAWYERR; CEO ISAAC KIRK KOFFI.

Water

The Volta Basin Authority (VBA) was created by Ghana, Benin, Burkina Faso, Côte d'Ivoire, Mali and Togo in 2006 to manage the resources of the Volta River basin.

Ghana Water Co Ltd (GWCL): 28th February Rd, POB MB194, Accra; tel. (30) 2666781; fax (30) 2663552; e-mail info@gwcl.com.gh; internet www.gwcl.com.gh; f. 1965 to provide, distribute and conserve water supplies for public, domestic and industrial use, and to establish, operate and control sewerage systems; jointly managed by Aqua Vitens (Netherlands) and Rand Water (South Africa); Chair. ARNOLD H. K. SESHIE; Man. Dir KWAKU GODWIN DOVLO (acting).

CO-OPERATIVES

Department of Co-operatives: POB M150, Accra; tel. (30) 2666212; fax (30) 2772789; f. 1944; govt-supervised body, responsible for registration, auditing and supervision of co-operative socs; Registrar R. BUACHIE-APHRAM.

Ghana Co-operatives Council Ltd (GACOCO): POB 4034, Accra; tel. 244267014 (mobile); fax (30) 2672014; e-mail gacopco@yahoo.com; f. 1951; co-ordinates activities of all co-operative socs and plays advocacy role for co-operative movement; comprises 11 active nat. asscns and 2 central orgs; Sec.-Gen. ALBERT AGYEMAN PREMPEH.

The national associations and central organizations include the Ghana Co-operative Marketing Asscn Ltd, the Ghana Co-operative Credit Unions' Asscn Ltd, the Ghana Co-operative Distillers' and Retailers' Asscn Ltd, and the Ghana Co-operative Poultry Farmers' Asscn Ltd.

TRADE UNIONS

Ghana Federation of Labour: POB Trade Fair 509, Accra; tel. (30) 2252105; fax (30) 2307394; e-mail gflgh@hotmail.com; Sec.-Gen. ABRAHAM KOOMSON; 10,540 mems.

Ghana Trades Union Congress (GTUC): Hall of Trade Unions, Liberia Rd, POB 701, Accra; tel. (30) 2662568; fax (30) 2667161; e-mail info@ghanatuc.org; internet www.ghanatuc.org; f. 1945; 17 affiliated unions; Chair. ALEX K. BONNEY; Sec.-Gen. KOFI ASAMOAH.

Transport

RAILWAYS

Ghana has a railway network of 977 km, which connects Accra, Kumasi and Takoradi. In 2010 a concessionary loan of US $4,000m. was secured from the Export-Import Bank of China to extend the Takoradi–Kumasi railway to Paga on the border with Burkina Faso.

Ghana Railway Co Ltd (GRC): POB 251, Takoradi; f. 1901; responsible for the operation and maintenance of all railways; to be run under private concession from April 2004; 947 km of track in use in 2003; Chair Dr CLEMENT HAMMAH; Man. Dir K. B. AMOFA (acting).

Ghana Railway Development Authority (GRDA): Ministry of Transport, PMB, Accra; tel. (21) 681780; fax (21) 681781; internet grda.gov.gh; f. 2005; regulatory and devt authority; Chair. PEACE JUDITH GEORGE; Man. Dir EMMANUEL OPOKU.

ROADS

In 2012 Ghana had a total road network of approximately 66,200 km, of which 41% was considered to be in 'good condition'.

Ghana Highway Authority: POB 1641, Accra; tel. (30) 2666591; fax (30) 2665571; e-mail eokonadu@highways.mrt.gov.gh; internet www.highways.gov.gh; f. 1974 to plan, develop, administer and maintain trunk roads and related facilities; Chair. JOE GIDISU (acting); Chief Dir TESCHMAKER ANTHONY ESSILFIE.

Intercity State Transport Company (STC) Coaches Ltd: POB 7384, 1 Adjuma Cres., Ring Rd West Industrial Area, Accra; tel. (30) 2221912; fax (30) 2221945; e-mail stc@ghana.com; internet beta.stcghana.com.gh; f. 1965; fmrly State Transport Co; 80% owned by the Social Security and National Insurance Trust, 20% state-owned; above name adopted in 2003; regional and international coach services; Chair. E. K. ASANTE; Man. Dir CHARLES THOMPSON (acting).

SHIPPING

The two main ports are Tema (near Accra) and Takoradi, both of which are linked with Kumasi by rail. There are also important inland ports on the Volta, Ankobra and Tano rivers. At 31 December 2013 the flag registered fleet comprised 125 vessels, totalling 112,854 grt.

Ghana Maritime Authority (GMA): E354/3 Third Ave, East Ridge, PMB 34, Ministries, Accra; tel. (30) 2662122; fax (30) 2677702; e-mail info@ghanamaritime.org; internet www.ghanamaritime.org; f. 2002; policy-making body; part of Ministry of Transport; regulates maritime industry; Dir-Gen. ISSAKA PETER AZUMA.

Ghana Ports and Harbour Authority (GPHA): POB 150, Tema; tel. (30) 3202631; fax (30) 3202812; e-mail headquarters@ghanaports.net; internet www.ghanaports.gov.gh; f. 1986; holding co for the ports of Tema and Takoradi; Dir-Gen. NESTER PERCY GALLEY.

Alpha (West Africa) Line Ltd: POB 451, Tema; operates regular cargo services to West Africa, the United Kingom, the USA, the Far East and northern Europe; shipping agents; Man. Dir AHMED EDGAR COLLINGWOOD WILLIAMS.

Liner Agencies and Trading (Ghana) Ltd: POB 214, Tema; tel. (30) 3202987; fax (30) 3202989; e-mail enquiries@liner-agencies

.com; international freight services; shipping agents; Dir J. OSSEI-YAW.

Maersk Ghana Ltd: Obourwe Bldg, Torman Rd, Fishing Harbour Area, POB 8800, Community 7, Tema; tel. (30) 3218700; fax (30) 3202048; e-mail gnamkt@maersk.com; internet www.maerskline.com/ghana; f. 2001; owned by Maersk Line (Denmark); offices in Tema, Takoradi and Kumasi; Man. Dir JEFF GOSCINIAK.

Scanship (Ghana) Ltd: Mensah Utreh Rd, Commercial Warehouse Area, POB 64, Tema; tel. (30) 3202561; fax (30) 3202571; e-mail scanship.ghana@gh.dti.bollore.com; shipping agents.

Shipping Association

Ghana Shippers' Authority: Enterprise House, 5th Floor, High St, POB 1321, Accra; tel. (30) 2666915; fax (30) 2668768; e-mail info@shippers-gh.com; internet shippers.org.gh; f. 1974; fmrly Ghana Shippers' Council, present name adopted 2010; represents interests of 28,000 registered Ghanaian shippers; also provides cargo-handling and allied services; Chair. G. M. GRIFFITHS; Chief Exec. KOFI MBIAH.

CIVIL AVIATION

The main international airport is at Kotoka (Accra). There are also airports at Kumasi, Takoradi, Sunyani, Tamale and Wa. The construction of a dedicated freight terminal at Kotoka Airport was completed in 1994; in 2001 44,779 metric tons of freight passed through the airport. In 2012 2.27m. passengers passed through Kotoka Airport. The rehabilitation of Kumasi Airport began in 2006, and, following upgrade work, Tamale Airport became the country's second international airport in December 2008.

Ghana Civil Aviation Authority (GCAA): PMB, Kotoka International Airport, Accra; tel. (30) 2776171; fax (30) 2773293; e-mail info@gcaa.com.gh; internet www.gcaa.com.gh; f. 1986; Chair. CHRISTIAN EDEM DOVLO; Dir-Gen. KWAME MAMPHEY.

Afra Airlines Ltd: 7 Nortei St, Airport Residential Area, Accra; tel. 244932488 (mobile); e-mail lukebutler@afraairlines.com; f. 2005; CEO LUKE BUTLER.

Antrak Air: 50 Senchi St, Airport Residential Area, Accra; tel. (30) 2782814; fax (30) 2782816; e-mail info@antrakair.com; internet www.antrakair.com; f. 2003; passenger and cargo services for domestic and international routes; Chair. ASOMA BANDA.

Gemini Airlines Ltd (Aero Gem Cargo): America House, POB 7238, Accra-North; tel. (30) 2771921; fax (30) 2761939; e-mail aerogemcargo@hotmail.com; f. 1974; operates weekly cargo flight between Accra and London; Gen. Man. ENOCH ANAN-TABURY.

Tourism

Ghana's attractions include fine beaches, game reserves, traditional festivals, and old trading forts and castles. In 2010 some 931,000 tourists visited Ghana. Revenue from tourism totalled US $694m. in 2011 (excluding passenger transport).

Ghana Tourist Board: POB GP3106, Accra-North; tel. (30) 2222153; fax (30) 2244611; e-mail gtb@africaonline.com.gh; internet www.touringghana.com; f. 1968; Exec. Dir JULIUS DEBRAH.

Ghana Association of Tourist and Travel Agencies (GATTA): Swamp Grove, Asylum Down, POB 7140, Accra-North; tel. (30) 2222398; fax (30) 2231102; e-mail info@gattagh.com; internet www.gattagh.com; Pres. HILLARIUS MCCASH AKPAH; Exec. Sec. TINA OSEI.

Ghana Tourist Development Co Ltd: POB 8710, Accra-North; tel. (30) 2770720; fax (30) 2770694; e-mail info@ghanatouristdevelopment.com; internet www.ghanatouristdevelopment.com; f. 1974; develops tourist infrastructure, incl. hotels, restaurants and casinos; operates duty-free shops; Man. Dir ALFRED KOMLADZEI.

Defence

As assessed at November 2013, Ghana's total armed forces numbered 15,500 (army 11,500, navy 2,000 and air force 2,000). In 2000 the Government restructured the armed forces; the army was subsequently organized into north and south commands, and the navy into western and eastern commands. In 2004 a peacekeeping training centre, which was primarily to be used by ECOWAS, was established in Accra. At November 2013 a total of 2,773 Ghanaian troops were stationed abroad, of whom 65 were observers.

Defence Expenditure: Estimated at 914m. new cedis for 2014.

Commander-in-Chief of the Armed Forces: Pres. JOHN DRAMANI MAHAMA.

Chief of Defence Staff: Rear Adm. MATTHEW QUARSHIE.

Chief of Air Staff: Air Vice-Marshall MICHAEL SAMSON-OJE.

Chief of Army Staff: Brig.-Gen. RICHARD OPOKU-ADUSEI.

Chief of Naval Staff: Rear Adm. GEOFFREY MAWULI BIEKRO.

Education

Education is officially compulsory and free of charge for eight years, between the ages of six and 14. Primary education begins at the age of six and lasts for six years, comprising two cycles of three years each. Secondary education begins at the age of 12 and lasts for a further seven years, comprising a first cycle of three years and a second of four years. Following three years of junior secondary education, pupils are examined to determine admission to senior secondary school courses, or to technical and vocational courses. In 2013, according to UNESCO, primary enrolment included 87% of children in the relevant age-group (boys 87%; girls 87%), while the comparable ratio for secondary enrolment in 2009 was estimated at 46% (boys 48%; girls 44%). Some 295,300 students were enrolled in tertiary education in 2011/12. There were seven universities in Ghana in 1998/99. In 2012/13 tertiary institutions also include 39 teacher-training colleges and 181 technical and vocational institutes. In 2012 spending on education was 24.4% of total budgetary expenditure.

GREECE

Introductory Survey

LOCATION, CLIMATE, LANGUAGE, RELIGION, FLAG, CAPITAL

The Hellenic Republic lies in south-eastern Europe. The country consists mainly of a mountainous peninsula between the Mediterranean Sea and the Aegean Sea, bounded to the north by Albania, the former Yugoslav republic of Macedonia and Bulgaria, and to the east by Turkey. To the south, east and west of the mainland lie numerous Greek islands, of which the largest is Crete. The climate is Mediterranean, with mild winters and hot summers. The average temperature in the capital is 28°C (82°F) in July and 9°C (48°F) in January. The language is Greek, of which there are two forms—the formal language (katharevoussa) and the language commonly spoken and taught in schools (demotiki). Almost all of the inhabitants profess Christianity, and the Greek Orthodox Church, to which about 97% of the population adhere, is the established religion. The national flag (proportions 2 by 3) displays nine equal horizontal stripes of blue and white, with a white cross throughout a square canton of blue at the upper hoist. The capital is Athens (Athinai).

CONTEMPORARY POLITICAL HISTORY

Historical Context

The liberation of Greece from the German occupation (1941–44) was followed by a civil war, which lasted until 1949. The communist forces were defeated, and the constitutional monarchy re-established. King Konstantinos (Constantine) II acceded to the throne on the death of his father, King Pavlos (Paul), in 1964. A succession of weak governments and conflicts between the King and his ministers culminated in a coup, led by right-wing army officers, in April 1967. An attempted counter-coup, led by the King, failed, and he went into exile. Col Georgios Papadopoulos became Prime Minister in December 1967 and Regent in March 1972.

Following an abortive naval mutiny, Greece was declared a republic in June 1973, and Papadopoulos was appointed President. Martial law was ended, and a civilian Government was appointed. A student uprising in Athens in November was violently suppressed by the army, and Papadopoulos was overthrown by another military coup. Lt-Gen. Phaidon Ghizikis was appointed President, and a mainly civilian Government, led by Adamantios Androutsopoulos, was installed, but effective power lay with a small group of officers and the military police under Brig.-Gen. Demetrios Ioannides. Following the failure of the military junta's attempt to overthrow President Makarios of Cyprus, and the Turkish invasion of the island, the Androutsopoulos administration collapsed in July 1974. Ghizikis summoned from exile a former Prime Minister, Konstantinos Karamanlis, who was invited to form a civilian Government of National Salvation. Martial law was ended, the press was released from state control and political parties were allowed to operate freely. A general election in November resulted in victory for Karamanlis's Nea Demokratia (ND—New Democracy), which won 220 of the 300 parliamentary seats. A referendum in December rejected proposals for a return to constitutional monarchy, and in June 1975 a new republican Constitution, providing for a parliamentary democracy, was promulgated. In the same month Prof. Konstantinos Tsatsos was elected President by the Vouli (Parliament).

At legislative elections in November 1977 ND was returned to power. In May 1980 Karamanlis was elected President; Georgios Rallis subsequently assumed the leadership of ND and was appointed Prime Minister. On 1 January 1981 Greece acceded to the European Community (EC, now the European Union—EU, see p. 273). The main opposition Panellinio Socialistiko Kinima (PASOK—Panhellenic Socialist Movement) secured an absolute majority at elections to Parliament in October, and the PASOK leader, Andreas Papandreou, became Prime Minister.

In March 1985 Karamanlis resigned in protest at plans by Papandreou to reduce his executive powers, and Parliament elected Christos Sartzetakis, a judge, as President. Legislative elections were held in June 1985 to enable the Government to secure support for the proposed constitutional changes. PASOK was returned to power, winning 161 seats in the 300-member Vouli. In March 1986 Parliament approved a series of constitutional amendments limiting the powers of the President. In May 1987, in response to ND accusations of mismanagement and corruption, Papandreou secured a parliamentary vote of confidence in his Government. However, in November 1988 several prominent ministers, having been implicated in a financial scandal, were forced to resign.

In January 1989 the Greek Left Party, led by Leonidas Kyrkos, formed an electoral alliance with the 'Exterior' faction of the Kommunistiko Komma Ellados (KKE—Communist Party of Greece), under the leadership of Charilaos Florakis, to create the Coalition of the Left and Progress (the Left Coalition). At elections in June, ND won the largest proportion of the votes cast, but failed to attain an overall majority in Parliament. The Left Coalition eventually agreed to form an interim administration with ND, on the condition that ND leader Konstantinos Mitsotakis renounced his claim to the premiership. Accordingly, Tzannis Tzannetakis, an ND deputy, was appointed Prime Minister of a Government that included two communist ministers. The coalition announced its intention to govern for only three months, and to implement a *katharsis* (campaign of purification) of Greek politics. The administration duly resigned in October, having initiated investigations into the alleged involvement of officials of the former socialist Government in various malpractices. (In 1991 Papandreou and three of his former ministers were tried on charges of complicity in large-scale embezzlement during their terms of office. In 1992 Papandreou was acquitted, and two of the former ministers received minor sentences; the third had died during the trial.) The President of the Supreme Court, Ioannis Grivas, was appointed Prime Minister of an interim Government comprising non-political figures, which was to oversee further legislative elections. The results of the elections, conducted in November 1989, were again inconclusive. In mid-November ND, PASOK and the Left Coalition agreed to form an interim coalition. However, following a dispute over military promotions in February 1990, the Government collapsed, and the former administration was reinstated on an interim basis. Further elections, conducted in April, resolved the impasse; ND secured 150 seats in Parliament. Mitsotakis secured the support of Konstantinos Stefanopoulos, the leader (and the sole parliamentary representative) of the Party of Democratic Renewal, thereby enabling him to form the first single-party Government since 1981. In May 1990 Karamanlis took office as President for a five-year term, following his election by 153 of the 300 members of Parliament. Stefanopoulos formally joined ND in June.

Domestic Political Affairs

In April 1992 the Prime Minister successfully sought a vote of confidence from Parliament, following the dismissal of the Minister of Foreign Affairs, Antonis Samaras, and Mitsotakis's assumption of the portfolio in order to address attempts by the former Yugoslav republic of Macedonia (FYRM—q.v.) to achieve international recognition as the Republic of Macedonia (see below). In August Michalis Papakonstantinou was allocated the foreign affairs portfolio. Industrial unrest continued throughout 1992 and 1993, in protest against government austerity measures.

In September 1993 two ND deputies resigned, following an appeal for support by Political Spring (POLAN), a centre-right party that had been established in July by Samaras. The consequent loss of Mitsotakis's one-seat majority in Parliament obliged him to offer the Government's resignation and schedule early legislative elections. At the elections, conducted in October, PASOK obtained 46.9% of the total votes cast and 170 of the 300 parliamentary seats, while ND received 39.3% of the votes and 111 seats, and POLAN 4.9% of the votes and 10 seats. In October Mitsotakis resigned as leader of ND.

In March 1995 Stefanopoulos was elected President by 181 of the 300 members of Parliament. From mid-1995 tensions within the governing PASOK became increasingly evident. A group of 'dissident' PASOK deputies, including Konstantinos Simitis and

Theodoros Pangalos, urged the resignation of Andreas Papandreou, and the implementation of further reforms within the party. In November the Prime Minister was admitted to hospital; Apostolos-Athanassios (Akis) Tsohatzopoulos assumed Papandreou's prime ministerial duties, in an acting capacity. On 15 January 1996 Papandreou submitted his resignation as Prime Minister. Three days later, Simitis was elected to the premiership by the PASOK parliamentary faction. Simitis awarded Pangalos the foreign affairs portfolio, while pro-European ministers replaced the majority of Papandreou's former associates.

Following Papandreou's death in June 1996, Simitis was elected leader of PASOK, defeating Tsohatzopoulos. In early legislative elections, held on 22 September, PASOK won 162 of the 300 parliamentary seats, with 41.5% of the votes cast, while ND obtained 108 seats (38.2%); POLAN failed to obtain parliamentary representation. Principal ministers in the outgoing Government were retained in the new PASOK administration. In March 1997 Konstantinos (Kostas) Karamanlis (a nephew of the former President and ND party leader) was elected leader of ND.

In February 1999 it emerged that dissident Kurdish leader Abdullah Öcalan, who had been charged with terrorism by Turkey, had been given refuge at the Greek embassy in Kenya, before being detained by the Turkish authorities. The Ministers of the Interior, Public Administration and Decentralization, of Foreign Affairs, and of Public Order subsequently resigned, prompting a government reorganization. Vasiliki Papandreou was appointed Minister of the Interior, Public Administration and Decentralization, and Georgios Papandreou (the son of the late Andreas Papandreou) replaced Pangalos as Minister of Foreign Affairs.

On 9 February 2000 Stefanopoulos was re-elected President by 269 of the 300 members of Parliament. At early legislative elections on 9 April, PASOK was returned to office, winning 43.8% of the votes cast and 158 parliamentary seats, narrowly defeating ND, with 42.7% of the votes and 125 seats. On 12 April Simitis formed a new Government. In October 2001 Simitis reorganized the Government, following his re-election as PASOK party leader.

In January 2004 Simitis announced his resignation from the leadership of PASOK, and scheduled early legislative elections for 7 March, asserting that an administration with a new mandate was necessary to address developments on the issue of Cyprus (see below). On 8 February Georgios Papandreou was elected unopposed as the President of PASOK.

The 2004 elections: ND Government

At the legislative elections held on 7 March 2004, ND secured 45.4% of the votes cast, thereby removing PASOK, which won 40.6% of the votes, from government. A new administration, headed by Karamanlis, was installed on 10 March. Greece's hosting of the summer Olympic Games in August was widely considered to be a success for the Government (although the cost was reported to have greatly exceeded projections). However, in November the Government publicly conceded that the PASOK administration had significantly understated public debt and budgetary deficit figures for several years in order for Greece to qualify for membership of the EU's economic and monetary union (EMU) in January 2001, after evidence to that effect emerged; it appeared that continued misrepresentation of defence expenditure had partially caused the discrepancies. The statement provoked a dispute between the ruling ND and PASOK, which criticized the revision of past official figures. On 8 February 2005 Karolos Papoulias, a member of PASOK and a former Minister of Foreign Affairs, was elected unopposed as President, receiving 279 votes in the 300-member Vouli; Papoulias was inaugurated as President on 12 March.

In early February 2006 the Government revealed that mobile cellular telephones belonging to Karamanlis, to prominent government and opposition members, and to public officials had been clandestinely monitored between June 2004 and March 2005. Later in February 2006 an extensive reorganization of the Government included the appointment of Dora Bakoyannis, a member of ND, the hitherto Mayor of Athens, and the daughter of former Prime Minister Mitsotakis, as Minister of Foreign Affairs. Local government elections took place on 15 and 22 October. ND retained control of some 30 prefectural councils and the municipalities of Athens and Thessaloníki, while PASOK increased its representation from 19 to 22 councils and gained control of the port towns of Piraeus and Patras. In December, following an independent inquiry, the mobile cellular telecommunications operator Vodafone Greece was ordered to pay €76m., after being held responsible for the illegal surveillance (believed to be linked to security concerns relating to the holding of the summer Olympic Games in 2004).

On 25 August 2007 Karamanlis declared a state of emergency after forest fires resulted in the deaths of some 65 people. Seven suspects were subsequently charged with arson. In late August an estimated 10,000 people held a protest in Athens at the perceived inadequacy of the Government's response to the emergency; it was further alleged that poor control of forests had prompted arsonists to take action to clear land for unauthorized building. At legislative elections conducted on 16 September ND was returned to power, securing 41.8% of the votes cast and 152 seats in Parliament. PASOK, with 38.1% of the votes, won a reduced number of seats (102), followed by the KKE (with 8.2% of votes and 22 seats) and the Synaspismós Rizospastikís Aristerás (SYRIZA—Coalition of the Radical Left—5.0% of votes and 14 seats); an extreme nationalist organization, Laikos Orthodoxos Synagermos (LAOS—Popular Orthodox Rally), received 3.8% of the votes and 10 seats, obtaining parliamentary representation for the first time. The rate of participation by the electorate was some 74.1%. Karamanlis subsequently established a smaller administration; the Ministry of Public Order was merged into the Ministry of the Interior.

PASOK's return to power

The international financial crisis from late 2008 exacerbated economic hardship and public discontent, and there were widespread skirmishes between police and disaffected youths. On 6 December a 15-year-old was shot and killed in Exarchia, an impoverished district of Athens. Two police officers were charged in connection with the killing, which precipitated rioting in Athens, Thessaloníki and other towns. Students occupied numerous universities and schools in Athens and Thessaloníki, benefiting from a constitutional provision that prohibited police from entering the grounds of certain educational establishments. A one-day national strike by public sector unions in protest against the Government's economic policies proceeded on 10 December, and developed into more general protests against further austerity measures planned by the Government. In early January 2009 a protest, organized mainly by students and teachers against the education reforms, police repression and the social system, was violently suppressed by police.

In January 2009 Karamanlis announced an extensive ministerial reorganization, in an effort to restore public confidence in the Government. At elections to the European Parliament on 7 June, PASOK secured 36.7% of the votes cast and eight seats, ND obtained 32.3% of the votes and eight seats, the KKE 8.4% and two seats, and LAOS 7.2% and two seats; 52.6% of the registered electorate participated in the elections. On 2 September Karamanlis requested the dissolution of Parliament, and announced that the legislative elections (due in September 2011) would be brought forward to October 2009. Parliament was officially dissolved on 9 September.

In the legislative elections held on 4 October 2009 PASOK secured victory, with 43.9% of the votes cast and 160 seats, while ND received 33.5% of the votes and 91 seats; the KKE received 7.5% and 21 seats, LAOS 5.6% and 15 seats, and SYRIZA 4.6% and 13 seats. The rate of participation was recorded at 70.9% of the registered electorate. In response to the party's defeat, Karamanlis resigned as President of ND; he was succeeded, in November, by Samaras, who had rejoined the party in 2004. The President of PASOK, Georgios Papandreou, appointed a new Government on 7 October 2009; Papandreou assumed the foreign affairs portfolio, in addition to the premiership, while former Minister of Foreign Affairs Theodoros Pangalos received the new position of Deputy Chairman of the Government, responsible for Co-ordination of the Foreign Policy and Defence Committee and the Economic and Social Policy Committee. The new administration, which also included two new ministries, won a motion of confidence in Parliament on 19 October. In December anti-Government demonstrations on the anniversary of the killing of the student in the previous year resulted in violence in central Athens and Thessaloníki; more than 150 people were arrested. Later in December the adoption of an austerity budget by Parliament prompted further public protests and days of national strike; these intensified from February 2010. A new programme of spending reductions and tax increases (which was opposed by ND) was adopted by Parliament on 5 March; a large trade union protest in central Athens was disrupted by members of extremist groups, resulting in violent clashes.

Meanwhile, on 3 February 2010 President Papoulias was elected, again unopposed, by Parliament for a further term of office, obtaining the support of 266 deputies. On 2 May the EU, the IMF and the European Central Bank (ECB) 'troika' reached agreement with Greece on an austerity programme intended to stabilize the Greek economy, which was adopted by Parliament four days later. (Three PASOK deputies who had opposed the motion were subsequently expelled from the party, thereby reducing its representation in the legislature to 157 seats.) Meanwhile, on 5 May, when a national strike was scheduled, a large-scale demonstration in Athens against the planned measures escalated into violence, and protesters attempted to occupy the parliamentary building; three people died in a fire at a bank that had been attacked.

In June 2010 trade unions organized a one-day strike against austerity measures (which included further extensive changes to the pension system), and a large-scale demonstration took place in Athens. Nevertheless, on 8 July (when a further one-day strike was held) the pension reforms were adopted, with the support of 159 votes in Parliament. A subsequent strike by truck drivers from late July, in protest at government plans to issue cheaper truck licences, resulted in nationwide fuel shortages and the suspension of transport services. The strike action was suspended on 1 August, after protesters agreed to enter into dialogue with the Government.

On 7 September 2010 Prime Minister Papandreou implemented an extensive government reorganization that was intended to support efforts to combat the debt crisis. Minister of Finance Georgios Papaconstantinou was retained, while Papandreou's additional portfolio of foreign affairs was reallocated to Deputy Prime Minister Pangalos. In the same month truck drivers resumed strike action, as Parliament adopted legislation liberalizing licensing regulations in the sector. Meanwhile, a police officer was sentenced to life imprisonment for the intentional killing of the student in December 2008, while his patrol partner received a custodial term of 10 years for complicity. The outcome of forthcoming local elections was regarded as a gauge of public support for the Government's economic programme. In the event, when the elections took place on 7 and 14 November 2010, PASOK won about 34.6% of the votes cast nationwide, narrowly defeating ND (which received 32.8% of the votes), despite registering a significant loss of support compared with the 2009 legislative elections; PASOK secured governorships in eight of the 13 regions and ND in five. (However, an exceptionally high rate of abstention was reported.)

During December 2010 public transport workers staged further one-day strikes in protest at salary reductions and the planned restructuring of state-owned transport companies. Later that month the adoption of the austerity budget for 2011 precipitated further protests in Athens. Public transport strikes continued in early 2011, despite a court order ruling the action to be illegal. Nevertheless, on 16 February Parliament adopted legislation providing for the reform of the public transport system. On 23 February, when a national strike and protests were organized, Parliament approved legislation liberalizing licensing regulations in a large number of professions.

Deepening fiscal crisis and new rescue plan

On 17 June 2011 Papandreou again reorganized the Government; notably, Papaconstantinou was removed from his position as Minister of Finance and replaced by Evangelos Venizelos, hitherto the Minister of National Defence, who also became a Deputy Chairman of the Government. Panos Beglitis was appointed as Minister of National Defence, and Stavros Lambrinidis replaced Dimitris Doutras as Minister of Foreign Affairs. At the end of June, amid a two-day national strike and violent protests outside the parliament building, Parliament approved a programme of austerity measures, deemed necessary by the EU and the IMF in order to mitigate the deepening financial crisis and provide for the release of further emergency funds; lending was duly approved by EU Ministers of Finance in early July. On 21 July, at an emergency summit meeting, held in Brussels, Belgium, eurozone leaders agreed the terms of a new, three-year rescue plan for Greece.

At the beginning of October 2011 the Government acknowledged that it would not meet budget deficit targets agreed with the EU and the IMF, and agreed further austerity measures, which included severe retrenchment in the state sector. On the following day eurozone Ministers of Finance, meeting in Luxembourg, agreed to postpone until November a decision on Greece's eligibility for continued funding under the EU-IMF package. On 20 October, amid a further two-day national strike and a protest staged by some 100,000 people outside the parliamentary building that escalated into violent clashes, Parliament adopted the new austerity measures (by 154 votes to 144), thereby allowing the disbursement of rescue funds to proceed. At a summit meeting in Brussels on 26–27 October, eurozone leaders reached a new agreement intended to reverse the escalating sovereign debt crisis. An emergency funding plan of €130,000m. for Greece was conditionally approved (after it had become evident that the programme agreed in July was no longer adequate to prevent a Greek debt default).

At the end of October 2011, however, Papandreou unexpectedly announced that the new rescue plan and accompanying economic measures would require endorsement at a national referendum. Papandreou's decision precipitated a further dramatic loss of confidence in international financial markets, and eurozone leaders demanded that he attend emergency discussions; disbursement of funds was again suspended, pending adoption of the rescue plan. The proposed referendum also prompted criticism and demands for Papandreou's resignation from within the Government and PASOK, with one PASOK parliamentarian resigning from the party. Convening an emergency cabinet meeting on 3 November, Papandreou agreed to abandon the planned referendum and to enter into dialogue with ND on the creation of an interim administration. On 5 November Papandreou's Government narrowly survived a vote of confidence in Parliament. Nevertheless, since ND remained unwilling to participate in a transitional government headed by Papandreou, he announced his resignation on the following day.

On 10 November 2011 Lucas Papademos, a former Governor of the Greek Central Bank and Vice-President of the ECB, received a mandate from President Papoulias to establish a transitional coalition administration. Several prominent members of the outgoing PASOK Government remained in the cabinet, while ND representatives received principal portfolios. Early legislative elections, initially scheduled for February 2012, were later postponed until May.

A general strike in protest against the austerity measures was organized by trade unions at the beginning of December 2011, and a protest, which resulted in clashes with police, was staged to coincide with the adoption of the 2012 budget by Parliament on 6 December 2011. In early 2012 the agreement of government party leaders to the implementation of spending reductions amounting to 1.5% of GDP and labour market reforms became an urgent priority in order to permit the rescue plan to proceed, and thereby avert a default on its debt by Greece. On 10 February LAOS withdrew its four representatives from the governing coalition and a PASOK deputy minister resigned, in protest against the austerity measures. The measures were formally adopted by 199 votes to 74 in Parliament on 12 February, while violent protests, with a number of arson attacks against shops and banks, took place in central Athens. On 21 February eurozone ministers responsible for finance formally agreed the second rescue plan, with a number of additional preconditions. Amid continuing anti-austerity protests, Parliament subsequently began to adopt reforms in accordance with EU requirements, and agreement was reached on debt-restructuring. In mid-March eurozone member states and the IMF approved a joint financing plan amounting to some €172,600m. (including unspent funds from the previous package) over four years, and the first critical EU instalment was subsequently released. On 20 March Venizelos announced his resignation as Minister of Finance, following his election as PASOK leader.

Legislative elections and revised rescue plan

The legislative elections were conducted on 6 May 2012: ND obtained 108 seats, SYRIZA 52 seats and PASOK 41 seats. After attempts by the main parties to form a governing coalition were unsuccessful, new elections were scheduled, and an interim administration was installed, headed by Panagiotis Pikrammenos (hitherto the President of the supreme administrative court, the Council of State). At the legislative elections held on 17 June ND won 29.7% of the votes and 129 seats in Parliament, while SYRIZA secured 71 seats and PASOK won 33 seats. Four smaller parties also obtained representation, among them the extreme nationalist Chrysi Avgi (Golden Dawn) party, which took 18 seats. The results were widely interpreted as a public endorsement of continued Greek membership of the eurozone. On 21 June a new Government was formed under the premiership of Antonis Samaras, the President of ND, who had succeeded in reaching a coalition agreement with PASOK and the small Dimokratiki Aristera (DIMAR—Democratic Left) party. Ioannis Stournaras, an independent economist, received the post of

Minister of Finance in early July, after the newly appointed minister resigned owing to illness. The new administration, principally comprising members of ND (PASOK and DIMAR each proposed two independent politicians) was approved by a vote of confidence in Parliament on 8 July.

During August 2012 Samaras sought to negotiate a two-year extension, to 2016, of the deadline for Greece to meet the fiscal targets agreed with the EU-IMF-ECB troika. In September discussions were suspended, pending the finalization of further austerity measures by the Government, resulting in a delay in the disbursement of a loan instalment required to avert the country's bankruptcy. Meanwhile, emergency workers staged protests outside Parliament against a planned 5%–10% reduction in wages for public sector workers, and a further general strike took place. Large anti-austerity demonstrations were organized to coincide with the visit to Athens of German Chancellor Angela Merkel on 9 October. Meanwhile, increasing dissension over austerity policies was reported within the ruling coalition, and essential legislation on privatization was only narrowly approved in Parliament at the end of October.

Despite further violent protests and strike action, in early November 2012 new, stringent measures, which included a two-year increase in the retirement age, were adopted by 153 deputies in Parliament. One ND representative and six PASOK deputies were subsequently expelled from their respective parties owing to their failure to support the programme; DIMAR also opposed the measures. Parliamentary approval of a revised budget for 2013 followed in November; however, eurozone Ministers of Finance subsequently delayed a decision on the release of funds, while approving the two-year extension for meeting fiscal targets. On 27 November the troika finally reached agreement on the disbursement of funds and also on further concessions for the reduction of Greece's debt (see Economic Affairs). In early December, in fulfilment of an additional condition, Greece succeeded in purchasing about €31,800m. of its debt from holders of sovereign bonds. On 13 December the troika confirmed the measures of 27 November, and the delayed EU tranche of €34,300m. was subsequently disbursed.

In February 2013 a former mayor of Thessaloníki and two other officials were sentenced to life imprisonment for the embezzlement of some €18m. in public funds. In early March former Minister of National Defence and prominent PASOK politician Akis Tsohatzopoulos received an eight-year term of imprisonment for failing to disclose his financial assets; three other former ministers were charged with similar offences.

In early June 2013 the Government announced the closure of the state radio and television broadcasting network, ERT, in an effort to satisfy redundancy targets imposed by the troika. Transmission was halted on the same day, under an emergency ministerial decree, despite the opposition of PASOK and DIMAR, prompting public protests. (ERT workers subsequently continued illicit broadcasts until the interim replacement service was established in early August.) Although PASOK subsequently reached consensus with ND, on 21 June DIMAR withdrew from the Government. On 24 June Samaras announced a government reorganization, in an effort to avert the necessity of scheduling new legislative elections; the new administration included 11 PASOK members, notably, PASOK leader Venizelos, who was appointed Deputy Prime Minister and Minister of Foreign Affairs.

In early July 2013 disbursement of the next tranche in aid to Greece was approved, after the Government agreed to implement further large-scale public sector dismissals demanded by the troika. Later that month Parliament voted to charge former Minister of Finance Papaconstantinou (who had been expelled from PASOK in December 2012) over his failure to investigate cases of alleged tax evasion, following the unauthorized publication, by investigative journalist Kostas Vaxevanis, of a list, which had been supplied to the Government by French officials, of more than 2,000 Greeks with Swiss bank accounts. Also in July Parliament approved reforms to the civil service and tax administration, in preparation for the dismissal of some 15,000 public sector workers by the end of 2014.

Recent developments: government measures against Chrysi Avgi

Amid reports that members of Chrysi Avgi were staging a campaign of intimidation against immigrants and committing other anti-social acts, in September 2013 an anti-fascist activist, Pavlos Fyssas, was killed by a self-declared sympathizer of Chrysi Avgi in the outskirts of Athens. Police raided Chrysi Avgi headquarters in Athens and at least 10 members of the organization were arrested in connection with the murder, which prompted nationwide protests. Minister of National Defence Dimitris Avramopoulos ordered an investigation into allegations that members of the armed forces were involved in the formation and training of a military wing by Chrysi Avgi, and two senior police officers were obliged to resign owing to suspected connections to the organization. Later in September some 19 members, including Chrysi Avgi's leader, Nikolaos Michaloliakos, and six prominent parliamentary deputies, were arrested; Michaloliakos and three of the deputies were subsequently detained on charges of organizing a criminal group. In October Parliament voted in favour of removing the parliamentary immunity of the six deputies, and of suspending state financing for political parties whose leaders were charged with serious crimes. (The suspension of state funding for Chrysi Avgi was approved by Parliament in December.)

Meanwhile, in September and November 2013 public sector workers staged further nationwide strike action in protest at government plans for continued retrenchment in the civil service in compliance with the demands of the troika. The Government survived a parliamentary vote of no confidence on 11 November, which had been proposed in response to a police raid on former ERT offices earlier that month; however, a PASOK deputy was expelled from the party after supporting the motion, while in December the Government's parliamentary majority was further reduced by the expulsion from ND of a deputy who had voted against the introduction of a controversial property tax. Amid concerns that elections to the European Parliament in May 2014 would precipitate increased political instability, the Government insisted in early January that the country was emerging from recession, and that the austerity programme would end that year. Later that month the Council of State ruled that members of the military and police be reimbursed for wage cuts implemented under the 2012 austerity measures. Greece (which had assumed the rotating presidency of the Council of the EU for a period of six months on 1 January 2014) continued negotiations with the troika on economic reform proposals for that year. Following a further delay in funding, on 18 March it was announced that agreement had been reached on the release of some €10,000m. in assistance; troika officials verified a primary budget surplus for 2013 projected by the Government, which announced that part of the surplus would be allocated to supplement the incomes of the most impoverished, including military and police personnel, and to meet a shortfall in the social insurance budget.

Domestic extremism

Throughout the 1990s and early 2000s numerous bomb attacks against military and commercial targets in Greece were carried out by dissident groups, in particular the extremist left-wing November 17 Revolutionary Organization (active since 1975) and the Revolutionary People's Struggle (ELA). In June 2000 a British defence attaché, Brig. Stephen Saunders, was assassinated by the November 17 group. The first arrest of a member of November 17 took place in June 2002, and the police subsequently arrested the movement's leader, Alexandros Giotopoulos. Shortly afterwards the Government announced that November 17 had been disbanded. By January 2003 a total of 19 suspected members of November 17 had been apprehended. The trial of all 19 alleged members of November 17 was concluded in December; Giotopoulos and five others were sentenced to life imprisonment, and eight defendants received lesser custodial sentences. In October five members of the ELA, including the movement's leader, were each sentenced to 25 years' imprisonment on charges relating to more than 100 bomb attacks.

Meanwhile, another extremist left-wing organization, Revolutionary Struggle (EA), which had emerged in 2003, claimed responsibility for numerous bomb attacks, including an assassination attempt against the Minister of Culture, Georgios Voulgarakis, in May 2006 and a rocket attack against the US Embassy in Athens in January 2007. Public disorder after December 2008 (see above) also gave rise to a resurgence in extremist activity. A group believed to be affiliated to the EA, the Sect of Revolutionaries (SE), issued threats to attack police and government facilities, and in June 2009 claimed responsibility for the killing of a police officer. In September four terrorist suspects, alleged to be members of the previously unknown Conspiracy of Fire Nuclei (SPF), were arrested on charges related to a bomb attack at the residence of a former Minister of Public Order in July, and against a PASOK parliamentary deputy earlier in September. In June 2010 an employee at the

Ministry of Civic Protection was killed by a parcel bomb. In November the SPF claimed responsibility for the dispatch of parcel bombs to a number of embassies in Athens, as well as to foreign government headquarters and embassies abroad. Following a police operation in December, a total of 26 suspected members of the SPF were arrested in connection with the parcel bombs and other attacks in Athens. In July 2011 six members of the SPF received prison sentences of between 11 and 25 years for bomb attacks in 2009. Amid continued social unrest, in January 2013 incendiary attacks were staged against party headquarters, the residences of journalists and commercial premises, while a gun attack took place at the office of Prime Minister Antonis Samaras; the incidents were widely attributed to left-wing anarchist groups. In November a previously unknown group, the Militant People's Revolutionary Forces, claimed responsibility for an attack in Athens in which two Chrysi Avgi members were shot and killed and a third was injured.

Regional Affairs

Relations with Turkey have been characterized by long-standing disputes concerning Cyprus (q.v.) and sovereignty over the continental shelf beneath the Aegean Sea. Tensions were exacerbated by the unilateral declaration of an 'independent' Turkish Cypriot state in Cyprus in November 1983 (the 'Turkish Republic of Northern Cyprus'—'TRNC'). In March 1987 a disagreement between Greece and Turkey over petroleum-prospecting rights in disputed areas of the Aegean Sea almost resulted in military conflict. In January 1988, however, the Greek and Turkish Prime Ministers, meeting (in the first formal contact between Greek and Turkish Heads of Government for 10 years) in Davos, Switzerland, agreed that joint committees should be established to negotiate peaceful solutions to disputes.

In 1994 Greece's stated intention of exercising its right, enshrined in the international Convention on the Law of the Sea (the International Seabed Authority, see p. 352), to extend its territorial waters from six to 12 nautical miles precipitated a further dispute with Turkey. Tensions intensified prior to the scheduled entry into force of the Convention in November, with both countries conducting concurrent military exercises in the Aegean. In early 1996 relations were exacerbated by conflicting claims of sovereignty over Imia (Kardak), a group of uninhabited islands in the Aegean Sea. In February Greece delayed the implementation of a financial protocol of the EU-Turkey customs union, claiming that Turkey's aggressive action in the Aegean violated the terms of the customs union agreement. In July Greece finally withdrew its opposition to Turkey's participation in an EU-Mediterranean assistance programme, in response to a joint statement by EU Heads of Government urging an end to Turkey's 'hostile policy' towards Greece; however, the block on funds from the customs union agreement remained in effect.

In July 1997 the Greek Prime Minister, Konstantinos Simitis, and the Turkish President, Süleyman Demirel, held direct talks, which led to an agreement, the Madrid Declaration, pledging not to use violence or the threat of violence to resolve bilateral disputes. However, relations remained strained, particularly concerning Greek support for Cyprus's application for membership of the EU. Relations between the two countries improved in August 1999, however, when Greece offered both financial and material assistance to Turkey, following a severe earthquake in the north-west of that country. Turkey reciprocated Greece's provision of emergency assistance when an earthquake struck Athens in September. At an EU summit, held in Helsinki, Finland, in December, Greece formally lifted its objections to Turkey's membership of the EU, although its consent remained dependent on the resolution of both the Cyprus issue and its dispute with Greece in the Aegean. In January 2000 the Greek Minister of Foreign Affairs, Georgios Papandreou, met Turkish government leaders for discussions in Ankara, the Turkish capital, during the first official visit by a Greek Minister of Foreign Affairs to Turkey since 1962.

The issue of Cyprus continued to dominate Greece's relations with Turkey (see the chapter on Cyprus). In February 2004 agreement was reached on proposals for reunification, which would allow Cyprus's accession to the EU as a single state. The final plan for reunification, submitted for approval in both the Republic of Cyprus and the 'TRNC' at referendums on 24 April, was endorsed in the latter with 64.9% of the votes cast, but rejected in the former with 75.8% of the votes (with the result that only that part of Cyprus administered by the principally Greek Cypriot Republic of Cyprus joined the EU on 1 May). In May the Turkish Prime Minister, Reçep Tayyip Erdoğan, made an official visit to Greece (the first by a Turkish premier in 16 years).

Following the installation of a new Greek Government in October 2009, Erdoğan proposed the establishment of a bilateral working group at ministerial level, in an effort to resolve outstanding issues of contention. In May 2010 Erdoğan, together with 10 Turkish ministers, made an official visit to Greece, where a joint government meeting was conducted, and 21 co-operation accords were signed. In March 2011 the Turkish Minister of Foreign Affairs and his Greek counterpart, meeting in Athens for discussions, pledged continued improvement in bilateral relations.

In 1985 Greece and Albania reopened their borders, which had remained closed since 1940, and Greece formally annulled claims to North Epirus (southern Albania), where there is a sizeable Greek minority. During the early 1990s, however, bilateral relations were severely strained by concerns over the treatment of ethnic Greeks residing in Albania (numbering an estimated 300,000) and over the illegal immigration of several thousand Albanians to Greece. In March 1996 President Stefanopoulos signed a treaty of friendship and co-operation with Albania's President, Sali Berisha. Albania agreed to provide Greek-language education in schools serving the ethnic Greek population, and Greece declared its willingness to issue temporary work permits for seasonal workers from Albania. A new border crossing was opened between Greece and Albania in May 1999. Following the stabilization of the political situation in Albania, the influx of Albanians into Greece decreased considerably.

Attempts after 1991 by the former Yugoslav republic of Macedonia (FYRM) to achieve international recognition as an independent state were strenuously opposed by the Greek Government, which insisted that 'Macedonia' was a purely geographical term (delineating an area that included a large part of northern Greece) and expressed fears that the adoption of such a name could imply ambitions on the Greek province of Macedonia. In early 1993 the Greek administration withdrew its former objection to the use of the word 'Macedonia', and its derivatives, as part of a fuller name for the new republic. At the end of March the Greek Government accepted a UN proposal that the title 'the former Yugoslav republic of Macedonia' should be used temporarily and agreed to hold direct talks with the FYRM to consider confidence-building measures. A subsequent government initiative to prevent any movement of goods, other than humanitarian aid, into the FYRM via the Greek port of Thessaloníki was widely criticized by the international community as effectively constituting an illegal trade embargo. In April the European Commission commenced legal proceedings against Greece at the Court of Justice of the European Communities. In April 1995 a preliminary opinion of the Court determined that the embargo was not in breach of Greece's obligations under the Treaty of Rome. In September the ministers responsible for foreign affairs of Greece and the FYRM, meeting in New York, USA, under UN auspices, signed an interim accord to normalize relations between the two countries, which included recognition of the existing international border. Under the terms of the agreement, Greece was to grant access to the port facilities at Thessaloníki and to remove all obstructions to the cross-border movement of people and goods, while the FYRM was to approve a new state flag; the measures were successfully implemented by October. Negotiations were to be pursued regarding the issue of a permanent name for the FYRM. In March 1997 the Greek Minister of Foreign Affairs visited the FYRM for the first time since its independence.

Greece strongly objected to the decision by the USA, announced in November 2004, that it would henceforth recognize the FYRM by its constitutional name of 'the Republic of Macedonia'. Negotiations on the issue, mediated by the UN, continued, while the Greek Government repeatedly threatened to obstruct the FYRM's aspirations to North Atlantic Treaty Organization (NATO, see p. 370) and EU accession, if it failed to agree to a compromise resolution. In January 2007 Greece protested at a decision by the FYRM Government to rename the international airport near Skopje after Alexander 'the Great' (who was considered by Greece to be integral to its cultural heritage). At a NATO conference convened in Bucharest, Romania, in April 2008, Greece vetoed the FYRM's application for membership, threatening similarly to obstruct the country's application to join the EU. In November the FYRM Government submitted legal proceedings against Greece to the International Court of Justice (ICJ, see p. 24) at The Hague, Netherlands, claiming that it had violated the terms of a UN-mediated interim accord regulating relations between the two countries, which stipulated that Greece would not veto the FYRM's accession to international institutions under that provisional name. Discussions were resumed in early 2009, but continued to be unproductive. On 5 December 2011 the ICJ ruled that Greece had contravened the interim accord by vetoing the FYRM's application to join NATO in 2008 and dismissed Greece's counterclaim that the FYRM had previously breached the accord. In November 2012 (by which time the FYRM Government urgently sought a settlement owing to its EU membership aspirations) negotiations were resumed, with mediation by Matthew Nimetz, the UN Secretary-General's Personal Envoy. In December 2013, however, the Prime Minister of the FYRM, Nikola Gruevski, declared that prospects for a resolution had not improved, and urged the international community to apply pressure on the Greek Government to comply with the ICJ ruling and refrain from impeding the FYRM's accession process.

CONSTITUTION AND GOVERNMENT

Under the Constitution of June 1975, and as subsequently revised, Greece is a parliamentary republic. The unicameral Vouli (Parliament) has 300 members, directly elected by universal adult suffrage for four years. The President is Head of State and is elected by Parliament for a five-year term. The President formally appoints the leader of the party with an absolute majority of seats in Parliament, or where no such party exists, the party with a plurality of seats, as Prime Minister, and upon his recommendation, the other members of the Government. Judicial power is exercised by the Supreme Court of Civil and Penal Law, courts of first instance and courts of justice of the peace. Greece comprises seven decentralized administrations, 13 administrative regions (perifereia) and 325 municipalities.

REGIONAL AND INTERNATIONAL CO-OPERATION

Greece is a member of the North Atlantic Treaty Organization (NATO, see p. 370), the Organisation for Economic Co-operation and Development (OECD, see p. 379) and the Organization of the Black Sea Economic Co-operation (see p. 401). Greece became a full member of the EC (now the European Union—EU, see p. 273) in 1981, having signed the Treaty of Accession in 1979.

Greece is a founding member of the UN. As a contracting party to the General Agreement on Tariffs and Trade, Greece joined the World Trade Organization (see p. 434) on its establishment in 1995.

ECONOMIC AFFAIRS

In 2012, according to estimates by the World Bank, Greece's gross national income (GNI), measured at average 2010–12 prices, was US $262,431m., equivalent to $23,260 per head (or $25,460 per head on an international purchasing-power parity basis). During 2003–12, it was estimated, the population increased at an average annual rate of 0.3%, while gross domestic product (GDP) per head decreased, in real terms, at an average annual rate of 1.0%. Overall GDP decreased, in real terms, at an average annual rate of 0.8% in 2003–12. Real GDP declined by 6.4% in 2012.

Agriculture (including hunting, forestry and fishing) contributed some 3.4% of GDP in 2012, and engaged 13.8% of the employed labour force in 2013. The principal cash crops are vegetable products and fruit (which, together, accounted for 4.5% of total export earnings in 2012), cereals, sugar beet and tobacco. According to the UN, real agricultural GDP declined at an average annual rate of 1.8% during 2003–12; the GDP of the sector decreased by 3.2% in 2012.

Industry (including mining, manufacturing, utilities and construction) provided 16.4% of GDP in 2012, and engaged 15.5% of the employed labour force in 2013. According to the UN, during 2003–12 real industrial GDP declined at an average annual rate of 3.1%; the GDP of the industrial sector decreased by 12.6% in 2011 and by 4.5% in 2012.

Mining and quarrying contributed 0.3% of GDP in 2011, and engaged 0.3% of the employed labour force in 2013. Mineral fuels and lubricants, iron and steel, and aluminium and aluminium alloys are the major mineral and metal exports. At the end of 2012, proven coal reserves stood at 3,020m. metric tons. Lignite, magnesite, silver ore and marble are also mined. In addition, Greece has small reserves of uranium, natural gas and gold.

Manufacturing provided 9.2% of GDP in 2011, and engaged 9.2% of the employed labour force in 2013. According to the UN, the GDP of the manufacturing sector decreased, in real terms, by an average annual rate of 0.6% in 2003–12; manufacturing GDP decreased by 13.1% in 2011 and by 1.0% in 2012.

Construction provided 2.1% of GDP in 2012, and engaged 4.6% of the employed labour force in 2013. According to the UN, the GDP of the construction sector decreased, in real terms, at an average annual rate of 10.6% in 2003–12; construction GDP decreased by 28.4% in 2011 and by 15.6% in 2012.

Energy is derived principally from lignite, which accounted for 55.8% of production in 2012, followed by natural gas (20.8%) and petroleum (7.6%). Greece is exploiting an offshore petroleum deposit in the north-eastern Aegean Sea. In April 2008 an agreement was signed on Greece's participation in the planned South Stream natural gas pipeline, which is intended to supply Russian natural gas to Europe by 2015. Solar power resources are also being developed. Mineral fuels represented 37.8% of the total value of imports in 2012.

The services sector contributed 80.2% of GDP in 2012, and engaged 70.7% of the employed labour force in 2013. Tourism is an important source of foreign exchange. There were 15.5m. visitor arrivals in 2012, according to official figures, while provisional figures from the World Tourism Organization indicated that receipts from the tourist sector totalled US $12,879m. in that year (excluding passenger transport). According to the UN, during 2003–12 the GDP of the services sector decreased, in real terms, at an average annual rate of 2.1%; sectoral GDP declined by 10.7% in 2012.

In 2012 Greece recorded a visible merchandise trade deficit of US $25,281m., and there was a deficit of $6,172m. on the current account of the balance of payments. In 2012 the principal source of imports was Russia (12.4%), followed by Germany; other major sources were Italy, Saudi Arabia, the People's Republic of China and the Netherlands. The principal market for exports in that year was Turkey (10.8%); other major purchasers were Italy, Germany, Bulgaria and Cyprus. The principal exports in that year were mineral fuels and lubricants (in particular, non-crude petroleum oils). Other major exports were base metals and articles thereof, mechanical and electrical equipment, and prepared foodstuffs, beverages, spirits, vinegar, tobacco, etc. The principal imports were mineral fuels and lubricants (mainly crude petroleum and petroleum products), chemicals and chemical products (mainly pharmaceutical products), mechanical and electrical equipment, transport equipment, and base metals and articles thereof.

According to provisional data, the budgetary deficit amounted to €39,744m. in 2012. Greece's general government gross debt was €303,918m. in 2012, equivalent to 156.9% of GDP. Greece's total external debt was estimated at €182,702m. at the end of 2004 (equivalent to 110.5% of that year's GDP). In 2003–12 the average annual rate of inflation was 3.0%; consumer prices increased by 1.5% in 2012. The rate of unemployment was 27.0% in 2013.

In 2004 the Government acknowledged that the previous administration had misrepresented public debt and budgetary deficit figures for several years in order for Greece to qualify for membership of the European Union's (EU) economic and monetary union in January 2001, and subsequently pledged to restrain the budgetary deficit to within the required limit. However, Greece's debt and budget deficit became unsustainable owing to the international financial crisis of 2008–09, and in May 2010 the EU, the IMF and the European Central Bank (ECB) 'troika' agreed a rescue programme for the country. After it became evident that this programme would not prevent an imminent Greek debt default, a second bailout plan, which provided for the disbursement of funds from the new European Financial Stability Facility (EFSF), was negotiated. Despite social unrest (see Domestic Political Affairs), the required austerity measures, which included a 22% reduction in the minimum wage and the loss of some 150,000 jobs in the public sector, were adopted by Parliament in February 2012. In March eurozone countries agreed funding for the new bailout plan, totalling up to €144,600m. from EFSF funds, and the IMF announced that it would contribute €28,000m. under its Extended Facility Fund; the first instalment of funds was disbursed later that month. In November, after new, stringent measures, which included a two-year increase in the retirement age and an austerity budget, were approved, the troika accepted a two-year extension, to 2016, for Greece to meet its fiscal targets. In December 2012, in fulfilment of a further condition, Greece succeeded in buying back about €31,800m. of its debt, with private sector holders of Greek sovereign bonds accepting a loss on the value of their investments. Further EU tranches were disbursed later that month and in early 2013. In July the disbursement of the next rescue instalment of €4,800m. for Greece was approved, after the Government agreed to implement further large-scale public sector dismissals demanded by the troika (amid a dramatic rise in unemployment). In December, however, the troika delayed the release of a further tranche, owing to Parliament's adoption, without consultation, of the budget for 2014. Later that month, in accordance with the troika's requirements, the Government adopted new measures to counter tax evasion, under which the state was empowered to seize the bank assets of offenders. Meanwhile, the European Commission announced a shortfall of €3,800m. in pledged bail-out funds. Greece's debt continued to rise (to an estimated 190% of GDP); however, the authorities announced a small primary budget surplus (of 1.6% of GDP—before debt repayments) for 2013, while yields on sovereign debt bonds had fallen to about 7.5% by January 2014, from 30.5% in March 2012. Although GDP again contracted, by a projected 4.4%, in 2013, a resumption in growth of 0.6% was forecast by the IMF for 2014. Following further negotiations with the troika on reforms for that year, in March it was announced that agreement had been reached on the release of some €10,000m. in bailout funds. In the same month Piraeus Bank successfully issued a €500m. bond (the first by a Greek bank in five years).

PUBLIC HOLIDAYS

2015: 1 January (New Year's Day), 6 January (Theophany), 23 February (Clean Monday), 25 March (Independence Day), 10–13 April (Greek Orthodox Easter), 1 May (Labour Day), 1 June (Whit Monday), 15 August (Assumption of the Virgin Mary), 28 October ('Ochi' Day, anniversary of Greek defiance of Italy's 1940 ultimatum), 25–26 December (Christmas).

Statistical Survey

Source (unless otherwise stated): National Statistical Service of Greece, Odos Lykourgou 14–16, 101 66 Athens; tel. (210) 4852084; fax (210) 4852552; e-mail info@statistics.gr; internet www.statistics.gr.

Area and Population

AREA, POPULATION AND DENSITY

Area (sq km)	131,957*
Population (census results)†	
18 March 2001	
Males	5,413,426
Females	5,520,671
Total	10,934,097
10–24 May 2011‡	10,815,197
Population (official estimates at 1 January)§	
2012	11,123,034
2013	11,062,508
Density (per sq km) at 1 January 2013	83.8

* 50,949 sq miles.

† Including armed forces stationed abroad, but excluding foreign forces stationed in Greece.

‡ Census total for resident population, not adjusted for underenumeration estimated at 2.84%.

§ Estimates not adjusted to take account of final results of the 2011 census.

POPULATION BY AGE AND SEX

(official estimates at 1 January 2013)

	Males	Females	Total
0–14	830,252	791,770	1,622,022
15–64	3,596,291	3,618,061	7,214,352
65 and over	986,747	1,239,387	2,226,134
Total	5,413,290	5,649,218	11,062,508

Note: Estimates not adjusted to take account of the final results of the 2011 census.

ADMINISTRATIVE DIVISIONS

(resident population at 2011 census)

Regions	Area (sq km)	Population	Density (per sq km)
Attica	3,808	3,827,624	1,005.2
East Macedonia and Thrace	14,156	608,182	43.0
Central Macedonia	18,810	1,880,058	99.9
Epirus	9,203	336,856	36.6
West Macedonia	9,451	283,689	30.0
Thessaly	14,036	732,762	52.2
Central Greece	15,549	547,390	35.2
Peloponnese	15,491	577,903	37.3
West Greece	11,350	679,796	59.9
Ionian Islands	2,307	207,855	90.1
North Aegean	5,286	308,975	58.5
South Aegean	3,836	199,231	51.9
Crete	8,336	623,065	74.7
Autonomous Monastic State			
'Holy Mountain' (Mount Athos)	336	1,811	5.4
Total	131,957	10,815,197	82.0

Note: Census data not adjusted for underenumeration estimated at 2.84%.

PRINCIPAL TOWNS

(population at 2011 census, provisional)

Athinai (Athens, the capital)	655,780	Larissa	163,380
Thessaloníki (Salonika)	322,240	Pésterion	138,920
Patras (Patrai)	214,580	Níkaia-Ágios Ioánnis Réndis	105,230
Iraklion	173,450	Kordelió-Évosmos	101,010
Piraeus	163,910	Calithèa	100,050

BIRTHS, MARRIAGES AND DEATHS

	Registered live births		Registered marriages		Registered deaths	
	Number	Rate (per 1,000)	Number	Rate (per 1,000)	Number	Rate (per 1,000)
2005	107,545	9.7	61,043	5.5	105,091	9.5
2006	112,042	10.1	57,802	5.2	105,476	9.5
2007	111,926	10.0	61,377	5.5	109,895	9.8
2008	118,302	10.5	53,500	4.8	107,979	9.6
2009	117,933	10.5	59,212	5.3	108,316	9.6
2010	114,766	10.2	56,338	5.0	109,084	9.7
2011	106,428	9.6	55,099	4.9	111,099	9.9
2012	100,371	9.0	49,710	4.5	116,670	10.5

Life expectancy (years at birth): 80.7 (males 78.5; females 83.1) in 2011 (Source: World Bank, World Development Indicators database).

ECONOMICALLY ACTIVE POPULATION
(sample surveys, '000 persons aged 15 years and over, July-September*)

	2011	2012	2013
Agriculture, hunting, forestry and fishing	504.1	491.5	503.2
Mining and quarrying	12.6	12.7	9.3
Manufacturing	419.0	356.9	336.1
Electricity, gas and water supply	51.7	50.2	51.0
Construction	241.8	204.8	166.5
Wholesale and retail trade; repair of motor vehicles, motorcycles and personal and household goods	744.8	664.6	650.5
Hotels and restaurants	317.4	296.0	286.7
Transport, storage and communications	267.6	253.2	255.7
Financial intermediation	115.2	106.1	112.6
Real estate, renting and business activities	293.7	294.5	277.5
Public administration and defence; compulsory social security	359.0	327.3	333.3
Education	304.3	287.6	276.5
Health and social work	241.3	219.9	210.5
Other community, social and personal service activities	136.1	118.2	116.9
Private households with employed persons	68.2	54.1	48.4
Extra-territorial organizations and bodies	2.6	1.6	1.1
Total employed	4,079.3	3,739.0	3,635.9
Unemployed	878.3	1,230.9	1,345.4
Total labour force	4,957.6	4,969.9	4,981.3
Males	2,867.6	2,846.2	2,856.1
Females	2,090.0	2,123.7	2,125.2

* Including members of the regular armed forces, but excluding persons on compulsory military service.

Note: Totals may not be equal to the sum of components, owing to rounding.

Health and Welfare

KEY INDICATORS

Total fertility rate (children per woman, 2011)	1.5
Under-5 mortality rate (per 1,000 live births, 2011)	4
HIV/AIDS (% of persons aged 15–49, 2009)	0.1
Physicians (per 1,000 head, 2009)	6.2
Hospital beds (per 1,000 head, 2009)	4.8
Health expenditure (2010): US $ per head (PPP)	3,069
Health expenditure (2010): % of GDP	10.8
Health expenditure (2010): public (% of total)	61.5
Total carbon dioxide emissions ('000 metric tons, 2010)	86,717.2
Carbon dioxide emissions per head (metric tons, 2010)	7.7
Human Development Index (2012): ranking	29
Human Development Index (2012): value	0.860

For sources and definitions, see explanatory note on p. vi.

Agriculture

PRINCIPAL CROPS
('000 metric tons)

	2010	2011	2012
Wheat	1,663	1,702	1,569
Rice, paddy	230	255	216
Barley	318	328	326
Maize	1,718	2,166	2,010
Oats	116	163	119
Potatoes	792	758	579
Sugar beet	762	324	435
Olives	1,810	1,874	2,081
Cabbages	188	180	186
Lettuce	129	130	128
Tomatoes	1,406	1,170	980
Cauliflowers and broccoli	73	86	89
Pumpkins, squash and gourds	73	77	82
Cucumbers and gherkins	104	175	142
Aubergines (Eggplants)	71	78	73
Chillies and peppers, green	141	131	168
Onions, dry	188	243	250
Beans, green	58	55	56*
Watermelons	493	648	565
Cantaloupes and other melons	116	127	119
Oranges	901	895	792
Tangerines, mandarins, clementines and satsumas	110	129	106
Lemons and limes	58	66	59
Apples	239	256	251
Pears	68	62	78
Apricots	77	83	90
Peaches and nectarines	738	690	760
Grapes	1,003	857	978
Figs	11	9	10
Tobacco, unmanufactured	22	24	22

* FAO estimate.

Aggregate production ('000 metric tons, may include official, semi-official or estimated data): Total cereals 4,094 in 2010, 4,658 in 2011, 4,277 in 2012; Total roots and tubers 795 in 2010, 762 in 2011, 583 in 2012; Total vegetables (incl. melons) 3,340 in 2010, 3,434 in 2011, 3,159 in 2012; Total fruits (excl. melons) 3,342 in 2010, 3,333 in 2011, 3,440 in 2012.

Source: FAO.

LIVESTOCK
('000 head, year ending 30 September)

	2010	2011	2012
Horses*	27	28	28
Asses*	40	40	40
Mules*	20	20	20
Cattle	679	681	680
Pigs	1,087	1,120	1,128
Sheep	8,966	9,781	9,585
Goats	4,850	4,296	4,219
Chickens*	32,000	33,000	33,500

* FAO estimates.

Source: FAO.

LIVESTOCK PRODUCTS
('000 metric tons)

	2010	2011	2012
Cattle meat*	77.4	79.0	74.9
Sheep meat	89.9*	89.8*	90.0†
Goat meat*	52.7	49.7	44.7
Pig meat*	100.2	100.1	100.9
Horse meat†	2.8	2.8	2.8
Chicken meat	114.3*	111.9*	104.0†
Cows' milk	852.0*	787.0*	800.0†
Sheep's milk*	770.0	773.0	699.5
Goats' milk	405.8*	402.1*	407.0†
Hen eggs	99.8	100.0†	102.0†
Honey	14.3†	14.5†	14.8
Wool, greasy†	7.6	7.8	7.8

* Unofficial figure(s).
† FAO estimate(s).

Source: FAO.

Forestry

ROUNDWOOD REMOVALS
('000 cubic metres, excl. bark)

	2005	2006	2007
Sawlogs, veneer logs and logs for sleepers	420	384	756
Other industrial wood	99	78	192
Fuel wood	1,004	1,100	795
Total	1,523	1,562	1,743

2008–12: Production assumed to be unchanged from 2007 (FAO estimates).

Source: FAO.

SAWNWOOD PRODUCTION
('000 cubic metres, incl. railway sleepers)

	2005	2006	2007
Coniferous (softwood)	74	64	64
Broadleaved (hardwood)	117	44	44
Total	191	108	108

2008–12: Production assumed to be unchanged from 2007 (FAO estimates).

Source: FAO.

Fishing

('000 metric tons, live weight)

	2009	2010	2011
Capture	83.3	71.0*	71.4*
European pilchard (sardine)	10.1	6.5	6.5*
European anchovy	14.5	12.0	12.0
Aquaculture	122.0	121.2	142.1*
European seabass	33.6	39.0	44.1*
Gilthead seabream	60.5	57.2	70.9
Mediterranean mussel	22.4	17.1	20.0*
Total catch	205.3	192.3*	213.5*

* FAO estimate.

Note: Figures exclude corals and sponges (metric tons, capture only): 6.0 in 2009; 7.0 in 2010; 6.8 in 2011 (FAO estimate).

Source: FAO.

Mining

('000 metric tons unless otherwise indicated)

	2010	2011	2012
Lignite	53,600	58,400	62,335
Crude petroleum ('000 barrels)	636	676	662
Natural gas*	11	11	n.a.
Iron ore*†	560	550	550
Bauxite	1,902	2,300*	1,816
Zinc†	20.0	39.1	41.8
Lead†	12.2*	16.6	18.1
Nickel†	13.8	14.1	14.0*
Silver (kilograms)*†	29.0	30.0	32.0
Magnesite (crude)	396	542	351
Salt (unrefined)	190*	175	192
Bentonite	1,382	1,188	1,235
Gypsum and anhydrite	700	587	746
Feldspar	23	10	12*
Perlite (crude)	760*	843	876
Pozzolan	850	350	285
Pumice	400	469	386
Marble ('000 cu m)	250*	285*	320

* Estimate(s).
† Figures refer to the metal content of ores and concentrates.

Source: US Geological Survey.

Industry

SELECTED PRODUCTS
('000 metric tons unless otherwise indicated)

	2010	2011	2012
Olive oil, virgin	353*	352*	352†
Wine	337*	295*	n.a.
Beer of barley	405*	400*	n.a.
Liquefied petroleum gas ('000 barrels)	8,030	8,000†	8,000†
Naphthas ('000 barrels)†	8,400	8,400	8,400
Motor spirit (petrol) ('000 barrels)	36,865	32,000†	32,000†
Jet fuels ('000 barrels)	12,775	14,000†	14,000†
Distillate fuel oils ('000 barrels)	51,468	47,000†	47,000†
Residual fuel oils ('000 barrels)	37,814	42,000†	42,000†
Cement (hydraulic)†	11,000	11,000	11,000
Crude steel (incl. alloys)	1,839	1,993	2,000†
Aluminium (primary, unwrought)	136.8	167.5	165.0

* Unofficial figure.
† Estimate(s).

Sources: FAO; US Geological Survey.

Electric energy (million kWh): 63,749 in 2008; 61,365 in 2009; 57,392 in 2010 (Source: UN Industrial Commodity Statistics Database).

Finance

CURRENCY AND EXCHANGE RATES

Monetary Units
100 cent = 1 euro (€).

Sterling, Dollar and Euro Equivalents (31 December 2013)
£1 sterling = 1.194 euros;
US $1 = 0.725 euros;
€10 = £8.37 = $13.79.

Average Exchange Rate (euros per US $)

2011	0.7194
2012	0.7783
2013	0.7532

Note: The national currency was formerly the drachma. Greece became a member of the euro area on 1 January 2001, after which a fixed exchange rate of €1 = 340.75 drachmae was in operation. Euro notes and coins were introduced on 1 January 2002. The euro and local currency circulated alongside each other until 28 February, after which the euro became the sole legal tender.

CENTRAL GOVERNMENT BUDGET

(€ million)*

Revenue	2011	2012†	2013‡
Ordinary budget	55,442	51,497	51,007
Tax revenue	48,950	47,178	44,403
Direct taxes	20,318	21,096	19,884
Personal income tax	8,285	9,968	7,982
Corporate income tax	2,736	1,715	1,640
Indirect taxes	28,632	26,082	24,519
Consumption taxes (fuels)	4,653	4,464	4,277
Value-added tax	16,887	14,955	13,644
Non-tax revenue	6,490	4,318	6,604
Investment budget	3,773	3,601	5,136
Statistical discrepancy	2	1	–1
Total	59,215	55,098	56,142

Expenditure§	2011	2012†	2013‡
Ordinary budget	75,429	64,823	56,301
Salaries and pensions	22,992	21,595	19,713
Interest payments	16,348	12,223	6,100
Investment budget	6,559	6,114	6,650
Total	81,988	70,937	62,951

* Figures refer to the budgetary transactions of the central Government, excluding the operations of social security funds and public entities (such as hospitals, educational institutions and government agencies) with individual budgets.

† Provisional figures.

‡ Budget estimates; expenditure figures exclude potential adjustments arising from the implementation of private sector investment in national debt servicing (PSI).

§ Excluding amortization payments (€ million): 28,843 in 2011; 23,905 in 2012 (provisional figure); 12,755 in 2013 (budget estimate). Also excluded is expenditure on military procurement (€ million): 360 in 2011; 410 in 2012 (provisional figure); 750 in 2013 (budget estimate).

2014 (€ million, budget estimates): *Revenue:* Ordinary budget 52,482 (Direct taxes 21,574, Indirect taxes 24,087, Non-tax revenue 6,821); Investment budget 5,002; Total revenue 57,484; *Expenditure:* Ordinary budget 52,237 (Salaries and pensions 19,244; Interest payments 6,150); Investment budget 6,800; Total expenditure 59,037 (excl. amortization payments 24,930).

Source: Bank of Greece, Athens.

INTERNATIONAL RESERVES

(US $ million at 31 December)*

	2010	2011	2012
Gold†	5,060.0	5,650.9	5,985.4
IMF special drawing rights	938.0	849.3	850.7
Reserve position in IMF	263.3	369.6	370.1
Foreign exchange	108.2	29.8	48.8
Total	6,369.5	6,899.6	7,255.0

* Figures exclude deposits made with the European Monetary Institute.

† Gold reserves are valued at market-related prices.

Source: IMF, *International Financial Statistics*.

MONEY SUPPLY

(incl. shares, depository corporations, national residency criteria, € '000 million at 31 December)

	2010	2011	2012
Currency issued	22.52	23.73	24.33
Bank of Greece	30.44	42.17	38.79
Demand deposits	90.30	73.97	64.38
Other deposits	123.74	104.87	102.13
Securities other than shares	3.43	1.57	3.17
Money market fund shares	1.18	0.73	0.83
Shares and other equity	45.83	54.77	56.03
Other items (net)	–15.47	–21.50	–28.39
Total	271.53	238.15	222.48

Source: IMF, *International Financial Statistics*.

COST OF LIVING

(Consumer Price Index; base: 2009 = 100)

	2010	2011	2012
Food	100.1	103.2	104.7
Fuel and light	136.2	161.8	181.2
Clothing	101.7	101.1	102.4
Rent	106.9	116.4	125.6
Transport	116.2	123.5	126.9
Communications	102.9	104.6	102.9
Health	101.5	100.9	99.2
Education	102.0	101.9	100.0
All items (incl. others)	104.7	108.2	109.8

Source: Bank of Greece.

NATIONAL ACCOUNTS

(€ million at current prices, provisional)

National Income and Product

	2010	2011	2012
Compensation of employees	80,493	73,288	63,968
Gross operating surplus	117,071	111,395	108,087
Gross domestic product (GDP) at factor cost	197,564	184,683	172,055
Taxes on production and imports	27,926	27,077	25,009
Less Subsidies	3,339	3,229	3,315
GDP in market prices	222,151	208,532	193,749
Primary incomes received from abroad	6,967	6,406	6,460
Less Primary incomes paid abroad	13,201	12,456	5,504
Gross national income (GNI)	215,917	202,482	194,705
Less Consumption of fixed capital	35,647	38,832	42,210
Net national income	180,270	163,651	152,495
Current transfers from abroad	2,064	1,655	1,815
Less Current transfers paid abroad	3,615	3,227	3,326
Net national disposable income	178,719	162,078	150,984

Expenditure on the Gross Domestic Product

	2010	2011	2012
Final consumption expenditure	203,803	191,812	177,154
Households	159,440	151,802	139,304
Non-profit institutions serving households	3,614	3,762	3,452
General government	40,749	36,248	34,398
Gross capital formation	38,955	33,591	26,339
Gross fixed capital formation	39,185	31,592	25,468
Changes in inventories	–230	1,999	871
Total domestic expenditure	242,758	225,403	203,493
Exports of goods and services	49,414	52,247	52,309
Less Imports of goods and services	70,020	69,119	62,053
GDP in purchasers' values	222,151	208,532	193,749

Gross Domestic Product by Economic Activity

	2010	2011	2012
Agriculture, forestry and fishing	6,300	6,175	5,751
Mining and quarrying	627	545	
Manufacturing	19,412	16,804	24,404
Electricity, gas and water supply	6,332	7,053	
Construction	6,772	4,561	3,616
Wholesale and retail trade; repair of motor vehicles and household goods; transport and storage; hotels and restaurants	49,980	45,723	39,801
Information and communications	9,464	8,894	8,309
Financial intermediation	9,245	8,958	8,326
Real estate, renting and business activities	38,421	37,763	36,684
Public administration and defence; compulsory social security; education; health and social work	39,628	37,469	35,520
Other service activities; private households with employed persons	9,041	9,191	8,110
Gross value added in basic prices	195,222	183,137	170,521
Taxes, less subsidies, on products	26,930	25,395	23,228
GDP in market prices	222,151	208,532	193,749

BALANCE OF PAYMENTS
(US $ million)

	2010	2011	2012
Exports of goods	22,410	27,954	28,088
Imports of goods	–59,962	–65,838	–53,369
Balance on goods	–37,552	–37,884	–25,281
Exports of services	37,667	40,168	35,343
Imports of services	–20,374	–19,624	–16,058
Balance on goods and services	–20,259	–17,339	–5,996
Primary income received	5,320	4,618	4,925
Primary income paid	–15,453	–16,599	–6,973
Balance on goods, services and primary income	–30,392	–29,320	–8,044
Secondary income received	6,053	6,116	6,628
Secondary income paid	–5,935	–5,379	–4,756
Current balance	–30,274	–28,583	–6,172
Capital account (net)	2,776	3,660	3,010
Direct investment assets	–1,697	–1,818	–679
Direct investment liabilities	534	1,092	1,663
Portfolio investment assets	17,061	6,846	–74,031
Portfolio investment liabilities	–43,932	–33,421	–54,284
Financial derivatives and employee stock options (net)	431	–985	–1,078
Other investment assets	10,272	9,939	17,998
Other investment liabilities	31,451	29,924	111,921
Net errors and omissions	–559	36	–494
Reserves and related items	–13,936	–13,310	–2,145

Source: IMF, *International Financial Statistics*.

External Trade

PRINCIPAL COMMODITIES
(distribution by HS, US $ million)

Imports c.i.f.	2010	2011	2012
Live animals and animal products	2,851.7	3,110.5	2,828.8
Vegetables and vegetable products	1,633.7	1,951.9	1,684.2
Prepared foodstuffs; beverages, spirits, vinegar; tobacco and articles thereof	3,259.7	3,241.3	2,931.2
Mineral products	15,690.8	16,912.7	23,585.3
Mineral fuels, oils, distillation products, etc.	15,543.6	16,698.6	23,477.8
Crude petroleum oils	11,075.4	10,016.1	16,522.3
Non-crude petroleum oils	2,697.4	4,301.2	4,284.4
Petroleum gases	1,197.7	1,886.3	2,105.9
Chemicals and related products	8,397.7	8,140.8	7,103.8
Pharmaceutical products	4,572.4	4,178.7	3,664.8
Medicaments put in dosage	3,883.6	3,528.8	3,109.5
Plastics, rubber, and articles thereof	2,313.8	2,414.6	2,076.3
Plastics and articles thereof	1,861.7	1,955.2	1,669.3
Textiles and textile articles	3,088.8	2,824.5	2,260.8
Iron and steel, other base metals and articles of base metal	3,942.2	4,449.9	3,586.2
Machinery and mechanical appliances; electrical equipment; parts thereof	7,807.2	7,354.5	6,677.4
Machinery, boilers, etc.	3,860.2	3,302.7	2,597.2
Electrical, electronic equipment	3,947.0	4,051.8	4,080.3
Vehicles, aircraft, vessels and associated transport equipment	7,582.5	4,002.0	4,208.1
Vehicles other than railway, tramway	2,764.7	2,060.9	1,348.7
Ships, boats and floating structures	3,919.6	1,707.6	2,525.7
Cruise ship, cargo ship, barges, etc.	3,827.7	1,664.3	2,475.6
Total (incl. others)	63,942.1	60,832.2	62,341.3

Exports f.o.b.	2010	2011	2012
Live animals and animal products	1,139.6	1,350.3	1,335.2
Fish, crustaceans, molluscs, aquatic invertebrates	680.8	807.9	773.8
Vegetables and vegetable products	1,419.7	1,454.2	1,571.4
Edible fruit, nuts, peel of citrus fruit, melons	898.1	909.2	974.7
Prepared foodstuffs; beverages, spirits, vinegar; tobacco and articles thereof	2,370.7	2,568.4	2,602.0
Vegetable, fruit, nut preparations	965.5	1,066.9	1,123.6
Mineral products	2,862.8	10,015.2	14,257.8
Mineral fuels, oils, distillation products, etc.	2,428.9	9,577.3	13,679.0
Non-crude petroleum oils	2,187.7	9,030.1	12,975.9
Chemicals and related products	2,346.6	2,399.0	2,355.8
Pharmaceutical products	1,341.4	1,212.7	1,230.5
Medicaments put in dosage	1,281.7	1,139.6	1,113.8

Exports f.o.b.—*continued*	2010	2011	2012
Plastics, rubber, and articles thereof	1,220.4	1,362.9	1,315.4
Plastics and articles thereof	1,112.2	1,234.9	1,170.6
Textiles and textile articles	1,899.9	1,693.9	1,687.7
Cotton	664.7	482.8	655.7
Iron and steel, other base metals and articles of base metal	3,055.7	4,530.1	3,755.1
Aluminium and articles thereof	1,207.1	1,730.0	1,539.6
Machinery and mechanical appliances; electrical equipment; parts thereof	2,067.5	2,413.3	2,381.3
Machinery, boilers, etc.	971.7	1,062.5	992.9
Electrical, electronic equipment	1,095.8	1,350.7	1,388.4
Total (incl. others)	21,750.0	31,711.1	35,179.7

Source: Trade Map-Trade Competitiveness Map, International Trade Centre, www.intracen.org/marketanalysis.

Total imports (incl. petroleum and value of ships, € '000 million): 50,740 in 2010; 48,350 in 2011 (provisional); 49,250 in 2012 (provisional).

Total exports (incl. petroleum and value of ships, € '000 million): 21,140 in 2010; 24,270 in 2011 (provisional); 27,560 in 2012 (provisional).

PRINCIPAL TRADING PARTNERS
(US $ million)

Imports c.i.f.	2010	2011	2012
Austria	705.6	580.8	516.3
Azerbaijan	13.2	162.5	634.8
Belgium	2,167.2	2,195.6	1,687.0
Bulgaria	1,375.5	1,609.0	1,669.3
China, People's Republic	3,815.8	3,591.4	2,944.6
Cyprus	718.7	927.9	721.3
Denmark	643.9	674.3	717.6
Egypt	386.4	908.3	571.2
France (incl. Monaco)	3,127.5	3,034.2	2,678.3
Germany	6,709.3	6,396.8	5,756.1
India	578.0	776.4	367.9
Iran	1,625.4	2,727.4	1,981.9
Iraq	890.1	805.0	2,269.3
Italy	6,161.2	5,569.5	4,879.9
Japan	737.5	447.0	166.5
Kazakhstan	1,412.2	1,196.5	1,636.7
Korea, Republic	2,437.1	1,459.7	2,416.5
Libya	1,854.1	440.4	2,173.3
Netherlands	3,367.8	3,289.1	2,865.6
Romania	607.4	660.4	613.7
Russia	6,361.4	5,776.1	7,731.3
Saudi Arabia	1,552.0	1,948.5	3,437.7
Spain	1,924.2	1,879.2	1,671.6
Switzerland-Liechtenstein	1,042.7	834.4	638.9
Turkey	1,539.5	1,604.1	1,424.7
United Kingdom	1,910.5	1,726.0	1,455.0
USA	1,554.4	1,146.6	735.2
Total (incl. others)	63,942.1	60,832.2	62,341.3

Exports f.o.b.	2010	2011	2012
Albania	523.2	592.4	537.1
Algeria	285.3	495.9	507.4
Belgium	318.0	394.4	414.6
Bulgaria	1,405.9	1,724.2	1,944.9
China, People's Republic	210.3	405.6	491.1
Cyprus	1,567.4	1,903.1	1,719.1
Egypt	276.9	482.5	444.1
France (incl. Monaco)	828.8	905.8	857.8
Germany	2,386.7	2,453.8	2,234.7
Israel	159.4	308.0	766.6
Italy	2,350.1	2,956.2	2,702.5
Lebanon	40.2	218.0	946.9
Libya	214.1	221.4	1,010.6
Macedonia, former Yugoslav republic	433.9	793.6	1,066.7
Netherlands	512.8	637.5	568.2
Poland	330.1	364.5	352.0
Romania	799.4	829.9	738.0
Russia	427.0	548.7	600.0
Saudi Arabia	123.7	349.4	495.6
Serbia	306.8	390.8	395.9
Singapore	136.5	817.6	698.4
Spain	517.5	639.6	691.7
Turkey	1,138.8	2,485.4	3,815.4
United Arab Emirates	225.0	632.6	599.2
United Kingdom	1,144.4	1,239.1	1,096.5
USA	873.9	1,711.6	1,325.0
Total (incl. others)	21,750.0	31,711.1	35,179.7

Source: Trade Map-Trade Competitiveness Map, International Trade Centre, www.intracen.org/marketanalysis.

Total imports (€ million, incl. petroleum products, provisional figures): 50,740 in 2010; 48,350 in 2011 (provisional); 49,250 in 2012 (provisional).

Total exports (€ million, incl. petroleum products, provisional figures): 21,140 in 2010; 24,270 in 2011 (provisional); 27,560 in 2012 (provisional).

Transport

RAILWAYS
(estimated traffic)

	2007	2008	2009
Passenger-kilometres (million)	1,954	2,003	1,413
Net ton-kilometres (million)	835	786	538

2010–11: Figures assumed to be unchanged from 2009.

Source: World Bank, World Development Indicators database.

ROAD TRAFFIC
(motor vehicles in use at 31 December)

	2010	2011	2012
Passenger cars	5,216,873	5,203,591	5,167,557
Buses and coaches	27,311	27,121	26,962
Lorries and vans	1,318,768	1,321,296	1,318,918
Motorcycles	1,499,133	1,534,902	1,556,435
Total	8,062,085	8,086,910	8,069,872

SHIPPING

Flag Registered Fleet
(at 31 December)

	2011	2012	2013
Number of vessels	1,487	1,454	1,397
Total displacement ('000 grt)	41,319.2	41,702.9	42,189.1

Source: Lloyd's List Intelligence (www.lloydslistintelligence.com).

International Sea-borne Freight Traffic
('000 metric tons)

	2010	2011	2012
Goods loaded	23,813	27,450	37,782
Goods unloaded	47,732	48,769	56,487

CIVIL AVIATION
(traffic on scheduled services)

	2010	2011
Kilometres flown (million)	79	72
Passengers carried ('000)	9,931	9,180
Passenger-kilometres (million)	7,560	7,177
Total ton-kilometres (million)	761	693

Source: UN, *Statistical Yearbook*.

2012: Passengers carried ('000) 7,937 (Source: World Bank, World Development Indicators database).

Tourism

FOREIGN TOURIST ARRIVALS BY NATIONALITY
(arrivals of non-resident tourists at national borders)

Country	2010	2011	2012
Albania	242,083	411,245	469,213
Austria	338,367	310,358	236,416
Belgium	339,836	432,625	326,937
Bulgaria	664,389	686,209	599,110
Cyprus	574,764	439,757	424,827
France	868,346	1,149,388	977,376
Germany	2,038,871	2,240,481	2,108,787
Italy	843,613	938,232	848,073
Netherlands	528,157	560,723	478,483
Poland	402,170	450,618	254,682
Russia	451,239	738,927	874,787
Serbia and Montenegro	706,635	692,059	620,450
Sweden	281,069	333,906	319,756
Switzerland	274,418	361,405	299,619
Turkey	561,198	552,090	602,306
United Kingdom	1,802,203	1,758,093	1,920,794
USA	498,301	484,708	373,831
Total (incl. others)	15,007,490	16,427,247	15,517,622

Tourism receipts (US $ million, excl. passenger transport): 12,742 in 2010; 14,623 in 2011; 12,879 in 2012 (provisional) (Source: World Tourism Organization).

Communications Media

	2010	2011	2012
Telephones ('000 main lines in use)	5,898.1	5,745.0	5,461.2
Mobile cellular telephones ('000 subscribers)	12,292.7	12,128.0	13,353.7
Internet subscribers ('000)	2,314.3	2,510.3	n.a.
Broadband subscribers ('000)	2,250.4	2,462.7	2,685.4

Source: International Telecommunication Union.

Education

(2011/12 unless otherwise indicated)

	Institutions	Teachers	Students
Pre-primary	5,861	14,018	165,931
Primary	4,746	67,314	633,291
Secondary: General	3,149	72,945	572,119
Secondary: Technical, vocational and ecclesiastical*	654	22,124	125,067
Higher: Universities	22†	11,508	168,804†
Higher: Technical, vocational and ecclesiastical	16	6,723	103,511

* 2005/06.

† Excludes Medical School of Athens.

Pupil-teacher ratio (primary education, UNESCO estimate): 10.3 in 2006/07 (Source: UNESCO Institute for Statistics).

Adult literacy rate (UNESCO estimates): 97.3% (males 98.4%; females 96.3%) in 2011 (Source: UNESCO Institute for Statistics).

Directory

The Government

HEAD OF STATE

President: KAROLOS PAPOULIAS (elected by vote of the Vouli 8 February 2005, inaugurated 12 March; re-elected by vote of the Vouli 3 February 2010, inaugurated 12 March).

GOVERNMENT

(April 2014)

A Government principally comprising members of Nea Demokratia (New Democracy—ND) and Panellinio Socialistiko Kinima (PASOK—Panhellenic Socialist Movement).

Prime Minister and Chairman of the Government: ANTONIS SAMARAS (ND).

Deputy Prime Minister and Minister of Foreign Affairs: EVANGELOS VENIZELOS (PASOK).

Minister of Finance: IOANNIS STOURNARAS (Independent).

Minister for Administrative Reform and e-Governance: KYRIAKOS MITSOTAKIS (ND).

Minister of the Interior: IOANNIS MICHELAKIS (ND).

Minister of National Defence: DIMITRIS AVRAMOPOULOS (ND).

Minister of Development and Competitiveness: KOSTIS HATZIDAKIS (ND).

Minister of Infrastructure, Transport and Networks: MICHAEL CHRYSSOCHOIDES (PASOK).

Minister of the Environment, Energy and Climate Change: YIANNIS MANIATIS (PASOK).

Minister of Education and Religious Affairs: KONSTANTINOS ARVANITOPOULOS (ND).

Minister of Culture and Sport: PANOS PANAGIOTOPOULOS (ND).

Minister of Labour, Social Security and Welfare: IOANNIS VROUTSIS (ND).

Minister of Health: ADONIS GEORGIADIS (ND).

Minister of Rural Development and Food: ATHANASIOS TSAFTSARIS (Independent).

Minister of Justice, Transparency and Human Rights: CHARALAMBOSO ATHANASSIOU (ND).

Minister of Public Order and Citizen Protection: NIKOLAOS DENDIAS (ND).

Minister of Tourism: OLGA KEFALOGIANNI (ND).

Minister of Maritime Affairs: MILTIADIS VARVITSIOTIS (ND).

Minister for Macedonia and Thrace: THEODOROS KARAOGLOU (ND).

Minister of State at the Office of the Prime Minister: DIMITRIS STAMATIS (ND).

MINISTRIES

Office of the President: Odos Vassileos Georgiou 2, 100 28 Athens; tel. (210) 7283111; fax (210) 7248938; internet www.presidency.gr.

Office of the Prime Minister: Maximos Mansion, Herodou Atticou 19, 106 74 Athens; tel. (210) 3385491; fax (210) 3238129; e-mail primeminister@primeminister.gr; internet www.primeminister.gr.

Ministry for Administrative Reform and e-Governance: Leoforos Vas. Sofias 15, 10674 Athens; tel. (213) 313000; internet www.ydmed.gov.gr.

Ministry of Culture and Sport: Rethymnou 1, Athens; tel. (210) 8201793; fax (210) 8201779; e-mail tep.dds@culture.gr; internet www.culture.gr/culture/eindex.jsp.

Ministry of Development, Competitiveness, Infrastructure, Transport and Networks: Odos Mesogeion 119, 101 92 Athens; tel. (210) 6974802; fax (210) 6969604; e-mail polites@mindev.gov.gr; internet www.mindev.gov.gr.

Ministry of Education and Religious Affairs: Andreas Papandreou 37, 151 80 Maroussi; tel. (210) 3442505; e-mail webmaster@ypepth.gr; internet www.minedu.gov.gr.

Ministry of the Environment, Energy and Climate Change: Odos Amalia 17, 115 23 Athens; tel. (210) 1515000; fax (210) 6447608; e-mail service@dorg.minenv.gr; internet www.ypeka.gr.

Ministry of Finance: Karageorgi Servias 10, 105 62 Athens; tel. (210) 3375000; fax (210) 3332608; e-mail kataggelies@sdoe.gr; internet www.minfin.gr.

Ministry of Foreign Affairs: Odos Sofias 1, 106 71 Athens; tel. (210) 3681000; fax (210) 3681717; e-mail mfa@mfa.gr; internet www.mfa.gr.

Ministry of Health: Odos Aristotelous 17, 101 87 Athens; tel. (210) 5232821; e-mail secretary.gen@yyka.gov.gr; internet www.yyka.gov.gr.

Ministry of the Interior: Odos Stadiou 27, 101 83 Athens; tel. (213) 1364000; fax (213) 1364130; e-mail info@ypes.gr; internet www.ypes.gr.

Ministry of Justice, Transparency and Human Rights: Odos Mesogeion 96, 115 27 Athens; tel. (210) 7767300; fax (210) 7767187; e-mail ypdipimi@otenet.gr; internet www.ministryofjustice.gr.

Ministry of Labour, Social Security and Welfare: Odos Pireos 40, 104 37 Athens; tel. (210) 5295248; fax (210) 5249805; e-mail info@ypakp.gr; internet www.ypakp.gr.

Ministry for Macedonia and Thrace: Administration Bldg, 541 23 Thessaloníki; tel. (2310) 379000; fax (2310) 263332; e-mail info@mathra.gr; internet www.mathra.gr.

Ministry of Maritime Affairs: Akti Vasiliadis 150, 18 510 Piraeus; tel. (210) 4191700; fax (210) 4220466; e-mail egov@yen.gr; internet www.yen.gr.

Ministry of National Defence: Odos Mesogeion 227–231, Holargos, 154 51 Athens; tel. (210) 6598100; fax (210) 6443832; e-mail minister@mod.mil.gr; internet www.mod.mil.gr.

Ministry of Public Order and Citizen Protection: P. Khanellopoulou 4, 101 77 Athens; tel. (210) 6924558; fax (210) 6929764; e-mail pressoffice@yptp.gr; internet www.mopocp.gov.gr.

Ministry of Rural Development and Food: Odos Acharnon 2, 104 32 Athens; tel. (210) 2124000; fax (210) 5240475; e-mail info@minagric.gr; internet www.minagric.gr.

Ministry of Tourism: Odos Mpoumpoulinas 20–22, 106 82 Athens; tel. (213) 1322100; fax (210) 8201138; e-mail grplk@culture.gr; internet www.culture.gr.

President

In voting by members of the Vouli (Parliament), held on 8 February 2005, the sole candidate for the presidency, KAROLOS PAPOULIAS, was elected to a five-year term of office, having obtained the support of 279 of the 300 legislative deputies. He was inaugurated on 12 March. He was elected, again unopposed, to a second five-year term on 3 February 2010, with the support of 266 legislative deputies. His inauguration took place on 12 March.

Legislature

Parliament (Vouli)

Parliament Bldg, Leoforos Vassilissis Sofias 2, 100 21 Athens; tel. (210) 3707000; fax (210) 3733566; e-mail infopar@parliament.gr; internet www.hellenicparliament.gr.

President: EVANGELOS-VASILEIOS MEIMARAKIS.

General Election, 17 June 2012

Parties	Votes	% of votes	Seats
Nea Demokratia	1,825,609	29.66	129
Synaspismós Rizospastikís Aristerás*	1,655,053	26.89	71
Panellinio Socialistiko Kinima	755,832	12.28	33
Anexartitoi Ellines	462,456	7.51	20
Chrysi Avgi	425,980	6.92	18
Dimokratiki Aristera	385,079	6.26	17
Kommunistiko Komma Ellados	277,179	4.50	12
Others	368,339	5.98	—
Total	6,155,527	100.00	300

* A coalition of left-wing parties, led by Synaspismós Tis Aristerás Ton Kinimáton Kai Tis Oikologias.

Election Commission

National Election Commission: 155 61 Athens; tel. (210) 6535522; fax (210) 6546886; controlled by the Ministry of the Interior.

Political Organizations

Anexartitoi Ellines (Independent Greeks): 2 Charokopu Ave, Kallithea, 176 71 Athens; tel. (210) 9545000; internet www.anexartitoiellines.gr; f. 2012 by fmr mems of Nea Demokratia (q.v.); Leader PANOS KAMMENOS.

Chrysi Avgi (Golden Dawn): Athens; tel. (210) 7521080; e-mail info@xryshaygh.com; internet xryshaygh.com; f. 1993; extreme nationalist; Leader NIKOLAOS MICHALOLIAKOS.

Dimokratiki Aristera (DIMAR) (Democratic Left): Kriezotou 4, 106 71 Athens; tel. (210) 3820790; fax (210) 3834831; internet www.dimokratikiaristera.gr; f. 2010 by fmr mems of SYN (q.v.); Pres. FOTIS KOUVELIS.

Dimokratiko Koinoniko Kinima (DIKKI) (Democratic Social Movement): Odos Karolou 28, 104 37 Athens; tel. (210) 5234288; fax (210) 5239856; e-mail info@dikki.org; internet www.dikki.org; f. 1995; leftist; contested Oct. 2009 legislative elections as part of SYRIZA; Co-ordinator, Steering Committee PANTAGIOTIS MANTAS.

Kommunistiko Komma Ellados (KKE) (Communist Party of Greece): Leoforos Irakliou 145, Perissos, Nea Ionia, 142 31 Athens; tel. (210) 2592111; fax (210) 2592298; e-mail cpg@int.kke.gr; internet inter.kke.gr; f. 1918; banned 1947, re-emerged 1974; Gen. Sec. ALEKA PAPARIGA.

Laikos Orthodoxos Synagermos (LAOS) (Popular Orthodox Rally): Leofoos Kallirrois 52, 117 45 Athens; tel. (210) 3665000; fax (210) 3665209; e-mail pr@laos.gr; internet www.laos.gr; f. 2000; nationalist; Pres. GEORGIOS KARATZAFERIS.

Nea Demokratia (ND) (New Democracy): Leoforos Syngrou 340, 176 73 Kallithea, Athens; tel. (210) 9444000; fax (210) 7251491; e-mail ndpress@nd.gr; internet www.nd.gr; f. 1974; broad-based centre-right party advocating social reform in the framework of a liberal economy; supports European integration and enlargement; Pres. ANTONIS SAMARAS; Sec. of the Policy Committee ANTONIS SAMARAS.

Oikologoi Prasinoi (OP) (Ecologist Greens): Plateia Eleytherias 14, 105 53 Athens; tel. (210) 3306301; fax (210) 3834390; e-mail ecogreen@otenet.gr; internet www.ecogreens-gr.org; f. 2002; mem. of European Green Party; Mems. of Executive Secretarial Committee MICHALIS TREMOPOULOS, THANASSIS PAPAKONSTANTINOU, VASSO NAKOU, GEORGE DIMITRIOU, ORESTIS KOLOKOROURIS, KONSTANTINA KOSMIDOU.

Panellinio Socialistiko Kinima (PASOK) (Panhellenic Socialist Movement): Odos Hippocrates 22, 106 80 Athens; tel. (210) 3665000; fax (210) 3665209; e-mail pasok@pasok.gr; internet www.pasok.gr; f. 1974; incorporates Democratic Defence and Panhellenic Liberation Movement resistance orgs; supports social welfare, decentralization and self-management, aims for Mediterranean socialist devt through international co-operation; Pres. EVANGELOS VENIZELOS; Sec. of the Nat. Council MICHAEL KARCHIMAKIS; 500 local orgs, 30,000 mems.

Synaspismós Rizospastikís Aristerás (SYRIZA) (Coalition of the Radical Left): Pl. Eleftherias 1, 105 53 Athens; tel. (210) 3378400; fax (210) 3217003; e-mail info@syriza.gr; internet www.syriza.gr; f. 2004; comprises Active Citizens, SYN, q.v., Communist Organization of Greece (KOE), (DIKKI, q.v.), Ecosocialists Greece (OE), Group Roza, Internationalist Workers Left (DEA), Movement for Unity of Action of the Left (KEDA), Red (Kokkino), Renewing Communist Ecological Left (AKOA) and Start (Xekinima); Leader ALEXIS TSIPRAS.

Synaspismós Tis Aristerás Ton Kinimáton Kai Tis Oikologias (SYN) (Coalition of the Left of Movements and Ecology): Pl. Eleftherias 1, 105 53 Athens; tel. (210) 3378400; fax (210) 3217003; e-mail info@syn.gr; internet www.syn.gr; f. 1991 on the basis of an alliance (f. 1989) of the nine political groups comprising the Greek Left Party and the KKE, q.v.; present name adopted 2003; contested legislative elections as part of the Coalition of the Radical Left; Pres. ALEXIS TSIPRAS.

Diplomatic Representation

EMBASSIES IN GREECE

Albania: Odos Vekiareli 7, Filothei, 152 37 Athens; tel. (210) 6876200; fax (210) 6876223; e-mail embassy.athens@mfa.gov.al; internet www.ambasadat.gov.al/greece; Ambassador DASHNOR DERVISHI.

Algeria: Leoforos Vassileos Konstantinou 14, 116 35 Athens; tel. (210) 7564191; fax (210) 7018681; e-mail embalg@otenet.gr; Ambassador TEDJINI SALAOUANDJI.

Angola: Odos El. Venizelou 24, 152 37 Filothei-Athens; tel. (210) 6898681; fax (210) 6898683; e-mail info@angolaembassy.gr; internet www.angolanembassy.gr; Ambassador ISAIAS JAIME VILINGA.

Argentina: Leoforos Vassilissis Sofias 59, 115 21 Athens; tel. (210) 7224753; fax (210) 7227568; e-mail egrec@mrecic.gov.ar; internet www.egrec.mrecic.gov.ar; Ambassador JORGE ALEJANDRO MASTROPIETRO.

Armenia: Leoforos Konstantinou Paleologou 95, 152 32 Khalandri; tel. (210) 6831130; fax (210) 6831183; e-mail embassy.athens@mfa.am; Ambassador GAGIK GHALATCHIAN.

Australia: Thon Bldg, Odos Kifisias & Odos Alexandras, POB 14070, 115 23 Ambelokipi-Athens; tel. (210) 8704000; fax (210) 8704111; e-mail ae.athens@dfat.gov.au; Ambassador JENNY BLOOMFIELD.

Austria: Leoforos Vassilissis Sofias 4, 106 74 Athens; tel. (210) 7257270; fax (210) 7257292; e-mail athen-ob@bmeia.gv.at; internet www.bmeia.gv.at/botschaft/athen; Ambassador MELITTA SCHUBERT.

Azerbaijan: Leoforos Vassilissis Sofias 25, 106 74 Athens; tel. (210) 3632721; fax (210) 3639087; e-mail embassy@azembassy.gr; internet www.azembassy.gr; Ambassador RAHMAN MUSTAFAYEV.

Bangladesh: Odos Marathonodromon 119, Palaio Psychiko, 154 52 Athens; tel. (210) 6720250; fax (210) 6754513; e-mail mission.athens@mofa.gov.bd; internet bdembassyathens.gr; Ambassador GOLAM MOHAMMAD.

Belgium: Odos Sekeri 3, 106 71 Athens; tel. (210) 3617886; fax (210) 3604289; e-mail athens@diplobel.fed.be; internet www.diplomatie.be/athens; Ambassador MARC VAN DEN REECK.

Bosnia and Herzegovina: Odos Filaellinon 25, 6th Floor, 105 57 Athens; tel. (210) 6410788; fax (210) 6411978; e-mail info@bhembassy.gr; internet www.bhembassy.gr; Ambassador DRAGAN BOŽANIĆ.

Brazil: Leoforos Vassilissis Sofias 23, 106 74 Athens; tel. (210) 7213039; fax (210) 7244731; e-mail brasemb.atenas@itamaraty.gov.br; Ambassador EDGARD ANTONIO CASCIANO.

Bulgaria: Odos Stratigou Kallari 33A, Palaio Psychiko, 154 52 Athens; tel. (210) 6748105; fax (210) 6748130; e-mail embassy.athens@mfa.bg; internet www.mfa.bg/embassies/greece; Ambassador EMILIYA KRALEVA.

Canada: Odos Ioannou Ghennadiou 4, 115 21 Athens; tel. (210) 7273400; fax (210) 7273480; e-mail athns@international.gc.ca; internet www.canadainternational.gc.ca/greece-grece; Ambassador ROBERT PECK.

Chile: Odos Rigillis 12, 106 74 Athens; tel. (210) 7292647; fax (210) 7252565; e-mail nvegab@minrel.gov.cl; Ambassador (vacant).

China, People's Republic: Odos Demokratias 10–12, Palaio Psychiko, 154 52 Athens; tel. (210) 6723282; fax (210) 6723819; e-mail chinaemb_gr@mfa.gov.cn; internet gr.chineseembassy.org; Ambassador ZOU XIAOLI.

Congo, Democratic Republic: Odos Kodrou 20, 152 31 Halandri; tel. (210) 6776123; fax (210) 6776124; e-mail ambardcathenes@yahoo.fr; Chargé d'affaires a.i. HENRI BENJAMIN NTIKALA BOOTO.

Croatia: Odos Tzavela 4, 154 51 Psychiko; tel. (210) 6777033; fax (210) 6711208; e-mail croemb.athens@mvpei.hr; Ambassador IVAN VELIMIR STRAČEVIĆ.

Cuba: Odos Sofokleos 5, 152 37 Filothei; tel. (210) 6855550; fax (210) 6842807; e-mail secretaria@embacuba.gr; internet www.cubadiplomatica.cu/grecia/en/Home.aspx; Ambassador OSVALDO JESÚS COBACHO MARTÍNEZ.

Cyprus: Odos Xenofontos 2A, 105 57 Athens; tel. (210) 3734800; fax (210) 7258886; e-mail athensembassy@mfa.gon.cy; Ambassador PHAEDON ANASTASIOU.

Czech Republic: Odos Georgiou Seferis 6, 154 52 Palaio Psychiko; tel. (210) 6713755; fax (210) 6710675; e-mail athens@embassy.mzv.cz; internet www.mzv.cz/athens; Ambassador HANA ŠEVČÍKOVÁ.

Denmark: Odos Mourouzi 10, 106 74 Athens; tel. (210) 7256440; fax (210) 7256473; e-mail athathen@um.dk; internet www.graekenland.um.dk; Ambassador METTE KNUDSEN.

Egypt: Leoforos Vassilissis Sofias 3, 106 71 Athens; tel. (210) 3618612; fax (210) 3603538; e-mail emb.egypt@yahoo.gr; Ambassador AHMAD FOUAD AL-BIDEWY.

Estonia: Leoforos Messoghion 2–4, Athens Tower, 23rd Floor, 115 27 Athens; tel. (210) 7475660; fax (210) 7475661; e-mail embassy.athens@mfa.ee; internet www.estemb.gr; Ambassador MARGUS RAVA.

Finland: Odos Hatziyianni Mexi 5, 115 28 Athens; tel. (210) 7255860; fax (210) 7255864; e-mail sanomat.ate@formin.fi; internet www.finland.gr; Ambassador PEKKA LINTU.

France: Leoforos Vassilissis Sofias 7, 106 71 Athens; tel. (210) 3391000; fax (210) 3391009; e-mail info@ambafrance-gr.org; internet www.ambafrance-gr.org; Ambassador JEAN-LOUP KUHN-DELFORGE.

Georgia: Odos Taygetou 27 & Marathonodromou, 154 52 Palaio Psychiko, Athens; tel. (210) 6742186; fax (210) 6716722; e-mail athens.emb@mfa.gov.ge; internet greece.mfa.gov.ge; Ambassador DAVID BAKRADZE.

Germany: Odos Karaoli & Dimitriou 3, Kolonaki, 101 10 Athens; tel. (210) 7285111; fax (210) 7285335; e-mail info@athen.diplo.de; internet www.athen.diplo.de; Ambassador Dr PETER SCHOOF.

Holy See: POB 65075, Odos Mavili 2, 154 52 Palaio Psychiko; tel. (210) 6722728; fax (210) 6742849; e-mail nunate@ath.forthnet.gr; Apostolic Nuncio EDWARD JOSEPH ADAMS.

Hungary: Leoforos Vassileos Konstantinou 38, Pangrati, 116 35 Athens; tel. (210) 7256800; fax (210) 7256840; e-mail mission.ath@kum.hu; internet www.mfa.gov.hu/emb/athens; Ambassador ESZTER SÁNDORFI.

India: Odos Kleanthous 3, 106 74 Athens; tel. (210) 7216227; fax (210) 7211252; e-mail embassy@indianembassy.gr; internet www.indianembassy.gr; Ambassador TSEWANG TOPDEN.

Indonesia: Odos Marathonodromou 99, 154 52 Palaio Psychiko; tel. (210) 6742345; fax (210) 6756955; e-mail athena.kbri@kemlu.go.id; internet www.indonesia.gr; Ambassador BENNY BAHANADEWA.

Iran: Odos Stratigou Kalari 16, 154 52 Palaio Psychiko; tel. (210) 6471436; fax (210) 6477945; e-mail irembatn@otenet.gr; internet www.iranembassy.gr; Ambassador BEHROUZ BEHNAM.

Iraq: Odos Mazaraki 4, Palaio Psychiko, 154 52 Athens; tel. (210) 6722330; fax (210) 6717185; e-mail iraqath@otenet.gr; internet www.iraqembassy-athens.com; Ambassador BURHAN JAF.

Ireland: Leoforos Vassileos Konstantinou 7, 106 74 Athens; tel. (210) 7232771; fax (210) 7293383; e-mail athensembassy@dfa.ie; internet www.embassyofireland.gr; Ambassador CHARLES SHEEHAN.

Israel: Odos Marathonodromou 1, 154 52 Palaio Psychiko; tel. (210) 6705500; fax (210) 6705555; e-mail pr@athens.mfa.gov.il; internet athens.mfa.gov.il; Ambassador ARYE MEKEL.

Italy: Odos Sekeri 2, 106 74 Athens; tel. (210) 3617260; fax (210) 3617330; e-mail ambasciata.atene@esteri.it; internet www.ambatene.esteri.it; Ambassador CLAUDIO GLAENTZER.

Japan: Odos Ethnikis Antistasseos 46, Halandri, 152 31 Athens; tel. (210) 6709900; fax (210) 6709980; e-mail embjapan@at.mofa.go.jp; internet www.gr.emb-japan.go.jp; Ambassador MASUO NISHIBAYASHI.

Jordan: Odos Papadiamanti 21, 154 52 Palaio Psychiko; tel. (210) 6744161; fax (210) 6740578; e-mail jor_emb1@otenet.gr; internet www.jordanembassy.gr; Ambassador (vacant).

Kazakhstan: Odos Imittou 122, 15 669 Papagou; tel. (210) 6515643; fax (210) 6516362; e-mail athens@kazembassy.gr; internet www.kazembassy.gr; Ambassador SERGEI NURTAEV.

Korea, Republic: Leoforos Messoghion 2–4, Athens Tower, A-Building, 19th Floor, 115 27 Athens; tel. (210) 6984080; fax (210) 6984083; e-mail gremb@mofat.go.kr; Ambassador GIL-SOU SHIN.

Kuwait: Odos Marathonodromou 27, 154 52 Palaio Psychiko; tel. (210) 6743593; fax (210) 6775875; e-mail info@kuwaitembassy.gr; Ambassador RAED ABDULLAH AL-RIFAI.

Latvia: Odos Vassilissis Constantinou 38, 116 35 Athens; tel. (210) 7294483; fax (210) 7294479; e-mail embassy.greece@mfa.gov.lv; internet www.mfa.gov.lv/greece; Ambassador IVARS PUNDURS.

Lebanon: Odos 25 Maritou 6, 154 52 Palaio Psychiko; tel. (210) 6755873; fax (210) 6755612; e-mail officesm@lebaneseembassygreece.gr; Ambassador GÉBRAN MICHEL SOUFAN.

Libya: Odos Vyronos 13, 154 52 Palaio Psychiko; tel. (210) 6472120; fax (210) 6742761; Ambassador AHMED YAGOB GZLLAL.

Lithuania: Leoforos Vassilissis Konstantinous 38, 116 35 Athens; tel. (210) 7294356; fax (210) 7294347; e-mail amb.gr@urm.lt; internet gr.mfa.lt; Ambassador ALFONSAS EIDINTAS.

Luxembourg: Leoforos Vassilissis Sofias 23A & Odos Neophytou Vamva 2, 106 74 Athens; tel. (210) 7256400; fax (210) 7256405; e-mail athenes.amb@mae.etat.lu; internet athenes.mae.lu; Ambassador CHRISTIAN MARC BIEVER.

Malta: Leoforos Vassilissis Sofias 96, 115 28 Athens; tel. (210) 7785138; fax (210) 7785242; e-mail maltaembassy.athens@gov.mt; Ambassador CHARLES STAFRACE.

Mexico: Plateia Filikis Etairias 14, 5th Floor, 106 73 Athens; tel. (210) 7294780; fax (210) 7294783; e-mail embgrecia@sre.gob.mx; Ambassador RICARDO-TARCISIO NAVARRETE-MONTES DE OCA.

Moldova: Odos Georgiou Bacu 20, 115 24 Athens; tel. (210) 6990372; fax (210) 6990660; e-mail atena@mfa.md; internet www.grecia.mfa.gov.md; Ambassador Dr VALENTIN CIUMAC.

Montenegro: Odos Loukianou 5, Kolonaki, 106 75 Athens; tel. (210) 7241212; fax (210) 7241076; e-mail greece@mfa.gov.me; Ambassador PETAR POPOVIĆ.

Morocco: Odos Marathonodromou 5, 154 52 Palaio Psychiko; tel. (210) 6744209; fax (210) 6749480; e-mail sifamath@otenet.gr; Ambassador ABDELKADER AL-ANSARI.

Netherlands: Leoforos Vassileos Konstantinou 5–7, 106 74 Athens; tel. (210) 7254900; fax (210) 7254907; e-mail ath@minbuza.nl; internet www.dutchembassy.gr; Ambassador JAN VERSTEEG.

Nigeria: Odos Strait 17, 152 37 Filothei, Athens; tel. (210) 8021168; fax (210) 8024208; e-mail nigeria.athens@mfa.gov.ng; Ambassador M. AYODEJI LAWRENCE AYODELE.

Norway: Leoforos Vassilissis Sofias 23, 106 74 Athens; tel. (210) 7246173; fax (210) 7244989; e-mail emb.athens@mfa.no; internet www.norway.gr; Ambassador SJUR LARSEN.

Pakistan: Odos Loukianou 6, Kolonaki, 106 75 Athens; tel. (210) 7290122; fax (210) 7257641; e-mail parepathen@otenet.gr; internet www.mofa.gov.pk/greece; Ambassador Dr SAEED KHAN MOHMAND.

Panama: Odos Filellinon 1-3 & Akti Miaouli, 185 36 Piraeus; tel. (210) 4286441; fax (210) 4286448; e-mail embassy@panamaembassy.gr; Ambassador AYMARD HIRAM JIMÉNEZ GRANDA.

Peru: Odos Koumbari 2, Kolonaki, 106 74 Athens; tel. (210) 7792761; fax (210) 7792905; e-mail lepruate@otenet.gr; internet www.peru.gr; Ambassador JORGE ROMÁN MOREY.

Philippines: Odos Antheon 26, 154 52 Palaio Psychiko; tel. (210) 6721883; fax (210) 6721872; e-mail athenspe@otenet.gr; internet www.philembathens.gr; Ambassador MEYNARDO L. B. MONTEALEGRE.

Poland: Odos Chryssanthemon 22, 154 52 Palaio Psychiko; tel. (210) 6797700; fax (210) 6797711; e-mail ateny.amb.sekretariat@msz.gov.pl; internet athens.mfa.gov.pl; Chargé d'affaires a.i. SANDRA HARMOZA.

Portugal: Leoforos Vassilissis Sofias 23, 106 74 Athens; tel. (210) 7290096; fax (210) 7245122; e-mail embportg@otenet.gr; Ambassador JOAQUIM JOSÉ MARQUES.

Qatar: Leoforos Kifissias 212 & Odos Perikleous 2, 154 51 Neo Psychiko Athens; tel. (210) 7255031; fax (210) 7255024; e-mail athens@mofa.gov.qa; internet www.qatarembassy.gr; Ambassador SOLTAN SAAD AL-MORAIKHI.

Romania: Odos Emmanuel Benaki 7, 154 52 Palaio Psychiko; tel. (210) 6728875; fax (210) 6728883; e-mail secretariat@romaniaemb.gr; internet atena.mae.ro; Ambassador LUCIAN FĂTU.

Russia: Odos Nikiforou Litra 28, 154 52 Palaio Psychiko; tel. (210) 6725235; fax (210) 6479708; e-mail embraf@otenet.gr; internet www.greece.mid.ru; Ambassador VLADIMIR I. CHKHIKVISHVILI.

Saudi Arabia: Odos Palaiologhou & Agias Annis 2, Halandri, 152 32 Athens; tel. (210) 6716911; fax (210) 6749833; e-mail gremb@mofa.gov.sa; Ambassador RAYED KRIMLY.

Serbia: Leoforos Vassilissis Sofias 106, 115 27 Athens; tel. (210) 7774344; fax (210) 7796436; e-mail beograd@hol.gr; internet www.embassyofserbia.gr; Ambassador (vacant).

Slovakia: Odos Georgiou Seferis 4, 154 52 Palaio Psychiko; tel. (210) 6771980; fax (210) 6771878; e-mail emb.athens@mzv.sk; internet www.mzv.sk/athens; Ambassador PETER MICHALKO.

Slovenia: Leoforos Kifissias 280 & Odos Dimokratias 1, 154 51 Neo Psychiko; tel. (210) 6720090; fax (210) 6775680; e-mail vat@gov.si; internet www.atene.veleposlanistvo.si; Ambassador ROBERT BASEJ.

South Africa: Leoforos Kifissias 60, 151 25 Maroussi; tel. (210) 6178020; fax (210) 6106640; e-mail athens.info@dirco.gov.za; Ambassador SOPHONIA RAPULANE MAKGETLA.

Spain: Odos D. Areopagitou 21, 117 42 Athens; tel. (210) 9213123; fax (210) 9213090; e-mail emb.atenas@maec.es; Ambassador ALFONSO LUCINI.

Sudan: Odos Mousson 6, 154 52 Palaio Psychiko, Athens; tel. (210) 6742520; fax (210) 6742521; Ambassador ABDELMONIEM AHMED EL-AMIN EL-HUSEIN.

Sweden: Leoforos Vassileos Konstantinou 7, 106 74 Athens; tel. (210) 7266100; fax (210) 7266150; e-mail ambassaden.athen@foreign.ministry.se; internet www.swedenabroad.com/athen; Ambassador HÅKAN MALMQVIST.

Switzerland: Odos Iassiou 2, 115 21 Athens; tel. (210) 7230364; fax (210) 7249209; e-mail ath.vertretung@eda.admin.ch; internet www.eda.admin.ch/athens; Ambassador LORENZO AMBERG.

Syria: Diamandidou 61, 154 52 Palaio Psychiko; tel. (210) 6725577; fax (210) 6716402; e-mail syrembas@otenet.gr; internet www.syrianembassy.gr; Ambassador (vacant).

Thailand: Odos Marathonodromou 25 & Odos Kyprou, 154 52 Palaio Psychiko; tel. (210) 6710155; fax (210) 6749508; e-mail thaiath@otenet.gr; Ambassador JOOMPOL MANASCHUANG.

Tunisia: Odos Antheon 2 & Odos Marathonodromou, 154 52 Palaio Psychiko; tel. (210) 6717590; fax (210) 6713432; e-mail atathina@otenet.gr; Ambassador TAREK SAADI.

Turkey: Odos Vassileos Gheorghiou II 8, 106 74 Athens; tel. (210) 7263000; fax (210) 7229597; e-mail embassy.athens@mfa.gov.tr; internet athens.emb.mfa.gov.tr; Ambassador KERIM URAS.

Ukraine: Odos Stefanou Delta 2, 152 37 Filothei; tel. (210) 6800230; fax (210) 6854154; e-mail emb_gr@mfa.gov.ua; internet www.mfa.gov.ua/greece; Ambassador VOLODYMYR SHKUROV.

United Arab Emirates: Leoforos Kifissias 280 & Odos Agriniou 3, 152 32 Halandri; tel. (210) 6770220; fax (210) 6770274; Ambassador SULTAN MUHAMMAD MAJID AL-ALI.

United Kingdom: Odos Ploutarchou 1, 106 75 Athens; tel. (210) 7272600; fax (210) 7272723; e-mail information.athens@fco.gov.uk; internet ukingreece.fco.gov.uk; Ambassador JOHN KITTMER.

Uruguay: Odos Menandrou 1, 145 61 Kifissia; tel. (210) 3602635; fax (210) 3613549; e-mail urugrec@otenet.gr; Ambassador ADRIANA LISSIDINI DOTTI.

USA: Leoforos Vassilissis Sofias 91, 106 10 Athens; tel. (210) 7212951; fax (210) 6456282; e-mail usembassy@usembassy.gr; internet athens.usembassy.gov; Ambassador DAVID DUANE PEARCE.

Venezuela: Odos Papadiamanti 15, 154 52 Palaio Psychiko; tel. (210) 6729169; fax (210) 6727464; e-mail emvenath@hol.gr; internet www.embavenez.gr; Ambassador FREDERIC F. STEPHAN GONZÁLEZ-FERNÁNDEZ-COUSTOLLE.

Viet Nam: Odos Yakinthon 50, Palaio Psychiko, 154 52 Athens; tel. (210) 6128733; fax (210) 6128734; e-mail vnemb.gr@mofa.gov.vn; internet www.mofa.gov.vn/vnemb.gr; Ambassador BINH VU.

Judicial System

SUPREME ADMINISTRATIVE COURTS

Special Supreme Tribunal: Odos Patision 30, Athens; consists of 11 members: three presidents (of the Supreme Court, Council of State and Court of Audit), four judges of the Supreme Court and four judges of the Council of State; has final jurisdiction in matters of constitutionality.

Council of State

Odos Panepistimiou 47-49, 105 64 Athens; tel. (210) 2132102; fax (210) 3710097; e-mail ste@ste.gr; internet www.ste.gr.

Has appellate powers over acts of the administration and final rulings of administrative courts; has power to rule upon matters of judicial review of laws.

President: RIZOS SOTIRIOS.

Supreme Court of Civil and Penal Law

Leoforos Alexandros 121, 115 10 Athens; tel. (210) 6411506; fax (210) 6433799; internet www.areiospagos.gr.

Supreme court in the State, also having appellate powers; consists of six sections (four Civil, two Penal) and adjudicates in quorum.

President: MICHAIL THEOCHARIDIS.

COURTS OF APPEAL

There are 12 Courts of Appeal with jurisdiction in cases of Civil and Penal Law of second degree, and, in exceptional penal cases, of first degree.

COURTS OF FIRST INSTANCE

There are 59 Courts of First Instance with jurisdiction in cases of first degree, and, in exceptional cases, of second degree. They function both as Courts of First Instance and as Criminal Courts. For serious crimes the Criminal Courts function with a jury.

In towns where Courts of First Instance sit there are also Juvenile Courts. Commercial Tribunals do not function in Greece, and all commercial cases are tried by ordinary courts of law. There are, however, Tax Courts in some towns.

OTHER COURTS

There are 360 Courts of the Justice of Peace throughout the country. There are 48 Magistrates' Courts (or simple Police Courts).

In all the above courts, except those of the Justice of Peace, there are District Attorneys. In Courts of the Justice of Peace, the duties of District Attorney are performed by the Public Prosecutor.

Religion

CHRISTIANITY

The Eastern Orthodox Church

The Greek branch of the Eastern Orthodox Church is the officially established religion of the country, to which nearly 97% of the population profess adherence.

Within the Greek State, there is also the semi-autonomous Church of Crete, which is under the spiritual jurisdiction of the Ecumenical Patriarchate of Constantinople (based in İstanbul, Turkey).

There are also four Metropolitan Sees of the Dodecanese, which are dependent on the Ecumenical Patriarchate, and, finally, the peninsula of Athos, which constitutes the region of the Holy Mountain (Mount Athos) and comprises 20 monasteries. These are dependent on the Ecumenical Patriarchate of Constantinople, but are autonomous and are safeguarded constitutionally.

The Orthodox Church of Greece: Odos Ioannou Gennadiou 14, 115 21 Athens; tel. (210) 7218381; e-mail contact@ecclesia.gr; internet www.ecclesia.gr; f. 1850.

Primate of Greece: IERONYMOS II (LIAPIS).

Archbishop of Crete: Archbishop IRENAIOS (whose See is in Heraklion).

The Roman Catholic Church

Greece comprises four archdioceses (including two, Athens and Rhodes, directly responsible to the Holy See), four dioceses, one Apostolic Vicariate and one Apostolic Exarchate for adherents of the Byzantine Rite. There is also an Ordinariate for Armenian Catholics. There are an estimated 180,637 adherents in the country, including 2,500 of the Byzantine Rite and 300 of the Armenian Rite.

Latin Rite

Bishops' Conference: G. Papandreou 15, 841 00 Syros; tel. (22) 81084783; fax (22) 8108684781; e-mail syrensis@otenet.gr; f. 1967; Pres. Rt Rev. FRAGKISKOS PAPAMANOLIS (Bishop of Syros and Milos, and of Santorini).

Archbishop of Athens: Archbishop Most Rev. NIKÓLAOS FÓSKOLOS, Odos Homirou 9, 106 72 Athens; tel. (210) 3624311; fax (210) 3618632.

Archbishop of Corfu, Zante and Cefalonia: Most Rev. IOANNIS SPITERIS, Montzeníkhou 3, 491 00 Kérkyra; tel. (26610) 30277; fax (26610) 31675; e-mail cathepco@otenet.gr.

Archbishop of Naxos, Andros, Tinos and Mykonos: Most Rev. NIKÓLAOS PRINTESIS, 842 00 Tinos; tel. (22830) 22382; fax (22830) 24769; e-mail kamipai@cathecclesia.gr.

Archbishop of Rhodes: (vacant), Odos Ionos Dragoumi 5, 851 00 Rhodes; tel. (22410) 21845; fax (22410) 26688.

Apostolic Vicariate of Thessaloníki: Kolokotroni 19B, 564 30 Thessaloníki; tel. (2310) 654256; fax (2310) 835780; e-mail ioas17@otenet.gr; Apostolic Vicar JOANNIS SPITERIS.

Byzantine Rite

Apostolic Exarchate for Greek Catholics of the Byzantine Rite: Odos Akarnon 246, 112 53 Athens; tel. (210) 8670170; fax (210) 8677039; e-mail grcathex@hol.gr; 3 parishes; 3,500 adherents (31 Dec. 2006); Apostolic Exarch Most Rev. DIMITRIOS SALACHAS (Titular Bishop of Carcabia).

Armenian Rite

Ordinariate for Catholics of the Armenian Rite in Greece: Odos René Pyo 2, 117 44 Athens; tel. (210) 9014089; fax (210) 9012109; 350 adherents (31 Dec. 2006); Ordinary (vacant); Apostolic Administrator Most Rev. NECHAN KARAKAHIAN (Titular Archbishop of Adana of the Armenian Rite).

Protestant Church

Greek Evangelical Church: Odos Markon Botsari 24, 117 41 Athens; tel. (210) 3231079; fax (210) 3316577; e-mail info@gec.gr; internet www.gec.gr; f. 1858; comprises 32 organized churches; 5,000 adherents (1996); Moderator Rev. MELETIS MELETIADIS.

ISLAM

The law provides a Chief Mufti as religious head of the Muslims; the Muslims in Greece possess a number of mosques and schools.

JUDAISM

The Jewish population of Greece, estimated in 1943 at 75,000 people, was severely reduced as a result of the Nazi German occupation. In 1994 there were about 5,000 Jews in Greece.

Central Board of the Jewish Communities of Greece: Odos Voulis 36, 105 57 Athens; tel. (210) 3244315; fax (210) 3313852; e-mail info@kis.gr; internet www.kis.gr; f. 1945; officially recognized representative body of the Jewish communities of Greece; Pres. DAVID SALTIEL.

The Press

PRINCIPAL DAILY NEWSPAPERS

Morning papers are not published on Mondays, nor afternoon papers on Sundays. The afternoon papers generally enjoy a wider circulation than do the morning ones.

Adesmeftos Typos (Rizos): Thiseseos 218, Kallithea, 176 75 Athens; tel. (210) 9405888; fax (210) 9407173; e-mail info@adesmeytos.gr; internet www.adesmeytos.gr; f. 1998; afternoon; publ. by Makedonikes Publications; Dir DIMITRIS RIZOS; Editor KOSTAS SARRIKOSTAS; circ. weekdays 12,973, Sun. 11,837 (2009).

Apogevmatini (The Afternoon): Odos Phidiou 12, 106 78 Athens; tel. (210) 6430011; fax (210) 3304800; e-mail info@apogevmatini.gr; internet www.apogevmatini.gr; f. 1956; independent; Editor MIHAIL VASILIADIS; circ. 12,815 (2009).

Avgi (Dawn): Odos Ag. Konstantiou 12, 104 31 Athens; tel. (210) 5231831; fax (210) 5231822; e-mail editors@avgi.gr; internet www.avgi.gr; f. 1952; morning; independent newspaper of the left; Dir NIKOS PHILES; circ. 2,791 (2012).

Ekathimerini (Every Day): Ethnarchou Makariou & Odos Falireos 2, Neo Faliro, 185 47, Piraeus, Athens; tel. (210) 4808000; fax (210) 4808205; e-mail info@ekathimerini.com; internet www.ekathimerini.gr; f. 1919; morning; conservative; Editor NIKOS KONSTADARAS; circ. 46,086 (2009).

Eleftherotypia (Press Freedom): Odos Minou 10–16, 117 43 Athens; tel. (211) 1096400; fax (210) 9028311; e-mail elef@enet.gr; internet www.enet.gr; f. 1974; afternoon; Publr HARRIS IKONOMOPOULOS; Chief Editor VANGELIS PANAGOPOULOS; circ. daily 41,511, Sun. 148,652 (2009).

Espresso: C. Averof 26–28, 142 32 Nea Ionia; tel. (210) 2503100; e-mail espresso@espressonews.gr; internet www.espressonews.gr; f. 2000; afternoon; publ. by Daily Press; Publr ANTONIS LIMBERIS; circ. daily 17,752, Sun. 10,453 (2012).

Ethnos (Nation): Odos Benaki 152, Metamorfosi Halandriou, 152 38 Athens; tel. (210) 6061000; fax (210) 6391337; e-mail editor@ethnos.gr; internet www.ethnos.gr; f. 1981; afternoon; Dir GIORGOS CHARVALIAS; Editor THANASIS TSEKOURAS; circ. daily 24,732, Sun. 102,241 (2012).

Exedra Ton Sports: Michalakopoulou 80, 115 28 Athens; tel. (211) 3657000; fax (211) 3659301; e-mail info@exedra.gr; internet www.exedra.gr; f. 2008; sport; circ. Tue.–Sun. 17,388, Mon. 18,199 (2009).

Express: 46 Leoforos Lavrion, POB 4814, Keratea, 190 01 Attica; tel. (213) 0161700; fax (213) 0161849; e-mail info@express.gr; internet www.express.gr; f. 1963; morning; financial; publ. by Kalofolia Group SA; Publr D. G. KALOFOLIAS; Editor G. DIAMANTOPOULOS; circ. 28,000.

Filathlos: Odos Dimitros 31, 177 78 Athens; tel. (210) 3489000; fax (210) 3489015; e-mail info@filathlos.gr; internet www.filathlos.gr; f. 1982; morning; sports; Publr and Editor G. KOLOKOTRONIS; circ. 8,879.

Goal News: Odos Benaki & Ag. Nektariou, Halandriou, 152 38 Athens; tel. (210) 6061800; fax (210) 6061801; internet www.sentragoal.gr; f. 2002; sport; publ. by Pegasus Publishing SA; circ. Tue.–Sun. 7,058, Mon. 9,911 (2013).

Imerissia (Daily): Odos Benaki & Ag. Nektariou, Metamorfosi Halandriou, 152 38 Athens; tel. (210) 6061000; fax (210) 6014636; e-mail imerissia@pegasus.gr; internet www.imerisia.gr; f. 1947; morning; financial; Dir ANTONIS DALIPIS; Editor ALEX KASIMATIS; circ. 39,000.

Kerdos (Profit): Rizariou 16, 152 33 Athens; tel. (210) 6747881; fax (210) 6747893; e-mail mail@kerdos.gr; internet www.kerdos.gr; f. 1985; morning; financial; Editor G. STEVIS; circ. 18,000.

Naftemporiki (Daily Journal): Odos Lenorman 205, 104 42 Athens; tel. (210) 5198000; fax (210) 5146013; e-mail info@naftemporiki.gr; internet www.naftemporiki.gr; f. 1924; morning; non-political journal of finance, commerce and shipping; Dir NIKOS FRANTZIS; Editor DIMITRIS PLAKOUTSIS; circ. 20,000.

Peloponnesos: Valtetsiou 1 & Maizonos, 262 23 Patras; tel. (2610) 312530; fax (2610) 312535; e-mail pelop@pelop.gr; internet www.pelop.gr; f. 1886; independent; conservative; Publr and CEO THEODOROS H. LOULOUDIS; circ. 7,000.

Protathlitis (Champions): Dimokratias 34, Melissia, 151 27 Athens; tel. (210) 8109000; fax (210) 8040149; e-mail info@championsday.gr; f. 1998; sport; circ. Tue.–Sun. 4,929, Mon. 4,995 (2013).

Rizospastis (Radical): Leoforos Heraklion 145, 142 32 Nea Ionia; tel. (210) 2592600; fax (210) 2592800; e-mail mailbox@rizospastis.gr; internet www.rizospastis.gr; f. 1974; morning; publ. by Modern Age Publishing SA; Editor PAVLOS ALEPIS; circ. 7,214 (2013).

Sport Day: Davaki 58, Kallithea, 176 72 Athens; tel. (210) 9508100; fax (210) 9508160; e-mail info@sday.gr; internet www.sday.gr; f. 2005; sport; circ. Tue.–Sun. 7,741, Mon. 9,812 (2013).

Ta Nea (News): Odos Michalakopoulou 80, 115 28 Athens; tel. (211) 3657000; fax (211) 3658301; e-mail info@tanea.gr; internet www.tanea.gr; f. 1944; liberal; afternoon; publ. by Lambrakis Press SA; Dir CHRISTOS MAMIS; circ. 28,764 (2013).

To Fos Ton Spor: Athinon 122, 104 42 Athens; tel. (210) 5154000; fax (210) 5141330; e-mail fos@otenet.gr; f. 1968; sport; circ. Tue.–Sun. 10,856, Mon. 14,032 (2013).

To Vima (Tribune): Odos Michalakopoulou 80, 115 28 Athens; tel. (210) 3657000; fax (210) 3658004; e-mail tovima@dolnet.gr; internet www.tovima.gr; f. 1922; liberal; publ. by Lambrakis Press SA; Dir and Editor STAVROS R. PSYCHARIS; circ. daily 38,712, Sun. 172,368 (2009).

WEEKLY PUBLICATIONS

I Aksia (Value): 3 Septemvriou 144, 112 51 Athens; tel. (210) 8254811; fax (210) 8814229; f. 1998; Publr ANTONIS PIKOULAS; circ. 13,165 (2009).

Athens News: Odos Doiranis 181, Kallithea, 176 73 Athens; tel. (213) 0087150; fax (210) 9431110; e-mail athensnews@athensnews.eu; internet www.athensnews.gr; f. 1952; weekly; in English; owned by NEP Publishing Company SA; Editor IOANNA PAPADIMITROPOULOU; circ. 10,000.

Kathimerini Tis Kiriakis (Every Day on Sunday): Minoos 10–16, 117 43 Athens; tel. (210) 9296001; fax (210) 9028311; e-mail ke@enet.gr; internet www.enet.gr; f. 1919; Dir JOHN VLASTARIS; Editors ALEXANDRA DALIANI, VAGELIS SIAFAKAS; circ. 134,665 (2009).

O Kosmos Tou Ependiti (The World of Investors): Leoforos 174, Kallithea, 176 71 Athens; tel. (210) 3721100; fax (210) 3721110; e-mail ependitis@kte.gr; internet www.kte.gr; f. 2002; politics, economics and social; Chair. and Man. Dir KOSTAS A. GIANNIKOS; Editor NIKOS FELEKIS; circ. 80,397 (2009).

Proto Thema (One Topic): Apostolou Pavlou 6, 15 123 Marousi; tel. (210) 6880700; fax (210) 6892778; e-mail protothemaonline@gmail.com; internet www.protothema.gr; f. 2005; Sunday; circ. 150,659 (2013).

Real News: Leoforos Kifisias 215, 151 24 Athens; tel. (211) 2008300; fax (211) 2008399; e-mail news@realnews.gr; internet www.real.gr; f. 2008; Sunday; Publr NIKOS HATZINIKOLAOU; circ. 88,719 (2013).

Sto Karfi Tou Savvatokyriakou (The Weekend Nail): Krimeas 2 & Mesogion 125, 115 26 Athens; tel. (210) 6901000; fax (210) 6915741; e-mail info@stokarfi.gr; internet digital.stokarfi.gr; f. 2004; Saturdays; left-wing; Dir KOSTAS GIANNOPOULOS; circ. 23,344 (2009).

Xrisi Efkeria (Golden Opportunity): Golden Opportunity Publ., Sakasomouli Hekataios 95 &73, 117 44 Athens; tel. (210) 9091333; fax (210) 9091420; e-mail contact@xe.gr; internet www.xe.gr; f. 1993; publ. by Golden Opportunity Publications; CEO DIMITRIS TRITARIS; circ. 41,293 (2009).

SELECTED PERIODICALS

Aktines (Rays): Odos Karytsi 14, 105 61 Athens; f. 1938; monthly; Christian publication on current affairs, science, philosophy, arts; circ. 10,000.

Asfalistikn Agora (The Insurance Market): Dionysus 126, 151 24 Maroussi; tel. (210) 6196879; fax (210) 6196943; e-mail aagora@aagora.gr; internet www.aagora.gr; f. 1977; publ. by Rouchotas D. & Co; monthly; Publr AMALIA ROUCHOTAS; Editor-in-Chief ATHANASIOS KORMA.

Computer Gia Olous (Computers for All): Capt. Dedousi 1 & Mesogion 304, Holargos, 155 62 Athens; tel. (210) 9238672; fax (210) 9216847; e-mail cpress@compupress.gr; internet www.cgomag.gr; monthly; Editor FORTIS KARATZIAS.

Deltion Diikiseos Epichiriseon Euro-Unial (Euro-Unial Business Administration Bulletin): Odos Alopekis 27-29, 106 75 Athens; tel. (210) 7235735; fax (210) 7240000; e-mail info@dde.gr; internet www.dde.gr; f. 1962; monthly; Editor IOANNIS N. PAPAMICHALAKIS; circ. 26,000 (2006).

Ebdomi (Seventh): Kanari 18, 153 51 Pallini; tel. (210) 6030655; fax (210) 9658949; e-mail scarabe@hol.gr; internet www.ebdomi.com; weekly; political-economic and cultural journal of Eastern Attica; Publr ANNA VENETSANOU.

Economiki Epitheorissi (Economic Review): Odos Vlahava 6–8, 105 51 Athens; tel. (210) 3314714; fax (210) 3230338; e-mail info@economia.gr; internet www.economia.gr; f. 1934; monthly; economy, business and politics; publ. by Group Economia-Kerkyra Publications; Dir and Publr ALEXANDRA VOVOLINI; Editors ANDREAS PETSINIS, SPYROS A. VRETOS; circ. 45,000.

Electrologos (Electrician): Odos Pileos & Leoforos Pentelis 3, Vrilissia, 152 35 Athens; tel. (210) 6800470; fax (210) 6800476; e-mail technoekdotiki@technoekdotiki.gr; internet www.electrologos.gr; f. 1991; monthly; technical; Publr VOULA MOURTA; Editor CHRISTINA SOURRA; circ. 11,500 (2009).

Elnavi (Greek Shipping Industry): Odos Aristidou 19, 185 31 Piraeus; tel. (210) 4522100; fax (210) 4282467; e-mail elnavi@elnavi.gr; internet www.elnavi.gr; f. 1974; monthly; shipping; Publr ELIAS KALAPOTHARAKOS; Dirs STEFANOS PAPANDREOU, THEANO KALAPOTHARAKOU; circ. 4,000 (2009).

Epiloghi (Selection): Kapodistrioy 2 & Demokratias 83, 154 51 Neo Psychiko; tel. (210) 6401850; fax (210) 6424850; e-mail press@allmedia.gr; internet www.epilogimag.gr; f. 1962; monthly; economics and business journal; publ. by All Media Publications; Dir CHRISTOS PAPAIOANNOU; Editor THOMI MELIDOU.

Greek Diplomatic Life: Giving Fountain 5, 106 78 Athens; tel. (210) 3806534; fax (210) 3818983; e-mail diplomat@otenet.gr; f. 1978; bi-monthly; Publr BOUTSIKOS NIKOLAOS; circ. 5,500 (2009).

Gynaika (Women): Odos Fragoklissias 7, Marousi, 151 25 Athens; tel. (210) 6199149; fax (210) 6104707; e-mail admin@e-gynaika.com; internet www.e-gynaika.gr; f. 1950; monthly; Publr CHRISTOS TERZOPOULOS; circ. 45,000.

Hot Doc: Athens; internet www.hotdoc.gr; f. 2012; politics and current affairs; every two weeks; Editor KOSTAS VAXEVANIS.

Idaniko Spiti (Ideal Home): Odos Benaki 5, Halandri, 152 38 Athens; tel. (210) 6061777; fax (210) 6061891; e-mail idanikospiti@pegasus.gr; internet www.idanikospiti.gr; f. 1990; monthly; interior decoration; Editor ALEXANDRA VAGENA; circ. 13,000 (2009).

Klik: Odos Fragoklisias 7, 151 25 Athens; fax (210) 6899153; internet www.klik.gr; f. 1987; monthly; popular music, media and fashion; Editor ARIS TERZOPUOLOS.

Kynigos Kai Fysi (Hunter and Nature): Kallirrois 85, 117 45 Athens; tel. (210) 7755464; fax (210) 7785776; e-mail onel@onel.gr; internet www.go-outdoor.gr; publ. by Onel SA; Publr KAKAVOULIS ELEFTHERIOS.

Mastoremata (Do-it-yourself): Odos Thorikou, Viopa Kalyvion, Kalyvia, 190 10 Attica; tel. (229) 9021360; fax (229) 9021359; e-mail info@mastoremata.gr; internet www.mastoremata.gr; monthly; publ. by Stefanos Karidakis SA; Publr PROKOPIS KARIDAKIS; Editor DIMITRIS GEORGOPOULOS.

Pantheon: Odos Christou Lada 3, 102 37 Athens; fax (210) 3228797; every two weeks; Publr and Dir N. THEOFANIDES.

Ptisi & Diastima (Flight & Space): Ioannou Metaxa 80, Koropi, 194 00 Athens; tel. (210) 9792500; fax (210) 9792528; e-mail ptisi@ptisi.gr; internet www.ptisi.gr; f. 1979; monthly; Editor FAITHON KARAIOSSIFIOIS; circ. 1,467.

Radiotileorasi (Radio-TV): Odos Rhigillis 4, 106 74 Athens; tel. (210) 7407252; fax (210) 7224812; e-mail radiotileorasi@ert.gr; internet www.radiotileorasi.gr; weekly; Editor DIMITRIS KOCHLATZIS; circ. 55,000.

Stigmes (Moments): Psaromiligkon 17, Heraklion, 712 02 Crete; tel. (281) 0288333; fax (281) 0301927; e-mail spiti@stigmes.gr; internet www.stigmes.gr; six a year; Cretan culture; Editor NIKOS KARELLIS.

Technika Chronika (Technical Times): Odos Nikis, Syndagma, 102 48 Athens; tel. (210) 3291200; fax (210) 3221772; e-mail tee@central.tee.gr; internet www.tee.gr; f. 1932; weekly; general technical subjects; Editor IOANNIS ALAVANOS; circ. 100,000.

Tilerama: Odos Voukourestiou 18, 106 71 Athens; tel. (210) 3607160; fax (210) 3607032; f. 1977; weekly; radio and television; circ. 189,406.

To Pontiki (The Mouse): Odos Massalias 10, 106 81 Athens; fax (210) 6898226; e-mail asfalistiko@topontiki.gr; internet www.topontiki.gr; weekly; humour; Dir and Editor K. PAPAIOANNOU.

NEWS AGENCY

Athens Macedonian News Agency (ANA-MPA): Odos Tsoha 36, 115 21 Athens; tel. (210) 6400560; fax (210) 6400581; e-mail sofia@amna.gr; internet www.amna.gr; f. 1895; as Athens News Agency; name changed to above following merger with Macedonian Press Agency in 2008; correspondents in leading capitals of the world and towns throughout Greece; Gen. Man. ANTONIS SKYLLAKOS; Gen. Dir SOFIA KRITHARA.

PRESS ASSOCIATIONS

Enosis Antapokriton Xenou Tipou (Foreign Press Association of Greece): Odos Valaoritou 9, 3rd Floor, 106 71 Athens; tel. (210) 3637318; fax (210) 3605035; e-mail fpa@fpa.gr; internet www.fpa.gr; f. 1916; Pres. IOANNA KOURELA; Gen. Sec. DIMITRIS MESSINS; 300 mems.

Enosis Demosiograpson Idioktiton Periodikou Tipou (Union of Journalists and Proprietors of the Periodical Press—EDIPT): Leoforos Vas Sofias 25, 3rd Floor, Athens; tel. (210) 7220875; fax (210) 7215128; e-mail info@edipt.gr; internet www.edipt.gr; f. 1939; Pres. KONSTANTINOS KALYVAS; Gen. Sec. MICHAEL SAVAKIS; 300 mems.

Enosis Idioktiton Imerission Ephimeridon Athinon (Athens Daily Newspaper Publishers' Association): Mourouzi 14, 106 74

Athens; tel. (210) 7209810; e-mail postmaster@eihea.gr; internet www.eihea.gr; f. 1951; Pres. DIMITRIS KALOFOLIAS; Sec. DIMITRIS RIZOS.

Enosis Syntakton Imerission Ephimeridon Athinon (Journalists' Union of Athens Daily Newspapers): Odos Akademias 20, 106 71 Athens; tel. (210) 3675400; fax (210) 3632608; e-mail info@esiea.gr; internet www.esiea.gr; f. 1914; Pres. DIMITRIS TRIMIS; Gen. Sec. MARIA ANTONIADES; 2,110 mems.

Enosis Syntakton Periodikou Tipou (Journalists' Union of the Periodical Press): Odos Valaoritou 9, 6th Floor, 106 71 Athens; tel. (210) 3633427; fax (210) 3638627; e-mail espit@otenet.gr; internet www.espit.gr; f. 1959; Pres. THEMIS K. BEREDIMAS; Gen. Sec. ALATAS THANASIS; 835 mems.

Publishers

Agkyra Publications: Odos Lamprou Katsoni 271, Aghi Anargyri, 135 62 Athens; tel. (210) 2693800; fax (210) 2693806; internet www.agyra.gr; f. 1890; general; Man. Dir DIMITRIOS PAPADIMITRIOU.

Akritas: Odos Chalkokondili 36, 104 32 Athens; tel. (210) 9334554; fax (210) 9404950; e-mail akritas@pkbooks.gr; internet www.akritas.net.gr; f. 1978; history, Orthodox Christianity, children's books.

Arsenides Publishers: Odos Akadimias 57, 106 79 Athens; tel. (210) 3629538; fax (210) 3633923; e-mail tarsen@otenet.gr; f. 1952; philosophy, psychology, sociology, history, biography, literature, children's books.

Ekdotike Athenon: Odos Hippokratous 13, 106 79 Athens; tel. (210) 3608911; fax (210) 3608914; e-mail info@ekdotikeathenon.gr; internet www.ekdotikeathenon.gr; f. 1962; history, archaeology, art.

Exandas Publications: Odos Didotou 57, 106 81 Athens; tel. (210) 3804885; fax (210) 3813065; e-mail info@exandasbooks.gr; internet www.exandasbooks.gr; f. 1974; fiction, literature, social sciences; Pres. MAGDA N. KOTZIA.

Govostis Publishing: Zoodohou Pigis 73, 106 81 Athens; tel. (210) 3815433; fax (210) 3816661; e-mail cotsos@govostis.gr; internet www.govostis.gr; f. 1926; arts, fiction, politics; Pres. COSTAS GOVOSTIS.

Denise Harvey: Katounia, 340 05 Limni, Evia; tel. and fax (22270) 31154; e-mail dhp@dharveypublisher.gr; internet www.deniseharveypublisher.gr; f. 1972; books concerned with post-Byzantine Greek culture, incl. literature, theology, history, travel, music, and social anthropology (English); Man. Dir DENISE HARVEY.

Hestia-I.D. Kollaros S.A. & Co: Odos Evripidou 84, 105 53 Athens; tel. (210) 3213704; fax (210) 220821; e-mail info@hestia.gr; internet www.hestia.gr; f. 1885; literature, history, politics, psychoanalysis, philosophy, children's books, political and philosophical essays; Gen. Dir EVA-MARIA KARAITIDI.

Kastaniotis Editions: Odos Zalogou 11, 106 78 Athens; tel. (210) 3301208; fax (210) 3822530; e-mail info@kastaniotis.com; internet www.kastaniotis.com; f. 1968; fiction and non-fiction, incl. arts, social sciences and psychology, children's books; Man. Dir ATHANASIOS KASTANIOTIS.

Kritiki Publishing: Odos Patission 75, 104 34 Athens; tel. (210) 8211811; fax (210) 8211026; e-mail biblia@kritiki.gr; internet www.kritiki.gr; f. 1987; economics, politics, literature, philosophy, business management, popular science; Publr THEMIS MINOGLOU.

Livani Publishing Organization: Odos Solonos 98, 106 80 Athens; tel. (210) 3661200; fax (210) 3617791; e-mail rights@livanis.gr; internet www.livanis.gr; f. 1972; fiction, non-fiction, children's books; Publr A. A. LIVANI.

Minoas: Odos Davaki Konstantinou 34, 144 51 Metamorfosi; tel. (210) 2711222; fax (210) 2711056; e-mail info@minoas.gr; internet www.minoas.gr; f. 1952; fiction, art, history; Man. Dir IOANNIS KONSTANTAROPOULOS.

Papazissis Publishers: Nikitara 2, 106 78 Athens; tel. (210) 3822496; fax (210) 3809150; e-mail papazisi@otenet.gr; internet www.papazisi.gr; f. 1929; economics, politics, law, history, school books; Man. Dir ALEXANDROS PAPAZISSIS.

Patakis Publishers: Pan. Tsaldari 38, 104 37 Athens; tel. (210) 3650000; fax (210) 3811940; e-mail bookstore@patakis.gr; internet www.patakis.gr; f. 1974; art, reference, fiction, educational, philosophy, psychology, sociology, religion, music, children's books, audiobooks; Pres. STEFANOS PATAKIS.

PUBLISHERS' ASSOCIATIONS

Book Publishers' Association of Athens: Odos Themistokleus 73, 106 83 Athens; tel. (210) 3303268; fax (210) 3823222; e-mail seva@otenet.gr; internet www.seva.gr; f. 1945; Pres. STELIOS ELLINIADIS; Sec. LOUCAS RINOPOULOS.

Hellenic Federation of Publishers and Booksellers: Odos Themistokleus 73, 106 83 Athens; tel. (210) 3804760; fax (210) 3301617; e-mail secretary@poev.gr; internet www.poev.gr; f. 1961; Pres. RAGIA ANNIE; Gen. Sec. STATHATOS NICHOLAS.

Broadcasting and Communications

TELECOMMUNICATIONS

By the end of 2009 some 531 licensed service providers were operating in the telecommunications sector: voice telephony and fixed-line networks (178); voice telephony (141); fixed-line networks (87); satellite networks (34); 2G and 3G mobile technology (13); terrestrial trunk radio (TETRA—five); and wireless local area network (W-LAN—73).

Forthnet: Odos Manis, 153 51 Pallini; tel. (1) 9559258; fax (1) 9559055; e-mail info@forthnet.gr; internet www.forthnet.gr; broadband and satellite telecommunications services; internet service provider; CEO PANAYIOTIS PAPADOPOULOS.

Hellenic Telecommunications Organization (OTE) (Organismos Telepikoinonion tis Elladas): Leoforos Kifissias 99, 151 24 Maroussi, Athens; tel. (210) 6117434; fax (210) 3405129; e-mail media-office@ote.gr; internet www.ote.gr; f. 1949; 10% owned by the Government, 40% by Deutsche Telekom (Germany); mobile cellular telecommunications and internet service provider; Chief Exec. and Chair. MICHAEL TSAMAZ.

COSMOTE: Leoforos Kifissias 99, 151 24 Marousi, Athens; tel. (210) 6177777; fax (210) 6177594; e-mail mediarelations@cosmote.gr; internet www.cosmote.gr; f. 1998; 59% owned by OTE; mobile cellular telecommunications and internet service provider; Pres. and CEO MICHAEL TSAMAZ.

Otesat-Maritel: Odos Egaleo 8, 185 45 Piraeus; tel. (210) 4599500; fax (210) 4599600; e-mail otesat-maritel@otesat-maritel.com; internet www.otesat-maritel.com; OTE subsidiary; marine telecommunications; Chair. THEODOROS VENIAMIS; CEO GEORGE POLYCHRONOPOULOS.

Vodafone Greece: 1–3 Tzavella St, 152 31 Halandri; tel. (210) 6702000; fax (210) 6703200; internet www.vodafone.gr; 55% owned by Vodafone Europe Holdings (UK); mobile cellular telecommunications and internet service provider; Chair. GLAUKOS PERSIANIS.

WIND Hellas Telecommunications: Leoforos Kifissias 66, 151 25 Marousi, Athens; tel. (210) 6158000; fax (210) 5100001; e-mail crm@wind.gr; internet www.wind.com.gr; f. 1992 as Telestet; renamed as above in 2007; fixed and mobile cellular telecommunications, internet services; Chair. and CEO NASSOS ZARKALIS.

Regulatory Authority

Hellenic Telecommunications and Post Commission: Leoforos Kifissias 60, 151 25 Athens; tel. (210) 6151000; fax (210) 6105049; e-mail info@eett.gr; internet www.eett.gr; regulatory body; Chair. CONSTANTINOS LOUROPOULOS.

RADIO AND TELEVISION

In June 2011, in addition to the publicly owned four national analogue terrestrial TV stations, three national digital TV stations and one satellite TV station, there were seven main national private TV networks and approximately 150 local and regional TV stations broadcasting across the country. The closure of the state broadcaster, Elliniki Radiophonia Tileorassi (ERT), was announced by the Government in June 2013. Following a court ruling a new temporary state broadcaster, Dimosia Tileorasi (EDT), commenced operations in the second half of 2013.

State Station

Dimosia Tileorasi (EDT) (Public Television): Leoforos Messoghion 136 & Odos Katechaki, Athens; f. 2013.

Private Stations

Antenna TV: Leoforos Kifissias 10–12, Maroussi, 151 25 Athens; tel. (210) 6886100; fax (210) 6834349; e-mail webmaster@antenna.gr; internet www.antenna.gr; f. 1989; Chair. M. X. KYRIAKOU.

City Channel: Leoforos Kastoni 14, 412 23 Larissa; tel. (241) 232839; fax (241) 232013.

Mega Channel: Roussou 4 & Mesogeion Ave, 115 26 Athens; tel. (210) 6903000; fax (210) 6983600; e-mail ngeorgiou@megatv.com; internet www.megatv.com; f. 1989; Chair. STAVROS PSYCHARIS; Man. Dir ELIAS E. TSIGAS.

Serres TV: Nigritis 27, 621 24 Serres; tel. (2321) 51688; fax (2321) 58020; e-mail info@serrestv.gr; internet www.serrestv.gr.

Star Channel: Odos Thermopylon 87, 351 00 Lamia; tel. (22310) 46725; fax (22310) 46728; e-mail star@star-online.gr; internet www.lamiastar.gr; f. 1988; Pres. NIKE CHEIMONIDIS.

Tele City: Praxitelous 58, 176 74 Athens; tel. (210) 9429222; fax (210) 9413589.

Traki TV: 30 Venizelos, 681 00 Alexandroupolis; tel. (2551) 52000; fax (2551) 37731; e-mail info@thrakinet.tv; internet www.thrakinet .tv.

TRT: Ferron 65, 383 34 Volos; tel. (2421) 28801; fax (2421) 36888; e-mail commercial@trttv.com; internet www.trttv.com; f. 1990; Pres. and CEO EVANGELOS ANTONIOU.

TV-100: Odos Aggelaki 16, 546 21 Thessaloníki; tel. (231) 265828; fax (231) 267532; e-mail depthe@fm100.gr; internet www.fm100.gr; f. 1988.

Finance

(cap. = capital; res = reserves; dep. = deposits; m. = million; brs = branches; amounts in euros)

BANKING

Following the restructuring of the banking sector, by 2013 four principal banks (the National Bank of Greece, Alpha Bank, Eurobank Ergasias SA and Piraeus Bank) held approximately 96% of deposits.

Central Bank

Bank of Greece: Leoforos E. Venizelos 21, 102 50 Athens; tel. (210) 3201111; fax (210) 3232239; e-mail sec.secretariat@bankofgreece.gr; internet www.bankofgreece.gr; f. 1927; cap. 111.2m., res 694.1m., dep. 10,266.6m. (Dec. 2009); Gov. GEORGIOS A. PROVOPOULOS; 17 branches and 33 agencies.

Commercial Banks

Alpha Bank: Stadiou 40, 102 52 Athens; tel. (210) 3260000; fax (210) 3265052; e-mail secretariat@alpha.gr; internet www.alpha.gr; f. 1879; present name adopted 2000; cap. 1,100.3m., res 3,025.9m., dep. 52,401.1m. (Dec. 2012); Chair. and Gen. Man. IOANNIS S. COSTOPOULOS; 713 brs.

Bank of Attica: Odos Omirou 23, 106 72 Athens; tel. (210) 3669000; fax (210) 3667245; e-mail info@atticabank.gr; internet www .atticabank.gr; f. 1925; cap. 185.9m., res 324.6m., dep. 3,648.6m. (Dec. 2012); Chair. of Bd and Exec. Dir IOANNIS GAMVRILIS; 80 brs.

Black Sea Trade and Development Bank: Odos Komninon 1, 546 24 Thessaloníki; tel. (231) 290400; fax (231) 221796; e-mail info@ bstdb.org; internet www.bstdb.org; f. 1997; owned by 11 member states: Greece, Russian Federation, Turkey (16.5% each); Bulgaria, Romania, Ukraine (13.5% each); Albania, Armenia, Azerbaijan, Georgia, Moldova (2.0% each); cap. 494.4m., res 44.2m., total assets 983.6m. (Dec. 2012); Pres. ANDREY KONDAKOV.

Eurobank Ergasias SA: Odos Leoforos Amalias 20, 105 57 Athens; tel. (210) 3337688; fax (210) 3337256; e-mail info@eurobank.gr; internet www.eurobank.gr; f. 1990; present name adopted 2000; 93.6% owned by the Hellenic Financial Stability Fund (HFSF); cap. 2,545m., res 2,636m., dep. 30,407m. (Dec. 2012); Pres. EYTHYMIOS N. CHRISTODOULOU; CEO NIKOLAS NANOPOULOS; 379 brs.

Geniki Bank—General Bank of Greece: Odos Messogeion 109–111, 115 10 Athens; tel. (210) 6975200; fax (210) 6975910; e-mail intdiv@geniki.gr; internet www.geniki.gr; f. 1937; present name adopted 1998; controlling stake acquired by Société Générale (France) in 2004, and obtained by Piraeus Bank in Dec. 2012; cap. 100.3m., res 1,056.6m., dep. 2,252.6m. (Dec. 2012); Chair. TRYFON KOUTALIDIS; 80 brs.

National Bank of Greece (NBG): Odos Aeolou 86, 102 32 Athens; tel. (210) 3341000; fax (210) 4806510; e-mail contact.center@nbg.gr; internet www.nbg.gr; f. 1841; state-controlled, but operates independently of the Govt; cap. 6,309.7m., res 2,702.7m., dep. 91,585.8m. (Dec. 2012); CEO ALEXANDROS TOURKOLIAS; 540 brs.

Piraeus Bank: Odos Amerikis 4, 105 64 Athens; tel. (210) 3335000; fax (210) 3335080; e-mail investor-relations@piraeusbank.gr; internet www.piraeusbank.gr; f. 1916; cap. 1,092.9m., res 2,957.9m., dep. 68,925.8m. (Dec. 2012); Chair. MICHALIS G. SALLAS; 85 brs.

STOCK EXCHANGE

Athens Stock Exchange: Odos Sophokleous 10, 105 59 Athens; tel. (210) 3211301; fax (210) 3213938; e-mail webmaster@ase.gr; internet www.ase.gr; f. 1876; Pres. CAPRALOS SPYROS; Vice-Pres. LAZARIDIS SOKRATIS.

PRINCIPAL INSURANCE COMPANIES

In 2012 there were 69 insurance companies operating in Greece, of which 13 provided life insurance, 45 provided non-life insurance, and 11 provided both life and non-life insurance.

ATE Insurance SA: Leoforos Syngrou 173, 171 21 Kallithea, Athens; tel. (210) 9379100; fax (210) 9358924; e-mail info@agroins .com; internet www.ateinsurance.gr; f. 1980; as Agrotiki Insurance SA Hellenic General Insurance Company; name changed as above in 2005; member of Piraeus Bank Group (Greece); Pres. SPYRIDON PAPASPYROU; CEO JORDAN HADJIOSIPH.

Atlantiki Enosis/Atlantic Union: Odos Messoghion 71 & Ilidos 36, 115 26 Athens; tel. (210) 7454000; fax (210) 7794446; e-mail atlantiki@atlantiki.gr; internet www.atlanticunion.gr; f. 1970; subsidiary of La Baloise (Switzerland); Pres. STASINOPOULOS SARANDOS.

Axa Insurance: Odos Michalakopoulou 48, 115 28 Athens; tel. (210) 7268000; fax (210) 7268408; e-mail info@axa-insurance.gr; internet www.axa-insurance.gr; f. 1999; fmrly Alpha Insurance; Pres. GRANIER JEAN-LAURENT RAYMONT MARIE; Man. Dir ERIC PIERRE KLEIJNEN.

Crédit Agricole Life: Odos Mitropoleos 45, 105 56 Athens; tel. (210) 3283545; fax (210) 3283520; e-mail info@ca-life.gr; f. 2001 as Emporiki Life; as a joint venture of Emporiki Bank and insurance arm of Crédit Agricole; became a subsidiary of Crédit Agricole Assurances in 2010; name changed as above in 2011; life insurance; Chair. PANAYIOTIS VARELAS; Man. Dir RICHARD SUTTON.

Dynamis: Leoforos Syngrou 320, 176 73 Kallithea, Athens; tel. (210) 9006900; fax (210) 9237768; e-mail info@dynamis.gr; internet www .dynamis.gr; f. 1977; Pres. and CEO PAUL G. KARAKOSTAS.

ERGO General Insurance Co SA: Odos Sofias 97, 115 21 Athens; tel. (210) 3705300; fax (210) 3244134; e-mail ergo@ergohellas.gr; internet www.ergohellas.gr; f. 1972; as Victoria General Insurance Co SA; Man. Dir G. ANDONIADIS.

Ethniki Hellenic General Insurance Co SA: Leoforos Syngrou 103–105, 117 45 Athens; fax (210) 9099111; internet www .ethniki-asfalistiki.gr; f. 1891; Pres. DEMETRIOS GEORGE DIMOPOULOS.

Groupama Phoenix: Leoforos Syngrou 213-215, N. Smirni, 171 21 Athens; tel. (210) 3295111; fax (210) 3239135; e-mail info@ groupama-phoenix.com; internet www.groupama-phoenix.com; f. 1928; general.

Horizon General Insurance Co: Leoforos Amalias 26A, 105 57 Athens; tel. (210) 3227932; fax (210) 3225540; e-mail info@horizonins .gr; f. 1965; Gen. Man THEODORE ACHIS.

Imperial: Leoforos Syngrou 253, N. Smirni, 171 22 Athens; tel. (210) 9426352; fax (210) 9426202; e-mail imperial@imperial.gr; internet www.imperial.gr; f. 1971; Gen. Man. GEORGE TZANIS.

ING: Leoforos Syngrou 198, 176 71 Kallithea, Athens; tel. (210) 9506000; fax (210) 9506076; e-mail info@ing.gr; internet www.ing.gr; f. 1980; CEO LUIS MIGUEL GOMEZ ORTIZ.

Interamerican Hellenic Life Insurance Co: Odos Sygrou 124–126, 176 80 Athens; tel. (210) 9462000; fax (210) 9461008; e-mail custserv@interamerican.gr; internet www.interamerican.gr; f. 1969; 79.4% owned by Eureko (the Netherlands); subsidiary cos provide medical, property, casualty, and automobile insurance; Chair. ADRIAN HEGARTY.

MetLife Alico: Leoforos Kifissias 119, 151 24 Maroussi, Athens; tel. (210) 8787000; fax (210) 6123722; e-mail contact@metlifealico.gr; internet www.metlifealico.gr; f. 1964; life insurance; Group Chair. and CEO STEVEN A. KANDARIAN.

Sideris Insurance Co: Odos Lekka 3–5, 105 63 Athens; tel. (281) 0301678; fax (281) 0301679; e-mail info@sideris-insurance.gr; internet www.sideris-insurance.gr; Dir G. SIDERIS.

Syneteristiki General Insurance Co: Leoforos Syngrou 367, 175 64 Kallithea, Athens; tel. (210) 9491280; fax (210) 9403148; e-mail com@syneteristiki.gr; internet www.syneteristiki.gr; Gen. Man. DIMITRIS ZORBAS.

Insurance Association

Hellenic Association of Insurance Companies: Odos Xenophontos 10, 105 57 Athens; tel. (210) 3334100; fax (210) 3334149; e-mail info@eaee.gr; internet www.eaee.gr; f. 1907; 71 mem cos; Pres. ALEXANDROS SARRIGEORGIOU; Gen. Man. MARGARITA ANTONAKI.

Trade and Industry

CHAMBERS OF COMMERCE

Athens Chamber of Commerce and Industry: Odos Akademias 7, 106 71 Athens; tel. (210) 3604815; fax (210) 3616464; e-mail info@ acci.gr; internet www.acci.gr; f. 1919; Pres. CONSTANTINOS MICHALOS; Sec.-Gen. NIKOS SOFIANOS; 70,000 mems.

Athens Chamber of Small and Medium-sized Industries: Odos Akademias 18, 106 71 Athens; tel. (210) 3680700; fax (210) 3614726; e-mail info@acsmi.gr; internet www.acsmi.gr; f. 1940; Pres. RAVANIS PAUL; Gen. Sec. LIAMETIS VASILIOS; c. 60,000 mems.

Piraeus Chamber of Commerce and Industry: Odos Loudovikou 1, Pl. Odessa, 185 31 Piraeus; tel. (210) 4177241; fax (210) 4178680; e-mail evep@pcci.gr; internet www.pcci.gr; f. 1919; Pres. VASSILIS KORKIDIS; Gen. Sec. DIMITRIOS MARKOMICHALIS.

Piraeus Chamber of Industry: Odos Karaiscou 111, 185 32 Piraeus; tel. (210) 4110443; fax (210) 4179495; e-mail info@bep.gr; internet www.bep.gr; f. 1925; Pres. ANDRIANOS MIHALARIAS; Gen. Sec. GERASIMOS MICHALAKIS.

Thessaloníki Chamber of Commerce and Industry (TCCI): Odos Tsimiski 29, 546 24 Thessaloníki; tel. (231) 0370100; fax (231) 0370166; e-mail root@ebeth.gr; internet www.ebeth.gr; f. 1918; Pres. DIMITRIOS BAKATSELOS; Sec.-Gen. KONSTANTINOS CHANTZARIDIS; 18,000 mems.

INDUSTRIAL AND TRADE ASSOCIATIONS

Federation of Industries of Northern Greece (FING): Morihovou 1, 546 25 Thessaloníki; tel. (231) 0539817; fax (231) 0541933; e-mail info@sbbe.gr; internet www.sbbe.gr; f. 1915; Pres. NIKOS PENTOZ; Gen. Sec. ATHANASIOS SAVAKIS.

Hellenic Cotton Board: Leoforos Syngrou 150, 176 71 Kallithea, Athens; tel. (210) 9225011; fax (210) 9243676; f. 1931; state org.; Pres. P. K. MYLONAS.

SEV Hellenic Federation of Enterprises: Odos Xenophontos 5, Syntagma, 105 57 Athens; tel. (211) 5006000; fax (210) 3222929; e-mail info@sev.org.gr; internet www.sev.org.gr; f. 1907; Chair. DIMITRIS DASKALOPOULOS.

Hellenic Organization of Small and Medium Enterprises and Handicrafts (EOMMEX): Odos Xenias 16, 115 28 Athens; tel. (210) 7491100; fax (210) 7491146; e-mail interel@eommex.gr; internet www.eommex.gr; f. 1977; Pres. CHRIS PITELIS.

UTILITIES

Regulatory Authority

Regulatory Authority for Energy (RAE): Leoforos Piraeus 132, 118 54 Athens; tel. (210) 3727400; fax (210) 3255460; e-mail info@rae.gr; internet www.rae.gr; f. 2000; Chair. Dr NIKOS VASILAKOS.

Electricity

Operator of the Electricity Market SA (LAGIE): Kastoros 72, 18545 Piraeus; tel. (210) 9466700; fax (210) 9466766; e-mail info@lagie.gr; internet www.lagie.gr; electric energy transmission; Pres. and CEO ANASTASIOS GARIS.

Public Power Corpn (DEI): Odos Chalkokondili 30, 104 32 Athens; tel. (210) 5293417; fax (210) 5238445; e-mail info@dei.com.gr; internet www.dei.gr; f. 1950; 51% state-owned; generating capacity of 96 power stations: 12,843 MW (2008); generation, transmission and distribution of electricity; Chair. and CEO ARTHOUROS ZERVOS.

Gas

Public Gas Corpn (DEPA): Marinou Antipa 92, Leoforos Antipa, 141 21 Athens; tel. (210) 2701000; fax (210) 2701010; e-mail pr@depa.gr; internet www.depa.gr; f. 1988; 35% owned by Hellenic Petroleum SA, 65% state-owned; began gas imports 1997, initially for industrial use; Chair. and CEO HARRIS SACHINIS.

Water

In 1980 a law was approved, creating Municipal Enterprises for Water Supply and Sewerage (DEYA) to manage drinking water and sewerage throughout Greece. Since then some 90 DEYA have been established.

The Hellenic Union of Municipal Enterprises for Water Supply and Sewerage (EDEYA): Odos Papakyriazi 37-43, 412 22 Larissa; tel. (241) 0258261; fax (241) 0532347; e-mail info@edeya.gr; internet www.edeya.gr; f. 1989; Dir GEORGE MARINAKIS; 155 mems.

TRADE UNIONS

There are about 5,000 registered trade unions, grouped together in 82 federations and 86 workers' centres, which are affiliated to the Greek General Confederation of Labour.

Greek General Confederation of Labour (GSEE): Odos Patission 69 & Aenian 2, 104 34 Athens; tel. (210) 8202100; fax (210) 8202186; e-mail info@gsee.gr; internet www.gsee.gr; f. 1918; Pres. IOANNIS PANAGOPOULOS; Sec.-Gen. KOSTAS POUPAKIS; 700,000 mems.

Pan-Hellenic Federation of Seamen's Unions (PNO): Akti Miaouli 47–49, 185 36 Piraeus; tel. (210) 4292958; fax (210) 4293040; e-mail info@pno.gr; internet www.pno.gr; f. 1920; confederation of 14 marine unions; Pres. IOANNIS CHELAS; Gen. Sec. JOHN HALAS.

Supreme Administration of Greek Civil Servants' Trade Unions (ADEDY): Odos Psylla Philellinon 2, 105 57 Athens; tel. (213) 1616900; fax (210) 3246165; e-mail adedyed@adedy.gr; internet www.adedy.gr; Pres. ANTONAKOS ANDONIS; Gen. Sec. AKRIBOS APOSTOLOS.

Transport

RAILWAYS

In 2009 there were 1,552 km of railway track in use. Construction of a 26-km electrified extension to the Athens–Piraeus line, in order to provide a three-line urban railway system for Athens, designated Metro Line 1, was completed in 2000. Metro Lines 2 and 3, each measuring some 9 km, opened prior to the holding of the Summer Olympic Games in 2004.

Attiko Metro: Leoforos Messoghion 191–93, 115 25 Athens; tel. (210) 6792399; fax (210) 6726126; e-mail info@ametro.gr; internet www.ametro.gr; f. 1991; operates lines 2 and 3 of underground railway in Athens; Chair. and CEO CHRISTOS TSITOURAS.

Organismos Sidirodromon Ellados (OSE) (Hellenic Railways Organization Ltd): Odos Karolou 1–3, 104 37 Athens; tel. (210) 5248395; fax (210) 5243290; internet www.ose.gr; f. 1971; state railways; Chair. NIKOLAOS BALTAS; Dir-Gen. A. LAZARIS.

Urban Rail Transport S.A. (STASY): Odos Athinas 67, 105 52 Athens; tel. (214) 4141140; fax (214) 4141378; e-mail pr@stasy.gr; internet www.stasy.gr; f. 2011; state-owned; Chair. and CEO NIKOLAOS C. PAPATHANASSIS.

ROADS

In 2010 there were 116,960 km of roads in Greece. Of this total, an estimated 9,299 km were main roads, and 1,197 km were motorways. The construction of the 680-km Egnatia highway, extending from the Adriatic coast to the Turkish border, was one of the largest road projects in Europe and was completed in 2009.

INLAND WATERWAYS

There are no navigable rivers in Greece.

Corinth Canal: built 1893; over six km long, links the Corinthian and Saronic Gulfs; shortens the journey from the Adriatic to Piraeus by 325 km; spanned by three single-span bridges, two for road and one for rail; can be used by ships of a maximum draught of 22 ft and width of 60 ft; managed since June 2001 by Sea Containers Group (UK).

SHIPPING

At the end of 2013 the Greek flag registered fleet totalled 1,397 vessels, with a combined aggregate displacement of 42.2m. grt., of which 244 were bulk carriers, 20 fishing carriers, 15 gas tankers and 90 general cargo ships. Greece controls one of the largest merchant fleets in the world. The principal ports are Piraeus, Patras and Thessaloníki.

Union of Greek Shipowners: Akti Miaouli 85, 185 38 Piraeus; f. 1916; Pres. NICOS EFTHYMIOU.

Port Authorities

Organismos Limenos Patras (Patras Port Authority): South Patras Port, Akti Dimeon, 26110 Patras; tel. (261) 0365113; fax (261) 0365110; e-mail info@patrasport.gr; internet www.patrasport.gr; Pres. and CEO KONSTANTINOS PLATIKOSTAS.

Organismos Limenos Piraeus (OLP) (Piraeus Port Authority): Piraeus Port Authority, Akti Miaouli 10, 185 38 Piraeus; tel. (210) 4550000; fax (210) 4550280; e-mail ceo@olp.gr; internet www.olp.gr; f. 1930; 25% privatized; Pres. and Man. Dir GIORGOS ANOMERITIS.

Organismos Limenos Thessaloníki (Port of Thessaloníki): Thessaloníki Port Authority, POB 10467, 541 10 Thessaloníki; tel. (231) 0593102; fax (231) 0593281; e-mail ceooffice@thpa.gr; internet www.thpa.gr; Pres. and CEO STYLIANOS AGGELOUDIS.

Shipping Companies

The following are among the largest or most important shipping companies.

Angel Shipping Enterprises: Akti Miaouli, POB 80004, 185 10 Piraeus; tel. (210) 4224500; fax (210) 4224819; f. 1971; subsidiary of Agelef Shipping Group (UK); Man. Dir J. PLATSIDAKIS.

Attica Holdings: Leoforos Syngrou 123–25 & Odos Torva 3, 117 45 Athens; tel. (210) 8919500; fax (210) 8919509; internet www.attica-group.com; f. 1918; subsidiary cos include Blue Star Ferries and Superfast.com; Chair. KYRIAKOS D. MAGEIRAS; CEO SPIROS PASCHALIS.

Blue Star Ferries: Leoforos Syngrou 123–25 & Odos Torva 3, 117 45 Athens; tel. (210) 8919800; fax (210) 8919829; e-mail bluestarferries@bluestarferries.com; internet www.bluestarferries.com; subsidiary of Attica Holdings (q.v.); operates passenger and cargo ferry services between the Greek mainland and islands, and between Greece and Italy.

Chandris (Hellas) Co: POB 80067, Akti Miaouli 95, 185 38 Piraeus; tel. (210) 4584000; fax (210) 4290256; e-mail chandris-hellas@chandris-group.gr; internet www.chandris-hellas.gr; f. 1915; Man. Dirs A. C. PIPERAS, M. G. SKORDIAS.

Costamare Shipping Co: Leoforos Syngrou & Odos Zephyrou 60, 175 64 Athens; tel. (210) 9390000; fax (210) 9409051; e-mail info@costamare.com; internet www.costamare.com; f. 1975; container-shipping; Pres. KONSTANTINOS KONSTANTAKOPOULOS.

Golden Union Shipping Co: Odos Aegales 8, 185 45 Piraeus; tel. (210) 4061000; fax (210) 4061199; e-mail infgusc@goldenunion.gr; internet www.goldenunion.gr; f. 1977; dry cargo bulk operations; Chair. and Man. Dir THEODORE VENIAMIS.

Marmaras Navigation Co: Odos Zephyrou 58B, 175 64 Palaio Faliro; tel. (210) 4589000; fax (210) 4589037; e-mail crew@marmaras-nav.gr; internet www.marmaras-nav.gr; Dir D. DIAMANTIDES.

Minoan Lines Shipping Co: Odos 25 August 17, 712 02 Heraklion; tel. (2810) 399800; fax (2810) 330308; e-mail info@minoan.gr; internet www.minoan.gr; f. 1972; operates passenger and cargo ferry services between the Greek mainland and Crete, and between Greece and Italy; Man. Dir ANTONIS MANIADAKIS.

Naftomar Shipping and Trading Co: Leoforos C. Karamanlis 243, 166 73 Voula; tel. (210) 8914200; fax (210) 8914235; e-mail naftomar@naftomar.gr; internet www.naftomar.gr; f. 1972; specializes in the shipping of liquid petroleum gas; Man. Dir RIAD ZEIN.

Thenamaris Ships Management Co: Odos Athinas 16 & Odos Vorreou, Kavouri, 166 71 Athens; tel. (210) 8909000; fax (210) 8909653; e-mail op@thenamaris.com; internet www.thenamaris.gr; f. 1970; Dir K. MARTINOS.

Tsakos Group: Macedonia House, Leoforos Syngrou 367, POB 79141, Paleon Faliron, 175 64 Athens; tel. (210) 9480700; fax (210) 9480710; e-mail mail@tsakoshellas.gr; internet www.tsakosgroup.com; f. 1970; subsidiary cos include: Tsakos Shipping and Trading; Tsakos Energy Navigation; Tsakos Industrias Navales; Dir Capt PANAGIOTIS N. TSAKOS.

CIVIL AVIATION

There are international airports at Athens, Eleftherios Venizelos-Spata, Thessaloníki, Alexandroupolis, Corfu, Lesbos, Andravida, Rhodes, Kos and Heraklion/Crete, and 24 domestic airports (of which 13 are authorized to receive international flights).

Aegean Airlines: Leoforos Viltanioti 31, 145 64 Kifissia Athens; tel. (210) 6261700; fax (210) 6261900; internet www.aegeanair.com; f. 1987; domestic and international services; Pres. and Chief Exec. THEODOROS VASSILAKIS.

Olympic Air: Eleftherios Venizelos Athens International Airport, Bldg 97, 190 19 Athens; tel. (210) 3550700; fax (210) 3550407; e-mail groups@olympicair.com; internet www.olympicair.com; f. 2009 in succession to state-owned Olympic Airways (f. 1957); owned by Aegean Airlines (q.v.); Chair. ANDREAS VGENOPOULOS.

Tourism

The sunny climate, the natural beauty of the country, and its history and traditions attract tourists to Greece. There are numerous islands and many sites of archaeological interest. The number of tourists visiting Greece increased from 1m. in 1968 to 15.5m. in 2012, according to provisional data; in 2012 provisional figures indicated receipts from tourism amounted to US $12,879m. (excluding passenger transport).

Ellinikos Organismos Tourismou (EOT) (Greek National Tourist Organization): Odos Tsoha 7, 115 21 Athens; tel. (210) 8707000; e-mail info@gnto.gr; internet www.visitgreece.gr; Pres. ZIKOS KONSTANTINOS.

Defence

Greece returned to the military structure of the North Atlantic Treaty Organization (NATO) in 1980, after an absence of six years. Military service is compulsory, and lasts for up to nine months. As assessed at November 2013, the armed forces numbered 143,350 (including conscripts), with an army of 86,150, a navy of 19,000, an air force of 26,600 and 11,600 joint-service troops; in addition, there were paramilitary forces of 4,000. Reservists, which included a national guard of 33,000, totalled 216,650. The USA occupied three military bases in Greece, with a total of 380 troops stationed there at November 2012.

Defence Expenditure: Budgeted at €3,830m. in 2014.

Chief of the General Staff of the National Defence: Lt-Gen. MICHALIS KOSTARAKOS.

Chief of the General Staff of the Army: Lt-Gen. CHRISTOS MANOLAS.

Chief of the General Staff of the Navy: Vice-Adm. EVANGELOS APOSTOLAKIS.

Chief of the General Staff of the Air Force: Lt-Gen. EVANGELOS TOURNAS.

Education

Education is available free of charge at all levels, and is officially compulsory for all children between the ages of six and 15 years. Primary education begins at the age of six and lasts for six years. Secondary education, beginning at the age of 12, is generally for six years, divided into two equal cycles. The vernacular language (demotiki) has replaced the formal version (katharevoussa) in secondary education. Pre-primary enrolment in 2009/10 included 76% of children in the relevant age-group. The comparable ratio in the same year at secondary schools was 99%. In 2003/04 the equivalent of 70% of the relevant age-group were enrolled in tertiary education (males 60%; females 79%). There were 22 universities in 2011/12 (excluding the Medical School of Athens), with a total enrolment of 168,804 students. In 2006 budgetary spending on education represented an estimated 9.9% of total expenditure, according to preliminary figures.

GRENADA

Introductory Survey

LOCATION, CLIMATE, LANGUAGE, RELIGION, FLAG, CAPITAL

Grenada, a mountainous, heavily forested island, is the most southerly of the Windward Islands, in the West Indies. The country also includes some of the small islands known as the Grenadines, which lie to the north-east of Grenada. The most important of these are the low-lying island of Carriacou and its neighbour, Petit Martinique. The climate is semi-tropical, with an average annual temperature of 28°C (82°F) in the lowlands. Annual rainfall averages about 1,500 mm (60 ins) in the coastal area and 3,800 mm to 5,100 mm (150 ins–200 ins) in mountain areas. Most of the rainfall occurs between June and December. The majority of the population speak English, although a French patois is sometimes spoken. According to the census of 1991, 82% of Grenada's population were of African descent, while 13% were of mixed ethnic origins. Most of the population profess Christianity, and the main denominations are Roman Catholicism (to which some 45% of the population adhered in 2006) and Anglicanism (about 14% of the population). The national flag (proportions 1 by 2) consists of a diagonally quartered rectangle (yellow in the upper and lower segments, green in the right and left ones) surrounded by a red border bearing six five-pointed yellow stars (three at the upper edge of the flag, and three at the lower edge). There is a red disc, containing a large five-pointed yellow star, in the centre, and a representation of a nutmeg (in yellow and red) on the green segment near the hoist. The capital is St George's.

CONTEMPORARY POLITICAL HISTORY

Historical Context

Grenada was initially colonized by the French but was captured by the British in 1762. The Treaty of Versailles recognized British control in 1783. Grenada continued as a British colony until 1958, when it joined the Federation of the West Indies, remaining a member until the dissolution of the Federation in 1962. Full internal self-government and statehood in association with the United Kingdom were achieved in March 1967. During this period, the political life of Grenada was dominated by Herbert Blaize, the leader of the Grenada National Party (GNP), and Eric Gairy, a local trade union leader, who in 1950 founded the Grenada United Labour Party (GULP), with the support of an associated trade union. Gairy became Premier after the elections of 1967 and again after those of 1972, which he contested chiefly on the issue of total independence.

Domestic Political Affairs

Grenada became independent, within the Commonwealth, on 7 February 1974, with Gairy as Prime Minister. Domestic opposition to Gairy was expressed in public unrest, and the formation by the three opposition parties—the GNP, the United People's Party and the New Jewel Movement (NJM)—of the People's Alliance, which contested the 1976 general elections and reduced GULP's majority in the lower house.

The opposition regarded the rule of Sir Eric Gairy, as he became in 1977, as increasingly autocratic and corrupt, and in 1979 he was replaced in a bloodless coup by the leader of the left-wing NJM, Maurice Bishop. The new People's Revolutionary Government (PRG) suspended the Constitution and announced the imminent formation of a People's Consultative Assembly to draft a new constitution. Meanwhile, Grenada remained a monarchy, with the British Queen as Head of State, represented in Grenada by a Governor-General. During 1980–81 there was an increase in repression, against a background of mounting anti-Government violence and the PRG's fears of an invasion by US forces.

By mid-1982 relations with the USA, the United Kingdom and the more conservative members of the Caribbean Community and Common Market (CARICOM, see p. 223) were becoming increasingly strained: elections had not been arranged, restrictions against the privately owned press had been imposed, many detainees were still awaiting trial, and Grenada was aligning more closely with Cuba and the USSR. Cuba was contributing funds and construction workers for the airport at Point Salines, a project that further strengthened the US Government's conviction that Grenada was to become a centre for Soviet manoeuvres in the area.

In June 1983 Bishop sought to improve relations with the USA, and announced the appointment of a commission to draft a new constitution. The more left-wing members of the PRG denounced this attempt at conciliation as an ideological betrayal. A power struggle developed between Bishop and his deputy, Bernard Coard. In October Bishop was placed under house arrest, allegedly for his refusal to share power with Coard. The commander of the People's Revolutionary Army (PRA), Gen. Hudson Austin, subsequently announced that Bishop had been expelled from the NJM. On 19 October thousands of Bishop's supporters stormed the house, freed Bishop, and demonstrated outside the PRA headquarters. PRA forces responded by firing into the crowd. Later in the day, Bishop, three of his ministers and two trade unionists were executed by the PRA. The Government was replaced by a 16-member Revolutionary Military Council (RMC), led by Gen. Austin and supported by Coard. The remaining NJM ministers were arrested and imprisoned, and a total curfew was imposed.

Regional and international outrage at the assassination of Bishop, in addition to fears of a US military intervention, was so intense that after four days the RMC relaxed the curfew, reopened the airport and promised a swift return to civilian rule. However, the Organisation of Eastern Caribbean States (OECS, see p. 467) resolved to intervene in an attempt to restore democratic order, and asked for assistance from the USA, which readily complied. (It is unclear whether the decision to intervene preceded or followed a request for help to the OECS by the Grenadian Governor-General, Sir Paul Scoon.) On 25 October 1983 some 1,900 US military personnel invaded the island, accompanied by 300 troops from Jamaica, Barbados and member countries of the OECS. Fighting continued for some days, and the USA gradually increased its troop strength, with further reinforcements waiting offshore with a US naval task force. The RMC's forces were defeated, while Coard, Austin and others who had been involved in the coup were detained.

In November 1983 Scoon appointed a non-political interim Council to assume responsibility for the government of the country until elections could be held. Nicholas Brathwaite, a former Commonwealth official, was appointed Chairman of this Council. The 1974 Constitution was reinstated and an electoral commission was created. By mid-December the USA had withdrawn all its forces except 300 support troops, who remained until September 1985.

Several political parties that had operated clandestinely or from exile during the PRG's rule re-emerged and announced their intention to contest the elections for a new House of Representatives. Sir Eric Gairy returned to Grenada in January 1984 to lead GULP, but did not stand as a candidate himself. In May three former NJM ministers formed the Maurice Bishop Patriotic Movement (MBPM). A number of centrist parties emerged or re-emerged, including Blaize's GNP. Fears that a divided opposition would allow GULP to win a majority of seats in the new House resulted in an agreement by several of these organizations, in August 1984, to form the New National Party (NNP), led by Blaize. The NNP achieved a convincing victory in the December election, and Blaize became Prime Minister.

The trial of 19 detainees (including Coard, his wife, Phyllis, and Gen. Austin), accused of murder and conspiracy against Bishop and six of his associates, opened in November 1984, although there were repeated adjournments. One of the detainees agreed to give evidence for the State in return for a pardon. Eventually, in December 1986, the jury returned verdicts on 196 charges of murder and conspiracy to murder. Fourteen of the defendants were sentenced to death, three received prison sentences of between 30 and 45 years, and one was acquitted. In 1991 the Court of Appeal upheld the original verdicts on the defendants in the Bishop murder trial, and further pleas for clemency were rejected. Preparations for the imminent hanging of the 14, however, provoked international outrage, and in

August Brathwaite announced that the death sentences were to be commuted to life imprisonment.

In 1987 breakaway members of the NNP launched a new party, the National Democratic Congress (NDC), led by George Brizan, who had earlier been appointed parliamentary opposition leader. In January 1989 Blaize was replaced as NNP leader by his cabinet colleague, Keith Mitchell, although he remained Prime Minister. In July, however, following allegations of corruption by the NDC, Blaize announced the dismissal of Mitchell and the Chairman of the NNP. Amid uncertainty as to whether the Blaize faction had formed a separate party, two more members of the Government resigned, thus reducing support for the Government to only five of the 15 members of the House of Representatives. Blaize did not officially announce the formation of a new party, the National Party, until late August, by which time he had advised the acting Governor-General to prorogue Parliament. Blaize died in December, and the Governor-General appointed Ben Jones, Blaize's former deputy, as Prime Minister. At the general election in March 1990 no party achieved an absolute majority in the House of Representatives, although the NDC achieved a working parliamentary majority. Nicholas Brathwaite became Prime Minister and appointed a new Cabinet. Brathwaite resigned as Prime Minister in February 1995, and was succeeded by Brizan.

The NNP's political domination

The NNP secured eight of the 15 seats in the House of Representatives at the general election of June 1995, while the NDC's representation was reduced to five seats. The remaining two seats were secured by GULP. Mitchell became Prime Minister.

In November 1998 the resignation of the Minister of Foreign Affairs, Raphael Fletcher, from the Government and NNP in order to join GULP, resulted in an early general election being called. The NNP obtained all of the 15 seats in the House of Representatives in the subsequent ballot in January 1999, thus becoming the first political party in the country's history to secure two successive terms in government.

In October 1999 Bernard Coard, serving a term of life imprisonment with 16 others for the 1983 murder of Prime Minister Maurice Bishop and a number of his associates (see above), issued a statement in which he accepted full responsibility for the crimes. In 2002 it was announced that three former soldiers gaoled in 1986 for Bishop's murder and that of seven others during the 1983 coup were to be released. Furthermore, in March 2004 the Court of Appeal ruled that the 17 prisoners would be resentenced, since the life sentences imposed on them were unconstitutional. However, the day before the resentencing, the Court of Appeal of the Eastern Caribbean Supreme Court, based in Saint Lucia, overturned the ruling. This decision was confirmed after a further hearing in 2005; lawyers for the men appealed against the judgment to the Privy Council, based in the United Kingdom, occasioning a ruling in February 2007 for the resentencing of 13 of the prisoners (three of their original number had been released in 2006, while Phyllis Coard had secured early release in 2000 in order to seek life-saving medical treatment). Subsequently, in June 2007 the Supreme Court ordered the release of three of the prisoners and reduced the sentences of the remaining 10. Three further prisoners secured an early release in December 2008, and in September 2009 the remaining seven, including Bernard Coard, were set free, prompting expressions of disapproval from large sections of the population.

The NNP secured a third successive term in office in the general election of November 2003, although its parliamentary majority was reduced to just one seat. The NDC won the seven remaining seats in the 15-seat House of Representatives. Keith Mitchell was sworn in again as Prime Minister.

Grenada was devastated by Hurricane Ivan in September 2004, which killed 39 Grenadians and destroyed 90% of the housing stock. According to the OECS, full rehabilitation would cost at least US $814m. Opposition deputies strenuously criticized the Government's relief efforts and the apparently slow progress of the recovery. In October the Agency for Reconstruction and Development was established to implement and monitor reconstruction projects and to manage the receipt of grants from international donors. Widespread looting and violent crime was brought under relative control after intervention from regional (primarily Trinidadian) security forces. The island was struck by another huge storm, Hurricane Emily, in July 2005. The cost of the damage was estimated at $200m.; the misfortune was compounded by the impact of Emily upon the recovery process from Hurricane Ivan. In January 2006 Mitchell announced that a 5% salary tax to help finance rebuilding efforts would be introduced; the levy was strenuously opposed by the Grenada Trade Union Congress.

The NDC in office

The NNP failed to secure a fourth successive term in office in a general election held on 8 July 2008, with the NDC winning 11 of the 15 legislative seats and 51% of the valid votes cast. The NNP won the remaining four seats and 48% of the ballot. Turnout was high, at 80%, and observers from the Organization of American States reported positively upon the procedure of the election. Tillman Thomas, the NDC leader, was sworn in as Prime Minister and the new Cabinet duly installed: notable appointments included Nazim Burke as Minister of Finance, Planning, Economy, Energy and Co-operatives, and Peter David as Minister of Foreign Affairs.

In October 2009 the High Court of Justice effected the liquidation of *Grenada Today*, following the newspaper's inability to pay compensation to former Prime Minister Keith Mitchell, who had successfully sued the newspaper for libel. The compensation award, at US $71,000, was generally viewed as excessive, and press freedom advocates appealed for a limit on libel damages.

Following a cabinet reorganization in November 2010, three ministers, Peter David, Glynis Roberts and Michael Church (who had been demoted as punishment for taking an unauthorized trip to Switzerland to attend a trade meeting), failed to attend the official ceremony to be sworn in to office. Their action prompted speculation about the unity of the Government and Church submitted his resignation shortly afterwards. Press reports alleged that the reorganization had led to divisions within the Cabinet, although Thomas rejected these claims.

Building upon earlier efforts to effect constitutional reform, in December 2010 a draft constitution was published, which advocated the removal of the British monarch as Head of State and the creation of a republic; the document also proposed that the Privy Council be replaced by the Caribbean Court of Justice as the nation's final appellate court. Consultations were expected to be prolonged, in advance of a proposed referendum on the draft constitution.

Thomas reorganized the Cabinet again in September 2011 amid press reports of rising factionalism within the ruling party. In January 2012 Joseph Gilbert, Minister of Environment, Foreign Trade and Export Development, was dismissed after allegedly concluding an unauthorized agreement with a US firm in relation to the establishment of a casino on the island. The resignations in April of Peter David, Minister of Tourism and Civil Aviation, and Karl Hood, Minister of Foreign Affairs, both of whom expressed dissatisfaction with the Government, prompted the opposition to call for a vote of no confidence in the administration. At the vote in mid-May the motion was defeated by eight votes to five. However, Hood sought to file a further motion of no confidence in the Government in August, prompting Thomas to ask the Governor-General to prorogue Parliament in order to avoid a second vote taking place. Increasing divisions within the ruling NDC, together with a weak economic situation, made the prospect of the Government's defeat in such a vote seem highly likely. As a result, Parliament did not convene for the remainder of 2012 and, in accordance with the Constitution (which states that the legislature must sit at least once in any six-month period), was dissolved in January 2013 in preparation for a general election. Three former cabinet members, Glynis Roberts, Peter David and Karl Hood, all of whom had been dismissed from the NDC by Thomas in September 2012, formed a new political party, the National United Party, in order to contest the election.

Recent developments: Mitchell's return to office

At a legislative election on 19 February 2013 the NNP won a resounding victory, securing all 15 seats in the House of Representatives and some 58.8% of total votes cast. Electoral participation was high, with an estimated 85% of eligible voters taking part in the poll. At his inauguration as Prime Minister the following day Keith Mitchell emphasized the need for national unity, in acknowledgement of the political instability that had characterized the latter period in office of the previous Government. The new Cabinet included Elvin Nimrod as Deputy Prime Minister and Attorney-General and Nickolas Steele as Minister of Foreign Affairs and International Business. Mitchell took responsibility for the finance, national security, energy and home affairs portfolios, among others.

In July 2013 the NNP Government came under criticism from the International Press Institute (IPI), based in Vienna, Austria, over controversial proposed legislation, the Electronic Crimes

Act, according to which (among other provisions) sending offensive electronic messages would become a criminal offence. Having commended Grenada for becoming the first Caribbean country to decriminalize libel, in July 2012, the IPI perceived this new bill as a step backwards. However, the Act was signed into law on 9 September, prompting international organization Reporters Without Borders to voice its concern. On 2 August Parliament approved the Grenada Citizen by Investment Act, which would enable Grenadian passports to be bought in exchange for a certain, unspecified amount of investment in the country. The scheme had already been introduced in a number of other Caribbean countries, although that in Grenada contained a residency requirement. In October the Governor-General announced plans to hold a referendum on a new constitution in 2014, the 40th anniversary of the country's independence. Issues for consideration in the plebiscite included the restructuring of Parliament and the replacement of the Privy Council by the Caribbean Court of Justice as the final Court of Appeal.

Foreign Affairs

Regional relations

Negotiations on the delimitation of Grenada's maritime border with Trinidad and Tobago had been in abeyance since 1993. However, a treaty demarcating the boundary was finally ratified in April 2010, allowing for the initiation of offshore petroleum and gas exploration. Discussions on finalizing an agreement on joint exploration operations took place in May 2013.

In 2005 Grenada became one of 13 Caribbean nations to sign the Petrocaribe accord, under which it was allowed to purchase petroleum from Venezuela at reduced prices.

Other external relations

In 1996 Grenada signed two treaties with the USA, relating to mutual legal assistance and extradition, as part of a regional campaign to combat drugs-trafficking. An agreement on maritime security co-operation was signed by Grenada and the USA in March 2011.

In 2000 Grenada restored diplomatic relations with Libya, suspended in 1983. From 1983 Grenada had maintained diplomatic relations with Taiwan instead of the People's Republic of China; however, in 2004 Taiwan recalled its ambassador to Grenada after Mitchell visited mainland China. Mitchell emphasized that the destruction caused by Hurricane Ivan had forced the Government to reconsider its international relationships and in January 2005 Grenada established official ties with China; Taiwan duly severed its relations with Grenada. In 2009 the Chinese Government provided Grenada with aid and loans amounting to some US $6m. Taiwan commenced legal proceedings against Grenada during 2011 to reclaim outstanding loan repayments totalling US $28m. Major airlines and cruise lines operating in Grenada were court ordered to deposit fees owed to the Taiwanese authorities into an escrow account, depriving the Grenadian Government, which launched a legal challenge against Taiwan's actions, of an important revenue source. In April 2013 it was announced that China would provide US $31.5m. for the reconstruction of the football stadium destroyed by Hurricane Ivan. In June, following talks between Mitchell and Chinese President Xi Jinping it was announced that Grenada would receive $8.7m. in grant assistance.

CONSTITUTION AND GOVERNMENT

The Constitution of Grenada was adopted upon independence in 1974. Grenada has dominion status within the Commonwealth. The British monarch is Head of State and is represented locally by a Governor-General. The Cabinet, led by the Prime Minister, holds executive power. Parliament comprises the Senate, made up of 13 Senators appointed by the Governor-General on the advice of the Prime Minister and the Leader of the Opposition, and the 15-member House of Representatives, elected by universal adult suffrage. The Cabinet is responsible to Parliament. Judicial power is vested in the Eastern Caribbean Supreme Court, although in certain cases further appeal can be made to the Privy Council in the United Kingdom.

REGIONAL AND INTERNATIONAL CO-OPERATION

Grenada is a member of the Caribbean Community and Common Market (CARICOM, see p. 223). It is also a member of the Economic Commission for Latin America and the Caribbean (ECLAC, see p. 33), the Organization of American States (OAS, see p. 394), the Association of Caribbean States (see p. 449), and of the Community of Latin American and Caribbean States (see p. 464), which was formally inaugurated in December 2011. Grenada is a member of the Eastern Caribbean Securities Exchange (based in Saint Christopher and Nevis), and of the Eastern Caribbean Central Bank (ECCB, see p. 455). In June 2010 Grenada was a signatory to the Revised Treaty of Basseterre, establishing an Economic Union among the member nations of the Organisation of Eastern Caribbean States (OECS, see p. 467). The Cabinet ratified the Treaty in mid-January 2011, and the Economic Union, which involved the removal of barriers to trade and the movement of labour as a step towards a single financial and economic market, came into effect on 21 January. Freedom of movement between the signatory states was granted to OECS nationals on 1 August. In January 2014 Grenada formally applied for membership of the Bolivarian Alliance for the Peoples of our America (Alianza Bolivariana para los Pueblos de Nuestra América—ALBA, see p. 463).

Grenada acceded to the UN in 1974, upon independence. It joined the World Trade Organization (see p. 434) in February 1996. The country is a member of the Commonwealth (see p. 236). Grenada is a signatory to the Cotonou Agreement (see p. 324), the successor arrangement to the Lomé Conventions between the African, Caribbean and Pacific (ACP) countries and the European Union.

ECONOMIC AFFAIRS

In 2012, according to estimates by the World Bank, Grenada's gross national income (GNI), measured at average 2010–12 prices, was US $750m., equivalent to $7,110 per head (or $10,300 per head on an international purchasing-power parity basis). During 2003–12 Grenada's population increased at an average rate of 0.3% per year, while gross domestic product (GDP) per head increased, in real terms, by an average of 0.4% per year. Overall GDP increased, in real terms, at an average annual rate of 0.7% in 2003–12, according to the Eastern Caribbean Central Bank (ECCB, see p. 455); real GDP increased by just 0.8% in 2011, and decreased by 1.8% in 2012.

Agriculture (including hunting, forestry and fishing) contributed 5.5% of GDP in 2012. The sector engaged an estimated 19.1% of the employed labour force in mid-2014, according to FAO estimates. Grenada is one of the world's largest producers of nutmeg (although Indonesia produces some 75% of the world's total). In the first nine months of 2012 exports of nutmeg and mace (the pungent red membrane around the nut) accounted for an estimated 19.1% of Grenada's total domestic export earnings. The importance of bananas to the economy has fallen in recent years; by 2012 FAO estimated output at only 3,400 metric tons. Livestock production, for domestic consumption, is important on Carriacou. There are extensive timber reserves on the island of Grenada; forestry development is strictly controlled and involves a programme of reafforestation. Exports of fish contributed an estimated 3.4% of domestic export earnings in 2012. According to the ECCB, agricultural GDP decreased at an average annual rate of 2.3% in 2003–12; the sector declined by 1.6% in 2011, but increased by 4.6% in 2012.

Industry (mining, manufacturing, construction and utilities) provided 13.8% of GDP in 2012 and engaged 23.9% of the employed labour force in 1998. According to the ECCB, industrial GDP decreased by an annual average of 2.6% during 2003–12; the sector's GDP declined by 8.9% in 2012.

The mining and quarrying sector accounted for only 0.2% of employment in 1998 and for 0.2% of GDP in 2012. Mining GDP decreased by an annual average of 11.2% in 2003–12; the sector contracted by 14.1% in 2012.

Manufacturing, which contributed 3.6% of GDP in 2012 and employed 7.7% of the working population in 1998, consists mainly of the processing of agricultural products and of cottage industries producing garments and spice-based items. Rum, soft drinks, paints and varnishes, household paper products and the tyre-retreading industries are also important. According to the ECCB, manufacturing GDP declined by an average of 0.9% per year in 2003–12; the sector's GDP declined by 0.2% in 2012.

The construction sector contributed 5.5% of GDP in 2012 and engaged 15.4% of the labour force in 1998. Construction GDP declined by an average of 5.5% per year in 2003–12, according to the ECCB; the sector's GDP declined by 18.0% in 2012.

Grenada is dependent upon imports for its energy requirements, and in 2012 mineral fuels and lubricants accounted for an estimated 30.4% of the total cost of imports. Electricity generation totalled 213.0m. kWh in 2010.

The services sector contributed 80.6% of GDP in 2012. Tourism and financial and business services were the main contributors to GDP. Receipts from tourism totalled an estimated EC $328.3m. in 2012, an increase on the previous year. Tourist arrivals decreased in 2012, by 15.6%, although this was mainly driven by a fall in cruise ship arrivals. These totalled 242,757, compared with 309,564 in 2011. The more lucrative stop-over market also contracted in 2012, but less dramatically, by 1.4%. The 'offshore' financial sector is also economically significant. Financial services contributed 7.0% to the economy in 2012. According to the ECCB, the GDP of the services sector increased at an average annual rate of 1.7% in 2003–12; the sector increased by 1.4% in 2011, but declined by 0.1% in 2012.

In 2012 Grenada reported a deficit on merchandise trade of EC $692.7m. and there was a deficit of $578.9m. on the current account of the balance of payments. In 2008 the principal source of imports was the USA, accounting for 30.9% of the total. The USA is also the principal market for exports, taking 16.4% of the total in 2008, along with Dominica. The principal export were food and live animals, accounting for 67.9% of total exports in 2012. The principal imports in that year were mineral fuels, oils and distillation products, food and live animals, machinery and transport equipment, manufactured goods, miscellaneous manufactured articles, and chemical and related products. The trade deficit is partly offset by earnings from tourism, capital receipts and remittances from the many Grenadians working abroad.

In 2012 there was an overall budgetary deficit of EC $120.4m., equivalent to 5.6% of GDP. Grenada's general government gross debt was EC $2,334m. in 2012, equivalent to 109.5% of GDP. Grenada's total external debt was US $567m. in 2011, of which US $487m. was public and publicly guaranteed debt. In 2011 the cost of servicing long-term public and publicly guaranteed debt and repayments to the IMF was equivalent to 13.3% of the value of exports of goods, services and income (excluding workers' remittances). The average annual rate of inflation was 3.6% in 2005–12; consumer prices increased by 1.8% in 2012, according to the IMF. The unemployment rate was 33.5% of the labour force in September 2013.

Following the contraction of Grenada's economy by 6.7% in 2009, as a result of the global economic downturn, a value-added tax (VAT) was introduced in 2010, resulting in increased revenues, although this was tempered by a subsequent reduction in VAT rates for key economic sectors. Economic contraction slowed to 0.5% in 2010 and economic expansion of 0.8% and 1.8% was recorded by the ECCB in 2011 and 2012, respectively. The country's poor economic situation was reflected in government wage arrears and several missed debt service payments to bilateral creditors in 2012. In March 2013 the World Bank suspended disbursements to Grenada until the country made good on overdue payments amounting to some US $750,000. In July, in an attempt to reduce the island's heavy dependence on tourism, which is particularly vulnerable to external economic conditions, the Government launched a farm labour subsidy programme that placed particular emphasis on the rehabilitation and replanting of nutmeg and cocoa. It was hoped that the scheme would provide employment for between 1,500 and 2,000 labourers. In October, following talks with IMF officials, Prime Minister Keith Mitchell announced the implementation of a three-year fiscal restructuring programme from 2014, which included new tax levels and improved tax collection. This was followed in March 2014 a three-year debt-restructuring agreement with the Fund worth US $21.9m. The budget for 2014 envisaged increased direct and indirect taxation and a growth in support for the private sector. The Citizenship by Investment programme (see Domestic Political Affairs) was also expected to generate government revenue. The ECCB estimated real GDP expansion of 1.6% in 2013 and 1.3% in 2014.

PUBLIC HOLIDAYS

2015: 1 January (New Year's Day), 7 February (Independence Day), 3 April (Good Friday), 6 April (Easter Monday), 1 May (Labour Day), 25 May (Whit Monday), 4 June (Corpus Christi), 3 August (Emancipation Holiday), 10–11 August (Carnival), 25 October (Thanksgiving Day), 25–26 December (Christmas).

Statistical Survey

AREA AND POPULATION

Area: 344.5 sq km (133.0 sq miles).

Population: 102,632 at census of 25 May 2001; 103,328 (males 52,651, females 50,677) at census of 12 May 2011 (preliminary). *Mid-2014* (UN estimate) 106,304 (Source: UN, *World Population Prospects: The 2012 Revision*).

Density (mid-2013): 307.4 per sq km.

Population by Age and Sex (UN estimates at mid-2014): *0–14:* 28,297 (males 14,498, females 13,799); *15–64:* 70,481 (males 35,726, females 34,755); *65 and over:* 7,526 (males 3,052, females 4,474); *Total* 106,304 (males 53,276, females 53,028) (Source: UN, *World Population Prospects: The 2012 Revision*).

Parishes (population at 2011 census, preliminary): Carriacou 5,354; St Andrew 25,722; St David 12,561; St George 36,823; St John 7,802; St Mark 4,086; St Patrick 10,980; *Total* 103,328.

Principal Town (population at 2011 census, preliminary): St George's (capital) 2,982. *Mid-2011* (UN estimate, incl. suburbs): St George's 41,054 (Source: UN, *World Urbanization Prospects: The 2011 Revision*).

Births and Deaths (registrations, 2001, provisional): Live births 1,899 (birth rate 18.8 per 1,000); Deaths 727 (death rate 7.2 per 1,000); *2012*: Birth rate 16.8 per 1,000; Death rate 8.0 per 1,000 (Source: Pan American Health Organization).

Life Expectancy (years at birth): 73.3 (males 70.8; females 76.1) in 2012. Source: Pan American Health Organization.

Employment (employees only, 1998): Agriculture, hunting, forestry and fishing 4,794; Mining and quarrying 58; Manufacturing 2,579; Electricity, gas and water 505; Construction 5,163; Wholesale and retail trade 6,324; Restaurants and hotels 1,974; Transport, storage and communications 2,043; Financing, insurance and real estate 1,312; Public administration, defence and social security 1,879; Community services 3,904; Other services 2,933; *Sub-total* 33,468; Activities not adequately defined 1,321; *Total employed* 34,789 (males 20,733, females 14,056). *Mid-2014* (estimates): Agriculture, etc. 9,000; Total labour force 47,000 (Source: FAO).

HEALTH AND WELFARE

Key Indicators

Total Fertility Rate (children per woman, 2011): 2.2.

Under-5 Mortality Rate (per 1,000 live births, 2011): 13.

Physicians (per 1,000 head, 2009): 0.8.

Hospital Beds (per 1,000 head, 2009): 2.4.

Health Expenditure (2010): US $ per head (PPP): 632.

Health Expenditure (2010): % of GDP: 5.8.

Health Expenditure (2010): public (% of total): 45.1.

Access to Water (% of persons, 2004): 95.

Access to Sanitation (% of persons, 2010): 97.

Total Carbon Dioxide Emissions ('000 metric tons, 2010): 260.4.

Total Carbon Dioxide Emissions Per Head (metric tons, 2010): 2.5.

Human Development Index (2012): ranking: 63.

Human Development Index (2012): value: 0.770.

For sources and definitions, see explanatory note on p. vi.

AGRICULTURE, ETC.

Principal Crops ('000 metric tons, 2012, FAO estimates unless otherwise indicated): Sugar cane 7.2; Pigeon peas 0.9; Coconuts 6.5; Bananas 3.4; Plantains 0.3; Oranges 0.6; Grapefruit and pomelos 1.5; Apples 0.6; Plums and sloes 0.7; Mangoes, mangosteens and guavas 1.2; Avocados 1.5; Cocoa beans 0.8 (unofficial figure); Nutmeg, mace and cardamom 0.6. *Aggregate Production* ('000 metric tons, may include official, semi-official or estimated data): Roots and tubers 2.4; Vegetables (incl. melons) 4.1 Fruits (excl. melons) 14.4.

Livestock ('000 head, year ending September 2012, FAO estimates): Cattle 4.6; Pigs 3.0; Sheep 13.2; Goats 7.2; Chickens 270.

Livestock Products ('000 metric tons, 2012, FAO estimates): Chicken meat 0.7; Cows' milk 0.7; Hen eggs 1.4.

Fishing (metric tons, live weight, 2011): Red hind 112; Coney 25; Snappers and jobfishes 70; Parrotfishes 120; Blackfin tuna 150; Yellowfin tuna 789; Atlantic sailfish 239; Swordfish 39; Common dolphinfish 189; *Total catch* (incl. others) 2,322.

Source: FAO.

INDUSTRY

Production (1994 unless otherwise indicated): Rum 300,000 litres; Beer 2,400,000 litres; Wheat flour 4,000 metric tons (1996); Cigarettes 15m.; Electricity 213.0 million kWh (2010). Source: UN, *Industrial Commodity Statistics Yearbook*.

FINANCE

Currency and Exchange Rates: 100 cents = 1 Eastern Caribbean dollar (EC $). *Sterling, US Dollar and Euro Equivalents* (31 December 2013): £1 sterling = EC $4.446; US $1 = EC $2.700; €1 = EC $3.724; EC $100 = £22.49 = US $37.04 = €26.86. *Exchange Rate:* Fixed at US $1 = EC $2.70 since July 1976.

Budget (EC $ million, 2012): *Revenue:* Tax revenue 403.2 (Taxes on income and profits 75.5, Taxes on property 16.4, Taxes on domestic goods and services 189.5, Taxes on international trade and transactions 121.8); Other current revenue 22.1; Total 425.3 (excluding grants received 20.8) *Expenditure:* Current expenditure 458.1 (Personal emoluments 227.2, Goods and services 86.4, Interest payments 73.6, Transfers and subsidies 70.9); Capital expenditure and net lending 108.4; Total 566.5. Source: Eastern Caribbean Central Bank.

International Reserves (US $ million at 31 December 2012): IMF special drawing rights 15.48; Foreign exchange 104.00; Total 119.49. Source: IMF, *International Financial Statistics*.

Money Supply (EC $ million at 31 December 2012): Currency outside depository corporations 112.88; Transferable deposits 333.30; Other deposits 1,528.32; *Broad money* 1,947.49. Source: IMF, *International Financial Statistics*.

Cost of Living (Consumer Price Index; base: 2005 = 100): 120.6 in 2010; 125.4 in 2011; 127.7 in 2012. Source: IMF, *International Financial Statistics*.

Gross Domestic Product (EC $ million at constant 2006 prices): 1,877.68 in 2010; 1,892.04 in 2011; 1,857.51 in 2012. Source: Eastern Caribbean Central Bank.

Expenditure on the Gross Domestic Product (EC $ million at current prices, 2012): Government final consumption expenditure 347.67; Private final consumption expenditure 1,974.21; Gross capital formation 353.00; *Total domestic expenditure* 2,674.88; Exports of goods and services 557.53; *Less* Imports of goods and services 1,068.35; *GDP in purchasers' values* 2,164.06. Source: Eastern Caribbean Central Bank.

Gross Domestic Product by Economic Activity (EC $ million at current prices, 2012): Agriculture and fishing 104.77; Mining and quarrying 4.25; Manufacturing 67.27; Electricity and water 85.51; Construction 104.83; Wholesale and retail trade 152.69; Hotels and restaurants 81.60; Transport and communications 227.74; Housing, real estate and business activities 255.47; Financial services 132.02; Public administration and defence 156.21; Other services 521.22; *Sub-total* 1,893.58; *Less* Financial intermediation services indirectly measured (FISIM) 25.28; *GDP at factor cost* 1,868.30; Taxes on products, less subsidies 295.76; *GDP in market prices* 2,164.06. Source: Eastern Caribbean Central Bank.

Balance of Payments (EC $ million, 2012): Goods (net) –692.68; Services (net) 151.18; *Balance of goods and services* –541.50; Other income (net) –103.26; Current transfers (net) 65.85; *Current balance* –578.91; Capital account (net) 110.99; Direct investment 81.62; Portfolio investment –17.65; Other investments 348.11; Net errors and omissions 50.44; *Overall balance* –5.40. Source: Eastern Caribbean Central Bank.

EXTERNAL TRADE

Principal Commodities (distribution by SITC, EC $ million, 2012): *Imports c.i.f.:* Food and live animals 193.34; Mineral fuels and related materials 280.19; Chemicals and related products 66.31; Manufactured goods 102.00; Machinery and transport equipment 148.05; Miscellaneous manufactured articles 87.89; Total (incl. others) 921.42. *Exports f.o.b:* Food and live animals 63.45; Chemicals and related products 2.81; Manufactured goods 11.28; Machinery and transport equipment 6.55; Miscellaneous manufactured articles 7.25; Total (incl. others) 93.43 (re-exports 11.42). Source: Eastern Caribbean Central Bank.

Principal Trading Partners (US $ million, 2008): *Imports c.i.f.:* Barbados 6.5; Brazil 9.2; Canada 10.1; China, People's Republic 12.0; France (incl. Monaco) 3.2; Germany 5.2; Guyana 3.9; Japan 13.0; Netherlands 4.8; Trinidad and Tobago 90.3; United Kingdom 16.1; USA 112.2; Venezuela 25.5; Total (incl. others) 363.3. *Exports f.o.b.:* Antigua and Barbuda 1.0; Barbados 2.9; Belgium 1.0; Canada 0.9; Dominica 5.0; France (incl. Monaco) 0.3; Guyana 0.6; Jamaica 0.5; Japan 6.5; Netherlands 1.1; Saint Christopher and Nevis 2.6; Saint Lucia 3.4; Saint Vincent and the Grenadines 1.0; Trinidad and Tobago 0.6; USA 5.0; Total (incl. others) 30.5. Source: Trade Map-Trade Competitiveness Map, International Trade Centre, www.intracen.org/marketanalysis. *2012* (EC $ million): Total imports 921.42; Total exports 93.43 (re-exports 11.42). (Source: Eastern Caribbean Central Bank).

TRANSPORT

Road Traffic ('000 motor vehicles in use, 2001): Passenger cars 15.8; Commercial vehicles 4.2. Source: UN, *Statistical Yearbook*.

Shipping: *Flag Registered Fleet* (at 31 December 2013): 8 vessels (total displacement 1,762 grt) (Source: Lloyd's List Intelligence—www.lloydslistintelligence.com). *International Sea-borne Freight Traffic* (estimates, '000 metric tons, 1995): Goods loaded 21.3; Goods unloaded 193.0. *Ship Arrivals* (1991): 1,254. *Fishing Vessels* (registered, 1987): 635.

Civil Aviation (aircraft arrivals, 1995): 11,310.

TOURISM

Visitor Arrivals: 445,622 (incl. 105,419 stop-over visitors and 333,291 cruise ship passengers) in 2010; 428,596 (incl. 113,947 stop-over visitors and 309,564 cruise ship passengers) in 2011; 361,673 (incl. 112,335 stop-over visitors and 242,757 cruise ship passengers) in 2012 (estimates).

Tourism Receipts (EC $ million): 301.4 in 2010; 315.3 in 2011; 328.3 in 2012 (estimate).

Source: Eastern Caribbean Central Bank.

COMMUNICATIONS MEDIA

Telephones (2012): 28,500 main lines in use.

Mobile Cellular Telephones (2012): 128,000 subscribers.

Internet Subscribers (2010): 14,400.

Broadband Subscribers (2012): 14,437.

Source: International Telecommunication Union.

EDUCATION

Pre-primary (2009/10 unless otherwise indicated): 74 schools (1994); 246 teachers; 3,562 pupils.

Primary (2009/10 unless otherwise indicated): 57 schools (1995); 851 teachers; 13,663 pupils.

Secondary (2009/10 unless otherwise indicated): 20 schools (2002); 566 teachers; 11,500 pupils.

Higher (excl. figures for the Grenada Teachers' Training College, 1993): 66 teachers; 651 students.

Source: partly UNESCO Institute for Statistics.

Pupil-teacher Ratio (primary education, UNESCO estimate): 16.1 in 2009/10 (Source: UNESCO Institute for Statistics).

Adult Literacy Rate: 96.0% in 2003. Source: UN Development Programme, *Human Development Report*.

Directory

The Government

HEAD OF STATE

Queen: HM Queen ELIZABETH II.

Governor-General: Dr CECILE LA GRENADE (took office 7 May 2013).

THE CABINET
(April 2014)

The Government was formed by the New National Party.

Prime Minister and Minister of Finance, Planning, Economic Development, Trade and Co-operatives, Energy and Co-operatives, National Security, Public Administration, Disaster Management, Home Affairs, and Implementation: KEITH MITCHELL.

Deputy Prime Minister, and Minister of Legal Affairs, Labour, Carriacou and Petite Martinique Affairs and Local Government: ELVIN NIMROD.

Minister of Economic Development, Trade, Planning and Co-operatives: OLIVER JOSEPH.

Minister of Communications, Works, Physical Development, Public Utilities and Information Communication Technology: GREGORY BOWEN.

Minister of Tourism, Civil Aviation and Culture: Dr ALEXANDRA OTWAY-NOEL.

Minister of Agriculture, Lands, Forestry, Fisheries and the Environment: ROLAND BHOLA.

Minister of Education and Human Resource Development: ANTHONY BOATSWAIN.

Minister of Health and Social Security: Dr CLARICE MODESTE-CURWEN.

Minister of Foreign Affairs and International Business: NICKOLAS STEELE.

Minister of Youth, Sports and Religious Relations: EMMALIN PIERRE.

Minister of Social Development and Housing: DELMA THOMAS.

MINISTRIES

Office of the Governor-General: Government House, Bldg 5, Financial Complex, The Carenage, St George's; tel. 440-6639; fax 440-6688; e-mail pato@spiceisle.com.

Office of the Prime Minister: Ministerial Complex, 6th Floor, Botanical Gardens, Tanteen, St George's; tel. 440-2255; fax 440-4116; e-mail pmsec@gov.gd; internet www.gov.gd/ministries/opm.html.

Ministry of Agriculture, Lands, Forestry, Fisheries and the Environment: Ministerial Complex, 3rd Floor, Botanical Gardens, Tanteen, St George's; tel. 440-2708; fax 440-4191; e-mail agriculture@gov.gd; internet www.agriculture.gov.gd.

Ministry of Carriacou and Petit Martinique Affairs and Local Government: Beauséjour, Carriacou; tel. 443-6026; fax 443-6040; e-mail minccoupm@spiceisle.com.

Ministry of Communications, Works, Physical Development, Public Utilities and Information Communication Technology: Ministerial Complex, 4th Floor, Botanical Gardens, Tanteen, St George's; tel. 440-2271; fax 440-4122; e-mail ministryofworks@gov.gd.

Ministry of Education and Human Resource Development: Ministry of Education Bldg, Ministerial Complex, Botanical Gardens, Tanteen, St George's; tel. 440-2737; fax 440-6650; internet www.grenadaedu.com.

Ministry of Finance, Planning, Economic Development, Trade and Co-operatives: Financial Complex, The Carenage, St George's; tel. 440-2731; fax 440-4115.

Ministry of Foreign Affairs and International Business: Ministerial Complex, 4th Floor, Botanical Gardens, Tanteen, St George's; tel. 440-2640; fax 440-4184; e-mail foreignaffairs@gov.gd.

Ministry of Health and Social Security: Ministerial Complex, Southern Wing, 1st and 2nd Floors, Botanical Gardens, Tanteen, St George's; tel. 440-2649; fax 440-4127; e-mail min-healthgrenada@spiceisle.com.

Ministry of Legal Affairs and Labour: Ministerial Complex, 3rd Floor, St George's; tel. 440-2532; fax 440-4923; e-mail ministry_labourga@hotmail.com.

Ministry of National Security, Disaster Management, Home Affairs, and Implementation: Ministerial Complex, 6th Floor, Botanical Gardens, Tanteen, St George's; tel. 440-2265; fax 440-4116; e-mail pmsec@gov.gd.

Ministry of Social Development and Housing: Ministerial Complex, 2nd Floor, Botanical Gardens, Tanteen, St George's; tel. 440-2103; fax 435-5864; e-mail mofhlcd@gov.gd.

Ministry of Tourism, Civil Aviation and Culture: Ministerial Complex, 4th Floor, Botanical Gardens, Tanteen, St George's; tel. 440-0366; fax 440-0443; e-mail tourism@gov.gd; internet www.grenada.mot.gd.

Ministry of Youth Empowerment, Sports and Religious Affairs: Ministerial Complex, 3rd Floor, Botanical Gardens, Tanteen, St George's; tel. 440-6917; fax 440-6924; e-mail sports@gov.gd.

Legislature

PARLIAMENT

Houses of Parliament: Office of the Houses of Parliament, Botanical Gardens, Tanteen, POB 315, St George's; tel. 440-2090; fax 440-4138; e-mail order.order@spiceisle.com.

Senate

President: LAWRENCE JOSEPH.

There are 13 appointed members.

House of Representatives

Speaker: GEORGE JAMES MCGUIRE.

General Election, 19 February 2013

	Votes	%	Seats
New National Party (NNP)	32,225	58.77	15
National Democratic Congress (NDC)	22,260	40.59	—
Others*	346	0.63	—
Total valid votes	54,831	100.00	15

* Comprising the Good Old Democracy Party (GOD), the Grenada Renaissance Party (GRP), the Grenada United Patriotic Movement (GUPM), the Movement for Independent Candidates (MIC), the National United Front (NUF) and the People's United Labor Party (PULP).

Political Organizations

Good Old Democracy Party (GOD): St George's; contested the 2013 elections; Leader JUSTIN MCBURNIE.

Grenada Renaissance Party (GRP): St George's; contested the 2013 elections; Leader DESMOND CUTHBERT SANDY.

Grenada United Labour Party (GULP): St George's; tel. 438-1234; e-mail gulp@spiceisle.com; f. 1950; merged with United Labour Congress in 2001; right-wing; did not contest 2013 elections; Pres. WILFRED HAYES; Leader (vacant).

Grenada United Patriotic Movement (GUPM): St George's; contested the 2013 elections.

National Democratic Congress (NDC): NDC Headquarters, Lucas St, St George's; tel. 440-3769; e-mail info@ndcgrenada.net; internet www.ndcgrenada.org; f. 1987 by fmr mems of the NNP and merger of Democratic Labour Congress and Grenada Democratic Labour Party; centrist; Leader NAZIM BURKE.

National United Front (NUF): St George's; e-mail info@nationalunitedfront.org; internet www.nationalunitedfront.org; f. 2012 by expelled mems of the NDP; Chair. SIDDIQUI SYLVESTER; Leader GLYNIS ROBERTS.

New National Party (NNP): Upper Lucas St, Mount Helicon, POB 646, St George's; tel. 440-1875; fax 440-1876; e-mail nnpadmin@spiceisle.com; internet www.nnpnews.com; f. 1984 following merger of Grenada Democratic Movt, Grenada National Party and National Democratic Party; centrist; Leader Dr KEITH MITCHELL; Dep. Leader GREGORY BOWEN.

People's United Labor Party (PULP): St George's; contested the 2013 elections; Leader WINSTON FREDERICK.

Diplomatic Representation

EMBASSIES IN GRENADA

Brazil: Mount Cinnamon Hill, Morne Rouge, POB 1226, Grand Anse, St George's; tel. 439-7162; fax 439-7165; e-mail brasemb .saintgeorges@mre.gov.br; Ambassador RICARDO ANDRE VIEIRA DINIZ.

China, People's Republic: Azar Villa, Calliste, POB 1079, St George's; tel. 439-6228; fax 439-6231; e-mail chinaemb_gd@mfa .gov.cn; internet gd.china-embassy.org; Ambassador OU BOQIAN.

Cuba: L'Anse aux Epines, St George's; tel. 444-1884; fax 444-1877; e-mail embacubagranada@caribsurf.com; internet www .cubadiplomatica.cu/granada; Ambassador MARIA CARIDAD BALAGUER LABRADA.

USA: L'Anse aux Epines, POB 54, St George's; tel. 444-1173; fax 444-4820; e-mail usembgd@caribsurf.com; Ambassador LARRY LEON PALMER (resident in Barbados).

Venezuela: Upper Lucas St, Belmont, POB 201, St George's; tel. 440-1721; fax 440-6657; e-mail vennes@caribsurf.com; Ambassador JORGE ALFONZO GUERRERO VELOZ.

Judicial System

Justice is administered by the Eastern Caribbean Supreme Court, based in Saint Lucia, composed of a High Court of Justice and a Court of Appeal. The Itinerant Court of Appeal consists of three judges and sits three times a year; it hears appeals from the High Court and the Magistrates' Court. Three judges of the High Court are resident in Grenada. The Magistrates' Court administers summary jurisdiction.

High Court Judges: MARGARET MOHAMMED, PAULA GILFORD, MARGARET PRICE FINDLAY.

Registrar: COLIN MEADE.

Office of the Attorney-General: Communal House, 414 H. A. Blaize St, St George's; tel. 440-2050; fax 435-2964; e-mail legalaffairs@spiceisle.com; Attorney-Gen. CAJETON HOOD.

Religion

CHRISTIANITY

The Roman Catholic Church

Grenada comprises the single diocese of Saint George's, suffragan to the archdiocese of Castries (Saint Lucia). The Bishop participates in the Antilles Episcopal Conference (based in Port of Spain, Trinidad and Tobago). Some 45% of the population are Roman Catholics.

Bishop of St George's in Grenada: Rev. VINCENT DARIUS, Bishop's House, Morne Jaloux, POB 375, St George's; tel. 443-5299; fax 443-5758; e-mail bishopgrenada@spiceisle.com; internet www.stgdiocese .org.

The Anglican Communion

Anglicans in Grenada are adherents of the Church in the Province of the West Indies. The country forms part of the diocese of the Windward Islands. The Bishop resides in Kingstown, Saint Vincent.

Other Christian Churches

The Presbyterian, Methodist, Plymouth Brethren, Baptist, Salvation Army, Jehovah's Witness, Pentecostal and Seventh-day Adventist faiths are also represented.

The Press

NEWSPAPERS

Barnacle: Mt Parnassus, St George's 3530; tel. 435-0981; e-mail barnacle@spiceisle.com; internet www.barnaclegrenada.com; f. 1991; business journal; every 2 weeks; Editor IAN GEORGE.

The Grenada Informer: Market Hill, POB 622, St George's; tel. 440-1530; fax 440-4119; e-mail grenada.informer@yahoo.com; internet www.thegrenadainformer.com; f. 1985; weekly.

The Grenadian Voice: Frequente Industrial Park, Bldg 1B, Maurice Bishop Hwy, POB 633, St George's; tel. 440-1498; fax 440-4117; e-mail gvoice@spiceisle.com; weekly; Man. Editor LESLIE PIERRE; circ. 3,000.

The New Today: POB 1970, St George's; tel. 435-9363; e-mail newtoday@spiceisle.com; internet thenewtoday.gd.

PRESS ASSOCIATION

Media Workers Association of Grenada: Bruce St, POB 1995, St George's; e-mail secretary@mwaggrenada.org; Pres. SHERE-ANN NOEL.

Publishers

Anansi Publications: Woodlands, St George's; tel. 440-0800; e-mail aclouden@spiceisle.com; f. 1986; Man. Dir ALVIN CLOUDEN.

Caribbean Publishing Co: Suite 5, Le Marquis Complex, POB 1744, Grand Anse, St George's; tel. 439-5000; fax 439-5003; e-mail vcharlemagne@globaldirectories.com; internet www.grenadayp .com; print and online directories.

St George's University Publications: Office of University Publications, University Centre, St George's; tel. 444-4175; fax 444-1770; e-mail mlambert@sgu.edu; internet www.sgu.edu/ university-communications; f. 2007; Dir MARGARET LAMBERT.

Broadcasting and Communications

TELECOMMUNICATIONS

Digicel Grenada Ltd: Point Salines, POB 1690, St George's; e-mail grenadacustomercare@digicelgroup.com; internet www .digicelgrenada.com; tel. 439-4463; fax 439-4464; f. 2003; owned by an Irish consortium; Chair. DENIS O'BRIEN; Man. (Grenada) PATRICIA MAHER.

Grenada Postal Corporation (GPC): Burns Point, St George's; tel. 440-2526; fax 440-4271; e-mail grenadapost@grenadapost.net; internet www.grenadapost.net; Chair. ADRIAN FRANCIS; Dir of Post LEO ROBERTS.

LIME: POB 119, The Carenage, St George's; tel. 440-1000; fax 440-4134; internet www.lime.com; f. 1989; fmrly Cable & Wireless Grenada Ltd; name adopted as above 2008; until 1998 known as Grenada Telecommunications Ltd (Grentel); 30% govt-owned; fixed lines, mobile telecommunications and internet services provider; CEO (Caribbean) MARTIN JOOS (acting).

Regulatory Authorities

Eastern Caribbean Telecommunications Authority: Vide Boutielle, Castries, POB 1886, Saint Lucia; tel. 458-1701; fax 458-1698; e-mail ectel@ectel.int; internet www.ectel.int; f. 2000 to regulate telecommunications in Grenada, Dominica, Saint Christopher and Nevis, Saint Lucia and Saint Vincent and the Grenadines.

National Telecommunications Regulatory Commission (NTRC): Maurice Bishop Highway, Grand Anse Shopping Centre, POB 854, St George's; tel. 435-6872; fax 435-2132; e-mail gntrc@ectel .int; internet www.ntrc.gd; Chair. Dr SPENCER THOMAS; Co-ordinator ALDWYN FERGUSON.

BROADCASTING

Radio

City Sound FM: River Rd, St George's; tel. 440-9616; e-mail citysound97i5@yahoo.com; internet www.citysoundfm.com; f. 1996.

Grenada Broadcasting Network (Radio): see Television.

HOTT FM: Observatory Rd, POB 535, St George's; tel. 444-5521; fax 440-4180; e-mail gbn@spiceisle.com; internet www.klassicgrenada .com; f. 1999 as Sun FM, present name adopted 2007; contemporary music.

Klassic AM: Observatory Rd, POB 535, St George's; tel. 444-5521; fax 440-4180; e-mail gbn@spiceisle.com; internet www .klassicgrenada.com.

Harbour Light of the Windwards: 400 Harbour Light Way, Tarleton Point, Carriacou; tel. and fax 443-7628; e-mail harbourlight@spiceisle.com; internet www.harbourlightradio.org; f. 1991; owned by Aviation Radio Missionary Services; Christian radio station; Man. Dir Dr RANDY CORNELIUS.

KYAK 106 FM: Church St, Hillsborough, Carriacou; tel. 443-6262; e-mail info@kyak106.com; internet www.kyak106.com; f. 1996; Office Man. DOREEN STANISLAUS.

Sister Isle Radio: Fort Hill, Hillsborough, Carriacou; tel. 443-8141; fax 443-8142; e-mail sisterisle@gmail.com; internet www .sisterisleradio.com; f. 2005.

Spice Capital Radio FM 90: Springs, St George's; tel. 440-3601.

WeeFM: Cross St, POB 555, St George's; tel. 440-4933; e-mail weefmradio@hotmail.com; internet www.weefmgrenada.com.

Television

Television programmes from Trinidad and Tobago and Barbados can be received on the island.

Grenada Broadcasting Network (GBN): Observatory Rd, POB 535, St George's; tel. 444-5521; fax 440-4180; e-mail gbn@spiceisle.com; internet www.klassicgrenada.com; f. 1972; 60% owned by One Caribbean Media Ltd, 40% govt-owned; 2 radio stations and 1 television station, GBN TV; Chair. CRAIG REYNALD; CEO VICTOR FERNANDES.

Finance

(cap. = capital; res = reserves; dep. = deposits; brs = branches; amounts in Eastern Caribbean dollars)

The Eastern Caribbean Central Bank, based in Saint Christopher and Nevis, is the central issuing and monetary authority for Grenada.

Eastern Caribbean Central Bank—Grenada Office: Monckton St, St George's; tel. 440-3016; fax 440-6721; e-mail eccbgnd@spiceisle.com; Country Dir LINDA FELIX-BERKLEY.

BANKING

Commercial Banks

FirstCaribbean International Bank (Barbados) Ltd: Church St, POB 37, St George's; tel. 440-3232; fax 440-4103; internet www.firstcaribbeanbank.com; f. 2002; adopted present name in 2002 following merger of Caribbean operations of CIBC and Barclays Bank PLC; Barclays relinquished its stake in 2006; Chair. MICHAEL MANSOOR; CEO RIK PARKHILL; 4 brs.

Grenada Co-operative Bank Ltd: 8 Church St, POB 135, St George's; tel. 440-2111; fax 440-6600; e-mail co-opbank@caribsurf.com; internet www.grenadaco-opbank.com; f. 1932; cap. 24.8m., res 11.2m., dep. 512.2m. (Sept. 2011); Chair. DERICK STEELE; Man. Dir and Sec. RICHARD W. DUNCAN; brs in St Andrew's, St George's, St Patrick's and Hillsborough.

Grenada Development Bank: Melville St, POB 2300, St George's; tel. 440-2382; fax 440-6610; e-mail gdbbank@spiceisle.com; internet www.grenadadevelopmentbank.com; f. 1965; govt-owned; Chair. MICHAEL ARCHIBALD.

RBTT Bank Grenada Ltd: Cnr of Cross and Halifax Sts, POB 4, St George's; tel. 440-3521; fax 440-4153; e-mail RBTTLTD@caribsurf.com; internet www.rbtt.com; f. 1983 as Grenada Bank of Commerce; name changed as above 2002; 10% govt-owned; national insurance scheme 15%; public 13%; RBTT Bank Caribbean Ltd, Castries 62%; cap. 11.0m., res 5.3m., dep. 487.8m. (Oct. 2010); Country Man. CHAMPA RAMPERSAD-BARNES; Regional CEO SURESH SOOKOO.

Republic Bank (Grenada) Ltd: Republic House, Maurice Bishop Hwy, Grand Anse, POB 857, St George's; tel. 444-2265; fax 444-5500; e-mail republichouse@republicgrenada.com; internet www.republicgrenada.com; f. 1979; fmrly National Commercial Bank of Grenada; name changed as above in 2006; 51% owned by Republic Bank Ltd, Port of Spain, Trinidad and Tobago; cap. 15.0m., res 18.3m., dep. 601.3m. (Sept. 2011); Chair. RONALD HARFORD; Man. Dir KEITH A. JOHNSON; 8 brs.

Scotiabank Grenada (Canada): Granby and Halifax Sts,POB 194, St George's; tel. 440-3274; fax 440-4173; e-mail bns.grenada@scotiabank.com; internet www.scotiabank.com/gd/en; f. 1963; Country Man. ELIE BENDALY; 3 brs.

REGULATORY AUTHORITY

Grenada Authority for the Regulation of Financial Institutions (GARFIN): POB 3973, Queens Park, St George's; tel. 440-6575; fax 440-4780; e-mail angus.smith@garfin.org; internet www.garfingrenada.org; f. 1999 as Grenada International Financial Services Authority; name changed to above in 2007; regulates non-banking financial sector; Chair. TIMOTHY ANTOINE; Exec. Dir ANGUS SMITH.

STOCK EXCHANGE

Eastern Caribbean Securities Exchange: Bird Rock, Basseterre, Saint Christopher and Nevis; tel. (869) 466-7192; fax (869) 465-3798; e-mail info@ECSEonline.com; internet www.ecseonline.com; f. 2001; regional securities market designed to facilitate the buying and selling of financial products for the 8 mem. territories—Anguilla, Antigua and Barbuda, Dominica, Grenada, Montserrat, Saint Christopher and Nevis, Saint Lucia, and Saint Vincent and the Grenadines; Chair. Sir K. DWIGHT VENNER; Gen. Man. TREVOR E. BLAKE.

INSURANCE

Several foreign insurance companies operate in Grenada and the other islands of the group. Principal locally owned companies include the following:

Gittens Insurance Brokerage Co Ltd: Benoit Bldg, Grand Anse, POB 1695, St George's; tel. 439-4408; fax 439-4462; internet www.cisgrenada.com/gittensinsurance; f. 2003; Chair. PHILLIP MCLAWRENCE GITTENS; CEO PHILLIP ARTHUR GITTENS.

Grenada Motor and General Insurance Co Ltd: Scott St, POB 152, St George's; tel. 440-3379; fax 440-7977; e-mail g500z@hotmail.com; Gen. Man. GABRIEL OLOUYNE.

Grenadian General Insurance Co Ltd: Cnr of Young and Scott Sts, POB 47, St George's; tel. 440-2434; fax 440-6618; e-mail ggicoltd@spiceisle.com; internet www.grenadiangeneralinsurance.com; Dir KEITH RENWICK.

Trade and Industry

CHAMBER OF COMMERCE

Grenada Chamber of Industry and Commerce, Inc (GCIC): Bldg 11, POB 129, Frequente, St George's; tel. 440-2937; fax 440-6627; e-mail gcic@grenadachamber.org; internet www.grenadachamber.org; f. 1921, incd 1947; 170 mems; Pres. AINE BRATHWAITE; Exec. Dir HAZELANN HUTCHINSON.

INDUSTRIAL AND TRADE ASSOCIATIONS

Grenada Cocoa Association (GCA): Kirani James Blvd, POB 3649, St George's; tel. 440-2234; fax 440-1470; e-mail gca@spiceisle.com; f. 1964; Chair. RAMSEY RUSH; Man. ANDREW HASTICK.

Grenada Co-operative Nutmeg Association (GCNA): Lagoon Rd, POB 160, St George's; tel. 440-2117; fax 440-6602; e-mail gcna.nutmeg@caribsurf.com; f. 1947; processes and markets all the nutmeg and mace grown on the island; includes the production of nutmeg oil; Chair. DENIS FELIX; Gen. Man. MARLON CLYNE.

Grenada Industrial Development Corporation (GIDC): Frequenté Industrial Park, Grand Anse, St George's; tel. 444-1035; fax 444-4828; e-mail invest@grenadaidc.com; internet www.grenadaidc.com; f. 1985; Chair. R. ANTHONY JOSEPH; Gen. Man. SONIA RODEN.

Marketing and National Importing Board (MNIB): Young St, POB 652, St George's; tel. 440-1791; fax 440-4152; e-mail mnib@spiceisle.com; internet www.mnib.gd; f. 1974; govt-owned; imports basic food items, incl. sugar, rice and milk; also exports fresh produce; Chair. CLAUDIA ALEXIS; Gen. Man. FITZROY JAMES.

EMPLOYERS' ORGANIZATION

Grenada Employers' Federation: Bldg 11, Frequenté Industrial Park, Grand Anse, POB 129, St George's; tel. 440-1832; fax 440-6627; e-mail gef@spiceisle.com; internet www.grenadaemployers.com; f. 1962; Pres. MICHAEL PHILBERT; Exec. Dir CECIL EDWARDS; 60 mems.

UTILITIES

Electricity

Grenada Electricity Services Ltd (Grenlec): Halifax St, POB 381, St George's; tel. 440-2097; fax 440-4106; e-mail customersupport@grenlec.com; internet www.grenlec.com; f. 1960; generation and distribution; majority privately owned (61% by WRB Enterprises, USA), 10% govt-owned; Chair. G. ROBERT BLANCHARD, Jr; Man. Dir and CEO VERNON LAWRENCE.

Water

National Water and Sewerage Authority (NAWASA): The Carenage, POB 392, St George's; tel. 440-2155; fax 440-4107; f. 1969; Chair. TERRENCE SMITH; Gen. Man. CHRISTOPHER HUSBANDS.

TRADE UNION

Grenada Trade Union Council (GTUC): Green St, POB 411, St George's; tel. and fax 440-3733; e-mail gtuc@caribsurf.com; Pres. MADONNA HARFORD; Gen. Sec. RAY ROBERTS; 8,000 mems (2011).

Transport

RAILWAYS

There are no railways in Grenada.

ROADS

There were approximately 1,127 km (700 miles) of roads, of which 61% were paved. Following the completion of the first phase of the Agricultural Feeder Roads Project, funded by the OPEC Fund for International Development, work on the second phase of the project, at a cost of EC $45.4m., began in May 2013. Funding for the second phase was provided by the Kuwait Fund for Arab Economic Development.

SHIPPING

The main port is St George's, with accommodation for two ocean-going vessels of up to 500 ft. A number of shipping lines call at St George's. The Melville Street Cruise Terminal became operational in 2004. Grenville, on Grenada, and Hillsborough, on Carriacou, are used mostly by small craft. An ambitious EC $1,600m. development at Port Louis, to include a 350-slipway marina with yachting facilities, was completed in 2009. In December 2013 Grenada's flag registered fleet comprised eight vessels, with an aggregate displacement of some 1,762 grt.

Grenada Ports Authority: POB 494, The Pier, St George's; tel. 440-7678; fax 440-3418; e-mail grenport@caribsurf.com; internet www.grenadaports.com; f. 1981; state-owned; Chair. NIGEL JOHN; Gen. Man. AMBROSE PHILLIP.

CIVIL AVIATION

Maurice Bishop International Airport (formerly Point Salines International Airport) is 10 km (6 miles) from St George's and has scheduled flights to most Eastern Caribbean destinations, including Venezuela, and to the United Kingdom and North America. There is an airfield at Pearls, 30 km (18 miles) from St George's, and Lauriston Airport, on the island of Carriacou, offers regular scheduled services to Grenada, Saint Vincent and Palm Island (Grenadines).

Grenada is a shareholder in the regional airline LIAT (see chapter on Antigua and Barbuda).

Grenada Airports Authority: Maurice Bishop Int. Airport, POB 385, St George's; tel. 444-4101; fax 444-4838; e-mail gaa@mbiagrenada.com; e-mail www.mbiagrenada.com; f. 1985; Chair. RODNEY GEORGE.

Tourism

Grenada has the attractions of white sandy beaches and a scenic, mountainous interior with an extensive rainforest. There are also sites of historical interest, and the capital, St George's, is a noted beauty spot. In 2012 there were 112,335 stop-over arrivals and 242,757 cruise ship passengers. In that year tourism earned EC $328.3m.

Grenada Hotel and Tourism Association Ltd: Ocean House Bldg, Morne Rouge Rd, Grand Anse, POB 440, St George's; tel. 444-1353; fax 444-4847; e-mail mail@ghta.org; internet www.ghta.org; f. 1961; Pres. IAN FIELDEN DA BREO; Exec. Dir PANCY CHANDLER CROSS.

Grenada Tourism Authority: Burns Point, POB 293, St George's; tel. 440-2279; fax 440-6637; e-mail gbt@spiceisle.com; internet www.grenadagrenadines.com; f. 1991 as Grenada Board of Tourism; upgraded to an authority in 2013; Chair. RICHARD STRACHAN.

Defence

A regional security unit was formed in 1983, modelled on the British police force and trained by British officers. A paramilitary element, known as the Special Service Unit and trained by US advisers, acts as the defence contingent and participates in the Regional Security System, a defence pact with other Eastern Caribbean states.

Commissioner of Police: WINSTON JAMES (acting).

Education

Education is free and compulsory for children between the ages of five and 16 years. Primary education begins at five years of age and lasts for seven years. Secondary education, beginning at the age of 12, lasts for a further five years. In 2009 enrolment at primary schools included 87% of children in the relevant age-group. In 2009/10 some 13,663 pupils attended primary school while 11,500 students attended secondary school. Enrolment at all secondary schools included 91% of pupils in the relevant age-group in 2008/09. In 2006 there were 2,710 full-time enrolled students at the T. A. Marryshow Community College. The Extra-Mural Department of the University of the West Indies has a branch in St George's and there is also St George's University, which had 5,880 students in 2012. The combined capital expenditure on education and human resources development was budgeted at EC $109.6m. in 2012 (equivalent to 10.7% of total capital expenditure).

GUATEMALA

Introductory Survey

LOCATION, CLIMATE, LANGUAGE, RELIGION, FLAG, CAPITAL

The Republic of Guatemala lies in the Central American isthmus, bounded to the north and west by Mexico, with Honduras and Belize to the east and El Salvador to the south. It has a long coastline on the Pacific Ocean and a narrow outlet to the Caribbean Sea. The climate is tropical in the lowlands, with an average temperature of 28°C (83°F), and more temperate in the central highland area, with an average temperature of 20°C (68°F). The official language is Spanish, but more than 20 indigenous languages are also spoken. Almost all of the inhabitants profess Christianity: the majority are Roman Catholics, while an estimated 40% are Protestants. A large proportion of the population also follows traditional Mayan beliefs. The national flag (proportions 5 by 8) has three equal vertical stripes, of blue, white and blue, with the national coat of arms (depicting a quetzal, the 'bird of freedom', and a scroll, superimposed on crossed rifles and sabres, encircled by a wreath) in the centre of the white stripe. The capital is Guatemala City.

CONTEMPORARY POLITICAL HISTORY

Historical Context

Under Spanish colonial rule, Guatemala was part of the Viceroyalty of New Spain. Independence was obtained from Spain in 1821, from Mexico in 1824 and from the Federation of Central American States in 1838. Subsequent attempts to revive the Federation failed and, under a series of dictators, there was relative stability, tempered by periods of disruption. A programme of social reform was begun by Juan José Arévalo (President in 1944–50) and his successor, Col Jacobo Arbenz Guzmán. In 1954 Arbenz was overthrown in a coup led by Col Carlos Castillo Armas, who invaded the country with US assistance. Castillo became President but was assassinated in 1957. The next elected President, Gen. Miguel Ydigoras Fuentes, took office in 1958 and ruled until he was deposed in 1963 by a military coup, led by Col Enrique Peralta Azurdia. He suspended the Constitution and dissolved the legislature. A Constituent Assembly introduced a new Constitution in 1965. Dr Julio César Méndez Montenegro was elected President in 1966, and in 1970 the candidate of the Movimiento de Liberación Nacional (MLN), Col (later Gen.) Carlos Araña Osorio, was elected President. Despite charges of fraud in the elections of 1974, Gen. Kjell Laugerud García of the MLN took office as President.

President Laugerud sought to discourage extreme right-wing violence and claimed some success, although it was estimated that 50,000–60,000 people were killed in political violence between 1970 and 1979. In 1978 Gen. Fernando Romeo Lucas García was elected President. The guerrilla movement increased in strength in 1980–81, while the Government was accused of the murder and torture of civilians and, particularly, persecution of the country's indigenous Indian inhabitants, who comprised 60% of the population.

Domestic Political Affairs

In the presidential election of March 1982, from which the left-wing parties were absent, the Government's candidate, Gen. Angel Aníbal Guevara, was declared the winner; however, the election was denounced as fraudulent. A coup followed on 23 March, in which Gen. José Efraín Ríos Montt was installed as leader of a three-man junta. The Congreso Nacional (National Congress) was closed, and the Constitution and political parties suspended. In June Gen. Ríos Montt dissolved the junta and assumed the presidency. He attempted to fight corruption, reorganized the judicial system and disbanded the secret police. The number of violent deaths diminished. However, after initially gaining the support of the national university, the Roman Catholic Church and the labour unions, Ríos Montt declared a state of siege and imposed censorship of the press. The war against the guerrillas intensified, and a civil defence force of Indians was established. Villages were burned, and many inhabitants killed, in order to deter the Indians from supporting the guerrillas. Ríos Montt's fragile hold on power was threatened in 1982 by several attempted coups, which he managed to forestall.

In January 1983 the US Government announced the resumption of arms sales to Guatemala, suspended since 1977 as a result of human rights violations. However, independent reports claimed that the human rights situation had deteriorated, and revealed that 2,600 people had been killed during the first six months of Ríos Montt's rule. In March the army was implicated in the massacre of 300 Indian peasants at Nahulá, and there was a resurgence in the activity of both left- and right-wing 'death squads'. The President declared a 30-day amnesty for guerrillas and political exiles, and lifted the state of siege. The Government's 'guns and beans' policy provided food and medicine in exchange for recruitment to the Patrullas de Autodefensa Civil (PAC), a pro-Government peasant militia.

By mid-1983 opposition to the President was widespread. In August Gen. Oscar Humberto Mejía Victores, the Minister of Defence, led a successful coup against Ríos Montt. Mejía ended press censorship and announced an amnesty for guerrillas. Urban and rural terrorism continued to escalate, however. Following the murder in northern Guatemala of six US aid workers, the USA suspended US $50m. in aid in 1984. Elections for a Constituent Assembly were held in July, at which the centre groups, including the newly formed Unión del Centro Nacional (UCN), obtained the greatest number of votes. Under the system of proportional representation, however, the right-wing coalition of the MLN and the Central Auténtica Nacionalista obtained a majority of seats in the Assembly.

Guatemala's new Constitution was promulgated in 1985. The main contest in the November presidential election was between Jorge Carpio Nicolle of the UCN and Mario Vinicio Cerezo Arévalo of the Partido Democracia Cristiana Guatemalteca (PDCG). As neither candidate obtained the requisite majority, a second round of voting was held in December, which Cerezo won. The PDCG won the majority of seats in the concurrent election to the new Congress. The US Administration increased economic aid and resumed military aid to Guatemala, in support of the new civilian Government.

Immediately prior to the transfer of power in January 1986, the outgoing military Government decreed a general amnesty for those suspected of involvement in abuses of human rights since 1982. A government commission to investigate 'disappearances' was created in 1987. In August a peace plan for the region was signed in Guatemala City by the Presidents of Costa Rica, El Salvador, Guatemala, Honduras and Nicaragua. Subsequently, a Commission of National Reconciliation (CNR) was formed. In October representatives of the Guatemalan Government and the main guerrilla grouping, the Unidad Revolucionaria Nacional Guatemalteca (URNG), met in Spain, but the peace negotiations ended without agreement. Right-wing pressure on the Government, and an attempted coup in May 1988, forced Cerezo to postpone further negotiations with the URNG. By this time there were also frequent reports of torture and killings by right-wing 'death squads' as discontent with the Government's liberal policies increased.

Guerrilla activity intensified in 1989. Many political figures and labour leaders fled the country after receiving death threats from paramilitary groups. Meanwhile, Cerezo refused to negotiate with the URNG while its members remained armed. In September the URNG made further proposals for negotiations, following the signing of the Tela Agreement (the Central American peace plan accord), but these were rejected. Despite Cerezo's promise to restrict the unlawful activities of the armed forces and right-wing 'death squads', the number of politically motivated assassinations and 'disappearances' escalated in 1990. Following discussions with the CNR, the URNG pledged not to disrupt the upcoming elections and agreed to participate in a constituent assembly to reform the Constitution.

None of the nominees obtained an absolute majority in the first round of the presidential election of November 1990. A second ballot in January 1991 between the two leading candidates was won by Jorge Serrano Elías of the Movimiento de Acción Solidaria (MAS). The MAS failed to secure a majority in the legislative election, however, and Serrano invited the Partido de Avanzada Nacional (PAN) and the Partido Socialista Democrático (PSD) to participate in a coalition Government.

In April 1991 direct talks between the URNG and the Government began in Mexico City. However, in an attempt to destabilize efforts at national reconciliation, some members of the state security forces launched a campaign of violence, directing death threats against leaders of trade unions and human rights organizations, and murdering a PSD politician. In late 1991 the ombudsman, Ramiro de León Carpio, secured the resignation of the Director of the National Police, Col Mario Enrique Paíz Bolanos, who was alleged to be responsible for the use of torture.

Further negotiations in Mexico City in 1992 led to concessions by the Government, which agreed to curb the expansion of the PAC. The URNG, which maintained that *campesinos* (peasants) were forcibly enlisted into the PAC, included in its conditions for a peace agreement the immediate dissolution of the patrols. In November the Government accepted renewed proposals by the URNG for the establishment of a commission on past human rights violations, but only if the rebels signed a definitive peace accord. Talks were suspended in May 1993. The URNG announced a unilateral ceasefire as a gesture of goodwill to the incoming President, Ramiro de León Carpio, in June (see below). In August, in a concession to the URNG, de León announced the reform of the Estado Mayor Presidencial, a military body accused of human rights offences. Preliminary talks were finally resumed in Mexico in January 1994.

Constitutional coup of 1993

Unrest at economic austerity measures escalated in May 1993. With the MAS no longer able to effect a constructive alliance in the Congress, on 25 May Serrano, with the support of the military, suspended parts of the Constitution and dissolved the Congress and the Supreme Court. A ban was imposed on the media and Serrano announced that he would rule by decree pending the drafting of a new constitution by a constituent assembly, to be elected within 60 days. The constitutional coup provoked almost unanimous international condemnation, with the USA immediately suspending aid. The military reappraised its position and forced the resignation of Serrano. The Minister of National Defence, Gen. José Domingo García Samayoa, assumed control of the country pending an election. The entire Cabinet, excluding García and the Minister of the Interior, Francisco Perdomo Sandoval, resigned on 3 June. Two days later the Congress reconvened to conduct a presidential ballot. The Instancia Nacional de Consenso (INC), a broad coalition of political parties, business leaders and trade unions, elected Ramiro de León Carpio, the former human rights ombudsman, as President. The USA subsequently restored its aid programme to the country.

In August 1993, as an initial measure in a campaign to eradicate corruption from state institutions, de León requested the voluntary resignation of the Congress and the Supreme Court. The request caused a serious division in the legislature, which separated into two main factions, the Gran Grupo Parlamentario (GGP), which included some 70 members of the MAS, UCN, PAN and the Frente Republicano Guatemalteco (FRG) and supported the dismissal of 16 deputies identified by the INC as corrupt, and a group of 38 deputies, including members of the PDCG and independents, who supported the resignation of all 116 deputies. In September the GGP defied a suspension of a legislative session and elected a new congressional President. The GGP also threatened to boycott any further sessions convened by the previous speaker, Fernando Lobo Dubón (a PDCG member). In November a compromise was reached between the Government and the legislature, involving a series of constitutional reforms. These were subsequently approved by a referendum, although less than 20% of the electorate participated, reflecting popular concern that more extensive reforms were necessary. The reforms took effect in April 1994, and fresh legislative elections were to be held in August. The new Congress, which was to serve until 14 January 1996, was to appoint the members of a new, enlarged Supreme Court of Justice. Other reforms included a reduction in the terms of office of the President, legislature and municipal authorities, and of the Supreme Court justices, and a reduction in the number of congressional seats.

In March 1994 the Government and the URNG agreed a timetable of formal negotiations aimed at achieving a definitive peace agreement by the end of the year. In addition, a general human rights agreement was signed, providing guarantees, including a government commitment to eliminate illegal security corps, strengthen national human rights institutions and cease obligatory military recruitment. Agreement was also reached on the establishment of a UN deputation, the Human Rights Verification Mission in Guatemala (MINUGUA), to verify the implementation of the accord. Further talks resulted in the signing, in June, of agreements on the resettlement of people displaced by the civil war (estimated to number some 1m.), and on the establishment of a Comisión para el Esclarecimiento Histórico (CEH—Commission for Historical Clarification) to investigate human rights violations committed during the 33-year conflict.

In August 1994 the URNG withdrew from the peace negotiations and accused the Government of failing to observe the agreed human rights provisions. Talks remained deadlocked until February 1995, when a new timetable for negotiations, achieved with UN mediation, was announced. The issue of the identity and rights of indigenous peoples was finally resolved, but talks continued beyond the agreed deadline without agreement on other substantive issues, including socio-economic reform and the incorporation of URNG guerrillas into civilian life.

At the legislative election of August 1994 only some 20% of the electorate exercised their vote. Despite winning the greatest number of seats in the 80-seat legislature, the FRG, led by Gen. (retd) José Efraín Ríos Montt, was excluded from the 12-member congressional directorate by an alliance of the PAN, PDCG, MLN and Unión Democrática. However, in December the PDCG transferred its allegiance to the FRG and Ríos Montt was subsequently elected President of the Congress. His inauguration in January 1995 provoked demonstrations by human rights organizations, which considered him responsible for the deaths of as many as 15,000 civilians as a result of counter-insurgency operations conducted during his period as de facto ruler in 1982–83.

The presidential and legislative elections of November 1995 were notable for the return to the electoral process, for the first time for more than 40 years, of the left wing, represented by the Frente Democrático Nueva Guatemala (FDNG). In addition, the URNG declared a unilateral ceasefire to coincide with the electoral campaign and urged people to vote. The two leading presidential candidates, Alvaro Enrique Arzú Irigoyen of the PAN and Alfonso Antonio Portillo Cabrera of the FRG, contested a second round of voting in January 1996, at which Arzú secured a narrow victory. The PAN also secured a majority of seats in the Congress.

The new President implemented a comprehensive reorganization of the military high command, replacing those officers who were not in favour of a negotiated peace settlement. In March 1996 the Congress ratified the International Labour Organization's Convention on the rights of indigenous peoples. However, the document was amended by the Congress, prompting protests by Indian organizations. On 20 March the URNG announced an indefinite unilateral ceasefire. Arzú immediately ordered the armed forces to suspend counter-insurgency operations. In May the Government and the URNG signed an agreement on agrarian and socio-economic reforms. In the following month the Congress adopted legislation that made members of the armed forces accountable to civilian courts for all but strictly military crimes. In September the Government and the URNG signed an agreement on the strengthening of civilian power and the role of the armed forces. Under the terms of the accord, all military and intelligence services were to be placed under the authority of the Government. The police force was to be reorganized, with the creation of a new national civilian force (Policía Nacional Civil—PNC). Also confirmed in the accord was the abolition of the PAC. A general amnesty law was approved by the Congress in December.

1996 peace treaty

On 29 December 1996 the Government and the URNG signed the definitive peace treaty in Guatemala City, bringing to an end some 36 years of civil war, during which an estimated 140,000 people had died. The demobilization of URNG guerrillas, estimated to number some 3,250, was supervised by MINUGUA and completed in May 1997. In the following month the URNG registered as a political party.

In April 1998 the auxiliary bishop of the metropolitan diocese of Guatemala City, Juan José Gerardi Conedera, was murdered. Gerardi had been a founder of the Roman Catholic Church's Oficina de Derechos Humanos del Arzobispado (ODHA—Archbishopric's Human Rights Office), and a prominent critic of the armed forces. Days before his death Gerardi had presented a report by the ODHA documenting human rights abuses during the civil conflict, of which army personnel were found responsible for some 80%. In what the Church and human rights groups interpreted as an attempt to conceal the truth, a priest, Mario Orantes Nájera, was formally charged with Gerardi's murder in October. In February 1999 the presiding judge ordered the release of Orantes on grounds of insufficient evidence; the judge withdrew from the case in the following month after allegedly receiving death threats. In 2001 former intelligence chief Col (retd) Disrael Lima Estrada, his son, Capt. Byron Lima Oliva, and a former member of the presidential guard, José Obdulio Villanueva, were convicted of Gerardi's murder; Orantes was convicted of conspiring in his death. However, in 2002 a Court of Appeal overturned the convictions and ordered a retrial. At the retrial in 2003 the sentences were upheld by the Supreme Court. Nevertheless, in 2005 a Court of Appeal amended the convictions of Lima Estrada and Lima Oliva to accessory to murder, reducing their sentences from 30 years' to 20 years' imprisonment, and in July 2012 Lima Oliva was released.

In August 1999, in what was widely regarded as a test case for the judicial system, 25 members of the armed forces convicted of the massacre in 1995 of 11 civilians in Xamán, Alta Verapaz, received minimum sentences of five years' imprisonment. The case was the first in which military personnel accused of killing civilians had been tried by a civilian court, and the decision, which provoked public outrage, greatly undermined confidence in the courts' ability to administer justice in the remaining 625 cases of massacres attributed to the security forces. A December 1999 MINUGUA report stated that commitments made by the Arzú administration under the 1996 peace treaty to reduce the influence of the military remained unfulfilled. In the following year MINUGUA asserted that the number of extrajudicial executions had doubled between 1996 and 2000.

In February 1999 the CEH published its final report, in which it attributed more than 93% of human rights violations committed during the civil conflict to the armed forces and state paramilitaries. It announced that 200,000 people had been killed or had 'disappeared' between 1962 and 1996, the majority of them Mayan Indians. It also concluded that the USA had financed and trained Guatemalan forces responsible for atrocities. The report recommended that compensation be provided for the families of victims, that prosecutions be brought against those suspected of crimes against humanity and that a purge of the armed forces be implemented. The Government described the Commission's findings as 'controversial', and did not express any intention of pursuing its recommendations.

In October 1998 the Congress approved constitutional reforms provided for in the 1996 peace accords. The reforms, which concerned the rights of indigenous peoples, the role of the armed forces and the police, and the strengthening of the courts, were subject to ratification in a referendum. However, at the plebiscite, in May 1999, 55.6% of participating voters rejected the constitutional amendments. The turnout was extremely low, at 18.6%, and observers attributed the result to a lack of information and to mistrust of the political establishment rather than to the rejection of the peace accords themselves. At presidential and legislative elections, conducted in November, voter participation, at some 40%, was greatly improved. The two leading presidential candidates, Alfonso Portillo of the FRG and Oscar Berger Perdomo of the PAN, contested a second round of voting on 26 December, in which Portillo secured victory. The FRG secured an outright majority in the election to the newly enlarged legislature.

The Portillo Government

The new administration of President Portillo, which took office in January 2000, immediately undertook the promised demilitarization of the upper echelons of government. However, disputes between the Government and the Congress resulted in virtual paralysis in policy-making. Furthermore, throughout 2001 the Government was beset by allegations of corruption. In March 2002 a congressional commission was formed to investigate claims that President Portillo and Vice-President Francisco Reyes López had established bank accounts in Panama for the purpose of money-laundering. The allegations provoked mass protests in Guatemala City. However, in June the investigation by the congressional commission collapsed, owing to a lack of evidence.

The US Government expressed its concern at levels of corruption, drugs-trafficking and continuing human rights abuses in Guatemala in 2002. In March the leader of the opposition Partido Patriótico, Jorge Rosal Zea, was assassinated. President Portillo subsequently announced a number of reforms to the security forces, including the dissolution of the Departamento de Operaciones Antinarcóticos (Department of Anti-Narcotics Operations) and the creation of a new unit, Unidades Móviles Operativas, to combat drugs-trafficking and terrorism. Nevertheless, in 2003 the USA added Guatemala to the list of nations it considered unco-operative in combating drugs-trafficking.

In May 2003 Óscar Berger Perdomo, hitherto the PAN's candidate in the forthcoming presidential election, announced that he would stand as the nominee of the Gran Alianza Nacional (GANA), a small, centre-right alliance comprising the Partido Patriota (PP), the Movimiento Reformador and the Partido Solidaridad Nacional. Ríos Montt was to be the FRG's nominee, but in July the Supreme Court barred his candidacy, prompting violent protests. At the end of the month the Constitutional Court overruled the supreme court decision and allowed Ríos Montt to register as a candidate.

Presidential and legislative elections of 2003

Presidential and legislative elections took place in November 2003. Berger and Alvaro Colom Caballeros of the Unidad Nacional de la Esperanza (UNE) contested a second round of voting in December, in which Berger narrowly secured the presidency. GANA won the largest number of seats in the expanded assembly, although it failed to secure a majority. In January 2004 GANA agreed a governability pact with the UNE and the PAN.

In February 2004 the Constitutional Court lifted the parliamentary immunity Ríos Montt had hitherto enjoyed. The following month he was charged with premeditated murder, coercion and threats in connection to the violence outside the Supreme Court in 2003 and placed under house arrest; the charges were dismissed in 2006. Also in February 2004, former President Portillo and former Vice-President Reyes similarly lost their immunity from prosecution. Shortly afterwards, Portillo left the country for Mexico. An injunction for his arrest on charges of money-laundering and misuse of public funds was requested and the US embassy revoked his visa. Reyes was arrested in July and charged with fraud, embezzlement and abuse of authority. However, in May 2007 the Constitutional Court ordered that the case against Portillo be abandoned. Nevertheless, in October 2008 Portillo surrendered himself to Mexican authorities to be extradited. On arrival in Guatemala, however, he was controversially released on bail. Portillo was arrested again in January 2010 after an extradition request by the USA (on money-laundering charges) was approved by a Guatemalan court. In August, however, Portillo was ordered to stand trial in Guatemala on the embezzlement charges. The trial of Portillo, together with his former Minister of National Defence, Eduardo Arévalo, and his former Minister of Public Finance, Manuel Maza, in 2011 resulted in all three men being exonerated, prompting criticism from CICIG (see below). (This judgment was upheld by a Court of Appeal in April 2013.) Nevertheless, in November 2011 Portillo's extradition to the USA was ratified by President Colom, and the former head of state was transferred to US custody in May 2013. In March 2014 Portillo admitted accepting US $2.5m. in bribes from Taiwan while in office; he was due to be sentenced in June.

Domestic security was one of the most pressing problems facing the Berger Government. Gang rivalry and vigilante groups were widely held to be responsible for the rising rates of murder and violent crime. In the first six months of 2004 the incidence of violent crime increased by 13%, prompting the resignation of the Minister of the Interior in July. Following the exposure of several senior police officers with links to criminal groups, in June Berger dismissed the head of the PNC. He also ordered the deployment of some 4,000 police and military officers in areas with particularly high crime rates. In spite of these initiatives, the murder rate increased by 25% in 2004.

Internal political conflicts and the defection of congressional deputies impeded the Berger Government's efforts to implement its legislative agenda. In an attempt to secure opposition support for proposed fiscal reforms, in May 2004 President Berger met with Ríos Montt. However, the meeting prompted the withdrawal of the UNE and the PAN from the governability pact and the PP left GANA in protest. In late 2004 a MINUGUA report noted that government efforts to reform the criminal justice system had been largely ineffective. Upon its withdrawal from Guatemala in December, MINUGUA reported that the Government still had to overcome three major challenges: public security; judicial reform; and discrimination against indigenous peoples. Following legislative approval, an office of the UN's

High Commission for Human Rights was opened in Guatemala in 2005.

Political tensions escalated into violence in early 2006. A number of political activists were assassinated, including a UNE deputy and the co-ordinator of the nascent political party Encuentro por Guatemala, Eleaza Tebalan. The lynching of four people in two separate attacks in April prompted the mobilization of 11,000 members of the armed forces to assist the police in maintaining order. In February 2007 the creation of an auxiliary police unit, composed of former members of the armed forces, to be deployed in areas experiencing the highest rates of violent crime, was announced. In the same month three Salvadorean deputies were found murdered on the outskirts of Guatemala City. Three days later four Guatemalan police officers who had confessed to the murders were arrested; however, they too were later killed. Following the incident 22 prison employees were arrested on suspicion of complicity in the crime. Notwithstanding the arrest of four further suspects in relation to the assassinations, a vote of no confidence in the Minister of the Interior, Carlos Vielmann, was approved by the Congress in March.

The crisis provoked by the assassinations facilitated, in August 2007, the overwhelming approval by the Congress of legislation to create the International Commission against Impunity in Guatemala (CICIG—Comisión Internacional contra la Impunidad en Guatemala). The independent body was to comprise a panel of international experts who would assist the Guatemalan authorities in the investigation and dismantling of paramilitary security forces and other criminal organizations linked to state institutions. CICIG officially began its operations in January 2008.

Presidential and legislative elections of 2007

Security issues dominated the campaign for the presidential and legislative elections held on 9 September 2007. The vote was preceded by the most violent electoral campaign since the end of the civil war, in which more than 40 people were killed. In the presidential ballot no candidate received enough votes for a first round victory. At a second round of voting on 4 November, the UNE's Colom defeated the PP candidate, Gen. (retd) Otto Fernando Pérez Molina, with 53% of the valid votes cast. In elections to the Congress the UNE increased its representation to 50 seats, becoming the largest party in the legislature. Colom was sworn in on 14 January 2008, becoming the first centre-left President since 1954.

Upon assuming office, Colom introduced the 'Plan Cuadrante', intended to reduce high crime rates. In February 2008 the Congress approved a PP proposal to restore the death penalty, suspended since 2002. The legislation, however, was vetoed by Colom. (Colom vetoed similar legislation in November 2010.) Investigations into the 2007 murders of the three Salvadorean deputies also progressed in 2008, with the arrest of two more suspects. In July a state prosecutor investigating the case was shot dead. The shooting took place the week after 13 gang members were acquitted of killing the police officers who had confessed to the murders.

Colom replaced the ministers responsible for the economy, the interior, health, and agriculture in mid-2008. The upheaval continued with the resignation of the Attorney-General, Juan Luis Florido, in August. Florido's departure was welcomed by CICIG, which had pressed for a change of personnel in the Attorney-General's office better to combat impunity. Furthermore, in the same month Eduardo Meyer Maldonado, the legislative speaker and a close ally of the President, was obliged to resign over his alleged involvement in the unauthorized transfer of congressional funds. (In 2010 Meyer was charged with embezzlement, dereliction of duty and failure to report a crime.)

Colom's electoral campaign included a pledge to improve internal security and reduce impunity. To this effect, in February 2008 the President announced that he planned gradually to decrease army participation in civilian security operations. In a decision welcomed by human rights activists, Colom also declared that previously unseen military archives would be released to the public. Reluctance from military personnel, however, led to delays in the files becoming available. (In June 2011 over 99% of the military's archives were finally declassified, although it had earlier been revealed that the documents covering 1980–85 had disappeared.) Nevertheless, in September 2008 the President announced plans to increase the size of the army to 25,000 to bolster the police force. Colom inaugurated a new security council, the Consejo Nacional de Seguridad, in November, to co-ordinate and supervise Guatemala's security institutions. In December Colom undertook further changes to the Guatemalan military with the dismissal of many important army officials and the replacement of the Minister of National Defence.

Efforts to improve security

CICIG's 2008 report conceded a lack of tangible progress in reducing crime and levels of impunity, largely owing to opposition from Guatemalan authorities. Colom replaced Francisco Jiménez Irungaray at the Ministry of the Interior with a more hard-line candidate, Salvador Gándara, in January 2009 and made renewed promises to improve security. In March the President announced the creation of an anti-impunity commission intended to complement CICIG's investigations, and in April he signed a national security and justice accord with the President of the Congress and the acting President of the Supreme Court. Notable provisions of the accord included the creation of a public security ministry and the extension of CICIG's mandate. Meanwhile, at the end of March the Congress approved long-awaited gun control legislation.

The President's efforts to reduce violent crime were overshadowed in May 2009 by allegations that he was involved in the killing of a prominent lawyer, Rodrigo Rosenberg Marzano, who, in a video recording made prior to his death, had claimed that Colom and other senior officials were plotting his murder. Colom requested that CICIG conduct an investigation into the allegations, which he vehemently denied, accusing his opponents of attempting to destabilize his Government. Thousands of people subsequently participated in protests in Guatemala City to demand Colom's resignation, while demonstrations in support of the President were also well attended. In January 2010 CICIG exonerated Colom, concluding that Rosenberg had orchestrated his own assassination. In July eight people were convicted in connection with Rosenberg's killing.

Meanwhile, CICIG continued to encounter resistance from officials while conducting its investigations. In June 2009 the commission filed a formal complaint against a judge who was seeking to terminate its involvement in the case against former President Portillo. The Congress approved a two-year extension of CICIG's mandate in July. With the violent murder rate continuing to rise, Gándara resigned as Minister of the Interior in the same month; he was succeeded by Raúl Antonio Velásquez Ramos. Gándara's decision to replace the leadership of the PNC with retired police officials in the previous month had been criticized by human rights groups. In August Velásquez dismissed the PNC officials appointed by Gándara for alleged involvement in drugs-trafficking. Following objections by CICIG to several of the Congress's nominees to the Supreme Court, as well as criticism from UN officials over a lack of transparency, in October the legislature revised the list of new judges. CICIG achieved a significant victory in January 2010, when it facilitated the arrest of Portillo (see above).

In the first such conviction since the end of the civil war, in August 2009 Felipe Cusanero Coj, a former member of the PAC, was found guilty of the forced 'disappearances' of six Mayan citizens in 1982–84 and sentenced to 150 years' imprisonment. In December a retired army officer, Marco Antonio Sánchez, received a 53-year prison sentence for the 'disappearances' of eight farm workers.

Three ministers were dismissed in February 2010: the Minister of Agriculture, Livestock and Food, Mario Aldana, owing to irregularities in the tendering process for the supply of fertilizers; the Minister of Education, Bienvenido Argueta, for failing to reveal information about the beneficiaries of Mi Familia Progresa, a social programme that some opposition members suspected had been used to reward government supporters; and Minister of the Interior Velásquez as a result of corruption allegations. Carlos Menocal, hitherto co-ordinator of the presidential anti-impunity commission, was appointed to replace Velásquez, becoming Colom's fifth Minister of the Interior. In March the PNC Director, Baltázar Gómez Barrios, the head of the PNC's counter-narcotics division, Nelly Bonilla, and the latter's deputy were arrested on suspicion of alleged collusion with drugs-traffickers. The resignation of Rubén Morales as Minister of the Economy in mid-June was followed later that month by those of the Minister of Energy and Mines, Carlos Meany, and the Minister of Public Finance, Juan Alberto Fuentes Knight. Fuentes cited disappointment with the Congress's repeated refusal to approve fiscal reforms aimed at increasing tax revenue. Fuentes' replacement, Edgar Balsells, was removed from the Government in November, owing to his failure to communicate with other ministers, although he reportedly claimed that he had been dismissed for seeking to reduce expenditure on social programmes overseen by Colom's wife, Sandra Torres de Colom. The Government's ability to pursue its legislative agenda had been severely hampered by the UNE's lack of a congressional majority, the party's position having been weakened further by the defection of a number of its deputies to Libertad Democrática Renovada (LIDER), a dissident legislative bloc created in 2009.

The director of CICIG, Carlos Castresana Fernández, resigned in June 2010, expressing frustration with the Government's failure to co-operate in the commission's efforts and urging Colom to dismiss the recently appointed Attorney-General, Conrado Reyes, who he alleged had strong links to organized crime. The Constitutional Court subsequently ruled that the selection process leading to the appointment of Reyes had been unconstitutional, resulting in his removal from the post. The naming of Claudia Paz y Paz Bailey, a lawyer and human rights activist, as Attorney-General in December was welcomed by civil society groups; she pledged to ensure effective co-ordination with CICIG. Also in that month, a further extension of CICIG's mandate, to 2013, was approved by the UN. (A further, final, extension of the mandate, to September 2015, was granted in 2013.)

President Colom declared a 30-day state of siege in the northern department of Alta Verapaz in December 2010, in response to reports that much of the department was under the control of a Mexican drugs cartel, Los Zetas. The state of siege, which suspended constitutional guarantees, allowing the army to detain suspects without warrants and curtail public gatherings, among other measures, was ended in February 2011. However, a further state of siege was enforced in Petén in May following the massacre of 27 people by Los Zetas members. (Nine members of the Los Zetas gang were sentenced to between 106 and 114 years' imprisonment for the murders in February 2014.) Also in May 2011 Brig.-Gen. Juan José Ruiz Morales was appointed as the new Minister of Defence.

The arrest in mid-2011 of several former high-ranking members of the security forces indicated that progress was being made in bringing to justice the alleged perpetrators of serious human rights violations during the civil conflict. Moreover, in an unprecedented ruling, four former soldiers were sentenced to life imprisonment in August after being found guilty of massacring over 200 villagers in 1982; a fifth suspect also received a life sentence in March 2012. Later in March four former PAC members and an ex-military officer were jailed for life for participating in a separate 1982 massacre, which claimed the lives of 256 indigenous Guatemalans. Meanwhile, a former high-ranking police official, Pedro García Arredondo, was handed a 70-year gaol term in August 2012 for orchestrating the 'disappearance' of a student in 1981.

Recent developments: Pérez Molina in office

Despite a constitutional provision barring those related to the incumbent President by blood or 'affinity' from contesting the presidency, in March 2011 Colom's wife, Sandra Torres de Colom, announced that she intended to compete in the upcoming election as the candidate of the UNE and GANA. Ostensibly to facilitate this objective, Torres and Colom divorced in the following month. However, the Supreme Electoral Tribunal regarded this move as a fraudulent attempt to bypass the Constitution and in June rejected Torres' candidacy. This ruling was endorsed by the Supreme Electoral Court and the Supreme Court in July and the Constitutional Court in August. With Torres' legal options exhausted and the registration deadline expired, the UNE-GANA coalition was unable to field a presidential candidate in the 11 September election.

The presidential and legislative polls took place peacefully, although the pre-election period had been marred by political violence. In the general election, the PP gained control of 56 seats in the 158-seat Congress, while the UNE-GANA (which terminated their alliance later that month) secured 48, LIDER and the Unión del Cambio Nacional 14 each, and Compromiso, Renovación y Orden 12; the remaining 14 seats were distributed among six smaller parties and coalitions. No candidate secured an outright victory in the presidential contest, so a second round of voting between the two leading contenders—the PP's Gen. (retd) Otto Fernando Pérez Molina and Manuel Antonio Baldizón Méndez of LIDER—was held 6 November. Pérez Molina triumphed in the run-off election, receiving 53.7% of the valid votes cast. The rate of participation by the electorate was recorded at 69.3% in the legislative poll and at 69.4% and 60.8% in the first and second rounds, respectively, of the presidential election.

Pérez Molina was sworn in as President on 14 January 2012, becoming the first head of state with a military background since the end of the civil conflict. His new Government was dominated by the PP, although the foreign affairs and agriculture portfolios were allocated to members of the Visión con Valores-Encuentro por Guatemala. A new Ministry of Social Development was also established, which was to focus on poverty reduction initiatives.

To address the country's crime problems, in January 2012 Pérez Molina announced plans for the further involvement of the military in police operations, in spite of the fact that this was in breach of the 1996 peace treaty. He also proposed recruiting an additional 10,000 police officers. Anti-crime measures introduced in mid-2012 included the establishment of a training facility for senior police officials to boost professionalism in the force, the creation of two additional military bases, and the temporary, but controversial, deployment of a contingent of US troops, who were to aid the Guatemalan authorities in combating drugs-smuggling. The PNC reported that the number of murders had declined to 5,174 in 2012, down from 5,681 in 2011 and 6,498 in 2009. However, provisional data indicated that the number of murders rose slightly in 2013.

In January 2012 Ríos Montt, whose immunity from prosecution had expired with the inauguration of the new Congress, was charged with genocide and other serious crimes dating from his 1982–83 presidency. This development, along with the concurrent ratification of the Rome Statute of the International Criminal Court, alleviated some of the concerns expressed by Pérez Molina's critics, who feared that the new President might obstruct the ongoing investigations into military abuses committed during the civil war. The trial of Ríos Montt finally began in March 2013, after delays caused by a series of appeals submitted by his defence team. In April, however, the trial was suspended after a further appeal by the former dictator's defence team. Nevertheless, in early May Ríos Montt was found guilty of crimes against humanity and sentenced to 80 years' imprisonment, although 10 days later the Constitutional Court overturned this verdict on the basis that the trial should not have resumed until all the defence appeals had been heard. The decision was condemned internationally and by human rights organizations. Nevertheless, the Court ruled that the proceedings of the trial remained valid. The trial of the former dictator was not scheduled to recommence until January 2015.

The death of an environmental activist in Santa Cruz Barillas, Huehuetenango, in May 2012 prompted rioting and the declaration of a 30-day state of siege in the municipality, although this was rescinded later that month following anti-Government demonstrations. There was also unrest in the capital in July, when a protest against proposed education reforms (which would increase the cost of teacher-training courses) turned violent; the Ministers of Education and the Interior were injured during the disturbances. In October the military resorted to the use of deadly force against six indigenous demonstrators during a march in Totonicapán organized by social activists and opponents of the Government's education plans. In spite of this atrocity, which generated widespread outrage as well as further questions regarding the propriety of the administration's hard-line security strategy, Pérez Molina continued to defend the use of soldiers as auxiliary police officers. Following violent clashes between anti-mining demonstrators and the police in San Rafael Las Flores, Santa Rosa, another 30-day state of siege was announced in May 2013, affecting several municipalities within Santa Rosa and Jalapa. Further social unrest was reported during 2013–14, with numerous demonstrations staged in protest against the Government's mining, energy and education policies; in August 2013 some 20,000 people participated in nationwide protests against high energy costs and to demand that the electricity network be renationalized.

Meanwhile, in August 2012 Pérez Molina proposed a series of constitutional changes, providing for judicial reform, a reduction in the number of congressional seats and the increased use of the military in civilian policing. However, political and popular reaction to these proposals was subdued, and in November Pérez Molina suspended the constitutional review process in the Congress, citing funding concerns. The President was more successful in his efforts to reduce high-level corruption, with an anti-graft bill receiving legislative approval in October. Pérez Molina reorganized the Cabinet in January 2013, appointing Luis Fernando Carrera Castro as Minister of Foreign Affairs and Elmer Alberto López Rodríguez as Minister of Agriculture, Livestock and Food. Ostensibly in response to an upturn in the murder rate, in July the President also replaced the Director-

General of the PNC and the Minister of National Defence; Brig.-Gen. Manuel Augusto López Ambrosio was given responsibility for defence. In a further cabinet reorganization in January 2014, María Concepción Castro Mazariegos was named as the new Minister of Public Finance and Michelle Martínez received the environment and natural resources portfolio. More controversially, in the following month the Constitutional Court upheld an appeal, submitted by a businessman with links to several right-wing parties, that would result in Attorney-General Paz y Paz's four-year mandate being reduced by seven months. A new Attorney-General was to be installed in May. The judgment elicited expressions of concern from CICIG and civil liberties groups, which feared that Paz y Paz's successor would be less willing to address the issue of impunity.

Presidential and legislative polls were due to be held by September 2015. The UNE selected Torres as its presidential candidate in mid-2013, while the ruling PP nominated Alejandro Sinibaldi, the minister responsible for communications, in early 2014. It was anticipated that Baldizón would again contest the presidential election as LIDER's representative.

Foreign Affairs

Until the return to civilian government in 1986, Guatemala remained steadfast in its claims to the neighbouring territory of Belize. However, Guatemala's new Constitution did not include Belize in its delineation of Guatemalan territory. In 1991 Guatemala and Belize signed an accord under the terms of which Belize pledged to legislate to reduce its maritime boundaries and to allow Guatemala access to the Caribbean Sea and use of its port facilities. In return, Guatemala officially recognized Belize as an independent state and established diplomatic relations. Nevertheless, in 1994 Guatemala formally reaffirmed its territorial claim to Belize. In 2000 the Organization of American States (OAS, see p. 394) established a panel of negotiators to supervise the process of bilateral negotiations. Talks in 2001 focused on the issue of Guatemalans living in the disputed border area; an agreement was later reached to relocate the families.

In 2002 relations with Belize appeared to improve following further OAS-mediated discussions on the border issue; proposals were outlined for a solution to the dispute. These included the provision that Guatemala would recognize Belize's land boundary as set out in the Treaty of 1859, and the creation of a model settlement for peasants and landless farmers in the disputed area. In 2003 the foreign ministers of both countries signed a co-operation agreement pending a final settlement of the dispute. In 2004 delegations from the two countries participated in OAS-sponsored negotiations to establish a series of initiatives designed to promote mutual confidence, and in 2005 Guatemala and Belize signed an Agreement on a Framework of Negotiation and Confidence Building Measures. Following almost two years of negotiations, in 2006 representatives of the two countries signed a partial free trade accord, which entered into force in October 2009. In December 2008 the ministers of foreign affairs of Guatemala and Belize signed an agreement, subject to ratification by referendum, to submit the dispute to the International Court of Justice (ICJ). In September 2010 the Guatemalan Congress approved the agreement. In November 2011 the ministers responsible for foreign affairs of Guatemala and Belize agreed that concurrent referendums on the issue would be conducted; the date for the plebiscite was set for 6 October 2013, although this was postponed at Guatemala's request in April. Bilateral discussions were ongoing in 2014, but it remained unclear when the referendums would be held.

In May 2013 Guatemala joined was granted permission to join Venezuela's Petrocaribe initiative, whereby Caribbean countries were able to purchase petroleum from Venezuela on preferential terms. However, in November Guatemala revealed that it was withdrawing from the accession proceedings owing to concerns over repayment rates.

CONSTITUTION AND GOVERNMENT

Under the 1986 Constitution (revised in 1994), legislative power is vested in the unicameral Congreso de la República (Congress), with 158 members elected for four years by universal adult suffrage. Of the total seats, 127 are filled by departmental representation and 31 according to national listing. Executive power is held by the President (also directly elected for four years), assisted by a Vice-President and an appointed Cabinet. Judicial power is exercised by the Supreme Court of Justice and other tribunals. For the purposes of local administration the country comprises 22 departments, which are divided into 330 municipalities.

REGIONAL AND INTERNATIONAL CO-OPERATION

Guatemala is a member of the Central American Common Market (see p. 229), of the Organization of American States (see p. 394), and of the Community of Latin American and Caribbean States (see p. 464), which was formally inaugurated in December 2011. Guatemala, El Salvador and Honduras signed a free trade agreement with Mexico in 2000, and a more expansive Central America-Mexico free trade pact came into force in September 2013. In 2004 the Presidents of Guatemala, El Salvador, Honduras and Nicaragua signed an agreement creating a Central American customs union. The Dominican Republic-Central American Free Trade Agreement (CAFTA-DR), between Guatemala, Costa Rica, El Salvador, Honduras, Nicaragua, the Dominican Republic and the USA, came into effect in 2006. CAFTA-DR entailed the gradual elimination of tariffs on most industrial and agricultural products over a period of 10 and 20 years, respectively. A free trade agreement between Guatemala, with other Central American countries, and the European Union entered into effect in December 2013. A similar agreement with Peru was ratified in July.

Guatemala was a founder member of the UN in 1945. As a contracting party to the General Agreement on Tariffs and Trade, Guatemala joined the World Trade Organization (see p. 434) shortly after its establishment in 1995.

ECONOMIC AFFAIRS

In 2012, according to estimates by the World Bank, Guatemala's gross national income (GNI), measured at average 2010–12 prices, was US $47,431m., equivalent to $3,140 per head (or $4,990 per head on an international purchasing-power parity basis). During 2003–12, it was estimated, the population increased by an average of 2.5% per year, while gross domestic product (GDP) per head increased, in real terms, by an average of 1.0% per year. Overall GDP increased, in real terms, at an average annual rate of 3.5% in 2003–12; according to official figures, GDP grew by an estimated 3.0% in 2012.

Agriculture, including hunting, forestry and fishing, contributed a preliminary 11.2% of GDP and engaged 32.3% of the employed population in 2012. The principal cash crops are coffee (which accounted for 9.6% of export earnings in 2012), sugar (8.0%) and bananas (5.0%). In recent years the country has successfully expanded production of less traditional crops, such as mangoes, berries and green beans. During 2003–12, according to official preliminary figures, agricultural GDP increased, in real terms, by an estimated average of 3.1% per year; agricultural GDP increased by 4.8% in 2012.

Industry, including mining, manufacturing, construction and power, contributed a preliminary 28.4% of GDP and engaged 19.5% of the working population in 2012. According to official preliminary figures, industrial GDP increased by an estimated average of 2.4% per year in 2003–12. Industrial GDP grew by an estimated 2.5% in 2012.

Mining contributed an estimated 2.2% of GDP in 2012 and employed 0.1% of the working population in 2006. The most important mineral exports are precious metals and stones, which accounted for 6.1% of total export earnings in 2012, and petroleum, which contributed 2.9% of the value of exports in 2012. In addition, copper, antimony, lead, zinc and tungsten are mined on a small scale. There are also deposits of nickel, gold and silver. It was estimated that mining GDP increased by an average of 1.0% per year during 2003–12. The sector increased by an estimated 18.5% in 2011, but decreased by 21.3% in 2012.

Manufacturing contributed an estimated 19.7% of GDP in 2012 and manufacturing and mining together employed 13.7% of the working population in the same year. Guatemala's *maquila*, or clothing assembly, sector, was an important economic contributor, accounting for 11.9% of the value of exports in 2012. Manufacturing GDP increased by an estimated average of 2.8% per year in 2003–12. The sector's GDP grew by an estimated 3.2% in 2012.

The construction sector contributed a preliminary 4.1% of GDP and engaged 5.8% of the employed labour force in 2012. During 2003–12 the GDP of the sector decreased at an estimated average annual rate of 0.6%. Construction GDP increased by an estimated 0.7% in 2012.

Energy is derived principally from mineral fuels and hydroelectric power. Petroleum provided 18.7% of electric energy in 2011. Hydroelectric power was responsible for a decreasing proportion of total power output, accounting for 39.8% of electricity generation in 2011, compared with 57.6% in 1997, while power generation from coal sources increased from 0.7% in 1999 to 14.4% in 2011. Guatemala is a marginal producer of petroleum and, in 2012, produced on average 14,580 barrels per day. According to estimates, proven petroleum reserves amounted to 80m. barrels in 2013, while reserves of natural gas totalled some 110,000m. cu ft in 2006. Imports of mineral products comprised 19.7% of the value of total imports in 2011. Efforts have been made in recent years to reduce Guatemala's dependency on oil; some US $1,800m. was invested in the construction of three coal-based generators and five hydroelectric plants by 2014. The Comision Nacional de Energía Eléctrica in 2013 announced plans to increase 'clean' energy use to 80% of total usage by 2026.

In 2012 the services sector contributed a preliminary 60.4% of GDP and employed 48.2% of the working population. The GDP of the services sector increased by an estimated average of 4.9% per year in 2003–12; growth in the sector was an estimated 3.9% in 2012.

In 2012 Guatemala recorded a visible merchandise trade deficit of US $5,731.1m., and there was a deficit of $1,488.5m. on the current account of the balance of payments. In 2012 the principal source of imports (38.0%) was the USA; other major suppliers were Mexico and the People's Republic of China. The USA was the principal market for exports (taking 39.6% of exports in that year); other significant purchasers were El Salvador, Honduras and Mexico. The main exports in 2012 were clothing, coffee, sugar, precious metals and stones, and bananas. The principal imports were electrical machinery and apparatus, vehicles and transport equipment, diesel oil, motor gas, and plastics. Remittances from citizens working abroad represented the second largest hard currency inflow into the country, after non-traditional exports. According to Banco de Guatemala, in 2013 remittances from the USA totalled $5,105.2m.

In 2012 there was a budgetary deficit of 9,533.9m. quetzales, equivalent to some 2.4% of GDP. Guatemala's general government gross debt was 87,852m. quetzales in 2011, equivalent to 23.7% of GDP. In 2011 Guatemala's total external debt stood at US $16,286m., of which $5,358m. was public and publicly guaranteed debt. In that year, the cost of servicing long-term public and publicly guaranteed debt and repayments to the IMF was equivalent to 15.6% of the value of exports of goods, services and income (excluding workers' remittances). In 2003–12 the average annual rate of inflation was 6.3%. Consumer prices increased by an average of 4.6% in 2013. An estimated 2.9% of the labour force were unemployed in 2012, and a further 17.8% were described as underemployed.

The Dominican Republic-Central American Free Trade Agreement (CAFTA-DR) with the USA was considered vital to the future development of the Guatemalan economy, which suffered from large trade deficits. The implementation of CAFTA-DR brought greater access to US markets and encouraged economic diversification. Given the price volatility of agricultural goods exported by Guatemala, the steady inflow of remittances from abroad (primarily the USA) tended to offset shortfalls in foreign exchange earnings. Major obstacles to economic growth included the country's weak human capital base, high rates of violent crime and rampant corruption, all of which deterred foreign investment. Exports, remittances, foreign direct investment (FDI) and tax revenues all rose during 2011, and real GDP expanded by 4.2%, according to official figures, in that year. In early 2012 the Congress approved legislation to restructure the taxation system, which was expected to lead to a further increase in tax receipts. Measures were also introduced to reduce the high levels of tax evasion. Remittances and FDI increased again in 2012, but exports declined slightly and growth slowed to 3.0%. The IMF estimated that real GDP growth would rise to 3.3% in 2013 owing to the strength of the tourism sector, remittance inflows and domestic consumption. The Fund expected the economy to grow by a further 3.4% in 2014.

PUBLIC HOLIDAYS

2015: 1 January (New Year's Day), 2–3 April (Maundy Thursday and Good Friday), 1 May (Labour Day), 29 June (for Anniversary of the Revolution), 15 August (Assumption, Guatemala City only), 15 September (Independence Day), 12 October (Columbus Day), 20 October (Revolution Day), 1 November (All Saints' Day), 24 December (Christmas Eve, afternoon only), 25 December (Christmas Day), 31 December (New Year's Eve, afternoon only).

Statistical Survey

Sources (unless otherwise stated): Banco de Guatemala, 7a Avda 22-01, Zona 1, Apdo 365, Guatemala City; tel. 2429-6000; fax 2253-4035; internet www.banguat.gob.gt; Instituto Nacional de Estadística, Edif. América, 4°, 8a Calle 9-55, Zona 1, Guatemala City; tel. 2232-6212; e-mail info-ine@ine.gob.gt; internet www.ine.gob.gt.

Area and Population

AREA, POPULATION AND DENSITY

Area (sq km)	
Land	108,429
Inland water	460
Total	108,889*
Population (census results)†	
17 April 1994	8,322,051
24 November 2002	
Males	5,496,839
Females	5,740,357
Total	11,237,196
Population (official estimates at mid-year)	
2012	15,073,375
2013	15,438,384
2014	15,806,675
Density (per sq km) at mid-2014	145.8

* 42,042 sq miles.

† Excluding adjustments for underenumeration.

POPULATION BY AGE AND SEX
(official estimates at mid-2012)

	Males	Females	Total
0–14	3,121,427	3,027,519	6,148,946
15–64	3,918,884	4,340,264	8,259,148
65 and over	312,558	352,723	665,281
Total	7,352,869	7,720,506	15,073,375

DEPARTMENTS
(official estimates at mid-2014)

Alta Verapaz	1,219,585	Quetzaltenango	844,906
Baja Verapaz	291,903	Quiché	1,053,737
Chimaltenango	666,938	Retalhuleu	325,556
Chiquimula	397,202	Sacatepéquez	336,606
El Progreso	166,397	San Marcos	1,095,997
Escuintla	746,309	Santa Rosa	367,569
Guatemala	3,306,397	Sololá	477,705
Huehuetenango	1,234,593	Suchitepéquez	555,261
Izabal	445,125	Totonicapán	521,995
Jalapa	345,926	Zacapa	232,667
Jutiapa	462,714		
Petén	711,585	**Total**	15,806,675

PRINCIPAL TOWNS
(official population estimates at mid-2014)

Guatemala City	993,815	San Juan Sacatepéquez	231,721
Villa Nueva	552,535	Escuintla	158,456
Mixco	491,619	Quetzaltenango	157,559
Cobán	250,675	Jalapa	156,419
San Pedro Carcha	235,213	Totonicapán	141,751

BIRTHS, MARRIAGES AND DEATHS

	Registered live births		Registered marriages		Registered deaths	
	Number	Rate (per 1,000)	Number	Rate (per 1,000)	Number	Rate (per 1,000)
2001	415,338	35.6	54,722	4.7	68,041	5.8
2002	387,287	32.3	51,857	4.3	66,089	5.5
2003	375,092	31.0	51,247	4.2	66,695	5.5
2004	383,704	31.0	53,860	4.3	66,991	5.4
2005	374,066	29.5	52,186	4.1	71,039	5.6
2006	368,399	28.3	57,505	4.4	69,756	5.4
2007	366,128	26.8	57,003	4.3	70,030	5.2
2008	369,769	26.4	52,315	3.8	70,233	5.1

2009: Registered live births 351,628.

2011: Registered live births 373,692; Registered deaths 72,354.

Sources: partly UN, *Demographic Yearbook* and *Population and Vital Statistics Report*.

Life expectancy (years at birth): 71.3 (males 67.9; females 74.9) in 2011 (Source: World Bank, World Development Indicators database).

ECONOMICALLY ACTIVE POPULATION
(population aged 15 years and over, January 2013)

	Males	Females	Total
Agriculture, forestry, hunting and fishing	1,547,973	191,895	1,739,868
Mining and quarrying; manufacturing	468,360	286,567	754,927
Construction	329,618	3,021	332,639
Wholesale and retail trade; transport and storage; hotels and restaurants	833,660	859,788	1,693,448
Information and communications	35,445	15,030	50,475
Financial and insurance services	36,736	37,675	74,411
Real estate activities	13,084	4,092	17,176
Professional, scientific, administrative and support services	130,747	45,704	176,451
Public administration and defence; education; health; social assistance	188,503	272,786	461,289
Other services	115,052	305,345	420,397
Total employed	3,699,178	2,021,903	5,721,081
Unemployed	91,212	97,481	188,693
Total labour force	3,790,390	2,119,384	5,909,774

Health and Welfare

KEY INDICATORS

Total fertility rate (children per woman, 2011)	3.9
Under-5 mortality rate (per 1,000 live births, 2011)	30
HIV/AIDS (% of persons aged 15–49, 2012)	0.7
Physicians (per 1,000 head, 2009)	0.9
Hospital beds (per 1,000 head, 2010)	0.6
Health expenditure (2010): US $ per head (PPP)	327
Health expenditure (2010): % of GDP	6.9
Health expenditure (2010): public (% of total)	34.9
Access to water (% of persons, 2011)	94
Access to sanitation (% of persons, 2011)	80
Total carbon dioxide emissions ('000 metric tons, 2010)	11,118.3
Carbon dioxide emissions per head (metric tons, 2010)	0.8
Human Development Index (2012): ranking	133
Human Development Index (2012): value	0.581

For sources and definitions, see explanatory note on p. vi.

Agriculture

PRINCIPAL CROPS
('000 metric tons)

	2010	2011	2012
Maize	1,634.0	1,672.2	1,690.0*
Potatoes	481.0	493.0	500.0†
Sugar cane	22,313.8	20,586.1	21,800.0†
Oil palm fruit†	1,213.0	1,653.0	2,067.0
Tomatoes	300.8	305.4	315.0
Watermelons†	125.2	128.3	130.0
Cantaloupes and other melons	480.4	497.2	500.0
Bananas	2,637.1	2,679.9	2,700.0
Plantains	192.6	188.8	195.0
Lemons and limes	107.8	109.1	112.0†
Guavas, mangoes and mangosteens	105.9	108.5	112.0
Pineapples	234.3	234.5	240.0†
Coffee, green	247.5	242.8	248.0†
Tobacco, unmanufactured†	18.6	22.4	24.0

* Unofficial figure.
† FAO estimate(s).

Aggregate production ('000 metric tons, may include official, semi-official or estimated data): Total cereals 1,723.6 in 2010, 1,760.3 in 2011, 1,771.4 in 2012; Total pulses 240.0 in 2010, 244.4 in 2011, 246.5 in 2012; Total roots and tubers 499.0 in 2010, 511.5 in 2011, 520.1 in 2012; Total vegetables (incl. melons) 1,553.9 in 2010, 1,592.0 in 2011, 1,626.0 in 2012; Total fruits (excl. melons) 3,968.4 in 2010, 4,013.3 in 2011, 4,069.1 in 2012.

Source: FAO.

LIVESTOCK
('000 head, year ending September)

	2010	2011	2012
Horses*	127	128	130
Asses*	9.9	9.9	10.0
Mules*	38.7	38.7	39.0
Cattle	3,306	3,388	3,400*
Sheep*	600	612	614
Pigs	2,733	2,799	2,800*
Goats*	128	130	132
Chickens*	33,000	34,000	35,000

* FAO estimate(s).

LIVESTOCK PRODUCTS
('000 metric tons)

	2010	2011	2012*
Cattle meat*	79.0	81.0	83.0
Pig meat*	58.7	60.0	61.5
Chicken meat	183.8	185.9	188.0
Cows' milk	463.1	463.1	465.0
Hen eggs	219.7†	224.6†	226.0
Honey*	3.5	3.5	3.6

* FAO estimate(s).
† Unofficial figure.

Source: FAO.

Forestry

ROUNDWOOD REMOVALS
('000 cubic metres, excl. bark, FAO estimates)

	2010	2011	2012
Sawlogs, veneer logs and logs for sleepers	677	837	705
Other industrial wood	15	15	15
Fuel wood	18,059	18,410	18,768
Total	18,751	19,262	19,488

Source: FAO.

SAWNWOOD PRODUCTION
('000 cubic metres, incl. railway sleepers, FAO estimates)

	2010	2011	2012
Coniferous (softwood)	43	40	39
Broadleaved (hardwood)	91	62	55
Total	134	102	94

Source: FAO.

Fishing

('000 metric tons, live weight)

	2009	2010	2011
Capture*	20.0	21.9	19.7
Freshwater fishes*	2.3	2.3	2.3
Skipjack tuna	7.6	7.0	6.7
Yellowfin tuna	5.9	5.6	6.3
Bigeye tuna	2.5	3.7	2.0
Penaeus shrimps	0.5	0.7	0.6
Pacific seabobs	0.1	1.3	0.9
Aquaculture	16.6*	22.8	21.5*
Other tilapias	3.0*	0.8	5.5
Penaeus shrimps	13.6	21.9	15.9
Total catch*	36.6	44.7	41.2

* FAO estimate(s).

Source: FAO.

Mining

('000 metric tons, unless otherwise indicated)

	2010	2011	2012
Crude petroleum ('000 barrels)	4,363	3,995	4,000*
Gold (kg)	9,213	11,898	6,473
Silver (kg)	194,683	272,771	204,555
Limestone	4,910	n.a.	2,000*
Sand and gravel ('000 cu m)	88	81	261

* Estimated figure.

Source: US Geological Survey.

Industry

SELECTED PRODUCTS
('000 metric tons unless otherwise indicated)

	2007	2008	2009
Sugar (raw)	2,364	2,145	2,382
Cement*	2,500	2,500	1,500
Electric energy (million kWh)	8,755	8,717	9,040

* Estimates from US Geological Survey.

2010: Cement ('000 metric tons) 1,500 (US Geological Survey estimate).

2011: Cement ('000 metric tons) 1,600 (US Geological Survey estimate).

2012: Cement ('000 metric tons) 1,700 (US Geological Survey estimate).

Source (unless otherwise indicated): UN Industrial Commodity Statistics Database.

Finance

CURRENCY AND EXCHANGE RATES

Monetary Units
100 centavos = 1 quetzal.

Sterling, Dollar and Euro Equivalents (31 December 2013)
£1 sterling = 12.931 quetzales;
US $1 = 7.852 quetzales;
€1 = 10.829 quetzales;
1,000 quetzales = £77.33 = $127.36 = €92.35.

Average Exchange Rate (quetzales per US dollar)
2011 7.7854
2012 7.8336
2013 7.8568

Note: In December 2000 legislation was approved to allow the circulation of the US dollar and other convertible currencies, for use in a wide range of transactions, from 1 May 2001.

BUDGET
(central government operations, million quetzales)

Revenue	2010	2011	2012
Current revenue	37,397.3	43,165.2	45,767.0
Tax revenue	34,772.0	40,292.2	42,819.8
Direct taxes	10,329.8	12,710.5	13,453.7
Excise taxes	24,442.1	27,581.7	29,366.1
Non-tax revenue	2,625.4	2,873.0	2,947.2
Social Security	1,069.1	1,214.4	1,273.6
Current transfers	548.9	587.8	498.8
Capital revenue	27.8	12.9	18.7
Total	37,425.1	43,178.1	45,785.7

Expenditure	2010	2011	2012
Current expenditure	34,656.6	38,774.2	42,307.5
Wages and salaries	12,528.8	14,155.7	15,080.6
Use of goods and services	6,287.6	7,218.2	8,760.5
Interest	4,939.6	5,475.7	6,022.3
Discounts and rewards	103.5	184.9	170.8
Transfers	7,818.1	8,592.6	8,967.5
Social benefits	2,979.2	3,147.1	3,305.9
Capital expenditure	13,728.7	14,736.8	13,012.0
Total	48,385.4	53,511.0	55,319.6

Source: Ministry of Finance, Guatemala City.

INTERNATIONAL RESERVES

(US $ million at 31 December)

	2010	2011	2012
Gold (national valuation)	312.9	348.9	368.8
IMF special drawing rights	267.4	266.4	267.6
Foreign exchange	5,369.4	5,568.5	6,057.4
Total	5,949.7	6,183.8	6,693.8

Source: IMF, *International Financial Statistics*.

MONEY SUPPLY

(million quetzales at 31 December)

	2010	2011	2012
Currency outside depository corporations	19,736.5	20,510.5	21,227.0
Transferable deposits	48,104.3	52,138.2	56,655.2
Other deposits	82,367.5	88,477.4	98,176.5
Securities other than shares	4,835.8	5,135.4	5,766.0
Broad money	155,044.1	166,261.5	181,824.7

Source: IMF, *International Financial Statistics*.

COST OF LIVING

(Consumer Price Index at November; base: December 2010 = 100)

	2011	2012	2013
Food and non-alcoholic beverages	111.6	118.2	129.2
Clothing and footwear	102.8	105.8	108.1
Housing, water and power	105.7	103.5	109.9
Health	103.2	106.3	108.9
Transport	106.6	108.2	108.4
Communications	100.8	100.6	100.6
Recreation and culture	101.2	104.7	107.1
Education	100.9	101.5	102.8
Restaurants and hotels	104.4	108.2	111.2
Miscellaneous items	102.6	107.7	111.0
All items	106.0	109.3	114.3

NATIONAL ACCOUNTS

(million quetzales at current prices)

Expenditure on the Gross Domestic Product

	2010	2011*	2012*
Government final consumption expenditure	34,894.4	38,311.2	42,195.2
Private final consumption expenditure	286,760.3	316,576.0	337,655.5
Increase in stocks	−2,899.5	1,575.7	−1,105.5
Gross fixed capital formation	49,324.5	54,637.1	57,730.0
Total domestic expenditure	368,079.7	411,100.0	436,475.2
Exports of goods and services	85,957.3	98,783.4	98,169.6
Less Imports of goods and services	120,943.5	138,605.4	141,133.3
GDP in purchasers' values	333,093.4	371,278.0	393,511.6
GDP at constant 2001 prices	199,473.8	207,930.8	214,085.1

Gross Domestic Product by Economic Activity

	2010	2011*	2012*
Agriculture, hunting, forestry and fishing	36,821.3	41,088.7	42,703.0
Mining and quarrying	6,616.0	10,512.2	8,511.8
Manufacturing	62,072.9	69,182.2	75,097.0
Electricity, gas and water	8,002.7	7,555.0	8,800.0
Construction	13,416.4	14,668.1	15,634.7
Trade, restaurants and hotels	56,719.3	67,118.0	72,269.3
Transport, storage and communications	26,290.0	29,115.3	30,549.4
Finance, insurance and real estate	10,819.7	11,518.4	12,853.2
Ownership of dwellings	29,142.9	30,448.4	31,781.8
General government services	24,407.9	26,782.3	28,925.6
Other community, social and personal services	47,539.2	50,582.0	53,500.6
Sub-total	321,848.3	358,570.6	380,626.4
Less Financial intermediation services indirectly measured (FISIM)	9,627.2	10,645.9	11,580.5
Gross value added in basic prices	312,221.1	347,924.7	369,045.9
Taxes on imports, less subsidies	20,872.3	23,353.3	24,465.6
GDP in purchasers' values	333,093.4	371,278.0	393,511.6

* Preliminary figures.

BALANCE OF PAYMENTS

(US $ million)

	2010	2011	2012
Exports of goods	8,535.7	10,518.7	10,107.0
Imports of goods	−12,806.4	−15,482.1	−15,838.1
Balance on goods	−4,270.7	−4,963.5	−5,731.1
Exports of services	2,291.4	2,267.4	2,342.6
Imports of services	−2,381.1	−2,386.0	−2,394.2
Balance on goods and services	−4,360.4	−5,082.1	−5,782.7
Primary income received	280.7	319.6	359.1
Primary income paid	−1,492.1	−1,970.0	−1,730.7
Balance on goods, services and primary income	−5,571.8	−6,732.4	−7,154.2
Secondary income received	4,917.9	5,092.7	5,692.9
Secondary income paid	−24.3	−32.0	−27.2
Current balance	−678.2	−1,671.7	−1,488.5
Capital account (net)	2.7	2.6	—
Direct investment assets	−63.2	−130.8	14.2
Direct investment liabilities	920.8	1,139.7	1,150.0
Portfolio investment assets	−45.8	−143.3	−6.7
Portfolio investment liabilities	−27.6	−342.1	−11.2
Other investment assets	131.5	−648.7	−36.2
Other investment liabilities	682.2	2,059.0	776.6
Net errors and omissions	−359.1	−225.1	−683.2
Reserves and related items	563.3	39.6	−285.0

Source: IMF, *International Financial Statistics*.

External Trade

PRINCIPAL COMMODITIES
(US $ million)

Imports c.i.f.	2010	2011	2012
Textile materials	581.4	667.0	635.7
Gas-diesel (distillate fuel) oil	878.2	1,178.2	1,248.6
Motor spirit (gasoline)	797.8	991.1	1,029.0
Other petroleum derivatives	416.5	622.4	599.4
Chemical products	538.2	625.7	661.2
Pharmaceutical products	449.9	503.2	528.3
Plastics and manufactures thereof	797.6	959.7	922.3
Transmitting and receiving apparatus	429.1	442.4	421.5
Electrical machinery and apparatus	1,152.3	1,405.1	1,531.4
Vehicles and transport equipment	961.9	1,133.7	1,273.7
Total (incl. others)	13,838.3	16,613.0	16,994.0

Exports f.o.b.	2010	2011	2012
Coffee	713.9	1,174.2	958.1
Cocoa	308.1	296.9	250.3
Bananas	353.3	475.3	499.9
Sugar	726.7	648.8	803.0
Edible fats and oils	201.3	330.9	361.0
Natural rubber	233.3	397.4	295.0
Crude petroleum	247.2	335.4	291.7
Articles of clothing	1,154.9	1,216.4	1,189.5
Plastics and manufactures thereof	223.6	270.7	299.2
Precious metals and stones	523.7	941.6	612.9
Total (incl. others)	8,462.5	10,400.9	9,977.6

PRINCIPAL TRADING PARTNERS
(US $ million, preliminary)

Imports c.i.f.	2010	2011	2012
Brazil	232.9	274.7	250.8
China, People's Republic	983.6	1,144.2	1,265.0
Colombia	394.0	596.8	551.4
Costa Rica	427.7	455.5	476.8
Ecuador	178.3	184.0	224.2
El Salvador	676.1	820.4	777.0
Germany	247.6	256.1	278.1
Honduras	307.0	344.7	367.1
Hong Kong	144.7	169.4	193.7
India	142.0	162.1	242.7
Japan	276.6	303.9	276.3
Korea, Republic	387.6	369.0	427.2
Mexico	1,542.8	1,858.9	1,915.7
Panama	441.1	476.8	544.4
Spain	151.4	171.9	186.5
USA	5,124.7	6,508.6	6,460.4
Total (incl. others)	13,838.3	16,613.0	16,994.0

Exports f.o.b.	2010	2011	2012
Belgium	52.7	110.2	75.1
Canada	136.0	158.7	149.4
Chile	91.6	135.6	130.1
Costa Rica	347.1	404.3	424.5
Dominican Republic	134.0	127.2	115.5
El Salvador	994.7	1,132.3	1,110.7
Germany	94.0	145.2	119.6
Honduras	700.2	814.7	795.5
Japan	146.8	212.2	176.7
Korea, Republic	79.3	125.0	53.1
Mexico	449.1	512.3	550.1
Netherlands	106.2	136.2	169.2
Nicaragua	352.7	459.1	473.4
Panama	217.9	247.4	246.4
Saudi Arabia	115.5	102.9	86.4
USA	3,258.7	4,307.5	3,955.0
Total (incl. others)	8,462.5	10,400.9	9,977.6

Transport

RAILWAYS
(traffic)

	1994	1995	1996
Passenger-km (million)	991	0	0
Freight ton-km (million)	25,295	14,242	836

Source: UN, *Statistical Yearbook*.

ROAD TRAFFIC
(motor vehicles in use)

	2008	2009	2010
Passenger cars	476,739	505,782	529,593
Buses and coaches	86,124	90,526	94,541
Lorries and vans	315,469	342,058	366,025
Motorcycles and mopeds	447,068	508,999	570,799
Total (incl. others)	1,760,013	1,912,469	2,051,945

SHIPPING

Flag Registered Fleet
(at 31 December)

	2011	2012	2013
Number of vessels	6	6	6
Total displacement ('000 grt)	3.0	3.0	3.0

Source: Lloyd's List Intelligence (www.lloydslistintelligence.com).

International Sea-borne Freight Traffic
('000 metric tons)

	1992	1993	1994
Goods loaded	2,176	1,818	2,096
Goods unloaded	3,201	3,025	3,822

CIVIL AVIATION
(traffic on scheduled services)

	1997	1998	1999
Kilometres flown (million)	5	7	5
Passengers carried ('000)	508	794	506
Passenger-km (million)	368	480	342
Total ton-km (million)	77	50	33

Source: UN, *Statistical Yearbook*.

Passengers carried ('000): 313.9 in 2010; 326.1 in 2011; 288.0 in 2012 (Source: World Bank, World Development Indicators database).

Tourism

TOURIST ARRIVALS BY COUNTRY OF ORIGIN

	2010	2011	2012
Belize	43,816	35,960	35,481
Canada	46,774	42,719	53,696
Costa Rica	48,088	42,039	44,984
El Salvador	485,888	542,316	604,871
Honduras	258,765	223,010	235,680
Mexico	127,691	132,661	144,076
Nicaragua	83,819	74,362	77,238
USA	471,056	429,216	434,175
Total (incl. others)	1,875,777	1,822,663	1,951,173

Tourism receipts (US $ million, excl. passenger transport): 985.6 in 2010; 937.2 in 2011; 986.8 in 2012.

Source: Guatemalan Institute of Tourism.

Communications Media

	2010	2011	2012
Telephones ('000 main lines in use)	1,498.6	1,626.3	1,743.8
Mobile cellular telephones ('000 subscribers)	18,068.0	19,479.1	20,787.1
Broadband subscribers ('000)	259.0	n.a.	n.a.

Internet users ('000) 2,279.4 in 2009.

Source: International Telecommunication Union.

Education

(2010/11 unless otherwise indicated)

	Institutions	Teachers	Students
Pre-primary	11,859*	26,126	537,265
Primary	17,499*	100,600	2,644,683
Secondary	4,874*	76,850	1,113,881
Tertiary	1,946†	3,843*	233,885‡

* 2005/06.

† 2003/04.

‡ 2006/07.

Source: mainly UNESCO Institute for Statistics.

Pupil-teacher ratio (primary education, UNESCO estimate): 26.3 in 2010/11 (Source: UNESCO Institute for Statistics).

Adult literacy rate (UNESCO estimates): 75.9% (males 81.2%; females 71.1%) in 2011 (Source: UNESCO Institute for Statistics).

Directory

The Government

HEAD OF STATE

President: Gen. (retd) OTTO FERNANDO PÉREZ MOLINA (took office 14 January 2012).

Vice-President: INGRID ROXANA BALDETTI ELÍAS.

CABINET
(April 2014)

The Government is formed by the Partido Patriota (PP) and the Visión con Valores-Encuentro por Guatemala (VIVA-EG) coalition.

Minister of Foreign Affairs: LUIS FERNANDO CARRERA CASTRO (Ind.).

Minister of the Interior: MAURICIO LÓPEZ BONILLA (PP).

Minister of National Defence: Brig.-Gen. MANUEL AUGUSTO LÓPEZ AMBROSIO (PP).

Minister of Public Finance: MARÍA CONCEPCIÓN CASTRO MAZARIEGOS.

Minister of the Economy: SERGIO DE LA TORRE (PP).

Minister of Public Health and Social Welfare: JORGE ALEJANDRO VILLAVICENCIO ALVAREZ (Ind.).

Minister of Communications, Infrastructure, Transport and Housing: ALEJANDRO SINIBALDI (PP).

Minister of Agriculture, Livestock and Food: ELMER ALBERTO LÓPEZ RODRÍGUEZ (Ind.).

Minister of Education: CYNTHIA DEL AGUILA (PP).

Minister of Energy and Mines: ERICK ARCHILA (PP).

Minister of Culture and Sport: CARLOS BATZÍN (PP).

Minister of the Environment and Natural Resources: MICHELLE MARTÍNEZ.

Minister of Social Development: EDGAR LEONEL RODRÍGUEZ LARA (PP).

Minister of Labour and Social Security: CARLOS CONTRERAS SOLÓRZANO (PP).

MINISTRIES

Ministry of Agriculture, Livestock and Food: Edif. Monja Blanca, Of. 306, 3°, 7a Avda 12-90, Zona 13, Guatemala City; tel. 2413-7000; fax 2413-7352; e-mail infoagro@maga.gob.gt; internet www.maga.gob.gt.

Ministry of Communications, Infrastructure, Transport and Housing: Edif. Antiguo Cocesna, 8a Avda y 15 Calle, Zona 13, Guatemala City; tel. 2223-4000; fax 2362-6059; e-mail relpublicas@micivi.gob.gt; internet www.civ.gob.gt.

Ministry of Culture and Sport: Calle 7, entre Avda 6 y 7, Centro Histórico, Palacio Nacional de la Cultura, Zona 1, Guatemala City; tel. 2239-5000; fax 2253-0540; e-mail info@mcd.gob.gt; internet www.mcd.gob.gt.

Ministry of the Economy: 8a Avda 10-43, Zona 1, Guatemala City; tel. 2412-0200; e-mail infonegocios@mineco.gob.gt; internet www.mineco.gob.gt.

Ministry of Education: 6a Calle 1-87, Zona 10, Guatemala City; tel. 2411-9595; fax 2361-0350; e-mail info@mineduc.gob.gt; internet www.mineduc.gob.gt.

Ministry of Energy and Mines: Diagonal 17, 29-78, Zona 11, Las Charcas, Guatemala City; tel. 2419-6464; fax 2476-2007; e-mail informatica@mem.gob.gt; internet www.mem.gob.gt.

Ministry of the Environment and Natural Resources: Edif. MARN, 20 Calle 28-58, Zona 10, Guatemala City; tel. 2423-0500; e-mail sip@marn.gob.gt; internet www.marn.gob.gt.

Ministry of Foreign Affairs: 2a Avda La Reforma 4-17, Zona 10, Guatemala City; tel. 2410-0010; fax 2410-0011; e-mail webmaster@minex.gob.gt; internet www.minex.gob.gt.

Ministry of the Interior: Antiguo Palacio de la Policía Nacional Civil, 6a Avda 13-71, Zona 1, Guatemala City; tel. 2413-8888; fax 2413-8587; e-mail info@mingob.gob.gt; internet www.mingob.gob.gt.

Ministry of Labour and Social Security: Edif. Torre Empresarial, 7 Avda 3-33, Zona 9, Guatemala City; tel. 2422-2500; fax 2422-2503; e-mail ministro@mintrabajo.gob.gt; internet www.mintrabajo.gob.gt.

Ministry of National Defence: Antiguas Escuela Politécnica, Avda La Reforma 1-45, Zona 10, Guatemala City; tel. 2269-4924; fax 2360-9919; e-mail dip@mindef.mil.gt; internet www.mindef.mil.gt.

Ministry of Public Finance: Centro Cívico, 8a Avda y 21 Calle, Zona 1, Guatemala City; tel. 2248-5005; fax 2248-5054; e-mail info@minfin.gob.gt; internet www.minfin.gob.gt.

Ministry of Public Health and Social Welfare: Escuela de Enfermería, 3°, 6a Avda 3-45, Zona 1, Guatemala City; tel. 2475-2121; fax 2475-1125; e-mail info@mspas.gob.gt; internet www.mspas.gob.gt.

Ministry of Social Development: 3a Avda 6-44, Zona 1, Guatemala City; tel. 2491-0900; internet www.mides.gob.gt.

President and Legislature

PRESIDENT

Presidential Election, 11 September and 6 November 2011

Candidate	First round % of votes	Second round % of votes
Gen. (retd) Otto Fernando Pérez Molina (PP)	36.10	53.74
Manuel Antonio Baldizón Méndez (LIDER)	22.68	46.26
José Eduardo Suger Cofiño (CREO)	16.62	—
Mario Amilcar Estrada Orellana (UCN)	8.72	—
Harold Osberto Caballeros López (VIVA-EG)	6.24	—

Candidate—*continued*	First round % of votes	Second round % of votes
Rigoberta Menchú Tum (WINAQ-URNG—MAIZ-ANN)	3.22	—
Juan Guillermo Gutiérrez Strauss (PAN)	2.76	—
Patricia de Arzú (Partido Unionista)	2.19	—
Alejandro Eduardo Giammattei Falla (CASA)	1.05	—
Adela Camacho de Torrebiarte (ADN)	0.42	—
Total valid votes	100.00	100.00

CONGRESS
(Congreso de la República)

President: ARÍSTIDES CRESPO.

General Election, 11 September 2011

	% of votes	Seats*
Partido Patriota (PP)	26.37	56
Unidad Nacional de la Esperanza-Gran Alianza Nacional (UNE-GANA)	22.24	48
Unión del Cambio Nacional (UCN)	9.48	14
Libertad Democrática Renovada (LIDER)	8.66	14
Compromiso, Renovación y Orden (CREO)	8.77	12
Visión con Valores-Encuentro por Guatemala (VIVA)	7.84	6
WINAQ-Unidad Revolucionaria Nacional Guatemalteca—Movimiento Amplio de Izquierdas-Alternativa Nueva Nación	3.20	3
Partido de Avanzada Nacional (PAN)	3.08	2
Frente Republicano Guatemalteco (FRG)†	2.72	1
Partido Unionista	2.67	1
VICTORIA	1.62	1
Centro de Acción Social	1.10	—
Acción de Desarrollo Nacional (ADN)	0.88	—
Frente de Convergencia Nacional (FCN)	0.53	—
Total valid votes (incl. others)	100.00	158

* Seats are distributed according to a combination of national lists and departmental and proportional representation.

† Succeeded by the Partido Republicano Institucional in 2013.

Election Commission

Tribunal Supremo Electoral: 6a Avda 0-32, Zona 2, Guatemala City; tel. 2413-0303; e-mail tse@tse.org.gt; internet www.tse.org.gt; f. 1983; independent; Pres. RUDY MARLÓN PINEDA RAMÍREZ.

Political Organizations

Acción de Desarrollo Nacional (ADN): Vía 7, 5-33 Zona 4, Guatemala City; tel. 2339-4000; internet www.adn.com.gt; registration cancelled by the Tribunal Supremo Electoral in May 2012; Sec.-Gen. ADELA CAMACHO DE TORREBIARTE.

Alternativa Nueva Nación (ANN): Avda 1-31, 8°, Zona 1, Guatemala City; tel. 2251-2514; e-mail corriente@intelnet.net.gt; contested the 2011 elections in coalition with the URNG—MAIZ (q.v.) and the Movimiento Político WINAQ (q.v.); Sec.-Gen. PABLO MONSANTO.

Bienestar Nacional (BIEN): 8a Avda 6-40, Zona 2, Guatemala City; tel. 2254-1458; internet www.bienestarnacional.org; Sec.-Gen. FIDEL REYES LEE.

Compromiso, Renovación y Orden (CREO): Vía 3, 5–27 Zona 4, Antiguo Edif. Manuel, Guatemala City; tel. 2339-4942; internet creo.org.gt; Pres. JOSÉ EDUARDO SUGER COFIÑO; Sec.-Gen. JOSÉ RODOLFO NEUTZE AGUIRRE.

Encuentro por Guatemala (EG): 9 Avda 0-71, Zona 4, Guatemala City; tel. 2231-9859; fax 2230-6463; e-mail izaveliz@yahoo.es; internet www.encuentroporguatemala.org; f. 2006; centre-left; promotes indigenous interests; contested the 2011 elections in coalition with Visión con Valores (q.v.); Sec.-Gen. NINETH VERENCA MONTENEGRO COTTOM.

Frente de Convergencia Nacional (FCN): Avda Centroamérica 13-45, Zona 1, Guatemala City; tel. 5908-7848; e-mail soporte@partidofcn.com; internet www.partidofcn.com; Sec.-Gen. JOSÉ LUIS QUILO AYUSO.

Gran Alianza Nacional (GANA): 6a Avda, 3-44, Zona 9, Guatemala City; tel. 2331-4811; fax 2362-7512; e-mail info@gana.com.gt; internet www.gana.com.gt; f. 2003 as electoral alliance of PP, Movimiento Reformador and Partido Solidaridad Nacional; registered as a party in 2005 following withdrawal of PP; Sec.-Gen. JAIME ANTONIO MARTÍNEZ LOHAYZA.

Libertad Democrática Renovada (LIDER): 13 Calle, 2-52 Zona 1, Guatemala City; tel. 2463-4942; Sec.-Gen. EDGAR AJCIP.

Movimiento Político WINAQ: 33 Avda 3-57, Zona 4 de Mixco Bosques de San Nicolás, Guatemala City; tel. 2436-0939; internet winaq.org.gt; promotes indigenous interests; contested the 2011 elections in coalition with the URNG—MAIZ (q.v.) and the Alternativa Nueva Nación (q.v.); Sec.-Gen. RIGOBERTA MENCHÚ TUM.

Partido de Avanzada Nacional (PAN): 3a Avda 18-28, Zona 14, Guatemala City; tel. 2366-1509; fax 2337-2001; e-mail pan.partidodeavanzadanacional@gmail.com; internet www.pan-gt.com; Sec.-Gen. JUAN GUILLERMO GUTIÉRREZ STRAUSS.

Partido Patriota (PP): 11 Calle 11-54, Zona 1, Guatemala City; tel. 2311-6886; e-mail comunicacion@partidopatriota.org; internet www.partidopatriota.com; f. 2002; contested 2003 elections as part of GANA (q.v.); withdrew from GANA in May 2004; right-wing; Leader Gen. (retd) OTTO FERNANDO PÉREZ MOLINA; Sec.-Gen. INGRID ROXANA BALDETTI ELÍAS.

Partido Republicano Institucional (PRI): Avda Las Américas 19-60, Zona 13, Guatemala City; tel. 2319-000; internet pri.gt; f. 2013 as successor party to Frente Republicano Guatemalteco (f. 1988); right-wing; Sec.-Gen. LUIS FERNANDO PÉREZ MARTÍNEZ.

Partido Unionista: 5a Avda 'A' 13-43, Zona 9, Guatemala City; tel. 2331-7468; fax 2331-6141; e-mail info@unionistas.com; internet www.unionistas.org; f. 1917; Sec.-Gen. ALVARO ENRIQUE ARZÚ IRIGOYEN.

Unidad Nacional de la Esperanza (UNE): 6a Avda 8-72, Zona 9, Guatemala City; tel. 2334-3451; e-mail ideas@une.org.gt; internet www.une.org.gt; f. 2001 following a split within the PAN; centre-left; Sec.-Gen. SANDRA TORRES DE COLOM.

Unidad Revolucionaria Nacional Guatemalteca—Movimiento Amplio de Izquierdas (URNG—MAIZ): 12a Avda 'B' 6-00, Zona 2, Guatemala City; tel. 2254-0704; fax 2254-7062; e-mail debate@urng-maiz.org.gt; internet www.urng-maiz.org.gt; f. 1982 following unification of principal guerrilla groups engaged in the civil war; formally registered as a political party in 1998; contested the 2011 elections in coalition with the Movimiento Político WINAQ (q.v.) and the Alternativa Nueva Nación (q.v.); Sec.-Gen. HÉCTOR ALFREDO NUILA ERICASTILLA.

Unión del Cambio Nacional (UCN): 5a Calle 5-27, Zone 9, Guatemala City; tel. 2361-6729; e-mail administracion.ucn@gmail.com; f. 2006; Sec.-Gen. MARIO AMILCAR ESTRADA ORELLANA.

Unión Democrática (UD): Casa 9, 5 Calle 12-00, Zona 14, Guatemala City; tel. 2363-5013; fax 2369-3062; e-mail info@uniondemocratica.info; f. 1983; Sec.-Gen. MANUEL EDUARDO CONDE ORELLANA.

Los Verdes (LV): 3a Avda 3-72, Zona 1, Guatemala City; tel. 570-3420; e-mail losverdesguatemala@gmail.com; Sec.-Gen. RODOLFO ROSALES GARCÍA SALAS.

VICTORIA: Edif. Crece Condado el Naranjo, Of. 607, 6°, 23 Calle 14-58, Zona 4 de Mixco, Guatemala City; Sec.-Gen. EDGAR ABRAHAM RIVERA SAGASTUME.

Visión con Valores (VIVA): 41 Calle 3-45, Zona 8, Guatemala City; tel. 2243-2999; e-mail contacto@visionconvalores.com; internet www.visionconvalores.com; contested the 2011 elections in coalition with Encuentro por Guatemala (q.v.); Sec.-Gen. HAROLD OSBERTO CABALLEROS LÓPEZ.

Diplomatic Representation

EMBASSIES IN GUATEMALA

Argentina: 5a Avda 6-50, Zona 14, Apdo 120, Guatemala City; tel. and fax 2464-5900; fax 2367-1091; e-mail eguat@mrecic.gov.ar; Ambassador ERNESTO JUSTO LÓPEZ.

Belize: Edif. Europlaza Torre II, Of. 1502, 5a Avda 5-55, Zona 14, Guatemala City; tel. 2207-4000; fax 2207-4001; e-mail infobelice@embajadadebelice.org; internet www.embajadadebelice.org; Ambassador ALFREDO MARTÍN MARTÍNEZ.

Brazil: Edif. Los Arcos, 2a Avda 20-13, Zona 10, Apdo 196-A, Guatemala City; tel. 2321-6800; fax 2366-1762; e-mail brascom@intelnet.net.gt; internet guatemala.itamaraty.gov.br; Ambassador JOSÉ ROBERTO DE ALMEIDA PINTO.

Canada: Edif. Edyma Plaza, 8°, 13a Calle 8-44, Zona 10, Apdo 400, Guatemala City; tel. 2363-4348; fax 2365-1210; e-mail gtmla@

international.gc.ca; internet www.canadainternational.gc.ca/guatemala; Ambassador HUGUES RÉAL ROUSSEAU.

Chile: 3a Avda 14-33, Zona 14, Guatemala City; tel. 2490-2323; fax 2334-8276; e-mail echilegu@intelnet.net.gt; Ambassador JUAN ALFONSO MANUEL MASFERRAR PELLIZARI.

Colombia: Edif. Europlaza, Torre I, Of. 1603, 5a Avda 5-55, Zona 14, Guatemala City; tel. 2385-3432; fax 2385-3438; e-mail embacolombia@intelett.com; internet www.embajadaenguatemala.gov.co; Ambassador FRANCISCO JOSÉ SANCLEMENTE MOLINA.

Costa Rica: 5a Avda 9-33, Zona 14, Guatemala City; tel. 2366-4215; fax 2337-1969; e-mail embacosta.gt@gmail.com; internet www.embajadacostaricaguatemala.com; Chargé d'affaires a.i. HEIZEL AMANDA ALPÍZAR OROZCO.

Cuba: Avda las Américas 20-72, Zona 13, Guatemala City; tel. 2332-5521; fax 2332-5525; e-mail embajador@gt.embacuba.cu; internet www.cubadiplomatica.cu/guatemala; Ambassador ROBERTO BLANCO DOMÍNGUEZ.

Dominican Republic: Centro Empresarial 'Zona Pradera', Torre II, Of. 1606, 18 Calle 24-69, Zona 10, Guatemala City; tel. 2261-7016; fax 2261-7017; e-mail embardgt@gmail.com; Ambassador RENÉ BIENVENIDO SANTANA GONZÁLEZ.

Ecuador: 4a Avda 12-04, Zona 14, Guatemala City; tel. 2368-0397; fax 2368-0397; e-mail embecuad@itelgua.com; Ambassador GALO ANDRÉS YÉPEZ HOLGUÍN.

Egypt: Edif. Cobella, 5°, 5a Avda 10-84, Zona 14, Apdo 502, Guatemala City; tel. 2333-6296; fax 2368-2808; e-mail embassy.guatemala@mfa.gov.eg; internet www.mfa.gov.eg/Guatemala_Emb; Ambassador MOSTAFA MAHMOUD MAHER ELREMALY.

El Salvador: Avda las Américas 16-40, Zona 13, Guatemala City; tel. 2360-7660; fax 2332-1228; e-mail emsalva@intelnet.net.gt; Ambassador JORGE ALBERTO PALENCIA MENA.

France: Edif. Cogefar, 5a Avda 8-59, Zona 14, Apdo 971-A, 01014 Guatemala City; tel. 2421-7370; fax 2421-7372; e-mail courrier@ambafrance-gt.org; internet www.ambafrance-gt.org; Ambassador PHILIPPE FRANC.

Germany: Edif. Reforma 10, 10°, Avda La Reforma 9-55, Zona 10, Guatemala City; tel. 2364-6700; fax 2365-2270; e-mail info@guat.diplo.de; internet www.guatemala.diplo.de; Ambassador MATTHIAS SONN.

Holy See: 10a Calle 4-47, Zona 9, Apdo 3041, Guatemala City (Apostolic Nunciature); tel. 2332-4274; fax 2334-1918; e-mail nuntius@itelgua.com; Apostolic Nuncio Most Rev. NICOLAS THEVENIN (Titular Archbishop of Aeclanum).

Honduras: 19 Avda A 20-19, Zona 10, Guatemala City; tel. 2366-5640; fax 2368-0062; e-mail embhond@intelnet.net.gt; Ambassador JORGE MIGUEL GABRIE LAGOS.

Israel: 13a Avda 14-07, Zona 10, Guatemala City; tel. 2333-6951; fax 2333-6950; e-mail info@guatemala.mfa.gov.il; internet guatemala.mfa.gov.il; Ambassador MOSHÉ BACHAR.

Italy: Edif. Santa Bárbara, 12a Calle 6-49, Zona 14, Guatemala City; tel. 2366-9271; fax 2367-3916; e-mail ambasciata.guatemala@esteri.it; internet www.ambguatemala.esteri.it; Ambassador FABRIZIO PIGNATELLI DELLA LEONESSA.

Japan: Edif. Torre Internacional, 10°, Avda de la Reforma 16-85, Zona 10, Guatemala City; tel. 2382-7300; fax 2382-7310; e-mail info@japon.net.gt; internet www.gt.emb-japan.go.jp; Ambassador EIICHI KAWAHARA.

Korea, Republic: Edif. Europlaza, Torre III, 7°, 5a Avda 5-55, Zona 14, Guatemala City; tel. 2382-4051; fax 2382-4057; e-mail korembsy@mofat.go.kr; internet gtm.mofat.go.kr; Ambassador CHOO YEON-GON.

Mexico: 2a Avda 7-57, Zona 10, Apdo 1455, Guatemala City; tel. 2420-3400; fax 2420-3410; e-mail embamexguat@itelgua.com; internet www.sre.gob.mx/guatemala; Ambassador CARLOS TIRADA ZAVALA.

Nicaragua: 13 Avda 14-54, Zona 10, Guatemala City; tel. 2333-4636; fax 2368-2284; e-mail embaguat@terra.com.gt; Ambassador SILVIO MORA MORA.

Norway: Edif. Murano Center, 15°, Of. 1501, 14 Calle 3-51, Zona 10, Apdo 1764, Guatemala City; tel. 2506-4000; fax 2366-5823; e-mail emb.guatemala@mfa.no; internet www.noruega.org.gt; Ambassador JAN GERHARD LASSEN.

Panama: 12a Calle 2-65, Zona 14, Apdo 929-A, Guatemala City; tel. 2366-3336; fax 2366-3338; e-mail panaguate@hotmail.com; internet www.panamaenelexterior.gob.pa/guatemala; Ambassador IRVING ORLANDO CENTENO SANSON.

Peru: 15a Avda A 20-16, Zona 13, Guatemala City; tel. 2339-1060; e-mail embajadadelperu@yahoo.com; Ambassador NILO JÉSUS FIGUEROA CORTAVARRIA.

Russia: 2a Avda 12-85, Zona 14, Guatemala City; tel. 2367-2765; fax 2367-2766; e-mail embajadarusa@gmail.com; internet www.guat.mid.ru; Ambassador NIKOLAY Y. BÁBICH.

Spain: 6a Calle 6-48, Zona 9, Guatemala City; tel. 2379-3530; fax 2379-3533; e-mail emb.guatemala@maec.es; internet www.maec.es/embajadas/guatemala; Ambassador MANUEL MARÍA LEJARRETA LOBO.

Sweden: Edif. Reforma 10, 11°, Avda de la Reforma 9-55, Zona 10, Apdo 966-A, Guatemala City; tel. 2384-7300; fax 2384-7350; e-mail ambassaden.guatemala@foreign.ministry.se; internet www.swedenabroad.com/guatemala; Ambassador JAN ANDERS MICHAEL FRUHLING.

Switzerland: Edif. Torre Internacional, 14°, 16a Calle 0-55, Zona 10, Apdo 1426, Guatemala City; tel. 2367-5520; fax 2367-5811; e-mail gua.vertretung@eda.admin.ch; internet www.eda.admin.ch/guatemala; Chargé d'affaires a.i. ALEXANDRE GUYOT.

Taiwan (Republic of China): 4a Avda A 13-25, Zona 9, Apdo 897, Guatemala City; tel. 2322-0168; fax 2332-2668; e-mail gtm@mofa.gov.tw; internet www.taiwanembassy.org/gt; Ambassador ADOLFO SUN.

United Kingdom: Edif. Torre Internacional, 11°, Avda de la Reforma, 16a Calle, Zona 10, Guatemala City; tel. 2380-7300; fax 2380-7339; e-mail embassy@intelnett.com; internet ukinguatemala.fco.gov.uk; Ambassador SARAH DICKSON.

USA: Avda de la Reforma 7-01, Zona 10, Guatemala City; tel. 2326-4000; fax 2326-4654; internet guatemala.usembassy.gov; Ambassador ARNOLD A. CHACON.

Uruguay: Centro Empresarial Pradera Torre IV, Of. 701, 18 Calle 24-69, Zona 10, Guatemala City; tel. 2261-8001; fax 2261-8003; e-mail uruguatemala@mrree.gub.uy; Ambassador RAÚL JUAN POLLAK GIAMPRIETO.

Venezuela: Edif. Atlantis, Of. 601, 13a Calle 3-40, Zona 10, Apdo 152, Guatemala City; tel. 2317-0703; fax 2317-0705; e-mail embavene@concyt.gob.gt; internet guatemala.embajada.gob.ve; Ambassador ORLANDO TORREALBA JÍMENEZ.

Judicial System

The judiciary comprises the Supreme Court, the Courts of Appeal, the Courts of the First Instance and the Justices of Peace. The Supreme Court is the highest court and is responsible for the administration of the judiciary. There are 20 Courts of Appeal throughout the country. There are 10 civil and 12 penal Courts of the First Instance in Guatemala City, and at least one civil and one penal in each of the 21 remaining departments.

Corte Suprema de Justicia: Centro Cívico, 21 Calle 7-70, Zona 1, Guatemala City; tel. 2426-7000; internet www.oj.gob.gt/csj; members are appointed by Congress; Pres. Dr GABRIEL ANTONIO MEDRANO VALENZUELA.

Attorney-General: CLAUDIA PAZ Y PAZ BAILEY.

Procurator-General: VLADIMIR AGUILAR GUERRA.

Religion

Almost all of the inhabitants profess Christianity, with a majority belonging to the Roman Catholic Church. In recent years the Protestant churches have attracted a growing number of converts.

CHRISTIANITY

The Roman Catholic Church

For ecclesiastical purposes, Guatemala comprises two archdioceses, 10 dioceses and the Apostolic Vicariates of El Petén and Izabal. Some 60% of the population are Roman Catholics.

Bishops' Conference: Conferencia Episcopal de Guatemala, Secretariado General del Episcopado, Km 15, Calzada Roosevelt 4-54, Zona 7, Mixco, Apdo 1698, Guatemala City; tel. 2433-1832; fax 2433-1834; e-mail ceguatemala@gmail.com; internet www.iglesiacatolica.org.gt; f. 1973; Pres. Rev. RODOLFO VALENZUELA NÚÑEZ (Bishop of La Verapaz).

Archbishop of Guatemala City: OSCAR JULIO VIAN MORALES, Palacio Arzobispal, 7a Avda 6-21, Zona 1, Apdo 723, Guatemala City; tel. 2231-9707; fax 2251-5068; e-mail arzobispadodeguatemala@gmail.com; internet www.arzobispadodeguatemala.com.

Archbishop of Los Altos, Quetzaltenango-Totonicapán: MARIO ALBERTO MOLINA PALMA, Arzobispado, 11 Avda 6-27, Zona 1, Apdo 11, 09001 Quetzaltenango; tel. 7761-2840; fax 7761-6049.

The Anglican Communion

Guatemala comprises one of the five dioceses of the Iglesia Anglicana de la Región Central de América.

Bishop of Guatemala: Rt Rev. ARMANDO ROMÁN GUERRA SORIA, Avda Castellana 40-06, Zona 8, Apdo 58, Guatemala City; tel. 2473-6828; fax 2472-0764; e-mail agepiscopal@yahoo.com; diocese founded 1967.

Protestant Churches

The largest Protestant denomination in Guatemala is the Full Gospel Church, followed by the Assembly of God, the Central American Church, and the Prince of Peace Church. The Baptist, Presbyterian, Lutheran and Episcopalian churches are also represented.

Convención de Iglesias Bautista de Guatemala (CIBG): Convention of Baptist Churches of Guatemala, 12 Calle 9-54, Zona 1, Apdo 322, 01901 Guatemala City; tel. and fax 2253-9194; e-mail convencion@cibg.org; internet cibg.org; f. 1946; Pres. OTTO ECHEVERRÍA VELÁSQUEZ; 43,876 mems.

Church of Jesus Christ of Latter-day Saints: 12a Calle 3-37, Zona 9, Guatemala City; e-mail contactos@mormones.org.gt; internet www.mormones.org.gt; 17 bishoprics, 9 chapels; Pres. THOMAS S. MONSON.

Conferencia de Iglesias Evangélicas de Guatemala (CIEDEG) (Conference of Protestant Churches in Guatemala): 7a Avda 1-11, Zona 2, Guatemala City; tel. 2232-3724; fax 2232-1609; internet www.nuevociedeg.org; f. 1987; Pres. VITALINO SIMILOX.

Congregación Luterana La Epifanía (Evangelisch-Lutherische Epiphanias-Gemeinde): 2a Avda 15-31, Zona 10, 01010 Guatemala City; tel. 2333-3697; fax 2366-4968; e-mail pfarrer@laepifania.org; internet www.laepifania.org; mem. of Lutheran World Federation; Pres. MARKUS BÖTTCHER; 200 mems.

Iglesia Evangélica Nacional Presbiteriana de Guatemala: Avda Simeón Cañas 7-13, Zona 2, Apdo 655, Guatemala City; tel. 2288-4441; fax 2254-1242; e-mail ienpg@yahoo.com; f. 1962; mem. of World Alliance of Reformed Churches; Pres. BENJAMIN YAC POZ; Sec. Pastor ISAÍAS GARCÍA CITALÁN; 25,000 mems.

Iglesia Luterana Castillo Fuerte: 19 Avda 6-64, Zona 11, Guatemala City; tel. 2472-0186; fax 2384-0703; e-mail castillofuerte@lycos.com; f. 2000.

Iglesia Luterana El Divino Salvador de Zacapa: 4a Calle, 9-34, Zona 1, Barrio San Marcos, Zacapa; tel. 7941-0574; e-mail hogarluterano@hotmail.com; f. 1946; Pastors GERARDO VENANCIO VÁSQUEZ SALGUERO, ARED RODRÍGUEZ.

Iglesia Nacional Evangélica Menonita Guatemalteca: Guatemala City; tel. 2339-0606; e-mail AlvaradoJE@ldschurch.org; Pres. ALFREDO SIQUIC ACTÉ; 12,000 mems.

Union Church: 12a Calle 7-37, Zona 9, 01009 Guatemala City; tel. 2361-2037; fax 2362-3961; e-mail unionchurchguatemala@gmail.com; internet www.unionchurchguatemala.com; f. 1943; English-speaking church; Pastor JOHN CONNER.

The Press

PRINCIPAL DAILIES

Diario de Centro América: Casa Editora Tipografía Nacional, 18 Calle 6-72, Zona 1, Guatemala City; tel. 2414-9600; e-mail lector@dca.gob.gt; internet www.dca.gob.gt; f. 1880; morning; official; Dir-Gen. HÉCTOR SALVATIERRA; Editor-in-Chief JUAN CARLOS RUIZ CALDERÓN.

Guía Interamericana de Turismo: Edif. Plaza los Arcos, 3°, 20 Calle 5-35, Zona 10, Guatemala City; tel. 2450-6431; e-mail info@guiainter.org; internet www.guiainter.org; f. 1989; online journal; Dir-Gen. MARIO ORINI; Editor ALFREDO MAYORGA.

La Hora: 9 Calle A 1-56, Zona 1, Apdo 1593, Guatemala City; tel. 2423-1800; fax 2423-1837; e-mail lahora@lahora.com.gt; internet www.lahora.com.gt; f. 1920; evening; ind.; Dir-Gen. OSCAR CLEMENTE MARROQUÍN; Editor-in-Chief JAVIER ESTRADA TOBAR; circ. 18,000.

Nuestro Diario: 15 Avda 24-27, Zona 13, Guatemala City; tel. and fax 2379-1600; fax 2379-1621; e-mail opinion@nuestrodiario.com.gt; internet www.nuestrodiario.com; Gen. Man. FERNANDO FAHSEN; Gen. Editor MARIO RECINOS.

El Periódico: 15 Avda 24-51, Zona 13, Guatemala City; tel. 2427-2300; fax 2427-2361; e-mail redaccion@elperiodico.com.gt; internet www.elperiodico.com.gt; f. 1996; morning; ind.; Pres. JOSÉ RUBÉN ZAMORA MARROQUÍN; Editor TULIO JUÁREZ; circ. 30,000.

Prensa Libre: 13 Calle 9-31, Zona 1, Apdo 2063, Guatemala City; tel. 2230-5096; fax 2251-8768; e-mail nacionales@prensalibre.com.gt; internet www.prensalibre.com.gt; f. 1951; morning; ind.; Gen. Man. LUIS ENRIQUE SOLÓRZANO; Editor GONZALO MARROQUÍN GODOY; circ. 120,000.

Siglo Veintiuno: 14 Avda 4-33, Zona 1, Guatemala City; tel. 2423-6100; fax 2423-6346; e-mail suscripciones@siglo21.com.gt; internet www.s21.com.gt; f. 1990; morning; Dir GUILLERMO FERNÁNDEZ; circ. 65,000.

PERIODICALS

Amiga: 13 Calle 9-31, Zona 1, Guatemala City; tel. 2412-5000; fax 2220-5123; e-mail revistas@prensalibre.com.gt; internet www.revistaamiga.com; f. 1988; health; Dir CAROLINA VÁSQUEZ ARAYA; Editor SILVIA LANUZA.

Gerencia: Torre Citigroup, Of. 402, 3a Avda 13-78, Zona 14, Guatemala City; tel. 2427-4900; fax 2427-4971; e-mail jaqueline@agg.org.gt; internet www.agg.org.gt/revista-gerencia-b; f. 1967; monthly; official organ of the Asscn of Guatemalan Managers; Man. ILEANA LÓPEZ AVILA.

El Metropolitano: Plaza Morumbi 7 y 8, 2°, 3a Calle 15-29, Zona 8, San Cristóbal, Guatemala City; e-mail info@elmetropolitano.net; internet www.elmetropolitano.net; Editor JORGE GARCÍA MONTENEGRO.

Mundo Motor: 13a Calle 9-31, Zona 1, Guatemala City; tel. 2412-5000; fax 2220-5123; e-mail evasquez@prensalibre.com.gt; internet www.mundoymotor.com; Dir CAROLINA VÁSQUEZ; Editor NÉSTOR A. LARRAZÁBAL B.

Revista Data Export: 15 Avda 14-72, Zona 13, Guatemala City; tel. 2422-3431; fax 2422-3434; e-mail portal@export.com.gt; internet revistadata.export.com.gt; monthly; foreign trade affairs; organ of the Asociacíon Guatemalteca de Exportadores; Editor FULVIA DONIS.

Revista Industria y Negocios: 6a Ruta 9-21, Zona 4, Guatemala City; tel. 2380-9000; e-mail contactemos@industriaguate.com; internet www.revistaindustria.com; monthly; official organ of the Chamber of Industry; Dir JAVIER ZAPEDA.

Revista Mundo Comercial: 10a Calle 3-80, Zona 1, 01001 Guatemala City; e-mail jbalcarcel@camaradecomercio.org.gt; internet www.negociosenguatemala.com; monthly; business; official organ of the Chamber of Commerce; Gen. Man. JEANNETTE BALCARCEL; circ. 11,000.

Viaje a Guatemala: 13 Calle 9-31, Zona 1, Guatemala City; tel. 2412-5000; fax 2220-5123; internet www.viajeaguatemala.com; Dir-Gen. CAROLINA VÁSQUEZ; Editor-in-Chief SILVIA LANUZA.

PRESS ASSOCIATION

Asociación de Periodistas de Guatemala (APG): 14 Calle 3-29, Zona 1, Guatemala City; tel. 2232-1813; fax 2238-2781; e-mail apege@intelnet.net.gt; internet www.apg-gt.org; f. 1947; affiliated to International Freedom of Expression Exchange and Fed. Latinoamericana de Periodistas; Pres. VICTOR HUGO DE LEÓN MOLLINEADO; Sec. ADBEL MARCO OSORIO ALVARADO.

NEWS AGENCY

Inforpress Centroamericana: Calle Mariscal o Diagonal 21, 6-58, Zona 11, 0100 Guatemala City; tel. and fax 2473-1704; e-mail inforpre@guate.net; internet www.inforpressca.com; f. 1972; ind.; publishes 2 weekly news bulletins, in English and Spanish; Dir NURIA VILLANOVA.

Publishers

Cholsamaj: Calle 5, 2-58, Zona 1, Iximulew, Guatemala City; tel. 2232-5402; fax 2232-5959; e-mail editorialcholsamaj@yahoo.com; internet www.cholsamaj.org; Mayan language publs; Pres. KIKAB' GERBER MUX; Exec. Dir ULMIL JOEL MEJÍA.

Ediciones Legales Comercio e Industria: 12a Avda 14-78, Zone 1, Guatemala City; tel. 2253-5725; fax 2220-7592; Man. Dir LUIS EMILIO BARRIOS.

Editorial Cultura: Avda 12 11-11, Zona 1, Guatemala City; tel. 2232-5667; fax 2230-0591; e-mail kaxin@tutopia.com; internet www.mcd.gob.gt/editorial-cultura; f. 1987; part of the Ministry of Culture and Sport; Chief Editor FRANCISCO MORALES SANTOS.

Editorial Palo de Hormigo: 0 Calle 16-40, Zona 15, Col. El Maestro, Guatemala City; tel. 2369-3089; fax 2369-8858; e-mail eph_info@palodehormigo.com; f. 1990; Man. Dir RICARDO ULYSSES CIFUENTES.

Editorial Santillana, SA: 7 Avda 11-11, Zona 9, Guatemala City; tel. 2429-4300; fax 2429-4301; e-mail santillana@santillana.com.gt; internet www.gruposantillana.com/gr_gu.htm; f. 1995; subsidiary of Grupo Santillana (Spain); Dir-Gen. ALBERTO POLANCO.

Editorial Universitaria: Universidad de San Carlos de Guatemala, Ciudad Universitaria, Zona 12, Guatemala City; tel. and fax 2476-9616; e-mail editorialusac@usac.edu.gt; internet editorial.usac.edu.gt; literature, social sciences, health, pure and technical sciences, humanities, secondary and university educational textbooks; Dir ANACLETO MEDINA GÓMEZ.

F & G Editores: 31a Avda 'C' 5-54, Zona 7, 01007 Guatemala City; tel. and fax 2439-8358; e-mail informacion@fygeditores.com; internet www.fygeditores.com; f. 1990 as Figueroa y Gallardo; changed name in 1993; law, literature and social sciences; Editor RAÚL FIGUEROA SARTI.

Piedra Santa: 37 Avda 1-26, Zona 7, Guatemala City; tel. 2422-7676; fax 2422-7610; e-mail info@piedrasanta.com; internet www.piedrasanta.com; f. 1947; education, culture; Man. Dir IRENE PIEDRA SANTA.

PUBLISHERS' ASSOCIATION

Consejo Nacional del Libro (CONALIBRO): 11 Avda 11-07, Zona 1, Guatemala City; tel. 2253-0536; fax 2253-0544; e-mail conalibro@gmail.com; f. 1989; Pres. LUIS EDUARDO MORALES.

Broadcasting and Communications

TELECOMMUNICATIONS

Comcel Guatemala (Tigo): Edif. Plaza Tigo, 3°, Km 9.5, Carretera al Salvador, Guatemala City; tel. 2428-0000; fax 2428-1140; e-mail servicioalcliente@tigo.com.gt; internet www.tigo.com.gt; f. 1990; provider of mobile telecommunications; 55% owned by Millicom International Cellular (Luxembourg); CEO VICTOR UNDA.

Telecomunicaciones de Guatemala, SA (Claro): Edif. Central Telgua, 7a Avda 12-39, Zona 1, Guatemala City; tel. 2230-2098; fax 2251-1799; e-mail clientes@claro.com.gt; internet www.claro.com.gt; fmrly state-owned Empresa Guatemalteca de Telecomunicaciones (Guatel); name changed as above to facilitate privatization; 95% share sold in 1998; owned by América Móvil, SA de CV (Mexico); Dir ANA BEATRIZ GODÍNEZ.

Telefónica Guatemala, SA (MoviStar): Edif. Iberoplaza, 1°, Blvd Los Próceres 20-09, Zona 10, Guatemala City; tel. 2379-7979; e-mail servicioalcliente@telefonica.com.gt; internet www.movistar.com.gt; owned by TelefónicaMóviles, SA (Spain); acquired BellSouth Guatemala in 2004; wireless, wireline and radio paging communications services; 298,000 customers; Dir SALVADOR MONTES DE OCA.

Regulatory Authority

Superintendencia de Telecomunicaciones de Guatemala: 4 Avda 15-51, Zona 10, Guatemala City; tel. 2321-1000; fax 2321-1074; e-mail informacion@sit.gob.gt; internet www.sit.gob.gt; f. 1996; Supt EDDIE PADILLA.

BROADCASTING

Radio

Central de Radio, SA: Edif. Canal 3, 30 Avda 3-40, Zona 11, Guatemala City; tel. 2410-3150; internet www.centralderadio.com.gt; owns and operates 7 radio stations; Pres. FERNANDO VILLANUEVA CARRERA.

Emisoras Unidas de Guatemala: 4a Calle 6-84, Zona 13, Guatemala City; tel. 2421-5353; fax 2475-3870; e-mail patrullajeinformativo@emisorasunidas.com; internet www.emisorasunidas.com; f. 1964; 6 stations: Yo Sí Sideral, Emisoras-Unidas, Kiss, Atmósfera, Fabustereo and La Grande; Pres. EDGAR ARCHILA MARROQUÍN.

La Marca: 30a Avda 3-40, Zona 11, Guatemala City; tel. 2410-3150; fax 2410-3151; e-mail lamarca@94fm.com.gt; internet www.94fm.com.gt.

Metro Stereo: 14a Avda 14-78, Zona 10, Guatemala City; tel. 2277-7686; fax 2368-2040; e-mail metrored@metrostereo.net; internet www.metrostereo.net; f. 1980; Dir RUGGIERO MAURO-RHODIO.

Radio Corporación Nacional (RCN): Torre Profesional I, Of. 903, 6 Avda 0-60, Centro Comercial Zona 4, Guatemala City; tel. 2411-2000; tel. 2411-2005; internet www.rcn.com.gt; owns and operates 12 radio stations; Pres. SERGIO ROBERTO ALCÁZAR SOLÍS.

Radio Cultural TGN: 4a Avda 30-09 Zona 3, Apdo 601, 01901 Guatemala City; tel. 2207-7700; fax 2207-7600; e-mail tgn@radiocultural.com; internet www.radiocultural.com; f. 1950; religious and cultural station; programmes in Spanish and English, Cakchiquel, Kekchi, Quiché and Aguacateco; Dir ESTEBAN SYWULKA.

Radio Grupo Alius, SA: Torre Profesional II, 10°, 6 Avda 0-60, Zona 4, Guatemala City; tel. 2412-8484; fax 2412-8448; e-mail exa@grupoalius.com; internet www.grupoalius.com; owns and operates 5 radio stations; Pres. EDUARDO ALFONSO LIU.

Radio Nacional TGW (La Voz de Guatemala): 18a Calle 6-72, Zona 1, Guatemala City; tel. 2323-8282; fax 2323-8310; e-mail info@radiotgw.gob.gt; internet www.radiotgw.gob.gt; f. 1930; govt station; Dir (vacant).

Television

Azteca Guatemala: 12 Avda 1-96, Zona 2 de Mixco, Col. Alvarado, Guatemala City; tel. 2411-1231; e-mail festrada@tvaguatemala.tv; internet www.azteca.com.gt; f. 2008; subsidiary by the merger of Televisión Azteca (Mexico) and Latitud TV; commercial; general; Dir-Gen. MARIO SAN ROMÁN.

Canal Antigua: Of. 12C, 12°, Avda Reforma 13-70, Zona 9, 01009 Guatemala City; tel. 2222-8800; e-mail info@canalantigua.com; internet www.canalantigua.com; f. 2009; commercial; news and opinions; Exec. Dir ANABEL BONAMI.

Guatevisión: Edif. Tikal Futura, Torre Sol, 4°, Calz Roosevelt 22-43, Zona 11, Guatemala City; tel. 2328-6000; e-mail info@guatevision.com; internet www.guatevision.com; f. 2000; Dir HAROLDO SÁNCHEZ.

Radio-Televisión Guatemala, SA: Edif. Canal 3, 30 Avda 3-40, Zona 11, Apdo 1367, Guatemala City; tel. 2410-3000; e-mail telediario@canal3.com.gt; internet www.canal3.com.gt; f. 1956; commercial; part of Albavisión; Pres. MAXIMILIANO KESTLER FARNÉS; Vice-Pres. J. F. VILLANUEVA; operates the following channels:

Teleonce: 20 Calle 5-02, Zona 10, Guatemala City; tel. 2469-0900; fax 5203-8455; e-mail jcof@canalonce.tv; internet canales11y13.blogspot.in; f. 1968; commercial; channel 11; Gen. Dir JUAN CARLOS ORTIZ.

Televisiete, SA: 30 Avda 3-40, Zona 11, Apdo 1242, Guatemala City; tel. 2410-3000; fax 2369-1393; internet www.canal7.com.gt; f. 1988; commercial; channel 7; Dir LUIS RABBÉ.

Trecevisión, SA: 20 Calle 5-02, Zona 10, Guatemala City; tel. 2368-2221; e-mail escribanos@canal7.com.gt; internet www.canaltrece.tv; f. 1978; commercial; channel 13; f. 1978; Dir FERNANDO VILLANUEVA.

Regulatory Authority

Dirección General de Radiodifusión y Televisión Nacional: Edif. Tipografía Nacional, 3°, 18 Calle 6-72, Zona 1, Guatemala City; tel. 2323-8282; e-mail contacto@radiotgw.gob.gt; internet www.radiotgw.gob.gt; f. 1931; govt supervisory body; Dir-Gen. JUAN JOSÉ RÍOS.

Finance

(cap. = capital; res = reserves; dep. = deposits; m. = million; brs = branches; amounts in quetzales)

BANKING

Superintendencia de Bancos: 9a Avda 22-00, Zona 1, Apdo 2306, Guatemala City; tel. 2429-5000; fax 2232-0002; e-mail info@sib.gob.gt; internet www.sib.gob.gt; f. 1946; Supt RAMÓN BENJAMÍN TOBAR MORALES.

Central Bank

Banco de Guatemala: 7a Avda 22-01, Zona 1, Apdo 365, Guatemala City; tel. 2429-6000; fax 2253-4035; e-mail webmaster@banguat.gob.gt; internet www.banguat.gob.gt; f. 1946; state-owned; cap. and res 504.1m., dep. 34,384.7m. (Dec. 2009); Pres. EDGAR BALTAZAR BARQUÍN DURÁN; Gen. Man. SERGIO FRANCISCO RECINOS RIVERA.

State Commercial Bank

Crédito Hipotecario Nacional de Guatemala (CHN): 7a Avda 22-77, Zona 1, Apdo 242, Guatemala City; tel. 2223-0333; fax 2238-2041; e-mail mercadeo@chn.com.gt; internet www.chn.com.gt; f. 1980; govt-owned; cap. 15m., res 418m., dep. 2,173.6m. (Dec. 2010); Pres. OSCAR EDGAR ESTUARDO RAMÍREZ SÁNCHEZ; Gen. Man. GUSTAVO ADOLFO DÍAZ LEÓN; 44 agencies.

Private Commercial Banks

Banco Agromercantil de Guatemala, SA: 7a Avda 7-30, Zona 9, 01009 Guatemala City; tel. 2338-6565; fax 2388-6566; e-mail bam@bam.com.gt; internet www.bam.com.gt; f. 1926; changed name to Banco Agrícola Mercantil in 1948; cap. 260.5m., res 25.6m., dep. 1,659.9m. (Feb. 2014); Pres. JOSÉ LUIS VALDÉS O'CONNELL; Man. CHRISTIAN ROBERTO SCHNEIDER WILL; 234 brs.

Banco de América Central, SA (BAC): Local 6-12, 1°, 7a Avda 6-26, Zona 9, Guatemala City; tel. 2360-9440; fax 2331-8720; internet www.bac.net; Pres. LUIS FERNANDO SAMAYOA DELGADO; Gen. Man. JUAN JOSÉ VIAUD PÉREZ; 20 brs.

Banco Citibank de Guatemala, SA: Torre Citibank, 1°, 3a Avda 13-78, Zona 10, 01010 Guatemala City; tel. 2333-6574; fax 2333-6860; internet www.citibank.com.gt; Citi acquired Banco Cuscatlan and Banco Uno in 2007; Pres. CONSTANTINO GOTSIS.

Banco de Desarrollo Rural, SA: Avda La Reforma 9-30, Zona 9, Guatemala City; tel. 2339-8888; fax 2360-9740; e-mail internacional4@banrural.com.gt; internet www.banrural.com.gt; f. 1971 as Banco de Desarrollo Agrícola; name changed as above in 1998; cap. 1,151.2m., res 1,623m., dep. 26,537.9m. (Dec. 2011); Pres. ADOLFO FERNANDO PEÑA PÉREZ; 640 brs.

Banco G & T Continental, SA: Plaza Continental, 6a Avda 9-08, Zona 9, Guatemala City; tel. 2338-6801; fax 2332-2682; e-mail subanco@gytcontinental.com.gt; internet www.gytcontinental.com.gt; f. 2000 following merger of Banco Continental and Banco Granai y Townson; total assets 11.4m. (2000); Gen. Man. FLAVIO MONTENEGRO; 151 brs.

Banco Industrial, SA (BAINSA): Edif. Centro Financiero, Torre 1, 7a Avda 5-10, Zona 4, Apdo 744, Guatemala City; tel. 2420-3000; fax 2331-9437; e-mail webmaster@bi.com.gt; internet www.bi.com.gt; f. 1964 to promote industrial devt; merged with Banco del Quetzal in 2007; cap. 1,377m., res 1,383.7m., dep. 34,998m. (Dec. 2011); Exec. Pres. DIEGO PULIDO ARAGÓN; 350 brs.

Banco Inmobilario, SA: Edif. Galerias España, 7a Avda 11-59, Zona 9, Apdo 1181, Guatemala City; tel. 2339-3777; fax 2332-1418; e-mail info@bcoinmob.com.gt; internet www.bancoinmobiliario.com.gt; f. 1958; cap. 77.6m., res 0.4m., dep. 738.6m. (Dec. 2002); Pres. ADEL ABED ANTON TURJUMAN; 44 brs.

Banco Promerica Guatemala: Edif. Reforma 10, 2°, Avda 9-55Z, 01010 Guatemala City; tel. 2413-9400; e-mail servicio@bancopromerica.com.gt; internet www.bancopromerica.com.gt; f. 1991 as Banco de la Producción, SA (BANPRO), adopted present name in 2007 following merger with Bancasol; Gen. Man. EDGAR BRAND.

Banco Reformador, SA: 7a Avda 7-24, Zona 9, 01009 Guatemala City; tel. 2362-0888; fax 2362-0847; internet www.bancoreformador.com; cap. 392.5m., res 220.4m., dep. 6,765.1m. (Dec. 2010); merged with Banco de la Construcción in 2000, acquired Banco SCI in 2007; Pres. LUIS MIGUEL AGUIRRE FERNÁNDEZ; Gen. Man. MARÍA ANTONIETA DE BONILLA; 100 brs.

Banco de los Trabajadores: Avda Reforma 6-20, Zona 9, 01001 Guatemala City; tel. 2410-2600; fax 2410-2616; e-mail webmaster@bantrab.net.gt; internet www.bantrab.com.gt; f. 1966; deals with loans for establishing and improving small industries as well as normal banking business; cap. 460.4m., dep. 2,119.5m., total assets 2,897.6m. (Dec. 2005); Pres. SERGIO HERNÁNDEZ; Gen. Man. RONALD GIOVANNI GARCÍA NAVARIJO; 52 brs.

Inter Banco, SA: Torre Internacional, Avda Reforma 15-85, Zona 10, Apdo 2588, Guatemala City; tel. 2277-3666; fax 2366-6743; e-mail info@bco.inter.com; internet www.interbanco.com.gt; f. 1976; cap. 217.7m., res 91m., dep. 3,545.8m. (Dec. 2011); Pres. CÉSAR JOSÉ ANTONIO CORRALES AGUILAR; Gen. Man. FRANCISCO NARANJO MARTÍNEZ; 44 brs.

Banking Association

Asociación Bancaria de Guatemala: Edif. Margarita 2, Torre II, 5°, Of. 502, Diagonal 6, No 10-11, Zona 10, Guatemala City; tel. 2382-7200; fax 2382-7201; internet www.abg.org.gt; f. 1961; represents all state and private banks; Pres. CHRISTIAN SCHNEIDER.

STOCK EXCHANGE

Bolsa de Valores Nacional, SA: Centro Financiero, Torre 2, 9°, 7a Avda 5-10, Zona 4, Guatemala City; tel. 2338-4400; fax 2332-1721; e-mail info@bvnsa.com.gt; internet www.bvnsa.com.gt; f. 1987; the exchange is commonly owned (1 share per associate) and trades stocks from private companies, govt bonds, letters of credit and other securities; Gen. Man. ROLANDO SAN ROMÁN.

INSURANCE

National Companies

Aseguradora La Ceiba, SA: 20 Calle 15-20, Zona 13, Guatemala City; tel. 2379-1800; fax 2334-8167; e-mail aceiba@aceiba.com.gt; internet www.aceiba.com.gt; f. 1978; Man. ALEJANDRO BELTRANENA.

Aseguradora General, SA: 10a Calle 3-71, Zona 10, Guatemala City; tel. 2285-7200; fax 2334-2093; e-mail servicio@generali.com.gt; internet www.aseguresemejor.com; f. 1968; subsidiary of Grupo Generali, Trieste, Italy; Pres. ENRIQUE NEUTZE AYCINENA; Man. ENRIQUE NEUTZE TORIELLO.

Aseguradora Guatemalteca, SA (ASEGUA): Edif. Torre Azul, 10°, 4a Calle 7-53, Zona 9, Guatemala City; tel. 2361-0206; fax 2361-1093; e-mail aseguate@guate.net; internet www.aseguate.com; f. 1974; Pres. Gen. FERNANDO ALFONSO CASTILLO RAMÍREZ; Man. JOSÉ GUILLERMO H. LÓPEZ CORDÓN.

Chartis Seguros Guatemala, SA: Edif. Etisa, 7a Avda 12-23, Plazuela España, Zona 9, Guatemala City; tel. 2285-5900; fax 2361-3032; e-mail cmg.servicios@chartisinsurance.com; internet www.chartisinsurance.com; f. 1967 as La Seguridad de Centroamérica; present name adopted 2010; Gen. Man. JUAN MANUEL FRIEDERICH LOPEZ.

Cía de Seguros El Roble, SA: Torre 2, 7a Avda 5-10, Zona 4, Guatemala City; tel. 2420-3333; fax 2361-1191; e-mail rerales@elroble.com; internet www.elroble.com; f. 1973; Pres. JUAN MIGUEL TORREBIARTE; Gen. Man. HERMANN GIRON.

Departamento de Seguros y Previsión del Crédito Hipotecario Nacional: Centro Cívico, 7a Avda 22-77, Zona 1, Guatemala City; tel. 2223-0333; fax 2253-8584; e-mail vjsc@chn.com.gt; internet www.chn.com.gt; f. 1942; Pres. OSCAR ERASMO VELASQUEZ RIVERA; Man. GUSTAVO ADOLFO DÍAZ LEÓN.

Mapfre Seguros Guatemala, SA: Edif. Europlaza, Torre IV, 5a Avda 5-55, Zona 14, Guatemala City; tel. 2328-5000; fax 2328-5001; e-mail roberto.ewel@mapfre.com.gt; internet www.mapfre.com.gt; Gen. Man. JOSÉ TULIO URRUTIA.

Pan-American Life Insurance de Guatemala Cía de Seguros, SA: Edif. Plaza Panamericana, 10°, Avda la Reforma 9-00, Zona 9, Guatemala City; tel. 2338-9800; e-mail servicioalclientegt@panamericanlife.com; internet www.palig.com/Regions/guatemala; f. 1968; Country Man. SALVADOR LEIVA MADRID.

Seguros Columna, SA: 5a. Calle 0-55, Zona 9, Apdo 01009, Guatemala City; tel. 2419-2020; e-mail info@seguroscolumna.com; internet www.seguroscolumna.com; f. 1994; part of Corporación Financiera Cooperativa FENACOAC; Pres. JOSÉ GUILLERMO PERALTA ROSA; Gen. Man. BORIS ESTUARDO QUIRDA PINTO.

Seguros G & T, SA: Edif. Mini, 6a Avda 1-73, Zona 4, Guatemala City; tel. 2338-5778; e-mail erodriguez@gyt.com.gt; internet www.segurosgyt.com.gt; f. 1947; Pres. MARÍO GRANAI ANDRINO; Gen. Man. ENRIQUE RODRÍGUEZ.

Seguros de Occidente, SA: Edif. Corporación de Occidente, 7a Avda 7-33, Zona 9, Guatemala City; tel. 2279-7000; e-mail seguros@occidentecorp.com.gt; internet www.occidente.com.gt/cdo; f. 1979; Pres. JOSÉ GÚZMAN; Gen. Man. MARIO ROBERTO VALDEAVELLANO MUÑOZ.

Seguros Universales, SA: 4a Calle 7-73, Zona 9, Apdo 01009, Guatemala City; tel. 2384-7400; fax 2332-3372; e-mail info@segurosuniversales.net; internet www.segurosuniversales.net; f. 1962; Pres. PEDRO NOLASCO SICILIA VALLS; Gen. Man. FELIPE SICILIA.

Insurance Association

Asociación Guatemalteca de Instituciones de Seguros (AGIS): Edif. Torre Profesional I, Of. 703, 4°, 6a Avda 0-60, Zona 4, Guatemala City; tel. 2335-2140; fax 2335-2357; e-mail info@agis.com.gt; internet www.agis.com.gt; f. 1953; 12 mems; Pres. JUAN RAÚL AGUILAR KAEHLER; Exec. Dir ENRIQUE MURILLO C.

Trade and Industry

DEVELOPMENT ORGANIZATIONS

Instituto de Fomento de Hipotecas Aseguradas (FHA): Edif. Aristos Reforma, 2°, Of. 207, Avda Reforma 7-62, Zona 9, Guatemala City; tel. 2323-5656; fax 2362-9491; e-mail promocion@fha.gob.gt; internet www.fha.gob.gt; f. 1961; insured mortgage institution; Pres. EDIN HOMERO VELASQUEZ ESCOBEDO; Man. SERGIO ARMANDO IRUNGARAY SUÁREZ.

Instituto Nacional de Administración Pública (INAP): Blvd Los Próceres 16-40, Zona 10, Apdo 2753, Guatemala City; tel. 2419-8181; fax 2419-8126; e-mail informacion@inap.gob.gt; internet www.inap.gob.gt; f. 1964; provides technical experts to assist in administrative reform programmes; provides training for govt staff; research programmes in administration, sociology, politics and economics; Pres. FERNANDO FUENTES MOHR; Man. HÉCTOR HUGO VÁSQUEZ BARREDA.

Secretaría de Planificación y Programación (SEGEPLAN): 9a Calle 10-44, Zona 1, Guatemala City; tel. 2232-6212; fax 2253-3127; e-mail segeplan@segeplan.gob.gt; internet www.segeplan.gob.gt; f. 1954; oversees implementation of the national economic devt plan; Sec. LUIS FERNANDO CARRERA CASTRO.

CHAMBERS OF COMMERCE AND INDUSTRY

Cámara de Comercio de Guatemala: 10a Calle 3-80, Zona 1, Guatemala City; tel. 2417-2700; fax 2220-9393; e-mail info@camaradecomercio.org.gt; internet www.negociosenguatemala.com; f. 1894; Pres. JORGE EDUARDO BRIZ ABULARACH; Exec. Dir JUAN JOSÉ CABRERA.

Cámara Empresarial de Comercio y Servicios (Cecoms): Guatemala City; Pres. GUILLERMO GONZÁLEZ.

Cámara de Industria de Guatemala: 6a Ruta 9-21, 12°, Zona 4, Apdo 214, Guatemala City; tel. 2380-9000; e-mail info@

industriaguate.com; internet www.industriaguate.com; f. 1959; Pres. ANDRÉS CASTILLO; Exec. Dir JAVIER ZEPEDA.

Cámara Oficial Española de Comercio de Guatemala: Edif. Paladium, 14°, 4 Avda 15-70, Zona 10, Guatemala City; tel. 2470-3301; fax 2470-3304; e-mail gerencia@camacoes.org.gt; internet www.camacoes.org.gt; f. 1928; Pres. Dr RAFAEL BRIZ; Gen. Man. SILVIA CAROLINA TAMAYAC MÁRQUEZ.

Comité Coordinador de Asociaciones Agrícolas, Comerciales, Industriales y Financieras (CACIF): Edif. Cámara de Industria de Guatemala, 6a Ruta 9-21, Zona 4, Guatemala City; tel. 2231-0651; fax 2334-7025; e-mail informacion@cacif.org.gt; internet www.cacif.org.gt; 6 mem. chambers; Pres. ANDRÉS CASTILLO; Exec. Dir ROBERTO ARDÓN.

INDUSTRIAL AND TRADE ASSOCIATIONS

Asociación de Azucareros de Guatemala (ASAZGUA): Edif. Europlaza, 178°, 5a Avda 5-55, Zona 14, Guatemala City; tel. 2386-2299; fax 2386-2020; e-mail asazgua@azucar.com.gt; internet www.azucar.com.gt; f. 1957; sugar producers' asscn; 15 mems; Pres. MARCO AUGUSTO GARCÍA; Gen. Man. ARMANDO BOESCHE.

Asociación General de Agricultores (AGA): Edif. Rodseguros, 6°, Via 1, 1-67, Zona 4, Guatemala City; tel. 2361-0654; fax 2332-4817; e-mail asistente@aga.org.gt; internet www.aga.org.gt; f. 1920; general farmers' asscn; Pres. PETER FRANK; 350 mems.

Asociación Guatemalteca de Exportadores (AGEXPORT): 15a Avda 14-72, Zona 13, Guatemala City; tel. 2422-3400; fax 2422-3434; e-mail portal@export.com.gt; internet www.export.com.gt; f. 1982; exporters' asscn; Pres. FRANCISCO MENENDEZ; Dir-Gen. LUIS GODOY.

Asociación Nacional de Avicultores (ANAVI): Edif. El Reformador, 4°, Of. 401, Avda La Reforma 1-50, Zona 9, Guatemala City; tel. 2360-3384; fax 2360-3161; e-mail anavi@anaviguatemala.org; internet www.anaviguatemala.com; f. 1964; national asscn of poultry farmers; 60 mems; Pres. MARIA DEL ROSARIO DE FALLA; Gen. Man. PEGGY CONTRERAS.

Asociación Nacional del Café—Anacafé: 5a Calle 0-50, Zona 14, Guatemala City; tel. 2421-3700; e-mail info@email.anacafe.org; internet www.anacafe.org; f. 1960; national coffee asscn; Pres. RICARDO VILLANUEVA CARRERA; Sec. MARTÍN ARÉVALO DE LEÓN.

Cámara del Agro: Edif. Géminis 10, Torre Norte, 9°, Of. 909, 12 Calle, 1-25, Zona 10, Guatemala City; tel. 2219-9021; e-mail camagro@intelnet.net.gt; internet www.camaradelagro.org; f. 1973; Pres. OTTO KUSIEK; Exec. Dir CARLA CABALLEROS.

Gremial de Empresarios Indígenas de Guatemala (GuateMaya): f. 2012; private sector org. representing 190 indigenous cos; mem. of CACIF (q.v.); Pres. LUIS TEPEU.

Gremial de Huleros de Guatemala: 6a Avda A 12-37, Zona 9, Guatemala City; tel. 2339-1752; fax 2339-1755; e-mail gremhuleger@guate.net.gt; internet www.gremialdehuleros.org; f. 1970; rubber producers' guild; 125 mems; Pres. JOSÉ MIGUEL EIZAGUIRRE; Gen. Man. CARLOS ALFREDO NÁJERA CASTILLO.

UTILITIES

Regulatory Authority

Comisión Nacional de Energía Eléctrica (CNEE): Edif. Paladium, 12°, 4 Avda 15-70, Zona 10, Guatemala City; tel. 2321-8000; fax 2321-8002; e-mail cnee@cnee.gov.gt; internet www.cnee.gob.gt; f. 1996; Pres. CARLOS EDUARDO COLOM BICKFORD.

Electricity

Empresa Eléctrica de Guatemala, SA: 6a Avda 8-14, Zona 1, Guatemala City; tel. 2277-7000; e-mail consultas@eegsa.net; internet www.eegsa.com; f. 1972; state electricity producer; 80% privatized in 1998; Gen. Man. JORGE ALONZO; subsidiaries include:

Comercializadora Eléctrica de Guatemala, SA (COMEGSA): Avda 6, 8-14, Zona 1, Guatemala City; tel. 2420-4200; fax 2230-5628; e-mail comegsaonline@comegsa.net; internet www.comegsa.com.gt; f. 1998; Gen. Man. ANGEL GARCÍA.

Trelec, SA: 2 Avda 9-27, Zona 1, Guatemala City; tel. 2420-4235; fax 2420-0409; e-mail trelec@trelec.net; f. 1999; Gen. Man. LEONEL FRANCISCO SANTIZO GONZÁLEZ.

Instituto Nacional de Electrificación (INDE): Edif. La Torre, 7a Avda 2-29, Zona 9, Guatemala City; tel. (2) 2422-1800; e-mail gerencia.general@inde.gob.gt; internet www.inde.gob.gt; f. 1959; fmr state agency for the generation and distribution of hydroelectric power; principal electricity producer; privatized in 1998; Pres. ERICK ESTUARDO ARCHILA DEHESA; Gen. Man. MARINUS ARIE BOER JOHANNESSEN.

CO-OPERATIVE

Instituto Nacional de Cooperativas (INACOP): Via 6, 6-72, Zona 4, Guatemala City; tel. 2339-1627; fax 2339-1648; e-mail macoadministrativa@inacop.gob.gt; internet www.inacop.gob.gt; technical and financial assistance in planning and devt of co-operatives; Gen. Man. LUIS ALBERTO MONTENEGRO.

TRADE UNIONS

Confederación General de Trabajadores de Guatemala (CGTG): 3 Avda 12-22, Zona 1, Guatemala City; tel. 2232-1010; fax 2251-3212; e-mail info@confederacioncgtg.org; internet www.confederacioncgtg.org; f. 1987; fmrly Central Nacional de Trabajadores (CNT); Sec.-Gen. JOSÉ E. PINZÓN SALAZAR; 60,000 mems (2007).

Federación Sindical de Trabajadores de la Alimentación Agro-Industrias y Similares de Guatemala (FESTRAS): 16 Avda 13-52, Zona 1, Guatemala City; tel. and fax 2251-8091; e-mail festras@gmail.com; internet festras.blogspot.in; f. 1991; Sec.-Gen. JOSÉ DAVID MORALES C.

Unidad de Acción Sindical y Popular (UASP): 10 Avda A 5-40, Zona 1, Guatemala City; tel. 2230-5423; fax 2230-3004; e-mail uaspgt@yahoo.es; internet www.uaspgt.es.tl; f. 1988; broad coalition of leading labour and peasant orgs; Co-ordinator NERY ROBERTO BARRIOS DE LEÓN; Sec. NÉLIDA CORADO; includes:

Comité de la Unidad Campesina (CUC) (Committee of Peasants' Unity): 31a Avda A 14-46, Zona 7, Ciudad de Plata II, Apdo 1002, Guatemala City; tel. 2434-9754; fax 2438-1424; e-mail cuc@intelnett.com; internet www.cuc.org.gt; f. 1978; Sec.-Gen. DANIEL PASCUAL HERNÁNDEZ.

Confederación de Unidad Sindical de Guatemala (CUSG): 12 Calle A, 0-66, Zona 1, Guatemala City; tel. and fax 2220-7875; fax 2238-3654; e-mail info@cusg.com.gt; internet www.cusg.com.gt; f. 1983; Sec.-Gen. CARLOS ENRIQUE MANCILLA GARCÍA; 30,000 mems (2011).

Unión Guatemalteca de Trabajadores (UGT): 13a Calle 11-40, Zona 1, Guatemala City; tel. and fax 2251-1686; e-mail ugt.guatemala@yahoo.com; Sec.-Gen. ADOLFO LACS.

Transport

RAILWAYS

In 2007 there were 885 km of railway track in Guatemala.

Ferrovías Guatemala: 24 Avda 35-91, Zona 12, 01012 Guatemala City; tel. 2412-7200; fax 2412-7205; e-mail info@ferroviasgt.com; internet www.rrdc.com/op_guatemala_fvg.html; f. 1968 as Ferrocarriles de Guatemala (FEGUA); 50-year concession awarded in 1997 to the US Railroad Devt Corpn (RDC); 784 km from Puerto Barrios and Santo Tomás de Castilla on the Atlantic coast to Tecún Umán on the Mexican border, via Zacapa, Guatemala City and Santa María; in 2007 services were suspended after arbitration claim filed by the RDC under the terms of the Dominican Republic-Central American Free Trade Agreement; claim resolved in 2013, but the services remained suspended in 2014; Pres. WILLIAM J. DUGGAN.

ROADS

In 2010 there were 14,118 km of roads, of which just over one-half were paved. The Guatemalan section of the Pan-American highway is 518.7 km long and totally asphalted. In 2009 construction began of the 362-km Franja Transversal del Norte highway, linking the departments of Huehuetenango and Izabal. The Banco Centroamericano de Integración Económica approved a US $203m. loan for the project.

SHIPPING

Guatemala's major ports are Puerto Barrios and Santo Tomás de Castilla on the Gulf of Mexico, San José and Champerico on the Pacific Ocean, and Puerto Quetzal. At 31 December 2013 the flag registered fleet comprised six vessels, totalling 2,990 grt.

Comisión Portuaria Nacional: 6 Avda A 8-66, Zona 9, Apdo 01009, Guatemala City; tel. 2419-4800; fax 2360-5457; e-mail info@cpn.gob.gt; internet www.cpn.gob.gt; f. 1972; Pres. VIOLETA LUNA; Exec. Dir CARLOS ENRIQUE DE LA CERDA.

Dacotrans de Centroamerica, SA: 24 Avda 41-81, Zona 12, Interior Almacenadora Integrada, Apdo 40, Guatemala City; tel. 2381-1200; fax 2381-1244; e-mail dacotrans@dacotrans.com.gt; internet www.dacotrans.com.gt; f. 1969; part of Grupo Dacotrans Grosskopf GMBH & Co (Germany); Gen. Man. MATHIAS REHE.

Empresa Portuaria Nacional de Champerico: Avda del Ferrocarril, frente a la playa, 1000101 Champerico, Retalhuleu; tel. 7773-7223; fax 7773-7221; e-mail vallejo.l@gmail.com; internet www.epnac.blogspot.com; f. 1955; Pres. LUIS ENRIQUE PRADO LUARCA; Man. MARGARITO FLORIAN ESCOBEDO.

Empresa Portuaria Nacional Santo Tomás de Castilla (EMPORNAC): Calle Real de la Villa, 17 Calle 16-43, Zona 10, Guatemala City; tel. 7720-4040; fax 7960-0584; e-mail mercadeo@

santotomasport.com.gt; internet www.santotomasport.com.gt; Pres. JOSÉ ROBERTO DÍAZ-DÚRAN QUEZADA; Gen. Man. EDGARDO LÓPEZ.

Empresa Portuaria Quetzal: Edif. Torre Azul, 1°, Of. 105, 4 Calle 7-53, Zona 9, 01009 Guatemala City; tel. 2312-5000; fax 2334-8172; e-mail mercadeo@puerto-quetzal.com; internet www.puerto-quetzal.com; port and shipping co; Pres. FELIPE CASTAÑEDA; Gen. Man. RODOLFO KUSHIEK.

Seaboard Marine Ltda: Edif. Galerias Reforma, 4°, Of. 411, Avda La Reforma 8-60, Zona 9, Guatemala City; tel. 2384-3900; fax 2334-0077; e-mail Guillermo_Ortiz@seaboardmarine.com.gt; internet www.seaboardmarine.com; subsidiary of Seaboard Corpn (USA); Rep. GUILLERMO ORTIZ.

Transmares, SA: Torre 2, 8°, Centro Gerencial Las Margaritas, Diagonal 6, 10-01, Zona 10, 01010 Guatemala City; tel. 2429-8100; fax 2429-8148; e-mail henneke.sieveking@transmares.net; internet www.transmares.org; ocean liner and cargo shipping; logistics services under Translogística, SA; Gen. Man. HENNEKE SIEVEKING.

CIVIL AVIATION

There are two international airports, La Aurora in Guatemala City and Mundo Maya in Santa Elena, El Petén.

Dirección General de Aeronáutica Civil: Aeropuerto La Aurora, Zona 13, 01013 Guatemala City; tel. 2362-0216; e-mail direccion@dgac.gob.gt; internet www.dgacguate.com; f. 1929; administers and regulates aviation services; Dir JUAN JOSÉ CARLOS SUÁREZ.

Aviones Comerciales de Guatemala (Avcom): Aeropuerto 'La Aurora', Avda Hincapié 18, Zona 13, Guatemala City; tel. 2331-5821; fax 2332-4946; domestic charter passenger services.

TACA: Aeropuerto 'La Aurora', Avda Hincapié 12-22, Zona 13, Guatemala City; tel. 2470-8222; e-mail scastillo@taca.com; internet www.taca.com; f. 1945 as Aerolíneas de Guatemala (AVIATECA); privatized in 1989; domestic services and services to the USA, Mexico, and within Central America; Gen. Man. MYNOR CORDON.

Transportes Aéreos Guatemaltecos, SA (TAG): Avda Hinapie y 18 Calle, Zona 13, Guatemala City; tel. 2380-9494; fax 2334-7205; e-mail tagsa@tag.com.gt; internet www.tag.com.gt; f. 1969; domestic and int. charter services; Gen. Man. JONATHAN LAYTON.

Tourism

Guatemala's main attraction lies in the ancient Mayan ruins. Other tourism highlights include its active steaming volcanos, mountain lakes, pristine beaches and a rich indigenous culture. The number of tourist arrivals rose steadily following the end of the civil war in 1996. By 2012 arrivals had reached 1,951,173. In the same year receipts from tourism, excluding passenger transport, were US $986.8m.

Instituto Guatemalteco de Turismo (INGUAT) (Guatemala Tourist Institute): Centro Cívico, 7a Avda 1-17, Zona 4, Guatemala City; tel. 2421-2800; fax 2331-4416; e-mail informacion@inguat.gob.gt; internet www.inguat.gob.gt; f. 1967; policy and planning council: 11 mems representing the public and private sectors; Dir PEDRO PABLO DUCHEZ.

Defence

As assessed in November 2013, Guatemala's active armed forces numbered an estimated 17,300: army 15,550, navy 900 and air force 850. Reserve forces totalled 63,850. In addition, there were paramilitary forces of 25,000. Military service is by selective conscription for 30 months.

Defence Budget: an estimated 2,040m. quetzales in 2013.

Chief of Staff of National Defence: Gen. RUDY ISRAEL ORTIZ RUIZ.

Education

Elementary education is free and compulsory between seven and 14 years of age. Primary education begins at the age of seven and lasts for six years. Secondary education, beginning at 13 years of age, lasts for up to six years, comprising two cycles of three years each. Enrolment at primary schools in 2011 included 93% of children in the relevant age-group. The comparable ratio for secondary education in that year was 46%. There are 12 universities, of which 11 are privately run. In 2012 expenditure on education by the central Government was projected at 11,097.7m. quetzales, equivalent to 18.6% of total spending.

GUINEA

Introductory Survey

LOCATION, CLIMATE, LANGUAGE, RELIGION, FLAG, CAPITAL

The Republic of Guinea lies on the west coast of Africa, with Sierra Leone and Liberia to the south, Senegal and Guinea-Bissau to the north, and Mali and Côte d'Ivoire inland to the east. The climate on the coastal strip is hot and moist, with temperatures ranging from about 32°C (90°F) in the dry season to about 23°C (73°F) in the wet season (May–October). The interior is higher and cooler. The official language is French, but Soussou, Manika and six other national languages are widely spoken. Most of the population are Muslims, but some follow traditional animist beliefs. Around 3% are Roman Catholics. The national flag (proportions 2 by 3) consists of three equal vertical stripes, of red, yellow and green. The capital is Conakry.

CONTEMPORARY POLITICAL HISTORY

Historical Context

The Republic of Guinea (formerly French Guinea, part of French West Africa) became independent on 2 October 1958, after 95% of voters rejected the Constitution of the Fifth Republic under which the French colonies became self-governing within the French Community. The new state was the object of punitive reprisals by the outgoing French authorities: all aid was withdrawn, and the administrative infrastructure destroyed. The Parti Démocratique de Guinée—Rassemblement Démocratique Africain (PDG—RDA) became the basis for the construction of new institutions. Its leader, Ahmed Sékou Touré, became President, and the PDG—RDA the sole political party. Sékou Touré pursued vigorous policies of socialist revolution. Opposition was ruthlessly crushed, and his administration perpetuated rumours of a 'permanent conspiracy' by foreign powers to overthrow the regime. Following an abortive invasion by Portuguese troops and Guinean exiles in 1970, many of those convicted of involvement were executed.

In November 1978 it was announced that the functions of the PDG—RDA and the state were to be merged, and the country was renamed the People's Revolutionary Republic of Guinea. There was, none the less, a general move away from rigid Marxism and a decline in relations with the USSR, as Guinea sought a political and economic rapprochement with its African neighbours, with France and with other Western powers.

Domestic Political Affairs

Sékou Touré died in March 1984, while undergoing surgery in the USA. In April, before a successor had been chosen by the ruling party, the armed forces seized power in a bloodless coup. A Comité Militaire de Redressement National (Military Committee for National Recovery—CMRN) was appointed, headed by Col (later Gen.) Lansana Conté; the PDG—RDA and the legislature were dissolved; and the Constitution was suspended. The Second Republic of Guinea was proclaimed in May. In December Conté, as President, assumed the posts of Head of Government and Minister of Defence.

In late 1989 Conté announced that, following a referendum on a proposed new constitution, a joint civilian and military Comité Transitoire de Redressement National (Transitional Committee for National Recovery—CTRN) would replace the CMRN. After a transitional period of not more than five years, civilian rule would be established, with an executive and legislature directly elected within a two-party system. The draft Constitution of what was designated the Third Republic was reportedly endorsed by 98.7% of the 97.4% of the electorate who voted in a referendum in December 1990; and the CTRN was inaugurated in February 1991, under Conté's chairmanship.

In October 1991 Conté announced that a law authorizing the registration of an unlimited number of political parties would come into effect in April 1992, and that legislative elections would be held before the end of 1992. The Constitution was promulgated on 23 December 1991, and in January 1992 Conté ceded the presidency of the CTRN, in conformity with the constitutional separation of powers. Most military officers, and all those who had returned from exile after the 1984 coup (termed *Guinéens de l'extérieur*), were subsequently removed from the Council of Ministers.

Some 17 political parties were legalized in April 1992; it was subsequently rumoured that the pro-Conté Parti pour l'Unité et du Progrès (PUP), established by prominent *Guinéens de l'extérieur*, was benefiting from state funds. In December the Government postponed indefinitely the legislative elections which had been scheduled for later that month.

In October 1993 the Supreme Court approved eight candidates for the forthcoming presidential election. According to official results, Conté was elected with 51.7% of the votes cast. His closest rival, Alpha Condé, of the Rassemblement du Peuple de Guinée (RPG), took 19.6% of the votes; Mamadou Boye Bâ, of the Union pour la Nouvelle République (UNR), won 13.4%; and Siradiou Diallo, of the Parti pour le Renouveau et le Progrès (PRP), 11.9%. Conté was inaugurated as President in January 1994.

The delayed legislative elections finally took place in June 1995. Some 846 candidates, from 21 parties, contested the 114 seats in the Assemblée Nationale (National Assembly). As preliminary results indicated that the PUP had won an overwhelming majority in the legislature, the parties of the 'radical' opposition (the RPG, the PRP and the UNR) announced their intention to boycott the assembly, protesting that voting had been conducted fraudulently. According to the final results, which were verified by the Supreme Court in July, the PUP won 71 seats—having taken 30 of the 38 single-member constituencies and 41 of the 76 seats elected on the basis of national lists. Of the eight other parties to win representation, the RPG secured 19 seats, while the PRP and the UNR each won nine. The new legislature was officially inaugurated on 30 August.

In February 1996 Conté was reportedly seized as he attempted to flee the presidential palace during a mutiny by disaffected elements of the military, and was held by rebels for some 15 hours until he made concessions including a doubling of salaries and immunity from prosecution for those involved in the uprising. The Minister of Defence, Col Abdourahmane Diallo, was dismissed, and Conté assumed personal responsibility for defence. In March it was announced that eight members of the military, including four senior officers, had been charged with undermining state security in connection with the coup attempt. In July Conté announced the appointment of a non-partisan economist, Sidya Touré, as Prime Minister, the first time that position had existed under the Third Republic. (The Constitution made no explicit provision for such a post.)

In June 1997 it was announced that a State Security Court was to be established to deal with matters of exceptional jurisdiction, and that its first task would be to try the alleged leaders of the previous year's mutiny. In September 38 people charged with offences related to the 1996 attempted coup were sentenced by the new court to custodial sentences of up to 15 years.

The official results of the December 1998 presidential election confirmed a decisive victory for Conté, with 56.1% of the valid votes cast. Bâ, contesting the election for the Union pour le Progrès et le Renouveau (UPR, formed by a merger of the UNR and the PRP), won 24.6%; and Condé, for the RPG, 16.6%. Condé was arrested shortly after the election and subsequently charged with plotting against the Conté regime. In March 1999 Lamine Sidimé, hitherto Chief Justice of the Supreme Court, was appointed Prime Minister.

Opposition groups and human rights organizations campaigned throughout 1999 and 2000 for the release of Condé and other activists detained at the time of the 1998 presidential election. In September 2000 Condé was found guilty of sedition by the State Security Court and sentenced to five years' imprisonment; a further seven defendants were given custodial sentences of between 18 months and three years.

In September 2000 an armed rebellion in the forest region of south-east Guinea reportedly resulted in at least 40 deaths. Instability subsequently intensified in regions near the borders with Sierra Leone and Liberia. By mid-October fighting between armed groups and Guinean soldiers was reported to have caused around 360 deaths. The Guinean authorities attributed the upsurge in violence to forces supported by the Governments of Liberia and Burkina Faso, and to members of the Sierra Leonean rebel Revolutionary United Front (RUF, see Sierra Leone), in alliance with Guinean dissidents. In November a series of cross-border attacks was reportedly conducted by former members of a faction of a dissolved Liberian dissident group, the United Liberation Movement of Liberia for Democracy (ULIMO), ULIMO—K (see Liberia), which President Conté had previously supported. In December rebel attacks on the southern towns of Guéckédou and Kissidougou led to more than 230 deaths, and the almost complete destruction of Guéckédou. The Government estimated that some 94,000 people had been displaced as a result of fighting in the region, and aid agencies withdrew from south-east Guinea later in the month as a result of the heightened instability.

Constitutional changes

A constitutional referendum took place in November 2001. According to official results, 98.4% of voters approved a series of amendments that removed the restriction on the number of terms the President could serve; allowed candidates aged over 70 years to contest the presidency; and extended the presidential term of office from five years to seven, with effect from the presidential election due in 2003. Turnout was put at 87.2% of the registered electorate. Prior to the vote, there were violent clashes between security forces and opponents of the proposed changes. Opposition members disputed the results, claiming that less than 20% of the electorate had voted.

In April 2002 President Conté issued decrees scheduling legislative elections, which had been repeatedly delayed, for 30 June; and establishing a supervisory Conseil National Electoral. Concerns were expressed that the short period between the establishment of the election council and the forthcoming polls would be insufficient to ensure transparency of conduct, and the European Union (EU, see p. 273) subsequently withheld funding for the elections. In May four opposition parties that had announced their intention to boycott the legislative elections—including the RPG and the Union des Forces Républicaines—formed a political alliance, the Front de l'Alternance Démocratique (FRAD). A split in the UPR became increasingly apparent between a faction led by the current party President, Siradiou Diallo, who sought to engage with the electoral process, and a group led by Mamadou Boye Bâ, its honorary President, who pledged allegiance to the FRAD.

At the June 2002 elections, the PUP increased its majority in the National Assembly, winning 85 of the 114 seats. The governing party was unopposed in all 38 single-member constituencies, and took 47 of the 76 seats allocated by proportional representation. The UPR became the second largest party in the legislature, with 20 seats. Opposition parties, both those that had contested the elections and those of the FRAD, alleged that there had been widespread fraud in the conduct of the polls, and the US ambassador to Guinea expressed concern at apparent electoral irregularities. In October Bâ became President of a new party, the Union des Forces Démocratiques de Guinée (UFDG).

In September 2003, shortly after the formal nomination of Conté as the presidential candidate of the PUP, the FRAD announced that negotiations between the Government and opposition parties on the conduct of the forthcoming election had broken down. In November both the FRAD and the UPR announced that they would boycott the election. Meanwhile, the National Assembly approved legislation providing for an amnesty for persons convicted of political crimes—notably including Alpha Condé, who would thereby nominally be permitted to contest the presidential election. In the event, however, the only candidate who was approved to challenge the incumbent was Mamadou Bhoye Barry, of the Union pour le Progrès National—Parti pour l'Unité et le Développement.

Voting in the presidential election proceeded in December 2003. In the absence of any significant opposition, Conté was re-elected for a further (now seven-year) term of office, with 95.3% of the votes cast, according to official results. Although the opposition claimed that turnout had been as low as 15%, official figures indicated a rate of participation of approximately 82% of the registered electorate. Barry alleged that the official results were fraudulent, and that he had in fact received a majority of the votes cast.

In February 2004 Conté dismissed Lamine Sidimé and appointed a substantially reorganized Government, with François Lonsény Fall as Prime Minister. In April, however, it was announced that Fall had resigned and had fled Guinea; the former premier subsequently claimed that his Government had been obstructed in its attempts to implement economic and judicial reforms. The post of Prime Minister remained vacant until the appointment in December of Cellou Dalein Diallo, previously Minister of Fisheries and Aquaculture.

Diallo announced a comprehensive government reorganization in April 2006, involving new appointments to most ministerial positions. Notably, responsibility for the economy and finance, for planning and international co-operation, and for economic and financial control was transferred to the office of the Prime Minister. However, it emerged that President Conté (constitutionally Head of Government, as well as Head of State) had not authorized the changes. Diallo was dismissed and the reorganization was countermanded. Conté restructured the Government in May, nominating six ministers of state with responsibility for key portfolios including foreign affairs, the economy and finance, and presidential affairs. No Prime Minister was appointed.

Domestic unrest

In June 2006 the country's two principal trade unions, the Confédération Nationale des Travailleurs de Guinée (CNTG) and the Union Syndicale des Travailleurs de Guinée (USTG), organized a widely observed general strike, demanding, *inter alia*, reductions in the prices of fuel and rice. Clashes between protesters and security forces reportedly resulted in the deaths of some 20 people. The strike was brought to an end after the Government agreed to increase public sector salaries and allowances for rent and transportation, as well as to lower the cost of rice.

The CNTG and the USTG commenced a further general strike in January 2007, supported by a number of opposition parties, non-governmental organizations (NGOs) and civil society groups. Initially, the action again focused on prices of basic foodstuffs and fuel, as well as the return to gaol of two former prominent politicians, accused of financial impropriety, whose release had been secured by the President in the previous month. However, following violent clashes between demonstrators and security forces, in which five people were killed and several hundred were arrested, the unions extended their demands to include the resignation of Conté and his administration. Conté dismissed the Minister of State for Presidential Affairs, El Hadj Fodé Bangoura, but protests continued, and further deaths were reported across the country. Both the UN and the African Union (AU, see p. 186) urged the Government to commence negotiations with the trade unions. After almost two weeks trade union leaders, who had been briefly detained meanwhile, were invited to talks with Conté, who indicated his willingness to appoint a 'consensus' Prime Minister. The strike was halted in late January, after Conté agreed to nominate a new Prime Minister. However, Conté's subsequent choice of Eugène Camara (who had succeeded Bangoura as Minister of State for Presidential Affairs) as Prime Minister was rejected by the trade unions and the political opposition, The unions recommenced the general strike in mid-February, again demanding the President's resignation. In response, the President declared a 'state of siege', imposing martial law and a nationwide curfew. In negotiations with the Government, the trade unions rejected Conté's proposal to maintain Camara as interim Prime Minister. The National Assembly subsequently voted to terminate martial law and the curfew; and in late February, following further negotiations brokered by the Economic Community of West African States (ECOWAS, see p. 260), Conté announced that he would select a new Prime Minister from a list of candidates drawn up by the trade unions and opposition parties. Lansana Kouyaté, a career diplomat and the former Executive Secretary of ECOWAS, was duly appointed Prime Minister, and the industrial action was brought to an end. By this time, at least 130 people were reported to have been killed in the violence since January.

Kouyaté was sworn in as Prime Minister at the beginning of March 2007. He subsequently named a Council of Ministers (composed largely of technocrats, notably excluding ministers from the previous administration), in which the former Deputy Chief of Staff of the Armed Forces, Gen. Arafan Camara, became Minister of National Defence. However, Camara was (together with the Chief of Staff of the Armed Forces) replaced following a two-week uprising by members of the armed forces in May, involving widespread intimidation of civilians. The military had been demanding the payment of salary arrears, in some cases dating back as far as 11 years, and protesting against several senior defence appointments made earlier in the year.

In January 2008 Conté dismissed the Minister of Communication and Information Technology, Justin Morel Junior, who had criticized the content of the President's New Year address—in which Conté referred to Prime Minister Kouyaté's administration as a 'disappointment'. Trade unions demanded the minister's reinstatement on the grounds that his dismissal was contrary to the agreement brokered in early 2007, threatening renewed industrial action. Following negotiations led by Kouyaté with trade unions and civil society representatives, a planned general strike was deferred pending further discussion of a presidential decree, issued in December 2007, whereby Conté had reassumed a number of powers previously devolved to the Prime Minister. Tensions escalated once again in May 2008 after Conté dismissed Kouyaté and replaced him with a close personal ally, Ahmed Tidiane Souaré. Conté also dismissed Gen. Bailo Diallo, the successor to Arafan Camara as Minister of National Defence, following a further uprising by soldiers to demand the payment of salary arrears. At least three people were killed in violence in Conakry, and it was reported that the army Chief of Staff had briefly been held hostage. There were renewed security concerns in June, when a protest by police in Conakry led to clashes with armed forces personnel. A civilian, Almany Kabèle Camara, was appointed in place of Gen. Diallo in the new Government named in that month. In October legislative elections were postponed for a third time, because of insufficient funds and incomplete preparations. In the following month at least four people were killed after security forces opened fire on demonstrators who were demanding lower fuel prices.

Military takeover following death of Lansana Conté

President Conté, who was thought to have been in poor health for some time, died on 22 December 2008. Although Aboubacar Somparé, the Speaker of the National Assembly, stated that he should assume the presidency pending an election, a group of junior army officers, led by Capt. Moussa Dadis Camara, swiftly seized power. Camara proclaimed the formation of a 32-member Conseil National pour la Démocratie et le Développement (National Council for Democracy and Development—CNDD), the suspension of the Constitution and the dissolution of all state institutions. The CNDD banned all political and trade union activities, and demoted all military generals of the former regime. The coup was widely condemned by the international community, and the AU, followed by ECOWAS, announced the suspension of Guinea's membership pending the return of constitutional order. At the end of December an economist, Kabiné Komara, was appointed as Prime Minister. A new Government was named in January 2009, including Gen. Sékouba Konaté as Minister at the Presidency, in charge of National Defence; Justin Morel Junior was notably reappointed as Minister of Information and Culture. Meanwhile, Camara, who pledged to eradicate corruption and improve living standards, made a commitment to hold legislative and presidential elections within 12 months, stating that he did not intend to contest the latter. A number of former ministers, including Ousmane Doré, and several prominent business executives appeared before a commission charged with investigating corruption during the Conté era. The ban on political and trade union activity was revoked in February. In April two army officers were detained, on suspicion of plotting a coup as Camara prepared to leave the country for the first time since taking power.

A revised election timetable was announced in August 2009, whereby the presidential election was to be held in January 2010, followed by legislative elections in March. Despite an earlier undertaking that members of the military would be precluded from seeking elected office, Camara subsequently indicated his intention to contest the presidency. Tensions had been increasing since the military's seizure of power, and, in response to Camara's announcement, opposition parties organized a protest rally at a stadium in Conakry in September 2009, attended by some 10,000 people. Security forces opened fire on demonstrators, leaving more than 150 dead and many more injured. In October the UN Secretary-General announced that an international Commission of Inquiry would be established to investigate the incident. Meanwhile, ECOWAS imposed an arms embargo on Guinea, and the AU, the EU and the USA imposed targeted sanctions on members of the CNDD. Several government ministers resigned in protest against the killings. The presidential election was subsequently rescheduled for July 2010, with legislative elections to follow at an unspecified date.

Camara's decision to delay the elections, and his apparent intention to stand as a presidential candidate, coupled with international pressure on Camara to bring to justice those believed to be responsible for the Conakry killings, led to growing disaffection within the military regime. In December 2009 there was an assassination attempt against Camara, who suffered a gunshot wound to the head and was transferred to Morocco for medical treatment. Gen. Sékouba Konaté was installed as interim President. The perpetrator of the attack, Lt Abubakar 'Toumba' Diakite—who, it was subsequently reported, was to have been handed over to the authorities to be prosecuted for his alleged role in the events of September—meanwhile evaded capture and fled the country.

The UN Commission of Inquiry into the September 2009 massacre submitted its report in December. The inquiry found that crimes against humanity had been committed, and that there were reasonable grounds to allege individual criminal responsibility on the part of key members of Guinea's military regime—including Capt. Camara and Lt Diakite. The investigation recorded 156 deaths, 109 documented rapes and 40 reported 'disappearances', together with widespread illegal arrests and detentions, and torture of detainees. The Commission recommended, *inter alia,* that cases of crimes against humanity be taken up by the International Criminal Court, and that the Office of the UN High Commissioner for Human Rights (OHCHR) monitor the situation in Guinea. (Accordingly, OHCHR began operations in Conakry in May 2010.)

In January 2010 Konaté pledged to restore civilian rule, and indicated the CNDD's willingness to appoint a transitional government of national unity with a Prime Minister from the political opposition. Following negotiations hosted by the President of Burkina Faso, Blaise Compaoré, involving Camara (who had now been transferred from Morocco to Burkina), senior members of the CNDD and representatives of the opposition, it was agreed that Camara would remain outside Guinea on a 'leave of absence' to continue his convalescence. Jean-Marie Doré, the leader of the Union pour le Progrès de la Guinée, was sworn in as Prime Minister in late January. His new Government, appointed in February, included a number of military members of the outgoing administration, together with representatives of opposition parties, trade unionists and members of civil society. Meanwhile, also in late January, Konaté installed the Secretary-General of the CNTG, Rabiatou Serah Diallo, as President of a Conseil National de Transition (National Transitional Council—CNT). This new body was to oversee the transition from military to civilian rule; its 155 members, including representatives of civil society, political parties and religious groups, as well as members of the CNDD, were appointed in March. Konaté announced in that month that the presidential election would be held on 27 June, and confirmed that he would not be a candidate.

The CNT presented a draft Constitution (replacing that suspended in December 2008) to Konaté in April 2010. Under the terms of the new document, which was adopted by decree on 7 May, a new President and legislature were to be elected for a term of five years, with the presidential mandate to be renewable only once; the minimum age for presidential candidates was set at 35 years.

Alpha Condé elected President

The first round of the presidential election proceeded on 27 June 2010, with 24 candidates. The following day the Commission Electorale Nationale Indépendante (CENI) acknowledged widespread technical failings, but ECOWAS observers assessed that the election had been conducted without malpractice. Provisional results, released by the CENI in early July, indicated that Cellou Dalein Diallo (the candidate of the UFDG) and Alpha Condé (representing the RPG) would proceed to a second round. Protests ensued from several other candidates, in particular from the third-placed Sidya Touré and his supporters. On 20 July the Supreme Court declared revised election results, according to which Diallo, with 43.7% of the votes, and Condé, with 18.3%, were to proceed to a second round. Voter turnout was recorded at about 52% of the registered electorate. Touré subsequently urged his supporters to vote for Diallo, while Lansana Kouyaté, who had been placed fourth in the first round, declared his support for Condé. Gen. Konaté subsequently announced that the second round of the presidential election (originally scheduled for 18 July) would take place on 19 September.

In September 2010 the head of the CENI, Ben Sékou Sylla, and its Director of Planning, Boubacar Diallo, were found guilty of fraudulent activity during the first round of the election, and sentenced to one year's imprisonment. The announcement of their conviction provoked violent clashes between supporters of Diallo and Condé, in which one person was killed and at least 50 others were injured. The authorities suspended the election process and banned all demonstrations. In October the second round was again deferred after Diallo accused the newly appointed head of the CENI, Lounceny Camara, of favouring Condé, prompting his replacement by a Malian general, Siaka Toumany Sangaré. The poll was finally rescheduled for 7 November.

International electoral observers declared that the second round of the presidential election, which duly took place on 7 November 2010, had been conducted successfully. In mid-November the CENI announced that Condé had been elected to the presidency, with about 52.5% of votes cast. Diallo again alleged malpractice, and announced that he would challenge the results at the Supreme Court. Following the declaration of the election results, violent clashes erupted between supporters of the two candidates in Conakry and the western cities of Pita and Labé, in which some 10 people were killed and 200 injured. The election of Condé, a member of the Malinké ethnic group, was reported to have exacerbated long-standing tensions between the Malinké and Peul (or Fulani), Diallo's ethnic group. In response to the deterioration in the security situation, Konaté imposed a national state of emergency.

The results of the presidential election were confirmed by the Supreme Court in early December 2010. The AU subsequently restored Guinea's membership and ended all other sanctions in force. The state of emergency was subsequently ended, and Konaté urged the country's armed forces to support the new President. Condé was inaugurated on 21 December. A hitherto relatively unknown economist, Mohamed Saïd Fofana, was appointed Prime Minister. Kerfala Yansané, the Minister of the Economy and Finance in the transitional administration, remained in post, while Condé assumed personal responsibility for defence.

In April 2011, in anticipation of the return of Diallo to Conakry, Condé imposed a ban on demonstrations. Protesters defied the ban, and there were violent clashes with security forces in which, according to the UFDG, three activists were killed and 60 wounded. In July there was an apparent assassination attempt against Condé, when a rocket-propelled grenade landed in the presidential residence, killing at least one bodyguard and wounding several others. The Government blamed the attacks on senior army officers close to the previous regime.

Meanwhile, in June 2011 the CENI stated that legislative elections would be held by the end of the year, contingent on the Government and opposition reaching agreement on the voters' register. The Government sought to compile a completely new list, while the opposition preferred a revision of the current list on the grounds that the Government would seek to manipulate a new list to its advantage. In September it was announced that the poll would be held on 29 December. Opposition groups objected that the schedule would not allow for required electoral reforms. In late September, on the eve of what had been planned as a day of national reconciliation in remembrance of the violent events of September 2009, opposition supporters clashed with police in demonstrations over the issues of the timing of the elections and voters' list reform. At least two protesters were reported to have been killed, and the authorities stated that 322 people had been arrested.

In December 2011 numerous casualties were reported when security forces dispersed a meeting of Lansana Kouyaté's Parti de l'Espoir pour le Développement National (PEDN) in Kankan. On 20 December it was announced that the scheduled legislative elections would be postponed. At the same time, 15 opposition activists convicted for their involvement in the violence in September were pardoned. Furthermore, the enforced retirement of some 4,600 members of the armed forces in late December was interpretive as a significant gesture towards reform on the part of Condé. Nevertheless, talks scheduled for early January 2012 to agree a date for elections were subsequently boycotted by the opposition.

It was stated in February 2012 that the legislative elections would take place in May, but in March Lounceny Camara (meanwhile reappointed head of the CENI) confirmed 8 July as the election date. The opposition again asserted that this did not allow sufficient time for the full revision of electoral lists, and in April President Condé announced a further postponement. In May the opposition held demonstrations to demand electoral reforms, and to protest against what they considered to be a pro-Condé bias on the part of the CENI; violent clashes with the security forces ensued, leading to mass arrests and the imposition of a ban on subsequent demonstrations. Further arrests of opposition activists were reported in August, following another anti-Government rally. Two PEDN cabinet ministers resigned in protest against the detentions. The taut political climate fuelled ethnic tensions, and there were outbreaks of violence between Malinké and Peul communities in Conakry during September. Camara, stood down as head of the CENI in September, thus fulfilling a key opposition demand. A new CENI, with increased opposition representation, was inaugurated in November, with Bokary Fofana as its President. In December the new CENI announced that the legislative elections would, provisionally, be held in May 2013.

Condé reorganized the Council of Ministers in October 2012, dismissing the remaining cabinet members who had been involved in the 2008 military coup as well as two ministers accused of corruption. Among new appointees was François Lonsény Fall (latterly Secretary-General at the Presidency), who took the foreign affairs portfolio.

The Chief of Staff of the Armed Forces, Gen. Souleymane Kelefa Diallo, was one of 11 people killed in February 2013, when the aircraft in which they were travelling crashed in Liberia. Gen. Diallo, who had been regarded as an important ally of President Condé, responsible for key armed forces reforms, was succeeded by Brig.-Gen. Namory Traoré, previously Deputy Chief of Staff.

Recent developments: the 2013 legislative elections

There was renewed violence from February 2013, an initial catalyst for which was an opposition-led demonstration in Conakry to demand transparency in the forthcoming legislative elections. Both the UN Secretary-General and OHCHR appealed for calm, but the situation escalated, apparently fuelled by inter-ethnic tensions between Malinké and Peul groups. In mid-April the Secretary-General's Special Representative for West Africa, Saïd Djinnit, was mandated to facilitate a dialogue between the Guinean Government and opposition (after the previous nominee, a Senegalese retired army general, failed to meet the approval of Guinea's opposition groups). Also in mid-April President Condé issued a decree whereby the elections were again postponed until 30 June. The announcement provoked renewed violence, as police intervened in the capital to disperse opposition activists who were protesting against what they considered to be a unilateral decision on the part of the administration. Among opposition demands were that the South African company awarded the contract for revising the electoral register, together with its local partner, be replaced; and that members of the Guinean diaspora be permitted to vote in the national elections. By the end of April at least 12 people were reported to have been killed, and more than 300 injured, in two months of unrest, and a further 12 people were killed, and 100 injured, during a further protest in late May. In response to these latest incidents, Condé dismissed the Minister of Security and Civil Protection, Mouramany Cissé, replacing him with Madifing Diané; a former senior police officer and latterly Guinea's ambassador to Senegal. In late June, by which time the number of deaths reportedly exceeded 50, Condé announced a further postponement of the elections until 28 July. Opposition parties, which had meanwhile withdrawn from the dialogue with the Government in protest against the shooting by police of three political activists at a demonstration by supporters of Cellou Dalein Diallo, returned to negotiations under Djinnit's mediation in early July, and in mid-July a presidential decree was issued setting an election date of 24 September. Agreement was reached whereby the existing contract for the electoral register would remain in place, and that Guineans abroad would be eligible to vote. A monitoring committee, led by the head of the Court of Appeal and including representatives of the CENI, the Government, political parties and representatives of the UN, the EU, the AU, ECOWAS and the Organisation Internationale de la Francophonie (La Francophonie), was established to support the CENI's work in ensuring that the elections were free, fair and credible.

Meanwhile, in late June 2013 a senior figure in the former CNDD, Col Claude Pivi, was indicted on charges including murder, rape, arson and destruction of property in connection with the 2009 stadium massacre. At the time of his indictment, Col Pivi was responsible for presidential security in the Condé administration. Hitherto, none of the seven members of the military who had been charged as a result of the investigation into the stadium incident and related events had been brought to trial.

In mid-July 2013, following a six-month trial, five people were sentenced to life imprisonment, having been convicted of involvement in the attempt to assassinate President Condé two years earlier. Among those sentenced were a former head of the late

Lansana Conté's presidential guard, Commdr Alpha Oumar Boffa Diallo, and Mamadou Oury Bah (a founder of the UFDG, now living in exile in France), who was one of three defendants convicted *in absentia*.

Security forces were deployed to N'Zérékoré, the country's second largest city, in the Forestière region of south-eastern Guinea, in mid-July 2013, following clashes between rival Guerze and Konianke groups in which at least 57 people were killed and more than 160 injured. OHCHR commended the authorities' efforts to restore calm, reminding them also of the need to uphold human rights during law enforcement operations

One week before the National Assembly elections were due to take place, the Government and opposition agreed, with UN mediation, to postpone voting for four days in order for final preparations to be completed. The opposition had threatened to renew street protests if the elections were to proceed without procedural grievances first being addressed. The legislative elections—the first in Guinea since 2002—finally proceeded according to this latest schedule on 28 September 2013, with some 33 parties presenting about 1,700 candidates for the National Assembly's 114 seats. Voting was reported to have taken place in an atmosphere of calm, despite further violence in preceding days, and early indications suggested that turnout was high. Cellou Dalein Diallo, whose UFDG was considered as presenting the greatest challenge to Condé's RPG Arc-en-ciel alliance, asserted that logistical problems and anomalies had not been resolved; and at the beginning of October the main opposition parties, alleging widespread fraud, withdrew their representatives from oversight of the counting process and demanded that the elections be annulled. The opposition also subsequently withdrew from the UN-facilitated dialogue once again. Initially, the ECOWAS observer mission had assessed that any logistical difficulties did not bring into question the integrity of the election, and that voting had taken place in acceptable conditions of freedom and transparency. In early October, however, a joint statement by the various observer groups—including representatives of ECOWAS, the UN and the EU, together with French and US diplomatic missions—expressed concern that the validity of certain results could be undermined by breaches and irregularities observed in eight of the 38 single-member constituencies. None the less, the UN Secretary-General and ECOWAS, along with other members of the international community, commended the release of provisional results by the CENI on 18 October. These showed that the RPG Arc-en-ciel alliance had won the largest number of seats (53, including 18 in the single-member constituencies), although not an overall majority of the 114 seats. The UFDG won 37 seats (including 14 single-member seats), and the Union des Forces Républicaines (UFR) of Sidya Touré 10 (of which five were in single-member constituencies); 12 other parties also secured representation. Turnout was recorded at some 64% of the eligible electorate. Opposition parties maintained their demand that the results be annulled on grounds of fraud. On 15 November, however, the Supreme Court rejected all complaints lodged against the outcome of the elections and formally declared the results unchanged from those previously announced by the CENI. A week later at least one person was killed in clashes with police during an opposition protest against the declared outcome. In mid-December opposition parties including the UFDG and the UFR confirmed that they would take up their seats in the National Assembly, despite their continued objections to the election results.

The new legislature was sworn in on 13 January 2014 (formally succeeding the CNT, a final task of which had been to approve the state budget for the new year), with deputies electing Claude Kory Kondiano, the preferred candidate of the RPG, as President of the National Assembly. Mohamed Saïd Fofana was reappointed as Prime Minister on 18 January, having formally resigned three days earlier. The composition of the new, 35-member Council of Ministers was announced on 20 January, including six members with the rank of Minister of State. Key ministers from the outgoing administration were retained in the RPG-dominated Government, among them Kerfala Yansané as Minister of State, Minister of Mines and Geology, a principal task for whom was expected to be the restoration of investors' confidence in the mining sector. He was succeeded as Minister of the Economy and Finance by Mohamed Diaré, previously a deputy minister responsible for the budget. François Lonsény Fall remained as Minister of Foreign Affairs and Guineans Abroad, with the rank of Minister of State; and Madifing Diané retained his post as Minister of Security and Civil Protection. Among 15 new appointees was Cheick Sakho, a lawyer latterly based in France, as Minister of State, Minister of Justice and Keeper of the Seals, and Idrissa Thiam, hitherto a special adviser at the presidency, as Minister of Energy and Water. President Condé retained personal responsibility for defence.

Despite a degree of optimism afforded by the end of the transitional period and the installation of the new National Assembly, concerns remained regarding the security situation and increasing frustration on the part of Guineans at the Condé administration's perceived failure to improve economic and social conditions. There were violent clashes in Conakry in mid-February 2014 as police intervened to disperse protests against power failures; at least two people were killed during one day of rioting. At the end of the month government buildings and a police station were ransacked by protesters in Fria, north of Conakry, following the death of a young man in police custody there. At this time, the aluminium smelter in Fria (Guinea's only refinery) had been closed for almost two years in response to what its Russian owner deemed to be illegal strike action.

In mid-March 2014 the Governor of Conakry, Commdr Sékou Resco Camara, was dismissed, apparently in connection with a judicial investigation—in response to a complaint brought in 2012 by the International Federation for Human Rights Leagues and the Organisation Guinéene de Défense des Droits de l'Homme et du Citoyen (OGDH), together with 17 individuals—into alleged acts of torture conducted in 2010. Commdr Camara had been indicted in February 2013; Gen. Nouhou Thiam (who remained in detention while awaiting trial in connection with the attack on the presidential residence in 2011) was charged in the same case later that month, and Commdr Aboubacar Sidiki Camara, head of the presidential guard under the interim administration of Sékouba Konaté, was indicted at the end of July.

There was an outbreak of Ebola virus disease in south-eastern Guinea from February 2014, with cases recorded in Conakry by late March. At the beginning of April the World Health Organization reported 122 confirmed and suspected cases, with 80 confirmed deaths. (A smaller number of cases was recorded in Liberia among nationals who had recently travelled to Guinea, and the border between the two countries was temporarily closed. Senegal also closed its border with Guinea as a precautionary measure.)

Foreign Affairs

Regional relations

Relations between Guinea and several of its neighbours have frequently been strained, most notably during the civil conflicts in Liberia and Sierra Leone. Relations between Guinea and Sierra Leone were further complicated in the early 2000s by an ongoing dispute over ownership of the border town of Yenga, in a reputedly diamond-rich region of Sierra Leone, which Guinean troops had occupied in 1998. In 2004 the two countries issued a joint statement that recognized Yenga as belonging to Sierra Leone, on the basis of a border agreement of 1912 between the British and French colonial powers. Guinea and Sierra Leone concluded an agreement in March 2012 to delineate their maritime boundaries, and in August the two countries pledged to withdraw all military personnel from Yenga and negotiate a peaceful settlement to the dispute.

The protracted conflicts in Liberia and Sierra Leone, as well as the civil conflict in Côte d'Ivoire from 2002, resulted in the presence in Guinea of large numbers of refugees, at times variously estimated to represent 5%–15% of the total population. At mid-2013 the office of the UN High Commissioner for Refugees recorded a population of concern of 11,020 refugees and asylum seekers in Guinea.

Other external relations

The risk of insecurity in Guinea undermining stabilization efforts in neighbouring countries has been of significant concern to the international community, particularly following the seizure of power by the military at the end of 2008. An International Contact Group on Guinea was formed in early 2009, comprising the permanent and African members of the UN Security Council, the EU, La Francophonie and the Mano River Union (see p. 452), and there was close co-operation with the AU and ECOWAS in the process culminating in the election of President Alpha Condé in late 2010. These organizations also worked together in facilitating and overseeing the legislative elections that eventually took place in September 2013, with the UN Secretary-General's Special Representative for West Africa assuming the role of mediator between the Government and opposition from April that year. The installation of the new National Assembly in January 2014 was welcomed by the country's international partners. In December 2013, meanwhile, the EU, which had partially suspended development co-operation in late 2008, announced that conditions had been fulfilled for the complete resumption of co-operation with Guinea. President Condé's stated intention of promoting good governance in the management of Guinea's resources received the support of the international community, although a review, from 2011, of the terms of existing mining contracts, together with the adoption of a new mining code (see Economic Affairs) were considered to have contributed to subsequent slow progress in major projects in the sector.

CONSTITUTION AND GOVERNMENT

The Constitution adopted on 7 May 2010 defines the clear separation of the powers of the executive, the legislature and the judiciary. The President of the Republic, who is Head of State, must be elected by an absolute majority of the votes cast, and a second round of voting is held should no candidate obtain such a majority at a first round. The duration of the presidential mandate is five years, renewable only once, and elections are by universal adult suffrage. The President appoints a Prime Minister, who is Head of Government, and proposes the structure and composition of the Government for approval by the President. Legislative power is vested in the National Assembly; 38 of its 114 members are elected in single-member constituencies, and 76 from national lists. The legislature is elected, by universal suffrage, with a five-year mandate.

Local administration is based on eight administrative entities (the city of Conakry and seven administrative regions) each under the authority of an appointed Governor; the country is sub-divided into 33 prefectures. Conakry, which comprises a separate administrative unit, is divided into five communes. The 33 prefectures outside of Conakry are sub-divided into 303 communes.

REGIONAL AND INTERNATIONAL CO-OPERATION

Guinea is a member of the African Union (see p. 186) and of the Economic Community of West African States (ECOWAS, see p. 260). Guinea is also a member of the Gambia River Basin Development Organization (OMVG, see p. 451), of the Africa Rice Center (AfricaRice, see p. 445) and of the Mano River Union (see p. 452).

Guinea became a member of the UN in 1958 and was admitted to the World Trade Organization (WTO, see p. 434) in 1995. Guinea is a member of the International Coffee Organization (see p. 446).

ECONOMIC AFFAIRS

In 2012, according to estimates by the World Bank, Guinea's gross national income (GNI), measured at average 2010–12 prices, was US $5,270m., equivalent to $460 per head (or $980 on an international purchasing-power parity basis). During 2003–12, it was estimated, the population increased at an average annual rate of 2.5%, while gross domestic product (GDP) per head increased, in real terms, by an average of 0.2% per year. Overall GDP increased, in real terms, at an average annual rate of 2.7% in 2003–12; it grew by 3.9% in 2012.

According to provisional figures from the African Development Bank (AfDB), agriculture (including hunting, forestry and fishing) contributed 21.2% of GDP in 2012. About 77.9% of the labour force were employed in the agricultural sector in mid-2014, according to FAO estimates. The principal cash crops are fruits, oil palm, groundnuts and coffee. Important staple crops include rice, cassava, maize and plantains. The attainment of self-sufficiency in rice and other basic foodstuffs remains a priority. The food supply is supplemented by the rearing of cattle and other livestock. The Government has made efforts towards the commercial exploitation of Guinea's forest resources and substantial fishing stocks. According to the World Bank, during 2003–11 agricultural GDP increased at an average annual rate of 3.2%; according to provisional figures from the AfDB, growth in agricultural GDP in 2012 was 3.8%.

Industry (including mining, manufacturing, construction and power) contributed an estimated 41.9% of GDP in 2012, according to provisional AfDB figures. An estimated 5.8% of the employed labour force were engaged in the industrial sector at the time of the 1996 census. According to the World Bank, industrial GDP increased at an average annual rate of 2.9% in 2003–11; growth in 2011 was 4.5%.

According to provisional AfDB figures, mining contributed an estimated 21.6% of GDP in 2012. Only 1.1% of the employed labour force were engaged in the sector at the time of the 1996 census. Guinea is the world's foremost exporter of bauxite and the second largest producer of bauxite ore (from which aluminium is extracted), possessing between one-quarter and one-third of known reserves of the mineral. However, in 2012, the aluminium ores and concentrates accounted for only 2.0% of the country's total export earnings, compared with 26.3% the previous year. Gold, which is also mined, accounted for 64.8% of total exports in 2012. Guinea also has valuable deposits of iron ore. Plans for the development of reserves of more than 2,000m. metric tons of high-grade ore at Simandou, in the south-east of the country—led by the multinational Rio Tinto, in a joint venture with the Aluminum Corporation of China (Chinalco), the International Financial Corporation and the Government of Guinea—include construction of a 650-km railway to transport mined ore to the coast, and development of a new deep-water port south of Conakry. However, the scheme has been subject to a series of delays owing to contractual and economic uncertainties, as well as security concerns. Development of reserves of high-grade iron ore at Mt Nimba, near the border with Liberia and Côte d'Ivoire, has similarly been long delayed. The Anglo-Australian BHP Billiton announced its intention to sell its 40% holding there in 2012. Guinea also has diamond deposits. The GDP of the mining sector increased at an average annual rate of 2.0% in 2000–06, according to the IMF. According to provisional figures from the AfDB, the sector's GDP increased by 4.3% in 2011, but declined by 3.8% in 2012.

The manufacturing sector remains largely undeveloped, contributing only a provisional 7.4% of GDP in 2012, according to the AfDB. At the time of the 1996 census, 2.8% of the employed labour force were engaged in the manufacturing sector. There is an alumina smelter at Fria; however, production there, which was halted by its operator, United Company RUSAL, in April 2012, in response to strike action, remained suspended in early 2014. Most other industrial companies are involved in import-substitution, including the processing of agricultural products and the manufacture of construction materials. According to the World Bank, manufacturing GDP increased at an average annual rate of 2.1% in 2003–11. It increased by 4.7% in 2012, according to provisional AfDB figures.

The construction sector contributed a provisional 12.4% of GDP in 2012, according to the AfDB. At the time of the 1996 census, the sector engaged 1.8% of the employed labour force. According to provisional figures from the AfDB, construction GDP grew by 8.7% in 2012.

Electricity generation is, at present, insufficient to meet demand, and power failures outside the mining and industrial sectors (in which the largest operators generate their own power supplies) have been frequent. However, Guinea possesses considerable hydroelectric potential. The 75-MW Garafiri dam project was inaugurated in 1999, and a further major scheme (with a capacity of 240 MW), at Kaléta, was scheduled for completion in the early 2010s. In the mean time, some 600,000 metric tons of hydrocarbons are imported annually, and in 2012 imports of mineral fuels accounted for 15.8% of the value of total merchandise imports.

According to the AfDB, the services sector contributed a provisional 36.9% of GDP in 2012. According to the World Bank, during 2003–11 the sector's GDP increased at an average annual rate of 1.5%; it increased by 3.1% in 2011.

In 2012 Guinea recorded a visible merchandise trade deficit of US $316.4m. and there was a deficit of $1,101.5m. on the current account of the balance of payments. The principal suppliers of imports in 2012 were the Netherlands (which supplied 14.7% of the total), the People's Republic of China, France, Belgium and India. The principal markets for exports in that year were Switzerland (which took 27.1% of exports), France, Belgium, the United Arab Emirates and Ireland. The principal exports in 2012 were gold, natural rubber and petroleum oils. The principal imports included machinery, mechanical appliances and electrical equipment, mineral fuels, rice, vehicles, aircraft, vessels and associated transport equipment, chemicals and related products, and iron and steel, other base metals and articles of base metal.

In 2013 Guinea's overall budget deficit was forecast to reach 1,364,000m. FG. Guinea's general government gross debt was 26,239,220m. FG in 2011, equivalent to 77.8% of GDP. The country's total external debt was US $3,139m. at the end of 2011, of which $2,849m. was public and publicly guaranteed debt. In that year the cost of debt-servicing long-term public and publicly guaranteed debt and repayments to the IMF was equivalent to 11.2% of the value of exports of goods, services and income (excluding workers' remittances). Annual inflation averaged 18.0% in 2003–12, according to the AfDB; consumer prices increased by an average of 21.3% in 2011 and by 13.1% in 2012.

Guinea's potential for the attainment of wealth is substantial, owing to its valuable mineral deposits (particularly bauxite, gold and iron ore), water resources and generally favourable climate; however, the economy remains overdependent on revenue from bauxite reserves and on external assistance, while the country's infrastructure is inadequate and its manufacturing base narrow. The inauguration of Alpha Condé as President in December 2010 allowed the reintegration of Guinea into the international community and the resumption of financial assistance. The IMF approved a three-year, SDR 128.52m. Extended Credit Facility in February 2012. The 'Paris Club' of sovereign creditors agreed to restructure the country's debt commitments in the same year; and extensive debt relief was confirmed by the IMF and the World Bank after Guinea successfully completed its obligations under the Heavily Indebted Poor Countries (HIPC) initiative. A new mining code was adopted in 2011, with terms enabling the Guinean Government to assume a 15% stake in any mining project without recompense, and to acquire a further 20% on commercial terms. In April 2013 the transitional administration made amendments to this code, including reductions in taxes and royalty obligations, but Guinea's acquisition rights were retained. A review of all mining licences contracted by previous administrations, initiated in 2011, was ongoing in early 2014. Meanwhile, all mining contracts were made available online from February 2013. In its third review under the ECF, released in February 2014, the IMF recorded that the fragile socio-political environment in Guinea, together with a sharp deceleration in investment in the mining sector, had contributed to lower GDP growth—estimated at 2.5%, substantially below the projected 4.5%—in 2013. Lower mining revenues and reduced economic activity more widely, together with difficulties in tax collection resulting from unrest related to the September legislative elections, and delays in the introduction of a fuel price adjustment mechanism, meant that there was a substantial shortfall in government revenue. Although subsidies to the state utility Electricité de Guinée (EDG) were higher than expected, and notwithstanding additional election-related spending, the IMF noted that the Government made compensatory cuts in current expenditure to offset the shortfall in revenues. Furthermore, capacity constraints meant that domestically financed investment spending was substantially lower than projected in the first half of 2013. As a result, the budget out-turn, with an overall deficit (including grants) at an estimated 5.3% of GDP, remained comparable with the 5.1% of GDP previously projected for the year. There was a further reduction in annual inflation, which averaged 11.9%. GDP growth was forecast to recover to 4.5% in 2014, but this was contingent on a return to political stability, an acceleration of investment in the mining sector, and an international economic climate supporting demand for iron ore and bauxite. Envisaged structural reforms for the year included progress with measures delayed from 2013, including reform of EDG and implementation, from early 2014, of a fuel price adjustment mechanism. Particularly critical to the mining sector would be settlement of the investment framework for the Simandou iron ore mega-project, some progress with which was reported in 2013. Uncertainty remained, however, regarding the rights to half of the Simandou reserves that had been reassigned by President Lansana Conté shortly before his death in 2008.

PUBLIC HOLIDAYS

2015: 1 January (New Year's Day), 2 January*† (Mouloud, Birth of Muhammad), 6 April (Easter Monday), 1 May (Labour Day), 17 July* (Id al-Fitr, end of Ramadan), 27 August (Anniversary of Women's Revolt), 28 September (Referendum Day), 2 October (Republic Day), 1 November (All Saints' Day), 22 November (Day of 1970 Invasion), 23 December*† (Mouloud, Birth of Muhammad), 25 December (Christmas).

* These holidays are determined by the Islamic lunar calendar and may vary by one or two days from the dates given.

† This festival occurs twice (in the Islamic years AH 1436 and 1437) within the same Gregorian year.

Statistical Survey

Source (unless otherwise stated): Direction Nationale de la Statistique, BP 221, Conakry; tel. 300-21-33-12; e-mail dnstat@biasy.net: internet www.stat-guinee.org.

Area and Population

AREA, POPULATION AND DENSITY

Area (sq km)	245,857*
Population (census results)	
4–17 February 1983	4,533,240†
31 December 1996‡	
Males	3,497,551
Females	3,658,855
Total	7,156,406
Population (UN estimates at mid-year)§	
2012	11,451,273
2013	11,745,190
2014	12,043,899
Density (per sq km) at mid-2014	49.0

* 94,926 sq miles.

† Excluding adjustment for underenumeration.

‡ Including refugees from Liberia and Sierra Leone (estimated at 640,000).

§ Source: UN, *World Population Prospects: The 2012 Revision*.

POPULATION BY AGE AND SEX

(UN estimates at mid-2014)

	Males	Females	Total
0–14	2,552,193	2,510,328	5,062,521
15–64	3,309,141	3,299,878	6,609,019
65 and over	171,964	200,395	372,359
Total	6,033,298	6,010,601	12,043,899

Source: UN, *World Population Prospects: The 2012 Revision*.

ETHNIC GROUPS

1995 (percentages): Peul 38.7; Malinké 23.3; Soussou 11.1; Kissi 5.9; Kpellé 4.5; Others 16.5 (Source: La Francophonie).

ADMINISTRATIVE DIVISIONS

('000 persons, official population estimates at 2011)

Region	Area (sq km)	Population	Density (per sq km)	Principal city
Conakry	450	1,659.1	3,687.0	Conakry
Basse-Guinée	47,063	2,217.3	47.1	Kindia
Moyenne-Guinée	52,939	2,489.0	47.0	Labé
Haute-Guinée	99,437	2,137.0	21.5	Kankan
Guinée Forestière	45,968	2,361.4	51.4	N'Zérékoré
Total	245,857	10,863.9	44.2	

Note: The regions were subsequently reorganized. The new regions (which in each case share their name with the regional capital) are: Boké; Conakry; Faranah; Kankan; Kindia; Labé; Mamou; and N'Zérékoré.

PRINCIPAL TOWNS
(population at 1996 census)

Conakry (capital)	1,092,936	Kindia	96,074
N'Zérékoré	107,329	Guéckédou	79,140
Kankan	100,192	Kamsar	61,526

Mid-2011 (incl. suburbs, UN estimate): Conakry 1,786,300 (Source: UN, *World Urbanization Prospects: The 2011 Revision*).

BIRTHS AND DEATHS
(annual averages, UN estimates)

	1995–2000	2000–05	2005–10
Birth rate (per 1,000)	43.2	41.1	39.2
Death rate (per 1,000)	15.3	14.9	12.7

Source: UN, *World Population Prospects: The 2012 Revision*.

Life expectancy (years at birth): 55.6 (males 54.8; females 56.4) in 2011 (Source: World Bank, World Development Indicators database).

ECONOMICALLY ACTIVE POPULATION
(at 1996 census)

	Males	Females	Total
Agriculture, hunting and forestry	1,140,775	1,281,847	2,422,622
Fishing	9,969	889	10,858
Mining and quarrying	26,599	8,376	34,975
Manufacturing	84,974	5,911	90,885
Electricity, gas and water supply	4,366	324	4,690
Construction	59,802	724	60,526
Wholesale and retail trade; repair of motor vehicles and motorcycles and personal and household goods	176,527	191,230	367,757
Restaurants and hotels	3,162	2,790	5,952
Transport, storage and communications	75,374	1,696	77,070
Financial intermediation	1,728	626	2,354
Real estate, renting and business activities	877	209	1,086
Public administration and defence; compulsory social security	50,401	12,791	63,192
Education	15,044	3,773	18,817
Health and social work	4,762	3,522	8,284
Other community, social and personal service activities	44,897	48,292	93,189
Private households with employed persons	5,553	6,202	11,755
Extra-territorial organizations and bodies	3,723	1,099	4,822
Total employed	1,708,533	1,570,301	3,278,834

Mid-2014 ('000 persons): Agriculture, etc. 4,188; Total labour force 5,373 (Source: FAO).

Health and Welfare

KEY INDICATORS

Total fertility rate (children per woman, 2011)	5.2
Under-5 mortality rate (per 1,000 live births, 2011)	126
HIV/AIDS (% of persons aged 15–49, 2012)	1.7
Physicians (per 1,000 head, 2005)	0.1
Hospital beds (per 1,000 head, 2011)	0.3
Health expenditure (2010): US $ per head (PPP)	67
Health expenditure (2010): % of GDP	6.2
Health expenditure (2010): public (% of total)	32.5
Access to water (% of persons, 2011)	74
Access to sanitation (% of persons, 2011)	18
Total carbon dioxide emissions ('000 metric tons, 2010)	1,235.8
Carbon dioxide emissions per head (metric tons, 2010)	0.1
Human Development Index (2012): ranking	178
Human Development Index (2012): value	0.355

For sources and definitions, see explanatory note on p. vi.

Agriculture

PRINCIPAL CROPS
('000 metric tons)

	2010	2011	2012
Rice, paddy	1,499.0	1,670.0*	1,919.0*
Maize	580.1†	611.0*	641.0*
Fonio	388.6†	409.0*	429.0*
Sweet potatoes†	235.0	227.1	230.0
Cassava (Manioc)	1,100.0†	1,112.6*	1,200.0†
Taro (Cocoyam)†	27.9	28.0	30.0
Yams†	24.4	24.5	26.0
Sugar cane†	283	283	295
Pulses†	55.9	56.0	57.0
Groundnuts, with shell*	291.7	290.0	300.0
Coconuts	33.3*	41.1*	41.5†
Oil palm fruit†	830.0	830.0	830.0
Bananas†	201.5	210.0	215.0
Plantains†	461.7	463.0	470.0
Guavas, mangoes and mangosteens	163.9†	157.7*	165.0†
Pineapples	107.5†	118.6*	120.0
Seed cotton†	37.1	40.0	42.0
Coffee, green	29.0	29.5†	30.0

* Unofficial figure(s).
† FAO estimate(s).

Aggregate production ('000 metric tons, may include official, semi-official or estimated data): Total cereals 2,743.0 in 2010, 2,947.0 in 2011, 3,260.0 in 2012; Total roots and tubers 1,398.1 in 2010, 1,403.2 in 2011, 1,498.0 in 2012; Total vegetables (incl. melons) 563.9 in 2010, 557.7 in 2011, 537.9 in 2012; Total fruits (excl. melons) 1,218.7 in 2010, 1,237.3 in 2011, 1,261.0 in 2012.

Source: FAO.

LIVESTOCK
('000 head, year ending September)

	2010	2011*	2012†
Cattle	4,906	4,672	4,965
Sheep	1,615	1,410	1,700
Goats	1,932	1,751	1,800
Pigs	95.2	91.0	103.0
Chickens	15,200†	15,090	15,000

* Unofficial figures.
† FAO estimate(s).

Source: FAO.

LIVESTOCK PRODUCTS
('000 metric tons, FAO estimates)

	2010	2011	2012
Cattle meat	54.9	52.3	52.8
Chicken meat	6.6	6.5	6.6
Sheep meat	6.7	6.0	6.1
Goat meat	9.3	8.7	9.3
Game meat	5.4	5.8	6.0
Cows' milk	115.0	115.2	116.0
Goats' milk	12.7	12.8	12.9
Hen eggs	23.6	24.5	24.5

Source: FAO.

Forestry

ROUNDWOOD REMOVALS
('000 cubic metres, excl. bark, FAO estimates)

	2010	2011	2012
Sawlogs, veneer logs and logs for sleepers	138	138	138
Other industrial wood	513	513	513
Fuel wood	11,959	12,010	12,063
Total	12,610	12,661	12,714

Source: FAO.

SAWNWOOD PRODUCTION
('000 cubic metres, incl. railway sleepers, FAO estimates)

	2005	2006	2007
Total (all broadleaved)	2.5	2.2	30.0

2008–12: Production assumed to be unchanged from 2007 (FAO estimates).

Source: FAO.

Fishing

('000 metric tons, live weight)

	2009	2010	2011
Freshwater fishes*	14.0	16.0	18.0
Sea catfishes	10.2	9.0	9.0*
Bobo croaker	8.6	6.9	7.0*
West African croakers	5.3	5.1	5.1*
Sardinellas	6.6	5.1	5.2*
Bonga shad	48.3	39.4	40.0*
Total catch (incl. others)*	127.8	113.5	115.0

* FAO estimate(s).

Source: FAO.

Mining

('000 metric tons unless otherwise indicated)

	2009	2010	2011
Bauxite (dry basis)*†	13,600	15,300	15,300
Gold (kilograms)	18,091	15,217	15,695
Salt (unrefined)†	15	15	15
Diamonds ('000 carats)‡	697	374	304

* Estimated to be 7% water.
† Estimates.
‡ Including artisanal production.

Source: US Geological Survey.

Industry

SELECTED PRODUCTS
('000 metric tons unless otherwise indicated)

	2009	2010	2011
Palm oil (unrefined)*†	50	50	50
Beer of barley*‡	13.0	7.9	23.2
Raw sugar§	25	n.a.	n.a.
Alumina (calcined equivalent)‖	530	597	574
Electric energy (million kWh)§	996	n.a.	n.a.

* Data from FAO.
† Unofficial figures.
‡ FAO estimates.
§ Data from UN Industrial Commodity Statistics Database.
‖ Data from the US Geological Survey.

Palm oil (unrefined) ('000 metric tons): 50 in 2012 (FAO estimate).

Finance

CURRENCY AND EXCHANGE RATES

Monetary Units
100 centimes = 1 franc guinéen (FG or Guinean franc).

Sterling, Dollar and Euro Equivalents (29 June 2012)
£1 sterling = 10,844.238 Guinean francs;
US $1 = 6,950.094 Guinean francs;
€1 = 8,750.170 Guinean francs;
100,000 Guinean francs = £9.22 = $14.39 = €11.43.

Average Exchange Rate (Guinean francs per US $)

2009	4,801.1
2010	5,726.1
2011	6,658.0

BUDGET
('000 million Guinean francs)

Revenue*	2011	2012†	2013‡
Mining-sector revenue	1,296	1,607	1,798
Other revenue	4,366	6,368	7,427
Tax revenue	3,882	5,993	7,033
Taxes on domestic production and trade	1,904	2,765	3,581
Taxes on international trade	978	1,452	1,734
Non-tax revenue	484	375	394
Total	5,662	7,975	9,225

Expenditure§	2011	2012†	2013‡
Current expenditure	5,490	6,291	7,175
Wages and salaries	1,764	1,757	2,284
Other goods and services	1,814	2,356	2,694
Subsidies and transfers	1,248	1,505	1,565
Interest due on external debt	293	216	55
Interest due on domestic debt	370	402	373
Capital expenditure	1,750	3,801	4,143
Domestically financed	984	2,674	2,576
Externally financed	753	1,113	1,551
Capital transfer	13	16	16
Total	7,240	10,092	11,318

* Excluding grants received ('000 million Guinean francs): 1,162 in 2011; 1,071 in 2012 (estimate); 1,098 in 2013 (budget figure).
† Estimates.
‡ Budget figures.
§ Excluding lending minus repayments ('000 million Guinean francs): 7 in 2011; 251 in 2012 (estimate); 369 in 2013 (budget figure).

Source: IMF, *Guinea: Second Review Under the Three-Year Arrangement Under the Extended Credit Facility, Requests for Modifications of Performance Criteria and Waiver of Nonobservance of Performance Criterion, and Financing Assurances Review* (July 2013).

INTERNATIONAL RESERVES
(US $ million at 31 December)

	2010	2011
Gold (national valuation)	10.02	8.60
IMF special drawing rights	116.16	94.34
Reserve position in IMF	0.12	0.12
Foreign exchange	n.a.	8.70
Total	n.a.	111.76

IMF special drawing rights: 120.60 in 2012.

Reserve position in IMF: 0.12 in 2012.

Source: IMF, *International Financial Statistics*.

MONEY SUPPLY
(million Guinean francs at 31 December)

	2009	2010	2011
Currency outside banks	2,123,925	3,987,512	3,296,217
Demand deposits at commercial banks	1,944,782	4,785,300	5,490,842
Total (incl. others)	4,398,032	8,814,784	9,783,878

Source: IMF, *International Financial Statistics*.

COST OF LIVING
(Consumer Price Index at December; base: 2002 = 100)

	2010	2011	2012
Foodstuffs, beverages and tobacco	651.0	786.8	891.8
Clothing and shoes	275.0	321.7	374.7
Housing, water, electricity and gas	336.0	370.4	440.0
Health	318.0	393.6	463.0
Transport	425.0	474.9	485.5
Education	238.0	313.7	325.1
Entertainment, culture and recreation	209.0	264.0	284.6
Restaurants and hotels	396.0	480.1	580.3
Miscellaneous goods and services	226.0	246.6	259.5
All items	445.0	529.8	597.8

NATIONAL ACCOUNTS
('000 million Guinean francs at current prices)

Expenditure on the Gross Domestic Product

	2010	2011	2012*
Government final consumption expenditure	3,550.8	3,355.3	4,118.2
Private final consumption expenditure	20,539.7	31,459.0	34,575.4
Gross fixed capital formation	4,634.4	6,741.4	9,286.4
Changes in inventories	2.4	5.1	5.4
Total domestic expenditure	28,727.3	41,560.8	47,985.4
Exports of goods and services	9,135.2	10 172.2	11,511.8
Less Imports of goods and services	10,780.7	18,036.3	20,597.6
GDP at market prices	27,081.6	33,696.7	38,899.7

Gross Domestic Product by Economic Activity

	2010	2011	2012*
Agriculture, livestock, forestry and fishing	5,490.6	6,349.5	7,511.9
Mining and quarrying	6,322.9	7,137.5	7,654.5
Manufacturing	1,806.4	2,268.7	2,614.1
Electricity, gas and water	109.8	126.9	172.6
Construction	2,883.2	3,620.7	4,368.6
Trade, restaurants and hotels	4,429.2	6,620.6	7,748.7
Transport and communications	1,428.3	1,734.3	2,039.5
Public administration and defence	1,691.5	1,848.0	1,956.0
Other services	708.4	1,109.5	1,289.9
GDP at factor cost	24,870.0	30,815.6	35,355.9
Indirect taxes	2,211.6	2,881.1	3,543.8
GDP at purchasers' values	27,081.6	33,696.7	38,899.7

* Provisional.

Notes: Deduction for imputed bank service charge assumed to be distributed at origin. Totals may not be equal to the sum of components, owing to rounding.

Source: African Development Bank.

BALANCE OF PAYMENTS
(US $ million)

	2010	2011	2012
Exports of goods	1,471.2	1,428.4	1,927.6
Imports of goods	–1,398.5	–2,097.1	–2,244.0
Balance on goods	72.7	–668.8	–316.4
Exports of services	62.4	77.4	159.1
Imports of services	–402.0	–576.1	–891.8
Balance on goods and services	–266.9	–1,167.5	–1,049.1
Primary income received	14.9	22.2	31.5
Primary income paid	–92.0	–155.6	–153.5
Balance on goods, services and primary income	–344.0	–1,300.8	–1,171.1
Secondary income received	81.5	353.7	242.4
Secondary income paid	–66.8	–268.0	–172.9
Current balance	–329.2	–1,215.2	–1,101.5
Capital account (net)	16.9	138.9	78.5
Direct investment assets	—	–0.8	–1.9
Direct investment liabilities	101.4	956.1	0.1
Portfolio investment assets	–0.1	211.6	–3.1
Other investment assets	–77.4	–186.5	–98.4
Other investment liabilities	289.5	755.6	126.6
Net errors and omissions	38.7	–40.1	235.8
Reserves and related items	39.8	619.6	–763.9

Source: IMF, *International Financial Statistics*.

External Trade

PRINCIPAL COMMODITIES
(distribution by HS, US $ million)

Imports c.i.f.	2010	2011	2012
Vegetables and vegetable products	223.8	255.7	269.2
Cereals	153.4	193.6	187.0
Rice	139.5	184.3	186.7
Milling products, malt, starches, inulin, wheat gluten	54.1	52.6	70.2
Wheat or meslin flour	40.0	48.5	67.3
Prepared foodstuffs; beverages, spirits, vinegar; tobacco and articles thereof	157.5	109.7	98.1
Mineral products	1,050.8	529.5	401.3
Salt, sulphur, earth, stone, plaster, lime and cement	97.0	54.4	68.8
Cements, portland, aluminous, slag, supersulfate and similar hydraulic materials	79.1	45.3	59.9
Mineral fuels, oils, distillation products, etc.	953.7	475.1	332.4
Petroleum oils, not crude	940.0	472.4	322.1
Chemicals and related products	204.5	144.9	163.4
Pharmaceutical products	93.7	58.9	71.1
Plastics, rubbers, and articles thereof	81.2	48.8	63.2

Imports c.i.f.—*continued*	2010	2011	2012
Iron and steel, other base metals and articles of base metal	108.1	105.8	117.6
Machinery and mechanical appliances; electrical equipment; parts thereof	371.3	422.6	548.1
Machinery, boilers, etc.	236.4	313.5	388.7
Self-propelled bulldozers, angledozers, graders, excavators, etc.	24.8	60.2	71.4
Machine parts	96.9	97.5	146.1
Electrical, electronic equipment	134.9	109.1	159.4
Vehicles, aircraft, vessels and associated transport equipment	180.5	156.8	173.5
Vehicles other than railway, tramway	180.5	156.8	173.5
Cars (incl. station wagons)	56.2	50.9	61.7
Total (incl. others)	2,618.8	1,952.5	2,038.9

Exports f.o.b.	2010	2011	2012
Mineral products	490.6	483.8	151.0
Ores, slag and ash	482.7	467.1	43.7
Aluminum ores and concentrates	482.7	467.1	43.3
Mineral fuels, oils, distillation products, etc.	7.9	16.6	107.1
Petroleum oils, not crude	7.9	16.6	107.0
Chemicals and related products	170.1	176.3	53.7
Inorganic chemicals, precious metal compound, isotopes	169.2	174.6	51.3
Aluminium oxide (incl. artificial corundum); aluminium hydroxide	169.1	174.6	51.3
Plastics, rubber, and articles thereof	28.1	34.6	303.1
Rubber and articles thereof	18.5	21.5	289.4
Natural rubber, balata, gutta-percha, etc.	18.5	21.4	289.4
Pulp of wood, paper and paperboard, and articles thereof	132.1	73.0	92.7
Printed books, newspapers, pictures, etc.	132.0	72.8	92.7
Unused stamps; cheque forms, banknotes, bond certificates, etc.	132.0	72.8	92.7
Pearls, precious stones, metals, coins, etc.	834.2	857.7	1,425.1
Gold, unwrought or in semi-manufactured forms	797.5	821.5	1,386.2
Machinery and mechanical appliances; electrical equipment; parts thereof	148.4	69.4	55.1
Machinery, boilers, etc.	146.0	24.0	54.0
Machine parts	135.2	4.1	6.8
Total (incl. others)	1,895.6	1,776.5	2,139.2

Source: Trade Map-Trade Competitiveness Map, International Trade Centre, www.intracen.org/marketanalysis.

PRINCIPAL TRADING PARTNERS
(US $ million)

Imports c.i.f.	2010	2011	2012
Australia	37.5	33.2	75.4
Belgium	198.5	146.9	131.8
Brazil	30.0	39.6	19.5
China, People's Republic	232.0	169.1	257.2
Côte d'Ivoire	53.3	26.2	11.7
France (incl. Monaco)	198.5	140.7	162.3
Greece	18.8	21.2	9.8
Germany	24.1	14.4	26.4
India	83.0	57.2	130.1
Italy	66.7	30.1	41.5
Japan	30.0	10.9	30.9

Imports c.i.f.—*continued*	2010	2011	2012
Malaysia	25.5	28.3	46.2
Korea, Republic	31.8	9.6	19.8
Mali	1.6	27.8	27.2
Malta	3.3	35.2	23.1
Morocco	29.9	40.5	69.5
Myanmar	22.7	17.7	41.3
Netherlands	696.0	353.7	300.4
Pakistan	64.2	60.1	19.4
Portugal	6.8	40.9	32.4
Senegal	27.3	24.2	17.8
Singapore	10.0	34.8	17.1
South Africa	35.2	38.7	59.7
Spain	89.6	13.4	35.8
Sweden	16.0	21.0	10.7
Thailand	4.1	21.5	9.7
Turkey	22.0	23.1	27.7
United Arab Emirates	58.4	51.9	45.8
United Kingdom	125.1	72.3	32.9
USA	65.9	86.6	75.8
Viet Nam	52.9	59.4	17.7
Total (incl. others)	2,618.8	1,952.5	2,038.9

Exports f.o.b.	2010	2011	2012
Belgium	24.9	48.9	355.7
Canada	56.6	55.1	0.9
China, People's Republic	43.0	6.1	5.3
France (incl. Monaco)	442.5	513.5	527.8
Germany	52.3	63.8	3.8
Iran	67.6	7.8	n.a.
Ireland	45.8	86.2	117.1
Italy	1.8	7.3	83.0
Mali	7.4	53.0	10.0
Nigeria	141.4	8.4	6.4
Russia	140.7	150.4	41.2
Sierra Leone	4.4	8.0	104.3
Spain	119.8	112.9	3.6
Switzerland	490.1	384.1	579.5
Ukraine	47.4	40.8	41.9
United Arab Emirates	53.9	56.2	124.8
USA	76.7	79.8	24.7
Total (incl. others)	1,895.6	1,776.5	2,139.2

Source: Trade Map-Trade Competitiveness Map, International Trade Centre, www.intracen.org/marketanalysis.

Transport

RAILWAYS
(estimated traffic)

	1991	1992	1993
Freight ton-km (million)	660	680	710

Source: UN Economic Commission for Africa, *African Statistical Yearbook*.

ROAD TRAFFIC
('000, motor vehicles in use, estimates)

	2010	2011
Private vehicles	150.0	190.0
Public vehicles	100.0	109.2
Total	250.0	299.2

SHIPPING

Flag Registered Fleet
(at 31 December)

	2011	2012	2013
Number of vessels	36	37	37
Total displacement ('000 grt)	25.2	28.8	28.8

Source: Lloyd's List Intelligence (www.lloydslistintelligence.com).

International Sea-borne Freight Traffic
(Port of Conakry, '000 metric tons)

	2009	2010	2011
Goods loaded	3,409	3,759	3,814
Goods unloaded	2,539	3,118	3,357

CIVIL AVIATION
(traffic on scheduled services)

	1997	1998	1999
Kilometres flown (million)	1	1	1
Passengers carried ('000)	36	36	59
Passenger-km (million)	55	55	94
Total ton-km (million)	6	6	10

Source: UN, *Statistical Yearbook*.

Passengers carried (Conakry-Gbèssia airport, '000): 248.5 in 2009; 247.6 in 2010; 325.3 in 2011.

Freight carried (Conakry-Gbèssia airport, '000 metric tons): 3.0 in 2009; 233.2 in 2010; 4.4 in 2011.

Tourism

FOREIGN VISITOR ARRIVALS*

Country of origin	2005	2006	2007
Belgium	1,126	970	685
Canada	1,135	1,023	798
China, People's Repub.	1,575	1,696	1,874
Côte d'Ivoire	2,453	1,261	1,103
France	7,984	7,376	4,488
Germany	1,029	1,114	603
Mali	1,295	818	870
Senegal	4,523	3,406	2,171
Sierra Leone	1,328	1,620	802
USA	3,237	380	911
Total (incl. others)†	45,330	46,096	30,194

* Arrivals of non-resident tourists at national borders, by nationality.
† Air arrivals at Conakry-Gbèssia airport.

Receipts from tourism (US $ million, excl. passenger transport): 3.0 in 2009; 2.0 in 2010; 2.0 in 2011.

Source: World Tourism Organization.

Communications Media

	2010	2011	2012
Telephones ('000 main lines in use)	18	18	18
Mobile cellular telephones ('000 subscribers)	4,000	4,500	4,781
Broadband subscribers ('000)	0.5	0.6	0.7

Internet users ('000): 95 in 2009.

Source: International Telecommunication Union.

Education

(2011/12 unless otherwise indicated)

	Institutions	Teachers	Students ('000) Males	Females	Total
Pre-primary	202*	3,599†	77.8‡	73.7‡	151.5‡
Primary	8,024	36,731	877.8	722.0	1,599.8
Secondary	1,130	21,501	412.9	256.1	669.0
General	n.a.	19,880	395.1	240.6	635.7
Tertiary	52	6,221	65.7	23.9	89.6

* 1996/97.
† 2009/10.
‡ 2010/11.

Source: partly UNESCO Institute for Statistics.

Pupil-teacher ratio (primary education, UNESCO estimate): 43.6 in 2011/12 (Source: UNESCO Institute for Statistics).

Adult literacy rate (UNESCO estimates): 25.3% (males 36.8%; females 12.2%) in 2010 (Source: UNESCO Institute for Statistics).

Directory

The Government

HEAD OF STATE

President and Minister of National Defence: ALPHA CONDÉ (inaugurated 21 December 2010).

COUNCIL OF MINISTERS
(April 2014)

Prime Minister: MOHAMED SAÏD FOFANA.

Minister of State, responsible for Mines and Geology: KERFALA YANSANÉ.

Minister of State, responsible for Justice: CHEICK SAKHO.

Minister of State, responsible for Foreign Affairs and Guineans Abroad: FRANÇOIS LONSÉNY FALL.

Minister of State, responsible for Telecommunications, Posts and New Information Technologies: OYÉ GUILAVOGUI.

Minister of State, responsible for the Economy and Finance: MOHAMED DIARÉ.

Minister of State, responsible for Higher Education and Scientific Research: BAILO TÉLIWEL DIALLO.

Minister of Health: Col REMY LAMAH.

Minister of Security and Civil Protection: Elhadj MADIFING DIANÉ.

Minister of Energy and Water: IDRISSA THIAM.

Minister of Territorial Administration and Decentralization: ALASSANE CONDÉ.

Minister of Agriculture: JACQUELINE SULTAN.

Minister of Employment, Labour, Technical Education and Vocational Training: ALBERT DAMANTANG CAMARA.

Minister of Urban Development and Territorial Management: IBRAHIMA BANGOURA.

Minister of the Civil Service, State Reform and Administrative Modernization: SÉKOU KOUROUMA.

Minister of Sport: DOMANI DORÉ.

Minister of International Co-operation: Dr KOUTOUB MOUSTAPHA SANO.

Minister of Communication: ALHOUSSENI KAKÉ MANAKANÉRA.

Minister of Commerce: MARC YOMBOUNO.

Minister of Fisheries and Aquaculture: MOUSSA CONDÉ.

Minister of Transport: ALIOUNE DIALLO.

Minister of Pre-university Education and Literacy: Dr IBRAHIMA KOUROUMA.

Minister of Public Works: MOHAMED TRAORÉ.

Minister of the Environment, Water and Forests: KADIATOU N'DIAYE.

Minister of Tourism, Hotels and Handicrafts: LOUSENY CAMARA.

Minister of Stockbreeding: THIERNO OUSMANE DIALLO.

Minister of Planning: SÉKOU TRAORÉ.

Minister of Industry, Small and Medium-sized Enterprises and the Promotion of the Private Sector: FATOUMATA BINTA DIALLO.

Minister of Culture, Arts and Heritage: AHMED TIDIANE CISSÉ.

Minister of Social Affairs, the Promotion of Women and Children: CAMARA SANABA KABA.

Minister of Human Rights and Public Freedom: KALIFA GASSAMA DIABY.

Minister of Youth and Youth Employment: MOUSTAPHA NAITÉ.

Minister-delegate for National Defence: Commdr ABDOUL KABÉLÉ CAMARA.

Minister-delegate for the Budget: ANSOUMANE CONDÉ.

Minister-delegate for Guineans Abroad: SANOUSSY BANTAMA SOW.

MINISTRIES

Office of the President: BP 1000, Boulbinet, Conakry; tel. 664-87-96-59 (mobile); fax 300-41-16-73; internet www.presidence.gov.gn.

Office of the Prime Minister: BP 5141, Conakry; tel. 300-41-51-19; fax 300-41-52-82.

Office of the Secretary-General at the Presidency: Conakry.

Ministry of Agriculture: face à la Cité du Port, BP 576, Conakry; tel. 601-55-36-76 (mobile); e-mail dourasano@hotmail.com.

Ministry of Commerce: Conakry.

Ministry of Communication: Conakry.

Ministry of Culture, Arts and Heritage: Conakry.

Ministry of the Economy and Finance: Boulbinet, BP 221, Conakry; tel. 300-45-17-95; fax 300-41-30-59.

Ministry of Employment, Technical Education and Vocational Training: Conakry; tel. 628-20-58-58 (mobile).

Ministry of Energy: route du Niger, Coléah, Conakry; tel. 601-22-50-54 (mobile).

Ministry of the Environment, Water and Forests: Conakry.

Ministry of Fisheries and Aquaculture: face à la Cité du Port, BP 307, Conakry; tel. 300-41-12-58; fax 300-41-43-10; e-mail minipaq.jpl@eti-bull.net; internet www.fis.com/guinea.

Ministry of Foreign Affairs and Guineans Abroad: Quartier Almamya, face au Port Autonome de Conakry, Commune de Kaloum, BP 2519, Conakry; tel. 657-16-45-05 (mobile); fax 300-41-16-21; internet www.mae.gov.gn.

Ministry of Health and Public Hygiene: blvd du Commerce, BP 585, Conakry; tel. 300-41-20-32; fax 300-41-41-38.

Ministry of Higher Education and Scientific Research: face à la Cathédrale Sainte-Marie, BP 964, Conakry; tel. 300-45-12-17; fax 300-41-20-12.

Ministry of Human Rights and Public Freedom: Conakry.

Ministry of Industry and Small and Medium-sized Enterprises: Conakry.

Ministry of Information: Conakry.

Ministry of International Co-operation: Conakry.

Ministry of Justice: face à l'Immeuble 'La Paternelle', Almamya, Conakry; tel. 300-41-29-60.

Ministry of Labour and the Civil Service: Boulbinet, Conakry; tel. 300-45-20-01.

Ministry of Literacy and the Promotion of National Languages: Conakry.

Ministry of Mines and Geology: BP 295, Conakry; tel. 300-41-38-33; fax 300-41-49-13.

Ministry of National Defence: Camp Samory-Touré, Conakry; tel. 300-41-11-54.

Ministry of Planning: BP 221, Conakry; tel. 300-44-37-15; fax 300-41-43-50.

Ministry of Pre-university Education: Boulbinet, BP 2201, Conakry; tel. 300-45-19-17.

Ministry of Public Works and Transport: BP 715, Conakry; tel. 300-41-36-39; fax 300-41-35-77.

Ministry of Security, Civil Protection and the Reform of Security Services: Coléah-Domino, Conakry; tel. 300-41-45-50.

Ministry of Social Affairs, the Promotion of Women and Children: Corniche-Ouest, face au Terminal Conteneurs du Port de Conakry, BP 527, Conakry; tel. 300-45-45-39; fax 300-41-46-60.

Ministry of Telecommunications, Posts and New Information Technologies: BP 3000, Conakry; tel. 300-43-17-81; fax 300-45-18-96.

Ministry of Territorial Administration and Decentralization: face aux Jardins du 2 Octobre, Tombo, BP 2201, Conakry; tel. 300-41-15-10; fax 300-45-45-07.

Ministry of Tourism, Hotels and Handicrafts: BP 1304, Conakry; tel. 300-44-26-06; fax 300-44-49-90.

Ministry of Urban Development, Housing and Construction: Conakry.

Ministry of Youth, Youth Employment and Sports: ave du Port Secrétariat, BP 262, Conakry; tel. 601-52-74-76 (mobile); fax 300-41-19-26.

President

Presidential Election, First Round, 27 June 2010

Candidate	% of votes
Cellou Dalein Diallo (UFDG)	43.69
Alpha Condé (RPG)	18.25
Sidya Touré (UFR)	13.02
Lansana Kouyaté (PEDN)	7.04
Papa Koly Kourouma (RDR)	5.74
Ibrahima Abe Sylla (NGR)	3.23
Jean-Marc Telliano (RDIG)	2.33
Others*	6.70
Total	100.00

* There were 17 other candidates.

Presidential Election, Second Round, 7 November 2010

Candidate	Votes	% of votes
Alpha Condé (RPG)	1,474,973	52.52
Cellou Dalein Diallo (UFDG)	1,333,666	47.48
Total	2,808,639	100.00

Legislature

National Assembly: Palais du Peuple, BP 414, Conakry; tel. 300-41-28-04; fax 300-45-17-00; e-mail s.general@assemblee.gov.gn; internet www.assemblee.gov.gn.

President: CLAUDE KORY KONDIANO.

General Election, 28 September 2013

Party	Constituency seats	National list seats	Total seats
Rassemblement du Peuple de Guinée Arc-en-ciel	18	35	53
Union des Forces Démocratiques de Guinée	14	23	37
Union des Forces Républicaines	5	5	10
Union pour le Progrès de la Guinée	1	1	2
Parti de l'Espoir pour le Développement National	–	2	2
Others*	–	10	10
Total	38	76	114

* The Génération pour la Réconciliation, l'Union et le Prospérité, Guinée pour Tous, Guinée Unie pour le Développement, the Nouvelle Génération pour la République, the Parti Guinéen pour la Renaissance et le Progrès, the Parti National pour le Renouveau, the Parti du Travail et de la Solidarité, the Rassemblement pour le Développement Intégré de la Guinée, the Union Guinéenne pour la Démocratie et le Développement and the Union pour le Progrès et le Renouveau were all allocated one national list seat each.

Election Commission

Commission Electorale Nationale Indépendante (CENI): Villa 17, Cité des Nations, Conakry; tel. 664-24-22-06 (mobile); e-mail bensekou@ceniguinee.org; internet www.ceniguinee.org; f. 2005; comprises 10 representatives of the parliamentary majority, 10 representatives of the parliamentary opposition, three representatives of civil society and two representatives of the state administration; Pres. BAKARY FOFANA; Sec.-Gen. BOKAR CISSOKO.

Advisory Council

Economic and Social Council: Immeuble FAWAZ, Corniche Sud, Coléah, Matam, BP 2947, Conakry; tel. 300-45-31-23; fax 300-45-31-24; e-mail ces@sotelgui.net.gn; f. 1997; 45 mems; Pres. MICHEL KAMANO; Sec.-Gen. MAMADOU BOBO CAMARA.

Political Organizations

Alliance Nationale pour le Progrès (ANP): Conakry; Leader Dr SAGNO MOUSSA.

Front Uni pour la Démocratie et le Changement (FUDEC): Ratoma, Conakry; tel. 601-22-76-71 (mobile); fax 666-87-28-62 (mobile); internet www.fudec.org; f. 2009; Pres. FRANÇOIS LOUNCENY FALL.

Génération pour la Réconciliation, l'Union et le Prospérité (GRUP): Conakry; Pres. PAPA KOLY KOUROUMA.

Guinée pour Tous (GPT): Conakry; Pres. IBRAHIMA KASSORY FOFANA.

Guinée Unie pour le Développement (GUD): Conakry; f. 2002; Pres. Dr SÉKOU BENNA CAMARA.

Nouvelle Génération pour la République (NGR): Kissosso; tel. 664-29-05-72 (mobile); Leader IBRAHIMA ABE SYLLA.

Parti Démocratique de Guinée—Rassemblement Démocratique Africain (PDG—RDA): Conakry; f. 1946; revived 1992; Sec.-Gen. El Hadj ISMAËL MOHAMED GASSIM GHUSSEIN.

Parti Dyama: Conakry; e-mail mansourkaba@yahoo.fr; internet www.guinea-dyama.com; moderate Islamist party; Pres. MOHAMED MANSOUR KABA.

Parti Écologiste de Guinée (PEG—Les Verts): BP 3018, Quartier Boulbinet, 5e blvd, angle 2e ave, Commune de Kaloum, Conakry; tel. 300-44-37-01; Leader OUMAR SYLLA.

Parti de l'Espoir pour le Développement National (PEDN): Commune Ratoma, BP 1403, Conakry; tel. 655-55-00-00 (mobile); e-mail info@pednespoirl.org; internet pednespoir.org; Pres. LANSANA KOUYATÉ.

Parti Guinéen pour la Renaissance et le Progrès (PGRP): Conakry; Pres. ALPHA IBRAHIMA SILA BAH.

Parti National pour le Renouveau: Conakry; Pres. ALPHA SOULEYMANE BAH FISHER.

Parti du Peuple de Guinée (PPG): BP 1147, Conakry; socialist; boycotted presidential election in 2003, following the Supreme Court's rejection of its nominated candidate; Leader CHARLES-PASCAL TOLNO.

Parti du Travail et de la Solidarité (PTS): Pres. MAMADOU DIAWARA.

Parti de l'Unité et du Progrès (PUP): Camayenne, Conakry; internet www.pupguinee.org; Pres. (vacant); Sec.-Gen. El Hadj Dr SÉKOU KONATÉ.

Rassemblement pour la Défense de la République (RDR): Leader PAPA KOLY KOUROUMA.

Rassemblement pour le Développement Intégré de la Guinée (RDIG): Leader JEAN-MARC TELLIANO.

Rassemblement du Peuple de Guinée (RPG): Conakry; e-mail admin@rpgguinee.org; internet www.rpgguinee.org; f. 1980 as the Rassemblement des Patriotes Guinéens; socialist; Pres. ALPHA CONDÉ.

Union Démocratique de Guinée (UDG): Dixinn Centre, Conakry; tel. 601-52-40-26 (mobile); f. 2009; Leader El Hadj MAMADOU SYLLA.

Union des Forces Démocratiques (UFD): BP 3050, Conakry; tel. 300-34-50-20; e-mail ufdconakry@yahoo.fr; internet www.ufd-conakry.com; Pres. MAMADOU BAADIKKO BAH.

Union des Forces Démocratiques de Guinée (UFDG): BP 3036, Conakry; e-mail baggelmalal@yahoo.fr; internet www.ufdg.org; f. 2002 by faction of UPR in protest at that party's participation in elections to National Assembly; Pres. CELLOU DALEIN DIALLO.

Union des Forces Républicaines (UFR): Immeuble 'Le Golfe', 4e étage, BP 6080, Conakry; tel. 664-30-47-50 (mobile); fax 300-45-42-31; e-mail ufrguinee@yahoo.fr; internet www.ufrguinee.org; f. 1992; liberal-conservative; Pres. SIDYA TOURÉ; Sec.-Gen. BAKARY G. ZOUMANIGUI.

Union Guinéenne pour la Démocratie et le Développement (UGDD): BP 4600, Conakry; tel. 640-00-00-23 (mobile); e-mail info@ugdd.org; internet ugdd.org; Sec.-Gen. KEAMOU BOGOLA HABA.

Union pour le Progrès de la Guinée (UPG): Conakry; Leader JEAN-MARIE DORÉ.

Union pour le Progrès et le Renouveau (UPR): BP 690, Conakry; tel. 300-25-26-01; e-mail basusmane@mirinet.net.gn; internet www.uprguinee.org; f. 1998 by merger of the Parti pour le Renouveau et le Progrès and the Union pour la Nouvelle République; Pres. OUSMANE BAH.

Union pour le Progrès National—Parti pour l'Unité et le Développement (UPN—PUD): Conakry; Leader MAMADOU BHOYE BARRY.

Diplomatic Representation

EMBASSIES IN GUINEA

Algeria: Cité des Nations, Quartiers Kaloum, BP 1004, Conakry; tel. 664-00-00-95 (mobile); fax 300-41-15-35; Ambassador RABAH FASSIH.

Angola: Conakry; tel. 664-56-24-21 (mobile); Ambassador EDUARDO RUAS DE JESUS MANUEL.

Brazil: Résidence 2000, Immeuble de ÍAdministration el de la DHL, 5e étage, Conakry; tel. 664-20-21-11 (mobile); e-mail brasemb.conacri@itamaraty.gov.br; Chargé d'affaires e.p. ALIRIO RAMOS.

China, People's Republic: Quartier Donka, Cité Ministérielle, Commune de Dixinn, BP 714, Conakry; tel. 664-00-80-00 (mobile); fax 300-46-95-83; e-mail chinaemb_gn@mfa.gov.cn; internet gn.chineseembassy.org; Ambassador BIAN JIANQIANG.

Congo, Democratic Republic: Quartier Almamya, ave de la Gare, Commune du Kaloum, BP 880, Conakry; tel. 300-45-15-01.

Côte d'Ivoire: blvd du Commerce, BP 5228, Conakry; tel. 622-13-38-01 (mobile); fax 300-45-10-79; e-mail acign@ambaci-guinee.org; Ambassador DIARRASSOUBA M. YOUSSOUF.

Cuba: Cité Ministérielle, Quartier Donka, Commune de Dixinn, Conakry; tel. 664-20-87-73 (mobile); fax 300-46-95-28; e-mail embagcon@sotelgui.net.gn; Ambassador MAITÉ RIVERO TORRES.

Egypt: Corniche Sud 2, BP 389, Conakry; tel. 300-46-85-08; fax 300-46-85-07; e-mail ambconakry@hotmail.com; Ambassador TAMER AL MAWAZINI.

France: ave du Commerce, BP 373, Conakry; tel. 621-00-00-10 (mobile); fax 300-47-10-15; e-mail ambafrance.conakry@diplomatie.gouv.fr; internet www.ambafrance-gn.org; Ambassador BERTRAND COCHERY.

Germany: 2e blvd, Kaloum, BP 540, Conakry; tel. 621-22-17-06 (mobile); fax 300-45-22-17; e-mail amball@sotelgui.net.gn; internet www.conakry.diplo.de; Ambassador HARTMUT KRAUSSER.

Ghana: Immeuble Ex-Urbaine et la Seine, BP 732, Conakry; tel. 622-66-47-45 (mobile); Ambassador BEATRICE ROSA BROBBEY.

Guinea-Bissau: Quartier Bellevue, Commune de Dixinn, BP 298, Conakry; tel. 628-97-13-05 (mobile); Ambassador Elhadj BRAIMA EMBALO.

Holy See: La Minière, DI 777, BP 2016, Conakry; tel. 664-58-49-59 (mobile); e-mail nunziaturaguinea@gmail.com; Apostolic Nuncio Most Rev. SANTO ROCCO GANGEMI.

Iran: Donka, Cité Ministérielle, Commune de Dixinn, BP 310, Conakry; tel. 300-01-03-19; fax 300-47-81-84; e-mail ambiran@yahoo.com; Ambassador KHALIL SADATI-AMIRI.

Japan: Lanseboundji, Corniche Sud, Commune de Matam, BP 895, Conakry; tel. 628-68-38-38 (mobile); fax 300-46-85-09; Ambassador NAOTSUGU NAKANO.

Korea, Democratic People's Republic: BP 723, Conakry; Ambassador RI KYONG SON.

Liberia: Cité Ministérielle, Donka, Commune de Dixinn, BP 18, Conakry; tel. 666-41-46-51 (mobile); Ambassador KRUBO KOLLIE.

Libya: Commune de Kaloum, BP 1183, Conakry; tel. 300-41-41-72; Ambassador B. AHMED.

Malaysia: Quartier Mafanco, Corniche Sud, BP 5460, Conakry; tel. 300-22-17-54; e-mail malconakry@kln.gov.my; internet www.kln.gov.my/web/gin_conakry/home; Ambassador MOHAMED SAMPIL.

Mali: rue D1–15, Camayenne, Corniche Nord, BP 299, Conakry; tel. 300-46-14-18; fax 300-46-37-03; e-mail ambamaliguinee@yahoo.fr; Ambassador HASSANE BARRY.

Morocco: Cité des Nations, Villa 12, Commune du Kaloum, BP 193, Conakry; tel. 300-41-36-86; fax 300-41-38-16; e-mail sifamgui@biasy.net; Ambassador MAJID HALIM.

Nigeria: Corniche Sud, Quartier de Matam, BP 54, Conakry; tel. 666-37-59-19 (mobile); fax 300-46-27-75; Ambassador Dr AISHA LARABA ABDULLAHI.

Russia: Matam-Port, km 9, BP 329, Conakry; tel. 631-70-15-75 (mobile); fax 300-47-84-43; e-mail ambrus@biasy.net; internet www.guinee.mid.ru; Ambassador ALEXANDER V. BREGADZE.

Saudi Arabia: BP 611, Conakry; tel. 300-46-70-75; e-mail gnemb@mofa.gov.sa; internet embassies.mofa.gov.sa/sites/Guinea; Ambassador AMJAD BIN HOSAIN BIN ABDUL HAMEED AL-BEDAIWI.

Senegal: bâtiment 142, Coléah, Corniche Che Sud, BP 842, Conakry; tel. 300-44-61-32; fax 300-46-28-34; Ambassador YAKHAM DIOP.

Sierra Leone: Quartier Bellevue, face aux cases présidentielles, Commune de Dixinn, BP 625, Conakry; tel. 631-35-82-03 (mobile); fax 300-41-23-64; Ambassador ADIKALIE FODAY SUMAH.

South Africa: Coléah, Mossoudougou, Conakry; tel. 664-29-92-33 (mobile); fax 300-49-08-79; e-mail conakrys@foreign.gov.za; Ambassador NOMASONTO MARIA SIBANDA-THUSI.

Spain: Plaza Almany Samory Touré, Immeuble R2000, BP 706, Conakry; tel. 631-35-87-30 (mobile); e-mail emb.conakry@maec.es; Ambassador GUILLERMO ARDIZONE GARCÍA.

Ukraine: Commune de Dixinn, Corniche Nord, Cité Ministérielle, Rue DI 256, BP 1350, Conakry; tel. 622-35-38-01 (mobile); fax 622-35-38-03 (mobile); e-mail ambukra@gmail.com; internet www.mfa.gov.ua/guinea; Ambassador ANDRIY ZAYATS.

United Kingdom: BP 6729, Conakry; tel. 631-35-53-29 (mobile); fax 631-35-90-59 (mobile); e-mail britembconakry@hotmail.com; Ambassador TIM BROWNBILL.

USA: Koloma, Ratoma, BP 603, Conakry; tel. 655-10-40-00 (mobile); fax 655-10-42-97 (mobile); e-mail conconakry@state.gov; internet conakry.usembassy.gov; Ambassador ALEXANDER MARK LASKARIS.

Judicial System

The Constitution of 7 May 2010 embodies the principle of the independence of the judiciary, and delineates the competencies of each component of the judicial system, including the Supreme Court and the Revenue Court.

Supreme Court (Cour Suprême): Corniche-Sud, Camayenne, Conakry; tel. 300-41-29-28; Pres. MAMADOU SYLLA.

Court of Appeal (Cour d'Appel): Conakry: First Pres. YAYA BOIRO; Kankan: First Pres. DOURA CHÉRIF.

Religion

It is estimated that 85% of the population are Muslims and 8% Christians, while 7% follow animist beliefs.

ISLAM

National Islamic League: BP 386, Conakry; tel. 300-41-23-38; f. 1988; Sec.-Gen. (vacant).

CHRISTIANITY

The Roman Catholic Church

Guinea comprises one archdiocese and two dioceses. About 3% of the population are Roman Catholics.

Bishops' Conference: Conférence Episcopale de la Guinée, BP 1006 bis, Conakry; tel. and fax 300-41-32-70; e-mail dhewara@eti.met.gn; Pres. Most Rev. VINCENT COULIBALY (Archbishop of Conakry).

Archbishop of Conakry: Most Rev. VINCENT COULIBALY, Archevêché, BP 2016, Conakry; tel. and fax 300-43-47-04; e-mail conakriensis@yahoo.fr.

The Anglican Communion

Anglicans in Guinea are adherents of the Church of the Province of West Africa, comprising 15 dioceses. The diocese of Guinea was established in 1985 as the first French-speaking diocese in the Province. The Primate and Metropolitan of the Province is the Bishop of The Gambia.

Bishop of Guinea: Rt Rev. JACQUES BOSTON, Cathédrale Toussaint, BP 1187, Conakry; tel. 631-20-46-60 (mobile); e-mail agomezd@yahoo.fr.

BAHÁ'Í FAITH

Assemblée Spirituelle Nationale: BP 2010, Conakry 1; e-mail asngunee@yahoo.fr; Sec. MAMMA TRAORE.

The Press

REGULATORY AUTHORITY

Haute Autorité de la Communication (HAC): en face Primature, BP 2955, Conakry; tel. 300-45-54-82; fax 300-41-23-85; f. 2010; regulates the operations of the press, and of radio and television; regulates political access to the media; nine mems; Pres. MARTINE CONDÉ.

NEWSPAPERS AND PERIODICALS

Le Démocrate: Quartier Ratoma Centre, Commune de Ratoma, BP 2427, Conakry; tel. 601-20-01-01 (mobile); e-mail mamadoudianb@yahoo.fr; weekly; Dir HASSANE KABA; Editor-in-Chief MAMADOU DIAN BALDÉ.

Le Diplomate: BP 2427, Conakry; tel. and fax 300-41-23-85; f. 2002; weekly; Dir SANOU KERFALLAH CISSÉ.

L'Enquêteur: Conakry; e-mail habib@boubah.com; internet enqueteur.boubah.com; f. 2001; weekly; Editor HABIB YAMBERING DIALLO.

Fonike: BP 341, Conakry; daily; sport and general; state-owned; Dir IBRAHIMA KALIL DIARE.

Horoya (Liberty): BP 191, Conakry; tel. 300-47-71-17; fax 300-45-10-16; e-mail info@horoyaguinee.net; govt daily; Dir OUSMANE CAMARA.

L'Indépendant: Quartier Ratoma Centre, Commune de Ratoma, BP 2427, Conakry; tel. 601-20-01-01 (mobile); e-mail lindependant@afribone.net.gn; weekly; also *L'Indépendant Plus*; Publr ABOUBACAR SYLLA; Dir HASSANE KABA; Editor-in-Chief MAMADOU DIAN BALDÉ.

Journal Officiel de Guinée: BP 156, Conakry; fortnightly; organ of the Govt.

La Lance: Immeuble Baldé Zaïre, BP 4968, Conakry; tel. and fax 300-41-23-85; weekly; general information; Dir SOULEYMANE E. DIALLO.

Le Lynx: Immeuble Baldé Zaïre Sandervalia, BP 4968, Conakry; tel. 300-41-23-85; fax 300-45-36-96; e-mail le-lynx@afribone.net.gn; internet www.afribone.net.gn/lynx; f. 1992; weekly; satirical; Editor SOULEYMANE DIALLO.

La Nouvelle Tribune: blvd Diallo Tally, entre 5e et 6e ave, BP 35, Conakry; tel. 300-22-33-02; e-mail abdcond@yahoo.fr; internet www.nouvelle-tribune.com; weekly, Tuesdays; independent; general information and analysis; Dir of Publ. and Editing ABDOULAYE CONDÉ.

L'Observateur: Immeuble Baldé, Conakry; tel. 300-40-05-24; e-mail ibrahimanouhou@yahoo.fr; internet www.observateur-guinee.com; weekly; independent; Dir NOUHOU BALDÉ.

L'Oeil du Peuple: BP 3064, Conakry; tel. 300-67-23-78; weekly; independent; Dir of Publishing ISMAËL BANGOURA.

Sanakou: Labé, Foutah Djallon, Moyenne-Guinée; tel. 300-51-13-19; e-mail sanakoulabe@yahoo.fr; f. 2000; monthly; general news; Publr IDRISSA SAMPIRING DIALLO; Editor-in-Chief YAMOUSSA SOUMAH; circ. 1,000.

Le Standard: Conakry; Dir of Publication HASSANE KABA.

3-P Plus (Parole-Plume-Papier) Magazine: 7e ave Bis Almamyah, BP 5122, Conakry; tel. 300-45-22-32; fax 300-45-29-31; e-mail 3p-plus@mirinet.net.gn; internet www.mirinet.net.gn/3p_plus; f. 1995; journal of arts and letters; supplements *Le Cahier de l'Economie* and *Mag-Plus: Le Magazine de la Culture*; monthly; Pres. MOHAMED SALIFOU KEÏTA; Editor-in-Chief SAMBA TOURÉ.

NEWS AGENCY

Agence Guinéenne de Presse: BP 1535, Conakry; tel. 300-41-14-34; e-mail info@agpguinee.net; f. 1960; Man. Dir NÈTÈ SOVOGUI.

PRESS ASSOCIATION

Association Guinéenne des Editeurs de la Presse Indépendante (AGEPI): Conakry; f. 1991; an asscn of independent newspaper publishers; Chair. HASSANE KABA.

Publishers

Les Classiques Guinéens (SEDIS sarl): 545 rue KA020, Mauquepas, BP 3697, Conakry; e-mail cheick.sedis@mirinet.net.gn; f. 1999; art, history, youth literature; Dir CHEICK ABDOUL KABA.

Editions du Ministère de l'Education Nationale: Direction nationale de la recherche scientifique et technique, BP 561, Conakry; tel. 300-43-02-66; e-mail dnrst@mirinet.net.gn; f. 1959; general and educational; Deputy Dir Dr TAMBA TAGBINO.

Editions Ganndal (Knowledge): BP 542, Conakry; tel. and fax 300-46-35-07; e-mail ganndal@mirinet.net.gn; f. 1992; educational, youth and children, general literature and books in Pular; Dir MAMADOU ALIOU SOW.

Société Africaine d'Edition et de Communication (SAEC): Belle-Vue, Commune de Dixinn, BP 6826, Conakry; tel. 300-29-71-41; e-mail dtniane@yahoo.fr; social sciences, reference, literary fiction; Editorial Assistant OUMAR TALL.

Broadcasting and Communications

TELECOMMUNICATIONS

In 2013 there were five providers of mobile cellular telephone services and one provider of fixed-line telephone services in Guinea.

Areeba Guinée: Quartier Almamya, Commune de Kaloum, BP 3237, Conakry; tel. 664-22-22-22 (mobile); fax 664-33-33-33 (mobile); internet www.areeba.com.gn; f. 2005; mobile cellular telephone provider; 75% owned by MTN (South Africa); Dir-Gen. P. J. PHIKE.

Cellcom Guinée: Immeuble WAQF-BID, Almamya, C/Kaloum, BP 6567, Conakry; tel. 655-10-01-00 (mobile); fax 655-10-01-01 (mobile); e-mail info@gn.cellcomgsm.com; internet www.gn.cellcomgsm.com; f. 2008; Dir-Gen. AVISHAY MARZIANO.

Intercel: Immeuble Intercel, Quartier Almamya, rue KA 038, BP 965, Conakry; tel. 631-35-35-35 (mobile); fax 300-40-92-92; e-mail info@gn.intercel.net; internet www.intercel-guinee.com; mobile cellular telephone operator; fmrly Telecel Guinée; acquired by Sudatel (Sudan) in 2011; Dir-Gen. DJIBRIL TOBE.

Orange Guinée: Conakry; tel. 622-77-00-00 (mobile); e-mail serviceclientguinee@orange-sonatel.com; internet www.orange-guinee.com; f. 2007; 85% owned by Groupe Sonatel (Senegal); Dir-Gen. ALASSANE DIÈNE.

Société des Télécommunications de Guinée (SOTELGUI): 4e blvd, BP 2066, Conakry; tel. 300-45-27-50; fax 300-45-03-06; e-mail vickycu@sotelgui.net.gn; f. 1992; state-owned; provides fixed-line services; 12,000 fixed-line subscribers and 549,713 mobile subscribers (2010); Dir-Gen. MOUSSA KEITA.

Lagui: Conakry; wholly owned subsidiary of SOTELGUI providing mobile telephone services.

Regulatory Authority

Autorité de Régulation des Postes et des Télécommunications (ARPT): BP 1500, Conakry; tel. 657-66-66-11 (mobile); e-mail contact@arptguinee.org; internet www.arpt.gov.gn; f. 2008; Dir-Gen. DIABY MOUSTAPHA MAMY.

BROADCASTING

Regulatory Authority

Haute Autorité de la Communication (HAC): see The Press.

Radio

Espace FM: Quartier Matoto, Immeuble Mouna, BP 256, Conakry; tel. 664-20-20-92 (mobile); e-mail services@espacefmguinee.info; internet espacefmguinee.info; Dir-Gen. LAMINE GUIRASSY.

Milo FM: BP 215, Kankan; tel. 300-72-00-82; e-mail info@milo-fm.com; internet www.milo-fm.com; Dir-Gen. LANCINÉ KABA.

Radiodiffusion-Télévision Guinéenne (RTG): BP 391, Conakry; tel. 300-44-22-01; fax 300-41-50-01; broadcasts in French, English, Créole-English, Portuguese, Arabic and local languages; Dir-Gen. YAMOUSSA SIDIBÉ; Dir of Radio ISSA CONDÉ.

Radio Rurale de Guinée: BP 391, Conakry; tel. 300-42-11-09; fax 300-41-47-97; e-mail ruralgui@mirinet.net.gn; network of rural radio stations.

Television

Radiodiffusion-Télévision Guinéenne (RTG): see Radio; transmissions in French and local languages; one channel; f. 1977.

Finance

(cap. = capital; res = reserves; dep. = deposits; m. = million; brs = branches; amounts in Guinean francs)

BANKING

In 2012 there were 14 banks operating in Guinea.

Central Bank

Banque Centrale de la République de Guinée (BCRG): 12 blvd du Commerce, BP 692, Kaloum, Conakry; tel. 300-41-26-51; fax 300-41-48-98; e-mail gouv.bcrg@eti-bull.net; internet www.bcrg-guinee.org; f. 1960; bank of issue; cap. 50,000m., res 20,881m., dep. 7,171,432m. (Dec. 2009); Gov. LOUNCENY NABÉ; First Deputy Gov. YÉRO BALDÉ BALDÉ.

Commercial Banks

Banque Internationale pour le Commerce et l'Industrie de la Guinée (BICIGUI): ave de la République, BP 1484, Conakry; tel. 300-41-45-15; fax 300-41-39-62; e-mail dg.bicigui@africa.bnpparibas.com; internet bicigui.org; f. 1985; 30.8% owned by BNP Paribas BDDI Participations (France), 15.1% state-owned; cap. and res 37,989.3m., total assets 315,689.5m. (Dec. 2003); Pres. IBRAHIMA SOUMAH; Dir-Gen. MANGA FODÉ TOURÉ; 20 brs.

Banque Populaire Maroco-Guinéenne (BPMG): Immeuble BPMG, blvd du Commerce, Kaloum, BP 4400, Conakry 01; tel. 300-41-36-93; fax 300-41-32-61; e-mail bpmg@sotelgui.net.gn; f. 1991; 55% owned by Crédit Populaire du Maroc, 42% state-owned; cap. and res 9,936m., total assets 65,549m. (Dec. 2004); Pres. EMMANUEL GNAN; Dir-Gen. AHMED IRAQUI HOUSSAINI; 3 brs.

Ecobank Guinée: Immeuble Al Iman, ave de la République, BP 5687, Conakry; tel. 631-70-14-34 (mobile); fax 300-45-42-41; e-mail ecobankgn@ecobank.com; internet www.ecobank.com; f. 1999; wholly owned by Ecobank Transnational Inc. (Togo); cap. 25,000.0m., res 27,667.3m., dep. 975,266.4m. (Dec. 2009); Pres. SAIKOU BARRY; Man. Dir MAMADOU MOUSTAPHA FALL; 9 brs.

First American Bank of Guinea: blvd du Commerce, angle 9e ave, BP 4540, Conakry; tel. 300-41-34-32; fax 300-41-35-29; f. 1994; jtly owned by Mitan Capital Ltd (Grand Cayman) and El Hadj Haidara Abdourahmane Chérif (Mali).

International Commercial Bank SA: Ex-cité Chemin de Fer, Immeuble Mamou, BP 3547, Conakry; tel. 300-41-25-90; fax 300-41-54-50; e-mail enquiry@icbank-guinea.com; internet www.icbank-guinea.com; f. 1997; total assets 19.6m. (Dec. 1999); Pres. JOSÉPHINE PREMLA; Man. Dir HAMZA BIN ALIAS; 3 brs.

Orabank Guinée: 6e ave de la République, angle 5e blvd, BP 324, Conakry; tel. 620-35-90-90 (mobile); fax 300-97-26-30; e-mail info-gn@orabank.net; f. 1988; fmrly the Union Internationale de Banques en Guinée, present name adopted in 2011; 54.0% owned by Oragroup SA (Togo), 14.3% owned by Orabank Tchad; cap. 25,000m., res –1,139.1m., dep. 259,713.9m. (Dec. 2009); Pres. PATRICK MESTRALLET; Dir-Gen. MAMADOU SENE; 7 brs.

Société Générale de Banques en Guinée (SGBG): Immeuble Boffa, Cité du Chemin de Fer, BP 1514, Conakry; tel. 300-45-60-00; fax 300-41-25-65; e-mail contact@sgbg.net.gn; internet www.sgbg.net; f. 1985; 53% owned by Société Générale (France); cap. and res 13,074m., total assets 228,196m. (Dec. 2003); Pres. GÉRALD LACAZE; Dir-Gen. JEAN-PHILIPPE EQUILBECQ; 8 brs.

Islamic Bank

Banque Islamique de Guinée: Immeuble Nafaya, 6 ave de la République, BP 1247, Conakry; tel. 664-00-44-66 (mobile); fax 300-41-50-71; e-mail bigconakry@biasy.net; internet www.big-bank.com; f. 1983; 50.01% owned by Dar al-Maal al-Islami Trust (Switzerland), 49.99% owned by Islamic Development Bank (Saudi Arabia); cap. and res 2,368.5m., total assets 26,932.1m. (Dec. 2003); Pres. SIDI MOHAMED OULD TALEB; Dir-Gen. YAYA DIONG.

INSURANCE

In 2011 there were eight insurance companies in Guinea.

Gras Savoye Guinée: 4e ave, angle 4e blvd, Quartier Boulbinet, Commune de Kaloum, BP 6441, Conakry; tel. 300-45-58-43; fax 300-45-58-42; e-mail gsguinee@sotelgui.net.gn; affiliated to Gras Savoye (France); Man. CHÉRIF BAH.

International Insurance Co: Conakry; tel. 622-03-81-05 (mobile); f. 2007; Dir-Gen. KABINET KONDÉ.

Mutragui: BP 1189, Conakry; tel. 657-05-00-00; e-mail info@mutragui.com; internet mutragui.com.

Société Nouvelle d'Assurances de Guinée (SONAG): Conakry; internet www.assurances-sonag.com.

Union Guinéenne d'Assurances et de Réassurances (UGAR): pl. des Martyrs, BP 179, Conakry; tel. 300-41-48-41; fax 300-41-17-11; e-mail ugar@ugar.com.gn; internet www.ugarassurance.com; f. 1989; 40% owned by AXA (France), 35% state-owned; cap. 2,000m.; Pres. ISMAËL BANGOURA; Man. Dir RENÉ BUÉE.

LGV: BP 1786, Conakry; tel. 601-52-99-10 (mobile); life insurance; Dir-Gen. MANGA FODÉ TOURÉ.

Trade and Industry

GOVERNMENT AGENCIES

Agence de Promotion des Investissements Privés-Guichet Unique (APIP–GUINEE): BP 2024, Conakry; tel. 300-41-49-85; fax 300-41-39-90; e-mail dg@apiguinee.org; internet www.apiguinee.org; f. 1992; promotes private investment; Dir-Gen. MOHAMED LAMINE BAYO.

Centre de Promotion et de Développement Miniers (CPDM): BP 295, Conakry; tel. 300-41-15-44; fax 300-41-49-13; e-mail cpdm@mirinet.net.gn; f. 1995; promotes investment and co-ordinates devt strategy in mining sector; Dir MOCIRÉ SYLLA.

Entreprise Nationale Import-Export (IMPORTEX): BP 152, Conakry; tel. 300-44-28-13; state-owned import and export agency; Dir MAMADOU BOBO DIENG.

DEVELOPMENT ORGANIZATIONS

Agence Française de Développement (AFD): 5e ave, KA022, BP 283, Conakry; tel. 300-41-25-69; fax 300-41-28-74; e-mail afdconakry@afd.fr; internet www.afd.fr; Country Dir YAZID BENSAID.

France Volontaires: BP 570, Conakry; tel. 300-35-08-60; internet www.france-volontaires.org; f. 1987; name changed as above in 2009; devt and research projects; Nat. Rep. ERIK HOUINSOU.

Service de Coopération et d'Action Culturelle: BP 373, Conakry; tel. 300-41-23-45; fax 300-41-43-56; administers bilateral aid; Dir in Guinea TOBIE NATHAN.

CHAMBERS OF COMMERCE

Chambre de Commerce, d'Industrie et de l'Artisanat de la Guinée (CCIAG): Quartier Tombo, Commune de Kaloum, BP 545, Conakry; tel. 601-26-02-31 (mobile); fax 300-47-70-58; e-mail cciag@sotelgui.net.gn; internet www.cciag.org; f. 1985; Pres. MORLAYE DIALLO.

Chambre Economique de Guinée: BP 609, Conakry.

Chambre des Mines: Conakry; internet chambredesminesgn.org; f. 1997; Pres. MAMADY YOULA; 66 mems.

TRADE AND EMPLOYERS' ASSOCIATIONS

Association des Commerçants de Guinée: BP 2468, Conakry; tel. 664-21-92-42; e-mail thouca_acic@yahoo.fr; f. 1976; Sec.-Gen. THIERNO OUMAR CAMARA.

Association des Femmes Entrepreneurs de Guinée (AFEG): BP 104, Kaloum, Conakry; tel. 657-28-02-95; e-mail afeguine@yahoo.fr; f. 1987; Pres. HADJA RAMATOULAYE SOW.

Conseil National du Patronat Guinéen (CNPG): Dixinn Bora, BP 6403, Conakry; tel. and fax 300-41-24-70; e-mail msylla@leland-gn.org; f. 1992; Pres. SÉKOU CISSÉ (acting).

UTILITIES

Electricity

Electricité de Guinée (EDG): BP 1463, Conakry; tel. 300-45-18-56; fax 300-45-18-53; e-mail di.sogel@biasy.net; f. 2001 to replace Société Guinéenne d'Electricité; majority state-owned; production, transport and distribution of electricity; Dir-Gen. NAVA TOURÉ.

Water

Service National d'Aménagement des Points d'Eau (SNAPE): BP 2064, Conakry; tel. 300-41-18-93; fax 300-41-50-58; e-mail snape@mirinet.net.gn; supplies water in rural areas; Dir-Gen. Dr ALPHA IBRAHIMA NABÉ.

Société des Eaux de Guinée (SEG): Quartier Almamya, BP 150, Conakry; tel. 601-29-01-50 (mobile); fax 300-41-43-69; e-mail info@segguinee.com; internet segguinee.com; f. 2001 to replace SONEG; national water co; Coordinator Gen. MAMADOU DIOULDÉ DIALLO.

TRADE UNIONS

Confédération Nationale des Travailleurs de Guinée (CNTG): Bourse du Travail, Corniche Sud 004, BP 237, Conakry; tel. 300-41-50-44; fax 11-45-49-96; e-mail cntg60@yahoo.fr; f. 1984; Sec.-Gen. AMADOU DIALLO.

Organisation Nationale des Syndicats Libres de Guinée (ONSLG): BP 559, Conakry; tel. 300-41-52-17; fax 300-43-02-83; e-mail onslguinee@yahoo.fr; 27,000 mems (1996); Sec.-Gen. YAMOUDOU TOURÉ.

Union Syndicale des Travailleurs de Guinée (USTG): BP 1514, Conakry; tel. 300-41-25-65; fax 300-41-25-58; e-mail fofi1952@yahoo.fr; independent; 64,000 mems (2001); Sec.-Gen. IBRAHIMA FOFANA.

Transport

RAILWAYS

There are 1,086 km of railways in Guinea, including 662 km of 1-m gauge track from Conakry to Kankan in the east of the country, crossing the Niger at Kouroussa. Three lines for the transport of bauxite link Sangaredi with the port of Kamsar in the west, via Boké, and Conakry with Kindia and Fria, a total of 383 km. In 2012 the Government announced plans to construct a new 670-km railway, which was to connect the iron ore deposits in the Simandou area with a new port in the Forecariah area (yet to be built); it was hoped that the project would be completed by 2015.

Office National des Chemins de Fer de Guinée (ONCFG): BP 589, Conakry; tel. 300-44-46-13; fax 300-41-35-77; f. 1905; Man. Dir NABY BADRA YOULA.

Chemin de Fer de Boké: BP 523, Boké; operations commenced 1973.

Chemin de Fer Conakry–Fria: BP 334, Conakry; operations commenced 1960; Gen. Man. A. CAMARA.

Chemin de Fer de la Société des Bauxites de Kindia: BP 613, Conakry; tel. 300-41-38-28; operations commenced 1974; Gen. Man. K. KEITA.

ROADS

The road network comprised 44,348 km of roads (of which 4,342 km were paved) in 2003. In 2009 an estimated 35% of all roads were paved. An 895-km cross-country road links Conakry to Bamako, in Mali, and the main highway connecting Dakar (Senegal) to Abidjan (Côte d'Ivoire) also crosses Guinea. The road linking Conakry to Freetown (Sierra Leone) forms part of the Trans West African Highway, extending from Morocco to Nigeria.

La Guinéenne-Marocaine des Transports (GUIMAT): Conakry; f. 1989; owned jtly by Govt of Guinea and Hakkam (Morocco); operates nat. and regional transport services.

Société Générale des Transports de Guinée (SOGETRAG): Conakry; f. 1985; 63% state-owned; bus operator.

SHIPPING

Conakry and Kamsar are the international seaports. The port of Conakry handled 6.9m. metric tons of freight in 2010. The country's flag registered fleet at 31 December 2013 numbered 37 vessels, totalling 28,809 grt.

Getma Guinée: Immeuble KASSA, Cité des Chemins de Fer, BP 1648, Conakry; tel. 300-41-26-66; fax 300-41-42-73; e-mail info@getmaguinee.com.gn; internet www.getma.com; f. 1979; fmrly Société Guinéenne d'Entreprises de Transports Maritimes et Aeriens; marine transportation; cap. 1,100m. FG; Chair. and CEO JEAN-JACQUES GRENIER; 135 employees.

Port Autonome de Conakry (PAC): BP 805, Conakry; tel. 300-41-27-28; fax 300-41-26-04; e-mail pac@eti-bull.net; internet www.biasy.net/~pac; haulage, porterage; Gen. Man. MAMADOUBA SAKHON.

Société Navale Guinéenne (SNG): BP 522, Conakry; tel. 300-44-29-55; fax 300-41-39-70; f. 1968; state-owned; shipping agents; Dir-Gen. MAMADI TOURÉ.

Transmar: 33 blvd du Commerce, Kaloum, BP 3917, Conakry; tel. 300-43-05-41; fax 300-43-05-42; e-mail elitegn@gmail.com; shipping, stevedoring, inland transport.

CIVIL AVIATION

There is an international airport at Conakry-Gbessia, and some 13 smaller airfields elsewhere in the country. In 2009 renovation and extension work was begun at Conakry airport, with the aim of increasing its annual handling capacity from some 300,000 passengers to more than 1m. passengers. In 2010 plans were under way for the construction of a new international airport at Matakang.

Air Guinée International: Conakry; f. 2010 to replace Air Guinée (f. 1960); regional and internal services; Dir-Gen. MOHAMED EL-BORAÏ.

Société de Gestion et d'Exploitation de l'Aéroport de Conakry (SOGEAC): BP 3126, Conakry; tel. 300-46-48-03; f. 1987; manages Conakry-Gbessia int. airport; 51% state-owned; Dir-Gen. OULABA KABASSAN KEÏTA.

Union des Transports Aériens de Guinée (UTA): scheduled and charter flights to regional and int. destinations.

Tourism

Some 30,194 tourists visited Guinea in 2007; receipts from tourism in 2011 totalled US $2.0m. (excluding passenger transport).

Office National du Tourisme: Immeuble al-Iman, 6e ave de la République, BP 1275, Conakry; tel. 300-45-51-63; fax 300-45-51-64; e-mail ibrahimabakaley@yahoo.fr; internet www.ontguinee.com; f. 1997; Dir-Gen. IBRAHIM A. DIALLO.

Defence

As assessed at November 2013, Guinea's active armed forces numbered 9,700, including an army of 8,500, a navy of 400 and an air force of 800. Paramilitary forces comprised a republican guard of 1,600 and a 1,000-strong gendarmerie, as well as a reserve 'people's militia' of 7,000. Military service is compulsory and lasts for two years.

Defence Expenditure: Estimated at 275,000m. Guinean francs in 2012.

Chief of Staff of the Armed Forces: Gen. NAMORY TRAORÉ.

Chief of Staff of the Army: Commdr MORIBA ABEL MARA.
Chief of Staff of the Air Force: Col NABY IBRAHIMA SOUMAH.
Chief of Staff of the Navy: Lt-Col LAMINE TOURÉ.
Chief of Staff of the National Gendarmerie: Gen. IBRAHIM BALDÉ.

Education

Education is provided free of charge at every level in state institutions. Primary education, which begins at seven years of age and lasts for six years, is officially compulsory. According to UNESCO estimates, in 2012 enrolment in primary education included 74% of children in the relevant age-group (males 80%; females 69%), while in 2011 enrolment at secondary schools included 30% of children in the appropriate age-group (boys 37%; girls 23%). Secondary education, from the age of 13, lasts for seven years, comprising a first cycle (collège) of four years and a second (lycée) of three years. There are universities at Conakry and Kankan, and other tertiary institutions at Manéyah, Boké and Faranah; a total of some 89,600 students were enrolled at tertiary institutions in 2011/12. In 2012 spending on education represented 11.8% of total budgetary expenditure.

GUINEA-BISSAU

Introductory Survey

LOCATION, CLIMATE, LANGUAGE, RELIGION, FLAG, CAPITAL

The Republic of Guinea-Bissau lies on the west coast of Africa, with Senegal to the north and Guinea to the east and south. The climate is tropical, although maritime and Sahelian influences are felt. The average temperature is 20°C (68°F). The official language is Portuguese, of which the locally spoken form is Creole (Crioulo). There are 19 local languages, of which the most widely spoken are Balanta-Kentohe, Pulaar (Fula), Mandjak, Mandinka and Papel. The principal religious beliefs are animism and Islam. There is a small minority of Roman Catholics and other Christian groups. The national flag (proportions 1 by 2) has two equal horizontal stripes, of yellow over light green, and a red vertical stripe, with a five-pointed black star at its centre, at the hoist. The capital is Bissau.

CONTEMPORARY POLITICAL HISTORY

Historical Context

Portuguese Guinea (Guiné) was colonized by Portugal in the 15th century. Nationalist activism began to emerge in the 1950s. Armed insurgency commenced in the early 1960s, and by 1972 the Partido Africano da Independência da Guiné e Cabo Verde (PAIGC) was in control of two-thirds of the country. The independence of the Republic of Guinea-Bissau was unilaterally proclaimed in September 1973, with Luís Cabral (the brother of the founder of the PAIGC, Amílcar Cabral) as President of the State Council. Hostilities ceased following the military coup in Portugal in April 1974, and on 10 September Portugal recognized the independence of Guinea-Bissau under the leadership of Luís Cabral.

The PAIGC regime introduced measures to establish a single-party socialist state. At elections in December 1976 and January 1977 voters chose regional councils from which a new Assembleia Nacional Popular (National People's Assembly—ANP) was later selected. In 1978 the Chief State Commissioner, Francisco Mendes, died; he was succeeded by Commdr João Vieira, hitherto State Commissioner for the Armed Forces and President of the ANP.

The PAIGC initially supervised both Cape Verde and Guinea-Bissau, the Constitutions of each remaining separate but with a view to eventual unification. These arrangements were terminated in November 1980, when President Cabral was deposed in a coup organized by Vieira, who was installed as Chairman of the Council of the Revolution. Diplomatic relations between Guinea-Bissau and Cape Verde were restored after the release of Cabral from detention in 1982.

Domestic Political Affairs

In May 1983 the ANP, which had been dissolved following the 1980 coup, was re-established, and the Council of the Revolution was replaced by a 15-member Conselho de Estado (Council of State), selected from among the members of the ANP. Vieira was subsequently elected as President of the Council of State and Head of State. The ANP immediately ratified a new Constitution, and formally abolished the position of Prime Minister.

In December 1990 the Central Committee of the PAIGC agreed to the adoption of a multi-party system, following a period of transition, and the holding of a presidential election in 1993. In May 1991 a series of constitutional amendments ending one-party rule were approved by the ANP, terminating the political monopoly of the PAIGC. In addition, all links between the PAIGC and the armed forces were severed, and the introduction of a free-market economy was guaranteed. New legislation in October accorded greater freedom to the press and permitted the formation of new trade unions. In November the Frente Democrática (FD) became the first opposition party to obtain official registration.

In December 1991 a major government reshuffle took place, in which the office of Prime Minister was restored. Carlos Correia was appointed to the post. In late 1991 and early 1992 three further opposition parties obtained legal status: the Resistência da Guiné-Bissau—Movimento Bah-Fatah (RGB—MB); the Frente Democrática Social (FDS); and the Partido Unido Social Democrático (PUSD). Following a split in the FDS, a further party, the Partido para a Renovação Social (PRS), was established in January 1992 by the former Vice-Chairman of the FDS, Kumba Yalá. In the same month four opposition parties—the PUSD, FDS, RGB—MB and the Partido da Convergência Democrática (PCD), led by Vítor Mandinga—agreed on the establishment of a 'democratic forum', whose demands included the dissolution of the political police, the creation of an electoral commission and an all-party consultation on the setting of election dates. Legislation preparing for the transition to a multi-party democracy was approved by the ANP in February 1993, and in the following month a commission was appointed to supervise the forthcoming presidential and legislative elections, which were later scheduled for March 1994.

The elections were subsequently postponed, owing to financial and technical difficulties, and in May 1994 it was announced that they would be held in July. In May six opposition parties, the FD, the FDS, the Movimento para a Unidade e a Democracia, the Partido Democrático do Progresso, the Partido de Renovação e Desenvolvimento and the Liga Guinéense de Protecção Ecológica (LIPE), formed a coalition, the União para a Mudança (UM). The elections took place on 3 July, although voting was extended for two days, owing to logistical problems. The PAIGC secured a clear majority in the ANP, winning 62 of the 100 seats, while in the presidential election Vieira obtained 46.3% of the votes, and his nearest rival, Yalá, secured 21.9%. The two candidates contested a second round of polling on 7 August in which Yalá was narrowly defeated, securing 48.0% of the votes. International observers declared the elections to have been free and fair. Vieira was inaugurated as President on 29 September and appointed Manuel Saturnino da Costa (the Secretary-General of the PAIGC) as Prime Minister in October. The Council of Ministers was appointed in November, comprising solely members of the PAIGC.

Guinea-Bissau attained membership of the Union Economique et Monétaire Ouest-Africaine (see p. 330) in March 1997 and entered the Franc Zone in April. The national currency was replaced by the franc CFA, and the Banque Centrale des Etats de l'Afrique de l'Ouest assumed central banking functions. In May da Costa was dismissed. Carlos Correia was subsequently again appointed Prime Minister, and a new Council of Ministers was inaugurated in June. In March 1998, following protests by opposition parties at delays in the organization of legislative elections, an independent national elections commission was established. The elections were due to be held in July.

Attempted coup

In June 1998 rebel troops, led by Brig. (later Gen.) Ansumane Mané, who had recently been dismissed as Chief of Staff of the Armed Forces, seized control of the Bra military barracks in the capital and the international airport. Mané subsequently formed a military junta and demanded the resignation of Vieira and his administration. With the support of Senegalese and Guinean soldiers, troops loyal to the Government attempted unsuccessfully to regain control of rebel-held areas of the city, and heavy fighting ensued. Some 200,000 residents of Bissau fled the city. Fighting continued in July, with many members of the Guinea-Bissau armed forces reportedly defecting to the side of the rebels.

On 26 July 1998, following mediation by a delegation from the lusophone commonwealth body, the Comunidade dos Países de Língua Portuguesa (CPLP, see below), the Government and the rebels agreed to implement a truce. In August representatives of the Government and the rebels met, under the auspices of the CPLP and the Economic Community of West African States (ECOWAS, see p. 260), and an agreement was reached to transform the existing truce into a ceasefire. However, the rebels' demand that all Senegalese and Guinean forces be withdrawn from the country as a prerequisite to a definitive peace agreement was rejected by the Government and in October the ceasefire collapsed. On 20 October the Government imposed a nationwide curfew, and on the following day Vieira declared a unilateral ceasefire. By that time almost all of the government troops had joined forces with the rebels, who were thought to control some 99% of the country. On 23 October Mané agreed to conform to a 48-hour truce, and agreement was subsequently reached for direct talks to be held. Further negotiations, held under the aegis of ECOWAS, resulted in the signing of a peace accord on 1 November. Under the terms of the accord, the two sides reaffirmed the ceasefire of August, and resolved that the withdrawal of Senegalese and Guinean troops be conducted simultaneously with the deployment of an ECOMOG (ECOWAS Ceasefire Monitoring Group) interposition force, which would guarantee security on the border with Senegal. It was also agreed that a government of national unity would be established, to include representatives of the rebel junta, and that presidential and legislative elections would be held no later than March 1999. In November 1998 agreement was reached on the composition of a Joint Executive Commission to implement the peace accord. In December Francisco José Fadul was appointed Prime Minister, and Vieira and Mané reached agreement on the allocation of portfolios to the two sides.

In January 1999 agreement was reached between the Government, the rebel military junta and ECOWAS on the strength of the ECOMOG interposition force, which was to comprise some 710 troops. A timetable for the withdrawal of Senegalese and Guinean troops from the country was also established. However, at the end of January hostilities resumed in the capital. In February talks between the Government and the rebels produced agreement on a ceasefire and provided for the immediate withdrawal of Senegalese and Guinean troops. On 20 February the new Government of National Unity was announced. The disarmament of rebel troops and those loyal to the President began in March and the withdrawal of Senegalese and Guinean troops was completed that month. On 30 April the UN Secretary-General established the UN Peacebuilding Support Office in Guinea-Bissau (UNOGBIS), with a mandate to support the consolidation of peace, democracy and the rule of law; its mandate was regularly extended in subsequent years.

Vieira overthrown

In early May 1999 Vieira announced that the elections would take place on 28 December. However, on 7 May, to international condemnation, Vieira was overthrown by the rebel military junta, which claimed that its actions had been prompted by Vieira's refusal to allow his presidential guard to be disarmed. Vieira signed an unconditional surrender and the President of the ANP, Malam Bacai Sanhá, was appointed acting President of the Republic pending a presidential election. In June Vieira went into exile in Portugal where he was offered political asylum. In July constitutional amendments were introduced limiting the tenure of presidential office to two terms and abolishing the death penalty. It was also stipulated that the country's principal offices of state could only be held by Guinea-Bissau nationals born of Guinea-Bissau parents. In September an extraordinary congress of the PAIGC voted to expel Vieira and six others from the party. The incumbent Minister of Defence and Freedom Fighters, Francisco Benante, was appointed President of the party. In October the Attorney-General, Amine Michel Saad, announced that he had sufficient evidence to prosecute Vieira for crimes against humanity and expressed his intention to seek Vieira's extradition from Portugal.

Presidential and legislative elections took place on 28 November 1999. Of the 102 seats in the enlarged legislature, the PRS secured 38, the RGB—MB 28, the PAIGC 24, the Aliança Democrática (AD, an alliance of the FD and the PCD) four, the UM three, the Partido Social Democrata (PSD) three, and the FDS and the União Nacional para Democracia e Progresso one each. As no candidate received the necessary 50% of the votes to win the presidential election outright, the leading candidates, Yalá of the PRS and Sanhá of the PAIGC, contested a second round of voting on 16 January 2000, at which Yalá secured victory with 72% of the votes cast. Yalá was inaugurated on the following day and installed a new Council of Ministers, which included members of several former opposition parties, later that month. Caetano N'Tchama of the PRS was appointed Prime Minister. The election was subsequently judged by international observers to have been 'free and fair'. In May tensions were reported between Yalá and certain elements in the army who viewed Mané as the rightful leader of the country, on the grounds that it was he who had ousted Vieira from power. In October Yalá appointed a State Council, comprising members of all parliamentary political parties, which was to have an advisory role.

Demonstrations organized by the PAIGC, in support of demands for the resignation of the Government, took place in Bissau in November 2000. In late November Mané declared himself Commander-in-Chief of the armed forces, following renewed violence in Bissau, instigated by soldiers loyal to him. However, government troops quickly suppressed the insurgency, and a number of opposition leaders were arrested. Mané fled the capital, and was subsequently killed by the security forces.

In October 2001 a motion of no confidence in Yalá was approved by the ANP; the vote had been instigated by opposition parties in response to what they considered to be increasingly unconstitutional actions by the President. A demonstration against Yalá in Bissau, attended by some 10,000 people, followed further demands for the President's resignation by a coalition of opposition parties. Prime Minister Faustino Fudut Imbali was dismissed in December and was replaced by Almara Nhassé, a member of the PRS and hitherto Minister of Internal Administration. Nhassé immediately formed a new Government, composed solely of members of the ruling coalition. Nhassé was subsequently elected President of the PRS, in place of Yalá.

The developing political uncertainty in the country intensified in November 2002, when Yalá dissolved the ANP and dismissed the Government, citing its incompetence in coping with the economic crisis. Legislative elections were scheduled for February 2003. Mario Pires was appointed as Prime Minister, to head a transitional Government that was dominated by the PRS. Several political coalitions opposing the PRS were formed in late 2002 and early 2003 in preparation for the legislative elections, which were subsequently subject to repeated postponements. In December 2002 the PSD, the LIPE, the Partido da Renovação e Progresso and the Partido Socialista Guinéense created the União Eleitoral (UE). In February 2003 the Plataforma Unida—Mufunessa Larga Guiné was formed by the AD, the FDS, the Frente para a Libertação e Independência da Guiné and the Grupo de Democratas Independentes, which had been established by former members of the RGB—MB.

Seabra deposes Yalá

On 14 September 2003 President Yalá was detained by the armed forces in a bloodless coup, which was widely welcomed within Guinea-Bissau. The Chief of Staff of the Armed Forces, Gen. Veríssimo Correia Seabra, who led the coup, stated that the seizure of power had been in response to the worsening political and economic situation. Seabra proclaimed himself interim President of Guinea-Bissau, and President of a Military Committee for the Restoration of Constitutional and Democratic Order. On 17 September Yalá officially resigned from the presidency, and on 28 September Henrique Pereira Rosa, a business executive, and Artur Sanhá were sworn in as interim President and Prime Minister, respectively. On 2 October a transitional civilian Government was appointed, in accordance with an agreement signed by political organizations and the military authorities. A 56-member National Transition Council, composed of representatives of political and civil groups and the army, was to monitor government policy. In November the Government resumed payment of civil servants' salaries, and schools were reopened, having been closed for much of the previous two years owing to a series of strikes by unpaid teachers. In December the Council announced that legislative elections would be held on 28 March 2004, with the presidential election expected to be held one year later (in accordance with a Transitional Charter drafted in October 2003).

Elections to the ANP took place on 28 and 30 March 2004, with a voter turnout of 74.6%. The PAIGC won 45 of the 100 seats while the PRS secured 35 and the PUSD 17. The PAIGC reached an agreement with the PRS, whereby the latter undertook to support the Government in return for senior positions in the ANP, governmental departments and other state institutions. PAIGC President Carlos Gomes Júnior took office as Prime Minister on 10 May. The new Council of Ministers was sworn in on 12 May.

On 6 October 2004 Seabra and another senior military official were taken hostage and killed by a group of disaffected soldiers, led by Maj. Buate Yanta Namam, in protest against their non-payment for a peacekeeping operation undertaken in Liberia. On 6 and 7 October the soldiers, who emphasized that they were not seeking to overthrow the Government, presented their demands, which included an improvement in army conditions, a salary increase and the payment of salary arrears. Gomes Júnior attributed the unrest to political forces dissatisfied with the outcome of the April elections (widely assumed as referring to members of the PRS). On 10 October a Memorandum of Understanding was signed by Gomes Júnior, Yanta Naman and

Maj.-Gen. Baptista Tagmé Na Wai, representing the armed forces, according to which the soldiers would return to their barracks and salary arrears would be paid. An amnesty was to be granted to the mutineers and later in October Gomes Júnior announced that nearly all salary arrears had been settled. A new military high command, reportedly chosen by the mutineers, was also installed. Na Wai became Chief of Staff of the Armed Forces, while José Americo Bubo Na Tchuto was appointed Navy Chief of Staff.

It was announced in March 2005 that a presidential election would take place on 19 June. Malam Bacai Sanhá, who served as acting President in 1999, was chosen as the candidate for the PAIGC. Meanwhile, both Vieira (who was standing as an independent) and Yalá, representing the PRS, announced their candidacies. According to the Transitional Charter, both Yalá and Vieira were subject to five-year bans from political activity; however, in April their candidacies were approved by the Supreme Court.

The return of Vieira

The presidential election took place, as scheduled, on 19 June 2005. Sanhá secured 35.5% of the votes cast, while Vieira took 28.9% and Yalá 25.0%. As none of the candidates had won an outright majority there followed on 24 July a second round of voting, contested by Sanhá and Vieira, at which Vieira received 52.4% of valid votes cast, while Sanhá took 47.7%. The rate of voter participation was recorded at 87.6% in the first round and 78.6% in the second round, and international observers declared the election to have been free and fair.

Despite allegations of widespread electoral fraud and Sanhá's demands that the results of the election be annulled, the outcome was upheld by the Supreme Court and Vieira took office on 1 October 2005. Tensions continued, however, among the pro-Vieira members of the PAIGC and the pro-Sanhá, governing faction of the party. In mid-October 14 PAIGC deputies resigned from the party and declared themselves independents, and several members of that party, together with the PRS and the PUSD, formed a pro-Vieira alliance, the Forúm de Convergência para o Desenvolvimento (FCD), with the intention of precipitating the collapse of Gomes Júnior's Government. Members of the FCD claimed to have a majority in the ANP, while the PAIGC could count on the support of only 31 of the 100 members of the legislature.

In late October 2005, following continued demands by the FCD for the dismissal of the Prime Minister, Vieira dissolved the Government. Aristides Gomes, the former Vice-President of the PAIGC, was appointed Prime Minister on 2 November. Meanwhile, civil unrest exacerbated tensions, resulting in the temporary allocation to Aristides Gomes of the economy and finance portfolios, in order to facilitate the payment of civil service salaries. The new Government was sworn in on 9 November and comprised members of five parties (the PAIGC, the PRS, the PUSD, the PCD and the UE) and independents, the majority of whom were former PAIGC members. The PAIGC challenged the constitutional legitimacy of the appointment of Aristides Gomes, claiming that as the party that held the largest number of seats in the legislature, it had the right to propose the new Prime Minister; however, in January 2006 the Supreme Court ruled that Vieira had acted in accordance with the Constitution.

In November 2006 Kumba Yalá was re-elected as leader of the PRS, following one year's absence from the country; he announced that he no longer recognized the FCD and sought early elections. In mid-March 2007 the PAIGC, the PRS and the PUSD announced that they had signed a National Stability Pact (NSP), which aimed to precipitate the formation of a new government of national unity. The PRS and the PUSD also confirmed their withdrawal from the FCD. President Vieira initially refused to accede to demands to dismiss the Government; however, on 19 March 54 deputies approved a motion of no confidence in Prime Minister Gomes, who tendered his resignation 10 days later. Also in late March it was reported that the PUSD had withdrawn its support for the NSP. On 10 April Vieira nominated Martinho N'Dafa Cabi, a senior member of the PAIGC, who had held the positions of Deputy Prime Minister and Minister of National Defence in the Gomes Júnior administration, as the new Prime Minister. A new 29-member unity Government was installed in mid-April. Legislative elections were subsequently scheduled for November 2008.

In August 2008 a number of senior ministers were dismissed, prompting the PAIGC to withdraw from the government of national unity. In anticipation of the forthcoming elections Vieira dissolved the ANP and appointed Carlos Correia as Prime Minister at the head of a new Government composed largely of former PAIGC members loyal to him. Political tensions remained high and later that month it was revealed that an attempted coup to overthrow the President had been averted. Nevertheless, preparations for the legislative elections continued and the ballot duly took place as scheduled on 16 November. According to official results, the PAIGC won 67 seats in the ANP, securing 49.8% of the votes cast, while the PRS took 28 seats with 25.3% of the votes. The newly formed Partido Republicano para a Independência e o Desenvolvimento, led by Aristides Gomes, took three seats and the Partido para a Nova Democracia and the AD won one seat each. Voter participation was reported to have been high. However, a further failed coup attempt in late November—a number of mutinous soldiers were reported to have forced their way into the presidential palace, killing one member of the presidential guard—highlighted the growing instability in the country. A new Council of Ministers was named in December, with Gomes Júnior returning to the post of Prime Minister.

The assassination of Vieira

President Vieira was assassinated in an attack on his private residence in the early hours of 2 March 2009, which was reported to have been carried out by soldiers seeking to avenge the killing of Na Wai, allegedly ordered by Vieira just hours earlier. Relations between the two had deteriorated in January when Na Wai ordered the disarming of the 400-member militia that had been recruited to protect the President after the November 2008 coup attempt. Na Wai had, in January 2009, reportedly escaped unharmed following an outbreak of gunfire at the presidential palace; three soldiers were held for questioning by military investigators, although it was strenuously denied that any attempt on Na Wai's life had been made. In the days immediately after Vieira's death senior army figures insisted that no coup had been carried out and stated that the armed forces reaffirmed their respect for the democratically elected institutions of state and the Constitution. On 3 March Raimundo Pereira, President of the ANP, was sworn in as Interim President, pending a presidential election that was, in accordance with the Constitution, to be held within 60 days. The Government subsequently announced that it would hold a judicial inquiry into the deaths of Na Wai and Vieira. The events in Guinea-Bissau were condemned by the African Union (AU), the UN, the European Union (EU, see p. 273) and ECOWAS, and the latter declared that it was to deploy a multi-disciplinary group to monitor and co-ordinate security sector reform in the country. In April Pereira issued a decree stipulating that the presidential election would take place on 28 June.

On 5 June 2009 Baciro Dabo, a close ally of Vieira and a former government minister who had announced his intention to contest the forthcoming presidential election as an independent candidate, was shot dead in his residence by armed men, and a second candidate, former Prime Minister Imbali, was reportedly abducted. With the security situation worsening—the former Minister of Defence, Helder Proenca, was also killed in early June—Pedro Nfanda withdrew from the presidential poll. Requests were filed with the Supreme Court for the election to be postponed and while the Constitution stipulated that the ballot should be delayed in the event of the death of a candidate, Interim President Pereira announced that the poll would proceed as scheduled. Malam Bacai Sanhá, again representing the PAIGC, won 39.6% of votes cast, while Mohamed Yalá Embaló (as Kumba Yalá, who had converted to Islam in 2008 had become known) took 29.4% and Henrique Rosa secured 24.2%. At a second round of voting, which took place on 26 July, Sanhá secured 63.3% of the votes cast, while Yalá Embaló, took 36.7%. Shortly after the election results were announced, Commdr José Zamora Induta, formerly the Navy Chief of Staff, was confirmed as Chief of Staff of the Armed Forces.

Sanhá was sworn in as President on 8 September 2009 and a new Council of Ministers, again headed by Gomes Júnior, was appointed in late October. Maria Adiatú Djaló Nandingna, Minister of Foreign Affairs in the outgoing administration, was appointed Minister of the Presidency of the Council of Ministers, Social Communication and Parliamentary Affairs, the most senior cabinet post after the Prime Minister.

In December 2009 former Navy Chief of Staff Na Tchuto, who had fled to The Gambia following his alleged involvement in the coup attempt of August 2008 (see The return of Vieira), returned to the country, prompting the Government to order that he be arrested and prosecuted. Claiming to fear for his personal safety, Na Tchuto was granted refuge in the headquarters of UNOGBIS (which upon completion of its mandate was formally replaced on

1 January 2010 by UNIOGBIS, the UN Integrated Peacebuilding Office in Guinea-Bissau).

Attempted military coup and continuing instability

On 1 April 2010 dissident members of the armed forces, led by the Deputy Army Chief of Staff, Gen. (later Maj.-Gen.) António Indjai, staged a coup attempt. Early that day rebel soldiers entered the UNIOGBIS compound to release Na Tchuto, who joined Indjai, subsequently bringing into question the extent to which he may have been involved in the planning of the coup. Induta was seized, together with the head of military intelligence, Samba Djaló, and a number of other officers, after which he was transferred to a military compound outside of Bissau, where he remained in detention. After assuming control over the armed forces, Indjai and his entourage arrested Prime Minister Gomes Júnior at the government headquarters. Upon news of his detention, demonstrations were staged in the capital to express support for Gomes Júnior and rejection of the attempted coup. Indjai responded by announcing in a radio broadcast that he would kill Gomes Júnior unless his supporters dispersed. Shortly afterwards, however, the Prime Minister was released, and returned to his office. The international community condemned the attempted coup and urged that the Constitution be respected. On 8 April the US Department of State issued a statement accusing Na Tchuto and Ibraima Papá Camara, the Chief of Staff of the Air Force, of involvement in drugs-trafficking, and announced the freezing of the two men's assets in the USA. Although both Na Tchuto and Camara denied the accusations, the decision increased speculation that the coup attempt was linked to resistance within some elements of the armed forces to efforts to reform the country's security forces, which potentially jeopardized their control over illegal sources of revenue.

Throughout April 2010 there were rumours of further attempts to arrest the Prime Minister. After reportedly seeking refuge in foreign embassies on more than one occasion, Gomes Júnior fled the country and remained abroad for over one month, allegedly for health reasons, returning in June. In late June Sanhá appointed Indjai as the new Chief of Staff of the Armed Forces (the post having been left officially vacant since the ousting of Induta). In the same month the EU announced that it was to end its security sector reform mission in Guinea-Bissau (with effect from the end of September), in view of Na Tchuto and Camara's alleged involvement in narcotics-trafficking and Indjai's appointment. On 1 June Na Tchuto was formally acquitted by a military court of all the charges pending against him, and in October he was reinstated by Sanhá as Navy Chief of Staff (prompting criticism from the USA). In October Gomes Júnior suspended the Minister of the Interior, Hadja Satu Camara Pinto, from office, after she appointed police officers in defiance of a decree issued by the Prime Minister prohibiting this on the grounds that it would disrupt reforms in the armed and security forces. In December Camara Pinto tendered her resignation, complaining that President Sanhá (who had been admitted to hospital in Paris, France) had failed to support her in the dispute with Gomes Júnior. (Dinis Na Fantchamena was subsequently appointed as the new Minister of the Interior.)

In November 2010 the UN Security Council approved a resolution authorizing the extension of UNIOGBIS's mandate in the country until the end of 2011 (subsequently renewed until February 2013), expressing its concern at continuing instability in Guinea-Bissau. The Government had also requested the deployment of an international stabilization force, which was to be established by the AU and ECOWAS to assist in post-conflict reconstruction and development. In December Induta, together with Djaló, were released from detention, shortly after the EU threatened to impose sanctions against the Government.

Following the withdrawal of EU support for Guinea-Bissau's security sector reform programme, a replacement plan proposed by ECOWAS and the CPLP was endorsed by the Council of Ministers in March 2011. In particular, the ECOWAS-CPLP 'roadmap' envisaged a reduction in the size of the military. In the same month Angola, which had assumed a leading role in the ECOWAS-CPLP mission, transferred some 200 troops to Guinea-Bissau to assist in the training and restructuring of the security forces—representing the first phase of an expected deployment of 600 ECOWAS-CPLP personnel.

In May 2011 the official investigation into the June 2009 murders of Dabo and Proenca was suspended, ostensibly because of insufficient evidence, while the judicial inquiry examining the deaths of Na Wai and Vieira in March 2009 had only made limited progress by mid-2011. Opposition parties organized several anti-Government demonstrations during July in response. Sanhá effected an extensive cabinet reorganization in the following month, but rejected opposition demands to replace Gomes Júnior as Prime Minister. Most notably, the President appointed Baciro Djá as Minister of National Defence and Fighters for the Country's Freedom.

The death of Sanhá and the subsequent military coup

Sanhá travelled to Senegal in September 2011, reportedly to receive medical treatment for diabetes. He returned to Guinea-Bissau three weeks later, but in late November was again hospitalized in Senegal, before being transferred to a French hospital shortly thereafter. Amid growing concern for Guinea-Bissau's stability, on 26 December reports emerged from the capital of intra-military clashes. Gomes Júnior fled to the Angolan embassy during the unrest, and at least one fatality was recorded. The Government declared on the following day that Na Tchuto and a number of his associates had been arrested after attempting to stage a coup (although they were released in June 2012). However, other sources claimed that a military pay dispute had precipitated the violence, rather than an attempt to overthrow the Government. There were also suspicions that the fighting had been related to the illegal narcotics trade. The Government announced its intention to launch an inquiry into the alleged uprising. Sanhá died in Paris on 9 January. In compliance with the Constitution, ANP President Raimundo Pereira again became Interim President. Pereira subsequently proclaimed that a presidential election would be held on 18 March.

In early February 2012 Gomes Júnior resigned the premiership and announced his intention to stand for the presidency as the candidate of the PAIGC; Djaló Nandingna was appointed Acting Prime Minister. Among the other eight candidates to contest the presidential election, which was duly held on 18 March, were Yalá Embaló and Henrique Rosa. According to official results, Gomes Júnior won 49.0%, while Yalá Embaló was placed second with 23.4% and Manuel Serifo Nhamadjo took 15.7%. The rate of voter participation was put at 55% of the registered electorate. A run-off election was scheduled to be held on 29 April. However, Yalá Embaló maintained that he would boycott the second round of voting, in protest at alleged irregularities that took place during the first round.

On 12 April 2012 members of the military seized power and detained Pereira and Gomes Júnior. It was reported that the coup was carried out in reaction to plans by Gomes Júnior to use Angolan troops to remove certain elements of the Guinea-Bissau armed forces. A 'Military Command' (Comando Militar) was formed, under the leadership of the army Deputy Chief of Staff, Gen. Mamadu Ture Kuruma, and on 18 April the establishment of a National Transitional Council (Conselho Nacional de Transição) was announced, after 22 political parties, although notably excluding the PAIGC, and the military junta agreed upon a timeframe towards new elections. The Government was dissolved. The AU announced the suspension of Guinea-Bissau from the organization, pending the restoration of democratic rule, while the World Bank and the African Development Bank also suspended their development programmes. On 21 April the junta stated that the transitional period would be reduced from two years to one. Despite this concession and the release from custody of Pereira and Gomes Júnior on 27 April, ECOWAS, which had also suspended Guinea-Bissau's membership, confirmed the imposition of diplomatic and financial sanctions on the country on 30 April. Although it was reported that Indjai had also been arrested in the immediate aftermath of the coup, by late April he had become a key figure in negotiations between the junta and ECOWAS, and was believed to have masterminded the overthrow of the institutions of state.

Following further dialogue with ECOWAS, in mid-May 2012 Nhamadjo was installed as interim President, while former Minister of Finance Rui Duarte de Barros was nominated as Prime Minister. On 19 May a roadmap agreement on the return to civilian rule was signed by the Military Command and 25 political parties (although the PAIGC again declined to participate), and on 22 May the junta formally transferred power to a transitional Government. Celestino de Carvalho, who had been involved in the coup, was controversially included in the new Council of Ministers as the minister responsible for defence; former Prime Minister Imbali received the foreign affairs portfolio. Gomes Júnior denounced the transitional administration as illegitimate. Indeed, some observers noted that, by supporting a Government that excluded Pereira, Gomes Júnior and the PAIGC, ECOWAS had, in effect, upheld the main objectives of the coup. The EU withheld official recognition of the transitional Government and on 31 May expanded its sanctions regime (first introduced on 3 May) against the coup leaders. UN Security Council Resolution 2048, approved earlier that month, also provided for sanctions against senior junta members. Meanwhile, the ECOWAS Mission in Guinea-Bissau (ECOMIB), comprising 629 security personnel, was deployed during 18–27 May. ECOMIB replaced the divisive Angolan military contingent (which was withdrawn in early June) and was given a six-month mandate to stabilize the security situation and monitor the transitional process.

A military base near the capital came under attack by armed men on 21 October 2012, resulting in the deaths of at least seven people. The transitional Government regarded the raid as an attempted counter coup and claimed that it had been orchestrated by Portugal and its allies in the CPLP, which had maintained a firmly pro-Gomes Júnior stance since the April coup. The Guinea-Bissau authorities suspected that Capt. Pansau N'Tchama had overseen the attack, and he was placed in detention in late October. It was also revealed at this time that Guinea-Bissau had requested the extradition of Gomes Júnior from Portugal.

ECOMIB's mandate was formalized and extended for a further six months in November 2012. Also in that month, an agreement on restarting the military reform programme was signed by the transitional Government and ECOWAS, which authorized US $63m. in funding for the initiative. In January 2013 the former President of Timor-Leste, José Ramos Horta, was named as the Special Representative of the Secretary-General to Guinea-Bissau and Head of UNIOGBIS; in February UNIOGBIS's mandate was extended until the end of May. Meanwhile, a multi-party political transition accord was concluded in January following negotiations between the transitional Government and the PAIGC, although a final decision on the electoral timetable was still pending.

In early April 2013 Na Tchuto was apprehended on a vessel in international waters close to Cape Verde, following an operation carried out by officials of the US Drugs Enforcement Administration. Na Tchuto was transferred to custody in New York, USA, along with two other detainees, where they were charged with drugs-trafficking offences. On 22 May the UN Security Council extended the mandate of the UNIOGBIS for a further year, while entasking the mission under an amended mandate to support the organization of elections.

Delays in the transitional programme

Political discussions conducted throughout May 2013 resulted in the signature and entry into force of a political agreement between the various parties and a new transitional programme. In early June Nhamadjo reorganized the transitional Government, notably appointing Fernando Delfim da Silva as Minister of Foreign Affairs and Gino Mendes as Minister of Finance; the military succeeded in retaining control over the ministries of national defence and of the interior. On 28 June Nhamadjo announced that the delayed presidential legislative and presidential elections would take place on 24 November.

In mid-November 2013 Nhamadjo announced that the legislative elections had been postponed until 16 March 2014, due to logistical difficulties. Later in November Ramos Horta reported a deterioration in the security situation in the country. In December da Silva and the Minister of the Interior, Antonio Suka Tchama, resigned their government posts after it emerged that a Portuguese national airline plane had been obliged to transport 74 Syrian refugees with false documentation from Bissau to Lisbon, Portugal. The Attorney-General subsequently ordered Tchama's arrest (although it was reported that police had not done so, citing security concerns). The Portuguese Government criticized the incident as a breach of security, while Portugal temporarily suspended flights to Guinea-Bissau.

In January 2014 Nhamadjo announced that a voter registration exercise scheduled to be conducted during December was still incomplete. On 21 February he issued a decree rescheduling the elections for 13 April. Later in February the UN Security Council urged the authorities to adhere to the transitional programme and again warned of the possible imposition of sanctions. Nhamadjo announced in early March that, in accordance with the transitional agreements, he would not seek the presidency. The PAIGC finally selected a former Minister of Finance, José Mário Vaz 'Jomav', as its presidential candidate, rather than former premier Gomes Júnior. Attorney-General Abdú Mané subsequently urged the Supreme Court to prohibit Vaz from contesting the poll, on the grounds that an investigation into embezzlement allegations against him was ongoing. However, in mid-March the Supreme Court released a list of 13 approved presidential candidates, including Vaz (eight applications had been rejected); 15 of 22 applicant parties had secured registration to contest the legislative elections.

Recent developments: presidential and legislative elections

The elections finally took place peacefully on 13 April 2014. According to official results, the PAIGC secured 57 seats in the 102-member National People's Assembly and the PRS 41. In the concurrent presidential election, Vaz secured about 40.9% of the votes cast, Nuno Gomes Nabiam, an independent candidate (and former head of the civil aviation authority) who was supported by the military, 24.8%, an independent and former World Bank official, Paulo Gomes, 10.4% and the PRS candidate, Abel Incada, 7.0%. A voter turnout of more than 88% was reported. Owing to the PAIGC's parliamentary majority, the party's President, Domingos Simões Pereira, was expected to become the next Prime Minister. A presidential second round between Vaz and Nabiam was scheduled for 18 May.

Foreign Affairs

Regional relations

In 1989 a dispute arose between Guinea-Bissau and Senegal over the demarcation of maritime borders. Guinea-Bissau began proceedings against Senegal in the International Court of Justice (ICJ) after rejecting an international arbitration tribunal's ruling in favour of Senegal. In November 1991 the ICJ ruled that a 1960 agreement regarding the demarcation of maritime borders between Guinea-Bissau and Senegal remained valid. In December 1992, in retaliation for the deaths of two Senegalese soldiers, the Senegalese air force and infantry bombarded alleged Casamance separatist bases in the São Domingos area of Guinea-Bissau. In October 1993 the Presidents of Guinea-Bissau and Senegal signed an agreement providing for the joint management and exploitation of the countries' maritime zones. In December 1995 the legislature authorized the ratification of the October 1993 accord. In the previous month the ICJ announced that Guinea-Bissau had halted all proceedings regarding the border dispute with Senegal.

During 1995 the Senegalese air force bombarded border villages in Guinea-Bissau on at least three occasions, apparently in error, prompting the Guinea-Bissau legislature to form a commission of inquiry to investigate such incidents. In April 2000 there were renewed reports of incidents on the border between Senegal and Guinea-Bissau. In August an agreement was signed by Yalá and President Abdoulaye Wade of Senegal providing for the establishment of a joint military force to patrol the border area. Following the signing of a peace accord between the Senegalese Government and the Casamance separatists in December 2004, security in the region improved. However, a dissident faction of the separatists renewed disruption and from mid-March 2006 further skirmishes occurred with Guinea-Bissau troops, causing the displacement of civilian population. Tensions between the two countries mounted again in October 2009, when a minor border dispute related to the construction of a hotel by a Guinean construction company in territory claimed by the two countries led to the deployment of troops, but were defused soon afterwards.

Relations between Guinea-Bissau and The Gambia were severely strained in June 2002, when President Yalá accused the Government of The Gambia of harbouring and training Casamance rebels and former associates of Gen. Mané, the leader of the coup of 1998 and attempted coup of 2000. With specific reference to the alleged attempted coup of May 2002, Yalá threatened invasion of The Gambia if support for the rebels continued; President Jammeh of The Gambia denied any such support was being provided. A visit to The Gambia by Guinea-Bissau's Minister of Foreign Affairs in mid-June eased tensions somewhat, and was followed by UN intervention in July, which recommended the reactivation of a joint commission of the two countries. An improvement in relations was signalled by a visit by Yalá to The Gambia in October.

Other external relations

The People's Republic of China has been active in promoting good economic relations with Guinea-Bissau since the mid-2000s and funded various public projects. This was regarded as undermining the unified approach of the rest of the international donor community in eliciting commitments to reform in return for aid.

China benefited from maritime treaties and fishing rights in Guinea-Bissau territorial waters.

In July 1996 Guinea-Bissau was among the five lusophone African nations that, along with Brazil and Portugal, officially established the CPLP, a lusophone grouping intended to benefit each member state by means of joint co-operation in technical, cultural and social matters. Portugal provided Guinea-Bissau with considerable funding and other aid. Guinea-Bissau was a signatory to the 'Luanda Declaration' in November 2011, which pledged greater co-operation between the CPLP member states in the fields of, *inter alia*, security, crime prevention and immigration.

CONSTITUTION AND GOVERNMENT

Under the terms of the 1984 Constitution (revised in 1991, 1996 and 1999), Guinea-Bissau is a multi-party state, although the formation of parties on a tribal or geographical basis is prohibited. Legislative power is vested in the Assembleia Nacional Popular (National People's Assembly), which comprises 102 members, elected by universal adult suffrage for a term of four years. Executive power is vested in the President of the Republic, who is Head of State and who governs with the assistance of an appointed Council of Ministers, led by the Prime Minister. The President is elected by universal adult suffrage for a term of five years.

REGIONAL AND INTERNATIONAL CO-OPERATION

Guinea-Bissau is a member of the African Union (see p. 186), of the Economic Community of West African States (ECOWAS, see p. 260) and of the West African organs of the Franc Zone (see p. 330). In 2004 Guinea-Bissau became a member of the Community of Sahel-Saharan States (see p. 450).

Guinea-Bissau became a member of the UN in 1974 and was admitted to the World Trade Organization (WTO, see p. 434) in 1995.

ECONOMIC AFFAIRS

In 2012, according to estimates by the World Bank, Guinea-Bissau's gross national income (GNI), measured at average 2010–12 prices, was US $916m., equivalent to $550 per head (or $1,190 on an international purchasing-power parity basis). During 2003–12, it was estimated, the population increased at an average annual rate of 2.3%, while gross domestic product (GDP) per head increased, in real terms, by an average of 0.5% per year. Overall GDP increased, in real terms, at an average annual rate of 2.8% in 2003–12; it increased by 5.7% in 2011, but decreased by 1.5% in 2012.

Agriculture (including forestry and fishing) contributed an estimated 47.8% of GDP in 2011, according to the African Development Bank (AfDB) and the sector engaged an estimated 77.9% of the economically active population in mid-2014, according to FAO. The main cash crops are cashew nuts (production of which in 2012 was estimated by FAO at 130,000 metric tons, with export earnings in that year totalling 66.4m. francs CFA) and cotton. Other crops produced include rice, cassava, oil palm fruit, plantains, coconuts, sorghum, maize and millet. Livestock and timber production are also important. The fishing industry developed rapidly during the 1990s, and earnings from fishing exports and the sale of fishing licences are a significant source of government revenue (revenue from fishing licences was 7,515m. francs CFA in 2005, equivalent to 26.9% of total revenue). A study conducted in 2004 revealed that the potential annual fishing catch was 96,000 tons, although in 2011 the total catch recorded by FAO amounted to only 6,800; in 2006 the Minister of Fisheries and the Maritime Economy estimated that 40,000 tons of fish were stolen from Guinea-Bissau waters annually. According to the World Bank, agricultural GDP increased, in real terms, by an average of 3.9% per year in 2000–08. Agricultural GDP increased by 5.0% in 2011, according to AfDB estimates.

Industry (including mining, manufacturing, construction and power) employed an estimated 4.1% of the economically active population at mid-1994 and, according to AfDB estimates, provided 13.0% of GDP in 2011. According to the World Bank, industrial GDP grew, in real terms, by an average of 4.2% per year in 2000–08; growth of 3.8% was recorded in 2008.

The mining sector is underdeveloped, although Guinea-Bissau possesses reserves of bauxite, phosphates, diamonds and gold. In 2003 recoverable petroleum reserves were estimated at 2,000m. barrels per day.

The sole branches of the manufacturing sector are food-processing, brewing and timber- and cotton-processing, while there are plans to develop fish-processing. According to the AfDB, manufacturing contributed 11.3% of GDP in 2011. According to the World Bank, manufacturing GDP increased, in real terms, by an average of 4.1% per year in 2000–08; growth of 4.9% was recorded in 2011, according to AfDB estimates.

The construction sector contributed 1.3% of GDP in 2011. According to estimates by the AfDB, the sector grew by 10.0% in 2011.

Energy is derived principally from thermal and hydroelectric power. Imports of petroleum and petroleum products comprised 17.1% of the value of total imports in 2011. Energy production since 1999 has been insufficient to supply demand in Bissau, mainly owing to fuel shortages caused by government-set low prices, and to equipment failures caused by poor maintenance. As a result, most energy is currently supplied by private generators.

Services employed an estimated 19.4% of the economically active population at mid-1994, and, according to AfDB estimates, provided 39.2% of GDP in 2011. According to the World Bank, the combined GDP of the service sectors increased by 1.4% in 2000–08; services GDP grew by 4.0% in 2008.

In 2012 Guinea-Bissau recorded a trade deficit of 31,600m. francs CFA, and there was a deficit of 27,400m. francs CFA on the current account of the balance of payments, according to the IMF. In 2011 the principal source of imports was Senegal (20.1%). In that year India was the principal market for exports (89.0%). In 2012 the principal export was cashew nuts. The principal imports in that year were petroleum and petroleum products.

According to the IMF, in 2012 there was a preliminary budgetary deficit of 12,900m. francs CFA. Guinea-Bissau's general government gross debt was 209,191m francs CFA in 2011, equivalent to 45.8% of GDP. Guinea-Bissau's total external debt was US $284m. at the end of 011, of which $219m. was public and publicly guaranteed debt. In 2009 the cost of servicing long-term public and publicly guaranteed debt and repayments to the IMF was equivalent to 6.4% of the value of exports of goods, services and income (excluding workers' remittances). In 2003–12 the average annual rate of inflation was 3.1%. Consumer prices increased by 2.2% in 2012.

Guinea-Bissau is one of the world's poorest countries. Its economy is largely dependent on the export of cashew nuts, and foreign financing accounts for a significant part of budget revenue. Relations with donors have, however, been uneasy since the early 2000s and support has periodically been withheld. The economy has also been negatively affected by chronic political instability and the growing use of the country as a route for the trafficking of illegal narcotics between South America and Europe. In May 2010 the IMF approved a three-year Extended Credit Facility of US $33.3m. to support the Government's economic programme, and in December Guinea-Bissau was pronounced by the IMF to have met the requirements to reach completion point under the initiative for heavily indebted poor countries. The IMF and the World Bank subsequently announced their decision to support $1,200m. in debt relief for Guinea-Bissau. In May 2011 the 'Paris Club' of creditor nations announced debt relief totalling $283m., while Angola, Brazil, France, the European Union and the African Development Bank also cancelled large proportions of Guinea-Bissau's debt during that year. However, following strong growth in 2011, the military coup of April 2012 led to widespread economic disruption, and a contraction in real GDP. The cashew sector was particularly affected, with production and exports both declining sharply in that year; lower levels of international demand for cashew nuts also had a negative impact on the industry. The suspension of financial assistance programmes by many of Guinea-Bissau's international partners compounded economic hardship. IMF expectations of a recovery in 2013 were not realized and GDP growth amounted to only 0.3% in that year, with a resurgence in cashew export volumes offset by a sharp decline in prices, a significant fiscal contraction, and frequent interruptions in electricity and water supplies. By early 2014 civil servants were owed three months' salary arrears and the humanitarian situation had deteriorated significantly. However, the prospects for economic stabilization improved significantly following the successful organization of elections in April (see Domestic Political Affairs). The International Crisis Group urged external donors to resume support for the payment of government expenses, including public sector wages, and long-term funding for development programmes.

PUBLIC HOLIDAYS

2015: 1 January (New Year's Day), 20 January (Death of Amílcar Cabral), 8 March (International Women's Day), 1 May (Labour Day), 17 July* (Korité, end of Ramadan), 3 August (Anniversary of the Killing of Pidjiguiti), 23 September* (Tabaski, Feast of the Sacrifice), 24 September (National Day), 14 November (Anniversary of the Movement of Readjustment), 25 December (Christmas Day).

* These holidays are dependent on the Islamic lunar calendar and may vary by one or two days from the dates given.

Statistical Survey

Source (unless otherwise stated): Instituto Nacional de Estatística Guiné-Bissau, Av. Amílcar Cabral, CP 6, Bissau; tel. 3225457; e-mail inec@mail.gtelecom.gw; internet www.stat-guinebissau.com.

Area and Population

AREA, POPULATION AND DENSITY

Area (sq km)	36,125*
Population (census results)	
1 December 1991	983,367
15–29 March 2009	
Males	737,634
Females	783,196
Total	1,520,830
Population (UN estimates at mid-year)†	
2012	1,663,558
2013	1,704,256
2014	1,745,798
Density (per sq km) at mid-2014	48.3

* 13,948 sq miles.
† Source: UN, *World Population Prospects: The 2012 revision*.

POPULATION BY AGE AND SEX

(UN estimates at mid-2014)

	Males	Females	Total
0–14	359,956	359,580	719,536
15–64	484,627	491,027	975,654
65 and over	23,322	27,286	50,608
Total	867,905	877,893	1,745,798

Source: UN, *World Population Prospects: The 2012 Revision*.

ETHNIC GROUPS

1996 (percentages): Balante 30; Fulani 20; Mandjak 14; Mandinka 12; Papel 7; Other 16 (Source: Comunidade dos Países de Língua Portuguesa).

POPULATION BY REGION

(2009 census)

Bafatá	210,007	Quinará	63,610
Biombo	97,120	Sector Autónomo Bissau (SAB)	387,909
Bolama/Bijagós	34,563	Tombali	94,939
Cacheu	192,508	**Total**	1,520,830
Gabú	215,530		
Oio	224,644		

PRINCIPAL TOWNS

(population at 2009 census)

Bissau (capital)	365,097*	Bigene	51,412
Gabú†	81,495	Farim	48,264
Bafatá	68,956	Mansôa	46,046
Bissorã	56,585	Pitche	45,594

* Figure for Sector Autónomo Bissau (SAB) administrative division.
† Formerly Nova Lamego.

BIRTHS AND DEATHS

	2009	2010	2011
Birth rate (per 1,000)	38.7	38.7	37.9
Death rate (per 1,000)	17.0	16.7	16.4

Source: African Development Bank.

Life expectancy (years at birth): 53.8 (males 52.3; females 55.4) in 2011 (Source: World Bank, World Development Indicators database).

ECONOMICALLY ACTIVE POPULATION

('000 persons at mid-1994)

	Males	Females	Total
Agriculture, etc.	195	175	370
Industry	15	5	20
Services	80	14	94
Total	290	194	484

Source: UN Economic Commission for Africa, *African Statistical Yearbook*.

Mid-2014 (estimates in '000): Agriculture, etc. 508; Total labour force 652 (Source: FAO).

Health and Welfare

KEY INDICATORS

Total fertility rate (children per woman, 2011)	5.0
Under-5 mortality rate (per 1,000 live births, 2011)	161
HIV/AIDS (% of persons aged 15–49, 2012)	3.9
Physicians (per 1,000 head, 2009)	0.1
Hospital beds (per 1,000 head, 2009)	1.0
Health expenditure (2010): US $ per head (PPP)	82
Health expenditure (2010): % of GDP	7.0
Health expenditure (2010): public (% of total)	33.1
Access to water (% of persons, 2011)	72
Access to sanitation (% of persons, 2011)	19
Total carbon dioxide emissions ('000 metric tons, 2010)	238.4
Carbon dioxide emissions per head (metric tons, 2010)	0.2
Human Development Index (2012): ranking	176
Human Development Index (2012): value	0.364

For sources and definitions, see explanatory note on p. vi.

Agriculture

PRINCIPAL CROPS
('000 metric tons)

	2010	2011	2012
Rice, paddy	209.2	175.2	198.5
Maize*	12.3	8.0	10.0
Millet	15.0	14.0	17.0
Sorghum	17.6	19.0*	24.0*
Cassava	68.3	60.3	68.3
Sugar cane†	6.3	6.3	6.3
Cashew nuts†	108.0	128.7	130.0
Groundnuts, with shell	36.2	35.4	45.2
Coconuts	42.1*	42.2*	34.0†
Oil palm fruit†	80.0	80.0	80.0
Plantains†	48.6	49.6	51.0
Oranges†	6.3	6.4	6.5

* Unofficial figure(s).
† FAO estimate(s).

Aggregate production ('000 metric tons, may include official, semi-official or estimated data): Total cereals 256.6 in 2010, 218.2 in 2011, 251.5 in 2012; Total roots and tubers 161.3 in 2010, 165.0 in 2011, 168.3 in 2012; Total vegetables (incl. melons) 37.0 in 2010, 34.6 in 2011, 35.5 in 2012; Total fruits (excl. melons) 96.2 in 2010, 100.1 in 2011, 103.5 in 2012.

Source: FAO.

LIVESTOCK
('000 head, year ending September)

	2010	2011	2012*
Cattle*	642	650	653
Pigs	394	462	480
Sheep*	454	460	465
Goats	689	732	735
Chickens	1,143	1,192	1,850

* FAO estimates.

Source: FAO.

LIVESTOCK PRODUCTS
('000 metric tons, FAO estimates)

	2010	2011	2012
Cattle meat	6.4	6.5	6.7
Pig meat	13.6	15.0	15.2
Cows' milk	17.3	17.3	17.5
Goats' milk	4.0	4.0	4.0

Source: FAO.

Forestry

ROUNDWOOD REMOVALS
('000 cubic metres, excluding bark, FAO estimates)

	2010	2011	2012
Sawlogs, veneer logs and logs for sleepers	1.9	1.9	1.9
Other industrial wood	130.0	130.0	130.0
Fuel wood	2,600.0	2,637.4	2,675.2
Total	2,731.9	2,769.3	2,807.1

Source: FAO.

SAWNWOOD PRODUCTION
('000 cubic metres, including railway sleepers, FAO estimates)

	1970	1971	1972
Total	10	16	16

1973–2012: Production assumed to be unchanged from 1972 (FAO estimates).

Source: FAO.

Fishing

(metric tons, live weight, FAO estimates)

	2007	2008	2009
Freshwater fishes	150	150	150
Marine fishes	2,650	2,866	2,862
Sea catfishes	340	385	385
Meagre	240	240	240
Mullets	1,500	1,500	1,500
Sompat grunt	200	230	230
Lesser African threadfin	370	420	420
Total catch (incl. others)	6,500	6,804	6,800

2010–11: Catch assumed to be unchanged from 2009 (FAO estimates).

Source: FAO.

Industry

SELECTED PRODUCTS
('000 metric tons unless otherwise indicated)

	2001	2002	2003
Hulled rice	69.1	68.4	67.7
Groundnuts (processed)	6.8	6.7	6.6
Bakery products	7.6	7.7	7.9
Frozen fish	1.7	1.7	1.7
Dry and smoked fish	3.6	3.7	3.8
Vegetable oils (million litres)	3.6	3.6	3.7
Beverages (million litres)	3.5	0.0	0.0
Dairy products (million litres)	1.1	0.9	0.9
Wood products	4.7	4.5	4.4
Soap	2.6	2.5	2.4
Electric energy (million kWh)	18.9	19.4	15.8

Source: IMF, *Guinea-Bissau: Selected Issues and Statistical Appendix* (March 2005).

Electric energy (million kWh, estimates): 30 in 2008; 31 in 2009; 32 in 2010 (Source: UN Industrial Commodity Statistics Database).

Finance

CURRENCY AND EXCHANGE RATES

Monetary Units

100 centimes = 1 franc de la Communauté Financière Africaine (CFA).

Sterling, Dollar and Euro Equivalents (31 December 2013)

£1 sterling = 783.286 francs CFA;
US $1 = 475.641 francs CFA;
€1 = 655.957 francs CFA;
10,000 francs CFA = £12.77 = $21.02 = €15.24.

Average Exchange Rate (francs CFA per US $)

2011 471.866
2012 510.290
2013 494.040

Note: An exchange rate of 1 French franc = 50 francs CFA, established in 1948, remained in force until January 1994, when the CFA franc was devalued by 50%, with the exchange rate adjusted to 1 French franc = 100 francs CFA. This relationship to French currency remained in effect with the introduction of the euro on 1 January 1999. From that date, accordingly, a fixed exchange rate of €1 = 655.957 francs CFA has been in operation.

BUDGET
('000 million francs CFA)

Revenue*	2011	2012†	2013‡
Tax revenue	40.3	38.9	45.2
Non-tax revenue	12.3	7.1	6.5
Fishing licences	7.1	0.2	0.1
Total	52.6	46.0	51.7

Expenditure	2011	2012†	2013‡
Current expenditure	56.6	62.3	55.5
Wages and salaries	23.6	25.1	25.6
Goods and services	7.6	12.8	8.1
Transfers	11.8	12.8	11.7
Other current expenditures	12.9	11.4	9.6
Scheduled interest payments	0.6	0.1	0.5
Capital expenditure and net lending	37.0	21.6	18.5
Total	93.6	83.9	74.1

* Excluding budget grants received ('000 million francs CFA): 34.4 in 2011; 25.0 in 2012 (preliminary figure); 22.1 in 2013 (projection).

† Preliminary figures.

‡ Projections.

Source: IMF, *Guinea-Bissau: Staff Report for the 2013 Article IV Consultation; Debt Sustainability Analysis; Informational Annex; Public Information Notice on the Executive Board Discussion; and Statement by the Executive Director for Guinea-Bissau* (July 2013).

CENTRAL BANK RESERVES
(US $ million at 31 December)

	2010	2011	2012
IMF special drawing rights	19.09	19.02	19.04
Reserve position in IMF	0.20	0.32	0.39
Foreign exchange	137.15	200.66	145.16
Total	156.43	220.00	164.59

Source: IMF, *International Financial Statistics*.

MONEY SUPPLY
(million francs CFA at 31 December)

	2010	2011	2012
Currency outside banks	64,086	85,912	83,385
Demand deposits at deposit money banks	40,400	69,032	48,195
Total money (incl. others)	104,871	156,519	131,731

Source: IMF, *International Financial Statistics*.

COST OF LIVING
(Consumer Price Index; base: 2003 = 100)

	2010	2011	2012
Food, beverages and tobacco	99.4	106.7	110.1
All items (incl. others)	122.2	128.3	131.1

Source: ILO.

NATIONAL ACCOUNTS

Expenditure on the Gross Domestic Product
(US $ million at current prices)

	2009	2010	2011*
Government final consumption expenditure	53,297	55,196	58,544
Private final consumption expenditure	359,627	373,123	402,828
Gross fixed capital formation	31,212	39,818	51,424
Change in inventories	400	422	953
Total domestic expenditure	444,536	468,559	513,749
Exports of goods and services	60,502	73,360	82,396
Less Imports of goods and services	114,523	118,523	125,651
GDP in purchasers' values	390,515	423,397	470,495

Gross Domestic Product by Economic Activity
(million francs CFA at current prices)

	2009	2010	2011*
Agriculture, hunting, forestry and fishing	170,411	189,900	212,688
Mining and quarrying	110	116	116
Manufacturing	44,936	46,899	50,177
Electricity, gas and water	1,636	1,670	1,770
Construction	3,227	5,030	5,634
Trade, restaurants and hotels	80,110	76,314	85,472
Finance, insurance and real estate	14,268	15,599	17,159
Transport, storage and communications	15,876	18,106	20,279
Public administration and defence	40,545	46,258	51,346
Sub-total	371,119	399,892	444,640
Indirect taxes	19,396	23,505	25,856
GDP at purchasers' values	390,515	423,397	470,495

* Estimates.

Source: African Development Bank.

BALANCE OF PAYMENTS
('000 million francs CFA)

	2011	2012
Exports of goods f.o.b.	114.2	65.3
Imports of goods f.o.b.	–119.7	–96.9
Trade balance	–5.5	–31.6
Exports of services	6.7	7.4
Imports of services	–38.6	–35.8
Balance on goods and services	–37.4	–60.0
Other income (net)	–0.3	–0.4
Balance on goods, services and income	–37.7	–60.4
Official current transfers	15.8	15.9
Private current transfers	16.6	17.0
Current balance	–5.3	–27.4
Capital account (net)	26.0	16.2
Financial account (net)	–3.9	–19.2
Statistical discrepancy	14.2	—
Overall balance	31.0	–30.4

Source: IMF, *Guinea-Bissau: Staff Report for the 2013 Article IV Consultation; Debt Sustainability Analysis; Informational Annex; Public Information Notice on the Executive Board Discussion; and Statement by the Executive Director for Guinea-Bissau* (July 2013).

External Trade

PRINCIPAL COMMODITIES
(million francs CFA)

Imports c.i.f.	2009	2010	2011
Cereals and cereal preparations	14,489	13,234	17,851
Beverages	5,899	7,596	12,065
Petroleum and petroleum products	24,677	13,252	24,031
Iron and steel	3,349	4,627	6,807
Road vehicles	3,397	4,376	5,029
Total (incl. others)	100,727	102,625	140,166

Exports f.o.b.	2009	2010	2011
Cashew nuts	46,600	51,800	104,400
Total (incl. others)	57,438	62,700	114,200

2012: Cashew nuts 66,400; Total exports (incl. others) 76,800.

Source: African Development Bank.

PRINCIPAL TRADING PARTNERS
(million francs CFA)

Imports	2009	2010	2011
China, People's Republic	7,470	4,374	6,815
Italy	3,389	4,361	5,077
Netherlands	8,431	4,300	5,333
Portugal	17,766	727	1,409
Senegal	19,133	22,330	28,118
Total (incl. others)	100,727	102,625	140,166

Exports	2009	2010	2011
India	50,503	52,471	101,627
Portugal	701	727	1,409
Singapore	1,333	1,374	2,664
USA	3,552	3,668	7,085
Total (incl. others)	57,438	62,700	114,200

2012: Total exports 76,800.

Source: African Development Bank.

Transport

ROAD TRAFFIC
(motor vehicles in use, estimates)

	1994	1995	1996
Passenger cars	5,940	6,300	7,120
Commercial vehicles	4,650	4,900	5,640

2008 (motor vehicles in use): Passenger cars 42,222; Buses and coaches 289; Vans and lorries 9,323; Motorcycles and mopeds 4,936.

Source: International Road Federation, *World Road Statistics*.

SHIPPING

Flat Registered Fleet
(at 31 December)

	2010	2011	2012
Number of vessels	12	12	12
Total displacement (grt)	2,903	2,903	2,903

Source: Lloyd's List Intelligence (www.lloydslistintelligence.com).

International Sea-Borne Freight Traffic
(UN estimates, '000 metric tons)

	1991	1992	1993
Goods loaded	40	45	46
Goods unloaded	272	277	283

Source: UN Economic Commission for Africa, *African Statistical Yearbook*.

CIVIL AVIATION
(traffic on scheduled services)

	1996	1997	1998
Kilometres flown (million)	1	0	0
Passengers carried ('000)	21	21	20
Passenger-km (million)	10	10	10
Total ton-km (million)	1	1	1

Source: UN, *Statistical Yearbook*.

Tourism

TOURIST ARRIVALS BY NATIONALITY

	2005	2006	2007
Cape Verde	159	401	1,498
China, People's Republic	46	659	1,488
Cuba	29	329	309
France	599	834	2,984
Italy	213	343	1,871
Korea, Republic	36	523	1,289
Portugal	1,552	2,599	2,245
Senegal	235	921	2,798
Spain	324	231	1,458
USA	57	320	265
Total (incl. others)	4,978	11,617	30,092

Receipts from tourism (US $ million, excl. passenger transport): 2.8 in 2006; 28.4 in 2007; 38.2 in 2008.

Source: World Tourism Organization.

Communications Media

	2010	2011	2012
Telephones ('000 main lines in use)	5.0	n.a.	5.0
Mobile cellular telephones ('000 subscribers)	715.0	869.1	1,097.0

Source: International Telecommunication Union.

Education

(2009/10 unless otherwise indicated, UNESCO estimates)

		Students		
	Teachers	Males	Females	Total
Pre-primary	309	4,360	4,590	8,950
Primary	5,371	144,075	134,815	278,890
Secondary: general	1,913*	46,445	31,581	78,026
Secondary: technical and vocational		656†	239†	895†
Tertiary†	32	399	74	473

* 1999.
† 2000/01.

Institutions (1999): Pre-primary 54; Primary 759.

Students (2005/06): Primary 269,287; Secondary 55,176; Tertiary 3,689.

Teachers (2005/06): Primary 4,327; Secondary 1,480; Tertiary 25.

Pupil-teacher ratio (primary education, UNESCO estimate): 51.9 in 2009/10 (Source: UNESCO Institute for Statistics).

Adult literacy rate (UNESCO estimates): 55.3% (males 68.9%; females 42.1%) in 2011.

Source: UNESCO Institute for Statistics.

Directory

The Government

HEAD OF STATE

Interim President: MANUEL SERIFO NHAMADJO.

COUNCIL OF MINISTERS
(April 2014)

Prime Minister: RUI DUARTE DE BARROS.

Minister of State, Minister of the Presidency of the Council of Ministers and Parliamentary Affairs: FERNANDO VAZ.

Minister of State, Minister of the Civil Service, State Reform, Labour and Social Security: ARISTIDES OCANTE DA SILVA.

Minister of State, Minister of Transport and Telecommunications: ORLANDO MENDES VIEGAS.

Minister of Foreign Affairs, International Co-operation and Communities: (vacant).

Minister of National Defence and Fighters for the Country's Freedom: CELESTINO DE CARVALHO.

Minister of the Interior: (vacant).

Minister of Finance: GINO MENDES.

Minister of the Economy and Regional Integration: SOARES SAMBÚ.

Minister of Territorial Administration and Local Government: Dr BAPTISTA TÉ.

Minister of Fisheries and Fishing Resources: MÁRIO LOPES DA ROSA.

Minister of National Education, Youth, Culture and Sport: ALFREDO GOMES.

Minister of Public Health: Dr AGOSTINHO CÁ.

Minister of Justice: Dr MAMADÚ SAIDO BALDÉ.

Minister of Energy and Industry: DANIEL GOMES.

Minister of Natural Resources: CERTÓRIO BIOTE.

Minister of Infrastructure: RUI ARAÚJO GOMES.

Minister of Trade, the Promotion of Local Products and Handicrafts: Dr ABUBACAR BALDÉ.

Minister of Agriculture: NICOLAU SANTOS.

Minister of Women, Families and Social Solidarity: Dr GABRIELA FERNANDES.

In addition there were 15 Secretaries of State.

MINISTRIES

Office of the President: Bissau; internet www.presidencia-gw.org.

Office of the Prime Minister: Av. dos Combatentes da Liberdade da Pátria, CP 137, Bissau; tel. 3211308; fax 3201671.

Ministry of Agriculture: Av. dos Combatentes da Liberdade da Pátria, CP 102, Bissau; tel. 3221200; fax 3222483.

Ministry of the Civil Service, State Reform, Labour and Social Security: Bissau.

Ministry of the Economy and Regional Integration: Av. dos Combatentes da Liberdade da Pátria, CP 67, Bissau; tel. 3203670; fax 3203496; e-mail info@mail.guine-bissau.org; internet www.guine-bissau.org.

Ministry of Energy and Industry: CP 311, Bissau; tel. 3215659; fax 3223149.

Ministry of Finance: Rua Justino Lopes 74A, CP 67, Bissau; tel. 3203670; fax 3203496; e-mail info@mail.guine-bissau.org.

Ministry of Fisheries and Fishing Resources: Bissau.

Ministry of Foreign Affairs, International Co-operation and Communities: Av. dos Combatentes da Liberdade da Pátria, Bissau; tel. 3204301; fax 3202378.

Ministry of Infrastructure: Av. dos Combatentes da Liberdade da Pátria, CP 14, Bissau; internet www.minisinfraestruturas-gov.com; tel. 3206575; fax 3203611.

Ministry of the Interior: Av. Unidade Africana, Bissau; tel. 3203781.

Ministry of Justice: Av. Amílcar Cabral, CP 17, Bissau; tel. 3202185; internet mj-gb.org.

Ministry of National Defence and Fighters for the Country's Freedom: Amura, Bissau; tel. 3223646.

Ministry of National Education, Youth, Culture and Sport: Rua Areolino Cruz, Bissau; tel. 3202244.

Ministry of Natural Resources: Bissau.

Ministry of the Presidency of the Council of Ministers and Parliamentary Affairs: Bissau.

Ministry of Public Health: CP 50, Bissau; tel. 3204438; fax 3201701.

Ministry of Territorial Administration and Local Government: Bissau.

Ministry of Trade, the Promotion of Local Products and Handicrafts: 34A Av. Pansau na Isna, Bissau; tel. and fax 3206062; e-mail turismom@yahoo.com; internet www.minturgb-gov.com.

Ministry of Transport and Telecommunications: Bissau.

Ministry of Women, Families and Social Solidarity: Bissau.

President

Presidential Election, First Round, 18 March 2012*

Candidate	Votes	% of votes
Carlos Gomes Júnior	154,797	48.97
Mohamed Yalá Embaló (PRS)	73,842	23.36
Manuel Serifo Nhamadjo	49,767	15.74
Henrique Rosa	17,070	5.40
Others*	20,631	6.53
Total	316,107	100.00

* Under the terms of the Constitution, a second round of the presidential election was scheduled to take place on 29 April in order to determine which of the two leading candidates from the first round would be elected. However, on 12 April members of the military seized power and announced the dissolution of the organs of state.

* There were five other candidates.

Legislature

Assembleia Nacional Popular: Palácio Colinas de Boé, Av. Francisco Mendes, CP 219, Bissau; tel. 3201991; fax 3206725; internet www.anpguinebissau.org.

President: IBRAIMA SORY DJALÓ.

General Election, 13 April 2014

Party	Valid votes	% of valid votes	Seats
Partido Africano da Independência da Guiné e Cabo Verde (PAIGC)	281,408	47.98	57
Partido para a Renovação Social (PRS)	180,432	30.76	41
Partido para a Nova Democracia (PND)	28,581	4.87	1
Partido da Convergência Democrática (PCD)	19,757	3.37	2
União para a Mudança (UM)	10,803	1.84	1
Others	65,543	11.17	—
Total	586,524	100.00	102

Election Commission

Comissão Nacional de Eleições (CNE): Av. 3 de Agosto 44, CP 359, Bissau; tel. 3203600; fax 3203601; e-mail cne-info@guinetel.com; internet www.cne-guinebissau.org; Pres. AUGUSTO MENDES.

Political Organizations

Aliança Democrática (AD): c/o Assembleia Nacional Popular, Bissau; f. 2008; Leader VÍTOR FERNANDO MANDINGA.

Frente Democrática (FD): Bissau; f. 1991; officially registered in Nov. 1991; Pres. JORGE FERNANDO MANDINGA.

Partido da Convergência Democrática (PCD): Bissau; Leader VÍTOR FERNANDO MANDINGA.

Aliança de Forças Patrióticas (AFP): Bissau; f. 2008; Pres. AMINE MICHEL SAAD.

Forum Cívico Guinéense-Social Democracia (FCG-SD): Bissau; Pres. ANTONIETA ROSA GOMES; Sec.-Gen. CARLOS VAIMAN.

Frente Democrática Social (FDS): c/o Assembleia Nacional Popular, Bissau; f. 1991; Pres. LUCAS DA SILVA.

Partido de Solidariedade e Trabalho (PST): Bissau; f. 2002; Leader IANCUBA INDJAI; Sec.-Gen. ZACARIAS BALDÉ.

União para a Mudança (UM): Bissau; f. 1994; Leader AGNELO REGALA.

Centro Democrático (CD): Bissau; tel. and fax 452517; e-mail empossaie@centrodemocratico.com; internet www.cd.empossaie.com; f. 2006; Pres. EMPOSSA IÉ; Sec.-Gen. VICTOR DJELOMBO.

Liga Guinéense de Protecção Ecológica (LIPE): Bairro Missirá 102, CP 1290, Bissau; tel. and fax 3252309; f. 1991; environmental party; Interim Pres. MAMADU MUSTAFA BALDÉ.

Movimento Democrático Guinéense (MDG): Bissau; f. 2003; Pres. SILVESTRE CLAUDINHO ALVES.

Partido Africano da Independência da Guiné e Cabo Verde (PAIGC): CP 106, Bissau; internet www.paigc.org; f. 1956; fmrly the ruling party in both Guinea-Bissau and Cape Verde; although Cape Verde withdrew from the PAIGC following the coup in Guinea-Bissau in Nov. 1980, Guinea-Bissau has retained the party name and initials; Pres. DOMINGOS SIMÕES PEREIRA; Sec. AUGUSTO OLIVAIS.

Partido da Convergência Democrática (PCD): Bissau; Pres. VICENTE FERNANDES.

Partido para Democracia, Desenvolvimento e Cidadania (PADEC): Bissau; f. 2005; Leaders FRANCISCO JOSÉ FADUL.

Partido Democrático Guinéense (PDG): f. 2007; Pres. EUSEBIO SEBASTIAO DA SILVA.

Partido Democrático Socialista (PDS): Bissau; f. 2006; Pres. JOÃO SECO MAMADÚ MANÉ.

Partido Democrático Socialista de Salvação Guineense: Leader SERIFO BALDÉ.

Partido para a Nova Democracia (PND): Bissau; f. 2007; Pres. IBRAIMA DJALÓ.

Partido Popular Democrático (PPD): Bissau; f. 2006; Pres. MARIA LUIZA EMBALÓ.

Partido de Progresso (PP): Bissau; f. 2004; Pres. IBRAHIMA SOW.

Partido da Reconciliação Nacional (PRN): Bissau; f. 2004; Leader ALMARA NHASSÉ; Sec.-Gen. OLUNDO MENDES.

Partido para a Renovação Social (PRS): c/o Assembleia Nacional Popular, Bissau; f. 1992; Pres. ALBERTO NAMBEIA EMBALÓ.

Partido Republicano para a Independência e o Desenvolvimento (PRID): Bissau; f. 2008; Pres. ARISTIDES GOMES.

Partido Social Democrata (PSD): c/o Assembleia Nacional Popular, Bissau; f. 1995; Pres. ANTONIO SAMBA BALDÉ.

Partido Socialista-Guiné Bissau (PS-GB): Bissau; f. 1994; Pres. CIRILO OLIVEIRA RODRIGUES.

Partido dos Trabalhadores (PT): Bissau; e-mail contact@nodjuntamon.org; internet www.nodjuntamon.org; f. 2002; left-wing; Pres. ARREGADO MANTENQUE TÉ.

Partido Unido Social Democrático (PUSD): Bissau; f. 1991; officially registered in Jan. 1992; Pres. AUGUSTO BARAI MANGO.

União para a Mudança (UM): Bissau; Pres. AGNELO REGALA.

União Nacional para Democracia e Progresso (UNDP): Bissau; f. 1998; Pres. ABUBACAR BALDÉ.

União Patriótica Guinéense (UPG): Bissau; f. 2004 by dissident members of the RGB; Pres. FRANCISCA VAZ TURPIN.

Diplomatic Representation

EMBASSIES IN GUINEA-BISSAU

Angola: Bissau; Ambassador FELICIANO DOS SANTOS.

Brazil: Rua São Tomé, Esquina Rua Moçambique, CP 29, Bissau; tel. 3212549; fax 3201317; e-mail emb_brasil_bxo@hotmail.com; Ambassador JORGE GERALDO KADRI.

China, People's Republic: Av. Francisco João Mendes, Bissau; tel. 3203637; fax 3203590; e-mail chinaemb_gw@mail.mfa.gov.cn; internet gw.china-embassy.org/chn; Ambassador LI BAOJUN.

Cuba: Rua Joaquim N'Com 1, y Victorino Costa, CP 258, Bissau; tel. 3213579; fax 3201301; e-mail embcuba@sol.gtelecom.gw; Ambassador ELIS ALBERTO GONZÁLEZ POLANCO.

France: Bairro de Penha, Av. dos Combatentes da Liberdade da Pátria, Bissau; tel. 3257400; fax 3257421; e-mail cad.bissao-amba@diplomatie.gouv.fr; internet www.ambafrance-gw.org; Ambassador MICHEL FLESCH.

The Gambia: 47 Victorino Costa, Chao de Papel, CP 529, 1037 Bissau; tel. 3205085; fax 3251099; e-mail gambiaembbissau@hotmail.com; Ambassador CHERNO B. TOURAY.

Guinea: Rua 14, No. 9, CP 396, Bissau; tel. 3212681; Ambassador TAMBA TIENDO MILLIMONO.

Korea, Democratic People's Republic: Bissau; Ambassador KIM KYONG SIN.

Nigeria: 6 Av. 14 de Novembro, CP 199, Bissau; tel. 3201018; fax 3202564; Ambassador AHMED MAIGIDA ADAMS.

Libya: Rua 16, CP 362, Bissau; tel. 3212006; Representative DOKALI ALI MUSTAFA.

Portugal: Av. Cidade de Lisboa, CP 76, 1021 Bissau; tel. 3201261; fax 3201269; e-mail embaixada@bissau.dgaccp.pt; Ambassador Dr ANTÓNIO MANUEL RICOCA FREIRE.

Russia: Av. 14 de Novembro, CP 308, Bissau; tel. 3251050; fax 3251028; e-mail russiagb@eguitel.com; Ambassador MIKHAIL VALINSKIY.

Senegal: Rua Omar Torrijos 43A, Bissau; tel. 3212944; fax 3201748; Ambassador Gen. ABDOULAYE DIENG.

South Africa: c/o Bissau Palace Hotel, Rm No. 9, Av. 14 de Novembro, CP 1334, Bissau; tel. 6678910; e-mail bissau@dirco.gov.za; Ambassador LOUIS MNGUNI.

Spain: Praza Dos Hèroes Naçionais; tel. 6722246; fax 3207656; e-mail emb.bissau@maec.es; Ambassador ALFONSO LÓPEZ PERONA.

Judicial System

The judicial system comprises a Supreme Court, a Court of Appeal, nine Regional Courts (of which five are functional) and 42 Sectoral Courts (of which 21 are functional). The Supreme Court is the final court of appeal in criminal and civil cases and consists of nine judges. The Regional Courts are courts of first instance and deal with felony cases and major civil cases. They also hear appeals from the Sectoral Courts. The Sectoral Courts hear minor civil cases with maximum fines of 1m. francs CFA and criminal cases punishable by sentences of up to three years' imprisonment. There are plans to establish a second Court of Appeal in Bafatá and other Regional and Sectoral Courts envisaged by law.

Supreme Court (Supremo Tribunal de Justiça): Rua Guerra Mendes, CP 341, Bissau; tel. 3211003; fax 3201365; Pres. PAULO SANHA.

Attorney-General of the Republic: ABDÚ MANÉ.

Religion

According to the 1991 census, 45.9% of the population were Muslims, 39.7% were animists and 14.4% were Christians, mainly Roman Catholics.

ISLAM

Associação Islâmica Nacional: Bissau; Sec.-Gen. Alhaji ABDÚ BAIO.

Conselho Superior dos Assuntos Islâmicos da Guiné-Bissau (CSAI-GB): Bissau; Exec. Sec. MUSTAFA RACHID DJALÓ.

CHRISTIANITY

The Roman Catholic Church

Guinea-Bissau comprises two dioceses, directly responsible to the Holy See. The Bishops participate in the Episcopal Conference of Senegal, Mauritania, Cape Verde and Guinea-Bissau, currently based in Senegal. Approximately 10% of the total population are adherents of the Roman Catholic Church.

Bishop of Bafatá: Rev. CARLOS PEDRO ZILLI, CP 17, Bafatá; tel. 3411507; e-mail domzilli@yahoo.com.br.

Bishop of Bissau: JOSÉ CÂMNATE NA BISSIGN, Av. 14 de Novembro, CP 20, 1001 Bissau; tel. 3251057; fax 3251058; e-mail diocesebissau@yahoo.it.

The Press

REGULATORY AUTHORITY

Conselho Nacional de Comunicação Social (CNCS): Bissau; f. 1994; dissolved in 2003, recreated in November 2004; Pres. AUGUSTO MENDES.

NEWSPAPERS AND PERIODICALS

Banobero: Rua José Carlos Schwarz, CP 760, Bissau; tel. 3230702; fax 3230705; e-mail banobero@netscape.net; weekly; Dir FERNANDO JORGE PEREIRA.

Comdev Negócios (Community Development Business): Av. Domingos Ramos 21, 1° andar, Bissau; tel. 3215596; f. 2006; independent; business; Editor FRANCELINO CUNHA.

Diário de Bissau: Rua Vitorino Costa 29, Bissau; tel. 3203049; daily; Owner JOÃO DE BARROS.

Expresso de Bissau: Rua Vitorino Costa 30, Bissau; tel. 6666647; e-mail expressobissau@hotmail.com.

Fraskera: Bairro da Ajuda, 1ª fase, CP 698, Bissau; tel. 3253060; fax 3253070; weekly.

Gazeta de Notícias: Av. Caetano Semeao, CP 1433, Bissau; tel. 3254733; e-mail gn@eguitel.com; internet www.gaznot.com; f. 1997; weekly; Dir HUMBERTO MONTEIRO; circ. 1,000.

Journal Nô Pintcha: Av. do Brasil, CP 154, Bissau; tel. 3213713; internet www.jornalnopintcha.com; Dir SRA CABRAL; circ. 6,000.

Kansaré: Edifico Sitec, Rua José Carlos Schwarz, Bissau; e-mail kansare@eguitel.com; internet www.kansare.com; f. 2003; Editor FAFALI KOUDAWO.

Última Hora: Av. Combatentes da Liberdade da Pátria (Prédio Suna Ker), Bissau; tel. 5932236; e-mail damil@portugalmail.com; Dir ATHIZAR PEREIRA; circ: 500.

Voz de Bissau: Rua Eduardo Mondlane, Apdo 155, Bissau; tel. 3202546; twice weekly.

Wandan: Rua António M'Bana 6, CP 760, Bissau; tel. 3201789.

NEWS AGENCY

Agência de Notícias da Guiné-Bissau (ANG): Av. Domingos Ramos, CP 248, Bissau; tel. 2605200; fax 2605256.

Publisher

Ku Si Mon Editora: Bairro d'Ajuda, Rua José Carlos Schwarz, CP 268, Bissau; tel. 6605565; e-mail kusimon@kusimon.com; internet www.kusimon.com; f. 1994; privately owned; Portuguese language; Dir ABDULAI SILA.

Broadcasting and Communications

REGULATORY AUTHORITY

Autoridade Reguladora Nacional das Tecnologias de Informação (ARN): Av. Domingos Ramos 53, Praça Cheguevara, CP 1372, Bissau; tel. 3204874; fax 3204876; e-mail geral@arn-gb.com; internet arn-gb.com; f. 2010 to replace Instituto das Comunicações da Guiné-Bissau; also manages radio spectrum; Pres. GIBRIL MANÉ.

TELECOMMUNICATIONS

In 2011 there was one fixed–line telephone operator (4,844 subscribers) and three mobile telephone operators (793,176 subscribers) in Guinea-Bissau.

Guiné Telecom (GT): Bissau; tel. 3202427; internet www.gtelecom.gw; f. 2003 to replace the Companhia de Telecomunicações da Guiné-Bissau (Guiné Telecom—f. 1989); state-owned; privatization pending; 4,844 subscribers (2011).

Guinetel: Bissau; f. 2003; mobile operator; CEO JOÃO FREDERICO DE BARROS; 104,749 subscribers (2011).

MTN Guinea Bissau: 7 Av. Unidade Africana, CP 672, Bissau; tel. 3207000; fax 6600111; e-mail contact@mtn-bissau.com; internet www.mtn-bissau.com; f. 2007; mobile operator; CEO ANTHONY MASOZERA; 110 employees; 443,750 subscribers (2011).

Orange Bissau: Praça dos Herois Nacionais, BP 1087, Bissau; tel. 5603030; e-mail abdul.dapiedadeTMP@orange-sonatel.com; internet orange-bissau.com; f. 2007; mobile operator; 244,677 (subscribers 2011).

RADIO AND TELEVISION

Radiodifusão Nacional da República da Guiné-Bissau (RDN): Av. Domingos Ramos, Praça dos Martires de Pindjiguiti, CP 191, Bissau; tel. 3212426; fax 3253070; e-mail rdn@eguitel.com; f. 1974; govt-owned; broadcasts in Portuguese on short-wave, MW and FM; Dir-Gen. LAMINE DJATA.

Rádio Bafatá: CP 57, Bafatá; tel. 3411185.

Rádio Bombolom: Bairro Cupelon, CP 877, Bissau; tel. 3201095; f. 1996; independent; Dir AGNELO REGALA.

Rádio Jovem: Bairro de Ajuda, Bissau; internet www.radiojovem.info.

Rádio Mavegro: Rua Eduardo Mondlane, CP 100, Bissau; tel. 3201216; fax 3201265.

Rádio Pindjiguiti: Bairro da Ajuda, 1ª fase, CP 698, Bissau; tel. 3253070; f. 1995; independent.

Televisão da Guiné-Bissau (TGB): Bairro de Luanda, CP 178, Bissau; tel. 3221920; fax 3221941; internet www.televisao-gb.net; f. 1997; Dir-Gen. LUÍS DOMINGOS CAMARÁ DE BARROS.

Finance

(cap. = capital; res = reserves; dep. = deposits; m. = million; amounts in francs CFA)

BANKING

Central Bank

Banque Centrale des Etats de l'Afrique de l'Ouest (BCEAO): Av. dos Combatentes da Liberdade da Pátria, Brá, CP 38, Bissau; tel. 3256325; fax 3256300; internet www.bceao.int; HQ in Dakar, Senegal; f. 1955; bank of issue for the mem. states of the Union Economique et Monétaire Ouest-Africaine (UEMOA, comprising Benin, Burkina Faso, Côte d'Ivoire, Guinea-Bissau, Mali, Niger, Senegal and Togo); cap. 134,120m., res 1,474,195m., dep. 2,124,051m. (Dec. 2009); Gov. KONÉ TIÉMOKO MEYLIET; Dir in Guinea-Bissau JOÃO ALAGE MAMADU FADIA.

Other Banks

Banco da África Ocidental, SARL: Rua Guerra Mendes 18, CP 1360, Bissau; tel. 3203418; fax 3203412; e-mail bao-info@eguitel.com; internet bancodaafricaocidental.com; f. 2000; 15% owned by International Finance Corporation, 15% Grupo Montepio Geral (Portugal), 15% Carlos Gomes Júnior; cap. and res 1,883m. (Dec. 2003); Chair. ABDOOL VAKIL; Man. Dir RÓMULO PIRES.

Banco Regional de Solidariedade: Rua Justino Lopes 70, Bissau; tel. 3207112; fax 3207113; e-mail zcassama@yahoo.fr; Man. Dir ZENAIDA MARIA LOPES CASSAMA.

Banco da União (BDU): Av. Domingos Ramos 3, CP 874, Bissau; tel. 3207160; fax 3207161; e-mail info@bdu-sa.com; internet www.bdu-sa.com; f. 2005; 30% owned by Banque de Développement du Mali; CEO HUGO DOS REIS BORGES.

Caixa de Crédito da Guiné: Bissau; govt savings and loan institution.

Caixa Económica Postal: Av. Amílcar Cabral, Bissau; tel. 3212999; postal savings institution.

Ecobank Guinea-Bissau: Av. Amílcar Cabral, BP 126, Bissau; tel. 3207360; fax 3207363; e-mail info@ecobankgw.com; Chair. JOÃO JOSÉ SILVA MONTEIRO; Man. Dir GILLES GUERARD.

STOCK EXCHANGE

In 1998 a regional stock exchange, the Bourse Régionale des Valeurs Mobilières, was established in Abidjan, Côte d'Ivoire, to serve the member states of the UEMOA.

INSURANCE

GUINEBIS—Guiné-Bissau Seguros: Rua Dr Severino Gomes de Pina 36, Bissau; tel. 3211458; fax 3201197.

Instituto Nacional de Previdência Social: Av. Domingos Ramos 12, CP 62, Bissau; tel. and fax 3211331; fax 3204396; e-mail inps_informatica@hotmail.com; internet www.inps-gb.com; state-owned; Dir-Gen. MAMADU IAIA DJALÓ.

NSIA Assurances: Bissau; tel. 5803131; e-mail amadou.thiam@groupensia.com; Dir-Gen. AMADOU THIAM.

Trade and Industry

DEVELOPMENT ORGANIZATION

Ajuda de Desenvolvimento de Povo para Povo ná Guiné Bissau (ADPP): CP 420, Bissau; tel. 6853323; e-mail adppartemisa@eguitel.com.

CHAMBER OF COMMERCE

Câmara de Comércio, Indústria, Agricultura e Serviços da Guiné-Bissau (CCIAS): Av. Amílcar Cabral 7, CP 361, Bissau; tel. 3212844; fax 3201602; f. 1987; Pres. BRAIMA CAMARÁ; Sec.-Gen. SALIU BA.

INDUSTRIAL AND TRADE ASSOCIATIONS

Associação Comercial, Industrial e Agricola (ACIA): CP 88, Bissau; tel. 3222276.

Direcção de Promoção do Investimento Privado (DPIP): Rua 12 de Setembro, Bissau Velho, CP 1276, Bissau; tel. 3205156; fax 3203181; e-mail dpip@mail.bissau.net.

Fundaçao Guineense para o Desenvolvimento Empresarial Industrial (FUNDEI): Rua Gen. Omar Torrijos 49, Bissau; tel. 3202470; fax 3202209; e-mail fundei@fundei.bissau.net; internet www.fundei.net; f. 1994; industrial devt org.; Pres. MACÁRIA BARAI.

Procajú: Bissau; private sector association of cashew producers.

UTILITIES

Gas

Empresa Nacional de Importação e Distribuição de Gás Butano: CP 269, Bissau; state gas distributor.

TRADE UNIONS

Confederação Geral dos Sindicatos Independentes da Guiné-Bissau (CGSI-GB): Rua nº10, Bissau Apartado 693, Bissau; tel. 3204110; fax 3204114; e-mail cgsi-gb@hotmail.com; internet www.lgdh.org/CONFEDERACAOGERALDOSSINDICATOSINDEPENDENTES.htm; Sec.-Gen. FILOMENO CABRAL.

União Nacional dos Trabalhadores da Guiné (UNTG): 13 Av. Ovai di Vievra, CP 98, Bissau; tel. and fax 3207138; e-mail untgcs.gb@hotmail.com; Pres. DESEJADO LIMA DA COSTA; Sec.-Gen. ESTÊVÃO GOMES CÓ.

Transport

RAILWAYS

There are no railways in Guinea-Bissau. However, the proposed construction of a railway line by Bauxite Angola, linking the bauxite extraction site in Boé with the future deep-water port at Buba, was announced in 2008. These plans were put on hold following the coup in April 2012.

ROADS

According to the Ministry of Infrastructure, there are 2,755 km of 'classified' roads in Guinea-Bissau, of which 770 km are paved. There are plans in place for a further 300 km to be paved by 2020.

SHIPPING

Plans have been announced to build a major deep-water port at Buba, the capacity of which will make it one of the largest in West Africa. However, following the coup in April 2012, these plans were postponed. At 31 December 2013 the flag registered fleet comprised 12 vessels, totalling 2,903 grt.

Empresa Nacional de Agências e Transportes Marítimos: Rua Guerva Mendes 4–4A, CP 244, Bissau; tel. 3212675; fax 3213023; state shipping agency; Dir-Gen. M. LOPES.

CIVIL AVIATION

There is an international airport at Bissau, which there are plans to expand, and 10 smaller airports serving the interior. TAP Portugal, Senegal Airlines, Royal Air Maroc and Transportes Aéreos de Cabo Verde (TACV) fly to Bissau.

Tourism

There were 30,092 tourist arrivals in 2007. Receipts from tourism totalled US $38.2m. in 2008.

Central de Informação e Turismo: CP 294, Bissau; tel. 3213905; state tourism and information service.

Direcção Geral do Turismo: CP 1024, Bissau; tel. 3202195; fax 3204441.

Defence

As assessed at November 2013, the armed forces officially totalled an estimated 4,450 men (army 4,000, navy 350, air force 100), and there was a paramilitary gendarmerie of 2,000 men. Military service was made compulsory from 2007, as part of a programme of reform for the armed forces. Following the seizure of power by the military in April 2012 the ECOWAS Mission in Guinea-Bissau (ECOMIB), comprising 629 security personnel, was deployed in May. ECOMIB's mandate was formalized and extended for a further six months in November 2012. In July 2013 the mission's mandate was renewed until May 2014.

Defence Expenditure: Budgeted at 13,000m. francs CFA in 2012.

Chief of Staff of the Armed Forces: Gen. ANTÓNIO INDJAI.

Army Chief of Staff: Gen. AUGUSTO MÁRIO CÓ.

Navy Chief of Staff: Capt. SANHA CLUSSÉ (acting).

Chief of Staff of the Air Force: Brig.-Gen. IBRAIMA PAPÁ CAMARA.

Education

Education is officially compulsory only for the period of primary schooling, which begins at six years of age and lasts for seven years. Secondary education, beginning at the age of 13, lasts for up to five years (a first cycle of three years and a second of two years). According to UNESCO estimates, in 2010 enrolment at primary schools included 70% of children in the relevant age-group (males 71%; females 68%), while enrolment at secondary schools in 2006 was equivalent to only 34% of children in the relevant age-group. In 2000/01 473 students were enrolled in tertiary education. There are three tertiary level institutions in Guinea-Bissau: the Universidade Amílcar Cabral (public); the Universidade Colinas do Boé (private); and the Faculdade de Direito de Bissau (a law school funded and run within the ambit of Portuguese co-operation). According to the 2005 budget, expenditure on education was forecast at 15.0% of total spending.

GUYANA

Introductory Survey

LOCATION, CLIMATE, LANGUAGE, RELIGION, FLAG, CAPITAL

The Co-operative Republic of Guyana lies on the north coast of South America, between Venezuela to the west and Suriname to the east, with Brazil to the south. The narrow coastal belt has a moderate climate with two wet seasons, from April to August and from November to January, alternating with two dry seasons. Inland, there are tropical forests and savannah, and the dry season lasts from September to May. The average annual temperature is 27°C (80°F), with average rainfall of 1,520 mm (60 ins) per year inland, rising to between 2,030 mm (80 ins) and 2,540 mm (100 ins) on the coast. English is the official language but Hindi, Urdu and Amerindian dialects are also spoken. The principal religions are Christianity (which is professed by about 50% of the population), Hinduism (about 28%) and Islam (7%). The national flag (proportions 3 by 5 when flown on land, but 1 by 2 at sea) is green, with a white-bordered yellow triangle (apex at the edge of the fly) on which is superimposed a black-bordered red triangle (apex in the centre). The capital is Georgetown.

CONTEMPORARY POLITICAL HISTORY

Historical Context

Guyana was formerly British Guiana, a colony of the United Kingdom, formed in 1831 from territories finally ceded to Britain by the Dutch in 1814. A new Constitution, providing for universal adult suffrage, was introduced in 1953. The elections of April 1953 were won by the left-wing People's Progressive Party (PPP), led by Dr Cheddi Bharat Jagan. In October, however, the British Government, claiming that a communist dictatorship was threatened, suspended the Constitution. An interim administration was appointed. The PPP split in 1955, and in 1957 a number of former members founded a new party, the People's National Congress (PNC), under the leadership of Forbes Burnham. The PNC drew its support mainly from the African-descended population, while PPP support came largely from the Asian-descended 'East' Indian community.

Domestic Political Affairs

A revised Constitution was introduced in December 1956 and an election was held in August 1957. The PPP won and Jagan became Chief Minister. Another Constitution, providing for internal self-government, was adopted in July 1961. The PPP won an election in August and Jagan was appointed premier. In the election of December 1964, held under the system of proportional representation, the PPP won the largest number of seats in the Legislative Assembly, but not a majority. A coalition Government was formed by the PNC and The United Force (TUF), with Burnham as Prime Minister. This coalition led the colony to independence, as Guyana, on 26 May 1966.

The PNC won elections in 1968 and in 1973, although the results of the latter, and every poll thenceforth until the defeat of the PNC in 1992, were disputed by the opposition parties. Guyana became a co-operative republic on 23 February 1970, and Arthur Chung was elected non-executive President in March. In 1976 the PPP, which had boycotted the National Assembly since 1973, offered the Government its 'critical support'. Following a referendum in July 1978 that gave the Assembly power to amend the Constitution, elections to the Assembly were postponed. The legislature assumed the role of a constituent assembly, established in November 1978, to draft a new constitution. In October 1980 Forbes Burnham declared himself executive President of Guyana, and a new Constitution was promulgated.

Internal opposition to the PNC Government increased after the assassination in 1980 of Walter Rodney, leader of the Working People's Alliance (WPA). The Government was widely believed to have been involved in the incident. All opposition parties except the PPP and TUF boycotted the December 1980 elections to the National Assembly. The PNC received 78% of the votes, according to official results, although allegations of substantial electoral malpractice were made, both within the country and by international observers. None the less, Burnham was inaugurated as President in January 1981.

In 1981 arrests and trials of opposition leaders continued, and in 1982 the Government's relations with human rights groups, and especially the Christian churches, deteriorated further. Editors of opposition newspapers were threatened, political violence increased, and the Government was accused of interference in the legal process. Industrial unrest and public discontent continued in 1983 and 1984, as Guyana's worsening economic situation increased opposition to the Government, and led to growing disaffection within the trade union movement and the PNC.

Burnham died in August 1985 and was succeeded as President by Desmond Hoyte, hitherto the First Vice-President and Prime Minister. The PNC won the December election, although opposition groups, including the PPP and WPA, denounced the poll as fraudulent. In 1986 five of the six opposition parties formed the Patriotic Coalition for Democracy (PCD).

Outside the formal opposition of the political parties, the Government also experienced pressure from members of the Guyana Human Rights Association, business leaders and prominent religious figures. This culminated, in 1990, in the formation of a movement for legal and constitutional change, Guyanese Action for Reform and Democracy (Guard), which initiated a series of mass protests, urging the Government to accelerate the process of democratic reform. To counter this civic movement, the PNC began mobilizing its own newly established Committees to Re-elect the President (Creeps). Guard accused the Creeps of orchestrating violent clashes at Guard rallies, and of fomenting racial unrest in the country in an attempt to regain support from the Afro-Guyanese population.

In January 1991 the date of the forthcoming general election was postponed, following the approval of legislation extending the term of office of the National Assembly by two months after its official dissolution date. In March a further two-month extension provoked the resignation of TUF and PPP members from the National Assembly (WPA members had resigned a month earlier). Similar extensions followed in May and July, owing to alleged continuing electoral reform problems. The National Assembly was finally dissolved in late September. The publication of a revised electoral register in that month, however, revealed widespread inaccuracies, including the omission of an estimated 100,000 eligible voters. In November several opposition parties announced a boycott of the general election, which had been rescheduled for mid-December. However, on 28 November Hoyte declared a state of emergency (subsequently extended until June 1992) in order to legitimize a further postponement of the poll. A further revised electoral register was approved by the Elections Commission in August 1992. The election finally took place on 5 October and resulted in a narrow victory for the PPP in alliance with the Civic alliance (a social and political movement of businessmen and professionals). The result, which signified an end to the PNC's 28-year period in government, provoked riots by the mainly Afro-Guyanese PNC supporters in Georgetown. However, international observers were satisfied that the elections had been fairly conducted, and Dr Cheddi Bharat Jagan took office as President. Jagan appointed Samuel Hinds, an industrialist who was not a member of the PPP, as Prime Minister.

In August 1995 a serious environmental incident resulted in the temporary closure of Omai Gold Mines Ltd (OGML). The company, which began production in the Omai District of Essequibo province in 1993, was responsible for an increase of some 400% in Guyana's gold production in subsequent years and was Guyana's largest foreign investor. However, a breach in a reservoir where residue from the gold extraction process was stored resulted in the spillage of some 3.5m. cu m of cyanide-tainted water, of which a large volume flowed into the Omai river, a tributary of the Essequibo river. OGML resumed operations in 1996 following the implementation of government-approved environmental safeguards.

In March 1997, following the death of Jagan, Prime Minister Hinds succeeded to the presidency, in accordance with the provisions of the Constitution. Hinds appointed Janet Jagan, the widow of the former President, to the post of Prime Minister. Following the PPP/Civic's success in the December general election, Jagan, who was that alliance's nominee, was inaugurated as President.

In January 1998 the Government accepted a proposal by private sector leaders for an international audit of the election to be conducted. However, the PNC rejected the proposal and demanded instead the holding of fresh elections. In mid-January the Chief Justice ruled that it was beyond the jurisdiction of the High Court to prohibit Jagan from exercising her presidential functions pending a judicial review of the election. The ruling provoked serious disturbances in Georgetown. Public protests by PNC supporters continued in defiance of a ban on demonstrations in the capital. However, following mediation by a three-member Caribbean Community and Common Market (CARICOM) commission, it was announced that an accord (the Herdmanston Agreement) had been signed by Jagan and Hoyte, which provided for the organization of fresh elections within 36 months and the creation of a constitutional commission to make recommendations on constitutional reform, subsequently to be submitted to a national referendum and a legislative vote. The agreement also made provision for an independent audit of the December 1997 election. In June 1998 the CARICOM commission upheld the published results of the December poll.

In January 1999 a 20-member Constitutional Reform Commission was established, comprising representatives of the country's principal political parties and community groups. The Commission's report included proposals (submitted by the PPP/Civic alliance) that the country should be renamed the Republic of Guyana, that the President should be limited to two consecutive terms of office, and that the President should no longer be empowered to dissolve the National Assembly should he/she be censured by the Assembly. The Commission further proposed that the President should no longer have the power to dismiss a public officer in the public interest, and the President and Cabinet should be collectively responsible to the National Assembly and should resign if defeated in a vote of no confidence.

President Jagan retired in August 1999. She was replaced by the erstwhile Minister of Finance, Bharrat Jagdeo. The appointment of Jagdeo, whose relative youth (he was 35 years of age), reported willingness to reach across the political divide, and strong background in economics all contributed to his popularity, was widely welcomed in Guyana and by the international community.

The general and regional elections of March 2001 were preceded by demonstrations over the late distribution of voter identification cards. The PPP/Civic obtained a majority in the National Assembly, with 34 seats, while the PNC (which contested the elections as the PNCReform) won 27 seats. Some 90% of the registered electorate participated. International observers declared the elections to be generally free and fair. Despite continued allegations of irregularities by the PNCReform, Jagdeo was inaugurated for a second term as President at the end of the month.

A period of social unrest, accompanied by a high incidence of violent crime, began in 2002, as a result of ongoing hostilities between the Government and opposition. During that period large numbers of people were killed or 'disappeared'. The disorder culminated in July in an attack by opposition protesters on the presidential offices during a meeting of CARICOM heads of government. The security forces opened fire on the protesters, killing two and wounding 15. While condemning the violence, the PNCReform leadership announced their support for the demonstrators' grievances of racial discrimination and police brutality.

Robert Corbin was elected leader of the PNCReform in February 2003 following the unexpected death of Hoyte. Corbin pledged a policy of 'constructive engagement' with the PPP and in May 2003 Jagdeo and Corbin signed an agreement on a number of issues, including local government reform and opposition representation on state bodies, particularly the government-owned media. In the same month the PNCReform ended its boycott of the National Assembly. Progress was slow and acrimonious throughout the year; none the less, in December agreement was reached by the two parties on the establishment of four constitutional commissions to oversee reform of the judiciary, the police, the civil service and the teaching sector.

Crime, in particular violent crime, continued to increase under Jagdeo's presidency. Following an increase in the number of abductions in early 2003, the National Assembly approved legislation to extend the terms of imprisonment for those convicted of kidnap. In December a parliamentary report referred to the possible existence of a clandestine, government-run paramilitary group. It was claimed that the group targeted suspected criminals and persons linked to known criminals. The allegations were supported in the following month by George Bacchus, who claimed he had been an informant for the so-called 'death squad', which had been allegedly responsible for more than 40 extra-judicial killings in 2003. Bacchus alleged that the Minister of Home Affairs, Ronald Gajraj, had orchestrated the group's operations. In May 2004 a three-member commission was appointed to investigate the allegations. However, on 24 June, the day that he was scheduled to testify before the commission, Bacchus was killed. In April 2005 a Presidential Commission of Inquiry cleared Gajraj of involvement in the activities of the 'death squads'. He was immediately reinstated to his cabinet post; however, following international pressure and vociferous criticism from the opposition PNCReform, at the end of the month Gajraj resigned.

The problem of violent crime remained a pressing concern in the months preceding the general election of August 2006 and was brought into dramatic focus in April when Minister of Agriculture Satyadeow Sawh was shot dead at his home.

The re-election of Jagdeo

The PPP/Civic secured a comfortable victory at the general election on 28 August 2006. The party increased its representation in the National Assembly to 36 seats, while the People's National Congress Reform-One Guyana (PNCR-1G, as PNCReform had been restyled) obtained 22 seats. The recently formed Alliance for Change (AFC) won five seats. The rate of voter participation, at 69%, was the lowest since independence. Jagdeo made nine new ministerial appointments, and appointed two ministers to each of the Ministries of Finance, Health and Education.

A series of strikes, reportedly involving up to 10,000 sugar industry workers, were organized during 2010 by the Guyana Agricultural and General Workers' Union (GAWU) to demand a 15% pay increase from the state-owned Guyana Sugar Corpn (GuySuCo). Following negotiations between GAWU and GuySuCo, in December sugar workers accepted 5% pay rise.

In December 2010 the National Assembly adopted legislation to postpone the local elections (due since 1997) for another year. Jagdeo argued that the state lacked the resources necessary to organize local elections, and blamed the opposition, holding them responsible for a lack of progress on local government reform—a prerequisite for the staging of fresh local elections. By early 2014 local elections had still not been held; in early March a joint statement was issued by foreign embassies in the country and civil society and legal organizations urging all political parties in Guyana to co-operate in holding local elections by 1 August.

Ramotar in office

The PPP/Civic secured a narrow victory and its fifth consecutive win at the general election of 28 November 2011. However, the party lost its overall majority in the National Assembly, securing 32 seats (four fewer than in the previous parliament). It garnered 48.6% of votes cast, while A Partnership for National Unity (APNU)—the coalition of opposition parties comprising the PNCR, the Guyana Action Party, the National Front Alliance and the Working People's Alliance, formed to contest the elections—obtained 26 seats and 40.8% of the ballot. The AFC won seven seats, with 10.3% of the votes cast. The rate of voter participation was 73%.

As Jagdeo was constitutionally prohibited from seeking a third term in office, the PPP/Civic's candidate was party Secretary-General Donald Ramotar. Ramotar was inaugurated as President on 3 December 2011. Given that the PPP/Civic would be forming a minority government (the first of its kind in Guyana), Ramotar emphasized the importance of national unity and co-operation. However, the new administration included only PPP/Civic members and remained largely unchanged from the previous administration. Significantly, the President created a new ministry—of Natural Resources and the Environment—to which he appointed former agriculture minister Robert Persaud.

Opposition supporters protested against the election results, leading to the police firing rubber bullets and injuring some demonstrators in the capital on 6 December 2011. Granger alleged irregularities in the election process, while the APNU called on the Chairman of the Guyana Elections Commission and the Chief Elections Officer to resign for failing to release the preliminary results on the day after the ballot, despite earlier pledges.

The two main opposition parties obtained a combined one-seat majority of one seat over the PPP/Civic, so they were able to control the legislative branch of government. Thus, in January 2012 AFC leader Raphael Trotman was installed as parliamentary Speaker. In April the opposition used their majority to reject the Government's proposed budget and to approve one with significantly lower levels of expenditure.

In July 2012 demonstrations took place in Linden, Guyana's second largest town, against the Government's decision to remove electricity subsidies, which was to result in increases of up to 300% in residents' bills. In clashes with police three protesters were shot dead and some 20 injured. On 31 July the National Assembly passed a vote of no confidence in the home affairs minister, Clement Rohee. Despite an agreement to reverse the proposed cuts, disturbances continued and led to the temporary suspension of bauxite production in the area, as roads remained blocked. The Government accused the opposition of prolonging the unrest in the area, which has strategic border crossings with Brazil, in an attempt to destabilize the administration. The final report of a Commission of Inquiry into the Linden shootings was issued in March 2013. It concluded that the police were responsible for the deaths of the three protesters, but also found that the use of firearms was justified and the event's organizers were also to blame.

Increasing animosity between the Government and the opposition during 2012 culminated in December in the submission of a government document to the Organization of American States (OAS), which warned of the threat of political instability to the country by the opposition's 'consistent undermining and subversion of parliamentary democracy'. It accused the opposition of using its one-seat majority to subvert a number of parliamentary conventions, such as the selection of committee members and appointments to key parliamentary positions, including Speaker and Deputy Speaker. The Government also repeated the assertion that the opposition leader David Granger was exploiting long-standing racial divisions within the country for political purposes.

Recent developments: the opposition wields its majority

In June 2013 it was announced that a deadline set by the Caribbean Financial Action Task Force (CFATF) for Guyana to conform to international anti-money laundering standards had been moved back to November, following the Government's failure to win majority support for its Anti-Money Laundering and Countering Financing of Terror Bill by the original deadline of 27 May. The opposition-dominated National Assembly also failed to pass four bills presented by Clement Rohee, having pledged never to support any proposed legislation from the home affairs ministry while he remained in office. In July the Government rejected a report on human trafficking by the US Department of State, declaring it to be 'riddled with fabrication'.

Guyana was accused by the CFATF on 20 November 2013 of not having taken sufficient measures to improve its compliance with international standards, following the defeat of the anti-money laundering legislation earlier that month. The opposition had prevented the law from being approved because the amendments that they had demanded had not been included in the final version. The proposed changes included the establishment of a Public Procurement Commission and the granting of increased powers to the country's Financial Intelligence Unit to monitor implementation of the legislation. While Minister of Finance Ashni Singh warned that the country's credibility in the international community could be severely damaged if the law was not passed, the CFATF advised its members to consider implementing countermeasures to protect their own financial system from the risks emanating from Guyana. On 20 December a new select committee was appointed with the aim of expediting the passage of the bill by February 2014. In mid-February the Financial Action Task Force (based in Paris, France) decided against blacklisting Guyana because the failure of the legislation was not the fault of the Government. However, a revised deadline of May was imposed.

In October 2013 the Cabinet rejected a Leadership and Democracy Project worth US $13.1m. to be funded by the US Agency for International Development. However, it was subsequently reported that aspects of the project were none the less being implemented, a move that was described by the head of the Presidential Secretariat as an affront to Guyana's sovereignty. On 23 January 2014 the Minister of Local Government and Regional Development, Ganga Persaud, resigned citing personal reasons.

Foreign Affairs

Regional relations

Guyana has been involved in long-running border disputes with Venezuela and Suriname. Following the restoration of diplomatic links with Suriname in 1979 relations improved as a result of increased trade between the countries. However, in 2000 Suriname formally claimed that Guyana had violated its territorial integrity by granting a concession to a Canadian company to explore for petroleum and gas. Negotiations to settle the dispute ended inconclusively, so in January 2002 the Presidents of the two countries met to discuss the possibility of a production-sharing agreement. However, in June the Surinamese navy forcibly ejected a rig that had been authorized by Guyana to drill in waters disputed by the two countries. Guyana referred the dispute to arbitration at the UN's International Tribunal for the Law of the Sea (ITLOS), in Hamburg, Germany, and in 2007 the Tribunal ruled in favour of Guyana, granting sovereignty over 33,152 sq km (12,800 sq miles) of coastal waters; Suriname was awarded 17,891 sq km (6,900 sq miles).

In October 2008 the seizure by the Surinamese military of a Guyanese ship provoked serious confrontation between the two countries. The ship, had been transporting sugar up the Corentyne river and was detained for allegedly entering Suriname illegally. The ship and its crew were eventually released after payment of a small fine. In September 2010 Jagdeo and new Surinamese President Desiré (Desi) Bouterse agreed to put aside any unresolved border issues and concentrate instead on enhancing bilateral co-operation in trade and security. In August 2012 foreign ministers from the two countries agreed to seek finance from the Inter-American Development Bank for a feasibility study of the construction of a bridge across the Corentyne river. In a further display of co-operation the two countries agreed to establish a joint border security committee in an attempt to deter cross-border crime, particularly that associated with the smuggling of gold. In December 2013 the announcement that Guyana had granted permission for a Brazilian company to conduct a geological and geographical survey of a disputed area, the New River Triangle (or Tigri, as it is known in Suriname), provoked a heightening of nationalist sentiment in both countries, although the two Governments remained silent on the issue.

In 1962 Venezuela renewed its claim to 130,000 sq km (50,000 sq miles) of land west of the Essequibo river (nearly two-thirds of Guyanese territory). The area was accorded to Guyana in 1899 by an international tribunal, but Venezuela based its claim on a papal bull of 1493. The Port of Spain Protocol of 1970 put the issue in abeyance until 1982. Guyana and Venezuela referred the dispute to the UN in 1983, and in 1989 the two countries agreed to a mutually acceptable intermediary. In 1999 Guyana and Venezuela established a joint commission, intended to expedite the resolution of the territorial dispute and to promote mutual co-operation. However, in October President Hugo Chávez of Venezuela, announced his Government's intention to reopen its claim to the territory. In 2004 Chávez visited Guyana and met President Jagdeo with the aim of increasing bilateral co-operation, and in the following year Guyana signed the Petrocaribe energy accord with Venezuela, which offered favourable terms on the price of petroleum. Moreover, Guyana was to settle its debt to Venezuela for energy imports by exporting crops such as rice. The agreement began in late 2010.

Relations became strained in 2007 when Guyana accused Venezuelan troops of crossing into its territory and blowing up two gold-mining dredges. The Venezuelan Government subsequently expressed regret for the incident and talks took place between the two countries to establish measures to prevent another military incursion. In mid-2010 Jagdeo and Chávez concluded a number of trade agreements and agreed to restart UN-mediated negotiations on their territorial dispute, which had been in abeyance since 2007.

In September 2011 relations between Guyana and Venezuela were strained further after Guyana applied to the UN to extend its continental shelf by 150 nautical miles (from 200 to 350 miles). (Owing to the long-standing territorial dispute the two countries' maritime boundaries had yet to be defined.) Guyana wanted to extend its underwater shelf to conduct seismic surveys, which could lead to wider access to potential mineral and hydrocarbon deposits. Venezuela objected on two fronts: that Guyana had not informed it of the application beforehand; and that Guyana had claimed that the area of the extension was not under dispute. In

August 2013, following the death of Chávez, new Venezuelan President Nicolas Maduro made an official visit to Guyana during which he expressed a commitment to strengthening ties between the two countries and resolving the territorial dispute. Two months later, however, bilateral relations were strained when the Venezuelan navy intercepted a research vessel conducting a survey of the sea floor on behalf of a US oil company. Although Venezuela claimed that the vessel had entered its territory Guyana declared that it was well within its own exclusive economic zone. Both sides expressed their commitment to reaching agreement by peaceful means and a UN envoy presented a plan to accelerate the resolution of the dispute. None the less it was announced that on 14 November the Guyanese Government had placed its troops on alert after reports that Venezuelan forces might enter Guyanese territory.

Guyana's relations with Brazil continued to improve through trade and military agreements. In 2003 the Government approved a request by the Brazilian authorities for a partial abolition of visas for both countries. A bridge across the Takutu river between the two countries was completed in 2009.

Other external relations

In January 2010 President Jagdeo held talks in Moscow with his Russian counterpart. The negotiations were aimed at furthering political dialogue, as well as extending trade and economic and humanitarian co-operation between the two countries. In the same month Jagdeo made an official visit to Iran during which he signed two co-operation agreements with that country; Iranian officials travelled to Guyana for further discussions later that year.

Guyana was the first CARICOM country to establish diplomatic relations with the People's Republic of China, in 1972. Political and economic co-operation between the two countries culminated in 2004 in the signing of a bilateral investment treaty. In 2010 legislation was passed whereby Chinese nationals who had resided in Guyana for more than seven years would automatically be granted citizenship. In 2012 two agreements were signed that would provide Guyana with a total of US$9.6m. in support from China, in addition to a $130m. concessional loan agreement for the improvement of the country's international airport. In February 2013 the Guyanese Government came under criticism from the APNU after reports that it had agreed to allow the Shanghai Construction Group to employ only Chinese workers on the US $61m. construction of the Marriott Hotel in Georgetown. The announcement was followed by a series of criminal attacks and robberies against the Chinese community in Guyana, prompting an appeal from the Chinese ambassador for positive media coverage regarding the two countries' bilateral relations.

CONSTITUTION AND GOVERNMENT

Guyana became a republic, within the Commonwealth, on 23 February 1970. A new Constitution was promulgated in October 1980, and amended in 1998, 2000 and 2001. Legislative power is held by the unicameral National Assembly, with 65 members elected for five years by universal adult suffrage, on the basis of proportional representation: 40 members are elected from national lists, and a further 25 members are elected from regional constituency lists. Executive power is held by the President, who leads the majority party in the Assembly and holds office for its duration. The President appoints and heads a Cabinet, which includes the Prime Minister, and may include up to four Ministers who are not elected members of the Assembly. The Cabinet is collectively responsible to the National Assembly. Guyana comprises 10 regions.

REGIONAL AND INTERNATIONAL CO-OPERATION

Guyana is a founder member of CARICOM (see p. 223). It was also one of the six founder members of CARICOM's Caribbean Single Market and Economy (CSME), established in 2006. Guyana became a member of the UN in 1966. As a contracting party to the General Agreement on Tariffs and Trade, Guyana joined the World Trade Organization (see p. 434) on its establishment in 1995. The country is a member of the Commonwealth (see p. 236). In 2001 Guyana was one of 11 Caribbean states to sign an agreement establishing a jointly administered regional court. The Caribbean Court of Justice, inaugurated in Trinidad and Tobago in 2005, replaced the Privy Council in the United Kingdom as Guyana's highest appellate body. Guyana also participated in the third meeting of South American Presidents in Cusco, Peru, in 2004, which created the Comunidad Sudamericana de Naciones (South American Community of Nations, which was renamed Unión de Naciones Suramericanas, UNASUR—Union of South American Nations, see p. 469—in 2007), intended to promote greater regional economic integration. In February 2011 Guyana was a signatory to the Caribbean Basin Security Initiative between CARICOM and the USA. The country is also a member of the Community of Latin American and Caribbean States (see p. 464), which was formally inaugurated in December 2011. In July 2013 Guyana (with Suriname) signed a framework agreement to join the Southern Common Market (Mercado Comum do Sul—Mercosul, see p. 429).

ECONOMIC AFFAIRS

In 2012, according to estimates by the World Bank, Guyana's gross national income (GNI), measured at average 2010–12 prices, was US $2,710m., equivalent to US $3,410 per head (or US $3,400 per head on an international purchasing-power parity basis). During 2003–12, it was estimated, the population increased at an average annual rate of 0.6%, while gross domestic product (GDP) per head increased, in real terms, by an average of 1.9% per year. Overall GDP increased, in real terms, at an average annual rate of 4.5% in 2006–12; real GDP increased by 4.8% in 2012.

Agriculture (including forestry and fishing) provided an estimated 20.2% of GDP in 2012 and, according to FAO, employed an estimated 13.4% of the total labour force in mid-2014. The principal cash crops are rice and sugar cane (sugar provided an estimated 9.5% of the value of total domestic exports in 2012). The sugar industry, which accounted for 4.6% of GDP in 2012, was affected by the gradual ending, from 2006, of the European Union's (EU) preferential price regime. In 2009 a US $180m. project, to be jointly financed by the Government, the state sugar company GuySuCo (Guyana Sugar Corpn Inc) and Chinese lenders, to upgrade the Skeldon sugar refinery in Berbice and to construct a 30-MW co-generation facility, was officially inaugurated. Nevertheless, sugar output continued to fall, reaching just 186,807 metric tons in 2013, below the 235,000 tons needed to meet local and EU needs. Vegetables and fruit are cultivated for the local market, and livestock-rearing is being developed. Fishing is also important (particularly shrimp), and accounted for an estimated 2.2% of GDP in 2012. Agricultural production increased by an average annual rate of 1.2% during 2006–12. The sector's GDP increased by 3.7% in 2012.

Timber resources in Guyana are extensive and underdeveloped. In 2012 the forestry sector contributed 2.6% of GDP. About three-quarters of the country's total land area consists of forest and woodland. In 2012 timber shipments provided an estimated 2.8% of total domestic exports. The forestry sector's GDP declined at an average annual rate of 3.4% in 2006–12; the output from the sector decreased by 4.4% in 2012.

Industry (including mining, manufacturing, construction and power) provided an estimated 32.7% of GDP in 2012 and engaged 25.4% of the employed labour force in 2002. Industrial GDP increased at an average annual rate of 3.7% in 2006–12. The sector's GDP increased by 2.6% in 2012.

Mining contributed an estimated 20.5% of GDP in 2012 and employed 4.1% of the total working population in 2002. The registered production of gold accounted for 51.4% of domestic exports in 2012 (compared with 45.8% in the previous year). In 2011 Guyana Goldfields Inc announced it had discovered up to 6m. troy ounces of high-quality gold in Aurora, in the north-west of the country. In 2000 the gold industry was estimated directly to employ some 32,000 people. Bauxite, which is used for the manufacture of aluminium, is also a valuable export. Production fluctuated following the withdrawal in 2002 of the US-based aluminium company Alcoa from the Aroaima bauxite and aluminium mine; nevertheless, in 2011 output increased by 68% and by a further 22% in 2012. In that latter year a total of 2.8m. metric tons of bauxite was exported, generating 10.8% of the total value of exports. There are also some petroleum reserves and significant diamond resources. In 2012 diamond production stood at 40,763 metric carats, compared with 52,273 metric carats in 2011. The GDP of the mining sector was estimated to have increased by an average of 6.3% per year in 2006–12; the sector increased by 14.8% in 2012.

Manufacturing accounted for an estimated 3.4% of GDP in 2012 and, in 2002, employed 13.3% of the total working population. The main activities are the processing of bauxite, sugar, rice and timber. Manufacturing GDP increased at an average annual rate of 2.0% in 2006–12. Output from the sector increased by 2.4% in 2012.

Construction accounted for an estimated 7.5% of GDP in 2012 and, in 2002, employed 7.0% of the total working population. According to official figures, construction GDP (including engineering) increased at an average annual rate of 1.8% in 2006–12. Output from the sector increased by 2.8% in 2011, but decreased by 11.0% in 2012.

Energy requirements are almost entirely met by imported hydrocarbon fuels. In 2012 fuels and lubricants constituted 31.4% of the total value of imports (mainly from Venezuela and Trinidad and Tobago). Guyana was a signatory to the Petrocaribe agreement, under which Venezuela accorded petroleum concessions. Guyana is believed to possess substantial petroleum deposits. In 2014 the Government was exploring the potential of bioenergy production; to this end it signed memorandums of understanding with foreign investors for feasibility studies in 2013.

The services sector contributed an estimated 46.7% of GDP in 2012 and engaged 52.4% of the employed labour force in 2002. The GDP of the services sector increased by an average of 6.5% per year in 2006–12. Services GDP increased, in real terms, by 7.3% in 2012.

In 2012 Guyana recorded a visible merchandise trade deficit of US $581.9m. and a deficit of US $394.8m. on the current account of the balance of payments. In 2012 the principal source of imports was the USA (24.7%), followed by Venezuela, the People's Republic of China and Suriname. Canada was the principal market for exports (35.9% of total exports in 2012), followed by the USA, Venezuela and the United Kingdom. The principal exports in 2012 were gold, rice, bauxite and sugar, and the principal imports were fuel and lubricants, and contractors' plant equipment.

In 2012 the overall budget deficit was an estimated $ G28,427.1m. (equivalent to 4.9% of GDP). Guyana's general government gross debt was $ G342,537m. in 2011, equivalent to 65.2% of GDP. According to World Bank estimates, by the end of 2011 Guyana's external debt totalled US $1,846m., of which US $1,054m. was public and publicly guaranteed debt. In 2010, the cost of servicing long-term public and publicly guaranteed debt and repayments to the IMF was equivalent to 2.7% of the value of exports of goods, services and income (excluding workers' remittances). According to the IMF, the annual rate of inflation averaged 4.6% in 2006–12. Consumer prices increased by some 2.4% in 2012. According to census figures the rate of unemployment in 2002 was 11.7%.

The Guyanese economy's reliance on sugar meant that the gradual withdrawal of the EU's Sugar Protocol in 2009 (combined with the removal of sugar duties in 2008) posed an enormous challenge to the authorities. Financial assistance provided by the EU in 2012, worth some US $40m., was intended for the modernization of sugar production facilities in the country and the revitalization of the industry. However, at the end of 2013 it was announced that sugar production had reached its lowest levels since 1990 as a result of industrial action, mechanical problems and the movement of workers to other sectors, leading to a growing debate about the future of the sugar industry. A source of further concern was the announcement in mid-2013 that the EU would abolish sugar quotas in 2017, three years earlier than agreed by the European Parliament earlier in the year. In mid-2013 the Government reached an agreement with the CARICOM Development Fund that would provide $7.32m. in funding for the country's agricultural sector. Compared with most of its neighbours in the region, Guyana demonstrated an impressive resilience when confronted by the global economic downturn, registering its seventh consecutive year of GDP growth in 2012. Moreover, real GDP growth of 5.3% was estimated for 2013 and the Government predicted growth of 5.6% for 2014, underpinned by rising gold and rice production and renewed services and construction sector expansion. Large infrastructure projects, most notably the Amaila Falls hydroelectric power project, which received finance totalling some $506m. from US and Chinese interests in 2012, were expected to stimulate the economy, although the project suffered a major reverse in August 2013 when the US developer withdrew from the venture, citing the failure of the National Assembly to reach a consensus on financing.

PUBLIC HOLIDAYS

2015: 1 January (New Year's Day), 2 January* (Yum an-Nabi, birth of the Prophet), 23 February (Mashramani, Republic Day), 3 April (Good Friday), 6 April (Easter Monday), 1 May (Labour Day), 5 May (Indian Heritage Day), 2 July (CARICOM Day), 17 July* (Id al-Fitr, end of Ramadan), 3 August (Freedom Day), 23 September* (Id al-Adha, feast of the Sacrifice), 23 December* (Yum an-Nabi, birth of the Prophet), 25–26 December (Christmas).

* These holidays are dependent on the Islamic lunar calendar and may vary by one or two days from the dates given.

In addition, the Hindu festivals of Holi Phagwah (usually in March) and Diwali (October or November) are celebrated. These festivals are dependent on sightings of the moon and their precise date is not known until two months before they take place.

Statistical Survey

(Sources (unless otherwise stated): Bank of Guyana, 1 Church St and Ave of the Republic, POB 1003, Georgetown; tel. 226-3250; fax 227-2965; e-mail communications@bankofguyana.org.gy; internet www.bankofguyana.org.gy; Bureau of Statistics, Ministry of Finance, Main and Urquhart Sts, Georgetown; tel. 227-1114; fax 226-1284; internet www.statisticsguyana.gov.gy.

AREA AND POPULATION

Area: 214,969 sq km (83,000 sq miles).

Population: 723,673 at census of 12 May 1991; 751,223 (males 376,034, females 375,189) at census of 15 September 2002. *2010* (official estimate): 778,099 (males 390,827, females 387,272). *2014* (UN estimate at mid-year): 803,677 (Source: UN, *World Population Prospects: The 2012 Revision*).

Density (at mid-2014): 3.7 per sq km.

Population by Age and Sex (UN estimates at mid-2014): *0–14:* 284,060 (males 149,836, females 134,224); *15–64:* 491,777 (males 248,913, females 242,864); *65 and over:* 27,840 (males 9,517, females 18,323); *Total* 803,677 (males 408,266, females 395,411) (Source: UN, *World Population Prospects: The 2012 Revision*).

Ethnic Groups (at 2002 census): 'East' Indians 326,277; Africans 227,062; Mixed 125,727; Amerindians 68,675; Portuguese 1,497; Chinese 1,396; White 477; Total (incl. others) 751,223.

Regions (population at 2002 census): Barima–Waini 24,275; Pomeroon–Supenaam 49,253; Essequibo Islands–West Demerara 103,061; Demerara–Mahaica 310,320; Mahaica–Berbice 52,428; East Berbice–Corentyne 123,695; Cuyuni–Mazaruni 17,597; Potaro–Siparuni 10,095; Upper Takutu–Upper Essequibo 19,387; Upper Demerara–Berbice 41,112; Total 751,223.

Principal Towns (population at 2002 census): Georgetown (capital) 134,497; Linden 29,298; New Amsterdam 17,033; Corriverton 11,494. *Mid-2011* ('000, incl. suburbs, UN estimate): Georgetown 127 (Source: UN, *World Urbanization Prospects: The 2011 Revision*).

Births, Marriages and Deaths (2010): Birth rate 19.2 per 1,000; Marriages 4,239 (marriage rate 5.4 per 1,000); Deaths 4,649 (death rate 6.4 per 1,000).

Life Expectancy (years at birth): 65.9 (males 63.4; females 68.5) in 2011. Source: World Bank, World Development Indicators database.

Economically Active Population (persons aged 15 years and over, census of 2002): Agriculture, hunting and forestry 45,378; Fishing 5,533; Mining and quarrying 9,374; Manufacturing 30,483; Electricity, gas and water 2,246; Construction 16,100; Trade, repair of motor vehicles and personal and household goods 37,690; Restaurants and hotels 5,558; Transport, storage and communications 16,790; Financial intermediation 3,074; Real estate, renting and business services 7,384; Public administration, defence and social security 14,995; Education 13,015; Health and social work 5,513; Other community, social and personal service activities 9,599; Private households with employed persons 6,156; Extra-territorial organizations and bodies 477; *Sub-total* 229,365; Activities not adequately defined 1,489; *Total employed* 230,854 (males 162,596, females 68,258); Unemployed 30,533; *Total labour force* 261,387 (males 180,946, females 80,441). *2009:* Central government 10,955; Rest of the public sector 17,027; Total public sector employment 27,982. *Mid-2014* ('000, estimates): Agriculture, etc. 48; Total labour force 357 (Source: FAO).

HEALTH AND WELFARE

Key Indicators

Total Fertility Rate (children per woman, 2011): 2.2.

Under-5 Mortality Rate (per 1,000 live births, 2011): 36.

HIV/AIDS (% of persons aged 15–49, 2012): 1.3.

Physicians (per 1,000 head, 2010): 0.2.

Hospital Beds (per 1,000 head, 2009): 2.0.

Health Expenditure (2010): US $ per head (PPP): 194.

Health Expenditure (2010): % of GDP: 5.6.

Health Expenditure (2010): public (% of total): 79.5.

Access to Water (% of persons, 2011): 95.

Access to Sanitation (% of persons, 2011): 84.

Total Carbon Dioxide Emissions ('000 metric tons, 2010): 1,701.5.

Total Carbon Dioxide Emissions Per Head (metric tons, 2010): 2.2.

Human Development Index (2012): ranking: 118.

Human Development Index (2012): value: 0.636.

For sources and definitions, see explanatory note on p. vi.

AGRICULTURE, ETC.

Principal Crops ('000 metric tons, 2012): Rice, paddy 600 (unofficial figure); Cassava (Manioc) 4 (FAO estimate); Sugar cane 2,900 (FAO estimate); Coconuts 80 (FAO estimate); Bananas 7; Plantains 5. *Aggregate Production* ('000 metric tons, may include official, semi-official or estimated data): Total cereals 605.0; Vegetables (incl. melons) 44.4; Fruits (excl. melons) 36.2.

Livestock ('000 head, year ending September 2012, FAO estimates): Horses 2.4; Asses 1.0; Cattle 113; Sheep 131; Pigs 14; Goats 82; Chickens 26,000.

Livestock Products ('000 metric tons, 2012, FAO estimates unless otherwise indicated): Cattle meat 1.9; Sheep meat 0.6; Pig meat 0.8; Chicken meat 30.4; Cows' milk 44.0; Hen eggs 1.1 (unofficial figure).

Forestry ('000 cubic metres, 2012, FAO estimates): *Roundwood Removals:* Sawlogs, veneer logs and logs for sleepers 370, Pulpwood 100, Other industrial wood 17, Fuel wood 843; Total 1,330. *Sawnwood Production:* Total (all broadleaved) 76.

Fishing ('000 metric tons, live weight, 2011): Capture 43.2 (Marine fishes 19.6; Atlantic seabob 19.6; Whitebelly prawn 0.8); Aquaculture 0.3 (FAO estimate); *Total catch* 43.4 (FAO estimate). Note: Figures exclude crocodiles: the number of spectacled caimans caught in 2011 was 28,058.

Source: FAO.

MINING

Production (2012): Bauxite 2,213,972 metric tons; Gold 12,435 kg; Diamonds 40,763 metric carats.

INDUSTRY

Selected Products (2012 unless otherwise indicated): Raw sugar 218,070 metric tons; Rice 422,057 metric tons; Rum 41,700 hl; Beer and stout 155,090 hl; Logs 264,536 cu m; Margarine 2,333 metric tons; Biscuits 1,250,000 kg; Paint 27,448 hl; Electricity 691m. kWh.

FINANCE

Currency and Exchange Rates: 100 cents = 1 Guyana dollar ($ G). *Sterling, US Dollar and Euro Equivalents* (31 December 2013): £1 sterling = $ G339.653; US $1 = $ G206.250; €1 = $ G284.439; $ G1,000 = £2.94 = US $4.85 = €3.52. *Average Exchange Rate* ($ G per US $): 204.018 in 2011; 204.358 in 2012; 205.386 in 2013.

Budget ($ G million, 2012): *Revenue:* Tax revenue 118,333.9 (Income tax 44,357.2; Value-added tax 34,105.6; Trade taxes 12,900.6); Other current revenue 11,055.6; Capital revenue (incl. grants) 13,509.5; Total 142,899.0. *Expenditure:* Current expenditure 114,914.6 (Personnel emoluments 34,793.9; Other goods and services 73,585.2; Interest 6,535.5); Capital expenditure 56,411.5; Total 171,326.1.

International Reserves (US $ million at 31 December 2012): IMF special drawing rights 1.81; Foreign exchange 862.22; *Total* 864.03. Source: IMF, *International Financial Statistics*.

Money Supply ($ G million at 31 December 2012): Currency outside depository corporations 60,107; Transferable deposits 71,948; Other deposits 258,173; *Broad money* 390,228. Source: IMF, *International Financial Statistics*.

Cost of Living (Consumer Price Index; base: 2000 = 100): All items 170.9 in 2009; 177.3 in 2010; 186.1 in 2011. Source: ILO.

Expenditure on the Gross Domestic Product ($ G million at current prices, 2012): Government final consumption expenditure 76,872; Private final consumption expenditure 526,634; Gross capital formation 145,204; *Total domestic expenditure* 748,709; Net imports of goods and services –166,053; *GDP in purchasers' values* 582,657.

Gross Domestic Product by Economic Activity ($ G million at current prices, 2012): Agriculture, forestry and fishing 109,711 (Sugar 24,578); Mining and quarrying 109,027; Manufacturing 18,271; Construction 39,764; Electricity, gas and water 6,437; Wholesale and retail trade 80,477; Transport, storage, information and communications 54,599; Finance and insurance 21,551; Real estate and renting 5,123; Public administration 43,201; Education 17,054; Health and social welfare 7,790; Other services 18,273; *Sub-total* 531,278; *Less* Financial intermediation services indirectly measured 19,942); *Gross value added in basic prices* 511,337; Indirect taxes, less subsidies 71,319; *GDP in purchasers' values* 582,657.

Balance of Payments (US $ million, 2012): Exports of goods f.o.b. 1,395.8; Imports of goods f.o.b. –1,977.7; *Trade balance* –581.9; Services (net) –232.1; *Balance on goods and services* –814.0; Transfers (net) 419.2; *Current balance* –394.8; Capital account (net) 428.5; Net errors and omissions –21.3; *Overall balance* 12.4.

EXTERNAL TRADE

Principal Commodities (US $ million, 2012): *Imports c.i.f.:* Articles of iron and steel 48.9; Contractors plant equipment 99.8; Fuel and lubricants 619.0; Goods and special purpose motor vehicles 42.9; Medicaments including veterinary medicine 40.9; Motor cars 48.6; Telecommunication equipment 38.9; Total (incl. others) 1,969.7. *Exports f.o.b.:* Bauxite 150.8; Sugar 132.1; Rice 196.2; Gold 716.9; Shrimps 48.4; Timber 39.0; Total (incl. others, incl. re-exports) 1,395.7.

Principal Trading Partners (US $ million, 2012): *Imports:* Canada 43.0; China, People's Republic 194.5; Japan 77.9; Suriname 143.8; Trinidad and Tobago 269.4; United Kingdom 48.9; USA 486.0; Venezuela 336.0; Total (incl. others) 1,969.7. *Exports:* Canada 501.3; Germany 60.0; Jamaica 42.7; Trinidad and Tobago 54.8; Ukraine 23.4; United Kingdom 118.8; USA 295.2; Venezuela 145.9; Total (incl. others) 1,395.7.

TRANSPORT

Road Traffic (vehicles in use, 2008): Passenger cars 44,739; Lorries and vans 28,122; Motorcycles and mopeds 37,069. Source: IRF, *World Road Statistics*.

Shipping: *International Sea-borne Freight Traffic* ('000 metric tons, estimates, 1990): Goods loaded 1,730; Goods unloaded 673 (Source: UN, *Monthly Bulletin of Statistics*). *Flag Registered Fleet* (at 31 December 2013): Vessels 60; Total displacement 32,127 grt (Source: Lloyd's List Intelligence—www.lloydslistintelligence.com).

Civil Aviation (traffic on scheduled services, 2001): Kilometres flown (million) 1; Passengers carried ('000) 48; Passenger-km (million) 175; Total ton-km (million) 17 (Source: UN, *Statistical Yearbook*). *2012:* Passengers carried ('000) 247.8 (Source: World Bank, World Development Indicators database).

TOURISM

Tourist Arrivals: 141,281 (USA 76,955) in 2009; 152,000 in 2010; 157,000 in 2011.

Tourism Receipts (US $ million, excl. passenger transport): 59 in 2008, 35 in 2009, 80 in 2010.

Source: World Tourism Organization.

COMMUNICATIONS MEDIA

Telephones (2012): 154,200 main lines in use.

Mobile Cellular Telephones (2012): 547,000 subscribers.

Internet Subscribers (2010): 16,400.

Broadband Subscribers (2012): 29,200.

Source: International Telecommunication Union.

EDUCATION

Pre-primary (2010/11): Institutions 441; Teachers 1,595 (males 7, females 1,588); Students 25,096 (males 12,825, females 12,271).

Primary (2010/11): Institutions 439; Teachers 3,596 (males 430, females 3,166); Students 92,321 (males 47,114, females 45,207).

General Secondary (2010/11): Institutions 109; Teachers 3,078 (males 809, females 2,269); Students 75,116 (males 37,221, females 37,895).

Special Education (2010/11): Institutions 6; Teachers 77 (males 8, females 69); Students 619 (males 397, females 222).

Technical and Vocational (2010/11): Institutions 8; Teachers 289 (males 160, females 129); Students 4,779 (males 2,540, females 2,239).

Teacher Training (2010/11): Institutions 1; Teachers 323 (males 86, females 237); Students 2,001 (males 278, females 1,723).

University (2010/11): Institutions 1; Teachers 473 (males 262, females 211); Students 6,546 (males 2,361, females 4,185).

Private Education (2010/11 unless otherwise indicated): Institutions 58 (2009/10); Teachers 1,112 (males 255, females 857); Students 16,455 (males 8,165, females 8,290).

Source: Ministry of Education.

Pupil-Teacher Ratio (primary education, UNESCO estimate): 24.6 in 2010/11 (Source: UNESCO Institute for Statistics).

Adult Literacy Rate (UNESCO estimates): 85.0% (males 82.4%; females 87.3%) in 2009. Source: UN Development Programme, *Human Development Report*.

Directory

The Government

HEAD OF STATE

President: DONALD RAMOTAR (sworn in 3 December 2011).

CABINET
(April 2014)

The PPP/Civic alliance forms the Government.

Prime Minister and Minister of Parliamentary Affairs and Energy: SAMUEL A. HINDS.
Minister of Foreign Affairs: Dr CAROLYN RODRIGUES-BIRKETT.
Minister of Finance: Dr ASHNI K. SINGH.
Minister of Agriculture: Dr LESLIE RAMSAMMY.
Minister of Amerindian Affairs: PAULINE CAMPBELL-SUKHAI.
Minister of Home Affairs: CLEMENT J. ROHEE.
Minister of Legal Affairs and Attorney-General: ANIL NANDLALL.
Minister of Education: PRIYA DEVI MANICKCHAND.
Minister of Health: Dr BHERI S. RAMSARAN.
Minister of Housing and Water: IRFAAN ALI.
Minister of Labour: Dr NANDA K. GOPAUL.
Minister of Human Services and Social Security: JENNIFER I. M. WEBSTER.
Minister of Local Government and Regional Development: (vacant).
Minister of Public Service: Dr JENNIFER WESTFORD.
Minister of Public Works: BRINDLEY H. R. BENN.
Minister of Culture, Youth and Sport: Dr FRANK C. S. ANTHONY.
Minister of Natural Resources and Environment: ROBERT M. PERSAUD.
Minister of Tourism, Industry and Commerce: IRFAAN ALI (acting).
Head of the Presidential Secretariat: Dr ROGER LUNCHEON.
Minister in the Ministry of Finance: JUAN A. EDGHILL.
Minister in the Ministry of Local Government and Regional Development: NORMAN WHITTAKER.
Minister in the Ministry of Agriculture: ALLI BAKSH.

MINISTRIES

Office of the President: New Garden St, Bourda, Georgetown; tel. 225-7051; fax 226-3395; e-mail opmed@op.gov.gy; internet www.op.gov.gy.

Office of the Prime Minister: Oranapai Towers, Wights Lane, Kingston, Georgetown; tel. 226-6955; fax 226-7573; e-mail opm@networksgy.gy.

Ministry of Agriculture: Regent Rd and Shiv Chanderpaul Dr., POB 1001, Bourda, Georgetown; tel. 227-5049; fax 227-2978; e-mail info@agriculture.gov.gy; internet www.agriculture.gov.gy.

Ministry of Amerindian Affairs: 251–252 Thomas and Quamina Sts, South Cummingsburg, Georgetown; tel. 227-5067; fax 223-1616; e-mail ministryofamerindian@networksgy.com; internet www.amerindian.gov.gy.

Ministry of Culture, Youth and Sport: 71 Main St, North Cummingsburg, Georgetown; tel. 227-7860; fax 225-5067; e-mail mincys@guyana.net.gy; internet www.mcys.gov.gy.

Ministry of Education: 26 Brickdam, Stabroek, POB 1014, Georgetown; tel. 226-3094; fax 225-5570; e-mail moegyweb@yahoo.com; internet www.education.gov.gy.

Ministry of Finance: 49 Main and Urquhart Sts, Kingston, Georgetown; tel. 225-6088; fax 226-1284; e-mail minister@finance.gov.gy; internet www.finance.gov.gy.

Ministry of Foreign Affairs: 254 South Rd and Shiv Chanderpaul Dr., Bourda, Georgetown; tel. 226-1606; fax 225-9192; e-mail minfor@guyana.net.gy; internet www.minfor.gov.gy.

Ministry of Health: Brickdam, Stabroek, Georgetown; tel. 226-5861; fax 225-4505; e-mail moh@sdnp.org.gy; internet www.health.gov.gy.

Ministry of Home Affairs: 6 Brickdam, Stabroek, Georgetown; tel. 225-7270; fax 227-4806; e-mail info@moha.gov.gy; internet moha.gov.gy.

Ministry of Housing and Water: 41 Brickdam and United Nations Pl., Stabroek, Georgetown; tel. 225-7192; fax 227-3455; e-mail minister_housing@yahoo.com; internet www.chpa.gov.gy.

Ministry of Labour, Human Services and Social Security: 1 Water St and Corhill St, Stabroek, Georgetown; tel. 225-0655; fax 227-1308; e-mail psmlhsss@yahoo.com; internet www.mlhsss.gov.gy.

Ministry of Legal Affairs and Office of the Attorney-General: 95 Carmichael St, North Cummingsburg, Georgetown; tel. 226-2616; fax 225-4809; e-mail legalaffairsps@yahoo.com; internet legalaffairs.gov.gy.

Ministry of Local Government and Regional Development: De Winkle Bldg, Fort St, Kingston, Georgetown; tel. 225-8621; fax 226-5070; e-mail mlgrdps@telsnetgy.net.

Ministry of Natural Resources and the Environment: Shiv Chanderpaul Dr., Bourda, Georgetown; tel. 225-5285; fax 223-0969; e-mail minister@nre.gov.gy; internet www.nre.gov.gy.

Ministry of Public Service: 164 Waterloo St, North Cummingsburg, Georgetown; tel. 227-1193; fax 227-2700; e-mail psm@sdnp.org.gy.

Ministry of Public Works: Wights Lane, Kingston, Georgetown; tel. 226-1875; fax 225-6954; e-mail minoth@networksgy.com.

Ministry of Tourism, Industry and Commerce: 229 South Rd, Lacytown, Georgetown; tel. 226-2505; fax 225-9898; e-mail ministry@mintic.gov.gy; internet www.mintic.gov.gy.

President and Legislature

NATIONAL ASSEMBLY

Speaker: RAPHAEL TROTMAN.
Deputy Speaker: DEBORAH BACKER.
Clerk: SHERLOCK ISAACS.

Election, 28 November 2011

Party	% of votes	Seats
People's Progressive Party/Civic	48.6	32
A Partnership for National Unity*	40.8	26
Alliance for Change	10.3	7
The United Force	0.2	—
Total	100.0	65

* A coalition comprising the Guyana Action Party, the National Front Alliance, the People's National Congress Reform and the Working People's Alliance.

Under Guyana's system of proportional representation, the nominated candidate of the party receiving the most number of votes is elected to the presidency. Thus, on 3 December 2011 the candidate of the PPP/Civic alliance, DONALD RAMOTAR, was inaugurated as President.

Election Commission

Guyana Elections Commission (GECOM): 41 High and Cowan Sts, Kingston, Georgetown; tel. 225-0277; fax 226-0924; e-mail gecomfeedback@webworksgy.com; internet www.gecom.org.gy; f. 2000; appointed by the Pres., partly in consultation with the leader of the opposition; Chair. Dr STEVE SURUJBALLY; Chief Elections Officer CALVIN BENN (acting).

Political Organizations

Alliance for Change (AFC): 77 Hadfield St, Werk-en-Rust, Georgetown; tel. 231-8183; fax 225-0455; e-mail office@voteafc.com; internet www.afcguyana.com; f. 2005; Leader KHEMRAJ RAMJATTAN; Chair. NIGEL HUGHES.

Justice For All Party (JFAP): 43 Robb and Wellington Sts, Lacytown, Georgetown; tel. 226-5462; fax 227-3050; e-mail cnsharma@guyana.net.gy; Leader CHANDRANARINE SHARMA.

A Partnership for National Unity (APNU): 121 Regent Rd, Bourda, Georgetown; e-mail info@apnuguyana.com; internet www.apnuguyana.com; f. 2011; fmrly the Jt Opposition of Political Parties (JOPP); presidential candidate Brig.-Gen. (retd) DAVID GRANGER; comprises the following parties:

Guyana Action Party (GAP): Georgetown; Leader EVERALL FRANKLIN.

National Front Alliance: Georgetown; f. 2000; comprises the National Democratic Movt and National Republican Party; Leader KEITH SCOTT; Sec. FIESAL FEROSE ALI.

People's National Congress Reform (PNCR): Congress Pl., Sophia, POB 10330, Georgetown; tel. 225-7852; fax 225-2704; e-mail pnc@guyana-pnc.org; internet www.guyanapnc.org; f. 1957 as People's National Congress following split with the PPP; present name adopted in 2006; Leader ROBERT H. O. CORBIN; Chair. BISHWAISHWAR RAMSAROOP; Gen. Sec. OSCAR E. CLARKE.

Working People's Alliance (WPA): Walter Rodney House, 80 Croal St, Stabroek, Georgetown; tel. and fax 225-3679; originally popular pressure group, became political party 1979; independent Marxist; Collective Leadership Dr CLIVE THOMAS, Dr RUPERT ROOPNARINE.

People's Progressive Party/Civic (PPP/Civic): Freedom House, 41 Robb St, Lacytown, Georgetown; tel. 227-2095; fax 227-2096; e-mail pr@ppp-civic.org; internet www.ppp-civic.org; f. 1950; Marxist-Leninist; Gen. Sec. CLEMENT ROHEE.

The United Force (TUF): Unity House, 95 Robb and New Garden Sts, Bourda, Georgetown; tel. 226-2596; fax 225-2973; f. 1960; right-wing; Leader MANZOOR NADIR; Dep. Leader MICHAEL ANTHONY ABRAHAM.

Diplomatic Representation

EMBASSIES AND HIGH COMMISSIONS IN GUYANA

Brazil: 308 Church St, Queenstown, POB 10489, Georgetown; tel. 225-7970; fax 226-9063; e-mail brasemb@networksgy.com; Ambassador LUIZ GILBERTO SEIXAS DE ANDRADE.

Canada: High and Young Sts, POB 10880, Georgetown; tel. 227-2081; fax 225-8380; e-mail grgtn@international.gc.ca; internet www.canadainternational.gc.ca/guyana; High Commissioner NICOLE GILES.

China, People's Republic: Lot 2, Botanic Gardens, Mandela Ave, Georgetown; tel. 227-1651; fax 225-9228; e-mail prcemb@networksgy.com; internet gy.china-embassy.org/eng; Ambassador ZHANG LIMIN.

Cuba: 46 High St, POB 10268, Kingston, Georgetown; tel. 225-1883; fax 226-1824; e-mail emguyana@networksgy.com; internet www.cubadiplomatica.cu/guyana; Ambassador JULIO CÉSAR GONZÁLES MARCHANTE.

India: 307 Church St, Queenstown, Georgetown; tel. 226-3996; fax 225-7012; e-mail hoc.georgetown@mea.gov.in; internet www.hcigeorgetown.org.gy; High Commissioner PURAN MAL MEENA.

Mexico: 44 Brickdam, Stabroek, Georgetown; tel. 226-3987; fax 226-3722; e-mail mexicoembassygy@gmail.com; internet embamex.sre.gob.mx/guyana; Ambassador FRANCISCO OLGUIN.

Russia: 3 Public Rd, Kitty, Georgetown; tel. 226-9773; fax 227-2975; e-mail embrus.guyana@mail.ru; internet www.guyana.mid.ru; Ambassador NIKOLAY SMIRNOV.

Suriname: 171 Peter Rose and Crown Sts, Queenstown, Georgetown; tel. 226-7844; fax 225-0759; e-mail surnmemb@gol.net.gy; Ambassador NISHA KURBAN-BABU.

United Kingdom: 44 Main St, POB 10849, Georgetown; tel. 226-5881; fax 225-3555; e-mail bhcguyana@networksgy.com; internet ukinguyana.fco.gov.uk; High Commissioner ANDREW AYRE.

USA: 100 Young and Duke Sts, POB 10507, Kingston, Georgetown; tel. 225-4900; fax 225-8497; e-mail usembassy@hotmail.com; internet georgetown.usembassy.gov; Ambassador BRENT HARDT.

Venezuela: 296 Thomas St, South Cummingsburg, Georgetown; tel. 226-1543; fax 225-3241; e-mail embveguy@gol.net.gy; Ambassador REINA MARGARITA ARRATIA DIAZ.

Judicial System

The Judicature of Guyana comprises the Supreme Court of Judicature, which consists of the Court of Appeal and the High Court (both of which are superior courts of record), and a number of Courts of Summary Jurisdiction.

The Court of Appeal consists of the Chancellor as President, the Chief Justice, and such number of Justices of Appeal as may be prescribed by the National Assembly.

The High Court of the Supreme Court consists of the Chief Justice as President of the Court and Puisne Judges. Its jurisdiction is both original and appellate. It has criminal jurisdiction in matters brought before it on indictment. The High Court of the Supreme Court has unlimited jurisdiction in civil matters and exclusive jurisdiction in probate, divorce and admiralty and certain other matters. In April 2005 the Caribbean Court of Justice was inaugurated, in Port of Spain, Trinidad and Tobago, as Guyana's highest court of appeal.

A magistrate has jurisdiction to determine claims where the amount involved does not exceed a certain sum of money, specified by law. Appeal lies to the Full Court.

Chancellor of the Judiciary: CARL SINGH (acting).

Chief Justice: IAN CHANG (acting).

Attorney-General: ANIL NANDLALL.

Religion

CHRISTIANITY

Guyana Council of Churches: 26 Durban St, Lodge, Georgetown; tel. 227-5126; e-mail bishopedghill@hotmail.com; f. 1967 by merger of the Christian Social Council (f. 1937) and the Evangelical Council (f. 1960); 15 mem. churches, 1 assoc. mem.; Chair. Rev. FRANCIS ALLEYNE.

The Anglican Communion

Anglicans in Guyana are adherents of the Church in the Province of the West Indies, comprising eight dioceses. The Archbishop of the Province is the Bishop of the North Eastern Caribbean and Aruba, resident in St John's, Antigua and Barbuda. The diocese of Guyana also includes French Guiana and Suriname. According to the latest available census figures, Anglicans constitute 7% of the population.

Bishop of Guyana: Rt Rev. CORNELL JEROME MOSS, Church House, 49 Barrack St, POB 10949, Georgetown 1; tel. and fax 226-4183; e-mail dioofguy@networksgy.com.

The Baptist Church

Baptist Convention of Guyana: POB 10149, Georgetown; tel. 226-0428; 33 mem. churches, 1,823 mems.

The Lutheran Church

Evangelical Lutheran Church in Guyana: Lutheran Courts, Berbice, POB 40, New Amsterdam; tel. and fax 333-6479; e-mail sjgoolsarran@gmail.com; internet www.elcguyana.org; f. 1947; 13,000 mems; Pres. Rev. MOSES PRASHAD.

The Roman Catholic Church

Guyana comprises the single diocese of Georgetown, suffragan to the archdiocese of Port of Spain, Trinidad and Tobago. According to the 2002 census, some 8% of the population are Roman Catholics. The Bishop participates in the Antilles Episcopal Conference Secretariat, currently based in Port of Spain, Trinidad.

Bishop of Georgetown: FRANCIS DEAN ALLEYNE, Bishop's House, 27 Brickdam, POB 101488, Stabroek, Georgetown; tel. 226-4469; fax 225-8519; e-mail rcbishop@networksgy.com; internet www.rcdiocesegy.org.

Seventh-day Adventists

According to the 2002 census, 5% of the population are Seventh-day Adventists. The Guyana Conference is a member of the Caribbean

Union Conference and comprises two congregations and 137 churches.

Guyana Conference: 222 Peter Rose and Lance Gibbs Sts, Queenstown, POB 10191, Georgetown; tel. 226-3313; fax 223-8142; e-mail info@guyanaconference.org; internet guyanaconference.org; 50,291 mems in 2007; 173 churches in 23 pastoral districts; Pres. Pastor RICHARD JAMES.

Other Christian Churches

According to the 2002 census, 17% of the population are Pentecostal Christians. Other denominations active in Guyana include the African Methodist Episcopal Church, the African Methodist Episcopal Zion Church, the Church of God, the Church of the Nazarene, the Ethiopian Orthodox Church, the Guyana Baptist Mission, the Guyana Congregational Union, the Guyana Presbyterian Church, the Hallelujah Church, the Methodist Church in the Caribbean and the Americas, the Moravian Church, and the Presbytery of Guyana.

HINDUISM

According to the 2002 census, Hindus constitute 28% of the population.

Guyana Hindu Dharmic Sabha (Hindu Religious Centre): 392–393 Ganges St, Prashad Nagar, Demerara-Mahaica; tel. 227-6181; e-mail ghds@ymail.com; f. 1974; Pres. REEPU DAMAN PERSAUD.

ISLAM

Muslims in Guyana comprise 7% of the population, according to the 2002 census.

Central Islamic Organization of Guyana (CIOG): M.Y.O. Bldg, Woolford Ave, Thomas Lands, POB 10245, Georgetown; tel. 225-8654; fax 227-2475; e-mail contact@ciog.org.gy; internet www.ciog.org.gy; Pres. Haji S. M. NASIR; Dir of Education QAYS ARTHUR.

Guyana United Sad'r Islamic Anjuman: 157 Alexander St, Kitty, POB 10715, Georgetown; tel. 226-9620; e-mail khalid@gusia.org; f. 1936; 120,000 mems; Pres. Haji A. HAFIZ RAHAMAN.

BAHÁ'Í FAITH

National Spiritual Assembly: 220 Charlotte St, Bourda, Georgetown; tel. and fax 226-5952; e-mail secretariat@gy.bahai.org; internet gy.bahai.org; incorporated in 1976; National Sec. KALA SEEGOPAUL.

The Press

DAILIES

Guyana Chronicle: 2A Lama Ave, Bel Air Park, POB 11, Georgetown; tel. 227-5204; fax 227-5208; e-mail gm@guyanachronicle.com; internet www.guyanachronicleonline.com; f. 1881; govt-owned; also produces weekly *Sunday Chronicle* (tel. 226-3243); Editor-in-Chief MAHENDRA (MARK) RAMOTAR; circ. 23,000 (weekdays), 43,000 (Sun.).

Guyana Times: 238 Camp and Quamina Sts, Georgetown; tel. 225-5128; fax 225-5134; e-mail news@guyanatimesgy.com; internet www.guyanatimesgy.com; f. 2008; owned by Queen's Atlantic Investment Inc; Editor NIGEL WILLIAMS.

Kaieteur News: 24 Saffon St, Charlestown, Georgetown; tel. 225-8465; fax 225-8473; e-mail kaieteurnews@yahoo.com; internet www.kaieteurnewsonline.com; f. 1994; independent; Editor-in-Chief ADAM HARRIS; Publr GLENN LALL; daily circ. 19,000, Fri. 25,000, Sun. 32,000.

Stabroek News: E1/2 46–47 Robb St, Lacytown, Georgetown; tel. 227-5197; fax 226-2549; e-mail stabroeknews@stabroeknews.com; internet www.stabroeknews.com; f. 1986; also produces weekly *Sunday Stabroek*; liberal independent; Editor-in-Chief ANAND PERSAUD; circ. 14,100 (weekdays), 26,400 (Sun.).

WEEKLIES AND PERIODICALS

The Catholic Standard: 222 South and Wellington Sts, Queenstown, POB 10720, Georgetown; tel. 226-2195; fax 226-2292; e-mail catholicstandardgy@gmail.com; f. 1905; organ of the Roman Catholic church; weekly; Editor COLIN SMITH; circ. 4,000.

The Official Gazette of Guyana: Guyana National Printers Ltd, Lot 1, Public Rd, La Penitence, Georgetown; tel. 226-2616; fax 225-4809; internet www.officialgazette.gov.gy; govt-owned; weekly; circ. 450.

PRESS ASSOCIATION

Guyana Press Association (GPA): 82C Duke St, Kingston, Georgetown; tel. 623-5430; fax 223-6625; e-mail gpaexecutive@gmail.com; f. 1945; affiliated with the Asscn of Caribbean Media Workers; Pres. GORDON MOSELEY.

NEWS AGENCY

Guyana Information Agency: Area B, Homestretch Ave, D'Urban Backlands, Georgetown; tel. 226-6715; fax 226-4003; e-mail gina@gina.gov.gy; internet www.gina.gov.gy; f. 1993; Dir NEAZ SUBHAN.

Publishers

Guyana National Printers Ltd: 1 Public Rd, La Penitence, POB 10256, Greater Georgetown; tel. 225-3623; e-mail gnpl@guyana.net.gy; f. 1939; govt-owned.

Guyana Publications Inc: E 1/2 46–47 Robb St, Lacytown, Georgetown; tel. 226-5197; fax 226-3237; e-mail info@stabroeknews.com; internet www.stabroeknews.com; publrs of *Stabroek News* and *Sunday Stabroek*; Chair. Dr IAN MCDONALD.

Broadcasting and Communications

TELECOMMUNICATIONS

Broadband Inc: Georgetown; tel. 226-4114; e-mail support@bbgy.com; internet www.bbgy.com; f. 2002; internet service provider; Exec. Dir NAVINDRA NARINE.

Digicel Guyana: Fort & Barrack St, Kingston, Georgetown; tel. 669-2677; fax 227-8184; e-mail guy_ccfrontoffice@digicelgroup.com; internet www.digicelguyana.com; f. 1999 as Trans-World Telecom; acquired Cel Star Guyana in 2003; acquired by Digicel Group in Nov. 2006; GSM cellular telecommunications network; operates Celstar and U-Mobile brands; CEO GREGORY DEAN.

E-Networks Inc: 220 Camp St, North Cummingsburg, Georgetown; tel. 225-1461; fax 225-1412; e-mail info@ewirelessgy.com; internet www.ewirelessgy.com; f. 2004; internet service provider; Man. Dir VISHOK PERSAUD.

Guyana Telephones and Telegraph Company (GT & T): 79 Brickdam, POB 10628, Georgetown; tel. 226-0053; fax 226-7269; e-mail pubcomm@gtt.co.gy; internet www.gtt.co.gy; f. 1991; fmrly state-owned Guyana Telecommunications Corpn; 80% ownership by Atlantic Tele-Network (USA); CEO JOSEPH GOVINDA SINGH.

Regulatory Authority

National Frequency Management Unit (NFMU): 68 Hadfield St, D'Urban Park, Georgetown; tel. 226-2233; fax 226-7661; e-mail info@nfmu.gov.gy; internet www.nfmu.gov.gy; f. 1990; following the Telecommunications Amendment Bill 2011, a new regulatory body, the Telecommunication Agency, was scheduled to be created; Man. Dir VALMIKKI SINGH.

BROADCASTING

Radio

Hits and Jams 94.1 Boom FM: 206 Lance Gibbs St, Queenstown, Georgetown; tel. 227-0580; f. 2013; part of the HJ Entertainment Group; Dirs RAWLE FERGUSON, KERWIN BOLLERS.

National Communications Network (NCN): see Television; operates 3 channels: Hot FM, Radio Roraima and Voice of Guyana.

Radio Guyana Inc. (RGI): TVG, Camp and Quamina St, South Cummingsburg, Georgetown; internet radioguyanafm89.com; f. 2012; part of Queens Atlantic Investment Inc (QAII); Pres. Dr RANJISINGHI (BOBBY) RAMROOP.

Television

CNS Television Six (CNS6): 43 Robb and Wellington Sts, Lacytown, Georgetown; tel. 226-5462; fax 227-3050; e-mail sharma@cns6.tv; internet www.cns6.tv; f. 1992; privately owned; Man. Dir CHANDRANARINE SHARMA.

National Communications Network (NCN): Homestretch Ave, D'Urban Park, Georgetown; tel. 227-1566; fax 226-2253; e-mail feedback@ncnguyana.com; internet www.ncnguyana.com; f. 2004 following merger of Guyana Broadcasting Corpn (f. 1979) and Guyana Television and Broadcasting Co (f. 1993); govt-owned; operates 3 radio channels and 6 TV channels; CEO MICHAEL GORDON (acting).

Regulatory Authority

Guyana National Broadcast Authority (GNBA): Georgetown; f. 2012; licensing authority; Chair. BIBI SAFORA SHADICK.

Finance

(cap. = capital; res = reserves; dep. = deposits; m. = million; brs = branches; amounts in Guyana dollars)

BANKING

Central Bank

Bank of Guyana: 1 Church St and Ave of the Republic, POB 1003, Georgetown; tel. 226-3250; fax 227-2965; e-mail communications@bankofguyana.org.gy; internet www.bankofguyana.org.gy; f. 1965; cap. 1,000m., res 1,125.8m., dep. 140,694.3m. (Dec. 2009); central bank of issue; acts as regulatory authority for the banking sector; Gov. LAWRENCE T. WILLIAMS.

Commercial Banks

Bank of Baroda (Guyana) Inc (India): 10 Ave of the Republic and Regent St, POB 10768, Georgetown; tel. 226-6423; fax 225-1691; e-mail bobinc@networksgy.com; internet www.bankofbaroda.com; f. 1966; Man. Dir AMIT KUMAR.

Citizens' Bank Guyana Inc (CBGI): 201 Camp St and Charlotte St, Lacytown, Georgetown; tel. 226-1705; fax 226-1719; e-mail info@citizensbankgy.com; internet www.citizensbankgy.com; f. 1994; 51% owned by Banks DIH; total assets 18,773m. (Sept. 2007); Chair. CLIFFORD B. REIS; Man. Dir ETON M. CHESTER; 4 brs.

Demerara Bank Ltd: 230 Camp and South Sts, POB 12133, Georgetown; tel. 225-0610; fax 225-0601; e-mail banking@demerarabank.com; internet www.demerarabank.com; f. 1994; cap. 450.0m., res 345.7m., dep. 17,899.9m. (Sept. 2007); Chair. YESU PERSAUD; CEO PRAVINCHANDRA S. DAVE.

Guyana Bank for Trade and Industry Ltd (GBTI): High and Young Sts, Kingston, POB 10280, Georgetown; tel. 231-4401; fax 231-4411; e-mail banking@gbtibank.com; internet www.gbtibank.com; f. 1987 to absorb the operations of Barclays Bank; cap. 800m., res 945m., dep. 66,566.9m. (Dec. 2011); Chair. ROBIN STOBY; CEO JOHN TRACEY; 9 brs.

Republic Bank (Guyana): Promenade Court, 155–156 New Market St, North Cummingsburg, Georgetown; tel. 223-7938; fax 227-2921; e-mail email@republicguyana.com; internet www.republicguyana.com; f. 1984; 51% owned by Republic Bank Ltd, Port of Spain, Trinidad and Tobago; acquired Guyana National Co-operative Bank in 2003; name changed from National Bank of Industry and Commerce in 2006; cap. 300m., res 1,414.1m., dep. 92,008.9m. (Sept. 2011); Chair. DAVID DULAL-WHITEWAY; Man. Dir JOHN N. ALVES; 10 brs.

Scotiabank (Canada): 104 Carmichael St, POB 10631, Georgetown; Georgetown; tel. 225-9222; fax 225-9309; e-mail bns.guyana@scotiabank.com; internet www.guyana.scotiabank.com; f. 1968; Country Man. AMANDA ST AUBYN; 5 brs.

Merchant Bank

Guyana Americas Merchant Bank Inc (GAMBI): GBTI Bldg, 138 Regent St, Lacytown, Georgetown; tel. 223-5193; fax 223-5195; e-mail gambi@networksgy.com; f. 2001; fmrly known as Guyana Finance Corpn Ltd; Man. Dir RICHARD ISAVA.

STOCK EXCHANGE

Guyana Association of Securities Companies and Intermediaries Inc (GASCI): Hand-in-Hand Bldg, 1 Ave of the Republic, Georgetown; tel. 223-6176; fax 223-6175; e-mail info@gasci.com; internet www.gasci.com; f. 2001; Chair. NIKHIL RAMKARRAN; Gen. Man. GEORGE EDWARDS.

INSURANCE

Supervisory Body

Office of the Commissioner of Insurance: Privatisation Unit Bldg, 126 Barrack St, Kingston, Georgetown; tel. 225-0318; fax 226-6426; e-mail mvanbeek@insurance.gov.gy; internet www.insurance.gov.gy; regulates insurance and pensions industries; Commr MARIA VAN BEEK.

Companies

Caricom General Insurance Co Inc: Lot A, Ocean View Dr., Ruimzeight Gardens, Ruimzeight, West Coast Demerara; tel. 269-0020; fax 269-0022; e-mail mail@guyanainsurance.com; internet www.guyanainsurance.com; f. 1997; fmrly Guyana Fire, Life & General Insurance Co Ltd; CEO SAISNARINE KOWLESSAR.

Demerara Mutual Life Assurance Society Ltd: 61–62 Robb St and Ave of the Republic, Georgetown; tel. 225-8991; fax 225-8995; e-mail demlife@demeraramutual.com; internet demeraramutual.net; f. 1891; Chair. RICHARD B. FIELDS; CEO KEITH CHOLMONDELEY.

Diamond Fire and General Insurance Inc: 44B High St, Kingston, Georgetown; tel. 223-9771; fax 223-9770; e-mail diamondins@solutions2000.net; f. 2000; privately owned; Man. PHILIP KOWLESSAR; cap. 100m.

Guyana Co-operative Insurance Service (GCIS): 47 Main St, Georgetown; tel. 225-9153; f. 1976; 67% owned by the Hand-in-Hand Group; Area Rep. SAMMY RAMPERSAUD.

Guyana and Trinidad Mutual Group of Insurance Companies: 27–29 Robb and Hinck St, Georgetown; tel. 225-7910; fax 225-9397; e-mail gtmgroup@gtm-gy.com; internet www.gtm-gy.com; f. 1880; Chair. RAM LALBAHADUR SINGH; Man. Dir ROGER YEE.

Hand-in-Hand Mutual Fire and Life Group: Hand-in-Hand Bldg, 1–4 Ave of the Republic, POB 10188, Georgetown; tel. 225-1865; fax 225-7519; e-mail info@hihgy.com; internet www.hihgy.com; f. 1865; fire and life insurance; Chair. JOHN G. CARPENTER; CEO KEITH EVELYN.

Association

Insurance Association of Guyana: South 0.5, 14 Pere St, Kitty, Georgetown; tel. 226-3514; f. 1968.

Trade and Industry

GOVERNMENT AGENCIES

Environmental Protection Agency, Guyana: Ganges St, Sophia, Georgetown; tel. 225-5467; fax 225-5481; e-mail epa@epaguyana.org; internet www.epaguyana.org; f. 1988 as Guyana Agency for the Environment; renamed 1996; formulates, implements and monitors policies on the environment; Exec. Dir INDARJIT RAMDASS.

Guyana Energy Agency (GEA): 295 Quamina St, POB 903, South Cummingsburg, Georgetown; tel. 226-0394; fax 226-5227; e-mail gea@gea.gov.gy; internet www.gea.gov.gy; f. 1998 as successor to Guyana National Energy Authority; CEO MAHENDRA SHARMA.

Guyana Marketing Corporation: 87 Robb and Alexander Sts, Lacytown, Georgetown; tel. 226-8255; fax 227-4114; e-mail info@newgmc.com; internet www.newgmc.com; Gen. Man. NIZAM HASSAN.

Guyana Office for Investment (Go-Invest): 190 Camp and Church Sts, Georgetown; tel. 225-0653; fax 225-0655; e-mail goinvest@goinvest.gov.gy; internet www.goinvest.gov.gy; f. 1994; CEO GEOFFREY DA SILVA.

National Industrial and Commercial Investment Ltd (NICIL): 126 Barrack St, Kingston, Georgetown; tel. 226-0576; e-mail winston.brassington@gmail.com; internet www.privatisation.gov.gy; f. 1991; state-run privatization unit; Exec. Dir WINSTON BRASSINGTON.

DEVELOPMENT ORGANIZATION

Institute of Private Enterprise Development (IPED): 253–254 South Rd, Bourda, Georgetown; tel. 225-8949; fax 226-4675; e-mail iped@solutions2000.net; internet www.ipedgy.com; f. 1986; total loans provided $ G1,400m. (2007); Chair. YESU PERSAUD; Exec. Dir RAMESH PERSAUD.

CHAMBER OF COMMERCE

Georgetown Chamber of Commerce and Industry (GCCI): 156 Waterloo St, North Cummingsburg, Georgetown; tel. 225-5846; fax 226-3519; e-mail info@gcci.gy; internet www.georgetownchamberofcommerce.org; f. 1889; Pres. CLINTON URLING; 90 mems.

INDUSTRIAL AND TRADE ASSOCIATIONS

Guyana Rice Development Board: 116–17 Cowan St, Kingston, Georgetown; tel. 225-8717; fax 225-6486; internet www.grdb.gy; f. 1994 to assume operations of Guyana Rice Export Board and Guyana Rice Grading Centre; Gen. Man. JAGNARINE SINGH.

National Dairy and Development Programme (NDDP): c/o Lands and Surveys Bldg, 22 Upper Hadfield St, Durban Backlands, POB 10367, Georgetown; tel. 225-7107; fax 226-3020; e-mail nddp@sdnp.org.gy; f. 1984; aims to increase domestic milk and beef production; Programme Dir MEER BACCHUS.

EMPLOYERS' ASSOCIATIONS

Consultative Association of Guyanese Industry Ltd: 157 Waterloo St, POB 10730, North Cummingsburg, Georgetown; tel. 225-7170; fax 227-0725; e-mail info@cagi.org.gy; internet www.cagi.org.gy; f. 1962; Chair. YESU PERSAUD; Exec. Dir SAMUEL JERRY GOOLSARRAN; 54 mems.

Forest Products Association of Guyana: 157 Waterloo St, Cummingsburg, Georgetown; tel. 226-9848; fax 226-2832; e-mail fpasect@guyana.net.gy; internet www.fpaguyana.org; f. 1944; 62 mem. cos; Pres. KHALAWAN CORT; Exec. Officer JANICE CRAWFORD.

Guyana Manufacturing and Services Association Ltd (GMSA): National Exhibition Centre, Sophia, Georgetown; tel. 219-0072; fax 219-0073; e-mail gma_guyana@yahoo.com; f. 1967 as the Guyana Manufacturers' Asscn; name changed in 2005 to reflect growth in services sector; 190 mems; Pres. CLINTON WILLIAMS.

Guyana Rice Producers' Association (GRPA): 126 Parade and Barrack St, Georgetown; tel. 226-4411; fax 223-7249; e-mail grpa.riceproducers@networksgy.com; f. 1946; non-govt org.; 18,500 mems; Pres. LEEKHA RAMBRICH; Gen. Sec. DHARAMKUMAR SEERAJ.

UTILITIES

Electricity

Guyana Power and Light Inc (GPL): 40 Main St, POB 10390, Georgetown; tel. 226-2606; fax 227-1978; e-mail bharat.dindyal@gplinc.com; internet www.gplinc.com; f. 1999; fmrly Guyana Electricity Corpn; state-owned; Chair. WINSTON BRASSINGTON; CEO BHARAT DINDYAL; 1,200 employees.

Water

Guyana Water Inc (GWI): Vllissengen Rd and Church St, Bel Air Park, Georgetown; tel. 227-8701; fax 227-8718; e-mail customercallcentre@gwi.gy; internet www.gwiguyana.com; f. 2002 following merger of Guyana Water Authority and Georgetown Sewerage and Water Comm.; operated by Severn Trent Water International (United Kingdom); Chair. Dr RAMESH DOOKHOO; CEO SHAIK BAKSH.

TRADE UNIONS

Federation of Independent Trade Unions of Guyana (FITUG): Georgetown; f. 1988; c. 35,000 mems; Pres. CARVIL DUNCAN; Gen. Sec. KENNETH JOSEPH.

Guyana Trades Union Congress (GTUC): Critchlow Labour College, Woolford Ave, Non-pareil Park, Georgetown; tel. 226-1493; fax 227-0254; e-mail gtucorg@yahoo.com; f. 1940; national trade union body; 13 affiliated unions; c. 15,000 mems; affiliated to the International Trade Union Confederation; Pres. NORRIS WITTER; Gen. Sec. LINCOLN LEWIS.

Transport

RAILWAY

There are no public railways in Guyana. Until the early 21st century the 15-km Linmine Railway was used for the transportation of bauxite from Linden to Coomaka.

ROADS

The coastal strip has a well-developed road system. There were an estimated 7,970 km (4,952 miles) of paved and good-weather roads and trails. A bridge across the Takutu river, linking Guyana to Brazil, was inaugurated in 2009, while a bridge over the Berbice river was completed in the previous year. In 2012 Guyana and Suriname asked the Inter-American Development Bank (IDB) to fund a feasibility study of a bridge across the Corentyne river. The IDB approved another $66m. for a road network upgrade and expansion programme in the same year.

SHIPPING

Guyana's principal ports are at Georgetown and New Amsterdam. The port at Linden serves for the transportation of bauxite products. A ferry service is operated between Guyana and Suriname. Communications with the interior are chiefly by river, although access is hindered by rapids and falls. There are 1,077 km (607 miles) of navigable rivers. At 31 December 2013 the flag registered fleet comprised 60 vessels, totalling 32,127 grt.

Transport and Harbours Department: Water St, Stabroek, Georgetown; tel. 225-9350; fax 227-8445; e-mail t&hd@solutions2000.net; Gen. Man. MARCLENE MERCHANT.

Shipping Association of Guyana Inc (SAG): 10–11 Lombard St, Werk-en-Rust, Georgetown; tel. 226-2169; fax 226-9656; e-mail saginc@networksgy.com; internet www.shipping.org.gy; f. 1952; non-governmental forum; Chair. ANDREW ASTWOOD; Sec. IAN D'ANJOU; members:

Guyana National Industrial Company Inc (GNIC): 1–9 Lombard St, Charlestown, POB 10520, Georgetown; tel. 225-5398; fax 226-0432; e-mail gnicadmin@futurenetgy.com; metal foundry, ship building and repair, agents for a number of international transport cos; privatized in 1995; CEO CLINTON WILLIAMS; Port Man. ALBERT SMITH.

Guyana National Shipping Corporation Ltd: 5–9 Lombard St, La Penitence, POB 10988, Georgetown; tel. 226-1840; fax 225-3815; e-mail agencydivision@gnsc.com; internet www.gnsc.com; fmrly Bookers Shipping Transport and Wharves Ltd; govt-owned since 1976; Man. Dir ANDREW ASTWOOD (acting).

John Fernandes Ltd: 24 Water St, POB 10211, Georgetown; tel. 227-3344; fax 226-1881; e-mail philip@jf-ltd.com; internet www.jf-ltd.com; f. 1959; ship agents, pier operators and stevedore contractors; part of the John Fernandes Group of Cos; Chair. and CEO CHRIS FERNANDES.

CIVIL AVIATION

The main airport, Cheddi Jaggan International Airport, is at Timehri, 42 km (26 miles) from Georgetown. Ogle International Airport, six miles east of Georgetown, also accepts international flights; construction of a 4,000-ft runway was completed in 2013. The regional airline LIAT (based in Antigua and Barbuda, and in which Guyana is a shareholder) provides scheduled passenger and cargo services.

Roraima Airways: R8 Epring Ave, Bel Air Park, Georgetown; tel. 225-9650; fax 225-9648; e-mail ral@roraimaairways.com; internet www.roraimaairways.com; f. 1992; flights to Venezuela and 4 domestic destinations; Man. Dir Capt. GERALD GOUVEIA.

Trans Guyana Airways: Ogle Aerodrome, Ogle, East Coast Demerara; tel. 222-2525; e-mail commercial@transguyana.net; internet www.transguyana.net; f. 1956; internal flights to 22 destinations; Dir Capt. GERARD GONSALVES.

Tourism

Despite the beautiful scenery in the interior of the country, Guyana has limited tourist facilities, although during the 1990s the country began to develop its considerable potential as an eco-tourism destination. The total number of visitors to Guyana in 2012 was 176,642. Expenditure by tourists amounted to some US $80m. in 2010.

Guyana Tourism Authority: National Exhibition Centre, Sophia, Georgetown; tel. 219-0094; fax 219-0093; e-mail info@guyana-tourism.com; internet www.guyana-tourism.com; f. 2003; state-owned; Dir INDRANAUTH HARALSINGH.

Tourism and Hospitality Association of Guyana (THAG): 157 Waterloo St, Georgetown; tel. 225-0807; fax 225-0817; e-mail thag@networksgy.com; internet www.exploreguyana.com; f. 1992; Pres. PAUL STEPHENSON; Exec. Dir TREINA BUTTS.

Defence

The armed forces are united in a single service, the Combined Guyana Defence Force, which consisted of some 1,100 men (of whom 900 were in the army, 100 in the air force and about 100 in the navy), as assessed at November 2013. In addition there were reserve forces numbering some 670 (army 500, navy 170). The Guyana People's Militia, a paramilitary reserve force, totalled about 1,500. The President is the Commander-in-Chief.

Defence Budget: An estimated $ G7,390m. (US $35m.) in 2013.

Chief-of-Staff: Brig.-Gen. MARK PHILLIPS.

Education

Education is free and compulsory for children aged between five years and 15 years of age. Children receive primary education for a period of six years; enrolment at primary schools in 2012 included 72% of children in the relevant age-group. Secondary education, beginning at 12 years of age, lasts for up to seven years in a general secondary school. In 2010/11 an estimated 75,116 pupils were enrolled in secondary schools. Higher education is provided by eight technical and vocational schools and one teacher training college, in all of which 6,780 students were enrolled in 2010/11. The state-run University of Guyana offers degrees, as does the private GreenHeart Medical University. An estimated $ G32,200m. was allocated to the education sector in 2014.

HAITI

Introductory Survey

LOCATION, CLIMATE, LANGUAGE, RELIGION, FLAG, CAPITAL

The Republic of Haiti occupies the western part of the Caribbean island of Hispaniola (the Dominican Republic occupies the remaining two-thirds) and some smaller offshore islands. Cuba, to the west, is less than 80 km away. The climate is tropical but the mountains and fresh sea winds mitigate the heat. Temperatures vary little with the seasons, and the annual average in Port-au-Prince is about 27°C (80°F). The rainy season is from May to November. The official languages are French and Creole. About 65% of the population belong to the Roman Catholic Church, the country's official religion, and other Christian churches are also represented. The folk religion is Voodoo (vodou), a fusion of beliefs involving communication with the spirit world through the medium of trance. The national flag (proportions variable) has two equal horizontal stripes, of dark blue and red. The state flag (proportions 3 by 5) has, in addition, a white rectangular panel containing the national coat of arms (a palm tree, surmounted by a Cap of Liberty and flanked by flags and cannons) in the centre. The capital is Port-au-Prince.

CONTEMPORARY POLITICAL HISTORY

Historical Context

Haiti was first colonized in 1659 by the French, who named the territory Saint-Domingue. French sovereignty was formally recognized by Spain in 1697. Following a period of internal unrest, a successful uprising, begun in 1794 by African-descended slaves, culminated in 1804 with the establishment of Haiti as an independent state, ruled by Jean-Jacques Dessalines, who proclaimed himself Emperor. Hostility between the black population and the mulattos continued throughout the 19th century until, after increasing economic instability, the USA intervened militarily and supervised the government of the country from 1915 to 1934. Mulatto interests retained political ascendancy until 1946, when a black President, Dumarsais Estimé, was installed following a military coup. Following the overthrow of two further administrations, Dr François Duvalier, a country physician, was elected President in 1957.

Domestic Political Affairs

The Duvalier administration soon became a dictatorship, maintaining its authority by means of a notorious private army, popularly called the Tontons Macoutes (Creole for 'Bogeymen'), who used extortion and intimidation to crush opposition to the President's rule. In 1964 Duvalier became President-for-Life, and at his death in April 1971 he was succeeded by his 19-year-old son and designated successor, Jean-Claude Duvalier.

At elections held in 1979 almost all seats were won by the official government party, the Parti de l'Unité Nationale. The first municipal elections for 25 years, in 1983, were overshadowed by allegations of fraud and Duvalier's obstruction of opposition parties. No opposition candidates were permitted to contest the general election of February 1984.

In April 1985 Duvalier announced a programme of constitutional reforms, including the eventual appointment of a Prime Minister and the formation of political parties, subject to certain conditions. In September Roger Lafontant, the minister most closely identified with the Government's acts of repression, was dismissed. However, protests organized by the Roman Catholic Church and other religious groups gained momentum, and further measures to curb continued disorder were adopted in January 1986. Duvalier declared martial law.

In February 1986, following intensified public protests, Duvalier fled to exile in France, leaving a National Council of Government (Conseil National Gouvernemental), led by the Chief of Staff of the army, Gen. Henri Namphy, to succeed him. The military-civilian Council appointed a new Cabinet. The National Assembly was dissolved, the Constitution was suspended, and the Tontons Macoutes were disbanded. Gen. Namphy announced a timetable to restore constitutional government by February 1988.

The election of members of a Constituent Assembly to revise the Constitution took place in October 1986. The new Constitution was approved by 99.8% of voters in a referendum held in March 1987. An independent Conseil Electoral Provisoire (CEP—Provisional Electoral Council) was subsequently appointed. Presidential and legislative elections were cancelled three hours after voting had begun on 29 November, owing to renewed violence, for which former members of the Tontons Macoutes were believed to be responsible. Elections were rescheduled for 17 January 1988. Leslie Manigat of the Rassemblement des Démocrates Nationaux et Progressistes (RDNP) was declared the winner of the presidential ballot. Opposition leaders alleged that there had been extensive fraud and malpractice.

The Manigat Government was overthrown by disaffected members of the army in June 1988. Gen. Namphy, whom Manigat had attempted to replace as army Chief of Staff, assumed the presidency and appointed a military Cabinet. The Constitution of 1987 was abrogated, and Duvalier's supporters returned to prominence, as did the Tontons Macoutes.

In September 1988 Gen. Namphy was ousted in a coup, led by Brig.-Gen. Prosper Avril. In March 1989 Avril partially restored the Constitution of 1987 and restated his intention to hold democratic elections. In the following month the Government survived two coup attempts by the Leopard Corps, the country's élite anti-subversion squadron, and the Dessalines battalion, based in Port-au-Prince. Avril resigned as President in March 1990 in response to sustained popular opposition, together with diplomatic pressure from the USA. Power was ceded to the Chief of the General Staff, Hérard Abraham, who subsequently transferred authority to Ertha Pascal-Trouillot, a member of the Supreme Court. Pascal-Trouillot shared power with a 19-member Council of State.

Presidential and legislative elections took place in December 1990. Fr Jean-Bertrand Aristide, a left-wing Roman Catholic priest representing the Front National pour le Changement et la Démocratie (FNCD), won an overwhelming victory in the presidential election. His closest rival was Marc Bazin, the candidate of the centre-right Mouvement pour l'Instauration de la Démocratie en Haïti (MIDH). However, the FNCD failed to win a majority of seats in either the Sénat (Senate) or the Chambre des Députés (Chamber of Deputies).

Aristide initiated proceedings in early 1991 to secure the extradition from France of Duvalier to face charges that included embezzlement, abuse of power and murder. Aristide also undertook the reform of the armed forces, and in July Gen. (later Lt-Gen.) Raoul Cédras replaced Abraham as Commander-in-Chief and René Garcia Préval was appointed Prime Minister.

Military coup of 1991

On 30 September 1991 a military junta, led by Gen. Cédras, overthrew the Government. Following international diplomatic intervention, Aristide was allowed to go into exile. The coup received international condemnation, and an economic embargo was imposed on Haiti by the Organization of American States (OAS, see p. 394). Many hundreds of people were reported to have been killed during the coup. On 7 October military units assembled 29 members of the legislature and coerced them into approving the appointment of Joseph Nerette as interim President.

During the following months the OAS, which continued to recognize Aristide as the legitimate head of state, attempted to negotiate a settlement. However, the two sides remained deadlocked over the conditions for Aristide's return. In February 1992, following OAS-supervised talks in Washington, DC, USA, between Aristide and members of a Haitian legislative delegation, an agreement was signed providing for the installation of René Théodore, leader of the Mouvement pour la Reconstruction Nationale, as Prime Minister. He was to govern in consultation with the exiled Aristide and facilitate his return. However, in March politicians opposed to the accord withdrew from a joint session of the legislature, leaving it inquorate. Following an appeal by Nerette, the Supreme Court declared the agreement null and void, on the grounds that it violated the Constitution by endangering the country's sovereignty. In response, the OAS increased economic sanctions against Haiti.

In May 1992 an agreement providing for the appointment of a new Prime Minister and a multi-party government of national consensus was ratified by the Senate. In June the legislature, in the absence of the FNCD, approved the nomination of Bazin to be Prime Minister. The presidency was left vacant, ostensibly to allow for Aristide's return. A Cabinet, comprising members of most major parties (with the exception of the FNCD), was installed, with the army retaining control of the interior and defence. The appointment of the new Government provoked worldwide condemnation. In September the Government agreed to allow the presence of an OAS commission in Haiti to help to guarantee human rights and assess progress towards a resolution of the prevailing political crisis.

In June 1993 the USA imposed sanctions against Haiti. Shortly afterwards Bazin resigned as Prime Minister following a loss of support in the legislature. In July, following OAS- and UN-sponsored talks between Cédras and Aristide, a peace accord was signed, delineating a 10-point agenda for Aristide's reinstatement. Under the terms of the accord, the embargo was to be revoked following the installation of a new Prime Minister (to be appointed by Aristide), Cédras would retire, and a new Commander-in-Chief of the armed forces would be appointed. The accord was approved by Haiti's main political parties. Legislation providing for a series of political and institutional reforms, as required by the accord, was to be enacted, including provision for the transfer of the police force to civilian control.

In August 1993 the legislature ratified the appointment by Aristide of Robert Malval as Prime Minister. In September a concerted campaign of political violence and intimidation by police auxiliaries, known as 'attachés', threatened to undermine the accord. With the upsurge of a Duvalierist tendency, largely embodied by the attachés, a new political party, the Front Revolutionnaire pour l'Avancement et le Progrès d'Haïti (FRAPH), was founded in opposition to any attempt to reinstate Aristide. In September the UN Security Council approved a resolution providing for the immediate deployment of a lightly armed UN Mission in Haiti. Cédras refused to resign his post in October. In that month the campaign of political violence by the attachés escalated. In response, the US Government ordered six warships into Haitian territorial waters to enforce the reimposed UN embargo. Malval resigned as Prime Minister in December.

A National Reconciliation Conference, proposed by Aristide and excluding the military, took place in Miami, Florida, USA, in January 1994. Following the military regime's failure to meet a revised UN deadline to comply with the terms of the accord, the USA unilaterally imposed further sanctions. In April the US Government abandoned its attempts to effect a compromise solution to the crisis in Haiti in favour of more rigorous economic sanctions with a view to forcing the military regime to relinquish power. In May the UN Security Council approved a resolution introducing sanctions banning all international trade with Haiti, excluding food and medicine, reducing air links with the country and preventing members of the regime from gaining access to assets held outside Haiti.

In early 1994 the Senate declared the presidency of the Republic vacant, invoking Article 149 of the Constitution, which provides that, in case of prolonged absence by the Head of State, the position may be assumed by the President of the Court of Cassation. In May, with the support of the armed forces, an inquorate legislature appointed Emile Jonassaint, provisional President. The appointment by Jonassaint of a new Cabinet was denounced as illegal by the international community. In the following month the USA increased sanctions against Haiti.

In July 1994 the Haitian junta issued an order providing for the expulsion of the UN/OAS international civil commission. On 31 July the UN Security Council approved a resolution authorizing 'all necessary means' to remove the military regime from power and providing for the deployment of a UN peacekeeping force once stability had been achieved, to remain in Haiti until February 1996, when Aristide's presidential term expired. In August leaders of the Caribbean Community and Common Market (CARICOM, see p. 223) agreed to support a US-led military invasion.

Agreement on a return to civilian rule, 1994

On 19 September 1994 a nominally multinational force composed almost entirely of US troops began a peaceful occupation of Haiti. Under a compromise agreement, the Haitian security forces were to co-operate with the multilateral force in effecting a transition to civilian rule. All sanctions were to be lifted and the military junta granted 'early and honourable retirement' following legislative approval of a general amnesty law, or by 15 October at the latest (the date when Aristide was to return from exile to resume his presidency). In September the USA announced the suspension of its unilateral sanctions. A few days later the UN Security Council approved a resolution ending all sanctions against Haiti with effect from the day after the return of Aristide. In October Aristide authorized the amnesty of those involved in the 1991 coup. Later that month the USA formally ended its freeze on the assets of the Haitian military regime. On 12 October Robert Malval resumed office as interim Prime Minister following the resignation of the Jonassaint administration.

Aristide returned to Haiti on 15 October 1994 and appointed Smarck Michel as premier. A new Cabinet, comprising mainly members of the pro-Aristide Organisation Politique Lavalas (OPL), was inaugurated in November. Later that month the legislature approved the separation of the police from the army. In December the formation of a new CEP was completed. In the following month two commissions were established for the restructuring of the armed forces and the new civilian police force.

In January 1995 the UN Security Council adopted a resolution authorizing the deployment of a UN force of 6,000 troops and 900 civil police to succeed the multinational force. The UN Mission in Haiti (UNMIH) was to be responsible for reducing the strength of the army and training both the army and the 4,000-strong (subsequently increased to 6,000) civilian police force, as well as maintaining the 'secure and stable' environment. On 31 March authority was officially transferred to UNMIH.

The first round of legislative, local and municipal elections was held on 25 June 1995. All of the seats were won by the Plateforme Politique Lavalas (PPL), a three-party alliance of the OPL, the Mouvement d'Organisation du Pays (MOP) and the Pati Louvri Baryè (PLB). The results were rejected by the majority of opposition parties, which announced a boycott of the electoral process. In early August the FNCD, MIDH and the Parti National Progressiste Révolutionnaire withdrew their respective representatives from the Government in protest against the unresolved electoral dispute. In October Michel resigned as Prime Minister, and was succeeded by Claudette Werleigh.

Presidential election of 1995

At a presidential election held on 17 December 1995, which was boycotted by all the main opposition parties, the candidate endorsed by Aristide, René Préval, was elected with some 88% of the votes cast. He was inaugurated as President in February 1996, and later that month the legislature approved the appointment of Rosny Smarth as Prime Minister.

Partial legislative elections were held in April 1997. The elections were boycotted by many opposition parties, and less than 5% of the electorate participated in the poll. Of the seats contested, only two, in the Senate, were decided, both of which were secured by a new political party established by Aristide, La Fanmi Lavalas (FL). The OPL, the majority party in the governing coalition, alleged that members of the CEP had manipulated the election results in favour of the FL. OAS observers supported the claims of electoral irregularities, and, following international pressure, the CEP postponed indefinitely the second round ballot.

Smarth resigned from office on 9 June 1997. However, Préval's nomination of Ericq Pierre as his replacement was rejected by the Chamber of Deputies. In November Préval nominated Hervé Denis, an economist and former minister in the Malval Government, as Prime Minister and announced the establishment of an electoral commission, comprising three independent legal experts, to resolve the electoral deadlock. In January 1998 the legislature rejected the nomination of Denis. In March, following negotiations with supporters of Aristide in the lower house, the OPL (renamed the Organisation du Peuple en Lutte) withdrew its demands for the annulment of the April 1997 elections as a precondition for the approval of a new Prime Minister, and proposed three candidates. However, Préval renominated Denis, whose candidacy was again rejected by the legislature in April. In July Préval finally agreed to OPL demands to replace the CEP, subsequently receiving the party's support for the nomination of the Minister of National Education, Jacques-Edouard Alexis, as Prime Minister. Conversely, Aristide's supporters opposed the nomination of Alexis. In August the FL announced that it had formally gone into opposition to the Préval administration.

In December 1998 Alexis was finally declared eligible to become Prime Minister, subject to his nomination being approved by the legislature (which did not occur until November 2000). On 25 March 1999 Préval appointed by decree a new Cabinet headed by Alexis and including representatives of five small opposition parties. The OPL was not included in the new administration. In June a new CEP announced that it would disregard the results of the flawed partial legislative elections of April 1997; Préval signed a decree annulling the elections in July.

Disputed legislative and presidential elections of 2000

The first round of legislative and municipal elections was held on 21 May 2000; an estimated 60% of the electorate participated. Opposition parties alleged that the results had been manipulated in favour of the FL and demanded the conduct of a fresh ballot. The CEP rejected these claims, but in June the CEP President, Léon Manus, fled to the Dominican Republic, claiming that he had received death threats following his refusal to validate the first round results. His flight prompted demonstrations by Aristide supporters, demanding the publication of the results. According to official first round results, the FL won 16 of the 19 contested seats in the Senate and 26 of the 83 seats in the lower house. The results were criticized as inaccurate by the UN, the OAS and numerous foreign governments. Nevertheless, a second round of voting went ahead on 9 July. A boycott by the 15-party opposition coalition, the Convergence Démocratique (CD), resulted in a low rate of voter participation (an estimated 10%). According to official results, the FL won 72 seats in the Chamber of Deputies and 18 of the 19 seats contested in the 27-seat upper house. The party also secured control of some 80% of the local councils.

Elections to the presidency and to renew the remaining eight senate seats were held on 20 November 2000 and boycotted by the CD. Aristide was elected President with some 92% of the votes cast. CARICOM estimated a 30% rate of voter participation. The FL also won the eight seats contested in the Senate and the one remaining seat in the Chamber of Deputies.

An eight-member Transition Committee was established in December 2000 to oversee the transfer of power. However, on 7 December the CD announced the formation of an alternative, provisional Government, the Front Alternatif, with the intention of holding fresh elections within two years, provoking widespread violent demonstrations by Aristide supporters. On 15 February 2001 seven of the senators controversially awarded seats in the May 2000 elections resigned. President Aristide named Jean-Marie Chérestal as Prime Minister, and in March a new Cabinet was appointed. In the same month, in an attempt to end the political impasse, Aristide appointed a new CEP to investigate the results of the disputed 2000 elections. The CD was not represented on the Council. In March 2001 it was announced that legislative elections would be held one year early, in November 2002, in order to satisfy international and opposition criticism and to restore the flow of foreign aid, suspended since May 2000. Three days later violent protests broke out in Port-au-Prince, which continued over the following months, and a number of opposition party members were arrested on treason and terrorism charges. In July 2001, following further OAS mediation, the Government stated that legislative and local elections would be held in 2002; an accord was also reached on the composition of the new CEP. The CEP would additionally organize an election to the seven Senate seats vacated in February.

In December 2001 an armed group, allegedly composed of former members of the military, attacked the presidential palace. At least four people were killed in the coup attempt, which prompted further outbreaks of violence. The opposition claimed that the coup attempt had been staged by the Government in order to justify further repression. In July 2002 an OAS Commission of Inquiry reported that no attempted coup had taken place.

On 23 January 2002 Prime Minister Chérestal resigned his post, following criticism over his inability to resolve the crisis. On 15 March Aristide appointed Senate speaker and prominent FL member Yvon Neptune as Prime Minister.In June Aristide met opposition leaders for the first time in two years, but the talks achieved little progress. Meanwhile, Haiti's accession to full membership of CARICOM in July increased international pressure on Aristide to bring about an end to political instability in the country.

Intensification of political unrest

Political unrest intensified as the November 2002 deadline for the creation of a new CEP passed unfulfilled. Five of the nation's civil groups chose representatives to the CEP in November, but the opposition continued to refuse to do so. In December a general strike led by the opposition was joined by members of Haiti's private sector. Opposition parties united in demanding the resignation of Aristide as the demonstrations continued. Frustrated by the continued political instability, some 184 business and civil society organizations formed the 'Group of 184', which subsequently emerged as a major element of the opposition to Aristide.

The political stalemate between the Government and the opposition remained unresolved in 2003, despite OAS efforts. Most nominees to the nine-member CEP refused to assume their posts, claiming that they were unconvinced that the Government would not resort to fraudulent practices in future legislative elections, as it had done in 2000. In October at least four people died as a result of violent clashes between police and anti-Government demonstrators in Gonaïves. In December three ministers resigned in protest at the Government's increasing use of violence to suppress the continuing demonstrations.

In January 2004 the mandates of all the members of the Chamber of Deputies and 12 of the 27 members of the Senate expired, leaving Haiti effectively without a legislature and entitling President Aristide to rule by decree. The President pledged to hold legislative elections within six months, an offer rejected by the opposition. CARICOM threatened to impose economic sanctions on Haiti unless President Aristide satisfied a number of conditions, including the formation of a new electoral council and the holding of elections. Following a meeting between Aristide, opposition members and CARICOM leaders, in Jamaica, Aristide agreed to implement a number of reforms within the following two months, including creating a neutral electoral council.

In February 2004, however, anti-Government forces took control of Gonaïves and several other cities in the north of the country. Shortly afterwards, former members of the Haitian armed forces, led by former police chief Guy Philippe and the former deputy commander of the FRAPH, Louis-Jodel Chamblain, joined the insurrection, enlisting with the rebels to form the Front pour la Libération et la Reconstruction Nationales (FLRN). President Aristide appealed to the international community for assistance in suppressing the rebellion. A plan to end the violence, proposed by France, CARICOM and the OAS, was rejected by the opposition as it failed to provide for the President's departure. At a meeting of the UN Security Council in late February, Caribbean nations called for a multilateral force to be sent to the country in an attempt to bring an end to the violence. However, the USA and France insisted that a political settlement would have to be reached before any forces were deployed to Haiti.

President Aristide finally resigned on 29 February 2004, largely owing to international pressure, and fled to the Central African Republic, where he claimed that he had been unconstitutionally removed from office by the USA. The USA maintained that Aristide had requested assistance to leave Haiti. In accordance with the Constitution, the President of the Supreme Court, Boniface Alexandre, was sworn in as interim President. On the same day the UN Security Council, acting in response to a request from Alexandre, authorized the establishment of a Multinational Interim Force (MIF) to help to secure law and order prior to the deployment of a larger peacekeeping mission. The MIF eventually comprised around 3,600 troops from the USA, France, Canada and Chile. On 9 March Alexandre and the recently established Council of Elders appointed Gérard Latortue as Prime Minister. The installation of a new Cabinet, composed of independents and technocrats, was generally welcomed by the international community, although CARICOM refused to recognize the Latortue Government.

In April 2004 Latortue, the seven members of the Council of Elders, representatives of the main political organizations (with the exception of the FL) and leaders of civil society organizations signed an agreement on political transition, which provided for the organization of presidential, legislative and municipal elections in 2005, leading to the inauguration of a new administration by February 2006. The agreement also provided for a new CEP, which was inaugurated in May 2004. The FL refused to designate a representative to the CEP, demanding that alleged persecution and repression of its supporters cease. In the same month Jocelerme Privert, the former Minister of the Interior, was arrested on suspicion of having ordered the killing of a number of anti-Aristide protesters in February.

In a report to the UN Security Council in April 2004, the UN Secretary-General, Kofi Annan, accused Aristide of having formed an alliance with armed groups, *chimères*, in order to reinforce his position in power and of having condoned their engagement in organized crime, including drugs-smuggling. Aristide went into exile in South Africa at the end of May.

UN peacekeeping force established, 2004

A UN peacekeeping force, the UN Stabilization Mission in Haiti (MINUSTAH), was officially established on 1 June 2004 and replaced the MIF later that month. MINUSTAH, which had an authorized strength of 6,700 military personnel and 1,622 civilian police, was to assist the interim administration with preparations for elections and the disarmament and demobilization of armed militias. Meanwhile, the OAS General Assembly approved a resolution declaring Aristide's removal from power to be unconstitutional, although it continued to recognize Latortue's Government.

Former Prime Minister Neptune was arrested in June 2004 in connection with the deaths of demonstrators in the uprising against Aristide's administration in February. In July the Latortue Government issued a deadline of 15 September for armed groups to surrender their weapons. The disarmament of the rebels was one of CARICOM's principal demands, but the deadline for the surrender of weapons passed unfulfilled.

At the end of September 2004 violence broke out between the police and supporters of Aristide at a rally in Port-au-Prince in support of the former President's return from exile. Clashes continued, and by early November at least 80 people had been killed. Tensions were exacerbated by the arrival in the capital of more than 200 former soldiers, who demanded to be allowed to confront the so-called *chimères*. Three members of the FL, including the former President of the Senate, Yvon Feuillé, were arrested in October on suspicion of inciting the violence and possessing illegal firearms, and 75 suspected members of the *chimères* were also detained by the national police and MINUSTAH troops in a joint operation. By mid-October only around 2,100 troops of the 6,700-strong authorized MINUSTAH force had actually been deployed.

In November 2004 the President of the CEP, Roselaure Julien, resigned, claiming that considerable pressure had been exerted on her, particularly by the Group of 184, to allow manipulation of the electoral process. Later that month a five-member Anti-Corruption Commission was established within the Ministry of the Economy and Finance to investigate alleged corruption between February 2001 and February 2004, as envisaged in the agreement on political transition signed in April. Also in November, CARICOM issued a 'consensus statement' reaffirming its decision not to recognize Latortue's Government. Later in the month the UN Security Council approved the extension of MINUSTAH's mandate until 1 June 2005. In December 2004, amid continuing political violence and civil unrest, MINUSTAH troops entered the Cité Soleil area of Port-au-Prince, a stronghold of the pro-Aristide gangs, and successfully seized control of two police stations and other official buildings occupied by the *chimères*. Meanwhile, following pressure from the UN Secretary-General to free politicians detained without formal charge, the authorities provisionally released the three FL members arrested in October.

In January 2005 the CEP announced a timetable for the forthcoming elections: the municipal elections were to take place on 9 October, followed by legislative and presidential elections in two rounds, on 13 November and 18 December. A permanent register of voters was to be compiled prior to the elections, and national identity cards were to be issued. It was hoped that proposed mediation by the African Union (see p. 186) would result in the participation of the FL, which continued to demand the release of former officials of the Aristide administration, such as Neptune and Privert, and other 'political' prisoners. In February the Government created a National Disarmament Commission to facilitate and monitor the recovery of illegal weapons.

Escalation of violence

A sharp escalation in fighting between MINUSTAH troops and rebel groups was evident from March 2005. Many of the rebels who had helped to oust Aristide from power had subsequently turned against the interim Government. A number of UN peacekeeping troops and rebels were killed in confrontations in the following months. The interim Government denied claims by local residents and human rights organizations that there had been civilian fatalities.

In May 2005 Neptune was formally charged, 11 months after being arrested, for his alleged role in political killings during the uprising against Aristide's administration; in the previous month Neptune had begun a hunger strike to protest against his detention without charge. Human rights organizations claimed that hundreds of Aristide supporters had similarly been detained without charge for almost a year.

In June 2005 Paul-Henri Mourral, the French honorary consul, was shot dead and numerous others were also killed as gangs ran amok in the capital. Later that month the UN Security Council decided both to extend MINUSTAH's mandate by a further eight months and to deploy an additional 1,000 peacekeeping troops to the country. MINUSTAH subsequently intensified military operations against the rebel gangs and denied allegations that civilians had been killed by UN troops. In July about 1,000 demonstrators marched through the capital to protest against the interim Government, MINUSTAH and the collective failure of both to address adequately the security situation within Haiti. (The protest was catalysed by the murder earlier that month of the prominent Haitian journalist Jacques Roche, at whose funeral the Minister of Culture and Communications, Magalie Comeau Denis, had alleged that Aristide supporters had orchestrated the killing in an attempt to disrupt the electoral process.)

In August 2005 local elections were postponed until December, so as to allow the authorities to concentrate on preparations for legislative and presidential elections, which in turn were delayed, on account of extremely low voter registration, divisions in the electoral council and general disorganization. The elections were further postponed on three subsequent occasions, with a revised date of 7 February 2006 eventually being announced; at the same time Latortue also announced that he was to resign as Prime Minister on that date, regardless of when elections were finally held.

Presidential and legislative elections of 2006

On 7 February 2006 presidential and legislative elections were finally held. Voter participation was higher than expected, at 60% of the total electorate, in the presidential poll. It was announced that former President Préval, representing Fwon Lespwa (Front de l'Espoir), had obtained 49% of the vote—far more than any other candidate, but marginally short of the overall majority required to avoid a second round of voting. Incensed by what they perceived to be an attempt by the interim Government to force a run-off vote, and with tempers further inflamed by the discovery of thousands of burnt ballot papers (many of which were reported to be marked in favour of Préval) in a dump near Port-au-Prince, thousands of Préval supporters marched through the capital in protest. Following calls from the UN Security Council, and amid allegations of vote manipulation from two members of the CEP itself, the interim Government ordered that the publication of official results be halted until a full inquiry could be held into the allegations of electoral fraud. It was announced on 16 February that Préval had in fact secured an outright victory and was consequently to be declared President. The announcement followed emergency talks between the interim Government and electoral officials, during which it was agreed to share out the 91,219 blank ballots (4.4% of the total votes cast) proportionately among the candidates, thereby increasing Préval's percentage of the vote to 51%. The RDNP representative, former President Leslie Manigat—the second-placed candidate (with only 12% of the vote)—denounced the outcome, as did the third-placed Respè nominee, Charles Henri Baker. However, the international community—including, significantly, the UN, CARICOM, the OAS and the USA—did recognize Préval's victory. Préval was formally sworn into office on 14 May.

Elections to a newly enlarged 30-seat Senate and 99-seat Chamber of Deputies were also held on 7 February 2006. However, most of the results were inconclusive, necessitating a second round of voting, to be held on 19 March. This was subsequently postponed until 21 April, a delay attributed by the CEP to the need to investigate numerous claims of voting irregularities. According to partial, provisional results following the second round of voting, Préval's Fwon Lespwa won the largest number of seats in both legislative chambers (13 in the Sénat and 24 in the Chamber of Deputies), although the party failed to secure a majority in either house. The Fusion des Sociaux-Démocrates Haïtiens alliance was placed second, with four seats in the upper house and 18 in the lower chamber, while the OPL won three senate seats and 11 seats in the Chamber of Deputies.

President Préval nominated Jacques-Edouard Alexis as Prime Minister. The proposed return of Alexis to his former role was subsequently approved by both legislative chambers, and in June 2006 a new 18-member coalition cabinet, with representatives from six political parties, was sworn into office. Alexis declared that he would give consideration to the plight of political prisoners enduring lengthy detentions without being put on trial. A few days later it was announced that Jocelerme Privert had been released on parole, and in July Yvon Neptune was released on health and humanitarian grounds (the charges against Neptune were withdrawn in 2009). Meanwhile, the period of relative calm that had followed Préval's election victory was fractured in June 2006, when a severe intensification of street violence and kidnappings prompted MINUSTAH to increase its presence in Port-au-Prince. Between June and August approximately 100 people were reported to have been killed in the capital, with a further 400 people wounded. In August the President and the Prime Minister issued an ultimatum to the gang leaders thought to be responsible for much of the violence, ordering them to hand in their weapons or be killed. In September the Government appointed a new commission designed to disarm gang members by offering them food, financial support and training.

In August 2006 the UN Security Council voted unanimously to extend MINUSTAH's mandate until February 2007. In November and December 2006 angry protesters amassed in the streets of Cité Soleil to demonstrate against the continued presence of MINUSTAH, accusing UN troops of using indiscriminate force to quell civil unrest, a claim the UN mission denied. Despite the opposition, MINUSTAH's mandate was extended until October 2008. Joint operations by MINUSTAH and Haitian police contributed to a significant improvement in security in Port-au-Prince during 2007, with a reported 70% reduction in kidnappings compared with the previous year. MINUSTAH's mandate was extended for a further 12 months in October 2008.

Continuing political unrest

In early April 2008 several days of violent demonstrations by thousands of protesters against a sharp increase in the cost of food resulted in the deaths of five people and the murder of a MINUSTAH peacekeeper. (It was reported that the prices of food staples had increased by some 50% in the previous year.) On 12 April the Senate approved a motion to dismiss Alexis as Prime Minister over his handling of the crisis. In late April Préval nominated Ericq Pierre as Prime Minister, for which role he had previously been designated in 1997 under Préval's first administration. Pierre was subsequently rejected once again by the Chamber of Deputies, as was Préval's subsequent nomination, Robert Manuel. In June Préval nominated Michèle Pierre-Louis, an economist and director of a charitable foundation, and, following legislative approval, she was eventually sworn in on 29 August, bringing to an end some four months without a functioning Government.

Delayed elections to renew one-third of the seats in the Senate were held in April 2009. In February it had been revealed by the CEP that all candidates from former President Aristide's FL were to be excluded from the elections on the grounds that it was not clear which nominees of the party were legitimate, as two rival FL factions had both submitted lists of candidates. Thousands of FL supporters took to the streets on 28 February in protest against the decision, which had also prompted expressions of concern from the OAS and the US embassy, and to mark the fifth anniversary of Aristide's exile. The first round of the elections, on 19 April, was marked by a low rate of voter participation, of only 11.8%, and violent demonstrations caused polling to be cancelled in the Centre department. As no candidate obtained the required 50% majority, a second round of voting was eventually conducted on 21 June. Fwon Lespwa won five of the 11 seats contested, giving the party a total of 12 of the Senate's 30 seats, with the remaining six seats divided between five parties and an independent. However, the turnout was reported to be even lower than in the first round, prompting the FL to declare that the results should be annulled.

At a conference held in Washington, DC, in April 2009, international donors pledged to disburse US $324m. in development aid for Haiti. Following a continued improvement in security in 2008–09, the UN began to broaden the focus of its activities in Haiti, and in May the UN Secretary-General, Ban Ki-Moon, appointed former US President Bill Clinton as his first Special Envoy for the country, with a remit to secure further international support for economic and social recovery.

The Senate adopted a motion to dismiss Pierre-Louis as Prime Minister on 30 October 2009, on the grounds that her Government's efforts to address Haiti's economic difficulties had been insufficient. Noting that Pierre-Louis had succeeded in securing the support of bilateral and multilateral donors during her 14 months in office, observers speculated that her removal was in fact politically motivated. Préval nominated Jean-Max Bellerive as Prime Minister. His new Cabinet retained 11 of the 18 ministers from the previous administration.

In November 2009 the CEP announced that the FL would not be permitted to contest the legislative elections scheduled to be held in 2010, citing the party's alleged failure to meet the legal requirements for registration. Meanwhile, following the dissolution of Fwon Lespwa (at Préval's behest), a new movement in support of the President, Inite (Unité), was formed by several organizations, including the MOP, the PLB and the Union Nationale Chrétienne pour la Reconstruction d'Haïti. Inite's main opposition was expected to come from the Alternative pour le Progrès et la Democratie (Altenativ), a new electoral alliance created by Alyans, the Fusion des Sociaux-Démocrates Haïtiens and the OPL.

Earthquake of January 2010

More than 230,000 people were estimated to have been killed and more than 300,000 injured in Port-au-Prince and surrounding areas on 12 January 2010 in an earthquake with a magnitude of 7.0. Damage to buildings and infrastructure was also extensive: the UN estimated that some 10% of the buildings in the capital had been destroyed, while at least 1.5m. people had been made homeless. On 15 January the UN appealed for US $562m. (subsequently raised to $577m.) in emergency relief to assist an estimated 3m. affected people over a period of six months; one-half of this amount was to be used to provide food aid. The Government's response to the disaster was hampered by the destruction of the presidential palace, the parliament building, the police headquarters and many of its ministries, as well as by the death of public officials and civil servants. International organizations based in the capital were similarly affected: the headquarters of MINUSTAH collapsed and the head of the mission and his deputy were among those killed. Logistical difficulties, resulting from the damage to transport infrastructure and also from the scale of the aid required, delayed the distribution of supplies. A state of emergency was declared on 17 January (and extended for a further 18 months in April). A resolution approved by the UN Security Council on 19 January authorized the deployment to Haiti of an additional 2,000 military personnel and 1,500 police officers. In late January FAO appealed to international donors to support an 18-month plan for the investment of $700m. in the Haitian agricultural sector in order to repair infrastructure, to stimulate food production and to create employment for people (subsequently estimated to number 661,000) fleeing the Port-au-Prince area. Those who did not leave the capital settled in more than 1,300 camps created around the earthquake-affected area.

A government report published in March 2010 estimated the total value of damage and losses caused by the earthquake at $7,860m. (equivalent to around 120% of gross domestic product) and the cost of the long-term reconstruction of the country at $11,500m., one-half of which would be required for the basic social services, such as health, education, nutrition, water and sanitation. The report also advocated a development strategy focused on greater decentralization, noting that 65% of Haiti's economic activity had hitherto been located in the Port-au-Prince area. At a conference held in New York at the end of March, international donors pledged $9,900m. in support of the Haitian Government's Action Plan for National Recovery and Development, including some $1,000.5m. in debt relief and $5,373.4m. in funding to be disbursed during 2010–12. An Interim Haiti Recovery Commission, co-chaired by Prime Minister Bellerive and Bill Clinton, was established in April to co-ordinate the implementation of the Plan and to monitor the distribution of funds.

The legislative elections were postponed indefinitely in February 2010. In May the Chamber of Deputies and the Senate approved legislation allowing President Préval, whose term was due to end on 7 February 2011, to remain in office until 14 May of that year if the presidential election had to be delayed. The extension of Préval's term prompted demands for the President's resignation at opposition-organized demonstrations in Port-au-Prince attended by some 2,000 people. In June 2010, however, Préval signed a decree scheduling both the legislative and the presidential elections for 28 November.

The UN Security Council approved a resolution authorizing the deployment of an additional 680 police officers in Haiti in June 2010, recognizing the need for MINUSTAH to assist the Haitian national police force in protecting the population, amid reports of increased crime and sexual violence in the temporary settlements for displaced people, particularly those adjacent to traditional slum areas such as Cité Soleil. There were also concerns about a rise in the activity of criminal gangs, which was partly linked to the escape following the earthquake of 5,409 prisoners, several hundred of whom had been detained on charges related to gang activity. (Joint operations between MINUSTAH and the Haitian police resulted in at least 629 prisoners being recaptured during 2010.) The UN Security Council extended MINUSTAH's mandate for a further year in October, maintaining its authorized strength at a military component of up to 8,940 troops and a police component of up to 4,391 officers.

Haiti suffered a further severe setback in October 2010, with the confirmation of an outbreak of cholera in the Artibonite and Centre departments, which subsequently spread throughout the country. Allegations that Nepalese peacekeepers were the source of the outbreak (after tests indicated that the strain of cholera affecting Haiti was most similar to one found in South Asia) led to unrest and demonstrations against MINUSTAH's presence in Haiti in November. One protester was killed in clashes with UN troops in the northern city of Cap-Haïtien, although the UN suggested that the violence had been orchestrated by those seeking to disrupt the forthcoming elections. In December Ban Ki-Moon announced the establishment of an independent panel to investigate the source of the cholera outbreak; the panel's report, issued in May 2011, concluded that it had originated from the contamination of the Artibonite river, near the base where the Nepalese peacekeepers were stationed, although a variety of factors had caused the disease to spread. Meanwhile, the UN appealed for some US $175m. in international aid to combat the cholera epidemic. By late November 2013 some 689,500 cases of cholera, including just under 8,500 fatalities, had been recorded.

In January 2013, in a speech to mark the third anniversary of the earthquake, the President claimed that the disaster had caused damages of nearly US $13,000m. and urged donors to co-operate more closely with the Haitian Government. Of the estimated total of $6,430m. in humanitarian and recovery funding that had been disbursed from all sources in 2010–12 to assist Haiti, only an estimated 9.1% had been channelled through the Haitian Government. In June 2013 it was reported that around 4,000 people displaced by the earthquake had been forced out of temporary camps since the start of the year, most of the camps being located on private property, with a further 75,000 facing threats of eviction. In late October, according to the UN, the number of Haitians living in camps was some 172,000 down from 1.5m. immediately following the disaster.

2010 and 2011 elections

The presidential and legislative elections were held, as scheduled, on 28 November 2010. Voter participation was extremely low, at just 22.8%. Immediately after the elections, 12 of the 19 presidential candidates alleged that fraud had been perpetrated in favour of Inite's candidate, Jude Célestin, but a joint OAS-CARICOM mission concluded that the irregularities that its officials had observed were not sufficiently serious to invalidate the vote. According to preliminary results released by the CEP on 7 December, the RDNP candidate, Mirlande Manigat, an academic and wife of former President Leslie Manigat, secured the largest share of the presidential ballot, with 31.4%, followed by Célestin, with 22.5%, and Michel Martelly, a musician representing Repons Peyizan (Réponse des Paysans), with 21.8%. A second round of voting between the two leading nominees was to be held on 16 January 2011. However, the US embassy cast doubt on the CEP's preliminary results, noting that they were 'inconsistent' with those published by a national election observation organization, which placed Martelly in second place, and violent protests by supporters of Martelly resulted in five deaths. In mid-December 2010, in response to increasing international pressure, President Préval requested OAS assistance in reviewing the disputed results. The second round of voting (in both the presidential and legislative elections) was consequently suspended by the CEP. The OAS electoral experts issued their report in January 2011, concluding that Martelly was the second-placed presidential candidate, ahead of Célestin. In early February, without releasing detailed results of the first round, the CEP announced that Manigat and Martelly would contest the run-off presidential ballot, which was to be held on 20 March, concurrently with the second round of the legislative elections (only four of the 11 seats contested in the Senate and 18 of the 99 seats in the lower house having thus far been filled). Meanwhile, former President Duvalier unexpectedly returned to Haiti in January, after 25 years in exile; he was swiftly charged with corruption and misappropriation of funds. Moreover, on the eve of the run-off ballot, Aristide, whose FL had been excluded from the elections, also returned from exile.

International observers asserted that the run-off presidential ballot of 20 March 2011 was better conducted than the first round of voting. Martelly defeated Manigat, winning 67.6% of the valid votes cast, his victory reflecting his popularity among younger voters and public disenchantment with more traditional politicians. The electoral turnout was again very low, at only 22.5%. Following voting in the second round of the legislative election, Inite was by far the largest party in the legislature, holding 17 of the 30 seats in the Sénat and 46 of the 99 seats in the Chamber of Deputies, according to final, official results. Martelly's Repons Peyizan took only three seats in the Chamber of Deputies and failed to gain representation in the upper chamber. However, the results of 19 legislative seats (17 in the lower house and two in the Senate), 16 of which had been allocated to Inite, were subsequently disputed. In late April, having examined each case at the request of President Préval, the joint OAS-CARICOM electoral observation mission recommended the reinstatement of preliminary results, which had attributed 33 seats in the Chamber of Deputies to Inite. On 11 May the CEP announced the reversal of 15 of the 19 challenged results, with Inite retaining just four of the seats in question. Later that month the Senate established a committee of inquiry to consider allegations of electoral wrongdoing, while a second round of voting finally took place in three constituencies.

Martelly in office

President Martelly took office on 14 May 2011, pledging to accelerate stalled reconstruction efforts, to address the cholera epidemic, to restore security, to boost employment and to introduce free education, which would be financed by the imposition of taxes on international telephone calls and money transfers to Haiti. More controversially, he also proposed the re-establishment of the armed forces, which had been disbanded by Aristide in 1995, suggesting that it could eventually replace MINUSTAH, and mooted granting amnesty to Aristide and Duvalier. Meanwhile, the legislature adopted a number of amendments to the Constitution, notably voting against a proposed change that would have allowed Presidents to serve two consecutive five-year terms, but voting in favour of a revision according dual nationality to Haitians living abroad, thereby allowing them to vote and own land in Haiti and to hold lower public office. However, despite having expressed support for the latter measure, Martelly subsequently vetoed the amendments, after it emerged that there were discrepancies between the constitutional text to be published in the official gazette and that adopted by parliament. The unamended Constitution thus remained in force.

The President's ability to implement his plans was constrained by his weak position in the legislature and consequent failure to secure approval for his choice of Prime Minister. Martelly designated businessman Daniel-Gérard Rouzier as premier, but this was rejected in June 2011 by the Chamber of Deputies, in which Inite had joined with other parties to form the Groupe des parlementaires pour le renouveau, an alliance claiming to comprise some 70 deputies. Martelly's second nominee, Bernard Gousse, a former Minister of Justice in the administration of Gérard Latortue (2004–06), was rejected by the Senate in early August. Finally, on 4 October, the appointment of Martelly's third nominee, Garry Conille, an official at the UN Development Programme and until recently chief of staff to UN Special Envoy Bill Clinton, was endorsed by the Senate, having been accepted by the Chamber of Deputies on 16 September. On 15 October the lower house approved Conille's programme for government—including plans to attract foreign aid and investment, to resettle the homeless, to modernize infrastructure, to establish urban and rural development zones, and to create 1.5m. jobs over a period of five years—as well as the composition of his Cabinet, which included three Inite ministers, and took office three days later.

In January 2012 President Martelly announced that a civilian commission that he had appointed had recommended the restoration of the army with a remit to safeguard territorial integrity, respond to natural disasters and combat drugs-trafficking and terrorism. However, there were concerns among the opposition, and internationally, regarding the financial burden involved (estimated at some US $95m.) and the poor human rights record of the previous military. Hundreds of uniformed former soldiers, many of them armed, began to occupy disused military bases from January, demanding the re-establishment of the army and the payment of some $15m. in wages and pension contributions that they claimed to be owed. Following a series of protest marches in May, one of which culminated in the firing of tear gas by UN peacekeepers, a number of former soldiers were arrested and charged with forming a rogue army, and police raided bases that they had refused to vacate. In November the Ministry of National Defence warned former soldiers not to take any action that would disrupt public order; in October 2013 it was announced by the defence ministry that no former members of the armed forces of Haiti would be part of the new civil defence force.

The mandate of the Interim Haiti Recovery Commission expired in October 2011. In August the Commission had notably approved a US $78m. project proposed by the President, which was expected to create some 4,500 jobs and to rehabilitate 16 neighbourhoods of Port-au-Prince to allow the return of some 30,000 people from six particularly vulnerable camps. In September President Martelly announced the creation of a 32-member Presidential Advisory Council on Economic Growth and Investment, comprising eight former heads of state of various countries, as well as business executives with expertise in a wide range of areas; co-chaired by Bill Clinton, the Council was charged with attracting foreign investment and to revitalize the country's economy.

The UN Security Council approved an extension of MINUSTAH's mandate for a further year in October 2011, but reduced its maximum authorized strength to pre-earthquakes levels (some 7,340 troops and 3,241 police officers), in view of the completion of the presidential and legislative elections and the gradual curtailment of large-scale humanitarian operations. In the previous month, meanwhile, clashes had occurred in Port-au-Prince between police and hundreds of protesters who were demanding MINUSTAH's withdrawal from Haiti, amid growing anger regarding the possibility that Nepalese peacekeepers had been the source of the ongoing cholera epidemic and following allegations that Uruguayan peacekeepers had sexually assaulted a Haitian man.

The Minister of Justice and Public Security, Josué Pierre-Louis, was forced to resign from office in November 2011, after he ordered the arrest of Arnel Bélizaire, an opposition member of the Chamber of Deputies, thereby further damaging relations between the legislative and executive branches of government. Pierre Michel Brunache was appointed to replace him in December. Also in December, the Senate established a committee of inquiry into the nationality of Martelly and members of his Government, following allegations that the President and several ministers held foreign citizenship, in contravention of the Constitution.

In late January 2012, in a report to the Attorney-General's office, the judge handling the case against Duvalier recommended that the former dictator should be tried on charges of embezzlement of public funds, but that the statute of limitations had expired with regard to human rights abuses committed during his regime. However, a group of alleged victims of such abuses and their relatives appealed against the latter ruling, arguing that, under international law, the statute of limitations did not apply to crimes against humanity. After several postponements, when Duvalier failed to attend court, a hearing into the appeal took place on 28 February at which the former President denied responsibility for abuses carried out during his time in office, including the murder and torture of political opponents. By early 2014 there had been little progress in bringing Duvalier to justice.

Prime Minister Conille resigned from office on 24 February 2012. His departure followed a deterioration in relations with President Martelly, particularly after Conille's decision to establish a commission to examine the awarding of construction contracts in the wake of the 2010 earthquake. On 1 March 2012 Martelly nominated close ally and Minister of Foreign Affairs and Religion Laurent Lamothe to succeed Conille, a nomination that received legislative approval. Lamothe formally took office on 16 May, retaining the foreign affairs and religion portfolio. The new Prime Minister pledged to improve transport infrastructure, to increase security measures and to introduce an anti-poverty strategy entailing free tuition for children of primary school age and monthly cash transfers to around 100,000 mothers living in disadvantaged neighbourhoods on condition that they agreed to the vaccination of their children. The Government revoked 39 construction contracts in July, following the completion of the investigation initiated by Conille.

The revised Constitution, as amended by the legislature in May 2011, was finally published in June 2012, allowing its entry into force. In addition to according dual nationality to Haitians living abroad, the changes provided for the creation of three new institutions: a constitutional court; a Supreme Council of Judicial Power (Conseil Supérieur du Pouvoir Judiciaire—CSPJ), which was duly inaugurated in July; and a Permanent Electoral Council (Conseil Electoral Permanent) to replace the discredited CEP, the members of which had been dismissed in December 2011. The establishment of a new electoral council was particularly urgent, as municipal polls and elections to renew one-third of the members of the Senate were overdue, with the mandates of 10 senators having expired in May 2012. Six of the nine members of the Permanent Electoral Council, representing the executive and the judiciary, were installed in August, but the two legislative chambers could not agree on a process to select its nominees, partly owing to the depleted nature of the Senate. The inclusion of former Minister of Justice and Public Security Josué Pierre-Louis as a representative of the executive was also controversial. In October, moreover, the CSPJ designated three new representatives to the electoral council, following complaints that its existing members had been elected by minority vote, although the installed members refused to stand aside for their replacements. In December, in an attempt to overcome the impasse, the executive and legislative branches of government signed an agreement on the formation of a Transitional College of the Permanent Electoral Council to organize the next elections, after which its mandate would end. This body would comprise the six members already nominated to the Permanent Electoral Council (with further negotiations to be held to decide which of the CSPJ representatives were legitimate) and three still to be appointed by the legislature. However, this arrangement appeared to be widely regarded as unsatisfactory.

Meanwhile, Lamothe announced a cabinet reorganization in August 2012, notably ceding the foreign affairs and religion portfolio to his erstwhile secretary of state, Pierre Richard Casimir, while assuming responsibility for planning and external co-operation. In September Lamothe announced the establishment of a new mechanism for co-ordinating international assistance: the Aid Effectiveness Committee (Comité de l'Efficacité de l'Aide, CEA). Chaired by the Prime Minister himself and involving the participation of donors, civil society, local government and the private sector, the CEA was to assume the role previously undertaken by the Interim Haiti Recovery Commission.

MINUSTAH's mandate was extended for a further year in early October 2012, although its maximum authorized strength was to be reduced to 6,270 troops and 2,601 police officers by June 2013; one of its principal priorities was to assist in the implementation of a plan to increase the Haitian national police force to a minimum of 15,000 serving officers by 2016 (from around 10,000 in 2012). Haiti's security situation was deemed to be stable but fragile by UN Secretary-General Ban Ki-Moon, who urged the Government to continue to strengthen institutions responsible for the rule of law and to intensify its efforts to combat unemployment and poverty. Also in early October, plans were announced to boost the government education fund created from levying taxes on international telephone calls and money transfers by some US $100m. through the imposition of additional taxes on alcohol, cigarettes and gambling. However, public discontent with the Government was evident in mid-October, when hundreds of protesters demonstrated in Port-au-Prince against the high cost of living, with some demanding the resignation of President Martelly, whom they accused of corruption, wasting resources and failing to alleviate poverty.

Haiti's difficulties were exacerbated later in October 2012 when Hurricane Sandy struck, killing 54 people, leaving more than 30,000 homeless and inflicting severe damage on the agricultural sector, with an estimated 70% of crops destroyed in the south of the country. The country had already suffered significantly as a result of Tropical Storm Isaac in August, when 24 people were killed, over 81,000 ha of crops damaged and 1,105 homes destroyed. A one-month state of emergency was declared in response to Sandy, while the UN and the Government appealed for an additional US $39.9m. in funding for humanitarian assistance over the following year, amid rising concerns regarding food insecurity in particular. An increase in the number of cholera cases was also reported. The recent revelation by a US cholera expert—who was a member of the panel established by the UN in December 2010 to investigate the outbreak of the disease in Haiti (see Earthquake of January 2010)—that newly available data demonstrated that the strain of cholera in Haiti exactly matched that prevalent in Nepal in 2010 appeared to strengthen the case of those seeking compensation from the UN. Some 5,000 victims and their families had lodged an official claim with the UN, on the grounds that Nepalese UN peacekeepers were the source of the cholera outbreak, demanding $100,000 for those who had died and $50,000 for those who had fallen ill. In February 2013, however, the UN formally rejected the compensation claims filed by victims of the cholera outbreak (which had caused more than 8,000 fatalities to date), invoking its legal immunity in the countries in which it operates under the Convention on the Privileges and Immunities of the UN (which was adopted by the UN General Assembly in 1946). In May the UN was informed by the Institute for Justice and Democracy (based in Boston, Massachusetts, USA) that it had 60 days in which to initiate compensation talks with the families of the cholera victims. The Institute filed a new complaint against the UN, in an attempt to lift its diplomatic immunity, in a federal court in New York on 9 October; however, the US Government rejected the claim in March 2014. In the same month a new class action was initiated against the UN. In October 2013 UN Security Council voted to extend MINUSTAH's mandate until 15 October 2014.

Amid mounting international concern regarding the continued delay in organizing the overdue municipal and partial senatorial elections, and persistent public discontent over rising food prices and alleged government corruption among other issues, the Cabinet was reorganized again in January 2013. Most significantly, Saint Cyr was succeeded as Minister of the Interior and Territorial Collectivities by David Bazile, an ally of Martelly who had served as Secretary of State for Public Security in 2004–06. Marie-Carmelle Jean-Marie, the Minister of the Economy and Finance, resigned in April, as did Minister of Communications Régine Godefroy; they were replaced, respectively, by Wilson Laleau and Josette Darguste (in an acting capacity).

Recent developments: the long road to elections

On 11 April 2013 a presidential decree was finally published on the formation of the Transitional College of the Permanent Electoral Council. The College was to comprise nine members, three each appointed by the executive, the legislature and the judiciary. In May the Senate approved the country's first ever anti-corruption law; by early 2014, however, the Chamber of Deputies had failed to approve the new legislation. In August it was reported that the President of the lower house was to introduce drastic measures to ensure that its members participated in the sessions; no law had been passed since early June owing to the lack of quorum. The preliminary draft of the electoral law was submitted to the President on 3 July; it was passed by the Senate on 2 October, ratified by the Chamber of Deputies, in an extraordinary session convened by Martelly, on 27 November and promulgated on 14 December. It was expected that the long overdue partial senatorial ballot would take place in 2014, but remained to be seen whether the election of 10 additional senators, as well as local elections and those of the members of the lower house, would be held simultaneously. (Had the electoral law not been promulgated by 13 January 2014 10 out of the 20 currently sitting senators would have been forced to leave office, leaving the upper house short of a quorum.) Apart from the passage of the electoral law, the work of the Chamber of Deputies in the second half of 2013 was obstructed by persistent absenteeism. Representatives of the executive, legislature and political parties began negotiations towards an agreement on the holding of elections began in late January 2014 in Pétionville, mediated by the Bishop of Les Cayes, Cardinal Chibly Langlois. On 14 March an accord was reached, which provided for elections to be held to two-thirds of the Senate and the entire Chamber of Deputies by the end of the year, but ideally by 26 October. This was approved by the legislature on 1 April.

The death of Judge Jean Serge Joseph on 13 July 2013 caused a huge amount of political controversy. At the time of his death the judge had been investigating charges of corruption against Martelly's wife and son. It was alleged that on 11 July in a secret meeting Joseph had been ordered to call off the investigation by, among others, the President, the Prime Minister and the Minister of Justice and Public Security, Jean Renel Sanon, all of whom denied that such a meeting took place. Joseph died of a brain haemorrhage, the causes of which were reported to be either stress or poison. A report published on 8 August, following a Senate inquiry into the judge's death, recommended that Lamothe and Sanon be removed from office and that Martelly be impeached for high treason for having lied to the nation. An inquiry conducted by the lower house made similar recommendations.

In January 2014 nine people were charged with the murder of Jean Dominique, a prominent radio broadcaster and political analyst, and a security guard in April 2000. The suspects included several allies of Aristide who was leader of the opposition when the murder took place. In May 2013 thousands of the former President's supporters defied a ban in order to greet him as he appeared in court to give evidence at the trial. Aristide was not indicted as having been part of the conspiracy despite evidence that the organizer of Dominique's murder, former FL senator Mirlande Libérus, had been acting on his orders.

As part of the so-called 'El Rancho' agreement (named after the hotel in which negotiations took place) on elections reached in March 2014, in early April President Martelly effected a cabinet reshuffle, in order that a wider range of political parties were represented in government. Notably, Marie-Carmelle Jean-Marie was reappointed to the economy and finance ministry.

Foreign Affairs

Regional relations

Relations between Haiti and its neighbour on the island of Hispaniola, the Dominican Republic, have traditionally been tense owing to the use of the border area by anti-Government guerrillas, smugglers and illegal migrants, resulting in the periodic closure of the border. In March 1996, following an official visit to the Dominican Republic by Préval, the first by a Haitian President since 1935, a joint communiqué was issued establishing a bilateral commission to promote improved co-operation. In 1998 agreement was reached to establish joint border patrols to combat the traffic of drugs and other contraband. In November 1999 Préval submitted a formal protest to the Dominican Republic following a spate of summary deportations of Haitians from the neighbouring country. A protocol was signed in December limiting the repatriations.

Relations between Haiti and the Dominican Republic suffered a marked deterioration in 2005. The Dominican Republic's army forcibly repatriated thousands of Haitian immigrants, a process that was intensified following the murder of a Dominican woman, allegedly at the hands of two Haitian men, in May. Human rights organizations alleged that the Dominican army was acting indiscriminately and had deported not only illegal immigrants but also many legal immigrants and Dominicans of Haitian origin; the army strenuously denied such claims. In December a visit to Haiti by Dominican President Leonel Fernández was abruptly curtailed after violent demonstrations in protest against the alleged abuse of Haitians in the Dominican Republic broke out. Tensions rose again in 2009, following the murder of a Haitian migrant in the Dominican capital. Following the earthquake in 2010, the Dominican authorities provided humanitarian assistance to the country and suspended the repatriation of Haitian immigrants. In 2011, however, deportations of illegal immigrants resumed and border controls were tightened, in an attempt to curtail the spread of cholera from Haiti, where several thousand deaths from the disease had been recorded (see Domestic Political Affairs). President-elect Martelly visited the Dominican Republic in May. Talks with President Fernández focused on border security issues and the status of the estimated 1m. undocumented Haitians living in the Dominican Republic. In June 2012 Haiti briefly recalled its ambassador from the Dominican Republic, amid concerns regarding the effect on Haitian migrants of new legislation regulating foreign workers in the Dominican Republic. However, relations subsequently improved and the new Dominican President, Danilo Medina, reaffirmed a desire to negotiate a free trade agreement with Haiti. In February 2013, moreover, the Haitian and Dominican Governments agreed to connect their electricity systems, with the aim of improving energy security and lowering prices, although work on the project, which would require external financing, was not expected to begin for two years. In June the Haitian authorities imposed a ban on the import of eggs and poultry from its neighbour, citing an outbreak of avian flu across the border, a claim that was strenuously denied by the Dominican Republic. The following month, despite assurances that there would be no reprisals for the ban, the

Dominican Republic expelled 157 Haitians without complying with repatriation procedures; further expulsions occurred over a period of several months. Relations between the two countries deteriorated further in September, following an order issued by the Dominican Republic's Constitutional Court whereby the citizenship of the descendants of Haitians born in the Dominican Republic after 1929 was to be removed, rendering thousands of people stateless. Tensions escalated further after the murder of an elderly Dominican couple in Neiba, Dominican Republic, allegedly by a group of Haitians, and the subsequent revenge killing of a Haitian. In November it was reported that more than 1,000 Haitian fugitives, who had escaped their country at the time of the 2010 earthquake, were still at large in the Dominican Republic. In January 2014 a series of talks between the two countries, attended by international observers, resulted in the lifting of the poultry ban and the expression of commitment on both sides to enact measures to safeguard the rights of Haitians living in the Dominican Republic.

Other external relations

The USA contributed some 1,900 troops to the Multinational Interim Force deployed in Haiti following the resignation of Aristide in February 2004. In 2006 President-elect Préval visited the USA, meeting US President George W. Bush and addressing the UN Security Council. In October, in recognition of government efforts to introduce peace and stability to the country, the USA partially lifted its arms embargo against Haiti, imposed in 1991. Préval sought to promote strong relations with the US Administration of Barack Obama, meeting Secretary of State Hillary Clinton in 2009. Clinton emphasized the Obama Administration's commitment to assisting Haiti during talks with Préval in Port-au-Prince in April. Following the earthquake of January 2010, the USA dispatched more than 22,000 military personnel to the country to assist in the distribution of relief supplies and temporarily to assume control of the international airport. Clinton expressed strong support for President-elect Martelly when he visited Washington, DC, in April 2011.

CONSTITUTION AND GOVERNMENT

The March 1987 Constitution was amended in June 2012. It provided for a bicameral legislature, elected by universal adult suffrage. Executive power is held by the President, who is elected by universal adult suffrage for a five-year term and cannot not stand for immediate re-election. The amended Constitution of 2012 provided for the creation of a constitutional court and a permanent electoral council to replace the discredited Provisional Electoral Council.

There are 10 departments, subdivided into arrondissements and communes.

REGIONAL AND INTERNATIONAL CO-OPERATION

Haiti is a member of the Caribbean Community and Common Market (see p. 223), the Association of Caribbean States (see p. 449), of the Latin American Economic System (see p. 452), and of the Community of Latin American and Caribbean States (see p. 464), which was formally inaugurated in December 2011. Haiti is also a member of the International Coffee Organization (see p. 446). Haiti was a founder member of the UN in 1945. Having been a contracting party to the General Agreement on Tariffs and Trade since 1950, Haiti joined the World Trade Organization (see p. 434) in 1996. Haiti is also a signatory to the European Union's Cotonou Agreement (see p. 324), which replaced the Lomé Convention in 2000.

ECONOMIC AFFAIRS

In 2012, according to estimates by the World Bank, Haiti's gross national income (GNI), measured at average 2010–12 prices, was US $7,691m., equivalent to $760 per head (or $1,240 per head on an international purchasing-power parity basis). In 2003–12 the population increased at an average annual rate of 1.4%, while gross domestic product (GDP) per head decreased, in real terms, by an average of 0.2% per year. Overall GDP increased, in real terms, at an average annual rate of 1.1% in 2003–12; according to official estimates, real GDP increased by 2.8% in 2011/12.

Agriculture (including hunting, forestry and fishing) contributed an estimated 23.0% of GDP, at constant prices, in 2011/12. About 56.7% of the total labour force were engaged in agricultural activities in mid-2014, according to FAO estimates. The principal cash crop, traditionally, was coffee, although production has decreased significantly in recent years and has been overtaken by mangoes and cocoa. The export of essential oils for cosmetics and pharmaceuticals has become increasingly important, and crayfish are also an important export commodity. The main food crops are sugar, cassava, bananas, yams, sweet potatoes, maize and rice. The World Bank released US $50m. in aid for the agriculture sector in 2012. According to official estimates, agricultural GDP increased at an average annual rate of 1.0% during 2007/08–2011/12. The sector's GDP increased by 1.1% in 2010/11, before decreasing by 2.2% in 2011/12.

Industry (including mining, manufacturing, construction and power) contributed an estimated 18.5% of GDP, at constant prices, in 2011/12. About 9.7% of the employed labour force were engaged in the sector in 2003. According to official estimates, industrial GDP increased at an average annual rate of 4.6% during 2007/08–2011/12; sectoral GDP increased by 6.4% in 2011/12.

Mining contributed 0.1% of GDP, at constant prices, in 2011/12. About 0.3% of the employed labour force were engaged in extractive activities in 2003. Marble, limestone and calcareous clay are mined. There are also unexploited copper, silver and gold deposits.

Manufacturing contributed a provisional 8.1% of GDP, at constant prices, in 2011/12. Some 6.5% of the employed population were engaged in the sector in 2003. The most important branches of manufacturing were food-processing, textiles (including apparel, leather and fur products, and footwear), chemicals (including rubber and plastic products) and tobacco. According to official estimates, manufacturing GDP increased at an average annual rate of 2.8% during 2007/08–2011/12; the sector's GDP increased by 7.1% in 2011/12.

Construction contributed an estimated 9.5% of GDP, at constant prices, in 2011/12. Some 2.7% of the employed population were engaged in the sector in 2003. According to official estimates, manufacturing GDP increased at an average annual rate of 5.5% during 2007/08–2011/12; the sector's GDP increased by 5.3% in 2011/12.

In 2011 some 79.0% of the country's public electricity came from petroleum, while 16.7% came from hydroelectric power. Overall electricity production was believed to amount to just one-10th of the capital's requirements. Haiti participated in the Petrocaribe initiative (whereby Caribbean countries were able to purchase petroleum from Venezuela on preferential terms). Imports of mineral fuels and related products accounted for 28.5% of the total value of imports in 2011/12.

The services sector contributed an estimated 58.5% of GDP, at constant prices, in 2011/12 and engaged 44.6% of the employed labour force in 2003. According to official estimates, services GDP increased by an average annual rate of 0.8% during 2007/08–2011/12; the sector's GDP increased by 3.7% in 2011/12.

In 2011/12 Haiti recorded a visible merchandise trade deficit of US $1,894.4m., and there was a deficit of $1,358.4m. on the current account of the balance of payments. The principal source of imports was the USA (35% in 2004); the USA was also the principal market for exports (81% in the same year). Other significant trading partners in recent years include France, Canada, Japan and the Dominican Republic. The principal export in 2011/12 was manufactured goods (83.3%); agricultural products were also significant. The principal imports in 2011/12 were mineral fuels and lubricants (28.5%), basic manufactures, food products and miscellaneous manufactured goods. The re-export, to the USA, of assembled goods (valued at $706.0m. in 2011/12) has become a significant source of revenue, with income rivalling that derived from domestic exports. Smuggling was estimated to have accounted for two-thirds of Haiti's imports in 2000.

In the financial year ending 30 September 2012 there was an estimated budgetary deficit of 9,779.4m. gourdes. Haiti's general government gross debt was 50,824m. gourdes in 2012, equivalent to 15.5% of GDP. At the end of 2011 Haiti's total external debt was US $783m., of which $635m. was public and publicly guaranteed debt. In that year the cost of servicing long-term public and publicly guaranteed debt and repayments to the IMF was equivalent to 0.5% of the total value of exports of goods, services and income (excluding workers' remittances). The annual rate of inflation averaged 17.7% per year in 2000–12. Consumer prices increased by an average of 6.3% in 2012. Some 60% of the labour force were estimated to be unemployed in 2001. Remittances from Haitians living abroad amounted to approximately $1,988m. in 2012 (equivalent to almost 20% of GDP in that year).

In terms of average income, Haiti is the poorest country in the Western hemisphere, and there is extreme inequality of wealth.

More than one-half of the population lives on less than US $1 a day, while in 2013, despite some improvements in food security, around one in five children was suffering from acute malnutrition. Economic progress has been impeded by political instability and a series of natural disasters, most notably the 2010 earthquake, which caused damage and losses equivalent to more than 120% of GDP. Substantial emergency assistance was pledged to Haiti, and the IMF immediately disbursed $102m., on highly concessionary terms, under its Extended Credit Facility (ECF). Moreover, the Group of Seven most industrialized nations agreed to cancel Haiti's bilateral debts, and international donors pledged to provide aid of $5,373m. by 2013. In July 2010 the IMF approved the cancellation of Haiti's outstanding liabilities to the Fund, as well as a new three-year ECF arrangement. There were concerns that much of the money allocated to Haiti by the international community was not reaching its target; in July 2013 it was reported that just 31% of the $651m. pledged by the US Agency for International Development to support relief and reconstruction had been spent. The attraction of foreign investment was a key government priority, as were the development of a nascent mining sector and the promotion of Haiti as a tourist destination, with the renovation of airports and the construction of new hotels (such as the Marriott Hotel in Port-au-Prince, scheduled to open in 2015) regarded as important advances in this regard. In October 2012, in a significant move towards economic decentralization, the Government inaugurated an industrial park in Caracol, near Cap-Haïtien. It was envisaged that the park would eventually provide jobs for 20,000 workers. GDP increased by 5.6% in 2010/11 and by 2.8% in 2011/12. The agricultural sector in 2012 suffered a drought and destruction caused by Hurricane Sandy, causing damage of an estimated $254m., with the loss of one-third of annual production. The effect of natural disasters on agricultural production resulted in the IMF forecasting GDP growth of 3.4% for 2013, significantly short of the original figure of 6.5% under the ECF arrangement, and 4.5% for 2014. In August of that year the IMF agreed to a further disbursement to Haiti of $2.5m. and an extension of the ECF arrangement until August 2014, in order to support the Government in its completion of key reforms, particularly in the fiscal area.

PUBLIC HOLIDAYS

2015: 1 January (Independence Day), 2 January (Heroes of Independence), 16 February (Shrove Monday, half-day), 17 February (Shrove Tuesday), 3 April (Good Friday), 14 April (Pan-American Day), 1 May (Labour and Agriculture Day), 18 May (Flag and University Day), 4 June (Corpus Christi), 15 August (Assumption), 17 October (Death of J.-J. Dessalines), 24 October (United Nations Day), 1 November (All Saints' Day), 2 November (All Souls' Day), 18 November (Army Day and Commemoration of the Battle of Vertières), 25 December (Christmas Day).

Statistical Survey

Sources (unless otherwise stated): Banque de la République d'Haïti, angle rues du Pavée et du Quai, BP 1570, Port-au-Prince; tel. 2299-1202; fax 2299-1145; e-mail brh@brh.net; internet www.brh.net; Institut Haitien de Statistique et d'Informatique, Ministère de l'Economie et des Finances, 1, angle rue Joseph Janvier et boulevard Harry S Truman, Port-au-Prince; tel. 2514-3789; fax 2221-5812; e-mail info@ihsi.ht; internet www.ihsi.ht.

Area and Population

AREA, POPULATION AND DENSITY

Area (sq km)	27,065*
Population (census results)	
30 August 1982†	5,053,792
7 July 2003	
Males	4,039,272
Females	4,334,478
Total	8,373,750
Population (UN estimates at mid-year)‡	
2012	10,173,774
2013	10,317,461
2014	10,461,408
Density (per sq km) at mid-2014	386.5

* 10,450 sq miles.

† Excluding adjustment for underenumeration.

‡ Source: UN, *World Population Prospects: The 2012 Revision*.

Note: It was estimated that as many as 230,000 people were killed as a result of a powerful earthquake that devastated the country's capital, Port-au-Prince, in January 2010. No reliable official estimates of total population have been published since the earthquake.

POPULATION BY AGE AND SEX
(UN estimates at mid-2014)

	Males	Females	Total
0–14	1,839,968	1,775,057	3,615,025
15–64	3,117,053	3,254,578	6,371,631
65 and over	212,031	262,721	474,752
Total	5,169,052	5,292,356	10,461,408

Source: UN, *World Population Prospects: The 2012 Revision*.

DEPARTMENTS
(official population projections at mid-2009)

	Area (sq km)	Population	Density (per sq km)	Capital
L'Artibonite (Artibonite)	4,886.9	1,571,020	321.5	Gonaïves
Centre	3,487.4	678,626	194.6	Hinche
Grand'Anse	1,911.9	425,878	222.8	Jérémie
Nippes	1,267.8	311,497	245.7	Miragoâne
Nord	2,115.2	970,495	458.8	Cap-Haïtien
Nord-Est	1,622.9	358,277	220.8	Fort Liberté
Nord-Ouest	2,102.9	662,777	315.2	Port-de-Paix
Ouest	4,982.6	3,664,620	735.5	Port-au-Prince
Sud	2,653.6	704,760	265.6	Les Cayes
Sud-Est	2,034.1	575,293	282.8	Jacmel
Total	27,065.3	9,923,243	366.6	—

PRINCIPAL TOWNS
(official projected population at mid-2009)

Port-au-Prince (capital)	897,859	Delmas	359,451
Carrefour	465,019		

Mid-2011 (urban population in city districts, UN estimate): Port-au-Prince 2,207,110 (Source: UN, *World Urbanization Prospects: The 2011 Revision*).

BIRTHS AND DEATHS
(UN estimates)

	1995–2000	2000–05	2005–10
Crude birth rate (per 1,000)	32.7	29.7	27.7
Crude death rate (per 1,000)	11.3	10.6	9.4

Source: UN, *World Population Prospects: The 2012 Revision*.

Life expectancy (years at birth): 62.3 (males 60.5; females 64.2) in 2011 (Source: World Bank, World Development Indicators database).

ECONOMICALLY ACTIVE POPULATION
(official estimates, persons aged 10 years and over, mid-1990)

	Males	Females	Total
Agriculture, hunting, forestry and fishing	1,077,191	458,253	1,535,444
Mining and quarrying	11,959	12,053	24,012
Manufacturing	83,180	68,207	151,387
Electricity, gas and water	1,643	934	2,577
Construction	23,584	4,417	28,001
Trade, restaurants and hotels	81,632	271,338	352,970
Transport, storage and communications	17,856	2,835	20,691
Financing, insurance, real estate and business services	3,468	1,589	5,057
Community, social and personal services	81,897	73,450	155,347
Sub-total	1,382,410	893,076	2,275,486
Activities not adequately defined	33,695	30,280	63,975
Total employed	1,416,105	923,356	2,339,461
Unemployed	191,333	148,346	339,679
Total labour force	1,607,438	1,071,702	2,679,140

Source: ILO, *Yearbook of Labour Statistics*.

2007/08 (national survey of employment and the informal economy, sample survey of persons aged 10 years and over, primary occupation, percentage distribution): Agriculture 36.8; Fishing 1.3; Mining and quarrying 0.3; Manufacturing 7.7; Electricity, gas and water 0.2; Construction 3.3; Wholesale and retail trade, vehicle repairs 27.2; Hotels and restaurants 3.8; Transport, storage and communications 3.0; Financial intermediation 0.6; Real estate, renting and other business activities 1.0; Public administration and compulsory social security 1.1; Education 4.8; Health and social welfare 1.9; Other community, social and personal services 2.3; Other services 4.7; Total employed 100.0.

Mid-2014 (estimates in '000): Agriculture, etc. 2,365; Total labour force 4,174 (Source: FAO).

Health and Welfare

KEY INDICATORS

Total fertility rate (children per woman, 2011)	3.3
Under-5 mortality rate (per 1,000 live births, 2011)	70
HIV/AIDS (% of persons aged 15–49, 2012)	2.1
Physicians (per 1,000 head, 1998)	0.3
Hospital beds (per 1,000 head, 2007)	1.3
Health expenditure (2010): US $ per head (PPP)	76
Health expenditure (2010): % of GDP	6.9
Health expenditure (2010): public (% of total)	40.0
Access to water (% of persons, 2011)	64
Access to sanitation (% of persons, 2011)	26
Total carbon dioxide emissions ('000 metric tons, 2010)	2,119.5
Carbon dioxide emissions per head (metric tons, 2010)	0.2
Human Development Index (2012): ranking	161
Human Development Index (2012): value	0.456

For sources and definitions, see explanatory note on p. vi.

Agriculture

PRINCIPAL CROPS
('000 metric tons)

	2010	2011	2012
Rice, paddy*	118	115	106
Maize†	340	360	202
Sorghum	116*	126*	92†
Sweet potatoes*	248	240	215
Cassava (Manioc)*	600	652	652
Yams*	353	323	323
Sugar cane*	1,110	1,150	1,200
Avocados*	49	52	53
Bananas*	255	265	270
Plantains*	239	265	267
Guavas, mangoes and mangosteens*	218	199	205

* FAO estimate(s).
† Unofficial figure(s).

Aggregate production ('000 metric tons, may include official, semi-official or estimated data): Total cereals 573 in 2010, 60 in 2011, 400 in 2012; Total roots and tubers 1,264 in 2010, 1,286 in 2011, 1,264 in 2012; Total vegetables (incl. melons) 158 in 2010, 149 in 2011, 155 in 2012; Total fruits (excl. melons) 901 in 2010, 930 in 2011, 950 in 2012.

Source: FAO.

LIVESTOCK
('000 head, year ending September, FAO estimates)

	2010	2011	2012
Horses	500	500	500
Asses	210	210	210
Mules	80	80	80
Cattle	1,455	1,460	1,465
Pigs	1,000	1,001	1,001
Sheep	153	153	154
Goats	1,910	1,920	1,950
Chickens	5,600	5,650	5,700
Turkeys	195	195	195
Ducks	190	190	190

Source: FAO.

LIVESTOCK PRODUCTS
('000 metric tons, FAO estimates)

	2010	2011	2012
Cattle meat	45.0	45.5	46.5
Goat meat	5.5	5.5	5.5
Pig meat	35.0	35.0	35.0
Horse meat	5.6	5.6	5.6
Chicken meat	8.0	8.0	8.0
Cows' milk	63.4	64.0	65.0
Goats' milk	28.1	28.1	28.2
Hen eggs	5.0	5.0	5.0

Source: FAO.

Forestry

ROUNDWOOD REMOVALS
('000 cubic metres, excl. bark, FAO estimates)

	2010	2011	2012
Sawlogs, veneer logs and logs for sleepers*	224	224	224
Other industrial wood*	15	15	15
Fuel wood	2,041	2,050	2,060
Total	2,280	2,289	2,299

* Production assumed to be unchanged since 1971.

Source: FAO.

SAWNWOOD PRODUCTION
('000 cubic metres, incl. railway sleepers)

	1969	1970	1971
Coniferous (softwood)	5	8	8
Broadleaved (hardwood)	10	5	6
Total	14	13	14

1972–2012: Annual production as in 1971 (FAO estimates).

Source: FAO.

Fishing

('000 metric tons, live weight)

	2009	2010*	2011
Capture	16.0	13.7	16.5
Freshwater fishes	0.6	0.5	0.6*
Marine fishes	14.4	12.5	15.2*
Marine crabs	0.2	0.1	0.2*
Caribbean spiny lobster	0.6	0.4	0.3
Natantian decapods	0.1	0.1	0.1*
Stromboid conchs	0.2	0.2	0.2*
Aquaculture	0.2	0.4	0.6
Total catch*	16.2	14.1	17.1

* FAO estimate(s).

Note: Figures exclude corals and madrepores (FAO estimates, metric tons): 10 in 2009–11.

Source: FAO.

Industry

SELECTED PRODUCTS
(metric tons, unless otherwise indicated, year ending 30 September)

	1999/2000
Edible oils	38,839.6
Butter	2,972.2
Margarine	2,387.4
Cornflour	104,542.6
Soap	30,069.9
Detergent	4,506.1
Beer ('000 cases of 24 bottles)	784.5
Beverages ('000 cases of 24 bottles)	1,807.7
Rum ('000 750 ml bottles)	2,009.5
Electric energy (million kWh)	698.0

Cement ('000 metric tons, estimates): 290.0 in 2004–10 (Source: US Geological Survey).

Electric energy (million kWh): 486 in 2008; 721 in 2009; 587 in 2010 (Source: UN Industrial Commodity Statistics Database).

Finance

CURRENCY AND EXCHANGE RATES

Monetary Units
100 centimes = 1 gourde.

Sterling, Dollar and Euro Equivalents (31 December 2013)
£1 sterling = 72.265 gourdes;
US $1 = 43.882 gourdes;
€1 = 60.518 gourdes;
1,000 gourdes = £13.84 = $22.79 = €16.52.

Average Exchange Rate (gourdes per US $)

2011	40.523
2012	41.950
2013	43.463

Note: The official rate of exchange was maintained at US $1 = 5 gourdes until September 1991, when the central bank ceased all operations at the official rate, thereby unifying the exchange system at the 'floating' free market rate.

BUDGET
(million gourdes, year ending 30 September)

Current revenue	2010	2011*	2012*
Internal receipts	19,489.6	24,613.1	28,330.7
Customs	11,493.8	13,764.9	13,843.2
Total (incl. others)	31,445.3	38,932.6	42,313.1

Expenditure	2010	2011*	2012*
Current expenditure	28,259.0	35,825.9	39,804.5
Wages and salaries	13,437.2	15,474.1	18,847.3
Capital expenditure	9,708.0	6,883.0	12,288.0
Total	37,967.0	42,709.0	52,092.5

* Provisional figures.

INTERNATIONAL RESERVES
(US $ million at 31 December)

	2010	2011	2012
IMF special drawing rights	106.1	105.7	105.8
Reserve position in IMF	0.1	0.1	0.1
Foreign exchange	1,288.8	1,088.9	1,178.6
Total	1,395.0	1,194.7	1,284.5

Source: IMF, *International Financial Statistics*.

MONEY SUPPLY
(million gourdes at 31 December)

	2010	2011	2012
Currency outside depository corporations	20,347.8	21,701.5	23,263.3
Transferable deposits	48,766.8	51,487.1	56,449.7
Other deposits	62,397.0	67,360.0	70,875.0
Broad money	131,511.6	140,548.6	150,588.0

Source: IMF, *International Financial Statistics*.

COST OF LIVING
(Consumer Price Index, year ending 30 September; base: 2000 = 100, metropolitan areas)

	2009	2010	2011
Food	378.5	397.4	438.1
Clothing and footwear	298.1	309.6	327.0
Rent	341.3	391.5	436.1
All items (incl. others)	359.6	380.1	411.9

2012: Food 467.3; All items (incl. others) 431.9.

Source: ILO.

NATIONAL ACCOUNTS
(million gourdes, year ending 30 September)

Expenditure on the Gross Domestic Product
(at current prices)

	2009/10*	2010/11†	2011/12†
Final consumption expenditure	328,993	337,695	347,850
Gross capital formation	67,154	83,338	95,619
Total domestic expenditure	396,147	421,033	443,469
Exports of goods and services	32,346	40,693	43,516
Less Imports of goods and services	164,454	164,045	157,949
GDP in purchasers' values	264,039	297,681	329,036
GDP at constant 1986/87 prices	13,255	13,996	14,392

Gross Domestic Product by Economic Activity
(at constant 1986/87 prices)

	2009/10*	2010/11†	2011/12†
Agriculture, hunting, forestry and fishing	3,289	3,326	3,253
Mining and quarrying	17	18	19
Manufacturing	910	1,074	1,150
Electricity and water	69	88	102
Construction	1,167	1,274	1,342
Trade, restaurants and hotels	3,600	3,766	3,906
Transport, storage and communications	963	1,034	1,085
Business services	1,536	1,577	1,639
Other services	1,540	1,586	1,629
Sub-total	13,091	13,743	14,125
Less Imputed bank service charge	839	810	854
Taxes, less subsidies, on products.	1,003	1,063	1,121
GDP in purchasers' values	13,255	13,996	14,392

* Provisional figures.
† Estimates.

BALANCE OF PAYMENTS
(US $ million, year ending 30 September)

	2009/10	2010/11	2011/12
Exports of goods	563.4	768.1	785.0
Imports of goods	–2,810.1	–3,014.0	–2,679.3
Balance on goods	–2,246.7	–2,245.9	–1,894.4
Exports of services	239.0	249.2	257.0
Imports of services	–1,277.3	–1,140.2	–1,170.1
Balance on goods and services	–3,284.9	–3,136.9	–2,807.5
Primary income received	32.7	44.2	72.4
Primary income paid	–10.4	–3.2	–3.7
Balance on goods, services and primary income	–3,262.6	–3,095.9	–2,738.8
Secondary income received	1,473.8	1,551.4	1,612.3
Secondary income paid	–167.0	–240.2	–231.9
Current balance	–1,955.8	–1,784.8	–1,358.4
Capital account (net)	658.0	170.0	75.7
Direct investment liabilities	150.0	181.0	178.8
Other investment assets	–334.7	–85.6	–69.7
Other investment liabilities	–595.6	–229.8	357.9
Net errors and omissions	461.6	–64.9	67.6
Reserves and related items	–1,616.6	–1,814.1	–748.2

Source: IMF, *International Financial Statistics*.

External Trade

PRINCIPAL COMMODITIES
(US $ million, year ending 30 September, provisional figures)

Imports c.i.f.	2009/10	2010/11	2011/12
Food products	578.7	551.3	523.0
Mineral fuels, lubricants, etc.	545.7	770.4	820.5
Chemical products	102.0	129.6	106.6
Basic manufactures	601.8	843.1	673.1
Machinery and transport equipment	482.8	292.5	224.4
Miscellaneous manufactured goods	541.8	525.2	450.5
Total (incl. others)	3,021.6	3,240.9	2,881.1

Exports f.o.b.*	2009/10	2010/11	2011/12
Cocoa	9.1	6.9	9.3
Mangoes	7.6	10.6	10.1
Essential oils	13.9	16.4	14.3
Manufactured goods	196.0	267.8	273.7
Total (incl. others)	236.7	321.7	328.7

* Excluding re-export of assembled goods to the USA (US $ million, year ending 30 September, provisional figures): 506.1 in 2009/10; 686.3 in 2010/11;706.0 in 2011/12.

Source: Administration Générale des Douanes, Port-au-Prince.

PRINCIPAL TRADING PARTNERS
(US $ million, year ending 30 September)*

Imports c.i.f.	1989/90	1990/91	1991/92
Belgium	3.4	3.7	2.9
Canada	22.0	31.9	15.2
France	24.5	32.4	17.2
Germany, Federal Republic	14.6	19.2	10.0
Japan	23.6	31.2	17.7
Netherlands	11.2	13.9	8.7
United Kingdom	5.6	6.7	4.2
USA	153.1	203.2	126.7
Total (incl. others)	332.2	400.5	277.2

Exports f.o.b.†	1989/90	1990/91	1991/92
Belgium	15.9	19.5	6.0
Canada	4.5	4.7	2.3
France	17.4	21.6	6.1
Germany, Federal Republic	5.4	6.6	2.4
Italy	16.5	20.7	8.7
Japan	2.4	2.9	0.9
Netherlands	3.4	4.3	1.4
United Kingdom	2.3	2.3	0.7
USA	78.3	96.3	39.7
Total (incl. others)	163.7	198.7	74.7

* Provisional figures.
† Excluding re-exports.

Source: Administration Générale des Douanes, Port-au-Prince.

Transport

ROAD TRAFFIC
('000 motor vehicles in use)

	1994	1995	1996
Passenger cars	30.0	49.0	59.0
Commercial vehicles	30.0	29.0	35.0

1999 ('000 motor vehicles in use): Passenger cars 93.0; Commercial vehicles 61.6.

Source: UN, *Statistical Yearbook*.

SHIPPING

Flag Registered Fleet
(at 31 December)

	2011	2012	2013
Number of vessels	4	4	4
Total displacement ('000 grt)	1.4	1.4	1.4

Source: Lloyd's List Intelligence (www.lloydslistintelligence.com).

International Sea-borne Freight Traffic
('000 metric tons)

	1988	1989	1990
Goods loaded	164	165	170
Goods unloaded	684	659	704

Source: UN, *Monthly Bulletin of Statistics*.

CIVIL AVIATION

Traffic (international flights, 2012): Passengers arriving 615,191; Passengers departing 639,946.

Tourism

TOURIST ARRIVALS BY COUNTRY OF ORIGIN

	2009	2010	2011
Canada	31,017	20,119	19,568
Dominican Republic	9,910	3,168	4,487
France	12,508	14,261	18,432
USA	268,224	183,243	267,422
Total (incl. others)	387,218	254,732	348,755

Receipts from tourism (US $ million, excl. passenger transport): 169 in 2010; 162 in 2011.

Source: World Tourism Organization.

Communications Media

	2010	2011	2012
Telephones ('000 main lines in use)	50.0	50.0	50.0
Mobile cellular telephones ('000 subscribers)	4,000.0	4,200.0	6,094.9
Broadband subscribers ('000)	16.5	16.7	n.a.

Internet users ('000): 1,000 in 2009.

Source: International Telecommunication Union.

Education

(1994/95)

	Institutions	Teachers	Students
Pre-primary	n.a.	n.a.	230,391*
Primary	10,071	30,205	1,110,398
Secondary	1,038	15,275	195,418
Tertiary	n.a.	654*	6,288*

* 1990/91 figure.

Adult literacy rate (UNESCO estimates): 62.1% (males 60.1%; females 64.0%) in 2007 (Source: UNESCO Institute for Statistics).

Directory

The Government

HEAD OF STATE

President: Michel Joseph Martelly (took office on 14 May 2011).

CABINET
(April 2014)

Prime Minister and Minister of Planning and External Co-operation: Laurent Salvador Lamothe.

Minister of Foreign Affairs and Religion: Duly Brutus.

Minister of Justice and Public Security: Jean Renel Sanon.

Minister of the Interior and Territorial Collectivities: Réginald Delva.

Minister of the Economy and Finance: Marie-Carmelle Jean-Marie.

Minister of Public Works, Transport and Communications: Jacques Rousseau.

Minister of Agriculture, Natural Resources and Rural Development: Thomas Jacques.

Minister of Trade and Industry: Wilson Laleau.

Minister of Tourism and Creative Industries: Stéphanie Balmir Villedrouin.

Minister of National Education and Vocational Training: Nesmy Manigat.

Minister of Public Health and the Population: Dr Florence Duperval Guillaume.

Minister of Social Affairs and Labour: Charles Jean-Jacques.

Minister of Culture: Monique Rocourt.

Minister of Communication: Rudy Hériveaux.

Minister of Women's Affairs and Women's Rights: Yannick Mézile.

Minister of National Defence: Lener Renauld.

Minister of Youth, Sports and Civic Action: Col (retd) Himler Rébu.

Minister of the Environment: Jean François Thomas.

Minister of Haitians Residing Abroad: François Guillaume, II.

Minister-delegate to the Prime Minister, in charge of Human Rights and the Fight Against Extreme Poverty: Rose Anne Auguste.

Minister-delegate to the Prime Minister, in charge of Promoting the Peasantry: Marie Mimose Félix.

Minister-delegate to the Prime Minister, in charge of Energy Security: René Jean-Jumeau.

Minister-delegate to the Prime Minister, in charge of Strengthening Political Parties: Patrick Sully Joseph.

MINISTRIES

Office of the President: Palais National, ave de la République, Champs de Mars, Port-au-Prince; tel. 2222-3024; e-mail webmestre@palaisnational.info; internet www.lapresidence.ht.

Office of the Prime Minister: 33 blvd Harry S Truman, BP 6114, Port-au-Prince; tel. 2221-0013; e-mail primature@primature.gouv.ht; internet www.primature.gouv.ht.

Ministry of Agriculture, Natural Resources and Rural Development: Route Nationale 1, Damien, BP 1441, Port-au-Prince; tel. 2510-3916; fax 2222-3591; internet www.agriculture.gouv.ht.

Ministry of Communication: 4 rue Magny, Port-au-Prince; tel. 2223-5514.

Ministry of Culture: angle des rues de la République et Geffrard 509, Port-au-Prince; tel. 2221-3238; fax 2221-7318; e-mail contact4@ministereculture.gouv.ht; internet www.ministereculture.gouv.ht.

Ministry of the Economy and Finance: Palais des Ministères, rue Mgr Guilloux, Port-au-Prince; tel. 2223-7113; fax 2223-1247; e-mail mef@mefhaiti.gouv.ht; internet www.mefhaiti.gouv.ht.

Ministry of the Environment: 11 rue Pacot, Port-au-Prince; tel. 2943-0520; fax 2943-0521; e-mail scmde.gouv.ht@hotmail.com; internet www.mde-h.gouv.ht.

Ministry of Foreign Affairs and Religion: blvd Harry S Truman, Cité de l'Exposition, Port-au-Prince; tel. 2222-8482; fax 2223-1668; e-mail webmaster@maehaitiinfo.org; internet www.mae.gouv.ht.

Ministry of Haitians Residing Abroad: 87 ave Jean-Paul II, Turgeau, BP 6113, Port-au-Prince; tel. 2245-1116; fax 2245-0287; e-mail info@mhave.gouv.ht; internet www.mhave.gouv.ht.

Ministry of the Interior and Territorial Collectivities: Palais des Ministères, Champs de Mars, Port-au-Prince; tel. 2223-0204; fax 2222-8057; e-mail info@mict.gouv.ht; internet www.mict.gouv.ht.

Ministry of Justice and Public Security: 19 ave Charles Summer, Port-au-Prince; tel. 2245-9737; fax 2245-0474; internet www.mjsp.gouv.ht.

Ministry of National Defence: 2 rue Bazelais, Delmas 60, BP 1106, Pétionville; tel. 3454-0501; e-mail haitidefense@gmail.com.

Ministry of National Education and Vocational Training: rue Dr Audain, Port-au-Prince; tel. 2222-1036; fax 2245-3400; e-mail menfp_info@eduhaiti.gouv.ht; internet www.eduhaiti.gouv.ht.

Ministry of Planning and External Co-operation: ave John Brown, route de Bourdon 347, Port-au-Prince; tel. 2228-2512; fax 2222-0226; e-mail info@mpce.gouv.ht; internet www.mpce.gouv.ht.

Ministry of Public Health and the Population: 111 rue Saint Honoré, Port-au-Prince; tel. 2223-6248; fax 2222-4066; e-mail info@mspp.gouv.ht; internet www.mspp.gouv.ht.

Ministry of Public Works, Transport and Communications: rue Toussaint Louverture, Delmas 33, Port-au-Prince; tel. 2222-2528; fax 2223-4519; e-mail secretariat.communications@mtptc.gouv.ht; internet www.mtptc.gouv.ht.

Ministry of Social Affairs and Labour: 16 rue de la Révolution, Port-au-Prince; tel. 2222-1244; fax 2221-0717.

Ministry of Tourism: 8 rue Légitime, Champs de Mars, Port-au-Prince; tel. 2949-2010; fax 2949-2011; e-mail info@haititourisme.gouv.ht; internet www.haititourisme.gouv.ht.

Ministry of Trade and Industry: Bureau du Ministre, 23 ave l'Amartinière, BP 6114, Port-au-Prince; tel. 2943-4488; fax 2943-1868; e-mail secretariatdumiistre@mci.gouv.ht; internet www.mci.gouv.ht.

Ministry of Women's Affairs and Women's Rights: ave Magny 4, Port-au-Prince; tel. 2224-9152; e-mail contact@mcfdf.ht; internet www.mcfdf.ht.

Ministry of Youth, Sports and Civic Action: Ranch de la Croix-des-Bouquets, route de Meyer, route Nationale 3, 18 route de Frères, Pétionville; tel. 2813-0268; internet www.jeunessetsports.gouv.ht.

Office of the Minister-delegate to the Prime Minister, in charge of Parliamentary Relations: Delmas 48, 5 rue François, Port-au-Prince; tel. 2246-9912.

President and Legislature

PRESIDENT

Election, first round, 28 November 2010*

Candidates	Valid votes cast	%
Mirlande Manigat (RDNP)	336,878	31.37
Jude Celéstin (Inite)	241,462	22.48
Michel Joseph Martelly (Repons Peyizan)	234,617	21.84
Jean Henry Ceant (Renmen Ayiti)	87,834	8.18
Jacques Edouard Alexis (MPH)	32,932	3.07
Charles Henri Baker (Respè)	25,512	2.38
Total (incl. others)	1,074,056	100.00

* Preliminary results from the Provisional Electoral Council. A report issued by the Organization of American States in January 2011 stated that Martelly, not Celéstin, was the second-placed candidate. In February the Provisional Electoral Council announced that Manigat would face Martelly in the run-off ballot, held on 20 March.

Election, second round, 20 March 2011

Candidates	Valid votes cast	%
Michel Joseph Martelly (Repons Peyizan)	716,986	67.57
Mirlande Manigat (RDNP)	336,747	31.74
Total*	1,061,089	100.00

* Including 7,356 blank ballots.

LEGISLATURE

Senate
(Sénat)

President: SIMON DIEUSEUL DESRAS (Oganizasyon Lavni).

Distribution of Seats, August 2012*

	Seats
Inite	15
Alternative pour le Progrès et la Democratie (Altenativ)	5
Fusion des Sociaux-Démocrates Haïtiens	3
Ayiti an Aksyon (AAA)	2
Konbit pou Bati Ayiti (KONBA)	1
Pou Nou Tout (PONT)	1
Organisation du Peuple en Lutte (OPL)	1
La Fanmi Lavalas (FL)	1
Oganizasyon Lavni (LAVNI)	1
Total	30

* The Senate has 30 members, three from each province. One-third of these seats are renewable every two years. The last elections to the Senate were held on 28 November 2010 and 20 March 2011.

Chamber of Deputies
(Chambre des Députés)

President: STEVENSON JACQUES TIMOLÉON.

Elections, 28 November 2010 and 20 March 2011

	Seats
Inite	32
Alternative pour le Progrès et la Democratie (Altenativ)	11
Ansanm Nou Fò	10
Ayiti an Aksyon (AAA)	8
Oganizasyon Lavni (LAVNI)	7
Rasanble	4
Repons Peyizan	3
Konbit pou Refè Haïti (KONBIT)	3
Pou Nou Tout (PONT)	3
Mouvement Chrétien pour une Nouvelle Haïti (MOCHRENHA)	3
Plateforme Liberation	2
Plateforme des Patriotes Haïtiens (PLAPH)	2
Mouvement Action Socialiste (MAS)	2
Mouvement Démocratique pour la Libération d'Haïti-Parti Revolutionnaire Démocratique d'Haïti (MODELH-PRDH)	1
Respè	1
Veye Yo	1
Independent	2
Vacant	4
Total	99

Election Commission

The Provisional Electoral Council was dissolved on 29 December 2011. A constitutional amendment of 19 June 2012 allowed for the formation of a new electoral body, the Permanent Electoral Council. According to the Constitution, the nine-member commission would comprise three representatives from each of the three branches of government. A Memorandum of Understanding on 24 December 2012 formed the Transitional College of the Permanent Electoral Council to temporarily manage the Permanent Electoral Council to organize the next elections. In April 2013 the nine members of the Transitional College were appointed. The mandate for this body was to expire following the publication of the final election results.

President of the Transitional College of the Permanent Electoral Council: EMMANUEL MÉNARD.

Political Organizations

Action Démocratique pour Bâtir Haïti (ADEBHA): 509 route de Delmas, entre Delmas 103 et 105, Port-au-Prince; tel. 2256-6739; fax 3446-6161; e-mail versun_etatdedroit@yahoo.fr; internet www.adebha.populus.org; f. 2004; Pres. René Julien.

Alliance Chrétienne Citoyenne pour la Reconstruction d'Haïti (ACCRHA): Port-au-Prince; Leader Jean Chavannes Jeune.

Alliance pour la Libération et l'Avancement d'Haïti (ALAH): Haut Turgeau 95, BP 13350, Port-au-Prince; tel. 2245-0446; fax 2257-4804; e-mail reynoldgeorges@yahoo.com; f. 1975; Leader Reynold Georges.

Alternative pour le Progrès et la Democratie (Altenativ): f. 2010 to contest the legislative elections; grouping of more than 70 legislative candidates; Mems of Exec. Cttee Rosny Smart, Edgard Leblanc Fils, Victor Benoît, Serge Gilles, Evans Paul.

Alyans (Alliance Démocratique): Port-au-Prince; centre-left coalition of Konvansyon Inite Demokratik (KID) and Popular Party for the Renewal of Haïti (PPRH); formed an alliance with the Fusion des Sociaux-Démocrates Haïtiens and the OPL in late 2009 to contest the 2010 legislative elections; Leader Evans Paul.

Ansanm Nou Fò: contested the 2010 elections; Leader Leslie Voltaire.

Ayisyen pou Ayiti: Port-au-Prince; contested the 2010 presidential election; Leader Yvon Néptune.

Ayiti an Aksyon (AAA): Port-au-Prince; internet ayitianaksyon.net; contested the 2010 legislative elections; Pres. Youri Latortue.

Congrès National des Mouvements Démocratiques (KONA-KOM): Bois Verna, Port-au-Prince; tel. 2245-6228; f. 1987; social democratic; Leader Victor Benoît.

La Fanmi Lavalas (FL): blvd 15 Octobre, Tabarre, Port-au-Prince; tel. 2256-7208; internet www.hayti.net; f. 1996 by Jean-Bertrand Aristide; barred from contesting the 2010 elections.

Fòs 2010 (Force 2010): Delmas; f. 2010; contested the 2010 presidential election; Leader Wilson Jeudi.

Fòs Patriotik ou Respè Konstitsyon an (FOPARK) (Patriotic Force for the Respect of the Constitution): Port-au-Prince; opposition coalition; Nat. Dir Biron Odige.

Front pour la Reconstruction Nationale (FRN): Gonaïves; f. 2004; Sec.-Gen. Guy Philippe.

Fusion des Sociaux-Démocrates Haïtiens: POB 381056, Miami, FL 33138, USA; e-mail fusion@pfsdh.org; internet www.pfsdh.org; formed an alliance with Alyans and the OPL in late 2009 to contest the 2010 legislative elections; Leader Serge Gilles.

Grand Rassemblement pour l'Evolution d'Haïti (GREH): Port-au-Prince; f. 2003; Leader Col (retd) Himler Rébu.

Inite (Unité): Port-au-Prince; f. 2009 to replace Lespwa (l'Espoir, f. 2005); supported Pres. René Préval; dissolution announced May 2012; Nat. Co-ordinator Levaillant Louis-Jeune.

Konbit pou Bati Ayiti (KONBA): Port-au-Prince; f. 2005.

Konbit pou Refè Haïti (KONBIT): Port-au-Prince; contested the 2010 legislative elections.

Konfyans: Port-au-Prince; centre-left; Rudy Hériveaux.

Mobilisation pour le Progrès Haïtien (MPH): Port-au-Prince; contested the 2010 presidential election; Leader Jacques Edouard Alexis.

Mouvement Action Socialiste (MAS): Hinche; contested the 2010 legislative elections.

Mouvement Chrétien pour une Nouvelle Haïti (MOCHRENHA): rue M 7 Turgeau, Carrefour, Port-au-Prince; tel. 3443-3120; e-mail mochrenha@hotmail.com; f. 1998; contested the 2010 legislative elections; Leaders Luc Mésadieu, Gilbert N. Léger.

Mouvement Démocratique pour la Libération d'Haïti-Parti Revolutionnaire Démocratique d'Haïti (MODELH-PRDH): contested the 2010 legislative elections; Leader François Latortue.

Mouvement Indépendant pour la Réconciliation Nationale (MIRN): Port-au-Prince; mem. of Inite; Leader Luc Fleurinord.

Mouvement pour l'Instauration de la Démocratie en Haïti (MIDH): 114 ave Jean Paul II, Port-au-Prince; tel. 2245-8377; f. 1986; centre-right; contested the 2010 legislative elections.

Mouvement Patriotique de l'Opposition Démocratique (MOPOD): Port-au-Prince; f. as umbrella opposition movt, registered as political party in 2014; Gen. Co-ordinator Jean André Victor.

Nouveau Parti Communiste Haïtien (NPCH): Grand Rue 1, Nan Gonmye; e-mail vanialubin@yahoo.fr; internet www.npch.net; Marxist-Leninist.

Oganizasyon Lavni (LAVNI): contested the 2010 presidential election; Leader Yves Christalin.

Organisation du Peuple en Lutte (OPL): 105 ave Lamartinière, Bois Verna, Port-au-Prince; tel. 2245-4214; f. 1991 as Organisation Politique Lavalas; name changed as above 1998; formed an alliance with Alyans and the Fusion des Sociaux-Démocrates Haïtiens in late 2009 to contest the 2010 legislative elections; Leader Sauveur Pierre Etienne; Nat. Co-ordinator Edgard Leblanc Fils.

Parti Agricole Industriel National (PAIN): f. 1956; Pres. Hébert Docteur.

Parti du Camp Patriotique et de l'Alliance Haïtienne (PACA-PALAH): Port-au-Prince; contested the 2010 legislative elections.

Parti pour l'Evolution Nationale d'Haïti (PENH): Port-au-Prince; contested the 2010 elections; Leader Eric Smarki Charles.

Parti des Industriels, Travailleurs, Agents du Développement et Commercants d'Haïti (PITACH): Port-au-Prince.

Parti Nationale Démocratique Progressiste d'Haïti (PNDPH): Port-au-Prince; reactivated 2014; Pres. Turneb Delpé.

Parti Social Rénové (PSR): Port-au-Prince; Leader Bonivert Claude.

Plateforme Liberation: Port-au-Prince; contested the 2010 legislative elections.

Plateforme des Patriotes Haïtiens (PLAPH): Cap-Haïtien; contested the 2010 legislative elections.

Pou Nou Tout (PONT): Port-au-Prince; contested the 2010 legislative elections.

Rasanble: contested the 2010 legislative elections.

Rassemblement des Démocrates Nationaux Progressistes (RDNP): 234 route de Delmas, Delmas, Port-au-Prince; tel. 2246-3313; f. 1979; centre party; Sec.-Gen. Mirlande Manigat.

Regwoupman Sitwayen pou Espwa (Respè): Port-au-Prince; f. 2009; centre party; Pres. Charles Henri Baker.

Renmen Ayiti: Port-au-Prince; e-mail info@renmenayiti.org; internet www.renmenayiti.org; Leader Jean Henry Ceant.

Repons Peyizan (Réponse des Paysans): Port-au-Prince; Leader Michel Joseph Martelly.

Solidarité: contested the 2010 elections; Leader Génard Joseph.

Union de Citoyens Ayisyen pour la Démocratie, le Développement et l'Education (UCADDE): Miragoâne; contested the 2010 legislative elections.

Veye Yo: Cap-Haïtien; contested the 2010 legislative elections.

Viv Ansanm: Port-au-Prince; Leader Daniel Jean Jacques.

Diplomatic Representation

EMBASSIES IN HAITI

Argentina: 48 rue Metellus, Pétionville, Port-au-Prince; tel. 2940-6711; fax 2940-6714; e-mail ehait@mrecic.gov.ar; internet ehait.mrecic.gov.ar; Ambassador Marcelo Raul Sebaste.

Bahamas: 12 rue Boyer, Pétionville, Port-au-Prince; tel. 2257-8782; fax 2256-5759; e-mail bahamasembassy@hainet.net; Ambassador Godfrey Gordon Rolle.

Brazil: Immeuble Héxagone, 3ème etage, angle des rues Clerveaux et Darguin, Pétionville, BP 15845, Port-au-Prince; tel. 2256-0900; fax 2510-6111; e-mail brasemb1@accesshaiti.com; internet portoprincipe.itamaraty.gov.br; Ambassador José Luiz Machado e Costa.

Canada: route de Delmas, entre Delmas 71 et 75, BP 826, Port-au-Prince; tel. 2249-9000; fax 2249-9920; e-mail prnce@international.gc.ca; internet www.canadainternational.gc.ca/haiti; Ambassador Henri-Paul Normandin.

Chile: 2 rue Coutilien et rue Delmas 60, Musseau, Port-au-Prince; tel. 2813-1613; fax 2813-1708; e-mail embajadachile_haiti@hotmail.com; internet chileabroad.gov.cl/haiti; Ambassador Raul Fernández Daza.

Cuba: 3 rue Marion, Peguy Ville, Pétionville, POB 15702, Port-au-Prince; tel. 2256-3503; fax 2257-8566; e-mail secretaria@ht.embacuba.cu; internet www.cubadiplomatica.cu/haiti; Ambassador Ricardo Sotero García Nápoles.

Dominican Republic: rue Panaméricaine 121, BP 56, Pétionville, Port-au-Prince; tel. 2813-0887; fax 3257-0383; e-mail embrepdomhai@yahoo.com; Ambassador Rubén Silié Valdez.

France: 51 rue de Capois, BP 1312, Port-au-Prince; tel. 2999-9000; fax 2999-9001; e-mail ambafrance@hainet.net; internet www.ambafrance-ht.org; Ambassador Patrick Nicoloso.

Germany: 2 impasse Claudinette, Bois Moquette, Pétionville, BP 1147, Port-au-Prince; tel. 2949-0202; fax 2257-4131; e-mail info@

port-au-prince.diplo.de; internet www.port-au-prince.diplo.de; Ambassador KLAUS PETER SCHICK.

Holy See: rue Louis Pouget, Morne Calvaire, BP 326, Port-au-Prince; tel. 2257-6308; fax 2257-3411; e-mail nonciatureap@hughes.net; Apostolic Nuncio Most Rev. BERNARDITO CLEOPAS AUZA (Titular Archbishop of Suacia).

Japan: Hexagone, 2ème étage, angle rues Clerveaux et Darguin, Pétionville, Port-au-Prince; tel. 2256-3333; fax 2256-9444; internet www.ht.emb-japan.go.jp; Ambassador KENJI KURATOMI (resident in the Dominican Republic).

Mexico: rue Métélus 48, Pétionville, BP 327, Port-au-Prince; tel. 2813-0089; fax 2256-6528; e-mail embhaiti@sre.gob.mx; internet embamex.sre.gob.mx/haiti; Ambassador JOSÉ LUIS ALVARADO GONZÁLEZ.

Panama: 73 rue Grégoire, Pétionville, Port-au-Prince; tel. 2513-1844; fax 3864-4881; e-mail panaembahaiti@yahoo.com; internet www.panamaenelexterior.gob.pa/Haiti; Ambassador JOHN EVANS ATHERLEY.

Spain: 50 rue Metellus, Pétionville, BP 386, Port-au-Prince; tel. 2940-0952; e-mail Emb.PuertoPrincipe@maec.es; internet www.maec.es/embajadas/puertoprincipe; Ambassador MANUEL HERNÁNDEZ RUIGÓMEZ.

Taiwan (Republic of China): 22 rue Lucien Hubert, Morne Calvaire, Pétionville, Port-au-Prince; tel. 3775-0109; fax 2256-8067; e-mail haiti888@gmail.com; internet www.taiwanembassy.org/HT; Ambassador PETER HWANG.

United Kingdom: rue Delmas 73–75, Port-au-Prince; tel. 2812-9191; Ambassador STEVEN FISHER (resident in the Dominican Republic).

USA: Tabarre 41, blvd 15 Octobre, Port-au-Prince; tel. 2229-8000; fax 2229-8028; internet haiti.usembassy.gov; Ambassador PAMELA WHITE.

Venezuela: blvd Harry S Truman, Cité de l'Exposition, BP 2158, Port-au-Prince; tel. 3443-4127; fax 2223-7672; e-mail embavenezhaiti@hainet.net; Ambassador PEDRO ANTONIO CANINO GONZÁLEZ.

Judicial System

Law is based on the French Napoleonic Code, substantially modified during the presidency of François Duvalier.

Courts of Appeal and Civil Courts sit at Port-au-Prince and the three provincial capitals: Gonaïves, Cap-Haïtien and Port de Paix. In principle each commune has a Magistrates' Court. Judges of the Supreme Court and Courts of Appeal are appointed by the President. Constitutional amendments in 2012 created a Supreme Council of Judicial Power and a constitutional court (which was yet to be appointed in 2014).

Conseil Supérieur du Pouvoir Judiciaire (Supreme Council of Judicial Power): la route de Frères, Port-au-Prince; f. July 2012 to oversee judicial system, ensure separation of powers; 9 mems; Pres. ANEL ALEXIS JOSEPH (Pres. of Supreme Court).

Cour de Cassation (Supreme Court): Port-au-Prince; Pres. ANEL ALEXIS JOSEPH; Vice-Pres. ANTOINE NORGAISSE.

Citizens' Rights Defender: FLORENCE ÉLIE.

Religion

Roman Catholicism and the folk religion Voodoo (vodou) are the official religions. There are various Protestant and other denominations.

CHRISTIANITY

The Roman Catholic Church

For ecclesiastical purposes, Haiti comprises two archdioceses and eight dioceses. Some 65% of the population are Roman Catholics.

Bishops' Conference: Conférence Episcopale de Haïti, angle rues Piquant et Lammarre, BP 1572, Port-au-Prince; tel. 222-5194; fax 223-5318; e-mail ceh56@hotmail.com; internet ceh.ht; f. 1977; Pres. Cardinal CHIBLY LANGLOIS (Bishop of Les Cayes).

Archbishop of Cap-Haïtien: Most Rev. LOUIS KÉBREAU, Archevêché, rue 19–20 H, BP 22, Cap-Haïtien; tel. 262-0071; fax 262-1278.

Archbishop of Port-au-Prince: GUIRE POULARD, Archevêché, rue Dr Aubry, BP 538, Port-au-Prince; tel. 2943-4446; e-mail guypoulard@hotmail.com; internet archidiocesedepaup.org.

The Anglican Communion

Anglicans in Haiti fall under the jurisdiction of a missionary diocese of Province II of the Episcopal Church in the USA.

Bishop of Haiti: Rt Rev. JEAN ZACHÉ DURACIN, Eglise Episcopale d'Haïti, BP 1309, Port-au-Prince; tel. 2257-1624; fax 2257-3412; e-mail epihaiti@egliseepiscopaledhaiti.org; internet www.egliseepiscopaledhaiti.org.

Protestant Churches

Baptist Convention: Route Nationale 1, Cazeau BP 2601, Port-au-Prince; tel. 2262-0567; e-mail conventionbaptiste@yahoo.com; f. 1964; Gen. Sec. EMMANUEL PIERRE.

Evangelical Lutheran Church of Haiti: Eglise Evangélique Luthérienne d'Haiti, 29 Route de Frére, Impasse Perpignant 8, Port-au-Prince; tel. 2947-2347; e-mail info@lutheranchurchofhaiti.org; internet www.lutheranchurchofhaiti.org; f. 1975; Pres. Rev. JOSEPH LIVENSON LAUVANUS; 9,000 mems.

Other denominations active in Haiti include Methodists, Church of the Latter-Day Saints (Mormons) and the Church of God 'Eben-Ezer'.

VOODOO

Konfederasyon Nasyonal Vodou Ayisyen (KNVA): Le Péristyle de Mariani, Mariani; tel. 3458-1500; f. 2008; Supreme Leader FRANÇOIS MAX GESNER BEAUVOIR.

The Press

DAILY

Le Nouvelliste: 198 rue du Centre, Port-au-Prince; tel. 2222-4754; fax 2224-2061; e-mail manigapier@lenouvelliste.com; internet www.lenouvelliste.com; f. 1898; evening; French; ind.; Editor-in-Chief FRANTZ DUVAL; Publr JEAN MAX CHAUVET; circ. 10,000.

PERIODICALS

Ayiti Fanm: Centre National et International de Documentation, d'Information et de Défense des Droits des Femmes en Haïti, 16 rue de La Ligue Féminine, BP 6114, Port-au-Prince; tel. 2245-0346; fax 2244-1841; e-mail ayitifanm@enfofanm.net; internet www.ayitifanm.org; f. 1991; monthly; publ. by ENFOFANM; Creole; Founder and Editor-in-Chief CLORINDE ZÉPHIR; Dir MYRIAM MERLET.

Haïti en Marche: 74 bis, rue Capois, Port-au-Prince; tel. 3454-0126; e-mail melodiefm@gmail.com; internet www.haitienmarche.com; f. 1986; weekly; Editors MARC GARCIA, ELSIE ETHÉART.

Haïti Observateur: 98 ave John Brown, 3ème étage, Port-au-Prince; tel. 2223-0782; e-mail contact@haiti-observateur.net; internet www.haiti-observateur.net; f. 1971; weekly; Editor RAYMOND JOSEPH; circ. 75,000.

Haïti Progrès: 61, Rue Capois, Port-au-Prince; tel. 3446-1957; fax 3680-9397; e-mail editor@haiti-progres.com; internet www.haiti-progres.com; f. 1983; weekly; French, English, Spanish and Creole; Dir MAUDE LEBLANC.

Le Matin: 3 rue Goulard, Pétionville, Port-au-Prince; tel. 4688-3876; e-mail lematinpublicite@gmail.com; internet www.lematinhaiti.com; f. 1907; French; publ. every other week from Jan. 2010; ind.; Editor-in-Chief DALY VALET; Publr RÉGINALD BOULOS; circ. 5,000.

Le Moniteur: Presses Nationales d'Haïti, rue Hammerton Killick 231, BP 1746 bis, Port-au-Prince; tel. 2222-1744; fax 2223-1026; e-mail pndh-moniteur@hainet.net; f. 1845; 2 a week; French; official state gazette; Dir-Gen. WILLEMS EDOUARD; circ. 2,000.

Le Septentrion: Cap-Haïtien; weekly; ind.; Editor NELSON BELL; circ. 2,000.

NEWS AGENCIES

Agence Haïtienne de Presse (AHP): 6 rue Fernand, Port-au-Prince; tel. 2245-7222; fax 2245-5836; e-mail ahp@yahoo.com; internet www.ahphaiti.org; f. 1989; publishes daily news bulletins in French and English; Dir-Gen. GEORGES VENEL REMARAIS.

AlterPresse: 38 Delmas 8, BP 19211, Port-au-Prince; tel. 2249-9493; e-mail alterpresse@medialternatif.org; internet www.alterpresse.org; f. 2001; independent; owned by Alternative Media Group; Dir GOTSON PIERRE.

Haiti Press Network: 14 rue Lamarre, Pétionville, Port-au-Prince; tel. 2511-6555; fax 2256-6197; e-mail hpnhaiti@yahoo.fr; internet www.hpnhaiti.com; Dir CLARENS RENOIS.

Publishers

Editions des Antilles: route de l'Aéroport, Delmas, Port-au-Prince; tel. 2940-0217; fax 2249-1225; e-mail editiondesantilles@yahoo.com.

Editions Caraïbes, SA: 57 rue Pavée, BP 2013, Port-au-Prince; tel. 2222-0032; e-mail piereli@yahoo.fr; Man. PIERRE J. ELIE.

Editions CUC-Université Caraïbe: 7, Delmas 29, Port-au-Prince; tel. 2246-5531; e-mail editions@universitecaraibe.com; internet www.editionsuniversitecaraibe.com.

Editions Les Presses Nationales d'Haïti: 223 rue du Centre, BP 1746, Port-au-Prince; tel. 2222-1744; fax 2223-1026; e-mail pnd-moniteur@hainet.net.

Imprimerie Roland Theodore, SA: Delmas 1A, No 19, Delmas; tel. 2940-7200; e-mail info@imprimerie-theodore.com; internet www.imprimerie-theodore.com; Gen. Man. HENRI THEODORE.

Maison Henri Deschamps—Les Entreprises Deschamps Frisch, SA: 25 rue Dr Martelly Seïde, BP 164, Port-au-Prince; tel. 2223-2215; fax 2223-4976; e-mail entdeschamps@gdfhaiti.com; internet www.maisonhenrideschamps.com; f. 1898; education and literature; divisions include Editions Hachette-Deschamps and Imprimerie Henri Deschamps; Man. Dir JACQUES DESCHAMPS, Jr; CEO HENRI R. DESCHAMPS.

Broadcasting and Communications

REGULATORY BODY

Conseil National des Télécommunications (CONATEL): 4 ave Christophe, BP 2002, Port-au-Prince; tel. 2511-3940; fax 2223-9229; e-mail info@conatel.gouv.ht; internet www.conatel.gouv.ht; f. 1969; govt communications licensing authority; Dir-Gen. JEAN MARIE GUILLAUME.

TELECOMMUNICATIONS

Digicel Haiti: 151 angle ave John Paul II et Impasse Duverger, BP 15516, Port-au-Prince; tel. 3711-3444; e-mail customercarehaiti@digicelgroup.com; internet www.digicelhaiti.com; f. 2005; owned by Digicel (Ireland); mobile telephone network provider; Group Chair. DENIS O'BRIEN; CEO, Haiti DAMIAN BLACKBURN.

HaiTel (Haiti Telecommunications International, SA): 17 rue Darguin, 3ème étage, Pétionville, Port-au-Prince; tel. 3510-1201; fax 3510-6273; f. 1999; part-owned by US-based MCI WorldCom; mobile telecommunications provider; Pres. FRANCK CINÉ.

Multilink Haiti: Autoroute de Delmas, angle Delmas 18, 1er étage, Port-au-Prince; tel. 2813-0231; fax 2949-2929; e-mail info@multilink.ht; internet www.multilink.ht; f. 1999; internet service provider; Gen. Man. PAOLO CHILOSI.

Natcom (National Télécom, SA): angle ave Martin Luther King et rue Fernand, Pont-Morin, BP 814, Port-au-Prince; tel. 2222-8888; fax 3939-3939; e-mail info@haititeleco.com; internet www.natcom.com.ht; fmrly Télécommunications d'Haiti (Haiti Téléco); renamed as above in 2010; 60% owned by Viettel (Viet Nam), 40% govt-owned; landline provider; Dir YVES ARMAND.

BROADCASTING

Radio

La Brise FM 104.9: Camp Perrin, Les Cayes, Sud; tel. 3709-6021; e-mail contact@labrisefm.com; internet www.labrisefm.com; f. 2007; music station; Dir MAX ALAIN LOUIS.

Radio Antilles International: 75 rue du Centre, BP 2335, Port-au-Prince; tel. 3433-0712; fax 2222-0260; e-mail jacquessampeur@yahoo.com; f. 1984; independent; Dir-Gen. JACQUES SAMPEUR.

Radio Caraïbes: 45 rue Chavannes, Port-au-Prince; tel. 3558-9110; e-mail radiocaraibesfm@yahoo.fr; internet radiotelevisioncaraibes.com; f. 1949; owned by Moussignac Group; broadcasts in Port-au-Prince area; Dir PATRICK MOUSSIGNAC.

Radio Galaxie: 17 rue Pavée, Port-au-Prince; tel. 2432-4473; e-mail info@radiogalaxiehaiti.com; internet www.radiogalaxiehaiti.com; f. 1990; independent; Dir YVES JEAN-BART.

Radio Ginen: 28 bis, Delmas 31, BP 6120, Port-au-Prince; tel. 2249-9292; fax 2511-1737; e-mail info@rtghaiti.com; internet www.rtghaiti.com; f. 1994; Dir JEAN LUCIEN BORGES.

Radio Ibo: 51 route du Canapé-Vert, BP 15174, Pétionville, Port-au-Prince; tel. 3557-5214; fax 2245-9850; e-mail ibo@radioibo.net; internet radioibo.net; Dir HÉROLD JEAN FRANÇOIS.

Radio Kiskeya: 42 rue Villemenay, Boisverna, Port-au-Prince; tel. 2244-6605; e-mail admin@radiokiskeya.com; internet radiokiskeya.com; f. 1994; Dir MARVEL DANDIN.

Radio Lumière: Côte-Plage 16, Carrefour, BP 1050, Port-au-Prince; tel. 2234-0331; fax 2234-3708; e-mail rlumiere@radiolumiere.org; internet www.radiolumiere.org; f. 1959; Protestant; independent; Dir VARNEL JEUNE.

Radio Mélodie: 74 bis, rue Capois, Port-au-Prince; tel. 2452-0428; e-mail melodiefm@gmail.com; internet radiomelodiehaiti.com; f. 1998; Dir MARCUS GARCIA.

Radio Metropole: 8 route de Delmas 52, BP 62, Port-au-Prince; tel. 2246-2626; fax 2249-2020; e-mail informations@naskita.com; internet www.metropolehaiti.com; f. 1970; independent; Pres. HERBERT WIDMAIER; Dir-Gen. RICHARD WIDMAIER.

Radio Nationale d'Haïti: see Télévision Nationale d'Haïti.

Radio Nirvana FM: Cap-Haïtien; tel. 2431-5784; e-mail pdg@radionirvanafm.com; internet www.radionirvanafm.com; Dir-Gen. RAPHAEL ABRAHAM.

Radio Port-au-Prince Plus: Stade Sylvio Cator, BP 863, Port-au-Prince; tel. 3927-3182; e-mail contactus@radioportauprinceplus.com; internet www.radioportauprinceplus.com; f. 1979; independent; broadcasts in Creole and English; religious programming; Dir-Gen. MAX PRINCE.

Radio Superstar: Delmas 68, angle rues Safran et C. Henri, Pétionville, Port-au-Prince; tel. 3734-2254; fax 2257-3015; e-mail info@radiosuperstarhaiti.com; internet www.superstarhaiti.com; f. 1987; independent; Dir ALBERT CHANCY, Jr.

Radio Tele Megastar: 106 rue de la Réunion, Port-au-Prince; tel. 3711-1197; e-mail jcharleus0@yahoo.com; internet www.radiotelemegastar.com; f. 1991; Pres. and Dir-Gen. JEAN-EDDY CHARLEUS.

Radio Télé Venus: 106 rue 5 et 6 E, Cap-Haïtien; tel. 2262-2742; fax 3780-8053; internet www.radiotelevenushaiti.com; f. 1994.

Radio Vision 2000: 184 ave John Brown, BP 13247, Port-au-Prince; tel. 2813-1875; e-mail info@radiovision2000.com; internet www.radiovision2000haiti.net; f. 1991; Dir LÉOPOLD BERLANGER.

Sans Souci FM: 57, rue 26, blvd Carénage, Cap-Haïtien; tel. 2813-1874; fax 3701-5913; e-mail sanssoucifm@radiosanssouci.com; internet www.radiosanssouci.com; f. 1998; Dir IVES MARIE CHANEL.

Signal FM: 127 rue Louverture, Pétionville, BP 391, Port-au-Prince; tel. 2256-4368; fax 2256-4396; e-mail info@signalfmhaiti.com; internet www.signalfmhaiti.com; f. 1991; independent; Dir-Gen. MARIO VIAU.

Television

CanalSat Haïti: angle des rues Faustin 1er et Chériez, Canapé-Vert, Port-au-Prince; tel. 2946-4141; internet www.emitelsa.com; f. 2011; satellite broadcaster, 46 European channels and 10 radio stations, mostly in French; Exec. Dir RÉGINALD BAKER.

NU TV: 57 rue Clerveaux, Pétionville, Port-au-Prince; tel. 4438-1204; e-mail ialerte@nu-tv.com; internet www.nu-tv.com; f. 2012; 90 Haitian, European, North American and Spanish-language TV channels via satellite; CEO PATRICE TURNIER.

Télé Caraïbes: 45 rue Chavannes, Port-au-Prince; tel. 3558-9110; e-mail radiocaraibesfm@yahoo.fr; internet www.radiotelevisioncaraibes.com; broadcasts in Port-au-Prince area; owned by Moussignac Group; Dir PATRICK MOUSSIGNAC; Exec. Dir WEIBERT ARTHUS.

Télé Eclair: 526 route de Delmas, Port-au-Prince; tel. 2256-4505; fax 2256-3828; f. 1996; independent; Dir PATRICK ANDRÉ JOSEPH.

Télé Ginen: 28 bis, Delmas 31, BP 6120, Port-au-Prince; tel. 2949-2407; fax 2511-1737; e-mail info@rtghaiti.com; internet www.rtghaiti.com; nationwide transmission; Owner, Dir and Gen. Man. JEAN LUCIEN BORGES.

Télé Haïti (Société Haïtienne de Télévision par Satellites, SA): blvd Harry S Truman, Bicentenaire, BP 1126, Port-au-Prince; tel. 2222-3887; fax 2222-9140; e-mail info@telhaiti.com; internet www.telehaiti.net; f. 1959; bldg destroyed by 2010 earthquake, recommenced broadcasts in 2012; pay cable station with 128 international channels; broadcasts in French, Spanish and English; Pres. ALLEN BAYARD.

Télé Metropole: 8 route de Delmas 52, BP 62, Port-au-Prince; tel. 2246-2626; fax 2249-2020; e-mail informations@naskita.com; internet www.metropolehaiti.com; f. 2007; broadcasts to Port-au-Prince area, mainly in French; Pres. HERBERT WIDMAIER; Dir-Gen. RICHARD WIDMAIER.

Télémax: 3 Delmas 19, Port-au-Prince; tel. 246-2002; fax 2246-1155; f. 1994; independent; Dir ROBERT DENIS.

Télévision Nationale d'Haïti: Delmas 33, BP 13400, Port-au-Prince; tel. 2246-2325; fax 2246-0693; e-mail info@tnh.ht; internet www.tnhtv.ht; f. 1979; merged with Radio Nationale d'Haïti in 1987; govt-owned; cultural; 4 channels in Creole, French and Spanish; administered by 4-mem. board; Dir-Gen.(Television) EMMANUEL MÉNARD; Dir-Gen. (Radio) HARRISON ERNEST.

Finance

(cap. = capital; m. = million; res = reserves; dep. = deposits; brs = branches; amounts in gourdes)

BANKING

Central Bank

Banque de la République d'Haïti: angle rues du Pavée et du Quai, BP 1570, Port-au-Prince; tel. 2299-1202; fax 2299-1145; e-mail webmaster@brh.net; internet www.brh.net; f. 1911 as Banque Nationale de la République d'Haïti; name changed as above in 1979; bank of issue; administered by 5-mem. board; cap. 50m., res 3,053.4m., dep. 55,355.2m. (Sept. 2009); Gov. CHARLES CASTEL; Dir-Gen. JEAN BADEN DUBOIS.

Commercial Banks

Banque Nationale de Crédit: angle rues du Quai et des Miracles, BP 1320, Port-au-Prince; tel. 2299-4081; fax 2299-4076; internet www.bnconline.com; f. 1979; cap. 25m., dep. 729.9m. (Sept. 1989); Pres. JEAN PHILIPPE VIXAMAR; Dir-Gen. JOSEPH EDY DUBUISSON.

Banque Populaire Haïtienne: angle rues Aubran et Gabart, Petionville, Port-au-Prince; tel. 2299-6080; fax 2299-6076; e-mail bphinfo@brh.net; f. 1973; state-owned; cap. and res 72.9m., dep. 819m. (Mar. 2007); Dirs-Gen. JESLY LÉVÊQUE, MYRIAM JEAN; 3 brs.

Banque de l'Union Haïtienne: angle rues du Quai et Bonne Foi, BP 275, Port-au-Prince; tel. 2299-8500; fax 2299-8517; e-mail buh@buhsa.com; internet www.buh.ht; f. 1973; cap. 30.1m., res 6.2m. (Sept. 1997), dep. 1,964.3m. (Sept. 2004); Pres. MARCEL FONTIN; 12 brs.

Capital Bank: 38 rue Flaubert, Pétionville, BP 2464, Port-au-Prince; tel. 2299-6700; fax 2299-6519; e-mail capitalbank@brh.net; internet www.capitalbankhaiti.com; f. 1986; fmrly Banque de Crédit Immobilier, SA; cap. 270m., res 141.9m., dep. 6,903.3m. (Sept. 2011); Pres. BERNARD ROY; Gen. Man. LILIANE C. DOMINIQUE.

Sogebank, SA (Société Générale Haïtienne de Banque, SA): route de Delmas, BP 1315, Port-au-Prince; tel. 2229-5000; fax 2229-5022; e-mail sogebanking@sogebank.com; internet www.sogebank.com; f. 1986; part of Groupe Sogebank; cap. 750m., res. 1,231m., dep 36,975.2m. (Sept. 2011); Pres. RALPH PERRY; 35 brs.

Scotiabank Haiti (Canada): 360 blvd J. J. Dessalines, BP 686, Port-au-Prince; tel. 2941-3001; e-mail bns.haiti@scotiabank.com; f. 1972; Country Man. MAXIME CHARLES; 4 brs.

Unibank: 157 rue Flaubert, Pétionville, BP 46, Port-au-Prince; tel. 2299-2057; fax 2299-2070; e-mail info@unibankhaiti.com; internet www.unibankhaiti.com; f. 1993; cap. 2,000m., res 265.3m., dep. 40,582.4m. (Sept. 2011); Pres. F. CARL BRAUN; Dir-Gen. FRANCK HELMCKE; 20 brs.

INSURANCE

Principal Companies

Alternative Insurance, SA: 4 rue Jean Gilles, blvd Toussaint Louverture, Port-au-Prince; tel. 2229-6300; fax 2250-1461; e-mail info@aic.ht; internet www.aic.ht; Dir-Gen. OLIVIER BARREAU.

Les Assurances Léger, SA (ALSA): 40 rue Lamarre, BP 2120, Port-au-Prince; tel. 2222-3451; fax 2223-8634; e-mail alsa@alsagroup.com; f. 1994; headquarters in France; Pres. (vacant).

Compagnie d'Assurances d'Haïti, SA (CAH): étage Dynamic Entreprise, route de l'Aéroport, BP 1489, Port-au-Prince; tel. 2250-0700; fax 2250-0236; e-mail info@groupedynamic.com; internet www.groupedynamic.com/cah.php; f. 1978; subsidiary of Groupe Dynamic SA; Group Chair. and CEO PHILIPPE R. ARMAND.

Excelsior Assurance, SA: rue 6, no 24, Port-au-Prince; tel. 2245-8881; fax 2245-8598; e-mail ingesanon@yahoo.fr; Dir-Gen. EMMANUEL SANON.

Haïti Sécurité Assurance, SA: 352 ave John Brown, BP 1754, Bourdon, Port-au-Prince; tel. 3489-3444; fax 3489-3423; e-mail admin@haiti-securite.com; internet www.haiti-securite.com; f. 1985; Dir-Gen. WILLIAM PHIPPS.

MAVSA Multi Assurances, SA: étage Dynamic Entreprise, route de l'Aéroport, BP 1489, Port-au-Prince; tel. 2250-0700; fax 2250-0236; e-mail info@groupedynamic.com; internet www.groupedynamic.com/mavsa.php; f. 1992; subsidiary of Groupe Dynamic SA; credit life insurance and pension plans; Group Chair. and CEO PHILIPPE R. ARMAND.

National d'Assurance, SA (NASSA): 25 rue Ferdinand Canapé-Vert, BP 532, Port-au-Prince, HT6115; tel. 2245-9800; fax 2245-9701; e-mail nassa@nassagroup.com; internet www.nassagroup.com; f. 1989; specializing in property, medical and life insurance; Pres. FRITZ DUPUY.

National Western Life Insurance: 13 rue Pie XII, Cité de l'Exposition, Port-au-Prince; tel. 2223-0734; e-mail intlmktg@globalnw.com; headquarters in USA; Chair. and CEO ROBERT L. MOODY; Agent VORBE BARRAU DUPUY.

Office National d'Assurance Vieillesse (ONA): 21 angle des rue Gregoire et Villate, Petion-Ville, Port-au-Prince; tel. 2256-6272; fax 2256-6274; e-mail ona@ona.ht; internet www.ona.ht; f. 1965; Dir-Gen. BERNARD DEGRAFF.

Société de Commercialisation d'Assurance, SA (SOCOMAS): étage Complexe STELO, 56 route de Delmas, BP 636, Port-au-Prince; tel. 2246-4768; fax 2246-4874; e-mail socomashaiti@hotmail.com; Dir-Gen. JEAN DIDIER GARDÈRE.

Insurance Association

Association des Assureurs d'Haïti: 40 rue Lamarre, Port-au-Prince; tel. 2816-8888; e-mail harold.cadet@alsagroup.com; Pres. HAROLD CADET.

Trade and Industry

GOVERNMENT AGENCIES

Centre de Facilitation des Investissements (CFI): 8 rue Légitime, Champs de Mars, BP 6110, Port-au-Prince; tel. 2514-5792; fax 2224-8990; e-mail fihaiti@gmail.com; internet www.cfihaiti.net; f. 2006; foreign investment promotion; Dir-Gen. NORMA POWELL.

Centre National des Équipements (CNE): Port-au-Prince; state-run construction co; Dir-Gen. JUDE CÉLESTIN.

Conseil de Modernisation des Entreprises Publiques (CMEP): Palais National, Port-au-Prince; tel. 2222-4111; fax 2222-7761; internet www.cmep.gouv.ht; f. 1996; oversees modernization and privatization of state enterprises; Dir-Gen. YVES BASTIEN.

DEVELOPMENT ORGANIZATIONS

Fonds de Développement Industriel (FDI): 12 angle rue Butte et impasse Chabrier, BP 2597, Port-au-Prince; tel. 2244-9728; fax 2244-9727; e-mail fdi@fdihaiti.com; internet www.fdihaiti.com; f. 1981; Dir-Gen. LHERMITE FRANÇOIS.

Mouvman Peyizan Papay (MPP): Papaye, Hinche; internet www.mpphaiti.org; f. 1973; peasant org., chiefly concerned with food production and land protection; Leader CHAVANNES JEAN-BAPTISTE.

Société Financière Haïtienne de Développement, SA (SOFIHDES): 11 blvd Harry S Truman, BP 1399, Port-au-Prince; tel. 2250-1427; fax 2250-1436; e-mail info@sofihdes.com; internet www.sofihdes.com; f. 1983; industrial and agro-industrial project-financing; Chair. FRANTZ BERNARD CRAAN; Man. Dir THONY MOÏSE.

Société Nationale des Parcs Industriels (SONAPI) (National Society of Industrial Parks): Port-au-Prince; manages industrial parks for housing cos; owns the Caracol Industrial Park (PIC) and the Metropolitan Industrial Park (PIM); Dir-Gen. BERNARD SCHETTINI.

CHAMBERS OF COMMERCE

Chambre Américaine de Commerce en Haïti (AMCHAM): 18 rue Moïse, Pétionville, Delmas, BP 13486, Port-au-Prince; tel. 2511-3024; fax 2940-3024; e-mail psaintcyr@amchamhaiti.com; internet amchamhaiti.com; f. 1979; Pres. PHILIPPE ARMAND; Exec. Dir PHILIPPE SAINT-CYR.

Chambre de Commerce et d'Industrie d'Haïti (CCIH): blvd Harry S Truman, Cité de l'Exposition, BP 982, Port-au-Prince; tel. and fax 3512-5141; e-mail ccih@ccih.ht; internet www.ccih.org.ht; f. 1895; 10 departmental chambers; Pres. HERVÉ DENIS; Sec. JOVENEL MOISE.

Chambre de Commerce et d'Industrie Haitiano-Canadienne (CCIHC): rue des Nimes, Port-au-Prince; tel. 2813-0773; e-mail direction@ccihc.com; internet ccihc.com; Pres. NATHALIE PIERRE-LOUIS LAROCHE; Exec. Dir LAROCHE CHANDLER.

Chambre Franco-Haïtienne de Commerce et d'Industrie (CFHCI): 5 rue Goulard, Pétionville, 6140 Port-au-Prince; tel. and fax 2510-8965; e-mail cfhci@yahoo.fr; internet www.chambrefrancohaitienne.com; f. 1987; Pres. GRÉGORY BRANDT; Exec. Dir KETTLY FOURON; 109 mems.

INDUSTRIAL AND TRADE ORGANIZATIONS

Association des Exportateurs de Café (ASDEC): rue Barbancourt, BP 1334, Port-au-Prince; tel. 2249-2160; fax 2249-2142; e-mail asdec@primexsa.com; Pres. JULIEN ETIENNE.

Association Haïtienne pour le Développement des Technologies de l'Information et de la Communication (AHTIC): 18 rue Moise, Pétionville, Port-au-Prince; tel. 2454-1498; e-mail sbruno@websystems.ht; Pres. REYNOLD GUERRIER; Exec. Dir STÉPHANE BRUNO.

Association Haïtienne des Economistes (AHE): rue Lamarre, 26 étage, BP 15567, Pétionville; tel. 2512-4605; e-mail haiti_economistes@yahoo.fr; Pres. EDDY LABOSSIÈRE.

Association des Industries d'Haïti (ADIH): 21 rue Borno, Pétionville, BP 15199, Port-au-Prince; tel. 3776-1211; fax 2514-0184; e-mail administration@adih.ht; internet www.adih.ht; f. 1980; Pres. NORMA POWELL; Exec. Dir GRÉGOR AVRIL.

Association Nationale des Distributeurs de Produits Pétroliers (ANADIPP): Centre Commercial Dubois, route de Delmas, Bureau 401, BP 1379, Port-au-Prince; tel. 2246-1414; fax 2245-0698; e-mail moylafortune@hotmail.com; f. 1979; Pres. MAURICE LAFORTUNE.

Association Nationale des Exporteurs de Mangues (ANEM): 5 Santo 20, Route Nationale 3, Croix des Bouquets; tel. 2510-2636; e-mail anem@mango-haiti.com; Pres. JEAN-MAURICE BUTEAU; Man. BERNARD CRAAN.

Association Nationale des Institutions de Microfinance d'Haïti (ANIMH): 87 rue Wallon, Plc Boyer, BP 15321, Pétionville; tel. 2257-3405; e-mail info@animhaiti.org; internet www.animhaiti.org; f. 2002; Pres. YVENS VARISTE; Exec. Dir SOPHIE VINCENT.

Association Professionnelles des Banques (APB): 133 rue Faubert, Pétionville; tel. 2299-3298; fax 2257-2374; e-mail apbhaiti@yahoo.com; Pres. MAXIME CHARLES; Exec. Dir VLADIMIR FRANÇOIS.

UTILITIES

Electricity

Electricité d'Haïti (Ed'H): rue Dante Destouches, Port-au-Prince; tel. 2222-4600; state energy co; Dir-Gen. SERGE RAPHAEL.

Péligre Hydroelectric Plant: Artibonite Valley.

Saut-Mathurine Hydroelectric Plant: Les Cayes.

Water

Direction Nationale d'Eau Potable et de l'Assainissement (DINEPA): angle rue Metellus et route Ibo lélé, No 4, Pétionville, 6140 Port-au-Prince; tel. 2256-4770; fax 2940-0873; e-mail communication@dinepa.gouv.ht; internet www.dinepa.gouv.ht; fmrly Service Nationale d'Eau Potable (SNEP); Dir-Gen. JOSEPH LIONEL DUVALSAINT.

TRADE UNIONS

Batay Ouvriye (Workers' Struggle): Delmas, BP 13326, Port-au-Prince; tel. 2222-6719; e-mail batay@batayouvriye.org; internet www.batayouvriye.org; f. 2002; independent umbrella org.; Co-ordinator YANNICK ETIENNE.

Centrale Autonome des Travailleurs Haïtiens (CATH): 93 rue des Casernes, Port-au-Prince; tel. 3875-1044; e-mail cath.cath17@yahoo.com; f. 1980; Sec.-Gen. LOUIS FIGNOLÉ SAINT-CYR.

Confédération Nationale des Educateurs d'Haïti (CNEH): impasse Noë 17, ave Magloire Ambroise, BP 482, Port-au-Prince; tel. 3421-5777; fax 3812-4576; e-mail cnehaiti@haitiworld.com; f. 1986; Sec.-Gen. LOURDES EDITH JOSEPH DÉLOUIS.

Confédération des Travailleurs Haïtiens (CTH): 138 route de Fréres, Pétionville; tel. 2223-9216; fax 2223-7430; e-mail cthhaiti@gmail.com; internet haiticth.org; f. 1989; comprises 11 federations; Sec.-Gen. LOULOU CHÉRY.

Transport

RAILWAYS

The railway service closed in the early 1990s.

ROADS

In 2001, according to International Road Federation estimates, there were 4,160 km (2,585 miles) of roads, of which 24.3% were paved. There are all-weather roads from Port-au-Prince to Cap-Haïtien, on the northern coast, and to Les Cayes, in the south. The Inter-American Development Bank in November 2013 approved a US $50m. grant for a five-year road improvement project.

SHIPPING

The two principal ports are Port-au-Prince and Cap-Haïtien. In December 2013 the flag registered fleet comprised four vessels, totalling 1,473 grt.

Autorité Portuaire Nationale: blvd La Saline, BP 616, Port-au-Prince; tel. 2223-2440; fax 2221-3479; e-mail apnpap@hotmail.com; internet www.apn.gouv.ht; f. 1978; Dir-Gen. JEAN EVENS CHARLES.

Adeko Enterprises: 33–35 blvd Harry S Truman, ave Marie-Jeanne, Port-au-Prince; tel. 3445-0617; e-mail info@adeko-ht.com; internet www.adeko-ht.com; air and sea freight forwarders and maritime agency; Pres. JEAN MARC ANTOINE; Gen. Man. MARC KINSON ANTOINE.

AI Shipping International: Apt No 1, Sonadim Bldg, blvd Toussaint Louverture and Patrice Lumumba, Port-au-Prince; tel. 2940-5476; fax 2941-5476; e-mail info@aishippingintl.com; internet www.aishippingintl.com; f. 1981; freight forwarder and maritime agency; Pres. ANTOINE ILANES.

CIVIL AVIATION

The international airport, situated 8 km (5 miles) outside Port-au-Prince, is the country's principal airport. There is also an airport at Cap-Haïtien, which opened to international flights in 2013 following an upgrade. In April of that year it was announced that the airport was to be named after the late Venezuelan President Hugo Chávez. Antoine-Simon airport at Les Cayes opened in 2005 and, following an extension of the runway and the building of a new terminal in 2013, was also expected to open to international flights. Construction of a new airport on the island of Ile à Vache began in 2013. There are smaller airfields at Jacmel, Jérémie and Port-de-Paix.

Autorite Aéroportuaire Nationale (AAN): Aéroport International Toussaint Louverture, Port-au-Prince; tel. 3443-0250; fax 2250-5866; e-mail dgaan@haitiworld.com; internet papaeroportauthority.org; Dir-Gen. PIERRE ANDRÉ LAGUERRE.

Office National de l'Aviation Civile (OFNAC): Aéroport International Toussiant Louverture, Delmas, BP 1346, Port-au-Prince; tel. 2246-0052; fax 2246-0998; e-mail lpierre@ofnac.org; Dir-Gen. JEAN MARC FLAMBERT.

Sunrise Airways: 12 Impasse Besse, rue Panamericaine, Pétionville; tel. 2816-0616; fax 2811-2222; e-mail info@sunriseairways.net; internet sunriseairways.net; f. 2009 as charter carrier; began scheduled flights within Haiti in 2012, flights to the Turks and Caicos in 2013; Pres. PHILIPPE BAYARD.

Vision Air Haiti: Aérogare Guy Malary, Port-au-Prince; tel. 3886-2420; internet visionairhaiti.com; f. 2010; domestic flights; Gen. Man. JEAN JIHA, Jr.

Tourism

Tourism was formerly Haiti's second largest source of foreign exchange. However, as a result of political instability, the number of cruise ships visiting Haiti declined considerably. In 2011 tourist arrivals totalled 348,755 and receipts from tourism totalled US $162m. In 2013 Best Western International opened a $15m. hotel in Pétionville. Further hotels, including a 173-room Marriott hotel in Port-au-Prince, were also under construction.

Association Haïtienne des Agences de Voyages (ASHAV): 17 rue des Miracles, Port-au-Prince; tel. 3445-5903; fax 2511-2424; e-mail ashav@hainet.net; f. 1988; Pres. PIERRE CHAUVET, Fils.

Association Touristique d'Haïti (ATH): rue Moise 18, Pétionville, BP 2562, Port-au-Prince; tel. 2946-8484; fax 3906-8484; e-mail athaiti@gmail.com; internet www.haiticherie.ht; f. 1951; Pres. RICHARD BUTEAU; Exec. Dir VALERIE LOUIS.

Defence

The armed forces were effectively dissolved in 1995, although officially they remained in existence pending an amendment to the Constitution providing for their abolition. As assessed at November 2013, the national police force numbered an estimated 2,000. There was also a coastguard of 50. In 2004 the UN Stabilization Mission in Haiti (MINUSTAH) assumed peacekeeping responsibilities in the country. Following the 2010 earthquake, MINUSTAH's authorized capacity was increased. As of February 2014, MINUSTAH comprised 6,355 troops, 2,240 civilian police, 1,629 international and local civilian staff (as of 30 November 2013), and 164 UN Volunteers. The MINUSTAH budget for 2013/14 was an estimated US $576.6m. In 2012 the Governments of Brazil and Ecuador agreed to assist Haiti in the formation of a new army, to number 1,500, which, it was hoped, would eventually replace MINUSTAH. In 2013 Haiti inaugurated a naval base at Les Cayes, intended primarily to counter drugs-trafficking activities.

Director-General of the Police Nationale: GODSON AURÉLUS.

Education

Education is provided by the state, by the Roman Catholic Church and by other religious organizations. Teaching is based on the French model, and French is the language of instruction. Primary education, which normally begins at six years of age and lasts for six years, is officially compulsory. Secondary education usually begins at 12 years of age and lasts for a further six years, comprising two cycles of three years each. According to UNICEF estimates, in 2011 the primary attendance ratio included 48% of male and 52% of female children in the relevant age-group, while at secondary schools it included 18% of male and 21% of female students in the relevant age-group. Higher education is provided by 18 technical and vocational centres, 42 domestic science schools, by the Université d'Etat d'Haïti and by the Université Roi Henri Christophe (inaugurated in 2012). More than 1,300 educational institutions were destroyed in the 2010 earthquake. In 2011 the National Fund for Education (FNE) was launched to provide more than 500,000 children with access to education. Some US $70m. was made available in 2012 to the FNE. In 2010/11 an estimated 8,504m. gourdes was allocated to education, representing 8% of the total spending.

HONDURAS

Introductory Survey

LOCATION, CLIMATE, LANGUAGE, RELIGION, FLAG, CAPITAL

The Republic of Honduras lies in the middle of the Central American isthmus. It has a long northern coastline on the Caribbean Sea and a narrow southern outlet to the Pacific Ocean. Its neighbours are Guatemala to the west, El Salvador to the south-west and Nicaragua to the south-east. The climate ranges from temperate in the mountainous regions to tropical in the coastal plains: temperatures in the interior range from 15°C (59°F) to 24°C (75°F), while temperatures in the coastal plains average about 30°C (86°F). There are two rainy seasons in upland areas, May–July and September–October. The national language is Spanish. Almost all of the inhabitants profess Christianity, and about 82% of the population are adherents of the Roman Catholic Church. The national flag (proportions 1 by 2) has three horizontal stripes, of blue, white and blue, with five blue five-pointed stars, arranged in a diagonal cross, in the centre of the white stripe. The capital is Tegucigalpa.

CONTEMPORARY POLITICAL HISTORY

Historical Context

Honduras was ruled by Spain from the 16th century until 1821 and became a sovereign state in 1838. From 1939 the country was ruled as a dictatorship by Gen. Tiburcio Carías Andino, leader of the Partido Nacional (PN), who had been President since 1933. In 1949 Carías was succeeded as President by Juan Manuel Gálvez, also of the PN. In 1954 the leader of the Partido Liberal (PL), Dr José Ramón Villeda Morales, was elected President, but was immediately deposed by Julio Lozano Díaz, himself overthrown by a military junta in 1956. The junta organized elections in 1957, when the PL secured a majority in Congress and Villeda was re-elected President. He was overthrown in 1963 by Col (later Gen.) Oswaldo López Arellano, who, following elections held on the basis of a new Constitution, was appointed President in June 1965.

A presidential election in 1971 was won by Dr Ramón Ernesto Cruz Uclés, the PN candidate. In December 1972, however, Cruz was deposed in a bloodless coup, led by former President López. In 1974 President López was replaced as Commander-in-Chief of the Armed Forces by Col (later Gen.) Juan Melgar Castro, who was appointed President in 1975. President Melgar was forced to resign in 1978, and was replaced by a military junta. The Commander-in-Chief of the Armed Forces, Gen. Policarpo Paz García, assumed the role of Head of State.

Domestic Political Affairs

Military rule was ended officially when, in April 1980, elections to a Constituent Assembly were held. The PL won 52% of the votes but was unable to assume power. Gen. Paz was appointed interim President. At a general election in 1981 the PL, led by Dr Roberto Suazo Córdova, secured an absolute majority in the Congreso Nacional (National Congress). Suazo was sworn in as President, but real power lay in the hands of Col (later Gen.) Gustavo Alvarez Martínez, who became Commander-in-Chief of the Armed Forces. Alvarez suppressed increasing political unrest by authorizing the arrests of trade union activists and left-wing sympathizers; 'death squads' were allegedly also used. In 1984 Gen. Alvarez was deposed as Commander-in-Chief by a group of army officers.

At the 1985 presidential election the leading candidate of the PN, Rafael Leonardo Callejas Romero, obtained 42% of the votes cast, but the PL's leading candidate, José Simeón Azcona del Hoyo (who had obtained only 27% of the votes cast), was declared the winner because, in accordance with a new electoral law, the combined votes of the PL's candidates secured the requisite majority of 51% of the total votes.

A report by the human rights organization Amnesty International in 1988 gave evidence of an increase in violations of human rights by the armed forces and by right-wing death squads. The Inter-American Court of Human Rights (an organ of the Organization of American States—OAS, see p. 394) found the Honduran Government guilty of the 'disappearances' of Honduran citizens during 1981–84. The PL secured a majority of seats in the National Congress at the November 1989 general election, while Callejas of the PN won the concurrent presidential ballot. The Callejas administration promptly adopted economic austerity measures, provoking widespread social unrest.

In 1993, in response to increasing pressure by human rights organizations, the Government established a special commission to investigate allegations of human rights violations by the armed forces. The commission recommended, *inter alia*, the replacement of the armed forces' much-criticized secret counter-intelligence organization, the División Nacional de Investigaciones (DNI), with a body under civilian control. Legislation replacing the DNI with a new ministry, the Dirección de Investigación Criminal, was approved in December.

At presidential and legislative elections in November 1993 Carlos Roberto Reina Idiáquez, the candidate of the PL, was elected President. The PL also obtained a clear majority in the Congress. Reina, a former President of the Inter-American Court of Human Rights, expressed his commitment to the reform of the judicial system and the armed forces. In 1994 the Congress approved a constitutional reform abolishing compulsory military service (the amendment was ratified in 1995). Also approved was the transfer of the police from military to civilian control. In July 4,000 members of indigenous organizations occupied the Congress building and succeeded in securing an agreement with the Government granting rights and social assistance to the country's indigenous community. The following months were characterized by growing social and political tension. Concern was raised by human rights organizations that instability was being fomented by the armed forces in an attempt to stem the rapid diminution of its powers. An increase in the incidence of crime and violent demonstrations forced the Government to declare a state of national emergency in August and to deploy the armed forces to maintain order.

In May 1997, following the killing of two ethnic minority leaders in the previous month, more than 3,000 members of the indigenous community conducted a march from the western departments of Copán and Ocotepeque to the capital to protest outside the presidential palace. As a result, Reina agreed to conduct a full investigation into the killings and to accelerate the distribution of some 7,000 ha of land to the indigenous community. However, the killing of a further two ethnic minority leaders later that month led to accusations by human rights groups that attempts were being made to eliminate minority autonomous organizations.

At the general election held in November 1997 Carlos Roberto Flores Facussé, the candidate of the ruling PL, was elected President. The PL also obtained a majority in the Congress. In May 1998 control of the police force, widely suspected of perpetrating human rights abuses, was transferred from the military to the civilian authorities. Nevertheless, reports of human rights abuses continued.

The Maduro presidency

The PN candidate, Ricardo Maduro Joest, emerged victorious in the presidential election of November 2001. The PN also gained a majority in the Congress in the concurrent legislative ballot.

President Maduro faced increasing industrial unrest during his term in office. Public dissatisfaction with reductions in public expenditure culminated with a 'March for Dignity', in which some 10,000 people converged on Tegucigalpa in August 2003 in protest at, *inter alia*, the decentralization of water services and plans for civil service reform. Intermittent unrest continued in 2004.

Despite the implementation of increased security measures by the Maduro administration, Honduras experienced rising levels of violent crime in the 2000s. In January 2003, in response to increasing conflict between street gangs (*maras*), 10,000 army troops had been deployed on to the streets of several cities. Controversial legislation approved in August introduced prison sentences of between nine and 12 years for members of the *maras*, which were held responsible for much of the crime in Honduras. In December 2004 the Government introduced further legislation, increasing the maximum prison sentence for gang membership and extending the period of detention without charge. However, President Maduro's strict policies towards criminals also raised fears of human rights abuses.

The 2005 elections

The presidential election held on 27 November 2005 was narrowly won by the PL's José Manuel Zelaya Rosales. In the concurrent legislative election the PL won 62 of the 128 seats in the National Congress, while the PN secured 55 seats. The delay in announcing the final results was severely criticized by observers, who denounced the electoral process as the worst in 25 years of democracy. Zelaya assumed the presidency on 27 January 2006 and a new Government was installed.

The assassination, in March 2007, of Rigoberto Aceituno, the second most senior police official in Honduras, served as a stark reminder of the continuing influence of the country's drugs gangs. Violent crime persisted as a serious problem in 2008, with the assassination of several political figures, including the Vice-President of the Congress, Mario Fernando Hernández, in November.

In April 2008 demonstrators began a hunger strike outside the Congress to protest against government corruption and impunity. They demanded a review of case files involving prominent figures from politics and business, accusing the Attorney-General of failing to investigate corruption charges. The Congress agreed to an audit of the cases, and the strike ended after 38 days.

The ratification, in October 2008, of Honduras' accession to what became known as the Bolivarian Alliance for the Peoples of our America-People's Trade Treaty (Alianza Bolivariana para los Pueblos de Nuestra América-Tratado de Comercio de los Pueblos—ALBA-TCP, see p. 463), a Venezuelan-led economic and social integration initiative, created some tension within the National Congress. In order to win the support of the legislature, President Zelaya agreed to endorse the campaign of the speaker, Roberto Micheletti Baín, for the presidential election due in November 2009, and created a development fund worth US $19.5m. to support the congressional campaigns of PL deputies who voted in favour of ratification. The PN decried the misuse of public funds and abstained from voting.

The 2009 constitutional crisis

President Zelaya provoked considerable controversy in March 2009 when he ordered the National Statistics Institute to organize a referendum on convening a constituent assembly to revise the Constitution. The PN and several prominent members of the PL opposed the proposal, amid speculation that Zelaya was seeking a reform that would allow him to remain in office beyond the expiry of his term in January 2010, while the office of the Attorney-General insisted that only the Tribunal Supremo Electoral (TSE—Supreme Electoral Court) had the power to conduct a referendum.

On 23 June 2009, five days before the plebiscite was scheduled to be held, political tensions escalated when the National Congress attempted to thwart Zelaya's plans by approving legislation prohibiting the holding of referendums 180 days before or after a general election. The Chairman of the Joint Chiefs of Staff, Gen. Romeo Vásquez Velásquez, consequently refused to provide logistical support for the vote on the grounds that it was unlawful, leading to his dismissal by Zelaya, which, in turn, prompted the resignation of several senior military officials and of Edmundo Orellana as Minister of National Defence. The Supreme Court, meanwhile, insisted that Vásquez be reinstated. However, Zelaya refused to comply with the Court's demand and proceeded with preparations for the non-binding referendum, without the support of the military and in defiance of both the judiciary and the legislature, which commenced discussions on the possibility of impeaching the President.

Shortly before voting was due to begin, on 28 June 2009, President Zelaya was seized at his residence by members of the armed forces and forced into exile in Costa Rica; it subsequently emerged that the Supreme Court had authorized the detention of Zelaya on 18 charges, including treason and abuse of authority. Later that day the Congress voted to remove Zelaya from the presidency, on the grounds that he had repeatedly violated the Constitution and failed to observe court orders, and Micheletti was sworn in to act as President until the end of the current term in January 2010; prior to the vote, the Congress had been read an alleged letter of resignation from Zelaya (which he denied having signed). An interim Cabinet was appointed on 29 June 2009. Micheletti, who maintained that Zelaya had been legally removed from office in what he termed a 'constitutional succession', declared that the presidential and legislative elections would be conducted, as scheduled, on 29 November. However, the ousting of Zelaya was denounced internationally, with both the UN General Assembly and the OAS adopting resolutions condemning what they deemed to be a coup and demanding the restoration of Zelaya to the presidency. The OAS also suspended the right of Honduras to participate in the Organization and designated Costa Rican President Oscar Arias Sánchez to lead diplomatic efforts to mediate a resolution to the country's political crisis. Meanwhile, demonstrations both for and against Zelaya's reinstatement as President took place nationwide. Zelaya attempted to return to Honduras on 5 July, but the aircraft in which he was travelling was prevented from landing; at least two people were reportedly killed in clashes between the security forces and supporters of the deposed President.

Arias brokered talks between the two sides in Costa Rica, in July 2009, but Micheletti's representatives repeatedly rejected a proposed arrangement that would involve Zelaya returning to serve the remainder of his presidential term as head of a unity government. An OAS delegation of foreign ministers visited Tegucigalpa in late August, but failed to persuade Micheletti's de facto Government to accept the US-supported accord devised by Arias. The Supreme Court also rejected the terms of the accord. The OAS and the US Department of State both announced that they would not recognize the outcome of polls conducted under Micheletti's administration.

Zelaya made an unexpected return to Honduras on 21 September 2009, taking refuge in the Brazilian embassy in Tegucigalpa, outside which thousands of his supporters subsequently gathered before being dispersed by the security forces. The de facto Government imposed a temporary curfew and, on the following day, adopted a decree suspending five constitutional articles, including those guaranteeing freedom of expression, freedom of association and of assembly, and freedom of movement, for a period of 45 days. The decree prompted widespread condemnation, not only internationally, but also from domestic political and business figures, many of whom had previously supported Zelaya's removal from office, including the two main presidential candidates, Porfirio Lobo Sosa of the PN and Elvin Santos for the PL. Micheletti repealed the decree in October.

Representatives of Micheletti and Zelaya held a series of talks in Tegucigalpa in October 2009, under the auspices of the OAS. The main point of contention was Zelaya's proposed restitution to office. On 30 October, following the intervention of the US Department of State, the Tegucigalpa/San José Accord was signed. Under the terms of the Accord, an interim government of unity and national reconciliation was to be formed to oversee the election on 29 November and the transition to a new administration. Also, a congressional vote was to be held on the restoration of executive power to those in office prior to 28 June. A Verification Commission was established to monitor compliance with the commitments contained in the Accord, and a Truth and Reconciliation Commission was to be created. However, amid dissent regarding the timing of the legislative vote on the potential reinstatement of Zelaya, Micheletti announced on 5 November that he was proceeding unilaterally with the appointment of the new interim government owing to the failure of the deposed President to nominate ministers. The US Department of State adopted a different approach from the OAS, meanwhile, stating that the Honduran state institutions should determine how to implement the agreement and confirming that it would recognize the forthcoming elections.

Lobo was victorious in the presidential election of November 2009, securing 57% of the valid votes cast, compared with 38% for Santos. In the concurrent legislative elections, Lobo's PN also won a large majority in the Congress, taking 71 of the 128 seats, while the PL obtained 45 seats, the Partido Demócrata Cristiano de Honduras (PDCH) five, the Partido de Unificación Democrática (PUD) four and the Partido Innovación y Unidad—Social Demócrata (PINU—SD) three. The PN's strong performance was largely attributed to public disenchantment with the divided PL, the party of both Micheletti and Zelaya. A turnout of some 50% of registered voters was recorded. The results were recognized by the USA and a number of Latin American countries, including Colombia, Costa Rica and Panama, although the OAS, ALBA-TCP, the Mercado Común del Sur (Mercosur) and other members of the international community refused to accept the legitimacy of the vote.

President-elect Lobo's most immediate challenge was to secure international support for his incoming administration, particularly in view of the urgent need for a resumption of foreign aid and lending to Honduras, largely suspended since June 2009. This task was made more difficult on 2 December, when the legislature voted overwhelmingly against the reinstatement of Zelaya (who remained in the Brazilian embassy), pending Lobo's inauguration in January 2010. Lobo subsequently came under significant international pressure to persuade Micheletti to resign as acting President in order to allow the formation of a government of national unity and reconciliation, and to secure a safe passage out of Honduras for Zelaya. However, Micheletti resolutely refused to stand down before Lobo's investiture and insisted that Zelaya would only be permitted to leave Honduras without answering the charges against him if he accepted political asylum in a country outside Central America. In early January the Chairman of the Joint Chiefs of Staff, Gen. Vásquez, and five other senior military officials were charged with abuse of authority in connection with the forced expulsion of Zelaya from Honduras. On 20 January Lobo signed an agreement with President Leonel Fernández Reyna of the Dominican Republic on the safe passage of the deposed President to that country following Lobo's investiture; Zelaya accepted the arrangement.

Lobo in office

Lobo was sworn in as President on 27 January 2010. The new Congress approved a decree granting amnesty for any political offences committed by Zelaya and those involved in his removal from power, while the Supreme Court acquitted the six senior military officials charged with abuse of authority. Lobo's Cabinet included the defeated presidential candidates of the PDCH, the PUD and the PINU—SD, although the most senior posts were allocated to members of the PN: notably, Mario Canahauti was appointed as Minister of Foreign Affairs, and William Chong Wong returned to the position of Minister of Finance, which he had formerly held during Maduro's presidency.

The primary focus of President Lobo's first months in office was the restoration of relations with the international community. To this end, he continued efforts to fulfil the requirements of the Tegucigalpa/San José Accord. The World Bank and the US Government subsequently announced that they would resume the provision of aid to Honduras. However, human rights groups expressed concern in March 2010 over the murder of several journalists and a series of attacks on political activists, particularly members of the Frente Nacional de Resistencia Popular (FNRP), a broad alliance of organizations and movements that had opposed Zelaya's removal from office. Lobo subsequently sought to demonstrate his commitment to protecting human rights by creating a new government post of Minister Adviser on Human Rights. Meanwhile, Zelaya and four former ministers and officials from his administration were charged in February with fraud, falsification of documents and abuse of authority in relation to the alleged misuse of 30m. lempiras from the Honduran social investment fund. The charges against Zelaya complicated Lobo's efforts to gain recognition of his administration from the countries of ALBA-TCP and Mercosur, which demanded that the former President be permitted to return to political life in Honduras. (The charge of abuse of authority was later dismissed, in accordance with the recently approved amnesty decree.)

The Truth and Reconciliation Commission commenced work in May 2010. The FNRP, which continued to seek Zelaya's return and to advocate the creation of a constituent assembly to amend the Constitution, questioned the independence of the Commission, claiming that its purpose was to exonerate the coup leaders, and established an alternative truth commission in June. An OAS commission tasked with assessing the political situation in Honduras issued its report in July. It recommended the termination of legal proceedings involving Zelaya and his associates; the application by Zelaya for membership of the Central American Parliament (Parlacen) in order to secure recognition of his status as Lobo's predecessor as constitutional President of Honduras; the adoption of measures to protect journalists, members of the FNRP and judges who had opposed the coup; the cessation of impunity for human rights violations; and the organization of a national dialogue with the participation of all political sectors. In May the Supreme Court had provoked controversy by dismissing four judges who had criticized the removal of Zelaya from office and the Court's role in this.

Meanwhile, in June 2010 a joint committee of the TSE and the National Congress was established to consider, and consult the public on, a range of proposed political reforms, including a constitutional amendment to ease the conditions for holding a referendum. In October Lobo initiated a national dialogue to discuss the convening of a constituent assembly to reform the Constitution. However, most FNRP members rejected the President's invitation to participate in the dialogue on the grounds that they would not engage with a Government that they did not recognize. A commission charged with drafting reforms to the article of the Constitution regulating referendums was subsequently created. In February 2011 the Congress adopted the proposed constitutional amendments, which not only eased the conditions for initiating a referendum, but also removed a restriction preventing referendums on a provision that forbade the revision of a number of other constitutional articles, including those relating to the length of the presidential term and the ban on presidential re-election. Despite favouring constitutional reform, the FNRP expressed opposition to the amendments, continuing to demand that a constituent assembly be convened. Also approved was the creation of a judicial council, which would assume responsibility for appointing and dismissing judges from the Supreme Court.

Amid mounting concern regarding increasing insecurity in Honduras, in early 2011 Lobo ordered some 2,000 troops to participate in joint patrols with the police force in an effort to combat organized crime, particularly drugs-trafficking. The murder rate had risen to 82 per 100,000 persons in 2010. In November 2011 the Government announced a further joint police-military deployment, and measures were introduced to address endemic police corruption. Nevertheless, the declining security situation led the Government in December to declare a 90-day state of emergency, which, in accordance with a controversial constitutional amendment adopted by the legislature in the previous month, granted the military extensive powers to carry out policing duties. (The military's mandate was extended during 2012.) Some observers raised questions about the appropriateness of using soldiers to perform functions usually conducted by trained police officers. Also in December 2011, the Congress approved legislation authorizing electronic surveillance, while in the following month the Constitution was modified again to permit the extradition of Hondurans accused of committing offences related to drugs-trafficking, organized crime and terrorism. In spite of these efforts, the UN reported that the murder rate increased to 92 per 100,000 persons in 2011. A commission of inquiry into police and judicial corruption and potential security reforms was established in early 2012, and a purge of corrupt police officers was effected during the second half of the year.

In May 2011, following pressure from the Government, the Supreme Court revoked the corruption charges against Zelaya, and shortly thereafter Lobo and Zelaya, with Colombian-Venezuelan mediation, concluded a formal reconciliation agreement. As a result, the former President returned to Honduras at the end of the month. This successful process of reconciliation fulfilled a key demand of Lobo's critics in the region, precipitating Honduras' readmission to the OAS in June and the normalization of the country's diplomatic relations. In July the Truth and Reconciliation Commission released its report on the events of 28 June 2009, concluding that Zelaya's letter of resignation had been fabricated and that his deposition had constituted a coup. The Commission therefore adjudged Micheletti's administration to have been illegal, but also criticized Zelaya for having increased institutional tensions prior to the coup. The report recommended that the Constitution be amended to permit presidential impeachment, thus providing the Honduran institutions with a legitimate alternative to military intervention in cases where the head of state was suspected of acting unlawfully. Six senior military officers accused of abuse of authority for their involvement in the 2009 coup were controversially exonerated by the Supreme Court in October 2011. Zelaya denounced this decision, claiming that those responsible for deposing him were being 'protected'.

With support from the FNRP and defectors from the PL, in October 2011 Zelaya established a new political party, the Partido Libertad y Refundación (LIBRE). However, even though the former President had been removed from power before the completion of his full term of office, the Constitution prohibited him from contesting another presidential election. Consequently, Zelaya's wife, Xiomara Castro de Zelaya, announced she would stand as LIBRE's candidate in the 2013 election. The Alianza Patriótica Hondureña was founded in November, with Gen. Vásquez, the former Chairman of the Joint Chiefs of Staff and a central figure in the ouster of Zelaya, as the party's presidential nominee.

With violent crime still prevalent, in September 2011 Lobo replaced Minister of Public Security Oscar Alvarez with Pompeyo Bonilla Reyes. In the same government reorganization, Arturo Corrales Alvarez was appointed Minister of Foreign Affairs. Further cabinet changes were implemented in February 2012: Héctor Guillén received the finance portfolio, Marlon Oniel Escoto Valerio became the new Minister of Education, and José Adonis Lavaire was given responsibility for industry and commerce. Guillén resigned in August and was replaced by Wilfredo Cerrato.

In an attempt to ease long-standing tensions between peasants and landowners in the north of the country, the Government announced a land redistribution scheme in June 2012, while in August a disarmament initiative was implemented in Colón. Nevertheless, land invasions and violent attacks against peasants continued to be reported in the region. In November primary elections were conducted to determine the main parties' representatives in the upcoming presidential poll, due to take place on 24 November 2013. Juan Orlando Hernández Alvarado, the President of the National Congress and a close associate of President Lobo, was elected as the PN's candidate, Mauricio Villeda was to represent the PL, and Castro de Zelaya was endorsed as LIBRE's nominee. Hernández became PN President in March 2013.

Tensions between the Lobo administration and the Supreme Court, which had been escalating since 2010 owing to the latter's repeated rejection of the Government's legislative initiatives, culminated in December 2012 when the Congress approved the replacement of four members of the Court's constitutional branch who had recently voted against legislation on police reform. Legislators claimed that the magistrates had not acted in the national interest. The domestic and international reaction to this politically motivated, and arguably unconstitutional, intervention in the functioning of the Supreme Court was largely subdued, however, and an appeal by the dismissed justices was denied in February 2013. The Constitution was modified in January to incorporate more robust procedures for the impeachment of the President and other high-ranking public figures; the amendments to the charter also, *inter alia*, provided for a reduction in the decision-making powers of the constitutional chamber.

The public security portfolio was reassigned again in April 2013; Corrales was named as Bonilla's replacement, while Mireya Agüero was given responsibility for foreign affairs. New anti-crime measures announced in 2013 included an increase in prison sentences for those convicted of violent crimes, the implementation of structural reforms within the police force and the formation of several specialized security units, while in early 2014 controversial aircraft interception legislation was also adopted by the outgoing Congress. The new law would allow the military to shoot down aircraft suspected of drugs-trafficking. Approval of the law prompted the USA to suspend radar co-operation with Honduras in March. In addition, in mid-2013 the Catholic Church and the OAS brokered a provisional truce between the major *maras*. The murder rate fell to 86 per 100,000 people in 2012 and to 79 per 100,000 in 2013. Honduras' murder rate remained, however, the highest in the world.

Recent developments: Hernández elected President

Hernández attracted 36.9% of the votes cast in the presidential election conducted on 24 November 2013, defeating Castro de Zelaya (28.8%), Villeda (20.3%) and Salvador Nasralla of the recently formed Partido Anticorrupción (PAC—13.4%). In the concurrent legislative polls, Hernández's PN garnered 48 of the 128 seats in the National Congress; LIBRE won 37 seats, the PL 27, the PAC 13 and smaller parties the remaining three. Despite some electoral irregularities and disquiet about campaign financing, the results were endorsed by international observers. LIBRE, however, denounced the presidential poll as illegitimate and mounted an unsuccessful legal challenge.

Hernández assumed the presidency on 27 January 2014, and several members of the Lobo administration—including Agüero, Cerrato and Corrales—were reappointed to the new Cabinet. In addition, complementary portfolios were to be grouped together into seven consolidated 'superministries' in an attempt to improve government efficiency. Jorge Ramón Hernández Alcerro was named as Co-ordinator-General of the Government and was tasked with overseeing the sectoral ministries. Although the PN had lost its majority in the Congress, commentators deemed it likely that the PL would provide the ruling party with the requisite votes to implement its manifesto.

The Minister of Agriculture and Livestock, Jorge Lobo (son of the former President), resigned in March 2014, reportedly following a disagreement with President Hernández. He was replaced by Jacobo Paz Bodden.

Foreign Affairs

Regional relations

From the early 1980s former members of the Nicaraguan National Guard (so-called 'Contras') established bases in Honduras, from which they conducted raids across the border, allegedly with support from the Honduran armed forces. In return for considerable military assistance from the USA, the Honduran Government permitted US military aid to be supplied to the Contras based there. Public opposition to US military presence in Honduras increased from 1984, and in December, following revelations that the USA had secretly sold weapons to the Government of Iran and that the proceeds had been used to finance the activities of the Contra rebels, President José Simeón Azcona requested the departure of the Contras from Honduras.

In 1987 Honduras, Costa Rica, El Salvador, Guatemala and Nicaragua signed a Central American peace plan, the 'Esquipulas agreement', the crucial provisions of which included the implementation of simultaneous ceasefires in Nicaragua and El Salvador, a halt to foreign assistance to rebel groups, and the establishment of national reconciliation commissions in each of the Central American nations. The Government agreed to the establishment by the UN and the OAS of an international commission to oversee the voluntary repatriation or removal to a third country of the rebel forces; in return, the Nicaraguan Government agreed to abandon the action that it had initiated against Honduras at the International Court of Justice (ICJ).

In 1995 Honduras and Nicaragua signed an accord providing for the visible demarcation of each country's territorial waters in the Gulf of Fonseca, and the establishment of a joint naval patrol to police the area. However, in 1999 Nicaragua severed commercial ties with Honduras following a dispute over the Caribbean Sea Maritime Limits Treaty, which granted Colombia territorial rights to areas of the Caribbean historically claimed by Nicaragua. In 2000, following OAS mediation, the two countries agreed to establish a maritime exclusion zone in the disputed area. Representatives of Honduras and Nicaragua also signed an accord on joint patrols in the Caribbean, pending a ruling by the ICJ, and on combined operations in the Gulf of Fonseca, as well as the withdrawal of forces from the land border area. Following further talks under OAS auspices, in 2001 the two countries agreed to allow monitors into the disputed area to verify troop deployment. In 2002, however, the situation deteriorated when the Nicaraguan Government announced plans to sell oil-drilling rights in the disputed area. The ICJ brought an end to the dispute in 2007, ruling on a revised maritime border approximately midway between the two countries. In November 2012 the ICJ settled a disagreement between Colombia and Nicaragua concerning their boundaries in the Caribbean Sea. The Honduran Government declared its support for the ICJ's judgment, even though, according to some interpretations, the settlement would entail the transfer of approximately 14,000 sq km of Caribbean waters from Honduras to Nicaragua.

A long-standing dispute between Honduras and El Salvador, regarding the demarcation of the two countries' common border and rival claims to three islands in the Gulf of Fonseca, caused hostilities to break out between the two countries in 1969. Although armed conflict soon subsided, the Honduran and Salvadorean Governments did not sign a peace treaty until 1980. In 1992 the ICJ awarded Honduras sovereignty over some two-thirds of the disputed mainland territory and over one of the disputed islands in the Gulf of Fonseca. A convention governing the acquired rights and nationality of those people was finally signed by the Presidents of both countries in 1998. In 2006 President Zelaya met his Salvadorean counterpart to ratify the border demarcation. Honduras, El Salvador and Nicaragua created a commission in December 2012 to support the peaceful development of the Gulf of Fonseca region. However, another boundary dispute in the Gulf of Fonseca resurfaced in August 2013 when the Honduran military landed on the tiny Conejo Island, sovereignty over which was asserted by both Honduras and El Salvador, and planted a Honduran flag. The Salvadorean authorities submitted a formal complaint to Honduras in September, but Honduran activity on the island increased during that month. El Salvador's acquisition of 10 attack aircraft in October further exacerbated the situation.

In 2002 Honduras restored diplomatic relations with Cuba, suspended since 1961. Meanwhile, relations with other Latin American countries, in particular Venezuela, were strengthened by the admission of Honduras, in 2007, to the Petrocaribe initiative (whereby Caribbean countries were able to purchase petroleum from Venezuela on preferential terms), and by the country's accession to ALBA-TCP (see above) in 2008. Petroleum supplies to Honduras under Petrocaribe were suspended in July 2009 in response to the removal from office of President Zelaya, which was condemned by regional leaders, most vigorously by Venezuelan President Hugo Chávez. Moreover, ALBA-TCP refused to recognize the November elections. In January 2010 the outgoing National Congress ratified a decree issued by de facto President Micheletti withdrawing Honduras from ALBA-TCP. President Lobo swiftly succeeded in gaining recognition for his administration from other Central American countries, with the notable exception of Nicaragua, but many South American countries, including Argentina, Brazil and Venezuela, continued to withhold their support for the restoration of OAS membership rights to Honduras. Following Venezuelan and Colombian mediation, in May 2011 a reconciliation agreement was signed by Lobo and Zelaya, which precipitated the latter's return to Honduras. This breakthrough led to the re-establishment of diplomatic relations between Honduras and its regional neighbours (excluding Ecuador), and the country was permitted to rejoin the OAS in June. Honduras was readmitted to the Petrocaribe programme in May 2013, and diplomatic relations with Ecuador were restored in March 2014.

Other external relations

The US Administration of Barack Obama condemned the removal from power of Zelaya in 2009, demanding his reinstatement and suspending all military co-operation and some development aid in response. In September further US aid to Honduras was cancelled and the visas of Micheletti, several other senior officials in his administration and the members of the Supreme Court were revoked. None the less, the USA opted to recognize the elections held in November, and the resumption of US aid was announced in March 2010. In September the USA included Honduras for the first time on its list of major illicit drugs-transit or drugs-producing countries. The US Drug Enforcement Administration (DEA) is involved in counter-trafficking operations in Honduras, although its activities in the country are often controversial. Violent demonstrations were staged in Gracias a Dios during May 2012 in protest against a DEA-backed drugs raid that, according to local residents, had resulted in the deaths of several innocent civilians.

CONSTITUTION AND GOVERNMENT

A new Constitution was approved by the legislature in November 1982, and amended in 1995 and 2011. Under the provisions of the Constitution, the President is elected by a simple majority of the voters. The President holds executive power and has a single four-year mandate. Legislative power is vested in the Congreso Nacional (National Congress), with 128 members elected by universal adult suffrage for a term of four years. Judicial power is exercised by the Supreme Court, the Courts of Appeal and various lesser tribunals. The country is divided into 18 local departments, which are subdivided into 298 autonomous municipalities.

REGIONAL AND INTERNATIONAL CO-OPERATION

Honduras is a member of the Central American Common Market (see p. 229), of the Organization of American States (OAS, see p. 394), of the Association of Caribbean States (see p. 449), and of the Community of Latin American and Caribbean States (see p. 464), which was formally inaugurated in December 2011. The Dominican Republic-Central American Free Trade Agreement (CAFTA-DR), between the Dominican Republic, the Central American countries of Costa Rica, Honduras, El Salvador, Guatemala and Nicaragua, and the USA, entered force in Honduras in 2006. CAFTA-DR, which aims to foster export-orientated growth in the region, was to entail the gradual elimination of tariffs on most industrial and agricultural products over a period of 10 and 20 years, respectively. In 2010 an association agreement, covering trade, political dialogue and co-operation, was concluded between Costa Rica, El Salvador, Guatemala, Honduras, Nicaragua and Panama and the European Union (EU). These countries also concluded a free trade agreement with the EU in 2012. A free trade agreement with Mexico entered into force in 2013 and Honduras concluded a free trade agreement with Canada at the end of that year. Honduras was a founder member of the UN in 1945. As a contracting party to the General Agreement on Tariffs and Trade, Honduras joined the World Trade Organization (see p. 434) on its establishment in 1995.

ECONOMIC AFFAIRS

In 2012, according to estimates by the World Bank, Honduras' gross national income (GNI), measured at average 2010–12 prices, was US $16,405m., equivalent to $2,070 per head (or $3,820 per head on an international purchasing-power parity basis). During 2003–12, it was estimated, the population increased at an average annual rate of 2.0%, while gross domestic product (GDP) per head increased, in real terms, by an average of 2.2% per year. Overall GDP increased, in real terms, at an average annual rate of 4.2% in 2003–12; real GDP increased by 3.9% in 2012, according to central bank estimates.

Agriculture (including hunting, forestry and fishing) contributed an estimated 14.0% of GDP and employed 38.2% of the economically active population in 2012. The principal cash crop is traditionally coffee, which contributed 32.8% of the total value of exports (excluding gold and *maquila* exports) in 2012. An outbreak of coffee leaf rust in 2013–14 severely affected the sector. Exports of bananas contributed 10.3% of total export earnings in 2012. The main subsistence crops include maize, plantains, beans, rice, sugar cane and citrus fruit. Exports of shellfish make a significant contribution to foreign earnings (lobsters and prawns provided 4.9% of total export earnings in 2012). According to official estimates, agricultural GDP increased at an average annual rate of 3.9% during 2003–12; the sector increased by 9.9% in 2012.

Industry (including mining, manufacturing, construction and power) contributed an estimated 26.4% of GDP and employed 19.5% of the economically active population in 2012. According to official estimates, industrial GDP increased at an average annual rate of 3.2% during 2003–12; it increased by 2.2% in 2012.

Mining contributed an estimated 0.9% of GDP and employed 0.4% of the economically active population in 2012. Gold was the major mineral export, contributing an estimated 1.3% of total export earnings in 2012. Lead, zinc, silver, copper and low-grade iron ore are also mined. In addition, small quantities of petroleum derivatives are exported. The GDP of the mining sector decreased by an average of 4.6% per year in 2003–12; it declined by an estimated 10.6% in 2011, but increased by 7.4% in 2012.

Manufacturing contributed an estimated 18.1% of GDP and employed 13.4% of the economically active population in 2012. Value added by the *maquila* sector contributed an estimated 21,691m. lempiras to the economy in 2012. According to official estimates, manufacturing GDP increased at an average annual rate of 2.9% during 2003–12. The sector's GDP increased by 1.9% in 2012.

Construction contributed an estimated 6.0% of GDP and employed 5.4% of the economically active population in 2012. According to official estimates, the GDP of the construction sector increased at an average annual rate of 1.3% during 2003–12; it increased by 2.6% in 2012.

Petroleum accounted for 54.7% of electrical energy output in 2011, while most of the remainder (39.5%) was derived from hydroelectric power. Imports of mineral fuels and lubricants accounted for 23.9% of the value of total imports in 2012. El Cajón dam, the largest in Central America, provided 300 MW of hydroelectricity. The 102 MW Cerro de Hula wind farm south of Tegucigalpa began operating in December 2011. A project to build two hydroelectric dams on sections of the Ulúa river in the north-western province of Santa Bárbara, valued at around US $600m., was initiated in 2009, jointly financed by international donors, and the state-owned electricity company. The dams were projected to become operational in 2014, although progress was slow. Construction of a hydroelectricity plant on the Patuca river in eastern Honduras was scheduled to recommence in 2014 after receiving Chinese funding.

The services sector contributed an estimated 59.6% of GDP and engaged 42.3% of the working population in 2012. The GDP of the services sector increased by an average of 7.5% per year in 2003–12, according to official estimates; it increased by 4.9% in 2012.

In 2012 Honduras recorded a visible merchandise trade deficit of US $4,288.9m., while there was a deficit of $1,586.9m. on the current account of the balance of payments. Workers' remittances from abroad constitute an important source of income: according to central bank estimates, remittances totalled some

$2,891.8m. in 2012. The majority of remittances came from the USA. The USA was the principal market for exports (34.1%, excluding *maquila* goods) in 2012; other significant purchasers were Germany, Belgium and El Salvador. In the same year the principal source of imports (44.0%) was also the USA; other major suppliers were Guatemala, El Salvador and Mexico. The principal exports (excluding *maquila* goods) in 2012 were coffee, bananas, and palm oil. The principal imports in that year were mineral fuels and lubricants, machinery and electrical appliances, and chemicals and related products.

In 2013 there was an estimated budgetary deficit of 13,682.8m. lempiras. Honduras' general government gross debt was 124,642m. lempiras in 2012, equivalent to 34.4% of GDP. Honduras' external debt totalled US $4,642m. at the end of 2011, of which $3,180m. was public and publicly guaranteed debt. In that year, the cost of servicing long-term public and publicly guaranteed debt and repayments to the IMF was equivalent to 16.0% of the value of the exports of goods, services and income (excluding workers' remittances). The annual rate of inflation averaged 6.7% in 2004–13. Consumer prices increased by an annual average of 5.2% in 2013. Some 3.6% of the labour force were registered as unemployed in May 2012; it was estimated that around one-quarter of the workforce was underemployed.

Honduras is among the poorest nations in the Americas, and poverty and violent crime are pervasive. The economy contracted in 2009, owing to the impact of the global financial crisis, exacerbated by political instability and the suspension of substantial amounts of financial assistance. After taking office in January 2010, President Porfirio Lobo secured a resumption of credit from multilateral lenders. Renewed growth of 3.7% was recorded in 2010, as the value of exports rose, partly owing to higher prices for coffee and bananas. Remittances, which traditionally account for a significant portion of GDP, increased as a result of improved conditions in the USA. Real GDP expanded by a further 3.8% in 2011. The economy benefited from continued high prices for export commodities, while the restoration of diplomatic relations with the country's regional trading partners was also a positive development. However, inflation, already high owing to rising international petroleum and food prices, continued to rise. Vigorous domestic consumption contributed to economic growth of 3.9% in 2012, although there was a downturn in the *maquila* sector and increased government spending undermined the fiscal position. IMF funding ended in March, and subsequent discussions with the Fund failed to yield a replacement stand-by arrangement. Consequently, the Government issued a US $500m. bond in early 2013. Honduras rejoined the Petrocaribe programme in mid-2013; regaining access to cheaper Venezuelan petroleum was expected to alleviate some of the pressure on the current account. Real GDP growth moderated to 2.6% in that year as the coffee sector was seriously undermined by an epidemic of the coffee leaf rust fungal disease. A series of fiscal austerity reforms was adopted by the legislature in December, although some of the measures envisaged were revoked by the incoming administration in January 2014 following public outcry. The IMF forecast economic growth of 2.8% in 2014.

PUBLIC HOLIDAYS

2015: 1 January (New Year's Day), 14 April (Pan-American Day/Bastilla's Day), 2–4 April (Easter), 1 May (Labour Day), 15 September (Independence Day), 3 October (Morazán Day), 12 October (Columbus Day), 21 October (Army Day), 25 December (Christmas).

Statistical Survey

Sources (unless otherwise stated): Department of Economic Studies, Banco Central de Honduras, Avda Juan Ramón Molina, 1a Calle, 7a Avda, Apdo 3165, Tegucigalpa; tel. 2237-2270; fax 2237-1876; e-mail jreyes@bch.hn; internet www.bch.hn; Instituto Nacional de Estadística, Edif. Plaza Guijarro, 5°, Lomas de Guijarro, Tegucigalpa; e-mail info@ine.hn.org; internet www.ine.gob.hn.

Area and Population

AREA, POPULATION AND DENSITY

Area (sq km)	112,492*
Population (census results)†	
29 May 1988	4,614,377
1 August 2001	
Males	3,230,958
Females	3,304,386
Total	6,535,344
Population (official estimates at mid-year)	
2011	8,215,313
2012	8,385,072
2013	8,555,072
Density (per sq km) at mid-2013	76.05

* 43,433 sq miles.

† Excluding adjustments for underenumeration, estimated to have been 10% at the 1974 census.

POPULATION BY AGE AND SEX

(UN estimates at mid-2014)

	Males	Females	Total
0–14	1,465,038	1,405,441	2,870,479
15–64	2,494,032	2,523,090	5,017,122
65 and over	174,480	198,667	373,147
Total	4,133,550	4,127,198	8,260,748

Source: UN, *World Population Prospects: The 2012 Revision*.

PRINCIPAL TOWNS

('000, official population estimates in 2012)

Tegucigalpa—Distrito Central (capital)	1,172.9	Juticalpa	126.0
San Pedro Sula	743.2	Comayagua	124.1
Choloma	305.2	Catacamas	119.4
El Progreso	216.8	Puerto Cortés	117.0
La Ceiba	196.5	Olanchito	98.6
Danlí	190.1	Siguatepeque	90.2
Choluteca	178.8	Tela	87.8
Villanueva	149.4	Tocoa	84.4

BIRTHS AND DEATHS

(UN estimates)

	1995–2000	2000–05	2005–10
Birth rate (per 1,000)	33.4	30.0	27.7
Death rate (per 1,000)	5.6	5.3	5.1

Source: UN, *World Population Prospects: The 2012 Revision*.

Life expectancy (years at birth): 73.2 (males 70.8; females 75.7) in 2011 (Source: World Bank, World Development Indicators database).

EMPLOYMENT
('000 persons)

	2010	2011	2012
Agriculture, hunting, forestry and fishing	1,222	1,180	1,240
Mining and quarrying	7	7	12
Manufacturing	411	433	434
Electricity, gas and water	17	16	14
Construction	168	169	174
Trade, restaurants and hotels	743	732	710
Transport, storage and communications	114	98	107
Financing, insurance, real estate and business services	107	101	95
Community, social, personal and other services	465	491	459
Total employed	3,254	3,226	3,244

Health and Welfare

KEY INDICATORS

Total fertility rate (children per woman, 2011)	3.1
Under-5 mortality rate (per 1,000 live births, 2011)	21
HIV/AIDS (% of persons aged 15–49, 2011)	0.5
Physicians (per 1,000 head, 2005)	0.4
Hospital beds (per 1,000 head, 2010)	0.8
Health expenditure (2010): US $ per head (PPP)	340
Health expenditure (2010): % of GDP	8.7
Health expenditure (2010): public (% of total)	49.8
Access to water (% of persons, 2011)	89
Access to sanitation (% of persons, 2011)	81
Total carbon dioxide emissions ('000 metric tons, 2010)	8,107.7
Carbon dioxide emissions per head (metric tons, 2010)	1.1
Human Development Index (2012): ranking	120
Human Development Index (2012): value	0.632

For sources and definitions, see explanatory note on p. vi.

Agriculture

PRINCIPAL CROPS
('000 metric tons)

	2010	2011	2012
Maize	509	583	600*
Sorghum	63	37*	40*
Sugar cane	7,819	7,671†	8,600†
Beans, dry	69	91	100†
Oil palm fruit	1,556	1,265	1,414
Tomatoes	158	153†	155†
Melons†	333	385	396
Bananas	751	755†	765†
Plantains	82	84†	86†
Oranges	266	280†	285†
Pineapples	125	138†	142†
Coffee, green	229	282	300†

* Unofficial figure.
† FAO estimate(s).

Aggregate production ('000 metric tons, may include official, semi-official or estimated data): Total cereals 607.9 in 2010, 670.0 in 2011, 688.0 in 2012; Total vegetables (incl. melons) 735.8 in 2010, 786.5 in 2011, 812.3 in 2012; Total fruits (excl. melons) 1,361.3 in 2010, 1,400.5 in 2011, 1,424.2 in 2012.

Source: FAO.

LIVESTOCK
('000 head, year ending September)

	2010	2011*	2012*
Cattle	2,695	2,650	2,660
Sheep*	16	16	16
Goats*	25	25	25
Pigs	470	478	480
Horses*	181	181	182
Mules*	70	70	70
Chickens	40,590	39,500	40,000

* FAO estimates.

Source: FAO.

LIVESTOCK PRODUCTS
('000 metric tons)

	2010	2011*	2012*
Cattle meat	58.6	60.0	62.0
Pig meat	9.6	12.0	13.0
Chicken meat	152.5	158.7	160.0
Cows' milk	739.4	825.0	830.0
Hen eggs	44.2	45.0	45.6

* FAO estimates.

Source: FAO.

Forestry

ROUNDWOOD REMOVALS
('000 cubic metres, excl. bark)

	2010	2011	2012
Sawlogs, veneer logs and logs for sleepers	424	485	386
Other industrial wood	10	14	14
Fuel wood*	8,575	8,535	8,497
Total	9,009	9,034	8,897

* FAO estimates.

Source: FAO.

SAWNWOOD PRODUCTION
('000 cubic metres, incl. railway sleepers)

	2009	2010	2011
Coniferous (softwood)	267	225	230
Broadleaved (hardwood)	10	4	4
Total	277	229	234

2012: Production assumed to be unchanged from 2011 (FAO estimates).

Source: FAO.

Fishing

('000 metric tons, live weight)

	2009	2010	2011
Capture*	11.3	11.1	9.2
Marine fishes*	2.0	2.0	2.1
Caribbean spiny lobster	2.1	3.2	3.3
Penaeus shrimps	1.4	2.1	2.0
Stromboid conchs	1.6	1.6	1.6
Aquaculture	28.9	27.5	37.0*
Nile tilapia	14.2	16.5	20.0*
Penaeus shrimps	14.6	11.1	17.0
Total catch*	40.2	38.6	46.1

* FAO estimate(s).

Source: FAO.

Mining

(metal content)

	2010	2011	2012
Lead (metric tons)	16,944	16,954	12,400
Zinc (metric tons)	33,839	26,000	26,000
Silver (kg)	58,158	53,167	50,605
Gold (kg)	2,197	1,893	1,858

Source: US Geological Survey.

Industry

SELECTED PRODUCTS

	2010	2011	2012
Raw sugar ('000 quintales)	9,543	9,410	10,649
Cement ('000 bags of 42.5 kg)	35,779	40,255	40,337
Cigarettes ('000 packets of 20)	268,665	286,568	267,605
Beer ('000 12 oz bottles)	236,196	257,031	256,198
Soft drinks ('000 12 oz bottles)	2,011,364	2,065,687	2,154,163
Wheat flour ('000 quintales)	3,274	3,319	3,623
Fabric ('000 sq m)	1,294,106	1,210,844	1,155,006
Liquor and spirits ('000 litres)	15,115	18,628	18,723
Vegetable oil and butter ('000 libras)	342,935	382,403	415,978
Electric energy (million kWh)	6,729	7,122	7,336

Finance

CURRENCY AND EXCHANGE RATES

Monetary Units
100 centavos = 1 lempira.

Sterling, Dollar and Euro Equivalents (30 September 2013)
£1 sterling = 33.189 lempiras;
US $1 = 20.547 lempiras;
€1 = 27.748 lempiras;
1,000 lempiras = £30.13 = $48.67 = €36.04.

Average Exchange Rate (lempiras per US $)
2010 18.895
2011 18.917
2012 19.502

GOVERNMENT FINANCE
(general government transactions, non-cash basis, million lempiras, preliminary)

Summary of Balances

	2009	2010	2011
Revenue	64,621.8	69,351.7	77,473.7
Less Expense	65,855.5	68,561.8	74,687.9
Gross operating balance	–1,233.7	789.9	2,785.7
Less Net acquisition of non-financial assets	12,176.1	10,880.1	12,644.4
Net lending/borrowing	–13,409.8	–10,090.2	–9,858.6

Revenue

	2009	2010	2011
Taxes	40,919.4	45,388.6	51,808.7
Taxes of income, profits and capital gains	12,502.8	13,241.3	16,677.7
Taxes of goods and services	24,076.3	26,432.2	29,640.1
Social contributions	8,122.1	8,671.1	9,653.5
Grants	5,096.6	4,162.6	3,676.7
Other revenue	10,483.7	11,129.4	12,334.8
Total	64,621.8	69,351.7	77,473.7

Expense by economic type*

	2009	2010	2011
Compensation of employees	37,197.4	39,585.8	39,971.7
Wages and salaries	36,243.6	36,232.2	37,097.6
Social contributions	953.8	3,353.6	2,874.1
Use of goods and services	12,900.8	10,961.8	12,183.9
Interest	1,780.4	2,560.5	4,072.4
Subsidies	363.3	318.2	557.5
Social benefits	387.0	406.3	364.8
Other expense	13,016.9	14,561.3	17,337.2
Statistical discrepancy	—	—	200.0
Total (incl. others)	65,855.5	68,561.8	74,687.9

* Including purchases of non-financial assets.

Source: IMF, *Government Finance Statistics Yearbook*.

2012 (general government budget, million lempiras, projections): *Revenue:* Current 60,316.4 (Taxes on profits and income 55,495.4); Other revenue 200.0; Grants 3,204.3; Total revenue 63,720.7; *Expenditure:* Current 64,879.4 (Wages and Salaries 34,974.0, Goods and services 8,931.7, Interest 6,466.6, Transfers and subsidies 14,507.1); Capital 15,004.0; Total expenditure 79,883.4 (excl. net lending –25.7).

2013 (general government budget, million lempiras, budget figures): *Revenue:* Current 63,603.7 (Taxes on profits and income 61,247.7); Other revenue 500.0; Grants 2,644.8; Total revenue 66,748.5; *Expenditure:* Current 67,394.8 (Wages and Salaries 36,651.1, Goods and services 9,268.2, Interest 8,391.5, Transfers and subsidies 13,084.0); Capital 13,010.7; Total expenditure 80,405.5 (excl. net lending –25.8).

CENTRAL BANK RESERVES
(US $ million at 31 December)

	2010	2011	2012
Gold (national valuation)	31.15	35.02	38.79
IMF special drawing rights	159.60	154.20	148.08
Foreign exchange	2,497.90	2,582.30	2,333.90
Reserve position in IMF	13.29	13.24	13.26
Total	2,701.94	2,784.76	2,534.03

Source: IMF, *International Financial Statistics*.

MONEY SUPPLY
(million lempiras at 31 December)

	2010	2011	2012
Currency outside depository corporations	14,686	16,199	16,426
Transferable deposits	28,422	30,804	29,102
Other deposits	108,322	122,947	136,336
Securities other than shares	2,135	2,222	2,411
Broad money	153,565	172,172	184,275

Source: IMF, *International Financial Statistics*.

COST OF LIVING
(Consumer Price Index, base: 1999 = 100)

	2011	2012	2013
Food and non-alcoholic beverages	216.2	222.7	233.9
Alcohol and tobacco	249.8	264.4	275.3
Rent, water, fuel and power	274.0	288.2	303.5
Clothing and footwear	208.1	218.9	232.0
Health	257.6	272.9	290.0
Transport	266.9	296.1	310.2
Communications	64.0	64.9	65.9
Culture and recreation	168.0	173.5	180.9
Education	353.1	379.4	401.3
Restaurants and hotels	247.1	263.2	277.4
All items (incl. others)	235.1	247.3	260.1

NATIONAL ACCOUNTS
(million lempiras at current prices)

Expenditure on the Gross Domestic Product

	2010	2011	2012*
Government final consumption expenditure	53,651	53,820	58,306
Private final consumption expenditure	233,795	260,106	281,802
Changes in inventories	970	5,224	5,730
Gross fixed capital formation	64,514	81,883	87,889
Total domestic expenditure	352,930	401,034	433,727
Exports of goods and services	136,950	171,728	182,441
Less Imports of goods and services	190,594	237,733	254,123
GDP in purchasers' values	299,286	335,028	362,044
GDP at constant 2000 prices	159,828	165,958	172,370

Gross Domestic Product by Economic Activity

	2010	2011	2012*
Agriculture, hunting, forestry and fishing	34,691	47,640	49,725
Mining and quarrying	2,932	3,329	3,290
Manufacturing	49,492	57,606	64,388
Electricity, gas and water	6,243	5,044	5,009
Construction	17,912	20,506	21,214
Wholesale and retail trade	40,006	46,247	50,036
Hotels and restaurants	9,100	9,874	10,820
Transport and storage	9,473	10,127	11,342
Communications	10,621	10,527	11,624
Finance and insurance	18,130	20,253	22,054
Owner-occupied dwellings	16,336	17,361	18,571
Business activities	13,899	15,247	16,905
Education services	23,012	23,692	26,029
Health	11,018	11,474	12,727
Public administration and defence	20,943	20,638	22,246
Other services	8,936	9,568	10,368
Sub-total	292,743	329,132	356,348
Less Financial intermediation services indirectly measured	15,020	17,745	19,697
GDP at factor cost	277,722	311,388	336,651
Indirect taxes, *less* subsidies	21,564	23,640	25,393
GDP in purchasers' values	299,286	335,028	362,044

* Preliminary.

BALANCE OF PAYMENTS
(US $ million)

	2010	2011	2012
Exports of goods	2,831.7	3,977.6	4,409.1
Imports of goods	–6,605.7	–8,355.9	–8,698.0
Balance on goods	–3,774.0	–4,378.4	–4,288.9
Exports of services	2,107.6	2,254.0	2,257.5
Imports of services	–1,169.5	–1,447.8	–1,515.0
Balance on goods and services	–2,835.9	–3,572.3	–3,546.4
Primary income received	53.6	58.6	80.3
Primary income paid	–781.4	–1,032.3	–1,355.5
Balance on goods, services and primary income	–3,563.8	–4,545.9	–4,821.5
Secondary income received	2,949.3	3,220.5	3,315.9
Secondary income paid	–67.7	–82.8	–81.3
Current balance	–682.1	–1,408.3	–1,586.9
Capital account (net)	84.7	166.2	101.2
Direct investment assets	363.2	–30.3	–63.7
Direct investment liabilities	484.8	1,042.6	1,067.6
Portfolio investment assets	–18.9	45.8	–11.8
Portfolio investment liabilities	–22.1	41.9	12.9
Other investment assets	65.8	–436.6	137.3
Other investment liabilities	468.9	428.1	315.6
Net errors and omissions	–174.8	184.4	–242.8
Reserves and related items	569.5	33.8	–270.6

Source: IMF, *International Financial Statistics*.

External Trade

PRINCIPAL COMMODITIES
(US $ million)

Imports c.i.f.*	2010	2011	2012
Vegetables and fruit	298.4	434.8	414.1
Food products	693.8	812.2	907.9
Mineral products	1,517.4	2,155.5	2,284.0
Fuels and lubricants	1,487.6	2,103.9	2,242.2
Chemicals and related products	1,031.3	1,227.8	1,281.9
Plastic and manufactures	433.6	508.2	558.6
Paper, paperboard and manufactures	364.2	395.5	352.7
Metal and manufactures	424.3	614.6	611.4
Machinery and electrical appliances	1,147.5	1,380.8	1,359.5
Transport equipment	411.6	497.3	573.4
Total (incl. others)	7,127.7	9,016.2	9,385.3

* Excluding imports destined for the *maquila* sector (US $ million): 2,393.4 in 2010; 2,879.7 in 2011; 2,780.8 in 2012.

Exports f.o.b.*	2010	2011	2012
Bananas	335.4	397.8	442.4
Cigars and cigarettes	73.5	81.4	92.2
Coffee	722.6	1,358.4	1,402.4
Lead and zinc	71.5	65.3	51.6
Melons and watermelons	42.9	54.0	50.9
Palm oil	165.7	270.1	304.2
Lobsters and prawns	176.3	205.8	211.5
Soaps and detergents	59.6	68.9	82.1
Tilapia	56.8	62.8	61.7
Paper and paperboard	71.2	63.7	148.7
Plastics and articles thereof	52.8	78.4	94.7
Total (incl. others)	2,734.8	3,866.4	4,281.3

* Excluding exports of gold, and of *maquila* goods (US $ million): 3,516.1 in 2010; 4,092.6 in 2011; 3,974.1 in 2012.

PRINCIPAL TRADING PARTNERS
(US $ million, excluding *maquila* goods)

Imports c.i.f.	2010	2011	2012
Brazil	107.5	83.9	95.5
China, People's Republic	540.2	337.2	436.1
Colombia	176.6	317.0	272.2
Costa Rica	282.0	364.5	384.8
Ecuador	84.8	226.8	238.3
El Salvador	313.9	485.7	554.9
Germany	107.0	143.0	132.2
Guatemala	558.9	798.4	801.0
Japan	143.7	111.1	119.0
Korea, Republic	79.2	85.8	90.0
Mexico	531.8	488.8	538.0
Panama	77.9	346.9	359.6
Peru	130.8	27.5	75.2
Spain	60.8	80.4	95.7
USA	2,883.3	4,207.2	4,131.1
Total (incl. others)	7,127.7	9,016.2	9,385.3

Exports f.o.b.*	2010	2011	2012
Belgium	130.9	256.0	305.4
Canada	62.1	106.5	50.0
China, People's Republic	62.1	88.6	117.4
Costa Rica	87.3	119.3	103.2
Dominican Republic	31.9	40.3	45.9
El Salvador	226.7	301.1	293.9
France	45.4	62.3	53.9
Germany	202.4	389.6	496.2
Guatemala	201.1	240.3	214.6
Italy	51.3	67.9	80.2
Japan	25.1	47.4	34.9
Mexico	93.7	131.9	126.1
Netherlands	47.2	61.5	149.8
Nicaragua	123.1	158.0	201.6
Panama	21.8	32.7	52.6
Spain	54.9	39.6	57.1
United Kingdom	53.6	95.2	77.1
USA	1,028.9	1,278.9	1,496.0
Total (incl. others)	2,818.8	3,959.8	4,391.0

* Including exports of gold (US $ million): 84.0 in 2010; 93.4 in 2011; 109.7 in 2012.

Transport

ROAD TRAFFIC
(licensed vehicles in use)

	2001	2002	2003
Passenger cars	345,931	369,303	386,468
Buses and coaches	20,380	21,814	22,514
Lorries and vans	81,192	86,893	91,230
Motorcycles and bicycles	36,828	39,245	41,852

2008 (vehicles in use): Passenger cars 213,643; Buses and coaches 51,233; Vans and lorries 427,503; Motorcycles and mopeds 122,397 (Source: IRF, *World Road Statistics*).

SHIPPING

Flag Registered Fleet
(at 31 December)

	2011	2012	2013
Number of vessels	690	677	664
Total displacement ('000 grt)	730.4	665.3	755.1

Source: Lloyd's List Intelligence (www.lloydslistintelligence.com).

International Sea-borne Freight Traffic
('000 metric tons)

	1988	1989	1990
Goods loaded	1,328	1,333	1,316
Goods unloaded	1,151	1,222	1,002

Source: UN, *Monthly Bulletin of Statistics*.

CIVIL AVIATION
(traffic on scheduled services)

	1993	1994	1995
Kilometres flown (million)	4	5	5
Passengers carried ('000)	409	449	474
Passenger-km (million)	362	323	341
Total ton-km (million)	50	42	33

Source: UN, *Statistical Yearbook*.

Passengers carried ('000): 501 in 2010; 424 in 2011; 421 in 2012 (Source: World Bank, World Development Indicators database).

Tourism

TOURIST ARRIVALS BY COUNTRY OF ORIGIN

	2009	2010	2011
Canada	19,062	16,838	18,530
Costa Rica	21,831	24,073	22,825
El Salvador	145,157	159,755	150,343
Guatemala	111,220	122,641	115,768
Italy	17,392	20,773	20,977
Mexico	23,513	20,613	22,968
Nicaragua	106,598	117,342	110,299
Panama	7,925	8,810	8,350
Spain	12,913	15,229	15,459
USA	282,667	248,137	275,117
Total (incl. others)	835,531	862,548	871,468

Total tourist arrivals ('000): 906 in 2012 (provisional).

Receipts from tourism (US $ million, excl. passenger transport): 627 in 2010; 639 in 2011; 661 in 2012 (provisional).

Source: World Tourism Organization.

Communications Media

	2010	2011	2012
Telephones ('000 main lines in use)	669.5	614.3	610.5
Mobile cellular telephones ('000 subscribers)	9,505.1	8,062.2	7,370.0
Broadband subscribers ('000)	1.0	57.9	61.3

Internet subscribers: 72,400 in 2009.

Education

(2011/12 unless otherwise indicated)

		Students		
	Teachers	Males	Females	Total
Pre-primary	8,837*	122,933	121,234	244,167
Primary	37,370*	622,119	594,620	1,216,739
Secondary	16,667†	303,340	356,218	659,558
Higher‡	8,593	79,911	89,967	169,878

* 2008/09.
† 2003/04.
‡ 2009/10.

Source: UNESCO Institute for Statistics.

Institutions (2006/07 unless otherwise indicated): Pre-primary 8,178; Primary and secondary (grades 1 to 9) 11,277; High school 938; Higher (incl. university) 16.

Pupil-teacher ratio (primary education, UNESCO estimate): 33.9 in 2008/09 (Source: UNESCO Institute for Statistics).

Adult literacy rate (UNESCO estimates): 85.1% (males 85.3%; females 84.9%) in 2011 (Source: UNESCO Institute for Statistics).

Directory

The Government

HEAD OF STATE

President: JUAN ORLANDO HERNÁNDEZ ALVARADO (took office 27 January 2014).

CABINET

(April 2014)

The Government is comprised of members of the Partido Nacional.

Minister, Co-ordinator-General of the Government: JORGE RAMÓN HERNÁNDEZ ALCERRO.

Minister of Human Rights, Justice, Government and Decentralization: RIGOBERTO CHANG CASTILLO.

Minister of the Presidency: REINALDO SÁNCHEZ.

Minister of Finance: WILFREDO CERRATO.

Minister of Health: YOLANY BATRES.

Minister of Public Security: ARTURO CORRALES ALVAREZ.

Minister of National Defence: SAMUEL ARMANDO REYES RENDÓN.

Minister of Foreign Affairs: MIREYA AGÜERO DE CORRALES.

Minister of Public Works, Transport and Housing: ROBERTO ORDÓÑEZ.

Minister of Industry and Commerce: ALDEN RIVERA.

Minister of Education: MARLON ESCOTO.

Minister of Energy, Natural Resources and Mines: JOSÉ ANTONIO GALDÁMEZ.

Minister of Agriculture and Livestock: JACOBO PAZ BODDEN.

Minister of Development and Social Inclusion: LISANDRO ROSALES.

Director of Communications and Strategy in the Office of the President: HILDA HERNÁNDEZ.

MINISTRIES

Office of the President: Palacio José Cecilio del Valle, Blvd Francisco Morazán, Tegucigalpa; tel. 2290-5010; fax 2231-0097; e-mail diseloalpresidente@presidencia.gob.hn; internet www.presidencia.gob.hn.

Ministry of Agriculture and Livestock: Avda La FAO, Blvd Centroamérica, Col. Loma Linda, Tegucigalpa; tel. 2232-5029; fax 2231-0051; e-mail infoagro@infoagro.hn; internet www.sag.gob.hn.

Ministry of Development and Social Inclusion: Edif. Ejecutivo, Las Lomas Anexo II, frente a Ferretería INDUFESA, Blvd Juan Pablo II, Tegucigalpa; tel. 2239-8005; internet sedis.gob.hn.

Ministry of Education: 1 Avda, entre 2 y 3 Calle, Comayagüela, Tegucigalpa; tel. 2238-4325; fax 2222-8571; e-mail webmaster@se.gob.hn; internet www.se.gob.hn.

Ministry of Energy, Natural Resources and Mines: 100 m al sur del Estadio Nacional, Apdo 1389, Tegucigalpa; tel. 2232-1386; fax 2232-6250; e-mail sdespacho@yahoo.com; internet www.serna.gob.hn.

Ministry of Finance: Edif. SEFIN, Avda Cervantes, Barrio El Jazmín, Tegucigalpa; tel. 2222-0112; fax 2238-2309; e-mail sgeneral@sefin.gob.hn; internet www.sefin.gob.hn.

Ministry of Foreign Affairs: Centro Cívico Gubernamental, Antigua Casa Presidencial, Blvd Kuwait, Contiguo a la Corte Suprema de Justicia, Tegucigalpa; tel. 2230-4156; fax 2230-5664; e-mail cancilleria.honduras@gmail.com; internet www.sre.gob.hn.

Ministry of Health: 2 Calle, Avda Cervantes, Tegucigalpa; tel. 2222-8518; fax 2238-6787; e-mail comunicacionessalud@yahoo.com; internet www.salud.gob.hn.

Ministry of Human Rights, Justice, Government and Decentralization: Residencia La Hacienda, Calle La Estancia, Tegucigalpa; tel. 2232-5995; fax 2232-0226; e-mail francis.caceres@seip.gob.hn; internet www.seip.gob.hn.

Ministry of Industry and Commerce: Edif. San José, Col. Humuya, Blvd José Cecilio del Valle, Tegucigalpa; tel. 2235-3699; fax 2235-3686; e-mail info@sic.gob.hn; internet www.sic.gob.hn.

Ministry of National Defence: Blvd Suyapa, Col. Florencia Sur, frente a Iglesia Colegio Episcopal, Tegucigalpa; tel. 2239-2330; e-mail transparencia@sedena.gob.hn; internet www.sedena.gob.hn.

Ministry of Public Security: Cuartel General de Casamata, subida al Picacho, Tegucigalpa; tel. 2220-4298; fax 2220-1711; e-mail info@seguridad.gob.hn; internet www.seguridad.gob.hn.

Ministry of Public Works, Transport and Housing: Barrio La Bolsa, Comayagüela, Tegucigalpa; tel. 2225-2690; fax 2225-5003; e-mail info@soptravi.gob.hn; internet www.soptravi.gob.hn.

In addition, President Hernández created seven sectoral ministries, responsible for the following areas: governability and decentralization, development and social inclusion, economic development, infrastructure, security and defence, competition and economic regulation, and foreign affairs.

President and Legislature

PRESIDENT

Election, 24 November 2013

Candidate	Valid votes cast	% of valid votes
Juan Orlando Hernández Alvarado (PN)	1,149,302	36.89
Xiomara Castro de Zelaya (LIBRE)	896,498	28.78
Mauricio Villeda (PL)	632,320	20.30
Salvador Nasralla (PAC)	418,443	13.43
Others	18,885	0.61
Total*	3,115,448	100.00

* In addition, there were 108,171 spoiled votes and 51,727 blank votes.

NATIONAL CONGRESS

(Congreso Nacional)

President: MAURICIO OLIVA.

General Election, 24 November 2013

	Seats
Partido Nacional (PN)	48
Partido Libertad y Refundación (LIBRE)	37
Partido Liberal (PL)	27
Partido Anticorrupción (PAC)	13
Partido Innovación y Unidad—Social Demócrata (PINU—SD)	1
Partido de Unificación Democrática (PUD)	1
Partido Demócrata Cristiano de Honduras (PDCH)	1
Total	128

Election Commission

Tribunal Supremo Electoral (TSE): Col. El Prado, frente a Edif. Syre, Tegucigalpa; tel. 2239-1058; fax 2239-3060; e-mail centroinformacion@tse.hn; internet www.tse.hn; f. 2004 as successor to Tribunal Nacional de Elecciones; Pres. DAVID ANDRÉS MATAMOROS BATSÓN.

Political Organizations

Alianza Patriótica Hondureña (La Alianza): Tegucigalpa; tel. 2213-8091; fax 2213-2367; e-mail contacto@laalianza.hn; internet www.laalianza.hn; f. 2011; right-wing; Pres. Gen. (retd) ROMEO VÁSQUEZ VELÁSQUEZ.

Frente Amplio Político Electoral en Resistencia (FAPER): Tegucigalpa; internet partido-faper.blogspot.co.uk; f. 2012; contested the 2013 elections; Pres. ANDRÉS PAVÓN.

Partido Anticorrupción (PAC): Tegucigalpa; e-mail honduras@salvadornasralla.com; f. 2012; centre-left; Pres. SALVADOR NASRALLA.

Partido Demócrata Cristiano de Honduras (PDCH): Col. San Carlos, Tegucigalpa; tel. 2236-5969; fax 2236-9941; e-mail pdch@hondutel.hn; internet www.pdch.hn; legally recognized in 1980; Pres. LUCAS EVANGELISTO AGUILERA PINEDA; Sec.-Gen. ARNOLD AMAYA.

Partido Innovación y Unidad—Social Demócrata (PINU—SD): 2a Avda, entre 9 y 10 calles, Apdo 105, Comayagüela, Tegucigalpa; tel. 2220-4224; fax 2220-4232; e-mail pinusd@amnettgu.com; internet pinusd.hn; f. 1970; legally recognized in 1978; Pres. JORGE RAFAEL AGUILAR PAREDES; Sec. IRIS ELIZABETH VIGIL.

Partido Liberal (PL): Col. Miramontes, atrás de Supermercado la Col. No 1, Tegucigalpa; tel. 2232-0822; e-mail info@partidoliberaldehonduras.hn; f. 1891; Pres. ELVIN SANTOS.

Partido Libertad y Refundación (LIBRE): Tegucigalpa; internet libertadyrefundacion.tumblr.com; f. 2011; party of 2013 presidential candidate Xiomara Castro de Zelaya; Pres. JOSÉ MANUEL ZELAYA ROSALES.

Partido Nacional (PN): Paseo el Obelisco, Comayagüela, Tegucigalpa; tel. 2237-7310; fax 2237-7365; e-mail partidonacional@partidonacional.net; internet www.partidonacional.net; f. 1902; traditional right-wing party; Pres. JUAN ORLANDO HERNÁNDEZ ALVARADO; Sec.-Gen. REINALDO SÁNCHEZ.

Partido de Unificación Democrática (PUD): Col. los Almendros, Blvd Morazón, atrás del Restaurante Las Reses, Tegucigalpa; tel. and fax 2236-6868; e-mail partidoudhonduras@yahoo.es; internet www.partidoud.com; f. 1992 following merger of Partido Revolucionario Hondureño, Partido Renovación Patriótica, Partido para la Transformación de Honduras and Partido Morazanista; left-wing; Pres. DAVID ADOLFO CÉSAR HAM PEÑA; Sec. MARTÍN PIÑEDA ENGELS.

Diplomatic Representation

EMBASSIES IN HONDURAS

Argentina: Calle Palermo 302, Col. Rubén Darío, Apdo 3208, Tegucigalpa; tel. 2232-3376; fax 2231-0376; e-mail ehond@mrecic.gov.ar; Ambassador GUILLERMO ROBERTO ROSSI.

Belize: Area Comercial del Hotel Honduras Maya, Col. Palmira, Tegucigalpa; tel. 2238-4614; fax 2238-4617; e-mail vesahonduras@gmail.com; Chargé d'affaires a.i. RICHARD CLARK VINELLI REISMAN.

Brazil: Col. Palmira, Calle República del Brasil, Apdo 341, Tegucigalpa; tel. 2221-4432; fax 2236-5873; e-mail brastegu@clarotv.com.hn; internet tegucigalpa.itamaraty.gov.br; Ambassador ZENIK KRAWCTSCHUK.

Chile: Torres Metrópolis 1, 16°, Of. 11608, Blvd Suyapa, Tegucigalpa; tel. 2232-4106; fax 2232-2114; e-mail embachilehonduras@clarotv.com.hn; internet chileabroad.gov.cl/honduras; Ambassador RODRIGO PÉREZ MANRÍQUEZ.

Colombia: Edif. Palmira, 3°, Col. Palmira, Apdo 468, Tegucigalpa; tel. 2239-9709; fax 2232-9324; e-mail ehonduras@cancilleria.gov.co; internet www.embajadaenhonduras.gov.co; Ambassador FRANCISCO CANOSSA GUERRERO.

Costa Rica: Residencial El Triángulo, Calle 3451, Lomas del Guijarro, Apdo 512, Tegucigalpa; tel. 2232-1768; fax 2232-1054; e-mail embacori@amnettgu.com; Ambassador MARÍA GUTIÉRREZ VARGAS.

Cuba: Col. Lomas del Guijarro, Calle Los Eucaliptos, No 3720, Tegucigalpa; tel. 2235-3349; fax 2235-7624; e-mail admon@hn.embacuba.cu; internet www.cubadiplomatica.cu/honduras; Chargé d'affaires a.i. SERGIO OLIVA GUERRA.

Dominican Republic: Plaza Miramontes, 2°, Local No 6, Col. Miramontes, Tegucigalpa; tel. 2239-0130; fax 2239-1594; e-mail joacosta@serex.gov.do; Ambassador JOSÉ OSVALDO LEGER AQUINO.

Ecuador: Bloque F, Casa 2968, Sendero Senecio, Col. Lomas del Castaños Sur, Apdo 358, Tegucigalpa; tel. 2221-4906; fax 2221-1049; e-mail mecuahon@multivisionhn.net; Chargé d'affaires a.i. CRISTINA GRANDA MENDOZA.

El Salvador: Col. Altos de Miramontes, Casa 2952, Diagonal Aguan, Tegucigalpa; tel. 2239-7015; fax 2239-6556; e-mail embasalhonduras@rree.gob.sv; internet embajadahonduras.rree.gob.sv; Ambassador CARLOS POZO.

France: Col. Palmira, Avda Juan Lindo, Callejón Batres 337, Apdo 3441, Tegucigalpa; tel. 2236-6800; fax 2236-8051; e-mail info@ambafrance-hn.org; internet www.ambafrance-hn.org; Ambassador PHILIPPE ARDANAZ.

Germany: Avda República Dominicana 925, Sendero Santo Domingo, Col. Lomas del Guijarro, Apdo 3145, Tegucigalpa; tel. 2232-3161; fax 2239-9018; e-mail info@tegucigalpa.diplo.de; internet www.tegucigalpa.diplo.de; Ambassador Dr JOHANNES TROMMER.

Guatemala: Casa No 0440, Bloque B, Calle Londres, Col. Lomas del Guijarro Sur, Tegucigalpa; tel. 2232-5018; fax 2239-9809; e-mail embhondurasgt@gmail.com; Ambassador HUGO RENÉ HEMMERLING GONZÁLEZ.

Holy See: Palacio de la Nunciatura Apostólica, Col. Palmira, Avda Santa Sede 401, Apdo 324, Tegucigalpa; tel. 2238-6013; fax 2238-6257; e-mail nunziohn@hotmail.com; Apostolic Nuncio Most Rev. LUIGI BIANCO (Titular Archbishop of Falerone).

Italy: Torre Lafise, 3°, Avda Los Próceres, Centro Corporativo, Col. San Carlos, Tegucigalpa; tel. 2221–4963; fax 2221–4953; e-mail ambasciata.tegucigalpa@esteri.it; internet www.ambtegucigalpa.esteri.it; Ambassador GIOVANNI ADORNI BRACCESI CHIASSI.

Japan: Col. San Carlos, Calzada Rep. Paraguay, Apdo 3232, Tegucigalpa; tel. 2236-5511; fax 2236-6100; e-mail keikyo1@multivisionhn.net; internet www.hn.emb-japan.go.jp; Ambassador KENJI OKADA.

Korea, Republic: Edif. Plaza Azul, 5°, Col. Lomas del Guijarro Sur, Tegucigalpa; tel. 2235-5561; fax 2235-5564; e-mail coreaembajada@mofat.go.kr; internet hnd.mofat.go.kr; Ambassador KIM RAI-HYUG.

Mexico: Col. Lomas del Guijarro, Avda Eucalipto 1001, Tegucigalpa; tel. 2232-4039; fax 2232-4719; e-mail embamexhonduras@gmail.com; internet www.sre.gob.mx/honduras; Ambassador VÍCTOR HUGO MORALES.

Nicaragua: Col. Tepeyac, Bloque M-1, Avda Choluteca 1130, Apdo 392, Tegucigalpa; tel. 2231-1966; fax 2231-1412; e-mail embanic@amnettgu.com; Ambassador MARIO JOSÉ DUARTE ZAMORA.

Panama: Edif. Palmira, 3°, Col. Palmira, Apdo 397, Tegucigalpa; tel. 2239-5508; fax 2232-8147; e-mail ephon@multivisionhn.net; Ambassador MARIO RUÍZ DOLANDE.

Peru: Col. Linda Vista, Calle Principal 3301, Tegucigalpa; tel. 2236-7994; fax 2221-4596; e-mail embajadadelperu@cablecolor.hn; Ambassador GUILLERMO GONZÁLEZ ARICA.

Spain: Col. Matamoros, Calle Santander 801, Apdo 3221, Tegucigalpa; tel. 2236-6875; fax 2236-8682; e-mail emb.tegucigalpa@maec.es; internet www.maec.es/Embajadas/Tegucigalpa; Ambassador MIGUEL ALBERO SUÁREZ.

Taiwan (Republic of China): Col. Lomas del Guijarro, Calle Eucaliptos 3750, Apdo 3433, Tegucigalpa; tel. 2239-5837; fax 2232-0532; e-mail hnd@mofa.gov.tw; internet www.taiwanembassy.org/hn; Ambassador JOSEPH Y. L. KUO.

USA: Avda La Paz, Apdo 3453, Tegucigalpa; tel. 2236-9320; fax 2236-9037; internet honduras.usembassy.gov; Ambassador LISA KUBISKE.

Venezuela: Col. Rubén Darío, 2116 Circuito Choluteca, Apdo 775, Tegucigalpa; tel. 2232-1879; fax 2232-1016; e-mail info@venezuelalabolivariana.com; internet venezuelalabolivariana.com; Chargé d'affaires a.i. ARIEL NICOLAS VARGAS ARDENCO.

Judicial System

Justice is administered by the Supreme Court, five Courts of Appeal, and departmental courts (which have their own local jurisdiction).

Tegucigalpa has two Courts of Appeal, the first of which has jurisdiction in the department of Francisco Morazán, and the second of which has jurisdiction in the departments of Choluteca Valle, El Paraíso and Olancho.

The Appeal Court of San Pedro Sula has jurisdiction in the department of Cortés; that of Comayagua has jurisdiction in the departments of Comayagua, La Paz and Intibucá; and that of Santa Bárbara in the departments of Santa Bárbara, Lempira and Copán.

Supreme Court: Edif. Palacio de Justicia, contiguo Col. Miraflores, Centro Cívico Gubernamental, Tegucigalpa; tel. 2275-7183; fax 2233-6784; e-mail comunicaciones@poderjudicial.gob.hn; internet www.poderjudicial.gob.hn; comprises 4 courts: constitutional, labour, civil and penal; Pres. JORGE RIVERA AVILÉS.

Attorney-General: OSCAR FERNANDO CHINCHILLA.

Religion

The majority of the population are Roman Catholics; the Constitution guarantees toleration of all forms of religious belief.

CHRISTIANITY

The Roman Catholic Church

Honduras comprises one archdiocese and seven dioceses. Some 82% of the population are Roman Catholics.

Bishops' Conference: Conferencia Episcopal de Honduras, Blvd Estadio Suyapa, Apdo 3121, Tegucigalpa; tel. 2229-1111; fax 2229-1144; e-mail ceh@unicah.edu; internet www.iglesiahn.org; f. 1929; Pres. Cardinal OSCAR ANDRÉS RODRÍGUEZ MARADIAGA (Archbishop of Tegucigalpa).

Archbishop of Tegucigalpa: Cardinal OSCAR ANDRÉS RODRÍGUEZ MARADIAGA, Arzobispado, 3a y 2a Avda 1113, Apdo 106, Tegucigalpa; tel. 2236-2849; fax 2236-2967; e-mail oficina@arquitegucigalpa.org; internet www.arquitegucigalpa.org.

The Anglican Communion

Honduras comprises a single missionary diocese, in Province IX of the Episcopal Church in the USA.

Bishop of Honduras: Rt Rev. LLOYD EMMANUEL ALLEN, Diócesis de Honduras, 23 Avda C, 21 St Colony Trejo, San Pedro Sula; tel. 2556-6155; fax 2556-6467; e-mail obispoallen@yahoo.com; internet honduras.fedigitales.org.

The Baptist Church

Convención Nacional de Iglesias Bautistas de Honduras (CONIBAH): Apdo 2176, Tegucigalpa; tel. and fax 2221-4024; e-mail conibah@sigmanet.hn; internet www.ublaonline.org/paises/honduras.htm; Pres. Pastor TOMÁS MONTOYA; 24,142 mems.

Other Churches

Church of Jesus Christ of Latter-Day Saints (Mormons): Residenciales Roble Oeste, Blvd Roble Oeste, 3ra Calle Sur, Comayagüela; tel. 2264-1212; internet www.lds.org; 154,207 mems.

Iglesia Cristiana Luterana de Honduras (Lutheran): Barrio Villa Adela, 19 Calle entre 5a y 6a Avda, Apdo 2861, Tegucigalpa; tel. 2225-4464; fax 2225-4893; e-mail iclh@cablecolor.hn; internet iclh.wordpress.com; Pres. Rev. JOSÉ MARTIN GIRÓN; 1,500 mems.

BAHÁ'Í FAITH

National Spiritual Assembly: Sendero de los Naranjos 2801, Col. Castaños, Apdo 273, Tegucigalpa; tel. 2232-6124; fax 2231-1343; e-mail sdooki@tropicohn.com; internet www.bahaihonduras.net; Co-ordinator SOHEIL DOOKI; 40,000 mems resident in more than 500 localities.

The Press

DAILIES

La Gaceta: Empresa Nacional de Artes Gráficas, Col. Miraflores, Tegucigalpa; tel. 2230-1339; fax 2230-3026; internet www.lagaceta.hn; f. 1830; morning; official govt paper; Gen. Man. MARTHA ALICIA GARCÍA CASCO; Co-ordinator MARCO ANTONIO RODRÍGUEZ CASTILLO; circ. 3,000.

El Heraldo: Avda los Próceres, Frente al Pani, Barrio San Felipe, Apdo 1938, Tegucigalpa; tel. 2236-6000; e-mail contactos@elheraldo.hn; internet www.elheraldo.hn; f. 1979; morning; independent; Editor FERNANDO BERRÍOS; circ. 50,000.

La Prensa: Guamilito, 3a Avda, 6–7 Calles No 34, Apdo 143, San Pedro Sula; tel. 2553-3101; fax 2553-0778; e-mail redaccion@laprensa.hn; internet www.laprensa.hn; f. 1964; morning; independent; Editor NELSON GARCÍA; Exec. Dir MARÍA ANTONIA MARTÍNEZ DE FUENTES; circ. 50,000.

El Tiempo: 1 Calle, 5a Avda 102, Barrio Santa Anita, Cortés, Apdo 450, San Pedro Sula; tel. 2553-3388; fax 2553-4590; e-mail web.tiempo@continental.hn; internet www.tiempo.hn; f. 1960; morning; left-of-centre; Pres. JAIME ROSENTHAL OLIVA; circ. 35,000.

La Tribuna: Col. Santa Bárbara, Carretera al Primer Batallón de Infantería, Comayagüela, Apdo 1501, Tegucigalpa; tel. 2234-3206; fax 2234-3050; e-mail tribuna@latribuna.hn; internet www.latribuna.hn; f. 1976; morning; independent; Dir ADÁN ELVIR FLORES; Editor OLMAN MANZANO; circ. 45,000.

PERIODICALS

Comercio Global: Cámara de Comercio e Industrias de Tegucigalpa, Blvd Centroamérica, Apdo 3444, Tegucigalpa; tel. 2232-4200; fax 2232-0759; e-mail mercadeo@ccit.hn; internet www.ccit.hn; f. 1970; 4 a year; commercial and industrial news; Publr DANIELA ZELAYA.

Cromos: Torre Libertad, Blvd Suyapa, Tegucigalpa; tel. 2239-3916; fax 2239-7008; e-mail editor@cromos.hn; internet www.cromos.hn; f. 1999; society; monthly; publishes specialized edns *Cromos Gourmet*, *Cromos Bodas*, *Cromos Seniors*, *Cromos Hogar*, *Cromos Fashion* and *Cromos Ellos* annually; Publr REGINA MARÍA WONG; Editors ALEJANDRA PAREDES, EMMA MIDENCE.

Estilo: Tegucigalpa; tel. 2553-3101; fax 2558-1273; e-mail revista@estilo.hn; internet www.estilo.hn; f. 1996; lifestyle; monthly; Pres. JORGE CANAHUATI LARACH; Editor BLANCA BENDECK.

Hablemos Claro: Edif. Torre Libertad, Blvd Suyapa, Residencial La Hacienda, Tegucigalpa; tel. 2232-8058; fax 2239-7008; e-mail rwa@hablemosclaro.com; internet www.hablemosclaro.com; f. 1990; weekly; Editor RODRIGO WONG ARÉVALO; circ. 9,000.

Honduras Weekly: Centro Comercial Villa Mare, Blvd Morazán, Apdo 1323, Tegucigalpa; tel. 2239-0285; fax 2232-2300; e-mail editor@hondurasweekly.com; internet www.hondurasweekly.com; f. 1988; weekly; English language; tourism, culture and the environment; Bureau Chief NICOLE MUÑOZ; Editor MARCO CÁCERES.

El Libertador: Tegucigalpa; internet www.ellibertador.hn; Dir JHONNY LAGOS; Editor DELMER MEMBREÑO.

PRESS ASSOCIATION

Asociación de Prensa Hondureña: Casa del Periodista, Avda Gutemberg 1525, Calle 6, Barrio El Guanacaste, Apdo 893, Tegucigalpa; tel. 2239-2970; fax 2237-8102; f. 1930; Pres. CARLOS ORTIZ; Sec.-Gen. FELA ISABEL DUARTE.

Publishers

Centro Editorial: Apdo 1683, San Pedro Sula; tel. and fax 2558-6282; e-mail centroeditorialhn@gmail.com; f. 1987; Dir JULIO ESCOTO.

Ediciones Ramses: Edif. Chiminike, 2°, Blvr Fuerzas Armadas de Honduras, Tegucigalpa; tel. 2225-6630; fax 2225-6633; e-mail servicioalcliente@edicionesramses.hn; internet www.edicionesramses.hn; educational material.

Editorial Coello: Avda 9, Calle 4, 64a, Barrio El Benque, San Pedro Sula; tel. 2553-1680; fax 2557-4362; e-mail tcoello@globalnet.hn; Dir AUGUSTO C. COELLO.

Editorial Pez Dulce: 143 Paseo La Leona, Barrio La Leona, Tegucigalpa; tel. and fax 222-1220; e-mail pezdulce@yahoo.com; Dir RUBÉN IZAGUIRRE.

Editorial Universitaria de la Universidad Nacional Autónoma de Honduras: Blvd Suyapa, Tegucigalpa; tel. and fax 2232-4772; f. 1847; Dir SEGISFREDO INFANTE.

Guaymuras: Avda Zaragoza, Apdo 1843, Barrio La Leona, Tegucigalpa; tel. 2237-5433; fax 2238-4578; e-mail ediguay@123.hn; internet www.guaymuras.hn; f. 1980; Dir ISOLDA ARITA MELZER.

Broadcasting and Communications

REGULATORY AUTHORITY

Comisión Nacional de Telecomunicaciones (Conatel): Edif. Conatel, Col. Modelo, 6 Avda Suroeste, Comayagüela, Apdo 15012, Tegucigalpa; tel. 2232-9600; fax 2234-8611; e-mail info@conatel.gob.hn; internet www.conatel.gob.hn; f. 1995; Pres. RICARDO CARDONA.

TELECOMMUNICATIONS

The monopoly of the telecommunications sector by Hondutel ceased at the end of 2005, when the fixed line and international services market was opened to domestic and foreign investment.

Claro Honduras: Col. San Carlos, Avda República de Colombia, Tegucigalpa; tel. 2205-4222; fax 2205-4337; e-mail clientes@claro.com.hn; internet www.claro.com.hn; f. 2003; operated by Servicios de Comunicaciones de Honduras (Sercom Honduras), a subsidiary of América Móvil, SA de CV (Mexico) since 2004; mobile cellular telephone operator; Gen. Man. LUIS DEL SID.

Empresa Hondureña de Telecomunicaciones (Hondutel): Edif. Gerencia Los Almendros, Residencial Montecarlo, Tegucigalpa; tel. 2221-0411; fax 2216-7800; e-mail miguel.velez@hondutelnet.hn; internet www.hondutel.hn; f. 1976; scheduled for privatization; Gen. Man. Gen. (retd) ROMEO VÁSQUEZ VELÁSQUEZ.

Multifon: Tegucigalpa; tel. 206-0607; e-mail sac@multifon.net; f. 2003; subsidiary of MultiData; awarded govt contract with UT Starcom (q.v.) for fixed telephone lines in 2003; Pres. JOSÉ RAFAEL FERRARI; CEO JOSÉ LUIS RIVERA.

Telefónica Celular (CELTEL) (Tigo): Edif. Celtel, contiguo a la Iglesia Episcopal, Blvd Suyapa, Col. Florencia Norte Hondureña, Tegucigalpa; tel. 2235-7966; fax 2220-7060; e-mail info@mail.celtel.net; internet www.tigo.com.hn; f. 1996; mobile cellular telephone company; wholly owned subsidiary of Millicom International Cellular (Luxembourg); Pres. ANTONIO TAVEL OTERO.

UT Starcom (USA): Edif. Plaza Azul, 6°, Calle Viena, Avda Berlin, Col. Lomas del Guijarro Sur, Tegucigalpa; tel. 2239-8289; fax 2239-9161; e-mail services@utstar.com; internet www.utstar.com; awarded govt contract with Multifon (q.v.) for fixed telephone lines in 2003; Pres. and CEO JACK LU.

BROADCASTING

Radio

HRN, La Voz de Honduras: Blvd Suyapa, contiguo a Televicentro, Apdo 642, Tegucigalpa; tel. 2232-5100; fax 2232-5109; e-mail contacto@radiohrn.hn; internet www.radiohrn.hn; commercial station; f. 1933; part of Grupo Emisoras Unidas; broadcasts 12 channels; 23 relay stations; Gen. Man. NAHÚN EFRAÍN VALLADARES.

Power FM: Edif. Power FM, Blvd del Norte Costado Sur, 105 Brigada, Apdo 868, San Pedro Sula; tel. 2564-0500; fax 2564-0529; e-mail info@powerfm.hn; internet www.powerfm.hn; Gen. Man. XAVIER SIERRA.

Radio América: Col. Alameda, frente a la Droguería Mandofer, Apdo 259, Tegucigalpa; tel. 2290-4950; fax 2232-1009; e-mail info@americamultimedios.net; internet www.radioamericahn.net; commercial station; broadcasts Radio San Pedro, Radio Continental, Radio Monderna, Radio Universal, Cadena Radial Sonora, Super Cien Stereo, Momentos FM Stereo and 3 regional channels; f. 1948; 13 relay stations; Gen. Man. JULIO ARÉVALO.

Radio Club Honduras: Salida Chamelecon, Apdo 273, San Pedro Sula; tel. 2556-6173; fax 2617-1151; e-mail hr2rch@yahoo.com; internet www.hr2rch.com; f. 1958; amateur radio club; Pres. NOE OLIVA.

Radio Juticalpa: Juticalpa, Olancho; tel. 2785-2277; fax 2785-5063; internet www.radiojuticalpa.com; Gen. Man. MARTHA ELENA RUBÍ H.

Radio Nacional de Honduras: Avda La Paz, Col. Lomas Del Mayab, detras del edif. del Ministerio de la Presidencia, Tegucigalpa; tel. 2235-6723; fax 2235-6678; e-mail radio@rnh.hn; internet www.rnh.hn; f. 1976; official station, operated by the Govt; Exec. Dir GUSTAVO BLANCO.

Radio la Voz del Atlántico: 12 Calle, 2–3 Avda, Barrio Copen, Apdo 21301, Puerto Cortés; tel. 2665-5166; fax 2665-2401; e-mail administracion@lavozdelatlantico.com; internet www.lavozdelatlantico.com; f. 1955; Dir FRANCISCO ANDRÉS GRIFFIN BOQUIN.

Super K: Entrada Principal, Barrio La Ceiba, San Lorenzo del Valle; tel. 2781-2001; e-mail superk_895fm@yahoo.com; internet www.lasuperkfm.com; f. 2008; Dir MARVIN ESTRADA.

Television

Televicentro: Edif. Televicentro, Blvd Suyapa, Col. Florencia, Apdo 734, Tegucigalpa; tel. 2207-5514; fax 2232-5514; e-mail tvcoperaciones@televicentro.hn; internet www.televicentrotv.net; f. 1987; 11 stations, including Telecadena 7 y 4 (f. 1985), Telesistema Hondureño, Canal 3 y 7 (f. 1967) and Megatv; Pres. JOSÉ RAFAEL FERRARI SAGASTUME.

Canal 5: tel. 2232-7835; fax 2232-0097; f. 1959; Gen. Man. RENATO ALVAREZ.

Televisión Nacional de Honduras (TNH): Edif. Ejecutivo 2, 4°, Frente Casa Presidencial, Tegucigalpa; e-mail info@tnh.gob.hn; internet www.tnh.gob.hn; f. 1962; channels include TVN–8, Telenacional, Cadena 1, Primera Cadena and TNH–8; Dir ARMANDO VALDÉZ.

VICA Television: 9a Calle, 10a Avda 64, Barrio Guamilito, Apdo 120, San Pedro Sula; tel. 2552-4478; fax 2557-3257; e-mail info@mayanet.hn; internet www.vicatv.hn; f. 1986; operates regional channels 2, 9 and 13; Pres. RIGEL SIERRA.

Finance

(cap. = capital; res = reserves; dep. = deposits; m. = million; brs = branches; amounts in lempiras unless otherwise stated)

BANKING

Central Bank

Banco Central de Honduras (BANTRAL): Avda Juan Ramón Molina, 7a Avda y 1a Calle, Apdo 3165, Tegucigalpa; tel. 2237-2270; fax 2237-1876; e-mail Carlos.Espinoza@bch.hn; internet www.bch.hn; f. 1950; bank of issue; cap. 212.5m., res 1,192m., dep. 39,232.9m. (Dec. 2009); Pres. MARLÓN TÁBORA; Gen. Man. HÉCTOR MENDÉZ.

Commercial Banks

BAC Honduras: Blvd Suyapa, frente a Emisoras Unidas, Apdo 116, Tegucigalpa; tel. 2216-0200; fax 2239-4509; internet www.bac.net/honduras; bought by Grupo Aval de Colombia in Dec. 2010; fmrly Banco Mercantil, SA, then BAC BAMER; Gen. Man. JACOBO ATALA.

Banco Atlántida, SA (BANCATLAN): Plaza Bancatlán, Blvd Centroamérica, Apdo 3164, Tegucigalpa; tel. 2232-1050; fax 2232-6120; e-mail webmaster@bancatlan.hn; internet www.bancatlan.hn; f. 1913; cap. 3,750m., res 22.7m. dep. 30,583.1m. (Dec. 2011); Exec. Pres. GUILLERMO BUESO ANDURAY; 179 brs.

Banco Continental, SA (BANCON): Centro Comercial Novaprisa, 9–10 Avda NO, Blvd Morazán, San Pedro Sula; tel. 2550-0880; fax 2550-2750; e-mail imontoya@continental.hn; internet www.bancon.hn; f. 1974; cap. 500m., res 14.7m., dep. 4,358.3m. (Dec. 2011); Pres. JAIME ROSENTHAL OLIVA; 77 brs.

Banco Davivienda Honduras, SA: Intersección Blvd Suyapa y Blvd Juan Pablo II, Apdo 344, Tegucigalpa; tel. 2240-0909; internet www.davivienda.com.hn; f. 1947 as Capitalizadora Hondureña, became BANCAHSA in 1968; known as Banco HSBC from 2007 until 2012, when it was bought by Banco Davivienda (Colombia); part of the Grupo Financiero Bolívar Honduras, SA; cap. 1,280m., res 257.9m., dep. 12,051.8m. (Dec. 2010); CEO EFRAÍN FORERO; 50 brs.

Banco Financiera Comercial Hondureña (Banco FICOHSA): Edif. Plaza Victoria, Col. Las Colinas, Blvd Francia, Tegucigalpa; tel. 2239-6410; fax 2239-6420; e-mail ficobanc@ficohsa.hn; internet www.ficohsa.com; Pres. JAVIER ATALA; 101 brs.

Banco de Honduras, SA: Blvd Suyapa, Col. Loma Linda Sur, Tegucigalpa; tel. 2232-6122; fax 2232-6167; internet www.bancodehonduras.citibank.com; f. 1889; subsidiary of Citibank NA (USA); cap. 250.0m., res 6.8m., dep. 1,940.9m. (2008); Gen. Man. CONSTANTINO GOTSIS; 2 brs.

Banco de Occidente, SA (BANCOCCI): 6a Avda, Calle 2–3, Apdo 3284, Tegucigalpa; tel. 2226-0027; fax 2263-8240; e-mail info@bancocci.hn; internet www.bancocci.hn; f. 1951; cap. 1,600m., res 277.8m., dep. 25,845.6m. (2010); Pres. and Gen. Man. JORGE BUESO ARIAS; Vice-Pres. EMILIO MEDINA R.; 146 brs.

Banco del País (BANPAIS): Edif. Torre del País, Blvd José Antonio Peraza, Calle Banpais esq., San Pedro Sula; tel. 2566-2020; fax 2566-2040; internet www.banpais.hn; f. 1969; acquired Banco Sogerin and client portfolio of Banco de las Fuerzas Armadas in 2003; cap. 1,400m., res 101.3m., dep. 13,072m. (Dec. 2010); Pres. JUAN MIGUEL TORREBIARTE; 109 brs.

Banco de los Trabajadores, SA (BANCOTRAB): 3a Avda, 13a Calle, Comayagüela, Apdo 3246, Tegucigalpa; tel. 2238-0017; fax 2238-0077; internet www.btrab.com; f. 1967; cap. 204.8m. (Dec. 2002); Pres. JOSÉ ADONIS LAVAIRE; Gen. Man. RENÉ ARDÓN MATUTE; 6 brs.

Development Banks

Banco Centroamericano de Integración Económica: Edif. Sede BCIE, Blvd Suyapa, Apdo 772, Tegucigalpa; tel. 2240-2231; fax 2240-2183; e-mail echinchi@bcie.hn; internet www.bcie.org; f. 1960 to finance the economic devt of the Central American Common Market and its mem. countries; mems: Costa Rica, El Salvador, Guatemala, Honduras, Nicaragua; cap. and res US $1,020.0m. (June 2003); Dir TANIA JOSELINA LOBO DE QUIÑÓNEZ; Man. FERNANDO ENRIQUE CHINCHILLA GARCÍA.

Banco Financiera Centroamericana, SA (FICENSA): Edif. FICENSA, Blvd Morazán, Apdo 1432, Tegucigalpa; tel. 2238-1661; fax 2221-3855; e-mail rrivera@ficensa.com; internet www.ficensa.com; f. 1974; private org. providing finance for industry, commerce and transport; Exec. Vice-Pres. and Gen. Man. ROQUE RIVERA RÍBAS.

Banco Hondureño del Café, SA (BANHCAFE): Calle República de Costa Rica, Blvd Juan Pablo II, Col. Lomas del Mayab, Apdo 583, Tegucigalpa; tel. 2232-8370; fax 2232-8782; e-mail banhcafe@banhcafe.hn; internet www.banhcafe.com; f. 1981 to help finance coffee production; owned principally by private coffee producers; cap. 300m., res 69.2m., dep. 2,249.2m. (Dec. 2010); Pres. MIGUEL ALFONSO FERNÁNDEZ RÁPALO; Gen. Man. CÉSAR A. ZAVALA L.; 50 brs.

Banco Nacional de Desarrollo Agrícola (BANADESA): 4 Avda y 5 Avda, 13 Calle, contiguo al Estado Mayor, Barrio el Obelisco, Apdo 212, Comayagüela; tel. 2237-2201; fax 2237-5187; e-mail banadesa@banadesa.hn; internet www.banadesa.hn; f. 1980; govt devt bank; loans to agricultural sector; cap. 354m., res 3.7m., dep. 841.3m. (Dec. 2008); Pres. JORGE JOHNY HANDAL HAWIT; 37 brs.

Banking Associations

Asociación Hondureña de Instituciones Bancarias (AHIBA): Edif. AHIBA, Blvd Suyapa, Apdo 1344, Tegucigalpa; tel. 2235-6770; fax 2239-0191; e-mail ahiba@ahiba.hn; internet www.ahiba.hn; f. 1957; 21 mem. banks; Pres. ROQUE RIBERA RIVAS; Exec. Dir MARÍA LYDIA SOLANO.

Comisión Nacional de Bancos y Seguros (CNBS): Edif. Santa Fé, Col. Castaño Sur, Paseo Virgilio Zelaya Rubí, Bloque C, Apdo 20074, Tegucigalpa; tel. 2290-4500; fax 2237-6232; e-mail rbarahona@cnbs.gov.hn; internet www.cnbs.gov.hn; Pres. VILMA CECILIA MORALES.

STOCK EXCHANGE

Bolsa Centroamericana de Valores: Edif. Torre Alianza 2, 5°, Frente a Gasolinera Puma, Blvd San Juan Bosco, Col. Lomas del Guijarro Sur, Apdo 3885, Tegucigalpa; tel. 2271-0400; fax 2271-0403; internet www.bcv.hn; Pres. JOSÉ ARTURO ALVARADO.

INSURANCE

American Home Assurance Co (Chartis Honduras): Edif. Los Castaños, 4°, Blvd Morazán, Apdo 3220, Tegucigalpa; tel. 2232-3938; fax 2239-9169; e-mail ask.chartis@chartisinsurance.com; internet www.chartisinsurance.com; f. 1958; Gen. Man. JOSÉ EDGARDO FLORES RIVEIRO.

Ficohsa Seguros, SA: Edif. Plaza Victoria, Torre II, Col. Las Colinas, Blvd Francia, Tegucigalpa; tel. 2232-4747; fax 2232-2255; internet www.ficohsaseguros.com; f. 1957; fmrly Interamericana de Seguros, SA; part of Grupo Financiero Ficohsa; Gen. Man. LUIS ALBERTO ATALA FARAJ.

Mapfre Honduras, SA: Edif. El Planetario, 4°, Avda París, Col. Lomas del Guijarro Sur, Calle Madrid, Apdo 312, Tegucigalpa; tel. 2216-2672; fax 2231-0982; e-mail info@mapfre.com.hn; internet www.mapfre.com.hn; f. 1954; fmrly Aseguradora Hondureña, SA; Gen. Man. GERARDO CORRALES.

Pan American Life Insurance Co (PALIC): Edif. PALIC, Avda República de Chile 804, Col. Palmira, Apdo 123, Tegucigalpa; tel. 2216-0909; fax 2239-3437; e-mail servicioalclientehn@panamericanlife.com; internet www.palig.com/Regions/honduras; f. 1944; Pres. SALVADOR ORTEGA (Central America); Gen. Man. MARÍA DEL ROSARIO ALVAREZ.

Seguros Atlántida: Edif. Sonisa, Costado Este de Plaza Bancatlan, Tegucigalpa; tel. 2232-4014; fax 2232-3688; e-mail info@seatlan.com; internet www.segurosatlantida.com; f. 1985; Pres. ROBERT VINELLI; Gen. Man. JUAN MIGUEL ORELLANA.

Seguros Continental, SA: Edif. Continental, 4°, 3a Avda SO, 2a y 3a Calle, Apdo 605, San Pedro Sula; tel. 2550-0880; fax 2550-2750; e-mail seguros@continental.hn; internet www.seguros.continental.hn; f. 1968; Pres. JAIME ROLANDO ROSENTHAL OLIVA; Gen. Man. MARIO ROBERTO SOLÍS DACOSTA.

Seguros Crefisa: Edif. Banco Ficensa, 1°, Blvd Morazán, Apdo 3774, Tegucigalpa; tel. 2238-1750; fax 2238-1714; e-mail info@crefisa.com; internet www.crefisa.com; f. 1993; Gen. Man. MARIO BATRES PINEDA.

Seguros del País: Edif. IPM Anexo, 4°, Blvd Centroamérica, Tegucigalpa; tel. 2239-7077; fax 2232-4216; internet www.segpais.com; f. 2000; Gen. Man. GERARDO RIVERA.

Insurance Association

Cámara Hondureña de Aseguradores (CAHDA): Edif. Casa Metromedia, 3°, Col. San Carlos, Apdo 3290, Tegucigalpa; tel. 2221-5354; fax 2221-5356; e-mail info@cahda.org; internet www.cahda.org; f. 1974; Pres. PEDRO BARQUERO; Gen. Man. TETHEY MARTINEZ.

Trade and Industry

GOVERNMENT AGENCY

Fondo Hondureño de Inversión Social (FHIS): Antiguo Edif. I.P.M., Col. Godoy, Comayagüela, Apdo 3581, Tegucigalpa; tel. 2234-5231; fax 2534-5255; e-mail dgarcia@fhis.hn; internet www.fhis.hn; social investment fund; Exec. Dir GUNTHER BUSTAMENTE.

DEVELOPMENT ORGANIZATIONS

Dirección Ejecutiva de Fomento a la Minería (DEFOMIN): Edif. DEFOMIN, 3°, Blvd Miraflores, Avda la FAO, Apdo 981, Tegucigalpa; tel. 2232-6721; fax 2232-6044; e-mail miguel.mejia@defomin.gob.hn; internet www.defomin.gob.hn; promotes the mining sector; Exec. Dir ALDO SANTOS.

Instituto Hondureño del Café (IHCAFE): Edif. El Faro, Col. Las Minitas, Apdo 40-C, Tegucigalpa; tel. 2237-3130; fax 2238-2368; e-mail gerencia@ihcafe.2hn.com; internet www.cafedehonduras.org; f. 1970; coffee devt programme; Pres. ASTERIO REYES; Gen. Man. VICTOR HUGO MOLINA.

Instituto Hondureño de Mercadeo Agrícola (IHMA): Apdo 727, Tegucigalpa; tel. 2235-3193; fax 2235-5719; e-mail yohanyleticia@yahoo.com; internet www.ihma.gob.hn; f. 1978; agricultural devt agency; Gen. Man. JOSÉ CARLOS ARÍSTIDES GIRÓN AYALA.

Instituto Nacional Agrario (INA): Col. La Almeda, 4a Avda, entre 10a y 11a Calles, No 1009, Apdo 3391, Tegucigalpa; tel. 2232-4893; fax 2232-7398; e-mail transparencia@ina.hn; internet www.ina.hn; agricultural devt programmes; Minister of the INA NEPTALÍ MEDINA AGURCIA.

Instituto Nacional de Conservación Forestal (INCF): Salida Carretera del Norte, Zona El Carrizal, Col. Brisas de Olancho, Comayagüela, Apdo 1378, Tegucigalpa; tel. 2223-7303; fax 2223-8587; e-mail direccion@icf.gob.hn; internet www.icf.gob.hn; f. 2008 to replace Corporación Hondureña de Desarrollo Forestal (f. 1974); control of the forestry industry and conservation of forest resources; Dir JOSÉ TRINIDAD SUAZO BULNES.

CHAMBERS OF COMMERCE

Cámara de Comercio e Industrias de Copán: Edif. Comercial Romero, 2°, Barrio Mercedes, Santa Rosa de Copán; tel. 2662-0843; fax 2662-1783; e-mail info@camaracopan.com; internet www.camaracopan.com; f. 1940; Pres. RAMÓN DE JESÚS FLORES.

Cámara de Comercio e Industrias de Cortés (CCIC): Barrio Las Brisas, 22 y 24 Calle, Apdo Postal 14, San Pedro Sula; tel. 2561-6100; fax 2566-0344; e-mail cie@ccichonduras.org; internet www.ccichonduras.org; f. 1931; 1,500 mems; Pres. EMÍN JORGE ABUFELE.

Cámara de Comercio e Industrias de Tegucigalpa (CCIT): Blvd Centroamérica, Apdo 3444, Tegucigalpa; tel. 2232-4200; fax 2232-5764; e-mail asuservicio@ccit.hn; internet www.ccit.hn; Pres. MIGUEL R. MOURRA; Exec. Dir MARIO BUSTILLO.

Cámara Hondureña de la Industria de la Construcción (Chico): Casa 2525, 2da Calle, entre 1era y 2da Avda, al par de Kinder Happy Faces, Col. Florencia Sur, Tegucigalpa; tel. 2239-2039; internet www.chicoorg.org; f. 1968; Pres. JOSÉ ALEJANDRO ALVAREZ ALVARADO; Gen. Man. SILVIO LARIOS BONES.

Federación de Cámaras de Comercio e Industrias de Honduras (FEDECAMARA): Edif. Castañito, 2°, 6a Avda, Col. Los Castaños, Apdo 3393, Tegucigalpa; tel. 2232-1870; fax 2232-6083; e-mail fedecamara.direccion@amnettgu.com; internet www.fedecamara.org; f. 1948; 1,200 mems; Pres. AMÍLCAR BULNES; Coordinator JUAN FERRERA LÓPEZ.

Fundación para la Inversión y Desarrollo de Exportaciones (FIDE) (Foundation for Investment and Development of Exports): Col. La Estancia, Plaza Marte, final del Blvd Morazán, Apdo 2029, Tegucigalpa; tel. 2221-6304; fax 2221-6316; e-mail vsierra@fidehonduras.com; internet www.hondurasinfo.hn; f. 1984; non-profit; Exec. Pres. VILMA SIERRA DE FONSECA.

Honduran American Chamber of Commerce (Amcham Honduras): Commercial Area Hotel Honduras Maya, POB 1838, Tegucigalpa; tel. 2232-6035; fax 2232-2031; e-mail amcham@amchanhonduras.org; internet www.amchamhonduras.org; f. 1981; Pres. JOSÉ EDUARDO ATALA; Exec. Dir ARACELY BATRES.

INDUSTRIAL AND TRADE ASSOCIATIONS

Asociación Hondureña de Maquiladores (AHM): Altia Business Park, 12°, Blvd Armenta, San Pedro Sula; tel. 2516-9100; internet www.ahm-honduras.com; f. 1991; non-profit asscn for the *maquila* industry; Pres. DANIEL FACUSSÉ.

Consejo Hondureño de la Empresa Privada (COHEP): Edif. 8, Calle Yoro, Col. Tepeyac, Apdo 3240, Tegucigalpa; tel. 2235-3336; fax 2235-3345; e-mail consejo@cohep.com; internet www.cohep.com; f. 1968; represents 52 private sector trade asscns; Pres. ALINE FLORES PAVÓN; Exec. Dir ARMANDO URTECHO.

Asociación Hondureña de Productores de Café (AHPROCAFE) (Coffee Producers' Association): Edif. AHPROCAFE, Avda La Paz, Apdo 959, Tegucigalpa; tel. 2236-8286; fax 2236-8310; e-mail ahprocafe@amnet.tgu.com; Pres. ASTERIO REYES.

Asociación Nacional de Acuicultores de Honduras (ANDAH) (Aquaculture Association of Honduras): Empacadora San Lorenzo, Puerto Viejo, contiguo a Banco de Occidente, San Lorenzo, Valle; tel. 2782-0986; fax 2782-3848; e-mail andahn@hondutel.hn; f. 1986; 136 mems; Pres. MARCO POLO MICHELETTI.

Asociación Nacional de Exportadores de Honduras (ANEXHON) (National Association of Exporters): Industrias Panavisión, salida nueva a la Lima Frente a Sigmanet, San Pedro Sula; tel. 2553-3029; fax 2557-0203; e-mail roberto@ipsa.hn; comprises 104 private enterprises; Pres. ROBERTO PANAYOTTI.

Asociación Nacional de Industriales (ANDI) (National Association of Manufacturers): Torre Alliance, 10°, Col. Lomas del Guijarro Sur, Blvd San Juan Bosco, Apdo 3447, Tegucigalpa; tel. 2271-0084; fax 2271-0085; e-mail andi@andi.hn; internet www.andi.hn; f. 1958; Pres. ADOLFO FACUSSÉ; Exec. Dir FERNANDO GARCÍA MERINO.

Asociación de Productores de Azúcar de Honduras (APAH): Edif. Palmira, 5°, Módulo E y B, Tegucigalpa; tel. 2239-4933; fax 2239-4934; e-mail apah@cablecolor.hn; internet www.azucar.hn; Pres. CARLOS MELARA.

Federación Nacional de Agricultores y Ganaderos de Honduras (FENAGH) (Farmers' and Livestock Breeders' Association): Col. Miramontes, Avda Principal, 7a Calle 1557, Tegucigalpa; tel. 2239-1303; fax 2231-1392; e-mail jlizardo@fenagh.net; internet www.fenagh.net; Pres. LEOPOLDO DÚRAN; Exec. Dir JOSÉ LIZARDO REYES.

UTILITIES

Electricity

Empresa Nacional de Energía Eléctrica (ENEE) (National Electrical Energy Co): Edif. EMAS, 4°, Bo El Trapiche, Tegucigalpa; tel. 2235-2934; fax 2235-2969; e-mail informatica@enee.hn; internet www.enee.hn; f. 1957; state-owned electricity co; Pres. RIGOBERTO CUELLAR; Man. EMIL HAWIT.

Luz y Fuerza de San Lorenzo, SA (LUFUSSA): Edif. Comercial Los Próceres, Final Avda Los Próceres 3917, Tegucigalpa; tel. 2236-6545; fax 2236-5826; e-mail lufussa@lufussa.com; internet www.lufussa.com; f. 1994; generates thermoelectric power; Pres. EDUARDO KAFIE.

TRADE UNIONS

Central General de Trabajadores de Honduras (CGTH) (General Confederation of Labour of Honduras): Barrio La Granja, antiguo Local CONADI, Apdo 1236, Comayagüela, Tegucigalpa; tel. 2239-7383; fax 2225-2525; e-mail cgt@123.hn; f. 1970; legally recognized from 1982; attached to Partido Demócrata Cristiano de Honduras; Sec.-Gen. DANIEL A. DURÓN; 250,000 mems (2011).

Confederación Hondureña de Cooperativas (CHC): Edif. I.F.C., 3001 Blvd Morazán, Apdo 3265, Tegucigalpa; tel. 2232-2890; fax 2231-1024; f. 1971; Pres. JOSÉ FRANCISCO ORDÓÑEZ.

Confederación de Trabajadores de Honduras (CTH) (Workers' Confederation of Honduras): Edif. Beige, 2°, Avda Juan Ramón Molina, Barrio El Olvido, Apdo 720, Tegucigalpa; tel. 2220-1757; fax 2237-8575; e-mail organizacioncth@yahoo.es; f. 1964; Sec.-Gen. JOSÉ HILARIO ESPINOZA; 55,000 mems (2007).

Confederación Unitaria de Trabajadores de Honduras (CUTH): Barrio Bella Vista, 10a Calle, 8a y 9a Avda, Casa 829, Tegucigalpa; tel. and fax 2220-4732; e-mail sgeneral@cuth.hn; f. 1992; Sec.-Gen. JOSÉ LUIS BAQUEDANO; 295,000 mems (2011).

Transport

RAILWAYS

The railway network is confined to the north of the country and most lines are used for fruit cargo. There are 995 km of railway track in Honduras, of which 349 km are narrow gauge. In 2010 the Government allocated 15m. lempiras to revive three railway routes serving San Pedro Sula, Choloma, Villanueva and Puerto Cortés. There are plans to restructure the train stations and coaches, as well as to set up additional railway routes to serve banana plantations.

Ferrocarril Nacional de Honduras (National Railway of Honduras): 1a Avda entre 1a y 2a Calle, Apdo 496, San Pedro Sula; tel. and fax 2552-8001; f. 1870; govt-owned; Gen. Man. LESTER AGUILAR.

ROADS

According to Fondo Vial de Honduras, in 2011 there were an estimated 14,044 km of roads in Honduras, of which only 21.2% were paved. A further 3,156 km of roads have been constructed by the Fondo Cafetero Nacional, and some routes have been built by the Corporación Hondureña de Desarrollo Forestal to facilitate access to coffee plantations and forestry development areas. In 2010 the Inter-American Development Bank (IDB) approved a US $30m. loan for a rapid bus transit system in Tegucigalpa. The IDB approved a further $17m. loan in 2013 to improve the main highway.

Dirección General de Carreteras: Barrio La Bolsa, Comayagüela, Tegucigalpa; tel. 2225-1703; fax 2225-2469; e-mail dgc@soptravi.gob.hn; internet www.soptravi.gob.hn/Carreteras; f. 1915; highways board; Dir WALTER MALDONADO.

SHIPPING

The principal port is Puerto Cortés on the Caribbean coast, which is the largest and best-equipped port in Central America. Other ports include Tela, La Ceiba, Trujillo/Castilla, Roatán, Amapala and San Lorenzo; all are operated by the Empresa Nacional Portuaria. There are several minor shipping companies. A number of foreign shipping lines call at Honduran ports. In December 2013 the flag registered fleet comprised 664 vessels, totalling 755,065 grt, of which three were gas tankers and 294 were general cargo ships.

Empresa Nacional Portuaria (National Port Authority): Apdo 18, Puerto Cortés; tel. 665-0987; fax 665-1402; e-mail gerencia@enp.hn; internet www.enp.hn; f. 1965; has jurisdiction over all ports in Honduras; a network of paved roads connects Puerto Cortés and San Lorenzo with the main cities of Honduras, and with the principal cities of Central America; Gen. Man. JOSÉ DARÍO GÁMEZ PANCHAMÉ.

CIVIL AVIATION

Local airlines in Honduras compensate for the deficiencies of road and rail transport, linking together small towns and inaccessible districts. There are four international airports: Golosón airport in La Ceiba, Ramón Villeda Morales airport in San Pedro Sula, Toncontín airport in Tegucigalpa and Juan Manuel Gálvaz airport in Roatán. A new airport at Río Amarillo, Copán, near the Copán Ruinas archaeological park, commenced operations in 2011.

Dirección General Aeronáutica Civil: Apdo 30145, Tegucigalpa; tel. 2234-0263; fax 2233-0258; e-mail contactos@dgachn.org; internet www.dgachn.org; airport infrastructure and security; Dir-Gen. MANUEL ENRIQUE CÁCERES.

Isleña Airlines: Edif. Taragon, 2°, Avda Circunvalacion, San Pedro Sula; tel. 2552-9910; fax 2552-9964; e-mail info.islena@taca.com; internet www.flyislena.com; subsidiary of TACA, El Salvador; domestic service and service to the Cayman Islands; Pres. and CEO ARTURO ALVARADO WOOD.

Tourism

Tourists are attracted by the Mayan ruins, the fishing and boating facilities in Trujillo Bay and Lake Yojoa, near San Pedro Sula, and the beaches on the northern coast. According to provisional figures, Honduras received 906,000 tourists in 2012, when tourism receipts (excluding passenger transport) totalled US $661m.

Asociación Hotelera y Afines de Honduras (AHAH): Hotel Escuela Madrid, Suite 402, Col. 21 de Octubre-Los Girasoles, Tegucigalpa; tel. 2221-5805; fax 2221-4789; e-mail asociacionhotelerahn@yahoo.com; Pres. LUZ MEJÍA AMADOR; Exec. Dir NORMA MENDOZA.

Asociación Nacional de Agencias de Viajes y Turismo de Honduras: Blvd Morazán, frente a McDonald's, Tegucigalpa; tel. 2232-2308; e-mail scarlethmoncada@yahoo.com; Pres. SCARLETH DE MONCADA.

Asociación de Operadores de Turismo Receptivo de Honduras (OPTURH): Col. San Carlos, Avda Ramon E. Cruz, Tegucigalpa; tel. 2236-9704; e-mail secretaria@opturh.com; internet www.opturh.com; f. 1996; Pres. ROBERTO BANDES.

Cámara Nacional de Turismo de Honduras: Calle Paris, Avda Niza, Casa 1233, Col. Lomas del Guijarro Sur, Tegucigalpa; tel. 2232-1937; fax 2235-8355; e-mail canaturh@canaturh.org; internet www.canaturh.org; f. 1976; Pres. EPAMINONDAS MARINAKYS.

Instituto Hondureño de Turismo: Edif. Europa, 5°, Col. San Carlos, Apdo 3261, Tegucigalpa; tel. and fax 2222-2124; e-mail tourisminfo@iht.hn; internet www.iht.hn; f. 1972; Exec. Vice-Pres. SYNTIA BENNETT SALOMON; Sec.-Gen. MÓNICA HÍDALGO.

Defence

Military service is voluntary. Active service lasts eight months, with subsequent reserve training. As assessed at November 2013, the armed forces numbered 12,000: army 8,300, navy 1,400 and air force some 2,300. Paramilitary public security and defence forces numbered 8,000. There were also 60,000 joint reserves. In addition, some 360 US troops were based in Honduras.

Defence Budget: 3,650m. lempiras (US $177m.) in 2013.

Chairman of the Joint Chiefs of Staff: Gen. FREDY SANTIAGO DÍAZ ZELAYA.

Commander-General of the Army: Col FRANCISCO ISAÍAS ALVAREZ URBINA.

Commander-General of the Air Force: Col JORGE ALBERTO FERNÁNDEZ LÓPEZ.

Commander-General of the Navy: Capt. HÉCTOR ORLANDO CABALLERO ESPINOZA.

Education

Primary education, beginning at six years of age and comprising three cycles of three years, is officially compulsory and is provided free of charge. Secondary education, which is not compulsory, begins at the age of 15 and lasts for three years. In 2012 enrolment at primary schools included 94% of children in the relevant age-group, while enrolment at secondary schools in 2012 was equivalent to 73% of children (66% of boys; 80% of girls) in the appropriate age-group. There are three universities, including the Autonomous National University in Tegucigalpa. Estimated spending on education in 2012 was 23,000m. lempiras, representing 15.9% of the total budget.

HUNGARY

Introductory Survey

LOCATION, CLIMATE, LANGUAGE, RELIGION, FLAG, CAPITAL

The Republic of Hungary (renamed Hungary in the Constitution that took effect on 1 January 2012) lies in central Europe, bounded to the north by Slovakia, to the east by Ukraine and Romania, to the south by Serbia and Croatia, and to the west by Slovenia and Austria. Its climate is continental, with long, dry summers and severe winters. Temperatures in Budapest are generally between −3°C (27°F) and 28°C (82°F). The language is Hungarian (Magyar). There is a large Romany community (numbering between 500,000 and 700,000 people), and also Croat, German, Romanian, Serb, Slovak, Slovene and Jewish minorities. Most of the inhabitants profess Christianity, and the largest single religious denomination is the Catholic Church, representing about 58% of the population. Other Christian groups include Calvinists (20%), Lutherans (5%), Pentecostals, and the Eastern Orthodox Church. The national flag (proportions 2 by 3) consists of three equal horizontal stripes, of red, white and green. The capital is Budapest.

CONTEMPORARY POLITICAL HISTORY

Historical Context

Although Hungary entered the Second World War on the side of Nazi Germany in 1941, when it sought to break the alliance in 1944 the country was occupied by German forces. In January 1945 Hungary was invaded by Soviet troops and signed an armistice, restoring pre-1938 frontiers. It became a republic in February 1946, and nationalization measures began in December. In the 1947 elections, the communists became the largest single party, with 22.7% of the votes. The communists merged with the Social Democrats to form the Hungarian Workers' Party in June 1948. A People's Republic was established in August 1949.

As First Secretary of the Workers' Party, Mátyás Rákosi became the leading political figure, and opposition was removed by means of purges and political trials. Rákosi became Prime Minister in 1952; in 1953 he was replaced by the more moderate Imre Nagy, and a short period of liberalization followed. Rákosi, however, remained as First Secretary, and in 1955 forced Nagy's resignation. Following increasing dissension between the Rákosi and Nagy factions, in July 1956 Rákosi was forced to resign, but was replaced by a close associate, Ernő Gerő. The consequent discontent provoked demonstrations against communist domination, and in October fighting broke out. Nagy was reinstated as Prime Minister; he renounced membership of the Warsaw Pact (the defence grouping of the Soviet bloc) and promised other controversial reforms. In November Soviet troops, stationed in Hungary under the 1947 peace treaty, intervened, and the uprising was suppressed. A new Soviet-supported Government, led by János Kádár, was installed. Some 20,000 participants in the uprising were arrested, of whom 2,000 were subsequently executed, including Nagy and four associates. Kádár, who was appointed the leader of the renamed Hungarian Socialist Workers' Party (MSzMP), held the premiership until January 1958, and from September 1961 until July 1965.

In March 1985 Kádár was re-elected as leader of the MSzMP, with the new title of General Secretary of the Central Committee. The legislative elections in June gave voters a wider choice of candidates under the system of mandatory multiple nominations. In May 1988 Kádár was replaced as General Secretary of the Central Committee by Károly Grósz (Chairman of the Council of Ministers since June 1987), and promoted to the new, ceremonial post of MSzMP President; he lost his membership of the Politburo (Political Bureau). About one-third of the members of the Central Committee were replaced by younger politicians. In June 1988 Dr Brunó Ferenc Straub, who was not a member of the MSzMP, was elected to the largely ceremonial post of President of the Presidential Council. In November Miklós Németh, a prominent member of the MSzMP, replaced Grósz as Chairman of the Council of Ministers.

Following Grósz's appointment as leader of the MSzMP, there was a relaxation of censorship laws, and independent political groups were formally established. In January 1989 the right to strike was fully legalized. In the same month the Országgyülés (National Assembly) enacted legislation guaranteeing the right to demonstrate and to form associations and political parties independent of the MSzMP. In February the MSzMP agreed to abandon the constitutional clause upholding the party's leading role in society.

During 1989 there was increasing evidence of dissension within the MSzMP between conservative and reformist members. In April the Politburo was replaced by a smaller body. In May the Council of Ministers declared its independence from the MSzMP; Kádár was removed from the presidency and the Central Committee of the party, officially for health reasons. After a radical restructuring of the MSzMP in June, the new Chairman, Rezső Nyers, emerged as the party's leading figure. At a provincial by-election in July 1989, a joint candidate of the centre-right Hungarian Democratic Forum (MDF), the liberal Szabad Demokraták Szövetsége (SzDSz—Alliance of Free Democrats) and the Federation of Young Democrats (Fidesz) became the first opposition deputy since 1947 to win representation in the legislature. Four further by-elections were won by opposition candidates in July–September 1989. Following popular pressure and continued anti-Government demonstrations, in September the MSzMP and the opposition agreed that the Constitution and electoral law be fundamentally amended, and that the Presidential Council be dissolved. At an MSzMP Congress in October, the party was reconstituted as Magyar Szocialista Párt (MSzP—Hungarian Socialist Party.

Domestic Political Affairs

On 18 October 1989 the National Assembly elected Mátyás Szűrös, the parliamentary President (Speaker), to the newly created post of President of the Republic, on an interim basis. On 23 October (the anniversary of the 1956 uprising) the Republic of Hungary was proclaimed. Multi-party elections were held, in two rounds, on 25 March and 8 April 1990. The MDF received the largest proportion of the total votes cast (42.7%) and 165 of the 386 seats in the National Assembly, followed by the SzDSz, with 23.8% of the votes and 92 seats. The Independent Smallholders' Party (FKgP) and Kereszténydemokrata Néppárt (KDNP—Christian Democratic People's Party), both of which contested the second round of polling in alliance with the MDF, secured 43 and 21 seats, respectively. The MSzP secured 33 seats, while Fidesz obtained 21 seats. The MSzMP failed to secure the 4% of the votes required for representation.

A coalition Government was formed in May 1990, comprising members of the MDF, the FKgP, the KDNP and three independents. József Antall, the Chairman of the MDF, had earlier been elected to chair the new Council of Ministers. The new Government declared commitment to membership of the European Community (now European Union—EU, see p. 273) and transition to a market economy. In the same month Gyula Horn, the outgoing Minister of Foreign Affairs, replaced Nyers as leader of the MSzP. In August Árpád Göncz, a member of the SzDSz, was elected President of the Republic by the legislature. At local elections in September and October, a coalition of the SzDSz and Fidesz won control of Budapest and many other cities.

In May 1991 the National Assembly approved legislation to provide compensation for persons killed, imprisoned or deported, or whose property had been expropriated for political reasons in 1939–89. Further legislation was approved in early 1993 allowing for prosecutions in connection with crimes committed under the communist regime.

In February 1992 the Chairman of the FKgP, József Torgyán, frustrated at his party's perceived lack of political influence, announced that it was to withdraw from the Government. However, many FKgP deputies disagreed with this decision; in June members loyal to the Government formed what became the United Historic Smallholders' Party, while the main faction renamed itself the Independent Smallholders' and Peasants' Party (retaining the acronym FKgP). In September some 50,000 people demonstrated in Budapest against extreme right-wing figures within the MDF, including the Vice-Chairman of the party, István Csurka. Csurka was expelled from the MDF in July 1993, and subsequently founded the Hungarian Justice and Life Party (MIÉP). Antall died in December, and was succeeded as Prime Minister by Dr Péter Boross, an independent, and hitherto the Minister of the Interior. In February 1994 Lajos Für was elected Chairman of the MDF.

Democratic consolidation

Elections to the National Assembly, held on 8 and 29 May 1994, resulted in a parliamentary majority for the MSzP, which received 33.0% of the votes cast for regional party lists and won 209 of the 386 legislative seats. The SzDSz won 19.8% of the votes and 70 seats, while the MDF won only 11.7% of the votes and 37 seats. The FKgP, the KDNP and Fidesz also secured parliamentary seats. The MSzP and the SzDSz signed a coalition agreement in June. Horn was invested as Prime Minister in July.

In January 1995 the Minister of Finance, László Bekesi, resigned, following disagreements with Horn regarding economic reform; he was replaced by Lajos Bokros. Economic austerity measures, adopted in March, prompted strong domestic criticism, and the ministers responsible for public health and for national security resigned shortly afterwards. On 19 June Göncz was re-elected as President of the Republic by the National Assembly. The economic programme continued to cause dissent within the Government, and the Minister of Labour tendered her resignation in October. Bokros resigned in February 1996, and a banker, Péter Medgyessy, was appointed as Minister of Finance. Following the election of Sándor Lezsák to the MDF leadership, a split in the party ensued in March, with the departure of those who discerned an increasingly nationalistic tendency. In December the MDF established an electoral alliance with the reconstituted Federation of Young Democrats—Hungarian Civic Party (which continued to be known as Fidesz) and the Hungarian Christian Democratic Federation, a new party formed by breakaway members of the KDNP.

Legislative elections took place, in two rounds, on 10 and 24 May 1998. Fidesz, with 147 seats, obtained the largest representation in the National Assembly; the MSzP received 134 seats, the FKgP 48, the SzDSz 24, the MDF 18 and the MIÉP 14. In June Fidesz signed a coalition agreement with the MDF and the FKgP (which was later renamed the Independent Smallholders', Agrarian Workers' and Civic Party). In July the National Assembly elected Viktor Orbán, the Chairman of Fidesz, as Prime Minister of a coalition Government dominated by Fidesz representatives. In September, following the resignation of Horn from the leadership of the MSzP, a former minister, László Kovács, was elected Chairman. In January 2000 László Kövér replaced Orbán as leader of Fidesz. On 6 June Ferenc Mádl, the sole candidate, secured the requisite two-thirds' majority to be elected President of the Republic. He took office on 4 August.

In the legislative elections held on 7 and 21 April 2002, although an alliance of Fidesz and the MDF won 48.7% of the total votes cast (188 seats), a left-wing coalition of the MSzP (46.1% of the votes and 178 seats) and the SzDSz (5.2% of the votes and 20 seats) secured an overall majority in the National Assembly. Péter Medgyessy of the MSzP was sworn in as Prime Minister on 27 May; the Council of Ministers comprised eight further members of the MSzP, four members of the SzDSz and three independents.

In June 2002 media allegations prompted Medgyessy to reveal that he had served as a counter-intelligence agent at the Ministry of Finance in 1977–82; he insisted that he had sought to protect sensitive economic information from the KGB (the Soviet secret service), in order to negotiate Hungarian membership of the IMF (which it joined in 1982). In July 2002 two parliamentary commissions were established to investigate the alleged links of post-communist government officials with the Soviet-era security service. Meanwhile, in early July the leader of Fidesz, Zoltán Pokorni, who had led demands for Medgyessy's resignation, relinquished his own party and parliamentary posts, after his father's role as a communist informer was revealed. It subsequently emerged that several members of Fidesz (which had emphasized its anti-communist past during campaigning for the legislative elections) had counter-intelligence associations. Local elections took place on 20 October, in which the governing coalition consolidated its position.

In December 2002 the National Assembly voted to adopt a number of constitutional amendments, which were required to permit the country to become a full member of the EU (see below). In May 2003 Fidesz was re-formed as Fidesz—Magyar Polgári Szöevetség (Fidesz, Fidesz—Hungarian Civic Alliance), with former premier Orbán as its leader.

In January 2004 the Minister of Finance, Csaba László, left office when it was revealed that the fiscal results for 2003 had failed to meet government targets. Tibor Draskovics (an independent), succeeded László in February, implementing a financial austerity plan shortly afterwards. On 1 May Hungary acceded to full membership of the EU.

On 18 August 2004 Medgyessy resigned as Prime Minister following a decline in support and a severe dispute with the SzDSz over proposed changes to the Council of Ministers. On 24 August the MSzP nominated one of the country's wealthiest business executives, Ferenc Gyurcsány, hitherto the Minister of Children, Youth and Sports, as Prime Minister. Following Gyurcsány's installation as Prime Minister on 4 October, he appointed seven new ministers, including a further Minister without Portfolio, Etele Baráth, with responsibility for EU issues. In February 2005 Gyurcsány appointed Andras Bozoki as Minister of Cultural Heritage to replace István Hiller, who had resigned his ministerial post after becoming Chairman of the MSzP. Gyurcsány made further adjustments to the Council of Ministers in April: Draskovics was dismissed as Minister of Finance, and replaced by a prominent MSzP member, János Veres. On 7 June László Sólyom, an independent politician endorsed by the main opposition parties, was elected as President, after three rounds of legislative voting. Sólyom took office on 5 August.

Left-wing coalition elected to second term

At the legislative elections, which were held on 9 and 23 April 2006, the governing MSzP-SzDSz coalition secured 210 of the 386 seats in the National Assembly and 54.4% of the votes. A coalition of Fidesz and the KDNP, with 42.5% of the votes, secured 164 seats, the MDF took 11 seats (with 2.9% of the votes) and one seat was won by an independent candidate. In early June, after several weeks of coalition negotiations, a new Government, led by Gyurcsány and comprising members of the MSzP and the SzDSz, was formed. On the following day Gyurcsány announced stringent fiscal adjustment measures, which were intended to reduce the unsustainable budget deficit.

On 17 September 2006 the media broadcast of a clandestine recording of a post-election speech by Gyurcsány to his party members, in which he admitted having misled the electorate during the campaign over the country's fiscal situation, precipitated mass anti-Government riots in Budapest. Protesters surrounded government buildings and temporarily seized control of the state television headquarters; some 300 people were injured in the rioting and the ensuing confrontations with the police. On 27 September Gyurcsány issued a public apology for the Government's delay in addressing the economic situation. At municipal elections on 2 October, Fidesz made significant gains, securing mayoralties in 15 of Hungary's 23 largest cities and majorities in 18 of the 19 county councils. Nevertheless, in early October a parliamentary motion of confidence in the Government, proposed by Gyurcsány, was supported by 207 votes in the National Assembly.

Official celebrations on 23 October 2006, the 50th anniversary of the 1956 uprising against Soviet rule, were marred by anti-Government demonstrations, organized by the leadership of Fidesz, which demanded Gyurcsány's resignation. Security forces suppressed ensuing violent riots, in which about 170 people were injured, and a total of 130 protesters were arrested. Gyurcsány subsequently accused Orbán of inciting the rioting, and the Budapest municipal authorities implemented measures to restrain continuing protests. In February 2007 a commission investigating the rioting issued a report strongly criticizing Fidesz's increasingly populist stance for implying support for the protesters, who were predominantly associated with extreme nationalist groups, and concluding that the police had employed excessive force in suppressing the violence.

In June 2007 Gyurcsány reorganized the Government in support of his reform programme. In December Csaba Kákossy became the new Minister of Economy and Transport, following the resignation of János Kóka, who had been elected as Chairman of the SzDSz in March. In November public sector workers staged strike action in protest against the Government's proposed health care reforms. In December legislation on the disputed reforms was approved in the National Assembly, but was vetoed by President Sólyom. On 11 February 2008 demonstrations were staged outside parliament to coincide with the repeated approval by the National Assembly of the health care legislation, which Sólyom was constitutionally obliged to endorse. Fidesz organized a national referendum to seek support for the abolition of newly introduced fees for doctors' visits and hospital stays, and of university fees. At the referendum, held on 9 March, more than 80% of the votes, cast by some 50.5% of the electorate, were in favour of the abolition of these fees. Gyurcsány duly announced that the fees would be abandoned from 1 April, but that the Government was unable to subsidize health and higher education institutions.

Minority Government

At the end of March 2008 Gyurcsány dismissed the Minister of Health, who was an SzDSz representative, prompting the party to withdraw from the governing coalition (which henceforth lacked a parliamentary majority). An extensive government reorganization was approved in the National Assembly in May, when Gordon Bajnai, a close associate of Gyurcsány and hitherto the Minister of Local Government and Regional Development, became Minister of National Development and the Economy. In June Gábor Fodor was elected as the new Chairman of the SzDSz, following divisions within the party and the emergence of a faction opposed to Kóka (who, however, remained leader of the party's parliamentary caucus).

The international financial crisis, which had a marked impact in Hungary, further exacerbated anti-Government sentiment. At an MSzP congress in March 2009, Gyurcsány announced his intention to resign as Prime Minister, citing concern that he had become an 'obstacle' to further economic reform, and relinquished the party leadership. (On 5 April he was succeeded as party leader by Ildikó Lendvai.) Bajnai, an independent candidate nominated by the MSzP, was formally elected Prime Minister by the National Assembly on 14 April; he affirmed his commitment to austerity measures, and subsequently formed a new Council of Ministers. However, Fidesz boycotted the parliamentary vote, and a demonstration was staged in Budapest to demand early legislative elections.

At elections to the European Parliament, held on 7 June 2009, Fidesz, in coalition with the KDNP, secured 56.4% of the votes cast and 14 of the 22 contested seats, the MSzP 17.4% of the votes cast and four seats, an extreme nationalist movement, Jobbik Magyarországért Mozgalom (Jobbik—Movement for a Better Hungary), obtained 14.8% of votes and three seats, and the MDF 5.3% of votes and one seat; the rate of electoral participation was recorded at 36.3% of the electorate. The relative success of Jobbik at these polls generated concern both domestically and internationally, particularly owing to the close association of the party with a proscribed nationalist group, the Hungarian Guard (see Minority affairs), and to the frequent public expression of anti-Semitic and anti-Roma sentiments by numerous senior party officials. (The party also incorporated a substantial number of former members of the MIÉP.) Fodor resigned as Chairman of the SzDSz, following the party's failure to obtain European representation; in July a party congress elected Attila Retkes as his successor. In December Draskovics resigned as Minister of Justice and Law Enforcement; he was succeeded by Imre Forgács.

Fidesz returns to power

In the elections to the National Assembly on 11 and 25 April 2010, Fidesz, again in coalition with the KDNP, secured 263 of the 386 elective seats (enabling it to adopt constitutional amendments). The MSzP was the second-placed party, with 59 seats, followed by Jobbik (which secured national representation for the first time), with 47 seats; a recently formed environmentalist party, Lehet Más a Politika! (LMP—Politics Can Be Different!), obtained 16 seats. Later in April President Sólyom confirmed the nomination of Orbán as Prime Minister. A new Government formed by Orbán, in which the number of ministries was reduced from 12 to eight, was approved by the National Assembly on 29 May. Tibor Navracsics of Fidesz became Deputy Prime Minister and Minister of Public Administration and Justice, and Zsolt Semjén of the KDNP Deputy Prime Minister and Minister without Portfolio. Other principal new appointments included an independent, Sándor Pintér, as Minister of the Interior and György Matolcsy of Fidesz as Minister of the National Economy. On 29 June the National Assembly voted to elect Pál Schmitt of Fidesz (the parliamentary Chairman since May), as President of the Republic, in succession to Sólyom. On 10 July Attila Mesterházy was elected as leader of the MSzP, replacing Lendvai. Schmitt formally assumed office on 6 August. In municipal elections, which were conducted on 3 October, Fidesz secured 22 of the 23 mayoralties, including in Budapest (where the long-standing SzDSz mayor was replaced by a Fidesz-supported candidate, István Tarlós), and majorities in all 19 county councils. Gyurcsány subsequently announced the establishment of a group, known as the Demokratikus Koalíció (DK—Democratic Coalition), within the MSzP, following the latter's defeat.

In October 2010 a dispute erupted between the Government, which had adopted a number of controversial fiscal measures through its parliamentary majority, and the Constitutional Court, after the Court reversed new legislation retroactively imposing a 98% tax on large severance payments in the public sector. In November the National Assembly adopted controversial legislation restricting the powers of the Constitutional Court to rule on the state budget, taxes and other financial matters. (Despite its reduced powers, the Constitutional Court ruled again, in May 2011, that the imposition of retroactive tax demands was unconstitutional.) In December 2010 new media legislation, whereby a regulatory authority, comprising five members nominated by the ruling coalition, was empowered to impose large fines on print, broadcast and internet outlets for violating 'public interest, public morals or order', prompted a protest by students in Budapest. The legislation, which entered into effect at the beginning of 2011, continued to attract strenuous criticism from civil liberty organizations, and the European Commission pronounced it to be in violation of EU regulations on freedom of expression. In December the Constitutional Court vetoed parts of the media legislation.

New Constitution and the resignation of President Schmitt

On 18 April 2011 the National Assembly approved a new Constitution, with 262 votes cast in favour, 44 against and one abstention. The text renamed the country 'Hungary', rather than the 'Republic of Hungary', with effect from January 2012. The Constitution included a new preamble, protecting human life from the moment of conception, and reaffirming the traditional definition of marriage as the union of one man and one woman. The opposition expressed concern that the new Constitution might prompt additional legislation to be introduced on contentious issues such as the legal position of minority citizens. Described as fiscally conservative, the new basic law also introduced financial restrictions, including a legal limit, equivalent to 50% of GDP, on the permitted level of national debt, causing further concern among political opponents. The non-governmental organization Human Rights Watch urged President Schmitt to refer the text back to the National Assembly for reconsideration; nevertheless, Schmitt signed the new Constitution on 25 April.

During 2011 a series of legislative reforms was introduced by Fidesz, and Orbán was re-elected as Chairman in July, as the ruling party attempted to consolidate its balance of power. In December new legislation was approved reducing the number of members of the National Assembly from 386 to 199. A new, two-tier (replacing a three-tier) parliamentary election system was introduced, providing for 106 seats to be filled in single-member districts and 93 from national party lists. Voting rights were introduced for Hungarian citizens not permanently resident in Hungary. Meanwhile, the split within the MSzP had deepened, and in October the DK broke away to become an independent political organization.

The new Constitution entered into force on 1 January 2012, amid large protests in Budapest. In February the European Parliament adopted a resolution expressing serious concerns about the new Constitution and announced that it was investigating whether the new legislation was in breach of 'common European values of freedom and democracy'. The European Commission requested that Hungary submit proposals for amendments to three specific laws affecting the independence of the Central Bank and the national data office, and imposing a mandatory retirement age on judges and prosecutors. The Commission also opened an inquiry against the Hungarian authorities, citing political interference in the judiciary, the Central Bank and data protection laws. In March, at a rally to commemorate the anniversary of the 1848 uprising against Austrian rule, Orbán denounced what he termed the 'colonialism' of the EU, shortly after the European Commission announced the suspension of funding to Hungary (see Economic Affairs).

Meanwhile, in late 2011 allegations emerged that the President had committed plagiarism in the composition of his doctoral thesis, which had been awarded by Semmelweis University in Budapest in 1992. The university conducted an investigation, and at the end of March 2012 announced that it had withdrawn Schmitt's doctoral award. On 2 April Schmitt, while continuing to deny the allegations, resigned as President. (In accordance with constitutional norms, the legislative President, Kövér, became acting President.) Later in the month Orbán nominated János Áder, a senior member of Fidesz, deputy of the European Parliament and former President of the National Assembly, as a presidential candidate. A presidential election took place in the National Assembly on 2 May, and Áder was duly elected as President, by 262 votes to 40.

Constitutional changes

In September 2012 Gyurcsány and two other members of the DK staged a one-week hunger strike outside the parliamentary building, in protest against a proposed change to the electoral law that would require voters to register no later than 15 days before an election. In the same month the Budapest Court of Appeals overturned a decision by the Media Council (a five-member body appointed by the National Assembly within the new media authority) rejecting an application by opposition radio station Klubradio for a broadcasting licence. In October the new electoral law (which, according to opposition parties, would deter large sections of the electorate and benefit the parties in government) was adopted by the ruling coalition in the National Assembly; however, it was subsequently referred by President Áder to the Constitutional Court. A large, pro-Government rally was staged on 23 October, the anniversary of the 1956 uprising against Soviet rule, while at a concurrent opposition demonstration Bajnai announced the creation of a new, centrist alliance, Együtt 2014 (Together 2014). During December 2012 students staged a series of protests against further government plans to abolish state financing for higher education. In January 2013 the Constitutional Court ruled against the new voter registration regulations, together with other proposed provisions in the electoral law that imposed restrictions on the broadcasting of political advertisements in the public media.

At the beginning of March 2013 Orbán nominated György Matolcsy, a close associate, as the new Governor of the Central Bank; a former Minister of Finance, Mihály Varga, was appointed to succeed Matolcsy as Minister of the National Economy. Meanwhile, radical constitutional changes proposed by the Government prompted mass protests in Budapest; in addition to the adoption of restrictions on political advertisements and the imposition of a number of social measures, rulings made by the Constitutional Court prior to 2012 were to be overturned and its future powers limited. Orbán dismissed criticism by the EU and the USA, amid concerns that the proposed constitutional amendments represented an attempt by the Government to reintroduce changes already deemed to be contrary to European law, and opposed by the Constitutional Court in 2012. The controversial amendments were approved in the National Assembly on 11 March 2013, with opposition deputies boycotting the vote. A further protest was staged in Budapest later that month. In April the Monitoring Committee of the Parliamentary Assembly of the Council of Europe (PACE) recommended that democracy in Hungary be formally monitored. In the same month the European Commission issued further warnings that legal action could be undertaken against the Hungarian Government unless it expedited the reform of the March amendments deemed to be in breach of EU standards. On 11 June the National Assembly adopted legislation that restricted citizens' access to information held by the State, including data on public expenditure.

In response to EU pressure, on 16 September 2013 the National Assembly adopted further constitutional amendments that, *inter alia*, permitted election campaigning by political parties in both state-funded and private media, thereby reversing a principal restrictive measure adopted in March. In November the European Commission officially ended legal proceedings that had been launched against Hungary over the forced early retirement of judges and public prosecutors, after the National Assembly, in March, amended legislation gradually to increase the retirement age to 65 (rather than 62).

Recent developments: electoral preparations

In January 2014 several leftist opposition parties, including the MSzP, Bajnai's Együtt 2014 and Gyurcsány's DK, signed an agreement to establish a coalition, the Unity Alliance, to contest legislative elections on 6 April. Electoral campaigning began in early February; by the end of that month opinion polls indicated that support for the Unity Alliance parties had declined to 18%, compared with a level of about 47% for the ruling parties, following corruption allegations involving a senior MSzP official. In March the trial began of Béla Biszku, a former Minister of the Interior in the Kádár administration, who was charged with responsibility for the shooting of protesters in 1956.

At the legislative elections, held as scheduled on 6 April 2014, a coalition of Orbán's Fidesz and the KDNP won 133 of the 199 seats in the National Assembly. The Unity Coalition, a coalition of the MSzP, Együtt 2014, the DK and two smaller parties, secured 38 seats, Jobbik obtained 23 seats and the LMP won five seats.

Minority affairs

There has been considerable activism within Hungary by the country's ethnic minorities for the protection of their rights. In July 1993 the National Assembly adopted legislation guaranteeing the cultural, civil and political rights of 12 minority groups and prohibiting ethnic discrimination. From 1994 ethnic minorities were able to elect their own local ethnic authorities, with consultative roles on cultural and educational issues affecting the community. In February 1995 Hungary signed the Council of Europe (see p. 252) Convention on the Protection of National Minorities. In April the Roma of Hungary elected their own governing body, the National Autonomous Authority of the Romany Minority (the first such body in the former Eastern bloc), which was empowered to administer funds and deliberate issues affecting the Roma. In December 2008 the Metropolitan Court in Budapest ordered the dissolution of the extreme nationalist Hungarian Guard (established in August 2007), which was responsible for attacks and discriminatory behaviour against the Roma community. This dissolution of the Hungarian Guard was confirmed by the Supreme Court in December 2010. (However, former Hungarian Guard members continued to convene, and attempted to reconstitute the movement as a civil service association.) In October 2012 fighting involving Roma residents in the western town of Devecser was followed by an anti-Roma rally organized by Jobbik that degenerated into violent rioting. In January 2013 two Roma men, who as children had been placed in a school for the education of those identified as having special needs, won a discrimination case against Hungary at the European Court of Human Rights. In August three nationalist extremists were sentenced to life imprisonment and a fourth received a 13-year term for killing six Roma in nine attacks in north-eastern Hungary during 2008–09.

In March 2010 legislation that criminalized the denial or 'questioning' of the Holocaust (*shoah*) of the Jews during the Second World War was signed into law in Hungary. Although the law was widely supported among the Jewish community of Hungary, concerns were expressed that the legislation might become a focus of extreme nationalist agitation. Remarks by a Jobbik parliamentary deputy in November 2012, suggesting that lists of citizens of Jewish ancestry should be compiled in the interests of national security, prompted protests outside the National Assembly. In April 2013 a protest against an increase in anti-Semitism in Hungary was staged in Budapest. In early May the annual World Jewish Congress, which was usually held in Jerusalem, Israel, was convened in Budapest to demonstrate concerns at anti-Semitism in the country. Around 1,000 people attended a rally that was organized by Jobbik in Budapest, in protest at the holding of the Congress in the capital, after an earlier government prohibition on the rally had been overturned by a court ruling; protesters demanded that officials holding dual Hungarian-Israeli citizenship should resign. In February 2014 a rally organized by Jobbik in a former synagogue in the northern town of Esztergom prompted further protests from Jewish groups.

Foreign Affairs

Regional relations

A principal factor governing Hungary's relations with several neighbouring states since the 1990s—particularly Romania and Slovakia—has been the presence in those countries of a substantial population of ethnic Hungarians. In September 1996 Hungary and Romania signed a bilateral treaty, guaranteeing the inviolability of the joint border between the two countries and the rights of minority ethnic groups. In May 1997 President Árpád Göncz made an official visit to Romania (the first by a Hungarian Head of State). In June 2001 the Hungarian National Assembly approved legislation that, with effect from January 2002, granted ethnic Hungarians living in adjacent countries education, employment and medical rights in Hungary. This legislation, referred to as the 'status' law, prompted protests from Romania (and Slovakia—see below) that it discriminated against their non-ethnic Hungarian populations and constituted a violation of sovereignty. In December 2001 a memorandum of understanding was signed by Viktor Orbán and Prime Minister Adrian Năstase of Romania, which extended the short-term employment rights offered to ethnic Hungarians under the terms of the law to all Romanian citizens. Finally, in September 2003 a bilateral agreement on the implementation of the 'status' law in Romania was signed in the Romanian capital, Bucharest, by Péter Medgyessy and Năstase.

Apart from issues arising from the presence of a large ethnic Hungarian minority in Slovakia, relations between Hungary and Slovakia were strained by a dispute over the Gabčíkovo-Nagymaros hydroelectric project (a joint Hungarian-Czechoslovak scheme initiated in 1977). In November 1989 Hungary announced that it was to abandon the scheme, following pressure from environmentalists. In July 1991 Czechoslovakia decided to proceed unilaterally with the project; the resumption of work, in February 1992, prompted the Hungarian Government to abrogate the 1977 treaty. In April 1993 it was agreed to refer the case to the International Court of Justice (ICJ).

In March 1995 Prime Minister Horn and his Slovak counterpart, Vladimír Mečiar, signed a Treaty of Friendship and Co-operation, according to which the two countries undertook to guarantee the rights of minority ethnic groups and to recognize the inviolability of their common border. The Treaty came into effect in May 1996. In August 1997 discussions between Horn and Mečiar resulted in an agreement that a joint committee be established to monitor the standard of human rights of ethnic Hungarians resident in Slovakia and the Slovak community in Hungary. In September the ICJ concluded proceedings regarding the dispute over the Gabčíkovo-Nagymaros hydroelectric project, ruling that both countries had contravened international law. Both Hungary and Slovakia were required to pay compensation for damages incurred, and to resume negotiations regarding the further implementation of the agreement. In February 2006 it was announced that Slovakia and Hungary had agreed to implement the 1997 ICJ ruling.

The entry into force of the Hungarian 'status' law (see above) in January 2002 also threatened to damage relations with Slovakia, although that country had in place a similar law, which granted privileges to the Slovak diaspora. Finally, in December 2003 the Ministers of Foreign Affairs of Hungary and Slovakia signed a bilateral agreement on the implementation of the status law in Slovakia.

Tensions between Hungary and Slovakia were again apparent in August 2009, when the Hungarian President, László Sólyom, was prohibited from entering Slovakia on the instructions of the Slovak Ministry of Foreign Affairs, despite EU regulations on freedom of movement between member states. Sólyom's intended visit to unveil a statue to St István (Stephen), the first King of Hungary, in a predominantly ethnically Hungarian town in southern Slovakia was condemned by the Slovakian Government, on the grounds that it was planned for 21 August, the anniversary of the 1968 invasion of Czechoslovakia by Warsaw Pact (including Hungarian) troops. Legislation that took effect in Slovakia from 1 September 2009 placing restrictions on the use of languages other than Slovak in an official context was a further source of controversy; some 10,000 people, believed to be mainly ethnic Hungarians, subsequently attended a protest rally in the southern Slovakian town of Dunajská Streda. Concern was expressed that the legislation might criminalize the use of minority languages in private, as well as official, conversation. Slovakia and Hungary subsequently agreed that the Organization for Security and Co-operation in Europe (OSCE, see p. 387) would oversee the implementation of the law to ensure that it complied with international norms.

On 26 May 2010 the National Assembly approved controversial legislation, regarded as an extension of the 'status' law, which would permit ethnic Hungarians resident outside the country to apply for Hungarian citizenship with effect from January 2011. The Prime Minister of Slovakia, Robert Fico, described the legislation as representing a security threat to his country, and prompted the amendment, on the same day, of that country's law on citizenship, with the proposed effect that anyone applying for citizenship of a second country would have their Slovak citizenship removed. Under an amendment to the status law, also effective from January, it was stipulated that ethnic Hungarians residing permanently in neighbouring states, with Hungarian as their first language, would remain eligible for benefits, regardless of whether they held Hungarian citizenship.

In November 1990 Hungary became a member of the Council of Europe. In March 1996 Hungary was admitted to the Organisation for Economic Co-operation and Development (OECD, see p. 379). Meanwhile, Hungary's associate membership of the EU came into effect on 1 February 1994, and in April Hungary became the first post-communist state to apply for full EU membership. In December 2002 Hungary was one of 10 countries formally invited to join the EU in May 2004. At a national referendum, held on 12 April 2003, Hungarian membership of the EU was endorsed by 83.8% of the votes cast (with 45.6% of the electorate participating). In December 2007 Hungary, together with eight other nations, implemented the EU's Schengen Agreement, enabling its citizens to travel to and from other member states, without border controls. In the same month Hungary became the first EU member state to ratify the draft Treaty of Lisbon.

Other external relations

Following a North Atlantic Treaty Organization (NATO, see p. 370) summit meeting in Madrid, Spain, in July 1997, Hungary was invited to enter into discussions regarding its application for membership of the Alliance. A national referendum on the country's entry into NATO was conducted in November, at which its accession was approved by 85.3% of the votes cast, with the participation of 49% of the electorate. Hungary was formally admitted to NATO in March 1999. In early 2003 an air base at Taszar, in south-western Hungary, was used by the USA for the training of Iraqi opposition forces, in relation to the US-led military campaign in Iraq. Hungary subsequently contributed 300 soldiers to the international peacekeeping force in Iraq. Following considerable public and political opposition, these were withdrawn from the region in March 2005.

In August 2012 Armenia suspended diplomatic relations with Hungary, following the Hungarian Government's extradition to Azerbaijan of an Azerbaijani soldier who had murdered an Armenian fellow participant during a NATO 'Partnership for Peace' course in Budapest in 2004. Hungary's action, at the request of the Azerbaijani President, prompted protests in Budapest and international criticism.

Prior to a visit to the Russian capital, Moscow, in March 2007, Prime Minister Ferenc Gyurcsány declared support for plans of the Russian gas producer Gazprom to extend its 'South Stream' pipeline, linking Novorossiisk in southern Russia, to Ankara, Turkey, further to central Europe. In March 2009 Gazprom signed an agreement in Moscow with the Hungarian Development Bank, in the presence of Gyurcsány and Russian premier Vladimir Putin, on the establishment of a joint venture for the 'South Stream' pipeline project on Hungarian territory. On the same occasion, the Hungarian Oil and Gas Company (MOL) signed an accord with Gazprom on the construction of a gas storage facility in Hungary. In July 2009 Hungary was also one of five countries to sign an agreement on the establishment of the proposed EU- and US-supported Nabucco pipeline, which was to supply gas from various Central Asian states to Europe. In April 2012, however, MOL announced that it was unable to continue financing the Nabucco consortium (and the Nabucco project was subsequently abandoned). In November the Hungarian Government finalized the investment agreement with Gazprom on the South Stream project, which involved construction of a 229-km section of the pipeline in Hungary. (However, in December 2013 the European Commission declared that Russia's bilateral agreements on South Stream were in breach of EU law and should be renegotiated.) Following discussions between Russian President Putin and Prime Minister Orbán in January 2014, it was announced that Russian nuclear agency Rosatom had secured the contract to construct a further two units at the nuclear power installation at Paks, in central Hungary. The nuclear co-operation agreement, under which the Russian Government was to provide 80% of the project's costs, was approved by the Hungarian legislature in early February.

CONSTITUTION AND GOVERNMENT

On 1 January 2012 a new Constitution entered into force, removing references to the 'Republic of Hungary' and referring only to 'Hungary'. Controversial new laws (see Domestic Political Affairs) were introduced on social and fiscal issues; additional constitutional amendments were approved by the legislature in March 2013. Legislative power is held by the unicameral National Assembly (Országgyülés), which, under the new Constitution comprises 199 members, rather than the previous 386, elected for a term of four years by universal adult suffrage, under a mixed system of proportional and direct representation. The

President of the Republic (Head of State) is elected by the National Assembly for a term of five years. The President may be re-elected for a second term. The Council of Ministers, the highest organ of state administration, is elected by the Assembly on the recommendation of the President. Judicial power is exercised by local courts, labour courts, county courts (or the Metropolitan Court) and the Supreme Court. All judicial offices are filled by election. For local administrative purposes, Hungary is divided into 19 counties (*megyei*) and the capital city (with 23 districts). A 53-member National Autonomous Authority of the Romany Minority is empowered to administer funds disbursed by the central Government.

REGIONAL AND INTERNATIONAL CO-OPERATION

Hungary became a full member of the European Union (EU, see p. 273) in May 2004. It is also a member of the North Atlantic Treaty Organization (NATO, see p. 370), the Council of Europe, the Organization for Security and Co-operation in Europe (OSCE, see p. 387) and the Organisation for Economic Co-operation and Development (OECD, see p. 379).

Hungary joined the UN in 1955 and became a member of the World Trade Organization (WTO, see p. 434) in 1995.

ECONOMIC AFFAIRS

In 2012, according to estimates by the World Bank, Hungary's gross national income (GNI), measured at average 2010–12 prices, was US $123,013m., equivalent to $12,370 per head (or $20,710 per head on an international purchasing-power parity basis). During 2003–12, it was estimated, the population decreased at an average annual rate of 0.2%, while gross domestic product (GDP) per head increased, in real terms, by an average of 1.1% per year. Overall GDP increased, in real terms, at an average annual rate of 0.8% during 2003–12; real GDP increased by 1.6% in 2011, but decreased by 1.7% in 2012.

Agriculture (including hunting, forestry and fishing) contributed 4.7% of GDP and engaged 5.2% of the employed labour force in 2012. The principal crops are maize, wheat, sunflower seeds, barley and sugar beet. Viticulture is also important. During 2003–12, according to UN estimates, real agricultural GDP increased at an average annual rate of 0.2%. The GDP of the sector increased by 11.8% in 2011, but decreased by 18.9% in 2012.

Industry (including mining, manufacturing, construction and power) contributed 30.6% of GDP in 2012, when the sector engaged 29.8% of the employed labour force. According to UN estimates, real industrial GDP increased at an average annual rate of 0.4% in 2003–12. Industrial GDP increased by 0.4% in 2011, but decreased by 2.0% in 2012.

Mining and quarrying accounted for 0.3% of GDP and engaged 0.2% of the employed labour force in 2012. Hungary's most important mineral resources are lignite (brown coal) and natural gas. Petroleum, bauxite and hard coal are also exploited. At the end of 2012 Hungary's proven coal reserves stood at 1,660m. metric tons. According to UN estimates, real mining GDP (along with utilities) decreased by 1.1% during 2003–12; GDP decreased by 3.8% in 2011 and by a further 7.0% in 2012.

The manufacturing sector contributed 22.7% of GDP in 2012, when it engaged 20.7% of the employed labour force. According to estimates by the UN, manufacturing GDP increased, in real terms, at an average annual rate of 1.5% in 2003–12. Manufacturing GDP increased by 0.8% in 2011, but decreased by 0.4% in 2012.

The construction sector contributed 3.8% of GDP in 2012, when it engaged 6.3% of the labour force. According to UN estimates, real construction GDP decreased by 3.5% in 2003–12. The GDP increased by 2.0% in 2011, but decreased by 6.3% in 2012.

In 2012 some 45.9% of Hungary's electricity production was generated by nuclear power, 26.7% by natural gas and 18.8% by coal. Imports of fuels and electricity represented 12.7% of the value of total imports in 2012.

The services sector has a significant role, contributing 64.7% of GDP in 2012, when it engaged 65.0% of the employed labour force. According to UN estimates, the GDP of the services sector increased, in real terms, at an average rate of 0.8% per year in 2003–12. The GDP of the services sector increased by 1.9% in 2011, but decreased by 0.3% in 2012.

In 2012 Hungary recorded a visible merchandise trade surplus of US $1,940m. and a surplus of $1,119m. on the current account of the balance of payments. In that year the principal source of imports was Germany (accounting for 24.6% of the total); other major sources were Russia, Austria, the People's Republic of China, Slovakia and Poland. Germany was also the principal market for exports in that year (25.0%); other important purchasers were Romania, Slovakia, Austria and Italy. The principal exports in 2012 were machinery and transport equipment, basic manufactures, and food, beverages and tobacco. The main imports in that year were machinery and transport equipment, basic manufactures, fuels and electricity, and food, beverages and tobacco.

According to official figures, in 2012 Hungary's overall budgetary deficit was estimated at 620.1m. forint, equivalent to 2.2% of GDP. Hungary's general government gross debt was 22,380,900m. forint in 2012, equivalent to 79.2% of GDP. The country's total external debt was an estimated US $107,677m. at the end of 2006, of which $28,017m. was long-term public debt. In that year the cost of debt-servicing was equivalent to 33.1% of the value of exports of goods and services. The annual rate of inflation averaged 5.2% in 2003–12; consumer prices increased by 5.7% in 2012. The rate of unemployment was 10.2% in 2013, according to official figures.

In early 2012 the European Union (EU, see p. 273) suspended the release of funds to Hungary on the grounds that it had failed to address excessive budgetary deficit and external debt levels. Although negotiations with the IMF continued on the provision of credit, in September the Government rejected fiscal adjustment measures, including the abolition of the high tax rates imposed on banks, which were stipulated as conditions for the approval of funding. In October the Government announced the extension of the tax measures in force in the financial sector, and the introduction of further taxes on foreign energy enterprises and public utilities, despite IMF opposition to these policies on the grounds that they inhibited private sector investment and growth. In April 2013 the new Governor of the Central Bank announced measures designed to encourage economic growth through the provision of credit at reduced rates of interest to small and medium-sized enterprises, and to mitigate foreign-exchange risks. The EU excessive deficit procedure against Hungary was officially ended in June, after the fiscal consolidation efforts had successfully reduced the general government deficit. In August 2013 (ahead of schedule) Hungary repaid outstanding obligations totalling US $2,850m. to the IMF. In the same month the European Commission suspended some €2,000m. in development assistance to Hungary, citing significant deficiencies in the management of operational programmes; however, the funds were released in September, after the Government finalized corrective measures. Meanwhile, the Central Bank announced in September that it had signed a three-year currency exchange agreement amounting to $1,620m. with the Central Bank of the People's Republic of China, which was to facilitate bilateral trade and investment. A nuclear co-operation agreement, under which Russian nuclear agency Rosatom was to construct a further two units at Hungary's only nuclear power installation, secured legislative approval in February 2014. After economic contraction in 2012, growth resumed, at an estimated annual rate of 1.2%, in 2013, reflecting a regional recovery.

PUBLIC HOLIDAYS

2015: 1 January (New Year's Day), 15 March (Anniversary of 1848 uprising against Austrian rule), 6 April (Easter Monday), 1 May (Labour Day), 25 May (Whit Monday), 15 August (Assumption), 20 August (Constitution Day), 23 October (Day of the Proclamation of the Republic), 1 November (All Saints' Day), 25–26 December (Christmas).

Statistical Survey

Source (unless otherwise stated): Központi Statisztikai Hivatal (Hungarian Central Statistical Office), 1525 Budapest, Keleti Károly u. 5–7; tel. (1) 345-6136; fax (1) 345-6378; e-mail erzsebet.veto@office.ksh.hu; internet www.ksh.hu.

Area and Population

AREA, POPULATION AND DENSITY

Area (sq km)	93,027*
Population (census results)	
1 February 2001	10,198,315
1 October 2011	
Males	4,718,479
Females	5,219,149
Total	9,937,628
Population (official estimates at 1 January)	
2012	9,931,925
2013	9,908,798
Density (per sq km) at 1 January 2013	106.5

* 35,918 sq miles.

POPULATION BY AGE AND SEX

(official estimates at 1 January 2013)

	Males	Females	Total
0–14	734,685	696,180	1,430,865
15–64	3,350,779	3,425,479	6,776,258
65 and over	630,489	1,071,186	1,701,675
Total	4,715,953	5,192,845	9,908,798

ADMINISTRATIVE DIVISIONS

(official population estimates at 1 January 2013)

	Area (sq km)	Population	Density (per sq km)	County town (with population)
Counties:				
Bács-Kiskun	8,445	519,930	61.6	Kecskemét (111,863)
Baranya	4,430	377,142	85.1	Pécs (147,719)
Békés	5,630	359,153	63.8	Békéscsaba (61,046)
Borsod-Abaúj-Zemplén	7,250	682,350	94.1	Miskolc (162,905)
Csongrád	4,263	409,571	96.1	Szeged (161,837)
Fejér	4,358	421,086	96.6	Székesfehérvár (99,247)
Győr-Moson-Sopron	4,208	448,312	106.5	Győr (128,567)
Hajdú-Bihar	6,211	541,352	87.2	Debrecen (204,333)
Heves	3,637	306,336	84.2	Eger (54,867)
Jász-Nagykun-Szolnok	5,582	386,654	69.3	Szolnok (73,193)
Komárom-Esztergom	2,265	302,451	133.5	Tatabánya (67,406)
Nógrád	2,546	200,755	78.9	Salgótarján (37,199)
Pest	6,391	1,218,172	190.6	Érd (63,333)
Somogy	6,036	318,096	52.7	Kaposvár (65,337)
Szabolcs-Szatmár-Bereg	5,937	563,653	94.9	Nyíregyháza (118,185)
Tolna	3,703	229,942	62.1	Szekszárd (33,599)
Vas	3,336	255,294	76.5	Szombathely (77,547)
Veszprém	4,493	351,165	78.2	Veszprém (60,876)
Zala	3,784	281,673	74.4	Zalaegerszeg (59,618)
Capital city				
Budapest*	525	1,735,711	3,306.1	—
Total	93,027	9,908,798	106.5	—

* Budapest has separate county status.

PRINCIPAL TOWNS

(official population estimates at 1 January 2013)

Budapest (capital)	1,735,711	Pécs	147,719
Debrecen	204,333	Győr	128,567
Miskolc	162,905	Nyíregyháza	118,185
Szeged	161,837	Kecskemét	111,863

BIRTHS, MARRIAGES AND DEATHS

	Registered live births		Registered marriages		Registered deaths	
	Number	Rate (per 1,000)	Number	Rate (per 1,000)	Number	Rate (per 1,000)
2005	97,496	9.7	44,234	4.4	135,732	13.5
2006	99,871	9.9	44,528	4.4	131,603	13.1
2007	97,613	9.7	40,842	4.1	132,938	13.2
2008	99,149	9.9	40,105	4.0	130,027	13.0
2009	96,442	9.6	36,730	3.7	130,414	13.0
2010	90,335	9.0	35,520	3.6	130,456	13.0
2011	88,050	8.8	35,812	3.6	128,795	12.9
2012	90,269	9.1	36,161	3.6	129,440	13.0

Life expectancy (years at birth): 74.9 (males 71.2; females 78.7) in 2011 (Source: World Bank, World Development Indicators database).

ECONOMICALLY ACTIVE POPULATION

(labour force surveys, '000 persons aged 15 to 74 years)

	2010	2011	2012
Agriculture, hunting, forestry and fishing	171.8	185.1	200.3
Mining and quarrying	11.1	11.1	9.0
Manufacturing	786.6	809.0	802.1
Electricity, gas and water supply	85.4	89.7	99.5
Construction	277.6	264.0	245.9
Wholesale and retail trade; repair of motor vehicles, motorcycles and personal and household goods	539.8	545.7	544.3
Hotels and restaurants	154.5	163.5	164.0
Transport, storage and communications	355.3	351.0	365.6
Financial intermediation	91.0	91.8	93.9
Real estate, renting and business activities	270.3	273.5	290.2
Public administration and defence; compulsory social security	317.2	309.6	326.8
Education	323.9	316.9	314.6
Health and social work	251.6	255.0	266.1
Other community, social and personal service activities	145.1	146.0	155.6
Total employed	3,781.2	3,811.9	3,877.9
Unemployed	474.8	467.9	475.6
Total labour force	4,256.0	4,279.8	4,353.4
Males	2,287.1	2,310.6	2,345.0
Females	1,968.9	1,969.3	2,008.5

2013 (labour force survey, '000 persons aged 15 to 74 years, July–September): Total employed 3,989.6 (males 2,169.7, females 1,819.9); Unemployed 434.2 (males 231.9, females 202.2); *Total labour force* 4,423.8 (males 2,401.6, females 2,022.1).

Health and Welfare

KEY INDICATORS

Total fertility rate (children per woman, 2011)	1.4
Under-5 mortality rate (per 1,000 live births, 2011)	6.0
HIV/AIDS (% of persons aged 15–49, 2011)	<0.1
Physicians (per 1,000 head, 2010)	3.4
Hospital beds (per 1,000 head, 2009)	7.1
Health expenditure (2010): US $ per head (PPP)	1,601
Health expenditure (2010): % of GDP	7.8
Health expenditure (2010): public (% of total)	64.8
Total carbon dioxide emissions ('000 metric tons, 2010)	50,582.6
Carbon dioxide emissions per head (metric tons, 2010)	5.1
Human Development Index (2012): ranking	37
Human Development Index (2012): value	0.831

For sources and definitions, see explanatory note on p. vi.

Agriculture

PRINCIPAL CROPS
('000 metric tons)

	2010	2011	2012
Wheat	3,745.2	4,107.0	3,740.0
Barley	943.8	988.0	995.7
Maize	6,984.9	7,992.0	4,741.5
Rye	78.2	75.0	78.0
Oats	117.9	129.0	140.4
Triticale (wheat-rye hybrid)	366.8	345.7	345.1
Potatoes	439.9	600.0	511.1
Sugar beet	818.9	856.0	769.7
Peas, dry	36.6	42.6	42.5
Soybeans (Soya beans)	85.4	95.0	67.8
Sunflower seed	969.7	1,374.8	1,316.5
Rapeseed	530.6	526.8	414.6
Cabbages and other brassicas	76.6	101.1	82.9
Tomatoes	134.3	163.3	108.8
Cucumbers and gherkins	38.0	35.9	33.9
Chillies and peppers, green	122.4	128.0	92.6
Onions, dry	40.9	57.6	57.2
Peas, green	61.1	99.1	92.4
Carrots and turnips	58.5	65.1	74.7
Maize, green	302.8	427.3	433.6
Watermelons	141.1	202.9	182.7
Apples	496.9	292.8	650.6
Sour (Morello) cherries	51.9	61.7	53.4
Peaches and nectarines	54.2	43.1	16.9
Plums and sloes	70.9	37.3	43.3
Grapes	294.8	450.9	356.4
Tobacco, unmanufactured	9.0	10.9	9.3

Aggregate production ('000 metric tons, may include official, semi-official or estimated data): Total cereals 12,269.4 in 2010, 13,692.0 in 2011, 10,082.7 in 2012; Total roots and tubers 439.9 in 2010, 600.0 in 2011, 511.1 in 2012; Total vegetables (incl. melons) 1,144.6 in 2010, 1,475.3 in 2011, 1,363.1 in 2012; Total fruits (excl. melons) 1,069.4 in 2010, 971.7 in 2011, 1,188.7 in 2012.

Source: FAO.

LIVESTOCK
('000 head, year ending September)

	2010	2011	2012
Cattle	700	682	694
Pigs	3,247	3,169	3,025
Sheep	1,223	1,181	1,081
Goats	58	75	80
Horses	61	65	74
Chickens	32,128	31,848	32,865
Ducks	3,713	5,813	4,436
Geese	1,405	1,384	1,187
Turkeys	3,018	3,168	2,999

Source: FAO.

LIVESTOCK PRODUCTS
('000 metric tons)

	2010	2011	2012
Cattle meat	27.6	26.4	25.4
Sheep meat	0.8	1.0	1.1
Pig meat	452.1	434.7	393.7
Chicken meat	221.4	235.7	253.8
Duck meat	52.4	59.3	61.4
Rabbit meat	5.4	5.7	6.5
Cows' milk	1,684.9	1,712.5	1,798.2
Sheep's milk	1.8	1.6	1.6*
Goats' milk	3.8	3.9	4.0*
Hen eggs	151.8	136.6	131.1
Other poultry eggs*	3.9	3.9	3.9
Honey	16.5	17.5	17.0*
Wool, greasy	4.1	3.8	3.8

* FAO estimate(s).

Source: FAO.

Forestry

ROUNDWOOD REMOVALS
('000 cu metres, excl. bark)

	2010	2011	2012
Sawlogs, veneer logs and logs for sleepers	1,079	1,232	1,196
Pulpwood	954	959	1,073
Other industrial wood	713	827	718
Fuel wood	2,994	3,215	2,959
Total	5,740	6,232	5,946

Source: FAO.

SAWNWOOD PRODUCTION
('000 cu metres, incl. railway sleepers)

	2010	2011	2012
Coniferous (softwood)	14	122	90
Broadleaved (hardwood)	119*	100	202†
Total	133*	222	292†

* Unofficial figure.
† FAO estimate.

Source: FAO.

Fishing

(metric tons, live weight)

	2009	2010	2011
Capture	6,366	6,216	7,048
Common carp	3,238	3,247	3,855
Silver carp	367	350	455
Other cyprinids	1,257	1,113	1,219
Aquaculture	14,825	14,245	15,584
Common carp	9,931	9,927	10,807
Grass carp	480	437	437
Silver carp	1,567	1,081	1,545
North African catfish	1,716	1,810	1,913
Freshwater fishes	743	619	407
Total catch	21,191	20,461	22,632

Source: FAO.

Mining

('000 metric tons unless otherwise indicated)

	2009	2010	2011
Brown coal	952	911	758
Lignite	8,025	8,203	8,801
Crude petroleum ('000 barrels)*	4,970	5,280	4,470
Bauxite	267	307	278
Natural gas (million cu metres)†	2,748	2,600	2,670

* Estimates.
† Marketed production.

Source: US Geological Survey.

Industry

SELECTED PRODUCTS

('000 metric tons unless otherwise indicated)

	2008	2009	2010
Crude steel*	2,160	1,401	1,681
Cement*	3,544	3,200†	2,560†
Nitrogenous fertilizers‡	190	232	242
Refined sugar	188	140	n.a.
Electric energy (million kWh)	40,025	35,908	37,371
Radio receivers ('000)	1,926	1,522	n.a.

* Source: US Geological Survey.
† Estimate.
‡ Production in terms of nitrogen (Source: FAO).

Non-rubber footwear ('000 pairs): 5,346 in 2007.

Source: mainly UN Industrial Commodity Statistics Database.

2011 ('000 metric tons): Crude steel 1,733; Cement 2,600 (estimate) (Source: US Geological Survey).

Finance

CURRENCY AND EXCHANGE RATES

Monetary Units
100 fillér = 1 forint.

Sterling, Dollar and Euro Equivalents (31 December 2013)
£1 sterling = 355.165 forint;
US $1 = 215.670 forint;
€1 = 297.430 forint;
1,000 forint = £2.82 = $4.64 = €3.36.

Average Exchange Rate (forint per US dollar)
2011 201.055
2012 225.104
2013 223.695

BUDGET

('000 million forint)

Revenue	2011	2012	2013*
Payments of economic units	1,210.2	1,157.2	1,451.3
Corporate taxes	316.6	342.3	320.8
Simplified business tax	172.3	146.5	108.1
Gambling tax	51.6	52.4	47.0
Other central payments	108.6	172.0	251.0
Taxes on consumption	3,132.3	3,702.7	4,286.9
Value-added tax	2,219.5	2,747.4	2,953.2
Excises and tax on consumption	909.6	943.1	961.1
Payments of households†	1,462.0	1,609.4	1,657.8
Personal income tax revenue of the central budget	1,382.8	1,498.4	1,501.6
Fees	75.3	109.6	111.0
Central budgetary institutions and chapter-administered appropriations	2,169.6	2,576.7	2,489.2
Payments of general government sub-systems	52.7	68.0	96.9
Payments of extra-budgetary funds	—	—	10.0
Payments related to state property	40.0	69.8	116.0
Revenue from the Pension Reform and Debt Reduction Fund	95.6	—	—
Revenue related to debt service and other revenues	147.1	172.0	107.9
Transfers from the European Union	32.6	20.8	26.4
Total	8,342.2	9,376.7	10,232.4

Expenditure	2011	2012	2013*
Subsidies to economic units	212.0	259.5	268.7
Support to the media	53.7	61.8	68.6
Social policy subsidy for fares	—	—	93.0
Consumer price subsidy	108.3	96.9	—
Housing grants	129.1	124.0	201.5
Family benefits and social subsidies	618.9	817.0	829.6
Family benefits	451.5	445.8	452.5
Income-supplement benefits	139.8	62.7	63.7
Payments of central budgetary institutions and chapter-administered appropriations	4,730.7	5,046.9	5,580.8
Transfers to general government sub-systems†	1,922.5	1,852.2	1,846.4
Contribution to social-security funds	637.8	690.9	1,066.5
Transfers to local governments	1,195.6	1,066.7	643.3
Transfer to non-profit organizations	3.8	3.8	3.8
Debt service related expenditures and interest expenditures	1,101.1	1,202.4	1,237.2
Reserves	—	—	511.4
Subsidy for local governments' debt repayments	—	76.0	30.0
State property expenditures	633.3	137.4	245.1
Extraordinary and other expenditures	43.4	43.4	52.5
Government guarantees redeemed	29.4	40.8	30.2
Debt assumptions	249.9	—	—
Contribution to the European Union budget	233.0	234.9	277.0
Total	10,069.3	9,996.8	11,275.8

* Budget estimates.
† Including personal income tax ceded to local governments.

INTERNATIONAL RESERVES

(US $ million at 31 December)

	2010	2011	2012
Gold (national valuation)	139	154	164
IMF special drawing rights	1,154	842	365
Reserve position in IMF	114	113	113
Foreign exchange	43,581	47,725	44,028
Total	44,988	48,834	44,670

Source: IMF, *International Financial Statistics*.

MONEY SUPPLY

('000 million forint at 31 December)

	2010	2011	2012
Currency outside depositary corporations	2,218.3	2,551.5	2,553.9
Transferable deposits	4,416.7	4,791.3	4,743.4
Other deposits	7,758.1	8,058.3	7,911.7
Securities other than shares	2,440.7	2,530.8	1,864.8
Broad money	16,833.7	17,931.8	17,073.8

Source: IMF, *International Financial Statistics*.

COST OF LIVING
(Consumer Price Index; base: 2000 = 100)

	2010	2011	2012
Food	191.7	204.3	216.4
All items (incl. others)	173.1	179.9	190.1

Source: ILO.

NATIONAL ACCOUNTS
('000 million forint at current prices)

Expenditure on the Gross Domestic Product

	2010	2011	2012
Government final consumption expenditure	5,827.5	5,815.4	5,720.1
Private final consumption expenditure*	14,073.7	14,725.9	15,372.4
Changes in inventories	190.3	359.3	13.9
Gross fixed capital formation	4,920.1	4,950.0	4,880.8
Total domestic expenditure	25,011.5	25,850.6	25,987.2
Exports of goods and services	22,551.5	25,320.1	26,551.7
Less Imports of goods and services	21,050.0	23,535.2	24,490.8
GDP in purchasers' values	26,513.0	27,635.4	28,048.1

* Includes non-profit institutions serving households.

Gross Domestic Product by Economic Activity

	2010	2011	2012
Agriculture, hunting, forestry and fishing	806.9	1,083.5	1,114.2
Mining and quarrying	50.6	57.9	59.3
Manufacturing	4,896.1	5,202.0	5,321.8
Electricity, gas and water supply	940.4	886.5	912.2
Construction	936.7	947.9	893.9
Wholesale and retail trade; repair of motor vehicles	2,248.5	2,417.9	2,349.7
Hotels and restaurants	364.8	357.8	336.2
Transport, storage and communications	2,526.9	2,677.4	2,682.1
Financial intermediation	1,059.1	1,070.7	1,024.3
Real estate, renting and business activities	3,898.9	4,056.0	4,089.5
Public administration, defence and compulsory social security	2,015.3	2,008.2	1,965.2
Education	1,069.2	1,063.7	1,073.2
Health and social work	912.0	929.2	1,015.2
Other community, social and personal service activities	655.0	669.2	654.9
Gross value added in basic prices	22,380.3	23,427.9	23,491.6
Taxes *less* subsidies on products	4,132.8	4,207.5	4,556.5
GDP in market prices	26,513.0	27,635.4	28,048.1

BALANCE OF PAYMENTS
(US $ million)

	2010	2011	2012
Exports of goods	85,685	97,770	88,412
Imports of goods	–81,960	–94,535	–86,472
Balance on goods	3,725	3,235	1,940
Exports of services	18,560	22,753	22,652
Imports of services	–15,244	–17,202	–15,704
Balance on goods and services	7,041	8,786	8,888
Primary income received	18,078	13,943	12,894
Primary income paid	–25,323	–22,841	–21,140
Balance on goods, services and primary income	–204	–112	642
Secondary income received	3,282	3,773	3,514
Secondary income paid	–2,816	–3,004	–3,037
Current balance	261	657	1,119
Capital account (net)	2,287	3,229	3,237

—*continued*	2010	2011	2012
Direct investment assets	24,807	–7,869	–6,477
Direct investment liabilities	–20,934	9,342	9,356
Portfolio investment assets	–833	2,289	937
Portfolio investment liabilities	456	6,392	1,339
Financial derivatives and employee stock options assets	6,593	7,016	6,038
Financial derivatives and employee stock options liabilities	–5,681	–8,053	–5,649
Other investment assets	–659	3,054	2,519
Other investment liabilities	–1,117	–7,967	–13,565
Net errors and omissions	–1,018	–2,540	1,768
Reserves and related items	4,162	5,550	621

Source: IMF, *International Financial Statistics*.

External Trade

PRINCIPAL COMMODITIES
('000 million forint)

Imports c.i.f.	2010	2011	2012
Food, beverages and tobacco	901.0	1,088.3	1,122.3
Crude materials	382.1	521.5	537.1
Fuels and electricity	1,948.6	2,511.4	2,759.6
Basic manufactures	5,790.1	6,800.1	7,096.1
Machinery and transport equipment	9,152.5	9,442.5	9,706.0
Total	18,174.3	20,363.9	21,221.0

Exports f.o.b.	2010	2011	2012
Food, beverages and tobacco	1,365.3	1,683.2	1,887.2
Crude materials	477.4	681.4	790.9
Fuels and electricity	558.6	810.3	935.6
Basic manufactures	5,435.5	6,537.5	7,192.9
Machinery and transport equipment	11,853.4	12,630.2	12,336.5
Total	19,690.0	22,342.5	23,143.1

PRINCIPAL TRADING PARTNERS
('000 million forint)*

Imports c.i.f.	2010	2011	2012
Austria	1,124.9	1,342.3	1,493.7
Belgium	401.5	427.4	451.8
China, People's Republic	1,284.5	1,226.4	1,218.9
Czech Republic	588.3	698.2	753.8
France	671.8	740.5	765.9
Germany	4,360.6	4,852.1	5,221.3
Italy	777.9	915.0	938.3
Japan	394.5	318.0	286.7
Korea, Republic	595.4	423.7	326.7
Netherlands	821.0	850.3	851.6
Poland	958.4	944.2	988.3
Romania	474.0	651.5	594.3
Russia	1,419.1	1,780.8	1,859.5
Slovakia	754.9	1,104.9	1,197.6
Slovenia	178.1	228.0	226.5
Spain	228.2	239.2	253.0
Sweden	165.6	224.9	230.5
Switzerland	136.7	154.0	141.6
Taiwan	281.8	263.7	265.1
Ukraine	182.4	275.3	352.0
United Kingdom	341.5	416.1	402.9
USA	327.8	390.7	428.5
Total (incl. others)	18,174.3	20,363.9	21,221.0

Exports f.o.b.	2010	2011	2012
Austria	965.3	1,260.1	1,329.3
Belgium	296.0	318.1	337.4
China, People's Republic	318.6	337.7	407.2
Croatia	238.5	322.9	367.4
Czech Republic	682.1	831.7	897.0
France	984.9	1,041.7	1,067.0
Germany	4,941.8	5,529.9	5,785.0
Italy	1,089.2	1,113.8	1,076.7
Netherlands	622.4	555.3	640.9
Poland	725.2	856.8	876.4
Romania	1,060.5	1,361.7	1,377.5
Russia	704.0	717.4	740.5
Serbia	232.5	301.7	360.3
Slovakia	1,053.1	1,312.3	1,359.2
Slovenia	208.1	247.7	265.0
Spain	625.2	587.1	540.2
Sweden	197.2	223.3	245.6
Switzerland	193.1	200.7	220.4
Turkey	332.6	375.4	351.1
Ukraine	401.5	456.0	514.6
United Arab Emirates	188.6	393.6	267.4
United Kingdom	1,070.5	1,023.0	961.0
USA	401.3	457.0	553.2
Total (incl. others)	19,690.0	22,342.5	23,143.1

* Imports by country of origin; exports by country of destination.

Transport

RAILWAYS
(traffic)

	2010	2011	2012
Passengers carried (million)	140.5	145.7	147.8
Passenger-kilometres (million)	7,692	7,806	7,806
Freight carried ('000 metric tons)	45,794	47,424	46,177
Net ton-kilometres (million)	8,809	9,118	9,093

ROAD TRAFFIC
(motor vehicles in use at 31 December)

	2010	2011	2012
Passenger cars	2,984,063	2,967,792	2,985,991
Buses and coaches	17,641	17,358	17,282
Lorries and vans	416,672	415,418	414,375
Motorcycles and mopeds	142,251	147,367	151,346
Road tractors	48,207	50,258	52,574

SHIPPING

Flag Registered Fleet
(at 31 December)

	2011	2012	2013
Number of vessels	2	2	3
Total displacement (grt)	15	15	1,315

Source: Lloyd's List Intelligence (www.lloydslistintelligence.com).

INLAND WATERWAYS
(traffic)

	2010	2011	2012
Freight carried ('000 metric tons)	9,951	7,175	8,135
Freight ton-km (million)	2,393	1,840	1,982

CIVIL AVIATION
(traffic)

	2010	2011
Kilometres flown (million)	127	142
Passengers carried ('000)	11,787	12,970
Passenger-km (million)	14,984	17,021
Total ton-km	1,377	1,562

Source: UN, *Statistical Yearbook*.

2012 ('000): Passengers carried 11,170 (Source: World Bank, World Development Indicators database).

Tourism

TOURISTS BY COUNTRY OF ORIGIN
('000 arrivals, including visitors in transit)

	2010	2011	2012
Austria	6,696	6,649	7,233
Croatia	868	934	756
Germany	3,135	3,026	3,188
Poland	1,540	1,331	1,603
Romania	7,614	7,575	7,901
Serbia	2,329	2,964	2,658
Slovakia	8,404	8,825	9,971
Ukraine	1,819	1,831	1,863
Total (incl. others)	39,904	41,304	43,565

Tourist receipts (million forint): 1,189,819 in 2010; 1,200,139 in 2011; 1,175,086 in 2012.

Communications Media

	2010	2011	2012
Telephones ('000 main lines in use)	2,977.2	2,933.3	2,960.6
Mobile cellular telephones ('000 subscribers)	12,011.8	11,689.9	11,579.4
Internet subscribers ('000)	1,971.4	2,221.5	n.a.
Broadband subscribers ('000)	2,057.8	2,208.1	2,281.1
Book production: titles	12,997	12,456	12,080
Book production: copies ('000)	34,416	34,251	30,649

Source: mainly International Telecommunication Union.

Education

(2012/13, full- and part-time education)

	Institutions	Teachers	Students
Pre-primary	4,321	30,449	340,204
Primary	3,251	72,048	745,058
Vocational	843	10,447	139,453
Secondary	1,807	37,305	486,548
General	877	17,851	228,315
Vocational	921	18,983	258,233
Tertiary	66	20,555	338,467

2013/14 (preliminary): *Students:* Pre-primary 330,109; Primary 750,333; Vocational 125,606; Secondary 459,738 (General 220,472, Vocational 239,266).

Pupil-teacher ratio (primary education, UNESCO estimate): 10.5 in 2011/12 (Source: UNESCO Institute for Statistics).

Adult literacy rate (UNESCO estimates): 99.0% (males 99.2%; females 98.9%) in 2011 (Source: UNESCO Institute for Statistics).

Directory

The Government

HEAD OF STATE

President of the Republic: JÁNOS ÁDER.

COUNCIL OF MINISTERS
(April 2014)

Following legislative elections, the Government, comprising members of Fidesz—Magyar Polgári Szöevetség (Fidesz, Federation of Young Democrats—Hungarian Civic Alliance), Kereszténydemokrata Néppárt (KDNP—the Christian Democratic People's Party) and Independents, remained in place pending the formation of a new Government under VIKTOR ORBÁN.

Prime Minister: VIKTOR ORBÁN (Fidesz).

Deputy Prime Minister, Minister without Portfolio: Dr ZSOLT SEMJÉN (KNDP).

Deputy Prime Minister, Minister of Public Administration and Justice: Dr TIBOR NAVRACSICS (Fidesz).

Minister of Rural Development: Dr SÁNDOR FAZEKAS (Fidesz).

Minister of National Development: ZSUZSA NÉMETH (Independent).

Minister of Defence: Dr CSABA HENDE (Fidesz).

Minister of Foreign Affairs: Dr JÁNOS MARTONYI (Fidesz).

Minister of the National Economy: MIHÁLY VARGA (Fidesz).

Minister of the Interior: Dr SÁNDOR PINTÉR (Independent).

Minister of Human Resources: ZOLTÁN BALOG (Fidesz).

MINISTRIES

Office of the President: 1014 Budapest, Sándor-Palace, Szent György tér 1; tel. (1) 224-5000; fax (1) 784-9181; e-mail ugyfelkapu@keh.hu; internet www.keh.hu.

Office of the Prime Minister: 1357 Budapest, pf. 6; tel. (1) 795-5000; fax (1) 795-0381; e-mail titkarsag@me.gov.hu; internet www.kormany.hu.

Ministry of Defence: 1055 Budapest, Balaton u. 7–11; tel. (1) 236-5111; fax (1) 474-1335; e-mail hmugyfelszolgalat@hm.gov.hu; internet www.kormany.hu/hu/honvedelmi-miniszterium.

Ministry of Foreign Affairs: 1027 Budapest, Bem rakpart 47; tel. (1) 458-1000; fax (1) 212-5918; e-mail kozkapcsolat@kum.gov.hu; internet www.kormany.hu/hu/kulugyminiszterium.

Ministry of Human Resources: 1055 Budapest, Szalay u. 10–14; tel. (1) 795-1200; fax (1) 795-0012; e-mail info@nefmi.gov.hu; internet www.kormany.hu/hu/emberi-eroforrasok-miniszteriuma.

Ministry of the Interior: 1051 Budapest, József Attila u. 2–4; tel. (1) 441-1000; fax (1) 441-1437; e-mail ugyfelszolgalat@bm.gov.hu; internet www.kormany.hu/hu/belugyminiszterium.

Ministry of National Development: 1011 Budapest, Fő u. 44–50; tel. (1) 795-1700; fax (1) 795-0697; e-mail ugyfelszolgalat@nfm.gov.hu; internet www.kormany.hu/hu/nemzeti-fejlesztesi-miniszterium.

Ministry of the National Economy: 1051 Budapest, József Nádor tér 2–4; tel. (1) 374-2700; fax (1) 374-2925; e-mail ugyfelszolgalat@ngm.gov.hu; internet www.kormany.hu/hu/nemzetgazdasagi-miniszterium.

Ministry of Public Administration and Justice: 1055 Budapest, Kossuth Lajos tér 4; tel. (1) 795-1000; fax (1) 795-0002; e-mail lakossag@kim.gov.hu; internet www.kormany.hu/hu/kozigazgatasi-es-igazsagugyi-miniszterium.

Ministry of Rural Development: 1055 Budapest, Kossuth Lajos tér 11; tel. (1) 795-2000; fax (1) 795-0200; e-mail miniszter@vm.gov.hu; internet www.kormany.hu/hu/videkfejlesztesi-miniszterium.

President

Following the resignation of PÁL SCHMITT on 2 April 2012, a presidential election was conducted in the National Assembly on 2 May. JÁNOS ÁDER, the sole candidate, was duly elected as President, receiving the support of 262 deputies; 40 deputies voted to oppose the nomination of ÁDER. Five invalid votes were cast, and 79 deputies did not vote.

Legislature

National Assembly (Országgyűlés)

1055 Budapest, Kossuth Lajos tér 1–3; 1357 Budapest, POB 2; tel. (1) 441-4000; fax (1) 441-5000; internet www.mkogy.hu.

President: LÁSZLÓ KÖVÉR.

General Election, 6 April 2014

Parties	Seats A*	Seats B*	Total
Fidesz—Magyar Polgári Szöevetség-Kereszténydemokrata Néppárt (Fidesz-KDNP) coalition	96	37	133
Unity†	10	28	38
Jobbik Magyarországért Mozgalom	—	23	23
Lehet Más a Politika! (LMP)	—	5	5
Total	106	93	199

* The 199 seats of the National Assembly comprise 106 elected in single-member constituencies (A) and 93 elected on the basis of national list.

† A coalition of Magyar Szocialista Párt (MSzP), Együtt 2014 (Together 2014), Demokratikus Koalíció (DK), Párbeszéd Magyarországért (PM) and Magyar Liberális Párt (MLP).

Election Commission

Országos Választási Iroda (OVI) (National Election Office): 1357 Budapest, POB 2; tel. (1) 795-3303; fax (1) 795-0143; e-mail visz@otm.gov.hu; internet www.valasztas.hu; Chair. VILMOS BORDÁS.

Political Organizations

Civil Mozgalom (Civil Movement): 1426 Budapest, POB 122; tel. (70) 231-6933; e-mail civilek@civilmozgalom.hu; internet www.civilmozgalom.hu; seeks to reduce government bureaucracy and eliminate corruption, and the strengthening of civil society; Leader MÁRIA SERES.

Demokratikus Koalíció (DK) (Democratic Coalition): 1081 Budapest, Népszínház u. 42–44; tel. (1) 300-1000; e-mail ugyfelszolgalat@dk365.hu; internet www.demokratikuskoalicio.hu; f. 2011 by fmr mems of Magyar Szocialista Párt (q.v.); social democratic; contested 2014 legislative elections as mem. of Unity; Chair. FERENC GYURCSÁNY.

Együtt 2014 (Together 2014): 1122 Budapest, Városmajor utca 48/b; tel. (1) 919-1414; e-mail info@hazaeshaladas.org; internet www.egyutt2014.hu; f. 2013; alliance of three civil society organizations: the Patriotism and Progress Association; One Million for Press Freedom; and the Hungarian Solidarity Movement; contested 2014 legislative elections as mem. of Unity; Pres. GORDON BAJNAI.

Fidesz—Magyar Polgári Szöevetség (Fidesz) (Fidesz (Federation of Young Democrats)—Hungarian Civic Alliance): 1062 Budapest, Lendvay u. 28; tel. (1) 555-2000; fax (1) 441-5463; e-mail fidesz@fidesz.hu; internet www.fidesz.hu; f. 1988 as the Federation of Young Democrats; renamed April 1995; re-formed as an alliance in 2003, with a new charter; Chair. VIKTOR ORBÁN; 10,000 mems.

Jobbik Magyarországért Mozgalom (Jobbik) (Jobbik—Movement for a Better Hungary): 1113 Budapest, Villányi út 20A; tel. and fax (1) 365-1488; e-mail jobbik@jobbik.hu; internet www.jobbik.hu; f. 2003; extreme nationalist; Pres. GÁBOR VONA.

Jólét és Szabadság Demokrata Közösség (JESz) (Democratic Community of Welfare and Freedom): 1026 Budapest, Szilágyi Erszébet fasor 73; tel. (1) 225-2280; fax (1) 225-2290; e-mail kis.jozsef@jesz.hu; internet www.jesz.hu; f. 1987; fmrly Hungarian Democratic Forum; present name adopted 2011; centre-right; Chair. ZSOLT MAKAY.

Kereszténydemokrata Néppárt (KDNP) (Christian Democratic People's Party): 1141 Budapest, Bazsarózsa u. 69; tel. (1) 489-0880; fax (1) 489-0879; e-mail kdnp@kdnp.hu; internet www.kdnp.hu; f. 1989 as revival of pre-communist-era party; formed an electoral alliance with Fidesz—Magyar Polgári Szöevetség (q.v.) to contest the 2010 and 2014 legislative elections; Chair. ZSOLT SEMJÉN.

Lehet Más a Politika! (LMP) (Politics Can Be Different!): 1136 Budapest, Hegedus Gyula u. 36; 1386 Budapest, POB 959; tel. and fax (30) 962-6868; e-mail info@lehetmas.hu; internet www.lehetmas.hu; f. 2009; environmentalist; Sec. ATTILA VIDA.

Magyar Liberális Párt (MLP) (Hungarian Liberal Party): 1051 Budapest, Sas u. 10-12; tel. (1) 784-3680; e-mail liberalisok@liberalisok.hu; internet liberalisok.hu; f. 2013; contested 2014 legislative elections as mem. of Unity; Chair. GÁBOR FODOR.

Magyarországi Szociáldemokrata Párt (MSzDP) (Hungarian Social Democratic Party): 1535 Budapest; tel. (1) 214-9496; fax (1) 214-9497; e-mail mszdp@mszdp.hu; internet www.mszdp.hu; f. 1890; absorbed by the Communist Party in 1948; revived 1988; affiliated with the Social Democratic Youth Movement; Chair. LÁSZLÓ KAPOLYI.

Magyar Szocialista Párt (MSzP) (Hungarian Socialist Party): 1066 Budapest, Jókai u. 6; tel. (1) 459-7200; fax (1) 210-0081; e-mail info@mszp.hu; internet www.mszp.hu; f. 1989 to replace the Hungarian Socialist Workers' Party; contested 2014 legislative elections as mem. of Unity; Pres. ATTILA MESTERHÁZY.

Párbeszéd Magyarországért (PM) (Dialogue For Hungary): Budapest; tel. (1) 441-5260; e-mail info@parbeszedmagyarorszagert.hu; internet parbeszedmagyarorszagert.hu; f. 2013 by fmr members of the LMP; environmentalist; contested 2014 legislative elections as mem. of Unity; Leader BENEDEK JÁVOR.

Szabad Demokraták Szövetsége (SzDSz) (Alliance of Free Democrats): 1092 Budapest, Ráday u. 50; tel. (1) 223-2050; fax (1) 222-3599; e-mail szerkesztoseg@szdsz.hu; internet www.szdsz.hu; f. 1988; Exec. Chair. VIKTOR SZABADAI.

Diplomatic Representation

EMBASSIES IN HUNGARY

Albania: 1062 Budapest, Andrássy u. 132; tel. and fax (1) 336-1098; e-mail embassy.budapest@mfa.gov.al; Ambassador MIRA HOXHA.

Algeria: 1121 Budapest, Zugligeti u. 27; tel. (1) 392-0510; fax (1) 200-6781; e-mail ambalbud@t-online.hu; internet www.algerianembassy.hu; Ambassador LOUNÈS MAGRAMANE.

Angola: 1124 Budapest, Sirály u. 3; tel. (1) 487-7680; fax (1) 487-7699; e-mail embanhun@angolaembassy.hu; internet www.angolaembassy.hu; Ambassador JOÃO MIGUEL VAHEKENI.

Argentina: 1023 Budapest, Vérhalom u. 12–16; tel. (1) 325-0492; fax (1) 326-0494; e-mail eungr@mrecic.gov.ar; Ambassador DOMINGO SANTIAGO CULLEN.

Austria: 1068 Budapest, Benczúr u. 16; tel. (1) 479-7010; fax (1) 352-8795; e-mail budapest-ob@bmeia.gv.at; internet www.aussenministerium.at/budapest; Ambassador Dr MICHAEL ZIMMERMANN.

Azerbaijan: 1067 Budapest, Eötvös u. 14; tel. (1) 374-6070; fax (1) 302-3535; e-mail budapest@azembassy.hu; internet www.azembassy.hu; Ambassador VILAYAT GULIYEV.

Belarus: 1126 Budapest, Agárdi u. 3B; tel. (1) 214-0553; fax (1) 214-0554; e-mail hungary@mfa.gov.by; internet www.hungary.mfa.gov.by; Ambassador ALEKSANDR KHAINOVSKY.

Belgium: 1015 Budapest, Toldy Ferenc u. 13; tel. (1) 457-9960; fax (1) 375-1566; e-mail budapest@diplobel.fed.be; internet www.diplomatie.be/budapest; Ambassador JOHAN INDEKEU.

Bosnia and Herzegovina: 1026 Budapest, Verseghy Ferenc u. 4; tel. (1) 212-0106; fax (1) 212-0109; e-mail bihambud@yahoo.com; Ambassador NIKOLA ĐUKIĆ.

Brazil: 1054 Budapest, Szabadság tér 7; tel. (1) 351-0060; fax (1) 202-0740; e-mail brasemb.budapeste@itamaraty.gov.br; internet budapeste.itamaraty.gov.br; Ambassador VALTER PECLY MOREIRA.

Bulgaria: 1062 Budapest, Andrássy u. 115; tel. (1) 322-0824; fax (1) 322-5215; e-mail embassy.budapest@mfa.bg; internet www.mfa.bg/embassies/hungary; Ambassador BISERKA BENISHEVA.

Canada: 1027 Budapest, Ganz u. 12–14; tel. (1) 392-3360; fax (1) 392-3390; e-mail bpest@international.gc.ca; internet www.canadainternational.gc.ca/hungary-hongrie; Ambassador LISA HELFAND.

Central African Republic: 1056 Budapest, Molnár u. 19; tel. (1) 484-7590; fax (1) 421-8558; e-mail ambassaderca@yahoo.fr; internet www.centrafricaine.info/hu; Ambassador BERNARD LECLERC.

Chile: 1024 Budapest, Rózsahegy u. 1B; tel. (1) 326-3054; fax (1) 326-3056; e-mail embajada@embachile.hu; internet chileabroad.gov.cl/hungria; Ambassador RODRIGO NIETO MATURANA.

China, People's Republic: 1068 Budapest, Városligeti fasor 20–22; tel. (1) 413-2400; fax (1) 413-2451; e-mail chinaemb_hu@mfa.gov.cn; internet hu.chineseembassy.org; Ambassador XIAO QIAN.

Croatia: 1063 Budapest, Munkácsy Mihály u. 15; tel. (1) 354-1315; fax (1) 354-1319; e-mail croemb.bp@mvep.hr; internet hu.mvp.hr; Ambassador GORDAN GRLIĆ RADMAN.

Cuba: 1121 Budapest, Normafa u. 55A; tel. (1) 325-7290; fax (1) 325-7586; e-mail recepcion@embacuba.hu; internet www.embacuba.hu; Ambassador SORAYA ELENA ÁLVAREZ NÚÑEZ.

Cyprus: 1051 Budapest, Dorottya u. 3; tel. (1) 266-1330; fax (1) 266-0538; e-mail cypembhu@axelero.hu; Ambassador ANTONIOS THEOCHAROUS.

Czech Republic: 1064 Budapest, Rózsa u. 61; tel. (1) 462-5011; fax (1) 351-9189; e-mail budapest@embassy.mzv.cz; internet www.mzv.cz/budapest; Ambassador HELENA BAMBASOVÁ.

Denmark: 1122 Budapest, Határőr u. 37; tel. (1) 487-9000; fax (1) 487-9045; e-mail budamb@um.dk; internet ungarn.um.dk; Ambassador TOM NØRRING.

Ecuador: 1061 Budapest, Andrássy u. 20 1/2; tel. (1) 315-2124; fax (1) 315-2104; e-mail embajada@ecuador.hu; Ambassador JAIME AUGUSTO BARBERIS MARTINEZ.

Egypt: 1124 Budapest, Istenhegyi u. 7B; tel. (1) 225-2150; fax (1) 225-8596; e-mail egyptembassybudapest@yahoo.com; Ambassador ALI EL-HEFNY.

Estonia: 1025 Budapest, Áldás u. 3; tel. (1) 354-2570; fax (1) 354-2571; e-mail embassy.budapest@mfa.ee; internet www.estemb.hu; Ambassador PRIIT PALLUM.

Finland: 1118 Budapest, Kelenhegyi u. 16A; tel. (1) 279-2500; fax (1) 385-0843; e-mail sanomat.bud@formin.fi; internet www.finland.hu; Ambassador PASI TUOMINEN.

France: 1062 Budapest, Lendvay u. 27; tel. (1) 374-1100; fax (1) 374-1140; e-mail consulat.budapest-amba@diplomatie.gouv.fr; internet www.ambafrance-hu.org; Ambassador ROLAND GALHARAGUE.

Georgia: 1125 Budapest, Virányos u. 6B; tel. (1) 202-3390; fax (1) 214-3299; e-mail budapest.emb@mfa.gov.ge; internet www.hungary.mfa.gov.ge; Ambassador ZAZA KANDELAKI.

Germany: 1014 Budapest, Úri u. 64–66; tel. (1) 488-3500; fax (1) 488-3505; e-mail info@budapest.diplo.de; internet www.budapest.diplo.de; Ambassador Dr MATEI I. HOFFMANN.

Greece: 1063 Budapest, Szegfű u. 3; tel. (1) 413-2621; fax (1) 342-1934; e-mail gremb.bud@mfa.gr; internet www.greekembassy.hu; Ambassador GIANNAKAKIS DIMITRIS.

Holy See: 1126 Budapest, Gyimes u. 1–3; tel. (1) 355-8979; fax (1) 355-6987; e-mail nuntbud@communio.hcbc.hu; Apostolic Nuncio JULIUSZ JANUSZ (Titular Archbishop of Opitergium).

India: 1025 Budapest, Búzavirág u. 14; tel. (1) 325-7742; fax (1) 325-7745; internet www.indianembassy.hu; Ambassador MALAY MISHRA.

Indonesia: 1068 Budapest, Városligeti fasor 26; tel. (1) 413-3800; fax (1) 322-8669; e-mail embassy@indonesianembassy.hu; internet www.indonesia.hu; Ambassador MARULI TUA SAGALA.

Iran: 1143 Budapest, Stefánia u. 97; tel. (1) 460-9260; fax (1) 460-9430; e-mail embiran@nextra.hu; internet www.iran-embassy.hu; Ambassador Dr REZA MORSHEDZADEH.

Iraq: 1146 Budapest, Bölöni György u. 3; tel. (1) 392-5120; fax (1) 392-5133; e-mail budemb@iraqmofamail.net; Ambassador QASIM ASKAR.

Ireland: 1054 Budapest, Szabadság tér, Bank Center; tel. (1) 301-4960; fax (1) 302-9599; e-mail budapestembassy@dfa.ie; internet www.embassyofireland.hu; Ambassador KEVIN DOWLING.

Israel: 1026 Budapest, Fullánk u. 8; tel. (1) 392-6200; fax (1) 200-0783; e-mail info@budapest.mfa.gov.il; internet embassies.gov.il/budapest; Ambassador ILAN MOR.

Italy: 1143 Budapest, Stefánia u. 95; tel. (1) 460-6200; fax (1) 460-6260; e-mail ambasciata.budapest@esteri.it; internet www.ambbudapest.esteri.it; Ambassador MARIA ASSUNTA ACCILI.

Japan: 1125 Budapest, Zalai u. 7; tel. (1) 398-3100; fax (1) 275-1281; e-mail administration@japanembassy.hu; internet www.hu.emb-japan.go.jp; Ambassador TADASHI YAMAMOTO.

Kazakhstan: 1025 Budapest, Kapy u. 59; tel. (1) 275-1300; fax (1) 275-2092; e-mail kazak@t-online.hu; internet www.kazembassy.hu; Ambassador NURBAKH RUSTEMOV.

Korea, Republic: 1062 Budapest, Andrássy u. 109; tel. (1) 462-3080; fax (1) 351-1182; e-mail korcom@t-online.hu; internet hun.mofat.go.kr; Ambassador NAM GWAN-PYO.

Kosovo: 1054 Budapest, Szabadság tér 7; tel. (1) 688-7872; fax (1) 688-7875; e-mail embassy.hungary@ks-gov.net; internet www.ambasada-ks.net/hu; Ambassador SAMI UKELLI.

Kuwait: 1122 Budapest, Székács u. 16; tel. (1) 202-3335; fax (1) 202-3387; e-mail kuwait.emb@kuwaitembassy.hu; Ambassador ABD AL-HAMID AL-FAILAKAWI.

Latvia: 1124 Budapest, Vas Gereben u. 20; tel. (1) 310-7262; fax (1) 249-2901; e-mail embassy.hungary@mfa.gov.lv; Ambassador IMANTS VIESTURS LIEĢIS.

Lebanon: 1112 Budapest, Sasadi u. 160; tel. (1) 249-0900; fax (1) 249-0901; e-mail amblib@t-online.hu; Ambassador NOEL FATTAL.

Libya: 1143 Budapest, Stefánia u. 111; tel. (1) 364-9336; fax (1) 364-9330; Ambassador AHMED MENESI.

Lithuania: 1052 Budapest, Deák Ferenc u. 15; tel. (1) 224-7910; fax (1) 202-3995; e-mail amb.hu@urm.lt; internet hu.mfa.lt; Ambassador (vacant).

Macedonia, former Yugoslav republic: 1062 Budapest, Andrássy u. 130, 1/1-2; tel. (1) 336-0510; fax (1) 315-1921; e-mail budapest@mfa.gov.mk; internet www.missions.gov.mk/budapest; Ambassador DARKO ANGELOV.

Malaysia: 1026 Budapest, Pasaréti u. 29; tel. (1) 488-0810; fax (1) 488-0824; e-mail malbdpest@kln.gov.my; internet www.kln.gov.my/perwakilan/budapest; Ambassador Dato' KAMILAN MAKSOM.

Mexico: 1024 Budapest, Rómer Flóris u. 58; tel. (1) 326-0447; fax (1) 326-0485; e-mail consulmex@t-online.hu; internet embamex.sre.gob.mx/hungria/; Ambassador ISABEL BÁRBARA TÉLLEZ ROSETE.

Moldova: 1024 Budapest, Ady Endre u. 16; tel. (1) 336-3450; fax (1) 209-1195; e-mail budapesta@mfa.md; internet www.ungaria.mfa.md; Ambassador ALEXANDRU CODREANU.

Mongolia: 1022 Budapest II, Bogár u. 14C; tel. (1) 212-5904; fax (1) 212-5731; e-mail mongolemb@t-online.hu; Ambassador TÖGSJARGALYN GANDI.

Montenegro: 1051 Budapest, Arany János 15; tel. (1) 373-0300; fax (1) 269-4475; e-mail hungary@mfa.gov.me; Ambassador MIRSAD BIBOVIĆ.

Morocco: 1026 Budapest, Sodrás u. 11; tel. (1) 391-4310; fax (1) 275-1437; e-mail sifamabudap@t-online.hu; Ambassador NOUREDDINE BENOMAR.

Netherlands: 1022 Budapest, Füge u. 5–7; tel. (1) 336-6300; fax (1) 326-5978; e-mail bdp@minbuza.nl; internet hungary.nlembassy.org; Ambassador GAJUS SCHELTEMA.

Nigeria: 1023 Budapest, Rómer Flóris u. 57; tel. (1) 212-2021; fax (1) 212-2025; e-mail embassy@nigerianembassy.hu; internet www.nigerianembassy.hu; Ambassador EDDY ONUOHA.

Norway: 1015 Budapest, Ostrom u. 13; tel. (1) 325-3300; fax (1) 325-3399; e-mail emb.budapest@mfa.no; internet www.norvegia.hu; Ambassador TOVE SKARSTEIN.

Pakistan: 1125 Budapest, Adonis u. 3A; tel. (1) 355-8017; fax (1) 375-1402; e-mail parepbudapest@yahoo.com; internet www.mofa.gov.pk/hungary; Ambassador IFTEKHAR AZIZ.

Philippines: 1026 Budapest, Gábor Áron u. 58; tel. (1) 391-4300; fax (1) 200-5528; e-mail phbuda@philembassy.hu; internet www.philippineembassy.hu; Ambassador ELEANOR L. JAUCIAN.

Poland: 1068 Budapest, Városligeti fasor 16; tel. (1) 413-8200; fax (1) 351-1722; e-mail budapeszt.amb.sekretariat@msz.gov.pl; internet budapeszt.msz.gov.pl; Ambassador ROMAN KOWALSKI.

Portugal: 1123 Budapest, Alkotás u. 53, MOM Park Bldg C, 4th Floor; tel. (1) 201-7617; fax (1) 201-7619; e-mail embport@t-online.hu; Ambassador ANTÓNIO AUGUSTO JORGE MENDES.

Qatar: 1025 Budapest, Cseppkő u. 27B; tel. (1) 392-1010; fax (1) 392-1020; e-mail budapest@mofa.gov.qa; internet www.qatarembassy.hu; Ambassador ABDULLAH HUSSAIN ALJABER.

Romania: 1146 Budapest, Thököly u. 72; tel. (1) 384-8394; fax (1) 384-5535; e-mail budapesta@mae.ro; internet budapest.mae.ro; Ambassador ALEXANDRU VICTOR MICULA.

Russia: 1062 Budapest, Bajza u. 35; tel. (1) 302-5230; fax (1) 353-4164; e-mail rusemb@t-online.hu; internet www.hungary.mid.ru; Ambassador ALEKSANDR A. TOLKACH.

Saudi Arabia: 1016 Budapest, Bérc u. 16; tel. (1) 436-9500; fax (1) 453-3554; e-mail huemb@mofa.gov.sa; internet www.saudiembassy.org.hu; Ambassador NABIL BIN KHALAF BIN AHMAD ASHOOR.

Serbia: 1068 Budapest, Dózsa György u. 92 B; tel. (1) 322-9838; fax (1) 322-1438; e-mail budapest@amb.srbije.net; internet budapest.mfa.gov.rs; Ambassador RADE DROBAC.

Slovakia: 1143 Budapest, Stefánia u. 22–24; tel. (1) 460-9010; fax (1) 460-9020; e-mail emb.budapest@mzv.sk; internet www.mzv.sk/budapest; Ambassador RASTISLAV KÁČER.

Slovenia: 1025 Budapest, Cseppkő u. 68; tel. (1) 438-5600; fax (1) 325-9187; e-mail vbp@goy.si; internet budimpesta.veleposlanistvo.si; Ambassador KSENIJA ŠKRILEC.

South Africa: 1026 Budapest, Gárdonyi Géza u. 17; tel. (1) 392-0999; fax (1) 200-7277; e-mail budapest.admin@dirco.gov.za; Ambassador J. MARX.

Spain: 1067 Budapest, Eötvös u. 11B; tel. (1) 202-4006; fax (1) 202-4206; e-mail emb.budapest@maec.es; internet www.maec.es/embajadas/budapest/es/home; Ambassador ENRIQUE PASTOR DE GANA.

Sweden: 1027 Budapest, Kapás u. 6–12; tel. (1) 460-6020; fax (1) 460-6021; e-mail ambassaden.budapest@gov.se; internet www.swedenabroad.com/budapest; Ambassador KARIN OLOFSDOTTER.

Switzerland: 1143 Budapest, Stefánia u. 107; tel. (1) 460-7040; fax (1) 384-9492; e-mail bud.vertretung@eda.admin.ch; internet www.swissembassy.hu; Ambassador JEAN-FRANÇOIS PAROZ.

Thailand: 1025 Budapest, Verecke u. 79; tel. (1) 438-4020; fax (1) 438-4023; e-mail info@thaiembassy.hu; internet www.thaiembassy.org/budapest; Ambassador KRIT KRAICHITTI.

Tunisia: 1021 Budapest, Pusztaszeri u. 24A; tel. (1) 336-1616; fax (1) 325-7291; e-mail at.budapest@t-online.hu; Chargé d'affaires a.i. ADNENE DAMERGI.

Turkey: 1062 Budapest, Andrássy u. 123; tel. (1) 478-9100; fax (1) 344-5143; e-mail embassy.budapest@mfa.gov.tr; internet budapest.emb.mfa.gov.tr; Ambassador ŞAKIR FAKILI.

Ukraine: 1125 Budapest, Istenhegyi u. 84B; tel. (1) 422-4120; fax (1) 220-9873; e-mail emb_hu@mfa.gov.ua; internet hungary.mfa.gov.ua; Ambassador YURIY MUSHKA.

United Kingdom: 1051 Budapest, Harmincad u. 6; tel. (1) 266-2888; fax (1) 266-0907; e-mail info@britemb.hu; internet ukinhungary.fco.gov.uk; Ambassador JONATHAN KNOTT.

USA: 1054 Budapest, Szabadság tér 12; tel. (1) 475-4400; fax (1) 475-4764; e-mail publicaffairsbudapest@state.gov; internet hungary.usembassy.gov; Chargé d'affaires a.i. M. ANDRÉ GOODFRIEND.

Venezuela: 1051 Budapest, Szegfű u. 6; tel. (1) 326-0460; fax (1) 326-0450; e-mail embavenezhu@t-online.hu; Ambassador RAÚL JOSÉ BETANCOURT SEELAND.

Viet Nam: 1146 Budapest, Thököly u. 41; tel. (1) 342-5583; fax (1) 352-8798; e-mail vp-budapest@mofa.gov.vn; internet www.vietnamembassy-hungary.org; Ambassador NGÔ DUY NGO.

Yemen: 1026 Budapest, Bimbó út 179/a; tel. (1) 212-3991; fax (1) 212-3883; e-mail yemen22may@t-online.hu.

Judicial System

The system of court procedure in Hungary is based on an act that came into effect in 1953 and that has since been updated frequently, and was revised by the Constitution that entered into effect in 2012, and further in 2013. Notably, on the latter occasion, all rulings of the Constitutional Court taken prior before the introduction of the 2012 Constitution were deemed to be of no legal effect.

The system of jurisdiction is based on local courts, labour courts, county courts (or the Metropolitan Court) and the Kúria. In the legal remedy system of two instances, appeals against the decisions of city and district courts can be lodged with the competent county court and the Metropolitan Court of Budapest, respectively. Against the judgment of first instance of the latter, appeal is to be lodged with the Kúria.

The President of the Kúria, which is the supreme judicial body, is elected from among its members by the National Assembly for a period of nine years. Judges are appointed by the President of Hungary for an indefinite period, but may not serve beyond the legal age of retirement. Assessors are elected by the local municipal councils.

In the interest of ensuring legality and a uniform application of the law, the Kúria exercises a principled guidance over the jurisdiction of courts. Judges are independent and subject only to the law and other legal regulations.

The Minister of Public Administration and Justice supervises the general activities of courts. The Supreme Prosecutor is elected by the National Assembly upon the recommendation of the President of Hungary.

Kúria: 1055 Budapest, Markó u. 16; tel. (1) 268-4500; fax (1) 268-4740; e-mail kuria@kuria.birosag.hu; internet www.kuria-birosag.hu; Pres. Dr PÉTER DARÁK.

Supreme Prosecutor: Dr PÉTER POLT.

Constitutional Court (Alkotmánybíróság): 1015 Budapest, Donáti u. 35–45; tel. (1) 488-3100; fax (1) 212-1170; internet www.mkab.hu; Pres. Dr PÉTER PACZOLAY.

Religion

CHRISTIANITY

The Roman Catholic Church

Hungary comprises four archdioceses, nine dioceses (including one for Catholics of the Byzantine Rite), one apostolic exarchate of the Byzantine Rite and one territorial abbacy (directly responsible to the Holy See).

Bishops' Conference: 1071 Budapest, Városligeti fasor 45, POB 79; tel. (1) 342-6959; fax (1) 342-6957; e-mail pkt@katolikus.hu; internet www.katolikus.hu; Pres. Cardinal PÉTER ERDŐ (Archbishop of Esztergom-Budapest).

Archbishop of Eger: Most Rev. CSABA TERNYÁK, 3301 Eger, Széchenyi u. 1; tel. (36) 517-589; fax (36) 517-751.

Archbishop of Esztergom-Budapest: Cardinal PÉTER ERDŐ, 1014 Budapest, Úri u. 62; tel. (33) 225-2590; fax (33) 202-5458; e-mail egombp@katolikus.hu.

Archbishop of Kalocsa-Kecskemét: Most Rev. BALÁZS BÁBEL, 6301 Kalocsa, Szentháromság tér 1; tel. (78) 462-166; fax (78) 465-279; e-mail hivatal@asztrik.hu.

Archbishop of Veszprém: Most Rev. GYULA MÁRFI, 8201 Veszprém, Vár u. 19; tel. (88) 462-088; fax (88) 466-287; e-mail ersekseg@ersekseg.veszprem.hu.

Apostolic Exarch of Miskolc for Catholics of the Byzantine Rite in the Hungarian Territories: OROSZ ATANÁZ (Titular Bishop of Panium), 4400 Nyíregyháza, Bethlen Gábor u. 5; tel. (42) 415-901; fax (42) 415-911.

Protestant Churches

Evangelical Lutheran Church in Hungary (Magyarországi Evangélikus Egyház): 1085 Budapest, Üllöi u. 24; tel. (1) 483-2260; fax (1) 486-3554; e-mail szerkesztoseg@lutheran.hu; internet www.lutheran.hu; Presiding Bishop PÉTER GÁNCS; 213,125 mems (2010).

Faith Church (Hit Gyülekezete): 1103 Budapest, Gyömröi u. 69; tel. (1) 432-2700; fax (1) 432-2711; e-mail hit@hit.hu; internet www.hit.hu; f. 1979; charismatic pentecostal church; Senior Pastor SÁNDOR NÉMETH.

Reformed Church in Hungary—Presbyterian (Magyarországi Református Egyház): 1146 Budapest, Abonyi u. 21; tel. (1) 343-7870; e-mail info@reformatus.hu; internet www.reformatus.hu; Pres. of Gen. Synod Bishop Dr GUSZTÁV BÖLCSKEI.

The Eastern Orthodox Church

The Bulgarian, Romanian, Russian and Serbian Orthodox Churches are all represented in Hungary.

ISLAM

There are about 3,000 Muslims in Hungary.

Hungarian Islamic Community (Magyar Iszlám Közösség): 1135 Budapest, Róbert Karoly krt. 104; tel. (30) 272-9865; internet www.magyariszlam.hu; Pres. ZOLTÁN BOLEK.

JUDAISM

The Jewish community in Hungary is estimated to number around 120,000 people. Some 80% of Hungary's Jewish community resides in Budapest.

Federation of Jewish Communities in Hungary (Magyarországi Zsidó Hitközségek Szövetsége): 1075 Budapest, Síp u. 12; tel. and fax (1) 413-5504; internet mazsihisz.hu; 120,000 mems; 40 active synagogues; Orthodox and Conservative; Exec. Dir GUSZTAV ZOLTAI; Chief Rabbi of Hungary ROBERT DEUTSCH.

The Press

Budapest dailies circulate nationally. The most popular are: *Népszabadság*, *Nemzeti Sport* and *Népszava*. *Népszabadság*, the most influential daily, was formerly the central organ of the Hungarian Socialist Workers' Party, but is now independent.

PRINCIPAL DAILIES

24 Óra (24 Hours): 2800 Tatabánya, Fő tér 4; tel. (34) 514-010; fax (34) 514-011; e-mail kemma@kemma.hu; internet www.24ora.hu; Editor-in-Chief ZOLTÁN TAKÁCS; circ. 17,023 (2010).

Békés Megyei Hírlap (Békés County News): 5600 Békéscsaba, Kiss Ernő u. 3; tel. (66) 527-226; fax (66) 527-231; e-mail beol@beol.hu; internet www.bmhirlap.hu; f. 1945; Editor-in-Chief JÁNOS NÁNÁSI; circ. 23,279 (2010).

Blikk: 1082 Budapest, Futó u. 35–37; tel. (1) 460-2400; fax (1) 460-2501; e-mail online@blikk.hu; internet www.blikk.hu; f. 1994; colour tabloid; Editor-in-Chief GERGELY KOMÁROMI; circ. 192,182 (2010).

Délmagyarország (Southern Hungary): 6740 Szeged, Szabadkai 20; tel. (62) 567-800; fax (62) 567-881; e-mail szerkesztoseg@delmagyar.hu; internet www.delmagyar.hu; Editor-in-Chief GÁBOR TÓTH; circ. 27,199 (2010).

Észak-Magyarország (Northern Hungary): 3526 Miskolc, Zsolcai kapu 3; tel. (46) 502-900; fax (46) 501-262; e-mail info@eszak.hu; internet www.eszak.hu; Editor-in-Chief LÁSZLÓ KISS; circ. 44,615 (2010).

Fejér Megyei Hírlap (Fejér County Journal): 8000 Székesfehérvár, Ady Endre u. 15; tel. (22) 542-703; fax (22) 542-719; e-mail szerk@fmh.plt.hu; internet www.fmh.hu; Editor-in-Chief ELEKES ANDRÁS; circ. 37,053 (2010).

Hajdú-Bihari Napló (Hajdú-Bihar Diary): 4031 Debrecen, Balmazújvárosi út 11; tel. (40) 424-424; e-mail info@naplo.hu; internet www.naplo.hu; f. 1944; Editor-in-Chief LÁSZLÓ KISS; circ. 60,000.

Heves Megyei Hírlap (Heves County Journal): 3301 Eger, Trinitárius u. 1; tel. (36) 513-600; e-mail heol@heol.hu; internet www.hevesmegyeihirlap.hu; Editor-in-Chief ISTVÁN STANGA; circ. 15,276 (2010).

Kisalföld: 9021 Győr, Újlak u. 4A; tel. (96) 504-555; fax (96) 504-414; e-mail szerkesztoseg@kisalfold.hu; internet www.kisalfold.hu; Editor-in-Chief CSABA NYERGES; circ. 70,257 (2010).

Magyar Hírlap (Hungarian Journal): 1145 Budapest, Thököly u. 105–107; tel. (1) 887-3230; fax (1) 887-3253; e-mail levelezes@magyarhirlap.hu; internet www.magyarhirlap.hu; f. 1968; Editor-in-Chief ISTVÁN STEFKA; circ. 13,858 (2010).

Magyar Nemzet (Hungarian Nation): Budapest; tel. (1) 476-2131; fax (1) 215-3197; e-mail szerk@mno.hu; internet www.mno.hu; Editor-in-Chief GÁBOR ÉLŐ; circ. 48,877 (2010).

Metropol: 1134 Budapest, Tüzér u. 39-41; tel. (1) 431-6422; fax (1) 431-6401; e-mail g.izbeki@metropol.hu; internet www.metropol.hu; fmrly *Metro*, current name adopted in Aug. 2008; five issues a week; distributed free of charge; Editor-in-Chief GÁBOR IZBÉKI; circ. 274,105 (2010).

Napló (Diary): 8200 Veszprém, Almádi u. 3; 8201 Veszprém, POB 161; tel. (20) 241-1655; fax (88) 579-432; e-mail bartak.peter@naplo.plt.hu; internet veol.hu; Editor-in-Chief PÉTER BARTÁK; circ. 40,744 (2010).

Nemzeti Sport (National Sport): 1082 Budapest, Futó u. 35-37; tel. (1) 460-2600; fax (1) 460-2601; e-mail szerkesztoseg@nemzetisport.hu; internet www.nemzetisport.hu; Editor-in-Chief JÓZSEF BUZGÓ; circ. 69,607 (2010).

Népszabadság (People's Freedom): 1591 Budapest, POB; tel. (1) 460-2740; fax (1) 436-4619; e-mail szerkesztoseg@nepszabadsag.hu; internet www.nol.hu; f. 1942; independent; Editor LEVENTE TÓTH (acting); circ. 72,502 (2010).

Népszava (Voice of the People): 1146 Budapest, Thököly u. 127; tel. (1) 688-7030; fax (1) 477-9033; e-mail online@nepszava.hu; internet www.nepszava.hu; f. 1873; Editor PÉTER NÉMETH; circ. 19,099 (2010).

Petőfi Népe: 1122 Budapest, Városmajor u. 11; tel. (76) 518-200; e-mail baon@baon.hu; internet www.petofinepe.hu; Editor-in-Chief ERNŐ KIRÁLY; circ. 27,938 (2010).

Somogyi Hírlap (Somogy Journal): 7400 Kaposvár, Kontrássy u. 2A; tel. (82) 528-104; fax (82) 528-155; e-mail sonline@sonline.hu; internet www.somogyihirlap.hu; Editor ATTILA CZENE; circ. 25,478 (2010).

Tolnai Népújság (Tolna News): 7100 Szekszárd, Liszt Ferenc tér 3; tel. (74) 511-510; fax (74) 511-500; e-mail teol@teol.hu; internet www.tolnainepujsag.hu; Editor-in-Chief FERENC NIMMERFROH; circ. 16,601 (2010).

Új Dunántúli Napló: 1122 Budapest, Városmajor u. 11; tel. (72) 505-060; fax (72) 505-034; e-mail hirportal_fejlesztes@axelspringer.hu; internet www.dunantulinaplo.hu; f. 1948; Editor FERENC NIMMERFROH; circ. 34,677.

Új Néplap (New People's Paper): 5000 Szolnok, Mészáros Lőrinc út 2; tel. (56) 516-753; e-mail szoljon@szoljon.hu; internet www.ujneplap.hu; Editor-in-Chief ATTILA MOLNÁR; circ. 22,338 (2010).

Vas Népe (Vas People): 9700 Szombathely, Moszkva tér 40; tel. (94) 528-309; fax (94) 522-596; e-mail vasnepe@vn.plt.hu; internet www.vasnepe.hu; Editor-in-Chief MIKLÓS HALMÁGYI; circ. 48,672 (2010).

Zalai Hírlap (Zala Journal): 8901 Zalaegerszeg, Ady Endre u. 62; tel. (92) 502-231; fax (92) 502-240; e-mail zalaihirlap@zh.plt.hu; internet www.zalaihirlap.hu; Editor-in-Chief ZSOLT VIRRASZTÓ; circ. 47,979 (2010).

WEEKLIES

The Budapest Times/Budapester Zeitung: 1037 Budapest, Kunigunda útja 18; tel. (1) 453-0752; fax (1) 240-7583; e-mail erlag@bzt.hu; internet www.budapesttimes.hu; internet www.budapester.hu; f. 1999 (*Budapester Zeitung*); f. 2003 (*The Budapest Times*); English and German edns; Editors ALLAN BOYKO (*The Budapest Times*), JAN MAINKA (*Budapester Zeitung*).

Élet és Irodalom (Life and Literature): 1089 Budapest, Rezsö tér 15; tel. (1) 303-9211; fax (1) 303-9241; e-mail es@es.hu; internet www.es.hu; f. 1957; literary and political; Editor ZOLTÁN KOVÁCS; circ. 22,000.

Élet és Tudomány (Life and Science): 1088 Budapest, Bródy u. 16; tel. (1) 327-8950; fax (1) 327-8969; e-mail eltud@eletestudomany.hu; internet www.eletestudomany.hu; f. 1946; popular science; Editor-in-Chief ÁKOS GÓZON; circ. 20,000.

Evangélikus Élet (Evangelical Life): 1085 Budapest, Üllői u. 24; tel. (1) 317-1108; fax (1) 486-1195; e-mail evelet@lutheran.hu; internet www.evangelikuselet.hu; f. 1933; Evangelical Lutheran Church newspaper; Editor KÁROLY T. PINTÉR; circ. 4,000 (2012).

Figyelő (Observer): 1053 Budapest, Kecskeméti u. 5; tel. (1) 437-3957; fax (1) 437-1420; e-mail online@figyelo.hu; internet www.figyelo.hu; f. 1957; Thursdays; business; Editor-in-Chief MIKLÓS KIS; circ. 15,932 (2010).

Heti Világgazdaság (World Economy Weekly): 1037 Budapest, Montevideo u. 14; tel. (1) 436-2000; fax (1) 436-2045; e-mail hvg.hu@hvg.hu; internet www.hvg.hu; f. 1979; Editor GÁBOR GAVRA.

Ľudové Noviny (People's News): 1135 Budapest, Csata u. 17; tel. (1) 878-1431; fax (1) 878-1432; e-mail ludove@luno.hu; internet www.luno.hu; in Slovak; for Slovaks in Hungary; Editor IVETT HORVÁTHOVÁ; circ. 1,700.

Magyar Mezőgazdaság (Hungarian Agriculture): 1141 Budapest, Mírtusz u. 2; tel. (1) 470-0411; fax (1) 470-0410; e-mail kiado@magyarmezogazdasag.hu; internet www.magyarmezogazdasag.hu; f. 1946; Editors LÁSZLÓ BÁRDOS, DÁNIEL HAFNER; circ. 24,000.

Neue Zeitung (New Paper): 1062 Budapest, Lendvay u. 22; tel. and fax (1) 302-6877; e-mail neuezeitung@t-online.hu; internet www.neue-zeitung.hu; f. 1957; in German; Editor-in-Chief JOHANN SCHÜTH; circ. 2,000 (2014).

Reformátusok Lapja: 1113 Budapest, Tas vezér u. 13; tel. (1) 217-6809; fax (1) 217-8386; e-mail szerk@reflap.hu; internet www.reflap.hu; f. 1957; Reformed Church paper for the laity; Editor-in-Chief and Publr LÁSZLÓ T. NÉMETH.

RTV Részletes (Radio and TV News): 1801 Budapest; tel. (1) 328-7905; fax (1) 328-7475; e-mail info@rtvreszletes.hu; internet www.rtvreszletes.hu; f. 1924; circ. 50,000 (2013).

Szabad Föld (Free Earth): 1036 Budapest, Lajos u. 48–66; tel. (1) 489-8800; e-mail info@szabadfold.hu; internet www.szabadfold.hu; f. 1945; Editor LÁSZLÓ HORVÁTH; circ. 720,000.

Új Ember (New Man): 1053 Budapest, Kossuth Lajos u. 1; tel. (1) 317-3933; fax (1) 317-3471; e-mail ujember@katolikus.hu; internet ujember.katolikus.hu; f. 1945; weekly; Roman Catholic; Editor TAMÁS PAPP; circ. 40,000.

OTHER PERIODICALS

(published monthly, unless otherwise indicated)

Beszélő (The Speaker): 1364 Budapest, POB 143; tel. (1) 756-4416; e-mail beszelo@enternet.hu; internet beszelo.c3.hu; f. 1981; political and cultural; Editor-in-Chief LÁSZLÓ NEMÉNYI.

Budapest Business Journal (BBJ): 1022 Budapest, Alsó-Törökvész u. 9; tel. (1) 398-0344; fax (1) 398-0345; e-mail recepcio@amedia.hu; internet www.bbj.hu; every two weeks; English; Man. Editor PATRICIA FISCHER; circ. 9,226 (2010).

Ezermester 2000 (Handyman 2000): 1145 Budapest, Mexikói u. 35A; tel. (1) 222-6392; fax (1) 220-9065; e-mail ezermester@ezermester.hu; internet www.ezermester2000.hu; f. 1957; do-it-yourself magazine; Editor JÓZSEF PERÉNYI; circ. 50,000.

Gramofon—Klasszikus: 1023 Budapest, Fergeteg u. 11; tel. (1) 430-2870; fax (1) 436-0101; e-mail kovacs.veronika@gramofon.hu; internet www.gramofon.hu; f. 1996; classical, jazz and 'world' music; 4 a year; Editor-in-Chief TAMÁS VÁRKONYI; circ. 3,000 (2009).

Közgazdasági Szemle (Economic Review): 1112 Budapest, Budaörsi u. 45; tel. (1) 319-3165; fax (1) 319-3166; e-mail kszemle@econ.core.hu; internet www.kszemle.hu; f. 1954; publ. by Cttee for Economic Sciences of Hungarian Academy of Sciences; Editor-in-Chief TAMÁS HALM; circ. 1,000.

Magyar Közlöny (Official Gazette): 1055 Budapest, Kossuth Lajos tér 4; tel. (1) 112-1236; e-mail info.magyarkozlony@kim.gov.hu; internet kozlony.magyarorszag.hu; publ. by Office of the Prime Minister; Chief of Editorial Bd Dr ANDRÁS LEVENTE GÁL; circ. 90,000.

Magyar Tudomány (Hungarian Science): Hungarian Academy of Sciences, 1051 Budapest, Nádor u. 7; tel. and fax (1) 317-9524; e-mail matud@hefka.iif.hu; internet www.matud.iif.hu; f. 1846; multi-disciplinary science review; Chief Editor VILMOS CSÁNYI.

Új Élet (New Life): Magyarországi Zsidó Hitközségek Szövetsége, 1075 Budapest, Síp u. 12; tel. (1) 413-5564; fax 413-5504; f. 1945; every two weeks; Jewish interest; Editor Dr PÉTER KARDOS; circ. 5,000.

NEWS AGENCIES

HavariaPress News Agency: 1152 Budapest, Vécsey u. 15; tel. (1) 321-5538; e-mail havaria@havaria.hu; internet www.havariapress.hu; f. 1994; independent.

Hungarian News Agency Co (Magyar Távirati Iroda Rt—MTI): 1016 Budapest, Naphegy tér 8; tel. (1) 441-9000; fax (1) 318-8297; e-mail info@mti.hu; internet www.mti.hu; f. 1880; 20 brs in Hungary; 10 bureaux abroad; CEO ISTVÁN GALAMBOS.

Independent News Agency (Független Hírügynökség—FH): 1137 Budapest, Szent István Park 3; tel. (1) 382-0310; fax (1) 382-0309; e-mail info@fuggetlenhir.hu; f. 2004; Editor-in-Chief PÉTER KÖVESDI.

PRESS ASSOCIATIONS

Hungarian Newspaper Publishers' Association: 1016 Budapest, Naphegy tér 8; tel. (1) 368-8674; fax (1) 212-5025; e-mail mle@t-online.hu; internet www.mle.org.hu; f. 1990; Gen. Sec. KATALIN HAVAS; 47 mems.

National Association of Hungarian Journalists (Magyar Újságírók Országos Szövetsége—MÚOSZ): 1064 Budapest, Vörösmarty u. 47A; tel. (1) 478-9040; e-mail info@muosz.hu; internet www.muosz.hu; f. 1896; Pres. TÓTH KÁROLY; 7,000 mems.

Publishers

PRINCIPAL PUBLISHING HOUSES

Akadémiai Kiadó: 1117 Budapest, Prielle Kornélia u. 19/D; tel. (1) 464-8200; fax (1) 464-8201; e-mail ak@akkrt.hu; internet www.akkrt.hu; f. 1828; economics, humanities, social, political, natural and technical sciences, dictionaries, textbooks and journals; Hungarian and English; Dir BUCSI SZABÓ ZSOLT.

Corvina Kiadó: 1086 Budapest, Dankó u. 4–8; tel. (1) 411-2410; fax (1) 318-4410; e-mail corvina@lira.hu; internet www.corvinakiado.hu; f. 1955; art and educational books, general non-fiction, tourist guides and cookery books; Dir LÁSZLÓ KUNOS.

EMB Music Publisher: 1132 Budapest, Victor Hugo u. 11–15; tel. (1) 236-1100; fax (1) 236-1101; e-mail emb@emb.hu; internet www.emb.hu; f. 1950; sheet music and books on musical subjects; Dir ANTAL BORONKAY.

Európa Könyvkiadó: 1055 Budapest, Kossuth Lajos tér 13–15; tel. (1) 353-2328; fax (1) 331-4162; e-mail info@europakiado.hu; internet www.europakiado.hu; f. 1946; world literature translated into Hungarian; Dir IMRE BARNA.

Helikon Kiadó: 1027 Budapest, Horvát u. 14–24/V; tel. (1) 225-4300; fax (1) 225-4320; e-mail helikon@helikon.hu; internet www.helikon.hu; bibliophile books; Dir KATALIN BERGER.

Kossuth Kiadó: 1043 Budapest, Csányi László u. 36; tel. (1) 370-0607; fax (1) 370-0602; f. 1944; social sciences, educational and philosophy publs, information technology books; Man. ANDRÁS SÁNDOR KOCSIS.

Közgazdasági és Jogi Könyvkiadó: Budapest; tel. (1) 112-6430; fax (1) 111-3210; f. 1955; business, economics, law, sociology, psychology, tax, politics, education, dictionaries; Man. Dir DAVID G. YOUNG.

Magvető Könyvkiadó: 1806 Budapest, Dankó u. 4–8; 1086 Budapest, POB 123; tel. (1) 235-5032; e-mail magveto@lira.hu; internet www.lira.hu/kiado/magveto; f. 1955; literature; Dir GÉZA MORCSÁNYI.

Medicina Könyvkiadó: 1072 Budapest, Rákóczi u. 16; tel. (1) 312-2650; fax (1) 312-2450; e-mail medkiad@euroweb.hu; internet www.medicina-kiado.hu; f. 1957; books on medicine, health care, tourism; Dir FRIGYESNÉ FARKASVÖLGYI.

Mezőgazda Kiadó: 1165 Budapest, Koronafürt u. 44; tel. (1) 407-1018; fax (1) 407-1012; e-mail mezoig@mezogazdakiado.hu; internet www.mezogazdakiado.hu; ecology, natural sciences, environmental protection, food industry; Man. Dr LAJOS LELKES.

Móra Könyvkiadó Zrt: 1134 Budapest, Váci u. 19; tel. (1) 320-4740; fax (1) 320-5382; e-mail mora@mora.hu; internet www.mora.hu; f. 1950; fiction and non-fiction; Pres. Dr JÁNOS JANIKOVSZKY.

Műszaki Könyvkiadó: 1033 Budapest, Szentendre u. 89–93; tel. (1) 437-2405; fax (1) 437-2404; e-mail lakatosz@muszakikiado.hu; internet www.muszakikiado.hu; f. 1955; scientific and technical, vocational, and general textbooks; Man. SÁNDOR BÉRCZI.

Nemzeti Tankönyvkiadó (National Textbook Publishing House): 1143 Budapest, Szobránc u. 6–8; tel. (1) 460-1800; fax (1) 460-1869; e-mail public@ntk.hu; internet www.ntk.hu; f. 1949; school and university textbooks, pedagogical literature and language books; Gen. Man. JÓZSEF PÁLFI.

PUBLISHERS' ASSOCIATION

Hungarian Publishers' and Booksellers' Association (Magyar Könyvkiadók és Könyvterjesztők Egyesülése): 1073 Budapest, Kertész u. 41 I/4; 1367 Budapest, POB 130; tel. (1) 343-2540; fax (1) 343-2541; e-mail mkke@mkke.hu; internet www.mkke.hu; f. 1795; Pres. LÁSZLÓ PÉTER ZENTAI; Sec.-Gen. MARTINA BUDAY.

Broadcasting and Communications

TELECOMMUNICATIONS

At May 2011 there were 11 fixed-line telephone operators and three providers of mobile cellular telecommunications services in Hungary. At that time 60.4% of households had a fixed-line telephone, while the rate of mobile network subscription was equivalent to 118% of the population.

Magyar Telekom: 1013 Budapest, Krisztina krt 55; tel. (1) 458-0000; fax (1) 458-7176; e-mail investor.relations@telekom.hu; internet www.telekom.hu; f. 1991 as Matáv Hungarian Telecommunications Co; name changed as above in May 2005; 59.2% owned by Deutsche Telekom AG (Germany); merged with T-Mobile Magyarország in Dec. 2005; mobile telecommunications and internet service provider; CEO CHRISTOPHER MATTHEISEN; 11,653 employees (2012).

Telenor Magyarorszag (Telenor Hungary): 2045 Törökbálint, Pannon u. 1; tel. (1) 464-6000; fax (1) 464-6100; e-mail sajto@telenor.hu; internet www.telenor.hu; f. 1994 as Pannon GSM Telecommunications; 100% stake acquired by Telenor (Norway) in 2002; rebranded as above in May 2010; mobile telecommunications and internet service provider; CEO CHRISTOPHER LASKA; 3.5m. subscribers (2013).

Vodafone Hungary: 1476 Budapest, POB 350; tel. (1) 288-3288; fax (1) 288-3149; e-mail ugyfelszolgalat.hu@vodafone.com; internet www.vodafone.hu; f. 1999; mobile cellular telecommunications and internet service provider; owned by Vodafone (UK); Chair. Dr GYÖRGY BECK; Chief Exec. DIEGO MASSIDDA; more than 2m. subscribers (May 2007).

Regulatory Authority

National Media and Communications Authority (Nemzeti Média- és Hírközlési Hatóság): 1525 Budapest, POB 75; tel. (1) 457-7100; fax (1) 356-5520; e-mail info@nmhh.hu; internet www.nmhh.hu; f. 2010, by the merger of the National Communications Authority and the National Radio and Television Commission; responsible to the legislature; Pres. Dr MONIKA KARAS.

BROADCASTING

Antenna Hungária Rt: 1119 Budapest, Petzvál József u. 31–33; tel. (1) 464-2464; fax (1) 464-2525; e-mail antennah@ahrt.hu; internet www.ahrt.hu; f. 1998; radio and television; 100% owned by TDF, SAS (France); Chief Exec. ANDRÁS PILLER.

Radio

Hungarian Radio (Magyar Rádió zrt): 1016 Budapest, Naphegy tér 8; tel. (1) 328-7000; fax (1) 328-7447; e-mail info@radio.hu; internet www.radio.hu; f. 1925; stations: Radio Kossuth, Radio Petőfi, Radio Bartók (classical music), MR4 (regional and minority interest), MR5 (parliamentary sessions) and MR6 (regional programmes); CEO ISTVÁN JÓNÁS.

Radio C: 1086 Budapest, Teleki László tér 7; tel. (1) 492-0240; e-mail radioc@radioc.hu; internet www.radioc.hu; f. 2001; Roma radio station; Man. Dir FÁTYOL TIVADAR.

Television

Hungarian Television Rt (Magyar Televízió): 1054 Budapest, Naphegy tér 8; tel. (1) 441-9353; fax (1) 373-4133; e-mail ujmedia@mti.hu; internet premier.mtv.hu; f. 1957; state-owned; three channels (M1, M2, M3); Editor ALEXANDER KORDA.

Finance

(cap. = capital; res = reserves; dep. = deposits; m. = million; brs = branches; amounts in forint)

In 2010 there were 30 commercial banks in operation in Hungary. Responsibility for bank supervision is held by the Central Bank of Hungary (into which the Hungarian Financial Supervisory Authority was absorbed in October 2013).

BANKING

Central Bank

Central Bank of Hungary (Magyar Nemzeti Bank): 1850 Budapest, Szabadság tér 8–9; tel. (1) 429-2600; fax (1) 428-8000; e-mail info@mnb.hu; internet www.mnb.hu; f. 1924; bank of issue; conducts international transactions; supervises banking system; Hungarian Financial Supervisory Authority merged with the Central Bank in October 2013; cap. 10,000m., res 261,768m., dep. 4,912,097m. (Dec. 2009); Gov. Dr GYÖRGY MATOLCSY.

Other Banks

Bank of Hungarian Savings Co-operatives (Magyar Takarékszövetkezeti Bank): 1122 Budapest, Pethényi köz 10, POB 775; tel. (1) 457-8907; fax (1) 225-4280; e-mail info@tbank.hu; internet www.takarekbank.hu; f. 1989; 63.72% owned by savings co-operatives, 31.27% owned by DZ Bank AG (Germany); cap. 2,735m., res 5,861m., dep. 40,632m. (Dec. 2012); Chair. of Bd IMRE HARTMANN; CEO PÉTER CSICSÁKY.

Budapest Credit and Development Bank: 1138 Budapest, POB 1852, Váci u. 188; tel. (1) 450-6000; fax (1) 450-6001; e-mail info@budapestbank.hu; internet www.budapestbank.hu; f. 1987; cap. 19,346m., res 21,919m., dep. 744,616m. (Dec. 2012); 99.7% owned by GE Capital International Financing Corpn (USA); Pres. and CEO SEAN MORRISSEY; 101 brs.

CIB Bank Ltd: 1027 Budapest, Medve u. 4–14, POB 394; tel. (1) 423-1000; fax (1) 489-6500; e-mail cib@cib.hu; internet www.cib.hu; f. 1979; 89.1% owned by Intesa Holding International, SA (Luxembourg); name changed as above Jan. 2008, following merger with Inter-Európa Bank Zrt; cap. 145,000m., res 101,692m., dep. 1,745,854m. (Dec. 2012); Chair. Dr GYÖRGY SURÁNYI; CEO TOMAS SPURNY.

Citibank Zrt: 1367 Budapest, POB 123; tel. (1) 374-5000; fax (1) 374-5100; internet www.citibank.hu; f. 1985; owned by Citibank Europe Plc; cap. 13,005m., res 7,295m., dep. 364,493m. (Dec. 2006); Country Chief Officer SAJJAD RAZVI.

Commerzbank Zrt: 1054 Budapest, Széchenyi rkp 8; tel. (1) 374-1000; fax (1) 269-4574; e-mail info.budapest@commerzbank.hu; internet www.commerzbank.hu; f. 1993; cap. 2,467m., res 19,976m., dep. 252,838m. (Dec. 2011); Pres. and Chair. of Supervisory Bd WILHELM NÜSE; Chair. and Chief Exec. KOZMA ANDRÁS.

Erste Bank Hungary Zrt: 1138 Budapest, Népfürdo u. 24–26; tel. (1) 298-0221; fax (1) 272-5160; e-mail uszolg@erstebank.hu; internet www.erstebank.hu; f. 1987; present name adopted 1998; absorbed Postbank and Savings Bank Corpn—Postabank in 2004; 99.9% owned by Erste Group Bank (Austria); cap. 101,000m., res 189,248m., dep. 2,457,567m. (Dec. 2012); CEO EDIT PAPP; 143 brs.

Hungarian Export-Import Bank (EXIMBANK): 1065 Budapest, Nagymezö u. 46–48; tel. (1) 374-9100; fax (1) 269-4476; e-mail eximh@eximbank.hu; internet www.eximbank.hu; f. 1994; state-owned; cap. 10,100m., res 7,154m., total assets 258,569m. (Dec. 2012); CEO ROLAND NÁTRÁN.

K&H Bank Zrt: 1095 Budapest, Lechner Ödön fasor 9; tel. (1) 328-9000; fax (1) 328-9696; e-mail bank@kh.hu; internet www.kh.hu; f. 1987 as Kereskedelmi és Hitelbank Nyrt; name changed as above 2008; owned by KBC Bank NV (Belgium); cap. 140,978m., res 61,329m., dep. 1,999,026m. (Dec. 2012); Chair. DANNY DE RAYMAEKER; CEO HENDRIK SCHEERLINCK; 219 brs.

MagNet Bank—Magyar Közösségi Bank (Hungarian Community Bank): 1062 Budapest, Andrássy u. 98; tel. (1) 428-8888; fax (1) 428-8889; e-mail info@magnetbank.hu; internet www.magnetbank.hu; f. 2006; fmrly HBW Express Bank; present name adopted 2010; cap. 2,000m., res 2,129m., dep. 76,152m. (Dec. 2012); Chair. ZSOLT FÁY.

MFB Hungarian Development Bank (Magyar Fejlesztési Bank): 1051 Budapest, Nádor u. 31; tel. (1) 428-1400; fax (1) 428-1490; e-mail mfb@mfb.hu; internet www.mfb.hu; f. 1991 as an investment company; authorized as a bank 1993; name changed as above 2007; state-owned; cap. 114,500m., res 112,529m., dep. 563,966m. (Dec. 2012); Pres. DÁNIEL LONTAI; CEO CSABA NAGY.

MKB Bank Zrt: 1056 Budapest, Váci u. 38; tel. (1) 327-8600; fax (1) 327-8700; e-mail mkb@mkb.hu; internet www.mkb.hu; f. 1950; commercial banking; 89.6% owned by Bayerische Landesbank (Germany); absorbed Konzumbank in 2003; present name adopted 2007; cap. 108,936m., res 224,350m., dep. 1,800,817m. (Dec. 2012); Chair. and CEO TAMÁS ERDEI; 80 brs.

OTP Bank (Országos Takarékpénztár Bank): 1051 Budapest, Nádor u. 16; tel. (1) 473-5000; fax (1) 473-5955; e-mail otpbank@otpbank.hu; internet www.otpbank.hu; f. 1949 as Hungarian National Savings Bank; name changed as above 2006; savings deposits, credits, foreign transactions; privatized in 1996; cap. 28,000m., res –98,418m., dep. 7,352,490m. (Dec. 2012); Chair. and Chief Exec. Dr SÁNDOR CSÁNYI; 405 brs.

Raiffeisen Bank Zrt: 1054 Budapest, Akadémia u. 6; tel. (1) 484-4400; fax (1) 484-4444; e-mail info@raiffeisen.hu; internet www.raiffeisen.hu; f. 1986; present name adopted 1999; 100% owned by Raiffeisen Banking Group (Austria); cap. 165,023m., res –4,405m., dep. 1,726,187m. (Dec. 2012); Pres. Dr HERBERT STEPIC; Man. Dir Dr PÉTER FELCSUTI; 120 brs.

UniCredit Bank Hungary Zrt: 1054 Budapest, Szabadság tér 5–6; tel. (1) 269-0812; fax (1) 353-4959; e-mail info@unicreditbank.hu; internet www.unicreditbank.hu; f. 2001 by merger of Bank Austria Creditanstalt Hungary RT and Hypovereinsbank Hungary RT; name changed as above 2007; 100% owned by Bank Austria

Creditanstalt AG; cap. 24,118m., res 47,308m., dep. 1,360,433m. (Dec. 2012); CEO Dr MIHÁLY PATAI.

STOCK EXCHANGE

Budapest Stock Exchange (Budapesti Értéktőzsde—BET): 1062 Budapest, Andrássy u. 93; tel. (1) 429-6700; fax (1) 429-6800; e-mail info@bse.hu; internet www.bse.hu; f. 1991; partly owned by a consortium comprising: UniCredit Bank Hungary (25.2%), Wiener Börse (Vienna Stock Exchange, Austria, 12.5%) and Österreichische Kontrollbank AG (Austria, 12.5%); allied with the Wiener Börse from May 2004; Pres. MIHÁLY PATAI; Chief Exec. GYÖRGY MOHAI.

INSURANCE

In 2013 there were 32 insurance companies. The following are among the most important:

AB-AEGON Általános Biztosító: 1091 Budapest, Üllői u. 1; tel. (1) 477-4800; fax (1) 476-5710; e-mail ugyfelszolg@aegon.hu; internet www.aegon.hu; f. 1949; present name adopted 1992; pensions, life and property insurance, insurance of agricultural plants, co-operatives, foreign insurance, etc.; Gen. Man. Dr GÁBOR KEPECS.

Allianz Hungária Insurance Co (Hungária Biztosító): 1087 Budapest, Könyves Kálmán u. 48-52; tel. (1) 301-6565; fax (1) 301-6100; e-mail ugyfelszolgalat@allianz.hu; internet www.allianz.hu; f. 1986; handles international insurance, industrial and commercial insurance, and motor car, marine, life, household, accident and liability insurance; cap. 4,266m.; Chair. and Chief Exec. PÉTER KISBENEDEK.

ERSTE Vienna Insurance Group Biztosító Zrt: 1134 Budapest, Váci u. 24-26; tel. (1) 484-1778; fax (1) 484-1799; e-mail info@erstebiztosito.hu; internet erstebiztosito.hu; f. 2000; life insurance; Chair. GÁBOR LEHEL; Pres. and CEO ZSOLT RAVECZKY.

Generali Esoport: 1066 Budapest, Teréz 39; tel. (1) 301-7100; fax (1) 452-3505; e-mail generali@generali.hu; internet www.generali.hu; f. 1832; CEO MIHÁLY ERDŐS.

Grawe Életbiztosító Zrt: 1126 Budapest, Istenhegyi u. 9B; tel. (1) 202-1211; fax (1) 355-5530; e-mail info@grawe.hu; internet www.grawe.hu; Pres. Dr OTHMAR EDERER.

ING Biztosító Zrt: 1068 Budapest, Dózsa György u. 84B; tel. (1) 255-5757; fax (1) 267-9093; e-mail ing@ing.hu; internet www.ing.hu; f. 2003.

K&H Insurance: 1068 Budapest, Benczúr u. 47; tel. (1) 461-5200; fax (1) 461-5276; e-mail biztosito@kh.hu; internet www.kh.hu; f. 2006; both life and non-life.

MetLife: 1138 Budapest, Népfürdő u. 22; tel. (40) 444-445; fax (1) 391-1660; e-mail info@metlife.hu; internet www.metlife.hu; f. 1996; 100% owned by MetLife, Inc.

UNION Biztosító: 1082 Budapest, Baross u. 1; tel. (1) 486-4343; fax (1) 486-4390; e-mail ugyfelszolgalat@unionbiztosito.hu; internet www.unionbiztosito.hu; f. 2000; mem. of Vienna Insurance Gp (registered in Austria); Pres. and CEO GÁBOR LEHEL.

UNIQA Biztosító Zrt: 1134 Budapest, Róbert Károly 70–74; tel. (1) 544-5555; fax (1) 238-6060; e-mail info@uniqa.hu; internet www.uniqa.hu; f. 1990; name changed as above in 2003; Pres. Dr WOLFGANG KINDL; CEO OTHMAR MICHL.

INSURANCE ASSOCIATION

Association of Hungarian Insurance Companies (Magyar Biztosítók Szövetsége—MABISZ): 1062 Budapest, Andrássy u. 100; tel. (1) 318-3473; fax (1) 337-5394; e-mail info@mabisz.hu; internet www.mabisz.hu; f. 1990; Pres. ANETT PANDURICS; Sec.-Gen. Dr DÁNIEL MOLNOS; 26 mem. cos.

Trade and Industry

GOVERNMENT AGENCY

Hungarian State Holding Co (Magyar Nemzeti Vagyonkezelő Zrt.—MNV Zrt): 1133 Budapest, Pozsonyi u. 56; tel. (1) 237-4400; fax (1) 237-4100; e-mail info@mnv.hu; internet www.mnv.hu; f. 2008; Chair. Dr TIBOR HALASI.

NATIONAL CHAMBERS OF COMMERCE AND OF AGRICULTURE

Hungarian Chamber of Agriculture (Magyar Agrárkamara): 1119 Budapest, Fehérvári u. 89-95; tel. (1) 802-6100; fax (1) 802-0600; e-mail info@agrarkamara.hu; internet www.agrarkamara.hu; f. 1994; Pres. Dr FORGÁCS BARNA.

Hungarian Chamber of Commerce and Industry (Magyar Kereskedelmi és Iparkamara): 1055 Budapest, Kossuth Lajos tér 6–8; tel. (1) 474-5100; fax (1) 474-5105; e-mail hcci@hcci.com; internet www.mkik.hu; f. 1850; central org. of the 23 Hungarian county chambers of commerce and industry; based on a system of voluntary membership; over 46,000 mems; Pres. Dr LÁSZLÓ PARRAGH; Sec.-Gen. PÉTER DUNAI.

REGIONAL CHAMBERS OF COMMERCE

There are regional chambers of commerce in each of the 20 principal administrative divisions of Hungary (comprising the 19 counties and the City of Budapest). The following are among the most important:

Borsod-Abaúj-Zemplén County Chamber of Commerce and Industry (Borsod-Abaúj-Zemplén Kereskedelmi és Iparkamara): 3525 Miskolc, Szentpáli u. 1; tel. (46) 501-090; fax (46) 501-099; e-mail bokik@bokik.hu; internet www.bokik.hu; f. 1990; membership of 1,100 cos; Pres. TAMÁS BIHALL.

Budapest Chamber of Industry and Commerce (Budapesti Kereskedelmi és Iparkamara): 1016 Budapest, Krisztina krt 99; tel. (1) 488-2000; e-mail ugyfelszolgalat@bkik.hu; internet www.bkik.hu; f. 1850; Chair. KRISTÓF SZATMÁRY; Sec.-Gen. ERVIN KISS.

Csongrád County Chamber of Commerce and Industry: 6721 Szeged, Párizsi krt 8-12; tel. (62) 426-343; fax (62) 426-149; e-mail info@csmkik.com; internet kamara.dravanet.hu; Pres. PÁL NEMESI; Sec. ZSUZSANNA TRÁSERNÉ OLÁH.

Hajdú-Bihar County Chamber of Commerce and Industry: 4025 Debrecen, Petőfi tér 10; tel. (52) 500-710; fax (52) 500-720; e-mail hbkik@hbkik.hu; internet www.hbkik.hu; Chair. FERENC MIKLÓSSY; Sec. Dr EVA SKULTÉTI.

Pécs-Baranya Chamber of Commerce and Industry: 7625 Pécs, Dr Majorossy I. u. 36; tel. (72) 507-148; fax (72) 507-152; e-mail pbkik@pbkik.hu; internet www.pbkik.hu; Pres. ISTVÁN KÉRI; Sec. TAMÁS SÍKFÔI.

Pest County Chamber of Commerce and Industry (Pest Megyei Kereskedelmi és Iparkamara): 1056 Budapest, Vàci u. 40; tel. (1) 317-7666; fax (1) 317-7755; e-mail titkarsag@pmkik.hu; internet www.pmkik.hu; Chair. Dr ZOLTÁN VERECZKEY; Sec.-Gen. Dr LAJOS KUPCSOK.

EMPLOYERS' ASSOCIATIONS

Confederation of Hungarian Employers and Industrialists (Munkaadók és Gyáriparosok Országos Szövetsége—MGYOSZ): 1055 Budapest, Kossuth L. tér 6–8; tel. (1) 474-2044; fax (1) 474-2065; e-mail mgyosz@mgyosz.hu; internet www.mgyosz.hu; f. 1902; re-est. 1990; 64 member asscns; Sec.-Gen. ISTVÁN WIMMER.

National Asscn of Entrepreneurs and Employers (Vállalkozók és Munkáltatók Országos Szövetsége—VOSZ): 1107 Budapest, Mázsa tér 2–6; tel. (1) 414-2181; fax (1) 414-2180; e-mail center@vosz.hu; internet www.vosz.hu; f. 1988; Sec.-Gen. DÁVID FERENC.

INDUSTRIAL AND TRADE ASSOCIATIONS

Hungarian Industrial Asscn (Magyar Iparszövetség—OKISZ): 1146 Budapest, Thököly u. 58–60; tel. (1) 343-5181; fax (1) 343-5521; e-mail okisz@okiszinfo.hu; internet www.okisz.hu; safeguards interests of over 1,100 mem. enterprises (all private); Pres. ISTVÁN TOKÁR.

HUNICOOP Foreign Trade Co for Industrial Co-operation: 1036 Budapest, Galagonya u. 7; tel. (1) 250-8117; fax (1) 250-8121; e-mail hunicoop@axelero.hu; internet www.hunicoop.hu; agency for foreign cos in Hungary, export and import; Dir GÁBOR TOMBÁCZ.

National Asscn of Industrial Corporations (Ipartestületek Országos Szövetsége—IPOSZ): 1054 Budapest, Kálmán Imre u. 20; tel. (1) 354-3140; e-mail titkarsag@iposz.hu; internet www.iposz.hu; Chair. GYÖRGY SZŰCS; 230 mem. orgs.

National Federation of Agricultural Co-operators and Producers (Mezőgazdasági Szövetkezők és Termelők Országos Szövetsége—MOSZ): 1125 Budapest, Istenhegyi u. 59–61; tel. (1) 332-1163; fax (1) 353-2552; e-mail mosztit@mosz.agrar.hu; internet www.mosz.agrar.hu; f. 1967; present name adopted 1989; Pres. TAMÁS NAGY; Sec.-Gen. GÁBOR HORVÁTH; c. 1,300 mem. orgs.

UTILITIES

Supervisory Organization

Hungarian Energy Office (Magyar Energia Hivatal): 1081 Budapest, II János Pál Pápa tér 7; tel. (1) 459-7777; fax (1) 459-7766; e-mail eh@eh.gov.hu; internet www.eh.gov.hu; f. 1994; regulation and supervision of activities performed by gas and electricity cos, price regulation and protection of consumer interest; Pres. PÉTER HORVÁTH.

Electricity

Budapest Electricity Co (Budapesti Elektromos Művek—ELMŰ): 1132 Budapest, Váci u. 72–74; tel. (1) 238-1000; fax (1) 238-2822; e-mail elmu@elmu.hu; internet www.elmu.hu; f. 1949; transmission and distribution of electricity; CEO Dr MARIE-THERES THIELL; Chair. of Supervisory Bd EMMERICH ENDRESZ; 3,000 employees.

Démász (South Hungarian Power Supply Co): 6720 Szeged, Klauzál tér 9; tel. (62) 565-565; fax (62) 482-500; e-mail info@edf.hu; internet www.edfdemasz.hu; f. 1951; distributes electricity to south-eastern Hungary; Pres. THIERRY LE BOUCHER.

EDF Émász (North Hungarian Electricity Supply Co): 3525 Miskolc, Dózsa Gy, u. 13; tel. (46) 411-875; fax (46) 411-871; e-mail emasz@emasz.hu; internet www.emasz.hu; majority share owned by EDF (France); Chair. Dr MARIE-THÉRÈSE THIELL.

E.ON Hungária Rt: 1051 Budapest, Széchenyi tér 7-8; tel. (1) 472-2300; e-mail info@eon-hungaria.com; internet www.eon-hungaria.com; f. 2000; 86% owned by E.ON Energie AG (Germany); subsidiary electicity supply cos incl. E.ON Del-dunántúli Áramszolgáltató (South-West Hungary), E.ON Észak-dunántúli Áramszolgáltató (North-West Hungary), E.ON Tiszántúli Áramszolgáltató (North-East Hungary); Chair. of Bd of Dirs KONRAD KRAUSER.

Mátrai Power Plant (Erőmű Részvénytársaság) Co: 3271 Visonta, Erőmű u. 11; tel. (37) 334-000; fax (37) 334-016; e-mail matra@mert.hu; internet www.mert.hu; f. 1965; electricity generation; Chair. JÓZSEF VALASKA; 3,645 employees.

MVM Hungarian Electricity Private Limited Company (MVM Magyar Villamos Művek Zrt.—MVM): 1031 Budapest, Szentendrei u. 207-209; tel. (1) 304-2000; fax (1) 202-1246; e-mail mvm@mvm.hu; internet www.mvm.hu; f. 1963; electricity wholesaler; CEO BAJI CSABA.

MVM Paks Nuclear Power Plant Ltd. (MVM Paksi Atomerőmű Zrt.): 7031 Paks, POB 71; tel. (75) 508-833; fax (75) 506-662; e-mail uzemlatogatas@npp.hu; internet www.npp.hu; f. 1992; electrical energy production; CEO ISTVÁN LÁSZLÓ HAMVAS; 2,500 employees.

Vértesi Power Plant (Erőmű) Co: 2841 Oroszlány, POB 23; tel. (34) 360-255; fax (34) 360-882; e-mail vert@vert.hu; internet www.vert.hu; electricity and heat generation; CEO ANDRÁS ZOLTÁN KOVÁCS.

Gas

Főgáz—Fővárosi Gázművek (Budapest Gas) Co: 1081 Budapest, II János Pál Pápa tér 20; tel. (1) 477-1111; fax (1) 477-1277; e-mail kommunikacio@fogaz.hu; internet www.fogaz.hu; f. 1856; gas distribution; Pres. Dr TAMÁS BÁN.

GDF SUEZ Energia Magyarország Zrt.: 6724 Szeged, Pulz u. 44; tel. (62) 569-600; fax (63) 473-943; e-mail ugyfel@degas.hu; internet www.gdfsuez-energia.hu; fmrly Égáz-Dégáz Zrt; present name adopted 2010; gas supply and services; 99.6% owned by Gaz de France (France); CEO PATRICK ECKELERS.

MOL Hungarian Oil and Gas PLC: 1117 Budapest, Október huszonharmadika u. 18; tel. (1) 209-0000; fax (1) 209-0005; e-mail webmaster@mol.hu; internet www.mol.hu; f. 1991; privatized in 1995; petroleum and gas exploration, processing, transportation and distribution; 34,000 employees; Chair. and CEO ZSOLT HERNÁDI.

Tigáz—Tiszántúli Gázszolgáltató (Tiszá Gas) Co: 4200 Hajdúszoboszló, Rákóczi u. 184; tel. (52) 333-338; fax (52) 361-149; e-mail titkarsaga@tigaz.hu; internet www.tigaz.com; f. 1950; majority share owned by ENI S.p.A (Italy); gas distribution in north-eastern regions of Hungary; Chair. of Bd CESARE CUNIBERTO.

TRADE UNIONS

From 1988, and particularly after the restructuring of the former Central Council of Hungarian Trade Unions (SzOT) as the National Confederation of Hungarian Trade Unions (MSzOSz) in 1990, several new union federations were created. Several unions are affiliated to more than one federation, and others are completely independent.

Trade Union Federations

Association of Hungarian Free Trade Unions (Magyar Szabad Szakszervezetek Szövetsége): 1068 Budapest, Városligeti fasor 46–48; tel. (1) 323-2686; fax (1) 323-2651; internet www.mszosz.com; f. 1994; Pres. BÉLA BALOGH.

Autonomous Trade Union Confederation (Autonóm Szakszervezetek Svövetsége): 1068 Budapest, Benczúr u. 45; tel. (1) 413-1934; fax (1) 461-2480; e-mail autonom@t-online.hu; internet www.autonomok.hu; Pres. LAJOS FŐCZE; 137,000 mems (2007).

Democratic League of Independent Trade Unions—LIGA (Független Szakszervezetek Demokratikus Ligája): 1146 Budapest, Ajtósi Dürer sor 27/A; tel. (1) 321-5262; fax (1) 321-5405; e-mail info@liganet.hu; internet www.liganet.hu; f. 1988; Pres. ISTVÁN GASKÓ; 110,000 mems (2011).

Federation of Unions of Intellectual Workers (Értelmiségi Szakszervezeti Tömörülés—ÉSzT): 1066 Budapest, Jókai u. 2; tel. (1) 473-1429; fax (1) 331-4577; e-mail eszt@eszt.hu; internet www.eszt.hu; Pres. Dr LÁSZLÓ KUTI.

National Confederation of Hungarian Trade Unions (Magyar Szakszervezetek Országos Szövetsége—MSzOSz): 1086 Budapest, Magdolna u. 5–7; tel. (1) 323-2660; fax (1) 323-2662; e-mail gykiss@mszosz.hu; internet www.mszosz.hu; f. 1898; reorganized 1990; Pres. Dr LÁSZLÓ SÁNDOR; 400,000 mems (2007).

Transport

RAILWAYS

In 2011 the length of railway lines in use totalled 7,906 km, of which 2,996 km were electrified. There is an underground railway in Budapest, which has a network of four lines totalling some 40 km.

Budapest Transport Company (BKV): 1072 Budapest, Akácfa u. 15; tel. (1) 461-6500; fax (1) 461-6557; e-mail bkv@bkv.hu; internet www.bkv.hu; f. 1968; operates metro system, suburban railway network, trams, trolley buses and conventional buses; Pres. Dr GYULA VÁRSZEGI; Chief Exec. TIBOR BOLLA.

Hungarian State Railways Co (Magyar Államvasutak—MÁV): 1087 Budapest, Kálmán krt. 54-60; tel. (1) 511-3186; fax (1) 511-4931; e-mail sajto@mav.hu; internet www.mav.hu; f. 1993; Pres. and Chief Exec. ZSOLT VÖLGYESI; Gen. Dir ILONA DÁVID.

ROADS

In 2010 there were 199,567 km of roads in Hungary, of which 1,477 km were motorways and 6,821 km were main roads.

SHIPPING AND INLAND WATERWAYS

MAHART—Magyar Hajózás (Hungarian Shipping) Co: 1211 Budapest, Weiss Manfréd ú. 5—7; tel. (20) 979-0152; fax (1) 278-3505; e-mail kabinet@mahart.hu; internet www.mahart.hu; f. 1895; transportation of goods on the Rhine–Main–Danube waterway; carries passenger traffic on the Danube; operates port activities at Budapest Csepel National and Free Port (port agency service, loading, storage, handling goods); management of multi-modal and combined transport (cargo-booking, oversized goods, chartering); shipbuilding and ship-repair services; Dir-Gen. Capt. LÁSZLÓ SOMLÓVÁRI.

CIVIL AVIATION

Budapest Ferenc Liszt International Airport (formerly Budapest Ferihegy International Airport) and Balatonkiliti airport, near Siófok, serve international traffic. Other airports are located at Nyíregyháza, Debrecen, Szeged, Pécs, Szombathely and Győr.

National Transport Authority (Nemzeti Közlekedési Hatóság—NKH): 1066 Budapest, Teréz krt. 38; tel. (1) 373-1400; fax (1) 332-6532; e-mail office@nkh.gov.hu; internet www.nkh.gov.hu; f. 2007; as a successor to Civil Aviation Authority; controls civil aviation; Pres. GYULA GYŐRI.

Wizz Air Hungary: 1185 Budapest; tel. (22) 351-9499; e-mail info@wizzair.com; internet www.wizzair.com; f. 2003; wholly owned subsidiary of Wizz Air (UK); mem. of European Low Fares Airline Asscn; Chair. and Chief Exec. JÓZSEF VÁRADI.

Tourism

Tourism has developed rapidly and is an important source of foreign exchange. Lake Balaton is the main holiday centre for boating, bathing and fishing. Hungary's cities have great historical and recreational attractions, and the annual Budapest Spring Festival is held in March. Budapest has numerous swimming pools watered by thermal springs, which are equipped with modern physiotherapy facilities. There were 43.6m. foreign visitors in 2011, when revenue from tourism amounted to 1,175,086m. forint.

Hungarian Tourism Office: 1115 Budapest, Bartók Béla u. 105-113; tel. (1) 488-8700; fax (1) 488-8600; e-mail info@itthon.hu; internet www.hungarytourism.hu; Gen. Man. DENÉNÉ TÓTH MARIANNA.

Defence

Compulsory military service was abolished in November 2004. As assessed at November 2013, the active armed forces numbered 26,500, including an army of 10,300, an air force of 5,900 and 10,300 joint-forces troops. Reservists totalled 44,000. Paramilitary forces comprised 12,000 border guards. In 1999 Hungary became a member of the North Atlantic Treaty Organization (NATO).

Defence Expenditure: Budgeted at 242,000m. forint for 2013.

Chief of the Defence Staff: Gen. TIBOR BENKŐ.

Education

Children under the age of three years attend crèches (bölcsődék), and those between the ages of three and six years attend kindergartens (óvodák). Education is compulsory between the ages of six and 16 years. Children attend basic or primary school (általános iskola) until the age of 14. In 2010/11 pre-primary enrolment included 84% of children in the relevant age-group. The comparable ratio in the same year for primary education was 93% and that for secondary education was 92%. In southern Hungary, bilingual schools have been established to promote the languages of the national minorities. The majority of children continue with their education after 16 years of age. The most popular types of secondary school are the grammar school (gimnázium) and the vocational school (szakközépiskola). The gimnázium provides a four-year course of mainly academic studies, although some vocational training does feature on the curriculum. The szakközépiskola offers full vocational training together with a general education, emphasis being laid on practical work. Apprentice training schools (szakmunkásképző intézetek) are attached to factories, agricultural co-operatives, etc., and lead to full trade qualifications.

In 1999–2000 the system of higher education underwent a major reorganization, as a result of which from 1 January 2000 there were 30 state-run universities and colleges, 26 church universities and colleges, and six colleges administered by foundations. In 2012/13 some 338,467 students attended 66 institutions of tertiary education. Expenditure on education in 2011 was some 1,077.6m. forint (equivalent to 3.86% of total government expenditure).

ICELAND

Introductory Survey

LOCATION, CLIMATE, LANGUAGE, RELIGION, FLAG, CAPITAL

The Republic of Iceland comprises one large island and numerous smaller ones, situated near the Arctic Circle in the North Atlantic Ocean. The main island lies about 300 km (190 miles) south-east of Greenland, about 1,000 km (620 miles) west of Norway and about 800 km (500 miles) north of Scotland. The Gulf Stream keeps Iceland warmer than might be expected, with average temperatures ranging from 10°C (50°F) in the summer to 1°C (34°F) in winter. Icelandic is the official language. Almost all of the inhabitants profess Christianity: the Evangelical Lutheran Church is the established church and embraces about 75% of the population. The civil flag (proportions 18 by 25) displays a red cross, bordered with white, on a blue background, the upright of the cross being towards the hoist; the state flag (proportions 9 by 16) bears the same design, but has a truncated triangular area cut from the fly. The capital is Reykjavík.

CONTEMPORARY POLITICAL HISTORY

Historical Context

Iceland became independent on 17 June 1944, when the Convention that linked it with Denmark, under the Danish crown, was terminated. Iceland became a founder member of the North Atlantic Treaty Organization (NATO, see p. 370) in 1949, joined the Council of Europe (see p. 252) in 1950, and has belonged to the Nordic Council (see p. 467) since its foundation in 1952. Membership of the European Free Trade Association (EFTA, see p. 451) was formalized in 1970.

From 1959 to 1971 Iceland was governed by a coalition of the Independence Party (IP) and the Social Democratic Party (SDP). Following the general election of June 1971, Ólafur Jóhannesson, the leader of the Progressive Party (PP), formed a coalition Government with the left-wing People's Alliance (PA) and the Union of Liberals and Leftists. At the general election held in June 1974 voters favoured right-wing parties, and the IP and the PP subsequently formed a coalition Government under the leader of the IP, Geir Hallgrímsson. However, failure adequately to address economic difficulties resulted in a decline in the coalition's popularity and the Government resigned in June 1978, following extensive electoral gains by the PA and the SDP. In September Jóhannesson formed a coalition of the PP with the PA and the SDP, but this Government resigned in October 1979, when the SDP withdrew from the coalition. An interim administration was formed by Benedikt Gröndal, the leader of the SDP. The results of a general election, held in December, were inconclusive, and in February 1980 Gunnar Thoroddsen of the IP formed a coalition Government with the PA and the PP.

Domestic Political Affairs

In June 1980 Vigdís Finnbogadóttir, a non-political candidate, achieved a narrow victory in the election for the mainly ceremonial office of President. She took office on 1 August 1980, becoming the world's first popularly elected female Head of State. The coalition Government lost its majority in the Lower House of the Alþingi (Althingi—parliament) in September 1982, and a general election took place in April 1983. The IP received the largest share of the votes cast, and a coalition was subsequently formed by the IP and the PP, with Steingrímur Hermannsson (the leader of the PP) as Prime Minister.

A general election for an enlarged, 63-seat Althingi was held in April 1987. The IP's representation decreased from 24 to 18 seats, and the PP lost one of its 14 seats. The SDP secured 10 seats, and the newly formed, right-wing Citizens' Party (CP) won seven. A coalition of the IP, the PP and the SDP was formally constituted in July. Thorsteinn Pálsson, the leader of the IP and hitherto the Minister of Finance, was appointed Prime Minister.

In September 1988 the SDP and the PP withdrew from the Government, following disagreements over economic policy. Later that month Hermannsson became Prime Minister in a centre-left coalition of the PP, the SDP and the PA. In September 1989 a new Government, based on a coalition agreement between the PP, the SDP, the PA, the CP and the Association for Equality and Social Justice, was formed. Hermannsson remained as Prime Minister.

In March 1991 Davíð Oddsson, the mayor of Reykjavík, successfully challenged Pálsson for the leadership of the IP. At a general election in April the IP emerged as the largest single party, securing 26 seats. Although the incumbent coalition would have retained an overall majority of seats, the SDP decided to withdraw from the coalition, chiefly as a result of the failure to reach agreement on Iceland's position in the discussions between EFTA and the European Community (EC, now European Union—EU, see p. 273), with regard to the creation of a European Economic Area (EEA). A new coalition Government was formed in April by the IP and the SDP, with Oddsson as Prime Minister.

In 1991 Iceland's Constitution was amended, ending the system whereby the Althingi was divided into an Upper House (one-third of the members) and a Lower House.

In June 1992 President Finnbogadóttir was elected unopposed for a fourth term in office (she had begun a second term, unopposed, in August 1984 and a third term in June 1988).

Although the IP secured the largest number of seats (25) at a general election in April 1995, the SDP obtained only seven seats, thus their governing coalition could not be renewed. A new coalition Government was subsequently formed, comprising the IP and the PP, with Oddsson continuing as Prime Minister. Halldór Ásgrímsson, the Chairman of the PP, became Minister of Foreign Affairs.

Ólafur Ragnar Grímsson, a former leader of the PA, won the presidential election of June 1996, with 41% of the votes cast. (Finnbogadóttir had decided not to seek re-election.) Grímsson secured a second term of office in August 2000, his candidacy being unopposed.

At a general election in May 1999 the governing coalition retained its majority in the Althingi: the IP and the PP won 26 and 12 seats, respectively. The Social Democratic Alliance (SDA), a left-wing electoral grouping composed of the PA, the SDP, the People's Movement and the Women's List, won 17 seats. Two new parties also secured representation in the legislature: the Left-Green Movement, established by three former PA deputies, won six seats, while the Liberal Party, founded by a former IP minister, secured two. A new coalition Government comprising the IP and the PP, was formed under Oddsson.

At a general election in May 2003, the IP remained the party with the largest representation in the Althingi, winning 22 seats. The IP renewed its coalition with the PP, which had won 12 seats, and Oddsson remained as Prime Minister. The two parties agreed that Oddsson would relinquish the premiership in September 2004 in favour of Ásgrímsson, who had been reappointed as Minister of Foreign Affairs. The SDA won 20 seats, the Left-Green Movement five, and the Liberal Party four.

In May 2004 the Althingi narrowly approved a bill to limit media ownership. The legislation provoked uncharacteristic public protests as many perceived the bill to be directed against a particular company, the Baugur Group, whose media outlets had been openly critical of Oddsson. In the first use of the presidential power of veto in the 60-year history of the Republic, President Grímsson refused to sign the bill, stating that it lacked the necessary consensus. Grímsson was re-elected President for a third term on 26 June, with 85.6% of the votes cast. The Althingi rejected an amended version of the media bill in July.

On 15 September 2004, in accordance with the post-election agreement between the IP and PP, Oddsson stood down as Prime Minister in favour of Ásgrímsson, whose post Oddsson assumed. Oddsson resigned from politics in September 2005 and assumed the chairmanship of the Central Bank of Iceland. He was replaced as Minister of Foreign Affairs by Geir Haarde, who was also elected leader of the IP in October.

In June 2006 Ásgrímsson resigned as Prime Minister, following the PP's poor performance in municipal elections, and was succeeded by Haarde. Ásgrímsson also resigned as Chairman of the PP in August and was replaced by Jón Sigurðsson, whom

Haarde had recently appointed Minister of Industry and Commerce.

At the general election of 12 May 2007 the IP remained the largest party in the Althingi, securing 25 seats. The PP, however, won just seven seats. The SDA won 18 seats, while the Left-Green Movement became the third largest party in the legislature, increasing its representation from five to nine seats. A new coalition Government comprising the IP and the SDA was subsequently formed. Haarde remained as Prime Minister, while the leader of the SDA, Ingibjörg Sólrún Gísladóttir, became Minister of Foreign Affairs. Meanwhile, Sigurðsson was succeeded as Chairman of the PP by Guðni Ágústsson. President Grímsson was sworn in to serve a fourth term of office in August 2008, his candidacy having been unopposed.

Collapse of the banking sector

By mid-2008 a sharp contraction of credit on the global financial markets had severely weakened confidence in Iceland's banking sector, which held assets reported to be worth 10 times the country's annual gross domestic product (GDP); meanwhile, the value of the króna declined rapidly during 2008, and the country experienced high levels of inflation. On 6 October the Althingi approved an emergency bill to give the Icelandic Financial Supervisory Authority (Fjármálaeftirlitið—FME) extensive powers to intervene in the country's financial system. The Government assumed control of Iceland's three largest banks—Glitnir Banki, Landsbanki Íslands and Kaupþing Banki—and placed all three in receivership. Relations between the United Kingdom and Iceland were strained when it emerged that, as a consequence of the action taken by the FME, the accounts of some 400,000 British and Dutch savers who had invested in Icesave, a savings brand operated by Landsbanki in the United Kingdom and the Netherlands, had been frozen. Amid doubts that the Icelandic Depositors' and Investors' Guarantee Fund had sufficient assets to compensate Landsbanki's foreign creditors, the British Government invoked anti-terrorism legislation in order to seize Landsbanki's assets in the United Kingdom. The measure, which was described by Haarde as 'hostile', caused significant popular resentment in Iceland. The Bank of England subsequently granted Landsbanki a loan of £100m. to assist Iceland in repaying British Icesave account holders. The IMF approved a loan of US $2,100m. to Iceland in November, following an announcement that Iceland and EU member states had reached an agreement over compensation for Icesave account holders in the United Kingdom and the Netherlands.

In November 2008 the Government defeated a motion of no confidence proposed by the opposition in the Althingi over its handling of the economic crisis. However, this did little to increase public confidence in the administration. A series of demonstrations were staged around Iceland throughout late 2008 and early 2009 calling for the Government to resign. In January Haarde scheduled an early general election for 9 May, and announced his intention to stand down as leader of the IP. Two days later the Minister of Business Affairs, Björgvin Sigurðsson, resigned, citing his resolve to take responsibility for the political role he had played in the country's financial decline. Prior to his resignation, he dismissed the director of the FME. The following day Haarde announced the resignation of the Government. On 1 February Jóhanna Sigurðardóttir of the SDA, hitherto Minister of Social Affairs, was sworn in as Iceland's first female Prime Minister and a minority interim coalition Government comprising the SDA, the Left-Green Movement and independents was appointed, pending the general election, which was brought forward to 25 April.

Sigurðardóttir began implementing measures aimed at alleviating Iceland's acute financial situation. In February 2009 the Althingi approved a bill on the reorganization of the senior management of the Central Bank of Iceland, facilitating the dismissal of the bank's Governor, Oddsson, whom many considered responsible for exacerbating the country's economic problems. In the event, Oddsson resigned. In March Gísladóttir resigned as leader of the SDA for health reasons; Sigurðardóttir was elected her successor. Meanwhile, Bjarni Benediktsson was appointed Chairman of the IP, replacing Haarde.

At the general election held on 25 April 2009 the interim coalition parties, the SDA and the Left-Green Movement, won 34 of the 63 seats in the Althingi, the first time left-wing parties had won a majority in parliament. The SDA replaced the IP as the largest party in the Althingi, winning 20 seats, while the Left-Green Movement won 14 seats. The IP won 16 seats, while the PP slightly increased its representation to nine seats. The success of the Citizens' Movement, founded just two months earlier by activists involved in the protests against the Government's handling of the economic crisis, also confounded expectations by winning four seats.

The SDA-Left-Green Movement Coalition

On 10 May 2009 a new Government, led by Sigurðardóttir and largely unchanged from the outgoing interim coalition, took office. Steingrímur J. Sigfússon, the leader of the Left-Green Movement, remained Minister of Finance. The new administration declared its principal aim to be the achievement of a balanced state budget by 2013. In July the Althingi voted narrowly in favour of applying for accession to the EU (which had gained increasing popular support since the onset of the economic crisis and which had been a central policy of the SDA). A formal application was duly submitted to the European Council. The Government emphasized that, should Iceland be admitted to the EU, the accession treaty would be subject to approval in a referendum.

Meanwhile, negotiations continued with the United Kingdom and the Netherlands over the consequences of the collapse of Landsbanki Íslands. In June 2009 it was agreed that the Icelandic Government would guarantee loans of some £2,350m. from the United Kingdom and €1,200m. from the Netherlands to the Depositors' and Investors' Guarantee Fund in respect of the compensation that the two countries' Governments had issued to savers who had lost deposits held in Icesave accounts; the loans were to be repaid by 2024, with repayment, at an interest rate of 5.55%, to commence in 2016. The agreement encountered domestic opposition on the grounds that it placed an unduly harsh burden on the Icelandic economy, the amount loaned being equivalent to some US $17,000 per head. None the less, in August 2009 the Althingi approved a bill to ratify the loan agreement, but added stipulations to the effect that Iceland would repay no more than 4% of its annual GDP growth to the United Kingdom and 2% to the Netherlands in any one year, and that any portion of the debt not repaid by 2024 would effectively be cancelled. The British and Dutch Governments objected to the amended bill (which was signed into law in September 2009) and demanded further negotiations with Iceland. A revised agreement with the United Kingdom and the Netherlands was concluded in October, which retained the Althingi's annual limits on repayment but allowed for payments to continue beyond the 2024 deadline if necessary. The new agreement was narrowly approved by the Althingi in December 2009. However, by 2 January 2010 more than 56,000 people—some 23% of the electorate—had signed a petition urging President Grímsson to veto the bill. In response, on 5 January Grímsson announced that he would not sign the legislation, and that, in accordance with the Constitution, it would thus be subject to a referendum.

In anticipation of a referendum defeat for the Icesave compensation bill, the Government held further talks with the British and Dutch authorities in February 2010. However, the talks collapsed after Iceland rejected as insufficient a British and Dutch offer, estimated to be worth €450m., to waive interest payments for the first two years and to replace the fixed interest rate of 5.55% with a variable one. Sigurðardóttir urged electors not to vote in the referendum, arguing that the offer of revised terms for the loans had already made the bill of December 2009 obsolete. None the less, 62.7% of registered voters participated in the referendum (the first since Iceland's independence) on 6 March 2010, at which 93.2% of votes cast were against the bill. As a result, the payment terms authorized in September 2009 were to remain in force pending further negotiations with the United Kingdom and the Netherlands.

A commission established by the Althingi to investigate the collapse of the banking sector in 2008 presented its report in April 2010, accusing the Icelandic Government and regulators of the financial sector of 'extreme negligence' in the period preceding the crisis and concluding that the failure of the banking system had become inevitable as early as the end of 2006. Seven former officials were specifically criticized: from the Government, then Prime Minister Haarde, Minister of Finance Árni Mathiesen and Minister of Business Affairs Björgvin Sigurðsson; from the Central Bank, former Governor Oddsson and two other officials; and from the FME, former Director-General Jónas Jónsson. The report was also highly critical of the management and largest shareholders of the three banks that failed, noting that the owners had 'abnormally easy access to loans in these banks' and were, indeed, their largest borrowers. In September the nine-member commission voted in favour of a recommendation to convene the Landsdómur, a special court for hearing cases against elected officials, to try Haarde, Mathiesen and Sigurðsson, as well as former Minister of Foreign Affairs Ingibjörg Gísladóttir. Later that month the Althingi voted to pursue charges of negligence against Haarde, but not the other three erstwhile ministers.

The Landsdómur was duly convened in February 2011, for the first time since its establishment in 1905. In June Haarde was formally charged on six counts of violating the laws on ministerial responsibility. Appearing before the Landsdómur in September, Haarde sought the dismissal of the charges against him, all of which he denied, claiming that they were a result of a 'political vendetta' against him by the current Government. The Landsdómur subsequently withdrew two of the six charges against Haarde. In April 2012 Haarde was found guilty of a minor charge—of failing to keep his government ministers properly informed of developments prior to the collapse of the banking sector in 2008, for which he faced no punishment—and was cleared of the more serious charges of negligence. Meanwhile, a special prosecutor appointed in early 2009 to investigate the collapse of the banking sector in 2008 began to file charges against former bank executives, including Lárus Welding, the former CEO of Glitnir Banki, and Gudmundur Hjaltason, Glitnir's former head of corporate finance, in December 2011, and Hreiðar Már Sigurðsson and Sigurður Einarsson, respectively the former CEO and Chairman of Kaupþing Banki, in February 2012; Sigurjón Árnason, the former CEO of Landsbanki Íslands, was also under investigation. Welding and Hjaltason were convicted of fraud and each sentenced to nine months' imprisonment in December 2012. Meanwhile, Welding and Jón Ásgeir Jóhannesson, the former head of Icelandic investment company Baugur and Glitnir's largest shareholder, were indicted by the special prosecutor in a separate case related to the approval of a 6,000m. krónur loan. Also in December, Welding's predecessor at Glitnir, Bjarni Ármannsson, was formally indicted for tax evasion. In July 2013 charges were filed against another four former employees of Glitnir bank for market manipulation and irregularities surrounding a 3,800m. krónur loan. to a company owned by a senior executive at the bank, while in December Sigurðsson and Einarsson of Kaupþing Banki were sentenced to five-and-a-half, and five years' imprisonment, respectively, for fraud.

The second Icesave referendum

Public discontent with the traditional parties was evident at the municipal elections of May 2010 with the success in Reykjavík of a new, satirical political organization, the Best Party, which had been established by a comedian, Jón Gnarr, in November 2009. The party won the largest number of seats on Reykjavík's city council, with Gnarr subsequently becoming mayor.

At a summit held in Brussels, Belgium, in June 2010, EU leaders agreed to open membership negotiations with Iceland, although it was made clear that accession would not be possible while the dispute with the United Kingdom and the Netherlands over compensation for savers who had lost Icesave deposits remained unresolved. In the previous month the EFTA Surveillance Authority had ruled that Iceland was obliged to ensure payment of the minimum compensation (€20,000) to British and Dutch savers. Negotiations on Iceland's accession to the EU formally opened in Brussels in July.

Direct elections to a constitutional parliament, which was to propose revisions to the Constitution, took place on 27 November 2010, but were marked by an extremely low turnout of around 36%. The Supreme Court declared the elections void in January 2011, owing to irregularities in the organization of the vote. In February a legislative committee recommended that, instead of holding new elections, the 25 people elected to the constitutional parliament should be appointed by the Althingi to a Constitutional Council, which would have a similar role to the planned parliament. The Constitutional Council was duly appointed and convened in April.

In December 2010 Iceland reached a new agreement with the Netherlands and the United Kingdom on the repayment of loans related to the compensation of savers who had lost deposits held in Icesave accounts. From Iceland's perspective, the terms of this accord represented a significant improvement on those of the previous one: repayments were to commence in 2016 and to be completed by 2046, while interest was to be paid at a fixed rate of 3.0% to the Netherlands and 3.3% to the United Kingdom (reflecting the differing cost to each country of raising funds). Annual repayments would also be limited to no more than the equivalent of 5% of government revenue in the preceding year or 1.3% of GDP (whichever was higher). In February 2011 the Althingi approved the ratification of the agreement, but President Grímsson again vetoed the accord, thus triggering the organization of a referendum, which took place on 9 April, at which the repayment agreement was rejected by 58.9% of those who voted. Opposition to the agreement appeared to centre on the rejection of the principle that the Icelandic taxpayer should be responsible for the debt. The dispute reverted to the EFTA Surveillance Authority, which decided in December to refer the matter to the Court of Justice of the European Free Trade Association States (EFTA Court). In January 2013 the EFTA Court ruled in Iceland's favour, judging that the relevant European directive did not require the Icelandic state itself to ensure payments to depositors in the Icesave branches in the Netherlands and the United Kingdom when the deposit guarantee scheme was unable to meet its obligations. Meanwhile, payments continued to be made from the estate of Landsbanki Íslands to the Governments of the United Kingdom and the Netherlands and to other priority creditors, including British and Dutch local authorities, having commenced in December 2011, following a ruling by the Supreme Court in October upholding emergency legislation adopted in 2008 that had given depositors priority status over other creditors for compensation. By January 2013 Landsbanki's estate had reportedly paid back the equivalent of more than 90% of the amount that the British and Dutch Governments had advanced to cover the minimum deposit guarantee.

Recent developments: EU negotiations and constitutional review

Iceland and the EU commenced formal negotiations on the first four of the 35 negotiating chapters of the *acquis communautaire*, the EU's body of law, on 27 June 2011. Two of the chapters were completed that day, an unprecedented development within the EU's enlargement history, which was attributed to the fact that Iceland already largely complied with some two-thirds of EU law through its membership of the EEA.

In July 2011 the Constitutional Council presented its draft bill on a new constitution to the Althingi. The bill notably provided for increased public participation in decision-making (allowing 10% of the electorate to demand a referendum on laws adopted by the Althingi and 2% to submit a legislative proposal); a strengthening of the role of the Althingi; the creation of a Law Council (Lögrétta) to examine the constitutionality of new legislation; and greater autonomy for local authorities. In addition, the President would be limited to serving a maximum of three terms in office and government ministers to holding the same office for eight years, while the Prime Minister would be directly elected by the Althingi following legislative elections.

The Minister of Fisheries and Agriculture, Jón Bjarnason of the Left-Green Movement, and the Minister of Economic Affairs, Árni Páll Árnason of the SDA, were dismissed in a cabinet reorganization effected in December 2011. Bjarnason's vocal opposition to Iceland's proposed membership of the EU had exacerbated tensions within the governing coalition, with the Left-Green Movement being officially against accession and the SDA in favour. Sigfússon, the leader of the Left-Green Movement, became Minister of Fisheries and Agriculture and of Economic Affairs, being replaced as Minister of Finance by Oddný G. Harðardóttir of the SDA. The changes thus reduced the number of ministers to nine; the number of ministers was further reduced to eight in 2012 with the merger of the Ministry of Industry, Energy and Tourism and the Ministry of Agriculture and Fisheries to form the Ministry of Industries and Innovation.

Grímsson was re-elected to serve a fifth term as President at an election held on 30 June 2012, securing 52.8% of the votes cast.

A non-binding national referendum on the Constitutional Council's draft bill on a new constitution was held on 20 October 2012. A majority of those who participated (48.9% of the electorate) responded positively to all six questions posed. A specific proposal that natural resources that are not privately owned should be declared national property received the strongest level of support. In November the Althingi submitted the bill for the consideration of the Venice Commission of the Council of Europe, which provided its legal opinion in February 2013, criticizing some provisions for being too general or unclear. In March, as it became clear that discussions on the draft constitution would not be completed prior to the forthcoming legislative elections, which were scheduled to take place on 27 April, a deputy representing the opposition The Movement (which had been created in 2009 by former members of the Citizens' Movement) submitted a parliamentary resolution for a vote of no confidence in the Government owing to the failure to finalize the constitutional review during the current parliamentary term. The Government narrowly survived the vote, with 32 deputies voting against the motion and 29 in favour. On the final day of its term in office a government amendment was adopted, stipulating that the draft constitution could be approved with the support of two-thirds of the Althingi and 40% of the electorate in a further referendum.

In January 2013 the Government announced that it was suspending the opening of negotiations on new chapters of the EU's *acquis* pending the elections to the Althingi in April. Popular support for EU accession had declined since the submission of Iceland's application for membership in July 2009, amid a recovery in the Icelandic economy and serious financial difficulties in the eurozone. National congresses held by the principal parties in February were dominated by discussions regarding EU accession negotiations, which the IP and PP wished to halt, while the SDA, the Left-Green Movement and Bright Future favoured their completion. The two governing parties also chose new leaders: Árni Páll Árnason, the former Minister of Economic Affairs, was elected to replace Prime Minister Sigurðardóttir as Chairman of the SDA, and Katrín Jakobsdóttir, the Minister of Education, Science and Culture, was elected to succeed Sigfússon at the head of the Left-Green Movement.

The governing coalition of the SDA and the Left-Green Movement—which had lost its narrow majority following a series of defections—was ousted at the legislative elections on 27 April 2013, with the IP and the PP each securing 19 seats. The Left-Green Movement won seven seats, while new groupings Bright Future, established in early 2012 by members of the Best Party and Guðmundur Steingrímsson, formerly of the PP, won six seats and the Pirate Party, campaigning for political transparency and internet freedom, won three seats. An electoral participation rate of 81.2% was the lowest recorded in the country's history. The PP and the IP agreed on coalition terms in May. Chairman of the PP Sigmundur Gunnlaugsson, whose party had more than doubled its representation at the election, became the youngest Prime Minister in Iceland's history, at 38 years old. Bjarni Benediktsson of the IP was appointed Minister of Finance and Economic Affairs. Both parties had campaigned against the country's bid to join the EU, and one of the first actions of the coalition Government was the announcement of the indefinite suspension of EU accession negotiations. There were protests outside the Althingi in February and March 2014, after members of the coalition parties in the Althingi voted in favour of suspending EU membership negotiations; opinion polls showed that some 82% of Icelanders wanted the issue of Iceland's application for membership put to the electorate in a referendum, as had been pledged by Benediktsson before the elections. The new administration announced its intention to ease the economic difficulties of ordinary householders by reducing taxes and providing mortgage debt relief, and also directed government ministries to submit proposals for cuts of 1.5% in their expenditure.

Ongoing negotiations with the foreign creditors of Iceland's failed banks were expected to be among the greatest challenges for the new Government. At a meeting in London in September 2013 representatives of Landsbanki asked the British and Dutch Governments for a more lenient repayment schedule, claiming that the regime due to commence in early 2014 was not workable. Moreover, the Central Bank of Iceland had publicly stated that the country's economy could not support the schedule. However, in November 2013 the British and Dutch financial authorities began legal proceedings against the Icelandic Depositors' and Investors' Guarantee Fund over the collapse of Icesave.

Foreign Affairs

Regional relations

Iceland has strong links to the EU through its participation in the EEA and its membership of the Schengen Agreement on border controls. Negotiations on Iceland's accession to the EU formally opened in July 2010, one year after the country applied for membership, and discussions on the first four of the 35 negotiating chapters of the *acquis communautaire*, the EU's body of legislation, commenced in July 2011. Negotiations on accession to the Union, however, were suspended indefinitely following the general election of April 2013.

The importance of fishing to Iceland's economy, and fears of excessive exploitation of the fishing grounds near Iceland by foreign fleets, caused the Icelandic Government to extend its territorial waters to 12 nautical miles (22 km) in 1964 and to 50 nautical miles (93 km) in 1972. British opposition to these extensions resulted in two 'cod wars'. In October 1975 Iceland unilaterally introduced a fishing limit of 200 nautical miles (371 km), both as a conservation measure and to protect Icelandic interests. The 1973 agreement on fishing limits between Iceland and the United Kingdom expired in November 1975, and failure to reach a new agreement led to the third and most serious 'cod war'. Casualties occurred, and in February 1976 Iceland temporarily severed diplomatic relations with the United Kingdom, the first diplomatic break between two NATO countries. In June an agreement was reached, and in December the British trawler fleet withdrew from Icelandic waters. In June 1979 Iceland declared its exclusive rights to the 200-mile fishing zone. Following negotiations between the EC and EFTA on the creation of the EEA, an agreement was reached (in October 1991) allowing tariff-free access to the EC for 97% of Iceland's fisheries products by 1997, while Iceland was to allow EC vessels to catch 3,000 metric tons of fish per year in its waters, in return for some access to EC waters. The EEA agreement was ratified by the Althingi in January 1993 and entered into force in January 1994.

In August 1993 a dispute developed between Iceland and Norway over fishing rights in an area of the Barents Sea fished by Iceland, over which Norway claimed jurisdiction. Iceland's case was weakened in January 1995, when Canada officially recognized Norway's sovereign rights over the disputed area (a fisheries protection zone extending 200 km around the Svalbard archipelago). A similar dispute arose in August 1996 between Iceland and Denmark over fishing rights in an area of the Atlantic Ocean between Iceland and Greenland (a self-governing province of Denmark).

Iceland's relations with the EU and Norway were strained from the second half of 2010 by a dispute over fishing quotas for mackerel in the north-east Atlantic Ocean. In April 2010 Iceland had unilaterally set itself a mackerel quota of 130,000 metric tons for that year, in the absence of an agreement on the issue between the interested states. Iceland and the Faroe Islands, which also set its own quota in July, maintained that they had been forced to take this action having been excluded from a bilateral quota arrangement between the EU and Norway and that stocks of mackerel had become more plentiful in their waters as a result of changing migration patterns. Negotiations between officials from the four parties, held in October and November, failed to reach a resolution on quotas for 2011. The Icelandic Government subsequently announced that its mackerel quota for 2011 would be 146,818 tons, prompting threats of sanctions from the European Commission. However, Icelandic officials claimed that the EU and Norway would be primarily responsible for overfishing of mackerel in 2011, having allocated themselves more than 90% of the recommended total allowable catch. Officials from the EU, Norway, Iceland and the Faroe Islands engaged in several rounds of negotiations during 2011–12, but these again ended without agreement. In September 2012 the European Parliament approved a regulation that would allow the imposition of sanctions against countries deemed to be engaging in unsustainable fishing practices, including restrictions on the import of fish from these countries to the EU. In January 2013 the continued dispute over quotas led the Marine Conservation Society to downgrade mackerel from its list of fish suitable to eat. In February the Icelandic Government announced a 15% reduction in its mackerel quota for 2013 (compared with 2012), citing its commitment to the long-term sustainability of stocks. As in previous years, the European Commission expressed regret at such unilateral action, and in July 2013 the EU's Fisheries and Maritime Affairs Commissioner threatened to commence infringement action against Iceland. However, no such measures were undertaken and a further meeting between officials from Iceland and the EU in Reykjavík in September ended without agreement.

Other external relations

Iceland has developed close relations with the USA, which was the first country officially to recognize Icelandic independence in 1944. Having joined NATO at its foundation in 1949, in 1951 Iceland concluded a bilateral defence agreement with the USA, which provided for the territorial defence of Iceland by the USA and led to the establishment of the Iceland Defence Force (IDF) at Keflavík airbase, near Reykjavík.

In May 2003 it emerged that the USA was planning to withdraw the four remaining fighter jet aircraft stationed at Keflavík, following a review of its international military commitments. The IDF, which was composed of 1,658 US troops, was traditionally viewed as providing protection for Iceland, which had no military of its own; moreover, many Icelanders in the nearby town of Reykjanesbær depended on the Keflavík airbase for their livelihood. Oddsson suggested that if the USA withdrew the aircraft it would have to end its military presence in Iceland altogether—an unpalatable proposition for the USA, which still regarded its reconnaissance of the North Atlantic as a high priority. Concern among Icelanders was such that the Government requested that the Secretary-General of NATO, Lord Robertson of Port Ellen, intervene on their behalf. Following Lord Robertson's subsequent non-partisan representations in July 2003, the US authorities announced that they had delayed their decision with regard to the aircraft at Keflavík.

In March 2006 the USA announced its intention to withdraw the remaining US troops from Keflavík airbase by October of that year. A subsequent offer by the Icelandic Government to contribute one-half of the annual cost of maintaining the US mission was rejected. In September the new coalition Government signed an agreement with the USA, under which the USA reaffirmed its commitment to defend Iceland as a NATO ally and agreed to return the Keflavík airbase to Icelandic ownership. For its part, Iceland would pay up to 5,000m. krónur to clean contaminated land at the former US airbase and return the site to civilian use. On 30 September the USA completed the withdrawal of its troops from Iceland.

At a meeting of the North Atlantic Council in July 2007 NATO members signed an agreement over the protection of Icelandic airspace, which had been proposed by the Prime Minister, Geir Haarde, in November 2006. Under the accord, the air forces of NATO member countries would undertake military exercises and patrols in Iceland on a rotating basis at intervals of no more than four months, while the Icelandic Government would pay for technical assistance and the use by visiting forces of the facilities at the Keflavík airbase. In May 2008 the Ministry of Foreign Affairs established the Iceland Defence Agency (IDA) to co-ordinate the country's security and defence policy and supervise all NATO matters pertaining to Iceland. In January 2011, however, the IDA was dissolved, with its duties integrated into the new Ministry of the Interior, although relations with NATO were to remain the responsibility of the Ministry for Foreign Affairs.

Iceland strongly criticized the moratorium on commercial whaling, imposed (for conservation purposes) by the International Whaling Commission (IWC, see p. 442) in 1986, and continued to catch limited numbers of whales for scientific purposes. However, in 1989 Iceland halted whaling, following appeals by environmental organizations for an international boycott of Icelandic products. In 1991 Iceland announced its withdrawal from the IWC (with effect from June 1992), claiming that certain species of whales were not only too plentiful to be in danger of extinction, but were also threatening Iceland's stocks of cod and other fish. In March 1999 the Althingi voted to end the self-imposed 10-year ban on whaling.

Iceland's application to rejoin the IWC, with an unprecedented exemption that would allow it to disregard the moratorium on commercial whaling, was rejected in July 2001. However, it was granted permission to attend discussions as an observer without voting rights. Iceland's bid for full membership was rejected again in May 2002, but it was readmitted in October 2002, when the Government undertook not to allow the resumption of commercial whaling until at least 2006 and after that not to resume commercial whaling while negotiations on a revised management plan were in progress. In August 2003, however, Iceland resumed whaling for research purposes, provoking widespread international criticism. Furthermore, in October 2006 Iceland resumed commercial whaling. However, in August 2007 the Minister of Fisheries and Agriculture, Einar Kristinn Guðfinnsson, announced the suspension of commercial whaling quotas during the forthcoming fishing season, owing to a lack of consumer demand, meat from the 2006/07 season having remained unsold. By May 2008, however, Guðfinnsson licensed the capture of 40 minke whales for the 2008/09 season, and in 2009 issued an annual whaling quota of 150 fin whales and 100 minke whales over a five-year period. At its annual meeting in June 2010, the IWC failed to reach agreement on a proposal that would have lifted the moratorium on commercial whaling, but allowed the Commission to set quotas for whaling countries. Iceland's whaling quota for 2011 and 2012 was 216 minke whales and 154 fin whales. The only company involved in capturing fin whales, Hvalur, suspended hunting for 2011, owing to weak demand from Japan, its main export market, but 58 minke whales were caught that season. Commercial hunting of minke whales continued in 2012, while hunting for fin whales, which are included on the International Union for the Conservation of Nature's 'red list' of endangered species, remained suspended. However, Hvalur resumed its commercial hunting of the fin whale in June 2013 and by September of that year it had killed 134 fin whales. The resumption of the practice provoked international outrage, with many freight operators refusing to ship the whale meat. A consignment of whale meat en route to Japan was sent back to Iceland from Hamburg, Germany, via Rotterdam, the Netherlands in July, when officials at the port refused to handle the cargo.

CONSTITUTION AND GOVERNMENT

The Constitution came into force in June 1944, when Iceland became an independent republic. Executive power is vested in the President (elected for four years by universal adult suffrage) and the Cabinet, consisting of the Prime Minister and other ministers appointed by the President. In practice, however, the President performs only nominally the functions ascribed in the Constitution to this office, and it is the Cabinet alone that holds real executive power. Legislative power is held jointly by the President and the unicameral Althingi (parliament), with 63 members elected by universal suffrage for four years (subject to dissolution by the President), using a system of proportional representation in eight multi-member constituencies. The Cabinet is responsible to the Althingi. Iceland is divided into 74 municipalities, each with a municipal council and executive. Municipal governments are responsible for education, infrastructure and social services.

REGIONAL AND INTERNATIONAL CO-OPERATION

Iceland is a member of the Nordic Council (see p. 467), the Arctic Council (see p. 448) and the European Free Trade Association (EFTA, see p. 451). It participates in the European Economic Area, and is thus integrated into the internal market of the European Union (EU, see p. 273); it is also a member the EU's Schengen Agreement on border controls by virtue of its membership of the Nordic passport union. Iceland applied for full membership of the EU in July 2009 and accession negotiations formally opened in July 2010. It is also participates in the Council of Europe (see p. 252) and the Organization for Security and Co-operation in Europe (OSCE, see p. 387).

Iceland joined the UN in 1946. As a contracting party to the General Agreement on Tariffs and Trade, it joined the World Trade Organization (WTO, see p. 434) on its establishment in 1995. Iceland was a founder member of the North Atlantic Treaty Organization (NATO, see p. 370) and is a member of the Organisation for Economic Co-operation and Development (OECD, see p. 379).

ECONOMIC AFFAIRS

In 2012, according to estimates by the World Bank, Iceland's gross national income (GNI), measured at 2010–12 prices, was US $12,393m., equivalent to $38,710 per head (or $33,840 per head on an international purchasing-power parity basis). During 2003–12, it was estimated, the population increased at an average annual rate of 1.1%, while gross domestic product (GDP) per head increased, in real terms, by an average of 1.1% per year. Iceland's overall GDP increased, in real terms, at an average annual rate of 2.2% during 2003–12; GDP increased by 1.6% in 2012.

Agriculture (including fishing) contributed 8.1% of GDP in 2011 (fishing contributed 7.0% of GDP and agriculture alone only 1.1%); in 2012 5.7% of the employed labour force were engaged in the agricultural and fishing sectors, with a further 2.4% employed in fish processing. The principal agricultural products are dairy produce and lamb. Marine products accounted for 34.1% of total export earnings in 2012. A cod quota system is in place to avoid the depletion of fish stocks through overfishing as happened in previous years. The decline in the catch of cod has been offset by an increase in the catch of other species, such as haddock and redfish. Capelin remains the most valuable species, accounting for 40.6% of the value of the total catch in 2012, followed by cod (13.8%), other pelagics (10.5%) and herring (6.8%). According to UN estimates, during 2003–12 agricultural GDP (including fishing) increased at an average annual rate of 0.4%; the sector grew by 5.9% in 2012.

Industry (including mining, manufacturing, construction and power) contributed 25.2% of GDP in 2011 and engaged 18.2% of the employed labour force (including the 2.4% employed in fish processing) in 2012. Mining activity is negligible. During 2003–12, according to UN estimates, industrial GDP increased at an average annual rate of 1.1%; industrial GDP increased by 1.5% in 2011, but declined by 1.0% in 2012.

Manufacturing contributed 14.5% of GDP in 2011, and employed 9.6% of the labour force in 2012. The most important sectors are fish processing (which contributed 4.0% of GDP in 2011), the production of aluminium, medical equipment, pharmaceuticals and ferrosilicon. Basic metal processing contributed 4.4% of GDP in 2011. A new aluminium smelter, Alcoa Fjardaál, fuelled by hydroelectric power plants, opened in 2007, with a production capacity of 346,000 metric tons per year. Construction of an aluminium smelter at Helguvík, with a planned production capacity of 360,000 tons, began in 2008, but was subject to delays. However, the Government announced in May 2013 that it planned to allow construction of the smelter to recommence. During 2003–12 the GDP of the manufacturing sector grew at an average annual rate of 2.4%, according to UN estimates; the sector grew by 3.8% in 2011, but declined by 0.2% in 2012.

The construction sector contributed 4.4% of GDP in 2011 and engaged 5.5% of the employed labour force in 2012. According to UN estimates, the GDP of the sector declined at an average annual rate of 2.6% during 2003–12; the GDP of the sector decreased by 0.4% in 2011, but increased by 1.5% in 2012.

Iceland is potentially rich in hydroelectric and geothermal power, although both energy sources have yet to be fully exploited. Hydroelectric power has promoted the development of the aluminium industry, while geothermal energy provides nearly all the country's heating and hot water. In 2012 hydroelectric power provided 70.9% of the country's electricity, geothermal energy 24.8% and fuel 4.3%. Fuel imports comprised 15.0% of the value of merchandise imports in 2012. In 2001 Iceland announced its intention to develop the world's first economy free of carbon dioxide emissions by using hydrogen or methanol-powered fuel cells. Two new hydroelectric power plants in the east of the country, the Kárahnjúkar Hydroelectric Project, built amid much controversy to fuel the Alcoa Fjardaál smelter, were officially opened in June 2007.

Services contributed 66.6% of GDP in 2011 and employed 76.0% of the labour force in 2012. Banking was an important sector in Iceland, with the financial sector providing 8.7% of GDP in 2007; however, the sector effectively collapsed in October 2008, when the three largest banks, Glitnir Banki, Landsbanki Islands and Kaupþing Banki, were placed in receivership. The tourism sector is becoming an increasingly significant source of revenue; the number of overnight stays by foreign visitors in hotels and guest houses totalled 2,231,963 in 2012. Receipts from tourism totalled US $845m. in 2012, according to provisional figures from the World Tourism Organization. According to UN estimates, the real GDP of the services sector grew at an average annual rate of 2.8% in 2003–12; the GDP of the sector increased by 2.8% in 2012.

In 2012 Iceland recorded a visible merchandise trade surplus of US $619.8m., while there was a deficit of $740.3m. on the current account of the balance of payments. In 2012 the principal sources of imports were Norway (providing 16.6% of total imports), followed by the USA, Germany, the People's Republic of China, the Netherlands, Denmark, Brazil and the United Kingdom; the principal market for exports was the Netherlands (accounting for 30.0% of total exports), followed by Germany and the United Kingdom. In 2012 member countries of the European Economic Area (EEA, see p. 451) provided 64.6% of Iceland's merchandise imports and took 86.3% of its exports. The principal imports in 2012 were petroleum and petroleum products, electrical equipment and machinery appliances, metalliferous ores, transport equipment and road vehicles. The principal exports in the same year were fish, crustaceans, molluscs, and non-ferrous metals.

In 2012 there was a budgetary deficit of 65,300m. krónur, equivalent to 3.8% of GDP. Iceland's total external debt was 13,150,098m. krónur at the end of 2012. Iceland's general government gross debt was 1,692,525m. krónur in 2012, equivalent to 99.1% of GDP. According to IMF estimates, the annual rate of inflation averaged 7.2% in 2005–12; consumer prices increased by 5.2% in 2012. The unemployment rate was 6.1% in 2012.

From the late 1990s the Icelandic economy expanded rapidly: the financial sector benefited from the liberalization of capital flows, while high-technology industries were developed and the tourism sector grew strongly. However, the over-extended banking sector experienced major difficulties in 2008 owing to a lack of availability of credit resulting from the international financial crisis, and in October the Government was forced to assume control of the three largest commercial banks. In November Iceland became the first Western nation since 1976 to receive IMF assistance. The stabilization of the currency, the króna, which had depreciated drastically, was the principal aim of the IMF's economic recovery programme. The Government that took office in May 2009 aimed to eliminate the fiscal deficit by 2013 (subsequently deferred until 2014). The deficit was reduced from 13.5% of GDP in 2008 to 3.8% in 2012, and was predicted to have contracted further to 1.8% in 2013. Meanwhile, the inflation rate decreased from 18.6% in January 2009 to 1.8% in January 2011 (before rising to an annual average of 5.2% in 2012, subsequently declining to 3.7% in November 2013), and the króna stabilized, as the central bank lowered interest rates and imposed restrictions on capital flows. However, unemployment rose significantly, peaking at 9.1% in the second quarter of 2009; it fluctuated thereafter, but had declined to 5.1% by mid-2013. Following contractions of 6.6% in 2009 and 4.0% in 2010, GDP increased by 2.9% and 1.6% in 2011 and 2012, respectively; GDP was expected to increase by 1.9% in 2013 and by a predicted 2.5% in 2014. Iceland returned to the international credit markets in June 2011, in its first bond issue since 2006, and successfully completed its IMF-supported programme in August 2011, announcing the early repayment of some of its loans in early 2012. The country's relatively rapid recovery was attributed in part to its refusal (and inability) to bail out the failed banks and their foreign creditors and its exchange rate flexibility, which allowed the devaluation of the króna, thereby increasing export competitiveness. In August 2013 the IMF, which had praised Iceland for its decisive response to the banking crisis, warned that slow progress in removing capital controls imposed in 2008 was creating a barrier for investors. It also cautioned that electoral pledges by the Government that took office in May 2013 to forgive household mortgage debt could affect the country's target of a balanced budget for 2014.

PUBLIC HOLIDAYS

2015: 1 January (New Year's Day), 2 April (Maundy Thursday), 3 April (Good Friday), 6 April (Easter Monday), 23 April (First Day of Summer), 1 May (Labour Day), 14 May (Ascension Day), 25 May (Whit Monday), 17 June (National Day), 3 August (Bank Holiday), 24*–26 December (Christmas), 31 December (New Year's Eve)*.

* Afternoon only.

Statistical Survey

Sources (unless otherwise stated): Statistics Iceland, Borgartúni 21A, 150 Reykjavík; tel. 5281000; fax 5281099; e-mail statice@statice.is; internet www.statice.is; Seðlabanki Íslands (Central Bank of Iceland), Kalkofnsvegur 1, 150 Reykjavík; tel. 5699600; fax 5699605; e-mail sedlabanki@sedlabanki.is; internet www.sedlabanki.is.

AREA AND POPULATION

Area: 103,000 sq km (39,769 sq miles).

Population: 321,857 (males 161,438, females 160,419) at 1 January 2013 (national population register).

Density (at 1 January 2013): 3.1 per sq km.

Population by Age and Sex (national population register at 1 January 2013): *0–14:* 66,466 (males 33,920, females 32,546); *15–64:* 213,714 (males 108,064, females 105,650); *65 and over:* 41,677 (males 19,454, females 22,223); *Total* 321,857 (males 161,438, females 160,419).

Principal Towns (population at 1 January 2013): Reykjavík (capital) 119,764; Kópavogur 31,726; Hafnarfjörður 26,808; Akureyri 17,966; Reykjanesbær 14,231.

Births, Marriages and Deaths (2012, unless otherwise indicated): Live births 4,533 (birth rate 14.1 per 1,000); Marriages 1,458 (marriage rate 4.6 per 1,000) in 2011; Deaths 1,955 (death rate 6.1 per 1,000).

Life Expectancy (years at birth): 82.4 (males 80.7; females 84.1) in 2011. Source: World Bank, World Development Indicators database.

Economically Active Population (2012, figures rounded to nearest 100 persons): Agriculture 4,800; Fishing 4,900; Manufacturing (excl. fish-processing) 16,300; Fish-processing 4,100; Electricity and water supply 1,100; Construction 9,300; Wholesale and retail trade, repairs 22,600; Restaurants and hotels 8,200; Transport, storage and communications 11,700; Financial intermediation 7,500; Real estate and business services 17,400; Public administration 9,000; Education 19,500; Health services and social work 19,300; Other services not specified 13,500; *Total employed* (incl. unclassified) 169,300; Unemployed 10,900; *Total labour force* 180,100. Note: Totals may not be equal to the sum of components, owing to rounding.

HEALTH AND WELFARE

Key Indicators

Total Fertility Rate (children per woman, 2011): 2.1.

Under-5 Mortality Rate (per 1,000 live births, 2011): 3.

HIV/AIDS (% of persons aged 15–49, 2011): 0.3.

Physicians (per 1,000 head, 2011): 3.5.

Hospital Beds (per 1,000 head, 2007): 5.8.

Health Expenditure (2010): US $ per head (PPP): 3,230.

Health Expenditure (2010): % of GDP: 9.3.

Health Expenditure (2010): public (% of total): 80.4.

Total Carbon Dioxide Emissions ('000 metric tons, 2010): 1,961.8.

Carbon Dioxide Emissions Per Head (metric tons, 2010): 6.2.

Human Development Index (2012): ranking: 13.

Human Development Index (2012): value: 0.906.

For sources and definitions, see explanatory note on p. vi.

AGRICULTURE, ETC.

Principal Crops (metric tons, 2012): Cereals 16,170; Carrots 682; Cabbages 408; Tomatoes 1,716; Cucumbers 1,673; Cauliflower 136; Turnips 1,265; Peppers 261; Chinese cabbages 196; Mushrooms 583.

Livestock (2012): Cattle 71,513; Sheep 476,262; Horses 77,380; Goats 875; Pigs 3,643; Hens 200,169; Other poultry 50,820; Mink 50,820.

Livestock Products (metric tons, 2012, unless otherwise indicated): Cattle meat 4,113; Goat meat 9,921; Pig meat 5,854; Chicken meat 5,854; Milk ('000 litres, processed) 123,178 (2010).

Fishing (metric tons, live weight, 2012): Atlantic cod 204,755; Saithe 50,994; Haddock 47,768; Atlantic redfish 5,940; Capelin 600,706; Atlantic herring 100,767; Total (incl. others) 1,480,472.

INDUSTRY

Selected Products ('000 metric tons, 2011, unless otherwise indicated): Frozen fish 462.8 (demersal catch, 2009); Salted, dried or smoked fish 875.6 (2007); Cement 140.0 (estimated figure); Ferrosilicon 120.1; Aluminium (unwrought) 780.9; Electric energy 17,549 million kWh (2012). Source: partly US Geological Survey.

FINANCE

Currency and Exchange Rates: 100 aurar (singular: eyrir) = 1 new Icelandic króna (plural: krónur). *Sterling, Dollar and Euro Equivalents* (31 December 2013): £1 sterling = 190.288 krónur; US $1 = 115.550 krónur; €1 = 159.355 krónur; 1,000 krónur = £5.26 = $8.65 = €6.28. *Average Exchange Rate* (krónur per US $): 115.954 in 2011; 125.083 in 2012; 122.179 in 2013.

Budget (general government finances, '000 million krónur, 2012): *Revenue:* Tax revenue 559.7 (Taxes on income, profits and capital gains 283.2, Taxes on payroll and workforce 5.4, Taxes on property 42.4, Taxes on goods and services 212.0, Taxes on international trade 7.7, Other taxes 8.9); Social contributions 64.9; Grants 3.7; Other revenue 112.1; Total 740.3. *Expenditure:* Current expenditure 808.1 (Compensation of employees 250.7, Use of goods and services 200.7, Consumption of fixed capital 37.1, Interest 95.8, Subsidies 30.5, Grants 3.8, Social benefits 135.3, Other expenditure 54.2); Non-financial assets –2.5; Total 805.6.

International Reserves (US $ million at 31 December 2012): Gold (national valuation) 106.9; IMF special drawing rights 13.7; Reserve position in IMF 28.8; Foreign exchange 4,042.8; Total 4,192.2. Source: IMF, *International Financial Statistics*.

Money Supply (million krónur at 31 December 2012): Currency outside banks 40,861; Transferable deposit 426,875; Other deposit 1,056,745; *Broad money* 1,524,481. Source: IMF, *International Financial Statistics*.

Cost of Living (Consumer Price Index; base: 2005 = 100): All items 149.1 in 2010; 155.0 in 2011; 163.1 in 2012. Source: IMF, *International Financial Statistics*.

Gross Domestic Product (million krónur at constant 2000 prices): 947,186 in 2008; 883,985 in 2009; 848,626 in 2010. Source: IMF, *International Financial Statistics*.

Expenditure on the Gross Domestic Product (million krónur at current prices, 2012, preliminary): Government final consumption expenditure 430,413; Private final consumption expenditure 912,861; Changes in inventories 4,340; Gross fixed capital formation 246,937; *Total domestic expenditure* 1,594,551; Exports of goods and services 1,009,455; *Less* Imports of goods and services 905,514; *Gross domestic product in market prices* 1,698,492.

Gross Domestic Product by Economic Activity (million krónur at current prices, 2011, preliminary): Agriculture, hunting and forestry 16,048; Fishing 100,433; Mining and quarrying 921; Manufacturing 207,428; Electricity, gas and water supply 90,957; Construction 62,782; Wholesale and retail trade and repair of vehicles and household goods 131,022; Hotels and restaurants 29,042; Transport, storage and communications 136,854; Financial intermediation 91,619; Real estate, renting and business services 240,661; Public administration and compulsory social security 116,933; Education 65,622; Health and social work 98,205; Other community, social and personal services 44,594; Private households with employed persons 1,027; *Sub-total* 1,434,148; Correction item, taxes and subsidies on products 12,767; *Gross value added at basic prices* 1,446,915; Taxes on production and imports 196,799; *Less* Subsidies 15,037; *GDP in market prices* 1,628,677.

Balance of Payments (US $ million, 2012): Exports of goods 5,060.3; Imports of goods –4,440.4; *Balance on goods* 619.8; Exports of services 3,009.3; Imports of services –2,794.7; *Balance on goods and services* 834.4; Primary income received 694.8; Primary income paid –2,188.3; *Balance on goods, services and primary income* –659.1; Secondary income received 4.7; Secondary income paid –85.9; *Current balance* –740.3; Capital account (net) –1.3; Direct investment assets 3,196.5; Direct investment liabilities 1,086.0; Portfolio investment assets –631.9; Portfolio investment liabilities –9,157.9; Other investment assets –2,070.3; Other investment liabilities –4,554.4; Net errors and omissions 157.9; *Reserves and related items* –12,715.6. Source: IMF, *International Financial Statistics*.

EXTERNAL TRADE

Principal Commodities (million krónur, 2012): *Imports c.i.f.:* Food and beverages 55,499.7; Fuels and lubricants 88,579.6 (Motor spirit 18,485.5); Capital goods 125,390.1; Transport equipment 75,604.3 (Passenger cars 21,988.1); Consumer goods 76,320.8 (Semi-durable goods 29,177.1; Non-durable goods 33,267.5); Miscellaneous industrial supplies 174,337.1; Total (incl. others) 597,262.2. *Exports f.o.b.:* Food and beverages 257,094.9; Fuels and lubricants 12,741.1; Capital goods 23,689.6; Consumer goods 23,993.9; Miscellaneous industrial supplies 301,801.9; Total (incl. others) 633,029.1.

Principal Trading Partners (million krónur, country of consignment, 2012): *Imports c.i.f.:* Belgium 7,928.1; Brazil 39,730.9; Canada 6,594.2; China, People's Republic 42,743.1; Denmark (incl. Faroe Islands and Greenland) 36,532.3; France 12,777.4; Germany 54,813.1; Ireland 8,699.3; Italy 17,912.9; Japan 8,830.8; Malaysia 6,482.5; Netherlands 36,120.9; Norway 99,315.6; Poland 7,167.1; Spain 7,048.6; Sweden 22,929.5; Switzerland 6,611.6; United Kingdom 27,753.6; USA 61,059.0; Total (incl. others) 597,262.2. *Exports f.o.b.:* Belgium 10,055.0; China, People's Republic 7,646.9; Denmark (incl. Faroe Islands and Greenland) 25,932.0; France 28,116.1; Germany 81,502.2; Italy 13,014.1; Japan 12,925.1; Lithuania 10,843.8; Netherlands 189,654.4; Nigeria 16,502.0; Norway 32,258.0; Poland 9,158.3; Portugal 9,241.4; Russia 24,200.4; Spain 22,076.1; Switzerland 10,639.1; United Kingdom 62,170.7; USA 28,338.1; Total (incl. others) 633,029.1.

TRANSPORT

Road Traffic (registered motor vehicles, 2012): Passenger cars 210,070; Buses and coaches 2,084; Goods vehicles 30,338; Motorcycles 10,135.

Shipping: *Flag Registered Fleet* (registered vessels, 31 December 2013): Vessels 203; Total displacement 156,018 grt (Source: Lloyd's List Intelligence—www.lloydslistintelligence.com). *International Freight Traffic* ('000 metric tons, 2006): Goods loaded 1,858.4; Goods unloaded 4,058.4.

Civil Aviation (scheduled traffic, 2011): Kilometres flown (million) 37; Passengers carried ('000) 1,804; Passenger-km (million) 4,970; Total ton-km (million) 566. Source: UN, *Statistical Yearbook*. *Passengers Carried* ('000): 2,057 in 2012 (Source: World Bank, World Development Indicators database).

TOURISM

Foreign Visitors by Country of Origin (overnight stays in hotels and guesthouses, 2012): Canada 44,685; Denmark 105,911; France 161,597; Germany 349,603; Italy 59,736; Netherlands 92,181; Norway 124,981; Spain 66,142; Sweden 103,639; Switzerland 59,968; United Kingdom 351,215; USA 309,228; Total (incl. others) 2,231,963.

Receipts from Tourism (US $ million, excl. passenger transport): 559 in 2010; 748 in 2011; 845 in 2012 (provisional) (Source: World Tourism Organization).

COMMUNICATIONS MEDIA

Telephones (2012): 189,000 main lines in use.

Mobile Cellular Telephones ('000 subscribers, 2012): 346.0.

Internet Subscribers ('000, 2011): 114.8.

Broadband Subscribers ('000, 2012): 113.1.

Books (published, 2010): 1,506 titles (incl. new editions).

Daily Newspapers (2010, unless otherwise specified): 3 (combined circulation 129,750 copies per issue in 2010).

Non-daily Newspapers (2010): 21 (combined circulation 230,792 copies).

Source: partly International Telecommunication Union.

EDUCATION

Institutions (2012 unless otherwise indicated): Pre-primary 262; Primary and secondary (lower level) 168; Secondary (higher level) 53 (2005); Tertiary (universities and colleges) 23 (2010).

Teachers (incl. part-time, 2012 unless otherwise indicated): Pre-primary 3,544; Primary and secondary (lower level) 4,784; Secondary (higher level) 1,915 (2011); Tertiary 2,070.

Students (2012): Pre-primary 19,615; Primary and Secondary (lower level) 42,320; Secondary (higher level) 25,460; Tertiary 18,619.

Pupil-teacher Ratio (primary education, UNESCO estimate): 10.3 in 2006/07 (Source: UNESCO Institute for Statistics).

Directory

The Government

HEAD OF STATE

President: ÓLAFUR RAGNAR GRÍMSSON (elected 29 June 1996, took office 1 August 1996; unopposed in 2000, began a second term 1 August 2000; re-elected 26 June 2004, began third term 1 August 2004; unopposed in 2008, began fourth term 1 August 2008; re-elected 30 June 2012, began a fifth term 1 August 2012).

THE CABINET
(April 2014)

A coalition of the Independence Party (IP) and the Progressive Party (PP).

Prime Minister: SIGMUNDUR DAVÍÐ GUNNLAUGSSON (PP).

Minister of Finance and Economic Affairs: BJARNI BENEDIKTSSON (IP).

Minister of Health: KRISTJÁN ÞÓR JÚLÍUSSON (IP).

Minister of Education, Science and Culture: ILLUGI GUNNARSSON (IP).

Minister of Industry and Trade: RAGNHEIÐUR ELÍN ÁRNADÓTTIR (IP).

Minister of Social Affairs and Housing: EYGLÓ HARÐARDÓTTIR (PP).

Minister of Fisheries and Agriculture and for the Environment and Natural Resources: SIGURÐUR INGI JÓHANNSSON (PP).

Minister for Foreign Affairs and External Trade: GUNNAR BRAGI SVEINSSON (PP).

Minister of the Interior: HANNA BIRNA KRISTJÁNSDÓTTIR (IP).

MINISTRIES

Office of the President: Stadastaður, Sóleyjargötu 1, 101 Reykjavík; tel. 5404400; fax 5624802; e-mail forseti@forseti.is; internet www.forseti.is.

Prime Minister's Office: Stjórnarráðshúsinu við Lækjartorg, 150 Reykjavík; tel. 5458400; fax 5624014; e-mail postur@for.stjr.is; internet www.forsaetisraduneyti.is.

Ministry of Education, Science and Culture: Sölvhólsgötu 4, 150 Reykjavík; tel. 5459500; fax 5623068; e-mail postur@mrn.is; internet www.menntamalaraduneyti.is.

Ministry for the Environment and Natural Resources: Skuggasundi 1, 150 Reykjavík; tel. 5458600; fax 5624566; e-mail postur@uar.is; internet www.umhverfisraduneyti.is.

Ministry of Finance and Economic Affairs: Arnarhvoli við Lindargötu, 150 Reykjavík; tel. 5459200; fax 5459299; e-mail postur@fjr.is; internet www.fjr.is.

Ministry for Foreign Affairs: Rauðarárstíg 25, 150 Reykjavík; tel. 5459900; fax 5622373; e-mail postur@utn.stjr.is; internet www.mfa.is.

Ministry of Industries and Innovation: Skúlagata 4, 150 Reykjavík; tel. 5459700; fax 5521160; e-mail postur@anr.is; internet www.atvinnuvegaraduneyti.is.

Ministry of the Interior: Sölvhólsgötu 7, 150 Reykjavík; tel. 5459000; fax 5527340; e-mail postur@irr.is; internet www.innanrikisraduneyti.is.

Ministry of Welfare: Hafnarhúsinu við Tryggvagötu, 101 Reykjavík; tel. 5458100; fax 5519165; e-mail postur@vel.is; internet www.velferdarraduneyti.is.

President and Legislature

PRESIDENT

Presidential Election, 30 June 2012

	% of votes
Ólafur Ragnar Grímsson	52.78
Thóra Arnórsdóttir	33.16
Ari Trausti Guðmundsson	8.64
Herdís Thorgeirsdóttir	2.63
Andrea Johanna Ólafsdóttir	1.80
Hannes Bjarnason	0.98

LEGISLATURE

Althingi
(Alþingi)

v/Austurvöll, 150 Reykjavík; tel. 5630500; fax 5630550; e-mail editor@althingi.is; internet www.althingi.is.

Speaker of the Althingi: EINAR K. GUÐFINNSSON.

Secretary-General (Clerk) of the Althingi: HELGI BERNÓDUSSON.

General Election, 27 April 2013

Party	Votes	% of votes	Seats
Sjálfstæðisflokkurinn (Independence Party)	50,454	26.70	19
Framsóknarflokkurinn (Progressive Party)	46,173	24.43	19
Samfylkingin (Social Democratic Alliance)	24,292	12.85	9
Vinstrihreyfingin–grænt framboð (Left-Green Movement)	20,546	10.87	7

Party—*continued*	Votes	% of votes	Seats
Björt framtíð (Bright Future)	15,583	8.25	6
Píratar (Pirate Party)	9,647	5.10	3
Dögun (Dawn)	5,855	3.10	—
Flokkur Heimilanna (Households Party)	5,707	3.02	—
Lýðræðisvaktin (The Democracy Watch)	4,658	2.46	—
Hægri Grænir Flokkur Fólksins (Right-Green People's Party)	3,262	1.73	—
Regnboginn (Rainbow)	2,021	1.07	—
Landsbyggðarflokkurinn (Rural Party)	326	0.17	—
Sturla Jónsson	222	0.12	—
Húmanistaflokkurinn (Humanist Party)	126	0.07	—
Alþýðufylkingin (People's Front of Iceland)	118	0.06	—
Total	188,990	100.00	63

Election Commission

Landskjörstjórn (National Electoral Commission): Kirkjustræti 8B, 150 Reykjavík; tel. 5630933; fax 5630905; e-mail thorhallurv@althingi.is; internet www.landskjor.is; Sec. ÞÓRHALLUR VILHJÁLMSSON.

Political Organizations

Alþýðufylkingin (People's Front of Iceland—PFI): Hverfisgata 82, 101 Reykjavík; e-mail althydufylkingin@gmail.com; f. 2013; anti-capitalist, anti-euro; Chair. ÞORVALDUR ÞORVALDSSON.

Besti Flokkurinn (Best Party): Holtsgata 20, 101 Reykjavík; e-mail heida@bestiflokkurinn.is; internet www.bestiflokkurinn.is; f. 2009; satirical; won the largest number of seats on Reykjavík city council at municipal elections in 2010; Leader JÓN GNARR.

Björt framtíð (Bright Future): Hverfisgata 98, 101 Reykjavík; e-mail tolvupostur@heimasidan.is; internet www.bjortframtid.is; f. 2012; Leader GUÐMUNDUR STEINGRÍMSSON.

Borgarahreyfingin (Citizens' Movement): Höfðatúni 12, 105 Reykjavík; tel. 5111944; e-mail info@borgarahreyfingin.is; internet www.xo.is; f. 2009; advocates economic reform and membership of the European Union; 3 mems of parliamentary group left the party in Sept. 2009 to form Hreyfingin (The Movement, q.v.); part of the Dögun alliance; Leader FRIÐRIK ÞÓR GUÐMUNDSSON.

Dögun (Dawn): e-mail xdogun@xdogun.is; internet www.xdogun.is; f. 2012 as an alliance of Borgarahreyfingin, Frjálslyndi flokkurinn and other small parties; Chair. BENEDIKT SIGURÐARSON.

Flokkur Heimilanna (Households Party): f. 2013; a coalition of 8 smaller parties formed to contest the 2013 general election.

Framsóknarflokkurinn (Progressive Party—PP): Hverfisgötu 33, POB 453, 101 Reykjavík; tel. 5404300; fax 5404301; e-mail framsokn@framsokn.is; internet www.framsokn.is; f. 1916 with a programme of social liberalism and co-operation; Chair. SIGMUNDUR DAVÍÐ GUNNLAUGSSON; Parliamentary Leader SIGRÚN MAGNÚSDÓTTIR.

Frjálslyndi flokkurinn (Liberal Party): Lyngháls 3, 110 Reykjavík; tel. 4452093; e-mail xf@xf.is; f. 1998 by Sverrir Hermannsson, a former IP cabinet minister; incorporated fmr mems of defunct Nýtt Afl (New Force) in 2006; part of the Dögun alliance; Leader SIGURJÓN ÞÓRÐARSON.

Hægri Grænir Flokkur Fólksins (Right-Green People's Party): Barónsstígur 47, 101 Reykjavík; tel. 5177740; e-mail stjornmalaflokkur@gmail.com; internet www.afram-island.is; f. 2010; Chair. GUÐMUNDUR FRANKLÍN JÓNSSON.

Hreyfingin (The Movement): Austurstræti 8–10, 150 Reykjavík; tel. 5630484; e-mail hreyfingin@hreyfingin.is; internet www.hreyfingin.is; f. 2009 by fmr mems of Borgarahreyfingin (Citizens' Movement); part of the Dögun alliance.

Húmanistaflokkurinn (Humanist Party): Brautarholt 4, 105 Reykjavík; tel. 6615621; f. 1984.

Landsbyggðarflokkurinn (Rural Party): f. 2013.

Lýðræðishreyfingin (Democracy Party): Vogasel 1, 109 Reykjavík; tel. 4962002; Leader ÁSTÞÓR MAGNÚSSON.

Lýðræðisvaktin (The Democracy Watch): e-mail xlvaktin@xlvaktin.is; f. 2013; Leader Dr THORVALDUR GYLFASON.

Píratar (Pirate Party): e-mail piratar@piratar.is; internet www.piratar.is; f. 2012; Leader BIRGITTA JÓNSDÓTTIR.

Regnboginn (Rainbow): Reykjavík; e-mail regnboginn@regnboginn.is; internet regnboginn.is; f. 2013; Spokesperson JÓN BJARNASON.

Samfylkingin (Social Democratic Alliance—SDA): Hallveigarstíg 1, 101 Reykjavík; tel. 4142200; fax 4142201; e-mail samfylking@samfylking.is; internet www.samfylkingin.is; f. 1999 by merger of Alþýðubandalagið (People's Alliance, f. 1956), Alþýðuflokkurinn (Social Democratic Party, f. 1916), Samtök um kvennalista (Women's List, f. 1983) and Þjóðvaki—hreyfing fólksins (Awakening of the Nation—People's Movement, f. 1994); Chair. ÁRNI PÁLL ÁRNASON; Parliamentary Leader MAGNÚS ORRI SCHRAM.

Sjálfstæðisflokkurinn (Independence Party—IP): Háaleitisbraut 1, 105 Reykjavík; tel. 5151700; fax 5151717; e-mail xd@xd.is; internet www.xd.is; f. 1929 by an amalgamation of the Conservative and Liberal Parties; advocates social reform within the framework of private enterprise and the furtherance of national and individual independence; Leader BJARNI BENEDIKTSSON; Parliamentary Leader RAGNHEIÐUR RÍKHARÐSDÓTTIR; Sec.-Gen. ÞÓRÐUR ÞÓRARINSSON.

Sturla Jónsson: f. 2013; fmrly called Forward Moving Party; Leader STURLA JÓNSSON.

Vinstrihreyfingin-grænt framboð (Left-Green Movement): Suðurgötu 3, POB 175, 101 Reykjavík; tel. 5528872; e-mail vg@vg.is; internet www.vg.is; f. 1999 by dissident mems of the People's Alliance, the Women's List, the Greens and independent left-wingers; around 3,000 mems; Leader KATRÍN JAKOBSDÓTTIR; Parliamentary Leader SVANDÍS SVAVARSDÓTTIR; Sec.-Gen. SÓLEY TÓMASDÓTTIR.

Diplomatic Representation

EMBASSIES IN ICELAND

Canada: Túngata 14, 101 Reykjavík; POB 1510, 121 Reykjavík; tel. 5756500; fax 5756501; e-mail rkjvk@international.gc.ca; internet www.canadainternational.gc.ca/iceland-islande; Ambassador STEWART WHEELER.

China, People's Republic: Bríetartún 1, 105 Reykjavík; tel. 5526751; fax 5626110; e-mail chinaemb@simnet.is; internet is .china-embassy.org; Ambassador MA JISHENG.

Denmark: Hverfisgata 29, 101 Reykjavík; tel. 5750300; fax 5750310; e-mail rekamb@um.dk; internet island.um.dk; Ambassador KJUEL NIELSEN.

Finland: Túngata 30, 101 Reykjavík; POB 1060, 121 Reykjavík; tel. 5100100; fax 5623880; e-mail sanomat.rey@formin.fi; internet www.finland.is; Ambassador IRMA ERTMAN.

France: Túngata 22, 101 Reykjavík; POB 1750, 121 Reykjavík; tel. 5759600; fax 5759604; e-mail ambafrance@ambafrance.is; internet ambafrance-is.org; Ambassador MARC BOUTEILLER.

Germany: Laufásvegur 31, 101 Reykjavík; tel. 5301100; fax 5301101; e-mail info@reykjavik.diplo.de; internet www.reykjavik.diplo.de; Ambassador THOMAS MEISTER.

India: Skúlagata 17, 101 Reykjavík; tel. 5349955; fax 5349959; e-mail gen@indianembassy.is; internet www.indianembassy.is; Ambassador ASHOK DAS.

Japan: Laugavegur 182, POB 5380, 105 Reykjavík; tel. 5108600; fax 5108605; e-mail japan@rk.mofa.go.jp; internet www.is.emb-japan.go.jp; Ambassador AKIO SHIROTA (resident in Oslo, Norway).

Norway: Fjólugötu 17, 101 Reykjavík; tel. 5200700; fax 5529553; e-mail emb.reykjavik@mfa.no; internet www.noregur.is; Ambassador DAG WERNØ HOLTER.

Poland: Þórunnartún 2, 105 Reykjavik; tel. 5205050; fax 5111120; e-mail reykjavik.info@msz.gov.pl; internet www.reykjavik.msz.gov.pl; Ambassador STEFAN CZMUR (Resident in Oslo, Norway).

Russia: Garðastræti 33, POB 380, 101 Reykjavík; tel. 5515156; fax 5620633; e-mail russemb@itn.is; internet www.iceland.mid.ru; Ambassador ANDREY V. TSYGANOV.

Sweden: Lágmúla 7, 108 Reykjavík; POB 8136, 128 Reykjavík; tel. 5201230; fax 5201235; e-mail ambassaden.reykjavik@foreign.ministry.se; internet www.swedenabroad.com/reykjavik; Ambassador BO WILLIAM HEDBERG.

United Kingdom: Laufásvegur 31, 101 Reykjavík; POB 460, 121 Reykjavík; tel. 5505100; fax 5505105; e-mail info@britishembassy.is; internet ukiniceland.fco.gov.uk; Ambassador STUART GILL.

USA: Laufásvegur 21, 101 Reykjavík; tel. 5629100; fax 5629139; e-mail reykjavikprotocol@state.gov; internet iceland.usembassy.gov; Ambassador ROBERT C. BARBER (acting).

Judicial System

All cases are heard in Ordinary Courts except those specifically within the jurisdiction of Special Courts. The Ordinary Courts include both a lower division of urban and rural district courts presided over by the district magistrates, and the Supreme Court.

Justices of the Supreme Court are appointed by the President and cannot be dismissed except by the decision of a court. The Justices elect the Chief Justice for a period of two years.

Supreme Court: Dómhúsið v. Arnarhól, 150 Reykjavík; tel. 5103030; fax 5623995; e-mail haestirettur@haestirettur.is; internet www.haestirettur.is; Chief Justice MARKÚS SIGURBJÖRNSSON.

Religion

At the beginning of 2014 some 75.1% of the total population were members of the Þjoðkirkja Íslands (Evangelical Lutheran Church of Iceland). The Free Lutheran Churches had a total membership of 5.0% of the population, while 3.5% were members of the Roman Catholic Church. Some 6.4% belonged to 'other and not specified' religious organizations' (including religions, such as Judaism, that have been practised in the country for years without requesting official recognition), while 5.3% were not part of any religious organization.

CHRISTIANITY

Protestant Churches

Þjoðkirkja Íslands (Evangelical Lutheran Church of Iceland): Biskupsstofa, Laugavegur 31, 150 Reykjavík; tel. 5284000; fax 5284099; e-mail kirkjan@kirkjan.is; internet www.kirkjan.is; the national church, endowed by the state; Iceland forms 1 diocese, with 2 suffragan sees; 272 parishes, 150 pastors (2011); 244,440 mems (2014); Bishop AGNES M. SIGURÐARDÓTTIR.

A further 19 Protestant churches are officially registered, the largest of which are the following:

Fríkirkjusöfnuðurinn í Hafnarfirði (Hafnarfjörður Free Lutheran Church): Linnetsstíg 6-8, 220 Hafnarfjörður; tel. 5653430; e-mail einar@frikirkja.is; internet www.frikirkja.is; f. 1913; 6,221 mems (2014); Head EINAR EYJÓLFSSON.

Fríkirkjusöfnuðurinn í Reykjavík (Reykjavík Free Lutheran Church): Laufásvegi 13, 101 Reykjavík; POB 1671, 121 Reykjavík; tel. 5527270; fax 5527287; e-mail frikirkjan@frikirkjan.is; internet www.frikirkjan.is; f. 1899; Free Lutheran denomination; 9,386 mems (2014); Head HJÖRTUR MAGNI JÓHANNSSON.

Hvítasunnukirkjan á Íslandi (Pentecostal Assemblies): Hátúni 2, 105 Reykjavík; tel. 5354700; e-mail filadelfia@filadelfia.is; internet www.filadelfia.is; f. 1936; 2,075 mems (2014); Head VÖRÐUR LEVÍ TRAUSTASON.

Óhádi söfnuðurinn (Independent Congregation): Háteigsvegi 56, 105 Reykjavík; tel. 5510999; e-mail postur@ohadisofnudurinn.is; internet www.ohadisofnudurinn.is; Free Lutheran denomination; 3,312 mems (2014); Head Rev. PÉTUR ÞORSTEINSSON.

The Roman Catholic Church

Iceland comprises a single diocese, directly responsible to the Holy See. At the beginning of 2014 there were 11,454 adherents in the country (3.5% of the total population).

Bishop of Reykjavík: Rt Rev. PIERRE BÜRCHER, Biskupsstofa, Hávallagata 14, 101 Reykjavík; POB 490, 121 Reykjavík; tel. 5525388; fax 5623878; e-mail catholica@catholica.is; internet www.catholica.is.

ISLAM

Félag múslima á Íslandi (Muslim Asscn of Iceland): Ármúli 38, 3 hæð, 108 Reykjavík; tel. 8951967; e-mail ibrahim@islam.is; internet www.islam.is; f. 1997; 481 mems (2014); Head IBRAHIM SVERRIR AGNARSSON.

BAHÁ'Í FAITH

Bahá'í samfélagið á Íslandi (Bahá'í Community of Iceland): Öldugötu 2, 101 Reykjavík; tel. 5670344; e-mail nsa@bahai.is; internet www.bahai.is; 399 mems (2014); Sec. RÓBERT BADÍ BALDURSSON.

BUDDHISM

Búddistafélag Íslands (Buddhist Association of Iceland): Víghólastíg 21, 200 Kópavogur; 964 mems (2014); Head PHAMAHAPRASIT BOONKAM.

Trúfélagið Zen á Íslandi, Nátthagi (Soto Zen Buddhist Asscn of Iceland): Grensásvegur 8, 108 Reykjavík; e-mail zen@zen.is; internet www.zen.is; 85 mems (2011); Head HELGA JÓAKIMSDÓTTIR.

The Press

PRINCIPAL DAILIES

DV (Dagblaðið-Vísir): DV ehf, Tryggvagötu 11,101 Reykjavík; tel. 5127000; e-mail ritstjorn@dv.is; internet www.dv.is; f. 1910; independent; Editors REYNIR TRAUSTASON, JÓN TRAUSTI REYNISSON; circ. 340,000 (2013).

Fréttablaðið (The Newspaper): Skaftahlíð 24, 105 Reykjavík; tel. 5125000; fax 5125301; e-mail ritstjorn@frettabladid.is; internet www.visir.is; f. 2001; distributed free of charge; owned by 365 miðlar ehf; Editor-in-Chief ÓLAFUR Þ. STEPHENSEN; circ. 88,000 (2010).

Morgunblaðið (Morning News): Hádegismóum 2, 110 Reykjavík; tel. 5691100; fax 5691110; e-mail morgunbladid@mbl.is; internet www.mbl.is; f. 1913; owned by Árvakur hf; Editors DAVÍÐ ODDSSON, HARALDUR JOHANNESSEN; circ. 43,250 (2010).

WEEKLIES

Bæjarins besta (BB): Sólgötu 9, 400 Ísafjörður; tel. 4564560; fax 4564564; e-mail bb@bb.is; internet www.bb.is; f. 1984; local; Editor SIGURJÓN J. SIGURÐSSON.

Fiskifréttir: Nóatúni 17, 105 Reykjavík; tel. 5116622; fax 5696692; e-mail vb@vb.is; internet www.fiskifrettir.is; f. 1983; weekly; for the fishing industry; Editor GUÐJÓN EINARSSON; circ. 6,000.

Séð & Heyrt: Lyngás 17, 210 Garðabær; tel. 5155500; fax 5155599; e-mail birtingur@birtingur.is; internet www.birtingur.is; showbusiness and celebrities; Editor LILJA KATRÍN GUNNARSDÓTTIR; circ. 23,000.

Skessuhorn: Kirkjubraut 56, 300 Akranesi; tel. 4335500; fax 4335501; e-mail skessuhorn@skessuhorn.is; internet www.skessuhorn.is; f. 1998; local; Editor MAGNÚS MAGNÚSSON.

Sunnlenska Fréttablaðið: Austurvegi 22, 800 Selfoss; tel. 4823074; fax 4823084; e-mail sunnlenska@sunnlenska.is; internet www.sunnlenska.is; f. 1991; local newspaper; Editor SIGMUNDUR SIGURDÓRSSON; circ. 6,300.

Vikan: Lynghåls 17, 210 Garðabær; tel. 5155500; fax 5155599; e-mail birtingur@birtingur.is; internet www.birtingur.is; f. 1938; publ. by Birtíngur; women's weekly; Editor ELÍN ARNAR; circ. 17,000.

Víkurfréttir: Grundarvegur 23, 260 Reykjanesbær; tel. 4210000; fax 4210020; e-mail pket@vf.is; internet www.vf.is; f. 1983; local newspaper; Editor PÁLL KETILSSON; circ. 8,700.

Viðskiptablaðið: Nóatún 17, 105 Reykjavík; tel. 5116622; fax 5116692; e-mail mottaka@vb.is; internet www.vb.is; f. 1994; publ. by Framtíðarsýn hf; business weekly in collaboration with the *Financial Times* (United Kingdom); Editor-in-Chief HARALDUR JOHANNESSEN.

OTHER PERIODICALS

Ægir: Hafnarstræti 82, 600 Akureyri; tel. 5155220; e-mail johann@athygli.is; internet www.athygli.is; f. 1905; owned by Athygli ehf; publ. by the Fisheries Asscn of Iceland; 10 a year; Editor JÓHANN ÓLAFUR HALLDÓRSSON; circ. 2,500.

Atlantica: Borgartún 23, 105 Reykjavík; tel. 5127575; fax 5618646; e-mail heimur@heimur.is; internet www.heimur.is; f. 1967; 6 a year; in-flight magazine of Icelandair; Editor PÁLL STEFÁNSSON.

Bændablaðið: 107 Reykjavík; tel. 5630300; fax 5623058; e-mail bbl@bondi.is; f. 1995; fortnightly; organ of the Icelandic farmers' union; Editor HÖRÐUR KRISTJÁNSSON; circ. 6,400.

Eiðfaxi: Nóatúni 17, 105 Reykjavík; tel. 5116622; e-mail eidfaxi@eidfaxi.is; internet www.eidfaxi.is; f. 1977; monthly (Icelandic edn, English and German edns every 2 months); horse-breeding and horsemanship; circ. 7,000.

Freyr, búnaðarblað: Bændahöllin við Hagatorg, 107 Reykjavík; tel. 5630300; fax 5623058; e-mail freyr@bondi.is; internet www.bondi.is; monthly; agriculture; Editor TJORVI BJARNASON; circ. 1,600.

Frjáls Verslun (Free Trade): Borgartún 23, 105 Reykjavík; tel. 5617575; fax 5618646; e-mail jgh@heimur.is; internet www.heimur.is; f. 1939; 10 a year; business magazine; Editor JÓN G. HAUKSSON; circ. 6,000–9,000.

Gestgjafinn: Lyngás 17, 210 Garðabær; tel. 5155500; fax 5155599; e-mail gestgjafinn@frodi.is; internet www.gestgjafinn.is; f. 1981; 12 a year; food and wine; Editor SIGRÍÐUR BJÖRK BRAGADÓTTIR.; circ. 13,000–16,000.

Hús og Híbýli: Lyngás 17, 210 Garðabær; tel. 5155500; fax 5155599; e-mail birtingur@birtingur.is; f. 1973; 17 a year; architecture, homes and gardens; Editor SIGRÍÐUR ELÍN ÁSMUNDSDÓTTIR; circ. 15,000–17,000.

Húsfreyjan (The Housewife): Túngata 14, 101 Reykjavík; tel. 5517044; e-mail husfreyjan@husfreyjan.is; f. 1949; quarterly; the organ of the Federation of Icelandic Women's Societies; Editor HRAFNHILDUR VALGARÐS; circ. 4,000.

Iceland Review: Borgartún 23, 105 Reykjavík; tel. 5127575; e-mail icelandreview@icelandreview.com; internet www.icelandreview.com; f. 1963; quarterly, in English; general; Editor PÁLL STEFÁNSSON.

Lifandi vísindi: Klapparstíg 25, 105 Reykjavík; tel. 5708300; fax 5703809; e-mail lifandi@visindi.is; internet www.visindi.is; popular science; Editor GUÐBJARTUR FINNBJÖRNSSON.

Mannlíf: Lyngháls 17, 210 Garðabær; tel. 5155500; fax 5155599; e-mail birtingur@birtingur.is; internet www.birtingur.is; f. 1984; 10 a year; general interest; Dir KARLS STEINARS ÓSKARSSONAR; circ. 16,000.

Myndbönd mánaðarins (Videos of the Month): Reykjavík; tel. 5811280; fax 5811286; e-mail myndmark@islandia.is; f. 1994; monthly; Editor BERGUR ÍSLEIFSSON; circ. 26,000.

Nýtt Líf: Lyngás 17, 210 Garðabær; tel. 5155555; fax 5155599; e-mail nyttlif@birtingur.is; f. 1978; 11 a year; fashion; Editor KOLBRÚN PÁLÍNA HELGADÓTTIR; circ. 13,000–17,000.

Peningamál: Kalkofnsvegur 1, 150 Reykjavík; tel. 5699600; fax 5699605; e-mail sedlabanki@sedlabanki.is; internet www.sedlabanki.is; f. 1999; 4 a year; bulletin published by the Central Bank; circ. 1,000; Editor THÓRARINN G. PÉTURSSON.

The Reykjavík Grapevine: Hafnarstræti 15, 101 Reykjavík; tel. 5403600; fax 5403609; e-mail grapevine@grapevine.is; internet www.grapevine.is; f. 2003; 18 a year; in English; distributed free of charge; owned by Fröken ehf; Publr HILMAR STEINN GRÉTARSSON; Editor HAUKUR S. MAGNÚSSON; circ. 30,000.

Skírnir: Skeifan 3B, 108 Reykjavík; tel. 5889060; fax 5814088; e-mail hib@islandia.is; internet www.hib.is; f. 1827; journal of Hið íslenska bókmenntafélag (Icelandic Literary Society); Editor HALLDÓR GUÐMUNDSSON.

Skutull (Harpoon): Miðtun 16, 400 Isafjörður; tel. 8958270; e-mail skutull@skutull.is; internet skutull.is; f. 1923; monthly; organ of the Social Democratic Alliance in Westfjords; Editor SIGURÐUR PÉTURSSON.

Ský: Borgartún 23, 105 Reykjavík; tel. 5127575; fax 5618646; e-mail benedikt@heimur.is; internet www.heimur.is; complimentary in-flight magazine of Air Iceland; Editors BENEDIKT JÓHANNESSON, JÓN G. HAUKSSON.

Tölvuheimur (PC World Iceland): Borgartún 23, 105 Reykjavík; tel. 5127575; fax 5618646; e-mail tolvuheimur@heimur.is; internet www.heimur.is; in collaboration with International Data Group; computers; Editor (vacant).

Veiðimaðurinn (The Angler): Borgartún 23, 105 Reykjavík; tel. 5127575; fax 5618646; e-mail heimur@heimur.is; internet www.heimur.is; f. 1984; 3 a year; angling; Editor BJARNI BRYNJÓLFSSON; circ. 5,000–7,000.

Vinnan (Labour): Sætún 1, 105 Reykjavík; tel. 5107500; fax 5107501; e-mail gra@asi.is; internet www.asi.is; 2 a year; f. 1943; publ. by Icelandic Federation of Labour; Editor Dr SNORRI MÁR SKÚLASON; circ. 5,000.

Vísbending: Borgartún 23, 105 Reykjavík; tel. 5127575; fax 5618646; e-mail heimur@heimur.is; internet www.heimur.is; f. 1983; weekly; business; Editor BENEDIKT JÓHANNESSON.

Publishers

Birtíngur útgáfufélag: Lyngháls 17, 110 Reykjavík; tel. 5155500; fax 5155599; e-mail birtingur@birtingur.is; internet www.birtingur.is; f. 2007; publ. 9 popular magazines: *Gestgjafinn*, *Hús & Híbýli*, *Júlía*, *Nýtt Líf*, *Sagan Öll*, *Séð & Heyrt*, *Vikan* and *WOW*; Dir HREINN LOFTSSON.

Bjartur: Bræðraborgarstíg 9, 101 Reykjavík; tel. 4141450; e-mail bjartur@bjartur.is; internet www.bjartur.is; f. 1990; contemporary fiction, illustrated and children's books; Publr PÉTUR MÁR ÓLAFSSON.

Edda útgáfa hf: Lynghálsi 4, 110 Reykjavík; tel. 5222000; fax 5222022; e-mail edda@edda.is; internet www.edda.is; imprints: Almenna bókafélagið, Forlagið, Iðunn, Mál og menning, Nýja bókafélagið-Þjoðsaga, Vaka-Helgafell; Icelandic fiction and non-fiction, translated fiction, biography, illustrated books, children's books on Iceland, maps; Man. Dir SÆMUNDUR BENEDIKTSSON; Editor GRÉTA BJÖRG JAKOBSDÓTTIR.

Forlagið: Bræðraborgarstíg 7, 101 Reykjavík; tel. 5755600; fax 5755601; e-mail forlagid@forlagid.is; internet www.forlagid.is; general, fiction, biography, reference, illustrated; Dir JÓHANN PÁLL VALDIMARSSON.

Háskólaútgáfan (University of Iceland Press): Dunhagi 18, 107 Reykjavík; tel. 5254003; fax 5255255; e-mail hu@hi.is; internet www.haskolautgafan.hi.is; f. 1988; non-fiction, science, culture, history; Man. Dir JÖRUNDUR GUÐMUNDSSON.

Hið íslenska bókmenntafélag (Icelandic Literary Society): Skeifan 3B, 108 Reykjavík; tel. 5889060; fax 5814088; e-mail hib@islandia.is; internet www.hib.is; f. 1816; literary criticism; Pres. SIGURÐUR LÍNDAL.

Hið íslenska Fornritafélag: Skeifan 3B, 108 Reykjavík; tel. 5889060; fax 5814088; e-mail hib@islandia.is; internet www.hib.is; f. 1928; Pres. J. NORDAL.

Hólar: Hagasel 14, 109 Reykjavík; tel. 5872619; fax 5871180; e-mail holar@holabok.is; internet www.holabok.is; f. 1995; general; Dir GUDJÓN INGI EIRÍKSSON.

Jentas ehf: Austurströnd 10, 170 Seltjarnarnes; tel. 5687054; internet www.jentas.is; f. 1997; formerly PP Forlag ehf Ísland; general; Dir SIGRÚN HALLDÓRSDÓTTIR.

Krydd í tilveruna: Heiðarhjalli 5, 200 Kópavogur; tel. 8923334; e-mail krydd@simnet.is; f. 1989; children's, cookery; Dir ÆVAR GUÐMUNDSSON.

Námsgagnastofnun (National Centre for Educational Materials): Víkurhvarf 3, 203 Kópavogur; tel. 5350400; fax 5350401; e-mail simi@nams,is; internet www.nams.is; f. 1979; state-owned; Man. Dir INGIBJÖRG ÁSGEIRSDÓTTIR.

Ormstunga: Ránargötu 20, 101 Reykjavík; tel. 5610055; e-mail books@ormstunga.is; internet www.ormstunga.is; f. 1992; Icelandic and foreign fiction and non-fiction; Dir GÍSLI MÁR GÍSLASON.

Salka: Skipholti 50C, 105 Reykjavík; tel. 5222250; fax 5528122; e-mail salka@salka.is; internet www.salka.is; f. 2000; non-fiction, books for, by and about women; Dir HILDUR HERMÓÐSDÓTTIR.

Samhjálp: Stangarhyl 3A, 110 Reykjavík; tel. 5611000; fax 5610050; e-mail heidar@samhjalp.is; internet www.samhjalp.is; religious, pentecostal; Dir HEIDAR GUÐNASON.

Setberg: Akralind 2, 203 Kópavogur; tel. 5517667; fax 5526640; e-mail setberg@setberg.is; internet www.setberg.is; f. 1950; fiction, cookery, juvenile, picture books, activity books and children's books; Dir ARNBJÖRN KRISTINSSON.

Skálholtsútgáfan (National Church Publishing): Laugavegi 31, 101 Reykjavík; tel. 5284200; fax 5621595; e-mail skalholtsutgafan@skalholtsutgafan.is; internet www.skalholtsutgafan.is; f. 1981; non-fiction, religion, children's; Man. Dir EDDA MÖLLER.

Skjaldborg ehf: Mörkin 1, POB 8427, 108 Reykjavík; tel. 5882400; fax 5888994; e-mail skjaldborg@skjaldborg.is; general; Dir BJÖRN EIRÍKSSON.

Skrudda: Eyjarslóð 9, 101 Reykjavík; tel. 5528866; fax 5528870; e-mail skrudda@skrudda.is; internet www.skrudda.is; f. 2003; fiction, non-fiction, translated fiction, biography, children's; Man. STEINGRIMUR STEINTHORSSON.

Sögufélagið: Skeifunni 3 B, 108 Reykjavík; tel. 5889060; e-mail sogufelag@sogufelag.is; internet www.sogufelag.is; f. 1902; non-fiction, history; Dir GUÐNI TH. JÓHANNESSON.

Stofnun Árna Magnússonar í íslenskum fræðum: Árnagarður, Suðurgötu, 101 Reykjavík; tel. 5254010; fax 5254035; e-mail arnastofnun@hi.is; internet www.arnastofnun.is; f. 1972; state-owned; non-fiction; Dir GUÐRÚN NORDAL.

Útgáfufélagið Heimur: Borgartún 23, 105 Reykjavík; tel. 5127575; fax 5618646; e-mail heimur@heimur.is; internet www.heimur.is; f. 2000; magazines, travel books; Man. Dir BENEDIKT JÓHANNESSON.

PUBLISHERS' ASSOCIATION

Félag íslenskra bókaútgefenda (Icelandic Publishers' Asscn): Barónsstíg 5, 101 Reykjavík; tel. 5118020; fax 5115020; e-mail baekur@simnet.is; internet www.bokautgafa.is; f. 1889; Pres. EGILL ÖRN JÓHANNSSON; Man. BENEDIKT KRISTJANSSON.

Broadcasting and Communications

TELECOMMUNICATIONS

IceCell ehf: Skúlagata 19, 101 Reykjavík; tel. 6666330; fax 6666331; e-mail info@icecell.is; internet www.icecell.is; mobile telecommunications; CEO ANDREAS FINK.

IMC Island ehf: Borgartún 31, 105 Reykjavík; tel. 6618540; e-mail info@worldcell.com; GSM mobile service provider; wholly owned subsidiary of WorldCell Inc., USA; CEO JEFFREY STARK.

Nova ehf: Lágmúla 9, 108 Reykjavík; tel. 5191000; fax 5190001; e-mail nova@nova.is; internet www.nova.is; f. 2006; mobile telecommunications and broadband internet access; Chair. TÓMAS OTTO HANSSON.

Síminn hf: Ármúla 25, 108 Reykjavík; tel. 5506000; fax 5506009; e-mail siminn@siminn.is; internet www.siminn.is; f. 1998 as Iceland Telecom Ltd; present name adopted 2005 following privatization; offers fixed-line telecommunications, digital TV services and broadband internet access; Pres. and CEO SÆVAR FREYR ÞRÁINSSON.

Vodafone Iceland: Skútuvogi 2, 104 Reykjavík; tel. 5999000; fax 5999001; e-mail vodafone@vodafone.is; internet www.vodafone.is; f. 2003 as Og Vodafone by merger of Tal, Íslandssími and Halló; renamed as above in 2006; provides mobile and fixed-line telecommunications; CEO ÓMAR SVAVARSSON.

Supervisory Authority

Póst- og Fjarskiptastofnun (Post and Telecom Administration): Suðurlandsbraut 4, 108 Reykjavík; tel. 5101500; fax 5101509; e-mail pfs@pfs.is; internet www.pfs.is; supervisory authority; Man. Dir HRAFNKELL V. GÍSLASON.

BROADCASTING

Ríkisútvarpið (Icelandic National Broadcasting Service—RÚV): Broadcasting Centre, Efstaleiti 1, 150 Reykjavík; tel. 5153000; fax 5153010; e-mail istv@ruv.is; internet www.ruv.is; f. 1930; Dir-Gen. PÁLL MAGNÚSSON.

Skjárinn: Skipholt 31, 105 Reykjavík; tel. 5956000; e-mail info@skjarinn.is; internet www.skjarinn.is; f. 2005; owned by Síminn hf; multi-channel digital television service; also operates 3 television channels: Skjáreinn, Skjárbíóand and Skjárheimur; Man. FRIÐRIK FRIÐRIKSSON.

365 miðlar ehf: Skaftahlíð 24, 105 Reykjavík; tel. 5125000; e-mail askrft@stod2.is; internet www.365.is; f. 2005; owns fmr broadcasting assets of Íslenska Sjónvarpsfélagið hf, as well as the daily newspaper *Fréttablaðið*; Chair. INGIBJÖRG STEFANÍA PÁLMADÓTTIR.

Radio

Ríkisútvarpið—Útvarpi (Icelandic National Broadcasting Service—Radio): Radio Division, Efstaleiti 1, 150 Reykjavík; tel. 5153000; fax 5153010; e-mail radionews@ruv.is; internet www.ruv.is; f. 1930; Programmes 1 and 2 are broadcast over a network of 89 transmitters each; Programme 1 is broadcast for 112 hours a week, with the remaining hours simulcast with Programme 2; Programme 2 is broadcast 168 hours a week; 2 long-wave transmitters broadcast the same programme, alternating between Programme 1 and Programme 2; Dir SIGRÚN STEFÁNSDÓTTIR.

Akraneskaupstaður: Stillholt 16–18, 300 Akranes; tel. 4331000; fax 4331090; e-mail akranes@akranes.is; internet www.akranes.is; broadcasts only in Akranes; Dir BJÖRN LÁRUSSON.

Bylgjan: Skaftahlíð 24, 105 Reykjavík; tel. 5125000; fax 5156900; e-mail ritstjorn@visir.is; internet bylgjan.visir.is; owned by 365 miðlar ehf; Dir ÁGÚST HEÐINSSON.

FM957: Skaftahlíð 24, 110 Reykjavík; tel. 5110957; e-mail fm957@fm957.is; internet www.fm957.is; owned by 365 miðlar ehf.

Kristilega útvarpsstöðin Lindin: Krókháls 4A, 110 Reykjavík; tel. 5671818; fax 5671824; e-mail lindin@lindin.is; internet lindin.is; Dir MICHAEL E. FITZGERALD.

Létt Bylgjan: Skaftahlíð 24, 105 Reykjavík; tel. 5125000; fax 5156830; e-mail lettbylgjan@lettbylgjan.is; internet www.bylgjan.is; owned by 365 miðlar ehf; Dir AGUST HEÐINSSON.

Útvarp Saga: Nóatún 17, 105 Reykjavík; tel. 5333943; fax 5881994; e-mail saga@utvarpsaga.is; internet www.utvarpsaga.is; Dir ARNÞRÚÐUR KARLSDÓTTIR.

Útvarp Vestmannaeyjar: Brekkugata 1, 900 Vestmannaeyjar; tel. 4811534; fax 4813475; broadcasts only in Vestmannaeyjar; Dir BJARNI JÓNASSON.

X 97.7: Skaftahlíð 24, 105 Reykjavík; tel. 5125000; e-mail x977@x977.is; internet www.x977.is; owned by 365 miðlar ehf.

Television

Ríkisútvarpið—Sjónvarp (Icelandic National Broadcasting Service—Television): Efstaleiti 1, 150 Reykjavík; tel. 5153000; fax 5153010; e-mail istv@ruv.is; internet www.ruv.is; f. 1966; covers 99% of the population; broadcasts daily, total 70 hours a week; Dir SIGRÚN STEFÁNSDÓTTIR.

Bíórásin: Skaftahlíð 24, 105 Reykjavík; tel. 5125000; owned by 365 miðlar ehf.

Kristniboðskirkjan: Grensásvegur 8, 108 Reykjavík; tel. 5683131; fax 5683741; f. 1995; broadcasts only in the Reykjavík area; religious; Dir EIRÍKUR SIGURBJÖRNSSON.

PoppTíví: Skaftahlíð 24, 105 Reykjavík; tel. 5156000; f. 1998; owned by 365 miðlar ehf; music station.

Stöð 2: Skaftahlíð 24, 105 Reykjavík; tel. 5125000; fax 5125100; e-mail askrift@stod2.is; internet www.stod2.is; f. 1986; owned by 365 miðlar ehf; 'pay-TV' station.

Sýn (Vision): Skaftahlíð 24, 105 Reykjavík; tel. 5125000; owned by 365 miðlar ehf.

Finance

(cap. = capital; res = reserves; dep. = deposits; m. = million; amounts in krónur; brs = branches)

BANKING

In 1989–90 the number of commercial banks was reduced from seven to three, by amalgamating four banks to form Íslandsbanki; a further restructuring of the banking sector commenced in 2000 with the merger of Íslandsbanki with the recently privatized investment bank FBA. Íslandsbanki was renamed Glitnir Banki in 2006. By early 2003 the Icelandic Government had withdrawn completely from the country's commercial banking sector, having sold its controlling stakes in Bunarðarbanki Íslands and Landsbanki Íslands.

In 2008 the banking sector suffered severe difficulties resulting from a reduction in the availability of credit on global financial markets, and the Icelandic Government was forced to intervene in an attempt to stabilize the economy. In October the Government acquired a 75% stake in Iceland's third largest retail bank, Glitnir Banki, and subsequently announced that it would guarantee the security of all domestic bank deposits held in Icelandic banks. The Althingi (parliament) approved legislation in the same month that granted wide-ranging powers to the Financial Supervisory Authority (Fjármálaeftirlitið—FME), allowing it to take control of financial institutions. The FME subsequently assumed control of Landsbanki Íslands, Glitnir Banki and Kaupþing Banki. Three new banks—Nýi Glitnir Banki (renamed Íslandsbanki in February 2009), Nýi Kaupþing Banki (renamed Arion Banki in November) and NBI (Landsbankinn)—which were fully owned by the Icelandic Government, were created to take control of domestic assets, ensure the provision of normal banking services and safeguard domestic deposits, while the foreign assets and liabilities were retained by the former banks, which were in receivership.

Central Bank

Seðlabanki Íslands (Central Bank of Iceland): Kalkofnsvegur 1, 150 Reykjavík; tel. 5699600; fax 5699605; e-mail sedlabanki@sedlabanki.is; internet www.sedlabanki.is; f. 1961; cap. 57,501m., res 11,878.2m., dep. 1,019,162.5m. (Dec. 2010); Chair., Supervisory Bd ÓLÖF NORDAL; Gov. MÁR GUÐMUNDSSON.

Principal Banks

Arion Banki: Borgartún 19, 105 Reykjavík; tel. 4446000; fax 4446009; e-mail arionbanki@arionbanki.is; internet www.arionbanki.is; f. 2008 as Nýi Kaupþing Banki hf to assume responsibility for domestic assets and deposits of Kaupþing Banki (f. 2003) after it was nationalized; adopted current name Nov. 2009; 87% owned by creditors of Kaupþing Banki, 13% by Icelandic Govt; cap. 2,000m., res 75,498m., dep. 506,155m. (Dec. 2011); Chair. MONICA CANEMAN; CEO HÖSKULDUR H. ÓLAFSSON; 35 brs.

Íslandsbanki hf: Kirkjusandur, 155 Reykjavík; tel. 4404000; fax 4404001; e-mail islandsbanki@islandsbanki.is; internet www.islandsbanki.is; f. 2008 as Nýi Glitnir Banki to assume responsibility for domestic assets and deposits of Glitnir Banki (f. 1990) after it was nationalized in Oct. 2008; adopted current name Feb. 2009; 95% owned by creditors of Glitnir Banki, 5% by Icelandic Govt; cap. 10,000m., res 57,471m., dep. 543,842m. (Dec. 2012); Chair. FRIÐRIK SOPHUSSON; CEO BIRNA EINARSDÓTTIR; 29 brs.

Landsbankinn hf (Nýi Landsbanki Íslands—Landsbankinn): Austurstræti 11, 155 Reykjavík; tel. and fax 5606600; e-mail info@landsbank.is; internet www.landsbanki.is; f. 2008; 81.3% owned by Icelandic Govt; established to assume responsibility for domestic assets and deposits of Landsbanki Íslands (f. 1885) after it was nationalized in Oct. 2008; present name adopted 2011; cap. 23,618m., res 127,746m., dep. 456,662m. (Dec. 2013); Chair. GUNNAR HELGI HÁLFDÁNARSON; CEO STEINÞÓR PÁLSSON; 33 brs.

MP Banki hf: Ármúli 13A, 108 Reykjavík; tel. 5403230; fax 5403201; e-mail info@mp.is; internet www.mp.is; f. 1999 as a brokerage firm under name MP Verdbref; status changed to investment bank in 2003 and name changed to MP Fjárfestingarbanki; granted a commercial licence in Oct. 2008 and adopted current name; cap. 5,550m., res 49.9m., dep. 42,402.4m. (Dec. 2012); Chair. ÞORSTEINN PÁLSSON; CEO SIGURÐUR ATLI JÓNSSON.

STOCK EXCHANGE

NASDAQ OMX Nordic Exchange Iceland: Laugavegur 182, 105 Reykjavík; tel. 5252800; fax 5252888; internet www.nasdaqomx

.com; f. 2006 by merger of Kauphöll Íslands and OMX AB (Sweden); part of OMX Nordic Exchange with Copenhagen (Denmark), Helsinki (Finland) and Stockholm (Sweden) exchanges; acquired by NASDAQ Stock Market, Inc (USA) in 2008; Group CEO ROBERT GREIFELD.

INSURANCE

Tryggingastofnun ríkisins (Social Insurance Administration): Laugavegi 114, 105 Reykjavík; tel. 5604400; fax 5604451; e-mail tr@tr.is; internet www.tr.is; f. 1936; Chair. STEFÁN ÓLAFSSON; Dir-Gen. SIGRIÐUR LILLÝ BALDURSDÓTTIR.

Private Insurance Companies

Líftryggingafélag Íslands hf (Lífís): Ármúla 3, 108 Reykjavík; tel. 5605100; fax 5605108; e-mail vis@vis.is; internet www.lifis.is; f. 1990; owned by holding co. of Vátryggingafélag Íslands hf (VÍS); life; CEO SIGRÚN RAGNA OLAFSDÓTTIR.

Líftryggingamiðstöðin hf: Síðumúla 24, 108 Reykjavík; tel. 5152000; fax 5152020; f. 2005; subsidiary of Tryggingamiðstöðin hf (TM); Gen. Man. HJÁLMAR SIGURÞÓRSSON.

Sjóvá-Almennar tryggingar hf (Marine-General Insurance Co): Kringlan 5, 103 Reykjavík; tel. 4402000; fax 4402020; e-mail sjova@sjova.is; internet www.sjova.is; f. 1988; all branches except life; Chair. ERNA GÍSLADÓTTIR; Gen. Man. HERMANN BJÖRNSSON.

Tryggingamiðstöðin hf (TM): Síðumúla 24, 108 Reykjavík; tel. 5152000; fax 5152020; e-mail tm@tm.is; internet www.tm.is; f. 1956; acquired Trygging hf in 1999; Chair. SIGURÐUR VIÐARSSON.

Vátryggingafélag Íslands hf (VÍS): Ármúla 3, 108 Reykjavík; tel. 5605000; fax 5605108; e-mail vis@vis.is; internet www.vis.is; f. 1989; non-life; Chair. FRIÐRIK HALLBJÖRN KARLSSON; CEO SIGRÚN RAGNA ÓLAFSDÓTTIR.

Viðlagatrygging Íslands: Borgartún 6, 105 Reykjavík; tel. 5753300; fax 5753303; e-mail vidlagatrygging@vidlagatrygging.is; internet www.vidlagatrygging.is; Chair. GUÐRÚN ERLINGSDÓTTIR.

Vörður tryggingar hf: Borgartún 25, 105 Reykjavík; tel. 5141000; fax 5141001; e-mail vordur@vordur.is; internet www.vordur.is; f. 1926; as Vörður; life and non-life; Chair. JENS ERIK CHRISTENSEN.

Supervisory Authority

Fjármálaeftirlitið (FME) (Financial Supervisory Authority): Höfðatún 2, 105 Reykjavík; tel. 5203700; fax 5203727; e-mail fme@fme.is; internet www.fme.is; f. 1999 by merger of Insurance Supervisory Authority and Bank Inspectorate of the Central Bank of Iceland; Chair. AÐALSTEINN LEIFSSON; Dir-Gen. UNNUR GUNNARSDÓTTIR.

Trade and Industry

GOVERNMENT AGENCIES

Íslandsstofa (Promote Iceland): Borgartún 35, 105 Reykjavík; POB 1000, 121 Reykjavík; tel. 5114000; fax 5114040; e-mail islandsstofa@islandsstofa.is; internet www.islandsstofa.is; promotes Icelandic exports; partnership between govt and private enterprise; Man. Dir JÓN ÁSBERGSSON.

Invest in Iceland: Sundagarðar 2, 104 Reykjavík; tel. 5114000; fax 5114040; e-mail info@invest.is; internet www.invest.is; f. 1995; promotes foreign investment; managed by Promote Iceland and Ministry of Industries and Innovation; Man. Dir THORDUR H. HILMARSSON.

Orkustofnun (National Energy Authority): Grensásvegur 9, 108 Reykjavík; tel. 5696000; fax 5688896; e-mail os@os.is; internet www.os.is; f. 1967; part of the Ministry of Industries and Innovation; 2 main divisions: hydrological research unit and energy administration unit; contracts and supervises energy research projects financed by the national budget, monitors energy consumption and publishes forecasts for energy market; operates United Nations Geothermal Training Programme as independent entity; licenses and monitors exploration for oil and gas in Icelandic waters; Dir-Gen. Dr GUÐNI A. JOHANNESSON.

CHAMBER OF COMMERCE

Viðskiptaráð Íslands (Iceland Chamber of Commerce): Hús Verslunarinnar, Kringlan 7, 103 Reykjavík; tel. 5107100; fax 5686564; e-mail mottaka@vi.is; internet www.vi.is; f. 1917; fmrly Verslunarráð Íslands; Man. Dir FINNUR ODDSSON; 370 mems.

INDUSTRIAL AND TRADE ASSOCIATIONS

Fiskifélag Íslands (Fisheries Asscn of Iceland): POB 8214, 128 Reykjavík; tel. 5910308; fax 5910301; e-mail fi@fiskifelag.is; internet www.fiskifelag.is; f. 1911; conducts technical and economic research and services for fishing vessels and for the fishing industry; Chair. KRISTJÁN LOFTSSON.

Landssamband Íslenskra Útvegsmanna (Icelandic Fishing Vessel Owners' Federation): Borgartúni 35, 105 Reykjavík; tel. 5910300; fax 5910301; e-mail liu@liu.is; internet www.liu.is; f. 1939; Chair. ADOLF GUÐMUNDSSON; CEO FRIÐRIK JÓN ARNGRÍMSSON.

Samtök Iðnaðarins (SI) (Federation of Icelandic Industries): Borgartúni 35, 105 Reykjavík; tel. 5910100; fax 5910101; e-mail mottaka@si.is; internet www.si.is; f. 1993 by merger of Federation of Icelandic Industries (f. 1933), Federation of Icelandic Crafts and Industries (f. 1932) and 4 other employers' orgs; Chair. SVANA HELEN BJÖRNSDÓTTIR; 1,200 mems.

EMPLOYERS' ORGANIZATION

Samtök atvinnulífsins (SA) (Confederation of Icelandic Employers): Borgartúni 35, 105 Reykjavík; tel. 5910000; fax 5910050; e-mail sa@sa.is; internet www.sa.is; f. 1934; 7 mem. asscns; Chair. VILMUNDUR JÓSEFSSON; Man. Dir Dr VILHJÁLMUR EGILSSON.

UTILITIES

Electricity

HS Orka hf: Brekkustíg 36, POB 225, 260 Reykjanesbær; tel. 5209300; fax 4214727; e-mail hsorka@hsorka.is; internet www.hsorka.is; f. 2008 by division of Hitaveita Suðurnesja hf (HS, f. 1974) into HS Orka hf and HS Veitur hf; produces and sells geothermal electricity; 66.6% shares owned by Magma Energy Sweden A.B. and 33.4% owned by Jarðvarmi slhf; Chair. ROSS BEATY; Man. Dir ÁSGEIR MARGEIRSSON.

HS Veitur hf: Brekkustíg 36, POB 225, 260 Reykjanesbær; tel. 4225200; fax 4214727; e-mail hs@hs.is; internet www.hsveitur.is; f. 2008 by division of Hitaveita Suðurnesja hf (HS); produces and distributes hot-water heating and electricity for the Suðurnes region; Chair. BÖÐVAR JÓNSSON.

Landsvirkjun (National Power): Háaleitisbraut 68, 103 Reykjavík; tel. 5159000; fax 5159007; e-mail landsvirkjun@lv.is; internet www.landsvirkjun.com; f. 1965; generates and sells electric power wholesale to public distribution systems and industrial enterprises; state-owned; Chair. BRYNDÍS HLÖDVERSDÓTTIR; Man. Dir HÖRDUR ARNARSON.

Orkubú Vestfjarða hf (Westfjord Power Co): Stakkanesi 1, 400 Isafjördur; tel. 4503211; fax 4563204; e-mail orkubu@ov.is; internet www.ov.is; f. 1977; produces, distributes and sells electrical energy in the Westfjords area; state-owned; Man. Dir KRISTJÁN HARALDSSON.

Orkuveita Reykjavíkur (OR) (Reykjavík Energy): Bæjarháls 1, 110 Reykjavík; tel. 5166000; fax 5166709; e-mail or@or.is; internet www.or.is; f. 1999; produces and distributes geothermal hot-water for central heating, cold water and electricity for the city of Reykjavík and regions in south-western Iceland; owned by city of Reykjavík and other local authorities; Chair. HARALDUR FLOSI TRYGGVASON; CEO BJARNI BJARNASON.

RARIK ohf (Iceland State Electricity): Bíldshöfða 9, 110 Reykjavík; tel. 5289000; fax 5289009; e-mail rarik@rarik.is; internet www.rarik.is; f. 1947 as Rafmagnsveitur Ríkisins; produces, procures, distributes and sells electrical energy; also provides consultancy services; Chair. ÁRNI STEINAR JOHANNSSON; Man. Dir TRYGGVI ÞÓR HARALDSSON.

TRADE UNIONS

Althýðusamband Íslands (ASÍ) (Icelandic Confederation of Labour): Sætún 1, 105 Reykjavík; tel. 5355600; fax 5355601; e-mail asi@asi.is; internet www.asi.is; f. 1916; affiliated to ITUC, ETUC and the Council of Nordic Trade Unions; Pres. GYLFI ARNBJÖRNSSON; c. 109,000 mems.

Bandalag Háskólamanna (BHM) (Asscn of Academics): Borgartún 6, 105 Reykjavík; tel. 5955100; fax 5955101; e-mail bhm@bhm.is; internet www.bhm.is; f. 1958; asscn of 26 trade unions; publishes *BHM-tíðindi* (annual); Chair. GUÐLAUG KRISTJÁNSDÓTTIR; Gen. Man. STEFÁN AÐALSTEINSSON; 10,000 mems.

Bandalag Starfsmanna Ríkis og Bæja (BSRB) (Municipal and Government Employees' Asscn): Grettisgötu 89, 105 Reykjavík; tel. 5658300; fax 5258309; e-mail bsrb@bsrb.is; internet www.bsrb.is; f. 1942; Chair. ELÍN BJÖRG JÓNSDÓTTIR; 21,000 mems.

Blaðamannafélag Íslands (Union of Icelandic Journalists): Síðumúla 23, 108 Reykjavík; tel. 5539155; fax 5539177; e-mail bi@press.is; internet www.press.is; f. 1897; Chair. HJÁLMAR JÓNSSON; 570 mems.

Transport

Samgöngustofa (Icelandic Transport Authority—ICETRA): POB 470, 202 Kópavogur; tel. 4806000; e-mail samgongustofa@samgongustofa.is; internet www.us.is; f. 2013; responsible for all areas of transport.

RAILWAYS

There are no railways in Iceland.

ROADS

Much of the interior is uninhabited and the main road largely follows the coastline. Regular motor coach services link the main settlements. In 2012 Iceland had 12,898 km of national roads, of which 4,425 km were main roads. Approximately one-third of the main roads are paved. The construction of three tunnels was approved in 2012, including a 7.5-km tunnel between Eskifjörður and Neskaupstaður in eastern Iceland, which was to be built by 2016 to replace a one-lane tunnel that was deemed to be hazardous.

Vegagerðin (Icelandic Road and Coastal Administration—ICERA): Borgartún 5-7, 105 Reykjavík; tel. 5221000; e-mail vegagerdin@vegagerdin.is; internet www.vegagerdin.is; part of the Icelandic Transport Authority (ICETRA); oversees the construction and maintenance of roads; since 2013 also responsible for harbour and lighthouse operations of the Icelandic Maritime Administration; Man. Dir JÓN HELGASON.

Bifreiðastöð Íslands hf (BSÍ) (Iceland Motor Coach Service): Umferðarmiðstöðinni, Vatnsmýrarveg 10, 101 Reykjavík; tel. 5621011; e-mail bsi@bsi.is; internet www.bsi.is; f. 1936; 45 scheduled bus lines throughout Iceland; also operates sightseeing tours and excursions; Chair. ÓSKAR SIGURJÓNSSON; Man. Dir GUNNAR SVEINSSON.

SHIPPING

Heavy freight is carried by coastal shipping. The principal seaport for international shipping is Reykjavík. At 31 December 2013 the Icelandic flag registered fleet numbered 203 vessels, with a combined displacement of 156,018 grt, of which 158 were fishing vessels and 4 were general cargo ships.

Port Authority

Faxaflóahafnir sf (Associated Icelandic Ports): POB 382, 121 Reykjavík; Harbour Bldg, Tryggvagata 17, 101 Reykjavík; tel. 5258900; fax 5258990; e-mail hofnin@faxaports.is; internet faxafloahafnir.is; f. 2005 by merger of ports of Akranes, Borgarnes, Grundartangi and Reykjavík; Chair. HJÁLMAR SVEINSSON; Dir GISLI GISLASON.

Principal Companies

Eimskip (Iceland Steamship Co Ltd): Korngörðum 2, 104 Reykjavík; tel. 5257000; fax 5257009; e-mail info@eimskip.com; internet www.eimskip.com; f. 1914 as Eimskipafélag Íslands; subsidiary of Avion Group; transportation and logistics services between Iceland and the United Kingdom, Scandinavia, the rest of Europe, the USA and Canada; Chair. BRAGI RAGNARSSON; Pres. and CEO GYLFI SIGFÚSSON.

Nesskip hf: Austurströnd 1, 170 Seltjarnarnes; tel. 5639900; fax 5639919; e-mail operations@nesskip.is; internet www.nesskip.is; f. 1974; bulk cargo shipping services to the USA, Canada, Russia, Scandinavia, the Baltic countries and other parts of Europe; agency and chartering for vessels in all Icelandic ports; Chair. OYVING GJERDE; Man. Dir GARÐAR JÓHANNSSON.

Samskip hf: Kjalarvogur, 104 Reykjavík; tel. 4588000; fax 4588100; e-mail samskip@samskip.is; internet www.samskip.is; services to Europe, the USA, South America and the Far East; Chair ÓLAFUR ÓLAFSSON.

CIVIL AVIATION

Air transport is particularly important to Iceland and is used to convey both people and agricultural produce from remote districts. More than 90% of passenger traffic between Iceland and other countries is by air. There are regular air services between Reykjavík and outlying townships. There is an international airport at Keflavík, 47 km from Reykjavík.

Flugmálastjórn Íslands (ICAA) (Icelandic Civil Aviation Administration): Skógarhlíð 12, 105 Reykjavík; tel. 5694100; fax 5623619; e-mail fms@caa.is; internet www.caa.is; f. 1945; regulatory authority; part of Icelandic Transport Authority (ICETRA); Dir-Gen. PÉTUR K. MAACK.

Air Atlanta Icelandic: Hlíðasmára 3, 201 Kópavogur; tel. 4584000; fax 4584001; e-mail info@airatlanta.com; internet www.airatlanta.com; f. 1986; leases cargo and passenger aircraft; CEO HANNES HILMARSSON.

Air Iceland: Reykjavík Airport, 101 Reykjavík; tel. 5703000; fax 5703001; e-mail service@airiceland.is; internet www.airiceland.is; part of Icelandair Group; scheduled regional flights; 96% owned by Icelandair; Man. Dir ÁRNI GUNNARSSON.

Eagle Air (Flugfélagið Ernir ehf): Reykjavík Airport, 101 Reykjavík; tel. 5624200; fax 5624202; e-mail info@eagleair.is; internet www.eagleair.is; f. 1970; charter and domestic scheduled services; Pres. and CEO HÖRÐUR GUÐMUNDSSON.

Icelandair (Flugleiðir hf): Reykjavík Airport, 101 Reykjavík; tel. 5050757; fax 5050758; e-mail postmaster@icelandair.is; internet www.icelandair.is; f. 1973 as the holding co for the 2 principal Icelandic airlines, Flugfélag Íslands (f. 1937) and Loftleiðir (f. 1944); took over all licences, permits and authorizations previously held by Flugfélag Íslands and Loftleiðir in 1979; operates flights from Reykjavík to 9 domestic airfields and more than 20 destinations in Europe and North America; CEO BIRKIR HÓLM GUÐNASON.

WOW Air: Höfðatún 12, 105 Reykjavík; tel. 5903000; e-mail wowair@wow.is; internet www.wowiceland.co.uk; f. 2011; took over Iceland Express flight operations in October 2012; Chair. LIV BERGÞÓRSDÓTTIR; Pres. and CEO SKÚLI MOGENSEN.

Tourism

Iceland's main attraction for tourists lies in the rugged beauty of the landscape, with its geysers and thermal springs. In 2012 receipts from tourism, excluding passenger transport, totalled US $845m. Overnight stays by foreign visitors in hotels and guesthouses amounted to 2.2m. in 2012.

Iceland Tourist Board: Sundagarðar 2, 104 Reykjavík; tel. 5114000; fax 5114040; e-mail visiticeland@promoteiceland.is; internet www.visiticeland.com; Gen. Dir ÓLÖF ÝRR ATLADÓTTIR.

Höfuðborgarstofa (Visit Reykjavík): Aðalstræti 2, 101 Reykjavík; tel. 5901500; fax 5901501; e-mail info@visitreykjavik.is; internet www.visitreykjavik.is; tourism marketing and events for the city of Reykjavík; Dir EINAR ÞÓR BÁRÐARSON.

Defence

Apart from a 180-strong coastguard, Iceland has no defence forces of its own, but it is a member of the North Atlantic Treaty Organization (NATO). Until 2006 there were units of US forces at Keflavík airbase, which was used for observation of the North Atlantic Ocean, under a bilateral agreement made in 1951 between Iceland and the USA. In September 2006 the USA withdrew its forces from Iceland, but maintained its commitment to defend Iceland as a fellow member of NATO. In November 2012 Denmark, Finland, Iceland, Sweden and Norway agreed to operate military transport aircraft jointly. (Iceland does not currently own military aircraft, but was to contribute funds towards joint purchases.)

Defence Expenditure: Budgeted at 4,640m. krónur (coastguard only) for 2013.

Education

Education starts at the pre-primary level, which is non-compulsory for pupils aged between one and six years of age. Education is compulsory and free for 10 years between six and 16 years of age (primary and lower secondary levels). Upper secondary education begins at 16 years of age and usually lasts for four years. In 2011/12, enrolment in pre-primary schools included 97% of children in the relevant age-group. In the same year, enrolment in primary schools included 98% of children in the relevant age-group, while enrolment in secondary education included 88% of children in the relevant age-group. Higher education is provided by universities and select institutions offering a limited number of study programmes. Iceland had 23 institutions providing tertiary-level education in 2010. In 2012 there were 18,619 students enrolled in tertiary-level education. Public expenditure on education was 7.22% of gross domestic product in 2012. Local communities finance compulsory education.

INDIA

Introductory Survey

LOCATION, CLIMATE, LANGUAGE, RELIGION, FLAG, CAPITAL

The Republic of India forms a natural sub-continent, with the Himalaya mountain range to the north. Two sections of the Indian Ocean—the Arabian Sea and the Bay of Bengal—lie to the west and east, respectively. India's neighbours are Tibet (the Xizang Autonomous Region of the People's Republic of China), Bhutan and Nepal to the north, Pakistan to the north-west and Myanmar (formerly Burma) to the north-east, while Bangladesh is surrounded by Indian territory except for a short frontier with Myanmar in the east. Near India's southern tip, across the Palk Strait, is Sri Lanka. India's climate ranges from temperate to tropical, with an average summer temperature on the plains of approximately 27°C (85°F). Annual rainfall varies widely, but the summer monsoon brings heavy rain over much of the country in June and July. The official language is Hindi, spoken by about 30% of the population. English is used as an associate language for many official purposes. The Indian Constitution also recognizes 18 regional languages, of which the most widely spoken are Telugu, Bengali, Marathi, Tamil, Urdu and Gujarati. In addition, many other local languages are used. According to the 2001 census, about 81% of the population are Hindus and 13% Muslims. There are also Christians, Sikhs, Buddhists, Jains and other minorities. The national flag (proportions 2 by 3) has three equal horizontal stripes, of saffron, white and green, with the Dharma Chakra (Wheel of the Law), in blue, in the centre of the white stripe. The capital is New Delhi.

CONTEMPORARY POLITICAL HISTORY

Historical Context

After a prolonged struggle against British colonial rule, India became independent, within the Commonwealth, on 15 August 1947. The United Kingdom's Indian Empire was partitioned, broadly on a religious basis, between India and Pakistan. The principal nationalist movement that had opposed British rule was the Indian National Congress (later known as the Congress Party). At independence the Congress leader, Jawaharlal Nehru, became India's first Prime Minister. Sectarian violence, the movement of 12m. refugees, the integration of the former princely states into the Indian federal structure and a territorial dispute with Pakistan over Kashmir presented major problems to the new Government.

India became independent as a dominion, with the British monarch as head of state, represented by an appointed Governor-General. In November 1949, however, the Constituent Assembly approved a republican Constitution, providing for a President (with mainly ceremonial functions) as head of state. Accordingly, India became a republic on 26 January 1950, although remaining a member of the Commonwealth. France transferred sovereignty of Chandernagore to India in May, and ceded its four remaining Indian settlements in 1954.

In December 1961 Indian forces overran the Portuguese territories of Goa, Daman and Diu, which were immediately annexed by India. Border disputes with the People's Republic of China escalated into a brief military conflict in 1962. Nehru died in May 1964 and was succeeded by Lal Bahadur Shastri. India and Pakistan fought a second war over Kashmir in 1965. Following mediation by the USSR, Shastri and President Ayub Khan of Pakistan signed a joint declaration, aimed at a peaceful settlement of the Kashmir dispute, on 10 January 1966. However, Shastri died on the following day and Nehru's daughter, Indira Gandhi, became Prime Minister.

Domestic Political Affairs

Indira Gandhi dominates Indian politics (1966–84)

Following the presidential election of August 1969, when two factions of Congress supported different candidates, the success of Indira Gandhi's candidate split the party. The Organization (Opposition) Congress, led by Morarji Desai, emerged in November, but at the next general election to the lower house of the legislature, the Lok Sabha (House of the People), held in March 1971, Indira Gandhi's wing of Congress won 350 of the 515 elective seats.

Border incidents led to a 12-day war with Pakistan in December 1971. The Indian army rapidly occupied East Pakistan, which India recognized as the independent state of Bangladesh. Indira Gandhi and President Zulfikar Ali Bhutto of Pakistan held a summit conference at Shimla in June–July 1972, when the two leaders agreed that their respective forces should respect the ceasefire line in Kashmir, and that India and Pakistan should resolve their differences through bilateral negotiations or other peaceful means. In 1975 the former protectorate of Sikkim became the 22nd state of the Indian Union, leading to tensions in India's relations with Nepal.

A general election to the Lok Sabha was held in March 1977, when the number of elective seats was increased to 542. The election resulted in victory for the Janata (People's) Party, chaired by Morarji Desai, who became Prime Minister. The Janata Party and an allied party, the Congress for Democracy, together won 298 of the 540 seats where polling took place. Congress obtained 153 seats. In January 1978 Indira Gandhi became leader of a new breakaway political group, the Congress (Indira) Party, known as Congress (I).

In 1979 the Government's ineffectual approach to domestic problems provoked a wave of defections by Lok Sabha members of the Janata Party. Many joined Raj Narain, who formed a new, secular party, the Lok Dal. Congress (I) lost its position as official opposition party after defections from its ranks to the then official Congress Party by members who objected to Indira Gandhi's perceived authoritarianism. The resignation of Desai's Government in July was followed by the departure from the Janata Party of Charan Singh, who became the leader of the Lok Dal and, shortly afterwards, Prime Minister in a coalition with both Congress parties. When Congress (I) withdrew its support, Singh's 24-day administration collapsed, and Parliament was dissolved. A general election to the Lok Sabha was held in January 1980. Congress (I) won an overwhelming majority (352) of the elective seats; the Janata Party and the Lok Dal won only 31 and 41 seats, respectively. Indira Gandhi was reinstated as Prime Minister. Presidential rule was imposed in nine states, hitherto governed by opposition parties, in February.

By-elections in June 1981 for the Lok Sabha and state assemblies (to which elections were held in June 1980) were notable for two reasons: the overwhelming victory that Rajiv Gandhi, the Prime Minister's son, obtained in the former constituency of his late brother (killed in an air crash in 1980); and the failure of the fragmented Janata Party to win any seats. In February 1983 Rajiv Gandhi became a General Secretary of Congress (I).

Indira Gandhi's Government faced serious problems, as inter-communal disturbances in several states (particularly Assam and Meghalaya) continued in 1982–83, with violent protests against the presence of Bengali immigrants. Election defeats in Andhra Pradesh, Karnataka and Tripura represented a series of setbacks for the Prime Minister. Alleged police corruption and the resurgence of caste violence (notably in Bihar and Gujarat) caused further problems for the Government.

There was also unrest in the Sikh community of the Punjab, despite the election to the Indian presidency in July 1982 of Giani Zail Singh, the first Sikh to hold the position. Demands were made for greater religious recognition, for the settlement of grievances over land and water rights, and over the sharing of the state capital at Chandigarh with Haryana; in addition, a minority called for the creation of a separate Sikh state ('Khalistan'). In October 1983 the state was brought under presidential rule. However, the violence continued, and followers of an extremist Sikh leader, Jarnail Singh Bhindranwale, established a terrorist stronghold inside the Golden Temple (the Sikh holy shrine) at Amritsar. An army assault against the extremists resulted in the death of Bhindranwale and hundreds of his supporters, and serious damage to sacred buildings.

Rajiv Gandhi assumes power (1984–89)

In October 1984 Indira Gandhi was assassinated by militant Sikh members of her personal guard. Her son, Rajiv Gandhi, was immediately sworn in as Prime Minister, despite his lack of ministerial experience. The widespread communal violence that erupted throughout India, resulting in more than 2,000 deaths, was curbed by prompt government action. Congress (I) achieved a decisive victory in elections to the Lok Sabha in December. Including the results of the January 1985 polling, the party won 403 of the 513 contested seats.

In February 1986 there were mass demonstrations and strikes throughout India in protest against government-imposed increases in the prices of basic commodities. The opposition parties united against Rajiv Gandhi's policies, and Congress (I) suffered considerable reversals in the indirect elections to the upper house of the legislature, the Rajya Sabha (Council of States), in March. In April Rajiv Gandhi attempted to purge Congress (I) of critics calling themselves 'Indira Gandhi loyalists', and, in a major government reorganization, he appointed Sikhs to two senior positions. The Prime Minister survived an assassination attempt by three Sikhs in October.

Laldenga, the leader of the Mizo National Front (MNF), signed a peace agreement with Rajiv Gandhi in June 1986, thus ending Mizoram's 25 years of rebellion. The accord granted Mizoram limited autonomy in the drafting of local laws, independent trade with neighbouring foreign countries and a general amnesty for all Mizo rebels. In February 1987 Mizoram and Arunachal Pradesh were officially admitted as the 23rd and 24th states of India, and in May the Union Territory of Goa became India's 25th state.

During 1987 Congress (I) sustained defeats in a number of state elections, and political tensions were intensified by an open dispute between the Prime Minister and the outgoing President, Giani Zail Singh. Public concern was aroused by various accusations of corruption and financial irregularities made against senior figures in the ruling party. Several ministers resigned from the Government, among them the Minister of Defence, Vishwanath Pratap (V. P.) Singh, who was also, with three other senior politicians, expelled from Congress (I) in July for 'anti-party activities'. V. P. Singh soon emerged as the leader of the Congress (I) dissidents, and in October formed a new political group, the Jan Morcha (People's Front), advocating radical social change.

In 1988 a more confrontational style was adopted by the central administration towards non-Congress (I) state governments, and presidential rule was imposed in states suffering political instability. The opposition forces attained a degree of unity when four major centrist parties, the Indian National Congress (S), the Jan Morcha, the Janata Party and the Lok Dal, and three major regional parties formed a coalition National Front (Rashtriya Morcha), to oppose Congress (I) at the next election. Three of the four centrist parties formed a new political grouping, the Janata Dal (People's Party), which was to work in collaboration with the National Front. V. P. Singh, who was widely regarded as Rajiv Gandhi's closest rival, was elected President of the Janata Dal.

The Janata Dal Government (1989–91)

At the general election to the Lok Sabha held in November 1989, Congress (I) lost its overall majority. Of the 525 contested seats, it won 193, the Janata Dal and its electoral allies in the National Front won 141 and three, respectively, and the right-wing Hindu nationalist Bharatiya Janata Party (BJP) won 88. In December, after the National Front had been promised the support of the communist parties and the BJP, V. P. Singh was sworn in as the new Prime Minister. He appointed Devi Lal, the populist Chief Minister of Haryana and President of Lok Dal (B), as Deputy Prime Minister, and a Kashmiri Muslim, Mufti Mohammed Sayeed, as Minister of Home Affairs. At elections held in February 1990, Congress (I) lost power in eight of 10 state assemblies that it had formerly controlled, and there was a notable increase in support for the BJP.

In July 1990 Devi Lal was dismissed from his post as Deputy Prime Minister, accused of nepotism and disloyalty, and making unsubstantiated accusations of corruption against ministerial colleagues. In August there were violent demonstrations in many northern Indian states against the Government's decision to implement the recommendations of the 10-year-old Mandal Commission and to raise the quota of government and public sector jobs reserved for disadvantaged sections of the population. In October the Supreme Court directed the Government to halt temporarily the implementation of the quota scheme, in an attempt to curb the caste violence.

The BJP withdrew its support for the National Front in October 1990, following the arrest of its President, Lal Krishna (L. K.) Advani, as he led a controversial procession of Hindu devotees to the holy town of Ayodhya, in Uttar Pradesh, to begin the construction of a Hindu temple on the site of a disused ancient mosque, the Babri Masjid. V. P. Singh accused the BJP leader of deliberately inciting inter-communal hatred by exhorting Hindu extremists to join him in illegally tearing down the mosque. Paramilitary troops were sent to Ayodhya, and thousands of Hindu activists were arrested, in an attempt to prevent a Muslim–Hindu confrontation. However, following repeated clashes between police and crowds, Hindu extremists stormed and slightly damaged the mosque and laid siege to it for several days.

In November 1990 one of the Prime Minister's leading rivals in the Janata Dal, Chandra Shekhar (with the support of Devi Lal), formed his own dissident faction, known as the Janata Dal (Socialist) or Janata Dal (S) (which merged with the Janata Party in April 1991 to become the Samajwadi Party). The Lok Sabha convened for a special session, at which the Government overwhelmingly lost a vote of confidence. V. P. Singh immediately resigned, and the President invited Rajiv Gandhi, as leader of the largest parliamentary party, to form a new government. Gandhi refused the offer, in favour of Shekhar. Although the strength of the Janata Dal (S) in the Lok Sabha comprised only about 60 deputies, Congress (I) had earlier offered it unconditional parliamentary support. On 10 November 1990 Chandra Shekhar was sworn in as Prime Minister. A new Council of Ministers was appointed, with Devi Lal becoming Deputy Prime Minister and President of the Janata Dal (S). Although Shekhar succeeded in initiating talks between the two sides in the Ayodhya dispute, violence between Hindus and Muslims increased throughout India in December.

In January 1991 the Prime Minister imposed direct rule in Tamil Nadu in response to the increased activity of Sri Lankan Tamil militants in the state, which had led to the breakdown of law and order. In the resultant riots more than 1,000 arrests were made. In February five members of the Council of Ministers were forced to resign when they lost their seats in the Lok Sabha for violating India's anti-defection laws: they had left the Janata Dal to join the Janata Dal (S). The fragility of the parliamentary alliance between the Janata Dal (S) and Congress (I) became apparent in March, when the Congress (I) deputies boycotted Parliament, following the revelation that Rajiv Gandhi's house had been kept under police surveillance. In an unexpected counter-move, Chandra Shekhar resigned, but accepted the President's request that he remain as head of an interim Government until the holding of a fresh general election.

The return of Congress to power (1991–96)

As the general election, which was scheduled to take place over three days in May 1991, approached, it seemed likely that no party would win an outright majority and that the political stalemate would continue. On 21 May, however, after the first day's polling had taken place, Rajiv Gandhi was assassinated while campaigning in Tamil Nadu, allegedly by members of the Tamil separatist group, the Liberation Tigers of Tamil Eelam (LTTE). Consequently, the remaining elections were postponed until June. The final result gave Congress (I) 227 of the 511 seats contested. The BJP, which almost doubled its share of the vote compared with its performance in the 1989 general election, won 119 seats, while the Janata Dal gained only 55 seats. P. V. Narasimha Rao, who had been elected as acting President of Congress (which had gradually shed its (I) suffix) following Rajiv Gandhi's assassination, assumed the premiership and appointed a new Council of Ministers. The new Government's main priority on assuming power was to attempt to solve the country's severe economic crisis, caused by an enormous foreign debt, high inflation, a large current account deficit and an extreme shortage of foreign exchange reserves. The new Minister of Finance, Dr Manmohan Singh, launched a far-reaching programme of economic liberalization and reform, including the dismantling of bureaucratic regulations and the encouragement of private and foreign investment. In September the Government announced the adoption of the recommendations of the Mandal Commission that 27% of government jobs and institutional places be reserved for certain lower castes, in addition to the 22.5% already reserved for those from a Dalit ('untouchable') background and tribal people. (In November 1992 the Supreme Court ruled that non-Hindus, such as Christians and Sikhs, who were socially disadvantaged were also entitled to job reservations.) In July 1992 the Congress candidate, Dr Shankar Dayal Sharma, was elected to the presidency.

Following the collapse of talks in November 1992 between the Vishwa Hindu Parishad (VHP—World Hindu Council) and the All India Babri Masjid Action Committee regarding the Ayodhya dispute—see The Janata Dal Government (1989–91)—the VHP and the BJP appealed for volunteers to begin the construction of a Hindu temple on the site of the existing mosque. Despite the dispatch of paramilitary troops to Ayodhya, in December the temple/mosque complex was stormed by large numbers of Hindu activists, who proceeded to tear down the remains of the ancient mosque. This highly inflammatory action provoked widespread communal violence throughout India, which resulted in more than 1,200 deaths and prompted worldwide condemnation, notably from the neighbouring Islamic states of Pakistan and Bangladesh, where violent anti-Hindu demonstrations were held. The central Government also strongly condemned the demolition of the holy building and pledged to rebuild it. The leaders of the BJP, including L. K. Advani and the party's President, Dr Murli Manohar Joshi, and those of the VHP were arrested. The BJP Chief Minister of Uttar Pradesh resigned, the state legislature was dissolved and Uttar Pradesh was placed under presidential rule. The security forces took full control of Ayodhya, including the disputed complex. The Government banned five communal organizations, including the VHP and two Muslim groups, on the grounds that they promoted disharmony among different religious communities. In mid-December the Government established a commission of inquiry into events in Ayodhya. In an attempt to prevent any further acts of Hindu militancy, the central Government dismissed the BJP administrations in Madhya Pradesh, Rajasthan and Himachal Pradesh and placed these states under presidential rule. In late December the Government announced plans to acquire all the disputed areas in Ayodhya. The land would be made available to two trusts, which would be responsible for the construction of a new Hindu temple and a new mosque.

However, in January 1993 there was a resurgence of Hindu–Muslim violence in India's commercial centre, Mumbai (then still known as Bombay), and in Ahmedabad, necessitating the imposition of curfews and the dispatch of extra paramilitary troops to curb the unrest. In an effort to prevent a proposed mass rally of Hindu activists taking place in the centre of New Delhi in February, thousands of BJP members were arrested throughout India and the crowds that did gather in the capital were dispersed by the security forces. In March there were a number of bomb explosions in Mumbai, resulting in some 250 casualties.

In July 1993 Narasimha Rao narrowly survived a vote of no confidence, which was proposed in the Lok Sabha by virtually all the opposition parties. However, an apparent decline in the BJP's popularity was highlighted by its inability in November to win state elections in three of the four northern states where BJP governments had been dismissed in December 1992. During 1994 the Government's economic reforms continued to show positive results and Narasimha Rao's premiership appeared fairly secure, with the opposition suffering from fragmentation. Nevertheless, in late 1994 and early 1995 Congress suffered damaging defeats in several state elections.

In January 1996 accusations of official corruption came to the fore when the Central Bureau of Investigation (CBI) charged seven leading politicians, including L. K. Advani and Devi Lal, and sought the prosecution of three Union ministers (who subsequently resigned) for allegedly accepting large bribes from a Delhi-based industrialist, Surendra Jain. The sheer scale of the scandal (known as the Hawala—illegal money transfer—case), in terms of the sums involved and the number of people implicated, led to widespread public disillusionment with politicians in general. At the end of January the President of the Janata Dal, S. R. Bommai, was also implicated in the scandal; he subsequently resigned from his post. In February Congress's hopes of retaining power in the forthcoming general election appeared increasingly fragile when three more ministers resigned from the Council of Ministers after their names had been linked to the Hawala case.

Political instability under the United Front (1996–98)

The results of the general election held in April–May 1996 gave no party or group an overall majority. The largest party was the BJP, which won 160 seats and, with the support of Shiv Sena (a right-wing Hindu nationalist party based in Mumbai) and other smaller allies, could count on an overall legislative strength of 194 seats. Congress secured 136 seats. The National Front (comprising the Janata Dal and its allies) and Left Front (representing the two major communist parties) together obtained 179 seats, with the remainder won by minor parties and independents. On 15 May the President asked the BJP under its new parliamentary leader, Atal Bihari Vajpayee, to form the new government and to prove its majority support within two weeks. The latter task proved impossible, and Vajpayee resigned on 28 May in anticipation of his Government's inevitable defeat in a parliamentary vote of confidence. In the mean time, the National and Left Fronts had merged to form an informal coalition known as the United Front (UF), which comprised a total of 13 parties, with the Janata Dal, the Samajwadi Party, the two communist parties and the regional Dravida Munnetra Kazhagam (DMK) and Telugu Desam as its major components. With Congress prepared to lend external support, the UF was able to form a Government at the end of May, led by former Chief Minister of Karnataka H. D. Deve Gowda.

In September 1996 Narasimha Rao resigned from the leadership of Congress after he was ordered to stand trial on charges of cheating and criminal conspiracy; separate charges of forgery and criminal conspiracy (dating back to his tenure of the external affairs ministry in the 1980s) were later made against Rao, who was replaced as Congress's president and parliamentary leader by the veteran politician Sitaram Kesri.

In April 1997 Deve Gowda resigned following the defeat of the UF administration in a vote of confidence. Inder Kumar Gujral, hitherto Minister of External Affairs, was chosen by the UF to replace Gowda as leader of the coalition; Gujral was sworn in as Prime Minister on 22 April. In May Sonia Gandhi, the widow of former Prime Minister Rajiv Gandhi, joined Congress as a 'primary member', and in the following month Kesri was re-elected President of the party in Congress's first contested leadership poll since 1977. In July 1997 Kocheril Raman Narayanan was elected as India's new President, notably the first person of Dalit origins to reach this position. In September the results of a five-year investigation into the destruction of the mosque at Ayodhya in 1992 led to charges of criminal conspiracy and incitement to riot being filed against senior BJP and religious leaders, including L. K. Advani and the leader of Shiv Sena, Balashaheb 'Bal' Thackeray.

Prime Minister Gujral was forced to resign in November 1997, when Congress withdrew its support for the Government over Gujral's refusal to expel the Tamil Nadu-based DMK (which was alleged to be indirectly implicated in the 1991 assassination of Rajiv Gandhi) from the coalition. President Narayanan dissolved the Lok Sabha in December following the inability of both Congress and the BJP to form an alternative coalition government. Gujral retained the premiership in an acting capacity pending the holding of a fresh general election in early 1998.

In an apparent attempt to halt the fragmentation of the Congress party, which had suffered internal discord and defections, Sonia Gandhi agreed to campaign in the run-up to the general election. Although she gained increasing popular support, she steadfastly refused to stand for parliamentary office. In January 1998 26 Tamil militants implicated in the murder of Rajiv Gandhi were sentenced to death by a court in Chennai (Madras). (In May 1999, however, the Supreme Court in New Delhi acquitted 19 defendants and commuted the sentences of three others. In February 2014 the Supreme Court commuted the final three death sentences in the case to life imprisonment, on the grounds of unreasonable delays in settling the convicts' pleas for clemency. However, the Court subsequently blocked a decision by the government of Tamil Nadu to release the remaining seven prisoners convicted in the case, including the three whose death sentences had just been commuted.)

The BJP heads coalition governments (1998–2004)

At the general election held in February–March 1998, the BJP won 182 of the 545 seats in the Lok Sabha, but failed to achieve an overall majority. Congress secured 142 seats, and shortly after the election Sonia Gandhi replaced Kesri as the party's President. BJP parliamentary leader Atal Bihari Vajpayee was appointed Prime Minister by the President and, with the support of the All-India Anna Dravida Munnetra Kazhagam (AIADMK), the Telugu Desam (which eventually left the UF) and a number of other minor groups, he formed a coalition Government that secured a legislative vote of confidence on 28 March. None the less, it was immediately apparent that Vajpayee's 14-party coalition had a fragile hold on power.

In May 1998 the Government shocked both India and the rest of the world by authorizing a series of underground nuclear test explosions. This provocative action was initially greeted with massive popular enthusiasm, but Pakistan's retaliatory tests and a rapid realization of the negative international consequences (particularly the imposition of economic sanctions by the USA) soon led to a more measured domestic assessment.

Two AIADMK ministers resigned from the Government in April 1999, following a dispute over the dismissal of the Chief of Staff of the Navy. When the Government narrowly lost a resultant parliamentary vote of confidence, the President invited Sonia Gandhi to assemble a new coalition, which she was unable to do. Consequently, the Lok Sabha was dissolved and fresh elections were called, with Vajpayee's Government remaining in power in an acting capacity.

In May 1999 Congress's erstwhile parliamentary leader, Sharad Pawar, who had earlier publicly criticized Sonia Gandhi's foreign (Italian) origins, announced the formation of a breakaway party, entitled the Nationalist Congress Party (NCP); the NCP absorbed the Indian National Congress (S) in the following month. Meanwhile, the assertion of Indian military dominance following an outbreak of hostilities between Indian and Pakistani troops in the Kargil area of Kashmir in mid-1999 (see Foreign Affairs) had a positive effect on the nationalist BJP's standing and, in particular, on that of acting premier Vajpayee, who was widely perceived to have responded with dignity, firmness and commendable restraint in the face of Pakistani provocation.

The BJP contested the general election, held in September–October 1999, at the head of the 24-member National Democratic Alliance (NDA), which comprised numerous minor regional and national parties with little shared ideology. The NDA won an outright majority in the Lok Sabha, with 299 of the 545 seats, while Congress and its electoral allies obtained 134 seats. Although Sonia Gandhi won both of the seats that she herself contested in Karnataka and Uttar Pradesh, her lack of political experience, weak grasp of Hindi and foreign birth all contributed to Congress's worst electoral defeat since India's independence. Following his appointment as leader of the NDA, Vajpayee was sworn in as Prime Minister, for a third term, at the head of a large coalition Government.

Legislation establishing the states of Chhattisgarh, Jharkhand and Uttaranchal was approved by Parliament in August 2000; the new states came into being in November. In the previous month former Prime Minister Narasimha Rao was convicted of corruption and sentenced to three years' imprisonment. (In March 2002, however, his conviction was overturned by the High Court in New Delhi.)

Following a devastating earthquake in Gujarat in January 2001, which claimed the lives of more than 30,000 people and rendered more than 1m. people homeless, both the central and state Governments were criticized for their tardy reaction to the disaster. During 2001 a new series of political and financial scandals exposed continuing corruption at the highest levels of government and commerce, and further undermined popular confidence in the BJP. In March videotaped evidence emerged of senior government and army officials accepting bribes from journalists posing as facilitators seeking to secure a bogus defence contract. Both Bangaru Laxman, President of the BJP, and Jaya Jaitly, leader of the Samata Party, resigned from their posts following the revelations, as did the Minister of Defence, George Fernandes. (Laxman was charged in connection with the case in mid-2006; in April 2012 he was convicted of bribery and sentenced to four years' imprisonment.) Elections to four state assemblies and one union territory assembly in May resulted in major gains for Congress and its electoral allies (in Kerala and Assam) at the expense of the parties of the NDA coalition. In September the Prime Minister expanded and reorganized the Council of Ministers, and in October George Fernandes (now leader of the Samata Party) was reappointed Minister of Defence.

In January 2002 Prime Minister Vajpayee resumed efforts to resolve the long-running dispute over the religious site in Ayodhya, with the All India Babri Masjid Action Committee continuing to refuse negotiations with the uncompromising VHP. As the mid-March deadline set by the Dharma Sansad (a religious parliament established by the VHP) to begin building the temple approached, hundreds of Hindu activists assembled in Ayodhya to take part in the illegal construction. In late February communal violence broke out in Gujarat after a train carrying members of the VHP returning from Ayodhya was attacked by a suspected group of Muslims in the town of Godhra. The attack, in which 60 Hindu activists were killed, provoked a cycle of communal violence throughout Gujarat that lasted for several weeks and resulted in the deaths of up to 2,000 people, the majority of whom were Muslims. The Indian army was drafted in to quell the riots. Opposition members demanded the resignation of the Minister of Home Affairs, L. K. Advani, and the Chief Minister of Gujarat, Narendra Modi, for failing to control the riots. In April the European Union's report on the situation in Gujarat, which corroborated a number of other reports published in that month, concluded that the riots and killings had been, contrary to the official account, not in reaction to the attack on the train, but in fact an organized massacre of Muslims, and that the security forces had been under orders not to intervene. Modi eventually resigned and recommended the dissolution of the state assembly in July; he was requested to continue as leader of an interim administration until state elections were held in December.

In April 2002 the federal Minister of Coal and Mines, Ram Vilas Paswan, resigned and withdrew his Lok Jan Shakti party from the NDA in protest against the Government's handling of the situation in Gujarat. In June L. K. Advani was assigned the additional portfolio of Deputy Prime Minister, prompting speculation that he had been nominated as Vajpayee's eventual successor. In the following month the Government's candidate, Aavul Pakkiri Jainulabidin Abdul Kalam, a South Indian Muslim who was closely involved in the development of the country's missile and nuclear programme, won a convincing victory in the presidential election.

Elections to the Gujarat state assembly took place on 12 December 2002. The BJP secured 126 of the 182 seats, while Congress won only 51 seats. Interim Chief Minister Narendra Modi was confirmed in the post. Meanwhile, controversy over the Gujarat riots continued as communal tensions persisted. In September two armed assailants forced entry into a Hindu temple in Gujarat and shot dead 29 worshippers; three commandos were also killed in the attack, which was believed to have been carried out in retaliation for the deaths of Gujarati Muslims in the recent riots. In September 2003, amid allegations of witness intimidation and inadequate police investigations, the Supreme Court openly challenged the Government of Gujarat's competence and integrity to pursue any case against alleged rioters. (In 2008 the Supreme Court appointed a special investigative team to examine the attack on the train in Godhra and the ensuing riots—for further details see below, Mounting corruption scandals put pressure on the Congress-led Government.)

In the mean time, in March 2003 the Allahabad High Court ordered the Archaeological Survey of India to carry out an excavation at the disputed site in Ayodhya to ascertain whether an earlier Hindu temple existed beneath the Babri Masjid; issued in August, the report indicated that there was indeed evidence of a temple-like structure existing from the 10th century. However, a group of independent archaeologists and historians claimed that the Survey had misused or falsified evidence supporting claims that a Hindu temple once stood on the site for political reasons. Meanwhile, in May the CBI filed new charges against L. K. Advani and seven other leading politicians in connection with the destruction of the Ayodhya mosque in 1992. In September 2003 a special court exonerated Advani of any role in inciting crowds, provoking the demolition of the mosque and encouraging communal agitation, but sustained the charges against the seven other defendants.

In January 2004, encouraged by the BJP's recent victories in state elections, a surging economy and an improvement in relations with Pakistan, Vajpayee announced that a general election would be held by the end of April, five months earlier than scheduled. Nevertheless, the BJP lost support from the DMK, the Marumalarchi Dravida Munnetra Kazhagam (MDMK) and Pattali Makkal Katchi; the AIADMK, meanwhile, announced that it would form an alliance with the BJP to contest the forthcoming election. In the same month the NCP split into two factions; the faction led by Sharad Pawar entered into an alliance with Congress, while Purno Shangma's group agreed to support the NDA.

Congress returned to power: the 2004 and 2009 general elections

At the general election held in April–May 2004, Congress defeated the NDA, securing, together with its allies, a total of 222 seats in the 545-member Lok Sabha, compared with 186 for the NDA. Congress alone won 145 seats, while the BJP secured 138. Left Front parties also performed well, with the Communist Party of India—Marxist (CPI—M) winning 43 seats. Shortly after the election Sonia Gandhi refused the appointment of

Prime Minister, despite being unanimously endorsed as a candidate by Congress, its allies and the Left Front. However, she remained President of Congress, and was elected as Chairwoman of the newly formed Congress-led coalition, the United Progressive Alliance (UPA). The respected Sikh economist and former Minister of Finance Dr Manmohan Singh was subsequently appointed as India's first non-Hindu Prime Minister by President Kalam on Gandhi's recommendation. Meanwhile, Congress secured victory at state elections in Andhra Pradesh in May, and in Maharashtra and Arunachal Pradesh later in the year.

At the first session of the newly elected Lok Sabha, held in June 2004, the BJP disrupted the meeting by protesting against the UPA's appointment of three ministers—all members of the Bihar-based Rashtriya Janata Dal—who had been charged variously with corruption and attempted murder, most notably the new Minister of Railways, Lalu Prasad Yadav, who continued to face corruption charges related to his tenure as Chief Minister of Bihar in 1997. (In April 2005 Yadav was formally charged with embezzlement during his tenure as Chief Minister; he received a five-year prison term in October 2013, having been found guilty of corruption and criminal conspiracy.) In July 2004 the Government dismissed the Governors of Goa, Gujarat, Haryana and Uttar Pradesh, owing to their alleged links to the fundamentalist Hindu group Rashtriya Swayamsevak Sangh (RSS—National Volunteer Organization).

India was one of the countries worst affected by the devastating tsunami generated by a huge earthquake in the Indian Ocean on 26 December 2004. The states of Tamil Nadu, Kerala and Andhra Pradesh and the Union Territory of Pondicherry on the east coast were all affected, together with the Andaman and Nicobar Islands, which were severely damaged. The disaster resulted in the loss of around 16,000 lives and numerous homes and livelihoods.

Subsequent to the general election, L. K. Advani took over as the BJP's parliamentary leader and later also as President of the party. However, in July 2005 charges were brought against Advani (and seven others) in connection with the riots at Ayodhya in 1992, overturning the ruling in September 2003 that had exonerated him of blame. Advani's resignation from the party leadership in December 2005 was believed to be largely a result of pressure from the RSS, which had close links with the BJP. Rajnath Singh, a former Chief Minister of Uttar Pradesh and a federal minister in the Government of Atal Bihari Vajpayee, was subsequently appointed as Advani's successor.

The Minister of External Affairs, K. Natwar Singh, was forced to resign from his post in November 2005, having been implicated as a beneficiary of corrupt practices following an investigation into the UN's 'oil-for-food' programme in Iraq; Prime Minister Manmohan Singh subsequently assumed the external affairs portfolio. In December a total of 11 legislators (10 from the Lok Sabha and one from the Rajya Sabha) were expelled from Parliament, having been filmed in the process of accepting bribes, apparently in exchange for asking certain questions in the chamber. Six of those expelled were BJP legislators. The expulsion was the largest to have taken place in India since independence.

In February 2006 the BJP assumed a position in government in a southern Indian state for the first time when, in coalition with the Janata Dal (Secular), it came to power in Karnataka. In March Sonia Gandhi resigned as a member of the Lok Sabha and as Chairperson of the National Advisory Council (NAC), following assertions made by her opponents regarding the alleged illegality of her holding both positions simultaneously. Legislation was subsequently approved that categorized the chairmanship of the NAC and numerous other posts as non-'office of profit' positions. In May Sonia Gandhi was re-elected to the Lok Sabha in a by-election in Rae Bareilly. At state elections in April and May Congress, with the support of its allies, retained power in Assam (Asom) and in Puducherry, but was defeated by a CPI—M alliance in Kerala and West Bengal. During 2007–08 Congress obtained mixed results at various state elections, being voted into government in states including Manipur, Rajasthan and Mizoram. The BJP appeared to experience a resurgence, with victories in several states including Uttarakhand, Himachal Pradesh and Gujarat and, significantly, the southern state of Karnataka.

In August 2006 the regional party Telangana Rashtra Samithi (TRS) withdrew from the UPA, expressing its dissatisfaction with the Government's apparent lack of commitment to creating an independent Telangana state in Andhra Pradesh. In February 2007 the Samajwadi Party also withdrew from the UPA coalition; this was followed by the withdrawal of the MDMK in March and the Bahujan Samaj Party (BSP) in June 2008. In July 2007, upon the expiry of A. P. J. Abdul Kalam's presidential term, the UPA candidate and erstwhile Governor of Rajasthan, Pratibha Patil, was sworn in to succeed him. Although Patil's election as the first female President of India represented a milestone in the country's history, the UPA's choice of nominee was not without controversy, with critics objecting to a perceived politicization of the office and Patil's reportedly unexceptional record. In September the rapid rise to political prominence of Rahul Gandhi, the son of Sonia Gandhi and Rajiv Gandhi, continued with his appointment as a General Secretary of Congress.

In July 2008 the Left Front bloc withdrew its parliamentary support from the UPA Government in protest against the ratification of a nuclear co-operation agreement with the USA (see Foreign Affairs). A parliamentary vote of confidence, swiftly called by Prime Minister Singh, took place later in the month amid an atmosphere of uncertainty and allegations of bribery. Ultimately the Government was able to ensure its survival, gaining the support of the Samajwadi Party and others to secure a total of 275 votes against the opposition's 256 votes.

Meanwhile, in 2007 the establishment of Special Economic Zones (SEZs) was a major point of controversy in a number of states, including West Bengal, where activists and local residents protested against the forcible seizure of land for industrial development. In May 2008 protests staged by Gujjar tribespeople in Rajasthan against their official caste status escalated into violence, resulting in the deaths of more than 40 people and causing disruption in other states. Violence against Christians increased dramatically in 2008, with attacks on churches in Orissa and Karnataka and the displacement of thousands of people.

In the general election held in five phases during April–May 2009, the UPA won a decisive victory, taking 262 seats in the 543-seat Lok Sabha, while the NDA achieved 159 seats and the Third Front (a newly formed electoral alliance comprising the Left Front and a number of major regional parties—including the AIADMK, the BSP and the Telugu Desam) garnered only 79 seats. Many observers interpreted Congress's comfortable victory as a sign of the Indian public's overriding wish for stability and continuity at a time of worldwide economic crisis. Manmohan Singh was reappointed Prime Minister (the first Indian premier since Jawaharlal Nehru to be returned to office following a full five-year term) and a new coalition Government, dominated by Congress members, was installed on 22 May. Following state legislative elections in Maharashtra, Haryana and Arunachal Pradesh in October, Congress retained power in all three states.

Angered by the Government's perceived failure adequately to address the issue of rising food prices, the opposition called a 12-hour general strike in April 2010, which severely affected transport services and business operations in a number of states, including West Bengal and Kerala. Another 12-hour strike, over rising fuel prices, was called by the opposition in July following the Government's decision to eliminate state petrol subsidies in a bid to tackle the fiscal deficit. The announcement in August that parliamentarians' salaries were to be almost tripled, from Rs 16,000 a month to Rs 50,000, while their parliamentary expenses allowances were to be doubled, further exacerbated a sense of public anger. Further protests against food price inflation and unemployment took place in February 2011, with at least 100,000 trade union members reported to have marched through the streets of New Delhi. Meanwhile, an historic piece of legislation came into effect in April 2010, which made free and elementary education a fundamental right for all children in India between the ages of six and 14 years.

In September 2010 the Allahabad High Court ruled that the disputed Ayodhya holy site should be divided equally between Hindus and Muslims within three months, and that the razed mosque should not be rebuilt, appearing to accept the findings of the August 2003 Archaeological Survey of India report—see The BJP heads coalition governments (1998–2004). However, both Hindu and Muslim groups filed appeals against the ruling. In May 2011 the Supreme Court suspended the High Court's verdict, noting that neither party had sought the partitioning of the site. Pending a final ruling, both sides were to be prohibited from engaging in any construction activities at the disputed site.

Mounting corruption scandals put pressure on the Congress-led Government

During 2010–11 the Government was beset by a number of corruption scandals that diminished public confidence in the Congress-led administration. In April 2010 allegations emerged that the Government had covertly monitored the mobile telephone calls of prominent political figures, including the Minister of Agriculture and of Food Processing Industries, Sharad Pawar, without the required authorization. Furore over the allegations, which the Government adamantly denied, precipitated the adjournment of both legislative chambers. In December, following further revelations concerning the widespread use of telephone surveillance measures by government agencies, Prime Minister Singh defended the use of such practices as essential to national security and the prevention of money-laundering and tax evasion; none the less, the premier ordered an inquiry into the use of telephone surveillance by law enforcement agencies.

The Government was criticized by the Supreme Court in October 2010 for alleged inaction in response to claims that in 2008 the Minister of Communications and Information Technology, Andimuthu Raja of the DMK, had sold mobile telephone licences at grossly undervalued rates to a select group of companies, instead of organizing appropriate commercial bidding processes. Critics claimed that the Prime Minister's reluctance to intervene was borne out of a fear of alienating the DMK, one of Congress's main coalition partners. A leaked report by the office of the Comptroller and Auditor General in November 2010 deemed Raja to be personally responsible for the scandal, which it alleged had cost the Government as much as US $37,000m. in lost revenue. Raja resigned later in November, but denied the accusations against him, insisting that he had merely sought to increase competition and reduce tariff prices in the burgeoning telecommunications industry. The Government resisted opposition demands for a full, joint inquiry into the allegations, underlining that impartial agencies—the CBI and the Supreme Court—were already investigating the case. In the same month a report published by the US-based Global Financial Integrity claimed that India had lost some US $462,000m. in illegal capital outflows since acceding to independence in 1947, with a marked increase since economic liberalization began in 1991.

Prime Minister Singh effected a cabinet reorganization in January 2011, amid rising public anger over the corruption scandals and food price inflation. The most prominent portfolios remained unchanged, however, and critics of the Government argued that the reorganization failed to remove ageing, ineffectual ministers or those most complicit in state corruption. During a rare press conference in February, Singh reiterated his commitment to eradicating corruption at all levels of the political system. On the following day, in a *volte-face* that was welcomed by the opposition, the Prime Minister announced that a joint parliamentary committee was to be launched to investigate the circumstances surrounding the telecommunications scandal.

In a further setback for the Government, in March 2011 the Supreme Court ruled that the appointment of P. J. Thomas as head of the Central Vigilance Commission, an organization charged with monitoring public corruption, had been inappropriate, in light of corruption allegations against him dating back to 1992, as well as his having worked in the Ministry of Communications and Information Technology during the telecommunications scandal. Thomas duly tendered his resignation, while refuting the charges against him as baseless. Further controversy was provoked following the online release, in March 2011, by WikiLeaks—an organization publishing leaked private and classified content—of a US diplomatic cable in which it was alleged that an aide to a senior Congress leader had shown a US embassy official cash that was intended to buy votes in advance of a vote of no confidence in 2008 over a controversial nuclear agreement with the USA (see Foreign Affairs). The opposition had claimed at the time that the Government had bought votes, but an investigation subsequently found insufficient evidence to corroborate the allegations. Two men were arrested in connection with the allegations in July 2011, while the Supreme Court dismissed the police investigation into the scandal as a 'shoddy probe'. In August four members of Parliament were charged with each having accepted bribes worth US $2.5m. in return for their support in the vote of no confidence, and in September a former aide of the BJP's L. K. Advani was arrested in connection with the scandal; all denied any wrongdoing.

In April 2011 Raja—who had been arrested by the CBI in February—was formally indicted on a series of charges including conspiracy, forgery and abuse of official position; eight other individuals, including two officials from the Ministry of Communications and Information Technology and senior executives from the telecommunications industry, were also indicted on similar charges. The trial of Raja and his co-accused commenced in November, with the proceedings still ongoing in early 2014. Meanwhile, the scandal led to a second ministerial resignation in July 2011, when the Minister of Textiles, Dayanidhi Maran of the DMK, left his post amid allegations of coercion in relation to the mis-selling of the mobile telephone licences during his tenure as Minister of Communications and Information Technology in 2004–08. In February 2012 the Supreme Court ordered the cancellation of 122 licences awarded by Raja during 2008—a ruling that was expected to cause considerable disruption to the telecommunications sector.

As a popular anti-corruption movement gained momentum, two figures rose to prominence: Swami Ramdev (popularly known as Baba Ramdev), a well-known yoga guru who had become increasingly renowned for his political and social activism, and Kisan Baburao Hazare (popularly known as Anna Hazare), a social campaigner. Ramdev and Hazare both used widely publicized hunger strikes to force action on corruption, and were able to attract large numbers of supporters for protests. In response to the public mood, in July 2011 the Government proposed the establishment of an independent ombudsman—the Lokpal—which would have the authority to investigate and prosecute public officials suspected of corruption; however, neither serving Prime Ministers, senior members of the judiciary nor the conduct of legislators within Parliament would fall within its remit. Hazare pledged to stage a new hunger strike at a rally in Delhi in August in support of more comprehensive anti-corruption reforms, but was arrested by the authorities. Hazare was released after three days, whereupon he commenced a 15-day hunger strike in the capital, again urging the Government to implement more stringent anti-graft legislation or to resign. In late August Hazare ended his hunger strike, on its 12th day, after members of Parliament, apparently taken aback by the extent of public support for the activist, approved a resolution in favour of tabling tougher anti-corruption legislation. The resulting Lokpal and Lokayuktas Bill (the jurisdiction of which was to cover most categories of government officials, including the Prime Minister) was approved by the Lok Sabha in December, but the legislation subsequently foundered in the Rajya Sabha. After the introduction of a number of amendments, the Bill was finally adopted by both houses of Parliament, with broad cross-party support, in late December 2013.

Meanwhile, the 2010 Commonwealth Games, which were hosted by New Delhi in October of that year (the largest international sporting event ever to be held in India), were plagued by poor planning and delays in the construction of stadiums and other amenities, highlighting India's infrastructural deficiencies and damaging its international reputation. Immediately after the event, Prime Minister Singh announced the creation of a special investigating committee that was to examine the allegations of corruption and mismanagement surrounding the Games. A number of senior members of the organizing committee for the event were arrested between November 2010 and April 2011 in connection with the ongoing investigations. (In February 2013 Suresh Kalmadi, the Chairman of the organizing committee, was charged with corruption, along with the Secretary-General and the Director-General of the Games, and seven others).

Legislative elections were held in several states in April–May 2011; notably, the CPI—M was defeated both in Kerala, where it lost to the Congress-led United Democratic Front, and in West Bengal, where its uninterrupted period of rule since 1977 was ended by the All India Trinamool Congress (AITC). The AITC Chairwoman and federal Minister of Railways, Mamata Banerjee, became West Bengal's first female Chief Minister, heading a coalition government that also comprised Congress. Dinesh Trivedi of the AITC succeeded Banerjee as Minister of Railways in July.

Rahul Gandhi's rise to political prominence continued in August 2011, when he was appointed to a committee charged with leading Congress while Sonia Gandhi underwent medical treatment in the USA. Moreover, following Sonia Gandhi's return to India, and to the helm of Congress, in September, Rahul Gandhi was named as one of five new appointees to Congress's Central Election Committee, which was responsible for finalizing the party's nominations for parliamentary and state assembly elections.

Corruption allegations against the Chief Minister of Karnataka, B. S. Yeddyurappa of the BJP, who in November 2010 had been accused of undervaluing state-owned land that had subsequently been purchased by his sons, intensified during 2011, and, following his indictment on charges pertaining to his alleged involvement in illegal mining operations, Yeddyurappa finally tendered his resignation in July. Yeddyurappa adamantly denied any connection with the fraudulent operations, which were estimated to have cost the treasury in excess of US $3,000m. during 2006–10 (he was acquitted in March 2012).

In February 2011 31 people were convicted on charges of criminal conspiracy and murder in connection with the 2002 Godhra train attack—see above, The BJP heads coalition governments (1998–2004)—of whom 11 were sentenced to death and 20 were imprisoned for life. Several trials relating to the communal violence in Gujarat that followed the train attack concluded during 2011 and 2012: more than 80 people, many of whom received life sentences, were convicted of involvement in the violence. In April 2012 the Chief Minister of Gujarat, Narendra Modi, was formally cleared of complicity in one of the worst atrocities of the 2002 riots, in which 69 mainly Muslim residents of the Gulbarg housing complex in Ahmedabad were killed. However, in August 2012 a former Gujarat state minister and aide to Modi, Maya Kodnani, was sentenced to 28 years' imprisonment for her involvement in the massacre of almost 100 Muslims in Naroda Patiya, a suburb of Ahmedabad.

In mid-September 2011 six people were killed when police in Tamil Nadu opened fire on a group of Dalit protesters in the town of Paramakudi who were demanding the release of the Tamizhaga Makkal Munnetra Kazhagam (TMMK—Tamil People's Progressive Federation) leader, John Pandian, who had been arrested earlier in the month. State authorities insisted that the police had acted in self-defence after coming under attack by the protesters. Later in the month 17 police and government officials were convicted of rape, while 252 others were convicted of 'atrocities against Dalits' in connection with an incident in the Tamil Nadu village of Vachathi in June 1992, when officials had raided the village following reports that villagers were involved in sandalwood-smuggling. More than 100 Dalits were reported to have been abused, 18 women were raped, and homes and livestock were destroyed.

Meanwhile, the majority of elected representatives from the northern Telangana region of Andhra Pradesh and 12 Telangana members of the national Parliament tendered their resignations in July 2011, in protest at the state government's failure to introduce a bill on the formation of the proposed new state of Telangana. The fact that the resignations cut across party lines increased pressure on the state and federal governments to address the issue. In the same month pro-Telangana activists staged a 48-hour strike in support of their demands for the new state, bringing Andhra Pradesh's capital city, Hyderabad, and other towns and cities in the state to a virtual standstill. In November the Speaker of the Lok Sabha rejected the resignations submitted by the 12 Telangana legislators in July, on the grounds that their resignation letters had not followed the correct format prescribed by parliamentary rules.

A session of the Lok Sabha in November 2011 was disrupted by angry protests following the approval by the Uttar Pradesh state assembly of a resolution, introduced by Chief Minister Kumari Mayawati, in support of the division of Uttar Pradesh into four smaller states—Avadh Pradesh, Bundelkhand, Paschim Pradesh and Purvanchal. Disagreements over the proposal (which was widely interpreted as an attempt by the ruling BSP to bolster its popular support in advance of state legislative elections due in February–March 2012) led to the temporary adjournment of both the Lok Sabha and the Rajya Sabha. Meanwhile, with effect from 1 November 2011, the state of Orissa was officially redesignated as Odisha, with the Oriya language henceforth to be known as Odia.

Recent developments: political events in advance of the 2014 general election

State elections during January–March 2012 were expected to provide an indication of the political prospects for Congress and its main rivals at the general election scheduled for 2014. Despite running an intensive election campaign, led by Rahul Gandhi, Congress recorded only a marginal increase of seats and remained a minor party in Uttar Pradesh, India's most populous state, where the left-wing Samajwadi Party ousted Mayawati's BSP. The BJP replaced Congress as Goa's government, and maintained a majority at municipal elections in Delhi; in the Punjab the ruling Shiromani Akali Dal-BJP coalition retained control of the state assembly. Congress stayed in power in Manipur and emerged as the largest party in Uttarakhand, forming a state administration with the support of independent candidates.

In March 2012, following objections from within his own party to the announcement of passenger fare increases, Dinesh Trivedi of the AITC resigned as federal Minister of Railways. Mukul Roy, also of the AITC, was appointed as his replacement, and it was expected that the proposed fare rises would be lessened. The incident provided a further illustration of the ability of junior partners in the UPA coalition to wield a disproportionate influence on government policy. In June further criticism was levelled at the Government when the Minister for Micro, Small and Medium Enterprises, Virbhadra Singh, resigned after having been charged with corruption during his tenure as Chief Minister of Himachal Pradesh (Singh was later acquitted). In July Pranab Mukherjee, the erstwhile Minister of Finance in the UPA cabinet, won a convincing victory in a presidential election. Mukherjee's extensive political experience was expected to transform the ceremonial post into a position of greater influence. However, in the same month the UPA faced internal rupture on a number of occasions. The AITC had initially been reluctant to support Mukherjee and only relented two days before the election. Soon after, the NCP's Sharad Pawar and Praful Patel, Minister of Agriculture and Minister of Heavy Industries and Public Enterprises, respectively, reportedly submitted their resignations, citing dissatisfaction with Congress's management of the coalition. In response, Congress agreed to the establishment of a coalition co-ordination committee, forestalling the ministers' departure. At the end of July the Prime Minister announced a cabinet reorganization, allocating the finance portfolio to P. Chidambaram, and appointing Sushilkumar Shinde, the erstwhile Minister of Power, to replace Chidambaram as Minister of Home Affairs. Chidambaram's appointment in particular was seen as addressing mounting criticism of government inertia in the area of economic policy-making.

In August 2012 a report published by the Comptroller and Auditor General (CAG) asserted that between 2005 and 2009 coalfields were allocated without the necessary auction procedure, resulting in losses of approximately US $33,000m. Prime Minister Singh, who had held responsibility for the coal portfolio at the time, was not accused of misconduct by the CAG; nevertheless, the BJP demanded his immediate resignation and the cancellation of the original allocations, causing an interruption to parliamentary proceedings that lasted 13 days. Discord within the UPA coalition was evident in September when the AITC withdrew its ministers, including Minister of Railways Mukul Roy, from Government in protest over the latter's decision to allow majority foreign investment in multi-sector retail, a policy that had also proved unpopular with the opposition; however, the Government did secure parliamentary support for the measure in December.

In October 2012, shortly before a planned cabinet reorganization, S. M. Krishna resigned as Minister of External Affairs. Singh subsequently announced major alterations to the composition of the Council of Ministers, introducing or promoting several younger Congress members. The external affairs portfolio was given to Salman Khurshid, who was replaced as Minister of Law and Justice by Ashwani Kumar.

Several missile tests were performed in 2012, including that of a long-range missile capable of reaching China or Europe; India was reported to have become the largest importer of military equipment in the world. The country was also financing a major expansion of its space programme, with an unmanned mission to Mars announced in August 2012. In July, meanwhile, a massive power failure resulted in an electricity 'blackout' for approximately 670m. Indians in 20 states in the north, west and east of the country, causing large-scale disruption and considerable embarrassment for the Government.

State elections were held in Himachal Pradesh in November 2012 and in Gujarat in December. Congress defeated the incumbent BJP government in Himachal Pradesh; former union minister Virbhadra Singh became Chief Minister of the state for the sixth time. In Gujarat the BJP retained power, winning almost twice as many seats as Congress. Narendra Modi was sworn in for a fourth term as Chief Minister amid heightened speculation over his potential as a future prime minister. At state elections in Meghalaya in February 2013, Congress won the largest number of seats, but required the support of independents or smaller parties to secure a parliamentary majority. In the same month elections were held in Tripura and Nagaland: in the former, the CPI—M's Left Front retained power with an increased majority, and in the latter the incumbent Democratic Alliance of Nagaland, led by the Nagaland People's Front, secured a third term. Congress's performance in all three of the north-eastern elections was poorer than anticipated and did not bode well for the forthcoming national election. In January the party had appointed Rahul Gandhi as its Vice-President, as he continued his expected trajectory towards prime ministerial candidate.

Meanwhile, in January 2013 the National President of the India National Lok Dal and former Chief Minister of Haryana, Om Prakash Chautala, was convicted of corruption and sentenced to 10 years' imprisonment. His son Ajay Singh Chautala, the Secretary-General of the party, received the same sentence. In the same month Rajnath Singh was elected as President of the BJP (having previously served in the position until 2009), to replace Nitin Gadkari, who was under investigation for alleged corruption.

In December 2012 the rape and murder of a woman on a private bus in Delhi by a group of men provoked large-scale protests and outrage, highlighting the mistreatment of women in Indian society and the shortcomings of the legal system. Five men and a juvenile male were subsequently arrested in connection with the case. In February 2013 the country's rape laws were amended, with longer minimum sentences and the provision of the death penalty in cases where rape leads to death. The amendments were adopted by Parliament in late March. However, earlier in March, in what was described as a 'major lapse in security', one of the suspects in the rape case died in prison, having reportedly committed suicide. In September four of the suspects were sentenced to death for their involvement in the Delhi rape and murder case. However, two of the executions were postponed in March 2014, pending appeal hearings with the Supreme Court; the two other men were expected to launch similar appeals against their sentences.

The Government suffered a further setback in March 2013, when the Tamil Nadu-based DMK—which held five cabinet posts—withdrew its support from the coalition. The regional party accused the Government of a weak response to ongoing allegations that the Government of Sri Lanka committed human rights violations against its Tamil citizens during that country's civil war. Although India voted in support of a US-sponsored resolution on Sri Lanka at the UN Human Rights Council (UNHRC) in the same month, which recommended an independent investigation into allegations of humanitarian violations, the DMK contended that the Indian authorities had failed to use their influence to secure a more forceful resolution.

Despite recent setbacks, Congress achieved an outright majority at state elections held in the formerly BJP-controlled state of Karnataka in May 2013. The party won 121 out of 224 seats, compared with 40 seats each for the BJP and the Janata Dal (Secular). K. Siddaramaiah was chosen by Congress as the new Chief Minister of Karnataka. In the same month the federal Minister of Railways, Pawan Kumar Bansal, and the Minister of Law and Justice, Ashwani Kumar, both tendered their resignations following allegations of corruption. The Minister of Road Transport and Highways, C. P. Joshi, assumed additional responsibility for the railways portfolio, while the Minister of Communications and Information Technology, Kapil Sibal, also took charge of the law and justice portfolio.

Prime Minister Singh carried out a significant reorganization of the Council of Ministers in June 2013, with eight new ministers (all of whom were members of Congress) being appointed to the Government. Among the changes, Mallikarjun Kharge, hitherto Minister of Labour and Employment, was accorded the railways portfolio, Oscar Fernandes was appointed Minister of Road Transport and Highways, while Girija Vyas and Sis Ram Ola were given charge of Housing and Urban Poverty Alleviation, and Labour and Employment, respectively.

At the end of July 2013 the UPA approved the division of Andhra Pradesh to create a separate state of Telangana, which would thereby become India's 29th state. The announcement led to a series of violent protests and strikes being held in coastal and southern districts of Andhra Pradesh by those opposed to the bifurcation of the state; many inhabitants of the existing state feared that the change would bring economic disruption and that Maoist insurgents in Telangana would threaten the region's security. In October several Congress ministers from Andhra Pradesh tendered their resignations from the federal cabinet (although these were not accepted), and several legislators from the Congress and Telugu Desam parties withdrew from Parliament in early October. The draft legislation was endorsed by the Lok Sabha in mid-February 2014, having received the support of the BJP as well as the UPA; it was approved by the Rajya Sabha in late February. Under the proposals, the neighbouring states would share the capital city of Hyderabad for an initial period of 10 years. Government officials denied opposition claims that the decision to proceed with the creation of Telangana was intended to attract regional votes at the forthcoming general election. At the Lok Sahba vote in February, there were violent disturbances in the chamber as legislators protested against the Government's proposals for the region; 17 legislators were suspended for their role in the uproar. After President Mukherjee signed the Telangana bill into law on 1 March, the Government announced that the new state of Telangana—to have 10 districts, compared with 13 in the remaining areas of Andhra Pradesh—would officially be created on 2 June.

State elections were held in Chhattisgarh, Madhya Pradesh and Rajasthan, and in the National Capital Territory of Delhi, during November–December 2013. The results represented a notable success for the BJP, which secured outright majorities in the three states, winning by significant margins in Madhya Pradesh and Rajasthan. The BJP also won the most seats in the Delhi territorial election, although no party achieved a majority in the capital and thus the formation of a new government proved to be problematic (see below). In a worrying sign for the party as it prepared for the 2014 legislative elections, Congress candidates fared extremely badly at the state assembly polls. Securing an absolute majority in the small state of Mizoram in early December provided little consolation for the Congress leadership. In mid-December the Minister of Labour and Employment, Sis Ram Ola, died after suffering years of ill health; Oscar Fernandes assumed additional responsibility for the labour portfolio.

While the BJP performed strongly in the December 2013 Delhi election—increasing its representation in the assembly to 31 seats, from 23 seats at the previous election in 2008—the most notable result of the polls was the success of the recently formed Aam Aadmi Party (AAP), which had emerged from the popular anti-corruption movement and was contesting its first-ever election; the AAP secured 28 seats in the assembly. Congress was relegated to third place with just eight seats (compared with 43 seats in 2008); Sheila Dixit of Congress, who since 1998 had served three consecutive terms as Chief Minister, tendered her resignation. Given the inconclusive outcome of the Delhi polls, Kejriwal's AAP formed a minority government in the territory, with conditional support from Congress. The AAP's leader Arvind Kejriwal, a social activist and former civil servant with no political experience, was sworn in as Chief Minister of Delhi in late December. The AAP subsequently announced plans to contest more than 70 seats across the country in the forthcoming general election; the party indicated that it would target seats that were held by legislators who had been accused of corruption. However, in mid-February 2014, after less than two months in office, Kejriwal resigned as Chief Minister of Delhi following the failure of both Congress and the BJP to support the introduction of tough anti-corruption legislation in the territory—the AAP's flagship policy; Kejriwal's resignation led to the imposition of presidential rule in Delhi.

In late February 2014 Kiran Kumar Reddy tendered his resignation as Chief Minister of Andhra Pradesh in protest against the imminent division of the state; Reddy also announced his departure from Congress. On 1 March, following the failure of Congress officials in the state to reach agreement on a successor to Reddy, presidential rule was imposed in Andhra Pradesh. In March Reddy formed the Jai Samaikyandhra Party, the main goal of which was to overturn the bifurcation of Andhra Pradesh.

Meanwhile, in June 2013 Narendra Modi was appointed Chairman of the BJP's election committee in preparation for the 2014 legislative elections, despite opposition from L. K. Advani, a senior BJP leader and one of the party's founders; Advani resigned from all his official BJP posts. In September 2013 Modi was officially named as the BJP's prime ministerial candidate. While Modi attracted extensive popular support, in particular for his record on promoting economic development in Gujarat, there were also concerns that his controversial handling of communal tensions in his home state would make him a divisive leader, who could alienate many of India's non-Hindu citizens. In January 2014 Manmohan Singh confirmed that he would not continue in political office after the forthcoming general election. In the same month Rahul Gandhi was appointed chief of Congress's general election campaign. However, despite widespread expectation that, as the latest representative of the influential Gandhi political dynasty, Rahul would be Congress's prime ministerial candidate, the leadership insisted that it was not party policy to nominate a candidate in advance of the election. According to some analysts, this approach reflected a desire by the party leadership to protect Rahul's political reputation in the event of a disastrous electoral performance by Congress. On 5 March the Election Commission announced that the legislative elections would be held in nine phases between 7 April and 12 May, with vote-counting to be completed on 16 May. Meanwhile, in February eleven left-leaning and regional parties—including the Samajwadi Party, the CPI—M, Janata Dal (Secular), Biju Janata Dal, Asom Gana Parishad and the AIADMK—announced the formation of a Third Front to contest the general election. While most analysts predicted that the BJP would emerge as the largest party, and that Congress would suffer a significant defeat, it remained far from certain that any single party or electoral alliance would secure sufficient seats to form a majority government—an outcome which had the potential to further increase the influence of smaller, regional parties in the Indian political landscape. Thus, the immediate political future of the world's biggest democracy remained uncertain as this book went press.

Internal Unrest and the Threat of Terrorism

In the aftermath of the devastating terrorist attacks on the US mainland on 11 September 2001, for which the USA held the militant Islamist al-Qa'ida organization responsible, the Indian Government sought to emphasize its own uncompromising response to the activities of illegal organizations. In October the Government promulgated the controversial Prevention of Terrorism Act 2001 (POTA), which broadened the definitions of terrorist activity and the preventative and retaliatory powers of the Government, and proscribed indefinitely 23 organizations engaged in principally separatist activities. A series of audacious terrorist attacks perpetrated by Kashmiri separatists severely tested the resolve of the Government in late 2001 and early 2002 (see Foreign Affairs), resulting in an unexpected consolidation of popular and political support for the ruling coalition.

A number of bomb explosions occurred in Mumbai in December 2002–August 2003, killing more than 65 people. In June 2004 five people were charged under the POTA in connection with the bombings. (The Government approved the repeal of the POTA in September, and stated its intention to amend the Unlawful Activities—Prevention—Act of 1967 by adding another ordinance in order to incorporate legislative provisions against terrorism. The Rajya Sabha gave its assent to the amended legislation in December.) During 2005–08 there was a series of terrorist attacks against civilian targets in various locations across India. In October 2005 a number of bomb attacks in the national capital, New Delhi, resulted in the deaths of more than 60 people. In November police announced that they had arrested a man suspected of having financed and planned the bombings; he was believed to be a member of the Pakistan-based militant group Lashkar-e-Taiba (LeT), which had previously denied responsibility for the attacks. In March 2006 a number of bombs exploded in the holy city of Varanasi in Uttar Pradesh, killing at least 14 people. Several suspects, allegedly linked to the Bangladesh-based Islamist militant group Harakat-ul-Jihad-i-Islami, were subsequently arrested. On 11 July about 180 people were killed and hundreds more injured in a series of bomb blasts on the Mumbai train network. In October 28 people were charged with involvement in the bombings, including 15 suspects who had not yet been apprehended. Among those charged *in absentia* was Azam Cheema, who was reported to be a member of LeT. Another series of bomb explosions, at a Muslim cemetery in Malegaon, Maharashtra, killed at least 37 people in September. By the end of November several suspects, with alleged links to the banned Students' Islamic Movement of India (SIMI—which was alleged to be linked to both al-Qa'ida and the militant Hizbul Mujahideen, see Foreign Affairs), had been arrested. In August 2007 two bomb explosions in the southern city of Hyderabad killed some 42 people. Six bomb explosions targeting three courts in Uttar Pradesh claimed the lives of 18 people in November; a previously little known group, the Indian Mujahideen (which was believed to comprise junior members of SIMI), claimed responsibility for the attacks.

Further attacks were carried out in May 2008 in Jaipur, Rajasthan, resulting in the deaths of more than 80 people. In July bombings in Bangalore, Karnataka, which caused two fatalities, were followed by a series of explosions in the Gujarati city of Ahmedabad, killing some 50 people. In September, a month after Prime Minister Singh had identified 'terrorism, extremism, communalism and fundamentalism' as the 'major challenges to the unity and integrity' of the country, bomb attacks resulted in the deaths of more than 20 people in Delhi. The Indian Mujahideen claimed responsibility for each of the four series of attacks.

In November 2008 some 166 people were killed in co-ordinated offensives carried out by 10 gunmen against public targets in Mumbai, including two hotels, a hospital, a railway station and a Jewish centre. Following the attacks and subsequent siege, which lasted for several days in some locations, and in which all but one of the gunmen were killed, the Minister of Home Affairs, Shivraj V. Patil, resigned on 30 November; he was replaced by the incumbent Minister of Finance, P. Chidambaram. As public criticism of the Government's handling of the attacks increased, in December the Chief Minister of Maharashtra, Vilasrao Deshmukh, was also forced to step down. In the same month the establishment of the National Investigation Agency was announced as part of a government campaign for greater internal security; anti-terrorism legislation was also expected to be reviewed. In May 2010 the sole surviving gunman of the 2008 Mumbai attacks, Pakistani national Mohammed Ajmal Amir Kasab—who was allegedly a member of LeT—was convicted on five charges, including murder, terrorist activity and waging war against the nation, and sentenced to death; he was hanged in November 2012.

From December 2008 the authorities in Pakistan arrested several militants suspected of involvement in planning the Mumbai attacks; these included Zaki-ur-Rehman Lakhvi, a senior leader of LeT. However, Pakistan resisted Indian demands for the suspects to be extradited to India. Seven suspects, including Lakhvi, were charged in connection with the attacks under Pakistani anti-terrorism laws in November 2009; all seven denied the charges against them. Nine others were charged *in absentia*. In December the Indian Government announced plans to overhaul and strengthen its security services by recruiting 400,000 more police officers, establishing a national intelligence database and creating a national counter-terrorism centre. In June 2012 another alleged planner of the attacks was arrested in New Delhi, while in January 2013 David Headley, a US-Pakistani associate of LeT, was sentenced in the USA to 35 years in prison for his part in the attacks.

Three co-ordinated bomb explosions in busy districts of Mumbai in July 2011 claimed the lives of 26 people and injured many others. No individuals or groups claimed responsibility for the attacks. In August Minister of Home Affairs P. Chidambaram disclosed that ongoing investigations into the bombings appeared to indicate the involvement of an 'Indian module', with some officials attributing the blame for the attacks to the Indian Mujahideen. However, some contended that the attacks had been orchestrated by LeT or other elements seeking to derail the Indo-Pakistani peace process, while others argued that the attacks were linked to the Indian criminal underworld.

In September 2011, while Prime Minister Singh was on a state visit to Bangladesh, a bomb exploded outside the High Court in Delhi, killing 12 people. The Indian Mujahideen and Harakat-ul-Jihad-e-al-Islami (HUJI—the Movement for Islamic Jihad, which was founded in 1984 and believed to have links to al-Qa'ida) both claimed responsibility for the attack; HUJI's senior leader, Ilyas Kashmiri, was reported to have died in a US unmanned drone strike in north-western Pakistan in June. Responding to the latest terrorist attack, Singh acknowledged that there were 'weaknesses' in India's security system and that the authorities needed comprehensively to address these. However, Nitin Gadkari, President of the BJP, accused the Singh administration of having failed to adopt a sufficiently firm stance both in its efforts to combat home-grown terrorism and in negotiations with Pakistan, and argued that the Government's approach was tantamount to 'appeasement of terrorism'. Later in September the Indian Mujahideen became the first Indian-based group to be formally designated as a foreign terrorist organization by the US Department of State.

In February 2013 17 people were killed and more than 100 injured following a pair of bomb attacks in Hyderabad. Although the identity of the perpetrators was unknown, numerous reports speculated that the attacks were related to an upsurge in unrest in Jammu and Kashmir in the same month (see Relations with Pakistan and the Kashmir issue).

Gurkha Separatist Movement

Regional issues continue to play an important role in Indian political affairs. In 1986 the Gurkhas (of Nepalese stock) in West Bengal launched a campaign for a separate autonomous homeland in the Darjiling (Darjeeling) region and the recognition of Nepali as an official language. The violent separatist campaign, led by the Gurkha National Liberation Front (GNLF), was prompted by the eviction of about 10,000 Nepalis from the state of Meghalaya, where the native residents feared that they were becoming outnumbered by immigrants. When violent disturbances and a general strike were organized by the GNLF in June 1987, the central Government agreed to hold tripartite talks with the GNLF's leader, Subhas Ghising, and the Chief Minister of West Bengal. The Prime Minister rejected the GNLF's demand for an autonomous Gurkha state, but Ghising agreed to the establishment of a semi-autonomous Darjiling Gorkha Hill Council (DGHC), which was inaugurated in August 1988. Following elections to the DGHC in November, the GNLF won 26 of the 28 elective seats (the 14 remaining members of the Council were to be nominated) and Ghising was elected Chairman of the Council. However, the GNLF continued to demand the establishment of a fully autonomous Gurkha state. In 1992 a constitutional amendment providing for the recognition of Nepali as an official language was adopted.

In February 2008 a splinter group of the GNLF, the Gorkha Janmukti Morcha (GJM), blockaded entry routes into Darjiling to protest against a new autonomy agreement drawn up between the DGHC and the state and federal authorities. Following the resignation and enforced exile from the region of Ghising in March, the GJM rapidly became the dominant force representing Gurkha separatism. A series of GJM-orchestrated strikes and protests severely disrupted the key tourism and tea industries in the area. In August 2009 the central Government initiated a series of tripartite talks involving the GJM and the West Bengal state authorities, following which the Government agreed to repeal the legislation creating the DGHC, while the GJM pledged to remain 'peaceful and democratic'. After Mamata Banerjee of the AITC became Chief Minister of West Bengal (see Domestic Political Affairs), an agreement was signed between the state government and the GJM in July 2011 providing for the creation of a semi-autonomous Gorkhaland Territorial Administration (GTA), which was to comprise Darjiling, Kalimpong and Kurseong and have various administrative, executive and financial powers, as well as the authority to regulate its tea plantations; legislative and tax levying responsibilities would remain vested in the central Government. The agreement was ratified by the West Bengal state assembly in September. In October the GJM proposed the enlargement of the GTA to include a number of subdivisions in Terai and Dooars inhabited primarily by Gurkhas or Adivasis (also of Nepalese stock), whereby the GTA's official designation would change to the Gorkhaland and Adivasi Territorial Administration. In March 2013 a GJM delegation travelled to Delhi to meet with President Pranab Mukherjee. The GJM reiterated its demands for an autonomous Gurkha state ('Gorkhaland'), and complained about the West Bengal state government's interference in GTA affairs. In August, as the Government was proceeding with plans to create an independent state of Telangana out of Andhra Pradesh, the GJM declared an indefinite strike in Darjiling to protest against the failure of the federal authorities to establish a separate Gurkha state; the strike again had a serious effect on the economy of West Bengal.

Unrest in Assam

In December 1985 an election for the state assembly in Assam was won by the Asom Gana Parishad (AGP—Assam People's Council), a newly formed regional party. This followed the signing, in August, of an agreement between the central Government and two groups of Hindu activists, concluded after five years of sectarian violence, which limited the voting rights of immigrants (mainly Bangladeshis) to Assam. When the accord was announced, Bangladesh stated that it would not take back Bengali immigrants from Assam and denied that it had allowed illegal refugees to cross its borders into Assam. Another disaffected Indian tribal group, the Bodos of Assam, demanded a separate state of Bodoland within India. In February 1989 the Bodos, under the leadership of the All Bodo Students' Union (ABSU), intensified their separatist campaign by organizing strikes, bombings and violent demonstrations. The central Government dispatched armed forces to the state. In August the ABSU held peace talks with the state government and central government officials, agreeing to suspend its violent activities, while the Assam government agreed to suspend emergency security measures.

The situation became more complicated in 1989, when a militant Maoist group, the United Liberation Front of Assam (ULFA), re-emerged. The ULFA demanded the outright secession of the whole of Assam from India. In 1990 the ULFA claimed responsibility for about 90 assassinations, abductions and bombings. In November, when the violence began to disrupt the state's tea industry, the central Government placed Assam under direct rule, dispatched troops to the state and outlawed the ULFA. In the 1991 state elections the AGP was defeated, and Congress (I) took power. In September, following the breakdown of prolonged talks with the ULFA, the Government launched a new offensive against the separatist guerrillas and declared the entire state a disturbed area. Meanwhile, following the suspension of violence by the ABSU, the Bodo Security Force assumed the leading role in the violent campaign for a separate state of Bodoland. The Bodo Security Force was outlawed by the central Government in November 1992. At a tripartite meeting attended by the Minister of State for Home Affairs, the Chief Minister of Assam and the President of the ABSU in Guwahati in February 1993, a memorandum was signed providing for the establishment of a 40-member Bodoland Autonomous Council, which would be responsible for the socio-economic and cultural affairs of the Bodo people. However, attacks leading to substantial loss of life were made by Bodo and ULFA activists in the second half of the 1990s, both on the security forces and on non-tribal groups in the area. In March 2000 the Government and the Bodo Liberation Tigers (BLT—a group that had waged a violent campaign for a separate state for the Bodo people since 1996) agreed to a ceasefire.

In February 2002 it was reported that the Assam state assembly had passed a resolution granting a degree of autonomy to the Bodo people through the creation of a territorial council for the Bodos of four western districts of the state. One year later the Union Government, state government and BLT signed a pact formally agreeing upon the introduction of a Bodoland Territorial Council. The Council was established in December 2003 and the Bodo militants surrendered their weapons to mark the formal disbanding of the BLT. However, the ULFA continued its campaign of violence and inter-tribal clashes also occurred in the state. In August 2004 the ULFA was believed to have been responsible for the bombing of an Independence Day parade in the town of Dhemaji, which killed 16 people (many of them children). In October a series of violent incidents in Assam and neighbouring Nagaland was attributed to the ULFA and the National Democratic Front of Bodoland (NDFB), another militant group operating in the region. In May 2005 the NDFB signed a one-year ceasefire agreement with both the government of Assam and the Union Government. In September the ULFA agreed to conduct peace negotiations with the Union Government, on condition that the army halted its counter-insurgency operation in the state; by September 2006, however, negotiations had collapsed, and in subsequent months the Government dispatched further troops to the region to curb the escalating violence. There was also an increase in attacks on migrant workers in Assam, allegedly perpetrated by the ULFA, together with a new strategy of targeting Congress officials.

Co-ordinated bomb attacks, most of them in Guwahati, resulted in more than 80 fatalities in October 2008. In the same month violence between Bodos and settlers caused dozens of deaths in the state. In early 2009 it was reported that the ULFA had split into two rival factions. In November several senior ULFA leaders were arrested by the Bangladeshi Government authorities and transferred into Indian custody. A marked reduction in militant activity was evident from 2010, and, to facilitate peace talks with the central Government, the ULFA announced a unilateral ceasefire in July 2011. Violence broke out between Bodos and Muslim settlers in July 2012, leading to some 95 deaths and the internal displacement of hundreds of thousands of people. Further displacement was reported in southern cities, including Bangalore and Chennai, as north-eastern migrants fearing further violence fled. In February 2013 the holding of local elections precipitated clashes between protesters and the police, resulting in 19 fatalities.

Nagaland

Elsewhere in north-eastern India, violence—separatist, inter-tribal (particularly against ethnic Bengali settlers) and anti-Government—continued in Nagaland, Tripura, Bihar, Mizoram and Manipur during the 2000s, leading to an alarming increase in the number of civilian deaths. In 1997 the central Government entered a ceasefire agreement with the National Socialist Council of Nagaland (Issak Muivah)—NSCN (IM)—a rebel organization that advocated the creation of a 'greater Nagaland', which, in addition to the state of Nagaland, would include districts in Assam, Manipur and Arunachal Pradesh. In June 2001 the Government extended the scope of the existing ceasefire in Nagaland to include the National Socialist Council of Nagaland (Khaplang)—NSCN (K)—along with all underground organizations in north-eastern India, and offered to involve the NSCN (K) and the NSCN (IM) in peace negotiations. The decision to extend the ceasefire to Naga groups in the neighbouring states of Assam, Manipur and Arunachal Pradesh gave rise to fears of the creation of a 'greater Nagaland' as part of an eventual settlement at the expense of the other states. Strikes and violent protests took place in Manipur. In July, in an effort to curb the violence, the national Government agreed to limit the ceasefire arrangement to the state of Nagaland. In November 2002 the central Government lifted its ban on the NSCN (IM) and agreed to hold negotiations on the political status of Nagaland. In February 2007, at India's request, security forces in Myanmar took action against NSCN (K) bases inside Myanma territory. In mid-2010 there was renewed conflict between Naga and non-Naga groups in Manipur, with a Naga student group linked to the NSCN (IM) conducting a blockade of all roads leading into Manipur.

Naxalite Insurgency

The Naxalites are a myriad group of Maoist insurgents who emerged in the late 1960s in West Bengal. Since then the rebels, who claim to be fighting for the rights of the rural poor, have spread into less developed areas of central and eastern India (popularly known as the 'Red Corridor'). According to India's intelligence agency, the Research and Analysis Wing, the total number of regular Naxalite cadres is estimated at around 50,000 and armed cadres at about 20,000.

In mid-2004 the state government of Andhra Pradesh agreed a ceasefire with the People's War Group, a faction of the Communist Party of India (Marxist-Leninist), which had been waging a sporadic violent campaign in the state since 1980. The Naxalite rebels demanded the creation of a communist state comprising tribal areas in Andhra Pradesh, Maharashtra, Orissa, Bihar and Chhattisgarh. In September 2004 the People's War Group merged with another militant separatist group, the Maoist Communist Centre, to become the Communist Party of India (Maoist)—CPI (Maoist). Peace negotiations commenced between the rebels and the Andhra Pradesh state authorities in October. However, they collapsed in early 2005, leading to escalating violence in the region. In August the state government imposed a fresh ban on the CPI (Maoist), after rebels murdered nine people in the town of Narayanpet.

In September 2005 an Inter-State Joint Task Force was established following an agreement among the chief ministers of 13 states affected by ongoing Naxalite insurgencies. The Force was intended to co-ordinate operations against guerrillas across state borders, and was to have the assistance of the Union Government. In the same month the government of Chhattisgarh outlawed all Naxalite organizations, following a recent increase in insurgent activity in the state. In April 2006 Prime Minister Manmohan Singh stated that the Naxalite insurgency posed the 'single biggest internal security challenge' to India, and called for further co-operation between the main affected states. In 2007 insurgents were allegedly involved in road blockades and attacks on infrastructure staged in protest against the establishment of Special Economic Zones in states such as West Bengal (see Domestic Political Affairs). During 2006–07 Naxalite attacks and clashes between rebels and security forces in Chhattisgarh reportedly resulted in several hundred deaths, including many civilians. In 2008 it was reported that Naxalites were operating in as many as 16 states and that the CPI (Maoist) remained active in at least seven states. In February 2009, in the run-up to the general election, the Union Government announced plans to launch simultaneous counter-operations in all of the states that were worst affected by Naxalite violence—Chhattisgarh, Orissa, Andhra Pradesh, Maharashtra, Jharkhand, Bihar, Uttar Pradesh and West Bengal—in an attempt to block all possible escape routes of the insurgents. In June the Government banned the CPI (Maoist) as a terrorist organization. Despite this concerted action, the number of deaths resulting from Naxalite violence increased from 794 in 2008 to 1,134 in 2009. By early 2010 it was estimated that the Naxalite insurgency had spread to at least 20 of India's 28 states.

In April 2010 more than 70 paramilitary troops were killed by Naxalite rebels in Chhattisgarh. After a landmine killed more than 30 people (the majority of whom were civilians) in the same state in May, the Government announced that it was reviewing its strategy against the rebels. In an apparent case of sabotage later that month, more than 80 people were killed when a train travelling from Calcutta to Mumbai derailed. Naxalite leaders denied involvement in the derailment (which, if proved to be a rebel operation, represented the most deadly attack of the Naxalites' 43-year insurgency), but pledged to launch an investigation and to punish any 'rogue' units found to have been involved; police claimed to have substantial evidence indicating the responsibility of a local Naxalite militia. In June Minister of Home Affairs P. Chidambaram set out the Government's preconditions for initiating peace talks with Naxalite rebels, demanding the total cessation of violent activities for a 72-hour period, following which security forces would refrain from targeting them; the initiative was reported to have been cautiously welcomed by Naxalite rebels, but the violence continued unabated, and a number of rebels were reported to have been killed during July–August. The number of deaths resulting from Naxalite violence increased to 1,005 in 2010 (according to revised figures reported by the Ministry of Home Affairs in 2013). However, the ministry noted a marked decline, to 611 persons, in 2011, and attributed this to the Government's ongoing counter-insurgency efforts. Enhanced co-operation between the various authorities across state borders and significant improvements in intelligence-gathering were believed to have played key roles in the significant reduction of casualties. Meanwhile, in November a senior CPI—M leader, Koteswara Rao (alias Kishenji), was killed by security forces in West Bengal.

Although the number of fatalities caused by Naxalite militants decreased further in 2012, to an estimated 415, violent incidents continued to be reported. In May 2013 Maoist militants attacked a convoy of political activists in Chhattisgarh, killing 12 senior Congress officials; a total of 28 people were killed as a result of the attack. The state's Chief Minister, Raman Singh, acknowledged subsequently that there had been a 'lapse' in security prior to the incident, while the Government ordered an official investigation into the exact circumstances of the attack. In June nine states that faced security threats from Maoist insurgents, including Bihar and Chhattisgarh, announced the implementation of a new, united policy to tackle the problem. An estimated 40,000 members of the security forces in eight of the states commenced a four-day military operation in December to attempt to defeat the insurgency. It became apparent in the second half of 2013, with further fatal Maoist attacks having taken place in Bihar and Jharkhand in June and July, respectively, that the insurgents were increasingly targeting the civilian population as well as government and military targets. Two attacks by Maoist rebels on groups of police officers in Chhattisgarh in late February and early March 2014 resulted in the deaths of 22 officers.

Foreign Affairs

Relations with Pakistan and the Kashmir issue

Relations with Pakistan had deteriorated in the late 1970s and early 1980s, owing to Pakistan's potential capability for the development of nuclear weapons and its significant purchases of US armaments. The Indian Government believed that such developments would upset the balance of power in the region and precipitate an 'arms race'. Pakistan's President, Gen. Mohammad Zia ul-Haq, visited India in 1985, when he and Rajiv Gandhi announced their mutual commitment not to attack each other's nuclear installations and to negotiate the sovereignty of the disputed Siachen glacier region in Kashmir. Pakistan continued to demand a settlement of the Kashmir problem in accordance with earlier UN resolutions, prescribing a plebiscite under UN auspices in the two parts of the state, now divided between India and Pakistan. India argued that the problem should be settled in accordance with the Shimla Agreement of 1972, which required that all Indo–Pakistani disputes be resolved through bilateral negotiations. The Indian decision to construct a barrage on the River Jhelum in Jammu and Kashmir, in an alleged violation of the 1960 Indus Waters Treaty, also created concern in Pakistan. In late 1989 the outlawed Jammu and Kashmir Liberation Front (JKLF) and several other militant Islamist groups intensified their campaigns of civil unrest, strikes and terrorism, demanding an independent Kashmir or unification with Pakistan. The Indian Government dispatched troops to the region and placed the entire Srinagar valley under curfew. Pakistan denied India's claim that the militants were trained and armed in Pakistan-held Kashmir (known as Azad Kashmir). In January 1990 Jammu and Kashmir was placed under Governor's rule, and in July under President's rule. By 1996 the total death toll resulting from the conflict in Jammu and Kashmir was estimated at up to 20,000. However, the situation improved somewhat when elections for the national parliamentary seats were held in the troubled state shortly after the general election of April–May 1996. State elections (the first to be held since 1987) were conducted in Jammu and Kashmir in September and attracted a turnout of more than 50%, despite being boycotted by the majority of the separatist groups. The moderate Jammu and Kashmir National Conference (JKNC), led by Dr Farooq Abdullah, won the majority of seats in the state assembly and subsequently offered to instigate talks with the separatist leaders.

Meanwhile, in June 1994 the Indian army had begun to deploy a new missile, *Prithvi*, which had the capacity to reach most of Pakistan. While the 'arms race' between the two countries continued, talks (which had been suspended since 1994) were resumed in March 1997. Tension increased in September when a large-scale outbreak of artillery exchanges along the Line of Control (LoC) in Kashmir (a ceasefire line drawn up in 1949) resulted in about 40 civilian deaths. After a hiatus of more than one year (during which time both countries carried out controversial nuclear test explosions—see Domestic Political Affairs), Indo-Pakistani talks at foreign secretary level regarding Kashmir and other issues were resumed in Islamabad in October 1998. In February 1999 Prime Minister Vajpayee made an historic bus journey over the border to Lahore, inaugurating the first passenger bus service between India and Pakistan. He and his Pakistani counterpart, Muhammad Nawaz Sharif, proceeded to hold a rare summit meeting, at which they signed the Lahore Declaration on peace and nuclear security. The contentious subject of Jammu and Kashmir was, however, largely avoided.

Despite the apparent rapprochement, in April 1999 both India and Pakistan carried out tests on their latest missiles, which were capable of carrying nuclear warheads. In May the situation deteriorated drastically after Islamist guerrilla groups, reinforced by regular Pakistani troops, occupied strategic positions on the Indian side of the LoC in the Kargil area of Kashmir. The Indian army was forced to wage an expensive and lengthy campaign, during which more than 480 Indian soldiers were killed, but in July Indian military dominance combined with US diplomatic pressure led to a Pakistani withdrawal.

In August 1999 the Hizbul Mujahideen, one of the main Kashmiri militant groups, ended a brief ceasefire because of the Indian Government's opposition to instigating tripartite negotiations including representatives of Pakistan. In April 2000 there were indications that the Indian Government was willing to re-establish dialogue with Kashmiri militants. Leaders of the All-Party Hurriyat Conference (APHC), an organization that, to an extent, acted as the political voice for some of the militant groups, were released in April and May. In November the Indian Government declared the suspension of combat operations against Kashmiri militants during the Muslim holy month of Ramadan, a unilateral ceasefire that was subsequently extended; Indian security forces were authorized to retaliate if fired upon. The majority of national parties and foreign governments supported the cessation of hostilities, but the militant groups refused to enter into tripartite discussions and continued their campaign of violence. In January 2001 the Indian High Commissioner to Pakistan visited the Pakistani President, Gen. Pervez Musharraf—the first high-level contact between the two countries since a military coup in Pakistan in 1999. In May 2001 the Indian Government announced the end of its unilateral ceasefire, during the course of which more than 1,000 people were estimated to have been killed in Kashmir-related violence.

Relations with Pakistan appeared to improve following the earthquake in Gujarat in January 2001, when Pakistan offered humanitarian relief to India. In May Vajpayee issued an unexpected invitation to Gen. Musharraf to attend bilateral negotiations in Agra in July. However, the two leaders failed to agree to a joint declaration on Kashmir; the divergent views of the two sides on the priority issue in the dispute (cross-border terrorism according to India, and Kashmiri self-determination in the opinion of Pakistan) appeared to be more firmly entrenched than ever. Violence increased in the region as a result of the disappointment engendered by the meeting. In October a guerrilla-style attack on the state assembly building in Srinagar resulted in an estimated 38 fatalities. The Indian Government attributed responsibility for the attack to the Pakistan-based militant groups Jaish-e-Mohammed (JeM) and Lashkar-e-Taiba (LeT).

On 13 December 2001 five armed assailants attempted to launch an apparent suicide attack on the Union Parliament building in New Delhi. Although no parliamentary deputies were hurt in the attack, 14 people (including the assailants) were killed. The Indian authorities again attributed responsibility for the attack to JeM and LeT, and suggested that the assailants appeared to be of Pakistani origin. Bilateral tensions continued to mount when a member of JeM arrested in Kashmir admitted his involvement in the incident and alleged publicly that Pakistani security and intelligence agencies had provided support to those directly responsible. India recalled its High Commissioner from Islamabad and announced the suspension of overground transport services between the two countries. As positions were reinforced with troops and weapons (including missiles) on both sides of the LoC, there was considerable international concern that such brinkmanship might propel the two countries into renewed armed conflict. Mindful of the potential detriment to security at Pakistan's border with Afghanistan that could result from an escalation in conflict in Kashmir, the USA applied increased pressure on the Pakistani Government to adopt a more conciliatory attitude towards India's security concerns, and in late December 2001 the Pakistani authorities followed the US Government's lead in freezing the assets of the two groups held responsible for the attack on India. The leaders of the two groups were later detained by the Pakistani authorities, but the Indian Government continued to dismiss much of the Pakistani response as superficial and demanded that the two leaders be extradited to stand trial in India. In December 2002 a special court established under the POTA (see Internal Unrest and the Threat of Terrorism) convicted three Kashmiri Muslims—two of whom were reportedly members of JeM and the third a member of the JKLF—of organizing the attack on the Union Parliament and sentenced them to death. (However, a High Court ruling overturned the convictions of two of the men following an appeal in October 2003.)

In January 2002 Musharraf yielded to relentless international pressure by publicly condemning the activities of militant extremists based in Pakistan and announcing the introduction of a broad range of measures to combat terrorist activity and religious zealotry, including the proscription of five extremist organizations (among them JeM and LeT). However, further attacks by suspected Islamist militants in January and May, which the Indian authorities linked to Pakistan, caused another stand-off along the LoC. Relations deteriorated further following the assassination of Abdul Ghani Lone, the leader of the APHC, in May, by suspected Islamist militants. As a result of international efforts to defuse the situation, in June India withdrew five naval ships from patrol of the coast of Pakistan and allowed Pakistani civilian aircraft to enter its airspace, in response to Pakistani pledges to halt cross-border infiltration, and both sides subsequently scaled down their troop numbers along the international border.

Meanwhile, the APHC declared that it would boycott the state elections due to be held in Jammu and Kashmir in September–October 2002, regarding them as meaningless unless a referendum on independence was held first. Violence continued throughout the election period, with at least 730 people reportedly being killed. Following the elections, in which no single party won an outright majority, Congress and the regional People's Democratic Party (PDP) reached a power-sharing arrangement, under which PDP leader Mufti Mohammed Sayeed was to be appointed Chief Minister for a three-year term, followed by local Congress President Ghulam Nabi Azad for the next three years. Sayeed pledged to seek a resolution to the Kashmir issue through a programme of dialogue and reconciliation.

Indo-Pakistani relations deteriorated in early 2003 amid mutual accusations of diplomatic espionage. Tensions were exacerbated by India's latest round of 'routine' ballistic missile tests without advance warning (Pakistan responded in kind), the violence in Kashmir, and India's recently signed military agreement with Russia (see Other external relations). The killing of 24 Kashmiri Hindus, including women and children, in a village south of Srinagar by suspected Islamists in March provoked widespread condemnation and posed a setback to Sayeed's reconciliation programme. Nevertheless, in May the Indian and Pakistani premiers agreed to restore the recently severed diplomatic relations and civil aviation links. Two months later the bus service between the Pakistani city of Lahore and New Delhi was restored.

The assassination of the militant leader Ghazi Baba at the end of August 2003 provoked a surge in violence in September. In the same month the APHC openly split after the new leadership of Maulvi Abbas Ansari, the first Shi'a Muslim to chair the organization, was challenged by a significant faction, which proceeded to elect former Chairman Syed Ali Shah Geelani instead. In October the Indian Minister of External Affairs, Yashwant Sinha, announced 12 confidence-building measures to improve and normalize relations with Pakistan, while emphasizing that no direct talks on Kashmir would take place until Pakistan halted cross-border infiltration by Islamist militants. In November a bilateral ceasefire along the LoC came into effect. In December Indian and Pakistani officials signed a three-year agreement on the restoration of a train service between New Delhi and Lahore. Direct aviation links between the two countries were resumed on 1 January 2004.

At a ground-breaking South Asian Association for Regional Cooperation (SAARC, see p. 420) summit meeting in Islamabad in January 2004, Musharraf assured Vajpayee that he would not permit any territory under Pakistan's control to be used to support terrorism; in return Vajpayee agreed to begin negotiations on all bilateral issues, including Kashmir. However, Islamist militants who were unhappy with what they perceived as a betrayal by Musharraf continued their violent campaign. The APHC called for a boycott of the general election, held in April–May, and a series of violent attacks directed at all politicians campaigning in Jammu and Kashmir over the election period resulted in several deaths. Overall electoral turnout in Kashmir was 35%, although this declined to less than 19% in Srinagar. In June several rounds of discussions took place between Indian and Pakistani officials in New Delhi, during which both sides agreed to restore their diplomatic missions to full strength. An agreement was also reached that each country would, in future, notify the other of any forthcoming missile tests. In September India and Pakistan held their first, official, ministerial-level talks in more than three years in New Delhi, agreeing to implement a series of confidence-building measures.

In November 2004 Prime Minister Manmohan Singh ordered a 'substantial' reduction in the number of Indian troops deployed in Kashmir. In early 2005 Jammu and Kashmir held its first municipal elections in 27 years. At the same time, tensions resurfaced, with India and Pakistan accusing each other of violating the ongoing ceasefire along the LoC. However, in February the two countries agreed to open a bus service across the LoC, linking Srinagar with Muzaffarabad. In April Musharraf travelled to New Delhi for further peace talks with Prime Minister Singh. In June a delegation of APHC leaders travelled to Muzaffarabad, where they held discussions with Pakistani Kashmiri leaders. The visit represented the first time since 1946 that Indian Kashmiri politicians had been permitted to traverse the LoC. In September, in a symbolic gesture, the Government began to withdraw paramilitary Border Security Force (BSF) troops from Srinagar; responsibility for security in the city was subsequently assumed by the Central Reserve Police Force (CRPF).

In October 2005 a massive earthquake centred in Azad Kashmir resulted in widespread loss of life and destruction, particularly on the Pakistani side of the LoC. Pakistan accepted an Indian offer of aid and, following a series of negotiations, the two countries subsequently agreed to open a number of crossing-points on the LoC, in order to permit the reunification of divided families. In February 2006 a second rail link was opened between India and Pakistan, linking the town of Munabao in Rajasthan to the Pakistani town of Khokrapar in Sindh.

Relations between India and Pakistan were strained by the Mumbai train bombings in July 2006 (see Internal Unrest and the Threat of Terrorism). Although President Musharraf condemned the attacks, Prime Minister Singh suggested that those responsible had links to Pakistan. Bilateral peace talks were postponed, and in September the Mumbai police claimed that LeT was responsible for the July bombings and had apparently been aided in the attacks by Pakistan's Inter-Services Intelligence agency (an accusation swiftly denied by the Pakistani authorities). In November India and Pakistan agreed to share information on anti-terrorism measures. In February 2007, however, explosions on the Samjhauta Express train, which was bound for Lahore, Pakistan, from Delhi, caused a devastating fire on board, killing at least 67 passengers, the majority of whom were Pakistani nationals. The attack was viewed by many as an attempt to hinder the peace process; none the less, later in the month India and Pakistan signed an agreement designed to prevent inadvertent nuclear conflict between the two countries.

In mid-2008 a decision by the state government of Jammu and Kashmir to transfer land (on a permanent basis) to a board managing a popular Hindu shrine precipitated considerable unrest in the region. Following large-scale protests, the government rescinded its offer, but the issue had already served to intensify hostility between Muslim separatists and Hindu nationalists. The episode culminated in the resignation of Chief Minister Ghulam Nabi Azad. Legislative elections were held in November, after which the JKNC was forced to form a coalition with Congress in order to secure a majority. Omar Abdullah, the son of Dr Farooq Abdullah, was sworn in as Chief Minister in January 2009. According to official statistics, militancy-related violence in Jammu and Kashmir in 2009 fell to its lowest level in 20 years; the number of militancy-related deaths totalled 386, compared with 3,035 in 1995.

While India accused Pakistan of border incursions in Kashmir, terrorist attacks on Indian targets also damaged relations with Pakistan in 2008. In July a suicide bombing at the Indian embassy in Kabul, Afghanistan, resulted in more than 40 fatalities; the Indian Government intimated that the plot had originated in Pakistan. In the aftermath of the November Mumbai attacks (see Internal Unrest and the Threat of Terrorism), the Indian Government suggested that the perpetrators were all from Pakistan, a claim that the Pakistani authorities initially denied; however, they subsequently conceded that the sole gunman captured alive was indeed a Pakistani national. Moreover, in an unexpected turnaround, a senior official of the Pakistan Government publicly admitted in February 2009 that the Mumbai attacks had been partly planned in Pakistan and stated that seven suspects belonging to LeT had been arrested. The Indian Government welcomed the admission but demanded that the suspects be extradited to India; however, Pakistan insisted that any prosecutions be carried out internally.

In February 2010 India and Pakistan held their first high-level direct talks since the 2008 Mumbai attacks; however, the discussions proved fruitless, with both sides accusing each other of supporting terrorism and of tolerating human rights abuses. In June 2010 the Indian Minister of Home Affairs, P. Chidambaram, visited Islamabad, urging the Pakistani Government to intensify its efforts against LeT members thought to have been involved in the planning of the attacks. In July a visit to Islamabad by the Indian Minister of External Affairs, S. M. Krishna, was initially hailed by both sides as having been a 'constructive' resumption of high-level talks, but the meeting culminated in mutual recriminations. Prior to the summit the Indian Home Secretary had accused Pakistan's intelligence agency of having co-ordinated the Mumbai attacks.

In March 2011 Pakistani Prime Minister Yousaf Raza Gilani accepted an invitation from his Indian counterpart to attend the semi-final of the Cricket World Cup, between India and Pakistan, in Mohali, India. During Gilani's visit, the premiers held positive discussions that apparently encompassed 'all outstanding issues' concerning bilateral relations. A two-day meeting involving the Indian and Pakistani Home Secretaries had preceded the summit, resulting in a range of measures to enhance co-operation in counter-terrorism; furthermore, security officials from India and Pakistan were to be granted access to each other's countries to facilitate investigations into the 2008 Mumbai attacks.

Following a ministerial summit in September 2011 in New Delhi, the two countries pledged to double bilateral trade (to around US $6,000m.) within three years. The decision by Pakistan to confer the status of 'most favoured nation' upon India in November (having previously insisted that this would require a resolution to the ongoing dispute over Kashmir) was hailed by both sides as a reflection of improving ties, and later in the month, during sideline talks at the SAARC summit meeting in the Maldives, Prime Ministers Singh and Gilani acknowledged 'positive movement' in bilateral relations. In April 2012, during what was ostensibly a private visit to India, Pakistani President Asif Ali Zardari met with Prime Minister Singh for informal discussions on bilateral issues. It was hoped that the meeting might serve as a precursor to formal, substantive dialogue between the respective leaders in the near future. However, relations again became strained in early 2013 over ceasefire violations in Kashmir. In January India accused the Pakistani army of beheading one of its soldiers; two Indian soldiers and three Pakistani soldiers were killed in that month. In early February unrest erupted in Kashmir following the execution, after a protracted legal contest, of Afzal Guru, a Kashmiri Muslim who had been convicted in 2002 of organizing the attack a year earlier on the parliament building in New Delhi (see above). Five CRPF officers and two militants were killed during a suicide attack in Srinagar a few days later.

Prime Minister Singh was swift to congratulate Muhammad Nawaz Sharif upon his victory in Pakistan's general election of May 2013, thereby securing an historic third term as Prime Minister. Many Indians hoped that the change of Pakistani leadership might lead to an easing of tensions between the two countries, since the new premier outlined improved relations with India as one of the priorities of his administration. However, bilateral ties continued to be threatened by actions carried out by militant Islamist groups from Pakistan and by mutual accusations of ceasefire violations in Kashmir. In late June eight Indian soldiers were killed by militants in Srinagar; a further five soldiers were killed in the territory in early August, with Indian military officials accusing members of an élite Pakistani military command of having ambushed an Indian army patrol. A few days later members of the Indian Parliament voted unanimously to attribute the blame for the growing tensions along the border to Pakistan's armed forces. A further militant attack that targeted security forces in India-held Kashmir in late September resulted in a reported 10 deaths. Nevertheless, a meeting between the Indian and Pakistani Prime Ministers at the UN General Assembly in New York at the end of that month was said by Indian sources to have been 'useful' in terms of the ongoing effort by both Governments to stem the violence.

Other regional relations

India's military intervention in the civil war involving East and West Pakistan in 1971 helped East Pakistan to break away and form Bangladesh. None the less, issues of border policing and demarcation, and water-sharing disputes have provoked sporadic tensions in Indo-Bangladeshi relations. In 1992 the Indian Government, under the provisions of an accord signed with Bangladesh in 1974, formally leased the Tin Bigha Corridor (a small strip of land covering an area of only 1.5 ha) to Bangladesh for 999 years. India maintained sovereignty over the Corridor, but the lease gave Bangladesh access to its enclaves of Dahagram and Angarpota. The transfer of the Corridor occasioned protests from right-wing quarters in India, who also made an issue over the presence in Delhi and other cities of illegal immigrants from Bangladesh and claimed that the Bangladeshi Government had done little to protect its Hindu minority. In December 1996 India signed an 'historic' treaty with Bangladesh, which was to be in force for 30 years, regarding the sharing of the Ganga waters. In April 2001 some 16 members of the Indian BSF and three members of the Bangladesh Rifles were killed during fighting on the Bangladeshi border with the Indian state of Meghalaya—the worst strife between the two countries since serious border clashes in 1976. As a result of subsequent negotiations, two joint working groups were established to review the undemarcated section of the border.

Senior Indian and Bangladeshi officials concurred on some aspects of water-sharing and co-ordination of border patrols at talks in Dhaka, the Bangladeshi capital, in September 2004. Nevertheless, existing tensions were exacerbated by India's decision not to attend a planned summit of SAARC in Bangladesh in February, citing security concerns; this forced the postponement of the meeting. Further clashes between the border patrols of the two countries aggravated the situation, which had deteriorated as a result of India's continued construction of a fence along the joint border, in contravention of its obligations under a 1974 treaty.

Relations between India and Bangladesh improved following the return to power of the Bangladesh Awami League in December 2008, partly because the new Bangladeshi Government began to take action against the Indian groups that maintained bases in Bangladesh (including the arrest and transfer to the Indian authorities of a number of ULFA leaders). Following a successful visit to New Delhi by the Bangladeshi Prime Minister, Sheikh Hasina, in January 2010, it was reported that Bangladesh and India aimed to remove all barriers to mutual trade in an effort to improve economic co-operation and as a precursor to the conclusion of a bilateral free trade agreement. The two countries later announced an agreement in August providing for a US $1,000m. loan by India to Bangladesh for infrastructural development. In October India eliminated tariffs on 61 local products imported by Bangladesh, including textiles. In November the two countries held the first bilateral border talks in five years, which was interpreted by some observers as a tacit acknowledgement from India of the importance of ensuring continued growth and development in Bangladesh in order to safeguard the development and security of India's north-eastern states. Following a joint border survey of disputed frontier areas, in August 2011 Bangladesh and India began the process of approving border maps, officially recognizing their 4,156-km frontier (a 6.5-km stretch of the border remained disputed). Meanwhile, in September 2010 Rajkumar Meghen, the leader of the militant United National Liberation Front (a separatist group in Manipur) was arrested in Dhaka and handed over to India.

An interim bilateral agreement on the sharing of waters from the Teesta river was one of several significant deals that had been expected to be concluded during an official visit to Dhaka in September 2011 by Prime Minister Singh—the first state visit to Bangladesh by an Indian Prime Minister in 12 years. However, reportedly due to objections from Mamata Banerjee, the Chief Minister of West Bengal, Singh withdrew the proposed deal. The two countries consequently failed to reach agreement on a land transit agreement that would have granted India overland access to its landlocked north-eastern states through Bangladeshi territory. Nevertheless, a border agreement, resolving demarcation of the remaining 6.5-km stretch of the bilateral frontier, and an agreement providing for the exchange of 111 Indian enclaves within Bangladesh and 51 Bangladeshi enclaves within India, were signed, formally concluding a dispute dating back to 1947. During a visit to Tripura in January 2012 Bangladeshi Prime Minister Sheikh Hasina urged the Indian Government to be more flexible in order to facilitate the resolution of outstanding bilateral issues, including the issue of water-sharing. However, no major progress was made on a water-sharing agreement in that year. In July it was announced that India would help to locate and return to Bangladesh the remains of some 2,400 Bangladeshi fighters who were believed to have been buried along the border during the Bangladesh war of liberation in 1971. Following a visit by Sheikh Hasina to New Delhi in January 2013, in April India and Bangladesh signed a major joint-venture agreement to build two coal-fired power stations in the south of Bangladesh by 2018; the project was estimated to cost some US $1,600m. A joint power transmission plant was also opened in October 2013 to enable India to supply electricity to Bangladesh. Also in 2013 plans were finalized for the construction of a 15-km rail link between eastern Bangladesh and Tripura, which would greatly improve rail connectivity between the Indian mainland and its north-eastern states.

Relations between India and Nepal deteriorated in 1989, when India decided not to renew two bilateral treaties determining trade and transit, insisting that a common treaty covering both issues be negotiated. Nepal refused, stressing the importance of keeping the treaties separate on the grounds that Indo-Nepalese trade issues were negotiable, whereas the right of transit was a recognized right of landlocked countries. India responded by closing most of the transit points through which Nepal's trade was conducted. The dispute was aggravated by Nepal's acquisition of Chinese-made military equipment, which, according to India, violated the Treaty of Peace and Friendship of 1950. However, in June 1990 India and Nepal signed an agreement restoring trade relations and reopening the transit points. Chandra Shekhar visited Kathmandu in February 1991 (the first official visit to Nepal by an Indian Prime Minister since 1977), shortly after it was announced that the first free elections in Nepal were to be held in May. In June 1997 the Indian Prime Minister, Inder Kumar Gujral, made a visit to Nepal and announced the opening of a transit route through north-eastern India between Nepal and Bangladesh.

In February 2005 relations with Nepal were seriously affected when the Nepalese King orchestrated a coup, dismissing the Government and declaring a state of emergency in the country. It was feared that Maoist rebels from Nepal might infiltrate the country's border with India's fractious north-eastern states, a concern borne out to an extent by a reported decision by the CPI (Maoist) and Nepalese rebels to co-operate in promoting the spread of communism in both countries. India subsequently ceased provision of all military aid to Nepal and intensified security along the shared border. In July India resumed non-lethal military aid to Nepal. In January 2006 the bilateral transit treaty expired and was automatically renewed pending a review, as was the bilateral trade treaty, which expired in March 2007. Meanwhile, in June 2006, following the reinstatement of Parliament, the newly appointed Nepalese Prime Minister, G. P. Koirala, paid an official visit to India, during which India pledged to increase aid to Nepal. In August 2009 the two countries signed a trade treaty and India pledged to assist its neighbour with development projects such as road and rail links and the establishment of a police academy. During a visit to New Delhi in October 2011, Baburam Bhattarai, who had assumed the Nepalese premiership in August, met with Prime Minister Singh, whereupon a 10-year Bilateral Investment Promotion and Protection Agreement was signed. It was announced in June 2013 that India and Nepal had pledged to co-operate in efforts to tighten border security and to tackle the problems of militancy and organized crime such as human- and drugs-trafficking.

Since 1983 India's relations with Sri Lanka have been threatened by conflicts between the latter's Sinhalese and Tamil communities, in which India has sought to arbitrate. In July 1987 Rajiv Gandhi and the Sri Lankan President, Junius Jayewardene, signed an accord aimed at settling the conflict. An Indian Peacekeeping Force (IPKF) was dispatched to Sri Lanka, but encountered considerable resistance from the Tamil separatist guerrillas. Following the gradual implementation of the peace accord, the IPKF troops completed their withdrawal in March 1990. However, violence flared up again and by late 1991 the number of Sri Lankans living in refugee camps in Tamil Nadu was estimated at more than 200,000. The assassination of Rajiv Gandhi in May 1991, allegedly by members of the Liberation Tigers of Tamil Eelam (LTTE), completed India's disenchantment with the latter organization. Measures were subsequently taken by the Tamil Nadu government to suppress LTTE activity within the state, and also to begin the slow and difficult process of repatriating refugees. In May 1992 the LTTE was officially banned in India. In December 1998 the Indian Prime Minister and Sri Lankan President signed a bilateral free trade agreement, which came into effect in March 2000. During the 2000s India refrained from any direct involvement in the Sri Lankan conflict, but, after the escalation in hostilities in 2008 following the collapse of a ceasefire, insisted that a negotiated political settlement rather than a military solution be sought. India subsequently extended its ban on the LTTE at regular intervals, most recently in mid-2012 for a further two-year period.

Following the defeat of the LTTE in 2009, India played a major role in the resettlement and rehabilitation of thousands of displaced Tamil civilians and in the reconstruction of the war-ravaged north-east of Sri Lanka. India opened two new consulates in Sri Lanka (in Hambantota and Jaffna) during 2010. During an official visit to India by Sri Lankan President Mahinda Rajapaksa in June, an agreement was signed regarding the possibility of Sri Lanka supplying India with electricity. The extension by India of an invitation to Rajapaksa to attend the closing ceremony of the Commonwealth Games hosted by New Delhi in October—the only invitation to be extended to a foreign head of state—was widely interpreted as being symptomatic of improved relations between the two countries. Bilateral relations were threatened by the shooting, allegedly by members of the Sri Lankan navy, of two Indian fishermen in separate incidents in January 2011. Nevertheless, ferry services between the two countries resumed in June, having been suspended in the 1980s as a result of the Sri Lankan conflict. In March 2012 India decided to support a US-sponsored resolution at the UN Human Rights Council (UNHRC), which urged the Sri Lankan Government to investigate allegations of human rights violations in the final stages of the Sri Lankan civil conflict. India's stance, which appeared to contravene a traditional policy of abstaining on country-specific UNHRC resolutions, was widely interpreted as a response to pressure exerted on the federal Government by its political partners in Tamil Nadu. President Rajapaksa paid an official visit to India in September, meeting with the Indian President, Pranab Mukherjee, and Prime Minister Singh. The leader of the Tamil MDMK party, Vaiko, was arrested for leading a protest march against Rajapaksa's visit. India supported a second US-sponsored resolution, adopted by UNHRC in March 2013, which recommended that an independent investigation be conducted into the claims of human rights violations. The DMK had withdrawn from India's coalition Government earlier that month in protest at its perceived weakness in dealing with its Sri Lankan counterpart on the issue. In November Singh decided to boycott a summit meeting of Commonwealth heads of government, due to be held in Colombo, Sri Lanka, in order to demonstrate India's dissatisfaction at Sri Lanka's recent record on human rights. However, in March 2014 the Indian authorities opted to abstain from a stronger UNHRC resolution, which demanded the establishment of an independent, international investigation into alleged human rights abuses in Sri Lanka.

During 1981 there was an improvement in India's relations with the People's Republic of China. Both countries agreed to try to resolve their Himalayan border dispute and to seek to normalize relations, and a number of working groups were subsequently established. Following an official visit to India by the Chinese Premier, Li Peng, in December 1991 (the first such visit by a Chinese Premier for 31 years), bilateral border trade was resumed in July 1992. Sino-Indian relations were further strengthened as a result of a three-day visit to India conducted by the Chinese President, Jiang Zemin, in November 1996 (the first ever visit by a Chinese head of state to India). However, despite the gradual improvement in relations, India has frequently expressed concern over the nuclear asymmetry between the two countries and what it perceives as China's willingness to transfer missiles and missile technology to Pakistan. Sino-Indian relations deteriorated following India's 1998 nuclear tests, partly because China believed that India was using a fabricated threat from China to justify its actions. In June 1999 the Indian Minister of External Affairs visited Beijing to restore Sino-Indian dialogue. Border negotiations between the two countries were held in November 2000. Prime Minister Vajpayee made a state visit to China in June 2003, during which a number of agreements were signed, the most significant being India's official recognition of Chinese sovereignty over Tibet (the Xizang Autonomous Region). China also agreed to trade with the north-eastern Indian state of Sikkim, thus implicitly acknowledging India's control of that area.

In January 2005 India and China held their first-ever strategic dialogue, in New Delhi, agreeing, *inter alia*, to attempt to resolve their boundary dispute in a fair and mutually satisfactory manner. In April Chinese Premier Wen Jiabao visited India, agreeing to plans for the resolution of the boundary dispute and the expansion of bilateral trade. In July 2006 the reopening of the historic border trading post of Nathu La (which was once part of the ancient Silk Road) highlighted the ongoing improvement in Sino-Indian relations, which was further strengthened when the Chinese President, Hu Jintao, paid an official visit to India in November; the two countries agreed to co-operate in several fields, including nuclear energy. Prime Minister Singh reciprocated with a visit to China in January 2008. However, a number of issues continued to undermine cordial relations, including India's deepening relations with the USA, and in August 2010 India suspended all bilateral defence exchanges, in protest at the refusal by the Chinese authorities to grant a visa to an Indian army general from Kashmir—China has long maintained a claim to the Shaksam Valley and Aksai Chin areas of Kashmir. Furthermore, during a state visit to India in December, Premier Wen's refusal to condemn the 2008 Mumbai attacks was widely interpreted as reflecting a wish not to alienate Pakistan, China's other firm ally in South Asia; in response, India refused to reiterate its adherence to the 'one China' policy. Nevertheless, during Wen's visit 48 bilateral commercial contracts, collectively worth an estimated US $16,000m., were signed and the two leaders pledged to increase bilateral trade to some $100,000m. by 2015. In April 2011 India and China agreed to resume bilateral defence exchanges, and in January 2012 an agreement was signed providing for the establishment of a joint border management mechanism. In March President Hu Jintao attended talks with Prime Minister Singh in Delhi; the two leaders declared 2012 to be the year of 'India-China friendship and co-operation'.

Shortly after becoming China's new Premier, Li Keqiang undertook an official visit to India in May 2013, during which eight bilateral agreements were signed covering various fields including culture, trade and water resources. It was reported that trade between the two countries had increased from US $2,090m. in 2001/02 to $67,830m. in 2012/13. In June 2013 representatives from India and China held the 16th round of talks intended to resolve their long-running Himalayan border dispute. In October a Border Defence Co-operation Agreement was signed in an effort to improve Sino-Indian understanding and minimize the risk of further incidents taking place such as had occurred in April, when a contingent of Chinese soldiers temporarily established a camp in the disputed territory of Aksai Ching. The incident had led to an increase in bilateral tensions prior to the withdrawal of the Chinese troops three weeks later. In a further sign of improving relations, the two countries' armed forces held 10 days of joint counter-terrorism exercises in

Chengdu, south-western China, in November—the first time that such exercises had been staged since 2008.

In October 2004 the Chairman of Myanmar's ruling body, the State Peace and Development Council, Field Marshal Than Shwe, paid the first visit to India by a Myanma head of state in 24 years. The visit was illustrative of improving relations between the two countries, deemed necessary if India was to combat successfully the problem of insurgents in north-eastern India establishing bases across the border in Myanmar. In April 2008 India signed an agreement worth US $120m. to construct a seaport at Sittway in north-western Myanmar and to improve roads and waterways elsewhere in the country. In return for its help with infrastructure development, it was widely believed that India was hoping for preferential access (as was China) to Myanmar's reserves of petroleum and natural gas. During Than Shwe's second visit to India in July 2010 the two countries signed five bilateral agreements intended to enhance co-operation in the fields of energy, defence, counter-terrorism and transnational crime prevention. In October 2011 Singh hosted a visit to India from Myanma President Thein Sein, who had been inaugurated in March, following controversial legislative elections in Myanmar in November 2010. During Thein Sein's visit, a series of agreements intended to bolster bilateral trade and investment, including the provision by India of a $500m. grant for infrastructural development projects in Myanmar, was signed; the two leaders also pledged to enhance co-operation in the field of oil and gas exploration. In November 2012 the Myanma opposition leader Aung San Suu Kyi attended talks with Singh in Delhi; she called for India's backing for Myanmar's nascent democratization process. India's Ministry of External Affairs proposed in August 2013 that India and Myanmar should establish a Joint Border Working Group in order to resolve any border incidents that occurred between the two countries.

As relations between Afghanistan and Pakistan deteriorated amid Afghan allegations of Pakistani support for a series of violent attacks against the Afghan authorities during 2011 (see the chapter on Afghanistan), India appeared keen to enhance its own ties with Afghanistan. In May, during his first visit to the Afghan capital, Kabul, since August 2005, Prime Minister Singh announced that India was to grant US $500m. over a six-year period (in addition to the $1,500m. that it had already pledged) to Afghanistan, to be disbursed on a range of development projects, with a focus on agriculture, infrastructure and social programmes. Bilateral relations were further consolidated during a reciprocal visit to India by Afghan President Hamid Karzai in October 2011 with the signing of a strategic partnership agreement, which was intended to enhance co-operation in the fields of trade, counter-terrorism, and political and cultural engagement. Under the terms of the accord, India also pledged to provide security training and equipment to support the Afghan authorities as they prepared to assume full responsibility for national security by the end of 2014, and to undertake efforts to facilitate Afghanistan's economic integration within South Asia as a whole. In 2013 the Afghan leadership was reported to be seeking closer military ties with India: during a visit to New Delhi in May, President Karzai discussed with Prime Minister Singh the possibility of India supplying Afghanistan with a range of heavy weaponry and other military equipment, including tanks and helicopters. However, the Indian Government kept to its long-standing pledge to provide only 'non-lethal military assistance' to the Karzai administration. In July India's Minister of External Affairs, Salman Khurshid, advocated dialogue with all groups in Afghanistan, including militant organizations such as the Taliban, thereby indicating a reversal of India's previous foreign policy with regard to Afghanistan.

Other external relations

Prior to its disintegration in December 1991, the USSR was a major contributor of economic and military assistance to India. The President of Russia, Boris Yeltsin, made an official visit to India in 1993, during which he signed an Indo-Russian Treaty of Friendship and Co-operation. In October 1996 India and Russia signed a defence co-operation agreement, and in December India signed a US $1,800m. contract to purchase 40 fighter aircraft from Russia. In June 1998 Russia defied a Group of Eight (G8) ban on exporting nuclear technology to India by agreeing to supply the latter with two nuclear reactors. In October 2000 the newly elected Russian President, Vladimir Putin, visited India. The two countries signed a declaration of 'strategic partnership', which involved co-operation on defence, economic matters and international terrorism issues. India signed a contract to purchase a further 50 fighter aircraft from Russia, with a licence to manufacture around 150 more, and in February 2001 India agreed to buy 310 Russian tanks. In June the two countries successfully conducted tests of a new, jointly developed supersonic cruise missile, the PJ-10. In November it was announced that Russia had been awarded a contract to construct a nuclear power reactor in Kudankulam in Tamil Nadu (this was later extended to two reactors). During a visit to India by the Russian President in January 2007, Putin and Prime Minister Singh focused on the key bilateral issues of energy and trade, and announced that Russia was to assist India with the construction of four more nuclear power reactors at Kudankulam; the latter was confirmed during the visit of the new Russian President, Dmitrii Medvedev, to New Delhi in December 2008. In March 2010 Putin, in his new role as Russia's Prime Minister, paid an official visit to India, during which an important agreement was signed by the two countries regarding Russia's pledge to construct 16 new nuclear reactors in India. A further 30 bilateral deals were signed during a visit to India by President Medvedev in December, including two framework agreements that provided for the construction of two additional nuclear reactors in India; Medvedev also offered Russian support for Indian aspirations to gain a permanent seat on the UN Security Council. (In October India, together with Colombia, Germany, Portugal and South Africa, had secured election to the 15-member Council for a two-year term commencing in January 2011; as a result of India's election, all four of the 'BRIC' emerging countries—Brazil, Russia, India and China—were for the first time seated together on the Council.) Following talks between Medvedev and Singh in Moscow in December 2011, the former expressed the support of the Russian Government for India's bid to secure full membership of the Shanghai Cooperation Organization. During a visit by President Putin to India in December 2012 the two countries signed further defence agreements, amid media reports that Russia was keen to preserve its position as India's primary weapons provider. Following protracted delays and widespread opposition to the plant within Tamil Nadu, the production of nuclear energy at the Kudankulam plant finally commenced in October 2013.

Meanwhile, in mid-1996, in a move that provoked widespread international condemnation, India decided not to be party to the Comprehensive Test Ban Treaty (CTBT), which it had earlier supported, so long as the existing nuclear powers were unwilling to commit themselves to a strict timetable for full nuclear disarmament. In May 1998 India's controversial decision to explode five nuclear test devices and to claim thereby its new status as a nuclear-weapons state led to a rapid escalation in the 'arms race' with Pakistan (which responded with its own series of nuclear tests). The USA, with limited support from other countries, subsequently imposed economic sanctions on both India and Pakistan until such time as they had signed the Nuclear Non-Proliferation Treaty (NPT) and the CTBT and taken steps to reverse their nuclear programmes. Immediately after the tests, India announced a self-imposed moratorium on further testing and launched itself into intense diplomatic activity. During 1998–99 the USA lifted some of the sanctions imposed on India and Pakistan, while reiterating its requests that the two countries sign the CTBT and exercise restraint in their respective missile programmes.

Following the collapse of the USSR, the Indian Government sought to strengthen its ties with the USA. In January 1992 discussions were held between Indian and US officials regarding military co-operation and ambitious joint defence projects. However, the USA remained concerned about the risks of nuclear proliferation across South Asia and India's ongoing refusal to sign the NPT. In addition, despite India's adoption of a programme of economic liberalization, conflicts over trade and related issues remained. During a visit to India by the US Secretary of Defense in January 1995, a 'landmark' agreement on defence and security co-operation was signed by the two countries. US President Bill Clinton made an official visit to India in March 2000 (the first by a US President since 1978), which was widely considered as the launch of a new era in bilateral relations. President Clinton appeared to endorse India's opinion that the Kashmir dispute was a regional issue and did not directly concern the international community. In September Prime Minister Vajpayee visited the USA, asserting that consensus among Indian ministers had to be reached before a decision on the CTBT could be made. In late September 2001 US President George W. Bush announced an end to the military and economic sanctions imposed against India and Pakistan in 1998. The decision followed the renewal of high-level military contacts between the USA and India in mid-2001, and Pakistan's co-operation with US counter-terrorism initiatives against neighbouring Afghanistan in the aftermath of the terrorist attacks carried out on US mainland targets on 11 September. In July 2003 India declined a request by the USA to contribute peacekeeping troops to the US-led forces in Iraq.

In July 2005 Prime Minister Manmohan Singh visited the USA, where he signed an historic outline agreement with President Bush regarding future nuclear co-operation. In return for an Indian pledge to separate its civilian and military nuclear programmes, to allow international monitoring of its civilian nuclear programme, and not to conduct further nuclear weapons tests or to transfer nuclear technology to other countries, the US Government proposed to share civilian nuclear technology with India. The agreement was finalized during a visit to India by President Bush in March 2006. In August 2007, however, the agreement met with opposition not only from the BJP, but from the UPA coalition's allies, the left-wing parties comprising the Left Front, which feared the possibility of US intervention in India's foreign policy and other areas. In July 2008, despite the withdrawal of support by the Left Front, the Government was able to win a parliamentary vote of confidence and to proceed with the agreement, which, having subsequently received the endorsement of the International Atomic Energy Agency and the Nuclear Suppliers Group, as well as the approval of the US Congress, was signed into law by President Bush in October. In November 2010, during his first state visit to India following his inauguration as US President in January 2009, Barack Obama furthered the promises of the civilian nuclear pact by announcing that export controls on sensitive dual-use technologies—those that have both civilian and military uses—were to be lifted, assuaging Indian concerns that the momentum built up during Bush's two presidential terms might be lost under the Obama Administration; the controls were formally rescinded in January 2011. In addition, Obama reiterated the US view that the Kashmir issue was an internal affair and pledged not to intervene unless requested to do so by India. A series of relatively minor bilateral agreements was signed during the visit, but Obama hailed the breadth and sheer number of deals, collectively estimated to be worth some US $10,000m., as a sign of burgeoning bilateral relations. During his visit, Obama also expressed US support for India's quest to attain a permanent seat on the UN Security Council—an endorsement that was denounced as 'incomprehensible' by Pakistan. Counter-terrorism operations, bilateral trade and investment, and Indian concerns about the USA's withdrawal from Afghanistan formed the focus of a visit to New Delhi by US Secretary of State Hillary Clinton in July. Clinton appealed for a deepening of bilateral security and nuclear energy co-operation, while noting the US Government's positive response to the renewed dialogue between India and Pakistan. Clinton paid another visit to India in May 2012, during which she urged India to decrease its oil imports from Iran. Despite a visit by Singh to the USA for talks with President Obama in September 2013, and evidence that diplomatic and economic relations were continuing to grow, India's relationship with the USA was damaged in December when the Indian Deputy Consul-General in New York was arrested on suspicion of visa fraud. The Indian authorities protested vociferously against the alleged harsh treatment of their envoy at the hands of US officials.

During a state visit to Delhi in December 2010 by French President Nicolas Sarkozy, India and France signed a co-operation deal providing for the construction by the French company Areva of two nuclear reactors, each worth approximately US $10,000m., and for a new nuclear plant in Jaitapur, in the western Indian state of Maharashtra. A range of other bilateral deals were signed during the visit, including agreements pertaining to atomic energy, civil aviation and defence. Meanwhile, India and Canada signed a nuclear co-operation deal in June 2010, which provided for the opening up of the Indian market to Canadian nuclear exports, as well as enhanced co-operation in the field of nuclear waste management.

CONSTITUTION AND GOVERNMENT

The Constitution of India, adopted by the Constituent Assembly on 26 November 1949, was inaugurated on 26 January 1950. India is a federal republic. Legislative power is vested in Parliament, consisting of the President and two Houses. The Council of States (Rajya Sabha) has 245 members, most of whom are indirectly elected by the state assemblies for six years (one-third retiring every two years), the remainder being nominated by the President for six years. The House of the People (Lok Sabha) has up to 550 elected members, serving for five years (subject to dissolution). A small number of members of the Lok Sabha may be nominated by the President to represent the Anglo-Indian community, while the 550 members are directly elected by universal adult suffrage in single-member constituencies. The President is a constitutional head of state, elected for five years by an electoral college comprising elected members of both Houses of Parliament and the state legislatures. The President exercises executive power on the advice of the Council of Ministers, which is responsible to Parliament. The President appoints the Prime Minister and, on the latter's recommendation, other ministers.

India contains 28 self-governing states, each with a governor (appointed by the President for five years), a legislature (elected for five years) and a council of ministers headed by the chief minister. Bihar, Jammu and Kashmir, Karnataka, Maharashtra and Uttar Pradesh have bicameral legislatures, the other 23 state legislatures being unicameral. Each state has its own legislative, executive and judicial machinery, corresponding to that of the Indian Union. In the event of the failure of constitutional government in a state, presidential rule can be imposed by the Union. There are also six Union Territories and one National Capital Territory, administered by lieutenant-governors or administrators, all of whom are appointed by the President. The territories of Delhi and Puducherry also have elected chief ministers and state assemblies. In February 2014 Parliament approved legislation drafted by the Government that would divide the state of Andhra Pradesh to create Telangana, India's 29th self-governing state, in June.

REGIONAL AND INTERNATIONAL CO-OPERATION

India is a member of the Asian Development Bank (ADB, see p. 207), the South Asian Association for Regional Cooperation (SAARC, see p. 420) and the Colombo Plan (see p. 449).

Having joined the UN on its foundation in 1945, India is a member of the Economic and Social Commission for Asia and the Pacific (ESCAP, see p. 28). As a contracting party to the General Agreement on Tariffs and Trade (GATT), India joined the World Trade Organization (WTO, see p. 434) on its establishment in 1995.

ECONOMIC AFFAIRS

In 2012, according to estimates by the World Bank, India's gross national income (GNI), measured at average 2010–12 prices, was US $1,890,363m., equivalent to $1,530 per head (or $3,840 per head on an international purchasing-power parity basis). During 2003–12, it was estimated, the population increased at an average annual rate of 1.4%, while gross domestic product (GDP) per head grew, in real terms, by an average of 6.1% per year. According to official figures, overall GDP increased, in real terms, at an average annual rate of 7.6% in 2003/04–2012/13; the rate of growth was 6.7% in 2011/12 and 4.5% in 2012/13.

Agriculture (including forestry and fishing) contributed an estimated 17.4% of GDP in 2012/13. According to FAO estimates, about 52.6% of the economically active population were expected to be engaged in agriculture in mid-2014. The principal cash crops are cotton (which accounted for 3.0% of total export earnings in 2012/13), sugar cane, rice, groundnuts, spices and tea. Coffee and jute production are also important. According to official figures, the average annual growth rate in the output of the agricultural sector was 3.3% in 2003/04–2012/13; agricultural GDP increased by 1.9% in 2012/13.

Industry (including mining, manufacturing, power and construction) contributed an estimated 25.8% of GDP in 2012/13. According to estimates by the Asian Development Bank (ADB), about 24.3% of the working population were employed in the industrial sector in 2011. According to official figures, industrial GDP increased at an average annual rate of 7.7% in 2003/04–2012/13; industrial GDP grew by 2.1% in 2012/13.

Mining contributed an estimated 2.3% of GDP in 2012/13, and employed an estimated 2.1% of the working population in 2010. Iron ore and cut diamonds are the major mineral exports. Coal, limestone, zinc and lead are also mined. In 2012 India was the third largest coal producer in the world after the People's Republic of China and the USA. Substantial uranium deposits have recently been discovered in Andhra Pradesh; according to the Atomic Energy Commission of India, following the completion of exploratory work total reserves at the Tumalapalli mine were estimated to amount to some 150,000 metric tons, which would render it the largest uranium mine in the world. According to official figures, mining GDP increased at an estimated average annual rate of 3.5% during 2003/04–2012/13; sectoral GDP decreased by an estimated 0.6% in 2012/13.

Manufacturing contributed an estimated 13.5% of GDP in 2012/13, and employed an estimated 8.9% of the working population in 2010. According to official figures, the GDP of the manufacturing sector increased at an average annual rate of 7.8% during 2003/04–2012/13; manufacturing GDP rose by an estimated 1.0% in 2012/13.

Construction contributed an estimated 8.1% of GDP in 2012/13, and employed 7.5% of the working population in 2010. According to official figures, the GDP of the construction sector increased at an average annual rate of 9.1% during 2003/04–2012/13; construction GDP rose by an estimated 4.3% in 2012/13.

Production of electricity rose from 808,404m. kWh in 2010/11 to 912,056m. kWh in 2012/13. In 2012/13 thermal plants (including renewable energy sources) accounted for an estimated 83.4% of total power generation and hydroelectric plants (often dependent on monsoons) for 12.5%. Nuclear plants accounted for 3.6% of total power generation. However, the Government has proposed plans to increase this to 25% of total power generation by 2050, which would involve the establishment of 30 nuclear reactors. Imports of mineral fuels, lubricants, etc., comprised 36.9% of the cost of total imports in 2012/13.

The services sector, which is dominated by the rapidly expanding data-processing business, the growing number of business call centres and the tourism industry, contributed an estimated 56.9% of GDP in 2012/13. According to estimates by the ADB, the service sector engaged 26.8% of the economically active population in 2011. By the early 2000s business call centres had become the fastest growing industry in India and an increasing number of multinational companies were transferring their call centre operations to the country, largely owing to cheaper labour costs and low long-distance telephone charges. More than 550,000 people were employed in the outsourcing industry in 2006/07. According to official figures, the GDP of the services sector increased by an average of 9.4% per year in 2003/04–2012/13; the rate of growth reached 7.1% in 2012/13.

In 2012/13 India reported a visible merchandise trade deficit of US $195,656m. and a deficit of $88,163m. on the current account of the balance of payments, according to preliminary official figures. In that year the principal source of imports was China (providing 10.7% of total imports), followed by the United Arab Emirates (UAE), Saudi Arabia, Switzerland and the USA. The principal market for exports (accounting for 12.1% of total exports) was the UAE. Other major trading partners were the USA, Singapore and China. The principal exports in 2012/13 were mineral fuels, mineral oils and products of their distillation, and natural or cultured pearls, precious and semi-precious stones and precious metals. The principal imports in that year were mineral fuels and lubricants, pearls, precious and semi-precious stones, and electrical machinery and equipment.

In the financial year ending 31 March 2014 there was a projected budgetary deficit of Rs 8,936,701m. According to the ADB, the overall fiscal deficit of the central Government amounted to the equivalent of 6.4% of GDP in 2012/13. In 2008, according to the UN Development Programme, India received a total of US $2,108m. in official development assistance. India's general government gross debt was Rs 59,569,728m. in 2011, equivalent to 66.4% of GDP. According to the ADB, India's total external debt was US $400,250m. at the end of 2013. The cost of debt-servicing in that year was equivalent to 6.2% of earnings from the exports of goods and services. According to figures by the International Labour Organization, the average annual rate of inflation was 7.6% in 2003–12. According to the ADB, consumer prices increased by 5.9% in 2013. A labour force survey for 2009/10 indicated that the rate of unemployment stood at about 9.4% (with the rate in urban areas at 7.3%, and that in rural areas in excess of 11%).

The process of wide-ranging economic reform initiated in 1991, including trade and investment liberalization, industrial deregulation, gradual privatization of public enterprises, and financial and tax reforms, has continued despite several changes in government. Following the creation in 2004 of an Investment Commission for the purpose of encouraging domestic and foreign investment, total foreign direct investment (FDI) inflows, according to data published by the Department of Industrial Policy and Promotion, increased from US $4,300m. in 2003/04 to a peak of $46,800m. in 2011/12, before decreasing to $36,860m. in 2012/13. In June 2013 a UN report again ranked India as third among most-favoured destinations for worldwide investors. In December 2012, despite strong public and political opposition, legislation permitting 51% FDI in the previously protected retail sector gained parliamentary approval. Meanwhile, in October 2011 the Council of Ministers approved a National Manufacturing Policy, which aimed to increase the sector's contribution to GDP from 13.5% in 2012/13 to around 25% by 2022 and envisaged the creation of some 100m. new jobs. According to a July 2012 World Trade Organization report, in 2011 India recorded the largest global increase in export growth. By 2013, however, export growth had stagnated, and the large trade and current account deficits as well as the significant depreciation of the currency during that year presented major challenges to the Government. Ongoing attempts to address India's unwieldy fiscal deficit (traditionally exacerbated by the country's modest tax base and cumbersome local government apparatus) have been largely frustrated by the repeated stalling of the divestment programme, internal security concerns, volatile foreign relations and the costs associated with natural disasters; nevertheless, the deficit declined to 4.9% of GDP in 2012/13 from in excess of 6% in 2009/10, with a further decline—to 4.6% of GDP—anticipated in 2013/14. Agriculture provides employment for more than 50% of the working population, but the performance of the sector is affected by volatile climatic conditions: after growth of 7.9% in 2010/11, the sector expanded by just 1.9% in 2012/13; however, with a good monsoon in 2013 agricultural growth of 4.6% was projected for 2013/14. Manufacturing growth also decelerated in 2012/13, to 1.3% (from 8.9% in 2010/11), and the mining sector contracted by 0.6% (compared with growth of 5.2% in 2010/11). This, combined with global market uncertainties—particularly in the euro area, the USA and China—and the effects of the imposition of some 13 separate increases to the national interest rate between March 2010 and February 2012, in an effort to control rising inflation, contributed to GDP growth of 6.7% in 2011/12 (compared with growth of 8.9% in 2010/11). Between April 2012 and May 2013 the central bank announced four reductions in the national interest rate in an attempt to stimulate economic growth; however, GDP growth slowed to 4.5% in 2012/13. The bank implemented an unexpected rise in the interest rate in January 2014, after India's inflation rate had reportedly exceeded 10%. In its 2014/15 national budget, the Government pledged to: invest heavily in infrastructure, focus on developing India's manufacturing sector, introduce further measures to encourage FDI, complete the necessary financial sector reforms, and pursue its urbanization and skills development programmes. According to Government projections, GDP growth was expected to recover marginally in 2013/14, to 4.9%.

PUBLIC HOLIDAYS

The public holidays observed in India vary locally. The dates given below apply to Delhi. There are, in addition, numerous restricted (or optional) holidays.

2015: 2 January (Milad-un-Nabi, Birth of the Prophet), 26 January (Republic Day), 6 March (Holi), 28 March (Ram Navami), 2 April (Mahavir Jayanti), 3 April (Good Friday), 4 May (Buddha Purnima), 17 July (Id al-Fitr, end of Ramadan), 15 August (Independence Day), 5 September (Janmashtami), 23 September (Id ul-Zuha, Feast of the Sacrifice), 2 October (Mahatma Gandhi's Birthday), 14 October (Muharram, Islamic New Year), 22 October (Dussehra), 11 November (Diwali), 6 November (Guru Nanak Jayanti), 23 December (Milad-un-Nabi, Birth of the Prophet), 25 December (Christmas).

Note: A number of Hindu, Muslim and Buddhist holidays depend on lunar sightings.

Statistical Survey

Source (unless otherwise stated): Central Statistical Organization, Ministry of Statistics and Programme Implementation, Sardar Patel Bhavan, Patel Chowk, New Delhi 110 001; tel. (11) 23742150; fax (11) 23344689; e-mail moscc@bol.net.in; internet mospi.nic.in.

Area and Population

AREA, POPULATION AND DENSITY*

Area (sq km)	3,166,414†
Population (census results)	
1 March 2001‡	1,028,610,328
1 March 2011	
Males	623,121,843
Females	587,447,730
Total	1,210,569,573
Population (official estimate at mid-year)§	
2012	1,213,370,000
Density (per sq km) at mid-2012	383.2

* Including the Indian-held part of Jammu and Kashmir.

† 1,222,559 sq miles.

‡ Including estimates for certain areas in the states of Gujarat and Himachal Pradesh where the census could not be conducted owing to recent natural disasters, but excluding data for Mao-Maram, Paomata and Purul sub-divisions of Senapati district of Manipur.

§ Official projection; data rounded to nearest thousand persons.

Source: Office of the Registrar General of India, Ministry of Home Affairs, New Delhi.

POPULATION BY AGE AND SEX

('000 persons at 2001 census)

	Males	Females	Total
0–14	189,488	174,123	363,611
15–64	316,987	296,168	613,155
65 and over	24,182	24,924	49,106
Total*	530,657	495,215	1,025,872

* Excluding persons of unknown or undeclared age: 2,738,000 (males 1,500,000, females 1,238,000).

2011 census (provisional): *0–6:* 158,789,287 (males 82,952,135, females 75,837,152); *7 and over:* 1,051,404,135 (males 540,772,113, females 510,632,022); *Total:* 1,210,193,422 (males 623,724,248, females 586,469,174).

STATES AND TERRITORIES

(population at 2011 census)

	Area (sq km)	Population ('000)	Density (per sq km)	Capital
States				
Andhra Pradesh	275,045	84,580.8	307.5	Hyderabad
Arunachal Pradesh	83,743	1,383.7	16.5	Itanagar
Assam	78,438	31,205.6	397.8	Dispur
Bihar	94,163	104,099.5	1,105.5	Patna
Chhattisgarh	135,191	25,545.2	189.0	Raipur
Goa	3,702	1,458.5	394.0	Panaji
Gujarat	196,024	60,439.7	308.3	Gandhinagar
Haryana	44,212	25,351.5	573.4	Chandigarh*
Himachal Pradesh	55,673	6,864.6	123.3	Shimla
Jammu and Kashmir†	101,387	12,541.3	123.7	Srinagar/Jammu
Jharkhand	79,714	32,988.1	413.8	Ranchi
Karnataka	191,791	61,095.3	318.6	Bangalore
Kerala	38,863	33,406.1	859.6	Thiruvananthapuram (Trivandrum)
Madhya Pradesh	308,245	72,626.8	235.6	Bhopal
Maharashtra	307,713	112,374.3	365.2	Mumbai (Bombay)
Manipur	22,327	2,570.4	115.1	Imphal
Meghalaya	22,429	2,966.9	132.3	Shillong
Mizoram	21,081	1,097.2	52.0	Aizawl
Nagaland	16,579	1,978.5	119.3	Kohima
Orissa‡	155,707	41,974.2	269.6	Bhubaneswar
Punjab	50,362	27,743.3	550.9	Chandigarh*
Rajasthan	342,239	68,548.4	200.3	Jaipur
Sikkim	7,096	610.6	86.0	Gangtok
Tamil Nadu	130,058	72,147.0	554.7	Chennai (Madras)
Tripura	10,486	3,673.9	350.4	Agartala
Uttarakhand§	53,483	10,086.3	188.6	Dehradun
Uttar Pradesh	240,928	199,812.3	829.3	Lucknow
West Bengal	88,752	91,276.1	1,028.4	Kolkata (Calcutta)
Territories				
Andaman and Nicobar Islands	8,249	380.6	46.1	Port Blair
Chandigarh*	114	1,055.5	9,258.8	Chandigarh
Dadra and Nagar Haveli	491	343.7	700.0	Silvassa
Daman and Diu	112	243.3	2,172.3	Daman
Delhi	1,483	16,787.9	11,320.2	Delhi
Lakshadweep	32	64.5	2,015.6	Kavaratti
Puducherry (Pondicherry)	479	1,248.0	2,605.4	Puducherry (Pondicherry)
Total‖	3,166,414	1,210,569.6	382.3	—

* Chandigarh forms a separate Union Territory, not within Haryana or the Punjab. As part of a scheme for a transfer of territory between the two states, Chandigarh was due to be incorporated into the Punjab on 26 January 1986, but the transfer was postponed.

† Figures refer only to the Indian-held part of the territory.

‡ Renamed Odisha from November 2011.

§ Uttaranchal prior to 2007.

‖ Area data exclude contested area of Jammu and Kashmir (120,849 sq km), a disputed area between Puducherry and Andhra Pradesh (13 sq km) and two as yet undemarcated areas of Madhya Pradesh (7 sq km) and Chhattisgarh (3 sq km).

Source: Office of the Registrar General of India, Ministry of Home Affairs, New Delhi.

PRINCIPAL TOWNS

(population at 2011 census, provisional*)

Greater Mumbai (Bombay)	12,478,447	Guwahati	963,429
Delhi	11,007,835	Chandigarh	960,787
Bangalore	8,425,970	Solapur	951,118
Hyderabad	6,809,970	Hubli-Dharwad	943,857
Ahmedabad	5,570,585	Bareilly	898,167
Chennai (Madras)	4,681,087	Moradabad	889,810
Kolkata (Calcutta)	4,486,679	Mysore	887,446
Surat	4,462,002	Gurgaon	876,824
Pune (Poona)	3,115,431	Aligarh	872,575
Jaipur (Jeypore)	3,073,350	Jalandhar	862,196
Lucknow	2,815,601	Tiruchirappalli	846,915
Kanpur (Cawnpore)	2,767,031	Bhubaneswar	837,737
Nagpur	2,405,421	Salem	831,038
Indore	1,960,631	Mira-Bhayander	814,655
Thane	1,818,872	Thiruvananthapuram	752,490
Bhopal	1,795,648	Bhiwandi	711,329
Visakhapatnam (Vizag)	1,730,320	Saharanpur	703,345
Pimpri-Chinchwad	1,729,359	Gorakhpur	671,048
Patna	1,683,200	Guntur	651,382
Vadodara (Baroda)	1,666,703	Bikaner	647,804
Ghaziabad	1,636,068	Amravati	646,801
Ludhiana	1,613,878	Noida	642,381
Agra	1,574,542	Jamshedpur	629,659
Nashik	1,486,973	Bhilai Nagar	625,697
Faridabad Complex	1,404,653	Warangal	620,116
Meerut	1,309,023	Cuttack	606,007
Rajkot	1,286,995	Firozabad	603,797
Kalyan-Dombivli	1,246,381	Kochi (Cochin)	601,574
Vasai Virar	1,221,233	Bhavnagar	593,768
Varanasi (Banaras)	1,201,815	Dehradun	578,420
Srinagar	1,192,792	Durgapur	566,937
Aurangabad	1,171,330	Asansol	564,491
Dhanbad	1,161,561	Nanded Waghala	550,564

Amritsar	1,132,761	Kolapur	549,283
Navi Mumbai	1,119,477	Ajmer	542,580
Allahabad	1,117,094	Gulbarga	532,031
Ranchi	1,073,440	Jamnagar	529,308
Haora	1,072,161	Ujjain	515,215
Coimbatore	1,061,447	Loni	512,296
Jabalpur (Jubbulpore)	1,054,336	Siliguri	509,709
Gwalior	1,053,505	Jhansi	507,293
Vijayawada (Vijayavada)	1,048,240	Ulhasnagar	506,937
Jodhpur	1,033,918	Nellore	505,258
Madurai	1,016,885	Jammu	503,690
Raipur	1,010,087	Sangli Miraj Kupwad	502,697
Kota	1,001,365		

* Figures refer to the city proper in each case.

Capital: New Delhi, provisional population 249,998 at 2011 census.

Population of principal urban agglomerations at 2011 census, provisional: Greater Mumbai 18,414,288; Delhi 16,314,838; Kolkata 14,112,536; Chennai 8,696,010; Bangalore 8,499,399; Hyderabad 7,749,334; Ahmedabad 6,352,254; Pune 5,049,968; Surat 4,585,367; Kanpur 2,920,067; Lucknow 2,901,474; Nagpur 2,497,777; Ghaziabad 2,358,525; Indore 2,167,447; Coimbatore 2,151,466; Kochi 2,117,990; Patna 2,046,652; Kozhikode 2,030,519; Bhopal 1,883,381; Thrissur 1,854,783; Vadodara 1,817,191; Agra 1,746,467; Malappuram 1,698,645; Thiruvananthapuram 1,687,406; Kannur 1,642,892; Nashik 1,562,769; Vijayawada 1,491,202; Madurai 1,462,420; Varanasi 1,435,113; Meerut 1,424,908; Rajkot 1,390,933; Jamshedpur 1,337,131; Srinagar 1,273,312; Jabalpur 1,267,564; Asansol 1,243,008; Allahabad 1,216,719; Dhanbad 1,195,298; Aurangabad 1,189,376; Amritsar 1,183,705; Jodhpur 1,137,815; Ranchi 1,126,741; Raipur 1,122,555; Kollam 1,110,005; Gwalior 1,101,981; Durg-Bhilainagar 1,064,077; Chandigarh 1,025,682; Tiruchirappalli 1,021,717.

BIRTHS AND DEATHS

(estimates based on Sample Registration Scheme)

	2010	2011	2012
Birth rate (per 1,000)	22.1	21.8	21.6
Death rate (per 1,000)	7.2	7.1	7.0

Life expectancy (years at birth): 66.0 (males 64.3; females 67.7) in 2011 (Source: World Bank, World Development Indicators database).

ECONOMICALLY ACTIVE POPULATION

(persons aged five years and over, 1991 census, excluding Jammu and Kashmir)

	Males	Females	Total
Agriculture, hunting, forestry and fishing	139,361,719	51,979,110	191,340,829
Mining and quarrying	1,536,919	214,356	1,751,275
Manufacturing	23,969,433	4,702,046	28,671,479
Construction	5,122,468	420,737	5,543,205
Trade and commerce	19,862,725	1,433,612	21,296,337
Transport, storage and communications	7,810,126	207,620	8,017,746
Other services	23,995,194	5,316,428	29,311,622
Total employed	221,658,584	64,273,909	285,932,493
Marginal workers	2,705,223	25,493,654	28,198,877
Total labour force	224,363,807	89,767,563	314,131,370

Unemployment (work applicants at 31 December, '000 persons aged 14 years and over): 41,466 (males 29,685, females 11,781) in 2006; 39,974 (males 27,972, females 12,002) in 2007; 39,112 (males 26,785, females 12,327) in 2008 (Source: ILO).

2001 census: Cultivators 127,312,851 (males 85,416,498, females 41,896,353); Agricultural labourers 106,775,330 (males 57,329,100, females 49,446,230); Household industry workers 16,956,942 (males 8,744,183, females 8,212,759); Other 151,189,601 (males 123,524,695, females 27,664,906); Total employed 402,234,724 (incl. 89,229,741 marginal workers).

Mid-2014 (FAO estimates in '000): Agriculture, etc. 281,225; Total labour force 535,123 (Source: FAO).

Health and Welfare

KEY INDICATORS

Total fertility rate (children per woman, 2011)	2.6
Under-5 mortality rate (per 1,000 live births, 2011)	61
HIV/AIDS (% of persons aged 15–49, 2012)	0.3
Physicians (per 1,000 head, 2009)	0.6
Hospital beds (per 1,000 head, 2005)	0.9
Health expenditure (2010): US $ per head (PPP)	126
Health expenditure (2010): % of GDP	3.7
Health expenditure (2010): public (% of total)	28.2
Access to water (% of persons, 2011)	92
Access to sanitation (% of persons, 2011)	35
Total carbon dioxide emissions ('000 metric tons, 2010)	2,008,822.9
Carbon dioxide emissions per head (metric tons, 2010)	1.7
Human Development Index (2012): ranking	136
Human Development Index (2012): value	0.554

For sources and definitions, see explanatory note on p. vi.

Agriculture

PRINCIPAL CROPS

('000 metric tons, year ending 30 June)

	2010/11	2011/12	2012/13*
Total cereals	226,250	242,200	236,920
Rice, milled	95,980	105,300	104,400
Sorghum (Jowar)	7,000	5,980	5,330
Cat-tail millet (Bajra)	10,370	10,280	8,740
Maize	21,730	21,760	22,230
Finger millet (Ragi)	2,190	1,930	1,590
Small millets	450	450	430
Wheat	86,870	94,880	92,460
Barley	1,660	1,620	1,740
Chick-peas (Gram)	8,220	7,700	8,880
Pigeon-peas (Tur)	2,860	2,650	3,070
Dry beans, dry peas, lentils and other pulses	7,160	6,740	6,490
Total food grains	244,490	259,290	255,360
Groundnuts (in shell)	8,265	6,964	4,749
Sesame seed	893	810	654
Rapeseed and mustard	8,179	6,604	7,820
Linseed	147	152	150
Castorseed	1,350	2,295	2,177
Total edible oilseeds (incl. others)	32,479	29,799	31,006
Cotton lint†	33,000	35,200	34,000
Jute and kenaf‡	10,620	11,399	11,296
Sugar cane: production cane	342,382	361,037	338,963

* Estimates.

† Production in '000 bales of 170 kg each.

‡ Production in '000 bales of 180 kg each.

Source: Directorate of Economics and Statistics, Ministry of Agriculture.

Tea ('000 metric tons): 991 in 2010; 967 in 2011; 1,000 in 2012 (FAO estimate) (Source: FAO).

Tobacco, unmanufactured ('000 metric tons): 690 in 2010; 830 in 2011; 875 in 2012 (FAO estimate) (Source: FAO).

Potatoes ('000 metric tons): 36,577 in 2010; 42,339 in 2011; 45,000 in 2012 (FAO estimate) (Source: FAO).

LIVESTOCK
('000 head, year ending September)

	2010	2011	2012
Cattle	210,384	210,824*	218,000†
Sheep†	73,991	74,500	75,000
Goats†	154,000	157,000	160,000
Pigs†	9,630	9,500	9,400
Horses†	524	520	525
Asses†	326	326	294
Mules†	112	105	105
Buffaloes	111,891	112,916*	115,400†
Camels†	446	440	438
Chickens	841,865	942,000†	947,000
Ducks†	26,000	26,500	27,000

* Unofficial figure.
† FAO estimate(s).

Source: FAO.

LIVESTOCK PRODUCTS
('000 metric tons)

	2010	2011	2012
Cattle meat*	1,076.3	1,086.5	1,096.8
Buffalo meat*	1,489.4	1,502.4	1,529.0
Sheep meat*	289.2	293.4	295.8
Goat meat*	586.5	596.6	603.7
Pig meat*	332.5	329.0	329.2
Chicken meat	2,193.0	2,206.0*	2,219.0
Duck meat*	37.7	39.0	39.0
Cows' milk	54,903	53,500†	54,000*
Buffaloes' milk	62,350	65,140†	66,000*
Goats' milk	4,594	4,760†	4,850*
Hen eggs	3,378	3,490†	3,600
Wool, greasy	43.0	44.4	45.5*

* FAO estimate(s).
† Unofficial figure.

Source: FAO.

Forestry

ROUNDWOOD REMOVALS
('000 cubic metres, excl. bark, FAO estimates)

	2010	2011	2012
Sawlogs, veneer logs and logs for sleepers	22,390	22,390	22,390
Pulpwood	624	624	624
Other industrial wood	178	178	178
Fuel wood	309,307	308,776	308,244
Total	332,499	331,968	331,436

Source: FAO.

SAWNWOOD PRODUCTION
('000 cubic metres, incl. railway sleepers)

	2005	2006	2007
Coniferous sawnwood	9,900	9,900	2,000
Broadleaved sawnwood	4,889	4,889	4,889
Total	14,789	14,789	6,889

2008–12: Figures assumed to be unchanged from 2007 (FAO estimates).
Source: FAO.

Fishing

('000 metric tons, live weight)

	2009	2010	2011
Capture	4,066.8	4,689.3	4,301.5
Bombay-duck (Bummalo)	194.1	156.2	136.6
Croakers and drums	245.5	238.5	262.9
Indian oil-sardine (Sardinella)	324.0	320.2	386.7
Giant tiger prawn	192.3	155.5	187.9
Aquaculture	3,791.9*	3,785.8	4,573.5
Roho labeo	495.7	279.0	579.8
Mrigal carp	304.8	87.7	117.5
Catla	2,191.8	2,705.2	2,121.4
Silver carp	285.6	129.8	1,323.0
Total catch	7,858.7*	8,475.1	8,875.0

* FAO estimate.

Source: FAO.

Mining

('000 metric tons, unless otherwise indicated)

	2010/11	2011/12	2012/13
Coal	532,694	539,950	557,158
Lignite	37,733	42,332	46,458
Iron ore*	207,157	168,582	136,019
Manganese ore*	3,056	2,412	2,322
Bauxite	12,723	13,600	15,360
Chalk (Fireclay)	178	179	167
Kaolin (China clay)	2,728	3,077	3,679
Dolomite	5,840	5,969	6,713
Gypsum	4,918	3,979	3,538
Limestone	246,336	262,568	279,736
Crude petroleum	37,712	38,090	37,868
Chromium ore*	4,326	2,923	2,950
Phosphorite	2,097	2,260	2,124
Kyanite	6	4	1
Magnesite	236	224	213
Steatite	903	998	939
Copper ore*	3,602	3,479	3,639
Lead concentrates*	148	162	184
Zinc concentrates*	1,427	1,414	1,493
Mica—crude (metric tons)	1,333	1,899	1,255
Gold (kg)	2,399	2,194	1,588
Diamonds (carats)	11,222	18,490	31,989
Natural gas (million cu m)†	52,222	47,559	39,733

* Figures refer to gross weight. The estimated metal content is: Iron 63%; Manganese 40%; Chromium 30%; Copper 1.2%; Lead 70%; Zinc 60%.
† Figures refer to gas utilized.

Source: Indian Bureau of Mines.

Industry

SELECTED PRODUCTS

('000 metric tons, unless otherwise indicated)

	2008/09	2009/10	2010/11
Refined sugar*	18,407	17,303	22,535
Cotton cloth (million sq metres)	26,898	28,517	30,659
Paper and paper board	6,543	7,067	n.a.
Soda ash	1,989	2,051	2,298
Fertilizers	14,334	16,224	n.a.
Motor spirit	16,020	15,970	17,509
Cement	181,400	200,651	209,660
Pig-iron	6,206	5,796	5,585
Stainless steel	2,680	2,881	3,737
Aluminium ingots (metric tons)	784,755	745,542	n.a.
Diesel engines—stationary (number)	3,337,682	3,377,819	n.a.
Television receivers (number)	7,574,271	9,622,186	n.a.
Electric fans (number)	11,541,791	14,074,284	n.a.
Passenger cars	1,516,791	1,910,465	2,452,819
Commercial vehicles (number)	416,491	566,585	752,597
Motorcycles, mopeds and scooters (number)	8,361,411	10,510,331	13,376,451
Bicycles (number)	11,123,734	12,651,846	n.a.

* Figures relate to crop year (beginning November) and are in respect of cane sugar only.

Finance

CURRENCY AND EXCHANGE RATES

Monetary Units

100 paise (singular: paisa) = 1 Indian rupee (R).

Sterling, Dollar and Euro Equivalents (31 December 2013)

£1 sterling = Rs 101.932;
US $1 = Rs 61.897;
€1 = Rs 85.362;
1,000 Indian rupees = £9.81 = $16.16 = €11.71.

Average Exchange Rate (rupees per US $)

2011	46.670
2012	53.437
2013	58.598

UNION BUDGET

(Rs million, rounded, year ending 31 March)

Revenue	2011/12	2012/13*	2013/14†
Tax revenue (net)	6,297,648	7,421,150	8,840,783
Customs receipts	1,493,275	1,648,530	1,873,080
Union excise duties	1,456,076	1,719,961	1,975,540
Corporation tax	3,228,162	3,588,740	4,195,200
Other taxes on income	1,703,426	2,060,950	2,476,390
Other taxes and duties	1,010,825	1,362,185	1,838,491
Less States' share of tax revenue	2,554,136	2,915,466	3,469,918
Less Surcharge transferred to National Calamity Contingency Fund	39,979	43,750	48,000
Other current revenue	1,216,723	1,297,126	1,722,524
Interest receipts (net)	202,523	165,949	177,644
Dividends and profits	506,081	554,428	738,664
Receipts of Union Territories	10,145	11,231	11,659
External grants	29,620	27,620	14,560
Other receipts (net)	468,350	537,900	780,000
Non-debt capital revenue	369,380	380,729	664,680
Total	7,883,751	9,099,005	11,227,987

Expenditure	2011/12	2012/13*	2013/14†
Central Ministries/Departments	11,959,259	13,142,427	15,242,031
Agriculture and co-operation (incl. agricultural research and education)	149,369	162,721	198,188
Atomic energy	83,041	68,286	98,333
Defence	2,136,733	2,230,035	2,533,459
Drinking water supply	99,977	130,053	152,657
Economic affairs	3,162,575	3,718,660	4,329,689
External affairs	78,548	100,620	117,190
Fertilizers	709,692	660,100	662,690
Food and public distribution	738,001	862,262	910,346
Health and family welfare	243,551	259,270	332,780
Home affairs	453,722	484,339	569,068
Education and literacy	406,414	455,420	527,010
Petroleum and natural gas	700,997	975,141	651,884
Railways	230,134	242,650	260,000
Road transport and highways	21,986	22,670	22,670
Rural development	642,635	520,448	744,777
Urban development	86,190	84,236	103,638
State plans	1,001,288	1,071,471	1,299,300
Union territories	83,103	94,354	111,642
Total	13,043,650	14,308,252	16,652,973
Current‡	11,457,853	12,630,721	14,361,687
Capital	1,585,797	1,677,531	2,291,286

* Estimates.

† Forecasts.

‡ Including interest payments (Rs million): 2,731,500 in 2011/12; 3,166,740 in 2012/13 (estimate); 3,706,840 in 2013/14 (forecast).

Source: Government of India, Union Budget 2013/14.

INTERNATIONAL RESERVES

(US $ million at 31 December)

	2010	2011	2012
Gold (national valuation)	22,470	26,620	27,220
IMF special drawing rights	5,078	4,429	4,436
Reserve position in IMF	2,385	3,923	4,494
Foreign exchange	267,814	262,933	261,656
Total	297,747	297,905	297,806

Source: IMF, *International Financial Statistics*.

MONEY SUPPLY

(Rs '000 million, last Friday of year ending 31 March)

	2010/11	2011/12	2012/13
Currency with the public	9,118.4	10,226.5	11,447.4
Demand deposits with banks	7,228.6	7,109.8	7,469.6
Other deposits with Reserve Bank	36.5	28.2	32.4
Time deposits	48,657.7	56,283.9	64,870.9
Broad money	65,041.2	73,648.4	83,820.2

Source: Reserve Bank of India.

COST OF LIVING

(Consumer Price Index for Industrial Workers; base: 2000 = 100)

	2010	2011	2012
Food (incl. beverages)	193.8	208.1	227.9
All items (incl. others)	182.7	198.9	217.4

Source: ILO.

NATIONAL ACCOUNTS

(Rs '000 million at current prices, year ending 31 March)

National Income and Product

	2010/11	2011/12	2012/13
Domestic factor incomes	65,041.66	74,767.65	84,676.06
Consumption of fixed capital	7,628.00	8,767.30	9,934.07
Gross domestic product at factor cost	72,669.66	83,534.95	94,610.13
Indirect taxes	8,215.72	9,703.34	5,596.07
Less Subsidies	2,932.25	3,488.82	
GDP in purchasers' values	77,953.13	89,749.47	100,206.20
Net factor income from abroad	–818.07	–768.30	–999.00
Gross national product	77,135.06	88,981.17	99,207.20
Less Consumption of fixed capital	7,628.00	8,767.30	9,934.07
National income in market prices	69,507.06	80,213.87	89,273.13

Expenditure on the Gross Domestic Product

	2010/11	2011/12	2012/13
Government final consumption expenditure	8,910.33	10,426.77	11,867.61
Private final consumption expenditure	43,498.89	50,562.19	56,943.62
Increase in stocks	2,451.13	1,893.84	3,541.54
Gross fixed capital formation	24,744.64	27,490.72	29,646.77
Acquisitions, less disposals, of valuables	1,628.36	2,429.68	2,501.11
Total domestic expenditure	81,233.35	92,803.20	104,500.65
Exports of goods and services	17,101.93	21,436.47	23,877.41
Less Imports of goods and services	20,501.82	27,224.54	31,601.59
Statistical discrepancy	119.67	2,734.35	3,429.73
GDP in purchasers' values	77,953.13	89,749.47	100,206.20
GDP at constant 2004/05 prices	52,961.08	56,313.79	58,136.64

Gross Domestic Product by Economic Activity

	2010/11	2011/12	2012/13
Agriculture	11,320.48	12,680.81	14,186.78
Forestry and logging	1,175.25	1,321.31	1,463.34
Fishing	573.69	655.41	798.22
Mining and quarrying	1,960.92	2,010.76	2,189.10
Manufacturing	10,807.50	12,020.86	12,799.66
Electricity, gas and water supply	1,310.08	1,448.17	1,702.38
Construction	5,954.54	6,852.04	7,673.88
Trade, hotels and restaurants	12,469.65	15,071.10	17,658.51
Transport, storage and communications	5,277.43	5,954.48	6,441.14
Banking and insurance	4,104.07	4,796.80	5,554.88
Real estate and business services	7,554.94	9,048.01	10,619.08
Public administration and defence	4,437.61	5,057.53	5,771.71
Other services	5,723.50	6,617.67	7,751.43
GDP at factor cost	72,669.66	83,534.95	94,610.13
Indirect taxes	8,215.72	9,703.34	5,596.07
Less Subsidies	2,932.25	3,488.82	
GDP in market prices	77,953.13	89,749.47	100,206.20

BALANCE OF PAYMENTS

(US $ million)

	2010/11	2011/12	2012/13*
Exports of goods f.o.b.	256,159	309,774	306,581
Imports of goods f.o.b.	–383,481	–499,533	–502,237
Trade balance	–127,322	–189,759	–195,656
Services (net)	44,081	64,098	64,915
Balance on goods and services	–83,241	–125,661	–130,741
Other income (net)	–17,952	–15,988	–21,455
Balance on goods, services and income	–101,193	–141,649	–152,196
Current transfers (net)	53,140	63,494	64,034
Current balance	–48,053	–78,155	–88,163
Direct investment abroad	–17,195	–10,892	–7,134
Direct investment from abroad	29,029	32,952	26,953
Portfolio investment assets	31,471	17,409	27,770
Portfolio investment liabilities	–1,179	–239	–878
Net loans	29,135	19,307	31,124
Banking capital (net)	4,962	16,226	16,570
Rupee debt service	–68	–79	–58
Other capital (net)	–12,416	–6,929	–5,047
Net errors and omissions	–2,636	–2,432	2,689
Overall balance	13,050	–12,831	3,826

* Preliminary figures.

Source: Reserve Bank of India.

External Trade

PRINCIPAL COMMODITIES

(Rs million, year ending 31 March)

Imports c.i.f.	2010/11	2011/12	2012/13
Animal and vegetable oils, fats and waxes	300,562	465,681	616,301
Mineral fuels, mineral oils and products of their distillation	5,277,877	8,279,657	9,860,856
Organic chemicals	575,498	691,442	854,391
Natural or cultured pearls, precious and semi-precious stones, precious metals and articles thereof; imitation jewellery; coin	3,503,964	4,345,985	4,558,560
Iron and steel	501,332	657,494	741,253
Boilers, machinery, mechanical appliances and parts thereof	1,321,619	1,800,016	741,253
Electrical machinery and equipment and parts thereof; sound and television apparatus	1,238,592	1,573,375	1,622,670
Aircraft, spacecraft, and parts thereof	156,756	198,111	256,914
Total (incl. others)	16,834,670	23,454,632	26,691,620

Exports f.o.b.	2010/11	2011/12	2012/13
Cereals	152,351	306,249	525,678
Ores, slag and ash	238,555	262,173	129,154
Mineral fuels, mineral oils and products of their distillation	1,939,162	2,743,870	3,375,673
Organic chemicals	413,180	561,793	659,150
Pharmaceutical products	303,832	408,169	547,737
Iron and steel	325,323	397,592	440,421
Articles of iron or steel	302,981	339,877	404,776
Cotton	314,285	436,017	485,143
Articles of apparel and clothing accessories, knitted or crocheted	225,557	276,385	302,382
Articles of apparel and clothing accessories, not knitted or crocheted	303,639	381,001	402,907
Natural or cultured pearls, precious and semi-precious stones, precious metals and articles thereof; imitation jewellery; coin	1,989,077	2,262,909	2,384,585
Boilers, machinery, mechanical appliances and parts thereof	408,046	520,508	628,467
Electrical machinery and equipment and parts thereof; sound and television apparatus	461,674	553,766	591,441
Vehicles other than railway or tramway rolling stock, and parts and accessories thereof	424,163	525,568	663,992
Total (incl. others)	11,429,219	14,659,594	16,343,188

Source: Ministry of Commerce and Industry.

PRINCIPAL TRADING PARTNERS
(Rs million, year ending 31 March)

Imports c.i.f.	2010/11	2011/12	2012/13
Angola	232,730	318,685	389,464
Australia	491,876	746,196	712,171
Belgium	391,787	497,573	545,368
China, People's Republic	1,980,791	2,654,656	2,843,846
Germany	541,360	748,406	779,337
Hong Kong	428,251	495,702	430,301
Indonesia	451,363	704,199	809,657
Iran	497,246	665,522	630,256
Iraq	409,772	905,315	1,045,964
Italy	193,947	245,094	256,524
Japan	393,093	576,710	675,472
Korea, Republic	477,125	615,703	713,373
Kuwait	469,760	794,495	901,843
Malaysia	297,459	453,850	541,988
Nigeria	490,051	701,039	656,222
Qatar	310,358	618,638	854,578
Saudi Arabia	928,549	1,531,099	1,846,848
Singapore	325,458	397,085	407,640
South Africa	325,251	524,460	483,196
Switzerland	1,127,396	1,663,834	1,745,118
Thailand	194,599	253,248	291,130
United Arab Emirates	1,491,234	1,756,375	2,129,233
United Kingdom	245,617	340,939	342,312
USA	913,585	1,123,629	1,372,386
Venezuela	237,482	321,301	768,345
Total (incl. others)	16,834,670	23,454,632	26,691,620

Exports f.o.b.	2010/11	2011/12	2012/13
Bangladesh	147,525	183,867	279,826
Belgium	263,470	342,061	299,264
Brazil	183,359	275,769	328,720
China, People's Republic	702,422	874,708	735,296
France	236,875	220,208	271,059
Germany	307,185	379,653	394,081
Hong Kong	470,384	618,772	668,982
Indonesia	259,244	321,007	289,961
Iran	113,369	115,117	182,548
Israel	132,826	193,266	203,467
Italy	206,907	232,717	237,793
Japan	231,790	305,113	332,142
Kenya	99,475	109,872	205,257
Korea, Republic	169,528	207,678	228,702
Malaysia	176,772	191,032	241,435
Nepal	98,708	131,302	168,056
Netherlands	349,497	439,073	573,726
Saudi Arabia	212,961	272,082	532,444

Exports f.o.b.—*continued*	2010/11	2011/12	2012/13
Singapore	447,317	803,630	739,950
South Africa	178,847	227,297	278,034
Sri Lanka	159,624	209,515	216,877
Taiwan	104,792	159,862	165,551
Thailand	103,463	142,535	203,102
Turkey	125,098	168,940	215,244
United Arab Emirates	1,538,661	1,722,685	1,978,321
United Kingdom	331,726	411,402	468,782
USA	1,151,945	1,664,554	1,967,408
Viet Nam	120,451	180,850	215,628
Total (incl. others)	11,429,219	14,659,594	16,343,188

Source: Ministry of Commerce and Industry.

Transport

RAILWAYS
(million, year ending 31 March)

	2009/10	2010/11	2011/12
Passengers	7,246	7,651	8,224
Passenger-km	903,465	978,508	1,046,522
Freight (metric tons)	892.2	926.4	975.5
Freight (metric ton-km)	601,290	626,473	668,618

Source: Railway Board, Ministry of Railways and Indian Railways.

ROAD TRAFFIC
('000 motor vehicles in use at 31 March)

	2010	2011	2012
Private cars, jeeps and taxis	17,109	19,231	21,568
Buses and coaches	1,527	1,604	1,677
Goods vehicles	6,432	7,064	7,658
Motorcycles and scooters	91,598	101,865	115,419
Others	11,080	12,102	13,169
Total	127,746	141,866	159,491

Source: Ministry of Road Transport and Highways.

SHIPPING

Flag Registered Fleet
(at 31 December)

	2011	2012	2013
Number of vessels	1,331	1,378	1,553
Total displacement ('000 grt)	10,043.0	9,587.8	9,740.1

Source: Lloyd's List Intelligence (www.lloydslistintelligence.com).

International Sea-borne Traffic
(year ending 31 March)

	2003/04	2004/05	2005/06
Vessels ('000 nrt):			
entered	68,111	66,943	44,320
cleared	88,733	41,634	23,891
Freight ('000 metric tons):			
loaded	n.a.	143,071	154,045
unloaded	n.a.	157,593	175,162

2006/07 ('000 nrt): Vessels entered 67,404; Vessels cleared 40,700.

CIVIL AVIATION
(all Indian carriers, traffic on scheduled services)

	2009/10	2010/11	2011/12
Passengers carried ('000)	56,949	67,001	75,217
Passenger-km (million)	89,443	103,171	112,794
Freight carried (metric tons)	513,706	620,000	602,200
Freight ton-km (million)	1,427	1,646	1,750
Mail carried (metric tons)	33,361	25,000	18,500
Mail ton-km (million)	58	48	45

Source: Directorate General of Civil Aviation.

Tourism

FOREIGN VISITORS BY COUNTRY OF ORIGIN

	2010	2011	2012
Australia	169,647	192,592	202,105
Bangladesh	431,962	463,543	487,397
Canada	242,372	259,017	256,021
China, People's Republic	119,530	142,218	168,952
France	225,232	231,423	240,674
Germany	227,720	240,235	254,783
Japan	168,019	193,525	220,015
Malaysia	179,077	208,196	195,853
Russia	122,048	144,312	177,526
Sri Lanka	266,515	305,853	296,983
United Kingdom	759,494	798,249	788,170
USA	931,292	980,688	1,039,947
Total (incl. others)	5,775,692	6,309,222	6,577,745

Receipts from tourism (US $ million, provisional): 14,193 in 2010; 16,564 in 2011; 17,737 in 2012.

Source: Ministry of Tourism.

Communications Media

	2010	2011	2012
Telephones ('000 main lines in use)	35,090.0	32,685.2	31,080.0
Mobile cellular telephones ('000 subscribers)	752,190.0	893,862.5	864,720.0
Internet subscribers ('000)	18,690	22,390	n.a.
Broadband subscribers ('000)	10,990	13,350	14,306

Daily newspapers (2009/10): 9,355 (circulation 162,313,000 copies).

Non-daily newspapers and other periodicals (2009/10): 68,029 (circulation 146,504,000 copies).

Sources: International Telecommunication Union; Register of Newspapers for India; Ministry of Information and Broadcasting.

Education

(2010/11 unless otherwise indicated, provisional)

	Institutions	Teachers	Students
Pre-primary	68,413	78,781	6,236,462
Primary	748,547	2,100,462	135,316,946
Middle	447,600	1,887,343	62,056,450
Secondary (high school); Higher secondary (new pattern); Intermediate/pre-degree/junior college	200,184	2,500,101	51,195,106
Higher education*	33,634†	817,000‡	25,191,000‡

* Includes colleges for general and professional education, universities and institutions of national importance.

† At August 2011.

‡ Rounded figure.

Source: Ministry of Human Resource Development.

Pupil-teacher ratio (primary education, UNESCO estimate): 35.2 in 2010/11 (Source: UNESCO Institute for Statistics).

Adult literacy rate (UNESCO estimates): 66.0% (males 76.9%; females 54.5%) in 2007 (Source: UNESCO Institute for Statistics).

Directory

The Government

HEAD OF STATE

President: PRANAB MUKHERJEE (sworn in 25 July 2012).

Vice-President: MOHAMMAD HAMID ANSARI (sworn in 12 August 2007; re-elected 7 August 2012).

COUNCIL OF MINISTERS

(April 2014)

The Government is formed by the United Progressive Alliance, a coalition of the Indian National Congress (Congress), the Nationalist Congress Party (NCP), the Jammu and Kashmir National Conference (JKNC) and the Rashtriya Lok Dal (RLD).

Prime Minister and Minister-in-charge of Personnel, Public Grievances and Pensions, of Planning, of Atomic Energy and of Space: Dr MANMOHAN SINGH (Congress).

Minister of Finance: P. CHIDAMBARAM (Congress).

Minister of Railways: MALLIKARJUN KHARGE (Congress).

Minister of Agriculture and of Food Processing Industries: SHARAD PAWAR (NCP).

Minister of Defence: A. K. ANTONY (Congress).

Minister of Home Affairs: SUSHILKUMAR SHINDE (Congress).

Minister of External Affairs: SALMAN KHURSHID (Congress).

Minister of Science and Technology and of Earth Sciences: JAIPAL S. REDDY (Congress).

Minister of Health and Family Welfare, and of Water Resources: GHULAM NABI AZAD (Congress).

Minister of New and Renewable Energy: Dr FAROOQ ABDULLAH (JKNC).

Minister of Petroleum and Natural Gas: M. VEERAPPA MOILY (Congress).

Minister of Overseas Indian Affairs: VAYALAR RAVI (Congress).

Minister of Urban Development and of Parliamentary Affairs: KAMAL NATH (Congress).

Minister of Civil Aviation: AJIT SINGH (RLD).

Minister of Human Resource Development: M. MANGAPATI PALLAM RAJU (Congress).

Minister of Communications and Information Technology: KAPIL SIBAL (Congress).

Minister of Commerce and Industry, and of Textiles: ANAND SHARMA (Congress).

Minister of Road Transport and Highways, and of Labour and Employment: OSCAR FERNANDES (Congress).

Minister of Housing and Urban Poverty Alleviation: GIRIJA VYAS (Congress).

Minister of Culture: CHANDRESH KUMARI KATOCH (Congress).

Minister of Shipping: G. K. VASAN (Congress).

Minister of Social Justice and Empowerment: KUMARI SELJA (Congress).

Minister of Tribal Affairs, and of Panchayati Raj: KISHORE CHANDRA DEO (Congress).

Minister of Steel: BENI PRASAD VERMA (Congress).

Minister of Coal: SHRIPRAKASH JAISWAL (Congress).

Minister of Law and Justice: KAPIL SIBAL (Congress).

Minister of Minority Affairs: K. RAHMAN KHAN (Congress).

Minister of Mines: DINSHA J. PATEL (Congress).

Minister of Heavy Industries and Public Enterprises: PRAFUL PATEL (NCP).

Minister of Rural Development: JAIRAM RAMESH (Congress).

Ministers of State with Independent Charge

Minister of State for Women and Child Development: KRISHNA TIRATH (Congress).

Minister of State for Youth Affairs and Sports, and for Defence: JITENDRA SINGH (Congress).

Minister of State for Consumer Affairs, Food and Public Distribution: Prof. K. V. THOMAS.

Minister of State for Statistics and Programme Implementation, and of Chemicals and Fertilizers: SRIKANT JENA.

Minister of State for Environment and Forests: JAYANTHI NATARAJAN (Congress).

Minister of State for Power: J. MADHAVRAO SCINDIA (Congress).

Minister of State for Micro, Small and Medium Enterprises: K. H. MANIYAPPA (Congress).

Minister of State for Drinking Water and Sanitation: B. M. SOLANKI (Congress).

Minister of State for Corporate Affairs: SACHIN PILOT (Congress).

Minister of State for Information and Broadcasting: MANISH TEWARI (Congress).

Minister of State for Tourism: Dr. K. CHIRANJEEVI (Congress).

Minister of State for the Development of the North-Eastern Region, and for Parliamentary Affairs: PABAN SINGH GHATOWAR (Congress).

There are, in addition, 33 Ministers of State without independent charge.

MINISTRIES AND GOVERNMENT OFFICES

President's Office: Rashtrapati Bhavan, New Delhi 110 004; tel. (11) 23015321; fax (11) 23017290; e-mail presidentofindia@rb.nic.in; internet www.presidentofindia.nic.in.

Vice-President's Office: 6 Maulana Azad Rd, New Delhi 110 011; tel. (11) 23016344; fax (11) 23018124; e-mail vpindia@nic.in; internet vicepresidentofindia.nic.in.

Prime Minister's Office: South Blk, Raisina Hill, New Delhi 110 011; tel. (11) 23012312; fax (11) 23016857; e-mail pmindia@pmindia.nic.in; internet www.pmindia.nic.in.

Ministry of Agriculture: Krishi Bhavan, Dr Rajendra Prasad Rd, New Delhi 110 001; tel. (11) 23383370; fax (11) 23384129; e-mail secy-agri@nic.in; internet agricoop.nic.in.

Ministry of Chemicals and Fertilizers: Shastri Bhavan, Dr Rajendra Prasad Rd, New Delhi 110 001; tel. (11) 23386519; fax (11) 23384020; e-mail mincf.cpc@sb.nic.in; internet chemicals.gov.in; internet fert.nic.in; internet pharmaceuticals.gov.in.

Ministry of Civil Aviation: Rajiv Gandhi Bhavan, Safdarjung Airport, New Delhi 110 023; tel. (11) 24610358; fax (11) 24602397; e-mail secy.moca@nic.in; internet civilaviation.nic.in.

Ministry of Coal: Shastri Bhavan, Dr Rajendra Prasad Rd, New Delhi 110 001; tel. (11) 23384884; fax (11) 23381678; e-mail secy.moc@nic.in; internet coal.nic.in.

Ministry of Commerce and Industry: 45C Udyog Bhavan, New Delhi 110 011; tel. (11) 23063664; fax (11) 23061796; e-mail csoffice@nic.in; internet commerce.nic.in.

Ministry of Communications and Information Technology: Electronic Niketan, CGO Complex, Lodhi Rd, New Delhi 110 003; tel. (11) 24364041; fax (11) 24363134; e-mail secretary@deity.gov.in; internet deity.gov.in.

Ministry of Consumer Affairs, Food and Public Distribution: 179 Krishi Bhavan, New Delhi 110 001; tel. (11) 23070637; fax (11) 23386098; e-mail secy-food@nic.in; internet fcamin.nic.in.

Ministry of Corporate Affairs: 'A' Wing, Shastri Bhavan, Dr Rajendra Prasad Rd, New Delhi 110 001; tel. (11) 23384660; fax (11) 23073806; e-mail hq.delhi@mca.gov.in; internet www.mca.gov.in.

Ministry of Culture: 'C' Wing, Shastri Bhavan, Dr Rajendra Prasad Rd, New Delhi 110 001; tel. (11) 23386995; fax (11) 23385115; e-mail secy-culture@nic.in; internet indiaculture.nic.in.

Ministry of Defence: South Blk, New Delhi 110 011; tel. (11) 23019030; fax (11) 23015403; e-mail ak.antony@sansad.nic.in; internet www.mod.nic.in.

Ministry of Development of North Eastern Region: Vigyan Bhavan Annexe, Maulana Azad Rd, New Delhi 110 011; tel. (11) 23022020; fax (11) 23022024; e-mail secydoner@nic.in; internet mdoner.gov.in.

Ministry of Drinking Water and Sanitation: 'A' Wing, 2nd Floor, Nirman Bhavan, New Delhi 110 001; tel. (11) 23061207; fax (11) 23062715; e-mail secydws@nic.in; internet ddws.gov.in.

Ministry of Earth Sciences: Prithvi Bhavan, IMD Campus, Lodhi Rd, New Delhi 110 003; tel. (11)24629771; fax (11) 24629777; e-mail secretary@moes.gov.in; internet moes.gov.in.

Ministry of Environment and Forests: Paryavaran Bhavan, CGO Complex, Lodhi Rd, New Delhi 110 003; tel. (11) 24361727; fax (11) 24362222; e-mail envisect@nic.in; internet moef.nic.in.

Ministry of External Affairs: South Blk, New Delhi 110 011; tel. (11) 23011127; fax (11) 23013254; e-mail eam@mea.gov.in; internet www.mea.gov.in.

Ministry of Finance: North Blk, 1st Floor, New Delhi 110 001; tel. (11) 23092611; fax (11) 23094075; e-mail secy-dea@nic.in; internet finmin.nic.in.

Ministry of Food Processing Industries: Panchsheel Bhavan, August Kranti Marg, New Delhi 110 049; tel. (11) 26493225; fax (11) 26493012; e-mail secy.hub@nic.in; internet mofpi.nic.in.

Ministry of Health and Family Welfare: Nirman Bhavan, Maulana Azad Rd, New Delhi 110 011; tel. and fax (11) 23061647; fax (11) 23062358; e-mail secyhfw@nic.in; internet mohfw.nic.in.

Ministry of Heavy Industries and Public Enterprises: Udyog Bhavan, New Delhi 110 011; tel. (11) 23061854; fax (11) 23062207; e-mail singh.rk1967@nic.in; internet dhi.nic.in.

Ministry of Home Affairs: North Blk, Central Secr., New Delhi 110 001; tel. (11) 23092011; fax (11) 23093750; e-mail websitemhaweb@nic.in; internet mha.nic.in.

Ministry of Housing and Urban Poverty Alleviation: Nirman Bhavan, Maulana Azad Rd, New Delhi 110 011; tel. (11) 23061444; fax (11) 23061991; e-mail secy-mhupa@nic.in; internet mhupa.gov.in.

Ministry of Human Resource Development: Shastri Bhavan, Dr Rajendra Prasad Rd, New Delhi 110 001; tel. (11) 23383936; fax (11) 23381355; e-mail dsel-mhrd@nic.in; internet mhrd.gov.in.

Ministry of Information and Broadcasting: 'A' Wing, Shastri Bhavan, Dr Rajendra Prasad Rd, New Delhi 110 001; tel. (11) 23382639; fax (11) 23386530; e-mail secy.inb@nic.in; internet mib.gov.in.

Ministry of Labour and Employment: Shram Shakti Bhavan, Rafi Marg, New Delhi 110 001; tel. (11) 23710265; fax (11) 23718730; e-mail m.sarangi@nic.in; internet labour.nic.in.

Ministry of Law and Justice: 'A' Wing, 4th Floor, Shastri Bhavan, Dr Rajendra Prasad Rd, New Delhi 110 001; tel. (11) 23387557; fax (11) 23384241; e-mail vnathan@nic.in; internet lawmin.nic.in.

Ministry of Micro, Small and Medium Enterprises: Udyog Bhavan, Rafi Marg, New Delhi 110 011; tel. (11) 23062107; fax (11) 23063045; e-mail secretary-msme@nic.in; internet msme.gov.in.

Ministry of Mines: 'A' Wing, 3rd Floor, Shastri Bhavan, Dr Rajendra Prasad Rd, New Delhi; tel. (11) 23385173; fax (11) 23384682; e-mail secy-mines@nic.in; internet mines.nic.in.

Ministry of Minority Affairs: Paryavaran Bhavan, 11th Floor, CGO Complex, Lodhi Rd, New Delhi 110 003; tel. (11) 24364272; fax (11) 24364285; e-mail secy-mma@nic.in; internet minorityaffairs.gov.in.

Ministry of New and Renewable Energy: Blk 14, CGO Complex, Lodhi Rd, New Delhi 110 003; tel. (11) 24361481; fax (11) 24367329; e-mail secy-mnre@nic.in; internet mnes.nic.in.

Ministry of Overseas Indian Affairs: Akbar Bhavan, Chanakya Puri, New Delhi 110 021; tel. (11) 24197900; fax (11) 24197919; e-mail info@moia.nic.in; internet moia.gov.in.

Ministry of Panchayati Raj: Krishi Bhavan, Dr Rajendra Prasad Rd, New Delhi 110 001; tel. (11) 23074309; fax (11) 23389028; e-mail secy-mopr@nic.in; internet www.panchayat.gov.in.

Ministry of Parliamentary Affairs: 87 Parliament House, New Delhi 110 001; tel. (11) 23017663; fax (11) 23017726; e-mail secympa@nic.in; internet mpa.nic.in.

Ministry of Personnel, Public Grievances and Pensions: North Blk, New Delhi 110 001; tel. (11) 23094848; fax (11) 23092432; e-mail secy_mop@nic.in; internet persmin.nic.in.

Ministry of Petroleum and Natural Gas: Shastri Bhavan, Dr Rajendra Prasad Rd, New Delhi 110 001; tel. (11) 23381462; fax (11) 23386118; e-mail vmoily@kar.nic.in; internet petroleum.nic.in.

Ministry of Power: Shram Shakti Bhavan, Rafi Marg, New Delhi 110 001; tel. (11) 23710271; fax (11) 23721487; e-mail p.umashankar@nic.in; internet powermin.nic.in.

Ministry of Railways: Rail Bhavan, Raisina Rd, New Delhi 110 001; tel. (11) 23385227; fax (11) 23382068; e-mail secyrb@rb.railnet.gov.in; internet www.indianrailways.gov.in.

Ministry of Road Transport and Highways: Parivahan Bhavan, 1 Parliament St, New Delhi 110 001; tel. (11) 23714104; fax (11) 23356669; e-mail ifcmost@nic.in; internet morth.nic.in.

Ministry of Rural Development: Krishi Bhavan, Dr Rajendra Prasad Rd, New Delhi 110 001; tel. (11) 23382230; fax (11) 23382408; e-mail secyrd@nic.in; internet rural.nic.in.

Ministry of Science and Technology: Technology Bhavan, New Mehrauli Rd, New Delhi 110 016; tel. (11) 26567373; fax (11) 26864570; e-mail dstinfo@nic.in; internet dst.gov.in.

Ministry of Shipping: Transport Bhavan, 1 Parliament St, New Delhi 110 001; tel. (11) 23714938; fax (11) 23716656; e-mail secyship@nic.in; internet shipping.gov.in.

Ministry of Social Justice and Empowerment: Shastri Bhavan, Dr Rajendra Prasad Rd, New Delhi 110 001; tel. (11) 23382683; fax (11) 23385180; e-mail secywel@nic.in; internet socialjustice.nic.in.

Ministry of Statistics and Programme Implementation: Sardar Patel Bhavan, Patel Chowk, New Delhi 110 001; tel. (11) 23340884; fax (11) 23340138; e-mail srikantjena3@gmail.com; internet mospi.gov.in.

Ministry of Steel: Udyog Bhavan, New Delhi 110 107; tel. (11) 23063417; fax (11) 23063236; e-mail ric-steel@nic.in; internet steel.nic.in.

Ministry of Textiles: Udyog Bhavan, New Delhi 110 011; tel. (11) 23061769; fax (11) 23063681; e-mail secy-ub@nic.in; internet texmin.nic.in.

Ministry of Tourism: Transport Bhavan, Rm 109, 1 Parliament St, New Delhi 110 001; tel. (11) 23711792; fax (11) 23717890; e-mail sectour@nic.in; internet tourism.gov.in.

Ministry of Tribal Affairs: Shastri Bhavan, Dr Rajendra Prasad Rd, New Delhi 110 001; tel. (11) 23388482; fax (11) 23070577; e-mail dirit@tribal.nic.in; internet www.tribal.nic.in.

Ministry of Urban Development: Nirman Bhavan, Maulana Azad Rd, New Delhi 110 011; tel. (11) 23062377; fax (11) 23061459; e-mail secyurban@nic.in; internet urbanindia.nic.in.

Ministry of Water Resources: Shram Shakti Bhavan, Rafi Marg, New Delhi 110 001; tel. and fax (11) 23715919; fax (11) 23731553; e-mail secy-mowr@nic.in; internet wrmin.nic.in.

Ministry of Women and Child Development: Shastri Bhavan, Dr Rajendra Prasad Rd, New Delhi; tel. (11) 23383586; fax (11) 23381495; e-mail secy.wcd@nic.in; internet wcd.nic.in.

Ministry of Youth Affairs and Sports: Shastri Bhavan, Dr Rajendra Prasad Rd, New Delhi 110 001; tel. (11) 23384183; fax (11) 23381898; e-mail minister.yas@nic.in; internet yas.nic.in.

Department of Atomic Energy: Anushakti Bhavan, Chatrapathi Shivaji Maharaj Marg, Mumbai 400 001; tel. (22) 22862500; fax (22) 22048476; e-mail info@dae.gov.in; internet www.dae.gov.in.

Department of Space: Antariksh Bhavan, New BEL Rd, Bangalore 560 231; tel. (80) 23415241; fax (80) 23415328; e-mail chairman@isro.gov.in; internet dos.gov.in.

Legislature

PARLIAMENT

Rajya Sabha

(Council of States)

Most of the members of the Rajya Sabha are indirectly elected by the state assemblies for six years, with one-third retiring every two years. The remaining members are nominated by the President.

Rajya Sabha: Parliament House Annexe, New Delhi 110 001; tel. (11) 23034695; fax (11) 23792940; e-mail secygen.rs@sansad.nic.in; internet rajyasabha.nic.in.

Chairman: Mohammad Hamid Ansari.

Deputy Chairman: P. J. Kurien.

Distribution of Seats, March 2014

Party	Seats
Congress	72*
Bharatiya Janata Party	47
Bahujan Samaj Party	15
Communist Party of India (Marxist)	11
All India Trinamool Congress	9
Janata Dal (United)	9
Samajwadi Party	9
All-India Anna Dravida Munnetra Kazhagam	7
Biju Janata Dal	6
Nationalist Congress Party	6
Dravida Munnetra Kazhagam	6
Telugu Desam	4
Shiv Sena	4
Shiromani Akali Dal	3
Communist Party of India	2
Jammu and Kashmir National Conference	2
Asom Gana Parishad	1
Rashtriya Janata Dal	1
Independents and others	18
Nominated	12
Total	244

* Including two nominated members.

Lok Sabha

(House of the People)

Lok Sabha: Parliament House Annexe, New Delhi 110 001; tel. (11) 23017465; fax (11) 23792107; e-mail vnathan@sansad.nic.in; internet loksabha.nic.in.

Speaker: Meira Kumar.

Deputy Speaker: Kariya Munda.

General Election, 16, 22, 23 and 30 April and 7 and 13 May 2009

Party	Seats
United Progressive Alliance	262
Congress	206
Dravida Munnetra Kazhagam	18
Nationalist Congress Party	9
All India Trinamool Congress	19
Jharkhand Mukti Morcha	2
Jammu and Kashmir National Conference	3
Viduthali Chiruthaigal Katch	1
All India Majlis-e-Ittehadul Muslimeen	1
Muslim League Kerala State Committee	2
Kerala Congress (Mani)	1
National Democratic Alliance	159
Bharatiya Janata Party	116
Shiv Sena	11
Rashtriya Lok Dal	5
Shiromani Akali Dal	4
Janata Dal (United)	20
Telangana Rashtra Samithi	2
Asom Gana Parishad	1
Third Front	79
Communist Party of India (Marxist)	16
Communist Party of India	4
All India Forward Bloc	2
Revolutionary Socialist Party	2
Bahujan Samaj Party	21
Biju Janata Dal	14
All-India Anna Dravida Munnetra Kazhagam	9
Telugu Desam Party	6
Janata Dal (Secular)	3
Haryana Janhit Congress	1
Marumalarchi Dravida Munnetra Kazhagam	1
Fourth Front	27
Samajwadi Party	23
Rashtriya Janata Dal	4
Independents and others	16
Nominated	2*
Total	545

* Nominated by the President to represent the Anglo-Indian community.

Note: the latest legislative elections were to be held in nine phases between 7 April and 12 May 2014, with vote-counting to be completed on 16 May.

State Governments

(Note: Distribution of seats in the state legislatures reflect the results of the most recent state election, except where otherwise indicated.)

ANDHRA PRADESH

(Capital—Hyderabad)

Governor: E. S. L. Narasimhan.

Chief Minister: (vacant); Chief Minister Kiran Kumar Reddy tendered his resignation on 20 February 2014; the state was placed under presidential rule in early March.

Legislative Assembly: 295 seats (at Feb. 2014: Congress 146, Telugu Desam 80, Telangana Rashtra Samithi 17, YSR Congress 17, All India Majlis-e-Ittehadul Muslimeen 7, Communist Party of India 4, Bharatiya Janata Party 3, Communist Party of India—Marxist 1, Lok Satta Party 1, independents 3, nominated 1, vacant 15); last election April 2009.

Legislative Council: revived April 2007; 90 seats (at 2013: Congress 29, Telugu Desam 14, Telangana Rashtra Samithi 4, All-India Majlis-e-Ittehadul Muslimeen 2, Communist Party of India 1, YSR Congress 1, independents 16, nominated 12, vacant 11).

ARUNACHAL PRADESH
(Capital—Itanagar)

Governor: NIRBHAY SHARMA.

Chief Minister: NABAM TUKI (Congress).

Legislative Assembly: 60 seats (Congress 42, Nationalist Congress Party 5, All India Trinamool Congress 5, People's Party of Arunachal 4, Bharatiya Janata Party 3, independent 1); last election Oct. 2009.

ASSAM (ASOM)
(Capital—Dispur)

Governor: JANAKI BALLAV PATNAIK.

Chief Minister: TARUN GOGOI (Congress).

Legislative Assembly: 126 seats (at March 2013: Congress 80, All India United Democratic Front 17, Bodoland Peoples Front 12, Asom Gana Parishad 9, Bharatiya Janata Party 5, All India Trinamool Congress 1, independents 2); last election April 2011.

BIHAR
(Capital—Patna)

Governor: D. Y. PATIL.

Chief Minister: NITISH KUMAR (Janata Dal—United).

Legislative Assembly: 243 seats (Janata Dal—United 115, Bharatiya Janata Party 91, Rashtriya Janata Dal 22, Lok Jan Shakti Party 3, Congress 4, independents 6, others 2); last election Oct.–Nov. 2010.

Legislative Council: 75 seats.

CHHATTISGARH
(Capital—Raipur)

Governor: SHEKHAR DUTT.

Chief Minister: Dr RAMAN SINGH (Bharatiya Janata Party).

Legislative Assembly: 91 seats (Bharatiya Janata Party 49, Congress 39, Bahujan Samaj Party 1, independent 1, nominated 1); last election Nov. 2013.

GOA
(Capital—Panaji)

Governor: B. V. WANCHOO.

Chief Minister: MANOHAR PARRIKAR (Bharatiya Janata Party).

Legislative Assembly: 40 seats (Bharatiya Janata Party 21, Congress 9, Maharashtrawadi Gomantak Party 3, Goa Vikas Party 2, independents 5); last election March 2012.

GUJARAT
(Capital—Gandhinagar)

Governor: Dr KAMLA BENIWAL.

Chief Minister: NARENDRA DAMODARDAS MODI (Bharatiya Janata Party).

Legislative Assembly: 182 seats (Bharatiya Janata Party 117, Congress 59, Nationalist Congress Party 3, Janata Dal—United 1, independents 2); last election Dec. 2012.

HARYANA
(Capital—Chandigarh)

Governor: JAGANNATH PAHADIA.

Chief Minister: BHUPINDER SINGH HOODA (Congress).

Legislative Assembly: 90 seats (Congress 40, Indian National Lok Dal 31, Haryana Janhit Congress 6, Bharatiya Janata Party 4, Bahujan Samaj Party 1, Shiromani Akali Dal 1, others 7); last election Oct. 2009.

HIMACHAL PRADESH
(Capital—Shimla)

Governor: URMILA SINGH.

Chief Minister: VIRBHADRA SINGH (Congress).

Legislative Assembly: 68 seats (Bharatiya Janata Party 41, Congress 23, Bahujan Samaj Party 1, independents 3); last election Nov. 2012.

JAMMU AND KASHMIR
(Capitals—Srinagar (Summer), Jammu (Winter))

Governor: NARENDRA NATH VOHRA.

Chief Minister: OMAR ABDULLAH (Jammu and Kashmir National Conference).

Legislative Assembly: 87 seats (Jammu and Kashmir National Conference 28, People's Democratic Party 21, Congress 17, Bharatiya Janata Party 11, Panther's Party 3, Communist Party of India—Marxist 1, People's Democratic Front 1, Jammu and Kashmir Democratic Party Nationalist 1, independents 4); last election Nov.–Dec. 2008.

Legislative Council: 36 seats.

JHARKHAND
(Capital—Ranchi)

Governor: Dr SYED AHMED.

Chief Minister: HEMANT SOREN (Jharkhand Mukti Morcha).

Legislative Assembly: 81 seats (Bharatiya Janata Party 18, Jharkhand Mukti Morcha 18, Congress 14, Jharkhand Vikas Morcha (Prajatantrik) 11, Rashtriya Janata Dal 5, Janata Dal—United 2, independents and others 13); last election Nov.–Dec. 2009.

KARNATAKA
(Capital—Bangalore)

Governor: HANS RAJ BHARDWAJ.

Chief Minister: K. SIDDARAMAIAH (Congress).

Legislative Assembly: 224 seats (Congress 122, Bharatiya Janata Party 40, Janata Dal—Secular 40, Karnataka Janata Paksha 6, Badavara Shramikara Raitara (Congress) Party 4, Maharashtra Ekikarana Samiti 2, others 3, independents 7); last election May 2013.

KERALA
(Capital—Thiruvananthapuram)

Governor: SHEILA DIXIT.

Chief Minister: OOMMEN CHANDY (Congress).

Legislative Assembly: 140 seats (Communist Party of India (Marxist) 45, Congress 38, Muslim League Kerala State Committee 20, Communist Party of India 13, Kerala Congress (M) 9, Janata Dal (Secular) 4, National Congress Party 2, Revolutionary Socialist Party 2 and others 7); last election April 2011.

MADHYA PRADESH
(Capital—Bhopal)

Governor: RAM NARESH YADAV.

Chief Minister: SHIVRAJ SINGH CHOUHAN (Bharatiya Janata Party).

Legislative Assembly: 230 seats (Bharatiya Janata Party 165, Congress 58, Bahujan Samaj Party 4, independents 3); last election Nov. 2013.

MAHARASHTRA
(Capital—Mumbai)

Governor: KATEEKAL SANKARANARAYANAN.

Chief Minister: PRITHVIRAJ CHAVAN (Congress).

Legislative Assembly: 288 seats (Congress 82, Nationalist Congress Party 62, Bharatiya Janata Party 46, Shiv Sena 44, Maharashtra Navnirman Sena 13, Samajwadi Party 4, Peasants' and Workers' Party of India 4, Bahujan Vikas Aghadi 2, Communist Party of India—Marxist 1, others 30); last election Oct. 2009.

MANIPUR
(Capital—Imphal)

Governor: VINOD KUMAR DUGGAL.

Chief Minister: OKRAM IBOBI SINGH (Congress).

Legislative Assembly: 60 seats (Congress 42, All India Trinamool Congress 7, Manipur State Congress Party 5, Naga People's Front 4, Lok Jan Shakti Party 1, Nationalist Congress Party 1); last election Jan. 2012.

MEGHALAYA
(Capital—Shillong)

Governor: K. K. PAUL.

Chief Minister: Dr MUKUL M. SANGMA (Congress).

Legislative Assembly: 60 seats (Congress 29, United Democratic Party 8, Hill State People's Democratic Party 4, Nationalist Congress Party 2, National People's Party 2, independents and others 15); last election Feb. 2013.

MIZORAM
(Capital—Aizawl)

Governor: VAKKOM PURUSHOTHAMAN.

Chief Minister: LAL THANHAWLA (Congress).

Legislative Assembly: 40 seats (Congress 34, Mizo National Front 5, Mizo People's Conference 1); last election Nov. 2013.

NAGALAND
(Capital—Kohima)

Governor: ASHWANI KUMAR.

Chief Minister: NEIPHIU RIO (Nagaland People's Front).

Legislative Assembly: 60 seats (Nagaland People's Front 38, Congress 8, Nationalist Congress Party 4, Bharatiya Janata Party 1, Janata Dal (United) 1, independents 8); last election Feb. 2013.

ODISHA
(Capital—Bhubaneswar)

Governor: S. C. JAMIR.

Chief Minister: NAVEEN PATNAIK (Biju Janata Dal).

Legislative Assembly: 147 seats (Biju Janata Dal 103, Congress 27, Bharatiya Janata Party 6, Nationalist Congress Party 4, Communist Party of India 1, independents 6); last election April 2009.

PUNJAB
(Capital—Chandigarh)

Governor: SHIVRAJ VISHWANATH PATIL (also Administrator of Chandigarh ex officio).

Chief Minister: PARKASH SINGH BADAL (Shiromani Akali Dal).

Legislative Assembly: 117 seats (Shiromani Akali Dal 56, Congress 46, Bharatiya Janata Party 12, independents 3); last election Jan. 2012.

RAJASTHAN
(Capital—Jaipur)

Governor: MARGARET ALVA.

Chief Minister: VASUNDHARA RAJE (Bharatiya Janata Party).

Legislative Assembly: 200 seats (Bharatiya Janata Party 163, Congress 21, National People's Party 4, Bahujan Samaj Party 3, National Unionist Zamindara Party 2, independents 7); last election Dec. 2013.

SIKKIM
(Capital—Gangtok)

Governor: SHRINIWAS PATIL.

Chief Minister: PAWAN KUMAR CHAMLING (Sikkim Democratic Front).

Legislative Assembly: 32 seats (Sikkim Democratic Front 32); last election April 2009.

TAMIL NADU
(Capital—Chennai)

Governor: KONIJETI ROSAIAH.

Chief Minister: J. JAYALALITHAA (All India Anna Dravida Munnetra Kazhagam).

Legislative Assembly: 234 seats, (All India Anna Dravida Munnetra Kazhagam 150, Desiya Murpokku Dravida Kazhagam 29, Dravida Munnetra Kazhagam 23, Communist Party of India (Marxist) 10, Communist Party of India 9, Congress 5, Pattali Makkal Katchi 3, All India Forward Bloc 1, others 4); last election April 2011.

TRIPURA
(Capital—Agartala)

Governor: DEVANAND KONWAR.

Chief Minister: MANIK SARKAR (Communist Party of India—Marxist).

Legislative Assembly: 60 seats (Communist Party of India—Marxist 49, Congress 10, Communist Party of India 1); last election Feb. 2013.

UTTAR PRADESH
(Capital—Lucknow)

Governor: B. L. JOSHI.

Chief Minister: AKHILESH YADAV (Samajwadi Party).

Legislative Assembly: 404 seats (Samajwadi Party 222, Bahujan Samaj Party 80, Bharatiya Janata Party 47, Indian National Congress 27, Rashtriya Lok Dal 8, Peace Party 4, Qaumi Ekta Dal 2, Apna Dal 1, Nationalist Congress Party 1, Ittehad-e-Millat Council 1, All India Trinamool Congress 1, independents 6, nominated 1); last election December 2013.

Legislative Council: 100 seats.

UTTARAKHAND
(Capital—Dehradun)

Governor: AZIZ QURESHI.

Chief Minister: HARISH RAWAT (Congress).

Legislative assembly: 70 seats (Congress 32, Bharatiya Janata Party 31, Bahujan Samaj Party 3, Uttarakhand Kranti Dal 1, independents 3); last election Jan. 2012.

WEST BENGAL
(Capital—Kolkata)

Governor: MAYANKOTE KELATH NARAYANAN.

Chief Minister: MAMATA BANERJEE (All India Trinamool Congress).

Legislative Assembly: 294 seats (All India Trinamool Congress 184, Congress 42, Communist Party of India—Marxist 40, All India Forward Bloc 11, Revolutionary Socialist Party 7, Gorkha Janmukti Morcha 3, Communist Party of India 2, others 5); last election April–May 2011.

UNION TERRITORIES

Andaman and Nicobar Islands (Headquarters—Port Blair): Lt-Gov. Lt-Gen. (retd) A. K. SINGH.

Chandigarh (Headquarters—Chandigarh): Administrator SHIVRAJ VISHWANATH PATIL (Governor of the Punjab *ex officio*); Chandigarh was to be incorporated into the Punjab state on 26 January 1986, but the transfer was postponed indefinitely.

Dadra and Nagar Haveli (Headquarters—Silvassa): Administrator BHUPINDER S. BHALLA.

Daman and Diu (Headquarters—Daman): Administrator BHUPINDER S. BHALLA.

Lakshadweep (Headquarters—Kavaratti): Administrator RAJESH PRASAD.

Puducherry (Capital—Puducherry): Lt-Gov. VIRENDRA KATARIA; Chief Minister THIRU. N. RANGASAMY (All India NR Congress); Legislative Assembly: 30 seats (Congress 7, All India Anna Dravida Munnetra Kazhagam 5, Dravida Munnetra Kazhagam 2 and others 16).

NATIONAL CAPITAL TERRITORY

Delhi (Headquarters—Delhi): Lt-Gov. NAJEEB JUNG; Chief Minister (vacant); following the resignation of Chief Minister Arvind Kejriwal in mid-February 2014, the capital territory was placed under presidential rule; Legislative Assembly: 70 seats (Bharatiya Janata Party 31, Aam Aadmi Party 28, Congress 8, Janata Dal (United) 1, Shiromani Akali Dal 1, independent 1); last election Dec. 2013.

Election Commission

Election Commission of India: Nirvachan Sadan, Ashoka Rd, New Delhi 110 001; tel. (11) 23717391; fax (11) 23717075; e-mail feedbackeci@gmail.com; internet eci.nic.in; f. 1950; independent; Chief Election Commr Dr SYED NASIM AHMAD ZAIDI.

Political Organizations

MAJOR NATIONAL POLITICAL ORGANIZATIONS

Bahujan Samaj Party (Majority Society Party): 12 Gurudwara Rakabganj Rd, New Delhi 110 001; internet www.bspindia.org; f. 1984; promotes the rights of the *Harijans* ('Untouchables') of India; Founder KANSHI RAM; Pres. KUMARI MAYAWATI.

Bharatiya Janata Party (BJP) (Indian People's Party): 11 Ashok Rd, New Delhi 110 001; tel. (11) 23005700; fax (11) 23005787; e-mail webmaster@bjp.org; internet www.bjp.org; f. 1980 as a breakaway group from Janata Party; right-wing Hindu party; Pres. and Chair. of Parliamentary Party RAJNATH SINGH; Gen. Secs RAM LAL, ANANTH KUMAR, THAWARCHAND GEHLOT, JAGAT P. NADDA, DHARMENDRA PRADHAN, TAPIR GAO, AMIT SHAH, VARUN GANDHI, RAJIV P. RUDDY, P. MURALIDHAR RAO; 10.5m. mems.

Communist Party of India (CPI): 15 Ajoy Bhavan, Indrajit Gupta Marg, New Delhi 110 002; tel. (11) 23235546; fax (11) 23235543; e-mail nationalcouncil@communistparty.in; internet www.communistparty.in; f. 1925; advocates the establishment of a socialist society led by the working class, and ultimately of a communist society; nine-mem. cen. secr; Leader GURUDAS DASGUPTA; Gen. Sec. S. SUDHAKAR REDDY; 486,578 mems (2004).

Communist Party of India—Marxist (CPI—M): A. K. Gopalan Bhavan, 27–29 Bhai Vir Singh Marg, New Delhi 110 001; tel. (11) 23344918; fax (11) 23747483; e-mail cc@cpim.org; internet www.cpim.org; f. 1964; est. after split in the CPI; maintains an ind. position; managed by a cen. cttee of 89 mems and a politburo of 15 mems; Leaders BUDDHADEV BHATTACHARYA, PRAKASH KARAT, SITARAM YECHURY; Gen. Sec. PRAKASH KARAT; 1,044,833 mems (2011).

Communist Party of India (Marxist-Leninist): U-90, Shakarpur, New Delhi 110 092; tel. and fax (11) 22521067; fax (11) 22442790; e-mail mail@cpiml.org; internet www.cpiml.org; f. 1969; Gen. Sec. DIPANKAR BHATTACHARYA.

Indian National Congress (Congress): 24 Akbar Rd, New Delhi 110 011; tel. (11) 23019080; fax (11) 23017047; e-mail connect@inc.in; internet www.inc.in; f. in 1885 as a forum for political debate; subsequently played an active role in the struggle for independence; following independence in 1947, the party remained the dominant force in Indian politics for three decades, under the leadership of Jawaharlal Nehru, Indira Gandhi and others; following a split in the party in 1969, a separate faction was est. under Indira Gandhi, originally known as Indian National Congress (R), then as Indian National Congress (I); name of party gradually reverted to Indian National Congress or, simply, Congress in the early to mid-1990s; Pres. SONIA GANDHI; Vice-Pres. RAHUL GANDHI; Gen. Secs MUKUL WASNIK, JANARDAN DWIVEDI, DIGVIJAYA SINGH, B. K. HARIPRASAD, MADHUSUDAN MISTRY, AJAY MAKEN, AMBIKA SONI, C. P. JOSHI, GURUDAS KAMAT, LUIZINHO FALEIRO , MOHAN PRAKASH, SHAKEEL AHMED; 35m. mems (1998).

Nationalist Congress Party (NCP): 10 Dr Bishambhar Das Marg, New Delhi 110 001; tel. (11) 23314414; fax (11) 23352112; e-mail info@ncp.org.in; internet www.ncp.org.in; f. 1999; est. as breakaway faction of Indian National Congress; split into two factions—one headed by Sharad Pawar and the other by Purno Sangma—in Jan. 2004, but was reunified in 2006; Pres. SHARAD PAWAR; Gen. Secs TARIQ ANWAR, T. P. PEETHAMBARAN MASTER, Prof. DEVI PRASAD TRIPATHI, Dr V. RAJESHWARAN, GOVINDRAO ADIK.

MAJOR REGIONAL POLITICAL ORGANIZATIONS

Aam Aadmi Party (AAP): Ground Floor, A-119, Kaushambi, Ghaziabad 201 010; tel. (971) 8500606; e-mail contact@aamaadmiparty.org; internet www.aamaadmiparty.org; f. 2012; campaigns on an anti-corruption platform; formed a minority government in the Delhi Legislative Assembly following Dec. 2013 territorial election; Leader ARVIND KEJRIWAL.

Akhil Bharat Hindu Mahasabha: Hindu Mahasabha Bhavan, Mandir Marg, New Delhi 110 001; tel. and fax (11) 23365354; e-mail info@akhilbharathindumahasabha.org; internet www.akhilbharathindumahasabha.org; f. 1915; seeks the establishment of a democratic Hindu state; Pres. CHANDRA PRAKASH KAUSHIK; Gen. Sec. MUNNA KUMAR SHARMA; 525,000 mems.

All-India Anna Dravida Munnetra Kazhagam (AIADMK) (All-India Anna Dravidian Progressive Asscn): 226 Avvai Shanmugam Salai, Roayapettah, Chennai 600 014; tel. (44) 28132266; fax (44) 28133510; e-mail aiadmk.tn@hotmail.com; internet www.aiadmkallindia.org; f. 1972; breakaway group from the DMK; Leader and Gen. Sec. JAYARAM JAYALALITHA.

All India Forward Bloc: 28 Gurudwara Rakab Ganj Rd, New Delhi 110 001; tel. and fax (11) 23714131; fax (11) 23714131; e-mail info@forwardbloc.org; internet www.forwardbloc.org; f. 1940; socialist aims, incl. nationalization of major industries, land reform and redistribution, and the establishment of a union of socialist republics through revolution; Chair. N. VELAPPAN NAIR; Gen. Sec. DEBABRATA BISWAS; 900,000 mems (1999).

All India Trinamool Congress (AITC): 30B Harish Chatterjee St, Kolkata 700 026; tel. (33) 24540881; fax (33) 24540880; e-mail aitmc@aitmc.org; internet aitmc.org; Chair. MAMATA BANERJEE; Gen. Secs MUKUL ROY.

Asom Gana Parishad (AGP) (Assam People's Council): Gopinath Bordoloi Rd, Guwahati 781 001; tel. and fax (361) 2600536; e-mail party.agp@gmail.com; internet www.asomganaparishad.org; f. 1985; draws support from All-Assam Gana Sangram Parishad and All-Assam Students' Union (Pres. SANKAR PRASAD ROY; Gen. Sec. TAPAN KUMAR GOGOI; internet www.aasu.org.in); advocates the unity of India in diversity and a united Assam; Pres. PRAFULLA KUMAR MAHANTA.

Biju Janata Dal: 6R/3, Unit 6, Forest Park, Bhubaneswar 751 006; tel. and fax (674) 2395979; e-mail president@bijujanatadal.net; internet www.bjdodisha.org.in; f. 1997; Pres. NAVEEN PATNAIK.

Dravida Munnetra Kazhagam (DMK): Anna Arivalayam, 367–369 Anna Salai, Chennai 600 018; e-mail thedmk@vsnl.com; internet www.dmk.in; f. 1949; aims at full autonomy for states (primarily Tamil Nadu) within the Union; Pres. MUTHUVEL KARUNANIDHI; Gen. Sec. K. ANBAZHAGAN; more than 4m. mems.

Indian National Lok Dal: 18 Janpath, New Delhi 110 001; e-mail inldchandigarh@gmail.com; internet indiannationallokdal.com; fmrly mem. of the National Democratic Alliance; promotes the cause of farmers and labourers of Haryana; Nat. Pres. OM PRAKASH CHAUTALA; Sec.-Gen. TELU RAM JOGI.

Jammu and Kashmir National Conference (JKNC): Mujahid Manzil, Nawa-i-Subh Complex Zero Bridge, Srinagar 190 002; tel. (194) 2452326; e-mail contact@jknc.in; internet www.jknc.in; fmrly All Jammu and Kashmir Nat. Conference; f. 1931; renamed 1939, reactivated 1975; state-based party campaigning for internal autonomy and responsible self-govt; Pres. Dr FAROOQ ABDULLAH; Gen. Sec. SHEIKH NAZIR AHMED; 1m. mems.

Janata Dal—Secular (People's Party—Secular): 5 Safdarjung Lane, New Delhi 110 003; tel. (11) 23794499; e-mail jdsecular2013@gmail.com; internet www.jds.ind.in; f. 2000 following split of Janata Dal; Pres. H. D. DEVE GOWDA; Sec.-Gen. KUNWAR DANISH ALI.

Janata Dal—United (People's Party—United): 7 Jantar Mantar Rd, New Delhi 110 001; tel. (11) 23368833; fax (11) 23368138; e-mail info@janatadalunited.org; internet www.janatadalunited.org; f. 2000; est. following split of Janata Dal; merged with Samata Party in 2003; mem. of National Democratic Alliance; advocates non-alignment, eradication of poverty, unemployment and wide disparities in wealth, and protection of minorities; Pres. SHARAD YADAV; Leader NITISH KUMAR.

Jharkhand Mukti Morcha: Bariatu Rd, Ranchi 834 008; tel. and fax (651) 2542009; aligned with national ruling coalition, the United Progressive Alliance; Leader SHIBU SOREN.

Lok Jan Shakti Party (LJSP): 12 Janpath, Firoz Shah Marg, New Delhi, 110 001; tel. (11) 23015249; fax (11) 23017681; e-mail lokjanshaktiparty@gmail.com; internet www.lokjanshaktiparty.org.in; f. 2000; est. as breakaway faction of Janata Dal—United; left-wing; Pres. RAM VILAS PASWAN; Sec. Gen. ABDUL KHALIQ.

Pattali Makkal Katchi (PMK): 63 Nattumuthu Naicken St, Teynampet, Chennai 600 118; tel. 9842775152; e-mail arunramv@yahoo.co.in; internet www.pmkparty.in; f. 1989; Tamil; Leader Dr ANBUMANI RAMDOSS; Pres. G. K. MANI.

Rashtriya Janata Dal (RJD) (National People's Party): 13 V. P. House, Rafi Marg, New Delhi 110 001; tel. (11) 23357182; e-mail info@rjd.co.in; internet www.rjd.co.in; f. 1997; est. by breakaway mems of Janata Dal; Leader LALU PRASAD YADAV.

Rashtriya Lok Dal: 12 Tughlaq Rd, New Delhi 110 011; tel. (11) 23792040; fax (11) 23792037; e-mail rld@rashtriyalokdal.com; internet rashtriyalokdal.com; Pres. AJIT SINGH.

Revolutionary Socialist Party: 17 Feroz Shah Rd, New Delhi 110 001; tel. (11) 23782167; fax (11) 23782342; f. 1940; Marxist-Leninist; Leader ABANI ROY; Gen. Sec. T. J. CHANDRACHOODAN.

Samajwadi Party (Socialist Party): 18 Copernicus Lane, New Delhi; tel. (11) 23386842; fax (11) 23382430; e-mail contact@samajwadipartyindia.com; internet www.samajwadiparty.in; f. 1991; Pres. MULAYAM SINGH YADAV.

Shiromani Akali Dal (SAD): Blk 6, Madhya Marg, Sector 28, Chandigarh; e-mail contact@shiromaniakalidal.org.in; internet www.shiromaniakalidal.org.in; f. 1920; largest of six splinter groups, each of which claims to be the 'real' Akali Dal; Pres. (Shiromani Akali Dal—Badal) SUKHBIR SINGH BADAL; Sec.-Gen. SUKHDEV SINGH DHINDSA.

Shiv Sena (Army of Shiv): Shiv Sena Bhavan, Ram Ganesh Gadkari Chowk, Dadar, Mumbai 400 028; tel. (22) 24328181; e-mail mazamaharashtra@shivsena.org; internet www.shivsena.org; f. 1966; militant Hindu group; Bharatiya Kamgar Sena (Indian Workers' Army) affiliated to the party; Pres. UDDHAV THACKERAY.

Sikkim Democratic Front: Upper Deorali, Gangtok, East Sikkim; internet sikkimdemocraticfront.org; f. 1993; Pres. Dr PAWAN KUMAR CHAMLING.

Telangana Rashtra Samithi: Telangana Bhavan, Rd 10, Banjara Hills, Hyderabad 500 034; f. 2001; campaigns for the creation of a new Telangana state through the bifurcation of Andhra Pradesh; Pres. K. CHANDRASEKHAR RAO.

Telugu Desam (Telugu Nation): NTR Bhavan, Rd 2, Banjara Hills, Hyderabad 500 034; tel. (40) 30699999; fax (40) 23542108; e-mail contact@telugudesam.org; internet www.telugudesam.org; f. 1983; state-based party (Andhra Pradesh); Pres. N. CHANDRABABU NAIDU; 8m. mems.

Diplomatic Representation

EMBASSIES AND HIGH COMMISSIONS IN INDIA

Afghanistan: 5/50F Shanti Path, Chanakyapuri, New Delhi 110 021; tel. (11) 24103331; fax (11) 26875439; e-mail delhi@afghanistan-mfa.net; internet www.afghanembassy.in; Ambassador SHAIDA MOHAMMAD ABDALI.

Albania: B2, West End, New Delhi 110 021; tel. and fax (11) 46108285; e-mail embassy.delhi@mfa.gov.al; Ambassador FATOS KERCIKU.

Algeria: 2/2 Shanti Niketan, New Delhi 110 021; tel. (11) 24117585; fax (11) 24117590; e-mail embalgindia@hotmail.com; internet www.embalgindia.com; Ambassador MOHAMMED HACENE ECHARIF.

Angola: 5 Poorvi Marg, Vasant Vihar, New Delhi 110 057; tel. (11) 26146195; fax (11) 26146184; e-mail angolaembassyindia@gmail.com; internet www.angolaembassyindia.com; Ambassador MANUEL EDUARDO DOS SANTOS E SILVA BRAVO.

Argentina: A-2/6 Vasant Vihar, New Delhi 110 057; tel. (11) 41661982; fax (11) 41661988; e-mail embargentindi@yahoo.com; Ambassador RAUL IGNACIO GUASTAVINO.

Armenia: D-133 Anand Niketan, New Delhi 110 057; tel. (11) 24112851; fax (11) 24112853; e-mail armemb@vsnl.com; internet www.armenian.co.in; Ambassador ARA HAKOBYAN.

Australia: 1/50G Shanti Path, Chanakyapuri, POB 5210, New Delhi 110 021; tel. (11) 41399900; fax (11) 41494490; e-mail austhighcom.newdelhi@dfat.gov.au; internet www.india.embassy.gov.au; High Commissioner PATRICK MICHAEL SUCKLING.

Austria: EP-13 Chandragupta Marg, Chanakyapuri, New Delhi 110 021; tel. (11) 24192700; fax (11) 26886929; e-mail new-delhi-ob@bmeia.gv.at; internet www.aussenministerium.at/newdelhi; Ambassador BERNHARD WRABETZ.

Azerbaijan: 41 Paschimi Marg, Vasant Vihar, New Delhi 110 057; tel. (11) 24652228; fax (11) 24652227; e-mail newdelhi@mission.mfa.gov.az; internet www.azembassy.in; Ambassador IBRAHIM ASSAD OGLU HAJIYEV.

Bahrain: 4 Olof Palme Marg, Vasant Vihar, New Delhi 110 057; tel. (11) 26154153; fax (11) 26146731; e-mail bahrainembindia@yahoo.com; internet www.bahrainembassyindia.com; Ambassador Maj. Gen. TARIQ MUBARAK BIN DAINEH.

Bangladesh: EP-39 Dr S. Radhakrishnan Marg, Chanakyapuri, New Delhi 110 021; tel. (11) 24121389; fax (11) 26878953; e-mail bdhcdelhi@gmail.com; internet www.bhcdelhi.org; High Commissioner TARIQ AHMAD KARIM.

Belarus: F-6/8B Vasant Vihar, New Delhi 110 057; tel. (11) 40529338; fax (11) 40529336; e-mail india@mfa.gov.by; internet india.mfa.gov.by/eng; Ambassador VITALY A. PRIMA.

Belgium: 50N Shanti Path, Chanakyapuri, New Delhi 110 021; tel. (11) 42428000; fax (11) 42428002; e-mail newdelhi@diplobel.fed.be; internet www.diplomatie.be/newdelhi; Ambassador PIERRE VAESEN.

Benin: K-26, Jangpura, New Delhi 110 014; tel. (11) 43074470; fax (11) 43074472; e-mail ambabenindelhi@yahoo.fr; internet www.beninembassy.in; Ambassador ANDRE SANRA.

Bhutan: Chandragupta Marg, Chanakyapuri, New Delhi 110 021; tel. (11) 26889807; fax (11) 26876710; e-mail bhutan@vsnl.com; Ambassador Maj.-Gen. VETSOP NAMGYEL.

Bolivia: A-2/7 Ground Floor, Vasant Vihar, New Delhi 110 057; tel. (11) 46060934; fax (11) 46060935; e-mail coco.cardenas@gmail.com; Ambassador JORGE CÁRDENAS ROBLES.

Bosnia and Herzegovina: E-9/11 Vasant Vihar, New Delhi 110 057; tel. (11) 41662481; fax (11) 41662482; e-mail abhind@gmail.com; Ambassador Dr SABIT SUBASIC.

Botswana: F-8/3 Vasant Vihar, New Delhi 110 057; tel. (11) 46537000; fax (11) 46036191; e-mail botind@gov.bw; internet www.botswanahighcom.in; High Commissioner LESEGO ETHEL MOTSUMI.

Brazil: 8 Aurangzeb Rd, New Delhi 110 011; tel. (11) 23017301; fax (11) 23793684; e-mail brasindi@eth.net; internet www.brazilembassy.in; Ambassador CARLOS SERGIO SOBRAL DUARTE.

Brunei: 4 Poorvi Marg, Vasant Vihar, New Delhi 110 057; tel. (11) 26148340; fax (11) 26142101; e-mail newdelhi.india@mfa.gov.bn; High Commissioner Haji SIDEK BIN Haji ALI.

Bulgaria: 16/17 Chandragupta Marg, Chanakyapuri, New Delhi 110 021; tel. (11) 26115549; fax (11) 26876190; e-mail embassy.delhi@mfa.bg; internet www.mfa.bg/embassies/india; Ambassador BORISLAV KOSTOV.

Burkina Faso: F2/4 Vasant Vihar, New Delhi 110 057; tel. (11) 26140641; fax (11) 26140630; e-mail embassy@burkinafasoindia.org; internet www.burkinafasoindia.org; Ambassador IDRISS RAOUA OUEDRAOGO.

Burundi: B-4/1, Vasant Vihar, New Delhi 110 057; tel. (11) 46151947; fax (11) 49503170; e-mail ambabudelhi@yahoo.fr; internet www.burundiembassy.in; Ambassador RUBUKA ALOYS.

Cambodia: W-112 Greater Kailash Part II, New Delhi 110 048; tel. (11) 29214435; fax (11) 29214438; e-mail camemb.ind@mfa.gov.kh; Ambassador YOUS MAKANA.

Canada: 7/8 Shanti Path, Chanakyapuri, New Delhi 110 021; tel. (11) 41782000; fax (11) 41782020; e-mail delhi@international.gc.ca; internet www.india.gc.ca; High Commissioner STEWART BECK.

Chile: A-16/1 Vasant Vihar, New Delhi 110 057; tel. (11) 43100400; fax (11) 43100431; e-mail embassy@chileindia.com; internet chileabroad.gov.cl/india; Ambassador CRISTIAN BARROS MELET.

China, People's Republic: 50D Shanti Path, Chanakyapuri, New Delhi 110 021; tel. (11) 26112345; fax (11) 26885486; e-mail chinaemb_in@mfa.gov.cn; internet in.chineseembassy.org; Ambassador WEI WEI.

Colombia: 85 Poorvi Marg, Vasant Vihar, New Delhi 110 057; tel. (11) 43202100; fax (11) 43202199; e-mail eindia@cancilleria.gov.co; internet india.embajada.gov.co; Ambassador MONICA LANZETTA MUTIS.

Congo, Democratic Republic: B-3/61 Safdarjung Enclave, New Delhi 110 029; tel. (11) 26183354; fax (11) 41663152; e-mail poliad@drcembassyinindia.org; internet www.drcembassyinindia.org; Ambassador BALUMUENE NKUNA FRANCOIS.

Costa Rica: C-25, 3rd Floor, Anand Niketan, New Delhi 110 021; tel. (11) 41080810; fax (11) 41080809; e-mail embajadacostarica.india@gmail.com; Ambassador (vacant).

Côte d'Ivoire: 63 Poorvi Marg, Vasant Vihar, New Delhi 110 057; tel. (11) 46043000; fax (11) 46043031; e-mail embassy@amb2ci-inde.org; internet www.amb2ci-inde.org; Ambassador SAINY TIEMELE.

Croatia: A-15 West End, New Delhi 110 021; tel. (11) 41663101; fax (11) 24116873; e-mail croemb.new-delhi@mvpei.hr; Chargé d'affaires a.i. MAJA PLANCIC LELAS.

Cuba: W-124A Greater Kailash Part I, New Delhi 110 048; tel. (11) 29242467; fax (11) 26232469; e-mail consular@embacubaindia.com; internet www.cubadiplomatica.cu/india; Ambassador ABELARDO RAFAEL CUETO SOSA.

Cyprus: D-67 Jor Bagh, New Delhi 110 003; tel. (11) 26111156; fax (11) 26111160; e-mail delhihc@mfa.gov.cy; internet www.mfa.gov.cy/mfa/highcom/highcom_newdelhi.nsf; High Commissioner MARIA MICHAEL.

Czech Republic: 50M Niti Marg, Chanakyapuri, New Delhi 110 021; tel. (11) 24155200; fax (11) 24155270; e-mail newdelhi@embassy.mzv.cz; internet www.mfa.cz/newdelhi; Ambassador MILOSLAV STAŠEK.

Denmark: 11 Golf Links, New Delhi 110 003; tel. (11) 42090700; fax (11) 24602019; e-mail delamb@um.dk; internet www.ambnewdelhi.um.dk; Ambassador FREDDY SVANE.

Djibouti: E-12/6 Vasant Vihar, New Delhi 110 057; tel. (11) 41354491; fax (11) 41354490; e-mail embassyofdjibouti@airtelmail.in; Ambassador YOUSSOUF OMAR DOUALEH.

Dominican Republic: 4 Munirka Marg, Vasant Vihar, New Delhi 110 057; tel. (11) 46015000; fax (11) 46015004; e-mail info@dr-embassy-india.com; internet www.dr-embassy-india.com; Ambassador FRANK HANS DANNENBERG CASTELLANOS.

Ecuador: B-9/1A Vasant Vihar, New Delhi 110 057; tel. (11) 46011801; fax (11) 46011804; e-mail eecuindia@mmrree.gov.ec; internet www.embassyofecuadortoindia.com; Ambassador CARLOS ABAD ORTIZ.

Egypt: 1/50M Niti Marg, Chanakyapuri, New Delhi 110 021; tel. (11) 26114096; fax (11) 26885355; e-mail india_emb@mfa.gov.eg; internet www.mfa.gov.eg/english/embassies/egyptian_embassy_india/pages/default.aspx; Ambassador KHALED EL-BAKLY.

El Salvador: E-5/1 F-48 Munirka Marg, Vasant Vihar, New Delhi 110 057; tel. (11) 46088400; fax (11) 46011688; e-mail esembassy@gmail.com; internet embajadaindia.rree.gob.sv; Ambassador GUILLERMO RUBIO FUNES.

Eritrea: C-7/9 Vasant Vihar, New Delhi 110 057; tel. (11) 26146336; fax (11) 26146337; e-mail eriindia@yahoo.co.in; internet www.eritreaembindia.com; Ambassador ALEM TSEHAYE WOLDEMARIAM.

Estonia: C-15 Malcha Marg, Chanakyapuri, New Delhi 110 021; tel. (11) 49488650; fax (11) 49488651; e-mail Embassy.New-Delhi@mfa.ee; internet www.newdelhi.vm.ee; Ambassador VILJAR LUBI.

Ethiopia: 7/50G Satya Marg, Chanakyapuri, New Delhi 110 021; tel. (11) 26119513; fax (11) 26875731; e-mail delethem@yahoo.com; internet www.ethiopiaembassy.in; Ambassador GENET ZEWDIE.

Fiji: C-1/10, Ground Floor, Vasant Vihar, New Delhi 110 057; tel. (11) 46564574; fax (11) 46564573; e-mail info@fijihc-india.in; internet www.fijihc-india.in; High Commissioner YOGESH KARAN.

Finland: E-3 Nyaya Marg, Chanakyapuri, New Delhi 110 021; tel. (11) 41497500; fax (11) 41497555; e-mail sanomat.nde@formin.fi; internet www.finland.org.in; Ambassador AAPO PÖLHÖ.

France: 2/50E Shanti Path, Chanakyapuri, New Delhi 110 021; tel. (11) 24196100; fax (11) 43196119; e-mail webmaster@france-in-india.org; internet www.ambafrance-in.org; Ambassador FRANÇOIS RICHIER.

Gabon: E-84 Paschimi Marg, Vasant Vihar, New Delhi 110 057; tel. (11) 41012513; fax (11) 41012512; e-mail gabonambainde@yahoo.fr; internet www.gabonembassynewdelhi.com; Ambassador DESIRE KOUMBA.

The Gambia: 7 Olof Palme Marg, 1st Floor, Vasant Vihar, New Delhi 110 057; tel. (11) 46120472; fax (11) 46120471; e-mail gamhighcomdel@hotmail.com; Ambassador DEMBO BADJIE.

Georgia: 115 Jor Bagh, New Delhi 110 003; tel. (11) 47078602; fax (11) 47078603; e-mail delhi.emb@mfa.gov.ge; internet india.mfa.gov.ge; Ambassador ZURAB KACHKACHISHVILI.

Germany: 6/50G Shanti Path, Chanakyapuri, POB 613, New Delhi 110 021; tel. (11) 44199199; fax (11) 26873117; e-mail info@new-delhi.diplo.de; internet www.new-delhi.diplo.de; Ambassador MICHAEL STEINER.

Ghana: 50N Satya Marg, Chanakyapuri, New Delhi 110 021; tel. (11) 24193500; fax (11) 24193525; e-mail ghcindia@vsnl.net; internet www.ghana-mission.co.in; High Commissioner ROBERT TACHIE-MENSON.

Greece: EP-32 Dr S. Radhakrishnan Marg, Chanakyapuri, New Delhi 110 021; tel. (11) 26880700; fax (11) 26888010; e-mail gremb.del@mfa.gr; internet www.greeceinindia.com; Ambassador IOANNIS E. RAPTAKIS.

Guinea-Bissau: 26 Poorvi Marg, Vasant Vihar, New Delhi 110 057; tel. (11) 46540211; fax (11) 46544440; e-mail ambaguineedelhi@gmail.com; Ambassador MALAM SAMBU.

Guyana: E-7/19 Vasant Vihar, New Delhi 110 057; tel. (11) 41669717; fax (11) 41669714; e-mail hcommguy.del@gmail.com; High Commissioner JAIRAM RONALD GAJRAJ.

Holy See: 50C Niti Marg, Chanakyapuri, New Delhi 110 021 (Apostolic Nunciature); tel. (11) 42492300; fax (11) 26874286; e-mail nuntius@apostolicnunciatureindia.com; internet www.apostolicnunciatureindia.com; Nuncio Most Rev. SALVATORE PENNACCHIO (Titular Archbishop of Montemarano).

Hungary: Plot 2, 50M Niti Marg, Chanakyapuri, New Delhi 110 021; tel. (11) 26114737; fax (11) 26886742; e-mail mission.del@kum.hu; internet www.mfa.gov.hu/emb/newdelhi; Ambassador Dr JÁNOS TERÉNYI.

Iceland: 10 Munirka Marg, Vasant Vihar, New Delhi 110 057; tel. (11) 43530300; fax (11) 43530311; e-mail emb.newdelhi@mfa.is; internet www.iceland.org/in; Ambassador GUDMUNDUR EIRIKSSON.

Indonesia: 50A Kautilya Marg, Chanakyapuri, New Delhi 110 021; tel. (11) 26118642; fax (11) 26886763; e-mail administrasi@indonesianembassy.in; internet www.kemlu.go.id/newdelhi; Ambassador RIZALI WILMAR INDRAKESUMA.

Iran: 5 Barakhamba Rd, New Delhi 110 001; tel. (11) 4247786; fax (11) 23325493; e-mail info@iran-embassy.org.in; internet www.iran-embassy.org.in; Ambassador GHOLAMREZA ANSARI.

Iraq: A-15/14 Vasant Vihar, New Delhi 110 057; tel. (11) 26150081; fax (11) 26150083; e-mail dlh1emb@iraqmfamail.com; Ambassador AHMAD TAHSIN AHMAD BERWARI.

Ireland: C-17, Malcha Marg, Chanakyapuri, New Delhi 110 021; tel. (11) 49403200; fax (11) 40591898; e-mail newdelhiembassy@dfa.ie; internet www.irelandindia.com; Ambassador FEILIM MCLAUGHLIN.

Israel: 3 Aurangzeb Rd, New Delhi 110 011; tel. (11) 30414500; fax (11) 30414555; e-mail info@newdelhi.mfa.gov.il; internet delhi.mfa.gov.il; Ambassador ALON USHPIZ.

Italy: 50E Chandragupta Marg, Chanakyapuri, New Delhi 110 021; tel. (11) 26114355; fax (11) 26873889; e-mail ambasciata.newdelhi@esteri.it; internet www.ambnewdelhi.esteri.it; Ambassador DANIELE MANCINI.

Japan: Plots 4–5, 50G Shanti Path, Chanakyapuri, New Delhi 110 021; tel. (11) 26876581; fax (11) 26885587; e-mail jpembjic@nd.mofa.go.jp; internet www.in.emb-japan.go.jp; Ambassador TAKESHI YAGI.

Jordan: 30 Golf Links, New Delhi 110 003; tel. (11) 24653318; fax (11) 24653353; e-mail jordan@jordanembassyindia.org; internet www.jordanembassyindia.org; Ambassador HASSAN MAHMOUD MUHAMMAD AL-JAWARNEH.

Kazakhstan: 61 Poorvi Marg, Vasant Vihar, New Delhi 110 057; tel. (11) 46007700; fax (11) 46007701; e-mail office@kazembassy.in; internet www.kazembassy.in; Ambassador DOULAT KUANYSHAEV.

Kenya: D-1/27 Vasant Vihar, New Delhi 110 057; tel. (11) 26146537; fax (11) 26146550; e-mail info@kenyahicom-delhi.com; internet www.kenyahicom-delhi.com; High Commissioner FLORENCE IMISA WECHE.

Korea, Democratic People's Republic: E-455 Greater Kailash Part II, New Delhi 110 048; tel. (11) 29219644; fax (11) 29219645; e-mail dprk194899@yahoo.com; Ambassador PAK KYONG SON.

Korea, Republic: 9 Chandragupta Marg, Chanakyapuri Ext., New Delhi 110 021; tel. (11) 42007000; fax (11) 26884840; e-mail india_visa@mofa.go.kr; internet ind.mofa.go.kr; Ambassador LEE JOON-GYU.

Kuwait: 5A Shanti Path, Chanakyapuri, New Delhi 110 021; tel. (11) 24100791; fax (11) 26873516; e-mail new_delhi@mofa.gov.kw; internet www.kuwaitembassy.in; Ambassador SAMI MOHAMMAD AL-SULAIMAN.

Kyrgyzstan: 78 Poorvi Marg, Vasant Vihar, New Delhi 110 057; tel. (11) 26149582; fax (11) 24118009; e-mail delhi@kgzembind.in; internet www.kgzembind.in; Chargé d'affaires a.i. EVGENY KABLUKOV.

Laos: A-104/7 Parmanand Estate, Maharani Bagh, New Delhi 110 065; tel. (11) 41327352; fax (11) 41327353; e-mail boualyrone_delhi@yahoo.com; Ambassador THONGPHANH SYACKHAPHOM.

Lebanon: H-1 Anand Niketan, New Delhi 110 021; tel. (11) 24110919; fax (11) 24110818; e-mail lebemb@bol.net.in; Ambassador WAJIB ABDEL SAMAD.

Lesotho: B-8/19 Vasant Vihar, New Delhi 110 057; tel. (11) 41660713; fax (11) 26141636; e-mail lesotho.newdelhi@gov.ls; Chargé d'affaires a.i. BOTHATA TSIKOANE.

Libya: 22 Golf Links, New Delhi 110 003; tel. (11) 24697717; fax (11) 24633005; e-mail libya_bu_ind@yahoo.com; Ambassador ALI ABD AL-AZIZ AL-ISAWI.

Lithuania: D-129 C-93 Anand Niketan, New Delhi 110 021; tel. (11) 43132200; fax (11) 43132222; e-mail amb.in@urm.lt; internet in.mfa.lt; Ambassador LAIMONAS TALAT KELPŠA.

Luxembourg: 84 Jor Bagh, New Delhi 110 003; tel. (11) 49986600; fax (11) 41525201; e-mail newdelhi.amb@mae.etat.lu; internet newdelhi.mae.lu; Ambassador GASTON STRONCK.

Macedonia, former Yugoslav republic: K-80A Hauz Khaz Enclave, New Delhi 110 016; tel. (11) 46142603; fax (11) 46142604; e-mail embassy.macedonia@gmail.com; internet www.macedoniaindia.com; Ambassador SLOBODAN TASHOVSKI.

Madagascar: 781 Nikka Singh Block, Asian Games Village, New Delhi 110 049; tel. (11) 41067747; fax (11) 66173222; e-mail contact@madagascar-embassy.in; Chargé d'affaires a.i. MARIE LEONTINE RAZANADRASOA.

Malawi: C-6/11, Vasant Vihar, New Delhi 110 057; tel. (11) 26706000; fax (11) 26706010; e-mail malawihcindia@gmail.com; internet www.malawi-india.org; High Commissioner Dr PERKS M. LIGOYA.

Malaysia: 50M Satya Marg, Chanakyapuri, New Delhi 110 021; tel. (11) 26111291; fax (11) 26881538; e-mail maldelhi@kln.gov.my; internet www.kln.gov.my/perwakilan/newdelhi; High Commissioner Datuk NAIMUN ASHAKLI MOHAMMAD.

Maldives: B-2 Anand Niketan, New Delhi 110 021; tel. (11) 41435701; fax (11) 41435709; e-mail admin@maldiveshighcom.in; internet www.maldiveshighcom.in; High Commissioner MOHAMED NASEER.

Mali: A-2/29 Safdarjung Enclave, New Delhi 110 029; tel. (11) 41090624; fax (11) 41090620; e-mail info@maliembassy.co.in; internet www.maliembassy.co.in; Ambassador OUSMANE TANDIA.

Malta: N-60 Panchsheel Park, New Delhi 110 017; tel. (11) 47674900; fax (11) 47674949; e-mail maltahighcommission.newdelhi@gov.mt; High Commissioner JOHN AQUILINA.

Mauritius: EP-41 Jesus and Mary Marg, Chanakyapuri, New Delhi 110 021; tel. (11) 24102161; fax (11) 24102194; e-mail mhcnd@bol.net.in; High Commissioner ARYE KUMAR JAGESSUR.

Mexico: C-8 Anand Niketan, New Delhi 110 021; tel. (11) 24107182; fax (11) 24117193; e-mail contact@embmexin.com; internet embamex.sre.gob.mx/india/index.php/en; Ambassador JAIME NUALART.

Mongolia: 34 Archbishop Makarios Marg, New Delhi 110 003; tel. (11) 24631728; fax (11) 24633240; e-mail mongemb@vsnl.net; Ambassador SANJAASÜRENGIIN BAYARA.

Morocco: 46 Sunder Nagar, New Delhi 110 003; tel. (11) 24355582; fax (11) 24355579; e-mail ambassador@moroccoembassyin.org; internet www.moroccoembassyin.org; Ambassador LARBI MOUKHARIQ.

Mozambique: B-3/24 Vasant Vihar, New Delhi 110 057; tel. (11) 26156663; fax (11) 26156665; e-mail hcmozind@hclinfinet.com; High Commissioner JOSÉ MARÍA DA SILVA VIEIRA MORAIS.

Myanmar: 3/50F Nyaya Marg, Chanakyapuri, New Delhi 110 021; tel. (11) 24678822; fax (11) 24678824; e-mail myandelhi@gmail.com; internet myanmedelhi.com; Ambassador AUNG KHIN SOE.

Namibia: E-86 Paschimi Marg, Vasant Vihar, New Delhi 110 057; tel. (11) 26140389; fax (11) 26146120; e-mail nam@nhcdelhi.com; internet www.nhcdelhi.com; Ambassador PIUS DUNAISKI.

Nepal: Barakhamba Rd, New Delhi 110 001; tel. (11) 23327361; fax (11) 23329647; e-mail mail@nepalembassy.in; internet www.nepalembassy.in; Chargé d'affaires a.i. KHAGA NATH ADHIKARI.

Netherlands: 6/50F Shanti Path, Chanakyapuri, New Delhi 110 021; tel. (11) 24197600; fax (11) 24197710; e-mail nde@minbuza.nl; internet india.nlembassy.org; Ambassador ALPHONSUS H. M. STOELINGA.

New Zealand: Sir Edmund Hillary Marg, Chanakyapuri, New Delhi 110 021; tel. (11) 26883170; fax (11) 26883165; e-mail nzhcindia@gmail.com; internet www.nzembassy.com/india; High Commissioner JAN HENDERSON.

Nigeria: EP-4 Chandragupta Marg, Chanakyapuri, New Delhi 110 021; tel. (11) 24122142; fax (11) 24122138; e-mail nhcnder@nigeriahighcommissionindia.org; internet www.nigeriahighcommissionindia.org; High Commissioner NDUBUISI VITUS AMAKU.

Norway: 50C Shanti Path, Chanakyapuri, New Delhi 110 021; tel. (11) 41779200; fax (11) 41680145; e-mail emb.newdelhi@mfa.no; internet www.norwayemb.org.in; Ambassador EIVIND S. HOMME.

Oman: EP-10/11 Chandragupta Marg, Chankyapuri, New Delhi 110 021; tel. (11) 26885622; fax (11) 26885621; e-mail newdelhi@mofa.gov.om; internet www.omanembassy.in; Ambassador Sheikh HAMED BIN SAIF BIN ABDUL AZIZ AL-RAWAHI.

Pakistan: 2/50G Shanti Path, Chanakyapuri, New Delhi 110 021; tel. (11) 26110601; fax (11) 26872339; e-mail pahicnewdelhi@mofa.gov.pk; High Commissioner ABDUL BASIT.

Panama: 3D Palam Marg, Vasant Vihar, New Delhi 110 057; tel. (11) 26148268; fax (11) 26148261; e-mail panaind@bol.net.in; Ambassador JULIO DE LA GUARDIA ARROCHA.

Papua New Guinea: B-2/19 Vasant Vihar, 1st Floor, New Delhi 110 057; tel. (11) 46012813; fax (11) 46012812; e-mail kundund@yahoo.com; internet www.pnghcdelhi.in; High Commissioner TARCISIUS A. ERI.

Paraguay: B-11 Vasant Marg, Vasant Vihar, New Delhi 110 057; tel. (11) 42705671; fax (11) 42705672; e-mail delhi@embaparindia.in; internet www.paraguayembassy.in; Ambassador GENARO VICENTE PAPPALARDO AYALA.

Peru: F-3/16, Vasant Vihar, New Delhi 110 057; tel. (11) 46163333; fax (11) 46163301; e-mail admin@embassyperuindia.in; internet www.embassyperuindia.in; Ambassador JAVIER MANUAL PAULINICH VELARDE.

Philippines: 50N Nyaya Marg, Chanakyapuri, New Delhi 110 021; tel. (11) 26889091; fax (11) 26876401; e-mail newdelhipe@bol.net.in; internet www.newdelhipe.com; Ambassador BENITO B. VALERIANO.

Poland: 50M Shanti Path, Chanakyapuri, New Delhi 110 021; tel. (11) 41496900; fax (11) 26871914; e-mail info@newdelhi.polemb.net; internet www.newdelhi.polemb.net; Ambassador Prof. PIOTR KLODKOWSKI.

Portugal: 4 Panchsheel Marg, Chanakyapuri, New Delhi 110 021; tel. (11) 46071001; fax (11) 4607103; e-mail embassy@portugal-india.com; internet www.portugal-india.com/en; Ambassador JORGE ROZA DE OLIVEIRA.

Qatar: EP-31A Chandragupta Marg, Chanakyapuri, New Delhi 110 021; tel. (11) 26117988; fax (11) 26886080; e-mail newdelhi@mofa.gov.qa; Ambassador AHMED IBRAHIM ABDULLA AL-ABDULLA.

Romania: D-6/6 Vasant Vihar, New Delhi 110 057; tel. (11) 26140447; fax (11) 26140611; e-mail newdelhi@mae.ro; internet www.newdelhi.mae.ro; Chargé d'affaires a.i. RADU OCTAVIAN DOBRE.

Russia: Shanti Path, Chanakyapuri, New Delhi 110 021; tel. (11) 26873799; fax (11) 26876823; e-mail emb@rusembassy.in; internet www.india.mid.ru; Ambassador ALEXANDER M. KADAKIN.

Rwanda: 41 Paschimi Marg, Vasant Vihar, New Delhi 110 057; tel. (11) 28661604; fax (11) 28661605; e-mail rwandaembassy@yahoo.com; internet india.embassy.gov.rw; High Commissioner ERNEST RWAMUCYO.

Saudi Arabia: 2 Paschimi Marg, Vasant Vihar, New Delhi 110 057; tel. (11) 43244444; fax (11) 26144244; e-mail inemb@mofa.gov.sa; internet www.saudiembassy.org.in; Ambassador SAUD BIN MOHAMMED AL-SATI.

Senegal: E-14/2 Vasant Vihar, New Delhi 110 057; tel. (11) 26734400; fax (11) 26142422; e-mail embassy@senindia.org; internet www.embsenindia.org; Ambassador AMADOU MOUSTAPHA DIOUF.

Serbia: 3/50G Niti Marg, Chanakyapuri, New Delhi 110 021; tel. (11) 26873661; fax (11) 26885535; e-mail embassyofserbianewdelhi@hotmail.com; internet www.newdelhi.mfa.gov.rs; Ambassador JOVAN MIRILOVIĆ.

Seychelles: F-4 Anand Niketan, New Delhi 110 021; tel. (11) 26658853; fax (11) 26658852; e-mail seychelleshighcommission@gmail.com; High Commissioner WAVEN WILLIAM.

Singapore: E-6 Chandragupta Marg, Chanakyapuri, New Delhi 110 021; tel. (11) 46000800; fax (11) 46016413; e-mail singhc_del@sgmfa.gov.sg; internet www.mfa.gov.sg/newdelhi; High Commissioner LIM THUAN KUAN.

Slovakia: 50M Niti Marg, Chanakyapuri, New Delhi 110 021; tel. (11) 26889071; fax (11) 26877941; e-mail emb.delhi@mzv.sk; internet www.newdelhi.mfa.sk; Ambassador ŽIGMUND BERTÓK.

Slovenia: A-5/4, Vasant Vihar, New Delhi 110 057; tel. (11) 41662891; fax (11) 41662895; e-mail vnd@gov.si; internet newdelhi.embassy.si; Ambassador DARJA BAVDAZ KURET.

Somalia: D-47, Anand Niketan, New Delhi 110 021; tel. (11) 28034177; fax (11) 45510250; e-mail webmaster@somaligov.net; internet www.india.somaligov.net; Ambassador EBYAN LADANE.

South Africa: B-18 Vasant Marg, Vasant Vihar, New Delhi 110 057; tel. (11) 26149411; fax (11) 26148605; e-mail highcommissioner@sahc-india.com; internet southafricainindia.wordpress.com; High Commissioner FRANCE KOSINYANE MORULE, (vacant).

South Sudan: Farm House, 50D Radhey Mohan Dr., Bandh Rd, Jonapur, New Delhi 110 047; tel. (11) 66545656; fax (11) 66545666; e-mail embassyssindia@gmail.com; Ambassador DANIEL PETER OTHOL.

Spain: 12 Prithviraj Rd, New Delhi 110 011; tel. (11) 41293000; fax (11) 41293020; e-mail emb.nuevadelhi@maec.es; Ambassador GUSTAVO MANUEL DE ARISTEGUI Y SAN ROMAN.

Sri Lanka: 27 Kautilya Marg, Chanakyapuri, New Delhi 110 021; tel. (11) 23010201; fax (11) 23793604; e-mail lankacomnd@mea.gov.lk; internet www.slhcindia.org; High Commissioner PRASAD KARIYAWASAM.

Sudan: Plot 3, Shanti Path, Chanakyapuri, New Delhi 110 021; tel. (11) 26873785; fax (11) 26883758; e-mail admin@sudanembassyindia.org; internet www.sudanembassyindia.org; Ambassador HASSAN EISA EL TALIB.

Suriname: A-15/27, Vasant Vihar, New Delhi 110 057; tel. (11) 26150153; fax (11) 26150150; e-mail amb.india@foreignaffairs.gov.sr; internet www.embsurnd.com; Ambassador AASHNA WANDANI RADHA KANHAI.

Sweden: 4–5 Nyaya Marg, Chanakyapuri, New Delhi 110 021; tel. (11) 44197100; fax (11) 44197101; e-mail ambassaden.new-delhi@foreign.ministry.se; internet www.swedenabroad.se/newdelhi; Ambassador HARALD SANDBERG.

Switzerland: Nyaya Marg, Chanakyapuri, New Delhi 110 021; tel. (11) 49959500; fax (11) 49959509; e-mail ndh.vertretung@eda.admin.ch; internet www.eda.admin.ch/newdelhi; Ambassador LINUS VON CASTELMUR.

Syria: D-5/8 Vasant Vihar, New Delhi 110 057; tel. (11) 26140233; fax (11) 26143107; e-mail embsyriadel@rediffmail.com; Ambassador RIAD KAMEL ABBAS.

Tajikistan: E-13/2 Vasant Vihar, New Delhi 110 057; tel. and fax (11) 26154282; fax 26154282; e-mail tajembindia@gmail.com; internet www.tajikembassy.in; Ambassador SAIDOV SAIDBEG BOYKHONOVICH.

Tanzania: EP-15C Chanakyapuri, New Delhi 110 021; tel. (11) 24122864; fax (11) 24122862; e-mail info@tanzrepdelhi.com; internet www.tanzrepdelhi.com; High Commissioner JOHN W. H. KIJAZI.

Thailand: D-1/3 Vasant Vihar, New Delhi 110 057; tel. (11) 26150130; fax (11) 26150128; e-mail thaidel@mfa.go.th; internet www.thaiemb.org.in; Ambassador CHALIT MANITYAKUL.

Trinidad and Tobago: B-3/26 Vasant Vihar, New Delhi 110 057; tel. (11) 46007500; fax (11) 46007505; e-mail info@hctt.in; internet www.hctt.net; High Commissioner CHANDRADATH SINGH.

Tunisia: B-1/2 Vasant Vihar, New Delhi 110 057; tel. (11) 26145346; fax (11) 26145301; e-mail tunisiaembassy@airtelbroadband.in; Ambassador TAREK AZOUZ.

Turkey: 50N Nyaya Marg, Chanakyapuri, New Delhi 110 021; tel. (11) 26889054; fax (11) 26881409; e-mail embassy.newdelhi@mfa.gov.tr; internet yenidelhi.be.mfa.gov.tr; Ambassador Dr BURAK AKCAPAR.

Turkmenistan: C-11 West End Colony, Chanakyapuri, New Delhi 110 021; tel. (11) 24116527; fax (11) 24116526; e-mail tmemb.ind2@gmail.com; internet www.turkmenembassy.in; Ambassador PARAKHAT HOMMADOVICH DURDYEV.

Uganda: B-3/26, Vasant Vihar, New Delhi 110 057; tel. (11) 26144413; fax (11) 26144405; e-mail ughcom@ndb.vsnl.net.in; High Commissioner ELIZABETH PAULA NAPEYOK.

Ukraine: E-1/8 Vasant Vihar, New Delhi 110 057; tel. (11) 26145093; fax (11) 26146043; e-mail emb_in@mfa.gov.ua; internet india.mfa.gov.ua; Ambassador OLEKSANDR D. SHEVCHENKO.

United Arab Emirates: EP-12 Chandragupta Marg, Chanakyapuri, New Delhi 110 021; tel. (11) 26111111; fax (11) 26873272; e-mail info.newdelhi@mofa.gov.ae; internet www.uaeembassy-newdelhi.com; Ambassador MUHAMMAD SULTAN ABDULLA AL-OWAIS.

United Kingdom: Shanti Path, Chanakyapuri, New Delhi 110 021; tel. (11) 24192100; fax (11) 24192411; e-mail web.newdelhi@fco.gov.uk; internet ukinindia.fco.gov.uk; High Commissioner JAMES BEVAN.

USA: Shanti Path, Chanakyapuri, New Delhi 110 021; tel. (11) 24198000; fax (11) 24190017; e-mail ndwebmail@state.gov; internet newdelhi.usembassy.gov; Ambassador NANCY J. POWELL.

Uruguay: B-8/3 Vasant Vihar, New Delhi 110 057; tel. (11) 26151991; fax (11) 26144306; e-mail uruind@del3.vsnl.net.in; Chargé d'affaires a.i. CARLOS OSVALDO BENTANCOUR FERNANDEZ.

Uzbekistan: EP-40 Dr S. Radhakrishnan Marg, Chanakyapuri, New Delhi 110 021; tel. (11) 24670774; fax (11) 24670773; e-mail info@uzbekembassy.in; internet www.uzbekembassy.in; Ambassador Dr SALIKH INAGAMOV.

Venezuela: E-106 Malcha Marg, Chanakyapuri, New Delhi 110 021; tel. (11) 41680218; fax (11) 41750743; e-mail embassy@embaveneindia.com; internet www.embaveneindia.com; Ambassador MILENA SANTANA-RAMÍREZ.

Viet Nam: 20 Kautilya Marg, Chanakyapuri, New Delhi 110 021; tel. (11) 26879852; fax (11) 26879869; e-mail ebsvnin@yahoo.com.vn; internet www.mofa.gov.vn/vnemb.india; Ambassador NGUYEN THANH TAN.

Yemen: D-2/5 Vasant Vihar, New Delhi 110 057; tel. (11) 42705723; fax (11) 42705725; e-mail info@yemeninindia.com; internet www.yemeninindia.com; Ambassador KHADIJA RADMAN MOHAMED GHANEM.

Zambia: D-5/4, Vasant Vihar, New Delhi 110 057; tel. (11) 26145883; fax (11) 26145764; e-mail zambiand@sify.com; High Commissioner Brig. Gen. PATRICK RUMEDYO TEMBO.

Zimbabwe: 4 Aradhana Enclave, Sector 13, R. K. Puram, New Delhi 110 066; tel. (11) 26110430; fax (11) 26114316; e-mail info@zimdelhi.com; internet zimdelhi.net; Ambassador JONATHAN WUTAWUNASHE.

Judicial System

THE SUPREME COURT

The Supreme Court, consisting of a Chief Justice and 28 other judges appointed by the President, exercises exclusive jurisdiction in any dispute between the Union and the states (although there are certain restrictions where an acceding state is involved). It has appellate jurisdiction over any judgment, decree or order of the High Court where that Court certifies that either a substantial question of law or the interpretation of the Constitution is involved. The Supreme Court can enforce fundamental rights and issue writs covering habeas corpus, mandamus, prohibition, quo warranto and certiorari. The Supreme Court is a court of record and has the power to punish for its contempt.

Provision is made for the appointment by the Chief Justice of India of judges of High Courts as ad hoc judges at sittings of the Supreme Court for specified periods, and for the attendance of retired judges at sittings of the Supreme Court. The Supreme Court has advisory jurisdiction in respect of questions which may be referred to it by the President for opinion. The Supreme Court is also empowered to hear appeals against a sentence of death passed by a State High Court in reversal of an order of acquittal by a lower court, and in a case in which a High Court has granted a certificate of fitness.

The Supreme Court also hears appeals which are certified by High Courts to be fit to be heard, subject to rules made by the Court. Parliament may, by law, confer on the Supreme Court any further powers of appeal.

The judges hold office until the age of 65 years.

Supreme Court: Tilak Marg, New Delhi 110 001; tel. (11) 23388942; fax (11) 23381508; e-mail supremecourt@nic.in; internet supremecourtofindia.nic.in; Chief Justice P. SATHASIVAM.

Attorney-General: GOOLAM ESSAJI VAHANVATI.

HIGH COURTS

The High Courts are the Courts of Appeal from the lower courts, and their decisions are final except in cases where appeal lies with the Supreme Court.

LOWER COURTS

Provision is made in the Code of Criminal Procedure for the constitution of lower criminal courts called Courts of Session and Courts of Magistrates. The Courts of Session are competent to try all persons duly committed for trial, and inflict any punishment authorized by the law. The President and the local government concerned exercise the prerogative of mercy.

The constitution of inferior civil courts is determined by regulations within each state.

Religion

BUDDHISM

The Buddhists in Ladakh (Jammu and Kashmir) are followers of the Dalai Lama. The Buddhists in Sikkim are also followers of Mahayana Buddhism. In 2001 there were 8.0m. Buddhists in India, representing 0.8% of the population.

Mahabodhi Society of India: 4-A, Bankim Chatterjee St, Kolkata 700 073; tel. and fax (33) 22415214; fax (33) 22199294; e-mail mbsi_kolkata@yahoo.co.in; internet mahabodhisocietyofindia.wordpress.com; f. 1891; 11 centres in India, 5 centres worldwide; Pres. JIGMI YOEZER THINLEY; Gen. Sec. P. SEEWALEE THERO.

HINDUISM

In 2001 there were 827.6m. Hindus in India, representing 80.5% of the population.

Rashtriya Swayamsevak Sangh (RSS) (National Volunteer Organization): Keshav Kunj, Jhandewala, D. B. Gupta Marg, New Delhi 110 055; tel. (11) 23611372; fax (11) 23611385; e-mail contactus@rss.org; internet www.rss.org; f. 1925; 934,000 service centres in tribal, rural and urban slum areas; 58,000 working centres; Pres. MOHAN BHAGWAT; Gen. Sec. SURESH SONI.

Sarvadeshik Arya Pratinidhi Sabha: 15 Hanuman Rd, New Delhi 110 001; tel. (11) 23274771; e-mail aryasabha@seshik.com; internet www.thearyasamaj.org/sarvadeshiksabha; f. 1875 by Maharishi Dayanand Saraswati; the international body for Arya Samaj temples propagating reforms in all fields on the basis of Vedic principles; Pres. ACHARYA BALDEV; Sec. PRAKASH ARYA ADV.

Vishwa Hindu Parishad (VHP) (World Hindu Council): Sankat Mochan Ashram, Ramakrishna Puram Sector 6, New Delhi 110 022; tel. (11) 26178992; fax (11) 26195527; e-mail info@vhp.org; internet www.vhp.org; f. 1964, banned in Dec. 1992–June 1993 for its role in the destruction of the Babri mosque in Ayodhya; Pres. PRAVINBHAI TOGADIYA; Sec.-Gen. CHAMPAT RAI.

ISLAM

Muslims are divided into two main sects, Shi'as and Sunnis. Most of the Indian Muslims are Sunnis. At the 2001 census Islam had 138.2m. adherents (13.4% of the population).

Jamiat Ulama-i-Hind (Assembly of Muslim Religious Leaders of India): 1 Bahadur Shah Zafar Marg, New Delhi 110 002; tel. (11) 23311455; fax (11) 23316173; e-mail jamiat@vsnl.com; internet www.jamiatulamaihind.net; f. 1919; Pres MAULANA QARI MOHAMMAD USMAN MANSOORPURI; Leader MAULANA MAHMOOD.

SIKHISM

In 2001 there were 19.2m. Sikhs (comprising 1.9% of the population), the majority living in the Punjab.

Shiromani Gurdwara Parbandhak Committee: Darbar Sahab, Amritsar 143 001; tel. (183) 2553957; fax (183) 2553919; e-mail info@sgpc.net; internet www.sgpc.net; f. 1925; highest authority in Sikhism; Pres. Jathedar AVTAR SINGH; Sec. SARDAR DALMEGH SINGH.

CHRISTIANITY

According to the 2001 census, Christians represented 2.3% of the population in India.

National Council of Churches in India: Christian Council Lodge, Civil Lines, POB 205, Nagpur 440 001; tel. (712) 2531312; fax (712) 2520554; e-mail ncci@nccindia.in; internet www.nccindia.in; f. 1914; mems: 30 protestant and orthodox churches, 17 regional Christian councils, 17 All-India ecumenical orgs, 7 related agencies and 3 autonomous bodies; represents c. 13m. mems; Pres. Bishop Dr TARANATH S. SAGAR; Gen. Sec. Bishop Dr ROGER GAIKWAD.

Orthodox Churches

Malankara Orthodox Syrian Church: Devalokam, Kottayam 686 038; tel. (481) 2578500; fax (481) 2570569; e-mail catholicos@mosc.in; internet malankaraorthodoxchurch.in; c. 3m. mems (2012); 31 bishops, 30 dioceses, 2,000 parishes; Catholicos of the East and Malankara Metropolitan HH BASELIOS MARTHOMA PAULOSE II.

Mar Thoma Syrian Church of Malabar: Tiruvalla 689 101; tel. (469) 2630449; fax (469) 2630327; e-mail sabhaoffice@marthoma.in; internet www.marthomasyrianchurch.org; c. 1m. mems (2001); Valiya Metropolitan Most Rev. Dr PHILIPOSE MAR CHRYSOSTOM; Sec. Rev. P. T. THOMAS.

The Malankara Jacobite Syrian Orthodox Church is also represented.

Protestant Churches

Church of North India (CNI): CNI Bhavan, 16 Pandit Pant Marg, New Delhi 110 001; tel. (11) 43214000; fax (11) 43214006; e-mail alwanmasih@cnisynod.org; internet www.cnisynod.org; f. 1970 by merger of the Church of India (Anglican—fmrly known as the Church of India, Pakistan, Burma and Ceylon), the Council of the Baptist Churches in Northern India, the Methodist Church (British and Australasian Conferences), the United Church of Northern India (a union of Presbyterians and Congregationalists, f. 1924), the

Church of the Brethren in India, and the Disciples of Christ; comprises 27 dioceses; c. 1.5m. mems (2012); Moderator Most Rev. Dr PHILIP P. MARANDIH (Bishop of Patna); Gen. Sec. ALWAN MASIH.

Church of South India (CSI): CSI Centre, 5 Whites Rd, Chennai 600 014; tel. (44) 28521566; fax (44) 28523528; e-mail info@csisynod.com; internet www.csisynod.com; f. 1947 by merger of the Weslyan Methodist Church in South India, the South India United Church (itself a union of churches in the Congregational and Presbyterian/Reformed traditions) and the 4 southern dioceses of the (Anglican) Church of India; comprises 22 dioceses (incl. one in Sri Lanka); c. 3.8m. mems (2009); Moderator Most Rev. G. DYVASIRVADAM; Gen. Sec. Rev. D. R. SADANANDA.

Methodist Church in India: Methodist Centre, 21 YMCA Rd, Mumbai 400 008; tel. (22) 23094316; fax (22) 23074137; e-mail gensecmci@vsnl.com; f. 1856 as the Methodist Church in Southern Asia; 648,000 mems (2005); Gen. Sec. Rev. MUNNAGI ALFRED DANIEL.

Samavesam of Telugu Baptist Churches: A. B. M. Compound, Kavali 524 201; tel. (8626) 241363; fax (8626) 241847; e-mail stbcpabc@yahoo.com; f. 1962; comprises 2,000 independent Baptist churches; 578,295 mems (1995); Gen. Sec. Dr J. M. FRANKLIN.

United Evangelical Lutheran Churches in India: Martin Luther Bhavan, 95 Purasawalkam High Rd, Kilpauk, Chennai 600 010; tel. (44) 26430008; fax (44) 26611364; e-mail augustinejkumar@uelci.org; internet www.uelci.org; f. 1975; 12 constituent denominations: Andhra Evangelical Lutheran Church, Arcot Lutheran Church, Evangelical Lutheran Church in Madhya Pradesh, Evangelical Lutheran Church in the Himalayan States, Good Shepherd Evangelical Lutheran Church, Gossner Evangelical Lutheran Church in Chotanagpur and Assam (Asom), India Evangelical Lutheran Church, Jeypore Evangelical Lutheran Church, Nepal Northern Evangelical Lutheran Church, Northern Evangelical Lutheran Church, South Andhra Lutheran Church and Tamil Evangelical Lutheran Church; more than 4.5m. mems; Pres. Rt Rev. GODWIN NAG; Exec. Sec. Rev. Dr A. G. AUGUSTINE JEYAKUMAR.

Other denominations active in the country include the Assembly of the Presbyterian Church in North East India, the Bengal-Odisha-Bihar Baptist Convention (6,000 mems), the Chaldean Syrian Church of the East, the Convention of the Baptist Churches of Northern Circars, the Council of Baptist Churches of North East India, the Council of Baptist Churches of Northern India, the Hindustani Convent Church and the Mennonite Church in India.

The Roman Catholic Church

India comprises 30 archdioceses and 134 dioceses. These include five archdioceses and 25 dioceses of the Syro-Malabar rite, and two archdioceses and six dioceses of the Syro-Malankara rite. The archdiocese of Goa and Daman is also the seat of the Patriarch of the East Indies. The remaining archdioceses are metropolitan sees. In 2011 there were an estimated 15.5m. adherents of the Roman Catholic faith in the country.

Catholic Bishops' Conference of India (CBCI): CBCI Centre, 1 Ashok Place, nr Gole Dakkhana, New Delhi 110 001; tel. (11) 23344470; fax (11) 23364615; e-mail cbci@vsl.com; internet www.cbcisite.com; f. 1944; Pres. Cardinal OSWALD GRACIAS (Archbishop of Bombay); Sec.-Gen. Most Rev. ALBERT D'SOUZA (Archbishop of Gandhinagar).

Latin Rite

Conference of Catholic Bishops of India (CCBI): CCBI Centre, 2nd Cross, Hutchins Rd, POB 8490, Bangalore 560 084; tel. (80) 25498282; fax (80) 25498180; e-mail ccbi@airtelmail.in; internet www.ccbi.in; f. 1994; Pres. Cardinal TELESPHORE TOPPO (Archbishop of Ranchi).

Syro-Malabar Rite

In 2012 there were some 4.2m. Syro-Malabar Catholics in India.

Major Archbishop of the Syro-Malabar Church: MAR GEORGE Cardinal ALENCHERRY (Archbishop of Ernakulam-Angamaly), Archdiocesian Curia, Mount St Thomas, POB 2580, Kakkand, Kochi 682 031; tel. (484) 2352629; fax (484) 2355010; e-mail curia@ernakulamarchdiocese.org; internet www.ernakulamarchdiocese.org.

Archbishop of Changanasserry: Most Rev. MAR JOSEPH PERUMTHOTTAM, Archbishop's House, POB 20, Changanasserry 686 101; tel. (481) 2420040; fax (481) 2422540; e-mail abpchry@sancharnet.in; internet www.archdiocesechanganacherry.org.

Archbishop of Kottayam: Most Rev. MATHEW MOOLAKKATTU, Archbishop's House, POB 71, Kottayam 686 001; tel. (481) 2563527; fax (481) 2563327; e-mail cbhktym@hotmail.com; internet www.kottayamad.org.

Archbishop of Tellicherry: Most Rev. GEORGE VALIAMATTAM, Archbishop's House, POB 70, Tellicherry 670 101; tel. (490) 2341058; fax (49) 2341412; e-mail archbishopgeorgev@gmail.com; internet www.archdioceseoftellicherry.org.

Archbishop of Trichur: Most Rev. MAR ANDREWS THAZHATH, Archbishop's House, Trichur 680 005; tel. (487) 2333325; fax (487) 2338204; e-mail carbit@sancharnet.in; internet www.trichurarchdiocese.org.

Syro-Malankara Rite

Major Archbishop of Trivandrum: Cardinal BASELIOS CLEEMIS CATHOLICOS, Major Archbishop's House, Pattom, Thiruvananthapuram 695 004; tel. (471) 2541643; fax (471) 2541635; e-mail malankaracc@gmail.com; internet www.malankaracatholicchurch.net.

BAHÁ'Í FAITH

National Spiritual Assembly: Bahá'í House, 6 Shrimant Madhavrao Scindia Rd, POB 19, New Delhi 110 001; tel. (11) 23387004; fax (11) 23782178; e-mail admin@bahai.in; internet www.bahai.in; f. 1923; c. 2m. mems; Sec.-Gen. Dr A. K. MERCHANT.

OTHER FAITHS

Jainism: 4.2m. adherents (2001 census), 0.4% of the population.

Zoroastrianism: In 2001 69,601 Parsis practised the Zoroastrian religion, compared with 76,382 in 1991.

The Press

The majority of publications in India are under individual ownership, and they claim a large part of the total circulation. The most powerful groups, owned by joint stock companies, publish most of the large English dailies and frequently have considerable private commercial and industrial holdings. Four of the major groups are as follows:

Ananda Bazar Patrika Group: controlled by AVEEK SARKAR and family; dailies: the *Ananda Bazar Patrika* (Kolkata) and the English *The Telegraph* (Guwahati, Kolkata and Siliguri); periodicals include: *Business World*, Bengali weekly *Anandamela*, Bengali fortnightly *Desh*, Bengali monthly *Anandalok* and the Bengali monthly *Sananda*.

Hindustan Times Group: controlled by the K. K. BIRLA family; dailies: the *Hindustan Times* (published from 6 regional centres), *Pradeep* (Patna) and the Hindi *Hindustan* (published from 13 regional centres); periodicals: the weekly *Overseas Hindustan Times* and the Hindi monthlies *Nandan* and *Kadambini* (New Delhi).

Indian Express Group: controlled by the family of the late RAMNATH GOENKA; publishes 9 dailies including the *Indian Express*, the Marathi *Lokasatta*, the Tamil *Dinamani*, the Telugu *Andhra Prabha*, the Kannada *Kannada Prabha* and the English *Financial Express*; 6 periodicals including the English weeklies the *Indian Express* (Sunday edition), *Screen*, the Telugu *Andhra Prabha Illustrated Weekly* and the Tamil *Dinamani Kadir* (weekly).

Times of India Group: controlled by family of the late ASHOK JAIN; dailies: *The Times of India* (published in 10 regional centres), *Economic Times*, the Hindi *Navbharat Times* and *Sandhya Times*, the Marathi *Maharashtra Times* (Mumbai); periodicals: the English fortnightly *Femina* and monthly *Filmfare*.

PRINCIPAL DAILIES

Circulation figs are for 2009, unless otherwise stated.

Delhi (incl. New Delhi)

The Asian Age: S-7, Green Park, Main Market, New Delhi 110 016; tel. (11) 26530001; fax (11) 26530027; e-mail delhidesk@asianage.com; internet www.asianage.com; f. 1994; morning; English; also publ. from Ahmedabad, Bangalore, Kolkata, Mumbai and London; Editor-in-Chief VENKATTRAM REDDY; circ. 46,895.

Business Standard: Nehru House, 4 Bahadur Shah Zafar Marg, New Delhi 110 002; tel. (11) 23720202; fax (11) 23720201; e-mail letters@business-standard.com; internet www.business-standard.com; morning; English; also publ. from Kolkata, Ahmedabad, Bangalore, Chennai, Hyderabad, Chandigarh, Pune, Kochi, Lucknow, Bhubaneswar and Mumbai; Editor Dr SANJAYA BARU; circ. 26,390.

Daily Milap: Milap Niketan, 8A Bahadur Shah Zafar Marg, New Delhi 110 002; tel. (11) 23317651; fax (11) 23319166; e-mail yogi@milap.com; internet www.milap.com; f. 1923; Urdu; nationalist; also publ. in Hindi; publ. also from Jullundur and Hyderabad; Man. Editor PUNAM SURI; Editor NAVIN SURI; circ. 36,295.

Daily Pratap: Pratap Bhavan, 5 Bahadur Shah Zafar Marg, New Delhi 110 002; tel. (11) 23317938; fax (11) 41509555; e-mail admin@

dailypratap.com; internet www.dailypratap.com; f. 1919; Urdu; Chief Editor ANIL NARENDRA; CEO S. M. AFIF AHSEN; circ. 65,866.

The Economic Times: 7 Bahadur Shah Zafar Marg, New Delhi 110 002; tel. (11) 23492234; fax (11) 23491248; internet economictimes.indiatimes.com; f. 1961; English; also publ. from Kolkata, Ahmedabad, Bangalore, Hyderabad, Chennai and Mumbai; Exec. Editor ROHIT SARAN; circ. 175,438.

Financial Express: Express Bldg, The Indian Express Online Media (Pvt) Ltd, 9–10 Bahadur Shah Zafar Marg, New Delhi 110 002; tel. (11) 23702100; fax (11) 26530114; e-mail editor@expressindia.com; internet www.financialexpress.com; f. 1961; morning; English; also publ. from Ahmedabad (in Gujarati), Mumbai, Bangalore, Kolkata and Chennai; Editor MYTHILI BHUSNURMATH; circ. 31,383.

The Hindu: PTI Bldg, 3rd Floor, 4 Parliament St, New Delhi 110 001; tel. (11) 43579797; fax (11) 23723808; e-mail letters@thehindu.co.in; internet www.thehindu.com; f. 1878; morning; English; also publ. from 12 other regional centres; Editor-in-Chief N. RAM; circ. 65,847 (2011).

Hindustan: 18–20 Kasturba Gandhi Marg, New Delhi 110 001; tel. (11) 23704600; fax (11) 66561445; e-mail feedback@hindustantimes.com; internet www.livehindustan.com; f. 1936; morning; Hindi; also publ. from Patna, Muzaffarpur, Bhagalpur, Ranchi, Jamshedpur, Dhanbad, Lucknow, Varanasi, Meerut, Agra, Kanpur and Chandigarh; Editor-in-Chief SHASHI SHEKHAR; circ. 429,759.

Hindustan Times: 18–20 Kasturba Gandhi Marg, New Delhi 110 001; tel. (11) 23361234; fax (11) 66561270; e-mail feedback@hindustantimes.com; internet www.hindustantimes.com; f. 1924; morning; English; also publ. from Mumbai, Lucknow, Patna, Ranchi and Kolkata; Editor-in-Chief SANJOY NARAYAN; circ. 993,349.

Indian Express: Express Bldg, The Indian Express Online Media (Pvt) Ltd, 9–10 Bahadur Shah Zafar Marg, New Delhi 110 002; tel. (11) 23702100; fax (11) 23702141; e-mail editor@expressindia.com; internet www.indianexpress.com; f. 1953; English; also publ. from 8 other cities; Chair. and Man. Dir VIVEK GOENKA; Editor-in-Chief SHEKHAR GUPTA; circ. 71,585.

Jansatta: 9–10 Bahadur Shah Zafar Marg, New Delhi 110 002; tel. (11) 23702100; fax (11) 23702141; e-mail jansatta@expressindia.com; f. 1983; Hindi; also publ. from Kolkata and Raipur; Editor OM THANVI; circ. 43,612.

Navbharat Times: 7 Bahadur Shah Zafar Marg, New Delhi 110 002; tel. (11) 23492041; fax (11) 23492168; internet navbharattimes.indiatimes.com; f. 1947; Hindi; also publ. from Mumbai; Editor RAM KRIPAL SINGH; circ. 409,584.

The Pioneer: Link House, 3 Bahadur Shah Zafar Marg, New Delhi 110 002; tel. (11) 23755271; fax (11) 23755275; e-mail info@dailypioneer.com; internet www.dailypioneer.com; f. 1865; also publ. from Lucknow, Bhopal, Bhubaneswar, Ranchi, Kochi, Chandigarh and Dehradun; Editor CHANDAN MITRA; circ. 96,332.

Punjab Kesari: Plot No. 2, Printing Press Complex, Ring Rd, nr Wazirpur Bus Depot, Delhi 110 035; tel. (11) 27193719; fax (11) 27194470; e-mail sales@punjabkesari.com; internet www.punjabkesari.com; f. 1983; Hindi; also publ. from Jalandhar and Ambala; circulated in Haryana, Rajasthan, Uttar Pradesh, Uttarakhand, Madhya Pradesh, Punjab, Himachal Pradesh, Maharashtra, Bihar and Gujarat; Resident Editor ASHWANI KUMAR; circ. 348,890.

Rashtriya Sahara: Navrang House, 12th Floor, 21 Kasturba Gandhi Marg, New Delhi 110 001; tel. (11) 43596017; fax (11) 23352370; e-mail rsahara@saharasamay.com; internet rashtriyasahara.samaylive.com; morning; Hindi; also publ. from Lucknow, Gorakhpur, Kanpur, Dehradun and Patna; Resident Editor AZIZ BURNEY; circ. 97,625 (2011).

Sandhya Times: 7 Bahadur Shah Zafar Marg, New Delhi 110 002; tel. (11) 23492162; fax (11) 23492047; f. 1979; Hindi; evening; Editor SAT SONI; circ. 34,756.

The Statesman: Statesman House, 148 Barakhamba Rd, New Delhi 110 001; tel. (11) 23315911; fax (11) 23315295; e-mail thestatesman@vsnl.com; internet www.thestatesman.net; f. 1931; English; also publ. from Bhubaneswar, Kolkata and Siliguri; Editor and Man. Dir RAVINDRA KUMAR; circ. 7,598.

The Times of India: 7 Bahadur Shah Zafar Marg, New Delhi 110 002; tel. (11) 23492049; fax (11) 23351606; internet timesofindia.indiatimes.com; f. 1838; English; also publ. from 9 other towns (Mumbai, Pune, Ahmedabad, Bangalore, Chennai, Hyderabad, Jaipur, Kolkata and Lucknow); Editor-in-Chief JAIDEEP BOSE; circ. 1,190,772.

Andhra Pradesh

Hyderabad

Andhra Jyothi: Andhra Jyothi Bldg, Plot No. 76, HUDA Heights, Rd No. 70, Journalist Colony, Jubilee Hills, Hyderabad 500 033; tel. (40) 23558233; fax (40) 23558288; e-mail editor@andhrajyothy.com; internet www.andhrajyothy.com; f. 1960; Telugu; also publ. from 13 other regional centres; Editor K. SRINIVAS; combined circ. 91,896.

Andhra Prabha: 16-1-28, Kolandareddy Rd, Poornanandampet, Vijayawada 520 003; tel. (866) 2571351; e-mail info@andhraprabha.com; internet www.andhraprabha.in; f. 1938; Telugu; also publ. from Bangalore, Hyderabad, Chennai and Visakhapatnam; Editor VASUDEV DEKSHITILU; circ. 68,590.

Deccan Chronicle: 36 Sarojini Devi Rd, Hyderabad 500 003; tel. (40) 27803930; fax (40) 27803870; e-mail thomas@deccanmail.com; internet www.deccanchronicle.com; f. 1938; English; also publ. from 6 other regional centres; Editor-in-Chief A. T. JAYANTI; circ. 45,748.

Eenadu: Somajiguda, Hyderabad 500 082; tel. (40) 23318181; fax (40) 23392530; e-mail editor@eenadu.net; internet www.eenadu.net; f. 1974; Telugu; also publ. from 22 other towns; Chief Editor RAHUL KUMAR; circ. 34,459.

Rahnuma-e-Deccan: 12-2-837/A/3, Asif Nagar, Hyderabad 500 028; tel. (40) 23534943; fax (40) 23534945; e-mail jameelnews@gmail.com; f. 1949; morning; Urdu; independent; Chief Editor SYED VICARUDDIN; circ. 26,293.

Siasat Daily: Jawaharlal Nehru Rd, Hyderabad 500 001; tel. (40) 24744180; fax (40) 24603188; e-mail contact@siasat.com; internet www.siasat.com; f. 1949; morning; Urdu; Editor ZAHID ALI KHAN; circ. 44,073.

Vijayawada

New Indian Express: 29-28-39, Dasarivari St, Suryaraopet, Vijayawada; tel. (866) 2444163; internet www.expressbuzz.com; English; also publ. from 7 other cities; Man. Editor MANOJ KUMAR SONTHALIA; circ. 9,588.

Assam (Asom)

Guwahati

Amar Asom: G. S. Rd, Ulubari, Guwahati 781 007; tel. (361) 2458395; fax (361) 2521620; e-mail glpghy2009@hotmail.com; internet amarasom.glpublications.in; f. 1997; Assamese; also publ. from Jorhat and Lakhimpur; Editor HOMEN BORGOHAIN; circ. 59,995.

Asomiya Pratidin: Maniram Dewan Rd, Chandmari, Guwahati 781 003; tel. (361) 2660420; fax (361) 2666377; e-mail pratidinedi@vsnl.net; internet www.asomiyapratidin.co.in; morning; Assamese; also publ. from Dibrugarh, Barpari and Kamrup; Editor HAIDAR HUSSAIN; circ. 74,460.

Assam Tribune: GNB Rd, Guwahati 781 003; tel. (361) 2661357; fax (361) 2666398; e-mail editoratribune@gmail.com; internet www.assamtribune.com; f. 1939; English; also publishes Assamese edn, Dainik Assam; Man. Dir and Editor P. G. BARUAH; circ. 90,815 (2011).

Dainik Agradoot: Agradoot Bhavan, Dispur, Guwahati 781 006; tel. (361) 2261923; fax (361) 2260655; e-mail agradoot@sify.com; internet www.dainikagradoot.com; f. 1995; Assamese; Editor K. S. DEKA; circ. 66,409.

Dainik Jugasankha: 13 Green Path, G. S. Rd, Guwahati 781 007; tel. (361) 2526670; fax (361) 2450496; e-mail dainikjugasankha@yahoo.com; f. 1950; Bengali; also publ. from Silchar; Editor-in-Chief BIJOY KRISHNA NATH; Editor AMAL GUPTA; circ. 75,650.

The North East Times: G.S. Rd, Ulubari, Guwahati 781 007; tel. (361) 2458395; fax (361) 2521620; e-mail guwahatiglpghy@hotmail.com; internet net.glpublications.in; English; Editor G. L. AGARWALLA; circ. 34,891.

The Sentinel: G. S. Rd, Six Mile, Dispur, Guwahati 781 022; tel. (361) 2229330; fax (361) 2229110; e-mail thesentinel@satyam.net.in; internet www.sentinelassam.com; f. 1983; English; Editor SHANKAR RAJKHEWA; circ. 58,751.

Jorhat

Dainik Janmabhumi: Tulsi Narayan Sarma Rd, Jorhat 785 001; tel. (376) 2320033; fax (376) 2321713; e-mail editordj@sify.com; internet www.dainikjanambhumi.co.in; f. 1972; Assamese; also publ. from Tinsukia, Guwahati and Tezpur; Editor HEMANTA BARMAN; Man. Partner SUBROTO SHARMA; circ. 29,163.

Bihar

Dainik Jagran: 172/92/11 B/2, 5th Floor, Rashmi Complex, Kidwaipuri, Patna 800001; tel. (612) 2520671; fax (612) 2534386; internet in.jagran.yahoo.com; f. 1942; Hindi; also publ. from 25 other cities; Man. Editor MAHENDRA MOHAN GUPTA; circ. 356,328.

Hindustan Times: Buddha Marg, Patna 800 001; tel. (612) 2223434; fax (612) 2226120; internet www.hindustantimes.com; f. 1918; morning; English; also publ. from 5 regional centres; Editor SHEKHAR BHATIA; circ. 17,285.

Chhattisgarh

Dainik Bhaskar: Press Complex, Rajbandha Maidan, G. E. Rd, Raipur 492 001; tel. (771) 2535277; fax (771) 2535255; e-mail editorbhaskar@bhaskar.com; internet www.bhaskar.com; Hindi; morning; also publ. from 18 other regional centres; Editor RAMESH CHANDRA AGRAWAL; circ. 184,587.

Deshbandhu: Deshbandhu Complex, Ramsagar Para, Raipur 492 001; tel. (771) 4288888; e-mail deshbandhuraipur@gmail.com; internet www.deshbandhu.co.in; f. 1959; Hindi; also publ. from Jabalpur, Satna, Bilaspur, Indore, New Delhi and Bhopal; publishes an evening edn, Highway Channel, from Raipur, Jabalpur and Bilaspur; Chief Editor LALIT SURJAN; circ. 84,357 (Raipur), 24,289 (Satna), 46,785 (Bhopal), 50,468 (Jabalpur), 59,013 (Bilaspur).

Nava Bharat: Nava Bharat Bhavan Press Complex, G. E. Rd, Raipur 492 001; tel. (771) 2535544; fax (771) 2534936; internet www.navabharat.biz; Hindi; also publ. from 6 other regional centres; Editor PRAKASH MAHESHWARI; circ. 189,186 (2011).

Goa

Gomantak Times: Gomantak Bhavan, St Inez, Panaji, Goa 403 001; tel. (832) 2422700; fax (832) 2422701; internet www.dainikgomantak.com; f. 1962; morning; Marathi and English edns; Exec. Editor DERRICK ALMEIDA; circ. 24,906 (Marathi).

Navhind Times: Navhind Bhavan, Rua Ismail Gracias, POB 161, Panaji, Goa 403 001; tel. (832) 6651111; fax (832) 2224258; e-mail advt@navhindtimes.com; internet www.navhindtimes.in; f. 1963; morning; English; Editor ARUN SINHA; circ. 34,835.

O Heraldo: Herald Publications Pvt Ltd, POB 160, Rua St Tome, Panjim 403 001; tel. (832) 2224202; fax (832) 2225622; e-mail info@oheraldo.in; internet www.heraldgoa.in; f. 1900; English; Editor-in-Chief R. F. FERNANDES; Editor SUJAY GUPTA; circ. 61,587 (2011).

Gujarat

Ahmedabad

Gujarat Samachar: Gujarat Samachar Bhavan, Khanpur, Ahmedabad 380 001; tel. (79) 30410000; fax (79) 5502000; e-mail editor@gujaratsamachar.com; internet www.gujaratsamachar.com; f. 1930; morning; Gujarati; also publ. from Surat, Rajkot, Baroda, Bhavnagar, Mumbai, London and New York; Editor SHREYANSH SHAH; circ. 537,029.

Lokasatta—Janasatta: Mirzapur Rd, POB 188, Ahmedabad 380 001; tel. (79) 25507307; fax (79) 25507708; f. 1953; morning; Gujarati; also publ. from Rajkot and Vadodara; Man. Editor VIVEK GOENKA; circ. 49,161.

Sandesh: Sandesh Bhavan, Lad Society Rd, Ahmedabad 380 054; tel. (79) 40004000; fax (79) 40004242; e-mail advt@sandesh.com; internet sandesh.com; f. 1923; Gujarati; also publ. from Bhavnagar, Vadodara, Rajkot and Surat; Editor FALGUNBHAI C. PATEL; circ. 346,553.

The Times of India: 139 Ashram Rd, POB 4046, Ahmedabad 380 009; tel. (79) 26553300; fax (79) 26583758; internet timesofindia.indiatimes.com; f. 1968; English; also publ. from 9 other towns; Chief Editor RAJESH KALRA; circ. 199,612.

Western Times: 301 Gala Argos, 3rd Floor, nr Kalgi Char Rasta, Gujarat College Rd, Ellisbridge, Ahmedabad 380 006; tel. (79) 26402880; fax (79) 26402882; e-mail gujarati@westerntimes.co.in; internet www.westerntimes.co.in; f. 1967; English and Gujarati edns; also publ. (in Gujarati) from 8 other towns; Editor NIKUNJ PATEL; total circ. more than 200,000.

Bhuj

Kutchmitra: Kutchmitra Bhavan, nr Indirabai Park, Bhuj 370 001; tel. (2832) 252090; fax (2832) 250271; e-mail info@kutchmitradaily.com; internet www.kutchmitradaily.com; f. 1947; Gujarati; Propr Saurashtra Trust; Editor KIRTI J. KHATRI; circ. 47,882 (2011).

Rajkot

Jai Hind: Jai Hind Press Bldg, Babubhai Shah Rd, POB 59, Rajkot 360 001; tel. (281) 3048684; fax (281) 2448677; e-mail editor@jaihinddaily.com; internet www.jaihinddaily.com; f. 1948; morning and evening (in Rajkot as Sanj Samachar); Gujarati; also publ. from Ahmedabad; Editor Y. N. SHAH; combined circ. 107,300.

Phulchhab: Phulchhab Bhavan, Phulchhab Marg, Rajkot 360 001; tel. (281) 2444611; fax (281) 2448751; e-mail editor@janmabhoominewspapers.com; internet phulchhab.janmabhoominewspapers.com; f. 1950; morning; Gujarati; Propr Saurashtra Trust; Editor DINESH RAJA; circ. 84,500.

Surat

Gujaratmitra and Gujaratdarpan: Gujaratmitra Bhavan, nr Old Civil Hospital, Sonifalia, Surat 395 003; tel. (261) 2599992; fax (261) 2599990; e-mail mitra@gujaratmitra.in; internet www.gujaratmitra.in/web; f. 1863; morning; Gujarati; Editor B. P. RESHAMWALA; circ. 91,000.

Haryana

Bharat Janani: Sonipat Rd, Rohtak; tel. and fax (1262) 427191; f. 1971; Hindi; morning; also publ. from Rewari; Editor Dr R. S. SANTOSHI; circ. 56,360.

Himachal Pradesh

Dainik Himachal Sewa: Hans Kutir, Khalini, Shimla 171 002; tel. (177) 2224119; fax (177) 2260187; f. 1986; Hindi; Editor-in-Chief Dr R. S. SANTOSHI; circ. 60,000.

Himachal Times: Himachal Times Complex, 64–66 The Mall, Shimla 171 001; tel. and fax (177) 2811555; e-mail devkpandhi@gmail.com; internet himachaltimesgroup.com; f. 1948; English; Chief Editor VIJAY PANDHI.

Jammu and Kashmir

Daily Excelsior: Excelsior House, Excelsior Lane, Janipura, Jammu Tawi 180 007; tel. (191) 2537055; fax (191) 2537831; e-mail editor@dailyexcelsior.com; internet www.dailyexcelsior.com; f. 1965; English; Publr and Editor S. D. ROHMETRA.

Greater Kashmir: 6 Pratap Park, Residency Rd, Srinagar 190 001; tel. (194) 2455435; fax (194) 2477782; e-mail editor@greaterkashmir.com; internet www.greaterkashmir.com; f. 1993; English; Chief Editor FAYAZ AHMED KALOO; circ. 81,068.

Kashmir Times: Residency Rd, Jammu 180 001; tel. (191) 2543676; fax (191) 2542028; e-mail jmt_prabodh@sancharnet.in; internet www.kashmirtimes.com; f. 1955; morning; English and Hindi; Editor-in-Chief PRABODH JAMWAL.

Srinagar Times: Badshah Bridge, Srinagar; f. 1969; Urdu; Editor S. F. MOHAMMED; circ. 14,000.

Jharkhand

Aaj: 15–16 Namkum Industrial Area, Ranchi; Hindi; morning; also publ. from 8 other cities; Publr AMITAV CHAKRAVORTHY; circ. 59,267 (Ranchi).

Hindustan: Circular Court, Circular Rd, Ranchi 834 001; tel. (651) 2205811; Hindi; morning; also publ. from Patna, Delhi, Bhagalpur, Lucknow, Varanasi and Muzaffarpur; Editor MRINAL PANDE; circ. 295,934 (2011).

Prabhat Khabar: 15-P, Kokar Industrial Area, Kokar, Ranchi 834 001; tel. (651) 3053100; fax (651) 254006; e-mail ranchi@prabhatkhabar.in; internet www.prabhatkhabar.com; f. 1984; Hindi; also publ. from Dhanbad, Kolkata, Jamshedpur, Siliguri, Deoghar and Patna; Chief Editor HARIVANSH; circ. 120,162 (Ranchi).

Ranchi Express: 55 Baralal St, Ranchi 834 001; tel. (651) 2206320; fax (651) 2206213; e-mail news@ranchiexpress.com; internet ranchiexpress.com; f. 1963; Hindi; morning; Editor AJAY MAROO; circ. 57,959.

Karnataka

Bangalore

Deccan Herald: 75 Mahatma Gandhi Rd, POB 5331, Bangalore 560 001; tel. (80) 25588000; fax (80) 25580523; e-mail ads@deccanherald.co.in; internet www.deccanherald.com; f. 1948; morning; English; also publ. from Hubli-Dharwar, Mangalore, Dhavangere and Gulbarga; Editor K. N. TILAK KUMAR; circ. 163,221.

Kannada Prabha: Express Bldgs, 1 Queen's Rd, Bangalore 560 001; tel. (80) 22866893; fax (80) 22866617; e-mail anisikeprabha@gmail.com; internet www.kannadaprabha.com; f. 2005; morning; Kannada; also publ. from Belgaum, Mangalore, Gulbarga, Hubali and Shimoga; Editor VISHWESHWAR BHAT; circ. 96,485 (2011).

New Indian Express: 1 Queen's Rd, Bangalore 560 001; tel. (80) 22256998; fax (80) 22256617; f. 1965; English; also publ. from Bhubaneswar, Kochi, Hyderabad, Chennai, Madurai, Vijayawada and Vizianagaram; Chair. and Man. Editor MANOJ KUMAR SONTHALIA; circ. 27,634.

Prajavani: 75 M. G. Rd, POB 5331, Bangalore 560 001; tel. (80) 25880000; fax (80) 25880165; e-mail ads@deccanherald.co.in; internet www.prajavani.net; f. 1948; morning; Kannada; also publ. from Mysore, Gulbarga, Mangalore and Dharwad; Editor-in-Chief K. N. SHANTH KUMAR; circ. 56,240.

Hubli-Dharwar

Samyukta Karnataka: POB 30, Koppikar Rd, Hubli 580 020; tel. (836) 2364303; fax (836) 2362760; e-mail skhubli@gmail.com; internet www.samyukthakarnataka.com; f. 1933; Kannada; also publ. from Bangalore, Davangere, and Gulbarga; Editor A. C. GOPAL; circ. 100,337.

Vijay Karnataka: Giriraj Annexe, Circuit House Rd, Hubli 580 029; tel. (836) 2237556; fax (836) 2253630; internet www.vijaykarnatakaepaper.com; f. 1999; Kannada; also publ. from Bangalore, Gangavati, Gulbarga, Mangalore, Mysore, Bagalkot, Chitradurga and Shimoga; Printer and Publr VIJAY SANKESHWAR; circ. 69,201.

Manipal

Udayavani: Manipal Media Network, New Udayavani Bldg, Manipal 576 119; tel. (820) 2571151; fax (820) 2570563; e-mail udayavanionline@manipalmedia.com; internet www.udayavani.com; f. 1970; Kannada; also publ. from Manipal-Udupi and Mumbai; Editor T. SATISH U. PAI; Regional Editors N. GURAJ (Manipal), R. POORNIMA (Bangalore), T. SATISH (Mumbai); circ. 21,739.

Kerala

Kottayam

Deepika: POB 7, Kottayam 686 001; tel. (481) 3012001; fax (481) 3012222; e-mail editor@deepika.com; internet www.deepika.com; f. 1887; Malayalam; independent; also publ. from Kannur, Kochi, Kozhikode, Thiruvananthapuram and Thrissur; Chief Editor Fr ALEXANDER PAIKADA; circ. 47,520.

Malayala Manorama: K. K. Rd, POB 26, Kottayam 686 001; tel. (481) 2563646; fax (481) 2562479; e-mail editor@malayalamanorama.com; internet www.manoramaonline.com; f. 1890; Malayalam; also publ. from 16 other regional centres; morning; Man. Dir and Editor MAMMEN MATHEW; circ. 308,985.

Kozhikode

Deshabhimani: Deshabhimani Bldg, Kaloor, Kochi 682 017; tel. (484) 253034; fax (484) 2530006; e-mail kochi@deshabhimani.com; internet www.deshabhimani.com; f. 1946; Malayalam; morning; publ. by the CPI (M); also publ. from Kochi, Kottayam, Thrissur, Calicut, Malappuram and Thiruvananthapuram; Chief Editor V. V. DAKSHINAMOORTHY; circ. 57,530.

Mathrubhumi: M. J. Krishnamohan Memorial Bldg, K. P. Kesava Menon Rd, POB 46, Kozhikode 673 001; tel. (495) 2366655; fax (495) 2366656; e-mail mbiclt@mpp.co.in; internet www.mathrubhumi.com; f. 1923; Malayalam; also publ. from Thiruvananthapuram, Kozhikode, Kannur, Thrissur, Kollam, Malappuram, Pallakad, Alappuzha, Kottayam, Kochi, Bangalore, Chennai, New Delhi and Mumbai; Editor M. KESAVA MENON; circ. 157,040 (2011).

Thiruvananthapuram

Kerala Kaumudi: Kaumudi Bldgs, Pettah, Thiruvananthapuram 695 024; tel. (471) 2461010; fax (471) 2461985; e-mail editor@ekaumudi.com; internet news.keralakaumudi.com; f. 1911; Malayalam; also publ. from Kollam, Alappuzha, Kochi, Kannur, Kozhikode and Bangalore; Editor-in-Chief M. S. MANI; Man. Editor DEEPU RAVI; circ. 60,036.

Madhya Pradesh

Dainik Bhaskar: 6 Dwarka Sadan, Press Complex, M. P. Nagar, Bhopal; tel. (755) 3988884; fax (755) 270466; e-mail editorbhaskar@bhaskar.com; internet www.bhaskar.com; f. 1958; morning; Hindi; also publ. from 18 other regional centres; Chief Editor SHRAVAN GARG; circ. 265,474.

Naidunia: 60/1 Babu Labhchand Chhajlani Marg, Indore 452 009; tel. (731) 4711000; fax (731) 4711111; e-mail response@naidunia.com; internet www.naidunia.com; f. 1947; morning; Hindi; also publ. from Jabalpur, Gwalior and Bhopal; CEO VINAY CHHAJLANI; combined circ. 412,904.

Maharashtra

Kolhapur

Pudhari: 2318, 'C' Ward, Kolhapur 416 002; tel. (231) 2543111; fax (231) 2543124; e-mail news.kop@pudhari.co.in; internet www.pudhari.com; f. 1974; Marathi; Editor P. S. JADHAV; circ. 361,176 (2011).

Mumbai (Bombay)

Afternoon Despatch & Courier: Janmabhoomi Bhavan, 3rd Floor, Janmabhoomi Marg, Fort, Mumbai 400 001; tel. (22) 40768999; fax (22) 40768916; e-mail afternoonnews@gmail.com; internet www.afternoondc.in; evening; English; Editor CAROL ANDRADE.

Bombay Samachar: Red House, S. A. Brelvi Rd, Horniman Circle, Fort, Mumbai 400 001; tel. (22) 22045531; fax (22) 22046642; e-mail samachar.bombay@gmail.com; internet www.bombaysamachar.com; f. 1822; morning and Sun.; Gujarati; political, social and commercial; Editor PINKY DALAL; circ. 77,774 (2011).

Daily News and Analysis (DNA): Oasis Bldg, 1st Floor, Lower Parel, Mumbai 400 013; tel. (22) 39888888; fax (22) 39801000; internet www.dnaindia.com; f. 2005; English; also publ. from Bangalore, Pune, Ahmedabad, Surat and Jaipur; Exec. Editor ADITYA SINHA; circ. 397,147.

Dainik Saamana: Sadguru Darshan, Nagu Sayaji Wadi, Dainik Saamana Marg, Prabhadevi, Mumbai 400 028; tel. (22) 24370591; fax (22) 24224181; f. 1989; Marathi; Exec. Editor SANJAY RAUT; circ. 102,900.

The Economic Times: Times of India Bldg, Dr Dadabhai Naoroji Rd, Mumbai 400 001; tel. (22) 22733535; fax (22) 22731344; e-mail etbom@timesgroup.com; internet economictimes.indiatimes.com; f. 1961; also publ. from New Delhi, Kolkata, Ahmedabad, Hyderabad, Chennai and Bangalore; English; Editor (Mumbai) SUDESHNA SEN; combined circ. 461,900, circ. 241,617 (Mumbai).

Financial Express: Express Towers, Nariman Point, Mumbai 400 021; tel. (22) 6740000; fax (11) 22022139; e-mail editor@expressindia.com; internet www.financialexpress.com; f. 1961; morning; English; also publ. from New Delhi, Bangalore, Kolkata, Coimbatore, Ahmedabad (Gujarati) and Chennai; Man. Editor VIVECK GOENKA; Editor SHOBHANA SUBRAMANIAN; circ. 22,427 (English).

The Free Press Journal: Free Press House, 215 Free Press Journal Rd, Nariman Point, Mumbai 400 021; tel. (22) 22874566; fax (22) 22874688; e-mail mail@fpj.co.in; internet www.freepressjournal.in; f. 1930; English; also publ. from Indore, Kolkata, Bhopal, Chennai and New Delhi; Man. Editor G. L. LAKHOTIA.

Hindustan Times: Mahalaxmi Industrial Estate, 2nd Floor, L. J. Coross Rd No. 1, Mumbai 400 016; tel. (22) 24368012; fax (22) 24303625; e-mail feedback@hindustantimes.in; internet www.hindustantimes.com; f. 1923; also publ. from Delhi, Lucknow, Bhopal, Kolkata and Chandigarh; Editor SOUMYA BHATTACHARYA; circ. 279,372.

Indian Express: Express Tower, 1st and 2nd Floors, Nariman Point, Mumbai 400 021; tel. (22) 67440000; fax (22) 22022139; f. 1940; English; also publ. from 8 regional centres; Man. Editor VIVECK GOENKA; Chief Editor SHEKHAR GUPTA; circ. 75,020.

Inquilab: 156 D. J. Dadajee Rd, Tardeo, Mumbai 400 034; tel. (22) 23522586; fax (22) 23510226; e-mail inquilab@mid-day.com; internet www.inquilab.com; f. 1938; morning; Urdu; Editor SHAHID LATIF; circ. 31,640.

Janmabhoomi: Janmabhoomi Bhavan, Janmabhoomi Marg, Fort, POB 62, Mumbai 400 001; tel. (22) 22870831; fax (22) 22874097; e-mail jbhoomi@yahoo.com; internet www.janmabhoominewspapers.com; f. 1934; evening; Gujarati; Propr Saurashtra Trust; Editor KUNDAN VYAS; circ. 18,464.

Lokasatta: Express Towers, Ramnath Goenka Marg, Nariman Point, Mumbai 400 021; tel. (22) 22022627; fax (22) 22822187; e-mail pratikriya@expressindia.com; internet www.loksatta.com; f. 1948; morning (incl. Sun.); Marathi; also produces editions for New Delhi, Pune, Thane, Nashik, Nagpur, Aurangabad, Navi Mumbai and Ahmedmangar; Editor GIRISH KUBER; circ. 206,975.

Maharashtra Times: Dr Dadabhai Naoroji Rd, POB 213, Mumbai 400 001; tel. (22) 22733636; fax (22) 22731175; internet maharashtratimes.indiatimes.com; f. 1962; Marathi; Editor ASHOK PANVALKAR; circ. 312,614.

Mid-Day: Peninsula Centre, Dr S. S. Rao Rd, opp. Mahatma Gandhi Hospital, Parel, Mumbai 400 012; tel. (22) 67017171; fax (22) 24150009; e-mail cs@mid-day.com; internet www.mid-day.com; f. 1979; daily and Sun.; English; also publ. from New Delhi, Pune and Bangalore; Editor AVIROOK SEN; circ. 121,342.

Mumbai Mirror: The Times of India Bldg., Dr Dadabhai Naoroji Rd, Mumbai 400 001; tel. (22) 26005555; e-mail mumbai.mirror@timesgroup.com; internet www.mumbaimirror.com; f. 2005; English; Editor MEENAL BAGHEL; circ. 708,687.

Navakal: 13 Shenviwadi, Khadilkar Rd, Girgaun, Mumbai 400 004; tel. (22) 23860978; fax (22) 23860989; f. 1923; Marathi; Editor N. Y. KHADILKAR; circ. 172,466.

Navbharat Times: Dr Dadabhai Naoroji Rd, Mumbai 400 001; tel. (22) 22733535; fax (22) 22731144; internet navbharattimes.indiatimes.com; f. 1950; Hindi; also publ. from New Delhi, Jaipur, Patna and Lucknow; Chief Editor VISHWANATH SACHDEV; circ. 159,578 (Mumbai).

Navshakti: Free Press House, 215 Nariman Point, Mumbai 400 021; tel. (22) 22853335; fax (22) 22874688; e-mail editor@navshakti.co.in; internet navshakti.co.in; f. 1932; Marathi; Chief Editor PRAKASH KULKARNI; circ. 16,719.

Sakal: Sakal Bhavan, Plot No. 42-B, Sector No. 11, CBD Belapur, Navi Mumbai 400 614; tel. (22) 66843000; fax (22) 27574280; e-mail editor.mumbai@esakal.com; internet www.esakal.com; f. 1970; Marathi; also publ. from Pune, Aurangabad, Nasik, Kolhapur and Solapur; Chief Editor SANJEEV LATKAR; circ. 88,094.

The Times of India: The Times of India Bldg, Dr Dadabhai Naoroji Rd, Mumbai 400 001; tel. (22) 56353535; fax (22) 22731444; e-mail toieditorial@timesgroup.com; internet www.timesofindia.com; f. 1838; morning; English; also publ. from 9 regional centres; Exec. Editor ARINDAM SENGUPTA; circ. 763,758.

Nagpur

The Hitavada: Pandit Jawaharlal Nehru Marg, POB 201, Dhantoli, Nagpur 440 012; tel. (712) 2435737; fax (712) 2422362; e-mail hitavada_ngp@sancharnet.in; internet www.ehitavada.com; f. 1911; morning; English; also publ. from Raipur and Jabalpur; Man. Editor BANWARILAL PUROHIT; Editor V. PHANSHIKAR; circ. 73,550.

Lokmat: Lokmat Bhavan, Wardha Rd, Nagpur 440 012; tel. (712) 2523527; fax (712) 2445555; e-mail lokmat@bom2.vsnl.net.in; internet onlinenews.lokmat.com; also publ. from Jalgaon, Pune and Nasik; Marathi; Lokmat Samachar (Hindi) publ. from Nagpur, Akola and Aurangabad; Lokmat Times (English) publ. from Nagpur and Aurangabad; Chair. VIJAY DARDA; circ. 205,990 (Marathi), 93,744 (Hindi).

Nava Bharat: Nava Bharat Bhavan, Cotton Market, Nagpur 440 018; tel. (712) 2726677; fax (712) 2723444; internet www.navabharat.biz; f. 1938; morning; Hindi; also publ. from 10 other cities; Editor-in-Chief R. G. MAHESWARI; circ. 133,495.

Tarun Bharat: 28 Farmland, Ramdaspeth, Nagpur 440 010; tel. (712) 6653102; fax (712) 2531758; e-mail ibharat_ngp@sancharnet.in; internet tarunbharat.net; f. 1941; Marathi; independent; also publ. from Belgaum; Man. Editor ANIL DANDEKAR; Chief Editor SUDHIR PATHAK; circ. 53,617 (Nagpur).

Pune

Kesari: 569 Narayan Peth, Pune 411 030; tel. (20) 4459250; fax (20) 4451677; e-mail kesari@giaspn01.vsnl.net.in; internet www.dailykesari.com; f. 1881; Marathi; also publ. from Solapur, Chiplun, Ahmednagar and Sangli; Editor ARVIND VYANKATESH GOKHALE; circ. 41,191.

Sakal: 595 Budhawar Peth, Pune 411 002; tel. (20) 24455500; fax (20) 24450583; e-mail webeditor@esakal.com; internet www.esakal.com; f. 1932; daily; Marathi; also publ. from 10 other regional centres; Chief Editor NAVNEET DESHPANDE (Pune); Man. Editor PRATAP PAWAR; circ. 410,932.

Manipur

Naharolgi Thoudang: Keishampat Airport Rd, Imphal 795 001; tel. (38) 52449086; fax (38) 52440353; e-mail nthoudang@yahoo.co.in; internet www.naharolgithoudang.com; f. 1996; daily; Manipuri; Editor LOYALAKPA KHOIROM; circ. 27,420.

Poknapham: Keishampat Junction, Keishampat Thiyam Leirak, Imphal 795 001; tel. (38) 52459175; fax (38) 52442981; e-mail poknafamdaily@rediffmail.com; internet www.poknapham.in; f. 1975; daily; Manipuri; also publ. from Silchar; Editor A. ROBINDRO SHARMA; Assoc. Editor BIJOY KAKCHINGTABAM; circ. 32,566.

The Sangai Express: Sega Rd, Thouda Bhabok Leikai, Imphal 795 001; tel. (38) 52458133; fax (38) 52444881; e-mail sangaiinfo@gmail.com; internet www.thesangaiexpress.com; f. 1999; daily; Manipuri and English; Editor RAJESH HIJAM; circ. 27,513 (Manipuri) and 11,817 (English).

Meghalaya

Mawphor: Mawkhar, Mavis Dunn Rd, Shillong 793 002; tel. (364) 2548433; e-mail mawphordailynews@yahoo.com; internet mawphor.com; f. 1989; Khasi; Editor D. L. SIANGSHAI; circ. 53,972.

The Shillong Times: Rilbong, Shillong 793 004; tel. (364) 2223488; fax (364) 2229488; e-mail letters@theshillongtimes.com; internet www.theshillongtimes.com; f. 1945; English; Editor PATRICIA MUKHIM; circ. 30,899.

Nagaland

The Morung Express: 4 Duncan Basti, Dimapur 797 112; tel. (386) 236871; fax (386) 235194; e-mail morung@gmail.com; internet www.morungexpress.com; f. 2005; Man. Dir AKUM LONGCHARI; Editor ALONG LONGKUMER; circ. 25,593.

Nagaland Post: Nagaland Post Bldg, POB 59, Circular Rd, Dimapur 797 112; tel. (386) 2230748; fax (386) 2225366; e-mail info@nagalandpost.com; internet www.nagalandpost.com; f. 1990; English; Editor GEOFFREY YADEN; circ. 50,450 (2011).

Odisha

Dharitri: 26B, Industrial Estate, POB 144, Bhubaneswar 751 010; tel. (674) 2580101; fax (674) 2586854; e-mail advt@dharitri.com; internet www.dharitri.com; f. 1974; evening and morning; Oriya; Editor TATHAGATA SATPATHY; circ. 210,986.

Pragativadi: 178B, Mancheswar Industrial Estate, Bhubaneswar 751 010; tel. (674) 2588297; fax (674) 2582709; e-mail pragativadi@yahoo.com; internet www.pragativadi.com; f. 1973; Exec. Editor SAMAHIT BAL; circ. 215,388.

Samaja: Gopabandhu Bhavan, Buxibazar, Cuttack 753 001; tel. (671) 2301994; fax (671) 2301086; e-mail samajactc@hotmail.com; internet www.thesamaja.com; f. 1919; Oriya; also publ. from Sambalpur, Vizag, Bhubaneswar, Rourkela, Baleswar, Berhampur and Kolkata; Editor GOPALA KRUSHNA MAHAPATRA; circ. 14,927.

The Samaya: Plot No. 44 and 54, Sector A, Zone D, Mancheswar Industrial Estate, Bhubaneswar 751 017; tel. (674) 2585740; fax (674) 2582565; e-mail thesamaya@yahoo.com; internet www.orissasamaya.com; f. 1966; Oriya; Editor SATAKADI HOTA; circ. 226,668.

Sambad: B-27 Industrial Estate, Rasulgarh, Bhubaneswar 751 010; tel. (674) 2585351; fax (674) 2588517; e-mail sambadadvt@easternmedia.in; internet sambadepaper.com; f. 1984; Oriya; also publ. from 7 other regional centres; Editor S. R. PATNAIK; circ. 94,903.

Punjab

Chandigarh

The Tribune: Sector 29C, Chandigarh 160 030; tel. (172) 2655066; fax (172) 2651293; e-mail letters@tribuneindia.com; internet www.tribuneindia.com; f. 1881 (English edn), f. 1978 (Hindi and Punjabi edns); Editor-in-Chief RAJ CHENGAPPA; Editor (Hindi edn) NARESH KAUSHAL; Editor (Punjabi edn) VARINDER WALIA; circ. 161,231–English, 59,846–Punjabi, 1,010–Hindi (2011).

Jalandhar

Ajit: Ajit Bhavan, Nehru Garden Rd, Jalandhar 144 001; tel. (181) 2455961; fax (181) 2455960; internet www.ajitjalandhar.com; f. 1955; Punjabi; Chief Editor SADHU SINGH HAMDARD; CEO SARVINDER KAUR; circ. 369,474.

Hind Samachar: Civil Lines, Jalandhar 144 001; tel. (181) 2280104; fax (181) 2280113; e-mail punjabkesari@vsnl.com; internet hindsamachar.in; f. 1948; morning; Hindi; also publ. from Ambala Cantt and Jammu; Editor-in-Chief VIJAY KUMAR CHOPRA; combined circ. 30,041.

Jag Bani: ER-129 Pucca Bagh, Jalandhar; tel. (181) 2280104; fax (181) 2280111; e-mail contact@thepunjabkesari.com; internet www.jagbani.in; f. 1978; morning; Punjabi; also publ. from Ludhiana; Publr JAGAT NARAIN; circ. 302,988.

Punjab Kesari: Civil Lines, Pucca Bagh, Jalandhar 144 001; tel. (181) 2280104; fax (181) 2280111; e-mail contact@thepunjabkesari.com; internet www.thepunjabkesari.com; f. 1965; morning; Hindi; also publ. from Ludhiana, Ambala, Panipat, Hisar, Palampur and Jammu; Editor-in-Chief VIJAY KUMAR CHOPRA; Jt Editor AVINASH CHOPRA; circ. 10,093 (2011).

Rajasthan

Rajasthan Patrika: Kesargarh, Jawaharlal Nehru Marg, Jaipur 302 004; tel. (141) 39404142; fax (141) 2566011; e-mail info@epatrika.com; internet www.rajasthanpatrika.com; f. 1956; Hindi edn also publ. from 17 other towns; Chief Editor GULAB KOTHARI; circ. 345,382 (Hindi).

Rashtradoot: M.I. Rd, POB 30, Jaipur 302 001; tel. (141) 2372634; fax (141) 2373513; f. 1951; Hindi; also publ. from Kota, Udaipur, Ajmer, Bikaner, Jalore, Hindaun and Churu; CEO SOMESH SHARMA; Chief Editor RAJESH SHARMA; circ. 204,878.

Tamil Nadu

Chennai (Madras)

Daily Thanthi: 86 E.V.K. Sampath Rd, POB 467, Chennai 600 007; tel. (44) 26618661; fax (44) 26618797; e-mail managerms@dt.co.in; internet www.dailythanthi.com; f. 1942; Tamil; also publ. from 14 other regional centres; Chief Gen. Man. (Admin.) RENGASAMY CHANDRASEKARAN; Editor J. P. VIJAYARAJ; circ. 1,690,608.

Dinakaran: 229 Kutchery Rd, Mylapore, POB 358, Chennai 600 004; tel. (44) 42209191; fax (44) 24951008; e-mail dotcom@dinakaran.com; internet www.dinakaran.com; f. 1977; Tamil; also publ. from Madurai, Tiruchirapalli, Vellore, Tirunelveli, Salem, Coimbatore and Puducherry (Pondicherry); Man. Dir KALANIDHI MARAN; Editor R. M. R. RAMESH; circ. 246,487.

Dinamalar: 219 Anna Salai, Chennai 600 002; tel. (44) 28413553; fax (44) 28523695; e-mail dmrae@dinamalar.in; internet www.dinamalar.com; f. 1951; Tamil; also publ. from 10 other towns; Editor Dr R. KRISHNAMURTHY; circ. 128,436.

Dinamani: Express Estates, Mount Rd, Chennai 600 002; tel. (44) 8520751; fax (44) 8524500; e-mail webmani@dinamani.com; internet www.dinamani.com; f. 1934; morning; Tamil; also publ. from

Madurai, Coimbatore, Thiruchirapalli, Vellore, Tirunelveli and Bangalore; Editor K. VAIDYANATHAN; circ. 37,981.

Financial Express: Vasanthi Medical Center, 30/20 Pycrofts Garden Rd, Chennai 600 006; tel. (44) 28231112; fax (44) 28231489; e-mail editor@expressindia.com; internet www.financialexpress.com; f. 1961; morning; English; also publ. from Mumbai, Ahmedabad (in Gujarati), Bangalore, Kochi, Kolkata and New Delhi; Man. Editor VIVECK GOENKA; combined circ. 13,909.

The Hindu: Kasturi Bldgs, 859/860 Anna Salai, Chennai 600 002; tel. (44) 28576300; fax (44) 28415325; e-mail letters@thehindu.co.in; internet www.thehindu.com; f. 1878; morning; English; independent; also publ. from 12 other regional centres; Editor-in-Chief SIDDHARTH VARADARAJAN; circ. 1,420,368.

The Hindu Business Line: 859 Anna Salai, Chennai 600 002; tel. (44) 28413344; fax (44) 28415325; e-mail bleditor@thehindu.co.in; internet www.thehindubusinessline.com; f. 1994; morning; English; also publ. from 12 other regional centres; Editor-in-Chief SIDDHARTH VARADARAJAN; circ. 178,520.

Murasoli: 93 Kodambakkam High Rd, Chennai 600 034; tel. (44) 28270044; fax (44) 28217515; internet www.murasoli.in; f. 1960; organ of the DMK; Tamil; Editor S. SELVAM; circ. 54,000.

New Indian Express: 29 Express Gardens, Ambattur Industrial Estate, Chennai 600 058; tel. (44) 23457601; fax (44) 23457619; e-mail info@expressbuzz.com; internet expressbuzz.com; f. 1932 as Indian Express; morning; English; also publ. from 7 other cities; Chair. and Man. Dir MANOJ KUMAR SONTHALIA; circ. 103,247.

Tripura

Dainik Sambad: 11 Jagannath Bari Rd, POB 2, Agartala 799 001; tel. (381) 2326676; fax (381) 2324845; e-mail dainik2@sanchar.net.in; internet www.dainiksambad.net; f. 1966; Bengali; morning; Editor SANJAY GUPTA; circ. 56,922.

Uttar Pradesh

Agra

Amar Ujala: Sikandra Rd, Agra 282 007; tel. (562) 2321600; fax (562) 2322181; e-mail editor@amarujala.com; internet www.amarujala.com; f. 1948; Hindi; also publ. from Bareilly, Allahabad, Jhansi, Kanpur, Moradabad, Chandigarh and Meerut; Editor AJAY K. AGARWAL; circ. 131,688.

Kanpur

Dainik Jagran: Jagran Bldg, 2 Sarvodaya Nagar, Kanpur 208 005; tel. (512) 2216161; fax (512) 2216972; e-mail jpl@jagran.com; internet in.jagran.yahoo.com; f. 1942; Hindi; also publ. from 26 other cities; Chair. and Man. Editor MAHENDRA MOHAN GUPTA; Editor SANJAY GUPTA; combined circ. 3,200,000.

I Next: Jagran Bldg, 2 Sarvodaya Nagar, Kanpur 208005; tel. (512) 2216161; fax (512) 2216972; internet epaper.inextlive.com; f. 2006; Hindi daily in bilingual format.

Lucknow

Hindustan: Vibhuti Khand, nr Picup Bhawan, Gomti Nagar, Lucknow 226 010; tel. (522) 6663296; e-mail hindustan.lucknow@gmail.com; internet www.livehindustan.com; f. 1996; Hindi; also publ. from Delhi, Muzaffarpur, Bhagalpur, Ranchi, Jamshedpur, Dhanbad, Varanasi, Meerut, Agra, Kanpur and Chandigarh; Editor NAVEEN JOSHI; circ. 214,928 (2011).

The Pioneer: Sahara Shopping Centre, Faizabad Rd, Lucknow 226 016; tel. (522) 2346444; fax (522) 2345582; internet www.dailypioneer.com; f. 1865; English; also publ. from Bhopal, Chandigarh, Dehradun, Ranchi and New Delhi; Editor CHANDAN MITRA; circ. 86,913.

Swatantra Bharat: 1 Jopling Rd, 2nd Floor, Lucknow 226 001; tel. (522) 2204306; fax (522) 2208071; e-mail swatantrabharat47@gmail.com; internet swatantrabharat.com; f. 1947; Hindi; also publ. from Kanpur; Editor K. K. SRIVASTAVA; circ. 73,317 (Lucknow), 73,689 (Kanpur).

The Times of India: 16 Rana Pratap Marg, Lucknow 226 001; tel. (522) 2206081; internet timesofindia.indiatimes.com; f. 1838; also publ. from 9 other towns (Mumbai, Pune, Ahmedabad, Bangalore, Chennai, Hyderabad, Jaipur, Kolkata and Delhi); Editor-in-Chief JAIDEEP BOSE; circ. 107,503 (2011).

Varanasi

Aj: Aj Bhavan, Sant Kabir Rd, Kabirchaura, Varanasi 221 001; tel. (542) 2393981; fax (542) 2393989; e-mail ajhindidaily@gmail.com; f. 1920; Hindi; also publ. from Gorakhpur, Patna, Allahabad, Ranchi, Agra, Bareilly, Lucknow, Jamshedpur, Haldwani and Kanpur; Editor SHARDUL VIKRAM GUPTA; circ. 45,314.

West Bengal

Kolkata (Calcutta)

Aajkaal: BP-7, Sector 5, Bidhannagar, Kolkata 700 091; tel. (33) 30110800; fax (33) 23675502; e-mail aajkaal@cal.vsnl.net.in; internet www.aajkaal.net; f. 1981; morning; Bengali; also publ. from Agartala and Siliguri; Chief Editor ASHOK DASGUPTA; circ. 152,123.

Ananda Bazar Patrika: 6 Prafulla Sarkar St, Kolkata 700 001; tel. (33) 22374880; fax (33) 22253241; internet www.anandabazar.com; f. 1922; morning; Bengali; also publ. from Mumbai; Chief Editor AVEEK SARKAR; circ. 1,263,259.

Bartaman: Bartaman Pvt Ltd, 6 J. B. S Haldane Ave, Kolkata 700 105; tel. (33) 23000291; fax (33) 23234030; e-mail info@bartamanpatrika.com; internet www.bartamanpatrika.com; f. 1984; also publ. from Barddhaman and Siliguri; Editor SUBHA DUTTA; circ. 534,603.

Business Standard: Saraf Bldg, 3rd Floor, 4/1 Red Cross Pl., Kolkata 700 001; tel. (33) 22101314; fax (33) 22101599; e-mail letters@business-standard.com; internet www.business-standard.com; f. 1975; morning; also publ. from Mumbai, Delhi, Patna, Lucknow, Bhopal and Chandigarh; English; Editor A. K. BHATTACHARYA; circ. 13,217.

Financial Express: 83 B. K. Pal Ave, Kolkata 700 005; e-mail editor@expressindia.com; internet www.financialexpress.com; morning; English; also publ. from Mumbai, Ahmedabad, Bangalore, Coimbatore, Kochi, Chennai and New Delhi; Man. Editor VIVECK GOENKA; circ. 12,312.

Ganashakti: 74A A. J. C. Bose Rd, Kolkata 700 016; tel. (33) 22278950; fax (33) 2278090; e-mail mail@ganashakti.co.in; internet www.ganashakti.com; f. 1967; owned by Communist Party of India (Marxist), West Bengal State Cttee; morning; Bengali; also publ. from Durgapur and Siliguri; Editor NARAYAN DATTA; circ. 176,812.

Sandhya Aajkaal: BP-7, Sector 5, Salt Lake City, Kolkata 700 091; tel. (33) 30110800; fax (33) 23675502; e-mail aajkaal@cal.vsnl.net.in; internet www.aajkaal.net; evening; Bengali; Chief Editor ASHOK DASGUPTA; circ. 12,815.

Sangbad Pratidin: 20 Prafulla Sarkar St, Kolkata 700 072; tel. (33) 22128400; fax (33) 22126031; e-mail mail@sangbadpratidin.org; internet sangbadpratidin.in; f. 1992; morning; Bengali; also publ. from Ranchi and Siliguri; Chief Editor SRINJOY BOSE; circ. 299,876.

Sanmarg: 160B Chittaranjan Ave, Kolkata 700 007; tel. (33) 30615000; fax (33) 22415087; e-mail sanmarghindi@gmail.com; internet www.sanmarg.in; f. 1948; Hindi; also publ. from Varanasi, Patna, Ranchi and Bhubaneswar; Editor HARI RAM PANDEY; circ. 115,049.

The Statesman: Statesman House, 4 Chowringhee Sq., Kolkata 700 001; tel. (33) 22127070; fax (33) 22126181; e-mail thestatesman@vsnl.com; internet www.thestatesman.net; f. 1875; morning; English; independent; also publ. from New Delhi, Siliguri and Bhubaneswar; Editor RAVINDRA KUMAR; circ. 177,113.

The Telegraph: 6 Prafulla Sarkar St, Kolkata 700 001; tel. (33) 22345374; fax (33) 22253243; e-mail ttedit@abpmail.com; internet www.telegraphindia.com; f. 1982; English; also publ. from Guwahati, Jamshedpur, Ranchi and Siliguri; Editor AVEEK SARKAR; circ. 555,869.

Uttar Banga Sambad: 7 Old Court House St, Kolkata 700 001; tel. (33) 22435663; fax (33) 22435618; e-mail uttarmail@sify.com; internet www.uttarbangasambad.com; f. 1980; Bengali; circ. 143,177.

Vishwamitra: 74 Lenin Sarani, Kolkata 700 013; tel. (33) 22651139; fax (33) 22656393; e-mail vismtra@vsnl.com; f. 1915; morning; Hindi; commercial; Editor PRAKASH CHANDRA AGRAWALLA; circ. 99,911.

SELECTED PERIODICALS

Delhi and New Delhi

Alive: Delhi Press Bldg, E-3 Jhandewala Estate, Rani Jhansi Rd, New Delhi 110 055; tel. (11) 23529557; fax (11) 23625020; e-mail delpress@bol.net.in; internet www.caravanalive.com; f. 1940 as *Caravan*; monthly; English; men's interests; Editor, Publr and Printer PARESH NATH; circ. 4,049.

Bal Bharati: Patiala House, Publications Division, Ministry of Information and Broadcasting, New Delhi; f. 1948; monthly; Hindi; for children; Editor VEDPAL; circ. 60,425.

Business Today: Videocon Towers, E-1 Jhandelwalan Extn, New Delhi 110 055; tel. (11) 23684800; fax (11) 23684819; e-mail Mukta.Saigal@intoday.com; internet businesstoday.intoday.in; f. 1992; fortnightly; English; Editor CHAITANYA KALBAG; circ. 111,806.

Catholic India: CBCI Centre, 1 Ashok Place, Goldakkhana, New Delhi 110 001; tel. and fax (11) 23344470; fax (11) 23364615; e-mail editor@cbci.in; internet cbci.in; bi-annual; Fr GEORGE PLATHOTTAM.

Champak: Delhi Press Bldg, E-3 Jhandewala Estate, Rani Jhansi Rd, New Delhi 110 055; tel. (11) 41398888; fax (11) 23625020; e-mail editorial@delhipressgroup.com; f. 1968; fortnightly (Hindi, English, Gujarati, Tamil, Telugu, Malayalam, Marathi and Kannada edns); children's; Editor, Publr and Printer PARESH NATH; circ. 65,220 (Hindi), 47,225 (English), 13,155 (Marathi), 5,812 (Gujarati), 1,934 (Malayalam), 1,652 (Telugu), 992 (Tamil), 8,393 (Kannada).

Children's World: Nehru House, 4 Bahadur Shah Zafar Marg, New Delhi 110 002; tel. (11) 23316970; fax (11) 23721090; e-mail cbtnd@cbtnd.com; internet www.childrensbooktrust.com; f. 1968; monthly; English; Editor NAVIN MENON; circ. 25,000.

Competition Refresher: 4739/23 UGF, Ansari Rd, Daryaganj, New Delhi 110 002; tel. (11) 23283226; fax (11) 23269227; e-mail editorial@brightpublications.com; internet www.brightpublications.com; f. 1984; monthly; English; Chief Editor, Publr and Man. Dir PRITAM SINGH BRIGHT; circ. 175,000.

Competition Success Review (CSR): 604 Prabhat Kiran Bldg, Rajendra Place, Delhi 110 008; tel. (11) 45113300; fax (11) 25825391; e-mail info@competitionreview.com; internet www.competitionreview.com; f. 1964; monthly; English; Editor S. K. SACHDEVA; circ. 185,955.

Cosmopolitan: Videocon Tower, 5th Floor, E-1 Jhandewalan Extn, New Delhi 110 055; tel. (11) 23684800; e-mail nandini.bhalla@intoday.com; internet cosmo.intoday.in; monthly; English; women's lifestyle; Editor NANDINI BHALLA; circ. 31,149.

Cricket Samrat: A6/1 Mayapuri Phase 1, New Delhi 110 064; tel. (11) 28115835; fax (11) 25469581; internet www.dewanpublications.com/magazine/index.php; f. 1978; monthly; Hindi; Editor ANAND DEWAN; circ. 9,645 (2011).

Employment News: Government of India, East Blk IV, Level 5, R. K. Puram, New Delhi 110 066; tel. (11) 26174975; fax (11) 26105875; e-mail empnews@bol.net.in; internet www.employmentnews.gov.in; f. 1976; weekly; Hindi, Urdu and English edns; Gen. Man. and Chief Editor VISHWANATH RAMESH; Editor HASAN ZIA; combined circ. 301,868.

Filmi Duniya: B-10 Shiv Apt, 7 Rajnarain Marg, Civil Lines, New Delhi 110 054; tel. (11) 23278087; fax (11) 23279341; e-mail filmiduniyaonline@yahoo.com; f. 1958; monthly; Hindi; Publr V. K. CHOPRA; circ. 35,550.

Grihshobha: Delhi Press Bldg, E-3 Jhandewala Estate, Rani Jhansi Rd, New Delhi 110 055; tel. (11) 51398888; fax (11) 51540714; e-mail editorial@delhipressgroup.com; internet www.grihshobhaindia.com; f. 1979; fortnightly Hindi and Bangla edns; monthly Tamil, Telugu, Kannada, Marathi, Malayalam and Gujarati edns; women's interests; Editor, Publr and Printer PARESH NATH; circ. 68,355 (Kannada), 41,334 (Gujarati), 88,119 (Marathi), 286,031 (Hindi), 11,111 (Telugu), 3,569 (Tamil), 4,700 (Malayalam), 3,144 (Bangla).

India Perspectives: Room 149B, 'A' Wing, Shastri Bhavan, New Delhi 110 001; tel. (11) 23389471; fax 23385549; internet meaindia.nic.in/mystart.php?id=2701; f. 1988; culture; publ. by Ministry of External Affairs; Editor NAVDEEP SURI.

India Today: F-14/15, Connaught Place, New Delhi 110 001; tel. (11) 23315801; fax (11) 23316180; e-mail ratnam@intoday.com; internet www.india-today.com; f. 1975; weekly; English, Tamil, Telugu, Malayalam, Bengali and Hindi; Editor M. J. AKBAR; Editor-in-Chief AROON PURIE; circ. 336,460 (English), 130,574 (Hindi), 28,355 (Tamil), 18,850 (Malayalam), 16,974 (Telugu), 4,981 (Bengali).

Indian Railways: 411 Rail Bhavan, Raisina Rd, New Delhi 110 001; tel. (11) 23384481; fax (11) 23383540; e-mail editorir@rb.railnet.gov.in; f. 1956; monthly; English; publ. by the Ministry of Railways (Railway Board); Editor M. R. KALYANI; circ. 7,000.

Junior Science Refresher: 4739/23 UGF, Ansari Road, Daryaganj, New Delhi 110 002; tel. (11) 23282226; fax (11) 23269227; e-mail editorial@brightpublications.com; internet www.brightpublications.com; f. 1987; monthly; English; Chief Editor, Publr and Man. Dir PRITAM SINGH BRIGHT; circ. 118,000.

Kadambini: Hindustan Times House, 18–20 Kasturba Gandhi Marg, New Delhi 110 001; tel. (11) 66561234; fax (11) 66561270; e-mail vnagar@hindustantimes.com; f. 1960; monthly; Hindi; Editor VIJAY KISHORE MANAV; Exec. Editor VISHNU NAGAR; circ. 31,530.

Krishak Samachar: Bharat Krishak Samaj, Dr Panjabrao Deshmukh Krishak Bhavan, A-1 Nizamuddin West, New Delhi 110 013; tel. (11) 24619508; fax (11) 24359509; e-mail publication@bks.org.in; f. 1957; monthly; English and Hindi edns; agriculture; Editor Dr KRISHAN BIR CHAUDHARY; circ. 6,970 (English), 22,728 (Hindi).

Kurukshetra: Soochna Bhawan, CGO Complex, Lodhi Rd, New Delhi 110 003; tel. (11) 23015014; fax (11) 23386879; monthly; English and Hindi; rural development; Publr KAILASH CHAND MEENA; circ. 18,056 (English), 21,146 (Hindi).

Liberation: U-90 Shakarpur, New Delhi 110 092; tel. and fax (11) 22521067; fax (11) 22442790; e-mail mail@cpiml.org; internet www.cpiml.org; f. 1967; monthly; organ of Communist Party of India (Marxist-Leninist).

Mainstream: 145/1D Shahpur Jat, 1st Floor, nr Asiad Village, New Delhi 110 049; tel. (11) 26497188; fax (11) 26569382; e-mail mainlineweekly@yahoo.com; internet www.mainstreamweekly.net; English; weekly; politics and current affairs; Editor SUMIT CHAKRAVARTTY.

Maxim India: Media Transasia (India) Ltd, K-35, Green Park, New Delhi 110 016; tel. (11) 26862687; fax (11) 26867641; internet www.maximindia.in; f. 2005; monthly; English; men's lifestyle; CEO and Publr PIYUSH SHARMA; Editor-in-Chief ANUP KUTTY.

Mayapuri: A-5, Mayapuri Phase 1, New Delhi 110 064; tel. (11) 28116120; fax (11) 41833139; e-mail info@mayapurigroup.com; internet www.mayapurigroup.com/mayapuri.htm; f. 1974; weekly; Hindi; cinema; Editor A. P. BAJAJ; circ. 146,144.

Nandan: Hindustan Times House, 18–20 Kasturba Gandhi Marg, New Delhi 110 001; tel. (11) 66561213; fax (11) 66561270; e-mail kshamasharma@livehindustan.com; f. 1964; monthly; Hindi; children's; Publr SHASHI SHEKHAR; circ. 57,694.

New Age Weekly: Ajoy Bhavan, 15 Comrade Indrajeet Gupta Marg, Delhi 110 002; tel. (11) 23230762; fax (11) 23235543; e-mail cpindia@del2.vsnl.net.in; internet www.newageweekly.com; f. 1953; main organ of the Communist Party of India; weekly; English; Editor SHAMEEM FAIZEE; Man. N. S. NEGI; circ. 215,000.

Organiser: Sanskriti Bhavan, D. B. Gupta Rd, Jhandewala, New Delhi 110 055; tel. (11) 47642022; fax (11) 47642023; e-mail editor@organiserweekly.com; internet www.organiser.org; f. 1947; weekly; English; Editor R. BALASHANKAR; circ. 44,100.

Outlook: AB-10 Safdarjung Enclave, New Delhi 110 029; tel. (11) 26191421; fax (11) 26191420; e-mail outlook@outlookindia.com; internet www.outlookindia.com; f. 1995; weekly; Hindi and English edns; Publr MAHESHWER PERI; Editor-in-Chief KRISHNA PRASAD; circ. 250,000.

Panchjanya: Sanskriti Bhavan, Deshbandhu Gupta Marg, Jhandewala, New Delhi 110 055; tel. (11) 47642013; fax (11) 47642015; e-mail editor.panchjanya@gmail.com; internet www.panchjanya.com; f. 1947; weekly; Hindi; general interest; nationalist; Editor BALDEV BHAI SHARMA; circ. 41,573.

Punjabi Digest: 209 Hemkunt House, 6 Rajendra Place, POB 2549, New Delhi 110 008; tel. (11) 25715225; fax (11) 25761053; e-mail info@punjabidigest.com; internet www.punjabidigest.com; f. 1971; literary monthly; Gurmukhi; Chief Editor Sardar S. B. SINGH; circ. 55,000.

Sainik Samachar: Blk L-1, Church Rd, New Delhi 110 001; tel. (11) 23094668; e-mail sainiksamachar@gmail.com; internet sainiksamachar.nic.in; f. 1909; pictorial fortnightly for India's armed forces; English, Hindi, Urdu, Tamil, Punjabi, Telugu, Marathi, Kannada, Gorkhali, Malayalam, Bengali, Assamese and Oriya edns; Editor-in-Chief DHIRENDRA OJHA; circ. 20,000.

Saras Salil: Delhi Press Bldg, E-3 Jhandewala Estate, Rani Jhansi Rd, New Delhi 110 055; tel. (11) 41398888; fax (11) 41540714; e-mail editorial@delhipressgroup.com; internet www.delhipress.in; f. 1993; fortnightly; Hindi, Telugu, Tamil, Gujarati and Marathi edns; Editor, Publr and Printer PARESH NATH; circ. 677,503 (Hindi), 4,066 (Marathi), 1,092 (Gujarati), 1,015 (Telugu).

Sarita: Delhi Press Bldg, E-3 Jhandewala Estate, Rani Jhansi Rd, New Delhi 110 055; tel. (11) 41398888; fax (11) 23625020; e-mail editorial@delhipressgroup.com; internet www.delhipress.in; f. 1945; fortnightly; Hindi; family magazine; Editor, Publr and Printer PARESH NATH; circ. 75,735.

Tehelka: M-76, M-Block Market, 2nd Floor, Greater Kailash Pt 2, New Delhi 110 048; tel. and fax (11) 40575757; e-mail editor@tehelka.com; internet www.tehelka.com; f. 2004; weekly; English; current affairs, business and culture; Editor (vacant).

Vigyan Pragati: CSIR-NISCAI, Dr K. S. Krishnan Marg, New Delhi 110 012; tel. (11) 25841769; fax (11) 25847062; e-mail vp@niscair.res.in; internet www.niscair.res.in; f. 1952; monthly; Hindi; popular science; Editor PRADEEP SHARMA; circ. 37,000.

Woman's Era: Delhi Press Bldg, E-3 Jhandewala Estate, Rani Jhansi Rd, New Delhi 110 055; tel. (11) 41398888; fax (11) 23625020; e-mail delpress@bol.net.in; internet www.womansera.com; f. 1973; fortnightly; English; women's interests; Editor, Publr and Printer PARESH NATH; circ. 66,200.

Yojana: Yojana Bhavan, Sansad Marg, New Delhi 110 001; tel. (11) 23717910; fax (11) 23359578; e-mail yojana@techpilgrim.com; internet www.yojana.gov.in; f. 1957; monthly; English, Tamil, Bengali, Marathi, Gujarati, Assamese, Malayalam, Telugu, Kannada, Punjabi, Urdu, Oriya and Hindi edns; Chief Editor RINA SONOWAL KOULI; circ. 29,032 (English).

Andhra Pradesh

Andhra Bhoomi Sachitra Masa Patrika: 36 Sarojini Devi Rd, Secunderabad 500 003; tel. (842) 27802346; fax (842) 27805256; f. 1977; fortnightly; Telugu; Editor T. VENKATRAM REDDY; circ. 34,817.

Andhra Jyoti Sachitra Vara Patrika: Vijayawada 520 010; tel. (866) 2474532; f. 1967; weekly; Telugu; Editor PURANAM SUBRAMANYA SARMA; circ. 59,000.

Andhra Prabha Weekly: 591 Lower Tank Bund Rd, Express Centre, Domalaguda, Hyderabad 500 029; tel. (40) 2233586; e-mail info@apweekly.com; internet www.apweekly.com; weekly; Telugu; publ. by Indian Express Group.

Swati Saparivara Patrika: Anil Bldgs, Suryaraopet, POB 339, Vijayawada 520 002; tel. (866) 2431862; fax (866) 2430433; e-mail advt_swati@sify.com; internet www.swatipublications.com; f. 1984; weekly; Telugu; Editor VEMURI BALARAM; circ. 252,100.

Assam (Asom)

Agradoot: Agradoot Bhavan, Dispur, Guwahati 781 006; tel. (361) 2261923; fax (361) 2260655; e-mail agradoot@sify.com; f. 1971; bi-weekly; Assamese; Editor KANAK SEN DEKA; circ. 29,463.

Asam Bani: Tribune Bldg, Guwahati 781 003; tel. (361) 2661356; fax (361) 2660594; e-mail assam@assamnet.org; internet www.assamtribune.com; f. 1955; weekly; Assamese; Editor DILEEP CHANDAN; circ. 6,153.

Sadin: Maniram Dewan Rd, Chandmari, Guwahati 781 003; tel. (361) 2524594; fax (361) 2524634; e-mail sadin@pratidinassam.com; internet www.pratidinassam.com/sadin; weekly; Assamese; Editor ANURADHA SHARMA PUJARI; circ. 33,082.

Bihar

Hamara Dinmaan: Trading Co Pvt Ltd, Bandhuk Bhawan, Station Rd, Patna; monthly; Hindi; Publr MAHESH KUMAR SINGH; circ. 53,700.

Kewal Sach: East Ashok Nagar, 14 Kankarbagh Rd, Patna 800 020; tel. (612) 3240075; e-mail info@kewalsach.com; internet www.kewalsach.com; monthly; Hindi; Publr BRAJESH MISHRA; circ. 24,035.

Ubharta Bihar: C-49 Housing Colony, Lohiya Nagar, Kankadbagh, Patna 800020; internet ubhartabihar.com; monthly; Hindi; Publr RAJIV RANJAN; circ. 23,550.

Chhattisgarh

Krishak Jagat: LIG-163, Sector 2, Shankar Nagar, Raipur; tel. (771) 2420449; e-mail info@krishakjagat.org; internet www.krishakjagat.org; f. 1946; weekly; Hindi; agricultural devt; Chief Editor VIJAY KUMAR BONDRIYA; circ. 35,460.

Gujarat

Akhand Anand: Anand Bhavan, Relief Rd, POB 123, Ahmedabad 380 001; tel. (79) 2357482; e-mail innitadi@sancharnet.in; f. 1947; monthly; Gujarati; Pres. ANAND AMIN; Editor Dr DILAVARSINH JADEJA; circ. 10,000.

Chitralok: Gujarat Samachar Bhavan, Khanpur, POB 254, Ahmedabad 380 001; tel. (79) 5504010; fax (79) 5502000; e-mail editor@gujaratsamachar.com; internet www.gujaratsamachar.com/20110624/purti/chitralok/chlokhome.html; f. 1952; weekly; Gujarati; films; Man. Editor SHREYANS S. SHAH; circ. 20,000.

Parmarth: Jai Hind Publications, Jai Hind Press Bldg, Babubhai Shah Marg, Rajkot 360 001; tel. (281) 2440511; fax (281) 2448677; e-mail info@jaihinddaily.com; monthly; Gujarati; philosophy and religion; Editor Y. N. SHAH; circ. 8,000.

Sakhi: Sakhi Publications, Jai Hind Press Bldg, nr Gujarat Chamber, Ashram Rd, Navrangpura, Ahmedabad 380 009; tel. (79) 26581734; fax (79) 26587681; f. 1984; fortnightly; Gujarati; women's interests; Man. Editor NITA Y. SHAH; Editor Y. N. SHAH; circ. 10,000.

Stree: Sandesh Bhavan, Lad Society Rd, Ahmedabad 380 054; tel. (79) 26765480; fax (79) 26753587; e-mail stree@sandesh.com; internet www.sandesh.com; f. 1962; weekly; Gujarati; Editor RITABEN PATEL; circ. 42,000.

Zagmag: Gujarat Samachar Bhavan, Khanpur, Ahmedabad 380 001; tel. (79) 30410000; fax 25502000; f. 1952; weekly; Gujarati; for children; Editor BAHUBALI S. SHAH; circ. 38,000.

Karnataka

Mayura: 75 Mahatma Gandhi Rd, Bangalore 560 001; tel. (80) 25588999; fax (80) 25587179; e-mail ads@deccanherald.co.in; f. 1968; monthly; Kannada; Editor-in-Chief K. N. SHANTH KUMAR; circ. 20,512 (2011).

Sudha: 75 Mahatma Gandhi Rd, Bangalore 560 001; tel. (80) 25588999; fax (80) 25587179; e-mail ads@deccanherald.co.in; f. 1965; weekly; Kannada; Editor-in-Chief K. N. HARI KUMAR; circ. 61,300.

Taranga: New Udayavani Bldg, Press Corner, Manipal 576 104; tel. (820) 2571151; fax (820) 2570563; e-mail tarangaonline@manipalmedia.com; internet www.udayavani.com; f. 1983; weekly; Kannada; Editor-in-Chief SANDHYA S. PAI; circ. 69,510.

Kerala

Arogya Masika: Mathrubhumi Bldgs, K. P. Kesava Menon Rd, Kozhikode 673 001; tel. (495) 2765381; fax (495) 2760138; e-mail arogyamasika@mpp.co.in; internet www.mathrubhumi.com; owned by Mathrubhumi Printing and Publishing Co Ltd; monthly; Malayalam; health; Man. Editor P. V. CHANDRAN; circ. 193,391 (2011).

Balabhumi: Matrabhumi Bldgs, K. P. Kesava Menon Rd, Kozhikode 673 001; tel. (495) 2366655; fax (495) 2366656; e-mail balabhumi@mpp.co.in; internet www.mathrubhumi.com; f. 1996; weekly; Malayalam; children's; Editor K. K. SREEDHARAN NAIR; circ. 126,580.

Balarama: MM Publications Ltd, POB 226, Kottayam 686 001; tel. (481) 2563721; fax (481) 2564393; e-mail childrensdivision@mmpublications.com; f. 1972; children's weekly; Malayalam; Chief Editor BINA MATHEW; Senior Gen. Man. V. SAJEEV GEORGE; circ. 245,898.

Chithrabhumi: Mathrubhumi Bldgs, K. P. Kesava Menon Rd, Kozhikode 673 001; tel. (495) 2366655; fax (495) 2366656; e-mail cinema@mpp.co.in; internet www.mathrubhumi.org; f. 1982; owned by Mathrubhumi Printing and Publishing Co; weekly; Malayalam; films; Editor K. K. SREEDHARAN NAIR; circ. 23,260.

Grihalakshmi: Mathrubhumi Bldgs, K. P. Kesava Menon Rd, POB 46, Kozhikode 673 001; tel. (495) 2366655; fax (495) 2366656; e-mail mathrclt@md2.vsnl.net.in; internet www.mathrubhumi.org; f. 1979; monthly; Malayalam; women's interests; Editor K. K. SREEDHARAN NAIR; circ. 204,674.

Kalakaumudi: Kaumudi Bldgs, Pettah, Thiruvananthapuram 695 024; tel. (471) 2443531; fax (471) 2442895; e-mail vellinakshatram@gmail.com; internet www.kalakaumudi.com; f. 1975; weekly; Malayalam; Chief Editor M. S. MANI; Editor N. R. S. BABU; circ. 73,000.

Kerala Sabdam: Andamukkam, Kollam 691 001; tel. (474) 2745772; fax (474) 2751010; e-mail sabdam@vsnl.com; internet www.nanaonline.in; f. 1962; weekly; Malayalam; Man. Editor B. A. RAJAKRISHNAN; circ. 66,600.

Malayala Manorama: K. K. Rd, POB 26, Kottayam 686 001; tel. (481) 2563646; fax (481) 2565398; e-mail editorial@mm.co.in; internet www.manoramaonline.com; f. 1937; weekly; Malayalam; also publ. from Kozhikode; Editor-in-Chief MAMMEN MATHEW; circ. 518,542 (2011).

Mathrubhumi Sports Masika: Mathrubhumi Bldgs, K. P. Kesava Menon Rd, Kozhikode 673 001; tel. (495) 2366655; fax (495) 2366656; e-mail sports@mpp.co.in; internet www.mathrubhumi.com/sports; monthly; Malayalam; sport; Editor M. KESAVA MENON; circ. 46,933 (2011).

Thozhilvartha: Mathrubhumi Bldgs, K. P. Kesava Menon Rd, Kozhikode 673 001; tel. (495) 2366655; fax (495) 2366656; e-mail mbiclt@mpp.co.in; internet www.mathrubhumi.org; f. 1992; weekly; Malayalam; employment; Editor K. K. SREEDHARAN NAIR; circ. 313,131.

Vanitha: MM Publications Ltd, POB 226, Kottayam 686 001; tel. (481) 2563721; fax (481) 2564393; e-mail vanitha@mmp.in; f. 1975; women's fortnightly; Malayalam (monthly) and Hindi editions; Chief Editor PREMA MAMMEN MATHEW, MARIAM MAMMEN MATHEW; Gen. Man. V. SAJEEV GEORGE; circ. 586,609 (Malayalam), 209,188 (Hindi).

Vellinakshatram: Kaumudi Bldgs, Pettah, Thiruvananthapuram 695 024; tel. (471) 2443531; fax (471) 2442895; e-mail kalakaumudi@vsnl.net; internet www.vellinakshatram.com; f. 1987; film weekly; Malayalam; Editor PRASAD LAKSHMANAN; Chief Editor SUKUMARAN MANI; circ. 65,000.

The Week: Malayala Manorama Bldgs, POB 4278, Kochi 682 036; tel. (484) 2316285; fax (484) 2315745; e-mail editor@the-week.com; internet week.manoramaonline.com; f. 1982; weekly; English; current affairs; Man. Editor PHILIP MATHEW; circ. 235,667.

Madhya Pradesh

Krishak Jagat: 14 Indira Press Complex, M. P. Nagar, POB 37, Bhopal 462 011; tel. (755) 3013605; fax (755) 2571449; e-mail info@krishakjagat.org; internet www.krishakjagat.org; f. 1946; weekly; Hindi; agriculture; also publ. in Jaipur and Raipur; Chief Editor VIJAY KUMAR BONDRIYA; Editor SUNIL GANGRADE; circ. 73,950.

Maharashtra

Mumbai (Bombay)

Abhiyaan: Sambhaav Media Ltd, 4 AB, Government Industrial Estate, Charkop, Kandivli (W), Mumbai 400 067; tel. (22) 28687515; fax (22) 28680991; e-mail rajeshpathak@sambhaav.com; internet www.sambhaav.com; f. 1986; weekly; Gujarati; Chief Man. Dir KIRAN VADODARIA; Group Editor DEEPAL TREVEDIE; circ. 68,883.

Arogya Sanjeevani: C-14 Royal Industrial Estate, 5-B Naigaum Cross Rd, Wadala, Mumbai 400 031; tel. (22) 24138723; fax (22) 24133610; e-mail woman17@zediffmail.com; f. 1990; quarterly; Hindi; Editor RAM KRISHNA SHUKLA; circ. 12,204 (2011).

Auto India: Nirmal, Nariman Point, Mumbai 400 021; tel. (22) 22883946; fax (22) 22883940; e-mail editor@auto-india.com; f. 1994; monthly; Editor RAJ WARRIOR; circ. 31,845.

Bhavan's Journal: Kulapati Dr K. M. Munshi Marg, Chowpatty, Mumbai 400 007; tel. (22) 23631261; fax (22) 23630058; e-mail bhavan@bhavans.info; internet www.bhavans.info; f. 1954; fortnightly; English; literature, philosophy, culture and spirituality; Exec. Sec. H. N. DASTUR; Editor V. N. NARAYANAN; circ. 40,000.

Bombay Samachar: Red House, Sayed Abdulla Brelvi Rd, Mumbai 400 001; tel. (22) 22045531; fax (22) 22046642; e-mail samachar.bombay@gmail.com; internet bombaysamachar.com; f. 1822; weekly; Gujarati; Editor P. D. DALAL (acting); circ. 77,774 (2011).

Business India: Nirmal, 14th Floor, Nariman Point, Mumbai 400 021; tel. (22) 22883943; fax (22) 22883940; e-mail biedit.mumbai@businessindiagroup.com; internet www.businessindiagroup.com; f. 1978; fortnightly; English; Publr ASHOK ADVANI; circ. 75,700.

Business World: B-2/C-2, Paragon Condominium Asscn, P. Budhkar Marg, Worli, Mumbai 400 013; tel. (22) 24962587; fax (22) 24962596; e-mail bwonline@bworldmail.com; internet www.businessworld.in; f. 1980; weekly; English; Editor PROSENJIT DATTA; circ. 146,500.

Chitralekha: 62 Vaju Kotak Marg, Fort, Mumbai 400 001; tel. (22) 40347777; fax (22) 22615895; e-mail mumbai@chitralekha.com; internet www.chitralekha.com; f. 1950 (Gujarati), f. 1989 (Marathi); weekly; Gujarati and Marathi; Editors BHARAT GHELANI, GYANESH MAHARAO; circ. 114,587 (Gujarati), 21,763 (Marathi).

Cine Blitz Film Monthly: A/3, Sangam Bhavan, Ground Floor, Brahma Kumaris Rd, nr Strand Cinema, Colaba, Mumbai 400 005; tel. (22) 22830668; fax (22) 22830672; e-mail cbedit@sify.com; f. 1974; fortnightly; English; Editor NISHI PREM; circ. 41,611.

Economic and Political Weekly: 320–321, A to Z Industrial Estate, Ganapatrao Kadam Marg, Lower Parel, Mumbai 400 013; tel. (22) 40638282; fax (22) 24934515; e-mail epw.mumbai@gmail.com; internet epw.in; f. 1966; English; Editor C. RAMMANOHAR REDDY; circ. 12,500.

Femina: Times of India Bldg, Dr Dadabhai Naoroji Rd, Mumbai 400 001; tel. and fax (22) 22733535; fax (22) 22731585; e-mail contactfemina@wwm.co.in; internet www.femina.in; f. 1959; fortnightly (English), monthly (Hindi); Editor-in-Chief PETTY S. FATIMAH; circ. 138,644 (English), 39,575 (Hindi).

Filmfare: Times of India Bldg, 4th Floor, Dr Dadabhai Naoroji Rd, Mumbai 400 001; tel. (22) 22733535; fax (22) 22731585; e-mail rahul.nanda@wwm.co.in; internet www.filmfare.com; f. 1952; monthly; English; Exec. Editor SHASHI BALIGA; circ. 93,127.

Janmabhoomi-Pravasi: Janmabhoomi Bhavan, Janmabhoomi Marg, Fort, POB 62, Mumbai 400 001; tel. (22) 22870831; fax (22) 22874097; e-mail bhoomi@bom3.vsnl.net.in; internet pravasi.janmabhoominewspapers.com; f. 1939; weekly; Gujarati; Propr Saurashtra Trust; Editor KUNDAN VYAS; circ. 27,709.

Meri Saheli: C-14 Royal Industrial Estate, 5-B Naigaum Cross Rd, Wadala, Mumbai 400 031; tel. (22) 24182797; fax (22) 24133610; e-mail woman17@zediffmail.com; internet www.merisaheli.com; f. 1987; monthly; Hindi; women's lifestyle; Editor HEMA MALINI; circ. 369,446.

New Woman: C-14 Royal Industrial Estate, 5-B Naigaum Cross Rd, Wadala, Mumbai 400 031; tel. (22) 43448000; fax (22) 43448080; e-mail newwomanmag@gmail.com; f. 1996; monthly; English; Editor HEMA MALINI; circ. 72,800.

Onlooker: Free Press House, 215 Free Press Journal Marg, Nariman Point, Mumbai 400 021; tel. (22) 22874566; f. 1939; fortnightly; English; news magazine; Exec. Editor K. SRINIVASAN; circ. 61,000.

Reader's Digest: 12th Floor, Tower 2A, One India Bulls, Parel West, Mumbai 400 001; tel. (22) 66523337; e-mail editor.india@rd.com; internet readersdigest.co.in; f. 1954; monthly; English; Editor-in-Chief MOHAN SIVANAND; circ. 450,389,378.

Savvy: Magna Publishing Co Ltd, Magna House, 100E Old Prabhadevi Rd, Prabhadevi, Mumbai 400 025; tel. (22) 24362270; fax (22) 24306523; e-mail savvy@magnamags.com; internet www.magnamags.com; f. 1984; monthly; English; Editor FAHEEM RUHANI; circ. 25,994.

Screen: Express Tower, Nariman Point, Mumbai 400 021; tel. (22) 22022627; fax (22) 22022139; e-mail iemumbai@expressindia.co.in; internet www.screenindia.com; f. 1950; film weekly; English; circ. 8,379.

Society: Magna Publishing Co Ltd, Magna House, 100E Old Prabhadevi Rd, Prabhadevi, Mumbai 400 025; tel. (22) 24362270; fax (22) 24306523; e-mail society@magnamags.com; internet www.magnamags.com; f. 1979; monthly; English; Editorial Dir FAHEEM RUHANI; circ. 29,302.

Stardust: Magna Publishing Co Ltd, Magna House, 100E Old Prabhadevi Rd, Prabhadevi, Mumbai 400 025; tel. (22) 24362270; fax (22) 24306523; e-mail stardust@magnamags.com; internet www.magnamags.com; f. 1985; monthly; English and Hindi; Editor FAHEEM RUHANI; circ. 84,186.

Vyapar: Janmabhoomi Bhavan, Janmabhoomi Marg, POB 62, Fort, Mumbai 400 001; tel. (22) 22870831; fax (22) 22874097; e-mail jbhoomi@yahoo.com; internet www.janmabhoominewspapers.com/Vyapar/Default.aspx; f. 1949; (Gujarati), 1987 (Hindi); Gujarati (2 a week) and Hindi (weekly); commerce; propr Saurashtra Trust; Editor RAJESH M. BHAYANI; circ. 8,933 (Gujarati), 5,017 (Hindi), 1,438 (English).

Nagpur

All India Reporter: AIR Ltd, Congress Nagar, POB 209, Nagpur 440 012; tel. (712) 2534321; fax (712) 2526283; e-mail info@airwebworld.com; internet www.airwebworld.com; f. 1914; weekly and monthly; English; law journals and court reports; Chief Editor V. R. MANOHAR; circ. 55,500.

Manipur

The Eastern Frontier: Kwakeithel Thiyam Leikai, Imphal; monthly; Manipuri; Editor LOITONGBAM BINODKUMAR SINGH.

Image: Keishampat Leimajam Leikai, Imphal 795001; tel. 9856114682 (mobile); e-mail imagemag@live.com; f. 2007; monthly; Manipuri; film; Editor RANJAN SALAM; circ. 5,500.

Rajasthan

Balhans: Kesargarh, Jawahar Lal Nehru Marg, Jaipur 302 004; tel. (141) 39404142; fax (141) 2566011; e-mail info@patrika.com; internet www.rajasthanpatrika.com; Hindi; children's fortnightly; circ. 345,382.

Itwari Patrika: Kesargarh, Jawahar Lal Nehru Marg, Jaipur 302 004; tel. (141) 2561582; fax (141) 2566011; e-mail ads@rajasthanpatrika.com; weekly; Hindi; circ. 12,000.

Krishak Jagat: D-97, Tulsi Marg, Bahi Park, nr Madhosingh Circle, Jaipur 302 016; tel. (141) 2282680; e-mail info@krishakjagat.org; internet www.krishakjagat.org; f. 2002; Hindi; agricultural and rural devt; weekly; Editor VIJAY BONDRIYA; circ. 41,633.

Rashtradoot Saptahik: M.I. Rd, POB 30, Jaipur 302 001; tel. (141) 2372634; fax (141) 2373513; e-mail info@rashtradoot.com; f. 1983; Hindi; also publ. from Kota and Bikaner; Chief Editor and Man. Editor RAJESH SHARMA; CEO SOMESH SHARMA; combined circ. 324,721.

Tamil Nadu

Chennai (Madras)

Ananda Vikatan: 757 Anna Salai, Chennai 600 002; tel. (44) 28524074; fax (44) 28523819; e-mail ennangal@vikatan.com; internet www.vikatan.com; f. 1924; weekly; Tamil; Editor R. KANNAN; Man. Dir B. SRINIVASAN; circ. 359,936.

Aval Vikatan: 757 Anna Salai, Chennai 600 002; tel. (44) 28524074; fax (44) 28523819; e-mail aval@vikatan.com; internet www.vikatan.com; f. 1998; fortnightly; Tamil; Editor and Man. Dir B. SRINIVASAN; circ. 233,560.

Chandamama: B-3, Lunic Industry, Cross Road B, M.I.D.C., Andheri East, Mumbai 4000093; tel. (22) 28311849; fax (22) 28311872; e-mail online@chandamama.com; internet www.chandamama.com; f. 1947; children's monthly; publ. in 13 languages incl. Hindi, Gujarati, Telugu, Kannada, English, Tamil, Malayalam; Editor PRASHANT MULEKAR; combined circ. 420,000.

Chutti Vikatan: 757 Anna Salai, Chennai 600 002; tel. (44) 28524074; fax (44) 28523819; e-mail chutti@vikatan.com; internet www.vikatan.com; f. 1999; fortnightly; Tamil; children's; Editor N. V. SANKARAN; Man. Dir B. SRINIVASAN; circ. 24,215.

Devi: 727 Anna Salai, Chennai 600 006; tel. (44) 28521428; f. 1979; weekly; Tamil; Editor B. RAMACHANDRA ADITYAN; circ. 24,498.

Frontline: Kasturi Bldgs, 859/860 Anna Salai, Chennai 600 002; tel. (44) 28413344; fax (44) 28415325; e-mail frontline@thehindu.co.in; internet www.flonnet.com; f. 1984; fortnightly; English; current affairs; independent; Editor and Publr N. RAM; circ. 73,442.

Junior Vikatan: 757 Anna Salai, Chennai 600 002; tel. (44) 28524074; fax (44) 28523819; e-mail junior@vikatan.com; internet www.vikatan.com; f. 1983; twice a week; Tamil; Editor and Man. Dir B. SRINIVASAN; circ. 180,447.

Kalki: Bharathan Publications (P) Ltd, Kalki Bldgs, 47-NP Jawaharlal Nehru Rd, Ekkaduthangal, Chennai 600 032; tel. (44) 43438888; fax (44) 43438899; e-mail onlines@kalkiweekly.com; internet www.kalkionline.com; f. 1941; weekly; Tamil; literary and cultural; circ. 25,933.

Kumudam: 151 Purasawalkam High Rd, Chennai 600 010; tel. (44) 26422146; fax (44) 26425041; e-mail kumudam@hotmail.com; internet www.kumudam.com; f. 1947; weekly; Tamil; Editor Dr S. A. P. JAWAHAR PALANIAPPAN; circ. 286,109.

Kungumam: 93A Kodambakkam High Rd, Chennai 600 034; tel. (44) 28268177; e-mail hariharan@dinakaran.com; internet www.kungumam.co.in; f. 1978; weekly; Tamil; Editor PARASAKTHI; circ. 184,323.

Rani Muthu: 86 Periyar E.V.R. High Rd, Chennai 600 007; tel. (44) 25324771; fax (44) 26426884; e-mail raniweekly@vsnl.net; f. 1969; fortnightly; Tamil; Editor RAGUPATHY BASKARAN; circ. 35,175.

Rani Weekly: 86 Periyar E.V.R. High Rd, Chennai 600 007; tel. (44) 25324771; fax (44) 26426884; e-mail raniweekly@vsnl.net; f. 1962; Tamil; Editor RAGUPATHY BASKARAN; circ. 141,911.

Sportstar: Kasturi Bldgs, 859/860 Anna Salai, Chennai 600 002; tel. (44) 28413344; fax (44) 28415325; e-mail wsvcs@thehindu.co.in; internet www.tssonnet.com; f. 1978; weekly; English; independent; Publr S. RANGARAJAN; Editor N. RAM; circ. 48,900.

Thuglak: 46 Greenways Rd, Chennai 600 028; tel. (44) 42606228; fax (44) 24936915; e-mail webmaster@thuglak.com; internet www.thuglak.com; f. 1970; weekly; Tamil; Editor CHO S. RAMASWAMY; circ. 66,087.

Uttar Pradesh

Manohar Kahaniyan: 1A Tagore Town, Hashimpur Rd, Allahabad 211 002; tel. (532) 2415549; fax (532) 2415533; f. 1940; monthly; Hindi; Editor ASHOK MITRA; circ. 34,130.

Nutan Kahaniyan: 15 Sheo Charan Lal Rd, Allahabad 211 003; tel. (532) 2400612; f. 1975; monthly; Hindi; Chief Editor K. K. BHARGAVA; circ. 31,655.

Satya Katha: 1A Tagore Town, Hashimpur Rd, Allahabad 211 002; f. 1974; monthly; Hindi; Editor ALOK MITRA; circ. 15,785.

West Bengal

Kolkata (Calcutta)

All India Appointment Gazette: 7 Old Court House St, Kolkata 700 001; tel. (33) 22435663; fax (33) 22435618; e-mail sambadmail@sify.com; f. 1973; weekly; English; circ. 22,713.

Anandalok: 6 Prafulla Sarkar St, Kolkata 700 001; tel. (33) 22374880; fax (33) 22253241; f. 1975; fortnightly; Bengali; film; Editor DULENDRA BHOWMIK; circ. 71,707.

Anandamela: 6 Prafulla Sarkar St, Kolkata 700 001; tel. (33) 22216600; fax (33) 22253240; f. 1975; weekly; Bengali; for children; Editor PAULAMI SENGUPTA SARKAR; circ. 56,721.

Contemporary Tea Time: c/o Contemporary Brokers Pvt Ltd, 1 Old Court House Corner, POB 14, Kolkata 700 001; tel. (33) 22307241; fax (33) 22435753; e-mail webmaster@contemporary.co.in; internet www.contemporarybrokers.com; f. 1988; quarterly; English; tea industry; Editor SAMAR SIRCAR; circ. 5,000.

Desh: 6 Prafulla Sarkar St, Kolkata 700 001; tel. (33) 22374880; fax (33) 22253240; e-mail desh@abpmail.com; f. 1933; fortnightly; Bengali; literary; Editor HARSHA DATTA; circ. 99,881.

Global Reach Newsletter: 7W The Millennium, 235/2A A. J. C. Bose Rd, Kolkata 700 020; tel. (33) 22835537; fax (33) 22835538; e-mail global.reach@vsnl.com; internet www.globalreach.in; f. 1991; monthly; English; education magazine for those planning to study abroad; Editor RAVI LOCHAN; circ. 4,500.

Naba Kallol: 11 Jhamapookur Lane, Kolkata 700 009; tel. (33) 23504294; f. 1960; monthly; Bengali; Editor P. K. MAZUMDAR; circ. 29,500.

Prabuddha Bharata (Awakened India): 5 Dehi Entally Rd, Kolkata 700 014; tel. (33) 22640898; e-mail mail@advaitaashrama.org; internet www.advaitaashrama.org; f. 1896; monthly; art, culture, religion, humanities and philosophy; Publr Swami BODHASARANANDA; Editor Swami SATYAMAYANANDA; circ. 7,500.

Sananda: 6 Prafulla Sarkar St, Kolkata 700 001; tel. (33) 22374880; fax (33) 22253241; f. 1986; monthly; Bengali; Editor MADHUMITA CHATTOPADHYAY; circ. 16,460.

Saptahik Bartaman: 6 J. B. S. Haldane Ave, Kolkata 700 105; tel. (33) 23000101; fax (33) 23234030; e-mail bartaman@satyam.net.in; f. 1988; weekly; Bengali; Editor KAKOLI CHAKRABORTY; circ. 120,025.

Suktara: 11 Jhamapukur Lane, Kolkata 700 009; tel. (33) 23504294; e-mail dev_sahityer@rediffmail.com; f. 1948; monthly; Bengali; juvenile; Editor ARUN CHANDRA MAZUMDER; circ. 41,541.

Unish-Kuri: 6 Prafulla Sarkar St, Kolkata 700 001; f. 2004; fortnightly; Bengali; youth; Editor PAULAMI SENGUPTA SARKAR; circ. 55,128.

NEWS AGENCIES

Press Trust of India Ltd: PTI Bldg, 4 Parliament St, New Delhi 110 001; tel. (11) 23716621; fax (11) 23718714; e-mail trans@pti.in; internet www.ptinews.com; f. 1947; re-established 1978; Editor-in-Chief and CEO M. K. RAZDAN.

United News of India (UNI): 9 Rafi Marg, New Delhi 110 001; tel. (11) 23710522; fax (11) 23355841; e-mail uninet@uniindia.com; internet www.uniindia.com; f. 1959; national and international news service in English, Hindi (UNIVARTA) and Urdu; photograph and graphics service; brs in 67 centres in India; Chair. PRAFULLA KUMAR MAHESHWARI; Chief Editor and Gen. Man. ARUN KUMAR BHANDARI.

CO-ORDINATING BODIES

Press Information Bureau: Shastri Bhavan, Dr Rajendra Prasad Rd, New Delhi 110 001; tel. (11) 23383643; fax (11) 23383203; e-mail pib@alpha.nic.in; internet www.pib.nic.in; f. 1946 to co-ordinate press affairs for the govt; represents newspaper managements, journalists, news agencies, parliament; has power to examine journalists under oath and may censor objectionable material; Prin. Information Officer DEEPAK SANDHU.

Registrar of Newspapers for India: Ministry of Information and Broadcasting, West Block 8, Wing 2, Ramakrishna Puram, New Delhi 110 066; tel. (11) 26107504; fax (11) 26189801; e-mail rni.hub@nic.in; internet rni.nic.in; f. 1956 as a statutory body to collect press statistics; maintains a register of all Indian newspapers; Press Registrar AMITABHA CHAKRABARTI.

PRESS ASSOCIATIONS

All-India Newspaper Editors' Conference: 36–37 Northend Complex, Rama Krishna Ashram Marg, New Delhi 110 001; tel. (11) 23364519; fax (11) 23317947; f. 1940; c. 300 mems; Pres. VISHWA BANDHU GUPTA; Sec.-Gen. BISHAMBER NEWAR.

All India Small and Medium Newspapers' Federation: 26-F Rajiv Gandhi Chowk (Connaught Pl.), New Delhi 110 001; tel. (11) 23326000; fax (11) 23320906; e-mail indian.observer@gmail.com; c. 9,200 mems; Pres. GURINDER SINGH; Gen. Secs B. C. GUPTA, B. M. SHARMA, VIJAY SOOD.

The Foreign Correspondents' Club of South Asia: AB-19 Mathura Rd, opp. Pragati Maidan Gate 3, New Delhi 110 001; tel. (11) 23385118; fax (11) 23385517; e-mail fccsouthasia@gmail.com; internet www.fccsouthasia.net; f. 1992; over 400 mems; Pres. JOHN ELLIOTT.

Indian Federation of Working Journalists: Garud Vihar, Connaught Place, New Delhi 110 001; tel. and fax (11) 23418871; e-mail ifwj.media@gmail.com; internet www.ifwj.in; f. 1950; 31,460 mems; Pres. K. VIKRAM RAO; Sec.-Gen. PARMANAND PANDEY.

Indian Journalists' Association: New Delhi; Pres. VIJAY DUTT; Gen. Sec. A. K. DHAR.

Indian Languages Newspapers' Association: Janmabhoomi Bhavan, Janmabhoomi Marg, POB 10029, Fort, Mumbai 400 001; tel. (22) 22870537; f. 1941; 320 mems; Pres. VIJAY KUMAR BONDRIYA; Hon. Gen. Secs PRADEEP G. DESHPANDE, KRISHNA SHEWDIKAR, LALIT SHRIMAL.

Indian Newspaper Society: INS Bldg, Rafi Marg, New Delhi 110 001; tel. (11) 23715401; fax (11) 23723800; e-mail indnews@sify.com; internet www.indiannewspapersociety.org; f. 1939; 685 mems; Pres. HORMUSJI N. CAMA.

National Union of Journalists (India): 7 Jantar Mantar Rd, 2nd Floor, New Delhi 110 001; tel. and fax (11) 23368610; e-mail nujindia@ndf.vsnl.in; internet education.vsnl.com/nujindia; f. 1972; 12,000 mems; Pres. J. K. GUPTA; Sec.-Gen. M. D. GANGWAR.

Press Club of India: 1 Raisina Rd, New Delhi 110 001; tel. (11) 23719844; fax (11) 23357048; internet www.pressclubofindia.org; f. 1958; Pres. PARVEZ AHMED; 4,500 mems.

Press Council of India: Soochna Bhavan, 8 C. G. O. Complex, Ground Floor, Lodhi Rd, New Delhi 110 003; tel. (11) 24366746; e-mail pcibpp@gmail.com; internet www.presscouncil.nic.in; est. under an Act of Parliament to preserve the freedom of the press and maintain and improve the standards of newspapers and news agencies in India; 28 mems; Chair. Justice GANENDRA NARAYAN RAY; Sec. VIBHA BHARGAVA.

Press Institute of India: Rind Premises, Second Main Rd, Taramani, CPT Campus, Chennai 600 113; tel. (44) 22542344; fax (44) 22542323; e-mail arunchacko@pressinstitute.org; internet www

.pressinstitute.org; f. 1963; 32 mem. newspapers and other orgs; Chair. O. P. BHATT; Dir and Editor V. MURALI.

Publishers

DELHI AND NEW DELHI

Affiliated East-West Press (Pvt) Ltd: G-1/16 Ansari Rd, Daryaganj, New Delhi 110 002; tel. (11) 23264180; fax (11) 23260538; e-mail affiliat@vsnl.com; internet www.aewpress.com; textbooks and reference books; also represents scientific societies; Dirs SUNNY MALIK, KAMAL MALIK.

Aleph Book Co: 161 B/4, Ground Floor, Gulmohar House, Yusuf Sarai Community Centre, New Delhi 110 049; tel. (11) 49226666; e-mail publicity@alephbookcompany.com; internet www.alephbookcompany.com; f. 2011; literary fiction, history, biography, popular culture; Man. Dir DAVID DAVIDAR.

Atlantic Publishers and Distributors (Pvt) Ltd: 7/22 Ansari Rd, Darya Ganj, New Delhi 110 002; tel. (11) 40775252; fax (11) 23285873; e-mail editorial@atlanticbooks.com; internet www.atlanticbooks.com; f. 1977; academic, professional and general non-fiction; co-publishing and distribution arrangements with numerous int. publrs; Man. Dir MANISH KUMAR GUPTA.

B. I. Publications Pvt Ltd: B. I. House, 54 Janpath, New Delhi 110 001; tel. (11) 46209999; fax (11) 23323138; e-mail bipgroup@vsnl.com; internet www.bipgroup.com; f. 1959; academic, general and professional; Man. Dir SHASHANK BHAGAT.

Book Circle: 19A Ansari Rd, Daryaganj, New Delhi 110 002; tel. (11) 23264444; fax (11) 23263050; e-mail bookcircle@vsnl.net; f. 2001; social sciences, art and architecture, technical, medical, scientific; Propr and Dir HIMANSHU CHAWLA.

Cambridge University Press India (Pvt) Ltd: Cambridge House, 4381/4 Ansari Rd, Daryaganj, New Delhi 110 002; e-mail cupdel@cambridge.org; internet cambridgeindia.org; branch offices in Mumbai, Kolkata, Chennai, Bengaluru, Hyderabad, Pune and Thiruvananthapuram; academic and educational books; Man. Dir MANAS SAIKIA.

S. Chand and Co Ltd: 7361 Ram Nagar, Qutab Rd, nr New Delhi Railway Station, New Delhi 110 055; tel. (11) 23672080; fax (11) 23677446; e-mail info@schandgroup.com; internet www.schandgroup.com; f. 1917; educational and general in English and Hindi; also book exports and imports; Man. Dir RAVINDRA KUMAR GUPTA.

Children's Book Trust: Nehru House, 4 Bahadur Shah Zafar Marg, New Delhi 110 002; tel. (11) 23316970; fax (11) 23721090; e-mail cbtnd@vsnl.com; internet www.childrensbooktrust.com; f. 1957; children's books in English and other languages of India; Editor C. G. R. KURUP; Gen. Man. RAVI SHANKAR.

Concept Publishing Co: A/15–16, Commercial Block, Mohan Garden, New Delhi 110 059; tel. (11) 25351794; fax (11) 25357109; e-mail publishing@conceptpub.com; internet www.conceptpub.com; f. 1974; social sciences, management, psychology, community development; Chair. and Man. Dir ASHOK KUMAR MITTAL; CEO NITIN MITTAL.

Delhi Press: E-3, Rani Jhansi Rd, Jhandewalan, New Delhi 110 055; tel. (11) 41398888; fax (11) 23625020; internet www.delhipress.in; f. 1939; publr of 32 magazine titles in nine languages, incl. Grihshobha, Sarita, Saras Salil and Champak; Dir ANANT NATH.

Frank Bros & Co (Publishers) Ltd: 4675A Ansari Rd, 21 Daryaganj, New Delhi 110 002; tel. (11) 23263393; fax (11) 23269032; e-mail connect@frankbros.com; internet www.frankbros.com; f. 1930; children's, educational and management; Chair. and Man. Dir R. C. GOVIL.

Heritage Publishers: 19A Ansari Rd, Daryaganj, New Delhi 110 002; tel. (11) 23266633; fax (11) 23263050; e-mail heritage@nda.vsnl.net.in; internet www.meditechbooks.com; f. 1973; social sciences, art and architecture, technical, medical, scientific; Propr and Dir B. R. CHAWLA.

Hindustan Publishing Corpn (India): 4805/24 Bharat Ram Rd, 102, Daryaganj, New Delhi 110 002; tel. (11) 43580512; e-mail hpcedu@rediffmail.com; archaeology, anthropology, business management, demography and population dynamics, economics, pure and applied sciences, geology, mathematics, physics, sociology; publ. *Demography India* and *Journal of Economic Geology and Georesource Management*; exporter of Indian journals and periodicals, Indian and foreign books; Man. Partner B. B. JAIN.

Lalit Kala Akademi: Rabindra Bhavan, New Delhi 110 001; tel. (11) 23009200; fax (11) 23009292; e-mail lka@lalitkala.gov.in; internet www.lalitkala.gov.in; books on Indian art; Chair. BALAN NAMBIAR.

Lancers Books: POB 4236, New Delhi 110 048; tel. (11) 26241617; fax (11) 26992063; e-mail lancersbooks@hotmail.com; internet www.lancersbooks.net; f. 1977; politics (with special emphasis on north-east India), defence; Propr S. KUMAR.

Motilal Banarsidass Publishers (Pvt) Ltd: A-44, Naraina Industrial Area, Phase 1, New Delhi 110 028; tel. (11) 25795180; fax (11) 25797221; e-mail web@mlbd.com; internet www.mlbd.com; f. 1903; religion, philosophy, astrology, yoga, linguistics, history, art, architecture, literature, music and dance, alternative medicine; English and Sanskrit; offices in Bangalore, Chennai, Kolkata, Mumbai, Patna, Pune and Varanasi; Man. Dir N. P. JAIN.

Munshiram Manoharlal Publishers Pvt Ltd: 54 Rani Jhansi Rd, POB 5715, New Delhi 110 055; tel. (11) 23671668; fax (11) 23612745; e-mail info@mrmlonline.com; internet www.mrmlonline.com; f. 1952; Indian art, architecture, archaeology, religion, music, law, medicine, dance, dictionaries, travel, history, politics, numismatics, Buddhism, philosophy, sociology, etc.; Man. Dir ASHOK JAIN.

National Book Trust: 5 Institutional Area, Vasant Kunj, Phase 2, New Delhi 110 070; tel. (11) 26707700; fax (11) 26121883; e-mail nbtindia@ndb.vsnl.net.in; internet www.nbtindia.org.in; f. 1957; autonomous organization established by the Ministry of Human Resources Development to produce and encourage the production of good literary works; Chair. Prof. BIPAN CHANDRA.

National Council of Educational Research and Training (NCERT): Sri Aurobindo Marg, New Delhi 110 016; tel. (11) 26560620; fax (11) 26868419; e-mail ncert.media@gmail.com; internet www.ncert.nic.in; f. 1961; school textbooks, teachers' guides, research monographs, journals, etc.; Dir Prof. P. SINCLAIR.

Neeta Prakashan: A-4 Ring Rd, South Extension Part I, POB 3853, New Delhi 110 049; tel. (11) 24636010; fax (11) 24636011; e-mail info@neetaprakashan.com; internet www.neetaprakashan.com; f. 1960; educational, children's, general; Dir RAJESH GUPTA.

New Age International Pvt Ltd: 4835/24 Ansari Rd, Daryaganj, New Delhi 110 002; tel. (11) 23276802; fax (11) 23267437; e-mail info@newagepublishers.com; internet www.newagepublishers.com; f. 1966; science, engineering, technology, management, humanities, social sciences; Man. Dir SAUMYA GUPTA.

Oxford University Press: YMCA Library Bldg, 1st Floor, 1 Jai Singh Rd, POB 43, New Delhi 110 001; tel. (11) 43600300; fax (11) 23360897; e-mail admin.in@oup.com; internet www.oup.co.in; f. 1912; educational, scientific, medical, general, humanities and social sciences, dictionaries and reference; Man. Dir MANZAR KHAN.

Penguin Books India (Pvt) Ltd: 11 Community Centre, Panchsheel Park, New Delhi 110 017; tel. (11) 26494401; fax (11) 26494403; e-mail penguin@del2.vsnl.net.in; internet www.penguinbooksindia.com; f. 1987; Indian literature and general non-fiction in English; CEO ANDREW PHILLIPS; Pres. THOMAS ABRAHAM.

PHI Learning: M-97 Connaught Circus, New Delhi 110 001; tel. (11) 22143344; fax (11) 23417179; e-mail phi@phindia.com; internet www.phindia.com; f. 1963 as Prentice-Hall of India (Pvt) Ltd; university-level text and reference books; Man. Dir A. K. GHOSH.

Pitambar Publishing Co Pvt Ltd: 888 East Park Rd, Karol Bagh, New Delhi 110 005; tel. (11) 23676058; fax (11) 23676058; e-mail pitambar@bol.net.in; academic, children's books, textbooks and general; Man. Dir ANAND BHUSHAN; 5 brs.

Pustak Mahal: J-3/16 Daryaganj, New Delhi 110 002; tel. (11) 23272783; fax (11) 23260518; e-mail pustak@pustakmahal.com; internet www.pustakmahal.com; children's, general, computers, religious, encyclopaedias; Chair. R. A. GUPTA; Man. Dir ASHOK GUPTA.

Rajkamal Prakashan (Pvt) Ltd: 1B Netaji Subhas Marg, Daryaganj, New Delhi 110 002; tel. (11) 23274463; fax (11) 23278144; e-mail info@rajkamalprakashan.com; internet www.rajkamalprakashan.com; f. 1947; Hindi; literary; also literary journal and monthly trade journal; Man. Dir ASHOK KUMAR MAHESHWARI.

Rajpal and Sons: 1590 Madrasa Rd, Kashmere Gate, Delhi 110 006; tel. (11) 23865483; fax (11) 23867791; e-mail mail@rajpalpublishing.com; internet www.rajpalpublishing.com; f. 1891; humanities, social sciences, art, juvenile; Hindi; Chair. MEERA JOHRI.

Research and Information System for Developing Countries: Zone IV-B, 4th Floor, India Habitat Centre, Lodhi Rd, New Delhi 100 003; tel. (11) 24682177; fax (11) 24682173; e-mail publication@ris.org.in; internet www.ris.org.in; f. 1983; trade and development issues; Dir-Gen. Dr BISWAJIT DHAR.

Roli Books (Pvt) Ltd: M-75 Greater Kailash Part II Market, New Delhi 110048; tel. (11) 40682000; e-mail info@rolibooks.com; internet www.rolibooks.com; f. 1978; general fiction and non-fiction, children's books; Publisher PRAMOD KAPOOR.

Rupa & Co: 7/16 Ansari Rd, Daryaganj, POB 7017, New Delhi 110 002; tel. (11) 23278586; fax (11) 23277294; e-mail info@rupapublications.com; internet www.rupapublications.com; f. 1936; Chief Exec. R. K. MEHRA.

Sage Publications India Pvt Ltd: B-1/I-1, Mohan Co-operative Industrial Estate, Mathura Rd, Post Bag 7, New Delhi 110 044; tel. (11) 40539222; fax (11) 40539234; e-mail info@sagepub.in; internet www.sagepub.in; f. 1981; social sciences, development studies, business and management studies; Man. Dir and CEO VIVEK MEHRA.

Sahitya Akademi: Rabindra Bhavan, 35 Ferozeshah Rd, New Delhi 110 001; tel. (11) 23386626; fax (11) 23382428; e-mail secy@ndb.vsnl.net.in; internet www.sahitya-akademi.gov.in; f. 1954; bibliographies, translations, monographs, encyclopaedias, literary classics, etc.; Pres. SUNIL GANGOPADHYAY; Sec. A. KRISHNA MURTHY.

Scholar Publishing House (Pvt) Ltd: 85 Model Basti, New Delhi 110 005; tel. (11) 23541299; fax (11) 23676565; e-mail info@scholar.ws; internet www.scholar.ws; f. 1968; educational; Man. Dir RAMESH RANADE.

Sterling Publishers (Pvt) Ltd: A-59 Okhla Industrial Area, Phase II, New Delhi 110 020; tel. (11) 26387070; fax (11) 26383788; e-mail mail@sterlingpublishers.com; internet www.sterlingpublishers.com; f. 1964; academic books on the humanities and social sciences, children's books, trade paperbacks; Chair. and Man. Dir S. K. GHAI; Dirs VIKAS GHAI, GAURAV GHAI.

Taylor & Francis Books India Pvt Ltd: 15–17 Tolstoy Marg, 912 Tolstoy House, New Delhi 110 001; tel. (11) 23712131; fax (11) 23712132; e-mail inquiry@tandfindia.com; internet www.taylorandfrancisgroup.com; f. 2004; Man. Dir NITASHA DEVASAR.

Vitasta Publishing: 2/15 Ansari Rd, New Delhi 110 002; tel. (11) 23283024; fax (11) 23263522; e-mail info@vitastapublishing.com; internet www.vitastapublishing.com; f. 2004; science, technology and management; Man. Dir RENU KAUL KUMAR.

Women Unlimited: K-36, Hauz Khas Enclave, Ground Floor, New Delhi 110 016; tel. (11) 26964947; fax (11) 26496597; e-mail womenunltd@vsnl.net; internet www.womenunlimited.net; f. 2003; feminism; Head RITU MENON.

Zubaan: 128B, 1st Floor, Shahpur Jat, New Delhi 110 019; tel. (11) 26494617; e-mail contact@zubaanbooks.com; internet www.zubaanbooks.com; f. 2003; women's studies, social sciences, humanities, general non-fiction, fiction, etc.; Dir URVASHI BUTALIA; Editor PREETI GILL.

CHENNAI (MADRAS)

Emerald Publishers: 15A Casa Major Rd, 1st Floor, Egmore, Chennai 600 008; tel. (44) 28193206; fax (44) 28192380; e-mail info@emeraldpublishers.com; internet www.emeraldpublishers.com; English textbooks, self-help and examination skills; CEO G. OLIVANNAN.

Eswar Press: Archana Arcade, 16 Natesan St, T. Nagar, Chennai 600 017; tel. (44) 24345902; fax (44) 24339590; e-mail enquiry@eswar.com; internet www.eswar.com; science and technology; CEO M. PERIYASAMY.

New Horizon Media: 177/103 Ambal's Bldg, 1st Floor, Lloyds Rd, Royapettah, Chennai 600 014; tel. (92) 44411119; fax (44) 43009701; e-mail nhm-shop@nhm.in; internet www.nhm.in; f. 2004; fiction and non-fiction in Tamil, English and Malayalam; Man. Dir BADRI SESHADRI.

Scitech Publications (India) (Pvt) Ltd: 7/3-C Madley Rd, T. Nagar, Chennai 600 017; tel. (44) 24311113; e-mail scitech@md5.vsnl.net.in; internet www.scitechpublications.com; f. 1998; science, technology, management, reference, etc.; Man. Dir M. R. PURUSHOTHAMAN.

Sura Books (Pvt) Ltd: 1620 J Block, 16th Main Rd, Anna Nagar, Chennai 600 040; tel. (44) 26162126; fax (44) 26162173; e-mail enquiry@surabooks.com; internet www.surabooks.com; children's books, dictionaries, examinations guides, tourist guides, Indology, etc.; Man. Dir V. K. SUBBURAJ.

JAIPUR

Neelkanth Publishers: C-93, Jagraj Marg, Bapu Nagar, Jaipur 302 015; tel. (141) 2702517; e-mail info@neelkanthpublishers.in; internet www.neelkanthpublishers.in; f. 2005; academic textbooks and reference books; Dir KULDEEP GOYAL.

Pointer Publishers: 807 Vyas Bldg, S.M.S. Highway, Jaipur 302 003; tel. and fax (141) 2578159; e-mail info@pointerpublishers.com; internet www.pointerpublishers.com; f. 1986; sciences, commerce, economics, education, literature, history, journalism, law, philosophy, psychology, sociology, tourism; in English and Hindi; Contact VIPIN JAIN.

Rajasthan Hindi Granth Akademi: Plot No. 1, Jhalana Institutional Area, Jaipur 302 004; tel. (141) 2711129; fax (141) 2710341; e-mail hindigranth@indiatimes.com; internet www.rajhga.com; engineering, agriculture, science, social sciences, law, education, fine arts and journalism; Dir Dr R. D. SAINI.

Shyam Prakashan: 1926 Nataniyon Ka Rasta, Jaipur 302 003; tel. (141) 2317659; fax (141) 2326554; e-mail ankit_146@sify.com; internet www.shyamprakashan.com; Propr OM PRAKASH AGRAWAL.

KOLKATA (CALCUTTA)

Academic Publishers: 5A Bhawani Dutta Lane, Kolkata 700 073; tel. (33) 22571071; fax (33) 22572489; e-mail info@academicpublishers.in; internet www.academicpublishers.in; f. 1958; textbooks, management, medical, technical; Man. Partner B. K. DHUR.

Advaita Ashrama: 5 Dehi Entally Rd, Kolkata 700 014; tel. (33) 22164000; e-mail mail@advaitaashrama.org; internet www.advaitaashrama.org; f. 1899; religion, philosophy, spiritualism, Vedanta; publication centre of Ramakrishna Math and Ramakrishna Mission; Editor PRABUDDHA BHARATA.

Ananda Publishers (Pvt) Ltd: 45 Beniatola Lane, Kolkata 700 009; tel. (33) 22414352; fax (33) 22193856; e-mail ananda@cal3.vsnl.net.in; internet www.anandapub.com; literature, general; owned by ABP Group (internet www.abp.in); Man. Dir S. MITRA.

Assam Review Publishing Co: 27A Waterloo St, 1st Floor, Kolkata 700 069; tel. (33) 22482251; fax (33) 22482251; e-mail assamrev@yahoo.co.in; f. 1926; publrs of *The Assam Review and Tea News* (monthly) and *The Assam Directory and Tea Areas Handbook* (annually); Chief Exec. GOBINDALAL BANERJEE.

Dev Sahitya Kutir: 21 Jhamapukur Lane, Kolkata 700 009; tel. (33) 23507887; e-mail dev_sahitya@rediffmail.com; children's, general; Dir ARUN CHANDRA MAZUMDER.

Dey's Publishing: 13 Bankim Chatterjee St, Kolkata 700 073; tel. (33) 22412330; fax (33) 22192041; e-mail deyspublishing@hotmail.com; internet deyspublishing.com; academic books, religion, philosophy, general; Dir SUDHANGSHU KUMAR DEY.

Eastern Law House (Pvt) Ltd: 54 Ganesh Chunder Ave, Kolkata 700 013; tel. (33) 22151989; fax (33) 22150491; e-mail elh.cal@gmail.com; internet www.easternlawhouse.com; f. 1918; legal, commercial and accountancy; Dir ASOK DE; br. in New Delhi.

Firma KLM Private Ltd: 257B B. B. Ganguly St, Kolkata 700 012; tel. and fax (33) 22217294; e-mail info@firmaklm.net; internet www.firmaklm.net; f. 1950; Indology, scholarly, alternative medicine; in English, Bengali, Sanskrit and Hindi; Man. Dir S. MUKHERJI.

Indian Museum: 27 Jawaharlal Nehru Rd, Kolkata 700 016; tel. (33) 22861702; fax (33) 22861696; e-mail imbot@cal12.vsnl.net.in; internet www.indianmuseumkolkata.org; social sciences and humanities; Dir ANUP K. MATILAL.

Naya Udyog: 206 Bidhan Sarani, Kolkata 700 006; tel. (33) 22413540; e-mail nayaudyog@yahoo.in; f. 1992; books in English and Bengali; agriculture, horticulture, social sciences, history, botany; distributes Naya Prokash publications; Man. Dir PARTHA SANKAR BASU.

Punthi Pustak: 136/4B Bidhan Sarani, Kolkata 700 004; tel. and fax (33) 25555573; e-mail info@punthipustak.com; f. 1956; religion, history, philosophy; Propr P. K. BHATTACHARYA.

Samya: 16 Southern Ave, Kolkata 700 026; tel. (33) 24660812; fax (33) 24644614; e-mail streesamya.manager@gmail.com; internet www.stree-samyabooks.com; f. 1996; owned by joint partnership, Bhatkal and Sen; social change, cultural studies, caste studies and Dalit writings; Dir MANDIRA SEN.

Seagull Books (Pvt) Ltd: 31A S. P. Mukherjee Rd, Kolkata 700 025; tel. (33) 24765869; fax (33) 22805143; e-mail books@seagullindia.com; internet www.seagullindia.com; f. 1982; academic, literary, general; CEO NAVIN KISHORE.

Shishu Sahitya Samsad: 32A Acharya Prafulla Chandra Rd, Kolkata 700 009; tel. (33) 23507669; fax (33) 23603508; e-mail contact@samsadbooks.com; internet www.samsadbooks.com; f. 1951; children's, reference, science, literature; Man. Dir DEBAJYOTI DATTA.

Stree-Samya: 16 Southern Ave, Kolkata 700 026; tel. (33) 24660812; fax (33) 24644614; e-mail streesamya@gmail.com; internet www.stree-samyabooks.com; f. 1990 (Stree), 1996 (Samya); imprints publ. by joint venture of Harsha Bhatkal, Popular Prakashan and Mandira Sen; social and women's issues and caste writings in English and Bengali; Dir MANDIRA SEN.

MUMBAI (BOMBAY)

Allied Publishers (Pvt) Ltd: 15 J. N. Heredia Marg, Mumbai 400 001; tel. (22) 42126969; fax (22) 22617928; e-mail arjunsachdev@alliedpublishers.com; internet alliedpublishers.com; f. 1934; academic and general; Dir ARJUN SACHDEV.

Bharatiya Vidya Bhavan: Munshi Sadan, Kulapati K. M. Munshi Marg, Mumbai 400 007; tel. (22) 23631261; fax (22) 23630058; e-mail bhavans@bhavans.info; internet www.bhavans.info; f. 1938; art, literature, culture, education, philosophy, religion, history of India; various periodicals in English, Hindi, Sanskrit and other Indian languages; Pres. SURENDRALAL G. MEHTA; Dir-Gen. H. N. DASTUR.

Himalaya Publishing House: Dr Bhalerao Marg (Kelewadi), Girgaon, Mumbai 400 004; tel. (22) 23860170; fax (22) 23877178; e-mail himpub@vsnl.com; internet www.himpub.com; f. 1976; textbooks and research work; Publr MEENA PANDEY.

India Books and Magazines Distributors (Pvt) Ltd: Arch No 30, Below Mahalaxmi Bridge, nr Race Course, Mahalaxmi; tel. (22)

40497401; e-mail contact@ibhworld.com; internet www.ibhworld.com; Man. Dir ABIZAR SHAIKH.

International Book House (Pvt) Ltd: Indian Mercantile Mansions (Extension), Madame Cama Rd, Mumbai 400 039; tel. (22) 66242222; fax (22) 22851109; e-mail info@ibhbookstore.com; internet www.ibhbookstore.com; f. 1941; children's, general, educational, scientific, technical, engineering, social sciences, humanities and law; Dir ROHIT GUPTA; Dir SANJEEV GUPTA.

Jaico Publishing House: A2, Jash Chambers, Sir P. M. Rd, Fort, Mumbai 400 001; tel. (22) 40306767; fax (22) 22656412; e-mail jaicowbd@vsnl.com; internet www.jaicobooks.com; f. 1947; general paperbacks, management, computer and engineering books, etc.; imports scientific, medical, technical and educational books; Man. Dir ASHWIN J. SHAH.

Popular Prakashan (Pvt) Ltd: 301 Mahalaxmi Chambers, 22 Bhulabhai Desai Rd, Mumbai 400 026; tel. (22) 23530303; fax (22) 24945294; e-mail info@popularprakashan.com; internet www.popularprakashan.com; f. 1968; sociology, biographies, religion, philosophy, fiction, arts, music, current affairs, medicine, history, politics and administration in English and Marathi; CEO HARSHA BHATKAL.

Sheth Publishing House: G-12 Suyog Industrial Estate, nr LBS Marg, Vikhroli (W), Mumbai 400 083; tel. (22) 25773707; fax (22) 25774200; e-mail shethpublishinghouse@gmail.com; internet www.indiamart.com/shethpublishinghouse; educational, children's; Man. PURVISH SHETH.

Somaiya Publications (Pvt) Ltd: 172 Mumbai Marathi Granthasangrahalaya Bldg, M.M.G.S. Marg, Dadar (E), Mumbai 400 014; tel. (22) 24130230; fax (22) 22047297; e-mail somaiyabooks@rediffmail.com; internet www.somaiya.com; f. 1967; economics, sociology, history, politics, mathematics, sciences, language, literature, education, psychology, religion, philosophy, logic; Chair. Dr S. K. SOMAIYA.

Vora Medical Publications: 6 Princess Bldg, E. R. Rd, Mumbai 400 003; tel. (22) 23754161; fax (22) 23704053; e-mail voramedpub@yahoo.co.in; internet www.voramedicalpublications.com; medicine, nursing, management, spiritualism, general knowledge; Propr R. K. VORA.

OTHER TOWNS

Anada Prakashan (Pvt) Ltd: 1756 Gandhi Rd, Ahmedabad 380 001; tel. (79) 2169956; fax (79) 2139900; e-mail anadaad1@sancharnet.in; internet www.anada.com; children's, educational, dictionaries; Man. Dir B. R. ANADA.

Bharati Bhawan: Thakurbari Rd, Kadamkuan, Patna 800 003; tel. (612) 2670325; fax (612) 2670010; e-mail sales.bbpddel@gmail.com; internet bharatibhawan.in; f. 1942; educational and juvenile; Man. Partner TARIT KUMAR BOSE.

Books for Change: 139 Richmond Rd, Bangalore 560 025; tel. (80) 25580346; fax (80) 25586284; e-mail bfc@bookforchange.info; internet www.booksforchange.info; f. 1997; operated by ActionAid Karnataka Projects; publr and distributor of books and other media relating to social issues; Publr and Chief Editor SHOBA RAMACHANDRAN.

DC Books: DC Kizhakemuri Edam, Good Shepherd St, POB 214, Kottayam 686 001; tel. (481) 2563114; fax (481) 2564758; e-mail info@dcbooks.com; internet www.dcbooks.com; f. 1974; fiction, general and reference books in Malayalam; CEO RAVI DEECEE.

HarperCollins Publishers India (Pvt) Ltd: A-53, Sector 57, Noida; tel. (120) 4044800; e-mail sapana.solanki@harpercollins-india.com; internet www.harpercollins.co.in; f. 2003; general fiction and non-fiction, children's and reference; imprints incl. Collins, Avon, Harper Vantage, Fourth Estate; CEO P. M. SUKUMAR.

Hind Pocket Books (Pvt) Ltd: B-13, Sector 81, Phase II, Noida 201305; tel. (120) 3093992; fax (120) 2563983; e-mail gbp@del2.vsnl.net.in; f. 1958; fiction and non-fiction paperbacks in English, Hindi, Punjabi, Malayalam and Urdu; Chair DINA NATH MALHOTRA; Man. Dir SHEKHAR MALHOTRA.

Indica Books: D-40/18 Godowlia, Varanasi 221 001; tel. (542) 3094999; fax (542) 2452258; e-mail indicainfo@indicabooks.com; internet www.indicabooks.com; Indology, philosophy, religion, culture; Propr DILIP KUMAR JAISWAL.

Kalyani Publishers: 1/1 Rajinder Nagar, Civil Lines, Ludhiana 141 008; tel. (161) 2745756; fax (161) 2745872; e-mail kalyanibooks@yahoo.co.in; textbooks; Dir RAJ KUMAR.

Krishna Prakashan Media (Pvt) Ltd: Krishna House, 11 Shivaji Rd, Meerut 250 001; tel. (121) 2644766; fax (121) 2642946; e-mail info@krishnaprakashan.com; internet www.krishnaprakashan.com; f. 1942; textbooks; Exec. Dir SUGAM RASTOGI; Dir S. K. RASTOGI.

Law Publishers: 18 A. Sardar Patel Marg, Civil Lines, POB 1077, Allahabad; tel. (532) 262374; fax (532) 2622781; e-mail sai@lawpublisherindia.com; internet www.lawpublisherindia.com; f. 1929; legal texts in English; Dir NARESH SAGAR.

Macmillan Publishers India Ltd: 315/316 Raheja Chambers, 12 Museum Rd, Bangalore 560 001; tel. (80) 25586563; fax (80) 25588713; e-mail rberi@macmillan.co.in; internet www.macmillanindia.com; school and university books in English; general; Pres. and Man. Dir RAJIV BERI.

Madhubun Educational Books: E-28, Sector 8, Noida 201 301; tel. (120) 4078900; fax (120) 4078999; e-mail info@madhubunbooks.com; internet madhubunbooks.com; f. 1969; school books, children's books; Dir SAJILI SHIRODKAR.

Mapin Publishing (Pvt) Ltd: 706B Kaivanna, Panchvati, Ellisbridge, Ahmedabad 380 006; tel. (79) 40228228; fax (79) 40228201; e-mail mapin@mapinpub.com; internet www.mapinpub.com; f. 1984; illustrated books on Indian art, culture, history, architecture, photography, crafts and literature; collaborates with art book publrs and museums to provide custom packaging services; Man. Dir BIPIN SHAH.

Navajivan Publishing House: PO Navajivan, Ahmedabad 380 014; tel. (79) 7540635; f. 1919; Gandhiana and related social sciences; in English, Hindi and Gujarati; Man. Trustee JITENDRA DESAI; Sales Man. KAPIL RAWAL.

Orient Blackswan (Pvt) Ltd: 3-6-752 Himayat Nagar, Hyderabad 500 029; tel. (40) 27665466; fax (40) 27645046; e-mail centraloffice@orientblackswan.com; internet www.orientblackswan.com; f. 1948 as Orient Longman (Pvt) Ltd; educational, technical, general and children's in English and almost all Indian languages; Chair. SHANTA RAMESHWAR RAO; Dirs Dr NANDINI RAO, J. KRISHNADEV RAO.

Parikalpana Prakashan: D-68 Nirala Nagar, Lucknow 226 010; tel. (522) 2786782; fax (522) 2786782; e-mail janchetna@rediffmail.com; internet janchetnaa.blogspot.in; f. 1996; fiction, poetry, literary criticism, history, political sciences, philosophy; Hindi and English; Pres. KATYAYANI.

Pilgrims Publishing: Pilgrims Book House, B27/98-A-8 Nawabganj Rd, Durga Kund, Varanasi 221 001; tel. (542) 2314060; fax (542) 2314059; e-mail pilgrims@satyam.net.in; internet www.pilgrimsbooks.com; f. 1986; publishes fiction and reference books on subjects including history, travel, Nepal, Tibet, India and the Himalayas; also operates Pilgrims Book House in India and Nepal; Editor CHRISTOPHER N. BURCHETT.

Punjabi University Publication Bureau: Punjabi University, Patiala 147 002; tel. (175) 3046093; fax (175) 2283073; e-mail head_publication@pbi.ac.in; internet www.punjabiuniversity.ac.in; f. 1966; university-level text and reference books, and other general interest books; Punjabi, English and other languages; Head of Bureau Dr S. K. SHARMA.

Ram Prasad and Sons: Hospital Rd, Agra 282 003; tel. (562) 2461904; fax (562) 2460920; e-mail rpsons@sancharnet.in; f. 1905; agricultural, arts, history, commerce, education, general, computing, engineering, pure and applied science, economics, sociology; Man. S. N. AGARWAL; br. in Bhopal.

Random House India: Windsor IT Park, 7th Floor, Tower-B, A-1, Sector 125, Noida 201 301; tel. (120) 4607500; fax (120) 4607518; e-mail contact@randomhouse.co.in; internet www.randomhouse.co.in; f. 2005; part of United Kingdom-based Random House Group; Man. Dir GAURAV SHRINAGESH.

Sahitya Bhawan Publications: Agra-Mathura Bypass Rd, Agra 282 002; tel. (562) 4042977; fax (562) 2858183; e-mail sbpd.publications@gmail.com; internet sahityabhawan.com; social sciences, humanities; Propr RAHUL BANSAL.

Samvad Prakashan: 233 Rajlaxmi Society, nr Shivmahal Palace, Old Padra Rd, Vadodara 390015; tel. (265) 2312747; e-mail samvadprakashan@yahoo.co.in; internet www.samvadprakashan.co.in; books and magazines in Gujarati; Propr YUYUTSU PANCHAL.

Simon and Schuster India: 2316, Tower A, The Corenthum, A-41, Sector 62, Noida 201 301; tel. (91) 9810173662 (mobile); e-mail rahul.srivastava@simonandschuster.com; f. 2011; Dir RAHUL SRIVASTAVA.

Tata McGraw-Hill Publishing Co Ltd: B-4, Sector 63, Noida 2010301; tel. (120) 4383400; fax (120) 4383401; e-mail editorial_india@mcgraw-hill.com; internet www.tatamcgrawhill.com; f. 1970; engineering, computers, sciences, medicine, management, humanities, social sciences; Chair. Dr F. A. MEHTA; Man. Dir Dr N. SUBRAHMANYAM.

Universities Press (India) (Pvt) Ltd: 3-6-747/1/A and 3-6-754/1 Himayat Nagar, Hyderabad 500 029; tel. (40) 27662849; fax (40) 27645046; e-mail info@universitiespress.com; internet www.universitiespress.com; academic and educational books on science, technology, management; Man. Dir MADHU REDDY.

Vikas Publishing House Pvt Ltd: E-28, Sector 8, Noida 201 301; tel. (120) 4078900; fax (120) 4078999; e-mail helpline@vikaspublishing.com; internet www.vikaspublishing.com; f. 1969; computers, management, commerce, sciences, engineering textbooks; Dir PIYUSH CHAWLA.

Vishwavidyalaya Prakashan: Vishalakshi Bldg, POB 1149, Chowk, Varanasi 221 001, Uttar Pradesh; tel. (542) 2413741; fax (542) 2413082; e-mail vvp@vsnl.com; internet www.vvpbooks.com; f. 1950; Hindu and Sanskrit literature, Indology, history, art and culture, spiritualism, religion, philosophy, education, sociology, psychology, music, journalism, mass communication, science and social science; Partner ANURAG KUMAR MODI.

GOVERNMENT PUBLISHING HOUSE

Publications Division: Ministry of Information and Broadcasting, Govt of India, Patiala House, New Delhi 110 001; tel. and fax (11) 24366670; e-mail dpd@sb.nic.in; internet publicationsdivision.nic.in; f. 1941; culture, art, literature, planning and development, general; also 21 periodicals in English and 13 Indian languages; Dir-Gen K. GANESAN.

PUBLISHERS' ASSOCIATIONS

Association of Publishers in India: c/o Cambridge University Press, Cambridge House, 4381/4, 3rd Floor, Ansari Rd, Daryaganj, New Delhi 110 002; e-mail info@api.org; internet www.publishers.org.in; f. 2001; represents the interests of foreign publishers operating in India; 27 mem. cos; Pres. P. M. SUKUMAR; Sec. ROHIT KUMAR.

Bombay Booksellers' and Publishers' Association: No. 25, 6th Floor, Bldg No. 3, Navjivan Commercial Premises Co-op Society Ltd, Dr Bhadkamkar Marg, Mumbai 400 008; tel. (22) 23088691; e-mail bbpassn@yahoo.co.in; f. 1961; 400 mems; Pres. ANIL KUMAR PANDEY; Hon. Gen. Sec. B. S. FERNANDES.

Delhi State Booksellers' and Publishers' Association: 4760-61/23 Ansari Rd, Daryaganj, New Delhi 110 002; tel. (11) 43502211; fax (11) 43502212; e-mail info@dsbpa.in; internet www.dsbpa.in; f. 1941; 450 mems; Pres. K. K. SAXENA; Sec. SURYA MITTAL.

Federation of Indian Publishers: Federation House, 18/1-C Institutional Area, nr JNU, New Delhi 110 067; tel. (11) 26964847; fax (11) 26864054; e-mail fipl@satyam.net.in; internet www.fipindia.org; 18 affiliated asscns; 190 mems; Pres. ANAND BHUSHAN; Hon. Gen. Sec. SHAKTI MALIK.

Federation of Publishers' and Booksellers' Associations in India: 84 Daryaganj, 2nd Floor, New Delhi 110 002; tel. (11) 23272845; fax (11) 23281227; e-mail fpbaidelhi@gmail.com; internet www.fpbai.org; f. 1955; 12 affiliated asscns; 507 mems; Pres. S. C. SETHI; Hon. Sec. J. L. KUMAR.

Publishers' and Booksellers' Guild: Guild House, 2B Jhamapukur Lane, Kolkata 700 009; tel. (33) 23544417; fax (33) 23604566; e-mail guildpb@gmail.com; internet www.kolkatabookfaironline.com; f. 1975; 39 mems; organizes annual internationally recognized Kolkata Book Fair; Pres. JAYANT MANAKTALA; Hon. Gen. Sec. TRIDIB KR. CHATTERJEE.

Broadcasting and Communications

TELECOMMUNICATIONS

The telecommunications sector has expanded rapidly in recent years. Mobile cellular subscriptions increased from 52.2m. in 2004 to 886.3m. at the end of December 2013 (representing the second largest market in the world in terms of subscribers); of these, 762.4m. were described as active subscriptions. The mobile telephone penetration rate was measured at 71.7% of the population. At that time there were an estimated 28.9m. fixed-line telephone subscribers and 55.2m. broadband internet subscribers.

Regulatory Authority

Telecom Regulatory Authority of India (TRAI): Mahanagar Doorsanchar Bhavan (next to Zakir Hussain College), Jawaharlal Nehru Marg (Old Minto Rd), New Delhi 110 002; tel. (11) 23236308; fax (11) 23213294; e-mail ap@trai.gov.in; internet www.trai.gov.in; f. 1997; Chair. RAHUL KHULLAR.

Service Providers

Aircel Ltd: Dishnet Wireless Ltd, Bldg 10A, 2nd Floor, DLF Cyber City, Phase II, Gurgaon 122 022; tel. (124) 4765000; fax (124) 4290524; e-mail care.haryana@aircel.co.in; internet www.aircel.com; f. 1999; 74% owned by Maxis Communications Bhd (Malaysia); 58m. subscribers (July 2011); Chair. SUNEETA REDDY.

Bharat Sanchar Nigam Ltd (BSNL): Bharat Sanchar Bhavan, Harish Chandra Mathur Lane, Janpath, New Delhi 110 001; tel. (11) 23372424; fax (11) 23372444; e-mail cmdbsnl@bsnl.co.in; internet www.bsnl.co.in; f. 2000; fmrly Dept of Telecom Operations; state-owned; 104.2m. subscribers (Jan. 2011); Chair. and Man. Dir R. K. UPADHYAY.

Bharti Airtel Ltd: Bharti Crescent, 1 Nelson Mandela Rd, Vasant Kunj, Phase 2, New Delhi 110 070; tel. (11) 46666100; fax (11) 41666137; internet www.airtel.in; f. 1995; India's first privately owned telephone network; provides mobile, fixed-line, direct-to-home and internet protocol TV services; 200m. subscribers (July 2011); Chair. and Man. Dir SUNIL BHARTI MITTAL.

Idea Cellular: Idea Cellular Ltd, 5th Floor, Windsor CST Rd, Kalina Santa Cruz (East), Mumbai 400 098; tel. 9594004000 (mobile); fax 9594003182 (mobile); e-mail rajat.mukarji@idea.adityabirla.com; internet www.ideacellular.com; f. 1995; 49% owned by Aditya Birla Group; 100m. subscribers (Sept. 2011); Chair. KUMAR MANGALAM BIRLA; Man. Dir HIMANSHU KAPANIA.

Mahanagar Telephone Nigam Ltd (MTNL): Jeevan Bharati Bldg, 124 Connaught Circus, New Delhi 110 001; tel. (11) 23719020; fax (11) 23314243; e-mail cmd@bol.net.in; internet www.mtnl.net.in; f. 1986; 56% state-owned; owns and operates telecommunications and information technology services in Mumbai and Delhi; 8.8m. subscribers (Jan. 2011); Chair. and Man. Dir A. K. GARG.

Reliance Communications Ltd: Blk H, 1st Floor, Dhirubhai Ambani Knowledge City, Navi Mumbai 400 709; tel. (22) 30373333; fax (22) 30388005; e-mail customercare@relianceada.com; internet www.rcom.co.in; f. 1999; provides mobile and fixed-line telephony services throughout India; 150m. subscribers (July 2011); Chair. and Man. Dir ANIL D. AMBANI.

Sistema Shyam TeleServices Ltd: MTS Towers, 334 Udyog Vihar, Phase IV, Gurgaon 122 001; tel. (12) 44812500; e-mail ceo@mtsindia.in; internet www.mtsindia.in; f. 1993; offers services under the brand MTS; 9.1m. subscribers (Jan. 2011); Pres. and CEO VSEVOLOD ROZANOV.

Tata Group: operates Tata Teleservices Ltd, Tata Communications (fmrly VSNL) and Tatanet; 87.2m. subscribers (Jan 2011); Chair. RATAN TATA.

Tata Communications: Plots C-21 and C-36, Blk G, Bandra Kurla Complex, Bandra (East), Mumbai 400 098; tel. (22) 66578765; fax (22) 66591912; e-mail ravindran.s@tatacommunications.com; internet www.tatacommunications.com; f. 1986 as Videsh Sanchar Nigam Ltd (VSNL); enterprise data services and overseas communications; Man. Dir VINOD KUMAR.

Tata Teleservices Ltd: A, E and F Blks, Voltas Premises, T. B. Kadam Marg, Chinchpokli, Mumbai 400033; tel. (22) 66671414; fax (22) 66605335; internet www.tatateleservices.com; f. 1996; Chair. RATAN N. TATA; Man. Dir and CEO SRINATH NARASIMHAN.

Telewings Communications Services Ltd (Uninor): Unitech Wireless (Tamil Nadu) Pvt Ltd, Ground Floor, Masterpiece, Sector 54, DLF Golf Course Rd, Gurgaon 122 002; tel. (12) 43329000; e-mail sharad.goswami@uninor.in; internet www.uninor.in; f. 2009; subsidiary of Telenor Group, Norway; 20.3m. subscribers (Jan. 2011); Man. Dir MORTEN KARLSEN SORBY.

Videocon Telecommunications Ltd: 248 Udyog Vihar, Phase IV, Gurgaon 122 015; e-mail 121@videocon.com; internet www.videocon.com; f. 2010; 6m. subscribers (Jan. 2011); Chair. VENUGOPAL DHOOT.

Vodafone Essar Ltd (Hutch): Peninsula Corporate Park, Ganpatrao Kadam Marg, Lower Parel, Mumbai 400 013; tel. 9619215000 (mobile); fax (22) 24963645; e-mail vodafonecare.mum@vodafone.com; internet www.vodafone.in; f. 1994; Vodafone (United Kingdom) acquired controlling 67% share from Hutchison Telecommunications International (Hong Kong) in Feb. 2007, 33% owned by Essar Group; 127.3m. subscribers (Jan. 2011); CEO MARTEN PIETERS.

Other mobile telephone operators include:Loop Mobile and S Tel.

Other Companies

ITI Ltd: ITI Bhavan, Doorvaninagar, Bangalore 560 016; tel. (80) 25614466; fax (80) 25617525; e-mail secretary@itiltd.co.in; internet www.itiltd-india.com; f. 1948; govt undertaking; mfrs of all types of telecommunication equipment, incl. telephones, automatic exchanges and long-distance transmission equipment; also produces optical-fibre equipment and microwave equipment; will manufacture all ground communication equipment for the 22 earth stations of the Indian National Satellite; in conjunction with the Post and Telegraph Department, a newly designed 2,000-line exchange has been completed; Chair. and Man. Dir K. L. DHINGRA.

BROADCASTING

Prasar Bharati (Broadcasting Corpn of India): Doordarshan Bhavan, Copernicus Marg, New Delhi 110 001; tel. (11) 23737603; fax (11) 23352549; e-mail webadmin@dd.nic.in; internet www.ddindia.gov.in/Prasar+Bharati; f. 1997; autonomous body; oversees operations of state-owned radio and television services; Chair. MRINAL PANDE; CEO RAJIV TAKRU.

Radio

By 2011 there were more than 245 privately owned FM radio channels in operation.

All India Radio (AIR): Akashvani Bhavan, Sansad Marg, New Delhi 110 001; tel. (11) 23710300; fax (11) 23421956; e-mail dgair@air.org.in; internet allindiaradio.org; broadcasting is controlled by the Ministry of Information and Broadcasting and is primarily govt-financed; operates a network of 208 stations and 380 transmitters (grouped into four zones—north, south, east and west), covering almost the entire population and over 90% of the total area of the country; Dir-Gen. LEELA DHAR MANDLOI; The News Services Division of AIR, centralized in New Delhi, is one of the largest news organizations in the world. It has 45 regional news units, which broadcast 469 bulletins daily in 75 languages. Daily broadcasts include: 178 bulletins in 33 languages in the Home Services; 187 regional bulletins in 65 languages and dialects; and 66 bulletins in 26 languages in the External Services.

Television

In late 2011 the Government introduced legislation that required the entire industry to convert to digital infrastructure by the end of 2014. The total number of television channels grew from 461 in 2009 to 626 in 2011. Cable and satellite penetration across the country had reached 80% by 2012.

Doordarshan India (Television India): Mandi House, Doordarshan Bhavan, Copernicus Marg, New Delhi 110 001; tel. (11) 23385958; fax (11) 23386507; e-mail webadmin@dd.nic.in; internet www.ddindia.gov.in; f. 1976; broadcasting is controlled by the Ministry of Information and Broadcasting and is govt-financed; programmes: 280 hours weekly; 5 all-India channels, 11 regional-language satellite channels, 5 state networks and 1 international channel; Dir-Gen. TRIPURARI SHARAN.

NDTV Network: NDTV Ltd, 207 Okhla Industrial Estate, Phase III, New Delhi 110 020; tel. (11) 26446666; fax (11) 41037119; e-mail feedback@ndtv.com; internet www.ndtv.com; f. 1988; 3 news channels: NDTV 24x7 (English), NDTV India (Hindi) and NDTV Profit (Business); also NDTV Lifestyle, NDTV Convergence and NDTV Good Times; 23 offices and studios; Chair. and Dir Dr PRANNOY ROY; CEO VIKRAMADITYA CHANDRA.

Network 18 Group: 503, 504 and 507, 5th Floor, Mercantile House, 15 Kasturba Gandhi Marg, New Delhi 110 001; tel. (11) 41506112; fax (11) 41506115; internet www.network18online.com; f. 1993; owns news channels, incl. CNN-IBN, CNBC-TV18, IBN 7 and IBN Lokmat (Marathi); also operates, in a jt venture with Viacom, Inc. of the USA, entertainment channels incl. Colors, MTV, VH1 and Nick; Chair. and Man. Dir RAGHAV BAHL; Exec. Dir SANJAY RAY CHAUDHURI.

Sony Entertainment Television (Multi Screen Media Pvt. Ltd): Multi Screen Media Pvt. Ltd, 3rd Floor, Bldg No. 7, Malad Link Rd, Malad (West), Mumbai 400 064; tel. (22) 67081111; fax (22) 66434748; e-mail feedback.set@setindia.com; internet www.setindia.com; f. 1995; channels incl. Sony Entertainment Television, SAB TV, SET Max, Sony Aath, SET PIX, Sony MIX, AXN and Animax India; owned by MSM Pvt. Ltd, fmrly SET India Pvt. Ltd; CEO MAN JIT SINGH.

Star TV: Star India Pvt. Ltd, Star House, Dr E. Moses Rd, Mahalaxmi, Mumbai 400 011; tel. (22) 66305555; fax (22) 66305050; e-mail info@startv.com; internet www.startv.com; f. 1991; 35 channels in 7 languages, incl. Star World, Star Movies, Star Plus, Star One, Star Utsav, Star Gold, Star News, ESPN, Star Sports, Channel [V], National Geographic Channel, etc.; CEO UDAY SHANKAR.

TV Today Network: Videocon Tower, 8th Floor, E-1 Jhandewalan Extn, New Delhi 110 055; tel. (11) 23684878; fax (11) 23684895; e-mail info@aajtak.com; internet www.indiatodaygroup.com; f. 1975; owns news channels incl. Aaj Tak (Hindi), Headlines Today (English), Tez (Hindi) and Dilli Aaj Tak (Hindi) news channel; Chair. AROON PURIE; CEO JOY CHAKRABORTHY.

Zee Entertainment Enterprises Ltd: 135 Continental Bldg, Dr Annie Beasant Rd, Worli, Mumbai 400 018; tel. (22) 66971234; fax (22) 24900302; e-mail inquiry@zeenetwork.com; internet www.zeetelevision.com; f. 1992; owns more than 30 news and entertainment channels, incl. Zee TV, Zee Cinema, Ten Sports, Zee Studio, Zee News, Zee Business, 9X, etc.; Chair. SUBHASH CHANDRA; CEO PUNIT GOENKA.

Finance

(cap. = capital; p.u. = paid up; res = reserves; dep. = deposits; m. = million; brs = branches; amounts in rupees, unless otherwise stated)

BANKING

Scheduled commercial banks are grouped under the following categories: the State Bank of India and its associates; state-owned commercial banks; foreign banks; regional rural banks; and private scheduled commercial banks. At the end of March 2011 there were 169 commercial banks in operation in India; of these, 165 were scheduled commercial banks (including 82 regional rural banks) and four were non-scheduled banks. At that time scheduled commercial banks held aggregate deposits of an estimated Rs 52,079,690m. and operated a network of 90,263 branches.

State Banks

Reserve Bank of India: Central Office Bldg, Shahid Bhagat Singh Rd, POB 10007, Mumbai 400 001; tel. (22) 22661602; fax (22) 22658269; e-mail helpprd@rbi.org.in; internet www.rbi.org.in; f. 1934; nationalized 1949; sole bank of issue; cap. 50m., res 65,000m., dep. 3,754,115m. (June 2010); Gov. RAGHURAM G. RAJAN; Dep. Govs Dr K. C. CHAKRABARTY, ANAND SINHA, URJIT PATEL, H. R. KHAN; 19 regional offices and 9 sub-offices.

State Bank of India: Corporate Centre, Madame Cama Rd, POB 10121, Mumbai 400 021; tel. (22) 22022426; fax (22) 22851391; e-mail gm.gbu@sbi.co.in; internet www.statebankofindia.com; f. 1955; cap. 6,710.5m., res 896,929.5m., dep. 14,146,894.0m. (March 2012); 7 associates, 7 domestic subsidiaries/affiliates, 3 foreign subsidiaries, 4 jt ventures abroad; Chair. ARUNDHATI BHATTACHARYA; Man Dirs HEMANT CONTRACTOR, DIWAKAR GUPTA, A. KRISHNA KUMAR; 9,593 brs (incl. 52 overseas brs and rep. offices in 34 countries).

State-owned Commercial Banks

Fourteen of India's major commercial banks were nationalized in 1969 and a further six in 1980. They are managed by 15-member boards of directors (two directors appointed by the central Government, one employee director, one representing employees who are not workmen, one representing depositors, three representing farmers, workers, artisans, etc., five representing persons with special knowledge or experience, one Reserve Bank of India official and one Government of India official). The Department of Banking of the Ministry of Finance controls all banking operations.

Allahabad Bank: 2 Netaji Subhas Rd, Kolkata 700 001; tel. (33) 22319144; fax (33) 22107425; e-mail gmpd@allahabadbank.in; internet www.allahabadbank.com; f. 1865; nationalized 1969; cap. 5,000.3m., res 81,008.5m., dep. 1,595,838.7m. (March 2012); Chair. and Man. Dir J. P. DUA; Exec. Dirs T. R. CHAWLA, ARUN TIWARI; 2,020 brs.

Andhra Bank: Andhra Bank Bldgs, Saifabad, 5-9-11 Secretariat Rd, Hyderabad 500 004; tel. (40) 23252000; fax (40) 23232419; e-mail customerser@andhrabank.co.in; internet www.andhrabank.in; f. 1923; nationalized 1980; cap. 5,595m., res 53,551.4m., dep. 1,058,331.2m. (March 2012); Chair. and Man. Dir B. A. PRABHAKAR; Exec. Dirs K. K. MISRA, A. A. TAJ; 1,128 brs and 113 extension counters.

Bank of Baroda: Baroda Corporate Centre, C-26, G Blk, Bandra-Kurla Complex, Bandra (East), Mumbai 400 051; tel. (22) 26985000; fax (22) 26523000; e-mail customerservice@bankofbaroda.com; internet www.bankofbaroda.com; f. 1908; nationalized 1969; merged with Benares State Bank in 2002; cap. 4,123.8m., res 227,166.8m., dep. 3,926,159.5m. (March 2012); Chair. and Man. Dir M. D. MALLYA; Exec. Dirs RAJIV KUMAR BAKSHI, SUDHIR KUMAR JAIN, P. SRINIVAS; 2,773 brs in India, 38 brs overseas.

Bank of India: Star House, C-5, G Blk, 3rd Floor, Bandra-Kurla Complex, Bandra (East), Mumbai 400 051; tel. (22) 66684444; fax (22) 56684558; e-mail headoffice.god@bankofindia.co.in; internet www.bankofindia.com; f. 1906; nationalized 1969; cap. 5,745.2m., res 181,146.2m., dep. 3,194,125.3m. (March 2012); Chair. and Man. Dir ALOK KUMAR MISRA; 2,883 brs in India, 21 brs overseas.

Bank of Maharashtra: 'Lokmangal', 1501 Shivajinagar, Pune 411 005; tel. (20) 25532731; fax (20) 25533246; e-mail bomcopln@mahabank.co.in; internet www.bankofmaharashtra.in; f. 1935; nationalized 1969; cap. 11,775.9m., res 27,573.1m., dep. 765,219.6m. (March 2012); Chair. and Man. Dir NARENDRA SINGH; Exec. Dir C. V. R. RAJENDRAN; 1,291 brs.

Canara Bank: 112 Jayachamarajendra Rd, POB 6648, Bangalore 560 002; tel. (80) 22221581; fax (80) 22223168; internet www.canarabank.com; f. 1906; nationalized 1969; cap. 4,430m., res 192,587m., dep. 3,268,940.4m. (March 2012); Chair. and Man. Dir S. RAMAN; Exec. Dirs ARCHANA S. BHARGAVA, ASHOK KUMAR GUPTA; 2,744 brs.

Central Bank of India: Chandermukhi, Nariman Point, Mumbai 400 021; tel. (22) 66387777; fax (22) 22044336; e-mail chairman@centralbank.co.in; internet www.centralbankofindia.co.in; f. 1911; nationalized 1969; cap. 23,531.1m., res 100,793.4m., dep. 1,962,353.2m. (March 2012); Chair. and Man. Dir M. V. TANKSALE; Exec. Dirs VIJAYALAKSHMI R. IYER, RAJIV KISHORE DUBEY; 3,130 brs.

Corporation Bank: Mangaladevi Temple Rd, POB 88, Mangalore 575 001; tel. (824) 2426416; fax (824) 2440964; e-mail query@

corpbank.co.in; internet www.corpbank.com; f. 1906; nationalized 1980; cap. 1,481.3m., res 66,786.1m., dep. 1,361,348.1m. (March 2012); Chair. and Man. Dir AJAI KUMAR; Exec. Dirs AMAR LAL DAULTANI, ASHWANI KUMAR; 617 brs.

Dena Bank: C-10, G Blk, Bandra-Kurla Complex, Bandra (East), Mumbai 400 051; tel. (22) 26545035; fax (22) 26545761; e-mail cmd@denabank.co.in; internet www.denabank.com; f. 1938 as Devkaran Nanjee Banking Co Ltd; nationalized 1969; cap. 3,500.6m., res 33,241.3m., dep. 771,668m. (March 2012); Chair. and Man. Dir NUPUR MITRA; Exec. Dir A. K. DUTT; 1,122 brs.

Indian Bank: 254 Avvai Shanmugam Salai, POB 5555, Royapettah, Chennai 600 014; tel. (44) 28134300; fax (44) 25231278; e-mail indmail@indianbank.co.in; internet www.indian-bank.com; f. 1907; nationalized 1969; cap. 8,297.7m., res 81,889.9m., dep. 1,207,157.1m. (March 2012); Chair. and Man. Dir T. M. BHASIN; Exec. Dirs B. RAJ KUMAR, RAJEEV RISHI; 1,960 brs.

Indian Overseas Bank: 763 Anna Salai, POB 3765, Chennai 600 002; tel. (44) 28524212; fax (44) 28523595; e-mail investor@iobnet.co.in; internet www.iob.in; f. 1937; nationalized 1969; merged with Bharat Overseas Bank Ltd in 2007; cap. 7,970m., res 100,805.3m., dep. 1,784,341.7m. (March 2012); Chair. and Man. Dir M. NARENDRA; Exec. Dirs A. D. M. CHAVALI, A. K. BANSAL; 1,496 brs.

Oriental Bank of Commerce: Harsha Bhavan, E Blk, Connaught Place, POB 329, New Delhi 110 001; tel. (11) 47651186; fax (11) 23321514; e-mail bdncmd@obcindia.com; internet www.obcindia.co.in; f. 1943; nationalized 1980; cap. 2,917.6m., res 116,502.5m., dep. 1,556,649.2m. (March 2012); Chair. and Man. Dir S. L. BANSAL; Exec. Dirs V. KANNAN, S. C. SINHA; 1,772 brs.

Punjab National Bank: 7 Bhikaiji Cama Place, Africa Ave, New Delhi 110 066; tel. (11) 26102303; fax (11) 26196456; e-mail cmd@pnb.co.in; internet www.pnbindia.com; f. 1895; nationalized 1969; merged with New Bank of India in 1993; cap. 3,391.8m., res 233,869.5m., dep. 3,844,082.2m. (March 2012); Chair. and Man. Dir Dr K. R. KAMATH; Exec. Dirs USHA ANANTHASUBRAMANIAN, RAKESH SETHI; 3,833 brs.

Punjab & Sind Bank: Bank House, 21 Rajendra Place, New Delhi 110 008; tel. (11) 25719082; fax (11) 25723793; e-mail ho.pr@psb.org.in; internet www.psbindia.com; f. 1908; nationalized 1980; cap. 4,342m., res 23,922.3m., dep. 631,239.8m. (March 2012); Chair. and Man. Dir DEVINDER PAL SINGH; Exec. Dir PARVEEN KUMAR ANAND; 866 brs.

Syndicate Bank: POB 1, Manipal 576 119; tel. (825) 2571181; fax (825) 2570266; e-mail idcb@syndicatebank.com; internet www.syndicatebank.com; f. 1925; est. as Canara Industrial and Banking Syndicate Ltd; name changed as above 1964; nationalized 1969; cap. 6,019.5m., res 71,286.6m., dep. 1,579,369.9m. (March 2012); Chair. and Man. Dir MADHUKANT GIRDHARLAL SANGHVI; Exec. Dirs M ANJANEYA PRASAD, RAVI CHATTERJEE; 2,127 brs.

UCO Bank: 10 Biplabi Trailokya Maharaj Sarani (Brabourne Rd), POB 2455, Kolkata 700 001; tel. (33) 22254120; fax (33) 22253986; e-mail ucobank@vsnl.net; internet www.ucobank.com; f. 1943; est. as United Commercial Bank Ltd; name changed as above 1985; nationalized 1969; cap. 24,877.1m., res 40,146.1m., dep. 1,540,034.9m. (March 2012); Chair. and Man. Dir ARUN KAUL; Exec. Dirs S. CHANDRASEKHARAN, N. R. BADRINARAYANAN; 1,849 brs.

Union Bank of India: Union Bank Bhavan, 239 Vidhan Bhavan Marg, Nariman Point, Mumbai 400 021; tel. (22) 22892000; fax (22) 22824689; e-mail ibd@unionbankofindia.com; internet www.unionbankofindia.co.in; f. 1919; nationalized 1969; cap. 6,615.5m., res 123,733.4m., dep. 2,227,765.1m. (March 2012); Chair. and Man. Dir ARUN TIWARI; Exec. Dirs SURESH KUMAR JAIN, K. SUBRAHMANYAM; 2,082 brs.

United Bank of India: 11 Hemant Basu Sarani, Kolkata 700 001; tel. (33) 2487471; fax (33) 2485852; e-mail homail@unitedbank.co.in; internet www.unitedbankofindia.com; f. 1950; nationalized 1969; cap. 11,610m., res 37,861.5m., dep. 891,162.6m. (March 2012); Chair. and Man. Dir BHASKAR SEN; Exec. Dirs D. NARANG, SANJAY ARYA; 1,354 brs.

Vijaya Bank: 41/2 Mahatma Gandhi Rd, Bangalore 560 001; tel. (80) 25584066; fax (80) 25584142; e-mail ibd@vijayabank.co.in; internet www.vijayabank.com; f. 1931; nationalized 1980; cap. 16,955.4m., res 38,631m., dep. 970,172m. (March 2013); Chair. and Man. Dir V. KANNAN; Exec. Dir K. RAMADAS SHENOY; 1,200 brs.

Principal Private Banks

Bombay Mercantile Co-operative Bank Ltd: 78 Mohammed Ali Rd, Mumbai 400 003; tel. (22) 23425961; fax (22) 23482387; e-mail bmcit@vsnl.net; internet bmcbankltd.com; f. 1939; cap. 382m., res 959.9m., dep. 21,150.7m. (March 2011); Man. Dir SHAIKH MUSHTAQUE ALI AHMED; 52 brs.

Catholic Syrian Bank Ltd: St Mary's College Rd, POB 502, Trichur 680 020; tel. (487) 2333020; fax (487) 2333435; e-mail pdd@csb.co.in; internet www.csb.co.in; f. 1920; cap. 314.1m., res 5,082.3m., dep. 106,048.7m. (March 2012); Chair. S. SANTHANAKRISHNAN; Man. Dir and CEO V. P. ISWARDAS; 380 brs.

City Union Bank Ltd: 149 TSR (Big) St, Kumbakonam 612 001; tel. (435) 2432322; fax (435) 2431746; e-mail co@cityunionbank.com; internet www.cityunionbank.com; f. 1904; cap. 408.2m., res 9,164.6m., dep. 163,407.5m. (March 2012); Chair. S. BALASUBRAMANIAN; Man. Dir and CEO N. KAMAKODI; 125 brs.

The Federal Bank Ltd: Federal Towers, POB 103, Alwaye 683 101; tel. (484) 2623620; fax (484) 2622672; e-mail nrihelp@federalbank.co.in; internet www.federalbank.co.in; f. 1931; cap. 1,710.4m., res 47,336.9m., dep. 489,347.3m. (March 2012); Man. Dir and CEO SHYAM SRINIVASAN; Exec. Dirs P. C. JOHN, ABRAHAM CHACKO; 606 brs.

HDFC Bank: HDFC Bank House, Senapati Bapat Marg, Lower Parel, Mumbai, 400 013; tel. (22) 66521000; fax (22) 24960739; e-mail corporatecommunications@hdfcbank.com; internet www.hdfcbank.com; merged with Centurion Bank of Punjab in 2008; cap. 4,693.3m., res 181,674.4m., dep. 2,465,395.7m. (March 2012); Chair. C. M. VASUDEV; Man. Dir ADITYA PURI; 1,412 brs.

ICICI Bank Ltd: ICICI Towers, South Tower, 4th Floor, Bandra-Kurla Complex, Bandra (East), Mumbai 400 051; tel. (22) 26531414; fax (22) 26531124; e-mail info@icicibank.com; internet www.icicibank.com; f. 1994; cap. 15,027.7m., res 484,730.3m., dep. 2,832,538.7m. (March 2012); merged with Sangli Bank in 2007 and with The Bank of Rajasthan Ltd in 2010; CEO and Man. Dir CHANDA D. KOCHHAR; Chair. K. V. KAMATH; 1,400 brs.

IndusInd Bank Ltd: One Indiabulls Centre, Tower 1, 8th Floor, 841 S. B. Marg, Elphinstone Rd, Mumbai 400 013; tel. (22) 24231999; fax (22) 24231998; e-mail mktg@indusind.com; internet www.indusind.com; f. 1994; cap. 4,677m., res 27,570.3m., dep. 423,615.5m. (March 2012); Chair. R. SESHASAYEE; Man. Dir ROMESH SOBTI; 209 brs.

ING Vysya Bank Ltd: 22 M. G. Rd, Bangalore 560 001; tel. (80) 25005000; fax (80) 25588442; e-mail ingvysyabank@ingvysyabank.com; internet www.ingvysyabank.com; f. 1930; cap. 1,501.2m., res 28,584.1m., dep. 351,908.7m. (March 2012); Chair. ARUN THIAGARAJAN; Man. Dir and CEO SHAILENDRA BHANDARI; 404 brs.

Jammu and Kashmir Bank Ltd: Corporate Headquarters, M. A. Rd, Srinagar 190 001; tel. (194) 2481930; fax (194) 2481923; e-mail jkbcosgr@jkbmail.com; internet jkbank.net; f. 1938; cap. 484.9m., res 32,417.2m., dep. 533,417.6m. (March 2012); Chair. MUSHTAQ AHMAD; 556 brs.

Karnataka Bank Ltd: POB 599, Kodialbail, Mangalore 575 003; tel. (824) 2228222; fax (824) 2228284; e-mail info@ktkbank.com; internet www.karnatakabank.com; f. 1924; cap. 1,882.9m., res 21,638.2m., dep. 316,083.2m. (March 2012); Chair. and CEO ANANTHAKRISHNA; Man. Dir and CEO P. JAYARAMA BHAT; 370 brs.

The Karur Vysya Bank Ltd: Erode Rd, POB 21, Karur, Tamil Nadu 639 002; tel. (4324) 226520; fax (4324) 225700; e-mail kvbpdd@kvbmail.com; internet www.kvb.co.in; f. 1916; cap. 1,071.8m., res 20,970m., dep. 321,115.9m. (March 2012); Chair. K. P. KUMAR; Man. Dir and CEO K. VENKATARAMAN; 312 brs.

Lakshmi Vilas Bank Ltd: Kathaparai, Salem Rd, POB 2, Karur 639 006; tel. (4324) 220051; fax (4324) 220068; e-mail info@lvbank.com; internet www.lvbank.com; f. 1926; cap. 975m., res 7,535.7m., dep. 141,141.4m. (March 2012); Man. Dir and CEO P. R. SOMASUNDARAM; 291 brs.

South Indian Bank Ltd: SIB House, T. B. Rd, Mission Quarters, Thrissur 680 001; tel. (487) 2420020; fax (487) 2442021; e-mail sibcorporate@sib.co.in; internet www.southindianbank.com; f. 1929; cap. 1,133.7m., res 16,368.9m., dep. 365,005.3m. (March 2012); Man. Dir and CEO V. A. JOSEPH; 450 brs.

Tamilnad Mercantile Bank Ltd: 57 Victoria Extension Rd, Tuticorin 628 002; tel. (461) 2321932; fax (461) 2322994; e-mail bd@tnmbonline.com; internet www.tmb.in; f. 1921; est. as Nadar Bank; name changed as above 1962; cap. 2.8m., res 13,201.4m., dep. 171,104.4m. (March 2012); Man. Dir and CEO K. B. NAGENDRA MURTHY; 304 brs.

Banking Organizations

Indian Banks' Association: World Trade Centre Complex, Centre I Bldg, 6th Floor, Cuffe Parade, Mumbai 400 005; tel. (22) 22174040; fax (22) 22184222; e-mail webmaster@iba.org.in; internet www.iba.org.in; 156 mems; Chair. ALOK K. MISRA.

Indian Institute of Banking and Finance: 2 Kohinoor City Commercial, Tower 1, 2nd and 3rd Floors, Kirol Rd, Kurla (West), Mumbai 400 070; tel. (22) 25039746; fax (22) 25037332; e-mail mem-services@iibf.org.in; internet www.iibf.org.in; f. 1928; 343,202 mems; four zonal offices; CEO R. BHASKARAN; Pres. M. D. MALLYA.

National Institute of Bank Management: NIBM Post Office, Kondhwe Khurd, Pune 411 048; tel. (20) 26716000; fax (20) 26834478; e-mail director@nibmindia.org; internet www.nibmindia.org; f. 1969; Gov. Dr D. SUBBARAO; Dir ALLEN C. A. PEREIRA.

DEVELOPMENT FINANCE ORGANIZATIONS

Agricultural Finance Corporation Ltd: Dhanraj Mahal, 1st Floor, Chhatrapati Shivaji Maharaj Marg, Mumbai 400 001; tel. (22) 22029517; fax (22) 22028966; e-mail afcl@afcindia.org.in; internet www.afcindia.org.in; f. 1968; est. by consortium of 45 public and private sector commercial banks incl. devt finance institutions; aims to increase the flow of investment and credit into agriculture and rural devt projects; provides project consultancy services to commercial banks, Union and state govts, public sector corpns, the World Bank, the ADB, FAO, the International Fund for Agricultural Development and other institutions, and to individuals; undertakes techno-economic and investment surveys in agriculture and agro-industries, etc.; publishes quarterly journal *Financing Agriculture*; Chair. Y. C. NANDA; Man. Dir A. K. GARG; 3 regional offices and 9 br. offices.

Export-Import Bank of India: Centre One Bldg, Floor 21, World Trade Centre Complex, Cuffe Parade, Mumbai 400 005; tel. (22) 22172600; fax (22) 22182572; e-mail cag@eximbankindia.in; internet www.eximbankindia.com; f. 1982; cap. 22,999.9m., res 32,301.7m., dep. 31,566.1m. (March 2012); Chair. and Man. Dir T. C. A. RANGANATHAN; 14 offices world-wide.

Housing Development Finance Corpn Ltd (HDFC): Ramon House, 169 Backbay Reclamation, Churchgate, Mumbai 400 020; tel. (22) 66316000; fax (22) 22048834; e-mail info@hdfc.com; internet www.hdfc.com; f. 1977; provides loans to individuals and corporate bodies; cap. p.u. 2,844.5m., res 128,529.4m., dep. 193,746.7m. (March 2009); Chair. C. M. VASUDEV; Man. Dir RENU SUD KARNAD; 173 brs (incl. one overseas br.).

IDBI Bank Ltd (Industrial Development Bank of India): IDBI Tower, World Trade Centre Complex, Cuffe Parade, Mumbai 400 005; tel. (22) 66553355; fax (22) 22188137; e-mail pro@idbi.co.in; internet www.idbi.com; f. 1964; reorg. 1976; merged with The United Western Bank Ltd in 2006; 52.68% govt-owned; provides direct finance, refinance of industrial loans and bills, finance to large- and medium-sized industries, extends financial services, such as merchant banking and forex services, to the corporate sector; cap. 12,783.8m., res 158,031m., dep. 2,102,441.7m. (March 2012); Chair. and Man. Dir R. M. MALLA; 5 zonal offices and 36 br. offices.

Small Industries Development Bank of India: SIDBI Tower, 15 Ashok Marg, Lucknow 226 001; tel. (522) 2288547; fax (522) 2288548; e-mail cmdsecttlho@sidbi.com; internet www.sidbi.in; f. 1990; wholly owned subsidiary of IDBI; promotes, finances and develops small-scale industries; cap. 4,500m., res 57,974.9m., dep. 157,342m. (March 2012); Chair. and Man. Dir SUSHIL MUHNOT; 39 offices.

IFCI Ltd: IFCI Tower, 61 Nehru Place, New Delhi 110 019; tel. (11) 41792800; fax (11) 26488471; e-mail helpdesk@ifciltd.com; internet www.ifciltd.com; f. 1948, as Industrial Finance Corpn of India; renamed as above in 1999; CEO and Man. Dir ATUL K. RAI.

Industrial Investment Bank of India: 19 Netaji Subhas Rd, Kolkata 700 001; tel. (33) 22209941; fax (33) 22208049; e-mail iibiho@vsnl.com; Chair. and Man. Dir BHASKAR SEN; Exec. Dir V. K. DHINGRA.

National Bank for Agriculture and Rural Development: Plot C-24, G Blk, Bandra-Kurla Complex, Bandra (East), Mumbai 400 051; tel. (22) 26525068; fax (22) 26530050; e-mail contact@nabard.org; internet www.nabard.org; f. 1982; est. to provide credit for agricultural and rural devt through commercial, co-operative and regional rural banks; cap. p.u. 20,000m., res 52,910m. (March 2004); held 50% each by cen. Govt and Reserve Bank; Chair. PRAKASH BAKSHI; 30 regional offices, 10 sub-offices and 4 training establishments.

STOCK EXCHANGES

At the end of December 2011 there were 25 stock exchanges in India. The two most important exchanges are the Bombay Stock Exchange and the National Stock Exchange.

Ahmedabad Stock Exchange: Kamdhenu Complex, opp. Sahajanand College, Panjarapole, Ambawadi, Ahmedabad 380 015; tel. (79) 26307971; fax (79) 26308877; e-mail info@agipt.org; internet www.aselindia.org; f. 1894; 2,000 mems; Chair. HEMANTSINGH JHALA; Man. Dir K. K. MISHRA.

Bangalore Stock Exchange Ltd: 51 Stock Exchange Towers, 1st Cross, J. C. Rd, Bangalore 560 027; tel. (80) 41575234; fax (80) 41575232; e-mail ed_secretary@bgse.co.in; internet www.bgse.co.in; 257 mems; Chair. MICHAEL BASTIAN; Exec. Dir MANJIT SINGH.

Bombay Stock Exchange (BSE): Phiroze Jeejeebhoy Towers, 25th Floor, Dalal St, Fort, Mumbai 400 001; tel. (22) 22721233; fax (22) 22721919; e-mail info@bseindia.com; internet www.bseindia.com; f. 1875; 5,112 listed cos (Dec. 2011); Chair. S. RAMADORAI; Man. Dir and CEO ASHISH KUMAR CHAUHAN.

Calcutta Stock Exchange Association Ltd: 7 Lyons Range, Kolkata 700 001; tel. (33) 40253000; fax (33) 22104500; e-mail cseadmn@cse-india.com; internet www.cse-india.com; f. 1908; 917 mems; Chair. SUNIL MITRA; Man. Dir and CEO B. MADHAV REDDY.

Delhi Stock Exchange Ltd: DSE House, 3/1 Asaf Ali Rd, New Delhi 110 002; tel. (11) 46470000; fax (11) 46740053; e-mail contact@dseindia.org.in; internet www.dseindia.org.in; f. 1947; some 2,750 listed cos (Feb. 2013); Sec. SUNIL BHATIA.

Ludhiana Stock Exchange Association Ltd: Feroze Gandhi Market, Ludhiana 141 001; tel. (161) 2405756; fax (161) 2404748; e-mail lse@satyam.net.in; internet lse.co.in; f. 1981; 295 mems; Chair. PADAM PARKASH KANSAL.

Madras Stock Exchange Ltd: Exchange Bldg, 30 Second Line Beach, POB 183, Chennai 600 001; tel. (44) 25228951; fax (44) 25244897; e-mail info@mseindia.in; internet www.mseindia.in; f. 1937; 222 mems; Man. Dir K. N. RAMANATH.

National Stock Exchange of India Ltd (NSE): Exchange Plaza, Bandra-Kurla Complex, Bandra (East), Mumbai 400 051; tel. (22) 26598100; fax (22) 26598120; e-mail cc_nse@nse.co.in; internet www.nseindia.com; f. 1994; 1,640 listed cos (Dec. 2011); New York Stock Exchange, Goldman Sachs, General Atlantic (all of the USA) and SoftBank Asian Infrastructure Fund (Hong Kong) each acquired a 5% share in Jan. 2007; Chair. VIJAY KELKAR; CEO CHITRA RAMKRISHNA.

Uttar Pradesh Stock Exchange Association Ltd (UPSE): Padam Towers, 14/113 Civil Lines, Kanpur 208 001; tel. (512) 2293115; fax (512) 2293175; e-mail upstockexchange@gmail.com; internet www.upse-india.com; 540 mems; Chair. K. D. GUPTA; Man. Dir BHARAT KUMAR NADHANI.

Other recognized stock exchanges include: Madhya Pradesh (Indore), Pune, Guwahati, Jaipur, Bhubaneswar (Odisha), Coimbatore, Meerut, Vadodara, the OTC Exchange and the Inter-connected Stock Exchange (ISE).

Regulatory Authority

Securities and Exchange Board of India: Plot No. C4-A,'G' Block, Bandra Kurla Complex, Bandra (East), Mumbai 400 051; tel. (22) 26449000; fax (22) 26449019; e-mail sebi@sebi.gov.in; internet www.sebi.gov.in; f. 1992; Chair. U. K. SINHA.

INSURANCE

In January 1973 all Indian and foreign insurance companies were nationalized. The Insurance Regulatory and Development Authority Bill, approved by the legislature in December 1999, established a regulatory authority for the insurance sector and henceforth permitted up to 26%investment by foreign companies in new domestic, private sector insurance companies. At the end of September 2013 there were 28 general insurance companies and 24 life insurance companies.

Bajaj Allianz: GE Plaza, Airport Rd, Yerawada, Pune 411 006; tel. (20) 66026777; fax (20) 66026789; e-mail info@bajajallianz.co.in; internet www.bajajallianz.com; f. 2001; life and general insurance; private sector; Chair. RAHUL BAJAJ; Man. Dir and CEO TAPAN SINGHEL.

General Insurance Corpn of India (GIC): 'Suraksha', 170 J. Tata Rd, Churchgate, Mumbai 400 020; tel. (22) 22867000; fax (22) 22899600; e-mail info@gicofindia.com; internet www.gicofindia.com; f. 1972; Chair. and Man. Dir ASHOK KUMAR ROY.

HDFC ERGO General: Leela Business Park, 6th Floor, Andheri Kurla Rd, Andheri (East), Mumbai 400 059; tel. (22) 66383600; fax (22) 66383699; e-mail care@hdfcergo.com; internet www.hdfcergo.com; f. 2002; general insurance; private sector; Chair. DEEPAK S. PAREKH; Man. Dir and CEO RITESH KUMAR; 78 brs.

ICICI Lombard: 401 and 402, Interface Bldg, 11 Link Rd, Malad (West), Mumbai 400 064; internet www.icicilombard.com; f. 2001; general insurance; private sector; Chair. CHANDA KOCHHAR; Man. Dir and CEO BHARGAV DASGUPTA; 350 brs.

ICICI Prudential: ICICI Pru Life Towers, 1,089 Appasaheb Marathe Marg, Prabhadevi, Mumbai 400 025; tel. (22) 40391600; e-mail lifeline@iciciprulife.com; internet www.iciciprulife.com; f. 2000; life insurance; private sector; Chair. CHANDA KOCHHAR; Man. Dir and CEO SANDEEP BAKHSHI.

IFFCO—Tokio: IFFCO Tower, 4th and 5th Floors, Plot 3, Sector 29, Gurgaon 122 001; internet www.iffcotokio.co.in; f. 2000; general insurance; private sector; Man. Dir YOGESH LOHIYA.

Life Insurance Corpn of India (LIC): 'Yogakshema', Jeevan Bima Marg, Mumbai 400 021; tel. (22) 26137545; fax (22) 22810680; e-mail co_pgs@licindia.com; internet www.licindia.in; f. 1956; leading insurance co; public sector; Chair. S. K ROY; Man. Dirs Thomas MATHEW, SUSHOBHAN SARKER; 109 divisional offices, 2,048 brs, 8 zonal offices and 992 satellite offices.

National Insurance Co Ltd: 3 Middleton St, Kolkata 700 071; tel. (33) 22831705; fax (33) 22831712; e-mail website.administrator@nic.co.in; internet www.nationalinsuranceindia.com; f. 1906; general insurance; public sector; Chair. and Man. Dir N. S. R. Chandra Prasad; 1,000 brs.

New India Assurance Co Ltd: 87 Mahatma Gandhi Rd, Fort, Mumbai 400 001; tel. (22) 22708220; fax (22) 22652811; e-mail cmd.nia@newindia.co.in; internet www.newindia.co.in; f. 1919; general insurance; public sector; 26 regional offices, 393 divisional offices, 614 br. offices, 34 direct agent brs and 19 overseas brs; Chair. and Man. Dir G. Srinivasan.

The Oriental Insurance Co Ltd: Oriental House, A-25/27 Asaf Ali Rd, New Delhi 110 002; tel. (11) 23279221; internet www.orientalinsurance.org.in; general insurance; public sector; Chair. and Man. Dir Dr A. K. Saxena.

Sahara India Life Insurance Co Ltd: Sahara India Centre, 2 Kapoorthala Complex, Lucknow 226 024; tel. (522) 2337777; fax (522) 2332683; e-mail life@life.sahara.co.in; internet www.saharalife.com; f. 2004; was the first wholly Indian-owned insurance co; pvt sector; Chair. Subrata Roy Sahara; Dir and CEO N. P. Bali.

SBI Life Insurance Co Ltd: Natraj, M.V. Rd and Western Express Highway Junction, Andheri (East), Mumbai 400 069; e-mail info@sbilife.co.in; internet www.sbilife.co.in; f. 2001; jt venture between State Bank of India and BNP Paribas Assurance; Man. Dir and CEO M. N. Rao; 430 brs.

United India Insurance Co Ltd: 24 Whites Rd, Chennai 600 014; tel. (44) 28520161; internet www.uiic.co.in; f. 1938; general insurance; public sector; Chair. and Man. Dir G. Srinivasan Garg; 1,340 brs.

Regulatory Authority

Insurance Regulatory and Development Authority: Parisrama Bhavan, 3rd Floor, Basheer Bagh, Hyderabad 500 004; tel. (40) 23381100; fax (40) 66823334; internet www.irda.gov.in; f. 2000; Chair. T. S. Vijayan.

Trade and Industry

GOVERNMENT AGENCIES AND DEVELOPMENT ORGANIZATIONS

Coal India Ltd: 10 Netaji Subhas Rd, Kolkata 700 001; tel. (33) 22488099; fax (33) 22435316; e-mail chairman@coalindia.in; internet www.coalindia.in; f. 1975; cen. govt holding co with 8 subsidiaries; responsible for almost total (more than 90%) exploration for, planning and production of coal mines; owns 462 coal mines throughout India; marketing of coal and its products; Chair. and Man. Dir S. Narsing Rao; 383,347 employees (2012).

Cotton Corpn of India Ltd: Plot No. 3A, Sector No. 10, CBD Belapur, Navi Mumbai 400 614; tel. (22) 27579217; fax (22) 27576030; e-mail headoffice@cotcorp.com; internet www.cotcorp.gov.in; f. 1970 as an agency in the public sector for the purchase, sale and distribution of home-produced cotton and imported cotton staple fibre; exports long staple cotton; Chair. and Man. Dir B. K. Mishra.

Export Credit Guarantee Corpn of India Ltd (ECGC): Express Towers, 10th Floor, Nariman Point, POB 11677, Mumbai 400 021; tel. (22) 66590500; fax (22) 66590517; e-mail webmaster@ecgc.in; internet www.ecgc.in; f. 1957 to insure for risks involved in exports on credit terms and to supplement credit facilities by issuing guarantees, etc.; Chair. and Man. Dir N. Shankar; 29 brs.

Food Corpn of India: DDA Complex, Ground Floor, Rajendra Pl., Rajendra Bhavan, New Delhi 110 008; tel. (11) 25710962; fax (11) 25750670; e-mail fci-gmhq@lsmgr.nic.in; internet www.fciweb.nic.in; f. 1965 to undertake trading in food grains on a commercial scale but within the framework of an overall govt policy; to provide farmers an assured price for their produce; to supply food grains to the consumer at reasonable prices; also purchases, stores, distributes and sells food grains and other foodstuffs and arranges imports and handling of food grains and fertilizers at the ports; distributes sugar in a number of states and has set up rice mills; Chair. and Man. Dir C. Viswanath; 59,800 employees (2002).

Handicrafts and Handlooms Exports Corpn of India Ltd: Jawahar Vyapar Bhavan Annexe, 5th Floor, 1 Tolstoy Marg, New Delhi 110 001; tel. (11) 23701086; fax (11) 23701051; e-mail hhecnd@bol.net.in; internet www.hhecworld.com; f. 1958; govt undertaking dealing in export of handicrafts, handloom goods, ready-to-wear clothes, carpets, jute, leather and precious jewellery, and import of bullion and raw silk; promotes exports and trade development; Chair. and Man. Dir Nirmal Sinha.

Housing and Urban Development Corpn Ltd: HUDCO Bhavan, India Habitat Centre, Lodhi Rd, New Delhi 110 003; tel. (11) 24649610; fax (11) 24625308; e-mail mail@hudco.org; internet www.hudco.org; f. 1970 to finance and undertake housing and urban development programmes including the establishment of new or satellite towns and building material industries; 21 brs; Chair. and Man. Dir V. P. Baligar.

India Trade Promotion Organisation (ITPO): Pragati Bhavan, Pragati Maidan, Lal Bahadur Shastri Marg, New Delhi 110 001; tel. (11) 23371540; fax (11) 23371492; e-mail info@itpo.gov.in; internet www.indiatradefair.com; f. 1992 following merger; promotes selective development of exports of high quality products; arranges investment in export-orientated ventures undertaken by India with foreign collaboration; organizes trade fairs; operates Trade Information Centre; regional offices in Bangalore, Mumbai, Kolkata and Chennai, and international offices in Frankfurt, New York, Moscow, São Paulo and Tokyo; Chair. and Man. Dir Rita Menon; Exec. Dir Malay Shrivastava.

Jute Corpn of India Ltd: 15-N, Nellie Sengupta Sarani, 7th Floor, Kolkata 700 087; tel. (33) 22527027; fax (33) 22526771; e-mail jutecorp@vsnl.net; internet www.jci.gov.in; f. 1971; objects: (i) to undertake price support operations in respect of raw jute; (ii) to ensure remunerative prices to producers through efficient marketing; (iii) to operate a buffer stock to stabilize raw jute prices; (iv) to handle the import and export of raw jute; (v) to promote the export of jute goods; Chair. and Man. Dir Arun Kumar Chakraborty.

Minerals and Metals Trading Corpn of India Ltd (MMTC): SCOPE Complex, Core 1, 7 Institutional Areas, Lodhi Rd, New Delhi 110 003; tel. (11) 24368426; fax (11) 24366274; e-mail mmtc@mmtclimited.com; internet www.mmtclimited.com; f. 1963; export of iron and manganese ore, ferro-manganese, finished stainless steel products, engineering, agricultural and marine products, textiles, leather items, chemicals and pharmaceuticals, mica, coal and other minor minerals; import of steel, non-ferrous metals, rough diamonds, fertilizers, etc. for supply to industrial units in the country; 13 regional offices in India; foreign offices in Japan, the Republic of Korea, Jordan and Romania; Chair. and Man. Dir D. S. Dhesi.

National Co-operative Development Corpn: 4 Siri Institutional Area, Hauz Khas, New Delhi 110 016; tel. (11) 26569246; fax (11) 26962370; e-mail editor@ncdc.in; internet www.ncdc.in; f. 1963 to plan, promote and finance country-wide programmes through co-operative societies for the production, processing, marketing, storage, export and import of agricultural produce, foodstuffs and notified commodities and minor forest produce; also programmes for the development of poultry, dairy, fish products, coir, handlooms, distribution of consumer articles in rural areas, industrial and service co-operatives, water conservation work, irrigation, micro-irrigation, animal care, health, disease prevention, agricultural insurance and credit, rural sanitation, etc.; 18 regional directorates; Pres. Sharad Pawar; Chair. Vasudha Mishra.

National Mineral Development Corpn Ltd: Khanij Bhavan, 10-3-311/A Castle Hills, Masab Tank, POB 1352, Hyderabad 500 028; tel. (40) 23538713; fax (40) 23538711; e-mail hois@nmdc.co.in; internet www.nmdc.co.in; f. 1958; cen. govt undertaking; to exploit minerals (excluding coal, atomic minerals, lignite, petroleum and natural gas) in public sector; may buy, take on lease or otherwise acquire mines for prospecting, development and exploitation; iron ore mines at Bailadila-11C, Bailadila-14 and Bailadila-5 in Madhya Pradesh, and at Donimalai in Karnataka State; new 5m. metric ton iron ore mine under construction at Bailadila-10/11A; diamond mines at Panna in Madhya Pradesh; research and development laboratories and consultancy services covering all aspects of mineral exploitation at Hyderabad; investigates mineral projects; Chair. and Man. Dir C. S. Verma.

National Productivity Council: Utpadakta Bhavan, 5–6 Institutional Area, Lodhi Rd, New Delhi 110 003; tel. (11) 24690331; fax (11) 24615002; e-mail npcinfo@npcindia.gov.in; internet www.npcindia.gov.in; f. 1958 to increase productivity and to improve quality by improved techniques which aim at efficient and proper utilization of available resources; autonomous body representing national orgs of employers and labour, govt ministries, professional orgs, local productivity councils, small-scale industries and other interests; 13 regional professional management groups, one training institute; 75 mems; Chair. Amitabh Kant; Sec. Harbhajan Singh.

National Research Development Corpn: 20–22 Zamroodpur Community Centre, Kailash Colony Extension, New Delhi 110 048; tel. (11) 29240401; fax (11) 29240409; e-mail write2@nrdcindia.com; internet www.nrdcindia.com; f. 1953 to stimulate development and commercial exploitation of new inventions with financial and technical aid; finances development projects to set up demonstration units in collaboration with industry; exports technology; Chair. and Man. Dir Rajendra Dobhal.

National Seeds Corpn Ltd: Beej Bhavan, Pusa, New Delhi 110 012; tel. (11) 25846292; fax (11) 25846462; e-mail nsc@indiaseeds.com; internet www.indiaseeds.com; f. 1963 to improve and develop the seed industry; Chair. and Man. Dir Vinod Kumar Gaur.

National Small Industries Corpn Ltd: NSIC Bhavan, Okhla Industrial Estate, New Delhi 110 020; tel. (11) 26926275; fax (11) 26932075; e-mail pro@nsic.co.in; internet www.nsic.co.in; f. 1955 to aid, advise, finance and promote the interests of small industries; establishes and supplies machinery for small industries in other developing countries on turnkey basis; all shares held by the Govt; Chair. and Man. Dir H. P. KUMAR.

PEC Ltd: 'Hansalaya', 15 Barakhamba Rd, New Delhi 110 001; tel. (11) 23316397; fax (11) 23314797; e-mail pec@peclimited.com; internet www.peclimited.com; f. 1971; export of engineering, industrial and railway equipment; undertakes turnkey and other projects and management consultancy abroad; countertrade, trading in agrocommodities, construction materials (steel, cement, clinkers, etc.) and fertilizers; Chair. and Man. Dir A. K. MIRCHANDANI.

Power Finance Corpn Ltd: Urjanidhi Bldg, 1 Barakhamba Lane, Connaught Pl., New Delhi 110 001; tel. (11) 23456000; internet www.pfcindia.com; f. 1986; provides funding for power sector projects; Chair. and Man. Dir M. K. GOEL.

State Farms Corpn of India Ltd: Farm Bhavan, 14–15 Nehru Place, New Delhi 110 019; tel. (11) 26446903; fax (11) 26226898; e-mail sfci-moa@nic.in; internet sfci.nic.in; f. 1969 to administer the central state farms; activities include the production of quality seeds of high-yielding varieties of wheat, paddy, maize, bajra and jowar; advises on soil conservation, reclamation and development of waste and forest land; consultancy services on farm mechanization; auth. cap. Rs 1,486.1m., res and surplus Rs 638.0m., sales Rs 1,952.7m. (March 2009); Chair. and Man. Dir Brig. VINOD KUMAR GAUR.

State Trading Corpn of India Ltd: Jawahar Vyapar Bhavan, Janpath Road, Tolstoy Marg, New Delhi 110 001; tel. (11) 23313177; fax (11) 23701191; e-mail co.stc@gov.in; internet stc.gov.in; f. 1956; govt undertaking dealing in exports and imports; 10 regional brs, 6 sub-brs and 1 office overseas; Chair. and Man. Dir KHALEEL RAHIM.

Steel Authority of India Ltd (SAIL): Ispat Bhavan, Lodhi Rd, POB 3049, New Delhi 110 003; tel. (11) 24367481; fax (11) 24367015; e-mail sail.co@vsnl.com; internet www.sail.co.in; f. 1973 to provide co-ordinated development of the steel industry in the public sector; integrated steel plants at Bhilai, Bokaro, Durgapur, Rourkela; stainless and alloy steel plants at Chhattisgarh, West Bengal, Odisha, Jharkhand, Tamil Nadu and Karnataka; five jt venture power- and steel-related cos; 86% govt-owned; subsidiaries: Bhilai Oxygen Ltd (Chhattisgarh), Indian Iron and Steel Co (West Bengal), Maharashtra Elektrosmelt Ltd; combined crude steel capacity is 12m. metric tons annually; Chair. CHANDRA SHEKHAR VERMA; 131,910 employees (March 2004).

Tea Board of India: 14 B. T. M. Sarani (Brabourne Rd), POB 2172, Kolkata 700 001; tel. (33) 22351331; fax (33) 22215715; internet teaboard.gov.in; provides financial assistance to tea research stations; sponsors and finances independent research projects in universities and tech. institutions to supplement the work of tea research establishments; also promotes tea production and export; Chair. SIDDHARTH.

CHAMBERS OF COMMERCE

Associated Chambers of Commerce and Industry of India (ASSOCHAM): 1 Community Centre, Zamrudpur Kailash Colony, New Delhi 110 048; tel. (11) 46550555; fax (11) 46536481; e-mail assocham@nic.in; internet www.assocham.org; f. 1920; central org. of 350 chambers of commerce and industry and industrial asscns representing more than 100,000 cos throughout India; five promoter chambers, 115 ordinary mems, 45 patron mems and 500 corporate associates; Pres. RAJKUMAR DHOOT; Sec.-Gen. D. S. RAWAT.

Federation of Indian Chambers of Commerce and Industry (FICCI): Federation House, Tansen Marg, New Delhi 110 001; tel. (11) 23738760; fax (11) 23320714; e-mail ficci@ficci.com; internet www.ficci.com; f. 1927; more than 1,500 corporate mems, 500 chamber of commerce and business asscn mems; Pres. R. V. KANORIA; Sec.-Gen. Dr RAJIV KUMAR.

International Chamber of Commerce (ICC) India: Federation House, Tansen Marg, New Delhi 110 001; tel. (11) 23322472; fax (11) 23320714; e-mail iccindia@iccindiaonline.org; internet www.iccindiaonline.org; f. 1929; 43 org. mems, 375 corporate mems, 8 patron mems, 130 cttee mems; Pres. RAJIV MEMANI; Exec. Dir ASHOK UMMAT.

Associated Chambers of Commerce and Industry of Uttar Pradesh: 2/302 Vikas Khand, Gomti Nagar, POB 17, Lucknow 226 010; tel. (522) 2301957; fax (522) 2301958; e-mail asochamup@yahoo.com; internet asochamup.org.in; f. 1994; 405 mems; Pres. ANIL RATHI; Sec.-Gen. S. B. AGRAWAL.

Bengal Chamber of Commerce and Industry: 6 Netaji Subhas Rd, Kolkata 700 001; tel. (33) 22303711; fax (33) 22301289; e-mail bencham@bengalchamber.com; internet www.bengalchamber.com; f. 1853; more than 300 mems; Pres. KALLOL DATTA.

Bengal National Chamber of Commerce and Industry: BNCCI House, 23 Sir R. N. Mukherjee Rd, Kolkata 700 001; tel. (33) 22482951; fax (33) 22487058; e-mail bncci@bncci.com; internet www.bncci.com; f. 1887; 500 mems, 35 affiliated industrial and trading asscns; Pres. AMIT KUMAR SEN; Sec. D. P. NAG.

Bharat Chamber of Commerce: 9 Park Mansions, 2nd Floor, 57-A Park St, Kolkata 700 016; tel. (33) 22299591; fax (33) 22294947; e-mail bcc@cal2.vsnl.net.in; internet www.bharatchamber.com; f. 1900; c. 500 mems; Pres. ASHOK AIKAT; Sec.-Gen. K. SARMA.

Bihar Chamber of Commerce: Judges Court Rd, Patna 800 001; tel. (612) 2673505; fax (612) 2689505; e-mail bcc_chamber@rediffmail.com; f. 1926; 552 ordinary mems; Pres. O. P. SAH.

Bombay Chamber of Commerce and Industry: Mackinnon Mackenzie Bldg, 3rd Floor, 4 Shoorji Vallabhdas Rd, Ballard Estate, POB 473, Mumbai 400 001; tel. (22) 49100200; fax (22) 49100213; e-mail bcci@bombaychamber.com; internet www.bombaychamber.com; f. 1836; 935 ordinary mems, 650 assoc. mems, 75 hon. mems; Pres. UDAY KHANNA; Vice-Pres. R. MUKUNDAN.

Calcutta Chamber of Commerce: 18H Park St, Stephen Court, Kolkata 700 071; tel. (33) 22290758; fax (33) 22298961; e-mail calchamb@cal3.vsnl.net.in; internet www.calcuttachamber.com; 300 mems; Pres. ALKA BANGUR; Sr Vice-Pres. R. K. CHHAJER.

Chamber of Commerce and Industry (Regd): OB 31, Rail Head Complex, Jammu 180 012; tel. (191) 2472266; fax (191) 2472255; e-mail ccijammu@yahoo.com; f. 1932; 1,069 mems; Pres. Y. V. SHARMA; Sec.-Gen. SATISH GUPTA.

Cochin Chamber of Commerce and Industry: Bristow Rd, Willingdon Island, POB 503, Kochi 682 003; tel. (484) 2668650; fax (484) 2668651; e-mail cochinchamber@eth.net; internet www.cochinchamber.org; f. 1857; 245 mems; Pres. P. NARAYAN; Vice-Pres. P. MAMMEN.

Delhi Chamber of Commerce: 49 Rani Jhansi Rd, New Delhi 110055; tel. (11) 23518994; fax (11) 23628847; e-mail dccnd@nda.vsnl.net.in; internet www.delhichamber.com; f. 1949; Pres. DAVINDER KUMAR; Sec.-Gen. JASBIRENDRA S. SODHBANS.

Federation of Andhra Pradesh Chambers of Commerce and Industry: Federation House, FAPCCI Marg, 11-6-841, Red Hills, POB 14, Hyderabad 500 004; tel. (40) 23395515; fax (40) 23395525; e-mail info@fapcci.in; internet www.fapcci.in; f. 1917; 3,300 mems; Pres. SRINIVAS AYYADEVARA; Sec.-Gen. P. VYDEHI.

Federation of Karnataka Chambers of Commerce and Industry: Federation House, K. G. Rd, POB 9996, Bangalore 560 009; tel. (80) 22262355; fax (80) 22251826; e-mail president@fkcci.in; internet www.fkcci.org; f. 1916; 2,100 mems; Pres. SHIVA SHANMUGAM; Sr Vice-Pres. R. SHIVA KUMAR.

Federation of Madhya Pradesh Chambers of Commerce and Industry: Udyog Bhavan, 129A Malviya Nagar, Bhopal 462 003; tel. (755) 2573612; fax (755) 2551451; e-mail fmpcci@yahoo.co.in; internet fmpcci.com; f. 1975; 500 ordinary mems, 58 asscn mems; Pres. RAMESH CHANDRA AGRAWAL.

Goa Chamber of Commerce and Industry: Narayan Rajaram Bandekar Bhavan, Rua de Ormuz, POB 59, Panaji 403 001; tel. (832) 2422635; fax (832) 2425560; e-mail goachamber@goachamber.org; internet www.goachamber.org; f. 1908 as Associacao Commercial da India Portuguesa; more than 500 mems; Pres. MANGUIRISH PAI RAIKAR; Dir-Gen. Air Cmmdr (retd) P. K. PINTO.

Gujarat Chamber of Commerce and Industry: Shri Ambica Mills, Gujarat Chamber Bldg, Ashram Rd, POB 4045, Ahmedabad 380 009; tel. (79) 26582301; fax (79) 26587992; e-mail gcci@gujaratchamber.org; internet www.gujaratchamber.org; f. 1949; 7,713 mems; Pres. MAHENDRABHAI N. PATEL; Sr Vice-Pres. PRAKASH BHAGWATI.

Indian Chamber of Commerce: ICC Towers, 4 India Exchange Place, Kolkata 700 001; tel. (33) 22203242; fax (33) 22213377; e-mail info@indianchamber.net; internet www.indianchamber.org; f. 1925; 500 corporate group mems, more than 1,200 mem. cos; Pres. RAJIV MUNDHRA; Dir-Gen. Dr RAJEEV SINGH.

Indian Chamber of Commerce and Industry—Cochin: POB 236, Indian Chamber Rd, Mattancherry, Kochi 682002; tel. (484) 2224335; fax (484) 2224203; e-mail info@iccicochin.com; internet www.iccicochin.com; f. 1897; Pres. P. L. PRAKASH JAMES; Sec. RAMAKRISHNAN S.

Indian Merchants' Chamber: IMC Bldg, IMC Marg, Churchgate, Mumbai 400 020; tel. (22) 22046633; fax (22) 22048508; e-mail imc@imcnet.org; internet www.imcnet.org; f. 1907; 185 asscn mems, 2,915 mem. firms; Pres. NIRANJAN HIRANANDANI; Sec.-Gen. ARVIND PRADHAN.

Karnataka Chamber of Commerce and Industry: G. Mahadevappa Karnataka Chamber Bldg, Jayachamraj Nagar, Hubli 580 020; tel. (836) 2218234; fax (836) 2360933; e-mail kccihble@sify.com; internet www.kccihubli.org; f. 1928; 2,500 mems; Pres. NIRMALKUMAR P. JAVALI; Hon. Sec. VISHWANATH S. GINIMAV.

Madhya Pradesh Chamber of Commerce and Industry: Chamber Bhavan, Sanatan Dharam Mandir Marg, Gwalior 474 009; tel. (751) 2382917; fax (751) 2323844; e-mail info@mpcci.com; internet www.mpcci.com; f. 1906; 1,705 mems; Pres. VISHNUPRASAD GARG; Hon. Sec. BHUPENDRA JAIN.

Madras Chamber of Commerce and Industry (MCCI): Karumuttu Centre, 1st Floor, 634 Anna Salai, Chennai 600 035; tel. (44) 24349452; fax (44) 24349164; e-mail madraschamber@madraschamber.in; internet www.madraschamber.in; f. 1836; 374 mem. firms, 20 affiliated, 8 hon.; Pres. T. SHIVARAMAN; Sec.-Gen. K. SARASWATHI.

Maharashtra Chamber of Commerce, Industry and Agriculture: Oricon House, 6th Floor, 12 K. Dubhash Marg, Fort, Mumbai 400 001; tel. (22) 22855859; fax (22) 22855861; e-mail sec.general@maccia.org.in; internet www.maccia.org.in; f. 1927; more than 3,500 mems; more than 800 affiliated trade asscns and professional bodies; Pres. ASHISH PEDNEKAR; Sr Vice Pres. RAMCHANDRA BHOGALE.

Mahratta Chamber of Commerce, Industries and Agriculture: MCCIA Trade Tower, 505, A-Wing, ICC Complex, 403 Senapati Pabat Rd, Pune 411 016; tel. (20) 25709000; fax (20) 25709021; e-mail info@mcciapune.com; internet www.mcciapune.com; f. 1934; more than 2,000 mems; Pres. SURENDRAKUMAR JAIN; Dir-Gen. ANANT SARDESHMUKH; Hon. Secs SATISH D. MAGAR, P. C. NAMBIAR.

Merchants' Chamber of Uttar Pradesh: 14/76 Civil Lines, Kanpur 208 001; tel. (512) 2530877; fax (512) 2531306; e-mail info@merchantschamber-up.com; internet www.merchantschamber-up.com; f. 1932; 222 mems; Pres. S. K. JHUNJHUNWALA; Sec. A. K. SINHA.

North India Chamber of Commerce and Industry: 9 Gandhi Rd, Dehra Dun; tel. (935) 223479; f. 1967; 105 ordinary mems, 29 asscn mems, seven mem. firms, 91 assoc. mems; Pres. ARVIND RAI; Hon. Sec. ASHOK K. NARANG.

PHD Chamber of Commerce and Industry (PHDCCI): PHD House, 4/2 Siri Institutional Area, August Kranti Marg, New Delhi 110 016; tel. (11) 26863801; fax (11) 26863135; e-mail phdcci@phdcci.in; internet www.phdcci.in; f. 1905; 1,760 mems, 150 asscn mems; Pres. SANDIP SOMANY; Sec.-Gen. SUSMITA SHEKHAR.

Rajasthan Chamber of Commerce and Industry: Rajasthan Chamber Bhavan, M. I. Rd, Jaipur 302 002; tel. (141) 2565163; fax (141) 2561419; e-mail info@rajchamber.com; internet www.rajchamber.com; 575 mems; Pres. Dr MAHENDRA S. DAGA; Hon. Sec.-Gen. Dr K. L. JAIN.

Southern India Chamber of Commerce and Industry (SICCI): Indian Chamber Bldgs, 6 Esplanade, POB 1208, Chennai 600 108; tel. (44) 25342228; fax (44) 25341876; e-mail info@sicci.in; internet sicci.in; f. 1909; 1,000 mems; Pres. JAWAHAR VADIVELU; Sec. S. RAGHAVAN.

Upper India Chamber of Commerce: 113/47, Swaroop Nagar, POB 63, Kanpur 208 002; tel. (512) 2543905; fax (512) 2531684; f. 1888; 52 mems; Pres. DILIP BHARGAVA; Sec. S. P. SRIVASTAVA.

Utkal Chamber of Commerce and Industry Ltd: N/6, IRC Village, Nayapalli, Bhubaneswar 751 015; tel. (674) 3296035; fax (674) 2557598; e-mail contact@utkalchamber.com; internet utkalchamber.com; f. 1963; 250 mems; Pres. RAMESH MOHAPATRA; Hon. Sec. DEBABRATA DASH.

INDUSTRIAL AND TRADE ASSOCIATIONS

Ahmedabad Textile Mills' Association: Ashram Rd, Navrangpura, POB 4056, Ahmedabad 380 009; tel. (79) 26582273; fax (79) 26588574; e-mail shukla@atmaahd.com; f. 1891; 12 mems; Pres. CHINTAN N. PARIKH; Sec.-Gen. ABHINAVA SHUKLA.

All India Federation of Master Printers: 605 Madhuban, 6th Floor, 55 Nehru Place, New Delhi 110 019; tel. (11) 26451742; fax (11) 26451743; e-mail fopaid11@gmail.com; internet www.aifmp.com; f. 1953; 59 affiliates, 900 mems; Pres. RANJAN KUTHARI; Hon. Gen. Sec. ASOK KUMAR PAL.

All India Manufacturers' Organization (AIMO): Jeevan Sahakar, 4th Floor, Sir P.M. Rd, Fort, Mumbai 400 001; tel. (22) 22661016; fax (22) 22660838; e-mail aimoindia@mtnl.net.in; f. 1941; 800 mems; Pres. AMITKUMAR SEN; Sr Vice-Pres. JAGDISH TODI.

All India Plastics Manufacturers' Association: AIPMA House, A-52, St No. 1, MIDC, Andheri (East), Mumbai 400 093; tel. (22) 28216390; fax (22) 28252295; e-mail office@aipma.net; internet www.aipma.net; f. 1947; 2,500 mems; Pres. JAYESH RAMBHIA.

All India Shippers' Council: Federation House, Tansen Marg, New Delhi 110 001; tel. (11) 23487492; fax (11) 23320736; e-mail aisc.india@gmail.com; internet www.aisc.in; f. 1967; 82 mems; Chair. RAMU S. DEORA; CEO and Sec. MANAB MAJUMDAR.

Association of Man-made Fibre Industry of India: Resham Bhavan, 78 Veer Nariman Rd, Mumbai 400 020; tel. (22) 22040009; fax (22) 22049172; e-mail amfiirayon@hotmail.com; internet www.viscoserayonindia.com; f. 1954; 7 mems; Pres. LALIT NAIK; Sec. M. P. JOSEPH.

Automotive Component Manufacturers' Association of India: The Capital Court, 6th Floor, Olof Palme Marg, Munirka, New Delhi 110 067; tel. (11) 26160315; fax (11) 26160317; e-mail acma@acma.in; internet www.acmainfo.com; 600 mems; Pres. ARVIND KAPUR; Exec. Dir VINNIE MEHTA.

Automotive Tyre Manufacturers' Association: PHD House, opp. Asian Games Village, Siri Fort Institutional Area, New Delhi 110 016; tel. (11) 26851187; fax (11) 26864799; e-mail atma@atmaindia.org; internet www.atmaindia.org; f. 1975; 10 mems; Chair. NEERAJ KANWAR; Dir-Gen. RAJIV BUDHRAJA.

Bharat Krishak Samaj (Farmers' Forum, India): Dr Panjabrao Deshmukh Krishak Bhavan, A-1 Nizamuddin West, New Delhi 110 013; tel. (11) 65650384; fax (11) 24359509; e-mail ho@bks.org.in; internet www.farmersforum.in; f. 1954; national farmers' org.; 5m. ordinary mems, 100,000 life mems; Chair. AJAY VIR JAKHAR; Pres. RAM NIWAS MIRDHA.

Bombay Metal Exchange Ltd: 88/90 Kika St, 1st Floor, Gulalwadi, Mumbai 400 004; tel. (22) 22421964; fax (22) 22422640; e-mail bme@bom8.vsnl.net.in; internet www.bme.in; f. 1950; promotes trade and industry in non-ferrous metals; 386 mems; Pres. ASHOK G. BAFNA; Sr Vice-Pres MAHENDRA H. SHAH.

Bombay Shroffs Association: 250 Sheikh Memon St, Mumbai 400 002; tel. (22) 23425588; f. 1910; 325 mems; Pres SEVANTILAL P. SHAH, KAMLESH C. SHAH.

Calcutta Tea Traders' Association: 6 Netaji Subhas Rd, Kolkata 700 001; tel. (33) 22301574; fax (33) 22301289; e-mail info@cttacal.org; internet www.cttacal.org; f. 1886; 1,300 mems; Chair. SANGEETA KICHLU; Vice-Chair. L. N. GUPTA.

Cement Manufacturers' Association: CMA Tower, A-2E, Sector 24, Noida 201 301; tel. (95120) 2411955; fax (95120) 2411956; e-mail cmand@vsnl.com; internet cmaindia.org; f. 1961; 54 mems; 126 major cement plants; Pres. M. A. M. R. MUTHIAH; Sec.-Gen. N. A. VISWANATHAN.

Confederation of Indian Industry (CII): 23 Institutional Area, Lodi Rd, New Delhi 110 003; tel. (11) 24629994; fax (11) 24626149; e-mail info@cii.in; internet www.cii.in; f. 1974; 7,500 mem. cos; Pres. AJAY S. SHRIRAM; Dir-Gen. CHANDRAJIT BANERJEE.

Consumer Electronics and Appliances Manufacturers' Association (CEAMA): PHD House, 5th Floor, 4/2 Siri Institutional Area, August Kranti Marg, New Delhi 110 016; tel. (11) 46070335; fax (11) 46070336; e-mail info@ceama.in; internet www.ceama.in; f. 1978; 106 mems; Pres. ANIRUDH V. DHOOT; Sec.-Gen. VIKAS MOHAN.

Cotton Association of India: Cotton Exchange Bldg, 2nd Floor, Cotton Green, Mumbai 400 033; tel. (22) 30063400; fax (22) 23700337; e-mail cai@caionline.in; internet www.caionline.in; f. 1921; 465 mems; Pres. DHIREN N. SHETH; Sec. AMAR SINGH.

Darjeeling Tea Association: Royal Exchange, 6 Netaji Subhas Rd, Kolkata 700 001; tel. and fax (33) 22102408; fax (33) 22102408; internet www.darjeelingtea.com; Chair. S. S. BAGARIA.

ELCINA Electronic Industries Association of India: ELCINA House, 422 Okhla Industrial Estate, New Delhi 110 020; tel. (11) 26924597; fax (11) 26923440; e-mail info@elcina.com; internet www.elcina.com; f. 1967; fmrly Electronic Component Industries Association; 255 mems; Pres. T. VASU; Sec.-Gen. RAJOO GOEL.

Federation of Automobile Dealers Associations: 805 Surya Kiran, 19 Kasturba Gandhi Marg, New Delhi 110 001; tel. (11) 23320095; fax (11) 23320093; e-mail fada@fada.in; internet www.fada.in; f. 1964; Pres. MOHAN HIMATSINGKA; Sec.-Gen. GULSHAN AHUJA; 1500 mems.

Federation of Gujarat Industries: Gotri-Sevasi Rd, Khanpur, Vadodara 390 101; tel. (265) 2372901; fax (265) 2372904; e-mail info@fgi.co.in; internet www.fgibaroda.com; f. 1918; Pres. AMIT PATEL; 415 mems.

Federation of Hotel and Restaurant Associations of India (FHRAI): B-82 Himalaya House, 23 Kasturba Gandhi Marg, New Delhi 110 001; tel. (11) 40780780; fax (11) 40780777; e-mail fhrai@vsnl.com; internet www.fhrai.com; f. 1955; 3,961 mems; Pres. VIVEK NAIR; Sec.-Gen. M. D. KAPOOR.

Federation of Indian Export Organisations: Niryat Bhavan, Rao Tula Ram Marg, opp. Army Hospital Research and Referral, New Delhi 110 057; tel. (11) 46042112; fax (11) 26150112; e-mail fieo@nda.vsnl.net.in; internet www.fieo.org; f. 1965; 17,500 mems; Pres. M. RAFEEQUE AHMED; Dir-Gen.and CEO AJAY SAHAI.

Federation of Indian Mineral Industries (FIMI): B-311, Okhla Industrial Area, Phase 1, New Delhi 110 020; tel. (11) 26814596; fax (11) 26814593; e-mail fimi@fedmin.com; internet www.fedmin.com; f. 1966; 350 mems; Pres. P. K. MUKHERJEE.

The Fertiliser Association of India: 10 Shaheed Jit Singh Marg, New Delhi 110 067; tel. (11) 26567144; fax (11) 26960052; e-mail general@faidelhi.org; internet www.faidelhi.org; f. 1955; 1,414 mems; Chair. A. VELLAYEN; Dir-Gen. S. NAND.

Indian Drug Manufacturers' Association: 102B Poonam Chambers, Dr A. B. Rd, Worli, Mumbai 400 018; tel. (22) 24944624; fax (22) 24950723; e-mail idma1@idmaindia.com; internet www.idma-assn

.org; f. 1961; 800 mems; Pres. MANISH U. DOSHI; Hon. Sec.-Gen. BAL KISHAN GUPTA.

Indian Electrical and Electronics Manufacturers' Association (IEEMA): 501 Kakad Chambers, 132 Dr Annie Besant Rd, Worli, Mumbai 400 018; tel. (22) 24930532; fax (22) 24932705; e-mail mumbai@ieema.org; internet www.ieema.org; f. 1948; 650 mems; Pres. RAMESH CHANDAK; Dir-Gen. P.V. KRISHNA.

Indian Jute Mills Association: Royal Exchange, 6 Netaji Subhas Rd, Kolkata 700 001; tel. (33) 22309918; fax (33) 22313836; e-mail ijma@cal2.vsnl.net.in; sponsors and operates export promotion, research and product development; regulates labour relations; 35 mems; Chair. MANISH PODDAR; Exec. Vice-Chair. S.K. BHATTACHARYA.

Indian Leather Products Association: Suite 6, Chatterjee International Centre, 14th Floor, 33-A, Jawaharlal Nehru Rd, Kolkata 700 071; tel. (33) 22267102; fax (33) 22468339; e-mail ilpa@cal2.vsnl.net.in; internet www.ilpaindia.org; 150 mems; Pres. DARSHAN SINGH SABHARWAL; Exec. Dir P. P. RAY CHAUDHURI.

Indian Machine Tool Manufacturers' Association: 10th Mile, Tumkur Rd, Madavara Post, Bangalore 562 123; tel. (80) 66246600; fax (80) 66246661; e-mail imtma@imtma.in; internet www.imtma.in; 500 mems; Pres. VIKRAM SIRUR; Dir-Gen. V. ANBU.

Indian Motion Picture Producers' Association: IMPPA House, Dr Ambedkar Rd, Bandra (West), Mumbai 400 050; tel. (22) 26486344; fax (22) 26480757; e-mail imppa1937@gmail.com; f. 1938; 14,400 mems; Pres. T. P. AGGARWAL.

Indian National Shipowners' Association: 22 Maker Tower F, Cuffe Parade, Mumbai 400 005; tel. (22) 22182105; fax (22) 22182104; e-mail insa@insa.org.in; internet insa.in; f. 1929; 36 mems; Pres. S. HAJARA; Sec.-Gen. S. S. KULKARNI.

Indian Oilseeds & Produce Export Promotion Council (IOPEA): 78/79 Bajaj Bhavan, Nariman Point, Mumbai 400 021; tel. (22) 22023225; fax (22) 22029236; e-mail info@iopepc.org; internet www.iopepc.org; f. 1956; export promotion council; 350 mems; Chair. KISHORE TANNA; CEO SURESH RAMRAKHIANI.

Indian Refractory Makers' Association: 5 Lala Lajpat Rai Sarani, 4th Floor, Kolkata 700 020; tel. (33) 22810868; fax (33) 22814357; e-mail irmaindia@hotmail.com; internet www.irmaindia.org; 85 mems; Chair. A. K. CHATTOPADHYAY; Exec. Dir P. DAS GUPTA.

Indian Soap and Toiletries Makers' Association: 614 Raheja Centre, 6th Floor, Free Press Journal Marg, Nariman Point, Mumbai 400 021; tel. (22) 22824115; fax (22) 22853649; e-mail istmamum@gmail.com; internet istma.internetindia.com/index.htm; f. 1937; 28 mems; Pres. HEMANT BAKSHI; Sec.-Gen. O. P. AGARWAL.

Indian Sugar Mills' Association: Ansal Plaza, 2nd Floor, C-Blk, Andrews Ganj, New Delhi 110 049; tel. (11) 26262294; fax (11) 26263231; e-mail isma@indiansugar.com; internet www.indiansugar.com; f. 1932; 250 mems; Pres. AJIT S. SHRIRAM.

Indian Tea Association: Royal Exchange, 6 Netaji Subhas Rd, Kolkata 700 001; tel. (33) 22102474; fax (33) 22434301; e-mail ita@indiatea.org; internet www.indiatea.org; f. 1881; 202 mem. cos; 482 tea estates; Chair. A. N. SINGH; Sec.-Gen. MONOJIT DASGUPTA.

Indian Woollen Mills' Federation: Churchgate Chambers, 7th Floor, 5 New Marine Lines, Mumbai 400 020; tel. (22) 22624372; fax (22) 22624675; e-mail mail@iwmfindia.com; internet www.iwmfindia.com; f. 1963; 50 mems; Chair. RAJ K. KHANNA; Sec.-Gen. MAHESH N. SANIL.

Industries and Commerce Association: ICO Association Rd, POB 70, Dhanbad 826 001; tel. (326) 2303147; fax (326) 2303787; e-mail ica_dnb_1@hotmail.com; f. 1933; represents manufacturers of metallurgical coke; 78 mems; Pres. B. N. SINGH; Sec. PRADEEP CHATTERJEE.

Millowners' Association, Mumbai: Elphinstone Bldg, 10 Veer Nariman Rd, Fort, Mumbai 400 001; tel. (22) 22040411; fax (22) 22832611; f. 1875; 23 mem. cos; Chair. R. K. DALMIA; Sec.-Gen. V. Y. TAMHANE.

Mumbai Textile Merchants' Mahajan: 250 Sheikh Memon St, Mumbai 400 002; tel. (22) 22411686; fax (22) 22400311; f. 1879; 1,900 mems; Pres. SURENDRA TULSIDAS SAVAI.

National Association of Software and Service Companies (NASSCOM): International Youth Centre, Teen Murti Marg, Chanakyapuri, New Delhi 110 021; tel. (11) 23010199; fax (11) 23015452; e-mail info@nasscom.in; internet www.nasscom.in; 1,200 mems; Pres. SOM MITTAL; Chair. N. CHANDRASEKARAN.

Organisation of Pharmaceutical Producers of India (OPPI): Peninsular Corporate Park, Peninsular Chambers, Ground Floor, Ganpatrao Kadam Marg, Lower Parel, Mumbai 400 013; tel. (22) 24918123; fax (22) 24915168; e-mail indiaoppi@vsnl.com; internet www.indiaoppi.com; f. 1965; 74 mems; Pres. RANJIT SHAHANI; Dir-Gen. TAPAN RAY.

Society of Indian Automobile Manufacturers: Core 4B, 5th Floor, India Habitat Centre, Lodhi Rd, New Delhi 110 003; tel. (11) 24647810; fax (11) 24648222; e-mail siam@vsnl.com; internet www.siamindia.com; f. 1960; 36 mems; Pres. S. SANDILYA; Dir-Gen. VISHNU MATHUR.

Southern India Mills' Association: 41 Race Course, Coimbatore 641 018; tel. (422) 4225333; fax (422) 4225366; e-mail info@simamills.com; internet www.simamills.com; f. 1933; 360 mems; Chair. T. DINAKARAN; Sec.-Gen. Dr K. SELVARAJAU.

Surgical Manufacturers' and Traders' Association: 60 Darya Ganj, New Delhi 110 002; tel. (11) 23271027; fax (11) 23258576; e-mail info@smta.in; internet www.smta.in; f. 1951; Pres. RAVI AWASTHI; Sec. S. B. SAWHNEY.

Synthetic and Art Silk Mills' Research Association Ltd (SASMIRA): Sasmira Bldg, Sasmira Marg, Worli, Mumbai 400 030; tel. (22) 24935351; fax (22) 24930225; e-mail sasmira@vsnl.com; internet www.sasmira.org; f. 1950; 100 mems; Pres. MAGANLAL H. DOSHI; Exec. Dir U. K. GANGOPADHYAY.

Telecom Equipment Manufacturers' Association of India (TEMA): PHD House, 4th Floor, Khel Gaon Marg, Hauz Khas, New Delhi 110 016; tel. (11) 26859621; fax (11) 26859620; e-mail tema@eth.net; internet tematelecom.in; f. 1990; Pres. RAJIV MEHROTRA; Sec.-Gen. SANJAY BAKAYA.

The United Planters' Association of Southern India (UPASI): Glenview, POB 11, Coonoor 643 101; tel. (423) 2230270; fax (423) 2232030; e-mail upasi@upasi.org; internet www.upasi.org; f. 1893; 749 mems; Pres. PETER MATHIAS; Sec.-Gen. ULLAS MENON.

EMPLOYERS' ORGANIZATIONS

Council of Indian Employers: Federation House, Tansen Marg, New Delhi 110 001; tel. (11) 23316121; fax (11) 23320714; e-mail secretariat@aioe.com; f. 1956; Pres. SAROJ KUMAR PODDAR; comprises:

All India Organisation of Employers (AIOE): Federation House, Tansen Marg, New Delhi 110 001; tel. (11) 23316121; fax (11) 23320714; e-mail aioe@ficci.com; internet www.aioe.in; f. 1932; 50 affiliated asscns and 149 corporate mems; Pres. SANJAY BHATIA.

Employers' Federation of India (EFI): Army and Navy Bldg, 148 Mahatma Gandhi Rd, Mumbai 400 023; tel. (22) 22844232; fax (22) 22843028; e-mail efisolar@mtnl.net.in; internet www.efionline.in; f. 1933; 28 asscn mems, 182 ordinary mems, 18 hon. mems; Pres. RAJEEV DUBEY; Sec.-Gen. SHARAD S. PATIL.

Standing Conference of Public Enterprises (SCOPE): Core 8, SCOPE Complex, 1st Floor, 7 Lodhi Rd, New Delhi 110 003; tel. (11) 24362604; fax (11) 24361371; e-mail scope_dg@yahoo.co.in; internet www.scopeonline.in; f. 1973; representative body of all central public enterprises in India; advises the Govt and public enterprises on matters of major policy and co-ordination; trade enquiries, regarding imports and exports of commodities, carried out on behalf of mems; 211 mems; Chair. C. S. VERMA.

Employers' Federation of Southern India: 33 Hindi Prachar Sabha St, T Nagar, Chennai 600 017; tel. (44) 24320801; fax (44) 24322750; e-mail efsi@vsnl.net; internet www.efsi.org.in; f. 1920; 735 mems; Pres. S. GOAPA KUMAR; Sec. T. M. JAWAHARLAL.

UTILITIES

Electricity

Central Electricity Authority (CEA): Sewa Bhavan, R. K. Puram, New Delhi 110 066; tel. (11) 26108476; fax (11) 26105619; e-mail cea-edp@hub.nic.in; internet www.cea.nic.in; responsible for technical co-ordination and supervision of electricity programmes; advises Ministry of Power on all technical, financial and economic issues; Chair. NEERJA MATHUR.

Essar Power Ltd: Essar House, 11 Keshavrao Khadye Marg, Mahalaxmi, Mumbai 400 034; tel. (22) 66601100; fax (22) 66601809; e-mail essarpower@essar.com; internet www.essar.com/power; Chair. T. N. THAKUR; Man. Dir RAMESH KUMAR.

National Hydroelectric Power Corpn: Sector 33, Faridabad 121 003; tel. (129) 2278421; fax (129) 2277941; e-mail webmaster@nhpc.nic.in; internet www.nhpcindia.com; f. 1975; Chair and Man. Dir G. SAI PRASAD.

NTPC Ltd: Core 7, SCOPE Complex, Lodhi Rd, New Delhi 110 003; tel. (11) 24360100; fax (11) 24361018; e-mail info@ntpc.co.in; internet www.ntpc.co.in; f. 1975 as National Thermal Power Corpn; renamed as above 2005; operates 11 coal-fired and five gas-fired power stations throughout India; Chair. and Man. Dir ARUP ROY CHOUDHURY; 24,000 employees.

Nuclear Power Corpn of India Ltd: Commerce Center-1, 16th Floor, World Trade Centre, Cuffe Parade, Mumbai 400 005; tel. (22) 22182171; fax (22) 22180109; e-mail info@npcil.co.in; internet www.npcil.org; Chair. and Man. Dir K. C. PUROHIT.

Power Grid Corpn of India Ltd: Saudamani, Plot No. 2, Sector 29, Gurgaon 122 001; tel. (124) 2571700; fax (124) 2571760; internet www.powergridindia.com; f. 1989; responsible for formation of national power grid; Chair. and Man. Dir R. N. NAYAK.

Reliance Energy: Reliance Energy Centre, Santacruz (East), Mumbai 400 055; tel. (22) 30099999; fax (22) 30099536; e-mail corporate.communication@relianceada.com; internet www.rel.co.in; f. 1929 as Bombay Suburban Electric Supply Ltd, merged with the Reliance Group in Jan. 2003; generates, transmits and distributes power in Maharashtra, Goa and Andhra Pradesh; Chair. and Man. Dir ANIL AMBANI.

Rural Electrification Corpn Ltd: Core-4, SCOPE Complex, 7 Lodhi Rd, New Delhi 110 003; tel. (11) 24365161; fax (11) 24360644; e-mail recorp@recl.nic.in; internet www.recindia.com; f. 1969; provides support to rural electrification projects; Chair. and Man. Dir RAJEEV SHARMA.

Tata Power Co Ltd: Bombay House, 24 Homi Mody St, Mumbai 400 001; tel. (22) 66658282; fax (22) 66658801; e-mail webadmin@tatapower.com; internet www.tatapower.com; generation, transmission and distribution of electrical energy; Chair. CYRUS MISTRY; Man. Dir ANIL SARDANA.

Gas

Gas Authority of India Ltd: 16 Bhikaji Cama Place, R. K. Puram, Delhi 110 066; tel. (11) 26172580; fax (11) 26185941; internet gail.nic.in; f. 1984; 80% state-owned; transports, processes and markets natural gas; constructing gas-based petrochemical complex; subsidiaries incl.: GAIL Gas Ltd, GAIL Global (Singapore) Pte Ltd; Chair. and Man. Dir B. C. TRIPATHI; 3,480 employees (2009).

Gujarat Gas Co Ltd: 2 Shanti Sadan Society, Ellis Bridge, Ahmedabad 380 006; tel. (79) 26462980; fax (79) 26466249; internet www.gujaratgas.com; Chair. VARESH SINHA; Man. Dir P. P. G. SHARMA.

Indraprastha Gas Ltd: IGL Bhavan Plot No. 4, Community Centre Sector 9, R. K. Puram, New Delhi 110 022; tel. (11) 46074607; fax (11) 26171860; internet www.iglonline.net; Chair. K. K GUPTA; Man. Dir NARENDRA KUMAR.

Water

Central Water Commission: Sewa Bhavan, R. K. Puram, New Delhi 110 066; tel. (11) 26187232; fax (11) 26195516; e-mail secy-cwc@nic.in; internet cwc.gov.in; responsible for co-ordination of nat. water policy and projects; provision of research, promotion and advice on water resources devt; Chair. ASHWIN PANDEY.

Chennai Metropolitan Water Supply and Sewerage Board: No. 1 Pumping Station Rd, Chintadripet, Chennai 600 002; tel. (44) 28451300; fax (44) 28458181; internet www.chennaimetrowater.tn.nic.in; f. 1978; Man. Dir B. CHANDRA MOHAN.

Delhi Jal Board: Varunalaya Phase II, Karol Bagh, New Delhi 110 005; tel. and fax (11) 23516261; e-mail prodjb306@gmail.com; internet www.delhijalboard.nic.in; f. 1957 as Delhi Water Supply and Sewage Disposal Undertaking, reconstituted as above in 1998; part of the Delhi Municipal Corpn; production and distribution of potable water and treatment and disposal of waste water in Delhi; Chair. (vacant).

Karnataka Rural Water Supply and Sanitation Agency: E Blk, 2nd Floor, KHB Complex, Cauvery Bhavan, K. G. Rd, Bangalore 560 009; tel. (80) 22246508; fax (80) 22240509; e-mail krwssa@gmail.com; internet www.jalnirmal.org; Dir SALMA K. FAHIM.

Karnataka Urban Water Supply and Drainage Board: 6 Jalabhavan 1st Stage, 1st Phase, BTM Layout, Bannerghatta Rd, Bangalore 560 029; tel. (80) 26539003; fax (80) 26539206; internet www.kuwsdb.org; Chair. S. N. KRISHNAIAH SETTY.

Kolkata Municipal Corpn (Water Supply Department): 5 S. N. Banerjee Rd, Kolkata 700 013; tel. (33) 22861239; fax (33) 22861444; e-mail dgwskmc@rediffmail.com; internet www.kolkatamycity.com; f. 1870; Dir-Gen. (Water Supply) BIBHAS KUMAR MAITI.

TRADE UNIONS

In 2008 there were 11 Central Trade Union Organizations (CTUO) recognized by the Indian Ministry of Labour and Employment. The major unions were:

All-India Trade Union Congress (AITUC): 24 Canning Lane, New Delhi 110 001; tel. (11) 23387320; fax (11) 23386427; e-mail aitucong@bol.net.in; internet www.aituc.org; f. 1920; affiliated to WFTU; 4.6m. mems, 2,272 affiliated unions; 28 state brs, 21 national feds; Pres. J. CHITHARANJAN; Gen. Sec. GURUDAS DASGUPTA.

All India United Trade Union Centre: 77/2/1 Lenin Sarani, Kolkata 700 013; tel. (33) 22659085; fax (33) 22645605; e-mail aiutuc@gmail.com; f. 1958; fmrly the United Trade Union Centre—Lenin Sarani (UTUC—LS); changed to present name in 2008; labour wing of the Socialist Unity Party of India; 600 affiliated unions; 1.3m. mems in 2002; Pres. KRISHNA CHAKRABORTY; Gen. Sec. SHANKAR SAHA.

Bharatiya Mazdoor Sangh: Dattopant Thengadi Bhawan, 27 Deen Dayal Upadhyay Marg, New Delhi 110 002; tel. (11) 23562654; fax (11) 23582648; e-mail bms@bms.org.in; internet www.bms.org.in; f. 1955; 4,700 affiliated unions with a total membership of 8.5m.; 27 state brs; 34 nat. feds; Pres. C. K. SAJINARAYANAN; Gen. Sec. BAIJ NATH RAI.

Centre of Indian Trade Unions: BTR Bhavan, 13 A Rouse Ave, New Delhi 110 002; tel. (11) 23221288; fax (11) 23221284; e-mail citu@bol.net.in; internet www.citucentre.org; f. 1970; 3.37m. mems; 25 state and union territory brs; 4,300 affiliated unions, 12 nat. feds; Major affiliated unions incl. All India Coal Workers' Fed., All India Road Transport Workers' Fed., Steel Workers' Fed. of India, Water Transport Workers' Fed. of India; Pres. A. K. PADMANABHAN; Gen. Sec. TAPAN SEN.

Hind Mazdoor Sabha (HMS): 120 Babar Rd, New Delhi 110 001; tel. (11) 23413519; fax (11) 23411037; e-mail hms1gs@gmail.com; internet www.hmsindia.org.in; f. 1948; affiliated to ITUC; 5.8m. mems from more than 2,775 affiliated unions; 25 state councils; 16 nat. industrial feds; Major affiliated unions incl. Mumbai Port Trust Dock and General Employees' Union, South Central Railway Mazdoor Union, Transport and Dock Workers' Union, Western Railway Employees' Union; Pres. SHARAD RAO; Gen. Sec. UMRAOMAL PUROHIT.

Indian National Trade Union Congress (INTUC): 4 Bhai Veer Singh Marg, New Delhi 110 001; tel. (11) 23747767; fax (11) 23364244; e-mail info@intuc.net; internet www.intuc.net; f. 1947; 4,411 affiliated unions with a total membership of 7.93m.; affiliated to ICFTU; 32 state brs and 29 nat. feds; Pres. G. SANJEEVA REDDY; Gen. Sec. RAJENDRA PRASAD SINGH.

Major affiliated unions include:

Indian National Mineworkers' Federation: CJ 49 Salt Lake, Kolkata 700 091; tel. and fax (33) 23372158; e-mail imme@vsnl.com; f. 1949; 351,454 mems in 139 affiliated unions; Pres. RAJENDRA P. SINGH; Sec.-Gen. S. Q. ZAMA.

Indian National Textile Workers' Federation: 27 Burjorji Bharucha Marg, Fort, Mumbai 400 023; tel. (22) 22671577; f. 1948; 400 affiliated unions; 363,790 mems; Pres. SACHINBHAU AHIR; Gen. Sec. P. L. SUBHAIH.

Indian National Transport Workers' Federation: Bus Mazdoor Karyalaya, L/1, Hathital Colony, Jabalpur 482 001; tel. (761) 2429210; 357 affiliated unions; 379,267 mems; Pres. G. SANJEEVA REDDY; Gen. Sec. K. S. VERMA.

United Trades Union Congress (UTUC): 249 Bipin Behari Ganguly St, 1st Floor, Kolkata 700 012; tel. (33) 22259234; fax (33) 22375609; f. 1949; 1.2m. mems from 387 affiliated unions; 12 state brs and 6 nat. feds; Pres. SHANKARAN NAIR; Gen. Sec. ABANI ROY.

Other principal trade unions:

All India Bank Employees' Association (AIBEA): Prabhat Nivas, Singapore Plaza, 164 Linghi Chetty St, Chennai 600 001; tel. (44) 25351522; fax (44) 25358853; e-mail aibeahq@gmail.com; internet www.bankunionaibea.in; 32 state units, 710 affiliated unions, 525,000 mems; Pres. RAJEN NAGAR; Gen. Sec. C. H. VENKATACHALAM.

All India Defence Employees' Federation (AIDEF): Survey No. 81, Elphinstone Rd, Khadki, Pune 411 003; tel. (20) 25818761; f. 1953; 358 affiliated unions; 200,000 mems; Pres. S. N. PATHAK; Gen. Secs S. BHATTACHARYA, C. SRIKUMAR.

All India Railwaymen's Federation (AIRF): 4 State Entry Rd, New Delhi 110 055; tel. (11) 23365912; fax (11) 23363167; e-mail airfindia@gmail.com; internet www.airfindia.com; f. 1924; 1.0m. mems (2010); 24 affiliated unions; Pres. UMRAOMAL PUROHIT; Gen. Sec. SHIVA GOPAL MISHRA.

Confederation of Central Government Employees and Workers: Manishinath Bhavan, A-2-95 Rajouri Garden, New Delhi 110 027; tel. (11) 25105324; e-mail confederation06@yahoo.co.in; internet confederationhq.blogspot.com; 1.2m. mems; Pres. S. K. VYAS; Sec.-Gen. K. K. N. KUTTY.

Affiliated union:

National Federation of Postal Employees (NFPE): D-7, North Ave Post Office Bldg, 1st Floor, New Delhi 110 001; tel. and fax (11) 23092771; e-mail nfpehq@gmail.com; internet nfpe.blogspot.com; f. 1954 as National Federation of Post and Telegraph Employees, reconstituted as above in 1986; 400,000 mems from 7 affiliated unions; Pres. R. N. CHAUDHARY; Sec.-Gen. M. KRISHNAN.

Electricity Employees' Federation of India (EEFI): B. T. R. Bhavan, 13A Rouse Ave, New Delhi 110 002; tel. 9830264170 (mobile); fax (11) 23219670; e-mail eefederation@gmail.com; internet www.eefi.org; f. 1984; largest electricity union in India; 45 affiliated unions; Pres. K. O. HABIB; Gen. Sec. PRASANTA N. CHOWDHURY.

National Federation of Indian Railwaymen (NFIR): 3 Chelmsford Rd, New Delhi 110 055; tel. (11) 23343305; fax (11) 23744013;

e-mail nfir@satyam.net.in; f. 1953; 26 affiliated unions; 925,500 mems (2003); Pres. GUMAN SINGH; Gen. Sec. M. RAGHAVAIAH.

Transport

RAILWAYS

India's railway system is the largest in Asia and the fourth largest in the world. In 2011/12 the total length of the railways was 64,600 route-km. In that year the network carried an estimated 8,224m. passengers and 975.2m. metric tons of freight traffic.The Government exercises direct or indirect control over all railways through the Railway Board. India's largest railway construction project of the 20th century, the 760-km Konkan railway line, was officially opened in 1998. The construction of a 345-km Jammu–Udhampur–Srinagar–Baramulla line, linking Jammu and Kashmir with the national rail network, was declared a project of national importance in 2002. By early 2010 two of the project's four phases had been completed. However, owing to technical challenges presented by the difficult terrain, the project was unlikely to be completed before 2016.

A 16.5-km underground railway was completed in Kolkata in 1995 and extended to 22.2 km in 2009. The network carries more than 1m. people daily. The country's second metro system, in New Delhi, became operational in 2004. Following the completion of work on the second phase of the system in early 2011, the network comprised 142 stations across a route length of 189 km, carrying 1.3m. people daily. A third metro system, in Bangalore, became operational in late 2011. On completion of the first phase of the project, the system was to comprise 41 stations across a route length of 42.3 km. The first phase of a 12–km metro rail system in Gurgaon, a fast-developing satellite city of New Delhi, was opened in November 2013. In February 2014 a 9-km metropolitan monorail line was inaugurated in Mumbai; a second line was also under construction.

Ministry of Railways (Railway Board): Rail Bhavan, Raisina Rd, New Delhi 110 001; tel. (11) 23384010; fax (11) 23384481; e-mail crb@rb.railnet.gov.in; internet www.indianrailways.gov.in; Chair. VINAY MITTAL.

Zonal Railways

The railways are grouped into 17 zones:

Central Railway: Chhatrapati Shivaji Terminus (Victoria Terminus), Mumbai 400 001; tel. (22) 22697311; fax (22) 22612354; e-mail gmcr@bom2.vsnl.net.in; internet www.cr.indianrailways.gov.in; Gen. Man. S. K. JAIN.

East Central Railway: Hajipur 844 101; tel. (6224) 274728; fax (6224) 274738; internet www.ecr.indianrailways.gov.in; f. 1996; Gen. Man. VARUN BHARTHUAR.

East Coast Railway: Rail Vihar, Chandrasekhar Pur, Bhubaneswar 751 023; tel. (674) 2300773; fax (674) 2300196; e-mail gm@eastcoastrailway.gov.in; internet www.eastcoastrail.indianrailways.gov.in; f. 1996; Gen. Man. INDRA GHOSH.

Eastern Railway: 17 Netaji Subhas Rd, Kolkata 700 001; tel. (33) 22307596; fax (33) 22480370; internet www.er.indianrailways.gov.in; Gen. Man. G. C. AGARWAL.

Metro Railway, Kolkata: Metro Rail Bhavan, 8th Floor, 33/1 J. L. Nehru Rd, Kolkata 700 071; tel. (33) 22267280; fax (33) 22264581; e-mail com@mtp.railnet.gov.in; internet www.mtp.indianrailways.gov.in; f. 1995; Gen. Man. P. B. MURTY.

North Central Railway: Allahabad 211 001; tel. (532) 2230200; fax (532) 2603900; e-mail secy@ncr.railnet.gov.in; internet www.ncr.indianrailways.gov.in; f. 1996; Gen. Man. H. C. JOSHI.

North Eastern Railway: Gorakhpur 273 012; tel. (551) 2201041; fax (551) 2201299; e-mail gm@ner.railnet.gov.in; internet www.ner.indianrailways.gov.in; Gen. Man. OM PRAKASH.

North Western Railway: Nr Jawahar Circle, Jaipur; tel. 9001195127 (mobile); fax (141) 2725833; e-mail cio@nwr.railnet.gov.in; internet www.nwr.indianrailways.gov.in; Gen. Man. ASHOK KUMAR GUPTA.

Northeast Frontier Railway: Maligaon, Guwahati 781 011; tel. (361) 2676000; fax (361) 2570580; e-mail gm@nfr.railnet.gov.in; internet www.nfr.indianrailways.gov.in; f. 1958; Gen. Man. K. CHANDRA.

Northern Railway: NOCR Bldg, State Entry Rd, New Delhi 110 001; tel. (11) 23363469; fax (11) 23363469; e-mail gm@nr.railnet.gov.in; internet www.nr.indianrailways.gov.in; Gen. Man. B. N. RAJASEKHAR.

South Central Railway: Rm 312, 3rd Floor, Rail Nilayam, Secunderabad 500 071; tel. (40) 27822874; fax (40) 27833203; e-mail gm@scr.railnet.gov.in; internet www.scr.indianrailways.gov.in; Gen. Man. G. N. ASTHANA.

South East Central Railway: R. E. Complex, Bilaspur 495 004; tel. (7752) 47102; e-mail webmaster@secr.railnet.gov.in; internet www.secr.indianrailways.gov.in; Gen. Man. ARUNENDRA KUMAR.

South Eastern Railway: 11 Garden Reach Rd, Kolkata 700 043; tel. (33) 24393532; fax (33) 24397831; e-mail cpro@ser.railnet.gov.in; internet www.ser.indianrailways.gov.in; Gen. Man. A. K. VERMA.

South Western Railway: Club Rd, Keshwapur, Hubli 580 023; tel. (836) 2360747; fax (836) 2365209; e-mail gm@southwesternrailway.in; internet www.swr.indianrailways.gov.in; f. 1996; Gen. Man. ASHOK KUMAR MITAL.

Southern Railway: Park Town, Chennai 600 003; tel. (44) 25353455; fax (44) 25354950; e-mail srailway@gmail.com; internet www.sr.indianrailways.gov.in; Gen. Man. DEEPAK KRISHAN.

West Central Railway: Jabalpur 482 001; tel. (761) 2627444; fax (761) 2607555; e-mail osdwcr@yahoo.com; internet www.wcr.indianrailways.gov.in; f. 1996; Gen. Man. S. V. ARYA.

Western Railway: Churchgate, Mumbai 400 020; tel. (22) 22005670; fax (22) 22068545; e-mail secygm@wr.railnet.gov.in; internet www.wr.indianrailways.gov.in; Gen. Man. MAHESH KUMAR.

ROADS

In 2011 there were an estimated 4.7m. km of roads in India, 234,832 km of which were national or state highways; 53.8% of the total road network was paved. In 1999 the Government launched the ambitious Rs 500,000m. National Highways Development Project, which included plans to build a circuit of roads linking the four main cities of Mumbai, Chennai, Kolkata and New Delhi (Phase I), as well as an east–west corridor linking Silchar with Porbandar and a north–south corridor linking Kashmir with Kanyakumari (Phase II). The majority of work on the first two phases had been completed by 2010. The third phase of the project, the widening and upgrading of an estimated 12,000 km of national highways, was scheduled for completion by 2016. Under four other organized plans (Phases III to VI), the Government has approved construction work on expressways and highways across the country.In 2007 the Government pledged Rs 480,000m. for the upgrade of India's rural road network with the stated aim of connecting 66,000 villages;the allocation represented part of the four-year Bharat Nirman initiative (at an estimated cost of Rs 1,740,000m.) to enhance infrastructure and rural incomes by increasing connectivity with roads, telecommunications and drinking water.

Ministry of Road Transport and Highways: Parivahan Bhavan, 1 Sansad Marg, New Delhi 110 001; tel. (11) 23753991; fax (11) 23719023; e-mail nr.gokarn@nic.in; internet morth.nic.in; responsible for the planning, development and maintenance of India's system of national highways connecting the state capitals and major ports and linking with the highway systems of neighbouring countries. This system includes 172 national highways, which constitute the main trunk roads of the country.

Border Roads Organisation: Seema Sadak Bhavan, Ring Road Naraina, Delhi 110 010; e-mail bro-edp@nic.in; internet www.bro.nic.in; f. 1960 to accelerate the economic development of the north and north-eastern border areas; it has constructed 31,061 km and improved 37,077 km of roads, and built permanent bridges totalling a length of 19,544 m in the border areas.

National Highways Authority of India: G-5 and 6, Sector 10, Dwarka, New Delhi 110 075; tel. (11) 25074100; fax (11) 25093507; e-mail chairman@nhai.org; internet www.nhai.org; f. 1995; planning, designing, construction and maintenance of national highways; implementation of the National Highways Development Project; under Ministry of Shipping, Road Transport and Highways; Chair. A. K. UPADHYAY.

INLAND WATERWAYS

About 14,500 km of rivers are navigable by power-driven craft, and 3,700 km by large country boats. Services are mainly on the Ganga and Brahmaputra and their tributaries, the Godavari, the Mahanadi, the Narmada, the Tapti and the Krishna. About 55m. metric tons of cargo is moved annually by certified vessels. In addition, a substantial volume of cargo and passengers is transported in the unorganized sector.

Central Inland Water Transport Corpn Ltd: 4 Fairlie Pl., Kolkata 700 001; tel. (33) 22435718; fax (33) 22436164; e-mail ciwtc@cal3.vsnl.net.in; internet www.ciwtcltd.com; f. 1967; inland water transport services in Bangladesh and the east and north-east Indian states; also ship-building and -repairing, general engineering, lightering of ships and barge services; Chair. and Man. Dir PRAFUL TAYAL.

Inland Waterways Authority of India: A-13, Sector 1, Noida 201 301; tel. (120) 2544036; fax (120) 2544041; e-mail iwainoi@nic.in; internet iwai.nic.in; f. 1986; devt and regulation of inland waterways for shipping and navigation; under Ministry of Shipping, Road Transport and Highways; Chair. S. P. GAUR.

SHIPPING

The major ports are Chennai, Haldia, Jawaharlal Nehru (at Nhava Sheva near Mumbai), Kandla, Kochi, Kolkata, Mormugao, Mumbai, New Mangalore, Paradip (Paradeep), Tuticorin and Visakhapatnam. At 31 December 2013 India's flag registered fleet had a total of 1,553 ships, including 209 general cargoes, 90 bulk carriers, 40 fishing tankers and 16 gas tankers, with a total displacement of 9.74m. grt.

Port Authorities and Supervisory Bodies

Chennai Port Trust: 1 Rajaji Salai, Chennai 600 001; tel. (44) 25362201; fax (44) 25361228; e-mail info@chennaiport.gov.in; internet www.chennaiport.gov.in; f. 1881; under the Ministry of Shipping; Chair. ATULYA MISRA.

Cochin Port Trust: Willingdon Island, Cochin 682 009; tel. (484) 2668200; fax (484) 2666417; e-mail mail@cochinport.gov.in; internet www.cochinport.com; f. 1926; owned by the Ministry of Shipping; manages infrastructure around Ernakulam and Mattancherry wharfs; Chair. PAUL ANTONY.

Indian Ports Association: South Tower, 1st Floor, NBCC Place, Bhisham Pitamah Marg, Lodi Rd, New Delhi 110 003; fax (11) 24365866; e-mail ipa@nic.in; internet ipa.nic.in; f. 1966; supervisory and advisory body; Man. Dir A. JANARDHANA RAO.

Indian Register of Shipping: 72 Maker Tower F, 7th Floor, Cuffe Parade, Mumbai 400 005; tel. (22) 40804080; fax (22) 22181241; e-mail mumbai@irclass.org; internet www.irclass.org; f. 1975; ship classification society; provides technical inspection and certification services for marine craft and structures; Chair. Capt. J. C. ANAND.

Kolkata Port Trust: 15 Strand Rd, Kolkata 700 001; tel. (33) 22303451; fax (33) 22304901; e-mail calport@kopt.in; internet www.kolkataporttrust.gov.in; f. 1870; operates Kolkata and Haldia dock systems; handles cargo and maintains vessel traffic; Chair. R. P. S. KAHLON.

Mumbai Port Trust: Port House, S. V. Marg, Mumbai 400 001; tel. (22) 22621234; fax (22) 66564011; e-mail chairman@mbptmail.com; internet www.mumbaiport.gov.in; f. 1873; works to improve infrastructure facilities and manages port traffic; Chair. RAJEEV GUPTA.

Visakhapatnam Port Trust: Port Area, Visakhapatnam 530 035; tel. (891) 2876001; fax (891) 2565023; e-mail info@vizagport.com; internet www.vizagport.com; f. 1964; handles 3 harbours: outer (200 ha with 6 berths), inner (100 ha with 18 berths) and a fishing harbour; Chair. AJEYA KALLAM.

Shipping Companies

Kolkata (Calcutta)

Apeejay Shipping Ltd: Apeejay House, 15 Park St, Kolkata 700 016; tel. (33) 44035455; fax (33) 22179596; e-mail solcal@apeejaygroup.com; internet www.apeejayshipping.com; f. 1948; shipowners; Chair. KARAN PAUL; CEO S. S. MAHAPATRA.

India Steamship Co Ltd: Birla Bldg, 9th Floor, 9/1 R. N. Mukherjee Rd, Kolkata 700 001; tel. (33) 71071000; fax (33) 22624191; e-mail iss@indiasteamship.com; internet www.indiasteamship.com; f. 1928; cargo services; Pres. K. SATISHCHANDRA; br in Delhi.

Mumbai (Bombay)

Chowgule Brothers (Pvt) Ltd: Malhotra House, 3rd Floor, POB 1770, Mumbai 400 001; tel. (22) 22675579; fax (22) 22610659; e-mail mumbai.cb@chowgule.co.in; internet www.chowgulebros.com; Dir JAYWANT CHOWGULE.

Essar Shipping Ltd: Essar House, 11 Keshavrao Khadye Marg, Mahalaxmi, Mumbai 400 034; tel. (22) 24950606; fax (22) 24954312; e-mail contactshipping@essar.com; internet www.essar.com; f. 1969; Chair. SHASHI RUIA; Man. Dir A. R. RAMAKRISHNAN.

The Great Eastern Shipping Co Ltd: Ocean House, 134A Dr Annie Besant Rd, Worli, Mumbai 400 018; tel. (22) 66613000; fax (22) 24920200; e-mail marketing@greatshipglobal.com; internet www.greatshipglobal.com; f. 1948; shipping; Exec. Chair. BHARAT K. SHETH; Man. Dir RAVI K. SHETH; brs in Singapore, Mauritius, Australia and the United Kingdom.

Mercator Ltd: Mittal Tower, 3rd Floor, B Wing, Nariman Point, Mumbai 400 021; tel. (22) 66373333; fax (22) 66373344; e-mail mercator@mercator.in; internet www.mercator.in; f. 1983; cargo shipping; fmrly Mercator Lines Ltd; Chair. H. K. MITTAL; Man. Dir ATUL J. AGARWAL.

Shipping Corpn of India Ltd: Shipping House, 245 Madame Cama Rd, Mumbai 400 021; tel. (22) 22026666; fax (22) 22026905; e-mail mail@sci.co.in; internet www.shipindia.com; f. 1961 as a govt undertaking; Chair. and Man. Dir S. HAJARA; brs in Kolkata, New Delhi, Chennai and London.

Tolani Shipping Co Ltd: 10A Bakhtawar, Nariman Point, Mumbai 400 021; tel. (22) 56568989; fax (22) 22870697; e-mail tmi@tolani.edu; internet www.tolanigroup.com; f. 1974; Chair. and Man. Dir Dr NANDLAL PRIBHDAS TOLANI.

Varun Shipping Co Ltd: Laxmi Bldg, 3rd Floor, 6 Shoorji Vallabhdas Marg, Ballard Estate, Mumbai 400 001; tel. (22) 66350100; fax (22) 66350274; e-mail isd@varunship.com; internet www.varunship.com; f. 1971; Chair. and Man. Dir ARUN MEHTA.

CIVIL AVIATION

In 2013 there were 19 designated international airports under the jurisdiction of the Airports Authority of India (AAI)—10 managed by the AAI, six operated by private consortiums and three civil enclaves. In addition, there were more than 80 domestic airports and seven customs airports. Overall annual passenger-handling capacity of AAI airports increased from 101.2m. in 2009 to 233m. in 2012. Net air traffic increased from 48.8m. in 2004 to 142.4m. in 2010. Since 2006 contracts to manage and modernize several international airports, including Mumbai, New Delhi and Hyderabad, have been awarded to public-private partnerships. A new terminal at Indira Gandhi International Airport in New Delhi was inaugurated in 2010, increasing the airport's annual handling capacity to 37m. passengers. In February 2014 a major new terminal was opened at Mumbai's Chhatrapati Shivaji International Airport with a handling capacity of some 40m. passengers annually.

Airports Authority of India: Rajiv Gandhi Bhavan, Safdarjung Airport, New Delhi 110 003; tel. (11) 24632950; fax (11) 24641088; e-mail aaichmn@vsnl.com; internet www.aai.aero; f. 1972; responsible for air traffic management and devt of airport infrastucture; manages 125 international and domestic airports; Chair. ALOK SINHA.

Directorate General of Civil Aviation (DGCA): Aurbindo Marg, New Delhi 110 003; tel. (11) 24643010; fax (11) 24616783; e-mail skumar.dgca@nic.in; internet www.dgca.nic.in; Dir-Gen. Dr PRABHAT KUMAR.

Air-India: Air-India Bldg, 218 Backbay Reclamation, Nariman Point, Mumbai 400 021; tel. (22) 22023031; fax (22) 22021096; e-mail eCommerce@airindia.in; internet www.airindia.in; f. 1932 as Tata Airlines; renamed Air-India in 1946; in 1953 became a state corpn responsible for international flights; merged with Indian Airlines in 2007 to form the National Aviation Company of India, operating as Air-India; operates domestic flights under the brand name Air India Regional and low-cost services under the Air India Express brand (internet www.airindiaexpress.in); carried an estimated 4.4m. passengers in 2011/12; Chair. and Man. Dir ROHIT NANDAN.

Blue Dart Express: 88–89 Old International Terminal, Meenambakkam Airport, Chennai 600 027; tel. (44) 22568200; fax (44) 22568385; e-mail radhag@bluedart.com; internet www.bluedart.com; f. 1983 as Blue Dart Courier Services; name changed as above in 1990; air express transport co; operates a fleet of 7 aircraft; Chair. SHARAD UPASANI; Man. Dir ANIL KHANNA.

Go Air: C-1, Wadia Int. Centre, 1st Floor, Pandurang Budhkar Marg, Worli, Mumbai 400 025; tel. (22) 67410000; fax (22) 67420001; e-mail feedback@goair.in; internet www.goair.in; f. 2005; low-cost passenger services to domestic destinations; Man. Dir JEHANGIR 'JEH' WADIA.

Indigo Airlines: Tower C, Level 1, Global Business Park, Mehrauli-Gurgaon Road, Gurgaon 122 002; tel. (124) 4352500; fax (124) 4068536; e-mail sakshi.batra@bm.com; internet www.goindigo.in; f. 2005; private co; passenger services to domestic destinations; int. services to Oman, Singapore, Thailand and the United Arab Emirates launched in 2011; Chair. RAHUL BHATIA; Pres. ADITYA GHOSH.

Jagson Airlines: Vandana Bldg, 3rd Floor, 11 Tolstoy Marg, New Delhi 110 001; tel. (11) 23721594; fax (11) 23324693; e-mail jagson-id@eth.net; f. 1991; scheduled and charter passenger services to domestic destinations; Chair. JAGDISH GUPTA.

Jet Airways (India) Ltd: Siroya Centre, Sahar Airport Rd, Andheri (East), Mumbai 400 099; tel. (22) 61211000; fax (22) 29201313; internet www.jetairways.com; f. 1992; commenced operations 1993; acquired Air Sahara in April 2007; private co; scheduled passenger services to domestic and regional destinations; operates flights to 50 domestic and international destinations; also operates low-cost JetLite service; Chair. and Man. Dir NARESH GOYAL; CEO (vacant).

JetLite: Siroya Centre, Sahar Airport Rd, Andheri (East), Mumbai 400 099; tel. (11) 61211000; fax (11) 23755510; internet www.jetlite.com; f. 1991 as Sahara India Airlines; name changed as above when acquired by Jet Airways (India) in April 2007; private co; scheduled passenger and cargo services to domestic and regional destinations; Chair. NARESH GOYAL.

Kingfisher Airlines: Kingfisher House, Western Express Highway, Vile Parle (East), Mumbai 400 099; tel. (22) 26262200; fax (22) 67020625; e-mail info@flykingfisher.com; internet www.flykingfisher.com; f. 2005; 100% owned by UB Group; national and international passenger service; also operates Kingfisher Red, a low-cost domestic passenger service; in March 2012, owing to ongoing financial difficulties, the airline announced that it was to suspend all international operations until further notice; Chair. and Man. Dir VIJAY MALLYA.

SpiceJet: 319 Udyog Vihar, Phase IV, Gurgaon 122 016; tel. 9871803333 (mobile); e-mail custrelations@spicejet.com; internet www.spicejet.com; f. 2005; low-cost domestic passenger service; Chair. KALANITHI MARAN; CEO (vacant).

Trans Bharat Aviation Ltd: 212–213, Somdutt Chamber I, 2nd Floor, Bhikaji Cama Place, Delhi 110 066; tel. (11) 26181824; fax (11) 26160146; e-mail qcmtba@rediffmail.com; f. 1990; commenced operations 1991; provides helicopter charter services throughout India; CEO PRADIP BISWAS.

Tourism

The tourist attractions of India include sub-Himalayan scenery in the north and the east; diverse fauna, including the Bengal tiger, the peacock and the Asiatic elephant; myriad wildlife sanctuaries and national parks; historic monuments, including forts, palaces and temples; various cultural and religious festivals; and many other vibrant urban and rural attractions. India possesses 28 UNESCO World Heritage sites, including the Taj Mahal. Tourism infrastructure has recently been expanded by the provision of additional luxury hotels and improved means of transport. In 2012 there were an estimated 6.6m. foreign visitors to India, an increase of 4.3% compared with the previous year. In that year revenue from tourism rose by 7.1%, compared with the previous year, to reach an estimated US $17,737m. In 2012 the USA and the United Kingdom were the most important sources of tourist arrivals, providing 15.8% and 12.0% of total arrivals, respectively.

Ministry of Tourism: (see Ministries and Government Offices); formulates and administers govt policy for promotion of tourism; plans the org. and devt of tourist facilities; operates tourist information offices in India and overseas; Sec. RAJEN HABIB KHWAJA.

India Tourism Development Corpn Ltd: SCOPE Complex, Core-8, 7 Lodhi Rd, New Delhi 110 003; tel. (11) 24360303; fax (11) 24360233; e-mail contact@itdc.com; internet www.theashokgroup.com; f. 1966; operates Ashok Group of hotels, resort accommodation, tourist transport services, duty-free shops and a travel agency and provides consultancy and management services; Chair. and Man. Dir Dr SHANKARSINH VAGHELA.

Travel Agents' Association of India: 2D Lawrence and Mayo House, 276 Dr D. N. Rd, Mumbai 400 001; tel. (22) 40836786; fax (22) 40836767; e-mail taai@taai.in; internet www.travelagentsofindia.com; 1,692 mems; Pres. IQBAL MULLA; Hon. Sec.-Gen. R. SUNIL KUMAR.

Defence

As assessed at November 2013, India's total armed forces numbered 1,325,000: army 1,129,900, navy 58,350 (incl. naval air force), air force 127,200, coast guard 9,550. Active paramilitary forces totalled 1,403,700 members, including the 230,000-strong Border Security Force (based mainly in the troubled state of Jammu and Kashmir). Military service is voluntary, although the Constitution states that every citizen has a fundamental duty to perform national service when called upon to do so.

Defence Budget (2013/14): Estimated at Rs 2,040,000.

Chief of the Air Staff: Air Chief Marshal ARUP RAHA.

Chief of the Army Staff: Gen. BIKRAM SINGH.

Chief of the Naval Staff: Adm. ROBIN DHOWAN.

Education

Under the Constitution, education in India is primarily the responsibility of the individual state governments, although the central Government has several direct responsibilities, including responsibility for the Central Universities, all higher institutions, promotion and propagation of Hindi, co-ordination and maintenance of higher education standards, scientific and technological research and welfare of Indian students abroad.

Education in India is administered centrally by the Ministry of Human Resources Development (Department of Education). At state level, there is an Education Minister. There are facilities for free primary education (lower and upper stages) in all the states. An amendment to the Constitution, which came into effect in April 2010, ensures free and compulsory education for children from the age of six to 14. In addition, the historic legislation seeks to ensure universal education by requiring private schools to reserve no less than one-quarter of placements for children from impoverished backgrounds, by creating new state-run neighbourhood schools, by removing school admission fees and by providing for the creation of schools for children with disabilities. Budgetary expenditure on education and literacy for 2013/14 was estimated at Rs 527,010m. (equivalent to 3.16% of total spending).

ELEMENTARY EDUCATION

The notable characteristic of elementary education in India is the use of what is known as basic education. There is an activity-centred curriculum which educates through socially useful, productive activities such as spinning, weaving, gardening, leather work, book craft, domestic crafts, pottery, elementary engineering, etc. Emphasis has been placed on introducing important features of basic education in non-basic schools. Basic education is the national pattern of all elementary education and all elementary schools will ultimately be brought over to the basic system.

In pre-primary and primary classes, for children between six and 11 years of age, the total number of pupils increased from 50m. in 1965 to an estimated 141.5m. in 2010/11. Enrolment in higher primary or middle schools (age-group 11–14 years) in that year was 62.1m. Similarly, the number of primary (lower and higher) schools increased from 466,862 in 1965/66 to more than 1.2m. in 2010/11. Enrolment at primary schools in 2011 included 93% of pupils in the relevant age-group.

SECONDARY EDUCATION

Education at this level is provided for those between the ages of 14 and 18. There were an estimated 200,184 secondary schools, higher secondary schools and junior colleges in 2010/11, with some 51.2m. pupils and 2.5m. teachers. In 2011 enrolment at secondary schools was equivalent to 69% of pupils in the relevant age-group (71% of boys; 66% of girls).

Most schools follow what is known as the 'three-language formula', which comprises teaching of the regional language or dialect, Hindi and English. Much emphasis is now also being laid on physical training, which has become a compulsory subject.

HIGHER AND ADULT EDUCATION

The universities are for the most part autonomous as regards administration. The University Grants Commission is responsible for the promotion and co-ordination of university education and has the authority to make appropriate grants and to implement development schemes.

India had a total of 564 universities and institutions with university status in 2010/11, and some 33,634 colleges of higher education by August 2011. In 2010/11, by some estimates, university enrolment was equivalent to some 14.1% of students in the relevant age-group. In that year an estimated 25.2m. students were enrolled in institutions of higher education.

INDONESIA

Introductory Survey

LOCATION, CLIMATE, LANGUAGE, RELIGION, FLAG, CAPITAL

The Republic of Indonesia consists of a group of about 18,108 islands (including rocks, reefs, sandbanks, etc.), lying between the mainland of South-East Asia and Australia. The archipelago is the largest in the world, and it stretches from the Malay peninsula to New Guinea. The principal islands are Java, Sumatra, Kalimantan (comprising more than two-thirds of the island of Borneo), Sulawesi (Celebes), Papua (formerly Irian Jaya, comprising the western part of the island of New Guinea), Maluku (the Moluccas) and West Timor (comprising part of the island of Timor). Indonesia's only land frontiers are with Papua New Guinea, to the east of Papua, with the Malaysian states of Sarawak and Sabah, which occupy northern Borneo, and with Timor-Leste (formerly East Timor), to the east of West Timor. The climate is tropical, with an annual average temperature of 26°C (79°F) and heavy rainfall during most seasons. Rainfall averages 706 mm (28 in) annually in Indonesia, although there are large variations throughout the archipelago; the heaviest annual rainfall (averaging 2,286 mm or 90 in) is along the equatorial rain belt, which passes through Sumatra, Borneo and Sulawesi. The official language is Bahasa Indonesia (a form of Malay); there are an estimated 583 other languages and dialects spoken in the archipelago, including Javanese, Sundanese, Arabic and Chinese. Around 88% of the inhabitants profess adherence to Islam. About 10% of the population are Christians, and most of the remainder are either Hindus or Buddhists. The national flag (proportions 2 by 3) has two equal horizontal stripes, of red and white. The capital is Jakarta, on the island of Java.

CONTEMPORARY POLITICAL HISTORY

Historical Context

Indonesia was formerly the Netherlands East Indies (except for the former Portuguese colony of East Timor, which became known as Timor-Leste following its accession to independence in 2002—see Provincial Affairs and Separatist Tensions). Dutch occupation began in the 17th century and gradually extended over the whole archipelago. Nationalist opposition to colonial rule emerged in the early 20th century. During the Second World War the territory was occupied by Japanese forces from March 1942. On 17 August 1945, three days after the Japanese surrender, a group of nationalists proclaimed the independence of Indonesia. The first President of the self-proclaimed republic was Dr Sukarno, a leader of the nationalist movement since the 1920s. The declaration of independence was not recognized by the Netherlands, which attempted to restore its pre-war control of the islands. After four years of intermittent warfare and negotiations between the Dutch authorities and the nationalists, agreement was reached on a formal transfer of power. On 27 December 1949 the United States of Indonesia became legally independent, with Sukarno continuing as President. Initially, the country had a federal Constitution, which gave limited self-government to the 16 constituent regions. In August 1950, however, the federation was dissolved, and the country became the unitary Republic of Indonesia. The 1949 independence agreement excluded West New Guinea (subsequently Irian Jaya and known as Papua from 1 January 2002), which remained under Dutch control until October 1962; however, following a brief period of UN administration, it was transferred to Indonesia in May 1963.

Domestic Political Affairs

Sukarno followed a policy of extreme nationalism, and his regime became increasingly dictatorial. His foreign policy was sympathetic to the People's Republic of China but, under his rule, Indonesia also played a leading role in the Non-aligned Movement (see p. 467). Inflation and widespread corruption provoked opposition to Sukarno's regime; in September–October 1965 there was an abortive military coup, in which the Partai Komunis Indonesia (PKI—Indonesian Communist Party) was strongly implicated. A massacre of alleged PKI members and supporters ensued. In March 1966 Sukarno was forced to transfer emergency executive powers to military commanders, led by Gen. Suharto, Chief of Staff of the Army, who outlawed the PKI. In February 1967 Sukarno transferred full power to Suharto. In March the Majelis Permusyawaratan Rakyat (MPR—People's Consultative Assembly) removed Sukarno from office and named Suharto acting President. He became Prime Minister in October 1967 and, following his election by the MPR, he was inaugurated as President in March 1968. In July 1971, in the first general election since 1955, the government-sponsored Sekretariat Bersama Golongan Karya (Joint Secretariat of Functional Groups), known as Golkar, won a majority of seats in the Dewan Perwakilan Rakyat (DPR—House of Representatives). Suharto was re-elected to the presidency in March 1973.

Under Suharto's 'New Order', real power passed from the legislature and the Cabinet to a small group of army officers and to the Operation Command for the Restoration of Order and Security (Kopkamtib), the internal security organization. Left-wing movements were suppressed, and a liberal economic policy was adopted. A general election in May 1977 gave Golkar a legislative majority, and Suharto was re-elected President (unopposed) in March 1978. Golkar won an increased majority in the election of May 1982. In March 1983 Suharto was re-elected, again unopposed, as President.

During 1984 Suharto's attempt to introduce legislation requiring all political, social and religious organizations to adopt *Pancasila*, the five-point state philosophy (belief in a supreme being; humanitarianism; national unity; democracy by consensus; social justice), as their only ideology encountered violent opposition, allegedly instigated by Muslim opponents of the proposed legislation; many Muslims were tried and imprisoned. All political parties had accepted *Pancasila* by July 1985. At the April 1987 general election, despite international allegations of corruption and human rights abuse, Golkar won 299 of the 500 seats in the DPR.

In February 1988 new legislation reaffirmed the *dwifungsi*, or 'dual (i.e. military and socio-economic) function', of the Angkatan Bersenjata Republik Indonesia (ABRI—Armed Forces of the Republic of Indonesia). In March Suharto was again re-elected unopposed as President. Lt-Gen. (retd) Sudharmono, the Chairman of Golkar, was subsequently appointed Vice-President, to the consternation of ABRI since, under Sudharmono's chairmanship of Golkar, there had been a shift away from military dominance in the grouping. In October Sudharmono resigned as party Chairman and was replaced by Gen. (retd) Wahono.

In 1989 Suharto promoted legislation whereby decisions made by Islamic courts no longer required confirmation by civil courts, and in December 1990 the President opened the symposium of the newly formed Ikatan Cendekiawan Muslim Indonesia (ICMI—Association of Indonesian Muslim Intellectuals), an organization that united a broad spectrum of Islamic interests. ABRI was opposed to the establishment of ICMI because it regarded the polarization of politics by religion as a threat to stability.

During 1991 several new organizations were formed to promote freedom of expression and other democratic values. As labour unrest grew, arrests and the alleged intimidation of political activists curbed expressions of dissent, and political campaigns were banned on university campuses. In September Suharto removed several of the most outspoken members of Golkar from the list of candidates to contest the next legislative elections. During the campaign period, political parties were prohibited from addressing religious issues, the question of the dominant role of the ethnic Chinese community in the economy, or any subject that might present a threat to national unity. However, the opposition parties did exploit the increasing public resentment about the rapidly expanding businesses of Suharto's children. In June 1992 90.4% of the electorate participated in the elections to the DPR; Golkar secured 282 of the 400 elective seats, the Partai Persatuan Pembangunan (PPP—United Development Party) won 62 seats (a gain of one seat from the 1987 elections) and the Partai Demokrasi Indonesia (PDI—Indonesian Democratic Party) won 56 seats (a gain of 16).

In March 1993 the DPR elected Suharto and Gen. Try Sutrisno, the former Commander-in-Chief of the Armed Forces, to the posts of President and Vice-President, respectively, the election of the latter appearing to consolidate ABRI's position following considerable public debate over its active involvement in political affairs and, in particular, concern over whether the appointment of 100 members of ABRI to the DPR remained justifiable. However, Suharto's new 41-member Cabinet reduced ABRI representation from 11 to eight members, and included several members of ICMI, whose Chairman, Prof. Dr Ir Bucharuddin Jusuf (B. J.) Habibie, was deeply unpopular with ABRI.

In October 1993, at the party Congress, the Minister of Information, Harmoko, became the first civilian to be elected to the chairmanship of Golkar. In an unprecedented development, Suharto had openly endorsed Harmoko's candidacy. Also at the Congress, Suharto's family entered active national politics; his son, Bambang Trihatmodjo, and daughter, Siti Hardijanti Rukmana (known as Mbak Tutut), who had both been appointed to the MPR in 1992, were elected to positions of responsibility within Golkar.

Meanwhile, in July 1993 the incumbent Chairman of the PDI, Soerjadi, was re-elected to the post at a fractious party Congress. However, the Government invalidated the election of Soerjadi, who had campaigned during the 1992 elections for a limited presidential term of office, and appointed a 'caretaker board' pending new elections. An extraordinary Congress of the PDI ended inconclusively in December owing to the unexpected candidacy for the chairmanship of Megawati Sukarnoputri, the daughter of former President Sukarno. Despite government pressure to elect a senior party official, Megawati received overwhelming support from the congressional participants, and the 'caretaker board' prevented a vote from taking place. The Government then ordered the holding of a new PDI Congress, at which Megawati was elected Chairman.

Suppression of political and civil unrest, 1993–98

In June 1993, in response to pressure from the USA for Indonesia to improve workers' rights or lose trade privileges under the Generalized System of Preferences, the Government adopted reforms to the only officially recognized trade union, the Serikat Pekerja Seluruh Indonesia (All Indonesia Workers' Union), substantially increased the minimum wage and revoked the controversial 1986 Labour Law, which allowed the intervention of the armed forces in labour disputes. However, workers subsequently went on strike, accusing employers of failing to pay the new minimum wage and demanding improved working conditions. In February 1994 the unrecognized Serikat Buruh Sejahtera Indonesia (SBSI—Indonesian Prosperous Labour Union) appealed for a one-hour national work stoppage. The General Secretary of the SBSI, Muchtar Pakpahan, was charged with inciting hatred against the Government and temporarily detained. In April riots broke out in Medan, Sumatra, over workers' continuing demands, rapidly degenerating into attacks on ethnic Chinese property and business executives, who were widely perceived to have benefited disproportionately from the country's rapid economic growth. Three members of the SBSI surrendered to the authorities in May and admitted to having organized the protests. Further strikes took place in other parts of northern Sumatra. In August Pakpahan was rearrested; he was given a three-year prison sentence in November for inciting labour unrest (later extended to four years).

In January 1995 the armed forces announced that 300 members of the PDI were to be investigated for links to the 1965 coup attempt, following allegations that many party members had relatives or contacts in the banned PKI. In a further apparent bid to discredit the opposition grouping, the authorities attempted to ascribe social unrest to communist subversion. In September the Chief of Staff of the Armed Forces named several prominent dissidents, including Pakpahan (whose conviction for incitement had been rescinded by the Supreme Court in that month), as members of 'formless organizations', which, he claimed, had infiltrated pressure groups to promote the revival of communism. In November 300 alleged subversives were arrested in Java.

In July 1995, in response to widespread condemnation of Indonesia's human rights violations, Suharto announced that three prisoners detained for their complicity in the 1965 coup attempt would be released to coincide with the 50th anniversary of independence in August. The administration also subsequently announced that the code ET (which stood for *Eks Tahanan Politik*—former political prisoner) was to be removed from identity papers following the anniversary. The measure affected about 1.3m. citizens, most of whom had been arrested following the 1965 coup attempt, but released without trial; ET status had subjected them to certain restrictions (for example, in employment) and to widespread discrimination. In October 1995 30 members of an extreme right-wing group, the Islamic State of Indonesia, were arrested in western Java for attempting to overthrow 'the unitary state of Indonesia'. In January 1996 in Bandung, West Java, thousands took part in demonstrations against the disproportionately wealthy ethnic Chinese.

In January 1996 the Government abolished permit requirements for political meetings (police permission was still necessary for public gatherings and demonstrations). In March a group of political activists established an Independent Election Monitoring Committee, which was declared unconstitutional by the Government. In April the Government restored voting rights to more than 1.1m. people who had been associated with the PKI. However, the Government's increasing concern over potential opposition resulted in a return to more authoritarian practices.

In June 1996, in response to the increasing popularity of Megawati's leadership of the PDI, government supporters within the party organized a party Congress in the northern Sumatran town of Medan, which removed Megawati as leader, and re-installed Soerjadi as Chairman. PDI members loyal to Megawati organized demonstrations in her support. In July members of Soerjadi's PDI faction and the armed forces forcibly removed Megawati and her supporters from the PDI headquarters, prompting violence in which five people were killed. The Government declared the minor, Marxist-influenced Partai Rakyat Demokrasi (PRD) to be responsible for the rioting, and renewed its campaign against communism. In September the Government proscribed the PRD, and Megawati's new party headquarters in eastern Jakarta were closed down.

In October 1996 Suharto ordered ABRI to suppress all political dissent. In November the Government declared that it would take action against non-governmental organizations (NGOs) that violated Indonesian law and the *Pancasila* ideology. In December the DPR ratified legislation granting the Government extensive powers to revoke the broadcasting permits of private television and radio stations. In the same month a government decree banned mass rallies during campaigning for the forthcoming legislative elections. In April 1997 thousands of supporters of Megawati rallied outside the DPR to protest against the exclusion from the final list of candidates of those nominated by her faction.

In the worst incident of pre-election violence, 125 people were killed when a shopping centre was set alight during clashes between supporters of Golkar and the PPP in the provincial capital of Kalimantan, Banjarmasin; more than 150 others were killed in various other incidents across the country. The elections were held in May 1997. However, riots in Madura, fuelled by PPP claims that ballots had not been counted, resulted in an unprecedented repeat of voting at 86 polling stations several days later. The final results of the elections, which continued to attract allegations of fraud, revealed that Golkar had secured 74.3% of the vote (compared with 68.1% in 1992), giving it control of 325 seats; the PPP had won 89 seats, while Soerjadi's PDI had secured only 11 seats (compared with 56 in 1992).

Widespread social unrest continued throughout 1997, as a result of religious tension, income disparity between social and ethnic groups and the repercussions of the central Government's transmigration programme, which had been initiated in 1971 in an effort to reduce population pressure on the most densely populated islands, particularly Java.

In August 1997 two Muslim leaders, Abdurrahman Wahid, the Chairman of the country's largest Islamic organization, the Nahdlatul Ulama (NU—Revival of the Islamic Scholars), and Amien Rais, the head of Indonesia's second largest Islamic grouping, Muhammadiyah, were excluded from the list of 500 civilian and military appointees to the MPR. Amien Rais had been forced to resign from a board of experts in ICMI in February for publicly criticizing the controversial Freeport mine in Irian Jaya (now Papua).

Following a massive decline in the value of the Indonesian currency between August and October 1997, President Suharto was forced to accept a rescue programme from the IMF. However, he subsequently failed to implement the requisite reforms, fearing that they would provoke unrest and adversely affect the business interests of his family and friends. At an unprecedented gathering of Muslim leaders and intellectuals (including members of ICMI) held in December, participants rejected Suharto's leadership and rallied around Amien Rais, who had already offered himself as a presidential candidate. Wahid subsequently joined Amien Rais and Megawati (who had entered an informal alliance) in demanding Suharto's resignation. In a largely symbolic gesture, in January 1998 Megawati also presented herself as a presidential candidate.

Nevertheless, at the presidential election, held in March 1998, Suharto was re-elected unopposed. He then endorsed the nomination of Habibie as the new Vice-President. Suharto's new Cabinet included a number of his immediate circle of friends and family. (Prior to his re-election, Suharto had also appointed his son-in-law, Lt-Gen. Prabowo Subianto, as Commander of Kostrad—the Indonesian army's strategic reserve.) In May riots erupted in Jakarta, precipitated by the announcement of a 70% increase in the price of fuel. The following month Indonesia's leading human rights group claimed that at least 1,188 people had died in Jakarta alone, while hundreds were believed to have perished during unrest elsewhere. Indonesia's ethnic Chinese minority was the target for much of the violence: an indeterminate number of Chinese were murdered, numerous Chinese women were raped, and Chinese homes and businesses were looted and burned.

The presidencies of Habibie and Wahid

On 21 May 1998, following sustained pressure (including an unprecedented demand for his resignation by Golkar Chairman Harmoko, and the resignation of 14 cabinet ministers), Suharto stepped down as President. Vice-President Habibie was sworn in as Suharto's successor, and subsequently appointed a new 'reform Cabinet', which nevertheless retained some ministers from the previous administration. The new President also announced the release of a number of political prisoners (including the union leader Pakpahan), encouraged government departments to sever links with enterprises owned by Suharto's family, and supported the dismissal of Suharto's son-in-law, Lt-Gen. Prabowo, from his position as Commander of Kostrad. In June an investigation into the assets of Suharto and other government officials was announced, and Habibie expelled 41 members of the MPR, including several close associates of Suharto, on account of alleged corruption, nepotism and collusion. Seven members of Suharto's family were removed from their seats in the MPR the following month.

Unrest continued across the archipelago throughout the latter half of 1998, exacerbated by dissatisfaction at the pace of change under the new administration and at severe food shortages. During a four-day special session of the MPR in Jakarta in November at least 16 people were killed and many injured when students and other civilians clashed with soldiers outside the building. At least 14 people died during clashes between Muslims and Christians in further riots. In the same month a report was published containing the findings of a panel appointed by the Government to investigate the riots that had occurred in May. The panel found that elements of the military had acted as 'provocateurs' during the riots, with particular suspicion falling on Kostrad. Lt-Gen. Prabowo had been formally dismissed from the army in August owing to the role that he had played as the then Commander of the unit. In December Suharto was questioned at the Higher Prosecutor's Office over allegations of corruption.

In December 1998 it was announced that legislative elections would be held in June 1999 and that the MPR (including 200 additional delegates) would convene in August to elect a new President (although this was subsequently postponed until November). Elections to the DPR would be conducted under a new electoral system, combining both district and proportional voting, but only parties presenting candidates in the requisite number of districts would be permitted to contest the poll. Civil servants were no longer to be obliged to support Golkar; the number of seats in the DPR allocated to the military was to be reduced from 75 to 38; and the membership of the MPR was to be reduced from 1,000 to 700.

At least 159 people were killed during clashes between Muslims and Christians on the island of Ambon, in the province of Maluku, in early 1999. The Habibie Government continued to pursue an extensive programme of reform. In April the police force—part of the Indonesian military since 1962—was formally separated from the armed forces (while remaining under the control of the Ministry of Defence), and the armed forces reassumed their revolutionary-era name, Tentara Nasional Indonesia (TNI—Indonesian National Defence Forces), instead of ABRI. The Subversion Law, introduced in 1963 and previously applied in the suppression of political dissidents, was repealed by the MPR (although some prohibitions were retained). In May 1999 a presidential decree removed a ban on the use and teaching of the Mandarin Chinese language and also outlawed discrimination on the grounds of ethnic origin.

President Habibie was nominated as the sole presidential candidate of Golkar in May 1999, despite some concerns regarding his close association with former President Suharto. The three leading opposition parties—Megawati's Partai Demokrasi Indonesia Perjuangan (PDI—P, Indonesian Democratic Struggle Party), Wahid's Partai Kebangkitan Bangsa (PKB—National Awakening Party), and Amien Rais's Partai Amanat Nasional (PAN—National Mandate Party)—created an informal electoral alliance to stand against Golkar; however, the alliance exhibited instability from an early stage. The turnout at the legislative elections in June was 91% of the electorate. As predicted, the PDI—P was victorious, securing 154 seats; the second largest share of the vote was unexpectedly won by Golkar, which received 120 seats, performing poorly in the cities but achieving a strong result in the outer islands. The PKB secured 59 seats, while the PAN won 35 seats.

Megawati and Habibie thus emerged initially as the main candidates for the presidency. However, in October 1999, following the rejection of his presidential record by the MPR in a secret ballot, Habibie withdrew his candidacy. Contrary to the expectations of many, Megawati failed to win the presidential contest, receiving 313 votes, compared with the 373 secured by Wahid, the only other serious candidate, who had received the endorsement of a number of Islamic parties, as well as the support of Golkar. Wahid's victory provoked outrage among Megawati's supporters, and violent protests ensued in Jakarta and elsewhere. The MPR voted to appoint Megawati as Vice-President. The new Cabinet reflected the conciliatory and inclusive approach of the incoming President, incorporating both Islamic and nationalist representatives, as well as representatives of non-Javanese groups. Gen. Wiranto was replaced as Minister of Defence by the former Minister of Education and Culture, Juwono Sudarsono, the first civilian to hold the post.

The newly appointed Attorney-General, Marzuki Darusman, announced that the investigation into the allegations of corruption made against former President Suharto was to be reopened. The apparent commitment of the new administration to addressing corruption was further emphasized in November 1999, when Wahid urged the investigation of three government ministers, one of whom, the Co-ordinating Minister for People's Welfare and leader of the PPP, Hamzah Haz, subsequently resigned from the Cabinet.

Following Wahid's election to the presidency, there was further unrest across the archipelago. Ethnic violence continued on the island of Ambon in Maluku province where, according to official estimates published in December 1999, more than 750 people had died and from where many thousands more had fled, since the renewal of violent clashes between Muslims and Christians in January. (Aid agencies estimated the total number of dead to be much higher.) In mid-December Wahid and Megawati (who was criticized for her failure to address the crisis, despite having been charged with special responsibility for Maluku) visited the region and appealed for an end to the conflict. Hundreds of additional troops were sent to Ambon to supplement the 2,500 already deployed in Maluku, following the occurrence of dozens more deaths. Although the predominantly Muslim northern districts of Maluku were formally separated as the new province of North Maluku in late 1999, at least 265 people were believed to have been killed in clashes between Christians and Muslims on the island of Halmahera at the end of December, with violence also reported on other islands.

In January 2000 Indonesia's National Human Rights Commission released the results of its investigation into the role of the Indonesian armed forces in human rights abuses in the former Indonesian province of East Timor (now Timor-Leste—see Provincial Affairs and Separatist Tensions). Thirty-three military officers, including Gen. Wiranto, who had been Commander-in-Chief of the armed forces in 1998–99, were implicated; Wiranto resigned from the Cabinet in May 2000. In January, meanwhile, a reorganization took place within the TNI, in which officers loyal to Wiranto were removed from positions of influence. A second reorganization of senior military personnel was announced in February. In August doubts concerning the commitment of the Indonesian Government to the trial of military personnel suspected of involvement in gross human rights violations in East Timor were provoked when the MPR introduced a constitutional amendment that excluded military personnel from prosecution for crimes committed prior to the enactment of the relevant legislation. In September, furthermore, Wiranto was not included on the Attorney-General's list of 19 suspects.

In April 2000 President Wahid dismissed from the Cabinet the Minister of State for Investment and Development of State Enterprises, Laksamana Sukardi of the PDI—P, and the Minister of Trade and Industry, Muhammad Jusuf Kalla of the pro-Habibie wing of Golkar, subsequently suggesting that both were guilty of corruption. In July Wahid was heavily criticized by the DPR for refusing to explain the reasons for these dismissals. Meanwhile, general misgivings about Wahid's style of government also increased. In August Wahid announced that he was to delegate the daily administration of the Government to Vice-President Megawati. Constitutional amendments approved by the MPR in that month included articles defining explicitly the authority of the DPR, particularly in relation to the body's questioning and investigating of government activities; legislation was also enacted to extend military representation in the MPR until 2009, four years after the date at which the military had been scheduled to relinquish its remaining 38 seats in the chamber. In August 2000 President Wahid announced the formation of a new Cabinet, which included considerably fewer representatives of Megawati's PDI—P and allocated a number of the most influential posts to Wahid loyalists: Gen. (retd) Susilo Bambang Yudhoyono was appointed Co-ordinating Minister for Political, Legal and Security Affairs.

In August 2000 Suharto was formally charged with corruption. In September, however, the charges against him were dismissed after an independent medical team declared the former President mentally and physically unfit to stand trial, provoking violent protests in Jakarta. (In May 2006 criminal charges against Suharto were formally abandoned on account of his deteriorating health, but a civil case was subsequently instigated—see The first direct presidential election.) In September 2000 President Wahid ordered the arrest of Suharto's youngest son, Hutomo Mandala Putra (commonly known as Tommy Suharto), in connection with a series of bomb threats and explosions in Jakarta. In one such attack in September at least 15 people were killed when a bomb exploded at the Jakarta Stock Exchange; two men were subsequently convicted of carrying out the bombing and were both sentenced to 20 years' imprisonment. At the end of September the Supreme Court overruled Tommy Suharto's previous acquittal from an unrelated charge of fraudulent activity in 1999, and sentenced him to 18 months' imprisonment. In July 2001 the judge who had presided over the proceedings, Justice Syafiuddin Kartasasmita, was shot dead. Two suspects subsequently confessed to the murder, but admitted in custody that Suharto's son had financed them and supplied the weapons used in the attack; both were convicted and sentenced to life imprisonment. In an unexpected development, a Supreme Court panel rescinded the original fraud charge in October. However, Tommy Suharto was arrested in the following month in connection with the murder of Syafiuddin. In July 2002 he was convicted of arranging Syafiuddin's murder, illegal possession of a weapon and attempting to evade justice, and was sentenced to 15 years' imprisonment. Following a successful appeal, this was subsequently reduced to a 10-year term, and in October 2006 he was granted conditional early release. Several further corruption cases against him were dismissed in 2008–09.

The transfer of power to Megawati

In September 2000 the DPR appointed a commission to investigate two financial scandals with which President Wahid had been linked: the first involved the irregular diversion of US $4.1m. from the funds of the Badan Urusan Logistic (BULOG—National Logistics Agency), allegedly to finance the Golkar party election campaign in 1999, while the second concerned a donation of $2m. made by Sultan Hassanal Bolkiah of Brunei. The President's refusal to be questioned on either matter provoked intense frustration among legislators. In January 2001 the commission concluded that Wahid 'could be suspected of playing a role' in the theft of BULOG funds by his personal masseur and that the President had been deliberately inconsistent in his explanations of how the donation from the Sultan (originally intended for social welfare) had been spent; however, the commission was unable to present clear evidence that Wahid had personally benefited from either situation. In February the DPR voted overwhelmingly to censure Wahid formally over his alleged involvement in the scandals. Wahid was given three months in which to provide a satisfactory explanation of his actions to the DPR. The President continued to deny any wrongdoing and stated his intention to complete his term of presidential office. Tens of thousands of pro-Wahid demonstrators took to the streets in Surabaya and elsewhere in East Java (President Wahid's home province), and protesters set fire to the regional offices of Golkar, which had supported the vote to censure Wahid. Later in the same month Wahid offered himself for questioning by police investigating the two scandals.

In March 2001 more than 12,000 students held a demonstration in Jakarta to demand the President's resignation. In view of Wahid's unsatisfactory reply to his first censure, in April the DPR issued a second censure and requested that the MPR convene a special session to begin impeachment proceedings. Violent pro-Wahid demonstrations took place in East Java. Despite the abandonment of all charges against Wahid in May, following the ruling by Attorney-General Marzuki Darusman that there was no evidence to suggest the President had been involved in either of the financial scandals, later that month the DPR voted by a huge majority to instruct the MPR to instigate an impeachment hearing. In response, in June the President reorganized his Cabinet, dismissing the Co-ordinating Minister for Political, Legal and Security Affairs, Yudhoyono. The Chief of Police, Gen. Surojo Bimantoro, was suspended. In the following month the President threatened to declare a state of emergency if no compromise were reached, and effected another cabinet reorganization. He also appointed a new Chief of Police without the support of the legislature. A special session of the MPR was convened to which the President was summoned to give an account of his 21 months in power. President Wahid deemed the session illegal and refused to attend. He suspended the legislature, declaring a state of civil emergency, and urged that new elections be held in one year's time. However, the military refused to support the declaration, and the MPR stated that the President did not have the constitutional authority to dissolve it.

On 23 July 2001 Wahid was deposed as President following an impeachment hearing. He was replaced by Vice-President Megawati. Legislators elected the leader of the PPP, Hamzah Haz, to act as the new President's deputy, and in August Megawati announced the composition of her first Cabinet. Of its 32 members, only four were former military men, in sharp contrast to previous practice, and Yudhoyono was reinstated as Co-ordinating Minister for Political, Legal and Security Affairs.

In October 2001 President Megawati assented to a prosecution request to question the Speaker of the DPR, Akbar Tandjung, over the alleged misappropriation of BULOG funds. In September 2002 Tandjung was convicted of corruption and sentenced to a three-year prison term; in February 2004, however, the Supreme Court overruled his conviction.

Meanwhile, on 1 January 2001 new legislation took effect devolving increased financial and administrative control to Indonesia's regional governments. The central Government was to retain control over justice, defence, foreign affairs and monetary policy.

The first direct presidential election

In August 2002 a series of constitutional amendments was approved by the MPR. These provided for the direct election of both the President and Vice-President at the next national poll, scheduled to be held in 2004, and for the abolition of all seats held by non-elected representatives, effectively terminating military involvement in the legislature five years earlier than originally intended. The amendments also provided for a bicameral legislature through the creation of the Dewan Perwakilan Daerah (DPD—House of Representatives of the Regions), which, together with the DPR, would form the MPR. A total of 14 amendments (constituting the 'Fourth Amendment' to the Constitution) received legislative assent, and were ratified by the DPR in 2003.

A total of 24 parties contested the legislative elections held in April 2004; turnout was estimated at 84% of the electorate. Golkar secured 128 of the 550 seats in the expanded DPR, replacing the PDI—P, which won 109 seats, as the largest parliamentary grouping. Of the smaller parties, the PPP won 58 seats, the Partai Democrat (PD—Democratic Party) 57, and the PAN and the PKB each secured 52 seats.

At the inaugural direct presidential and vice-presidential election held in July 2004, the presidential candidate of the PD, Yudhoyono secured 33.6% of the votes cast, followed by the incumbent Megawati, with 26.6%, and Golkar's candidate, Gen. (retd) Wiranto, with 22.2%; Amien Rais and Vice-President Hamzah Haz also contested the election on behalf of their respective parties, the PAN and the PPP. As no candidate won more than 50% of the votes, Yudhoyono and Megawati proceeded to a second round of voting, which was held in September: despite Golkar's declared support for the incumbent, Yudhoyono (whose vice-presidential candidate was Muhammad Jusuf Kalla, the Co-ordinating Minister for People's Welfare) emerged victorious, securing 60.6% of the votes cast. Estimated voter turnout in the second round was 75%, compared with 78% in the first. The new President, who was inaugurated in October, included representatives of several political organizations in his Cabinet. Among the notable new appointees were Adm. (retd) Widodo Adi Sutjipto, the former Commander-in-Chief of the TNI, as Co-ordinating Minister for Political, Legal and Security Affairs, and Aburizal Bakrie, of Golkar, as Co-ordinating Minister for Economic Affairs; Hassan Wirajuda, the Minister of Foreign Affairs, was one of five ministers retained from Megawati's administration.

Vice-President Kalla was elected as Chairman of Golkar in December 2004, defeating the incumbent, Akbar Tandjung. As a result, it was anticipated that Golkar would henceforth broadly support the Government, enabling Yudhoyono to secure legislative approval for his policies. In late December Abdullah Puteh, the Governor of Aceh, became the first person to be prosecuted by the recently formed Komisi Pemberantasan Korupsi (KPK—Corruption Eradication Commission). Puteh, who was suspended from office by Yudhoyono, was charged with corruption in relation to the purchase of a Russian helicopter in 2002. He was convicted in April 2005 and was sentenced to 10 years' imprisonment.

Meanwhile, in August 2004 an Indonesian court acquitted the head of the Kopassus special forces regiment, Maj.-Gen. Sriyanto Muntrasan, who had been accused of human rights violations in connection with the shooting of several Muslim activists near Jakarta's Tanjung Priok port in 1984, despite having sentenced Sriyanto's immediate superior, Maj.-Gen. (retd) Rudolf Butar-Butar, to 10 years' imprisonment in April 2004 for failing to prevent the shooting; later in August 11 soldiers received prison terms, having been found guilty in the same case of systematic attacks against civilians. However, in July 2005 the convictions of Butar-Butar and the soldiers were overruled on appeal by the High Court, which deemed the shootings to have been accidental.

In November 2004 it emerged that Munir Said Thalib, a leading Indonesian human rights activist who had died during a flight to the Netherlands in September, had been poisoned with arsenic. Munir had been an outspoken critic of Indonesia's military and Badan Inteligen Negara (BIN—State Intelligence Agency). In March 2005 Pollycarpus Priyanto, an airline pilot of the state-owned Garuda Indonesia who had been on Munir's flight while off duty, was arrested and charged with the activist's murder. Pollycarpus was convicted and sentenced to 14 years' imprisonment in December, but was acquitted on appeal by the Supreme Court in September 2006. However, the case was reopened after prosecutors argued that Indra Setiawan, the former CEO of Garuda, had played a significant part in the murder of Munir by allowing the off-duty pilot the opportunity to carry out the poisoning. In January 2008 Pollycarpus was convicted of pre-meditated murder and forgery, and sentenced to 20 years' imprisonment, and in February Setiawan was convicted of assisting in Munir's murder and given a 12-month sentence; both men claimed to have been carrying out orders issued to them by BIN. In August Maj.-Gen. Muchdi Purwopranjono, the deputy head of BIN at the time of Munir's murder, went on trial, charged with ordering the killing of Munir. Human rights groups welcomed the development, which represented the first prosecution of a senior BIN official. However, Purwopranjono was acquitted in December owing to a lack of evidence.

Meanwhile, Indonesia, in particular the region of Aceh, was devastated by a series of tsunamis caused by a massive earthquake in the Indian Ocean on 26 December 2004. The regional capital, Banda Aceh, was severely damaged, while the town of Meulaboh, 150 km from the epicentre of the earthquake, was completely destroyed. UN agencies and other organizations commenced operations to distribute food, medical supplies and shelter to survivors. Aceh had been under emergency rule prior to the disaster, owing to a separatist insurgency (see Provincial Affairs and Separatist Tensions), and largely closed to foreign agencies and the international media. Most official estimates subsequently concurred that in Aceh alone as many as 170,000 people had died; more than 400,000 were made homeless.

In July 2005 the Majelis Ulama Indonesia (MUI—Indonesian Ulama Council) issued 11 *fatwa* (religious edicts), the most controversial of which outlawed secularism, pluralism and liberal Islamic teachings. The issue of the *fatwa* was thought to be in response to the activities of two moderate, progressive Islamic organizations: the Jaringan Islam Liberal (JIL—Liberal Islam Network) and the Muhammadiyah Youth Intellectuals Network. Meanwhile, ongoing criticism of the Ahmadiyah sect (which maintained that its founder, Mirza Ghulam Ahmad, rather than the Prophet Muhammad, was the final prophet) continued; although deemed an heretical group, the sect was believed to have 200,000 followers in Indonesia. In July thousands of members of the so-called Indonesian Muslim Solidarity group attacked the Ahmadiyah compound in Jakarta, citing an edict issued in 1980 by the MUI, which had declared members of Ahmadiyah to be deviants. The edict was renewed in August 2005. Ahmadis in Bandung and other Javanese cities were also targeted. In April 2008, after a government panel recommended that the group be banned, a large protest was held in Jakarta demanding the expulsion of Ahmadis from Indonesia. A series of attacks on Ahmadiyah mosques prompted the Government to demand that Ahmadis cease 'spreading interpretations and activities which deviate from the principal teachings of Islam' and to warn of prison terms for offenders. It was subsequently reported that the police had helped local Islamic extremists forcibly to shut down several mosques owned by the sect in a village in West Java. The leniency of sentences handed down by a district court in July 2011 to the perpetrators of a violent mob attack against a group of Ahmadis at a mosque in another West Javan village, during which three Ahmadis had been killed (attendant police officers having apparently failed to intervene), elicited much criticism from human rights groups and the wider international community. The defendants, none of whom were charged with murder, received short prison terms, having been convicted only of relatively minor offences.

In December 2005, meanwhile, President Yudhoyono effected a cabinet reorganization, which focused predominantly on economic personnel. Co-ordinating Minister for Economic Affairs Aburizal Bakrie, who had attracted much criticism for his failure to halt the rapid decline in the value of the rupiah, was replaced by Prof. Dr Boediono, Minister of Finance during Megawati's presidency. Minister of State for National Development Planning Dr Sri Mulyani Indrawati was transferred to the finance portfolio, in place of Jusuf Anwar. Further ministerial changes were required in May 2007 following the dismissal of the Minister of Justice and Human Rights Affairs, Hamid Awaluddin, and State Secretary Yusril Ihza Mahendra, as a result of their alleged involvement in the illegal transfer of US $10m. to Tommy Suharto from a bank account in the United Kingdom.

In July 2007 a civil case was filed against former President Suharto, in the hope of recovering some US $440m. that he had allegedly misappropriated from funds ostensibly allocated to an educational foundation. However, Suharto died in January 2008, prompting the Government to declare a week of mourning. Although the former President was posthumously acquitted in March, his charitable foundation, Supersemar, was found guilty and directed to reimburse some $100m. to the state. In August the Government seized $150m. from Timor Putra Nasional, a now-defunct motor vehicle company belonging to Tommy Suharto, amid ongoing investigations into allegations that he had illegally sold assets from Timor Putra Nasional to five of his other companies.

Meanwhile, Jakarta's first direct gubernatorial election took place in August 2007. The election, which attracted a turnout of 65%, was won by the incumbent Deputy Governor, Fauzi Bowo, who received nearly 58% of the votes cast, there being only one other candidate. In June 2008 Minister of Finance and State Enterprises Development Dr Indrawati assumed concurrent responsibility for the economic affairs portfolio, following the departure of Prof. Dr Boediono from the Cabinet.

In October 2008 Burhanuddin Abdullah, the former Governor of Bank Indonesia, was sentenced to five years' imprisonment, after being convicted of embezzling funds in order to bribe legislators and to engage lawyers in an attempt to defend officials of the central bank against corruption allegations.

The 2009 legislative and presidential elections

In April 2008 it was announced that the legal status of 24 new political parties had been recognized. A total of 38 national parties were now deemed eligible to participate in the 2009 legislative elections. Under new legislation approved in October 2008, political parties were required to secure at least 20% of the seats or 25% of the votes cast in the legislative elections in order to nominate a presidential candidate.

At the legislative elections in April 2009, the number of seats in the DPR was increased from 550 to 560. For the first time, under

Indonesia's system of proportional representation, electors were able to vote for specific candidates within each party. Polling for the 132 (hitherto 128) regional delegates of the DPD also took place, along with local elections. A major issue was the rapid deterioration in the country's economy. The PD won 20.8% of the votes cast (nearly tripling the share of the votes it received at the 2004 elections) to secure 148 of the 560 seats in the DPR, thereby enabling the incumbent President Yudhoyono formally to present his candidacy for the presidential election scheduled for July. Golkar secured 108 seats (14.4% of the vote), reduced from 128 at the last elections, while the PDI—P won 93 seats (14.0%), compared with 109 five years previously. Turnout was estimated at 71% of the electorate, a decline of 13 percentage points from that recorded in 2004, although still comparatively high by international standards.

In May 2009, having failed to fulfil the criteria required to nominate a presidential candidate, Golkar and the PDI—P announced the formation of a 10-party electoral coalition, thus enabling them to present Kalla and Megawati as their respective candidates for the presidential election, which was held in July. Incumbent President Yudhoyono, with Prof. Dr Boediono as his vice-presidential candidate, achieved a resounding victory, attracting 60.8% of the votes cast. Megawati and Lt-Gen. Prabowo secured 26.8% of the ballot, while Kalla and Gen. (retd) Wiranto obtained just 12.4%. Yudhoyono was sworn in for his second consecutive term as President in October. The incoming Cabinet retained 10 ministers from the previous administration, including Dr Indrawati as Minister of Finance. Notable new appointees included Air Chief Marshal (retd) Djoko Suyanto as Co-ordinating Minister for Political, Legal and Security Affairs and Hatta Radjasa as Co-ordinating Minister for Economic Affairs.

Aburizal Bakrie was elected as the new Chairman of Golkar at a party Congress in October 2009; the former Co-ordinating Minister for People's Welfare defeated three other candidates, including Tommy Suharto (who failed to secure a single vote).

Declining support for Yudhoyono

An alleged plot to sabotage the KPK was a significant contributory factor in a rapid decline in the popularity of President Yudhoyono from late 2009. In October the integrity of the KPK had been called into question when two of its Deputy Chairmen were detained by the police on suspicion of bribery. However, both were released in November, and the charges against them were withdrawn in December, after the pair submitted covert recordings of conversations between several people widely accepted to have been senior police officers and the Attorney-General's office, which revealed that those speaking, angered by the KPK's successful investigation and charging of numerous officials, intended to destroy the reputation of the anti-corruption commission. Two of the officials linked to the plot, Deputy Attorney-General Abdul Hakim Ritonga and Chief Detective Susno Duadji, tendered their resignations, following numerous protests demanding the dismissal of those involved. In March 2011 Susno Duadji was sentenced to three-and-a-half years' imprisonment, having been convicted of accepting bribes and embezzling public funds. However, as of early 2014, no proceedings appeared to have been instigated against Susno—or any other individual—in connection with the alleged plot against the KPK. Many Indonesians were disillusioned by the perceived failure of Yudhoyono to intervene, and questioned his commitment to his pre-election pledge to take firm action against vice and corruption.

Meanwhile, the controversy surrounding the alleged plot against the KPK intensified further in February 2010 when the former head of the commission, Antasari Azhar, was convicted of arranging the murder of an Indonesian businessman and sentenced to 18 years' imprisonment. The conviction of Antasari (who had been Chairman of the KPK at the time of his arrest in May 2009) came despite claims made by a witness during the trial that he had been forced to co-operate with a police-instigated plot to incriminate the former KPK head. An appeal lodged by Antasari was rejected by the Supreme Court in September 2010. However, his many supporters continued to insist that he had been the victim of an ongoing attempt by the police to discredit the KPK and obstruct anti-corruption efforts.

The Government's controversial rescue programme for a failing financial institution, PT Bank Century Tbk, was another source of considerable contention. Legislators and the general public alike were angered by the revelation in late 2009 that the takeover of the bank in November 2008 had cost taxpayers the equivalent of US $720m., more than four times the amount originally agreed by the Government and the DPR. Opposition parliamentarians argued that Vice-President Boediono (Governor of Bank Indonesia at the time of the intervention) and Minister of Finance Indrawati had abused their positions to protect the interests of Bank Century, which was renamed PT Bank Mutiara Tbk in October 2009, without first securing the approval of the DPR. (Subsequently, many of the bank's wealthy clients were alleged to have made sizeable donations to the election campaign of Yudhoyono and Boediono.) A parliamentary inquiry into 'Centurygate', as the scandal had become known, was initiated in late 2009. In March 2010 the committee published its final report: although it stated that it had found no evidence of Bank Century money being used to support any political campaign, it did criticize the decision-making process, including the actions of Boediono and Indrawati, and urged the Government to pursue the possibility of prosecutions. However, Yudhoyono contested that the rescue programme had been 'essential to saving the banking system' and declared that he saw no need for any action to be taken against Boediono or Indrawati, who both denied any wrongdoing. A forensic audit of the bank was carried out by the Badan Pemeriksa Keuangan (BPK—Supreme Audit Agency) in mid-2011 at the request of the House of Representatives. However, the report submitted by the BPK in December was inconclusive and was widely criticized for its perceived failure fully to explain how all of the rescue programme funding had been spent.

In April 2010 Megawati secured re-election to a third consecutive five-year term as PDI—P Chairperson, but failed to deliver on a pledge to introduce a new generation of PDI—P members to the party's senior leadership. The decision attracted much criticism, with many observers contending that the PDI—P's poor performance in the 2009 elections had been largely attributable to the party's 'old guard', and that the conservative nature of the appointments would likely damage the party's chances at the next legislative elections, due to be held in 2014.

Also in April 2010 the Constitutional Court rejected appeals to overrule controversial legislation implemented in 1967 allowing for criminal penalties and bans on individuals or groups that 'distort' the central tenets of Indonesia's six officially recognized religions—Buddhism, Christianity (both Catholicism and Protestantism), Confucianism, Hinduism and Islam—declaring that the law was in accordance with the Constitution and was vital to religious harmony. It had been hoped that the legislation might be reviewed to allow the official establishment of new religions and sects. According to a local human rights organization, there was a notable rise in the number of reported attacks on religious freedom in Indonesia in the first half of 2010; many of the attacks were attributed to the Front Pembela Islam (FPI—Islamic Defenders' Front), which demanded the implementation of Islamic law (*Shari'a*) across the archipelago. Critics of the Yudhoyono Government claimed that the President had failed to intervene since Islamic parties formed the core of his parliamentary support.

In May 2010 Indrawati, who was widely credited for the macroeconomic reforms that had helped Indonesia to withstand the effects of the international financial crisis of 2008/09, tendered her resignation as Minister of Finance in order to assume a senior position at the World Bank; she was replaced by former banking executive Agus Martowardojo.

Yudhoyono's reputation as an anti-corruption reformist suffered a further reverse during the trial of former tax official Gayus Tambunan, who in January 2011 was convicted of corruption; the defendant's testimony during court proceedings suggested endemic levels of corruption within the judiciary, the police force and the prison service. Also in January, the Minister of Home Affairs, Gamawan Fauzi, expressed concern at the apparent escalation in corruption, noting that some 155 regional leaders had been named as suspects in investigations since 2004; of these, 17 were either current or former governors.

In a more positive development, in October 2010 the Constitutional Court rescinded legislation that allowed the Attorney-General's office unilaterally to prohibit the publication and supply of books that were deemed to be 'offensive' or a 'threat to public order', ruling that the power to impose such bans should henceforth be accorded to the judicial system. The revocation of the legislation, which had been implemented in 1963 and had been used to silence opposition during the Suharto era, was welcomed as symbolically significant.

Also in October 2010, the Government came under intense criticism following a tsunami that claimed the lives of more than 400 people and left some 13,000 homeless. Indonesia's early warning system, which had been implemented at great expense after the 2004 disaster, failed to alert the authorities to the impending tsunami, generated by a major earthquake off the coast of Sumatra; the system was reported to have fallen into disrepair owing to inadequate maintenance. Yudhoyono curtailed a state visit to Viet Nam and returned to Indonesia to oversee the subsequent rescue operation, together with a separate operation to provide relief to those affected by the eruption of a volcano one day after the tsunami; a series of eruptions by Mount Merapi over the course of several weeks killed more than 200 people. However, the authorities' perceived mishandling of the response to the tsunami disaster, with reports of shortages of basic medical and food supplies, prompted widespread anger.

New, more stringent, legislation to combat human-trafficking was approved by the legislature in April 2011. Under the new laws, those convicted of transporting illegal migrants into the country could be sentenced to up to 15 years in prison. The development was widely welcomed, both domestically and further afield, particularly by the Australian Government, which had for some time been pressing Indonesia to adopt a firmer stance on the issue, with many thousands of migrants and asylum seekers using Jakarta as a transit point en route to Australia. None the less, concerns were raised as to how the new legislation might be effectively implemented, amid widespread reports of Indonesian immigration officials accepting bribes on a frequent basis.

Further corruption allegations emerged in April 2011, with the Treasurer of the PD, Muhammad Nazaruddin, accused of soliciting bribes amounting to US $2.8m. from a construction company, in exchange for a contract to build athletes' accommodation for the Southeast Asian Games, which Indonesia hosted in November. However, Nazaruddin refuted the claims, alleging that other legislators and PD officials—including the Secretary-General of the PD, Edhie 'Ibas' Baskoro Yudhoyono (the President's son), and PD Chairman Anas Urbaningrum—had been involved in the scandal. Having fomented division with the PD leadership, Nazaruddin was eventually dismissed from his role as party Treasurer, although he was allowed to retain his parliamentary seat pending further investigation by the KPK. He fled the country in May, but was arrested in Colombia in August and was extradited to Indonesia. Following the conclusion of the KPK investigation, Nazaruddin was formally charged with bribery in December. Having been found guilty in April 2012, he was sentenced to four years and 10 months in prison. The episode, and particularly concerns regarding how Nazaruddin had been able to flee the country despite the gravity of the claims against him, wreaked considerable damage upon the reputation of both the PD and the Yudhoyono administration, and cast further doubt on the latter's commitment to tackling corruption.

Meanwhile, the appointment in June 2011 of Gen. Pramono Edhie Wibowo, Yudhoyono's brother-in-law, as Chief of Staff of the Army provoked accusations of nepotism. Of further consternation to critics of the appointment was the alleged involvement of Gen. Wibowo in human rights abuses in East Timor in 1999 (see Provincial Affairs and Separatist Tensions).

A cabinet reorganization effected by Yudhoyono in October 2011 was widely interpreted as an attempt to restore public confidence in the President's administration, particularly its handling of economic concerns. However, critics described the ministerial changes as 'superficial', with around two-thirds of the incumbent ministers retaining their positions—including, notably, Co-ordinating Minister for Economic Affairs Hatta Rajasa and Minister of Finance Agus Martowardojo. Opinion polls conducted in that month suggested that Yudhoyono's popularity had sunk to its lowest ebb; the President's perceived failure effectively to combat corruption and to address the country's economic challenges were two of the principal factors cited in the decline.

In December 2011 a student activist, Sondang Hutagalung, set himself on fire outside the presidential buildings; he subsequently died from his injuries. While Sondang's motivation remained unclear, the local media was quick to speculate that the student's self-immolation had been driven by deep discontent with the Government and the 'corrupted' state of Indonesian society. President Yudhoyono suffered a further setback in December 2012 when the Minister of State for Youth and Sports Affairs, Andi Mallarangeng, was forced to resign following allegations of his complicity in financial irregularities surrounding the construction of a large sports complex in Bogor in West Java. Mallarangeng's suspected involvement in the scandal was of particular embarrassment to Yudhoyono since he was the first serving government minister to be accused of corruption by the KPK since the commission's establishment in 2003. The President's problems mounted in February 2013 when the Chairman of the PD, Anas Urbaningrum, stood down from his post following accusations by the KPK that he too had been involved in the sports complex scandal; Yudhoyono was elected unopposed to the chairmanship at an extraordinary party congress the following month.

Meanwhile, Jakarta's second direct gubernatorial election was held in September 2012. The candidate supported by the majority of the opposition parties, Joko Widodo, defeated the incumbent Fauzi Bowo (who had the backing of the central Government) in a fiercely contested poll. In January 2013 the new, populist Governor was forced to declare a temporary state of emergency in the capital following severe flooding that left 32 people dead and inundated much of the city.

In October 2012 the number of provinces in Indonesia increased from 33 to 34 following the establishment of Kalimantan Utara (North Kalimantan), which was formed from four regencies of Kalimantan Timur (East Kalimantan) on the island of Borneo.

Following his assumption of the governorship of the central bank in May 2013, Agus Martowardojo was replaced as Minister of Finance by Dr Muhammad Chatib Basri. The reputation of the Government was once again tarnished by allegations of high-level corruption when Rudi Rubiandini, the chairman of the state petroleum and gas regulatory agency, SKK Migas, and former cabinet minister, was arrested by the KPK in August 2013 on suspicion of bribery. Furthermore, in September a former senior police officer, Inspector Gen. Djoko Susilo, was sentenced to 10 years in prison on corruption charges, and in the following month the Chief Justice of the Constitutional Court, Dr Akil Mochtar, was forced to resign following allegations of bribery.

Recent developments: the 2014 legislative elections

The legislative elections of 9 April 2014 were contested by 12 political parties nationally, with a further three local parties running in the province of Aceh (see below). Polling for the 132 regional delegates of the DPD, along with local elections, took place concurrently. According to provisional results (the official results and seat allocations were not due to be announced until May), there was no outright winner in the elections to the DPR; the PDI—P won some 18.9% of the votes cast, Golkar 14.6% and the Partai Gerakan Indonesia Raya (Gerindra—Great Indonesia Movement Party)—headed by the former Commander of Kostrad, Lt-Gen. Prabowo Subianto—12.0% (compared with just 4.5% in 2009). Support for the PD of the outgoing President, Yudhoyono, who, in accordance with the Constitution, was barred from seeking a third presidential term, was halved to around 9.8% of the vote. Since none of the parties achieved the requisite 25% of the vote to be eligible to present, on its own, a candidate for the presidential election, which was due to be held on 9 July, a series of intensive negotiations was undertaken during April in an attempt to establish parliamentary alliances that would enable a number of presidential nominees to be put forward. An early pledge by the Partai NasDem (National Democratic Party), which secured around 6.8% of the vote, to support the PDI—P ensured that the presidential nominee of the latter party, the populist Governor of Jakarta, Joko Widodo ('Jokowi'), would be able to contest the forthcoming poll.

The Threat of Terrorism

An ongoing challenge for successive Indonesian governments has been the threat posed by terrorist activity, at both a domestic and regional level. In October 2002 the Government's response to this threat was tested when two bombs exploded outside a nightclub in the tourist resort of Kuta, on the island of Bali. The explosions resulted in the deaths of 202 people, many of whom were Australian tourists. In its first admission that Islamist fundamentalists were operative within Indonesia, the Government initially attributed the attack to the international network of al-Qa'ida, which it believed had collaborated with local terrorists. The DPR authorized two emergency decrees, bringing into effect several previously delayed anti-terrorism measures, including a law permitting suspects to be detained for up to seven days without charge. The Muslim cleric Abu Bakar Bashir, commander of the Majelis Mujahidin Indonesia (MMI—Indonesian Mujahideen Council) and alleged to be the spiritual head of the regional Islamist organization Jemaah Islamiah (JI), was detained in connection with the attack. (He had been questioned by police in January over alleged links to al-Qa'ida but had been released without charge.) The USA and the UN announced that they had designated JI a terrorist entity and frozen its financial assets. The police made several further arrests as the investigation into the bombings proceeded and in November 2002 one of the suspects, Amrozi bin Nurhasyim, confessed to his involvement and to having strong links to JI, as well as implicating several others in the attack. Later in the same month Imam Samudra was arrested on suspicion of having organized the attack. He confessed to being a member of JI and to having planned earlier attacks, including the bombing of churches across the archipelago in December 2000 (see Provincial Affairs and Separatist Tensions), together with the operational leader of JI, Riduan Isamuddin (alias Hambali). In December 2002 Ali Gufron (alias Mukhlas), who apparently had succeeded Hambali as JI operational leader, was also arrested and confessed to having helped to plan the Bali attack.

In March 2003 the DPR gave its assent to legislation specifically designating terrorism as a crime and providing for detention without trial for terrorist suspects. The legislation was enacted retrospectively in order to cover the Bali bombings. In April the trial of Bashir on charges of, *inter alia*, subversion, immigration violations, and involvement in several terrorist attacks, including the December 2000 church bombings, began in Jakarta. In September 2003 Bashir was convicted of the subversion charges against him but, owing to insufficient evidence, was acquitted of any involvement in terrorist attacks and of being the spiritual leader of JI. He was sentenced to a four-year prison term, which on appeal was later reduced to three years, although the remaining charges against him were upheld. Bashir's sentence was further reduced to 18 months by the Supreme Court in March 2004. In the following month, immediately after his release from prison, Bashir was rearrested on suspicion of terrorism. Meanwhile, Idris (alias Jhoni Hendrawan), suspected of involvement in the Bali bombings, was reported to have been arrested in June 2003, and in August the Thai authorities announced that they had finally captured Hambali, who was subsequently taken into custody by the USA. Also in August Amrozi became the first person to be convicted in connection with the Bali bombings; his appeal against the death sentence was subsequently rejected. In the following month Imam Samudra was also convicted and sentenced to death; a further suspect, Ali Imron, was sentenced to life imprisonment, having expressed some remorse for his actions. In October Mukhlas was convicted of having helped to plan the attacks and was sentenced to death. (Amrozi, Imam Samudra and Mukhlas were executed in November 2008, their final appeals against the death sentence having been rejected by the Supreme Court during 2007.) In July 2004 the Constitutional Court declared that the counter-terrorism legislation approved in 2003 and used to convict a number of those responsible for the Bali bombings should not have been applied retroactively. The Minister of Justice and Human Rights Affairs stated that the ruling did not rescind the convictions already secured, but made it impossible to apply the law in future cases for crimes committed before its enactment.

In August 2003 an explosive device detonated by a suicide bomber outside the Marriott Hotel in Jakarta resulted in the deaths of 12 people. The police apprehended a number of suspects, all of whom were believed to be members of JI. In February 2004 Sardono Siliwangi was convicted of involvement in the attack; he was sentenced to a 10-year prison term. A second suspect, Mohammed Rais, was convicted in May and sentenced to seven years in prison. In August Idris was sentenced to 10 years' imprisonment for his part in the hotel bombing, but charges against him in connection with the Bali bombings were withdrawn, owing to the Constitutional Court's July ruling, despite an earlier confession of his involvement.

A bomb exploded outside the Australian embassy in Jakarta in September 2004, killing nine people and injuring more than 180 others. JI was held responsible for the attack, and a number of suspects were subsequently detained. In October the trial of Bashir on charges of conspiring and inciting acts of terrorism, including the Bali and Marriott bombings, commenced in Jakarta; he was again accused of being the spiritual leader of JI. In relation to the Bali attacks, Bashir was to be tried under the criminal code. In March 2005 Bashir was found guilty of conspiracy over the Bali attacks and sentenced to a prison term of two-and-a-half years, although he was acquitted of involvement in the Marriott bombing. Australia and the USA immediately expressed their disappointment at the leniency of the sentence. An appeal by Bashir against the verdict was rejected by the Supreme Court in August. However, Bashir's sentence was reduced as part of Indonesia's 60th anniversary of independence celebrations, and he was released from prison in June 2006. He again appealed against the original verdict, and in January 2007 his conviction was overruled by the Supreme Court on the grounds of insufficient evidence. Meanwhile, in July 2005 the first suspect to be tried in connection with the bombing of the Australian embassy in September 2004, the Islamist militant Irun Hidayat, was convicted of being an accessory to the attack and was sentenced to three-and-a-half years' imprisonment. In September three men were found guilty of helping to organize the attack; two of them received the death penalty, while the third was sentenced to 10 years' imprisonment.

In October 2005 Bali was again seriously affected by terrorist activity. Three bombs were detonated at tourist locations on the island, killing 23 people, including the bombers, and injuring more than 100 others. In November one of JI's senior leaders, the Malaysian bomb-maker Azahari Husin, who was suspected of organizing the previous month's bombings with fellow Malaysian Noordin Mohammad Top, was killed during an Indonesian police operation in Batu, near Malang, in East Java. In January 2006 Noordin released a statement claiming responsibility for the 2005 Bali attacks. In his message, Noordin also claimed to have formed a new South-East Asian Islamist militant organization, Tanzim Qaedat al-Jihad (Organization for the Basis of Jihad). In September 2006 four suspects were convicted of involvement in the 2005 Bali bombings and were sentenced to between eight and 18 years' imprisonment. In November eight members of JI were found guilty of carrying out and supporting terrorist activity; they received prison terms of between six years and life. In March 2007 police arrested several suspected JI members in the Javanese city of Yogyakarta; the militants were believed to have links to Abu Dujana, who, according to some reports, had become the commander of JI's military operations. In June Abu Dujana was one of eight suspects apprehended by the authorities in Central Java. On the same day, Zarkasih (also known as Nuaim or Mbah, among other aliases), who had acted as the head of JI since 2004, was also arrested. Both members of JI admitted their involvement with the organization and in April 2008 were sentenced to 15 years' imprisonment: Abu Dujana on charges of plotting terrorist activities and of sheltering other militants; and Zarkasih on charges of conspiring to commit terrorism and of supplying weapons and training to JI members. Meanwhile, two senior members of JI—Abdul Rohim, who was alleged to have replaced Zarkasih as JI leader following the latter's arrest, and Agus Purwanto—were apprehended in Malaysia in January and subsequently extradited to Indonesia.

In July 2009 the Marriott Hotel suffered a second terrorist attack when suicide bombers launched near-simultaneous strikes on the Marriott and Ritz-Carlton hotels in Jakarta. Six foreign tourists and one Indonesian were killed, as well as the two bombers themselves; more than 50 others were seriously injured. The bombers were widely believed to have links to JI, although no claim of responsibility was reported. In September the Indonesian authorities announced that Noordin Mohammad Top had been killed during a police operation in Central Java. The trials of three men accused of involvement in the Marriott and Ritz-Carlton bombings commenced in February 2010; in June the defendants each received prison sentences of between 18 months and eight years.

In July 2010 the Government formally established a new national anti-terrorism agency, which was to be responsible for all existing anti-terrorism divisions across the Government, the police force and the military. Meanwhile, in early 2010 the authorities announced the discovery in Aceh of a military training camp with purported links to Jemaah Ansharut Tauhid (JAT), a new terrorist network thought to have been established by Amar Usman (alias Dulmatin), a senior JI leader suspected of involvement in the 2002 Bali bombings. In February 2010 members of the cell were reported to have shot dead three police officers, and in the following month three suspected militants (one of whom was later confirmed to be Dulmatin) were killed in two separate police operations near Jakarta. Abdullah Sonata was subsequently reported to have replaced Dulmatin as leader of JAT, but was arrested in Java, together with two other suspected militants, in June. More than 100 other individuals had already been detained on suspicion of connection with the network. In August Abu Bakar Bashir was rearrested on suspicion of having helped to establish and fund JAT; in December he was charged with multiple counts of terrorist involvement.

Bashir was convicted in June 2011 and sentenced to 15 years' imprisonment. Following an appeal, in October the Jakarta High Court reduced Bashir's prison term to nine years 'on humanitarian grounds', prompting widespread anger. However, in February 2012 the Supreme Court overturned the High Court ruling, reinstating Bashir's 15-year sentence.

One of the main suspects in the 2002 Bali bombings, Umar Patek, an Indonesian national, was arrested in Pakistan in January 2011, and was extradited to Indonesia in August. Patek, who was alleged to have made the explosives used in the Bali attacks and to have had close links with Dulmatin, was charged with murder rather than terrorism in connection with the 2002 bombings, owing to the Constitutional Court's outlawing of the retroactive use of the 2003 counter-terrorism legislation (see above); however, he was also charged with, *inter alia*, assisting JAT in terrorist activities. Patek's trial commenced in February 2012, and in June, having been found guilty of murder, bomb-making and complicity in the church attacks of December 2000, he was sentenced to 20 years in prison.

Another suspect in the 2002 Bali bombings, Heru Kuncoro, was arrested in Central Java in June 2011, after the authorities uncovered a new terrorist plot against the police force, in which cyanide was to have been used to poison officers in revenge for their killing prominent terrorist leaders. Although the Government's crackdown on JI following the Bali bombings in 2002 was generally held to have proved relatively successful, a number of new, smaller terrorist organizations were reported to have been established and there were also incidents of attacks being organized by lone extremists. In October 2012 11 people were arrested on suspicion of planning bomb attacks on Western targets in Indonesia, including the US embassy in Jakarta and the offices of the mining company Freeport. The detainees were allegedly members of an Islamic group known as the Harakah Sunniyah Untuk Masyarakat Islami (HASMI—Sunni Movement for Islamic Society), which had been established in around 2009. HASMI denied any involvement in terrorism activity, claiming that it was engaged solely in peaceful activities such as education. The trial of five Islamist activists accused of plotting to carry out a bomb attack on the Myanma embassy in Jakarta in May 2013 commenced in November; the defendants, who were allegedly part of a network called the Negara Islam Indonesia (Islamic State of Indonesia), were reported to have been seeking revenge for the deaths of Rohingya Muslims during a period of prolonged communal unrest in Myanmar in 2012. In January 2014 the ringleader of the group was convicted of committing an act of terrorism and was sentenced to seven-and-a-half years in prison.

Provincial Affairs and Separatist Tensions

From 2000 a major challenge confronting successive governments was the escalation of communal violence across the archipelago, together with separatist tensions in individual regions such as Aceh and Irian Jaya (now Papua). Some of the worst such violence occurred in the provinces of Maluku and North Maluku, arising from the ongoing conflict between the region's Christian and Muslim populations. By mid-2000 more than 4,000 people were reported to have been killed and some 300,000 displaced. In June President Wahid declared a state of civil emergency in the two provinces and it was announced that around 1,400 of the 10,200 members of the armed forces in the region were to be replaced because they had become involved in the conflict. In the case of at least one outbreak of serious violence it was reported that evidence had emerged of the military's collusion with elements of the militant Muslim paramilitary organization Laskar Jihad, which had travelled to the region to participate in the campaign of violence. On 24 December 18 people were reported to have been killed and more than 80 others injured in a series of bombings of Christian churches in nine towns and cities across Indonesia, including Jakarta. In June 2002 an Iraqi citizen, Omar al-Faruq, who claimed to be the South-East Asian representative of al-Qa'ida, was arrested and allegedly confessed to having participated in carrying out the bombings. Following the bombings in Bali, a senior operative of JI also confessed to involvement in the church attacks. In a television broadcast in April 2004 four Malaysians detained in Indonesia admitted involvement in the church bombings and membership of JI. However, human rights groups claimed that the statements had been obtained through coercion.

Following negotiations between the warring Muslim and Christian factions in Maluku and North Maluku, the 'Malino II Agreement', which urged the expulsion of external groups such as Laskar Jihad from the area, was signed in February 2002. A series of bombings in the city of Ambon between February and April was condemned by the Government, but it insisted that it did not signify the failure of the peace agreement. In the latter month Alex Manuputty, the leader of the Christian separatist organization Front Kedaulatan Maluku (FKM—the Maluku Sovereignty Front), was arrested and charged with treason for planning to raise a flag to commemorate the 52nd anniversary of the proclamation of the South Maluku Republic. On 25 April FKM members raised flags in Ambon in remembrance of the anniversary, prompting the leader of Laskar Jihad, Ja'far Umar Thalib, to urge all Muslims in the region to renew their war against the Christian community. (In October 14 FKM members were sentenced to terms of imprisonment for raising the flags.) Violence broke out again in Ambon at the end of April, resulting in the deaths of 14 Christians. Thalib was arrested in May and was subsequently charged with inciting hatred and rebellion and defaming the President and Vice-President; he was later acquitted of all charges. In October, following the Bali bombings, Laskar Jihad reportedly disbanded and left the region; Thalib claimed that the decision had been taken owing to the group's increasing political involvement and denied that it had any connection to events in Bali. In January 2003 Manuputty and another Christian leader, Samuel Waileruny, were convicted of subversion and sentenced *in absentia* to three-year prison terms, later increased to four years. In late 2003, following the rejection of his appeal against his conviction by the Supreme Court, Manuputty fled to the USA; the Government's subsequent request for his deportation to Indonesia was turned down.

In April 2003 supporters of the separatist movement in Maluku were again alleged to have flown flags in commemoration of the anniversary of the proclamation of the South Maluku Republic; more than 120 people were subsequently prosecuted on charges of subversion. However, owing to the relative peace that had been maintained in the province since the signing of the Malino II Agreement, in September it was reported that the Government had revoked the state of civil emergency in Maluku; several battalions of peacekeeping troops would continue to be stationed in the province. The civil emergency status in North Maluku had been revoked in the previous year. In January 2004 nine men were sentenced to prison terms of up to 15 years for membership of the FKM. At least 40 people were killed and around 150 injured in violent clashes in Ambon in April, following a rally by a predominantly Christian separatist group on the island. More than 1,000 police officers and troops were dispatched in an attempt to quell the unrest. In May one person was killed and at least 22 others injured in a series of bomb explosions on Ambon. These events led some observers to question the long-term success of the peace treaty. In November Moses Tuanakotta, an FKM leader, was convicted of subversion and sentenced to nine years in prison for instigating the rally in April.

Meanwhile, in late 2001 violence also broke out on the island of Sulawesi, where ongoing religious tensions had caused approximately 1,000 deaths over the previous two years. In the first week of December at least seven people were killed and thousands left homeless following clashes between armed Muslim groups and Christians. The violence was believed to have been precipitated by the recent arrival of members of Laskar Jihad on the island, and more than 2,000 police and troop reinforcements were sent to the area. A peace agreement was concluded between the involved parties in late December, but explosions at four churches in the capital of Central Sulawesi, Palu, during New Year celebrations highlighted the continuing political instability on the island. In June 2002 a bomb exploded on a bus travelling towards Poso, Central Sulawesi, killing four people, and in December, two bombs exploded in Makassar, the capital of South Sulawesi, resulting in the deaths of three people.

In October 2003 an estimated 11 people died as a result of an outbreak of sectarian violence in Poso. There was speculation that the renewal of violence in Sulawesi had been co-ordinated by JI to coincide with the anniversary of the bombings in Bali. In the following month at least four more people died following an outbreak of anti-Christian violence in the city. In January 2004 a bomb exploded in the town of Palopo, South Sulawesi, killing four people. A subsequent series of attacks in Central Sulawesi included a bomb explosion on a bus in Poso in November 2004, which killed six people, and two explosions in a busy market in the predominantly Christian town of Tentena in May 2005, which claimed the lives of 21 people and injured dozens more. In July 24 alleged members of JI were arrested in connection with these attacks, as well as with the Bali bombings of 2002. In

October 2005 religious tensions were further exacerbated in Central Sulawesi by the beheading, allegedly by Islamist militants, of three Christian schoolgirls near Poso. In 2007 six suspected Islamist militants were convicted in connection with the murders and sentenced to terms of imprisonment ranging from 10 to 20 years.

In September 2006 three Christian men were executed following their convictions on charges of inciting an attack on an Islamic school in Poso, in which approximately 200 people had been killed in May 2000. Many Christians alleged that the three men were not the perpetrators of the attack, and demonstrations ensued. In October 2006 a Christian priest who had been one of the leaders of the protests against the executions was shot dead in Palu. In late 2007 several Muslim militants were convicted of carrying out attacks in Central Sulawesi—including the murder of the priest in October 2006 and the Tentena market bombings in May 2005—and were sentenced to lengthy terms in prison.

In April 2011 19 people were arrested on suspicion of planning a terrorist attack on Good Friday, following the discovery of a large unexploded bomb near a Catholic church in Jakarta. A suicide bomb attack at a church in Solo, Central Java, in September claimed the lives of at least two people and injured several others. In April 2012 the authorities in the Singkil region of southern Aceh ordered the closure of 20 Christian churches, and later that year the provincial government demanded the closure of nine more churches and five Buddhist temples. In a further indication of the rising levels of religious intolerance in Indonesia, two members of a minority Shi'a community in Madura, East Java, were killed and more than a dozen wounded in August in an unprovoked attack by several hundred anti-Shi'a fanatics armed with machetes. The previous month the religious leader of Madura's Shi'a community had been sentenced to two years' imprisonment after having been found guilty of blasphemy on the grounds of his religious teachings. Human rights groups claimed that the Indonesian Government was failing adequately to clamp down on the perpetrators of religious violence and that the relatively small number of individuals who were actually convicted of such offences were given overly lenient sentences.

East Timor (Timor-Leste)

During 1974 several parties emerged within the small Portuguese colony of East Timor (which became known as Timor-Leste following its accession to independence on 20 May 2002), with aims ranging from full independence to integration with Indonesia or Australia. Indonesia, which had never presented a claim to East Timor, initially showed little interest in the territory. In 1975 Portuguese forces withdrew from the colony, and the territory's capital, Dili, was occupied by the forces of the left-wing Frente Revolucionária do Timor Leste Independente (Fretilin), which advocated independence for East Timor. To prevent Fretilin from gaining full control of the island of Timor, Indonesian troops intervened and established a provincial government. (In December 2001 the declassification of US state papers relating to the Indonesian occupation revealed that the US Government had endorsed the invasion in the belief that it would curb the spread of communism in the region.) In July 1976 East Timor was declared the 27th province of Indonesia. Human rights organizations subsequently claimed that as many as 200,000 people, from a total population of 650,000, might have been killed by the Indonesian armed forces during the annexation. The UN continued officially to recognize Portugal as the administrative power in East Timor. In February 1983 the UN Commission on Human Rights adopted a resolution affirming East Timor's right to independence and self-determination. In November 1990 the Indonesian Government rejected proposals by the military commander of Fretilin, José Alexandre (Xanana) Gusmão, for unconditional peace negotiations aimed at ending the armed struggle in East Timor. In August 1992 the UN General Assembly adopted its first resolution condemning Indonesia's violations of human rights in East Timor.

Following the downfall of President Suharto, in August 1998 it was announced that Indonesia and Portugal had agreed to hold discussions on the possibility of 'wide-ranging' autonomy for East Timor. In January 1999 the Indonesian Government unexpectedly announced that, if the East Timorese were to vote to reject Indonesia's proposals for autonomy, it would consider granting independence to the province. Although the Government was initially opposed to a referendum on the issue of independence for East Timor, it signed an agreement with Portugal in May, giving its assent to a process of 'popular consultation' to take the form of a UN-supervised poll. The referendum proceeded on 30 August, and resulted in an overwhelming rejection, by 78.5% of voters, of the Indonesian Government's proposals for autonomy and in an endorsement of independence for East Timor. The announcement of the result of the referendum led to a rapid deterioration in the territory's security situation. In late September Indonesia and Portugal reiterated their agreement for the transfer of authority in East Timor to the UN. Also in late September the Indonesian armed forces formally relinquished responsibility for security in the territory to the UN peacekeeping force, the International Force for East Timor (Interfet); the last Indonesian troops left East Timor in late October. In the same month the result of the referendum was ratified by the Indonesian MPR, thus permitting East Timor's accession to independence to proceed (see Timor-Leste). In September 2000 Indonesia drew criticism from the UN and the international community following the murder of three UN aid workers by pro-Jakarta militias in West Timor. The militia groups were widely believed to be receiving the support of the Indonesian military. In December 2001 10 members of a pro-Indonesia militia became the first individuals to be convicted by the UN-sponsored Special Panel for Serious Crimes (SPSC) in Dili of crimes against humanity in connection with the violence of 1999. However, the Indonesian Government continued to obstruct efforts to bring all those culpable to justice, blocking attempts to extradite an 11th suspect, a special forces officer, to stand trial.

In January 2002 the Government established a special court in Jakarta to try those suspected of contravening human rights in East Timor in 1999. A total of 18 pro-Jakarta militiamen and Indonesian soldiers were prosecuted by the tribunal, the first trials of which began in March. Prior to its disbandment the tribunal passed just six convictions, prompting widespread international condemnation, with many observers insisting that the acquittal of 12 of the 18 defendants represented a gross miscarriage of justice. The six convicted men included former Governor of East Timor Abílio Soares, who was found guilty of failing to prevent violence involving his subordinates; Eurico Guterres, head of the youth wing of President Megawati's PDI—P; Lt-Col Soejarwo, Indonesia's military commander in Dili in 1999; and Maj.-Gen. Adam Damiri, the most senior military officer to have been charged. However, by August 2004 all six convictions had been overturned.

Meanwhile, in February 2003 the SPSC in Dili indicted Gen. (retd) Wiranto, Abílio Soares and 56 other Indonesian generals for crimes committed in East Timor; the Indonesian Government continued to refuse to hand over any of the accused for trial. The SPSC issued an arrest warrant for Wiranto in May 2004. In December Indonesia and Timor-Leste announced the establishment of a joint Commission of Truth and Friendship (CTF) to investigate human rights violations during the violence in East Timor in 1999. In the previous month the UN Security Council had expressed concern at Indonesia's failure to punish those responsible. The first hearing of the CTF opened on Bali in February 2007. Its 10 members were drawn from both Indonesia and Timor-Leste and included experts in the fields of law and human rights. In its final report, which was published in July 2008, the CTF concluded that the Indonesian Government, military and police bore 'institutional responsibility for gross human rights violations'. President Yudhoyono responded by stating his remorse, but critics were dissatisfied with the lack of a clear apology or of punishment for the perpetrators.

Aceh

In the mid-1970s dissent re-emerged in Aceh, which, at the end of the war of independence, had held the status of a full province of the Republic of Indonesia but which had subsequently had this status removed before being made a 'special district' (Daerah Istimewa) with considerable autonomy in religious and educational affairs. The dissent was provoked by the central Government's exploitation of Aceh's natural resources and the subsequent lack of benefits from these operations received by the region itself. A sense of the erosion of Aceh's autonomy was heightened by the migration and transmigration of other Indonesians into the region and by the increasing power of the central Government, and in 1976 the Gerakan Aceh Merdeka (GAM—Free Aceh Movement) was formed by Hasan di Tiro, who declared independence in 1977. This small-scale rebellion was swiftly suppressed by the armed forces; Tiro later established a government-in-exile in Sweden.

In 1989 opposition to the central Government arose again, this time led by the National Liberation Front Acheh Sumatra. The region was made a 'military operations zone' in 1990, thus allowing the armed forces far greater freedom to counter the uprising. By mid-1991 the rebellion had been largely suppressed; however, it was estimated that about 1,000 Acehnese had been killed in the process. The number of deaths continued to rise in subsequent years, and in 1993 the human rights organization Amnesty International estimated that about 2,000 Acehnese had been killed since 1989, with hundreds of others having 'disappeared'.

Aceh's status as a 'military operations zone' was revoked in June 1998, following the downfall of President Suharto in May, and an apology for past military excesses was made by Gen. Wiranto. However, the subsequent intended withdrawal of Indonesian troops from the territory was suspended following rioting in Aceh in September. Decentralization measures introduced by President Habibie failed to defuse resentment in the region, and public opinion in Aceh became increasingly sympathetic towards the notion of independence. In 1999 the discovery of several mass graves of people killed by the armed forces during security operations further exacerbated tension in the territory. Violence continued to escalate following the legislative elections in June as GAM guerrillas intensified their campaign for independence for Aceh.

In early November 1999, following the rejection by legislators in the regional assembly of demands for the holding of a referendum on self-determination for Aceh, a local government building in western Aceh was set on fire during a demonstration by 5,000 protesters. While much of the ongoing widespread violence in the territory was attributed to the separatist movement, some believed that a degree of the unrest was being initiated by 'provocateurs' acting to destabilize Aceh and undermine the separatist movement. Despite the Indonesian Government and Acehnese rebel negotiators reaching agreement in May 2000 on a ceasefire, which took effect the following month and was subsequently extended indefinitely, violence continued throughout the territory; Acehnese human rights groups estimated that more than 1,000 civilians died in clashes between the Indonesian military and Acehnese rebels during 2000. In December thousands of Acehnese protesters rallied peacefully in Banda Aceh, demanding independence for the territory. However, it was reported that at least 34 (and possibly as many as 200, according to human rights groups) unarmed civilians had been killed in the days preceding the rally as the result of military action to target Acehnese en route to the demonstration.

In April 2001 President Abdurrahman Wahid signed a decree authorizing the security forces to assist the military in restoring law and order in Aceh by targeting armed separatist organizations. This brought an end to the uneasy truce prevailing in the region. In July one of President Megawati's first official actions was to sign into law a special autonomy plan for Aceh intended to assuage the separatist movement. However, while generous in its scope, the legislation was criticized for failing to address the problems posed by the continued military presence in the area. Critics' concerns were borne out when some 30 civilians were massacred on an Aceh palm oil plantation in August. According to GAM, the military had carried out the attack as retribution for an earlier assault on a military post that had left several soldiers dead.

In January 2002 the commander of GAM, Abdullah Syafei, was killed during a gun battle with security forces on Sumatra; six other GAM members also died. Further fighting prompted the Government to resume a separate military command for Aceh, a decision denounced by both GAM and human rights groups. In May, following the instigation of peace discussions in Geneva, Switzerland, the Government and GAM agreed to work towards a ceasefire. However, the violence continued. Aceh's Legal Aid Institute reportedly claimed that 771 people had been killed in the region's conflict during the first six months of 2002.

In December 2002 government and GAM representatives finally signed a peace agreement in Geneva. As well as establishing an immediate ceasefire, the deal provided for free elections (to be held in 2004), which would establish an autonomous, although not independent, government, and included the granting of permission by the central Government to the Acehnese authorities to implement partial *Shari'a* law (Aceh's first *Shari'a* court was inaugurated in March 2003). The new regional government would retain 70% of all fuel revenues. In return, all rebels in the territory would disarm in designated areas. Following the signing of the peace accord, international peace monitors arrived in Aceh and established a Joint Security Committee. In February 2003 GAM rebels began surrendering their weapons, but by April the peace agreement was close to collapsing. Offices occupied by the international monitors had been attacked and, in one instance, burned down. At peace talks held in May in Tokyo, Japan, GAM negotiators refused to accept the Government's demands that the movement abandon its goal of independence, accept a special autonomy agreement and complete the disarmament of its forces. President Megawati immediately authorized the imposition of martial law in Aceh, initially for a six-month period, and the recommencement of military action against GAM. Owing to the restrictions placed on media reporting of the conflict, little independent information was available as to its progress throughout the succeeding months. In November the Government announced that it would extend its military operations in Aceh indefinitely, prompting international criticism. In December a bomb exploded at a market in the eastern town of Pereulak, killing 10 people.

The Government downgraded the status of martial law in Aceh to a state of civil emergency in May 2004, restoring power to the civilian Governor. The security forces, which were to remain in the territory, claimed to have killed some 2,000 suspected GAM rebels and arrested a further 3,000 since launching the military offensive against the separatist movement a year earlier. Human rights groups alleged that at least 300 of those killed had been civilians. In November President Yudhoyono extended the state of civil emergency in Aceh by up to six months and, during a visit to the territory, offered an amnesty to all GAM rebels who surrendered their weapons.

Following the tsunami disaster that devastated Aceh in December 2004, GAM and the Government agreed to an informal ceasefire to facilitate relief efforts. In mid-January 2005, however, the Chief of Staff of the Army announced that during the previous two weeks the security forces had killed 120 GAM rebels who had been stealing aid intended for victims of the tsunamis; GAM dismissed the claims of theft. None the less, the natural disaster appeared to have provided a new impetus for GAM and the Indonesian Government to seek a resolution to their conflict, and in late January formal talks between the two sides were held in Helsinki, Finland. After several rounds of negotiations, the two sides reached agreement in July upon the terms of a draft accord, which was formally signed on 15 August. GAM agreed to discard its long-standing claims for independence and the Indonesian Government was to allow GAM to operate as an official political party, a concession that would require constitutional change (current laws decreed that all political parties be based in Jakarta and that branches be maintained in at least one-half of the country's then 33 provinces). Furthermore, as agreed in 2002, Aceh was to be allocated up to 70% of the revenues earned from the exploitation of its natural resources (including petroleum and natural gas). In late August 2005 the Indonesian authorities released approximately 200 Acehnese detainees, including four senior GAM members, and the Government began a phased withdrawal of its 24,000 troops based in the region; by the end of the year almost 10,000 troops had departed. Meanwhile, GAM effected a process of complete disarmament within three months of the signing of the agreement. In July 2006 legislation was introduced granting Aceh partial autonomy and allowing for the formation of political parties in the territory. Although GAM agreed to its terms, critics argued that the law was strongly biased in favour of the central Government, which was to monitor all the affairs of the Acehnese administration; furthermore, management of petroleum and gas in Aceh was to be conducted jointly by the regional administration and the central Government.

In December 2006 Aceh held its first direct gubernatorial and district elections, formally marking the culmination of the peace process. The polls, which attracted a turnout of 85%, passed without incident. Irwandi Yusuf, an independent candidate and former GAM spokesman, secured the position of regional Governor, obtaining 38% of the total votes cast. In the same month the Indonesian Government finalized draft legislation providing for the establishment of local political parties in Aceh, although candidates would only be allowed to stand for seats within the House of Representatives in Jakarta if they secured the support of national parties and would be required to relinquish membership of their local party once nominated. In October 2008 Hasan di Tiro, the founder of GAM, returned to Aceh, thereby ending three decades of self-imposed exile; he died in June 2010. Zaini Abdullah, the former GAM 'foreign minister', was elected as Aceh's second Governor in gubernatorial and district elections held in April 2012, securing nearly 56% of the votes cast, and defeating the incumbent Yusuf (who won some 29% of the vote) and three other candidates. In March 2013 the Acehnese authorities approved the use of the former GAM flag as the official flag of Aceh, prompting tensions with the central Government, which subsequently demanded that the flag be changed on the grounds that it violated a law banning separatist symbols. A report published by Amnesty International in April claimed that the failure of the central Government to establish a 'truth commission' to investigate alleged human rights abuses perpetrated by both sides during the conflict between GAM and the Indonesian military constituted a breach of the commitments made under the 2005 peace accord. In December the newly elected Wali Nanggroe ('guardian of the state') of Aceh, Malik Mahmud al-Haytar, who was reportedly a former leader of GAM, was inaugurated as the head of a new bureaucracy set up to safeguard Acehnese culture and values.

Three local parties from Aceh were authorized to take part in the elections of 9 April 2014, in accordance with the 2005 peace agreement. Both the dominant local party, the Partai Aceh (PA—Aceh Party), which controls the Provincial Assembly in Aceh, and Irwandi Yusuf's Partai Nasional Aceh (PNA—Aceh National Party), comprised many former combatants from GAM. Rivalry between the PA and the PNA led to the deaths of several people in politically motivated violence during the campaign period. As local parties were unable to field candidates at national level, the PA formed an alliance with Gerindra to contest the national elections. (In the 2009 election it had allied itself with Yudhoyono's PD.)

Papua

In May 1977 a rebellion in the province of Irian Jaya (annexed to Indonesia in 1963—see Historical Context) was reported to have been organized by the Organisasi Papua Merdeka (OPM—Free Papua Movement), which sought unification with Papua New Guinea. Fighting continued until December 1979, when Indonesia and Papua New Guinea finalized a new border administrative agreement. However, frequent border incidents ensued, and in early 1984 fighting broke out in Jayapura, the capital of Irian Jaya. As a result, about 10,000 refugees fled over the border into Papua New Guinea. In October Indonesia and Papua New Guinea signed a five-year agreement establishing a joint border security committee; at the end of 1985 Indonesians were continuing to cross into Papua New Guinea, but a limited number of repatriations took place in 1986. There was also concern among native Irian Jayans (who are of Melanesian origin) at the introduction of large numbers of Javanese into the province, under the central Government's transmigration scheme. This was interpreted as an attempt to reduce the Melanesians to a minority and thus to stifle opposition. In 1986 it was announced that the Government intended to resettle 65m. people over a 20-year period, despite protests by human rights and conservation groups. Relations with Papua New Guinea improved when the Prime Minister, Paias Wingti, visited Suharto in January 1988. However, cross-border action by the Indonesian armed forces during October and November, in an attempt to capture Melanesian separatists operating on the border, led to renewed tension between the two countries. In October 1990 the Governments of Indonesia and Papua New Guinea renewed the basic accord on border arrangements, which included an agreement on the formation of a joint defence committee and a formal commitment to share border intelligence. In September 1992 the two countries agreed to facilitate the passage of border trade, and in the following month an Indonesian consulate was established in Vanimo, Papua New Guinea.

In April 1995 the Australian Council for Overseas Aid (ACFOA) alleged that 37 Irian Jayans had been killed by security forces near the copper and gold mine operated by PT Freeport Indonesia (a subsidiary of the US conglomerate Freeport-McMoran) between June 1994 and February 1995. In August the ACFOA's claims were reiterated by NGOs, which lodged a complaint with the National Commission on Human Rights in Jakarta about summary executions, arbitrary detentions and torture in the province between mid-1994 and mid-1995. In November 1995 four members of the Indonesian armed forces were arrested in an investigation into the killing in May of 11 unarmed civilians at a prayer meeting. Also in November the Overseas Private Investment Corporation (a US government agency) cancelled political risk insurance valued at US $100m. for Freeport, citing environmental concerns. Freeport's perceived responsibility for the situation in Irian Jaya arose from its role as civil administrator in the area of the mine and also because the indigenous inhabitants' campaigns against Freeport's indiscriminate exploitation of natural resources in the area often resulted in their being killed by security forces as suspected members of the OPM.

In December 1995 clashes between Indonesian forces and the OPM intensified, forcing hundreds of refugees to cross into Papua New Guinea. Four people were killed in riots in Jayapura in March 1996. Riots near the Grasberg mine in the same month were the result of problems similar to those experienced by residents in the area around the Freeport mine (relating principally to the lack of any benefit from the mining project to the local community and to the potential adverse impact of the project on the local environment). There were also tensions among the local Irianese, Indonesians from other provinces and commercial operators. In April Freeport agreed to allocate 1% of revenue over a period of 10 years to community development programmes for tribal groups living around the mine, and to improve environmental safeguards.

Seven people were reported to have been killed in outbreaks of violence in Jayapura and the island of Biak in July 1998. In October the Government revoked the status of Irian Jaya as a 'military operations zone' following the conclusion of a ceasefire agreement with the OPM in September, but this was not followed by the withdrawal of troops from the region. In February 1999 Irian Jayan tribal leaders raised the issue of independence for the province at a meeting with President Habibie. (A referendum on self-determination for the province had been promised by the Indonesian Government prior to the territory's annexation in 1963; however, while a vote was eventually held in 1969, only tribal chiefs selected by Jakarta were allowed to participate and the result was widely discredited.) The independence movement in the province continued to strengthen throughout 1999, and was encouraged by the achievements of the East Timorese independence movement. In December independence demonstrations took place throughout Irian Jaya. A delegation from the DPR visited the province and announced that the administration of the newly elected President Abdurrahman Wahid had agreed to the popular demand that the province's name be changed from Irian Jaya to West Papua, although it was emphasized that this decision should not be construed as implying the Government's approval of any action towards the province's secession from Indonesia. (However, it was subsequently reported that the proposed change had not been approved by the Indonesian legislature.)

In mid-2000 the Papuan People's Congress, held in Jayapura, adopted a five-point resolution reinstating a unilateral declaration of independence for West Papua originally made in 1961, before the province's annexation to Indonesia. However, the declaration was immediately rebuffed by the Indonesian Government. In October 2000 30–40 people were killed and many others injured in clashes between police and West Papuan separatists in the town of Wamena when police attempted to remove a Morning Star independence flag being flown by the separatists. Although President Wahid had previously decreed that the flying of the Morning Star flag was allowed, provided that the flag was flown alongside, and slightly lower than, the Indonesian flag, following the violence the Government introduced a ban on the flying of the flag. In November and December the Indonesian military took severe action against separatists; seven people were shot dead by the armed forces in an outbreak of violence in the town of Merauke, and dozens of separatist sympathizers, including the pro-independence leader of the Presidium Dewan Papua (PDP—Papua Presidium Council), Theys Eluay, were arrested.

In March 2001 five West Papuan separatist leaders, including Theys Eluay, were released on bail to await trial on charges of treason. In October the DPR approved legislation giving Irian Jaya greater autonomy and a larger share of tax revenues. Furthermore, the so-called Special Autonomy Law for Papua also proposed that the region be officially known as Papua and made provision for a bicameral Papuan People's Council, intended to safeguard indigenous interests. However, the separatist PDP swiftly rejected the legislation as it failed to grant Irian Jaya complete independence. In November Theys Eluay was found dead in his car. He was believed to have been assassinated and military involvement was suspected. In December hundreds of students occupied the parliament building in Jayapura to demand a referendum on independence and to express their anger at the authorities' failure to find the killer of Theys Eluay. The protest took place just days before the autonomy reforms came into force on 1 January 2002, when the province officially became known as Papua.

In August 2002 two US citizens and an Indonesian were killed following an ambush near the Freeport mine. In November it was alleged by police that Kopassus soldiers had been involved in the attack. (In June 2004 the US authorities indicted *in absentia* Anthonius Wamang, an Indonesian, for murdering the two US citizens, describing him as an operational commander for the OPM, although human rights groups reportedly claimed that Wamang had close links to the Kopassus special forces.) In April 2003 four Kopassus officers and three soldiers were convicted of the abduction, torture and murder of Theys Eluay and were sentenced to brief prison terms. However, the trial was criticized both for the leniency of the verdicts and for its failure to investigate the reasons behind the murder of Eluay. Meanwhile, in January 2003 the central Government approved legislation that would lead to the division of Papua into three smaller provinces—Central Papua, East Papua and West Irian Jaya. The proposal angered local leaders, who claimed that such action would threaten the region's autonomy. Following reports that six people had died during fighting in Timika, the designated capital of Central Papua, the formal creation of Central Papua was postponed. However, the appointment of a Governor for West Irian Jaya was approved in November. In November 2004 the Constitutional Court simultaneously overruled the law dividing Papua province into three and ratified the creation of the province of West Irian Jaya (which was formally renamed West Papua—or Papua Barat—in April 2007) as an established fact; the original province of Papua was, therefore, now composed of two constituent parts—the provinces of West Irian Jaya and Papua. Meanwhile, in the latter half of 2003 it was reported that 10 members of the OPM had been killed in clashes with government troops in Papua. In December the appointment of Brig.-Gen. Timbul Silaen to the post of regional police commander was criticized by the USA, owing to Silaen's indictment for crimes against humanity in East Timor. In March 2004 it was reported that Leo Warisman, a leader of the OPM, had been killed in a gunfight with security forces in Papua. Another OPM leader, Yance Hembring, was sentenced to 10 years' imprisonment by a court in Jayapura in August for advocating Papua's independence. In December at least five people were injured and 18 arrested during violent clashes between protesters and police at a pro-independence rally in Jayapura.

In October 2005 the Papuan People's Council (Majelis Rakyat Papua—MRP) was formally established; it was charged primarily with the issue of the partition of Papua and with the forthcoming gubernatorial elections. Originally scheduled to be held in November, the elections were twice postponed, owing to poor administrative planning, but finally proceeded in March 2006. Barnabas Suebu was subsequently pronounced Governor of Papua. In January 2006 more than 200 demonstrators forced their way into the local legislative building and demanded the immediate withdrawal of all Indonesian military personnel from the province. In February the Minister of Defence, Juwono Sudarsono, conceded that some members of the Indonesian military and police force had committed human rights abuses, including torture and rape, against local residents in Papua. In the same month the Constitutional Court officially reaffirmed the legitimacy of West Irian Jaya's status as a separate province, maintaining that the 2001 Special Autonomy Law for Papua could not be applied retroactively. In March 2006 five members of the security forces were killed in Jayapura by demonstrators reiterating demands for the closure of the Freeport mine, which continued to be regarded locally as a symbol of oppression, and in the following month four people, including two soldiers, were killed in an assault on an army post in Papua.

In February 2007 the international NGO Human Rights Watch drew attention to the continued imprisonment of 18 Papuan activists, who were reported to have received substantial sentences following their peaceful protests in support of Papuan self-determination. The organization urged the Indonesian Government to release these prisoners and to abandon charges against other political detainees who had yet to be brought to trial. In July Human Rights Watch accused the Papuan police force of perpetrating, with apparent impunity, extrajudicial killings and other serious abuses.

A number of people were killed and dozens injured during several days of fighting in October 2007 between rival tribal groups near the Freeport mine. The mine was the scene of another attack, in July 2009, when an Indonesian police officer and an Australian security guard were fatally shot in an attack attributed by the police to the OPM (although subsequent revelations cast doubt on this theory and the OPM denied any involvement). In December a senior leader of the OPM, Kelly Kwalik, who the authorities claimed had been involved in a series of attacks, including the 2002 Freeport ambush, was killed during a police operation in Timika; his death prompted a wave of anti-Indonesian protests and demands for self-determination for Papuans. A three-month strike by employees at the Freeport mine in late 2011, which severely hindered production, was finally concluded in December after the company agreed to a substantial increase in staff wages, together with improved housing and retirement benefits.

Meanwhile, in June 2010 the lower house of the MRP voted to reject Special Autonomy status. In July an estimated 50,000 Papuans took to the streets of Jayapura, and urged the upper house of the provincial legislature to endorse the decision. Demands for full autonomy intensified following the release on the internet in October of a video recording purporting to show two men in military uniforms torturing indigenous Papuan civilians; the central Government subsequently confirmed that the aggressors in the footage were members of the Indonesian army, and in January 2011 a military tribunal sentenced the two men to prison terms of eight and nine months, respectively, while their sergeant was sentenced to 10 months' imprisonment. Meanwhile, in December 2010 four Indonesian soldiers were sentenced to up to seven months' imprisonment after being convicted of torturing Papuan civilians in a separate incident.

In early August 2011 thousands of Papuans marched on the parliament building in Jayapura, demanding the holding of a referendum on the question of Papuan self-determination. In October Indonesian troops fired tear gas and warning shots at members of the Third Papuan People's Congress gathered in Abepura and arrested dozens of those in attendance; the authorities claimed that the Congress had issued a declaration of independence and announced the formation of a transitional government for Papua. Although it was reported that three people had been killed, the authorities denied that there had been any casualties. The trial of five activists accused of treason in connection with the incident began in January 2012; having been convicted in March, they each received sentences of three years' imprisonment. The situation in Papua remained tense throughout the remainder of the year and into 2013, with a series of violent incidents reportedly taking place between separatists and the security forces. The apparently unprovoked fatal shooting by police of an activist in June 2012 led to a riot in Jayapura during which cars and buildings were set alight. In November three police officers were killed in an attack by unidentified gunmen on a police outpost in Pirime in the Jayawija district of Papua. The OPM was widely believed to have been responsible for the deaths of eight soldiers in two separate attacks on military posts in the Puncak Jaya district in February 2013. According to Australian media reports, at least 11 OPM supporters were killed by Indonesian counter-terrorist troops in a village in the central highlands of Papua in May. It was reported that in November at least one person was killed and others injured when Indonesian police opened fire on a crowd of around 800 demonstrators in Jayapura. The protest had been staged by the Komite Nasional Papua Barat (KNPB—West Papua National Committee), which demanded the holding of a referendum on Papuan independence. In February 2014 five men who had been arrested in May 2013 for raising the banned Morning Star flag at a ceremony commemorating the 50th anniversary of Indonesia's annexation of West Papua were sentenced to terms of imprisonment ranging from 22 months to three years.

During an official visit to Indonesia by Prime Minister Peter O'Neill of Papua New Guinea in June 2013, the two countries signed a controversial extradition treaty, which, some claimed, would be used by Indonesia primarily to demand the extradition of separatist activists from Papua province seeking refuge in Papua New Guinea.

Foreign Affairs

Regional relations

Indonesia's foreign policy has focused on its leading role in the regional grouping of the Association of Southeast Asian Nations (ASEAN, see p. 211), which it founded, together with Malaysia, the Philippines, Singapore and Thailand, in 1967. Indonesia supported the organization's opposition to Viet Nam's military presence in Cambodia and played a prominent role in attempts to find a political solution to the situation in Cambodia (q.v.). In 1989 Indonesia was also one of the founding members of the Asia-Pacific Economic Cooperation (APEC, see p. 201). In October 2008 Indonesia became the final member state to ratify the

ASEAN charter, which declared among its purposes the promotion of democracy and good governance, and the creation of a single market. Indonesia assumed the annually rotating chair of ASEAN in 2011. At the ASEAN summit meeting held in Bali in November, President Susilo Bambang Yudhoyono asserted that the regional grouping had recorded a number of positive developments under Indonesia's chairmanship, including the signing of the Bali Declaration on the ASEAN Community in a Global Community of Nations (commonly known as the Bali Concord III), which pledged increased co-operation in the fields of, *inter alia*, politics, security, economics and culture, at both regional and global level; the agreement also defined development issues pertaining to the implementation, by 2015, of an ASEAN Economic Community and the promotion of ASEAN's full integration into the global economy. The 25th summit meeting of APEC was held in Bali in October 2013.

Diplomatic relations with China, suspended since 1967 owing to its alleged complicity in the 1965 attempted coup in Indonesia, were finally restored in 1990 following an Indonesian undertaking to settle financial debts incurred with China by the Sukarno regime. Bilateral relations suffered a reverse in 1998 following the violence perpetrated against ethnic Chinese Indonesians at the time of the removal of President Suharto in May. China issued a strong diplomatic protest; President Habibie publicly expressed his sympathy for the plight of the ethnic Chinese victims of violence. Subsequently, in May 1999, as part of a programme of general reform, Habibie removed a ban that had existed on the use and teaching of the Mandarin Chinese language within Indonesia. The two countries signed a strategic partnership agreement, intended to promote bilateral trade, investment and maritime co-operation, in April 2005; a further agreement, aimed at enhancing co-operation in the political, legal and security fields, was signed in January 2010. Between 2003 and 2010 Sino-Indonesian bilateral trade increased almost tenfold. The strengthening ties between Indonesia and China were clearly illustrated when, during a visit to Jakarta in October 2013, the new Chinese President, Xi Jinping, became the first foreign leader ever to address the Indonesian legislature.

Indonesia and Australia restored defence co-operation links in April 1990, following a four-year hiatus. In September 1994 Vice-President Sutrisno became the first senior Indonesian official to visit Australia since Suharto's last visit in 1975. In July 1995 Indonesia withdrew the nomination of Lt-Gen. Herman Mantiri, a former Chief of the General Staff, as ambassador to Australia, owing to widespread protests there concerning his defence of the actions of the Indonesian armed forces in the 1991 Dili massacre of unarmed civilians (see Timor-Leste). Relations with Australia were also strained by, *inter alia*, Australia's decision to investigate claims of new evidence about the killing of six Australia-based journalists, in two separate incidents, during the annexation of East Timor in 1975. The Indonesian Government claimed that the journalists had died in crossfire. However, separate reports published by the Australian Government, in June 1996, and by Switzerland-based human rights organization International Commission of Jurists, in 1998, concluded that the journalists had been killed by Indonesian troops, in order to conceal Indonesia's invasion of East Timor; in October 1998 it was announced that Australia was to reopen a judicial inquiry into the killings. In November 2007 the Deputy State Coroner of New South Wales ruled that five of the Australia-based journalists (the 'Balibo five') had been deliberately killed by Indonesian special forces, declaring that there was sufficient evidence for the case to constitute a war crime.

Meanwhile, in October 1996 the Australia-Indonesia Development Area was created to develop bilateral economic links, and in March 1997 Indonesia and Australia signed a treaty defining permanent maritime boundaries between the two countries. Following the downfall of Suharto in May 1998, relations between Indonesia and Australia continued to be affected by the issue of East Timor. In January 1999 the Indonesian Government expressed its 'deep regret' at Australia's announcement earlier in that month that it was to change its policy on East Timor and actively promote 'self-determination' in the territory. Following the vote in favour of independence held in East Timor in August, Australia committed 4,500 peacekeeping troops to Interfet, which was formed by the UN to restore order in the territory following the violence perpetrated by pro-Jakarta militias after the announcement of the result of the poll. A military co-operation agreement signed between Indonesia and Australia in December 1995 was reported, in October 1999, to have been cancelled as a result of the Indonesian Government's displeasure at Australia's leading involvement in the peacekeeping operation.

In November 2000 the Australian ambassador to Indonesia, John McCarthy, was physically attacked by a pro-Jakarta mob in Makassar, Sulawesi. The Australian Government accepted the Indonesian Government's apology for the incident. In June 2001, following several postponements, President Abdurrahman Wahid paid an official visit to Australia, the first by an Indonesian head of state for 26 years. In August the Australian Prime Minister, John Howard, became the first foreign leader to make an official visit to Indonesia following President Megawati's assumption of power.

However, relations were strained once again later in August 2001 when a cargo ship carrying hundreds of mainly Afghan asylum seekers became stranded in the international waters between the two countries. Neither country agreed to accept responsibility for the refugees. In September the Australian Minister for Foreign Affairs, Alexander Downer, arrived in Jakarta for discussions with Indonesian ministers on the problems raised by illegal trafficking of immigrants. In October more than 350 refugees, believed to be heading for Australia, drowned when their boat sank off the Indonesian coast, and in the same month a missing boat carrying approximately 170 Iraqi and Afghan asylum seekers was found on the Indonesian island of Wera. In February 2002 Indonesia and Australia co-hosted the inaugural 'Bali Process' regional ministerial summit on people-smuggling, human-trafficking and related transnational crime. (Four further summit meetings were co-hosted by Indonesia and Australia between 2003 and 2013, by which time more than 50 countries, as well as numerous international organizations, participated in the 'Bali Process'.)

Both the Speaker of the DPR and the Speaker of the MPR cancelled scheduled meetings with Howard during his visit to Indonesia in February 2002; during the Australian Prime Minister's stay, students protested in response to allegations that Australia was providing funding for separatist groups in Aceh and Papua. Howard denied such charges and signed an agreement with President Megawati concerning counter-terrorism measures. In May, following an initiative proposed during Howard's visit, the inaugural Australia-Indonesia dialogue was held in Bogor, where Minister of Foreign Affairs Hassan Wirajuda met with his Australian counterpart, Downer.

In October 2002 Indonesia's relations with Australia were seriously affected by the bomb attacks on the island of Bali, a popular destination for Australian tourists, which resulted in the deaths of almost 90 Australian citizens. While the Australian Government immediately offered assistance to Indonesia, a subsequent series of raids on the homes of Indonesian Muslims resident in Australia prompted Vice-President Hamzah Haz to warn that such an offensive could damage bilateral relations. In February 2004 Australia and Indonesia co-hosted the Bali Regional Ministerial Meeting on Counter-Terrorism on Bali; a second conference was co-hosted by the two countries in Jakarta in March 2007. In December 2004, however, bilateral relations were strained by the Australian Government's announcement that it was to create a coastal security zone extending five times as far as its territorial waters.

Following the tsunami disaster of December 2004, Australia dispatched some 1,000 troops to assist with relief operations in the province of Aceh and pledged US $773m. in aid to the Indonesian Government. Prime Minister Howard visited Aceh in February 2005. In the same month, however, the lenience of Abu Bakar Bashir's sentence for his role in the 2002 Bali bombings (see The Threat of Terrorism) was heavily criticized by the Australian Government. In April 2005 President Yudhoyono and Prime Minister Howard signed a Comprehensive Partnership Agreement, which addressed economic, trade, security and reconstruction issues.

Indonesia's relations with Australia were threatened in February 2006 by the conviction of the 'Bali nine'—a group of nine Australians who had been arrested by the Indonesian authorities in April 2005 for attempting to smuggle a large quantity of heroin into Australia from the Indonesian island. The two ringleaders of the group were sentenced to death by firing squad, while the seven drugs couriers were all sentenced to life imprisonment. At April 2014 the two ringleaders, having lost a number of judicial appeals, were still awaiting execution.

In January 2006 a dispute arose over the case of 43 Papuans who had fled to Australia by boat in search of asylum from alleged human rights abuses; the refugees claimed that they had been tortured while imprisoned without charge, and that they had witnessed the shooting of friends and relatives. Following the Australian Government's announcement in March that all but one of the asylum seekers were to be granted temporary visas, Indonesia recalled its ambassador from Canberra, accusing Australia of giving tacit support to the Papuan separatist movement. The ambassador returned to Australia in June, prior to Prime Minister Howard's visit to the Indonesian island of Batam to meet with President Yudhoyono, and in July the remaining detainee was finally granted a temporary visa.

In November 2006 Indonesian Minister of Foreign Affairs Wirajuda and his Australian counterpart, Downer, signed a security pact to promote co-operation in law enforcement and counter-terrorism. Yudhoyono met with the new Australian Prime Minister, Kevin Rudd, during the latter's visit to Indonesia in June 2008, when the two leaders agreed to collaborate in the areas of defence, the economy and the environment. Relations were further consolidated by a number of senior-level bilateral visits during 2010, including that of Yudhoyono to Australia in March, and a reciprocal visit by Prime Minister Julia Gillard (who had replaced Rudd in June) in November. Under the terms of a disaster management plan agreed between the two countries in late 2011, Australia was to provide US $1m. towards a secretariat in Jakarta to help to co-ordinate the region's response to natural disasters and to supply Indonesia with four aircraft intended to help that country's humanitarian assistance efforts. Negotiations on a proposed Indonesia-Australia Comprehensive Economic Partnership Agreement commenced in Jakarta in September 2012. In November Prime Minister Gillard organized an historic trilateral meeting in Bali between herself, President Yudhoyono and the Prime Minister of Timor-Leste, Kay Rala (Xanana) Gusmão, on the sidelines of the fifth annual Bali Democracy Forum.

Following his resumption of the Australian premiership in June 2013, Prime Minister Rudd travelled to Indonesia to hold talks with President Yudhoyono, including on the pressing issue of people-smuggling and deepening trade ties. In response to the recent sharp increase in asylum seekers arriving in Australia via Indonesia, Yudhoyono offered to host a regional meeting—involving countries of origin, transit and destination—to attempt to address the problem. However, relations between Indonesia and Australia soured somewhat when, shortly after assuming power in September, the new Australian Prime Minister, Tony Abbott, announced that asylum seekers setting out for Australia from Indonesia by boat would now be intercepted en route by the Australian navy and returned to their point of departure. The Indonesian authorities claimed that such action could potentially constitute a violation of their country's sovereignty. During an official visit by Abbott to Jakarta in late September (notably, his first official foreign visit) the new Australian Prime Minister attempted to assuage these concerns by stressing that his country respected Indonesia's sovereignty and territorial integrity. Relations deteriorated markedly in November, however, following allegations that Australian embassies (including that in Jakarta) had been used as part of a US-led spying network in Asia; the Australian Government declined to comment on the reports, which were based on leaked official US documents. In the wake of further revelations later that month that Australian espionage agencies had monitored the telephone calls of President Yudhoyono, his wife, Vice-President Boediono and other senior ministers in 2009, the Indonesian ambassador to Australia was recalled and Indonesia suspended co-ordinated military co-operation (including anti-people-smuggling operations) with Australia. In January 2014 the Indonesian authorities alleged that the Australian navy had violated Indonesia's sovereignty on several occasions during operations to turn back boats carrying asylum seekers.

The forced repatriation in early 1998 of thousands of Indonesian workers from Malaysia as a result of the regional economic crisis placed a strain on relations between the two countries. Relations were further exacerbated in October when the Indonesian Government condemned the treatment received in custody by the former Malaysian Deputy Prime Minister and Minister of Finance, Anwar Ibrahim (see Malaysia), breaking with a tradition among ASEAN countries of non-interference in the internal affairs of other member countries. In May 2002 Indonesia signed a trilateral security pact with Malaysia and the Philippines, enabling the signatories to exchange intelligence and launch joint police operations in an attempt to combat terrorism in the region; Cambodia and Thailand later also acceded to the agreement.

In August 2002 relations with Malaysia were affected by that country's introduction of stringent anti-immigration laws, which resulted in the forced deportation of many illegal immigrants, most of whom were Indonesian, and provoked protests outside the Malaysian embassy in Jakarta. In early February 2005 Malaysia extended an amnesty for illegal immigrants to leave the country if they were to avoid legal action, in response to a written request from President Yudhoyono. In the same month Yudhoyono visited both Malaysia and Singapore to meet with Malaysian Prime Minister Abdullah Badawi and Singaporean Prime Minister Lee Hsien Loong; this was the first visit to Singapore by an Indonesian head of state since 1974. In April 2007 Indonesia concluded agreements with Singapore relating to extradition and defence co-operation.

Indonesia's diplomatic relations with both Malaysia and Singapore were placed under considerable strain in mid-2013 as a result of the record high levels of air pollution experienced in the two countries caused by a persistent smog from the fires used in illegal land-clearing practices in Sumatra. President Yudhoyono offered an official apology to both countries for the hazardous haze and stated that extensive efforts were being made to extinguish the fires.

Meanwhile, in May 2002 President Megawati attracted criticism when she attended celebrations in Timor-Leste to mark the territory's official accession to nation status; in February Indonesia and East Timor had agreed to establish full diplomatic relations following independence. The inaugural meeting of the Indonesia-Timor-Leste Joint Ministerial Commission for Bilateral Co-operation took place in Jakarta in October. In April 2005, during an official visit to Timor-Leste, President Yudhoyono met with Timorese President Gusmão; the two heads of state signed a border agreement resolving the demarcation of approximately 96% of the land borders between the two countries.

Indonesia signed an important free trade agreement with Japan in August 2007 during a state visit by Prime Minister Shinzo Abe to Jakarta. The agreement envisaged the eventual removal of most bilateral import taxes (with the notable exception of Japanese imports of rice). Indonesia also confirmed its supplies of liquefied natural gas to Japan. The Japan-Indonesia Economic Partnership Agreement entered into force in July 2008.

Other external relations

In response to the Dili massacre in November 1991, the US Congress imposed a ban on International Military Education and Training (IMET) to Indonesia in 1992; in March 1996 the ban was relaxed to allow members of ABRI, excluding military officers, to attend IMET courses. However, in September 1999 US President Bill Clinton announced the suspension of military assistance to Indonesia following ABRI's 'campaign of destruction' in East Timor. Later that month the US Senate passed legislation banning all military co-operation, including IMET, for Indonesia until that country honoured the results of the August 1999 referendum and allowed independence to be granted to East Timor. In late October 2000 and early November Muslim groups rallied outside the US embassy in Jakarta, calling for *jihad*; threats were made against US citizens in Indonesia; US companies in the country were attacked; and it was reported that the Indonesian Government had requested the immediate removal and replacement of the recently appointed US ambassador, Robert Gelbard, for his alleged interference in Indonesian domestic affairs.

President Megawati visited Washington, DC, in mid-September 2001, becoming the first leader of a predominantly Muslim country to meet with US President George W. Bush in the aftermath of the terrorist attacks of 11 September 2001; the two heads of state issued a joint statement in which they agreed to 'strengthen bilateral co-operation on counter-terrorism'. However, following the commencement of air strikes against the Taliban regime in Afghanistan in October, fundamentalist Muslims in Indonesia threatened violence if the Indonesian Government did not sever diplomatic relations with the USA. In October the Front Pembela Islam (FPI—Islamic Defenders' Front) warned that if British and US citizens did not leave the country immediately their safety could not be guaranteed. Megawati, under pressure from Muslim groups and Vice-President Hamzah Haz, indirectly condemned the US attacks in Afghanistan for the first time.

In April 2002 Indonesia and the USA held sensitive security talks, during which measures to combat terrorism and to strengthen civilian control over the armed forces were discussed. In July the US Congress approved legislation awarding

US $16m. to the Indonesian police forces; this included $12m. for the establishment of a dedicated anti-terrorism unit, and followed a vote by the Senate to remove restrictions on the provision of IMET to Indonesia, pending congressional approval. In August, during a two-day visit to Indonesia, US Secretary of State Colin Powell granted some $50m. of funding for Indonesia's police and counter-terrorism units over a three-year period. However, following the murders in the same month of two US citizens in Papua and the 'insufficient co-operation' with the resultant investigation on the part of the Indonesian Government and military, the US Congress voted against the restoration of normal military relations, including any further relaxation of IMET. In early 2003 the USA placed Indonesia on a list of countries whose citizens were required to register with the US immigration authorities if they visited the country. Nevertheless, in October President Bush visited Indonesia and announced plans for a $157m. programme to improve education in the country in an attempt to create a system that would discourage the development of Islamist extremism.

The USA took an active part in relief operations in Indonesia following the tsunami disaster of December 2004, notably deploying some 13,000 military personnel in the region. In February 2005 US Secretary of State Condoleezza Rice announced a full resumption of IMET for Indonesia (although this excluded the training of Indonesia's élite special forces, Kopassus), stating that Indonesian co-operation in the investigation of the two murdered US citizens in Papua had 'met the conditions set by Congress'. In May President Yudhoyono made an official visit to the USA, during which he met with President Bush. In a joint communiqué, the two heads of state stressed their common commitment to work towards the establishment of normal military relations; to improve economic co-operation and trade relations; and to strengthen co-operation and investment in the fields of counter-terrorism, energy and education. Bush reiterated the US Administration's support for Indonesia's territorial integrity and its opposition to secessionist movements within the archipelago. In the same month the USA resumed the export of non-lethal defence articles to Indonesia. In November the USA resumed the export of lethal defence articles and Foreign Military Financing (FMF) for Indonesia, thereby achieving the normalization of military bilateral relations.

The election in November 2008 of US President Barack Obama, who had lived in Indonesia for several years during childhood, was warmly welcomed by the Indonesian Government and public alike. In February 2009 the new US Secretary of State, Hillary Clinton, visited Indonesia, holding discussions with Indonesian Minister of Foreign Affairs Wirajuda on a range of issues, including security, trade and counter-terrorism. In June 2010 Indonesia and the USA signed the Framework Arrangement on Cooperative Activities in the Field of Defense, a wide-ranging agreement that was intended to integrate existing collaboration between the two countries.

In July 2010 US Secretary of Defense Robert Gates announced that the USA was gradually to resume the training of Kopassus, owing to positive reforms within Indonesia's military and assurances that further such measures were to be implemented. Human Rights Watch and other rights organizations expressed reservations about the announcement, claiming that individuals still active within Kopassus were guilty of human rights transgressions and did not appear likely ever to be brought to justice. During a short visit to Indonesia by Obama in the course of a tour of Asia in November, the US President emphasized Indonesia's global importance as a rising economic power, while appealing for increased co-operation on efforts to address the challenge posed by religious extremism. In September 2012, as part of an extensive tour of South-East Asia, US Secretary of State Clinton held talks with President Yudhoyono and her Indonesian counterpart in Jakarta.

Meanwhile, in December 1999, with the issue of the status of East Timor having been resolved, Indonesia and Portugal formally re-established full diplomatic relations. In August 1995 Queen Beatrix of the Netherlands, the former colonial power in Indonesia, visited Indonesia (the first Dutch monarch to do so for 24 years) and spoke of her regret for the suffering caused to Indonesians by Dutch rule. In March 2010 Indonesia and the Netherlands signed a formal commitment to intensify bilateral co-operation in the field of trade and investment. In December 2011 the Dutch Government extended a formal apology for a massacre perpetrated by its soldiers in the Indonesian village of Rawagede (subsequently renamed Balongsari) in 1947, which claimed the lives of several hundred Indonesian men, and pledged financial compensation for the surviving widows of those killed in the atrocity. At an official ceremony held in the Dutch embassy in Jakarta in September 2013 the Dutch ambassador made another, more general, formal apology for the 'excesses committed by Dutch forces' in Indonesia between 1945 and 1949.

During a visit to Moscow in April 2003 President Megawati signed an agreement to buy Russian defence equipment to the value of US $197m., which was to be partly financed by the bartering of Indonesian palm oil. In September 2007 President Vladimir Putin of Russia visited Jakarta, where he concluded an agreement with President Yudhoyono providing for further purchases of Russian armaments and fighter aircraft. This arrangement was to be financed by a 10-year loan of $1,000m. from Russia. Various other agreements, relating to co-operation in economic relations, counter-terrorism measures and environmental protection, were also signed.

Indonesia has appeared keen in recent years to develop its relations with a number of Middle Eastern and South Asian countries. In October 2005 King Abdullah of Jordan undertook a state visit to Jakarta where he had discussions with President Yudhoyono on bilateral relations and issues pertaining to the international Islamic community. In the following month Yudhoyono paid an official visit to Pakistan, during which he signed a framework agreement on bilateral economic co-operation with his Pakistani counterpart, Pervez Musharraf. In July 2010 the Indonesian Minister of Defence and his Pakistani counterpart signed a defence co-operation agreement, entailing joint military exercises between the armed forces of both countries, intelligence sharing on terrorism and military student exchanges. During a tour of the Middle East in April–May 2006, Yudhoyono reached preliminary energy and investment agreements, worth many millions of dollars, and expressed Indonesia's support for the creation of an independent Palestinian state. In July demonstrations were held outside the US embassy in Jakarta in protest at Israel's ongoing military activity against the Palestinians in Gaza, while Muslim protesters accused the US Administration of bias towards Israel. During his first official visit to Indonesia, in October 2007, the Palestinian President, Mahmud Abbas, signed several co-operation agreements with his host country, covering areas such as education and communications.

Relations with Saudi Arabia were threatened in November 2010 by the publicizing of the case of an Indonesian maid working in Saudi Arabia who had received horrific injuries, reportedly inflicted by her employer. Later in November the body of another Indonesian maid employed in Saudi Arabia was found in the Saudi town of Abha; the maid had allegedly been tortured to death by her employer. In the wake of the ensuing public anger, President Yudhoyono voiced his desire for the law to be upheld by the Saudi authorities. Bilateral tensions were exacerbated by the execution in June 2011 of an Indonesian maid who had been convicted of murdering her Saudi employer, after allegedly suffering months of abuse at her hands and having been denied permission to leave her employment and return to her family in Indonesia. The Minister of Foreign Affairs, Marty Natalegawa, expressed particular displeasure at the Saudi Government's failure to inform the Indonesian authorities or the woman's family that she was to be executed until after the event. Despite assurances by Saudi officials that such an occurrence would not be repeated, at the end of June the Indonesian Government announced a moratorium prohibiting its nationals from working as domestic servants in Saudi Arabia, effective from 1 August. In response, the Saudi Government announced that it was to cease issuing new work permits to Indonesian domestic workers, effective from 2 July. In June 2012 around 17,000 Indonesian migrant workers were imprisoned in Saudi Arabia, and at April 2014, according to the Indonesian foreign ministry, some 41 Indonesian maids faced possible death sentences there. In February 2014 Indonesia and Saudi Arabia signed an agreement which guaranteed better terms of employment for Indonesian domestic servants working in the Gulf state; however, the Indonesian authorities planned to retain the moratorium on the recruitment of new domestic workers from Indonesia until they were certain that the new agreement was being properly implemented.

CONSTITUTION AND GOVERNMENT

Executive power rests with the President, who is elected for five years by the Majelis Permusyawaratan Rakyat (MPR—People's Consultative Assembly), which is the highest authority of the state. The President governs with the assistance of an appointed Cabinet; the Cabinet is responsible to the President. In 2002 the

MPR approved a series of amendments to the Constitution. These provided for: the direct election of the President and Vice-President; the termination of all non-elected representation in the Dewan Perwakilan Rakyat (DPR—House of Representatives) and the MPR; and the creation of the Dewan Perwakilan Daerah (DPD—House of Representatives of the Regions), which, together with the DPR, henceforth comprised the MPR. The MPR consists of 692 members serving for five years. The MPR incorporates all 560 (increased in 2009 from 550) members of the DPR, the country's legislative organ, and the 132 (previously 128) elected regional representatives of the DPD.

There are 34 provinces, and local government is through a three-tier system of provincial, regency and village assemblies. Each province is headed by a Governor, who is elected to a five-year term of office by the Provincial Assembly. Provincial Governors must be confirmed by the President. The Governor of Jakarta, which is designated as a 'special district' (as are Aceh and Yogyakarta), was chosen by direct election for the first time in August 2007.

REGIONAL AND INTERNATIONAL CO-OPERATION

Indonesia is a member of the Association of Southeast Asian Nations (ASEAN, see p. 211), of the Asian Development Bank (ADB, see p. 207) and of Asia-Pacific Economic Cooperation (APEC, see p. 201). It is also a member of the UN's Economic and Social Commission for Asia and the Pacific (ESCAP, see p. 28) and of the Colombo Plan (see p. 449), which promotes economic and social development in Asia and the Pacific.

Indonesia became a member of the UN in 1950. As a contracting party to the General Agreement on Tariffs and Trade (GATT), Indonesia joined the World Trade Organization (WTO, see p. 434) upon its establishment in 1995. The country is a member of the International Labour Organization (ILO, see p. 137) and of the Non-aligned Movement (see p. 467). In January 2009 Indonesia suspended its membership of the Organization of the Petroleum Exporting Countries (OPEC, see p. 408).

ECONOMIC AFFAIRS

In 2012, according to estimates by the World Bank, Indonesia's gross national income (GNI), measured at average 2010–12 prices, was US $844,007m., equivalent to $3,420 per head (or $4,810 per head on an international purchasing-power parity basis). During 2003–12, it was estimated, the population increased at an average annual rate of 1.4%, while gross domestic product (GDP) per head grew, in real terms, by an average of 4.3% per year. According to figures from the Asian Development Bank (ADB), overall GDP increased, in real terms, by an average of 5.8% per year in 2003–12; GDP expanded by 5.8% in 2013.

Agriculture, forestry and fishing contributed 14.4% of GDP in 2012, according to preliminary figures, and engaged 35.0% of the employed labour force at February 2013. Principal crops for domestic consumption include rice, cassava and maize. Although Indonesia remains a major exporter of rubber and palm oil, these commodities' contributions to the country's export earnings have declined. Other important cash crops are sugar cane, coconut, banana, coffee, spices, tea, cocoa and tobacco. A large percentage of Indonesia's land area remains covered by tropical rainforests. However, illegal logging practices have been widespread, leading to serious environmental damage. During 2003–12, according to figures from the ADB, agricultural GDP increased by an average of 3.5% per year; the GDP of the agricultural sector expanded by 3.5% in 2013.

Industry (including mining, manufacturing, construction and utilities) provided 46.9% of GDP in 2012, according to preliminary figures, and engaged 20.6% of the employed labour force at February 2013. During 2003–12, according to ADB data, industrial GDP increased by an average of 4.5% per year; the GDP of the industrial sector grew by 5.0% in 2013.

Mining contributed 11.8% of GDP in 2012, according to preliminary figures, but engaged just 1.4% of the employed labour force at February 2013. Indonesia's principal mineral resource is petroleum, and the country is a leading exporter of liquefied natural gas. At the end of 2012 proven reserves of petroleum amounted to 4,000m. barrels, sufficient to sustain production at that year's rate for nearly 11 years. Indonesia suspended its membership of the Organization of the Petroleum Exporting Countries (OPEC) in January 2009 on the grounds that the country was no longer a net oil exporter. Prior to that, Indonesia was subject to annual quotas for petroleum production as agreed within OPEC. The Government aimed to increase crude petroleum production from an estimated 978,000 barrels per day (b/d) in 2008 to 1.1m. b/d by 2015; however, crude petroleum output fell to 826,000 b/d in 2013, according to the ADB. In 2012, according to industry sources, natural gas production was 71,100m. cu m, from proven reserves amounting to 300,000m. cu m at the end of that year, sufficient to sustain production at that year's rate for more than 41 years. In 2012 coal production reached 386m. metric tons. Indonesia is one of the world's largest producers of tin, with output of ore amounting to 44,409 tons in 2012. Bauxite, nickel, copper, gold and silver are also mined. During 2003–12, according to figures from the ADB, mining GDP increased at an average annual rate of 1.6%; the GDP of the sector expanded by 1.3% in 2013.

Manufacturing contributed 23.9% of GDP in 2012, according to preliminary figures, and engaged 13.0% of the employed labour force at February 2013. Apart from petroleum refineries, the main branches of the sector include food products, textiles, clothing and footwear, transport equipment, electrical machinery and electronic equipment. According to ADB data, manufacturing GDP increased by an average of 4.7% per year in 2003–12; sectoral GDP grew by 5.6% in 2013.

Construction contributed 10.4% of GDP in 2012, according to preliminary figures, and engaged 6.0% of the employed labour force at February 2013. According to figures from the ADB, construction GDP increased by an average of 7.5% per year in 2003–12; the sector's GDP grew by 7.5% in 2012.

From the 1980s Indonesia broadened the base of its energy supplies to include gas, coal, hydroelectricity and geothermal energy, in addition to the traditional dependence on petroleum. In 2011, of total electricity produced, coal accounted for 44.4%, petroleum 23.2% and natural gas 20.3%. In 2012 imports of mineral fuels and lubricants comprised 22.3% of the total value of merchandise imports. Plans for the construction of two nuclear power plants on the island of Bangka, to the east of Sumatra, were confirmed in 2011. It was anticipated that construction work on the plants, which were expected to supply 40% of electricity needs in Sumatra, Java and Bali, would commence in 2015.

Services (including trade, transport and communications, finance and tourism) provided 38.6% of GDP in 2012, according to preliminary figures, and engaged 44.4% of the employed labour force at February 2013. Tourism is normally a major source of foreign exchange. Revenue from tourism (excluding passenger transport) reached an estimated US $8,325m. in 2012. The number of tourist arrivals totalled 8m. in that year. According to figures from the ADB, the GDP of the services sector expanded by an average of 7.8% per year in 2003–12; the sector's GDP increased by 7.1% in 2013.

In 2012, according to IMF figures, Indonesia recorded a visible merchandise trade surplus of US $8,676.2m. and a deficit of $24,073.9m. on the current account of the balance of payments. In 2012 the principal source of imports was the People's Republic of China (which supplied 15.3% of the total), followed by Singapore, Japan, Malaysia, the Republic of Korea, the USA and Thailand. Japan was the principal market for exports in that year (purchasing 15.9%). Other major purchasers were China, Singapore, the Republic of Korea, the USA, India and Malaysia. The principal exports in 2012 were solid fuels manufactured from coal, petroleum gases, palm oil and its fraction, crude petroleum oils, electrical and electronic equipment, and rubber and rubber products. The principal imports were mineral fuels and lubricants, machinery, nuclear reactors and boilers, electrical and electronic equipment, iron and steel, and vehicles other than railway and tramway.

Budget proposals for 2013 projected revenue of Rp. 1,525,190,000m. and expenditure of Rp. 1,154,381,000m. According to the ADB, a budget deficit of Rp. 15,139,700m. was recorded in 2012, equivalent to 1.9% of GDP; the deficit widened to 2.3% of GDP in 2013. Indonesia's general government gross debt was Rp. 2,022,935,585m. in 2012, equivalent to 24.6% of GDP; according to the ADB, this ratio increased to an estimated 26.1% of GDP in 2013. According to the ADB, Indonesia's external debt was estimated at US $264,060m. at the end of 2013. In that year the cost of servicing external public debt was equivalent to 42.7% of the value of exports of goods and services. The annual rate of inflation averaged 7.2% in 2003–12. According to the ADB, consumer prices increased by 6.4% in 2013. The rate of unemployment rose to 6.3% of the labour force in August 2013 (the first such increase since 2005), while the level of underemployment (those working fewer than 35 hours a week) remained very high, at 29% at August 2012.

Amid declining international commodity prices and export demand resulting from the emerging global financial crisis, in February 2009 the Government announced a Rp. 73,300,000m. stimulus programme, which aimed to maintain consumer spending and to create employment opportunities through infrastructure projects. Following a sharp decrease, from US $9,318m. in 2008 to $4,877m. in 2009, foreign direct investment (FDI) recovered strongly thereafter, reaching $19,400m. in 2012 before declining slightly to $18,400m. in 2013. Indonesia has a large domestic market, and consumer demand strengthened during 2010, while the rupiah appreciated in value. Although GDP contracted in the fourth quarter of 2008, for the year as a whole the economy recorded positive growth, which was maintained in 2009 and 2010. Following GDP growth of 6.5% in 2011 (the highest annual rise in 15 years), there was a slight deceleration to 6.2% in 2012. Despite weaker export growth in 2012, resulting from a slowdown in the key market of the People's Republic of China and the generally sluggish recovery of the global economy (notably in the USA and the eurozone), the Indonesian economy remained robust, with FDI and government expenditure continuing to rise and private consumption remaining buoyant. Following the Government's postponement of fuel price increases in April, inflation was more subdued than forecast, falling to a 12-year low of 4.3%. The implementation of capital projects became more efficient in 2012 as budgetary disbursement accelerated; furthermore, tax revenue increased at a faster rate than predicted. Strong economic growth helped to generate thousands of new jobs in the formal sector, and there was a slight fall in the incidence of poverty. The rate of growth of GDP moderated to 5.8% in 2013 as levels of both FDI and external demand decreased, the current account deficit widened to a record high, and the rate of inflation rose to 6.4% (largely owing to increases in fuel and food prices and a sharp depreciation in the rupiah). According to the IMF, the medium-term prospects of the Indonesian economy were dependent on increased productivity through a faster rate of structural reform (including more flexibility within the labour market), the creation of new export markets and the achievement of greater social equality through more inclusive growth. In January 2014 the Government announced measures to boost FDI, including tax incentives and the opening up of a number of profitable market sectors that had previously been closed to overseas investment. According to ADB projections based on the successful conduct of legislative and presidential elections in that year, GDP was forecast to grow by a further 5.7% in 2014.

PUBLIC HOLIDAYS

2015: 1 January (New Year's Day), 2 January*† (Mouloud, Prophet Muhammad's Birthday), 18 February (Chinese New Year), 3 April (Good Friday), 3 May (Waisak Day), 14 May (Ascension Day), 15 May* (Ascension of the Prophet Muhammad), 17 July* (Id al-Fitr, end of Ramadan), 17 August (Independence Day), 23 September* (Id al-Adha, Feast of the Sacrifice), 14 October* (Muharram, Islamic New Year), 23 December*† (Mouloud, Prophet Muhammad's Birthday), 25 December (Christmas Day).

* These holidays are dependent on the Islamic lunar calendar and may vary by one or two days from the dates given.

† This holiday occurs twice in 2015.

Statistical Survey

Source (unless otherwise stated): Badan Pusat Statistik (Central Bureau of Statistics/Statistics Indonesia), Jalan Dr Sutomo 6–8, Jakarta 10710; tel. (21) 3507057; fax (21) 3857046; e-mail bpshq@bps.go.id; internet www.bps.go.id.

Area and Population

AREA, POPULATION AND DENSITY

Area (sq km)	1,910,931*
Population (census results)	
30 June 2000	206,264,595
31 May 2010	
Males	119,630,913
Females	118,010,413
Total	237,641,326
Population (UN estimates at mid-year)†	
2012	246,864,192
2013	249,865,631
2014	252,812,245
Density (per sq km) at mid-2014	132.3

* 737,814 sq miles.

† Source: UN, *World Population Prospects: The 2012 Revision*.

POPULATION BY AGE AND SEX
(UN estimates at mid-2014)

	Males	Females	Total
0–14	36,955,774	35,028,654	71,984,428
15–64	84,245,035	83,161,957	167,406,992
65 and over	5,962,369	7,458,456	13,420,825
Total	127,163,178	125,649,067	252,812,245

Source: UN, *World Population Prospects: The 2012 Revision*.

ISLANDS AND PROVINCES
(population at census of May 2010)*

	Area (sq km)	Population ('000)	Density (per sq km)
Jawa (Java) and Madura	129,438	136,610.6	1,055.4
DKI Jakarta†	664	9,607.8	14,469.6
Jawa Barat	35,378	43,053.7	1,217.0
Jawa Tengah	32,801	32,382.7	987.2
DI Yogyakarta†	3,133	3,457.5	1,103.6
Jawa Timur	47,800	37,476.8	784.0
Banten	9,663	10,632.2	1,100.3
Sumatera (Sumatra)	480,793	50,630.9	105.3
Nanggroe Aceh Darussalem†	57,956	4,494.4	77.5
Sumatera Utara	72,981	12,982.2	177.9
Sumatera Barat	42,013	4,846.9	115.4
Riau	87,024	5,538.4	63.6
Jambi	50,058	3,092.3	61.8
Sumatera Selatan	91,592	7,450.4	81.3
Bangkulu	19,919	1,715.5	86.1
Lumpung	34,624	7,608.4	219.7
Kepulauan Bangka-Belitung	16,424	1,223.3	74.5
Kepulauan Riau	8,202	1,679.2	204.7
Sulawesi (Celebes)	188,522	17,371.8	92.1
Sulawesi Utara	13,852	2,270.6	163.9
Sulawesi Tengah	61,841	2,635.0	42.6
Sulawesi Selatan	46,717	8,034.8	172.0
Sulawesi Tenggara	38,068	2,232.6	58.6
Gorontalo	11,257	1,040.2	92.4
Sulawesi Barat	16,787	1,158.7	69.0
Kalimantan	544,150	13,787.8	25.3
Kalimantan Barat	147,307	4,396.0	29.8
Kalimantan Tengah	153,565	2,212.1	14.4
Kalimantan Selatan	38,744	3,626.6	93.6
Kalimantan Timur	204,534	3,553.1	17.4
Nusa Tenggara and Bali‡	73,070	13,074.8	178.9
Nusa Tenggara Barat	18,572	4,500.2	242.3
Nusa Tenggara Timur	48,718	4,683.8	96.1
Bali	5,780	3,890.8	673.1

—*continued*	Area (sq km)	Population ('000)	Density (per sq km)
Maluku (Moluccas) and Papua§	494,957	6,165.4	12.5
Maluku	46,914	1,533.5	32.7
Maluku Utara	31,983	1,038.1	32.5
Papua Barat†	97,024	760.4	7.8
Papua†	319,036	2,833.4	8.9
Total	1,910,931	237,641.3	124.4

* Figures refer to provincial divisions, organized according to geography, island or island groupings.
† Province with special status.
‡ The Nusa Tenggara provinces comprise most of the Lesser Sunda Islands, principally Flores, Lombok, Sumba, Sumbawa and part of Timor.
§ The Papua provinces were formerly known as Irian Jaya (West Papua).

A new province, Kalimantan Utara, was created in October 2012 from part of the former territory of the province of Kalimantan Timur.

PRINCIPAL TOWNS
(population at 2010 census)

Jakarta (capital)	9,607,787	Depok	1,738,570
Surabaya	2,765,487	Semarang	1,555,984
Bandung	2,394,873	Palembang	1,455,284
Bekasi	2,334,871	Ujung Pandang (Makassar)	1,338,663
Medan	2,097,610	Tangerang Selatan	1,290,322
Tangerang	1,798,601	Padang	833,562

Mid-2011 (incl. suburbs, UN estimate): Jakarta 9,769,010 (Source: UN, *World Urbanization Prospects: The 2011 Revision*).

BIRTHS AND DEATHS
(annual averages, UN estimates)

	1995–2000	2000–05	2005–10
Birth rate (per 1,000)	21.9	21.5	21.0
Death rate (per 1,000)	6.9	6.7	6.4

Source: UN, *World Population Prospects: The 2012 Revision*.

Life expectancy (years at birth): 70.4 (males 68.4; females 72.5) in 2011 (Source: World Bank, World Development Indicators database).

ECONOMICALLY ACTIVE POPULATION
(persons aged 15 years and over, at February)

	2011	2012	2013
Agriculture, hunting, forestry and fishing	42,475,329	41,205,030	39,959,073
Mining and quarrying	1,352,219	1,620,028	1,555,564
Manufacturing	13,696,024	14,211,562	14,784,843
Electricity, gas and water	257,270	297,805	254,528
Construction	5,591,084	6,103,457	6,885,341
Trade, restaurants and hotels	23,239,792	24,020,934	24,804,705
Transport, storage and communications	5,585,124	5,191,771	5,231,775
Financing, insurance, real estate and business services	2,058,968	2,779,201	3,012,770
Public services	17,025,934	17,373,017	17,532,590
Total employed	111,281,744	112,802,805	114,021,189
Unemployed	8,117,631	7,614,241	7,170,523
Total labour force	119,399,375	120,417,046	121,191,712

Health and Welfare

KEY INDICATORS

Total fertility rate (children per woman, 2011)	2.1
Under-5 mortality rate (per 1,000 live births, 2011)	32
HIV/AIDS (% of persons aged 15–49, 2012)	0.4
Physicians (per 1,000 head, 2012)	0.20
Hospital beds (per 1,000 head, 2010)	0.60
Health expenditure (2010): US $ per head (PPP)	123
Health expenditure (2010): % of GDP	2.8
Health expenditure (2010): public (% of total)	36.1
Access to water (% of persons, 2011)	89
Access to sanitation (% of persons, 2011)	59
Total carbon dioxide emissions ('000 metric tons, 2010)	433,989.5
Carbon dioxide emissions per head (metric tons, 2010)	1.8
Human Development Index (2012): ranking	121
Human Development Index (2012): value	0.629

For sources and definitions, see explanatory note on p. vi.

Agriculture

PRINCIPAL CROPS
('000 metric tons)

	2010	2011	2012
Rice, paddy	66,469	65,741	69,045
Maize	18,328	17,629	19,377
Potatoes	1,061	995	1,069
Sweet potatoes	2,051	2,192	2,483
Cassava (Manioc)	23,918	24,010	23,922
Beans, dry	292	341	288
Sugar cane	26,600*	24,000*	26,342
Cashew nuts, with shell	115	115	117
Soybeans (Soya beans)	907	844	852
Groundnuts, with shell	779	691	713
Coconuts	18,000*	17,500*	18,000†
Oil palm fruit†	97,800	101,700	109,000
Cabbages and other brassicas	1,385	1,364	1,488
Tomatoes	892	954	888
Pumpkins, squash and gourds	370	428	430
Cucumbers and gherkins	547	522	512
Aubergines (Eggplants)	482	519	519
Chillies and peppers, green	1,332	1,903	1,657
Onions, dry	1,048	893	964
Beans, green	942	885	871
Carrots and turnips	404	527	466
Oranges	2,029	1,819	1,612
Avocados	224	276	294
Mangoes, mangosteens and guavas	1,287	2,131	2,376
Pineapples	1,406	1,541	1,781
Bananas	5,775	6,133	6,189
Papayas	676	958	906
Coffee, green	684	639	657
Cocoa beans	845	712	936
Tea	150	150	150
Cinnamon	88	90	91
Cloves	98	72	73
Ginger	108	95	114
Tobacco, unmanufactured	136	215	227
Natural rubber	2,735	2,990	3,040

* Unofficial figure.
† FAO estimate(s).

Aggregate production ('000 metric tons, may include official, semi-official or estimated data): Total cereals 84,797.0 in 2010, 83,370.0 in 2011, 88,422.2 in 2012; Total roots and tubers 27,395.0 in 2010, 27,577.4 in 2011, 27,874.3 in 2012; Total vegetables (incl. melons) 9,780.2 in 2010, 10,518.0 in 2011, 10,507.8 in 2012; Total fruits (excl. melons) 14,881.1 in 2010, 17,572.6 in 2011, 17,744.4 in 2012.

Source: FAO.

LIVESTOCK
('000 head)

	2010	2011	2012
Cattle	13,582	14,824	16,035
Sheep	10,725	11,372	12,768
Goats	16,620	17,483	17,862
Pigs	7,477	7,758	7,831
Horses	419	416	422
Buffaloes	2,005	1,305	1,378
Chickens	1,349,626	1,442,331	1,552,131
Ducks	44,302	49,392	46,990

Source: FAO.

LIVESTOCK PRODUCTS
('000 metric tons)

	2010	2011	2012
Cattle meat	436.5	485.3	505.5
Buffalo meat	35.9	35.3	35.3
Sheep meat	44.9	46.8	46.5
Goat meat	68.8	66.3	68.6
Pig meat*	695.0	721.1	728.8
Chicken meat	1,539.6	1,664.8	1,751.8
Cows' milk	909.5	974.6	1,017.9
Goats' milk*	281.3	281.4	282.0
Hen eggs	1,121.1	1,027.8	1,059.3
Other poultry eggs	260.7	256.2	276.2
Wool, greasy*	30.8	30.8	30.8

* FAO estimates.

Note: Figures for meat refer to inspected production only, i.e. from animals slaughtered under government supervision.

Source: FAO.

Forestry

ROUNDWOOD REMOVALS
('000 cubic metres, excl. bark, FAO estimates)

	2010	2011	2012
Sawlogs, veneer logs and logs for sleepers	25,200	28,000	28,000
Pulpwood	24,700	28,000	29,900
Other industrial wood	4,206	4,706	4,706
Fuel wood	59,743	57,288	54,917
Total	113,849	117,994	117,523

Source: FAO.

SAWNWOOD PRODUCTION
('000 cubic metres, incl. railway sleepers)

	2006	2007	2008
Total (all broadleaved)	4,330	4,330	4,169

2009–12: Production assumed to be unchanged from 2008 (FAO estimates).

Source: FAO.

Fishing

('000 metric tons, live weight)

	2009	2010	2011
Capture	5,103.6	5,380.3	5,707.7
Scads	330.7	351.2	405.8
Goldstripe sardinella	237.1	255.6	246.2
'Stolephorus' anchovies	193.0	175.7	204.8
Skipjack tuna	357.1	351.8	359.2
Indian mackerels	18.6	17.8	19.7
Aquaculture	1,733.4	2,304.8*	2,718.4
Common carp	249.3	282.7	332.2
Milkfish	328.3	422.1	467.3
Total catch	6,837.0	7,685.1*	8,426.1

* FAO estimate.

Note: Figures exclude aquatic plants ('000 metric tons): 2,966.6 (capture 3.0, aquaculture 2,963.6) in 2009; 3,917.7 (capture 2.7, aquaculture 3,915.0) in 2010; 5,175.7 (capture 5.5, aquaculture 5,170.2) in 2011. Also excluded are crocodiles, recorded by number rather than by weight. The number of crocodiles caught was: 12,251 in 2009; 11,752 in 2010; 15,780 in 2011.

Source: FAO.

Mining

('000 metric tons unless otherwise indicated)

	2009	2010	2011
Crude petroleum (million barrels)*	346.0	341.0†	340.0†
Natural gas (million cu m)	73,587	77,741	80,000†
Bauxite†	15.0	27.0	40.0
Coal (bituminous)	196,209	137,801	150,000†
Nickel‡	202.8	235.8	218.2
Copper‡	998.5	878.4	542.7
Tin ore (metric tons)‡	46,078	43,258	42,000†
Gold (kg)§	140,488	106,316	96,100
Silver (kg)§	359,451	271,534	310,400

* Including condensate.
† Estimate(s).
‡ Figures refer to the metal content of ores and concentrates.
§ Including gold and silver in copper concentrate.

Source: US Geological Survey.

2012 ('000 metric tons unless otherwise indicated, preliminary): Crude petroleum (million barrels) 314.7; Bauxite 28.0; Tin ore (metric tons) 44,409.

Industry

SELECTED PRODUCTS
('000 metric tons unless otherwise indicated)

	2008	2009	2010
Raw sugar (centrifugal)[1]	3,263	2,740	2,450
Palm oil[12,]	17,540	19,324	19,760
Veneer sheets ('000 cu m)[1]	427	685	737
Plywood ('000 cu m)[12,]	4,150	4,150	4,850
Paper and paperboard[1,3]	89	86	86
Jet fuel	1,445	1,911	1,791
Motor spirit (petrol)	8,155	9,243	8,350
Naphthas	2,663	1,921	1,731
Kerosene	6,182	3,794	2,478
Gas-diesel oil	12,766	13,769	13,338
Residual fuel oils	9,471	2,803	2,271
Lubricating oils	439	388	283

—*continued*	2008	2009	2010
Liquefied petroleum gas	910	1,425	1,825
Rubber tyres ('000)[4]	37,826	36,811	n.a.
Cement (hydraulic)[5,3]	36,000	22,195	28,000
Aluminium (unwrought)[5,6]	243	258	253
Tin (unwrought, metric tons)[5,6]	53,471	51,418	43,832
Electric energy (million kWh)	149,437	157,516	186,594

2011 ('000 metric tons unless otherwise stated): Palm oil 21,449 (unofficial figure)[1,2]; Veneer sheets ('000 cu m) 816[1]; Plywood ('000 cu m) 4,850[1,2]; Paper and paperboard 87[1]; Cement (hydraulic) 29,000[3,5]; Aluminium (unwrought) 244[5]; Tin (unwrought, metric tons) 43,000[3,5].

2012 ('000 metric tons unless otherwise stated): Palm oil 23,672 (unofficial figure)[1,2]; Veneer sheets ('000 cu m) 891[1]; Plywood ('000 cu m) 5,178[1]; Paper and paperboard 89[1]; Cement (hydraulic) 29,000[3,5]; Aluminium (unwrought) 244[5]; Tin (unwrought, metric tons) 43,000[3,5].

[1] Source: FAO.
[2] Unofficial figure.
[3] Provisional or estimated production.
[4] For road motor vehicles, excluding bicycles and motorcycles.
[5] Source: US Geological Survey.
[6] Primary metal production only.

Source (unless otherwise indicated): UN Industrial Commodity Statistics Database.

Finance

CURRENCY AND EXCHANGE RATES

Monetary Units
100 sen = 1 rupiah (Rp.).

Sterling, Dollar and Euro Equivalents (31 December 2013)
£1 sterling = 20,072.8 rupiah;
US $1 = 12,189.0 rupiah;
€1 = 16,809.8 rupiah;
100,000 rupiah = £4.98 = $8.20 = €5.95.

Average Exchange Rate (rupiah per US $)
2011 8,770.4
2012 9,386.6
2013 10,461.2

GOVERNMENT FINANCE
(central government operations, '000 million rupiah)

Summary of Balances

	2011	2012*	2013*
Revenue	1,205,346	1,357,380	1,525,190
Less Expenditure and net lending	883,722	954,137	1,154,381
Overall balance	321,624	403,243	370,809

Revenue and Grants

	2011	2012*	2013*
Tax revenue	873,874	1,016,237	1,192,994
Income tax	431,122	513,650	584,890
Value-added tax (VAT) on goods and services, and tax on sales of luxury goods	277,800	336,057	423,708
Tax of rights in land and building	29,893	29,687	27,344
Excise duties	77,010	83,267	92,004
Import duties	25,266	24,738	27,003
Export taxes	28,856	23,206	31,702
Other taxes	3,928	5,632	6,343
Non-tax revenue	331,472	341,143	332,196
Total	1,205,346	1,357,380	1,525,190

Expenditure and Net Lending

	2011	2012*	2013*
Personnel expenditure	175,738	215,725	241,606
Material expenditure	124,640	138,482	200,735
Interest payments	93,262	123,072	113,244
Domestic interest	66,825	89,358	80,703
External interest	26,437	33,714	32,541
Subsidies	295,358	208,850	317,219
Petroleum subsidies	255,609	168,560	274,743
Non-petroleum subsidies	39,749	40,290	42,476
Social expenditure	71,104	63,572	73,609
Capital expenditure	117,855	168,126	184,364
Other expenditure	5,465	34,513	19,983
Grant expenditures	300	1,797	3,621
Total	883,722	954,137	1,154,381

* Budget proposals.

INTERNATIONAL RESERVES
(US $ million at 31 December)

	2010	2011	2012
Gold (market prices)	3,303	3,598	3,940
IMF special drawing rights	2,714	2,704	2,707
Reserve position in IMF	224	223	224
Foreign exchange	89,970	103,611	105,907
Total	96,211	110,136	112,778

Source: IMF, *International Financial Statistics*.

MONEY SUPPLY
('000 million rupiah at 31 December)

	2010	2011	2012
Currency outside depository corporations	260,227	307,760	361,967
Transferable deposits	484,312	568,499	662,060
Other deposits	1,717,592	1,986,573	2,270,198
Securities other than shares	9,075	14,388	10,420
Broad money	2,471,206	2,877,220	3,304,645

Source: IMF, *International Financial Statistics*.

COST OF LIVING
(Consumer Price Index; base: 2000 = 100)

	2010	2011	2012
Food	247.0	268.1	283.8
All items (incl. others)	227.2	239.3	249.6

Source: ILO.

NATIONAL ACCOUNTS
('000 million rupiah at current prices)

Expenditure on the Gross Domestic Product

	2010	2011*	2012*
Government final consumption expenditure	587,283	668,583	732,345
Private final consumption expenditure	3,643,425	4,053,364	4,496,373
Changes in inventories	18,364	70,774	178,190
Gross fixed capital formation	2,064,994	2,372,765	2,733,180
Total domestic expenditure	6,314,066	7,165,486	8,140,089
Exports of goods and services	1,584,674	1,955,821	1,999,380
Less Imports of goods and services	1,476,620	1,851,070	2,127,545
Statistical discrepancy	24,732	152,544	229,940
GDP in purchasers' values	6,446,852	7,422,781	8,241,864
GDP at constant 2000 prices	2,314,459	2,464,677	2,618,139

Gross Domestic Product by Economic Activity

	2010	2011*	2012*
Agriculture, forestry and fishing	985,471	1,091,447	1,190,412
Mining and quarrying	719,710	879,505	970,600
Manufacturing	1,599,073	1,806,141	1,972,847
Electricity, gas and water	49,119	56,789	65,125
Construction	660,891	754,484	860,965
Trade, hotels and restaurants	882,487	1,024,009	1,145,601
Transport, storage and communications	423,172	491,283	549,116
Finance, insurance, real estate and business services	466,564	535,153	598,523
Public administration	359,841	432,785	485,535
Other services	300,525	351,185	403,141
Total	6,446,852	7,422,781	8,241,864

* Preliminary figures.

BALANCE OF PAYMENTS
(US $ million)

	2010	2011	2012
Exports of goods	149,965.8	191,108.7	187,346.5
Imports of goods	–118,962.7	–157,283.7	–178,670.3
Balance of goods	31,003.1	33,825.0	8,676.2
Exports of services	17,006.8	21,844.1	23,627.3
Imports of services	–26,706.1	–31,518.7	–34,459.5
Balance on goods and services	21,303.9	24,150.4	–2,156.0
Primary income received	1,889.7	2,516.6	2,626.9
Primary income paid	–22,679.6	–29,192.4	–28,574.2
Balance on goods, services and primary income	514.0	–2,525.4	–28,103.3
Secondary income received	7,571.3	7,635.6	8,001.8
Secondary income paid	–2,941.0	–3,425.1	–3,972.4
Current balance	5,144.3	1,685.1	–24,073.9
Capital account (net)	49.8	32.9	37.5
Direct investment assets	–2,664.2	–7,712.9	–5,308.8
Direct investment from liabilities	13,770.6	19,241.3	19,618.0
Portfolio investment assets	–490.3	–1,189.4	–5,467.0
Portfolio investment liabilities	15,713.3	4,995.8	14,665.6
Other investment assets	–1,725.3	–6,754.5	–5,178.0
Other investment liabilities	3,987.5	4,953.7	6,576.2
Net errors and omissions	–3,501.2	–3,396.2	–654.8
Reserves and related items	30,284.4	11,855.6	214.8

Source: IMF, *International Financial Statistics*.

External Trade

PRINCIPAL COMMODITIES
(distribution by HS, US $ million)

Imports c.i.f.	2010	2011	2012
Vegetables and vegetable products	5,052.5	8,906.0	7,611.8
Prepared foodstuffs; beverages, spirits, vinegar; tobacco and articles thereof	4,534.9	5,903.7	6,741.6
Mineral products	28,665.6	42,337.8	44,218.9
Mineral fuels, oils, distillation products, etc.	27,530.7	40,840.2	42,764.2
Crude petroleum oils	8,531.2	11,154.5	10,803.3
Non-crude petroleum oils	17,654.3	27,721.8	28,038.2
Chemicals and related products	12,545.0	16,359.3	17,519.3
Organic chemicals	5,326.4	6,634.8	6,883.0
Plastics, rubber, and articles thereof	6,487.8	9,034.2	9,615.2
Plastics and articles thereof	4,817.1	6,687.5	6,990.9
Textiles and textile articles	6,186.4	8,530.5	8,143.6
Iron and steel, other base metals and articles of base metal	13,773.1	17,247.7	20,481.1
Iron and steel	6,371.5	8,580.5	10,138.9
Machinery and mechanical appliances; electrical equipment; parts thereof	35,652.2	42,974.0	47,334.3
Machinery, boilers, etc.	20,019.0	24,728.8	28,429.6
Electrical and electronic equipment	15,633.2	18,245.2	18,904.7
Vehicles, aircraft, vessels and associated transport equipment	11,310.0	13,108.6	16,192.0
Vehicles other than railway and tramway	7,737.4	7,602.8	9,757.0
Total (incl. others)	135,663.3	177,435.6	191,690.9

Exports f.o.b.	2010	2011	2012
Animal, vegetable fats and oils, cleavage products, etc.	16,312.2	21,655.3	21,299.8
Palm oil and its fraction	13,469.0	17,261.2	17,602.2
Mineral products	55,078.4	76,428.8	68,580.8
Ores, slag and ash	8,148.0	7,342.6	5,082.6
Copper ores and concentrates	6,882.2	4,700.4	2,594.7
Mineral fuels, oils, distillation products, etc.	46,765.3	68,921.1	63,385.1
Solid fuels manufactured from coal	18,169.7	25,523.2	24,293.2
Crude petroleum oils	10,402.9	13,828.7	12,293.4
Petroleum gases	13,669.5	22,871.5	20,520.5
Chemicals and related products	7,142.0	10,689.7	10,239.6
Plastics, rubber, and articles thereof	11,523.5	16,865.9	12,911.7
Rubber and articles thereof	9,373.3	14,352.2	10,475.2
Natural rubber, balata, gutta-percha, etc.	7,329.1	11,766.2	7,864.5
Pulp of wood, paper and paperboard, and articles thereof	5,708.1	5,769.4	5,517.8
Textiles and textile articles	11,224.0	13,256.8	12,461.7
Iron and steel, other base metals and articles of base metal	10,139.6	11,965.8	9,387.4
Machinery and mechanical appliances; electrical equipment; parts thereof	15,359.9	16,894.9	16,867.9
Machinery, boilers, etc.	4,986.7	5,749.5	6,103.1
Electrical and electronic equipment	10,373.2	11,145.4	10,764.8
Total (incl. others)	157,779.1	203,496.6	190,031.8

Source: Trade Map-Trade Competitiveness Map, International Trade Centre, www.intracen.org/marketanalysis.

PRINCIPAL TRADING PARTNERS
(US $ million)*

Imports c.i.f.	2010	2011	2012
Australia	4,099.0	5,177.1	5,297.6
Brazil	1,717.5	1,898.1	1,971.0
Canada	1,108.4	2,015.8	1,810.7
China, People's Republic	20,424.2	26,212.2	29,387.1
France (incl. Monaco)	1,340.9	2,007.4	1,926.2
Germany	3,006.7	3,393.8	4,188.5
Hong Kong	1,860.4	2,465.2	1,930.2
India	3,294.8	4,322.0	4,305.6
Japan	16,965.8	19,436.6	22,767.8
Korea, Republic	7,703.0	12,999.8	11,970.4
Kuwait	1,372.7	1,407.9	2,181.5
Malaysia	8,648.7	10,404.9	12,243.6
Saudi Arabia	4,360.8	5,426.6	5,199.4
Singapore	20,240.8	25,964.7	26,087.3
Taiwan	3,241.9	4,259.5	4,692.8
Thailand	7,470.7	10,405.1	11,437.2
Viet Nam	1,142.3	2,382.9	2,595.0
USA	9,416.0	10,834.0	11,614.2
Total (incl. others)	135,663.3	177,435.6	191,690.9

Exports f.o.b.	2010	2011	2012
Australia	4,244.4	5,582.5	4,905.4
China, People's Republic	15,692.6	22,941.0	21,659.5
Germany	2,984.7	3,304.7	3,075.0
Hong Kong	2,501.4	3,215.4	2,633.9
India	9,915.0	13,335.7	12,496.3
Italy	2,370.5	3,168.3	2,277.0
Japan	25,781.8	33,714.7	30,135.1
Korea, Republic	12,574.6	16,388.8	15,049.9
Malaysia	9,362.3	10,995.8	11,280.3
Netherlands	3,722.5	5,132.5	4,664.3
Philippines	3,180.7	3,699.0	3,707.6
Singapore	13,723.3	18,443.9	17,135.0
Spain	2,328.7	2,427.9	2,069.3
Taiwan	4,837.6	6,584.9	6,242.5
Thailand	4,566.6	5,896.7	6,635.1
United Arab Emirates	1,475.3	1,734.5	1,619.0
United Kingdom	1,693.2	1,719.7	1,696.8
USA	14,301.9	16,497.6	14,910.2
Viet Nam	1,946.2	2,354.2	2,273.7
Total (incl. others)	157,779.1	203,496.6	190,031.8

* Imports by country of production, exports by country of consumption; figures include trade in gold.

Source: Trade Map-Trade Competitiveness Map, International Trade Centre, www.intracen.org/marketanalysis.

Transport

RAILWAYS
(traffic)

	2010	2011	2012
Passengers embarked ('000)	203,270	199,337	102,200
Passenger-km (million)	20,340	19,024	7,692
Freight loaded ('000 tons)	19,114	20,438	11,497
Total ton-km (million)	6,559	6,643	3,393

ROAD TRAFFIC
(motor vehicles registered)

	2010	2011	2012
Passenger cars	8,891,041	9,548,866	10,432,259
Trucks	4,687,789	4,958,738	5,286,061
Buses	2,250,109	2,254,406	2,273,821
Motorcycles	61,078,188	68,839,341	76,381,183
Total	76,907,127	85,601,351	94,373,324

SHIPPING

Flag Registered Fleet
(at 31 December)

	2011	2012	2013
Number of vessels	5,684	6,138	6,781
Displacement ('000 grt)	13,714.3	15,085.0	16,547.9

Source: Lloyd's List Intelligence (www.lloydslistintelligence.com).

Sea-borne Freight Traffic
('000 metric tons)

	2010	2011	2012
International:			
goods loaded	232,222	376,652	488,264
goods unloaded	65,641	78,836	69,645
Domestic:			
goods loaded	182,486	238,940	312,599
goods unloaded	221,675	284,292	327,715

CIVIL AVIATION
(traffic on scheduled services)

	2010	2011
Kilometres flown (million)	440	518
Passengers carried ('000)	56,774	67,795
Passenger-km (million)	60,649	73,098
Total ton-km (million)	5,797	6,964

Source: UN, *Statistical Yearbook*.

Passengers carried ('000): 77,157 in 2012 (Source: World Bank, World Development Indicators database).

Tourism

FOREIGN TOURIST ARRIVALS

Country of residence	2010	2011	2012
Australia	769,585	933,376	981,539
China, People's Republic	511,188	594,997	625,699
France	160,193	171,736	180,598
Germany	144,441	149,110	156,804
India	159,373	181,791	191,172
Japan	416,151	423,113	444,946
Korea, Republic	296,060	320,596	337,139
Malaysia	1,171,737	1,173,351	1,233,897
Netherlands	158,957	163,268	171,693
Philippines	171,181	210,029	220,867
Singapore	1,206,360	1,324,839	1,393,202
Taiwan	214,192	228,922	240,735
United Kingdom	192,335	201,221	211,604
USA	177,677	203,205	213,691
Total (incl. others)	7,002,944	7,649,731	8,044,462

Receipts from tourism (US $ million, excl. passenger transport): 6,957 in 2010; 7,997 in 2011; 8,325 in 2012 (provisional) (Source: World Tourism Organization).

Communications Media

	2010	2011	2012
Telephones ('000 main lines in use)	40,928.9	38,617.5	37,982.9
Mobile cellular telephones ('000 subscribers)	211,290.2	236,799.5	281,963.7
Broadband subscribers ('000)	2,280.3	2,736.4*	2,983.0

* Estimate.

Internet subscribers: 1,707,200 in 2008.

Source: International Telecommunication Union.

Education

(2011/12)

	Institutions	Teachers	Pupils and Students
Kindergarten	70,917	204,406	3,612,441
Primary schools	146,826	1,401,581	27,583,919
General junior secondary schools	33,668	482,264	9,425,336
General senior secondary schools	11,654	252,858	4,196,467
Vocational senior secondary schools	10,256	164,074	4,019,157
Tertiary institutions	3,170	192,944	5,616,670

Source: Ministry of National Education.

Pupil-teacher ratio (primary education, UNESCO estimate): 15.9 in 2010/11 (Source: UNESCO Institute for Statistics).

Adult literacy rate (UNESCO estimates): 92.8% (males 95.6%; females 90.1%) in 2011 (Source: UNESCO Institute for Statistics).

Directory

The Government

HEAD OF STATE

President: Gen. (retd) SUSILO BAMBANG YUDHOYONO (elected 5 July 2004; re-elected 8 July 2009).

Vice-President: Prof. Dr BOEDIONO.

CABINET
(April 2014)

Note: No party won an outright majority in the legislative elections that took place on 9 April 2014. It, therefore, appeared highly likely that, following the presidential election, which was due to be held on 9 July, another coalition government would be appointed.

The outgoing Government listed below includes members of the Partai Demokrat (PD), Partai Golongan Karya (Golkar), Partai Amanat Nasional (PAN), Partai Damai Sejahtera (PDS), Partai Persatuan Pembangunan (PPP) and Partai Kebangkitan Bangsa (PKB), along with numerous unaffiliated members.

Co-ordinating Minister for Political, Legal and Security Affairs: Air Chief Marshal (retd) DJOKO SUYANTO.

Co-ordinating Minister for Economic Affairs: HATTA RAJASA.

Co-ordinating Minister for People's Welfare: Dr AGUNG LAKSONO.

Minister of Home Affairs: GAMAWAN FAUZI.

Minister of Foreign Affairs: Dr RADEN (MARTY) MOHAMMAD MULIANA NATALEGAWA.

Minister of Defence: Dr Ir PURNOMO YUSGIANTORO.

Minister of Justice and Human Rights: AMIR SYAMSUDDIN.

Minister of Finance: Dr MUHAMMAD CHATIB BASRI.

Minister of Energy and Mineral Resources: Ir JERO WATJIK.

Minister of Industry: MOHAMAD S. HIDAYAT.

Minister of Trade: MUHAMMAD LUTFI.

Minister of Agriculture: Ir H. SUSWONO.

Minister of Forestry: ZULKIFLI HASAN.

Minister of Transportation: E. E. MANGINDAAN.

Minister of Marine Affairs and Fisheries: SYARIF C. SUTARDJO.

Minister of Manpower and Transmigration: Drs MUHAIMIN ISKANDAR.

Minister of Public Works: Ir DJOKO KIRMANTO.

Minister of Health: NAFSIAH MBOI.

Minister of Education and Culture: Dr Ir MUHAMMAD NUH.

Minister of Social Affairs: Dr SALIM SEGAF AL-JUFRIE.

Minister of Religious Affairs: Drs SURYADHARMA ALI.

Minister of Tourism and Creative Economy: Dr MARI ELKA PANGESTU.

Minister of Communications and Information Technology: Ir TIFATUL SEMBIRING.

Minister of State for Research and Technology: Dr Ir GUSTI MUHAMMAD HATTA.

Minister of State for Co-operatives and Small and Medium-Sized Businesses: Dr SYARIFUDDIN HASAN.

Minister of State for the Environment: BALTAZAR KAMBUAYA.

Minister of State for Women's Empowerment: LINDA AMALIA SARI.

Minister of State for Administrative and Bureaucratic Reform: AZWAR ABUBAKAR.

Minister of State for State Enterprises: DAHLAN ISKAN.

Minister of State for Development of Disadvantaged Regions: Ir AHMAD HELMI FAISAL ZAINI.

Minister of State for National Development Planning: Dr ARMIDA ALISJAHBANA.

Minister of State for Public Housing: DJAN FARIDZ.

Minister of State for Youth and Sports Affairs: ROY SURYO NOTODIPROJO.

Officials with the rank of Minister of State:

Attorney-General: BASRIEF ARIEF.

State Secretary: Lt-Gen. (retd) SUDI SILALAHI.

MINISTRIES

Office of the President: Istana Merdeka, 2nd Floor, Jakarta 10110; tel. (21) 3840946; internet www.presidenri.go.id.

Office of the Vice-President: Istana Wakil Presiden, Jalan Medan Merdeka Selatan 14, Jakarta 10110; tel. (21) 34830565; fax (21) 3503940; e-mail tirta_hidayat@yahoo.go.id; internet www.setwapres.go.id.

Office of the Attorney-General: Jalan Sultan Hasanuddin 1, Kebayoran Baru, Jakarta Selatan; tel. (21) 7221269; fax (21) 7392576; e-mail webmaster@kejaksaan.go.id; internet www.kejaksaan.go.id.

Office of the Cabinet Secretary: 4th Floor, Jalan Veteran 18, Jakarta Pusat 10110; tel. (21) 3846463; fax (21) 3866579; e-mail itcp@setkab.go.id; internet www.setkab.go.id.

Office of the Co-ordinating Minister for Economic Affairs: Jalan Lapangan Banteng Timur 2–4, Jakarta 10710; tel. (21) 3521974; fax (21) 3521985; e-mail humas@ekon.go.id; internet www.ekon.go.id.

Office of the Co-ordinating Minister for People's Welfare: Jalan Merdeka Barat 3, Jakarta Pusat; tel. (21) 3459444; fax (21) 3453289; internet www.menkokesra.go.id.

Office of the Co-ordinating Minister for Political, Legal and Security Affairs: Jalan Medan Merdeka Barat 15, Jakarta 10110; tel. (21) 3521121; fax (21) 3450918; e-mail dkpt@polkam.go.id; internet www.polkam.go.id.

Office of the State Secretary: Jalan Veteran 17–18, Jakarta 10110; tel. (21) 3849043; fax (21) 3452685; e-mail webmaster@setneg.go.id; internet www.setneg.go.id.

Ministry of Agriculture: Gedung D, 4th Floor, Jalan Harsono R. M. 3, Ragunan, Pasar Minggu, Jakarta Selatan 12550; tel. (21) 7804056; fax (21) 7804237; e-mail webmaster@deptan.go.id; internet www.deptan.go.id.

Ministry of Communications and Information Technology: Jalan Medan Merdeka Barat 9, Jakarta Pusat 10110; tel. (21) 3844227; fax (21) 3867600; e-mail info@depkominfo.go.id; internet www.depkominfo.go.id.

Ministry of Defence: Jalan Medan Merdeka Barat 13–14, Jakarta Pusat 10200; tel. (21) 3456184; fax (21) 3440023; e-mail webmaster@dephan.go.id; internet www.dephan.go.id.

Ministry of Education and Culture: Jalan Jenderal Sudirman, Senayan, Jakarta Pusat 10270; tel. (21) 57950226; fax (21) 5733125; e-mail pengaduan@kemdikbud.go.id; internet www.kemdiknas.go.id.

Ministry of Energy and Mineral Resources: Jalan Medan Merdeka Selatan 18, Jakarta 10110; tel. and fax (21) 3519881; e-mail pie@esdm.go.id; internet www.esdm.go.id.

Ministry of Finance: Jalan Lapangan Banteng Timur 2–4, Jakarta 10710; tel. (21) 3841067; fax (21) 3808395; e-mail helpdesk@depkeu.go.id; internet www.depkeu.go.id.

Ministry of Foreign Affairs: 10th Floor, Jalan Taman Pejambon 6, Jakarta Pusat 10110; tel. (21) 3441508; fax (21) 3857316; e-mail dipten@deplu.go.id; internet www.deplu.go.id.

Ministry of Forestry: Gedung Manggala Wanabakti, Blok I, 3rd Floor, Jalan Jenderal Gatot Subroto, Senayan, Jakarta 10270; tel. (21) 5704501; fax (21) 5720216; e-mail pusdata@dephut.go.id; internet www.dephut.go.id.

Ministry of Health: Blok X5, Jalan H. R. Rasuna Said, Kav. 4–9, Jakarta 12950; tel. (21) 5201590; fax (21) 5201591; internet www.depkes.go.id.

Ministry of Home Affairs: Gedung Utama, 4th Floor, Jalan Medan Merdeka Utara 7, Jakarta Pusat 10110; tel. (21) 3450038; fax (21) 3851193; e-mail pusdatinkomtel@depdagri.go.id; internet www.depdagri.go.id.

Ministry of Industry: Jalan Jenderal Gatot Subroto, Kav. 52–53, Jakarta Selatan 12950; tel. (21) 5252194; fax (21) 5261086; internet www.depperin.go.id.

Ministry of Justice and Human Rights: Jalan H. R. Rasuna Said, Kav. 6–7, Kuningan, Jakarta Selatan; tel. (21) 5253004; fax (21) 5253139; e-mail pullahta@depkumham.go.id; internet www.depkumham.go.id.

Ministry of Manpower and Transmigration: Jalan Jenderal Gatot Subroto, Kav. 51, Jakarta Selatan 12950; tel. (21) 5255683; fax (21) 7974488; e-mail redaksi_balitfo@nakertrans.go.id; internet www.depnakertrans.go.id.

Ministry of Marine Affairs and Fisheries: Gedung Humpus, Jalan Medan Merdeka Timur 16, Jakarta 10110; tel. (21) 3500023; fax (21) 3519133; e-mail mail@kkp.go.id; internet www.kkp.go.id.

Ministry of Public Works: Jalan Pattimura 20, Kebayoran Baru, Jakarta Selatan 12110; tel. (21) 7392262; fax (21) 7200793; e-mail sekjen@pu.go.id; internet www.pu.go.id.

Ministry of Religious Affairs: Jalan Lapangan Banteng Barat 3–4, Jakarta Pusat 10710; tel. (21) 3843005; fax (21) 3812306; e-mail pikda@depag.go.id; internet www.depag.go.id.

Ministry of Social Affairs: Jalan Salemba Raya 28, Jakarta 10430; tel. (21) 3103591; fax (21) 3103783; e-mail setjend@kemsos.go.id; internet www.depsos.go.id.

Ministry of Tourism and Creative Economy: Gedung Sapta Pesona, Jalan Medan Merdeka Barat 17, Jakarta Pusat 10110; tel. (21) 3838167; fax (21) 3849715; e-mail pusdatin@budpar.go.id; internet www.budpar.go.id.

Ministry of Trade: 2nd Floor, Jalan Jenderal Gatot Subroto, Kav. 52–53, Jakarta 12950; tel. (21) 5256548; fax (21) 5229592; internet www.depdag.go.id.

Ministry of Transportation: Jalan Medan Merdeka Barat 8, Jakarta 10110; tel. (21) 3811308; fax (21) 3862371; e-mail pusdatin@dephub.go.id; internet www.dephub.go.id.

Office of the Minister of State for Administrative and Bureaucratic Reform: Jalan Jenderal Sudirman, Kav. 69, Jakarta Selatan 12190; tel. (21) 7398381; internet www.menpan.go.id.

Office of the Minister of State for Co-operatives and Small and Medium-Sized Businesses: Jalan H. R. Rasuna Said, Kav. 3–5, POB 177, Jakarta Selatan 12940; tel. (21) 5204366; fax (21) 5204378; e-mail bagdat@depkop.go.id; internet www.depkop.go.id.

Office of the Minister of State for Development of Disadvantaged Regions: Jalan Abdul Muis 7, Jakarta Pusat 10110; tel. (21) 3500334; internet www.kemenegpdt.go.id.

Office of the Minister of State for the Environment: Gedung A, 6th Floor, Jalan D. I. Panjaitan, Kav. 24, Kebon Nanas, Jakarta 13410; tel. (21) 8580067; fax (21) 8517184; e-mail edukom@menlh.go.id; internet www.menlh.go.id.

Office of the Minister of State for Research and Technology: Gedung BPP Teknologi II, 5th–8th Floors, Jalan M. H. Thamrin 8, Jakarta Pusat 10340; tel. (21) 3169119; fax (21) 3101952; e-mail webmstr@ristek.go.id; internet www.ristek.go.id.

Office of the Minister of State for State Enterprises: Jalan Medan Merdeka Selatan 13, Jakarta 10110; e-mail sekretariat@bumn.go.id; internet www.bumn.com.

Office of the Minister of State for Women's Empowerment: Jalan Medan Merdeka Barat 15, Jakarta 10110; tel. (21) 3805563; fax (21) 3805562; e-mail biroren@menegpp.go.id; internet www.menegpp.go.id.

Office of the Minister of State for Youth and Sports Affairs: Jalan Gerbang Pemuda Senayan, Jakarta 10270; internet www.kemenpora.go.id.

OTHER GOVERNMENT BODIES

Badan Pemeriksa Keuangan (BPK) (Supreme Audit Board): Jalan Gatot Subroto 31, Jakarta 10210; tel. (21) 25549000; fax (21) 57854096; internet www.bpk.go.id; Chair. Drs HADI POERNOMO; Vice-Chair. HASAN BISRI.

National Economic Council: Jakarta; f. 1999; 13-mem. council formed to advise the President on economic policy; Chair. EMIL SALIM.

President and Legislature

PRESIDENT

Presidential Election, 8 July 2009

Candidate	Votes	% of votes
Gen. (retd) Susilo Bambang Yudhoyono (PD)	73,874,562	60.80
Megawati Sukarnoputri (PDI—P)	32,548,105	26.79
Muhammad Jusuf Kalla (Golkar)	15,081,814	12.41
Total	121,504,481	100.00

LEGISLATURE

People's Consultative Assembly (Majelis Permusyawaratan Rakyat)

Jalan Jenderal Gatot Subroto 6, Jakarta 10270; tel. (21) 57895049; fax (21) 57895048; e-mail kotaksurat@mpr.go.id; internet www.mpr.go.id.

In late 2002 the Constitution was amended to provide for the direct election of all members of the Majelis Permusyawaratan Rakyat (MPR—People's Consultative Assembly) at the next general election, held in 2004. The MPR thus became a bicameral institution comprising the Dewan Perwakilan Daerah (DPD—House of Representatives of the Regions) and the Dewan Perwakilan Rakyat (DPR—House of Representatives). The MPR subsequently consisted of the 550 members of the DPR and 128 regional delegates, increasing to 560 and 132 respectively at the 2009 election.

Speaker: SIDARTO DANUSUBROTO.

	Seats
Members of the Dewan Perwakilan Rakyat	560
Regional representatives	132
Total	692

House of Representatives (Dewan Perwakilan Rakyat)

Jalan Gatot Subroto 16, Jakarta; tel. (21) 586833; e-mail humas@dpr.go.id; internet www.dpr.go.id.

Speaker: MARZUKI ALIE.

Legislative Elections, 9 April 2009

	Seats
Partai Demokrat (PD)	148
Partai Golongan Karya (Golkar)	108
Partai Demokrasi Indonesia Perjuangan (PDI—P)	93
Partai Keadilan Sejahtera (PKS)	59
Partai Amanat Nasional (PAN)	42
Partai Persatuan Pembangunan (PPP)	39
Partai Gerakan Indonesia Raya (Gerindra)	30
Partai Kebangkitan Bangsa (PKB)	26
Partai Hati Nurani Rakyat (Hanura)	15
Total	560

Note: According to provisional results for the legislative elections that were held on 9 April 2014, PDI—P won some 18.9% of the votes cast, Golkar 14.6%, Gerindra 12.0%, the PD 9.8%, the PKB 9.0%, PAN 7.5%, the PKS 6.9%, the Partei NasDem 6.8%, the PPP 6.4% and Hanura 5.3%. The official results and seat allocations were due to be announced in May and a presidential election was scheduled for 9 July.

Election Commission

Komisi Pemilihan Umum (KPU): Jalan Imam Bonjol 29, Jakarta 10310; tel. (21) 31937223; fax (21) 3157759; e-mail redaktur@kpu.go.id; internet www.kpu.go.id; f. 1999; govt body; Chair. HUSNI KAMIL MANIK.

Political Organizations

All parties must adhere to the state philosophy of *Pancasila* and reject communism. A total of 12 national parties contested the legislative elections of April 2014.

Partai Amanat Nasional (PAN) (National Mandate Party): Rumah PAN, Jalan Raya Warung Buncit 17, Jakarta Selatan; tel. (21) 7975588; fax (21) 7975632; internet www.pan.or.id; f. 1998; aims to achieve democracy, progress and social justice, to limit the length of the presidential term of office and to increase autonomy in the provinces; Chair. HATTA RAJASA; Sec.-Gen. TAUFIK KURNIAWAN.

Partai Bulan Bintang (PBB) (Crescent Moon and Star Party): Jalan Raya Pasar Minggu 1B, Km 18, Jakarta Selatan; tel. (21) 79180734; fax (21) 79180765; internet bulan-bintang.org; f. 1998; Leader M. S. KABAN; Sec.-Gen. B. M. WIBOWO.

Partai Demokrasi Indonesia Perjuangan (PDI—P) (Indonesian Democratic Struggle Party): Jalan Lenteng Agung 99, Jakarta Selatan; tel. (21) 7806028; fax (21) 7814472; internet www.pdiperjuangan.or.id; est. by Megawati Sukarnoputri, fmr PDI leader, following her removal from PDI leadership by Govt in 1996; Chair. MEGAWATI SUKARNOPUTRI; Sec.-Gen. TJAHJO KUMOLO.

Partai Demokrat (PD): Jalan Kramat Raya 146, Jakarta Pusat 10450; tel. (21) 31907999; fax (21) 31908999; internet www.demokrat.or.id; f. 2001; Chair. Gen. (retd) SUSILO BAMBANG YUDHOYONO; Sec.-Gen. EDHIE 'IBAS' BASKORO YUDHOYONO.

Partai Gerakan Indonesia Raya (Gerindra) (Great Indonesia Movement Party): Jalan Harsono R. M. 54, Ragunan, Jakarta Selatan 12160; tel. (21) 7892377; fax (21) 7819712; e-mail badankomunikasi@partaigerindra.or.id; internet www.partaigerindra.or.id; f. 2008; Chair. SUHARDI; Sec.-Gen. AHMAD MUZANI.

Partai Golongan Karya (Golkar) (Party of Functional Groups): Jalan Anggrek Nellimurni, Jakarta 11480; tel. (21) 5302222; fax (21) 5303380; e-mail info@golkar.or.id; internet www.golkar.or.id; f. 1964; reorg. 1971; Pres. and Chair. ABURIZAL BAKRIE; Sec.-Gen. IDRUS MARHAM.

Partai Hati Nurani Rakyat (Hanura) (People's Conscience Party): Jalan Tanjung Karang 7, Menteng, Jakarta 10310; tel. (21) 31935334; fax (21) 3922054; e-mail info@hanura.or.id; internet www.hanura.com; f. 2006; Chair. WIRANTO; Sec.-Gen. YUS USMAN SUMANEGARA.

Partai Keadilan dan Persatuan Indonesia (PKPI) (Justice and Unity Party): Jalan Diponegoro 63, Menteng, Jakarta Pusat 10310; tel. (21) 31922733; fax (21) 31922822; e-mail info@pkpindonesia.or.id; internet pkpindonesia.or.id; f. 2002; Chair. SUTIYOSO; Sec.-Gen. LUKMAN F. MOKOGINTA.

Partai Keadilan Sejahtera (PKS) (Prosperous Justice Party): Jalan T. B. Simatupang 82, Pasar Minggu, Jakarta 21520; tel. (21) 78842176; fax (21) 78846456; e-mail partai@pks.or.id; internet www.pks.or.id; f. 2002; Islamic party; Chair. ANIS MATTA; Sec.-Gen. MUHAMMAD TAUFIK RIDHO.

Partai Kebangkitan Bangsa (PKB) (National Awakening Party): Jalan Raden Saleh 9, Jakarta Pusat 10430; tel. (21) 3145328; fax (21) 3145329; e-mail dpp@pkb.or.id; internet www.dpp.pkb.or.id; f. 1998; nationalist Islamic party; Chair. MUHAIMIN ISKANDAR.

Partai NasDem: Jalan R. P. Soeroso 44, Menteng, Jakarta 10350; tel. (21) 31927141; fax (21) 31927039; internet www.partainasdem.org; f. 2011; supports the creation of a welfare state; Chair. SURYA PALOH; Sec.-Gen PATRICE RIO CAPELLA.

Partai Persatuan Pembangunan (PPP) (United Development Party): Jalan Diponegoro 60, Jakarta Pusat 10310; tel. (21) 31936338; fax (21) 3142558; e-mail info@ppp.or.id; internet www.ppp.or.id; f. 1973; est. by merger of 4 Islamic parties; Leader SURYADHARMA ALI; Sec.-Gen. ROMAHURMUZIY.

In accordance with the 2005 peace agreement, Aceh is the only province that permits local parties. Three local parties were authorized to contest the elections of 9 April 2014 in the province: the Partai Aceh (PA—Aceh Party; f. 2008; Leader Muzakkir Manaf), the Partai Nasional Aceh (PNA—Aceh National Party; f. 2012; Chair. Irwansyah; Sec.-Gen. Muharram Idris) and the Partai Damai Aceh (PDA—Aceh Peace Party). The PA and the PNA both comprised many former combatants of the separatist group the Gerakan Aceh Merdeka (GAM—Free Aceh Movement). Since local parties could not field candidates at national level, the dominant local party, the PA, formed an alliance with Gerindra for the national elections.

Diplomatic Representation

EMBASSIES IN INDONESIA

Afghanistan: Jalan Dr Kusuma Atmaja 15, Jakarta Pusat 10310; tel. (21) 3143169; fax (21) 31935390; e-mail afghanembassy_jkk@yahoo.com; Ambassador FAZLURRAHMAN FAZIL.

Algeria: Jalan H. R. Rasuna Said, Kav. 10-1, Kuningan, Jakarta 12950; tel. (21) 5254719; fax (21) 5254654; e-mail ambaljak@cbn.net.id; internet www.embalgeria-id.org; Ambassador ABDELKRIM BELARBI.

Argentina: Menara Thamrin, Suite 1705, 17th Floor, Jalan M. H. Thamrin, Kav. 3, Jakarta 10250; tel. (21) 2303061; fax (21) 2303962; e-mail eisia@mrecic.gov.ar; internet www.eisia.mrecic.gov.ar; Ambassador RICARDO LUIS BOCALANDRO.

Armenia: Jakarta; Ambassador ANNA AGHAJANYAN.

Australia: Jalan H. R. Rasuna Said, Kav. C15–16, Kuningan, Jakarta 12940; tel. (21) 25505555; fax (21) 25505467; e-mail public-affairs-jakt@dfat.gov.au; internet www.indonesia.embassy.gov.au; Ambassador GREG MORIARTY.

Austria: Jalan Diponegoro 44, Menteng, Jakarta 10310; tel. (21) 23554005; fax (21) 31904881; e-mail jakarta-ob@bmeia.gv.at; internet www.austrian-embassy.or.id; Ambassador Dr ANDREAS KARABACZEK.

Azerbaijan: Jalan Karang Asem Tengah, Blok C-5, Kav. 20, Kuningan Timur, Jakarta 12950; tel. (21) 25554408; fax (21) 25554409; e-mail jakarta@mission.mfa.gov.az; internet www.azembassy.or.id; Ambassador TAMERLAN KARAYEV.

Bangladesh: Jalan Karang Asem Utara, Blok C4, No.12, Kav.42, Jakarta Selatan 12950; tel. (21) 5262173; fax (21) 5262174; e-mail bdootjak@yahoo.com; internet www.bdembassyjakarta.org; Ambassador NIZAMUL QUAUNINE.

Belarus: Jalan Patra Kuningan VII 3, Kuningan, Jakarta Selatan 12950; tel. (21) 5251388; fax (21) 52960207; e-mail indonesia@mfa.gov.by; internet www.belembassy.org/eng/06.html; Ambassador VLADIMIR LOPATO-ZAGORSKY.

Belgium: Deutsche Bank Bldg, 16th Floor, Jalan Imam Bonjol 80, Jakarta 10310; tel. (21) 3162030; fax (21) 3162035; e-mail jakarta@diplobel.fed.be; internet www.diplomatie.be/jakarta; Ambassador FILIP CUMPS.

Bosnia and Herzegovina: Menara Imperium, 11th Floor, Suite D-2, Metropolitan Kuningan Super Blok, Kav. 1, Jalan H. R. Rasuna Said, Jakarta 12980; tel. (21) 83703022; fax (21) 83703029; Ambassador TARIK BUKVIC.

Brazil: Menara Mulia, Suite 1602, Jalan Jenderal Gatot Subroto, Kav. 9–11, Jakarta 12390; tel. (21) 5265656; fax (21) 5265659; e-mail brasemb.jacarta@itamaraty.gov.br; Ambassador PAULO ALBERTO DA SILVEIRA SOARES.

Brunei: Jalan Teuku Umar 9, Menteng, Jakarta Pusat 10350; tel. (21) 31906080; fax (21) 31905070; e-mail kbjindo@cbn.net.id; Ambassador Dato' Paduka MAHMUD Haji SAIDIN.

Bulgaria: Jalan Imam Bonjol 34–36, Menteng, Jakarta Pusat 10310; tel. (21) 3904048; fax (21) 3904049; e-mail embassy.jakarta@mfa.bg; internet www.mfa.bg/embassies/indonesia; Chargé d'affaires a.i. KATINA NOVKOVA.

Cambodia: Jalan T. B. Simatupang, Kav. 13, Jakarta Selatan 12520; tel. (21) 7812523; fax (21) 7812524; e-mail camemb.jkt@mfa.gov.kh; Ambassador KAN PHARITH.

Canada: World Trade Center, 6th Floor, Jalan Jenderal Sudirman, Kav. 29–31, POB 8324/JKS.MP, Jakarta 12920; tel. (21) 25507800; fax (21) 25507811; e-mail canadianembassy.jkrta@international.gc.ca; internet www.canadainternational.gc.ca/indonesia-indonesie; Ambassador DONALD BOBIASH.

Chile: City Tower Bldg, 27th Floor, Jalan M.H. Thamrin 81, Jakarta Pusat 10310; tel. (21) 31997201; fax (21) 31997204; e-mail emchijak@cbn.net.id; internet chileabroad.gov.cl/indonesia; Ambassador EDUARDO RUIZ ASMUSSEN.

China, People's Republic: Jalan Mega Kuningan 2, Karet Kuningan, Jakarta 12950; tel. (21) 5761039; fax (21) 5761034; e-mail chinaemb_id@mfa.gov.cn; internet id.china-embassy.org; Ambassador LIU JIANCHAO.

Colombia: Plaza Central Bldg, 12th Floor, Jalan Jenderal Sudirman, Kav. 47, Jakarta 12190; tel. (21) 57903560; fax (21) 52905217; e-mail eindonesia@cancilleria.gov.co; Ambassador ALFONSO GARZÓN MÉNDEZ.

Croatia: Menara Mulia, Suite 2801, Jalan Gatot Subroto, Kav. 9–11, Jakarta 12930; tel. (21) 5257822; fax (21) 5204073; e-mail jakarta@mvep.hr; internet www.croatemb.or.id; Ambassador ŽELJKO CIMBUR.

Cuba: Jalan Logan, Blok D-58, Permata Hijau, Jakarta 12210; tel. (21) 5485902; fax (21) 5328174; e-mail cubaindo@cbn.net.id; Ambassador ENNA ESTHER VIANT VALDÉS.

Cyprus: c/o Jalan Purwakarta 8, Menteng, Jakarta Pusat; tel. (21) 3106367; fax (21) 3919256; e-mail nicpanayi@yahoo.com; Ambassador NICOS PANAYI.

Czech Republic: Jalan Gereja Theresia 20, Menteng, Jakarta Pusat 10350; tel. (21) 2396112; fax (21) 3904078; e-mail jakarta@embassy.mzv.cz; internet www.mfa.cz/jakarta; Ambassador TOMÁŠ SMETÁNKA.

Denmark: Menara Rajawali, 25th Floor, Jalan Mega Kuningan, Lot 5.1, Jakarta 12950; tel. (21) 5761478; fax (21) 5761535; e-mail jktamb@um.dk; internet indonesien.um.dk; Ambassador MARTIN BILLE HERMANN.

Ecuador: World Trade Center, 16th Floor, Jalan Jenderal Sudirman, Kav. 31, Jakarta 12920; tel. (21) 5211484; fax (21) 5226954; e-mail ecuadorinindonesia@gmail.com; Ambassador EDUARDO ALBERTO CALDERÓN LEDESMA.

Egypt: Jalan Teuku Umar 68, Menteng, Jakarta Pusat 10310; tel. (21) 3143440; fax (21) 3145073; e-mail Jakarta_emb@mfa.gov.eg; internet www.mfa.gov.eg/Jakarta_Emb; Ambassador BAHAA BAHGAT IBRAHIM DESSOUKI AL DEEN.

Fiji: Menara Topaz, 14th Floor, Jalan M. H. Thambrin, Kav. 9, Jakarta 10350; tel. (21) 3902543; fax (21) 3902544; e-mail stui_cavuilati@yahoo.com; Ambassador RATU SEREMAIA TUI CAVUILATI.

Finland: Menara Rajawali, 9th Floor, Lot 5.1, Jalan Mega Kuningan, Kawasan Mega Kuningan, Jakarta 12950; tel. (21) 5761650; fax (21) 5761631; e-mail sanomat.jak@formin.fi; internet www.finland.or.id; Ambassador PÄIVI HILTUNEN-TOIVIO (designate).

France: Jalan M. H. Thamrin, 40th Floor, 1 Jakarta Pusat 10310; tel. (21) 23557600; fax (21) 23557602; e-mail contact@ambafrance-id.org; internet www.ambafrance-id.org; Ambassador CORINNE BREUZE.

Georgia: Jalan Karang Asem Tengah, Block C5, No. 22, Kuningan, Jakarta Selatan 12950; tel. (21) 29410842; fax (21) 29410694; e-mail jakarta.emb@mfa.gov.ge; internet www.indonesia.mfa.gov.ge; Ambassador ZURAB ALEKSIDZE.

Germany: Jalan M. H. Thamrin 1, Jakarta Pusat 10310; tel. (21) 39855000; fax (21) 39855130; e-mail kontakt-pr@jaka.diplo.de; internet www.jakarta.diplo.de; Ambassador Dr GEORG WITSCHEL.

Greece: Plaza 89, 12th Floor, Suite 1203, Jalan H. R. Rasuna Said, Kav. X-7 No. 6, Kuningan, Jakarta Selatan 12940; tel. (21) 5207776;

fax (21) 5207753; e-mail grembas@cbn.net.id; internet www.greekembassy.or.id; Ambassador GEORGIOS VEIS.

Holy See: Jalan Merdeka Timur 18, POB 4227, Jakarta Pusat (Apostolic Nunciature); tel. (21) 3841142; fax (21) 3841143; e-mail vatjak@cbn.net.id; Apostolic Nuncio ANTONIO GUIDO FILIPAZZI (Titular Archbishop of Sutrium).

Hungary: Jalan H. R. Rasuna Said 36, Kav. X-3, Kuningan, Jakarta 12950; tel. (21) 5203459; fax (21) 5203461; e-mail mission.jkt@kum.hu; internet www.mfa.gov.hu/kulkepviselet/id; Ambassador SZILVESZTER BUS.

India: Jalan H. R. Rasuna Said, Kav. S-1, Kuningan, Jakarta 12950; tel. (21) 5204150; fax (21) 5204160; e-mail ambasador@net-zap.com; internet www.indianembassyjakarta.com; Ambassador GURJIT SINGH.

Iran: Jalan Hos Cokroaminoto 110, Menteng, Jakarta Pusat 10310; tel. (21) 31931378; fax (21) 3107860; e-mail irembjkt@indo.net.id; internet www.iranembassy.or.id; Ambassador MAHMOUD FARAZANDER.

Iraq: Jalan Teuku Umar 38, Jakarta 10350; tel. (21) 3904067; fax (21) 3904066; e-mail iraqembi@rad.net.id; Ambassador ISMAEL SHAFIQ MUHSIN.

Italy: Jalan Diponegoro 45, Menteng, Jakarta Pusat 10310; tel. (21) 31937445; fax (21) 31937422; e-mail ambasciata.jakarta@esteri.it; internet www.ambjakarta.esteri.it; Ambassador FEDERICO FAILLA.

Japan: Jalan M. H. Thamrin 24, Jakarta Pusat 10350; tel. (21) 31924308; fax (21) 31925460; internet www.id.emb-japan.go.jp; Ambassador YOSHINORI KATORI.

Jordan: Artha Graha Tower, 9th Floor, Sudirman Central Business District, Jalan Jenderal Sudirman, Kav. 52–53, Jakarta 12190; tel. (21) 5153483; fax (21) 5153482; e-mail jordanem@scbd.net.id; internet www.jordanembassy.or.id; Ambassador MUHAMMAD HASSAN DAWODIEH.

Korea, Democratic People's Republic: Jalan Teluk Betung 1–2, Jakarta Pusat 12050; tel. (21) 31908425; fax (21) 31908427; e-mail dprkorea@rad.net.id; Ambassador RI JONG RYUL.

Korea, Republic: Plaza Office Tower, 30th Floor, Jalan M. H. Thamrin, Kav. 28-30, Jakarta Pusat 10350; tel. (21) 5201915; fax (21) 5254159; e-mail koremb_in@mofat.go.kr; internet idn.mofat.go.kr; Ambassador KIM YOUNG-SUN.

Kuwait: Jalan Mega Kuningan Barat III, Kav. 16–17, Jakarta; tel. (21) 5764159; fax (21) 5764561; e-mail jakarta@mofa.gov.kw; Ambassador NASER BAREH SHAHER EL-ENEZI.

Laos: Jalan Patra Kuningan XIV 1A, Kuningan, Jakarta 12950; tel. (21) 5229602; fax (21) 5229601; e-mail laoembjktof@hotmail.com; Ambassador PRASITH SAYASITH.

Lebanon: Jalan YBR V 82, Kuningan, Jakarta 12950; tel. (21) 5253074; fax (21) 5207121; e-mail lebanon_embassy_jkt@yahoo.com; Ambassador VICTOR ZMETER.

Libya: Jalan Kintamani Raya II, Blok C-17, Kav. 6–7, Kuningan Timur, Jakarta Selatan 12950; tel. (21) 52920033; fax (21) 52920036; e-mail gsplaj@cbn.net.id; Chargé d'affaires a.i. ABDUSSAMEE HARB.

Malaysia: Jalan H. R. Rasuna Said, Kav. X-6 Nos 1–3, Kuningan, Jakarta 12950; tel. (21) 5224947; fax (21) 5224974; e-mail maljakarta@kln.gov.my; internet www.kln.gov.my/web/idn_jakarta; Ambassador Datuk Seri ZAHRAIN MOHAMED HASHIM.

Mexico: Menara Mulia, Suite 2306, Jalan Jenderal Gatot Subroto, Kav. 9–11, Jakarta Selatan 12930; tel. (21) 5203980; fax (21) 5203978; e-mail embmexico@gmail.com; internet embamex.sre.gob.mx/indonesia; Ambassador MARY MELBA PRIA OLAVARRIETA.

Morocco: Jalan Denpasar Raya, Blok A-13, Kav. 1, Kuningan, Jakarta 12950; tel. (21) 5200773; fax (21) 5200586; e-mail sifamaind@gmail.com; Ambassador MOHAMED MAJDI.

Mozambique: Jalan Karang Asem II, Blok C-10, Kav. 2–3, Kuningan Timur, Jakarta 12950; tel. (21) 5227955; fax (21) 5227954; e-mail embamoc@cbn.net.id; Ambassador CARLOS AGUSTINHO DO ROŞARIO.

Myanmar: Jalan Haji Agus Salim 109, Menteng, Jakarta 10350; tel. (21) 327684; fax (21) 327204; e-mail myanmar@cbn.net.id; Ambassador MIN LWIN.

Netherlands: Jalan H. R. Rasuna Said, Kav. S-3, Kuningan, Jakarta 12950; tel. (21) 5248200; fax (21) 5700734; e-mail jak@minbuza.nl; internet indonesia.nlembassy.org; Ambassador TJEERD DE ZWAAN.

New Zealand: Sentral Senayan 2, 10th Floor, Jalan Asia Afrika 8, Gelora Bung Karno, Jakarta Pusat 10270; tel. (21) 29955800; fax (21) 57974578; e-mail nzembjak@cbn.net.id; internet www.nzembassy.com/indonesia; Ambassador DAVID TAYLOR.

Nigeria: Jalan Taman Patra XIV 11, Kuningan Timur, POB 3649, Jakarta Selatan 12950; tel. (21) 5260922; fax (21) 5260924; e-mail embnig@centrin.net.id; Ambassador ABDUL RAHMAN SALLAHDEEN.

Norway: Menara Rajawali, 20th Floor, Kawasan Mega Kuningan, Jakarta 12950; tel. (21) 29650000; fax (21) 29650001; e-mail emb.jakarta@mfa.no; internet www.norway.or.id; Ambassador STIG INGEMAR TRAAVIK.

Pakistan: Jalan Mega Kuningan, Blok E-3.9, Kav. 5–8, Kawasan Mega Kuningan, Jakarta Selatan 12950; tel. (21) 57851836; fax (21) 57851645; e-mail embassy@parepjakarta.com; internet www.mofa.gov.pk/indonesia; Ambassador ATTIYA MAHMOOD.

Panama: World Trade Center, 13th Floor, Jalan Jenderal Sudirman, Kav. 29–31, Jakarta 12920; tel. (21) 5711867; fax (21) 5711933; e-mail panaemb@net2cyber.web.id; Ambassador ROSEMARY SACETH DE LEÓN.

Papua New Guinea: Panin Bank Centre, 6th Floor, Jalan Jenderal Sudirman 1, Jakarta 10270; tel. (21) 7251218; fax (21) 7201012; e-mail kdujkt@cbn.net.id; Ambassador Cdre PETER ILAU.

Peru: Menara Rajawali, 12th Floor, Jalan Mega Kuningan, Lot 5.1, Kawasan Mega Kuningan, Jakarta Selatan 12950; tel. (21) 5761820; fax (21) 5761825; e-mail embaperu@cbn.net.id; Ambassador ROBERTO SEMINARIO PORTOCARRERO.

Philippines: Jalan Imam Bonjol 6–8, Jakarta Pusat 10310; tel. (21) 3100334; fax (21) 3151167; e-mail phjkt@indo.net.id; internet philembjkt.com; Ambassador MARIA ROŞARIO C. AGUINALDO.

Poland: Jalan H. R. Rasuna Said, Blok IV-3, Kav. X, Jakarta Selatan 12950; tel. (21) 2525938; fax (21) 2525958; e-mail dzakarta.amb.sekretariat@msz.gov.pl; internet www.dzakarta.msz.gov.pl; Ambassador TADEUSZ ANDRZEJ SZUMOWSKI.

Portugal: Jalan Indramayu 2A, Menteng, Jakarta 10310; tel. (21) 31908030; fax (21) 31908031; e-mail porembjak@cbn.net.id; internet www.embassyportugaljakarta.or.id; Ambassador JOAQUIM MOREIRA DE LEMOS.

Qatar: Lot E 2.3, Jalan Mega Kuningan Barat, Kawasan Mega Kuningan, Jakarta 12950; tel. (21) 57906065; fax (21) 57906564; e-mail jakarta@mofa.gov.qa; Ambassador MUHAMMAD KHATER IBRAHIM AL-KHATER.

Romania: Jalan Teuku Cik Di Tiro 42A, Menteng, Jakarta Pusat; tel. (21) 3900489; fax (21) 3106241; e-mail romind@indosat.net.id; internet jakarta.mae.ro; Ambassador VALERICA EPURE.

Russia: Jalan H. R. Rasuna Said, Kav. X-7 Nos 1–2, Jakarta 12940; tel. (21) 5222912; fax (21) 5222916; e-mail rusemb.indonesia@mid.ru; internet www.indonesia.mid.ru; Ambassador MIKHAIL Y. GALUZIN.

Saudi Arabia: Jalan M. T. Haryono, Kav. 27, Cawang Atas, Jakarta 13630; tel. (21) 8011533; fax (21) 8011527; e-mail idemb@mofa.gov.sa; Ambassador MUSTAFA IBRAHIM AL-MUBARAK.

Serbia: Jalan Hos Cokroaminoto 109, Jakarta Pusat 10310; tel. (21) 3143560; fax (21) 3143613; e-mail embjakarta@serbian-embassy.org; internet www.jakarta.mfa.rs; Ambassador JOVAN JOVANOVIĆ.

Singapore: Jalan H. R. Rasuna Said, Blok X-4, Kav. 2, Kuningan, Jakarta 12950; tel. (21) 5201489; fax (21) 5201486; e-mail singemb_jkt@sgmfa.gov.sg; internet www.mfa.gov.sg/jkt; Ambassador ANIL KUMAR NAYAR.

Slovakia: Jalan Prof. Mohammed Yamin 29, POB 1368, Menteng, Jakarta Pusat 10310; tel. (21) 3101068; fax (21) 3101180; e-mail emb.jakarta@mzv.sk; internet www.mzv.sk/jakarta; Ambassador MICHAL SLIVOVIČ.

Somalia: Jalan Permata Hijau Raya, Blok T, No. 8, Kebayoran Lama, Jakarta Selatan 12210; tel. (21) 8311506; fax (21) 8352586; e-mail somalirep_jkt@yahoo.com; internet www.indonesia.somaligov.net; Ambassador MOHAMED OLOW BAROW.

South Africa: Wisma GKBI, Suite 705, Jalan Jenderal Sudirman 28, Jakarta 10210; tel. (21) 5740660; fax (21) 5740655; e-mail saembpol@centrin.net.id; internet www.dirco.gov.za/jakarta; Ambassador NOEL NOA LEHOKO.

Spain: Jalan H. Agus Salim 61, Menteng, Jakarta 10350; tel. (21) 3142355; fax (21) 31935134; e-mail emb.yakarta@mae.es; Ambassador RAFAEL CONDE DE SARO.

Sri Lanka: Jalan Diponegoro 70, Jakarta 10320; tel. (21) 3161886; fax (21) 3107962; e-mail lankaemb@telkom.net; Ambassador Maj.-Gen. (retd) NANDA MALLAWAARACHCHI.

Sudan: Jalan Lembang 7, Menteng, Jakarta Pusat 10310; tel. (21) 3908234; fax (21) 3908235; e-mail sudanind@cbn.net.id; Ambassador ABD AL-RAHIM AL-SIDDIQ MOHAMED OMAR.

Suriname: Jalan Padalarang 9, Menteng, Jakarta Pusat 10310; tel. (21) 3154437; fax (21) 3154556; e-mail ambassador@srembassyjkt.org; Ambassador TITI AMINA PARDI.

Sweden: Menara Rajawali, 9th Floor, Jalan Mega Kuningan, Lot 5.1, Kawasan Mega Kuningan, Jakarta Selatan 12950; tel. (21) 55535900; fax (21) 5762691; e-mail ambassaden.jakarta@foreign.ministry.se; internet www.swedenabroad.com/jakarta; Ambassador EWA POLANO.

Switzerland: Jalan H. R. Rasuna Said, Blok X-3 No. 2, Kuningan, Jakarta Selatan 12950; tel. (21) 5256061; fax (21) 5202289; e-mail jak

.vertretung@eda.admin.ch; internet www.eda.admin.ch/jakarta; Ambassador HEINZ WALKER-NEDERKOORN.

Syria: Jalan Karang Asem I 8, Jakarta 12950; tel. (21) 5255991; fax (21) 5202511; e-mail syrianemb@cbn.net.id; internet syrianembassy.or.id; Chargé d'affaires a.i. BASSAM AL-KHATIB.

Thailand: Jalan Imam Bonjol 74, Jakarta Pusat 10310; tel. (21) 3904052; fax (21) 3107469; e-mail thaijkt@indo.net.id; internet www.thaiembassy.org/jakarta; Ambassador PASKORN SIRIYAPHAN.

Timor-Leste: Gedung Surya, 11th Floor, Jalan M. H. Thamrin, Kav. 9, Jakarta Pusat 10350; tel. (21) 3902678; fax (21) 3902660; e-mail manser_tl@yahoo.com; Ambassador MANUEL SERRANO.

Tunisia: Jalan Karang Asem Tengah, Blok C-5, Kav. 15, Kuningan, Jakarta Selatan 12950; tel. (21) 52892328; fax (21) 5255889; e-mail atjkt@uninet.net.id; Ambassador MOURAD BELHASSEN.

Turkey: Jalan H. R. Rasuna Said, Kav. 1, Kuningan, Jakarta 12950; tel. (21) 5256250; fax (21) 5226056; e-mail embassy.jakarta@mfa.gov.tr; internet jakarta.emb.mfa.gov.tr; Ambassador ZEKERIYA AKÇAM.

Ukraine: Jalan Jenderal Sudirman, Kav. 27, Mayapada Tower 2, 8th Floor, Jakarta 12920; tel. (21) 2500801; fax (21) 2500802; e-mail emb_id@mfa.gov.ua; internet www.mfa.gov.ua/indonesia; Ambassador VOLODYMYR PAKHIL.

United Arab Emirates: Jalan Prof. Dr Satrio, Blok C-4, Kav. 16–17, Jakarta 12950; tel. (21) 5206518; fax (21) 5206526; e-mail jakarta@mofa.gov.ae; internet www.uaeembassyjakarta.org/index.php; Ambassador AHMED ABDULLAH MUHAMMED AL-MUSALLI.

United Kingdom: Jalan Patra Kuningan Raya, Blok L5-6, Jakarta 12950; tel. (21) 23565200; fax (21) 23565351; e-mail Jakarta.MCS@fco.gov.uk; internet ukinindonesia.fco.gov.uk; Ambassador MARK CANNING.

USA: Jalan Medan Merdeka Selatan 3–5, Jakarta 10110; tel. (21) 34359000; fax (21) 3862259; e-mail jakconsul@state.gov; internet jakarta.usembassy.gov; Ambassador ROBERT BLAKE.

Uzbekistan: Jalan Daksa III 14, Kebayoran Baru, Jakarta; tel. (21) 7200950; fax (21) 5222582; e-mail inbox@uzbemb.or.id; internet www.uzbemb.or.id; Ambassador SHAVKAT DJAMOLOV.

Venezuela: Menara Mulia, 20th Floor, Suite 2005, Jalan Jenderal Gatot Subroto, Kav. 9–11, Jakarta Selatan 12930; tel. (21) 5227547; fax (21) 5227549; e-mail evenjakt@indo.net.id; Chargé d'affaires a.i. MARÍA VIRGINIA MENZONES LICCIONI.

Viet Nam: Jalan Teuku Umar 25, Jakarta Pusat 10350; tel. (21) 3100358; fax (21) 3149615; e-mail jakarta@mofa.gov.vn; internet www.vietnamembassy-indonesia.org; Ambassador NGUYEN XUAN THUY.

Yemen: Jalan Subang 18, Menteng, Jakarta Pusat 10310; tel. (21) 3108029; fax (21) 3904946; e-mail yemb-jakarta@mofa.gov.ye; Ambassador ALI AL-SOSWA.

Zimbabwe: Jalan Patra Kuningan VII 5, Jakarta Selatan 12950; tel. (21) 5221378; fax (21) 5250365; e-mail zimjakarta@yahoo.com; Ambassador ALICE MAGEZA.

Judicial System

There is one codified criminal law for the whole of Indonesia. In December 1989 the Islamic Judicature Bill, giving wider powers to *Shari'a* courts, was approved by the Dewan Perwakilan Rakyat (House of Representatives). The new law gave Muslim courts authority over civil matters, such as marriage. Muslims may still choose to appear before a secular court. Europeans are subject to the Code of Civil Law published in the State Gazette in 1847. Alien orientals (i.e. Arabs, Indians, etc.) and Chinese are subject to certain parts of the Code of Civil Law and the Code of Commerce. The work of codifying this law has started, but, in view of the great complexity and diversity of customary law, it may be expected to take a considerable time to achieve. In June 2005 a judicial commission was established; the seven-member body, appointed by the House of Representatives, was charged with reforming the judiciary and with nominating Supreme Court justices, including the Chief Justice.

Supreme Court (Mahkamah Agung): Jalan Merdeka Utara 9–13, Jakarta 10110; tel. (21) 3843348; fax (21) 3811057; e-mail info@ma-ri.go.id; internet www.mahkamahagung.go.id; final court of appeal; comprised 49 judges at Nov. 2012; Chief Justice HATTA ALI.

Constitutional Court (Mahkamah Konstitusi): Jalan Medan Merdeka Barat 6, Jakarta 10110; tel. (21) 23529000; fax (21) 3520177; e-mail humas@mahkamahkonstitusi.go.id; internet www.mahkamahkonstitusi.go.id; f. 2003; adjudicates the following matters: constitutionality of a law; impeachment; dissolution of a political party; disputes between state agencies; and disputes concerning election results; composed of nine justices, of whom three each are appointed by the President, the Supreme Court and the House of Representatives; Chief Justice HAMDAN ZOELVA.

High Courts in Jakarta Surabaya, Medan, Makassar, Banda Aceh, Padang, Palembang, Bandung, Semarang, Banjarmasin, Menado, Denpasar, Ambon and Jayapura deal with appeals from the District Courts. District Courts deal with marriage, divorce and reconciliation.

Religion

All citizens are required to state their religion. The Ministry of Religion accords official status to six religions—Islam, the Christian faiths of Protestantism and Catholicism, Hinduism, Buddhism and Confucianism. According to a survey in 2000, 88.2% of the population were Muslims, while 5.9% were Protestant, 3.1% were Roman Catholic, 1.8% were Hindus, 0.8% were Buddhists and 0.2% professed adherence to other religions, such as other Christian denominations and Judaism, which remains unrecognized.

National religious councils—representing the official religious traditions—were established to serve as liaison bodies between religious adherents and the Government and to advise the Government on the application of religious principles to various elements of national life.

ISLAM

Indonesia has the world's largest Muslim population.

Majelis Ulama Indonesia (MUI) (Indonesian Ulama Council): Jalan Proklamasi 51, Menteng, Jakarta Pusat; tel. (21) 31902666; fax (21) 31905266; e-mail mui-online@mui.or.id; internet www.mui.or.id; central Muslim org.; Chair. Dr SAHAL MAHFUDH; Sec.-Gen. ICHWAN SAM.

Muhammadiyah: Jalan Menteng Raya 62, Jakarta Pusat 10340; tel. (21) 3903021; fax (21) 3903024; e-mail pp_muhammadiyah@yahoo.com; internet www.muhammadiyah.or.id; f. 1912; 28m. mems; second largest Muslim org. in Indonesia; incorporates the Muhammadiyah Youth Asscn and 'Aisyiyah', a women's org.; religious, charitable and educational activities; has established more than 5,000 Islamic schools; Chair. Dr DIN SYAMSUDDIN; Sec.-Gen. Dr AGUNG DANARTO.

Nahdlatul Ulama (NU) (Revival of the Islamic Scholars): Jalan Kramat Raya 164, Jakarta 10430; tel. (21) 3914014; fax (21) 3914013; internet www.nu.or.id; f. 1926; 30m. mems; largest Muslim org. in Indonesia; promotes Islamic teachings, as well as culture, education and economic devt; directly involved in politics from the mid-1950s until 1984; Chair. Dr SAID AQIL SIRADJ; Sec.-Gen. Dr MARSUDI SYUHUD.

CHRISTIANITY

Persekutuan Gereja-Gereja di Indonesia (Communion of Churches in Indonesia): Jalan Salemba Raya 10, Jakarta Pusat 10430; tel. (21) 3150451; fax (21) 3150457; e-mail pgi@bit.net.id; internet www.pgi.or.id; f. 1950; 81 mem. churches; Chair. Rev. ROYKE OCTAVIAN RORING; Gen. Sec. GOMAR GULTOM.

The Roman Catholic Church

Indonesia comprises 10 archdioceses and 27 dioceses. At 31 December 2007 there were an estimated 6,537,062 adherents in Indonesia, representing 3.9% of the population.

Bishops' Conference: Konferensi Waligereja Indonesia (KWI), Jalan Cut Meutia 10, POB 3044, Jakarta 10340; tel. and fax (21) 31925757; e-mail dokpen@kawali.org; internet www.kawali.org; f. 1973; Pres. IGNATIUS SUHARYO.

Archbishop of Ende: Most Rev. VICENTIUS SENSI, Keuskupan Agung, POB 210, Jalan Katedral 5, Ndona-Ende 86312, Flores; tel. (381) 21176; fax (381) 21606; e-mail uskup@ende.parokinet.org.

Archbishop of Jakarta: Most Rev. IGNATIUS SUHARYO HARDJOATMODJO, Keuskupan Agung, Jalan Katedral 7, Jakarta 10710; tel. (21) 3813345; fax (21) 3855681.

Archbishop of Kupang: Most Rev. PETER TURANG, Keuskupan Agung Kupang, Jalan Thamrin, Oepoi, Kupang 85111, Timor NTT; tel. (380) 826199; fax (380) 833331.

Archbishop of Makassar: Most Rev. JOHANNES LIKU ADA', Keuskupan Agung, Jalan Thamrin 5–7, Makassar 90111, Sulawesi Selatan; tel. (411) 315744; fax (411) 326674; e-mail sekr_kams@yahoo.com.

Archbishop of Medan: Most Rev. BONGSU ANTONIUS SINAGA, Jalan Imam Bonjol 39, POB 1191, Medan 20152, Sumatra Utara; tel. (61) 4519768; fax (61) 4145745; e-mail sekrkam@hotmail.com.

Archbishop of Merauke: Most Rev. NICOLAUS ADI SEPTURA, Keuskupan Agung, Jalan Mandala 30, Merauke 99602, Papua; tel. (971) 321011; fax (971) 321311.

Archbishop of Palembang: Most Rev. ALOYSIUS SUDARSO, Keuskupan Agung, Jalan Tasik 18, Palembang 30135; tel. (711) 350417; fax (711) 314776; e-mail alva@mdp.net.id.

Archbishop of Pontianak: Most Rev. HIERONYMUS HERCULANUS BUMBUN, Keuskupan Agung, Jalan A. R. Hakin 92A, POB 1119, Pontianak 78011, Kalimantan Barat; tel. (561) 732382; fax (561) 738785; e-mail kap@pontianak.wasantara.net.id.

Archbishop of Samarinda: Most Rev. FLORENTINUS SULUI HAJANG HAU, Keuskupan Agung, POB 1062, Jalan Gunung Merbabu 41, Samarinda 75010; tel. (541) 741193; fax (541) 203120.

Archbishop of Semarang: Most Rev. JOHANNES MARIA TRILAKSYANTA PUJASUMARTA, Keuskupan Agung, Jalan Pandanaran 13, Semarang 50244; tel. (24) 8312276; fax (24) 8414741; e-mail uskup@semarang.parokinet.org.

Other Christian Churches

Protestant Church in Indonesia (Gereja Protestan di Indonesia): Jalan Medan Merdeka Timur 10, Jakarta 10110; tel. (21) 3519003; fax (21) 34830224; consists of 12 churches of Calvinistic tradition; 3,047,300 mems, 4,808 congregations; Chair. Rev. Dr SAMUEL B. HAKH.

Numerous other Protestant communities exist throughout Indonesia, mainly organized on a local basis.

BUDDHISM

All-Indonesia Buddhist Association: Jakarta.

Indonesian Buddhist Council: Jakarta.

HINDUISM

Hindu Dharma Council: Jakarta.

The Press

PRINCIPAL DAILIES

Bali

Harian Pagi Umum (Bali Post): Jalan Kepundung 67A, Denpasar 80232; tel. (61) 225764; fax (61) 249483; e-mail iklan@balipost.co.id; internet www.balipost.co.id; f. 1948; daily (Indonesian edn), weekly (English edn); Editor-in-Chief NYOMAN WIRATA; circ. 25,000.

Java

Angkatan Bersenjata: Jalan Kramat Raya 94, Jakarta Pusat; tel. (21) 46071; fax (21) 366870; armed forces newspaper.

Bandung Post: Jalan Lodaya 38A, Bandung 40264; tel. (22) 305124; fax (22) 302882; f. 1979; Chief Editor AHMAD SAELAN; Dir AHMAD JUSACC.

Berita Buana: RT 14/9, Johar Baru Village, District Johar Baru, Central Jakarta; tel. (21) 95316544; fax (21) 4203376; internet beritabuana.co; f. 1970; relaunched 1990; Indonesian; Editor-in-Chief DADA SUGANDI; Editor MUFI AL AKHYARI; circ. 150,000.

Bisnis Indonesia: Wisma Bisnis Indonesia, Jalan K. H. Mas Mansyur 12A, Karet, Jakarta 10220; tel. (21) 57901023; fax (21) 57901025; e-mail redaksi@bisnis.co.id; internet www.bisnis.com; f. 1985; available online; Indonesian; Editor-in-Chief ARIF BUDISUSILO; circ. 72,000.

Harian Pelita: Jalan Minangkabau 35B-C Manggarai, Jakarta Selatan 12970; tel. (21) 83706765; fax (21) 83706771; e-mail redaksi@pelitaonline.com; internet www.harianpelita.com; f. 1974; 6 a week; Indonesian; Muslim; Chief Editor A. BASORI.

Harian Terbit: Jalan Pulogadung 15, Kawasan Industri Pulogadung, Jakarta 13920; tel. (21) 4603973; fax (21) 4603970; e-mail terbit@harianterbit.com; internet www.harianterbit.com; f. 1972; Indonesian; Editor-in-Chief TARMAN AZZAM; Man. Editor ALI AKBAR COAL; circ. 120,000.

Harian Umum AB: CTC Bldg, 2nd Floor, Kramat Raya 94, Jakarta Pusat; f. 1965; official armed forces journal; Dir GOENARSO; Editor-in-Chief N. SOEPANGAT; circ. 80,000.

The Jakarta Post: Jalan Palmerah Barat 142–143, Jakarta 10270; tel. (21) 5300476; fax (21) 5350050; e-mail editorial@thejakartapost.com; internet www.thejakartapost.com; f. 1983; English; Exec. Dir RIYADI SUPARNO; Chief Editor MEIDYATAMA SURYODININGRAT; circ. 85,000.

Jawa Pos: Graha Pena Bldg, 4th Floor, Achmad Yani 88, Surabaya 60234; tel. (31) 8283333; fax (31) 8285555; e-mail digital@jawapos.co.id; internet www.jawapos.co.id; f. 1949; Indonesian; Pres. Dir AZRUL ANANDA; Chief Editor LEAK KUSTIYA; circ. 400,000.

Kedaulatan Rakyat: Jalan P. Mangkubumi 40–44, Yogyakarta; tel. (274) 565685; fax (274) 563125; internet krjogja.com; f. 1945; Indonesian; independent; Chief Editor OCTO LAMPITO; circ. 50,000.

Kompas: Gedung Kompas Gramedia, Unit II, Lantai 5, Jalan Palmerah Selatan 26–28, Jakarta 10270; tel. (21) 5350377; fax (21) 5360678; e-mail redaksikcm@kompas.co.id; internet www.kompas.com; f. 1965; Indonesian; Man. Editor TRI WAHONO; circ. 550,000.

Koran Tempo: Gedung Tempo, Jalan H. R. Rasuna Said, Kav. C-17, Kuningan, Jakarta 10270; tel. (21) 5201022; fax (21) 5200092; e-mail interaktif@tempo.co.id; internet www.korantempo.com; f. 2001; Indonesian; Editor-in-Chief BAMBANG HARYMURTI.

Media Indonesia Daily: Jalan Pilar Mas Raya, Kav. A–D, Kedoya Selatan, Kebon Jeruk, Jakarta 11520; tel. (21) 5812088; fax (21) 5812105; e-mail miol@mediaindonesia.co.id; internet www.mediaindo.co.id; f. 1989; fmrly *Prioritas*; Indonesian; Publr SURYA PALOH; Editor DJAFAR H. ASSEGAFF; circ. 2,000.

Pikiran Rakyat: Jalan Asia-Afrika 77, Bandung 40111; tel. (22) 51216; e-mail pdr@pikiran-rakyat.com; internet www.pikiran-rakyat.com; f. 1950; Indonesian; independent; Editor BRAM M. DARMAPRAWIRA; circ. 150,000.

Pos Kota: Yayasan Antar Kota, Jalan Gajah Mada 100, Jakarta 10130; tel. and fax (21) 5652603; e-mail editor@poskotanews.com; internet www.poskota.co.id; f. 1970; Indonesian; Editor-in-Chief H. JOKO LESTERI; circ. 500,000.

Rakyat Merdeka: Graha Pena, 9th Floor, Jalan Raya Kebayoran Lama 12, Jakarta Selatan 12210; tel. (21) 5348460; fax (21) 53671716; e-mail redaksi@rakyatmerdeka.co.id; internet www.rakyatmerdeka.co.id; f. 1945; Indonesian; independent; Chief Editor TEGUH SANTOSA; circ. 300,000.

Republika: Jalan Warung Buncit Raya 37, Jakarta Selatan 12510; tel. (21) 7803747; fax (21) 7800649; e-mail sekretariat@republika.co.id; internet www.republika.co.id; f. 1995; organ of the Asscn of Indonesian Muslim Intellectuals (ICMI); Chief Editor NASIHIN MASHA.

Sin Chew Daily Indonesia: Jalan Toko Tiga Seberang 21, POB 4755, Jakarta 11120; tel. (21) 6295948; fax (21) 6297830; internet indonesia.sinchew.com.my; f. 1966; Chinese; fmrly *Harian Indonesia*; Indonesia's first Chinese language newspaper; Editor W. D. SUKISMAN; Dir HADI WIBOWO; circ. 50,000.

Solo Pos: Griya SOLOPOS, Jalan Adisucipto 190, Solo 57145; tel. (271) 724811; fax (271) 724833; internet www.solopos.co.id; Editor-in-Chief SUNYOTO YA.

Suara Karya: Jalan Bangka Raya 2, Kebayoran Baru, Jakarta Selatan 12720; tel. (21) 7192656; fax (21) 71790746; e-mail redaksi@suarakarya-online.com; internet www.suarakarya-online.com; f. 1971; Indonesian; Chief Editor RICKY RACHMADI; Man. Editor DJUNAEDI TJUNTI AGUS; circ. 300,000.

Suara Merdeka: Jalan Pandanaran 30, Semarang 50241; tel. (24) 8412600; fax (24) 8411116; e-mail redaksi@suaramerdeka.info; internet www.suaramerdeka.com; f. 1950; Indonesian; Publr Ir H. TOMMY HETAMI; Editor-in-Chief IWAN KELANA; circ. 200,000.

Suara Pembaruan: Citra Graha Bldg, 11th Floor, Jalan Jenderal Gatot Subroto Kav 35-36, Jakarta 12950; tel. (21) 57851555; fax (21) 5200072; e-mail koransp@suarapembaruan.com; internet www.suarapembaruan.com; f. 1987; Chief Editor PRIMUS DORIMULU; CEO SACHIN GOPALAN.

Surabaya Post: Ruko Rich Palace, Kav. 19–20, Jalan Mayjend Sungkono 149–150, Surabaya; tel. (31) 5667000; fax (31) 5635000; e-mail redaksi@surabayapost.co.id; internet www.surabayapost.co.id; f. 1953; independent; afternoon; Chief Editor and Dir BAMBANG HARIAWAN; Man. Editor AGUSTINA WIDYAWATI; circ. 120,000.

Surya: Jalan Rungkut Industri III, 68 & 70 SIER, Surabaya 60293; tel. (31) 8419000; fax (31) 8414024; e-mail redaksi.suryaonline@gmail.com; internet www.surya.co.id; Editor-in-Chief DAHLAN DAHI.

Kalimantan

Banjarmasin Post: Gedung HJ Djok Mentaya, Jalan AS Musyaffa 16, Banjarmasin 70111; tel. (511) 3354370; fax (511) 4366123; e-mail redaksi@banjarmasinpost.co.id; internet www.banjarmasinpost.co.id; f. 1971; Indonesian; Editor-in-Chief YUSRAN PARE; circ. 48,000.

Kaltim Post: Jalan Jenderal Sudirman RT XVI 82, Balikpapan 76144; tel. (542) 736459; fax (542) 735242; e-mail redaksi@kaltimpost.net; internet www.kaltimpost.co.id; f. 1988; fmrly *Manuntung*; Editor-in-Chief Drs H. BAMBANG ISNOTO.

Lampung Post: Jalan Pangkal Pinang, Lampung; e-mail webmaster@metrotvnews.com; internet www.lampungpost.com; Editor DJADJAT SUDRADJAT.

Pontianak Post: Pontianak Post Group, Jalan Gajah Mada 2–4, Pontianak 78121; tel. (561) 735071; fax (561) 736607; e-mail redaksi@pontianakpost.com; internet www.pontianakpost.com; f. 1972; CEO Dr UNTUNG SUKARTI.

Maluku

Pos Maluku: Jalan Raya Pattimura 19, Ambon; tel. (911) 44614; daily.

Suara Maluku: Komplex Perdagangan Mardikas, Blok D3/11A, Ternate; tel. (911) 44590.

Nusa Tenggara

Pos Kupang: Jalan Kenari 1, Kupang 85115; tel. (380) 833820; fax (380) 831801; e-mail poskpg@yahoo.com; internet kupang.tribunnews.com; Chief Editor DION D. B. PUTRA.

Papua

Cenderawasih Post: Jalan Cenderawasih 10, Kelapa II, Entrop, Jayapura 99013; tel. (967) 532417; fax (967) 532418; e-mail cepos_jpr@yahoo.com; internet www.cenderawasihpos.com; Editor-in-Chief N. LUCKY IREEUW; Man. Editor WENNY FIRMAN.

Teropong: Jalan Soeprapto Sintuvu 38, Palu 94000; tel. (451) 427783; e-mail majalahteropong@ymail.com; internet www.teropongpapua.com.

Riau

Batam Pos: Gedung Graha Pena, 2nd Floor, Jalan Raya Batam Centre, Batam 29461; tel. (778) 460000; fax (778) 462162; e-mail redaksi@batampos.co.id; internet www.batampos.co.id; Editor-in-Chief HASAN ASPAHANI.

Riau Pos: Jalan H. R. Subrantas, Km 10.5, Pekanbaru, Riau 28294; tel. (761) 64633; fax (761) 64640; e-mail redaksi@riaupos.com; internet www.riaupos.co.id; Group Head Editor RAJA ISYAM ANWAR; Editor-in-Chief NAZIR MUHAMMAD FAHMI; circ. 40,000.

Sulawesi

Bulletin Sulut: Jalan Korengkeng 38, 2nd Floor, Manado 95114, Sulawesi Utara.

Cahaya Siang: Jalan Kembang II 2, Manado 95114, Sulawesi Utara; tel. (431) 61054; fax (431) 63393.

Fajar (Dawn): Gedung Graha Pena, Lantai 4, Jalan Urip Sumoharjo 21, Makassar 90231; tel. (411) 441441; fax (411) 441224; e-mail redaksi@fajar.co.id; internet www.fajar.co.id; Editor-in-Chief ALWI HAMU; circ. 35,000.

Manado Post: Manado Post Centre, Manado Town Sq., Blok B, Kav. 14–15, Manado; tel. (431) 855558; fax (431) 860398; e-mail editor@mdopost.com; internet www.mdopost.com; Editor-in-Chief SUHENDRO BOROMA.

Pedoman Rakyat: Jalan H. A. Mappanyukki 28, Makassar; f. 1947; independent; Editor M. BASIR; circ. 30,000.

Suluh Merdeka: Jalan R. W. Mongsidi 4/96, POB 1105, Manado 95110; tel. and fax (431) 866150.

Tegas: Jalan H. A. Mappanyukki 28, Makassar; tel. (411) 3960.

Sumatra

Harian Analisa: Jalan Ahmad Yani 35–49, Medan 20111; tel. (61) 4513554; fax (61) 4151436; internet www.analisadaily.com; f. 1972; Indonesian; Editor H. ALI SOEKARDI; circ. 75,000.

Harian Berita Sore: Jalan Letjen Suprapto 1, Medan 20151; tel. (61) 4158787; fax (61) 4150383; e-mail redaksi@beritasore.com; internet www.beritasore.com; Indonesian; Publr SAID PRABUDI SAID; Editor-in-Chief H. TERUNA JASA SAID.

Harian Haluan: Komplek Bandara Tabing, Jalan Hamka, Padang; tel. (51) 4488700; e-mail aluanpadang@gmail.com; internet www.harianhaluan.com; f. 1948; Publr BASRIZAL KOTO; Editor-in-Chief YON ERIZON; circ. 54,000.

Harian Umum Nasional Waspada: Jalan Letjen Suprapto, cnr Jalan Brigjenderal Katamso 1, Medan 20151; tel. (61) 4150858; fax (61) 4510025; e-mail redaksi.online@waspada.co.id; internet www.waspada.co.id; f. 1947; Indonesian; Editor-in-Chief AVIAN E. TUMENGKOL.

Mimbar Umum: Merah, Medan; tel. (61) 517807; e-mail mimbarumum@yahoo.com; internet www.mimbarumumberita.com; f. 1947; Indonesian; independent; Editor MOHD LUD LUBIS; circ. 55,000.

Padang Ekspres: Jalan Proklamasi Tarandam 5D, Padang, Sumatra Barat; tel. (751) 841300; fax (751) 841904; e-mail redaksi@padang-today.com; internet www.padang-today.com; Indonesian; Editor SHI MUSLIM.

Serambi Indonesia: Jalan Raya Lambaro, Km 4.5, Tanjung Permai, Manyang PA, Banda Aceh; tel. (651) 635544; fax (651) 637180; e-mail redaksi@serambinews.com; internet www.serambinews.com; Editor-in-Chief MAWARDI IBRAHIM.

Sinar Indonesia Baru: Jalan Brigjenderal Katamso 66, Medan 20151; tel. (61) 4512530; fax (61) 4538150; e-mail redaksi@hariansib.com; internet www.hariansib.com; f. 1970; Indonesian; Chief Editor G. M. PANGGABEAN; circ. 150,000.

Sriwijaya Post: Jalan Jenderal Basuki Rahmat 1608 B–D, Palembang; tel. (711) 310088; fax (711) 312888; e-mail redaksi@sripoku.com; internet www.suararakyat.net; f. 2002; Editor-in-Chief HADI PRAYOGO.

Suara Rakyat Semesta: Jalan K. H. Ashari 52, Palembang; Indonesian; Editor DJADIL ABDULLAH; circ. 10,000.

Waspada: Jalan Letjen Suprapto, cnr Jalan Brigjenderal Katamso 1, Medan 20151; tel. (61) 4150868; fax (61) 4510025; e-mail waspada@waspada.co.id; internet www.waspada.co.id; f. 1947; Indonesian; Editor-in-Chief AVIAN TUMENGKOL; circ. 60,000 (daily), 55,000 (Sun.).

PRINCIPAL PERIODICALS

Amanah: Jalan Garuda 69, Kemayoran, Jakarta; tel. (21) 410254; fortnightly; Indonesian; Muslim current affairs; Man. Dir MASKUN ISKANDAR; circ. 180,000.

Ayahbunda: Jalan H. R. Rasuna Said, Blok B, Kav. 32–33, Jakarta 12910; tel. (21) 5253816; fax (21) 5262131; e-mail kontak@ayahbunda.co.id; internet www.ayahbunda.co.id; fortnightly; family magazine.

Berita Negara: Jalan Pertjetakan Negara 21, Kotakpos 2111, Jakarta; tel. and fax (21) 4207251; f. 1951; 2 a week; official gazette.

Bobo (PT Penerbitan Sarana Bobo): Gramedia Magazine Bldg, 2nd Floor, Jalan Panjang 8A, Kebon Jeruk, Jakarta 11530; tel. (21) 5330150; fax (21) 5320681; f. 1973; subsidiary of Gramedia Group; weekly; children's magazine; Editor KOES SABANDIYAH; circ. 85,315.

Bola: Gedung Kompas Gramedia, Jalan Palmerah Barat 33–37, Jakarta 10270; tel. (21) 53677835; fax (21) 5303400; e-mail redaksi@bolanews.com; internet www.bolanews.com; f. 1984; 3 a week; Mon., Thur. and Sat.; Indonesian; Chief Editor ARIEF KURNIAWAN; circ. 715,000.

Buana Minggu: Jalan Tanah Abang Dua 33–35, Jakarta Pusat 10110; tel. (21) 364190; weekly; Sun.; Indonesian; Editor WINOTO PARARTHO; circ. 193,450.

Business News: Jalan H. Abdul Muis 70, Jakarta 10160; tel. (21) 3848207; fax (21) 3454280; f. 1956; 3 a week (Indonesian edn), 2 a week (English edn); Chief Editor SANJOTO SASTROMIHARDJO; circ. 15,000.

Cita Cinta: Jalan H. R. Rasuna Said, Blok B, Kav. 32–33, Jakarta 12910; tel. (21) 5254206; fax (21) 5262131; e-mail citacinta@feminagroup.com; internet www.citacinta.com; f. 2000; teenage lifestyle magazine.

Citra: Gramedia Bldg, Unit 11, 5th Floor, Jalan Palmerah Selatan 24–26, Jakarta 10270; tel. (21) 5483008; fax (21) 5494035; e-mail citra@gramedia-majalah.com; f. 1990; weekly; TV and film programmes, music trends and celebrity news; Chief Editor H. MAMAN SUHERMAN; circ. 239,000.

Depthnews Indonesia: Jalan Jatinegara Barat III/6, Jakarta 13310; tel. (21) 8194994; fax (21) 8195501; f. 1972; weekly; publ. by Press Foundation of Indonesia; Editor SUMONO MUSTOFFA.

Dunia Wanita: Jalan Brigjenderal 1 Katamso, Medan; tel. (61) 4150858; fax (61) 4510025; e-mail waspada@indosat.net.id; internet www.dunia-wanita.com; f. 1949; fortnightly; Indonesian; women's tabloid; Chief Editor Dr RAYATI SYAFRIN; circ. 10,000.

Economic Review: Bank BNI, Strategic Planning Division, Gedung Bank BNI, Jalan Jenderal Sudirman, Kav. 1, POB 2955, Jakarta 10220; tel. (21) 5728692; fax (21) 5728456; e-mail renkek01@bni.co.id; f. 1946; 3 a year; English; economic and business research and analysis; Editor-in-Chief DARWIN SUZANDI.

Ekonomi Indonesia: Jalan Merdeka, Timur 11–12, Jakarta; tel. (21) 494458; monthly; English; economic journal; Editor Z. ACHMAD; circ. 20,000.

Eksekutif: Jalan R. S. Fatmawati 20, Jakarta 12430; tel. (21) 7659218; fax (21) 7504018; internet eksekutif.com.

Femina: Jalan H. R. Rasuna Said, Blok B, Kav. 32–33, Jakarta Selatan 12910; tel. (21) 5209370; fax (21) 5209366; e-mail redaksi@feminagroup.com; internet www.femina.co.id; f. 1972; weekly; women's magazine; CEO SVIDA ALISJAHBANA; Editor-in-Chief PETTY S. FATIMAH; circ. 170,000.

Gadis: Jalan H. R. Rasuna Said, Blok B, Kav. 32–33, Jakarta 12910; tel. (21) 5253816; fax (21) 5262131; e-mail palupi.ambardini@feminagroup.com; internet www.gadis.co.id; f. 1973; 3 a month; Indonesian; teenage lifestyle magazine; Editor-in-Chief PALUPI AMBARDINI; circ. 150,000.

Gatra: Gedung Gatra, Jalan Kalibata Timur IV/15, Jakarta 12740; tel. (21) 7973535; fax (21) 79196941; e-mail redaksi@gatra.com; internet www.gatra.com; est. by fmr employees of Tempo (banned 1994–98); Man. Editor NUR HIDAYAT; Editor-in-Chief HEDDY LUGITO.

Gugat (Accuse): Surabaya; politics, law and crime; weekly; circ. 250,000.

Hai: Jalan Panjang 8A, Kebon Jeruk, Jakarta Barat; tel. (21) 5330170; fax (21) 5220070; e-mail hai_magazine@gramedia-majalah.com; internet www.hai-online.com; f. 1973; weekly; youth magazine; Man. Editor JUNIOR EKA PUTRO; circ. 42,000.

Indonesia Business News: Wisma Bisnis Indonesia, 7th Floor, Jalan K. H. Mas Mansyur 12A, Karet, Jakarta 10220; tel. (21) 57901023; fax (21) 57901025; e-mail redaksi@bisnis.co.id; internet www.bisnis.co.id; Indonesian and English.

Indonesia Business Weekly: Wisma Bisnis Indonesia, Jalan Letjenderal S. Parman, Kav. 12, Slipi, Jakarta 11410; tel. (21) 5304016; fax (21) 5305868; English; Editor TAUFIK DARUSMAN.

Indonesia Magazine: Jalan Merdeka Barat 20, Jakarta; tel. (21) 352015; f. 1969; monthly; English; Chair. G. DWIPAYANA; Editor-in-Chief HADELY HASIBUAN; circ. 15,000.

Intisari (Digest): Gramedia Bldg, Unit II, 5th Floor, Jalan Palmerah Selatan 24–26, Jakarta 10270; tel. (21) 5483008; fax (21) 53696525; e-mail intisari@gramedia-majalah.com; internet www.intisari-online.com; f. 1963; monthly; Indonesian; popular science, health, technology, crime and general interest; Editors AL. HERU KUSTARA, IRAWATI; circ. 141,000.

Jakarta Jakarta: Gramedia Bldg, Unit II, 5th Floor, Jalan Palmerah Selatan 24–26, Jakarta 10270; tel. (21) 5483008; fax (21) 5494035; f. 1985; weekly; food, fun, fashion and celebrity news; circ. 70,000.

Jurnal Indonesia: Jalan Hos Cokroaminoto 49A, Jakarta 10350; tel. (21) 31901774; fax (21) 3916471; e-mail jurnal@cbn.net.id; monthly; political, economic and business analysis.

Keluarga: Jalan Sangaji 11, Jakarta; fortnightly; women's and family magazine; Editor S. DAHONO.

Kontan: Gedung Kontan, Jalan Kebayoran Lama 3119, Jakarta 12210; tel. (21) 5357636; fax (21) 5357633; e-mail red@kontan.co.id; internet www.kontan.co.id; weekly; Indonesian; business newspaper; Editor-in-Chief ARDIAN TAUFIK GESURI.

Majalah Ekonomis: POB 4195, Jakarta; monthly; English; business; Chief Editor S. ARIFIN HUTABARAT; circ. 20,000.

Majalah Kedokteran Indonesia (Journal of the Indonesian Medical Asscn): Jalan Kesehatan 111/29, Jakarta 11/16; tel. (21) 31937910; fax (21) 3900465; e-mail yapenidi@yahoo.com; internet mki.idionline.org; f. 1951; monthly; Indonesian, English.

Manglé: Jalan Lodaya 19–21, 40262 Bandung; tel. (22) 411438; f. 1957; weekly; Sundanese; Chief Editor Drs OEJANG DARAJATOEN; circ. 74,000.

Matra: Grafity Pers, Kompleks Buncit Raya Permai, Kav. 1, Jalan Warung, POB 3476, Jakarta; tel. (21) 515952; f. 1986; monthly; men's magazine; general interest and current affairs; Editor-in-Chief SRI RUSDY; circ. 100,000.

Mimbar Kabinet Pembangunan: Jalan Merdeka Barat 7, Jakarta; f. 1966; monthly; Indonesian; publ. by Dept of Information.

Mutiara: Jalan Dewi Sartika 136D, Cawang, Jakarta Timur; general interest; Publr H. G. RORIMPANDEY.

Nova: Gedung Kompas Gramedia, Lantai 3, Jalan Panjang 8A, Kebon Jeruk, Jakarta Barat 11530; tel. (21) 5330150; fax (21) 5321020; e-mail admin@tabloidnova.com; internet www.tabloidnova.com; weekly; Wed.; Indonesian; women's interest; Publr SAMINDRA UTAMA; circ. 618,267.

Oposisi: Jakarta; weekly; politics; circ. 400,000.

Otomotif: Gedung Kompas Gramedia, Lantai 7, Jalan Panjang 8A, Kebon Jeruk, Jakarta Barat 11530; tel. (21) 5330170; fax (21) 5330185; e-mail otomotifnet@gramedia-majalah.com; internet www.otomotifnet.com; f. 1990; weekly; automotive specialist tabloid; Editor-in-Chief AGUS SULISTRIYONO; circ. 215,763.

PC Magazine Indonesia: Jalan H. R. Rasuna Said, Blok B, Kav. 32–33, Jakarta 12910; tel. (21) 5209370; fax (21) 5209366; computers; Editor-in-Chief SVIDA ALISJAHBANA.

Peraba: Bintaran Kidul 5, Yogyakarta; weekly; Indonesian and Javanese; Roman Catholic; Editor W. KARTOSOEHARSONO.

Pertani PT: Jalan Pasar Minggu, Kalibata, POB 247/KBY, Jakarta Selatan; tel. (21) 793108; f. 1974; monthly; Indonesian; agricultural; Pres. Dir Ir RUSLI YAHYA.

Petisi: Surabaya; weekly; Editor CHOIRUL ANAM.

Rajawali: Jakarta; monthly; Indonesian; civil aviation and tourism; Dir R. A. J. LUMENTA; Man. Editor KARYONO ADHY.

Selecta: Kebon Kacang 29/4, Jakarta; fortnightly; illustrated; Editor SAMSUDIN LUBIS; circ. 80,000.

SWA Sembada: Jalan Taman Tanah Abang, III/23, Jakarta 10610; tel. (21) 3523839; fax (21) 3457338; internet www.swa.co.id; business information; Editor-in-Chief KEMAL EFFENDI GANI.

Tempo: Gedung Temprint, Lantai 2, Jalan Palmerah Barat 8, Jakarta 12210; tel. (21) 5360409; fax (21) 5360412; e-mail interaktif@tempo.co.id; internet www.tempointeractive.com; f. 1971; weekly; Editor-in-Chief ARIEF ZULKIFLI.

Tiara: Gramedia Bldg, Unit 11, 5th Floor, Jalan Palmerah Selatan 24–26, Jakarta 10270; tel. (21) 5483008; fax (21) 5494035; f. 1990; fortnightly; lifestyles, features and celebrity news; circ. 47,000.

Ummat: Jakarta; Islamic; sponsored by ICMI.

Wenang Post: Jalan R. W. Mongsidi 4/96, POB 1105, Manado 95115; tel. and fax (431) 866150; weekly.

NEWS AGENCIES

ANTARA (Indonesian News Agency): Wisma Antara, Lantai 19, 17 Jalan Medan Merdeka Selatan, POB 1257, Jakarta 10110; tel. (21) 3802383; fax (21) 3522178; e-mail newsroom@antaranews.com; internet www.antaranews.com; f. 1937; 33 brs in Indonesia, 5 overseas brs; 800 bulletins in Indonesian and in English; monitoring service of stock exchanges world-wide; photo service; CEO M. SAIFUL HADI; Chief Editor AHMAD KUSAENI.

Kantorberita Nasional Indonesia (KNI News Service): Jalan Jatinegara Barat III/6, Jakarta Timur 13310; tel. (21) 811003; fax (21) 8195501; f. 1966; independent national news agency; foreign and domestic news in Indonesian; Dir and Editor-in-Chief Dr SUMONO MUSTOFFA; Exec. Editor HARIM NURROCHADI.

PRESS ASSOCIATIONS

Aliansi Jurnalis Independen (AJI) (Alliance of Independent Journalists): Jalan Kembang Raya 6 Kwitang, Senen, Jakarta Pusat 10420; tel. (21) 3151214; fax (21) 3151261; e-mail office@ajiindonesia.org; internet www.ajiindonesia.org; f. 1994; unofficial; aims to promote freedom of the press; Pres. EKO MARYADI; Sec.-Gen. SUWARJONO.

Jakarta Foreign Correspondents' Club: Plaza Gani Djemat, Lantai 4, Jalan Imam Bonjol 76–78, Jakarta 10310; tel. (21) 3903628; fax (21) 3917453; e-mail office@jfcc.info; internet www.jfcc.info; more than 400 mems; Pres. JOE COCHRANE; Exec. Dir THEODORA TRISNAWATI.

Persatuan Wartawan Indonesia (PWI) (Indonesian Journalists' Asscn): Gedung Dewan Pers, Lantai 4, Jalan Kebon Sirih 34, Jakarta 10110; tel. (21) 3453131; fax (21) 3453175; e-mail pwi@pwi.or.id; internet www.pwi.or.id; f. 1946; govt-controlled; 14,000 mems (Feb. 2009); Chair. MARGIONO; Gen. Sec. HENDRY BANGUN.

Serikat Penerbit Suratkabar (SPS) (Indonesian Newspaper Publishers' Asscn): Gedung Dewan Pers, 6th Floor, Jalan Kebon Sirih 34, Jakarta 10110; tel. (21) 3459671; fax (21) 3862373; e-mail spspusat@spsindonesia.or.id; f. 1946; mems: 451 publrs; Exec. Chair. DAHLAN IKSAN; Sec.-Gen. SUKARDI DARMAWAN.

Publishers

JAKARTA

Aries Lima/New Aqua Press PT: Jalan Rawagelan II/4, Jakarta Timur; tel. (21) 4897566; general and children's; Pres. TUTI SUNDARI AZMI.

Aya Media Pustaka PT: Wijaya Grand Centre C/2, Jalan Wijaya II, Jakarta 12160; tel. (21) 7206903; fax (21) 7201401; e-mail ayamedia@cbn.net.id; f. 1985; children's; Dir Drs ARIANTO TUGIYO.

PT Balai Pustaka Peraga: Jalan Gunung Sahari Raya 4, Gedung Balai Pustaka, 7th Floor, Jakarta 10710; tel. (21) 3451616; fax (21) 3855735; e-mail con_bpustaka@bumn-ri.com; f. 1917; children's, school textbooks, literary, scientific publs and periodicals; Dir R. SISWADI.

Bhratara Niaga Media PT: Jalan Cipinang Bali 17, Jakarta Timur 13420; tel. (21) 8520319; fax (21) 8191858; f. 1986; fmrly Bhratara Karya Aksara; university and educational textbooks; Man. Dir ROBINSON RUSDI.

Bina Rena Pariwara PT: Jalan Pejaten Raya 5E, Pasar Minggu, Jakarta 12510; tel. (21) 7901931; fax (21) 7901939; e-mail hasanbas@softhome.net; f. 1988; financial, social sciences, economic, Islamic, children's; Dir Drs HASAN BASRI.

Bulan Bintang PT: Jalan Kramat Kwitang I/8, Jakarta 10420; tel. (21) 3901651; fax (21) 3901652; e-mail bukubulanbintang@gmail.com; internet www.bulanbintang.co.id; f. 1954; Islamic, social sciences, natural and applied sciences, art; Man. Dir FAUZI AMELZ.

Bumi Aksara PT: Jalan Sawo Raya 18, Rawamanguu, Jakarta 13220; tel. (21) 4717049; fax (21) 4700989; e-mail info@bumiaksara.co.id; internet www.bumiaksara.co.id; f. 1990; university textbooks; Dir LUCYA ANDAM DEWI.

Cakrawala Cinta PT: Jalan Minyak I/12B, Duren Tiga, Jakarta 12760; tel. (21) 7990725; fax (21) 7974076; f. 1984; science; Dir Drs M. TORSINA.

Centre for Strategic and International Studies (CSIS): Jalan Tanah Abang III 23-27, Jakarta 10160; tel. (21) 3865532; fax (21) 3847517; e-mail csis@csis.or.id; internet www.csis.or.id; f. 1971; economic, political and social sciences; Exec. Dir RIZAL SUKMA.

Cipta Adi Pustaka: Graha Compaka Mas Blok C 22, Jalan Cempaka Putih Raya, Jakarta Pusat; tel. (21) 4213821; fax (21) 4269315; f. 1986; encyclopaedias; Dir BUDI SANTOSO.

Dian Rakyat PT: Jalan Rawa Girang 8, Kawasan Industri Pulogadung, Jakarta; tel. (21) 4604444; fax (21) 4609115; f. 1966; general; Pres. Dir MARIO ALISJAHBANA.

Djambatan PT: Jalan Paseban 29, Jakarta 10440; tel. (21) 7203199; fax (21) 7227989; e-mail djam@dnet.net.id; f. 1954; children's, textbooks, social sciences, fiction; Dir SJARIFUDIN SJAMSUDIN.

Dunia Pustaka Jaya: Jalan Kramat Raya 5K, Komp. Maya Indah, Jakarta 10450; tel. (21) 3909322; fax (21) 3909320; f. 1971; fiction, religion, essays, poetry, drama, criticism, art, philosophy and children's; Man. A. RIVAI.

EGC Medical Publishers: Jalan Agung Timur 4, No. 39 Blok 0–1, Jakarta 14350; tel. (21) 65306283; fax (21) 6518178; e-mail contact@egc-arcan.com; f. 1978; medical and public health, nursing, dentistry; Dir IMELDA DHARMA.

PT Elex Media Komputindo: Gramedia Bldg, 6th Floor, Jalan Palmerah Selatan 22, Jakarta 10270; tel. (21) 5483008; fax (21) 5326219; e-mail langganan@elexmedia.co.id; internet www.elexmedia.co.id; f. 1985; management, computing, software, children's, parenting, self-development and fiction; Dir ADHI MARDHIYONO.

Erlangga PT: Kami Melayani II, Pengetahuan, Jalan H. Baping 100, Ciracas, Jakarta 13740; tel. (21) 8717006; fax (21) 87794609; internet www.erlangga.co.id; f. 1952; secondary school and university textbooks; Man. Dir GUNAWAN HUTAURUK.

Gaya Favorit Press: Jalan H. R. Rasuna Said. Kav. B 32–33, Jakarta 12910; tel. (21) 5209370; fax (21) 5209366; f. 1971; fiction, popular science, lifestyle and children's; Vice-Pres. MIRTA KARTOHADIPRODJO; Man. Dir WIDARTI GUNAWAN.

Gema Insani Press: Jalan Kalibata Utara II/84, Jakarta 12740; tel. (21) 7984391; fax (21) 7984388; e-mail penerbitan@gemainsani.co.id; internet www.gemainsani.co.id; f. 1986; Islamic; Dir UMAR BASYARAHIL.

Ghalia Indonesia: Jalan Pramuka Raya 4, Jakarta 13140; tel. (21) 8581814; fax (21) 8564784; f. 1972; children's and general science, textbooks; Man. Dir LUKMAN SAAD.

Gramedia Widyasarana Indonesia: Gramedia Bldg, 3rd Floor, Jalan Palmerah Barat 33–37, Jakarta 10270; tel. (21) 53650110; fax (21) 53698095; internet www.grasindo.co.id; f. 1973; university textbooks, general non-fiction, children's and magazines; Man. JAROT YUDHOPRATOMO.

Gunung Mulia PT: Jalan Kwitang 22–23, Jakarta 10420; tel. (21) 3901208; fax (21) 3901633; e-mail publishing@bpkgm.com; internet www.bpkgm.com; f. 1946; general, children's, Christian; Chair. IWAN ARKADY; Pres. Dir STEPHEN Z. SATYAHADI.

Hidakarya Agung PT: Jalan Percetakan Negara D51, Jakarta Pusat; tel. (21) 4219786; fax (21) 4247128; Dir MAHDIARTI MACHMUD.

Ichtiar: Jalan Majapahit 6, Jakarta Pusat; tel. (21) 3841226; f. 1957; textbooks, law, social sciences, economics; Dir JOHN SEMERU.

Indira PT: Jalan Borobudur 20, Jakarta 10320; tel. (21) 3148868; fax (21) 3921079; f. 1953; general science, general trade and children's; Dir BAMBANG P. WAHYUDI.

Kinta CV: Jalan Kemanggisan Ilir V/110, Pal Merah, Jakarta Barat; tel. (21) 5494751; f. 1950; textbooks, social sciences, general; Man. Drs MOHAMAD SALEH.

Midas Surya Grafindo PT: Jalan Kesehatan 54, Cijantung, Jakarta 13760; tel. (21) 8400414; fax (21) 8400270; f. 1984; children's; Dir Drs FRANS HENDRAWAN.

Mutiara Sumber Widya PT: Gedung Maya Indah, Jalan Kramat 55C, Jakarta 10450; tel. (21) 3909864; fax (21) 3160313; f. 1951; textbooks, Islamic, social sciences, general and children's; Pres. FADJRAA OEMAR.

Penebar Swadya PT: Jalan Gunung Sahari III/7, Jakarta Pusat; tel. (21) 4204402; fax (21) 4214821; agriculture, animal husbandry, fisheries; Dir Drs ANTHONIUS RIYANTO.

Penerbit Universitas Indonesia: Jalan Salemba Raya 4, Jakarta; tel. (21) 335373; f. 1969; science; Man. S. E. LEGOWO.

Pradnya Paramita PT: Jalan Bunga 8–8A, Matraman, Jakarta 13140; tel. (21) 8504944; fax (21) 8583369; e-mail pradnya@centrin.net.id; f. 1973; children's, general, educational, technical and social sciences; Pres. Dir KONDAR SINAGA.

Pustaka Antara PT: Jalan Perdagangan 99, Bintaro, Jakarta 12330; tel. (21) 7361711; fax (21) 7351079; e-mail nacelod@indo.net.id; f. 1952; textbooks, political, Islamic, children's and general; Man. Dir AIDA JOESOEF AHMAD.

Pustaka Binaman Pressindo: Jalan Kembang Raya 8, Jakarta Pusat 10030; tel. (21) 2303157; fax (21) 2302051; e-mail pustaka@bit.net.id; f. 1981; management; Dir Ir MAKFUDIN WIRYA ATMAJA.

Pustaka LP3ES Indonesia: Jalan Letjen. S. Parman 81, Jakarta 11420; tel. (21) 5663527; fax (21) 56964691; e-mail puslp3es@indo.net.id; f. 1971; general; Dir M. D. MARUTO.

Pustaka Sinar Harapan PT: Jalan Dewi Sartika 136D, Jakarta 13630; tel. and fax (21) 8006982; internet penerbitsinarharapan.co.id; f. 1981; general science, fiction, comics, children's; Dir W. M. NAIDEN.

Pustaka Utma Grafiti PT: 25 Jalan Kramat VI, Jakarta Pusat 10250; tel. (21) 31903006; fax (21) 31906649; f. 1981; social sciences, humanities and children's books; Dir ZULKIFLY LUBIS.

Rajagrafindo Persada PT: Jalan Pelepah Hijau IV TN-1 14–15, Kelapa Gading Permai, Jakarta 14240; tel. (21) 4520951; fax (21) 4529409; f. 1980; general science and religion; Dir Drs ZUBAIDI.

Rineka Cipta PT: Kompang Perkantoran Mitra Matraman, 148 Jalan Matraman Raya B 1–2, Jakarta; tel. (21) 85918080; fax (21) 85918143; f. 1990; est. by merger of Aksara Baru (f. 1972) and Bina Aksara; general science and university texts; Dir Dr H. SUARDI.

Rosda Jayaputra PT: Jalan Kembang 4, Jakarta 10420; tel. (21) 3904984; fax (21) 3901703; f. 1981; general science; Dir H. ROZALI USMAN.

Sastra Hudaya: Jalan Kalasan 1, Jakarta Pusat; tel. (21) 882321; f. 1967; religious, textbooks, children's and general; Man. ADAM SALEH.

Tintamas Indonesia: Jalan Kramat Raya 60, Jakarta 10420; tel. and fax (21) 3911459; f. 1947; history, modern science and culture, especially Islamic; Man. MARHAMAH DJAMBEK.

Tira Pustaka: Jalan Cemara Raya 1, Kav. 10D, Jaka Permai, Jaka Sampurna, Bekasi 17145; tel. (21) 8841277; fax (21) 8842736; e-mail Tirapus@cbn.net.id; f. 1977; translations, children's; Dir ROBERT B. WIDJAJA.

Toko Buku Walisongo PT: Gedung Idayu, Jalan Kwitang 13, Jakarta 10420; tel. (21) 3154890; fax (21) 3154889; e-mail edp@tokowalisongo.com; f. 1986; fmrly Masagung Group; general, Islamic, textbooks, science; Pres. H. KETUT ABDURRAHMAN MASAGUNG.

Widjaya: Jalan Pecenongan 48C, Jakarta Pusat; tel. (21) 3813446; f. 1950; textbooks, children's, religious and general; Man. DIDI LUTHAN.

Yasaguna: Jalan Minangkabau 44, POB 422, Jakarta Selatan; tel. (21) 8290422; f. 1964; agricultural, children's, handicrafts; Dir HILMAN MADEWA.

BANDUNG

Alma'arif: Jalan Tamblong 48–50, Bandung; tel. (22) 4207177; fax (22) 4239194; e-mail almaarif@bdg.centrin.net.id; f. 1949; textbooks, religious and general; Man. H. M. BAHARTHAH.

Alumni PT: Jalan Bukit Pakar Timur II/109, Bandung 40197; tel. (22) 2501251; fax (22) 2503044; f. 1968; university and school textbooks; Dir EDDY DAMIAN.

Angkasa: Jalan Kiara Condong 437, Bandung; tel. (22) 7320383; fax (22) 7320373; e-mail akspst@centrin.net.id; Dir H. FACHRI SAID.

Armico: Jalan Madurasa Utara 10, Cigereleng, Bandung 40253; tel. (22) 5202234; fax (22) 5201972; f. 1980; school textbooks; Dir Ir ARSIL TANJUNG.

Citra Aditya Bakti PT: Jalan Geusanulun 17, Bandung 40115; tel. (22) 438251; fax (22) 438635; e-mail cab@citraaditya.com; internet www.citraaditya.com; f. 1985; general science; Dir Ir IWAN TANUATMADJA.

Diponegoro Publishing House: Jalan Mohammad Toha 44–46, Bandung 40252; tel. and fax (22) 5201215; e-mail dpnegoro@indosat.net.id; internet www.penerbitdiponegoro.com; f. 1963; Islamic, textbooks, fiction, non-fiction, general; Dir HADIDJAH DAHLAN.

Epsilon Group: Jalan Marga Asri 3, Margacinta, Bandung 40287; tel. (22) 7567826; f. 1985; school textbooks; Dir Drs BAHRUDIN.

Eresco PT: Jalan Megger Girang 98, Bandung 40254; tel. (22) 5205985; fax (22) 5205984; f. 1957; scientific and general; Man. Drs ARFAN ROZALI.

Ganeca Exact Bandung: Kawasan Industri MM 2100, Jalan Selayar Kav A5, Bekasi 17520; tel. (22) 89981946; fax (22) 89981947; e-mail presdir@ganeca-exact.com; internet www.ganeca-exact.com; f. 1982; school textbooks; Dir Ir KETUT SUARDHARA LINGGIH.

Mizan Pustaka PT: Jalan Cinambo 135, Bandung 40294; tel. (22) 7834310; fax (22) 7834311; e-mail info@mizan.com; internet www

.mizan.com; f. 1983; Islamic and general books; Pres. Dir HAIDAR BAGIR.

Penerbit ITB: Jalan Ganesa 10, Bandung 40132; tel. and fax (22) 2504257; e-mail itbpress@bdg.centrin.net.id; f. 1971; academic books; Dir EMMY SUPARKA; Chief Editor SOFIA MANSOOR-NIKSOLIHIN.

Putra A. Bardin: Jalan Kembar Timur II 3, Bandung 40254; tel. (22) 5208305; fax (22) 7300879; f. 1998; textbooks, scientific and general; Dir NAI A. BARDIN.

Remaja Rosdakarya PT: Jalan Ibu Inggit Garnasih 40, Bandung 40252; tel. (22) 5200287; fax (22) 5202529; e-mail rosda@indosat.net.id; textbooks and children's fiction; Pres. ROZALI USMAN.

Sarana Panca Karya Nusa PT: Jalan Kopo 633, Km 13/4, Bandung 40014; e-mail spkn641@yahoo.com; f. 1986; general; Dir WIMPY S. IBRAHIM.

Tarsito PT: Jalan Guntur 20, Bandung 40262; tel. (22) 7304915; fax (22) 7314630; academic; Dir T. SITORUS.

FLORES

Nusa Indah: Jalan El Tari, Ende 86318, Nusa Tenggara Timur, Flores; tel. (381) 21502; fax (381) 23974; e-mail namkahu@yahoo.com; f. 1970; religious and general; Dir LUKAS BATMOMOLIN.

KUDUS

Menara Kudus: Jalan Menara 4, Kudus 59315; tel. (291) 437143; fax (291) 436474; f. 1958; Islamic; Man. CHILMAN NAJIB.

MEDAN

Hasmar: Jalan Letjenderal Haryono M. T. 1, POB 446, Medan 20231; tel. (61) 4144581; fax (22) 4533673; f. 1962; primary school textbooks; Dir FAUZI LUBIS; Man. AMRAN SAID RANGKUTI.

Impola: Jalan H. M. Joni 46, Medan 20217; tel. (61) 711415; f. 1984; school textbooks; Dir PAMILANG M. SITUMORANG.

Madju Medan Cipta PT: Jalan Amaliun 37, Medan 20215; tel. (61) 7361990; fax (61) 7367753; e-mail koboi@indosat.net; f. 1950; textbooks, children's and general; Pres. H. MOHAMED ARBIE; Man. Dir Drs DINO IRSAN ARBIE.

Masco: Jalan Sisingamangaraja 191, Medan 20218; tel. (61) 713375; f. 1992; school textbooks; Dir P. M. SITUMORANG.

Monora: Jalan Letjenderal Jamin Ginting 583, Medan 20156; tel. (61) 8212667; fax (61) 8212669; e-mail monora_cv@plasa.com; f. 1962; school textbooks; Dir CHAIRIL ANWAR.

SEMARANG

Aneka Ilmu: Jalan Raya Semarang Demak, Km 8.5, Sayung, Demak; tel. (24) 6580335; fax (24) 6582903; e-mail pemasaran@anekailmu.com; internet www.anekailmu.com; f. 1983; general and school textbooks; Dir H. SUWANTO.

Effhar COY PT: Jalan Dorang 7, Semarang 50173; tel. (24) 3511172; fax (24) 3551540; e-mail dahara@indosat.net.id; f. 1976; general books; Dir H. DARADJAT HARAHAP.

Intan Pariwara: Jalan Ki Hajar Dewantoro, Kotak Pos III, Kotif Klaten, Jawa-Tengah; tel. (272) 322441; fax (272) 322607; e-mail intan@intanpariwara.co.id; internet www.intanpariwara.co.id; school textbooks; Pres. CHRIS HARJANTO.

Mandira PT: Jalan Letjenderal M. T. Haryono 501, Semarang 50241; tel. (24) 8316150; fax (24) 8415092; f. 1962; Dir Ir A. HARIYANTO.

Mandira Jaya Abadi PT: Jalan Kartini 48, Semarang 50241; tel. (24) 3519547; fax (24) 3542189; e-mail mjabadi@indosat.net.id; f. 1981; Dir Ir A. HARIYANTO.

SOLO

Pabelan PT: Jalan Raya Solo, Kertasura, Km 8, Solo 57162; tel. (271) 743975; fax (271) 714775; f. 1983; school textbooks; Dir AGUNG SASONGKO.

Tiga Serangkai Pustaka Mandiri, PT: Jalan Dr Supomo 23, Solo 57141, Central Java; tel. (271) 714344; fax (271) 713607; internet www.tigaserangkai.com; e-mail tspm@tigaserangkai.co.id; f. 1959; school textbooks, general textbooks; Pres. Commr ABDULLAH SITI AMINAH.

SURABAYA

Airlangga University Press: Kampus C, Jalan Mulyorejo, Surabaya 60115; tel. (31) 5992246; fax (31) 5992248; e-mail aupsby@rad.net.id; academic; Dir Dr ISMUDIONO.

Bina Ilmu PT: Jalan Tunjungan 53E, Surabaya 60275; tel. (31) 5323214; fax (31) 5315421; f. 1973; school textbooks, Islamic; Pres. ARIEFIN NOOR.

Bintang: Jalan Potroagung III/41C, Surabaya; tel. (31) 3770687; fax (31) 3715941; school textbooks; Dir AGUS WINARNO.

Grip PT: Jalan Rungkut Permai II/C11, Surabaya; tel. (31) 22564; f. 1958; textbooks and general; Man. SURIPTO.

Jaya Baya: Jalan Embong Malang 69H, POB 250, Surabaya 60001; tel. (31) 41169; f. 1945; religion, philosophy and ethics; Man. TADJIB ERMADI.

Sinar Wijaya: Jalan Raya Sawo VII/58, Bringin-Lakarsantri, Surabaya; tel. (31) 7406616; general; Dir DULRADJAK.

YOGYAKARTA

Andi Publishers: Jalan Beo 38–40, Yogyakarta 55281; tel. (274) 561881; fax (274) 588282; e-mail andi_pub@indo.net.id; f. 1980; Christian, computing, business, management and technical; Dir J. H. GONDOWIJOYO.

BPFE PT: Jalan Gambiran 37, Yogyakarta 55161; tel. (274) 373760; fax (274) 380819; f. 1984; university textbooks; Dir Drs INDRIYO GITOSUDARMO.

Centhini Yayasan: Gedung Bekisar UH V/716 E1, Yogyakarta 55161; tel. (274) 383148; f. 1984; Javanese culture; Chair. H. KARKONO KAMAJAYA.

Gadjah Mada University Press: Jalan Grafika 1, Kampus UGM, Bulaksumur, Yogyakarta 55281; tel. and fax (274) 561037; e-mail gmupress@ugm.ac.id; internet www.gmup.ugm.ac.id; f. 1971; university textbooks; Dir S. MUNANDAR.

Indonesia UP: Gedung Bekisar UH V/716 E1, Yogyakarta 55161; tel. (274) 383148; f. 1950; general science; Dir H. KARKONO KAMAJAYA.

Kanisius Printing and Publishing: Jalan Cempaka 9, Deresan, Yogyakarta 55281; tel. (274) 588783; fax (274) 563349; e-mail office@kanisiusmedia.com; internet www.kanisiusmedia.com; f. 1922; philosophy, children's, textbooks, Christian and general; Pres. Dir AUGUSTINUS SARWANTO.

Kedaulatan Rakyat PT: Jalan P. Mangkubumi 40–42, Yogyakarta; tel. (274) 2163; Dir DRONO HARDJUSUWONGSO.

Penerbit Tiara Wacana Yogya: Jalan Kaliurang, Km 7, 8 Kopen 16, Banteng, Yogyakarta 55581; tel. and fax (274) 880683; f. 1986; university textbooks and general science; Dir SITORESMI PRABUNINGRAT.

Government Publishing House

Balai Pustaka PT (Persero) (State Publishing and Printing House): 1 Jalan Pulokambing, Kav. 15, Kawasan Industri Pulogadung, Jakarta; tel. (21) 4613519; fax (21) 4613520; e-mail humas@balaipustaka.co.id; internet balaipustaka.co.id; history, anthropology, politics, philosophy, medical, arts and literature; Pres. Dir ZAIM UCHROWI.

PUBLISHERS' ASSOCIATION

Ikatan Penerbit Indonesia (IKAPI) (Asscn of Indonesian Book Publishers): Jalan Kalipasir 32, Jakarta Pusat 10330; tel. (21) 31902532; fax (21) 31926124; e-mail sekretariat@ikapi.org; internet www.ikapi.org; f. 1950; 1,009 mems (July 2011); Pres. LUYA ANDAM DEWI; Gen. Sec. HUSNI SYAWIE.

Broadcasting and Communications

TELECOMMUNICATIONS

PT AXIS Telekom Indonesia (AXIS): Jalan Jenderal Gatot Subroto, Kav. 35–36, Jakarta Selatan 12950; tel. (21) 5760880; fax (21) 5760809; e-mail cs@axisworld.co.id; internet www.axisworld.co.id; f. 2001; cellular telephone network operator; provides GSM 1800 and 3G video services; 80.1% owned by Saudi Telecom Co; Pres. Dir and CEO ERIK AAS.

PT Hutchison CP Telecommunications (HCPT): Wisma Barito Pacific, Tower II, 2nd Floor, Jalan Letjenderal S. Parman, Kav. 62–63, Slipi, Jakarta 11410; tel. (21) 53650000; fax (21) 53660000; internet www.three.co.id; f. 2003; est. as PT Cyber Access Communications; present name adopted 2005; 60% owned by Hutchison Telecom Int. Ltd (Hong Kong); 40% owned by Charoen Pokphand Group (Thailand); cellular telephone network operator providing GSM 1800 and third generation (3G) video services; CEO LAURENTIUS BULTERS.

PT Indonesian Satellite Corporation Tbk (INDOSAT): Jalan Medan Merdeka Barat 21, POB 2905, Jakarta 10110; tel. (21) 54388888; fax (21) 5449501; e-mail publicrelations@indosat.com; internet www.indosat.com; f. 1967; telecommunications; partially privatized in 1994; 41.94% stake sold to Singapore Technologies Telemedia in 2002; 40.81% share sold to QTEL in 2008; Pres. Dir HARRY SASONGKO TIRTOTJONDRO; Pres. Commr Sheikh ABDULLAH BIN MUHAMMAD BIN SAUD AL-THANI.

PT Satelit Palapa Indonesia (SATELINDO): Jalan Daan Mogot Km 11, Jakarta 11710; tel. (21) 5455121; fax (21) 5418548; e-mail palapa-c@satelindo.co.id; internet satelindo.boleh.com; f. 1993; owned by INDOSAT; telecommunications and satellite services; Pres. Dir DJOKO PRAJITNO.

PT SmartFren Telecom Tbk: Jalan H. Agus Salim 45, Sabang, Jakarta Pusat 10340; e-mail customercare@smartfren.com; internet www.smartfren.com; f. 2010 by merger of PT Mobile-8 and PT Smart Telecom; Pres. Dir RUDOLFO PANTOJA.

PT Telekomunikasi Indonesia Tbk (TELKOM): Corporate Office, Jalan Japati 1, Bandung 40133; tel. (22) 2500000; fax (22) 4240313; internet www.telkom.co.id; domestic telecommunications; 24.2% of share capital was transferred to the private sector in 1995; Pres. Commr JUSMAN DJAMAL; Pres. Dir ARIEF YAHYA.

PT Telekomunikasi Selular (TELKOMSEL): Wisma Mulia, 12th Floor, Jalan Jenderal Gatot Subroto, Kav. 42, Jakarta Selatan 12710; tel. (21) 5240811; fax (21) 52906121; e-mail investor@telkomsel.co.id; internet www.telkomsel.com; f. 1995; provides domestic cellular services with international roaming available through 356 network partners; jt venture between PT Telekomunikasi Indonesia Tbk (65%) and Singapore Telecommunications Ltd (35%); Pres. Commr RINALDI FIRMANSYAH; Pres. Dir SARWOTO ATMOSUTARNO.

PT XL Axiata Tbk (XL Axiata): Jalan Dr Ide Anak Agung Gde Agung, Blok 6.2, Kawasan Mega Kuningan, Jakarta 12950; tel. (21) 5761881; fax (21) 5761880; e-mail corpcomm@xl.co.id; internet www.xl.co.id; f. 1996; fixed-line and cellular telephone network provider; Pres. Dir HASNUL SUHAIMI.

Regulatory Authority

Directorate-General of Posts and Informatics Resources (SDPPI): Gedung Sapta Pesona, Jalan Medan Merdeka Barat 17, Jakarta 10110; tel. (21) 3835955; fax (21) 3860754; e-mail admin@postel.go.id; internet www.postel.go.id; Dir-Gen. MUHAMMAD BUDI SETIAWAN.

BROADCASTING

Radio

KBR68H: Jalan Utan Kayu 68H, Jakarta Timur 13120; tel. (21) 8513386; fax (21) 8513002; e-mail redaksi@kbr68h.com; internet www.kbr68h.com; Man. Dir TOSCA SANTOSO.

PT Radio Prambors 102.2 FM: Jalan Adityawarman 71, Kebayoran Baru, Jakarta 12160; tel. (21) 7202238; fax (21) 7222058; e-mail info@pramborsfm.com; internet pramborsfm.com; Gen. Man. JUNAS MIRADIARSYAH.

Radio Republik Indonesia (RRI): Jalan Medan Merdeka Barat 4–5, Jakarta 10110; tel. (21) 3846817; fax (21) 3457134; internet rri.co.id; f. 1945; 49 stations; Pres. Dir ROSARITA NIKEN WIDIASTUTI.

Voice of Indonesia: Jalan Medan Merdeka Barat 4–5, POB 1157, Jakarta; tel. (21) 3456811; fax (21) 3500990; e-mail voi@rri-online.com; internet www.voi.co.id; f. 1945; international service provided by Radio Republik Indonesia; daily broadcasts in Arabic, English, French, German, Bahasa Indonesia, Japanese, Bahasa Malaysia, Mandarin, Spanish and Thai.

Television

In March 1989 Indonesia's first private commercial television station began broadcasting to the Jakarta area. In 2009 there were 10 privately owned television stations in operation and 54 local television stations.

PT Cakrawala Andalas Televisi (ANTEVE): Gedung Sentra Mulia, 18th Floor, Jalan H. R. Rasuna Said, Kav. X-6 No. 8, Jakarta Selatan 12940; tel. (21) 5222086; fax (21) 5229174; e-mail humas@an.tv; internet www.an.tv; f. 1993; private channel; broadcasting to 10 cities; Pres. Commr ANINDYA N. BAKRIE; Pres. Dir DUDI HENDRAKUSUMA.

MNCTV: Jalan Pintu II—Taman Mini Indonesia Indah, Pondok Gede, Jakarta Timur 13810; tel. (21) 8412473; fax (21) 8412470; e-mail info@tpi.tv; internet www.mnctv.com; f. 1991; private channel funded by commercial advertising.

PT Rajawali Citra Televisi Indonesia (RCTI): Jalan Raya Pejuangan 3, Kebon Jeruk, Jakarta 11000; tel. (21) 5303540; fax (21) 5320906; e-mail webmaster@rcti.tv; internet www.rcti.tv; f. 1989; first private channel; 22-year licence; Pres. Dir HARY TANOESOEDIBJO; Vice-Pres. Commr POSMA LUMBAN TOBING.

PT Surya Citra Televisi (SCTV): SCTV Tower, Senayan City, Jalan Asia Afrika, Lot 19, Jakarta 10270; tel. (21) 27935555; fax (21) 27935444; e-mail stephanus@sctv.co.id; internet www.sctv.co.id; f. 1990; private channel broadcasting nationally; Pres. Dir SUTANTO HARTONO.

Televisi Republik Indonesia (TVRI): TVRI Senayan, Jalan Gerbang Pemuda, Senayan, Jakarta 10270; tel. (21) 5704720; fax (21) 5733122; e-mail daffa2000@tvri.co.id; internet www.tvri.co.id; f. 1962; fmrly state-controlled; became independent in 2003; Pres. Dir Maj.-Gen. (retd) I GDE NYOMAN ARSANA.

Regulatory Authority

Komisi Penyiaran Indonesia—KPI (Indonesian Broadcasting Commission): Lantai 6, Jalan Gajah Mada 8, Jakarta 10120; tel. (21) 6340713; fax (21) 6340667; internet www.kpi.go.id; f. 2002; ind. broadcasting regulatory authority; Dir-Gen. DADANG RAHMAT HIDAYAT.

Finance

(cap. = capital; p.u. = paid up; res = reserves; dep. = deposits; m. = million; brs = branches; amounts in rupiah)

BANKING

In October 2013 there were four state banks and 117 private banks operating in Indonesia.

Central Bank

Bank Indonesia (BI): Jalan M. H. Thamrin 2, Jakarta Pusat 10350; tel. (21) 2310108; fax (21) 3501867; e-mail humasbi@bi.go.id; internet www.bi.go.id; f. 1828; nationalized as central bank in 1953; cap. 16,876,926m., res 41,555,776m. (Dec. 2011); Gov. AGUS MARTOWARDOJO; 42 brs.

State Banks

PT Bank Mandiri (Persero): Plaza Mandiri, Jalan Jenderal Gatot Subroto, Kav. 36–38, Jakarta 12190; tel. (21) 52997777; fax (21) 52997735; internet www.bankmandiri.co.id; f. 1998; est. following merger of 4 state-owned banks—PT Bank Bumi Daya, PT Bank Dagang Negara, PT Bank Ekspor Impor Indonesia and PT Bank Pembangunan Indonesia; cap. 11,666,667m., res 16,833,988m., dep. 497,582,793m. (Dec. 2012); Chair. EDWIN GERUNGAN; Pres. Dir BUDI GUNADI SADIKIN; 909 local brs, 6 overseas brs.

PT Bank Negara Indonesia (Persero) Tbk: Jalan Jenderal Sudirman, Kav. 1, Jakarta 10220; tel. (21) 2511946; fax (21) 5728805; e-mail investor.relations@bni.co.id; internet www.bni.co.id; f. 1946; commercial bank; specializes in credits to the industrial sector; cap. 9,054,807m., res 18,936,953m., dep. 260,906,084m. (Dec. 2012); Pres. Commr PETER B. STOK; Pres. Dir and CEO GATOT MUDIANTORO SUWONDO; 919 local brs, 5 overseas brs.

PT Bank Rakyat Indonesia (Persero): Gedung BRI 1, Jalan Jenderal Sudirman, Kav. 44–46, POB 94, Jakarta 10210; tel. (21) 2510244; fax (21) 2500077; internet www.bri.co.id; f. 1895; present name since 1946; commercial and foreign exchange bank; specializes in agricultural smallholdings and rural devt; cap. 6,167,291m., res 11,971,824m., dep. 442,465,775m. (Dec. 2012); Pres. Commr BUNASOR SANIM; Pres. Dir SOFYAN BASIR; 326 brs.

PT Bank Tabungan Negara (Persero): Menara Bank BTN, 10th Floor, Jalan Gajah Mada 1, Jakarta 10130; tel. (21) 26533555; e-mail webadmin@btn.co.id; internet www.btn.co.id; f. 1964; commercial bank; state-owned; cap. 5,178.2m., res 3,736,689m., dep. 81,483,537m. (Dec. 2012); Pres. Commr ZAKI BARIDWAN; Pres. Dir MARYONO; 44 brs.

PT BPD Jawa Timur (Bank Jatim): Jalan Basuki Rachmad 98–104, Surabaya; tel. (31) 5310090; fax (31) 5470159; e-mail humas@bankjatim.co.id; internet www.bankjatim.co.id; f. 1961; cap. 942,123m., res 1,437,417m., dep. 20,388,367m. (Dec. 2011); Pres. Commr MULJANTO; Pres. Dir HADI SUKRIANTO.

Indonesia Eximbank: Gedung Bursa Efek, Menara II, Lantai 8, Jalan Jenderal Sudirman, Kav. 52–53, Jakarta 12190; tel. (21) 5154638; fax (21) 5154639; e-mail intbank@indonesiaeximbank.go.id; internet www.indonesiaeximbank.go.id; fmrly PT Bank Ekspor Indonesia (Persero); cap. 6,321,586m., res 629,035m., dep. 1,856,763m. (Dec. 2012); Chair. MADE GDE ERATA; Man. Dir ARIFIN INDRA SULISTYANTO.

Commercial Banks

PT Bank ANZ Indonesia: ANZ Tower, Ground Floor, Jalan Jenderal Sudirman (Senayan), Kav. 33A, Jakarta 10220; tel. (21) 5750300; fax (21) 5727447; e-mail products@anz.com; internet www.anz.com/indonesia; f. 1990; est. as Westpac Panin Bank; present name adopted 1993; 85% owned by Australia and New Zealand Banking Group Ltd; cap. 1,650,000m., res 14,690m., dep. 22,503m. (Dec. 2012); Pres. Dir JOSEPH ABRAHAM.

PT Bank Artha Graha Internasional Tbk: Bank Artha Graha Tower, 5th Floor, Jalan Jenderal Sudirman, Kav. 52–53, Jakarta 12190; tel. (21) 5152168; fax (21) 5153470; e-mail agraha@rad.net.id; internet www.arthagraha.com; f. 1967; est. as PT Bank Bandung; merged with PT Bank Arta Pratama in 1999 and with PT Bank Inter-Pacific in 2005; cap. 950,804.4m., res 418,787.2m., dep. 16,889,059m.

(Dec. 2011); Pres. Dir ANDY KASIH; Pres. Commr KIKI SYAHNAKRI; 78 brs.

PT Bank Central Asia Tbk (BCA): Menara BCA, Grand Indonesia, Jalan M. H. Thamrin 1, Jakarta 10310; tel. (21) 23588000; fax (21) 23588300; e-mail halobca@bca.co.id; internet www.bca.co.id; f. 1957; 51% share sold to Farallon Capital Management (USA) in March 2002; cap. 1,540,938m., res 4,751.6m., dep. 373,866.3m. (Dec. 2012); Pres. Commr DJOHAN EMIR SETIJOSO; Pres. Dir JAHJA SETIAATMADJA; 760 local brs.

PT Bank Chinatrust Indonesia: Wisma Tamara, Lantai 15–17, Jalan Jenderal Sudirman, Kav. 24, Jakarta 12920; tel. (21) 5206848; fax (21) 5206767; e-mail ctcbjak@rad.net.id; internet www.chinatrust.co.id; f. 1995; cap. 150,000m., dep. 3,675,976m. (Dec. 2011); Pres. Commr JACK LEE; Pres. Dir JOSEPH SHIH.

PT Bank CIMB Niaga Tbk: Graha Niaga, Jalan Jenderal Sudirman, Kav. 58, Jakarta 12190; tel. (21) 5460555; fax (21) 2505205; e-mail corsec@cimbniaga.co.id; internet www.cimbniaga.com; f. 1955; cap. 1,612,257m., res 7,715,582m., dep. 133,568,414m. (Dec. 2011); Pres. Commr Dato' Sri NAZIR RAZAK; Pres. Dir ARWIN RASYID; 227 brs.

PT Bank Danamon Indonesia Tbk: Menara Danamon, Lantai 6, Jalan Prof. Dr Satrio 6, Kav. E-4, Mega Kuningan, Jakarta 12950; tel. (21) 57991001; fax (21) 57991445; e-mail danamon.access@danamon.co.id; internet www.danamon.co.id; f. 1956; placed under supervision of Indonesian Bank Restructuring Agency in April 1998; merged with PT Bank Tiara Asia, PT Tamara Bank, PT Bank Duta and PT Bank Nusa Nasional in 2000; 51% share sold to consortium led by Singapore's Temasek Holdings in May 2003; cap. 5,901,122m., res 7,556,830m., dep. 91,340,427m. (Dec. 2011); Pres. Commr NG KEE CHOE; Pres. Dir HENRY HO HON CHEONG; 483 brs.

PT Bank ICB Bumiputera Tbk: Menara ICB Bumiputera, Jalan Probolinggo 18, Menteng, Jakarta Pusat 10350; tel. (21) 3919898; fax (21) 3919797; e-mail bank@icbbumiputera.co.id; internet www.icbbumiputera.co.id; f. 1989; cap. 548,607m., res 130,230m., dep. 6,413,520m. (Dec. 2011); Pres. Commr Dato MAT AMIR BIN JAFFAR; Pres. Dir RAJUENDRAN MARRAPAN (acting).

PT Bank Internasional Indonesia Tbk (BII): Gedung Sentral Senayan 3, Jalan Asia Afrika 8, Gelora Bung Karno, Jakarta 10270; tel. (21) 29228888; fax (21) 29039051; e-mail cs@bii.co.id; internet www.bii.co.id; cap. 3,407,411m., res 2,147.1m., dep. 88,491.2m. (Dec. 2012); Pres. Commr Tan Sri Dato' MEGAT ZAHARUDDIN BIN MEGAT MOHAMMAD NOR; Pres. Dir (vacant); 368 local brs; 3 overseas brs.

PT Bank KEB Indonesia: Wisma GKBI, Lantai 20, Suite 2002, Jalan Jenderal Sudirman, Kav. 28, Jakarta 10210; tel. (21) 5741030; fax (21) 5741031; e-mail contact.center@kebi.co.id; owned by KEB Seoul (99%) and PT Clemont Finance Indonesia (1%); f. 1990; fmrly PT Korea Exchange Bank Danamon; cap. 150,000m., res 30,000m., dep. 2,522,105m. (Dec. 2011); Pres. Commr OO YEOUNG JEONG; Pres. Dir CHO YONG WOO.

PT Bank Mayapada Internasional Tbk: Menara Mayapada, Jalan Jenderal Sudirman, Kav. 28, Jakarta 12920; tel. (21) 5212288; fax (21) 5211965; e-mail mayapada@bankmayapada.com; internet www.bankmayapada.com; f. 1989; cap. 464,486m., res 836m., dep. 15,165.6m. (Dec. 2012); Chair. Dato' Sri JONATHAN TAHIR; Pres. Dir HARIYONO TJAHJARIJADI; 41 brs.

PT Bank Mizuho Indonesia: Plaza BII, Lantai 24, Menara 2, Jalan M. H. Thamrin 51, Jakarta 10350; tel. (21) 3925222; fax (21) 3926354; internet www.mizuhobank.co.id; f. 1989; fmrly PT Bank Fuji International Indonesia; name changed as above in 2001; cap. 1,323,574m., res 7,847.6m., dep. 10,501.6m. (Dec. 2012); Pres. Commr RUSDI ABDULLAH DJAMIL; Pres. Dir SAMBUTAN DARI.

PT Bank Muamalat Indonesia (BMI): Gedung Arthaloka, Jalan Jenderal Sudirman 2, Jakarta 10220; tel. (21) 2511414; fax (21) 2511453; internet www.muamalatbank.com; Indonesia's first Islamic bank; cap. 821,843m., res 515,251.9m., dep. 39,669,316.8m. (Dec. 2012); Pres. Dir Ir ARVIYAN ARIFIN; Pres. Commr WIDIGDO SUKARMAN.

PT Bank Mutiara Tbk: Gedung International Financial Centre, Jalan Jenderal Sudirman, Kav. 22–23, Jakarta 12920; tel. (21) 29261111; fax (21) 5224670; e-mail corsec@mutiarabank.co.id; internet www.mutiarabank.co.id; f. 1989 as PT Bank Century Tbk; renamed as above in 2009; cap. 8,973,675m., res 274,862m., dep. 13,475,784m. (Dec. 2012); Pres. Commr PONTAS RIYANTO SIAHAAN; Pres. Dir SUKORIYANTO SAPUTRO.

PT Bank OCBC NISP Tbk: Menara Bank OCBC NISP, Jalan Prof. Dr Satrio, Kav. 25, Jakarta 12940; tel. (21) 25533888; fax (21) 57944000; internet www.ocbcnisp.com; f. 1941; 81.9% owned by OCBC Bank, Singapore; cap. 1,068,615m., res 3,711,000m., dep. 61,309,975m. (Dec. 2012); Pres. Commr PRAMUKTI SURJAUDAJA; Pres. Dir PARWATI SURJAUDAJA; 168 brs.

PT Bank Permata Tbk: Menara PermataBank I, Lantai 17, Jalan Jenderal Sudirman, Kav. 27, Jakarta 12920; tel. (21) 5237899; fax (21) 5237253; e-mail isaptono@permatabank.co.id; internet www.permatabank.com; f. 1954; est. as Bank Persatuan Dagang Indonesia; became PT Bank Bali in 1971 and PT Bank Bali Tbk in 1990; name changed as above Sept. 2002 following merger with PT Bank Prima Express, PT Bank Universal Tbk, PT Arthamedia Bank and PT Bank Patriot; cap. 1,667,159m., res 9,454,526m., dep. 106,919,167m. (Dec. 2012); Pres. Commr NEERAJ SWAROOP; Pres. Dir DAVID MARTIN FLETCHER; 288 brs.

PT Bank Rabobank International Indonesia: Plaza 89, Lantai 9, Jalan H. R. Rasuna Said, Kav. X-7 No. 6, Jakarta 12940; tel. (21) 2520876; fax (21) 2520875; e-mail indonesia@rabobank.com; internet www.rabobank.co.id; f. 1990; est. as PT Rabobank Duta Indonesia; name changed as above in 2001 when Rabobank Nederland secured sole ownership; cap. 715,000m., res 1,990m., dep. 11,441,190m. (Dec. 2012); Pres. Commr ROELOF JAN DEKKER; Pres. Dir HENK MULDER.

PT Bank Sumitomo Mitsui Indonesia: Gedung Summitmas II, Lantai 10, Jalan Jenderal Sudirman, Kav. 61–62, Jakarta 12190; tel. (21) 5227011; fax (21) 5227022; f. 1989; fmrly PT Bank Sumitomo Indonesia; merged with PT Bank Sakura Swadharma in April 2001; cap. 2,873,942m., res 107,095m., dep. 12,585,800m. (Dec. 2012); Pres. Commr MASAYUKI SHIMURA; Pres. Dir MASAYA HIRAYAMA; 1 br.

PT Bank UOB Indonesia: UOB Plaza, Jalan M. H. Thamrin 10, Jakarta 10230; tel. (21) 23506000; fax (21) 29936682; e-mail squ@uob.co.id; internet www.uob.co.id; f. 1956; est. as PT Bank Buana Indonesia Tbk; name changed to PT Bank UOB Buana in 2009; above name adopted in 2011; cap. 2,388,471m., res 2,105,419m., dep. 44,219,714m. (Dec. 2011); Pres. Commr WEE CHO YAW; Pres. Dir ARMAND B. ARIEF; CEO WEE EE CHEONG; 32 brs.

PT Pan Indonesia Tbk (Panin Bank): Panin Bank Centre, Lantai 11, Jalan Jenderal Sudirman, Kav. 1, Senayan, Jakarta 10270; tel. (21) 2700545; fax (21) 2700340; e-mail panin@panin.co.id; internet www.panin.co.id; f. 1971; est. as a result of the merger of 3 private national banks; cap. 2,408,765m., res 3,452,496m., dep. 109,477,500m. (Dec. 2012); Pres. Commr JOHNNY N. WIRAATMADJA; Pres. Dir Drs H. ROSTIAN SJAMSUDIN; 250 local brs, 2 overseas brs.

PT Woori Bank Indonesia: Jakarta Stock Exchange Bldg, Lantai 16, Jalan Jenderal Sudirman, Kav. 52–53, Jakarta 12190; tel. (21) 5151919; fax (21) 5151477; e-mail indonesia@wooribank.com; internet id.wooribank.com; fmrly PT Hanvit Bank Indonesia; cap. 170,000m., res 34,000m., dep. 3,561,858m. (Dec. 2011); Pres. Dir LIM CHOL-JIN.

Banking Association

The Association of Indonesian National Private Commercial Banks (Perhimpunan Bank-Bank Umum Nasional Swasta—PERBANAS): Griya Perbanas, Lantai 1, Jalan Perbanas, Karet Kuningan, Setiabudi, Jakarta 12940; tel. (21) 5223038; fax (21) 5223037; e-mail sekretariat@perbanas.org; internet www.perbanas.org; f. 1952; 78 mems; Chair. SIGIT PRAMONO; Sec.-Gen. FARID RAHMAN.

STOCK EXCHANGE

Indonesia Stock Exchange (IDX): Indonesia Stock Exchange Bldg, Menara 1, Jalan Jenderal Sudirman, Kav. 52–53, Jakarta 12190; tel. (21) 5150515; fax (21) 5150330; e-mail callcenter@idx.co.id; internet www.idx.co.id; fmrly Jakarta Stock Exchange; name changed as above upon merger with Surabaya Stock Exchange in 2007; 125 securities houses constitute the mems and the shareholders of the exchange, each company owning one share; CEO ITO WARSITO.

Regulatory Authority

Badan Pengawas Pasar Modal (BAPEPAM) (Capital Market Supervisory Agency): Gedung Sumitro Djojohadikusumo, Jalan Lapangan Banteng Timur 1–4, Jakarta 10710; tel. (21) 3858001; fax (21) 3857917; e-mail bapepam@bapepam.go.id; internet www.bapepam.go.id; Chair. A. FAUD RAHMANY; Exec. Sec. NGALIM SAWEGA.

INSURANCE

In September 2012 there were 235 insurance companies, including 101 non-life companies, 83 general insurance, 45 life companies, four reinsurance companies and two social insurance companies.

Insurance Supervisory Authority of Indonesia: Directorate of Financial Institutions, Jalan Dr Wahidin, Jakarta 10710; tel. (21) 3451210; fax (21) 3849504; wing of the Ministry of Finance and State Enterprises Devt; Dir H. FIRDAUS DJAELANI.

Selected Life Insurance Companies

PT AIA Financial: Menara Matahari, Lantai 8, Jalan Bulevar Palem Raya 7, Lippo Karawaci 1200, Tangerang 15811; tel. (21) 54218777; fax (21) 5475409; e-mail id.customer@aia.com; internet www.aia-financial.co.id; f. 1983; CEO and Pres. Dir PETER J. CREWE.

PT Asuransi Allianz Life Indonesia: Gedung Summitmas II, Lantai 1, Jalan Jenderal Sudirman, Kav. 61–62, Jakarta 12190; tel.

(21) 25989999; fax (21) 30003400; e-mail contactus@allianz.co.id; internet www.allianz.co.id; f. 1996; CEO JOACHIM WESSLING.

Asuransi Jiwa Bersama Bumiputera 1912: Wisma Bumiputera, Lantai 18–21, Jalan Jenderal Sudirman, Kav. 75, Jakarta 12910; tel. (21) 2512154; fax (21) 2512172; e-mail bp1912@bumiputera.com; internet www.bumiputera.com; Chair. Dr H. SUGIHARTO; Pres. Dir DIRMAN PARDOSI.

PT Asuransi Jiwa Central Asia Raya: Blue Dot Center, Blok A–C, Jalan Gelong Baru Utara 5–8, Jakarta Barat 11440; tel. (21) 56961929; fax (21) 56961939; e-mail lancar@car.co.id; internet www.car.co.id; Chair. SOEDONO SALIM.

PT Asuransi Jiwa 'Panin Putra': Jalan Pintu Besar Selatan 52A, Jakarta 11110; tel. (21) 672586; fax (21) 676354; f. 1974; Pres. Dir SUJONO SOEPENO; Chair. NUGROHO TJOKROWIRONO.

PT Asuransi Jiwasraya (Persero): Jalan H. Juanda 34, Jakarta 10120; tel. (21) 3444444; fax (21) 3862344; e-mail asuransi@jiwasraya.co.id; internet www.jiwasraya.co.id; f. 1959; Pres. Commr DJONNY WIGUNA; Pres. Dir HENDRISMAN RAHIM.

PT Asuransi Panin Life: Panin Life Center, Lantai 6, Jalan Letjenderal S. Parman, Kav. 91, Jakarta 11420; tel. (21) 25566888; fax (21) 25566711; e-mail customer@paninlife.co.id; internet www.paninlife.co.id; Pres. Dir HERU YUWONO.

Bumi Asih Jaya Life Insurance Co Ltd: Jalan Matraman Raya 165–167, Jakarta 13140; tel. (21) 2800700; fax (21) 8509669; e-mail baj@bajlife.com; internet www.bajlife.co.id; f. 1967; Chair. P. SITOMPUL; Pres. VIRGO HUTAGALUNG.

Selected Non-Life Insurance Companies

PT Asuransi Bina Dana Arta Tbk: Plaza ABDA, Lantai 27, Jalan Jenderal Sudirman, Kav. 59, Jakarta 122190; tel. (21) 51401688; fax (21) 51401698; e-mail contactus@abda.co.id; internet www.abda.co.id; Pres. Commr TJAN SOEN ENG; Pres. Dir CANDRA GUNAWAN.

PT Asuransi Bintang Tbk: Jalan R. S. Fatmawati 32, Jakarta Selatan 12430; tel. (21) 75902777; fax (21) 7656287; e-mail bintang@asuransibintang.com; internet www.asuransibintang.com; f. 1955; general insurance; Pres. Commr SHANTI POESPOSOETJIPTO; Pres. Dir ZAFAR DINESH IDHAM.

PT Asuransi Buana Independen: Jalan Pintu Besar Selatan 78, Jakarta 11110; tel. (21) 6266286; fax (21) 6263005; e-mail headoffice@buanaindependent.co.id; internet buanaindependent.co.id; Pres. Commr ISHAK SUMARNO; Pres. Dir MADE MARKA.

PT Asuransi Central Asia: Wisma Asia, Lantai 12–15, Jalan Letjenderal S. Parman, Kav. 79, Slipi, Jakarta Barat 11420; tel. (21) 56998288; fax (21) 5638029; e-mail info@aca.co.id; internet www.aca.co.id; Pres. Commr ANTHONY SALIM; Pres. Dir TEDDY HAILAMSAH.

PT Asuransi Dayin Mitra: Jalan Raden Saleh Raya, Kav. 1B–1D, Jakarta 10430; tel. (21) 3153577; fax (21) 3912902; e-mail nuning@dayinmitra.co.id; internet www.dayinmitra.co.id; f. 1982; general insurance; Man. Dir LARSOEN HAKER.

PT Asuransi Indrapura: Menara Chase Plaza, Lantai 4, Jalan Jenderal Sudirman, Kav. 21, Jakarta 12920; tel. (21) 5200338; fax (21) 5200175; e-mail insure@indrapura.co.id; internet www.indrapura.co.id; f. 1954; Pres. Commr A. WAHYUHADI; Pres. Dir MINTARTO HALIM.

PT Asuransi Jasa Indonesia: Jalan Letjenderal M. T. Haryono, Kav. 61, Jakarta 12041; tel. (21) 7994508; fax (21) 7995364; e-mail jasindo@jasindo.co.id; internet www.jasindo.co.id; Pres. Commr MOELYADI; Pres. Dir Drs EKO BUDIWIYONO.

PT Asuransi Jasa Tania: Wisma Jasa Tania, Jalan Teuku Cik Ditiro 14, Jakarta 10350; tel. (21) 3101850; fax (21) 31923089; e-mail ajstania@jasatania.co.id; internet www.jasatania.co.id; Pres. Dir BASRAN DAMANIK (acting).

PT Asuransi Maipark Indonesia: Gedung Setiabudi Atrium, Lantai 4, Suite 408, Jalan H. R. Rasuna Said, Kav. 62, Jakarta 12920; tel. (21) 5210803; fax (21) 5210738; e-mail maipark@maipark.com; internet www.maipark.com; fmrly PT Maskapai Asuransi Indonesia; Chair. and CEO KORNELIUS SIMANJUNTAK.

PT Asuransi Parolamas: Komplek Golden Plaza, Blok G 39–42, Jalan R. S. Farmawati 15, Jakarta 12420; tel. (21) 7508983; fax (21) 7506339; internet www.parolamas.co.id; Chief Commr TJUT ROEKMA RAFFLI; Pres. Dir Drs SYARIFUDDIN HARAHAP.

PT Asuransi Ramayana: Jalan Kebon Sirih 49, Jakarta 10340; tel. (21) 31937148; fax (21) 31934825; e-mail info@ramayanains.com; internet ramayanainsurance.com; f. 1965; Pres. Commr A. WINOTO DOERIAT; Pres. Dir SYAHRIL.

PT Asuransi Tri Pakarta: Jalan Paletehan I/18, Jakarta 12160; tel. (21) 7222717; fax (21) 7394748; internet www.tripakarta.co.id; Chair. SAIFUDIEN HASAN; Pres. TEDDY PUSPITO.

PT Asuransi Wahana Tata: Jalan H. R. Rasuna Said, Kav. C-4, Jakarta 12920; tel. (21) 5203145; fax (21) 5203149; e-mail aswata@aswata.co.id; internet www.aswata.co.id; Chair. RUDY WANANDI; Pres. Dir CHRISTIAN WANANDI.

PT Berdikari Insurance: Jalan Merdeka Barat 1, Jakarta 10110; tel. (21) 3440266; fax (21) 3440586; e-mail ho@berdikariinsurance.com; internet www.berdikariinsurance.com; Pres. ANGGIAT ISIDORUS SITOHANG.

PT Tugu Pratama Indonesia: Wisma Tugu I, Jalan H. R. Rasuna Said, Kav. C8–9, Kuningan, Jakarta Selatan 12920; tel. (21) 52961777; fax (21) 52961555; e-mail tpi@tugu.com; internet www.tugu.com; f. 1981; general insurance; Pres. Commr FEREDERICK SIAHAAN; Pres. Dir EVITA M. TAGOR.

Joint Ventures

PT Asuransi AIG Life: Matahari AIG Lippo Cyber Tower, 5th–7th Floors, Jalan Bulevar Palem Raya 7, Lippo Karawaci 1200, Tangerang 15811; tel. (21) 54218888; fax (21) 5475415; e-mail service@aig-life.co.id; internet www.aig-life.co.id; jt venture between American International Group, Inc, and PT Asuransi Lippo Life; life insurance; Dep. Pres. Dir S. BUDISUHARTO.

PT Asuransi Allianz Utama Indonesia: Gedung Summitmas II, 9th Floor, Jalan Jenderal Sudirman, Kav. 61–62, Jakarta Selatan 12190; tel. (21) 2522470; fax (21) 2523246; e-mail general@allianz.co.id; internet www.allianz.co.id; f. 1989; non-life insurance; Chair. EDI SUBEKTI; Pres. Dir VOLKER MISS.

PT Asuransi Jiwa Manulife Indonesia: Menara Selatan, Lantai 3, Jalan Jenderal Sudirman, Kav. 45, Jakarta 12930; tel. (21) 25557788; fax (21) 25557799; e-mail communication_id@manulife.com; internet www.manulife-indonesia.com; f. 1985; life insurance; Pres. Dir ALAN MERTEN.

PT Asuransi Jiwa Sinarmas: Wisma EKA Jiwa, Lantai 8, Jalan Mangga Dua Raya, Jakarta 10730; tel. (21) 6257808; fax (21) 6257837; e-mail cs@sinarmaslife.co.id; internet www.sinarmaslife.com; fmrly PT Asuransi Jiwa EKA Life; Pres. Commr INDRA WIDJAJA; Pres. Dir IVENA WIDJAJA.

PT Asuransi MSIG Indonesia: Gedung Summitmas II, Lantai 15, Jalan Jenderal Sudirman, Kav. 61–62, Jakarta 12190; tel. (21) 2523110; fax (21) 2524307; e-mail msig@id.msig-asia.com; internet www.msig.co.id; f. 1975; est. as PT Asuransi Mitsui Marine Indonesia; name changed to PT Asuransi Mitsui Sumitomo Indonesia in 2003, following merger with PT Asuransi Sumitomo Marine and Pool; present name adopted 2007; Chair. RUDY WANANDI; Pres. Dir TADASHI MAEKAWA.

PT Asuransi Tokio Marine Indonesia: Sentral Senayan I, Lantai 4, Jalan Asia Afrika 8, Jakarta 10270; tel. (21) 5725772; fax (21) 5724005; e-mail cp@tokiomarine.co.id; internet www.tokiomarine.co.id; jt venture between Tokio Marine Asia Pte Ltd and PT Asuransi Jasa Indonesia; Pres. Dir MITSUTAKA SATO.

PT Chartis Insurance Indonesia: Indonesia Stock Exchange Bldg, Menara II, Lantai 3A, Jalan Jenderal Sudirman, Kav. 52–53, Jakarta 12190; tel. (21) 52914888; fax (21) 52914889; e-mail contact.us@chartisinsurance.com; internet www.chartisinsurance.co.id; f. 1970; fmrly PT Asuransi AIU Indonesia; Pres. Dir MICHAEL BLAKEWAY.

Insurance Associations

Asosiasi Asuransi Jiwa Indonesia (Indonesia Life Insurance Association): The Plaza Office Tower, Lantai 19, Jalan M. H. Thamrin, Kav. 28–30, Jakarta 10350; tel. (21) 29922929; fax (21) 29922828; e-mail aaji.info@aaji.or.id; internet www.aaji.or.id; f. 2002; 49 mems; Chair. EVELINA PEITRUSCKHA; Exec. Dir STEPHEN JUWONO.

Asosiasi Asuransi Umum Indonesia (General Insurance Association of Indonesia): Permata Kuningan Bldg, 2nd Floor, Jalan Kuningan Mulia, Kav. 9C, Jakarta 12960; tel. (21) 2906980; fax (21) 29069828; e-mail secretary@aaui.or.id; f. 1957; est. as Dewan Asuransi Indonesia (Insurance Council of Indonesia); present name adopted 2003; Chair. KORNELIUS SIMANJUNTAK; Exec. Dir JULIAN NOOR.

Trade and Industry

GOVERNMENT AGENCIES

Badan Pengatur Hilir Minyak dan Gas Bumi (BPH Migas): Gedung BPH Migas, Jalan Captain P. Tendean 28, Jakarta Selatan 12710; tel. (21) 5255500; fax (21) 5223210; e-mail humas@bphmigas.go.id; internet www.bphmigas.go.id; f. 2002; regulates downstream petroleum and gas industry; Chair. TUBAGUS HARYONO.

Badan Pengembangan Industri Strategis (BPIS) (Agency for Strategic Industries): Gedung Arthaloka, 3rd Floor, Jalan Jenderal Sudirman 2, Jakarta 10220; tel. (21) 5705335; fax (21) 3292516; f. 1989; co-ordinates production of capital goods.

Badan Pengkajian dan Penerapan Teknologi (BPPT) (Agency for the Assessment and Application of Technology): Jalan M. H.

Thamrin 8, Jakarta 10340; tel. (21) 3168200; fax (21) 3904573; e-mail humas@bppt.go.id; internet www.bppt.go.id; Chair. Dr Ir MARZAN A. ISKANDAR.

Badan Tenaga Nuklir Nasional (BATAN) (National Nuclear Energy Agency): Jalan Kuningan Barat, Mampang Prapatan, Jakarta 12710; tel. (21) 5251109; fax (21) 5251110; e-mail humas@batan.go.id; internet www.batan.go.id; Chair. Dr SOEDYARTOMO.

Badan Urusan Logistik (BULOG) (National Logistics Agency): Jalan Jenderal Gatot Subroto, Kav. 49, Jakarta 12950; tel. and fax (21) 5256482; e-mail redaksiweb@bulog.co.id; internet www.bulog.co.id; Dir-Gen. SUTARTO ALIMOESO.

National Agency for Export Development (NAFED): Jalan M. I. Ridwan Rais 5, 3rd Floor, Jakarta 10110; tel. (21) 3858171; fax (21) 23528662; e-mail nafed@nafed.go.id; internet www.nafed.go.id; Chair. HESTI INDAH KRESNARINI.

National Economic Council: Jakarta; f. 1999; 13-mem. council formed to advise the President on economic policy; Chair. EMIL SALIM.

Satuan Kerja Khusus Sementara Pelaksana Kegiatan Usaha Hulu Minyak dan Gas Bumi (SKK Migas) (Special Task Force for Upstream Oil and Gas Business Activities): Gedung Wisma Mulia, Lantai 35, 42 Jalan Gatot Subroto, Jakarta 12710; tel. (21) 29241607; fax (21) 29249999; e-mail hupmas@skspmigas-esdm.go.id; internet www.skspmigas-esdm.go.id; f. 2012 to replace Badan Pelaksana Kegiatan Usaha Hulu Minyak dan Gas Bumi (BP Migas), disbanded by a ruling of the Constitutional Court; regulates upstream petroleum and natural gas industry; Chair. RUDI RUBIANDINI.

DEVELOPMENT ORGANIZATIONS

Badan Koordinasi Penanaman Modal (BKPM) (Investment Co-ordinating Board): Jalan Jenderal Gatot Subroto 44, POB 3186, Jakarta 12190; tel. (21) 52921334; fax (21) 5264211; e-mail info@bkpm.go.id; internet www.bkpm.go.id; f. 1976; Chair. MUHAMAD CHATIB BASRI.

Badan Perencanaan Pembangunan Nasional (Bappenas) (National Development Planning Board): Jalan Taman Suropati 2, Jakarta 10310; tel. (21) 3905650; fax (21) 3145374; e-mail admin@bappenas.go.id; internet www.bappenas.go.id; formulates Indonesia's economic devt plans; Chair. Dr ARMIDA ALISJAHBANA.

CHAMBER OF COMMERCE

Kamar Dagang dan Industri Indonesia (KADIN) (Indonesian Chamber of Commerce and Industry): Menara Kadin Indonesia, Lantai 29, Jalan H. R. Rasuna Said X5, Kav. 2–3, Jakarta 12950; tel. (21) 5274484; fax (21) 5274331; e-mail kadin@kadin-indonesia.or.id; internet www.kadin-indonesia.or.id; f. 1968; 33 provincial-level chambers and 442 district-level chambers; Chair. SURYO BAMBANG SULISTO; Exec. Dir Drs RAHARDJO JAMTOMO.

INDUSTRIAL AND TRADE ASSOCIATIONS

Association of Indonesian Automotive Industries (GAIKINDO): Jalan Hos Cokroaminoto 6, Jakarta Pusat 10350; tel. (21) 3157178; fax (21) 3142100; e-mail gaikindo@cbn.net.id; internet www.gaikindo.org; Chair. BAMBANG TRISULO.

Association of Indonesian Beverage Industries (ASRIM): 8/F, Wisma GKBI, Jalan Jenderal Sudirman 28, Jakarta 10210; tel. (21) 5723838; fax (21) 5740817; e-mail sekertariat.asrim@gmail.com; 22 mems; Chair. WILLY SIDHARTA; Sec.-Gen. SUROSO NATAKUSUMA.

Association of Indonesian Coffee Exporters (AIKE): Gedung AIKE, Lantai 3, Jalan R. P. Soeroso 20, Jakarta 10350; tel. (21) 3106765; fax (21) 3144115; e-mail bphaeki@yahoo.com; 800 mems; Chair. HASSAN WIDJAYA; Sec.-Gen. RACHIM KARTABRATA.

Association of State-Owned Companies: CTC Bldg, Jalan Kramat Raya 94–96, Jakarta; tel. (21) 346071; co-ordinates the activities of state-owned enterprises; Pres. ODANG.

BANI Arbitration Center (BANI): Wahana Graha, Lantai 2, Jalan Mampang Prapatan 2, Jakarta 12760; tel. (21) 7940542; fax (21) 7940543; e-mail bani-arb@indo.net.id; internet www.bani-arb.org; f. 1977; resolves business disputes; Chair. Prof. Dr H. PRIYATNA ABDURRASYID; Sec.-Gen. N. KRISNAWENDA.

Electric and Electronic Appliance Manufacturers' Association: Jalan Pangeran, Blok 20A-1D, Jakarta; tel. (21) 6480059.

Importers' Association of Indonesia (GINSI): Wisma Kosgoro Bldg, 8th Floor, Jalan M. H. Thamrin 53, Jakarta 10350; tel. (21) 39832510; fax (21) 39832540; f. 1956; 2,921 mems (1996); Chair. AMIRUDIN SAUD; Sec.-Gen. DEDDY BINTANG.

Indonesia National Shippers' Council (INSC): Jalan Cempaka Putih, Barat 6, Jakarta Pusat 10520; tel. (21) 4254677; fax (21) 4206303; e-mail depalindo@yahoo.com; Chair. SUARDI ZEN; Sec.-Gen. RACHIM KARTABRATA.

Indonesian Cement Association (ICA): Graha Irama Bldg, Lantai 11, Suite 11G, Jalan H. R. Rasuna Said, Blok X-1, Kav. 1–2, Jakarta Selatan 12950; tel. (21) 5261105; fax (21) 5261108; e-mail info@asi.or.id; internet www.asi.or.id; f. 1969; Chair. URIP TIMURYONO.

Indonesian Coal Mining Association (APBI-ICMA): Menara Kuningan, Lantai 1, Jalan H. R. Rasuna Said, Blok X-7, Kav. 5, Jakarta 12940; tel. (21) 30015935; fax (21) 30015936; e-mail apbi-icma@indo.net.id; internet www.apbi-icma.com; 109 mems; Chair. BOB KAMANDANU; Exec. Dir SUPRIATNA SUHALA.

Indonesian Cocoa Association (ASKINDO): Jalan Pungkur 115, Bandung 40262; tel. (22) 4262235; fax (22) 4214084; e-mail info@askindo.or.id; internet www.askindo.or.id; Chair. ZULHEFI SIKUMBANG.

Indonesian Exporters' Federation: Menara Sudirman, 8th Floor, Jalan Jenderal Sudirman, Kav. 60, Jakarta 12190; tel. (21) 5226522; fax (21) 5203303; Chair. HAMID IBRAHIM GANIE.

Indonesian Food and Beverages Association (GAPMMI): Kantor Pusat Kementerian Pertanian, Ground Floor, Lot 2, Jalan Harsono, Rm 3, 224A Ragunan, Pasarminggu, Jakarta 12550; tel. (21) 70322627; fax (21) 7804347; e-mail gapmmi@cbn.net.id; internet www.gapmmi.or.id; f. 1976; 260 mems; Chair. ADHI SISWAJA LUKMAN.

Indonesian Footwear Association (APRISINDO): Gedung Adis Dimension Footwear, Jalan Tanah Abang III/18, Jakarta Pusat 10160; tel. (21) 3447575; fax (21) 3447572; e-mail aprisindo@vision.net.id; internet www.aprisindo.info; 95 mems; Chair. EDDY WIJANARKO; Sec.-Gen. YUDHI KOMARUDIN.

Indonesian Furniture Industry and Handicraft Association (ASMINDO): Jalan Pegambiran 5A, 3rd Floor, Rawamangun Jakarta 13220; tel. (21) 47864028; fax (21) 47864031; e-mail asmindo@indo.net.id; f. 1988; Chair. AMBAR TJAHYONO; Sec.-Gen. TANANGGA KARIM.

Indonesian Nutmeg Exporters' Association: c/o PT Berdirari (Persero) Trading Division, Jalan Yos Sudarso 1, Jakarta; tel. (21) 4301625; e-mail bnuina@indosat.net.id.

Indonesian Palm Oil Producers' Association (GAPKI): Sudirman Park Rukan, Blok B, Jalan K. H. Mas Mansyur 18, Kav. 35, Jakarta 10220; tel. (21) 57943871; fax (21) 57943872; internet www.gapki.or.id; Chair. JOEFLY J. BAHROENY.

Indonesian Precious Metals Association: Galva Bldg, 5th Floor, Jakarta Pusat, Jakarta 10120; tel. (21) 3451202; fax (21) 3812713.

Indonesian Pulp and Paper Association: Jalan Cimandiri 6, Flat I/2, Jakarta 10330; tel. (21) 326084; fax (21) 3140168; Chair. M. MANSUR.

Indonesian Tea Association (ATI): Jalan Polombangkeng 15, Kebayoran Baru, Jakarta; tel. (21) 7260772; fax (21) 7205810; e-mail insyaf@hotmail.com; internet www.indotea.org; Chair. SUGIAT; Gen. Sec. ATIK DHARMADI.

Indonesian Textile Association (API): Panin Bank Centre, 3rd Floor, Jalan Jenderal Sudirman 1, Jakarta Pusat 10270; tel. (21) 7396094; fax (21) 7396341; f. 1974; Sec.-Gen. DANANG D. JOEDONAGORO.

Indonesian Tobacco Association: Jalan H. Agus Salim 85, Jakarta 10350; tel. (21) 3140627; fax (21) 325181; Pres. H. A. ISMAIL.

Masyarakat Perhutanan Indonesia (MPI) (Indonesian Forestry Community): Gedung Manggala Wanabakti, 9th Floor, Wing B, Blok IV, Jalan Jenderal Gatot Subroto, Jakarta Pusat 10270; tel. (21) 5733010; fax (21) 5732564; f. 1974; 9 mems; Pres. M. HASAN.

Rubber Association of Indonesia (Gapkindo): Jalan Cideng Barat 62A, Jakarta 10150; tel. (21) 3501510; fax (21) 3500368; e-mail karetind@indosat.net.id; internet www.gapkindo.org; 161 mems; Chair. DAUD HUSNI BASTARI; Exec. Dir Dr RUSDAN DALIMUNTHE.

UTILITIES

Electricity

PT Perusahaan Listrik Negara (Persero) (PLN): Jalan Trunojoyo, Blok M1/135, Kebayoran Baru, Jakarta Selatan 12160; tel. (21) 7251234; fax (21) 7204929; e-mail kontakkami@pln.co.id; internet www.pln.co.id; state-owned electricity co; Pres. Dir NUR PAMUDJI.

Gas

PT Perusahaan Pertambangan Minyak dan Gas Bumi Negara (PERTAMINA): Jalan Medan Merdeka Timur 1A, Jakarta 10110; tel. (21) 3815111; fax (21) 3843882; e-mail pcc@pertamina.com; internet www.pertamina.com; f. 1968; state-owned petroleum and natural gas mining enterprise; Pres. Dir and CEO KAREN AUGUSTIAWAN.

Perusahaan Gas Negara (PGN) (Public Gas Corporation): Jalan K. H. Zainul Arifin 20, Jakarta 11140; tel. (21) 6334838; fax (21) 6333080; e-mail contact.center@pgn.co.id; internet www.pgn.co.id; monopoly of domestic gas distribution; Pres. Dir HENDI PRIO SANTOSO.

Water

PDAM DKI Jakarta (PAM JAYA): Jalan Penjernihan II, Pejompongan, Jakarta 10210; tel. (21) 5704250; fax (21) 5711796; internet www.pamjaya.co.id; f. 1977; responsible for the water supply systems of Jakarta; govt-owned; Pres. Dir SRIWIDAYANTO KADERI.

PDAM Kodya Dati II Bandung: Jalan Badaksinga 10, Bandung 40132; tel. (22) 2509030; fax (22) 2508063; e-mail pdambdg@elga.net.id; f. 1974; responsible for the water supply and sewerage systems of Bandung; Pres. Dir Ir SOENITIYOSO HADI PRATIKTO.

PDAM Tirtanadi Medan: Jalan Sisingamangaraja 1, Medan 20212; tel. (61) 4571666; fax (61) 4572771; e-mail tirtanadi@pdamtirtanadi.co.id; internet www.pdamtirtanadi.co.id; f. 1979; manages the water supply of Medan and nearby towns and cities; Man. Dir Ir AZZAM RIZAL.

TRADE UNIONS

Konfederasi Serikat Pekerja Seluruh Indonesia (KSPSI) (Confederation of All Indonesian Trades Unions): Jalan Raya Pasar Minggu 9, Km 17, Jakarta Selatan 12740; tel. (21) 7974359; fax (21) 7974361; f. 1973; renamed 2001; sole officially recognized Nat. Industrial Union; 5.1m. mems in June 2005; Gen. Chair. JACOB NUWA WEA; Gen. Sec. LATIEF NASUTION.

Konfederasi Serikat Buruh Sejahtera Indonesia (KSBSI) (Confederation of Indonesia Prosperity Trade Unions): Jalan Cipinang Muara Raya 33, Jatinegara, Jakarta Timur 13420; tel. (21) 70984671; fax (21) 8577646; e-mail ksbsi@pacific.net.id; internet www.ksbsi.or.id; f. 1998; application for official registration rejected in May 1998; 1,228,875 mems in 168 branches in 27 provinces throughout Indonesia; Pres. REKSON SILABAN; Sec.-Gen. IDIN ROSIDIN.

Transport

RAILWAYS

There are railways on Java, Madura and Sumatra. In 2006 the Japanese Government agreed to provide a US $741m. loan to finance a Mass Rapid Transport (MRT) rail system in Jakarta. Construction commenced in May 2013, with completion expected by 2016.

Directorate General of Railways: Ministry of Transportation, Jalan Medan Merdeka Barat 8, Jakarta 10110; tel. (21) 3800349; fax (21) 3860758; e-mail bagrenka_dephub@yahoo.com; internet perkeretaapian.dephub.go.id; Dir-Gen. TUNDJUNG INDERAWAN.

PT Kereta Api Indonesia (Persero) (KAI): Jalan Perintis Kermedekaan 1, Bandung 40117; tel. (22) 4230031; fax (22) 4203342; e-mail kontak_pelanggan@kereta-api.co.id; internet www.kereta-api.co.id; 6 regional offices; transferred to the private sector in 1991; Chief Commr IMAN HARYATNA; Chief Dir IGNASIUS JONAN.

ROADS

There is an adequate road network on Java, Sumatra, Sulawesi, Kalimantan, Bali and Madura, but on many of the other islands traffic is by jungle track or river boat. In 2010 Indonesia had a total road length of 487,314 km, of which some 57% was asphalted. In 2013 the Ministry of Public Works announced the allocation of US $399m. for the improvement of regional road networks, proposing to construct up to 281.4 km of new national roads and 7,164 m of bridges.

Directorate General of Land Transportation: Ministry of Transportation, Jalan Medan Merdeka Barat 8, Jakarta 10110; tel. (21) 3502971; fax (21) 3503013; e-mail info@hubdat.web.id; internet www.hubdat.web.id; Dir-Gen. SUROYO ALIMOESO.

SHIPPING

In December 2013 Indonesia's flag registered fleet numbered 6,781 vessels, with a combined displacement of 16.5m. grt, including 1,056 general cargo carriers, 463 tank ships, 31 gas tankers and 55 fishing vessels. The four main ports are Tanjung Priok (near Jakarta), Tanjung Perak (near Surabaya), Belawan (near Medan) and Makassar (formerly Ujung Pandang, in South Sulawesi). More than 100 of Indonesia's ports and harbours are classified as capable of handling ocean-going shipping.

Directorate-General of Sea Transportation: Ministry of Transportation, Jalan Medan Merdeka Barat 8, Jakarta 10110; tel. (21) 3456332; internet kemhubri.dephub.go.id/hubla.

Indonesian National Ship Owners' Association (INSA): Jalan Tanah Abang III, No. 10, Jakarta Pusat; tel. (21) 3850993; fax (21) 3849522; e-mail info@insa.or.id; internet insa.or.id; Chair. CARMELITA HARTOTO; Sec.-Gen. PAULIS A. DJOHAN.

Shipping Companies

PT Admiral Lines: POB 1476, Jakarta 10014; tel. (21) 4247908; fax (21) 4206267; e-mail setper@admiral.co.id; internet admirallines.net; f. 1966; fmrly PT Pelayaran Samudera Admiral Lines; Pres. Dir BOBBY ADI PRABAWA MOELJADI.

PT Djakarta Lloyd: Jalan Senen Raya 44, Jakarta 10410; tel. (21) 3456208; fax (21) 3441401; internet www.djakartalloyd.co.id; f. 1950; services to USA, Europe, Japan, Australia and the Middle East; Commr Dr Ir TJUK SUKARDIMAN; Dir SYRAHIL JAPARIN.

PT Karana Line: Wisma Kalimanis, 12th and 13th Floors, Jalan M. T. Haryono, Kav. 33, Jakarta 12770; tel. (21) 7985914; fax (21) 7985913; Pres. Dir BAMBANG EDIYANTO.

PT Pelayaran Bahtera Adhiguna (Persero): Jalan Kalibesar Timur 10–12, POB 4313, Jakarta 11110; tel. (21) 6912547; fax (21) 6901450; e-mail pelba@bahteradhiguna.co.id; internet www.bahteradhiguna.co.id; f. 1971; Pres. Commr BINARTO BEKTI MAHARDJANA; Pres. Dir BIMA PUTRAJAYA.

PT Pelayaran Nasional Indonesia (PELNI): Jalan Gajah Mada 14, Jakarta 10130; tel. (21) 6334342; fax (21) 63854130; e-mail humas@pelni.co.id; internet www.pelni.co.id; state-owned; national shipping co; Pres. Dir JUSSABELLA SAHEA.

PT Pertamina (Persero): Downstream Directorate for Shipping, Jalan Yos Sudarso 32–34, POB 14020, Tanjung Priok, Jakarta Utara 14320; tel. (21) 43930325; fax (21) 4370161; e-mail pcc@pertaminashipping.com; internet www.pertaminashipping.com; f. 1959; state-owned; maritime business services; Pres. Dir KAREN AGUSTIAWAN.

PT Perusahaan Pelayaran Gesuri Lloyd: Gesuri Lloyd Bldg, Jalan Tiang Bendera IV/45, Jakarta 11230; tel. (21) 6904000; fax (21) 6925987; e-mail operation_agency@gesuri.co.id; internet www.gesuri.co.id; f. 1963; Pres. Dir ANTONIUS NURIMBA.

PT Perusahaan Pelayaran Nusantara (PANURJWAN): Jalan Raya Pelabuhan Nusantara, POB 2062, Jakarta 10001; tel. (21) 494344; internet www.panurjwan.co.id; Pres. Dir A. J. SINGH.

PT Perusahaan Pelayaran Samudera 'Samudera Indonesia': Jalan Yos Sudarso 1, Blok A1-7, Tanjung Priok, Jakarta 14320; tel. (21) 4301150; fax (21) 43930116; internet www.samudera.com; Chair. SHANTI L. POESPOSOETJIPTO; Pres. Dir MASLI MULIA.

PT Perusahaan Pelayaran Samudera Trikora Lloyd: Graha Satria, 4th Floor, Jalan R. S. Fatmawati 5, Jakarta Selatan, Jakarta 12430; tel. (21) 75915381; fax (21) 75915385; e-mail tkldir@cbn.net.id; internet www.boedihardjogroup.com/shipping/trikora_lloyd.htm; f. 1964; Pres. Dir GANESHA SOEGIHARTO; Man. Dir P. R. S. VAN HEEREN.

CIVIL AVIATION

Sukarno-Hatta Airport, at Cengkareng, serves Jakarta. An extensive expansion to increase passenger capacity at Ngurah Rai Airport, in Denpasar (Bali), was completed in September 2013. Other international airports include Kuala Namu Airport, replacing Polonia Airport, in Medan (North Sumatra), Juanda Airport, near Surabaya (East Java), Sam Ratulangi Airport, in Manado (North Sulawesi), Hasanuddin Airport, near Makassar (formerly Ujung Pandang, South Sulawesi), and Frans Kaisepo Airport, in Papua (formerly Irian Jaya). Construction of a new international airport in Buleleng (Bali) was scheduled to commence in late 2013, while Syamsudin Noor Airport, in Banjarbaru (South Kalimantan), was to begin international operations in 2014. There are numerous other commercial airports. In 2000 the Government announced a policy of liberalization for the airline industry, and by January 2005 there were 29 domestic airlines in operation, compared with only five in 2000. Four new airlines, Batik Air, Jatayu Air, Kartika Airlines and Nam Air, also began operations in 2013.

Directorate General of Civil Aviation: Jalan Medan Merdeka Barat 8, Jakarta Pusat 10110; tel. (21) 3505550; fax (21) 3505139; e-mail hubud@dephub.go.id; internet hubud.dephub.go.id; Dir-Gen. HERRY BAKTI.

Batik Air: Lion Air Tower, Jaland Gajah Mada 7, Jakarta Pusat; tel. (21) 6338345; fax (21) 6335669; internet www.batikairlines.com; f. 2013; subsidiary of PT Lion Mentari Airlines; licensed to provide long-haul services to 66 domestic and 20 int. destinations, incl. to Australia and East Asia; Pres. Dir ACHMAD LUTHFIE.

Citilink: Juanda Business Centre, Jalan Juanda 1, Blok C2, Gedangan, Sidoarjo; tel. (31) 8549860; internet www.citilink.co.id; f. 2001; subsidiary of PT Garuda Indonesia; low-cost carrier providing shuttle services between 7 domestic destinations.

Deraya Air Taxi (DRY): Terminal Bldg, 1st Floor, Rm 150/HT, Halim Perdanakusuma Airport, Jakarta 13610; tel. (21) 80899401; fax (21) 8095770; e-mail admderaya@deraya.co.id; internet www.deraya.co.id; f. 1967; scheduled and charter passenger and cargo services to domestic and regional destinations; Pres. Dir ATTY BOEDIMILYARTI.

Dirgantara Air Service (DAS): POB 6154, Terminal Bldg, Halim Perdanakusuma Airport, Rm 231, Jakarta 13610; tel. (21) 8093372; fax (21) 8094348; charter services from Jakarta, Barjarmas and

Pontianak to destinations in West Kalimantan; Pres. MAKKI PERDANAKUSUMA.

PT Garuda Indonesia: Gedung Area Perkantoran, Jalan M1, Garuda City Center, Sukarno-Hatta Airport, Cenkareng; tel. (21) 25601001; fax (21) 55915639; e-mail cs@garuda-indonesia.com; internet www.garuda-indonesia.com; f. 1949; 67% state-owned; operates scheduled domestic, regional and international services to destinations in Europe, the USA, the Middle East, Australasia and the Far East; Pres. and CEO EMIRSYAH SATAR; Chair. HADIYANTO.

PT Lion Mentari Airlines (Lion Air): Lion Air Tower, Jalan Gajah Mada 7, Jakarta Pusat; tel. (21) 6338345; fax (21) 6335669; e-mail info@lionair.co.id; internet www.lionair.co.id; f. 1999; budget carrier providing domestic and international services; Pres. Dir RUSDI KIRANA.

PT Mandala Airlines: Jalan Tomang Raya, Kav. 33–37, Jakarta 11440; tel. (21) 56997000; fax (21) 5663788; e-mail widya@mandalaair.com; internet www.mandalaair.com; f. 1969, temporarily grounded in 2011, resumed service in 2012; partner of Tiger Airways (Singapore); scheduled regional and domestic passenger and cargo services; CEO WARWICK BRADY.

PT Merpati Nusantara Airlines: Jalan Angkasa, Blok B-15, Kav. 2–3, Jakarta 10720; tel. (21) 6548888; fax (21) 6540620; e-mail contactcenter@merpati.co.id; internet www.merpati.co.id; f. 1962; subsidiary of PT Garuda Indonesia; domestic and regional services to Australia and Malaysia; Pres. Dir EKANUGRAHA EKANUGRAHA; Chief Commr EDDI HARIYADHI.

Pelita Air Service: Jalan Abdul Muis 52–56A, Jakarta 10160; tel. (21) 2312030; fax (21) 2312216; e-mail marketing@pelita-air.com; internet www.pelita-air.com; f. 1970; subsidiary of state oil co Pertamina; domestic scheduled and charter passenger and cargo services; Pres. Dir ANDJAR WIBAWANUN.

Premiair: Halim Perdanakusuma Airport Terminal Bldg, Ground Floor, Jakarta 13610; tel. (21) 8091255; fax (21) 8002060; e-mail sales@flypremiair.com; internet www.flypremiair.com; f. 1989; domestic and international charter services; CEO Capt. ARI DARYATA SINGGIH.

Sriwijaya Air: No. 13, Blok B8–10, Jalan Gunung Sahari Raya, Jakarta; tel. (21) 6396006; internet www.sriwijayaair-online.com; f. 2003; domestic services; Pres. Dir CHANDRA LIE; Pres. Commr HENDRY LIE.

Wings Abadi Airlines (Wings Air): Lion Air Tower, Jalan Gajah Mada 7, Jakarta Pusat; tel. (21) 6326039; fax (21) 6348744; f. 2003; subsidiary co of Lion Air; budget carrier providing scheduled domestic and international passenger services.

Tourism

Indonesia's tourism industry is based mainly on the islands of Java, famous for its volcanic scenery and religious temples, and Bali, renowned for its scenery and Hindu/Buddhist temples and religious festivals. Lombok, Sumatra and Sulawesi are also increasingly popular. Domestic tourism within Indonesia has also increased significantly. Revenue from tourism (excluding passenger transport) was a provisional US $8,325m. in 2012. The number of tourist arrivals exceeded 8.0m. in 2012.

Indonesia Tourism Promotion Board: Wisma Nugra Santana, 9th Floor, Jalan Jenderal Sudirman 8, Jakarta 10220; tel. (21) 5704879; fax (21) 5704855; e-mail itpb@cbn.net.id; private body; promotes national and international tourism; Chair. WIRYANT SUKAMDANI.

Defence

As assessed at November 2013, the total strength of the armed forces was an estimated 395,500: army 300,400, navy 65,000, and air force 30,100; paramilitary forces comprised some 281,000, including a police 'mobile brigade' of 14,000 and an estimated 40,000 trainees of KAMRA (People's Security). Reserve forces numbered 400,000. Military service, which is selective, lasts for two years. In support of international peacekeeping efforts, 1,288 Indonesian troops were stationed in Lebanon in November 2013 and 177 in the Democratic Republic of the Congo.

Defence Expenditure: Rp. 77,700,000m. for 2013.

Commander-in-Chief of the Armed Forces: Gen. MOELDOKO.

Chief of Staff of the Army: Gen. BUDIMAN.

Chief of Staff of the Navy: Adm. MARSETIO.

Chief of Staff of the Air Force: Air Chief Marshal IDA BAGUS PUTU DUNIA.

Education

Education is administered mainly by the Ministry of National Education, but the Ministry of Religious Affairs also operates Islamic religious schools (*madrasahs*) at the primary level.

Primary education, beginning at seven years of age and lasting for six years, was made compulsory in 1987. In 1993 it was announced that compulsory education was to be expanded to nine years. Secondary education begins at 13 years of age and lasts for a further six years, comprising three years of junior secondary education and a further three years of senior secondary education. A further three years of academic level or five years of higher education may follow. In May 2010 the Government announced plans to implement compulsory 12-year education for all Indonesian children by 2014.

In 2010/11 there were 27,580,215 pupils enrolled at 146,804 primary schools, 9,346,454 pupils enrolled at 30,290 general junior secondary schools, and 4,105,139 pupils at 11,306 general senior secondary schools. Enrolment at primary level in 2010/11 included 94% of pupils in the relevant age-group; enrolment at secondary level in the same year included 75% of children in the relevant age-group. Vocational subjects have been introduced in the secondary schools. There were 3,737,158 pupils at 9,164 vocational senior secondary schools in 2010/11. In the same year there were 3,185 tertiary institutions, with enrolment totalling 4,787,785. The Government's budget for 2009 allocated Rp. 244,440,000m., representing 20% of total expenditure, to education.

IRAN

Introductory Survey

LOCATION, CLIMATE, LANGUAGE, RELIGION, FLAG, CAPITAL

The Islamic Republic of Iran lies in western Asia, bordered by Armenia, Azerbaijan and Turkmenistan to the north, by Turkey and Iraq to the west, by the Persian (Arabian) Gulf and the Gulf of Oman to the south, and by Pakistan and Afghanistan to the east. The climate is one of great extremes. Summer temperatures of more than 55°C (131°F) have been recorded, but in the winter the great altitude of much of the country results in temperatures of −18°C (0°F) and below. The principal language is Farsi (Persian), spoken by about 50% of the population. Turkic-speaking Azeris form about 27% of the population, and Kurds, Arabs, Baluchs and Turkomans form less than 25%. The great majority of Persians and Azeris are Shi'a Muslims, while the other ethnic groups are mainly Sunni Muslims. There are also small minorities of Christians (mainly Armenians), Zoroastrians and Jews. The Bahá'í faith, which originated in Iran, has been severely persecuted, being denied rights given to other recognized religious minorities. The national flag (proportions 4 by 7) comprises three unequal horizontal stripes, of green, white and red, with the emblem of the Islamic Republic of Iran (the stylized word Allah) centrally positioned in red, and the inscription '*Allaho Akbar*' ('God is Great') written 11 times each in white Kufic script on the red and green stripes. The capital is Tehran.

CONTEMPORARY POLITICAL HISTORY

Historical Context

Iran, called Persia until 1935, was formerly a monarchy, ruled by a Shah (Emperor). In 1925, having seized power in a military coup, Reza Khan, a Cossack officer, was elected Shah, adopting the title Reza Shah Pahlavi. In 1941 British and Soviet forces occupied Iran, and the Shah (who favoured Nazi Germany) was forced to abdicate in favour of his son, Muhammad Reza Pahlavi. British and US forces left Iran in 1945, and Soviet forces in 1946. The United Kingdom retained considerable influence through the Anglo-Iranian Oil Co, which controlled much of Iran's extensive petroleum reserves. In March 1951, however, the Majlis (National Consultative Assembly) approved the nationalization of the petroleum industry. The leading advocate of nationalization, Dr Muhammad Mussadeq, who became Prime Minister in May 1951, was deposed in August 1953 in a military coup engineered by the US and British intelligence services. The Shah assumed dictatorial powers in 1963 with the so-called 'White Revolution'. Large estates were redistributed to small-scale farmers, and women were granted the right to vote. In 1965 Prime Minister Hassan Ali Mansur was assassinated, reportedly by a follower of Ayatollah Ruhollah Khomeini, a fundamentalist Shi'a Muslim leader strongly opposed to the Shah. (Khomeini had been deported in 1964 for his opposition activities, and was living in exile in Iraq.)

There followed a period of political stability and strong economic growth, based on substantial petroleum revenues which funded expenditure on defence equipment and infrastructure projects. However, a declining economy from late 1977 and the repressive nature of the Shah's rule led to widespread anti-Government protests by the end of 1978. These involved both left-wing and liberal opponents of the Shah, as well as Islamist activists, but the most effective opposition came from supporters of Ayatollah Khomeini (who was now based in France). The growing unrest forced the Shah to leave Iran in January 1979. Khomeini arrived in Tehran on 1 February, and effectively assumed power 10 days later. A 15-member Islamic Revolutionary Council was formed to govern the country, in co-operation with a Provisional Government, and on 1 April Iran was declared an Islamic republic. Supreme authority was vested in the Wali Faqih, a religious leader (initially Khomeini) appointed by the Shi'a clergy. Executive power was to be vested in a President, to which post Abolhasan Bani-Sadr was elected in January 1980. Elections to a 270-member Majlis—renamed the Majlis-e-Shura-e Islami (Islamic Consultative Assembly)—took place in March and May. The Islamic Republican Party (IRP), which was identified with Khomeini and traditionalist Muslims, won some 60 seats, but subsequently increased its support base.

Domestic Political Affairs

In November 1979 Iranian students seized 63 hostages at the US embassy in Tehran. The original purpose of the siege was to force the USA (where the Shah was undergoing medical treatment) to return the former ruler to Iran to face trial. The Shah died in Egypt in July 1980, by which time Iran had made other demands, notably for a US undertaking not to interfere in its affairs. Intense diplomatic activity led to the release of the 52 remaining hostages in January 1981, others having been freed two weeks into the siege. However, a failed rescue operation by the US military in April 1980 had resulted in the deaths of eight US servicemen.

The prolonged hostage crisis had forced the resignation of the moderate Provisional Government, and during 1980 a rift became apparent between President Bani-Sadr and his modernist allies on the one hand, and the IRP and traditionalist elements on the other. In June 1981 clashes between their rival supporters escalated into sustained fighting between members of the Mujahidin-e-Khalq (an Islamist guerrilla group that supported Bani-Sadr) and troops of the Islamic Revolutionary Guards Corps. The Majlis voted to impeach the President, who was subsequently dismissed by Khomeini. Bani-Sadr fled to France, as did the leader of the Mujahidin, Massoud Rajavi. A presidential election in July resulted in victory for the Prime Minister, Muhammad Ali Rajani, who was himself replaced by Muhammad Javar Bahonar. In August, however, both the President and Prime Minister were killed in a bomb attack attributed to the Mujahidin-e-Khalq. A further presidential election, held in October, was won by Hojatoleslam Sayed Ali Khamenei. Mir Hossein Mousavi was appointed Prime Minister.

Mousavi's attempts to implement nationalization and land reform were continually obstructed by the predominantly conservative, clerical Majlis. Elections to the second Majlis in April and May 1984 resulted in an easy victory for the IRP. The elections were boycotted by the sole opposition party to have a degree of official recognition, Nehzat-e Azadi-ye Iran (Liberation Movement of Iran), led by Dr Mehdi Bazargan (Prime Minister in the 1979 Provisional Government), which cited the undemocratic conditions prevailing in Iran. Prior to the August 1985 presidential election, the Council of Guardians (responsible for the supervision of elections) rejected almost 50 candidates, including Bazargan. Khamenei was elected President for a second four-year term, with 85.7% of the votes cast. Mousavi was reconfirmed as Prime Minister in October.

The Iran–Iraq War

For most of the 1980s Iran's domestic and foreign policy was dominated by the war with Iraq. In September 1980, ostensibly to assert a claim of sovereignty over the disputed Shatt al-Arab waterway, Iraqi forces invaded Iran along a 500-km front. The Iranian military offered strong resistance, and began a counter-offensive in early 1982; by June Iraq had been forced to withdraw from Iranian territory, and Iranian troops subsequently entered Iraq. A conflict of attrition thus developed, in which petroleum reserves, installations and transshipment facilities were targeted. From 1984 Iraq began attacking tankers using Iran's Kharg Island oil terminal in the Persian (Arabian) Gulf, and Iran retaliated by targeting Saudi Arabian and Kuwaiti tankers, as well as neutral vessels using Kuwait. Despite UN efforts to broker peace negotiations, Iran's conditions for peace were the removal from power of the Iraqi President, Saddam Hussain, as well as agreement by Iraq to pay war reparations. The war had left Iran in virtual diplomatic isolation, although in late 1986 it emerged that the USA had made secret shipments of weapons, allegedly in exchange for Iranian assistance in securing the release of US hostages held by Shi'a groups in Lebanon and an Iranian undertaking to relinquish involvement in international terrorism.

In April 1988 Iraq recaptured the Faw peninsula, forcing the Iranian military to withdraw across the Shatt al-Arab; in June Iraq also retook Majnoun Island. In July an IranAir passenger flight, apparently mistaken for an attacking fighter jet, was shot down by a US aircraft carrier in the Strait of Hormuz; all 290 people on board were killed. In that month Iraqi troops crossed into Iranian territory for the first time since 1986, and the last Iranian troops on Iraqi territory were dislodged. On 18 July 1988 Iran unexpectedly announced its unconditional acceptance of UN Security Council Resolution 598, adopted one year earlier. This urged an immediate ceasefire, the withdrawal of military forces to international boundaries, and the co-operation of Iran and Iraq in mediation efforts to achieve a peace settlement. More than 1m. people were estimated to have died in the eight-year conflict. A ceasefire came into effect on 20 August, and UN-sponsored peace negotiations began shortly afterwards in Geneva, Switzerland. In the same month a UN Iran-Iraq Military Observer Group (UNIIMOG) was deployed in the region. However, the negotiations soon became deadlocked in disputes regarding the sovereignty of the Shatt al-Arab waterway, the exchange of prisoners of war and the withdrawal of armed forces to within international boundaries. The pursuit of a comprehensive peace settlement was rapidly overshadowed by Iraq's invasion of Kuwait at the beginning of August 1990. Saddam Hussain sought an immediate, formal peace with Iran, accepting all the claims that Iran had pursued since the ceasefire declaration (including the reinstatement of the Algiers Agreement of 1975, dividing the Shatt al-Arab), and Iraq immediately began to redeploy troops from its border with Iran to Kuwait. Prisoner exchanges took place, and Iran and Iraq restored diplomatic relations in September 1990. In February 1991 the withdrawal of all armed forces to internationally recognized boundaries was confirmed by UNIIMOG, the mandate of which was terminated shortly afterwards.

Iran denounced Iraq's invasion of Kuwait, and observed the economic sanctions imposed by the UN on Iraq. However, it was unequivocal in its condemnation of the deployment of a US-led multinational force in the Gulf region. Relations between Iran and Iraq deteriorated after the liberation of Kuwait in February 1991. Iran protested strongly against the Baathist regime's suppression of the Shi'a-led rebellion in southern and central Iraq, and renewed its demand for Saddam Hussain's resignation. Iraq, in turn, accused Iran of supporting the rebellion. Nevertheless, in late 1993 high-level bilateral talks recommenced on the exchange of remaining prisoners of war, under the terms of Resolution 598.

Political developments following the death of Ayatollah Khomeini

Elections to the Majlis in April and May 1988 apparently provided a stimulus to more reformist elements in the Government (identified with Ali Akbar Hashemi Rafsanjani, since 1980 the Speaker of the Majlis, and Prime Minister Mousavi) by producing an assembly strongly representative of their views. (The elections were the first not to be contested by the IRP, which had been dissolved in 1987.) In June 1988 Rafsanjani was re-elected as Speaker, and Mousavi was overwhelmingly endorsed as Prime Minister. In February 1989, however, Ayatollah Khomeini referred explicitly to a division in the Iranian leadership between reformers (who sought a degree of Western participation in Iran's post-war reconstruction) and conservatives (who opposed such involvement), and declared that he would never permit the reformers to prevail. A number of prominent reformists, among them Ayatollah Ali Hossein Montazeri (who had been designated as Khomeini's successor by the Assembly of Experts in 1985), subsequently resigned from the Iranian leadership.

Ayatollah Khomeini died on 3 June 1989. In an emergency session on 4 June the Assembly of Experts elected President Khamenei to succeed Khomeini as Iran's spiritual leader (Wali Faqih). The presidential election, scheduled for mid-August, was brought forward to 28 July, to be held simultaneously with a referendum on proposed amendments to the Constitution. Both conservatives and reformers within the leadership apparently united in support of Rafsanjani's candidacy for the presidency, and Rafsanjani (opposed only by a 'token' candidate) was overwhelmingly elected with 95.9% of the votes cast. A similar proportion of voters approved the constitutional amendments, which included the abolition of the post of Prime Minister (and a consequent increase in the powers of the President).

President Rafsanjani appointed a Government balancing conservatives, reformers and technocrats, and its endorsement by the Majlis in August 1989 was viewed as a mandate for Rafsanjani to conduct a more conciliatory policy towards the West. In October 1990, with the co-operation of Ayatollah Khamenei, Rafsanjani was able to prevent the election of many powerful conservatives to the Assembly of Experts. An estimated 70% of deputies elected to the fourth Majlis in April–May 1992 were, broadly speaking, pro-Rafsanjani. However, economic reform was lowering the living standards of the traditional constituency of the Islamic regime, the urban lower classes, leading to serious rioting in several cities. Rafsanjani was re-elected in June 1993, but his share of the vote (against three ostensibly 'token' candidates) fell to 63.2%. In August 1995 it was reported that political parties, associations and groups were free to conduct political activities in Iran on condition that they honoured the country's Constitution, although Nehzat-e Azadi was subsequently refused formal registration as a political party.

Elections to the fifth Majlis, in March–April 1996, provided an important measure of the shifting balance of power between more reformist, or liberal, and conservative elements in Iranian politics. At the first round of voting, candidates of the pro-Rafsanjani Servants of Iran's Construction faction were reported to have won some 70% of the seats. However, the conservative Society of Combatant Clergy, with the unofficial patronage of Ayatollah Khamenei, claimed that its candidates had achieved an equally conclusive victory. After the second round of voting, unofficial sources suggested that the Society of Combatant Clergy would command the loyalty of 110–120 deputies in the 270-seat Majlis, and the Servants of Iran's Construction that of 90–100 deputies.

President Khatami's first term of office

In March 1997 Rafsanjani, whose presidential mandate was due to expire, was appointed Chairman of the Council to Determine the Expediency of the Islamic Order for a further five-year term. (He was reappointed as head of the Expediency Council—which arbitrates in disputes between the Majlis and the Council of Guardians—in 2002, 2007 and March 2012.) In May 1997 the Council of Guardians approved four candidatures for that month's presidential election, rejecting 234. It had been widely expected that Ali Akbar Nateq Nouri, the Majlis Speaker favoured by the Society of Combatant Clergy, would secure an easy victory, but the more liberal Sayed Muhammad Khatami (a presidential adviser and former Minister of Culture and Islamic Guidance) emerged as a strong contender immediately prior to the election. Khatami—supported by the Servants of Iran's Construction as well as by intellectuals, professionals, and women's and youth groups—took some 69.1% of the total votes cast; Nateq Nouri took 24.9%.

Taking office in August 1997, President Khatami emphasized his commitment to fostering sustained and balanced growth in the political, economic, cultural and educational spheres. In foreign affairs, he undertook to promote the principle of mutual respect, but pledged that Iran would stand up to any power that sought to subjugate Iranian sovereignty. Two notable liberal, or moderate, appointees in Khatami's first Council of Ministers were Abdollah Nuri as Minister of the Interior (a post he had previously held in 1989–93) and Dr Massoumeh Ebtekar as Vice-President and Head of the Organization for the Protection of the Environment (the first woman to be appointed to such a senior government post since the Islamic Revolution). In the months following his election, President Khatami appeared conciliatory towards the West, while Khamenei continued to denounce the West's military and cultural ambitions, particularly those of the USA and Israel.

The Khatami administration moved to formalize its support base during 1998, primarily through the registration or establishment of reformist parties such as the Servants of Construction, the Islamic Iran Solidarity Party (Hezb-e Hambastegi-ye Iran-e Islami) and the Islamic Iran Participation Front (Jebbeh-ye Mosharekat-e Iran-e Islami—which counted Ebtekar among its leaders). In June the Majlis voted to dismiss Abdollah Nuri as Minister of the Interior, a group of conservative deputies having initiated impeachment on the grounds that he had made provocative statements and permitted dissident rallies. Conservatives retained overwhelming control of the Assembly of Experts at elections in October. Khatami's Government suffered a further setback in February 1999 with the resignation of Qorbanali Dorri Najafabadi, the Minister of Information, after it was admitted that agents of his ministry had been responsible for the murder of several intellectuals and dissident writers in late 1998.

Iran's first local government elections since the Islamic Revolution took place in February 1999. Reformist candidates had notable success in Tehran, Shiraz and Esfahan, while conservatives secured control of councils in their traditional strongholds of Qom and Mashad.

During 1998–99 Ayatollah Khamenei and conservative Majlis deputies sought action against journalists and publications that they perceived as abusing freedom of speech to weaken Islamic beliefs. A small demonstration by students at the University of Tehran, to protest against the closure, in July 1999, of a newspaper with close links to President Khatami, was dispersed with considerable violence by police. This action, in conjunction with a raid on student dormitories by security forces, aided by vigilantes of the semi-official Ansar-e Hezbollah paramilitary (in which at least one student died), provoked five days of rioting in Tehran and other cities, resulting in some 1,400 arrests. Within a year both the national and Tehran chiefs of police had been dismissed, and as many as 100 police officers had been arrested for their role in the campus raid.

Pro-reform candidates secured notable victories at elections to the newly expanded, 290-seat Majlis in February 2000: by mid-2000 reformist or liberal deputies were believed to hold some 200 seats. Reformist deputies immediately drafted legislation to replace a new law, endorsed by the outgoing Majlis, that would further restrict freedom of the press. However, Ayatollah Khamenei instructed the new Majlis not to debate proposed amendments to the press law, on the grounds that these would endanger state security and religious faith.

Khatami's second presidential term

Khatami was re-elected as President in June 2001, with some 76.9% of the total votes cast. Despite this apparent endorsement of his programme of political and economic reforms, there were evident conflicts of interest between Khatami's more reformist supporters in the Majlis and ultra-conservative elements, particularly in the Council of Guardians. Furthermore, the judiciary intensified its actions against pro-reform activists, with mass arrests, public floggings and even public executions in the ostensible interests of reducing crime and encouraging stronger morality. Following what was reported to be the largest political trial in Iran since 1979, 33 activists of Nehzat-e Azadi received custodial sentences of up to 10 years in July 2002, and the movement was formally banned. In early 2003 the Council refused to ratify two reform bills that aimed to reduce the powers of the ultra-conservatives, including by transferring to the Ministry of the Interior the prerogative of the Council of Guardians to approve or disqualify election candidates.

At the beginning of 2004 the Council of Guardians announced that more than 2,000 candidates (from a preliminary list of around 8,200) for the forthcoming elections to the seventh Majlis would be barred from standing. Khatami and several of his ministers threatened to resign in protest, as did Iran's 27 regional governors, and about 100 deputies joined a sit-in at the Majlis, but attempts to reverse the disqualifications were largely unsuccessful. Voting proceeded in February, but turnout was estimated to be as low as 51%. A second round was held in May for 61 of the 290 seats that remained vacant after the first round. Conservatives were confirmed as having achieved a majority in the legislature, with some 195 seats overall; reformists held fewer than 50, with the remainder being held by nominally independent deputies. In June Gholam-Ali Haddad-Adel was elected as the country's first non-clerical Speaker since the Islamic Revolution. In May, meanwhile, the Council of Guardians formally approved new legislation that had been adopted by the Majlis to ban the use of torture.

Mahmoud Ahmadinejad's first term of office

Voting to elect President Khatami's successor took place in June 2005. As generally forecast, former President Rafsanjani, who had projected himself in the middle ground between reformers and hardliners, received the largest number of votes, with 21.0% of the total. Less expected was the success of Mahmoud Ahmadinejad, the mayor of Tehran, who was placed second with 19.5% of votes cast. Since none of the seven candidates received an outright majority, the election proceeded to an unprecedented second round. Meanwhile, the Council of Guardians announced that, following a partial recount of first-round votes in response to allegations of fraud, no evidence of malpractice had been uncovered. At the second round, Ahmadinejad—whose populist campaign promising greater economic equality, reduced corruption and a return to the values of the Islamic Revolution was strongly supported by poorer Iranians—was elected with a decisive 61.7% of votes cast. He was inaugurated in August.

Elections took place in December 2006 both to the Assembly of Experts and for more than 113,000 municipal councillors. By November more than two-thirds of candidates for the Assembly of Experts, hitherto dominated by hardliners, had reportedly been disqualified by the Council of Guardians, as a result of which only one person ran for office in some constituencies. Unexpectedly, associates of the President failed to win control of any municipal council. In Tehran, notably, Ahmadinejad's allies secured just two of the 15 council seats; allies of the hard-line mayor Muhammad Baqir Qalibaf won eight seats, reformists' four, and an independent candidate one. Former President Rafsanjani was among candidates elected to the Assembly of Experts; he was elected as Speaker of the Assembly in September 2007.

In January 2007 it was reported that 50 members of the Majlis had signed a document demanding that President Ahmadinejad answer questions in the legislature concerning his increasingly confrontational stance on the issue of Iran's nuclear programme. Moreover, 150 Majlis deputies were said to have signed a letter holding Ahmadinejad responsible for the country's high levels of inflation and unemployment, and condemning him for failing to deliver the state budget on time. The introduction of petrol rationing in June, following price increases the previous month, in an effort to reduce the burden of fuel subsidies on the budget, provoked a number of attacks on petrol stations and other state buildings in Tehran and elsewhere. In early 2008 Ayatollah Khamenei overruled the President's decision not to supply subsidized gas to Iranians in rural areas who were suffering shortages owing to extreme weather conditions.

Prior to the 2008 elections to the eighth Majlis, it was reported that the political conservatives had divided into separate electoral lists: the United Principlist Front was formed by traditionalists who supported Ahmadinejad's policies; while the Broad Principlist Coalition included those who were more critical of the President's foreign and economic policies (among them so-called 'revisionists' Ali Larijani, Mohsen Rezai and Muhammad Baqir Qalibaf). Meanwhile, at least 1,700 reformist candidates (of 7,168 registered candidates) were disqualified. At the first legislative ballot, held on 14 March, 208 of the 290 seats were reportedly filled. However, reformists asserted that the election had been neither free nor fair, since so many of their candidates had been disqualified; the opposition also considered that Iran's state-controlled media had been noticeably biased in favour of pro-Ahmadinejad candidates during the election campaign. Both the USA and the European Union (EU, see p. 273) were also strongly critical of the conduct of the election. A second round of voting for the undecided seats was held on 25 April. Three seats remained vacant following both rounds, after the results were annulled for unspecified reasons. Overall, according to official reports, conservatives consolidated their control of the Majlis, with some 198–200 seats (including 29 of the 30 seats for Tehran); reformists secured 46–50 seats, and 40–43 seats were held by independents. Around one-third of the conservatives were understood to be members of the Broad Principlist Coalition. Larijani was elected Speaker of the Majlis in May, in succession to Gholam-Ali Haddad-Adel; he was subsequently re-elected to the post four times, most recently in June 2012.

Ministerial appointments approved by the Majlis in August 2008 included Sayed Shamseddin Hosseini as Minister of Economic Affairs and Finance; and Ali Kordan as Minister of the Interior to replace Mostafa Pour-Muhammadi, whom Ahmadinejad had dismissed in May. However, Kordan was himself dismissed in November, after the Majlis impeached him for possessing a forged law degree. Sadeq Mahsouli was subsequently appointed as Minister of the Interior.

It was reported in January 2009 that 16 police officers who had been kidnapped in Sistan and Baluchestan province in mid-2008 had all been killed by the militant Sunni People's Resistance Movement of Iran (PRMI); the group had demanded the release from detention of 200 of its members. More than 20 people were killed in a suicide bomb attack on a Shi'a mosque in Zahedan in May 2009. Responsibility for the attack was claimed by the PRMI, which stated that a secret meeting involving senior members of the Revolutionary Guards had been taking place at the mosque. Assertions by the Iranian Government that the attack had been sponsored by the USA were vehemently denied by President Barack Obama. On 30 May three members of the PRMI were publicly executed, having allegedly confessed to involvement in planning the Zahedan bombing. In June 14 suspected PRMI members were extradited from Pakistan; 13 were executed in July for involvement in militant activity (although they were not specifically charged in connection with the Zahedan mosque bombing). The 14th suspect,

Abdolhamid Rigi—brother of the group's leader, Abdolmalek Rigi—was executed in May 2010. Abdolmalek Rigi was executed in June, having been found guilty of 79 charges relating to the PRMI's campaign of violence against the Iranian military, police, other establishment figures and civilians.

The 2009 presidential election

The Council of Guardians approved just four of 475 prospective candidates for the June 2009 presidential election. These were: Mahmoud Ahmadinejad; Mir Hossein Mousavi, the former Prime Minister who was supported by former President Khatami; former Majlis Speaker Mahdi Karrubi, considered a reformist; and Mohsen Rezai, a conservative former Revolutionary Guards commander opposed to the President's economic policies. Following the election, on 12 June, at which an estimated 85% of registered voters participated, Ahmadinejad was officially pronounced to have won 62.6% of the vote. Mousavi took 33.8%, Rezai 1.7% and Karrubi 0.9%. The defeated candidates demanded that the result be annulled, alleging irregularities in the conduct of the election. Violent clashes broke out between anti-Government protesters and security forces in Tehran, and hundreds of thousands of opposition supporters in Tehran defied an official ban on unauthorized demonstrations to march in protest against what they believed was a rigged election. The protests also spread to cities including Shiraz and Esfahan. The unprecedented wave of public protests in Iran in the following weeks became known as the 'Green Movement', with demonstrators wearing green items of clothing in reference to the predominant colour in Mousavi's election campaign material. There were reports of members of the Basij paramilitary volunteer force being deployed to suppress the protests; internet and mobile communications services were disrupted; and foreign journalists were officially prevented from reporting on the unrest. Official Iranian figures subsequently put the number of deaths as a result of the post-election protests at 36, while the opposition claimed that more than 80 supporters of the Green Movement had been killed.

Meanwhile, on 19 June 2009 Ayatollah Khamenei declared the election valid. He ordered an immediate end to the demonstrations, accusing foreign powers of fomenting unrest within Iran. Following an inquiry into allegations of voting irregularities, the Council of Guardians announced that the number of votes cast had exceeded the number of eligible voters in as many as 50 constituencies. However, the Council ruled that these and other discrepancies were insufficient to affect the outcome of the election. On 24 June Rezai withdrew his opposition to the election result. Intermittent violent clashes between protesters and security forces continued in subsequent weeks, although the numbers of demonstrators decreased progressively. Established divisions within the Iranian political hierarchy were apparently deepened as a result of the disputed election. In July, notably, Rafsanjani—now head of both the Expediency Council and the Assembly of Experts—alleged that the authorities had lost the trust of the people, and urged the lifting of restrictions on the media and the release of hundreds of detainees. Ahmadinejad was sworn in for a second term as President on 5 August, but the inauguration ceremony was boycotted by Mousavi and Karrubi (Rezai had withdrawn his opposition to the election result), as well as by former Presidents Rafsanjani and Khatami, and by as many as 50 parliamentary deputies.

Ahmadinejad's appointment of a close ally, Esfandiar Rahim-Mashai, to the position of First Vice-President in July 2009 caused some controversy. Rahim-Mashai, a former head of the Cultural Heritage, Handicrafts and Tourism Organization, had attracted severe criticism in the previous year, when he was reported to have referred to Iran as being 'a friend of the Israeli people'. Following an intervention by Ayatollah Khamenei, Rahim-Mashai swiftly tendered his resignation, although he was retained by Ahmadinejad as an adviser and head of the presidential office. The subsequent dismissal of the Minister of Intelligence and Security, Gholam-Hossein Mohseni Ejeie, and the resignation of the Minister of Culture and Islamic Guidance, Muhammad Hossein Saffar-Harandi, were widely reported to have resulted from the ministers' strong opposition to Rahim-Mashai's appointment. In September the Majlis approved 18 of Ahmadinejad's 21 ministerial nominees, five of whom retained the posts they had held in the outgoing cabinet. Marzieh Vahid Dastjerdi, the new Minister of Health and Medical Education, became the first woman to join the Council of Ministers since the Islamic Revolution. The appointment of Brig.-Gen. Ahmad Vahidi as Minister of Defence and Armed Forces Logistics provoked international criticism: Vahidi, a former Revolutionary Guards commander, was accused by the authorities in Argentina of involvement in the bombing of a Jewish cultural centre in Buenos Aires in 1994, which caused the deaths of 85 people. Nominees for the three outstanding ministerial positions received parliamentary approval in November 2009.

Meanwhile, in August 2009 the trial took place of more than 100 detainees, including numerous prominent reformist figures (among them a former Vice-President, Muhammad Ali Abtahi, and former Deputy Minister of Foreign Affairs Mohsen Aminzadeh, as well as journalists, student activists and lawyers), during which several defendants were reported to have confessed to involvement in fomenting the post-election unrest. Further, televised confessions were elicited as the trial proceeded, with defendants apparently giving details of a conspiracy to overthrow the Islamic Republic in collusion with various foreign agencies. Many of Ahmadinejad's critics and political rivals, including Mousavi, Khatami and Rafsanjani, were implicated in the alleged conspiracy. Opposition leaders and international human rights organizations protested that the confessions had been extracted under duress and that the proceedings were unconstitutional. In October three defendants were reported to have been sentenced to death for their role in the unrest; another five received the death sentence in November. Abtahi was sentenced to six years' imprisonment, having been convicted on charges including plotting against national security and insulting the President. Two dissidents who had been convicted in August were executed in January 2010. Both were alleged to have participated in a pro-royalist plot to overthrow the Islamic Republic. In February Aminzadeh and another former government minister, Mohsen Behzad, were sentenced to six and five years' imprisonment, respectively. A report published by the non-governmental organization Human Rights Watch in that month accused the Iranian authorities of committing widespread human rights abuses since the presidential election. In June Ayatollah Khamenei pardoned, or commuted the prison sentences of 81 people who had been convicted of crimes during the post-election unrest; the opposition considered this to be an attempt to pre-empt any large-scale protests on the first anniversary of Ahmadinejad's re-election. In January 2011 two further dissidents were executed, having been convicted of distributing footage of the 2009 demonstrations via the internet, and of promoting the proscribed Mujahidin-e-Khalq.

It was reported in October 2009, meanwhile, that Karrubi was to be investigated by a special judicial committee, after he alleged that security forces had tortured and sexually abused political prisoners following the post-election unrest. In November, on the 30th anniversary of the storming of the US embassy, more than 100 people were arrested following violent clashes in Tehran between security forces and participants in a Green Movement protest: demonstrators demanded the removal of Ahmadinejad, and some chanted slogans against Ayatollah Khamenei. It was subsequently disclosed that Khamenei, in response to the civil unrest, had sanctioned the creation of a new intelligence agency under the auspices of the Revolutionary Guards. Amid repeated demands from hardliners that the leaders of the anti-Government movement should be put on trial, Mousavi was removed from his post as President of the Iranian Academy of the Arts in December. There were further large demonstrations in Tehran at the end of December, on the occasion of the Ashoura festival; eight opposition activists (including a nephew of Mousavi) were reported to have died during clashes with security forces.

More than 40 people, including at least five senior Revolutionary Guards commanders, were killed in a suicide bomb attack in Sistan and Baluchestan province in October 2009, responsibility for which was claimed by the PRMI. The Iranian Government again accused the USA and the United Kingdom of providing support to the Baluchi militants, and also claimed that the militants maintained bases in Pakistan and had received assistance from Pakistani intelligence agents. In July 2010 28 people, again including Revolutionary Guards personnel, were reported to have been killed in a suicide bombing at a Shi'a mosque in Zahedan. The PRMI claimed that it had carried out the attack in revenge for the execution of its leader, Abdolmalek Rigi, in the previous month. Three Majlis deputies from Sistan and Baluchestan subsequently announced their resignation, in protest against the authorities' failure to prevent the attack. In November the US Department of State formally designated the PRMI as a terrorist organization. At least 33 people were killed in a bomb attack at a mosque in the south-eastern port city of

Chabahar in December 2010, responsibility for which was claimed by the PRMI.

The Islamic Iran Participation Front, which had denounced Ahmadinejad's victory in the 2009 election as a *'coup d'état'*, complained in March 2010 that the judiciary had barred it from holding its annual party conference. Marking the Iranian New Year in that month, Mousavi urged his supporters to ensure that the year would be a one of resistance against the current regime. In April both the Participation Front and the Organization of the Mujahidin of the Islamic Revolution, which had also supported Mousavi in the presidential election, were said to have been 'dissolved' for reasons of undermining national security.

Increased tensions within the political establishment

In April 2010 the Majlis approved legislation to reduce its powers to review orders issued by the Council of Guardians, the Assembly of Experts, the Expediency Council and the Supreme National Security Council (SNSC). This apparently exemplified the growing influence of these mainly non-elected bodies over the elected parliament. As the year progressed, however, it became apparent that even conservative politicians were becoming increasingly concerned by the authoritarianism of Ahmadinejad's regime. In December it was announced that the Minister of Foreign Affairs, Manouchehr Mottaki, had been removed from office and replaced on an interim basis by the Vice-President and Head of the Atomic Energy Organization, Ali Akbar Salehi. Mottaki was reported to have disagreed with Ahmadinejad over the ongoing negotiations concerning Iran's nuclear programme. In January 2011 the formal nomination of Salehi as Minister of Foreign Affairs was approved by the Majlis, and in February Fereydoun Abbasi Davani, a leading nuclear scientist who had been the target of an attempted assassination in 2010, assumed Salehi's former post.

In February 2011 two people were reportedly killed after Green Movement activists took part in protests in Tehran, apparently in support of the popular uprisings in Tunisia and Egypt. Karrubi and Mousavi were reportedly placed under house arrest in an attempt to prevent their participation in the protests. Both men remained in detention in early 2014, as did Mousavi's wife, Zahra Rahnavard, although the terms of their detention had partially eased by this time (see below).

In March 2011 Ayatollah Muhammad Reza Mahdavi Kani became Speaker of the Assembly of Experts. Rafsanjani had declined to seek a further term, citing concern for national unity. In April it was reported that Ahmadinejad had forced the resignation of the Minister of Intelligence and Security, Heydar Moslehi, but that Ayatollah Khamenei had intervened to order that Moslehi remain in office. In apparent protest, Ahmadinejad declined to attend meetings of the Council of Ministers for several days. In May Ahmadinejad dismissed the Ministers of Petroleum, of Industries and Mines, and of Welfare and Social Security, stating that he wished to reduce the number of government ministers; however, many observers considered that the dismissals were politically motivated. Incumbent ministers were given temporary charge of the latter two ministries, but Ahmadinejad named himself as interim Minister of Petroleum. He was prevented from formally assuming the post, on grounds of unconstitutionality, both by the Council of Guardians and by a large majority in the Majlis. The Majlis did, however, endorse Ahmadinejad's plan eventually to reduce the number of ministries from 21 to 17, despite strong opposition from conservative deputies. In August Brig.-Gen. Rostam Ghasemi was named as Minister of Petroleum. As a member of the Revolutionary Guards, Ghasemi was subject to US and EU sanctions. (For details of sanctions imposed against Iran, see The Nuclear Issue.)

In June 2011, meanwhile, the resignation was announced of the newly appointed Deputy Minister of Foreign Affairs, Muhammad Sharif Malekzadeh. A close ally of both the President and his adviser Rahim-Mashai (who had been replaced as head of the presidential office by Hamid Baqai in April), Malekzadeh was accused by conservative deputies of acting against the clerical hierarchy. Shortly after resigning, he was arrested in connection with a financial scandal that reportedly involved some of the country's largest banks. In October the Deputy Governor of the central bank, Sayed Hamid Pour-Mohammadi (another close associate of the President), was detained by police on suspicion of involvement in the alleged fraud. A number of Majlis deputies formally requested that President Ahmadinejad be examined by a parliamentary committee in relation to the affair. Deputies also requested the impeachment of the Minister of Economic Affairs and Finance, Shamseddin Hosseini, although he survived a vote in parliament in November. The trial of 39 defendants accused of involvement in the alleged fraud began in February 2012. In July four were given death sentences for their role in the scandal (their identities were not disclosed); two others were sentenced to life imprisonment; and the remaining defendants received gaol terms of up to 25 years.

A Green Movement rally in Tehran in June 2011, on the second anniversary of the disputed presidential election, was forcibly disrupted by security forces using tear gas and batons, and a number of protesters were reportedly arrested. Human rights groups monitoring the situation in Iran noted a significant increase in the number of executions during 2011: more than 600 people were reported to have been executed (a figure rejected by the Iranian Government), many of whom had been convicted of crimes in connection with drugs-trafficking.

In November 2011 an apparent bomb attack at a Revolutionary Guards missile base in Bigdaneh, east of Tehran, was reported to have killed 17 members of the corps; among the dead was Maj.-Gen. Hassan Moghaddam, who was said to be a leading figure in Iran's missiles programme. Although the Iranian authorities described the explosion as an accident, there was widespread speculation regarding the possible involvement of Israel's foreign intelligence agency, Mossad.

In March 2012 Mahmoud Ahmadinejad became the first serving President since the establishment of the Islamic Republic to appear before the Majlis for questioning. Principally under scrutiny was his management of the economy, although it was reported that some deputies also intended to question him about the state of relations with Ayatollah Khamenei and about recent disputes concerning the appointment or dismissal of government officials.

The 2012 legislative elections

A number of dissidents, journalists and intellectuals were reportedly arrested in early 2012, in advance of elections to the ninth Majlis, scheduled for March, and the Government apparently tried to block public internet access to sites critical of the regime. At the first round of voting, on 2 March, around 3,400 candidates contested the 290 parliamentary seats. At least one-third of the original 5,000 candidates had been barred from standing by the Council of Guardians; many of these were mainly reformist deputies in the outgoing Majlis, and several prominent supporters of President Ahmadinejad were also understood to have been disqualified. Iran's most prominent pro-reform parties boycotted the elections, in continuing protest against the disputed presidential election of 2009 and the subsequent crackdown on opposition groups, as well as ongoing abuses of human rights. It was reported that conservatives won 143 seats, while reformists took 59. Candidates representing religious minorities secured 14 seats, and independents nine. A second round of voting took place for the remaining 65 seats on 4 May, at which conservatives won 41 further seats, reformists 13, and independents 11. According to the Ministry of the Interior, the rate of voter participation was 64.2%. The outcome suggested that Ayatollah Khamenei was likely to receive more support from the new Majlis than was Ahmadinejad. At the end of May Ahmadinejad made changes at vice-presidential level, notably appointing Behrouz Moradi as Vice-President for Strategic Planning and Supervision Affairs.

In July 2012 it was reported that a group of Majlis deputies was seeking to initiate a debate concerning the introduction of a parliamentary, rather than presidential, system of government in Iran, which would involve the revival of the post of Prime Minister (which had been abolished in 1989). In December the Majlis adopted a bill proposing to introduce more stringent requirements for presidential candidates, in advance of the election scheduled to take place (concurrently with municipal elections) in June 2013. Ahmadinejad criticized the bill as handing too much power to the legislature concerning the election process. In January 2013 the Council of Guardians rejected the proposals concerning presidential candidates. The revised election reform bill notably transferred responsibility for the organization and monitoring of elections from the Ministry of the Interior to a central election board, to include, *inter alia*, representatives of the executive, legislature and judiciary. In late 2012, meanwhile, both Rafsanjani and former President Khatami made public declarations that the forthcoming presidential election should be free, fair and competitive. In response, Ayatollah Khamenei asserted strongly that all elections since the Islamic Revolution had been free.

As part of government changes in December 2012, Ahmadinejad appointed Esfandiar Rahim-Mashai as head of the Secretariat of the Non-Aligned Movement (of which Iran currently held the rotating chairmanship). The appointment increased speculation that the President was seeking to assist his close ally in a bid for the presidency in 2013. Ahmadinejad was also reported to have dismissed the Minister of Health and Medical Education, Marzieh Vahid Dastjerdi (who had remained the only woman in the Council of Ministers), as a result of a disagreement over government policy.

In early February 2013 the Majlis voted to impeach the Minister of Labour and Social Affairs, Abdolreza Sheikholeslami, in connection with his role in appointing former prosecutor-general Saeed Mortazavi as head of the country's social security fund. Mortazavi, who was regarded as a supporter of the President, had in 2010 been identified by a parliamentary investigation as being principally responsible for the deaths of three students at the Kahrizak detention centre in Tehran after the Green Movement protests in 2009. Also associated with the suppression of opposition media, and a subject of US sanctions, Mortazavi had been removed from his position at the social security fund in January 2013, following pressure by the Majlis. During the session at which the impeachment vote was taken, there was a verbal confrontation between Ahmadinejad, who spoke in support of Sheikholeslami, and Majlis Speaker Ali Larijani, in which the President accused Larijani and members of his family of corruption. Ahmadinejad subsequently appointed Sheikholeslami as Vice-President for Social Affairs. Meanwhile, Mortazavi was arrested shortly after the confrontation between Ahmadinejad and Larijani. He was released two days later, but his trial began in late February, before a closed court, on charges of participation in the murder of anti-Government protesters, in the illegal arrest of protesters, and in the falsification of reports in the Kahrizak case. The court's ruling, issued at the beginning of July, indicated that Mortazavi and two other defendants had been permanently dismissed from positions within the judiciary, and had been barred from holding any government office for five years. Mortazavi was acquitted of participation in murder, but was fined for false reporting.

Recent developments: the 2013 presidential election

It was announced in late May 2013 that the Council of Guardians had approved eight candidates (of 686 who had registered) for the following month's presidential election. The approved candidates were: Saeed Jalili, the Secretary of the SNSC and Iran's principal negotiator on the nuclear issue; Hassan Rouhani, head of the SNSC in 1989–2005 and also, in this capacity, chief nuclear negotiator; former Minister of Foreign Affairs Ali Akbar Velayati; Muhammad Baqir Qalibaf, the mayor of Tehran; former Revolutionary Guards commander Mohsen Rezai; former Majlis Speaker Gholam-Ali Haddad-Adel; Muhammad Reza Aref, who had served as First Vice-President under President Khatami; and Muhammad Gharazi, who had held ministerial office under Presidents Khamenei and Rafsanjani. Notable among the disallowed candidates were both former President Rafsanjani and Ahmadinejad's ally Rahim-Mashai. (The Council had also previously announced that, under the terms of the Constitution, women were ineligible to stand as candidates—30 women having registered.) With Rafsanjani disallowed, and with both Mir Hossein Mousavi and Mahdi Karrubi remaining in detention, initially it was widely assumed that the election would be dominated by conservative or principlist candidates loyal to Ayatollah Khamenei. As the election approached, however, moderate and reformist support coalesced around the centrist cleric Hassan Rouhani, who in campaigning urged greater engagement with the West, and undertook to ease economic hardship as a result of international sanctions and mismanagement under the Ahmadinejad regime, release political prisoners and institute media reforms. Muhammad Reza Aref, hitherto regarded as the most reformist of the approved candidates, withdrew from the contest shortly before the poll—apparently at the request of Khatami, who, together with Rafsanjani, urged support for Rouhani. (The conservative Haddad-Adel had also meanwhile withdrawn.)

Voting in the presidential election (held concurrently with municipal elections) proceeded on 14 June 2013, with, according to official figures, a turnout of 72.7% of the registered electorate. According to the official results, announced by the Ministry of the Interior the following day, Rouhani was elected outright with 50.7% of votes cast. Muhammad Baqir Qalibaf was placed second, with 16.6%, and Saeed Jalili third, with 11.4%. Conservatives performed strongly in the municipal elections, reportedly securing control of 70% of some 1,230 local councils nationwide; reformists took 20%, and about 9% came under moderate control. In the elections for Tehran's city council, conservative or principlist candidates were reported to have won as many as 18 of the 31 seats, and reformists 13. (In September the council elected Qalibaf to serve a third term as mayor of Tehran—although he only narrowly defeated Mohsen Hashemi Rafsanjani, the oldest son of the former President.)

Rouhani was sworn in as President on 4 August 2013, having been formally endorsed by Ayatollah Khamenei the previous day. In his inaugural address before the Majlis, Rouhani emphasized that voters had chosen moderation, and pledged, *inter alia*, to promote women's rights and to reduce state interference in the lives of the Iranian people. In international affairs, he urged engagement through dialogue rather than sanctions. Notably, representatives of the international community were invited to attend the inauguration for the first time since the Islamic Revolution.

On the day of his inauguration, Rouhani presented his first list of ministerial nominations for parliamentary approval. All but three of his 18 nominees were endorsed by the Majlis in mid-August 2013. (The rejected candidates were deemed principally to have been too close to the Green Movement protests in 2009.) Notable appointees included Bijan Namdar Zanganeh as Minister of Petroleum, Ali Tayebnia as Minister of Economic Affairs and Finance, and Muhammad Javad Zarif as Minister of Foreign Affairs. Most prominent among the nine Vice-Presidents appointed by Rouhani was Ali Akbar Salehi, who became Vice-President and Head of the Atomic Energy Organization. Expectations that the new President was likely to accord greater authority in international nuclear talks to Zarif, who had been Iran's permanent representative at the UN in 2002–07, were confirmed in September 2013, when Rouhani announced that the Ministry of Foreign Affairs—rather than the SNSC, regarded as close to Ayatollah Khamenei—would lead future nuclear negotiations on behalf of Iran. In October Rouhani's second nominations for the education and the science, research and technology portfolios were approved by the Majlis; two further nominations for the sport and youth affairs ministry were rejected before a fourth nominee was eventually approved in November.

In late September 2013, meanwhile, prior to the new President's highly anticipated visit to address the UN General Assembly in New York, USA, it was officially announced that 80 prisoners had been pardoned. These were understood to include a group of 11 political prisoners, among them Mohsen Aminzadeh and a prominent human rights lawyer, Nasrin Sotoudeh, whose release had been reported the previous week. Meanwhile, there were indications that the terms of house arrest of Mahdi Karrubi, Mir Hossein Mousavi and Zahra Rahnavard had eased somewhat; and in early February 2014 it was reported that Karrubi had been transferred from a government-owned property to his own home. (Mousavi and Rahnavard were at this time already being held in their home.) In its 2014 annual report, issued in January, the non-governmental organization Human Rights Watch drew attention to the continued detention of civil society activists and civil society leaders in Iran, and urged President Rouhani to press for a moratorium on the death penalty. Human Rights Watch noted that official sources put the number of judicial executions at around 270 in the year to October 2013, but stated that the actual number was thought to be much higher.

Despite some early signs of cautious change under Rouhani—including a degree of official engagement with social media, and suggestions by the Minister of Culture and Islamic Guidance, Ali Jannati, that internet social networks should be made more freely accessible to the Iranian public—uncertainty remained as to the likely tolerance within Iran's conservative institutions of such measures. In January 2014, notably, the Prosecutor-General, Gholam-Hossein Mohseni Ejeie, criticized comments made by Jannati concerning the need to ease restrictions on areas such as the media and arts, stating that it was not within the minister's authority to define the responsibilities of the judiciary. Meanwhile, the judiciary continued to curtail the activities of reformist news media outlets. By late February 2014 four reformist or pro-Rouhani newspapers had been banned for alleged violations of Islamic principles.

The Nuclear Issue

Following President Khatami's announcement in February 2003 regarding the discovery and successful extraction of uranium, the USA urged the International Atomic Energy Agency (IAEA) to declare Iran to be in violation of the nuclear non-proliferation treaty (NPT), and appealed for Russia to end its collaboration with Iran on construction of the Bushehr nuclear power plant, in south-western Iran. In June the Director-General of the IAEA, Dr Mohammed el-Baradei, called on Iran to open its nuclear programme to a more rigorous system of inspections. Iran responded that it would only comply with this request if it were given access to the nuclear technology it required. Despite Khatami's assurances that Iran's nuclear programme was 'entirely peaceful', the IAEA (with US support) adopted a resolution in September giving Iran until the end of October to disclose full details of its programme in order to prove that it was not developing nuclear weapons. This followed the discovery of enriched uranium at a processing plant south of Tehran. In late October 2003 it was announced that Iran would accept a more rigorous system of inspections at its nuclear facilities.

However, the IAEA reported in February 2004 that it had found evidence of undeclared facilities that could be used for the enrichment of uranium. The Agency adopted a resolution condemning Iran for the secrecy of its nuclear activities in March, and a further resolution on 18 June criticizing Iran for failing to co-operate with the inspections process. In late June the Iranian leadership announced that, although it would adhere to its pledge to suspend actual uranium enrichment, it would resume manufacturing parts for centrifuges and would also recommence the testing and assembly of centrifuges. Moreover, Iran criticized France, Germany and the United Kingdom for not supplying it with the technology and trade they had promised in return for this pledge. In October 2004 Russia and Iran completed the construction of the Bushehr nuclear plant, although Russian officials also pressed the Islamic regime to cease uranium enrichment. (The plant was not formally opened until 2011.) Iran also tested a long-range satellite-launching rocket, the *Shahab-4*, asserting that it would only use its missiles in self-defence. In November, following talks with French, German and British officials in Paris, France, Iran complied with IAEA demands to suspend temporarily its enrichment programme.

In August 2005 Iran resumed the conversion of uranium to gas (the stage before enrichment) at the Esfahan conversion facility, having previously rejected as 'worthless' a set of compensatory proposals put forward by France, Germany and the United Kingdom in exchange for abandoning its enrichment programme. The IAEA subsequently adopted a resolution in mid-August expressing 'serious concern' at the resumption of nuclear activities at Esfahan, and urging Iran to reinstate suspension. Also in August President Ahmadinejad appointed Ali Larijani, believed to be a close ally of Ayatollah Khamenei, as Secretary of the SNSC and chief nuclear negotiator. A further IAEA resolution in late September found Iran guilty of 'non-compliance' and asserted that it should increase the transparency of its nuclear programme. However, Iran announced in January 2006 that it had reopened its uranium enrichment research facility at Natanz, south of Tehran, after a two-year moratorium; it subsequently confirmed that small-scale uranium enrichment had recommenced. In early March el-Baradei transmitted his latest IAEA report on Iran's nuclear programme to the UN Security Council, which, later that month, approved a statement calling on Iran to suspend all uranium enrichment activities within 30 days. In April Ahmadinejad announced that Iran had successfully enriched uranium for the first time, although he insisted that his country had no intention of developing nuclear weapons. Meanwhile, the US Administration revealed that it was allocating US $75m. to fund Iranian dissident groups.

In late April 2006 el-Baradei delivered a report to the UN Security Council which concluded that Iran had failed to comply with the 30-day deadline imposed by the Council to halt its uranium enrichment activities, and that there could be no guarantee that its nuclear activities were purely peaceful. In response, the US ambassador to the UN, John Bolton, called on the Security Council to invoke Chapter VII of the UN Charter, which contained provision for the use of military action—a demand that was immediately rejected by the People's Republic of China and Russia. Meeting in Brussels, Belgium, in mid-May, EU ministers responsible for foreign affairs responded by proposing a 'bold' package of trade and technical incentives for Iran to halt its nuclear programme. However, the offer was firmly rejected by the Iranian leadership. Further economic incentives were offered by the EU's High Representative for Common Foreign and Security Policy, Javier Solana, in June, following an agreement reached by the five permanent members of the UN Security Council—China, France, Russia, the United Kingdom and the USA—together with Germany (the so-called P5+1 group), concerning new proposals to encourage Iran to renounce enrichment. These included an offer of nuclear technical assistance, the removal of certain US economic sanctions and the possible opening of direct discussions between Iran and the USA.

In July 2006 the UN Security Council approved a resolution (No. 1696), which expressed 'serious concern' regarding Iran's refusal to co-operate with the IAEA and warned that the country could face 'appropriate measures' unless it halted its uranium enrichment programme by 31 August. In late August 2006 Larijani presented a formal response to the package of economic incentives offered by the P5+1 group in June, describing Iran's enrichment activities as an 'inalienable right'. The IAEA reported to the UN Security Council on 31 August that Iran had failed to meet its requirement to cease uranium enrichment and that Iranian officials had not co-operated with the Agency's investigators. In late December the UN Security Council adopted Resolution 1737, which imposed a series of limited sanctions on the Iranian regime—including a ban on the trade of nuclear-related technology and materials, and a freeze on the assets of leading individuals and companies involved in the nuclear programme. Iran was granted 60 days in which to cease all enrichment activities and thus avoid further sanctions. However, President Ahmadinejad rejected the terms of Resolution 1737, and the Majlis adopted legislation that urged an acceleration of Iran's nuclear energy programme. In January 2007 Iran announced that it was barring 38 IAEA inspectors from the country, in retaliation for the imposition of sanctions.

In his report to the IAEA in February 2007, el-Baradei affirmed that Iran had failed to meet the deadline of the previous day to cease uranium enrichment and had actually expanded the programme from 'research-scale' to 'industrial-scale' enrichment. On 24 March the UN Security Council adopted Resolution 1747, which again required Iran to suspend all enrichment-related and reprocessing activities and to agree to grant IAEA inspectors full access to its nuclear sites. Resolution 1747 imposed, *inter alia*, an embargo on the sale of arms to and from Iran, and a ban on the transfer of funds to Iran by state and international financial institutions (excluding those intended for humanitarian or development aid). The UN granted Iran 60 days to comply with the measures or face 'further appropriate measures'. However, in April Ahmadinejad boasted that Iran had joined the 'nuclear club of nations'. Following an inspection of the Natanz nuclear facility, IAEA inspectors asserted that Iran had commenced the process of enriching uranium on an 'industrial scale', but were uncertain as to whether all of the 1,300 centrifuges at Natanz were actually in operation. The day before the Security Council's deadline of 24 May, and with Iran continuing to defy international demands to suspend its enrichment programme, el-Baradei declared that he believed Iran to possess the capability to build a nuclear weapon in between three to eight years. However, the IAEA Director-General asserted that he did not have evidence to support the claim that Iran was seeking to produce such weapons of mass destruction.

Following a meeting between Iranian and IAEA officials in Vienna, Austria, in July 2007, Iran agreed to provide information about previous nuclear experiments, to allow inspectors to visit a plutonium-producing reactor being built at Arak and to decelerate its uranium enrichment programme at Natanz. In August el-Baradei agreed a 'work plan' with Iranian officials, whereby Iran was given a three-month deadline by which to end any technical ambiguities concerning its nuclear programme. However, the US Administration continued to demand a complete and immediate cessation of uranium enrichment. In late October Saeed Jalili, Iran's Deputy Foreign Minister for European and American Affairs, replaced Larijani as Secretary of the SNSC and principal negotiator on the nuclear issue. Towards the end of October the USA imposed further unilateral sanctions against Iran, which principally targeted Iranian state-owned banks, organizations and agencies deemed to be involved in a clandestine nuclear programme or to sponsor terrorism abroad, and in particular named affiliates of the Revolutionary Guards and its élite Qods Force.

In November 2007 el-Baradei informed the IAEA that, despite improvements as far as transparency in the programme laid out in the 'work plan' was concerned, the Iranian authorities were continuing to restrict inspectors' access to nuclear plants. He also confirmed that Iran now had an estimated 3,000 centrifuges in operation. The US Administration insisted in December that a joint report (entitled the National Intelligence Estimate—NIE) published by the 16 US intelligence agencies, in which they disclosed their findings that Iran had in fact suspended its nuclear weapons development programme in 2003, would not lead his country to re-evaluate its policy towards the Islamic Republic. Ahmadinejad reiterated his assertion that Iran had never sought to develop a clandestine nuclear weapons programme.

In March 2008 the UN Security Council adopted Resolution 1803, which tightened the sanctions already imposed on Iran with regard to the financial assets and ability to travel of officials and institutions allegedly involved in nuclear activities. The resolution required UN member states to monitor the activities of two state-owned banks with suspected links to nuclear proliferation, Bank Melli and Bank Saderat. It also prohibited the trade in so-called 'dual-use' goods or technologies which could be employed for civilian or military purposes. In May the latest IAEA report issued by el-Baradei—as requested by the UN Security Council within 90 days of Resolution 1803—affirmed that Iranian officials had again failed to co-operate with the Agency in answering vital questions about its nuclear programme, and indeed that 500 centrifuges had been added to the 3,000 already in place at Natanz.

In an effort to resolve the ongoing dispute between Iran and the international community, Solana led a delegation from the P5+1 group to Tehran in mid-June 2008 to offer Iran a new package of incentives. Solana proposed that the UN Security Council would delay any further imposition of sanctions against the Iranian regime in return for Iran's agreement to suspend the installation of extra centrifuges at its nuclear facilities, while continuing current levels of uranium enrichment for a six-week period only. Under the proposals, which sought the cessation of Iran's expansion of its enrichment programme as a precondition for the start of formal negotiations, the international community would also assist with the construction of light-water reactors for electricity generation. Further talks were held by Solana and Jalili in Geneva in mid-July, notably in the presence of the USA's Undersecretary of State for Political Affairs, William Burns; these represented the most senior diplomatic contacts between the USA and Iran since 1979. However, by early August 2008 Iran had not sufficiently clarified its stance towards the incentives offered by the international delegation. After the EU had imposed new financial and trade sanctions against Iran, in mid-August further US sanctions were introduced targeting companies with links to the nuclear industry.

In late September 2008 the UN Security Council adopted Resolution 1835, requiring Iran to 'comply fully and without delay' with its obligations concerning its nuclear programme as outlined in earlier UN resolutions. This followed a report by the IAEA Director-General five days earlier, in which he maintained that Iran had failed to provide sufficient evidence that it was enriching uranium for peaceful purposes alone. In his subsequent report to the IAEA Board in November, el-Baradei stated that Iran's stockpiles of enriched uranium were growing at a rapid rate, and therefore that by early 2009 the country might achieve nuclear 'breakout capacity'—meaning that in theory it had the capability to produce a sufficient level of enriched uranium to build a nuclear weapon.

President Ahmadinejad inaugurated Iran's first nuclear fuel manufacturing plant at Esfahan in April 2009. The new facility was expected to produce uranium fuel pellets for use in the nuclear reactor under construction at Arak. Ahmadinejad also announced that tests had commenced on new centrifuges with enhanced enrichment capacity. In June an IAEA quarterly report on Iran revealed that the number of installed centrifuges had increased to 7,221, with almost 5,000 in operation at that time. A subsequent report, issued in August, revealed that IAEA inspectors had been granted access to the Arak reactor site for the first time in more than a year, and that improved monitoring arrangements had been introduced at the Natanz facility. None the less, the report noted Iran's continuing refusal to suspend its enrichment activity, as required by five Security Council resolutions, and highlighted its failure to co-operate with the Agency in connection with several issues of concern regarding a possible military dimension to its nuclear programme. In early September el-Baradei described the IAEA's relations with Iran as having reached a 'stalemate'.

International concern that the Iranian regime had a covert nuclear agenda was heightened considerably in late September 2009 following the revelation that a second uranium enrichment facility, the Fordo plant, was close to completion at a site near Qom. The Iranian authorities, who had hitherto concealed the plant, informed the IAEA of its existence just days before the leaders of the USA, the United Kingdom and France planned to disclose details of the facility at a meeting of the Group of 20 leading industrialized and developing nations (G20) in Pittsburgh, USA. The site had reportedly been monitored by Western intelligence agencies for two years. Ahmadinejad insisted that, as the facility was more than six months from completion, Iran was not obliged to report its existence to the IAEA. Later that month the Revolutionary Guards test-fired a number of *Shahab-3* and *Sajjil-2* rockets, which have a range of up to 1,300 miles and could thus reach targets in Israel as well as US military bases in the Gulf region.

Direct negotiations involving Jalili and the international negotiating group took place in Geneva at the beginning of October 2009. The international negotiators stipulated that Iran should suspend its enrichment programme immediately in order to forestall the introduction of further economic sanctions. They also detailed a proposal for the transfer of a large proportion of Iran's stock of low-enriched uranium to Russia and France for conversion into the higher-grade fuel that Iran claimed it required for medical research purposes. Iran's negotiators confirmed that they would facilitate an IAEA inspection of the Fordo enrichment plant and agreed to enter into substantive negotiations on the nuclear issue. However, Jalili insisted that these should be linked to a broad package of agreements on regional and international security and global nuclear disarmament. In the first direct senior-level engagement between US and Iranian officials since the Islamic Revolution, Jalili held bilateral talks with Burns during the summit. On 3 October the *New York Times* newspaper published details of a confidential IAEA dossier which alleged that Iran was in possession of sufficient knowledge to create an effective nuclear missile. However, the following day el-Baradei emphasized that there was still no concrete evidence of an Iranian military nuclear programme. El-Baradei hosted further talks in Vienna on 20–21 October, involving US, Russian, French and Iranian officials, during which a draft agreement on the uranium transfer proposal was finalized. An Iranian counter-proposal was received by the IAEA on 29 October; this involved Iran retaining most of its stock of low-enriched uranium and being granted permission to import higher-grade fuel from abroad. Meanwhile, in its November report the IAEA confirmed that around 3,000 centrifuges had been installed at the Fordo nuclear facility.

In late November 2009 the IAEA adopted a resolution calling on Iran to suspend construction of the Fordo facility and to confirm whether any other nuclear facilities were under development. In a defiant response, President Ahmadinejad announced plans for a major escalation of Iran's nuclear programme: some 10 new uranium enrichment plants were reportedly scheduled for construction (although analysts suggested that Iran lacked the resources to implement such a programme). In early February 2010, in response to the stalled uranium transfer negotiations, Salehi confirmed that Iran had commenced production of 20%-enriched uranium. Previously, Iran had processed only 3.5%-enriched uranium, a grade sufficient for the production of nuclear power, while the higher-grade fuel was required for the production of isotopes for use in medical research and diagnosis. (Uranium enriched to 90% would be required for the production of atomic weapons.) In mid-February the new Director-General of the IAEA, Yukiya Amano, expressed concerns that the Iranian nuclear programme had 'possible military dimensions', noting that the regime was still refusing to co-operate regarding IAEA inspections, and was continuing to expand its uranium enrichment activities in contravention of previous UN and IAEA resolutions. In late May Amano additionally stated that, with further enrichment, Iran now had sufficient nuclear fuel ultimately to produce two atomic weapons.

The acceleration of Iran's nuclear activities resulted in further international pressure on the Government either to accept the terms of the original IAEA uranium transfer proposal or to cease enrichment entirely. On 17 May 2010 the so-called Tehran Declaration, signed by Iran, Turkey and Brazil, agreed a new uranium transfer proposal whereby Iran would send 1,200 kg of its stockpile of low-enriched uranium to be stored in Turkey, in exchange for 120 kg of nuclear reactor fuel (the uranium having been processed further into fuel rods within one year). Yet the deal, which would still require further agreement to be reached with the Western negotiating governments, failed to prevent a fourth round of sanctions against Iran from being adopted by the UN Security Council in early June, by 12 votes to two (Turkey and Brazil opposed the motion). Resolution 1929, which expressed 'serious concern' regarding Iran's failure to comply with previous resolutions and to stop enriching uranium, involved more stringent military and economic penalties against Iran, focusing on the possible transport by Iranian-owned ships of proscribed materials and on financial institutions suspected of having links with nuclear activities, as well as freezing the assets of, and imposing travel bans on, 41 companies and individuals connected with the Revolutionary Guards and Iran's wider defence establishment. The resolution also asked the UN Secretary-General to establish a panel of experts charged with monitoring Iran's compliance with the new measures. China and Russia had apparently been persuaded to support a new round of sanctions following reassurances that their bilateral trade relations with Iran, in particular concerning the oil and gas sector, would not be jeopardized.

President Obama promulgated further unilateral US sanctions against Iran at the beginning of July 2010. The latest US measures specifically targeted the Post Bank of Iran (making it the 16th Iranian bank to be blacklisted by the US Administration), shipping and financial companies, and those providing the country with much needed fuel imports. The EU also announced new economic sanctions against Iran later that month: these included prohibiting investment in Iran's hydrocarbons sector by EU-based firms and increasing the number of goods which EU governments were prevented from exporting to Iran. On the same day Iran informed the IAEA that it was prepared to resume discussions regarding the proposed transfer of uranium without preconditions. In August the US Administration extended its sanctions to include several institutions suspected of assisting radical organizations in the region such as the Islamic Resistance Movement (Hamas) in the Palestinian territories and Hezbollah in Lebanon.

At the end of November 2010 the Iranian authorities declared that the loading of fuel into the nuclear reactor at the Bushehr power plant was complete, the reactor having finally been launched in August. Further talks between negotiators from the P5+1 group of countries and the Iranian team led by Jalili were held in Geneva in December and in İstanbul, Turkey, in January 2011; however, no breakthrough was achieved. Earlier that month Salehi had announced that Iran now possessed the capability to manufacture fuel plates and rods to be used in its nuclear reactors. In Amano's sixth report to the IAEA board in May, the Director-General suggested that an Iranian nuclear weapons programme might be under development; Iran was asked to clarify details of specific nuclear experiments that it was carrying out. In July the authorities stated that the installation of a new range of centrifuges would accelerate the process by which uranium could be enriched. The declaration further alarmed many regional and Western leaders, since analysts had already stated that Iran was potentially only months away from enriching uranium to the level required to produce a nuclear weapon. Nevertheless, after a visit to Iran's nuclear sites by IAEA inspectors in August, the Agency did refer to more 'transparency' from Iranian officials. In early September Amano's seventh report to the IAEA, which again included suggestions of a possible military dimension to Iran's past and present nuclear programme, prompted Abbasi Davani, Vice-President and Head of the Atomic Energy Organization of Iran, to promise full access to Iran's nuclear sites by IAEA inspectors if the sanctions in place against Tehran were lifted. On 12 September, a week after it had been connected to the national grid, the Bushehr plant was officially opened.

The IAEA issued a report in early November 2011 which used detailed evidence to indicate that the Islamic regime had, as recently as 2010, been involved in research and other testing processes required specifically for the 'development of a nuclear explosive device'. Crucially, the Agency found that some of these actions 'may still be ongoing'. This was the first time that the Agency had indicated directly that Iran was engaged in such efforts. A resolution passed by the IAEA Board in mid-November sought to increase the pressure against Iran by urging it to comply with the terms of previous UN Security Council resolutions and to engage in renewed dialogue with negotiators. Iranian officials swiftly repeated assertions that the programme was solely for civilian purposes. However, in that month both the USA and the United Kingdom announced a new range of sanctions affecting Iranian banks and the energy sector. (For further details on sanctions imposed in late 2011 and 2012, see Foreign Affairs.)

IAEA officials confirmed in early January 2012 that scientists at the Fordo enrichment plant near Qom had begun to enrich uranium to the higher level of 20% and thus were getting closer to reaching weapons-grade capacity. The US Administration described Iran as 'further escalating' its violation of UN Security Council resolutions. In late January President Ahmadinejad surprised some Western observers by offering to resume discussions on its nuclear programme, although he was not specific about the details of such talks. It was reported in mid-February that the Turkish Government had again offered to host negotiations between Iranian and P5+1 officials. Iran's ambassador to the UN, Muhammad Khazaii, declared in February that Iran would enter new talks without preconditions, but he reiterated the fact that his country would not give up any of its 'inalienable rights'. Later that month Ahmadinejad was present at a ceremony held at the Tehran research reactor (which manufactures isotopes for medical usage), where for the first time the reactor was loaded with domestically produced nuclear fuel rods. During the early part of 2012 Iran again prevented IAEA inspectors from carrying out their work without hindrance, and the Agency expressed further concerns that the country's nuclear activities could possess a military dimension.

Discussions finally resumed between the P5+1 group, under the leadership of Catherine Ashton, the EU High Representative for Foreign Affairs and Security Policy, and the Iranian delegation, led by Jalili, in İstanbul in mid-April 2012. Further high-level talks were held in Baghdad, Iraq, in late May and in Moscow, Russia, in mid-June. However, although the early stages of the negotiations were described by Ashton as 'constructive and useful', Iranian officials rejected the Western nations' offer to ease certain sanctions and provide fuel rods for the research reactor in Tehran in exchange for transporting its 20% enriched uranium to a foreign country, agreeing to end such enrichment and shutting down the Fordo facility. Moreover, in his 10th report to the IAEA concerning Iran's nuclear activities, issued in June, Amano stated that in the previous month IAEA inspectors examining the Fordo plant had found evidence of uranium enrichment up to the higher level of 27%. A meeting of technical experts from the Western nations and Iran was held in İstanbul in early July; however, no further high-level discussions were scheduled.

In mid-September 2012 the IAEA again reported Iran's non-compliance with its nuclear inspections team, adopting a resolution expressing 'serious concern' over the country's continued enrichment of uranium. Moreover, a report published by the US-based Institute for Science and International Security in early October, using evidence taken from IAEA inspections of Iran's nuclear facilities, found that the Iranian authorities—should this be their intention—were probably between two to four months away from producing a sufficient quantity of highly enriched uranium to manufacture a nuclear bomb and a further eight to 10 months away from the actual construction of such a device. In mid-November the IAEA's quarterly report on Iran's nuclear programme alleged that, based on recent inspections by Agency officials, the number of centrifuges in operation at the underground Fordo facility could be rapidly doubled by the Iranian authorities from some 700 to around 1,400 (of a total 2,784 centrifuges). Following his re-election to the US presidency in early November, Obama had pledged that his Administration would seek to revive the stalled negotiations between Iran and the international negotiators early in his second term so that a diplomatic solution to the escalating crisis could be found. There was also speculation in the US media that Iranian and US officials might be prepared to begin direct talks on the nuclear issue, although in early February 2013 Ayatollah Khamenei reportedly rejected the offer of such talks. Jalili had, in early January, stated Iran's willingness in principle to resume negotiations with the P5+1 group towards the end of that month; however, the talks were subsequently postponed until February. Further talks duly took place in Almatı, Kazakhstan, in late February. It was reported that the P5+1 group had presented an offer to remove some economic sanctions currently imposed on Iran in return for the suspension of uranium enrichment activity at the Fordo plant. However, despite the meeting being described as 'useful', no agreement was reached. Meanwhile, in mid-January IAEA officials resumed their discussions with their Iranian counterparts, amid growing frustration over the Iranian authorities' refusal to allow them access to Parchin, a military complex close to Tehran, where it was alleged that research into parts used in the manufacture of nuclear weapons had taken place; in March the head of the Agency declared that it would need 'convincing proof' from the IAEA before allowing inspectors to enter the complex. Following a round of expert level talks in İstanbul in March the EU announced that it had issued a series of proposals to Iran designed to end the stand-off. Iran submitted its own proposals at a meeting in Almatı in April; Ashton described the talks as constructive, while acknowledging that the two sides remained 'far apart'.

In June 2013, following initial denials by the Iranian authorities that a series of earthquakes in April and May had caused any damage, it was announced that cracks had appeared in one section of the Bushehr power plant. An earthquake in November was reported to have passed without causing further damage. In August President Rouhani appointed Ali Akbar Salehi as head of the Atomic Energy Organization (see Recent Developments). At the end of the month the UN announced that Iran had increased its nuclear capacity, having completed the installation of a further 1,000 advanced uranium enrichment centrifuges. In September Rouhani announced that nuclear negotiations would be led by the Ministry of Foreign Affairs, in place of the SNSC, which was under the control of Khamenei, thus allowing Rouhani greater influence over Iran's stance in the talks. Iran presented a new set of proposals specifying an 'endgame' to the dispute at a round of talks with the P5+1 group in Geneva in November. Although the position of neither side was made public, it was reported that the P5+1 negotiators' demand for the suspension of construction at Arak was the most contentious, with France in particular pursuing a hard line on the issue. Despite the talks being extended, no deal was reached. On 11 November, however, Iran and the IAEA reached an agreement on future co-operation that would allow the IAEA to send inspectors to the Arak site and the Gachin uranium mine. On 24 November Iran and the P5+1 group announced an interim agreement whereby Iran pledged to halt all uranium enrichment above 5% and to neutralize its existing stock of nearly 20% enriched uranium to below 5%. In addition, Iran pledged not to install new centrifuges for enrichment or to commission the Arak reactor, while also permitting the strict monitoring of its programme. For its part, the P5+1 agreed to relieve some US $7,200m. of economic sanctions, primarily pertaining to the trading of gold and precious metals, and the petrochemical and automobile sectors. Sanctions would also be eased on the purchase of aircraft components. It was envisaged that implementation of the interim agreement would begin in January 2014 and that a final, comprehensive agreement would be concluded by the end of July. An IAEA monitoring team duly arrived in Tehran in January. Iran subsequently began disabling centrifuges at two of its nuclear facilities and later that month the technical points of contention that remained, including those regarding the order in which sanctions should be revoked and uranium enrichment slowed down, were resolved following two days of talks in Geneva. Preliminary negotiations on a final settlement began in Vienna in mid-February, in advance of a meeting between the senior negotiators in late March.

Foreign Affairs

Relations with the USA

Relations with the USA since the end of the Iran–Iraq War have continued to be characterized by mutual suspicion. In April 1995 US efforts to isolate Iran internationally culminated in the announcement that all US companies and their overseas subsidiaries would be banned from investing in, or trading with, Iran (with the subsequent exception of US oil companies in the Caucasus and Central Asia involved in marketing petroleum from the countries of the former USSR). In mid-1996 the US Congress approved legislation (termed the Iran-Libya Sanctions Act—ILSA) to penalize companies operating in US markets that were investing US $40m. (subsequently amended to $20m.) or more in energy projects in prescribed countries deemed to be sponsoring terrorism. However, these 'secondary' economic sanctions received little international support.

A notable development following Khatami's election to the Iranian presidency in mid-1997 was the designation by the USA, in October, of the opposition Mujahidin-e-Khalq as one of 30 proscribed terrorist organizations. (The Mujahidin-e-Khalq's parent organization, the National Council of Resistance of Iran, also based in France, was proscribed by the USA in October 1999.) In December 1997 Khatami expressed his desire to engage in a 'thoughtful dialogue' with the American people, and in the following month publicly advocated the development of closer cultural links between Iran and the USA. However, the announcement, in July 1998, that Iran had successfully test-fired a new ballistic missile, the *Shahab-3*, capable of striking targets at a distance of 1,300 km (thus potentially Israel or US forces in the Gulf), caused renewed tensions. US concerns regarding what it perceived as Iran's efforts to acquire weapons of mass destruction remained a principal cause of mutual suspicion.

Addressing the American-Iranian Council in Washington, DC, USA, in March 2000, US Secretary of State Madeleine Albright announced an end to restrictions on imports from Iran of several non-hydrocarbons items. This substantive step towards the normalization of relations was in recognition of what the US Administration under President Bill Clinton regarded as trends towards democracy under President Khatami. Albright furthermore offered what amounted to an apology for the role played by the USA in the coup of 1953, as well as for US support for Iraq in the Iran–Iraq War. Relations between Iran and the USA deteriorated in June 2001 after 14 men (13 Saudi Arabians and one Lebanese) were indicted *in absentia* by the US Government, having been charged in connection with the bomb attack at al-Khobar, Saudi Arabia in 1996 (see Regional relations). US officials reiterated allegations that members of the Iranian Government were behind the bombing. In August 2001 the new Administration of President George W. Bush, inaugurated in January, confirmed that ILSA was to be extended for a further five years. However, in March 2005 President Bush announced a series of economic incentives, including the withdrawal of its veto on Iran's membership of the World Trade Organization (WTO), provided that Iran agreed permanently to suspend its nuclear energy programme. Subsequently, with Iran still at that time maintaining the suspension of its nuclear activities, a working party concerning Iran's WTO application was established, although accession negotiations had not begun by early 2014.

President Khatami offered his condolences to the USA following the suicide attacks in New York and Washington, DC, on 11 September 2001. Although Ayatollah Khamenei also condemned the terrorist attacks, he and Iran's 'conservative' press warned against any large-scale US military offensive targeting the Taliban regime and militants of the radical Islamist al-Qa'ida network—widely believed to have perpetrated the attacks—in Afghanistan. In 2002 the Iranian administration denied accusations by the USA that it was permitting fleeing al-Qa'ida and Taliban fighters to cross the Afghan border into Iran. Relations deteriorated abruptly in January, when, in his annual State of the Union address, the US President referred to Iran as forming (together with Iraq and the Democratic People's Republic of Korea—North Korea) an 'axis of evil', explicitly accusing Iran of aggressively pursuing the development of weapons of mass destruction and of 'exporting terror'. Khatami accused his US counterpart of 'warmongering', and in May urged reformist deputies in the Majlis not to attempt to hold discussions with US officials. Meanwhile, the US Department of State again designated Iran as the world's 'most active' sponsor of terrorism (as the country was also termed during 2003–12). President Khatami, for his part, openly condemned US plans to use military force to bring about 'regime change' in Iraq, warning that such action posed a serious risk to regional stability. The announcement made by Iranian officials in February 2003 that the country was to extract recently discovered deposits of uranium in order to produce nuclear fuel heightened fears within the US Administration that Iran was secretly involved in the manufacture of nuclear weapons.

Iran had been host to many Iraqi groups-in-exile, most notably the Shi'a-dominated Supreme Council for the Islamic Revolution in Iraq (renamed the Islamic Supreme Council of Iraq in 2007) and its military wing, the Badr Brigade (subsequently renamed the Badr Organization). Therefore, following the conflict in Iraq which began in March 2003 and the removal from power of President Saddam Hussain by the US-led coalition in April, the US Administration warned Iran not to meddle in Iraqi affairs, fearing that the Iranian leadership sought a political settlement that would favour the Shi'a Muslim majority and lead to the formation of a Shi'ite bloc in the Middle East antipathetic to US interests. However, in May it became necessary for the USA and Iran to instigate UN-sponsored talks in Geneva to discuss the return of Iraqi exiles and refugees in Iran, as well as the presence in Iraq of the Mujahidin-e-Khalq and its military wing, the National Liberation Army (NLA—see Regional relations). The talks collapsed after Ayatollah Khamenei described them as 'tantamount to surrender', and when US officials accused Iran of interfering in Iraqi internal affairs and of sheltering al-Qa'ida militants suspected of masterminding suicide bombings at expatriate compounds in Saudi Arabia, earlier that month.

After a devastating earthquake in the city of Bam in December 2003, the US Administration agreed to ease financial sanctions and restrictions on the export of technical apparatus to Iran in order to facilitate the reconstruction process. In April 2004 Iranian officials rejected suggestions that the USA had asked Iran for assistance in its struggle to defeat the insurgency in Iraq or that any Iranian element was supporting the radical Shi'a movement led by Hojatoleslam Muqtada al-Sadr. An Iranian diplomatic mission, supposedly dispatched upon the request of the United Kingdom to mediate between US troops and al-Sadr's forces around the Iraqi city of Najaf, was withdrawn following the assassination of the first secretary of the Iranian embassy in Baghdad. In July Iran criticized the USA's decision to declare a group of 3,800 members of the Mujahidin-e-Khalq interned in Iraq to be protected persons under the Geneva Convention, although US officials emphasized that they would not protect any individuals suspected of carrying out terrorist attacks. The introduction to the US Senate in August of the Iran Freedom and Support Act of 2004, which was designed to promote 'regime change' in Iran and to provide US $10m. in support of pro-democracy opposition groups, was seen as further evidence of the desire of President Bush's Administration to use military force against Iran. Meanwhile, despite its vehement opposition to the US-led invasion and occupation of Iraq, the Iranian regime undoubtedly benefited from the success of Shi'a parties in the elections to Iraq's new permanent legislature in December 2005.

The election of the 'ultra-conservative' Mahmoud Ahmadinejad to the Iranian presidency in June 2005 caused concern in US political circles. Rumours circulated in the US media that Ahmadinejad had, as a student, been involved in the taking of hostages at the US embassy in Tehran in 1979, although the Iranian Government denied the allegations. Bilateral tensions also increased markedly as a result of Iran's resumption of uranium enrichment. In May 2006 President Ahmadinejad sent an 18-page letter to Bush, proposing 'new solutions' for the two states to settle their differences. The letter, which was dismissed by US officials, was reported to be the first direct communication between an Iranian President and his US counterpart since the 1979 Islamic Revolution. In September 2006 the US Administration blacklisted the state-owned Bank Saderat Iran, following accusations that the bank was involved in the transfer of money to terrorist organizations, including Hezbollah in Lebanon.

In January 2007 US troops detained five Iranians during a raid on an Iranian liaison office in the northern Iraqi town of Irbil (Arbil). The USA accused the officials of being linked to the Revolutionary Guards, whom they alleged to be training insurgents within Iraq. The Iranian Government, for its part, accused the USA of having made illegal arrests, stating that, since the liaison office was in the process of being registered as a consulate, the officials enjoyed diplomatic immunity. Also in January the US Administration froze the assets of Iran's Bank Sepah, accusing the bank of acting as the conduit for an agreement with a North Korean organization that allegedly provided missile technology to Iran. Yet, despite the considerable tension in Iranian–US relations during mid-2007, exacerbated by military exercises being carried out by US naval forces in the Gulf, three rounds of direct talks concerning the sectarian conflict in Iraq were held by the US and Iranian ambassadors to Baghdad. (These discussions were halted by Iran in May 2008, in response to a recent operation by US and Iraqi forces against Shi'a militias in Iraq.)

After the inauguration of Barack Obama as US President in late January 2009, President Ahmadinejad stated in early February that he was willing to enter into a dialogue with the new US Administration provided that such a dialogue was based on 'mutual respect'. Later that month the Turkish Prime Minister, Recep Tayyip Erdoğan, claimed that Iran had sought Turkey's intervention as a mediator in future negotiations with the USA. President Obama had indicated during his election campaign that his Administration would be far more open to constructive discussions with Iran than had the Bush Administration. Nevertheless, the USA continued to view Iran as a threat to its national security and extended the sanctions against the Islamic regime for another year from mid-March.

President Obama condemned the violent repression of demonstrators during the unrest that followed the presidential election in June 2009 and rejected persistent allegations that the USA was complicit in fomenting the unrest. However, his Administration continued to pursue a policy of engagement with Iran and did not dispute the legitimacy of Ahmadinejad's presidency. The USA's engagement policy was most evident in its participation in direct negotiations over Iran's nuclear programme, initiated in October, during which US and Iranian officials held their most senior-level summit since the Islamic Revolution. However, from late 2009, following a lack of progress in the nuclear talks, the Obama Administration actively campaigned for a new package of UN Security Council sanctions against Iran. In February 2010 the US Administration extended its unilateral sanctions against businesses connected to the Revolutionary Guards. Meanwhile, earlier that month Gen. David Petraeus, Commander of the US Central Command, confirmed that the imminent deployment of major new US-manufactured missile defence systems in Bahrain, Kuwait, Qatar and the United Arab Emirates (UAE) was designed to counter the growing threat of a military conflict with Iran. Gen. Petraeus also revealed that US warships equipped with advanced anti-missile systems had been stationed in the Mediterranean and the Gulf. The USA imposed two further packages of unilateral sanctions against Iran in July and August, as bilateral relations continued to be dominated by US suspicions of a covert Iranian nuclear agenda and objections to Iranian interference in Iraq.

In early October 2011 the US Administration accused Iran of having plotted to assassinate Saudi Arabia's ambassador to Washington, DC, and to have planned to detonate bombs at the embassies of both Saudi Arabia and Israel in the US capital; Iranian officials strongly rejected the claims. Following further suggestions by the IAEA that Iran might have a covert nuclear agenda, in late November the USA extended its bilateral sanctions to target firms engaged in business deals with the Iranian oil and petrochemical sectors. Although the Obama Administration was keen to continue pursuing diplomatic means as a way of pressurizing the regime into changing its nuclear policy, some US officials appeared unwilling to rule out the possibility that the USA would engage in military action should Iran persist with the programme's rapid expansion. Further sanctions imposed at the end of 2011 were intended to make it harder for Iran to sell petroleum by placing restrictions on foreign companies that engage in business with the Central Bank. The Central Bank sanctions were further expanded in February 2012, while President Obama also announced a freeze on all Iranian government assets in the USA. Specific sanctions were imposed on Iran's Ministry of Intelligence, which was alleged by the US Administration to be sponsoring militant Islamist groups and violating Iranians' human rights. Meanwhile, in early 2012 the USA twice sent an aircraft carrier through the Strait of Hormuz, in an apparent gesture of defiance in response to Iran's recent threats that it would close the vital transit route. Sanctions introduced in June sought to prevent foreign companies from assisting Iran in defying the embargo on oil and petrochemical exports; an Iraqi and a Chinese bank were reported to have been included in the new measures. By late September, as the likelihood of Israel launching a pre-emptive military strike against Iran's nuclear facilities was thought to be increasing, the US Administration had sent a significant number of military vessels to the Gulf. In that month naval forces from some 25 countries—including the USA, the United Kingdom, Saudi Arabia and the UAE—held large-scale naval exercises to prepare for a possible Iranian retaliation in the form of closing the Strait of Hormuz.

In the run-up to the 2013 presidential election, Hassan Rouhani expressed his willingness to establish direct relations with the USA. In late August, following the release of declassified documents of the US Central Intelligence Agency, the Majlis approved a bill requiring the Iranian Government to sue the USA over its role, along with the British intelligence services, in the overthrow of Muhammad Mussadeq in 1953. In November 2013 the Obama Administration successfully persuaded the US Congress to reject a proposal by some of its members to impose further sanctions, citing the potential of such measures to undermine the USA's position in negotiations over the nuclear issue. (For further details of Iranian–US relations, see The Nuclear Issue.)

Regional relations

In October 2000 Kamal Kharrazi became the first Iranian Minister of Foreign Affairs to visit Iraq for a decade, and the two countries agreed to reactivate a 1975 border and security agreement that had been in abeyance since 1980. However, tensions between the two sides increased in April 2001, when Iran launched a heavy missile attack against Iraqi military bases used by the Mujahidin-e-Khalq, apparently in response to repeated attacks by the armed opposition group on Iranian targets. By early 2002 a general thaw in bilateral relations was evident, despite a protest lodged with the UN by Iraq in June stating that Iran was continuing to violate agreements reached at the end of the Iran–Iraq War.

Following the removal from power of the Iraqi regime under Saddam Hussain by the US-led coalition in early 2003, large numbers of Iraqis-in-exile returned to their homeland. Indeed, the UN High Commissioner for Refugees (UNHCR) estimated that, by December 2004, an estimated 107,000 Iraqi refugees—more than one-half of the pre-conflict total in Iran—had returned home; a further 56,000 returned to Iraq in 2005. After US-led coalition aircraft had launched attacks against training camps of the NLA, in April 2003 the Mujahidin-e-Khalq and its military wing (which had been based in Iraq since 1986) agreed a ceasefire with the occupying forces in Iraq, a move that was condemned by Iran. In November 2005 President Jalal Talabani became the first Iraqi head of state for over 30 years to visit Iran, and a high-profile reciprocal visit by President Ahmadinejad to Iraq in March 2008 was hailed by the Iranian President as heralding the start of a new era in bilateral relations. In November Iran and Iraq exchanged the remains of 241 troops (200 Iraqi, 41 Iranian) killed in the 1980–88 conflict. However, in December 2009 the Iraqi Government accused Iranian troops of occupying a section of the al-Fakkah oilfield in south-eastern Iraq. Moreover, following Iraq's legislative elections of March 2010, Iran was accused of interference in the protracted negotiations to form a new coalition government in order to guarantee the success of certain Shi'a parties. In December 2011 an agreement was reached between the Iraqi Government and the UN whereby some 3,000 members of the Mujahidin-e-Khalq who had been living at Camp Ashraf near Baghdad would be relocated to enable officials to verify their refugee status. In September 2012 the US Department of State formally removed the Mujahidin-e-Khalq from its list of proscribed terrorist organizations, in recognition of the group's decision to renounce violence. In July 2013 Iran and Iraq signed an agreement whereby Iran was to supply natural gas via a new pipeline to Basra province over four years. The value of the agreement to Iran was estimated at some US $3,700m. per year. In March 2014 Iranian officials indicated that exports would commence by the middle of that year. Meanwhile, in September 2013 some 52 members of the Mujahidin-e-Khalq were killed in an attack on Camp Ashraf. It was alleged by the residents of the camp—whose number had earlier been estimated at around 100—that Iraqi security forces had carried out the attack, although the Iraqi authorities denied involvement, claiming that the deaths had occurred during a dispute among the camp's residents.

Amid the continuing international disquiet over the country's nuclear ambitions in recent years, Iran has fuelled further outrage by its frequent statements about Israel and the Holocaust. Remarks by President Ahmadinejad in October 2005, in which he reiterated the demand of Ayatollah Khomeini that Israel be 'wiped off the map', were condemned in a statement by the UN Security Council. Subsequent public statements by Ahmadinejad in December, to the effect that the Holocaust was a 'fabrication' and that the Jewish state should be moved outside the Middle East, were similarly condemned by Israel, the USA and the EU as illustrating the dangers of allowing Iran to develop military nuclear capabilities. Hostility between Iran and Israel was exacerbated by the victory of Hamas in the Palestinian legislative elections of January 2006 and Iran's subsequent offer of financial support to the Hamas-led administration.

Iran was also viewed as having played a leading role in the conflict between Israel and the militant Lebanese organization Hezbollah in July–August 2006; however, while the Iranian leadership admitted its support for Hezbollah, it denied that Iran was providing the group with military assistance. In November a spokesman from the Iranian Ministry of Foreign Affairs warned that any pre-emptive military strikes launched by Israel against Iran's nuclear facilities would be met with a swift and powerful military response. In July 2008 the Iranian regime apparently responded to Israeli military exercises being held over the Mediterranean Sea by conducting a series of missile tests, which included testing a new *Shahab-3* ballistic missile. A new long-range missile, the *Sajjil*, was test-fired by Iran in November, and further tests conducted in May 2009 demonstrated that the country possessed missiles with sufficient range to target Israel and the USA's military bases in the region.

Meanwhile, following his appointment as Prime Minister of Israel in February 2009, Binyamin Netanyahu indicated that significant progress in the stalled Middle East peace process would not be possible until the threat posed by Iran's nuclear programme had been negated. In November it was announced that Israeli forces had intercepted a cargo ship in the Mediterranean Sea, en route to Syria, which Israel claimed was carrying a large consignment of Iranian armaments destined for Hezbollah militants in Lebanon. During his first official visit to Lebanon in October 2010, President Ahmadinejad provoked controversy—both within Israel and among members of Lebanon's pro-Western coalition Government—by visiting towns near the country's border with Israel, where fighting had been most intense during the war between Israel and Hezbollah in 2006.

Iran has accused Israel's external intelligence service, Mossad, of being responsible—together with the USA's Central Intelligence Agency and the British Secret Intelligence Service—for the actual and attempted assassinations of several of its leading nuclear scientists. For example, Mostafa Ahmadi-Roshan, who worked at the Natanz nuclear plant, was killed in a car bomb explosion in Tehran in January 2012. In mid-February a spokesman for Iran's Ministry of Foreign Affairs denied allegations by Netanyahu that Iran and Hezbollah were jointly responsible for a bomb attack in the Indian capital, New Delhi, and an attempted bombing in the Georgian capital, Tbilisi; in both cases, Israeli diplomats were the apparent targets. Police in the Thai capital, Bangkok, also accused Iran of being behind the attempted assassination of two Israeli diplomats on the following day. A suicide bombing carried out on a bus in Bulgaria in July, in which five Israeli tourists and a Bulgarian died, was similarly blamed on Iran and Hezbollah; a report published by Bulgarian investigators in January 2013 found that at least two of the three men suspected of carrying out the attack were connected to Hezbollah. During 2012 there were growing international concerns that, should the expansion of Iran's nuclear programme continue at such a rapid rate—with the possibility of development of an atomic bomb potentially only a few months away—Israel might launch unilateral pre-emptive military action against Iran. Netanyahu reiterated his Government's stance that Israel had the right to take such action in the interests of national security, urging other Governments attending the UN General Assembly in New York in September to ensure that a 'red line' would not be crossed as far as Iran's potential development of a nuclear bomb was concerned, although US President Barack Obama was known to favour delaying any military action until all diplomatic means had been exhausted. In September 2013, during an address to the UN General Assembly, President Rouhani condemned the Holocaust as a 'reprehensible crime', prompting hopes among some observers of a relaxation of tensions on the part of Iran. In March 2014, however, the interception of a ship in the Red Sea by Israeli security forces provoked further tension. It was claimed by Israel that the ship had been transporting surface-to-air missiles and other materiel from Iran, bound ultimately for use by Islamic Jihad and other Palestinian militant groups in the Gaza Strip. Iran denied any knowledge of the shipment.

Despite Iran's extremely close relationship with Syria and its military and financial support for the regime of President Bashar al-Assad, President Ahmadinejad surprised many in the West by urging Assad, in September 2011, to end the violence being perpetrated by Syrian government forces in their crackdown on the political uprising against Assad's rule, and to begin talks with representatives of the Syrian opposition. However, in September 2012 the Commander of Iran's Revolutionary Guards, Brig.-Gen. Muhammad Ali Jafari, admitted publicly that some members of the Guards' élite Qods Force were assisting President Assad's forces in their efforts to halt the anti-Government rebellion. This admission confirmed long-held fears among Western governments that the civil conflict in Syria was developing into a proxy war between those countries that were continuing to support the Syrian regime—such as Russia and Iran—and those that were providing military support to the opposition forces—namely the USA's and EU's regional allies Saudi Arabia, Qatar and Turkey. At a summit meeting of the Non-Aligned Movement held in Tehran at the end of August 2012, during which the newly elected President of Egypt, President Muhammad Mursi, became the first Egyptian head of state to visit Iran since 1979, many of the leaders in attendance (including Mursi) expressed support for the rebellion against Assad's rule. In November 2013 it was reported that hundreds of Iranians were fighting in Syria in support of President Assad's regime. At the end of that month some 25 people were killed in a suicide bomb attack outside the Iranian embassy in Beirut. Responsibility for the attack was claimed by a Sunni militant group, the Abdullah Azzam Brigades, which was thought to have been involved in other attacks against both Iranian and Lebanese Shi'a interests, amid fears that the Syria conflict was becoming increasingly characterized by sectarian divisions and was spreading into neighbouring states. Despite expressions of support for Assad by President Rouhani following his election, in January 2014 the Iranian Government was formally invited to participate in the Syrian peace talks in Geneva under UN auspices. On the conclusion of that round of talks, it was announced that an understanding had been reached that the goal of the negotiations would be to establish a transitional governing body in Syria, an objective that Iran had previously been opposed to on the grounds that it was likely to exclude Assad.

Relations between Iran and Saudi Arabia were frequently strained after the Islamic Revolution of 1979. A period of particularly hostile relations, following the deaths of 275 Iranian pilgrims as a result of clashes with Saudi security forces in the Islamic holy city of Mecca during the *Hajj* (annual pilgrimage) in July 1987, culminated in the suspension of diplomatic relations in April 1988. Links were not restored until March 1991. Allegations of Iranian involvement in the bombing of a US military housing complex at al-Khobar, Saudi Arabia, in June 1996 again strained relations. However, the installation of a new Iranian Government in August 1997 facilitated further rapprochement, perhaps reflecting the desire of the two countries, as the region's principal petroleum producers, to co-operate in maintaining world oil prices and in efforts to curtail over-production by members of the Organization of the Petroleum Exporting Countries (OPEC). An Iranian delegation led by former President Rafsanjani began a 10-day visit to Saudi Arabia in February 1998, at the end of which the formation of a joint ministerial committee for bilateral relations was announced. Several co-operation agreements were subsequently signed, including a Saudi-Iranian security accord in April 2001. During late 2003 Iran countered US accusations that certain suspected al-Qa'ida militants who remained in Iranian custody had been involved in plotting suicide attacks against expatriate compounds in Riyadh in May.

In March 2007 President Ahmadinejad undertook his first state visit to Saudi Arabia, where he held discussions with King Abdullah; the two leaders were apparently seeking to demonstrate that perceived differences between their countries as a result of recent sectarian tensions in Iraq and Lebanon had been exaggerated. Nevertheless, Saudi officials have outlined their opposition to Iran's nuclear activities, expressing deep concerns regarding regional security, and have warned that Saudi Arabia would also seek to develop a nuclear weapons capability should it be discovered that Iran had done so. Diplomatic relations were damaged following the dispatch by the Cooperation Council of the Arab States of the Gulf (Gulf Cooperation Council—GCC) of a contingent of (principally Saudi) military forces to assist the Sunni Muslim authorities in Bahrain in quelling the largely Shi'a anti-Government protests which erupted there in February 2011. Saudi Arabia, for its part, accused Iran of being behind much of the unrest in Bahrain. Bilateral tensions have also been heightened by the ongoing conflict between government and opposition forces in Syria, with Iran continuing to support the Assad regime and Saudi Arabia providing military assistance to the anti-Government rebels. Moreover, the Saudi Government has accused the Iranian authorities of encouraging dissent among its Shi'a minority, who staged several anti-Government demonstrations in Saudi Arabia's Eastern Province during 2011–12.

Both the Khatami and Ahmadinejad administrations have sought improved relations with Saudi Arabia's fellow members of the GCC, although a long-standing territorial dispute with the UAE remains unresolved. In March 1992 Iran occupied those parts of Abu Musa island and the Greater and Lesser Tunbs that had remained under the control of the emirate of Sharjah since the original occupation in 1971. In December 1994 the UAE announced its intention to refer the dispute to the International Court of Justice (ICJ) in The Hague, Netherlands. In June 1997, after Iran had in 1996 opened an airport on Abu Musa and a power station on Greater Tunb, the UAE complained to the UN about Iran's construction of a pier on Greater Tunb; UAE officials protested that Iran was repeatedly violating the emirates' territorial waters. During the 2000s the UAE remained an important trading partner of Iran and, although both countries continued to assert their sovereignty over the three disputed areas—with Iran angering the UAE leadership by establishing two maritime offices on Abu Musa in August 2008—political relations generally improved. Reports in July 2010 that the UAE's ambassador to the USA, Yousuf al-Otaiba, had appeared to encourage the idea of a pre-emptive US military strike against Iran in order to prevent the Islamic regime from building a nuclear weapon precipitated a deterioration in diplomatic relations. Difficulties persisted in 2011–12, amid allegations of Iranian meddling in Bahrain and the UAE's support for the international sanctions imposed against Iran; however, joint economic initiatives continued to be pursued. In April 2012 the UAE withdrew its ambassador from Tehran in protest against a controversial visit by President Ahmadinejad to Abu Musa, which holds a strategic location in the Strait of Hormuz, during which he revived Iran's historical claim of ownership over the island. Iranian military officials subsequently declared that the regime would be prepared to defend Abu Musa by force if the ongoing dialogue at the ICJ failed to resolve the dispute; in November Iran was reported to have opened a new naval base close to the island.

Victories achieved by the Sunni fundamentalist Taliban in the Afghan civil war in September 1996 prompted Iran, which supported the Government of President Burhanuddin Rabbani, to express fears for its national security, and to accuse the USA of interference in Afghanistan's internal affairs. In June 1997 the Taliban accused Iran of espionage, and ordered the closure of the Iranian embassy in Kabul and the withdrawal of all Iranian diplomats. Iran retaliated by halting all trade across its land border with Afghanistan. In September 1998, as it emerged that nine Iranian diplomats missing since August had been murdered by Taliban militia as they stormed the city of Mazar-i-Sharif, 500,000 Iranian troops were reportedly placed on full alert in readiness for open conflict with Afghanistan. In an attempt to defuse the crisis, in October the Taliban agreed to free all Iranian prisoners being held in Afghanistan and to punish those responsible for the killing of the nine diplomats. Following the suicide attacks on the USA in September 2001, as the USA began preparations for military action against al-Qa'ida and its Taliban hosts, Iran closed its eastern border with Afghanistan and sent a large contingent of troops there in order to prevent a further influx of Afghan refugees. In October, however, when the US-led military action began, Iran reportedly agreed to the establishment of eight refugee camps within its borders to provide shelter for some 250,000 Afghan refugees. Although Iran refused to give military assistance to the US-led coalition, it actively supported the Western-backed opposition forces, collectively known as the United National Islamic Front for the Salvation of Afghanistan (the Northern Alliance), and welcomed their swift victory over the Taliban.

A programme allowing for voluntary repatriations of Afghan refugees under the auspices of UNHCR was inaugurated by the Iranian and Afghan authorities in April 2002, although UNHCR put the number of 'spontaneous' repatriations prior to that date at 57,000. At the end of 2003, according to data published by UNHCR, the number of refugees in Iran was 984,896, of whom 834,699 were from Afghanistan and 150,196 from Iraq. More than 1.5m. Afghan refugees in Iran were estimated by UNHCR to have returned to Afghanistan by November 2005. By the end of 2011 the total number of refugees in Iran had fallen slightly, to 882,700; those fleeing Afghanistan (840,200) now accounted for virtually all of the refugees, with the number of Iraqis totalling 42,500. In August 2002 President Khatami became the first Iranian head of state to visit Afghanistan for 40 years. In June 2011 Brig.-Gen. Ahmad Vahidi, the Minister of Defence and Armed Forces Logistics, undertook an historic visit to Kabul for discussions with his Afghan counterpart, as the Afghan Government was preparing to assume control of some aspects of national security in advance of the planned departure of all foreign forces by the end of 2014. In August 2013 activists in the western Afghan province of Herat protested against what they claimed was Iranian interference in the region. The following month a protest against visa delays outside the Iranian consulate in Herat turned violent; at least one person was killed.

Closer relations were developed with Turkey during the 1990s, despite periodic tensions arising, particularly from Turkish allegations of Iranian support for the Kurdish separatist Kurdistan Workers' Party (Partiya Karkeren Kurdistan—PKK) in its conflict with the armed forces in south-eastern Turkey. In 1997 Iran was a founder member of the Developing Eight (D-8) group of Islamic countries, based in İstanbul. In May 2004 Tehran's Imam Khomeini International Airport, which the Turkish-led consortium Tepe-Akfen-Vie (TAV) was contracted to operate, was closed by the Revolutionary Guards after only one flight had landed because it was seen as a danger to national security, and apparently owing to Iran's hostility towards Turkey for its links with Israel and the USA. The airport reopened in May 2005, following complex negotiations that reportedly resulted in TAV rescinding control of operations to IranAir. Since 2010 the Turkish Government has played a more significant role in attempts to resolve the dispute between Iran and Western countries concerning Iran's nuclear programme, even hosting formal discussions in Istanbul between Iran and international negotiators in January 2011 and April 2012. Discussions concerning the signing of a preferential trade agreement between Iran and Turkey were reported to be at an advanced stage in November. However, tensions in the bilateral relationship were evident in the latter part of 2012 as a result of Iran's continued support for the Syrian regime under President Assad and Turkey's growing military assistance to Syrian opposition forces. In January 2014 Turkish premier Recep Tayyip Erdoğan visited Tehran, in an attempt to ease recent tensions between the two countries, capitalizing ostensibly upon the apparent rapprochement between Iran and Western governments over the Syrian conflict and the Iranian nuclear programme.

Meanwhile, considerable political and economic advantage has been perceived arising from Iran's potential as a transit route for hydrocarbons from the former Soviet republics of Central Asia, and since the early 1990s Iran has sought to strengthen its position in Central Asia through bilateral economic, security and cultural agreements as well as institutions such as the Tehran-based Economic Cooperation Organization. Relations between Iran and Azerbaijan—already tense owing to disagreement over a contested section of the Caspian Basin—deteriorated in July 2001, when Iran ordered a military patrol boat into the disputed waters in order to prevent foreign companies from undertaking oil exploration there. Subsequent meetings of the five littoral states (Iran, Russia, Azerbaijan, Kazakhstan and Turkmenistan) failed to resolve the dispute regarding the legal status of the Caspian. An improvement in relations between Iran and Azerbaijan was evident later in the decade, and moves towards the imposition of wider economic sanctions against Iran were of concern to Azerbaijan, owing to Iran's large ethnic Azeri population, as well as the energy agreements in place between the two countries. However, in February 2012 bilateral relations deteriorated after Azerbaijan announced that it was to purchase military equipment valued at some US $1,600m. from Israel. The following month the Azerbaijani Government denied international reports that it had agreed to allow the Israeli air force access to airfields within Azerbaijan in the event of Israeli military action against Iranian nuclear facilities. In early November 2013 Azerbaijan closed a section of its border with Iran following an incident in which an Azerbaijani government vehicle was reported to have been fired upon from the Iranian side of the border; Iran reciprocated later that month with the closure of two further crossings.

Other external relations

The EU pursued a policy of 'critical dialogue' with Iran during the 1990s, despite US pressure as well as tensions between Iran and certain EU states. Notably, a lengthy period of strained relations with the United Kingdom developed after Ayatollah Khomeini issued a *fatwa* (edict) in February 1989, imposing a death penalty against a British writer, Salman Rushdie, for material deemed offensive to Islam in his novel *The Satanic Verses*. 'Critical dialogue' was suspended in April 1997, after a German court ruled that the Iranian authorities had ordered the assassination of four prominent members of the dissident Democratic Party of Iranian Kurdistan in Berlin in September 1992. Germany withdrew its ambassador to Tehran (as did other EU members) and expelled four Iranian diplomats. In November 1997, following the inauguration of President Khatami, a compromise arrangement was finally reached allowing the readmission of all EU ambassadors, and in February 1998 EU foreign ministers agreed to resume senior-level ministerial contacts with Iran. Despite assurances given to the British Secretary of State for Foreign and Commonwealth Affairs, Robin Cook, in September by the Iranian Minister of Foreign Affairs that the Iranian Government had no intention of threatening the life of Rushdie or anyone associated with his work, 'conservative' clerics maintained that the *fatwa* issued by Ayatollah Khomeini was irrevocable, and the Qom-based 15 Khordad Foundation subsequently increased its financial reward offered for the writer's murder. President Khatami became the first Iranian head of state to visit the West since the Islamic Revolution when, in March 1999, he travelled to Italy and the Vatican. In December 2002 the EU commenced negotiations with Iran regarding a trade and co-operation agreement, with the stipulation that the accord be linked with consideration of political issues (notably human rights and terrorism).

A crisis erupted in relations with the United Kingdom in June 2004, when Iran captured three British patrol craft and detained eight Royal Navy personnel on the Shatt al-Arab waterway dividing Iran from Iraq. Iran asserted that the vessels had entered Iranian territorial waters, but the sailors, who were released four days later, alleged that they had been 'forcibly escorted' into Iranian waters. In October 2005, two years after the removal by the US-led coalition of Saddam Hussain's regime in Iraq, British officials accused the Iranians of supplying explosives to and running training camps for Iraqi Shi'a insurgents operating in the British-controlled region of southern Iraq. In March 2007 15 British Royal Navy and Royal Marines personnel were captured and detained by Iranian Revolutionary Guards while patrolling the Shatt al-Arab waterway. As in 2004, Iran claimed that the sailors had trespassed into Iranian territorial waters, and showed television footage of them in Tehran apparently admitting to their 'intrusion'; however, British naval officials insisted that the two crews were operating in Iraqi waters at the time of their arrest. Following discussions between Iranian and British officials in April 2007, the 15 sailors were finally released from detention 13 days after their capture. President Ahmadinejad stated that he had granted them a pardon as a 'gift to the British people', while the British Government denied that a deal had been agreed with Iran to secure the sailors' release. However, several commentators noted that shortly before the pardon five diplomats who had been seized by US forces at the Iranian consulate in Arbil, Iraq, in January had been granted consular access; moreover, a senior diplomat at the Iranian embassy in Baghdad, who had been abducted by gunmen in February, had also recently been released.

Relations between Iran and the United Kingdom deteriorated in the aftermath of the disputed Iranian presidential election in June 2009. The Iranian authorities alleged that British agents had travelled to Iran prior to the election to plan civil unrest, and that the British Broadcasting Corporation's Persian-language service had encouraged protests against the result of the election. Following allegations that they had engaged in activities 'inconsistent with their diplomatic status', two British diplomats were expelled from Iran on 22 June. The British Government retaliated with the expulsion of two Iranian diplomats. On 27 June nine Iranian employees from the British embassy in Tehran were arrested for their alleged role in the post-election unrest. Although by mid-July all had been released from custody, trial proceedings subsequently began against one senior employee, political counsellor Hossein Rassam. During a court hearing in early August, he reportedly admitted collecting and distributing information on the post-election unrest. The hearing was one of a series of mass trials of political prisoners that took place during August, which were described as 'show trials' by international observers. In October Rassam was convicted of espionage and fomenting unrest, and sentenced to four years' imprisonment; however, following an appeal, his prison term was commuted to a suspended sentence in October 2010.

Amid an intensification of the dispute concerning Iran's nuclear programme during 2011, the EU continued to extend its list of Iranian individuals and companies whose assets were frozen. On 29 November, two days after Iranian legislators voted to downgrade Iran's diplomatic ties with the United Kingdom, hundreds of Iranian demonstrators attacked the British embassy in Tehran to protest against the imposition by the British Government on 22 November of further economic sanctions—which included a virtual ban on British banks doing business with Iranian banks and on firms involved in Iran's energy sector. This followed the IAEA's strongly worded report detailing suspicions that Iran was engaged in the development of a nuclear weapons programme (see The Nuclear Issue). In response, on 30 November the United Kingdom closed its embassy, ordered all British diplomatic staff to leave Iran, and gave Iranian diplomats in London two days to leave the country. The British Government expressed outrage that the Iranian authorities had not prevented the protesters from entering the embassy compound. On 23 January 2012 the EU (which accounts for some 20% of Iranian oil exports) banned imports of crude petroleum from the Islamic Republic with effect from 1 July; existing agreements were to be honoured until that date. The Union also froze assets belonging to the Central Bank. The Iranian leadership warned that it would close the Strait of

Hormuz if the country was 'seriously threatened', and in February 2012 announced that it was ending all oil exports to the United Kingdom and France with immediate effect. In mid-October, after no breakthrough had been made in discussions between the international negotiating group and Iranian officials on how to resolve the nuclear crisis, EU member states introduced tougher sanctions against the Iranian regime. The measures included further asset freezes on Iranian companies, as well as a ban on imports of natural gas and on transactions with Iranian banks, unless these were for the purpose of providing food or medicines. In mid-March 2013 it was announced that the Iranian Government was in discussions with the United Kingdom regarding the resumption of consular activities between the two countries; representatives of both governments met at the nuclear talks in Geneva in October, following which it was announced that chargés d'affaires would be appointed. In December Iran's chargé d'affaires travelled to London to discuss the restoration of bilateral relations; a British delegation visited Tehran the following month. In September the European Court of Justice voted to reject sanctions imposed by the EU on a number of Iranian companies for their alleged links to Iran's nuclear energy programme.

In March 2001 Russia pledged to assist Iran with the completion of the nuclear plant at Bushehr (see The Nuclear Issue), and in May Russian officials reportedly agreed to supply Iran with advanced ship-borne cruise missiles. The two countries signed a military co-operation pact in October, believed to amount to annual sales to Iran of Russian weapons worth some US $300m. In July 2002 Russia and Iran concluded a draft 10-year development and co-operation accord, which was reported to include the construction of a further three nuclear reactors at Bushehr. Construction of the Bushehr plant was completed in October 2004, and in February 2005 Russia agreed to supply Iran with nuclear fuel for the plant; however, following international pressure, the deal required that Iran return to Russia spent fuel rods, which could be used to produce nuclear weapons, from the site. As the diplomatic crisis over Iran's nuclear programme intensified during that year, Russia developed an alternative proposal whereby the sensitive elements of Iran's nuclear programme, such as uranium enrichment, could be conducted on Russian territory; this proposal was rejected by the Iranian administration in early 2006.

It was reported in January 2007 that Russia had recently sold some 30 air defence missile systems to Iran, in a contract that was estimated to be worth US $700m. In March the Russian Government rejected a deadline by which it was to deliver nuclear fuel to the Bushehr plant, claiming that Iran had failed to make the requisite payments; Russia also warned Iran that it would continue to withhold the provision of fuel until Iran agreed to suspend uranium enrichment, as demanded by the UN Security Council. However, in October President Vladimir Putin expressed his opposition to any US-led military strike against Iran's nuclear facilities. The first shipment of Russian nuclear fuel to the Bushehr reactor arrived in December, after Russia and Iran had finally agreed on a timetable for completion of the project (for further details, see The Nuclear Issue). After a fourth round of UN sanctions were adopted against Iran in June 2010, the Russian Government declared that it was required, under the terms of Resolution 1929, to cancel the planned delivery of an *S-300* air defence missile system to the Iranian regime. By early 2012 senior Russian officials were expressing the view that any new sanctions imposed against Iran would merely harm the Iranian people rather than persuade the Government to end its nuclear programme. In January the two countries agreed henceforth to use their respective currencies, rather than the US dollar, for the purposes of bilateral trade. In July Iranian officials stated their intention to double the level of Iran's trade with Russia from the equivalent of US $4,000m. to $8,000m., and in February 2013 mutual pledges were made to increase co-operation in the fields of agriculture and energy.

Political and economic relations between Iran and China have been steadily improving in recent years. Iranian exports to the People's Republic (including oil exports) have risen considerably as Chinese demand has increased, and a growing number of Chinese companies are now investing in large-scale Iranian infrastructure projects, often replacing Western businesses which have withdrawn their interests as a consequence of sanctions imposed by the UN, the USA and the EU. Although China has voted for certain UN Security Council resolutions imposing stricter penalties against the Iranian regime, the Chinese have expressed support for Iran's right to develop a civil nuclear energy programme, and the official Chinese position is that negotiations and constructive dialogue are a more effective way of dealing with international concerns regarding the exact nature of Iranian nuclear ambitions. In 2009 China was reported to have become Iran's largest trading partner, with the value of bilateral trade estimated at US $21,200m. in that year, compared with a mere $400m. 15 years previously. In June 2012 China was among 20 oil importers that were given a temporary exemption from new US sanctions against foreign hydrocarbons firms which traded with Iran, provided that they purchased a reduced amount of the commodity.

Iran's relations with South and Central America grew in importance during 2006, not least owing to the election of new leaders in that region who shared President Ahmadinejad's hostility towards the US Administration under President Bush. In January 2007 Ahmadinejad embarked on a four-day tour of Venezuela—whose President, Hugo Chávez, had consistently supported Ahmadinejad's insistence on Iran's right to nuclear energy—together with Nicaragua, Ecuador and Bolivia. During Ahmadinejad's visit the Iranian delegation signed 11 bilateral agreements with its Venezuelan counterpart, with the aim of increasing the price of petroleum and furthering co-operation on energy, trade, industry and construction. The two leaders also agreed to expedite the creation of a US $2,000m. fund to invest in countries joining their anti-US alliance. A further 200 economic co-operation accords were signed when President Chávez visited Tehran in September 2009. During a tour of South American countries in November, President Ahmadinejad met with his Brazilian counterpart, Luiz Inácio Lula da Silva, in the Brazilian capital, Brasília. It was agreed to increase the volume of bilateral trade to some $25,000m. within the next five years. Following the death of Chávez in March 2013, Ahmadinejad attended the former President's funeral in the Venezuelan capital, Caracas.

CONSTITUTION AND GOVERNMENT

A draft constitution for the Islamic Republic of Iran was published on 18 June 1979. It was submitted to an Assembly of Experts, elected by popular vote on 3 August, to debate the various clauses and to propose amendments. The amended Constitution was approved by a referendum on 2–3 December 1979. A further 45 amendments to the Constitution were approved by a referendum on 28 July 1989.

Legislative power is vested in the Islamic Consultative Assembly (Majlis-e-Shura-e Islami), with 290 members. The chief executive of the administration is the President. The Majlis and the President are both elected by universal adult suffrage for a term of four years. There is no limit on the total number of terms a President may serve. However, no candidate may hold office for more than two consecutive terms. A 12-member Council of Guardians supervises elections and ensures that legislation is in accordance with the Constitution and with Islamic precepts. The Council to Determine the Expediency of the Islamic Order, created in February 1988 and formally incorporated into the Constitution in 1989, rules on legal and theological disputes between the Majlis and the Council of Guardians. In October 2005 the powers of the Expediency Council were extended, allowing it to supervise all branches of government. The executive, legislative and judicial wings of state power are subject to the authority of the Wali Faqih (supreme religious leader). Iran is divided into 30 provinces, each with an appointed Governor.

REGIONAL AND INTERNATIONAL CO-OPERATION

Iran became a member of the UN upon its foundation in October 1945. A working party was established in May 2005 to examine Iran's application to join the World Trade Organization (WTO); however, accession negotiations had not begun by early 2014. Iran is also a member of the Organization of Islamic Cooperation (OIC), of the Organization of the Petroleum Exporting Countries (OPEC), of the Developing Eight group of Islamic countries (D-8), and of the Group of 15 developing countries (G15). The headquarters of the Economic Cooperation Organization (ECO) are located in Tehran.

ECONOMIC AFFAIRS

In 2009, according to estimates by the World Bank, Iran's gross national income (GNI), measured at average 2007–09 prices, was US $330,400m., equivalent to $4,520 per head (or $11,380 per head on an international purchasing-power parity basis). During 2003–12, it was estimated, the population increased at an average annual rate of 1.2%, while gross domestic product (GDP) per head increased, in real terms, by an average of 3.3% per year during 2003–09. According to the Central Bank of Iran, overall GDP increased, in real terms, at an average annual rate of 3.6% between 2003/04 and 2012/13. GDP increased by a provisional 3.0% in 2011/12, but, largely owing to the impact of economic sanctions imposed on key sectors, declined by 5.8% in 2012/13 (Iranian year to March).

Agriculture (including forestry and fishing) contributed a provisional 11.4% of GDP in 2012/13. About 17.5% of the employed labour force were engaged in agriculture in the third quarter of 2013/14 (Iranian year to March), according to official estimates. The principal cash crops are fresh and dried fruit and nuts, which accounted for 6.5% of non-petroleum export earnings in 2011/12. Wheat, rice, sugar cane potatoes, sugar beet and barley are the main subsistence crops. Imports of cereals comprised some 4.9% of the value of total imports in 2011/12. Production of fruit and vegetables is also significant. According to the central bank, agricultural GDP increased by an average of 5.0% per year in 2001/02–10/11; the sector's GDP grew by 8.8% in 2010/11.

Industry (including manufacturing, construction and power, but excluding mining) contributed a provisional 21.6% of GDP in 2012/13, and, according to official estimates, engaged some 34.5% of the employed labour force in the third quarter of 2013/14. In 2001/02–10/11 industrial GDP increased by an average of 8.1% per year; growth was recorded at 9.2% in 2010/11, according to the central bank.

Mining (including petroleum-refining) contributed 22.7% of GDP in 2010/11, although the sector engaged only an estimated 0.5% of the working population in 2010. Metal ores are the major non-hydrocarbon mineral exports, and coal, magnesite and gypsum are also mined. The sector is dominated by the hydrocarbons sector, which contributed a provisional 17.2% of GDP in 2012/13. At the end of 2012 Iran's proven reserves of petroleum were estimated at 157,000m. barrels, sufficient to maintain the 2012 rate of production—estimated at 3.7m. barrels per day (b/d)—for more than 100 years. As a member of the Organization of the Petroleum Exporting Countries (OPEC, see p. 408), Iran is subject to production quotas agreed by the Organization's Conference. Iran's proven reserves of natural gas (33,620,000m. cu m at the end of 2012) are the second largest in the world, after those of Russia. Since late 2008 Iran, Russia and Qatar have increased their co-operation on gas projects. A deal was concluded in June 2010 for the construction of a pipeline, at a cost of US $7,600m., through which Iran would export natural gas from its South Pars offshore gasfield (an extension of Qatar's North Field) to Pakistan's southern provinces of Balochistan and Sindh. The project was officially inaugurated in March 2013, at which time the Iranian section of the pipeline was nearing completion. However, the Pakistani section was delayed until at least 2016 owing to financial difficulties. In July 2011 an agreement worth $10,000m. was signed by Iran, Iraq and Syria, involving the construction, by 2014–16, of a pipeline that would transport gas from the South Pars field to the latter countries and eventually via Lebanon to the Mediterranean Sea. The Iran–Iraq section of the pipeline was expected to be completed in 2014. According to the central bank, the GDP of the mining sector increased by an average of 3.0% per year in 2001/02–10/11; mining GDP declined by 3.6% in 2009/10, but increased by 2.6% in 2010/11.

Manufacturing (excluding petroleum-refining) contributed 11.4% of GDP in 2010/11, and engaged about 17.1% of the employed labour force in 2010. The most important sectors, in terms of value added, are textiles, food-processing and transport equipment. The sector's GDP increased by an average of 8.6% per year in 2001/02–10/11, growth of 10.0% was recorded in 2010/11, according to the central bank.

The construction sector contributed a provisional 4.8% of GDP in 2012/13, and engaged 13.7% of the employed labour force in 2010. The GDP of the sector increased at an average annual rate of 6.4% during 2001/02–10/11; the sector contracted by 4.9% in 2009/10, but expanded by 7.3% in 2010/11, according to the central bank.

Principal sources of energy are natural gas (providing around 66.8% of total electricity production in 2011) and petroleum (some 27.8% in the same year). Imports of mineral fuels and lubricants comprised just 1.4% of the value of total imports in 2011. The first phase of Iran's South Pars gasfield was brought on stream in 2004, and a total of 29 phases are planned. Gas reserves in the South Pars field are estimated at more than 14,000,000m. cu m, with a production capacity in late 2012 of 300m. cu m of gas per day.

The services sector contributed a provisional 49.9% of GDP in 2012/13, and engaged an estimated 48.0% of the employed labour force in the third quarter of 2013/14, according to official estimates. According to the Central Bank of Iran, during 2001/02 and 2010/11, the GDP of the services sector increased by an average of 5.3% per year; growth in the sector was about 4.0% in 2010/11.

According to preliminary figures from the Central Bank of Iran, in the year ending March 2013 Iran recorded a visible trade surplus of US $30,975m., and there was a surplus of $26,271m. on the current account of the balance of payments. In 2009/10 the principal source of imports was the United Arab Emirates (UAE, which supplied 29.3% of total imports); other major suppliers included the People's Republic of China, Germany and the Republic of Korea (South Korea). Iraq and China (taking 20.8% and 14.3%, respectively) were the principal market for Iranian exports in 2009/10; the UAE and India were also important export markets. Other than petroleum and natural gas, Iran's principal exports in 2011/12 were fruit and nuts, iron and steel, and carpets. Exports of petroleum and gas comprised 77.8% of the value of total exports in that year, according to preliminary figures. The principal imports in that year were machinery and transport equipment, basic manufactures, chemicals and related products, and food and live animals.

According to IMF estimates, the budget surplus for the financial year ending March 2011 totalled IR 71,049m. Iran's general government gross debt was IR 766,570,375m. in 2011, equivalent to 13.7% of GDP. Iran's total external debt was US $19,113m. at the end of 2011, of which $4,859m. was public and publicly guaranteed debt. The annual rate of inflation averaged 17.2% in 2003/04–12/13; consumer prices increased by an estimated average of 30.5% in 2012/13. According to the Central Bank, the rate of unemployment was 10.3% in the third quarter of 2012/13.

At the time of the presidential election in 2013, Iran's economy was facing a number of significant challenges, as weaknesses including the over-reliance on revenue from the petroleum sector, high rates of inflation and unemployment (at more than 24%) were compounded by the effects of the steadily tightening economic and technological sanctions imposed by the UN, the USA and the EU. Thus, while Iran possessed the world's second largest proven reserves of both crude oil and natural gas, new sanctions on its hydrocarbons industry required the Government to reduce its dependency on the sector, and to seek new export markets for its petroleum sales, offer attractive credit terms or use a bartering system. The EU, which accounted for some 20% of Iran's oil exports, banned the import of Iranian crude petroleum from July 2012, while other important markets also drastically reduced their import levels. The rapid decline in oil production and exports, the latter accounting for around 80% of foreign revenue, together with US and EU restrictions placed on firms dealing with Iran's financial institutions—including the Central Bank in late 2011 and early 2012—also had a dramatic impact on the value of Iran's currency. The rial reached a record low against the US dollar in early October 2012: it declined by 15% in a single day, and lost an estimated 50% of its value as a result of sanctions. Oil production, meanwhile, fell to 2.6m. b/d in 2013; its lowest rate since 1989. An average annual growth rate of 8% was projected in the Government's Fifth Five-Year Development Plan (2010–15). However, as the effects of the economic sanctions intensified, GDP growth rates remained below this target: the IMF recorded growth of only 2.0% in 2011, down from 5.9% in the previous year. In its World Economic Outlook, published in October 2013, the Fund estimated that GDP contracted by 1.5% in 2013. The election of Hassan Rouhani as President of Iran in June 2013, and the signing of an interim agreement on the country's nuclear programme in November between Iran and the P5+1 group of countries (which included the five permanent members of the UN Security Council—China, France, Russia, the United Kingdom and the USA—and Germany), went some way towards improving prospects for the economy. Exports of oil were expected to reach 1.4m. b/d in 2014, compared with 1.1m. b/d in 2013. The IMF forecast a return to GDP growth, at 1.3%, in 2014, while the rate of inflation was expected to be less than 30%. None the less, despite limited sanctions relief as a result of the November agreement, restrictions on oil exports and on the banking sector remained in place at March 2014, pending the conclusion of a permanent agreement.

PUBLIC HOLIDAYS

The Iranian year 1393 runs from 21 March 2014 to 20 March 2015, and the year 1394 from 21 March 2015 to 20 March 2016.

2015: 8 January (Birth of Prophet Muhammad and Birth of Imam Jafar Sadegh), 11 February (Victory of the Islamic Revolution), 20 March (Day of Oil Industry Nationalization), 21–24 March† (Norouz, Iranian New Year), 24 March (Martyrdom of Hazrat Fatemeh), 1 April (Islamic Republic Day), 2 April (Sizdah-bedar, Nature Day—13th Day of Norouz), 2 May (Birth of Imam Ali), 16 May* (Prophet Muhammad receives his calling), 3 June* (Birth of Imam Mahdi), 4 June (Death of Imam Khomeini), 5 June (1963 Uprising), 8 July* (Martyrdom of Imam Ali), 18–19 July* (Eid-e Fitr, end of Ramadan), 11 August* (Martyrdom of Imam Jafar Sadeq), 24 September* (Qorban, Feast of the Sacrifice), 2 October* (Eid-e Ghadir Khom), 23 October* (Tassoua), 24 October* (Ashoura), 3 December* (Arbain), 11 December (Demise of Prophet Muhammad and Martyrdom of Imam Hassan), 12 December* (Martyrdom of Imam Reza), 12 December (Birth of Prophet Muhammad and Birth of Imam Jafar Sadegh),

* These holidays are dependent on the Islamic lunar calendar and may vary by one or two days from the dates given.

† This festival begins on the date of the Spring Equinox.

Statistical Survey

The Iranian year runs from approximately 21 March to 20 March

Sources (except where otherwise stated): Statistical Centre of Iran, POB 14155-6133, Dr Fatemi Ave, Tehran 14144; tel. (21) 88965061; fax (21) 88963451; e-mail sci@sci.org.ir; internet www.amar.org.ir; Bank Markazi Jomhouri Islami Iran (Central Bank), POB 15875-7177, 144 Mirdamad Blvd, Tehran; tel. (21) 29954855; fax (21) 29954780; e-mail g.secdept@cbi.ir; internet www.cbi.ir.

Area and Population

AREA, POPULATION AND DENSITY

Area (sq km)	1,648,195*
Population (census results)	
28 October 2006	70,495,782
24 October 2011	
Males	37,905,669
Females	37,244,000
Total	75,149,669
Population (UN estimates at mid-year)†	
2012	76,424,440
2013	77,447,170
2014	78,470,223
Density (per sq km) at mid-2014	47.6

* 636,372 sq miles.

† Source: UN, *World Population Prospects: The 2012 Revision*.

POPULATION BY AGE AND SEX

(UN estimates at mid-2014)

	Males	Females	Total
0–14	9,607,518	9,184,196	18,791,714
15–64	27,774,417	27,670,879	55,445,296
65 and over	2,052,011	2,181,202	4,233,213
Total	39,433,946	39,036,277	78,470,223

Source: UN, *World Population Prospects: The 2012 Revision*.

PROVINCES

(population at 2011 census)

Province (Ostan)	Area (sq km)*	Population	Density (per sq km)	Provincial capital
Tehran (Teheran)†	13,692	12,183,391	889.8	Tehran (Teheran)
Markazi (Central)	29,127	1,413,959	48.5	Arak
Gilan	14,042	2,480,874	176.7	Rasht
Mazandaran	23,842	3,073,943	128.9	Sari
Azarbayejan-e-Sharqi (East Azerbaijan)	45,651	3,724,620	81.6	Tabriz
Azarbayejan-e-Gharbi (West Azerbaijan)	37,411	3,080,576	82.3	Orumiyeh
Bakhtaran (Kermanshah)	25,009	1,945,227	77.8	Bakhtaran
Khuzestan	64,055	4,531,720	70.7	Ahvaz
Fars	122,608	4,596,658	37.5	Shiraz
Kerman	180,726	2,938,988	16.3	Kerman
North Khorasan	28,434	867,727	30.5	Bojnurd
South Khorasan	95,385	662,534	6.9	Birjand
Razavi Khorasan	118,851	5,994,402	50.4	Mashhad
Esfahan	107,018	4,879,312	45.6	Esfahan
Sistan and Baluchestan	181,785	2,534,327	13.9	Zahedan
Kordestan (Kurdistan)	29,137	1,493,645	51.3	Sanandaj
Hamadan	19,368	1,758,268	90.8	Hamadan
Chaharmahal and Bakhtiyari	16,328	895,263	54.8	Shahr-e-Kord
Lorestan	28,294	1,754,243	62.0	Khorramabad
Ilam	20,133	557,599	27.7	Ilam
Kohgiluyeh and Boyerahmad	15,504	658,629	42.5	Yasuj
Bushehr	22,743	1,032,949	45.4	Bushehr
Zanjan	21,773	1,015,734	46.7	Zanjan
Semnan	97,491	631,218	6.5	Semnan
Yazd	129,285	1,074,428	8.3	Yazd
Hormozgan	70,697	1,578,183	22.3	Bandar Abbas
Ardebil	17,800	1,248,488	70.1	Ardebil
Qom	11,526	1,151,672	99.9	Qom
Qazvin	15,567	1,201,565	77.2	Qazvin
Golestan	20,367	1,777,014	87.2	Gorgan
Alborz†	5,122	2,412,513	471.0	Karaj
Total	1,628,771	75,149,669	46.1	—

* Excluding inland water; densities are calculated on basis of land area only.

† In June 2010 the legislature enacted a law dividing the existing province of Tehran to create a new province, Alborz, with the city of Karaj as its capital.

PRINCIPAL TOWNS

(population at 2011 census)

Tehran (Teheran, the capital)	8,154,051	Kerman	534,441
Mashad (Meshed)	2,766,258	Hamadan	525,794
Esfahan (Isfahan)	1,756,126	Yazd	486,152
Karaj	1,614,626	Arak	484,212
Tabriz	1,494,998	Ardabil (Ardebil)	482,632
Shiraz	1,460,665	Bandar Abbas	435,751
Ahvaz	1,112,021	Eslamshahr (Islam Shahr)	389,102
Qom	1,074,036	Zanjan	386,851
Bakhtaran (Kermanshah)	851,405	Qazvin	381,598
Orumiyeh	667,499	Sanandaj	373,987
Rasht	639,951	Khorramabad	348,216
Zahedan	560,725		

BIRTHS, MARRIAGES AND DEATHS
(annual averages, UN estimates)

	1995–2000	2000–05	2005–10
Birth rate (per 1,000)	20.7	18.9	18.8
Death rate (per 1,000)	5.4	5.2	5.3

Source: UN, *World Population Prospects: The 2012 Revision*.

Births ('000): 1,154 in 2004/05; 1,239 in 2005/06; 1,254 in 2006/07; 1,287 in 2007/08; 1,300 in 2008/09; 1,349 in 2009/10; 1,364 in 2010/11; 1,382 in 2011/12; 1,422 in 2012/13.

Marriages ('000): 724 in 2004/05; 788 in 2005/06; 778 in 2006/07; 841 in 2007/08; 882 in 2008/09; 890 in 2009/10; 892 in 2010/11; 875 in 2011/12; 830 in 2012/13.

Deaths ('000): 369 in 2003/04; 355 in 2004/05; 364 in 2005/06; 409 in 2006/07; 413 in 2007/08; 418 in 2008/09; 394 in 2009/10; 441 in 2010/11; 341 in 2011/12; 332 in 2012/13.

Life expectancy (years at birth): 73.4 (males 71.6; females 75.4) in 2011 (Source: World Bank, World Development Indicators database).

ECONOMICALLY ACTIVE POPULATION
('000 persons aged 10 years and over, excl. armed forces, 2010)

	Males	Females	Total
Agriculture, hunting and forestry	2,939.7	966.1	3,906.0
Fishing	63.8	0.4	64.0
Mining and quarrying	102.4	9.5	111.8
Manufacturing	2,727.3	795.0	3,522.3
Electricity, gas and water supply	188.5	9.1	197.7
Construction	2,789.5	30.9	2,820.4
Wholesale and retail trade; repair of motor vehicles, motorcycles and personal and household goods	3,006.5	226.2	3,232.7
Hotels and restaurants	231.2	15.3	246.5
Transport, storage and communications	2,084.5	41.1	2,125.6
Financial intermediation	205.2	37.3	242.5
Real estate, renting and business activities	523.0	141.4	664.4
Public administration and defence; compulsory social security	1,143.8	110.5	1,254.3
Education	607.0	626.3	1,233.4
Health and social work	255.6	236.4	492.0
Other community, social and personal service activities	327.0	183.0	510.0
Private households with employed persons	28.4	2.8	31.2
Extra-territorial organizations and bodies	0.6	—	0.6
Sub-total	17,198.4	3,457.0	20,655.4
Activities not adequately defined	1.3	—	1.3
Total employed	17,199.7	3,457.0	20,656.7
Unemployed	2,326.0	892.4	3,218.3
Total labour force	19,525.7	4,349.4	23,875.0

Source: ILO.

2013 (labour force survey, September–December 2013, '000 persons aged 10 years and over, incl. armed forces and unpaid family workers): Agriculture 3,661.8; Industry 7,195.5; Services 10,008.5; Total employed 20,865.8 (males 17,999.4, females 2,866.4); Unemployed 2,401.2 (males 1,668.9, females 732.3); Statistical discrepancy 1.8; Total labour force 23,268.8 (males 19,670.0, females 3,598.8).

Health and Welfare

KEY INDICATORS

Total fertility rate (children per woman, 2011)	1.6
Under-5 mortality rate (per 1,000 live births, 2011)	25
HIV/AIDS (% of persons aged 15–49, 2012)	0.2
Physicians (per 1,000 head, 2005)	0.9
Hospital beds (per 1,000 head, 2009)	1.7
Health expenditure (2010): US $ per head (PPP)	797
Health expenditure (2010): % of GDP	5.3
Health expenditure (2010): public (% of total)	41.6
Access to water (% of persons, 2011)	95
Total carbon dioxide emissions ('000 metric tons, 2010)	571,612.0
Carbon dioxide emissions per head (metric tons, 2010)	7.7
Human Development Index (2012): ranking	76
Human Development Index (2012): value	0.742

For sources and definitions, see explanatory note on p. vi.

Agriculture

PRINCIPAL CROPS
('000 metric tons)

	2010	2011	2012
Wheat	13,500.0	12,339.4	13,800.0*
Rice, paddy	3,012.7	2,746.6	2,400.0*
Barley	3,579.6	2,853.6	3,400.0*
Maize	2,144.9	2,746.6	1,223.0*
Potatoes	4,274.5	5,577.6	5,400.0†
Sugar cane	5,685.1	5,850.0†	6,000.0†
Sugar beet	4,095.6	4,100.0†	4,150.0†
Beans, dry	267.8	257.7	250.0†
Chick-peas	267.8	290.2†	315.0†
Lentils	100.2	71.8	85.0†
Almonds, with shell	158.1	92.5	100.0†
Walnuts, with shell	433.6	390.0	450.0†
Pistachios	446.6	472.1†	472.1†
Soybeans (Soya beans)	162.7	170.0*	200.0*
Cabbages and other brassicas†	391.7	508.6	550.0
Lettuce and chicory†	424.2	550.8	570.0
Tomatoes	5,256.1	5,565.2	6,000.0†
Pumpkins, squash and gourds†	732.7	951.2	965.0
Cucumbers and gherkins	1,811.6	1,532.8	1,600.0†
Aubergines (Eggplants)†	935.8	1,215.0	1,300.0
Chillies and peppers, green†	38.6	50.1	52.0
Onions, dry	1,923.0	2,168.0	2,260.0
Garlic†	69.5	90.2	90.0
Watermelons	3,466.9	3,786.3	3,800.0†
Cantaloupes and other melons†	1,387.8	1,400.0	1,450.0
Oranges	1,502.8	1,412.2	1,285.0†
Tangerines, mandarins, clementines and satsumas†	726.0	800.0	825.0
Lemons and limes†	689.8	560.1	600.0
Apples	1,662.4	1,843.0	1,700.0†
Pears	153.4	106.7	147.0†
Apricots	371.8	226.5	460.0†
Sweet cherries	242.7†	241.1	n.a.
Peaches and nectarines	496.1	476.4	500.0†
Plums and sloes	269.1	288.7	295.0†
Grapes	2,255.7	2,112.7	2,150.0†
Figs	76.4	67.4	78.0†
Dates	1,023.1	1,053.9	1,066.0†
Tea	165.7	103.9	158.0†

* Unofficial figure.
† FAO estimate(s).

Aggregate production ('000 metric tons, may include official, semi-official or estimated data): Total cereals 22,247.0 in 2010, 20,695.8 in 2011, 20,833.0 in 2012; Total roots and tubers 4,274.5 in 2010, 5,577.6 in 2011, 5,400.0 in 2012; Total vegetables (incl. melons) 20,038.9 in 2010, 22,471.8 in 2011, 23,485.7 in 2012; Total fruits (excl. melons) 12,020.5 in 2010, 11,695.9 in 2011, 11,971.7 in 2012.

Source: FAO.

LIVESTOCK
('000 head, FAO estimates)

	2010	2011	2012
Horses	140	140	140
Asses	1,600	1,600	1,600
Mules	175	175	175
Cattle	8,500	8,600	8,650
Buffaloes	375	375	375
Camels	153	152	152
Sheep	49,500	49,000	48,750
Goats	23,000	23,500	24,000
Chickens	880,000	900,000	925,000
Ducks	1,600	1,600	1,600
Geese and guinea fowl	1,000	1,000	1,000
Turkeys	2,000	2,000	2,000

Source: FAO.

LIVESTOCK PRODUCTS
('000 metric tons)

	2010	2011	2012
Cattle meat	222	250	248
Buffalo meat	3	3*	3*
Sheep meat	90	104	126
Goat meat*	140	142	143
Chicken meat	1,863	1,907	1,950*
Turkey meat*	6	6	6
Cows' milk*	6,391	6,425	6,550
Buffaloes' milk*	140	140	14
Goats' milk	270	205	225*
Hen eggs	687	559	625*
Honey*	47	47	48
Wool: greasy*	60	61	62

* FAO estimate(s).

Source: FAO.

Forestry

ROUNDWOOD REMOVALS
('000 cubic metres, excl. bark)

	2010	2011	2012
Sawlogs, veneer logs and logs for sleepers	263	254	286
Pulpwood	199	176	196
Other industrial wood	235	230	248
Fuel wood	53	46	52
Total	750	706	782

Source: FAO.

SAWNWOOD PRODUCTION
('000 cubic metres, incl. railway sleepers)

	2010	2011	2012
Total (all broadleaved)	32	31	33

Source: FAO.

Fishing

('000 metric tons, live weight)

	2009	2010	2011
Capture	419.9	443.7	487.8
Caspian sprat	25.5	27.1	20.7
Indian oil sardine	21.2	20.8	35.4
Kawakawa	17.8	16.3	22.2
Skipjack tuna	44.8	22.3	17.4
Longtail tuna	49.5	64.5	80.9
Yellowfin tuna	22.6	31.5	28.8
Aquaculture	179.6	220.0	247.3
Silver carp	55.2	66.9	72.7
Rainbow trout	73.6	91.5	106.4
Total catch	599.5	663.7	735.1

Source: FAO.

Production of caviar (metric tons, year ending 20 March): 7 in 2010/11; 6 in 2011/12; 5 in 2012/13.

Mining

CRUDE PETROLEUM
('000 barrels per day, year ending 20 March)

	2009/10	2010/11	2011/12
Total production	3,557	3,536	3,619

Total production ('000 barrels per day, estimate): 3,680 in 2012 (Source: BP, *Statistical Review of World Energy*).

NATURAL GAS
(excluding reinjection gas; million cu metres, year ending 20 March)

	2005/06	2006/07	2007/08
Consumption (domestic)*	102,200	109,800	122,500
Flared	15,800	15,100	15,000
Regional uses and wastes	7,400	5,000	7,300
Gas for export	4,800	5,700	5,600
Less Net imports	5,200	6,300	6,200
Total production	125,000	129,300	144,200

* Includes gas for household, industrial, generator and refinery consumption.

Natural gas consumption (domestic): 141,200 in 2009/10; 150,800 in 2010/11; 152,700 in 2011/12.

Gas injection (year ending 20 March, million cu metres): 26,663 in 2006/07; 25,971 in 2007/08; 28,448 in 2008/09; 28,840 in 2009/10.

OTHER MINERALS
('000 metric tons, unless otherwise indicated, year ending 20 March)

	2008/09	2009/10	2010/11*
Iron ore: gross weight	34,034	35,000*	35,000
Iron ore: metal content*	16,000	16,500	16,500
Copper concentrates*†	260	265	255
Bauxite	522	681	600
Lead concentrates*†	20	35	35
Zinc concentrates†	72	80*	80
Manganese ore‡	126	132	130
Chromium concentrates§	225	45	100
Molybdenum concentrates (metric tons)*†	2,500	3,900	3,900
Silver (metric tons)*†	15	15	15
Gold (kilograms)†	2,000	2,000	2,000
Bentonite	387	350	350
Kaolin	907	1,480	1,400
Other clays*	530	550	550
Magnesite	131	130*	130

—continued	2008/09	2009/10	2010/11*
Fluorspar (Fluorite)	71	72*	70
Feldspar	635	652	650
Barite (Barytes)	361	326	330
Salt (unrefined)	2,816	3,291	3,000
Gypsum (crude)	13,000	11,914	12,000
Pumice and related materials*	1,500	1,500	1,500
Mica (metric tons)	6,797	2,860	2,900
Talc	66	96*	90
Turquoise (kilograms)*	19,000	20,000	20,000
Coal	2,181	2,300*	2,300

* Estimate(s).

† Figures refer to the metal content of ores and concentrates.

‡ Figures refer to gross weight. The estimated metal content ('000 metric tons) was: 45 in 2008/09, 46 in 2009/10, 46 in 2010/11.

§ Figures refer to gross weight. The estimated chromic oxide content ('000 metric tons) was: 110 in 2008/09, 22 in 2009/10, 50 in 2010/11.

Source: US Geological Survey.

Industry

PETROLEUM PRODUCTS
(average cu m per day, year ending 20 March)

	2007/08	2008/09	2009/10
Liquefied petroleum gas	7,723	8,071	8,362
Motor spirit (petrol)	45,080	51,496	59,515
Burning oil (for electricity)	21,680	21,347	18,519
Jet fuel	3,426	3,519	4,188
Gas-diesel (distillate fuel) oil	81,549	84,957	88,702
Residual fuel oils	73,020	77,132	76,101
Petroleum bitumen (asphalt)	976	616	698

OTHER PRODUCTS
(year ending 20 March)

	2007/08	2008/09	2009/10
Refined sugar ('000 metric tons)	1,841	1,656	1,409
Soft drinks (million bottles)	4,252	4,471	3,849
Malt liquor (million bottles)	356	597	870
Cigarettes (million)	17,387	22,436	26,898
Threads ('000 metric tons)	417	348	324
Finished fabrics (million metres)	325	338	293
Machine-made carpets ('000 sq m)	30,583	57,935	75,642
Hand-woven carpets (moquette—'000 sq m)	68,510	62,699	71,995
Paper ('000 metric tons)	455	502	466
Detergent powder ('000 metric tons)	584	505	594
Soap (metric tons)	72,616	72,791	57,750
Cement ('000 metric tons)	40,189	44,253	49,471
Washing machines ('000)	774	807	667
Radio receivers ('000)	702	637	656
Television receivers ('000)	355	298	389
Water meters ('000)	823	877	1,611
Electricity meters ('000)	689	1,294	1,757
Passenger cars and jeeps ('000)	946	1,258	1,442
Electric energy (million kWh)	203,983	214,530	221,314

Electric energy (million kWh): 232,994 in 2010/11; 240,064 in 2011/12; 248,200 in 2012/13.

Finance

CURRENCY AND EXCHANGE RATES

Monetary Units
100 dinars = 1 Iranian rial (IR).

Sterling, Dollar and Euro Equivalents (31 December 2013)
£1 sterling = 40,797.8 rials;
US $1 = 24,774.0 rials;
€1 = 34,165.8 rials;
100,000 Iranian rials = £2.45 = $4.04 = €2.93.

Average Exchange Rate (rials per US $)
2011 10,616.31
2012 12,175.55
2013 18,414.45

Note: In March 1993 the former multiple exchange rate system was unified, and since then the exchange rate of the rial has been market-determined. The foregoing information on average exchange rates refers to the base rate, applicable to receipts from exports of petroleum and gas, payments for imports of essential goods and services, debt-servicing costs and imports related to large national projects. There was also an export rate, set at a mid-point of US $1 = 3,007.5 rials in May 1995, which applied to receipts from non-petroleum exports and to all other official current account transactions not effected at the base rate. In addition, a market rate was determined by transactions on the Tehran Stock Exchange: at 31 January 2002 it was US $1 = 7,924 rials. The weighted average of all exchange rates (rials per US $, year ending 20 December) was: 3,206 in 1997/98; 4,172 in 1998/99; 5,731 in 1999/2000. A new unified exchange rate, based on the market rate, took effect from 21 March 2002.

BUDGET
(consolidated accounts of central government and Oil Stabilization Fund—OSF, '000 million rials, year ending 20 March)

Revenue	2007/08	2008/09*	2009/10†
Oil and gas revenue	578,708	569,951	436,159
Budget revenue	444,278	559,589	498,071
Transfers from OSF	209,098	184,235	223,099
Revenues transferred to OSF	134,430	10,362	–61,912
Non-oil budgetary revenue	237,893	283,918	354,315
Tax revenue	162,579	203,042	240,454
Taxes on income, profits and capital gains	97,097	130,453	153,994
Domestic taxes on goods and services	16,663	15,900	29,771
Taxes on international trade and transactions	48,819	56,689	56,689
Non-tax revenue	75,314	80,876	113,861
Non-oil OSF revenues	4,551	6,038	6,223
Total	821,152	859,906	796,697

Expenditure	2007/08	2008/09*	2009/10†
Central government expenditures	710,022	841,093	884,798
Current expenditure	562,306	595,254	676,682
Wages and salaries	151,583	211,000	229,000
Interest payments	7,371	5,982	5,982
Subsidies	62,862	61,000	68,000
Goods and services	39,119	55,000	71,600
Grants	13,823	50,800	28,700
Social benefits	64,492	139,605	181,000
Gasoline imports	33,820	60,867	34,300
Other expenses	189,236	11,000	58,100
Capital expenditure	147,716	245,839	208,116
OSF expenditures	40,289	19,148	—
Total	750,311	860,240	884,798

* Estimates.
† Projections.

Source: IMF, *Islamic Republic of Iran: 2009 Article IV Consultation—Staff Report; Staff Supplement; Public Information Notice on the Executive Board Discussion; and Statement by the Executive Director for Iran* (March 2010).

2010/11 ('000 million rials, estimates): *Revenue:* Tax revenue 272,382 (Taxes on income, profits and capital gains 145,470; Domestic taxes on goods and services 37,894; Taxes on international trade and transactions 77,886); Other revenue 714,731; Total 987,113. *Expenditure:* Current expenditure 710,957 (Compensation of employees 204,463; Goods and services 79,147; Subsidies 118,720; Social benefits 191,272); Net acquisition of non-financial assets 205,107; Total 916,064 (Source: IMF—see below).

2011/12 ('000 million rials, projections): *Revenue:* Tax revenue 344,867 (Taxes on income, profits and capital gains 180,355; Domestic taxes on goods and services 59,072; Taxes on international trade and transactions 91,639); Other revenue 1,115,309; Total 1,460,176. *Expenditure:* Current expenditure 1,032,775 (Compensation of employees 278,355; Goods and services 107,750; Subsidies 166,600; Social benefits 260,397); Net acquisition of non-financial assets 278,600; Total 1,311,375 (Source: *Islamic Republic of Iran: 2011 Article IV Consultation—Staff Report; Public Information Notice on the Executive Board Discussion; and Statement by the Executive Director for Iran*—August 2011).

INTERNATIONAL RESERVES

(US $ million at 31 December)*

	1993	1994	1995
Gold (national valuation)	229.1	242.2	251.9
IMF special drawing rights	144.0	142.9	133.6
Total	373.1	385.1	385.5

* Excluding reserves of foreign exchange, for which no figures have been available since 1982 (when the value of reserves was US $5,287m.).

IMF special drawing rights (US $ million at 31 December): 2,365 in 2010; 2,359 in 2011; 2,368 in 2012.

Source: IMF, *International Financial Statistics*.

MONEY SUPPLY

('000 million rials at 20 December)

	2008	2009	2010
Currency outside banks	122,603	147,878	210,289
Non-financial public enterprises' deposits at Central Bank	16,978	15,496	18,353
Demand deposits at commercial banks	300,451	317,415	150,432
Total money	440,031	480,790	379,073

Source: IMF, *International Financial Statistics*.

COST OF LIVING

(Consumer Price Index in urban areas, year ending 20 March; base: 2004/05 = 100)

	2009/10	2010/11	2011/12
Food and beverages	218.6	254.1	320.0
Clothing	179.7	200.9	245.4
Housing, water, electricity, gas, and other fuels	220.2	236.2	279.3
All items (incl. others)	203.0	228.2	277.2

2012/13 (base: 2011/12 = 100): Food and beverages 144.6; Clothing 147.8; Housing, water, electricity, gas, and other fuels 112.9; All items (incl. others) 130.5.

NATIONAL ACCOUNTS

('000 million rials at current prices, year ending 20 March, preliminary)

Expenditure on the Gross Domestic Product

	2008/09	2009/10	2010/11
Final consumption expenditure	1,812,176	1,985,948	2,248,482
Private	1,420,657	1,540,628	1,767,132
Public	391,519	445,320	481,350
Changes in inventories	313,386	475,472	639,312
Gross fixed capital formation	957,271	949,354	1,146,917
Total domestic expenditure	3,082,833	3,410,774	4,034,711
Exports of goods and services	1,015,562	923,411	1,194,391
Less Imports of goods and services	741,949	756,788	896,016
GDP at market prices	3,356,447	3,577,397	4,333,087
GDP at constant 1997/98 prices	492,520	511,975	542,174

2011/12 ('000 million rials at current prices, provisional): Final consumption expenditure 2,937,915 (Private 2,306,264, Public 631,651); Changes in inventories 1,006,620; Gross fixed capital formation 1,523,304; *Total domestic expenditure* 5,467,839; Net exports 653,165; *GDP at market prices* 6,121,004; *GDP at constant 1997/98 prices* 555,436.

2012/13 ('000 million rials at current prices, provisional): Final consumption expenditure 3,670,222 (Private 2,999,816, Public 670,406); Changes in inventories 1,238,594; Gross fixed capital formation 1,609,966; *Total domestic expenditure* 6,518,782; Net exports 274,388; *GDP at market prices* 6,793,170; *GDP at constant 1997/98 prices* 522,957.

Gross Domestic Product by Economic Activity

	2008/09	2009/10	2010/11
Hydrocarbon GDP	850,642	729,282	977,799
Non-hydrocarbon GDP	2,528,082	2,833,007	3,326,466
Agriculture	302,210	365,976	436,975
Industry	632,263	653,751	837,475
Mining	27,919	26,696	31,903
Manufacturing	345,806	374,950	509,150
Construction	215,877	210,176	244,337
Electricity, gas and water	42,660	41,930	52,085
Services	1,691,955	1,919,083	2,200,733
Transport and communication	317,512	350,949	389,426
Banking and insurance	102,718	120,059	167,403
Trade, restaurants and hotels	364,661	411,353	503,048
Ownership and dwellings	506,828	558,834	607,934
Public services	312,611	380,926	411,745
Private services	87,624	96,962	121,177
Less Imputed bank service charge.	98,344	105,803	148,717
GDP at factor prices	3,378,724	3,562,289	4,304,264
Net indirect taxes	−22,277	15,108	28,823
GDP at market prices	3,356,447	3,577,397	4,333,087

2011/12 ('000 million rials at current prices, provisional): Hydrocarbon GDP 1,663,621; Agriculture 534,858; Industry 1,296,912 (Mining and manufacturing 845,700, Construction 302,351, Electricity, gas and water 148,861); Services 2,825,922; *Less* Imputed bank service charge 216,445; *GDP at factor prices* 6,104,868; Net indirect taxes (figure obtained as residual) 16,136; *GDP at market prices* 6,121,004.

2012/13 ('000 million rials at current prices, provisional): Hydrocarbon GDP 1,196,803; Agriculture 794,263; Industry 1,505,698 (Mining and manufacturing 1,008,990, Construction 338,230, Electricity, gas and water 158,478); Services 3,480,059; *Less* Imputed bank service charge 219,733; *GDP at factor prices* 6,757,090; Net indirect taxes (figure obtained as residual) 36,080; *GDP at market prices* 6,793,170.

BALANCE OF PAYMENTS
(US $ million, year ending 20 March)

	2010/11	2011/12	2012/13*
Exports of goods f.o.b.	112,788	144,874	98,033
Petroleum and gas	90,191	118,232	68,135
Non-petroleum and gas exports	22,596	26,642	29,899
Imports of goods f.o.b.	–75,458	–77,805	–67,058
Trade balance	37,330	67,069	30,975
Exports of services	8,853	8,621	6,687
Imports of services	–18,893	–17,053	–12,979
Balance on goods and services	27,263	58,637	24,683
Income received	1,952	2,171	2,469
Income paid	–1,873	–1,849	–1,431
Balance on goods, services and income	27,369	58,960	25,722
Transfers (net)	185	423	552
Current balance	27,554	59,383	26,271
Capital account (net)	–986	–684	
Financial account (net)	–23,310	–37,291	–22,048
Overall balance	3,259	21,409	4,223

* Preliminary.

External Trade

PRINCIPAL COMMODITIES
(US $ million, year ending 20 March)

Imports c.i.f. (distribution by SITC)	2009/10	2010/11	2011/12
Food and live animals	6,409	6,790	7,388
Cereals and cereal preparations	3,517	2,278	2,998
Crude materials (inedible) except fuels	2,055	2,156	2,300
Animal and vegetable oils and fats	989	1,444	1,625
Vegetable oils and fats	983	1,440	1,620
Chemicals and related products	6,029	7,011	7,441
Chemical elements and compounds	1,248	1,434	1,440
Plastic, cellulose and artificial resins	1,835	2,190	2,536
Basic manufactures	12,590	14,231	13,442
Iron and steel	8,166	9,235	8,357
Machinery and transport equipment	18,060	20,713	22,136
Non-electrical machinery	9,552	10,692	10,291
Electrical machinery, apparatus, etc.	3,973	4,400	5,456
Transport equipment	4,535	5,620	6,388
Miscellaneous manufactured articles	1,867	1,788	1,809
Total (incl. others)	55,287	64,450	61,808

Exports f.o.b.*	2009/10	2010/11	2011/12
Agricultural and traditional goods	4,133	5,056	5,181
Carpets	495	557	559
Fruits (fresh and dried)	1,779	2,194	2,204
Industrial manufactures	17,017	20,194	27,590
Oil and gas products	3,925	4,892	8,485
Iron and steel	1,041	1,015	1,522
Total (incl. others)	21,891	26,551	33,819

* Excluding exports of crude petroleum and associated gas (US $ million): 69,957 in 2009/10; 90,191 in 2010/11; 118,232 in 2011/12 (preliminary).

Note: Imports include registration fee, but exclude defence-related imports and imports of refined petroleum products.

2012/13: Total imports 53,451; Total exports 32,567.

PRINCIPAL TRADING PARTNERS
(US $ million, year ending 20 March)

Imports c.i.f.	2007/08	2008/09	2009/10
Austria	1,071	1,131	736
Belgium	536	994	569
Brazil	563	570	614
Canada	149	672	312
China, People's Republic	4,292	4,945	4,846
France	1,894	1,992	1,688
Germany	5,328	5,369	4,688
India	1,457	1,819	1,793
Italy	1,902	1,979	1,898
Japan	1,325	1,344	1,423
Korea, Republic	2,456	3,105	3,468
Netherlands	537	535	1,092
Russia	863	1,405	1,016
Saudi Arabia	500	n.a.	n.a.
Singapore	575	882	1,015
Sweden	451	716	600
Switzerland	2,779	3,542	2,137
Taiwan	519	464	467
Turkey	1,246	1,508	2,025
United Arab Emirates	11,509	13,491	16,187
United Kingdom	2,002	2,039	1,654
Total (incl. others)	48,439	56,042	55,287

Exports f.o.b.	2007/08	2008/09	2009/10
Afghanistan	543	633	1,047
Azerbaijan	350	369	374
Belgium	223	406	509
China, People's Republic	1,244	2,051	3,126
Ecuador	20	224	n.a.
Germany	374	319	349
Hong Kong	292	150	200
India	837	1,159	1,264
Indonesia	206	321	368
Iraq	1,842	2,762	4,560
Italy	522	325	436
Japan	927	589	360
Korea, Republic	552	821	543
Kuwait	319	133	138
Malaysia	31	186	97
Netherlands	234	346	298
Pakistan	274	296	435
Philippines	47	108	222
Russia	367	358	333
Saudi Arabia	310	388	177
Spain	234	175	169
Syria	330	316	379
Taiwan	205	376	184
Tajikistan	171	187	163
Turkey	566	530	593
Turkmenistan	189	249	358
United Arab Emirates	2,166	2,322	2,934
Total (incl. others)	15,312	18,334	21,891

Note: Exports exclude crude petroleum and associated gas.

Transport

RAILWAYS
(traffic, year ending 20 March)

	2010/11	2011/12	2012/13
Passengers carried ('000)	28,814	28,560	27,015
Passenger-km (million)	17,611	17,877	17,172
Freight carried ('000 metric tons)	33,458	33,104	34,276
Freight ton-km (million)	21,779	21,008	22,604

ROAD TRAFFIC
(registered motor vehicles, year ending 20 March)

	2009/10	2010/11	2011/12
Passenger cars*	1,170,581	1,104,304	1,378,860
Pick-ups and light trucks	202,200	189,302	200,035
Motorcycles	591,318	835,711	813,386
Total (incl. others)	2,005,475	2,179,517	2,482,718

* Including ambulances.

SHIPPING

Flag Registered Fleet
(at 31 December)

	2011	2012	2013
Number of vessels	533	619	757
Total displacement ('000 grt)	787.6	2,394.7	3,416.9

Source: Lloyd's List Intelligence (www.lloydslistintelligence.com).

International Sea-borne Freight Traffic
(year ending 20 March, '000 metric tons)*

	2010/11	2011/12	2012/13
Goods loaded	54,910	57,188	57,439
Crude petroleum and petroleum products	18,014	21,029	16,877
Goods unloaded	72,102	64,471	66,673
Petroleum products	24,045	20,605	21,302

* Cargo loaded onto and from vessels with a capacity of 1,000 metric tons or greater only.

CIVIL AVIATION
(year ending 20 March)

	2010/11	2011/12	2012/13
Passengers ('000):			
domestic flights	16,104	16,481	16,655
international arrivals	3,847	4,379	4,079
international departures	4,053	4,404	4,138
Freight (excl. mail, metric tons):			
domestic flights	47,158	56,413	13,581
international arrivals	65,274	61,221	41,230
international departures	30,762	24,806	26,017
Mail (metric tons):			
domestic flights	5,785	3,843	3,005
international arrivals	8,708	7,842	1,124
international departures	3,038	4,180	1,271

Tourism

FOREIGN TOURIST ARRIVALS

Country of nationality	2009	2010	2011
Afghanistan	175,155	214,649	202,369
Armenia	331,868	566,932	533,820
Azerbaijan	383,588	690,333	732,201
Iraq	440,989	548,008	589,074
Pakistan	115,459	173,068	187,920
Saudi Arabia	14,601	60,107	74,275
Turkey	299,828	288,031	419,853
Turkmenistan	80,533	95,000	135,683
Total (incl. others)	2,116,244	2,938,054	3,353,713

Tourism receipts (US $ million, excl. passenger transport): 2,012 in 2009; 2,707 in 2010; 2,381 in 2011 (provisional).

Source: World Tourism Organization.

Total arrivals (year ending 20 March): 3,294,126 in 2011/12; 4,070,415 in 2012/13.

Communications Media

	2010	2011	2012
Telephones ('000 main lines in use)	25,815.2	27,766.9	28,758.5
Mobile cellular telephones ('000 subscribers)	54,051.8	56,043.0	58,157.5
Internet subscribers ('000)	n.a.	5,240.2	n.a.
Broadband subscribers ('000)	962.2	1,772.9	3,076.2
Book production*:			
titles	64,606	61,724	61,724
copies ('000)	198,593	173,592	152,135

* Twelve months beginning 21 March of year stated.

Newspapers and periodicals (number of titles, year ending 20 March 2006): Daily 183; Other 4,528.

Source: partly International Telecommunication Union.

Education

(2012/13 unless otherwise indicated)

	Institutions	Teachers	Students ('000) Males	Females	Total
Special	1,418	12,660	45.1	28.0	73.1
Pre-primary	13,419	1,898*	232.0	227.0	459.0
Primary	58,816	260,999	3,523.0	3,328.1	6,851.0
Lower secondary:					
mainstream	23,285	154,713	1,110.5	1,002.4	2,112.9
adult	979		11.0	10.0	21.0
Upper secondary:					
mainstream	21,671	188,070	1,683.3	1,594.7	3,278.0
adult	5,284		175.0	256.5	431.4
Pre-university:					
mainstream	8,593	n.a.	177.3	263.3	440.6
adult	1,068		24.1	19.3	43.4
Teacher training*	98	n.a.	16.6	18.9	35.5
Islamic Azad University	n.a.	84,134	972.9	609.5	1,582.4
Other higher	n.a.	184,854	1,326.9	1,526.6	2,853.5

* 2011/12.

Pupil-teacher ratio (primary education, UNESCO estimate): 20.5 in 2008/09 (Source: UNESCO Institute for Statistics).

Adult literacy rate (UNESCO estimates): 85.0% (males 89.3%; females 80.7%) in 2008 (Source: UNESCO Institute for Statistics).

Directory

The Government

SUPREME RELIGIOUS LEADER

Wali Faqih: Ayatollah SAYED ALI KHAMENEI.

HEAD OF STATE

President: HASSAN ROUHANI (assumed office 3 August 2013).

First Vice-President: ESHAQ JAHANGIRI.

Head of the Presidential Office and Chief of Staff: MUHAMMAD NAHVANDIAN.

Executive Vice-President: MUHAMMAD SHARIATMADARI.

Vice-President in charge of Legal Affairs: ELHAM AMINZADEH.

Vice-President for Legal and Parliamentary Affairs: MAJEAD ANSARI.

Vice-President for Science and Technology: SORENA SATTARI.

Vice-President for Women and Family Affairs: SHAHINDOKHT MOLAVERDI.

Vice-President for Supervision and Strategic Affairs: MUHAMMAD BAGHER NOBAKHT.

Vice-President and Head of the Cultural Heritage, Handicrafts and Tourism Organization: MASSOUD SULTANIFAR.

Vice-President and Head of the Atomic Energy Organization: ALI AKBAR SALEHI.

Vice-President and Head of the Martyrs' and Self-Sacrificers' Affairs Foundation: SEYED MUHAMMAD ALI SHAHIDI.

Vice-President and Head of the Organization for the Protection of the Environment: MASSOUMEH EBTEKAR.

COUNCIL OF MINISTERS
(April 2014)

Minister of Education: ALI ASGHAR FANI.

Minister of Communications and Information Technology: MAHMOUD VAEZI.

Minister of Intelligence: MAHMOUD ALAVI.

Minister of Economic Affairs and Finance: ALI TAYEBNIA.

Minister of Foreign Affairs: MUHAMMAD JAVAD ZARIF.

Minister of Health and Medical Education: HASSAN QAZIZADEH HASHEMI.

Minister of Agricultural Jihad: MAHMOUD HOJJATI.

Minister of Justice: MOSTAFA POUR-MUHAMMADI.

Minister of Defence: HOSSEIN DEHQAN.

Minister of Roads and Urban Development: ABBAS AHMAD AKHOUNDI.

Minister of Science, Research and Technology: REZA FARAJI-DANA.

Minister of Culture and Islamic Guidance: ALI JANNATI.

Minister of Labour, Co-operatives and Social Affairs: ALI RABEI.

Minister of the Interior: ABDOLREZA RAHMANI FAZLI.

Minister of Petroleum: BIJAN NAMDAR ZANGANEH.

Minister of Energy: HAMID CHITCHIAN.

Minister of Sport and Youth Affairs: MAHMOUD GOUDARZI.

Minister of Industries, Mines and Trade: MUHAMMAD REZA NEMATZADEH.

MINISTRIES

Office of the President: POB 1423-13185, Pasteur Ave, Tehran 13168-43311; tel. (21) 64451; e-mail webmaster@president.ir; internet www.president.ir.

Ministry of Agricultural Jihad: 20 Malaei Ave, Vali-e-Asr Sq., Tehran; tel. (21) 64583101; fax (21) 66412123; e-mail pr@maj.ir; internet www.maj.ir.

Ministry of Communications and Information Technology: POB 15875-4415, Shariati St, Tehran 16314; tel. (21) 88114315; fax (21) 88467210; e-mail khajeh@ict.gov.ir; internet www.ict.gov.ir.

Ministry of Culture and Islamic Guidance: POB 5158, Baharestan Sq., Tehran 11365; tel. (21) 38512583; fax (21) 33117535; e-mail info@ershad.gov.ir; internet www.farhang.gov.ir.

Ministry of Defence: Shahid Yousuf Kaboli St, Sayed Khandan Area, Tehran; tel. (21) 26126988; e-mail info@mod.ir; internet www.mod.ir.

Ministry of Economic Affairs and Finance: Bab Homayoon St, Imam Khomeini Sq., Tehran; tel. (21) 39909; fax (21) 33967205; e-mail mzandi22@yahoo.com; internet mefa.ir.

Ministry of Education: Si-e-Tir St, Imam Khomeini Sq., Tehran; tel. (21) 82282124; fax (21) 88894052; e-mail negah@medu.ir; internet www.medu.ir.

Ministry of Energy: POB 19968-32611, Niayesh Highway, Vali-e-Asr Ave, Tehran; tel. (21) 81606000; fax (21) 81606132; e-mail info@moe.org.ir; internet www.moe.gov.ir.

Ministry of Foreign Affairs: Imam Khomeini Sq., Tehran; tel. (21) 61151; fax (21) 66743149; e-mail info@mfa.gov.ir; internet www.mfa.gov.ir.

Ministry of Health and Medical Education: POB 310, Jomhouri Islami Ave, Hafez Crossing, Tehran 11344; tel. (21) 88363560; fax (21) 88364111; e-mail webmaster@mohme.gov.ir; internet www.mohme.gov.ir.

Ministry of Industries, Mines and Trade: Shahid Kalantari, Ostad Negatollahi St, Ferdosi Sq., Tehran; tel. (21) 88906563; fax (21) 88903650; e-mail intl@mim.gov.ir; internet www.mim.gov.ir.

Ministry of Intelligence: POB 16765-1947, Second Negarestan St, Pasdaran Ave, Tehran; tel. (21) 233031; fax (21) 23305.

Ministry of the Interior: Jahad Sq., Fatemi St, Tehran; tel. (21) 84861; fax (21) 88964678; e-mail ravabetomomi@moi.gov.ir; internet www.moi.ir.

Ministry of Justice: Panzdah-e-Khordad Sq., Tehran 14158-55139; tel. (21) 88383201; fax (21) 3904986; e-mail info@justice.ir; internet www.justice.ir.

Ministry of Labour, Co-operatives and Social Affairs: Azadi St, Tehran; tel. (21) 66580031; e-mail infopack@mcls.gov.ir; internet www.mcls.gov.ir.

Ministry of Petroleum: Hafez Crossing, Taleghani Ave, Tehran 15936-57919; tel. (21) 61651; fax (21) 61623949; e-mail info@mop.ir; internet www.mop.ir.

Ministry of Roads and Urban Development: Dadman Tower, Africa Blvd, Tehran; tel. (21) 88646130; internet www.mrud.ir.

Ministry of Science, Research and Technology: POB 15875-4375, Central Bldg, Ostad Nejatollahi Ave, Tehran; tel. (21) 82231000; fax (21) 88827234; e-mail zahedi@msrt.ir; internet www.msrt.ir.

Ministry of Sport and Youth Affairs: Tehran.

President

Presidential Election, 14 June 2013

Candidates	Votes	%
Hassan Rouhani	18,613,329	50.71
Muhammad Baqir Qalibaf	6,077,292	16.56
Saeed Jalili	4,168,946	11.36
Mohsen Rezai	3,884,412	10.58
Ali Akbar Velayati	2,268,753	6.18
Muhammad Gharazi	446,015	1.22
Total	36,704,156*	100.00

* Including 1,245,409 invalid votes (3.39% of total votes cast).

Legislature

MAJLIS-E-SHURA-E ISLAMI—ISLAMIC CONSULTATIVE ASSEMBLY

Elections to the eighth Majlis took place in early 2008. Prior to the elections the Council of Guardians and the Ministry of the Interior barred at least 1,700 of the 7,168 registered candidates from standing, including a number of current Majlis deputies. The majority of the barred candidates were recognized as being 'reformists'. At the first round of voting, held on 14 March, 208 deputies received a sufficient number of votes to be elected directly to the Majlis; at the second round, on 25 April, a further 79 deputies were elected. Three seats remained vacant following both rounds, after election officials had annulled the results for unspecified reasons; by-elections for these seats were to be held at a later date. According to official reports, 'conservatives' controlled the eighth Majlis, with an estimated 198–200 seats; 'reformists' secured around 46–50 seats, and some 40–43 seats were held by 'independents'. A reported 29 of the 30 seats in Tehran were filled by 'conservatives', with only one seat going to a 'reformist' candidate. However, despite the 'conservatives' having consolidated their control of the Majlis, some of the new deputies were reported to be critical of President Mahmoud Ahmadinejad's policies. On 2 March 2012 the first round of elections to the ninth Majlis took place. Of the 290 seats, 'conservatives' secured 143 seats, while 'reformists' took 59 seats. Candidates representing religious minorities held 14 seats and nine seats went to 'independents'. A second round of voting for the 65 remaining seats was held on 4 May, at which 'conservatives' secured 41 seats, 'reformists' secured 13 seats and 11 seats went to 'independents'.

Islamic Consultative Assembly: Baharestan Sq., Tehran; tel. (21) 33440236; fax (21) 33440309; internet www.parliran.ir.

Speaker: ALI ARDESHIR LARIJANI.

SHURA-YE ALI-YE AMNIYYAT-E MELLI—SUPREME NATIONAL SECURITY COUNCIL

Formed in July 1989 (in place of the Supreme Defence Council) to coordinate defence and national security policies, the political programme and intelligence reports, and social, cultural and economic activities related to defence and security. The Council is chaired by the President and includes a representative of the Wali Faqih, the Minister of the Interior, the Speaker of the Majlis, the Head of the Judiciary, the Chief of the Supreme Command Council of the Armed Forces, the Minister of Foreign Affairs, the Head of the Management and Planning Organization, and the Minister of Intelligence.

Secretary: Rear Adm. ALI SHAMKHANI.

MAJLIS-E KHOBREGAN—ASSEMBLY OF EXPERTS

Elections were held on 10 December 1982 to appoint an Assembly of Experts which was to choose an eventual successor to the Wali Faqih (then Ayatollah Khomeini) after his death. The Constitution provides for a three- or five-man body to assume the leadership of the country if there is no recognized successor on the death of the Wali Faqih. The Council comprises 86 clerics, who are elected by direct suffrage for an eight-year term. Elections to a fourth term of the Council were held on 15 December 2006.

Assembly of Experts: Tehran; e-mail info@majleskhobregan.com; internet www.majlesekhobregan.ir.

Speaker: Ayatollah MUHAMMAD REZA MAHDAVI KANI.

SHURA-E-NIGAHBAN—COUNCIL OF GUARDIANS

The Council of Guardians, composed of six qualified Muslim jurists appointed by Ayatollah Khomeini and six lay Muslim lawyers, appointed by the Majlis from among candidates nominated by the Head of the Judiciary, was established in 1980 to supervise elections and to examine legislation adopted by the Majlis, ensuring that it accords with the Constitution and with Islamic precepts.

Chairman: Ayatollah AHMAD JANNATI.

SHURA-YE TASHKHIS-E MASLAHAT-E NEZAM—COUNCIL TO DETERMINE THE EXPEDIENCY OF THE ISLAMIC ORDER

Formed in February 1988, by order of Ayatollah Khomeini, to arbitrate on legal and theological questions in legislation approved by the Majlis, in the event of a dispute between the latter and the supervisory Council of Guardians. Its permanent members, defined in March 1997, are Heads of the Legislative, Judiciary and Executive Powers, the jurist members of the Council of Guardians, and the Minister or head of organization concerned with the pertinent arbitration. In October 2005 the powers of the Expediency Council were extended, allowing it to supervise all branches of government. Former President Ali Akbar Hashemi Rafsanjani was reappointed as Chairman of the Council in March 2012; the members of the Council are appointed for a term of five years.

Chairman: Hojatoleslam ALI AKBAR HASHEMI RAFSANJANI.

Political Organizations

Numerous political organizations were registered in the late 1990s, following the election of former President Khatami, and have tended to be regarded as either 'conservative' or 'reformist', the principal factions in the legislature. There are also a small number of centrist political parties. Under the Iranian electoral system, parties do not field candidates *per se* at elections, but instead back lists of candidates, who are allowed to be members of more than one party. In the mid-2000s there were estimated to be more than 100 registered political organizations, some of which are listed below:

Democratic Coalition of Reformists: Tehran; f. 2010; Sec.-Gen. MASSOUMEH EBTEKAR.

Eslahteleban-e Motedel (Moderate Reformists): Tehran; Leader ALI MOTAHARI.

Jebhe-ye Besiret ve Bidari-ye Eslami (Insight and Islamic Awakening Front): Tehran; Leader SHAHABEDDIN SADRI.

Jebhe-ye Istadegi (Resistance Front): Tehran.

Jebhe-ye Mottehed-e Osulgeraian (United Front of Principalists): Tehran; officially formed in 2008; reformed in 2012; Leader MUHAMMAD REZA MAHDAVI KANI.

Jebhe-ye Paydari-ye Enghelab-e Eslami (Front of Islamic Revolution Stability): Tehran; internet www.jebhepaydari.ir; f. 2011; Leader GHOLAM-HUSSEIN ELHAM; Sec.-Gen. MORTEZA AGHA-TEHRANI.

Jebhe-ye Seda-ye Mellet (People's Voice Front): Tehran; f. 2011; Leader MOHSEN REZAI; Sec.-Gen. ALI MOTAHARI.

Jebhe-ye Touhid ve Edalet (Monotheism and Justice Front): Tehran; f. 2012; Leader MANOUCHEHR MOTTAKI; Sec.-Gen. ESFANDIAR RAHIM MASHAI.

Labour Coalition (LC): Tehran; f. 2000; Leader HOSSEIN KAMALI; Sec.-Gen. SOHEILA JOLODARZADEH.

Most of the following are either registered political parties that have boycotted elections to the Majlis-e-Shura-e Islami (Islamic Consultative Assembly) in the 2000s, or are unregistered organizations or guerrilla groups:

Ansar-e Hezbollah (Helpers of the Party of God): f. 1995; militant, ultra-conservative youth movement; pledges allegiance to the Wali Faqih (supreme religious leader).

Daftar-e Tahkim-e Vahdat (Office for Strengthening Unity): Tehran; f. 1979; org. of Islamist university students who supported Khatami in the presidential election of 1997 and reformist candidates in the Majlis elections of 2000; Sec.-Gen AHMAD ZEIDABADI.

Democratic Party of Iranian Kurdistan: 17 ave d'Italie, Paris 75013, France; tel. 1-45-85-64-31; fax 1-45-85-20-93; e-mail pdkiran@club-internet.fr; internet www.pdki.org; f. 1945; seeks a federal system of govt in Iran, in order to secure the national rights of the Kurdish people; consultative mem. of the Socialist International; 95,000 mems; Sec.-Gen. MUSTAFA HIJRI.

Fedayin-e-Khalq (Organization of the Iranian People's Fedayeen—Majority): Postfach 260268, 50515 Köln, Germany; e-mail info@fadai.org; internet www.fadai.org; f. 1971; Marxist; Leader BEHROUZ KHALIQ.

Fraksion-e Hezbollah: f. 1996 by deputies in the Majlis who had contested the 1996 legislative elections as a loose coalition known as the Society of Combatant Clergy; Leader ALI AKBAR HOSSAINI.

Free Life Party of Kurdistan (Parti Jiyani Azadi Kurdistan—PJAK): f. 2004; militant org. that operates in mountainous areas of Iran and northern Iraq; apparently has close links with the Kurdistan Workers' Party (PKK—Partiya Karkeren Kurdistan) of Turkey; seeks a federal, secular system of govt in Iran, in order to secure the national rights of the Kurdish people; Sec.-Gen. RAHMAN HAJI AHMADI.

Hezb-e Etemad-e Melli (National Confidence Party—NCP): Tehran; tel. (21) 88373305; fax (21) 88373306; e-mail info@etemademelli.ir; f. 2005 by Mahdi Karrubi, fmrly of the Militant Clergy Association, shortly after his defeat in the presidential election of June; reformist, centrist; Sec.-Gen. MAHDI KARRUBI.

Hezb-e Hambastegi-ye Iran-e Islami (Islamic Iran Solidarity Party): f. 1998; reformist; Sec.-Gen. EBRAHIM ASGHARZADEH.

Hezb-e-Komunist Iran (Communist Party of Iran): POB 70445, 107 25 Stockholm, Sweden; e-mail cpi@cpiran.org; internet www.cpiran.org; f. 1979 by dissident mems of Tudeh Party; Sec.-Gen. 'AZARYUN'.

Iran National Front (Jebhe Melli Iran): US Section, POB 136, Audubon Station, New York, NY 10032, USA; e-mail contact@jebhemelli.net; internet www.jebhemelli.net; f. late 1940s by the late Dr Muhammad Mussadeq; secular, pro-democracy opposition group, which also seeks to further religious freedom within Iran; Leader ADIB BOROUMAND.

Jame'e-ye Eslaami-e Mohandesin (Islamic Society of Engineers): f. 1988; conservative; mems incl. fmr President Mahmoud Ahmadinejad; Sec.-Gen. MUHAMMAD REZA BAHONAR.

Jebbeh-ye Mosharekat-e Iran-e Islami (Islamic Iran Participation Front): e-mail mail.emrooz@gmail.com; f. 1998; reformist, leftist; reportedly proscribed by the Iranian authorities in March 2010; Sec.-Gen. MOHSEN MIRDAMADI.

Komala Party of Iranian Kurdistan: e-mail secretariat@komala.org; internet www.komala.org; f. 1969; Kurdish wing of the Communist Party of Iran; Marxist-Leninist; Sec.-Gen. ABDULLAH MOHTADI.

Marze Por Gohar (Glorious Frontiers Party): 1351 Westwood Blvd, Suite 111, Los Angeles, CA 90024, USA; tel. (310) 473-4763; fax (310) 477-8484; e-mail info@marzeporgohar.org; internet www.marzeporgohar.org; f. 1998 in Tehran; nationalist party advocating a secular republic in Iran; Chair. ROOZBEH FARAHANIPOUR.

Mujahidin-e-Khalq (Holy Warriors of the People): e-mail mojahed@mojahedin.org; internet www.mojahedin.org; Marxist-Islamist guerrilla group opposed to clerical regime; since June 1987 comprising the National Liberation Army; mem. of the National Council of Resistance of Iran; based in Paris, France 1981–86 and in Baghdad, Iraq, 1986–2003; Leaders MARYAM RAJAVI, MASSOUD RAJAVI.

Nehzat-e Azadi-ye Iran (Liberation Movement of Iran): e-mail nehzateazadi1340@gmail.com; f. 1961; emphasis on basic human rights as defined by Islam; Sec.-Gen. Dr IBRAHIM YAZDI.

Pan-Iranist Party: POB 31535-1679, Karaj; e-mail iran@paniranism.info; internet www.paniranist.org; calls for a Greater Persia; Leader REZA KERMANI.

Sazeman-e Mujahidin-e Enqelab-e Islami (Organization of the Mujahidin of the Islamic Revolution): reformist; Sec.-Gen. MUHAMMAD SALAMATI.

Sazmane Peykar dar Rahe Azadieh Tabaqe Kargar (Organization Struggling for the Freedom of the Working Class): Marxist-Leninist.

Tudeh Party of Iran (Party of the Masses): POB 100644, 10566 Berlin, Germany; tel. and fax (30) 3241627; e-mail mardom@tudehpartyiran.org; internet www.tudehpartyiran.org; f. 1941; declared illegal 1949; came into open 1979; banned again April 1983; First Sec., Cen. Cttee ALI KHAVARI.

The National Council of Resistance (NCR) was formed in Paris, France, in October 1981 by former President Abolhasan Bani-Sadr and Massoud Rajavi, the leader of the Mujahidin-e-Khalq in Iran. In 1984 the Council comprised 15 opposition groups, operating either clandestinely in Iran or from exile abroad. Bani-Sadr left the Council in that year because of his objection to Rajavi's growing links with the Iraqi Government. The French Government asked Rajavi to leave Paris in June 1986 and he moved his base of operations to Baghdad, Iraq. In June 1987 Rajavi, Secretary of the NCR, announced the formation of a 10,000–15,000-strong National Liberation Army as the military wing of the Mujahidin-e-Khalq. However, the status of the Mujahidin was initially uncertain following the invasion of Iraq by the US-led coalition in March 2003 (see the chapter on Iraq) and firmer measures being taken against the activities of the organization by the authorities in Paris in mid-2003. In July 2004 the USA declared a group of 3,800 members of the Mujahidin-e-Khalq interned in Iraq to have 'protected status' under the Geneva Convention. There is also a National Movement of Iranian Resistance, based in Paris.

Diplomatic Representation

EMBASSIES IN IRAN

Afghanistan: Dr Beheshti Ave, cnr of 4th St, Pakistan St, Tehran; tel. (21) 88737050; fax (21) 88735600; e-mail info@afghanembassy.ir; internet www.afghanembassy.ir; Ambassador Dr NASIR AHMADNOUR.

Algeria: No. 6, 16th Alley, Velenjak Ave, Velenjak, Tehran; tel. (21) 22420015; fax (21) 22420017; e-mail ambalg_teheran@yahoo.fr; Ambassador SOFIANE MIMOUNI.

Argentina: POB 15875-4335, 11 Ghoo Alley, Yar Mohammadi Ave, Darrous, Tehran; tel. (21) 22577433; fax (21) 22577432; e-mail eiran@mrecic.gov.ar; internet www.eiran.mrecic.gob.ar; Chargé d'affaires GUILLERMO NICOLÁS.

Armenia: 32 Ostad Shahriar St, Razi St, Jomhouri Islami Ave, Tehran 11337; tel. (21) 66740199; fax (21) 66700657; e-mail armiranembassy@mfa.am; Ambassador GRIGOR ARAKELYAN.

Australia: POB 15875-4334, No. 2, 23rd St, Khalid Islambuli Ave, Tehran 15138; tel. (21) 83863666; fax (21) 88720484; e-mail dfat-tehran@dfat.gov.au; internet www.iran.embassy.gov.au; Ambassador PAUL FOLEY.

Austria: 6–8 Bahonar St, Moghaddasi St, Ahmadi Zamani St, Tehran; tel. (21) 22750040; fax (21) 22705262; e-mail teheran-ob@bmeia.gv.at; internet www.bmeia.gv.at/botschaft/teheran; Ambassador Dr FRIEDRICH STIFT.

Azerbaijan: 16 Ratovan St, Sherzad Ave, Ehteshamie, Tehran; tel. (21) 22563146; fax (21) 22558183; e-mail az.embassy.ir@gmail.com; internet www.iranembassy.az; Ambassador JAVANSHIR AKHUNDOV.

Bahrain: POB 33111-15186, Tehran; tel. (21) 88773383; fax (21) 88880276; e-mail tehran.mission@mofa.gov.bh; internet www.mofa.gov.bh/tehran; Ambassador RASHID BIN SAAD AL-DOSARI.

Bangladesh: POB 11365-3711, Bldg 58, cnr Maryam Alley, Vanak St, Tehran; tel. (21) 88063073; fax (21) 88039965; e-mail info@bangladoot.ir; Ambassador KHANDAKAR ABDUS SATTAR.

Belarus: House 1, Azar Alley, Shahid Taheri St, Fallahi St, Zafaranieyeh Ave, Tehran 19887; tel. (21) 22752229; fax (21) 22751382; e-mail iran@mfa.gov.by; internet iran.mfa.gov.by; Ambassador VIKTOR RYBAK.

Belgium: POB 11365-115, 82–157 Shahid Fayyaz Bakhsh Ave, Elahieh, Tehran 16778; tel. (21) 22391909; fax (21) 22247313; e-mail teheran@diplobel.fed.be; internet www.diplomatie.be/tehran; Ambassador FRANÇOIS DEL MARMOL.

Bosnia and Herzegovina: No. 485, Aban Alley, 4th St, Iran Zamin Ave, Shahrak-e-Ghods, Tehran; tel. (21) 88086929; fax (21) 88092120; e-mail bhembasy@parsonline.net; Ambassador EMIR HADŽIKADUNIĆ.

Brazil: POB 19886-33854, 2 Yekta St, Vali-e Asr Ave, Zafaranieh, Tehran; tel. (21) 22753010; fax (21) 22752009; e-mail brasemb.teera@itamaraty.gov.br; internet teera.itamaraty.gov.br; Ambassador SANTIAGO IRAZABAL MOURÃO.

Brunei: No. 7 Mina Blvd, Africa Ave, Tehran; tel. (21) 88797946; fax (21) 88770162; e-mail tehran.iran@mfa.gov.bn; Ambassador Pengiran Haji SAHARI Pengiran Haji SALEH.

Bulgaria: POB 11365-7451, Vali-e-Asr Ave, Tavanir Ave, 40 Nezami-e-Ganjavi St, Tehran; tel. (21) 88775662; fax (21) 88779680; e-mail embassy.tehran@mfa.bg; internet www.mfa.bg/embassies/iran; Chargé d'affaires a.i. STILIYAN VARBANOV.

China, People's Republic: POB 11365-3937, 13 Narenjestan 7th, Pasdaran Ave, Tehran; tel. (21) 22291240; fax (21) 22290690; e-mail chinaemb_ir@mfa.gov.cn; internet ir.china-embassy.org; Ambassador YU HONGYANG.

Comoros: No. 10 Malek St, Shariati Ave, Tehran; tel. (21) 77624400; fax (21) 77624411; e-mail ambacomoresthn@yahoo.fr; Ambassador AHMAD NADJID AL-MARZOUQI.

Croatia: No. 25, 1st Behestan, Pasdaran St, Tehran; tel. (21) 22589923; fax (21) 22549199; e-mail vrhteh@mvpei.hr; Chargé d'affaires SAŠA MOMČINOVIĆ.

Cuba: Bldg 54, 17th West, Khodaverdi St, Niavaran Sq., Tehran; tel. and fax (21) 22282749; e-mail embajada@embacuba.ir; internet www.cubadiplomatica.cu/iran; Ambassador WILLIAM CARBÓ RICARDO.

Cyprus: POB 18348-44681, 328 Shahid Karimi, Dezashib, Tajrish, Tehran; tel. (21) 22219842; fax (21) 22219843; e-mail cyprus@parsonline.net; internet www.mfa.gov.cy/embassytehran; Ambassador ANDREAS IGNATIOU.

Czech Republic: POB 11365-4457, No. 36, Nastaran Alley, Bostan St, North Pasdaran Ave, Upper Farmaniyeh Crossroads, Tehran; tel. (21) 26118851; fax (21) 22802079; e-mail teheran@embassy.mzv.cz; internet www.mfa.cz/tehran; Chargé d'affaires PETR ŠTĚPÁNEK.

Denmark: POB 19395-5358, 10 Dashti St, Dr Shariati Ave, Hedayat St, Tehran 1914861144; tel. (21) 28155000; fax (21) 22640007; e-mail thramb@um.dk; internet iran.um.dk; Ambassador ANDERS CHRISTIAN HOUGÅRD.

Finland: POB 19395-1733, No. 2, Haddadian Alley, Mirzapour St, Dr Shariati Ave, Tehran 19336; tel. (21) 23512000; fax (21) 22215822; e-mail sanomat.teh@formin.fi; internet www.finland.org.ir; Ambassador HARRI KÄMÄRÄINEN.

France: 64–66, rue Neauphle-le-Château, Tehran; tel. (21) 64094000; fax (21) 64094092; e-mail contact@ambafrance-ir.org; internet www.ambafrance-ir.org; Ambassador BRUNO FOUCHER.

The Gambia: No. 10, Malek St, Shariati Ave, Tehran; tel. (21) 77500074; fax (21) 77529515; e-mail gambiaembassy_tehran@yahoo.co.uk; Ambassador SAEED ZARE.

Georgia: 92, 2nd Golestan St, Pasdaran Ave, Tehran; tel. and fax (21) 22782386; fax (21) 22542692; e-mail tehran.emb@mfa.gov.ge; internet www.iran.mfa.gov.ge; Ambassador IOSEB CHAKHVASHVILI.

Germany: POB 11365-179, 320–324 Ferdowsi Ave, Tehran; tel. (21) 39990000; fax (21) 39991890; e-mail info@tehe.diplo.de; internet www.teheran.diplo.de; Ambassador MICHAEL FREIHERR VON UNGERN-STERNBERG.

Greece: POB 11155-1151, 43 Esfandiar Ave, Africa Expressway, Tehran 19679; tel. (21) 22050533; fax (21) 22057431; e-mail gremb.teh@mfa.gr; internet www.mfa.gr/tehran; Ambassador NIKOLAOS GARILIDIS.

Guinea: POB 11365-4716, Dr Shariati Ave, Malek St, No. 10, Tehran; tel. (21) 77535744; fax (21) 77535743; e-mail ambaguinee_thr@hotmail.com; Ambassador BANGALI DIAKHABI.

Holy See: Apostolic Nunciature, POB 11155-178, 84 Razi Ave, Crossroad Neauphle-le-Château Ave, Tehran; tel. (21) 66403574; fax (21) 66419442; e-mail nuntius_fars@fastmail.fm; Apostolic Nuncio LEO BOCCARDI (Titular Archbishop of Bittetum).

Hungary: POB 6363-19395, No. 16, Shadloo St, Hedayat Sq., Darrous, Tehran; tel. (21) 22550460; fax (21) 22550503; e-mail mission.thr@mfa.gov.hu; internet www.mfa.gov.hu/kulkepviselet/ir; Ambassador GYULA PETHŐ.

India: POB 15875-4118, 22 Mir-Emad St, cnr of 9th St, Dr Beheshti Ave, Tehran; tel. (21) 88755103; fax (21) 88755973; e-mail hoc

.tehran@mea.gov.in; internet www.indianembassy-tehran.ir; Ambassador DINKAR PRAKASH SRIVASTAVA.

Indonesia: POB 11365-4564, Ghaem Magham Farahani Ave, No. 210, Tehran; tel. (21) 88716865; fax (21) 88718822; e-mail kbritehran@safineh.net; internet www.indonesian-embassy.ir; Ambassador DIAN WIRENGJURIT.

Iraq: Vali-e-Asr Ave, Vali-e-Asr Sq., Tehran; tel. (21) 88938865; fax (21) 88938877; e-mail info@iraqembassy.ir; internet www.iraqembassy.ir; Ambassador MUHAMMAD MAJID ABBAS AL-SHEIKH.

Italy: POB 4813-4863, 81 Neauphle-le-Château Ave, Tehran 1134834814; tel. (21) 66726955; fax (21) 66726961; e-mail segreteria.teheran@esteri.it; internet www.ambteheran.esteri.it; Ambassador LUCA GIANSANTI.

Japan: POB 11365-814, Bucharest Ave, cnr of 5th St, Tehran; tel. (21) 88717922; fax (21) 88713515; e-mail infoeoj@th.mofa.go.jp; internet www.ir.emb-japan.go.jp; Ambassador KOJI HANEDA.

Jordan: No. 1553, 2nd Alley, North Zarafshan, Phase 4, Shahrak-e-Ghods, Tehran; tel. (21) 88088356; fax (21) 88080496; e-mail tehran@fm.gov.jo; Chargé d'affaires JANTI GLAZOGA.

Kazakhstan: 82 North Hedayet St, cnr of Masjed Alley, Darrous, Tehran; tel. (21) 22565933; fax (21) 22546400; e-mail iran@mfa.kz; Ambassador BAGDAD K. AMREYEV.

Kenya: POB 19395-4566, 46 Golshar St, Africa Ave, Tehran; tel. (21) 22049355; fax (21) 22025792; e-mail info@kenyaemb-tehran.com; Ambassador Dr RASHID ALI.

Korea, Democratic People's Republic: 349 Shahid Dastjerdi Ave, Africa Ave, Tehran; tel. (21) 22357300; fax (21) 22089718; Ambassador JO IN CHOL.

Korea, Republic: POB 11155-3581, No. 2, West Daneshvar St, Shaikhbahai Ave, Vanak Sq., Tehran; tel. (21) 88054900; fax (21) 88064899; e-mail emb-ir@mofa.go.kr; internet irn.mofa.go.kr; Ambassador SONG WOONG-YEOB.

Kuwait: Africa Ave, Mahiyar St, No. 15, Tehran; tel. (21) 88785997; fax (21) 88788257; Ambassador MAJDI AL-DHUFAIRI.

Kyrgyzstan: POB 19579-35611, Bldg 12, 5th Naranjestan Alley, Pasdaran St, Tehran; tel. (21) 22830354; fax (21) 22281720; e-mail krembiri.mydatak@gmail.com; Chargé d'affaires AKYLBEK KYLYCHEV.

Lebanon: POB 11365-3753, No. 31, Shahid Kalantari St, Gharani Ave, Tehran; tel. (21) 88908451; fax (21) 88907345; Ambassador FADI HAJALI.

Libya: 2 Maryam Alley, South Kamranieh St, Tehran; tel. (21) 22201677; fax (21) 22236649; Ambassador SAAD MOJBAR.

Macedonia, former Yugoslav republic: No. 7, 4th Alley, Intifada Ave, Tehran; tel. and fax (21) 88720810; Ambassador CVETKO SOFKOVSKI.

Malaysia: No. 6, Changizi Alley, Alef St, Mahmoodieh, Tehran; tel. (21) 22046873; fax (21) 22046972; e-mail malthran@kln.gov.my; internet www.kln.gov.my/web/irn_tehran; Ambassador MUHAMMAD SADIK KETHERGANY.

Mali: No. 16, Aroos Alley, Istanbul St, Shariati Ave, Tehran; tel. (21) 22207278; fax (21) 22234631; e-mail malimissiontehran@yahoo.com; Ambassador (vacant).

Mexico: POB 19156, No. 12, Golfam St, Africa Ave, Tehran; tel. (21) 22012921; fax (21) 22057589; e-mail embiran@sre.gob.mx; internet embamex.sre.gob.mx/iran; Ambassador ULISES CANCHOLA GUTIÉRREZ.

Netherlands: POB 11155-138, No. 7 Sonbol, Tehran; tel. (21) 23660000; fax (21) 23660190; e-mail teh@minbuza.nl; internet iran.nlambassade.org; Ambassador JOS DOUMA.

New Zealand: No. 1, 2nd Park Alley, 34 Sousan St, North Golestan Complex, Aghdassiyeh Ave, Niavaran, Tehran; tel. (21) 26122175; fax (21) 26121973; e-mail nzembassytehran@hotmail.co.nz; internet www.nzembassy.com/iran; Ambassador BRIAN SANDERS.

Nicaragua: Tehran; tel. (21) 88685070; fax (21) 88685073; e-mail mbarquero@cancilleria.gob.ni; Ambassador MARIO BARQUERO.

Nigeria: 11 Sarvestan St, Elahieh, Tehran; tel. (21) 22009119; fax (21) 88799783; e-mail ngrembtehran@yahoo.com; Ambassador TUKUR MANI.

Norway: No. 54, Dr Lavasani St, cnr of Salmanpoor Zahir St, Tehran 1953694483; tel. (21) 22291333; fax (21) 22292776; e-mail emb.tehran@mfa.no; internet www.norway-iran.org; Ambassador JENS-PETTER KJEMPRUD.

Oman: No. 12, Tandis Alley, Africa Ave, Tehran; tel. (21) 22128352; fax (21) 22044672; e-mail tehran@mofa.gov.om; Ambassador SAUD BIN AHMAD BIN KHALID AL-BIRWANI.

Pakistan: No. 1, Ahmed Eitmadzadeh St, West Dr Fatemi Ave, Tehran 14118; tel. (21) 66941388; fax (21) 66944898; e-mail eoptehran@gmail.com; Ambassador NOOR MOHAMMAD JADMANI.

Philippines: POB 19395-4797, 5 Khayyam St, Vali-e-Asr Ave, Tehran; tel. (21) 22668774; fax (21) 22668990; e-mail tehranpe@yahoo.com; Chargé d'affaires a.i. ROSARIO P. LEMQUE.

Poland: POB 11155-3489, No. 2, Pirouz St, Africa Expressway, Tehran; tel. (21) 88787262; fax (21) 88788774; e-mail teheran.amb.sekretariat@msz.gov.pl; internet teheran.msz.gov.pl; Ambassador JULIUSZ JACEK GOJŁO.

Portugal: No. 13, Rouzbeh St, Hedayat Ave, Darrous, Tehran; tel. (21) 22582760; fax (21) 22552668; e-mail teerao@mne.pt; internet www.portugueseembassy.ir; Ambassador Dr MARIO FERNANDO DAMAS NUNES.

Qatar: POB 11155-1631, No. 4, Golazin St, Africa Ave, Tehran; tel. (21) 22029336; fax (21) 22058478; e-mail tehran@mofa.gov.qa; Ambassador Dr ALI BIN HAMAD AL-SULAITI.

Romania: 89 Shahid Meshki, Baharestan Ave, Tehran; tel. (21) 77647570; fax (21) 77535291; e-mail teheran@mae.ro; Ambassador CRISTIAN TEODORESCU.

Russia: 32 Neauphle-le-Château Ave, Tehran; tel. (21) 66728873; fax (21) 66701676; e-mail teheran@dks.ru; internet www.rusembiran.ru; Ambassador LEVAN S. DZHAGARYAN.

Saudi Arabia: No. 1, Niloufar St, Boustan St, Pasdaran Ave, Tehran; tel. (21) 22288543; fax (21) 22294691; e-mail iremb@mofa.gov.sa; Ambassador MUHAMMAD BIN ABBAS AL-KILABI.

Serbia: POB 11365-118, Velenjak Ave, No. 9, 9th St, Tehran 19858; tel. (21) 22412571; fax (21) 22402869; e-mail serbembteh@parsonline.net; Ambassador ALEXANDER TASIĆ.

Sierra Leone: POB 11365-1689, No. 4, Bukan St, Sadeghi Ghomi St, Bahonar Ave, Niavaran, Tehran; tel. (21) 22721474; fax (21) 22721485; e-mail slembsy_tehran@yahoo.com; Ambassador MUHAMMAD FUFANA.

Slovakia: POB 19395-6341, 34 Sarlashgar Fallahi St, Tehran 19887; tel. (21) 22666601; fax (21) 22666605; e-mail emb.tehran@mzv.sk; internet www.tehran.mfa.sk; Ambassador JÁN BÓRY.

Slovenia: POB 19575-459, 30 Narenjestan 8th Alley, Pasdaran Ave, Tehran 19576; tel. (21) 22836042; fax (21) 22290853; e-mail vte@gov.si; internet tehran.embassy.si; Chargé d'affaires KRISTINA RADEJ.

Somalia: 1 Hadaiyan St, Mirzapour St, Dr Shariati Ave, Tehran; tel. and fax (21) 22245146; e-mail safarian@hotmail.com; Ambassador KHALIFA MOUSSA.

South Africa: POB 11365-7476, 5 Yekta St, Bagh-e-Ferdows, Vali-e-Asr Ave, Tehran; tel. (21) 22702866; fax (21) 22719516; e-mail tehran.admin@foreign.gov.za; Ambassador WILLIAM MAX WHITEHEAD.

Spain: No. 10 Shadi St Abbas Asadi St, Sharzad Blvd, Darrous, Tehran; tel. (21) 22568681; fax (21) 22568018; e-mail emb.teheran@maec.es; internet www.exteriores.gob.es/embajadas/teheran/es/paginas/inicio.aspx; Ambassador PEDRO ANTONIO VILLENA PÉREZ.

Sri Lanka: No. 66, Kafiabadi Alley, Shahid Fallahi St, Zafaranieh, Tehran; tel. (21) 22569179; fax (21) 22175471; e-mail slemb@aframail.com; Ambassador MUHAMMAD FEISAL RAZIN.

Sudan: No. 39, Babak Bahrami St, Africa Ave, Tehran; tel. (21) 88781183; fax (21) 88792331; e-mail sudanembassy_tehran@yahoo.com; internet www.sudanembassyir.com; Ambassador SULEIMAN ABD AL-TAWAB ZEIN.

Sweden: POB 19575-458, 27 Nastaran St, Boostan Ave, Tehran; tel. (21) 23712200; fax (21) 22296451; e-mail ambassaden.teheran-visum@gov.se; internet www.swedenabroad.com/tehran; Ambassador PETER TEJLER.

Switzerland: POB 19395-4683, 2 Yasaman St, Sharifimanesh Ave, Elahieh, Tehran 19649; tel. (21) 22008333; fax (21) 22006002; e-mail teh.vertretung@eda.admin.ch; internet www.eda.admin.ch/tehran; Ambassador GIULIO HAAS; also represents interests of the USA in Iran.

Syria: 19 Iraj St, Africa Ave, Tehran; tel. (21) 22052780; fax (21) 22059409; e-mail tehran@mofa.gov.sy; Ambassador Dr ADNAN MAHMOUD.

Tajikistan: No. 10, 3rd Alley, Shahid Zeynali St, Niavaran, Tehran; tel. (21) 22299584; fax (21) 22809299; e-mail tajemb-iran@tajikistanir.com; internet www.tajembiran.tj; Ambassador DAVLATALI HOTAMOV.

Thailand: POB 11495-111, No. 4 Esteghlal Alley, Baharestan St, Tehran; tel. (21) 77531433; fax (21) 77532022; e-mail info@thaiembassy-tehran.org; internet www.thaiembassy-tehran.org; Ambassador ADISORNDEJ SUKHASVASTI.

Tunisia: No. 12, Shahid Lavasani Ave, Farmanieh, Tehran; tel. (21) 2706699; fax (21) 22631994; e-mail at-teheran@neda.net; Ambassador KHALED ZITOUNI.

Turkey: POB 11365-8758, No. 337 Ferdowsi Ave, Africa Ave, Tehran; tel. (21) 35951100; fax (21) 33117928; e-mail embassy.tehran@mfa.gov.tr; internet tehran.emb.mfa.gov.tr; Ambassador ÜMIT YARDIM.

Turkmenistan: 5 Barati St, Vatanpour St, Tehran; tel. (21) 22206731; fax (21) 22206732; e-mail tmnteh@afranet.com; Ambassador AKHMED GURBANOV.

Uganda: 3rd Floor, 10 Malek St, Shariati Ave, Tehran; tel. (21) 77643335; fax (21) 77643337; e-mail uganda_teh@yahoo.com; Ambassador Dr MUHAMMAD AHMAD KISULE.

Ukraine: 101 Vanak St, Vanak Sq., Tehran; tel. (21) 22404081; fax (21) 22417921; e-mail emb_ir@mfa.gov.ua; internet mfa.gov.ua/iran; Ambassador OLEKSANDR SAMARSKY.

United Arab Emirates: POB 19395-4616, No. 355, Vahid Dastjerdi Ave, Vali-e-Asr Ave, Tehran; tel. (21) 88788515; fax (21) 88789084; e-mail tehran@mofa.gov.ae; Ambassador SAIF MUHAMMAD OBAID AL-ZAABI.

Uruguay: POB 19395-4718, No. 6, Mina Blvd, Africa Ave, Tehran; tel. (21) 88679690; fax (21) 88782321; e-mail uruter@uruter.com; Ambassador JUAN CARLOS OJEDA VIGLIONE.

Uzbekistan: No. 6, Nastaran Alley, Boustan St, Pasdaran Ave, Tehran; tel. (21) 22299780; fax (21) 22299158; internet www.uzbekembassy.ir; Ambassador ELHAM AKRAMOV.

Venezuela: No. 17 Tajiki St, Kamranieh St North, Tehran; tel. (21) 22284450; fax (21) 26124886; e-mail embve.irthr@mre.gob.ve; internet emveniran.net; Ambassador AMENHOTEP ZAMBRANO CONTRERAS.

Viet Nam: No. 6, East Ordibehesht, Zaferanieh, Peysian St, M. Ardabili Vali-e-Asr Ave, Tehran; tel. (21) 22411670; fax (21) 22416045; e-mail vnemb.ir@mofa.gov.vn; internet www.vietnamembassy-iran.org; Chargé d'affaires HO ANH THAI.

Yemen: No. 15, Golestan St, Africa Ave, Tehran; tel. (21) 22042701; e-mail yem.emb.ir@neda.net; Ambassador JAMAL ABDULLAH AL-SOLAL.

Zimbabwe: 6 Shad Avar St, Mogghadas Ardabili, Tehran; tel. (21) 22027555; fax (21) 22049084; e-mail zimtehran@yahoo.com; Ambassador NICHOLAS KITIKITI.

Judicial System

In August 1982 the Supreme Court revoked all laws dating from the previous regime that did not conform with Islam; in October all courts set up prior to the Islamic Revolution of 1979 were abolished. In June 1987 Ayatollah Khomeini ordered the creation of clerical courts to try members of the clergy opposed to government policy. A new system of *qisas* (retribution) was established, placing the emphasis on swift justice. Islamic codes of correction were introduced in 1983, including the amputation of a hand for theft, flogging for fornication and violations of the strict code of dress for women, and stoning for adultery. The Islamic revolutionary courts try those accused of crimes endangering national security, corruption, drugs-trafficking, and moral and religious offences. The Supreme Court has 33 branches, each of which is presided over by two judges.

Supreme Court: Chief Justice Ayatollah MOHSENI GORKANI.

Head of the Judiciary: Hojatoleslam SADEQ ARDESHIR LARIJANI.

Prosecutor-General: GHOLAM-HOSSEIN MOHSENI EJEIE.

Religion

According to the 1979 Constitution, the official religion is Islam of the Ja'fari sect (Shi'a), but other Islamic sects, including Zeydi, Hanafi, Maleki, Shafe'i and Hanbali, are valid and will be respected. Zoroastrians, Jews and Christians will be recognized as official religious minorities. According to the 2006 census, there were 70,097,741 Muslims, 109,415 Christians (mainly Armenian), 19,823 Zoroastrians and 9,252 Jews in Iran.

ISLAM

The great majority of the Iranian people are Shi'a Muslims, but there is a minority of Sunni Muslims. Persians and Azerbaijanis are mainly Shi'a, while the other ethnic groups are mainly Sunni.

CHRISTIANITY

The Roman Catholic Church

Armenian Rite

Bishop of Esfahan: (vacant), Armenian Catholic Bishopric, POB 11318, Khiaban Ghazzali 65, Tehran; tel. (21) 66707204; fax (21) 66727533; e-mail arcaveso@yahoo.com.

Chaldean Rite

Archbishop of Ahvaz: HANNA ZORA, Archbishop's House, 334 Suleiman Farsi St, Ahvaz; tel. (61) 2224980.

Archbishop of Tehran: RAMZI GARMOU, Archevêché, Enghelab St, Sayed Abbas Moussavi Ave 91, Tehran 15819; tel. (21) 88823549; fax (21) 88308714.

Archbishop of Urmia (Rezayeh) and Bishop of Salmas (Shahpour): THOMAS MERAM, Khalifagari Kaldani Katholiq, POB 338, 7 Mirzaian St, Orumiyeh 57135; tel. (441) 2222739; fax (441) 2236031; e-mail thmeram@yahoo.com.

Latin Rite

Archbishop of Esfahan: IGNAZIO BEDINI, Consolata Church, POB 11155-445, 73 Neauphle-le-Château Ave, Tehran; tel. (21) 66703210; fax (21) 66724749; e-mail latin.diocese@gmail.com.

The Anglican Communion

Anglicans in Iran are adherents of the Episcopal Church in Jerusalem and the Middle East, formally inaugurated in January 1976. The Bishop in Cyprus and the Gulf is resident in Cyprus.

Bishop in Iran: Rt Rev. AZAD MARSHALL, POB 135, 81465 Esfahan; tel. (21) 88801383; fax (21) 88906908; internet dioceseofiran.org; diocese founded 1912.

Presbyterian Church

Synod of the Evangelical (Presbyterian) Church in Iran: POB 14395-569, Assyrian Evangelical Church, Khiaban-i Hanifnejad, Khiaban-i Aramanch, Tehran; tel. (21) 88006135; Moderator Rev. ADEL NAKHOSTEEN.

OTHER COMMUNITIES

Communities of Armenians, and somewhat smaller numbers of Zoroastrians, Jews, Assyrians, Greek Orthodox Christians, Uniates and Latin Christians are also found as officially recognized faiths. The Bahá'í faith, which originated in Iran, has about 300,000 Iranian adherents, although at least 10,000 are believed to have fled since 1979 in order to escape persecution. The Government banned all Bahá'í institutions in August 1983.

The Press

Tehran dominates the media, as many of the daily papers are published there, and the bi-weekly, weekly and less frequent publications in the provinces generally depend on the major metropolitan dailies as a source of news. A press law announced in August 1979 required all newspapers and magazines to be licensed, and imposed penalties of imprisonment for insulting senior religious figures. Offences against the Act will be tried in the criminal courts. Under the Constitution, the press is free, except in matters that are contrary to public morality, insult religious belief, or slander the honour and reputation of individuals. An intense judicial campaign since the late 1990s has sought to curb freedom of the press; some sources estimate that more than 100 publications were closed down during Muhammad Khatami's presidency (1997–2005).

PRINCIPAL DAILIES

Aftab-e-Yazd (Sun of Yazd): POB 13145-1134, Tehran; tel. (21) 66495833; fax (21) 66495835; internet www.aftab-yazd.com; f. 2000; Farsi; pro-reform; Chief Editor SAYED MOJTABA VAHEDI; circ. 100,000.

Alik: POB 11365-953, 26 Shahid Mohebi Ave, North Sohrevardi Ave, Tehran 155588; tel. (21) 88768567; fax (21) 88760994; e-mail alikmail@hyenet.ir; internet www.alikonline.com; f. 1931; afternoon; Armenian; political, literary, cultural, social, sport; Editor DERENIK MELIKIAN; circ. over 4,500.

Donya-e-Eqtesad (Economic World): POB 14157-44344, Tehran; tel. (21) 87762511; fax (21) 87762516; e-mail info@donya-e-eqtesad.com; internet www.donya-e-eqtesad.com; Farsi; Editor Dr MOUSA GHANINEJAD.

Entekhab (Choice): 12 Noorbakhsh Ave, Vali-e-Asr Ave, Tehran; tel. (21) 88893954; fax (21) 88893951; e-mail info@tiknews.net; online only; Farsi; centrist; Man. Dir Dr TAHA HASHEMI.

Etemad (Confidence): e-mail info@etemaad.com; internet www.etemaad.ir; Farsi; pro-reform; Man. Dir ELIAS HAZRATI; Editor BEHROUZ BEHZADI.

Ettela'at (Information): Ettela'at Bldg, Mirdamad Ave, South Naft St, Tehran 15499; tel. (21) 29999; fax (21) 22258022; e-mail ettelaat@ettelaat.com; internet www.ettelaat.com; f. 1925; evening; Farsi; political and literary; operates under the direct supervision of *wilayat-e-faqih* (religious jurisprudence); Editor SAYED MAHMOUD DO'AYI; circ. 500,000.

Hambastegi (Solidarity): Tehran; e-mail info@hambastegi-news.com; internet www.hambastegidaily.com; Farsi; pro-reform; Editor SALEH ABADI.

Ham-Mihan (Compatriot): Tehran; e-mail info@hammihan.com; internet www.hammihan.com; f. 2000; Farsi; independent, pro-reform; Founder and Man. Dir GHOLAMHOSSEIN KARBASCHI; Chair. of Bd MUHAMMAD ATRIANFAR; Editor MUHAMMAD GHOUCHANI.

Hamshahri (Citizen): POB 19395-5446, Tehran; tel. (21) 23023453; fax (21) 23023455; e-mail adjigol@hamshahri.org; internet www.hamshahrilinks.org; f. 1993; Farsi; conservative; economics, society and culture; owned by the Municipality of Tehran; Editor-in-Chief HOSSEIN GORBANZADEH; circ. 400,000.

Iran: POB 15875-5388, Tehran; tel. (21) 88761720; fax (21) 88761254; e-mail iran-newspaper@iran-newspaper.com; internet www.iran-newspaper.com; Farsi; conservative; connected to the Islamic Republic News Agency; Man. Dir HOSSEIN ZIYAEI; Editor-in-Chief BIJAN MOGHADDAM.

Iran Daily: Iran Cultural and Press Institute, 208 Khorramshahr Ave, Tehran; tel. (21) 88755761; fax (21) 88761869; e-mail iran-daily@iran-daily.com; internet www.iran-daily.com; English.

Iran News: POB 15875-8551, No. 13, Pajouhesh Lane, Golestan St, Marzdaran Blvd, Tehran; tel. (21) 44253450; fax (21) 44253478; e-mail info@irannewsdaily.com; internet www.irannewsdaily.com; f. 1994; English; Man. Dir MAJID AQAZADEH; circ. 35,000.

Jam-e Jam: Tehran; tel. (21) 22222511; fax (21) 22226252; e-mail info@jamejamonline.ir; internet www.jamejamonline.ir; online only; Farsi, English and French; conservative; linked to Islamic Republic of Iran Broadcasting; Man. Editor B. MOGHADDAM.

Jomhouri-e-Eslami (Islamic Republic): tel. (21) 33916111; fax (21) 33117552; e-mail info@jomhourieslami.com; internet www.jomhourieslami.com; f. 1980; Farsi; conservative; Man. Dir MASIH MOHAJERI.

Kalameh-ye Sabz (Green Word): f. 2009; Man. Dir MIR HOSSEIN MOUSAVI; Editor-in-Chief SAYED ALI REZA BEHESHTI.

Kayhan (Universe): Institute Kayhan, POB 11365-3631, Shahid Shahcheraghi Alley, Ferdowsi Ave, Tehran 11444; tel. (21) 33110251; fax (21) 33111120; e-mail kayhan@kayhannews.ir; internet www.kayhannews.ir; f. 1941; evening; Farsi; political; also publishes *Kayhan International* (f. 1959; daily; English; Editor HAMID NAJAFI), *Kayhan Arabic* (f. 1980; daily; Arabic), *Kayhan Persian* (f. 1942; daily; Farsi), *Zan-e Rooz* (Today's Woman; f. 1964; weekly; Farsi), *Kayhan Varzeshi* (World of Sport; f. 1955; daily and weekly; Farsi), *Kayhan Bacheha* (Children's World; f. 1956; weekly; Farsi), *Kayhan Farhangi* (World of Culture; f. 1984; monthly; Farsi); owned and managed by Mostazafin Foundation from October 1979 until January 1987, when it was placed under the direct supervision of *wilayat-e-faqih* (religious jurisprudence); Editor-in-Chief HOSSEIN SHARIATMADARI; circ. 350,000.

Khorasan: Mashad; Head Office: Khorasan Daily Newspapers, 14 Zohre St, Mobarezan Ave, Tehran; tel. (511) 7634000; fax (511) 7624395; e-mail info@khorasannews.com; internet www.khorasannews.com; f. 1948; Farsi; Propr MUHAMMAD SADEGH TEHERANIAN; Editor MUHAMMAD SAEED AHADI; circ. 40,000.

Quds Daily: POB 91735-577, Khayyam Sq., Sajjad Blvd, Mashad; tel. (51) 7685011; fax (511) 7684004; e-mail info@qudsdaily.com; internet www.qudsdaily.com; f. 1987; Farsi; owned by Astan Quds Razavi, the org. that oversees the shrine of Imam Reza at Mashad; also publ. in Tehran; Man. Dir GHOLAMREZA GHALANDARIAN; Editor-in-Chief MUHAMMAD HADI ZAHEDI.

Resalat (The Message): POB 11365-777, 53 Ostad Nejatollahi Ave, Tehran; tel. (21) 88902642; fax (21) 88900587; e-mail info@resalat-news.com; internet www.resalat-news.com; f. 1985; organ of right-wing group of the same name; Farsi; conservative; political, economic and social; Propr Resalat Foundation; Man. Dir SAYED MORTEZA NABAVI; circ. 100,000.

Shargh (East): Tehran; f. 2003; Farsi; reformist; publ. suspended in August 2009, allowed to resume in March 2010; Man. Dir MEHDI RAHMANIAN; Editor AHMAD GHOLAMI.

Tehran Times: POB 14155-4843, 32 Bimeh Alley, Ostad Nejatollahi Ave, Tehran; tel. (21) 88800789; fax (21) 88800788; e-mail info@tehrantimes.com; internet www.tehrantimes.com; f. 1979; English; independent; Man. Dir REZA MOGHADASI; Editor-in-Chief ABOLFAZI AMOUEI.

PRINCIPAL PERIODICALS

Acta Medica Iranica: Bldg No. 8, Faculty of Medicine, Tehran University of Medical Sciences, Poursina St, Tehran 14174; tel. (21) 88973667; fax (21) 88962510; e-mail acta@sina.tums.ac.ir; internet acta.tums.ac.ir; f. 1956; monthly; English; Editors-in-Chief AHMAD REZA DEHPOUR, M. SAMINI; circ. 2,000.

Ashur (Assyria): Ostad Motahari Ave, 11–21 Kuhe Nour Ave, Tehran; tel. (21) 622117; f. 1969; Assyrian; monthly; Founder and Editor Dr WILSON BET-MANSOUR; circ. 8,000.

Bukhara: POB 15655-166, Tehran; tel. 9121300147 (mobile); fax (21) 88958697; e-mail dehbashi.ali@gmail.com; internet www.bukharamag.com; bi-monthly; Farsi; arts, culture and humanities; Editor ALI DEHBASHI.

Bulletin of the National Film Archive of Iran: POB 11155, Baharestan Sq., Tehran 11499-43381; tel. (21) 38512583; fax (21) 38512710; e-mail khoshnevis_nfai@yahoo.com; f. 1989; English; Editor M. H. KHOSHNEVIS.

Daneshmand (Scientist): POB 15875-3649, Tehran; tel. (21) 88497883; fax (21) 88497880; e-mail info@daneshmandonline.ir; f. 1963; monthly; Farsi; owned by Mostazafari Foundation; science and technology in Iran and abroad; CEO YAGHOUB MOSHFEGH; Editor-in-Chief MINOO MEHRALI.

Donyaye Varzesh (World of Sports): Tehran; tel. (21) 3281; fax (21) 33115530; weekly; sport; Editor G. H. SHABANI; circ. 200,000.

The Echo of Iran: POB 14155-1168, 4 Hourtab Alley, Hafez Ave, Tehran; tel. (21) 22930477; e-mail info@iranalmanac.com; internet www.iranalmanac.com; f. 1952; monthly; English; news, politics and economics; Man. FARJAM BEHNAM; Editor JAHANGIR BEHROUZ.

Echo of Islam: POB 14155-3899, Tehran; tel. (21) 88897663; fax (21) 88902725; e-mail info@echoofsalam.com; internet www.echoofsalam.com; quarterly; English; publ. by the Islamic Thought Foundation; Man. Dir Dr MAHDI GOLJAN; Editor-in-Chief S. MOUSAVI.

Economic Echo: POB 14155-1168, 4 Hourtab Alley, Hafez Ave, Tehran; tel. (21) 22930477; e-mail info@iranalmanac.com; internet www.iranalmanac.com; f. 1998; English; Man. FARJAM BEHNAM.

Ettela'at Haftegi: 11 Khayyam Ave, Tehran; tel. (21) 311238; fax (21) 33115530; f. 1941; general weekly; Farsi; Editor F. JAVADI; circ. 150,000.

Ettela'at Javanan: POB 15499-51199, Ettela'at Bldg, Mirdamad Ave, South Naft St, Tehran; tel. (21) 29999; fax (21) 22258022; f. 1966; weekly; Farsi; youth; Editor M. J. RAFIZADEH; circ. 120,000.

Farhang-e-Iran Zamin: POB 19575-583, Niyavaran, Tehran; tel. (21) 283254; annual; Farsi; Iranian studies.

Film International, Iranian Film Quarterly: POB 11365-875, Tehran; tel. (21) 66709374; fax (21) 66719971; e-mail info@film-international.com; internet www.film-international.com; f. 1993; quarterly; English; Editor-in-Chief MASSOUD MEHRABI; circ. 15,000.

Iran Almanac: POB 14155-1168, 4 Hourtab Alley, Hafez Ave, Tehran; tel. and fax (932) 9139201; e-mail behnam.f@iranalmanac.com; internet www.iranalmanac.com; f. 2000; English; reference; history, politics, trade and industry, tourism, art, culture and society; Researcher and Editor FARJAM BEHNAM.

Iran Tribune: POB 111244, Tehran; e-mail matlab@iran-tribune.com; internet www.iran-tribune.com; monthly; English and Farsi; socio-political and cultural.

Iran Who's Who: POB 14155-1168, 4 Hourtab Alley, Hafez Ave, Tehran; e-mail info@iranalmanac.com; internet www.iranalmanac.com; annual; English; Editor FARJAM BEHNAM.

Iranian Cinema: POB 11155, Baharestan Sq., Tehran 11499-43381; tel. (21) 35812583; fax (21) 35812710; e-mail khoshnevis-nfai@yahoo.com; f. 1985; annual; English.

Kayhan Bacheha (Children's World): Institute Kayhan, POB 11365-3631, Shahid Shahcheraghi Alley, Ferdowsi Ave, Tehran 11444; tel. (21) 33110251; fax (21) 33111120; f. 1956; weekly; illustrated magazine for children; Editor AMIR HOSSEIN FARDI; circ. 150,000.

Kayhan Varzeshi (World of Sport): Institute Kayhan, POB 11365-3631, Shahid Shahcheraghi Alley, Ferdowsi Ave, Tehran 11444; tel. (21) 33110246; fax (21) 33114228; e-mail info@kayhanvarzeshi.com; internet www.kayhanvarzeshi.com; f. 1955; weekly; Farsi; Dir MAHMAD MONSETI; circ. 125,000.

Mahjubah: POB 14155-3899, Tehran; tel. (21) 88897662; fax (21) 88902725; e-mail mahjubah@iran-itf.com; internet www.itf.org.ir; Islamic family magazine; publ. by the Islamic Thought Foundation; Editor-in-Chief TURAN JAMSHIDIAN.

Soroush: POB 15875-1163, Soroush Bldg, Motahari Ave, Mofatteh Crossroads, Tehran; tel. and fax (21) 88847602; e-mail cultural@soroushpress.com; internet www.soroushpress.com; f. 1972; one weekly magazine; four monthly magazines, one for women, two for adolescents and one for children; one quarterly review of philosophy; all in Farsi; Editor-in-Chief ALI AKBAR ASHARI.

Tavoos: POB 19395-6434, 6 Asgarian St, East Farmanieh Ave, Tehran 19546-44755; tel. (21) 22817700; fax (21) 22825447; e-mail info@tavoosmag.com; internet www.tavoosmag.com; quarterly; Farsi and English; arts; Man. Dir MANIJEH MIREMADI; circ. 5,000.

Tchissta: POB 13145-593, Tehran; tel. (21) 678581; e-mail daneshvamardom@tchissta.com; internet tchissta.com; Farsi; politics, society, science and literature; Editor-in-Chief PARVIZ SHAHRIARI.

ZamZam: POB 14155-3899, Tehran; tel. (21) 88897663; fax (21) 88902725; internet www.itf.org.ir; children's magazine; English;

publ. by the Islamic Thought Foundation; Man. Dir Dr MAHDI GOLJAN; Editor-in-Chief SHAGHAYEGH GHANDEHARI.

Zan-e Rooz (Today's Woman): Institute Kayhan, POB 11365-3631, Shahid Shahcheraghi Alley, Ferdowsi Ave, Tehran 11444; tel. (21) 33911575; fax (21) 33911569; e-mail kayhan@istn.irost.com; f. 1964; weekly; women's; circ. over 60,000.

NEWS AGENCIES

Fars News Agency: Tehran; e-mail info@farsnews.com; internet www.farsnews.com; f. 2003; independent; news in Farsi and English; Man. Dir HAMID REZA MOQADDAMFAR.

Iranian Quran News Agency (IQNA): 97 Bozorgmehr St, Qods Ave, Tehran; tel. (21) 66470212; fax (21) 66970769; e-mail info@iqna.ir; internet www.iqna.ir; f. 2003; general news and news on Koranic activities.

Islamic Republic News Agency (IRNA): POB 764, 873 Vali-e-Asr Ave, Tehran; tel. (21) 88902050; fax (21) 88905068; e-mail irna@irna.com; internet www.irna.com; f. 1934; state-controlled; Man. Dir MAJID OMIDI SHARAKI.

Mehr News Agency: 32 Bimeh Alley, Nejatollahi St, Tehran; tel. (21) 88809500; fax (21) 88805801; e-mail info@mehrnews.com; internet www.mehrnews.com; f. 2003; news in Farsi, English and Arabic; Man. Dir PARVIZ ESMAEILI.

PRESS ASSOCIATION

Association of Iranian Journalists: No. 87, 7th Alley, Shahid Kabkanian St, Keshavarz Blvd, Tehran; tel. (21) 88956365; fax (21) 88963539; e-mail generalsecretary@aoij.org; Pres. RAJABALI MAZROOEI; Sec. BADRALSADAT MOFIDI.

Publishers

Amir Kabir Book Publishing and Distribution Co: POB 11365-4191, Jomhouri Islami Ave, Esteghlal Sq., Tehran; tel. (21) 33900751; fax (21) 33903747; e-mail info@amirkabir.net; internet www.amirkabir.net; f. 1948; historical, philosophical, social, literary and children's books; Dir AHMAD NESARI.

Avayenoor Publications: 31 Roshan Alley, Vali-e-Asr Ave, Tehran; tel. (21) 55136353; fax (21) 88907452; e-mail info@avayenoor.com; internet www.avayenoor.com; f. 1988; sociology, politics and economics; Editor-in-Chief SAYED MUHAMMAD MIRHOSSEINI.

Caravan Books Publishing House: POB 186-14145, 18 Salehi St, Sartip Fakouri Ave, Northern Karegar Ave, Tehran 14136; tel. (21) 88007421; fax (21) 88029486; e-mail info@caravan.ir; internet caravan.ir; f. 1997; fiction and non-fiction; Chief Editor ARASH HEJAZI.

Echo Publishers & Printers: POB 14155-1168, 4 Hourtab Alley, Hafez Ave, Tehran; tel. and fax (21) 22930477; e-mail info@iranalmanac.com; internet www.iranalmanac.com; f. 2000; politics, economics and current affairs; Man. FARJAM BEHNAM.

Eghbal Publishing Organization: 273 Dr Ali Shariati Ave, Tehran 16139; tel. (21) 77500973; fax (21) 7768113; f. 1903; Man. Dir SAEED EGHBAL.

Farhang Moaser: 43 Khiaban Daneshgah, Tehran 13147; tel. (21) 66465520; fax (21) 66417018; e-mail info@farhangmoaser.com; internet www.farhangmoaser.com; dictionaries.

Gooya Publications: 139 Karimkhan-e Zand Ave, Tehran 15856; tel. (21) 8838453; fax (21) 8842987; e-mail info@gooyabooks.com; internet www.gooyabooks.com; f. 1981; art; Dir NASER MIR BAGHERI.

Iran Chap Co: Ettela'at Bldg, Mirdamad Ave, South Naft St, Tehran; tel. (21) 29999; fax (21) 22258022; e-mail ettelaat@ettelaat.com; internet www.ettelaat.com; f. 1966; newspapers, books, magazines, book-binding and colour printing; Man. Dir MAHMOUD DOAEI.

Iran Exports Publication Co Ltd: POB 16315-1773, 41 First Mehr Alley, Mirzapour St, Shariati Ave, Tehran; tel. (21) 22200646; fax (21) 22888505; e-mail info@iranexportsmagazine.com; internet www.iranexportsmagazine.com; f. 1987; business and trade publs in English; Editor-in-Chief and Dir of Int. Affairs AHMAD NIKFARJAM.

Ketab Sara Co: POB 15117-3695, Tehran; tel. (21) 88711321; fax (21) 88717819; e-mail ketabsara@ketabsara.org; internet www.ketabsara.org; f. 1980; Dir SADEGH SAMII.

Kowkab Publishers: POB 19575-511, Tehran; tel. (21) 22949834; fax (21) 22949834; e-mail info@kkme.com; internet www.kkme.com; engineering, science, medicine, humanities, reference; Man. Dir Dr AHMAD GHANDI.

The Library, Museum and Documentation Center of the Islamic Consultative Assembly (Ketab-Khane, Muze va Markaz-e Asnad-e Majlis-e-Shura-e Islami): POB 11365-866, Ketab-Khane Majlis-e-Shura-e Islami No. 2, Baharestan Sq., Tehran; tel. (21) 33130911; fax (21) 33130920; e-mail info@majlislib.com; internet www.majlislib.com; f. 1912 as Majlis Library; renamed as above in 1996; arts, humanities, social sciences, politics, Iranian and Islamic studies; Dir SAYED MOHAMMAD ALI AHMADI ABHARI.

Ofoq Publishers: 181 Nazari St, 12th Farvardin St, Tehran 13145-1135; tel. (21) 66413367; fax (21) 66414285; e-mail info@ofoqco.com; internet www.ofoqco.com; f. 1990; illustrated books for children and teenagers, adult fiction and non-fiction; Dir REZA HASHEMINEJAD.

Qoqnoos Publishing House: 111 Shohadaye Jandarmeri St, Enghelab Ave, Tehran; tel. (21) 66408640; fax (21) 66413933; e-mail qoqnoos@morva.net; internet www.qoqnoos.ir; f. 1977; fiction, history, philosophy, law, sociology and psychology; privately owned; Owner and Gen. Man. AMIR HOSSEINZADEGAN; Editor-in-Chief ARSALAN FASIHI.

Sahab Geographic and Drafting Institute: POB 11365-617, 30 Somayeh St, Hoquqi Crossroads, Dr Ali Shariati Ave, Tehran 16517; tel. (21) 77535651; fax (21) 77535876; internet www.sahabmap.com; f. 1936; maps, atlases, and books on geography, science, history and Islamic art; Man. Dir MUHAMMAD REZA SAHAB.

Soroush Press: POB 15875-1163, Soroush Bldg, Motahari Ave, Mofatteh Crossroads, Tehran; tel. and fax (21) 88847602; fax (21) 88300760; e-mail cultural@soroushpress.com; internet www.soroushpress.ir; part of Soroush Publication Group, the publs dept of Islamic Republic of Iran Broadcasting; publishes books, magazines and multimedia products on a wide range of subjects; Man. Dir ALI AKBAR ASHARI.

Tehran University Press: 16th St, North Karegar St, Tehran; tel. (21) 88012080; fax (21) 88012077; e-mail press@ut.ac.ir; internet press.ut.ac.ir; f. 1944; univ. textbooks; Man. Dir Dr MUHAMMAD SHEKARCIZADEH.

Broadcasting and Communications

TELECOMMUNICATIONS

The Mobile Communications Company of Iran, a subsidiary of the Telecommunications Company of Iran, previously had a monopoly over the provision of mobile cellular telecommunications services in the country. However, in February 2004 Iran's second GSM licence was awarded to Irancell, a consortium led by Turkcell (Turkey). The contract was subsequently revised by the Majlis and the Council of Guardians to require that domestic firms hold a majority stake in the consortium, and Turkcell was replaced as the foreign partner by the second-placed bidder, the South African company MTN. The licence award was eventually signed in November 2005, and initial services commenced in October 2006. A consortium led by the Emirates Telecommunications Corpn (Etisalat—United Arab Emirates) was named as the successful bidder for Iran's third GSM licence in January 2009. However, in May the award was revoked by the regulatory authority. In April 2010 the third GSM licence was reallocated to Tamin Telecom, an Iranian company that had formed part of the previous Etisalat-led consortium. Tamin began offering third-generation mobile telecommunications services, under the brand name RighTel, in 2013.

Telecommunications Company of Iran (TCI): POB 3316-17, Dr Ali Shariati Ave, Tehran; tel. (21) 88113938; fax (21) 88405055; e-mail info@tci.ir; internet tci.ir; fmrly 100% state-owned; 51% stake acquired by Etemad-e-Mobin consortium Sept. 2009; 24.3m. fixed-line subscribers (Sept. 2008); Chair. SEYYED MUSTAFA SEYYED HASHEMI; Man. Dir MUZAFAR POURRANJBAR.

Mobile Communications Company of Iran (MCCI): 88 Hamrah Tower, Vanak St., Vanak Sq., Tehran, 1991954651; fax (21) 88641012; e-mail info@mci.ir; internet www.mci.ir; f. 2004; wholly owned subsidiary of TCI; 27.8m. subscribers (Sept. 2008); CEO VAHID SADOUGHI.

MTN Irancell: 12 Anahita Alley, Africa St, Tehran; internet www.irancell.ir; f. 2004 as Irancell, name changed as above 2005; mobile telecommunications; consortium of Iran Electronic Devt Co (51%) and MTN (South Africa—49%); 18.2m. subscribers (March 2009); Chair. Dr IBRAHIM MAHMOUDZADEH; Man. Dir ALIREZA GHALAMBOR DEZFOULI.

Regulatory Authority

Radio Communications and Regulations Organization: f. 2005; affiliated to the Ministry of Communications and Information Technology (see Ministries).

BROADCASTING

Article 175 of Iran's Constitution prohibits the establishment of private television channels and radio stations that are deemed to be 'un-Islamic'. However, in addition to the channels operated by the state-controlled Islamic Republic of Iran Broadcasting, many

Iranians have access to foreign television programmes transmitted via satellite dishes (although ownership of these is officially banned).

Islamic Republic of Iran Broadcasting (IRIB): POB 19395-3333, Jam-e Jam St, Vali-e-Asr Ave, Tehran; tel. (21) 22041093; fax (21) 22014802; e-mail infopr@irib.ir; internet www.irib.ir; semi-autonomous authority, affiliated with the Ministry of Culture and Islamic Guidance; non-commercial; operates seven national and 30 provincial television stations, and nine national radio networks; broadcasts worldwide in 27 languages; launched Al-Alam (international Arabic-language news channel) in 2002 and Press TV (English-language satellite channel) in 2007; Pres. SAYED EZZATOLLAH ZARGHAMI.

Radio

Radio Network 1 (Voice of the Islamic Republic of Iran): Covers the whole of Iran and also reaches Europe, Asia, Africa and part of the USA via short-wave and the internet; medium-wave regional broadcasts in local languages: Arabic, Armenian, Assyrian, Azerbaijani, Balochi, Bandari, Dari, Farsi, Kurdish, Mazandarani, Pashtu, Turkish, Turkoman and Urdu; external broadcasts in English, French, German, Spanish, Italian, Turkish, Bosnian, Albanian, Russian, Georgian, Armenian, Azeri, Tajik, Kazakh, Arabic, Kurdish, Urdu, Pashtu, Dari, Hausa, Bengali, Hindi, Japanese, Mandarin, Kiswahili, Indonesian and Hebrew.

Television

Television Network 1 (Vision of the Islamic Republic of Iran): 625-line, System B; Secam colour; two production centres in Tehran producing for national networks and 30 local television stations.

Finance

(cap. = capital; res = reserves; dep. = deposits; brs = branches; m. = million; amounts in rials, unless otherwise stated)

BANKING

Banks were nationalized in June 1979 and a revised commercial banking system was introduced consisting of nine banks (subsequently expanded to 11). Three banks were reorganized, two (Bank Tejarat and Bank Mellat) resulted from mergers of 22 existing small banks, three specialize in industry and agriculture, and one, the Islamic Bank of Iran (now Islamic Economy Organization), set up in May 1979, was exempt from nationalization. The 10th bank, the Export Development Bank, specializes in the promotion of exports. Post Bank of Iran became the 11th state-owned bank upon its establishment in 2006. A change-over to an Islamic banking system, with interest (forbidden under Islamic law) being replaced by a 4% commission on loans, began on 21 March 1984. All short- and medium-term private deposits and all bank loans and advances are subject to Islamic rules.

A partial liberalization of the banking sector was implemented by the administration of former President Khatami during 1997–2005, beginning with the establishment of four private banks after 2001. Two further private banks were granted licences to commence operations in 2005. Notable banks included in the Government's privatization programme are Mellat, Refah, Saderat, Tejarat and Post Bank of Iran.

Central Bank

Bank Markazi Jomhouri Islami Iran (Central Bank): POB 15875-7177, 144 Mirdamad Blvd, Tehran; tel. (21) 29954855; fax (21) 29954780; e-mail g.secdept@cbi.ir; internet www.cbi.ir; f. 1960; Bank Markazi Iran until Dec. 1983; issuing bank, govt banking; cap. 15,000,000m., res 102,794,098m., dep. 782,499,933m. (March 2009); Gov. Dr VALIOLLAH SEIF.

State-owned Commercial Banks

Bank Keshavarzi (Agricultural Bank): POB 14155-6395, 247 Patrice Lumumba Ave, Jalal al-Ahmad Expressway, Tehran 14454; tel. (21) 84895593; fax (21) 88253625; e-mail icd@agri-bank.com; internet www.agri-bank.com; f. 1980 by merger of Agricultural Co-operative Bank of Iran and Agricultural Devt Bank of Iran; cap. 8,021,118m., res 10,660,488m., dep. 328,337,431m. (March 2013); Chair. and Man. Dir Dr MUHAMMAD TALEBI; 1,870 brs.

Bank Mellat (Nation's Bank): Head Office Bldg, 327 Taleghani Ave, Tehran 15817; tel. (21) 82962043; fax (21) 88834417; e-mail info@bankmellat.ir; internet www.bankmellat.ir; f. 1980 by merger of 10 fmr private banks; cap. 16,000,000m., res 5,685,685m., dep. 534,498,512m. (March 2011); Chair. and Man. Dir ALI DIVANDARI; 1,905 brs in Iran, 5 abroad.

Bank Melli Iran (National Bank of Iran): POB 11365-171, Ferdowsi Ave, Tehran; tel. (21) 66731382; fax (21) 66738606; e-mail intlrel@bankmelli-iran.com; internet www.bankmelli-iran.com; f. 1928; present name since 1943; cap. 22,400,000m., res 7,460,824m., dep. 508,409,899m. (March 2009); Chair. and Man. Dir Dr ABDOLNASER HEMMATI; 3,300 brs in Iran, 16 abroad.

Bank Refah Kargaran: 186 Northern Shiraz Ave, Molla Sadra Ave, Vanak Sq., Tehran 19917; tel. and fax (21) 88653991; fax (21) 42504292; e-mail info@bankrefah.ir; internet www.refah-bank.ir; f. 1960; cap. 895,000m., res 302,259m., dep. 56,545,320m. (March 2008); Chair. and Man. Dir SAYYED ZIA IMANI; 1,117 brs.

Bank Saderat Iran: POB 15745-631, Bank Saderat Tower, 43 Somayeh Ave, Tehran; tel. (21) 88302699; fax (21) 88839539; e-mail info@bsi.ir; internet www.bsi.ir; f. 1952; cap. 20,164,000m., res 8,445,000m., dep. 465,818,000m. (March 2011); Chair. MUHAMMAD REZA PISHRO; 3,300 brs in Iran, 21 abroad.

Bank Sepah: 7 Africa Ave, Argentina Sq., Tehran 15149-47111; tel. (21) 84433161; fax (21) 88646951; e-mail info@banksepah.ir; internet www.banksepah.ir; f. 1925; nationalized in June 1979; cap. 8,559,365m., res 1,870,563m., dep. 328,705,912m. (March 2013); Chair. and Man. Dir KAMEL TAGHAVI NEJAD; 1,891 brs in Iran, 3 abroad.

Bank Tejarat (Commercial Bank): POB 11365-5416, 130 Taleghani Ave, Nejatoullahie, Tehran 15994; tel. (21) 88826690; fax (21) 88893641; internet www.tejaratbank.ir; f. 1979 by merger of 12 banks; cap. 13,568,599m., res 6,345,677m., dep. 361,381,210m. (March 2011); Chair. and Man. Dir Dr MAJID REZA DAVARI; 1,971 brs in Iran, 2 abroad.

Post Bank of Iran (PBI): 229 Motahari Ave, Tehran 15876-18118; tel. (21) 88502024; fax (21) 88502025; e-mail info@postbank.ir; internet www.postbank.ir; f. 2006; cap. 561,143m., res 11,559m., dep. 8,236,617m. (March 2009); Chair. MAHMOUD HASSANZADEH; Man. Dir ALI ZIAEI.

Private Commercial Banks

Bank Pasargad: POB 19697-74511, 430 Mirdamad Ave, Tehran; tel. (21) 88649502; fax 88649501; e-mail info@bankpasargad.com; internet fa.bpi.ir; f. 2005; cap. 27,258,000m., res 4,841,393m., dep. 172,188,341m. (March 2012); Chair. SAYED KAZEM MIRVALAD; CEO Dr MAJID GHASEMI; 233 brs.

Bank Sarmaye: POB 19395-6415, 24 Arak St, Gharani Ave, Tehran; tel. (21) 88803632; fax (21) 88890839; e-mail info@sbank.ir; internet www.sbank.ir; f. 2005; cap. 3,535,000m., res 965,425m., dep. 37,242,086m. (March 2012); Chair. PARVIZ KAZEMI; CEO ALI BAKHSHAYESH; 61 brs.

Eghtesad Novin Bank (EN Bank): 28 Esfandiar Blvd, Vali-e-Asr Ave, Tehran 196865-5944; tel. (21) 82330000; fax (21) 88880166; e-mail info@enbank.ir; internet www.en-bank.com; f. 2001; granted operating licence in 2001; cap. 5,500,000m., res 1,585,908m., dep. 120,235,940m. (March 2011); Chair. BAHRAM FATHALI; CEO Dr HASSAN MOTAMEDI; 280 brs.

Karafarin Bank: POB 1966916461, No. 97, West Nahid St, Valiasr Ave, Tehran; tel. (21) 26215000; fax (21) 26214995; e-mail info@karafarinbank.com; internet www.karafarinbank.com; f. 1999 as Karafarin Credit Institute; converted into private bank in 2001; cap. 3,000,000m., res 1,026,021m., dep. 33,776,307m. (March 2011); Chair. ATAOLAH AYATOLAHI; Man. Dir FAZLOLAH MOAZAMI; 81 brs.

Parsian Bank: 4 Zarafshan St, Farahzadi Blvd, Shahrak Ghods, Tehran 146779-3811; tel. (21) 81151000; fax (21) 88362744; e-mail info@parsian-bank.ir; internet www.parsian-bank.com; f. 2002; cap. US $897m., res $567m., dep. $21,764m. (March 2012); Chair. Dr GHOLAMREZA SULEIMANI AMIRI; Man. Dir ALI DIVANDARI; 155 brs.

Saman Bank Corpn: Bldg No. 1, 879 Kaledge Junction, Engheleb St, Tehran; tel. (21) 23095100; fax (21) 26210911; e-mail info@sb24.com; internet www.sb24.com; f. 2001; cap. 6,573,503m., res 979,056m., dep. 118,659,330m. (March 2013); Chair. ALLAHVERDI RAJAEE SALMASI; 54 brs.

Development Banks

Bank of Industry and Mine (BIM): POB 15875-4456, Firouzeh Tower, 2917 Vali-e-Asr Ave (above Park Way Junction), Tehran; tel. (21) 22029811; fax (21) 22031904; e-mail info@bim.ir; internet w3.bim.ir; f. 1979 by merger of Industrial Credit Bank, Industrial and Mining Devt Bank of Iran, Devt and Investment Bank of Iran, and Iranian Bankers Investment Co; state-owned; cap. 20,722,472m., res 3,749,028m., dep. 48,449,128m. (March 2012); Chair. and Man. Dir ALI ASHRAF AFKHAMI; 31 brs.

Export Development Bank of Iran (EDBI): POB 151674-7913, Tose'e Tower, 15th St, Ahmad Ghasir Ave, Argentina Sq., Tehran; tel. (21) 88702130; fax (21) 88798259; e-mail info@edbi.ir; internet www.edbi.ir; f. 1991; state-owned; cap. 16,418,554m., res 6,325,389m., dep. 41,972,684m. (March 2012); Chair. and Man. Dir BAHMAN VAKILI; 34 brs.

Housing Bank

Bank Maskan (Housing Bank): POB 19947-63811, 14 Attar St, Vanak Sq., Tehran; tel. (21) 88797822; fax (21) 82932735; e-mail intl_div@bank-maskan.ir; internet bank-maskan.ir; f. 1979; state-owned; cap. 30,735,134m., res 3,615,729m., dep. 766,090,576m. (March 2013); provides mortgage and housing finance; Chair. and Man. Dir GHODRATOLLAH SHARIFI; 1,214 brs.

STOCK EXCHANGE

Tehran Stock Exchange: 192 Hafez Ave, Tehran 11355; tel. (21) 66719535; fax (21) 66710111; e-mail int@tse.ir; internet www.tse.ir; f. 1967; cap. US $164,722m. (Nov. 2013); 314 listed cos (2012); Chair. HAMID REZA RAFIEI KESHTELI; CEO and Pres. Dr HASSAN GHALIBAF ASL.

INSURANCE

The nationalization of insurance companies was announced in June 1979. However, as part of the reforms to the financial sector undertaken by the former Khatami administration, four new private insurance companies were licensed to commence operations in May 2003. In 2011 there were 24 privately owned insurance and reinsurance companies operating in Iran. There was also one state-owned insurance company in operation, Bimeh Iran.

Bimeh Alborz (Alborz Insurance Co): POB 4489-15875, Alborz Bldg, 234 Sepahbood Garani Ave, Tehran; tel. (21) 88803821; fax (21) 88908088; e-mail info@alborzins.com; internet www.alborzinsurance.ir; f. 1959; all types of insurance; Chair. and Man. Dir MUHAMMAD EBRAHIM AMIN; 39 brs.

Bimeh Asia (Asia Insurance Co): POB 15815-1885, Asia Insurance Bldg, 299 Taleghani Ave, Tehran; tel. (21) 88800950; fax (21) 88898113; e-mail info@bimehasia.ir; internet www.bimehasia.com; f. 1959; all types of insurance; Man. Dir A. HAJFATALIHA; 83 brs.

Bimeh Dana (Dana Insurance Co): 25 15th St, Ghandi Ave, Tehran 151789-5511; tel. (21) 88770971; fax (21) 88792997; e-mail info@dana-insurance.com; internet www.dana-insurance.com; f. 1988; 56% govt-owned; life, personal accident and health insurance; Chair. and Man. Dir H. O. HOSSEIN.

Bimeh Day (Day Insurance Co): 241 Mirdamad Blvd, Tehran; tel. (21) 22900551; fax (21) 22900516; e-mail info@dayins.com; internet www.dayins.com; f. 2004; privately owned; all types of insurance.

Bimeh Iran (Iran Insurance Co): POB 14155-6363, 107 Dr Fatemi Ave, Tehran; tel. (21) 88954712; e-mail info@iraninsurance.ir; internet www.iraninsurance.ir; f. 1935; state-owned; all types of insurance; Chair. and Man. Dir JAVAD SAHAMIAN MOGHADDAM; 246 brs in Iran, 14 brs abroad.

Bimeh Karafarin (Karafarin Insurance Co): POB 15875-8475, No. 9, 17th St, Ahmad Ghasir Ave, Argentina Sq., Tehran; tel. (21) 88723830; fax (21) 88723840; e-mail karafarin@karafarin-insurance.com; internet www.karafarin-insurance.com; f. 2003; privately owned; all types of insurance; 14 brs; Chair. Dr PARVIZ AGHILI-KERMANI; Man. Dir ABDOLMAHMOUD ZARRABI.

Bimeh Novin (Novin Insurance Co): POB 19119-33183, 11 Behrouz St, Madar (Mohseni) Sq., Mirdamad Blvd, Tehran; tel. (21) 22258046; fax (21) 22923844; e-mail info@novininsurance.com; internet www.novininsurance.com; f. 2006; privately owned; all types of insurance; Chair. Dr GHOLAMALI GHOLAMI.

Bimeh Saman (Saman Insurance Co): 113 Khaled Eslamboli Ave, Tehran 15138-13119; tel. (21) 88700205; fax (21) 88700204; e-mail info@samaninsurance.com; internet www.samaninsurance.com; f. 2005; privately owned; Chair. MUHAMMAD ZRABYH.

Bimeh Sina (Sina Insurance Co): 343 Beheshti Ave, Tehran; tel. (21) 88706701; fax (21) 88709654; e-mail info@sinainsurance.com; internet www.sinainsurance.com; f. 2003; privately owned.

Mellat Insurance Co: 48 Shahid Haghani Expressway, Vanak Sq., Tehran; tel. and fax (21) 88878814; e-mail info@mellatinsurance.com; internet www.mellatinsurance.com; privately owned; property, life, engineering, aviation and marine insurance; Chair. ABDOLHOSSEIN SABET; Man. Dir MASOUD HAJJARIAN KASHANI.

Regulatory Authority

Bimeh Markazi Iran (Central Insurance of Iran): POB 19395-5588, 72 Africa Ave, Tehran 19157; tel. (21) 22050001; fax (21) 22054099; e-mail pr@centinsur.ir; internet www.centinsur.ir; f. 1971; regulates and supervises the insurance market and tariffs for new types of insurance cover; the sole state reinsurer for domestic insurance cos, which are obliged to reinsure 50% of their direct business in life insurance and 25% of business in non-life insurance with Bimeh Markazi Iran; Pres. Dr JAVAD FARSHBAF MAHERIYAN.

Trade and Industry

CHAMBERS OF COMMERCE

Iran Chamber of Commerce, Industries and Mines: 254 Taleghani Ave, Tehran 15875-4671; tel. (21) 88846031; fax (21) 88825111; e-mail dsg@iccim.ir; internet www.iccim.ir; supervises the affiliated 32 local chambers; Pres. Dr MUHAMMAD NAHAVANDIAN.

Esfahan Chamber of Commerce, Industries and Mines: POB 81656-336, Feyz Sq., Tehran; tel. (311) 6611467; fax (311) 6615099; e-mail m.eslamian@eccim.com; internet www.eccim.com; Pres. KHORSO KARAEIYAN.

Shiraz Chamber of Commerce, Industries and Mines: Zand St, Shiraz; tel. (711) 6294901; fax (711) 6294910; e-mail info@sccim.org; internet www.sccim.ir; Chair. FERIDOUN FORGHANI.

Tabriz Chamber of Commerce, Industries and Mines: 65 North Artesh Ave, Tabriz; tel. (411) 5264111; fax (411) 5264115; e-mail info@tzccim.ir; internet www.tzccim.ir; f. 1906; privately owned; Chair. RAHIM SADEGHIAN.

Tehran Chamber of Commerce, Industries and Mines: 285 Motahari Ave, Tehran; tel. (21) 88701912; fax (21) 88715661; e-mail into@tccim.ir; internet www.tccim.ir; Chair. Dr YAHYA ALE-ESHAGH.

INDUSTRIAL AND TRADE ASSOCIATIONS

National Iranian Industries Organization (NIIO): POB 15875-1331, No. 11, 13th Alley, Miremad St, Tehran; tel. (21) 88744198; fax (21) 88757126; f. 1979; owns 400 factories in Iran; Man. Dir ALI TOOSI.

National Iranian Industries Organization Export Co (NECO): No. 8, 2nd Alley, Bucharest Ave, Tehran; tel. (21) 44162384; fax (21) 212429.

STATE HYDROCARBONS COMPANIES

The following are subsidiary companies of the Ministry of Petroleum:

National Iranian Gas Co (NIGC): POB 6394-4533, 7th Floor, No. 401, Saghitaman, Taleghani Ave, Tehran; tel. (21) 88133347; fax (21) 88133456; e-mail webmaster@nigc.org; internet www.nigc.ir; f. 1965; Chair. BIJAN NAMDAR ZANGANEH (Minister of Petroleum); Man. Dir JAVAD OJI.

National Iranian Oil Co (NIOC): POB 1863, Taleghani Ave, Tehran 15875-1863; tel. (21) 66154975; fax (21) 66154977; e-mail public-relations@nioc.com; internet www.nioc.com; f. 1948; controls all upstream activities in the petroleum and natural gas industries; incorporated April 1951 on nationalization of petroleum industry to engage in all phases of petroleum operations; in Feb. 1979 it was announced that in future Iran would sell petroleum directly to the petroleum companies, and in Sept. 1979 the Ministry of Petroleum assumed control of the NIOC; Chair. BIJAN NAMDAR ZANGANEH (Minister of Petroleum); Man. Dir SEIFOLLAH JASHNSAZ; subsidiary cos include the following:

Iranian Offshore Oil Co (IOOC): POB 5591, 38 Tooraj St, Vali-e-Asr Ave, Tehran 19395; tel. (21) 22664402; fax (21) 22664216; e-mail M.Khandan@iooc.co.ir; internet www.iooc.co.ir; f. 1980; devt, exploitation and production of crude petroleum, natural gas and other hydrocarbons in all offshore areas of Iran in the Persian (Arabian) Gulf and the Caspian Sea; Chair. Dr MUHAMMAD JAVAD ASEMI POOR; Man. Dir MAHMOUD ZIRAKCHIAN ZADEH.

Pars Oil and Gas Co (POGC): POB 14141-73111, 1 Parvin Etesami Alley, Dr Fatemi Ave, Tehran; tel. (21) 88966031; fax (21) 88989273; e-mail info@pogc.ir; internet www.pogc.ir; f. 1999; Man. Dir ALI VAKILI.

National Iranian Oil Refining and Distribution Co (NIORDC): POB 15815-3499, NIORDC Bldg, 140 Ostad Nejatollahi Ave, Tehran 15989; tel. (21) 88801001; fax (21) 66152138; e-mail info@niordc.ir; internet www.niordc.ir; f. 1992 to assume responsibility for refining, pipeline distribution, engineering, construction and research in the petroleum industry from NIOC; Chair. BIJAN NAMDAR ZANGANEH (Minister of Petroleum); Man. Dir NOUREDDIN SHAHNAZIZADEH.

National Iranian Petrochemical Co (NIPC): POB 19395-6896, North Sheikh Bahaei St, Tehran; tel. (21) 88620000; fax (21) 88059702; e-mail webmaster@nipc.net; internet www.nipc.net; f. 1964; oversees the devt and operation of Iran's petrochemical sector; directs activities of over 50 subsidiaries; Chair. BIJAN NAMDAR ZANGANEH (Minister of Petroleum); Man. Dir ABDOLHOSSEIN BAYAT.

CO-OPERATIVES

Central Union of Rural and Agricultural Co-operatives of Iran: POB 14155-6413, 78 North Palestine St, Opposite Ministry of Energy, Tehran; tel. (21) 88978150; fax (21) 88964166; internet www.trocairan.com; f. 1963; educational, technical, commercial and credit assistance to rural co-operative societies and unions; Chair. and Man. Dir SAYED MUHAMMAD MIRMUHAMMADI.

UTILITIES

Electricity

Iran Power Generation, Transmission and Distribution Co (Tavanir): POB 19988-36111, Tavanir Blvd, Rashid Yasami St, Vali-e-Asr Ave, Tehran; tel. (21) 88774088; fax (21) 88778437; e-mail info@tavanir.org.ir; internet www.tavanir.org.ir; f. 1979; state-owned; operates a network of 16 regional electricity cos, 27 generating cos and 42 distribution cos; also responsible for electricity transmission; Man. Dir HOMAYOUN HAERI.

Water

Iran Water Resources Management Co: 517 Felestin Ave, Tehran; tel. (21) 88905003; fax (21) 88801555; e-mail waterpr@wrm.ir; internet www.wrm.ir; f. 2003; govt agency reporting to the Ministry of Energy; in charge of Iran's Regional Water Authorities; Man. Dir MUHAMMAD HAJRASOULIHA.

Transport

RAILWAYS

In 2010 the total length of Iranian railways was 6,073 route-km. In 2007 it was reported that the Government planned to expand the rail network to 28,000 km by 2020. However, the expansion programme has been severely impeded by a shortage of foreign investment and the impact of US-led sanctions. None the less, construction of a 506-km rail link between Esfahan and Shiraz was completed in June 2009. In the same month a 250-km Zahedan–Kerman line was inaugurated, linking the rail networks of Iran and Pakistan and facilitating the launch of a direct Islamabad (Pakistan)–Tehran–İstanbul (Turkey) freight service in August. Construction of a 1,350-km railway along Iran's eastern border, linking Mashad, in the north-east, with Chabahar on the Persian (Arabian) Gulf, commenced in May 2010. A 51-km railway linking Khorramshahr with Basra in southern Iraq was also under construction. In February 2011 a US $12,860m. contract to build eight new lines—totalling some 5,300 km—was awarded to the People's Republic of China.

Islamic Republic of Iran Railways: Railways Central Bldg, Argentina Sq., Africa Blvd, Tehran; tel. (21) 88646568; fax (21) 88646570; e-mail iranrai@rai.ir; internet www.rai.ir; f. 1934; affiliated to Ministry of Roads and Urban Development; Pres. ABDOL-ALI SAHEB MUHAMMADI.

Raja Passenger Trains Co: POB 15875-1363, 1 Sanaie St, Karimkhan Zand Ave, Tehran; tel. (21) 88310880; fax (21) 88834340; e-mail info@raja.ir; internet www.raja.ir; f. 1996; state-owned; affiliated to Iranian Islamic Republic Railways; Chair. and Man. Dir NASER BAKHTIARI.

Underground Railway

Construction of the Tehran underground railway system commenced in 1977. By 2014 the system consisted of five lines: Line 1, a 34-km line linking north and south Tehran; Line 2, a 24-km line running east–west across the city; Line 3, initially a 7–km line between two stations in the city centre (eventually to become a 35–km line running south-east to north-east); Line 4, a 16-km line running east–west through the centre; and Line 5, a 41.5-km suburban line, linking Tehran with the satellite city of Karaj. A further two lines—6 and 7—were under construction. In March 2010 the Tehran Urban and Suburban Railway Company announced plans for an additional six underground lines—8 and 9, and four suburban lines linking central Tehran to satellite cities. It was envisaged that construction work on these additional lines would commence in 2018, following the completion of existing projects.

Tehran Urban and Suburban Railway Co (Tehranmetro) (TUSRC): 37 Mir Emad St, Tehran 15878-13113; tel. (21) 88740110; fax (21) 88740114; e-mail info@tehranmetro.com; internet www.tehranmetro.com; f. 1976; CEO HABIL DARVISH.

ROADS

In 2010 there were an estimated 198,866 km of roads, including 1,957 km of motorways, 31,945 km of highways, main or national roads, 43,264 km of secondary or regional roads and 121,700 km of other roads. There is a paved highway (A1, 2,089 km) from Bazargan on the Turkish border to the Afghanistan border. The A2 highway runs 2,473 km from the Iraq border to Mir Javeh on the Pakistan border. A new highway linking the eastern city of Dogharun to Herat in Afghanistan was opened in January 2005.

INLAND WATERWAYS

Lake Urmia (formerly Lake Rezaiyeh): 80 km west of Tabriz in north-western Iran; from Sharafkhaneh to Golmankhaneh there is a regular service of tugs and barges for the transport of passengers and goods.

Karun River: Flowing south through the oilfields into the Shatt al-Arab waterway, and thence to the head of the Persian (Arabian) Gulf near Abadan; there is a regular cargo service, as well as daily motor-boat services for passengers and goods.

SHIPPING

At 31 December 2013 Iran's flag registered fleet comprised 757 vessels, with an aggregate displacement of 3.4m. grt, of which 21 were bulk carriers, 23 were fish carriers and 93 were general cargo ships.

The main oil terminal on the Persian (Arabian) Gulf is at Kharg Island. The principal commercial non-oil ports are Bandar Shahid Rajai (which was officially inaugurated in 1983 and handles a significant proportion of the cargo passing annually through Iran's Gulf ports), Bandar Imam Khomeini, Bushehr, Bandar Abbas and Chabahar. The Bandar Abbas port complex, which predates the 1979 Islamic Revolution, comprises two separate ports, Shahid Rajai and Shahid Bahonar. A major expansion of Chabahar port, which was expected to increase annual handling capacity from 100,000 to 500,000 20-ft equivalent units, was under way in 2014. Iran's principal ports on the Caspian Sea include Bandar Anzali (formerly Bandar Pahlavi) and Bandar Nowshahr.

Port Authority

Ports and Maritime Organization (PMO): POB 158754574-158753754, South Didar St, Shahid Haghani Highway, Vanak Sq., Tehran; tel. (21) 88809280; fax (21) 88651191; e-mail info@pmo.ir; internet www.pmo.ir; f. 1960 as Ports and Shipping Org.; affiliated to Ministry of Roads and Urban Development; Man. Dir ATAOLLAH SADR.

Principal Shipping Companies

Bonyad Shipping Agencies Co (BOSCO): POB 15875-3794, 24 Gandhi Ave, 15177 Tehran; tel. (21) 88795211; fax (21) 88776951; e-mail bosaco@bosaco.ir; internet www.bosacoir.com; f. 1991; Man. Dir ALI SAFARALI.

Iran Marine Services: 151 Mirdamad Blvd, Tehran 19116; tel. (21) 22222249; fax (21) 22223380; e-mail center@ims-ir.com; internet www.ims-ir.com; f. 1981; Chair. and Man. Dir MUHAMMAD HASSAN ASHRAFIAN LAK.

Irano–Hind Shipping Co (IHSC): POB 15875-4647, 18 Sedaghat St, Vali-e-Asr Ave, Tehran; tel. (21) 22058095; fax (21) 22057739; e-mail admin@iranohind.com; internet www.iranohind.com; f. 1974; jt venture between Islamic Republic of Iran and Shipping Corpn of India; Man. Dir Capt. C. P. ATHAIDE.

Islamic Republic of Iran Shipping Lines (IRISL): POB 19395-1311, 37 Asseman Tower, Sayyad Shirazee Sq., Pasdaran Ave, Tehran; tel. (21) 20100369; fax (21) 20100367; e-mail e-pr@irisl.net; internet www.irisl.net; f. 1967; Man. Dir MUHAMMAD HOSSEIN DAJMAR.

National Iranian Tanker Co (NITC): POB 19395-4833, 67–68 Atefis St, Africa Ave, Tehran; tel. (21) 23803325; fax (21) 22058761; e-mail souri@nitc.co.ir; internet www.nitc.co.ir; Chair. and Man. Dir MUHAMMAD SOURI.

CIVIL AVIATION

The principal international airport is the Imam Khomeini International Airport (IKIA), to the south of Tehran. IKIA opened fully in May 2005, and, by mid-2006, had taken over all international flights from Mehrabad airport (west of Tehran). There are several other international airports, including those at Esfahan, Mashad, Shiraz and Tabriz.

Civil Aviation Organization (CAO): POB 13445-1798, Taleghani Ave, Tehran; tel. (21) 66025131; fax (21) 44665496; e-mail info@cao.ir; internet www.cao.ir; affiliated to Ministry of Roads and Urban Development; Pres. HAMID REZA PAHLEVANI.

Caspian Airlines: 5 Sabonchi St, Shahid Beheshti Ave, Tehran; tel. (21) 88751671; fax (21) 887516676; internet www.caspian.aero; f. 1992; operates more than 50 flights per week from Tehran to other cities in Iran, as well as scheduled flights to the United Arab Emirates, Lebanon, Syria, Turkey and several European destinations; rep. offices abroad; Gen. Dir Capt. ASGAR RAZZAGHI.

IranAir (Airline of the Islamic Republic of Iran): POB 13185-755, IranAir HQ, Mehrabad Airport, Tehran; tel. (21) 46624256; fax (21) 46628222; e-mail pr@iranair.com; internet www.iranair.com; f. 1962; serves the Middle East and Persian (Arabian) Gulf area, Europe, Asia and the Far East; Chair. and Man. Dir FARHAD PARVARESH.

Iran Airtours: POB 1587997811, 183 Motahari St, Dr Mofatteh Cross Rd, Tehran; tel. (21) 88755535; fax (21) 88755884; e-mail info@iranairtours.com; internet iranairtours.ir; f. 1992; low-cost subsidiary of IranAir, offering flights from Tehran and Mashad;

serves domestic routes and the wider Middle East; Chair. ABBAS POUR-MUHAMMADI; Man. Dir SAYED MAHDI SADEGHI.

Iran Aseman Airlines: POB 141748, Mehrabad Airport, Tehran 13145-1476; tel. (21) 66035310; fax (21) 66002810; e-mail public@iaa.ir; internet www.iaa.ir; f. 1980 as result of merger of Air Taxi Co (f. 1958), Pars Air (f. 1969), Air Service Co (f. 1962) and Hoor Asseman; domestic routes and charter services to destinations in Central Asia and the Middle East; Man. Dir ABBAS RAHMATIAN.

Kish Air: POB 19395-4639, 215 Africa Ave, Tehran 19697; tel. (21) 44665639; fax (21) 44665221; e-mail info@kishairline.com; internet www.kishairline.com; f. 1989, under the auspices of the Kish Devt Org.; domestic routes and flights to the United Arab Emirates and Turkey; Chair. and CEO Capt. REZA NAKHJAVANI.

Mahan Air: POB 14515-411, Mahan Air Tower, 21 Azadegan St, Karaj Highway, Tehran 14816-55761; tel. (21) 48041111; fax (21) 48041112; e-mail international@mahanairlines.com; internet www.mahan.aero; f. 1992; domestic routes and charter services to other Middle Eastern, Asian and European destinations; Man. Dir HAMID ARABNEJAD.

Qeshm Air: 17 Ghandi Ave, Tehran; tel. (21) 88776012; fax (21) 88786252; e-mail qeshmair@farazqeshm.com; operates regular flights from Qeshm Island to the Iranian mainland and the United Arab Emirates.

Saha Airlines: POB 13865-164, Karadj Old Rd, Tehran 13873; tel. (21) 66696200; fax (21) 66698016; e-mail saha2@iran-net.com; f. 1990; owned by the Iranian Air Force; operates passenger and cargo charter domestic flights and services to Europe, Asia and Africa; Man. Dir Capt. MANSOUR NIKUKAR.

Tourism

Iran's principal attraction for tourists is its wealth of historical sites, notably Esfahan, Shiraz, Persepolis, Tabriz and Shush (Susa). The country also possesses a wide variety of natural landscapes, and skiing or hiking are popular activities in the Alborz Mountains close to Tehran. In 2006 it was announced that Iran was seeking to attract tourists from neighbouring Muslim countries by developing the tourism industry on Kish island, declared a free trade zone in 1992. The Government plans to attract 20m. foreign tourists each year to Iran by 2018. Tourist arrivals totalled 4m. in 2012/13 (year ending 20 March). Receipts from tourism in 2011 were provisionally recorded at US $2,381m. (excluding passenger transport).

Iran Tourism and Touring Organization (ITTO): 154 Keshavarz Blvd, Tehran; tel. (21) 88737065; fax (21) 88736800; e-mail info@itto.org; internet www.itto.org; f. 1985; administered by Ministry of Culture and Islamic Guidance.

Defence

Secretary of the Supreme National Security Council: Rear Adm. ALI SHAMKHANI.

Chief of Staff of the Armed Forces: Maj.-Gen. HASSAN FIROUZABADI.

Commander of the Army: Brig.-Gen. ATAOLLAH SALEHI.

Commander of the Air Force: Brig.-Gen. HASSAN SHAHSAFI.

Commander of the Navy: Rear-Adm. HABIBOLLAH SAYYARI.

Chief of Staff of the Islamic Revolutionary Guards Corps (Pasdaran Inqilab): Brig.-Gen. MUHAMMAD ALI JAFARI.

Commander of the Islamic Revolutionary Guards Corps Ground Forces: Brig.-Gen. MUHAMMAD PAKPOUR.

Commander of the Islamic Revolutionary Guards Corps Air Force: Brig.-Gen. AMIR ALI HEJIZADEH.

Commander of the Islamic Revolutionary Guards Corps Navy: Rear-Adm. ALI FADAVI.

Commander of Basij (Mobilization) War Volunteers Corps: Brig.-Gen. MUHAMMAD REZA NAGHDI.

Budgeted defence expenditure (2013): (year ending 20 March) est. IR 366,000,000m.

Total armed forces: As assessed at November 2013, Iran's regular armed forces totalled an estimated 523,000 (excluding 350,000 reserves): army 350,000 men; navy 18,000; air force 30,000; Islamic Revolutionary Guards Corps (*Pasdaran Inqilab*, which has its own land, navy and marine units) some 125,000; membership of Basij War Volunteers Corps estimated to include up to 1m. combatants; there were also some 40,000 paramilitary forces under the command of the Ministry of the Interior.

Education

PRIMARY AND SECONDARY EDUCATION

Primary education, beginning at the age of six and lasting for five years, is compulsory for all children and provided free of charge. Secondary education, from the age of 11, lasts for up to seven years, comprising a first cycle of three years and a second of four years. According to the Government, 24,000 schools were built between the 1979 Revolution and 1984. According to official figures, 6,851,000 pupils were enrolled in primary education in 2012/13, while 5,843,300 were engaged in secondary education. In 2006/07, according to UNESCO estimates, primary enrolment included 99% of children in the relevant age-group, while in 2011 enrolment at secondary schools included 79% of the appropriate age-group.

HIGHER EDUCATION

Iran has 39 universities, including 16 in Tehran. Universities were closed by the Government in 1980 but have been reopened gradually since 1983. According to official sources, some 2,853,300 students were enrolled at Iran's public colleges and universities in the 2012/13 academic year, in addition to the 1,582,400 students enrolled at the Islamic Azad University. Apart from Tehran, there are universities in Bakhtaran, Esfahan, Hamadan, Tabriz, Ahwaz, Babolsar, Meshed, Kermanshah, Rasht, Shiraz, Zahedan, Kerman, Shahrekord, Urmia and Yazd. There are c. 50 colleges of higher education, c. 40 technological institutes, c. 80 teacher-training colleges, several colleges of advanced technology, and colleges of agriculture in Hamadan, Zanjan, Sari and Abadan. Vocational training schools also exist in Tehran, Ahwaz, Meshed, Shiraz and other cities. Budgetary expenditure on education by the central Government in the financial year 2004/05 was IR 31,518,000m. (8.2% of total spending).

IRAQ

Introductory Survey

LOCATION, CLIMATE, LANGUAGE, RELIGION, FLAG, CAPITAL

The Republic of Iraq is an almost landlocked state in western Asia, with a narrow outlet to the sea on the Persian (Arabian) Gulf. Its neighbours are Iran to the east, Turkey to the north, Syria and Jordan to the west, and Saudi Arabia and Kuwait to the south. The climate is extreme, with hot, dry summers, when temperatures may exceed 43°C (109°F), and cold winters, especially in the highlands. Summers are humid near the Gulf coast. The official language is Arabic, spoken by about 80% of the population; about 15% speak Kurdish, while there is also a small Turkoman-speaking minority. Some 95% of the population are Muslims, of whom about 60% belong to the Shi'a sect. In January 2008 the Council of Representatives approved the design of a new, temporary national flag, which was to be replaced by a permanent one within one year. However, by early 2014 a permanent flag had not been selected, largely owing to political differences between the Arab and Kurdish parties. The temporary flag (proportions 2 by 3) has three equal horizontal stripes, of red, white and black, and the inscription *'Allahu Akbar'* ('God is Great') written in green Kufic script on the central white stripe. The capital is Baghdad.

CONTEMPORARY POLITICAL HISTORY

Historical Context

Iraq was formerly part of Turkey's Ottoman Empire. During the First World War (1914–18), when Turkey was allied with Germany, the territory was captured by British forces. In 1920 Iraq was placed under a League of Nations mandate, administered by the United Kingdom. In 1921 Amir Faisal ibn Hussain, a member of the Hashimi (Hashemite) dynasty of Arabia, was proclaimed King of Iraq. After prolonged negotiations, a 25-year Anglo-Iraqi Treaty of Alliance was signed in 1930. The British mandate ended on 3 October 1932, when Iraq became fully independent.

During its early years the new kingdom was confronted with Kurdish revolts (1922–32) and with border disputes in the south. Gen. Nuri al-Said became Prime Minister in 1930 and held the office for seven terms over a period of 28 years. He strongly supported Iraq's close links with the United Kingdom and with the West in general. After the death of King Faisal I in 1933, the Iraqi monarchy remained pro-British in outlook, and in 1955 Iraq signed the Baghdad Pact, a British-inspired agreement on collective regional security. However, following the overthrow of King Faisal II (the grandson of Faisal I) during a military revolution on 14 July 1958, which brought to power a left-wing, nationalist regime headed by Brig. (later Lt-Gen.) Abd al-Karim Kassem, the 1925 Constitution was abolished, the legislature was dissolved, and in March 1959 Iraq withdrew from the Baghdad Pact. Kassem, who had become increasingly isolated, was assassinated in February 1963 during a coup by members of the armed forces. The new Government of Col (later Field Marshal) Abd al-Salem Muhammad Aref was more pan-Arab in outlook, and sought closer relations with the United Arab Republic (Egypt). Following his death in March 1966, President Aref was succeeded by his brother, Maj.-Gen. Abd al-Rahman Muhammad Aref, who was deposed on 17 July 1968 by members of the Arab Renaissance (Baath) Socialist Party. Maj.-Gen. (later Field Marshal) Ahmad Hassan al-Bakr, a former Prime Minister, became President and Prime Minister, and supreme authority was vested in the Revolutionary Command Council (RCC), of which President al-Bakr was also Chairman.

Domestic Political Affairs

On 16 July 1979 the Vice-Chairman of the RCC, Saddam Hussain, who had long exercised real power in Iraq, replaced al-Bakr as RCC Chairman and as President of Iraq. Shortly afterwards several members of the RCC were executed for their alleged role in a coup plot. The suspicion of Syrian involvement in the attempted putsch, exacerbated by the rivalry between both countries' Baathist movements, resulted in the suspension of discussions concerning political and economic union between Iraq and Syria. During 1979 the Iraqi Communist Party (ICP) broke away from the National Progressive Front, an alliance of Baathists, Kurdish groups and Communists, claiming that the Baathists were conducting a 'reign of terror'. In February 1980 Saddam Hussain announced a National Charter, reaffirming the principles of non-alignment. In June elections took place for a 250-member legislative National Assembly; these were followed in September by the first elections to a 50-member Kurdish Legislative Council in the Kurdish Autonomous Region (which had been established in 1970).

In 1982 Saddam Hussain consolidated his positions as Chairman of the RCC and Regional Secretary of the Baath Party by conducting a purge throughout the administration. Kurdish rebels became active in northern Iraq, occasionally supporting Iranian forces in the war with Iraq. Another threat was posed by the Supreme Council for the Islamic Revolution in Iraq (SCIRI, renamed the Islamic Supreme Council of Iraq—ISCI—in May 2007), formed in the Iranian capital, Tehran, in November 1982 by the exiled Shi'a leader Hojatoleslam Muhammad Baqir al-Hakim. None the less, the majority of Iraq's Shi'a community was not attracted by the fundamentalist Shi'a doctrine of Ayatollah Khomeini of Iran, remaining loyal to Iraq and its Sunni President, while Iranian-backed militant groups (such as the predominantly Shi'a Islamic Dawa Party—Hizb al-Da'wa al-Islamiya—which made numerous attempts to assassinate Saddam Hussain) were ineffective.

Relations with Iran, precarious for many years, descended into full-scale war in September 1980. Iraq had become increasingly dissatisfied with the 1975 Algiers Agreement, which had defined the southern border between Iran and Iraq as the mid-point of the Shatt al-Arab waterway, and also sought the withdrawal of Iranian forces from Abu Musa and the Tunb islands, which Iran had occupied in 1971. The Iranian Revolution of 1979 exacerbated these grievances, and Iran accused Iraq of encouraging Arab demands for autonomy in Iran's Khuzestan ('Arabistan') region. In September 1980, following clashes on the border, Iraq abrogated the Algiers Agreement and its forces advanced into Iran. Fierce Iranian resistance led to military deadlock until mid-1982, when Iranian counter-offensives led to the retaking of the port of Khorramshahr and the withdrawal of Iraqi troops from territory occupied in 1980. In July 1982 the Iranian army crossed into Iraq. However, the balance of military power in the war moved in Iraq's favour in 1984, and the USA and the USSR provided financial aid. (Diplomatic relations between the USA and Iraq were restored in November 1984, having been suspended since the Arab–Israeli War of 1967.) In July 1988 Iraqi forces crossed into Iran for the first time since 1986. Iran announced its unconditional acceptance of UN Security Council Resolution 598, and by August a UN-monitored ceasefire was in force. However, negotiations on the full implementation of the resolution had made little progress by the time of Iraq's invasion of Kuwait in August 1990, at which point Saddam Hussain abruptly sought a formal peace agreement with Iran—accepting all the claims that Iran had pursued since the ceasefire, including the reinstatement of the Algiers Agreement. (For a fuller account of the 1980–88 Iran–Iraq War and of subsequent bilateral relations, see the chapter on Iran.)

In the second half of the 1980s Saddam Hussain consolidated his control over the country. In 1988 the President announced political reforms, including the introduction of a multi-party system, and in January 1989 declared that these would be incorporated into a new permanent constitution. In April 1989 elections took place to the 250-seat National Assembly, as a result of which more than 50% of deputies were reported to be Baathists. In July the National Assembly approved a new draft Constitution, under the terms of which a 50-member Consultative Assembly was to be established; both institutions would assume the duties of the RCC, which was to be abolished after a presidential election.

During the 1980s representatives of Iraq's 2.5m.–3m. Kurds demanded greater autonomy. Resources were repeatedly diverted from the war with Iran to control Kurdish insurgency in the north-east of Iraq. Saddam Hussain sought an accommodation with the Kurds, and, after a ceasefire had been agreed with Jalal Talabani, the leader of the Patriotic Union of Kurdistan (PUK), discussions began in December 1983. However, they excluded the other main Kurdish group, the Kurdistan Democratic Party (KDP), led by Masoud Barzani. Negotiations collapsed in May 1984, and armed conflict resumed in Kurdistan in January 1985 between PUK guerrillas and government troops, with Kurdish and Iranian forces repeatedly collaborating in raids against Iraqi military and industrial targets. In February 1988 KDP and PUK guerrillas (assisted by Iranian forces) made inroads into government-controlled territory in Iraqi Kurdistan. In March the Iraqi Government retaliated by using chemical weapons against the Kurdish town of Halabja, killing up to 5,000 people and wounding about 10,000. In May the KDP and the PUK announced the formation of a coalition of six organizations to continue the struggle for Kurdish self-determination and to co-operate militarily with Iran. The ceasefire in the Iran–Iraq War in August allowed Iraq to launch a new offensive to overrun guerrilla bases near the borders with Iran and Turkey, again allegedly employing chemical weapons. By September there were reported to be more than 200,000 Kurdish refugees in Iran and Turkey. In that month the Iraqi Government offered a full amnesty to all Iraqi Kurds inside and outside the country, excluding only Jalal Talabani. By October 1989 it had also created a 30-km uninhabited 'security zone' along the whole of Iraq's border with Iran and Turkey by evacuating inhabitants of the Kurdish Autonomous Region to the interior of Iraq, prompting the PUK to announce a nationwide urban guerrilla campaign against the Government. In September elections had proceeded to the legislative council of the Kurdish Autonomous Region.

The 1990–91 Gulf War

In mid-1990 the Iraqi Government criticized countries (principally Kuwait and the United Arab Emirates—UAE) that had persistently produced petroleum in excess of the quotas imposed by the Organization of the Petroleum Exporting Countries (OPEC, see p. 408). Iraq also accused Kuwait of violating the Iraqi border in order to secure petroleum resources, and demanded that Kuwait waive repayments of Iraq's vast debt to the emirate, incurred during the Iran–Iraq War. Direct negotiations between Iraq and Kuwait concerning their territorial and debt disputes failed, and on 2 August Iraqi forces invaded Kuwait, taking control of the country and establishing a provisional 'free government'. The UN Security Council unanimously adopted Resolution 660, demanding the immediate and unconditional withdrawal of Iraqi forces from Kuwait. Subsequent resolutions imposed mandatory economic sanctions against Iraq and occupied Kuwait (No. 661), and declared Iraq's annexation of Kuwait null and void (No. 662). At a meeting of the League of Arab States (the Arab League, see p. 362) on 3 August, 14 of the 21 members condemned the invasion and demanded an unconditional withdrawal by Iraq; after Iraq announced its formal annexation of Kuwait on 8 August, 12 member states voted to send an Arab deterrent force to the region of the Persian (Arabian) Gulf. On 7 August the US Government dispatched troops and aircraft to Saudi Arabia, at the request of King Fahd, in order to secure the country's border with Kuwait against a possible Iraqi attack; other countries quickly lent their support to what was designated 'Operation Desert Shield', and a multinational force was formed to defend Saudi Arabia.

In November 1990 the UN Security Council adopted Resolution 678, authorizing member states to use 'all necessary means' to enforce an Iraqi withdrawal if all Iraqi forces had not left Kuwait by 15 January 1991. 'Operation Desert Storm'—in effect, war with Iraq—began on the night of 16–17 January, with air attacks on Baghdad by the multinational force, and by the end of January the allied force had achieved air supremacy. Although Iraq managed to launch Scud missiles against Saudi Arabia and Israel, the latter's refusal to retaliate was the result of considerable diplomatic pressure aimed at ensuring Arab unity in the coalition. In February Iraq formally severed diplomatic relations with Egypt, France, Italy, Saudi Arabia, Syria, the United Kingdom and the USA. During the night of 23–24 February the multinational force began a successful ground offensive for the liberation of Kuwait: Iraqi troops surrendered in large numbers. A ceasefire was declared by the US Government on 28 February. Iraq agreed to renounce its claim to Kuwait, to release prisoners of war and to comply with all pertinent UN Security Council resolutions. Resolution 687, adopted in April, provided for the establishment of a commission to demarcate the border between Iraq and Kuwait. The resolution also linked the removal of sanctions imposed on Iraq following its invasion of Kuwait to the elimination of non-conventional weaponry, to be certified by a UN Special Commission (UNSCOM), and required that Iraq accept proposals for the establishment of a war reparation fund to be derived from Iraqi petroleum reserves. Later that month the UN Security Council approved Resolution 689, which established a demilitarized zone between the two countries, to be monitored by the UN Iraq-Kuwait Observation Mission (UNIKOM).

Within Iraq, the war was followed by domestic unrest: in March 1991 rebel forces, including Shi'a Muslims and disaffected soldiers, were reported to have taken control of Basra and other southern cities, although the rebellion was soon crushed by troops loyal to Saddam Hussain. In the north, Kurdish separatists overran a large area of Kurdistan. However, the Kurdish guerrillas were unable to resist the onslaught of the Iraqi armed forces and an estimated 1m.–2m. Kurds fled across the mountains into Turkey and Iran. UN Security Council Resolution 688, adopted in April 1991, condemned the repression of Iraqi civilians and provided for the establishment of an international repatriation and relief effort—co-ordinated by a multinational task force, designated 'Operation Provide Comfort', and based in south-eastern Turkey—to provide relief to displaced persons and to secure designated 'safe havens' on Iraqi territory north of latitude 36°N. In support of Resolution 688, a corresponding air exclusion zone was established by the USA, with the support of France and the United Kingdom.

A second air exclusion zone, south of latitude 32°N, was established by those countries plus Russia in August 1992, with the aim of protecting the southern Iraqi Shi'a communities, including the semi-nomadic Ma'dan (Marsh Arabs). In July 1993 Iraqi armed forces were reported to have renewed the Government's offensive against the inhabitants of the marshlands. In May 1996 government forces launched a major offensive against the Shi'a opposition and tribes in Basra governorate, which led to armed clashes between Iraqi security forces and the Shi'a opposition throughout the southern regions.

Conflict in the Kurdish Autonomous Region

Meanwhile, in April 1991 the PUK leader, Jalal Talabani, announced that President Saddam Hussain had agreed in principle to implement the provisions of a 15-point peace plan concluded by Kurdish leaders and the Iraqi Government in 1970. However, negotiations subsequently became deadlocked over the Kurdish demand for the inclusion of Kirkuk in the Kurdish Autonomous Region. In October 1991 the Iraqi Government effectively subjected the Kurds to an economic blockade. The various Kurdish factions proceeded to organize elections, in May 1992, to a 105-member Iraqi Kurdistan National Assembly, and for a paramount Kurdish leader. The outcome of voting, in which none of the smaller Kurdish parties achieved representation, was that the KDP and the PUK agreed to share equally the number of seats in the new assembly. The election for an overall Kurdish leader was deemed inconclusive, with Masoud Barzani, the KDP leader, receiving 47.5% of the votes cast, and Jalal Talabani 44.9%.

In December 1993 armed conflict broke out between militants of the PUK and the Islamic League of Kurdistan (or Islamic Movement of Iraqi Kurdistan—IMIK). Following mediation by the Iraqi National Congress (INC—a broad coalition of largely foreign-based opposition groups), the two parties signed a peace agreement in February 1994. However, more serious armed conflict between partisans of the PUK and the KDP led, in May, to the division of the northern Kurdish-controlled enclave into two zones. In June 1995 the IMIK withdrew from the INC, and in July there was renewed fighting between PUK and KDP forces, as a result of which scheduled elections to the Iraqi Kurdistan National Assembly were postponed. The two parties finally agreed, in October, to hold the elections in May 1996.

However, hostilities escalated in August 1996, as the PUK contested the KDP's monopoly of duties levied on Turkish traders. At the end of the month Iraqi military support for the KDP in the recapture of the PUK-held towns of Irbil (Arbil) and Sulaimaniya in the Kurdish area of northern Iraq provoked a new international crisis. In September the USA unilaterally launched retaliatory 'limited' air strikes on air defence and communications targets in southern Iraq, and extended the southern air exclusion zone from latitude 32°N to latitude 33°N (thereby incorporating some southern suburbs of Baghdad). Turkey, which had refused to allow the use of its air bases for the US operation, deployed some 20,000 troops to reinforce its border with Iraq. Meanwhile, the KDP gained control of all three

Kurdish provinces. The Iraqi Government subsequently announced the restoration of Iraqi sovereignty over Kurdistan, and offered an amnesty to its Kurdish opponents. In late September the KDP formed a coalition administration which included the IMIK, the Kurdistan Communist Party and representatives of the northern Assyrian and Turkoman communities. In October PUK fighters were reported to have recaptured much of the territory that they had ceded to the KDP, having regained control of Sulaimaniya and Halabja. Concern that Iran's alleged involvement in the conflict would provoke direct Iraqi intervention in the north prompted renewed diplomatic efforts on the part of the USA and Turkey, and US-sponsored peace talks in Ankara, Turkey, in late October resulted in a truce agreement. Following the termination of Operation Provide Comfort, a new air surveillance programme—'Northern Watch', based in south-eastern Turkey and conducted by British, Turkish and US forces—began in January 1997.

The KDP withdrew from the peace negotiations in March 1997, and in May around 50,000 Turkish troops entered northern Iraq, where, apparently in co-operation with the KDP, they launched a major offensive against bases maintained by the Kurdistan Workers' Party (Partiya Karkeren Kurdistan—PKK). As Turkey began to withdraw its armed forces in October, the PUK launched a massive military offensive against the KDP, targeting several strategic points along the 1996 ceasefire line. The KDP (which subsequently claimed to have regained most of the territory recently lost to the PUK) alleged that the assault had been co-ordinated by Iran and supported by the PKK. By mid-1998, amid a fragile ceasefire between the PUK and the KDP, the two organizations agreed to exchange prisoners. In September a formal peace agreement was signed in Washington, DC, USA, which, *inter alia*, provided for: Kurdish legislative elections in 1999 (although these did not take place); a unified regional administration; the sharing of local revenues; and an end to hostilities. A new Kurdish coalition government was appointed by the Iraqi Kurdistan National Assembly in December 1999.

Political developments after the Gulf War

After Iraq's defeat by the US-led coalition forces in 1991, Saddam Hussain strengthened his control over the country by placing family members and close supporters in the most important government positions. In September Hussain was re-elected Secretary-General of the Baath Party's powerful Regional Command at its 10th Congress, and in May 1994 he assumed the post of Prime Minister. Unsuccessful coups reportedly took place in January and March 1995; the latter was instigated by the former head of Iraqi military intelligence and supported by Kurdish insurgents in the north and Shi'a rebels in the south. In September the RCC approved an interim amendment of the Constitution whereby its elected Chairman would automatically assume the presidency of the Republic, subject to approval by the National Assembly and endorsement by national plebiscite. Saddam Hussain's candidature was duly approved by the Assembly, and endorsed by 99.96% of the votes cast at a referendum held on 15 October.

The first elections to the Iraqi National Assembly since 1989 took place in March 1996, when 689 government-approved candidates contested 220 of the Assembly's 250 seats: the remaining 30 seats were reserved for representatives of the Autonomous Regions of Arbil, D'hok and Sulaimaniya, and were filled by presidential decree. The elections were denounced by the INC, based in London, United Kingdom, and by other groups opposed to the Government.

Following reports in late 1997 that Saddam Hussain had ordered the execution of a number of senior military officers, Baath Party members and prisoners, internal unrest continued during 1998. According to SCIRI, a renewed government offensive against the Shi'a in southern Iraq resulted in the execution of some 60 people during March. Later in 1998 two senior Shi'a religious leaders, Ayatollah Murtada al-Burujirdi and Grand Ayatollah Mirza Ali al-Gharawi, were both assassinated. In February 1999 the killing of Iraq's Shi'a leader, Grand Ayatollah Muhammad Sadiq al-Sadr, provoked widespread demonstrations that were brutally suppressed by units of the Sunni-dominated Iraqi Special Republican Guard. Meanwhile, in October 1998 the US Congress approved the Iraq Liberation Act, permitting the US President to provide up to US $97m. in military assistance to Iraqi opposition groups in exile. In April 1999 11 opposition groups gathered in London, where they undertook to reform the moribund INC and to prepare a plan to oust Saddam Hussain's regime, while several INC leaders relocated to the USA.

Elections took place on 27 March 2000 for 220 seats in the National Assembly. Official results stated that 165 seats had been won by members of the Baath Party, and the remaining 55 elective seats by independent candidates; a further 30 independents were nominated by the Government to fill the seats reserved for representatives of the Kurdish areas of the north, which the Iraqi authorities described as being 'occupied' by the USA. Saddam Hussain's elder son, Uday, was elected to the legislature for the first time. In May 2001 Saddam Hussain was re-elected Secretary-General of the Baath Party Regional Command at the organization's 12th Congress, while his younger son, Qusay, was elected to the party Command and later appointed as a deputy commander of the party's military section.

At a national referendum held on 15 October 2002 to decide whether President Saddam Hussain should remain in office for a further seven-year term, the Iraqi leader was officially reported to have received 100% of the votes. A general amnesty for prisoners held in Iraqi gaols was subsequently announced by the authorities; however, opposition groups maintained that there were still thousands of political prisoners in Iraq. This proved to be the last major internal political development under the Baath regime prior to the US-led coalition's military campaign of early 2003, which led to the removal of Saddam Hussain's Government, and which was the de facto culmination of more than a decade of international diplomatic manoeuvring on the issues of 'oil-for-food' and banned weapons programmes.

The UN's sanctions regime and international monitoring of Iraq's weapons programme

Issues of the maintenance of sanctions originally imposed under UN Security Council Resolution 661 and of Iraqi non-compliance with its obligations under Resolution 687 with regard to its weapons capabilities remained inextricably linked in the decade following the Gulf conflict. Resolution 692, adopted in May 1991, provided for the establishment of the UN Compensation Commission (UNCC) for victims of Iraqi aggression (both governments and individuals), to be financed by a levy (subsequently fixed at 30%) on Iraqi petroleum revenues. In August the Security Council adopted Resolution 706 (approved in Resolution 712 in September), proposing that Iraq should be allowed to sell petroleum worth up to US $1,600m. over a six-month period, the revenue from which would be controlled by the UN. Part of this revenue was to be made available to Iraq for the purchase of food, medicines and essential supplies. Iraq rejected the UN's terms for the resumption of petroleum exports, and in February 1992 withdrew from further negotiations, but in October Resolution 778 permitted the confiscation of oil-related Iraqi assets to the value of $500m.

UN Security Council Resolution 707, adopted in August 1991, condemned Iraq's failure to comply with UN weapons inspectors, and demanded that Iraq: disclose details of all non-conventional weaponry; allow members of UNSCOM and of the International Atomic Energy Agency (IAEA) unrestricted access to necessary areas and records; and halt all nuclear activities. Resolution 715, adopted in October, established the terms under which UNSCOM was to inspect Iraq's weapons capabilities. In early 1994, having reportedly agreed to co-operate with UN weapons inspectors, the Iraqi Government engaged in a campaign of diplomacy to obtain the removal of economic sanctions. However, the USA and the United Kingdom refused to join the other members of the UN Security Council—Russia, France and the People's Republic of China—in acknowledging Iraq's increased co-operation with UN agencies. Following a stand-off between Iraq and the US and British military, prompted by the movement of Iraqi forces near the border with Kuwait, the Iraqi National Assembly voted in November to recognize Kuwait within the border defined by the UN in April 1992.

Economic sanctions imposed on Iraq were renewed on a 60-day basis from 1995. In May 1996 the Iraqi Government accepted a revised UN proposal (contained in Security Council Resolution 986) for the partial resumption of crude petroleum exports to generate funds for humanitarian supplies under what was designated an 'oil-for-food' programme. The memorandum of understanding (MOU) signed by the two sides permitted Iraq to sell some 700,000 barrels per day (b/d) of petroleum over an initial period of six months. Of every US $1,000m. realized through the sales, $300m. would be paid into the UN reparations fund; $30m.–$50m. would contribute to the costs of UN operations in Iraq; and $130m.–$150m. would go towards funding UN humanitarian operations in Iraq's Kurdish governorates. Remaining revenues would be used for the purchase and distribution of humanitarian goods in Iraq. The UN emphasized that the embargo on sales of Iraqi petroleum would not be fully revoked until all the country's weapons of mass destruction had been accounted for and destroyed.

In October 1997 the initial report of the new head of UNSCOM, Richard Butler, to the UN Security Council asserted that Iraq had failed to produce a credible account of its biological, chemical and nuclear warfare programmes and was continuing to hinder UNSCOM's work. In November the Security Council unanimously adopted a resolution (No. 1137) that imposed a travel ban on Iraqi officials deemed to be responsible for obstructing UNSCOM weapons inspectors. The confrontation deepened in January 1998, when Iraq prohibited inspections by an UNSCOM team led by a former US marine officer, Scott Ritter, claiming that Ritter was spying for the US Central Intelligence Agency.

However, the UN Security Council remained divided on the issue of weapons inspections: the USA, supported by the United Kingdom, indicated that it was prepared to respond militarily to Iraq's continued non-co-operation, while China, France and Russia opposed the use of force. Moreover, Kuwait was the only country in the region to announce its approval of force if diplomatic efforts should fail. In February 1998 the five permanent members of the Security Council approved a compromise formula whereby a group of diplomats, specially appointed by the UN Secretary-General, Kofi Annan, in consultation with experts from UNSCOM and the IAEA, would be allowed unconditional and unrestricted access to the eight so-called presidential sites. The compromise was accepted by Iraq, and in March the Security Council unanimously approved Resolution 1154 endorsing the MOU and warning of 'extreme consequences' should Iraq renege on the agreement. Members of the special group began visiting the presidential sites later in the month, but in April the head of UNSCOM concluded that there had been no progress in the disarmament verification process since October 1997, and that the destruction of Iraq's chemical and biological weapons was incomplete.

Butler reportedly informed the UN Security Council in June 1998 that US military tests on weaponry recently dismantled showed that Iraq had loaded missile warheads with a chemical weapon component prior to the Gulf conflict. In August negotiations between the UNSCOM head and Iraqi Deputy Prime Minister Tareq Aziz collapsed, Iraq suspended arms inspections, and Saddam Hussain announced new terms and conditions for their resumption, including the establishment of a new executive bureau to supervise UNSCOM's operations. In September the Security Council unanimously adopted a resolution (No. 1194) demanding that the Iraqi Government co-operate fully with UNSCOM and suspending for an indefinite period any review of the sanctions regime. This prompted the Government to halt all co-operation with UNSCOM indefinitely. Reporting to the Security Council in October, Butler asserted that, while Iraq was close to fulfilling its obligations with regard to missiles and chemical weapons programmes, UNSCOM remained concerned about the country's capacity for biological warfare. In November the Security Council unanimously adopted a British-drafted resolution (No. 1205) demanding that Iraq immediately and unconditionally resume co-operation with UNSCOM. US and British military enforcements were again dispatched to the Gulf region to prepare for possible air strikes against Iraqi targets. Egypt, Saudi Arabia and Syria, while opposing the threat of force, urged Iraq to resume co-operation. Later in November Iraq declared that UNSCOM would be permitted unconditionally to resume the weapons inspection programme.

However, in early December 1998 a weapons inspection team conducting a new series of what were termed 'surprise' or 'challenge' inspections was denied access to the Baath Party headquarters in Baghdad. On the night of 16–17 December, following the withdrawal from Iraq of UNSCOM and IAEA personnel, the USA and the United Kingdom commenced a campaign of air strikes against Iraqi targets; 'Operation Desert Fox' was terminated on 20 December, with US and British forces claiming to have caused significant damage to Iraqi military installations. France, Russia and China contended that the military action had been undertaken without UN Security Council authorization; however, the USA and the United Kingdom maintained that Resolution 1154, adopted in March, provided sufficient legitimacy. In January 1999 Iraqi ground forces launched attacks on US aircraft engaged in policing the air exclusion zone over southern Iraq.

The US Administration of President George W. Bush, which assumed office in January 2001, swiftly adopted an uncompromising stance with regard to Iraq. In February US and British fighter aircraft launched a renewed attack on air defence targets near Baghdad, in what Bush described as a 'routine mission' to enforce the northern and southern air exclusion zones. Iraq protested that the air strikes had targeted residential areas of Baghdad, while Western media reports suggested that three people had been killed in the attacks. US and British military aircraft launched air strikes against Iraqi air defence installations in both exclusion zones during late 2001 and in September 2002, in response to what they claimed were continuing Iraqi attacks on allied aircraft patrolling the zones; Iraqi officials claimed that a number of civilians had died in the raids.

Meanwhile, the campaign of air strikes conducted against Iraqi targets in December 1998 was regarded as marking the collapse of UNSCOM's mission. Later that month the Security Council adopted a resolution (No. 1284) providing for the establishment of a UN Monitoring, Verification and Inspection Commission (UNMOVIC) as a successor body to UNSCOM. The resolution also provided for the suspension of the economic sanctions in force against Iraq for renewable 120-day periods (on the condition that Iraq co-operated fully with the new weapons inspectorate and the IAEA), and effectively removed restrictions on the maximum amount of petroleum that Iraq was permitted to sell under the oil-for-food programme. In January 2000 the Security Council endorsed the appointment of Hans Blix, a former Director-General of the IAEA, as head of UNMOVIC. Meanwhile, IAEA personnel undertook the first routine inspection of Iraqi facilities since their withdrawal in December 1998. In his first report to the UN Security Council in March 2000, Blix emphasized that, should Iraq permit the return of weapons inspectors, UNMOVIC would resume 'challenge' inspections of Iraqi sites. In the same month Tareq Aziz decisively rejected the terms of Resolution 1284. In March 2001 it was reported that, according to a recent UNMOVIC assessment, Iraq might still have the ability to build and use biological and chemical weapons, and might possess stocks of mustard gas, biological weapons and anthrax, as well as having the capability to deliver Scud missiles.

The 'oil-for-food' programme

Exports of Iraqi crude petroleum, under the terms of Resolution 986, had recommenced in December 1996, and continued until immediately prior to the US-led military intervention to remove the regime of Saddam Hussain in March 2003. The first supplies of food purchased with the revenues from these exports arrived in Iraq in March 1997. In February 1998 the UN Security Council raised the maximum permitted revenue from exports of petroleum to US $5,200m. in the six months to the end of July, of which Iraq would be permitted to spend some $3,550m. on humanitarian goods. The remainder would be used to finance reparations and UN operations. Following concerns about the deterioration of its oil production facilities, in June the Security Council approved a resolution allowing Iraq to import essential spare parts to the value of $300m. for the oil sector. Under the ninth phase of the oil-for-food programme from December 2000, Iraq was allocated a maximum of $525m. for the local costs of maintaining the oil industry. In September 2000 the UN Security Council approved the payment to Kuwait of $15,900m. in compensation for lost production and sales of petroleum as a result of the 1990–91 occupation. However, it was agreed to reduce the levy on Iraq's petroleum revenues destined for reparations under the oil-for-food programme from 30% to 25%.

In early 2001 the Bush Administration emphasized its commitment to maintaining the sanctions regime pending the full implementation of Resolution 1284. The USA swiftly undertook to secure implementation of a revised sanctions regime, with a view to resolving humanitarian concerns, by means of allowing the direct sale or supply to Iraq of most consumer goods without prior UN approval, while at the same time maintaining strict controls on the supply of goods with potential military applications. In November, after Iraq had threatened to end its participation in the oil-for-food programme if revisions to the sanctions regime were adopted, the UN Security Council unanimously approved Resolution 1382. This was essentially a compromise whereby Russia agreed to adopt an annexed list of embargoed items with military and civilian purposes before the expiry of the new (11th) phase, while the USA consented to review Resolution 1284. The Security Council continued to extend the oil-for-food programme every six months. In May 2002 the Security Council implemented a mechanism to accelerate the processing of contracts not subject to inclusion on the Goods Review List, while Resolution 1454, approved in December, expanded the list of goods subject to review to include certain items with a potential military use. In mid-March 2003, immediately prior to the start of the US-led military campaign in Iraq, the UN announced a temporary suspension of the oil-for-food programme. However, amid a sharp deterioration in the living conditions of Iraqi citizens following the outbreak of hostilities, at the end of March the UN Security Council adopted Resolution 1472, granting Secretary-General Kofi Annan the authority to implement existing contracts and to facilitate the delivery of aid for an initial 45-day period, which was subsequently extended until the beginning of June. On 22 May the UN Security Council passed Resolution 1483, which removed sanctions against Iraq; the oil-for-food programme was formally discontinued on 21 November.

Negotiations with UNMOVIC and the increasing threat of military intervention

After the defeat of the Taliban regime in Afghanistan (q.v.) in late 2001, there was considerable speculation that the USA would seek 'regime change' in Iraq as part of its declared 'war on terror'. In response to demands by George W. Bush that Iraq readmit UN inspectors to prove that it was not developing weapons of mass destruction, or otherwise be 'held accountable', the Iraqi authorities reiterated that UN sanctions should first be ended and the air exclusion zones revoked. Tensions were heightened in January 2002 when, in his State of the Union address, President Bush assessed Iraq as forming what he termed an 'axis of evil' (with Iran and the Democratic People's Republic of Korea) seeking to develop weapons of mass destruction, specifically accusing Iraq of plotting to develop anthrax, nerve gas and nuclear weapons.

In March 2002 Annan met with the Iraqi Minister of Foreign Affairs, Naji Sabri, in New York, USA (with the UNMOVIC head, Hans Blix, also in attendance), for talks focusing on the implementation of pertinent Security Council resolutions adopted since 1990. In August 2002 the UN Security Council declined an offer by the Iraqi Government to resume negotiations on the return of weapons inspectors, stating that Iraq should not impose any preconditions on the resumption of inspections. At the same time the USA pursued attempts to secure a UN resolution that would authorize military action in Iraq, while indicating that it would be prepared to act unilaterally. In late September the British Government published a dossier outlining its case against the regime of Saddam Hussain and the perceived threat posed by Iraq's 'illicit weapons programmes' to the security of both the West and the Middle East. Shortly afterwards the US Secretary of Defense, Donald Rumsfeld, reiterated US claims that Iraq had provided assistance in the training of Islamist militants from the al-Qa'ida network. In early October Blix stated that Iraq had agreed to allow inspectors 'unconditional and unrestricted access' to all relevant sites, but that no new agreement had been reached concerning access to the presidential palaces. The USA and the United Kingdom were keen for the Security Council to approve a new resolution that would strengthen the mandate under which the UN inspectors were to operate. China, France and Russia all maintained that—in the event of Iraq's failure to comply with the terms of a future resolution concerning Iraqi disarmament—a second UN resolution should be adopted prior to any military action being taken against the Iraqi regime.

In mid-October 2002 President Bush signed a resolution approved by the US Congress authorizing the use of force, if necessary unilaterally, to disarm Saddam Hussain's regime. On 8 November, after a compromise had been reached between the five permanent members, the UN Security Council unanimously adopted Resolution 1441, which demanded, *inter alia*, that Iraq permit weapons inspectors from UNMOVIC and the IAEA unrestricted access to sites suspected of holding illegal weapons (including the presidential palaces) and required the Iraqi leadership to make a full declaration of its chemical, biological, nuclear and ballistic weapons, as well as related materials used in civilian industries, within 30 days. The resolution warned that this represented a 'final opportunity' for Baghdad to comply with its disarmament obligations under previous UN resolutions, affirming that Iraq would face 'serious consequences' in the event of non-compliance with the UN inspectors or of any 'false statements and omissions' in its weapons declaration. On 13 November the RCC announced its formal and unconditional acceptance of the terms of the resolution. Iraqi officials, however, repeatedly stated that they did not possess any weapons of mass destruction.

Iraq presented UNMOVIC officials with a 12,000-page declaration of its weapons programmes in early December 2002. In mid-December, however, the USA stated that Iraq was in 'material breach' of UN Resolution 1441 since it had failed to give a complete account of its weapons capabilities, citing in particular Iraq's failure to account for stocks of biological weapons such as anthrax. In January 2003 UNMOVIC personnel to the south of Baghdad reported the discovery of several empty chemical warheads, which had reportedly not been included in Iraq's recent declaration. Meanwhile, Iraqi officials dismissed suggestions by some Arab states (including Saudi Arabia and Egypt) that Saddam Hussain either stand down or go into exile. At an emergency summit meeting of the Arab League in Cairo, Egypt, at the beginning of March, the UAE presented a plan for the Iraqi President to stand down and for the Arab League and UN to assume temporary control of Iraq.

During January 2003 the USA and the United Kingdom ordered a massive deployment of troops to the Gulf region, while asserting that a conflict was not inevitable if Iraq complied with the UN's disarmament terms. Both the French and German Governments, meanwhile, were vociferous in their opposition to military action and advocated an extension of the UN inspectors' mandate. In late January the ministers responsible for foreign affairs of Turkey, Syria, Iran, Jordan, Egypt and Saudi Arabia, meeting in İstanbul, Turkey, issued a joint communiqué urging Iraq to co-operate fully with UN inspectors in order to avoid a new conflict in the region. On 27 January, 60 days after the resumption of UN weapons inspections in Iraq (as stipulated under Resolution 1441), Blix and the Director-General of the IAEA, Muhammad el-Baradei, briefed the UN Security Council on the progress of inspections. El-Baradei stated that IAEA inspectors had found no evidence that Iraq had restarted its nuclear weapons programme, but requested more time for the organization to complete its research. Blix, for his part, claimed that there was no evidence that Iraq had destroyed known stocks of illegal chemical and long-range ballistic weapons, and announced that he was sceptical about Baghdad's willingness to disarm. Following the briefing, the British Secretary of State for Foreign and Commonwealth Affairs, Jack Straw, declared Iraq to be in 'material breach' of Resolution 1441.

Eight European countries (including the United Kingdom, Italy and Spain) signed a joint statement at the end of January 2003 expressing support for the USA's militant stance with regard to Iraq. In February the British Prime Minister, Tony Blair, accelerated his efforts to secure a second UN Security Council resolution authorizing a US-led campaign in Iraq should UNMOVIC inspectors continue to report Baghdad's non-compliance. President Bush asserted that, although he favoured the adoption of a second resolution, Resolution 1441 had given the USA the authority to disarm Iraq by military means. The US Secretary of State, Colin Powell, had, on 5 February, presented to the Security Council what the USA claimed to be overwhelming evidence of Iraq's attempts to conceal its possession of weapons of mass destruction, and outlined its alleged links with international terrorist groups, including al-Qa'ida. Despite signs of progress being reported by Hans Blix in his report on UNMOVIC's inspections to the Security Council on 14 February, the UN inspectorate chief stated that the monitoring process should continue in order to determine whether Iraq did possess undeclared weapons of mass destruction.

On 24 February 2003 the USA, the United Kingdom and Spain presented a draft resolution to the UN Security Council effectively proposing a US-led military campaign against Saddam Hussain's regime, in response to Baghdad's failure to disarm peacefully. The resolution stated that a deadline of 17 March would be set, by which time Iraq should prove that it was disarming; however, no specific mention was made of consequent military action in the event of the deadline not being met, apparently in an effort by the US-led coalition to persuade France, Russia and China not to exercise their right of veto. Officials from France, Russia and Germany presented an alternative proposal involving an extended timetable of weapons inspections in order to avert a war. At the beginning of March Turkey's Grand National Assembly voted to allow US military aircraft to enter Turkish airspace in the event of a campaign being waged against the Iraqi regime, while rejecting a plan for US forces to use Turkey's military bases. Shortly afterwards France and Russia pledged to veto a second UN resolution authorizing the use of force to disarm Saddam Hussain. In an attempt to encourage wavering countries in the Security Council to support an amended resolution, on 12 March Tony Blair proposed six new conditions that Iraq must meet in order to prove its intention to disarm. The British proposals came a day after President Bush had rejected a suggested 45-day postponement of any decision to go to war by six countries that had the power to influence the Security Council vote. On 15 March, in anticipation of a probable US-led invasion, Iraq's RCC issued a decree dividing the country into four military commands, under the overall leadership of Saddam Hussain. On 16 March a summit meeting was held in the Azores, Portugal, between Bush, Blair and the Spanish Prime Minister, José María Aznar. On the following day the USA, the United Kingdom and Spain withdrew their draft resolution from the UN, stating that they reserved the right to take their own action to ensure Iraqi disarmament. On the same day President Bush issued an ultimatum giving Saddam Hussain and his two sons 48 hours to leave Baghdad or face military action; the Iraqi National Assembly rejected the ultimatum.

The overthrow of Saddam Hussain

Shortly after the expiry of President Bush's deadline, on 20 March 2003 US and British armed forces launched a 'broad and concerted campaign' (code-named 'Operation Iraqi Freedom') to oust the regime of Saddam Hussain. An initial series of air strikes intended to target leading members of the regime in the suburbs of Baghdad were unsuccessful. Meanwhile, US-led coalition forces crossed into Iraq from Kuwait and began a steady advance towards the capital. At the same time a a series of air strikes were launched against selected military bases, government buildings, and broadcasting and communications headquarters in and around Baghdad. US and British forces adopted a simultaneous campaign of distributing leaflets and broadcasting radio messages, in an effort to persuade Iraqi citizens to abandon their support for the Baath regime: their declared intention was that Operation Iraqi Freedom would precipitate the disintegration of the regime 'from within'. British troops were principally engaged in securing towns in southern Iraq, including Iraq's second city of Basra, after the US-led coalition had seized control of the key southern port of Umm Qasr and the Al-Faw Peninsula. The coalition hoped that the Shi'a Muslim population of Basra would initiate an uprising against the regime of Saddam Hussain, as had occurred following the Gulf War in 1991. Although fighting between US-led troops and Iraqi armed forces was often intense, resistance from the Iraqi army and from a number of *fedayeen* (martyrs) and volunteers from other Arab countries was generally lighter than had been anticipated by the allies. Moreover, there were widespread reports of Iraqi soldiers surrendering to the advancing forces. In late March 2003 US forces opened a second front in the Kurdish-controlled regions of northern Iraq, where Kurdish forces joined US troops in targeting bases of Ansar al-Islam, a militant Islamist group suspected of having links with al-Qa'ida.

At an emergency summit meeting of Arab League states in Cairo on 24 March 2003, representatives of the 17 member states in attendance (except Kuwait) issued a resolution condemning the US-led invasion of Iraq and demanding the withdrawal of all foreign forces. By 7 April US armed forces had entered central Baghdad, including its presidential palaces. The disintegration of the Baath regime appeared to be complete on 9 April, when crowds of Iraqis staged street demonstrations denouncing Saddam Hussain and destroying images and statues of the President. Kurdish *peshmerga* fighters gained control of the northern town of Kirkuk on 10 April, while the town of Mosul was seized by Kurdish and US forces on the following day. Also on 11 April the USA issued a 'most wanted' list of 55 members of the deposed regime whom it sought to arrest: one of the most high-profile of these, Tareq Aziz, surrendered to US forces two weeks later. The seizure by US troops of Saddam Hussain's birthplace and power base, Tikrit (to the north of Baghdad), on 14 April was widely viewed as the last strategic battle of the US-led campaign to remove the Baathist regime. On 1 May President Bush officially declared an end to 'major combat operations' in Iraq.

On 15 April 2003 a US-sponsored meeting of Iraqi opposition groups took place in the southern city of Nasiriya. However, while the participants produced a 13-point resolution detailing proposals for a transition to a democratic, sovereign government, it became clear that in the interim period the practical day-to-day responsibilities of repairing, rebuilding and maintaining the material infrastructure of Iraq, as well as combating guerrilla supporters of the ousted regime and emerging 'resistance' groups, would fall to the US-led coalition. Retired US army general Jay Garner, Director of the USA's Office of Reconstruction and Humanitarian Assistance (ORHA), arrived in the country on 21 April to manage the restoration of basic services to the Iraqi population and to enforce law and order. However, the ORHA was subsequently replaced by the Coalition Provisional Authority (CPA), headed by US diplomat L. Paul Bremer, III. Bremer assumed his responsibilities on 12 May, his first act being to outlaw the Baath Party and related organizations, and to demobilize the Iraqi armed forces and security apparatus. The Ministries of Defence, of Information and of Military Affairs were all dissolved.

UN Security Council Resolution 1483, adopted on 22 May 2003, recognized the CPA as the legal occupying power in Iraq, and mandated it to establish a temporary Iraqi governing authority. On 13 July the inaugural meeting of the 25-member Iraqi Governing Council was held in Baghdad; members of the Governing Council were appointed in direct proportion to the principal ethnic and religious groups in Iraq: 13 Shi'a Arabs, five Sunni Arabs, five Kurds, one Assyrian Christian and one Turkoman. They were mostly drawn from the main parties that had been in opposition to Saddam Hussain's regime, notably Ahmad Chalabi of the INC, Dr Ayad Allawi of the Iraqi National Accord (INA), Jalal Talabani of the PUK, Masoud Barzani of the KDP and Abd al-Aziz al-Hakim of SCIRI. The Governing Council had no executive powers, but could appoint ministers and diplomatic representatives, set a date for the holding of free elections, and formulate a new constitution. At the end of July the Governing Council adopted a system of rotating presidency, under which Ibrahim al-Ja'fari, a leading member of the predominantly Shi'a Islamic Dawa Party, was chosen as Iraq's first President of the post-Baathist era. In August the UN Security Council approved a resolution 'welcoming', but not formally recognizing, the establishment of the Iraqi Governing Council. On 1 September the Governing Council announced the formation of a 25-member interim Cabinet, appointed along the same ethnic and religious lines, which was to administer the country until the holding of legislative elections. Finally, on 15 November a timetable for the transition of power to an elected, sovereign government was published by the CPA and the Governing Council. The plan was threefold: these two authorities were to be dissolved and replaced by an Iraqi Transitional National Assembly by 30 June 2004; a constitutional convention was to take place by mid-2005, after which a popular referendum would be held on the new constitution; and, by the end of 2005, national elections were to be held to select a new Iraqi government.

Increasing violence following the end of US-led combat operations

In the aftermath of the war, Iraq's security situation remained extremely volatile. Armed resistance to US-led coalition forces was waged by militants loyal to the former Baathist regime, even despite the arrest or elimination of several leading establishment figures. Moreover, the UN, diplomatic missions, Shi'a clergy and members of the interim Cabinet were also targeted by militant groups. In early August 2003 the Jordanian embassy in Baghdad was severely damaged by a car bomb, which killed up to 19 people. The militant Islamist group Ansar al-Islam was initially held to be responsible. (In November 2007 a military court in Jordan sentenced to death a Jordanian national found to have plotted the embassy bombing on the orders of al-Qa'ida in Iraq.) The UN Special Representative for Iraq, Sergio Vieira de Mello, and some 20 others were killed in late August 2003, when explosives hidden inside a truck were detonated in front of the UN compound in Baghdad. A previously unknown Islamist group, the Armed Vanguards of the Second Muhammad Army, claimed responsibility for the explosion, which resulted in most of the UN's foreign personnel being withdrawn from Iraq. At the end of that month a car bomb exploded in the holy city of Najaf, killing the Shi'a cleric Hojatoleslam Muhammad Baqir al-Hakim and up to 125 of his followers. The murdered cleric (who had only recently returned to Iraq from exile) was succeeded as leader of SCIRI by his brother Abd al-Aziz al-Hakim. It was evident from mid-2003 that Iraq's various Shi'a factions were fighting among themselves in order to establish a dominant position among the majority Shi'a population.

In July 2003 US special forces shot dead Saddam Hussain's two sons, Uday and Qusay, at a house in Mosul where they had apparently been hiding. In December Saddam Hussain was captured by US special forces in the village of al-Dawr, near the former President's hometown of Tikrit. Saddam Hussain was accorded prisoner-of-war status and detained in US military custody. In July 2004 Hussain, along with 11 co-defendants, appeared in front of a special US-appointed court in Baghdad to face seven charges, including the use of chemical weapons against Kurds in Halabja in 1988 and the invasion of Kuwait in 1990. However, the former Iraqi leader declared the proceedings to be illegal. In October 2004 US investigators seeking evidence as part of preparations for war crime trials against Saddam Hussain and former senior Iraqi officials found a mass grave in Hatra, near the ancient city of Nineveh, in which they uncovered the bodies of hundreds of Kurds apparently killed in late 1987–early 1988.

Meanwhile, in September 2004 a report issued by the Iraq Survey Group, a team of experts appointed by the US-led coalition to locate Iraq's alleged weapons of mass destruction, concluded that the Baathist regime's involvement with chemical or biological agents prior to the 2003 invasion had been restricted to small quantities of poisons, probably for use in assassinations. According to the report, while no illegal stockpiles of weapons had been found, and there was no evidence of any attempts to recommence Iraq's nuclear weapons programme, it did appear that Saddam Hussain's regime had intended to reintroduce its illegal weapons programmes if the UN lifted sanctions against the country. However, subsequent to the release of the report, the IAEA announced that buildings used during Iraq's nuclear programme prior to the Gulf War in 1991 had been dismantled, and that specialized equipment and material inside them that could be utilized to produce nuclear weapons had disappeared. The US Administration officially announced an end to the search for weapons of mass destruction in January 2005.

By January 2004 US-led forces had apprehended or killed 42 of the 55 'most wanted' former Baathists. However, during the final weekend of the month some 105 people, mostly Kurds, were killed in suicide bomb attacks directed against the offices of the principal Kurdish parties—the KDP and the PUK—in Arbil. Meanwhile, the insurgents were now targeting any Iraqis working with the occupying forces: in February 2004 nearly 100 people were killed in two separate attacks against the Iraqi police and army in Iskandariya and Baghdad, respectively. In early March a series of bombs exploded among crowds of Shi'a who had gathered in Baghdad and Karbala to celebrate the festival of Ashoura, resulting in more than 180 deaths. The CPA claimed that Abu Musab al-Zarqawi, a Jordanian national believed to have ties with al-Qa'ida, was responsible for the bombings and was also the mastermind behind the majority of attacks on coalition and civilian targets in Iraq. Bremer announced the re-establishment of the Ministry of Defence in March.

Following protracted negotiations, the Transitional Administrative Law (TAL) was signed by the Governing Council on 8 March 2004; it outlined a new timetable for the establishment of a permanent legislature and sovereign government (see Constitution and Government), which superseded that previously set out in the agreement published on 15 November 2003. This development was interpreted as evidence of the growing influence on the political process of Iraq's most senior Shi'a cleric, Grand Ayatollah Ali al-Husaini al-Sistani: in particular, plans to elect a transitional national assembly by regional caucuses were replaced by proposals to hold national elections to an interim (and likely Shi'a-dominated) legislature.

In May 2004 the Independent Electoral Commission of Iraq (IECI) was formed by the CPA to organize elections to a 275-member Transitional National Assembly (TNA), which were subsequently scheduled for 30 January 2005. Seats within the TNA were to be allocated on the basis of proportional representation. Key functions of the TNA were to draft, by 15 August 2005, a permanent constitution, to be submitted to a popular referendum by 15 October; and to elect a state Presidency Council (comprising a President and two Vice-Presidents) responsible for appointing a Prime Minister and cabinet. Under the timetable for Iraq's political transition, constitutionally elected organs of government were to be installed by 15 December. Voting for the TNA was to be held simultaneously with elections to 18 provincial assemblies and to a new Iraqi Kurdistan National Assembly. In early December 2004 the two main Kurdish parties, the PUK and the KDP, announced that they had agreed to form a joint list—the Kurdistan Alliance List (or Democratic Patriotic Alliance of Kurdistan). Subsequently, major Shi'a groups, backed by al-Sistani, announced that they too would be campaigning on a shared list, to be known as the United Iraqi Alliance (UIA). In late December, after failing to secure a delay in the holding of the ballot (citing security concerns), the Sunni Iraqi Islamic Party (IIP—al-Hizb al-Islami al-Iraqi) and various other Sunni groups and clerics withdrew from the campaign, advocating a boycott of the polls.

Meanwhile, the CPA closed down the Baghdad newspaper *Al-Hawza al-Natiqa* in March 2004 for allegedly inciting violence against the US-led coalition. The newspaper was closely associated with Hojatoleslam Muqtada al-Sadr, a Shi'a cleric whose father had been assassinated by the previous regime in February 1999 and who was a suspect in the murder of a moderate Shi'a cleric in Najaf in 2003. Several of al-Sadr's supporters had formed a militia known as the 'Mahdi Army', and protests outside the newspaper offices were the precursor to a nationwide upsurge in violence against coalition forces. After four US private security contractors were killed in an ambush in the Sunni-dominated town of Fallujah, to the west of Baghdad in Anbar province, in early April 2004, US forces surrounded and effectively blockaded the town; around 450 Iraqis (including many civilians) and 40 US soldiers died in the ensuing violence. A scandal developed in late April, when photographs taken by US guards of US soldiers coercing Iraqi prisoners into performing degrading acts were broadcast worldwide. One soldier received a 10-year gaol sentence in January 2005 in connection with the abuse of prisoners at the Abu Ghraib prison, west of Baghdad, while other implicated officers received lesser sentences. In early 2005 four British soldiers were discharged from the army and sentenced to short prison terms, having been convicted of the abuse of Iraqi prisoners at a military base near Basra in May 2003.

The transfer of power to the Iraqi Interim Government

In mid-May 2004 Sunni insurgents in central Baghdad assassinated the President of the Governing Council, Izzadine Salim, who was replaced by the Sunni Sheikh Ghazi Mashal Ajil al-Yawar. The INA Secretary-General, Dr Ayad Allawi, was appointed interim Prime Minister of Iraq in late May, and in early June Ghazi al-Yawar was named as President of the Interim Government, to which power was to be transferred from the CPA on 30 June. However, amid security fears following an intensification of insurgent attacks, and the kidnapping and killing of foreign workers, the date for the granting of sovereignty to the Interim Government was secretly moved forward to 28 June. Shortly after the ceremony in Baghdad, Bremer left Iraq; the CPA and the Governing Council were both dissolved. Around 140,000 US soldiers remained in Iraq following the handover of power. In August delegates to a national conference in Baghdad declared the appointment of a 100-member transitional national council that was to govern Iraq in conjunction with the Interim Government until the January 2005 elections.

Following a decision by the CPA to re-employ former Baathist security officials, the US military had, in April 2004, arranged for an Iraqi security force led by one of Saddam Hussain's ex-generals to replace the US Marine Corps in Fallujah. In May coalition forces launched major assaults against Muqtada al-Sadr's Mahdi Army, and particularly heavy fighting was reported in Sadr City (a predominantly Shi'a suburb of Baghdad), Karbala and Najaf. In June nine of Iraq's leading political factions reached agreement with Dr Allawi to disband their militias by January 2005. According to the agreement, some 100,000 fighters (but excluding members of the Mahdi Army) would join the security forces or return to civilian life. Meanwhile, after US forces reached an accommodation with al-Sadr to end his insurgency, in July 2004 the ban on the *Al-Hawza al-Natiqa* newspaper was lifted. However, a Sunni uprising in Najaf, where the Mahdi Army seized the Imam Ali Mosque, and in other southern cities from early August led to renewed fighting in that month, with many fatalities being reported. Grand Ayatollah al-Sistani, accompanied by thousands of Iraqi Shi'a, travelled to Najaf, where he negotiated a ceasefire with al-Sadr. Meanwhile, Abu Musab al-Zarqawi declared that he had managed a spate of co-ordinated attacks across Iraq in June, including five car bomb explosions in Mosul, which had killed about 100 people. In July the Interim Government introduced new legislation granting it wider powers to control the insurgency by enabling the Prime Minister to declare a state of emergency for periods of up to 60 days. The death penalty was reintroduced for certain crimes in August, having been suspended by the CPA in early 2003.

Al-Sadr's Mahdi Army announced a ceasefire in October 2004 and stated that it would begin to disarm, provided that the Interim Government released its prisoners and agreed not to arrest or harm any of its supporters. In mid-October insurgents managed to penetrate central Baghdad's heavily fortified International Zone—an area still commonly known by its original name, the Green Zone —and launch a suicide attack, which killed at least 10 people (including four US civilians). The Green Zone contained the headquarters of the Iraqi Government and the US and British embassies. Al-Zarqawi's group, which had recently named itself Tanzim Qa'idat al-Jihad fi Bilad al-Rafidain (Base of Holy War in Mesopotamia, also known as al-Qa'ida in Iraq), claimed responsibility for the attack, and for the killing in late October of 49 unarmed National Guard soldiers in Diyala province, near the Iranian border. It was estimated later in the month that 100,000 Iraqi civilians had died in the period since the US-led invasion, principally as a result of air strikes by coalition forces.

Allawi declared a 60-day state of emergency in early November 2004, closing Baghdad airport and imposing martial law across most of the country as an estimated 15,000 US troops and 3,000 Iraqi troops attempted to end the ongoing insurgency in Fallujah. By mid-November US troops claimed to be in control of the city, having killed an estimated 1,200 insurgents, with losses of a reported 38 US and six Iraqi military. Heavy civilian and military casualties were recorded during a spate of suicide car bomb attacks and insurgent raids in Karbala, Najaf, Mosul and the area around Baghdad in December 2004 and early January 2005. The number of insurgents at this time was estimated at 200,000, greater than the number of coalition troops. In response to the growing violence and in advance of the forthcoming legislative elections, in January the Interim Government extended the state of emergency for another month, closed Iraq's borders and imposed a strict curfew. Al-Zarqawi, who had castigated Shi'a Muslims for assisting the occupying forces, vowed in the week before the poll to launch a violent battle against the elections. Five days before the scheduled ballot, 37 US troops were killed—the highest single death toll for US forces since March 2003.

The January 2005 election to the Transitional National Assembly

Despite the boycott by many Sunni political groups and the poor security situation, the legislative election took place as scheduled on 30 January 2005. At least 44 people died in attacks across Iraq during polling. In the election to the TNA, the UIA took 47.6% of the total votes, winning 140 of the 275 seats, the Kurdistan Alliance List won 75 seats (with 25.4% of the votes) and the Iraqi List, a bloc led by Dr Allawi, secured 40 seats (with 13.6% of the votes); nine other parties achieved representation in the interim legislature. Voting for the TNA was held simultaneously with elections to 18 provincial assemblies and to a new Iraqi Kurdistan National Assembly, where the Kurdistan Democratic List won 104 of the 111 seats. As militants sought further to aggravate the division between Shi'a and Sunni communities, in February some 125 people were killed in a suicide bomb attack in the predominantly Shi'a city of Hilla.

Following protracted negotiations over the formation of the transitional government, on 6 April 2005 the TNA voted to appoint the PUK leader, Jalal Talabani, to the post of President. A Sunni, Ghazi al-Yawar (previously the President of the Interim Government), and a Shi'a, Adil Abd al-Mahdi (hitherto the Minister of Finance), were appointed Vice-Presidents. The three, together constituting a state Presidency Council, were sworn in on 7 April, whereupon they appointed Ibrahim al-Ja'fari to the post of Prime Minister. On 28 April the TNA overwhelmingly approved al-Ja'fari's new Council of Ministers, which was sworn in on 3 May. However, in large part owing to disagreements regarding the level of ministerial representation for Sunnis, seven posts remained unallocated, including those of defence (which was to be assumed on an interim basis by al-Ja'fari) and oil (temporarily allocated to Deputy Prime Minister Ahmad Chalabi). Six of the seven vacancies were filled later in May, when Saadoun al-Dulaimi, a Sunni Arab, was appointed Minister of Defence, while the oil portfolio was awarded to Dr Ibrahim Bahr al-Ulum, a Shi'a. By the end of May more than 1,000 people were reported to have been killed in various insurgent attacks across the country following the approval of the new Transitional Government. On 12 June the Iraqi Kurdistan National Assembly voted unanimously to appoint Masoud Barzani, leader of the KDP, to the post of President of the Kurdish Autonomous Region.

Meanwhile, under the schedule outlined by the TAL, a draft constitution drawn up by the transitional administration was to be agreed by a constitutional committee and submitted to the TNA for approval by 15 August 2005. Sunni representation on the committee was increased in an attempt to reach an agreeable consensus. Significant points of disagreement included: the degree of federalism to be incorporated into the new state; the distribution of oil revenue; the question of 'de-Baathification' of the official sphere; and the role of Islam as a source of legislation. The agreed deadline was twice missed, largely because of Sunni objections on these key issues, before a final text was submitted to the TNA for approval on 28 August. The text was subsequently submitted to the UN on 14 September. On the same day a series of car bombings in Baghdad, apparently perpetrated by al-Zarqawi's al-Qa'ida in Iraq, caused the deaths of some 150 people. At a nationwide referendum held on 15 October, the Constitution was ratified with the support of 78.6% of the valid votes cast.

On 19 October 2005 the new Supreme Iraqi Criminal Tribunal began trial proceedings against former Iraqi President Saddam Hussain. Together with his seven co-defendants, Hussain pleaded not guilty to charges of organizing the killing of 148 Iraqi Shi'a in the town of Dujail, where he had survived an assassination attempt in 1982. The trial was adjourned until late November 2005, by which time two defence lawyers had been killed. In January 2006 the appointment of a Kurd from Halabja (where Hussain's Government had used chemical weapons in 1988) as the new presiding judge compounded the objections of the defence team that the trial was incapable of impartiality.

In November 2005 US troops discovered more than 170 prisoners, many malnourished and showing signs of torture, in the basement of the Shi'a-dominated Ministry of the Interior. The IIP, with the support of the USA, demanded an inquiry into the practices of the Ministry's officials. In January 2006 some 28 people were killed in a suicide bomb attack on the Ministry building, which al-Qa'ida in Iraq announced it had carried out in revenge for the maltreatment of Sunni prisoners.

The formation of a permanent Council of Representatives

Following the approval of the Constitution, several Sunni groups that had boycotted the elections of January 2005 declared that they would participate in the elections to the first permanent Council of Representatives, which were now due to be held on 15 December. Three major Sunni groups, including the IIP, formed the Iraqi Accord Front (IAF—Jabhat al-Tawafuq al-Iraqiya) in October, in a bid to engage Sunnis in the political process. Another Sunni coalition, the Iraqi Front for National Dialogue (Hewar National Iraqi Front), was formed from parties that disagreed with the IIP's acceptance of the Constitution. Meanwhile, the UIA announced a 17-party list dominated once again by Shi'a, including supporters of al-Sadr alongside the Islamic Dawa Party and SCIRI. However, the INC, which had been transformed since 2003 from a multi-party coalition into a political party headed by Ahmad Chalabi, declined to run on the UIA list, creating instead the National Congress Coalition. In contrast to his support for the UIA in January 2005, Grand Ayatollah al-Sistani indicated his neutrality in the elections. Former Prime Minister Ayad Allawi established a secular coalition, the Iraqi National List (INL), including his own INA, the Iraqis party of Ghazi al-Yawar and the ICP, while the PUK and the KDP maintained the Kurdistan Alliance List. The voting on 15 December was only marginally disrupted by violence. The final election results, released on 10 February 2006, gave the UIA 41.2% of votes cast and 128 of the Council's 275 seats. The Kurdistan Alliance List secured 53 seats with 21.7% of votes, while the IAF won 15.1% of the votes and 44 seats. Allawi's INL won 25 seats, and 11 seats were allocated to the Iraqi Front for National Dialogue. Chalabi's coalition failed to win a seat.

On 22 February 2006, with negotiations ongoing over the composition of the new government, two bombs were exploded inside the al-Askari Mosque (or Golden Mosque) in Samarra, destroying the dome of one of Iraq's holiest Shi'a shrines. The attack caused a sharp increase in sectarian violence across the country (including retaliatory attacks on Sunni mosques), which resulted in the deaths of at least 300 people within a week, according to official sources; independent media reports suggested that more than 1,000 had died. Following the upsurge in violence, Kurdish, Sunni and secular factions increased their opposition to the continued premiership of al-Ja'fari, who had narrowly won the nomination of the UIA to the post of Prime Minister in February. On 13 March some 85 bodies were reportedly discovered by Iraqi police in various parts of Baghdad, apparently the victims of increasingly common execution-style killings by sectarian 'death squads'. The Council of Representatives eventually convened for the first time in Baghdad's Green Zone on 16 March.

Seeking to resolve the impasse in negotiations over the new government, on 20 April 2006 al-Ja'fari withdrew his candidacy for the post of Prime Minister. On the following day the UIA nominated Nuri Kamal (Jawad) al-Maliki, another prominent member of the Islamic Dawa Party, as their replacement candidate, a compromise apparently accepted by Sunni and Kurdish factions. At the second session of the Council of Representatives on 22 April, President Talabani was elected for a second term; two Vice-Presidents, Tariq al-Hashimi of the IIP and incumbent Adil Abd al-Mahdi, were also appointed, and Mahmoud al-Mashhadani was chosen as the chamber's Speaker. Talabani subsequently invited al-Maliki to form a permanent government within 30 days. Meanwhile, the Kurdish region's first unified Cabinet, led by Masoud Barzani, assumed office on 7 May.

On 20 May 2006 the Council of Representatives approved a list of ministerial nominees submitted by Prime Minister-designate al-Maliki, and the Council of Ministers was sworn into office. This Government of national unity represented the first permanent Iraqi Government since the removal of Saddam Hussain's regime in 2003, and it constituted the first administration since that date to include the principal Sunni factions. However, the portfolios of the interior and defence remained unfilled, and thus were assumed on an interim basis, respectively, by Prime Minister al-Maliki and Deputy Prime Minister Salam al-Zubaie. The position of Minister of State for National Security Affairs was also filled temporarily by the Deputy Prime Minister, Dr Barham Salih. Dr Hussain al-Shahristani, an independent Shi'a member of the UIA, became Minister of Oil. In all, the new Council of Ministers included 20 Shi'a, eight Kurds, eight Sunni Arabs and one Christian. Of the 275 seats in the Council of Representatives, the Government—composed principally of the UIA, the Kurdish Alliance, the IAF and the INL—plus three smaller parties, controlled 240. On 8 June 2006 the Council of Representatives approved al-Maliki's nominations for three key positions: Lt-Gen. Abd al-Qadir Muhammad Jasim Obeidi, a Sunni who had served in Saddam Hussain's armed forces, was appointed Minister of Defence; Jawad al-Bulani and Shirwan al-Waili, both Shi'a, were named as Minister of the Interior and Minister of State for National Security Affairs, respectively.

The new Government appeared initially to have been strengthened by reports on 7 June 2006 that Abu Musab al-Zarqawi, the leader of al-Qa'ida in Iraq, had been killed during a US air strike close to the town of Baquba. It was claimed by the Ministry of Health on the day before al-Zarqawi's death that almost 1,400 civilians had been killed in Baghdad during the previous month. On 14 June al-Maliki's administration ordered a new military strategy involving thousands of Iraqi and US forces, code-named 'Operation Together Forward'. Meanwhile, it was claimed that Abu Ayyub al-Masri, also known as Abu Hamza al-Muhajir, had been appointed to succeed al-Zarqawi as the leader of al-Qa'ida in Iraq. Al-Maliki also appealed for a dialogue with Sunni insurgents, and on 25 June announced a 'national reconciliation plan' offering an amnesty to members of certain militant groups who renounced violence, and outlining plans to disarm the country's various militias. However, the violence perpetrated by both Sunni insurgents and Shi'a militias continued relentlessly, prompting Grand Ayatollah al-Sistani to declare that he would no longer act as a political leader and was powerless to prevent civil war. Nevertheless, the formal handover of control of Iraq's armed forces from the US-led coalition to the Iraqi Government did occur on 7 September.

Also in September 2006 the Council of Representatives began to debate the controversial issue of federal devolution, which some feared might eventually lead to Iraq's dissolution along ethnic lines. The UIA, which submitted a draft federalism law to the Council, stated that it favoured the division of Iraq into autonomous regions, thereby permitting the oil-rich Shi'a south to be governed along the lines of the Kurdish north. While Sunni politicians had previously opposed the move, fearing that it would leave them only with the resource-poor centre and west of the country, they now hinted that they might support the 'administrative application of federalism' so long as a strong central Government remained in place. By late September a compromise had emerged: a parliamentary committee was to be set up immediately to draft constitutional amendments to ensure that national oil revenues were shared fairly and to limit the potential of regions to secede from the central state. Moreover, parliament agreed that any legislation on federalism could only be implemented after an 18-month delay. On 26 September both Kurdish and Shi'a legislators tabled federalism bills. The Kurdish bill (which showed the disputed, oil-rich city of Kirkuk as belonging to the Kurdish Autonomous Region) was rejected, but the Shi'a-proposed draft was given a first reading. The draft made provisions for Iraq's 18 provinces to hold referendums on whether they wanted to merge with neighbouring areas, thus forming larger areas with powers of self-rule. On 11 October a law was adopted unanimously by the Council of Representatives; however, only 138 of the 275 legislators attended the session, the two largest Sunni blocs and two factions making up the Shi'a alliance having refused to attend.

A UN report issued in late September 2006 showed that some 6,600 Iraqi civilians had been killed during July and August. British and Iraqi forces operating in Basra initiated a campaign, code-named 'Operation Sinbad', which was aimed at preventing the infiltration of some of the city's police units by Shi'a militants. In October al-Maliki announced the establishment of local security committees to monitor the violence in their respective areas. However, amid worsening violence, Sunni leaders from Anbar province, west of Baghdad, began to form their own security forces. Many Iraqis fled their homes and sought refuge either in other parts of the country or in neighbouring states.

The trial of Saddam Hussain and seven co-defendants accused of involvement in the murder of 148 Iraqi Shi'a in Dujail in 1982 was marred by numerous setbacks during 2006, including the murder of a third defence lawyer in June. On 5 November Hussain and two of his co-defendants—Awad Hamed al-Bandar (former head of the Revolutionary Court under the Baathist regime) and Barzan Ibrahim al-Tikriti (half-brother of the former President)—were found guilty of crimes against humanity in connection with the killing of the 148 Shi'a, and were sentenced to death. Former Vice-President Taha Yassin Ramadan was sentenced to life imprisonment, while three others received 15-year custodial sentences; one defendant was acquitted owing to a lack of evidence. The verdict provoked a mixed reaction in Iraq, with thousands defying a curfew to express publicly either their support for Hussain or to celebrate the verdict. Nevertheless, many commentators and human rights organizations questioned the impartiality of the trial, and Hussain's lawyers immediately lodged an appeal against the verdict.

In November 2006 at least 215 people died when a series of car bombs and mortar rounds exploded in Sadr City, followed by mortar attacks on Sunni areas of Baghdad. Prime Minister al-Maliki imposed an indefinite curfew in the capital, but the killings continued, prompting a group led by Muqtada al-Sadr to threaten withdrawal from the unity Government, in which his followers held six cabinet posts. This threat was carried out when al-Maliki flew to the Jordanian capital, Amman, to discuss Iraq's security situation with US President Bush—a move that al-Sadr's group described as 'a provocation to the Iraqi people and a violation of their constitutional rights'. On 6 December the US cross-party Iraq Study Group published a report demanding 'urgent action' to prevent Iraq from sliding towards chaos. The report recommended that, rather than conducting a combat mission and massively increasing troop numbers, US forces should be used to train Iraqis; it also appealed for direct dialogue on Iraq's future with Syria and Iran.

The execution of Saddam Hussain

Saddam Hussain was executed by hanging on 30 December 2006, following the rejection of his appeal against the death sentence imposed by the Supreme Iraqi Criminal Tribunal in November. The manner of his killing was extremely contentious: news reports apparently revealed that the former Iraqi President had been taunted by onlookers as he approached the gallows, and that his execution had been filmed on a mobile telephone, resulting in footage of the event soon appearing on the internet. Fearing a rise in sectarian violence as a result of this development, the Iraqi Government immediately launched an investigation into the circumstances of the execution. While some in Iraq celebrated the death of the deposed leader, many Sunnis described Saddam Hussain as a martyr, and protests against the hanging were held in Baghdad, Samarra and his hometown of Tikrit. A statement issued by the Baath Party at the start of January 2007 named Izzat Ibrahim al-Douri as its new Secretary-General. In mid-January Saddam Hussain's two aides, al-Bandar and al-Tikriti, were hanged, and in March former Vice-President Ramadan was also executed, after the Court of Appeal recommended that his sentence of life imprisonment was too lenient.

At the time of Saddam Hussain's death, trial proceedings (initiated in August 2006) were ongoing against the former

President and six co-defendants on charges of genocide and crimes against humanity in relation to an offensive in the Anfal region during 1987–88 in which, according to the prosecution, more than 180,000 Iraqi Kurds were killed. When the trial resumed in January 2007, the charges against Hussain were abandoned. In June Gen. Ali Hassan al-Majid, a cousin of Saddam Hussain and former regional commander, was sentenced to death by the Supreme Iraqi Criminal Tribunal, having been convicted of genocide, war crimes and crimes against humanity for his role in the Anfal operation. Two of al-Majid's co-defendants were handed down the same sentence, while a further two were sentenced to life imprisonment; the sixth defendant was acquitted owing to a lack of evidence. In August al-Majid received an additional death sentence following his conviction on charges of involvement in the violent suppression of thousands of Shi'a rebels in southern Iraq following the Gulf conflict of 1990–91. Al-Majid received a third death sentence in March 2009 for the killing of Shi'as protesting against the assassination of Grand Ayatollah Muhammad Sadiq al-Sadr in 1999. In mid-January 2010 al-Majid received a further death sentence for his role in the attacks involving chemical weapons that killed thousands of Kurds in Halabja in 1988, and he was executed by hanging on 25 January.

In 2007 there were growing fears concerning the large exodus of Iraqi citizens, both to neighbouring states and through regional displacement. According to estimates by the office of the UN High Commissioner for Refugees (UNHCR), by September between 2.1m. and 2.5m. Iraqis had become refugees in neighbouring countries, notably Syria (1.2m.–1.4m.) and Jordan (500,000–750,000), while around 2.3m. Iraqis were displaced internally. (An estimated 1m. of these had been displaced before the 2003 conflict, and although a reported 300,000 Iraqis did return to their homes principally from Iran, Jordan, Lebanon and Saudi Arabia, an increasing number were choosing to flee the violence.) Aid agencies, meanwhile, warned that many neighbouring countries were starting to impose severe limitations on the number of Iraqi refugees allowed to enter. UNHCR also expressed concern in September 2007 regarding the estimated 13,000 Palestinian refugees who were believed to remain in Iraq, as well as the Christian and other minority communities.

Prime Minister al-Maliki announced a new security plan for Baghdad on 9 January 2007; this centred on the deployment of additional Iraqi forces, including Kurdish troops, with US backing. Sunni leaders denounced the plan as unconstitutional since it had not been referred to the Council of Representatives for debate. The following day US President Bush confirmed that the USA would send an additional 21,000 troops to Iraq. Bush's new so-called 'surge' strategy also included the following provisions: the Iraqi Government was to appoint a new military commander for Baghdad; there was to be accelerated training of Iraqi security forces, leading to them being brought under Iraqi control by November; provincial elections were to be held later that year; and increased diplomacy was to be sought with Iraq's neighbours, excluding Iran and Syria (from where insurgents were allegedly crossing into Iraq).

On 16 January 2007 at least 70 people—most of them female students—were killed in a double bomb attack at Baghdad's Mustansiriyah University. Six days later more than 130 people were killed in and around the capital. None the less, the ending of the two-month political boycott by followers of al-Sadr appeared to suggest a greater unity among Iraq's Shi'a factions. Security forces subsequently claimed to have captured 600 members of al-Sadr's reportedly 60,000-strong Mahdi Army. In late January officials announced that some 300 insurgents, reportedly from a militant group called the Army of Heaven, had been killed in battles near Najaf. Some news reports, however, claimed that those killed were Shi'a pilgrims. In early February more than 130 people were killed in a lorry bombing at a central Baghdad marketplace. The attack coincided with the launch of the new Iraqi-US security initiative in the capital, 'Operation Law and Order' (or the Baghdad Security Plan). In the second week of February insurgents marked the first anniversary of the bombing of the Samarra shrine by launching a series of fatal explosions in Baghdad. In the first week of March more than 110 Shi'a pilgrims on their approach to Karbala were killed by militants in central Iraq.

The six cabinet ministers of Muqtada al-Sadr's faction resigned their posts in mid-April 2007, in protest against Prime Minister al-Maliki's failure to agree a timetable for the withdrawal of coalition forces from Iraq. Four days earlier at least one Iraqi legislator was killed in a suicide bomb attack inside the Council of Representatives building, adjacent to Baghdad's Green Zone. An international conference to discuss reconstruction and security in Iraq was convened in the Egyptian resort of Sharm el-Sheikh in May. At the conference, a five-year framework for the country's future development, the International Compact with Iraq, was launched by al-Maliki. By June it appeared that Operation Law and Order was not achieving significant results in curbing sectarian violence in Baghdad. Moreover, in that month suspected Sunni insurgents again targeted the al-Askari Mosque in Samarra, destroying two minarets of the Shi'a shrine. During July violence also intensified in the north of the country, particularly in Kirkuk, possibly as a result of the tightening of security by Iraqi-US forces in the capital. In one incident, the headquarters of the PUK were targeted, with militants clearly attempting to influence any future decision regarding the status of Kirkuk (where tensions between the ethnic Kurdish, Arab and Turkmen communities were growing in advance of a proposed referendum—initially scheduled to be held by 31 December, but later postponed). Meanwhile, on 29 June 2007 the UN Security Council adopted Resolution 1762, which, *inter alia*, ended the mandate of UNMOVIC, on the grounds that Iraq's known weapons of mass destruction had now been rendered harmless and that the new Iraqi Government had declared itself to be in favour of non-proliferation.

The perilous state of the Iraqi administration was demonstrated on 1 August 2007, when the IAF withdrew its six ministers from the national unity Government, resulting in an even weaker participation by Sunni politicians in the country's decision-making processes. Moderate Kurdish and Shi'a political parties responded to this announcement by establishing a new alliance aimed at assisting the Prime Minister in pushing forward important legislation; this new grouping included the PUK and the KDP, together with al-Maliki's Islamic Dawa Party and the Islamic Supreme Council of Iraq (ISCI—as SCIRI had been renamed in May).

The UN Security Council voted on 10 August 2007 to expand the organization's operations in Iraq, having played a minimal role in Iraq's political affairs following the attack against its Baghdad headquarters in August 2003. The mandate of the UN Assistance Mission for Iraq was subsequently extended at regular intervals, most recently for 12 months in late July 2013. On 14 August 2007 an estimated 400–500 people from the minority (primarily Kurdish) Yazidi community in northern Iraq were killed as the result of co-ordinated suicide bombings; US military officials asserted that al-Qa'ida in Iraq had been responsible for the blasts. Muqtada al-Sadr, meanwhile, declared at the end of the month that his Mahdi Army was to suspend its campaign against rival militias and US-led forces for a six-month period; this truce was extended for a further six months in February 2008. By the end of November 2007 two of the portfolios left vacant by the departure of al-Sadr's Shi'a faction in April had been filled.

The withdrawal of British troops from Basra

British armed forces withdrew from their remaining base in the city of Basra on 3 September 2007, transferring military control of the city centre to Iraqi troops and police. The formal handover of security from British to Iraqi forces in the remainder of Basra province took place on 16 December, thereby transferring to Iraqi authority the last of the four southern provinces controlled by the British military since 2003. An independent monitoring group, Iraq Body Count, estimated that 25,063 civilians had died as a result of violence during 2007, compared with 28,250 in 2006. US officials attributed the significant decline in the number of fatalities in Baghdad to the effectiveness of the Bush Administration's 'surge' strategy. Moreover, large numbers of Iraqi refugees were returning to the country, particularly from neighbouring countries such as Syria. In December the UN Secretary-General's Special Representative for Iraq, Staffan de Mistura, launched a plan worth US $11,400m. to provide assistance to thousands of refugees and internally displaced families who had chosen to return home. Nevertheless, it was reported in October 2007 that 22 Iraqi insurgent groups had agreed to establish a new coalition, the Supreme Command for Jihad and Liberation, to be led by the Baath Party's Izzat Ibrahim al-Douri.

After a period of lesser violence in Baghdad, on 1 February 2008 an estimated 100 people were killed in two massive suicide bomb attacks. Despite Basra having been noticeably calmer since the withdrawal of British forces, in March al-Maliki ordered a major offensive—code-named 'Operation Charge of the Knights'—against Shi'a militias in the city (including factions of Muqtada al-Sadr's Mahdi Army) in an effort to reduce levels of criminal and militant activity. Some 210 people reportedly died during the operation, which involved more than 40,000 Iraqi troops assisted by coalition forces, and was concluded on 30 March when a truce was agreed between the Government and al-Sadr. Meanwhile, fierce fighting was reported in several cities in southern Iraq and also in the Sadr City district of Baghdad. A joint Iraqi-US military operation against the Mahdi Army in Sadr City began on 6 April and, after seven weeks—when al-Sadr again declared a ceasefire—had led to around 1,000 (mainly civilian) deaths. On 12 May al-Sadr agreed to allow Iraqi troops to enter Sadr City, pledging that his forces would end mortar and rocket attacks against Baghdad's Green Zone.

By mid-2008 violence across the country had generally shown a significant decline since the overthrow of Saddam Hussain in 2003. One explanation given for the decline in sectarian killings in Baghdad was that the capital was now essentially divided into separate Shi'a and Sunni districts. Another reason for the improved security in Sunni provinces of Iraq (such as Anbar) was the policy adopted by the US Administration whereby former Sunni militias involved in the insurgency against coalition forces were encouraged to form so-called Awakening Councils, receiving the logistical and financial support of US troops in order to fight extremist Islamist groups such as al-Qa'ida in Iraq.

Meanwhile, on 12 January 2008 the Council of Representatives approved a law permitting former middle- and low-ranking members of the Baath Party who had not been charged with crimes to reclaim positions of public office, effectively repealing the CPA's de-Baathification legislation adopted in 2003, which had resulted in the dismissal of thousands of Baathist officials. In July 2008 the six IAF ministers who had left the national unity Government in August 2007 rejoined the cabinet. The IAF had reportedly been satisfied by recent government actions such as the approval of an amnesty law involving thousands of Sunni prisoners and the clampdown on Shi'a militias. Moreover, four independent members of the UIA replaced the ministers from al-Sadr's faction, who continued to boycott the Government.

Following numerous delays, on 24 September 2008 the Council of Representatives approved legislation stipulating that provincial elections originally scheduled to have taken place by 1 October should now be held in most parts of Iraq by the end of January 2009, and that a parliamentary committee would review the status of Kirkuk. The new law was approved by the Presidency Council on 3 October 2008. Meanwhile, in July 2008 Kirkuk council members voted to permit a referendum to be held among the province's population to decide whether or not the city would join the Kurdish Autonomous Region; Turkmen and Arab members boycotted the vote.

Discussions between US and Iraqi officials were ongoing regarding the proposed Status of Forces Agreement (SOFA), which would determine the long-term status of US troops in the country. President Bush declared in September 2008 that some 8,000 US forces would leave Iraq by February 2009—far fewer than had been anticipated—with some 138,000 troops remaining after that date. On 1 October 2008 the Iraqi Government assumed responsibility for directing and funding members of the Sunni Awakening Councils in Baghdad; by the end of that month 13 of Iraq's 18 provinces were under Iraqi security control. Meanwhile, on 9 October Saleh al-Auqaeili, a Shi'a member of the Council of Representatives affiliated with Muqtada al-Sadr, died in a roadside explosion in Sadr City. There was speculation that the ISCI's armed faction, the Badr Organization (founded in Tehran in 1983 as the Badr Brigade, but renamed upon its relocation to Iraq following the overthrow of the Baathist regime), might have been responsible for al-Auqaeili's murder, owing to the rivalry between its umbrella group and al-Sadr's followers. On 15 October US military chiefs claimed recently to have killed Abu Qaswarah (also known as Abu Sara), the second-in-command of al-Qa'ida in Iraq, during a military offensive in Mosul. In late 2008 al-Sadr was reported to have fled to Iran following the issuing of a warrant for his arrest.

The Status of Forces Agreement

The SOFA was signed by the US ambassador in Baghdad, Ryan Crocker, and the Iraqi Minister of Foreign Affairs, Hoshyar al-Zibari, on 17 November 2008, and subsequently endorsed by the Council of Representatives and Presidency Council. Under the terms of the security pact, which was to be put to a nationwide referendum by the end of July 2009, all US armed forces were to withdraw from urban areas of the country by 30 June 2009; the remaining forces would leave by 31 December 2011. However, this timetable was dependent on the successful assumption of control by Iraqi security forces. The Sadrist bloc insisted that the US military should withdraw from Iraq immediately. On 23 December 2008 the Iraqi parliament agreed to allow the Government to extend the mandate for non-US foreign forces to remain in the country after the expiry on 31 December of the UN mandate for the US-led multinational force, provided that these troops were withdrawn by July 2009. The British Government confirmed at this time that its 4,100 armed forces would leave Iraq by mid-2009. The number of US troops killed in Iraq was reported to have declined to some 314 in 2008, compared with 904 in 2007. On 1 January 2009, when the SOFA entered effect, control of the Green Zone in Baghdad was handed from the Iraqi to US authorities. At the same time, responsibility for the 145,700 US forces was transferred to the Iraqi Government. In February the newly renovated Abu Ghraib prison was officially reopened under the name of Baghdad Central Prison.

At the elections finally held on 31 January 2009 in 14 of Iraq's 18 provinces (the three Kurdish provinces and Kirkuk being excluded from the vote), the official rate of voter participation was just 51%; however, turnout in certain mainly Sunni areas was higher than expected, and the elections were hailed as demonstrating the return of Sunni Arab political parties to the democratic system. The vote was relatively free of violence, compared with 2005, although six prospective candidates were killed in advance of polling. Allies of Prime Minister Nuri al-Maliki—standing as the State of Law coalition—secured notable successes, particularly in southern Shi'a areas of Iraq; the poll was widely seen as representing a vote of confidence in the premier's recent policies and in more secular nationalist, as opposed to overtly religious, groupings. While al-Maliki's coalition won a majority of votes in Baghdad and nine other provinces, the ISCI—previously dominant in Shi'a areas—failed to win in any provinces. Ayad al-Samarrai, the Sunni leader of the IAF and a senior member of the IIP, was elected as Speaker of the Council of Representatives on 19 April 2009.

In February 2009 the recently inaugurated US President, Barack Obama, declared that his Administration intended to withdraw the majority of US troops from Iraq by the end of August 2010, referring to this date as the official end of the USA's combat mission. President Obama stated that between 35,000 and 50,000 US forces would remain in the country after that date in order to advise Iraqi security forces and protect US interests. All US forces would have withdrawn from Iraq by the end of 2011, as stipulated under the terms of the SOFA. During April 2009 scores of Iraqis were killed in violent attacks perpetrated by al-Qa'ida in Iraq and other militant groups in Baghdad and elsewhere; many Iranian pilgrims also died in an explosion targeting the revered Shi'a Imam Musa al-Kadhim shrine in the capital.

The withdrawal of coalition forces and continuing violent insurgency

On 30 April 2009 the United Kingdom's combat mission in Iraq was officially declared to have been completed. By the end of July the withdrawal had been effected of the majority of the 4,100-strong British force in southern Iraq, as well as all other non-US coalition forces in the country. An estimated 400 British troops were to remain to provide specialist training to the Iraqi security forces. A bilateral maritime agreement under which the United Kingdom's navy would protect offshore petroleum facilities and provide training for Iraq's navy entered into force in November. (In May 2011 the last remaining British navy personnel were withdrawn from Iraq, signalling the formal end of the British military's operations in Iraq, during which a total of 179 British troops had been killed.) Meanwhile, on 30 June 2009, according to the terms of the SOFA, US combat forces initiated their withdrawal from Baghdad and other urban centres. Henceforth, US forces would fulfil a non-combative support role in the cities, while serving as a partner in Iraqi-led combat operations elsewhere.

Frequent attacks and incidents of sectarian violence occurred in mid-2009, particularly in the environs of Baghdad and Mosul. Confidence in the Iraqi security forces was severely undermined following a series of co-ordinated bomb and mortar attacks on 19 August, which targeted official buildings near Baghdad's Green Zone, including the Ministries of Foreign Affairs and of Finance. At least 101 people were killed in the attacks. On 23 August a former Baathist police officer claimed responsibility for organizing one of the bombs, and alleged that the operation had been directed by two senior Iraqi Baath party officials exiled in Syria, a claim that provoked a diplomatic confrontation with

Syria (see Regional relations). Nevertheless, in late August Islamic State of Iraq, a network of Sunni militant groups suspected of links with al-Qa'ida, claimed that it had perpetrated the attacks. Islamic State of Iraq also alleged that it had organized two suicide car bombs in Baghdad on 25 October, one of which targeted the Ministry of Justice. At least 155 people died in the bombings, which raised concerns that the security forces were susceptible to infiltration by insurgents. By the end of October more than 60 security officers had reportedly been arrested and questioned in connection with the attacks. Meanwhile, in that month the Ministry of Human Rights issued the first comprehensive Iraqi government report on war casualties. It found that 85,694 people had been killed in violence between the beginning of 2004 and October 2008, almost 150,000 people had been injured and an estimated 10,000 were missing.

Amid reports of divisions in the Shi'a UIA coalition, the largest parliamentary grouping, in August 2009 the formation was announced of a new Shi'a electoral list, the Iraqi National Alliance. This new grouping, which excluded Prime Minister al-Maliki's Islamic Dawa Party, was dominated by supporters of al-Sadr (who remained in self-imposed exile in Iran) and also included the ISCI. In the same month the death was announced of the ISCI leader, Abd al-Aziz al-Hakim; he was succeeded by his son, Ammar al-Hakim, in September.

Meanwhile, on 24 June 2009 a draft Constitution for the Kurdish Autonomous Region was approved by the Iraqi Kurdistan Parliament (the National Assembly having adopted the name Parliament in February). The document, which identified Islamic *Shari'a* as the basis for the region's legal system, also included territorial claims to Kirkuk and other disputed regions. However, a planned referendum on the draft Constitution was subsequently postponed, owing to opposition from the Independent High Electoral Commission (IHEC) and the Iraqi Council of Representatives, as well as demands by Kurdish opposition parties for the document to be amended; no date had been set for the referendum by early 2014. Following elections to the Iraqi Kurdistan Parliament held on 25 July 2009, the Kurdistani List—comprising the PUK and the KDP—secured 59 of the 111 seats. A new reformist party, the Movement for Change (Gorran), which had been established by former PUK members in 2006, received 25 seats. In a concurrent election for the regional presidency, Barzani was re-elected with 69.6% of the valid votes cast. In August 2009 Barham Salih, of the PUK, resigned as Deputy Prime Minister in the central Government to assume the post of Prime Minister of the Kurdish Autonomous Region.

The March 2010 legislative elections

Revised legislation concerning the forthcoming national legislative elections was approved by the Council of Representatives on 7 November 2009. The negotiations had been protracted owing to disagreement over voter registration in the disputed city of Kirkuk. According to the new legislation, election results from Kirkuk would be subject to review by a parliamentary committee. The law also provided for: an increase in the number of Council seats from 275 to 323, partly to accommodate claims for increased representation by Kurds and Sunnis; an allocation of 5% of seats for representatives of minorities (including Christians) and displaced Iraqis; and the adoption of an open list system, which would allow voters to choose individual candidates from electoral lists. However, on 18 November Vice-President Tariq al-Hashimi vetoed the bill on the grounds that it provided inadequate representation for the vast numbers of Iraqis displaced in Syria and Jordan, many of whom were Sunnis. (According to figures published by the respective Governments, by January 2010 there were an estimated 1,054,466 Iraqi refugees living in Syria, and a further 450,756 in Jordan.) As a result, the IHEC declared that it would not be possible to hold the election by the constitutional deadline of the end of January 2010. An amended electoral law, which increased the number of seats in the Council to 325 and accorded displaced Iraqis the right to vote for candidates in their province of origin, received parliamentary approval on 7 December 2009. Al-Hashimi rescinded his veto, and the election was subsequently rescheduled for 7 March 2010. On 8 December 2009 five car bombs, three of which were suicide attacks, were directed at targets in Baghdad including the Ministry of the Interior and a university campus; at least 127 people were killed in the attacks, for which Islamic State of Iraq again claimed responsibility.

In mid-January 2010 the IHEC announced that it was to bar more than 500 candidates and up to 15 political organizations from participating in the forthcoming election. The proscribed list reportedly included more than 170 candidates who had been identified by the Justice and Accountability Commission (JAC), which oversees Iraq's de-Baathification policy, as having alleged links to the Baath Party or to Saddam Hussain's former security apparatus. Prominent Sunni politicians affected by the ruling included the Minister of Defence, Abd al-Qadir Muhammad Jasim Obeidi, and Saleh al-Mutlaq, the leader of the influential Iraqi Front for National Dialogue. Following claims by Sunni Arab leaders that the ruling would exacerbate sectarian tensions and diminish the legitimacy of the election, in early February a special appeals panel ruled that, instead, any elected candidates with Baath Party associations should be scrutinized after the election. However, the Government insisted that candidates be fully investigated prior to the ballot. On 11 February the JAC announced the reinstatement of 26 previously barred candidates, although al-Mutlaq remained ineligible.

A day of early voting on 4 March 2010 was marked by three separate attacks on polling stations in Baghdad, in which at least 17 people died. Nevertheless, some 62.4% of eligible voters participated in the election on 7 March. Final results were announced by the IHEC on 26 March. Following the allocation of compensatory seats, the Iraqi National Movement of former interim Prime Minister Ayad Allawi emerged as the largest party, with 89 seats (plus two compensatory seats) in the 325-seat Council of Representatives. This new electoral bloc, widely known as Iraqiya, had replaced Allawi's INL, and included the INA and the Iraqi Front for National Dialogue. The State of Law alliance of incumbent premier Nuri al-Maliki won 87 seats (plus two compensatory seats). The Shi'a Iraqi National Alliance secured 68 seats (with an additional two seats subsequently being allocated) and the Kurdistan Alliance list of the PUK and KDP 42 (plus one compensatory seat). UN and other international observers confirmed that the conduct of the poll had been fair. However, al-Maliki refused to accept the declared outcome and demanded a full manual recount of the votes; the IHEC announced on 19 April that a recount would take place in the Baghdad area. Meanwhile, owing to the lack of overall majority for either of the leading coalitions, lengthy coalition negotiations ensued. On 25 March 2010 the Federal Supreme Court had confirmed that, constitutionally, the leader of the largest coalition in parliament was entitled to form a new administration, leaving open the possibility of a post-election merger of the State of Law alliance with former allies in the Iraqi National Alliance. On 26 April the JAC upheld a ruling that a further 52 former Baathist candidates should not have been permitted to contest the elections. Only two of these, both from Iraqiya, had won seats, and they were subsequently replaced by other members of Iraqiya.

The political uncertainty, as well as the approach to the end of US combat operations in August 2010, again prompted a deterioration in Iraq's security situation. On 19 April 2010 the respective leaders of Islamic State of Iraq and of al-Qa'ida in Iraq, Abu Omar al-Baghdadi and Abu Ayyub al-Masri, were reportedly killed in a joint Iraqi-US security operation near Tikrit. Another al-Qa'ida leader, Ahmad al-Obeidi (also known as Abu Suhaib), was also reported killed in Nineveh on 20 April. The killing of these leading insurgents led to a wave of fatal revenge attacks across Iraq, and militants sought to widen the divisions between the country's Sunni and Shi'a communities. On 10 May more than 100 people were killed as bombs were detonated at a textiles factory in Hilla, gunmen attacked Iraqi soldiers and police officers in Baghdad, and attacks were carried out in Basra, Fallujah and Mosul. On 14 May Islamic State of Iraq announced the appointment of al-Masri's successor, Abu Suleiman al-Nasser (also known as Noman Salman), as its new 'Minister of War', and warned that the organization had begun a new military campaign against Iraqi Shi'a and security forces in revenge for the deaths of the al-Qa'ida commanders and alleged official abuse of Sunni detainees. (On 25 February 2011 Iraqi security forces claimed to have killed Abu Suleiman during a military raid near Baghdad.)

Meanwhile, in an effort to defeat Allawi's winning Iraqiya faction in its attempt to form Iraq's next government, on 4 May 2010 al-Maliki's State of Law alliance agreed to form a unified parliamentary bloc with the Iraqi National Alliance, to be called the National Alliance (NA). The merger of the two Shi'a alliances into a new 'super-bloc' was formally announced on 11 June, shortly before the first session of the new legislature. Al-Maliki was also reported to be participating in coalition discussions with the Kurdistan Alliance. However, Iraqiya insisted that, as the winner of the largest number of seats, it should be entitled to seek to form an administration first. Moreover, despite commanding a total of 159 seats in the Council of Representatives—and thus requiring only four more seats to hold a parliamentary majority of 163 in the 325-seat legislature—the constituent parties of the NA were unable to agree on a prime ministerial candidate, with the ISCI and the Sadrists refusing to accept al-Maliki's continuation in that role.

On 16 May 2010 the IHEC announced that it was upholding the results of the March legislative elections, confirming that the Baghdad recount had not found any evidence of fraudulent activity. An inaugural session of the Council of Representatives took place on 14 June. However, although Iraq's new deputies were sworn in, the session was declared to be left open but suspended, pending an agreement between the various political factions on the formation of a new government. (On 24 October the Supreme Court ordered the parliament to resume its functions, after a number of civic groups launched legal proceedings claiming that Fouad Masoum, who had replaced Ayad al-Samarrai to become interim Speaker on 14 June, had violated the Constitution by leaving the session open.) Meanwhile, on 17 May 2010 a court of appeal reinstated nine successful electoral candidates, eight of whom belonged to Allawi's faction, after they had previously been barred as part of the JAC's de-Baathification process. On 24 May a deputy from Iraqiya was attacked by unidentified gunmen outside his house in Mosul and subsequently died from his injuries.

The formation of a new Government

As the US Administration sought to exert pressure on Allawi's Iraqiya faction and al-Maliki's State of Law alliance in order to reach a power-sharing deal before the USA withdrew its combat troops, the agreement between al-Maliki's bloc and the Iraqi National Alliance began to falter in August 2010. Smaller Shi'a movements in the NA, such as the Sadrists, still refused to back al-Maliki's renomination as Prime Minister. For his part, Allawi—whose Iraqiya coalition also ruled out joining a government under al-Maliki—had held a meeting with al-Sadr in Damascus, Syria, in July, in an effort to accelerate the formation of a viable administration. On 16 August it was reported that discussions between Iraqiya and the State of Law alliance had been suspended, after the incumbent Prime Minister described Iraqiya as being a 'Sunni bloc'. A spokesman for Allawi insisted that his was a secular nationalist movement, although it had predominantly Sunni support. Moreover, al-Maliki refused to step down as Prime Minister in favour of Allawi.

President Obama formally declared the end of the US combat mission in Iraq, known as Operation Iraqi Freedom, on 31 August 2010. He confirmed that almost 50,000 US forces would remain in the country in order to 'advise and assist' Iraq's security forces and defend US interests, but that the US military would be completely withdrawn by 31 December 2011, under the terms of the SOFA. (The Iraqi Chief of Staff of the Joint Armed Forces, Lt-Gen. Babakir Zebari, had warned in early August 2010 that Iraqi troops might not be adequately prepared to guarantee the security of Iraq until 2020, and suggested that US forces should in fact remain until that date.) A ceremony was held in Baghdad on 1 September 2010 to commemorate the start of the 'final phase' of the USA's mission in Iraq, code-named 'Operation New Dawn'. The weeks preceding the end of US combat operations had been notably violent in several parts of the country, with a wave of attacks being perpetrated against Iraqi police and security targets, financial institutions and ordinary civilians; the continuing pattern of Sunni–Shi'a violence was also evident.

During the latter part of 2010 the campaign being waged by radical Islamist organizations against Iraq's Christian community intensified, resulting in a further exodus of Christians either to the relative safety of northern Iraq or abroad. On 3 November Islamic State of Iraq issued a statement threatening to 'extirpate and disperse' all Christians from the country, describing all institutions and followers of the Christian religion as 'legitimate targets' for Islamist attacks. This followed an incident on 31 October 2010 when gunmen entered the Syrian Catholic church in central Baghdad during a mass, holding around 100 worshippers hostage and reportedly demanding the release of al-Qa'ida detainees from Iraqi prisons. At least 58 people (including two priests and a reported six militants) were killed, most as a result of suicide bombs detonated by the attackers as security forces entered the church in an attempt to free the hostages.

Meanwhile, on 1 October 2010 it was announced that the NA had finally decided to support al-Maliki's continuing as Prime Minister at the head of a new administration, amid reports that a deal had been brokered by the Iranian Government. On 10 November the leaders of Iraq's principal factions in the Council of Representatives formally signed a power-sharing agreement under which a coalition government would again be led by al-Maliki (a Shi'a), while a new foreign policy and security council, the National Council for Strategic Policies (NCSP), would be run by Allawi (a secular Shi'a). The coalition agreement followed a power-sharing deal which had been reached between the NA and both the Kurdistan Alliance and Iraqiya in early November. On 11 November a session of the Council of Representatives was duly held, at which Jalal Talabani (a Kurd) was re-elected as President, while a Sunni Arab member of Iraqiya, Osama al-Nujaifi, was elected as the chamber's Speaker. Al-Maliki was officially named by President Talabani as Prime Minister-designate on 25 November and given 30 days to form a new government. Meanwhile, it emerged in late October 2010 that, apparently as part of the Iranian-brokered agreement reached between al-Maliki and al-Sadr, large numbers of militants from the latter's Mahdi Army had been released from gaol; the cleric was also believed to have been promised certain ministerial portfolios. The Mahdi Army was reported to have been dissolved by al-Sadr in mid-2008 and succeeded by a civilian organization, Al-Mumahidun (Supporters of the Mahdi). (Al-Sadr returned to Iraq in January 2011, after more than three years' self-imposed exile in Iran.)

On 17 November 2010 President Talabani refused to approve the execution order for Saddam Hussain's former Deputy Prime Minister, Tareq Aziz, after Aziz had on 26 October been sentenced to death by the Federal Supreme Court for his involvement in the persecution of Shi'a politicians during the 1980s; two other senior Baathists, including the former Minister of the Interior and Director of Iraqi Intelligence, Saadoun Shaker, were also given a death sentence. (Aziz had already been sentenced to a 15-year gaol term for having ordered the killing of 42 merchants found guilty of profiteering in 1992, and a further seven-year term for the forced displacement of a group of Iraqi Kurds from the north of the country in the 1980s.) Announcing his decision, Talabani cited the fact that Aziz was 74 years old and a Christian. Although a prime ministerial aide indicated in December 2011 that Aziz would in fact be executed during the course of 2012, following the completion of the US troop withdrawal, the execution had yet to occur by early 2014. Meanwhile, on 29 November 2010 Shaker was given a further death sentence for his role in the execution of Iraqi Kurds during the 1980s.

The legislature finally approved the new Council of Ministers submitted by al-Maliki, in which all the major blocs were represented, on 21 December 2010. However, 13 of the 42 government ministers were interim appointments; al-Maliki was to take temporary charge of the defence, national security and interior portfolios, amid disagreement about possible nominees to these crucial ministries. Saleh al-Mutlaq (a Sunni Arab who had renounced his former Baathist affiliation) was named as one of three Deputy Prime Ministers; Dr Rozh Nuri Shawais (a Kurd) was named as Deputy Prime Minister and Acting Minister of Trade, while Hussein al-Shahristani (a Shi'a) became Deputy Prime Minister for Energy Affairs. The Minister of Foreign Affairs, Hoshyar al-Zibari (a Kurd), retained his post, while Abd al-Karim al-Luaibi (a Shi'a) and Dr Rafie al-Issawi (a Sunni Arab) became Ministers of Oil and of Finance, respectively. On 13 February 2011 eight further nominees, including a permanent Minister of Trade, received parliamentary approval. In May agreement was finally reached on the appointment of three Vice-Presidents—Dr Adil Abd al-Mahdi, Tariq al-Hashimi and Khudhair al-Khuzai—with the former being chosen by President Talabani as First Vice-President. However, the resignation of al-Mahdi, who sought a more streamlined cabinet, was confirmed in July. In August 12 ministries were disbanded, including those of marsh lands and tribal affairs.

Meanwhile, the Federal Supreme Court issued a controversial ruling in mid-January 2011 that placed Iraq's independent commissions such as the IHEC and the Central Bank under executive, rather than legislative, control. Following protracted disagreements between the leading parliamentary groups regarding the establishment and authority of the new foreign policy and security council, Allawi announced in early March that he no longer wished to preside over the NCSP, citing the Prime Minister's decision to assume interim responsibility for the defence, national security and interior portfolios, together with the protracted delay in appointing permanent ministers, as evidence of his 'lack of commitment to national partnership'. Coalition disagreements regarding the allocation of these key portfolios remained unresolved by early 2014, with the posts being held by other cabinet ministers in an interim capacity.

Meanwhile, despite an apparent breakthrough in August 2011 during negotiations, mediated by President Talabani, between the State of Law alliance and Iraqiya—with al-Maliki reported to have agreed to honour the terms of the power-sharing agreement and to accelerate the formation of the NCSP—the Council had yet to be formed as of early 2014.

During February 2011, as social and political unrest spread across large parts of the Middle East and North Africa, spontaneous protests were held in several Iraqi cities—including Baghdad, Basra, Sulaimaniya and Karbala—by people demonstrating against official corruption, poor provision of basic services, high unemployment and the lack of civil liberties. The protesters called for 25 February to be a 'day of rage', and at least nine people were reportedly killed in clashes with security forces in cities outside the capital. Al-Maliki, who apparently described the demonstrations as a 'Baathist plot', had attempted to prevent the uprisings in Tunisia and Egypt—which had resulted in the ouster of both countries' governing regimes—from spreading to Iraq by announcing in early February that he would not stand for a third term of office in 2014. He also pledged to pursue constitutional reform, particularly by implementing legislation to prevent any Prime Minister from serving more than two consecutive terms of office, while the Government agreed to reduce the price of electricity. In late February 2011 al-Maliki warned government ministers that he would reorganize the Council of Ministers if there had not been a tangible improvement in ministerial performance after 100 days. The Prime Minister also announced that US $900m. of funds that had been allocated to the purchase of fighter aircraft were to be redirected towards the provision of food for the poor, with a further $400m. reserved for the purchase of generator fuel to power air conditioners during the hot summer months, and initiated a series of infrastructure projects intended to improve Iraq's dilapidated road and sewerage systems.

However, the protests continued into April 2011, principally in the Kurdish Autonomous Region. In late April security forces in Sulaimaniya opened fire on protesters who were demanding the resignation of the regional administration. Days later Iraqi troops and *peshmerga* fighters entered the city in an attempt to quell the protests. By the end of April it was reported that up to 36 people had been killed across Iraq as a result of the unrest. In June, as al-Maliki's deadline for ministerial improvements expired with no government minister having been dismissed owing to poor performance, hundreds of demonstrators converged in Baghdad. They protested against the Government's failure to achieve meaningful reform, and demanded an improvement in public services, particularly the supply of electricity. In early August the Minister of Electricity was forced to resign, after a government investigation discovered procedural irregularities on the part of his ministry pertaining to power plant contracts signed with two foreign firms.

Completion of the withdrawal of US troops

There was an escalation of attacks targeting US troops ahead of the scheduled completion of the military withdrawal, due by 31 December 2011 under the terms of the SOFA. Some 18 US soldiers were killed in eight separate attacks during a six-week period in June–July 2011, forcing the US military back into active combat despite the formal conclusion of the combat operation in August 2010. In mid-August 2011 13 apparently co-ordinated bomb attacks by Islamic State of Iraq, targeting largely Shi'a areas across Iraq as well as government compounds in Karbala and Najaf, killed more than 70 people; the attacks led to renewed concern about the Iraqi authorities' ability to manage national security in the absence of US assistance. In September Muqtada al-Sadr marked the imminent end to the US mission by ordering his supporters to halt attacks on US troops.

In July 2011 the Iraqi authorities assumed control of the Development Fund for Iraq, which had been established following the ouster of Saddam Hussain's regime in 2003 and contained billions of dollars of oil revenues set aside by the UN. Responsibility for the Fund was henceforth to be controlled by a panel of Iraqi financial experts operating under terms approved by the Council of Ministers. Meanwhile, in June 2011 a US official investigating the disappearance of US $6,600m. from the Fund, which had been airlifted into Iraq by the Bush Administration during 2003–04 as part of a $20,000m. reconstruction package, suggested that the money might have been stolen by elements within the Iraqi interim administration at the time.

During a joint press conference held on 12 December 2011, al-Maliki and President Obama reaffirmed their mutual commitment to a long-term comprehensive partnership between Iraq and the USA, including plans to bolster co-operation in the fields of counter-terrorism, defence and security, as well as trade and economic development, institution-building, education and energy. Although al-Maliki hailed the imminent completion of the US withdrawal as an indication of the successful defeat of terrorism and the beginning of a 'new chapter' for Iraq, Obama cautioned of the heightened risk of attacks in the coming months by elements seeking to 'derail Iraq's progress'. Many observers also noted that the US withdrawal would render Iraq more susceptible to increasing Iranian influence. Following the completion of its withdrawal, the USA was to have no military bases within Iraq, although a small number of military personnel would remain in the country to assist with arms sales, together with some 16,000 personnel to assist in the establishment of effective diplomatic, civilian and military ties.

A ceremony was staged in Baghdad on 15 December 2011 to mark the formal end of the US mission, attended by the US Secretary of Defense, Leon Panetta. On 18 December the final convoy of 500 US troops withdrew from Iraq, crossing the border into Kuwait, and thereby concluding a campaign that had claimed the lives of 4,484 US troops and cost the US Government an estimated US $800,000m. since its inception in March 2003. According to Iraq Body Count, an estimated 4,144 civilians died as a result of violence during 2011, representing a slight increase on the previous year.

The feared escalation in sectarian violence soon became apparent across Iraq. Moreover, the tensions between Iraq's various political factions which were heightened from early 2012 (see Recent developments) led many Iraqis to fear a return to the intense sectarian conflict seen in the country during 2006–07. According to Iraqi security officials, by late January 2012 some 434 people (mainly Shi'as) had been killed since the completion of the US withdrawal. Attacks against the national security forces also intensified, with a spate of attacks targeting police officers in January. A series of fatal gun and bomb attacks was launched by Sunni insurgents during 2012, with reciprocal attacks by militant Shi'a groups also being reported.

Meanwhile, in mid-December 2011 Prime Minister al-Maliki signed a warrant for the arrest of Vice-President al-Hashimi on charges of terrorism, and issued a concurrent request to the Council of Representatives to remove Deputy Prime Minister al-Mutlaq from office on the grounds of incompetence. Al-Mutlaq had recently referred to al-Maliki as a 'dictator', and he was barred from participating in cabinet meetings. Al-Hashimi, who subsequently fled to northern Iraq, was alleged by an investigative committee established by the Ministry of the Interior to have ordered bodyguards to carry out terrorist attacks against government and security officials, as well as Shi'a pilgrims, for a number of years. Al-Maliki demanded that the President of the Kurdistan Autonomous Region, Masoud Barzani, and Iraqi President Jalal Talabani transfer al-Hashimi to the custody of the Iraqi judiciary in Baghdad. In protest at the action taken against two of its members, who were both Sunnis, Iraqiya subsequently withdrew its participation from the Council of Ministers and announced a concomitant boycott of the Council of Representatives. Representatives of Iraqiya, which controlled 82 parliamentary seats and nine cabinet posts, accused al-Maliki of attempting to centralize power, of disregarding the terms of the power-sharing agreement signed in November 2010, and of arbitrarily arresting aides and security guards employed by Iraqiya leaders. Iraqiya also blamed al-Maliki for the authorities' failure to stem recent unrest in the largely Sunni province of Diyala. The dispute between the Shi'a Prime Minister and the nominally secular but Sunni-dominated Iraqiya threatened further to exacerbate sectarian divisions. Iraqiya ended its parliamentary boycott at the end of January 2012, and in early February also resumed its participation in cabinet meetings. However, in April the Higher Judicial Council announced that al-Hashimi—who had sought refuge in İstanbul, Turkey—would be tried *in absentia* on charges of murder from 3 May.

In late January 2012 the UN Office of the High Commissioner for Human Rights stated that at least 63 people had been executed by the Iraqi authorities in the preceding two months, while the High Commissioner, Navi Pillay, expressed reservations about the 'due process and fairness of trials' in Iraq. Pillay's comments echoed concerns expressed in an Amnesty International report in late 2011, which claimed that at least 1,300 prisoners were on death row in Iraq at that time, that trials 'consistently failed to satisfy international standards for fair trial', and that torture and other abuse of detainees within Iraqi prisons was 'rife'. At the beginning of February 2012 the Ministry of Justice confirmed that more than 50 people had been executed in Iraq during January—although some human rights groups claimed that the actual figure might be significantly higher.

Recent developments: renewed sectarian violence amid rising political tensions

The pressure on the al-Maliki Government increased in late April 2012, when the leaders of the Kurdistan Alliance, Iraqiya and the Sadrist movement held talks in Arbil in an effort to force the Prime Minister from office. Following the meeting, they presented a nine-point ultimatum letter to al-Maliki, which included the demands that a premier be permitted to serve only two consecutive terms of office and that the role of the Council of Representatives be expanded. In the absence of a satisfactory response from the Prime Minister within 15 days, the opposition leaders warned that they would seek a parliamentary vote of no confidence. However, the subsequent lack of political consensus among the various opposition groups meant that they were deemed to be unable to achieve a sufficient number of votes to remove al-Maliki from office.

It was announced in late May 2012 that al-Maliki and his deputy, Saleh al-Mutlaq, had resolved their dispute and that al-Mutlaq would resume his participation in the Government. In early September Vice-President al-Hashimi was found guilty *in absentia* of two charges of planning and facilitating murder, and sentenced to death by hanging by a court in Baghdad. However, al-Hashimi rejected the verdict, claiming that the proceedings had been instigated by the Prime Minister for political reasons. The Turkish Prime Minister, Recep Tayyip Erdoğan, indicated that Turkey would refuse any request by Iraq to extradite al-Hashimi. By mid-December al-Hashimi had been given a total of five death sentences, all *in absentia*, having additionally been convicted of crimes including plotting to explode a car bomb targeting Shi'a pilgrims, planning to assassinate an official at the Ministry of the Interior, and weapons offences; al-Hashimi's son-in-law, Ahmad Qahtan, was also sentenced to death on similar charges. It was reported in mid-October 2012 that Dr Sinan al-Shabibi, Governor of the Central Bank since 2003, had been suspended from his post and a warrant issued for his arrest, together with at least 15 other employees of the bank. Al-Shabibi and members of his staff were alleged by an investigative parliamentary committee to have been involved in financial impropriety concerning the Central Bank's handling of Iraq's foreign exchange markets. In mid-October 2013 al-Hashimi stated that he would be prepared to return to Iraq, provided that officials from the European Union could help to ensure that he received a fair trial.

During 2012 Iraq Body Count estimated the number of violent civilian deaths to be 4,573—representing a 10% increase compared with the previous year. In June a series of bomb attacks targeted Shi'a districts of Baghdad and other cities, with some estimates claiming that 280 people had been killed. Many of the victims were Shi'a pilgrims, and Islamic State of Iraq claimed responsibility for a significant number of the deaths. In a single day in early September more than 100 Iraqis were reportedly killed as a result of the co-ordinated bombings of principally Shi'a targets; the same militant group was again held responsible. In early February 2013 militants launched a series of car bombings in Shi'a-dominated areas of Baghdad and other Iraqi towns, apparently to disrupt preparations for the country's first ballot to be held since the legislative polls of March 2010. Provincial elections were scheduled to take place across Iraq, with the exclusion of the three Kurdish provinces, on 20 April 2013. On 19 March, 10 years after the commencement of the US-led invasion, at least 60 people were killed in a series of co-ordinated bombings and shootings in Shi'a districts of Baghdad. Later that day the Government announced that provincial elections in Anbar and Nineveh provinces were to be postponed, owing to concerns over security; these polls were later scheduled for June. Meanwhile, President Talabani was reported to have suffered a serious stroke in mid-December 2012 and was flown to Germany for emergency medical treatment. By January 2014 he had yet to return to his duties.

From late 2012 there was an escalation of protests being held by Sunni Iraqis against the Shi'a-led Government; some observers noted the evident loss of Talabani's ability to mediate between Iraq's rival Shi'a, Sunni and Kurdish groups. Supporters of the Iraqiya movement had begun anti-Government protests in cities including Fallujah and Ramadi in late December, following the arrest by the authorities of 10 bodyguards employed to protect the Sunni Minister of Finance, Dr Rafie al-Issawi, a senior member of Iraqiya; the men were all accused of involvement in terrorism. However, al-Maliki denied that he had personally ordered the arrests. The protests subsequently spread to majority Sunni districts of Baghdad, as well as Baquba, Mosul and Kirkuk, with demonstrators accusing al-Maliki's Government of anti-Sunni discrimination and demanding changes to the country's anti-terrorism laws. Counter-demonstrations were held by Shi'a supporters of the Government across Iraq, including in Basra and Karbala, in early January 2013. In mid-January a Sunni member of the Council of Representatives was killed, together with two of his bodyguards, in a suicide bombing in Fallujah. In late February demonstrators gathered in central Baghdad to protest at the failure of parliament to approve the Government's draft budget for that year, which risked inflicting further damage to Iraq's economy. The various political factions disagreed about several aspects of the budget proposals: Iraqiya demanded that a certain level of funding was allocated to develop Iraq's provinces, while the Kurdistan Alliance sought financial assistance from the central Government to pay the foreign oil firms operating in the region, as well as to carry out vital reconstruction projects. The budget was finally approved by the Council of Representatives on 7 March 2013, although the parliamentary session was boycotted by Kurdish deputies in protest at what they regarded as the unfair distribution of oil revenues. Meanwhile, at the beginning of March it was reported that al-Issawi had resigned from the Government, citing his opposition to the 'sectarian' nature of al-Maliki's administration. A week later Minister of Agriculture Ezz al-Din Ahmad Hussein al-Dawla—also a member of Iraqiya—announced his resignation, following allegations that the security forces had shot dead a Sunni demonstrator in Mosul. At least 40 people were killed in Hawija, close to Kirkuk, on 23 April, as clashes erupted between protesters and Iraqi security forces who had entered a protest camp in response to an attack on a police checkpoint. This latest round of violence, in which officers were alleged to have used excessive force against non-armed protesters, provoked further resignations of Sunni ministers—the Ministers of Education and of Science and Technology left their posts—but also prompted fears of a descent into civil and sectarian conflict. In late April the Government suspended the operating licences of some 10 television channels, including the Qatar-based Al Jazeera, accusing them of inciting violence and spreading misinformation about the nature of the protests in Iraq. At the end of April the Government claimed to have evidence that senior officials from the former Baathist regime, including Izzat Ibrahim al-Douri, were leading the protests.

Despite the ongoing unrest, provincial elections were held as scheduled in 12 of Iraq's 18 provinces on 20 April 2013; they were the first elections to take place since the completion of the US troop withdrawal in December 2011. Polls in the majority Sunni provinces of Anbar and Nineveh were held on 20 June 2013, while no elections were held in the three Kurdish provinces or in Kirkuk, the status of which continued to be disputed by Iraq's various political factions. Some violent incidents were reported at polling stations, but the elections were largely peaceful. The IHEC recorded an overall voter turnout of 50%; however, the rate was said to be as low as 33% in Baghdad. Although al-Maliki's State of Law coalition received the largest number of council seats and won a majority of votes in seven provinces (including Baghdad and Basra), it fared significantly worse than in the 2009 polls and was required to govern in coalition with other, smaller parties. Commentators attributed the State of Law's loss of votes to other Shi'a parties and the Sadrist movement to public disillusionment with the Prime Minister, notably his failure to reduce unemployment and improve public services, and to stem the tide of sectarian violence across Iraq. Meanwhile, a new grouping led by the Speaker of the Council of Representatives, Osama al-Nujaifi, called the Uniters, took a significant number of votes from Allawi's Iraqiya coalition. During 15–21 May 2013 an estimated 450 people died as the result of sectarian bomb and gun attacks in northern and central areas of the country. A double bomb attack at a Sunni mosque in Baquba on 17 May resulted in at least 43 deaths, while car bombings in Basra and Shi'a districts of Baghdad killed some 76 people (including 12 Iranian pilgrims).

By the second half of 2013 the violence had reached a level of intensity not seen since the 2006–08 period. There was a notable increase in the number of bomb attacks being reported, with a number of these attacks being perpetrated by extremist Sunni militant groups against both Shi'a and Christian targets. On

21 July more than 500 detainees, many of whom were said to be senior members of al-Qa'ida in Iraq, escaped from Baghdad Central Prison and the nearby Taji prison in a co-ordinated assault by the militant group using both gunmen and suicide bombers. An estimated 41 people (20 security guards and 21 prisoners) died during the operation, which was claimed by the umbrella group Islamic State of Iraq and the Levant—formed in April by jihadist fighters to co-ordinate militant attacks in both Iraq and Syria. On 22 July the group was also held responsible for the deaths of 25 people (including 22 soldiers) in a suicide bomb attack in Mosul. On 29 July a series of bomb attacks perpetrated by Sunni militants in predominantly Shi'a areas of Baghdad and other cities in central and southern Iraq killed more than 60 people. A further 80 people reportedly died in car bombings targeting Shi'as across Iraq as they celebrated the end of Ramadan on 10 August. Five days later a crossing on Iraq's border with Syria was opened, allowing some 50,000 (mainly Kurdish) Syrian refugees who were escaping fighting between Kurdish groups and Islamist rebels to enter the Kurdish Autonomous Region of northern Iraq. By November there were reported to be more than 200,000 Syrian refugees in Iraq. Meanwhile, many Iraqis who had fled to Syria during the Iraqi conflict and subsequent period were returning to the country, with Iraqi Red Cross officials stating that more than 70,000 had returned to Iraq since the start of the Syrian uprising in early 2011.

Iraq Body Count assessed on 1 September 2013 that between 120,809 and 133,960 civilians had died as a result of violence during the entire period since the US-led invasion in 2003. It was alleged on the same day that Iraqi security forces had entered Camp Ashraf, north-east of Baghdad, and killed some 52 members of the Iranian dissident group Mujahidin-e-Khalq. However, the Iraqi authorities, who were in the process of closing down the camp, denied the claims and attributed the deaths to 'infighting', while different sources disputed the actual death toll. In mid-September 2013 it was revealed that the remaining inhabitants of the camp had been moved to another centre close to the capital, from where they would be permanently resettled. Later that month Arbil, in the Kurdish Autonomous Region, became the target of further bombings by militant Islamists. Islamic State of Iraq and the Levant claimed that it was waging a campaign of violence against the Kurdish people as a result of their support for Syrian Kurds who were engaged in fighting Islamist groups in that country's civil conflict.

At elections to the Iraqi Kurdistan Parliament on 21 September 2013, the KDP emerged as the leading party, securing 38 seats. Gorran became the second largest party, with 24 seats, while the PUK came third, winning only 18 seats. However, although these polls were expected to have been held concurrently with a presidential ballot, on 30 June 2013 the Kurdish legislature had voted to postpone elections for the regional presidency until August 2015. The decision was condemned by Kurdish opposition parties, who insisted that Kurdish President Masoud Barzani (elected in 2005 and re-elected in 2009) had now served the permitted two terms in office. However, KDP and PUK officials asserted that the delay would enable an agreement to be reached on the new Kurdish constitution prior to the vote taking place. After Prime Minister al-Maliki had convened a cabinet meeting in Arbil for the first time in June 2013, in early July Barzani held talks in Baghdad with al-Maliki in an effort to reduce tensions between the Iraqi and the Kurdish authorities; their discussions reportedly focused on disputes concerning the exploitation of Iraq's vast hydrocarbon resources and the way in which oil and gas revenues were to be apportioned.

It was announced in early October 2013 that elections to the Iraqi Council of Representatives would take place in April 2014; following the passage of the electoral law on 4 November 2013, the vote was scheduled for 30 April 2014. Meanwhile, the sectarian violence continued: during 5–6 October 2013 more than 100 people died as a result of militant attacks, including 51 Shi'a pilgrims in a Baghdad suicide bombing and 12 children in a car bomb attack on their school in Mosul. Further attacks launched by Sunni militants in Shi'a areas of the Iraqi capital throughout the month led to scores of fatalities. In late December a group of Christians attending Christmas Day services in two churches in Baghdad were the victims of bomb attacks, with more than 35 worshippers being killed.

According to UN estimates, 7,157 people died as the result of violent incidents in Iraq during 2013—more than double the figure of 3,238 recorded in 2012. UN figures for January 2014 showed that at least 1,013 people had been killed—795 civilians, 122 soldiers and 96 police officers—while around 2,024 people were wounded. The number of fatalities was thus three times greater in that month than during January 2013, and indicated that the sectarian violence had deteriorated to a level last seen in 2008. The anti-Government protests led by Sunnis continued into 2014, and were met with a harsh response from the Iraqi authorities, who were widely criticized for failing to address the underlying causes of the unrest. In January security forces in the western province of Anbar, assisted by local Sunni tribesmen from the province's Awakening Council, were engaged in fierce gun battles with Sunni militias allied with Islamic State of Iraq and the Levant, who had seized control of parts of Fallujah and Ramadi in the previous month. The Government regained control of Ramadi, but struggled to defeat the militants in Fallujah. It was again apparent that some of the violence was being fuelled by sectarian tensions arising from the ongoing civil war in neighbouring Syria. (It had been reported in mid-2013 that the US Administration was preparing to send specialist forces to Iraq to assist the al-Maliki Government in its struggle to defeat militant groups allied with al-Qa'ida in Iraq, who were believed to be acting together with extremist Sunni groups seeking to topple the Syrian regime of President Bashar al-Assad.) However, the unrest in Anbar had also been provoked by the arrest on terrorism charges of a leading Sunni member of the Iraqiya faction in the legislature, Ahmad al-Alwani, in Ramadi on 28 December 2013. Al-Alwani had supported the anti-Government protests, while his brother—whom the security forces alleged to have been responsible for recent fatal attacks on Iraqi soldiers in the province (15 were killed during a battle with al-Qa'ida militants on 21 December)—was among those killed in the fighting that surrounded the legislator's arrest. The parliamentary Speaker, al-Nujaifi, denounced al-Alwani's arrest as a 'blatant violation' of Iraq's Constitution. On 30 December the Government forcibly ended the sit-in that had been initiated by Sunni protesters in Ramadi in late 2012; at least 10 people died as a result of this action, leading 44 (mainly Sunni) members of the Iraqi parliament to tender their resignations in protest. Meanwhile, in November 2013 it was announced that legislative elections would take place on 30 April. However, concerns were raised over the apparent rise in violence in the country in the months preceding the poll. In early March the UN published a report estimating that some 703 people (including 139 members of the police force) had been killed in Iraq during February. That figure did not take account of the ongoing violence in Anbar province, where it was estimated by late March that a total of 156 people had been killed as a result of acts of violence.

Regional relations

In June 2005 Egypt became the first Arab state to nominate an ambassador to Baghdad since the US-led invasion; however, the abduction and murder of the ambassador, Ihab al-Sherif, in July made other Arab countries unwilling to send envoys to Iraq. Al-Qa'ida in Iraq claimed responsibility for the killing of al-Sherif, together with the subsequent abduction and killing of two Algerian diplomats later in July. However, as the security situation improved, by mid-2008 several Arab countries had chosen to resume full diplomatic relations with Iraq and to return ambassadors to Baghdad. The UAE also cancelled some US $7,000m. of Iraqi debt in July. In November 2009 the new Egyptian ambassador to Iraq, Sherif Kamal Shahin, arrived in Baghdad. Saudi Arabia finally appointed a non-resident ambassador to Iraq, Fahd al-Zaid (its envoy to Jordan), in February 2012. On 29 March a historic summit meeting of the Arab League was held in the Iraqi capital, amid tight security following a recent intensification of sectarian violence. However, many Arab governments opted to send a low-level delegation to the summit, in protest at the Iraqi Government's close relations with Iran and its apparently 'neutral' position on the Syrian crisis. Iraq's relations with Saudi Arabia subsequently deteriorated amid disagreement over the Saudi authorities' decision to advocate the provision of weapons to rebels engaged in fighting government forces in Syria. However, in January 2014 the Saudi Government sought to reassure its Iraqi counterpart that the country's failure to open an embassy in Baghdad was for technical, rather than political, reasons.

In October 2008 Ali Muhammad al-Momen became the first Kuwaiti ambassador to Iraq since diplomatic relations were abruptly severed in 1990. In February 2010 the UN confirmed that it had been engaged in intensive efforts to promote progress on all outstanding issues between Iraq and Kuwait, including the issue of Kuwaiti missing persons. At the end of May Muhammad Hussain Bahr al-Ulum, Iraq's first ambassador to Kuwait since 1990, assumed his diplomatic post. In May 2010 the Iraqi

Government had announced the gradual dissolution of the national airline, Iraqi Airways, in an effort to avoid paying US $1,200m. in compensation to Kuwait for 10 Kuwait Airways planes that it had appropriated after the 1990 invasion; however, in May 2011 it announced that the dissolution had been halted. Having frequently attempted to seize Iraqi Airways planes at foreign airports, later that month the Kuwaiti authorities took control of the airline's office in Amman, after obtaining a court ruling in Jordan. Despite the removal of Iraq's Baathist regime in 2003, the Kuwaiti Government has consistently refused to agree to the cancellation of this debt. The attendance of Sheikh Sabah al-Ahmad al-Jaber al-Sabah, the Amir of Kuwait, at the Arab League summit held in Baghdad in March 2012 was widely heralded as marking a significant breakthrough in bilateral relations. In November the Iraqi Government endorsed the terms of a financial settlement agreed with its Kuwaiti counterpart in the previous month; according to the agreement, Iraq would pay $500m. to Kuwait Airways to resolve the long-running dispute, in return for which the Kuwaiti authorities would cancel all legal action currently in place against Iraqi Airways. Of the amount agreed, $300m. was in compensation to Kuwait for Iraq's actions in 1990, while $200m. was to be invested in the establishment of a new joint-venture airline. Following ratification of the deal by the Kuwaiti National Assembly in late January 2013, the $500m. payment was duly transferred at the end of that month.

In August 2008 King Abdullah of Jordan made the first visit to Baghdad by an Arab head of state since the fall of Saddam Hussain in 2003, and in the following month a new deal governing the supply of subsidized Iraqi oil to Jordan was announced. In October Nayef al-Zaidan took up his post as Jordan's ambassador to Iraq—the previous ambassador having been withdrawn following the bombing of the Jordanian embassy in August 2003. In January 2009 the Iraqi Government welcomed a directive from King Abdullah to ease the restrictions on Iraqis entering and residing in Jordan. The two countries also agreed, in June 2011, to increase the volume of bilateral trade, with Iraq pledging to raise the volume of oil supply to Jordan. In January 2013 the Iraqi and Jordanian authorities pledged to expedite the creation of a free trade zone that had been agreed in 2009. In January 2014 the respective Governments launched a joint project involving the construction of a double pipeline to transport oil and gas between Basra and the Jordanian city of Aqaba; the project, costing an estimated US $18,000m., was expected to be completed in 2017.

After Iraq and Syria declared in November 2006 that they would restore diplomatic ties that had been severed in 1982, in the following month they opened embassies in each other's capitals. Iraqi officials hoped that the resumption in relations with Syria would assist in stemming the flow of insurgents across their joint border. In January 2007 Talabani became the first Iraqi President to visit Syria for nearly three decades. In February Iraq accused Syria of harbouring fugitive militants and refusing refuge for genuine Iraqi refugees. Syria finally named an ambassador to Baghdad, Nawaf al-Fares, in September 2008. However, al-Fares and the newly appointed Iraqi ambassador in Syria, Dr Ala'a al-Jawadi, were both temporarily recalled from their respective embassies in August 2009, following Iraqi allegations that the latter was harbouring two men suspected of involvement in a series of bombings that had targeted government buildings in Baghdad earlier that month, killing more than 100 people (see Domestic Political Affairs); Syria adamantly denied the claims. Despite a number of conciliatory gestures by the Iraqi Government during 2011 in response to mounting international calls for President Assad to tender his resignation amid widespread popular protests in Syria (q.v.), in September Prime Minister al-Maliki urged Assad to step down. Nevertheless, as the Syrian authorities' harsh crackdown on the opposition protests had, by 2012, led to a civil war, the Iraqi Government was fearful that a more radical Sunni Islamist government might replace the Assad regime in the event of his ouster. During the Arab League summit held in Baghdad in March, al-Maliki sought to dissuade member states from providing military assistance to either side in the Syrian conflict, warning that such action risked turning it into a 'regional and international proxy war'. Nevertheless, during 2013 Western governments claimed to have evidence that the Iraqi authorities were permitting Iranian planes to use Iraqi airspace in order to provide military assistance to Syrian government forces.

Iraq and Iran resumed diplomatic relations in September 2004, although many issues relating to the 1980–88 War remained unresolved. In November 2005 President Talabani became the first Iraqi head of state to visit Tehran in over 30 years. In the same month an Iraqi passenger flight landed in the Iranian capital for the first time since 1980. Iran hosted security talks on Iraq in November 2006. Although the Iranian leadership pledged to assist Iraq by any possible means, it warned that the restoration of security was dependent on the withdrawal of US troops. Following discussions between the US and Iranian ambassadors to Baghdad concerning co-operation to end the sectarian violence, the first meeting of their joint sub-committee was held in August 2007. The Iranian President, Mahmoud Ahmadinejad, undertook an official visit to Baghdad in March 2008, where he signed seven MOUs relating to bilateral co-operation with his Iraqi counterpart. During the visit Ahmadinejad denied persistent US claims that Iran was providing military and financial assistance to Iraqi Shi'a militias. In July 2011 Iranian forces crossed the border into northern Iraq in pursuit of fighters belonging to the separatist group the Party of Free Life in Kurdistan. Several Iraqi Kurds were reportedly killed and hundreds displaced during the offensive. Also in July Iraq, Iran and Syria signed an MOU providing for the construction of a 6,000-km natural gas pipeline, which would extend under Iraqi, Syrian and Lebanese territory and transport gas from Assalouyeh, in southern Iran, to the European market. Construction of the Iranian section of the US $10,000m. pipeline project reportedly commenced in November 2012; Iraq was expected to receive its first supplies of Iranian gas during 2014. As the extent of trading between Iran and Iraq continued to increase, it was reported in January 2014 that the value of this bilateral trade had exceeded US $13,000m. in 2013 and was expected to rise to $15,000m. in 2014.

In September 2007 Turkey and Iraq signed a security co-operation pact intended to curb the military activities of the Kurdish separatist organization the Kurdistan Workers' Party (Partiya Karkeren Kurdistan—PKK). However, although the pact did not include Turkey's principal demand that its military be permitted to enter Iraqi territory in pursuit of Kurdish fighters, in December Turkish troops began an offensive against PKK bases in Iraq's northern region, in response to a series of cross-border raids by armed separatists to carry out bomb attacks against Turkish soldiers in south-eastern Turkey. The President of the Kurdish Autonomous Region, Masoud Barzani, described Turkey's actions as a violation of Iraqi sovereignty. In February 2008 Turkey ordered a further military incursion into northern Iraq, with the additional launching of air strikes against PKK militant bases. Dozens of PKK militants were killed in the week-long offensive, together with several Turkish soldiers. (The Turkish military claimed by this time to have killed 240 PKK fighters, and to have lost 27 of its soldiers; however, PKK sources alleged that around 90 Turkish soldiers had died in the recent incursion.) The Iraqi Government again asserted that it had not given its approval for the offensive. However, during a visit to Iraq by Turkey's Prime Minister, Recep Tayyip Erdoğan, in July 2008, the two sides agreed to form a strategic co-operation council to improve bilateral relations; several accords on energy and border security were also signed. The inaugural meeting of the Iraq-Turkey High-Level Strategic Co-operation Council was convened in İstanbul in September 2009.

In March 2011 Erdoğan became the first Turkish premier to visit Iraq's Kurdish Autonomous Region, where he held talks with Barzani regarding co-operation in combating the PKK. In May the Iraqi Government declared that the Turkish authorities' restriction of water supply from Turkey to Iraq via the Euphrates and Tigris rivers was 'unacceptable', claiming that a series of dams constructed on both rivers allowed Turkey to monopolize the waters, to the detriment of both Iraq and Syria. An Iraqi government spokesperson insisted that the Council of Representatives would not recognize the strategic co-operation council with Turkey until a bilateral water-sharing agreement was successfully concluded. Bilateral relations deteriorated in late 2011, after the Iraqi authorities' issuing of an arrest warrant for Vice-President al-Hashimi and his subsequent arrival in Turkey (see Domestic Political Affairs). Moreover, the Turkish Government was strongly criticized by its Iraqi counterpart in May 2012, when it agreed to begin importing crude petroleum from Iraq's Kurdish Autonomous Region via a new pipeline from 2013; the decision by the Kurdish regional government to bypass central government control over the allocation of the country's oil revenues was denounced as illegal by the Iraqi authorities. During mid-2012 Turkey intensified its military campaign against the PKK, launching air strikes against militant bases in northern Iraq in response to a series of fatal PKK attacks against its soldiers. The Turkish Government claimed that the civil conflict in Syria had made it easier for the PKK, assisted by affiliated Kurdish groups inside Syria, to launch operations against Turkey from the border areas. However, despite ongoing tensions, there were signs of mutual efforts by the Iraqi and Turkish authorities to improve bilateral relations from late 2013. In October the respective Ministers of Foreign Affairs, Hoshyar al-Zibari and Ahmet Davutoğlu, pledged henceforth to hold more intensive discussions on contentious issues.

CONSTITUTION AND GOVERNMENT

Prior to the ousting of Saddam Hussain's regime by the US-led coalition in April 2003, Iraq was divided into 18 governorates (including three Autonomous Regions). In the immediate aftermath of the war, a US-led Coalition Provisional Authority (CPA) was established to govern the country in the absence of an elected sovereign government. On 13 July the CPA formed a 25-member interim Governing Council, the members of which were selected in proportion to Iraq's main ethnic and religious groups. It had no executive power, but could appoint ministers and diplomatic representatives, draw up a new constitution and set a date for free elections. The Governing Council decided upon a rotating presidency, commencing in September, with nine members of the council each serving for one month. In the same month 25 ministers were appointed to serve in an interim Cabinet, also chosen according to ethnicity and creed. On 15 November the CPA and Governing Council published a plan for the creation of a democratically elected, sovereign government and constitution by the end of 2005. However, this plan was superseded by the Transitional Administrative Law (TAL) signed on 8 March 2004. Under the terms of the TAL, an Iraqi Interim Government assumed power on 28 June 2004 (two days earlier than planned), and the CPA and Governing Council were dissolved. The Interim Government was replaced by an Iraqi Transitional Government, consisting of a state Presidency Council and a Prime Minister and Cabinet to be appointed by the Council, in April 2005, following elections to the 275-member Transitional National Assembly (TNA), which took place on 30 January. Members of the TNA were required to produce a draft constitution by 15 August 2005, to be approved by national referendum by 15 October. In the event, disagreements over key issues delayed the submission of the draft Constitution to the TNA until 28 August 2005, and a further amended text was presented to the UN on 14 September. The draft Constitution was ratified following its endorsement at a national referendum on 15 October. National elections for a permanent legislature, the Council of Representatives, took place on 15 December.

REGIONAL AND INTERNATIONAL CO-OPERATION

Iraq is a member of the League of Arab States (the Arab League) and the Organization of Arab Petroleum Exporting Countries. It joined the UN on 21 December 1945. The country was granted observer status at the World Trade Organization (WTO) in February 2004, and working party discussions to negotiate the country's eventual membership of the WTO began in May 2007. Iraq also participates in the Organization of Islamic Cooperation (OIC), the Organization of the Petroleum Exporting Countries (OPEC), and the Group of 77 developing countries (G77).

ECONOMIC AFFAIRS

In 2012, according to estimates by the World Bank, Iraq's gross national income (GNI), measured at average 2010–12 prices, was US $191,181m., equivalent to $5,870 per head (or $4,300 per head on an international purchasing-power parity basis). During 2003–12, it was estimated, the population increased at an average annual rate of 2.6%, while gross domestic product (GDP) per head increased, in real terms, by an average of 5.9% per year. Overall GDP increased, in real terms, at an average annual rate of 8.6% during 2003–12; real GDP increased by 8.4% in 2012.

Agriculture (including hunting, forestry and fishing) contributed 4.1% of GDP in 2012. According to FAO estimates, 4.4% of the labour force was engaged in agriculture in mid-2014. Dates are the principal cash crop. Other crops include wheat, barley, maize, potatoes, tomatoes, cucumbers and gherkins, aubergines and melons. Production of eggs, milk and poultry meat is also important. According to official estimates, during 2003–10, the real GDP of the agricultural sector increased by an average of 7.1% per year; agricultural GDP increased by an estimated 38.8% in 2010.

Industry (including mining, manufacturing, construction and power) provided 61.2% of GDP in 2012, according to official figures. The sector engaged 18.2% of the employed population in 2008. During 2000–03 industrial GDP decreased by an average of 17.6% per year; the GDP of the sector contracted by an estimated 37.7% in 2003. According to official estimates, industrial GDP increased, in real terms, by an average annual rate of 9.8% in 2003–10; the sector's GDP increased by an estimated 5.5% in 2010.

The mining sector accounted for 52.9% of GDP in 2012 and employed 0.4% of the working population in 2008. Iraq had proven reserves of 150,000m. barrels of petroleum at the end of 2012 (the fifth largest in the world, after Venezuela, Saudi Arabia, Canada and Iran), as well as 3,587,745m. cu m of natural gas. In addition, Iraq is believed to possess considerable undiscovered reserves of petroleum. It was reported by the Ministry of Oil in January 2013 that the production rate had reached 2.92m. barrels per day (b/d). According to oil industry data, the rate of petroleum production in 2012 was 3.12m. b/d. Reserves of phosphates, sulphur, gypsum and salt are also exploited. According to official estimates, during 2003–10 the sector's GDP increased, in real terms, by an average annual rate of 8.1%; the sector's GDP increased by an estimated 0.1% in 2010.

Manufacturing contributed just 1.7% of GDP in 2012 and engaged 4.9% of the employed population in 2008. Since the outbreak of conflict in Iraq in 2003, the development of the manufacturing sector has been severely hindered by issues such as fuel shortages, damaged and outdated equipment, poor security, and communication problems. According to official estimates, manufacturing GDP increased, in real terms, at an average annual rate of 1.8% during 2003–10; sectoral GDP increased by an estimated 6.9% in 2010.

Construction contributed 5.6% of GDP in 2012 and employed 10.8% of the working population in 2008. During 2003–10, according to official estimates, the sector's GDP increased at an average annual rate of 46.2%. As reconstruction efforts increased following the end of the conflict, the sector expanded rapidly; construction GDP increased by some 64.8% in 2010.

Energy is derived principally from natural gas, which accounted for an estimated 62.1% of total electricity generation in 2011. Since 2003 power shortages and rationing have been a persistent feature in Iraq, particularly in Baghdad. Actual electricity-generating capacity has been lower than Iraq's official installed capacity, owing to outdated technology, insurgent attacks on power stations and disruptions in fuel supplies. In order to meet demand, additional electricity has been imported from Iran and Turkey. In 2012 the Iraqi Government launched a master plan for the energy sector, which involved the renovation of existing power plants and the installation of new ones to provide an additional 24,400 MW of electricity-generating capacity by 2017. With ongoing reconstruction of the means of generation, transmission and distribution, the country's installed generating capacity had reached an estimated 13,000 MW by the end of 2013. Iraq had become self-sufficient in electricity production by October 2013, according to the Ministry of Electricity, which pledged to provide 24-hour power supplies to households for the first time in two decades.

The services sector contributed 34.7% of GDP in 2012 and engaged 58.3% of the working population in 2008. During 2003–10, according to official estimates, the sector's GDP increased, in real terms, by an average annual rate of 17.0%; services GDP increased by an estimated 10.7% in 2010.

In 2012, according to IMF figures, Iraq recorded a visible merchandise trade surplus of US $44,052.0m., and there was a surplus of $29,541.0m. on the current account of the balance of payments. Crude petroleum was by far the most important export prior to the imposition of international economic sanctions in 1990. According to figures from the Central Bank, mineral fuels and lubricants constituted 99.2% of Iraqi exports in 2012. The principal imports in the same year were machinery and transport equipment, miscellaneous manufactured articles, basic manufactures, mineral fuels and lubricants, chemicals, animal and vegetable oils and fats, and food and live animals.

Budget proposals for 2013 forecast expenditure of ID 121,800,000m. and revenue of ID 126,100,000m. Iraq's general government gross debt was ID 114,806,794m. in 2010, equivalent to 116.7% of GDP. According to Central Bank estimates, Iraq's total external debt was US $87,700m. in 2010, equivalent to 106.7% of GDP. During 2000–12 the average annual rate of inflation was 18.1%, according to ILO figures. Consumer prices increased by an average of 6.1% in 2012. Iraq's official rate of unemployment was recorded at around 16% in mid-2012; however, the rate of youth unemployment was reported to be twice this figure, and many sources suggested that the real unemployment rate was in fact much higher.

In December 2010 the Government outlined details of a US $186,000m., five-year National Development Plan, the principal objectives of which were economic diversification, job creation, poverty reduction and sustained GDP growth through the completion of some 2,800 projects focusing on the agricultural, hydrocarbons, construction, power and transport sectors. Increased oil output coupled with rising global oil prices contributed to strong GDP growth of 9.9% in 2011, and growth of 8.4% was recorded in 2012. According to the Ministry of Planning and Development Co-operation, the economy grew by 9% in 2013. However, by early 2014 the Government's draft hydrocarbons law, proposed in February 2007, had still to be approved by the Iraqi parliament, owing to its complex and politically sensitive nature. In August 2007 the Kurdish regional government adopted a separate oil law; limited exports of oil from Iraqi Kurdistan commenced in June 2009, but have frequently been halted owing to an ongoing dispute with the national authorities regarding the legality of contracts awarded by the regional administration and over what the Kurdish authorities claim is the Ministry of Oil's decision to withhold payments owed to the international oil companies operating there. In November 2013 the Turkish Government reportedly signed a deal concerning the construction of oil and gas pipelines with the Kurdish administration; the agreement was expected to provide for the export of some 2m. b/d of oil from northern Iraq to Turkey (and thereafter Europe) and 10,000m. cu m of natural gas per year. The opening of the Iraqi oil sector to international oil companies from October 2008, including the award in June 2009 of a 20-year development contract for the giant Rumaila oilfield to British-based BP and the China National Petroleum Co, led the Ministry of Oil to forecast that production capacity could be increased from its 2010 level of 2.5m. b/d to about 12m. b/d by 2017. However, many industry analysts claimed that this was an unrealistic target, owing to Iraq's ongoing political, security and infrastructural problems, and in January 2014 the Deputy Prime Minister announced a new target of 4.7m. b/d by 2015 and 9.0m. b/d by 2020. Although by the end of 2012 oil production had risen to 3.1m. b/d, the International Energy Agency predicted that output would increase to only around 6.1m. b/d in 2020; production was estimated at 3.4m. b/d at the end of 2013. Oil exports were forecast to increase to 3.4m. b/d in 2014, from 2.4m. b/d in 2013; this latter figure represented a small decline from 2012. In recent years Asia has become an increasingly important market for Iraqi oil exports, while European demand has declined. Iraq's budget for 2014, approved by the Council of Ministers in mid-January, amounted to an estimated $150,120m. and projected a fiscal deficit of around $18,000m. Notwithstanding predictions of robust growth, increased oil production and exports, and rising inflows of foreign investment, at early 2014—almost 11 years since the US-led invasion which removed the former Baathist regime from office—political and security instabilities remained significant obstacles to hopes of a sustained economic recovery.

PUBLIC HOLIDAYS

2015: 1 January (New Year's Day), 2 January* (Mouloud, Birth of Muhammad), 6 January (Army Day), 17 April (FAO Day), 1 May (Labour Day), 15 May* (Leilat al-Meiraj, ascension of Muhammad), 14 July (Republic Day, commemorating overthrow of the Hashemite monarchy in 1958), 17 July* (Id al-Fitr, end of Ramadan), 8 August (Ceasefire Day, commemorating end of the Iran–Iraq War in 1988), 23 September* (Id al-Adha, Feast of the Sacrifice), 3 October (National Iraqi Day, commemorating Iraq joining League of Nations in 1932), 14 October* (Muharram, Islamic New Year), 23 October* (Ashoura), 23 December* (Mouloud, Birth of Muhammad).

* These holidays are dependent on the Islamic lunar calendar and may vary by one or two days from the dates given.

Statistical Survey

Sources (unless otherwise indicated): Central Organization for Statistics and Information Technology (COSIT), Ministry of Planning, 929/29/6 Arrasat al-Hindiya, Baghdad; tel. and fax (1) 885-3653; e-mail iraqmop@mop.gov.iq; internet cosit.gov.iq; Central Bank of Iraq, POB 64, al-Rashid St, Baghdad; tel. (1) 816-5170; fax (1) 816-6802; e-mail cbi@cbi.iq; internet www.cbi.iq.

Area and Population

AREA, POPULATION AND DENSITY

Area (sq km)	434,128*
Population (census results)	
17 October 1987	16,335,199
17 October 1997	
Males	10,987,252
Females	11,058,992
Total	22,046,244
Population (UN estimates at mid-year)†	
2012	32,778,033
2013	33,765,232
2014	34,768,760
Density (per sq km) at mid-2014	80.1

* 167,618 sq miles. This figure excludes 924 sq km (357 sq miles) of territorial waters and also the Neutral Zone, of which Iraq's share is 3,522 sq km (1,360 sq miles). The Zone lies between Iraq and Saudi Arabia, and is administered jointly by the two countries. Nomads move freely through it, but there are no permanent inhabitants.

† Source: UN, *World Population Prospects: The 2012 Revision*.

2011 (official estimate): Total population 33,330,512 (males 16,758,448, females 16,572,064).

POPULATION BY AGE AND SEX

(UN estimates at mid–2014)

	Males	Females	Total
0–14	7,085,386	6,699,285	13,784,671
15–64	10,001,592	9,882,175	19,883,767
65 and over	485,863	614,459	1,100,322
Total	17,572,841	17,195,919	34,768,760

Source: UN, *World Population Prospects: The 2012 Revision*.

GOVERNORATES

(official population estimates at 2011)

	Area (sq km)*	Population	Density (per sq km)
Nineveh	35,899	3,270,422	91.1
Salah al-Din	26,175	1,408,174	53.8
Al-Ta'meem (Kirkuk)	10,282	1,395,614	135.7
Diyala	19,076	1,443,173	75.7
Baghdad	734	7,055,196	9,612.0
Al-Anbar (Anbar)	138,501	1,561,407	11.3
Babylon	6,468	1,820,673	281.5
Karbala	5,034	1,066,567	211.9
Al-Najaf (Najaf)	28,824	1,285,484	44.6
Al-Qadisiya	8,153	1,134,314	139.1
Al-Muthanna	51,740	719,069	13.9
Thi-Qar	12,900	1,836,181	142.3
Wasit	17,153	1,210,591	70.6
Maysan	16,072	971,448	60.4
Al-Basrah (Basra)	19,070	2,531,997	132.8

—continued	Area (sq km)*	Population	Density (per sq km)
Kurdish Autonomous Region			
D'hok	6,553	1,128,745	172.2
Irbil (Arbil)	14,471	1,612,693	111.4
Al-Sulaimaniya (Sulaimaniya)	17,023	1,878,764	110.4
Total	434,128	33,330,512	76.8

* Excluding territorial waters (924 sq km).

PRINCIPAL TOWNS
(population at 1987 census)

Baghdad (capital)	3,841,268	Al-Sulaimaniya (Sulaimaniya)	364,096
Al-Mawsil (Mosul)	664,221	Al-Najaf (Najaf)	309,010
Irbil (Arbil)	485,968	Karbala	296,705
Kirkuk	418,624	Al-Hillah (Hilla)	268,834
Al-Basrah (Basra)	406,296	Al-Nasiriyah (Nasiriya)	265,937

Source: UN, *Demographic Yearbook*.

Mid-2011 (incl. suburbs, UN estimate): Baghdad 6,035,580 (Source: UN, *World Urbanization Prospects: The 2011 Revision*).

BIRTHS AND DEATHS
(annual averages, UN estimates)

	1995–2000	2000–05	2005–10
Birth rate (per 1,000)	36.4	35.2	33.3
Death rate (per 1,000)	5.1	5.1	5.6

Source: UN, *World Population Prospects: The 2012 Revision*.

Registered marriages: 249,430 in 2009; 245,022 in 2010.

Life expectancy (years at birth): 69.0 (males 65.4; females 72.8) in 2011 (Source: World Bank, World Development Indicators database).

EMPLOYMENT
(labour force survey, '000)

	2006	2007	2008
Agriculture, hunting and forestry	1,925.7	1,066.2	1,759.9
Fishing	22.8	10.0	21.7
Mining and quarrying	43.4	84.4	32.4
Manufacturing	376.3	522.3	369.4
Electricity, gas and water	76.6	130.5	161.6
Construction	665.0	797.2	823.5
Wholesale and retail trade; repair of motor vehicles, motorcycles and personal and household goods	961.8	1,117.6	1,167.2
Hotels and restaurants	52.9	105.4	62.6
Transport, storage and communications	616.5	707.5	608.1
Financial intermediation	26.9	26.4	20.8
Real estate, renting and business activities	40.6	285.8	35.1
Public administration and defence; compulsory social security	727.3	677.6	1,003.3
Education	556.1	612.9	686.7
Health and social work	146.2	196.8	218.2
Community, social and personal services	312.7	520.8	618.5
Households with employed persons	1.5	—	9.7
Extra-territorial organizations and bodies	4.7	—	7.3
Sub-total	6,557.2	6,861.4	7,606.1
Activities not adequately defined	—	255.3	—
Total employed	6,557.2	7,116.7	7,606.1

Source: ILO.

Mid-2014 (estimates in '000): Agriculture, etc. 414; Total labour force 9,397 (Source: FAO).

Health and Welfare

KEY INDICATORS

Total fertility rate (children per woman, 2011)	4.6
Under-5 mortality rate (per 1,000 live births, 2011)	38
HIV/AIDS (% of persons aged 15–49, 2003)	<0.1
Physicians (per 1,000 head, 2010)	0.6
Hospital beds (per 1,000 head, 2010)	1.3
Health expenditure (2010): US $ per head (PPP)	346
Health expenditure (2010): % of GDP	8.5
Health expenditure (2010): public (% of total)	81.2
Access to water (% of persons, 2011)	85
Access to sanitation (% of persons, 2011)	84
Total carbon dioxide emissions ('000 metric tons, 2010)	114,667.1
Carbon dioxide emissions per head (metric tons, 2010)	3.7
Human Development Index (2012): ranking	131
Human Development Index (2012): value	0.590

For sources and definitions, see explanatory note on p. vi.

Agriculture

PRINCIPAL CROPS
('000 metric tons)

	2010	2011	2012
Wheat	2,749	2,809	2,400
Rice, paddy	156	235	200*
Barley	1,137	820	500*
Maize	267	336	340*
Potatoes	205	557	560†
Sugar cane	13	11	12†
Chick peas	0.8	0.9	1.0†
Tomatoes	1,013	1,060	1,100†
Cauliflowers and broccoli	26	25	26†
Pumpkins, squash and gourds	145	165	170†
Cucumbers and gherkins	432	496	505†
Aubergines (Eggplants)	387	452	460†
Onions, dry	45	90	96†
Watermelons	304	340	350†
Canteloupes and other melons	177	161	165†
Grapes	213	227	227†
Oranges	98	91	95†
Tangerines, mandarins, clementines and satsumas	4	4	4†
Apples	40	46	47†
Apricots	19	21	23†
Peaches and nectarines	2	2	2†
Plums	10	10	10†
Dates	567	619	650†

* Unofficial figure.
† FAO estimate.

Aggregate production ('000 metric tons, may include official, semi-official or estimated data): Total cereals 4,362 in 2010, 4,270 in 2011, 3,513 in 2012; Total roots and tubers 205 in 2010, 557 in 2011, 560 in 2012; Total vegetables (incl. melons) 3,532 in 2010, 3,851 in 2011, 3,983 in 2012; Total fruits (excl. melons) 1,054 in 2010, 1,127 in 2011, 1,167 in 2012.

Source: FAO.

LIVESTOCK
('000 head, year ending September)

	2010	2011	2012
Horses	48	49	50*
Asses*	380	380	380
Mules*	11	11	11
Cattle	2,629	2,707	2,720*
Buffaloes	295	300	305*
Camels	60†	62*	65*
Sheep	7,945	8,183	8,200*
Goats	1,519	1,565	1,580*
Chickens*	34,000	38,000	38,000

* FAO estimate(s).
† Unofficial figure.

Source: FAO.

LIVESTOCK PRODUCTS
('000 metric tons)

	2010	2011	2012
Cattle meat	50.0*	50.1*	54.0†
Buffalo meat†	1.0	1.3	1.3
Sheep meat†	42.0	44.0	47.2
Goat meat†	11.6	11.4	11.5
Chicken meat	52.8	87.2	87.2†
Cows' milk†	226.5	233.0	234.9
Buffaloes' milk	23.8†	27.2	28.5†
Sheep's milk	58.9†	55.8	60.0†
Goats' milk	18.4†	18.8	20.0†
Hen eggs	46.3	50.9	53.0†
Wool, greasy†	17.2	17.0	17.0
Cattle and buffalo hides†	3.8	3.7	3.7

* Unofficial figure.
† FAO estimate(s).

Source: FAO.

Forestry

ROUNDWOOD REMOVALS
('000 cubic metres, excl. bark, FAO estimates)

	1996	1997	1998
Sawlogs, veneer logs and logs for sleepers	20.0	20.0	25.0
Other industrial wood	30.0	30.0	34.0
Fuel wood	49.3	110.0	118.0
Total	99.3	161.0	177.0

1999–2012: Annual production assumed to be unchanged from 1998 (FAO estimates).

Source: FAO.

SAWNWOOD PRODUCTION
('000 cubic metres, incl. railway sleepers, FAO estimates)

	1996	1997	1998
Total (all broadleaved)	8	8	12

1999–2012: Annual production as in 1998 (FAO estimates).

Source: FAO.

Fishing

('000 metric tons, live weight)

	2009	2010	2011
Capture	28.2	19.3	31.5
Cyprinids (incl. Common carp)	10.0	1.2	10.5
Freshwater siluroids	2.7	3.0	1.1
Other freshwater fishes	9.6	8.0	3.6
Marine fishes	0.9	1.7	0.2
Aquaculture	18.7	20.3	20.3*
Common carp	15.2	16.8	16.8*
Total catch	46.9	39.6	51.8*

* FAO estimate.

Source: FAO.

Mining

('000 metric tons unless otherwise indicated)

	2009	2010	2011
Crude petroleum	119,929	121,479	136,678
Natural gas (million cu m)*	16,577	16,885	18,692
Ammonia (nitrogen content)	30	126	143
Sulphur†	20	20	20‡
Salt (unrefined)‡	113	102	136

* Figures refer to gross production.
† Figures refer to native production and by-products of petroleum and natural gas processing.
‡ Estimated figure(s).

2012: Crude petroleum 152,449.

Sources: BP, *Statistical Review of World Energy*; US Geological Survey.

Industry

SELECTED PRODUCTS
('000 metric tons unless otherwise indicated)

	2007	2008	2009
Naphtha	364	483	464
Motor spirit (petrol)	2,212	2,937	2,822
Kerosene	739	981	943
Jet fuel	409	543	522
Gas-diesel (distillate fuel) oil	4,995	6,633	6,373
Residual fuel oils	5,595	7,430	7,138
Paraffin wax	65	86	83
Petroleum bitumen (asphalt)	340	451	433
Liquefied petroleum gas:			
from natural gas plants	918	954	976
from petroleum refineries	121	161	155
Cement*†	4,500	6,453	7,000
Electric energy (million kWh)	33,183	36,779	46,063

* Source: US Geological Survey.
† Estimated figures.

Cement ('000 metric tons, estimates): 8,000 in 2010; 10,000 in 2011.

Source (unless otherwise indicated): UN Industrial Commodity Statistics Database.

Finance

CURRENCY AND EXCHANGE RATES

Monetary Units
1,000 fils = 20 dirhams = 1 new Iraqi dinar (ID).

Sterling, Dollar and Euro Equivalents (31 December 2013)
£1 sterling = 1,920.2 Iraqi dinars;
US $1 = 1,166.0 Iraqi dinars;
€1 = 1,608.0 Iraqi dinars;
10,000 Iraqi dinars = £5.21 = $8.58 = €6.22.

Average Exchange Rate (Iraqi dinars per US $)
2011 1,170.00
2012 1,166.17
2013 1,166.00

Note: Following the overthrow of the regime of Saddam Hussein in 2003, the new Coalition Provisional Authority established an exchange rate of US $1 = 1,400 dinars. A new dinar currency, the new Iraqi dinar (ID), was introduced on 15 October to replace both the 'Swiss' dinar (at ID 1 = 150 'Swiss' dinars), the currency in use in the Kurdish autonomous regions of northern Iraq since 1991, and the 'Saddam' dinar (at par), the official currency of the rest of Iraq. The new currency was to be fully convertible.

BUDGET
(ID '000 million)

Revenue	2011	2012*	2013†
Revenues	102,400	119,400	126,100
Crude petroleum export revenues	93,400	109,400	117,900
Grants	2,100	0	0
Total	104,600	119,400	126,100

Expenditure	2011	2012*	2013†
Current expenditure	66,800	75,800	81,800
Salaries and pensions	33,900	34,900	41,000
Goods and services	12,000	17,500	17,600
Transfers	14,700	16,600	15,200
Interest payments	1,600	1,000	1,900
War reparations	4,600	5,500	5,500
Capital expenditure	27,400	33,600	40,000
Total	94,300	109,400	121,800

* Preliminary.
† Budget projections.

Source: IMF, *Iraq: 2013 Article IV Consultation* (July 2013).

INTERNATIONAL RESERVES
(US $ million at 31 December)

	2010	2011	2012
Gold (national valuation)	266.0	296.9	1,593.6
IMF special drawing rights	1,773.9	1,743.8	1,724.4
Reserve position in IMF	263.5	262.7	263.0
Foreign exchange	48,319.6	58,737.9	66,746.1
Total	50,623.0	61,041.3	70,327.1

Source: IMF, *International Financial Statistics*.

MONEY SUPPLY
(ID '000 million at 31 December)

	2010	2011	2012
Currency outside depository corporations	24,342.2	28,296.0	30,593.7
Transferable deposits	30,039.2	37,991.9	37,059.4
Other deposits	7,011.6	7,810.1	9,489.1
Broad money	61,393.1	74,098.0	77,142.2

Source: IMF, *International Financial Statistics*.

COST OF LIVING
(Consumer Price Index; base: 2007 = 100)

	2010	2011	2012
Food and non-alcoholic beverages	134.3	138.4	147.4
Alcoholic beverages and tobacco	121.5	127.5	132.1
Clothing and footwear	123.2	126.7	136.3
Housing, water, electricity, gas and other fuels	126.1	140.9	153.6
Household goods	114.9	116.3	118.9
Health	136.4	148.3	157.3
Transport	111.3	109.2	106.9
Communications	90.0	86.5	82.4
Recreation and culture	108.8	106.4	105.2
Education	129.2	138.4	150.6
Restaurants and hotels	125.3	133.3	141.2
Miscellaneous goods and services	130.8	147.4	157.4
All items	125.1	132.1	140.1

NATIONAL ACCOUNTS

National Income and Product
(ID '000 million at current prices, provisional estimates)

	2004	2005	2006
Compensation of employees	7,866.1	10,394.6	16,573.7
Operating surplus	33,857.9	45,296.7	67,543.7
Domestic factor incomes	41,723.9	55,691.2	84,117.4
Consumption of fixed capital	6,234.6	8,308.9	11,470.6
Gross domestic product (GDP) at factor cost	47,958.6	64,000.1	95,588.0
Indirect taxes (net)	−10,909.3	−14,009.4	−15,128.5
GDP in purchasers' values	37,049.3	49,990.7	80,459.4
Net factor income from abroad*	76.2	1,089.0	1,314.1
Gross national product (GNP)	37,125.5	51,079.7	81,773.6
Less Consumption of fixed capital	6,234.6	8,308.9	11,470.6
National income in market prices	30,890.8	42,770.8	70,303.0

* Figures obtained as residuals.

Gross Domestic Product by Economic Activity
(ID '000 million at current prices, provisional estimates)

	2004	2005	2006
Agriculture, hunting, forestry and fishing	3,539.4	4,248.8	5,569.0
Mining and quarrying	30,543.0	39,366.3	53,030.9
Crude petroleum	30,496.0	39,316.0	n.a.
Manufacturing	770.9	1,220.9	1,473.2
Electricity and water	263.3	393.1	779.4
Construction	468.3	2,932.4	3,449.7
Trade, restaurants and hotels	3,070.5	4,083.5	6,350.0
Transport, storage and communications	3,687.7	4,911.3	6,742.9
Finance, insurance and real estate	663.0	931.4	7,945.8
Government, community, social and personal services	5,200.4	6,139.9	10,726.2
Sub-total	48,206.5	64,227.6	96,067.2
Less Imputed bank service charge	248.0	227.5	479.2
GDP at factor cost	47,958.5	64,000.1	95,588.0
Indirect taxes / *Less* Subsidies	−10,909.3	−14,009.4	−15,128.5
GDP in market prices	37,049.3	49,990.7	80,459.4

2010 (ID '000 million at current prices): Agriculture, hunting, forestry and fishing 8,366.2; Mining and quarrying 73,569.9; Manufacturing 3,678.7; Construction 10,263.2; Electricity and water 2,909.7; Transport, storage and communications 9,452.3; Trade, restaurants and hotels 12,458.7; Finance, insurance and real estate 15,367.6; Government, community, social and personal services 31,771.9; *Sub-total* 167,838.2; *Less* Imputed bank service charge 745.0; *Gross domestic product at factor cost* 167,093.2.

2011 (ID '000 million at current prices): Agriculture, hunting, forestry and fishing 8,808.6; Mining and quarrying 116,184.9; Manufacturing 3,879.9; Construction 10,486.2; Electricity and water 2,671.6; Transport, storage and communications 10,323.6; Trade, restaurants and hotels 13,941.6; Finance, insurance and real estate 18,075.7; Government, community, social and personal services 27,882.8; *Sub-total* 212,254.9; *Less* Imputed bank service charge 945.0; *Gross domestic product at factor cost* 211,310.0.

2012 (ID '000 million at current prices): Agriculture, hunting, forestry and fishing 9,990.7; Mining and quarrying 130,064.4; Manufacturing 4,221.5; Construction 13,785.6; Electricity and water 2,429.2; Transport, storage and communications 11,582.9; Trade, restaurants and hotels 15,626.5; Finance, insurance and real estate 21,506.7; Government, community, social and personal services 36,527.8; *Sub-total* 245,735.2; *Less* Imputed bank service charge 1,232.5; *Gross domestic product at factor cost* 244,502.6.

BALANCE OF PAYMENTS
(US $ million)

	2010	2011	2012
Exports of goods	51,760.3	79,684.0	94,207.0
Imports of goods	–37,328.0	–40,633.0	–50,155.0
Balance on goods	14,432.3	39,051.0	44,052.0
Exports of services	2,833.6	2,822.0	2,833.0
Imports of services	–9,863.5	–11,124.0	–13,291.0
Balance on goods and services	7,402.4	30,749.0	33,594.0
Primary income received	2,079.9	1,172.0	2,080.0
Primary income paid	–486.7	–1,409.0	–1,021.0
Balance on goods, services and primary income	8,995.6	30,512.0	34,653.0
Secondary income received	240.8	371.0	413.0
Secondary income paid	–2,748.1	–4,757.0	–5,525.0
Current balance	6,488.3	26,126.0	29,541.0
Capital account (net)	25.3	11.0	7.0
Direct investment assets	–124.9	–366.0	–490.0
Direct investment liabilities	1,396.2	2,082.0	3,400.0
Portfolio investment assets	727.1	–6,573.0	–5,679.0
Portfolio investment liabilities	56.5	43.0	7.0
Other investment assets	5,310.4	–8,226.0	–4,976.0
Other investment liabilities	337.8	566.0	–8,448.0
Net errors and omissions	–9,150.6	–3,738.0	–4,116.2
Reserves and related items	5,066.1	9,924.2	9,254.8

Source: IMF, *International Financial Statistics*.

External Trade

PRINCIPAL COMMODITIES
(US $ million)

Imports c.i.f.	2010	2011	2012
Food and live animals	2,371	2,581	3,036
Beverages and tobacco	571	622	731
Crude materials (inedible) except fuels	790	860	1,125
Mineral fuels, lubricants, etc.	4,304	4,685	5,511
Animal and vegetable oils and fats	2,811	3,059	3,599
Chemicals	2,942	3,203	3,543
Basic manufactures	5,006	5,450	6,411
Machinery and transport equipment	16,907	18,404	21,650
Miscellaneous manufactured articles	6,939	7,553	8,997
Total (incl. others)	43,915	47,803	56,234

Exports c.i.f.	2010	2011	2012
Food and live animals	145	223	264
Crude materials (inedible) except fuels	78	120	141
Mineral fuels, lubricants, etc.	51,376	79,083	93,465
Chemicals	5	8	10
Basic manufactures	26	40	47
Machinery and transport equipment	124	191	226
Total (incl. others)	51,764	79,681	94,172

PRINCIPAL TRADING PARTNERS
(US $ million)

Imports c.i.f.	1988	1989	1990
Australia	153.4	196.2	108.7
Austria	n.a.	1.1	50.9
Belgium-Luxembourg	57.6	68.2	68.3
Brazil	346.0	416.4	139.5
Canada	169.9	225.1	150.4
China, People's Republic	99.2	148.0	157.9
France	278.0	410.4	278.3
Germany	322.3	459.6	389.4
India	32.3	65.2	57.5
Indonesia	38.9	122.7	104.9
Ireland	150.4	144.9	31.6
Italy	129.6	285.1	194.0
Japan	533.0	621.1	397.2
Jordan	164.3	210.0	220.3
Korea, Republic	98.5	123.9	149.4
Netherlands	111.6	102.6	93.8
Romania	113.3	91.1	30.1
Saudi Arabia	37.2	96.5	62.5
Spain	43.4	129.0	40.5
Sri Lanka	50.1	33.5	52.3
Sweden	63.0	40.6	64.8
Switzerland	65.7	94.4	126.6
Thailand	22.3	59.2	68.9
Turkey	874.7	408.9	196.0
USSR	70.7	75.7	77.9
United Kingdom	394.6	448.5	322.1
USA	979.3	1,001.7	658.4
Yugoslavia	154.5	182.0	123.1
Total (incl. others)	5,960.0	6,956.2	4,833.9

Exports f.o.b.	1988	1989	1990*
Belgium-Luxembourg	147.5	249.6	n.a.
Brazil	1,002.8	1,197.2	n.a.
France	517.4	623.9	0.8
Germany	122.0	76.9	1.7
Greece	192.5	189.4	0.3
India	293.0	438.8	14.7
Italy	687.1	549.7	10.6
Japan	712.1	117.1	0.1
Jordan	28.4	25.2	101.6
Netherlands	152.9	532.3	0.2
Portugal	120.8	125.8	n.a.
Spain	370.0	575.7	0.7
Turkey	1,052.6	1,331.0	83.5
USSR	835.7	1,331.7	8.9
United Kingdom	293.1	167.0	4.4
USA	1,458.9	2,290.8	0.2
Yugoslavia	425.4	342.0	10.4
Total (incl. others)	10,268.3	12,333.7	392.0

* Excluding exports of most petroleum products.

Source: UN, *International Trade Statistics Yearbook*.

2010 (US $ million): *Imports by regions:* Arab nations 10,399; North and South America 5,248; European Union 5,885; Other Europe 13,253; Asia 8,432; Other countries 698; Total imports 43,915. *Exports by region:* Arab nations 1,155; North and South America 15,886; European Union 11,155; Other Europe 1,289; Asia 21,953; Other countries 326; Total exports 51,764.

2011 (US $ million): *Imports by regions:* Arab nations 11,903; North and South America 4,101; European Union 4,881; Other Europe 13,925; Asia 12,615; Other countries 378; Total imports 47,803. *Exports by region:* Arab nations 2,853; North and South America 24,024; European Union 13,801; Other Europe 2,279; Asia 36,310; Other countries 414; Total exports 79,681.

2012 (US $ million): *Imports by regions:* Arab nations 14,002; North and South America 4,836; European Union 5,736; Other Europe 16,364; Asia 14,846; Other countries 450; Total imports 56,234. *Exports by region:* Arab nations 3,371; North and South America 28,393; European Union 16,311; Other Europe 2,693; Asia 42,914; Other countries 490; Total exports 94,172.

Transport

RAILWAYS
(traffic)

	2008	2009	2010
Passengers carried ('000)	107.0	219.8	212.3
Freight carried ('000 tons)	432.0	644.0	995.0
Passenger-km (million)	53.7	102.6	99.7
Freight ton-km (million)	121.0	170.0	249.0

ROAD TRAFFIC
(estimates, '000 motor vehicles in use)

	1995	1996
Passenger cars	770.1	773.0
Buses and coaches	50.9	51.4
Lorries and vans	269.9	272.5
Road tractors	37.2	37.2

2006: Passenger cars 784,794; Buses and coaches 112,114; Vans and lorries 1,345,361; *Total* 2,242,269.

Source: IRF, *World Road Statistics*.

SHIPPING

Flag Registered Fleet
(at 31 December)

	2011	2012	2013
Number of vessels	78	78	83
Total displacement ('000 grt)	149.4	128.0	149.5

Source: Lloyd's List Intelligence (www.lloydslistintelligence.com).

CIVIL AVIATION
(revenue traffic on scheduled services)

	1991	1992	1994*
Kilometres flown (million)	0	0	0
Passengers carried ('000)	28	53	31
Passenger-km (million)	17	35	20
Freight ton-km (million)	0	3	2

* Figures for 1993 unavailable.

Source: UN, *Statistical Yearbook*.

Passengers carried: 641,129 in 2010; 761,778 in 2011; 784,944 in 2012 (Source: World Bank, World Development Indicators database).

Tourism

ARRIVALS AT FRONTIERS OF VISITORS FROM ABROAD*

Country of nationality	2008	2009	2010
India	6,031	13,876	13,860
Iran	840,362	1,161,541	1,413,792
Lebanon	129	1,916	4,466
Pakistan	5,771	18,004	13,815
Total (incl. others)	863,657	1,261,921	1,517,766

* Including same-day visitors.

Tourism receipts (US $ million, excl. passenger transport): 1,660 in 2010; 1,544 in 2011.

Source: World Tourism Organization.

Communications Media

	2010	2011	2012
Telephones ('000 main lines in use)	1,720.6	1,794.0	1,871.0
Mobile cellular telephones ('000 subscribers)	23,264	25,519	26,756
Internet subscribers ('000)	0.3	n.a.	n.a.
Broadband subscribers ('000)	100	n.a.	n.a.

Source: International Telecommunication Union.

Education

(2011/12 unless otherwise indicated)

	Institutions	Teachers	Students
Pre-primary	919	7,221	175,835
Primary	14,674	271,734	5,124,257
Secondary:			
academic	6,041	141,355	2,211,421
vocational	295	12,553	56,301
Teacher training	106	3,172	22,823
Higher*	65	14,700	240,000†

* 2002/03.

† Figure for undergraduates only.

Sources: Ministries of Education, and of Higher Education and Scientific Research.

Pupil-teacher ratio (primary education, UNESCO estimate): 17.0 in 2006/07 (Source: UNESCO Institute for Statistics).

Adult literacy rate (UNESCO estimates): 78.5% (males 86.0%; females 71.2%) in 2011 (Source: UNESCO Institute for Statistics).

Directory

As a result of the US-led military campaign to oust the regime of Saddam Hussain in early 2003, and the ensuing insurgency, buildings occupied by a number of government ministries and other institutions were reported to have been damaged or destroyed.

The Government

HEAD OF STATE

President: JALAL TALABANI (assumed office 7 April 2005, re-elected by the Council of Representatives 22 April 2006 and 11 November 2010).

Vice-President: KHUDHAIR AL-KHUZAI.

COUNCIL OF MINISTERS
(April 2014)

Prime Minister and Acting Minister of the Interior: NURI KAMAL (JAWAD) AL-MALIKI.

Deputy Prime Minister for Economic Affairs: DR ROZH NURI SHAWAIS.

Deputy Prime Minister for Energy Affairs: HUSSEIN AL-SHAHRISTANI.

Deputy Prime Minister: SALEH AL-MUTLAQ.

Minister of Agriculture: EZZ AL-DIN AHMAD HUSSEIN AL-DAWLA.

Minister of Communications and Minister of State for Provincial Affairs: TORHAN MUDHER HASSAN AL-MUFTI.

Minister of Construction and Housing: MUHAMMAD SAHEB AL-DARRAJI.

Minister of Culture and Acting Minister of Defence: SAADOUN AL-DULAIMI.

Minister of Displacement and Migration: DINDAR NAJMAN SHAFIQ DUSKI.
Minister of Education: (vacant).
Minister of Electricity: ABD AL-KARIM AFTAN AL-JUMAILI.
Minister of the Environment: SARKOUN SLIWA.
Minister of Foreign Affairs: HOSHYAR AL-ZIBARI.
Minister of Health: MAJID HAMAD AMIN.
Minister of Higher Education and Scientific Research: ALI AL-ADIB.
Minister of Human Rights: MUHAMMAD SHAYYAA AL-SUDANI.
Minister of Industry and Minerals: AHMAD NASSER AL-DALI.
Minister of Justice: HASSAN AL-SHUMMARI.
Minister of Labour and Social Affairs: NASSAR AL-RUBAI.
Minister of Municipalities and Public Works: ADEL MHODER AL-RADHI.
Minister of Oil: ABD AL-KARIM AL-LUAIBI.
Minister of Planning and Acting Minister of Finance: ALI YOUSUF ABD AL-NABI AL-SHUKRI.
Minister of Science and Technology: (vacant).
Minister of Trade: KHAIRALLAH HASSAN BABAKR MUHAMMAD.
Minister of Transportation: AMIR HADI AL-AMIRI.
Minister of Tourism and Antiquities: LIWA SUMAYSIM.
Minister of Water Resources: MUHANNAD SALMAN AL-SAADI.
Minister of Youth and Sports: JASIM MUHAMMAD JA'FAR.
Minister of State for Civil Society Affairs: DAKHIL QASSIM.
Minister of State for Council of Representatives Affairs: SAFA AL-DIN MUHAMMAD AL-SAFI.
Minister of State for Foreign Affairs: ALI AL-SAJRI.
Minister of State for National Reconciliation: AMER HASSAN AL-KHUZAI.
Minister of State for Tribal Affairs: JAMAL AL-BATIKH.
Minister of State and Government Spokesperson: ALI AL-DABBAGH.
Minister of State for Women's Affairs: IBTIHAL AL-ZAIDI.
Acting Minister of State for National Security: FALIH AL-FAYYAD.
Ministers of State: DIYAA NAJEM AL-ASADI, SALAH MUZAHIM DARWISH, YASSIN HASSAN MUHAMMAD, HASSAN AL-MUTAIRI, ABD AL-SAHIB QAHRAMAN, HASSAN AL-RADI, BUSHRA HUSSEIN SALEH.

MINISTRIES

Ministry of Agriculture: Khulafa St, Khullani Sq., Baghdad; tel. (1) 717-9440; e-mail minis_of_agr@moagr.org; internet www.zeraa.gov.iq.
Ministry of Civil Society Affairs: Baghdad.
Ministry of Communications: Baghdad; tel. (1) 717-7552; e-mail info@moc.gov.iq; internet www.moc.gov.iq.
Ministry of Construction and Housing: Baghdad; e-mail moch@imariskan.gov.iq; internet www.moch.gov.iq.
Ministry of Culture: POB 624, Qaba bin Nafi Sq., Sadoun St, Baghdad; tel. (1) 538-3171; internet www.mocul.gov.iq.
Ministry of Defence: Baghdad; e-mail webmaster@mod.mil.iq; internet www.mod.mil.iq.
Ministry of Displacement and Migration: Baghdad; tel. (1) 537-0842; fax (1) 537-2497.
Ministry of Economic Affairs: Baghdad.
Ministry of Education: Saad State Enterprises Bldg, nr the Convention Centre, Baghdad; tel. (1) 883-2571; e-mail general@moedu.gov.iq; internet www.moedu.gov.iq.
Ministry of Electricity: Baghdad; e-mail infocen@moelc.gov.iq; internet www.moelc.gov.iq.
Ministry of Energy Affairs: Baghdad.
Ministry of the Environment: POB 10026, Baghdad; e-mail enviro_center@yahoo.com; internet www.moen.gov.iq.
Ministry of Finance: Khulafa St, nr al-Russafi Sq., Baghdad; tel. (1) 887-4871; e-mail iraqmof@mof.gov.iq; internet www.mof.gov.iq.
Ministry of Foreign Affairs: opp. State Organization for Roads and Bridges, Karradat Mariam, Baghdad; tel. (1) 537-0091; e-mail press@iraqmfamail.com; internet www.mofa.gov.iq.
Ministry of Health: Baghdad; e-mail hedmoh@moh.gov.iq; internet www.moh.gov.iq.
Ministry of Higher Education and Scientific Research: 52 Rusafa St, Baghdad; tel. and fax (1) 717-0709; e-mail info@mohesr.gov.iq; internet www.mohesr.gov.iq.
Ministry of Human Rights: Baghdad; e-mail minister1@humanrights.gov.iq; internet www.humanrights.gov.iq.
Ministry of Industry and Minerals: POB 5815, Baghdad; tel. (1) 816-2006; e-mail admin@industry.gov.iq; internet www.industry.gov.iq.
Ministry of the Interior: Baghdad; tel. (1) 817-3101; e-mail media@moi.gov.iq; internet www.moi.gov.iq.
Ministry of Justice: Baghdad; fax (1) 537-2269; internet www.moj.gov.iq.
Ministry of Labour and Social Affairs: Baghdad; e-mail info@molsa.gov.iq; internet www.molsa.gov.iq.
Ministry of Municipalities and Public Works: Baghdad; e-mail office_minister@mmpw.gov.iq; internet www.mmpw.gov.iq.
Ministry of National Reconciliation: Baghdad.
Ministry of Oil: Oil Complex Bldg, Port Said St, Baghdad; tel. (1) 817-7000; e-mail minister.office@oil.gov.iq; internet www.oil.gov.iq.
Ministry of Planning: 929/29/6 Arrasat al-Hindiya, Baghdad; tel. (1) 778-3899; e-mail iraqmop@mop.gov.iq; internet www.mop.gov.iq.
Ministry of Science and Technology: Baghdad; e-mail inprb@most.gov.iq; internet www.most.gov.iq.
Ministry of State for Council of Representatives Affairs: Baghdad.
Ministry of State for National Security: North Gate, Baghdad; tel. (1) 888-9071.
Ministry of State for Provincial Affairs: Baghdad.
Ministry of State for Tribal Affairs: Baghdad.
Ministry of State for Women's Affairs: Baghdad.
Ministry of Tourism and Antiquities: Baghdad.
Ministry of Trade: POB 5833, Khullani Sq., Baghdad; tel. (1) 887-2681; fax (1) 790-1907; e-mail motcenter@motiraq.org; internet www.mot.gov.iq.
Ministry of Transportation: nr Martyr's Monument, Karradat Dakhil, Baghdad; tel. (1) 776-6041; e-mail mt_office@motrans.gov.iq; internet www.motrans.gov.iq.
Ministry of Water Resources: Palestine St, Baghdad; tel. (1) 772-0240; fax (1) 774-0672; e-mail waterresmin@yahoo.co.uk; internet www.mowr.gov.iq.
Ministry of Youth and Sports: Baghdad; internet www.moys.gov.iq.

Legislature

Council of Representatives

Baghdad International Zone Convention Center, Baghdad; e-mail press@parliament.iq; internet www.parliament.iq.

Elections to the Council of Representatives were held on 7 March 2010. The rate of participation by eligible voters was recorded at 62.4%. According to final results (including compensatory seats) published by the Independent High Electoral Commission (IHEC) on 26 March, the Iraqi National Movement, led by former interim Prime Minister Dr Ayad Allawi, with 91 seats, emerged as the largest group in the 325-seat legislature. The State of Law coalition of incumbent Prime Minister Nuri al-Maliki won 89 seats. The Iraqi National Alliance obtained 70 seats and the Kurdistan Alliance 43 seats. Meanwhile, the Kurdish Movement for Change won eight seats, the Iraqi Accord six, the Kurdistan Islamic Union List and the Iraqi Unity Coalition each four, and the Islamic Group of Kurdistan two. Of the remaining eight seats, five were reserved for Christian parties and one each for the Sabian, Shebek and Yazidi communities. (On 1 June the declared outcome was ratified by the Higher Judicial Council, following a manual recount of the votes cast in the capital, Baghdad.) Legislative elections were held on 30 April 2014.

Speaker: OSAMA AL-NUJAIFI.

Kurdish Autonomous Region

A 15-article accord signed by the Iraqi Government and Kurdish leaders in 1970 provided for: the creation of a unified autonomous area for the Kurdish population, comprising the administrative departments of al-Sulaimaniya (Sulaimaniya), D'hok and Irbil (Arbil), and the Kurdish sector of the city of Kirkuk; and the establishment of a 50-member Kurdish Legislative Council. Following the recapture of Kuwait from Iraqi forces by a multinational military coalition in early 1991, renewed negotiations between the Iraqi Government (under Saddam Hussain) and Kurdish groups stalled over the status of Kirkuk, and in October 1991 the Government effectively severed all economic and administrative support to the region. In May 1992 the Kurdish Iraqi Front (KIF), an alliance of several Kurdish factions—including the two largest, the Patriotic Union of Kurdistan (PUK) and the Kurdistan Democratic Party (KDP)—established in 1988, organized elections to a new 105-member Iraqi Kurdistan National Assembly. However, by September 1996 bitter factional disputes had led to the effective disintegration of the KIF, and prompted the Government to reassert full Iraqi sovereignty over the Kurdish areas. At a meeting in Washington, DC, USA, in September 1998, representatives of the PUK and the KDP reached a formal peace agreement, which provided for a unified regional administration, the sharing of local revenues and co-operation in implementing the UN-sponsored 'oil-for-food' programme. In December 1999 the KDP announced the composition of a new 25-member coalition administration (comprising the KDP, the Iraqi Communist Party, the Assyrian Movement, the Independent Workers' Party of Kurdistan, the Islamic Union and independents) for the areas under its control, principally the departments of Arbil and D'hok. Municipal elections (to select 571 officials) were conducted in the KDP-administered region in May 2001; according to official KDP sources, KDP candidates received 81% of votes cast. Negotiations between representatives of the KDP and the PUK for the full implementation of the Washington accord were held during 2002, and resulted in the resumption of a transitional joint session of the Iraqi Kurdistan National Assembly in October. The autonomous regions retained their status following the removal of the regime of Saddam Hussain in early 2003, but the status of Kirkuk remained highly controversial.

THE GOVERNMENT OF THE KURDISH AUTONOMOUS REGION

President: MASOUD BARZANI.

THE CABINET
(April 2014)

A coalition Government comprising the Kurdistan Democratic Party (KDP), the Patriotic Union of Kurdistan (PUK), the Kurdistan Islamic Movement, Turkmen representatives, the Kurdistan Communist Party and independents.

Following the confirmation by the Independent High Electoral Commission of the KDP's victory at legislative elections held in September 2013, it began discussions with other parties regarding the formation of a new coalition government. Those talks were ongoing in early April 2014.

Prime Minister: NECHIRVAN IDRIS BARZANI.

Deputy Prime Minister: IMAD AHMAD SAYFOUR.

Minister of Agriculture and Water Resources: SERWAN BABAN.

Minister of Culture and Youth: KAWA MAHMOUD SHAKIR.

Minister of Education: ASMAT MUHAMMAD KHALID.

Minister of Electricity: YASIN SHEIKH ABU BAKIR MUHAMMAD MAWATI.

Minister of Endowment and Religious Affairs: KAMIL ALI AZIZ.

Minister of Finance and the Economy: BAYIZ SAEED MUHAMMAD TALABANI.

Minister of Health: REKAWT HAMA RASHEED.

Minister of Higher Education and Scientific Research: ALI SAEED.

Minister of Housing and Reconstruction: KAMARAN AHMAD ABDULLAH.

Minister of Justice: SHERWAN HAIDARI.

Minister for the Interior: ABD AL-KARIM SULTAN SINJARI.

Minister of Labour and Social Affairs: ASOS NAJIB ABDULLAH.

Minister of Martyrs and Anfal Affairs: SABAH AHMAD MUHAMMAD.

Minister of Municipalities and Tourism: DILSHAD SHAHAB.

Minister of Natural Resources: ABDULLAH ABD AL-RAHMAN ABDULLAH.

Minister of Peshmerga Affairs: JAFAR MUSTAFA ALI.

Minister of Planning: ALI SINDI.

Minister of Trade and Industry: SINAN ABD AL-KHALQ AHMAD CHALABI.

Minister of Transport and Communications: JONSON SIYAOOSH.

The President of the Divan of the Council of Ministers, the Secretary of the Cabinet, the Chief of Staff of the Presidency, the Head of the Department of Foreign Relations and the Chairman of the Investment Board also have full ministerial status.

LEGISLATURE

Iraqi Kurdistan Parliament

Erbil (Hewlêr) Kurdistan, Iraq; e-mail office@perleman.org; internet www.perleman.org.

In May 1992 negotiations with the Iraqi Government over the full implementation of the 1970 accord on Kurdish regional autonomy having stalled, the KIF unilaterally organized elections to a 105-member Iraqi Kurdistan National Assembly, in which almost the entire electorate of 1.1m. participated. The KDP and the PUK were the only parties to achieve representation in the new Assembly, and subsequently agreed to share seats equally (50 seats each—five having been reserved for two Assyrian Christian parties). However, the subsequent disintegration of the KIF and prolonged armed conflict between elements of the KDP and the PUK prevented the Assembly from becoming properly instituted. Relations between the KDP and the PUK improved following the Washington, DC, agreement of September 1998, and on 8 September 2002 representatives of the two parties signed an agreement providing for the inauguration of a transitional joint parliamentary session (with representation based on the results of the May 1992 elections) before the end of the year. On 4 October 2002 a joint session of the Iraqi Kurdistan National Assembly was convened for the first time since 1996. Following the removal of the regime of Saddam Hussain by US-led forces in early 2003, elections to a new Iraqi Kurdistan National Assembly took place on 30 January 2005, concurrently with elections to the Transitional National Assembly. The Kurdistan Democratic List won 104 of the 111 seats. On 12 June the new Kurdish legislature voted unanimously to appoint Masoud Barzani, leader of the KDP, to the post of President of the Kurdish Autonomous Region. The Government, led by Barzani, assumed office on 7 May 2006, and represented the region's first unified Cabinet. Prior to a unification agreement signed in January 2006, Sulaimaniya had been governed by the PUK, while Arbil and D'hok were administered by the KDP. In February 2009 the Iraqi Kurdistan National Assembly was renamed the Iraqi Kurdistan Parliament. A draft Constitution for the Kurdish Autonomous Region, which included territorial claims to Kirkuk and other disputed regions, was approved by the Iraqi Kurdistan Parliament on 24 June 2009. However, a planned referendum on the draft Constitution was subsequently postponed, owing to opposition from the Independent High Electoral Commission and the Iraqi parliament. At elections to the Iraqi Kurdistan Parliament held on 25 July, the Kurdistani List, which comprised the PUK and the KDP, secured 59 of the 111 seats in the legislature. The significant reduction in the two main parties' majority was largely due to the success of the Movement for Change (Gorran), which received 25 seats; the group had been established in 2006 by former members of the PUK, and campaigned on a pro-reform and anti-corruption platform. Meanwhile, in a concurrent election for the regional presidency, Barzani was re-elected with 69.6% of the valid votes cast. At legislative elections held on 21 September 2013, the KDP emerged as the leading party, winning 38 seats, according to official results announced on 2 October. Gorran became the second largest party, with 24 seats, surpassing the PUK, which took just 18 seats.

Speaker: MUHAMMAD SALEH SAEED (ad interim).

Election, 21 September 2013

	Seats
Kurdistan Democratic Party (KDP)	38
Movement for Change (Gorran)	24
Patriotic Union of Kurdistan (PUK)	18
Kurdistan Islamic Union	10
Islamic Group of Kurdistan	6
Islamic Movement in Iraqi Kurdistan	1
Kurdistan Communist Party	1
Kurdistan Socialist Democratic Party	1
Kurdistan Toilers Party	1
Seats reserved for minority groups*	11
Total	111

* Includes five seats reserved for parties representing the Assyrian, Chaldean and Syriac communities, five seats for representatives of the Turkoman community and one seat for the Armenian community.

Election Commission

Independent High Electoral Commission (IHEC): POB 55074, Baghdad; tel. (1) 743-2519; e-mail inquiries@ihec.iq; internet www.ihec.iq; f. 2004 as Independent Electoral Comm. of Iraq by fmr Coalition Provisional Authority; renamed as above 2007; Chair. SARBAST RASHEED.

Political Organizations

Following the removal from power of the Baathist regime, restrictions were effectively lifted on opposition political organizations that were either previously declared illegal, forced to operate clandestinely within Iraq or were based abroad. Some 306 political parties were reported to have participated in the election to the Council of Representatives held on 7 March 2010.

Arab Baath Socialist Party: revolutionary Arab socialist movement founded in Damascus, Syria, in 1947; governed Iraq during 1968–2003 as principal constituent of ruling coalition, the Nat. Progressive Front (NPF); the NPF was removed from power by US-led forces in May 2003, whereupon membership of the Baath Party was declared illegal and former party mems were barred from govt and military posts; subsequently thought to be involved in insurgent activities in Iraq; in Feb. 2008 new legislation was ratified permitting certain former Baathists to be reinstated to official posts; in Jan. 2007, following the execution of former Iraqi President Saddam Hussain, former Vice-President IZZAT IBRAHIM AL-DOURI was named as the party's new leader.

Assyrian Democratic Movement (Zowaa Dimuqrataya Aturaya—Zowaa): e-mail info@zowaa.org; internet www.zowaa.org; f. 1979; seeks recognition of Assyrian rights within framework of democratic national govt; Sec.-Gen. YOUNADAM YOUSUF KANNA.

Assyrian Socialist Party: Baghdad; e-mail gaboatouraya@yahoo.co.uk; internet asp2.no.sapo.pt; f. 2002 (refounded); advocates the establishment of an Assyrian nation.

Constitutional Party: Baghdad; f. 2004; Shi'ite; contested the March 2010 legislative election as part of the Iraqi Unity Coalition; Founder and Leader JAWAD AL-BULANI.

Al-Ezediah Movement for Progress and Reform: Yazidi grouping; Leader AMIN FARHAN JEJO.

Independent Democratic Gathering: f. 2003; seeks a secular and democratic govt of Iraq; contested March 2010 legislative election as part of the State of Law alliance; Leader MAHDI AL-HAFEZ.

Iraqi Accord (Jabhat al-Tawafuq al-Iraqiya): f. 2005 as the Iraqi Accord Front; reformed to contest the March 2010 legislative elections; mainly Sunni; secular; coalition of the Iraqi Islamic Party and the Nat. Gathering of the People of Iraq.

Iraqi Communist Party (ICP): Baghdad; e-mail info@iraqicp.com; internet www.iraqicp.com; f. 1934; became legally recognized in July 1973 on formation of NPF; left NPF March 1979; First Sec. HAMID MAJID MOUSSA.

Iraqi Constitutional Movement: Baghdad; f. 1993; fmrly Constitutional Monarchy Movement; contested March 2010 legislative election as part of Iraqi Nat. Alliance.

Iraqi Front for National Dialogue (Hewar National Iraqi Front): f. 2005 as breakaway party from Iraqi Nat. Dialogue Council; coalition of minor Sunni parties; contested the March 2010 legislative election as part of the Iraqi Nat. Movement list, although al-Mutlaq was himself banned from participating by the Justice and Accountability Comm; Founder and Leader SALEH AL-MUTLAQ.

Iraqi Islamic Party (IIP) (al-Hizb al-Islami al-Iraqi): e-mail iraqiparty@iraqiparty.com; internet www.iraqiparty.com; f. 1960; Sunni; branch of the Muslim Brotherhood; contested March 2010 legislative election as part of the Iraqi Accord list; Sec.-Gen. AYAD AL-SAMARRAI.

Iraqi National Accord (INA): e-mail wifaq_ina@hotmail.com; internet www.wifaq.com; f. 1990; contested March 2010 legislative election as mem. of Iraqi Nat. Movement; Founder and Sec.-Gen. Dr AYAD ALLAWI .

Iraqi National Alliance: list of mainly Shi'a parties, incl. the ISCI, the Sadr II Movement, the Iraqi Nat. Congress, the Nat. Reform Movement and the Islamic Virtue Party, which contested the March 2010 legislative elections as a single coalition; Leader IBRAHIM AL-JA'FARI.

Iraqi National Congress (INC): e-mail info@inciraq.com; internet inciraq.com; f. 1992 in London, United Kingdom, as a multi-party coalition supported by the US Govt; following the removal of the regime of Saddam Hussain, the INC moved to Baghdad and was transformed into a distinct political party; formed Nat. Congress Coalition before 2005 legislative elections, at which it failed to win any seats; contested March 2010 election as part of the Iraqi Nat. Alliance; Leader AHMAD CHALABI.

Iraqi National Foundation Congress (INFC): Baghdad; f. 2004; multi-party coalition incl. Nasserites, pre-Saddam Hussain era Baathists, Kurds, Christians, Sunnis and Shi'ites; seeks secular govt of national unity; opposed to presence of US-led coalition in Iraq, and consequently boycotted the electoral process initiated by the coalition; led by 25-mem. secretariat; Gen. Sec. Sheikh JAWAD AL-KHALISI.

Iraqi National Movement (Iraqiya): secular electoral list formed to contest the March 2010 legislative election, comprising a no. of political orgs, incl. the INA, the Iraqi Front for Nat. Dialogue, the Renewal List and Iraqis; Leader Dr AYAD ALLAWI.

Iraqi Turkmen Front (Irak Türkmen Cephesi): Arbil; internet www.kerkuk.net; f. 1995; coalition of Turkmen groups; seeks autonomy for Turkmen areas in Iraq and recognition of Turkmen as one of main ethnic groups in Iraq, and supports establishment of multi-party democratic system in Iraq; contests status of Kirkuk with Kurds; Leader ERŞAT SALIH; Sec.-Gen. YUNUS BAYRAKTAR.

Iraqi Unity Coalition: f. 2009 to contest the March 2010 legislative election; electoral alliance comprising 38 parties, incl. the Constitutional Party and the Iraqi Awakening Conference.

Iraqis (Iraqiyun): f. 2004; moderate; includes both Sunnis and Shi'ites; contested March 2010 legislative election as part of Iraqi National Movement list; Leader Sheikh GHAZI MASHAL AJIL AL-YAWAR.

Islamic Dawa Party (Hizb al-Da'wa al-Islamiya): Baghdad; e-mail info@islamicdawaparty.org; internet www.islamicdawaparty.org; f. 1957 in Najaf; banned 1980; fmrly based in Tehran, Iran, and London, United Kingdom; re-established in Baghdad 2003; contested March 2010 legislative election as part of State of Law coalition; predominantly Shi'a, but with Sunni mems; advocates govt centred on the principles of Islam; Gen. Sec. NURI KAMAL (JAWAD) AL-MALIKI.

Islamic Group of Kurdistan (Komaleh Islami): Khurmal; f. 2001; splinter group of IMIK; moderate Islamist, aligned with the PUK; contested March 2010 legislative election independently; Founder and Leader Mullah ALI BAPIR.

Islamic Movement in Iraqi Kurdistan (IMIK): Halabja; e-mail bzotnawa@yahoo.com; f. 1987; Islamist movement seeking to obtain greater legal rights for Iraqi Kurds; Founder and Leader Sheikh UTHMAN ABD AL-AZIZ.

Islamic Supreme Council of Iraq (ISCI): Najaf; e-mail info@almejlis.org; internet www.almejlis.org; f. 1982 as the Supreme Council for the Islamic Revolution in Iraq; name changed as above in 2007; Shi'a; seeks govt based on principle of *wilayat-e-faqih* (guardianship of the jurisprudent); armed faction, the Badr Organization (fmrly Badr Brigade), assisted coalition forces in Iraq after the removal of Saddam Hussain's regime; contested March 2010 legislative election as part of the Iraqi Nat. Alliance; Leader AMMAR AL-HAKIM.

Islamic Virtue Party (Hizb al-Fadhila al-Islamiya—IVP): Basra; internet www.alfadhela.net.iq; Shi'ite; an offshoot of the Sadrist movement; follows the spiritual leadership of Ayatollah al-Sayyid Muhammad al-Ya'qubi; contested March 2010 legislative election as part of Iraqi Nat. Alliance; Sec.-Gen. HASHIM AL-HASHIMI.

Kurdistan Alliance List (Democratic Patriotic Alliance of Kurdistan—DPAK): f. 2004 as a coalition of the PUK, the KDP and smaller Kurdish parties to contest Jan. 2005 legislative elections; participated in March 2010 legislative election as a two-party coalition of the PUK and the KDP; the PUK and the KDP formed a separate electoral list, the Kurdistan List, to contest elections to the Iraqi Kurdistan Parliament in July 2009.

Kurdistan Democratic Party (KDP): European Office (Germany), 10749 Berlin, POB 301516; tel. (30) 79743741; fax (30) 79743746; e-mail party@kdp.se; internet www.kdp.se; f. 1946; seeks to protect Kurdish rights and promote Kurdish culture and interests through regional political and legislative autonomy, as part of a federative republic; see also Kurdistan Alliance List; Pres. MASOUD BARZANI; Vice-Pres. NECHIRVAN BARZANI.

Kurdistan Islamic Union (Yakgrtui Islami Kurdistan): e-mail info@kurdiu.org; internet kurdiu.org; f. 1991; seeks establishment of an Islamic state in Iraq that recognizes the rights of Kurds; branch of the Muslim Brotherhood; contested July 2009 elections to the Iraqi Kurdistan Parliament as part of the Service and Reform List; participated in the March 2010 legislative election independently; Sec.-Gen. MUHAMMAD FARAJ.

Kurdistan Socialist Democratic Party (KSDP): Sulaimaniya; e-mail info@psdkurdistan.org; internet www.psdkurdistan.com; f. 1994; splinter group of the KDP, aligned with the PUK; contested July 2009 elections to the Iraqi Kurdistan Parliament as part of the Service and Reform List; Sec.-Gen. MUHAMMAD HAJI MAHMOUD.

Kurdistan Toilers Party (Hizbi Zahmatkeshani Kurdistan): f. 1985; advocates a federal Iraq; closely associated with the KSDP; contested July 2009 elections to the Iraqi Kurdistan Parliament as part of the Social Justice and Freedom List; Sec.-Gen. BALEN ABDULLAH.

Movement for Change (Gorran): e-mail info@gorran.net; internet gorran.net; f. 2006; established by fmr members of the PUK; advocates political and economic reform, anti-corruption measures and the independence of the judiciary; advocates a federal Iraq; contested July 2009 elections to the Iraqi Kurdistan Parliament as the Change List; contested the March 2010 legislative election independently; Leader NAWSHIRWAN MUSTAFA.

National Gathering of the People of Iraq: f. 2004 as the Iraqi People's Conference; name changed in 2009; Sunni; contested March

2010 legislative elections as part of the Iraqi Accord; Leader KHALED AL-BARAA.

National Rafidain List: e-mail info@alrafedainlist.com; internet www.alrafedainlist.com; f. 2004; Assyrian-Christian list headed by the Assyrian Democratic Movement; Leader YOUNADAM KANA.

National Reform Movement: f. 2008 by fmr mems of Islamic Dawa Party; Shi'ite; contested March 2010 legislative election as part of Iraqi Nat. Alliance; Leader IBRAHIM AL-JA'FARI.

National Tribal Gathering: f. 2007; Sunni; participated in March 2010 election as mem. of the Iraqi Accord list; Leader OMAR AL-HAYKAL.

Patriotic Union of Kurdistan (PUK): European Office (Germany), 10502 Berlin, POB 210213; tel. (30) 34097850; fax (30) 34097849; e-mail puk@puk.org; internet www.puk.org; f. 1975; seeks to protect and promote Kurdish rights and interests through self-determination; see also Kurdistan Alliance List; Pres. JALAL TALABANI.

Reconciliation and Liberation Bloc (Kutla al-Musalaha wa't-Tahrir): Mosul; f. 1995 in Jordan as Iraqi Homeland Party (Hizb al-Watan al-Iraqi); moved to Damascus, Syria, and to Mosul in 2003; liberal, secular Sunni; advocates withdrawal of coalition troops and partial rehabilitation of mems of the former Baathist regime; publishes *Al-Ittijah al-Akhar* newspaper; Leader MISHAAN AL-JUBURI.

Renewal List (Tajdeed): f. 2009 by Vice-Pres. Tariq al-Hashimi, following his resignation from the IIP; Sunni; contested March 2010 legislative election as part of the Iraqi Nat. Movement list; Leader TARIQ AL-HASHIMI.

Sadr II Movement (Jamaat al-Sadr al-Thani): Najaf; f. 2003; Shi'ite; opposes presence of US-led coalition in Iraq; mems of the Movement participated in the March 2010 legislative election as part of the Iraqi Nat. Alliance; military wing is Imam al-Mahdi Army; Leader Hojatoleslam MUQTADA AL-SADR.

Service and Reform List: alliance of Islamist and left-wing parties formed prior to the July 2009 elections to the Iraqi Kurdistan Parliament, comprising the Islamic Group of Kurdistan, the Kurdistan Islamic Union, the Kurdistan Socialist Democratic Party and the Future Party.

State of Law (Dawlat al-Kanoon): f. prior to 2009 provincial elections; contested March 2010 legislative election as a predominantly Shi'a alliance of parties and independent candidates, incl. the Islamic Dawa Party, the Independent Arab Movement and the Anbar Salvation Nat. Front.

Major militant groups that have launched attacks against Iraqis and the US-led coalition include: **Fedayeen Saddam** (Saddam's Martyrs; f. 1995 by mems of the former Baathist regime; paramilitary group); **Ansar al-Islam** (f. 1998; splinter group of IMIK; Islamist; suspected of having links with al-Qa'ida); **Hezbollah** (Shi'ite Marsh Arab; Leader ABD AL-KARIM MAHMOUD MOHAMMEDAWI—' ABU HATEM'); **Ansar al-Sunnah** (f. 2003 by mems of Ansar al-Islam; Islamist); **Imam al-Mahdi Army** (armed wing of the Sadr II Movement—Jamaat al-Sadr al-Thani); **Base of Holy War in Mesopotamia** (Tanzim Qa'idat al-Jihad fi Bilad al-Rafidain; Sunni insurgent network, also known as al-Qa'ida in Iraq; Leader AL-NASSER LIDEEN ALLAH ABU SULEIMAN, who was reported to have been killed in Feb. 2011); **Islamic State of Iraq** (Dawlat al-Iraq al-Islamiyya; network of Sunni insurgent groups; suspected of links with al-Qa'ida in Iraq; Leader ABU BAKR AL-BAGHDADI AL-HUSSEINI AL-QURASHI).

Diplomatic Representation

EMBASSIES IN IRAQ

Algeria: Hay al-Mansour, Baghdad; tel. (1) 543-4137; fax (1) 542-5829; Ambassador ABD AL-QADIR BIN SHA'A.

Australia: International Zone, Baghdad; tel. (1) 538-2100; e-mail austemb.baghdad@dfat.gov.au; internet www.iraq.embassy.gov.au; Ambassador LYNDALL SACHS.

Bahrain: 41/6/605 Hay al-Mutanabi, Baghdad; tel. (1) 580-8306; fax (1) 541-2027; e-mail baghdad.mission@mofa.gove.bh; internet www.mofa.gov.bh/baghdad; Ambassador SALAH AL-MALIKI.

Bangladesh: 6/14/929 Hay Babel, Baghdad; tel. (1) 719-0068; fax (1) 718-6045; Ambassador REZA NOOR RAHMAN KHAN.

Bulgaria: 12/25/624 al-Ameriya, Baghdad; tel. (1) 556-8197; fax (1) 556-4182; e-mail embassy.baghdad@mfa.bg; Chargé d'affaires a.i. IVAYLO HRISTOV.

Canada: International Zone, Baghdad; Chargé d'affaires STEPHANIE DUHAIME.

China, People's Republic: POB 2386, al-Jadryaa Post Office, Baghdad; tel. 7901912315 (mobile); e-mail chinaemb_iq@mfa.gov.cn; internet iq.chineseembassy.org; Ambassador WANG YONG.

Czech Republic: POB 27124, 37/11/601 Hay al-Mansour, Baghdad; tel. (1) 542-4868; fax (1) 214-2621; e-mail baghdad@embassy.mzv.cz; internet www.mzv.cz/baghdad; Ambassador ALEXANDR LANGER.

Egypt: 103/11/601 Hay al-Mansour, Baghdad; tel. (1) 543-0572; fax (1) 556-6346; e-mail egypt@uruklink.net; Ambassador AHMAD HASSAN IBRAHIM.

France: POB 118, 7/55/102 Abu Nawas, Baghdad; tel. (964) 718-1996; fax (964) 718-1997; e-mail info@ambafrance-iq.org; internet www.ambafrance-iq.org; Ambassador DENYS GAUER.

Germany: POB 2036, Hay al-Mansour, Baghdad; tel. (1) 543-1470; fax (1) 543-5840; e-mail info@bagdad.diplo.de; internet www.bagdad.diplo.de; Ambassador BRITA WAGENER.

Greece: 63/31/913, Jadriyah University Sq., Hay Babel, Baghdad; tel. (1) 778-2273; e-mail gremb.bag@mfa.gr; Ambassador MIRKORIOZ KARAVOTHIAS.

Holy See: Apostolic Nunciature, POB 2090, 904/2/46 Saadoun St, Baghdad; tel. (1) 718-2083; e-mail nuntiusiraq@yahoo.com; Apostolic Nuncio Most Rev. GIORGIO LINGUA (Titular Archbishop of Tuscania).

India: House 18, St 16, Mohalla 609, Al-Mansour, Baghdad; tel. 7704439731 (mobile); e-mail amb.baghdad@mea.gov.in; Ambassador SURESH K. REDDY.

Iran: POB 39095, Salehiya, Karadeh Maryam, Baghdad; tel. (1) 884-3033; fax (1) 537-5636; Ambassador HASSAN DANAFAR.

Italy: International Zone, Baghdad; tel. 7505010505 (mobile); e-mail ambasciata.baghdad@esteri.it; internet www.ambbaghdad.esteri.it/ambasciata_baghdad; Ambassador MASSIMO MAROTTI.

Japan: International Zone, Baghdad; tel. (1) 776-6791; e-mail azza_fh@yahoo.com; internet www.iraq.emb-japan.go.jp; Ambassador KAZUYA NASHIDA.

Jordan: POB 6314, 145/49/617 Hay al-Andalus, Baghdad; tel. (1) 541-2892; fax (1) 541-2009; e-mail jordan@uruklink.net; Ambassador MUHAMMAD QARAAN.

Korea, Republic: House 11, Babylon Hotel St, al-Jadriya, Baghdad; tel. 7707252006 (mobile); e-mail kembiraq@mofat.go.kr; internet irq.mofat.go.kr; Ambassador KIM HYUN-MYUNG.

Kuwait: Baghdad; Ambassador GHASSAN YOUSEF AL-ZAWAWI.

Lebanon: Bldg 51, al-Askari St, 116 al-Sarafiya Area, Baghdad; tel. (1) 414-2711; fax (1) 885-6731; e-mail lebembbaghadad@yahoo.com; Chargé d'affaires NAWAF SHARIF HAZZA.

Netherlands: POB 2064, 7/15/215 International Zone, Baghdad; tel. (1) 778-2571; fax (1) 776-3513; e-mail bag@minbuza.nl; internet iraq.nlembassy.org; Ambassador JEANNETTE SEPPEN.

Pakistan: 14/7/609 Hay al-Mansour, Baghdad; fax (1) 542-8707; e-mail pakembbag@yahoo.com; Ambassador SHAH M. JAMAL.

Philippines: POB 3236, 4/22/915 Hay al-Jamiyah, al-Jadriya, Baghdad; tel. (1) 788-9761; fax (1) 719-3228; e-mail baghdad.pe@dfa.gov.ph; Ambassador EDSEL BARBA BOUMBERADA.

Poland: 38/75 Karadat Mariam International Zone, Baghdad; tel. (1) 7902354765 (mobile); fax (1) 719-0296; e-mail bagdad.amb.sekretariat@msz.gov.pl; internet www.bagdad.msz.gov.pl; Ambassador LECH STEFANIAK.

Romania: POB 2571, Arassat al-Hindia St, 452A/31/929 Hay Babel, Baghdad; tel. (1) 778-2860; fax (1) 778-7553; e-mail bagdad@mae.ro; Ambassador IACOB PRADA.

Russia: 4/5/605 Hay al-Mutanabi, Baghdad; tel. and fax (1) 541-4749; e-mail rusiraq@mail.ru; internet www.iraq.mid.ru; Ambassador ILYA A. MORGUNOV.

Serbia: POB 2061, 16/35/923 Hay Babel, Baghdad; tel. (1) 778-7887; fax (1) 778-0489; e-mail embsrbag@yahoo.com; internet www.baghdad.mfa.rs; Ambassador RADISAV PETROVIĆ.

Slovakia: 94/28/923 Hay Babel, Baghdad; tel. (1) 776-7367; fax (1) 776-7368; Ambassador MILOSLAV NAD.

Spain: POB 2072, 50/1/609 al-Mansour, Baghdad; e-mail emb.bagdad@maec.es; Ambassador JOSÉ TURPÍN MOLINA.

Sweden: POB 3475, Karadat Mariam, Baghdad; tel. 7801987450; e-mail ambassaden.bagdad@gov.se; internet www.swedenabroad.com/baghdad; Ambassador JÖRGEN LINDSTRÖM.

Syria: Hay al-Mansour, Baghdad; Ambassador SATTAM JAD'AN AL-DANDAH.

Tunisia: 1/49/617 Hay al-Andalus, Baghdad; tel. (1) 542-4569; Ambassador SAMIR JUMAIE ABDULLAH.

Turkey: POB 14001, 2/8 Waziriya, Baghdad; tel. (312) 218-6010; fax (312) 218-6110; e-mail embassy.baghdad@mfa.gov.tr; internet www.baghdad.emb.mfa.gov.tr; Ambassador FARUK KAYMAKCI.

Ukraine: POB 15192, 50/1/609 al-Mansour, al-Yarmouk, Baghdad; tel. 7904167152 (mobile); fax 543-9849; e-mail emb_iq@mfa.gov.ua; internet iraq.mfa.gov.ua; Ambassador ANATOLII MARYNETS.

United Arab Emirates: 81/34/611 Hay al-Andalus (al-Daoudi), Baghdad; tel. (1) 543-9174; fax (1) 543-9093; Ambassador ABDULLAH IBRAHIM AL-SHEHHI.

United Kingdom: International Zone, Baghdad; e-mail britishconsulbaghdad@yahoo.co.uk; tel. 7901926280 (mobile); internet www.gov.uk/government/world/iraq; Ambassador SIMON COLLIS.

USA: Al-Kindi St, International Zone, Baghdad; e-mail baghdadirc@state.gov; internet iraq.usembassy.gov; Ambassador ROBERT STEPHEN BEECROFT.

Yemen: 4/36/904 Hay al-Wahada, Baghdad; tel. (1) 718-6682; fax (1) 717-2318; Ambassador ZAID HASSAN AL-WARITH.

Judicial System

Supreme Iraqi Criminal Tribunal: Following the ousting of the Baath regime, the judicial system was subject to a process of review and de-Baathification. In June 2003 the former Coalition Provisional Authority (CPA) established a **Judicial Review Committee**, the task of which was to review and repair the material status of the courts and to assess personnel. In December the Governing Council created the **Iraqi Special Tribune**, in order to bring to trial those senior members of the former regime accused of war crimes, crimes against humanity and genocide. The statute of the Tribune was amended by the former Transitional National Assembly in October 2005, when it was renamed the **Supreme Iraqi Criminal Tribunal**.

Central Criminal Court of Iraq: Consists of an **Investigative Court** and a **Trial Court**. It was created by the CPA in July 2003 as the senior court in Iraq, with jurisdiction over all crimes committed in the country since 19 March 2003. With a few exceptions, the application of justice was to be based upon the 1969 Penal Code of Iraq and the 1971 Criminal Proceedings Code of Iraq.

Higher Judicial Council: tel. (1) 538-4406; fax (1) 537-2267; e-mail iraqinfocenter@yahoo.com; internet www.iraqja.iq; Pres. HASSAN IBRAHIM HUSSEIN HUMAIRI.

Religion

ISLAM

About 95% of the population are Muslims, some 60% of whom are of the Shi'ite sect. The Arabs of northern Iraq, the Bedouins, the Kurds, the Turkomans and some of the inhabitants of Baghdad and Basra are mainly of the Sunni sect, while the remaining Arabs south of the Diyali are Shi'a.

CHRISTIANITY

There are Christian communities in all the principal towns of Iraq, but their main villages lie mostly in the Mosul district. The Christians of Iraq comprise three groups: the free Churches, including the Nestorian, Gregorian and Syrian Orthodox; the churches known as Uniate, since they are in union with the Roman Catholic Church, including the Armenian Uniates, Syrian Uniates and Chaldeans; mixed bodies of Protestant converts, New Chaldeans and Orthodox Armenians. There are estimated to be 500,000–700,000 Christians of various denominations in Iraq; however, there has been an exodus to neighbouring countries such as Syria and Jordan since the mid-2000s, as a result of the ongoing sectarian conflict.

The Assyrian Church

Assyrian Christians, an ancient sect having sympathies with Nestorian beliefs, were forced to leave their mountainous homeland in northern Kurdistan in the early part of the 20th century. The estimated 550,000 members of the Apostolic Catholic Assyrian Church of the East are now exiles, mainly in Iraq (about 50,000 adherents), Syria, Lebanon and the USA. Their leader is the Catholicos Patriarch, His Holiness MAR DINKHA IV.

The Orthodox Churches

Armenian Apostolic Church: Diocese of the Armenian Church of Iraq, POB 2280, al-Jadriya, Tayaran Sq., Baghdad; tel. (1) 815-1856; fax (1) 815-1857; e-mail iraqitem@yahoo.com; internet www.iraqitem.org; f. 1639; Primate Archbishop AVAK ASADOURIAN; 13 churches (four in Baghdad); 18,419 mems.

Syrian Orthodox Church: Syrian Orthodox Archbishopric, POB 843, al-Seenah St, Baghdad; tel. (1) 719-6320; fax (1) 719-7583; Archbishop of Baghdad and Basra SEVERIUS JAMIL HAWA; 12,000 adherents in Iraq.

The Greek Orthodox Church is also represented in Iraq.

The Roman Catholic Church

Armenian Rite

Archbishop of Baghdad: Most Rev. EMMANUEL DABBAGHIAN, 27/903 Archevêché Arménien Catholique, POB 2344, Karrada Sharkiya, Baghdad; tel. (1) 719-2461; e-mail dabbaghianemm@hotmail.com.

Chaldean Rite

Iraq comprises the patriarchate of Babylon, five archdioceses (including the patriarchal see of Baghdad) and five dioceses (all of which are suffragan to the patriarchate). Altogether, the Patriarch has jurisdiction over 21 archdioceses and dioceses in Iraq, Egypt, Iran, Lebanon, Syria, Turkey and the USA, and the Patriarchal Vicariate of Jerusalem.

Patriarch of Babylon of the Chaldeans: Cardinal EMMANUEL III DELLY, POB 6112, Patriarcat Chaldéen Catholique, al-Mansour, Baghdad; tel. (1) 537-9164; fax (1) 537-8556; e-mail info@st-addayyahoo.com.

Archbishop of Arbil: Most Rev. BASHAR WARDA, Archevêché Catholique Chaldéen, Ainkawa, Arbil; tel. (665) 225-0009.

Archbishop of Baghdad: the Patriarch of Babylon (q.v.).

Archbishop of Basra: Most Rev. IMAD AZIZ AL-BANNA, Archevêché Chaldéen, POB 217, Ashar-Basra; tel. (40) 613427; e-mail efather2006@yahoo.com.

Archbishop of Kirkuk: Most Rev. LOUIS SAKO, Archevêché Chaldéen, POB 490, Kirkuk; tel. (50) 220525; fax (50) 213978; e-mail luis_sako2@yahoo.com.

Archbishop of Mosul: Most Rev. EMIL SHIMOUN NONA, Archevêché Chaldéen, POB 757, Mayassa, Mosul; tel. (60) 815831; fax (60) 816742; e-mail archdioceseofmossul@yahoo.com.

Latin Rite

The archdiocese of Baghdad is directly responsible to the Holy See.

Archbishop of Baghdad: Most Rev. JEAN BENJAMIN SLEIMAN, Archevêché Latin, POB 35130, Hay al-Wahda—Mahallat 904, rue 8, Immeuble 44, 12906 Baghdad; tel. (1) 719-9537; fax (1) 717-2471; e-mail jbsleiman@yahoo.com.

Melkite Rite

The Greek-Melkite Patriarch of Antioch (GRÉGOIRE III LAHAM) is resident in Damascus, Syria.

Patriarchal Exarchate of Iraq: Exarchat Patriarchal Grec-Melkite, Karradat IN 903/10/50, Baghdad; tel. (1) 719-1082; 100 adherents (2006); Exarch Patriarchal (vacant).

Syrian Rite

Iraq comprises two archdioceses and the Patriarchal Exarchate of Basra.

Archbishop of Baghdad: Most Rev. ATHANASE MATTI SHABA MATOKA, Archevêché Syrien Catholique, 903/2/1 Baghdad; tel. (1) 719-1850; fax (1) 719-0166; e-mail mattishaba@yahoo.com.

Archbishop of Mosul: Most Rev. BOUTROS MOSHE, Archevêché Syrien Catholique, Hosh al-Khan, Mosul; tel. (60) 762160; fax (60) 771439; e-mail syrcam2003@yahoo.com.

The Anglican Communion

Within the Episcopal Church in Jerusalem and the Middle East, Iraq forms part of the diocese of Cyprus and the Gulf. Expatriate congregations in Iraq meet at St George's Church, Baghdad. The Bishop in Cyprus and the Gulf is resident in Cyprus.

JUDAISM

A tiny Jewish community, numbering only eight people in late 2008, remains in Baghdad.

OTHERS

About 550,000 Yazidis and a smaller number of Sabians and Shebeks reside in Iraq.

Sabian Community: al-Nasiriyah (Nasiriya); 20,000 adherents; Mandeans, mostly in Nasiriya; Head Sheikh DAKHIL.

Yazidis: Ainsifni; Leader TASHIN SAID ALI.

The Press

Since the overthrow of the regime of Saddam Hussain by US-led coalition forces in early 2003, the number of publications has proliferated: by the end of 2003 an estimated 250 newspapers and periodicals were in circulation, although only some 100 of these were reportedly still being published in 2008. Many newspapers are affiliated with political or religious organizations; however, the daily *Al-Sabah* is controlled by the Iraqi Government, with coalition backing. Security issues have resulted in severe distribution problems, and some newspaper offices have either relocated or chosen to publish online-only editions following threats being issued against journalists by militant groups, militias and security forces. A selection of publications is given below.

DAILIES

Al-Adala (Justice): Baghdad; e-mail aliisadik@yahoo.com; internet www.aladalanews.net; f. 2004; twice weekly; Arabic; organ of the Islamic Supreme Council of Iraq; publ. by the Al-Adala Group for Press, Printing and Publishing; Owner Dr Adil Abd al-Mahdi.

Baghdad: al-Zeitoun St, al-Harthiya, Baghdad; e-mail baghdadwifaq@yahoo.com; f. 1991; organ of the Iraqi Nat. Accord; Publr Ayad Allawi.

Al-Bayan (The Manifesto): Baghdad; f. 2003; Arabic; organ of Islamic Dawa Party; Man. Editor Sadiq al-Rikabi.

Dar al-Salam (House of Peace): Baghdad; Arabic; organ of Iraqi Islamic Party.

Al-Dustur (The Constitution): Baghdad; f. 2003; Arabic; politics; independent; publ. by Al-Dustur Press, Publishing and Distribution House; Chair. Basim al-Sheikh; Editor-in-Chief Ali al-Sharqi.

Al-Jarida (The Newspaper): Baghdad; f. 2003; Arabic; organ of the Iraqi Arab Socialist Movement; Editor Prof. Qays al-Azzawi.

Kul al-Iraq (All Iraq): Baghdad; e-mail info@kululiraq.com; internet www.kululiraq.com; f. 2003; Arabic; independent; Editor-in-Chief Dr Abbas al-Siraf.

Al-Mada: 41/1 Abu Nuwas St, Baghdad; fax (1) 881-3256; e-mail fakhri_kareem@almadapaper.com; internet www.almadapaper.com; f. 2004; Arabic; independent; publ. by Al-Mada Foundation for Media, Culture and Arts; Editor-in-Chief Fakhri Karim.

Al-Mannarah (Minarets): Basra; tel. (40) 315758; e-mail almannarah@almannarah.com; internet www.almannarah.com; Arabic; publ. by South Press, Printing and Publishing Corpn; Editor-in-Chief Dr Khalaf al-Manshadi.

Al-Mashriq: Baghdad; internet www.al-mashriq.net; f. 2004; Arabic; independent; publ. by Al-Mashriq Institution for Media and Cultural Investments; circ. 25,000.

Al-Mutamar (Congress): Baghdad; e-mail almutamer@yahoo.com; internet www.inciraq.com/index_paper.php; f. 1993; Arabic; publ. by Iraqi Nat. Congress; Editor-in-Chief Luay Baldawi.

Al-Sabah: Baghdad; e-mail sabah@alsabaah.com; internet www.alsabaah.com; f. 2003; Arabic and English; state-controlled; publ. by the Iraqi Media Network; Deputy Editor-in-Chief Adnan Sherkhan.

Al-Sabah al-Jadid (New Morning): Baghdad; e-mail info@newsabah.com; internet www.newsabah.com; f. 2004; Arabic; independent; Editor-in-Chief Ismail Zayer.

Sawt al-Iraq (Voice of Iraq): Baghdad; e-mail admin@sotaliraq.com; internet www.sotaliraq.com; online only; Arabic; independent.

Al-Taakhi (Brotherhood): e-mail badirkhansindi@yahoo.com; internet www.taakhinews.org; f. 1967; Kurdish and Arabic; organ of the Kurdistan Democratic Party (KDP); publ. by Al-Taakhi Publishing and Printing House; Editor-in-Chief Dr Badirkhan Sindi; circ. 20,000 (Baghdad).

Tariq al-Sha'ab (People's Path): Saadoun St, Baghdad; e-mail altareeq_1934@yahoo.com; internet www.iraqcp.org; f. 1974; Arabic and English; organ of the Iraqi Communist Party; Editor Abd al-Razzak al-Safi.

Xebat: Arbil; e-mail info@xebat.net; internet www.xebat.net; f. 1959; Arabic and Kurdish; organ of the KDP; Editor-in-Chief Nazhad Aziz Surme.

Al-Zaman (Time): Baghdad; tel. (1) 717-7587; e-mail postmaster@azzaman.com; internet www.azzaman.com; f. 1997 in the United Kingdom, f. 2003 in Baghdad; Arabic, with some news translated into English; Editor-in-Chief Saad al-Bazzaz.

WEEKLIES

Al-Ahali (The People): Baghdad; e-mail info@ahali-iraq.net; internet www.ahali-iraq.net; Arabic; politics; Editor Haval Zakhoubi.

Alif Baa al-Iraq: Baghdad; Arabic and English; general, social and political affairs.

Habazbuz fi Zaman al-Awlamah (Habazbuz in the Age of Globalization): Baghdad; f. 2003; Arabic; satirical; Editor Ishtar al-Yasiri.

Iraq Today: Baghdad; f. 2003; English; current affairs; Founder and Editor-in-Chief Hussain Sinjari.

Al-Iraq al-Yawm (Iraq Today): Baghdad; e-mail iraqtoday@iraqtoday.net; Arabic and English; Editor Isra Shakir.

Al-Ittihad (Union): Baghdad and Sulaimaniya; tel. (1) 543-8954; e-mail alitthad@alitthad.com; internet www.alitthad.com; Arabic and Kurdish; publ. by the Patriotic Union of Kurdistan; Editor Abd al-Hadi; circ. 30,000 (Baghdad).

Al-Ittijah al-Akhar (The Other Direction): Baghdad; tel. (1) 776-3334; fax (1) 776-3332; e-mail alitijahalakhar@yahoo.com; internet www.alitijahalakhar.com; Arabic; organ of Reconciliation and Liberation Bloc; Chair. and Editor Mishaan al-Juburi.

Kurdish Globe: Salah al-Din Highway, Pirzeen, Arbil; tel. (66) 2526792; e-mail info@kurdishglobe.net; internet www.kurdishglobe.net; f. 2005; English; Kurdish news and issues; Exec. Editor Jawad Qadir; circ. 40,000.

Majallati: POB 8041, Children's Culture House, Baghdad; Arabic; children's newspaper; Editor-in-Chief Dr Shafiq al-Mahdi.

Al-Muajaha (The Witness): 6/41/901, Karrada Dakhil, Baghdad; e-mail almuajaha@riseup.net; f. 2003; Arabic and English; current affairs; independent; Editor Ramzi Majid Jarrar.

Al-Nahda (Renaissance): Basra; f. 2003; Arabic; organ of the Independent Democratic Gathering; Publr Adnan Pachachi.

Regay Kurdistan: Arbil; e-mail dwalapere@regaykurdistan.com; internet www.regaykurdistan.com; Arabic and Kurdish; organ of the Iraqi and Kurdistan Communist Parties; Editor-in-Chief Handren Ahmad.

Al-Sina'i (The Industrialist): Baghdad; Arabic; general; publ. by the Nat. Industrialist Coalition; Editor-in-Chief Dr Zayd Abd al-Majid Bilal.

Al-Waqai al-Iraqiya (Official Gazette of the Republic of Iraq): Ministry of Justice, Baghdad; tel. (1) 537-2023; e-mail Hashim_Jaffar_alsaieg@yahoo.com; f. 1922; Arabic and English; Dir Hashim N. Jaffar; circ. 5,000.

PERIODICALS

Hawlati: e-mail hawlati2000@yahoo.com; internet www.hawlati.info; f. 2001; fortnightly; Kurdish, Arabic and English; independent, privately owned; mainly Kurdish politics; Publr Tariq Fatih; Editor Kamal Raouf.

Majallat al-Majma' al-'Ilmi al-Iraqi (Journal of the Academy of Sciences): POB 4023, Waziriya, Baghdad; tel. (1) 422-4202; fax (1) 422-2066; e-mail iraqacademy@yahoo.com; internet www.iraqacademy.iq; f. 1950; quarterly; Arabic; scholarly magazine on Arabic Islamic culture; Editor-in-Chief Prof. Dr Ahmad Matloub.

Al-Sa'ah (The Hour): Baghdad; twice weekly; Arabic; organ of the Iraqi Unified Nat. Movement; Publr Ahmad al-Kubaysi; Editor Ni'ma Abd al-Razzaq.

Sawt al-Talaba (Voice of the Students): Baghdad; fortnightly; Arabic; publ. by New Iraq Youth and Students' Org; Editor Mustafa al-Hayim.

NEWS AGENCIES

Aswat al-Iraq (Voices of Iraq): e-mail aswat.info@gmail.com; internet www.aswataliraq.info; f. 2004; Arabic, English and Kurdish; independent news agency with contributions from Iraqi correspondents and three Iraqi newspapers; Editor-in-Chief Zuhair al-Jezairi.

National Iraqi News Agency: Baghdad; tel. (1) 719-3459; e-mail news@ninanews.com; internet www.ninanews.com; f. 2005; Arabic and English; independent; Chair. Dr Farid Ayar; Man. Dir Abd al-Muhsen Hussain Jawad.

PRESS ORGANIZATION

Iraqi Union for Journalists: POB 14101, nr al-Resafah Bldg, al-Waziriya, Baghdad; tel. (1) 537-0762; fax (1) 422-6011; e-mail iraqiju@yahoo.com; Chair. Muaid al-Lami.

Publishers

Afaq Arabiya Publishing House: POB 4032, Adamiya, Baghdad; tel. (1) 443-6044; fax (1) 444-8760; publr of literary monthlies, periodicals and cultural books; Chair. Dr Mohsin al-Musawi.

Dar al-Ma'mun for Translation and Publishing: POB 24015, Karradat Mariam, Baghdad; tel. (1) 538-3171; publr of newspapers and magazines.

Al-Hurriyah Printing Establishment: Karantina, Sarrafiya, Baghdad; f. 1970.

Al-Jamaheer Press House: POB 491, Sarrafiya, Baghdad; tel. (1) 416-9341; fax (1) 416-1875; f. 1963; publr of a number of newspapers and magazines; Pres. Saad Qassem Hammoudi.

Kurdish Culture and Publishing House: Baghdad; f. 1976.

Al-Ma'arif Ltd: Mutanabi St, Baghdad; f. 1929; publishes periodicals and books in Arabic, Kurdish, Turkish, French and English.

Al-Mada Foundation for Media, Culture and Arts: 141 Abu Nuwas St, Baghdad; tel. 7702799999 (mobile); e-mail info@almadapaper.net; internet www.almadapaper.net; f. 1994; Dir FAKHRI KARIM.

Al-Muthanna Library: POB 14019, Mutanabi St, Baghdad; tel. 770-3649664 (mobile); e-mail mail@almuthannabooks.com; internet www.almuthannabooks.com; f. 1936; booksellers and publrs of books and monographs in Arabic and oriental languages; Propr ANAS AL-RAJAB; Dir IBRAHIM AL-RAJAB.

Al-Nahdah: Mutanabi St, Baghdad; tel. (1) 416-2689; e-mail yehya_azawy@yahoo.com; politics, Arab affairs.

National House for Publishing, Distribution and Advertising: POB 624, al-Jumhuriya St, Baghdad; tel. (1) 425-1846; f. 1972; publishes books on politics, economics, education, agriculture, sociology, commerce and science in Arabic and other Middle Eastern languages; Dir-Gen. M. A. ASKAR.

Al-Thawra Printing and Publishing House: POB 2009, Aqaba bin Nafi's Sq., Baghdad; tel. (1) 719-6161; f. 1970; Chair. (vacant).

PUBLISHERS' ASSOCIATION

Iraqi Publishers' Association: Baghdad; tel. (1) 416-9279; fax (1) 416-7584; e-mail al_nasheren@yahoo.com; Chair. Dr ABD AL-WAHAB AL-RADI.

Broadcasting and Communications

REGULATORY AUTHORITY

Communications and Media Commission (CMC): POB 2044, Hay Babel, al-Masbah, Baghdad; tel. (1) 718-0009; fax (1) 719-5839; e-mail enquiries@cmc.iq; internet www.cmc.iq; f. 2004 by fmr Coalition Provisional Authority; independent telecoms and media regulator; responsibilities include the award and management of telecommunications licences, broadcasting, media and information services, as well as spectrum allocation and management; CEO BURHAN AL-SHAWI.

TELECOMMUNICATIONS

Under the former Baathist regime, the Iraqi Telecommunications and Posts Co was the sole provider of telecommunications and postal services. Following the removal from power of Saddam Hussain, in 2003 the Coalition Provisional Authority issued three short-term licences for the provision of mobile telephone services to stimulate competition in the sector. Asiacell, led by the Iraqi Kurdish Asiacell Co for Telecommunication Ltd, was awarded the licence for the northern region; the licence for Baghdad and the central region was won by Orascom Telecom Iraq Corpn (Iraqna), led by Orascom Telecom of Egypt; and Atheer Telecom Iraq (MTC Atheer), led by the Mobile Telecommunications Co of Kuwait, won the licence for Basra and the southern region. In August 2007 Asiacell, Korek Telecom Ltd and MTC Atheer (which subsequently acquired 100% of Iraqna shares and was renamed Zain) won the auction launched by the Government for three new national licences to provide mobile telephone services over a 15-year period; Iraqna withdrew from the bidding process.

Asiacell: Headquarters Bldg, Sulaimaniya; e-mail customercare@asiacell.com; internet www.asiacell.com; f. 1999; 51% owned by Asiacell Co for Telecommunication Ltd, 40% by Wataniya Telecom (Kuwait) and 9% owned by United Gulf Bank (Bahrain); 6.0m. subscribers (Dec. 2008); Chair. of Bd FAROUK MUSTAFA RASOUL.

Iraqi Telecommunications and Posts Co (ITPC): POB 2450, Abu Nuwas St, Baghdad; tel. (1) 886-2372; e-mail itpcmedia@yahoo.com; internet www.itpc.gov.iq; state-owned; Dir-Gen. SALEH HASSAN ALI.

Korek Telecom: Kurdistan St, Pirmam, Arbil; tel. (66) 243-3455; e-mail media.pr@korektel.com; internet korektel.com; f. 2001; 44% owned by jt-venture of Agility Logistics (Kuwait) and France Telecom—Orange; CEO GHADA GEBARA.

Zain: Basra; e-mail info@iq.zain.com; internet www.zain.com; f. 2003 as MTC Atheer, a subsidiary of Mobile Telecommunications Co (Kuwait); acquired Iraqna Co for Mobile Phone Services Ltd (operated by Orascom Telecom Holding—Egypt) in Dec. 2007; name changed to above in Jan. 2008; 9.7m. subscribers (Dec. 2008); Chair. and Acting CEO MUHAMMAD AL-CHARCHAFCHI.

BROADCASTING

The **Iraqi Media Network (IMN)** was established by the former Coalition Provisional Authority (CPA) to replace the Ministry of Information following the ousting of the former regime. The IMN established new television and both FM and AM radio stations. In January 2004 the CPA announced that a consortium led by the US-based Harris Corpn had been awarded the contract to take over from the IMN the control of 18 television channels, two radio stations and the *Al-Sabah* daily newspaper.

Iraqi Media Network (IMN): Baghdad; e-mail info@imn.iq; internet www.imn.iq; f. 2003.

Al-Iraqiya Television: Baghdad; internet www.imn.iq/pages/iraqia-tv; terrestrial and satellite television.

Iraq Media Network—Southern Region: internet www.imnsr.com.

Republic of Iraq Radio: Baghdad; e-mail rir.info@iraqimedianet.net; internet www.imn.iq/pages/radio-iraqia/.

Radio

Hawler Radio: Shorsh St., Next to Shangri-La Hotel, Erbil; tel. 7507361177 (mobile); e-mail hawlerradio@yahoo.com; internet www.hawlerradio.com; Kurdish—language; covers Arbil, D'hok, Kirkuk and Sulaimaniya.

Radio Dijla: House 3, Hay al-Jamia Zone 635/52, Baghdad; tel. (0) 533-271-901; e-mail post@radiodijla.com; internet www.radiodijla.com; f. 2004; privately owned; first talk radio station to be established in post-invasion Iraq; also broadcasts music programmes; Founder Dr AHMAD AL-RIKABI.

Voice of Iraq: Baghdad; e-mail admin@voiraq.com; internet www.voiraq.com; f. 2003; privately owned AM radio station; broadcasts music, news and current affairs programmes in Arabic, Turkmen and English.

Other independent radio stations include Radio Al Bilad, Radio Nawa, Radio Shafak and Sumer FM.

Television

Al Sharqiya: 10/13/52 Karrada Kharj, Baghdad; tel. (88216) 6775-1380 (satellite); e-mail alsharqiya@alsharqiya.com; internet www.alsharqiya.com; f. 2004; privately owned; independent; broadcasts news and entertainment programming 24 hours a day terrestrially and via satellite; Founder and CEO SAAD AL-BAZZAZ.

Alsumaria TV: POB 3311, Baghdad; tel. and fax (1) 717-6023; e-mail communication-department@alsumaria.tv; internet www.alsumaria.tv; f. 2004; privately owned, independent satellite network; broadcasts news, entertainment and educational programming 24 hours a day.

Finance

(cap. = capital; res = reserves; dep. = deposits; brs = branches; m. = million; amounts in Iraqi dinars, unless otherwise stated)

All banks and insurance companies in Iraq, including all foreign companies, were nationalized in July 1964. The assets of foreign companies were taken over by the state. In May 1991 the Government announced its decision to end the state's monopoly in banking, and during 1992–2000 17 private banks were established; however, they were prohibited by the former regime from conducting international transactions. Following the establishment of the Coalition Provisional Authority in 2003, efforts were made to reform the state-owned Rafidain and Rashid Banks, and in October the Central Bank allowed private banks to begin processing international transactions. In January 2004 the Central Bank of Iraq announced that three foreign banks—HSBC and Standard Chartered (both of the United Kingdom), and the National Bank of Kuwait—had been awarded licences to operate in Iraq, the first such licences awarded for 40 years. A further five foreign banks had also been granted licences by mid-2005. There were six public sector and 37 private sector banks operating in Iraq in 2011.

BANKING

Central Bank

Central Bank of Iraq (CBI): POB 64, al-Rashid St, Baghdad; tel. (1) 816-5170; fax (1) 816-6802; e-mail cbi@cbi.iq; internet www.cbi.iq; f. 1947 as Nat. Bank of Iraq; name changed as above 1956; has the sole right of note issue; cap. 100,000m., res 246,026m., dep. 28,479,125m. (Dec. 2009); Gov. Dr ABD AL-BASET TURKI SAEED; 4 brs.

State-owned Commercial Banks

Rafidain Bank: POB 11360, Banks St, Baghdad; tel. (1) 816-0287; fax (1) 816-5035; e-mail emailcenter9@yahoo.com; internet www.rafidain-bank.org; f. 1941; cap. 25,000m., res 203,198m., dep. 30,021,687m. (Dec. 2012); Dir-Gen. HABIB ZIA ALCKHEON; 147 brs in Iraq, 8 brs abroad.

Rashid Bank: al-Rashid St, Baghdad; tel. (1) 818-8921; fax (1) 882-6201; e-mail natbank@uruklink.net; internet www.rasheedbank

.gov.iq; f. 1988; cap. 2,000m., res 39,628m., dep. 15,938,638m. (Dec. 2011); total assets US $750m. (2003); Chair. KADHIM M. NASHOOR; 161 brs.

Private Commercial Banks

Babylon Bank: al-Amara St, Baghdad; tel. (1) 717-3686; fax (1) 719-1014; e-mail info@babylonbank-iq.com; internet www.babylonbank-iq.com; f. 1999; cap. and res 31,310m., total assets 89,981m. (Dec. 2007); Chair. MUHAMMAD QASSIM AL-NADOSI; Gen. Dir TARIQ ABD AL-BAKI ABOUD; 6 brs.

Bank of Baghdad: POB 3192, al-Karada St, Alwiya, Baghdad; tel. (1) 717-5007; fax (1) 717-5006; internet www.bankofbaghdad.com; f. 1992; 50.6% stake owned by Burgan Bank (Kuwait); cap. 175,000m., res 7,153m., dep. 1,046,719m. (Dec. 2012); Chair. IMAD ISMAEL SHARIF; Man. Dir ADNAN AL-CHALABI; 5 brs.

Commercial Bank of Iraq PSC (CBIQ): Saadoun St, Alwiya, Baghdad; tel. (1) 740-5583; fax (1) 718-4312; e-mail cb.iraq@ahliunited.com; internet www.ahliunited.com/bh_aub_cbiq.html; f. 1992; Ahli United Bank BSC (Bahrain) acquired 49% stake in Dec. 2005; cap. US $60m., dep. $59.6m., total assets $124.3m. (2006); Chair. FAHAD AL-RAJAAN; CEO and Man. Dir ADEL A. AL-LABBAN; 10 brs.

Credit Bank of Iraq: POB 3420, Saadoun St, Alwiya, Baghdad; tel. (1) 718-2198; fax (1) 717-0156; e-mail creditbkiq@yahoo.com; internet www.creditbankofiraq.com; f. 1998; 75% owned by Nat. Bank of Kuwait SAK, 10% by World Bank's Int. Finance Corpn and 15% by private investors; cap. 1,250m., res 528m., dep. 16,376.9m. (Dec. 2002); Chair. FOUAD M MUSTAFA; Man. Dir BASIL H. AL-DHAHI; 12 brs.

Gulf Commercial Bank: POB 3101, nr Baghdad Hotel, Saadoun St, Alwiya, Baghdad; tel. (1) 719-8534; fax (1) 778-8251; e-mail admn@gulfbankiraq.com; f. 2000; cap. 37,500m. (Jan. 2009); Chair. ABU TALIB HASHIM; 14 brs.

National Bank of Iraq (al-Ahli al-Iraqi Bank): Saadoun St, nr Firdos Sq., Baghdad 11194; tel. (1) 717-7735; fax (6) 569-5942; e-mail Info@nbirq.com; internet www.nbirq.com; f. 1995; 59% owned by Capital Bank of Jordan; Chair. TALAL FANAR AL-FAISAL; 4 brs.

Sumer Commercial Bank: POB 3876, Hay al-Riad, Section 908, St 16, Baghdad; tel. (1) 719-6472; internet www.sumerbankiq.com; cap. 10,200m., res 531m., dep. 7,500m. (Aug. 2005); Chair. KHALIL KHAIRALLAH S. AL-JUMAILI; Man. Dir FOUAD HAMZA AL-SAEED; 9 brs.

Specialized Banks

Agricultural Co-operative Bank of Iraq: POB 2421, al-Rashid St, Baghdad; tel. (1) 886-4768; fax (1) 886-5047; e-mail agriculturalcoopbank@yahoo.com; internet www.agriculturalbank.gov.iq; f. 1936; state-owned; Dir-Gen. MUHAMMAD H. AL-KHAFAJI; 32 brs.

Basra International Bank for Investment: Watani St, Ashar, Basra; tel. (40) 616955; internet www.basrahbank.net; cap. 55,000m., res 10,320m., dep. 110,850m. (Dec. 2007); Chair. HUSSEIN GHALIB KUBBA; Man. Dir HASSAN GHALIB KUBBA; 12 brs.

Dar el-Salaam Investment Bank: POB 3067, al-Saadoun Park 103/41/3, Alwiya, Baghdad; tel. (1) 719-6488; e-mail info@desiraq.com; internet www.desiraq.com; f. 1999; 70.1% share acquired by HSBC (United Kingdom) in 2005; total assets 35,562m. (Aug. 2005); 14 brs.

Economy Bank for Investment and Finance (EBIF): 14 Ramadan St, al-Mansour Sq., Baghdad; tel. (1) 298-7712; fax (1) 298-7713; e-mail info@economybankiraq.com; internet www.economybankiraq.com; f. 1997; CEO HOUSSAM OBEID ALI; 23 brs.

Industrial Bank of Iraq: POB 5825, al-Sinak, Baghdad; tel. (1) 887-2181; fax (1) 888-3047; e-mail bank2004@maktoob.com; f. 1940; state-owned; total assets US $34.7m. (2003); Dir-Gen. BASSIMA ABD AL-HADDI AL-DHAHIR; 9 brs.

Investment Bank of Iraq: POB 3724, 902/2/27 Hay al-Wahda, Alwiya, Baghdad; tel. (1) 719-9042; fax (1) 719-8505; e-mail info@ibi-bankiraq.com; internet www.ibi-bankiraq.com; f. 1993; cap. 100,000m., res 7,819m., dep. 193,307m. (Dec. 2012); Chair. HUSSEIN SALIH SHARIF; Gen. Man. HAMZA DAWOUD SALMAN HALBOUN; 18 brs.

Iraqi Islamic Bank for Investment and Development: 609/18/67, al-Mansour, Baghdad; tel. (1) 416-4939; fax (1) 414-0697; e-mail info@iraqiislamicb.com; internet www.iraqiislamicb.com; f. 1992; Chair. Dr TARIQ KHALAF AL-ABDULLAH.

Iraqi Middle East Investment Bank: POB 10379, Bldg 65, Hay Babel, 929 Arasat al-Hindiya, Baghdad; tel. (1) 717-5545; e-mail cendep@iraqimdlestbank.com; internet www.iraqinet.net/com/3/mdlestbank.htm; f. 1993; cap. 100,000m., res 12,172m., dep. 505,117m. (Dec. 2011); Man. Dir M. F. AL-ALOOSI; Exec. Man. SUDAD A. AZIZ; 19 brs.

Kurdistan International Bank for Investment and Development: 70 Abd al-Salam Barzani St, Arbil; tel. (66) 223-0822; fax (66) 253-1369; e-mail info@kibid.com; internet www.kibid.com; f. 2005; private bank; cap. 300,000m., res 67,912m., dep. 574,719m. (Dec. 2012); Chair. SALAR MUSTAFA HAKIM; 4 brs.

Mosul Bank for Development and Investment: POB 1292, al-Markaz St, Mosul; tel. (60) 813-090; fax (60) 815-411; e-mail mosul_bank@yahoo.com; internet www.mosulbank.com.

Real Estate Bank of Iraq: POB 8118, 29/222 Haifa St, Baghdad; tel. (1) 885-3212; fax (1) 884-0980; e-mail estatebank194@yahoo.com; internet www.reb-iraq.com; f. 1949; state-owned; gives loans to assist the building industry; acquired the Co-operative Bank in 1970; total assets US $10m. (2003); Dir-Gen. ABD AL-RAZZAQ AZIZ; 25 brs.

United Bank for Investment: 906/14/69, al-Wathiq Sq., Hay al-Wehda, Baghdad; tel. (1) 888-112; e-mail unitedbank2004@yahoo.com; internet www.unitedbank–iq.net; f. 1995; cap. 250,000m., res 9,717m., dep. 246,693m. (Dec. 2012); Chair. IBRAHIM HASSAN AL-BADRI; Man. Dir ZIAD ABBAS HASHEM; 8 brs.

Warka Bank for Investment and Finance: POB 3559, 902/14/50, Hay al-Wehda, Baghdad; tel. (1) 717-4970; fax (1) 717-9555; e-mail info@warka-bank-iq.com; internet www.warka-bank.com; f. 1999; private bank; cap. 24,000m. (2006); Chair. and CEO SAAD SAADOUN AL-BUNNIA; 130 brs.

Trade Bank

Trade Bank of Iraq (TBI): POB 28445, Bldg 20, St 1, 608 al-Yarmouk District, Baghdad; tel. (1) 543-3561; fax (1) 543-3560; e-mail info@tbiraq.com; internet www.tbiraq.com; f. 2003 by fmr Coalition Provisional Authority to facilitate Iraq's exports of goods and services and the country's reconstruction; independent of Cen. Bank of Iraq; cap. US $427m., res $240m., dep. $13,700m. (Dec. 2011); Chair. HAMDIYAH MAHMOOD FARAJ AL-JAFF; 7 brs.

INSURANCE

Iraqi Insurance Diwan: Ministry of Finance, 147/6/47 Hay al-Eloom, Baghdad; tel. (1) 416-8030; e-mail IraqiInsuranceDiwan@iraqinsurance.org; internet www.iraqinsurance.org; f. 2005 as independent regulator for the insurance sector.

Ahlia Insurance Co: al-Tahreeat Sq., Baghdad; tel. (790) 4565829 (mobile); e-mail info@aic-iraq.com; internet www.aic-iraq.com; f. 2001; privately owned; general, marine, engineering, motor, health and life insurance; Chair. SAADOUN KUBBA; Gen. Man. SAADOUN M. KHAMIS AL-RUBAI.

Al-Hamra'a Insurance Co: POB 10491, Karrada, Baghdad; tel. (1) 717-7573; fax (1) 717-7574; e-mail info@alhamraains.com; internet www.alhamraains.com; f. 2001; private co; general and life insurance; CEO Dr YASIR RAOOF.

Iraq Insurance Co: POB 989, Khaled bin al-Walid St, Aqaba bin Nafi Sq., Baghdad; tel. (1) 719-2185; fax (1) 719-2606; state-owned; life, fire, accident and marine insurance.

Iraq Reinsurance Co: POB 297, Aqaba bin Nafi Sq., Khalid bin al-Waleed St, Baghdad; tel. (1) 719-5131; fax (1) 719-1497; e-mail iraqre@yahoo.com; f. 1960; state-owned; transacts reinsurance business on the international market; Chair. and Gen. Man. SAID ABBAS M. A. MIRZA.

National Insurance Co: POB 248, National Insurance Co Bldg, al-Khullani St, Baghdad; tel. (1) 885-3026; fax (1) 886-1486; f. 1950; state-owned; cap. 20m.; all types of general and life insurance, reinsurance and investment; Chair. and Gen. Man. MUHAMMAD HUSSAIN JAAFAR ABBAS.

STOCK EXCHANGE

Iraq Stock Exchange (ISX): Baghdad; tel. 7711211522 (mobile); e-mail info-isx@isx-iq.net; internet www.isx-iq.net; f. 2004, following the closure of the fmr Baghdad Stock Exchange by the Coalition Provisional Authority in March 2003; 84 cos listed in Oct. 2013; CEO TAHA AHMAD ABD AL-SALAM.

Trade and Industry

DEVELOPMENT ORGANIZATION

Iraq Foreign Investment Board: e-mail info@ishtargate.org; internet www.ishtargate.org; seeks to attract inward private sector investment into Iraq and to stimulate domestic capital resources for growth and innovation, as well as promote Iraqi businesses; Senior Advisor WILLIAM C. DAHM.

CHAMBERS OF COMMERCE

Federation of Iraqi Chambers of Commerce: POB 3388, Saadoun St, Alwiya, Baghdad; tel. (1) 717-1798; fax (1) 719-2479; e-mail ficcbaghdad@yahoo.com; internet www.ficciraqbag.org; f. 1969; all 18 Iraqi chambers of commerce are affiliated to the Federation; Chair. JAAFAR AL-HAMADANI.

Arbil Chamber of Commerce and Industry: Chamber of Commerce and Industry Bldg, Aras St, Arbil; tel. (66) 2222014; e-mail erbilchamberofcommerce@yahoo.com; internet www.erbilchamber.org; f. 1966; Chair. Dara Jalil Khayat.

Baghdad Chamber of Commerce: POB 5015, al-Sanal, Baghdad; tel. (1) 880-220; fax (1) 816-3347; e-mail baghdad_chamber@yahoo.com; internet www.baghdadchamber.com; f. 1926; Chair. Amjad Abd al-Karim al-Juburi.

Basra Chamber of Commerce: Manawi Pasha, Ashar, Basra; tel. (40) 614630; e-mail info@bcoc-iraq.net; internet www.bcoc-iraq.net; f. 1926; Chair. Makki Hassan Hamadi al-Sudani.

Kirkuk Chamber of Commerce: Kirkuk; e-mail kirkukchamber@yahoo.com; f. 1957; Chair. Sabah al-Din Muhammad al-Salihi.

Mosul Chamber of Commerce: POB 35, Mosul; tel. (60) 774771; fax (60) 771359; e-mail mcc19262000@yahoo.com; Chair. Mukbil Sidiq al-Dabagh.

Sulaimaniya Chamber of Commerce and Industry: Sulaimaniya; e-mail info@sulcci.com; internet www.sulcci.com; Chair. Hassan Baqi Horami.

EMPLOYERS' ORGANIZATION

Iraqi Federation of Industries: 191/22/915 al-Zaweya, Karada, Baghdad; tel. (1) 778-3502; fax (1) 776-3041; e-mail info@fediraq.org; internet www.fediraq.org; f. 1956; 35,000 mems; Pres. Hashim Thanoun al-Atrakchi.

PETROLEUM AND GAS

Ministry of Oil: Oil Complex Bldg, Port Said St, Baghdad; tel. (1) 727-0710; e-mail oilministry@oil.gov.iq; internet www.oil.gov.iq; merged with INOC in 1987; affiliated cos: Oil Marketing Co, Oil Projects Co, Oil Exploration Co, Oil Products Distribution Co, Iraqi Oil Tankers Co, Gas Filling Co, Oil Pipelines Co, Iraqi Drilling Co, North Oil Co, South Oil Co, Missan Oil Co, North Refineries Co, Midland Refineries Co, South Refineries Co, North Gas Co, South Gas Co.

Iraq National Oil Co (INOC): POB 476, Khullani Sq., Baghdad; tel. (1) 887-1115; f. 1964; reorg. upon nationalization of Iraq's petroleum industry, and became solely responsible for exploration, production, transportation and marketing of Iraqi crude petroleum and petroleum products; merged with Ministry of Oil in 1987, and remained under its authority following the overthrow of the regime of Saddam Hussain in 2003; draft legislation providing for the reconstitution of INOC as an independent entity was approved by the Council of Ministers in July 2009; under the proposed reorganization, INOC would be responsible for the management and development of Iraq's petroleum industry and would assume control of the existing state-run oil and gas cos.

UTILITIES

Electricity

Electricity production in Iraq has been greatly diminished as a result of the US-led military campaign in 2003, subsequent looting and sabotage by Baathist loyalists, and disruptions in fuel supplies to power stations. Power outages are common, especially in Baghdad and the surrounding area, and the Government has resorted to power-rationing. With ongoing reconstruction of the means of generation, transmission and distribution, the Ministry of Electricity was achieving peak production levels of 6,750 MW by early 2009, supplying intermittent power for only 14 hours a day.

Water

The Ministry of Water Resources manages the supply of water throughout Iraq. Water resources are diminishing, and a large-scale investment programme is currently under way, which includes funding for new dam and irrigation projects, repairs to damaged facilities, and improvements in technology. Following years of neglect during the period of UN sanctions, infrastructure has also been damaged since the US-led military campaign in 2003, largely as a result of vandalism and looting. The Baghdad Water Authority is responsible for the management of water resources in the capital.

TRADE UNIONS

General Federation of Iraqi Workers (GFIW): POB 3049, Tahrir Sq., al-Rashid St, Baghdad; fax (1) 670-4200; e-mail abdullahmuhsin@iraqitradeunions.org; internet www.iraqitradeunions.org; f. 2005 by merger of Gen. Fed. of Trade Unions, Gen. Fed. of Trade Unions of Iraq (an offshoot of the former) and Iraqi Fed. of Workers' Trade Unions; covers all of Iraq's provinces except the three Kurdish Autonomous Regions; Pres. Ali Raheem Ali; Vice-Pres. Hadi Ali Lafta.

There are also unions of doctors, pharmacologists, jurists, writers, journalists, artists, engineers, electricity and railway workers.

Transport

RAILWAYS

In 2010 the total length of Iraqi railways was 2,025 route-km. A line covers the length of the country, from Rabia, on the Syrian border, via Mosul, to Baghdad (534 km), and from Baghdad to Basra and Umm Qasr (608 km), on the Persian (Arabian) Gulf. A 404-km line links Baghdad, via Radi and Haditha, to Husaibah, near the Iraqi–Syrian frontier. Baghdad is linked with Arbil, via Khanaqin and Kirkuk, and a 252-km line (designed to serve industrial projects along its route) runs from Kirkuk to Haditha, via Baiji (though this was rendered out of action in mid-2006, as a result of bombing by US forces). A 638-km line runs from Baghdad, via al-Qaim (on the Syrian border), to Akashat (with a 150-km line linking the Akashat phosphate mines and the fertilizer complex at al-Qaim). A regular international service between Baghdad and İstanbul, Turkey, was suspended following the US-led invasion in 2003; however, services on a section of the line, between Mosul and Gaziantep, resumed in early 2010. Passenger rail services between Mosul and Aleppo, Syria, resumed in August 2000 after an interruption of almost 20 years, but were closed again in 2004 after repeated insurgent attacks. Passenger rail services between Baghdad and Basra resumed in late 2007, and a Baghdad–Ramadi passenger service recommenced in May 2009. The railway system was due to be repaired and upgraded as part of the reconstruction of Iraq following the removal from power of Saddam Hussain's regime in 2003. Eventually, it was planned that the system would be divided, with the infrastructure being kept as a state asset, while operations were to be privatized. It was reported in 2006 that the Ministry of Transportation hoped to add an additional 2,300 km to the existing rail network, although concerns remained over funding. In May 2010 the Government announced that it had invited bids from eight short-listed foreign consortia for the contract to construct a 25-km, two-line metro system in Baghdad; the French company Alstom signed a memorandum of understanding to undertake the project in January 2011.

General Co for Railways: Ministry of Transportation, nr Martyr's Monument, Karradat Dakhil, Baghdad; e-mail iraqitransport@yahoo.com; internet www.scr.gov.iq.

Iraqi Republic Railways Co (IRRC): West Station, Baghdad; tel. (1) 537-0011; e-mail d1_g_office@iraqrailways.com; internet www.iraqrailways.com; f. 1914; Dir-Gen. Rafil Yussef Abbas.

ROADS

In 2010, according to estimates by the International Road Federation, Iraq's road network extended over 41,716 km, of which 1,006 km were highways, main or national roads, and 29,420 km were secondary or regional roads.

The most important roads are: Baghdad–Mosul–Tel Kotchuk (Syrian border), 521 km; Baghdad–Kirkuk–Arbil–Mosul–Zakho (border with Turkey), 544 km; Kirkuk–Sulaimaniya, 160 km; Baghdad–Hilla–Diwaniya–Nasiriya–Basra, 586 km; Baghdad–Kut–Nasiriya, 186 km; Baghdad–Ramadi–Rurba (border with Syria), 555 km; Baghdad–Kut–Umara–Basra–Safwan (border with Kuwait), 660 km; and Baghdad–Baqaba–Kanikien (border with Iran). Most sections of the six-lane, 1,264-km international Express Highway, linking Safwan (on the Kuwaiti border) with the Jordanian and Syrian borders, had been completed by June 1990. Studies have been completed for a second, 525-km Express Highway, linking Baghdad and Zakho on the Turkish border. A complex network of roads was constructed behind the war front with Iran in order to facilitate the movement of troops and supplies during the 1980–88 conflict. The road network was included in the US-led coalition's programme of reconstruction following the ousting of the Baathist regime in 2003.

Iraqi Land Transport Co: Baghdad; internet sclt.gov.iq; f. 1988 to replace State Org. for Land Transport; fleet of more than 1,000 large trucks; Dir-Gen. Aysar al-Safi.

State Organization for Roads and Bridges: POB 917, Karradat Mariam, Karkh, Baghdad; tel. (1) 32141; responsible for road and bridge construction projects under the Ministry of Construction and Housing.

SHIPPING

The ports of Basra and Umm Qasr are usually the commercial gateway of Iraq. They are connected by various ocean routes with all parts of the world, and constitute the natural distribution centre for overseas supplies. The Iraqi State Enterprise for Maritime Transport maintains a regular service between Basra, the Persian (Arabian) Gulf and north European ports. There is also a port at Khor al-Zubair, which came into use in 1979.

For the inland waterways, there are 1,036 registered river craft, 48 motor vessels and 105 motorboats.

The port at Umm Qasr was heavily damaged during the early part of the US-led coalition's campaign to oust Saddam Hussain. A large-scale project to redevelop the port is under way. In July 2009 contracts to lease and develop new commercial berths at Umm Qasr were awarded to two foreign port operators. In February 2011 the UAE-based firm Gulftainer signed a US $150m. contract to construct and operate a dry port north of Umm Qasr. In August 2012 16 bids were received for the first phase in the construction of a new deep-sea port at Faw in Basra province. It was anticipated that the new $6,300m. facility would, upon completion, replace Umm Qasr as Iraq's main commercial port.

At 31 December 2013 Iraq's flag registered fleet totalled 83 vessels, with an aggregate displacement of 149,460 grt, of which two were fish carriers and six were general cargo ships.

Port and Regulatory Authorities

General Co of Iraqi Ports (IPA): Malik bin Dinar St, Basra; tel. (40) 041-3211; e-mail anmarbasrah@gmail.dom; internet scp.gov.iq; Dir-Gen. SALEH QADIR ABOUD.

State Enterprise for Iraqi Water Transport: POB 23016, Airport St, al-Furat Quarter, Baghdad; f. 1987, when State Org. for Iraqi Water Transport was abolished; responsible for the planning, supervision and control of six nat. water transportation enterprises, incl. General Co for Maritime Transport (see below).

Principal Shipping Companies

Arab Bridge Maritime Navigation Co: Aqaba, Jordan; tel. (3) 2092000; fax (3) 2092001; internet www.abmaritime.com.jo; f. 1987; jt venture by Egypt, Iraq and Jordan to improve economic co-operation; an expansion of the co established a ferry link between the ports of Aqaba, Jordan, and Nuweibeh, Egypt, in 1985; six vessels; cap. US $75m. (2010); Chair. Eng. OSAMA MUHAMMAD AL-SADER; Vice-Chairs. MOHANNAD SALMAN AL-QDAH, HISHAM OMAR AL-SARSAWI; Man. Dir HUSSEIN AL-SOUOB.

General Co for Maritime Transport: POB 13038, al-Jadriya al-Hurriya Ave, Baghdad; Basra office: POB 766, 14 July St, Basra; tel. (1) 776-3201; e-mail watertrans@motrans.gov.iq; internet scmt.gov.iq; f. 1952 as State Enterprise for Maritime Transport; renamed as above 2009; Dir-Gen. SAMIR ABD AL-RAZZAQ.

Gulf Shipping Co: POB 471, Basra; tel. (40) 776-1945; fax (40) 776-0715; f. 1988; imports and exports goods to and from Iraq.

Al-Masar al-Iraqi Co LLC: Manawi Pasha St, nr Manawi Pasha Hotel, POB 85885, Basra; tel. 7704926113 (mobile); e-mail operation@iraqilogistic.com; internet www.iraqilogistic.com; provides a range of freight and shipping agency services.

CIVIL AVIATION

There are international airports at Baghdad, Basra and Mosul. Baghdad's airport, previously named Saddam International Airport, reopened in August 2000, after refurbishment necessitated by damage sustained during the war with the multinational force in 1991. However, international air links were virtually halted by the UN embargo imposed in 1990. Internal flights, connecting Baghdad to Basra and Mosul, recommenced in November 2000. In April 2003 the capital's airport was renamed Baghdad International Airport by US forces during their military campaign to oust the regime of Saddam Hussain. Following a programme of reconstruction, the airports at Baghdad and Basra were reopened to commercial flights from late 2003; Mosul International Airport reopened for civilian flights in December 2007. The expansion of Arbil International Airport (including the construction of a new passenger terminal and runway) was completed in mid-2010. In July 2008 Al-Hamza airport in Najaf (formerly a military airport) was inaugurated for civilian use, as increasing numbers of pilgrims were visiting the shrines of that holy city. Construction work on a new airport in Karbala, with a projected annual capacity of 30m. passengers, commenced in March 2010.

Iraq Civil Aviation Authority (ICAA): Baghdad; tel. 7901 448827 (mobile); fax (1) 543-0764; e-mail info@iraqcaa.com; internet www.iraqcaa.com; f. 1987; Dir-Gen. Capt. NASER HUSSEIN BANDAR.

Iraqi Airways Co: Baghdad International Airport, Baghdad; tel. (1) 537-2002; e-mail info@iraqiairways.co.uk; internet www.iraqiairways.co.uk; f. 1945; operates flights to other Arab countries, Iran, Turkey, Greece and Sweden; Dir-Gen. Capt. KIFAH HUSSEIN JABBAR.

Tourism

Arrivals of foreign nationals totalled 1.5m. in 2010; tourist receipts in 2011 were estimated at US $1,544m. Following the US-led invasion of Iraq in 2003, the site housing the ruins of the ancient civilization of Babylon became part of a US military base; several other places of interest became military or refugee camps, and, amid the protracted period of conflict since 2003, tourists have been deterred from visiting the country's many cultural and religious sites. Nevertheless, in August 2006 the relatively peaceful Kurdish Autonomous Region launched a tourism campaign, with advertisements broadcast on US television. Since 2008 religious tourism has been growing, with increasing numbers of pilgrims using the newly renovated airport in Najaf (see Transport) to visit the Islamic holy shrines of both that city and nearby Karbala.

Iraq Tourism Board: POB 7783, Haifa St, Baghdad; tel. (1) 543-3912; Chair. HAMOUD MOHSEN AL-YACOUBI.

Defence

The US-led Coalition Provisional Authority (CPA) dissolved Iraq's armed forces and security organizations in place under Saddam Hussain in May 2003, following the ousting of the regime in the previous month. In August the CPA promulgated the establishment of the New Iraqi Army.

Chief of Staff of the Joint Armed Forces: Lt-Gen. BABAKIR SHAWKAT ZEBARI.

Commander of the Ground Forces: Lt-Gen. ALI GHAIDAN.

Commander of the Air Force: Lt-Gen. ANWAR HAMAD AMIN AHMAD.

Commander of the Navy: Rear Adm. ALI HUSSEIN ALI.

Defence Budget (2013): ID 19,700,000m.

Total Armed Forces (as assessed at November 2013): 271,400: army 193,400; navy 3,600; air force 5,050; plus 69,350 support. In addition, there were 531,000 Ministry of the Interior Forces, including 302,000 members of the Iraqi Police Service, 44,000 members of the Iraqi Federal police, 95,000 members of the Facilities Protection Service, 60,000 members of the Border Enforcement forces and 30,000 members of the Oil Police.

Education

After the establishment of the Republic in 1958, there was a marked expansion in education at all levels, and spending on education increased substantially. During the mid-1970s free education was established at all stages from pre-primary to higher, and private education was abolished; all existing private schools were transformed into state schools. However, military conflict and economic sanctions during the 1980s and 1990s undermined much of the progress made in education during the previous two decades. Primary education, beginning at six years of age, lasts for six years. Enrolment at primary schools of children in the relevant age-group had declined to 76% by 1995, but reportedly rose again, to 91%, in 2000/01. According to UNESCO estimates, in 2006/07 enrolment at primary schools included 88% of pupils in the relevant age-group. Secondary education, from 12 years of age and lasting for up to six years, is divided into two cycles of three years each. Enrolment at secondary schools in 2006/07 included some 43% of children in the appropriate age-group, according to UNESCO. Following the change of regime in Iraq in April 2003, a comprehensive reform of the country's education system was implemented. In the 2011/12 academic year there were estimated to be 20,715 primary and secondary schools in Iraq, with a total enrolment of 7,335,678 pupils. There are 43 technical institutes and colleges, two postgraduate commissions and 20 universities. In 2002/03 there were approximately 240,000 undergraduates attending institutions of higher education. In 2010 government expenditure on education amounted to US $4,310m., equivalent to 6.0% of total government spending.

IRELAND

Introductory Survey

LOCATION, CLIMATE, LANGUAGE, RELIGION, FLAG, CAPITAL

Ireland consists of 26 of the 32 historic counties that comprise the island of Ireland. The remaining six counties, in the north-east, form Northern Ireland, which is part of the United Kingdom. Ireland lies in the Atlantic Ocean, about 80 km (50 miles) west of Great Britain. The climate is mild and equable, with temperatures generally between 0°C (32°F) and 21°C (70°F). Irish (Gaeilge) is the official first language, but its use as a vernacular is now restricted to certain areas, collectively known as the Gaeltacht, mainly in the west of Ireland. English is the second official language and is almost universally spoken. The majority of the inhabitants profess Christianity: about 84% of the population are Roman Catholics. The national flag (proportions 1 by 2) consists of three equal vertical stripes, of green, white and orange. The capital is Dublin.

CONTEMPORARY POLITICAL HISTORY

Historical Context

The whole of Ireland was formerly part of the United Kingdom. In 1920 the island was partitioned, the six north-eastern counties remaining part of the United Kingdom, with their own government. In 1922 the 26 southern counties achieved dominion status, under the British Crown, as the Irish Free State. The dissolution of all remaining links with Great Britain culminated in 1937 in the adoption of a new Constitution, which gave the Irish Free State full sovereignty within the Commonwealth. Formal ties with the Commonwealth were ended in 1949, when the 26 southern counties became a republic. The partition of Ireland remained a contentious issue, and in 1969 a clandestine organization, calling itself the Provisional Irish Republican Army (IRA—see United Kingdom), initiated a violent campaign to achieve reunification.

Domestic Political Affairs

In the general election of February 1973, the Fianna Fáil party, which had held office, with only two interruptions, since 1932, was defeated. Jack Lynch, who had been Prime Minister (Taoiseach) since 1966, resigned, and Liam Cosgrave formed a coalition between his own party, Fine Gael, and the Labour Party. The Irish Government remained committed to power-sharing in the six counties, but opposed any British military withdrawal from Northern Ireland. Following the assassination of the British Ambassador to Ireland by the Provisional IRA in July 1976, the Irish Government introduced stronger measures against terrorism. Fianna Fáil won the general election of June 1977 and Lynch again became Prime Minister. Following his resignation in December 1979, he was succeeded by Charles Haughey. In June 1981, following an early general election, Dr Garret FitzGerald of Fine Gael became Prime Minister in a coalition of Fine Gael and the Labour Party. However, the rejection by the Dáil (the lower house of the legislature) of the coalition's budget proposals precipitated a further general election in February 1982, in which Haughey was returned to power. The worsening economic situation, however, made the Fianna Fáil Government increasingly unpopular, and in November Haughey lost the support of two independent members of the Dáil, precipitating an early general election, at which Fianna Fáil failed to gain an overall majority. In December FitzGerald formed a new Fine Gael-Labour Party coalition.

During 1986 FitzGerald's coalition lost support, partly due to the formation of a new party, the Progressive Democrats (PD), by disaffected members of Fianna Fáil. In June a government proposal to end a constitutional ban on divorce was defeated by national referendum. Shortly afterwards, as a result of a series of defections, the coalition lost its parliamentary majority. In January 1987 the Labour Party refused to support Fine Gael's budget proposals and the coalition collapsed. Following a general election in February, Fianna Fáil, led by Haughey, formed a minority Government.

Prior to the general election of June 1989 Fine Gael and the PD concluded an electoral pact to oppose Fianna Fáil. Although the Haughey administration had achieved significant economic improvements, severe reductions in public expenditure and continuing problems of unemployment and emigration adversely affected Fianna Fáil's electoral support, and it obtained only 77 of the 166 seats in the Dáil, while Fine Gael won 55 seats and the PD six seats. Following nearly four weeks of negotiations, a Fianna Fáil-PD coalition Government, led by Haughey, was formed.

In October 1991 the Government narrowly defeated a motion of no confidence, which had been introduced following a series of financial scandals involving public officials. In November, however, a group of Fianna Fáil members of the Dáil proposed a motion demanding Haughey's removal as leader of the party. Albert Reynolds, the Minister for Finance and a former close associate of Haughey, and Pádraig Flynn, the Minister for the Environment, announced their intention to support the motion, and were immediately dismissed from office. The attempt to depose Haughey was defeated by a substantial majority of the Fianna Fáil parliamentary grouping.

In January 1992 allegations arose that, contrary to his previous denials, Haughey had been aware of the secret monitoring, in 1982, of the telephone conversations of two journalists perceived to be critical of the Government. The PD made their continued support of the Government conditional on Haughey's resignation. In February 1992 Reynolds replaced Haughey as leader of Fianna Fáil and assumed the premiership.

In June 1992 the leader of the PD, Desmond O'Malley, criticized Reynolds' conduct as Minister for Industry and Commerce before a parliamentary inquiry into allegations of fraud and political favouritism during 1987–88. In October 1992, in his testimony to the inquiry, the Prime Minister accused O'Malley of dishonesty. Following Reynolds' refusal to withdraw the allegations, in early November the PD left the coalition, and the Government was defeated on the following day in a motion of no confidence. A general election took place in November, concurrent with three constitutional referendums on abortion. Fianna Fáil and Fine Gael both suffered a substantial loss of support, while the Labour Party more than doubled its number of seats; the PD also increased its representation. Following prolonged negotiations, in January 1993 Fianna Fáil and the Labour Party agreed to form a coalition Government. Reynolds retained the premiership, while Dick Spring, the leader of the Labour Party, was allocated the foreign affairs portfolio, as well as the post of Deputy Prime Minister (Tánaiste).

In November 1994 the Labour Party withdrew from the coalition after Reynolds and the Fianna Fáil members of the Cabinet approved the appointment of the Attorney-General, Harry Whelehan, to the High Court, in the absence of the Labour Party ministers, who had opposed Whelehan's nomination. Reynolds, while remaining as Prime Minister of a 'caretaker' Government, relinquished the Fianna Fáil leadership and was succeeded by the Minister for Finance, Bertie Ahern. Whelehan, meanwhile, resigned as President of the High Court. Following extensive talks, a new coalition of Fine Gael, the Labour Party and a small party, the Democratic Left, took office in December. The leader of Fine Gael, John Bruton, became Prime Minister, while Spring regained the role of Deputy Prime Minister and Minister for Foreign Affairs.

In November 1996 the Minister for Transport, Energy and Communications, Michael Lowry, resigned following allegations that he had received personal financial gifts from a business executive, Ben Dunne. During 1997 an inquiry into other political donations by Dunne revealed that payments totalling some IR£1.3m. had been made to Haughey during his premiership. Haughey later admitted the allegations, although he insisted that he had no knowledge of the donations until he resigned from office.

The Government of Bertie Ahern

At a general election held in June 1997 none of the main political parties secured an overall majority in the Dáil. Sinn Féin (the political wing of the IRA) won its first seat in the Dáil at the election. After Bruton conceded that he could not form a majority coalition administration, Ahern formed a Government composed of Fianna Fáil and the PD. The leader of the PD, Mary Harney, was appointed Deputy Prime Minister. In September the President, Mary Robinson, who had been elected in November 1990 as an independent candidate, resigned from her position in order to assume her new functions as the United Nations High Commissioner for Human Rights. In the ensuing election, conducted on 30 October 1997, the Fianna Fáil candidate, Dr Mary McAleese, was elected President (the country's first head of state from Northern Ireland), receiving 45.2% of the first-preference votes cast.

During 2000 independent judicial inquiries investigating corruption among politicians implicated many senior political figures. In April an inquiry into planning irregularities in County Dublin in the early 1990s, headed by Justice Feargus Flood, was told that the Fine Gael leader, Bruton, was aware that a member of his party had demanded payment for voting in favour of a planning decision, and had himself benefited from the decision. Despite his denials, in January 2001 Fine Gael members of the Dáil passed a motion of no confidence in Bruton, who resigned as party leader with immediate effect. He was replaced by Michael Noonan, a former Minister for Health and Children. In March 2001 investigations by the Flood tribunal revealed that Ray Burke, who had resigned as Minister for Foreign Affairs in October 1997, had held money in 'offshore' accounts during the 1980s while a minister, and had conducted international financial transactions without first requesting permission from the Central Bank (as the law stipulated). He also admitted to misleading the Dáil regarding his financial affairs. In September 2002 Justice Flood reported that Burke had received several 'corrupt payments' between 1974 and 1989. Ahern came under intense political pressure regarding his appointment of Burke as Minister for Foreign Affairs. Justice Alan Mahon replaced Flood as chairman of the Tribunal in June 2003. In December Burke was formally charged with making false tax returns, and in January 2005 he was sentenced to six months' imprisonment.

Meanwhile, a new tribunal chaired by Justice Michael Moriarty was established to investigate further payments made to politicians and the sources of specific offshore bank accounts that had been used by Haughey. In May 2000 the tribunal heard that between 1979 and 1996 Haughey had received payments totalling IR£8.5m., a much larger figure than had previously been acknowledged. In March 2003 Haughey agreed to pay the Revenue Commissioners €5m. in settlement of his outstanding tax liabilities resulting from undisclosed payments made to him. Haughey died in June 2006. In December a report by Justice Moriarty stated that, between 1979 and 1996, funds totalling IR£9.1m. had been made available for Haughey's personal use.

In June 2001 a referendum was held on the ratification of the Treaty of Nice, which proposed structural reforms to the institutions of the European Union (EU, see p. 273) prior to the enlargement of the Union from 2004. The endorsement of the treaty was rejected by 53.9% of those who voted, an embarrassing reverse for the Government, which had campaigned in favour of the treaty. The voter participation rate was only 34.8%. The defeat was attributed to fears that ratification of the treaty would result in Irish participation in the EU's proposed rapid reaction force, thus undermining Ireland's neutrality, and concerns that Ireland would receive reduced funding and assistance from the EU. The Government suffered a further reverse when, at a referendum on abortion held in early March 2002, 50.4% of the electorate voted against proposed changes, which would have removed the constitutional protection accorded by the Supreme Court to the lives of suicidal pregnant women wishing to terminate their pregnancies, and would have made abortion a criminal offence.

The elections of 2002 and 2007

At the general election in May 2002 Fianna Fáil increased its parliamentary representation to 81 seats, and thus only narrowly failed to achieve an overall majority in the Dáil. Fine Gael suffered a significant loss of support, winning just 31 seats. The PD and Sinn Féin increased their representation to eight seats and five seats, respectively, while the ecologist Green Party obtained six seats. Noonan resigned as leader of Fine Gael and was succeeded by Enda Kenny. In the same month Fianna Fáil and the PD concluded a new coalition agreement, following which Ahern was duly re-elected Prime Minister, with Harney continuing as his deputy.

In June 2002 the Government won support at an EU summit meeting for a declaration that formally stated that Ireland's participation in the EU rapid reaction force would be limited to those operations with a UN mandate, approved by the Government and sanctioned by the Dáil. For their part, Ireland's EU partners issued a complementary declaration reiterating that neither the Treaty of Nice nor previous EU treaties compromised Ireland's traditional neutrality and that no member state envisaged the rapid reaction force as a future European army. In September the Irish Government announced that a second constitutional referendum which, as well as providing for the final ratification of the Treaty of Nice, would now explicitly prohibit Irish participation in any future common European defence force, would take place on 19 October. At the referendum, 62.9% of those who voted approved the treaty's ratification, with voter turnout recorded at 49.5%.

At a referendum held in June 2004 a constitutional amendment removing the automatic entitlement to Irish citizenship of children born in Ireland (including Northern Ireland) was approved by 79.2% of voters. The plebiscite followed a ruling issued in January 2003 by the Irish Supreme Court, which declared that non-national parents of Irish-born children were not entitled to live in Ireland by virtue of having an Irish-born child. The Government had endorsed the amendment, citing the need to deter immigrants from exploiting Irish law to gain entitlement to residency in any EU member state. Ireland was the only EU country with an automatic right to citizenship at birth, which had been enshrined in the Constitution in 1999 as a consequence of the Good Friday Agreement for peace in Northern Ireland (see The peace process in Northern Ireland). In October 2004, as the sole nominee for the post, McAleese was deemed to be re-elected as President.

At the general election held on 24 May 2007 Fianna Fáil remained the largest party in the Dáil, with its representation declining slightly, to 78 seats. Fine Gael increased its representation substantially, to 51 seats, while the Labour Party won 20 seats and the Green Party six. Sinn Féin's representation declined from five to four seats, and that of the PD from eight seats to only two. Having failed to win re-election, John McDowell—who had replaced Harney as leader of the PD and Deputy Prime Minister in September 2006—was obliged (by the terms of the PD's Constitution) to resign as party leader. He was replaced, initially in an interim capacity, by Harney. In June 2007 a coalition agreement was signed between Fianna Fáil, the PD and (despite an undertaking before the election by the party leader, Trevor Sargent, not to join an administration with Fianna Fáil) the Green Party; Sargent subsequently resigned as party leader. A new Government was formed, again headed by Ahern, and in which many senior appointments in the outgoing administration remained unchanged. Brian Cowen retained the post of Minister for Finance, to which he had been appointed in September 2004, and was concurrently designated Deputy Prime Minister. Harney was reappointed as Minister for Health and Children, as the sole PD minister, while two ministers from the Green Party were appointed: John Gormley as Minister for the Environment, Heritage and Local Government; and Eamon Ryan as Minister for Communications, Energy and Natural Resources. The only new minister appointed from Fianna Fáil was Brian Lenihan, as Minister for Justice, Equality and Law Reform. Three of the five independent members of the Dáil also agreed to support the new coalition.

In July 2007 Gormley was elected as leader of the Green Party. In September Eamon Gilmore was elected as leader of the Labour Party, succeeding Pat Rabbitte, who had resigned in August. On 25 September a vote of no confidence in Ahern, brought by Fine Gael and the Labour Party in response to concerns about the veracity of evidence he had presented to the Mahon tribunal, concerning his personal finances, was defeated. (From September 2006 the tribunal had investigated allegations that, during his period of office as Minister for Finance between 1991 and 1993, Ahern had granted favours in return for loans or donations.) In January 2008 Kenny and Gilmore, as leaders of the two principal opposition parties, both demanded Ahern's resignation as Prime Minister.

The Government of Brian Cowen

In early April 2008 Ahern announced that he was to resign from the positions of Prime Minister and leader of Fianna Fáil with effect from 6 May. On 9 April the Deputy Prime Minister and Minister for Finance, Brian Cowen, was elected unopposed to succeed Ahern as leader of Fianna Fáil; he was duly elected as Prime Minister by the Dáil on 7 May. Cowen reorganized the Cabinet, reallocating those posts held by members of Fianna Fáil. Mary Coughlan (previously Minister for Agriculture, Fisheries and Food) was appointed Deputy Prime Minister and Minister for Enterprise, Trade and Employment, while Brian

Lenihan succeeded Cowen as Minister for Finance. Micheál Martin became Minister for Foreign Affairs, replacing Dermot Ahern, who assumed the role of Minister for Justice, Equality and Law Reform.

On 12 June 2008 a referendum was held on the ratification of the Treaty of Lisbon, which sought to reform the institutions of the EU and was intended to supersede the defunct EU constitutional treaty. Despite a campaign in favour of ratification led by Cowen, with the support of all the principal political parties except Sinn Féin, the treaty was rejected by 53.4% of those who voted. The result was attributed to the low rate of participation (53.1% of the electorate), widespread public uncertainty about the implications of the treaty, and concerns that it might compromise Ireland's neutrality or affect its policies on taxation or ethical issues such as abortion.

In November 2008 the PD voted at its conference to dissolve the party, after the leadership argued that it had no viable future. The PD, which had espoused many controversial liberal policies, on issues such as divorce and contraception, was formally disbanded in November 2009. The sole PD member of the Cabinet, Harney, declined to join any other party and retained her ministerial position as an independent.

During 2008 it became clear that the economic prosperity enjoyed by Ireland over the previous decade was coming to an end. Affected by the international credit crisis and the economic decline that was being experienced throughout much of the developed world, the Irish economy moved into recession, the first country in the eurozone to do so. Property prices, which had increased dramatically during the decade to 2006, when Irish banks made large loans to developers and builders for speculative projects, now declined rapidly. In September 2008 the Government announced that it would guarantee the deposits in six banks and building societies. In January 2009 it was obliged to nationalize Anglo Irish Bank (which had specialized in large-scale lending for property development) in order to maintain market confidence, and in February it agreed to provide new capital for Allied Irish Banks and the Bank of Ireland. In April the Government announced the establishment of a National Asset Management Agency (NAMA), which would purchase non-performing loans at a discount. Meanwhile, unpopular austerity measures were announced in October 2008 as part of the budget for 2009. In February 2009, despite failing to reach an agreement with the Irish Congress of Trade Unions, the Government announced further austerity measures, including a pension levy on the wages of public sector workers. Public disapproval of the Government's response to the economic crisis continued to increase, and Fianna Fáil and the Green Party both suffered heavy losses in local elections held in June, while Fine Gael performed strongly, becoming the largest party in local government.

In June 2009 Cowen announced that a second referendum on the Treaty of Lisbon would be held in October. The European Council had agreed on a document intended to address Irish concerns over the treaty, including formal guarantees, which were to be given force of law by their incorporation into the next EU accession treaty, to the effect that the Treaty of Lisbon would in no way affect any member state's neutrality or its competencies in relation to taxation or family law. At the referendum, which was held on 2 October, ratification of the treaty was approved by 67.1% of voters, with 59.0% of the electorate participating. It was believed that the economic crisis contributed to the strong increase in support for the treaty since June 2008 by strengthening popular enthusiasm for EU membership.

In October 2009 the Chairman (Ceann Comhairle) of the Dáil, John O'Donoghue of Fianna Fáil, was forced to resign as a result of pressure from the opposition parties over his extravagant official expenses. Séumas Kirk, also of Fianna Fáil, was elected to replace him. The incident represented a further loss of authority for the Government, which in August 2009 had lost its official majority in the Dáil after two Fianna Fáil members resigned from the parliamentary party in protest at the closure of a hospital unit in their constituency. Public disaffection with the Government was manifested in November in a strike by some 250,000 public sector workers protesting against proposed pay reductions and other austerity measures. The Government was weakened further in February 2010 by the resignation of Willie O'Dea, the Minister for Defence, and Trevor Sargent, a Minister of State and the former leader of the Green Party, over improprieties. In March Cowen carried out a government reorganization, in which O'Dea was replaced by Tony Killeen, among other changes.

Financial assistance from the EU and the IMF

During 2010 hopes of an economic recovery proved premature: levels of unemployment, and also of emigration, remained high, and the enormous cost to taxpayers of alleviating the banking crisis, necessitating substantial reductions in other budgetary spending, caused considerable resentment. In September fresh assistance for Allied Irish Banks, Anglo Irish Bank and the Irish Nationwide Building Society brought the total cost of supporting the financial system to at least €45,000m.; in addition, Irish banks owed some €130,000m. to the European Central Bank. By October the total budgetary deficit for 2010, including support for the banks, was estimated to be equivalent to 32% of gross domestic product (GDP—compared with the limit of 3% required by the EU). Meanwhile, the cost to Ireland of borrowing on the international bond markets increased as a result of uncertainty over the country's financial stability. The Minister for Finance, Lenihan, insisted that the programme of support for the banks was now complete and that the cost was manageable, that a four-year austerity programme would restore the budgetary deficit to acceptable levels, and that Ireland was not about to default on its debts. Nevertheless, under pressure from other EU governments, anxious to ensure the stability of the euro, in late November 2010 the Irish Government finally made a formal application for financial assistance from the EU and the IMF, and announced that agreement had been reached on the provision of financial support totalling €85,000m. from the EU and the IMF, as well as from the United Kingdom, Sweden and Denmark in the form of bilateral loans. Of this total, Ireland itself was to provide €17,500m. from its National Pension Reserve Fund and from cash reserves. The assistance was conditional upon a reorganization of the banking system, intensifying measures already adopted, and upon the four-year budgetary adjustment programme that had already been proposed by the Government, aiming to save €15,000m. over the period and to reduce the budgetary deficit to less than 3% of GDP by 2015. As part of this programme, the Government's proposed budget for 2011 envisaged savings of €6,000m. for that year alone, with reductions in welfare and other spending, in public sector pensions and in the minimum wage, together with tax increases and the introduction of taxation for the lower-paid. The 'bailout' agreement was widely perceived as a national humiliation and as imposing an unfair burden on the least well-off.

The 2011 general election

In November 2010 the Green Party, deploring the proposed economic adjustment programme, announced that it would leave the coalition by the end of January 2011. Cowen refused to accede to demands by the opposition parties and from within his own party that he should resign before the budget was adopted, but undertook to hold a general election early in the following year. Despite the success of a Sinn Féin candidate in a by-election in late November 2010, further reducing the Government's support in the Dáil, the budget was adopted in early December with the support of independent members. In January 2011 Cowen's principal critic within Fianna Fáil, the Minister for Foreign Affairs, Micheál Martin, resigned from his post and urged Cowen to resign, following revelations about previously undisclosed contacts with Sean Fitzpatrick, the former chairman of Anglo Irish Bank, prior to the Government's controversial guarantee to the banks in September 2008. However, Cowen, who denied any impropriety, retained the leadership of Fianna Fáil in a self-imposed vote of confidence among party members in the legislature. Cowen temporarily assumed responsibility for foreign affairs himself. Later in January Cowen attempted to reorganize the Cabinet, replacing five other ministers who had resigned on the grounds that they would not be candidates in the forthcoming election. He also announced that a general election would be held on 11 March. However, the Green Party, which had not been consulted on the reorganization, refused to accept it, and Cowen was obliged to withdraw the appointments and transfer the former ministers' portfolios to other members of the Cabinet. Following further loss of support within Fianna Fáil, on 22 January he resigned as leader of the party, while stating that he would remain as Prime Minister until the election. The Green Party then withdrew from the coalition, although it undertook to support the remaining budgetary legislation (on which depended the release of funds from the emergency assistance provided by the EU and the IMF). Later in January Martin was elected leader of Fianna Fáil. On 1 February Cowen announced the dissolution of the legislature and the holding of a general election on 25 February.

At the general election in February 2011, Fine Gael won 76 seats, compared with 51 at the previous election in 2007, while the Labour Party increased its representation from 20 to 37 seats. Fianna Fáil secured only 20 seats (having won 78 in 2007), and its former coalition partner, the Green Party, lost all six of the seats it had held. Sinn Féin won 14 seats (compared with four in 2007): the party's President, Gerry Adams (who had resigned as a member of the United Kingdom Parliament) was one of the successful candidates. Negotiations between Fine Gael and the Labour Party concluded on 6 March 2011 with an agreement to form a coalition Government, with Enda Kenny, the leader of Fine Gael, as Prime Minister. Kenny announced the formation of a Cabinet with 10 Fine Gael and five Labour members. Eamon Gilmore, the leader of the Labour Party, became Deputy Prime Minister and Minister for Foreign Affairs and Trade. Michael Noonan (Fine Gael) was appointed Minister for Finance, while some of the previous responsibilities of this post were transferred to a new Ministry for Public Expenditure and Reform, allocated to Brendan Howlin (Labour). Several other departments were reconfigured or combined. The new administration undertook to renegotiate the terms of the assistance programme that had been agreed with the EU and the IMF (in particular the high interest rates being charged on some of the loans), while implementing for at least two years most of the austerity measures introduced by the previous Government in order to reduce the budget deficit.

Recent developments: the Enda Kenny Government

During 2011 the IMF acknowledged the Irish Government's 'resolute implementation' of the economic adjustment programme, reporting that the reduction of the budgetary deficit and the restructuring of the banking sector were proceeding according to schedule. Moderate economic growth was resumed in 2011, although unemployment remained at a high level. In February 2012 it was announced that it would be legally necessary to hold a referendum in Ireland on a proposed EU 'fiscal compact' (the Treaty on Stability, Co-ordination and Governance) whereby participating countries would accept legally binding limits on future budgetary deficits, and incur penalties imposed by the European Court of Justice if they exceeded the limits. Kenny urged approval of the treaty (which he signed in early March, as did representatives of all other EU governments except the Czech Republic and the United Kingdom) as being in the national interest, and Fianna Fáil and the Green Party also declared their support. Sinn Féin urged voters to reject the treaty, declaring that approval would represent a vote for austerity. At the referendum, in late May, the treaty was approved by just over 60% of those voting.

In October 2011 a presidential election was held, to replace Mary McAleese after the expiry of her second term of office. The successful candidate was Michael D. Higgins, a former Labour member of the Dáil, who had held the post of Minister for Arts, Culture and the Gaeltacht in 1993–97. Higgins' closest rivals in the election (among a total of seven candidates) were a prominent businessman, Sean Gallagher (a former member of Fianna Fáil standing as an independent candidate), and Martin McGuinness, the Sinn Féin Deputy First Minister of Northern Ireland. Higgins took office on 11 November 2011 for a seven-year term.

In July 2011, meanwhile, the latest in a series of reports on the sexual abuse of children by Roman Catholic clergy in Ireland was published. The report, dealing with the Cloyne diocese, stated that diocesan officials, including the former bishop, had not followed the Church's own guidelines on reporting suspected abusers to the police. In the same month, speaking in the Dáil, Kenny strongly criticized the Vatican's alleged role in concealing the extent of the abuse. His speech, and the widespread support that it received, was perceived as indicating a profound change in the nation's traditionally deferential attitude to the Church. The Papal Nuncio (the diplomatic representative of the Holy See in Ireland) was recalled for consultations and later replaced. In May 2012 the leader of the Roman Catholic Church in Ireland, Cardinal Sean Brady, was criticized by senior politicians following accusations that he had failed to respond adequately to allegations of child abuse perpetrated by a priest in the 1970s; the Cardinal made a public apology to the victims, but rejected demands that he should resign his post. In November a referendum was held on amending the Irish Constitution to include provisions on the state's responsibilities in protecting the rights and welfare of children: some 58% of those voting approved the amendment, which was supported by all the main political parties. In February 2013, following the publication of an official report into the Magdalene Laundries (workhouses run by religious orders), Kenny made a formal apology on behalf of the state for its role in consigning women and girls to work in the laundries, where between 1922 and 1996 some 10,000 had been forcibly employed without pay.

In March 2012 the report of the Mahon tribunal on allegations of corruption in development planning (originally the Flood tribunal, initiated in 1997) was finally published: it found that corrupt payments had been received by the former minister and European Commissioner Pádraig Flynn and by two former Fianna Fáil members of the Dáil. Although the tribunal did not find that the former Prime Minister, Bertie Ahern, had received corrupt payments, it stated that he had failed truthfully to explain the source of money in his bank accounts. Ahern reiterated that he was innocent of any wrongdoing, but after Fianna Fáil began proceedings later in March to expel him for 'conduct unbecoming', he resigned from the party, as did Flynn. The Government referred the tribunal's report to the police.

During 2013 there was controversy over proposed changes to Ireland's legislation on abortion, which had hitherto only permitted the aborting of a foetus when the mother's physical or mental health was endangered; a credible threat of suicide was now proposed as additional grounds for abortion. Bishops of the Roman Catholic Church condemned the proposal as morally unacceptable, but the Government maintained that it was intending to clarify, rather than change, the law; supporters of the bill pointed out that, in any case, hundreds of Irish women were travelling to Britain for abortions every year. The legislation was approved by the Dáil in July. In October a referendum took place on a proposed constitutional change, namely the abolition of the upper house of the legislature, the Seanad (Senate). The Government argued that the body was ineffectual and the selection process for members unsatisfactory, while abolition would save some €20m. a year in public expenditure; opponents argued that the Seanad played a useful role in amending legislation. All the main political parties except Fianna Fáil supported abolition, but in the event 51.7% of those voting rejected the proposal, a result viewed as an embarrassment for the Government. In response to a separate question in the referendum, voters approved the establishment of a Court of Appeal to hear appeals from the High Court (hitherto heard by the Supreme Court).

During 2012 and 2013 representatives of the EU and the IMF continued to report favourably on Ireland's restructuring of its banking system and on the implementation of austerity measures to reduce its budgetary deficit, but the social cost of this success was high, with the rate of unemployment remaining at well above 12% during 2013, while some 300,000 people had emigrated from Ireland during the four years to mid-2013. In December Ireland made a formal exit from the 'bailout' programme: the Minister for Finance, Noonan, while celebrating the fact that Ireland had been 'handed back her purse' warned that austerity policies would have to continue in order to reduce the still unacceptably high public debt and budgetary deficit (see Economic Affairs).

The peace process in Northern Ireland

Consultations between the United Kingdom and Ireland on the future of Northern Ireland resulted, in November 1985, in the signing of the Anglo-Irish Agreement, which provided for regular participation in Northern Ireland affairs by the Irish Government on political, legal, security and cross-border matters. The Agreement maintained that no change in the status of Northern Ireland would be made without the assent of the majority of its population. The terms of the Agreement were approved by both the Irish and the United Kingdom Parliaments. Under the provisions of the Agreement, the Irish Government pledged co-operation in enhanced cross-border security, in order to suppress IRA operations. Despite underlying tensions, the ensuing co-ordination between the Garda Síochána (Irish police force) and the Northern Ireland police force, the Royal Ulster Constabulary (RUC), was broadly successful. In February 1989 a permanent joint consultative assembly, comprising 25 British MPs and 25 Irish members of the Dáil, was established. The representatives were selected in October. The assembly's meetings, the first of which began in February 1990, were to take place twice a year, alternately in Dublin and London.

In January 1990 the British Government launched an initiative to convene meetings between representatives from the major political parties in Northern Ireland, and the British and Irish Governments, to discuss the restoration of devolution to Northern Ireland, which had been abandoned in 1974. In May 1990 the unionists agreed to hold direct discussions with the Irish Government, an unprecedented concession. Discussions between the Northern Ireland parties commenced in June 1991, with the inclusion of the Irish Government in April and September 1992. The principal point of contention was the unionists' demand that Ireland hold a referendum on Articles 2 and 3 of its Constitution, which laid claim to the territory of Northern Ireland. Ireland was unwilling to make such a concession except as part of an overall settlement. The negotiations formally ended in November.

In October 1993 the new Irish Prime Minister, Albert Reynolds, and his British counterpart, John Major, issued a joint statement setting out the principles on which future negotiations were to be based, including, notably, that Sinn Féin permanently renounce violence before being admitted to the negotiations. In December the Prime Ministers issued a joint declaration, known as the Downing Street Declaration, which referred to the possibility of a united Ireland and accepted the legitimacy of self-determination, but insisted on majority consent within Northern Ireland. While Sinn Féin and the unionist parties considered their response to the Declaration, Reynolds received both groups' conditional support for his proposal to establish a 'Forum for Peace and Reconciliation', which was to encourage both sides to end violent action. In August 1994 the IRA announced that it had ceased all military operations; this was followed in October by a similar suspension on the part of loyalist organizations.

An international panel, under the chairmanship of George Mitchell (a former US Senator), began work in December 1995 to consider the merits of decommissioning of arms in Northern Ireland. Its findings, announced in January 1996, recommended that weapons decommissioning should take place in parallel with all-party talks, and that their destruction should be monitored by an independent commission. The British and Irish Governments accepted those recommendations, but the Irish Government deemed unacceptable proposals put forward by the British Government for elections to be held to a Northern Ireland assembly, which would provide the framework for all-party negotiations. In February 1996, following a bomb explosion in London, marking the termination of the IRA ceasefire, the British and Irish Governments suspended official contacts with Sinn Féin.

In May 1997 the Irish Prime Minister, John Bruton, met the newly elected British premier, Tony Blair, and the new Secretary of State for Northern Ireland, Mo Mowlam, and in June the two Governments announced a new initiative to proceed with weapons decommissioning, while simultaneously pursuing negotiations for a constitutional settlement. In July the newly elected Irish Prime Minister, Bertie Ahern, confirmed his commitment to the peace initiative during a meeting with Blair in London. Following the IRA's subsequent restoration of its ceasefire, the Irish Government restored official contacts with Sinn Féin and resumed the policy of considering convicted IRA activists for early release from prison. In September Sinn Féin announced that it would accept the outcome of the peace process and would renounce violence as a means of punishment or resolving problems, providing for the party's participation in all-party talks when they resumed in the middle of that month. A procedural agreement to pursue negotiations in parallel with the decommissioning of weapons (which was to be undertaken by an Independent International Commission on Decommissioning—IICD, led by Gen. John de Chastelain of Canada) was signed by all the main parties later in September.

On 10 April 1998 the two Governments and eight political parties involved in the talks signed the Good Friday (or Belfast) Agreement at Stormont Castle in the Northern Irish capital. Immediately thereafter the two Governments signed a new British-Irish Agreement, replacing the Anglo-Irish Agreement, committing them to enact the provisions of the Good Friday Agreement, subject to its approval at referendums to be held in Ireland and Northern Ireland in May. The peace settlement provided for changes to the Irish Constitution (notably Articles 2 and 3) and to British constitutional legislation to enshrine the principle that a united Ireland could be achieved only with the consent of the majority of the people of both Ireland and Northern Ireland. The Good Friday Agreement provided for a new Northern Ireland Assembly and Executive Committee, together with North/South and British-Irish institutions. In addition, provision was made for the early release of paramilitary prisoners affiliated to organizations that established a complete and unequivocal ceasefire. On 22 May, at referendums held simultaneously in Ireland and Northern Ireland, 94.4% and 71.1% of voters, respectively, voted in favour of the Good Friday Agreement.

Elections to the Assembly were conducted in June 1998; the Assembly convened in July and elected the leader of the Ulster Unionist Party (UUP), David Trimble, as First Minister. The peace process was threatened with disruption by sectarian violence in July and by the detonation of an explosive device in August in Omagh, Northern Ireland; the device was planted by a republican splinter group, the Real IRA, and caused 29 deaths, more than any other single incident since the beginning of unrest related to Northern Ireland. A dispute between unionists and Sinn Féin concerning weapons decommissioning meant that the deadlines for the formation both of the Executive Committee and the North/South body, and for the devolution of powers to the new Northern Ireland institutions, were not met. In June 1999 the two Prime Ministers presented a compromise plan that envisaged the immediate establishment of the Executive Committee prior to the surrender of paramilitary weapons, with the condition that Sinn Féin guarantee that the IRA complete decommissioning by May 2000. Negotiations effectively collapsed in July 1999 and a review of the peace process, headed by George Mitchell, began in September. In November Mitchell succeeded in producing an agreement providing for the devolution of powers to the Executive Committee, after the IRA issued a statement announcing that it would appoint a representative to enter discussions with the IICD. On 2 December power was officially transferred to the new Northern Ireland Executive. On the same day, in accordance with the Good Friday Agreement, the Irish Constitution was amended to remove the state's territorial claim over Northern Ireland.

In December 1999 the Irish Cabinet attended the inaugural meeting, in Armagh, of the North/South Ministerial Council. The British-Irish Council met for the first time later that month. With the failure of the IRA to undertake disarmament threatening to result in the collapse of the peace process the British and Irish Governments engaged in intensive negotiations. Despite assurances given by the IRA that its ceasefire would not be broken, in February legislation came into effect returning Northern Ireland to direct rule. The IRA subsequently announced its withdrawal from discussions with the IICD. Direct talks between the Irish and British Governments and the principal parties resumed in May 2000, with the British Government pledging to restore the Northern Ireland institutions and postpone the deadline for decommissioning until June 2001, subject to a commitment by the IRA on the arms issue. The IRA responded by offering to 'initiate a process that will completely and verifiably put arms beyond use'. On 30 May power was again transferred to the Northern Ireland institutions.

In July 2001 Trimble resigned as First Minister in protest at the lack of progress on IRA decommissioning; Sir Reg Empey assumed the role of acting First Minister. In August Ahern and Blair announced that they would formulate a package of non-negotiable proposals to be presented to the pro-Agreement parties. The ensuing proposals did not meet with the approval of the major political parties, and on 10 August the British Government suspended the Assembly for 24 hours in order to delay the necessity to appoint a new First Minister for a further six weeks. Following the temporary suspension, the IRA retracted its earlier offer to put arms 'beyond use'. The Assembly was again suspended on 22 September as the deadlock continued, and in October the three UUP ministers and two Democratic Unionist Party (DUP) ministers resigned. Later in the month, however, the IRA announced that it had begun a process of 'putting arms beyond use', and the IICD revealed that it had witnessed the 'significant' disposal of IRA weapons. The unionist ministers therefore reassumed their posts and Trimble was re-elected as First Minister. In November the RUC was replaced by the Police Service of Northern Ireland (PSNI).

In October 2002 Sinn Féin's offices at the Assembly were raided by police, who suspected that the IRA had infiltrated the Northern Ireland Office and gained access to large numbers of confidential documents. In consequence, Northern Ireland was returned to direct rule. In a joint statement, Blair and Ahern announced that the devolved institutions would only be restored if Sinn Féin ended its link with paramilitary organizations. Later in October the IRA announced that it had suspended all contact with the IICD.

Talks aimed at resolving the impasse continued between the major parties during late 2002 and early 2003. The IRA failed to respond to the British Government's demand for a definitive cessation of paramilitary activities, and in May 2003 Blair postponed the elections to the Assembly until an unspecified date. In the same month the British and Irish Governments published a Joint Declaration containing their proposals for reinstating the Northern Ireland institutions and demanding a full and permanent cessation of all paramilitary activity. Blair and Ahern stressed that political talks would continue to address the impasse over the holding of elections, and pledged that aspects of the Joint Declaration not conditional upon IRA acts of complete disarmament would be implemented. Talks between the British and Irish Governments and the major Northern Ireland political parties continued during late 2003, and in October, following further acts of decommissioning of IRA weapons, elections to the Assembly were scheduled for the following month.

At elections to the Assembly in November 2003, the DUP secured 30 of the 108 seats, thus becoming the largest party. In talks with Ahern in January 2004 the leader of the DUP, Rev. Ian Paisley, remained insistent that his party would not conduct direct talks with Sinn Féin until the IRA had disbanded. In May Blair and Ahern agreed the basis of a 'roadmap' to restore the suspended Northern Ireland Assembly and Executive by October. In September further talks became deadlocked, following a DUP demand for changes to the functioning of the Assembly and the Executive before it would enter a government with Sinn Féin. In October Paisley met Ahern in Dublin, his first formal political meeting with the Irish Prime Minister, to try to break the impasse. In the following month the British and Irish Governments passed their proposals for restoring the power-sharing Executive to the DUP and Sinn Féin for consultation.

In February 2005 Ahern and Blair warned the IRA that its failure to demilitarize was the only obstacle to reaching an agreement on power-sharing; the following day the IRA withdrew its commitment to decommissioning. However, in July the IRA announced the end of its armed campaign and renewed its commitment to decommissioning. In September the IICD confirmed that the IRA's weapons had been fully decommissioned. The British Secretary of State for Northern Ireland, Peter Hain, and the Irish Minister for Foreign Affairs, Dermot Ahern, chaired talks with the Northern Ireland parties in February 2006, while Blair and Bertie Ahern met to discuss plans for the restoration of the institutions in March. Dermot Ahern subsequently announced that if attempts to restore the institutions of Northern Ireland in accordance with the Good Friday Agreement failed, then the British and Irish Governments would adopt an intergovernmental approach.

On 15 May 2006 the Assembly was restored; however, no further progress was made regarding the nomination of candidates for the roles of First Minister and Deputy First Minister. In October the four-member International Monitoring Commission (IMC) reported that the IRA was no longer engaged in terrorist activity and was committed to the peace process, but noted that members both of loyalist and republican paramilitary groups continued to engage in criminal activity. The DUP remained sceptical concerning the progress of the disbandment of the IRA. On 13 October, following talks in St Andrews, Scotland, Ahern and Blair announced an agreement (the St Andrews Agreement) that was intended to precipitate the restoration of a power-sharing Executive, and set a deadline of 10 November by which the Northern Ireland main parties were to agree to adhere to its provisions, which included support by all parties for the PSNI and the Northern Ireland Policing Board, and the formation of a North-South Inter-parliamentary Forum, including an equal number of representatives from both the Assembly and the Irish Parliament. Devolution was to be restored on 24 November, when the DUP and Sinn Féin would nominate candidates for the posts of First Minister and Deputy First Minister, respectively. The Assembly duly convened on 24 November; however, Paisley refused to accept his nomination as First Minister, while hinting that he would assume the role after elections to the Assembly, scheduled to be held in early March 2007, should Sinn Féin formally signal its support for the PSNI and the Policing Board. Following a long period of consultation among Sinn Féin members, in January 2007 delegates to a special conference voted in favour of a proposal to support the policing institutions. Despite the DUP's scepticism concerning Sinn Féin's commitment, the two Governments insisted that the deadline of 26 March was binding and that, in the absence of an agreement, the Assembly would be dissolved.

In elections to the Assembly, held on 7 March 2007, the DUP secured 36 seats and Sinn Féin 28, thereby confirming their status as the main parties in Northern Ireland. As the deadline approached, the Irish Government and Hain indicated that the date could be flexible, should the two parties agree an alternative arrangement. On 26 March Paisley and the Sinn Féin President, Gerry Adams, held their first direct meeting, during which an agreement was reached for a power-sharing Executive, which was duly installed on 8 May. Paisley became First Minister and Sinn Féin's Martin McGuinness was appointed as Deputy First Minister. Meanwhile, in April Bertie Ahern met Paisley in Dublin to discuss arrangements for future co-operation between the Executive and the Irish Government.

From mid-2009 the functioning of the Executive was disrupted by disagreements between Sinn Féin and the DUP (led since June 2008 by Peter Robinson, who had also succeeded Paisley as First Minister) over a timetable for the transfer of powers over policing and justice, which constituted the final area of responsibility due to be devolved under the Good Friday Agreement. In January 2010, following the collapse of negotiations between the two parties aimed at ending the impasse, Brian Cowen (Irish Prime Minister from May 2008) and his British counterpart, Gordon Brown, travelled to Belfast in order to mediate in the dispute. After intensive talks involving Cowen, Brown and all the main parties, in February 2010 the DUP and Sinn Féin concluded an agreement that envisaged the transfer of policing and justice powers to the Executive on 12 April; the agreement also addressed other issues of contention between the parties, including a mechanism for resolving disputes over the routes of traditional parades by Protestant orders. The transfer of powers took place as scheduled on 12 April, when the Assembly elected a Minister of Justice to form part of the Executive.

During 2010–13 police in the Irish Republic seized weapons and explosives in a number of raids on suspected dissident republicans who were believed to be planning violent attacks in Northern Ireland in protest at the peace process. The Irish Prime Minister, Enda Kenny, was among senior politicians who attended the funeral of a member of the Northern Ireland police force, who died in an explosion in Omagh in April 2011: former members of the Provisional IRA claimed responsibility for the murder. In September 2012 Robinson urged Kenny to issue an official apology for the role played by previous Irish Governments in allegedly failing to discourage the development of the IRA in the 1970s, and in the same month a motion proposed by the DUP, demanding such an apology, was passed in the Northern Ireland Assembly; the demands were rejected by the Irish Government. In November 2012 a Northern Ireland prison officer was murdered by a group calling itself the IRA, believed to be an amalgamation of dissident republican groups. The murder was condemned by the North South Ministerial Council, and the Irish Minister of Justice attended the victim's funeral. Also in November the Irish Minister for Agriculture, Simon Coveney, became the first Irish government minister to attend and address a conference of the DUP. During 2012 there were several postponements of the publication of the report of a long-running inquiry into the murder of two senior RUC officers by the Provisional IRA in 1989: the inquiry, chaired by Justice Peter Smithwick, had been established by the Irish legislature in 2005 to investigate allegations that one or more members of the Garda Síochána had colluded in the killings by alerting the perpetrators to the whereabouts of the RUC officers. The report of the Smithwick inquiry was finally submitted to the Dáil in November 2013: the report concluded that there had been collusion by the Garda, but did not identify any individual officer as responsible.

Continuing sectarian tension in Northern Ireland was illustrated by violent street protests in Belfast in December 2012 after the city council voted to fly the Union flag on official buildings only for 18 days per year, instead of daily: the Union flag and the Irish tricolour flag, displayed officially and unofficially, had become emotive symbols for unionists and nationalists respectively. Violent actions attributed to dissident republicans continued in 2013, and stocks of weapons, ammunition and explosives believed to have been amassed by them were discovered on various occasions by police on both sides of the border. In May the First Minister and Deputy First Minister announced the formation of a panel comprising members of the five parties represented in the Northern Ireland Executive, to consider ways of reducing sectarianism and promoting reconciliation. The panel began its work in July under the chairmanship of Richard Haass, an American diplomat who had been the US special envoy to Northern Ireland in 2001–03. It considered three sources of division, namely parades, commemorations and related protests; flags and emblems; and contending with the past (referring chiefly to the lack of prosecutions for almost 3,300 of the killings, totalling some 3,500, that had taken place during the 'Troubles'). At the end of December, following months of negotiations, meetings with different groups and submissions from the public, a seventh and final draft agreement was produced. It proposed the replacement of the existing Parades Commission by an Office for Parades, Select Commemorations and Related Protests, which could refer contentious events to an Authority for Public Events Adjudication. The panel admitted failure to reach consensus on the display of flags and emblems, but proposed establishing a Commission on Identity, Culture and Tradition to hold public discussions on these and related matters. The panel recommended the establishment of a Historical Investigations Unit to take over investigation of past sectarian violence, leading to prosecution where the evidence warranted it, and an Independent Commission for Information Retrieval, which would allow victims and survivors to obtain information about conflict-related events, but would provide informants with limited immunity from prosecution, since the information provided would not be admissible as evidence in court. An Implementation and Reconciliation Group would be established to monitor the agreement's implementation.

The Haass agreement was accepted by the SDLP and Sinn Féin, but elements of it were rejected by the unionist parties: discussions between the parties continued, however, in January 2014. The Irish Deputy Prime Minister, Eamon Gilmore, expressed disappointment that the agreement had not been accepted, but acknowledged that progress had been made, while Enda Kenny promised to support further efforts towards reconciliation in the north. The process was severely affected in February when a judge at the High Court in London ruled that a former IRA member, John Downey, could not be prosecuted in connection with the deaths of four members of the Household Cavalry in a bomb attack in Hyde Park, London, in July 1982, because Downey had received a letter from the British Northern Ireland Office in 2007 stating that he would not face criminal charges in Northern Ireland and (mistakenly) that he was not wanted for questioning by any other police force in the United Kingdom. To the outrage of unionists it was then revealed that, under an agreement between the British Government and Sinn Féin, similar letters had been sent to more than 180 paramilitary republicans who were suspected of having committed conflict-related crimes before the Good Friday Agreement (or had been convicted and later escaped): the aim was to clarify the legal status of so-called 'On the Runs'. The British Prime Minister, David Cameron, announced an independent review of the 'On the Run' letters scheme, to report in May 2014.

Foreign Affairs

Ireland became a member of the European Community (EC—now the European Union—EU, see p. 273) in 1973. In May 1987 the country affirmed its commitment to the EC when, in a referendum, 69.9% of Irish voters supported adherence to the Single European Act, which provided for closer economic and political co-operation between EC member states (including the creation of a single market by 1993). In December 1991 Ireland agreed to the far-reaching Treaty on European Union (the Maastricht Treaty). Ireland secured a special provision within the treaty (which was signed by all parties in February 1992), guaranteeing that Ireland's constitutional position on abortion would be unaffected by any future EC legislation. Despite opposition, from both pro- and anti-abortion campaigners, to the special provision within the treaty and the threat to Ireland's neutrality perceived in the document's proposals for a common defence policy, ratification of the treaty was endorsed at a referendum held in June 1992. A referendum conducted in May 1998 approved the Amsterdam Treaty, which had been signed by EU ministers in October 1997, amending the Maastricht Treaty. The common European currency, the euro, was adopted by Ireland at the beginning of 2002. In October of that year the Treaty of Nice, which provided for the impending enlargement of the EU, was approved in a national referendum, despite having been rejected in an earlier referendum held in 2001. In early 2004 Ahern, as President of the Council of the European Union, led negotiations between the leaders of the member states over a draft constitutional treaty, which was eventually agreed in June. It was formally signed in October, but required ratification by all 25 member states either by parliamentary vote or referendum. Following the treaty's rejection in national referendums in France and the Netherlands in mid-2005, further referendums in EU countries yet to ratify the treaty, including Ireland, were postponed indefinitely. During 2007 agreement was reached on a treaty to replace the constitutional treaty. The resulting Treaty of Lisbon was signed in December, but was rejected at a referendum in Ireland in June 2008. However, the ratification process continued across Europe, and at an EU summit meeting in Brussels in June 2009 Cowen achieved a series of formal guarantees from the European Council addressing Irish concerns regarding certain aspects of the treaty. The treaty was approved by a substantial majority at a second referendum in October, and subsequently entered into force across the EU in December.

In July 2006 an amendment to previous defence legislation was promulgated following a vote in the Dáil. Under the amended legislation, Irish troops could join EU 'battlegroups' in emergency humanitarian, reconnaissance and training missions prior to receiving a UN mandate or approval from the Dáil, thus circumventing the so-called 'triple-lock' that required any deployment of Irish troops abroad to be mandated by the UN and approved by the Irish Government and Parliament. However, if either or both declined to approve such a mission, troops would be withdrawn.

In November 2010 the Irish Government accepted emergency assistance from the EU after the country's budgetary deficit exceeded by far the limits stipulated by the EU (see Economic Affairs). In March 2012 the Government signed the EU Treaty on Stability, Co-ordination and Governance (more often referred to as the 'fiscal compact'), and adherence to the treaty, which envisaged legally binding limits on national budgetary spending, was approved by a national referendum in May.

In May 2011 Queen Elizabeth II paid a state visit to Ireland, becoming the first British monarch to visit the country since its independence. In acts perceived as being of great symbolic importance, the Queen laid wreaths at memorials to those who had died in the struggle for Irish independence, and in the First World War, and in a speech she expressed 'deep sympathy' with victims of the 'troubled past'. The visit was regarded as indicating the development of a more mature and cordial relationship between the two countries, following the successful outcome of the peace process in Northern Ireland. In March 2012, during a visit to the United Kingdom by the Irish Prime Minister, Enda Kenny, a Joint Statement of Co-operation was signed by Kenny and his British counterpart, David Cameron: the statement referred to a 'uniquely close' relationship between the two countries, and the two Governments undertook to reinforce their co-operation over the next decade, especially with regard to economic recovery, research, energy supply, EU relations and the implementation of the peace agreements for Northern Ireland. In December 2013 Kenny and Cameron jointly visited memorials in Belgium to the dead of the First World War, including those from Ireland who had fought in the British army. In March 2014 Kenny visited London to discuss with Cameron, among other matters, the implementation of the Haass agreement (see The peace process in Northern Ireland) and proposals for the import by the United Kingdom of wind-generated electricity from Ireland. President Higgins paid a state visit to the United Kingdom in April, the first such visit by an Irish head of state.

Ireland has strong historic links with the USA through emigration, and from 1995 the special envoy of the US President undertook an important diplomatic role in negotiations on the future of Northern Ireland (see The peace process in Northern Ireland). The USA is a major trading partner (Ireland's largest individual export market in 2012) and the country's principal source of foreign direct investment, attracted by a skilled English-speaking labour force and a low corporate tax rate: in 2012 there were more than 700 US companies operating in Ireland, employing some 115,000 people. In May 2011 President Barack Obama became the sixth US President to pay an official visit to Ireland since John F. Kennedy in 1963. During 2012 Kenny paid three visits to the USA, promoting investment and tourism.

A visit by the Chinese Vice-President, Xi Jinping, in February 2012, during which various agreements on trade and investment were concluded, indicated that the Chinese Government regarded Ireland as an important entry point in its dealings with the EU. In March Kenny led a trade mission to China.

CONSTITUTION AND GOVERNMENT

The Constitution took effect in 1937. Legislative power is vested in the bicameral National Parliament (Oireachtas), comprising the Senate (Seanad Éireann) and the House of Representatives (Dáil Éireann). The Senate has 60 members, including 11 nominated by the Prime Minister (Taoiseach) and 49 indirectly elected for five years. The House of Representatives has 166 members, elected by universal adult suffrage for five years (subject to dissolution) by means of the single transferable vote, a form of proportional representation.

The President (Uachtarán) is the constitutional head of state, elected by direct popular vote for seven years; re-election is permitted only once. Executive power is effectively held by the Cabinet, led by the Prime Minister, who is appointed by the President on the nomination of the Dáil. The President appoints other Ministers on the nomination of the Prime Minister with the previous approval of the Dáil. The Cabinet is responsible to the Dáil.

Local government in Ireland consists of a number of democratically elected local and regional authorities at three levels: two regional assemblies, eight regional authorities and 29 county councils, five city councils, five borough councils and 75 town councils.

REGIONAL AND INTERNATIONAL CO-OPERATION

Ireland is a member of the European Union (EU, see p. 273) and uses the single currency, the euro; however, it does not participate in the Schengen Agreement on open borders. It is a member of the Council of Europe (see p. 252) and the Organization for Security and Co-operation in Europe (OSCE, see p. 387).

Ireland joined the UN in 1955. As a contracting party to the General Agreement on Tariffs and Trade, it joined the World Trade Organization (WTO, see p. 434) on its establishment in 1995. Ireland is also a member of the Organisation for Economic Co-operation and Development (OECD, see p. 379) and participates in the Partnership for Peace framework of the North Atlantic Treaty Organization (NATO, see p. 370).

ECONOMIC AFFAIRS

In 2012, according to estimates by the World Bank, Ireland's gross national income (GNI), measured at average 2010–12 prices, was US $178,838m., equivalent to $38,970 per head (or $35,870 on an international purchasing-power parity basis). During 2003–12, it was estimated, the population increased at an average annual rate of 1.5%, while gross domestic product (GDP) per head increased, in real terms, by an average of 0.1% per year. According to the World Bank, overall GDP increased, in real terms, at an average annual rate of 1.6% in 2003–12; in 2012 GDP increased by 0.9%, measured at constant prices, and increased by 0.2% according to chain-linked methodologies.

Agriculture (including forestry and fishing) contributed a preliminary 2.4% of GDP in 2012 and employed an estimated 5.8% of the working population in the third quarter of 2013. Beef and dairy production dominate Irish agriculture. Principal crops include barley, wheat and potatoes. According to UN estimates, agricultural GDP decreased by an average of 2.8% per year during 2003–12; sectoral GDP decreased by 10.0% in 2012. In 2012, according to chain-linked methodologies, agricultural GDP decreased by 12.6%.

Industry (comprising mining, manufacturing, construction and utilities) provided a preliminary 27.2% of GDP in 2012 and employed 18.3% of the working population in the third quarter of 2013. Industrial GDP, according to UN estimates, decreased by an average of 1.4% per year during 2003–12; it decreased by 1.5% in 2012. According to chain-linked methodologies, in 2012 industrial GDP decreased by 0.8%

Mining (including quarrying and turf production) provided employment to 0.4% of the working population in 2006. Ireland possesses substantial deposits of lead-zinc ore and recoverable peat, both of which are exploited. Natural gas is produced from the Kinsale field off the south coast of Ireland (although production is declining) and from the Seven Heads field that came on stream in 2003. Substantial gas supplies were discovered at the Corrib field situated off the west coast of Ireland; the project was delayed owing to local objections to a proposed pipeline to bring the gas onshore. Small quantities of coal are also extracted. Offshore reserves of petroleum have also been located and several licences awarded to foreign-owned enterprises to undertake further exploration.

According to World Bank estimates, manufacturing contributed 24.2% of GDP in 2009. The manufacturing sector comprises many high-technology, largely foreign-owned, capital-intensive enterprises. In the year to February 2010 the value of manufacturing output declined by 2.6%.

Construction engaged 5.6% of the employed labour force in the third quarter of 2013. According to UN estimates, construction GDP decreased, in real terms, at an average annual rate of 3.1% in 2003–12; sectoral GDP decreased by 7.4% in 2012. The construction sector contracted by 7.7% in 2012, according to chain-linked methodologies.

Electricity is derived principally from natural gas, which provided 49.7% of total requirements in 2012, while coal provided 20.0% and petroleum 1.5%. There was potential for the further development of wind-generated energy, which was increasing in importance. In 2012 imports of mineral fuels were 14.3% (by value) of total merchandise imports.

Service industries (including commerce, finance, transport and communications and public administration) contributed a preliminary 69.5% of GDP in 2012 and employed 75.9% of the working population in the third quarter of 2013. The financial sector expanded rapidly in the 2000s. However, in 2008–11 there was a crisis in the banking system, following the global financial crisis and the collapse in domestic property prices. Tourism is one of the principal sources of foreign exchange. Revenue from the tourism and travel sector amounted to an estimated €4,118m. in 2010; it increased to €4,567m. in 2011, but decreased to €4,078 in 2012. The GDP of the services sector increased by an average of 2.4% per year during 2003–12, but declined by 0.8% in 2012, according to UN estimates.

In 2012, according to IMF statistics, Ireland recorded a visible merchandise trade surplus of US $50,779m. with a surplus of $9,245m. on the current account of the balance of payments. In 2012 the principal source of imports was the United Kingdom (31.5%). The European Union (EU, see p. 273) as a whole accounted for 60.0% of imports; the USA, Germany and the People's Republic of China were also important suppliers. The USA was the principal market for exports (19.7%); the EU accounted for 59.0% of exports, while other major purchasers included the United Kingdom, Belgium, Germany and Switzerland. In 2012 principal imports included machinery and transport equipment, chemicals and related products, mineral fuels and lubricants, miscellaneous manufactured articles, and food and live animals. Principal exports included chemicals and related products, miscellaneous manufactured articles, machinery and transport equipment, and food and live animals.

There was an estimated general government deficit of €13,500m. in 2012, equivalent to 8.2% of GDP. Ireland's general government gross debt was €192.459m. at the end of 2012, equivalent to 117.4% of GDP. The annual rate of inflation averaged 2.0% in 2002–12. Consumer prices decreased by 2.5% in 2011 and by 1.7% in 2012. The unemployment rate averaged 13.0% in the third quarter of 2013.

In the late 1990s the Irish economy enjoyed an unprecedentedly high rate of growth, which was attributed largely to prudent fiscal and monetary management and low taxation, aided by a substantial increase in foreign direct investment. Continuing high levels of growth were sustained in 2004–07 by the rapid expansion of the construction sector (assisted by banks and building societies which provided loans on extremely liberal terms) and high levels of consumer spending. However, in 2008 the Irish economy became the first in the eurozone to enter recession, as the effects of the global financial crisis coincided with, and exacerbated, a correction in domestic property prices. The subsequent collapse in property prices and marked fall in investment, owing to the decline in building activity, led to a contraction in consumer spending, while the decrease in external demand and the high value of the euro against the pound sterling resulted in a decline in exports. Moreover, Ireland's banking sector, which was affected by the lack of available credit caused by the global financial crisis, was also exposed to the collapse in domestic property prices, which resulted in borrowers' inability to meet repayment obligations on lending. In September 2008 the Government announced that it would guarantee deposits in six financial institutions, in order to maintain confidence, and over the next two years it was obliged to provide support for the banking system totalling at least €45,000m. Meanwhile, the effects of the downturn led to a rapid deterioration of government finances; the budgetary deficit was equivalent to an estimated 31.9% of GDP in 2010 (compared with the maximum of 3% stipulated by the EU under its Stability and Growth Pact for countries belonging to the eurozone). Ireland's GDP declined by 5.5% in 2009, according to the IMF, and with persistent high unemployment and low consumer demand, GDP continued to contract, by 0.8%, in 2010. During that year uncertainty over the country's financial stability meant that the cost to Ireland of borrowing on the international bond markets increased to levels that were widely regarded as unsustainable. In November, under pressure from fellow members of the EU, concerned for the stability of the euro, the Irish Government was finally obliged to make a formal application for assistance from the EU and the IMF. Under the resulting 'bailout' agreement a total of €85,000m. was made available to Ireland, including €10,000m. for the recapitalization of the banks, with a further €25,000m. as a contingency reserve for the banking system. The assistance was conditional upon the restructuring of the banking system, and the adoption of a four-year programme of austerity measures, involving reductions in expenditure amounting to €10,000m. and increases in taxation totalling €5,000m., in order to reduce the budgetary deficit to the equivalent of 3% of GDP by 2015. Successive annual budgets, therefore, imposed reductions in social benefits, health services and public sector pay, and increases in tax income (including the introduction of income tax for the lower-paid). Ireland's traditionally low rate of corporation tax (12.5%) was maintained, however (despite pressure from other EU member states), in order to encourage foreign investment. In 2011 Ireland's GDP increased by 1.4%, after three years of decline. In February 2012 the Government announced plans to raise €3,000m. through the sale of state-owned assets, including gas and electricity suppliers and a stake in the national airline. Monitoring by the European Commission, the European Central Bank (ECB) and the IMF in 2011–13 showed that Ireland was consistently meeting its targets for restructuring the banking system and reducing the budgetary deficit: a reduction in bond yields on Ireland's sovereign debt during 2012 indicated growing confidence among investors. Growth in GDP in 2012 slowed to 0.2%, reflecting a decline in demand for exports caused by the economic problems of Ireland's trading partners, particularly in the eurozone, while high levels of unemployment (at more than 14% of the labour force) and of household debt also weakened domestic demand. The budgetary deficit remained high in 2012, at more than 8% of GDP. The Government's capital investment programme for 2012–16 aimed to stimulate growth and provide employment, envisaging public and private investment amounting to more than €19,000m., particularly for construction in the education, health and transport sectors. In March 2013 Ireland returned to the international bond markets with a successful sale of 10-year bonds, and in December the country made a formal exit from the EU/IMF assistance programme, a significant step in its economic recovery. However, GDP declined by 0.3% in 2013, and the rate of unemployment, although improving, was still 11.9% in February 2014. The budgetary deficit still amounted to about 7% of GDP in 2013, while public debt was equivalent to some 124% of GDP. Irish banks continued to register losses, remaining burdened by a high proportion of non-performing loans (with more than 17% of household mortgages being in arrears for more than 90 days). The budget for 2014 made further reductions in social welfare benefits, aiming to reduce the fiscal deficit to below 5% of GDP, while the Government hoped to reduce its debt to the equivalent of 116% of GDP in that year. The Central Bank predicted that increases both in exports and in consumer spending would lead to GDP growth of 2.1% in 2014.

PUBLIC HOLIDAYS

2015: 1 January (New Year), 17 March (St Patrick's Day), 6 April (Easter Monday), 4 May (May Bank Holiday), 1 June (June Bank Holiday), 4 August (August Bank Holiday), 26 October (October Bank Holiday), 25 December (Christmas Day), 26 December (St Stephen's Day).

Statistical Survey

Source (unless otherwise stated): Central Statistics Office, Skehard Rd, Cork; tel. (21) 4535000; fax (21) 4535555; e-mail information@cso.ie; internet www.cso.ie.

Area and Population

AREA, POPULATION AND DENSITY

Area (sq km)	70,182*
Population (census results)	
23 April 2006	4,239,848
28 April 2011	
Males	2,272,699
Females	2,315,553
Total	4,588,252
Population (official estimates at 30 April)†	
2012	4,585,407
2013	4,593,125
Density (per sq km) at 30 April 2013	65.4

* 27,097 sq miles.

† Preliminary.

POPULATION BY AGE AND SEX

(official estimates at 30 April 2013, preliminary)

	Males	Females	Total
0–14	513,919	493,764	1,007,683
15–64	1,498,657	1,518,682	3,017,339
65 and over	261,270	306,833	568,103
Total	2,273,846	2,319,279	4,593,125

ADMINISTRATIVE DIVISIONS

(population at 2011 census)

Province/County	Area (sq km)	Population	Density (per sq km)
Connacht	17,713	542,547	30.6
Galway	6,151	250,653	40.7
Galway City	51	75,529	1,481.0
Galway County	6,010	175,124	29.1
Leitrim	1,589	31,798	20.0
Mayo	5,588	130,638	23.4
Roscommon	2,548	64,065	25.1
Sligo	1,837	65,393	35.6
Leinster	19,774	2,504,814	126.7
Carlow	898	54,612	60.8
Dublin	921	1,273,069	1,382.3
Dublin City	118	527,612	4,471.3
Dún Laoghaire-Rathdown	127	206,261	1,624.1
Fingal	453	273,991	604.8
South Dublin	223	265,205	1,189.3
Kildare	1,694	210,312	124.2
Kilkenny	2,072	95,419	46.1
Laoighis	1,719	80,559	46.9
Longford	1,091	39,000	35.7
Louth	832	122,897	147.7
Meath	2,335	184,135	78.9
Offaly	1,990	76,687	38.5
Westmeath	1,825	86,164	47.2
Wexford	2,365	145,320	61.4
Wicklow	2,033	136,640	67.2
Munster	24,608	1,246,088	50.6
Clare	3,442	117,196	34.0
Cork	7,508	519,032	69.1
Cork City	40	119,230	2,980.8
Cork County	7,468	399,802	53.5
Kerry	4,735	145,502	30.7
Limerick	2,760	191,809	69.5
Limerick City*	20	57,106	2,855.3
Limerick County*	2,740	134,703	49.2
Tipperary	4,304	158,754	36.9

Province/County—*continued*	Area (sq km)	Population	Density (per sq km)
Tipperary North	2,046	70,322	34.4
Tipperary South	2,258	88,432	39.2
Waterford	1,859	113,795	61.2
Waterford City	42	46,732	1,112.7
Waterford County	1,817	67,063	36.9
Ulster (part)	8,087	294,803	36.5
Cavan	1,932	73,183	37.9
Donegal	4,860	161,137	33.2
Monaghan	1,296	60,483	46.7
Total	70,182	4,588,252	65.4

* The boundary of Limerick City was expanded at the 2011 census to include the electoral division Limerick North Rural, but revised area details were not available.

PRINCIPAL TOWNS
(population at 2011 census)

Dublin (capital)	527,612	Limerick	57,106
Cork	119,230	Waterford	46,732
Galway	75,529		

BIRTHS, MARRIAGES AND DEATHS

	Registered live births		Registered marriages		Registered deaths	
	Number	Rate (per 1,000)	Number	Rate (per 1,000)	Number	Rate (per 1,000)
2005	61,042	14.8	21,355	5.2	27,441	6.6
2006	64,237	15.2	22,089	5.2	27,479	6.5
2007	70,620	16.3	22,756	5.2	28,050	6.5
2008	75,724	17.1	22,187	5.0	28,192	6.4
2009	74,928	16.8	21,627	4.8	28,898	6.5
2010	74,976	16.8	20,635	4.6	27,565	6.2
2011	74,650	16.3	19,879	4.3	28,995	6.3
2012	72,225	15.8	21,245	4.6	28,848	6.3

Life expectancy (years at birth): 80.5 (males 78.3; females 82.8) in 2011 (Source: World Bank, World Development Indicators database).

IMMIGRATION AND EMIGRATION
('000, year ending April, official estimates unless otherwise indicated)

Immigrants

Country of origin	2010/11*	2011/12†	2012/13†
United Kingdom	11.9	8.4	9.7
Other EU	19.5	19.5	22.1
USA	3.3	4.9	3.6
Rest of the world	18.6	19.9	20.5
Total	53.3	52.7	55.9

Emigrants

Country of destination	2010/11	2011/12†	2012/13†
United Kingdom	20.0	19.0	21.9
Other EU	24.3	24.0	25.7
USA	4.7	8.6	6.2
Rest of the world	31.7	35.6	35.2
Total	80.6	87.1	89.0

* Census data.
† Preliminary figures.

Note: Data for immigrants include large number of Irish nationals returning from permanent residence abroad ('000): 19.6 in 2010/11 (census figure); 20.6 in 2011/12 (preliminary); 15.7 in 2012/13 (preliminary).

ECONOMICALLY ACTIVE POPULATION
('000 persons, quarterly labour force survey, July–September, estimates)

	2011	2012	2013
Agriculture, forestry and fishing	82.4	85.6	110.6
Mining and quarrying; Manufacturing; Electricity, gas and water	238.9	231.1	242.0
Construction	108.5	101.1	105.4
Wholesale and retail trade; repair of motor vehicles and motorcycles	276.5	272.7	273.3
Hotels and restaurants	121.1	123.1	137.7
Transport, storage and communications	173.8	168.5	170.2
Finance, insurance and real estate activities	99.1	102.3	101.5
Professional, scientific and technical activities	96.6	100.4	111.3
Administrative and support service activities	69.4	66.6	64.7
Public administration and defence; compulsory social security	99.3	99.7	96.1
Education	137.2	140.6	140.8
Health and social work	243.5	245.0	243.6
Other services	95.5	101.9	99.9
Sub-total	1,841.8	1,838.6	1,897.1
Activities not adequately defined	3.8	2.7	2.2
Total employed	1,845.6	1,841.3	1,899.3
Unemployed	328.1	324.5	282.9
Total labour force	2,173.7	2,165.8	2,182.2

Health and Welfare

KEY INDICATORS

Total fertility rate (children per woman, 2011)	2.1
Under-5 mortality rate (per 1,000 live births, 2011)	4
HIV/AIDS (% of persons aged 15–49, 2011)	0.3
Physicians (per 1,000 head, 2010)	3.2
Hospital beds (per 1,000 head, 2008)	4.9
Health expenditure (2010): US $ per head (PPP)	3,720
Health expenditure (2010): % of GDP	9.2
Health expenditure (2010): public (% of total)	69.2
Total carbon dioxide emissions ('000 metric tons, 2010)	39,999.6
Carbon dioxide emissions per head (metric tons, 2010)	8.9
Access to sanitation (% of persons, 2011)	99
Human Development Index (2012): ranking	7
Human Development Index (2012): value	0.916

For sources and definitions, see explanatory note on p. vi.

Agriculture

PRINCIPAL CROPS
('000 metric tons)

	2010	2011	2012
Wheat	669.0	929.0	618.0
Oats	148.0	168.0	145.0
Barley	1,223.0	1,412.0	1,152.0
Potatoes	419.7	357.8	232.0
Carrots and turnips*	25.6	25.5	27.0
Cabbages and other brassicas*	44.6	59.5	62.0

* FAO estimates.

Aggregate production ('000 metric tons, may include official, semi-official or estimated data): Total cereals 2,043.2 in 2010, 2,511.8 in 2011, 1,917.4 in 2012; Total roots and tubers 419.7 in 2010, 356.0 in 2011, 232.0 in 2012; Total vegetables (incl. melons) 209.0 in 2010, 226.3 in 2011, 235.4 in 2012; Total fruits (excl. melons) 48.9 in 2010, 51.6 in 2011, 52.6 in 2012.

Source: FAO.

LIVESTOCK
('000 head at June)

	2010	2011	2012
Cattle	6,606.6	6,493.0	6,754.1
Sheep	4,565.7	4,694.7	5,170.0
Pigs	1,516.3	1,549.0	1,570.6
Chickens*	13,800	14,000	14,500

* FAO estimates.

Source: FAO.

LIVESTOCK PRODUCTS
('000 metric tons)

	2010	2011	2012
Cattle meat	558.2	545.9	495.4
Sheep meat	47.8	48.1	54.0*
Pig meat	215.0	234.7	241.5
Chicken meat*	85.0	87.0	88.0
Cows' milk	5,327.0	5,536.7	5,379.7
Hen eggs*	45.0	46.0	46.5

* FAO estimate(s).

Source: FAO.

Forestry

ROUNDWOOD REMOVALS
('000 cubic metres, excluding bark)

	2010	2011	2012
Sawlogs, veneer logs and logs for sleepers	1,425	1,391	1,418
Pulpwood	893	936	831
Other industrial wood	119	113	126
Fuel wood	181	195	205
Total	2,618	2,635	2,580

Source: FAO.

SAWNWOOD PRODUCTION
('000 cubic metres, including railway sleepers)

	2010	2011	2012
Coniferous (softwood)	772	760	781
Broadleaved (hardwood)	0	1	1
Total	772	761	782

Source: FAO.

Fishing

('000 metric tons, live weight)

	2009	2010	2011
Capture	269.1	318.9	214.0
Blue whiting	9.3	8.3	1.2
Atlantic herring	26.3	26.7	24.8
Atlantic horse mackerel	40.7	44.5	38.5
Atlantic mackerel	61.4	58.2	61.7
Edible crab	5.7	8.2	6.7
Norway lobster	7.2	7.8	7.9
Aquaculture	47.5	46.5	44.3
Atlantic salmon	12.2	15.7	12.2
Blue mussel	26.8	22.2	22.7
Total catch	316.6	365.4	258.2

Note: Figures exclude aquatic plants ('000 metric tons, FAO estimates): 29.5 (North Atlantic rockweed 28.0) in 2009–11.

Source: FAO.

Mining

('000 metric tons unless otherwise indicated)

	2009	2010	2011
Natural gas (million cu m)	413	402	356
Lead*	43.0	39.1	50.7
Zinc*	357.0	342.5	344.0
Peat†‡	3,800	4,991	3,707

* Figures refer to the metal content of ores mined.

† Excluding peat for horticultural use ('000 metric tons, estimates): 500 in 2009–11.

‡ Estimates.

Source: US Geological Survey.

Industry

SELECTED PRODUCTS
('000 metric tons unless otherwise indicated)

	2008	2009	2010
Motor spirit (gasoline)	570	481	463
Gas-diesel oil (distillate fuel oil)	1,132	975	n.a.
Mazout (residual fuel oil)	1,161	949	969
Electric energy (million kWh)	29,685	28,242	n.a.

Source: UN Industrial Commodity Statistics Database.

Finance

CURRENCY AND EXCHANGE RATES

Monetary Units
100 cent = 1 euro (€).

Sterling and Dollar Equivalents (31 December 2013)
£1 sterling = €1.194
US $1 = €0.725;
€10 = £8.37 = $13.79.

Average Exchange Rate (euros per US $)
2011 0.7194
2012 0.7783
2013 0.7532

Note: The national currency was formerly the Irish pound (or punt). From the introduction of the euro, with Irish participation, on 1 January 1999, a fixed exchange rate of €1 = 78.7564 pence was in operation. Euro notes and coins were introduced on 1 January 2002. The euro and local currency circulated alongside each other until 9 February, after which the euro became the sole legal tender.

BUDGET
(€ '000 million)

Revenue	2012	2013*	2014*
Tax revenue	39.5	41.4	43.3
Personal income tax	15.2	15.7	16.3
Corporate income tax	4.0	4.4	4.7
Value-added tax	10.2	10.4	10.5
Excise tax	4.7	4.7	4.9
Others	5.4	6.2	6.9
Social contributions	9.7	9.9	10.3
Non-tax revenue	7.4	7.2	6.8
Total	56.5	58.5	60.4

Expenditure†	2012	2013*	2014*
Current expenditure	67.0	67.7	66.4
Interest payments	6.1	7.6	8.2
Wages and salaries	18.8	18.7	18.4
Goods and services	8.4	8.3	8.1
Social benefits	29.0	28.4	27.9
Subsidies	1.5	1.3	1.3
Other expenses	3.1	3.3	2.5
Gross fixed capital formation	3.1	3.0	2.6
Total	70.0	70.7	69.0

* Projections.

† Excluding bank support costs (€ '000 million): 0.0 in 2012; 0.0 in 2013 (projection); 0.1 in 2014 (projection).

Source: IMF, *Ireland: Twelfth Review Under the Extended Arrangement and Proposal for Post-Program Monitoring; Staff Report; Staff Supplements; and Press Release on the Executive Board discussion* (December 2013).

INTERNATIONAL RESERVES

(US $ million at 31 December)

	2010	2011	2012
Gold (Eurosystem valuation)	272	304	321
IMF special drawing rights	1,104	976	986
Reserve position in IMF	237	397	397
Foreign exchange	502	27	3
Total	2,115	1,704	1,707

Source: IMF, *International Financial Statistics*.

MONEY SUPPLY

(incl. shares, depository corporations, national residence criteria, € million at 31 December)

	2010	2011	2012
Currency issued	12,966	13,673	13,999
Central Bank of Ireland	27,923	29,062	29,940
Demand deposits	85,501	77,719	79,377
Other deposits	84,512	86,141	88,842
Securities other than shares	119,811	95,484	81,363
Money market fund shares	65,192	49,846	64,925
Shares and other equity	112,858	129,376	138,608
Other items (net)	–16,956	–10,088	–16,552
Total	463,884	442,151	450,562

Source: IMF, *International Financial Statistics*.

COST OF LIVING

(Consumer Price Index; base: December 2006 = 100)

	2010	2011	2012
Food and non-alcoholic beverages	100.7	101.8	102.4
Alcoholic beverages and tobacco	110.2	110.1	114.0
Clothing and footwear	71.5	70.2	70.1
Housing, water, electricity, gas and other fuel	95.2	104.4	105.1
Furnishings, household equipment and routine household maintenance	89.8	87.7	85.6
Health	112.6	116.4	116.9
Transport	106.2	109.8	116.1
Communications	103.3	105.7	104.1
Recreation and culture	99.9	99.1	97.9
Education	122.2	123.1	133.3
Restaurants and hotels	103.4	102.7	103.2
Miscellaneous goods and services	111.7	119.0	124.7
All items	101.2	103.8	105.6

NATIONAL ACCOUNTS

(€ million at current prices)

National Income and Product

	2010	2011	2012*
Gross domestic product in market prices	158,097	162,600	163,938
Net factor income from abroad	–26,285	–31,938	–31,289
Gross national product in market prices	131,812	130,662	132,649
Subsidies paid by the EU	1,494	1,700	1,632
Less Taxes paid to the EU	400	416	417
Gross national income in market prices	132,905	131,947	133,864
Net current transfers from abroad (excl. EU subsidies and taxes)	–2,508	–2,467	–2,420
Gross national disposable income	130,398	129,479	131,444

Expenditure on the Gross Domestic Product

	2010	2011	2012*
Government final consumption expenditure	26,196	25,701	25,096
Private final consumption expenditure	82,200	82,380	82,634
Changes in inventories	–567	984	376
Gross fixed capital formation	19,293	17,266	17,434
Total domestic expenditure	127,122	126,332	125,540
Exports of goods and services	157,810	166,964	176,736
Less Imports of goods and services	–128,326	–131,840	–136,990
Statistical discrepancy	1,490	1,144	–1,347
GDP in market prices	158,097	162,600	163,938

Gross Domestic Product by Economic Activity

	2010	2011	2012*
Agriculture, forestry and fishing	3,358	3,935	3,635
Mining and quarrying; Manufacturing; Electricity, gas and water supply; Construction	37,528	41,005	40,394
Wholesale and retail trade, repair and hotels and restaurants; Transport, storage and communications	35,895	35,582	36,186
Public administration and defence	6,751	6,498	6,036
Other services	60,801	61,676	61,062
Statistical discrepancy	–1,490	–1,144	1,347
Gross value added at factor cost	142,842	147,552	148,661
Taxes (excl. taxes on products)	2,300	2,356	2,340
Less Subsidies (excl. subsidies on products)	2,075	2,055	2,210
Gross value added in basic prices	143,066	147,853	148,791
Taxes on products	16,025	15,742	16,109
Less Subsidies on products	995	994	962
GDP in market prices	158,097	162,600	163,938

* Preliminary figures.

BALANCE OF PAYMENTS
(US $ million)

	2010	2011	2012
Exports of goods f.o.b.	118,792	127,471	119,321
Imports of goods f.o.b.	–62,124	–67,195	–63,628
Balance on goods	56,668	60,277	55,693
Exports of services	89,096	104,146	107,041
Imports of services	–107,301	–115,641	–111,955
Balance on goods and services	38,462	48,782	50,779
Primary income received	75,669	79,471	73,559
Primary income paid	–109,973	–123,734	–113,555
Balance on goods, services and primary income	4,158	4,519	10,783
Secondary transfers received	6,615	7,448	7,164
Secondary transfers paid	–8,455	–9,139	–8,701
Current balance	2,319	2,828	9,245
Capital account (net)	–915	–357	–2,634
Direct investment assets	–16,832	1,536	–21,340
Direct investment liabilities	37,764	23,665	40,962
Portfolio investment assets	17,740	–4,170	–95,816
Portfolio investment liabilities	101,615	41,379	94,077
Financial derivatives and employee stock options (net)	–16,024	554	–14,536
Other investment assets	–35,408	4,234	91,754
Other investment liabilities	–80,478	–71,043	–102,435
Net errors and omissions	–9,823	–16,266	–7,747
Reserves and related items	–42	–17,640	–8,470

Source: IMF, *International Financial Statistics*.

External Trade

PRINCIPAL COMMODITIES
(distribution by SITC, € million)

Imports c.i.f.	2010	2011	2012
Food and live animals	4,579	5,018	5,549
Mineral fuels, lubricants, etc.	5,602	6,946	7,016
Petroleum and petroleum products	4,285	5,324	5,336
Chemicals and related products	8,758	10,415	10,192
Organic chemicals	2,100	2,456	2,480
Medicinal and pharmaceutical products	3,464	4,387	4,127
Basic manufactures	3,499	3,712	3,698
Machinery and transport equipment	12,324	12,426	12,486
Office machines and automatic data-processing equipment	2,701	2,693	2,635
Telecommunications and sound equipment	1,129	1,058	1,193
Other electrical machinery, apparatus, etc.	2,146	2,102	1,910
Road vehicles and parts (excl. tyres, engines and electrical parts)	1,558	1,711	1,607
Other transport equipment	2,618	2,347	2,491
Miscellaneous manufactured articles	6,152	6,013	6,040
Total (incl. others)*	45,764	48,315	49,024

* Including transactions not classified by commodity.

Exports f.o.b.	2010	2011	2012
Food and live animals	6,983	7,874	8,064
Chemicals and related products	52,227	56,031	55,000
Organic chemicals	19,064	19,969	20,123
Medicinal and pharmaceutical products	24,206	26,393	24,447
Essential oils, perfume materials and toilet and cleansing preparations	5,462	5,777	6,245
Machinery and transport equipment	11,001	10,370	10,406
Office machines and automatic data-processing equipment	4,516	3,562	3,597
Telecommunications and sound equipment	829	708	963
Electrical machinery, apparatus, etc.	3,080	2,873	2,609
Miscellaneous manufactured articles	10,471	10,231	10,809
Professional, scientific and controlling apparatus	3,260	3,380	3,615
Total (incl. others)*	89,193	91,228	92,009

* Including transactions not classified by commodity.

PRINCIPAL TRADING PARTNERS
(€ million)*

Imports c.i.f.	2010	2011	2012
Belgium	1,084	1,166	955
China, People's Republic (incl. Hong Kong and Macao)	2,756	2,714	2,860
Denmark	779	605	460
France	1,842	1,994	1,902
Germany	3,493	3,706	3,414
Italy	780	775	772
Japan	798	796	728
Korea, Republic	244	384	333
Netherlands	2,226	2,434	2,311
Norway	1,291	1,165	938
Singapore	508	310	297
Spain	666	668	649
Sweden	341	480	361
Switzerland	847	762	958
Taiwan	163	184	252
United Kingdom	13,823	15,638	15,419
USA	6,427	5,907	6,397
Total (incl. others)	45,764	48,315	49,024

Exports f.o.b.	2010	2011	2012
Belgium	13,531	13,227	13,548
China, People's Republic (incl. Hong Kong and Macao)	2,494	2,330	2,167
France	4,482	4,951	4,428
Germany	6,354	6,285	7,526
Italy	2,709	2,992	2,684
Japan	1,754	1,743	2,101
Malaysia	693	385	241
Netherlands	3,091	3,123	3,346
Spain	3,359	3,049	2,767
Sweden	672	874	804
Switzerland	3,557	3,686	5,070
United Kingdom	12,436	12,845	13,794
USA	20,761	21,601	18,160
Total (incl. others)	89,193	91,228	92,009

* Imports by country of origin; exports by country of final destination.

Transport

RAILWAYS
(traffic, '000)

	2010	2011	2012
Passengers carried	38,070	37,222	36,837
Freight tonnage	568	611	567

ROAD TRAFFIC
(licensed motor vehicles at 31 December)

	2010	2011	2012
Passenger cars	1,872,715	1,887,810	1,882,550
Lorries and vans	327,096	320,966	309,219
Buses and coaches	34,925	33,405	32,446
Motorcycles and mopeds	38,145	36,582	35,106

Source: Department of Transport, Dublin.

SHIPPING

Flag Registered Fleet
(at 31 December)

	2011	2012	2013
Number of vessels	193	191	186
Total displacement (grt)	227,486	217,456	239,090

Source: Lloyd's List Intelligence (www.lloydslistintelligence.com).

Sea-borne Freight Traffic
('000 metric tons)

	2010	2011	2012
Goods loaded	14,359	15,240	16,458
Goods unloaded	30,712	29,838	31,191

CIVIL AVIATION
(traffic on scheduled services)

	2010	2011
Kilometres flown (million)	127	128
Passengers carried ('000)	84,784	89,956
Passenger-km (million)	97,834	109,948
Total ton-km (million)	8,959	10,101

Source: UN, *Statistical Yearbook*.

Passengers carried ('000): 92,053 in 2012 (Source: World Bank, World Development Indicators database).

Tourism

FOREIGN TOURIST ARRIVALS BY ORIGIN
('000)

	2007	2008	2009
France	394	412	390
Germany	436	456	408
Netherlands	155	151	134
United Kingdom*	4,369	4,170	3,665
Other continental Europe	1,592	1,542	1,395
Canada	96	103	82
USA	975	849	809
Other areas	316	343	306
Total	8,333	8,026	7,189

* Including residents of Northern Ireland.

2010: Germany 368; Italy 214; Spain 214; United Kingdom 3,356 (incl. residents of Northern Ireland); Total (incl. others) 6,515.

Total arrivals ('000): 7,630 in 2011.

Tourism receipts (€ million, excl. passenger transport, estimates): 4,118 in 2010; 4,567 in 2011; 4,078 in 2012 (provisional).
Source: World Tourism Organization.

Communications Media

	2010	2011	2012
Telephone lines ('000 in use)*	2,078.0	2,046.6	2,007.7
Mobile cellular telephones ('000 subscribers)*	4,701.5	4,906.4	4,905.9
Internet subscribers ('000)*	1,074.6	1,089.5	n.a.
Broadband subscribers ('000)	941.4	993.7	1,039.6

* At December.

Personal computers: 2,480,000 (582.1 per 1,000 persons) in 2006.

Source: International Telecommunication Union.

Education

(2012/13 unless otherwise indicated)

	Institutions	Teachers (full-time)	Students (full-time)
National schools*	3,293	32,175	526,422
Secondary schools	375	13,373†	187,709
Vocational schools	253	8,538†	118,860
Community and comprehensive schools	93	4,274†	56,278
Teacher (primary and home economics) training colleges	7	127‡	6,335
Technology colleges§	15	3,347‡	64,946
Universities and other Higher Education Authority Institutions	7	3,507‡	90,277
Other aided institutions	4	71‡	3,285

* State-aided primary schools; includes Special National Schools (numbering 141 in 2012/13).

† 2010/11.

‡ 2000/01.

§ Comprising 13 Institutes of Technology, the Tipperary Institute and the Hotel Training and Catering College, Killybegs, Co Donegal.

Sources: Central Statistics Office, and Department of Education and Skills.

Pupil-teacher ratio (primary education, UNESCO estimate): 15.6 in 2010/11 (Source: UNESCO Institute for Statistics).

Directory

The Government

HEAD OF STATE

Uachtarán (President): MICHAEL D. HIGGINS (assumed office 11 November 2011).

THE CABINET
(April 2014)

A coalition of Fine Gael (FG) and the Labour Party (LP)

Taoiseach (Prime Minister): ENDA KENNY (FG).

Tánaiste (Deputy Prime Minister), Minister for Foreign Affairs and Trade: EAMON GILMORE (LP).

Minister for Finance: MICHAEL NOONAN (FG).

Minister for Education and Skills: RUAIRÍ QUINN (LP).

Minister for Public Expenditure and Reform: BRENDAN HOWLIN (LP).

Minister for Jobs, Enterprise and Innovation: RICHARD BRUTON (FG).

Minister for Social Protection: JOAN BURTON (LP).

Minister for Arts, Heritage and the Gaeltacht: JIMMY DEENIHAN (FG).

Minister for Communications, Energy and Natural Resources: PAT RABBITTE (LP).

Minister for the Environment, Community and Local Government: PHIL HOGAN (FG).

Minister for Justice, Equality and Defence: ALAN SHATTER (FG).

Minister for Agriculture, Food and the Marine: SIMON COVENEY (FG).

Minister for Children and Youth Affairs: FRANCES FITZGERALD (FG).

Minister for Health: Dr JAMES REILLY (FG).

Minister for Transport, Tourism and Sport: LEO VARADKAR (FG).

MINISTRIES

Office of the President: Áras an Uachtaráin, Phoenix Park, Dublin 8; tel. (1) 6171000; fax (1) 6171001; e-mail info@president.ie; internet www.president.ie.

Department of the Taoiseach: Government Bldgs, Upper Merrion St, Dublin 2; tel. (1) 6194000; fax (1) 6194297; e-mail webmaster@taoiseach.gov.ie; internet www.taoiseach.gov.ie.

Department of Agriculture, Food and the Marine: Agriculture House, Kildare St, Dublin 2; tel. (1) 6072000; fax (1) 6616263; e-mail info@agriculture.gov.ie; internet www.agriculture.gov.ie.

Department of Arts, Heritage and the Gaeltacht: 23 Kildare St, Dublin 2; tel. (1) 6313800; e-mail press.office@ahg.gov.ie; internet www.ahg.gov.ie.

Department of Children and Youth Affairs: 43–49 Mespil Rd, Dublin 4; tel. (1) 6473000; fax (1) 6473101; e-mail omc@dcya.gov.ie; internet www.dcya.gov.ie.

Department of Communications, Energy and Natural Resources: 29–31 Adelaide Rd, Dublin 2; tel. (1) 6782000; fax (1) 6782449; e-mail press.office@dcenr.gov.ie; internet www.dcenr.gov.ie.

Department of Defence: Station Rd, Newbridge, Co Kildare; tel. (45) 492000; fax (45) 492017; e-mail info@defence.ie; internet www.defence.ie.

Department of Education and Skills: Marlborough St, Dublin 1; tel. (1) 8896714; fax (1) 8896788; e-mail info@education.gov.ie; internet www.education.ie.

Department of the Environment, Community and Local Government: Custom House, Dublin 1; tel. (1) 8882403; fax (1) 8882888; e-mail minister@environ.ie; internet www.environ.ie.

Department of Finance: Government Bldgs, Upper Merrion St, Dublin 2; tel. (1) 6767571; fax (1) 6789936; e-mail webmaster@finance.gov.ie; internet www.finance.gov.ie.

Department of Foreign Affairs and Trade: 80 St Stephen's Green, Dublin 2; tel. (1) 4082000; fax (1) 4082400; internet www.dfa.ie.

Department of Health: Hawkins House, Hawkins St, Dublin 2; tel. (1) 6354000; fax (1) 6354001; internet www.dohc.ie.

Department of Jobs, Enterprise and Innovation: 23 Kildare St, Dublin 2; tel. (1) 6312121; fax (1) 6312827; e-mail info@entemp.ie; internet www.enterprise.gov.ie.

Department of Justice and Equality: 94 St Stephen's Green, Dublin 2; tel. (1) 6028202; fax (1) 6615461; e-mail info@justice.ie; internet www.justice.ie.

Department of Public Expenditure and Reform: Government Bldgs, Upper Merrion St, Dublin 2; tel. (1) 6767571; fax (1) 6789936; e-mail webmasterper@per.gov.ie; internet per.gov.ie.

Department of Social Protection: Áras Mhic Dhiarmada, Store St, Dublin 1; tel. (1) 7043000; fax (1) 7043870; e-mail info@welfare.ie; internet www.welfare.ie.

Department of Transport, Tourism and Sport: 44 Kildare St, Dublin 2; tel. (1) 6707444; fax (1) 6041185; e-mail info@dttas.ie; internet www.dttas.ie.

Legislature

NATIONAL PARLIAMENT (OIREACHTAS)

Parliament comprises two Houses: Dáil Éireann (House of Representatives), with 166 members (Teachtaí Dála), elected for a five-year term by universal adult suffrage; and Seanad Éireann (Senate), with 60 members serving a five-year term, of whom 11 are nominated by the Taoiseach (Prime Minister) and 49 elected (six by the universities and 43 from specially constituted panels).

Dáil Éireann

Leinster House, Kildare St, Dublin 2; tel. (1) 6183000; fax (1) 6184118; e-mail communications@oireachtas.ie; internet www.oireachtas.ie.

Ceann Comhairle (Chairman): SEÁN BARRETT.

Leas-Cheann Comhairle (Deputy Chairman): MICHAEL KITT.

General Election, 25 February 2011

Party	Votes*	% of votes*	Seats
Fine Gael	801,628	36.10	76
Labour Party	431,796	19.45	37
Fianna Fáil	387,358	17.45	20†
Independents	279,459	12.58	15
Sinn Féin	220,661	9.94	14
Socialist Party	26,770	1.21	2
People Before Profit Alliance	21,551	0.95	2
Green Party	41,039	1.85	—
Total (incl. others)	2,220,359	100.00	166

* The election was conducted by means of the single transferable vote. Figures refer to first-preference votes.

† Including the Ceann Comhairle (Chairman), who is automatically re-elected.

Seanad Éireann

Leinster House, Dublin 2; tel. (1) 6183000; fax (1) 6184118; e-mail info@oireachtas.ie; internet www.oireachtas.ie.

Cathaoirleach (Chairman): PADDY BURKE.

Leas-Chathaoirleach (Deputy Chairman): DENIS O'DONOVAN.

Elections were held to the Seanad Éireann in April 2011, with the closing date for the receipt of votes from the members of five vocational panels (Administrative, Agricultural, Cultural and Educational, Industrial and Commercial, and Labour) being 26 April, and that for the two university panels (National University of Ireland, and University of Dublin) being 27 April. Following the nomination of 11 members by the Taoiseach (Prime Minister) on 20 May, the strength of the parties was as follows:

Party	Elected	Appointed	Total seats
Fianna Fáil	18	1	19
Fine Gael	14	—	14
Labour Party	9	3	12
Sinn Féin	3	—	3
Independents	5	7	12
Total	49	11	60

Political Organizations

Communist Party of Ireland (Páirtí Cumannach na hÉireann): James Connolly House, 43 East Essex St, Dublin 2; tel. and fax (1)

6708707; e-mail cpoi@eircom.net; internet www.communistpartyofireland.ie; f. 1933; advocates a united, socialist, independent Ireland; Chair. LYNDA WALKER; Gen. Sec. EUGENE MCCARTAN.

Fianna Fáil (The Republican Party) (Soldiers of Destiny): 65–66 Lower Mount St, Dublin 2; tel. (1) 6761551; fax (1) 6785690; e-mail info@fiannafail.ie; internet www.fiannafail.ie; f. 1926; centrist; Pres. and Leader MICHEÁL MARTIN; Gen. Sec. SEÁN DORGAN.

Fine Gael (United Ireland Party) (Family of the Irish): 51 Upper Mount St, Dublin 2; tel. (1) 6198444; e-mail finegael@finegael.com; internet www.finegael.ie; f. 1933; centrist; Leader ENDA KENNY; Chair CHARLIE FLANAGAN; Gen. Sec. TOM CURRAN.

Green Party (Comhaontas Glas): 16–17 Suffolk St, Dublin 2; tel. (1) 6790012; fax (1) 6797168; e-mail info@greenparty.ie; internet www.greenparty.ie; f. 1981 as the Ecology Party of Ireland; name changed as above in 1983; advocates a humane, ecological society, freedom of information and political decentralization; Leader EAMON RYAN; Chair. RODERIC O'GORMAN; Asst Gen. Sec. ALISON MARTIN.

The Labour Party: 17 Ely Place, Dublin 2; tel. (1) 6784700; fax (1) 6612640; e-mail head.office@labour.ie; internet www.labour.ie; f. 1912; merged with Democratic Left (f. 1992) in 1999; democratic socialist party; affiliated to the Party of European Socialists; Leader EAMON GILMORE; Gen. Sec. ITA MCAULIFFE.

Sinn Féin (We Ourselves): 44 Parnell Sq., Dublin 1; tel. (1) 8726100; fax (1) 8733441; e-mail admin@sinnfein.ie; internet www.sinnfein.ie; f. 1905; advocates the termination of British rule in Northern Ireland; seeks a mandate to establish a democratic socialist republic in a reunified Ireland; Pres. GERRY ADAMS; Chair. DECLAN KEARNEY; Gen. Sec. DAWN DOYLE.

Socialist Party: 141 Thomas St, Dublin 8; tel. (1) 6772592; fax (1) 6772686; e-mail info@socialistparty.net; internet www.socialistparty.net; f. 1996; mem. of the Committee for a Workers' International (CWI); advocates a socialist Ireland as part of a free and voluntary socialist federation of Ireland, Scotland, England and Wales; anti-EU; Leader JOE HIGGINS.

The Workers' Party: 48 North Great George's St, Dublin 1; tel. (1) 8740716; fax (1) 8748702; e-mail wpi@indigo.ie; internet www.workerspartyireland.net; f. 1905; fmrly Sinn Féin The Workers' Party; name changed as above in 1982; aims to establish a unitary socialist state on the island of Ireland; Pres. MICHAEL FINNEGAN; Gen. Sec. JOHN LOWRY.

Diplomatic Representation

EMBASSIES IN IRELAND

Argentina: 15 Ailesbury Dr., Dublin 4; tel. (1) 2691546; fax (1) 2600404; e-mail embassyofargentina@eircom.net; Ambassador SILVIA PISANO MARÍA MEREGA.

Australia: Fitzwilton House, 7th Floor, Wilton Terrace, Dublin 2; tel. (1) 6645300; fax (1) 6623566; e-mail austremb.dublin@dfat.gov.au; internet www.ireland.embassy.gov.au; Ambassador Dr RUTH P. ADLER.

Austria: 15 Ailesbury Court, 93 Ailesbury Rd, Dublin 4; tel. (1) 2694577; fax (1) 2830860; e-mail dublin-ob@bmeia.gv.at; Ambassador THOMAS NADER.

Belgium: 2 Shrewsbury Rd, Dublin 4; tel. (1) 6315283; fax (1) 6675665; e-mail dublin@diplobel.fed.be; internet www.diplomatie.belgium.be/ireland; Ambassador PHILIPPE ROLAND.

Brazil: Harcourt Centre, Block 8, Charlotte Way, Dublin 2; tel. (1) 4756000; fax (1) 4751341; e-mail info@brazil.ie; internet dublin.itamaraty.gov.br/en-us; Ambassador AFONSO JOSÉ SENA CARDOSO.

Bulgaria: 22 Burlington Rd, Dublin 4; tel. (1) 6603293; fax (1) 6603915; e-mail bulgarianembassydublin@eircom.net; internet www.mfa.bg/embassies/ireland; Ambassador BRANIMIR ZAIMOV.

Canada: 7–8 Wilton Terrace, 3rd Floor, Dublin 2; tel. (1) 2344000; fax (1) 2344001; e-mail dubln@international.gc.ca; internet www.canadainternational.gc.ca/ireland-irlande; Ambassador LOYOLA HEARN.

Chile: 44 Wellington Rd, Dublin 4; tel. (1) 6675094; fax (1) 6675156; e-mail echile.irlanda@minrel.gov.cl; internet www.chileabroad.gov.cl/irlanda; Ambassador LEONEL SEARLE.

China, People's Republic: 40 Ailesbury Rd, Dublin 4; tel. (1) 2691707; fax (1) 2839938; e-mail chinaemb_ie@mfa.gov.cn; internet ie.china-embassy.org; Ambassador XU JIANGUO.

Croatia: Adelaide Chambers, Peter St, Dublin 8; tel. (1) 4767181; fax (1) 4767183; e-mail croemb.dublin@mvep.hr; internet ie.mfa.hr; Ambassador JASNA OGNJANOVAC.

Cuba: 32B, Westland Sq., Pearse St, Dublin 2; tel. (1) 4752999; e-mail infocubadublin@eircom.net; internet www.cubadiplomatica.cu/irlanda; Ambassador HERMES HERRERA HERNÁNDEZ.

Cyprus: 71 Lower Leeson St, Dublin 2; tel. (1) 6763060; fax (1) 6763099; e-mail dublinembassy@mfa.gov.cy; internet www.mfa.gov.cy/embassydublin; Ambassador MICHALIS STAVRINOS.

Czech Republic: 57 Northumberland Rd, Dublin 4; tel. (1) 6681135; fax (1) 6681660; e-mail dublin@embassy.mzv.cz; internet www.mfa.cz/dublin; Ambassador HANA MOTTLOVÁ.

Denmark: Block E, 7th Floor, Iveagh Court, Harcourt Rd, Dublin 2; tel. (1) 4756404; fax (1) 4784536; e-mail dubamb@um.dk; internet www.irland.um.dk; Ambassador NIELS CHRISTEN PULTZ.

Egypt: 12 Clyde Rd, Ballsbridge, Dublin 4; tel. (1) 6606566; fax (1) 6683745; e-mail info@embegyptireland.ie; internet www.embegyptireland.ie; Ambassador SHERIF ELKHOLI.

Estonia: Block E, 3rd Floor, Iveagh Court, Harcourt Rd, Dublin 2; tel. (1) 4788888; fax (1) 4788887; e-mail embassy.dublin@mfa.ee; internet www.estemb.ie; Ambassador MAIT MARTINSON.

Ethiopia: 26 Upper Fitzwilliam St, Dublin 2; tel. (1) 6787062; fax (1) 6787065; e-mail info@ethiopianembassy.ie; internet www.ethiopianembassy.ie; Ambassador LELA-ALEM GEBREYOHANNES TEDLA.

Finland: Russell House, Stokes Pl., St Stephen's Green, Dublin 2; tel. (1) 4781344; fax (1) 4783727; e-mail sanomat.dub@formin.fi; internet www.finland.ie; Ambassador HILKKA NENONEN.

France: 36 Ailesbury Rd, Ballsbridge, Dublin 4; tel. (1) 2775000; fax (1) 2775001; e-mail chancellerie@ambafrance.ie; internet www.ambafrance-ie.org; Ambassador JEAN-PIERRE THÉBAULT.

Georgia: 5 Marine Rd, Dun Laoghaire, Co Dublin; tel. (1) 4067956; Chargé d'affaires IRAKLI KOPLATADZE.

Germany: 31 Trimleston Ave, Booterstown, Blackrock, Co Dublin; tel. (1) 2693011; fax (1) 2693800; e-mail info@dublin.diplo.de; internet www.dublin.diplo.de; Ambassador Dr ECKHARD LÜBKEMEIER.

Greece: 1 Upper Pembroke St, Dublin 2; tel. (1) 6767254; fax (1) 6618892; e-mail amboffice.dub@mfa.gr; internet www.mfa.gr/dublin; Ambassador CONSTANTINA ZAGORIANOU-PRIFTI.

Holy See: 183 Navan Rd, Dublin 7; tel. (1) 8380577; fax (1) 8380276; e-mail nuncioirl@eircom.net; Apostolic Nuncio Most Rev. CHARLES J. BROWN (Titular Archbishop of Aquileia).

Hungary: 2 Fitzwilliam Pl., Dublin 2; tel. (1) 6612902; fax (1) 6612880; e-mail mission.dub@kum.hu; internet www.mfa.gov.hu/kulkepviselet/ie; Ambassador Dr TAMÁS MAGYARICS.

India: 6 Leeson Park, Dublin 6; tel. (1) 4966792; fax (1) 4978074; e-mail indembassy@eircom.net; internet www.indianembassy.ie; Ambassador RADHIKA LAL LOKESH.

Iran: 72 Mount Merrion Ave, Blackrock, Co Dublin; tel. (1) 2880252; fax (1) 2834246; e-mail iranembassy@indigo.ie; Ambassador HOSSEIN PANAHIAZAR.

Israel: 122 Pembroke Rd, Ballsbridge, Dublin 4; tel. (1) 2309400; fax (1) 2309446; e-mail info@dublin.mfa.gov.il; internet dublin.mfa.gov.il; Ambassador BOAZ MODAI.

Italy: 63–65 Northumberland Rd, Dublin 4; tel. (1) 6601744; fax (1) 6682759; e-mail ambasciata.dublino@esteri.it; internet www.ambdublino.esteri.it; Ambassador GIOVANNI ADORNI BRACCESI CHIASSI.

Japan: Nutley Bldg, Merrion Centre, Nutley Lane, Dublin 4; tel. (1) 2028300; fax (1) 2838726; e-mail cultural@embjp.ie; internet www.ie.emb-japan.go.jp; Ambassador CHIHIRO ATSUMI.

Kenya: 11 Elgin Rd, Dublin 4; tel. (1) 6136380; fax (1) 6685506; e-mail info@kenyaembassyireland.net; internet www.kenyaembassyireland.net; Chargé d'affaires a.i. IMMACULATE N. WAMBUA.

Korea, Republic: Clyde House, 15 Clyde Rd, POB 2101, Dublin 4; tel. (1) 6608800; fax (1) 6608716; e-mail irekoremb@mofat.go.kr; internet irl.mofat.go.kr; Ambassador PARK HAE-YUN.

Latvia: 92 St Stephen's Green, Dublin 2; tel. (1) 4780161; fax (1) 4780162; e-mail embassy.ireland@mfa.gov.lv; internet www.am.gov.lv/en/ireland; Ambassador GINTS APALS.

Lesotho: 2 Clanwilliam Sq., Grand Canal Quay, Dublin 2; tel. (1) 6762233; fax (1) 6762258; e-mail info@lesothoembassy.ie; internet www.lesothoembassy.ie; Ambassador PARAMENTE PHAMOTSE.

Lithuania: 47 Ailesbury Rd, Ballsbridge, Dublin 4; tel. (1) 2035757; fax (1) 2839354; e-mail amb.ie@urm.lt; internet ie.mfa.lt; Ambassador VIDMANTAS PURLYS.

Malaysia: Level 3A–5A Shelbourne House, Shelbourne Rd, Dublin 4; tel. (1) 6677280; fax (1) 6677283; e-mail mwdublin@mwdublin.ie; Ambassador Dato' RAMLI NAAM.

Malta: 15 Leeson St Lower, Dublin 2; tel. (1) 6762340; fax (1) 6766066; e-mail maltaembassy.dublin@gov.mt; Chargé d'affaires CHANTAL SCIBERRAS.

Mexico: 19 Raglan Rd, Dublin 4; tel. (1) 6673105; fax (1) 6641013; e-mail info@embamex.ie; internet www.sre.gob.mx/irlanda; Ambassador CARLOS EUGENIO GARCIA DE ALBA.

Morocco: 39 Raglan Rd, Dublin 4; tel. (1) 6609449; fax (1) 6609468; e-mail sifamdub@indigo.ie; Ambassador ANAS KHALES.

Netherlands: 160 Merrion Rd, Dublin 4; tel. (1) 2693444; fax (1) 2839690; e-mail dub-info@minbuza.nl; internet www.netherlandsembassy.ie; Ambassador PAUL SCHELLEKENS.

Nigeria: 56 Leeson Park, Dublin 6; tel. (1) 6604366; fax (1) 6604092; e-mail enquiries@nigerianembassydublin.org; internet www.nigerianembassydublin.org; Ambassador FELIX YUSUFU PWOL.

Norway: 34 Molesworth St, Dublin 2; tel. (1) 6621800; fax (1) 6621890; e-mail emb.dublin@mfa.no; internet www.norway.ie; Ambassador ROALD NÆSS.

Pakistan: Ailesbury Villa, 1B Ailesbury Rd, Dublin 4; tel. (1) 2613032; fax (1) 2613007; e-mail pakembassydublin@gmail.com; internet www.pakembassydublin.com; Ambassador G. R. MALIK.

Poland: 5 Ailesbury Rd, Ballsbridge, Dublin 4; tel. (1) 2830855; fax (1) 2698309; e-mail dublin@msz.gov.pl; internet www.dublin.msz.gov.pl; Ambassador MARCIN NAWROT.

Portugal: 15 Leeson Park, Dublin 6; tel. (1) 4127040; fax (1) 4970299; e-mail embport@dublin.dgaccp.pt; internet www.embassyportugal.ie; Ambassador BERNARDO FUTSCHER PEREIRA.

Romania: 26 Waterloo Rd, Dublin 4; tel. (1) 6681085; fax (1) 6681761; e-mail ambrom@eircom.net; internet dublin.mae.ro; Ambassador MANUELA BREAZU.

Russia: 184–186 Orwell Rd, Rathgar, Dublin 14; tel. (1) 4922048; fax (1) 4923525; e-mail info@russianembassy.ie; internet www.ireland.mid.ru; Ambassador MAXIM ALEXANDROVICH PESHKOV.

Saudi Arabia: 6–7 Fitzwilliam Sq. East, Dublin 2; tel. (1) 6760704; fax (1) 6760715; e-mail prsedi@gmail.com; Ambassador ABD AL-AZIZ ABD AL-RAHMAN ALDRISS.

Slovakia: 80 Merrion Sq., Dublin 2; tel. (1) 6619594; fax (1) 6619553; e-mail emb.dublin@mzv.sk; internet www.mzv.sk/dublin; Ambassador DUŠAN MATULAY.

South Africa: Alexandra House, 2nd Floor, Earlsfort Centre, Earlsfort Terrace, Dublin 2; tel. (1) 6615553; fax (1) 6615590; e-mail dublin.info@dirco.gov.za; Ambassador AHLANGENE CYPRIAN SIGCAU.

Spain: 17A Merlyn Park, Dublin 4; tel. (1) 2691640; fax (1) 2691854; e-mail emb.dublin.inf@maec.es; internet www.maec.es/embajadas/dublin; Ambassador JAVIER GARRIGUES FLÓREZ.

Switzerland: 6 Ailesbury Rd, Dublin 4; tel. (1) 2186382; fax (1) 2830344; e-mail dub.vertretung@eda.admin.ch; internet www.eda.admin.ch/dublin; Ambassador MARIE-CLAUDE MEYLAN.

Turkey: 8 Raglan Rd, Ballsbridge, Dublin 4; tel. (1) 6144590; fax (1) 6685014; e-mail embassy.dublin@mfa.gov.tr; internet www.dublin.be.mfa.gov.tr; Ambassador NECIP EGÜZ.

Ukraine: 16 Elgin Rd, Ballsbridge, Dublin 4; tel. (1) 6685189; fax (1) 6697917; e-mail ukrembassy@eircom.net; internet www.mfa.gov.ua/ireland; Ambassador SERGII REVA.

United Arab Emirates: 45–47 Pembroke Rd, Dublin 4; tel. (1) 6600000; fax (1) 2375920; e-mail dublin@mofa.gov.ae; Ambassador KHALID NASSER RASHED LOOTAH.

United Kingdom: 29 Merrion Rd, Dublin 4; tel. (1) 2053700; fax (1) 2053885; e-mail chancery.dublx@fco.gov.uk; internet www.britishembassy.ie; Ambassador. DOMINICK JOHN CHILCOTT.

USA: 42 Elgin Rd, Dublin 4; tel. (1) 6688777; fax (1) 6689946; e-mail dublinrsvp@state.gov; internet dublin.usembassy.gov; Chargé d'affaires STUART DWYER.

Judicial System

Justice is administered in public by judges appointed by the President on the advice of the Government. The judges of all courts are completely independent in the exercise of their judicial functions. The jurisdiction and organization of the courts are dealt with in the Courts (Establishment and Constitution) Act, 1961, and the Courts (Supplemental Provisions) Acts, 1961 to 1981. An amendment to the Constitution, approved by a referendum held in October 2013, created a new Court of Appeal, which was expected to be established by October 2014.

Attorney-General: MÁIRE WHELAN.

SUPREME COURT

An Chúirt Uachtarach (The Supreme Court): Four Courts, Inns Quay, Dublin 7; tel. (1) 8886569; fax (1) 8732332; e-mail supremecourt@courts.ie; internet www.supremecourt.ie; consisting of the Chief Justice and seven other judges, the Supreme Court has appellate jurisdiction from all decisions of the High Court; the President of Ireland may, after consultation with the Council of State, refer a bill that has been passed by both Houses of the Oireachtas (other than a money bill or certain others) to the Court to establish whether it or any other provisions thereof are repugnant to the Constitution; the President of the High Court is ex officio a member of the Supreme Court; Chief Justice SUSAN DENHAM.

COURT OF CRIMINAL APPEAL

The Court of Criminal Appeal, consisting of the Chief Justice or an ordinary judge of the Supreme Court and two judges of the High Court, deals with appeals by persons convicted on indictment, where leave to appeal has been granted. The Court has jurisdiction to review a conviction or sentence on the basis of an alleged miscarriage of justice. The Director of Public Prosecutions may appeal against an unduly lenient sentence. The decision of the Court of Criminal Appeal is final unless the Court or Attorney-General or the Director of Public Prosecutions certifies that a point of law involved should, in the public interest, be taken to the Supreme Court.

HIGH COURT

An Ard-Chúirt (The High Court): Four Courts, Inns Quay, Dublin 7; tel. (1) 8886442; fax (1) 8725669; e-mail highcourtcentraloffice@courts.ie; internet www.courts.ie; comprising the President of the High Court and 36 ordinary judges, the High Court has full original jurisdiction in, and power to determine, all matters and questions whether of law or fact, civil or criminal; the High Court on circuit acts as an appeal court from the Circuit Court; the Central Criminal Court sits as directed by the President of the High Court to try criminal cases outside the jurisdiction of the Circuit Court; the duty of acting as the Central Criminal Court is assigned to a judge, or judges, of the High Court; the Chief Justice and the President of the Circuit Court are ex officio additional Judges of the High Court; Pres. NICHOLAS KEARNS; Master of the High Court EDMUND HONOHAN.

CIRCUIT AND DISTRICT COURTS

The civil jurisdiction of the Circuit Court is limited to €38,092.14 in contract and tort and in actions founded on hire-purchase and credit-sale agreements and to a rateable value of €252.95 in equity, and in probate and administration, but where the parties consent the jurisdiction is unlimited. In criminal matters the Court has jurisdiction in all cases except murder, rape, treason, piracy and allied offences. One circuit court judge is permanently assigned to each of the eight circuits with the exception of Dublin, which has 10 judges, and Cork, which has three. The remainder of the 38 judges are not permanently assigned to any circuit. The President of the District Court is ex officio an additional Judge of the Circuit Court. The Circuit Court acts as an appeal court from the District Court, which has a summary jurisdiction in a large number of criminal cases where the offence is not of a serious nature. In civil matters the District Court has jurisdiction in contract and tort (except slander, libel, seduction, slander of title, malicious prosecution and false imprisonment) where the claim does not exceed €6,348.69 and in actions founded on hire-purchase and credit-sale agreements.

All criminal cases, except those dealt with summarily by a judge in the District Court, are tried by a judge and a jury of 12 members. Juries are also used in some civil cases in the High Court. In a criminal case 10 members of the jury may, in certain circumstances, agree on a verdict, and in a civil case the agreement of nine members is sufficient.

President of An Chúirt Chuarda (the Circuit Court): RAYMOND GROARKE.

President of An Chúirt Dúiche (the District Court): ROSEMARY HORGAN.

Religion

CHRISTIANITY

The organization of the churches takes no account of the partition of the island of Ireland into two separate political entities; both Northern Ireland and Ireland are subject to a unified ecclesiastical jurisdiction. The Roman Catholic Primate of All Ireland and the Church of Ireland (Protestant Episcopalian) Primate of All Ireland have their seats in Northern Ireland, at Armagh, and the headquarters of the Presbyterian Church in Ireland is at Belfast, Northern Ireland.

Adherents of the Roman Catholic Church were enumerated at 3,861,335 in the 2011 census, representing some 84% of the population. In the same year there were 129,039 adherents of the Church of Ireland, 24,600 of the Presbyterian Church and 6,842 of the Methodist Church. There were 45,223 adherents of Orthodox churches in that year.

Irish Council of Churches: Inter-Church Centre, 48 Elmwood Ave, Belfast, BT9 6AZ, Northern Ireland; tel. (28) 9066-3145; e-mail info@irishchurches.org; internet www.irishchurches.org; f. 1922;

present name adopted 1966; Pres. Fr GODFREY O'DONNELL; Exec. Officer MERVYN MCCULLAGH; 15 mem. churches.

The Roman Catholic Church

The island of Ireland comprises four archdioceses and 22 dioceses. Numerous Roman Catholic religious orders are strongly established in the state; these play an important role, particularly in the spheres of education, health and social welfare.

Irish Episcopal Conference: Ara Coeli, Cathedral Rd, Armagh, BT61 7QY, Northern Ireland; tel. (28) 3752-2045; fax (28) 3752-6182; e-mail admin@aracoeli.com; Pres. Cardinal SEÁN B. BRADY (Archbishop of Armagh).

Archbishop of Armagh and Primate of All Ireland: Cardinal SEÁN B. BRADY, Ara Coeli, Cathedral Rd, Armagh, BT61 7QY, Northern Ireland; tel. (28) 3752-2045; fax (28) 3752-6182; e-mail admin@aracoeli.com; internet www.armagharchdiocese.org.

Archbishop of Cashel and Emly: Most Rev. DERMOT CLIFFORD, Archbishop's House, Thurles, Co Tipperary; tel. (504) 21512; fax (504) 22680; e-mail office@cashel-emly.ie; internet www.cashel-emly.ie.

Archbishop of Dublin and Primate of Ireland: Most Rev. Dr DIARMUID MARTIN, Archbishop's House, Drumcondra, Dublin 9; tel. (1) 8379253; fax (1) 8360793; e-mail communications@dublindiocese.ie; internet www.dublindiocese.ie.

Archbishop of Tuam: Most Rev. Dr MICHAEL NEARY, Archbishop's House, St Jarlath's, Tuam, Co Galway; tel. (93) 24166; fax (93) 28070; e-mail archdiocesetuam@gmail.com; internet www.tuamarchdiocese.org.

Church of Ireland

(The Anglican Communion)

Ireland (including Northern Ireland) comprises two archdioceses and 10 dioceses.

The Representative Body of the Church of Ireland: Church of Ireland House, Church Ave, Rathmines, Dublin 6; tel. (1) 4978422; fax (1) 4978821; e-mail office@rcbdub.org; internet rcb.ireland.anglican.org; Chief Officer and Sec. ADRIAN CLEMENTS.

Archbishop of Armagh and Primate of All Ireland and Metropolitan: Most Rev. Dr RICHARD CLARKE, The See House, Cathedral Close, Armagh, BT61 7EE, Northern Ireland; tel. (28) 3752-2858; fax (28) 3751-0596; e-mail archbishop@armagh.anglican.org; internet armagh.anglican.org.

Archbishop of Dublin and Bishop of Glendalough, Primate of Ireland and Metropolitan: Most Rev. Dr MICHAEL JACKSON, The See House, 17 Temple Rd, Milltown, Dublin 6; tel. (1) 4977849; fax (1) 4976355; e-mail archbishop@dublin.anglican.org; internet www.dublin.anglican.org.

Orthodox Churches

Greek Orthodox Church in Ireland: Greek Orthodox Church of the Annunciation, 46 Arbour Hill, Dublin 7; tel. and fax (1) 6779020; Pres. Very Rev. Dr IRENEU IOAN CRACIUN.

Russian Orthodox Church (Moscow Patriarchate) in Ireland: Harold's Cross Rd, Dublin 6; tel. (86) 7347934; e-mail stpeterstpaul@stpeterstpaul.net; internet www.stpeterstpaul.net; f. 2001; Parish Priest Very Rev. Fr MIKHAIL NASONOV.

Other Christian Churches

Association of Baptist Churches in Ireland: The Baptist Centre, 19 Hillsborough Rd, Moira, BT67 0HG, Northern Ireland; tel. (28) 9261-9267; e-mail abc@thebaptistcentre.org; internet www.baptistsinireland.org; Pres. Pastor PHILIP BROWN.

Lutheran Church in Ireland: Lutherhaus, 24 Adelaide Rd, Dublin 2; tel. and fax (1) 6766548; e-mail info@lutheran-ireland.org; internet www.lutheran-ireland.org; f. 1698; Pastors Dr JOACHIM DIESTELKAMP, CORINNA DIESTELKAMP.

Methodist Church in Ireland: 1 Fountainville Ave, Belfast, BT9 6AN, Northern Ireland; tel. (28) 9032-4554; fax (28) 9023-9467; e-mail secretary@irishmethodist.org; internet www.irishmethodist.org; Pres. Rev. KENNETH LINDSAY.

Presbyterian Church in Ireland: Church House, Fisherwick Place, Belfast, BT1 6DW, Northern Ireland; tel. (28) 9032-2284; fax (28) 9041-7301; e-mail info@presbyterianireland.org; internet www.presbyterianireland.org; Moderator of Gen. Assembly Rev. Dr ROB CRAIG; Clerk of Assembly and Gen. Sec. Rev. Dr DONALD WATTS.

Religious Society of Friends (Quakers) in Ireland: Quaker House, Stocking Lane, Rathfarnham, Dublin 16; tel. (1) 4998003; fax (1) 4998005; e-mail office@quakers.ie; internet www.quakers.ie; Recording Clerk ROSEMARY CASTAGNER.

ISLAM

The Muslim population of Ireland stood at 49,204 at the 2011 census.

Irish Council of Imams: 19 Roebuck Rd, Clonskeagh, Dublin 14; tel. (1) 2080000; e-mail imamhalawa@islamireland.ie; f. 2006; comprises 14 imams from across Ireland; Chair. Imam Sheikh HUSSEIN HALAWA; Vice-Chair. Sheikh YAHYA AL-HUSSEIN.

Islamic Cultural Centre of Ireland: 19 Roebuck Rd, Clonskeagh, Dublin 14; tel. (1) 2080000; fax (1) 2080001; e-mail info@islamireland.ie; internet www.islamireland.ie; f. 1996; CEO Dr NOOH AL-KADDO; Imam Sheikh HUSSEIN HALAWA.

Islamic Foundation of Ireland: 163 South Circular Rd, Dublin 8; tel. (1) 4533242; fax (1) 4532785; e-mail info@islaminireland.com; internet www.islaminireland.com; f. 1959; religious, cultural, educational and social org.; Imam YAHYA MUHAMMAD AL-HUSSEIN.

JUDAISM

At the 2011 census, the Jewish community numbered 1,984. In 2008 there were a total of three synagogues operating, of which two were Orthodox and one was progressive.

Chief Rabbi: ZALMAN LENT, Herzog House, Zion Rd, Rathgar, Dublin 6; tel. (1) 4923751; fax (1) 4920888; e-mail rabbilent@jewishireland.org; internet www.jewishireland.org.

The Press

A significant feature of the Irish press is the number of weekly and twice-weekly newspapers published in provincial centres.

DAILIES

(Average net circulation figures, including Ireland and the United Kingdom, as at December 2011, unless otherwise stated)

Cork

Evening Echo: City Quarter, Lapps Quay, Cork; tel. (21) 4272722; fax (21) 4273846; e-mail news@eecho.ie; internet www.eveningecho.ie; f. 1892; Editor MAURICE GUBBINS; circ. 17,556 (2012).

Irish Examiner: City Quarter, Lapps Quay, Cork; tel. (21) 4272722; fax (21) 4273846; e-mail editor@examiner.ie; internet www.irishexaminer.com; f. 1841; Editor TIM VAUGHAN; circ. 42,083.

Dublin

Evening Herald: Independent House, 27–32 Talbot St, Dublin 1; tel. (1) 7055333; fax (1) 7055497; e-mail hnews@independent.ie; internet www.herald.ie; f. 1891; Editor CLAIRE GRADY; circ. 62,411.

Irish Daily Mail: Embassy House, 3rd Floor, Herbert Park Lane, Dublin 4; tel. (1) 6375800; fax (1) 6375880; internet www.dailymail.co.uk; Propr Associated Newspapers (United Kingdom); Editor-in-Chief SEBASTIAN HAMILTON; circ. 50,486.

Irish Daily Star: Bldg 4, Level 5, Dundrum Town Centre, Sandyford Rd, Dublin 16; tel. (1) 4993400; fax (1) 4902193; e-mail info@thestar.ie; internet www.thestar.ie; Editor GERARD COLLERAN; circ. 81,105 (Ireland only).

Irish Independent: 27–32 Talbot St, Dublin 1; tel. (1) 7055333; fax (1) 8720304; internet www.independent.ie; f. 1905; Editor CLAIRE GRADY; circ. 131,161.

The Irish Times: Irish Times Bldg, 24–28 Tara St, Dublin 2; tel. (1) 6758000; fax (1) 6758035; e-mail newsdesk@irishtimes.com; internet www.irishtimes.com; f. 1859; Editor KEVIN O'SULLIVAN; circ. 96,150.

Metro Herald: Independent House, 1st Floor, 27–32 Talbot St, Dublin 1; tel. (1) 7055055; fax (1) 7055044; e-mail info@metroherald.ie; internet www.metroherald.ie; f. 2009 by merger of *Metro* and *Herald AM* (both f. 2005); distributed free of charge in the Greater Dublin area; Man. Dir PAUL CROSBIE; circ. 60,151.

OTHER NEWSPAPERS

(Average net circulation figures, including Ireland and the United Kingdom, as at December 2011, unless otherwise stated)

An Phoblacht: 58 Parnell Sq., Dublin 1; tel. (1) 8733611; fax (1) 8733074; e-mail editor@anphoblacht.com; internet www.anphoblacht.com; f. 1970; organ of Sinn Féin; monthly; Editor JOHN HEDGES; circ. 15,000 (2007).

Anglo-Celt: Station House, Cavan, Co Cavan; tel. (49) 4331100; fax (49) 4332280; e-mail linda@anglocelt.ie; internet www.anglocelt.ie; f. 1846; Thur.; Editor LINDA O'REILLY; circ. 12,310.

Argus: Partnership Court, Park St, Dundalk, Co Louth; tel. (42) 9334632; fax (42) 9331643; e-mail editorial@argus.ie; internet www.argus.ie; f. 1835; Thur.; circ. 11,507 (2007).

Clare Champion: Barrack St, Ennis, Co Clare; tel. (65) 6828105; fax (65) 6820374; e-mail editor@clarechampion.ie; internet www.clarechampion.ie; f. 1903; Thur.; Editor AUSTIN HOBBS; circ. 15,742.

Connacht Tribune: 15 Market St, Galway; tel. (91) 536222; fax (91) 567970; e-mail cormac@ctribune.ie; internet www.galwaynews.ie; f. 1909; Fri.; Group Editor DAVE O'CONNELL; circ. 20,702.

Connaught Telegraph: Cavendish Lane, Castlebar, Co Mayo; tel. (94) 9021711; fax (94) 9024007; e-mail info@con-telegraph.ie; internet www.con-telegraph.ie; f. 1828; Tue.; independent; Editor TOM GILLESPIE; circ. 14,900.

Donegal Democrat: Larkin House, Oldtown Rd, Donegal, Co Donegal; tel. (7491) 28000; e-mail editorial@donegaldemocrat.com; internet www.donegaldemocrat.com; f. 1919; Tue. and Thur.; Editor MICHAEL DALY; circ. 6,618 (Tue.); 9,191 (Thur.).

Drogheda Independent: 9 Shop St, Drogheda, Co Louth; tel. (41) 9838658; fax (41) 9834271; e-mail editorial@drogheda-independent.ie; internet www.drogheda-independent.ie; f. 1884; Thur.; circ. 10,328 (2007).

Dundalk Democrat: 7 Crowe St, Dundalk, Co Louth; tel. (42) 9334058; fax (42) 9331399; e-mail editor@dundalkdemocrat.ie; internet www.dundalkdemocrat.ie; f. 1849; Wed.; Editor ANTHONY MURPHY; circ. 6,500 (2007).

Dungarvan Observer: Shandon, Dungarvan, Co Waterford; tel. (58) 41205; fax (58) 41559; e-mail news@dungarvanobserver.ie; internet www.dungarvanobserver.ie; f. 1912; Editor JAMES A. LYNCH.

The Echo: Slaney Pl., Enniscorthy, Co Wexford; tel. (53) 9259900; fax (53) 9233506; e-mail editor@theecho.ie; internet www.theecho.ie; f. 1902; Wed.; edns for Enniscorthy, Gorey, New Ross and Wexford; Editor TOM MOONEY; circ. 7,210.

Iris Oifigiúil (Official Irish Gazette): 52 St Stephen's Green, Dublin 2; tel. (1) 6476636; fax (1) 6476843; e-mail irisoifigiuil@opw.ie; internet www.irisoifigiuil.ie; f. 1922; twice weekly (Tue. and Fri.); Editor DEIRDRE CARROLL.

Irish Mail on Sunday: Embassy House, 3rd Floor, Herbert Park Lane, Dublin 4; tel. (1) 6375800; fax (1) 4179830; Propr Associated Newspapers (United Kingdom); fmrly *Ireland on Sunday*; name changed as above in 2006; Editor-in-Chief CONOR O'DONNELL; circ. 122,231.

The Kerryman: Denny St, Tralee, Co Kerry; tel. (66) 7145500; fax (66) 7145572; e-mail dmalone@kerryman.ie; internet www.kerryman.ie; f. 1904; Thur.; Editor DECLAN MALONE; circ. 26,392 (2007).

Kilkenny People: 34 High St, Kilkenny; tel. (56) 7721015; fax (56) 7721414; e-mail editor@kilkennypeople.ie; internet www.kilkennypeople.ie; f. 1892; weekly; Editor BRIAN KEYES; circ. 11,536.

Leinster Express: Dublin Rd, Portlaoise, Co Laois; tel. (57) 8621666; fax (57) 8620491; e-mail conor.ganly@leinsterexpress.ie; internet www.leinsterexpress.ie; f. 1831; weekly; Editor PAT SOMERS; circ. 11,070 (incl. *Offaly Express*).

Leinster Leader: 19 South Main St, Naas, Co Kildare; tel. (45) 897302; fax (45) 897647; e-mail editor@leinsterleader.ie; internet www.leinsterleader.ie; f. 1880; Tue.; Editor DAVID POWER; circ. 6,497.

Limerick Leader: 54 O'Connell St, Limerick; tel. (61) 214500; fax (61) 401424; e-mail admin@limerick-leader.ie; internet www.limerick-leader.ie; f. 1889; 4 a week; Editor ALAN ENGLISH; circ. 14,851 (weekend edn).

Limerick Post: 97 Henry St, Limerick; tel. (61) 413322; fax (61) 417684; e-mail news@limerickpost.ie; internet www.limerickpost.ie; f. 1986; owned by Carnbeg Limited; distributed free of charge; Thur.; Dir JOHN RYAN; circ. 52,011.

The Mayo News: The Fairgreen, Westport, Co Mayo; tel. (98) 25311; fax (98) 26108; e-mail info@mayonews.ie; internet www.mayonews.ie; f. 1892; Tue.; Man. Editor NEILL O'NEILL; circ. 10,569 (2007).

Midland Tribune: Main St, Birr, Co Offaly; tel. (57) 9120003; fax (57) 9120588; e-mail editor@midlandtribune.ie; internet www.midlandtribune.ie; f. 1881; Wed.; Editor JOHN O'CALLAGHAN; circ. 10,105 (2007).

The Nationalist: Hanover House, Hanover, Carlow; tel. (59) 9170100; fax (59) 9130301; e-mail news@carlow-nationalist.ie; internet www.carlow-nationalist.ie; f. 1883; owned by Thomas Crosbie Holdings; Editor CONAL O'BOYLE.

Offaly Express: Bridge St, Tullamore, Co Offaly; tel. (57) 9321744; fax (57) 9351930; e-mail alan@offalyexpress.ie; internet www.offalyexpress.ie; weekly; Editor ALAN WALSH; circ. 11,070 (incl. *Leinster Express*).

Sligo Champion: Connacht House, Markievicz Rd, Sligo; tel. (71) 9169222; fax (71) 9169040; e-mail editor@sligochampion.ie; internet www.sligochampion.ie; f. 1836; Tue.; Editor JENNY MCCUDDEN; circ. 12,574 (2007).

The Southern Star: Ilen St, Skibbereen, Co Cork; tel. (28) 21200; fax (28) 21071; e-mail info@southernstar.ie; internet www.southernstar.ie; f. 1889; Sat.; Editor CON DOWNING; circ. 14,500 (2007).

Sunday Business Post: 80 Harcourt St, Dublin 2; tel. (1) 6026000; fax (1) 6796496; e-mail info@sbpost.ie; internet www.businesspost.ie; f. 1989; Editor CLIFF TAYLOR; circ. 39,416.

Sunday Independent: Independent House, 27–32 Talbot St, Dublin 1; tel. (1) 7055333; fax (1) 7055779; e-mail sunday.letters@independent.ie; internet www.independent.ie; f. 1905; Editor ANNE HARRIS; circ. 250,641.

Sunday World: Independent House, 27–32 Talbot St, Dublin 1; tel. (1) 8848900; fax (1) 8849002; e-mail news@sundayworld.com; internet www.sundayworld.com; f. 1973; Editor COLM MCGINTY; circ. 251,455.

Tipperary Star: Friar St, Thurles, Co Tipperary; tel. (504) 21122; e-mail info@tipperarystar.ie; internet www.tipperarystar.ie; f. 1909; Wed.; Editor ANNE O'GRADY; circ. 7,115.

Tuam Herald: Dublin Rd, Tuam, Co Galway; tel. (93) 24183; fax (93) 24478; e-mail editor@tuamherald.ie; internet www.tuamherald.ie; f. 1837; Wed.; Editor DAVID BURKE; circ. 8,482.

Tullamore Tribune: William St, Tullamore, Co Offaly; tel. (5793) 21152; fax (5793) 21927; e-mail editor@tullamoretribune.ie; internet www.tullamoretribune.ie; f. 1978; Wed.; Editor GERARD SCULLY.

Waterford News & Star: Gladstone House, Gladstone St, Waterford; tel. (51) 874951; fax (51) 855281; e-mail editor@waterford-news.ie; internet www.waterford-news.ie; f. 1848; Thur.; Editor FRANCES RYAN.

Western People: Tone St, Ballina, Co Mayo; tel. (96) 60999; fax (96) 70208; e-mail info@westernpeople.ie; internet www.westernpeople.ie; f. 1883; Tue.; Editor JAMES LAFFEY; circ. 14,166.

Westmeath Examiner: Blackhall Pl., Mullingar, Co Westmeath; tel. (44) 9346700; fax (44) 9330765; e-mail editor@westmeathexaminer.ie; internet www.westmeathexaminer.ie; f. 1882; weekly; Editor BRIAN O'LOUGHLIN; circ. 5,799.

Wicklow People: Channing House, Upper Row St, Wicklow, Co Wexford; tel. (53) 9140100; fax (53) 9140192; e-mail front.office@peoplenews.ie; internet www.wicklowpeople.ie; weekly; circ. 13,122 (2007).

SELECTED PERIODICALS

Afloat: 2 Lower Glenageary Rd, Dún Laoghaire, Co Dublin; tel. (1) 2846161; fax (1) 2846192; e-mail info@afloat.ie; internet www.afloat.ie; monthly; sailing and boating; Man. Editor DAVID O'BRIEN.

Banking Ireland: 1 North Wall Quay, Dublin 1; tel. (1) 6116500; fax (1) 6116565; e-mail info@bankers.ie; internet www.instbankers.com/bi/index.html; f. 1898; quarterly; journal of the Inst. of Bankers in Ireland; circ. 15,500 (Dec. 2006).

Books Ireland: Unit 9, 78 Furze Rd, Sandyford Industrial Estate, Dublin 18; tel. (1) 2933568; e-mail booksireland@wordwellbooks.com; f. 1976; owned by Wordwell Books Ltd; 6 a year; reviews Irish-interest books; Editor ANTHONY CANAVAN; circ. 2,350 (Dec. 2013).

Business & Finance: Unit 1A, Waters Edge, Charlotte Quay, Dublin 4; tel. (1) 2377000; fax (1) 6602504; e-mail info@businessandfinance.com; internet www.businessandfinance.com; f. 1964; bi-monthly; Publr IAN HYLAND; Editor NIAMH MAC SWEENEY; circ. 10,000.

Food & Wine: Rosemount House, Dundrum Rd, Dundrum, Dublin 16; tel. (1) 2405300; fax (1) 6619486; e-mail ross@harmonia.ie; internet www.harmonia.ie; f. 1997; publ. by Harmonia Ltd; Editor ROSS GOLDEN-BANNON; circ. 8,607 (2012).

Hot Press: 13 Trinity St, Dublin 2; tel. (1) 2411500; fax (1) 2411538; e-mail info@hotpress.com; internet www.hotpress.com; fortnightly; music, leisure, current affairs; Editor NIALL STOKES; circ. 17,178 (2012).

House and Home: Cunningham House, 130 Francis St, Dublin 8; tel. (1) 4167930; fax (1) 4167901; e-mail info@dyflin.ie; internet www.houseandhome.ie; bi-monthly; published by Dyflin Media Ltd; interior decor.

Image: 22 Crofton Rd, Dún Laoghaire, Co Dublin; tel. (1) 2808415; fax (1) 2808309; e-mail info@image.ie; internet www.image.ie; f. 1975; bi-monthly; women's fashion, lifestyle; Editor MELANIE MORRIS; circ. 21,511.

Ireland's Own: Channing House, Rowe St, Co Wexford; tel. (53) 9140140; fax (53) 9140192; e-mail irelands.own@peoplenews.ie; f. 1902; weekly; family interest; Editors PHILIP MURPHY, SEAN NOLAN; circ. 38,033 (2011).

The Irish Catholic: St Mary's, Bloomfield Ave, Donnybrook, Dublin 4; tel. (1) 6874020; fax (1) 4276450; e-mail news@irishcatholic.ie; internet www.irishcatholic.ie; f. 1888; publ. by Grace Communications; weekly; Man. Editor MICHAEL KELLY; circ. 30,000 (2012).

Irish Computer: Media House, South County Business Park, Leopardstown, Dublin 18; tel. (1) 2947777; fax (1) 2947799; e-mail info@mediateam.ie; internet www.techcentral.ie; f. 1977; monthly; Editor BILLY HUGGARD; circ. 4,000 (+1,500 to Irish Computer Society members).

Irish Farmers' Journal: Irish Farm Centre, Bluebell, Dublin 12; tel. (1) 4199599; fax (1) 4520876; e-mail jmccarthy@farmersjournal.ie; internet www.farmersjournal.ie; f. 1948; weekly; Editor JUSTIN MCCARTHY; weekly circ. 70,111 (July–Dec 2012).

The Irish Field: Irish Farm Centre, Bluebell, Dublin 12; tel. (1) 4051100; fax (1) 4554008; e-mail info@theirishfield.ie; internet www.theirishfield.ie; f. 1870; publ. by the Agricultural Trust; weekly; horse racing, breeding and equine leisure; Man. Editor LEO POWELL; circ. 11,117 (July–Dec 2012).

Irish Historical Studies: c/o Dept of History, Trinity College, Dublin 2; tel. (1) 6081020; e-mail info@irishhistoricalstudies.ie; internet www.irishhistoricalstudies.ie; f. 1938; 2 a year; publ. by Irish Historical Studies Publications Ltd; Editors Dr ROBERT ARMSTRONG, Dr ROBERT MCNAMARA.

Irish Journal of Medical Science: Royal Academy of Medicine in Ireland, Setanta House, 2nd Floor, Setanta Pl., Dublin 2; tel. (1) 6334820; fax (1) 6334918; e-mail helenmoore@rcpi.ie; internet www.ijms.ie; f. 1832; quarterly; organ of the Royal Academy of Medicine; Editor Prof. JAMES JONES.

Irish Law Times: Round Hall, 43 Fitzwilliam Pl., Dublin 2; tel. (1) 6625301; fax (1) 6625302; e-mail maura.smyth@thomsonreuters.com; internet www.roundhall.ie; f. 1983; 20 a year; Editor DAVID BOYLE.

Irish Medical Journal: 10 Fitzwilliam Pl., Dublin 2; tel. (1) 6767273; fax (1) 6612758; e-mail lduffy@imj.ie; internet www.imj.ie; f. 1867; 10 a year; journal of the Irish Medical Org; Editor Dr JOHN F. A. MURPHY.

The Irish Skipper: Unit 5, Teach na Rosann, Annagry, Co Donegal; tel. (74) 9548935; fax (74) 9548940; e-mail hugh@maramedia.ie; internet www.irishskipper.net; f. 1964; monthly; journal of the commercial fishing and aquaculture industries; Editor HUGH BONNER.

Irish Tatler: Rosemount House, Dundrum Rd, Dundrum, Dublin 16; tel. (1) 2405300; fax (1) 6619486; internet www.irishtatler.com; f. 1890; monthly; Editor SHAUNA O'HALLORAN (acting); circ. 24,919 (July–Dec 2012).

Irish University Review: School of English, Drama and Film, University College Dublin, Belfield, Dublin 4; tel. (1) 7168181; fax (1) 7161174; e-mail john.brannigan@ucd.ie; internet www.irishuniversityreview.ie; f. 1970; 2 a year; literature, history, fine arts, politics, cultural studies; Editor Dr JOHN BRANNIGAN.

Law Society Gazette: Law Society of Ireland, Blackhall Pl., Dublin 7; tel. (1) 6724800; fax (1) 6724801; e-mail gazette@lawsociety.ie; internet www.gazette.ie; f. 1907; 10 a year; publ. by the Law Society of Ireland; Editor MARK MCDERMOTT.

Motoring Life: 48 North Great George's St, Dublin 1; tel. (1) 8780444; fax (1) 8787740; e-mail info@motoringlife.ie; internet www.motoringlife.ie; f. 1946; bi-monthly; Editor GERALDINE HERBERT.

The Phoenix: 44 Lower Baggot St, Dublin 2; tel. (1) 6611062; fax (1) 6624532; e-mail editor@thephoenix.ie; internet www.thephoenix.ie; f. 1983; fortnightly; news and comment, satirical; Editor PADDY PRENDIVILLE; circ. 14,013 (July–Dec 2012).

Poetry Ireland (Éigse Éireann): 32 Kildare St, Dublin 2; tel. (1) 6789815; fax (1) 6789782; e-mail info@poetryireland.ie; internet www.poetryireland.ie; quarterly; Editor JOHN F. DEANE.

RTÉ Guide: Radio Telefís Éireann, Donnybrook, Dublin 4; tel. (1) 2083111; fax (1) 2083080; internet www.rteguide.ie; weekly; programmes of the Irish broadcasting service; Editor CATHERINE LEE; circ. 61,881 (2012).

ShelfLife: Media House, South County Business Park, Leopardstown, Dublin 18; tel. (1) 2947777; fax (1) 2947799; e-mail shelflife@mediateam.ie; internet www.shelflife.ie; monthly; food, drinks, grocery, consumer goods sectors; owned by Mediateam LTD; Man. Dir JOHN MCDONALD; Editor FIONNUALA CAROLAN; circ. 7,795 (2012).

Studies: An Irish Quarterly Review: 35 Lower Leeson St, Dublin 2; tel. (1) 6766785; fax (1) 7758598; e-mail studies@jesuit.ie; internet www.studiesirishreview.ie; f. 1912; published by the Jesuits In Ireland; quarterly review of letters, history, religious and social questions; Editor Fr BRUCE BRADLEY.

U Magazine: Rosemount House, Dundrum Rd, Dundrum, Dublin 14; tel. (1) 2405300; fax (1) 6619757; e-mail jstevens@harmonia.ie; internet www.harmonia.ie/#/20; f. 1979; every 2 weeks; for young women; Editor JENNIFER STEVENS; circ. 27,819 (2012).

Village Magazine: 6 Ormond Quay Upper, Dublin 7; tel. (1) 8735824; fax (1) 6425001; e-mail editor@villagemagazine.ie; internet www.villagemagazine.ie; f. 2004; monthly; current affairs; Editor MICHAEL SMITH.

Woman's Way: Rosemount House, Dundrum Rd, Dundrum, Dublin 14; tel. (1) 2405300; fax (1) 6628719; e-mail atoner@harmonia.ie; internet www.harmonia.ie/#/21; f. 1963; 51 a year; Editor AINE TONER; circ. 22,120 (2012).

NEWS AGENCY

Ireland International News Agency: 51 Wellington Quay, Dublin 2; tel. (1) 6712442; fax (1) 6796586; e-mail iina@eircom.net; Man. Dir DIARMAID MACDERMOTT.

PRESS ORGANIZATIONS

National Newspapers of Ireland: Clyde Lodge, 15 Clyde Rd, Dublin 4; tel. (1) 6689099; fax (1) 6689872; e-mail info@nni.ie; internet www.nni.ie; f. 1985; 16 mems; Chair. MATT DEMPSEY; Co-ordinating Dir FRANK CULLEN.

Regional Newspapers and Printers Association of Ireland: Latt, Cavan; tel. and fax (1) 6779116; e-mail johanlon@regionalnewspapers.ie; internet www.regionalnewspapers.ie; f. 1917; 35 mems; Pres. SEAN MAHON; Dir JOHNNY O'HANLON.

Publishers

Blackhall Publishing: Lonsdale House, Avoca Ave, Dublin; tel. (1) 2785090; fax (1) 2784800; e-mail info@blackhallpublishing.com; internet www.blackhallpublishing.com; f. 1997; law, business, marketing, management.

Boole Press: 19 Silchester Rd, Glenageary, Co Dublin; e-mail info@boolepress.com; internet www.boolepress.com; f. 1979; scientific, technical, medical, scholarly; Man. Dir Dr J. MILLER.

Cló Iar-Chonnachta: Inverin, Connemara, Co Galway; tel. (91) 593307; fax (91) 593362; e-mail eolas@cic.ie; internet www.cic.ie; f. 1985; music, children's books; Gen. Man. DEIRDRE NÍ THUATHAIL.

The Columba Press: 55A Spruce Ave, Stillorgan Industrial Park, Blackrock, Co Dublin; tel. (1) 2942556; fax (1) 2942564; e-mail info@columba.ie; internet www.columba.ie; f. 1985; sport, health, food, music, history, religion, memoirs, politics and fiction; Publr FEARGHAL O'BOYLE.

Comhairle Bhéaloideas Éireann (Folklore of Ireland Council): University College, Belfield, Dublin 4; tel. (1) 7168216; fax (1) 17161144; e-mail info@comhairlebheal.ie; internet comhairlebheal.ie; Editor Prof. SÉAMAS Ó CATHÁIN.

Cork University Press: Youngline Industrial Estate, Pouladuff Rd, Togher, Cork; tel. (21) 4902980; internet www.corkuniversitypress.com; f. 1925; owned by University College Cork; academic, art, music, geography, literature, history; imprints include Attic Press and Atrium; Publications Dir MIKE COLLINS.

Dedalus Press: 13 Moyclare Rd, Baldoyle, Dublin 13; tel. (1) 8392034; e-mail editor@dedaluspress.com; internet www.dedaluspress.com; f. 1985; Irish and some international poetry, occasional prose; Publr and Editor PAT BORAN.

Dominican Publications: 42 Parnell Sq., Dublin 1; tel. (1) 8731355; fax (1) 8731760; e-mail sales@dominicanpublications.com; internet www.dominicanpublications.com; f. 1897; religious affairs in Ireland and the developing world, pastoral-liturgical aids; Man. Rev. BERNARD TREACY.

CJ Fallon: Block B, Ground Floor, Liffey Valley Office Campus, Dublin 22; tel. (1) 6166400; fax (1) 6166499; e-mail editorial@cjfallon.ie; internet www.cjfallon.ie; f. 1927; educational; CEO BRIAN GILSENAN.

Four Courts Press: 7 Malpas St, Dublin 8; tel. (1) 4534668; fax (1) 4534672; e-mail info@fourcourtspress.ie; internet www.fourcourtspress.ie; f. 1970; philosophy, theology, Celtic and Medieval studies, art, literature, modern history; Editorial Dir MARTIN FANNING; Publr MARTIN HEALY.

The Gallery Press: Loughcrew, Oldcastle, Co Meath; tel. and fax (49) 8541779; e-mail gallery@indigo.ie; internet www.gallerypress.com; f. 1970; poetry, plays, prose by Irish authors; Publr and Editor PETER FALLON.

Gill and Macmillan: Hume Ave, Park West, Dublin 12; tel. (1) 5009500; fax (1) 5009597; e-mail sales@gillmacmillan.ie; internet www.gillmacmillan.ie; f. 1968; literature, biography, history, social sciences, current affairs and textbooks; Chair. MICHAEL GILL.

Goldsmith Press: Newbridge, Co Kildare; tel. (45) 433613; fax (45) 434648; f. 1972; poetry, Irish art, plays, foreign language, general; Dirs DESMOND EGAN, VIVIENNE ABBOTT.

Hachette Ireland: Unit 8, Castlecourt Centre, Dublin 15; tel. (1) 8246288; e-mail info@hbgi.ie; internet www.hachette.ie; f. 2002 as Hodder Headline Ireland; fiction, non-fiction; div. of Hachette UK; Editorial Dir CIARA DOORLEY.

Irish Academic Press: 8 Chapel Lane, Sallins, Co. Kildare; tel. (45) 895562; fax (45) 895563; e-mail info@iap.ie; internet www.iap.ie; f. 1974; academic and popular, mainly history and Irish studies; Publr CONOR GRAHAM; Man. Editor LISA HYDE.

Liberties Press: 140 Terenure Rd North, Dublin 6; tel. (1) 4151286; fax (1) 4100985; e-mail info@libertiespress.com; internet www

.libertiespress.com; f. 2003; sport, health, food, music, history, religion, politics and fiction; Publr SEAN O'KEEFFE.

Lilliput Press: 62/63 Sitric Rd, Arbour Hill, Dublin 7; tel. (1) 6711647; fax (1) 6711233; e-mail info@lilliputpress.ie; internet www.lilliputpress.ie; f. 1985; ecology and environment, literary criticism, biography, memoirs, fiction, Irish history, general; Publr ANTONY FARRELL.

Mentor Books: 43 Furze Rd, Sandyford Industrial Estate, Dublin 18; tel. (1) 2952112; fax (1) 2952114; e-mail admin@mentorbooks.ie; internet www.mentorbooks.ie; f. 1979; adult and children's fiction and non-fiction, educational; Man. Dir DANIEL MCCARTHY.

Mercier Press Ltd: Unit 3B, Oak House, Bessboro Rd, Blackrock, Co Cork; tel. (21) 4614700; fax (21) 4614802; e-mail info@mercierpress.ie; internet www.mercierpress.ie; f. 1944; folklore, history, biography, current affairs, fiction, politics, humour, religious; Man. Dir CLODAGH FEEHAN.

O'Brien Press Ltd: 12 Terenure Rd East, Rathgar, Dublin 6; tel. (1) 4923333; fax (1) 4922777; e-mail books@obrien.ie; internet www.obrien.ie; f. 1974; biography, history, sport, Celtic, politics, travel, crime, children's; Man. Dir IVAN O'BRIEN.

Poolbeg Press: 123 Grange Hill, Baldoyle Industrial Estate, Dublin 13; tel. (1) 8321477; fax (1) 8321430; e-mail info@poolbeg.com; internet www.poolbeg.com; f. 1976; general, poetry, politics, children's; Publr PAULA CAMPBELL.

Royal Irish Academy (Acadamh Ríoga na hÉireann): 19 Dawson St, Dublin 2; tel. (1) 6762570; fax (1) 6762346; e-mail admin@ria.ie; internet www.ria.ie; f. 1785; humanities and sciences; Man. Editor RUTH HEGARTY; Exec. Sec. LAURA MAHONEY.

Thomson Reuters/Round Hall: 43 Fitzwilliam Pl., Dublin 2; tel. (1) 6625301; fax (1) 6625302; e-mail catherine.dolan@thomsonreuters.com; internet www.roundhall.ie; f. 1980 as The Round Hall Press; law books and journals and Westlaw IE online; part of Thomson Reuters; Publr CATHERINE DOLAN.

Veritas Publications: 7–8 Lower Abbey St, Dublin 1; tel. (1) 8788177; fax (1) 8786507; e-mail publications@veritas.ie; internet www.veritas.ie; f. 1969; Christian, religious and educational, theological, liturgical; Dir MAURA HYLAND.

GOVERNMENT PUBLISHING HOUSE

Oifig an tSoláthair/Stationery Office: Government Publications, Office of Public Works, 52 St Stephen's Green, Dublin 2; tel. (1) 6476834; fax (1) 6476843; e-mail publications@opw.ie; internet www.opw.ie; Asst Principal Officer GERRY BURKE.

PUBLISHERS' ASSOCIATION

Publishing Ireland/Foilsiú Éireann: 25 Denzille Lane, Dublin 8; tel. (1) 6394868; e-mail info@publishingireland.com; internet www.publishingireland.com; f. 1970 as CLÉ—Irish Book Publishers' Association; 100 mem. publishers; Pres. MICHAEL MCLOUGHLIN.

Broadcasting and Communications

TELECOMMUNICATIONS

eircom: 1 Heuston South Quarter, St John's Rd, Dublin 8; tel. (1) 6714444; fax (1) 6716916; e-mail press-office@eircom.ie; internet www.eircom.ie; f. 1984; fmrly Telecom Éireann; offers fixed-line telecommunications and internet access; partially privatized in 1999, acquired by BCM Ireland Holdings Ltd in August 2006; Chair. NED SULLIVAN; CEO HERB HRIBAR.

Meteor Mobile Communications Ltd: 1 Heuston South Quarter, St John's Rd, Dublin 8; tel. (1) 4307085; fax (1) 4307013; e-mail info@meteor.ie; internet www.meteor.ie; f. 2001; mobile cellular telecommunications; subsidiary of eircom; 1,065,000 subscribers (March 2010).

Hutchison 3G Ireland Ltd (3 Ireland): 1 Clarendon Row, 3rd Floor, Dublin 2; tel. (1) 5426300; fax (1) 5426301; e-mail customer.services.ie@3mail.com; internet www.three.ie; f. 2005; mobile cellular telecommunications; owned by Hutchison Whampoa Ltd (Hong Kong); 500,000 subscribers (June 2010); CEO ROBERT FINNEGAN.

Telefónica O_2 Ireland Ltd: 28–29 Sir John Rogerson's Quay, Dublin 2; tel. (1) 6095000; e-mail customercare@o2.ie; internet www.o2.ie; f. 1997; mobile cellular telecommunications and broadband internet access; acquired by Telefónica, SA (Spain) 2006; CEO TONY HANWAY.

Vodafone Ireland: Mountainview, Leopardstown, Dublin 18; tel. (1) 2038232; fax (1) 6708465; e-mail custcare@vodafone.ie; internet www.vodafone.ie; f. 2001, following acquisition of Eircell; mobile cellular telecommunications; subsidiary of Vodafone Group PLC (UK); Chief Exec. ANNE O'LEARY.

Regulatory Authority

Commission for Communications Regulation (ComReg): Block DEF, Abbey Court, Irish Life Centre, Lower Abbey St, Dublin 1; tel. (1) 8049600; fax (1) 8049680; e-mail info@comreg.ie; internet www.comreg.ie; f. 2002; regulatory authority for Ireland's postal and telecommunications sectors; issues licences to service providers; manages the interconnection of telecommunications networks; approves equipment and oversees national telephone numbering; Chair. KEVIN O'BRIEN.

BROADCASTING

The Radio and Television Act of 1988 provided for the establishment of an independent television station, an independent national radio service and a series of local radio stations.

Broadcasting Authority of Ireland (BAI): 2–5 Warrington Pl., Dublin 2; tel. (1) 6441200; fax (1) 6441299; e-mail info@bai.ie; internet www.bai.ie; f. 2009 to replace the Broadcasting Commission of Ireland (f. 1988) and the Broadcasting Complaints Commission (f. 1977); responsible for regulating public service and independent broadcasting in Ireland; also responsible for the licensing of new broadcasting services, as well as the development of codes of programming and advertising standards for television and radio services; Chair. BOB COLLINS.

Radio

Raidió Teilifís Éireann (RTÉ): Donnybrook, Dublin 4; tel. (1) 2083111; fax (1) 2083080; e-mail info@rte.ie; internet www.rte.ie; f. 1960; national public service broadcasting corpn; financed by net licence revenue and sale of advertising time; governed by Board of 12 mems; operates 4 radio networks; Chair. TOM SAVAGE; Dir-Gen. NOEL CURRAN; Man. Dir of Radio JIM JENNINGS; Man. Dir of Television GLEN KILLANE; Man. Dir. of News KEVIN BAKHURST.

RTÉ lyric fm: Cornmarket Sq., Limerick, Co Limerick; tel. (61) 207300; fax (61) 207390; e-mail lyric@rte.ie; internet www.rte.ie/lyricfm; broadcasts classical and traditional music, jazz, opera; Dir AODÁN Ó DUBHGHAILL.

RTÉ Radio 1: Donnybrook, Dublin 4; tel. (1) 2083111; e-mail info@rte.ie; internet www.rte.ie/radio1; music news, drama and entertainment programmes; Dir TOM MCGUIRE.

RTÉ Raidió na Gaeltachta: Casla, Connemara, Co Galway; tel. (91) 506677; fax (91) 506666; e-mail rnag@rte.ie; internet www.rte.ie/rnag; f. 1972; broadcasts in Irish.

RTÉ 2FM: Donnybrook, Dublin 4; tel. (1) 2083111; e-mail info@rte.ie; internet 2fm.rte.ie; popular music; Head DAN HEALY.

Classic Hits 4FM: Castleforbes House, Ground Floor, Castleforbes Rd, Dublin 1; tel. (1) 4255400; fax (1) 4255444; e-mail info@4fm.ie; internet www.4fm.ie; f. 2009; broadcasting popular music programmes in Co Clare, Co Cork, Co Dublin, Co Galway and Co Limerick; Chief Exec. SEAN ASHMORE.

FM104: Macken House, Mayor St Upper, North Wall, Dublin 1; tel. (1) 5006600; fax (1) 6689401; e-mail sales@fm104.ie; internet www.fm104.ie; broadcasts popular music and entertainment programmes in Co Dublin; owned by UTV (UK); Chief Exec. MARGARET NELSON.

NewsTalk 106–108 FM: Marconi House, Digges Lane, Dublin 2; tel. (1) 6445100; fax (1) 6445101; e-mail info@newstalk.ie; internet www.newstalk.ie; f. 2002; began broadcasting news and talk programmes nationally in 2006; Propr Communicorp Group; Chair. DENIS O'BRIEN; Chief Exec. (vacant).

98 FM: South Block, The Malt House, Grand Canal Quay, Dublin 2; tel. (1) 4398800; fax (1) 4398899; e-mail info@98fm.com; internet www.98fm.com; f. 1989; provides news service to independent local radio stations under contract from the BAI; Propr Communicorp Group; CEO CHRIS DOYLE; Head of News TEENA GATES.

100-102 Today FM: Marconi House, Digges Lane, Dublin 2; tel. (1) 8049000; fax (1) 8049099; e-mail live@todayfm.com; internet www.todayfm.com; f. 1998; national, independent station; acquired by Communicorp Group 2007; Chair. JOHN MCCOLGAN; CEO WILLIE O'REILLY.

There are also local radio stations operating under the supervision of the Independent Radio and Television Commission.

Television

Four television channels, RTÉ 1, RTÉ 2, TV3 and TG4 owned by RTÉ NL (RTÉ Transmissions Network Ltd) transmit free-to-air channels. In October 2012 the transition from analogue to digital broadcasting was completed.

Raidió Teilifís Éireann (RTÉ): see above; operates 2 television channels: RTÉ 1 and RTÉ 2; Man. Dir of Television GLEN KILLANE.

Sky Ireland: Alexandra House, Earlsfort Terrace, Dublin 2; tel. (1) 6147776; internet www.sky.com/ireland; Man. Dir J. D. BUCKLEY.

TG4 (Teilifís na Gaeilge): Baile na hAbhann, Connemara, Co Galway; tel. (91) 505050; fax (91) 505021; e-mail pol.o.gallchoir@tg4.ie;

internet www.tg4.ie; f. 1996; national public service Irish-language broadcaster; fmrly operated under RTÉ, became an independent statutory authority in April 2007; financed by the Govt and sales of commercial airtime; Chief Exec. PÓL Ó GALLCHÓIR.

TV3: Westgate Business Park, Ballymount, Dublin 24; tel. (1) 4193333; fax (1) 4193300; e-mail info@tv3.ie; internet www.tv3.ie; f. 1998; first national, commercial, independent television network; also broadcasts entertainment channel, 3e; CEO DAVID MCREDMOND; Dir of Programming BEN FROW; Dir of News ANDREW HANLON.

Finance

(cap. = capital; res = reserves; dep. = deposits; m. = million; brs = branches; amounts in euros, unless otherwise indicated)

BANKING

Under the Central Bank Reform Act 2010, which took effect on 1 October, the Central Bank of Ireland was created as a new unitary body responsible for both central banking and financial regulation. The new structure replaced the previous related entities, the Central Bank and the Financial Services Authority of Ireland and the Financial Regulator.

Central Bank

Central Bank of Ireland (Banc Ceannais na hÉireann): Dame St, POB 559, Dublin 2; tel. (1) 2246000; fax (1) 6716561; e-mail enquiries@centralbank.ie; internet www.centralbank.ie; f. 1942; bank of issue; responsible for regulation of the banking and financial services industry; cap. and res 1,740.1m., dep. 108,408.4m. (Dec. 2009); Gov. PATRICK HONOHAN; Deputy Gov. (Financial Regulation) CYRIL ROUX; Deputy Gov. (Central Banking) STEFAN GERLACH.

Principal Banks

AIB Group (Allied Irish Banks PLC): Bankcentre, POB 452, Ballsbridge, Dublin 4; tel. (1) 6600311; fax (1) 6604715; e-mail aibtoday@aib.ie; internet www.aib.ie; f. 1966; 18.6% shares held by the Govt; nationalized in Dec. 2010; cap. 5,206m., res 5,039m., dep. 63,645m. (Dec. 2012); Exec. Chair. DAVID HODGKINSON; Man. Dir DAVID DUFFY; over 750 brs and offices.

Bank of Ireland Group: Lower Baggot St, Dublin 2; tel. (1) 6615933; fax (1) 6615193; e-mail careline@boimail.com; internet www.bankofireland.ie; f. 1783; cap. 2,452m., res 1,532m., dep. 83,220m. (Dec. 2012); Chair. ARCHIE KANE; CEO RICHIE BOUCHER; 357 brs.

Barclays Bank Ireland PLC: 2 Park Pl., Hatch St, Dublin 2; tel. (1) 6182600; internet www.barclays.ie; CEO ANDREW STEWART HASTINGS.

Danske Bank A/S: National House, Airton Close, Tallaght, Dublin 24; tel. (1) 4840000; fax (1) 6385198; internet www.danskebank.ie; f. 1986 as Northern Bank (Ireland) Ltd; name changed to present in 2012; subsidiary of Danske Bank Group (Denmark); began withdrawal from personal banking in Ireland in early 2014; Chair. PETER STRAARUP; CEO ANDREW HEALY; 61 brs.

DEPFA Bank PLC: 1 Commons St, Dublin 1; tel. (1) 7922222; fax (1) 7922211; e-mail info@depfa.com; internet www.depfa.com; subsidiary of Hypo Real Estate Holding AG (Germany); cap. 1,242m., res 2,602m., dep. 20,032m. (Dec. 2012); CEO TOM GLYNN.

DZ BANK Ireland PLC: International House, 3 Harbourmaster Pl., IFSC, Dublin 1; tel. (1) 6700715; fax (1) 8290298; e-mail info@dzbank.ie; internet www.dzbank.ie; f. 1994; present name adopted 2001; subsidiary of DZ BANK AG Deutsche Zentral-Genossenschaftsbank, (Germany); cap. 6.5m., res 200.8m., dep. 1,521m. (Dec. 2012); Man. Dirs Dr TILMANN GERHARDS, MARK JACOB.

EAA Covered Bond Bank PLC: IFSC House, Dublin 1; tel. (1) 6127133; fax (1) 6127175; e-mail bond@westlb.ie; f. 2002 as WestLB Covered Bond Bank PLC; name changed as above following acquisition in 2010; public sector finance; owned by Erste Abwicklungsanstalt (Germany); cap. 6.4m., res 669.8m., dep. 820.4m. (Dec. 2012); Chair. DIETRICH VOIGTLÄNDER; Man. Dir MICHAEL DOHERTY.

Intesa Sanpaolo Bank Ireland PLC: KBC House, 3rd Floor, 4 St George's Dock, IFSC, Dublin 1; tel. (1) 6726720; fax (1) 6726727; e-mail dublin.ie@intesasanpaolo.com; internet www.intesasanpaolo.com; f. 1987; present name adopted 2007; subsidiary of Intesa Sanpaolo SpA (Italy); cap. 400.5m., res 517.2m., dep. 7,709.2m. (Dec. 2012); Chair. STEFANO DEL PUNTA; Man. Dir ENRICO CUCCHIANI.

KBC Bank Ireland PLC: Sandwith St, Dublin 2; tel. (1) 6646000; fax (1) 6646199; e-mail info@kbc.ie; internet www.kbc.ie; f. 1973; fmrly IIB Bank PLC; present name adopted 2008; subsidiary of KBC Bank NV (Belgium); cap. 1,024m., res 407.7m., dep. 2,741.3m. (Dec. 2012); Chair. LUC PHILIPS; CEO JOHN H. REYNOLDS; 5 brs.

JP Morgan Bank (Ireland) PLC: JP Morgan House, IFSC, Dublin 1; tel. (1) 6123000; fax (1) 6123123; internet www.chase.com; f. 1968 as Chase and Bank of Ireland (International) Ltd; name changed as above 2001; owned by JP Morgan International Finance Ltd (USA); cap. US $56.6m., res US $238.1m., dep. US $1,421.9m. (Dec. 2011); Chair. and CEO JAMES DIMON; 1 br.

permanent tsb PLC: Irish Life Centre, Lower Abbey St, Dublin 1; tel. (1) 7041010; fax (1) 7041900; internet www.permanenttsbgroup.ie; f. 1884; present name adopted 2012; brought under state control in 2011; cap. 89m., res 5,255m., dep. 32,894m. (Dec. 2012); Chair. ALAN COOK; Group CEO JEREMY MASDING.

permanent tsb: 56–59 St Stephen's Green, Dublin 2; tel. (1) 2124101; e-mail info@permanenttsb.ie; internet www.permanenttsb.ie; formed by merger of Irish Permanent and TSB Bank; subsidiary of permanent tsb PLC; Group CEO JEREMY MASDING; 101 brs.

Rabobank Ireland PLC: George's Dock House, IFSC, Dublin 1; tel. (1) 6076100; fax (1) 6701724; e-mail fm.ie.dublin.information@rabobank.com; internet www.rabobank.ie; f. 1994; corporate and investment banking; owned by Rabobank International Holding BV (Netherlands); cap. 7.1m., res 308.4m., dep. 12,442.3m. (Dec. 2012); CEO KEVIN KNIGHTLY.

Ulster Bank Ireland Ltd: Ulster Bank Group Centre, George's Quay, Dublin 2; tel. (1) 6777623; fax (1) 6775035; internet www.ulsterbank.com; merged with First Active PLC in early 2010; mem. of Royal Bank of Scotland Group (United Kingdom); cap. 3,592m., res 13,648m., dep. 26,208m. (Dec. 2012); Chair. SEAN DORGAN; Chief Exec. JIM BROWN; 132 brs.

UniCredit Bank Ireland PLC: La Touche House, IFSC, Dublin 1; tel. (1) 6702000; fax (1) 6702100; e-mail enquiry@unicreditgroup.ie; internet www.unicreditbank.ie; f. 1995; present name adopted 2007; subsidiary of UniCredit SpA (Italy); cap. 1,343.1m., res 89.8m., dep. 10,964.3m. (Dec. 2012); Man. Dir and CEO STEFANO VAIANI.

Banking Association

Irish Banking Federation: Nassau House, Nassau St, Dublin 2; tel. (1) 6715311; fax (1) 6796680; e-mail info@ibf.ie; internet www.ibf.ie; approx. 70 mems; CEO NOEL BRETT.

STOCK EXCHANGE

Irish Stock Exchange: 28 Anglesea St, Dublin 2; tel. (1) 6174200; fax (1) 6776045; e-mail info@ise.ie; internet www.ise.ie; f. 1793; formed as limited co. 1995; operates under supervision of the Central Bank of Ireland; Chair. PADRAIC O'CONNOR; CEO DEIRDRE SOMERS; 50 listed cos.

INSURANCE

Principal Companies

Allianz PLC: Allianz House, Elm Park, Merrion Rd, Dublin 4; tel. (1) 6133000; fax (1) 6134444; internet www.allianz.ie; f. 1998; 66.4% owned by Allianz AG (Germany), 30.4% by Irish Life and Permanent PLC; Chief Exec. BRENDAN MURPHY.

Aviva Group Ireland PLC: 1 Park Place, Hatch St, Dublin 2; tel. (1) 8988000; internet www.aviva.ie; f. 1908; subsidiary of Aviva PLC (UK); life and non-life; Chief Exec. ALISON BURNS.

AXA Insurance Ltd: Wolfe Tone House, Wolfe Tone St, Dublin 1; tel. (1) 8726444; fax (1) 8729703; e-mail axa.dublincity@axa.ie; internet www.axa.ie; f. 1967; Chief Exec. JOHN O'NEILL.

Bank of Ireland Life: 40 Mespil Rd, Dublin 4; tel. (1) 6615933; fax (1) 6615671; e-mail info@bankofirelandlife.ie; internet www.bankofirelandlife.ie; f. 1987; present name adopted 2002; part of New Ireland Assurance Co; Group CEO RICHIE BOUCHER.

FBD Insurance PLC: FBD House, Bluebell, Dublin 12; tel. (1) 4639820; e-mail info@fbd.ie; internet www.fbd.ie; motor, property, business; Group CEO ANDREW LANGFORD.

Irish Life Assurance PLC: Lower Abbey St, POB 129, Dublin 1; tel. (1) 7041010; fax (1) 7041900; e-mail customerservice@irishlife.ie; internet www.irishlife.ie; f. 1939; life and non-life; bought by Great-West Lifeco (Canada) and merged with Canada Life (Ireland) in 2014; Chief Exec. GERRY HASSETT.

Liberty Insurance: Dublin Rd, Cavan, Co Cavan; tel. (49) 4324000; fax (49) 4368101; e-mail info@libertyinsurance.ie; internet www.libertyinsurance.ie; f. 1996 as Quinn Insurance; fmrly Quinn Insurance Ltd; acquired by Liberty Mutual Group, Inc (USA) in 2011 and renamed as above; property, motor, health; Chief Exec. PATRICK O'BRIEN.

New Ireland Assurance Co PLC: 9–12 Dawson St, Dublin 2; tel. (1) 6172000; fax (1) 6172075; e-mail info@newireland.ie; internet www.newireland.ie; f. 1918; wholly owned subsidiary of Bank of Ireland Group; Chair. JOHN COLLINS; Man. Dir SEAN CASEY.

permanent tsb: see Banking.

RSA Insurance Ireland Ltd: RSA House, Sandyford Rd, Dundrum, Dublin 16; tel. (1) 2901000; fax (1) 2901001; e-mail patrick

.nally@ie.rsagroup.com; internet www.rsagroup.ie; f. 1721; fmrly Royal & Sun Alliance; non-life; CEO Stephen Hester.

Standard Life Ireland: 90 St Stephen's Green, Dublin 2; tel. (1) 6397300; e-mail marketing@standardlife.ie; internet www.standardlife.ie; f. 1834; life assurance, pensions, investments and annuities; Chief Exec. Nigel Dunne.

Zurich Insurance PLC: Zurich House, Ballsbridge Park, Dublin 4; tel. (1) 6670666; fax (1) 6670644; e-mail customerhelp@zurich.ie; internet www.zurichinsurance.ie; f. 1919 as Eagle Star Insurance; present name adopted 2009; mem. of the Zürich Financial Services Group (Switzerland); CEO Ken Norgrove.

Insurance Associations

Insurance Institute of Ireland: 39 Molesworth St, Dublin 2; tel. (1) 6456600; fax (1) 6772621; e-mail info@iii.ie; internet www.iii.ie; f. 1885; Pres. Ken Norgrove; CEO Eamon Shackleton; c. 15,000 mems.

Insurance Ireland: Insurance House, 39 Molesworth St, Dublin 2; tel. (1) 6761820; fax (1) 6761943; e-mail info@insuranceireland.eu; internet www.insuranceireland.eu; f. 1986; Pres. Philip Smith; CEO Kevin Thompson; 63 mems.

Irish Brokers' Association: 87 Merrion Sq., Dublin 2; tel. (1) 6613067; fax (1) 6619955; e-mail info@iba.ie; internet www.iba.ie; f. 1990; Pres. (2013–14) John Bissett; CEO Ciaran Phelan; 500 mems.

Professional Insurance Brokers' Association (PIBA): Unit 14B, Cashel Business Centre, Cashel Rd, Crumlin, Dublin 1; tel. (1) 4922202; fax (1) 4991569; e-mail info@piba.ie; internet www.piba.ie; f. 1995; Chair. Liam Carberry; CEO Diarmuid Kelly; c. 880 mems.

Trade and Industry

GOVERNMENT AGENCIES

An Post (The Irish Post Office): General Post Office, O'Connell St, Dublin 1; tel. (1) 7057000; fax (1) 8723553; e-mail press.office@anpost.ie; internet www.anpost.ie; f. 1984; provides national postal, communications and financial services through c. 1,100 outlets; Chair. John Fitzgerald; CEO Donal Connell.

Food Safety Authority of Ireland (FSAI): Abbey Court, Lower Abbey St, Dublin 1; tel. (1) 8171300; fax (1) 8171301; e-mail info@fsai.ie; internet www.fsai.ie; f. 1998; takes all reasonable steps to ensure that food produced, distributed or marketed in Ireland meets the highest standards of food safety and hygiene reasonably available, and to ensure that food complies with legal requirements, or, where appropriate, with recognized codes of good practice; Chair. Prof. Michael Gibney; Chief Exec. Prof. Alan Reilly.

Forfás: Wilton Park House, Wilton Pl., Dublin 2; tel. (1) 6073000; fax (1) 6073030; e-mail info@forfas.ie; internet www.forfas.ie; f. 1994; the national policy advisory board for enterprise, trade, science, technology and innovation; Chair. Eoin O'Driscoll; Chief Exec. Martin D. Shanahan.

National Economic and Social Council (NESC): 16 Parnell Sq., Dublin 1; tel. (1) 8146300; fax (1) 8146301; e-mail info@nesc.ie; internet www.nesc.ie; f. 1973; analyses and reports on strategic issues relating to the efficient development of the economy and the achievement of social justice; Chair. Martin Fraser; Dir Dr Rory O'Donnell.

DEVELOPMENT ORGANIZATIONS

Enterprise Ireland: East Point Business Park, Dublin 3; tel. (1) 7272000; fax (1) 7272020; e-mail client.service@enterprise-ireland.com; internet www.enterprise-ireland.com; f. 1998; combines the activities of the fmr An Bord Tráchtála, Forbairt and the in-company training activities of FÁS; Chair. Terence O'Rourke; Chief Exec. Julie Sinnamon.

IDA Ireland: Wilton Park House, Wilton Pl., Dublin 2; tel. (1) 6034000; fax (1) 6034040; e-mail idaireland@ida.ie; internet www.idaireland.com; f. 1993; govt agency with national responsibility for securing new investment from overseas in manufacturing and international services and for encouraging existing foreign enterprises in Ireland to expand their businesses; Chair. Frank Ryan; CEO Barry O'Leary.

Sustainable Energy Ireland (SEAI): Wilton Park House, Wilton Pl., Dublin 2; tel. (1) 8082100; fax (1) 8082002; e-mail info@seai.ie; internet www.seai.ie; promotes and assists environmentally and economically sustainable production, supply and use of energy, in support of govt policy, across all sectors of the economy; Chair. Brendan Halligan; CEO Dr Brian Motherway.

Teagasc (Agriculture and Food Development Authority): Oak Park, Carlow; tel. (59) 9170200; fax (59) 9182097; e-mail info@hq.teagasc.ie; internet www.teagasc.ie; f. 1988; provides research, educational and training services to agri-food sector and rural communities; Chair. Dr Noel Cawle; Nat. Dir Prof. Gerry Boyle.

CHAMBERS OF COMMERCE

Chambers Ireland (CI): Newmount House, 22–24 Lower Mount St, Dublin 2; tel. (1) 4004300; e-mail info@chambers.ie; internet www.chambers.ie; f. 1923; Pres. Dónall Curtin; represents over 13,000 businesses nationwide; 60 chamber mems; CEO Ian Talbot.

Cork Chamber: Fitzgerald House, Summerhill North, Cork; tel. (21) 4509044; fax (21) 4508568; e-mail info@corkchamber.ie; internet www.corkchamber.ie; f. 1819; Pres. John Mullins; Chief Exec. Conor Healy; 1000 mems.

Dublin Chamber of Commerce: 7 Clare St, Dublin 2; tel. (1) 6647200; fax (1) 6766043; e-mail info@dubchamber.ie; internet www.dubchamber.ie; f. 1783; Pres. Patrick Coveney; Chief Exec. Gina Quin.

INDUSTRIAL AND TRADE ASSOCIATIONS

Construction Industry Federation (CIF): Construction House, Canal Rd, Dublin 6; tel. (1) 4066000; fax (1) 4966953; e-mail cif@cif.ie; internet www.cif.ie; Pres. Philip Crampton; Dir-Gen. Tom Parlon; 37 asscns representing 1,500 mems.

Irish Creamery Milk Suppliers' Association (ICMSA): John Feely House, Dublin Rd, Castletroy, Limerick; tel. (61) 314677; fax (61) 315737; e-mail info@icmsa.ie; internet www.icmsa.ie; f. 1950; Pres. John G. Comer; Gen. Sec. John Enright.

Irish Farmers' Association (IFA): Irish Farm Centre, Bluebell, Dublin 12; tel. (1) 4500266; fax (1) 4551043; e-mail postmaster@ifa.ie; internet www.ifa.ie; Pres. Eddie Downey; Gen. Sec. Pat Smith; 87,000 mems.

Irish Fishermen's Organisation Ltd: Cumberland House, Fenian St, Dublin 2; tel. (1) 6612400; fax (1) 6612424; e-mail irishfish@eircom.net; f. 1974; representative body for Irish commercial fishermen; Chair. Ebbie Sheehan.

Irish Grain and Feed Association (IGFA): Lower Main St, Abbeyleix, Co Laois; tel. (57) 8730350; e-mail info@eorna.ie; internet www.igfa.ie; Pres. Michael Phelan; Dir Deirdre Webb.

EMPLOYERS' ORGANIZATIONS

Irish Business and Employers Confederation (IBEC): Confederation House, 84–86 Lower Baggot St, Dublin 2; tel. (1) 6051500; fax (1) 6381500; e-mail info@ibec.ie; internet www.ibec.ie; f. 1993; represents c. 7,000 cos and orgs; Pres. Julie O'Neill; Dir-Gen. Danny McCoy.

Irish Exporters' Association (IEA): 28 Merrion Sq., Dublin 2; tel. (1) 6612182; fax (1) 6612315; e-mail iea@irishexporters.ie; internet www.irishexporters.ie; f. 1951; Pres. Mark Fitzgerald; CEO John Whelan.

UTILITIES

Regulatory Authority

An Coimisiún um Rialáil Fuinnimh/Commission for Energy Regulation (CER): The Exchange, Belgard Sq. North, Tallaght, Dublin 24; tel. (1) 4000800; fax (1) 4000850; e-mail info@cer.ie; internet www.cer.ie; f. 1999; responsible for licensing and regulating the generation and supply of electricity and natural gas, and authorizing construction of new generating plants; designed and implemented cross-border Single Electricity Market with Northern Ireland Authority for Utility Regulation; Chair. Dermot Nolan.

Electricity and Gas

Airtricity: Airtricity House, Ravenscourt Office Park, Sandyford, Dublin 18; tel. (1) 6556400; fax (1) 6556444; e-mail info@airtricity.com; internet www.airtricity.com; f. 1997; generator and supplier of electricity, using renewable sources; acquired by Scottish and Southern Energy PLC (United Kingdom) in 2008; Man. Dir Kevin Greenhorn.

Bord Gáis Éireann (BGÉ) (The Irish Gas Board): 6 Lapps Quay, POB 835, Cork, Co Cork; tel. (21) 4658700; fax (21) 4658701; e-mail gasinfo@bge.ie; internet www.bordgais.ie; f. 1975; natural gas transmission and distribution, gas and electricity supply, electricity generation; Chair. Rose Hynes; CEO Michael McNicholas.

EirGrid PLC: 160 Shelbourne Rd, Dublin 4; tel. (1) 6771700; fax (1) 6615375; e-mail info@eirgrid.com; internet www.eirgrid.com; f. 2006; manages transmission of Ireland's electricity; state-owned; Chair. Bernie Gray; CEO Fintan Slye.

Electricity Supply Board (ESB): 27 Lower Fitzwilliam St, Dublin 2; tel. (1) 6765831; fax (1) 6760727; e-mail service@esb.ie; internet www.esb.ie; f. 1927; reorg. 1988; supplier of electricity and operator of 15 generating stations; 95% state-owned; Chair. LOCHLANN QUINN; CEO PAT O'DOHERTY.

Energia: Mill House, 3rd Floor, Ashtowngate, Navan Rd, Dublin 15; fax (1) 8692050; e-mail customer.service@energia.ie; internet www.energia.ie; f. 1999; generator and supplier of electricity and gas to business customers across Ireland; subsidiary of Viridian Group Ltd (UK); Chief Exec. GARY RYAN.

Flogas Natural Gas Ltd: Knockbrack House, Matthews Lane, Donore Rd, Drogheda, Co Louth; tel. (41) 9831041; fax (41) 9834652; e-mail info@flogas.ie; internet www.flogasnaturalgas.ie; supplier of natural gas to residential customers across Ireland; Man. Dir RICHARD MARTIN.

Water

Responsibility for water supply rests with the City and County councils. The Department of the Environment, Community and Local Government is responsible for improving and maintaining water supply infrastructure.

CO-OPERATIVES

Irish Co-operative Organisation Society (ICOS): The Plunkett House, 84 Merrion Sq., Dublin 2; tel. (1) 6764783; fax (1) 6624502; e-mail info@icos.ie; internet www.icos.ie; f. 1894; 3 operating divisions; offices in Dublin, Cork and Brussels (Belgium); Pres. BERTIE O'LEARY; CEO SEAMUS O'DONOHOE; over 130 mem. co-operatives representing c. 150,000 farmers.

Irish Dairy Board: Grattan House, Lower Mount St, Dublin 2; tel. (1) 6619599; fax (1) 6612778; e-mail idb@idb.ie; internet www.idb.ie; f. 1961; reorg. 1973 as a farmers' co-operative; principal exporter of Irish dairy products; Chair. VINCENT BUCKLEY; Chief Exec. KEVIN LANE.

TRADE UNIONS

Central Organization

Irish Congress of Trade Unions (ICTU): 31–32 Parnell Sq., Dublin 1; tel. (1) 8897777; fax (1) 8872012; e-mail congress@ictu.ie; internet www.ictu.ie; f. 1894; represents some 787,000 workers in 50 affiliated unions in Ireland and Northern Ireland (2012); Pres. JOHN DOUGLAS; Gen. Sec. DAVID BEGG.

Unions not Affiliated to the ICTU

National Bus and Rail Union (NBRU): 54 Parnell Sq., Dublin 1; tel. (1) 8730411; fax (1) 8730137; e-mail nbru@eircom.net; internet www.nbru.ie; f. 1963; Gen. Sec. DERMOT O'LEARY; 3,000 mems.

Transport

Córas Iompair Éireann (CIÉ) (The Irish Transport Co): Heuston Station, Dublin 8; tel. (1) 7032008; fax (1) 7032276; internet www.cie.ie; f. 1945; state corpn operating rail and road transport services; 3 operating cos: Iarnród Éireann (Irish Rail), Bus Éireann (Irish Bus) and Bus Átha Cliath (Dublin Bus); Chair. VIVIENNE JUPP.

RAILWAYS

In 2013 there were some 2,400 km of track. Railway services are operated by Iarnród Éireann.

Iarnród Éireann (Irish Rail): Connolly Station, Dublin 1; tel. (1) 8363333; fax (1) 8364760; e-mail info@irishrail.ie; internet www.irishrail.ie; f. 1987; division of CIÉ; Chair. PHIL GAFFNEY; Chief Exec. DAVID FRANKS.

INLAND WATERWAYS

The Grand and Royal Canals and the canal link into the Barrow Navigation system are controlled by CIÉ. The Grand Canal and Barrow are open to navigation by pleasure craft, and the rehabilitation and restoration of the Royal Canal is proceeding. The River Shannon, which is navigable from Limerick to Lough Allen, includes stretches of the Boyle, Suck, Camlin and Inny Rivers, the Erne Navigation and the Shannon–Erne Waterway. The total length of Irish navigable waterways is about 700 km.

ROADS

At 31 December 2008 there were an estimated 96,424 km of roads; at 31 December 2010 there were 5,413 km of national roads, of which 2,697 km were national primary roads (including 900 km of motorways) and 2,716 km were national secondary roads.

National Roads Authority: St Martin's House, Waterloo Rd, Dublin 4; tel. (1) 6602511; fax (1) 6680009; e-mail info@nra.ie; internet www.nra.ie; f. 1994; responsible for the planning, supervision and maintenance of national road network; Chair. CORMAC O'ROURKE; Chief Exec. FRED BARRY.

Bus Éireann (Irish Buses): Heuston Station, Dublin 8; internet www.buseireann.ie; f. 1987; provides bus and coach services across Ireland, except Dublin area; subsidiary of CIÉ; Chair. PAUL MALLEE; Chief Exec. MARTIN NOLAN.

Dublin Bus (Bus Átha Cliath): 59 Upper O'Connell St, Dublin 1; tel. (1) 8734222; fax (1) 7033177; e-mail info@dublinbus.ie; internet www.dublinbus.ie; f. 1987; provides bus services in Dublin area; subsidiary of CIÉ; Chair. KEVIN BONNER; Chief Exec. PADDY DOHERTY.

SHIPPING

The principal seaports are Dublin, Dún Laoghaire, Cork, Waterford, Rosslare, Limerick, Foynes, Galway, New Ross, Drogheda, Dundalk, Fenit and Whiddy Island. At 31 December 2013 the Irish flag registered fleet numbered 186 vessels, with a combined displacement of 239,090 grt, of which 105 were fishing vessels and 30 were general cargo ships.

Arklow Shipping: North Quay, Arklow, Co Wicklow; tel. (402) 39901; fax (402) 39902; e-mail chartering@asl.ie; internet www.asl.ie; f. 1966; Man. Dir JAMES S. TYRRELL; 37 carriers.

Fastnet Line: Ferry Port, Ringaskiddy, Co Cork; tel. (21) 4378892; fax (21) 4378893; e-mail info@fastnetline.com; internet www.fastnetline.com; f. 2009; owned by West Cork Tourism Co-op; operates car ferry service between Cork and Swansea (Wales, United Kingdom); Chair. CONOR BUCKLEY; CEO PHIL JONES.

Irish Continental Group PLC: Ferryport, Alexandra Rd, Dublin 1; tel. (1) 6075700; fax (1) 8552268; e-mail info@icg.ie; internet www.icg.ie; f. 1972; controls Irish Ferries, operating passenger vehicle and ro-ro freight ferry services between Ireland, the United Kingdom and continental Europe; Chair. JOHN B. MCGUCKIAN; Man. Dir EAMONN ROTHWELL.

Irish Ferries: Ferryport, Alexandra Rd, POB 19, Dublin 1; tel. (81) 8300400; fax (1) 8193942; e-mail info@irishferries.com; internet www.irishferries.com; drive-on/drive-off car ferry and ro-ro freight services between Ireland, the United Kingdom and continental Europe, operating up to 109 sailings weekly; Group Man. Dir EAMONN ROTHWELL.

Stena Line: Ferry Terminal, Dún Laoghaire Harbour, Co Dublin; tel. (1) 2047777; fax (1) 2047620; e-mail info.ie@stenaline.com; internet www.stenaline.ie; services between Dún Laoghaire and Dublin Port–Holyhead (Wales, United Kingdom) including high-speed catamaran, Rosslare–Fishguard (Wales, United Kingdom), Belfast (Northern Ireland) and Stranraer (Scotland, United Kingdom), Larne–Fleetwood (England, United Kingdom), passengers, drive-on/drive-off car ferry, ro-ro freight services; Man. Dir GUNNAR BLOMDAHL.

Associations

Irish Chamber of Shipping: Port Centre, Alexandra Rd, Dublin Port, Dublin 1; tel. (1) 8559011; fax (1) 8559022; e-mail bks@iol.ie; Pres. JOHN TONER; Dir B. W. KERR.

Irish Ship Agents' Association: Conway House, East Wall Road, Dublin 3; tel. (1) 8556221; fax (1) 8557234; e-mail info@irishshipagents.com; internet www.irishshipagents.com; Pres. MICHAEL COLLINS.

CIVIL AVIATION

There are international airports at Dublin, Shannon, Cork, Kerry and Knock (Ireland West Airport).

Commission for Aviation Regulation: Alexandra House, 3rd Floor, Earlsfort Terrace, Dublin 2; tel. (1) 6611700; fax (1) 6611269; e-mail info@aviationreg.ie; internet www.aviationreg.ie; f. 2001; responsible for licensing the travel trade in Ireland as well as airlines; approves providers of ground handling services under EU regulations; Commissioner CATHAL GUIOMARD.

Dublin Airport Authority PLC (DAA): Dublin Airport, Dublin; tel. (1) 8141111; e-mail info@daa.ie; internet www.daa.ie; state-controlled; responsible for the management of Dublin and Cork airports; Chair. PÁDRAIG Ó. RÍORDÁIN; Chief Exec. KEVIN TOLAND.

Irish Aviation Authority: The Times Bldg, 11–12 D'Olier St, Dublin 2; tel. (1) 6718655; fax (1) 6792934; e-mail info@iaa.ie; internet www.iaa.ie; f. 1994; provides air traffic management, engineering and communications in airspace controlled by Ireland and related air traffic technological infrastructure; also regulates aircraft airworthiness certification and registration, the licensing of personnel and orgs involved in the maintenance of aircraft, as well as the licensing of pilots and aerodromes; Chair. ANNE NOLAN; Chief Exec. EAMONN BRENNAN.

Airlines

Aer Arann: 1 Northwood Ave, Santry, Dublin 9; tel. (1) 8447700; fax (1) 8447701; e-mail info@aerarann.com; internet www.aerarann.com; f. 1970; regional airline operating flights on 37 routes throughout Ireland, United Kingdom and France; CEO Seán Brogan (acting).

Aer Lingus Group PLC: Dublin Airport, Dublin; tel. (1) 8868202; fax (1) 8863832; internet www.aerlingus.com; f. 1936; reorg. 1993; 29.88% owned by Ryanair Holdings PLC, 25.1% govt-owned; domestic and international scheduled services; Chair. Colm Barrington; CEO Christoph Mueller.

CityJet: Swords Business Campus, Balheary Rd, Swords, Co Dublin; tel. (1) 8700100; fax (1) 8700115; e-mail info@cityjet.com; internet www.cityjet.com; f. 1994; operates chartered and scheduled passenger routes between Dublin and Belfast (Northern Ireland), London (United Kingdom) and destinations in continental Western Europe; 100% owned by Air France; CEO Christine Ourmières.

Ryanair: Dublin Airport, Dublin; tel. (1) 8121212; fax (1) 8121213; internet www.ryanair.com; f. 1985; scheduled and charter passenger services to European and North African destinations; Chair. David Bonderman; CEO Michael O'Leary.

Tourism

Intensive marketing campaigns have been undertaken in recent years to develop new markets for Irish tourism. In addition to many sites of historic and cultural interest, the country has numerous areas of natural beauty, notably the Killarney Lakes and the west coast. In 2011 a total of 7.6m. foreign tourists (including residents of Northern Ireland) visited Ireland. Receipts from tourism (including passenger transport) totalled an estimated €4,078m. in 2012.

Dublin Regional Tourism Authority Ltd (Dublin Tourism): Suffolk St, Dublin 2; tel. (1) 6057700; fax (1) 6057757; e-mail reservations@dublintourism.ie; internet www.visitdublin.com; Chair. Ann Riordan.

Fáilte Ireland (National Tourism Development Authority): 88–95 Amiens St, Dublin 1; tel. (1) 8847700; fax (1) 8556821; e-mail info@failteireland.ie; internet www.failteireland.ie; f. 2003; Chair. Redmond O'Donaghue; Chief Exec. Shaun Quinn.

Irish Tourist Industry Confederation (ITIC): Sandyford Office Park, Unit 5, Ground Floor, Dublin 18; tel. (1) 2934950; fax (1) 2934991; e-mail itic@eircom.net; internet www.itic.ie; Chair. Paul Carty; CEO Eamonn McKeon.

Tourism Ireland: Bishop's Sq., 5th Floor, Redmond's Hill, Dublin 2; tel. (1) 4763400; fax (1) 4763666; e-mail corporate.dublin@tourismireland.com; internet www.tourismireland.com; f. 1998; promotes Ireland and Northern Ireland as a tourist destination; jointly funded by the Irish Government and the Northern Ireland Executive; Chair. Brian Ambrose; Chief Exec. Niall Gibbons.

Defence

As assessed at November 2013, the regular armed forces totalled 9,350. The army comprised 7,500, the navy 1,050 and the air force 800. There was also a reserve of 4,630. Military service is voluntary. In November 2004 the European Union (EU) ministers responsible for defence agreed to create a number of 'battlegroups' (each comprising about 1,500 men), which could be deployed at short notice to crisis areas around the world. The EU battlegroups, two of which were to be ready for deployment at any one time, following a rotational schedule, reached full operational capacity from 1 January 2007. From January 2008 Ireland was a participant in the EUFOR mission to eastern Chad and the Central African Republic and by February 2009 was the second largest contributor to the mission (which was taken over by the UN in March), with 476 troops. In 2013 Irish troops contributed to the United Nations Interim Force in Lebanon (UNIFIL).

Defence Expenditure: budgeted at €898m. in 2014.

Chief of Staff of the Defence Forces: Maj.-Gen. Conor O'Boyle.

Education

The Irish state has constitutional responsibility for the national education system. An aided system is in operation: Irish schools are funded by the state, but are under the management (with a few minor exceptions) of community bodies, usually religious groups. Pre-primary education is non-compulsory and aimed at children aged between one and six years. Primary and lower secondary education in Ireland is compulsory for nine years between six and 16 years of age. Primary education may begin at the age of four and lasts for up to eight years, comprising a two-year infant cycle and a six-year primary cycle. In 2005/06 aided primary schools accounted for the education of 98.9% of children in the primary sector. In 2011/12 enrolment at primary level included 99% of children in the relevant age-group, while enrolment at secondary level in 2010/11 included 99% of children in the relevant age-group. Post-primary education begins at 12 years of age and lasts for up to six years, comprising a junior cycle of three years and a senior cycle of two or three years. The Junior Certificate examination is taken after three years in post-primary (second-level) education. The Leaving Certificate examination is taken after a further two or three years and is a necessary qualification for entry into university education. Accreditation for higher education is provided by the Department of Education and Skills. There are four universities in Ireland: the University of Dublin (Trinity College); the National University of Ireland (comprising the University Colleges of Cork, Dublin, Maynooth and Galway); Dublin City University; and the University of Limerick (which obtained university status in 1989). In 2012/13, there were seven university-level institutions, 15 institutes of technology and four other higher education providers.

Government expenditure on education and skills was budgeted at €8,759m. in 2014.

ISRAEL

Introductory Survey

LOCATION, CLIMATE, LANGUAGE, RELIGION, FLAG, CAPITAL

Israel lies in western Asia, occupying a narrow strip of territory on the eastern shore of the Mediterranean Sea. The country also has a narrow outlet to the Red Sea at the northern tip of the Gulf of Aqaba. All of Israel's land frontiers are with Arab countries, the longest being with Egypt to the west and with Jordan to the east. Lebanon lies to the north, and Syria to the north-east. The climate is Mediterranean, with hot, dry summers, when the maximum temperature in Jerusalem is generally between 30°C and 35°C (86°F to 95°F), and mild, rainy winters, with a minimum temperature in the city of about 5°C (41°F). The climate is sub-tropical on the coast but more extreme in the Negev Desert, in the south, and near the shores of the Dead Sea (a lake on the Israeli–Jordanian frontier), where the summer temperature may exceed 50°C (122°F). The official languages are Hebrew and Arabic. Hebrew is spoken by about two-thirds of the population, including most Jews. About 15% of Israeli residents, including Muslim Arabs, speak Arabic, while many European languages (notably Russian) are also spoken. Some 75.1% of the population profess adherence to Judaism, the officially recognized religion of Israel, while 17.4% are Muslims. The national flag (proportions 8 by 11) has a white background, with a six-pointed blue star composed of two overlapping triangles (the 'Shield of David') between two horizontal blue stripes near the upper and lower edges. Although the Israeli Government has designated the city of Jerusalem (part of which is Jordanian territory annexed by Israel in 1967) as the country's capital, this is not recognized by the UN, and most foreign governments maintain their embassies in Tel-Aviv.

CONTEMPORARY POLITICAL HISTORY

Historical Context

The Zionist movement emerged in Europe in the 19th century in response to the growing sense of insecurity among Jewish minorities in many European countries as a result of racial and religious persecution. The primary objective of Zionism was defined at the 1897 Basle Congress, when Dr Theodor Herzl stated that Zionism sought 'to create for the Jewish people a home in Palestine secured by public law'. Zionists aimed to re-establish an autonomous community of Jews in what was their historical homeland.

Palestine was almost entirely populated by Arabs, and had become part of the Turkish Ottoman Empire in the early 16th century. During the First World War the Ottoman Empire's Arab subjects launched the so-called Arab Revolt, and, following the withdrawal of the Turks, in 1917–18 British troops occupied Palestine. In November 1917 the British Foreign Secretary, Arthur Balfour, declared British support for the establishment of a Jewish national home in Palestine, on condition that the rights of 'the existing non-Jewish communities' there were safeguarded; this became known as the Balfour Declaration and was confirmed by the governments of other countries then at war with Turkey. The British occupation of Palestine continued after the war under the terms of a League of Nations mandate, which also incorporated the Balfour Declaration. (In 1920 Palestine was formally placed under British administration.) British rule in Palestine was hampered by the conflict between the declared obligations to the Jews and the rival claims of the Arab majority. In accordance with the mandate, Jewish settlers were admitted to Palestine only on the basis of limited annual quotas. There was serious anti-Jewish rioting by Arabs in 1921 and 1929. Attempts to restrict immigration led to Jewish-sponsored riots in 1933. The extreme persecution of Jews by Nazi Germany caused an increase in the flow of Jewish immigrants, both legal and illegal, which intensified the unrest in Palestine. In 1937 a British proposal to establish separate Jewish and Arab states, while retaining a British-mandated area, was accepted by most Zionists but rejected by the Arabs, and by the end of that year hostilities between the two communities had descended into open conflict. A British scheme offering eventual independence for a bi-communal Palestinian state was postponed because of the Second World War, during which the Nazis caused the deaths of an estimated 6m. Jews in central and eastern Europe (more than one-third of the world's total Jewish population). The enormity of the Holocaust greatly increased international sympathy for Jewish claims to a homeland in Palestine.

After the war there was strong opposition by Palestinian Jews to continued British occupation. Numerous terrorist attacks were made by Jewish groups against British targets. In November 1947 the UN approved a plan for the partition of Palestine into two states, one Jewish (covering about 56% of the area) and one Arab. The plan was, however, rejected by Arab states and by Palestinian Arab leaders. Meanwhile, the conflict in Palestine escalated into full-scale war.

On 14 May 1948 the United Kingdom terminated its mandate, and Jewish leaders immediately proclaimed the State of Israel, with David Ben-Gurion as Prime Minister. Despite the absence of recognized borders, the new state quickly received international recognition. Neighbouring Arab countries attempted to conquer Israel by military force, and fighting continued until January 1949, when ceasefire agreements left Israel in control of 75% of Palestine, including West Jerusalem. The de facto territory of Israel was thus nearly one-third greater than the area assigned under the original UN partition plan. Jordanian forces controlled most of the remainder of Palestine, the area eventually known as the West Bank (or, to Israelis, as Judea and Samaria) and which was fully incorporated into Jordan in April 1950.

At the end of the British mandate the Jewish population of Palestine was about 650,000 (or 40% of the total). The new State of Israel encouraged further Jewish immigration: the Law of Return, adopted in July 1950, established a right of immigration for all Jews, and resulted in a rapid influx of Jewish settlers. Many former Arab residents of Palestine, meanwhile, had become refugees in neighbouring countries, mainly Jordan and Lebanon. About 400,000 Arabs had evacuated their homes prior to May 1948, and a similar number fled subsequently. In 1964 exiled Palestinian Arabs formed the Palestine Liberation Organization (PLO), with the aim, at that time, of overthrowing Israel.

Israel, with the United Kingdom and France, launched an attack on Egypt in October 1956 following the nationalization of the Suez Canal by President Nasser; Israel seized the Gaza Strip (part of Palestine occupied by Egypt since 1949) and the Sinai Peninsula. After pressure from the UN and the USA, Israeli forces evacuated these areas in 1957, when a UN Emergency Force (UNEF) was established in Sinai. In 1967 the United Arab Republic (Egypt) secured the withdrawal of UNEF from its territory. Egyptian forces immediately reoccupied the garrison at Sharm el-Sheikh, near the southern tip of Sinai, and closed the Straits of Tiran to Israeli shipping, effectively (as in 1956) blockading the Israeli port of Eilat. In retaliation, Israeli forces attacked Egypt, Jordan and Syria, swiftly making substantial territorial gains. The so-called Six-Day War left Israel in possession of all Jerusalem, the West Bank area of Jordan, the Sinai Peninsula in Egypt, the Gaza Strip and the Golan Heights in Syria. East Jerusalem was almost immediately integrated into the State of Israel, while the other conquered areas were regarded as Occupied Territories. In November 1967 the UN Security Council adopted Resolution 242, urging Israel to withdraw from all the recently occupied Arab territories.

Domestic Political Affairs

Ben-Gurion resigned in June 1963 and was succeeded by Levi Eshkol. Three of the parties in the ruling coalition merged to form the Israel Labour Party in 1968. On the death of Eshkol in 1969, Golda Meir was elected Prime Minister. A ceasefire between Egypt and Israel was arranged in August 1970, but other Arab states and Palestinian guerrilla (mainly PLO) groups continued hostilities. Another Arab–Israeli war began on 6 October 1973, as Arab forces invaded Israeli-held territory on the Jewish holy day of Yom Kippur (the Day of Atonement). Egyptian forces crossed the Suez Canal and reoccupied part of Sinai, while Syrian troops launched an offensive on the Golan Heights.

Having successfully repelled these advances, Israel made ceasefire agreements with Egypt and Syria on 24 October. The UN Security Council adopted Resolution 338 in that month, urging a ceasefire and reaffirming the principles of Resolution 242. Gen. Itzhak Rabin succeeded Meir as Prime Minister of a Labour Alignment coalition in 1974. The Labour Alignment was defeated at the May 1977 general election, and the Likud (Consolidation) bloc, led by Menachem Begin of the Herut (Freedom) Party, formed a new coalition Government.

In November 1977 the Egyptian President, Anwar Sadat, visited Israel, indicating tacit recognition of the Jewish State. In September 1978 President Jimmy Carter of the USA, President Sadat and Prime Minister Begin met at the US presidential retreat at Camp David, Maryland, and concluded two agreements: a 'framework for peace in the Middle East', providing for autonomy for the West Bank and Gaza Strip after a transitional period of five years; and a 'framework for the conclusion of a peace treaty between Egypt and Israel'. A formal peace treaty was signed in March 1979 in Washington, DC, USA. In 1980 Egypt became the first Arab country to grant diplomatic recognition to Israel. However, approval by the Israeli Knesset (parliament) of legislation stating explicitly that Jerusalem should be forever the undivided capital of Israel, and, in 1981, Israel's formal annexation of the Golan Heights, impeded prospects of agreement on Palestinian autonomy.

Israel's phased withdrawal from Sinai was completed in April 1982. In June Israeli forces, under 'Operation Peace for Galilee', advanced through Lebanon and surrounded west Beirut, trapping 6,000 PLO fighters. Egypt withdrew its ambassador from Tel-Aviv in protest. Diplomatic efforts resulted in the evacuation of 14,000–15,000 PLO and Syrian fighters from Beirut to various Arab countries. In September Lebanese Phalangists massacred Palestinian refugees in the Sabra and Chatila camps in Beirut (see the chapter on Lebanon); an official Israeli inquiry found the Israeli leadership to be indirectly responsible through negligence, forcing the resignation of Gen. Ariel Sharon as Minister of Defence. In May 1983 Israel and Lebanon concluded a peace agreement, declaring an end to hostilities and envisaging the withdrawal of all foreign forces from Lebanon within three months. However, Syria's refusal to withdraw some 30,000 troops, and the continued presence of about 7,000 PLO fighters in the Beqa'a valley and northern Lebanon, delayed the Israeli withdrawal, although by the end of 1983 the number of Israeli troops in Lebanon had been reduced from 30,000 to 10,000.

In August 1983 Itzhak Shamir succeeded Begin as leader of the Likud bloc and Prime Minister. However, economic difficulties further undermined the Government, and the Labour Party forced a general election in July 1984. Since neither the Labour Alignment nor Likud could form a viable coalition, President Chaim Herzog invited the Labour leader, Shimon Peres, to form a government of national unity with Likud.

Israel's forces finally completed their withdrawal from Lebanon in June 1985, leaving responsibility for policing the occupied southern area of Lebanon to the Israeli-controlled 'South Lebanon Army' (SLA). During 1986 Palestinian guerillas resumed rocket attacks on settlements in northern Israel, provoking Israeli air assaults on Palestinian targets in southern Lebanon. Meanwhile, the Shi'a fundamentalist group Hezbollah intensified attacks on SLA positions within the southern buffer zone. The conflict escalated following the abduction, in July 1989, of a local Shi'a Muslim leader by Israeli agents, and in February 1992, after the assassination by the Israeli air force of the Hezbollah Secretary-General, Sheikh Abbas Moussawi.

In July 1988 King Hussein abrogated Jordan's legal and administrative responsibilities in the West Bank, and declared that he would no longer represent the Palestinians in any international conference on the Palestinian question. King Hussein's decision strengthened the PLO's negotiating position as the sole legitimate representative of the Palestinian people. International attention had been focused on the Palestinian cause since December 1987, following an *intifada* (uprising) against Israeli rule in the Occupied Territories and Israeli attempts to suppress the rebellion. In November 1988 the PLO declared an independent Palestinian state (notionally the West Bank and Gaza Strip), and endorsed UN Security Council Resolution 242, thereby implicitly granting recognition to Israel. The USA refused to accept proposals for a two-state solution put forward by the PLO Chairman, Yasser Arafat, in December, but it did open a dialogue with the organization. Prime Minister Itzhak Shamir (the Likud leader had assumed the Israeli premiership in October 1986, in accordance with the 1984 coalition agreement) would not negotiate, distrusting the PLO's undertaking to abandon violence. Instead, he appeared to favour the introduction of limited self-rule for the Palestinians of the West Bank and Gaza, as outlined in the 1978 Camp David accords. At the November 1988 general election neither Likud nor Labour secured enough seats in the Knesset to form a viable coalition. A further Government of national unity was formed under Shamir, with Shimon Peres as Deputy Prime Minister and Minister of Finance.

In April 1989 Shamir presented a peace proposal that included plans for the holding of democratic elections in the West Bank and Gaza for Palestinian delegates who would be empowered to negotiate self-rule under Israeli authority. The proposals were unacceptable to the PLO, with which direct talks were precluded. In September President Hosni Mubarak of Egypt offered to host a meeting between Israeli and Palestinian representatives, but Likud ministers rejected any direct contact with PLO delegates. In November Israel provisionally accepted a proposal by the US Secretary of State, James Baker, for a preliminary meeting to discuss the holding of elections in the West Bank and Gaza, on condition that Israel would not be required to negotiate with the PLO and that the talks would concern only Israel's election proposals. The PLO continued to demand a direct role, and the Baker initiative foundered.

The Likud-Labour coalition was beset in early 1990 with disputes and dismissals, and in March the Knesset adopted a motion of no confidence in Prime Minister Shamir. Shimon Peres was unable to form a new, Labour-led coalition, and in June, after several weeks of political bargaining, Shamir formed a new Government—a narrow, right-wing coalition of Likud, smaller parties and independents. In a policy document, Shamir emphasized the right of Jews to settle in all parts of 'Greater Israel', his opposition to the creation of an independent Palestinian state and his refusal to negotiate with the PLO—or with any Palestinians other than those resident in the Occupied Territories (excluding East Jerusalem).

Meanwhile, also in March 1990 US President George Bush opposed the granting to Israel of a loan of some US $400m. for the housing of Jewish immigrants from the USSR, since Israel would not guarantee to refrain from constructing new settlements in the Occupied Territories. Violence erupted throughout Israel and the Occupied Territories in May. The PLO's refusal to condemn the violence caused the USA to suspend its dialogue with the organization and to veto a UN Security Council resolution urging that international observers be dispatched to the Occupied Territories. In October some 17 Palestinians were shot dead by Israeli police, following clashes with Jewish worshippers. International outrage at the shootings prompted a UN Security Council vote to send an investigative mission, although Israel agreed only to receive a UN emissary. The invasion of Kuwait by Iraq in August had brought about an improvement in US-Israeli relations. However, Iraqi missile attacks on Israel in January 1991, shortly after the US-led multinational force had begun its offensive against Iraq, threatened the cohesion of the force. US diplomatic efforts, and the installation in Israel of US air defence systems, averted an immediate Israeli response.

The Madrid Peace Conference and the launch of the Middle East peace process

By August 1991 intensive diplomacy by US Secretary of State Baker had secured the agreement of the Israeli, Syrian, Egyptian, Jordanian and Lebanese Governments, and of Palestinian representatives, to attend a regional peace conference, the terms of reference for which would be a comprehensive peace settlement based on UN Security Council Resolutions 242 and 338. An initial, 'symbolic' session was held in Madrid, Spain, in October. However, subsequent talks soon became deadlocked over procedural issues. Israel repeatedly questioned the status of the Palestinian-Jordanian delegation, and the right of the Palestinian component to participate separately in negotiations; furthermore, the Government refused to end construction of new settlements in the Occupied Territories. In February 1992, immediately prior to the fourth session of peace talks, to be held in Washington, DC, Baker demanded a complete halt to Israel's settlement-building programme as a precondition for the granting of loan guarantees to the value of US $10,000m. for the housing of Jewish immigrants from the former USSR. A fifth round of negotiations was held in Washington in April 1992. Israeli representatives presented proposals for the holding of municipal elections in the West Bank and Gaza, and for the transfer of control of health care provision there to the

Palestinian authorities. In May the first multilateral negotiations commenced between the parties to the Middle East peace conference; however, the sessions were boycotted by Syria and Lebanon, considering them futile until progress had been made in the bilateral negotiations.

A general election was held in June 1992, following the collapse of Shamir's coalition Government in January. The new Chairman of the Labour Party, Itzhak Rabin, subsequently formed a new coalition. This alliance, comprising Labour, Meretz and the ultra-Orthodox Shas, held a total of 62 of the 120 Knesset seats, and also commanded the unofficial support of the two Arab parties. Although international observers generally regarded the installation of the Labour-led coalition as having improved the prospects for peace in the Middle East, the sixth and seventh rounds of bilateral negotiations between Israeli, Syrian, Lebanese and Palestinian-Jordanian delegations, in September–November, failed to achieve any progress.

An eighth round of bilateral negotiations between Israeli and Arab delegations commenced in Washington, DC, in December 1992, but were soon overshadowed by violent confrontations between Palestinians and the Israeli security forces in the Occupied Territories, which led to the withdrawal of the Arab participants. In mid-December, in response to the deaths of five members of the Israeli security forces, and the abduction and murder by the Islamic Resistance Movement (Hamas) of an Israeli policeman, the Rabin Government ordered the deportation to Lebanon of 413 alleged Palestinian supporters of Hamas. The expulsions provoked international outrage, and the UN Security Council, in Resolution 799, demanded the return of the deportees to Israel. Consequently, the ninth round of peace talks was formally suspended, with Palestinian delegates insisting on the full implementation of Resolution 799 as a precondition for resumed discussions. In March 1993, amid a sharp escalation of violence in the West Bank and Gaza, Israel sealed off the territories indefinitely.

The suspended ninth round of bilateral negotiations resumed in Washington, DC, in April 1993. The Palestinian delegation apparently agreed to attend the sessions following pressure by Arab governments, and after Israel had agreed to allow Faisal Husseini, the nominal leader of the Palestinian delegation and a resident of East Jerusalem, to participate. Israel was also reported to have undertaken to halt punitive deportations, and, with the USA, to have reaffirmed its commitment to Resolutions 242 and 338 as the terms of reference for the peace process.

In March 1993, meanwhile, Binyamin Netanyahu was chosen to replace Shamir as the Likud leader. In May Ezer Weizman was inaugurated as Israeli President. In July Israeli armed forces mounted the most intensive air and artillery attacks on targets in Lebanon since Operation Peace for Galilee in 1982, in retaliation for attacks by Hezbollah fighters on settlements in northern Israel.

Declaration of Principles on Palestinian Self-Rule (the Oslo accords)

Following the 10th round of bilateral negotiations, convened in Washington, DC, in June 1993, on 13 September Israel and the PLO signed a Declaration of Principles on Palestinian Self-Rule in the Occupied Territories. The agreement, which entailed mutual recognition by Israel and the PLO, had been elaborated during a series of secret negotiations mediated by Norway (and thus became known as the Oslo accords). The Declaration of Principles established a detailed timetable for Israel's disengagement from the Occupied Territories, stipulating that a permanent settlement of the Palestinian question be in place by December 1998. From 13 October 1993 Palestinian authorities were to assume responsibility for education and culture, health, social welfare, direct taxation and tourism in the Gaza Strip and the Jericho area of the West Bank, and a transitional period of Palestinian self-rule was to begin on 13 December. Although the Declaration of Principles was ratified by the Knesset on 23 September 1993, there was widespread opposition, particularly to Israel's recognition of the PLO, from right-wing Israelis. Rabin and Arafat held their first meeting in the context of the Oslo accords in Cairo, Egypt, on 6 October. A joint PLO-Israeli liaison committee was convened for the first time a week later, with delegations headed, respectively, by Mahmud Abbas and Shimon Peres.

Meanwhile, in September 1993 allegations of corruption against Shas leader Aryeh Der'i prompted the resignation of Shas ministers from the Government, thus reducing the coalition to an alliance between the Labour Party and Meretz (and the Government's Knesset majority to just two). A new coalition agreement was signed with Yi'ud, a breakaway group from the Tzomet party, in July 1994.

Meeting in Cairo on 4 May 1994, Israel and the PLO signed an accord providing for Israel's military withdrawal from the Gaza Strip and Jericho, and for the deployment of a 9,000-strong Palestinian police force. A nominated Palestinian (National) Authority (PA) was to assume control of these areas, with the exception of external security and foreign affairs. Elections for a Palestinian Council (which, under the terms of the Oslo accords, were to have taken place in Gaza and the West Bank in July) were postponed until October. Israel's military withdrawal from Gaza and Jericho was completed on 13 May 1994, and on 17 May the PLO formally assumed control of the Israeli Civil Administration's departments there. On 26–28 May the PA held its first meeting in the Tunisian capital, Tunis. Arafat made a symbolic return to Gaza City on 1 July—his first visit for 25 years—and the PA was formally inaugurated in Jericho on 5 July. In August Israel and the PLO signed an agreement extending the authority of the PA to include education, health, tourism, social welfare and taxation.

In October 1994 an Israeli soldier was abducted near Tel-Aviv by Hamas fighters, who subsequently demanded that Israel release the detained Hamas spiritual leader, Sheikh Ahmad Yassin, and other Palestinian prisoners. Despite Palestinian action to detain some 300 Hamas members in the Gaza Strip, the kidnapped soldier was subsequently killed in the West Bank. Shortly afterwards an attack by a Hamas suicide bomber in Tel-Aviv, in which 22 people died, prompted Israel to close its borders with the Palestinian territories. In November a member of another militant Palestinian organization, Islamic Jihad, was killed in a car bomb attack in Gaza. Three Israeli soldiers were subsequently killed in a suicide bombing in the Gaza Strip, for which Islamic Jihad claimed responsibility. It became clear that Israel's security concerns would continue to delay the redeployment of its armed forces in the West Bank and the holding of Palestinian elections (see The assassination of Itzhak Rabin). In January 1995 a further suicide bombing apparently carried out by Islamic Jihad at Beit Lid, in which 21 Israeli soldiers and civilians died, seriously jeopardized the peace process. The Israeli Government again closed the country's borders with the West Bank and Gaza, and postponed the planned release of some 5,500 Palestinian prisoners. In early February, meanwhile, Israeli armed forces completed their withdrawal from Jordanian territories, in accordance with the October 1994 bilateral peace treaty.

Despite intensive negotiations, an agreement on the expansion of Palestinian self-rule in the West Bank was not achieved by the target date of 1 July 1995. The principal obstacles remained the question of precisely to where Israeli troops in the West Bank would redeploy, and the exact nature of security arrangements for some 130,000 Jewish settlers who were to remain there. On 28 September the Israeli-Palestinian Interim Agreement on the West Bank and the Gaza Strip was finally signed by Israel and the PLO. Its main provisions were the withdrawal of Israeli armed forces from a further six West Bank towns (Nablus, Ramallah, Jenin, Tulkaram, Qalqilya and Bethlehem) and a partial redeployment from the town of Hebron; national Palestinian legislative elections to an 82-member Palestinian Council and for a Palestinian Executive President; and the phased release of Palestinians detained by Israel. In anticipation of a violent reaction against the Interim Agreement by 'rejectionist' groups within the Occupied Territories, Israel immediately sealed its borders with the West Bank and Gaza.

Meanwhile, bilateral negotiations between Israeli and Syrian delegations resumed in Washington, DC, in January 1994. In September Rabin announced details of a plan for a partial withdrawal of Israeli armed forces from the occupied Golan Heights, to be followed by a three-year trial period of Israeli-Syrian 'normalization'. The proposals were rejected by President Assad of Syria, although he did state his willingness to work towards peace with Israel. Eventually, in May 1995 Israel and Syria were reported to have concluded a 'framework understanding on security arrangements', intended to facilitate discussions on security issues. Also in January 1994 Morocco and Tunisia became the second and third Arab states, respectively, to establish diplomatic ties with Israel; the six members of the Cooperation Council for the Arab States of the Gulf (the Gulf Cooperation Council, see p. 246) agreed to revoke the subsidiary elements of the Arab economic boycott of Israel. On 25 July Israel and Jordan signed a joint declaration formally ending the state of war between them and further defining arrangements for future bilateral negotiations. On 26 October the two countries signed a formal peace treaty, defining their common border and providing for a normalization of relations.

The assassination of Itzhak Rabin

On 4 November 1995 Itzhak Rabin was assassinated in Tel-Aviv by a Jewish student opposed to the peace process, in particular the Israeli withdrawal from the West Bank. The Minister of Foreign Affairs, Shimon Peres, was, with the agreement of Likud, invited to form a new government. The members of the outgoing administration—Labour, Meretz and Yi'ud—subsequently signed a new coalition agreement, and the Cabinet was formally approved by the Knesset in late November. In February 1996 Peres announced that elections to the Knesset, and (for the first time) the direct election of the Prime Minister, would take place in May.

Israeli armed forces completed their withdrawal from the West Bank town of Jenin in November 1995, and in December they withdrew from Tulkaram, Nablus, Qalqilya, Bethlehem and Ramallah. With regard to Hebron, Israel and the PA signed an agreement transferring jurisdiction in some 17 areas of civilian affairs from Israel to the PA. At talks with Arafat in December, Peres confirmed that Israel would release some 1,000 Palestinian prisoners before the forthcoming Palestinian elections.

Peace negotiations between Israel and Syria resumed in December 1995 in Maryland, USA, and were followed by a second round in January 1996. However, the talks were swiftly undermined by a series of suicide bombings in Israel in early 1996, and in March the Israeli negotiators returned home. Meanwhile, King Hussein of Jordan made a visit to Tel-Aviv in January, during which Israel and Jordan signed a number of agreements relating to the normalization of economic and cultural relations.

Palestinian legislative and presidential elections were held in January 1996, leading in principle to the final stage of the peace process, when Palestinian and Israeli negotiators would address such issues as Jerusalem, the rights of Palestinian refugees and the status of Jewish settlements in the Palestinian territories. In February and March, however, more than 50 Israelis died as a result of suicide bomb attacks in Jerusalem, Ashkelon and Tel-Aviv, and talks were suspended. Israel again ordered the closure of its borders with the Palestinian territories, and demanded that the PA suppress the activities of Hamas and Islamic Jihad in the areas under its control. A hitherto unknown group, the 'Yahya Ayyash Units', claimed responsibility for the attacks, to avenge the assassination—by Israeli agents—of Ayyash, a leading Hamas activist. Arafat, now the elected Palestinian President, condemned the bombings, and in late February more than 200 members of Hamas were detained by Palestinian security forces. Israel asserted the right of its armed forces to enter PA-controlled areas when Israeli security was at stake, and an agreement to redeploy troops from Hebron by 20 March was rescinded.

In April 1996 Israeli armed forces began a sustained campaign of intense air and artillery attacks on alleged Hezbollah positions in southern Lebanon and the southern suburbs of Beirut. The declared aim of the operation (code-named 'Grapes of Wrath') was to achieve the complete cessation of rocket attacks by Hezbollah on settlements in northern Israel. Some 400,000 Lebanese were displaced northwards, after the Israeli military authorities warned that they would be endangered by the offensive against Hezbollah. Moreover, the shelling by Israeli forces of a base of the UN peacekeeping force at Qana resulted in the deaths of more than 100 Lebanese civilians who had been sheltering there, and of four UN peacekeepers. A ceasefire 'understanding' took effect in late April; this was effectively a compromise confining the conflict to the area of the security zone in southern Lebanon, recognizing both Hezbollah's right to resist Israeli occupation and Israel's right to self-defence; the 'understanding' also provided for an Israel-Lebanon Monitoring Group (ILMG), comprising Israel, Lebanon, Syria, France and the USA, to supervise the ceasefire.

Israel welcomed the decision of the Palestine National Council (PNC) in late April 1996 to amend the Palestinian National Charter (or PLO Covenant), removing all clauses demanding the destruction of Israel: the Israeli Government had required that the Covenant be amended as a precondition for participation in the final stage of peace negotiations with the PLO.

The first term of Prime Minister Binyamin Netanyahu

The Likud leader, Binyamin Netanyahu, achieved a marginal victory over Shimon Peres in the direct prime-ministerial election, held on 19 May 1996. At the parallel legislative election, an alliance of Likud, the Tzomet party and Gesher secured 32 of the 120 Knesset seats, and Labour 34. Netanyahu proceeded to sign agreements between the Likud alliance and Shas, the National Religious Party (NRP), Israel B'Aliyah, United Torah Judaism and the Third Way, to form a coalition that would command the support of 66 deputies in the Knesset. The new Government's statement of policy excluded the possibility of granting Palestinian statehood or, with regard to Syria, of relinquishing de facto sovereignty of the occupied Golan Heights. Moreover, Netanyahu apparently postponed further discussion of the withdrawal of Israeli armed forces from the West Bank town of Hebron, where they provided security for some 400 Jewish settlers.

In September 1996 it was announced that Israel's Ministry of Defence had approved plans to construct some 1,800 new homes at existing Jewish settlements in the West Bank. Violent confrontations erupted between Palestinian security forces and civilians, and the Israeli armed forces, in which at least 50 Palestinians and 18 Israelis were killed. The decision of the Israeli Government to open the north end of the Hasmonean tunnel running beneath the al-Aqsa Mosque in Jerusalem was cited as the immediate cause of the disturbances, although it appeared to be the inevitable culmination of Palestinian frustration at Israel's failure to implement agreements previously signed with the PA. Nevertheless, in January 1997 Israel and the PA finally concluded an agreement on the withdrawal of Israeli forces from Hebron. Israel was to withdraw from 80% of the town within 10 days; the first of three subsequent redeployments would take place six weeks after the signing of the agreement, and the remaining two by August 1998. As guarantor of the Hebron agreement, the USA undertook to obtain the release of Palestinian prisoners, and to ensure that Israel continued to engage in negotiations for a Palestinian airport in the Gaza Strip, and on safe passage for Palestinians between the West Bank and Gaza. The USA also undertook to ensure that the PA would continue to combat terrorism, complete the revision of the Palestinian National Charter, and consider Israeli requests to extradite Palestinians suspected of involvement in attacks in Israel.

Progress achieved through the agreement on Hebron was severely undermined in February 1997, when Israel announced that it was to proceed with the construction of 6,500 housing units at Har Homa (Jabal Abu Ghunaim in Arabic) in East Jerusalem. Tensions escalated in March, after Israel decided unilaterally to withdraw its armed forces from only 9% of the West Bank. Israeli intransigence over the Har Homa settlement prompted Palestinians to abandon the 'final status' talks on borders, the Jerusalem issue, Jewish settlements and Palestinian refugees, scheduled to begin on 17 March, and construction at the site began the following day. Riots erupted among Palestinians, and shortly afterwards Hamas carried out a bomb attack in Tel-Aviv, killing four people. In late March the League of Arab States (the Arab League, see p. 362) voted to resume its economic boycott of Israel, suspend moves to establish diplomatic relations, and withdraw from multilateral peace talks. (Jordan, the PA and Egypt were excluded from the resolution, owing to their binding bilateral agreements with Israel.)

In June 1997 Ehud Barak, a former government minister and army chief of staff, was elected to replace Peres as Labour Party Chairman. In July two Hamas suicide bombers killed 14 civilians in Jerusalem, prompting Israel to suspend payment of tax revenues to the PA and again close off the Gaza Strip and the West Bank. Further suicide bombings in West Jerusalem in early September resulted in eight deaths. Following a visit by US Secretary of State Madeleine Albright in mid-September, Israel released further Palestinian assets (one-third of tax revenues owed to the PA had been released in August), while the Palestinians announced the closure of 17 institutions affiliated to Hamas.

Renewed hostilities erupted in northern Israel in August 1997, after Hezbollah launched a rocket attack on civilians in Kiryat Shmona. The attack, made following raids by Israeli commandos in which five Hezbollah members were killed, provoked further air strikes by Israel in southern Lebanon. Violence escalated, with the shelling by the SLA of the Lebanese port of Sidon resulting in at least six deaths. Domestic pressure for an Israeli withdrawal from southern Lebanon increased after 12 Israeli marines were killed south of Sidon in September.

Relations between Jordan and Israel deteriorated in September 1997, after members of the Israeli intelligence force, Mossad, attempted to assassinate Hamas's political leader, Khalid Meshaal, in the Jordanian capital, Amman. Following intensive negotiations between Netanyahu, Crown Prince Hassan of Jordan and US officials, several agreements were reached regarding the release of prisoners: in October Israel freed the Hamas spiritual leader, Sheikh Ahmad Yassin, in return for the release by Jordan of two Mossad agents arrested in connection with the attack on Meshaal; a further 12 Mossad agents were expelled by the Jordanian authorities following the release by Israel of 23 Jordanian and 50 Palestinian prisoners.

Bilateral negotiations between Israel and the PA resumed in November 1997. Israel offered to decelerate its construction of Jewish settlements in return for Palestinian approval of a plan to delay further redeployments of Israeli troops from the West Bank. However, the Israeli Government also announced plans to build 900 new housing units in the area. This prompted several Arab states to boycott the Middle East and North Africa economic conference, held in Doha, Qatar, in mid-November, which an Israeli delegation was scheduled to attend. At the end of November the Israeli Cabinet agreed in principle to a partial withdrawal from the West Bank, but specified neither the timing nor the scale of this. In January 1998 Netanyahu announced that he would not make any further decisions regarding the peace process until the Palestinians had demonstrated further efforts to combat terrorism, reduced their security forces from 40,000 to 24,000, and amended their National Charter to recognize Israel's right to exist.

In June 1998 President Weizman (who had been elected for a second term in March) angered Netanyahu by publicly demanding the dissolution of the Knesset and early elections, so that Israelis might choose the future direction of peace talks. Meanwhile, the Cabinet approved Netanyahu's draft plan whereby the municipal boundaries of Jerusalem would be extended to incorporate seven West Bank Jewish settlements—to create a 'Greater Jerusalem' covering six times the current area of the city. Arab leaders accused Netanyahu of seeking formally to annex parts of the West Bank, and the UN Security Council urged Israel to abandon the proposals.

After nine days of intensive talks with US President Bill Clinton at the Wye Plantation, Maryland, on 23 October 1998 Netanyahu and Arafat signed an agreement (the Wye River Memorandum) that outlined a three-month timetable for the implementation of the 1995 Interim Agreement and signalled the commencement of 'final status' talks—which should have begun in May 1996. With the mediation of Clinton and King Hussein, Israel agreed to redeploy its troops from 13.1% of the West Bank, while the PA agreed to intensify measures to prevent terrorism and to rewrite the Palestinian National Charter. On 11 November 1998, after the postponement of four scheduled meetings (owing to a bombing by Islamic Jihad in Jerusalem and Israeli fears of further attacks by Palestinian militant groups), the Israeli Cabinet approved the Wye Memorandum. Netanyahu subsequently reiterated that a number of conditions would first have to be met by the Palestinians, and threatened effective Israeli annexation of areas of the West Bank if a Palestinian state were to be declared on 4 May 1999. (Arafat continued to reassert his right to declare a Palestinian state on the expiry date of the interim stage defined in Oslo.) The Knesset ratified the Wye Memorandum on 17 November 1998. Three days later the Israeli Government implemented the first stage of renewed redeployment from the West Bank, also releasing 250 Palestinian prisoners and signing a protocol allowing for the opening of an international airport at Gaza.

During December 1998 it became increasingly evident that divisions within Netanyahu's coalition over implementation of the Wye Memorandum were making government untenable. The administration effectively collapsed when the Minister of Finance, Yaacov Ne'eman, announced his resignation. Shortly afterwards the Knesset voted to hold elections to the legislature and premiership in early 1999.

In December 1998 US President Clinton attended a session of the PNC, at which the removal from the Palestinian National Charter of all clauses seeking Israel's destruction was re-affirmed. Following a meeting between Clinton, Arafat and Netanyahu, the Israeli premier reiterated accusations that the Palestinians had not adequately addressed their security commitments, and announced that he would not release Palestinian prisoners considered to have 'blood on their hands'. Netanyahu announced that the second phase of Israeli troop deployment envisaged by the Wye Memorandum, scheduled for 18 December, would not be undertaken. The Knesset subsequently voted to suspend implementation of the Wye Memorandum, thereby effectively suspending the peace process. In late December Arafat freed the Hamas spiritual leader, Sheikh Ahmad Yassin, from house arrest, prompting further Israeli claims that agreed anti-terrorism measures were not being implemented. The US Administration threatened to withhold US $1,200m. promised to Israel to fund its redeployment in the West Bank unless it complied with the terms of the Wye Memorandum. For several months President Clinton refused to hold a private meeting with Netanyahu, while agreeing to meet Arafat in March 1999 to discuss his threatened unilateral declaration of statehood on 4 May; following intense international pressure, the declaration was postponed at the end of April.

Hostilities in southern Lebanon between Israeli forces and Hezbollah persisted throughout 1998. In that year some 23 Israeli soldiers were killed, and there was increasing pressure on Netanyahu for a unilateral withdrawal from the territory. On 1 April the Israeli Security Cabinet voted unanimously to adopt UN Security Council Resolution 425 (of March 1978), urging an immediate withdrawal of Israeli troops from all Lebanese territory provided that the Lebanese army gave security guarantees. However, both Lebanon and Syria demanded an unconditional withdrawal. Fighting escalated in August, when Hezbollah launched rocket attacks on northern Israel in retaliation for an Israeli helicopter attack in which a senior Lebanese military official was killed. Seven Israeli soldiers died in two attacks in November, leading Netanyahu to curtail a European tour in order to hold an emergency cabinet meeting on a possible withdrawal. In December an Israeli air attack in which eight Lebanese civilians were killed provoked condemnation from the ILMG, which declared it to be a violation of the ceasefire 'understanding' reached in April 1996. In February 1999 the commander of the Israeli army unit for liaison with the SLA became the most senior Israeli officer to be killed in southern Lebanon since 1982. Israel responded with its heaviest air raids against Lebanon since the 1996 Grapes of Wrath operation.

The election of Ehud Barak as Prime Minister

At the general election held on 17 May 1999, Ehud Barak was elected Prime Minister with 56.1% of the total votes cast. In the elections to the Knesset, Barak's One Israel alliance (including Gesher and the moderate Meimad) secured 26 seats, while Likud's representation fell from 32 seats to 19. Shas won 17 seats. Netanyahu subsequently resigned from both the Knesset and the Likud leadership, and in September Ariel Sharon was elected as Likud's new Chairman. Barak stated that he would observe four 'security red lines' concerning negotiations with the Palestinians: Jerusalem would remain under Israeli sovereignty; there would be no return to the pre-1967 borders; most West Bank settlers would remain in settlements under Israeli sovereignty; and no 'foreign armies' would be based west of the Jordan river. Following complex negotiations, Barak forged a broad coalition with the Centre Party, Shas, Meretz, Israel B'Aliyah and the NRP, which was endorsed by the Knesset in July 1999. Barak himself took the defence portfolio. David Levy, the Gesher leader, became Minister of Foreign Affairs, and Shimon Peres Minister of Regional Co-operation.

In early September 1999, during a visit to the region by US Secretary of State Albright, Barak and Arafat travelled to Egypt for talks at Sharm el-Sheikh. On 4 September the two leaders signed the Sharm el-Sheikh Memorandum (or Wye Two accords), which outlined a revised timetable for implementation of the outstanding provisions of the original Wye Memorandum in order to facilitate the resumption of 'final status' talks: a new target date—13 September 2000—was set for the conclusion of a comprehensive 'final status' settlement (with a framework agreement to be in place six months prior to this). One important change was the reduction, to 350, of the number of Palestinian prisoners to be released by Israel. On 8 September 1999 the Knesset ratified the Wye Two accords; the following day Israel released some 200 Palestinian prisoners, and on 10 September a further 7% of the West Bank was transferred to Palestinian civilian control. A further 151 Palestinian prisoners were released from Israeli custody in mid-October. On 25 October a southern 'safe passage' for Palestinians travelling between Gaza and Hebron was finally opened.

Despite this apparent progress, Barak encountered severe criticism in late 1999 among left-wing groups and Palestinians over his Government's apparent intention to continue to approve the expansion of Jewish settlements in the West Bank. (Since coming to power, the Government had issued tenders for some 2,600 new homes in such settlements.) Barak subsequently angered settler groups with a ruling that several of the 42 'outpost settlements' established in the West Bank under the Likud Government had been built illegally; 12 of the 'outposts' were dismantled in October.

On 8 November 1999 representatives of Israel and the PA commenced talks on 'final status' issues in the West Bank city of Ramallah, although the redeployment of Israeli armed forces from a further 5% of the West Bank on 15 November was delayed owing to a dispute over which areas were to be transferred. In December Barak and Arafat met on Palestinian territory for the first time, and at the end of the month Israel released some 26 Palestinian 'security' prisoners as a gesture of goodwill. On 6–7 January 2000 Israeli troops withdrew from a further 5% of the West Bank. However, Israel subsequently announced the postponement of a third redeployment (scheduled for 20 January) until Barak had returned from talks with Syrian representatives in the USA. In early February PA officials suspended peace negotiations, following the decision by the Israeli Cabinet to withdraw its armed forces from a sparsely populated 6.1% of the West Bank. The redeployment from a further 6.1% took place on 21 March, facilitating an official resumption of 'final status' talks. In that month a ruling by Israel's Supreme Court that the allocation of state-owned land on the basis of religion, nationality or ethnicity was illegal allowed Israeli Arabs to purchase land for the first time.

Meanwhile, in June 1999 the SLA completed a unilateral withdrawal from the Jezzine enclave. Later that month the outgoing Netanyahu administration launched a series of air attacks on Lebanon, destroying Beirut's main power station and other infrastructure, in response to Hezbollah rocket attacks on northern Israel. In December Israel and Syria reached an 'understanding in principle' to limit the fighting in southern Lebanon. However, the informal ceasefire did not endure, and in February 2000 Israel retaliated for a series of attacks by Hezbollah with further bombing raids on Lebanese infrastructure. Israel also announced a unilateral withdrawal from the 1996 ceasefire agreement.

In March 2000 the Israeli Cabinet voted unanimously to withdraw its forces from southern Lebanon by 7 July, even in the absence of a peace agreement with Syria. The Lebanese Government responded by demanding that Israel also depart from the Shebaa Farms area on the Syrian border. (Shebaa Farms has been designated by the UN as being part of Syria, and thus subject to the Syrian track of the peace process; Hezbollah, however, considers it to be part of southern Lebanon.) In April Israel released 13 Lebanese prisoners who had been detained without trial for more than a decade, apparently as 'bargaining chips' for Israeli soldiers missing in Lebanon. Fighting between Israeli troops and Hezbollah intensified in May, and on 23 May Israel's Security Cabinet voted to accelerate the withdrawal of its remaining troops from southern Lebanon. By this date Hezbollah had taken control of about one-third of the territory, following the evacuation by the SLA of outposts transferred to its control by the Israeli army, and mass defections from the SLA were reported. The rapid departure of all Israeli forces from southern Lebanon was completed on 24 May; about 900 Israelis had been killed there since 1978. After the withdrawal several thousand SLA members and their families fled across the border into northern Israel. In June 2000 the UN Security Council confirmed that Israel had completed its withdrawal from Lebanon in compliance with Resolution 425. Following the withdrawal, personnel from the UN Interim Force in Lebanon (UNIFIL) began patrolling the area vacated by Israeli forces, monitoring the line of withdrawal and providing humanitarian assistance.

A third round of 'final status' discussions opened in Eilat on 30 April 2000, but maps presented by Israeli officials to the PA in early May, defining Barak's interpretation of a future Palestinian state, were firmly rejected by the Palestinians. Barak and Arafat held a crisis meeting in Ramallah, at which Barak proposed that Israel transfer to full PA control three Arab villages situated close to Jerusalem, on condition that the third West Bank redeployment (scheduled for June) was postponed until after the conclusion of a final peace settlement. The Knesset subsequently approved the transfer. However, Barak later announced that an Israeli withdrawal from the Arab villages would not be implemented until the PA took appropriate measures to curb unrest in the West Bank, where Palestinians had been protesting in support of gaoled Palestinians on hunger strike.

In May 2000, following an inconclusive police investigation into allegations of fraud, President Weizman announced his intention to resign. In the ensuing presidential election, held on 31 July, Likud's Moshe Katsav unexpectedly secured a narrow victory over Barak's nominee, Shimon Peres. Katsav was duly sworn in as the eighth President of Israel on 1 August, to serve an exceptional seven-year term. In early July, meanwhile, the three right-wing parties (Israel B'Aliyah, the NRP and Shas) withdrew from the coalition Government in protest against what they perceived to be Barak's willingness to concede to PA territorial claims. Despite the loss of six ministers (two from Meretz had earlier resigned following a dispute with Shas), Barak survived a motion of no confidence in the Knesset. He survived another vote of no confidence immediately after the presidential election. In early August, however, the Minister of Foreign Affairs, David Levy, announced his resignation, citing disagreements with Barak over the peace process; he was subsequently replaced by the Minister of Public Security, Shlomo Ben-Ami.

US President Clinton opened the Camp David talks, aimed at reaching a framework agreement for a final peace settlement, on 11 July 2000. Despite intensive mediation efforts, the summit ended on 25 July without agreement. Progress had reportedly been made on the issues of the borders of a future Palestinian entity (to comprise all of the Gaza Strip and at least 90% of the West Bank) and the status of Palestinian refugees, but the two sides were unable to reach a compromise regarding the future status of Jerusalem. In the summit's final communiqué, both sides vowed to continue the pursuit of a 'final status' settlement and to avoid 'unilateral actions'—thereby implying that Arafat would not declare a Palestinian state on 13 September. Shortly before that date the Palestinian legislature voted to delay such a declaration for an indefinite period.

The al-Aqsa intifada

In late September 2000 Barak and Arafat met for the first time since the Camp David summit. The resumption of contacts was swiftly overshadowed by a renewed uprising by Palestinians against Israeli occupation, which resulted in the suspension of the Middle East peace process. On 28 September the Likud leader, Ariel Sharon, made a highly controversial visit to the Temple Mount/Haram al-Sharif compound in Jerusalem (the site of the Dome of the Rock and the al-Aqsa Mosque). Protests there by Palestinians triggered violent unrest throughout the Palestinian territories. For the first time, notably, Israeli Arabs clashed with security forces within Israel. On 7 October the UN Security Council adopted a resolution condemning the 'excessive use of force' by Israeli security forces against Palestinian demonstrators. Israel closed the borders of the Palestinian territories and Gaza airport, and Barak demanded that Arafat rearrest some 60 militant Islamists who had recently been freed from Palestinian detention.

The crisis escalated in mid-October 2000, after Israeli forces launched rocket attacks on the headquarters of Arafat's Fatah movement in Ramallah and on other PA offices, in response to the murder of two Israeli army reservists by a Palestinian crowd. Despite an emergency summit meeting between Barak and Arafat, convened by President Clinton, and hosted by President Mubarak at Sharm el-Sheikh, at which measures were agreed to end the fighting (including the formation of an international commission to investigate its causes), violence intensified, and on 22 October Barak announced that Israel was to take a 'time-out' from the peace process. This came as Barak undertook discussions with Likud on the formation of a national unity government prior to the reconvening of the Knesset for the new parliamentary session; however, no compromise was reached, apparently owing to Sharon's demand for a veto on all decisions relating to national security. Barak's decision formally to suspend Israel's participation in the peace process was precipitated by the final communiqué issued by Arab leaders after an emergency summit meeting of the Arab League in Cairo, which declared that Israel bore full responsibility for the recent violence. Morocco, Tunisia and Oman announced that they had severed relations with Israel, and Qatar broke off ties in November.

A suicide bomb attack by Islamic Jihad on an Israeli military target in Gaza at the end of October 2000 led the Israeli army to declare a new strategy of 'initiated attacks', or 'targeted killings', of the leaders of such groups, as well as senior Fatah commanders, whom it held responsible for 'terrorist' actions. In early November the Israeli Minister of Regional Co-operation, Shimon

Peres, held crisis talks with Arafat in Gaza, at which a ceasefire was agreed, based on the provisions defined the previous month at Sharm el-Sheikh. However, the truce was broken almost immediately, when a car bomb planted by Islamic Jihad exploded in Jerusalem, killing two Israelis. In mid-November Israel effectively imposed a complete economic blockade of the Palestinian areas. Later in the month the explosion of a bomb close to a bus carrying Israeli schoolchildren (as a result of which two people died and several children were injured) provoked public outrage, and led Israel to launch further air raids against Fatah targets in Gaza. Egypt responded by announcing that it was recalling its ambassador from Tel-Aviv. (Egypt suspended all direct contact with the Israeli Government in April 2002, other than for negotiations aimed at restoring peace in the region, and did not return an ambassador to Israel until March 2005.)

The accession of Prime Minister Ariel Sharon

At the end of November 2000, in an apparent attempt to secure his increasingly beleaguered Government, Ehud Barak unexpectedly called early prime ministerial elections for 2001. The election, held on 6 February 2001, resulted in an overwhelming victory for the Likud leader, Ariel Sharon, with 62.4% of the votes cast. Barak had notably lost the Israeli Arab vote—as the Arab parties had urged their supporters to boycott or abstain in the poll—and his defeat was interpreted as a decisive rejection of the Oslo peace process by the majority of Israelis. Sharon immediately sought the formation of a broad-based government of national unity, essentially to secure a political base in the Knesset (where Likud held only 19 of the 120 seats). Barak announced his resignation as Labour leader; he subsequently declared that he would not enter a government led by Sharon, and that he would withdraw from political life. In late February Labour's Central Committee voted to join a coalition administration, enabling Sharon to conclude agreements principally with the religious and right-wing parties. The national unity Government, approved by the Knesset in early March, included the ultra-Orthodox Shas (the leader of which, Eliyahu Yishai, became Deputy Prime Minister and Minister of the Interior), Israel B'Aliyah and the extreme right-wing National Union-Israel Beytenu bloc.

Following his election victory, Sharon rejected an appeal by the new US Administration of President George W. Bush, who had been inaugurated in January 2001, for Israel to end its blockade on the West Bank and Gaza Strip and to deliver overdue tax transfers to the PA. In March Arab League heads of state, meeting in Amman, resolved to reinstate the 'secondary' economic boycott of Israel. It was announced in early April that the Israeli Government had issued tenders for the construction of a further 708 housing units in the West Bank. In the same month, in response to a Palestinian mortar attack on the Israeli town of Sderot, Israeli armed forces imposed road blockades, which effectively divided the Gaza Strip into three sections, and sent tanks and bulldozers into the Gazan town of Beit Hanoun; this was Israel's first armed incursion into territory that it had transferred to PA control under the terms of the Oslo accords. Under heavy pressure from the USA, Israel withdrew its forces less than 24 hours later. Hopes of a resumption of the Oslo peace talks were raised in mid-April amid a revival of the 'Egyptian-Jordanian initiative' or Taba plan. Based on the fragile understanding reached at Sharm el-Sheikh in October 2000, the initiative required that the situation on the ground be restored to that prior to the start of the al-Aqsa *intifada*. It also stipulated that negotiations be resumed from the point at which they stalled in January 2001, and that Israel agree to halt its settlement programme in the Occupied Territories. Sharon stated that Israel would endorse the Taba plan, on condition that the PA end its demand for a complete freeze on the construction of Jewish settlements, and that all Palestinian violence cease prior to the resumption of peace talks.

In May 2001 the Sharm el-Sheikh Fact-Finding Committee, under the chairmanship of former US Senator George Mitchell, published its recommendations relating to the causes of the Israeli–Palestinian violence. The Mitchell Report referred to the visit of Ariel Sharon to the Islamic holy sites in September 2000 as 'provocative', but declined to single out for blame either Sharon or the PA leadership (which Israeli officials had accused of having orchestrated the violence). The Mitchell Report also demanded that Arafat undertake further measures to curb Palestinian 'terrorist operations', and appealed to Israel to end its economic blockade of the West Bank and Gaza and to halt its settlement expansion programme. At the beginning of June 21 Israelis were killed in an attack on a Tel-Aviv nightclub by a Palestinian suicide bomber. In mid-June proposals for a comprehensive ceasefire, brokered by the USA, were approved by Israel and the PA; however, although Israel began to implement provisions to pull back troops from PA-controlled towns and to ease the economic blockade, the process was hindered by the murder of two West Bank settlers by Palestinian gunmen and the killing of two Israeli soldiers in a suicide bombing in the Gaza Strip.

At the end of July 2001 two leading Hamas members, alleged by Israel to have been involved in the Tel-Aviv nightclub bombing, were killed during an air raid on Hamas media offices in Nablus. In early August the Israeli administration published a 'most wanted' list of seven Palestinians whom it alleged to be prominent in the preparation of 'terrorist' attacks. Only days later at least 15 Israelis (including six children) were killed by a Palestinian suicide bomber at a Jerusalem restaurant. The Israeli Government responded to the bombing by taking temporary control of Orient House, the de facto headquarters of the PA in East Jerusalem. At the end of August Abu Ali Moustafa, leader of the Popular Front for the Liberation of Palestine (PFLP), was killed by Israeli security forces at the party's offices in Ramallah. In September the PFLP claimed responsibility for four bomb attacks in Jerusalem. On several occasions during the latter part of the year Israel ordered its forces into PA-controlled towns—among them Hebron, Bethlehem, Jenin and Beit Jala—in response to violent clashes between Israelis and Palestinians. By the time of the first anniversary of the outbreak of the al-Aqsa *intifada*, on 28 September, the violence had led to the deaths of more than 160 Israelis, and at least 600 Palestinians. The massive suicide attacks against New York and Washington, DC, on 11 September 2001 accelerated US and European Union (EU, see p. 273) efforts to urge Israel and the PA to effect a lasting ceasefire.

In October 2001 two ministers resigned after the right-wing National Union-Israel Beytenu bloc withdrew from the governing coalition in protest at the Sharon administration's decision to pull back Israeli armed forces from the West Bank town of Hebron. Two days later one of these outgoing ministers, the Minister of Tourism, Rechavam Ze'evi, was assassinated in Arab East Jerusalem by a PFLP militant, in apparent retaliation for the recent assassination of the group's leader. Following the murder of Ze'evi, the National Union-Israel Beytenu bloc maintained its presence in the Government, with Avigdor Lieberman retaining his post as Minister of National Infrastructure and Rabbi Binyamin Elon named as Ze'evi's successor. Sharon suspended all contact with the PA, holding Arafat personally responsible for Ze'evi's death. The Israeli Government also reversed its recent moves to ease the economic restrictions on Palestinians in the West Bank and Gaza, and demanded that the PA immediately extradite the PFLP militants implicated in the assassination. Israeli armed forces entered six Palestinian towns in the West Bank (including Ramallah, Jenin, Nablus and Bethlehem), leading US officials to urge Israel to pull back its troops from PA-controlled areas. Although Israeli forces duly withdrew from two of the towns (Bethlehem and Beit Jala) at the end of October, Sharon announced that the withdrawal from the remaining four would not take place until the PA arrested more Islamist militants.

The Israeli–Palestinian crisis escalated in December 2001, when Palestinian militants launched suicide attacks in Haifa and Jerusalem, in reprisal for the 'targeted killing' of a Hamas leader: over one weekend some 25 Israelis were killed, and scores wounded. Sharon ordered heavy military strikes against Palestinian security targets, and Israel escalated its operations in the Palestinian territories in mid-December after 10 Israelis died in a bomb attack in the West Bank. The Government demanded 'concrete action' from the PA, despite a recent speech in which Arafat had told Palestinian militant groups to end their armed campaign against Israel. Israeli armed forces undertook a 'tactical' withdrawal from areas around Nablus and Ramallah to permit Arafat's security forces to arrest wanted Palestinian militants. However, Arafat remained confined to his headquarters in Ramallah after Israel imposed a travel ban on the Palestinian leader.

In early January 2002 the Israeli administration ordered the partial withdrawal of its forces from some West Bank towns, and the easing of certain restrictions against Palestinians there. Meanwhile, it was announced that Israeli forces in the Red Sea had intercepted a freighter ship, the *Karine-A*, which Israel asserted was carrying Iranian-made heavy weaponry destined for the Gaza Strip. In response to claims by Israeli and US officials of the PA's involvement in the trafficking of arms into the Occupied Territories, Arafat (who denied all knowledge of the shipment) instituted an internal inquiry into the *Karine-A* affair. In mid-January Israeli forces assassinated a leader of the Fatah-affiliated Al-Aqsa Martyrs' Brigades, provoking retaliatory attacks by that organization in Hadera and Jerusalem in which six Israelis died. Israeli forces proceeded to tighten the blockade around Arafat's Ramallah offices. At the end of the month Sharon approved a security plan involving the physical 'separation' of Jerusalem from the West Bank, in order to prevent attacks by Palestinian Islamist groups on Israeli territory.

In early March 2002 the UN Security Council adopted Resolution 1397, affirming its 'vision' of both Israeli and Palestinian states 'within secure and recognized borders'. A peace initiative put forward by Crown Prince Abdullah of Saudi Arabia at the Arab League summit in Beirut in late March, whereby Israel would withdraw from all Arab lands occupied since 1967 in exchange for full recognition of the State of Israel by the Arab states, was rejected by the Israeli Government. Towards the end of March 2002 a Hamas suicide bombing at a Passover celebration in Netanya resulted in the deaths of 30 Israelis and injured 140 others. In response, Israeli forces, on 29 March, began a massive campaign of military incursions into West Bank towns—code-named 'Operation Defensive Shield'—with the declared aim of dismantling the Palestinian 'terrorist infrastructure'. Arafat's presidential compound at Ramallah was surrounded by Israeli troops, leaving the Palestinian leader isolated.

During the first two weeks of April 2002 intense fighting between the Israeli army and Palestinian militias occurred in the Jenin refugee camp—considered by Israel to be a base for Palestinian militants opposed to the Oslo accords. Some 23 Israeli soldiers and an estimated 53 Palestinians were reportedly killed in ambushes and gun battles at the camp. US Secretary of State Colin Powell arrived in Israel in mid-April in an attempt to broker a ceasefire, and the Bush Administration repeated demands for Israel to withdraw from PA-controlled towns. There was a subsequent redeployment of Israeli forces from areas of the West Bank, and Arafat was freed at the beginning of May, after the PA agreed to hand over five men suspected of involvement in the assassination of Rechavam Ze'evi. (For further details of events in the West Bank and Gaza Strip in March–May 2002, see the chapter on the Palestinian Territories.)

The National Union-Israel Beytenu bloc withdrew from the governing coalition in March 2002, in protest against recent concessions made towards the Palestinians. However, the Government was strengthened a month later by the appointment of David Levy of Gesher and two ministers from the NRP as ministers without portfolio. The Central Committee of Likud voted in May categorically to reject the creation of a Palestinian state; this was interpreted as a reverse for Ariel Sharon, who publicly accepted the possibility of Palestinian independence.

In June 2002 Israel commenced the construction of a 'security fence', to extend the entire length of its border with the West Bank, to prevent Palestinian militants from infiltrating Israeli territory. The barrier was to be constructed using sections of barbed wire, electrified metal and concrete wall. Despite international efforts to bring about a new round of peace talks between Israel and the PA, and reports of a potential US initiative involving the creation of an 'interim' Palestinian state, there was a marked increase in violence at this time. Israel launched a new offensive, code-named 'Operation Determined Path', ordering troops into several West Bank and Gaza towns, in retaliation for another series of suicide attacks by Palestinian militants; and Arafat's headquarters in Ramallah were again blockaded by the Israeli military. In late June senior-level talks resumed between Israel and the PA, while the Quartet group (comprising the USA, Russia, the UN and the EU) held discussions in London, United Kingdom, with the aim of reactivating the Oslo peace process.

Several Israelis died in an attack on a bus near a Jewish settlement in the West Bank in July 2002, for which three Palestinian militant groups all claimed responsibility. The Israeli response to the latest assaults included suspending plans to ease some of the restrictions imposed on Palestinians in the Territories and proposing to deport a number of relatives of suspected Palestinian militants to the Gaza Strip. In late July an Israeli air strike on a residential building in Gaza City, targeting a leader of Hamas's military wing, reportedly resulted in the deaths of 15 Palestinians. The Gaza air strike precipitated a new round of violence, with four Jewish settlers being killed near Hebron. Israel responded by ordering tanks into the Gaza Strip. At the end of July at least seven Israelis were killed in a suicide bomb attack at the Hebrew University in Jerusalem, for which Hamas claimed responsibility. Following at least 15 further Israeli fatalities in early August, as a result of Palestinian militant attacks, the Israeli Government ordered a total ban on freedom of movement for Palestinians in most West Bank cities, and targeted a number of leading Gazan militants. Israel and the PA agreed at this time to implement a security plan (the 'Gaza, Bethlehem First' plan), whereby Israel would withdraw from the Gaza Strip and Bethlehem in return for Palestinian security guarantees and a crackdown on militants. Israel began to withdraw its forces from Bethlehem the following day; however, violence continued and further talks were cancelled. In September the Israeli Ministry of the Interior took the unprecedented step of revoking the citizenship of an Arab Israeli who was accused of assisting Palestinian militants in plotting suicide attacks against Israelis. Following two suicide bombings in Um al-Fahm and Tel-Aviv in that month, Israeli forces began demolishing buildings in Arafat's Ramallah compound, claiming that some 20 Palestinian militants were being sheltered there.

Elections to the Knesset were held on 28 January 2003, a few months earlier than scheduled. In October 2002 the Labour Party had withdrawn from Sharon's governing coalition in opposition to provisions in the 2003 budget that allocated funds to Jewish settlements in the West Bank. Sharon and his Likud party won a resounding victory over the left-wing parties at the polls, securing 38 seats in the Knesset. A new coalition Government was announced at the end of February 2003: it comprised Likud, the secularist Shinui party (part of the Meretz alliance from 1992, but re-formed as an independent party in 1997), and the right-wing and religious NRP, National Union and Israel B'Aliyah parties. The former Likud premier, Binyamin Netanyahu, was named as Minister of Finance. In May Amram Mitzna resigned as Labour leader (to which post he had been elected in late 2002, in succession to Binyamin Ben-Eliezer); he was subsequently replaced, initially in an acting capacity, by Shimon Peres.

The 'roadmap' peace plan

President George W. Bush announced in mid-April 2003 that he would publish the Quartet-sponsored 'roadmap' for achieving peace in the Middle East once the newly appointed Palestinian Prime Minister, Mahmud Abbas, had announced a new cabinet. On 30 April the USA presented both the Israeli and Palestinian Prime Ministers with copies of the 'roadmap'—despite a suicide bombing in Tel-Aviv the previous day, as a result of which five people were killed. The three-phase initiative envisaged the creation of a sovereign Palestinian state by 2005–06. The first phase would deal largely with Palestinian issues, namely the cessation of militant operations against Israel and the establishment of a civilian and government infrastructure. Israel would be required to withdraw from areas that it had occupied since 2000, and to dismantle Jewish settlements constructed since 2001. In phase two, Israel would hold peace talks with Lebanon and Syria regarding Palestinian borders. The third and final phase would deal with the issues of Jerusalem and refugees. The roadmap emphasized the importance of UN Security Council Resolutions 242, 338 and 1397 in establishing a two-state settlement, and also reiterated that the Arab states must recognize Israel's right to exist. On 25 May the Israeli Cabinet accepted the terms of the roadmap, and at the end of the month Sharon made the unprecedented admission that Israel was in occupation of the Palestinian areas.

In early June 2003 Ariel Sharon, Mahmud Abbas and President Bush met in Aqaba, Jordan, to discuss the implementation of the roadmap, particularly the contentious issue of Jewish settlements. On 9 June Israeli troops commenced the dismantlement of settlements in the West Bank, but the renewed peace process was immediately thwarted by a resumption of violence. An attempt by Israel to kill a prominent Hamas leader, Abd al-Aziz al-Rantisi, prompted a suicide attack against a bus in Jerusalem, in which 16 people died. Israeli helicopter gunships were subsequently ordered to attack targets in Gaza. In all, 26 people were killed in the renewed hostilities. However, Israel continued to dismantle the settlements; it also instigated troop withdrawals from the West Bank and Gaza Strip, as well as the release of a number of Palestinian prisoners. Although this last was not a condition of the roadmap, it was regarded as an important expression of support for Abbas. By mid-August more than 400 prisoners had been released, including members of Hamas and Islamic Jihad who were deemed not to have been involved in planning or executing attacks against Israeli targets.

These two groups, along with Arafat's Fatah movement, had declared a three-month ceasefire at the end of June.

Meanwhile, there was growing international concern regarding Israel's construction of its 'security fence' in the West Bank: Israel was accused of using the 'fence' to annex Palestinian territory, and it was feared that it would become a permanent border in any future peace settlement. President Bush had urged Sharon to remove the 'security fence' when the two leaders met in July, and the US Administration further threatened to withhold nearly US $10,000m. of essential loan guarantees unless construction ceased. Israel none the less continued to erect the barrier, as well as to maintain its policy of 'initiated attacks' against senior Palestinian militants. In mid-August Israeli forces killed a senior Islamic Jihad commander in Hebron, and both Hamas and Islamic Jihad subsequently claimed responsibility for a suicide bomb attack on a bus in Jerusalem, in which 20 Israelis were killed. In retaliation, Israel reimposed road-blocks on the main north–south highway in the Gaza Strip, reversing one of the earliest roadmap initiatives.

In October 2003 the Israeli Cabinet approved the next phase of the 'security fence'; although this was not contiguous to sections of the barrier already built, it was to enclose settlements in the West Bank completely. Additionally, a tender was issued for the construction of 550 new homes in a settlement close to Jerusalem. The USA announced in November its intention to cut US $290m. from a set of loan guarantees for Israel as a penalty for renewed settlement construction in the West Bank and Gaza. The issue of the settlements was further raised by the authors of a new peace plan, launched by senior Palestinian and Israeli political figures in Geneva, Switzerland, on 1 December. The Geneva Accords, which did not have the official approval of either the Israeli or Palestinian administrations, outlined a two-state solution, including proposals that Palestinians would receive compensation for giving up the right of return; that most settlements in the West Bank and Gaza (except those neighbouring Jerusalem) would be dismantled; and that Jerusalem (which would be the capital of two states) would be divided administratively rather than physically. On 8 December the UN General Assembly adopted a resolution asking the International Court of Justice (ICJ) in The Hague, Netherlands, to issue a (non-binding) ruling on the legality of Israel's 'security fence'; hearings began in February 2004.

Sharon's disengagement plan

In December 2003 Ariel Sharon warned the PA that unless it began disarming and disbanding Palestinian militant groups, Israel would adopt a 'disengagement plan' that would effectively accelerate the construction of the 'security fence' in the West Bank and physically separate Israel from the Palestinian territories. Sharon's speech attracted criticism from right-wing and ultra-Orthodox settler groups when it became clear that disengagement would involve the evacuation of 17 settlements in the Gaza Strip, considered beyond the reach of the 'security fence'. The roadmap—which Sharon asserted he was willing to implement if the Palestinians also carried out their obligations—required at least 60 settlements in the West Bank and Gaza to be dismantled.

Sharon confirmed in an interview published in *Ha'aretz* newspaper in February 2004 that he had drawn up a plan to evacuate all Jewish settlements in the Gaza Strip. The evacuation would reportedly affect 7,500 settlers in 17 settlements (although details of the plan were subsequently amended—see below). Although the plan was welcomed by the recently appointed Palestinian Prime Minister, Ahmad Quray, the proposed disengagement was overshadowed by the 'targeted killing' of Sheikh Ahmad Yassin, the founder and spiritual leader of Hamas, by Israeli helicopter gunships in March. The action to kill Yassin, which provoked international condemnation, followed a double suicide bombing at the southern port of Ashdod, responsibility for which was claimed jointly by Hamas and the Al-Aqsa Martyrs' Brigades, in which 10 Israelis died. Yassin's successor as leader of Hamas in Gaza, Abd al-Aziz al-Rantisi, was also killed in April in a rocket attack by Israeli helicopter gunships. Hamas kept secret the identity of al-Rantisi's successor, reportedly adopting a policy of 'collective leadership' in order to prevent future known leaders of the organization from being similarly targeted.

The Israeli Prime Minister secured the endorsement of President Bush for his proposal to 'disengage' from Gaza, which also involved the consolidation of six settlements in the West Bank. In May 2004, however, members of his own Likud party overwhelmingly rejected the plan. Sharon subsequently made limited modifications to the proposals, and in June dismissed two ministers of the far-right National Union party—the Minister of Transport, Avigdor Lieberman, and the Minister of Tourism, Binyamin Elon—both of whom were opposed to disengagement from Gaza. A few days later the NRP Minister of Construction and Housing, Efraim Eitam, resigned, after the Cabinet approved in principle Sharon's broad proposals. However, Sharon subsequently lost his Knesset majority when National Union's six deputies resigned, and he entered into negotiations with the Labour Party.

Meanwhile, attacks by Palestinian militants against Israeli soldiers in the Gaza Strip intensified, and in May 2004 Israel launched a large military offensive, code-named 'Operation Rainbow'. The aims of the operation were to locate and dismantle tunnels in the Rafah refugee camps through which militants were able to smuggle weapons from Egypt, and to arrest Palestinians wanted for involvement in attacks against Israelis. Some 40 Palestinians, whom Israel claimed to be terrorists, were reported to have been killed. In June the Israeli Supreme Court ordered the Government to alter the route of part of the 'security fence', including a 30-km section around the Palestinian village of Beit Sourik. In July the ICJ advised that the barrier contravened international law and effectively constituted the annexation of Palestinian land, and that it disrupted thousands of civilians' lives, frustrating Palestinian attempts to achieve self-determination. The ICJ urged Israel to remove parts of the fence and pay compensation to affected Palestinians. Sharon rejected the ruling, which he asserted was politically motivated and detrimental to the US-led 'war on terror'. The UN General Assembly subsequently voted to demand that Israel comply with the ICJ ruling and dismantle the barrier. In August Sharon approved the construction of 1,000 new homes in the West Bank.

In October 2004 the Knesset voted to accept Sharon's proposal to dismantle all 21 Israeli settlements in Gaza, and four in the northern West Bank. In November the Cabinet approved a plan to compensate Jewish settlers due to be evacuated from Gaza, and to imprison settlers who resisted evacuation. The NRP's six parliamentary members withdrew from the coalition, in opposition to Sharon's proposals. In early December Sharon dismissed Shinui's five ministers, who had voted against the first reading of the 2005 budget because it pledged US $98m. in subsidies to projects supported by United Torah Judaism. Likud was left with only 40 out of the Knesset's 120 seats. Following negotiations, Labour agreed to form a coalition with Likud. In January 2005 the Knesset narrowly approved the new coalition Government, to be composed principally of Likud, Labour and United Torah Judaism, thereby restoring Sharon's parliamentary majority; the Labour leader, Shimon Peres, was awarded the title of Vice-Premier.

In mid-October 2004, meanwhile, the Israeli army ended a 16-day assault, code-named 'Operation Days of Penitence', in northern and southern Gaza; according to UN figures, 135 Palestinians were killed and an estimated 95 homes destroyed. The operation had been prompted by a Hamas rocket that killed two children in Sderot, close to the Gaza Strip. Egypt undertook to provide 750 border guards to replace Israeli troops along the Egypt–Gaza frontier, in an effort to stem arms-smuggling, and to prevent Hamas and other Palestinian militants from firing rockets into Israel in the event of Israeli disengagement.

Following the death of Yasser Arafat in November 2004, Mahmud Abbas was elected Executive President of the PA in January 2005. On 8 February a summit meeting was convened in Sharm el-Sheikh between Sharon, Abbas, Egypt's President Mubarak and King Abdullah of Jordan in Sharm el-Sheikh. Sharon and Abbas shook hands, and issued verbal declarations to end hostilities between their two peoples; however, despite hopes of a breakthrough in the Middle East peace process, no formal ceasefire was agreed, and Hamas and Islamic Jihad refused to be bound by Abbas's declaration. Israel none the less agreed to hand over to PA security control the towns of Jericho, Tulkaram, Bethlehem, Qalqilya and Ramallah in the coming weeks; its forces duly withdrew from Jericho and Tulkaram in March. Moreover, shortly after the Sharm el-Sheikh summit Israel allowed 56 deported Palestinians to return to the West Bank, and also transferred the bodies of 15 Palestinian bombers to the PA. In late February Israel began the release of 500 Palestinian prisoners; a further 400 prisoners were to be freed after a three-month period. Jordan returned its ambassador to Israel in March, as did Egypt.

The Israeli Cabinet gave its final approval in late February 2005 to the Government's planned disengagement from all settlements in the Gaza Strip and four in the West Bank. In March 13 armed Palestinian factions, including Hamas and Islamic Jihad, declared a ceasefire until the end of the year, on the condition that Israel refrained from attacks and released 8,000 Palestinian prisoners. The Knesset voted in late March to reject a bill that would require a national referendum to be held prior to any implementation of Sharon's Disengagement Plan, and approved the 2005 budget, thus avoiding the need to call a general election and preventing a delay to the planned disengagement.

In July 2005 Israeli and Palestinian officials were reported to have agreed in principle to the establishment of a 'safe passage' between the West Bank and the Gaza Strip following the implementation of Israel's Disengagement Plan. In early August, shortly before the Cabinet voted to implement the first stage of the disengagement, Binyamin Netanyahu announced his resignation as Minister of Finance, denouncing the plan as a threat to the security of the country and the unity of the nation. Sharon appointed the Vice-Prime Minister and Minister of Industry, Trade and Labour, Ehud Olmert, to replace Netanyahu in an acting capacity. Despite public protests, and the need forcibly to evacuate settlers who refused to leave the territories after the deadline of 17 August, the disengagement was completed ahead of schedule, on 12 September, when the last Israeli forces left Gaza. On 22 September Israeli forces completed their withdrawal from the northern West Bank. In late August, meanwhile, Israel had approved the deployment of Egyptian troops along the Egypt–Gaza frontier. In November Israeli and Egyptian officials agreed to reopen the Rafah border crossing, which was to be managed by the PA with support from European monitors.

Soon after the completion of the withdrawal, and in response to a series of rocket attacks on Israel by Hamas militants from Gaza, Israel carried out air strikes on the Gaza Strip, targeting the Hamas leadership, and made a series of arrests. Several fatal attacks against Israelis during October 2005 resulted in the suspension of security contacts with the PA. In November Hamas announced that it would not renew its ceasefire at the end of the year. Sharon continued to assert that Israeli operations against Hamas targets would not cease until Abbas disarmed militants and destroyed the 'terrorist infrastructure'.

The Israeli Supreme Court voted in September 2005 to reject the non-binding ICJ ruling of July 2004 that the 'security fence' contravened international law, considering that the verdict did not take into account Israel's security needs. The Government had approved the final route of its 'fence' in July 2005, which was to result in four Arab areas of Jerusalem being separated from local schools and hospitals. (New amenities were apparently to be built on the Palestinian side, and transport and crossing-points were to be provided.) Despite the Supreme Court's rejection of the ICJ ruling, justices ordered that a section of the barrier around the settler village of Alfei Menashe in the West Bank be removed, asserting that due consideration had not been given for the rights of Palestinians living in the area. Moreover, following complaints from residents of Palestinian villages near Qalqilya that the 'security fence' isolated them from the rest of the West Bank, the Supreme Court ordered a review of the barrier's route. (After the Supreme Court ruled in 2006 that the route around Qalqilya should be revised, in July 2008 the Israeli Ministry of Defence agreed to remove a section of the barrier to allow Palestinian residents better access to their farmland.)

Formation of Kadima

Having defeated Vice-Premier Shimon Peres in a ballot for the leadership of the Labour Party in November 2005, the Chairman of the Histadrut trade union confederation, Amir Peretz, announced that he would seek the party's withdrawal from the coalition Government, which he claimed had mismanaged the peace process as well as domestic social issues. Eight Labour-Meimad ministers subsequently resigned their posts, among them Peres and the Minister of National Infrastructure, Binyamin Ben-Eliezer.

At the same time Prime Minister Ariel Sharon announced that he was leaving Likud to establish a new party, Kadima (Forward), asserting that the constant distraction of political struggles meant that Likud could not achieve what he considered to be national objectives. The new party, he declared, would aim to pursue a peace agreement with the Palestinians in accordance with the roadmap, and to combat economic and social problems. The Vice-Prime Minister, Ehud Olmert, and the Minister of Immigrant Absorption and of Justice, Tzipi Livni, were among prominent Likud figures to join Kadima. Following a request from the Prime Minister, in late November 2005 President Katsav issued a decree dissolving the legislature, and calling legislative elections (due by November 2006) for 28 March 2006. Shimon Peres announced that he would leave the Labour Party in order to campaign for Kadima, without stating whether he would actually join the new party. Both the acting Chairman of Likud and Minister without Portfolio, Tzachi Hanegbi, and the Minister of Defence, Lt-Gen. Shaul Mofaz, joined Kadima in December 2005. Binyamin Netanyahu was confirmed as the new Likud Chairman later that month, and announced plans to withdraw Likud from the Government.

In early January 2006 Sharon suffered a stroke (his second in a month), which was to leave him in a coma for eight years (see Recent developments). In mid-January, following the withdrawal of Likud members, the Cabinet approved the appointment of three new ministers and the reallocation of various portfolios among existing government members. Acting Prime Minister Olmert adopted the interior portfolio (he additionally held those of industry, trade and labour, finance, and social affairs), while Livni replaced Silvan Shalom as Minister of Foreign Affairs. Olmert was also appointed acting leader of Kadima on the same day.

Also in January 2006, the Israeli Cabinet voted unanimously to permit Arab residents of East Jerusalem to participate in that month's elections to the Palestinian Legislative Council (PLC). Hamas—which was contesting the polls as the Change and Reform list in order to circumvent a ban on its direct participation—secured a decisive majority in the PLC. Abbas subsequently confirmed that he would ask Hamas to form a new administration. The president's own Fatah movement announced that it would not join Hamas in government.

Olmert declared that Israel would not deal with what he termed an 'armed terror organization that calls for Israel's destruction'. The Quartet group appealed to Hamas to reject violence and recognize Israel, and President Bush declared that the USA would not negotiate with a Hamas-led administration unless the organization renounced its call to destroy Israel. However, Khalid Meshaal, the head of Hamas's political bureau, asserted that violence was a legitimate form of resistance to Israeli occupation. Hamas was willing to negotiate a long-term truce only if Israel agreed to certain conditions, including a return to the pre-1967 borders. Olmert pledged, under a Kadima administration, to separate Israel from the Palestinians within permanent borders, and to preserve a Jewish majority in Israel: Israel would retain the whole of Jerusalem and the main West Bank settlement blocs of Ma'aleh Adumim, Ariel and Gush Etzion, in addition to the Jordan Valley, but would be willing to relinquish parts of the West Bank where the majority of the population were Palestinian. He added that Israel would attempt to secure an internationally backed peace plan with Hamas, and would pursue a unilateral solution only if such attempts should fail, and after giving Hamas time to reform, disarm and observe past interim peace agreements. Meshaal rejected the so-called Convergence Plan as allowing Israel to retain illegally its possession of the largest section of the West Bank and its 'security fence', reject concessions on the status of Jerusalem, and thwart the 'right of return' of Palestinian refugees.

Following the inauguration of the new PLC, in February 2006, Israel approved a series of measures intended to weaken the future Hamas-led administration, including withholding monthly tax payments to the PA and a ban on the transfer of equipment to Palestinian security forces. In early March Hamas leaders announced that it would never accept Israel's right to exist. However, they pledged to extend the ceasefire with Israel for another year, on the condition that Israel refrained from the use of force.

At the general election of 28 March 2006, Kadima obtained the largest share of the valid votes cast (22.0%), to win 29 of the 120 seats in the Knesset. Labour-Meimad retained 19 seats, while the depleted Likud held only 12. Shas also secured 12 seats, Israel Beytenu 11 and the Pensioners' Party seven. At 63.2% of the eligible electorate, the rate of participation was the lowest in the country's history. The new Knesset was sworn in on 17 April. On the same day a suicide bomber launched an attack in Tel-Aviv, killing himself and nine others; Islamic Jihad claimed responsibility for the attack. Meanwhile, the Government voted to change the status of Acting Prime Minister Olmert (whom President Katsav had asked to form a new coalition government) to Interim Prime Minister, in accordance with legislation stipulating that an interim premier must be appointed, from the governing faction, if the Prime Minister is unable to discharge the duties of that office for 100 days. In late April Labour-Meimad agreed to join the new, Kadima-led administration, and a coalition agreement with Shas and the Pensioners' Party was concluded in May. Likud, which strongly opposed Olmert's plans for Israel to withdraw from large areas of the West Bank, had ruled out the possibility of joining the coalition. The Knesset voted to approve the new Government, which commanded 67 seats, on 4 May. Olmert became Prime Minister and Minister of Social Affairs. Other notable appointees from Kadima included Shimon Peres as Vice-Premier and Minister for the Development of the Negev and Galilee, and Tzipi Livni as Vice-Prime Minister and Minister of Foreign Affairs. The Labour leader, Amir Peretz, was appointed Deputy Prime Minister and Minister of Defence.

Olmert made immediate efforts to secure diplomatic support for his unilateralist Convergence Plan. However, the likely success of his strategy was severely challenged as violence broke out in the Gaza Strip in late June 2006, following the kidnapping of an Israeli soldier, Corporal Gilad Shalit, in a cross-border raid by Hamas militants (in which two other soldiers were killed). Palestinian militant groups issued a statement demanding that Israel release all female Palestinian prisoners and all Palestinian detainees under 18 years of age in exchange for Shalit. Israel responded by launching air strikes on Gaza and entering the southern part of the Strip, in a military operation code-named 'Summer Rains'; Israeli security forces detained dozens of Hamas officials, including cabinet ministers and parliamentarians, in connection with their alleged involvement in attacks against Israeli targets.

Israel's military campaign in southern Lebanon

Regional tensions escalated further in mid-July 2006, after Hezbollah militants kidnapped two Israeli soldiers and killed three others in a raid across Lebanon's border with northern Israel. Rockets were also fired at Israeli communities and military posts. Five further Israeli soldiers were killed when troops crossed into Lebanon on a rescue mission. Hezbollah declared that it would free the abducted soldiers in exchange for the release of Lebanese prisoners in Israeli gaols. Olmert secured the approval of his Cabinet to undertake a military campaign against Hezbollah targets and Lebanese infrastructure with the aim of securing the release of the soldiers, and forcing the Lebanese Government to act to disarm Hezbollah. During the month-long conflict Hezbollah, having declared 'open war' on Israel, launched thousands of rockets into Israeli territory. Israel, meanwhile, systematically targeted Lebanese infrastructure, blockading seaports, destroying numerous roads and bridges, and bombing strategic targets such as Beirut International Airport. Prime Minister Olmert expressed his 'deep sorrow' when at least 28 Lebanese (many of them children) died in a bombing raid on an apartment building in Qana, Lebanon, at the end of July; Israeli military chiefs stated that Hezbollah had been using the building in order to launch missile attacks against Israel. In early August the Israeli Cabinet approved a plan to send ground troops deeper into Lebanon, as far as the Litani river—some 30 km north of the Israeli border. (For further details regarding the conflict, see the chapter on Lebanon.)

On 11 August 2006 the UN Security Council adopted Resolution 1701, which sought an immediate and full cessation of hostilities, the extension of the Lebanese Government's authority over the whole country, and the delineation of Lebanon's international boundaries, with particular regard to disputed areas such as Shebaa Farms. The resolution urged the parties involved to address the underlying causes of the conflict, including making efforts towards settling the issue of Lebanese prisoners in Israeli gaols, and pressed Hezbollah to release unconditionally the kidnapped Israeli soldiers. In line with earlier Security Council resolutions, Resolution 1701 also required that all armed groups in Lebanon should disarm. A ceasefire between Israel and Hezbollah took effect on 14 August. By this time, 43 Israeli civilians and 119 soldiers had been killed in the conflict, and more than 1,000 Lebanese had died; the number of Hezbollah militants killed was unknown. Under the terms of the ceasefire, Lebanese government forces and an enhanced UNIFIL contingent were to be deployed in southern Lebanon, while Israel was simultaneously to withdraw its forces from the territory. Israel removed restrictions on air travel to and from Lebanon, and lifted its naval blockade, in September. The final Israeli ground forces were withdrawn from Lebanon on 1 October.

Meanwhile, Israel had established a commission of inquiry under the chairmanship of a retired judge, Dr Eliyahu Winograd, into the military campaign in Lebanon. The Winograd Commission published the initial results of its investigation, covering the period between Israel's withdrawal from southern Lebanon in 2000 to mid-July 2006, at the end of April 2007. This interim report found Olmert and other senior Israeli officials to have demonstrated 'very serious failings' in their handling of the 2006 war with Hezbollah, and to have neglected to devise a comprehensive plan prior to the conflict. The Commission also found that the declared aims of the Israeli military—i.e. the defeat of Hezbollah—were 'overly ambitious and impossible to achieve'. The report singled out the Deputy Prime Minister and Minister of Defence, Peretz, and the former Chief of Staff of the Armed Forces, Lt-Gen. Dan Halutz, as being responsible for Israel's military failures. (Lt-Gen. Halutz had resigned in January 2007, following the conclusion of military investigations into the Israeli armed forces' conduct during the conflict.) Following the publication of the Commission's interim report, there were mass protests in Israel to demand the resignation of the Government, while Olmert was subject to three votes of no confidence (all of which he survived) in the Knesset in May.

Political developments after the war in Lebanon

In October 2006 the ultra-nationalist Avigdor Lieberman, of Israel Beytenu, was appointed as Deputy Prime Minister and Minister of Strategic Affairs. In January 2007 the Knesset voted to declare President Moshe Katsav 'temporarily incapacitated' for a three-month period, following a police recommendation that he be charged in connection with a number of serious offences, including rape and sexual harassment, fraud, bribery and obstruction of justice. The Knesset Speaker, Dalia Itzik, was named as acting President. In April Katsav's leave of absence was extended by a further three months, or until the scheduled end of his presidential term in July. Meanwhile, also in January the former Minister of Justice, Haim Ramon, was found guilty of sexual harassment; he was subsequently sentenced to 120 hours of community service. Ramon had resigned in August 2006, in view of charges against him, and the Vice-Prime Minister and Minister of Foreign Affairs, Tzipi Livni, had assumed additional responsibility for the justice portfolio in November.

Police began investigations in early 2007 into the role played by Ehud Olmert in the privatization of Bank Leumi in 2005, at which time he had held the finance portfolio in the Government of Ariel Sharon. It was alleged that Olmert had promoted the interests of two foreign businessmen in the sale of a controlling stake in the bank. In April 2007 Olmert assumed the finance portfolio in an acting capacity, after the Minister of Finance, Abraham Hirchson, took a temporary leave of absence as a result of police investigations into his failure to report an embezzlement of funds by a former employee. Shortly afterwards the State Comptroller recommended that the Prime Minister be subject to a criminal investigation into allegations that he arranged investment opportunities for an associate while serving as Minister of Industry, Trade and Labour. A new police investigation into Olmert's personal dealings began in September, after it was alleged that, while in office as mayor of Jerusalem, he had acquired a property in the city at a price significantly below its market value, in exchange for the accelerated provision of building permits to a property developer. The office of the Prime Minister strenuously denied the claims. In November the police recommended that there was insufficient evidence to begin criminal proceedings against Olmert in the case concerning the privatization of Bank Leumi.

On 13 June 2007 Shimon Peres was elected by the Knesset as President of Israel; he was officially inaugurated on 15 July. As part of a government reorganization in early July 2007, Haim Ramon returned to the Cabinet as Vice-Premier. Hirchson was succeeded as Minister of Finance by Ronnie Bar-On, whose previous post as Minister of the Interior was allocated to Meir Sheetrit.

Engagement between Olmert and Abbas

Towards the end of November 2006—following an intensification of Operation Summer Rains from October, and by which time hundreds of Palestinians had been killed in the military campaign—PA President Abbas brokered a ceasefire between Palestinian fighters and Israeli forces, resulting in an Israeli withdrawal from Gaza. Prime Minister Olmert subsequently made it clear that he now favoured the resumption of Middle East peace talks with a view to the eventual creation of a Palestinian state, rather than any further unilateral Israeli withdrawals from the West Bank, and indicated that Israel was prepared to free a substantial number of Palestinian prisoners, in exchange for the release, unharmed, of Corporal Gilad Shalit, whose abduction had precipitated several months of conflict.

Further to an agreement signed between representatives of Hamas and Fatah, in February 2007, to form a Palestinian government of national unity, Israeli officials maintained that they would refuse to have contact with any administration that failed to: recognize Israel's right to exist; renounce violence; and respect existing agreements between Israel and the PA. While Israel maintained its boycott of the Palestinian administration, the USA and some EU governments revealed that they would initiate contacts with non-Hamas ministers. In April 2007 Abbas and Olmert held discussions regarding a future Palestinian state and a possible prisoner exchange, in what was intended to be the first of a series of regular fortnightly meetings between the two. Later in the month, however, Hamas declared the ceasefire brokered five months earlier to be at an end, and launched a number of rockets into Israel from the Gaza Strip. Israel responded with air strikes against alleged militant targets in Gaza. Several Hamas ministers, PLC members and local government officials were detained by Israeli security forces at this time.

President Abbas dissolved the national unity government and appointed an emergency administration in its place in June 2007, after Hamas militants seized control of the Gaza Strip. Although Israel was swift to recognize the new administration (and to show its support for Abbas by agreeing to transfer tax revenues that it had withdrawn following Hamas's election victory in January 2006), the fact that governance of the Palestinian territories was now effectively split between a Cabinet backed by President Abbas of Fatah in the West Bank and a Hamas-led administration in Gaza made the likelihood of a resumption of peace negotiations more remote. In late June, at a meeting in Sharm el-Sheikh, Olmert announced that Israel was to release from gaol 250 Fatah activists.

Olmert and Abbas held discussions in the West Bank town of Jericho in early August 2007—the first meeting on Palestinian territory between Israeli and Palestinian leaders since May 2000. Further talks took place on 'fundamental issues' later in August 2007, and again in early September. Israel released another 57 Palestinian prisoners to the West Bank and 29 to the Gaza Strip in October. Later that month, in response to the launching of rockets into northern Israel by Palestinian militants from the Gaza Strip, Israel confirmed a strategy of reducing fuel supplies to Gaza, which it now classified as a 'hostile entity'. Meanwhile, Israel and the USA signed a memorandum of understanding in August 2007 concerning the provision to Israel of some US $30,000m. in military assistance during 2008–18.

The Annapolis conference

An international peace meeting, intended officially to relaunch the Middle East peace process, was convened under US auspices in Annapolis, Maryland, on 27 November 2007, following preparatory meetings between US officials and Israeli and Palestinian delegations in the preceding weeks. Representatives of the international Quartet group and the Arab League attended the talks, and Syria notably sent a low-level delegation. At the end of the meeting US President Bush read a statement of Joint Understanding on Negotiations between Olmert and Abbas, both of whom expressed their commitment to achieving a final settlement of the outstanding issues of contention by the end of 2008.

Following the Annapolis meeting, the Israeli authorities released a further 429 Palestinian prisoners as a renewed gesture of support for President Abbas. In December 2007, however, Israel issued tenders for more than 300 new housing units at the Har Homa settlement in East Jerusalem. Moreover, Olmert appeared to indicate that Israel would not be required to conclude a peace treaty with the PA by the end of 2008 if it considered that the Palestinians had not met their security obligations. In mid-December 2007 Israeli forces conducted a series of air strikes against militants in the Gaza Strip, and sent tanks into the southern part of the Strip, in an attempt to prevent the continuing rocket fire against Sderot in northern Israel.

Israel intensified its military offensive in the Gaza Strip after a Palestinian rocket assault on the city of Ashkelon in early January 2008. In response to international criticism regarding the number of Palestinians killed during the offensive, Israel claimed that militants were deliberately firing on Israeli troops from civilian areas. In that month President Bush visited Israel and the West Bank, holding discussions with both Olmert and Abbas. Bush asserted that a future Palestinian state should comprise contiguous territory, and not be a 'Swiss cheese' of separate cantons. He again urged Israel to cease the expansion of existing settlements in the West Bank and to remove illegal outposts, while also stating that the PA must ensure that militant groups be dismantled. Bush surprised some commentators by issuing a firm statement urging Israel to withdraw from Arab territory that its forces had occupied in 1967. Israel's actions to impose virtually a complete blockade on the Gaza Strip prompted vehement international criticism. Amid concerns about a potential humanitarian crisis in Gaza, the Olmert administration subsequently agreed to allow the supply of food, medicine and necessary fuel to the territory.

Also in January 2008 the Deputy Prime Minister and Minister of Strategic Affairs, Avigdor Lieberman, withdrew Israel Beytenu from the governing coalition, in protest at Olmert's policy of engaging in peace negotiations with the PA. This left Olmert with a reduced majority in the Knesset, and resulted in the resignation from the Cabinet of Lieberman and the Minister of Tourism, Yitzhak Aharonovitch.

The final report of the Winograd Commission was released at the end of January 2008. Although the Commission described Israel's ground offensive in Lebanon in mid-2006 as a 'serious failure' in both military and political terms, it assessed Prime Minister Olmert as having acted 'in the sincere interest of Israel' in ordering the military action. Many observers expressed surprise at the lack of serious direct criticism of the Prime Minister, particularly since he ordered Israeli armed forces to undertake a large-scale ground offensive in southern Lebanon only hours before the agreed ceasefire was scheduled to take effect: some 33 Israeli soldiers had died during this final stage of the war. However, the Commission did notably acknowledge Israel's failure to secure a clear military victory over Hezbollah. Thus, it was widely acknowledged that Olmert, who was already under investigation for alleged corrupt practices, had been further weakened by the Commission's findings.

Despite an incident in March 2008, in which a Palestinian gunman killed eight students at a Jewish religious college in West Jerusalem, talks between Olmert and Abbas resumed in April. Shortly after the Jerusalem shooting, Olmert approved a plan to construct a further 330 homes for settlers in the West Bank, and in June 2008 Israel announced two new building projects in East Jerusalem, involving the construction of some 2,200 new homes.

In May 2008 Israeli police began questioning Olmert with regard to the alleged receipt of some US $150,000 in donations from a US businessman to support past election campaigns for both the mayoralty of Jerusalem and the Likud leadership. The Prime Minister subsequently admitted to having received funds, but insisted that these had not been for personal gain. In July 2008, after investigators stated that they intended also to examine allegations that Olmert had been involved in 'serious fraud and other offences', he officially declared his intention to resign as Prime Minister in September, following the election of a new Kadima leader.

After lengthy negotiations under Egyptian auspices, in mid-June 2008 a formal ceasefire was agreed between Israeli and Hamas representatives in the Gaza Strip. Israel was to end its economic blockade, and cease military action in the territory, on condition that Hamas and other Palestinian militant groups halt cross-border attacks on Israeli targets. The truce was to remain in place for at least six months, and was to take effect in stages. Later in June, however, Israel responded to a rocket attack against the town of Sderot by closing border crossings into Gaza. The rocket attack was apparently carried out by Islamic Jihad in retaliation for the deaths of two Palestinian militants in an Israeli military raid in the West Bank. In early July Hamas stated that, since Israel was not abiding by the terms of the truce, it had suspended negotiations concerning a proposed prisoner exchange involving the release of Corporal Gilad Shalit.

In August 2008 Olmert was reported to have proposed a new peace plan whereby Israel would, *inter alia*, offer Palestinians 93% of the West Bank, provided that Abbas's security forces regained control of the Gaza Strip from Hamas. In that month the Israeli Government released 198 Palestinian prisoners in a goodwill gesture to Abbas. Among those freed were two of the longest-serving Palestinian detainees, who had been responsible for the deaths of two Israeli citizens in the 1970s. In September 2008 the Vice-Prime Minister and Minister of Foreign Affairs, Tzipi Livni, won the leadership of Kadima, narrowly defeating the Deputy Prime Minister and Minister of Transport and Road Safety, Shaul Mofaz. Accordingly, Olmert formally resigned as

Prime Minister (although he continued to serve on an interim basis), in order to contest the various corruption charges against him, and President Shimon Peres asked Livni to form a new government. In late October, however, Livni announced that negotiations with potential coalition partners had been unsuccessful, and a general election was thus scheduled for 10 February 2009.

Direct clashes took place in November 2008 between Israeli armed forces and Hamas militants in the Gaza Strip for the first time since the June ceasefire agreement. Israel launched a renewed military campaign in Gaza and reimposed its blockade, to prevent what it claimed to be Hamas's attempts to kidnap Israeli soldiers. Hamas and Islamic Jihad fighters responded by firing rockets into northern Israel. In December, following a meeting between Olmert and Abbas, Israel released some 227 Palestinian prisoners (none of whom were from Hamas or Islamic Jihad) as a confidence-building measure. On 16 December the UN Security Council approved Resolution 1850, which endorsed a two-state solution to the Israeli–Palestinian conflict and affirmed that the peace process was 'irreversible'. The resolution urged all parties involved in the negotiations to intensify their efforts to achieve a comprehensive and lasting peace in the Middle East.

'Operation Cast Lead'

On 19 December 2008 Hamas formally declared an end to its six-month truce with Israel, asserting that Israel had not adhered to its obligations. Rocket and mortar attacks by Palestinian militants against towns in northern Israel resumed. On 27 December Prime Minister Olmert ordered a campaign of intensive air strikes against targets in the Strip, as the first phase of a new offensive code-named 'Operation Cast Lead'. The military campaign initially targeted security headquarters and police stations, as well as the tunnels through which weapons were smuggled into the territory. At least 225 Palestinians were reported to have been killed on the first day of the operation. A meeting of the UN Security Council expressed 'serious concern' regarding the escalation of the situation in Gaza, and urged 'an immediate halt to all violence'.

Having declared an 'all-out war against Hamas', the Deputy Prime Minister and Minister of Defence, Ehud Barak, sanctioned a wider campaign of air strikes, which now targeted government offices, presidential buildings and the Islamic University in Gaza. On 3 January 2009 the Israeli Government ordered a major ground assault into the Strip. The declared aim of the operation, which effectively divided the enclave into two, was to guarantee the long-term security of Israel's citizens by preventing the continued firing of rockets and mortars by Hamas militants against towns in southern Israel; the Israeli military sought to destroy Hamas's infrastructure, weapons factories and supplies. Israeli army reservists were called up to join the ground offensive, and heavy fighting occurred in densely populated districts of Gaza City and other urban centres. There was condemnation from the international community when an Israeli mortar attack close to a UN-administered school in the Jabalia refugee camp resulted in the deaths of 43 Palestinians. In mid-January Israeli forces bombed the headquarters in Gaza City of the UN Relief and Works Agency for Palestine Refugees in the Near East (UNRWA). Israel insisted that, in both instances, the buildings were being used by Hamas militants in order to fire rockets and mortars into Israel.

UN Security Council Resolution 1860, adopted on 8 January 2009, called for an immediate and durable ceasefire between Israeli armed forces and Hamas militants, a complete withdrawal of Israeli forces from the Gaza Strip, the unimpeded provision of humanitarian aid within Gaza and intensified international arrangements to prevent the smuggling of weapons into the territory. (The USA abstained in the vote.) Eventually, on 17 January the Israeli Government declared a unilateral ceasefire, with Olmert asserting that the objectives of Operation Cast Lead had been achieved. The following day Hamas announced a week-long cessation of hostilities against Israeli targets, in order to permit Israel to withdraw its armed forces from the Gaza Strip. Palestinian sources claimed that more than 1,400 Palestinians had been killed, and some 5,000 wounded, during the 22-day offensive; 13 Israelis (including 10 soldiers) were reported to have died. Thousands of Palestinian homes, as well as commercial and industrial buildings, had also been destroyed by Israeli forces. There was a brief re-escalation towards the end of January when an Israeli soldier was killed in a bomb attack while patrolling the border with Gaza. The death in a militant bomb attack led the Israeli Government to order renewed military action against Hamas targets in Gaza, during which at least one Palestinian was killed.

During January 2009 several countries, including Mauritania, suspended relations with Israel, and the Qatari Government announced that it was closing Israel's trade office in Doha and was suspending political and economic ties. Meanwhile, international diplomatic efforts were ongoing in the region to secure a formal, permanent truce between Israel and Hamas, with the aim of ensuring that arrangements be put in place to prevent the smuggling of weapons into Gaza, and to allow for the unimpeded provision of humanitarian aid within Gaza and the reconstruction of the territory's infrastructure. In April the UN Human Rights Council appointed a committee led by a South African judge and former war crimes prosecutor, Richard Goldstone, to lead an investigation into 'all violations of international humanitarian law' before, during and in the aftermath of Operation Cast Lead.

Netanyahu returns as Prime Minister

Following the general election to the Knesset held on 10 February 2009, Tzipi Livni, of Kadima (which held 28 of the 120 Knesset seats), and Binyamin Netanyahu, of Likud (which, on a joint list with the right-wing, nationalist Ahi party, won 27 seats), each declared their ability to undertake successful coalition negotiations. In general, there had been a notable shift in voting towards the more right-wing, nationalist parties: Israel Beytenu won 15 seats, pushing the Labour Party, with 13 seats, into fourth place; the ultra-Orthodox Shas and United Torah Judaism secured 11 and five seats, respectively. A decision made in January by the Knesset and its Central Elections Committee to prevent two Israeli Arab political groupings—Balad (the National Democratic Assembly) and the United Arab List-Arab Movement for Renewal—from contesting the election was later overturned by the Supreme Court. Both groups had been accused, after protests by Israeli Arabs against the Israeli invasion of Gaza, of failing to recognize Israel's right to exist, and of supporting 'terrorist' groups.

President Peres, considering the Likud leader the most likely to forge a coalition agreement, appointed Netanyahu as Prime Minister-designate. The new Knesset was sworn in on 24 February 2009. At the end of March Netanyahu presented his Cabinet to parliament. The new administration was a coalition of Likud, Israel Beytenu, Labour, Shas and Jewish Home (HaBayit HaYehudi—a right-wing, nationalist party formed in 2008 as a successor to the NRP). United Torah Judaism also formed part of the Government, although none of its members were appointed to cabinet posts. Prime Minister Netanyahu himself took the post of Minister of Economic Strategy, of Pensioner Affairs, of Health, and of Science, Culture and Sport. The Israeli Beytenu leader, Avigdor Lieberman, became Deputy Prime Minister and Minister of Foreign Affairs, and Yuval Steinitz, of Likud, Minister of Finance. The Labour leader, Ehud Barak, remained as Deputy Prime Minister and Minister of Defence, while the Chairman of Shas, Eliyahu Yishai, remained as a Deputy Prime Minister, additionally assuming the interior portfolio. Likud's Dan Meridor was appointed to the new post of Deputy Prime Minister and Minister of Intelligence and Atomic Energy. Silvan Shalom, also of Likud, became Vice-Prime Minister and Minister for Regional Co-operation and the Development of the Negev and Galilee.

Netanyahu visited Washington, DC, in May 2009 for his first meeting with the new US President, Barack Obama, who affirmed his determination to foster a revival of the stalled peace process, and declared his commitment to a two-state settlement. Obama identified the expansion of settlements as the chief obstacle to the resumption of peace negotiations. For his part, Netanyahu identified Iran's nuclear ambitions as the main threat to regional peace, and insisted that negation of this threat should form an integral part of any Middle East peace agreement. In March, meanwhile, the new US Secretary of State, Hillary Clinton, had declared her support for the creation of a Palestinian state in the West Bank and Gaza. In a speech at Bar-Ilan University in June, Netanyahu presented his vision for the resolution of the Arab–Israeli conflict. Netanyahu indicated his acceptance of the idea of a sovereign Palestinian state. However, he insisted that the formation of such a state would be conditional on a complete demilitarization of the Palestinian territories, Arab recognition of Israel as a Jewish state, and an undivided, Israeli capital in Jerusalem. Furthermore, he rejected the 'right of return' of Palestinian refugees. An invitation to resume direct negotiations, issued to the PA Executive President, Abbas, in July, was rejected: the Palestinians refused to resume peace talks, suspended since the launch of the Israeli offensive in the Gaza Strip in December 2008, pending the complete cessation of Israeli settlement activity.

In late July 2009 George Mitchell, the US special envoy to the Middle East, and other senior-level US diplomats visited Israel for discussions on reviving the peace process. Mitchell held further talks with Netanyahu in London in August, during which the principal topic was reported to be the settlements issue. In early September the Israeli Ministry of Defence announced that approval had been granted for the construction of 455 new housing units in settlements in the West Bank. Later that month President Obama hosted a tripartite meeting involving Netanyahu and Abbas at the UN General Assembly in New York, although all parties acknowledged that the meeting did not signal the resumption of negotiations. During a visit to Jerusalem at the end of October, Clinton praised Netanyahu's stance on restraining settlement activity, describing his proposed concessions as 'unprecedented'. Abbas had already rejected a resumption of talks based on a partial suspension of settlement activity.

The Goldstone Report

The UN Fact Finding Mission on the Gaza Conflict, headed by Richard Goldstone, issued its final report in September 2009. The report found evidence of potential war crimes committed by both the Israeli armed forces and Palestinian militants, and of possible crimes against humanity perpetrated by both sides. The report proposed that the authorities in Israel and Gaza should conduct fully independent inquiries into the findings within six months. Failure to comply with this last would result in the referral of the report's findings to the UN Security Council for further investigation. The Israeli authorities, who had refused to co-operate with the investigation, rejected the report as 'propaganda'. Hamas also denied the allegations contained within the report pertaining to its own conduct, although it supported the document's referral to the Security Council. The Goldstone Report was endorsed by the UN Human Rights Council in October, and in November the UN General Assembly adopted a resolution demanding that Israel conduct an investigation into allegations that its forces had committed war crimes. In February 2010 the UN Secretary-General confirmed that Israel had submitted a formal response to the Goldstone Report. (In April 2011, in an article published in the US *Washington Post* newspaper, Goldstone expressed misgivings about some of the report's findings, suggesting that it had in some respects been too harsh in its allegations against Israel. However, Goldstone did not disclose any new information that appeared significantly to challenge the report's findings. In a statement issued later in April, the other members of the UN Fact Finding Mission reiterated their continued support for the report's conclusions and rejected Israeli appeals for it to be retracted.)

Israel's relations with several Western allies were strained by allegations of Israeli involvement in the assassination, in January 2010 in Dubai, United Arab Emirates, of senior Hamas member Mahmoud al-Mabhouh. The Dubai authorities issued details of 11 suspects, all of whom had travelled to the emirate using false British, Australian, Irish, French and German passports. Hamas accused the Israeli intelligence service, Mossad, of involvement in al-Mabhouh's death. In June the Polish authorities were reported to have arrested, at Germany's request, a suspected Mossad agent on charges relating to the assassination. The Israeli Government, for its part, insisted that there was no proof that its intelligence service had been involved in the incident.

In December 2009 Prime Minister Netanyahu announced a 10-month moratorium on settlement-building activity in the West Bank. However, the moratorium applied only to private homes, and excluded as many as 3,000 housing units that were already under construction or for which permission had previously been granted. Moreover, the initiative did not apply to settlements within East Jerusalem, which Netanyahu described as part of Israel's 'sovereign capital'. In February 2010 the Israeli Ministry of Defence confirmed that construction work had continued in some 29 West Bank settlements. The announcement in March that two further developments, in Bethlehem and East Jerusalem, had been approved coincided with a visit to Israel by the US Vice-President, Joe Biden, who criticized the decision and warned that it would undermine efforts by the USA to renew peace talks. A scheduled visit to Israel by George Mitchell was subsequently postponed, and no progress was reported on the issue of settlement-building following talks in Washington, DC, between Netanyahu and President Obama during separate visits by the Israeli premier in late March and in June.

In February 2010 Hamas suspended its participation in negotiations over the release of Gilad Shalit, which had resumed in early 2009, in part owing to the allegations of Israel's involvement in the killing of al-Mabhouh. In June, following five days of protests led by relatives of Shalit (by now promoted to the rank of staff-sergeant), it was announced that Israel had agreed to a prisoner exchange deal, whereby Hamas would release Shalit in exchange for some 1,000 Palestinian detainees. However, negotiations broke down, following disagreements over which detainees would be released by Israel, which refused to accede to demands by Hamas that the exchange include 450 Palestinians detained on suspicion of violent attacks.

Resumption and suspension of direct Israeli-Palestinian peace talks

Following a period of intense, US-led diplomatic activity, on 2 September 2010 Netanyahu and Abbas met in Washington, DC, for the first direct Israeli-Palestinian talks since December 2008; the sessions were chaired by US Secretary of State Clinton, and were also attended by George Mitchell. Hamas refused to recognize the legitimacy of the talks, which had been preceded by further violence in the West Bank in July–August. A second round of direct negotiations began in Sharm el-Sheikh on 14 September and continued in Jerusalem the following day. Progress was reported to have been made in some areas; for example, the two leaders agreed to hold further fortnightly meetings. However, following the expiry of Israel's 10-month moratorium on settlement-building in late September, the PA suspended its involvement in the peace process, stating that it would resume talks only when Israel had agreed to end the construction of settlements and the blockade of Gaza. It was reported in October that construction work had commenced on more than 600 new homes in settlements in the West Bank.

Also in October 2010 the Cabinet endorsed controversial draft legislation, promoted by the Deputy Prime Minister and Minister of Foreign Affairs, Avigdor Lieberman, that would require non-Jewish applicants for Israeli citizenship to pledge their loyalty to Israel as a 'Jewish and democratic state'. Some observers speculated that Netanyahu had supported the measure in exchange for Lieberman's acquiescence on further limits to settlement expansion. Three Likud ministers—including Dan Meridor, the Deputy Prime Minister and Minister of Intelligence and Atomic Energy—joined their Labour colleagues in voting against the legislation, which went on to receive Knesset approval in March 2011. Meanwhile, in November 2010 the Knesset approved legislation requiring any proposed withdrawal from territory under Israeli sovereignty—including East Jerusalem and the Golan Heights—to be endorsed by a two-thirds' parliamentary majority, or, failing that, at a national referendum.

Increasing criticism of the Netanyahu administration

In December 2010, following a year-long trial conducted behind closed doors, former President Moshe Katsav was convicted on charges of rape and of sexual assault, perpetrated against former employees during his term of office. Katsav was sentenced to seven years' imprisonment in March 2011, and was ordered to pay compensation costs totalling US $35,000. An appeal against his conviction was rejected by the Supreme Court in November 2011, and the original sentence was upheld.

Meanwhile, the trial began in February 2010 of former premier Ehud Olmert on corruption charges relating to his tenure as Minister of Industry, Trade and Labour and his two earlier terms as mayor of Jerusalem; the charges included fraud, breach of the public trust and failure to report income. In July 2012 Olmert was acquitted of the two most serious charges of corruption, although he was found to have granted illegal favours to a business associate and ordered to serve four months' community service. In January, meanwhile, Olmert was indicted on fresh charges pertaining to allegations that he had accepted bribes amounting to nearly US $1m. during his tenure as mayor of Jerusalem, in order to facilitate a construction project. Some 17 others, including Olmert's successor as mayor of Jerusalem, Uri Lupolianski, were also charged with offering or receiving associated bribes.

In January 2011 the Deputy Prime Minister and Minister of Defence, Ehud Barak, tendered his resignation as Labour Chairman in order to form a new party, Ha'atzmaut (Independence). The remaining Labour members of the Cabinet also subsequently resigned. A renewed coalition agreement, facilitating the appointment of further Ha'atzmaut representatives to the Government, was approved by the Knesset two days later. The revised Cabinet included four members of Ha'atzmaut, among them Barak, who retained the defence portfolio, and Shalom Simhon, hitherto Minister of Agriculture and Rural Development, who was appointed Minister of Industry, Trade and Labour and of Minority Affairs. A new Ministry of Home Front Defence was established, under Ha'atzmaut's Matan Vilnai. Barak's withdrawal from the Labour Party followed months of internal division concerning the party's future involvement in the coalition, prompted by Netanyahu's stance in the peace process. In September Shelly Yachimovich was announced as the new Labour leader, having defeated former party leader Amir Peretz in a run-off ballot.

In response to mass social protests which began in Tel-Aviv in July 2011 and rapidly spread to other cities, Netanyahu ordered the establishment of a committee, chaired by Prof. Manuel Trajtenberg, to examine the issues raised by the protesters, which mainly concerned escalating living costs. The Trajtenberg Committee for Social and Economic Change submitted its recommendations at the end of September, including proposed reforms in areas of taxation, housing and education. Among proposals adopted were taxation reforms, including the introduction of tax benefits for working parents of children under the age of three, and the extension of free education to pre-primary level.

In November 2011, in the context of elevated tensions between Israel and Iran (see Regional Relations), the opposition leader, Tzipi Livni, accused Netanyahu of being overly preoccupied with the perceived threat posed to Israel by Iran, urging him to heed the advice of the country's defence chiefs in this regard. Her comments appeared to confirm reports that Israel's leading military and security experts had made clear their opposition to a possible Israeli attack on Iranian nuclear facilities.

At the end of January 2012 Netanyahu was decisively re-elected as Likud Chairman, securing some 77% of the vote. In March 2012 Shaul Mofaz was elected to replace Livni as leader of Kadima. Livni resigned as a member of the Knesset in May. Meanwhile, amid growing anticipation of an early general election, a new, secular centrist party, Yesh Atid (There's a Future), was registered at the end of April by a prominent media personality, Yair Lapid.

In early May 2012 Netanyahu, apparently seeking to take advantage of a relatively favourable standing in opinion polls, stated that he would request Knesset approval for a general election to take place in early September. Almost immediately, however, he announced that a new agreement had been reached whereby Kadima would join a broad coalition government, with Shaul Mofaz appointed vice premier and minister without portfolio, ensuring a stable administration until the scheduled end of the Knesset's term in October 2013. Under the new arrangement, commitment was given to revive the peace process with the Palestinians, and to address the issue of legislation, commonly known as the Tal Law, allowing principally ultra-Orthodox students to defer military conscription. In February the High Court of Justice, under outgoing President Dorit Beinisch, had ruled the law in its current form to be unconstitutional: the legislation, introduced in 2002 and renewable every five years, was due to expire in August 2012, and had been deemed by the secular parties to be inequitable. The new administration, which was to command 94 seats in the 120-member Knesset, was subsequently endorsed by the legislature.

Kadima's participation in the coalition was, however, short-lived. The party withdrew from the Government in mid-July 2012, in disagreement with Netanyahu's proposed compromise arrangement to replace the provisions of the Tal Law: ultra-Orthodox members of the coalition had notably threatened to withdraw their support if seminary students were to lose their exemption from military service. Deeming the compromise, which envisaged a phased drafting into the Israeli military and civil service, insufficient, Kadima's Knesset members voted decisively to leave the coalition, again fuelling expectation of an early general election. In the absence of an agreement, the provisions of the Tal Law formally lapsed at the beginning of August.

In early October 2012 Netanyahu finally announced that a general election would take place early the following year. Ehud Barak subsequently confirmed that conscription of those previously exempted under the Tal Law would be deferred pending the election.

Developments in Israeli-Palestinian relations, 2011–12

In May 2011 the Israeli Government announced the temporary suspension of the transfer of tax revenues to the PA, in response to the conclusion of a 'unity' agreement between Fatah and Hamas. The Netanyahu administration stated that the funds could be used to finance Hamas operations against Israeli interests. Reports emerged in July that the Israeli Government had threatened to renounce all previous agreements concluded with the Palestinians, including the Oslo accords, in response to Palestinian proposals unilaterally to seek, through the UN, formal recognition of an independent Palestinian state, on the basis of its pre-1967 borders, and with East Jerusalem as its capital. Tensions were further heightened in September 2011, when the PA formally submitted an application for full membership of the UN as an independent state. (For further details, see the chapter on the Palestinian Territories.) In early November Israel and the USA both announced that they were to freeze their funding to UNESCO, in response to the organization's decision, the previous month, to admit 'Palestine' as a full member. Israel again announced that it was to halt the transfer of tax and customs revenues to the PA, and further stated that it was to accelerate the construction of 2,000 new homes in settlements in East Jerusalem and the West Bank. However, Israel subsequently agreed, under international pressure, to resume revenue transfers to the PA.

In mid-October 2011, in an Egyptian-brokered prisoner exchange, Gilad Shalit (now promoted to the rank of sergeant-major) was released after more than five years in Palestinian detention. The arrangement between Israel and Hamas provided for the release by Israel of 477 predominantly Palestinian prisoners immediately following that of Shalit, and of a further 550 prisoners (including 300 members of Fatah) in December. Of the total, some 280 were reported to have been serving life sentences for planning or perpetrating terrorist attacks against Israeli targets. PA President Abbas welcomed the exchange, but emphasized that the Palestinian authorities would continue to press for the release of all remaining Palestinian prisoners detained within Israel.

In early January 2012 the first meetings between Israeli and Palestinian peace negotiators in more than a year were held in Amman, under the auspices of King Abdullah; however, the exploratory talks, which it had been hoped might lead to the resumption of formal direct peace negotiations, were reported to have ended without any significant progress. At a press conference held shortly afterwards, the UN Secretary-General, Ban Ki-Moon, commended both sides for their participation in the talks, urging them to cease all provocative acts and to pursue confidence-building measures. However, the stalemate persisted, with the PA continuing to insist that it would not resume formal peace talks until Israel had suspended all settlement-building activity, and Israel maintaining that it would not participate until the PA had abandoned all preconditions to the resumption of formal negotiations.

The principal focus of discussions in Washington, DC, between President Obama and Netanyahu, in early March 2012, was Iran, with scant reference apparently being made to relations between Israel and the Palestinians. Shortly afterwards, the Secretary-General of the Hamas-aligned Popular Resistance Committees was among several militants killed in what were stated to be preventive Israeli air strikes on Gaza. In the ensuing exchange of retaliatory rocket attacks on Israel and further strikes on Gaza, some 25 Palestinians were killed. In late March the Israeli Government announced the suspension of co-operation with the UN Human Rights Council, after the body voted in favour of sending a mission to Israel to investigate the impact of Israeli settlements on Palestinians' civil, political, economic, social and cultural rights.

At the beginning of April 2012 a female Palestinian detainee from Jenin was released from Israeli custody and exiled to Gaza, under an arrangement whereby she ended a hunger strike begun following her detention without trial (so-called 'administrative detention') in mid-February. The detainee, a supporter of Islamic Jihad, had previously been among prisoners released under the terms of the October 2011 agreement, but had been rearrested for alleged involvement in planned attacks by Islamic Jihad. Her forced exile was condemned by the Palestinian authorities, as well as by Israeli human rights activists, while the International Committee of the Red Cross, which facilitated a meeting of the released woman with her family at the Erez crossing-point, urged Israel to comply with international humanitarian law, which prohibits such forcible transfer. The protest against administrative detention (under which some 300 Palestinians were held in custody) escalated during April 2012, with a mass hunger strike extending to some 1,500 Palestinians in Israeli detention by the end of the month. In early May the Supreme Court rejected an appeal against the terms of their imprisonment by two Palestinians, held in administrative detention on security grounds, who had maintained a hunger strike for more than 70 days. In mid-May, following a direct request by President Abbas and mediation assistance by Egypt and Jordan, an agreement was reached to end the mass protest. Among its terms, Israel undertook not to renew detentions without charge in the absence of further evidence, while prisoners would be required to sign a commitment to refrain while in custody from activities liable to contravene security. At the end of May, also under terms of the agreement ending the hunger strike, Israel transferred to the PA the remains of 91 Palestinians killed in suicide bombings and other attacks on Israel over a period of more than 35 years. The Israeli Government hoped that the operation, which it described as a humanitarian gesture, would allow for the resumption of peace talks.

However, direct confrontation was renewed in the second half of June 2012, as a series of Israeli air strikes on targets in Gaza provoked retaliatory rocket attacks for which Hamas's military wing—which had effectively refrained from such operations over a prolonged period—claimed responsibility. At least seven Palestinians were killed in the engagements; while the Israeli strikes were targeting militants preparing to launch rocket attacks. In late June Hamas stated that a senior member of the organization, Kamal Ghanaja, who had reportedly been a close associate of Mahmoud al-Mabhouh (killed in Dubai in 2010) had been assassinated in the Syrian capital, Damascus. In early August it was reported that an air strike on the Gaza Strip had targeted a militant held responsible for an exchange in June on Israel's border with Egypt, in which an Israeli civilian working on the border fence was killed in an attack from Sinai; two assailants had also been killed in the June engagement.

There was a major escalation in the situation from mid-November 2012, when, in response to protracted rocket fire from Gaza into southern Israel, Israeli forces began an intense series of strikes from the air and sea against Hamas, Islamic Jihad and other militant groups, and their missile capabilities and weapons storage facilities. Among the targets of 'Operation Pillar of Defence' was the head of Hamas's military wing, Ahmed Said Khalil al-Jabari, who, together with another Hamas official, was killed in an air strike on his vehicle in Gaza City on 14 November. As the confrontation deepened, Egypt led efforts to bring about a ceasefire. US Secretary of State Clinton travelled to Israel for talks with Netanyahu and other government officials, reaffirming US support for Israel's right to self-defence, and subsequently went on to Ramallah for discussions with Abbas, before meeting with President Muhammad Mursi in Cairo. The Israeli authorities were reported to have come under intense international pressure not to begin a ground offensive in Gaza. The diplomatic initiative was also joined by the UN Secretary-General, and a ceasefire eventually took effect on 21 November. Under its terms, Israel was to cease hostilities and targeted killings, enter discussions on the reopening of border crossings with Gaza, and ease restrictions on the movement of goods and people, while the Palestinian militant organizations were required to halt rocket attacks and border assaults. At the conclusion of hostilities, according to initial reporting by the UN Office for the Co-ordination of Humanitarian Affairs, there had been 158 deaths in Gaza, including 103 civilian deaths; at least 30 children were killed. Six Israelis were killed, four of them civilians. The relatively low numbers of Israeli casualties were ascribed to the efficacy of Israel's missile-defence systems in destroying missiles, particularly those targeted at populated areas.

Israel led opposition to the vote of the UN General Assembly, on 29 November 2012, which accorded (by 138 votes to nine, with 41 abstentions) Palestine the status of non-member observer state. Netanyahu denounced the decision as meaningless, and reiterated that there could be no establishment of a Palestinian state in the absence of a settlement guaranteeing Israel's security. The USA voted against the resolution, and Clinton termed the vote counter-productive. In early December the Israeli Ministry of Finance announced its intention to appropriate some NIS 460m. in tax and customs revenues due to the PA, in partial payment for debts owed for the supply of energy. Also in early December Israel confirmed its intention to proceed with its project to construct 3,000 settlement homes on land effectively separating East Jerusalem from the West Bank; plans also proceeded later in the month with regard to 1,500 housing units announced during US Vice-President Biden's visit in 2010; and planning approval was given for more than 2,600 homes on land between southern Jerusalem and Bethlehem.

The 2013 Knesset election and the new coalition Government

Likud and Israel Beytenu announced in late October 2012 that they would contest the forthcoming general election in alliance, presenting a joint list of candidates. In late November Tzipi Livni returned to active politics with the establishment of a new, centre-left party, Hatnua (The Movement); among its founder members were the former Labour leaders Amram Mitzna and Amir Peretz. In the same month Naftali Bennett, a former chief of staff to Netanyahu, became leader of the right-wing nationalist Jewish Home. Also in late November the Deputy Prime Minister and Minister of Defence, Ehud Barak, announced his intention to retire from party politics; the Ha'atzmaut party subsequently stated that it would not contest the 2013 general election.

In mid-December 2012 Avigdor Lieberman resigned as Deputy Prime Minister and Minister of Foreign Affairs, and waived his right of parliamentary immunity, after it was announced that he was to be prosecuted on charges—which he denied—of breach of trust. The Israel Beytenu leader was accused in connection with the promotion of an Israeli diplomat from whom he had allegedly received confidential documents pertaining to investigations, which had first begun more than a decade earlier, into his activities. However, the principal charges, including alleged money-laundering and bribery, were abandoned on grounds of lack of evidence. He was indicted at the end of December, and his trial formally opened in mid-February 2013.

The Likud-Israel Beytenu alliance, with 23.3% of valid votes cast, won the largest number of seats at the general election, which took place on 22 January 2013; however, the two parties' joint representation, at 31 of 120 seats, was significantly below their combined representation (43 seats) in the outgoing Knesset, and Netanyahu's own standing was considered to be somewhat weakened by the result. The greatest challenge came from Yair Lapid's Yesh Atid, which won 19 seats with 14.3% of the vote; the party had focused its campaign on an end to deferred military service and on a revival of the peace process with the Palestinians. The Labour Party won 15 seats (with 11.4%), while the populist rhetoric of Jewish Home's new leader saw its representation increase to 12 seats (with 9.1%). Shas retained 11 seats, and United Torah Judaism returned seven deputies. Tzipi Livni's Hatnua won six seats. The outcome of the election was particularly poor for Kadima, which retained just two of its previous 28 seats. The rate of participation by voters was officially recorded at 67.8%.

Members of the 19th Knesset were sworn in on 5 February 2013. Three days previously President Shimon Peres had asked Netanyahu, as the leader of the largest grouping in the legislature, to form a new coalition. Among Netanyahu's stated priorities for his new administration were security, fiscal and political responsibility, and a reduction in the cost of living, notably housing (which had been the focus of mass protests in mid-2011). Early tasks for the new Government included securing Knesset approval of the budget for 2013, and to achieve consensus on the issue of conscription. In mid-February 2013 it was announced that Netanyahu had reached an agreement with Livni whereby the Hatnua leader would join a new coalition as Minister of Justice, and as Israel's chief negotiator in the peace process (the key focus of her election campaign). At the beginning of March, following the expiry of the original, one-month deadline for the formation of a new government, Peres granted Netanyahu two more weeks to conclude an agreement, and, on 18 March, a new coalition administration, including members of Likud, Israel Beytenu, Yesh Atid, Jewish Home and Hatnua, took office. Prime Minister Netanyahu continued to hold the foreign affairs portfolio previously held by Lieberman, and also took personal responsibility for public diplomacy and diaspora affairs. The Yesh Atid leader, Yair Lapid, became Minister of Finance, in place of Yuval Steinitz (who now took the strategic affairs, intelligence and international relations portfolios), while Naftali Bennett became Minister of Industry, Trade and Labour, of Religious Services, and Minister for Jerusalem and the Diaspora. The defence portfolio was allocated to Moshe Ya'alon, of Likud. Gideon Sa'ar, also of Likud, was transferred to the post of Minister of the Interior, while Yesh Atid's Shai Piron succeeded him as Minister of Education. Jewish Home's Uri Yehuda Ariel was appointed Minister of Housing and Construction, while Livni was joined in the Cabinet by her Hatnua colleague Amir

Peretz, as Minister of Environmental Protection. Shas and United Torah Judaism were, notably, to remain outside the coalition for the first time since 2005.

Recent developments: relaunch of direct Israeli-Palestinian peace talks

The outcome of the election suggested a clear shift in voter sentiment away from the policies of the outgoing administration, not least with regard to Israeli-Palestinian relations. This, in conjunction with the inauguration for a second term of US President Obama, allowed for muted optimism among some commentators regarding the prospect of a renewed impetus in the peace process. The new US Secretary of State, John Kerry, was generally considered to favour a new US-led effort to restart negotiations. Livni's agreement, in February 2013, to join Israel's new coalition Government with a mandate to lead negotiations with the Palestinians was also recognized as a development likely to expedite renewed contacts. At the end of January, none the less, Israel became the first country to fail to attend a mandatory review of the UN Human Rights Council. The Council, in a report published at the end of the month, stated that the outgoing Netanyahu administration had contributed to the consolidation and expansion of settlements, and emphasized that the transfer of Israeli citizens to occupied territory was in violation of both international humanitarian and international criminal law. The Israeli Government responded that the report was a reminder of the Council's bias against Israel. Meanwhile, the PA had indicated that, should the new Israeli Government proceed with plans to construct settlements east of Jerusalem, it might seek recourse to the International Criminal Court (which it had become eligible to join upon adoption as a non-member observer state at the UN in November 2012).

The US President made his first official visit to Israel in March 2013, shortly after the inauguration of Netanyahu's new Government, before proceeding to Ramallah to meet with President Abbas. While in Israel, Obama notably spoke of the need for a viable, independent Palestinian state, and stated that the continued expansion of settlements on occupied land did not advance the cause of peace. However, he emphasized the strength of US-Israeli ties, not least in military and intelligence co-operation, and efforts were apparent to project a more cordial relationship between Obama and Netanyahu. The US President offered no new proposals for reviving peace talks, but stated that Secretary of State Kerry would take up the task of narrowing differences between Israel and the Palestinians with the aim of renewing negotiations; Kerry thus began a new programme of intense 'shuttle' diplomacy between the two sides.

In February 2013 violent clashes had broken out between Palestinian protesters and Israeli armed forces in West Bank towns. The protesters were demanding the release of four Palestinians in administrative detention, who were on hunger strike. According to figures published by the Israeli Prison Service in December 2012, a total of 4,517 Palestinians were being held in Israel, of whom 1,031 were awaiting the conclusion of legal proceedings, and 178 were in administrative detention. Tensions escalated in late February, following the sudden death in custody of a Palestinian from the West Bank who had been arrested on suspicion of stone-throwing. The Israeli authorities stated that the detainee had suffered a heart attack, but Palestinians claimed that there was evidence that he had died as a result of torture; in protest, most Palestinian detainees observed a one-day hunger strike.

Meanwhile, after the expiry of the Tal Law in 2012, a ministerial commission set up to look into the question of the gradual induction of ultra-Orthodox students into the Israeli military and civil service had recommended that only 1,800 of an estimated 40,000 seminary students should be exempted from military conscription. On 23 July 2013 draft legislation to replace the provisions of the Tal Law passed its first reading in the Knesset (by 64 votes to 21). Ultra-Orthodox students, with the exception of these 1,800, were thus required to enter military or civil service within a four-year period. Ultra-Orthodox parties in the legislature responded angrily to the vote, declaring that they would refuse to adhere to the terms of the draft law.

On 29–30 July 2013 preliminary discussions regarding a permanent status accord between Israel and the PA were held in Washington, DC. The talks were hosted by Kerry, and led by Minister of Justice Livni for Israel and Saeb Erakat for the PA. Having reportedly pledged to seek to reach a final status agreement within nine months, Israeli and Palestinian representatives began formal peace negotiations in Jerusalem on 14 August, with President Obama's newly appointed Special Envoy for Israeli-Palestinian Negotiations, Martin Indyk, in attendance. The talks were expected to take place weekly, and to alternate between Jerusalem and the West Bank town of Jericho. It was agreed at the initial discussions that, provided that progress was being made in the talks, Israel would release 104 long-serving Palestinian prisoners in four stages by 29 April 2014, the scheduled deadline for a preliminary agreement to be signed. The PA, for its part, was required to delay any applications for the Palestinian Territories' membership of UN agencies to be upgraded. However, no breakthrough in the peace process had been achieved by the end of February 2014, with Israel's Ministry of Housing and Construction continuing to approve tenders for the building of new Jewish settlements in the West Bank and East Jerusalem. (Shortly before the talks held on 14 August 2013 the Israeli Government freed the first 26 of the Palestinian prisoners; however, it was also announced that the construction of a further 2,000 new settler homes was planned. A further 26 detainees were released on 30 October, despite a recent upsurge in violence between Israeli forces and Hamas militants in the Gaza Strip, and a third group of 26 on 30 December.) In mid-February 2014 Erakat warned that, in the event of a failure in the negotiations by 29 April, the PA would push the international community to impose economic sanctions against Israel, and would bring a series of lawsuits against the Israeli Government in international courts such as the ICJ and the International Criminal Court, both based in The Hague. Meanwhile, the release of Palestinian prisoners remained a controversial issue among the Israeli electorate, since many of those being freed had been convicted of committing acts of terrorism against Israelis; many Palestinians also complained that the number of prisoners involved was too insignificant to represent a major concession to the PA. Netanyahu was also required to reassure several members of his own Government that he would put any eventual peace deal with the PA to a nationwide referendum; legislation to this effect was approved on 28 July 2013. However, in April 2014 the negotiations appeared to be faltering. In early April Israel announced that it was to suspend the transfer of around US$100m. per month in tax revenues to the PA, in response to the latter's formal accession to some 13 UN institutions. Later that month, following the announcement of a further national unity agreement between Hamas and Fatah, Netanyahu suspended Israel's participation in the peace process just days in advance of the scheduled deadline for a preliminary agreement to be concluded.

At the conclusion of his trial, on 6 November 2013 Avigdor Lieberman was cleared of the charges of breach of trust that had led to his resignation as Deputy Prime Minister and Minister of Foreign Affairs in December 2012. The Israel Beytenu leader therefore rejoined the Cabinet on 11 November 2013, again taking responsibility for the foreign affairs portfolio. Commentators noted that the reappointment of such a 'hardline' Minister of Foreign Affairs was unlikely to assist the diplomatic efforts aimed at securing a preliminary Israeli-Palestinian peace deal by April 2014. On 11 January 2014 it was announced that Ariel Sharon had died; the former Prime Minister had been in a coma since suffering a stroke in January 2006.

In late February 2014 the Jordanian Prime Minister and Minister of Defence, Abdullah Ensour, suggested that his country might reconsider the peace treaty it had signed with Israel in 1994, after members of the Knesset debated a bill brought to the legislature by a Likud member concerning the highly controversial issue of declaring Israeli sovereignty over the Temple Mount/Haram al-Sharif compound in Jerusalem (currently administered by Jordan). The debate, which had led a majority of Jordanian members of parliament to demand the expulsion of the Israeli ambassador and the recall of Jordan's envoy to Tel-Aviv, also provoked anger in a number of other neighbouring Arab states, including Egypt—the only other Arab country to have signed a peace deal with Israel. Amid heightened tensions at the Jerusalem compound, violent clashes between Israelis and Palestinians had been reported at the site in late September 2013.

Regional Relations

In July 1999 Prime Minister Ehud Barak undertook to negotiate a bilateral peace agreement with Syria, based on UN Resolutions 242 and 338: this was interpreted as a signal of his intention to return most of the occupied Golan Heights in exchange for peace and normalized relations. On 20 July Syria ordered a 'ceasefire' with Israel. In December, apparently as a result of diplomatic efforts by US President Bill Clinton and secret meetings between

Israeli and Syrian officials, the two sides agreed to a resumption of negotiations from the point at which they had broken off in 1996. Clinton inaugurated peace negotiations between Barak and the Syrian Minister of Foreign Affairs, Farouk al-Shara', in Washington, DC, on 15 December 1999. The talks commenced in the context of rising tensions in southern Lebanon, and resulted only in an agreement to resume discussions in January 2000. Barak, meanwhile, was encountering growing domestic opposition to a possible return of the Golan Heights to Syria. In late December 1999 Israel and Syria agreed an informal 'ceasefire' to curb hostilities in Lebanon. Barak and al-Shara' attended further discussions in January 2000 in Shepherdstown, West Virginia, USA. As a preliminary to the talks, it was agreed that four committees would be established to discuss simultaneously the issues of borders, security, normalization of relations and water sharing. The US Administration presented a 'draft working document' to both sides as the basis for a framework agreement. However, Syria announced that it required a commitment from Israel to withdraw from the Golan Heights before negotiations could resume. In mid-January a further scheduled round of talks between Israel and Syria was postponed indefinitely. Amid an intensification of the conflict in southern Lebanon, the Knesset voted in March to change the majority required in the event of a referendum on an Israeli withdrawal from the Golan Heights from 50% of participants to 50% of the registered electorate. In April Barak declared that the Israeli Government would resume the construction of settlements in the Golan Heights (following a declared suspension prior to the December 1999 talks).

Following the death of President Hafiz al-Assad in June 2000, his son, Bashar, who assumed the Syrian presidency in July, promised a continuation of his father's policies towards Israel. The Israeli-Syrian track remained deadlocked after Ariel Sharon became Israeli Prime Minister in 2001, and bilateral tensions were subsequently compounded by the US Administration of George W. Bush's references to Syria as a possible target in its 'war on terror'. In October 2003 Israel launched an air strike against an alleged training camp for Palestinian militants in Syria. The attack on the Ein Saheb camp, near Damascus, was prompted by a suicide bombing in Haifa a few days previously that killed 19 Israelis.

In late 2003 and early 2004 the Israeli President, Moshe Katsav, proposed to President Bashar al-Assad that Syria should commence direct negotiations with Israel 'without preconditions'. However, the Syrian leadership dismissed the offer as being 'not serious'. In February 2005 Israeli officials stated that they would not resume negotiations with Syria regarding the Golan Heights until Syria had implemented a complete withdrawal of its forces from Lebanon (for further details, see the chapters on Lebanon and Syria). A report published in Israel's *Ha'aretz* newspaper in January 2007 alleged that secret discussions had taken place between Israeli and Syrian representatives between September 2004 and the start of the conflict between Israel and Hezbollah in July 2006, as a result of which important mutual understandings had been reached with regard to the Golan Heights and other contentious issues. The claim was denied by officials from both countries.

Relations between Israel and Syria deteriorated further in September 2007, following an Israeli air strike on a military installation at al-Kibar in Syria. US intelligence indicated in April 2008 that the Israeli military had targeted a covert nuclear facility that was being built with assistance from the Democratic People's Republic of Korea (North Korea). Representatives of the UN International Atomic Energy Agency (IAEA) subsequently undertook investigations of the al-Kibar site, and an IAEA report published in February 2009 asserted that there was a 'low probability' that Israeli missiles used to bomb the installation were the source of traces of uranium that had been found there.

Israeli and Syrian officials confirmed in May 2008 that indirect negotiations aimed at concluding a 'comprehensive peace' between the two countries were being held in the city of İstanbul, Turkey. By the second week of August four rounds of Turkish-mediated talks had taken place, although no significant progress had apparently been reached in resolving the principal outstanding issues. Despite subsequent claims by President Assad that Israel and Syria were within 'touching distance' of reaching a peace deal, a fifth round, scheduled for September, was postponed owing to the political uncertainty in Israel, following the resignation of Ehud Olmert, as Prime Minister and that of his chief negotiator in the indirect talks, Yoram Turbowicz. Apparently in response to Israel's large-scale military offensive against Hamas targets in the Gaza Strip in December 2008 and January 2009 (which also led to a deterioration in relations between Israel and Turkey), Assad formally suspended the talks with Israel. Following the inauguration of a new Government under Binyamin Netanyahu in March 2009, the new Minister of Foreign Affairs, Avigdor Lieberman, ruled out any Israeli withdrawal from the Golan Heights.

Prospects for a resumption of direct negotiations were further impeded by the popular uprising in Syria from early 2011, and the subsequent descent into civil war. In May Israeli troops clashed with hundreds of pro-Palestinian protesters who had broken through a security fence to enter the Golan Heights from Syria. Syrian state media reported in the following month that 12 Palestinians and two Syrians had been killed when Israeli soldiers opened fire at another group of protesters attempting to enter the Golan Heights from across the Syrian border; some 225 others were reportedly injured in the incident. The Israeli authorities accused the Assad regime of orchestrating the violence as a means of diverting international attention from Syria's domestic unrest. As the Syrian conflict deepened, Israel was concerned to avoid a mass influx of refugees, but was notably generally cautious in its stance towards both the incumbent Assad regime and the armed opposition. In July 2012, none the less, the then Deputy Prime Minister and Minister of Defence, Ehud Barak, stated that Israel was ready to intervene in Syria should Hezbollah or other militant groups acquire chemical weapons. There was an escalation in tension in February 2013, when President Assad stated that Israel was attempting to destabilize Syria. In late January Syria had accused Israel of carrying out an air strike on Syrian territory, understood to involve the targeting of a weapons convoy bound for Hezbollah's use in Lebanon; the Syrian military itself stated that a military research facility had been hit. In subsequent months Israeli officials became increasingly concerned about the emergence of a number of radical Islamist groups among Syria's armed opposition; these fears increased during 2013, when it became evident that the Syrian civil war was also destabilizing Lebanon. In mid-2013 the Israeli leadership denied claims by the Syrian regime that its military planes had attacked a number of sites in Syria that were being used to store weapons. Meanwhile, in February 2014, following several incidents during the preceding months in which the violence from Syria had crossed into the Golan Heights (see Occupied Territories), the Israeli military announced that it was sending a new, specialized army division to the border area in order to increase Israel's preparedness to respond to further security threats originating from Syria.

Israel's strategic and commercial co-operation with Turkey increased following the upgrading of diplomatic relations to ambassadorial level in 1991. A Security and Secrecy Agreement concerning military and intelligence co-operation was signed in 1994. During 1996 the two countries signed a number of military accords, providing for joint military-training exercises, reciprocal access to airspace and co-operation in the provision of armaments. The arrangements, which received support from the USA, stemmed from common concerns about Iran, Iraq and Syria. A bilateral free trade agreement came into force in 1997. In 2002 a 20-year agreement was signed, whereby Turkey would supply Israel with 50m. cu m of water annually.

The Turkish Prime Minister, Recep Tayyip Erdoğan, described the Israeli offensive in Gaza of May 2004 as 'state-sponsored terrorism'. Turkey, which had acted as host and mediator for indirect peace talks between Syria and Israel during 2008, also voiced strong condemnation of Israel's military offensive against Hamas which began in Gaza in December of that year, and which led to the formal suspension of negotiations by Syria. Nevertheless, in March 2009 the foreign ministers of Israel and Turkey held talks on bilateral relations and regional stability during a North Atlantic Treaty Organization (NATO) summit in Brussels, Belgium. Turkey subsequently announced its willingness to resume the role of mediator in Syrian-Israeli peace negotiations. In October, however, Turkey announced the cancellation of Israel's involvement in a scheduled military exercise, as well as plans for a further bilateral military exercise. Despite initial official statements that the cancellation was for technical reasons, Turkey's Minister of Foreign Affairs, Ahmet Davutoğlu, subsequently acknowledged that the decision had been motivated by disapproval of Israel's operation in Gaza.

Tensions between Israel and Turkey escalated again following a raid, in May 2010, by Israeli naval forces on a ship in international waters. The vessel was part of a flotilla attempting to breach the Israeli blockade of Gaza, purportedly to deliver humanitarian aid and materials to the population there; nine pro-Palestinian Turkish activists were killed in the incident, and many more were injured. Foreign governments and international organizations condemned the Israeli action, despite Israel's claim that its forces had acted in self-defence. An Israeli commission established to investigate the raid subsequently determined that the actions of the Israeli soldiers had 'regrettable consequences of human life losses and physical injuries' but were, none the less, compliant with international law. In June Turkey suspended diplomatic and military ties with Israel, withdrawing its ambassador from Tel-Aviv and insisting that it would not restore full relations until Israel publicly apologized for the incident, compensated the relatives of the victims and agreed to the holding of a full and independent international inquiry.

Relations deteriorated further following the publication by the UN, in September 2011, of the report of an inquiry into the raid. The report criticized the conduct of both countries over the incident, determining that the decision by the Israeli military to board the vessel with substantial force and with no final warning constituted an 'excessive and unreasonable' action, while recognizing the 'legitimacy' of Israel's blockade as a means of stemming the flow of weapons into Gaza by sea. The Turkish Government, citing Israel's continued refusal formally to apologize for the incident, expelled the Israeli ambassador and his deputy from Ankara and recalled its remaining senior diplomats from its embassy in Tel-Aviv, as diplomatic relations with Israel were downgraded to the level of second secretary. Bilateral military and commercial ties were also suspended. Remarks in February 2013 by the Turkish Prime Minister in which he characterized Zionism (along with anti-Semitism, fascism and Islamophobia) as a 'crime against humanity' drew strong condemnation from Israel, the UN and the USA. In March, however, at the conclusion of US President Obama's visit to Israel, it was announced that Prime Minister Binyamin Netanyahu had issued an apology to Turkey for errors that could have resulted in the loss of life in the May 2010 raid, and agreed to conclude compensation arrangements. The apology, which was accepted by Erdoğan, was deemed to be an initial step towards the normalization of relations between Israel and Turkey. The Israeli Government stated that it had been agreed to exchange ambassadors, and that Turkey would withdraw legal proceedings against members of the Israeli armed forces with regard to the incident. However, despite reports in May 2013 that the two sides had reached a draft agreement concerning compensation for the Turkish victims, precise details of the arrangements were not released and bilateral discussions were ongoing in early 2014. Sources claimed in February that Netanyahu had rejected the terms of the proposed deal since he believed the amounts due to be paid to the victims to be excessively high.

Israel's relations with Iran have been characterized, particularly under the presidency of Mahmoud Ahmadinejad, by often violent anti-Israeli rhetoric on the part of the Iranian regime; and by intense suspicion within Israel of Iran's nuclear ambitions, and of Iranian support for Hamas and Hezbollah. From 2006 Israeli government officials repeatedly urged international leaders to act in order to prevent Iran from developing a nuclear weapons capability, emphasizing that a military attack against Iran's nuclear facilities remained a strategic option. Iran countered with warnings that any pre-emptive military strikes launched by Israel would be met with a swift and powerful military response. In May 2009 Iran conducted tests that appeared to demonstrate that it possessed missiles with sufficient range to target Israel, as well as US military bases in the region. In November it was announced that Israeli forces in the Mediterranean Sea had intercepted a cargo ship en route to Syria, which Israel claimed was carrying a large consignment of Iranian-made weapons destined for Hezbollah militants in Lebanon. In February 2010 the Israeli air force announced the development of a fleet of unmanned aircraft able to launch missile attacks or conduct surveillance operations. Ahmadinejad stated that the aircraft were intended to target Iran, but Prime Minister Netanyahu insisted that Israel had no intention of instigating military action.

In February 2011 two Iranian warships passed through the Suez Canal, for the first time since the 1979 Islamic Revolution, sailing past the Israeli coast en route to Syria; their passage was condemned by the Israeli Government as a deliberate act of provocation. In November Israel test-fired a ballistic missile (assumed to be a long-range missile capable of delivering warheads), intensifying speculation that Israel might be planning to launch a pre-emptive military strike against Iranian nuclear facilities. Such concerns were heightened following the publication by the IAEA of a report noting serious concerns regarding possible military dimensions to Iran's nuclear programme. (For fuller details, see the chapter on Iran.) Israel held Iran and Hezbollah responsible for a series of bomb explosions in February 2012 that apparently targeted staff at the Israeli embassies in New Delhi (India), Tbilisi (Georgia) and Bangkok (Thailand); the Iranian Government denied any involvement in the attacks. Addressing the Knesset in mid-March, Netanyahu again gave indications of Israel's willingness to act unilaterally against Iran's nuclear facilities. Netanyahu held Hezbollah responsible for the deaths of five Israeli tourists in a suicide bombing of a bus in Bulgaria in July, and warned Iran of a strong response to acts of terrorism.

In an address at the UN General Assembly in September 2012, Netanyahu stated that a critical point in the development of the Iranian nuclear programme was unlikely to be reached until 2013; this was widely interpreted as confirmation that Israel had opted to defer any decision on pre-emptive action until after the forthcoming US presidential election, allowing the opportunity for a further tightening of sanctions against Iran. Subsequently, the composition of the new Israeli Government appointed in March 2013 was interpreted by some observers as signalling a change in regional policy. The new Israeli Minister of Defence, Moshe Ya'alon, was initially considered to favour a less confrontational stance with regard to Iran; and some significance was attached to the agreement of Tzipi Livni, who had previously been highly critical of Netanyahu's rhetoric on Iran, to join his new administration. In February 2013 Israel announced that it had successfully tested its new Arrow 3 defensive interceptor system, capable of destroying incoming missiles (potentially including those with nuclear or chemical warheads) beyond the Earth's atmosphere. In November Netanyahu denounced in the strongest terms the interim agreement concerning Iran's nuclear programme that had been reached after intensive negotiations between Iran (since August under the presidency of Hassan Rouhani) and the Western negotiating powers in Geneva. The interim accord permitted the Government in Tehran to continue the enrichment of uranium, provided that this was not to a sufficiently high grade to permit Iran to construct a nuclear weapon. In return for Iran's commitment regarding uranium enrichment, the five permanent members of the UN Security Council (France, Russia, the People's Republic of China, the United Kingdom and the USA) plus Germany agreed to lift some of the sanctions imposed on the Iranian Government in recent years. (For further details on developments concerning the Iranian nuclear programme in 2013, see the chapter on Iran.) In early March 2013 Israeli naval forces intercepted a cargo ship in the Red Sea, claiming that the Panamanian-registered vessel was carrying surface-to-air missiles and other weapons from Iran that were intended, ultimately, for use by militant groups in the Gaza Strip.

Tensions between Israel and Lebanon remained high following Israel's military campaign in southern Lebanon in mid-2006. In August 2010 there were clashes between Israeli and Lebanese soldiers near the 'Blue Line' (the UN's name for the border between the two countries); this constituted the most serious confrontation between the two countries since 2006. The UN determined that a group of Israeli soldiers attempting to cut down a tree on the Lebanese side of the border fence (but on the Israeli side of the Blue Line) had not strayed into Lebanese territory, and urged both sides to exercise restraint. Israel and Lebanon acted swiftly to reduce tensions: Israel's Deputy Prime Minister and Minister of Defence, Ehud Barak, emphasized that the clash had not arisen as a result of any orders given by the Lebanese military command, nor had it involved Hezbollah.

The discovery of two huge natural gas reserves in the Mediterranean Sea off the coast of Israel, a short distance from the disputed maritime border with Lebanon, in 2009–10 further complicated relations. Israel contended that Lebanon's proposals for the delineation of its maritime border with Israel, submitted to the UN in August 2010, and with Cyprus, submitted in November, encroached upon Israeli territory. Furthermore, while the proposed boundaries did not include the recently discovered Tamar and Leviathan gasfields, they potentially contained significant oil and gas reserves, and contradicted previous maritime border agreements. In July 2011 Israel submitted its own proposal to the UN, rejecting the prospect of indirect negotiations and insisting that Lebanon agree to bilateral negotiations on all border issues. Lebanon filed a formal complaint with the UN over Israel's proposal for the maritime border in September, stating that it infringed on some 860 sq km of Lebanese sovereign territory. In November there was renewed tension at the land border, when four rocket attacks were launched into northern Israel from Lebanon, in response to which the Israeli military fired artillery shells into Lebanese territory. The militant Islamist organization Abdullah Azzam Brigades, reported to be affiliated with al-Qa'ida, subsequently claimed responsibility for the attacks. The Israeli Government was reported in early 2012 to have begun preparations for the construction of a wall along the northern cease-line with Lebanon, in order to bolster border security. In October Israeli officials stated that an unarmed drone, of Iranian origin, had been shot down over southern Israel, and that it was likely to have been launched from Lebanon by Hezbollah for the purposes of intelligence-gathering.

Following the removal from power of Egyptian President Hosni Mubarak in February 2011, there were fears of a significant deterioration in Israeli-Egyptian relations, which had remained generally stable during Mubarak's tenure. In Egypt the now increasingly influential Muslim Brotherhood, which had close links with Hamas, urged a review of the 1978 peace treaty signed between Israel and Egypt, insisting that it be submitted to a freely elected parliament for approval, and appealing for an end to normalization with Israel. In June 2011 the arrest in Egypt of a student of dual Israeli and US citizenship, Ilan Grapel, on suspicion of espionage and of working to foment unrest in the aftermath of Mubarak's removal from office prompted angry protests in Israel. In October, following the successful conclusion of the first phase of the prisoner exchange programme involving Gilad Shalit (see Developments in Israeli-Palestinian relations, 2011–12), Grapel was released in exchange for 25 Egyptian prisoners detained in Israeli gaols. Meanwhile, following the killing in August of five Egyptian soldiers by Israeli troops during an exchange of gunfire with suspected Palestinian militants close to the Israeli–Egyptian border, Egypt announced that it was to recall its ambassador from Tel-Aviv pending the completion of a full investigation into the incident by the Israeli Government (although, in the event, this was not carried out). In September protesters, who gathered outside the Israeli embassy in Cairo to demand the expulsion of the Israeli ambassador, penetrated the embassy's security wall, replaced the Israeli flag with that of Egypt and ransacked the premises, forcing the emergency evacuation to Israel of embassy staff and their families.

Relations with Egypt were further undermined by the success of the Freedom and Justice Party (FJP—founded by the Muslim Brotherhood) at legislative elections held in November 2011–January 2012, and by the election, in June 2012, of the FJP candidate, Muhammad Mursi, as President. However, the Egyptian authorities notably mediated in efforts to end both the mass hunger strike by Palestinian detainees in May and the confrontations between Israeli forces and Palestinian militants in Gaza in June. President Mursi, furthermore, drew praise internationally for his role in bringing about the ceasefire that ended the Israeli offensive and Palestinian counter-strikes in November. However, Mursi was removed from office by the Egyptian military in early July 2013 and replaced by an interim administration. The new Government proceeded to order a total crackdown on the Muslim Brotherhood: in September a court banned the Brotherhood from engaging in any activities within Egypt, and in December the group was designated as a 'terrorist organization'. Thus, the ousting of Mursi and handover of power to the new, military-backed authorities brought a swift end to the burgeoning relationship between Egypt and the Hamas administration in the Gaza Strip. In September, for example, Israeli officials welcomed measures taken by Egypt's interim administration to reduce the presence of militant Islamist groups in the Sinai Peninsula and to prevent the smuggling of weapons into Gaza.

CONSTITUTION AND GOVERNMENT

Israel does not have a formal, written constitution. However, in June 1950 the Knesset (parliament) voted to adopt a state constitution by evolution over an unspecified period. A number of laws, including the Law of Return (1950), the Nationality Law (1952), the State President (Tenure) Law (1952), the Education Law (1953) and the 'Yad-va-Shem' Memorial Law (1953), are considered as incorporated into the state Constitution. Other constitutional laws are: the Law and Administration Ordinance (1948), the Knesset Election Law (1951), the Law of Equal Rights for Women (1951), the Judges Act (1953), the National Service and National Insurance Acts (1953), and the Basic Law (the Knesset—1958).

Supreme authority in Israel rests with the Knesset, with 120 members elected by universal suffrage for four years (subject to dissolution), on the basis of proportional representation. The President, a constitutional head of state, is elected by the Knesset for a maximum of one seven-year term. Executive power lies with the Cabinet, led by a Prime Minister. The Cabinet takes office after receiving a vote of confidence in the Knesset, to which it is responsible. Ministers are usually members of the Knesset, but non-members may be appointed. The country is divided into six administrative districts. Local authorities are elected at the same time as elections to the Knesset. In 2012 there were 75 municipal councils, 126 local councils and 996 regional councils.

REGIONAL AND INTERNATIONAL CO-OPERATION

Israel became a member of the UN on 11 May 1949. As a contracting party to the General Agreement on Tariffs and Trade, Israel joined the World Trade Organization (WTO, see p. 434) on its establishment in 1995. The country officially acceded to the Organisation for Economic Co-operation and Development (OECD, see p. 379) on 7 September 2010.

ECONOMIC AFFAIRS

In 2011, according to estimates by the World Bank, Israel's gross national income (GNI), measured at average 2009–11 prices, was US $220,424m., equivalent to $28,380 per head (or $28,070 per head on an international purchasing-power parity basis). During 2003–12, it was estimated, the population increased at an average annual rate of 1.9%, while gross domestic product (GDP) per head increased, in real terms, by an average of 2.4% per year. Overall GDP increased, in real terms, at an average annual rate of 4.4% in 2003–12. GDP grew by 3.1% in 2012, according to official figures.

Agriculture (including hunting, forestry and fishing) contributed a preliminary 1.4% of GDP in 2013, and in 2012 engaged 1.6% of the employed labour force. Most agricultural workers live in large co-operatives (*kibbutzim*), of which there were 267 at December 2012, or co-operative smallholder villages (*moshavim*), of which there were 442. Israel is largely self-sufficient in foodstuffs. Citrus fruits constitute the main export crop. Other important crops are tomatoes, vegetables (particularly potatoes, carrots and turnips, chillies and peppers, and cucumbers and gherkins), wheat, melons and apples. The export of exotic fruits, winter vegetables and flowers has increased significantly in recent years. Poultry, livestock and fish production are also important. According to official data, the GDP of the agricultural sector increased at an estimated average annual rate of 3.4% in 2003–09; according to official estimates, it remained constant in 2009.

Industry (comprising mining, manufacturing, construction and power) contributed a preliminary 22.0% of GDP in 2013, and engaged 18.1% of the employed labour force in 2012. According to official figures, in 2003–08 industrial GDP increased at an average annual rate of 6.2%; it expanded by an estimated 4.2% in 2009. The state plays a major role in all sectors of industry, and there is a significant co-operative sector.

The mining and manufacturing sectors together contributed a preliminary 14.9% of GDP in 2013, and engaged 12.9% of the employed labour force in 2012; mining and quarrying employed about 0.2% of the working population in 2008. Israel has small proven reserves of petroleum (of some 3.9m. barrels), from which less than 500 barrels per day are currently produced; however, in 1999 potential new reserves were discovered in central Israel and off the southern coast. Israel's Petroleum Commission has estimated that the country could possess around 5,000m. barrels of oil reserves, most likely located underneath gas reserves, and that offshore gas could supply its short-term energy needs. Production at the offshore Tamar gasfield, the reserves of which were estimated at some 250,000m. cu m, began in March 2013; Tamar was expected to supply 50%–80% of Israel's natural gas consumption within the next decade. Reserves at the offshore Leviathan field, discovered in December 2010, are estimated at some 450,000m. cu m. Phosphates, potash, bromides, magnesium and other salts are mined, and Israel is the world's largest exporter of bromine. According to official estimates, in 2003–09 sectoral GDP increased by an average annual rate of 3.9%; it expanded by 6.2% in 2008, before declining by an estimated 6.2% in 2009. The principal branches of manufacturing, measured by gross revenue, are: chemical, petroleum and coal products; food products; scientific, photographic, optical equipment, etc.; metal products; pharmaceutical products; and rubber and plastic products.

The construction sector contributed a preliminary 5.4% of GDP in 2013. In 2012 the sector engaged 4.6% of the employed labour force. During 2003–09 the GDP of the sector increased at an average annual rate of 1.2%; however, construction GDP declined by 1.0% in 2009, according to official estimates.

Energy is derived principally from coal (accounting for 69.9% of total electricity output in 2012); however, it is intended that natural gas should eventually become Israel's principal energy source. Energy derived from natural gas contributed 20.9% of total electricity output in 2012, up from just 0.1% in 2003. Imports of mineral fuels comprised 22.0% of the total value of imports in 2012.

Services contributed a preliminary 76.6% of GDP in 2013, and engaged 80.3% of the employed labour force in 2012. Tourism is an important source of revenue, although the sector has at times been severely damaged by regional instability. A decline in the number of militant attacks in the late 2000s resulted in an increase in tourist numbers: in 2013 some 3.0m. tourists visited Israel (increased from 2.3m. in 2009), while receipts from tourism were estimated at US $5,493m. in 2012. Financial services are also important: banking, insurance, real estate and business services together contributed a preliminary 22.2% of GDP in 2013, and employed 17.3% of the working population in 2012. According to official data, in 2003–08 the GDP of the services sector increased at an average annual rate of 6.5%; it grew by an estimated 4.4% in 2009.

In 2012 Israel recorded a visible merchandise trade deficit of US $9,344.9m.; however, there was a surplus of $849.7m. on the current account of the balance of payments. Excluding trade with the West Bank and Gaza Strip, in 2012 the principal source of imports was the USA, which supplied 12.9% of imports to Israel; other major suppliers were the People's Republic of China, Germany and Switzerland-Liechtenstein. The USA was also the principal market for exports, taking 27.8% of Israeli exports in that year; other important purchasers were Hong Kong and the United Kingdom. Israel is the world's largest supplier of polished diamonds. The principal exports in 2012 were basic manufactures (chiefly non-metallic mineral manufactures), machinery and transport equipment, chemicals and related products, and miscellaneous manufactured articles. The principal imports in that year were machinery and transport equipment, mineral fuels and lubricants (mainly petroleum and petroleum products), basic manufactures (mainly non-metallic mineral manufactures), chemicals and related products, miscellaneous manufactured articles, and food and live animals.

Government revenue each year normally includes some US $8,632m. in economic and military aid from the USA. The Government planned for balanced budgets for 2014, with revenue and expenditure both totalling NIS 406,265m. in that year. Israel's general gross government debt was NIS 664,779m. in 2012, equivalent to 64.9% of GDP. During 2003–12 consumer prices rose at an average annual rate of 2.1%; consumer prices increased by 1.7% in 2012. The unemployment rate was reported to be 6.9% in 2012.

A principal task for the new coalition Government which took office in March 2013 was to secure approval of a budget that would balance the need to reduce spending obligations, with the electorate's demands for the reduction of living costs, and the highly sensitive issue of defence commitments. In May the Cabinet approved the new Minister of Finance's austerity budget for the August 2013–December 2014 period, which, *inter alia*, increased personal and corporate taxation, reduced child allowances and imposed a limited cut in defence expenditure; the budget received Knesset approval in July. Annual inflation in 2012 had averaged 1.7%, below the 2% centre of the target range: inflationary pressures came principally from housing, fuel and food, but were in part offset by the implementation of state-funded provision of pre-primary education, and by lower prices arising from increased competition in the mobile telephone sector. The continued growth in housing prices—a key focus of the mass social protests of 2011—reflected the shortage of homes relative to demand, as well as the impact of low interest rates in fuelling demand for property investment. In view of a widening in the government deficit to 4.2% of GDP at the end of 2012, the outgoing Governor of the Bank of Israel identified as critical the need to address the structural deficit, and for the Government to keep its commitments in line with its own spending target. He also emphasized the necessity of continued efforts to integrate Arab and ultra-Orthodox workers in the labour market; of promoting increased labour productivity; and of ensuring the allocation of profits from the long-term exploitation of the country's natural gas reserves through the establishment of a sovereign wealth fund. The Government approved draft legislation to create such a fund in April 2013. In its report published in February 2014, the IMF commended the authorities' 'bold fiscal consolidation measures'; the Fund estimated the budget deficit to have declined to 3.5% of GDP in 2013. Moreover, the commencement of natural gas production from the Tamar field in March of that year was expected to reduce Israel's dependence on fuel imports, including for refining; the country was expected to become a net exporter of natural gas by the end of the decade. In June 2013 the Government voted to permit the export of 40% of Israel's gas reserves, with the remaining 60% to be retained for domestic consumption; the decision was ratified by the Supreme Court in October. Following GDP growth of an estimated 3.4% in 2013, the IMF forecast the Israeli economy to grow at the same rate in 2014, with unemployment expected to rise from 6.4% to 6.7%.

PUBLIC HOLIDAYS

The Sabbath starts at sunset on Friday and ends at nightfall on Saturday. The Jewish year 5775 begins on 25 September 2014 and the year 5776 on 14 September 2015.

2015: 4–10 April (Pesach, Passover—public holidays on first and last days of festival), 23 April (Yom Ha'atzmaut, Independence Day), 24 May (Shavuot, Feast of Weeks), 14–15 September (Rosh Hashanah, Jewish New Year), 23 September (Yom Kippur, Day of Atonement), 28 September–4 October (Succot, Feast of the Tabernacles), 5 October (Shemini Atzeret, Assembly of the Eighth Day/Simchat Torah, Celebration of the Torah),

(Observance of the Jewish festivals and fast days begins at sunset in the evening prior to the dates given.)

Islamic holidays are observed by Muslim Arabs, and Christian holidays by the Christian Arab community.

Statistical Survey

Source (unless otherwise indicated): Central Bureau of Statistics, POB 13015, Hakirya, Romema, Jerusalem 91130; tel. 2-6592037; fax 2-6521340; e-mail yael@cbs.gov.il; internet www.cbs.gov.il.

Area and Population

AREA, POPULATION AND DENSITY

Area (sq km)	
Land	21,643
Inland water	429
Total	22,072*
Population (*de jure*; census results)†	
4 November 1995	5,548,523
27 December 2008	
Males	3,663,910
Females	3,748,270
Total	7,412,180
Population (*de jure*; official estimates at 31 December)†	
2010	7,695,100
2011	7,836,600
2012	7,984,500
Density (per sq km) at 31 December 2012	368.9§

* 8,522 sq miles. Area includes East Jerusalem, annexed by Israel in June 1967, and the Golan sub-district (1,154 sq km), annexed by Israel in December 1981.

† Including the population of East Jerusalem and Israeli residents in certain other areas under Israeli military occupation since June 1967. Figures also include non-Jews in the Golan sub-district, an Israeli-occupied area of Syrian territory. Census results exclude adjustment for under-enumeration.

§ Land area only.

POPULATION BY AGE AND SEX

('000, official population estimates at 31 December 2012)

	Males	Females	Total
0–14	1,470.1	1,399.3	2,869.4
15–64	2,118.8	2,163.4	4,282.2
65 and over	364.5	468.4	832.9
Total	3,953.4	4,031.1	7,984.5

POPULATION BY RELIGION

(31 December 2012)

	Number	%
Jews	5,999,600	75.1
Muslims	1,387,500	17.4
Christians*	158,400	2.0
Druze	131,500	1.6
Unclassified†	307,500	3.9
Total	7,984,500	100.0

* Including Arab Christians.

† Including Lebanese not classified by religion.

DISTRICTS

(31 December 2012)

	Area (sq km)*	Population (rounded)†	Density (per sq km)
Jerusalem‡	653	987,400	1,512.0
Northern§	4,473	1,320,800	295.3
Haifa	866	939,000	1,084.3
Central	1,294	1,931,000	1,492.3
Tel-Aviv	172	1,318,300	7664.5
Southern	14,185	1,146,600	80.8
Total	21,643	7,984,500	368.9

* Excluding lakes, with a total area of 429 sq km.

† Components exclude, but total includes, Israelis residing in Jewish localities in the West Bank totalling some 341,400 at 31 December 2012.

‡ Including East Jerusalem, annexed by Israel in June 1967.

§ Including the Golan sub-district (area 1,154 sq km, population an estimated 44,100 at 31 December 2012), annexed by Israel in December 1981.

PRINCIPAL TOWNS

(population at 31 December 2012)

Jerusalem (capital)*	815,300	Beersheba	197,300
Tel-Aviv—Jaffa	414,600	Netanya	192,200
Haifa	272,200	Holon	185,300
Rishon LeZiyyon	235,100	Bene Beraq	168,800
Ashdod	214,900	Ramat-Gan	148,400
Petach-Tikva	213,900	Bat Yam	129,400

* The Israeli Government has designated the city of Jerusalem (including East Jerusalem, annexed by Israel in June 1967) as the country's capital, although this is not recognized by the UN.

BIRTHS, MARRIAGES AND DEATHS*

	Registered live births		Registered marriages		Registered deaths†	
	Number	Rate (per 1,000)	Number	Rate (per 1,000)	Number	Rate (per 1,000)
2005	143,913	20.8	41,029	5.9	39,038	5.6
2006	148,170	21.0	44,685	6.3	38,765‡	5.5‡
2007	151,679	21.1	46,448	6.5	40,081	5.6
2008	156,923	21.5	50,038	6.8	39,484	5.4
2009	161,042	21.5	48,997	6.5	38,812	5.2
2010	166,255	21.8	47,855	6.2	39,613	5.2
2011	166,296	21.4	51,271	6.6	40,889	5.3
2012	170,940	21.6	n.a.	n.a.	42,073	5.3

* Including East Jerusalem.

† Including deaths abroad of Israelis residing outside of Israel less than one year.

‡ Excluding 116 deaths of military personnel resulting from hostilities with militant factions based in Lebanon.

Note: From 2006 data include marriages involving a spouse not resident in Israel and those in which spouses may be of different religions.

Life expectancy (years at birth): 81.8 (males 80.0; females 83.6) in 2011 (Source: World Bank, World Development Indicators database).

IMMIGRATION*

	2010	2011	2012
Immigrants on immigrant visas	13,679	14,332	13,497
Immigrants on tourist visas†	2,955	2,561	3,061
Total	16,634	16,893	16,558

* Excluding immigrating citizens (5,058 in 2010; 4,027 in 2011; 3,501 in 2012) and Israeli residents returning from abroad.

† Figures refer to tourists who changed their status to immigrants or potential immigrants.

ECONOMICALLY ACTIVE POPULATION

(sample surveys, '000 persons aged 15 years and over, excluding armed forces)*

	2010	2011	2012
Agriculture, hunting, forestry and fishing	47.8	42.6	51.5
Industry†	416.7	417.4	424.5
Electricity, gas and water supply	20.3	22.9	19.4
Construction	157.4	162.5	150.3
Wholesale and retail trade; repair of motor vehicles, motorcycles and personal and household goods	388.5	402.3	406.9
Hotels and restaurants	134.7	139.5	144.6
Transport, storage and communications	191.2	196.6	207.8
Financial intermediation	116.1	118.7	116.4
Real estate, renting and business activities	429.2	429.2	451.4
Public administration and defence; compulsory social security	134.6	146.3	342.5
Education	367.5	385.4	417.2

—*continued*	2010	2011	2012
Health and social work	303.7	306.8	329.1
Other community, social and personal service activities	147.2	154.2	161.5
Private households with employed persons	55.3	55.3	60.8
Extra-territorial organizations and bodies	2.3	2.5	1.5
Sub-total	2,907.9	2,979.1	3,285.4
Not classifiable by economic activity	25.8	45.6	73.7
Total employed	2,938.2	3,024.7	3,359.0
Unemployed	208.9	179.5	247.1
Total labour force	3,147.1	3,204.2	3,606.0
Males	1,664.3	1,698.8	1,917.8
Females	1,482.8	1,505.4	1,688.3

* Figures are estimated independently, so the totals may not be the sum of the component parts.

† Comprising mining and quarrying, and manufacturing.

Health and Welfare

KEY INDICATORS

Total fertility rate (children per woman, 2011)	2.9
Under-5 mortality rate (per 1,000 live births, 2011)	4
HIV/AIDS (% of persons aged 15–49, 2011)	0.2
Physicians (per 1,000 head, 2011)	3.1
Hospital beds (per 1,000 head, 2010)	3.5
Health expenditure (2010): US $ per head (PPP)	2,041
Health expenditure (2010): % of GDP	7.7
Health expenditure (2010): public (% of total)	61.7
Total carbon dioxide emissions ('000 metric tons, 2010)	70,655.8
Carbon dioxide emissions per head (metric tons, 2010)	9.3
Human Development Index (2012): ranking	16
Human Development Index (2012): value	0.900

For sources and definitions, see explanatory note on p. vi.

Agriculture

PRINCIPAL CROPS
('000 metric tons)

	2010	2011	2012
Wheat	112.3	122.0	189.5
Maize	86.5	96.4	85.4
Potatoes	548.7	621.1	565.6
Olives	73.5	66.0	63.0
Cabbages and other brassicas	52.4	57.7	59.8
Lettuce and chicory	28.7	32.2	32.9
Tomatoes	446.6	411.0	392.1
Cucumbers and gherkins	115.8	105.4	100.8
Aubergines (Eggplants)	45.3	46.1	43.1
Chillies and peppers, green	204.0	226.1	240.7
Onions, dry	83.3	91.8	82.8
Carrots and turnips	234.3	289.3	282.9
Watermelons	107.3	100.6	103.2
Cantaloupes and other melons	41.5	41.5	37.6
Bananas	112.7	101.3	129.5
Oranges	134.8	90.5	111.9
Tangerines, mandarins, clementines and satsumas	152.2	130.6	184.9
Grapefruit and pomelos	204.4	183.7	246.6
Apples	131.5	119.2	131.6
Peaches and nectarines	65.8	54.2	102.3
Grapes	95.1	89.5	94.0
Avocados	69.5	75.3	73.4

Aggregate production ('000 metric tons, may include official, semi-official or estimated data): Total cereals 241.1 in 2010, 253.7 in 2011, 323.4 in 2012; Total roots and tubers 568.7 in 2010, 641.3 in 2011, 582.9 in 2012; Total vegetables (incl. melons) 1,655.2 in 2010, 1,744.4 in 2011, 1,718.5 in 2012; Total fruits (excl. melons) 1,273.1 in 2010, 1,194.2 in 2011, 1,454.2 in 2012.

Source: FAO.

LIVESTOCK
('000 head, year ending September)

	2010	2011	2012
Cattle	430	432	435
Pigs*	223	224	224
Sheep	445	486	540
Goats	100	107	100
Chickens	42,599	40,717	40,247
Geese and guinea fowls†	1,000	1,050	1,050
Turkeys	3,800	3,685	3,503
Ducks†	200	200	200

* Unofficial figures.

† FAO estimates.

Source: FAO.

LIVESTOCK PRODUCTS
('000 metric tons)

	2010	2011	2012
Cattle meat	108.1	116.7	116.9
Sheep meat*	8.1	9.5	9.7
Pig meat	18.9	19.2	19.4
Chicken meat	450.0	480.0	480.0
Goose and guinea fowl meat*	3.6	3.6	3.6
Turkey meat	90.0	90.0	92.0
Cows' milk	1,292.1	1,355.7	1,366.4
Sheep's milk	16.8	16.5	18.1
Goats' milk	23.4	22.3	25.9
Hen eggs	102.5	120.9	120.3
Honey	2.5	2.9	3.1

* FAO estimates.

Source: FAO.

Forestry

ROUNDWOOD REMOVALS
('000 cubic metres, excl. bark)

	1999*	2000†	2001†
Sawlogs, veneer logs and logs for sleepers	36	28	11
Pulpwood	32	22	7
Other industrial wood	32	22	7
Fuel wood	13	8	2
Total	113	81	27

* FAO estimates.

† Unofficial figures.

2002–12: Figures assumed to be unchanged from 2001 (FAO estimates).

Source: FAO.

Fishing

(metric tons, live weight)

	2009	2010	2011
Capture	2,712	2,588	2,650*
Carps, barbels, etc.	294	294	258
Aquaculture*	19,177	19,895	20,107
Common carp	5,892	5,629	5,840
Tilapias	7,789	7,662	7,390
Gilthead seabream	1,072	1,240	1,440
Flathead grey mullet	2,048*	2,125	2,169
Total catch*	21,889	22,483	22,757

* FAO estimate(s).

Source: FAO.

Mining

('000 metric tons unless otherwise indicated)

	2009	2010	2011
Crude petroleum ('000 barrels)	14.7	12.4	12.0*
Natural gas (million cu m)	2,825	3,234	4,300*
Phosphate rock†	2,697	3,135	3,105
Potash salts‡	1,900	2,080	2,100*
Salt (unrefined, marketed)	357	421	430*
Gypsum	9	99.7	100.0*
Bromine (elemental)	128	185	202

* Estimate.

† Figures refer to beneficiated production; the phosphoric acid content (in '000 metric tons) was: 740 in 2009; 860 in 2010 (estimate); 850 in 2011 (estimate).

‡ Figures refer to K_2O content.

Source: US Geological Survey.

Industry

SELECTED PRODUCTS

('000 metric tons unless otherwise indicated)

	2009	2010	2011
Wine*	4.8	5.0	5.0
Sulphuric acid†	520	630	630
Cement	4,759	5,139	5,200
Electric energy (million kWh)	53,179	56,102	57,145

* FAO estimates.

† Sulphuric content; US Geological Survey estimates.

2012: Electric energy (million kWh) 61,074.

Sources: mainly FAO; US Geological Survey.

Finance

CURRENCY AND EXCHANGE RATES

Monetary Units

100 agorot (singular: agora) = 1 new sheqel (plural: sheqalim) or shekel (NIS).

Sterling, Dollar and Euro Equivalents (31 December 2013)

£1 sterling = NIS 5.716;
US $1 = NIS 3.471;
€1 = NIS 4.787;
NIS 100 = £17.49 = $28.81 = €20.89.

Average Exchange Rate (NIS per US $)

2011 3.5781
2012 3.8559
2013 3.6107

STATE BUDGET*

(NIS million)

Revenue and grants†	2012	2013‡	2014‡
Current receipts	258,804	279,846	286,932
Taxes and compulsory payments	233,826	235,953	259,166
Income and property taxes	111,800	112,800	126,300
Taxes on expenditure	122,026	123,153	132,866
Interest, royalties, etc.	4,366	2,693	2,782
Transfer from loans and capital account receipts	20,613	41,200	24,984
Receipts from loans and capital account	107,111	115,187	119,333
Collection of principal	6,240	5,160	4,983
Miscellaneous	40	13	14
Privatization	1,813	1,132	1,132
Domestic loans	99,786	128,305	118,254
Loans and grants from overseas	17,672	20,546	18,432
Less Transfer to current receipts	18,440	39,968	23,482
Total	365,916	395,033	406,265

Expenditure§	2012	2013‡	2014‡
Civilian consumption	71,155	80,691	84,157
Domestic	46,632	49,998	52,980
Defence consumption	66,610	58,622	57,840
Transfer and support payments	102,736	110,505	113,114
Investments and credit granting	19,335	25,159	27,569
Interest payments and credit subsidies	38,049	39,473	41,762
Miscellaneous	9,295	9,879	10,859
Reserves	—	7,076	7,401
Debt repayment (principal)	88,384	85,489	86,003
Less Revenue-dependent expenditure	19,171	21,860	22,441
Total	376,392	395,033	406,265

* Excluding Bank of Israel.

† Revenue includes grants received from abroad (NIS million): 8,672 in 2012; 8,746 in 2013 (forecast); 8,632 in 2014 (forecast).

‡ Forecasts.

§ Expenditure includes the central Government's credit issuance (NIS million): 1,214 in 2012; 1,943 in 2013 (forecast); 2,030 in 2014 (forecast).

Source: Ministry of Finance, Budget Division.

INTERNATIONAL RESERVES

(excluding gold, US $ million at 31 December)

	2010	2011	2012
IMF special drawing rights	1,323.4	1,269.5	1,276.7
Reserve position in IMF	319.0	552.6	591.0
Foreign exchange	69,265.0	73,052.0	74,040.0
Total	70,907.3	74,874.1	75,907.6

Source: IMF, *International Financial Statistics*.

MONEY SUPPLY

(NIS '000 million at 31 December)

	2010	2011	2012
Currency held by public	38.3	43.1	48.2
Current account deposits	63.5	58.7	68.6
Total means of payment	101.8	101.8	116.8

COST OF LIVING

(Consumer Price Index, annual averages; base: 2000 = 100)

	2010	2011	2012
Food	138.6	143.4	144.4
All items (incl. others)	123.6	127.9	130.1

Source: ILO.

NATIONAL ACCOUNTS

(NIS million at current prices)

National Income and Product

	2011	2012	2013*
Gross domestic product in market prices	923,900	993,365	1,053,291
Net income paid abroad	–15,543	–30,951	–28,856
Gross national income (GNI)	908,357	962,414	1,024,435
Less Consumption of fixed capital	122,440	130,996	133,684
Net national income	785,916	788,062	890,752

Expenditure on the Gross Domestic Product

	2011	2012	2013*
Final consumption expenditure	742,010	785,996	833,405
Private	529,208	558,525	592,670
General government	212,802	227,470	240,734
Changes in inventories	–2,297	2,553	5,338
Gross fixed capital formation	188,777	202,841	204,340
Total domestic expenditure	928,490	991,390	1,043,083
Exports of goods and services	328,001	359,361	343,104
Less Imports of goods and services	332,592	357,386	332,895
GDP in market prices	923,900	993,365	1,053,291

Gross Domestic Product by Economic Activity

	2011	2012	2013*
Agriculture, hunting, forestry and fishing	13,351	12,386	12,760
Manufacturing, mining and quarrying	116,625	137,935	139,997
Electricity, gas and water supply	11,825	11,015	15,622
Construction	44,885	48,542	50,733
Wholesale, retail trade, repair of motor vehicles, motorcycles and personal and household goods; hotels and restaurants	82,941	89,998	96,105
Transport, storage and communications	109,894	117,455	121,762
Financial intermediation; real estate, renting and business activities	184,410	195,570	208,035
Public administration and community services†	134,335	143,769	152,840
Housing services	106,105	112,945	119,702
Other community, social and personal services	17,584	18,986	20,807
Sub-total	821,955	888,601	938,363
Net taxes on products	101,945	104,761	114,931
GDP in market prices	923,900	993,365	1,053,291

* Preliminary.

† Including non-profit institutions serving households.

BALANCE OF PAYMENTS
(US $ million)

	2010	2011	2012
Exports of goods	56,413.4	64,293.9	62,320.6
Imports of goods	–58,367.3	–72,482.1	–71,665.5
Balance on goods	–1,953.9	–8,188.2	–9,344.9
Exports of services	24,769.5	27,409.2	30,879.4
Imports of services	–18,772.8	–20,537.2	–21,041.7
Balance on goods and services	4,042.8	–1,316.2	492.8
Primary income received	6,280.8	7,768.6	7,226.6
Primary income paid	–11,431.3	–12,122.2	–15,246.5
Balance on goods, services and primary income	–1,107.7	–5,669.8	–7,527.1
Secondary income received	9,688.4	10,132.3	9,600.4
Secondary income paid	–1,409.1	–1,209.1	–1,223.6
Current balance	7,171.6	3,253.4	849.7
Capital account (net)	982.7	1,234.0	672.6
Direct investment assets	–9,088.1	–5,329.0	–2,352.4
Direct investment liabilities	5,509.6	10,765.1	9,481.0
Portfolio investment assets	–9,370.2	–3,120.1	–8,778.1
Portfolio investment liabilities	8,985.5	–5,796.3	–3,512.1
Financial derivatives and employee stock options (net)	29.7	–12.3	296.3
Other investment assets	242.4	–351.9	2,249.9
Other investment liabilities	3,674.0	2,014.3	–3,646.2
Net errors and omissions	3,938.4	2,079.9	4,613.1
Reserves and related items	12,075.6	4,737.1	–126.2

Source: IMF, *International Financial Statistics*.

External Trade

PRINCIPAL COMMODITIES
(US $ million)

Imports c.i.f.	2010	2011	2012
Food and live animals	3,457.8	4,356.3	4,242.0
Mineral fuels, lubricants, etc.	10,441.2	13,635.9	16,078.8
Petroleum, petroleum products, etc.	8,700.0	11,709.4	14,309.0
Chemicals and related products	6,843.9	7,961.4	8,344.3
Basic manufactures	14,477.6	18,041.5	15,179.8
Non-metallic mineral manufactures	9,126.9	11,589.0	9,113.7
Machinery and transport equipment	16,751.0	21,146.7	21,039.6
General industrial machinery, equipment and parts	1,974.9	2,403.2	2,722.1
Machinery for particular industries	968.9	2,893.1	2,172.3
Office machines and automatic data-processing machines	1,844.5	1,937.5	1,842.8
Telecommunications and sound equipment	2,259.9	2,751.8	2,320.8
Other electrical machinery, apparatus, etc.	3,822.2	4,455.9	4,974.5
Road vehicles and parts	4,383.4	4,824.0	4,206.6
Miscellaneous manufactured articles	5,175.8	6,082.1	6,175.1
Total (incl. others)	59,199.4	73,536.2	73,121.4

Exports f.o.b.	2010	2011	2012
Food and live animals	1,726.1	1,925.8	1,944.7
Mineral fuels, lubricants and related products	2,796.1	4,046.6	3,257.9
Chemicals and related products	13,477.6	15,398.0	14,735.9
Organic chemicals	1,481.7	1,891.6	2,026.0
Medical and pharmaceutical products	6,475.2	7,083.1	6,598.9
Basic manufactures	19,568.2	24,105.4	20,755.7
Non-metallic mineral manufactures	16,696.3	20,991.0	17,884.4
Machinery and transport equipment	14,710.9	15,013.2	15,404.2
Telecommunications and sound equipment	3,424.2	3,202.2	3,002.4
Other electrical machinery, apparatus, etc.	5,395.3	5,691.1	6,085.9
Road vehicles and other transport equipment and parts	2,294.0	2,131.3	1,903.6
Miscellaneous manufactured articles	4,876.6	5,873.2	5,760.6
Professional, scientific and controlling instruments, etc.	2,354.8	2,849.7	2,806.7
Total (incl. others)	58,415.9	67,802.2	63,145.3

PRINCIPAL TRADING PARTNERS
(US $ million)*

Imports (excl. military goods) c.i.f.	2010	2011	2012
Belgium-Luxembourg	3,576.4	4,465.0	3,544.9
China, People's Republic	4,736.8	5,450.5	5,322.2
Cyprus	152.6	318.9	964.7
France	1,517.2	1,625.5	1,646.2
Germany	3,678.8	4,566.5	4,621.8
Hong Kong	1,398.6	1,856.2	1,563.9
India	1,845.6	2,154.5	1,936.2
Italy	2,425.8	3,055.9	2,779.5
Ireland	519.5	994.5	1,006.0
Japan	1,779.6	2,402.1	1,727.3
Korea, Republic	1,100.7	1,607.7	1,663.0
Netherlands	2,102.1	2,761.5	2,746.9
Russia	784.6	1,052.9	819.4
Singapore	702.8	794.5	773.4
Spain	975.4	1,183.4	1,201.9
Switzerland-Liechtenstein	3,220.2	3,970.2	4,055.4
Taiwan	709.1	761.5	782.1
Turkey	1,800.1	2,171.1	2,082.7
United Kingdom	2,246.4	2,776.7	2,598.1
USA	6,701.0	8,706.7	9,398.7
Total (incl. others)	59,199.4	73,536.2	73,121.4

Exports f.o.b.	2010	2011	2012
Belgium-Luxembourg	3,116.8	3,767.5	2,929.7
Brazil	934.8	892.6	1,138.7
Canada	749.5	807.1	767.7
China, People's Republic	2,046.8	2,718.3	2,758.2
Cyprus	755.6	937.4	905.1
France	1,266.5	1,542.0	1,450.9
Germany	1,701.4	1,950.0	1,638.9
Hong Kong	3,915.2	5,339.1	4,882.8
India	2,890.4	3,036.4	2,495.3
Italy	1,253.2	1,390.5	1,164.3
Japan	657.2	900.8	831.8
Korea, Republic	850.3	724.1	704.8
Malaysia	798.0	717.2	763.3
Netherlands	1,818.0	2,160.6	2,248.6
Russia	818.2	954.3	1,053.1
Spain	1,031.8	984.2	1,039.1
Switzerland-Liechtenstein	1,047.5	1,438.4	1,133.0
Taiwan	726.2	776.6	699.4
Turkey	1,310.7	1,855.7	1,421.4
United Kingdom	2,268.1	3,424.7	3,588.7
USA	18,488.2	19,432.4	17,561.7
Total (incl. others)	58,415.9	67,802.2	63,145.3

* Imports by country of purchase; exports by country of destination.

Transport

RAILWAYS
(traffic)

	2010	2011	2012
Passengers carried ('000 journeys)	35,877	35,930	40,511
Passenger-km (million)	1,986	1,927	2,133
Freight carried ('000 metric tons)	7,023	6,229	6,265
Freight ton-km (million)	1,062	1,099	1,011

ROAD TRAFFIC
(motor vehicles in use at 31 December)

	2010	2011	2012
Private passenger cars	2,053,248	2,164,385	2,246,053
Taxis	18,878	19,020	19,222
Minibuses	15,026	14,848	14,492
Buses and coaches	14,762	15,382	15,625
Lorries, vans and road tractors	347,152	347,980	341,859
Special service vehicles	4,118	4,318	4,433
Motorcycles and mopeds	113,007	117,254	119,295

SHIPPING

Flag Registered Fleet
(at 31 December)

	2011	2012	2013
Number of vessels	37	38	39
Displacement ('000 grt)	318.6	272.0	273.1

Source: Lloyd's List Intelligence (www.lloydslistintelligence.com).

International Sea-borne Freight Traffic
('000 metric tons)

	2010	2011	2012
Goods loaded	19,270	19,554	19,401
Goods unloaded*	24,142	25,392	26,947

* Including traffic between Israeli ports.

CIVIL AVIATION
(traffic on scheduled services)

	2010	2011
Kilometres flown (million)	109	109
Passengers carried ('000)	5,085	5,151
Passenger-km (million)	18,178	17,926
Total ton-km (million)	2,687	2,688

Source: UN, *Statistical Yearbook*.

Passengers carried ('000): 5,335 in 2012 (Source: World Bank, World Development Indicators database).

Tourism

TOURIST ARRIVALS
('000)*

Country of residence	2011	2012	2013†
Canada	64.4	62.0	65.3
France	269.5	263.5	292.3
Germany	171.0	158.5	159.8
Italy	113.3	126.2	127.7
Netherlands	58.7	62.0	52.0
Poland	60.4	58.9	67.3
Russia	353.4	380.8	405.0
Spain	51.0	50.1	47.9
Ukraine	106.8	109.2	108.0
United Kingdom	168.0	165.1	173.3
USA	581.0	583.6	597.2
Total (incl. others)	2,820.2	2,885.8	2,961.7

* Excluding arrivals of Israeli nationals residing abroad.
† Provisional.

Tourism receipts (US $ million, excl. passenger transport): 5,106 in 2010; 5,305 in 2011; 5,493 in 2012 (provisional) (Source: World Tourism Organization).

Communications Media

	2010	2011	2012
Telephones ('000 main lines in use)	3,408	3,500	3,594
Mobile cellular telephones ('000 subscribers)	9,111	9,200	9,225
Broadband subscribers ('000)	1,762	1,879	1,711

Internet subscribers ('000): 1,714.0 in 2008.

Source: International Telecommunication Union.

Education

(2012/13 unless otherwise indicated, provisional figures)

	Schools	Pupils	Teachers
Hebrew			
Kindergarten	n.a.	399,543	17,323
Primary schools	2,202	681,087	59,699
Special needs*	198	10,635	n.a.
Intermediate schools†	502	183,414	24,489
Secondary schools	1,453	484,804	64,847
Vocational schools‡	112	23,485	n.a.
Teacher training colleges	56‡	33,893‡	5,359§
Arab			
Kindergarten	n.a.	96,162	3,822
Primary schools	582	250,726	20,219
Special needs	58	3,334	n.a.
Intermediate schools†	138	70,463	5,195
Secondary schools	384	172,494	16,034
Vocational schools‡	24	4,376	n.a.
Teacher training colleges	4‡	2,827‡	491§

* 2011/12 provisional data.

† 2007/08 provisional data.

‡ 2008/09 provisional data.

§ 2006/07 data.

Pupil-teacher ratio (primary education, UNESCO estimate): 13.1 in 2009/10 (Source: UNESCO Institute for Statistics).

Adult literacy rate (UNESCO estimates): 96.9% (males 98.3%; females 95.6%) in 2003 (Source: UN Development Programme, *Human Development Report*).

Directory

The Government

HEAD OF STATE

President: SHIMON PERES (took office 15 July 2007).

THE CABINET
(April 2014)

A coalition of Likud, Israel Beytenu, Yesh Atid, Jewish Home and Hatnua.

Prime Minister and Minister of Public Diplomacy and Diaspora Affairs: BINYAMIN NETANYAHU (Likud).

Minister for Senior Citizens: URI ORBACH (Jewish Home).

Minister of Strategic Affairs, Minister of Intelligence and Minister Responsible for International Relations: YUVAL STEINITZ (Likud).

Minister of Defence: MOSHE YA'ALON (Likud).

Minister of Interior: GIDEON SA'AR (Likud).

Minister of Finance: YAIR LAPID (Yesh Atid).

Minister of Foreign Affairs: AVIGDOR LIEBERMAN (Israel Beytenu).

Minister of Health: YAEL GERMAN (Yesh Atid).

Minister of Home Front Defence and Minister of Communications: GILAD ERDAN (Likud).

Minister of Industry, Trade and Labour, Minister of Religious Services and Minister for Jerusalem and the Diaspora: NAFTALI BENNETT (Jewish Home).

Minister of Immigrant Absorption: SOFA LANDVER (Israel Beytenu).

Minister of Energy and Water Resources, Minister of Regional Co-operation and Minister for the Development of the Negev and Galilee: SILVAN SHALOM (Likud).

Minister of Welfare and Social Services: MEIR COHEN (Yesh Atid).

Minister of Public Security: YITZHAK AHARONOVITCH (Israel Beytenu).

Minister of Environmental Protection: AMIR PERETZ (Hatnua).

Minister of Justice: TZIPI LIVNI (Hatnua).

Minister of Housing and Construction: URI YEHUDA ARIEL (Jewish Home).

Minister of Transport, National Infrastructures and Road Safety: YISRAEL KATZ (Likud).

Minister of Agriculture and Rural Development: YAIR SHAMIR (Israel Beytenu).

Minister of Tourism: UZI LANDAU (Israel Beytenu).

Minister of Education: SHAI PIRON (Yesh Atid).

Minister of Science and Technology: YAAKOV PERRY (Yesh Atid).

Minister of Culture and Sport: LIMOR LIVNAT (Likud).

Note: The Prime Minister automatically assumes responsibility for any portfolio which becomes vacant, until a permanent or acting minister is appointed.

MINISTRIES

Office of the President: 3 Hanassi St, Jerusalem 92188; tel. 2-6707211; fax 2-5887225; e-mail public@president.gov.il; internet www.president.gov.il.

Office of the Prime Minister: POB 187, 3 Kaplan St, Kiryat Ben-Gurion, Jerusalem 91950; tel. 2-6705555; fax 2-5664838; e-mail pm_eng@pmo.gov.il; internet www.pmo.gov.il.

Ministry of Agriculture and Rural Development: POB 50200, Agricultural Centre, Beit Dagan 50250; tel. 3-9485555; fax 3-9485858; e-mail bellay@moag.gov.il; internet www.moag.gov.il.

Ministry of Communications: 23 Jaffa St, Jerusalem 91999; tel. 2-6706301; fax 2-6240029; e-mail dovrut@moc.gov.il; internet www.moc.gov.il.

Ministry of Culture and Sport: POB 49100, Kiryat Hamemshala, Hamizrachit, Bldg 3, Jerusalem 91490; tel. 3-6367223; fax 3-6883430; e-mail ministerts@most.gov.il; internet www.mcs.gov.il.

Ministry of Defence: Kirya, Tel-Aviv 64734; tel. 3-6975540; fax 3-6976711; e-mail pniot@mod.gov.il; internet www.mod.gov.il.

Ministry for the Development of the Negev and Galilee: 8 Shaul Hamelech Blvd, Tel-Aviv 64733; tel. 3-6060700; fax 3-6958414; e-mail hilap@pmo.gov.il; internet www.vpmo.gov.il.

Ministry of Education: POB 292, 34 Shivtei Israel St, Jerusalem 91911; tel. 2-5602222; fax 2-5602223; e-mail info@education.gov.il; internet www.education.gov.il.

Ministry of Energy and Water Resources: POB 36148, 216 Yaffo St, Jerusalem 91360; tel. 2-5006780; fax 2-5006720; e-mail pniot@energy.gov.il; internet www.energy.gov.il.

Ministry of Environmental Protection: POB 34033, 5 Kanfei Nesharim St, Givat Shaul, Jerusalem 95464; tel. 2-6495802; fax 2-6495892; e-mail pniot@environment.gov.il; internet www.environment.gov.il.

Ministry of Finance: POB 13195, 1 Kaplan St, Kiryat Ben-Gurion, Jerusalem 91030; tel. 2-5317111; fax 2-5695344; e-mail webmaster@mof.gov.il; internet www.mof.gov.il.

Ministry of Foreign Affairs: 9 Yitzhak Rabin Blvd, Kiryat Ben-Gurion, Jerusalem 91950; tel. 2-5303111; fax 2-5303367; e-mail pniot@mfa.gov.il; internet www.mfa.gov.il.

Ministry of Health: POB 1176, 2 Ben-Tabai St, Jerusalem 91010; tel. 2-5081222; fax 2-6787982; e-mail pniot@moh.health.gov.il; internet www.health.gov.il.

Ministry of Home Front Defence: Jerusalem; tel. 3-6977155; fax 3-6976990.

Ministry of Housing and Construction: POB 18110, 3 Clermont Ganneau St, Kiryat Hamemshala (East), Jerusalem 91180; tel. 2-5847654; fax 2-5824111; e-mail sar@moch.gov.il; internet www.moch.gov.il.

Ministry of Immigrant Absorption: 6 Ester Hamalka St. Tel-Aviv; tel. 3-5209127; fax 3-5209161; e-mail sar@moia.gov.il; internet www.moia.gov.il.

Ministry of Industry, Trade and Labour: 5 Bank of Israel St, Jerusalem 91009; tel. 2-6662252; fax 2-6662908; internet www.moit.gov.il.

Ministry of Intelligence: Jerusalem; tel. 2-6705360; fax 2-6703377.

Ministry of Interior: POB 6158, Kiryat Ben-Gurion, Jerusalem 91061; tel. 2-6701400; fax 2-566376; e-mail meda@moin.gov.il; internet www.moin.gov.il.

Ministry of Jerusalem Affairs and the Diaspora: Jerusalem; tel. 2-6587100; fax 2-6587118; e-mail yaels@it.pmo.gov.il.

Ministry of Justice: POB 49029, 29 Salahadin St, Jerusalem 91010; tel. 2-6466527; fax 2-6285438; e-mail pniot@justice.gov.il; internet www.justice.gov.il.

Ministry of Public Security: POB 18182, Bldg 3, Kiryat Hamemshala (East), Jerusalem 91181; tel. 2-5418083; fax 2-5428500; e-mail sar@mops.gov.il; internet www.mops.gov.il.

Ministry of Regional Co-operation: Jerusalem.

Ministry of Religious Services: POB 13059, 7 Kanfei Nesharim St, Jerusalem 95464; tel. 2-5311101; fax 2-5311308; e-mail keren@dat.gov.il; internet www.dat.gov.il.

Ministry of Science and Technology: POB 49100, Kiryat Hamemshala, Hamizrachit, Bldg 3, Jerusalem 91490; tel. 2-5411101; fax 2-5811613; e-mail minister@most.gov.il; internet www.most.gov.il.

Ministry of Senior Citizens: 3 Kaplan St, Kiryat Ben-Gurion, Jerusalem 91919; tel. 02-6547020; fax 02-6547035; internet vatikim.gov.il.

Ministry of Social Affairs and Social Services: POB 915, 2 Kaplan St, Kiryat Ben-Gurion, Jerusalem 91008; tel. 2-6752523; fax 2-5666385; e-mail sar@molsa.gov.il; internet www.molsa.gov.il.

Ministry of Strategic Affairs: Jerusalem; tel. 2-6773750; fax 2-6517299.

Ministry of Tourism: POB 1018, 5 Bank of Israel St, Jerusalem 91009; tel. 2-6664331; fax 2-6514629; e-mail sar@tourism.gov.il; internet www.tourism.gov.il.

Ministry of Transport, National Infrastructures and Road Safety: POB 867, Government Complex, 5 Bank of Israel St, Jerusalem 91008; tel. 2-6663333; fax 2-6663195; e-mail sar@mot.gov.il; internet www.mot.gov.il.

GOVERNMENT AGENCY

The Jewish Agency for Israel

POB 92, 48 King George St, Jerusalem 91000; tel. 2-6202222; fax 2-6202303; e-mail pniyottzibor@jafi.org; internet www.jewishagency.org.

f. 1929; reconstituted in 1971 as a partnership between the World Zionist Organization and the fund-raising bodies United Israel Appeal, Inc (USA) and Keren Hayesod.

Organization: The governing bodies are: the Assembly, which determines basic policy; the Board of Governors, which sets policy for the Agency between Assembly meetings; and the Executive, responsible for the day-to-day running of the Agency.

Chairman of Executive: NATAN SHARANSKY.

Chairman of Board of Governors: JAMES S. TISCH.

Director-General: ALAN HOFFMANN.

CEO and President of Jewish Agency International Development: MISHA GALPERIN.

Functions: According to the Agreement of 1971, the Jewish Agency undertakes the immigration and absorption of immigrants in Israel, including: absorption in agricultural settlement and immigrant housing; social welfare and health services in connection with immigrants; education, youth care and training; and neighbourhood rehabilitation through project renewal.

Legislature

Knesset

Kiryat Ben-Gurion, Jerusalem 91950; tel. 2-6753809; fax 2-6753566; e-mail shmulikhh@knesset.gov.il; internet www.knesset.gov.il.

Speaker: YULI-YOEL EDELSTEIN.

General Election, 22 January 2013

Party	Valid votes cast	% of valid votes	Seats
Likud Israel Beytenu*	885,163	23.34	31
Yesh Atid	543,458	14.33	19
Israel Labour Party	432,118	11.39	15
Jewish Home	345,985	9.12	12
Shas	331,868	8.75	11
United Torah Judaism	195,892	5.16	7
Hatnua	189,167	4.99	6
Meretz–Yahad	172,403	4.55	6
United Arab List	138,450	3.65	4
Hadash	113,439	2.99	4
Balad	97,030	2.56	3
Kadima	78,974	2.08	2
Others	268,795	7.09	0
Total	3,792,742†	100.00	120

* Likud and Israel Beytenu contested the election on a joint list.
† Excluding 40,904 invalid votes.

Election Commission

Central Elections Committee: Knesset, Kiryat Ben-Gurion, Jerusalem 91950; tel. 2-6753407; e-mail doverd@knesset.gov.il; internet www.bechirot.gov.il; independent; Supreme Court elects a Justice as Chair; each parliamentary group nominates representatives to the Cttee in proportion to the group's level of representation in the Knesset; Chair. Justice ELYAKIM RUBENSTEIN; Dir-Gen. ORLY ADAS.

Political Organizations

Agudat Israel (Union of Israel): POB 513, Jerusalem; tel. 2-5385251; fax 2-5385145; f. 1912; mainly Ashkenazi ultra-Orthodox Jews; stands for introduction of laws and institutions based on Jewish religious law (the Torah); contested 2009 legislative elections as part of the United Torah Judaism list (with Degel Hatorah).

Arab Movement for Renewal (Tnua'a Aravit le'Hitkadshut—Ta'al): Jerusalem; tel. 2-6753333; fax 2-6753927; e-mail atibi@knesset.gov.il; f. 1996 following split from Balad; contested March 2006 and Feb. 2009 legislative elections on joint list with United Arab List; Leader Dr AHMAD TIBI.

Balad (National Democratic Assembly): POB 2248, Nazareth Industrial Zone, Nazareth 16000; tel. 4-6455070; fax 4-6463457; e-mail balad@zahav.net.il; f. 1999; united Arab party; Leader Dr JAMAL ZAHALKA.

Communist Party of Israel (Miflagah Kommonistit Yisraelit—Maki): POB 26205, 5 Hess St, Tel-Aviv 61261; tel. 3-6293944; fax 3-6297263; e-mail info@maki.org.il; internet www.maki.org.il; f. 1948; Jewish-Arab party descended from the Socialist Workers' Party of Palestine (f. 1919); renamed Communist Party of Palestine 1921, Jewish and Arab sections split 1945, reunited as Communist Party of Israel (Maki) 1948; further split 1965: pro-Soviet predominantly Arab anti-Zionist group formed New Communist Party of Israel (Rakah) 1965, while predominantly Jewish bloc retained name Maki; Rakah joined with other leftist orgs as Hadash 1977; name changed to Maki 1989, as the dominant component of Hadash (q.v.); Gen. Sec. MUHAMMAD NAFA'H.

Degel Hatorah (Flag of the Torah): 103 Rehov Beit Vegan, Jerusalem; tel. 2-6438106; fax 2-6418967; f. 1988 by Lithuanian Jews as breakaway faction from Agudat Israel; mainly Ashkenazi ultra-Orthodox (Haredi) Jews; contested 2009 legislative elections as part of the United Torah Judaism list (with Agudat Israel).

Hadash (Hachazit Hademokratit Leshalom Uleshivyon—Democratic Front for Peace and Equality): POB 26205, Tel-Aviv 61261; tel. 3-6293944; fax 3-6297263; e-mail info@hadash.org.il; internet hadash.org.il; f. 1977 by merger of the New Communist Party of Israel (Rakah) with other leftist groups; party list, the principal component of which is the Communist Party of Israel (q.v.); Jewish-Arab membership; aims for a socialist system in Israel and a lasting peace between Israel, Arab countries and the Palestinian Arab people; favours full implementation of UN Security Council Resolutions 242 and 338, Israeli withdrawal from all Arab territories occupied since 1967, formation of a Palestinian Arab state in the West Bank and Gaza Strip (with East Jerusalem as its capital), recognition of national rights of State of Israel and Palestinian people, democratic rights and defence of working-class interests, and demands an end to discrimination against Arab minority in Israel and against oriental Jewish communities; Chair. MUHAMMAD BARAKEH.

Hatnua (The Movement): 8 HaArb'a St, Tel-Aviv; tel. 3-6333000; internet www.hatnua.org.il; f. 2012; centrist; supports revival of peace talks with the Palestinian (National) Authority based on a two-state solution, increase to the minimum wage, environmental sustainability, extension of national service to all citizens; Leader TZIPI LIVNI.

Israel Beytenu (Israel Is Our Home/Nash dom Izrail): 78 Yirmiyahu St, Jerusalem 94467; tel. 2-5012999; fax 2-5377188; e-mail gdv7191@hotmail.com; internet www.beytenu.org.il; f. 1999; right-wing immigrant party; joined Nat. Union in 2000, but left to contest March 2006 and Feb. 2009 legislative elections alone; contested 2013 elections on joint list with Likud; seeks resolution of the Israeli–Palestinian conflict through the exchange of territory and population with the Palestinians, incl. the transfer of Arab Israelis to territory under Palestinian control; membership largely drawn from fmr USSR; 18,000 mems (2006); Leader AVIGDOR LIEBERMAN.

Israel Labour Party (Mifleget HaAvoda HaYisraelit): POB 62033, Tel-Aviv 61620; tel. 3-6899444; fax 3-6899420; e-mail mifkad@havoda.org.il; internet www.havoda.org.il; f. 1968 as a merger of the three Labour groups, Mapai, Rafi and Achdut Ha'avoda; Am Ehad (One Nation) merged with Labour in 2004; a Zionist democratic socialist party; Chair. ISSAC HERZOG; Sec.-Gen. YECHIEL BAR.

Jewish Home (HaBayit HaYehudi): Jerusalem; internet baityehudi.org.il; f. 2008 by merger of Nat. Religious Party (NRP; f. 1956), Moledet and Tekuma; however, Moledet and some Tekuma mems subsequently withdrew from new party; right-wing nationalist, Zionist; opposes further Israeli withdrawals from the West Bank and the creation of a Palestinian state; favours strengthening of the state and system of religious education; Leader NAFTALI BENNETT.

Kadima (Forward): Petach Tikva, Tel-Aviv; tel. 3-9788000; fax 3-9788115; e-mail dovrutkadima@gmail.com; internet www.kadima.org.il; f. 2005; liberal party formed as a breakaway faction from Likud by fmr party Chairman Ariel Sharon; aims to pursue a peace agreement with the Palestinians in accordance with the 'roadmap' peace plan, and to establish Israel's permanent borders, if necessary unilaterally; seeks to combat economic and social problems; Leader SHAUL MOFAZ.

Likud (Consolidation): 38 Rehov King George, Tel-Aviv 61231; tel. 2-2754231; fax 2-5605000; internet www.likud.org.il; f. Sept. 1973; fmrly a parliamentary bloc of Herut (f. 1948), the Liberal Party of Israel (f. 1961), Laam (For the Nation—f. 1976), Ahdut, Tami (f. 1981; joined Likud in June 1987) and an ind. faction led by Itzhak Modai (f. 1990), which formed the nucleus of a new Party for the Advancement of the Zionist Idea; Herut and the Liberal Party formally merged in Aug. 1988 to form the Likud-Nat. Liberal Movement; Israel B'Aliyah merged with Likud in 2003; contested Feb. 2009 legislative elections on joint list with Ahi (right-wing nationalist; Leader EFRAIM EITAM); contested 2013 elections on joint list with Israel Beytenu; aims: territorial integrity; absorption of newcomers; a social order based on freedom and justice, elimination of poverty and want; economic devt and environmental reforms to improve living standards; Chair. BINYAMIN NETANYAHU.

Meimad: POB 53139, 19 Yad Harutzim St, Jerusalem 91533; tel. 2-6725134; fax 2-6725051; f. 1988; moderate democratic Jewish party; ended alliance with Israel Labour Party and joined list with Green Movement (HaTnuah Hayeruka—f. 2008) prior to Feb. 2009 legislative elections, at which it failed to achieve representation in the Knesset; Leader Rabbi MICHAEL MELCHIOR.

Meretz (Social Democratic Party of Israel): Beit Amot Mishpat, 8th Shaul Hamelech Blvd, Tel-Aviv 64733; tel. 3-6098998; fax 3-6961728; e-mail siatmeretz@knesset.gov.il; internet www.meretz.org.il; f. 2003 as Yahad (Together—Social Democratic Israel) from a merger of Meretz (f. 1992; an alliance of Ratz, Shinui and the United Workers' Party) and Shahar (f. 2002; a breakaway faction of the Israel Labour Party); name changed to above in 2005; formed joint list with New Movement (Hatnua Hahadasha) prior to Feb. 2009 legislative elections; Jewish-Arab social democratic party; stands for: civil rights; welfarism; Palestinian self-determination and a return to the 1967 borders, with minor adjustments; a divided Jerusalem, but no right of return for Palestinian refugees to Israel; separation of religion from the state; Chair. ZAHAVA GAL-ON.

Moledet (Homeland): 14 Yehuda Halevi St, Tel-Aviv; tel. 3-654580; e-mail moledet@moledet.org.il; internet www.m-moledet.org.il; f. 1988; right-wing nationalist party; aims include the expulsion ('transfer') of Palestinians living in the West Bank and Gaza Strip; united with Tehiya—Zionist Revival Movement in June 1994 as the Moledet—the Eretz Israel Faithful and the Tehiya; contested Feb. 2009 legislative elections as part of the Nat. Union; Chair. URI BANK.

National Union (Haichud Haleumi): e-mail info@leumi.org.il; f. 1999 as right-wing coalition comprising Herut, Moledet and Tekuma parties; contested March 2006 legislative elections on joint list with Nat. Religious Party, but stood alone (comprising Moledet, Hatikva, Eretz Yisrael Shelanu and fmr Tekuma mems) in Feb. 2009 elections; believes in a 'Greater Israel'; opposed to further withdrawals from the Occupied Territories; stated aim of joint list was the creation of an Israeli society based on the spiritual and social values of Judaism and the retention of an undivided Israel; Leader YAAKOV DOV KATZ.

Pensioners' Party (Gimla'ey Yisrael LaKneset—Gil) (Pensioners of Israel to the Knesset—Age): 100 Ha' Hashmonaim, Tel-Aviv; tel. 3-5611900; fax 3-5611909; e-mail info@gimlaim.org.il; internet www.gimlaim.org.il; stands for pensioners' rights; failed to achieve representation in the Knesset at 2013 legislative elections; Leader RAFI EITAN.

Shas (Sephardic Torah Guardians): POB 34263, Jerusalem 91341; tel. 2-5008888; fax 2-5380226; e-mail p@shas.org.il; internet shas.org.il; f. 1984 by splinter groups from Agudat Israel; ultra-Orthodox Sephardic party; Chair. ARYEH DER'I.

United Arab List (Reshima Aravit Me'uchedet—Ra'am): Jerusalem; tel. 9-7997088; fax 9-7996295; e-mail media.amc@gmail.com; internet www.a-m-c.org; f. 1996 by merger of the Arab Democratic Party and individuals from the Islamic Movement and Nat. Unity Front (left-wing Arab parties); supports establishment of a Palestinian state, with East Jerusalem as its capital, and equality for all Israeli citizens; contested March 2006 and Feb. 2009 legislative elections on joint list with Arab Movement for Renewal; Chair. AHMAD TIBI.

United Torah Judaism (Yahadut Hatorah): f. prior to 1992 election; electoral list of four minor ultra-Orthodox parties (Moria, Degel Hatorah, Poale Agudat Israel and Agudat Israel) established to overcome the increase in election threshold from 1% to 1.5% and to seek to counter the rising influence of the secular Russian vote; contested 2003 election composed of Degel Hatorah and Agudat Israel, into which constituent parties it split in early 2005; two parties reunited in late 2005 and contested March 2006 and Feb. 2009 legislative elections together; represents Ashkenazi ultra-Orthodox Jews and advocates the application of religious precepts in all areas of life and government; Chair., Parliamentary Group ISRAEL EICHLER.

Yesh Atid (There's a Future): Tel-Aviv; e-mail s_yeshatid@knesset.gov.il; internet en.yeshatid.org.il; f. 2012; proposes reduction in the size of the Cabinet, reform of the education system, expansion of mandatory national service to include all citizens, increase in housing provision; Founder and Leader YAIR LAPID.

Diplomatic Representation

EMBASSIES IN ISRAEL

Albania: 54/26 Pinkas St, Tel-Aviv 62261; tel. 3-5465866; fax 3-5444545; e-mail embassy.telaviv@mfa.gov.al; internet www.ambasadat.gov.al/israel; Ambassador (vacant).

Angola: 14 Simtat Beit Hashoeva St, Tel-Aviv; tel. 3-6912093; fax 3-6912094; e-mail embangi@zahav.net.il; internet www.angolaembassy.org.il; Ambassador JOSÉ JOÃO MANUEL.

Argentina: 85 Medinat Hayehudim St, 3rd Floor, Herzliya Pituach 46120; tel. 9-9702744; fax 9-9702748; e-mail embarg@netvision.net.il; Ambassador CARLOS FAUSTINO GARCÍA.

Australia: POB 29108, Discount Bank Tower, 28th Floor, 23 Yehuda Halevi St, Tel-Aviv 65136; tel. 3-6935000; fax 3-6935002; e-mail telaviv.embassy@dfat.org.au; internet www.israel.embassy.gov.au; Ambassador DEVANAND NOEL (DAVE) SHARMA.

Austria: Sason Hogi Tower, 12 Abba Hillel St, 4th Floor, Ramat-Gan 52506; tel. 3-6120924; fax 3-7510716; e-mail tel-aviv-ob@bmeia.gv.at; internet www.aussenministerium.at/telaviv; Ambassador Dr FRANZ JOSEF KUGLITSCH.

Belarus: POB 11129, 3 Reines St, Tel-Aviv 64381; tel. 3-5231069; fax 3-5231273; e-mail israel@mfa.gov.by; internet www.israel.mfa.gov.by; Ambassador VLADIMIR SKVORTSOV.

Belgium: 12 Abba Hillel St, 15th Floor, Ramat-Gan 52506; tel. 3-6138130; fax 3-6138160; e-mail telaviv@diplobel.fed.be; internet www.diplomatie.be/telaviv; Ambassador JOHN CORNET D'ELZIUS.

Bosnia and Herzegovina: Yachin Bldg, 10th Floor, 2 Kaplan St, Tel-Aviv; tel. 3-6124499; fax 3-6124488; e-mail embtelaviv@bezeqint.net; Ambassador BRANKO KESIC.

Brazil: 23 Yehuda Halevi St, 30th Floor, Tel-Aviv 65136; tel. 3-7971500; fax 3-6916060; e-mail brasemb.telaviv@itamaraty.gov.br; internet telaviv.itamaraty.gov.br; Ambassador HENRIQUE DA SILVEIRA SARDINHA PINTO.

Bulgaria: 21 Leonardo da Vinci St, Tel-Aviv 64733; tel. 3-6961379; fax 3-6961430; e-mail embassy.telaviv@mfa.bg; internet www.mfa.bg/en/118; Ambassador DIMITAR MIHAILOV.

Cameroon: 28 Moshe Sharet St, Ramat-Gan 52425; tel. 3-5298401; fax 3-6370583; e-mail activ50@yahoo.fr; Ambassador HENRI ETOUNDI ESSOMBA.

Canada: POB 9442, 3/5 Nirim St, Tel-Aviv 67060; tel. 3-6363300; fax 3-6363380; e-mail taviv@international.gc.ca; internet www.canadainternational.gc.ca/israel; Ambassador VIVIAN BERCOVICI.

Chile: 34 Habarzel St, Bldg B, Floor 1, Ramat Hahayal, Tel-Aviv 69710; tel. 3-5102751; fax 3-5100102; e-mail echileil@inter.net.il; internet chileabroad.gov.cl/israel; Ambassador JORGE MONTERO FIGUEROA.

China, People's Republic: POB 6067, 222 Ben Yehuda St, Tel-Aviv 61060; tel. 3-5442638; fax 3-5467251; e-mail chinaemb_il@mfa.gov.cn; internet il.china-embassy.org; Ambassador GAO YANPING.

Colombia: Hogi Sason Bldg, 8th Floor, Abba Hillel St, Ramat-Gan 12; tel. 3-6953384; fax 3-6957847; e-mail emcolis@netvision.net.il; Ambassador Dr FERNANDO ALZATE DONOSO.

Congo, Democratic Republic: 1 Rachel St, 2nd Floor, Tel-Aviv 64584; tel. 3-5248306; fax 3-5292623; e-mail ambardc_il@yahoo.fr; Chargé d'affaires a.i. KIMBOKO MA MAKENGO.

Congo, Republic: POB 12504, 9 Maskit St, Herzliya Pituach 46120; tel. 9-9577130; fax 9-9577216; e-mail guy_itoua@yahoo.fr; Chargé d'affaires a.i. JEAN MARIE NGAKALA.

Costa Rica: Paz Tower, 5-7 Shoham St, 6th Floor, Ramat-Gan 52521; tel. 3-6135061; fax 3-6134779; e-mail emcri@netvision.net.il; Ambassador RODRIGO X. CARRERAS.

Côte d'Ivoire: South Africa Bldg, 12 Menachim Begin St, Ramat-Gan 52521; tel. 3-6126677; fax 3-6126688; e-mail ambacita@netvision.net.il; Ambassador JEAN-BAPTISTE GOMIS.

Croatia: 2 Weizman St, Migdal Amot, Tel-Aviv 64239; tel. 3-6403000; fax 3-6438503; e-mail croemb.israel@mvep.hr; Ambassador PJER ŠIMUNOVIĆ.

Cyprus: Top Tower, 14th Floor, Dizengoff Centre, 50 Dizengoff St, Tel-Aviv 64322; tel. 3-9273000; fax 3-6290535; e-mail ambassador@cyprusembassytelaviv.com; internet www.mfa.gov.cy/embassytelaviv; Ambassador DIMITRIS HATZIARGYROU.

Czech Republic: POB 16361, 23 Zeitlin St, Tel-Aviv; tel. 3-6918282; fax 3-6918286; e-mail telaviv@embassy.mzv.cz; internet www.mzv.cz/telaviv; Ambassador TOMÁŠ POJAR.

Denmark: POB 21080, Museum Tower, 11th Floor, 4 Berkowitz St, Tel-Aviv 61210; tel. 3-6085850; fax 3-6085851; e-mail tlvamb@um.dk; internet israel.um.dk; Ambassador JESPER VAHR.

Dominican Republic: Beit Ackerstein, 3rd Floor, 103 Medinat Hayehudim St, Herzliya Pitauch 46766; tel. 9-9515529; fax 9-9515528; e-mail israel@embajadadominicana.net; Ambassador ALEXANDER DE LA ROSA.

Ecuador: POB 34002, Asia House, 5th Floor, 4 Weizman St, Tel-Aviv 64239; tel. 3-6958764; fax 3-6913604; e-mail eecuisrael@mmrree.gov.ec; Ambassador GUILLERMO BASSANTE RAMÍREZ.

Egypt: 54 Basel St, Tel-Aviv 62744; tel. 3-5464151; fax 3-5441615; e-mail egypem.ta@zahav.net.il; internet www.mfa.gov.eg/english/embassies/Egyptian_Embassy_TelAviv/Pages/default.aspx; Ambassador ATEF SALEM EL-AHL.

El Salvador: 6 Hamada St, 4th Floor, Herzliya Pituach 46733; tel. 9-9556237; fax 9-9556603; e-mail embassy@elsalvador.org.il; internet www.el-salvador.org.il; Ambassador SUZANA GUN DE HASENSON.

Eritrea: 1 Twin Towers, 33 Jabotinsky St, 11th Floor, Ramat-Gan 52511; tel. 3-6120039; fax 3-5750133; Ambassador TESFAMARIAM TEKESTE.

Estonia: POB 7166, 24th Floor, Menachem Begin Rd 125, 44 Kaplan St, HaYovel Tower, Tel-Aviv 61071; tel. 3-7103910; fax 3-7103919; e-mail embassy.telaviv@mfa.ee; internet www.telaviv.vm.ee; Ambassador MALLE TALVET-MUSTONEN.

Ethiopia: Bldg B, Floor 8B, 48 Darech Menachem Begin St, Tel-Aviv 66184; tel. 3-6397831; fax 3-6397837; e-mail info@ethioemb.org.il; internet www.ethioemb.org.il; Ambassador HELAWE YOSEF.

Finland: POB 39666, Canion Ramat Aviv, 9th Floor, 40 Einstein St, Tel-Aviv 61396; tel. 3-7456600; fax 3-7440314; e-mail sanomat.tel@formin.fi; internet www.finland.org.il; Ambassador LEENA-KAISA MIKKOLA.

France: 112 Tayelet Herbert Samuel, Tel-Aviv 63572; tel. 3-5208300; fax 3-5208340; e-mail diplomatie@ambafrance-il.org; internet www.ambafrance-il.org; Ambassador PATRICK MAISONNAVE.

Georgia: 3 Daniel Frisch St, Tel-Aviv 64731; tel. 3-6093206; fax 3-6093205; e-mail israel.emb@mfa.gov.ge; internet israel.mfa.gov.ge; Chargé d'affaires a.i. NIKOLOZ REVAZISHVILI.

Germany: POB 16038, 3 Daniel Frisch St, 19th Floor, Tel-Aviv 64731; tel. 3-6931313; fax 3-6969217; e-mail info@tel-aviv.diplo.de; internet www.tel-aviv.diplo.de; Ambassador ANDREAS MICHAELIS.

Ghana: 12 Abba Hillel St, 7th Floor, Ramat-Gan 52506; tel. 3-5766000; fax 3-7520827; e-mail chancery@ghanaemb.co.il; internet www.ghanaembassy.co.il; Ambassador ERNEST SOWATEY LOMOTEY.

Greece: POB 64731, 3 Daniel Frisch St, Tel-Aviv; tel. 3-6953060; fax 3-6951329; e-mail gremb.tlv@mfa.gr; internet www.mfa.gr/telaviv; Ambassador SPYRIDON LAMPRIDIS.

Guatemala: Beit Ackerstein, 4th Floor, 103 Medinat Hayehudim St, Herzliya Pituach 46766; tel. 9-9568707; fax 9-9518506; e-mail embguate@netvision.net.il; Ambassador ALFREDO VASQUEZ RIVERA.

Holy See: 1 Netiv Hamazalot, Old Jaffa 68037; tel. 2-6835658; fax 2-6835659; e-mail vatge@netvision.net.il; Apostolic Nuncio Most Rev. GIUSEPPE LAZZAROTTO (Titular Archbishop of Numana).

Honduras: Aharon Karon St, 3 Rishon le Zion 75262; tel. 3-9642092; fax 9-9577457; e-mail honduras@netvision.net.il; Ambassador JOSÉ ISAIAS BARAHONA HERRERA.

Hungary: POB 21095, 18 Pinkas St, Tel-Aviv 62661; tel. 3-5466985; fax 3-5467018; e-mail mission.tlv@kum.hu; internet www.mfa.gov.hu/emb/telaviv; Ambassador ANDOR NAGY.

India: POB 3368, 140 Hayarkon St, Tel-Aviv 61033; tel. 3-5291999; fax 3-5291953; e-mail indemtel@indembassy.co.il; internet www.indembassy.co.il; Ambassador JAIDEEP SARKAR.

Ireland: The Tower, 17th Floor, 3 Daniel Frisch St, Tel-Aviv 64731; tel. 3-6964166; fax 3-6964160; e-mail telavivembassy@dfa.ie; internet www.embassyofireland.co.il; Ambassador EAMONN CHRISTOPHER MCKEE.

Italy: Trade Tower, 25 Hamered St, Tel-Aviv 68125; tel. 3-5104004; fax 3-5100235; e-mail info.telaviv@esteri.it; internet www.ambtelaviv.esteri.it; Ambassador FRANCESCO MARIA TALÒ.

Japan: Museum Tower, 19th and 20th Floors, 4 Berkowitz St, Tel-Aviv 64238; tel. 3-6957292; fax 3-6910516; e-mail info@tl.mofa.go.jp; internet www.israel.emb-japan.go.jp; Ambassador HIDEO SATO.

Jordan: 14 Abba Hillel, Ramat-Gan 52506; tel. 3-7517722; fax 3-7517712; Ambassador WALID OBAIDAT.

Kazakhstan: 52A Hayarkon St, Tel-Aviv 63432; tel. 3-5163411; fax 3-5163437; e-mail tel-aviv@mfa.kz; internet www.kazakhemb.org.il; Ambassador BOLAT NURGALIYEV.

Kenya: 15 Aba Hillel Silver St, Ramat-Gan 52136; tel. 3-5754633; fax 3-5754788; e-mail kenya7@netvision.net; Ambassador Lt-Gen. AUGUSTIONO NJOROGE.

Korea, Republic: 4 Hasadna'ot St, 3rd Floor, Herzliya Pituach 46278; tel. 9-9510318; fax 9-9569853; e-mail israel@mofat.go.kr; internet isr.mofat.go.kr; Ambassador KIM IL-SOO.

Latvia: Amot Investments Tower, 15th Floor, 2 Weizman St, Tel-Aviv 64239; tel. 3-7775800; fax 3-6953101; e-mail embassy.israel@mfa.gov.lv; internet www.mfa.gov.lv/en/israel/; Ambassador VILCĀNS ANDRIS.

Lithuania: Amot Mishpat Bldg, 8 Shaul Ha Meleh, Tel-Aviv 64733; tel. 3-6958685; fax 3-6958691; e-mail amb.il@urm.lt; internet il.mfa.lt; Ambassador DARIUS DEGUTIS.

Macedonia, former Yugoslav republic: Paz Tower, 9th Floor, 5 Shoham St, Ramat-Gan 52136; tel. 3-7154900; fax 3-6124789; e-mail telaviv@mfa.gov.mk; internet www.missions.gov.mk/telaviv; Chargé d'affaires ZORAN TODOROV.

Mexico: Trade Tower, 5th Floor, 25 Hamered St, Tel-Aviv 68125; tel. 3-5163938; fax 3-5163711; e-mail communication1@embamex.org.il; internet www.sre.gob.mx/israel; Ambassador FEDERICO SALAS.

Moldova: 38 Rembrandt St, Tel-Aviv 64045; tel. 3-5231000; fax 3-5233000; e-mail moldova@barak.net.il; internet www.israel.mfa.md; Ambassador ANATOL VANGHELI.

Myanmar: Textile Centre, 12th Floor, 2 Kaufman St, Tel-Aviv 68012; tel. 3-5170760; fax 3-5163512; e-mail myanmar@zahav.net.il; internet www.metelaviv.co.il; Ambassador MYO AYE.

Nepal: Textile Centre, 7th Floor, 2 Kaufman St, Tel-Aviv 68012; tel. 3-5100111; fax 3-5167965; e-mail nepal.embassy@012.net.il; internet www.nepalembassy-israel.org; Ambassador PRAHLAD KUMAR PRASAI.

Netherlands: Beit Oz, 13th Floor, 14 Abba Hillel St, Ramat-Gan 52506; tel. 3-7540777; fax 3-7540751; e-mail nlgovtel@012.net.il; internet www.netherlands-embassy.co.il; Ambassador CASPAR VELDKAMP.

Nigeria: POB 3339, 34 Gordon St, Tel-Aviv 61030; tel. 3-5222144; fax 3-5248991; e-mail support@nigerianembassy.co.il; internet www.nigerianembassy.co.il; Ambassador DAVID OLADIPO OBASA.

Norway: POB 17575, Canion Ramat Aviv, 13th Floor, 40 Einstein St, Tel-Aviv 69101; tel. 3-7401900; fax 3-7441498; e-mail emb.telaviv@mfa.no; internet www.norway.org.il; Ambassador SVEIN SEVJE.

Panama: 10/3 Hei Be'Iyar St, Kikar Hamedina, Tel-Aviv 62998; tel. 3-6960849; fax 3-6910045; Ambassador HECTOR APARICIO.

Peru: 60 Medinat Hayehudim St, Entrance B, 2nd Floor, Herzliya Pituach 46766; tel. 9-9578835; fax 9-9568495; e-mail emperu@012.net.il; Ambassador JOSÉ LUIS SALINAS MONTES.

Philippines: 18 Bnei Dan St, Tel-Aviv 62260; tel. 3-6010500; fax 3-6041038; e-mail filembis@netvision.net.il; internet www.philippine-embassy.org.il; Ambassador GENEROSO DE GUZMAN CALONGE.

Poland: 16 Soutine St, Tel-Aviv 64684; tel. 3-7253111; fax 3-5237806; e-mail telaviv.amb.sekretariat@msz.gov.pl; internet www.telawiw.msz.gov.pl; Ambassador JACEK CHODOROWICZ.

Portugal: 3 Daniel Frisch St, 12th Floor, Tel-Aviv 64731; tel. 3-6956373; fax 3-6956366; e-mail eptel@012.net.il; Ambassador MIGUEL DE ALMEIDA E SOUSA.

Romania: 24 Adam Hacohen St, Tel-Aviv 64585; tel. 3-5229472; fax 3-5247379; e-mail office_romania@bezeqint.net; internet telaviv.mae.ro; Ambassador ANDREEA PĂSTÂRNAC.

Russia: 120 Hayarkon St, Tel-Aviv 63573; tel. 3-5226736; fax 3-5226713; e-mail consul@russianembassy.org.il; internet russianembassy.org.il; Ambassador SERGEY YA. YAKOVLEV.

Serbia: 10 Bodenheimer St, Tel-Aviv 62008; tel. 3-6045535; fax 3-6049456; e-mail srbambil@netvision.net.il; internet www.telaviv.mfa.gov.rs; Ambassador MILUTIN STANOJEVIC.

Slovakia: POB 6459, 37 Jabotinsky St, Tel-Aviv 62287; tel. 3-5449119; fax 3-5449144; e-mail emb.telaviv@mzv.sk; Ambassador RADOVAN JAVORČIK.

Slovenia: POB 23245, Top Tower, 19th Floor, 50 Dizengoff St, Tel-Aviv 64332; tel. 3-6293563; fax 3-5282214; e-mail vta@gov.si; internet telaviv.veleposlanistvo.si; Ambassador ALENKA SUHADOLNIK.

South Africa: POB 7138, Sason Hogi Tower, 17th Floor, 12 Abba Hilel Silver St, Ramat-Gan 52520; tel. 3-5252566; fax 3-5253230; e-mail info@saemb.org.il; internet www.safis.co.il; Ambassador SISA NGOMBANE.

Spain: Dubnov Tower, 18th Floor, 3 Daniel Frisch St, Tel-Aviv 64731; tel. 3-6965218; fax 3-6965217; e-mail emb.telaviv@maec.es; internet www.exteriores.gob.es/embajadas/telaviv; Ambassador FERNANDO CARDERERA SOLER.

Sri Lanka: 4 Jean Jaurès St, Tel-Aviv 63412; tel. 3-5277635; fax 3-5277634; e-mail srilanka@013.net; Ambassador SARATH DEVESENA WIJESINGHE.

Sweden: Asia House, 4 Weizman St, Tel-Aviv 64239; tel. 3-7180000; fax 3-7180005; e-mail ambassaden.tel-aviv@ gov.se; internet www.swedenabroad.com/telaviv; Ambassador CARL MAGNUS NESSER.

Switzerland: POB 6068, 228 Hayarkon St, Tel-Aviv 6106001; tel. 3-5464455; fax 3-5464408; e-mail tel.vertretung@eda.admin.ch; internet www.eda.admin.ch/telaviv; Ambassador ANDREAS BAUM.

Thailand: Mercazim Bldg 2001, 1 Abba Eban Blvd, Herzliya Pituach 46120; tel. 9-9548412; fax 9-9548417; e-mail thaisr@netvision.co.il; internet www.thaiembassy.org/telaviv; Ambassador JURK BOON-LONG.

Turkey: 202 Hayarkon St, Tel-Aviv 63405; tel. 3-35241101; fax 3-5241390; e-mail turkemb.telaviv@mfa.gov.tr; relations downgraded since Sept. 2011; Chargé d'affaires a.i. DOĞAN FERHAT IŞIK.

Ukraine: 50 Yirmiyahu St, Tel-Aviv 62594; tel. 3-6040242; fax 3-6042512; e-mail emb_il@mfa.gov.ua; internet www.mfa.gov.ua/israel; Ambassador HENNADII NADOLENKO.

United Kingdom: 192 Hayarkon St, Tel-Aviv 63405; tel. 3-7251222; fax 3-5278574; e-mail webmaster.telaviv@fco.gov.uk; internet ukinisrael.fco.gov.uk; Ambassador MATTHEW GOULD.

USA: 71 Hayarkon St, Tel-Aviv 63903; tel. 3-5197575; fax 3-5108093; e-mail nivtelaviv@state.gov; internet israel.usembassy.gov; Ambassador DANIEL B. SHAPIRO.

Uruguay: G.R.A.P. Bldg, 1st Floor, 4 Shenkar St, Industrial Zone, Herzliya Pituach 46725; tel. 9-9569611; fax 9-9515881; e-mail secretaria@emburuguay.co.il; Ambassador BERNARDO GREIVER.

Uzbekistan: 31 Moshe Sharet St, Ramat-Gan 52413; tel. 3-6722371; fax 3-6722621; e-mail admindep@uzbembassy.org.il; internet www.uzbembassy.org.il; Ambassador OYBEK I. ESHONOV.

Viet Nam: Asia Bldg, 4th Floor, 4 Weizman St, Tel-Aviv; tel. 3-6966304; fax 3-6966243; e-mail vnembassy.il@mofa.gov.vn; internet www.vietnamembassy-israel.org; Ambassador TA DUY CHINH.

Judicial System

The law of Israel is composed of the enactments of the Knesset and, to a lesser extent, of the acts, orders-in-council and ordinances that remain from the period of the British Mandate in Palestine (1922–48). The pre-1948 law has largely been replaced, amended or reorganized, in the interests of codification, by Israeli legislation. This legislation generally follows a very similar pattern to that operating in England and the USA. However, there is no jury system.

The Supreme Court: Sha'arei Mishpat St, Kiryat David Ben-Gurion, Jerusalem 91950; tel. 2-6759666; fax 2-6759648; e-mail marcia@supreme.court.gov.il; internet www.court.gov.il; This is the highest judicial authority in the state. It has jurisdiction as an Appellate Court over appeals from the District Courts in all matters, both civil and criminal (sitting as a Court of Civil Appeal or as a Court of Criminal Appeal). In addition, it is a Court of First Instance (sitting as the High Court of Justice) in actions against governmental authorities, and in matters in which it considers it necessary to grant relief in the interests of justice and which are not within the jurisdiction of any other court or tribunal. The High Court's exclusive power to issue orders in the nature of *habeas corpus, mandamus*, prohibition and *certiorari* enables the court to review the legality of, and redress grievances against, acts of administrative authorities of all kinds; Pres. ASHER D. GRUNIS.

District Courts: There are five District Courts (Jerusalem, Tel-Aviv, Haifa, Beersheba, Nazareth). They have residual jurisdiction as Courts of First Instance over all civil and criminal matters not within the jurisdiction of a Magistrates' Court (e.g. civil claims exceeding NIS 1m.), all matters not within the exclusive jurisdiction of any other tribunal, and matters within the concurrent jurisdiction of any other tribunal so long as such tribunal does not deal with them. In addition, the District Courts have appellate jurisdiction over appeals from judgments and decisions of Magistrates' Courts and judgments of Municipal Courts and various administrative tribunals.

Magistrates' Courts: There are 29 Magistrates' Courts, having criminal jurisdiction to try contraventions, misdemeanours and certain felonies, and civil jurisdiction to try actions concerning possession or use of immovable property, or the partition thereof, whatever may be the value of the subject matter of the action, and other civil claims not exceeding NIS 1m.

Labour Courts: Established in 1969. Regional Labour Courts in Jerusalem, Tel-Aviv, Haifa, Beersheba and Nazareth, composed of judges and representatives of the public; a National Labour Court in Jerusalem; the Courts have jurisdiction over all matters arising out of the relationship between employer and employee or parties to a collective labour agreement, and matters concerning the National Insurance Law and the Labour Law and Rules.

Religious Courts: The Religious Courts are the courts of the recognized religious communities. They have jurisdiction over certain defined matters of personal status concerning members of their respective communities. Where any action of personal status involves persons of different religious communities, the President of the Supreme Court decides which Court will decide the matter. Whenever a question arises as to whether or not a case is one of personal status within the exclusive jurisdiction of a Religious Court, the matter must be referred to a Special Tribunal composed of two Justices of the Supreme Court and the President of the highest court of the religious community concerned in Israel. The judgments of the Religious Courts are executed by the process and offices of the Civil Courts. Neither these Courts nor the Civil Courts have jurisdiction to dissolve the marriage of a foreign subject; Jewish Rabbinical Courts have exclusive jurisdiction over matters of marriage and divorce of Jews in Israel who are Israeli citizens or residents. In all other matters of personal status they have concurrent jurisdiction with the District Courts; Muslim Religious Courts have exclusive jurisdiction over matters of marriage and divorce of Muslims who are not foreigners, or who are foreigners subject by their national law to the jurisdiction of Muslim Religious Courts in such matters. In all other matters of personal status they have concurrent jurisdiction with the District Courts; Christian Religious Courts have exclusive jurisdiction over matters of marriage and divorce of members of their communities who are not foreigners. In all other matters of personal status they have concurrent jurisdiction with the District Courts; Druze Courts, established in 1963, have exclusive jurisdiction over matters of marriage and divorce of Druze in Israel, who are Israeli citizens or residents, and concurrent jurisdiction with the District Courts over all other matters of personal status of Druze.

Attorney-General: YEHUDA WEINSTEIN.

Religion

JUDAISM

Judaism, the religion of the Jews, is the faith of the majority of Israel's inhabitants. On 31 December 2012 Judaism's adherents totalled 5,999,600, equivalent to 75.1% of the country's population. Its basis is a belief in an ethical monotheism.

There are two main Jewish communities: the Ashkenazim and the Sephardim. The former are the Jews from Eastern, Central or Northern Europe, while the latter originate from the Balkan countries, North Africa and the Middle East.

There is also a community of Ethiopian Jews, the majority of whom have been airlifted to Israel from Ethiopia at various times since the fall of Emperor Haile Selassie in 1974.

The supreme religious authority is vested in the Chief Rabbinate, which consists of the Ashkenazi and Sephardi Chief Rabbis and the Supreme Rabbinical Council. It makes decisions on interpretation of the Jewish law, and supervises the Rabbinical Courts. There are eight regional Rabbinical Courts, and a Rabbinical Court of Appeal presided over by the two Chief Rabbis.

According to the Rabbinical Courts Jurisdiction Law of 1953, marriage and divorce among Jews in Israel are exclusively within the jurisdiction of the Rabbinical Courts. Provided that all the parties concerned agree, other matters of personal status can also be decided by the Rabbinical Courts.

There are over 170 Religious Councils, which maintain religious services and supply religious needs, and about 400 religious committees with similar functions in smaller settlements. Their expenses are borne jointly by the state and the local authorities. The Religious Councils are under the administrative control of the Ministry of Religious Services. In all matters of religion, the Religious Councils are subject to the authority of the Chief Rabbinate. There are 365 officially appointed rabbis. The total number of synagogues is about 7,000, most of which are organized within the framework of the Union of Israel Synagogues.

Head of the Ashkenazi Community: The Chief Rabbi YONA METZGER.

Head of the Sephardic Community: The Chief Rabbi SHLOMO AMAR, Jerusalem; tel. 2-5313131.

Two Jewish sects still loyal to their distinctive customs are:

The Karaites: a sect which recognizes only the Jewish written law and not the oral law of the Mishna and Talmud. The community of about 12,000, many of whom live in or near Ramla, has been augmented by immigration from Egypt.

The Samaritans: an ancient sect mentioned in 2 Kings xvii, 24. They recognize only the Torah. The community in Israel numbers about 500; about one-half of this number live in Holon, where a Samaritan synagogue has been built, and the remainder, including the High Priest, live in Nablus, near Mt Gerazim, which is sacred to the Samaritans.

ISLAM

The Muslims in Israel belong principally to the Sunni sect of Islam, and are divided among the four rites: the Shafe'i, the Hanbali, the Hanafi and the Maliki. Before June 1967 they numbered approximately 175,000; in 1971 some 343,900. On 31 December 2012 the total Muslim population of Israel was 1,387,500, equivalent to 17.4% of the country's population.

Mufti of Jerusalem: POB 17412, Jerusalem; tel. 2-283528; Sheikh MUHAMMAD AHMAD HUSSEIN (also Chair. Supreme Muslim Council for Jerusalem); appointed by the Palestinian (National) Authority (PA).

There was also a total of 131,500 Druzes in Israel at 31 December 2012. The official spiritual leader of the Druze community in Israel is Sheikh MUWAFAK TARIF, but his leadership is not widely recognized.

CHRISTIANITY

The total Christian population of Israel (including East Jerusalem) at 31 December 2012 was 158,400.

United Christian Council in Israel: POB 116, Jerusalem 91000; tel. and fax 2-6259012; e-mail ucci@ucci.net; internet www.ucci.net; f. 1956; member of World Evangelical Alliance; over 30 mems (evangelical churches and social and educational insts); Chair. Rev. CHARLES KOPP.

The Roman Catholic Church

Armenian Rite

The Armenian Catholic Patriarch of Cilicia is resident in Beirut, Lebanon.

Patriarchal Exarchate of Jerusalem and Amman: POB 19546, 36 Via Dolorosa, Jerusalem 91190; tel. 2-6284262; fax 2-6272123; e-mail acpejerusalem@yahoo.com; f. 1885; Exarch Patriarchal Mgr RAPHAEL FRANÇOIS MINASSIAN.

Chaldean Rite

The Chaldean Patriarch of Babylon is resident in Baghdad, Iraq.

Patriarchal Exarchate of Jerusalem: Chaldean Patriarchal Vicariate, POB 20108, 7 Chaldean St, Saad and Said Quarter, Jerusalem 91200; tel. 2-6844519; fax 2-6274614; e-mail kolin-p@zahav.net.il; Exarch Patriarchal Mgr MICHEL KASSARJI.

Latin Rite

The Patriarchate of Jerusalem covers Palestine, Jordan and Cyprus.

Bishops' Conference: Conférence des Evêques Latins dans les Régions Arabes, Notre Dame of Jerusalem Center, POB 20531, Jerusalem 91204; tel. 2-6288554; fax 2-6288555; e-mail evcat@palnet.com; f. 1967; Pres. His Beatitude FOUAD TWAL (Patriarch of Jerusalem).

Patriarchate of Jerusalem: Latin Patriarchate of Jerusalem, POB 14152, Jerusalem 91141; tel. 2-6282323; fax 2-6271652; e-mail chancellery@latinpat.org; internet www.lpj.org; Patriarch His Beatitude FOUAD TWAL; Auxiliary Bishop of Jerusalem WILLIAM SHOMALI; Vicar-General for Israel GIACINTO-BOULOS MARCUZZO (Titular Bishop of Emmaus Nicopolis); Vicariat Patriarcal Latin, Street 6191/3, Nazareth 16100; tel. 4-6554075; fax 4-6452416; e-mail latinpat@rannet.com.

Maronite Rite

The Maronite community is under the jurisdiction of the Maronite Patriarch of Antioch (resident in Lebanon).

Patriarchal Exarchate of Jerusalem: Maronite Patriarchal Exarchate, POB 14219, 25 Maronite Convent St, Jaffa Gate, Jerusalem 91141; tel. 2-6282158; fax 2-6272821; Exarch Patriarchal Mgr PAUL NABIL SAYAH (also the Maronite Archbishop of Haifa).

Melkite Rite

The Greek-Melkite Patriarch of Antioch and all the East, of Alexandria and of Jerusalem (GRÉGOIRE III LAHAM) is resident in Damascus, Syria.

Patriarchal Vicariate of Jerusalem

Patriarcat Grec-Melkite Catholique, POB 14130, Porte de Jaffa, Jerusalem 91141; tel. 2-6282023; fax 2-6289606; e-mail gcpjer@p-ol.com; Protosyncellus Archim. Archbishop GEORGES MICHEL BAKAR.

Archbishop of Akka (Acre): ELIAS CHACOUR, Archevêché Grec-Catholique, POB 9450, 33 Hagefen St, 31094 Haifa; tel. 4-8508105; fax 4-8508106; e-mail chacoure@netvision.net.il.

Syrian Rite

The Syrian Catholic Patriarch of Antioch is resident in Beirut, Lebanon.

Patriarchal Exarchate of Jerusalem: Vicariat Patriarcal Syrien Catholique, POB 19787, 6 Chaldean St, Jerusalem 91197; tel. 2-6282657; fax 2-6284217; e-mail st_thomas@bezeqint.net; Exarch Patriarchal Mgr GRÉGOIRE PIERRE MELKI.

The Armenian Apostolic (Orthodox) Church

Patriarch of Jerusalem: Archbishop NOURHAN MANOUGIAN, Armenian Patriarchate of St James, POB 14235, Jerusalem; tel. 2-6264853; fax 2-6264862; e-mail webmaster@armenian-patriarchate.org; internet www.armenian-patriarchate.org.

The Greek Orthodox Church

The Patriarchate of Jerusalem includes Israel, the Occupied Territories, Jordan, Kuwait, Saudi Arabia and the United Arab Emirates.

Patriarch of Jerusalem: THEOPHILOS III, POB 14518, Jerusalem 91145; tel. 2-6274941; fax 2-6282048; e-mail secretariat@jerusalem-patriarchate.info; internet www.jerusalem-patriarchate.info.

The Anglican Communion

Episcopal Diocese of Jerusalem and the Middle East: POB 19122, St George's Cathedral Close, Jerusalem 91191; tel. 2-6271670; fax 2-6273847; e-mail info@j-diocese.org; internet www.j-diocese.org; Bishop The Rt Rev. SUHEIL DAWANI (Anglican Bishop in Jerusalem).

Other Christian Churches

Other denominations include the Coptic Orthodox Church, the Russian Orthodox Church, the Ethiopian Orthodox Church, the Romanian Orthodox Church, the Baptist Church, the Lutheran Church and the Church of Scotland.

The Press

Tel-Aviv is the main publishing centre. Largely for economic reasons, no significant local press has developed away from the main cities; hence all newspapers have tended to regard themselves as national. Friday editions, issued on Sabbath eve, are increased to as much as twice the normal size by special weekend supplements, and experience a considerable rise in circulation. No newspapers appear on Saturday.

Most of the daily papers are in Hebrew, and others appear in Arabic, English, Russian, Polish, Hungarian, Yiddish, French and German. The total daily circulation is 500,000–600,000 copies, or 21 papers per hundred people, although most citizens read more than one daily paper.

Most Hebrew morning dailies have strong political or religious affiliations, and the majority of newspapers depend on subsidies from political parties, religious organizations or public funds. The limiting effect on freedom of commentary entailed by this party press system has provoked repeated criticism. There are around 400 other newspapers and magazines, including some 50 weekly and 150 fortnightly; over 250 of them are in Hebrew, the remainder in 11 other languages.

Ha'aretz is the most widely read of the morning papers, exceeded only by the popular afternoon press, *Ma'ariv* and *Yedioth Ahronoth*. *The Jerusalem Post* gives detailed news coverage in English.

DAILIES

Calcalist (Economist): Tel-Aviv; internet www.calcalist.co.il; f. 2008; Hebrew; business; publ. by Yedioth Ahronoth Group; Founder and Publr YOEL ESTERON; CEO STEVE SCHUMACHER.

Globes: POB 5126, Rishon le Zion 75150; tel. 3-9538611; fax 3-9525971; e-mail mailbox@globes.co.il; internet www.globes.co.il; f. 1983; evening; Hebrew; business and economics; owned by the Monitin Group; CEO EITAN MADMON; Editor-in-Chief HAGGAI GOLAN; circ. 45,000.

Ha'aretz (The Land): 21 Schocken St, Tel-Aviv 61001; tel. 3-5121212; fax 3-6810012; e-mail contact@haaretz.co.il; internet www.haaretz.co.il; f. 1919; morning; Hebrew and English; liberal; independent; 25% stake acquired by M. DuMont Schauberg (Germany) in 2006; Man. Dir RAMI GUEZ; Editor-in-Chief ALUF BENN; Publr AMOS SCHOCKEN; circ. 72,000 (weekdays), 100,000 (Fri.).

Hamodia (The Informer): POB 1306, 5 Yehudah Hamacabi St, Jerusalem 91012; tel. 2-5389255; fax 2-5003384; e-mail english@hamodia.co.il; internet www.hamodia.com; f. 1950; morning; Hebrew, English and French edns; Orthodox; organ of Agudat Israel; Editor HAIM MOSHE KNOPF; international circ. 250,000.

Israel HaYom (Israel Today): 2 Hashlosha St, Tel-Aviv; e-mail hayom@israelhayom.co.il; internet israelhayom.co.il; f. 2007; free daily publ. Sun.–Thur; Hebrew; Publr ASHER BAHARAV; Editor-in-Chief AMOS REGEV; CEO ZIPPI KOREN; circ. 255,000.

Israel Nachrichten (News of Israel): POB 28397, Tel-Aviv 61283; tel. 3-5372059; fax 3-5376166; e-mail info@israelnachrichten.de; f. 1935 as Neueste Nachrichten, renamed as above 1948; morning; German; Editor HELGA MÜLLER-GAZMAWE; circ. 1,500.

Israel Post: 15 HaAchim MeSalvita, Tel-Aviv; f. 2007 as Metro Israel; free daily; afternoon; Hebrew; publ. by Metro Israel Ltd; Co-owners ELI AZUR, DAVID WEISMAN; Editor-in-Chief GOLAN BAR-YOSEF.

Al-Itihad (Unity): POB 104, Haifa; tel. 4-8666301; fax 4-8641407; e-mail aletihad@bezeqint.net; internet www.aljabha.org; f. 1944; Arabic; organ of Hadash; Editor-in-Chief AIDA TOUMA-SLIMAN; circ. 60,000.

The Jerusalem Post: POB 81, The Jerusalem Post Bldg, Romema, Jerusalem 91000; tel. 2-5315666; fax 2-5389527; e-mail feedback@jpost.com; internet www.jpost.com; f. 1932 as The Palestine Post, renamed as above 1950; morning; English; independent; CEO RONIT HASIN-HOCHMAN; Editor-in-Chief STEVE LINDE; circ. 15,000 (weekdays), 40,000 (weekend edn); there is also a weekly international edn (circ. 70,000), and a weekly French edn.

Ma'ariv (Evening Prayer): 2 Carlebach St, Tel-Aviv 61200; tel. 3-5632111; fax 3-5610614; internet www.nrg.co.il; f. 1948; mid-morning; Hebrew; independent; publ. by Modiin Publishing House; Editor-in-Chief YOAV TZUR; circ. 150,000 (weekdays), 250,000 (weekends).

Nasha strana (Our Country): 52 Harakeret St, Tel-Aviv 67770; tel. 3-370011; fax 3-5371921; f. 1970; morning; Russian; Editor S. HIMMELFARB; circ. 35,000.

Novosti nedeli (The Week's News): 15 Ha-Ahim Mi-Slavita St, Tel-Aviv; tel. 3-6242225; fax 3-6242227; Russian; Editor-in-Chief DMITRII LODYZHENSKII.

Al-Quds (Jerusalem): POB 19788, Jerusalem; tel. 2-6272663; fax 2-6272657; e-mail hani@alquds.com; internet www.alquds.com; f. 1968; Arabic; Founder and Publr MAHMOUD ABU ZALAF; Gen. Man. Dr MARWAN ABU ZALAF; circ. 55,000.

Viata Noastra: 49 Tchlenor St, Tel-Aviv 66048; tel. 3-5372059; fax 3-6877142; e-mail viatanoastra2001@yahoo.com; internet viatanoastra.1colony.com; f. 1950; morning; Romanian; Editor NANDO MARIO VARGA; circ. 30,000.

Yated Ne'eman: POB 328, Bnei Brak; tel. 3-6170800; fax 3-6170801; e-mail let-edit@yatedneman.co.il; f. 1986; morning; Hebrew; religious; Editors Rabbi ITZHAK ROTH, Rabbi NOSSON ZE'EV GROSSMAN; circ. 25,000.

Yedioth Ahronoth (The Latest News): 2 Yehuda and Noah Mozes St, Tel-Aviv 61000; tel. and fax 3-6082222; e-mail service@y-i.co.il; internet www.ynet.co.il; f. 1939; evening; Hebrew; independent; Editor-in-Chief SHILO DE BEER; circ. 350,000, Fri. 600,000.

WEEKLIES AND FORTNIGHTLIES

Akhbar al-Naqab (News of the Negev): POB 426, Rahat 85357; tel. 8-9919202; fax 8-9917070; e-mail akhbar@akhbarna.com; internet www.akhbarna.com; f. 1988; weekly; Arabic; educational and social issues concerning the Negev Bedouins; Editor-in-Chief MUHAMMAD YOUNIS.

Aurora: Aurora Ltd, POB 57416, Tel-Aviv 61573; tel. 3-5625216; fax 3-5625082; e-mail aurora@aurora-israel.co.il; internet www.aurora-israel.co.il; f. 1963; weekly; Spanish; Editor-in-Chief ARIE AVIDOR; Director MARIO WAINSTEIN; circ. 20,000.

Bamahane (In the Camp): Military POB 1013, Tel-Aviv; f. 1948; illustrated weekly of the Israel Defence Forces; Hebrew; Editor-in-Chief YONI SHANFELD; circ. 70,000.

B'Sheva: Petach Tikva; internet www.inn.co.il/Besheva; f. 2002; Hebrew; religious Zionist newspaper, distributed freely in religious communities; owned by Arutz Sheva (Channel Seven) media network; Editor EMANUEL SHILO; circ. 140,000.

Etgar (The Challenge): POB 35252, Ha'aliyah St, 2nd Floor, Tel-Aviv 61351; tel. 3-5373268; fax 3-5373269; e-mail nirhanitzoz.org.il; internet www.etgar.info; twice weekly; Hebrew; publ. by Hanitzotz Publishing House; Editor NATHAN YALIN-MOR.

InformationWeek: POB 1161, 13 Yad Harutzim St, Tel-Aviv 61116; tel. 3-6385858; fax 3-6889207; e-mail world@pc.co.il; internet www.pc.co.il; weekly; Hebrew and English; Man. Dirs DAHLIA PELED, PELI PELED; Editor-in-Chief PELI PELED.

The Jerusalem Post International Edition: POB 81, Romema, Jerusalem 91000; tel. 2-5315666; fax 2-5389527; e-mail liat@jpost.com; internet www.jpost.co.il; f. 1959; weekly; English; overseas edn of *The Jerusalem Post* (q.v.); circ. 70,000 to 106 countries; Editor LIAT COLLINS.

Jerusalem Report: POB 1805, Jerusalem 91017; tel. 2-5315440; fax 2-5379489; e-mail jrep@jreport.co.il; internet www.jrep.com; f. 1990; bi-weekly; English; publ. under umbrella of *The Jerusalem Post*; Editor-in-Chief EETTA PRINCE-GIBSON.

Laisha (For Women): POB 28122, 35 Bnei Brak St, Tel-Aviv 66021; tel. 3-6386977; fax 3-6386933; e-mail laisha@laisha.co.il; internet laisha.co.il; f. 1949; Hebrew; women's magazine; Editor-in-Chief MIRIAM NOFECH-MOSES; circ. 100,000.

My Tour-Il Magazine: 15 Lamdan St, Tel-Aviv 6941415; tel. 3-6486611; fax 3-6486622; e-mail ilan777@gmail.com; internet www.mytour-il.co.il; f. 1994; weekly; Hebrew and English; Publr and Editor ILAN SHCHORI; circ. 50,000.

Reshumot: Ministry of Justice, POB 1087, 29 Rehov Salahadin, Jerusalem 91010; f. 1948; Hebrew, Arabic and English; official govt gazette.

Al-Sabar: POB 2647, Nazareth 16126; tel. 4-6462156; fax 4-6462152; e-mail alsabar.mag@gmail.com; internet www.alsabar-mag.com; publ. by the Org. for Democratic Action; Arabic; political and cultural Israeli-Palestinian affairs.

Vesti (News): 2 Homa U'Migdal, Tel-Aviv 67771; tel. 3-6383444; fax 3-6383440; f. 1992; publ. Sun.–Thur; Russian; Editor-in-Chief SERGEI PODRAZHANSKII.

OTHER PERIODICALS

Bitaon Heyl Ha'avir (Israel Air Force Magazine): Military POB 01560, Zahal; tel. 3-6067729; fax 3-6067735; e-mail iaf@inter.net.il; internet www.iaf.org.il; f. 1948; bi-monthly; Hebrew and English; Dep. Editor U. ETSION; Editor-in-Chief MERAV HALPERIN; circ. 30,000.

Al-Bushra (Good News): POB 6228, Haifa 31061; tel. 4-8385002; fax 4-8371612; f. 1935; monthly; Arabic; organ of the Ahmadiyya movement; Editor MUSA ASA'AD O'DEH.

Challenge: POB 35252, Tel-Aviv 61351; tel. 3-5373268; fax 3-5373269; e-mail oda@netvision.net.il; internet www.challenge-mag.com; f. 1989; magazine on the Israeli–Palestinian conflict, publ. by Hanitzotz Publishing House; online only; English; Editor-in-Chief RONI BEN EFRAT; Editor STEPHEN LANGFUR.

Diamond Intelligence Briefs: POB 3442, Ramat-Gan 52136; tel. 3-5750196; fax 3-5754829; e-mail office@tacy.co.il; internet www

.diamondintelligence.com; f. 1985; English; Publr CHAIM EVEN-ZOHAR.

Eastern Mediterranean Tourism/Travel: Israel Travel News Ltd, POB 3251, Tel-Aviv 61032; tel. 3-5251646; fax 3-5251605; e-mail office@itn.co.il; internet www.itn.co.il; f. 1979; monthly; English; Editor GERRY AROHOW; circ. 20,000.

Hamizrah Hehadash (The New East): Israel Oriental Society, The Hebrew University, Mount Scopus, Jerusalem 91905; tel. 2-5883633; e-mail ios49@hotmail.com; f. 1949; annual of the Israel Oriental Society; Middle Eastern, Asian and African Affairs; Hebrew with English summary; Editors HAIM GERBER, ELIE PODEH; circ. 1,500–2,000.

Harefuah (Medicine): POB 3566, 2 Twin Towers, 35 Jabotinsky St, Ramat-Gan 52136; tel. 3-6100444; fax 3-5753303; e-mail tguvot@ima.org.il; internet www.ima.org.il/harefuah; f. 1920; monthly journal of the Israel Medical Asscn; Hebrew with English summaries; also publishes *Israel Medical Asscn Journal*; Editor Prof. YEHUDA SHOENFELD; circ. 16,000.

Hed Hachinuch (Echoes of Education): 2 Tashach St, Tel-Aviv 62093; tel. 3-6091819; fax 3-6094521; e-mail hed@itu.org.il; internet www.itu.org.il; f. 1926; monthly; Hebrew; also publishes Arabic edn; educational; publ. by the Israel Teachers Union; Editor DALIA LACHMAN; circ. 40,000.

Hed Hagan (Echoes of Kindergarten): 8 Ben Saruk St, Tel-Aviv 62969; tel. 3-6922958; e-mail hedhagan@morim.org.il; internet www.itu.org.il; f. 1935; quarterly; Hebrew; early education issues; publ. by the Israel Teachers Union; Editor ILANA MALCHI; circ. 9,000.

Historia: POB 4179, Jerusalem 91041; tel. 2-5650444; fax 2-6712388; e-mail shazar@shazar.org.il; internet www.shazar.org.il/historia.htm; f. 1998; bi-annual; Hebrew, with English summaries; general history; publ. by the Historical Society of Israel; Editors Prof. YITZHAK HEN, Prof. ISRAEL SHATZMAN, Prof. GIDEON SHELACH; circ. 1,000.

Israel Environment Bulletin: Ministry of Environmental Protection, POB 34033, 5 Kanfei Nesharim St, Givat Shaul, Jerusalem 95464; tel. 2-6553777; fax 2-6535934; e-mail shoshana@environment.gov.il; internet www.environment.gov.il; f. 1973; bi-annual; English; environmental policy, legislation and news; Editor SHOSHANA GABBAY; circ. 3,500.

Israel Exploration Journal: POB 7041, 5 Avida St, Jerusalem 9107001; tel. 2-6257991; fax 2-6247772; e-mail ies@vms.huji.ac.il; internet israelexplorationsociety.huji.ac.il/iej.htm; f. 1950; bi-annual; English; general and biblical archaeology, ancient history and historical geography of Israel and the Holy Land; Editors SHMUEL AHITUV, AMIHAI MAZAR; circ. 2,500.

Israel Journal of Chemistry: POB 34299, Jerusalem 91341; tel. 2-6522226; fax 2-6522277; e-mail info@israelsciencejournals.com; internet www.sciencefromisrael.com; f. 1951; quarterly; English; publ. by Science from Israel; Editor Prof. HAIM LEVANON.

Israel Journal of Earth Sciences: POB 34299, Jerusalem 91341; tel. 2-6522226; fax 2-6522277; e-mail info@israelsciencejournals.com; internet www.sciencefromisrael.com; f. 1951; quarterly; English; publ. by Science from Israel; Editor-in-Chief Y. ENZEL.

Israel Journal of Ecology and Evolution: POB 34299, Jerusalem 91341; tel. 2-6522226; fax 2-6522277; e-mail info@israelsciencejournals.com; internet www.sciencefromisrael.com; f. 1951 as *Israel Journal of Zoology*; name changed in 2006; quarterly; English; publ. by Science from Israel; Editors LEON BLAUSTEIN, BURT P. KOTLER.

Israel Journal of Mathematics: The Hebrew University Magnes Press, POB 39099, Jerusalem 91390; tel. 2-6586656; fax 2-5633370; e-mail iton@math.huji.ac.il; internet www.ma.huji.ac.il/~ijmath; f. 1951; bi-monthly; English; Editor-in-Chief NATI LINIAL.

Israel Journal of Plant Sciences: POB 34299, Jerusalem 91341; tel. 2-6522226; fax 2-6522277; e-mail info@israelsciencejournals.com; internet www.sciencefromisrael.com; f. 1951 as *Israel Journal of Botany*; quarterly; English; publ. by Science from Israel; Editor-in-Chief EFRAIM LEWINSOHN.

Israel Journal of Psychiatry and Related Sciences: Gefen Publishing House Ltd, 6 Hatzvi St, Jerusalem 94386; tel. 2-5380247; fax 2-5388423; e-mail ijp@gefenpublishing.com; f. 1963; quarterly; English; Editor-in-Chief Dr DAVID GREENBERG.

Israel Journal of Veterinary Medicine: POB 22, Ra'nana 43100; tel. 9-7419929; fax 9-7431778; e-mail ivma@zahav.net.il; internet www.ijvm.org.il; f. 1943; fmrly *Refuah Veterinarith*; quarterly of the Israel Veterinary Medical Asscn; English; Editor-in-Chief TREVOR WANER.

Israel Law Review: Israel Law Review Asscn, Faculty of Law, Hebrew University of Jerusalem, Mt Scopus, Jerusalem 91905; tel. 2-5881156; fax 2-5819371; e-mail ilr@savion.huji.ac.il; internet law.huji.ac.il/eng/pirsumim.asp; f. 1966; 3 a year; English; Editors-in-Chief Sir NIGEL RODLEY, YUVAL SHANY.

Israel Medical Asscn Journal (IMAJ): POB 3604, 2 Twin Towers, 11th Floor, 35 Jabotinsky St, Ramat-Gan 52136; tel. 3-6100418; fax 3-7519673; e-mail imaj@ima.org.il; internet www.ima.org.il/imaj; f. 1999; monthly English-language journal of the Israel Medical Asscn; also publishes *Harefuah*; Editor-in-Chief Prof. YEHUDA SHOENFELD.

Journal d'Analyse Mathématique: The Hebrew University Magnes Press, POB 39099, Jerusalem 91390; tel. 2-6586656; fax 2-5633370; e-mail magnes@vms.huji.ac.il; internet www.ma.huji.ac.il/jdm; f. 1955; 3 vols a year; French; Exec. Editor A. LINDEN.

Leshonenu: Academy of the Hebrew Language, Givat Ram Campus, Jerusalem 91904; tel. 2-6493555; fax 2-5617065; e-mail ivrit@hebrew-academy.org.il; internet hebrew-academy.huji.ac.il; f. 1929; quarterly; Hebrew; for the study of the Hebrew language and cognate subjects; Editor MOSHE BAR-ASHER.

Leshonenu La'am: Academy of the Hebrew Language, Givat Ram Campus, Jerusalem 91904; tel. 2-6493555; fax 2-5617065; e-mail ivrit@heberw-academy.org.il; internet hebrew-academy.huji.ac.il; f. 1945; quarterly; Hebrew; popular Hebrew philology; Editor MOSHE FLORENTIN.

Lilac: Nazareth; f. 2000 for Christian and Muslim Arab women in the region; monthly; Arabic; Israel's first magazine for Arab women; Founder and Editor-in-Chief YARA MASHOUR.

MB-Yakinton (Yakinton): POB 1480, Tel-Aviv 61014; tel. 3-5164461; fax 3-5164435; e-mail info@irgun-jeckes.org; internet www.irgun-jeckes.org; f. 1932; 8 a year; monthly journal of the Irgun Jotsei Merkaz Europa (Asscn of Israelis of Central European Origin); Hebrew and German; Editor MICHA LIMOR.

Moznaim (Balance): POB 7098, Tel-Aviv; tel. 3-6953256; fax 3-6919681; f. 1929; monthly; Hebrew; literature and culture; publ. by Hebrew Writers Asscn; Editors ASHER REICH, AZRIEL KAUFMAN; circ. 2,500.

News from Within: POB 31417, Jerusalem 91313; tel. 2-6241159; fax 2-6253151; e-mail bryan@alt-info.org; internet www.alternativenews.org; monthly; joint Israeli-Palestinian publ; political, economic, social and cultural; publ. by the Alternative Information Centre.

PC Plus: PC Media, POB 11438, 13 Yad Harutzim St, Tel-Aviv 61114; tel. 3-7330733; fax 3-7330770; e-mail tigerlove@pc.co.il; internet www.pc.co.il; f. 1992; monthly; Hebrew; information on personal computers; CEO and Man. Editor DAHLIA PELED; CEO and Editor-in-Chief PELI PELED; circ. 23,000.

Proche-Orient Chrétien: St Anne's Church, POB 19079, Jerusalem 91190; tel. 2-6281992; fax 2-6280764; e-mail mafrpoc@steanne.org; f. 1951; quarterly on churches and religion in the Middle East; publ. in asscn with St Joseph University, Beirut, Lebanon; French; circ. 1,000.

Terra Santa: POB 14038, Jaffa Gate, Jerusalem 91142; tel. 2-6272692; fax 2-6286417; e-mail cicts@netmedia.net.il; internet www.cicts.org; f. 1973; bi-monthly; publ. by the Christian Information Centre, which is sponsored by the Custody of the Holy Land (the official custodians of the Holy Shrines); Italian, Spanish, French, English and Arabic edns publ. in Jerusalem by the Franciscan Printing Press, German edn in Munich, Maltese edn in Valletta; Dir Fr JERZY KRAJ.

WIZO Review: Women's International Zionist Organization, 38 Sderot David Hamelech Blvd, Tel-Aviv 64237; tel. 3-6923805; fax 3-6923801; e-mail wreview@wizo.org; internet www.wizo.org; f. 1926; English (3 a year); Man. Editor INGRID ROCKBERGER; Asst Editor ZOHAR FRIEDMAN; circ. 6,000.

NEWS AGENCY

Jewish Telegraphic Agency (JTA): Mideast Bureau, Jerusalem Post Bldg, Romema, Jerusalem 91000; tel. 2-610579; fax 2-536635; e-mail info@jta.org; internet www.jta.org; Man. Editor URIEL HEILMAN.

PRESS ASSOCIATIONS

Daily Newspaper Publishers' Asscn of Israel: POB 51202, 74 Petach Tikva Rd, Tel-Aviv 61200; fax 3-5617938; safeguards professional interests and maintains standards, supplies newsprint to dailies; negotiates with trade unions; mems all daily papers; affiliated to International Federation of Newspaper Publishers; Pres. SHABTAI HIMMELFARB; Gen. Sec. BETZALEL EYAL.

Foreign Press Asscn: Beit Sokolov, 4 Kaplan St, Tel-Aviv 64734; tel. 3-6916143; fax 3-6961548; e-mail fpa@netvision.net.il; internet www.fpa.org.il; f. 1957; represents journalists employed by international news orgs who report from Israel, the West Bank and the Gaza Strip; private, non-profit org.; almost 500 mems from 30 countries; Dep. Chair. GWEN ACKERMAN.

Israel Association of Periodical Press (IAPP): 17 Keilat Venezia St, Tel-Aviv 69400; tel. 3-6449851; fax 3-6449852; e-mail iapp@zahav

.net.il; internet www.iapp.co.il; f. 1962; 600 mems; Chair. JOSEPH FRENKEL.

Israel Press Council: Beit Sokolov, 4 Kaplan St, Tel-Aviv; tel. 3-6951437; fax 3-6951145; e-mail moaza@m-i.org.il; internet www.m-i.org.il; f. 1963; deals with matters of common interest to the Press such as drafting the code of professional ethics, which is binding on all journalists; Chair. ORNA LIN; Gen. Sec. AVI WEINBERG.

National Federation of Israeli Journalists (NFIJ): POB 585, 37 Hillet St, Jerusalem 91004; tel. 2-6254351; fax 3-6254353; e-mail office@jaj.org.il; internet www.jaj.org.il; affiliated to International Federation of Journalists; Chair. AHIA HIKA GINOSAR.

Publishers

Achiasaf Publishing House Ltd: 3, Bney Binyamin St, Netanya 4201959; tel. 9-8851390; fax 9-8851391; e-mail info@achiasaf.co.il; internet www.achiasaf.co.il; f. 1937; general; Pres. MATAN ACHIASAF.

Am Oved Publishers Ltd: 22 Mazeh St, Tel-Aviv 65213; tel. 3-6288500; fax 3-6298911; e-mail info@am-oved.co.il; internet www.am-oved.co.il; f. 1942; fiction, non-fiction, reference books, school and university textbooks, children's books, poetry, classics, science fiction; Man. Dir YAAKOV BREY.

Amihai Publishing House Ltd: POB 8448, 19 Yad Harutzim St, Netanya Darom 42505; tel. 9-8859099; fax 9-8853464; e-mail ami1000@bezeqint.net; internet www.amichaibooks.co.il; f. 1948; fiction, general science, linguistics, languages, arts; Dir ITZHAK ORON.

Arabic Publishing House: 93 Arlozorof St, Tel-Aviv; tel. 3-6921674; f. 1960; established by the Histadrut; periodicals and books; Gen. Man. GHASSAN MUKLASHI.

Ariel Publishing House: POB 3328, Jerusalem 91033; tel. 2-6434540; fax 2-6436164; e-mail elysch@netvision.net.il; internet www.arielp.co.il; f. 1976; history, archaeology, religion, geography, folklore; CEO ELY SCHILLER.

Astrolog Publishing House: POB 1231, Hod Hasharon 45111; tel. 3-9190957; fax 3-9190958; e-mail abooks@netvision.net.il; f. 1994; general non-fiction, religion, alternative medicine; Man. Dir SARA BEN-MORDECHAI.

Carta, The Israel Map and Publishing Co Ltd: POB 2500, 18 Ha'uman St, Industrial Area, Talpiot, Jerusalem 91024; tel. 2-6783355; fax 2-6782373; e-mail carta@carta.co.il; internet www.carta-jerusalem.com; f. 1958; the principal cartographic publr; Pres. and CEO SHAY HAUSMAN.

Eliner Library—The World Zionist Organization: POB 10615, Jerusalem 91104; tel. 2-6202137; fax 2-6202792; e-mail eliner@wzo.org.il; internet www.eliner.co.il; f. 1945; education, Jewish philosophy, studies in the Bible, children's books publ. in Hebrew, English, French, Spanish, German, Swedish and Portuguese, Hebrew teaching material; Dir of Publication Division ORIT AVITAL.

Gefen Publishing House Ltd: 6 Hatzvi St, Jerusalem 94386; tel. 2-5380247; fax 2-5388423; e-mail info@gefenpublishing.com; internet www.israelbooks.com; f. 1981; largest publr of English-language books in Israel; also publishes wide range of fiction and non-fiction; Publr ILAN GREENFIELD.

Globes Publishers: POB 5126, Rishon le Zion 75150; tel. 3-9538611; fax 3-9525971; e-mail mailbox@globes.co.il; internet www.globes.co.il; business, finance, technology, law, marketing; CEO EITAN MADMON; Editor-in-Chief HAGGAI GOLAN.

Gvanim: POB 11138, 29 Bar-Kochba St, Tel-Aviv 61111; tel. 3-5281044; fax 3-6202032; e-mail traklinm@zahav.net.il; internet gvanim-books.com; f. 1992; poetry, belles lettres, fiction; Man. Dir MARITZA ROSMAN.

Hakibbutz Hameuchad—Sifriat Poalim Publishing Group: POB 1432, Bnei Brak, Tel-Aviv 51114; tel. 3-5785810; fax 3-5785811; e-mail info@kibutz-poalim.co.il; internet www.kibutz-poalim.co.il; f. 1939 as Hakibbutz Hameuchad Publishing House Ltd; subsequently merged with Sifriat Poalim; general; Gen. Dir UZI SHAVIT.

Hanitzotz Publishing House: POB 35252, Tel-Aviv 61351; tel. 3-5373268; fax 3-5373269; e-mail oda@netvision.net.il; internet www.hanitzotz.com; f. 1985; 'progressive' booklets and publications, incl. the periodicals *Challenge* (in English), *Etgar* (Hebrew), and *Al-Sabar* (Arabic); also produces documentary films on human and workers' rights; Contact RONI BEN EFRAT.

The Hebrew University Magnes Press: The Hebrew University, The Sherman Bldg for Research Management, POB 39099, Givat Ram, Jerusalem 91390; tel. 2-6586656; fax 2-5660341; e-mail info@magnespress.co.il; internet www.magnespress.co.il; f. 1929; academic books and journals on many subjects, incl. biblical, classical and Jewish studies, social sciences, language, literature, art, history and geography; Dir HAI TSABAR.

Hed Arzi (Ma'ariv) Publishing Ltd: 3A Yoni Netanyahu St, Or-Yehuda, Tel-Aviv 60376; tel. 3-5383333; fax 3-6343205; e-mail shimoni@hed-arzi.co.il; f. 1954 as Sifriat-Ma'ariv Ltd; later known as Ma'ariv Book Guild Ltd; general; Man. Dir ELI SHIMONI.

Hod-Ami—Computer Books Ltd: POB 6108, Herzliya 46160; tel. 9-9564716; fax 9-9571582; e-mail info@hod-ami.co.il; internet www.hod-ami.co.il; f. 1984; information technology, management; translations from English into Hebrew and Arabic; CEO ITZHAK AMIHUD.

Jerusalem Center for Public Affairs: 13 Tel Hai St, Jerusalem 92107; tel. 2-5619281; fax 2-5619112; e-mail info@jcpa.org; internet www.jcpa.org; f. 1976; Jewish political tradition; publishes *Jerusalem Viewpoints*, *Jerusalem Issue Brief*, *Jewish Political Studies Review* and other books; Pres. DORE GOLD; Chair. Dr MANFRED GERSTENFELD.

The Jerusalem Publishing House: 2B HaGai St, Beit Hakerem, Jerusalem 96262; tel. 2-6537966; fax 2-6537988; e-mail mh2@017.net.il; internet jerpub.com; f. 1966; biblical research, history, encyclopedias, archaeology, arts of the Holy Land, cookbooks, guidebooks, economics, politics; CEO MOSHE HELLER; Man. Editor RACHEL GILON.

Jewish History Publications (Israel 1961) Ltd: POB 1232, 29 Jabotinsky St, Jerusalem 92141; tel. 2-5632310; f. 1961; encyclopedias, World History of the Jewish People series.

Keter Publishing House Ltd: POB 7145, Givat Shaul B, Jerusalem 91071; tel. 2-6557822; fax 2-6536811; e-mail info@keterbooks.co.il; internet www.keterbooks.co.il; f. 1959; original and translated works of fiction, encyclopedias, non-fiction, guidebooks and children's books; publishing imprints: Israel Program for Scientific Translations, Keter Books, Domino, Shikmona, Encyclopedia Judaica; Man. Dir YIPHTACH DEKEL.

Kinneret Zmora-Bitan Dvir Publishing House: 10 Hataasiya St, Or-Yehuda 60210; tel. 3-6344977; fax 3-6340953; internet www.kinbooks.co.il; f. 2002 following merger between Kinneret and Zmora Bitan-Dvir publishing houses; adult and children's fiction and non-fiction, history, science, sociology, psychology, current affairs and politics, dictionaries, architecture, travel; Man. Dir YORAM ROZ.

MAP-Mapping and Publishing Ltd (Tel-Aviv Books): POB 56024, 17 Tchernikhovski St, Tel-Aviv 61560; tel. 3-6210500; fax 3-5257725; e-mail info@mapa.co.il; internet www.mapa.co.il; f. 1985; maps, atlases, travel guides, textbooks, reference books; Man. Dir HEZI LEVY.

Ministry of Defence Publishing House: POB 916, Yaakov Dori Rd, Kiryat Ono 55108; tel. 3-7380738; fax 3-7380645; e-mail minuy@inter.net.il; f. 1958; military literature, Judaism, history and geography of Israel; Dir JOSEPH PERLOVITZ.

M. Mizrachi Publishing House Ltd: 67 Levinsky St, Tel-Aviv 66855; tel. 3-6870936; fax 3-6888185; e-mail mizrahi.co@jmail.com; f. 1960; children's books, fiction, history, medicine, science; Dirs MEIR MIZRACHI, ISRAEL MIZRACHI.

Mosad Harav Kook: POB 642, 1 Maimon St, Jerusalem 91006; tel. 2-6526231; fax 2-6526968; e-mail mosad-haravkook@neto.bezeqint.net; f. 1937; editions of classical works, Torah and Jewish studies; Dir Rabbi YOSEF MOVSHOVITZ.

Otsar Hamoreh: c/o Israel Teachers Union, 8 Ben Saruk, Tel-Aviv 62969; tel. 3-6922983; fax 3-6922988; f. 1951; educational; Man. Dir JOSEPH SALOMAN.

People and Computers Ltd: POB 11438, 53 Derech Asholom St, Givatayim 53454; tel. 3-7330733; fax 3-7330703; e-mail info@pc.co.il; internet www.pc.co.il; information technology; Editor-in-Chief and CEO PELI PELED; Man. Editor and CEO DAHLIA PELED.

Rodney Franklin Agency: POB 37727, 53 Mazeh St, Tel-Aviv 65789; tel. 3-5600724; fax 3-5600479; e-mail rodneyf@netvision.net.il; internet www.rodneyagency.com; f. 1974; exclusive representative of various British, other European and US publrs; e-marketing services for academic and professional journal publrs in 15 countries; Dir RODNEY FRANKLIN.

Rubin Mass Ltd: POB 990, 7 Ha-Ayin-Het St, Jerusalem 91009; tel. 2-6277863; fax 2-6277864; e-mail rmass@barak.net.il; internet www.rubinmass.com; f. 1927; Hebraica, Judaica, export of all Israeli books and periodicals; Man. OREN MASS.

Schocken Publishing House Ltd: POB 57188, 24 Nathan Yelin Mor St, Tel-Aviv 61571; tel. 3-5610130; fax 3-5622668; e-mail gila_g@haaretz.co.il; internet www.schocken.co.il; f. 1938; general; Publr RACHELI EDELMAN.

Shalem Press: 3 Ha'askan St, Jerusalem 9378010; tel. 2-5605586; fax 2-5605565; e-mail shalempress@shalem.ac.il; internet www.shalempress.co.il; f. 1994; economics, political science, history, philosophy, cultural issues; Pres. DANIEL POLISAR.

Sinai Publishing: 24 Rambam St, Tel-Aviv 65813; tel. 3-5163672; fax 3-5176783; e-mail sinaipub@zahav.net.il; internet www.sinaibooks.com; f. 1853; Hebrew books and religious articles; Dir MOSHE SCHLESINGER.

Steinhart-Katzir: POB 8333, Netanya 42505; tel. 9-8854770; fax 9-8854771; e-mail mail@haolam.co.il; internet www.haolam.co.il; f. 1991; travel; Man. Dir OHAD SHARAV.

Tcherikover Publishers Ltd: 12 Hasharon St, Tel-Aviv 66185; tel. 3-6396099; fax 3-6874729; e-mail barkay@inter.net.il; education, psychology, economics, psychiatry, literature, literary criticism, essays, history, geography, criminology, art, languages, management; Man. Editor S. TCHERIKOVER.

Yachdav United Publishers Co Ltd: POB 20123, 29 Carlebach St, Tel-Aviv 67132; tel. 3-5614121; fax 3-5611996; e-mail info@tbpai.co.il; f. 1960; educational; Chair. EPHRAIM BEN-DOR; Exec. Dir AMNON BEN-SHMUEL.

Yavneh Publishing House Ltd: POB 4781, 4 Mazeh St, Tel-Aviv 65213; tel. 3-6297856; fax 3-6293638; e-mail publishing@yavneh.co.il; internet www.yavneh.co.il; f. 1932; general; Man. Dir NIRA PREISKEL.

Yedioth Ahronoth Books: POB 53494, 10 Kehilat Venezia, Tel-Aviv 61534; tel. 3-7683333; fax 3-7683300; e-mail info@ybook.co.il; internet www.ybook.co.il; f. 1952; non-fiction, politics, Judaism, health, music, dance, fiction, education; Man. Dir DOV EICHENWALD.

S. Zack: 31 Beit Hadfus St, Jerusalem 95483; tel. 2-6537760; fax 2-6514005; e-mail zackmt@bezeqint.net; internet www.zack.co.il; f. 1935; fiction, science, philosophy, Judaism, children's books, educational and reference books, dictionaries, languages; Dir MICHAEL ZACK.

PUBLISHERS' ASSOCIATION

The Book Publishers' Association of Israel: POB 20123, 29 Carlebach St, Tel-Aviv 67132; tel. 3-5614121; fax 3-5611996; e-mail info@tbpai.co.il; internet www.tbpai.co.il; f. 1939; mems: 84 publishing firms; Chair. YARON SADAN; Man. Dir AMNON BEN-SHMUEL.

Broadcasting and Communications

TELECOMMUNICATIONS

013 Netvision: Omega Center, Matam, Haifa 3190501; tel. 4-8560660; fax 4-5201960; e-mail service@netvision013.net.il; internet www.013netvision.net.il; f. 2007 after merger with 013 Barak and GlobCall; CEO RAVIT BARNIV.

Bezeq—The Israel Telecommunication Corpn Ltd: Azrieli Center 2, Tel-Aviv 61620; tel. 3-6262600; fax 3-6262609; e-mail dover@bezeq.co.il; internet www.bezeq.co.il; f. 1984; privatized in May 2005; launched own cellular network, Pelephone Communications Ltd, in 1986; total assets NIS 15,156m. (Dec. 2007); CEO STELLA HANDLER; Chair. SHAUL ELOVITCH.

Pelephone Communications Ltd: 33 Hagvura St, Givatayim, Tel-Aviv 53483; tel. 3-5728881; fax 3-5728111; internet www.pelephone.co.il; f. 1986; launched Esc brand in 2003; 2.85m. subscribers (2010); CEO GIL SHARON.

Cellcom Israel: POB 4060, 10 Hagavish St, Netanya 42140; tel. 529990052 (mobile); fax 529989700; e-mail investors@cellcom.co.il; internet www.cellcom.co.il; f. 1994; mobile telecommunications operator; 3.19m. subscribers (Dec. 2012); Chair. AMI EREL; Pres. and CEO NIR SZTERN.

ECI Telecom Ltd: POB 3038, 30 Hasivim St, Petach-Tikva, Tel-Aviv 49133; tel. 3-9266555; fax 3-9266500; e-mail web.inquiries@ecitele.com; internet www.ecitele.com; f. 1961; Pres. and CEO DARRYL EDWARDS.

MagicJack VocalTec Ltd (Vocal Tec): 14 Beni Ga'on St, Bldg B2-Rakefet, Netanya 42504; tel. 9-9703888; fax 9-9558175; e-mail info@vocaltec.com; internet www.vocaltec.com; suppliers of VOIP software; Chair. DONALD A. BURNS; Pres. and CEO GERALD VENTO.

Partner Communications Co Ltd: POB 435, 8 Amal St, Afeq Industrial Park, Rosh Ha'ayin 48103; tel. 54-7814888; fax 54-7814999; e-mail deborah.margalit@orange.co.il; internet www.orange.co.il; f. 1999; provides mobile telecommunications and Wi-Fi internet services under the Orange brand name; represents about one-third of the mobile-cellular market in Israel; Chair. SHLOMO RODAV; CEO HAIM ROMANO.

BROADCASTING

In 1986 the Government approved the establishment of a commercial radio and television network to be run in competition with the state system.

Radio

Israel Broadcasting Authority (IBA) (Radio): POB 28080, 161 Jaffa Rd, Jerusalem 94342; tel. 2-5015555; e-mail dover@iba.org.il; internet www.iba.org.il; f. 1948; state-owned station in Jerusalem with additional studios in Tel-Aviv and Haifa; broadcasts six programmes for local and overseas listeners on medium-wave, shortwave and VHF/FM in 16 languages: Hebrew, Arabic, English, Yiddish, Ladino, Romanian, Hungarian, Moghrabi, Farsi, French, Russian, Bukharian, Georgian, Portuguese, Spanish and Amharic; Chair. AMIR GILAT; Dir-Gen. YONI BEN-MENACHEM.

Galei Zahal: MPOB, Zahal; tel. 3-5126666; fax 3-5126760; e-mail radio@galatz.co.il; internet glz.co.il; f. 1950; Israel Defence Force broadcasting station, Tel-Aviv, with studios in Jerusalem; broadcasts 24-hour news, current affairs, music and cultural programmes in Hebrew on FM, medium and short waves; Dir YARON DEKEL.

Kol Israel (The Voice of Israel): POB 1082, 21 Heleni Hamalka, Jerusalem 91010; tel. 1-599509510; e-mail radiodirector@iba.org.il; internet www.iba.org.il/kolisrael; broadcasts music, news and multilingual programmes within Israel and overseas on short wave, AM and FM stereo, in 15 languages, incl. Hebrew, Arabic, French, English, Spanish, Ladino, Russian, Yiddish, Romanian, Hungarian, Amharic and Georgian; Dir SHMUEL BEN-ZVI; Gen. Dir YONI BEN-MENACHEM.

Television

Israel Broadcasting Authority (IBA) (Television): 161 Jaffa Rd, Jerusalem; tel. 2-5301333; fax 2-292944; internet www.iba.org.il; broadcasts began in 1968; station in Jerusalem with additional studios in Tel-Aviv; one colour network (VHF with UHF available in all areas); one satellite channel; broadcasts in Hebrew, Arabic and English; Chair. AMIR GILAT; Dir-Gen. YONI BEN-MENACHEM.

The Council of Cable TV and Satellite Broadcasting: 23 Jaffa Rd, Jerusalem 91999; tel. 2-6702210; fax 2-6702273; e-mail inbard@moc.gov.il; f. 1982; Chair. NATI SCHUBERT.

Israel Educational Television: Ministry of Education, 14 Klausner St, Tel-Aviv 69011; tel. 3-646227; fax 3-6466164; e-mail webmaster@ietv.gov.il; internet www.23tv.co.il; f. 1966 by Hanadiv (Rothschild Memorial Group) as Instructional Television Trust; began transmission in 1966; school programmes form an integral part of the syllabus in a wide range of subjects; also adult education; Dir-Gen. ELDAD KOBLENTZ.

Second Authority for Television and Radio: POB 3445, 20 Beit Hadfus St, Jerusalem 95464; tel. 2-6556222; fax 2-6556287; e-mail rashut@rashut2.org.il; internet www.rashut2.org.il; f. 1991; responsible for providing broadcasts through two principal television channels, Channel 2 and Channel 10, and some 14 radio stations; Chair. ILAN AVISHAR.

Finance

(cap. = capital; res = reserves; dep. = deposits; m. = million; brs = branches; amounts in shekels)

BANKING

Central Bank

Bank of Israel: POB 780, Bank of Israel Bldg, Kiryat Ben-Gurion, Jerusalem 91007; tel. 2-6552211; fax 2-6528805; e-mail webmaster@bankisrael.gov.il; internet www.bankisrael.gov.il; f. 1954 as Cen. Bank of the State of Israel; cap. 60m., res 3,925m., dep. 212,688m. (Dec. 2009); Gov. Dr KARNIT FLUG; 1 br.

Principal Commercial Banks

Arab-Israel Bank Ltd: POB 207, 48 Bar Yehuda St, Tel Hanan, Nesher 36601; tel. 4-8205222; fax 4-8205250; e-mail aravi@bll.co.il; internet www.bank-aravi-israeli.co.il; res 315m., dep. 4,948m., total assets 5,761m. (Dec. 2011); subsidiary of Bank Leumi le-Israel BM; Chair. SHMUEL ZUSMAN; Gen. Man. ITZHAK EYAL.

Bank Hapoalim: 50 Rothschild Blvd, Tel-Aviv 61000; tel. 3-5673333; fax 3-5607028; internet www.bankhapoalim.co.il; f. 1921 as Workers' Bank; name changed as above 1961; mergers into the above: American-Israel Bank in 1999, Maritime Bank of Israel in 2003, Mishkan-Hapoalim Mortgage Bank and Israel Continental Bank in 2004; privatized in June 2000; cap. 8,010m., res 851m., dep. 278,055m. (Dec. 2012); Chair. YAIR SEROUSSI; Pres. and CEO ZION KENAN; 325 brs in Israel and 10 brs abroad.

Bank of Jerusalem Ltd: POB 2255, 2 Herbert Samuel St, Jerusalem 91022; tel. 2-6706018; fax 2-6234043; e-mail webmaster@bankjerusalem.co.il; internet www.bankjerusalem.co.il; private bank; cap. 127m., res 100m., dep. 9,877m. (Dec. 2012); Chair. JONATHAN IRONI; CEO PAZ URI; 14 brs.

Bank Leumi le-Israel BM: 34 Yehuda Halevi St, Tel-Aviv 65546; tel. 3-5148111; fax 3-5148656; e-mail pniot@bll.co.il; internet www.bankleumi.co.il; f. 1902 as Anglo-Palestine Co; renamed Anglo-Palestine Bank 1930; reincorporated as above 1951; 34.78% state-owned; cap. 7,059m., res 1,566m., dep. 294,062m. (Dec. 2012); Chair. DAVID BRODET; 242 brs in Israel and 2 abroad.

Bank Otsar Ha-Hayal Ltd: POB 52136, 11 Menachem Begin St, Ramat-Gan 52136; tel. 3-7556000; fax 3-7556007; e-mail ozfrndep@netvision.net.il; internet www.bankotsar.co.il; f. 1946; 68% owned by First Int. Bank of Israel, 24% by Hever Veterans & Pensions Ltd, 8% by Provident Fund of the Employees of IAILTD; dep. 11,214.8m., total assets 13,638m. (Dec. 2008); Chair. SMADAR BARBER-TSADIK; Gen. Man. ISRAEL TRAU.

First International Bank of Israel Ltd (FIBI): 42 Rothschild Blvd, Tel-Aviv 66883; tel. 3-5196111; fax 3-5100316; e-mail zucker.d@fibi.co.il; internet www.fibi.co.il; f. 1972 by merger between Foreign Trade Bank Ltd and Export Bank Ltd; cap. 927m., res −16m., dep. 82,519m. (Dec. 2010); Chair. RONI HIZKIYAHU; CEO SMADAR BARBER-TSADIK; 182 brs in Israel and abroad (incl. subsidiaries).

Israel Discount Bank Ltd: POB 456, 27–31 Yehuda Halevi St, Tel-Aviv 61003; tel. 3-5145555; fax 3-5146954; e-mail intidb@discountbank.co.il; internet www.discountbank.co.il; f. 1935; name changed as above in 1957; cap. 665m., res 3,970m., dep. 156,660m., total assets 200,880m. (Dec. 2012); Chair. Dr JOSEPH BACHAR; Pres. and CEO LILACH ASHER-TOPILSKY; 126 brs in Israel and abroad.

Mercantile Discount Bank Ltd: POB 1292, 103 Allenby Rd, Tel-Aviv 61012; tel. 3-710550; fax 3-7105532; e-mail fec@mdb.co.il; internet www.mercantile.co.il; f. 1971 as Barclays Discount Bank Ltd, to take over (from Jan. 1972) the Israel brs of Barclays Bank Int. Ltd; Barclays Bank PLC, one of the joint owners, sold its total shareholding to the remaining owner, Israel Discount Bank Ltd, in Feb. 1993, and name changed as above that April; Mercantile Bank of Israel Ltd became branch of the above in March 1997; cap. 51m., res 246m., dep. 22,558m. (Dec. 2012); Chair. Dr JOSEPH BACHAR; Pres. and CEO REUVEN SPIEGEL; 66 brs.

Mizrahi Tefahot Bank Ltd: POB 3450, 7 Jabotinsky St, Ramat-Gan 52136; tel. 3-7559468; fax 3-6234819; e-mail lernerh@umtb.co.il; internet www.mizrahi-tefahot.co.il; f. 1923 as Mizrahi Bank Ltd; mergers into the above: Hapoel Hamizrahi Bank Ltd, as United Mizrahi Bank Ltd; Finance and Trade Bank Ltd in 1990; Tefahot Israel Mortgage Bank Ltd in 2005, when name changed as above; Adanim Mortgage Bank merged into above bank in 2009; cap. 2,058m., res 63m., dep. 130,300m. (Dec. 2012); Chair. MOSHE VIDMAN; Pres. and CEO ELDAD FRESHER; 166 brs.

UBank Ltd: POB 677, 38 Rothschild Blvd, Tel-Aviv 61006; tel. 3-5645645; fax 3-5645285; e-mail gsteiger@u-bank.net; internet www.u-bank.net; f. 1934 as Palestine Credit Utility Bank Ltd; renamed Israel General Bank Ltd 1964; ownership transferred to Investec Bank Ltd (South Africa) 1996; name changed to Investec Clali Bank Ltd 1999, and to Investec Bank (Israel) Ltd 2001; control of bank transferred to First Int. Bank of Israel 2004 and name changed as above 2005; cap. 60m., res 346m., dep. 6,684m. (Dec. 2012); Chair. YORAM SIRKIS; CEO BEDNY RON; 8 brs.

Union Bank of Israel Ltd: 6–8 Ahuzat Bayit St, Tel-Aviv 65143; tel. 3-5191222; fax 3-5191344; e-mail info@ubi.co.il; internet www.ubi.co.il; f. 1951; cap. 952m., res 100m., dep. 32,048m. (Dec. 2012); Chair. ZEEV ABELES; Pres. and CEO HAIM FREILICHMAN; 35 brs.

Mortgage Banks

Discount Mortgage Bank Ltd: POB 2844, 16–18 Simtat Beit Hashoeva, Tel-Aviv 61027; tel. 3-5643311; fax 3-5661704; e-mail contact@discountbank.net; internet www.discountbank.net; f. 1959; subsidiary of Israel Discount Bank Ltd; total assets 10,355m. (Dec. 2005); Chair. SHLOMO ZOHAR; Pres. and CEO GIORA OFFER; 3 brs.

Leumi Mortgage Bank Ltd: POB 69, 31–37 Montefiore St, Tel-Aviv 65201; tel. 3-5648444; fax 3-5648334; f. 1921 as Gen. Mortgage Bank Ltd; subsidiary of Bank Leumi le-Israel BM; res 2,567m., dep. 48,605m., total assets 56,532m. (Dec. 2011); Chair. AVI ZELDMAN; Gen. Man. R. ZABAG; 9 brs.

STOCK EXCHANGE

The Tel-Aviv Stock Exchange: 54 Ahad Ha'am St, Tel-Aviv 65202; tel. 3-5677411; fax 3-5105379; e-mail info@tase.co.il; internet tase.co.il; f. 1953; Chair. SAUL BRONFELD; CEO ESTER LEVANON.

INSURANCE

The Israel Insurance Asscn lists 14 member companies; a selection of these are listed below, as are some non-members.

Clal Insurance Enterprise Holdings Ltd: POB 326, 46 Petach Tikva Rd, Tel-Aviv 66184; tel. 3-6387777; fax 3-6387676; e-mail avigdork@clal-ins.co.il; internet www.clalbit.co.il; f. 1962; 55% owned by IDB Group, 10% by Bank Hapoalim and 35% by the public; insurance, pensions and finance; Chair. KAPLAN AVIGDOR.

Dikla Insurance Co Ltd: 1 Ben Gurion Rd, BSR-2 Tower, Bnei Brak 51201; tel. 3-6145555; fax 3-6145566; internet www.dikla.co.il; f. 1976; health and long-term care insurance; Chair. YAIR HAMBURGER.

Eliahu Insurance Co Ltd: 2 Ibn Gvirol St, Tel-Aviv 64077; tel. 3-6920911; fax 3-6952117; e-mail gad.nussbaum@eliahu.com; internet www.eliahu.co.il; f. 1966; Chair. SHLOMO ELIAHU; Man. Dir OFER ELIAHU.

Harel Insurance Investments and Financial Services Ltd: Tel-Aviv; tel. 3-7547000; e-mail infonet@harel-group.co.il; internet www.harel-group.co.il; f. 1935 as Hamishmar Insurance Service; Harel est. 1975, became Harel Hamishmar Investments Ltd 1982, Harel Insurance Investments Ltd 1998 and current name adopted 2007; 39.9% owned by Hamburger family, 20.2% by Sampoerna Capital; Chair. GIDEON HAMBURGER.

Menorah Mivtachim Insurance Co Ltd: POB 927, 15 Allenby St, Tel-Aviv 61008; tel. 3-7107777; fax 3-7107402; e-mail anat-by@bezeqint.net; internet www.menoramivt.co.il; f. 1935; Chair. MENACHEM GUREWITZ; Gen. Man. SHABTAI ENGEL.

Migdal Insurance Co Ltd: POB 37633, 26 Sa'adiya Ga'on St, Tel-Aviv 67135; tel. 3-5637637; fax 3-9295189; e-mail marketing@migdal-group.co.il; internet www.migdal.co.il; 70% owned by Generali Group; 10% by Bank Leumi and 20% by the public; f. 1934; Chair. AHARON FOGEL; CEO YONEL COHEN.

Phoenix Insurance Co Ltd: 53 Derech Hashalom St, Givatayim 53454; tel. 3-7332222; fax 3-5735151; e-mail ir@fnx.co.il; internet www.fnx.co.il; f. 1949; controlled by Delek Group; Pres. and CEO EYAL LAPIDOT.

Trade and Industry

DEVELOPMENT ORGANIZATIONS

Galilee Development Authority: POB 2511, Acco 24316; tel. 4-9552426; fax 4-9552440; e-mail judith@galil.gov.il; internet www.galilee.gov.il; f. 1993; statutory authority responsible for the social and economic devt of the Galilee region; Man. Dir MOSHE DAVIDOVITZ.

Jerusalem Development Authority (JDA): 2 Safra Sq., Jerusalem 91322; tel. 2-6297627; e-mail moty@jda.gov.il; internet www.jda.gov.il; f. 1988; statutory authority responsible for the economic devt of Jerusalem; CEO MOTY HAZAN.

Negev Development Authority: Negev; e-mail negev_de@netvision.net.il; internet www.negev.co.il; f. 1991; statutory authority responsible for the economic and social devt of the Negev region, and co-ordination between govt offices; Chair SHMUEL RIFMAN.

CHAMBERS OF COMMERCE

Federation of Israeli Chambers of Commerce: POB 20027, 84 Ha' Hashmonaim St, Tel-Aviv 67132; tel. 3-5631020; fax 3-5619027; e-mail chamber@chamber.org.il; internet www.chamber.org.il; co-ordinates the Tel-Aviv, Jerusalem, Haifa, Nazareth and Beersheba Chambers of Commerce; Pres. URIEL LYNN.

Israel Federation of Bi-National Chambers of Commerce and Industry with and in Israel: POB 50196, 29 Hamered St, Tel-Aviv 61500; tel. 3-5177737; fax 3-5142881; e-mail felixk@export.gov.il; Chair. JAIME ARON; Man. Dir FELIX KIPPER.

Beersheba Chamber of Commerce: POB 5278, 7 Hamuktar St, Beersheba 84152; tel. 8-6234222; fax 8-6234899; e-mail chamber7@zahav.net.il; internet www.negev-chamber.org.il.

Chamber of Commerce and Industry of Haifa and the North: POB 33176, 53 Ha'atzmaut Rd, Haifa 31331; tel. 4-8302100; fax 4-8645428; e-mail main@haifachamber.org.il; internet www.haifachamber.com; f. 1921; 850 mems; Pres. GAD SCHAFFER; Man. Dir DOV MAROM.

Israel-British Chamber of Commerce: POB 50321, Industry House, 13th Floor, 29 Hamered St, Tel-Aviv 61502; tel. 3-5109424; fax 3-5109540; e-mail info@ibcc.co.il; internet www.ibcc.co.il; f. 1951; 350 mems; annual bilateral trade of more than US $3,000m. Chair. LEN JUDES; Exec. Dir FELIX KIPPER.

Jerusalem Chamber of Commerce: POB 2083, Jerusalem 91020; tel. 2-6254333; fax 2-6254335; e-mail jerccom@inter.net.il; internet www.jerccom.co.il; f. 1908; 200 mems; Pres. NAHUM WISSMANN.

INDUSTRIAL AND TRADE ASSOCIATIONS

Agricultural Export Co (AGREXCO): POB 2061, 121 Ha'Hashmonaim St, Tel-Aviv 61206; tel. 3-5630940; fax 3-5630988; e-mail info@agrexco.com; internet www.agrexco.co.il; state-owned agricultural marketing org.; CEO SHLOMO TIROSH.

The Centre for International Agricultural Development Cooperation (CINADCO): POB 30, Beit Dagan 50250; tel. 3-9485760; fax 3-9485761; e-mail cinadco@moag.gov.il; shares agricultural experience through the integration of research and project devt; runs specialized training courses, advisory missions and feasibility projects in Israel and abroad, incl. those in co-operation with developing countries; Dir YACOV POLEG.

Citrus Marketing Board of Israel: POB 54, Beit Dagan 50280; tel. 3-9595654; fax 3-9501495; e-mail info@jaffa.co.il; internet www.jaffa.co.il; f. 1941; central co-ordinating body of citrus growers and exporters in Israel; represents the citrus industry in international orgs; licenses private exporters; controls the quality of fruit; has responsibility for Jaffa trademarks; mounts advertising and promotion campaigns for Jaffa citrus fruit worldwide; carries out research and devt of new varieties of citrus and environmentally friendly fruit.

Fruit Board of Israel: POB 20117, 119 Rehov Ha' Hashmonaim, Tel-Aviv 61200; tel. 3-5632929; fax 3-5614672; e-mail fruits@fruit.org.il; internet www.fruit.org.il.

Israel Dairy Board (IDB): POB 97, 4 Derech Hahoresh, Yahud 56100; tel. 3-9564750; fax 3-9564766; e-mail office@milk.org.il; internet www.israeldairy.com; regulates dairy-farming and the dairy industry; implements govt policy on the planning of milk production and marketing; Man. Dir SHYKE DRORI.

Israel Diamond Exchange Ltd: 3 Jabotinsky Rd, Ramat-Gan 52130; tel. 3-5760300; fax 3-5750652; e-mail ella@isde.co.il; internet www.isde.co.il; f. 1937; production, export, import and finance facilities; exports: polished diamonds US $6,610m., rough diamonds $2,701m. (2006); Pres. and Chair. AVI PAZ; Man. Dir YAIR COHEN-PRIVA.

Israel Export and International Co-operation Institute: POB 50084, 29 Hamered St, Tel-Aviv 68125; tel. 3-5142900; fax 3-5162810; e-mail galit@export.gov.il; internet www.export.gov.il; f. 1958; jt venture between the state and private sectors; Dir-Gen. AVI HEFETZ.

The Israeli Cotton Board: POB 384, Herzlia B 46103; tel. 9-9604000; fax 9-9604030; e-mail cotton@cotton.co.il; internet www.cotton.co.il; f. 1956 as the Israel Cotton Production and Marketing Board.

Kibbutz Industries' Asscn: POB 40012, 13 Leonardo da Vinci St, Tel-Aviv 61400; tel. 3-6955413; fax 3-6951464; e-mail kia@kia.co.il; internet www.kia.co.il; f. 1962; liaison office for marketing and export of the goods produced by Israel's kibbutzim; Chair. JONATHAN MELAMED; Man. Dir AMOS RABIN.

Manufacturers' Assen of Israel: POB 50022, Industry House, 29 Hamered St, Tel-Aviv 61500; tel. 3-5198832; fax 3-5103154; e-mail leor@industry.org.il; internet www.industry.org.il; 1,700 mem. enterprises employing nearly 85% of industrial workers in Israel; Dir LEOR APPELBAUM; Pres. SHRAGA BROSH.

National Federation of Israeli Journalists: POB 585, Beit Agron, 37 Hillet St, Jerusalem 91004; tel. 2-6254351; fax 3-6254353; e-mail office@jaj.org.il; Chair. AHIYA GENOSAR.

Plants Production and Marketing Board: 46 Derech Ha'maca-bim, Rishon le Zion 75359; tel. 3-9595666; fax 3-9502211; e-mail plants@plants.org.il; internet www.plants.org.il.

UTILITIES

Israel Electric Corporation Ltd (IEC): POB 58003, Halechi 17, Bnei-Brak IT School, Haifa 1200; tel. 3-6174944; fax 3-6174922; e-mail ucgia@iec.co.il; internet www.iec.co.il; state-owned; total assets US $21,065m. (Dec. 2009); Chair. YIFTAH RON TAL; Pres. and CEO ELI GLIKMAN.

Mekorot (Israel National Water Co): POB 2012, 9 Lincoln St, Tel-Aviv 61201; tel. 3-6230555; fax 3-6230833; e-mail m-doveret@mekorot.co.il; internet www.mekorot.co.il; f. 1937; state-owned; sales more than US $700m. (2006); Chair. ALEX WIZNITZER; CEO SHIMON BEN HAMO.

The Histadrut

Histadrut (General Federation of Labour in Israel): 93 Arlozorof St, Tel-Aviv 62098; tel. 3-6921511; fax 3-6921512; e-mail avitals@histadrut.org.il; internet www.histadrut.org.il; f. 1920; Chair. OFER EINI.

The Histadrut is the largest labour organization in Israel. It strives to ensure the social security, welfare and rights of workers, and to assist in their professional advancement, while endeavouring to reduce the divisions in Israeli society. Membership of the Histadrut is voluntary, and open to all men and women of 18 years of age and above who live on the earnings of their own labour without exploiting the work of others. These include the self-employed and professionals, as well as housewives, students, pensioners and the unemployed. Workers' interests are protected through a number of occupational and professional unions affiliated to the Histadrut (see below). The organization operates courses for trade unionists and new immigrants, as well as apprenticeship classes. It maintains an Institute for Social and Economic Issues and the International Institute, one of the largest centres of leadership training in Israel, for students from Africa, Asia, Latin America and Eastern Europe, which includes the Levinson Centre for Adult Education and the Jewish-Arab Institute for Regional Co-operation. Attached to the Histadrut is Na'amat, a women's organization which promotes changes in legislation, operates a network of legal service bureaux and vocational training courses, and runs counselling centres for the treatment and prevention of domestic violence; women joining the Histadrut automatically become members of Na'amat.

ORGANIZATION

In 2006 the Histadrut had a membership of 700,000. In addition, over 100,000 young people under 18 years of age belong to the Organization of Working and Student Youth, HaNoar HaOved VeHalomed, a direct affiliate of the Histadrut.

All members take part in elections to the Histadrut Convention (Veida), which elects the General Council (Moetsa) and the Executive Committee (Vaad Hapoel). The latter elects the 41-member Executive Bureau (Vaada Merakezet), which is responsible for day-to-day implementation of policy. The Executive Committee also elects the Secretary-General, who acts as its chairman as well as head of the organization as a whole and chairman of the Executive Bureau. Nearly all political parties are represented on the Histadrut Executive Committee.

The Executive Committee has the following departments: Trade Union, Organization and Labour Councils, Education and Culture, Social Security, Industrial Democracy, Students, Youth and Sports, Consumer Protection, Administration, Finance and International.

TRADE UNION ACTIVITIES

Collective agreements with employers fix wage scales, which are linked with the retail price index; provide for social benefits, including paid sick leave and employers' contributions to sick and pension and provident funds; and regulate dismissals. Dismissal compensation is regulated by law. The Histadrut actively promotes productivity through labour management boards and the National Productivity Institute, and supports incentive pay schemes.

There are unions for the following groups: clerical workers, building workers, teachers, engineers, agricultural workers, technicians, textile workers, printing workers, diamond workers, metal workers, food and bakery workers, wood workers, government employees, seamen, nurses, civilian employees of the armed forces, actors, musicians and variety artists, social workers, watchmen, cinema technicians, institutional and school staff, pharmacy employees, medical laboratory workers, X-ray technicians, physiotherapists, social scientists, microbiologists, psychologists, salaried lawyers, pharmacists, physicians, occupational therapists, truck and taxi drivers, hotel and restaurant workers, workers in Histadrut-owned industry, garment, shoe and leather workers, plastic and rubber workers, editors of periodicals, painters and sculptors, and industrial workers.

Histadrut Trade Union Department: Chair. DANIEL AVI NISSENKORN.

Transport

RAILWAYS

In 2011 Israel's active railway network, including sidings, comprised an estimated 1,079 km of track. Freight traffic consists mainly of grain, phosphates, potash, containers, petroleum and building materials. A rail route serves Haifa and Ashdod ports on the Mediterranean Sea, while a combined rail-road service extends to Eilat port on the Red Sea. Passenger services operate between the main towns: Nahariya, Haifa, Tel-Aviv and Jerusalem. Construction of a high-speed rail link between Jerusalem and Tel-Aviv commenced in 2001. However, owing to technical and financial difficulties, completion of the project was not expected before 2017. The first line of a light railway network intended to ease traffic congestion in Jerusalem was inaugurated in August 2011. The project was a source of considerable controversy owing to the incorporation within the network of disputed Jewish developments in East Jerusalem.

Israel Railways (IR): POB 18085, Central Station, Tel-Aviv 61180; tel. 3-5774000; fax 3-6937443; e-mail israelrailways@tservice.co.il; internet www.rail.co.il; f. 2003 as an ind. govt-owned corpn; prior to that date IR had operated as a unit of the Ports and Railways Authority; CEO BOAZ ZAFRIR.

Underground Railway

Haifa Underground Funicular Railway: 122 Hanassi Ave, Haifa 34633; tel. 4-8376861; fax 4-8376875; e-mail orna@carmelit.com; internet www.carmelit.com; opened 1959; 2 km in operation.

ROADS

In 2010 there were 18,470 km of roads, of which 447 km were motorways, 6,068 km were highways, main or national roads and 11,955 km were other roads.

Ministry of Transport, National Infrastructures and Road Safety: see The Government—Ministries.

Egged Bus Co-operative: POB 43, Egged Bldg, Airport City 70150; tel. 3-9142000; fax 3-9142237; internet www.egged.co.il; f. 1933; operates 2,980 bus routes throughout Israel; Chair. GIDEON MIZRACHI.

SHIPPING

At 31 December 2013 Israel's flag registered fleet consisted of 39 vessels, with a combined aggregate displacement of 273,089 grt, of which one was a fish carrier and three were general cargo ships.

Haifa and Ashdod are the main ports in Israel. The former is a natural harbour, enclosed by two main breakwaters and dredged to 45 ft below mean sea level. Haifa handled 24.0m. metric tons of cargo and 1.4m. 20-ft equivalent units (TEUs) in 2012. The deep-water port at Ashdod was completed in 1965. A new NIS 3,000m. container terminal, Eitan Port, was inaugurated at Ashdod in 2005. Ashdod handled 19.5m. tons of cargo and 1.2m. TEUs in 2012. In 2009 the Government approved proposals to sell minority stakes in the Haifa and Ashdod port companies. The three-stage privatization process commenced in early 2010, with 15% of the shares in each company to be sold via a public offering.

The port of Eilat, Israel's gateway to the Red Sea, has storage facilities for crude petroleum. It is a natural harbour, operated from a wharf. In April 2011 the Government announced its intention fully to privatize the Eilat Port Company. The plan was approved by the Knesset in May 2012.

Port Authority and Companies

Israel Ports Development and Assets Co Ltd (IPC): POB 20121, 74 Menachem Begin Rd, Tel-Aviv 61201; tel. 3-5657060; fax 3-5622281; e-mail dovf@israports.co.il; internet www.israports.co.il; f. 1961 as the Israel Ports Authority (PRA); the IPC was established by legislation in 2005 as part of the Israeli Port Reform Program, whereby the PRA was abolished and replaced by four govt-owned cos: the IPC as owner and developer of port and infrastructure, and three port-operating cos responsible for handling cargo in each of Israel's three commercial seaports; responsible for devt and management of Israel's port infrastructure on behalf of the Govt and carries out some of the largest infrastructure projects in the country; CEO SHLOMO BRIEMAN.

Ashdod Port Co Ltd: POB 9001, Ashdod 77191; tel. 8-8517605; fax 8-8517632; e-mail igalbz@ashdodport.co.il; internet www.ashdodport.co.il; provides full range of freight and passenger services; f. 1965; CEO SHUKI SAGIS.

Haifa Port Co Ltd: Haifa; tel. 4-8518365; fax 4-8672872; internet www.haifaport.co.il; 6.5-km dock, 10.5m–14m draught; f. 1933; CEO MENDI ZALTZMAN.

Principal Shipping Companies

Ofer Shipping Group: POB 15090, 9 Andre Saharov St, Matam Park, Haifa 31905; tel. 4-8610610; fax 4-8501515; e-mail mail@oferg.com; internet www.oferg.com; f. 1956 as shipping agency, Mediterranean Seaways; part of the Ofer Group; runs cargo and container services; Chair. UDI ANGEL.

ZIM Integrated Shipping Services Ltd: POB 1723, 9 Andrei Sakharov St, MATAM Park, Haifa 31016; tel. 4-8652111; fax 4-8652956; e-mail shats.avner@il.zim.com; internet www.zim.co.il; f. 1945; 100% owned by the Israel Corpn; international integrated transportation system providing door-to-door services around the world; operates about 100 vessels; estimated 2m. TEUs of cargo carried in 2006; Chair. of Bd NIR GILAD; Pres. and CEO RAFI DANIELI.

CIVIL AVIATION

The principal airport is Ben-Gurion International Airport, situated about 15 km from the centre of Tel-Aviv. Limited international services also operate from Ovda Airport in the Negev Desert. The busiest domestic airports are located at Eilat, Haifa, Rosh Pina and Sde Dov (Tel-Aviv). In 2011 the Government approved a proposal to build a new international airport with a capacity of 1.5m. passengers at Timna, north of Eilat, at a projected cost of NIS 1,700m. Construction of the airport, which was to replace the existing airports at Eilat and Ovda, was expected to be completed in 2014.

Israel Airports Authority: POB 137, Ben-Gurion Airport, Tel-Aviv 70100; tel. 3-9752386; fax 3-9752387; internet www.iaa.gov.il; f. 1977; Chair. ELI OVADIA.

El Al Israel Airlines Ltd: 32 Ben-Yehuda St, Tel-Aviv; tel. 3-9771111; fax 3-6292312; e-mail customer@elal.co.il; internet www.elal.co.il; f. 1948; over 40% owned by Knafaim-Arkia Holdings Ltd; about 31% state-owned; regular services to many European cities, as well as to destinations in North America, Africa and Asia; direct flights to Brazil, with connecting flights to other South American destinations, launched in early 2009; Chair. of Bd AMIKAM COHEN; Pres. and CEO Gen. (retd) ELIEZER SHKEDI.

Arkia Israeli Airlines Ltd: POB 39301, Dov Airport, Tel-Aviv 61392; tel. 3-6902210; fax 3-6903311; e-mail customer.service@arkia.co.il; internet www.arkia.co.il; f. 1980 by merger of Kanaf-Arkia Airlines and Aviation Services; scheduled passenger services linking Tel-Aviv, Jerusalem, Haifa, Eilat, Rosh Pina, Kiryat Shmona and Yotveta; charter services to many European destinations, Turkey and Jordan; CEO GAD TEPPER.

Israir Airlines: POB 26444, 23 Ben Yehuda St, Tel-Aviv 63806; tel. 3-7954038; fax 3-7954051; e-mail israir@israir.co.il; internet www.israir.co.il; f. 1996; domestic flights between Tel-Aviv and Eilat, and international flights to destinations in Europe and the USA; Pres. and CEO DAVID KAMINITZ.

Tourism

Israel possesses a wealth of antiquities and cultural attractions, in particular the historic and religious sites of Jerusalem. The country has a varied landscape, with a Mediterranean coastline, as well as desert and mountain terrain. The Red Sea resort of Eilat has become an important centre for diving holidays, while many tourists visit the treatment spas of the Dead Sea. In 2013 an estimated 3.0m. tourists visited Israel, compared with 2.9m. the previous year. Tourism receipts, including passenger transport, in 2012 totalled US $5,493m., according to provisional figures.

Ministry of Tourism: See The Government—Ministries; Dir-Gen. NOAZ BAR NIR.

Defence

The General Staff: This consists of the Chiefs of the General Staff, Personnel, Technology and Logistics, Intelligence, Operations, and Plans and Policy Branches of the Defence Forces, the Commanders-in-Chief of the Air Force and the Navy, and the officers commanding the four Territorial Commands (Northern, Central, Southern and Home Front). It is headed by the Chief of Staff of the Armed Forces.

Chief of Staff of the Armed Forces: Lt-Gen. BINYAMIN (BENNY) GANTZ.

Chief of Ground Forces Command: Maj.-Gen. GUY ZUR.

Commander-in-Chief of the Air Force: Maj.-Gen. AMIR ESHEL.

Commander-in-Chief of the Navy: Vice Adm. RAM ROTHBERG.

Defence Budget (2013): NIS 58,400m.

Military Service (Jewish and Druze population only; Christians, Circassians and Muslims may volunteer): Officers are conscripted for regular service of 48 months, men 36 months, women 24 months. Annual training as reservists thereafter, to age 40 for men (54 for some specialists), 38 (or marriage/pregnancy) for women.

Total Armed Forces (as assessed at November 2013): 176,500: army 133,000 (107,000 conscripts); navy 9,500 (2,500 conscripts); air force 34,000. Reserves 465,000.

Paramilitary Forces (as assessed at November 2013): est. 8,000.

Education

Israel has high standards of literacy and advanced educational services. Free, compulsory education is provided for all children between five and 15 years of age. Following the recommendations of a committee set up in 2011 to investigate ways to improve socio-economic conditions within Israel, the Government announced that pre-primary education for children aged three and four years in public institutions would be provided free of charge. The changes entered into effect in August 2012, at the beginning of the new academic year. Primary education is provided for all those between five and 10 years of age. There is also secondary, vocational and agricultural education. Post-primary education comprises two cycles of three years. According to UNESCO estimates, enrolment at primary schools in 2010 included 97% of pupils in the relevant age-group, while 98% of pupils in the appropriate age-group were enrolled at secondary schools. There are six universities, as well as the Technion (Israel Institute of Technology) in Haifa and the Weizmann Institute of Science in Rehovot. In 2010 general government expenditure on education totalled NIS 55,015m. (some 15.9% of total spending).

OCCUPIED TERRITORIES

THE GOLAN HEIGHTS

LOCATION AND CLIMATE

The Golan Heights, a mountainous plateau that formed most of Syria's Quneitra Province (1,710 sq km) and parts of Dar'a Province, was occupied by Israel after the Arab–Israeli War of June 1967. Following the Disengagement Agreement of 1974, Israel continued to occupy some 70% of the territory (1,176 sq km), valued for its strategic position and abundant water resources (the headwaters of the Jordan river have their source on the slopes of Mount Hermon). The average height of the Golan is approximately 1,200 m above sea level in the northern region and about 300 m above sea level in the southern region, near Lake Tiberias (the Sea of Galilee). Rainfall ranges from about 1,000 mm per year in the north to less than 600 mm per year in the southern region.

DEMOGRAPHY

As a consequence of the Israeli occupation, an estimated 93% of the ethnically diverse Syrian population of 147,613, distributed across 163 villages and towns and 108 individual farms, was expelled. The majority were Arab Sunni Muslims, but the population also included Alawite and Druze minorities and some Circassians, Turkmen, Armenians and Kurds. Approximately 9,000 Palestinian refugees from the 1948 Arab–Israeli War also inhabited the area. At the time of the occupation, 64% of the labour force was employed in agriculture. Only one-fifth of the population resided in the administrative centres. By 1991 the Golan Heights had a Jewish population of about 12,000 living in 21 Jewish settlements (four new settlements had been created by the end of 1992), and a predominantly Druze population of some 16,000 living in the only six remaining villages, of which Majd al-Shams is by far the largest. According to official figures, at the end of 2012 the Golan Heights had a total population of 44,100, of whom 18,900 were Jews, 2,300 were Muslims and 21,500 Druze.

ADMINISTRATION

Prior to the Israeli occupation, the Golan Heights were incorporated by Syria into a provincial administration of which the city of Quneitra, with a population at the time of 27,378, was the capital. The Disengagement Agreement that was mediated by US Secretary of State Henry Kissinger in 1974 (after the 1973 Arab–Israeli War) provided for the withdrawal of Israeli forces from Quneitra. Before withdrawal, however, Israeli army engineers destroyed the city. In December 1981 the Israeli Knesset enacted the Golan Annexation Law, whereby Israeli civilian legislation was extended to the territory of Golan, now under the administrative jurisdiction of the Commissioner for the Northern District of Israel. The Arab-Druze community of the Golan responded immediately by declaring a strike and appealed to the UN Secretary-General to force Israel to rescind the annexation decision. At the seventh round of multilateral talks between Israeli and Arab delegations in Washington, DC, USA, in August 1992, the Israeli Government of Itzhak Rabin for the first time accepted that UN Security Council Resolution 242, adopted in 1967, applied to the Golan Heights. In January 1999 the Knesset approved legislation stating that any transfer of land under Israeli sovereignty (referring to the Golan Heights and East Jerusalem) must be approved by both an absolute majority of Knesset members and by the Israeli electorate at a national referendum. Following the election of Ehud Barak as Israel's Prime Minister in May 1999, peace negotiations between Israel and Syria were resumed in December. However, in January 2000 the talks were postponed indefinitely after Syria demanded a written commitment from Israel to withdraw from the Golan Heights. In July 2001 Israel's recently elected premier, Ariel Sharon, stated that he would be prepared to resume peace talks with Syria, but Sharon also declared that the Israeli occupation of the Golan was 'irreversible'.

Syrian President Bashar al-Assad claimed in March 2007 that Syrian representatives had been conducting secret, unofficial discussions with Israeli officials during recent years. Despite official denials of any such talks, in July a spokesman for the Israeli Ministry of Foreign Affairs confirmed that messages had been relayed between Israel and Syria by third parties for some time. Although Israel carried out an airstrike on a military installation 'deep within' Syrian territory in September, both countries confirmed in May 2008 that indirect negotiations aimed at concluding a 'comprehensive peace' were being held through Turkish intermediaries in İstanbul. By the second week of August four rounds of the Turkish-mediated discussions had taken place, although no significant progress had apparently been reached as far as resolving the principal outstanding issues was concerned. Despite subsequent claims by President Assad that Israel and Syria were within 'touching distance' of reaching a peace deal, a fifth round of talks, scheduled for September, was delayed owing to the political uncertainty in Israel following Ehud Olmert's resignation as premier. Moreover, Assad apparently responded to Israel's large-scale military offensive against Hamas targets in the Gaza Strip between December and January 2009 by formally suspending the indirect discussions with Israel.

The inauguration, in March 2009, of a new Israeli Government under Prime Minister Binyamin Netanyahu of Likud, with the right-wing Israel Beytenu leader, Avigdor Lieberman, being appointed as Minister of Foreign Affairs, was widely perceived as an obstacle to hopes of a resumption of bilateral negotiations: both have declared their opposition to the surrender of the Golan Heights as part of any Israeli-Syrian peace agreement. In November the Knesset approved legislation stating that any Israeli withdrawal from the Golan Heights would require the prior endorsement of Israeli voters in a national referendum. Hopes of further progress towards a resumption of direct negotiations were put on hold as a result of the popular uprising that emerged in Syria (q.v.) from early 2011. In May Israeli troops clashed with hundreds of pro-Palestinian protesters who had broken through a security fence to enter the Golan Heights from Syria. Syrian state media reported in the following month that 12 Palestinians and two Syrians had been killed when Israeli soldiers opened fire at another group of protesters attempting to enter the Golan Heights from across the Syrian border; according to hospital reports, some 225 others were injured in the incident. The Israeli authorities accused the Assad regime of orchestrating the violence as a means of diverting international attention from the harsh measures employed by Syrian government forces against opposition activists. From late 2012, with the Syrian domestic unrest having descended into civil conflict, fears increased that the violence could spill over into the Golan Heights. In November a campaign by Syria against opposition fighters located near the border resulted in mortar shells landing close to Israeli army posts in the north of the territory, prompting retaliatory attacks on Syrian government positions by Israeli troops. Several further instances of mortar shells from Syria falling in the Golan Heights were reported during 2013 and early 2014, as the conflict between government and opposition forces intensified. In a report published at the end of June 2013, UN Secretary-General Ban Ki-Moon recommended that the UN Disengagement Observer Force (UNDOF) be expanded and that it be given additional self-defence capabilities. Earlier in that year there had been two separate instances in which UNDOF troops had been abducted by Syrian militant groups, while in early June Austria had announced the withdrawal of its troops from UNDOF (representing one-third of the total), citing concerns over their safety.

EAST JERUSALEM

LOCATION

Greater Jerusalem includes: Israeli West Jerusalem (99% Jewish); the Old City and Mount of Olives; East Jerusalem (the Palestinian residential and commercial centre); Arab villages declared to be part of Jerusalem by Israel in 1967; and Jewish neighbourhoods constructed since 1967, either on land expropriated from Arab villages or in areas requisitioned as 'government land'. Although the area of the Greater Jerusalem district is 627 sq km, the Old City of Jerusalem covers just 1 sq km.

DEMOGRAPHY

In June 1993 the Deputy Mayor of Jerusalem, Avraham Kahila, declared that the city now had 'a majority of Jews', based on population forecasts that estimated the Jewish population at 158,000 and the Arab population at 155,000. For the Israeli administration this signified the achievement of a long-term objective. Immediately prior to the 1967 Arab–Israeli War, East Jerusalem and its Arab environs had an Arab population of approximately 70,000, and a small Jewish population in the old Jewish quarter of the city. By contrast, Israeli West Jerusalem had a Jewish population of 196,000. As a result of this imbalance, in the Greater Jerusalem district as a whole the Jewish population was in the majority even prior to the occupation of the whole city in 1967. Israeli policy following the occupation of East Jerusalem and the West Bank consisted of encircling the eastern sector of the city with Jewish settlements. In contrast to the more politically sensitive siting of Jewish settlements in the old Arab quarter of Jerusalem, the Government of Itzhak Rabin concentrated on the outer circle of settlement building. Official statistics for the end of 2012 reported that Greater Jerusalem had a total population of 987,400, of whom 660,200 were Jews, 298,600 were Muslims and 15,700 were Christians. The Jerusalem Institute for Israel Studies (JIIS) estimated in August 2007 that the growth rate for the Arab population of Greater Jerusalem was almost double that of the Jewish population. According to the JIIS, if this trend continued, the city's population would have a Jewish-Arab ratio of 60:40 by 2020, and of 50:50 by 2035. In May 2007 the mayor of Jerusalem, Uri Lupolianski, suggested easing the restrictions on family reunification for the estimated 10,000 Christian Arabs in Jerusalem, in order to prevent a further decline in their number.

The Old City, within the walls of which are found the ancient quarters of the Jews, Christians, Muslims and Armenians, is predominantly Arab. According to JIIS, the Old City had a total population of 39,865 in 2011.

ADMINISTRATION

Until the 1967 Arab–Israeli War, Jerusalem had been divided into the new city of West Jerusalem—captured by Jewish forces in 1948—and the old city, East Jerusalem, which was part of Jordan. Israel's victory in 1967, however, reunited the city under Israeli control. Two weeks after the fighting had ended, on 28 June, Israeli law was applied to East Jerusalem and the municipal boundaries were extended by 45 km (28 miles). Jerusalem had effectively been annexed. Israeli officials, however, still refer to the 'reunification' of Jerusalem.

Immediately following the occupation, all electricity, water and telephone grids in West Jerusalem were extended to the east. Roads were widened and cleared, and the Arab population immediately in front of the 'Wailing Wall' was forcibly evicted. Arabs living in East Jerusalem became 'permanent residents' and could apply for Israeli citizenship if they wished (in contrast to Arabs in the West Bank and Gaza Strip). However, few chose to do so. None the less, issued with identity cards (excluding the estimated 25,000 Arabs from the West Bank and Gaza living illegally in the city), the Arab residents were taxed by the Israeli authorities, and their businesses and banks became subject to Israeli laws and business regulations. Now controlling approximately one-half of all land in East Jerusalem and the surrounding Palestinian villages (previously communally, or privately, owned by Palestinians), the Israeli authorities allowed Arabs to construct buildings on only 10%–15% of the land in the city, and East Jerusalem's commercial district has been limited to three streets.

Since the 1993 signing of the Declaration of Principles on Palestinian Self-Rule, the future status of Jerusalem and the continuing expansion of Jewish settlements in East Jerusalem have emerged as two of the most crucial issues affecting the peace process. In May 1999 the Israeli Government announced its refusal to grant Israeli citizenship to several hundred Arabs living in East Jerusalem, regardless of their compliance with the conditions stipulated under the Citizenship Law. In October, however, Israel ended its policy of revoking the right of Palestinians to reside in Jerusalem if they had spent more than seven years outside the city. Moreover, the Israeli Government announced in March 2000 that Palestinian residents of Jerusalem whose identity cards had been revoked could apply for their restoration.

At the Camp David talks held between Israel and the Palestinian (National) Authority (PA) in July 2000, the issue of who would have sovereignty over East Jerusalem in a future 'permanent status' agreement proved to be the principal obstacle to the achievement of a peace deal. It was reported that the Israeli Government had offered the PA municipal autonomy over certain areas of East Jerusalem (including access to the Islamic holy sites), although sovereignty would remain in Israeli hands; the proposals were rejected by PA President Yasser Arafat. In September the holy sites of East Jerusalem were the initial focal point of a renewed uprising by Palestinians against the Israeli authorities, which became known as the al-Aqsa *intifada* (after Jerusalem's al-Aqsa Mosque). Although the publication of the internationally sponsored 'roadmap' peace plan in April 2003 offered directions for talks on the Jerusalem issue, the resumption of attacks by Palestinian militants against Israeli citizens in mid-2003 and Israeli counter-strikes against Palestinian targets, made any such discussions untenable at that time.

Following a lengthy period during which all negotiations between Israel and the PA were effectively stalled, owing to the continued Israeli–Palestinian violence as well as political instability in the Palestinian territories, some optimism was expressed in August 2007 when the Israeli Prime Minister, Ehud Olmert, held direct talks with the PA President, Mahmud Abbas, in the West Bank town of Jericho in preparation for an international Middle East peace conference, which was convened in Annapolis, Maryland, USA, in November. The US Administration of President George W. Bush declared its intention that a permanent Israeli-Palestinian settlement, including the establishment of a Palestinian state, could be reached by the end of the year. However, an increase in attacks being perpetrated by Palestinian militants from the Gaza Strip into northern Israel from January 2008, and a consequent military campaign by Israeli forces in Gaza, resulted in a stalling of negotiations. In February the Israeli Prime Minister angered Palestinians by declaring that talks concerning the final status of Jerusalem, and the key Palestinian demand that East Jerusalem become their capital, would be the last 'core issue' on the agenda to be negotiated by the two parties. Moreover, the Israeli Government continued to issue tenders for hundreds of new housing units at Jewish settlements in East Jerusalem and the West Bank, thereby contravening its obligations under the terms of the roadmap.

Renewed diplomatic efforts aimed at facilitating a resumption of the peace process followed the inauguration of Barack Obama as US President in January 2009. The Obama Administration demanded a temporary halt to Israel's settlement-building programme as a precondition for the resumption of negotiations. However, although in December the Israeli Government announced the imposition of a 10-month moratorium on settlement-building in the West Bank, building activity in East Jerusalem was exempted. In March 2010 Netanyahu asserted that the settlements were an 'integral and inextricable' part of the city and that building activity in all areas of Jerusalem would continue. Following the expiry in September of the temporary ban on Israeli settlement-building, the PA suspended its involvement in the peace process, stating that it would resume talks only when the Israeli Government had agreed to end both settlement construction and the blockade of Gaza. In August 2011 the Israeli Government approved plans for the construction of 1,600 new homes at Ramat Shlomo, announced in March 2010, and in the following month indicated its intention to authorize the construction of a brand new settlement at Givat Hamatos, to the south of Jerusalem; the settlement was to incorporate some 2,600 homes. Following the PA's acceptance at the end of October as a full member of UNESCO, the Israeli Government announced that it was to accelerate the construction of around 2,000 new homes in East Jerusalem and the West Bank. Further plans for expansion at the Har Homa and Pisgat Ze'ev settlements were published in January and April 2012. In October the Israeli Government gave its final approval to plans for 797 new homes at Gilo. After the UN General Assembly's decision in November to upgrade the PA's status in the organization to that of a non-member observer state (Abbas having applied for full UN membership in September), Netanyahu announced his Government's intention to accelerate plans for the construction of some 3,000 new homes in the so-called E-1 area between Jerusalem and the Ma'ale Adumim settlement to the east of the city. The Israeli general election held in January 2013 was characterized by the success of the centrist Yesh Atid party and the pro-settlement Jewish Home party; upon the appointment of a new Cabinet in early March the latter was allocated responsibility for the Jerusalem affairs and housing portfolios. During a visit to Jerusalem in March, President Obama appealed for Israel to resume negotiations with the PA. Following subsequent repeated visits to the region by the newly appointed US Secretary of State, John F. Kerry, preliminary talks were held in Washington, DC, in July between Israel's chief negotiator, Minister of Justice Tzipi Livni, and her PA counterpart, Saeb Erakat. The stated aim of the latest round of talks was for both parties to reach a limited peace agreement within nine months. Formal discussions, moderated by President Obama's Special Envoy for Israeli-Palestinian Negotiations, Martin Indyk, commenced in Jerusalem and Jericho in August. However, the prospects of an agreement being reached by the end of April were diminished by ongoing instances of Israeli–Palestinian violence and by the Israeli Government's continuation of its controversial settlement-building programme in East Jerusalem and the West Bank. Moreover, in mid-April Israel suspended the transfer of tax revenues to the PA over the latter's accession to UN institutions, and later that month Prime Minister Netanyahu suspended Israel's participation in the process following the announcement of a national unity agreement between Hamas and Fatah.

ITALY

Introductory Survey

LOCATION, CLIMATE, LANGUAGE, RELIGION, FLAG, CAPITAL

The Italian Republic comprises a peninsula, extending from southern Europe into the Mediterranean Sea, and a number of adjacent islands. The two principal islands are Sicily, to the south-west, and Sardinia, to the west. The Alps form a natural boundary to the north, where the bordering countries are France to the north-west, Switzerland and Austria to the north and Slovenia to the north-east. The climate is temperate in the north and Mediterranean in the south, with mild winters and long, dry summers. The average temperature in Rome is 7.4°C (45.3°F) in January and 25.7°C (78.3°F) in July. The principal language is Italian. German and Ladin are spoken in the Trentino-Alto Adige (South Tyrol) region on the Austrian border, and French in the Valle d'Aosta region (bordering France and Switzerland), while in southern Italy there are Greek-speaking and Albanian minorities. A dialect of Catalan is spoken in north-western Sardinia. Almost all of the inhabitants profess Christianity: more than 90% are adherents of the Roman Catholic Church. The national flag (proportions 2 by 3) has three equal vertical stripes, of green, white and red. The capital is Rome.

CONTEMPORARY POLITICAL HISTORY

Historical Context

The Kingdom of Italy, under the House of Savoy, was proclaimed in 1861 and the country was unified in 1870. Italy subsequently acquired an overseas empire, comprising the African colonies of Eritrea, Italian Somaliland and Libya. Benito Mussolini, leader of the Fascist Party, became President of the Council (Prime Minister) in October 1922 and assumed dictatorial powers in 1925–26. Relations between the Italian state and the Roman Catholic Church, a subject of bitter controversy since Italy's unification, were codified in 1929 by a series of agreements, including the Lateran Pact, which recognized the sovereignty of the state of the Vatican City (q.v.), a small enclave within the city of Rome, under the jurisdiction of the Pope. Under Mussolini, Italian forces occupied Ethiopia in 1935–36 and Albania in 1939. Italy supported the fascist forces in the Spanish Civil War of 1936–39, and from June 1940 supported Nazi Germany in the Second World War. In 1943, however, as forces from the allied powers invaded Italy, the fascist regime collapsed. In July of that year King Victor Emmanuel III dismissed Mussolini, and the Fascist Party was dissolved.

In April 1945 German forces in Italy surrendered and Mussolini was killed. In June 1946, following a referendum, the monarchy was abolished and Italy became a republic. Until 1963 the Partito della Democrazia Cristiana (DC—Christian Democratic Party) held power continuously, while industry expanded rapidly, supported by capital from the USA. By the early 1960s, however, public discontent was increasing, largely owing to low wage rates and a lack of social reform. In the general election of 1963 the Partito Comunista Italiano (PCI—Italian Communist Party), together with other parties of the extreme right and left, made considerable gains at the expense of the DC. During the next decade there was a rapid succession of mainly coalition Governments, involving the DC and one or more of the other major non-communist parties.

Domestic Political Affairs

Aldo Moro's coalition Government of the DC and the Partito Repubblicano Italiano (PRI—Italian Republican Party), formed in 1974, resigned in January 1976, following the withdrawal of support by the Partito Socialista Italiano (PSI—Italian Socialist Party). After the failure of a minority DC administration, the PCI won 228 seats at elections to the 630-member Chamber of Deputies (Camera dei Deputati) in June. The DC remained the largest party, but could no longer govern against PCI opposition in the legislature. However, the DC continued to insist on excluding the PCI from power, and in July formed a minority Government, with Giulio Andreotti as premier. He relied on the continuing abstention of PCI deputies to introduce severe austerity measures in response to the economic crisis. In January 1978 the minority Government was forced to resign under pressure from the PCI, which demanded more active participation in government. However, the new Government that Andreotti subsequently formed with support from the PCI was almost identical to the previous administration. In May former Prime Minister Moro was kidnapped and murdered by the extreme left-wing Brigate Rosse (Red Brigades).

The Andreotti administration collapsed in January 1979, when the PCI withdrew from the official parliamentary majority. A new coalition Government, formed by Andreotti in March, lasted only 10 days before being defeated in a vote of no confidence. Following elections in June, at which its representation in the Chamber of Deputies declined to 201 seats, the PCI returned to opposition. In August Francesco Cossiga of the DC formed a minority coalition Government. However, the new Government was continually thwarted by obstructionism in Parliament. In April 1980 Cossiga established a majority coalition, comprising members of the DC, the PRI and the PSI. In September, however, the Government resigned after losing a vote on its economic programme. The subsequent four-party coalition Government, assembled by Arnaldo Forlani, the Chairman of the DC, was beset with allegations of corruption; it too was forced to stand down, in May 1981, following revelations that more than 1,000 of Italy's foremost establishment figures belonged to a secret masonic lodge, P-2 ('Propaganda Due'), which had extensive criminal connections both in Italy and abroad. The lodge was linked with many political and financial scandals and with right-wing terrorism, culminating in 1982 with the collapse of one of Italy's leading banks, Banco Ambrosiano, and the death of its President, Roberto Calvi.

In June 1981 the leader of the PRI, Giovanni Spadolini, formed a coalition Government, thus becoming the first non-DC Prime Minister since 1946. Spadolini resigned in November 1982. Amintore Fanfani, a former DC Prime Minister, assembled a new coalition in December which lasted until the PSI withdrew its support in April 1983. A general election was held in June, at which the DC lost considerable support, winning only 33% of the votes for the Chamber of Deputies. The PSI increased its share of the votes to 11%, and its leader, Bettino Craxi, was subsequently appointed Italy's first socialist Prime Minister, at the head of a coalition. However, Craxi resigned in June 1986 when his Government lost a vote of confidence in the Chamber of Deputies; Andreotti began talks to form a new government. However, the refusal of other parties to support Andreotti led to Craxi's return to power in July, on condition that he transfer the premiership to a DC member in March 1987. Craxi accordingly submitted his resignation, and that of his Government, as scheduled. After several unsuccessful attempts to form a coalition, a general election was held in June, at which the DC won 34% of the votes cast and the PSI 14%. The PCI suffered its worst post-war electoral result, securing 27% of the votes. Giovanni Goria of the DC was appointed Prime Minister of a coalition Government. By the end of the year, however, the Government had lost considerable support, and in March 1988 Goria resigned. Ciriaco De Mita, the Secretary-General of the DC, formed a coalition with the same five parties that had served in Goria's administration.

Severe criticism by Craxi of De Mita's premiership led to the collapse of the coalition Government in May 1989. In July the coalition partners of the outgoing Government agreed to form a new administration, with Andreotti as Prime Minister. Andreotti resigned the premiership in March 1991, following criticism from the PSI. President Francesco Cossiga (who had taken office in July 1985) none the less nominated Andreotti to form a new government (Italy's 50th since 1945), which comprised the same coalition partners as the outbound administration, apart from the PRI.

In early 1991 the PCI was renamed the Partito Democratico della Sinistra (PDS—Democratic Party of the Left), having transformed itself into a social democratic party. A minority of members of the former PCI refused to join the PDS, and in May they formed the Partito della Rifondazione Comunista (PRC—Party of Communist Refoundation).

At the general election held in April 1992, support for the DC declined to less than 30% of the votes cast. The PDS won 16.1% of the votes cast, while the PSI received 13.6%. The Lega Nord (LN—Northern League), a grouping of regionalist parties led by Umberto Bossi, performed well in northern Italy. In May Giuliano Amato of the PSI was appointed Prime Minister; the new Government, which was appointed the following month, was composed of the same four parties that had formed the outgoing administration.

The 'Tangentopoli' affair

The uncovering of a corruption scandal in Milan in 1992, which became known as 'Tangentopoli' ('Bribesville'), subsequently assumed wider implications. It was alleged that politicians (mainly of the PSI and DC) and government officials had accepted bribes in exchange for the awarding of large public contracts. In February 1993 the Minister of Justice, Claudio Martelli of the PSI, was obliged to resign, having been placed under formal investigation for alleged complicity in the collapse of Banco Ambrosiano. Shortly afterwards, Craxi stood down as Secretary-General of the PSI, although he continued to deny accusations of fraud. In March 1993 five DC politicians, including Andreotti, were placed under investigation over their alleged links with the Mafia.

Despite the collapse of confidence in his Government, Amato agreed to remain in office until after nationwide referendums had been held in April 1993 on a number of proposed legislative amendments, including a reform of the electoral system for the upper legislative chamber, the Senate of the Republic (Senato della Repubblica), and the end of state funding of political parties. These amendments, intended to prevent electoral malpractice and, in particular, interference by organized crime, were overwhelmingly approved. (In August Parliament endorsed a similar system for elections to the Chamber of Deputies.) Amato resigned as Prime Minister shortly after the referendums, and Carlo Azeglio Ciampi was invited by President Oscar Luigi Scalfaro, who had taken office in May 1992, to form a new government. Ciampi, hitherto Governor of the Banca d'Italia (the central bank), was the first non-parliamentarian to be appointed to the premiership. His coalition comprised the four parties of the outgoing administration and the PRI.

In May 1993 the Chamber of Deputies voted overwhelmingly to abolish parliamentary immunity in cases of corruption and serious crime. Furthermore, the Senate approved the removal of Andreotti's parliamentary immunity, to allow investigations into his alleged association with the Mafia, although his arrest remained prohibited. Meanwhile, investigations began in April into the activities of former DC Prime Minister Forlani. The investigations were subsequently extended to encompass politicians of the PDS and PRI, as arrests of leading political and business figures multiplied. In August the Chamber of Deputies voted to allow Craxi to be investigated by magistrates on four charges of corruption. The following month Andreotti was charged with providing the Sicilian Mafia with political protection in exchange for votes in Sicily, and with complicity in the murder of an investigative journalist, Mario Francese, who had allegedly discovered evidence linking Andreotti with the Mafia.

Ciampi resigned in January 1994. President Scalfaro dissolved the legislature and scheduled a general election for March. In January Silvio Berlusconi, the principal shareholder in and former manager of the media-based Fininvest, Italy's third largest private business group, announced the formation of a right-wing organization, Forza Italia (Come on, Italy!), to contest the election. In subsequent weeks, in response to the collapse in popular support for the previously dominant DC and PSI largely due to the Tangentopoli affair, parties of all leanings formed electoral alliances with an aim to securing a majority in the Chamber of Deputies. Seven left-wing parties—including the PDS and the PRC—established I Progressisti (the Progressives); the Polo delle Libertà e del Buon Governo (commonly known as the Polo delle Libertà—the Freedom Alliance), under the leadership of Berlusconi, was set up by the LN, Forza Italia and the Alleanza Nazionale (AN—National Alliance), which incorporated members of the neo-fascist Movimento Sociale Italiano-Destra Nazionale (MSI-DN—Italian Social Movement-National Right); and the centre-right Patto per l'Italia (Pact for Italy) included the Partito Popolare Italiano (PPI—Italian People's Party), formed from the liberal wing of the DC. The Polo delle Libertà won an outright majority in the Chamber of Deputies and was only three seats short of a majority in the Senate. In May Berlusconi formed a new Government, which included members of the AN, the LN and the MSI-DN.

In November 1994 Berlusconi was placed under investigation for bribery. In the following month Antonio Di Pietro, a high-profile magistrate in Milan who had led the investigation into political corruption in 1992, resigned in protest at increasing government interference in the work of the judiciary. The failure of the Prime Minister to resolve his conflict of business and political interests, together with the growing tension between the Government and the judiciary, precipitated the disintegration of the coalition and Berlusconi's resignation in January 1995. Lamberto Dini, the Minister of the Treasury, formed an interim Government composed of technocrats. In March it was announced that Berlusconi was to be subject to further investigation on charges of financial irregularities.

In October 1995 the Minister of Justice, Filippo Mancuso, refused to resign despite a successful motion of no confidence in him, which had been prompted by his alleged vendetta against anti-corruption magistrates in Milan. President Scalfaro revoked Mancuso's mandate, and transferred responsibility for the justice portfolio to Dini. Shortly afterwards, the Government narrowly defeated a motion of no confidence proposed by Berlusconi and Mancuso, following an agreement whereby PRC deputies abstained from the vote on condition that Dini resign as premier by the end of the year. Dini's resignation, submitted in late December, was, however, rejected by Scalfaro. In January 1996 the AN proposed a resolution demanding Dini's resignation, which it was expected to win with the support of parties of the extreme left. Scalfaro was thus obliged to accept Dini's resignation, which he submitted prior to the vote. In February Scalfaro dissolved Parliament and requested that Dini remain as interim Prime Minister until a general election in April.

Meanwhile, in July 1994 Craxi and the former Deputy Prime Minister and Minister of Justice, Martelli, were both sentenced for fraudulent bankruptcy in relation to the collapse of Banco Ambrosiano. Craxi, who claimed to be too ill to return from his residence in Tunisia, was sentenced *in absentia*; in July 1995 he was formally declared a fugitive from justice. In October all 22 defendants were convicted in a trial concerning illegal funding of political parties. Among those convicted were former Prime Ministers Craxi, who was sentenced *in absentia* to four years' imprisonment, and Forlani, sentenced to 28 months' custody; Bossi received a suspended sentence.

The centre-left in power: 1996–2001

The legislative elections held in April 1996 were won by L'Ulivo (The Olive Tree), a centre-left electoral alliance dominated by the PDS, but also including the PPI and Dini's newly formed, centrist Rinnovamento Italiano (RI—Italian Renewal). The alliance narrowly defeated the Polo per le Libertà (as the Polo delle Libertà had been renamed), securing 284 of the 630 seats in the Chamber of Deputies and 157 of the 315 elective seats in the Senate. President Scalfaro invited Romano Prodi, the leader of L'Ulivo, to form a government.

In December 1997 Berlusconi and four associates were convicted on charges of false accounting with regard to the purchase of a film group in 1988. Later that month Berlusconi and Cesare Previti, a former Minister of Defence and a lawyer for Fininvest, were ordered to stand trial on charges relating to their planned bribery of judges. In two separate trials in July 1998 Berlusconi was convicted of bribing tax inspectors involved in Fininvest audits and of making illicit payments to Craxi and the PSI in 1991.

In June 1998 the Chamber of Deputies approved legislation endorsing the admission to the North Atlantic Treaty Organization (NATO, see p. 370) of Hungary, Poland and the Czech Republic. The vote, which had become an issue of confidence in the Prodi Government as the PRC (on which the coalition relied in parliamentary votes) opposed the eastward expansion of the alliance and thus withdrew its support, was carried with the backing of the new, centrist Unione Democratica per la Repubblica (UDR—Democratic Union for the Republic) and with the abstention of Forza Italia. There was a further political crisis in October, when the PRC again withdrew its support for the Government on the issue of the 1999 budget. The Government lost an ensuing confidence motion by one vote, and Prodi was forced to resign. Massimo D'Alema, the leader of the Democratici di Sinistra (DS—Democrats of the Left—as the PDS had been renamed), was asked to assume the premiership. The new Government comprised members of seven political parties. In May 1999 former Prime Minister Ciampi was elected to succeed Scalfaro as President of the Republic.

In October 1999 Berlusconi's 1998 conviction for making illicit payments to Craxi and the PSI was overturned. In the following month, however, Berlusconi was ordered to stand trial in two cases involving charges of bribery and false accounting. Meanwhile, in June a new trial had been ordered against Craxi on charges of illegal party financing; however, in January 2000 Craxi died in exile in Tunisia.

D'Alema tendered his resignation as Prime Minister in December 1999, following the withdrawal of support by a number of the coalition parties. President Ciampi asked D'Alema to form a new government; D'Alema forged a new coalition of parties of the left and centre, including I Democratici per l'Ulivo (The Democrats for the Olive Tree), founded earlier in that year by Prodi, and the Unione Democratici per l'Europa (UDEUR—Union of Democrats for Europe). However, following the defeat of the new centre-left coalition by a centre-right alliance of Forza Italia and LN at regional elections in April 2000, D'Alema resigned. In late April a new, eight-party, centre-left coalition Government, led by Amato, was sworn in.

In May 2000, at a first appeal, Berlusconi was acquitted of one charge of bribing tax inspectors involved in Fininvest audits on which he had been convicted in 1998; the appeals court also invoked the statute of limitations (which, under Italian law, continued to apply even after proceedings had begun) to overturn his convictions on three similar counts. In June 2000 Berlusconi was further acquitted at a pre-trial hearing of bribery charges relating to his acquisition of the Mondadori publishing company in 1991.

Berlusconi's second premiership: 2001–06

At the general election held in May 2001, Berlusconi's Casa delle Libertà (House of Freedoms) alliance—the successor to the Polo per le Libertà—won majorities in both legislative chambers. Following his nomination as premier by Ciampi, in June Berlusconi formed a coalition Government composed of Forza Italia, the AN, the LN, the Cristiani Democratici Uniti (CDU—United Christian Democrats), the Centro Cristiano Democratico (CCD—Christian Democratic Centre) and independents. The AN leader, Gianfranco Fini, became Deputy Prime Minister, and the Government also included three members of LN, one being Bossi.

The issue of apparent conflict of interest between Berlusconi's political role and business interests was heightened by the general election. Berlusconi's new position as Prime Minister placed him in effective control of the state broadcasting company, Radiotelevisione Italiana (Rai), and this, coupled with his ownership of the media company Fininvest (which operated Italy's principal private television concern, Mediaset), potentially gave him control over the majority of the Italian television network.

In August 2001 legislation to decriminalize fraud associated with false accounting was approved by the Chamber of Deputies. Furthermore, in October legislation was adopted by the Senate which altered regulations governing the use of evidence in criminal cases. Opposition parties protested that Berlusconi would directly benefit from the new regulations, which were likely to invalidate legal proceedings against himself and Previti in respect of allegations that they had bribed judges in return for a favourable court judgment over the sale of state-owned food company SME Meridionale. Prior to the trial's commencement, in January 2002, an attempt by the Minister of Justice to remove one of the three judges on the case caused public and judicial consternation. In October 2001 the Supreme Court of Cassation overturned Berlusconi's 1998 conviction on charges of bribing tax inspectors in exchange for favourable audits of Fininvest.

In April 2002 a 'conflict of interest' bill was passed in the Chamber of Deputies. The legislation prohibited a figure in public office from active involvement in running a company, but did not forbid ownership, thus permitting Berlusconi's continued possession of Mediaset. (The bill finally became law in July 2004.)

Following the rejection of an appeal by Berlusconi in May 2002 to have his bribery trial moved from Milan (where, he alleged, the judicial system was dominated by communists), several draft bills proposing judicial reform provoked controversy in the legislature and the judiciary, most notably a trial bill, which would allow proceedings to be rescheduled and relocated if there was 'legitimate suspicion' of prosecutorial bias on the part of the judge. Nevertheless, the trial bill was passed by Parliament in November. In the same month Bossi presented a draft bill that provided for the devolution of powers to the regions in matters of education, the health service and the police. Despite attempts by the opposition to hinder its progress, the devolution bill was passed in December.

In November 2002 an appeals court in Palermo overturned the acquittal of Andreotti on charges of conspiracy to murder the journalist Mario Francese in 1979, and sentenced the former Prime Minister to 24 years' imprisonment. In October 2003 the Supreme Court of Cassation overturned this ruling, acquitting Andreotti of the murder. Meanwhile, in May of that year an appeals court in Sicily upheld a 1999 ruling exonerating Andreotti of charges of association with the Mafia. In October 2004 Andreotti was acquitted by the Supreme Court of Cassation of collusion with the Mafia while in office.

In January 2003, after a further bid to relocate his bribery trial was rejected by the Supreme Court, Berlusconi announced the possible reintroduction of immunity from prosecution for members of Parliament (abolished in 1993), arousing opposition protest. In April Berlusconi's trial opened in Milan. Later that month Previti was sentenced to 11 years' imprisonment for bribing judges to influence two corporate takeovers in the 1990s. However, in June Berlusconi's trial was halted, following the adoption of a bill granting immunity while in office to Italy's five most senior politicians (the President, the Prime Minister, the head of the Constitutional Court and the leaders of the two chambers of Parliament). However, the Constitutional Court declared in January 2004 that this legislation was illegal, thus permitting the resumption in April of Berlusconi's bribery trial. Berlusconi was acquitted on one charge in December, and the court ruled that the statute of limitations had expired on the second charge.

In December 2003 President Ciampi refused to sign legislation designed to reduce restrictions on media ownership. Opponents of the bill maintained that it would allow Berlusconi—who, through his direct influence over Rai and his Mediaset company, already controlled more than 90% of Italy's television media—to expand his media holdings and thereby reduce further the freedom of the press. However, the bill was approved by the Chamber of Deputies in February 2004, as the Government linked the vote to a motion of confidence, and received final approval in the Senate in April; Ciampi was constitutionally obliged to sign it into law in May. The President of Rai consequently resigned.

In November 2004 employees in the legal profession organized a strike to protest against planned judicial reform which, it was claimed, would reduce the independence of the judiciary and the power of the legal professionals to prosecute politicians for corruption. Although it was adopted by Parliament, on 16 December President Ciampi refused to sign the legislation, stating that it was unconstitutional.

The ruling coalition performed poorly at regional elections in April 2005. The Unione dei Democratici Cristiani e di Centro (UDC—Union of Christian and Centre Democrats, formed in 2002 from a merger of the CDU and the CCD) subsequently withdrew from the governing coalition and the AN threatened to do likewise. Berlusconi resigned in order to form a new Government, which was duly inaugurated on 23 April. The new administration comprised representatives of the four parties in the previous Government, the PRI, the Nuovo Partito Socialista Italiano (Nuovo PSI—New Italian Socialist Party) and independents.

Legislation providing for a return to total proportional representation prior to the elections in 2006 and setting a threshold for the percentage of votes a party needed to win to be eligible for seats in Parliament was approved by the Chamber of Deputies in October 2005. The opposition abstained from voting, claiming that the legislation was designed to reduce the representation of L'Unione (a nine-party coalition created by Prodi and incorporating members of L'Ulivo and the PRC) in the next parliament. The legislation was approved by the Senate in December.

In November 2005 the two chambers of Parliament approved legislation reducing the statute of limitations for business-related crimes, including fraud and corruption, and lengthening it for Mafia-related crimes. In January 2006 President Ciampi refused to sign legislation, approved earlier in the month by Parliament, that abolished the right of prosecutors to appeal against an acquittal, claiming that it was unconstitutional. The legislation was widely regarded as being designed to exempt Berlusconi from further prosecution since a court in Milan was due to begin hearing an appeal of a case in which Berlusconi had been acquitted on four charges of bribing judges; the appeal was rejected in April 2007.

In March 2006 Berlusconi went on trial in Milan, along with 13 other defendants, on charges of tax fraud relating to the purchase of television and film rights by Mediaset in the 1990s. In

November a separate trial opened involving Berlusconi and his former lawyer, David Mills (the estranged husband of British government minister Tessa Jowell), in which Berlusconi was accused of paying Mills at least US $600,000 after the latter gave favourable testimony in two corruption trials involving Berlusconi in 1997 and 1998.

Prodi's second Government

At the general election held in April 2006, Prodi's L'Unione coalition won a narrow victory in both houses of Parliament. In the Senate L'Unione obtained 158 seats, while the Casa delle Libertà took 156 seats. New legislation, which automatically awarded 55% of the seats in the lower house to the party or group with the largest number of votes, meant that L'Unione secured 348 seats in the Chamber of Deputies, while Berlusconi's coalition won 281 seats. In May Giorgio Napolitano of the DS was elected to succeed Ciampi as President of the Republic, following which Prodi was inaugurated as Prime Minister. His Government included two former Prime Ministers: D'Alema as Minister of Foreign Affairs and Amato as Minister of Internal Affairs.

In June 2006 a referendum was held on controversial constitutional reforms, introduced by the previous administration and approved by Parliament in November 2005, aimed at granting greater autonomy to Italy's regions and extending the powers of the Prime Minister. The reforms were rejected, by 61.7% of the votes cast. President Ciampi and the centre-left had been severely critical of the proposed measures, claiming that the power of the legislature would be diminished and that the devolution of power to the regions, promoted by the LN, favoured the more affluent northern regions at the expense of their southern counterparts.

In February 2007 the Government was defeated in the Senate on the continued presence of Italian troops in Afghanistan and the expansion of a US military base near Vicenza. Although the vote was not tied to a motion of confidence, Prodi submitted his resignation to the President; however, this was not accepted by Napolitano, who asked the Prime Minister to call confidence votes in Parliament. Prodi went on to win the votes in the Senate in February and the Chamber of Deputies in March, after persuading all parties in the coalition to agree to a programme that included support for the peacekeeping mission in Afghanistan, as well as measures to liberalize the economy.

In October 2007, in an attempt to consolidate support for the main left-wing parties and to promote a more centrist agenda, the two largest parties in L'Unione—the DS and Democrazia è Libertà—La Margherita (Democracy is Freedom—The Daisy)—and a number of smaller parties merged to form the Partito Democratico (PD—Democratic Party); the Mayor of Rome, former Deputy Prime Minister Walter Veltroni, was elected as National Secretary of the new party.

The ongoing struggle to maintain stability within L'Unione culminated in January 2008 with the resignation of the Minister of Justice, Clemente Mastella, following the arrest of his wife on charges of corruption. Days later Mastella announced the withdrawal from the governing coalition of his UDEUR party, thereby divesting the Government of its narrow majority in the upper house. On 24 January the Government lost a vote of confidence in the Senate that had been prompted by the perceived inadequacy of its response to an ongoing refuse collection crisis in Naples. Prodi immediately submitted the Government's resignation, which was accepted by President Napolitano, who, nevertheless, requested that Prodi remain in office on an interim basis pending the appointment of a new Council of Ministers. Napolitano subsequently asked the President of the Senate, Franco Marini, to lead discussions over the formation of a cross-party interim administration with a mandate to pursue electoral reform. However, the main opposition parties refused to agree such measures, which would have reversed reforms implemented during Berlusconi's second term as Prime Minister, and urged Napolitano to call an early general election. In February Napolitano dissolved Parliament and scheduled a general election for April. Berlusconi and Fini announced that Forza Italia and the AN were to present a joint list of candidates at the election as the Popolo della Libertà, a coalition that was subsequently joined by numerous smaller parties. While ruling out a formal merger, the LN and the Movimento per l'Autonomia agreed to ally themselves with the Popolo della Libertà. The UDC was to contest the election as part of a new coalition, the Unione di Centro (UdC), which it had formed with other centrist, Christian-democratic parties in December 2007.

Meanwhile, in January 2008 a court in Milan acquitted Berlusconi on charges of false accounting, on the grounds that, according to the reforms promulgated in 2001 under Berlusconi's premiership, it was no longer a criminal offence.

Berlusconi's third premiership: 2008–11

At the general election conducted on 13 and 14 April 2008, the number of parties represented in Parliament was greatly reduced, partly owing to the consolidation of the main, centrist alliances. Berlusconi's Popolo della Libertà and its allies secured a majority in both the Chamber of Deputies and the Senate. In the lower house the Popolo della Libertà won 276 seats, while its allies the LN and the Movimento per l'Autonomia obtained 60 and eight seats, respectively, compared with 217 seats for the PD. The Popolo della Libertà won 147 seats in the upper chamber, while the LN and the Movimento per l'Autonomia secured 25 and two seats, respectively; the PD took 118 seats. The UdC, Antonio Di Pietro's Italia dei Valori (Italy of Principals) and a number of small parties also gained representation in both houses. A high voter turnout of 81.4% was recorded. A coalition Government, led by Berlusconi and comprising the Popolo della Libertà and the LN, was sworn in on 7 May. Franco Frattini (hitherto European Commissioner for Justice) was appointed as Minister of Foreign Affairs, and Roberto Maroni of the LN became Minister of the Interior. Other notable appointments included that of Bossi as Minister without Portfolio for Federal Reform.

The new Government embarked upon a controversial programme of judicial reform, despite fierce criticism from the centre-left opposition, which claimed that the measures were intended to protect Berlusconi against the possibility of conviction in the two ongoing trials in which he was a defendant. In June 2008 both houses of Parliament approved a bill providing for the suspension of all trials involving crimes committed before 2002 for which the maximum sentence was less than 10 years' imprisonment; the Government claimed that this measure was designed to prioritize cases involving serious or violent crimes. Following the promulgation of the legislation, the proceedings against Berlusconi begun in 2006 were suspended. In July 2008 legislation was approved by both houses of Parliament that granted immunity from prosecution while in office, for one legislative term, to the President, the Prime Minister, and the Presidents of the Chamber of Deputies and the Senate. The Government maintained that the new law would overcome the objections raised by the Constitutional Court to similar legislation, enacted in 2003, that had been annulled by the Court in 2004.

Meanwhile, immigration and crime continued to dominate the political agenda. In June 2008 the European Union (EU) and several non-governmental organizations denounced the Government's proposals to introduce compulsory fingerprinting for all people of Roma origin, accusing it of racial discrimination. The proposals reflected growing anti-Roma sentiment, which followed a number of widely reported violent incidents involving Roma immigrants. In July Maroni declared a national state of emergency, citing statistics indicating that the number of migrants arriving in Italy had doubled during the first half of 2008, compared with the same period in the previous year. Earlier in July the Government had proposed measures designed to curb illegal immigration and reduce violent crime, under which illegal immigrants convicted of crimes would receive prison sentences of up to one-third longer than those imposed on Italian and other EU citizens. More controversially, the measures also included powers to deploy up to 3,000 troops to patrol strategic locations in major cities, including railway stations and detention centres for illegal immigrants. The measures received final approval from the Senate later that month, and the deployment of troops commenced in August. In February 2009, following several widely publicized incidents of rape allegedly perpetrated by immigrants, the Government promulgated a decree which provided for a mandatory life sentence for certain categories of rape and introduced other measures relating to sexual violence and harassment; controversially, it also sanctioned the creation of civilian street patrols to apprehend criminals, and extended the period for which illegal immigrants could be held in detention centres. The decree secured parliamentary approval in April, but only after amendments had been adopted removing the provisions relating to civilian patrols and detention centres. However, these measures were incorporated into a bill also before Parliament that, in addition, sought to make illegal immigration a criminal offence. This legislation was adopted in July. It was criticized by the opposition, the Roman Catholic Church and human rights groups on the grounds that it was likely to increase the growing number of racist and anti-immigrant attacks, as it was liable to promote the creation of vigilante groups who would target immigrants.

The trend for consolidation among the main parties continued in late 2008, as Forza Italia and the AN prepared to formalize the creation of a single, right-wing party. In November the national executive committee of Forza Italia agreed to dissolve the party into a new party to be named the Popolo della Libertà (PdL), after the existing coalition. In March 2009 AN officials confirmed the party's dissolution prior to joining the new party. The PdL was finally established as a single party, under the leadership of Berlusconi, at the end of the month. Eleven small parties joined the new organization, but the LN remained independent. Meanwhile, following its defeat at the April 2008 general election, the centre-left opposition struggled to make an impact. In February 2009 Veltroni resigned as National Secretary of the PD, citing his failure to establish the party as an effective opposition movement; he was replaced by Pier Luigi Bersani in October.

In October 2009 the Constitutional Court overturned the legislation of July 2008 granting immunity from prosecution to the holders of the highest offices of state, principally on the grounds that it violated the constitutional principle that all citizens were equal before the law. The court's ruling was given in response to an appeal by the prosecutors in the two corruption trials in which Berlusconi was a defendant. As a result, both trials (one relating to the purchase of film rights by Mediaset and the other to the alleged bribery of Mills) resumed in November 2009. Meanwhile, the Government introduced draft legislation in that month which sought to limit the length of trials for which the maximum sentence was less than 10 years' imprisonment, by imposing time limits on each of the three stages of a trial (the initial hearing and two appeals). The bill, which would apply retroactively, and which the Government described as a much-needed reform of Italy's notoriously slow judicial system, was approved by the Senate in January 2010, but subsequently stalled in the Chamber of Deputies. In April both trials involving Berlusconi were suspended again, pending a ruling from the Constitutional Court on the legitimacy of a law passed by Parliament in March, under which the Prime Minister and members of the Council of Ministers were to be granted the automatic suspension of legal process for a maximum of 18 months if they certified that their official commitments constituted a 'legitimate impediment' to their attendance at a trial. Also in April, in a second case involving Mediaset, Berlusconi was accused of tax fraud and embezzlement related to the purchase of film rights by the company's Mediatrade division.

Regional elections held in March 2010 resulted in gains for the centre-right parties—particularly the LN—at the expense of the centre-left. Although the PdL's performance declined slightly in relation to recent elections, the popularity of the party and of the Prime Minister appeared not to have been significantly damaged by the recent controversies surrounding Berlusconi's confrontation with the judiciary, nor by a series of sex and corruption scandals in which he had been involved since mid-2009.

Internal divisions (notably between Berlusconi and Gianfranco Fini, the erstwhile leader of the AN and the President of the Chamber of Deputies) and further corruption scandals threatened the stability of the Government in the months following the regional elections. Claudio Scajola resigned as Minister of Economic Development in May 2010, following allegations that he had purchased a property with financial assistance from an allegedly corrupt businessman. In June the appointment as a Minister without Portfolio of Aldo Brancher, a former business associate of Berlusconi who had been charged with embezzlement, was widely condemned, particularly after he invoked the so-called 'legitimate impediment' law in order to avoid a court hearing. Brancher resigned after just 17 days in office, shortly before an opposition-proposed motion of no confidence in him was due to be debated in Parliament. In July Nicola Cosentino, an under-secretary in the Ministry of the Economy and Finance, also stood down, after being placed under investigation in connection with his alleged involvement in a secret association of PdL officials and supporters seeking to influence political appointments and judicial decisions.

Proposed legislation to restrict the use of telephone-tapping in judicial investigations and to prevent pre-trial reporting of intercepted conversations provoked considerable controversy and further divisions within the PdL in mid-2010. It was claimed that the measures were designed to shield Berlusconi and other government officials from adverse media coverage rather than to protect the privacy of ordinary citizens; the bill was amended in July to allow the publication of transcripts of intercepted conversations when considered relevant by magistrates. However, the Chamber of Deputies subsequently postponed a vote on the proposed legislation (the unamended version of which had been approved by the Senate in June).

Continued tensions between the Prime Minister and the President of the Chamber of Deputies culminated at the end of July 2010 in the adoption by the executive committee of the PdL of a motion censuring Fini for fomenting internal dissent within the PdL and criticizing party decisions. Legislators loyal to Fini consequently formed a new parliamentary group, Futuro e Libertà per l'Italia (FLI—Future and Freedom for Italy). The Government was thus deprived of a majority in the Chamber of Deputies, although Fini stated that the FLI would support government proposals that fulfilled electoral pledges made by the PdL.

In a significant reverse for Berlusconi's administration, the FLI withdrew its four members from the Council of Ministers in mid-November 2010 in response to Berlusconi's rejection of an ultimatum issued by Fini that he should resign to form a new, broader coalition. Opposition demands for the Prime Minister's resignation had been precipitated by further revelations regarding his personal life. In mid-December the Government defeated motions of no confidence in Berlusconi tabled in both chambers of Parliament, although the margin of victory in the Chamber of Deputies was only three votes. Following Berlusconi's narrow survival in the lower house, some 50 police officers and 40 anti-Government protesters were injured during violent clashes in Rome.

In January 2011 the Constitutional Court delivered its verdict on the validity of the 'legitimate impediment' law, ruling that the suspension of legal process should not be automatic but should be decided by individual judges. The three corruption trials in which Berlusconi was a defendant (one relating to the alleged bribery of Mills and the other two to the acquisition of film rights by Mediaset and its Mediatrade division) resumed in early 2011. Berlusconi attended court (for the first time since 2003) for proceedings relating to all three cases. In February, moreover, the Prime Minister was ordered to stand trial in a fourth case, in which he was accused of paying for sex with an underage prostitute and of abusing his power by intervening to seek her release from custody after she was arrested on suspicion of theft in May 2010. The trial, which Berlusconi did not attend, opened in April 2011, but was immediately adjourned. In the same month the Government suffered a further setback when its proposals regarding amendments to the tax system were rejected by a parliamentary committee.

In April 2011 the Chamber of Deputies passed a bill to shorten the statute of limitations on trials of defendants with no previous convictions. The legislation, which required approval by the Senate, formed part of a broader proposed reform of the judiciary, which Berlusconi insisted was necessary to limit political interference by politically biased magistrates but which critics claimed was to protect Berlusconi from prosecution and would weaken judicial independence. In October the Prime Minister was cleared of all charges in one of the Mediaset cases, and in February 2012 the Mills case was abandoned, having expired under the statute of limitations.

Berlusconi's political future appeared increasingly uncertain following poor performances (at the expense of the centre-left) by the PdL and the LN in local elections in May 2011; notably, the PdL mayor of Milan was unexpectedly ousted from office by the left-wing candidate, thus ending almost 18 years of centre-right rule in the Prime Minister's home town. Since his return to power in 2008 Berlusconi's approval rating had fallen dramatically, and the problems arising from the ongoing sex scandals and trials were compounded by Italy's ailing economy and its mounting debt crisis. In June 2011 the Prime Minister's political standing suffered a further serious blow when the electorate voted against government policy in a referendum tabled by the opposition. Despite Berlusconi's appeals for a boycott of the poll, in the first referendum since 1995 to achieve the requisite quorum of more than 51% of the electorate (actual turnout was around 57%), the Italian people overwhelmingly rejected the Government's plans to revive nuclear power production and partially to privatize water utilities, and voted to repeal the controversial 'legitimate impediment' law.

In early July 2011 the Minister of the Economy and Finance, Giulio Tremonti, introduced an austerity package aimed at lowering the country's budget deficit; the proposals, which included a range of expenditure cuts and a new series of privatizations, were approved by the Chamber of Deputies on

15 July. However, later that month Tremonti's political credibility was threatened by revelations of his links to a number of individuals who were under investigation for suspected corruption involving official appointments and state tenders. Also in July, Berlusconi's weakening authority was highlighted by the lower house voting, for the first time, to divest a legislator (Alfonso Papa of the PdL) accused of corruption of his immunity from arrest.

In August 2011 concern mounted that Italy's increasing debt would necessitate an EU bailout or, at worst, lead to the collapse of the eurozone. In response to growing pressure from the European Central Bank, an emergency austerity package was approved by the Government on 12 August; however, much internal dissension ensued regarding the details of the proposals and numerous revisions were enacted before a compromise package was agreed upon. In early September there were further damaging revelations regarding Berlusconi's personal life and the Prime Minister's problems were exacerbated by a general strike called by the Confederazione Generale Italiana del Lavoro in protest at the proposed austerity measures. On 14 September the Chamber of Deputies passed the much-amended austerity package (approved earlier by the Senate), which included a pledge to balance the budget by 2013.

Mario Monti's Government of technocrats

Amid widespread doubts that the Prime Minister was capable of resolving Italy's financial crisis, and following a number of defections from the PdL and the loss of the Government's majority in the Chamber of Deputies in October 2011, Berlusconi—Italy's longest-serving post-war Prime Minister—resigned from office on 12 November. (Parliament had previously approved a stability law incorporating the urgent economic reforms demanded by the EU.) On 13 November President Napolitano appointed Mario Monti, a renowned economist and former EU commissioner, as the country's new Prime Minister. On 16 November Monti announced the formation of a new Council of Ministers, composed of a team of technocrats tasked with addressing the deepening financial crisis. Monti assumed responsibility for the economy and finance portfolio (although he transferred responsibility for the ministry to Vittorio Grilli in July 2012). In December 2011 Parliament approved a new package of stringent austerity measures drawn up by Monti.

In early April 2012 the treasurer of the LN and close associate of Bossi, Francesco Belsito, was forced to resign following allegations of his improper use of party subsidies (large amounts of which had reportedly been transferred for the personal use of Bossi and his immediate family); Belsito was replaced by Stefano Stefani. While denying any wrongdoing on his part, Bossi resigned as Federal Secretary of the LN and was replaced by former Minister of the Interior Maroni. Bossi was appointed to the honorary position of Federal President for Life of the LN in July.

The extent of the discontent arising from the Government's austerity drive was reflected in the gains made by various protest groups and parties of the centre-left (including the PD), at the expense mainly of the PdL and the scandal-hit LN, in mayoral and local elections held throughout Italy in May 2012. One protest group that performed particularly strongly in northern Italy (notably in Parma) was the MoVimento 5 Stelle (M5S, Five Star Movement), an anti-establishment group founded by the popular comedian and activist Beppe Grillo in 2009. M5S, which attracted much of its support from among the younger electorate, had no traditional party structure and operated mainly through the internet.

In October 2012 Berlusconi was convicted of tax fraud relating to the purchase of film rights by Mediaset; he was sentenced to four years' imprisonment (subsequently reduced to one year, although, according to legislation introduced by the former Prime Minister, no one older than 70 years could be incarcerated in Italy) and barred from holding political office for five years. Having immediately launched an appeal against the verdict, in December Berlusconi announced that he intended to stand as the prime ministerial candidate of the PdL in the forthcoming elections. (In March 2013 Berlusconi was convicted and sentenced to one year in prison for illegally tapping the telephone of a political rival in 2005.)

The general election of February 2013

On 21 December 2012, following the PdL's withdrawal of parliamentary support earlier that month on the grounds that the Government's austerity measures were harming Italy, Prime Minister Monti resigned, having first overseen, as promised, the approval of the 2013 budget by Parliament. At the President's request, Monti remained as head of an interim administration pending the holding of a general election on 24–25 February 2013, two months ahead of schedule. Not surprisingly, the main focus of the election campaign was Italy's ongoing economic crisis: Berlusconi, adopting an anti-austerity stance, pledged to cut (and even refund) taxes, while his party's two main rivals—a centrist coalition, Con Monti per l'Italia (With Monti for Italy), headed by Monti and a centre-left coalition led by Bersani's PD, Italia. Bene Comune (Italy Common Good)—advocated the retention, to varying degrees, of the austerity programme. In the final stages of the campaign M5S rallies attracted large crowds, as many Italians appeared to have become disillusioned with the country's mainstream political parties; Grillo (who did not stand for election himself, owing to a previous conviction) vehemently protested against corruption and austerity, and pledged to hold a referendum on Italy's continued membership of the eurozone.

As widely predicted, there was no clear victor in the general election, which attracted a turnout of around 75%, and the country was confronted by political deadlock, with no single party or coalition able to form a government (since to do so required the attainment of a working majority in both houses of the legislature). The PD and its allies secured a majority of 345 seats in the Chamber of Deputies, while the PdL and its centre-right allies won 125 seats, the M5S 109 seats and the centrist coalition headed by Monti 47 seats. However, no party or coalition won a majority in the Senate: the PD and its allies obtained 123 seats in the upper house, the PdL and its allies 117 seats, the M5S 54 seats and Monti's coalition 19 seats. The widespread unpopularity of Monti's austerity programme was vividly illustrated by his coalition's poor performance in the polls and, conversely, by the extraordinary success achieved by Grillo's protest movement (whose new parliamentarians had little or no previous political experience).

In March 2013 the Minister of Foreign Affairs, Giulio Terzi di Sant'Agata, resigned in protest at the Government's sending back to India for trial of two Italian marines, who were accused of killing two Indian fishermen off the coast of Kerala in February 2012 (the marines, who had been guarding an Italian oil tanker, claimed to have mistaken the fishermen for pirates). The marines had been allowed to return to Italy in February 2013 for a four-week period in order to vote in the legislative elections. The Italian Government, which had originally insisted that the marines should be tried in Italy since the incident took place in international waters, agreed to their rendition following the imposition by the Indian Supreme Court of a travel ban on the Italian ambassador, Daniele Mancini, in New Delhi. The diplomatic dispute intensified in February 2014 when the Italian Government recalled Mancini to Italy in protest at the Indian authorities' decision to try the two defendants under anti-piracy law.

Meanwhile, as political deadlock persisted, with Bersani failing to form a coalition Government in late March 2013 (largely as a result of his refusal to work with Berlusconi), President Napolitano appointed a commission of 10 experts from the fields of politics, the judiciary and business, the so-called 'wise men', who reported in April on possible political and economic reforms. At presidential elections held on 18–20 April, the first five rounds of voting failed to produce a clear winner. In response to a cross-party appeal, the widely respected incumbent, Napolitano, who was due to retire in mid-May, presented himself as a candidate in the sixth round. The veteran politician was elected to an unprecedented second term of office, defeating the M5S candidate, Stefano Rodotà, by 738 votes to 217. Bersani resigned as leader of the PD immediately after the eventual conclusion of the presidential election, which had exposed the lack of unity between factions of the PD—many of the parliamentary deputies of the party, including the young mayor of Florence, Matteo Renzi (who had stood against Bersani in the PD leadership contest in October 2009), had refused to support Bersani's preferred presidential candidate. (Guglielmo Epifani replaced Bersani as National Secretary of the PD, on an interim basis, in May.) The re-elected President continued efforts to break the political impasse by requesting that the deputy leader of the PD, Enrico Letta, attempt to form a broad coalition. A new 'grand coalition' Government was finally sworn in on 28 April headed by Letta and comprising the PD, PdL, UdC, Scelta Civica (Civic Choice), Radicali Italiani and independent experts; the M5S refused to form part of the coalition. Noteworthy appointments included that of the Secretary of the PdL, Angelino Alfano, as Deputy

Prime Minister and Minister of the Interior and that of the Director-General of the Banca d'Italia, Fabrizio Saccomanni, as Minister of the Economy and Finance.

Recent developments: further political upheaval

An apparent decline in support for the M5S was indicated by its extremely poor performance in local elections held throughout Italy in May/June 2013; there were also reports of growing internal dissatisfaction with Grillo's leadership: by March 2014 13 M5S members of the Senate had either resigned from or had been expelled from the organization. The following month Alfano comfortably survived a vote of no confidence held in the Senate in the wake of allegations that he had been involved in the extradition from Italy of a Kazakh dissident and his family.

In late June 2013 Berlusconi was convicted of paying for sex with an underage prostitute in 2010 and of abuse of office; he was sentenced to seven years' imprisonment and a life-long ban from holding public office. Berlusconi suffered a more serious setback the following month when the Supreme Court of Cassation rejected his final appeal against the custodial sentence imposed on him (for tax fraud) in 2012; the Court also ordered a further judicial review on whether the former Prime Minister should be banned from holding public office. This ruling represented the first of Berlusconi's convictions to be confirmed on appeal in more than 20 years of fighting legal cases; however, rather than being incarcerated, the former Prime Minister was expected to serve house arrest or community service. In accordance with an anti-corruption law passed in 2012, Berlusconi now faced being expelled from the Senate. In protest against such an action, in September 2013 Berlusconi threatened to bring Letta's fragile administration to the verge of collapse by ordering the withdrawal of all PdL deputies from Parliament. The crisis was further compounded at the end of the month when, in an attempt to pre-empt the planned holding of a vote of confidence in the Government (as called for by Letta), Berlusconi ordered the resignation of the five PdL members of the Council of Ministers, citing his party's opposition to a proposed increase in the sales tax. However, Letta refused to accept the resignations. In the event, amid reports of the ministers' unwillingness to comply with their leader's order that they stand down and of threatened defections from the ranks of the more moderate PdL parliamentarians, Berlusconi carried out a dramatic *volte-face* when he supported the crucial vote of confidence in Letta's Government in early October. Later that month Berlusconi was ordered to stand trial on charges of bribing a senator to defect to his party in 2006 (the trial commenced in February 2014). Berlusconi's political standing appeared further diminished in mid-November 2013 when a group of some 60 PdL dissidents, led by Deputy Prime Minister Alfano, announced the establishment of a new party, the Nuovo Centrodestra (NC—New Centre-Right). The following day Berlusconi officially relaunched the PdL under his party's founding name, Forza Italia. At the end of November Berlusconi formally withdrew Forza Italia from the coalition, while the NC remained as a constituent party. A few days later the Senate voted to expel Berlusconi with immediate effect and barred him from standing in any election for six years; furthermore, without parliamentary immunity, the veteran politician now confronted the possibility of being arrested on other criminal charges. In March 2014 the Supreme Court of Cassation upheld a two-year ban on standing for public office which was imposed on Berlusconi after his conviction for tax fraud. None the less, Berlusconi defiantly pledged to continue his political career from outside parliamentary confines.

In early December 2013 Renzi won an overwhelming victory in a leadership contest for the PD. In the same month a series of protests were held across the country to protest against the Government's continuing programme of economic austerity. The demonstrations, which, in several instances were forcibly dispersed by riot police, attracted a disparate selection of the population, including framers, road hauliers, students and the unemployed. Also in December Prime Minister Letta announced that state funding of political parties was to be abolished.

The new PD leader, Renzi, made his debut in national politics by announcing in January 2014 his party's proposals for comprehensive reform of the electoral system and Constitution in a bid to end political instability and weak governance. The proposals, which—controversially—had earlier been discussed with and had won the approval of Berlusconi and his party, included changes to the proportional electoral system and the replacement of the Senate by a consultative body comprising regional and local representatives. Following a decision by the PD to support Renzi's demands for the installation of a new government and against a background of increasing pressure over the country's foundering economy, Letta resigned on 14 February. As widely predicted, President Napolitano asked Renzi to form a new government: the new coalition of the PD, NC, UdC, Scelta Civica and independents took office later that month. Notable new appointments to the Council of Ministers (one-half of which was female) included Federica Mogherini as Minister of Foreign Affairs, Roberta Pinotti as Minister of Defence and Pier Carlo Padoan, OECD Chief Economist, as Minister of the Economy and Finance. Alfano kept his position as Minister of the Interior.

Organized Crime

Despite mass trials of Mafia suspects in the late 1980s, the Italian Government continued to experience problems in dealing with organized crime. In 1992 the murders of Salvatore Lima, a Sicilian politician and member of the European Parliament, Giovanni Falcone, a prominent anti-Mafia judge, and Paolo Borsellino, a colleague of Falcone, provoked renewed public outrage, and later that year, following an increase in the powers of the police and the judiciary, hundreds of suspects were detained. In 1993 the judiciary mounted a campaign to seize Mafia funds, and in the course of the year several suspected leading figures in the world of organized crime, including Salvatore Riina, the alleged head of the Sicilian Mafia ('Cosa Nostra'), were arrested. In September 1997 24 influential members of the Mafia, including Riina, were sentenced to life imprisonment for their part in the murder of Falcone. The following July Riina received another conviction, along with 17 others, for complicity in the murder of Lima in 1992; this constituted Riina's 13th sentence of life imprisonment. In April 1999 an official of the treasury ministry was arrested on charges of external complicity with the Mafia; he was the first serving government member to be taken into preventive detention. In December 17 Mafia members were sentenced to life imprisonment for the murder of Borsellino. Emergency measures were decreed in November 2000 in an attempt to prevent the early release from prison of those accused of Mafia-related crimes. The laws followed the discharge, on technical grounds, of 10 detainees accused of involvement in murders attributed to the Mafia. Magistrates were granted greater powers in determining the length of preventive detention for suspects and a ban on plea-bargaining was introduced. Benedetto Spera, reputedly the closest colleague of the head (since 1995) of the Sicilian Mafia, Bernardo Provenzano, had also been arrested at the end of January; Spera had been convicted *in absentia* for his role in the murders of Falcone and Borsellino. In April 2001 Riina, along with six others, was sentenced to 30 years' imprisonment for the murder, in 1979, of the investigative journalist Mario Francese.

Organized crime continued to be problematic during Berlusconi's second term as Prime Minister. Provenzano's closest accomplice, Antonino Giuffrè, was arrested in April 2002 near Palermo. In December Giuffrè directly implicated Berlusconi in the bribing of the Mafia for votes in Sicily in 1993. (In April 2006 Provenzano himself, who had been in hiding since 1963, was arrested in Sicily.) Although a murder charge against Berlusconi was dropped in May 2002, a nine-year prison sentence (later reduced to seven years) for Mafia collusion was imposed on his close friend Marcello Dell'Utri in December 2004. Further allegations about Berlusconi's links with the Mafia emerged during Dell'Utri's trial in January 2003, when it was alleged by a Mafia informer that the Mafia had transferred its allegiance from the DC to Berlusconi's Forza Italia after the latter's formation in 1994.

In September 2004 an investigation into the President of the Sicilian regional administration, Salvatore Cuffaro of the UDC, concluded that he had indirectly aided the Mafia by transmitting sensitive information. In January 2008 Cuffaro was convicted and sentenced to five years' imprisonment. Later that month Cuffaro was forced to resign, despite having refused to do so in the aftermath of his conviction. However, pending the appeal process, Cuffaro was re-elected to the Senate in April. Cuffaro's sentence was increased to seven years in January 2010 by an appeals court in Palermo, which convicted him of the additional charge of favouring the Mafia. This verdict was confirmed by the Supreme Court of Cassation a year later, resulting in Cuffaro's imprisonment and the loss of his seat in the Senate.

During 2010–11 the Italian authorities focused their activities against organized crime on seizing control of the various assets of the Mafia (including properties, bank accounts, land, football clubs, vehicles, etc.) in an attempt to weaken the syndicate's financial structure. One of the most powerful organized crime networks in Italy, the 'Ndrangheta, which is based in the southern region of Calabria, suffered a serious setback in 2010 when police arrested more than 300 suspected members. In March 2012, in a major anti-Mafia operation centred on Naples, the police seized assets worth some US $1,300m. and arrested 16 judges who were alleged to have accepted bribes to issue rulings in favour of the Camorra organized crime group. In an attempt to prevent it from being overrun by suspected Mafia associates, the entire city council of Reggio Calabria was dismissed by the central authorities in October. The alleged head of the 'Ndrangheta, Roberto Pannunzi, who had escaped from custody in Rome in 2010, was arrested in Colombia in July 2013; the Colombian police described Pannunzi as 'Europe's most wanted drugs trafficker'. In January 2014 the Government was reportedly considering deploying the army to tackle the long-running problem of the illegal dumping of toxic waste in Naples and its environs, allegedly by members of the Camorra.

Foreign Affairs

Regional relations

Italy's foreign policy has traditionally been governed by its firm commitment to Europe, notably through its membership of the European Community (now European Union—EU, see p. 273) and NATO (see p. 370). The heads of state and of government of the EU formally approved the Treaty establishing a Constitution for Europe in October 2004, which required ratification by all 25 member states. Italy ratified the constitutional treaty by parliamentary vote in April 2005. However, the process of ratification was stalled, following the treaty's rejection in national referendums in France and the Netherlands in May and June, respectively. A reform treaty, to replace the constitutional treaty, was signed by EU heads of state and of government, including Prodi, at a summit meeting in Lisbon, Portugal, on 13 December 2007. The Treaty of Lisbon was ratified by the Italian Parliament in August 2008 and entered into force in December 2009.

Italy's extended coastline and geographical position attracts many illegal immigrants from South-Eastern Europe and North Africa. Following Italy's accession to the EU's Schengen Agreement on cross-border travel in October 1997, large numbers of refugees, mainly Turkish and Iraqi Kurds, began arriving in southern Italy, provoking concern from Italy's EU partners. On 1 April 1998 the Schengen Agreement, which had previously only been applicable to air travel between Italy and the other EU member states, was fully implemented, opening the borders with Austria and France. In order to comply with the terms of the agreement, a new law had been promulgated in February, providing for the detention, prior to forcible repatriation, of illegal immigrants. In February 1999 legislation was approved allowing for the detention of illegal immigrants arriving in Italy without first making an asylum application. In March 2002 a state of emergency was declared following the arrival of 1,000 Kurdish refugees in Sicily. In June legislation was passed allowing for the fingerprinting of non-EU nationals and requiring residence permits to be renewed every two years. Further increases in arrivals of immigrants prompted a government decree in June 2003 enabling the Italian navy to board ships carrying illegal immigrants and divert them away from the Italian coast.

In August 2004 an agreement was reached with Libya on controlling immigration through that country, and in October the Italian Government commenced returning would-be immigrants to Libya by aircraft. In September 2006 the Italian and Libyan Governments were accused of abusing the human rights of African migrants through forced repatriations. Italy signed an agreement with Libya in December 2007, with regard to establishing joint maritime patrols, although little progress was initially made. In August 2008, however, the two countries signed an accord under which Italy was to invest US $5,000m. in Libya over the following 20 years, in recognition of the injustices Libyans suffered in the colonial era, for which Berlusconi offered an official apology. In May 2009 it was announced that, in accordance with the terms of the so-called 'friendship agreement', joint maritime patrols had begun. The number of boats carrying illegal immigrants from Libya to Italy subsequently declined sharply. Given its extensive business and trade links with Libya, the Italian Government's response to a popular uprising in that country in February 2011 was initially cautious. A threat by the Libyan leader, Col Muammar al-Qaddafi, to end co-operation with the EU on illegal migration from North Africa if the EU supported anti-Government protesters in Libya was of particular concern to Italy, which had received an influx of some 5,000 migrants from Tunisia that month, in the wake of a revolution there. Nevertheless, the Italian Government condemned the violent repression of the anti-Government demonstrations in Libya and, following the evacuation of its citizens from that country, suspended the 2008 friendship agreement and announced its support for EU sanctions against Qaddafi's regime. During 2011 thousands of migrants from Tunisia, Libya and Egypt arrived by boat on the Italian island of Lampedusa following the civil unrest in those countries. Relations between Italy and France deteriorated as France objected to Italy providing thousands of Tunisian migrants with temporary residence permits, which enabled them to travel within the EU (often to France). In April, however, Italy and France agreed to launch joint sea and air patrols in an attempt to limit the influx from North Africa. In the same month the Italian Government committed Italy to joining France, the United Kingdom and the USA in mounting air strikes against Libya. In retaliation, the Italian embassy in Tripoli was attacked by Qaddafi loyalists in early May. Despite this, talks between 22 countries supporting the rebels in Libya took place in Rome later that month, chaired by Italy and Qatar; it was agreed to establish a non-military fund to help the rebels. Following the collapse of Qaddafi's regime in September and the death of the former dictator the following month, relations between Italy and Libya began to be normalized. Prime Minister Monti visited Tripoli in January 2012 to hold discussions with the transitional administration.

During 2013 thousands of migrants continued to attempt the dangerous crossing from North Africa across the Mediterranean to Sicily and other Italian islands. According to official figures, the number of migrants who reached Italy by sea in 2013 totalled almost 43,000, representing an increase of some 325% compared with the previous year. In October at least 366 African migrants (mainly from Eritrea and Somalia) died when the overcrowded boat that was carrying them sank off the coast of Lampedusa. In response to this disaster, the Italian Government announced an increase in the number of sea and air patrols.

Other external relations

Under the premiership of Berlusconi in 2001–06 increasing emphasis on promoting national interests was accompanied by a repositioning of Italian foreign policy towards support for the USA in its 'war on terror'. The deployment of some 2,700 Italian troops to assist US military efforts following the September 2001 suicide attacks on New York and Washington, DC, USA, was approved by the Italian Parliament in November. An investigation into the existence of terrorist cells possibly connected with the al-Qa'ida organization headed by the Saudi-born dissident Osama bin Laden led to a number of arrests in Italy in 2002–03. Berlusconi's increasing political allegiance with the so-called 'coalition of the willing' (the group of powers, including the USA, the United Kingdom and Spain, which was in favour of military action against the regime of Saddam Hussain in Iraq), gave rise to massive nationwide protests in February 2003. Owing to the level of popular dissent, the Italian Government did not at this stage agree to supply troops for the US-led military campaign in Iraq; it did, however, offer the USA the use of Italy's bases and airspace for logistical purposes. At the onset of armed conflict in Iraq in March, the anti-war movement in Italy gained momentum. In April the Government approved the provision of humanitarian support for Iraq; however, by November Italy had approximately 2,400 troops stationed in the country. In that month a suicide bombing took place at an Italian base in Nasiriyah, Iraq, killing 19 Italian soldiers; this led to renewed calls for Italy to pull out of Iraq. Pressure for the withdrawal of troops increased following the kidnapping and murder of an Italian journalist by Islamist extremists in Iraq in August 2004. In January 2006 the Italian Government announced that all 3,000 Italian troops then stationed in Iraq would be withdrawn by the end of the year; the last Italian troops left Iraq in early December.

Following the conflict in Lebanon between Israeli forces and the militant group Hezbollah in mid-2006, Italy sent some 2,500 peacekeeping troops to form part of the UN Interim Force in Lebanon (UNIFIL); at February 2013 the Italian contingent of UNIFIL numbered 1,097 troops. In early 2013 Italy also had around 4,000 troops stationed in Afghanistan as part of the NATO-led peacekeeping force (the International Security Assistance Force—ISAF).

CONSTITUTION AND GOVERNMENT

Under the 1948 Constitution, legislative power was held by the bicameral Parliament (Parlamento), elected by universal suffrage for five years (subject to dissolution) on the basis of proportional representation. A referendum held in 1993 supported the amendment of the Constitution to provide for the election of 75% of the members of the Senate of the Republic (Senato della Repubblica) by a simple plurality and the remainder under a system of proportional representation, and provided for further electoral reform. In August Parliament approved a similar system for elections to the Chamber of Deputies (Camera dei Deputati). In December 2005 new legislation was enacted providing for the return to full proportional representation. The Senate has 315 elected members (seats allocated on a regional basis) and up to five life Senators appointed by the President. The Chamber of Deputies has 630 members. The minimum voting age is 25 years for the Senate and 18 years for the Chamber of Deputies. The two houses have equal power.

The President of the Republic is a constitutional head of state elected for seven years by an electoral college comprising both houses of Parliament and 58 regional representatives. Executive power is exercised by the Council of Ministers. The head of state appoints the President of the Council (Prime Minister) and, on the latter's recommendation, other ministers. The Council is responsible to Parliament.

The country is divided into 20 regions, of which five (Sicily, Sardinia, Trentino-Alto Adige/Südtirol, Friuli-Venezia Giulia and Valle d'Aosta) enjoy a special autonomous status. There is a large degree of regional autonomy. Each region has a Regional Council elected every five years by universal suffrage and a Giunta Regionale responsible to the Regional Council. The Regional Council is a legislative assembly, while the Giunta holds executive power. At February 2014 the regions were subdivided into a total of 109 provinces and 8,058 municipalities. The Government planned to carry out a substantial reorganization of the provinces later that year which would result in a considerable reduction in their number. In 2009 legislation was passed establishing 10 metropolitan cities (città metropolitane); however, at early 2014 these new administrative divisions were not yet operational.

REGIONAL AND INTERNATIONAL CO-OPERATION

Italy was a founder member of the European Community, now the European Union (EU, see p. 273), and uses the single currency, the euro. It is a member of the Council of Europe (see p. 252), the Central European Initiative (see p. 464) and the Organization for Security and Co-operation in Europe (OSCE, see p. 387).

Italy joined the UN in 1955. As a contracting party to the General Agreement on Tariffs and Trade, Italy joined the World Trade Organization (WTO, see p. 434) on its establishment in 1995. Italy is also a member of the North Atlantic Treaty Organization (NATO, see p. 370), the Organisation for Economic Co-operation and Development (OECD, see p. 379), the Group of Eight major industrialized nations (G8, see p. 465) and the Group of 20 major industrialized and systemically important emerging market nations (G20, see p. 456).

ECONOMIC AFFAIRS

In 2012, according to estimates by the World Bank, Italy's gross national income (GNI), measured at average 2010–12 prices, was US $2,061,253m., equivalent to $33,840 per head (or $32,870 per head on an international purchasing-power parity basis). During 2003–12, it was estimated that the population increased by an average of 0.6% per year, while Italy's gross domestic product (GDP) per head decreased, in real terms, at an average annual rate of 0.7%. Overall GDP decreased, in real terms, at an average annual rate of 0.1% in 2003–12; GDP increased by 0.4% in 2011, but decreased by 2.4% in 2012.

Agriculture (including forestry and fishing) contributed 2.0% of GDP in 2012, and engaged 3.8% of the employed labour force in July–September 2013. The principal crops are maize, grapes, wheat, tomatoes and sugar beet. Italy is a leading producer and exporter of wine. According to the World Bank, during 2003–10 the real GDP of the agricultural sector increased at an average rate of 1.0% per year. According to chain-linked methodologies, agricultural GDP grew by 0.5% in 2011, but decreased by 4.4% in 2012.

Industry (including mining, manufacturing, construction and power) contributed 24.2% of GDP in 2012, and engaged 27.1% of the employed labour force in July–September 2013. According to the World Bank, real industrial GDP fell by an average of 1.4% per year during 2003–10; the GDP of the sector declined by 13.9% in 2009, but increased by 2.9% in 2010.

The mining sector contributed just 0.4% of GDP in 2012, and engaged 0.2% of the employed labour force in 2008. The major product of the mining sector is petroleum, followed by talc, feldspar, rock salt and gypsum. Italy also has reserves of lignite, lead and zinc. According to chain-linked methodologies, mining GDP increased by 3.5% in 2012.

Manufacturing contributed 15.6% of GDP in 2012, and engaged 20.5% of the employed labour force in 2008. The most important branches of manufacturing are metals and metal products, non-electrical machinery, food products, textiles and wearing apparel, rubber and plastic products, wood and paper products, and transport equipment. According to the World Bank, in 2003–10 the GDP of the manufacturing sector declined, in real terms, at an average annual rate of 1.7%. According to chain-linked methodologies, manufacturing GDP increased by 1.7% in 2011, but fell by 3.7% in 2012.

Construction contributed 5.9% of GDP in 2012, and engaged 8.4% of the employed labour force in 2008. According to chain-linked methodologies, the construction sector contracted by 5.8% in 2012.

More than 80% of energy requirements are imported. According to World Bank figures, in 2012 natural gas-fired stations provided 46.1% of electricity production, coal-fired electricity generating stations 16.0%, hydroelectric power stations 14.2% and petroleum 6.3%. In 2004 Libya began delivering natural gas to Sicily through a pipeline financed by Ente Nazionale Idrocarburi (Eni), the main—formerly wholly state-owned—gas provider, and its Libyan counterpart. In 2011, according to the World Bank, fuel imports accounted for 19.9% of the value of total merchandise imports.

Services accounted for 73.8% of GDP in 2012, and engaged 69.1% of the employed labour force in July–September 2013. Tourism is an important source of income; in 2012 48.7m. foreigners visited Italy, compared with 47.5m. in the previous year. Tourism receipts totalled US $41,185m. in 2012. According to the World Bank, the combined GDP of the services sector increased, in real terms, at an estimated average rate of 0.8% per year in 2003–10; sectoral GDP grew by 1.8% in 2012.

In 2012, according to IMF data, Italy recorded a visible merchandise trade surplus of US $25,402m., while there was a deficit of $8,054m. on the current account of the balance of payments. According to official provisional figures, in 2012 the principal source of imports was Germany (14.6%); other major suppliers were France, the People's Republic of China and the Netherlands. Germany was also the principal market for exports (12.5%); other major purchasers in that year were France, the USA, Switzerland and the United Kingdom. In 2012 Italy's fellow members of the European Union (EU, see p. 273) were the source of 52.9% of Italy's imports and purchased 53.7% of its exports. The principal exports in 2012 were machinery and mechanical equipment, metals and metal products, textile products, chemicals and artificial fibres, transport equipment, electrical equipment, food, beverages and tobacco, rubber, plastic products and non-metallic minerals, and refined oil products. The principal imports were chemicals and artificial fibres, crude petroleum, electrical equipment, metals and metal products, transport equipment, textile products, natural gas, food, beverages and tobacco, and machinery and mechanical equipment.

According to preliminary figures, the budgetary deficit for 2012 was €45,700m., equivalent to 2.9% of annual GDP. Italy's general government gross debt was €1,988,363m. in 2012, equivalent to 127.0% of GDP. According to the International Labour Organization the average annual rate of inflation in 2003–12 was 2.2%. Consumer prices increased by 3.1% in 2012. The rate of unemployment averaged 11.3% in July–September 2013.

Although Italy's economy is the fourth largest in Europe, the country suffers from significant structural problems, including low productivity, an inefficient public sector, and considerable economic disparity between the more industrialized, prosperous north and the impoverished south. Following the deterioration in global economic conditions in 2008, Italy officially entered a recession. Real GDP contracted by 1.3% in 2008 and by a further 5.1% in 2009, largely owing to declines in domestic demand, investment and the value of exports, while the budget deficit widened to 2.7% of GDP in 2008 and to 5.4% in 2009. In contrast to other advanced economies, the Italian Government was able to introduce only limited fiscal stimulus owing to the country's high public debt. Moderate growth of 1.3% in 2010 was driven mainly by an increase in the value of exports, as global demand recovered, and the budget deficit narrowed to 4.6% of GDP in that year. However, the debt-to-GDP ratio continued to rise, reaching 119.0% in 2010 (the second highest in the eurozone after Greece), and unemployment remained high, at 8.6% in December. A number of austerity packages were implemented by Silvio Berlusconi's Government in 2011 as the financial crisis deepened and Italy's borrowing costs soared to unsustainable levels. Although the budget deficit fell to 3.8% of GDP in that year, the rate of overall growth decelerated to 0.4% and the debt-to-GDP ratio had increased to 120.1% by the end of December. Following Berlusconi's resignation in November 2011, Prime Minister Mario Monti introduced an emergency package of fiscal adjustments in December, including new taxes, drastic cuts in public expenditure, the sale of state assets, a rise in fuel costs and controversial changes to the pension system. However, although these stringent measures led in 2012 to a further reduction in the budget deficit to match the EU ceiling of 3.0% of GDP, the situation deteriorated in other aspects, with the debt-to-GDP ratio rising to 127.0%, a contraction of 2.4% in real GDP, a significant downturn in the property market, and an increase in the unemployment rate to 10.8% at mid-year. Against a background of political instability and falling output and consumer demand, Italy's economic prospects remained bleak in 2013, with unemployment reaching 12.5% in September (the highest level since official records began in 1977). The high rate of youth unemployment (exceeding 40%) was a source of particular concern. Real GDP was projected to decline by a further 1.7% in 2013 and the debt-to-GDP ratio was forecast to reach a record high of 130.4%. Prime Minister Matteo Renzi announced in April 2014 that GDP was forecast to increase by just 0.8% in 2014. However, owing to the continuing austerity programme, the budget deficit was expected to decrease to 2.9% of GDP in 2013 and further to 2.6% in 2014.

PUBLIC HOLIDAYS

2015: 1 January (New Year's Day), 6 January (Epiphany), 6 April (Easter Monday), 25 April (Liberation Day), 1 May (Labour Day), 2 June (Republic Day), 15 August (Assumption), 1 November (All Saints' Day), 8 December (Immaculate Conception), 25 December (Christmas Day), 26 December (St Stephen's Day).

There are also numerous local public holidays, held on the feast day of the patron saint of each town.

Statistical Survey

Source (unless otherwise stated): Istituto Nazionale di Statistica, Via Cesare Balbo 16, 00184 Roma; tel. (06) 46731; fax (06) 467313101; e-mail info@istat.it; internet www.istat.it.

Area and Population

AREA, POPULATION AND DENSITY

Area (sq km)	301,336*
Population (census results)†	
21 October 2001	56,995,744
9 October 2011	
Males	28,745,507
Females	30,688,237
Total	59,433,744
Population (official estimates at 1 January)	
2012	59,394,207
2013	59,685,227
Density (per sq km) at 1 January 2013	198.1

* 116,346 sq miles.

† Census figures are *de jure*, in 2001 the de facto population was 57,110,144 (males 27,617,335, females 29,492,809).

POPULATION BY AGE AND SEX
(official population estimates at 1 January 2013)

	Males	Females	Total
0–14	4,289,923	4,058,415	8,348,338
15–64	19,218,339	19,478,721	38,697,060
65 and over	5,381,335	7,258,494	12,639,829
Total	28,889,597	30,795,630	59,685,227

REGIONS
(official population estimates at 1 January 2013)

Region	Area (sq km)	Population	Density (per sq km)	Regional capital(s)
Abruzzo	10,763	1,312,507	121.9	L'Aquila
Basilicata	9,995	576,194	57.6	Potenza
Calabria	15,081	1,958,238	129.8	Catanzaro
Campania	13,590	5,769,750	424.6	Napoli (Naples)
Emilia-Romagna	22,117	4,377,487	197.9	Bologna
Friuli-Venezia Giulia	7,858	1,221,860	155.5	Trieste
Lazio	17,236	5,557,276	322.4	Roma (Rome)
Liguria	5,422	1,565,127	288.7	Genova (Genoa)
Lombardia (Lombardy)	23,863	9,794,525	410.4	Milano (Milan)
Marche	9,694	1,545,155	159.4	Ancona
Molise	4,438	313,341	70.6	Campobasso
Piemonte (Piedmont)	25,402	4,374,052	172.2	Torino (Turin)
Puglia	19,358	4,050,803	209.3	Bari
Sardegna (Sardinia)	24,090	1,640,379	68.1	Cagliari
Sicilia (Sicily)	25,711	4,999,932	194.5	Palermo
Toscana (Tuscany)	22,994	3,692,828	160.6	Firenze (Florence)
Trentino-Alto Adige/Südtirol	13,607	1,039,934	76.4	Bolzano/Trento*
Umbria	8,456	886,239	104.8	Perugia
Valle d'Aosta	3,263	127,844	39.2	Aosta
Veneto	18,399	4,881,756	265.3	Venezia (Venice)
Total	301,336	59,685,227	198.1	—

* Bolzano (Bozen) and Trento (Trent) are joint regional capitals of Trentino-Alto Adige/Südtirol.

PRINCIPAL TOWNS
(official population estimates at 1 January 2013, measured by *comune*)

Roma (Rome, the capital)	2,638,842	Livorno (Leghorn)	156,998
Milano (Milan)	1,262,101	Ravenna	154,288
Napoli (Naples)	959,052	Cagliari	149,575
Torino (Turin)	872,091	Foggia	148,573
Palermo	654,987	Rimini	143,731
Genova (Genoa)	582,320	Salerno	131,925
Bologna	380,635	Ferrara	131,842
Firenze (Florence)	366,039	Sassari	125,672
Bari	313,213	Monza	120,440
Catania	290,678	Latina	119,426
Venezia (Venice)	259,263	Siracusa (Syracuse)	118,644
Verona	253,409	Pescara	117,091
Messina	242,267	Forlí	116,029
Padova (Padua)	207,245	Trento (Trent)	115,540
Trieste	201,148	Bergamo	115,072
Taranto	198,728	Vicenza	113,639
Brescia	188,520	Giugliano in Campania	110,473
Prato	187,159	Terni	109,382
Reggio di Calabria	180,686	Bolzano	103,891
Modena	179,353	Novara	101,933
Parma	177,714	Piacenza	100,843
Reggio nell'Emilia	163,928	Andria	100,432
Perugia	162,986	Ancona	100,343

BIRTHS, MARRIAGES AND DEATHS

	Registered live births		Registered marriages		Registered deaths	
	Number	Rate (per 1,000)	Number	Rate (per 1,000)	Number	Rate (per 1,000)
2005	554,022	9.7	247,740	4.2	567,304	9.8
2006	560,010	9.5	245,992	4.2	557,892	9.5
2007	563,933	9.5	250,360	4.2	570,801	9.6
2008	576,659	9.6	246,613	4.1	585,126	9.8
2009	568,857	9.5	230,613	3.8	591,663	9.8
2010	561,944	9.3	217,700	3.6	587,488	9.7
2011	546,607	9.0	204,830	3.5	593,404	9.7
2012	534,186	9.0	207,138	3.5	612,883	10.3

Life expectancy (years at birth): 82.1 (males 79.6; females 84.7) in 2011 (Source: World Bank, World Development Indicators database).

IMMIGRATION AND EMIGRATION

Immigrants by country of last residence	1998	1999	2000
European Union (EU)	24,140	24,088	25,955
France	4,160	3,892	4,328
Germany	9,435	9,608	10,054
United Kingdom	3,587	3,604	3,844
Other European countries	49,585	69,650	86,477
Albania	19,973	28,838	32,181
Poland	3,012	3,165	5,086
Romania	7,119	10,986	19,710
Switzerland	5,027	5,507	5,687
former Yugoslavia	7,813	11,926	11,991
Africa	30,930	41,967	48,925
Morocco	12,984	19,526	20,344
Senegal	2,167	3,458	4,681
Middle East and Asia	30,406	25,362	36,513
China, People's Republic	7,224	6,119	9,451
India	3,162	3,607	4,759
Philippines	9,089	4,898	7,003
Sri Lanka	3,463	2,942	4,243
Americas	21,287	23,491	28,485
Peru	4,893	3,935	5,279
USA	3,619	3,631	4,055
Oceania	537	494	613
Total	156,885	185,052	226,968

Emigrants by country of destination	1998	1999	2000
European Union (EU)	19,844	28,595	24,493
France	2,848	4,052	3,394
Germany	9,128	13,372	11,413
United Kingdom	3,187	4,535	3,919
Other European countries	9,881	13,677	12,245
Switzerland	6,127	8,850	7,416
former Yugoslavia	1,102	1,163	1,310
Africa	3,185	4,441	4,149
Middle East and Asia	2,849	3,613	3,423
Americas	9,677	13,912	11,740
Argentina	2,141	3,188	2,685
Brazil	953	1,349	1,168
USA	3,555	4,973	4,156
Oceania	453	635	551
Total	45,889	64,873	56,601

Total immigrants: 326,673 in 2005; 297,640 in 2006; 558,019 in 2007; 534,712 in 2008; 442,940 in 2009; 458,856 in 2010; 412,344 in 2011; 350,772 in 2012.

Total emigrants: 65,029 in 2005; 75,230 in 2006; 65,196 in 2007; 80,947 in 2008; 80,597 in 2009; 78,771 in 2010; 96,308 in 2011; 106,216 in 2012.

ECONOMICALLY ACTIVE POPULATION

('000 persons aged 15 years and over)

	2006	2007	2008
Agriculture, hunting and forestry	948	888	860
Fishing	34	35	35
Mining and quarrying	42	39	36
Manufacturing	4,826	4,870	4,805
Electricity, gas and water	159	139	144
Construction	1,900	1,955	1,970
Wholesale and retail trade; repair of motor vehicles, motorcycles and personal and household goods	3,522	3,541	3,540
Restaurants and hotels	1,114	1,154	1,179
Transport, storage and communications	1,224	1,257	1,294
Financial intermediation	675	664	653
Real estate, renting and business activities	2,434	2,542	2,618
Public administration and defence; compulsory social security	1,443	1,418	1,436
Education	1,597	1,606	1,584
Health and social work	1,570	1,575	1,659
Other community, social and personal service activities	1,164	1,167	1,136
Private households with employed persons	324	349	419
Extra-territorial bodies and organizations	12	22	36
Total employed	22,988	23,222	23,405
Unemployed	1,673	1,506	1,692
Total labour force	24,661	24,728	25,097
Males	14,740	14,779	14,884
Females	9,922	9,949	10,213

Source: ILO.

2011 ('000 persons aged 15 years and over, average of quarterly surveys): Agriculture 850; Industry 6,538; Services 15,579; *Total employed* 22,967 (males 13,619, females 9,349); Unemployed 2,108; *Total labour force* 25,075 (males 14,733, females 10,342).

2012 ('000 persons aged 15 years and over, average of quarterly surveys): Agriculture 849; Industry 6,362; Services 15,688; *Total employed* 22,899 (males 13,441, females 9,458); Unemployed 2,744; *Total labour force* 25,642 (males 14,909, females 10,733).

2013 ('000 persons aged 15 years and over, July-September): Agriculture 851; Industry 6,085; Services 15,493; *Total employed* 22,430; Unemployed 2,844; *Total labour force* 25,273.

Health and Welfare

KEY INDICATORS

Total fertility rate (children per woman, 2011)	1.4
Under-5 mortality rate (per 1,000 live births, 2011)	4
HIV/AIDS (% of persons aged 15–49, 2011)	0.4
Physicians (per 1,000 head, 2009)	3.8
Hospital beds (per 1,000 head, 2009)	3.6
Health expenditure (2010): US $ per head (PPP)	3,046
Health expenditure (2010): % of GDP	9.5
Health expenditure (2010): public (% of total)	77.6
Total carbon dioxide emissions ('000 metric tons, 2010)	406,307.3
Carbon dioxide emissions per head (metric tons, 2010)	6.7
Human Development Index (2012): ranking	25
Human Development Index (2012): value	0.881

For sources and definitions, see explanatory note on p. vi.

Agriculture

PRINCIPAL CROPS
('000 metric tons)

	2010	2011	2012
Wheat	6,850	6,642	7,767
Rice, paddy	1,516	1,490	1,583
Barley	991	949	960
Maize	8,496	9,753	8,195
Oats	289	297	283
Sorghum	271	300	158
Potatoes	1,558	1,547	1,598
Sugar beet	3,550	3,548	2,501
Almonds, with shell	108	105	90
Hazelnuts (Filberts)	90	129	85
Soybeans (Soya beans)	553	565	422
Olives	3,171	3,182	3,018
Sunflower seed	213	274	186
Cabbages	349	334	312
Artichokes	480	475	365
Lettuce	843	819	324
Tomatoes	6,025	5,950	5,132
Cauliflowers and broccoli	427	421	414
Pumpkins, squash and gourds	508	539	520*
Aubergines (Eggplants)	303	243	218
Chillies and peppers, green	294	229	191
Onions, dry	381	414	337
Beans, green	183	164	134
Carrots and turnips	489	543	482
Watermelons	478	378	347
Cantaloupes and other melons	666	536	461
Oranges	2,394	2,470	1,771
Tangerines, mandarins, clementines and satsumas	812	864	760
Lemons and limes	522	483	346
Apples	2,205	2,411	1,991
Pears	737	927	646
Apricots	253	263	247
Sweet cherries	115	113	105
Peaches and nectarines	1,591	1,637	1,332
Plums	207	192	172
Strawberries	154	150*	41
Grapes	7,788	7,445	5,819
Kiwi fruit	416	432	385
Tobacco, unmanufactured	89	82*	84*

* FAO estimate.

Aggregate production ('000 metric tons, may include official, semi-official or estimated data): Total cereals 18,502 in 2010, 19,521 in 2011, 19,046 in 2012; Total roots and tubers 1,567 in 2010, 1,557 in 2011, 1,603 in 2012; Total vegetables (incl. melons) 14,214 in 2010, 14,242 in 2011, 12,298 in 2012; Total fruits (excl. melons) 17,479 in 2010, 17,693 in 2011, 13,889 in 2012.

Source: FAO.

LIVESTOCK
('000 head, year ending September)

	2010	2011	2012
Horses*	300	305	306
Asses*	24	24	24
Mules*	9	9	9
Cattle	6,103	5,832	6,092
Buffaloes	365	354	349
Pigs	9,157	9,321	9,351
Sheep	8,013	7,900	7,016
Goats	961	983	960
Chickens*	130,000	138,000	140,000
Turkeys*	24,000	24,500	25,000

* FAO estimates.

Source: FAO.

LIVESTOCK PRODUCTS
('000 metric tons)

	2010	2011	2012
Cattle meat	1,069	1,000	958
Buffalo meat	6	11	24
Sheep meat	52	47	46
Pig meat	1,673	1,602	1,651
Horse meat	18	17	18
Chicken meat	865	889	922
Turkey meat	298	309	322
Rabbit meat*	255	255	263
Cows' milk	10,500	10,479	10,580
Buffaloes' milk	177	193	192
Sheep's milk	432	418	406
Goats' milk	25	24	28
Hen eggs*	737	755	765

* FAO estimates.

Source: FAO.

Forestry

ROUNDWOOD REMOVALS
('000 cubic metres, excl. bark)

	2009	2010	2011
Sawlogs, veneer logs and logs for sleepers	1,236	1,549	1,000
Pulpwood	594	370	645
Other industrial wood	898	728	711
Fuel wood	5,352	5,197	5,388
Total	8,080	7,844	7,744

2012: Production assumed to be unchanged from 2011 (FAO estimates).

Source: FAO.

SAWNWOOD PRODUCTION
('000 cubic metres, incl. railway sleepers)

	2010	2011	2012
Coniferous (softwood)	700	750	850
Broadleaved (hardwood)	500	500	520
Total	1,200	1,250	1,370

Source: FAO.

Fishing

('000 metric tons, live weight)

	2009	2010	2011
Capture	253.0	234.1	216.5*
European hake	12.5	12.0	10.5
European anchovy	54.4	54.1	46.2
Striped venus	17.3	19.7	19.7
Aquaculture	162.4	153.5	160.3*
Rainbow trout	35.8	33.2	38.0*
Mediterranean mussel	76.8	64.3	64.3*
Clams (Carpet shells)	32.8	36.7	36.8*
Total catch	415.4	387.6	376.8*

* FAO estimate.

Note: Figures exclude aquatic plants (FAO estimates, all capture, '000 metric tons): 1.4 in 2009; 1.4 in 2010; 1.2 in 2011. Also excluded are aquatic mammals (recorded by number rather than weight) and corals. The number of whales and dolphins caught was: nil in 2009; 3 in 2010; 2 in 2011. Corals landed (metric tons): 9.8 in 2009; 10.3 in 2010; 10.5 in 2011.

Source: FAO.

Mining

('000 metric tons unless otherwise indicated)

	2009	2010	2011
Crude petroleum ('000 barrels)	30,215	35,040	36,201
Natural methane gas (million cu m)	8,127	8,296	8,438
Copper (refined, all kinds)	6.5	25.2	23.9
Lead (metric tons)*†	800	800	800
Barite (Barytes)	3.5	3.5	3.5
Feldspar*	4,700	4,700	4,700
Bentonite	146	111	102
Kaolin	5	6	8
Salt	3,471	4,006	2,912
Gypsum	5,101	4,441	5,939
Pumice*‡	30	30	30
Pozzolan*	4,000	4,000	4,000
Talc and steatite	112.0*	110.0	110.0*

* Estimate(s).
† Metal content of ores and concentrates.
‡ Including pumiceous lapilli.

Source: US Geological Survey.

2004 ('000 metric tons unless otherwise indicated): Manganese (metric tons) 714; Fluorspar 17.9; Loam (rock) 13,821.1; Gold (kg) 100 (Source: US Geological Survey).

Industry

SELECTED PRODUCTS

('000 metric tons, unless otherwise indicated)

	2002	2003	2004
Wine (thousand hl)*	44,604.1	44,086.1	53,135.2
Cotton yarn	231.8	212.0	193.9
Cotton woven fabrics	209.8	197.1	186.9
Wood pulp, mechanical	309.2	341.4	364.8
Newsprint†	175.1	182.0	193.0
Magazine print	780.0	830.0	945.1
Other printing and writing paper	2,104.5	2,091.2	2,164.7
Washing powders and detergents	1,982.0	2,123.8	2,174.5
Jet fuels	2,458.8	2,626.8	2,550.9
Benzene	20,999.1	20,759.4	n.a.
Motor gasoline	37,297.0	38,349.5	38,025.0
Naphthas	3,243.3	4,287.7	3,938.8
Gas-diesel oil	12,286.3	12,166.5	13,278.2
Bitumen	2,942.3	3,274.8	3,496.3
Coke	3,973.9	3,663.1	3,964.6
Tyres for road motor vehicles	258.6	265.4	278.9
Glass bottles and other containers of common glass	2,939.8	3,139.5	3,171.1
Cement	41,722.3	43,580.0	45,342.9
Steel	26,301.4	26,832.1	28,385.4
Rolled iron	24,165.6	25,608.6	28,710.6
Other iron and steel-finished manufactures	3,260.2	3,133.9	3,164.8
Refrigerators for household use ('000 units)	7,088.8	6,715.3	6,444.1
Washing machines for household use ('000 units)	8,884.0	9,666.8	9,679.9
Passenger motor cars ('000 units)	1,125.8	1,026.5	839.2
Lorries (Trucks) ('000 units)	266.4	267.4	283.9
Motorcycles, scooters, etc. ('000 units)	588.9	572.5	622.3
Bicycles ('000 units)	597.7	581.6	501.5
Hydroelectric power (million kWh)‡	47,262	44,277	n.a.
Thermoelectric power (million kWh)‡	231,069	242,784	n.a.
Other electric power (million kWh)‡	6,066	6,799	n.a.

* Provisional data.
† Source: FAO.
‡ Net production.

2009 ('000 metric tons): Newsprint 211.3; Mechanical wood pulp 259.9; Other printing and writing paper 2,635 (Source: FAO); Crude steel 19,848; Cement 36,317 (Source: US Geological Survey).

2010 ('000 metric tons): Newsprint 181.3; Mechanical wood pulp 278.0; Other printing and writing paper 2,852 (Source: FAO); Crude steel 25,750; Cement 34,408 (Source: US Geological Survey).

2011 ('000 metric tons): Newsprint 193.2; Mechanical wood pulp 281.0; Other printing and writing paper 2,858 (Source: FAO); Crude steel 28,735; Cement 33,120 (Source: US Geological Survey).

2012 ('000 metric tons): Newsprint 127.1; Mechanical wood pulp 269.0; Other printing and writing paper 2,778 (Source: FAO).

Electrical energy (million kWh, including San Marino): 303,699 in 2005; 314,121 in 2006; 313,888 in 2007; 319,130 in 2008; 292,642 in 2009; 302,062 in 2010; 302,570 in 2012.

Finance

CURRENCY AND EXCHANGE RATES

Monetary Units

100 cent = 1 euro (€).

Sterling, Dollar and Euro Equivalents (31 December 2013)

£1 sterling = 1.194 euros;
US $1 = 0.725 euros;
€10 = £8.37 = $13.79.

Average Exchange Rate (euros per US $)

2011	0.7194
2012	0.7783
2013	0.7532

Note: The national currency was formerly the Italian lira (plural: lire). From the introduction of the euro, with Italian participation, on 1 January 1999, a fixed exchange rate of €1 = 1,936.27 lire was in operation. Euro notes and coins were introduced on 1 January 2002. The euro and local currency circulated alongside each other until 28 February, after which the euro became the sole legal tender.

STATE BUDGET

(€ '000 million)

Revenue	2011	2012*	2013†
Taxes	455.0	472.2	472.3
Social contributions	217.0	216.7	216.7
Grants	3.0	3.0	3.0
Other revenue	53.9	55.0	55.0
Total	728.8	746.8	747.0

Expenditure	2011	2012*	2013†
Expense	790.8	794.4	794.9
Compensation of employees	169.2	165.4	163.6
Use of goods and services	91.2	86.6	81.6
Consumption of fixed capital	31.2	31.4	33.6
Interest	76.5	84.8	84.0
Social benefits	348.9	357.1	366.9
Other expense	73.8	69.2	65.2
Net acquisition of non-financial assets	−3.8	−1.9	2.6
Total	787.0	792.5	797.4

* Preliminary figures.
† Projections.

Source: IMF, *Italy: 2013 Article IV Consultation* (September 2013).

INTERNATIONAL RESERVES
(US $ million at 31 December)

	2010	2011	2012
Gold (Eurosystem valuation)	111,169	124,116	131,171
IMF special drawing rights	9,549	9,184	9,458
Reserve position in IMF	2,457	5,844	6,225
Foreign exchange	35,678	34,158	34,816
Total	158,853	173,302	181,670

Source: IMF, *International Financial Statistics*.

MONEY SUPPLY
(incl. shares, depository corporations, national residency criteria, € '000 million at 31 December)

	2010	2011	2012
Currency issued	142.32	150.16	154.16
Banca d'Italia	142.32	150.16	154.16
Demand deposits	757.75	736.30	733.23
Other deposits	642.23	626.33	741.33
Securities other than shares	807.08	914.23	958.32
Money market fund shares	38.41	26.97	9.14
Shares and other equity	442.53	477.89	492.98
Other items (net)	–343.87	–463.00	–496.76
Total	2,486.44	2,468.87	2,592.40

Source: IMF, *International Financial Statistics*.

COST OF LIVING
(Consumer Price Index; annual averages, base: 2010 = 100)

	2011	2012
Food (incl. non-alcoholic beverages)	102.4	105.0
Alcohol and tobacco	103.5	109.6
Rent and utilities	105.1	112.6
Clothing (incl. footwear)	101.7	104.3
Household goods	101.7	103.8
Health services	100.5	100.5
Transport	106.2	113.1
Communications	98.8	97.3
Recreation, entertainment and culture	100.3	100.7
Education	102.3	104.6
Hotels, restaurants and public services	102.2	103.7
Miscellaneous goods and services	103.2	105.6
All items (incl. others)	102.8	105.9

NATIONAL ACCOUNTS
(€ million at current prices)

National Income and Product

	2010	2011	2012
Compensation of employees	658,427	670,048	668,917
Operating surplus and mixed income (net)	428,153	432,440	401,593
Domestic factor incomes	1,086,580	1,102,488	1,070,510
Consumption of fixed capital	265,693	273,690	278,964
Gross domestic product (GDP) at factor cost	1,352,273	1,376,178	1,349,473
Taxes on production and imports	221,807	225,766	238,139
Less Subsidies	22,195	21,534	20,602
GDP in market prices	1,551,886	1,580,410	1,567,010
Net primary income received from abroad	–7,321	–9,401	–10,229
Gross national product	1,544,565	1,571,009	1,556,781
Less Consumption of fixed capital	265,693	273,690	278,964
Net national income	1,278,871	1,297,319	1,277,818
Net current transfers from abroad	–16,951	–16,773	–15,862
Net national disposable income	1,261,920	1,280,545	1,261,955

Expenditure on the Gross Domestic Product

	2010	2011	2012
Final consumption expenditure	1,270,966	1,289,963	1,268,632
Households	937,611	961,412	947,080
Non-profit institutions serving households	6,352	6,498	6,596
General government	327,003	322,053	314,956
Gross capital formation	311,163	312,532	280,715
Changes in inventories	7,280	8,689	–2,417
Acquisitions, less disposals, of valuables	2,453	2,535	2,444
Gross fixed capital formation	301,429	301,308	280,688
Total domestic expenditure	1,582,129	1,602,495	1,549,347
Exports of goods and services	412,509	455,569	473,472
Less Imports of goods and services	442,752	477,654	455,809
GDP in market prices	1,551,886	1,580,410	1,567,010
GDP at constant 2005 prices	1,418,376	1,425,142	1,389,043

Gross Domestic Product by Economic Activity

	2010	2011	2012
Agriculture, hunting, forestry and fishing	26,328	28,150	28,168
Mining and quarrying	4,434	5,251	5,341
Manufacturing	229,664	233,115	219,399
Construction	83,587	84,576	82,354
Electricity, gas and water	30,603	28,552	32,878
Wholesale and retail trade; repair of motor vehicles, motorcycles and personal and household goods	147,879	151,541	151,972
Hotels and restaurants	57,035	58,740	58,521
Transport, storage and communications	139,673	141,144	137,811
Financial intermediation	75,884	78,974	76,022
Real estate, renting and business activities	305,065	314,450	321,048
Public administration and defence; compulsory social security	95,060	95,336	93,883
Education	64,678	62,481	62,183
Health and social work	80,994	81,764	80,896
Other community, social and personal service activities	33,766	35,120	35,447
Private households with employed persons	15,713	16,014	16,849
Gross value added in basic prices	1,390,363	1,415,207	1,402,773
Net taxes on products	161,523	165,203	164,237
GDP in market prices	1,551,886	1,580,410	1,567,010

BALANCE OF PAYMENTS
(US $ million)

	2010	2011	2012
Exports of goods	430,809	503,079	478,932
Imports of goods	–456,936	–524,032	–453,531
Balance on goods	–26,127	–20,953	25,402
Exports of services	96,740	105,922	103,324
Imports of services	–111,036	–116,893	–107,081
Balance on goods and services	–40,423	–31,924	21,642
Primary income received	74,100	84,983	69,403
Primary income paid	–84,889	–98,176	–79,201
Balance on goods, services and primary income	–51,213	–45,117	11,844
Secondary income received	23,690	27,639	25,324
Secondary income paid	–45,111	–49,665	–45,221
Current balance	–72,633	–67,143	–8,054

—continued	2010	2011	2012
Capital account (net)	–740	778	4,949
Direct investment assets	–17,707	–47,522	–14,549
Direct investment liabilities	–5,289	28,003	6,686
Portfolio investment assets	–43,163	48,889	79,018
Portfolio investment liabilities	94,026	–95,335	–42,845
Financial derivatives and employee stock options (net)	–6,657	10,338	–7,388
Other investment assets	64,899	–59,315	–49,440
Other investment liabilities	29,312	217,819	44,371
Net errors and omissions	–40,709	–35,342	–10,867
Reserves and related items	1,338	1,169	1,881

Source: IMF, *International Financial Statistics*.

External Trade

Note: Figures refer to the trade of Italy, San Marino and the Vatican City.

PRINCIPAL COMMODITIES
(€ million)

Imports c.i.f.	2010	2011	2012*
Agriculture and fishing	11,123	13,013	12,291
Food, beverages and tobacco	25,320	23,933	23,696
Crude petroleum	34,746	41,577	44,290
Natural gas	19,299	21,201	24,111
Textiles, clothing, leather and leather products	25,960	28,876	26,478
Wood and wood products; paper and paper products, printing and publishing	9,991	10,158	9,220
Chemicals and man-made fibres	49,466	55,663	55,364
Rubber, plastics and non-metal mineral ore products	11,312	12,404	11,490
Metals and metal products	36,107	42,468	37,753
Machinery and mechanical equipment	22,416	24,138	22,502
Computers, electrical appliances and electrical equipment	47,163	44,743	37,958
Transportation means	37,901	38,334	30,213
Total (incl. others)	367,390	401,428	378,759

Exports f.o.b.	2010	2011	2012*
Food, beverages and tobacco	22,179	24,419	26,059
Textiles, clothing, leather and leather products	37,339	41,979	43,064
Wood and wood products; paper and paper products, printing and publishing	7,151	7,503	7,628
Refined oil products	14,794	16,845	20,513
Chemicals and man-made fibres	36,549	40,239	42,558
Rubber, plastics and non-metal mineral ore manufactures	20,854	22,516	22,574
Metals and metal products	39,350	48,386	50,779
Machinery and mechanical equipment	60,061	68,447	70,483
Computers, electrical appliances and electrical equipment	30,984	33,244	32,535
Transportation means	34,507	36,518	36,142
Total (incl. others)	337,346	375,904	389,725

* Provisional data.

PRINCIPAL TRADING PARTNERS
(€ million)*

Imports c.i.f.	2010	2011	2012†
Algeria	8,060	8,311	8,972
Austria	8,452	9,439	8,839
Belgium	13,359	14,568	14,381
Brazil	3,314	4,148	3,402
China, People's Republic	28,789	29,574	24,695
Czech Republic	4,482	4,901	4,457
France	32,171	33,603	31,318
Germany	58,986	62,388	55,219
India	3,823	4,780	3,751
Iran	4,745	5,327	2,240
Japan	4,288	4,218	3,191
Libya	12,277	3,973	12,874
Netherlands	19,965	21,037	20,388
Poland	7,222	7,518	7,125
Romania	4,667	5,295	4,851
Russia	14,633	16,904	18,331
Saudi Arabia	3,235	7,031	7,483
Spain	16,737	18,111	16,848
Switzerland	10,203	11,294	11,018
Turkey	5,158	5,979	5,257
United Kingdom	10,012	10,943	9,554
USA	11,139	13,026	12,666
Total (incl. others)	367,390	401,428	378,759

Exports f.o.b.	2010	2011	2012†
Austria	8,002	8,724	8,630
Belgium	8,678	9,633	10,300
Brazil	3,877	4,782	4,997
China, People's Republic	8,609	9,996	9,003
Czech Republic	3,582	4,173	4,201
France	39,237	43,593	43,169
Germany	43,867	49,267	48,713
Greece	5,473	4,782	4,163
Japan	4,011	4,732	5,637
Netherlands	8,368	9,119	9,269
Poland	8,553	9,418	9,213
Romania	5,191	6,135	5,825
Russia	7,906	9,305	9,993
Slovenia	3,590	3,989	4,123
Spain	19,595	19,890	18,291
Sweden	3,412	3,892	3,774
Switzerland	15,823	20,640	22,878
Turkey	8,029	9,634	10,618
United Arab Emirates	3,685	4,729	5,511
United Kingdom	17,576	17,542	18,964
USA	20,329	22,831	26,656
Total (incl. others)	337,346	375,904	389,725

* Imports by country of production; exports by country of consignment.
† Provisional data.

Transport

STATE RAILWAYS
(traffic)

	2009	2010	2011
Passenger journeys (million)	799.9	838.9	847.3
Passenger-km (million)	48,124	47,172	46,845
Freight carried ('000 metric tons)	76,337	84,435	91,811
Freight ton-km (million)	17,791	18,616	19,787

ROAD TRAFFIC
(vehicles in use at 31 December)

	2008	2009	2010
Passenger cars	35,673,416	35,871,854	35,871,854
Buses and coaches	99,750	98,244	98,666
Lorries and vans	4,467,476	4,505,348	4,556,648
Motorcycles and mopeds	6,015,606	6,309,992	6,525,820

Source: IRF, *World Road Statistics*.

SHIPPING

Flag Registered Fleet
(at 31 December)

	2011	2012	2013
Number of vessels	2,235	2,232	2,221
Total displacement ('000 grt)	18,884.9	18,963.9	18,522.8

Source: Lloyd's List Intelligence (www.lloydslistintelligence.com).

International Sea-borne Traffic

	2002	2003	2004
Goods loaded ('000 metric tons)	73,402	74,479	79,222
Goods unloaded ('000 metric tons)	260,986	266,914	270,811
Passengers embarked ('000)	2,841	2,863	3,041
Passengers disembarked ('000)	2,873	2,831	3,187

Source: Ministry of Transport.

CIVIL AVIATION
(traffic on scheduled and charter services)

	2009	2010	2011
Passengers carried ('000):			
domestic	56,265	59,619	63,708
international	73,530	79,237	84,307
Freight carried ('000 metric tons):*	750.0	878.8	890.1

* Includes mail.

Tourism

TOURIST ARRIVALS BY COUNTRY OF ORIGIN
(arrivals in registered accommodation establishments)

	2010	2011	2012
Austria	2,011,317	2,115,524	2,110,605
Belgium	1,013,042	1,079,541	1,103,629
China, People's Republic	965,857	1,342,518	1,583,479
France	3,449,866	3,689,634	3,700,775
Germany	9,302,743	9,873,213	10,192,697
Japan	1,363,444	1,410,677	1,449,115
Netherlands	1,851,034	1,933,447	1,959,306
Poland	888,472	989,436	919,013
Russia	1,140,432	1,474,137	1,707,998
Spain	1,867,774	1,929,832	1,711,807
Switzerland-Liechtenstein	1,810,501	1,994,976	2,151,675
United Kingdom	2,676,121	2,746,752	2,890,015
USA	4,235,520	4,466,672	4,442,549
Total (incl. others)	43,794,338	47,460,809	48,738,575

Tourism receipts (US $ million, excl. passenger transport): 38,786 in 2010; 43,000 in 2011; 41,185 in 2012 (provisional) (Source: World Tourism Organization).

Tourist beds: 4,498,910 in 2006; 4,485,581 in 2007; 4,649,050 in 2008; 4,598,682 in 2009.

Communications Media

	2010	2011	2012
Telephones ('000 main lines in use)	22,466	22,105	21,656
Mobile cellular telephones ('000 in use)	93,666	96,041	97,226
Internet subscribers ('000)	13,400	n.a.	n.a.
Broadband subscribers ('000)	13,062	13,432	13,483

Source: International Telecommunication Union.

Education

(state education, 2007/08, unless otherwise indicated)

	Schools	Teachers	Students
Pre-primary	13,629	83,586	975,757
Primary	16,018	245,727	2,579,938
Secondary:			
Scuola Media	7,104	163,159	1,625,651
Scuola Secondaria Superiore	5,128	230,881	2,570,010
of which:			
Technical	1,802	78,411	870,708
Professional	1,425	43,950	540,794
Art Licei and institutes	271	9,261	96,812
Classical, linguistic and scientific Licei	1,630	70,040	1,061,696
Higher*	74	61,929	1,820,221†‡

* Includes private institutions.
† Undergraduates only.
‡ 2006/07 figure.

Source: Ufficio di Statistica, Ministero dell'Istruzione, dell'Università e della Ricerca.

2011/12: Pre-primary (schools 24,101, teachers 81,049, students 1,694,912); Primary (schools 17,541, teachers 201,269, students 2,818,734); Lower secondary (schools 7,931, teachers 139,191, students 1,792,379); Upper secondary (schools 7,058, teachers 204,369, students 2,655,134).

Pupil-teacher ratio (primary education, UNESCO estimate): 10.3 in 2006/07 (Source: UNESCO Institute for Statistics).

Adult literacy rate (UNESCO estimates): 99.0% (males 99.2%; females 98.7%) in 2011 (Source: UNESCO Institute for Statistics).

Directory

The Government

HEAD OF STATE

President of the Republic: GIORGIO NAPOLITANO (took office 15 May 2006; re-elected 20 April 2013).

COUNCIL OF MINISTERS
(April 2014)

A coalition comprising the Partito Democratico (PD), Nuovo Centrodestra (NC, which was formed after the dissolution of Popolo della Libertà (PdL) in November 2013), Unione di Centro (UdC), Scelta Civica (SC) and independents.

Prime Minister: MATTEO RENZI (PD).

Minister of Foreign Affairs: FEDERICA MOGHERINI (PD).

Minister of the Interior: ANGELINO ALFANO (NC).

Minister of Justice: ANDREA ORLANDO (PD).

Minister of Defence: ROBERTA PINOTTI (PD).

Minister of the Economy and Finance: PIER CARLO PADOAN (Ind.).

Minister of Economic Development: FEDERICA GUIDI (Ind.).

Minister of Infrastructure and Transport: MAURIZIO LUPI (NC).

Minister of Agricultural, Food and Forestry Policies: MAURIZIO MARTINA (PD).

Minister of the Environment, Land Management and the Sea: GIANLUCA GALLETTI (UdC).

Minister of Labour and Social Policies: GIULIANO POLETTI (Ind.).

Minister of Education, Universities and Research: STEFANIA GIANNINI (SC).

Minister of Cultural Assets and Activities and of Tourism: DARIO FRANCESCHINI (PD).

Minister of Health: BEATRICE LORENZIN (NC).

Minister of Regional Affairs: MARIA CARMELA LANZETTA (Ind.).

Minister for Constitutional Reforms and Relations with Parliament: MARIA ELENA BOSCHI (PD).

Minister for Legislative Simplification and Public Administration: MARIA ANNA MADIA (PD).

MINISTRIES

Office of the President: Palazzo del Quirinale, 00187 Roma; tel. (06) 46991; fax (06) 46993125; internet www.quirinale.it.

Office of the Prime Minister: Palazzo Chigi, Piazza Colonna 370, 00187 Roma; tel. (06) 67791; internet www.governo.it.

Ministry of Agricultural, Food and Forestry Policies: Via XX Settembre 20, 00187 Roma; tel. (06) 46651; fax (06) 4742314; e-mail urp@pec.politicheagricole.gov.it; internet www.politicheagricole.gov.it.

Ministry of Cultural Assets and Activities and of Tourism: Via del Collegio Romano 27, 00186 Roma; tel. (06) 67232980; fax (06) 6798441; e-mail urp@beniculturali.it; internet www.beniculturali.it.

Ministry of Defence: Palazzo Baracchini, Via XX Settembre 8, 00187 Roma; tel. (06) 46911; internet www.difesa.it.

Ministry of Economic Development: Via Molise 2, 00187 Roma; tel. (06) 47051; fax (06) 47887770; e-mail segreteria.capogabinetto@sviluppoeconomico.gov.it; internet www.sviluppoeconomico.gov.it.

Ministry of the Economy and Finance: Via XX Settembre 97, 00187 Roma; tel. (06) 476111; fax (06) 5910993; e-mail portavoce@tesoro.it; internet www.mef.gov.it.

Ministry of Education, Universities and Research: Via Trastevere 76A, 00153 Roma; tel. (06) 58491; e-mail urp@istruzione.it; internet www.istruzione.it.

Ministry of the Environment, Land Management and the Sea: Via Cristoforo Colombo 44, 00147 Roma; tel. (06) 57221; e-mail segr.ufficiostampa@minambiente.it; internet www.minambiente.it.

Ministry of Foreign Affairs: Piazzale della Farnesina 1, 00194 Roma; tel. (06) 36911; fax (06) 3236210; e-mail ministero.affariesteri@cert.esteri.it; internet www.esteri.it.

Ministry of Health: Viale Giorgio Ribotta 5, 00144 Roma; tel. (06) 59941; fax (06) 59942376; e-mail urpminsalute@sanita.it; internet www.salute.gov.it.

Ministry of Infrastructure and Transport: Piazzale Porta Pia 1, 00198 Roma; tel. (06) 44121; fax (06) 44123205; e-mail ufficio.stampa@mit.gov.it; internet www.mit.gov.it.

Ministry of the Interior: Piazzale del Viminale, Via Agostino Depretis 7, 00184 Roma; tel. (06) 4651; fax (06) 46549599; e-mail segreteriaufficiostampa@interno.it; internet www.interno.it.

Ministry of Justice: Via Arenula 71, 00186 Roma; tel. (06) 68851; fax (06) 68891493; e-mail centrocifra.gabinetto@giustiziacert.it; internet www.giustizia.it.

Ministry of Labour and Social Policies: Via Veneto 56, 00187 Roma; tel. (06) 46831; fax (06) 48161451; e-mail ufficiostampa@lavoro.gov.it; internet www.lavoro.gov.it.

President

The President of the Republic is elected by the members of both parliamentary chambers, in addition to representations (Grand Electors) of each administrative region, and is required to receive the support of at least two-thirds of the votes cast in the first three rounds of voting, or a simple majority thereafter. GIORGIO NAPOLITANO was elected President for a second term in a sixth round of voting conducted on 20 April 2013, receiving 738 votes (from 1,007 possible voters present at the session).

Legislature

PARLIAMENT
(Parlamento)

Chamber of Deputies
(Camera dei Deputati)

Palazzo di Montecitorio, Piazza Montecitorio, 00186 Roma; tel. (06) 67601; e-mail dlwebmast@camera.it; internet www.camera.it.

President: LAURA BOLDRINI.

General Election, 24 and 25 February 2013

Parties/Alliances	Total seats
Italia. Bene Comune	345
Partito Democratico (PD)	297
Sinistra Ecologia Libertà (SEL)	37
Centro Democratico (CD)	6
Südtiroler Volkspartei (SVP)	5
Centre-right coalition	125
Popolo della Libertà (PdL)*	98
Lega Nord (LN)	18
Fratelli d'Italia—Centrodestra Nazionale	9
MoVimento 5 Stelle (M5S)	109
Con Monti per l'Italia	47†
Scelta Civica (SC)	37
Unione di Centro (UdC)	8
Movimento Associativo Italiani all'Estero	2
USEI‡	1
Valle d'Aosta	1
Total	630

* In November 2013 the PdL split to form two parties: Nuovo Centrodestra and Forza Italia.

† Includes two seats won by Con Monti per l'Italia from expatriate votes.

‡ Unione Sudamericana Emigrati Italiani (South American Union of Italian Emigrants).

Senate
(Senato)

Piazza Madama, 00186 Roma; tel. (06) 67061; e-mail infopoint@senato.it; internet www.senato.it.

President: PIETRO GRASSO.

General Election, 24 and 25 February 2013

Parties/Alliances	Elective seats
Italia. Bene Comune	123
Partito Democratico (PD)*	113
Sinistra Ecologia Libertà	7
Il Megafono—Lista Crocetta	1
Südtiroler Volkspartei (SVP)*	2
Centre-right coalition	117
Popolo della Libertà (PdL)†	99
Lega Nord (LN)	17
Grande Sud	1
MoVimento 5 Stelle (M5S)	54
Con Monti per l'Italia	19
Movimento Associativo Italiani all'Estero	1
Valle d'Aosta	1
Total‡	315

* Partito Democratico (PD), Partito Autonomista Trentino Tirolese (PATT), Südtiroler Volkspartei (SVP) and Unione per il Trentino (UpT) contested the election in alliance in Trentino Tyrol. The PD won four seats while the SVP won two seats in that region.

† In November 2013 the PdL split to form two parties: Nuovo Centrodestra and Forza Italia.

‡ In addition to the 315 elected members, there were, as at March 2014, five life members.

Political Organizations

NATIONAL PARTIES AND COALITIONS

Alleanza per l'Italia (ApL) (Alliance for Italy): Largo Fontanella Borghese 84, 00186 Roma; tel. (06) 91712000; fax (06) 68802560; e-mail info@alleanzaperlitalia.it; internet www.alleanzaperlitalia.it; f. 2009; Pres. FRANCESCO RUTELLI; Co-ordinator LORENZO DELLAI.

Centro Democratico–Diritti e Libertà (Democratic Centre–Rights and Freedom): Via Giovanni Pierluigi da Palestrina 63, 00193 Roma; tel. (06) 93570168; e-mail info@ilcentrodemocratico.it; internet www.ilcentrodemocratico.it; f. 2012; centre-left coalition led by the party Diritti e Libertà; contested the 2013 legislative elections as part of Italia. Bene Comune; Pres. BRUNO TABACCI.

Federazione dei Liberali Italiani (Federation of Italian Liberals): Studio Sgobbo, Corso Trieste 61, 00198 Roma; tel. (06) 8418007; fax (06) 8416975; e-mail info@liberali.it; internet www.liberali.it; f. 1994; Pres. RAFFAELLO MORELLI.

Federazione dei Verdi (I Verdi) (Green Party): Via Antonio Salandra 6, 00187 Roma; tel. (06) 4203061; fax (06) 42004600; e-mail federazione@verdi.it; internet www.verdi.it; f. 1986; advocates environmentalist and anti-nuclear policies; contested the 2013 legislative elections as part of Rivoluzione Civile; branch of the European Green movement; Co-Pres ANGELO BONELLI, LUANA ZANELLA.

Forza Italia (FI) (Forward Italy): Via dell'Umiltà 36, 00187 Roma; tel. (06) 6731381; internet www.forzaitalia.it; f. 2013 following the splitting of Popolo della Libertà into two parties; Pres. SILVIO BERLUSCONI.

Fratelli d'Italia—Alleanza Nazionale (Brothers of Italy—National Centre-right): Via Quattro Cantoni 16, 00184 Roma; tel. (06) 4880690; fax (06) 48907931; e-mail info@fratelli-italia.it; internet www.fratelli-italia.it; f. 2012; contested the 2013 legislative elections as part of the centre-right coalition; Pres. GIORGIA MELONI.

Futuro e Libertà per l'Italia (FLI) (Future and Freedom for Italy): Via Poli 29, 00187 Roma; tel. (06) 69773701; internet www.futuroeliberta.it; f. 2011; liberal; contested the 2013 legislative elections as part of Con Monti per l'Italia; Nat. Co-ordinator ROBERTO MENIA.

Italia dei Valori—Lista Di Pietro (IdV) (Italy of Principals—Di Pietro List): Via Santa Maria in Via 12, 00187 Roma; tel. (06) 97848144; fax (06) 97848355; e-mail info@italiadeivalori.it; internet www.italiadeivalori.it; anti-corruption; contested the 2013 legislative elections as part of Rivoluzione Civile; Nat. Sec. IGNATIUS MESSINA.

Liberal Democratici (LD) (Liberal Democrats): Largo della Fontanella di Borghese 84, 00186 Roma; tel. (06) 68808380; fax (06) 68808500; e-mail liberal-democratici@libero.it; internet www.liberal-democratici.it; f. 2007; liberal centrist; Pres. ITALO TANONI; Co-ordinator ENZO MARRAZZO.

Lista Consumatori (Consumers' List): Via Tagliamento 3, Ardea, 00040 Roma; tel. (06) 23328286; e-mail info@listaconsumatori.it; f. 2004; Pres. RENATO CAMPIGLIA; Nat. Sec. DAVID BADINI.

Il Megafono—Lista Crocetta (The Megaphone—List of Crocetta): e-mail larivoluzionecontinua@gmail.com; f. 2012; contested the 2013 legislative elections as part of Italia. Bene Comune; Leader ROSARIO CROCETTA.

MoVimento 5 Stelle (M5S) (Five Star Movement): internet www.movimento5stelle.it; f. 2009; populist, anti-corruption; Leader BEPPE GRILLO.

Movimento Cristiano sociali (Christian-Social Movement): Via Calabria 56, 00198 Roma; tel. (06) 3210694; fax (06) 68300539; e-mail movcso@alice.it; internet www.cristianosociali.it; f. 1993; Pres. MIMMO LUCÀ.

Movimento Sociale—Fiamma Tricolore (Tricolour Flame): Via Flaminia Vecchia 732I, 00191 Roma; tel. (06) 33221128; fax (06) 233235547; e-mail info@fiammatricolore.com; internet www.fiammatricolore.com; f. 1996; electoral alliance incorporating fmr mems of neo-fascist Movimento Sociale Italiano-Destra Nazionale; Nat. Sec. ATTILIO CARELLI.

Nuovo Centrodestra (NC) (New Centre-Right): Roma; e-mail info@nuovocentrodestra.it; internet www.nuovocentrodestra.it; f. 2013 following the splitting of Popolo della Libertà into two parties; Leader ANGELINO ALFANO.

Partito dei Comunisti Italiani (PdCI) (Party of Italian Communists): Piazza Augusto Imperatore 32, 00186 Roma; tel. (06) 686271; fax (06) 68627230; e-mail direzionenazionale@comunisti-italiani.org; internet www.comunisti-italiani.it; f. 1998; contested the 2013 legislative elections as part of Rivoluzione Civile; Gen. Sec. CESARE PROCACCINI.

Partito Democratico (PD): Via Sant'Andrea delle Fratte 16, 00187 Roma; tel. (06) 695321; e-mail redazione@partitodemocratico.it; internet www.partitodemocratico.it; f. 2007 by merger of Democratici di Sinistra, Democrazia è Libertà—La Margherita and other leftwing and centrist parties; centre-left; contested the 2013 legislative elections as part of Italia. Bene Comune; Co-Vice-Pres MATTEO RICCI, SANDRA ZAMPA; Nat. Sec. MATTEO RENZI.

Partito Liberale Italiano (PLI) (Italian Liberal Party): Via Uffici del Vicario 43, 2°, 00186 Roma; tel. (06) 45505081; e-mail segretaria@partitoliberale.it; internet www.partitoliberale.it; Pres. PAOLO GUZZANTI; Nat. Sec. GIANCARLO MORANDI.

Partito Repubblicano Italiano (PRI) (Italian Republican Party): Corso Vittorio Emanuele II 326, 00186 Roma; tel. (06) 6865824; fax (06) 68210234; e-mail info@pri.it; internet www.pri.it; Nat. Pres. FRANCESCO NUCARA.

Partito della Rifondazione Comunista (PRC) (Party of Communist Refoundation): Viale del Policlinico 131, 00161 Roma; tel. (06) 441821; fax (06) 44182332; e-mail segretario@rifondazione.it; internet www.rifondazione.it; f. 1991 by fmr mems of the Partito Comunista Italiano (Italian Communist Party); contested the 2013 legislative elections as part of Rivoluzione Civile; Nat. Sec. PAOLO FERRERO.

Partito Socialista Italiano (PSI) (Italian Socialist Party): Via di Santa Caterina da Siena 57, 00186 Roma; tel. (06) 6878688; fax (06) 68307659; e-mail info@partitosocialista.it; internet www.partitosocialista.it; f. 2007 by fmr leadership of Socialisti Democratici Italiani; contested the 2013 legislative elections as part of Italia. Bene Comune; Nat. Sec. RICCARDO NENCINI.

Patto—Partito dei Liberaldemocratici (The Pact—Liberal Democratic Party): Via Vittorio Veneto 169, 00187 Roma; tel. and fax (06) 4744916; f. 1993 as Patto Segni; liberal party, advocating institutional reform; Nat. Sec. Prof. MARIO SEGNI.

Popolari—UDEUR (Alleanza Popolare—Unione Democratici per l'Europa) (Union of Democrats for Europe): Via Gaetano Donizetti 2, 82100 Benevento; tel. (0824) 24500; e-mail info@popolariudeur.it; internet www.popolariudeur.it; f. 1999; Sec. CLEMENTE MASTELLA.

Radicali Italiani (RI): Via di Torre Argentina 76, 00186 Roma; tel. (06) 689791; fax (06) 68210375; e-mail segreteria.roma@radicali.it; internet www.radicali.it; f. 2001 as Partito Radicale; Pres. LAURA ARCONTI; Gen. Sec. RITA BERNARDINI.

Scelta Civica (SC) (Civic Choice): tel. (06) 67486222; e-mail info@sceltacivica.it; internet www.sceltacivica.it; f. 2013; contested the 2013 legislative elections as part of Con Monti per l'Italia; Pres. (vacant).

Sinistra Ecologia Libertà (SEL) (Left Ecology Freedom): Via Goito 39, 00185 Roma; tel. (06) 44700403; fax (06) 4455832; e-mail redazione@sxmail.it; internet www.sinistraecologialiberta.it; f. 2010; socialist party advocating social progressivism; contested the 2013 legislative elections as part of Italia. Bene Comune; Pres. NICHI VENDOLA.

Unione di Centro (UdC) (Union of the Centre): Via dei Due Macelli 66, 00182 Roma; tel. (06) 69791001; fax (06) 6791574; f. 2008; coalition includes Unione dei Democratici Cristiani e di Centro and Rosa Bianca; contested the 2013 legislative elections as part of Con Monti per l'Italia; Leader PIER FERDINANDO CASINI.

Unione dei Democratici Cristiani e di Centro (UDC) (Union of Christian and Centre Democrats): Via dei Due Macelli 66, 00182 Roma; tel. (06) 69791001; fax (06) 6791574; e-mail info@udc-italia.it; internet www.udc-italia.it; f. 2002 from merger of Centro Cristiano Democratico (f. 1994) and Cristiani Democratici Uniti (f. 1995 after split from Partito Popolare Italiano); Pres. GIANPIERO D'ALIA; Nat. Sec. LORENZO CESA.

Political organizations for Italians abroad include **Alternativa Indipendente Italiani all'Estero (AIIE)**, the **Associazioni Italiane in Sud America**, the **Movimento Associativo Italiani all'Estero**, the **Partito degli Italiani nel Mondo** and the **Unione Sudamericana Emigranti Italiani**.

REGIONAL PARTIES AND COALITIONS

Autonomie Liberté Démocratie (ALD) (Autonomy Liberty Democracy): f. 2006; coalition of parties active in the Aosta valley.

Lega Nord per l'Indipendenza della Padania (LN) (Northern League for the Independence of Padania): Via Carlo Bellerio 41, 20161 Milano; tel. (02) 662341; fax (02) 6454475; e-mail webmaster@leganord.org; internet www.leganord.org; f. 1991; advocates federalism and transfer of control of resources to regional govts; in 1996 declared the 'Independent Republic of Padania'; opposes immigration; contested the 2013 legislative elections as part of the centre-right alliance; Pres. UMBERTO BOSSI; Sec. MATTEO SALVINI.

Liga Veneta Repubblica (Venetian Republic League): Via Antonio Provolo 2B, 37060 Verona; tel. and fax (045) 8601344; e-mail info@ligavenetarepubblica.org; internet www.ligavenetarepubblica.org; f. 2001 by merger of Liga Veneta Repubblica—Veneti d'Europa and Fronte Marco Polo; advocates independence for Veneto region; Pres. GIAN PIETRO PIOTTO; Gen. Sec. FABRIZIO COMENCINI.

Movimento per l'Autonomia (MPA) (Autonomy Movement): Via dell'Oca 27, Roma; tel. (06) 3220836; fax (06) 32647632; e-mail sede.roma@autonomia.info; internet www.mpa-italia.it; pro-regional autonomy in the south; Fed. Sec. GIOVANNI PISTORIO.

Partito Autonomista Trentino Tirolese (PATT) (Autonomist Party of Trento and the Tyrol): Via Roma 7, 38100 Trento; tel. (0461) 391399; fax (0461) 394940; e-mail info@patt.tn.it; internet www.patt.tn.it; advocates autonomy for South Tyrol region; Pres. WALTER KASWALDER; Pol. Sec. FRANCO PANIZZA.

Partitu Sardu—Partito Sardo d'Azione (Sardinian Action Party): Piazza Repubblica 18, 09125 Cagliari; tel. and fax (070) 3481434; e-mail info@psdaz.net; internet www.psdaz.net; Pres. GIACOMO SANNA; Nat. Sec. GIOVANNI ANGELO COLLI.

Südtiroler Volkspartei (SVP) (South Tyrol People's Party): Brennerstr. 7A, 39100 Bozen/Bolzano; tel. (0471) 304040; fax (0471) 981473; e-mail info@svp.eu; internet www.svpartei.org; regional party of the German and Ladin-speaking people in the South Tyrol; contested the 2013 legislative elections as part of Italia. Bene Comune; Pres. RICHARD THEINER; Gen. Sec. MARTIN ALBER.

Union Autonomista Ladina (Autonomist Ladin Movement): Strada Dolomites 111, 38036 Pozza di Fassa; tel. and fax (0462) 763396; e-mail ualdefascia@virgilio.it; internet www.movimentual.it; Pres. MICHELE ANESI; Pol. Sec. MANUEL FARINA.

Union Valdôtaine (Aosta Valley Union): Ave des Maquisards 29, 11100 Aosta; tel. (0165) 235181; fax (0165) 364289; e-mail siegecentral@unionvaldotaine.org; internet www.unionvaldotaine.org; f. 1945; promotes interests of the Aosta valley; contested the 2013 legislative elections as part of the Valle d'Aosta list; Pres ENNIO PASTORET.

Other regional parties and coalitions include the **Alleanza Lombarda**, **Die Freiheitlichen** (South Tyrol), the **Federazione per l'Autodeterminazione della Sicilia-Noi Siciliani**, **iRS—indipendèntzia Repùbrica de Sardigna**, **Moderati per il Piemonti**, the **Movimento Triveneto**, **Nuova Sicilia**, **Per il Sud**, **Progetto Nordest**, **Progetto Sud** and **Sardigna Natzione Indipendentzia.**

Diplomatic Representation

EMBASSIES IN ITALY

Afghanistan: Via Nomentana 120, 00161 Roma; tel. (06) 8611009; fax (06) 86322939; e-mail info@afghanistanembassyitaly.com; Ambassador ZIA UDDIN NEZAM.

Albania: Via Asmara 5, 00199 Roma; tel. (06) 8622414; fax (06) 86224120; e-mail embassy.rome@mfa.gov.al; internet www.ambasadat.gov.al/italy; Ambassador NERITAN CEKA.

Algeria: Via Bartolomeo Eustachio 12, 00161 Roma; tel. (06) 44202533; fax (06) 44292744; e-mail embassy@algerianembassy.it; internet www.algerianembassy.it; Ambassador RACHID MARIF.

Angola: Via Druso 39, 00184 Roma; tel. (06) 7726951; fax (06) 77590009; e-mail info@embangola.com; internet www.ambasciatangolana.com; Ambassador FLORÊNCIO MARIANO DA CONCEIÇÃO DE ALMEIDA.

Argentina: Piazza dell'Esquilino 2, 00185 Roma; tel. (06) 48073300; fax (06) 48073331; e-mail eital@mrecic.gov.ar; internet www.ambasciatargentina.it; Ambassador TORCUATO SALVADOR DI TELLA.

Armenia: Via XX Settembre 98E, scala A, 00187 Roma; tel. (06) 3296638; fax (06) 3297763; e-mail info@ambasciataarmena.it; Ambassador SARGIS GHAZARYAN.

Australia: Via A. Bosio 5, 00161 Roma; tel. (06) 852721; fax (06) 85272300; e-mail info-rome@dfat.gov.au; internet www.italy.embassy.gov.au; Chargé d'affaires DOUG TRAPPETT.

Austria: Via G. B. Pergolesi 3, 00198 Roma; tel. (06) 8440141; fax (06) 8543286; e-mail rom-ob@bmeia.gv.at; Chargé d'affaires a.i. GERDA VOGL.

Azerbaijan: Via Regina Margherita 1, II piano, 00198 Roma; tel. (06) 85305557; fax (06) 85231448; e-mail rome@mission.mfa.gov.az; internet www.azembassy.it; Ambassador VAGIF SADIQOV.

Bangladesh: Via Antonio Bertoloni 14, 00197 Roma; tel. (06) 8078541; fax (06) 8084853; e-mail embangrm@mclink.it; Ambassador SHAHDAT HOSSAIN.

Belarus: Via delle Alpi Apuane 16, 00141 Roma; tel. (06) 8208141; fax (06) 82084099; e-mail italy@mfa.gov.by; internet italy.mfa.gov.by; Ambassador YEVGENII A. SHESTAKOV.

Belgium: Via dei Monti Parioli 49, 00197 Roma; tel. (06) 3609511; fax (06) 3610197; e-mail rome@diplobel.fed.be; internet www.diplomatie.be/romeit; Ambassador VINCENT MERTENS DE WILMARS.

Belize: Piazza di Spagna 81, 00187 Roma; tel. (06) 69190776; fax (06) 69925794; e-mail ambasciatabelize@yahoo.it; internet www.ambasciatabelize.com; Ambassador NUNZIO ALFREDO D'ANGIERI.

Benin: Via dei Settemetri 11E, int. 6, 00118 Roma; tel. (06) 79846567; fax (06) 79810197; e-mail ambr201@tiscalinet.it; Ambassador MARIE ROSEMONDE YAKOUBOU.

Bolivia: Via Brenta 2A, int. 18, 00198 Roma; tel. (06) 8841001; fax (06) 8840740; e-mail infobolit@yahoo.it; internet www.embajadabolivia.it; Ambassador ANTOLIN AYAVIRI GÓMEZ.

Bosnia and Herzegovina: Piazzale Clodio 12, int. 17/18, 00195 Roma; tel. (06) 39742817; fax (06) 39030567; e-mail ambasciata@ambih.191.it; Ambassador NERKEZ ARIFHODZIC.

Brazil: Palazzo Pamphili, Piazza Navona 14, 00186 Roma; tel. (06) 683981; fax (06) 6867858; e-mail info@ambrasile.it; Ambassador RICARDO NEIVA TAVARES.

Bulgaria: Via Pietro Paolo Rubens 21, 00197 Roma; tel. (06) 3224643; fax (06) 3226122; e-mail embassy@bulemb.it; internet www.mfa.bg/en/107; Chargé d'affaires a.i. TODOR STOYANOV.

Burkina Faso: Via XX Settembre 86, 00187 Roma; tel. (06) 42010611; fax (06) 42016701; e-mail ambabf.roma@tin.it; Ambassador RAYMOND BALIMA.

Burundi: Via Enrico Accinni 63, scala B, int. 10, 00195 Roma; tel. (06) 36381786; fax (06) 36381171; e-mail ambaburoma@yahoo.fr; Chargé d'affaires a.i. JEAN-BOSCO NDINDURUVUGO.

Cameroon: Via Siracusa 4–6, 00161 Roma; tel. (06) 44291285; fax (06) 44291323; e-mail segreteriaambcam@virgilio.it; internet www.cameroonembassy.it; Ambassador DOMINIQUE AWONO ESSAMA.

Canada: Via Salaria 243, 00199 Roma; tel. (06) 854441; fax (06) 854443947; e-mail rome@international.gc.ca; internet www.canadainternational.gc.ca/italy-italie; Ambassador PETER MCGOVERN.

Cape Verde: Via Giosuè Carducci 4, 1°, 00187 Roma; tel. (06) 4744678; fax (06) 4744643; Ambassador MANUEL AMANTE DA ROSA.

Chile: Via Po 23, 00198 Roma; tel. (06) 844091; fax (06) 8841452; e-mail embajada@chileit.it; internet www.chileit.it; Ambassador OSCAR FRANCISCO ARCAYA.

China, People's Republic: Via Bruxelles 56, 00198 Roma; tel. (06) 96524200; fax (06) 96524200; e-mail segreteria.china@gmail.com; internet it.china-embassy.org; Ambassador LI RUIYU.

Colombia: Via Giuseppe Pisanelli 4, 00196 Roma; tel. (06) 3612131; fax (06) 3225798; e-mail eitalia@cancilleria.gov.co; internet www.emcolombia.it; Ambassador JUAN SEBASTIÁN BETANCUR ESCOBAR.

Congo, Democratic Republic: Via Barberini 3, 00187 Roma; tel. and fax (06) 42010779; Ambassador ALBERT TSHISELEKA FELHA.

Congo, Republic: Via Ombrone 8–10, 00198 Roma; tel. and fax (06) 8417422; e-mail ambacorome@gmail.com; internet www.ambasciatadelcongobrazzaville.it; Ambassador MAMADOU KAMARA DEKAMO.

Costa Rica: Viale Liegi 2, int. 8, 00198 Roma; tel. (06) 84242853; fax (06) 85355956; e-mail embcr.italia@gmail.com; Ambassador JAIME FENZAIG ROSENSTEIN.

Côte d'Ivoire: Via Guglielmo Saliceto 6–10, 00161 Roma; tel. (06) 44231129; fax (06) 44292531; e-mail ambassadecotedivoire61@rocketmail.com; Ambassador JANINE ADELE TAGLIANTE-SARACINO.

Croatia: Via Luigi Bodio 74–76, 00191 Roma; tel. (06) 36307650; fax (06) 36303405; e-mail vhrim@mvpei.hr; internet it.mfa.hr; Ambassador DAMIR GRUBIŠA.

Cuba: Via Licinia 7, 00153 Roma; tel. (06) 5717241; fax (06) 5745445; e-mail embajada@ecuitalia.it; Ambassador MILAGROS CARINA SOTO AGÜERO.

Cyprus: Via Ludovisi 35, V piano, scala A, int. 10, 00187 Roma; tel. (06) 8088365; fax (06) 8088338; e-mail cancelleria@ambasciatacipro.it; Ambassador LEONIDAS MARKIDES.

Czech Republic: Via dei Gracchi 322, 00192 Roma; tel. (06) 36309571; fax (06) 3244466; e-mail rome@embassy.mzv.cz; internet www.mzv.cz/rome; Ambassador PETR BURIÁNEK.

Denmark: Via dei Monti Parioli 50, 00197 Roma; tel. (06) 9774831; fax (06) 97748399; e-mail romamb@um.dk; internet www.italien.um.dk; Ambassador BIRGER RIIS-JØRGENSEN.

Dominican Republic: Via Giuseppe Pisanelli 1, int. 8, 00196 Roma; tel. (06) 45434789; fax (06) 45448452; e-mail embajadadominicana@tiscali.it; internet www.embajadadominicanaitalia.org; Ambassador VINICIO ALFONSO TOBAL URENA.

Ecuador: Via Antonio Bertoloni 8, 00197 Roma; tel. (06) 89672820; fax (06) 8076271; e-mail mecuroma@flashnet.it; Ambassador JUAN FERNANDO HOLGUÍN FLORES.

Egypt: Villa Savoia, Via Salaria 267, 00199 Roma; tel. (06) 84401921; fax (06) 8554424; e-mail ambegitto@yahoo.com; Ambassador AMR MOSTAFA KAMAL HELMY.

El Salvador: Via G. Castellini 13, 00197 Roma; tel. (06) 8076605; fax (06) 8079726; e-mail embasalvaroma@tiscali.it; internet www.embasalvaroma.com; Ambassador AIDA LUZ SANTOS DE ESCOBAR.

Equatorial Guinea: Via Bruxelles 59A, 00198 Roma; tel. (06) 8555428; fax (06) 85305685; Ambassador CECILIA OBONO NDONG.

Eritrea: Via Boncompagni 16B, int. 6, 00187 Roma; tel. (06) 42741293; fax (06) 42086806; e-mail segretaria@embassyoferitrea.it; Ambassador ZEMEDE TEKLE WOLDETATIOS.

Estonia: Viale Liegi 28, int. 5, 00198 Roma; tel. (06) 84407510; fax (06) 84407519; e-mail embassy.rome@mfa.ee; internet www.estemb.it; Ambassador MERIKE KOKAJEV.

Ethiopia: Via Andrea Vesalio 16, 00161 Roma; tel. (06) 4416161; fax (06) 4403676; e-mail embethrm@rdn.it; Ambassador MULUGETA ALEMSEGED GESSESE.

Finland: Via Lisbona 3, 00198 Roma; tel. (06) 852231; fax (06) 8540362; e-mail sanomat.roo@formin.fi; internet www.finlandia.it; Ambassador PETRI TUOMAS TUOMI-NIKULA.

France: Piazza Farnese 67, 00186 Roma; tel. (06) 686011; fax (06) 68601360; internet www.ambafrance-it.org; Ambassador ALAIN LE ROY.

Gabon: Via San Marino 36A, 00198 Roma; tel. (06) 85358970; fax (06) 8417278; e-mail cab.cdm@ambagabonrome.it; Ambassador CHARLES ESSONGHE.

Georgia: Corso Vittorio Emanuele II 21, scala A, 00186 Roma; tel. (06) 69925809; fax (06) 69941942; e-mail amgeorgia@libero.it; internet www.italy.mfa.gov.ge; Ambassador KARLO SIKHARULIDZE.

Germany: Via San Martino della Battaglia 4, 00185 Roma; tel. (06) 492131; fax (06) 4452672; e-mail info@rom.diplo.de; internet www.rom.diplo.de; Ambassador REINHARD SCHÄFERS.

Ghana: Via Ostriana 4, 00199 Roma; tel. (06) 86217191; fax (06) 86325762; e-mail info@ghanaembassy.it; internet www.ghanaembassy.it; Ambassador EVELYN ANITA STOKES-HAYFORD.

Greece: Viale G. Rossini 4, 00198 Roma; tel. (06) 8537551; fax (06) 8415927; e-mail gremb.rom@mfa.gr; Ambassador THEMISTOKLIS DEMIRIS.

Guatemala: Via Colli della Farnesina 128, 00194 Roma; tel. (06) 36381143; fax (06) 3291639; e-mail embitalia@minex.gob.gt; Ambassador STEPHANIE HOCHSTETTER SKINNER-KLÉE DE TOWARA.

Guinea: Via Adelaide Ristori, 9B 13, 00197 Roma; tel. (06) 8078989; fax (06) 8077588; e-mail ambaguineerome1@virgilio.it; Ambassador. MAMADY CONDE.

Haiti: Via di Villa Patrizi 7/7A, 00161 Roma; tel. (06) 44254106; fax (06) 44254208; e-mail segreteria@ambhaiti.it; Chargé d'affaires a.i. CARL BENNY RAYMOND.

Holy See: Via Po 27A–29, 00198 Roma; tel. (06) 8546287; fax (06) 8549725; e-mail nunzio@nunziatura.it; Apostolic Nuncio Most Rev. ADRIANO BERNARDINI (Titular Archbishop of Falerii).

Honduras: Via Giambattista Vico 40, int. 8, 00196 Roma; tel. (06) 3207236; fax (06) 3207973; e-mail honduras@embajada.it; Ambassador CARMELO RIZZO.

Hungary: Via dei Villini 12–16, 00161 Roma; tel. (06) 4402032; fax (06) 4403270; e-mail mission.rom@kum.hu; internet www.huembit.it; Ambassador JÁNOS BALLA.

India: Via XX Settembre 5, 00187 Roma; tel. (06) 4884642; fax (06) 4819539; e-mail gen.email@indianembassy.it; internet www.indianembassy.it; Ambassador BASANT K. GUPTA.

Indonesia: Via Campania 55, 00187 Roma; tel. (06) 4200911; fax (06) 4880280; e-mail indorom@uni.net; Ambassador AUGUST PARENGKUAN.

Iran: Via Nomentana 361–363, 00162 Roma; tel. (06) 86328485; fax (06) 86328492; Ambassador JAHANBAKHSH MOZAFFARI.

Iraq: Via della Camilluccia, 355, 00135 Roma; tel. (06) 3014508; fax (06) 3014445; e-mail iraqembroma@yahoo.com; Ambassador SAYWAN SABIR MUSTAFA BARZANI.

Ireland: Via Giacomo Medici 1, 00153 Roma; tel. (06) 5852381; fax (06) 5813336; e-mail romeembassy@dfa.ie; internet www.embassyofireland.it; Ambassador BOBBY MCDONAGH.

Israel: Via Michele Mercati 14, 00197 Roma; tel. (06) 36198500; fax (06) 36198555; e-mail caoassist@roma.mfa.gov.il; internet embassies.gov.il/rome; Ambassador NAOR GILON.

Japan: Via Quintino Sella 60, 00187 Roma; tel. (06) 487991; fax (06) 4873316; e-mail giappone@ro.mofa.go.jp; internet www.it.emb-japan.go.jp; Ambassador MASAHARU KOHNO.

Jordan: Via Giuseppe Marchi 1B, 00161 Roma; tel. (06) 86205303; fax (06) 8606122; e-mail embroma@jordanembassy.it; Ambassador ZAID MUFLEH FALEH AL-LOZI.

Kazakhstan: Via Cassia 471, 00189 Roma; tel. (06) 36301130; fax (06) 36292675; e-mail roma@mfa.kz; internet www.embkaz.it; Ambassador ANDRIAN YELEMESSOV.

Kenya: Via Luca Gaurico 205, 00143 Roma; tel. (06) 8082717; fax (06) 8082707; e-mail kenroma@rdn.it; internet www.embassyofkenya.it; Ambassador JOSEPHINE WANGARI GAITA.

Korea, Democratic People's Republic: Via dell'Esperanto 26, 00144 Roma; tel. (06) 54220749; fax (06) 54210090; e-mail permerepun@hotmail.com; Ambassador KIM CHUN GUK.

Korea, Republic: Via Barnaba Oriani 30, 00197 Roma; tel. (06) 802461; fax (06) 802462259; e-mail consul-it@mofat.go.kr; internet ita.mofat.go.kr; Ambassador JAE-HYUN BAE.

Kosovo: Via Tolmino 12, 00198 Roma; tel. (06) 85355316; fax (06) 8552212; e-mail embassy.italy@ks-gov.net; Ambassador BUKURIJE GJONBALAJ.

Kuwait: Via Archimede 124, 00197 Roma; tel. (06) 8078415; fax (06) 8076651; e-mail kwembrome@hotmail.com; Ambassador JABER DUAJI AL-SABAH.

Latvia: Via Giovanni Battista Martini 13, 00198 Roma; tel. (06) 8841227; fax (06) 8841239; e-mail embassy.italy@mfa.gov.lv; internet www.mfa.gov.lv/rome; Ambassador ARTIS BERTULIS.

Lebanon: Via Giacomo Carissimi 38, 00198 Roma; tel. (06) 8537211; fax (06) 8411794; e-mail ambalibano@hotmail.com; internet www.liban.it; Chargé d'affaires a.i. KARIM KHALIL.

Lesotho: Via Serchio 8, 00198 Roma; tel. (06) 8542496; fax (06) 8542527; e-mail secretary@lesothoembassyrome.com; Ambassador JOSEPH SEMPE LEJAHA.

Liberia: Piazza delle Medaglie d'Oro 7, scala A, int. 5, 00136 Roma; tel. (06) 35453399; fax (06) 35344729; e-mail liberiaembassy@hotmail.com; Chargé d'affaires a.i. MOHAMMED S. L. SHERIFF.

Libya: Via Nomentana 365, 00162 Roma; tel. (06) 86320951; fax (06) 86205473; e-mail ambasciatadilibia@libero.it; Chargé d'affaires a.i. SALAHEDDIN N. M. ELAYEB.

Lithuania: Viale di Villa Grazioli 9, 00198 Roma; tel. (06) 8559052; fax (06) 8559053; e-mail amb.it@urm.lt; internet it.mfa.lt; Ambassador PETRAS ZAPOLSKAS.

Luxembourg: Via Santa Croce in Gerusalemme 90, 00185 Roma; tel. (06) 77201177; fax (06) 77201178; e-mail rome.amb@mae.etat.lu; internet rome.mae.lu; Ambassador JANINE FINCK.

Macedonia, former Yugoslav republic: Viale Bruxelles 73–75, 00198 Roma; tel. (06) 84241109; fax (06) 84241131; e-mail rome@mfa.gov.mk; Chargé d'affaires a.i. MARJAN BARTON.

Madagascar: Via Riccardo Zandonai 84A, 00194 Roma; tel. (06) 66620089; fax (06) 66621905; e-mail ambamad@hotmail.com; Ambassador JEAN PIERRE RAZAFY ANDRIAMIHAINGO.

Malaysia: Via Nomentana 297, 00162 Roma; tel. (06) 8415764; fax (06) 8555040; e-mail mw.rome@flashnet.it; Ambassador Datin Paduka HALIMAH ABDULLAH.

Mali: Via Antonio Bosio 2, 00161 Roma; tel. (06) 44254068; fax (06) 44254029; e-mail amb.malirome@tiscalinet.it; Ambassador MOHAMED GAOUSSOU DRABO.

Malta: Lungotevere Marzio 12, 00186 Roma; tel. (06) 6879990; fax (06) 6892687; e-mail maltaembassy.rome@gov.mt; Ambassador VANESSA FRAZIER.

Mauritania: Via Giovanni Paisiello 26, 00198 Roma; tel. (06) 85351530; fax (06) 85351441; Chargé d'affaires a.i. MOCTAR MOULAYE AHMED LABEID.

Mexico: Via Lazzaro Spallanzani 16, 00161 Roma; tel. (06) 4416061; fax (06) 44292703; e-mail correo@emexitalia.it; internet www.sre.gob.mx/italia; Ambassador MIGUEL RUÍZ-CABAÑAS IZQUIERDO.

Moldova: Via Montebello 8, 00185 Roma; tel. (06) 4740210; fax (06) 47881092; e-mail roma@mfa.md; internet www.italia.mfa.md; Ambassador STELA STINGACI.

Monaco: Via Antonio Bertoloni 36, 00197 Roma; tel. (06) 8083361; fax (06) 8077692; e-mail monaco@ambasciatadimonaco.it; internet www.ambasciatadimonaco.it; Ambassador ROBERT FILLON.

Mongolia: Via Vincenzo Bellini 4, 00198 Roma; tel. and fax (06) 8540536; e-mail italy@mfa.gov.mn; Ambassador SHIJIKHÜÜGIIN ODONBAATAAR.

Montenegro: Via Antonio Gramsci 9, 00197 Roma; tel. (06) 88857745; fax (06) 88857743; e-mail montenegro-roma@libero.it; Ambassador VOJIN VLAHOVIĆ.

Morocco: Via Lazzaro Spallanzani 8–10, 00161 Roma; tel. (06) 4402524; fax (06) 44004458; e-mail sifamaroma@ambasciatadelmarocco.it; internet www.ambasciatadelmarocco.it; Ambassador HASSAN ABOUYOUB.

Mozambique: Via Filippo Corridoni 14, 00195 Roma; tel. (06) 37514675; fax (06) 37514699; e-mail sec@ambasciatamozambico.it; Ambassador CARLA ELISA LUIS MUCAVI.

Myanmar: Viale di Villa Grazioli 29, 00198 Roma; tel. (06) 36303753; fax (06) 36298566; e-mail merome2010@gmail.com; Ambassador TINT SWAI.

Netherlands: Via Michele Mercati 8, 00197 Roma; tel. (06) 32286001; fax (06) 32286256; e-mail rom@minbuza.nl; internet italy.nlembassy.org; Ambassador DEN HOND.

New Zealand: Via Clitunno 44, 00198 Roma; tel. (06) 8537501; fax (06) 4402984; e-mail rome@nzembassy.it; internet www.nzembassy.com/italy; Ambassador Dr TREVOR MATHESON.

Nicaragua: Via Ruffini 2A, 00195 Roma; tel. (06) 32110020; fax (06) 3203041; e-mail embanicitalia@cancilleria.gob.ni; Chargé d'affaires a.i. MARTHA IRENE ZUNIGA GUTIERREZ.

Niger: Via Antonio Baiamonti 10, 00195 Roma; tel. (06) 3720164; fax (06) 3729013; e-mail ambasciatadelniger@virgilio.it; Ambassador AMADOU TOURÉ.

Nigeria: Via Orazio 14–18, 00193 Roma; tel. (06) 683931; fax (06) 68393264; e-mail chancery@nigerianrome.org; internet www.nigerianrome.org; Ambassador ERIC TONYE AWORABHI.

Norway: Via delle Terme Deciane 7, 00153 Roma; tel. (06) 45238100; fax (06) 45238199; e-mail emb.rome@mfa.no; internet www.amb-norvegia.it; Ambassador BJØRN TRYGVE GRYDELAND.

Oman: Via della Camilluccia 625, 00135 Roma; tel. (06) 36300517; fax (06) 3296802; e-mail embassyoman@virgilio.it; Ambassador Dr AHMED BIN SALIM BA OMAR.

Pakistan: Via della Camilluccia 682, 00135 Roma; tel. (06) 36301775; fax (06) 36301936; e-mail pareprome1@tiscali.it; Ambassador TEHMINA JANJUA.

Panama: Largo di Torre Argentina 11 00186 Roma; tel. (06) 44252173; fax (06) 44252237; e-mail embajadapanamaroma@embajadadepanama.it; Ambassador GUIDO JUVENAL MARTINELLI ENDARA.

Paraguay: Via Firenze 43, scala A, 00187 Roma; tel. (06) 4741715; fax (06) 4745473; e-mail embaparoma@virgilio.it; Chargé d'affaires a.i. CARLOS RAMÓN VERA AGUILERA.

Peru: Via Francesco Siacci 2B, 00197 Roma; tel. (06) 80691510; fax (06) 80691777; e-mail embperu@ambasciataperu.it; tel. www.ambasciataperu.it; Chargé d'affaires a.i. PEDRO ROBERTO REÁTEGUI GAMARRA.

Philippines: Viale delle Medaglie d'Oro 114, 00136 Roma; tel. (06) 39746621; fax (06) 39740872; Ambassador VIRGILIO A. REYES, Jr.

Poland: Via Pietro Paolo Rubens 20, 00197 Roma; tel. (06) 36204200; fax (06) 3217895; e-mail roma.ufficio.stampa@msz.gov.pl; internet www.rzym.polemb.net; Ambassador WOJCIECH PONIKIEWSKI.

Portugal: Via della Camilluccia 701, 00135 Roma; tel. (06) 844801; fax (06) 36309827; e-mail emb@embportroma.it; internet www.embportroma.it; Ambassador MANUEL LOBO ANTUNES.

Qatar: Via Antonio Bosio 14, 00161 Roma; tel. (06) 44249450; fax (06) 44245273; e-mail qatar.embassy@gmail.com; internet www.qatarembassy.it; Ambassador ABDULLAH EID SALMAN AL-SULAITI.

Romania: Via Nicolo Tartaglia 36, 00197 Roma; tel. (06) 8084529; fax (06) 8084995; e-mail amdiroma@roembit.org; internet roma.mae.ro; Ambassador DANA-MANUELA CONSTANTINESCU.

Russia: Via Gaeta 5, 00185 Roma; tel. (06) 4941680; fax (06) 491031; e-mail rusembassy@libero.it; internet www.ambrussia.com; Ambassador SERGEY RAZOV.

San Marino: Via Eleonora Duse 35, 00197 Roma; tel. (06) 8072511; fax (06) 8070072; e-mail asmarino@ambrsm.it; Ambassador DANIELA ROTONDARO.

Saudi Arabia: Via G. B. Pergolesi 9, 00198 Roma; tel. (06) 844851; fax (06) 8551781; e-mail segretaria@arabia-saudita.it; internet www.arabia-saudita.it; Ambassador SALEH BIN MOHAMMED BIN GHURMALLAH AL-GHAMDI.

Senegal: Via delle Cave Fiscali 15, 00141 Roma; tel. (06) 6872381; fax (06) 68219294; e-mail ambasenequiri@tiscali.it; Ambassador SEYNABOU BADIANE.

Serbia: Via dei Monti Parioli 20, 00197 Roma; tel. (06) 3211950; fax (06) 3200868; e-mail info@ambroma.com; internet www.roma.mfa.gov.rs; Ambassador ANA HRUSTANOVIĆ.

Slovakia: Via dei Colli della Farnesina 144, 00194 Roma; tel. (06) 36715200; fax (06) 36715265; e-mail emb.roma@mzv.sk; internet www.mzv.sk/rim; Ambassador MÁRIA KRASNOHORSKÁ.

Slovenia: Via Leonardo Pisano 10, 00197 Roma; tel. (06) 80914310; fax (06) 8081471; e-mail vri@gov.si; internet rim.veleposlanistvo.si; Ambassador IZTOK MIROŠIČ.

Somalia: Via dei Gracchi 305, 00192 Roma; tel. (06) 3220651; fax (06) 32541832; e-mail somalrep@gmail.com; Ambassador MUSSA HASSAN ABDULLE.

South Africa: Via Tanaro 14, 00198 Roma; tel. (06) 852541; fax (06) 85254300; e-mail sae@sudafrica.it; internet www.sudafrica.it; Ambassador NOMATEMBA TAMBO.

Spain: Palazzo Borghese, Largo Fontanella Borghese 19, 00186 Roma; tel. (06) 6840401; fax (06) 6872256; e-mail emb.roma@maec.es; internet www.maec.es/embajadas/roma; Ambassador FRANCISCO JAVIER ELORZA CAVENGT.

Sri Lanka: Via Adige 2, 00198 Roma; tel. (06) 8554560; fax (06) 84241670; e-mail embassy@srilankaembassyrome.org; internet www.srilankaembassyrome.org; Ambassador NAWALAGE BENNET COORAY.

Sudan: Via Panama 48, 00198 Roma; tel. (06) 33222138; fax (06) 3340841; e-mail info@sudanembassy.it; Ambassador AMIRA DAOUD HASSAN GORNASS.

Sweden: Piazza Rio de Janeiro 3, 00161 Roma; tel. (06) 441941; fax (06) 44194760; e-mail ambassaden.rom@gov.se; internet www.swedenabroad.com/rom; Ambassador RUTH EVELYN JACOBY.

Switzerland: Via Barnaba Oriani 61, 00197 Roma; tel. (06) 809571; fax (06) 8088510; e-mail rom.vertretung@eda.admin.ch; internet www.eda.admin.ch/roma; Ambassador BERNARDINO REGAZZONI.

Syria: Piazza dell'Ara Coeli, 00186 Roma; tel. (06) 6749801; fax (06) 6794989; e-mail uffstampasyem@hotmail.it; Chargé d'affaires a.i. DIMA HARIRI.

Tanzania: Viale Cortina d'Ampezzo 185, 00135 Roma; tel. (06) 33485801; fax (06) 33485828; e-mail info@tanzania-gov.it; internet www.tanzania-gov.it; Ambassador JAMES ALEX MSEKELA.

Thailand: Via Nomentana 132, 00162 Roma; tel. (06) 86220524; fax (06) 86220555; e-mail thai.em.rome@wind.it.net; internet www.thaiembassy.org/rome; Ambassador SURAPIT KIRTIPUTRA.

Tunisia: Via Asmara 7, 00199 Roma; tel. (06) 8603060; fax (06) 86218204; e-mail at.roma@tiscali.it; Ambassador NACEUR MESTIRI.

Turkey: Palazzo Gamberini, Via Palestro 28, 00185 Roma; tel. (06) 445941; fax (06) 4941526; e-mail roma.be@libero.it; internet www.roma.be.mfa.gov.tr; Ambassador (vacant).

Uganda: Viale Giulio Cesare 71, II piano, scala A–B, 00192 Roma; tel. (06) 3225220; fax (06) 3213688; e-mail ugandaembassyrome@hotmail.com; internet www.ugandaembassy.it; Ambassador DINAH GRACE AKELLO.

Ukraine: Via Guido d'Arezzo 9, 00198 Roma; tel. (06) 8412630; fax (06) 8547539; e-mail emb_it@mfa.gov.ua; internet www.mfa.gov.ua/italy; Ambassador YEVHEN PERELYGIN.

United Arab Emirates: Via della Camilluccia 492, 00135 Roma; tel. (06) 36306100; fax (06) 36306155; e-mail uaeroma@tin.it; Ambassador ABD AL-AZIZ AL-SHAMSI.

United Kingdom: Via XX Settembre 80A, 00187 Roma; tel. (06) 42202431; fax (06) 42202333; e-mail romepoliticalsection@fco.gov.uk; internet www.ukinitaly.fco.gov.uk; Ambassador CHRISTOPHER PRENTICE.

USA: Palazzo Margherita, Via Vittorio Veneto 121, 00187 Roma; tel. (06) 46741; fax (06) 46742217; internet rome.usembassy.gov; Ambassador JOHN R. PHILLIPS.

Uruguay: Via Vittorio Veneto 183, 00187 Roma; tel. (06) 4821776; fax (06) 4823695; e-mail uruit@ambasciatauruguay.it; Ambassador ALBERTO BRECCIA.

Uzbekistan: Via Pompeo Magno 1, 00192 Roma; tel. (06) 87860310; fax (06) 87860309; e-mail ambasciata@uzbekistanitalia.org; internet www.uzbekistanitalia.org; Chargé d'affaires a.i. ZAFAR MUHTAROV.

Venezuela: Via Nicolò Tartaglia 11, 00197 Roma; tel. (06) 8079797; fax (06) 8084410; e-mail embaveit@ambavene.org; Ambassador JULIAN ISAIAS RODRIGUEZ DIAZ.

Viet Nam: Via di Bravetta 156, 00164 Roma; tel. (06) 66160726; fax (06) 66157520; e-mail vnemb.it@mofa.gov.vn; internet www.vnembassy.it; Ambassador NGUYEN HOANG LONG.

Yemen: Via Antonio Bosio 10, 00161 Roma; tel. (06) 44231679; fax (06) 44234763; e-mail info@yemenembassy.it; internet www.yemenembassy.it; Ambassador KHALID ABD AL-RAHMAN MUHAMMAD AL-AKWA.

Zambia: Via Ennio Quirino Visconti 8, VI piano, 00193 Roma; tel. (06) 36002590; fax (06) 97613035; e-mail info@zambianembassy.it; internet www.zambianembassy.it; Ambassador FRANK MUTUBILA.

Zimbabwe: Via Virgilio 8, 00193 Roma; tel. (06) 68308282; fax (06) 68308324; e-mail zimrome-wolit@tiscali.it; Chargé d'affaires a.i. SHEPHARD SHINGIRAI GWENZI.

Judicial System

The Constitutional Court was established in 1956 and is an autonomous constitutional body, standing apart from the judicial system. Its most important function is to pronounce on the constitutionality of legislation both subsequent and prior to the present Constitution of 1948. It also judges accusations brought against the President of the Republic or ministers.

At the base of the system of penal jurisdiction are the District Courts (Preture), where offences carrying a sentence of up to four years' imprisonment are tried. Above the Preture are the Tribunals (Tribunali) and the Assize Courts attached to the Tribunals, Corti di Assise presso i Tribunali, where graver offences are dealt with. From these courts appeal lies to the Courts of Appeal (Corti d'Appello) and the parallel Assize Courts of Appeal (Corti di Assise d'Appello). Final appeal may be made, on juridical grounds only, to the Supreme Court of Cassation (Corte Suprema di Cassazione).

Civil cases may be taken in the first instance to Justices of the Peace (Giudici Conciliatori), Preture or Tribunali, according to the economic value of the case. Appeal from the Giudici Conciliatori lies to the Preture, from the Preture to the Tribunali, from the Tribunali to the Corti d'Appello, and finally, as in penal justice, to the Corte Suprema di Cassazione on juridical grounds only.

Special divisions for cases concerning labour relations are attached to civil courts. Cases concerned with the public service and its employees are tried by Tribunali Amministrativi Regionali and the Consiglio di Stato. Juvenile courts have criminal and civil jurisdiction.

A new penal code was introduced in late 1989.

CONSTITUTIONAL COURT

Corte Costituzionale: Palazzo della Consulta, Piazza del Quirinale 41, 00187 Roma; tel. (06) 46981; fax (06) 4698916; e-mail ccost@cortecostituzionale.it; internet www.cortecostituzionale.it; consists of 15 judges, one-third appointed by the President of the Republic, one-third elected by Parliament in joint session, and one-third by the ordinary and administrative supreme courts; Pres. GAETANO SILVESTRI.

ADMINISTRATIVE COURTS

Consiglio di Stato: Palazzo Spada, Piazza Capo di Ferro 13, 00186 Roma; tel. (06) 68271; fax (06) 68272282; e-mail urp.cds@giustizia-amministrativa.it; internet www.giustizia-amministrativa.it; established in accordance with Article 10 of the Constitution; has both consultative and judicial functions; Pres. Dott. GIORGIO GIOVANNINI.

Corte dei Conti: Via Giuseppe Mazzini 105, 00195 Roma; tel. (06) 38761; fax (06) 38763477; e-mail urp@corteconti.it; internet www.corteconti.it; functions as the court of public auditors for the state; Pres. RAFFAELE SQUITIERI.

SUPREME COURT OF CASSATION

Corte Suprema di Cassazione: Palazzo di Giustizia, Piazza Cavour, 00193 Roma; tel. (06) 68831; e-mail cortedicassazione@giustizia.it; internet www.cortedicassazione.it; supreme court of civil and criminal appeal; First Pres. Dott. GIORGIO SANTACROCE.

SUPERVISORY BODY

Consiglio Superiore della Magistratura (CSM): Piazza Indipendenza 6, 00185 Roma; tel. (06) 444911; fax (06) 4457175; e-mail protocollo.csm@giustiziacert.it; internet www.csm.it; f. 1958; 27

mems; Pres. GIORGIO NAPOLITANO (President of the Republic); Vice-Pres. MICHELE VIETTI.

Religion

More than 90% of the population of Italy are adherents of the Roman Catholic Church. Under the terms of the Concordat formally ratified in June 1985, Roman Catholicism was no longer to be the state religion, compulsory religious instruction in schools was abolished and state financial contributions reduced. The Vatican City's sovereign rights as an independent state, under the terms of the Lateran Treaty of 1929, were not affected.

Several Protestant churches also exist in Italy, with a total membership of about 65,000. There is a small Jewish community, and in 1987 an agreement recognized certain rights for the Jewish community, including the right to observe religious festivals on Saturdays by not attending school or work. There is also a substantial Islamic population.

CHRISTIANITY

The Roman Catholic Church

For ecclesiastical purposes, Italy comprises the Papal See of Rome, the Patriarchate of Venice, 60 archdioceses (including three directly responsible to the Holy See), two eparchies, 153 dioceses (including seven within the jurisdiction of the Pope, as Archbishop of the Roman Province, and 11 directly responsible to the Holy See), two territorial prelatures and seven territorial abbacies (including four directly responsible to the Holy See). Almost all adherents follow the Latin rite, but there are two dioceses and one abbacy (all directly responsible to the Holy See) for Catholics of the Italo-Albanian (Byzantine) rite.

Bishops' Conference: Conferenza Episcopale Italiana, Circonvallazione Aurelia 50, 00165 Roma; tel. (06) 663981; fax (06) 6623037; e-mail segrgen@chiesacattolica.it; internet www.chiesacattolica.it; f. 1965; Pres. Cardinal ANGELO BAGNASCO (Archbishop of Genova); Sec.-Gen. Rt Rev. MARIANO CROCIATA.

Primate of Italy, Archbishop and Metropolitan of the Roman Province and Bishop of Rome: His Holiness Pope FRANCIS.

Patriarch of Venice: FRANCESCO MORAGLIA.

Archbishops

Acerenza: Most Rev. GIOVANNI RICCHIUTI.
Agrigento: Most Rev. FRANCESCO MONTENEGRO.
Amalfi-Cava de' Tirreni: Most Rev. ORAZIO SORICELLI.
Ancona-Osimo: Most Rev. EDOARDO MENICHELLI.
L'Aquila: Most Rev. GIUSEPPE PETROCCHI.
Bari-Bitonto: Most Rev. FRANCESCO CACUCCI.
Benevento: Most Rev. ANDREA MUGIONE.
Bologna: Cardinal CARLO CAFFARRA.
Brindisi-Otsuni: Most Rev. DOMENICO CALIANDRO.
Cagliari: Most Rev. ARRIGO MIGLIO.
Camerino-San Severino Marche: Most Rev. FRANCESCO GIOVANNI BRUGNARO.
Campobasso-Boiano: Most Rev. GIANCARLO MARIA BREGANTINI.
Capua: Most Rev. SALVATORE VISCO.
Catania: Most Rev. SALVATORE GRISTINA.
Catanzaro-Squillace: Most Rev. VINCENZO BERTOLONE.
Chieti-Vasto: Most Rev. BRUNO FORTE.
Cosenza-Bisignano: Most Rev. SALVATORE NUNNARI.
Crotone-Santa Severina: Most Rev. DOMENICO GRAZIANI.
Fermo: Most Rev. LUIGI CONTI.
Ferrara-Comacchio: Most Rev. LUIGI NEGRI.
Firenze (Florence): Most Rev. GIUSEPPE BETORI.
Foggia-Bovino: Most Rev. FRANCESCO PIO TAMBURRINO.
Gaeta: Most Rev. FABIO BERNARDO D'ONORIO.
Genova (Genoa): Cardinal ANGELO BAGNASCO.
Gorizia: Most Rev. CARLO ROBERTO MARIA REDAELLI.
Lanciano-Ortona: Most Rev. EMIDIO CIPOLLONE.
Lecce: Most Rev. DOMENICO UMBERTO D'AMBROSIO.
Lucca: Most Rev. BENVENUTO ITALO CASTELLANI.
Manfredonia-Vieste-San Giovanni Rotondo: Most Rev. MICHELE CASTORO.
Matera-Irsina: Most Rev. SALVATORE LIGORIO.
Messina-Lipari-Santa Lucia del Mela: Most Rev. CALOGERO LA PIANA.
Milano (Milan): Cardinal ANGELO SCOLA.
Modena-Nonantola: Most Rev. ANTONIO LANFRANCHI.
Monreale: Most Rev. MICHELE PENNISI.
Napoli (Naples): Cardinal CRESCENZIO SEPE.
Oristano: Most Rev. IGNAZIO SANNA.
Otranto: Most Rev. DONATO NEGRO.
Palermo: Cardinal PAOLO ROMEO.
Perugia-Città della Pieve: Cardinal GUALTIERO BASSETTI.
Pesaro: Most Rev. PIERO COCCIA.
Pescara-Penne: Most Rev. TOMMASO VALENTINETTI.
Pisa: Most Rev. GIOVANNI PAOLO BENOTTO.
Potenza-Muro Lucano-Marsico Nuovo: Most Rev. AGOSTINO SUPERBO.
Ravenna-Cervia: Most Rev. LORENZO GHIZZONI.
Reggio Calabria-Bova: Most Rev. GIUSEPPE FIORINI MOROSINI.
Rossano-Cariati: Most Rev. SANTO MARCIANÒ.
Salerno-Campagna-Acerno: Most Rev. LUIGI MORETTI.
Sant'Angelo dei Lombardi-Conza-Nusco-Bisaccia: Most Rev. PASQUALE CASCIO.
Sassari: Most Rev. PAOLO MARIO VIRGILIO ATZEI.
Siena-Colle di Val d'Elsa-Montalcino: Most Rev. ANTONIO BUONCRISTIANI.
Siracusa (Syracuse): Most Rev. SALVATORE PAPPALARDO.
Sorrento-Castellamare di Stabia: Most Rev. FRANCESCO ALFANO.
Spoleto-Norcia: Most Rev. RENATO BOCCARDO.
Taranto: Most Rev. FILIPPO SANTORO.
Torino (Turin): Most Rev. CESARE NOSIGLIA.
Trani-Barletta-Bisceglie: Most Rev. GIOVAN BATTISTA PICHIERRI.
Trento: Most Rev. LUIGI BRESSAN.
Udine: Most Rev. ANDREA BRUNO MAZZOCATO.
Urbino-Urbania-Sant'Angelo in Vado: Most Rev. GIOVANNI TANI.
Vercelli: Most Rev. MARCO ARNOLFO.

Protestant Churches

Federazione delle Chiese Evangeliche in Italia (Federation of the Protestant Churches in Italy): Via Firenze 38, 00184 Roma; tel. (06) 4825120; fax (06) 4828728; internet www.fcei.it; f. 1967; total mems c. 65,000; Pres. MASSIMO AQUILANTE; 9 mem. churches, incl. the following:

Chiesa Evangelica Luterana in Italia (Lutheran Church): Via Aurelia Antica 391, 00165 Roma; tel. (06) 66030104; fax (06) 66017993; e-mail decanato@chiesaluterana.it; internet www.chiesaluterana.it; Pres. CHRISTIANE GROEBEN; 7,000 mems.

Chiesa Evangelica Valdese (Unione delle Chiese Metodiste e Valdesi) (Waldensian Evangelical Church): Via Firenze 38, 00184 Roma; tel. (06) 4743695; fax (06) 47885308; e-mail info@chiesavaldese.org; internet www.chiesavaldese.org; in 2002 the Tavola Valdese merged with the Chiese Evangeliche Metodiste in Italia (Methodists); Moderator MARIA BONAFEDE; 27,465 mems.

ISLAM

Associazione Musulmani Italiani (AMI) (Italian Muslim Association): CP 7167, Roma; tel. and fax (06) 44360619; e-mail info@amimuslims.org; internet www.amimuslims.org; f. 1982; Pres. Prince BARZANGI AHMED ABUCAR SULDAN.

Unione delle Comunità Islamiche d'Italia (UCOII): Via delle 4, Fontane, Roma; tel. (0183) 48939934; fax (0183) 764735; e-mail alessandro.paolantoni@ucoii.org; internet www.ucoii.org; f. 1990; Pres. IZZEDDIN ELZIR; Sec. AHMED ALESSANDRO PAOLANTONI.

JUDAISM

Unione delle Comunità Ebraiche Italiane (UCEI) (Union of Italian Jewish Communities): Lungotevere Sanzio 9, 00153 Roma; tel. (06) 45542200; fax (06) 5899569; e-mail info@ucei.it; internet www.ucei.it; f. 1930; represents 21 Jewish communities in Italy; Pres. RENZO GATTEGNA; Gen. Sec. Dott. GLORIA ARBIB.

The Press

Relative to the size of Italy's population, the number of daily newspapers is rather small. Rome and Milan are the main press centres. The most important national dailies are *Corriere della Sera* in Milan and *La Repubblica* in Rome, followed by Turin's *La Stampa* and Milan's *Il Sole 24 Ore*, the economic and financial newspaper with the highest circulation in Europe. Among the most widely read newspapers are *La Gazzetta dello Sport* and *Il Corriere dello Sport—Stadio*, both of which exclusively cover sports news.

PRINCIPAL DAILIES

(Average net circulation figures, for January–December 2011, unless otherwise stated.)

Ancona

Il Corriere Adriatico: Via Berti 20, 60126 Ancona; tel. (071) 4581; fax (071) 42980; e-mail info@corriereadriaticonline.it; internet www.corriereadriatico.it; f. 1860; Editorial Dir PAOLO TRAINI; circ. 23,549.

Bari

La Gazzetta del Mezzogiorno: Viale Scipione l'Africano 264, 70124 Bari; tel. (080) 5470200; fax (080) 5502130; e-mail direzione.politica@gazzettamezzogiorno.it; internet www.lagazzettadelmezzogiorno.it; f. 1887; independent; Editor MICHELE PARTIPILO; circ. 46,804.

Il Quotidiano di Bari: Piazza Aldo Moro 31, 70121 Bari; tel. (080) 5240473; fax (080) 5245486; e-mail redazione@quotidianodibari.it; internet www.quotidianodibari.it; Dir MATTEO TATARELLA.

Bergamo

L'Eco di Bergamo: Viale Papa Giovanni XXIII 118, 24121 Bergamo; tel. (035) 386111; fax (035) 386217; e-mail redazione@eco.bg.it; internet www.ecodibergamo.it; f. 1880; Catholic; Dir GIORGIO GANDOLA; circ. 57,986.

Bologna

Il Resto del Carlino: Via Enrico Mattei 106, 40138 Bologna; tel. (051) 6006111; fax (051) 536111; e-mail segreteria.redazione.bologna@monrif.net; internet www.ilrestodelcarlino.it; f. 1885; publr Poligrafici Editoriale, SpA; Dir GIOVANNI MORANDI; circ. 180,914.

Bolzano/Bozen

Alto Adige: Via Volta 10, 39100 Bozen; tel. (0471) 904111; fax (0471) 904263; e-mail bolzano@altoadige.it; internet www.altoadige.it; f. 1945; publr Gruppo Editoriale L'Espresso, SpA; Dir ALBERTO FAUSTINI; circ. 36,951.

Dolomiten: Weinbergweg 7, 39100 Bozen; tel. (0471) 925111; fax (0471) 925440; e-mail dolomiten@athesia.it; internet www.stol.it/dolomiten; f. 1882; independent; German language; Dir Dott. TONI EBNER; circ. 55,654.

Brescia

Il Giornale di Brescia: Via Solferino 22, 25121 Brescia; tel. (030) 37901; fax (030) 3790289; e-mail info@giornaledibrescia.it; internet www.giornaledibrescia.it; f. 1947; Dir GIACOMO SCANZI; circ. 54,624.

Cagliari

L'Unione Sarda: Viale Regina Elena 12, 9100 Cagliari; tel. (070) 60131; fax (070) 6013306; e-mail unione@unionesarda.it; internet www.unionesarda.it; f. 1889; independent; Editor-in-Chief PAOLO FIGUS; circ. 70,699.

Catania

La Sicilia: Viale Odorico da Pordenone 50, 95126 Catania; tel. (095) 330544; fax (095) 336466; e-mail segreteria@lasicilia.it; internet www.lasicilia.it; f. 1945; independent; Man. Dott. MARIO CIANCIO SANFILIPPO; circ. 63,255.

Como

La Provincia di Como: Via Pasquale Paoli 21, 22100 Como; tel. (031) 582311; fax (031) 505003; e-mail laprovincia@laprovincia.it; internet www.laprovinciadicomo.it; f. 1892; independent; Dir DIEGO MINONZIO; circ. 56,000 (2003).

Firenze
(Florence)

La Nazione: Viale Giovine Italia 17, 50121 Firenze; tel. (055) 249511; fax (055) 2478207; e-mail segreteria@lanazione.it; internet www.lanazione.it; f. 1859; publr Poligrafici Editoriale, SpA; Dir JOSEPH MASCAMBRUNO; circ. 149,393.

Foggia

Quotidiano di Foggia: Via Gramsci 73A, 71100 Foggia; tel. (0881) 686967; fax (0881) 632247; e-mail redazione@quotidianodifoggia.it; internet www.quotidianodifoggia.it; Dir MATTEO TATTARELLA; circ. 25,000 (2007).

Genova
(Genoa)

Il Secolo XIX: Piazza Piccapietra 21, 16121 Genova; tel. (010) 53881; fax (010) 5388426; e-mail redazione@ilsecoloxix.it; internet www.ilsecoloxix.it; f. 1886; independent; Dir CARLO PERRONE; circ. 96,419.

Lecce

Nuovo Quotidiano di Puglia: Via dei Mocenigo 29, 73100 Lecce; tel. (0832) 3382000; fax (0832) 338244; e-mail redazioneweb@quotidianodipuglia.it; internet www.quotidianodipuglia.it; f. 1979 as *Il Quotidiano di Lecce*; 3 local edns covering Lecce, Brindisi and Taranto; Dir CLAUDIO SCAMARDELLA; circ. 24,109.

Livorno
(Leghorn)

Il Tirreno: Viale Alfieri 9, 57124 Livorno; tel. (0586) 220111; fax (0586) 402066; e-mail redazione.li@iltirreno.it; internet iltirreno.repubblica.it; f. 1978; publr Gruppo Editoriale L'Espresso, SpA; Dir ROBERTO BERNABÒ; circ. 93,939.

Mantova
(Mantua)

Gazzetta di Mantova: Piazza Cesare Mozzarelli 7, 46100 Mantova; tel. (0376) 3031; fax (0376) 303263; e-mail redazione.mn@gazzettadimantova.it; internet www.gazzettadimantova.it; f. 1664; publr Gruppo Editoriale L'Espresso, SpA; Dir ANDREA FILIPPI; circ. 34,114.

Messina

Gazzetta del Sud: Uberto Bonino 15C, 98124 Messina; tel. (090) 2261; fax (090) 2936359; e-mail amministrazione@gazzettadelsud.it; internet www.gazzettadelsud.it; f. 1952; independent; Dir NINO CALARCO; circ. 59,227.

Milano
(Milan)

Avvenire: Piazza Carbonari 3, 20125 Milano; tel. (02) 67801; fax (02) 6780208; e-mail lettere@avvenire.it; internet www.avvenire.it; f. 1968; Catholic; organ of the Italian Bishops' Conference; Dir MARCO TARQUINIO; circ. 145,754.

Corriere della Sera: Via Solferino 28, 20121 Milano; tel. (02) 6339; fax (02) 29009668; internet www.corriere.it; f. 1876; independent; contains weekly supplement, *Sette*; Dir FERRUCIO DE BORTOLI; circ. 622,070.

Il Foglio Quotidiano: Via Carroccio 12, 20123 Milano; tel. (02) 7712951; fax (02) 782511; e-mail lettere@ilfoglio.it; internet www.ilfoglio.it; Dir GIULIANO FERRARA.

La Gazzetta dello Sport: RCS Editoriale Quotidiani, SpA, Via Solferino 28, 20121 Milano; tel. (02) 6339; fax (02) 62827917; e-mail segretgaz@rcs.it; internet www.gazzetta.it; f. 1896; sport; Dir ANDREA MONTI; circ. 427,933.

Il Giornale: Via Gaetano Negri 4, 20123 Milano; tel. (02) 85661; fax (02) 72023880; e-mail segreteria@ilgiornale.it; internet www.ilgiornale.it; f. 1974; Editor ALESSANDRO SALLUSTI; circ. 258,941.

Il Giorno: Via Stradivari 4, 20123 Milano; tel. (02) 277991; fax (02) 27799537; e-mail ilgiorno@ilgiorno.it; internet www.ilgiorno.it; f. 1956; publr Poligrafici Editoriale, SpA; Dir GIOVANNI MORANDI; circ. 87,479.

Italia Oggi: Class Editori, Via M. Burigozzo 5, 20122 Milano; tel. (02) 58219256; e-mail italiaoggi@class.it; internet www.italiaoggi.it; f. 1991; economic daily; Dir PIERLUIGI MAGNASCHI; circ. 133,024.

Libero: Viale L. Majno 42, 20129 Milano; tel. (02) 99966300; fax (02) 99966305; e-mail redazione@libero-news.eu; internet www.libero-news.it; f. 2000; Dir EGREGIO MAURIZIO BELPIETRO; circ. 194,818.

MF (Milano Finanza): Class Editori, Via M. Burigozzo 5, 20122 Milano; tel. (02) 582191; internet www.milanofinanza.it; f. 1989; economic daily; Dir ENRICO ROMAGNA MANOJA.

Il Sole 24 Ore: Via Monte Rosa 91, 20149 Milano; tel. (02) 30221; fax (02) 312055; internet www.ilsole24ore.com; f. 1865; financial, political, economic; Dir ROBERTO NAPOLETANO; circ. 334,519.

Napoli
(Naples)

Corriere del Mezzogiorno: Vico II San Nicola alla Dogana 9, 80133 Napoli; tel. (081) 7602001; fax (081) 5802779; e-mail m.demarco@corrieredelmezzogiorno.it; internet www.corrieredelmezzogiorno.it; f. 1997; publr RCS MediaGroup; Dir MARCO DEMARCO.

Il Denaro: Via Kennedy 54, 800125 Napoli; tel. (081) 421900; fax (081) 422212; e-mail denaro@denaro.it; internet www.denaro.it; economic daily; Dir ALFONSO RUFFO.

Il Mattino: Via Chiatamone 65, 80121 Napoli; tel. (081) 7947111; fax (081) 7947288; e-mail redazioneinternet@ilmattino.it; internet www.ilmattino.it; f. 1892; reformed 1950; independent; Dir-Gen. MASSIMO GARZILLI; Editor VIRMAN CUSENZA; circ. 99,776.

Padova
(Padua)

Il Mattino di Padova: Via N. Tommaseo, 65B, 35131 Padova; tel. (049) 8083411; fax (049) 8070067; e-mail mattino@mattinopadova.it; internet www.mattinopadova.it; f. 1978; publr Gruppo Editoriale L'Espresso, SpA; Dir ANTONIO RAMENGHI; circ. 34,282.

Palermo

Giornale di Sicilia: Via Lincoln 21, 90122 Palermo; tel. (091) 6627111; fax (091) 6627280; e-mail gds@gestelnet.it; internet www.gds.it; f. 1860; independent; Dir ANTONIO ARDIZZONE; circ. 73,269.

Parma

Gazzetta di Parma: Via Mantova 68, 43100 Parma; tel. (0521) 2251; fax (0521) 225522; e-mail gazzetta@gazzettadiparma.net; internet www.gazzettadiparma.it; f. 1735; Dir GIULIANO MOLOSSI; circ. 47,186.

Perugia

Corriere dell'Umbria: Via Pievaiola 166F, 06132 Perugia; tel. (075) 52731; fax (075) 5273400; e-mail info@corrieredellumbria.it; f. 1983; independent; Editor ANNA MOSSUTO; circ. 30,097.

Pescara

Il Centro: Via Tiburtina 91, 65129 Pescara; tel. (085) 20521; fax (085) 4318050; e-mail lettere@ilcentro.it; internet www.ilcentro.it; f. 1986; publr Gruppo Editoriale L'Espresso, SpA; Dir SERGIO BARALDI; circ. 29,063.

Piacenza

Libertà: Via Benedettine 68, 29100 Piacenza; tel. (0523) 393939; fax (0523) 321723; e-mail info@liberta.it; internet www.liberta.it; f. 1883; Dir RIZZUTO GAETANO; circ. 33,690.

Rimini

Corriere di Romagna: Piazza Tre Martiri 43A, 47900 Rimini; tel. (0541) 354111; fax (0541) 351499; e-mail lega@corriereromagna.it; internet www.corriereromagna.it; also distributed in San Marino; Dir MARIA PATRIZIA LANZETTI.

Roma
(Rome)

Conquiste del Lavoro: Via Po 22, 00198 Roma; tel. (06) 8473430; fax (06) 85412333; e-mail conquiste_lavoro@cisl.it; internet www.conquistedellavoro.it; owned by Confederazione Italiana Sindacati Lavoratori (CISL); Dir RAFFAELE BONANNI; circ. 90,000 (2008).

Il Corriere dello Sport—Stadio: Piazza Indipendenza 11B, 00185 Roma; tel. (06) 49921; fax (06) 4992275; e-mail segrdirgen@corsport.it; internet www.corsport.it; f. 1924; Editor ALESSANDRO VOCALELLI; circ. 314,576.

Il Manifesto: Via Tomacelli 146, 00186 Roma; tel. (06) 687191; fax (06) 68719573; e-mail redazione@ilmanifesto.it; internet www.ilmanifesto.it; f. 1971; splinter communist; Dir NORMA RANGERI; circ. 69,152.

Il Messaggero: Via del Tritone 152, 00187 Roma; tel. (06) 47201; fax (06) 4720300; e-mail posta@ilmessaggero.it; internet www.ilmessaggero.it; f. 1878; independent; Pres. FRANCO G. CALTAGIRONE; Editor NORMA RANGERI; circ. 265,063.

La Repubblica: Via Cristoforo Colombo 149, 00147 Roma; tel. (06) 49821; fax (06) 49822923; e-mail larepubblica@repubblica.it; internet www.repubblica.it; f. 1976; left-wing; publr Gruppo Editoriale L'Espresso, SpA; Dir EZIO MAURO; circ. 576,216.

Il Riformista: Via Trinità dei Pellegrini 12, 00186 Roma; tel. (06) 427481; fax (06) 42748215; e-mail redazione@ilriformista.it; internet www.ilriformista.it; political; Dir EMANUELE MACALUSO.

Il Tempo: Piazza Colonna 366, 00187 Roma; tel. (06) 675881; fax (06) 6758869; internet www.iltempo.it; f. 1944; independent; right-wing; Editor MARIO SECHI; circ. 57,922.

L'Unità: Via Ostiense 131L, 00154 Roma; tel. (06) 585571; fax (06) 58557219; e-mail unitaonline@unita.it; internet www.unita.it; f. 1924; Dir LUCA LANDÒ; circ. 118,662.

Salerno

La Città: Via San Leonardo 51, 84131 Salerno; tel. (089) 2783111; fax (089) 2783236; e-mail redazione@lacittadisalerno.it; internet www.lacittadisalerno.it; Dir ANGELO DI MARINO.

Sassari

La Nuova Sardegna: Strada 30–31, Predda Niedda, 07100 Sassari; tel. (079) 222400; fax (079) 2674086; e-mail redazione@lanuovasardegna.it; internet lanuovasardegna.repubblica.it; f. 1891; publr Gruppo Editoriale L'Espresso, SpA; Dir ANDREA FILIPPI; circ. 163,175.

Torino
(Turin)

La Stampa: Via Marenco 32, 10126 Torino; tel. (011) 656811; fax (011) 655306; e-mail lettere@lastampa.it; internet www.lastampa.it; f. 1867; independent; Dir MARIO CALABRESI; circ. 381,423.

Trento

L'Adige: Via Missioni Africane 17, 38100 Trento; tel. (0461) 886111; fax (0461) 886264; e-mail p.giovanetti@ladige.it; internet www.ladige.it; f. 1946; independent; Dir Dott. PIERANGELO GIOVANETTI; circ. 30,646.

Trieste

Il Piccolo: Via Guido Reni 1, 34123 Trieste; tel. (040) 3733111; fax (040) 3733262; e-mail ufficio.centrale@ilpiccolo.it; internet ilpiccolo.repubblica.it; f. 1881; publr Gruppo Editoriale L'Espresso, SpA; Dir PAOLO POSSAMAI; circ. 41,999.

Primorski Dnevnik: Via dei Montecchi 6, 34137 Trieste; tel. (040) 7786300; fax (040) 7786339; e-mail redakcija@primorski.eu; internet www.primorski.eu; f. 1945; Slovene; Editor-in-Chief DUŠAN UDOVIČ; circ. 11,282 (2010).

Udine

Il Messaggero Veneto: Viale Palmanova 290, 33100 Udine; tel. (0432) 5271; fax (0432) 523072; e-mail ufficio.centrale@messaggeroveneto.it; internet www.messaggeroveneto.it; f. 1946; publr Gruppo Editoriale L'Espresso, SpA; Dir ANDREA FILIPPI; circ. 56,496.

Varese

La Prealpina: Viale Tamagno 13, 21100 Varese; tel. (0332) 275700; fax (0332) 275701; e-mail direttore@prealpina.it; internet www.prealpina.it; f. 1888; Dir PAOLO PROVENZI; circ. 40,000 (2007).

Venezia
(Venice)

Il Gazzettino: Via Torino 110, 30172 Venezia-Mestre; tel. (041) 665111; fax (041) 665413; e-mail segredazione@gazzettino.it; internet www.gazzettino.it; f. 1887; independent; Dir ROBERTO PAPETTI; circ. 103,797.

Verona

L'Arena: Corso Porta Nuova 67, 37122 Verona; tel. (045) 9600111; fax (045) 597966; e-mail redazione@larena.it; internet www.larena.it; f. 1866; independent; Editor-in-Chief MAURIZIO CATTANEO; Man. Dir Ing. ALESSANDRO ZELGER; circ. 54,411.

Vicenza

Il Giornale di Vicenza: Via Enrico Fermi 205, 36100 Vicenza; tel. (0444) 396311; fax (0444) 396333; internet www.ilgiornaledivicenza.it; f. 1945; Dir ARIO GERVASUTTI; circ. 48,276.

SELECTED PERIODICALS

Art, Architecture and Design

Abitare: Via Angelo Rizzoli 8, 20132 Milano; tel. (02) 25841; e-mail mario.piazza@rcs.it; internet www.abitare.it; f. 1962; monthly; architecture and design; in Italian and English; publr RCS MediaGroup; Editor-in-Chief MARIO PIAZZA.

Casabella: Arnoldo Mondadori Editore, SpA, Via Mondadori 1, 20090 Segrate, Milano; tel. (02) 75421; fax (02) 75422706; e-mail casabella@mondadori.it; internet casabellaweb.eu; f. 1928; 11 a year; architecture and interior design; publr Mondadori Editore SpA; Editor FRANCESCO DAL CO; circ. 40,000 (2014).

Domus: Via Gianni Mazzocchi 1/3, 20089 Rozzano, Milano; tel. (02) 824721; fax (02) 82472386; e-mail editorialedomus@edidomus.it; internet www.domusweb.it; f. 1928; 11 a year; architecture, interior design and art; Editor NICOLA DI BATTISTA; circ. 53,000.

Interni: Via D. Trentacoste 7, 20134 Milano; tel. (02) 215631; fax (02) 26410847; e-mail interni@mondadori.it; internet www.internimagazine.it; monthly; interior decoration and design; Editor GILDA BOJARDI; circ. 50,000 (2013).

Lotus International: Via Santa Marta 19A, 20123 Milano; tel. (02) 45475745; fax (02) 45475746; e-mail lotus@editorialelotus.it; internet www.editorialelotus.it; f. 1963; quarterly; architecture, town planning; Editor PIERLUIGI NICOLIN.

Storia dell'Arte: CAM Editrice, Srl, Via Capodiferro 4, 00186 Roma; tel. and fax (06) 68300889; e-mail info@cameditrice.com; internet www.cameditrice.com; f. 1968; quarterly; art history; Dir MAURIZIO CALVESI; circ. 2,500.

Education

Cooperazione Educativa: Via dei Sabelli 119, 00185 Roma; tel. (06) 4457228; fax (06) 4460386; e-mail mceroma@tin.it; f. 1952; 4 a year; education; Dir MIRELLA GRIECO.

Il Maestro: Clivo di Monte del Gallo 48, 00165 Roma; tel. (06) 634651; fax (06) 39375903; e-mail aimc@aimc.it; internet www.aimc.it; f. 1945; monthly; Catholic teachers' magazine; Dir GIUSEPPE DESIDERI; circ. 40,000.

Scuola e Didattica: Via Antonio Gramsci 26, 25121 Brescia; tel. (030) 29931; fax (030) 2993299; e-mail sdid@lascuola.it; internet www.lascuola.it; f. 1904; 18 a year; education; Editor PIERPAOLO TRIANI; circ. 40,000.

General, Political and Economic

Economy: Arnoldo Mondadori Editore, SpA, Via Mondadori 1, 20090 Segrate, Milano; tel. (02) 75421; fax (02) 75422302; e-mail economy@mondadori.it; f. 2003; weekly; economics and finance; Dir SERGIO LUCIANO; circ. 85,000.

L'Espresso: Via Cristoforo Colombo 90, 00147 Roma; tel. (06) 84781; fax (06) 84787220; e-mail espresso@espressoedit.it; internet espresso.repubblica.it; weekly; independent left; political; Editor BRUNO MANFELLOTTO; circ. 244,545 (2013).

Famiglia Cristiana: Piazza San Paolo 14, 12051 Alba; tel. (02) 48072777; fax (02) 48072778; e-mail famigliacristiana@stpauls.it; internet www.famigliacristiana.it; f. 1931; weekly; Catholic; illustrated; Dir ANTONIO SCIORTINO; circ. 392,645 (2013).

Gente: Via Roberto Bracco 6, 20159 Milano; tel. (02) 66191; e-mail abbonamenti@hearst.it; internet www.abbonationline.it; f. 1957; weekly; illustrated current events and general interest; Dir MONICA MOSCA; circ. 269,382 (2013).

Il Mulino: Strada Maggiore 37, 40125 Bologna; tel. (051) 256011; fax (051) 6486014; e-mail rivistailmulino@mulino.it; internet www.rivistailmulino.it; f. 1951; every 2 months; culture and politics; Dir MICHELE SALVATI.

Oggi: Via Angelo Rizzoli 8, 20132 Milano; tel. (02) 25841; fax (02) 27201485; internet www.oggi.it; f. 1945; weekly; current affairs, culture, family life; illustrated; publr RCS MediaGroup; Dir UMBERTO BRINDANI; circ. 353,681 (2013).

Panorama: Arnoldo Mondadori Editore, SpA, Via Mondadori 1, 20090 Segrate, Milano; tel. (02) 75421; fax (02) 75422302; e-mail info@panorama.it; internet www.panorama.it; f. 1962; weekly; current affairs; Dir GIORGIO MULÈ; circ. 300,240 (2013).

Visto: Via Angelo Rizzoli 8, 20132 Milano; tel. (02) 25841; f. 1989; weekly; entertainment, celebrities, current events; Dir FRANCO BONERA; circ. 69,368 (2013).

Zett—Die Zeitung am Sonntag: Weinbergweg 7, 39100 Bozen; tel. (0471) 925500; fax (0471) 200462; e-mail zett@athesia.it; internet www.stol.it/athesia/medien/zett; f. 1989; Sun; German language; Dir KLAUS INNERHOFER; circ. 34,000.

History, Literature and Music

Giornale della Libreria: Corso di Porta Romana 108, 20122 Milano; tel. (02) 89280802; fax (02) 89280862; e-mail redazione@giornaledellalibreria.it; internet www.giornaledellalibreria.it; f. 1888; monthly; organ of the Associazione Italiana Editori; bibliographical; Editor MARCO POLILLO; circ. 5,000.

Lettere Italiane: Via Beato Pellegrino 1, 35137 Padova; tel. (049) 8274861; fax (055) 8274840; e-mail pizzamig@unive.it; internet www.olschki.it/riviste/lettital.htm; f. 1949; quarterly; literary; Dirs CARLO OSSOLA, CARLO DELCORNO.

Il Pensiero Politico: Via Pascoli, 33, 06123 Perugia; tel. (075) 5855440; fax (055) 5855449; e-mail penspol@unipg.it; internet www.olschki.it/riviste/penspol.htm; f. 1968; every 4 months; political and social history; Dirs VITTOR IVO COMPARATO, CARLO CARINI.

Rivista di Storia della Filosofia: VVia De Togni 7, 20123 Milano; tel. (02) 28371433; fax (02) 2613268; e-mail redazioni@francoangeli.it; internet www.francoangeli.it/riviste/sommario.asp?idrivista=45; f. 1946; quarterly; philosophy; Editor ENRICO I. RAMBALDI.

Leisure and Sport

Ciak: Arnoldo Mondadori Editore, SpA, Via Mondadori 1, 20090 Segrate, Milano; tel. (02) 75421; fax (02) 75422302; e-mail ciak@mondadori.it; f. 1985; monthly; cinema; Dir PIERA DETASSIS; circ. 36,571 (2013).

Cucina Moderna: Arnoldo Mondadori Editore SpA, Via Mondadori 1, 20090 Segrate, Milano; tel. (02) 75421; fax (02) 75422302; e-mail cucinamoderna@mondadori.it; f. 1996; monthly; cookery; Dir LAURA MARAGLIANO; circ. 309,547 (2013).

Dove: Via Angelo Rizzoli 8, 20132 Milano; tel. (02) 50951; e-mail marina.poggi@rcs.it; internet doveviaggi.corriere.it; f. 1991; monthly; lifestyle and travel; publr RCS MediaGroup; Dir CARLO MONTANARO; circ. 80,000 (2013).

Gambero Rosso: GRH, SpA, Via E. Fermi 161, 00146 Roma; tel. (06) 551121; fax (06) 55112260; e-mail gambero@gamberorosso.it; internet www.gamberorosso.it; f. 1987; monthly; food and wine; Dir LUIGI SALERNO.

Max: Via Solferino 28, 20121 Milano; tel. (02) 62821; fax (02) 62827917; e-mail max@rcs.it; internet max.corriere.it; f. 1985; monthly; men's lifestyle; Dir ANDREA ROSSI; circ. 132,412.

OK: Via Angelo Rizzoli 8, 20132 Milan; tel. (02) 62291; e-mail redazione@ok.rcs.it; internet ok.corriere.it; f. 2005; monthly; health; publr RCS MediaGroup; Editor SIMONA TEDESCO; circ. 277,931.

Quattroruote: Via Gianni Mazzocchi 1/3, 20089 Rozzano, Milano; tel. (02) 824721; fax (02) 57500416; e-mail redazione@quattroruote.it; internet www.quattroruote.it; f. 1956; motoring; monthly; Editor CARLO CAVICCHI; circ. 226,344 (2013).

Starbene: Arnoldo Mondadori Editore SpA, Via Mondadori 1, 20090 Segrate, Milano; tel. (02) 75421; fax (02) 75422302; e-mail starbene@mondadori.it; internet www.starbene.it; f. 1978; monthly; health and beauty; Dir CRISTINA MERLINO; circ. 165,592 (2013).

Telesette: Corso di Porta Nuova 3A, 20121 Milano; tel. (02) 63675415; fax (02) 63675524; e-mail segreteria@casaeditriceuniverso.com; f. 1978; weekly; television; Editor NICOLA DE FEO; circ. 551,601.

TV Sorrisi e Canzoni: Arnoldo Mondadori Editore, SpA, Via Mondadori 1, 20090 Segrate, Milano; tel. (02) 75421; fax (02) 75422302; e-mail sorrisi@mondadori.it; internet www.sorrisi.com; f. 1952; weekly; television, entertainment; Dir ALDO VITALI; circ. 682,033.

Vita in Campagna: Via Bencivenga/Biondani 16, 37133 Verona; tel. (045) 8057511; fax (045) 8009240; e-mail vitaincampagna@vitaincampagna.it; internet www.vitaincampagna.it; publr Editoriale L'Informatore Agrario, SpA; f. 1983; 11 a year; horticulture and smallholding; Dir GIORGIO VINCENZI; circ. 110,553 (2013).

Religion

Città di Vita: Piazza Santa Croce 16, 50122 Firenze; tel. and fax (055) 242783; e-mail info@cittadivita.org; internet www.cittadivita.org; f. 1946; every 2 months; cultural review, theology, art and science; Dir MASSIMILIANO G. ROSITO; circ. 2,000.

La Civiltà Cattolica: Via di Porta Pinciana 1, 00187 Roma; tel. (06) 6979201; fax (06) 69792022; e-mail info@laciviltacattolica.it; internet www.laciviltacattolica.it; f. 1850; fortnightly; Catholic; Editor DOMENICO RONCHITELLI; circ. 17,000.

Humanitas: Via Gabriele Rosa 71, 25121 Brescia; tel. (030) 46451; fax (030) 2400605; e-mail redazione@morcelliana.it; internet www.morcelliana.it; f. 1946; every 2 months; religion, philosophy, science, politics, history, sociology, literature, etc.; Dir ILARIO BERTOLETTI.

Protestantesimo: Via Pietro Cossa 42, 00193 Roma; tel. (06) 3207055; fax (06) 3201040; e-mail protestantesimo@facoltavaldese.org; internet www.facoltavaldese.org; f. 1946; quarterly; Waldensian review; Dir Prof. FULVIO FERRARIO.

Rivista di Storia della Chiesa in Italia: Via Merulana 124A, 00185 Roma; e-mail maria.lupi@uniroma3.it; internet www.vitaepensiero.it; f. 1947; 2 a year; Editor AGOSTINO PARAVICINI BAGLIANI.

Science, Technology and Medicine

Alberi e Territorio: Via Goito 13, 40126 Bologna; tel. (051) 65751; e-mail redazione.edagricole@ilsole24ore.com; internet www.edagricole.it; f. 2004 as successor to *Monti e Boschi* (f. 1949); 6 a year; ecology and forestry; Editor ELIA ZAMBONI; circ. 4,500.

Focus: Via Battistotti Sassi 11A, 20133 Segrate, Milano; tel. (02) 762101; fax (02) 76013379; e-mail redazione@focus.it; internet www.focus.it; f. 1992; monthly; popular science and sociology; publr Gruner+Jahr/Mondadori; Editor-in-Chief FRANCESCA FOLDA; circ. 296,668.

Il Nuovo Medico d'Italia: Via Valpolicella 19, 00141 Roma; tel. and fax (06) 86398937; e-mail redazione@numedionline.it; internet www

.numedionline.it; monthly; medical science; Dir Dott. MARIO BERNARDINI.

Newton: Corso Venezia 6, 20121 Milano; e-mail info@ridoservizieditoriali.it; internet newton.corriere.it; f. 1997; monthly; popular science; circ. 91,124.

Rivista Geografica Italiana: Via S. Gallo 10, 50129 Firenze; tel. and fax (055) 2757956; fax (055) 2725956; e-mail redazione@rivistageograficaitaliana.it; internet www.rivistageograficaitaliana.it; f. 1894; quarterly geographical review; owned by Società di Studi Geografici; Dir BRUNO VECCHIO.

Women's Interest

A—Anna: Via San Marco 21, 20121 Milano; tel. (02) 25843213; f. 1933; weekly; Editor MARIA LATELLA; circ. 125,495 (2013).

Amica: Via Angelo Rizzoli 2, 20132 Milano; tel. (02) 25841; f. 1962; monthly; Dir DANIELA BIANCHINI; circ. 188,905(2013).

Chi: Arnoldo Mondadori Editore, SpA, Via Mondadori 1, 20090 Segrate, Milano; tel. (02) 75421; fax (02) 75422302; e-mail chiposta@mondadori.it; f. 1995; weekly; celebrities, fashion; Dir ALFONSO SIGNORINI; circ. 286,068.

Confidenze: Arnoldo Mondadori Editore, SpA, Via Mondadori 1, 20090 Segrate, Milano; tel. (02) 75421; fax (02) 75422302; e-mail braccif@mondadori.it; f. 1946; weekly; Dir ANNALISA MONFREDA; circ. 93,339 (2013).

Cosmopolitan: Via Roberto Bracco, 6, 20159 Milano; tel. (02) 66191; internet www.cosmopolitan.it; f. 2000; monthly; Dir ANNALISA MONFREDA; circ. 124,419.

Donna Moderna: Arnoldo Mondadori Editore, SpA, Via Mondadori 1, 20090 Segrate, Milano; e-mail donnamoderna@mondadori.it; internet www.donnamoderna.com; f. 1988; weekly; Dir ANNALISA MONFREDA; circ. 277,600 (2013).

Gioia: Via Roberto Bracco, 6, 20159 Milano; tel. (02) 66191; f. 1937; weekly; Dir VERA MONTANARI; circ. 116,566 (2013).

Grazia: Arnoldo Mondadori Editore, SpA, Via Mondadori 1, 20090 Segrate, Milano; tel. (02) 75421; fax (02) 75422302; e-mail graziamagazine@mondadori.it; internet www.graziamagazine.it; f. 1938; weekly; Dir SILVIA GRILLI; circ. 160,254 (2013).

Intimità: Piazza Aspromonte 13, 20131 Milano; tel. (02) 70642307; fax (02) 70642306; e-mail intimita@quadratum.it; internet www.quadratum.it; f. 1946; weekly; Dir ANNA GIUSTI; circ. 210,363 (2013).

Vanity Fair: Condé Nast S.p.A., Piazza Castello 27, 20121 Milano; e-mail abbonati@condenast.it; internet www.vanityfair.it; f. 2003; monthly; fashion, women's interest; Editor-in-Chief ROBERTO DELERA; circ. 243,406 (2013).

Vogue Italia: Piazza Castello 27, 20121 Milano; tel. (02) 85611; fax (02) 8055716; internet www.vogue.it; monthly; Editor FRANCA SOZZANI; circ. 84,863 (2013).

NEWS AGENCIES

AdnKronos: Palazzo dell'Informazione, Piazza Mastai 9, 00153 Roma; tel. (06) 58017; fax (06) 5807807; e-mail comunicazione@adnkronos.com; internet www.adnkronos.it; Dir-Gen. MASSIMO CICATIELLO.

Agenzia Giornalistica Italia (AGI): Via Ostiense 72, 00154 Roma; tel. (06) 519961; fax (06) 51996362; e-mail info@agi.it; internet www.agi.it; f. 1950; Pres. MASSIMO MONDAZZI.

Agenzia Nazionale Stampa Associata (ANSA): Via della Dataria 94, 00187 Roma; tel. (06) 67741; fax (06) 67746383; e-mail redazione.internet@ansa.it; internet www.ansa.it; f. 1945; co-operative, owned by 34 Italian newspapers; 22 regional offices in Italy and 79 brs internationally; service in Italian, Spanish, French, English; Pres. GIULIO ANSELMI; Dir-Gen. GIUSEPPE CERBONE.

Asca (Agenzia Stampa Quotidiana Nazionale): Via Ennio Quirino Visconti 8, 00193 Roma; tel. (06) 361484; e-mail agenzia@asca.it; internet www.asca.it; f. 1969; Dir CLAUDIO SONZOGNO.

Documentazioni Informazioni Resoconti (Dire): Via Guiseppe Marchi 4, 00161 Roma; tel. (06) 45499500; fax (06) 45499509; e-mail segr.direzione@dire.it; internet www.dire.it; Dir NICOLA PERRONE.

Inter Press Service International Association (IPS): Viale delle Terme di Caracalla, 00153 Roma; tel. (06) 57050053; fax (06) 57050052; e-mail headquarters@ips.org; internet www.ips.org; f. 1964; non-profit asscn; international daily news agency; Dir-Gen. MARIO LUBETKIN.

TM News: Via di Santa Maria 6, 00187 Roma; tel. (06) 695391; fax (06) 69539522; e-mail rcc@tmnews.it; internet www.tmnews.it; f. 2009; 60% owned by Gruppo Abete and 40% by Telecom Italia Media; Pres. BRUNETTO TINI.

PRESS ASSOCIATIONS

Associazione della Stampa Estera in Italia: Via della Umiltà 83C, 00187 Roma; tel. (06) 675911; fax (06) 67591262; e-mail segreteria@stampa-estera.it; internet www.stampa-estera.it; foreign correspondents' asscn; Pres. MAARTEN VAN AALDEREN; Sec. CONSTANZE REUSCHER.

Federazione Italiana Editori Giornali (FIEG): Via Piemonte 64, 00187 Roma; tel. (06) 4881683; fax (06) 4871109; e-mail info@fieg.it; internet www.fieg.it; f. 1950; asscn of newspaper publishers; Pres. GIULIO ANSELMI; 268 mems.

Federazione Nazionale della Stampa Italiana (FNSI): Corso Vittorio Emanuele II 349, 00186 Roma; tel. (06) 680081; fax (06) 6871444; e-mail segreteria.fnsi@fnsi.it; internet www.fnsi.it; f. 1908; 19 affiliated unions; Pres. GIOVANNI ROSSI; Sec.-Gen. FRANCESCO ANGELO SIDDI; 16,000 mems.

Unione Stampa Periodica Italiana (USPI): Viale Bardanzellu 95, 00155 Roma; tel. (06) 4071388; fax (06) 4066859; e-mail uspi@uspi.it; internet www.uspi.it; Pres. ANTONIO BARBIERATO; Gen. Sec. FRANCESCO SAVERIO VETERE; 4,500 mems.

Publishers

There are more than 300 major publishing houses and many smaller ones.

Adelphi Edizioni, SpA: Via S. Giovanni sul Muro 14, 20121 Milano; tel. (02) 725731; fax (02) 89010337; e-mail info@adelphi.it; internet www.adelphi.it; f. 1962; classics, philosophy, biography, music, art, psychology, religion and fiction; Pres. ROBERTO CALASSO.

Franco Angeli Editore Srl: Viale Monza 106, 20127 Milano; tel. (02) 2613268; fax (02) 26144793; e-mail redazione@francoangeli.it; internet www.francoangeli.it; f. 1955; academic and general non-fiction.

Armando Editore: Viale Trastevere 236, 00153 Roma; tel. (06) 5894525; fax (06) 5818564; e-mail info@armando.it; internet www.armando.it; f. 1950; philosophy, psychology, social sciences, languages, ecology, education; Man. Dir ENRICO IACOMETTI.

Bollati Boringhieri Editore: Corso Vittorio Emanuele II 86, 10121 Torino; tel. (011) 5591711; fax (011) 543024; e-mail info@bollatiboringhieri.it; internet www.bollatiboringhieri.it; f. 1957; owned by Gruppo Editoriale Mauri Spagnol; history, economics, natural sciences, psychology, social and human sciences, fiction and literary criticism; Chair. ROMILDA BOLLATI; Editorial Dir RENZO GUIDIERI.

Bulzoni Editore: Via dei Liburni 14, 00185 Roma; tel. (06) 4455207; fax (06) 4450355; e-mail bulzoni@bulzoni.it; internet www.bulzoni.it; science, arts, fiction, textbooks; Man. Dir IVANA BULZONI.

Caltagirone Editore, SpA: Via Barberini 28, 00187 Roma; tel. (06) 45412200; fax (06) 45412299; e-mail invrel@caltagironegroup.it; internet www.caltagironeeditore.com; f. 1999; news publisher; Pres. FRANCESCO GAETANO CALTAGIRONE.

Cappelli Editore: Via Farini 14, 40124 Bologna; tel. (051) 239060; fax (051) 239286; f. 1880; medical science, history, politics, literature, textbooks; Chair. and Man. Dir MARIO MUSSO.

Casa Editrice Bonechi: Via dei Cairoli 18B, 50131 Firenze; tel. (055) 576841; fax (055) 5000766; e-mail info@bonechi.it; internet www.bonechi.com; f. 1973; art, travel, cooking; Pres. GIAMPAOLO BONECHI.

Casa Editrice Clueb Scarl (Cooperativa Libraria Universitaria Editrice Bologna): Via Marsala 31, 40126 Bologna; tel. (051) 220736; fax (051) 237758; e-mail vendite@clueb.it; internet www.clueb.com; f. 1959; university education, arts, business, history, literature; Man. Dir LUIGI GUARDIGLI.

Casa Editrice Edumond-Le Monnier, SpA: Via A. Meucci 2, 50015 Grassina, Firenze; tel. (055) 64910; fax (055) 6491310; e-mail informazioni.lemonnier@lemonnier.it; internet www.lemonnier.it; f. 1837; from 1999, part of Gruppo Mondadori; academic and cultural books, textbooks, dictionaries; Pres. GIUSEPPE DE RITA.

Casa Editrice Idelson Gnocchi Srl: Via Michele Pietravalle 85, 80131 Napoli; tel. (081) 5464991; fax (081) 5453443; e-mail info@idelson-gnocchi.com; internet www.idelson-gnocchi.com; f. 1908; medical and scientific; CEO GUIDO GNOCCHI.

Casa Editrice Leo S. Olschki: Via del Pozzetto 8, CP 66, 50126 Firenze; tel. (055) 6530684; fax (055) 6530214; e-mail info@olschki.it; internet www.olschki.it; f. 1886; reference, periodicals, textbooks, humanities; Editorial Dir DANIELE OLSCHKI.

Casa Editrice Luigi Trevisini Srl: Via Tito Livio 12, 20137 Milano; tel. (02) 5450704; fax (02) 55195782; e-mail trevisini@trevisini.it; internet www.trevisini.it; f. 1859; school textbooks; Dirs LUIGI TREVISINI, GIUSEPPINA TREVISINI.

Casa Editrice Marietti, SpA: Via Donizetti 41, 20122 Milano; tel. (02) 778899; fax (02) 76003491; e-mail mariettieditore@mariettieditore.it; internet www.mariettieditore.it; f. 1820; religion, liturgy, theology, fiction, history, literature, philosophy, poetry, art; Editor GIOVANNI UNGARELLI.

Casa Ricordi, SpA: Via Benigno Crespi 19, 20159 Milano; tel. (02) 80282811; fax (02) 80282882; e-mail promozione.ricordi.Italy@umusic.com; internet www.ricordi.it; f. 1808; music; Chair. GIANNI BABINI.

CEDAM, SpA: Via Jappelli 5/6, 35121 Padova; tel. (049) 8239111; fax (049) 8752900; e-mail info@cedam.com; internet www.cedam.com; f. 1903; law, economics, political and social sciences, engineering, science, medicine, literature, philosophy, textbooks; Dirs ANTONIO MILANI.

De Agostini Editore: Via Giovanni da Verrazano 15, 28100 Novara; tel. (0321) 4241; fax (0321) 471286; internet www.deagostini.it; f. 1901; geography, maps, encyclopaedias, dictionaries, art, literature, textbooks, science; Pres. PIETRO BOROLI; CEO LORENZO PELLICIOLI.

Editori Laterza: Via di Villa Sacchetti 17, 00197 Roma; tel. (06) 45465311; fax (06) 3223853; e-mail glaterza@laterza.it; internet www.laterza.it; f. 1885; belles-lettres, biography, reference, religion, art, classics, history, economics, philosophy, social sciences; Editorial Dirs ALESSANDRO LATERZA, GIUSEPPE LATERZA.

Editrice Àncora: Via G. B. Niccolini 8, 20154 Milano; tel. (02) 3456081; fax (02) 34560866; e-mail editrice@ancoralibri.it; internet www.ancoralibri.it; f. 1934; religious, educational; Dir GILBERTO ZINI.

Editrice Ave (Anonima Veritas Editrice): Via Aurelia 481, 00165 Roma; tel. (06) 661321; fax (06) 6620207; e-mail info@editriceave.it; internet www.editriceave.it; f. 1935; theology, sociology, pedagogy, psychology, essays, learned journals, religious textbooks; Pres. ARMANDO OBERTI.

Editrice Ciranna: Via G. Besio 143, 90145 Palermo; tel. (091) 224499; fax (091) 311064; e-mail info@ciranna.it; internet www.ciranna.it; f. 1950; school textbooks; Editorial Dir LUCA POMARA.

Editrice La Scuola, SpA: Via Antonio Gramsci 26, 25121 Brescia; tel. (030) 29931; fax (030) 2993299; e-mail redazione@lascuola.it; internet www.lascuola.it; f. 1904; educational magazines, educational textbooks, audiovisual aids and toys; Chair. Dott. Ing. ELIA ZAMBONI.

Edizioni Borla Srl: Via delle Fornaci 50, 00165 Roma; tel. (06) 39375379; fax (06) 39376620; e-mail borla@edizioni-borla.it; internet www.edizioni-borla.it; f. 1853; religion, philosophy, psychoanalysis, ethnology, literature; Man. Dir JESSICA D'AGOSTINO.

Edizioni Lavoro: Via G. M. Lancisi 25, 00161 Roma; tel. (06) 44251174; fax (06) 44251177; e-mail info@edizionilavoro.it; internet www.edizionilavoro.it; f. 1982; history, politics, political philosophy, sociology, religion, Islamic, African, Arab and Caribbean literature; Chair. ANTONIO LOMBARDI.

Edizioni Mediterranee Srl: Via Flaminia 109, 00196 Roma; tel. (06) 32235433; fax (06) 3236277; e-mail info@edizionimediterranee.net; internet www.edizionimediterranee.it; f. 1953; alchemy, astrology, esoterism, meditation, natural medicine, parapsychology, hobbies, martial arts, zen.

Edizioni Rosminiane Sodalitas Sas: Corso Umberto I 15, 28838 Stresa; tel. (0323) 30091; fax (0323) 31623; e-mail info@rosmini.it; internet www.rosmini.it; f. 1925; philosophy, theology, *Rivista Rosminiana* (quarterly); Dir Prof. PIER PAOLO OTTONELLO.

Edizioni San Paolo: Piazza Soncino 5, 20092 Cinisello Balsamo—Milano; tel. (02) 660751; fax (02) 66075211; e-mail sanpaoloedizioni@stpauls.it; internet www.edizionisanpaolo.it; f. 1914; Catholic; Gen. Man. VINCENZO SANTARCANGELO.

Edizioni Scientifiche Italiane, SpA (ESI): Via Chiatamone 7, 80121 Napoli; tel. (081) 7645443; fax (081) 7646477; e-mail info@edizioniesi.it; internet www.edizioniesi.it; f. 1945; law, economics, literature, arts, history, science; Pres. PIETRO PERLINGIERI.

Edizioni Studium: VVia Crescenzio 25, 00193 Roma; tel. (06) 6865846; fax (06) 6875456; e-mail info@edizionistudium.it; internet www.edizionistudium.it; f. 1927; philosophy, literature, sociology, pedagogy, religion, economics, law, science, history, psychology; Pres. VINCENZO CAPPELLATTI.

Giulio Einaudi Editore, SpA: Via Umberto Biancamano 2, 10121 Torino; tel. (011) 56561; fax (011) 542903; e-mail einaudi@einaudi.it; internet www.einaudi.it; f. 1933; fiction, classics, general; CEO ENRICO SELVA CODDÈ.

Giangiacomo Feltrinelli Editore, SpA: Via Andegari 6, 20121 Milano; tel. (02) 725721; fax (02) 72572500; e-mail ufficio.stampa@feltrinelli.it; internet www.feltrinelli.it; f. 1954; fiction, juvenile, science, technology, history, literature, political science, philosophy; Chair. CARLO FELTRINELLI.

Garzanti Libri, SpA: Via Giuseppe Parini, 14 20121 Milano; tel. (02) 00623201; fax (02) 00623260; e-mail info@garzantilibri.it; internet www.garzantilibri.it; f. 1938; owned by Gruppo Editoriale Mauri Spagnol; literature, poetry, science, art, history, politics, encyclopaedias; Chair. GHERARDO COLOMBO; CEO STEFANO MAURI.

Ghisetti e Corvi Editori: Corso Concordia 7, 20129 Milano; tel. (02) 76006232; fax (02) 76009468; e-mail redazione@ghisettiecorvi.it; internet www.ghisettiecorvi.it; f. 1936; educational textbooks.

G. Giappichelli Editore Srl: Via Po 21, 10124 Torino; tel. (011) 8153511; fax (011) 8125100; e-mail contabilit@giappichelli.it; internet www.giappichelli.it; f. 1921; university publications on law, economics, politics and sociology.

Giunti Editore, SpA: Via Bolognese 165, 50139 Firenze; tel. (055) 50621; fax (055) 2985062; e-mail info@giunti.it; internet www.giunti.it; f. 1841; art, psychology, literature, science, law; CEO MARTINO MONTANARINI.

Gruppo Editoriale Mauri Spagnol, SpA: Via Gherardini 10, 20145 Milano; internet www.maurispagnol.it; f. 2005; owns Bollati Boringhieri Editore, La Cocinella, Casa Editrice Corbaccio, Garzanti Libri, Guanda, Longanesi, Editrice Nord, Ponte alle Grazie, Adriano Salani Editore, TEA (Tascabili degli Editori Associati), Antonio Vallardi Editore, and 50% of SuperPocket; Pres. STEFANO MAURI; CEO LUIGI SPAGNOL.

Gruppo Editoriale il Saggiatore: Via Melzo 9, 20129 Milano; tel. (02) 201301; fax (02) 29513061; e-mail commerciale@saggiatore.it; internet www.saggiatore.it; f. 1958; art, fiction, social sciences, history, travel, current affairs, popular science; Pres. LUCA FORMENTON.

Gruppo Ugo Mursia Editore, SpA: Via Melchiorre Gioia 45, 20124 Milano; tel. (02) 84251100; fax (02) 84251137; e-mail info@mursia.com; internet www.mursia.com; f. 1955; general fiction and non-fiction, reference, art, history, nautical books, philosophy, biography, sports, children's books; Gen. Man. FIORENZA MURSIA.

Guida Monaci, SpA: Via Salaria 1319, 00138 Roma; tel. (06) 8887777; fax (06) 8889996; e-mail infoitaly@italybygm.it; internet www.italybygm.it; f. 1870; commercial and industrial, financial, administrative and medical directories; Dir Ing. GIANCARLO ZAPPONINI.

Hearst Magazines Italia: Via Roberto Bracco 6, 20159 Milano; tel. (02) 66191; e-mail abbonamenti@hachette.it; internet www.hearst.it; f. 1969 as Rusconi Libri Srl; magazines; Pres. DIDIER QUILLOT.

S. Lattes e C. Editori, SpA: Via Confienza 6, 10121 Torino; tel. (011) 5625335; fax (011) 5625070; e-mail info@latteseditori.it; internet www.latteseditori.it; f. 1893; technical, textbooks; Pres. CATERINA BOTTARI LATTES; Man. Dir RENATA LATTES.

Levrotto e Bella, Libreria Editrice Universitaria: Via Pigafetta Antonio 2E, 10129 Torino; tel. (011) 5097367; fax (011) 504025; e-mail ammin@levrotto-bella.net; internet www.levrotto-bella.net; f. 1911; university textbooks; Man. Dir Dott. ELISABETTA GUALINI.

Libreria Editrice Gregoriana: Via Roma 82, 35122 Padova; tel. (049) 661033; fax (049) 663640; e-mail l.gregoriana@mclink.it; f. 1922; Lexicon Totius Latinitatis, religion, philosophy, psychology, social studies; Dir GIANCARLO MINOZZI.

Liguori Editore Srl: Via Posillipo 394, 80123 Napoli; tel. (081) 5751272; fax (081) 5751231; e-mail info@liguori.it; internet www.liguori.it; f. 1949; linguistics, mathematics, engineering, economics, law, history, philosophy, sociology; Man. Dir Dott. GUIDO LIGUORI.

Loescher Editore: Via Vittorio Amedeo II 18, 10121 Torino; tel. (011) 5654111; fax (011) 5625822; e-mail mail@loescher.it; internet www.loescher.it; f. 1861; school textbooks, general literature, academic books; Chair. LORENZO ENRIQUES.

Longanesi e C., SpA: Via Gherardini 10, 20145 Milano; tel. (02) 34597620; fax (02) 34597212; e-mail info@longanesi.it; internet www.longanesi.it; f. 1946; owned by Gruppo Editoriale Mauri Spagnol; art, archaeology, culture, history, philosophy, fiction; Man. Dir STEFANO MAURI.

Arnoldo Mondadori Editore, SpA: Via Mondadori 1, 20090 Segrate, Milano; tel. (02) 75421; fax (02) 75422302; e-mail redazione.internet@mondadori.it; internet www.mondadori.it; f. 1907; books, magazines, printing, radio, advertising; CEO ERNESTO MAURI.

Neri Pozza Editore, SpA: Via E. Fermi 205, 36100 Vicenza; tel. (0444) 396323; fax (0444) 396325; e-mail info@neripozza.it; internet www.neripozza.it; f. 1946; art, fiction, history, politics; Pres. VITTORIO MINCATO; Dir ALESSANDRO ZELGER.

Palombi & Partner Srl: Via Gregorio VII 224, 00165 Roma; tel. (06) 636970; fax (06) 635746; e-mail info@palombieditori.it; internet www.palombieditori.it; f. 1914; history, art, etc. of Rome; Man. Dir Dott. FRANCESCO PALOMBI.

Pearson Italia, SpA: Via Archimede 10/23/51, 20129 Milano; tel. (02) 748231; fax (02) 74823278; internet www.pearson.it; f. 1946; school and university textbooks.

Petrini Editore: Strada del Portone 179, 10095 Grugliasco, Torino; tel. (011) 2098741; fax (011) 2098765; e-mail redazione@petrini.it; internet www.petrini.it; f. 1872; school textbooks.

Piccin Nuova Libraria, SpA: Via Altinate 107, 35121 Padova; tel. (049) 655566; fax (049) 8750693; e-mail info@piccinonline.com;

internet www.piccinonline.com; f. 1952; scientific and medical textbooks and journals; Man. Dir Dott. MASSIMO PICCIN.

RCS Libri, SpA: Via San Marco 21, 20121 Milano; tel. (02) 25841; fax (02) 50952647; internet www.rcslibri.it; f. 1947; imprints include Rosellina Archinto Editore, Bompiani, BUR (Biblioteca Universale Rizzoli), Etas Srl, Fabbri, Marsilio Editore, La Nuova Editrice, SpA, Rizzoli, Sansoni, Sonzogno; fiction, juveniles, education, textbooks, reference, literature, art books; Chair. ANGELO PROVASOLI.

Rosenberg & Sellier: Via Andrea Doria 14, 10123 Torino; tel. (011) 8127820; fax (011) 8127808; e-mail info@rosenbergesellier.it; internet www.rosenbergesellier.it; f. 1883; economics, history, gender studies, social sciences, philosophy, linguistics, Latin, dictionaries, scientific journals; Chair. and Man. Dir UGO GIANNI ROSENBERG.

Adriano Salani Editore Srl: Via Gherardini 10, 20145 Milano; tel. (02) 34597624; fax (02) 34597206; e-mail info@salani.it; internet www.salani.it; f. 1988; fiction, children's books; Editor LUIGI SPAGNOL.

Skira Editore: Palazzo Casati Stampa, Via Torino 61, 20123 Milano; tel. (02) 724441; fax (02) 72444211; e-mail skira@skira.net; internet www.skira.net; f. 1928; arts and literature; Pres. MASSIMO VITTA ZELMAN.

Società Editrice Dante Alighieri Srl: Via Somalia 5, 00199 Roma; tel. (06) 3725870; fax (06) 37514807; e-mail nuovarivistastorica@dantealighierisrl.191.it; internet www.nuovarivistastorica.it; f. 1917; school textbooks, science and general culture; Dir GIGLIOLA SOLDI RONDININI.

Società Editrice Internazionale, SpA (SEI): Corso Regina Margherita 176, 10152 Torino; tel. (011) 52271; fax (011) 5211320; e-mail editoriale@seieditrice.com; internet www.seieditrice.com; f. 1908; textbooks, religion, history, education, multimedia; Head of Editorial Dept ULISSE JACOMUZZI.

Società Editrice Il Mulino: Strada Maggiore 37, 40125 Bologna; tel. (051) 256011; fax (051) 6486014; e-mail info@mulino.it; internet www.mulino.it; f. 1954; politics, history, philosophy, social sciences, linguistics, literary criticism, law, psychology, economics, journals; Pres. ALESSANDRO CAVALLI.

Il Sole 24 Ore Edagricole: Via Goito 13, 40126 Bologna; tel. (051) 65751; fax (051) 6575800; e-mail redazione.edagricole@ilsole24ore.com; internet www.edagricole.it; group includes Calderini (f. 1960; art, sport, electronics, mechanics, university and school textbooks, travel guides, nursing, architecture) and Edagricole (f. 1935; agriculture, veterinary science, gardening, biology, textbooks); Pres. Prof. GIANCARLO CERUTTI; Man. Dir DONATELLA TREU.

Sugarco Edizioni Srl: Via don Gnocchi 4, 20148 Milano; tel. (02) 4078370; fax (02) 4078493; e-mail info@sugarcoedizioni.it; internet www.sugarcoedizioni.it; f. 1957; fiction, biography, history, philosophy, Italian classics, catholic apologetics; Gen. Man. ATTILIO TRENTINI.

Ulrico Hoepli Casa Editrice Libraria, SpA: Via Hoepli 5, 20121 Milano; tel. (02) 864871; fax (02) 864322; e-mail libreria@hoepli.it; internet www.hoepli.it; f. 1870; grammars, art, technical, scientific and school books, encyclopaedias; Chair. Dott. CARLO HOEPLI; Man. Dir GIOVANNI ENRICO HOEPLI.

UTET, SpA (Unione Tipografico-Editrice Torinese): Lungo Dora Colletta 67, 10153 Torino; tel. (011) 2099111; fax (011) 2099394; e-mail assistenza@utet.it; internet www.utet.it; f. 1791; part of Gruppo De Agostini; university and specialized editions on history, geography, art, literature, economics, sciences, encyclopaedias, dictionaries, etc.; Pres. ANTONIO BELLONI.

Vallecchi Editore, Srl: Via Ponte All'Asse 7, 50144 Firenze; tel. (055) 324761; fax (055) 3980561; e-mail ufficiostampa@vallecchi.it; internet www.vallecchi.it; f. 1903; art, fiction, literature, essays, media; Pres. FERNANDO CORONA.

Vita e Pensiero: Largo A. Gemelli 1, 20123 Milano; tel. (02) 72342335; fax (02) 72342260; e-mail editrice.vp@unicatt.it; internet www.vitaepensiero.it; f. 1918; publisher of the Catholic University of the Sacred Heart, Milan; philosophy, literature, social science, theology, history; Dir AURELIO MOTTOLA.

GOVERNMENT PUBLISHING HOUSE

Istituto Poligrafico e Zecca dello Stato (IPZS): Via Salaria 1027, 00138 Roma; tel. (06) 85081; fax (06) 85082517; e-mail informazioni@ipzs.it; internet www.ipzs.it; f. 1928; art, literary, scientific, technical books and reproductions; Pres. and CEO Dott. MAURIZIO PRATO.

PUBLISHERS' ASSOCIATION

Associazione Italiana Editori (AIE): Corso di Porta Romana 108, 20122 Milano; tel. (02) 89280800; fax (02) 89280860; e-mail aie@aie.it; internet www.aie.it; f. 1869; Dir ALFIERI LORENZON; 420 mems.

Broadcasting and Communications

REGULATORY AUTHORITY

Autorità per le Garanzie nelle Comunicazioni (AGCOM): Centro Direzionale, Isola B5, Torre Francesco, 80143 Napoli; tel. (081) 7507111; fax (081) 7507616; e-mail info@agcom.it; internet www.agcom.it; f. 1997; regulatory authority with responsibility for telecommunications, broadcasting and publishing; Pres. CORRADO CALABRÒ; Sec.-Gen. ROBERTO VIOLA.

TELECOMMUNICATIONS

3 Italia: Via Leonardo da Vinci 1, 20090 Trezzano sul Naviglio, Milano; tel. (02) 44581; fax (02) 445812713; internet www.tre.it; f. 2003; owned by Hutchison Whampoa Ltd (Hong Kong); mobile cellular telecommunications; CEO VINCENZO NOVARI.

FASTWEB: Via Caracciolo 51, 20155 Milano; tel. (02) 45451; fax (02) 45454811; internet www.fastweb.it; f. 2004 by merger of FastWeb and e.Biscom; offers fixed-line and mobile cellular telecommunications services, digital television and broadband internet services; 82.1% stake owned by Swisscom AG; Chair. (vacant); Dir-Gen. ALBERTO CALCAGNO.

Tele2 Italia: Via Cassanese 210, 20090 Segrate, Milano; e-mail ufficio-stampa.tele2@tele2.it; internet www.tele2.it; f. 1999; fixed-line telecommunications and broadband internet services; owned by Vodafone Italia; Chair. SAVERIO TRIDICO; CEO MARCO BRAGADIN.

Telecom Italia: Piazza Affari 2, 20123 Milano; tel. (02) 85951; e-mail investitori.individuali@telecomitalia.it; internet www.telecomitalia.it; Italy's leading telecommunications operator; controlling stake owned by Telco, a consortium of Telefónica (Spain) and four Italian cos; Pres. GIUSEPPE RECCHI; CEO MARCO PATUANO.

TIM (Telecom Italia Mobile): Via Luigi Rizzo 22, 00136 Roma; tel. (06) 39001; internet www.tim.it; f. 1995; owned by Telecom Italia; mobile cellular telecommunications.

Tiscali Italia: Ioc. Sa Illetta, SS 195 Km 2300, 09122 Cagliari; tel. (070) 46011; fax (070) 4601296; e-mail info@tiscali.com; internet www.tiscali.it; f. 1998; internet service provider; Pres. and CEO RENATO SORU; Dir-Gen. LUCA SCANO.

Vodafone Italia: Via Caboto 15, 20094 Corsico, Milano; tel. (02) 41431; internet www.vodafone.it; f. 1995; mobile cellular telecommunications; Pres. PIETRO GUINDANI; CEO PAOLO BERTOLUZZO.

WIND Telecomunicazioni, SpA: Via Cesare Giulio Viola 48, 00148 Roma; tel. (06) 83111; internet www.windgroup.it; f. 1997; brands include WIND (mobile cellular telecommunications services) and Infostrada (fixed-line telecommunications and broadband internet services); Pres. KHALED BICHARA; CEO OSSAMA BESSADA.

BROADCASTING

Radio

Rai—Radiotelevisione Italiana: Viale Mazzini 14, 00195 Roma; tel. (06) 38781; fax (06) 3725680; e-mail radio@rai.it; internet www.radio.rai.it; f. 1924; a public share capital co; programmes comprise Radio Uno (general), Radio Due (recreational), Radio Tre (cultural); there are also regional programmes in Italian and in the languages of minority ethnic groups, and a foreign service, Rai International; Pres. PAOLO GARIMBERTI; Dir-Gen. LORENZA LEI.

Independent Stations

Radio Deejay: CP 314, Milano; tel. (02) 342522; e-mail diretta@deejay.it; internet www.deejay.it; f. 1982; propr Gruppo Editoriale L'Espresso, SpA; popular music; Dir GUIDO QUINTINO MARIOTTI.

Radio Italia Solo Musica Italiana: Viale Europa 49, 20093 Cologno Monzese, Milano; tel. (02) 254441; fax (02) 25444230; e-mail diretta@radioitalia.it; internet www.radioitalia.it; f. 1982.

Radio Maria: Via Milano 12, 22036 Erba, Como; tel. (031) 610610; e-mail info.ita@radiomaria.org; internet www.radiomaria.it; f. 1987; Roman Catholic; founder mem. of World Family of Radio Maria, comprising 40 national asscns; Dir Fr LIVIO FANZAGA.

RDS Radio Dimensione Suono: Via Pier Ruggero Piccio 55, 20122 Roma; tel. (06) 377041; e-mail customercare@rds.it; internet www.rds.it; f. 1978.

RTL 102.5: Via Piemonte 61/63, 20093 Cologno Monzese, Milano; tel. (02) 251515; fax (02) 25096201; e-mail ufficiostampa@rtl.it; internet www.rtl.it; Pres. LORENZO SURACI.

Rundfunk Anstalt Südtirol (RAS): Europaallee 164A, 39100 Bozen; tel. (0471) 546666; fax (0471) 200378; e-mail info@ras.bz.it; internet www.ras.bz.it; f. 1975; relays television and radio broadcasts from Germany, Austria and Switzerland to the population of South Tyrol; Pres. RUDI GAMPER; Dir GEORG PLATTNER.

Television

There are two main national television channels: the state-owned Rai—Radiotelevisione Italiana and the Gruppo Mediaset. The process to switch from analogue to digital broadcasting began in 2009 and was completed in 2012.

Rai—Radiotelevisione Italiana: Viale Mazzini 14, 00195 Roma; tel. (06) 38781; fax (06) 3725680; e-mail rai-tv@rai.it; internet www.rai.it; f. 1924; operates 3 terrestrial channels, Rai Uno, Rai Due and Rai Tre; satellite and digital channels include RaiNews24, Rai Sport and Rai Gulp (children's programmes); also broadcasts local programmes in Italian and in German for the South Tyrol; Pres. PAOLO GARIMBERTI; Dir-Gen. LORENZA LEI.

Independent Television Companies

Gruppo Mediaset: Piazza SS Giovanni e Paolo 8, 00184 Roma; tel. (06) 77081; e-mail mediaset@mediaset.it; internet www.gruppomediaset.it; f. 1993; operates Canale 5, Italia 1 and Rete 4; 38.8% stake owned by Fininvest; Pres. FEDELE CONFALONIERI; Vice-Pres. PIER SILVIO BERLUSCONI; Man. Dir GIULIANO ADREANI.

Rundfunk Anstalt Südtirol (RAS): see Radio.

Sky Italia: CP 13057, 20141 Milano; tel. (02) 70027300; e-mail info@sky.it; internet www.sky.it; f. 2003; owned by News Corporation (USA); broadcasts digital satellite channels; Chief Exec. ANDREA ZAPPIA.

Telecom Italia Media: Via della Pineta Sacchetti 229, 00168 Roma; tel. (06) 355841; e-mail carlo.demartino@telecomitalia.it; internet www.telecomitaliamedia.it; subsidiary of Telecom Italia, SpA; digital terrestrial broadcaster; operates 2 channels, La7 and MTV Italia; Pres. SEVERINO SALVEMINI; Man. Dir GIOVANNI STELLA.

Finance

(cap. = capital; res = reserves; dep. = deposits; m. = million; amounts in euros; brs = branches)

In September 2008, of the 815 banks in existence, 251 were private banks, 438 were co-operative banks, 38 were *banche popolari* (a form of savings bank) and 88 were branches of foreign banks. In that year 83 banking groups were operating in Italy.

BANKING

Central Bank

Banca d'Italia: Via Nazionale 91, 00184 Roma; tel. (06) 47921; fax (06) 47922983; e-mail email@bancaditalia.it; internet www.bancaditalia.it; f. 1893; cap. 0.2m., res 20,078.7m., dep. 64,061.9m. (Dec. 2009); Gov. IGNAZIO VISCO; Dir-Gen. FABRIZIO SACCOMANNI; 74 brs.

Major Banks

Banca Carige, SpA (Cassa di Risparmio di Genova e Imperia): Via Cassa di Risparmio 15, 16123 Genova; tel. (010) 5791; fax (010) 5794000; e-mail carige@carige.it; internet www.gruppocarige.it; f. 1846; name changed as above in 1991; cap. 2,177.2m., res 1,510.7m., dep. 21,357.3m. (Dec. 2012); Chair. Dott. GIOVANNI BERNESCHI; Gen. Man. ENNIO LA MONICA.

Banca Carime, SpA: Viale Crati, 87100 Cosenza; tel. (0984) 8011; fax (0984) 806988; internet www.carime.it; f. 1998 as a result of merger of Carical, Carisal and Caripuglia savings banks; 92.8% owned by Gruppo Unione di Banche Italiane (UBI Banca); cap. 1,468.2m., res 75.7m., dep. 5,275.9m. (Dec. 2012); Chair. ANDREA PISANI MASSAMORMILE; Gen. Man. RAFFAELE AVANTAGGIATO; 255 brs.

Banca CR Firenze, SpA: Via Carlo Magno 7, 50127 Firenze; tel. (055) 26121; fax (055) 2613872; e-mail estero@bancacrfirenze.it; internet www.bancacrfirenze.it; f. 1829; name changed as above in 2003; 89.7% stake owned by Intesa Sanpaolo, SpA; cap. 831.4m., res 581.8m., dep. 19,244.7m. (Dec. 2012); Chair. and Pres. AURELIANO BENEDETTI; Gen. Man. and CEO LUCIANO NEBBIA; 367 brs and agencies.

Banca Fideuram, SpA: Piazzale Giulio Douhet 31, 00143 Milano; tel. (06) 59021; fax (06) 59022634; internet www.bancafideuram.it; f. 1913; name changed as above in 1992; owned by Intesa Sanpaolo, SpA; cap. 186.3m., 536.2m., dep. 7,239.9m. (Dec. 2012); Pres. SALVATORE MACCARONE; Gen. Man. MATTEO COLAFRANCESCO; 53 brs.

Banca IMI: Piazza Giordano dell'Amore 3, 20121 Milano; tel. (02) 72611; fax (02) 77512030; e-mail info@bancaimi.it; internet www.bancaimi.it; f. 2007 by merger of Banca d'Intermediazione Mobiliare, SpA and Banca Caboto, SpA; owned by Intesa Sanpaolo, SpA; cap. 962.5m., res 1,872.2m., dep. 10,883.9m. (Dec. 2012); Chair. EMILIO OTTOLENGHI; Man. Dir ANDREA MUNARI.

Banca delle Marche, SpA: Via Alessandro Ghislieri 6, 60035 Jesi; tel. (0731) 5391; fax (0731) 539695; e-mail info@bancamarche.it; internet www.bancamarche.it; f. 1994; cap. 662.7m., res 822.9m., dep. 14,078m. (Dec. 2012); Chair. MICHELE AMBROSINI; Gen. Man. MASSIMO BIANCONI; 293 brs.

Banca del Mezzogiorno–MedioCredito Centrale: Via Piemonte 51, 00187 Roma; tel. (06) 47911; fax (06) 47913130; e-mail mcc@mcc.it; internet www.mcc.it; f. 1952; renamed as above following demerger with Unicredit, SpA in 2011; cap. 132.5m., res 5.9m., dep. 117.3m. (Dec. 2012); Chair. MASSIMO SARMI; Man. Dir PIETRO D'ANZI.

Banca Monte dei Paschi di Siena, SpA (Mps): Piazza Salimbeni 3, 53100 Siena; tel. (0577) 294111; fax (0577) 294313; e-mail info@banca.mps.it; internet www.mps.it; f. 1472; jt-stock co; Part of Gruppo Montepaschi, which also includes Banca Antonveneta and Biverbanca (Cassa di Risparmio di Biella e Vercelli); cap. 7,484.5m., res 2,137.6m., dep. 104,941m. (Dec. 2012); Chair. ALESSANDRO PROFUMO; CEO FABRIZIO VIOLA; 2,744 brs.

Banca Nazionale del Lavoro, SpA: Via Vittorio Veneto 119, 00187 Roma; tel. (06) 47021; fax (06) 47027336; e-mail redazionebnl@bnlmail.com; internet www.bnl.it; f. 1913; owned by BNP Paribas (France); cap. 2,076.9m., res 3,280.1m., dep. 50,289.5m. (Dec. 2012); Chair. Dott. LUIGI ABETE; Gen. Man. FABIO GALLIA; 864 brs.

Banca Popolare di Bergamo: Piazza Vittorio Veneto 8, 24122 Bergamo; tel. (035) 392111; fax (035) 392910; e-mail info@bpb.it; internet www.bpb.it; f. 1869; co-operative bank; name changed as above in 2003 following merger; 93% owned by Unione di Banche Italiane (UBI Banca); cap. 1,350.5m., res 812.6m., dep. 13,429.6m. (Dec. 2012); Chair. EMILIO ZANETTI; Man. Dir GIUSEPPE MASNAGA; 357 brs.

Banca Popolare Commercio e Industria, SpA: CP 10167, Via della Moscova 33, 20121 Milano; tel. (02) 62755; fax (02) 62755640; e-mail intbkg@bpci.it; internet www.bpci.it; f. 1888; 64.4% stake owned by Unione di Banche Italiane (UBI Banca); cap. 934.2m., res 226.3m., dep. 6,102.7m. (Dec. 2012); Chair. MARIO CERA; Gen. Man. FRANCESCO IORIO; 234 brs.

Banca Popolare dell'Emilia Romagna Società Cooperativa: Via San Carlo 8/20, 41121 Modena; tel. (059) 2021111; fax (059) 220537; e-mail relest@bper.it; internet www.bper.it; f. 1867; cap. 998.2m., res 3,075.8m., dep. 38,557.4m. (Dec. 2012); Chair. ETTORE CASELLI; Gen. Man. FABRIZIO TOGNI; 323 brs.

Banca Popolare di Milano Scarl: Piazza F. Meda 4, 20121 Milano; tel. (02) 77001; fax (02) 77002993; e-mail bipiemme@bpm.it; internet www.bpm.it; f. 1865; cap. 2,865.7m., res 1,579.1m., dep. 28,641.3m. (Dec. 2012); Pres., Supervisory Bd DINO PIERO GIARDA; Pres., Management Bd MARIO ANOLLI; 495 brs.

Banca Popolare di Sondrio Società Cooperativa per Azioni: Piazza Garibaldi 16, 23100 Sondrio; tel. (0342) 528111; fax (0342) 528204; e-mail info@popso.it; internet www.popso.it; f. 1871; cap. 924.4m., res 911.2m., dep. 25,579.5m. (Dec. 2012); Chair. and CEO PIERO MELAZZINI; Gen. Man. MARIO ALBERTO PEDRANZINI; 282 brs.

Banca Popolare di Vicenza: Via Battaglione Framarin 18, 36100 Vicenza; tel. (0444) 339111; fax (0444) 907125; e-mail intdep@popvi.it; internet www.popolarevicenza.it; f. 1866; cap. 296.9m., res 2,393.4m., dep. 23,323.5m. (Dec. 2012); Chair. GIOVANNI ZONIN; Gen. Man. SAMUELE SORATO; 544 brs.

Banca Regionale Europea, SpA: Via Monte di Pietà 7, 20121 Milano; tel. (02) 721211; fax (02) 865413; internet www.brebanca.it; f. 1995 by merger of Cassa di Risparmio di Cuneo and Banca del Monte di Lombardia; 56.5% stake owned by Unione di Banche Italiane (UBI Banca); cap. 587.9m., res 763.6m., dep. 5,662.2m. (Dec. 2012); Chair. LUIGI ROSSI DI MONTELERA; Gen. Man. ROBERTO TONIZZO; 229 brs.

Banco di Brescia San Paolo Cab, SpA (Banco di Brescia): Corso Martiri della Libertà 13, 25171 Brescia; tel. (030) 29921; fax (030) 2992470; e-mail info@bancodibrescia.com; internet www.bancodibrescia.com; f. 1999; 96.4% owned by Unione di Banche Italiane (UBI Banca); cap. 615.6m., res 775.1m., dep. 8,215.2m. (Dec. 2012); Chair. FRANCO POLOTTI; Dir-Gen. ELVIO SONNINO; 322 brs.

Banco di Sardegna, SpA: Viale Umberto 36, 07100 Sassari; tel. (079) 226000; fax (079) 226015; e-mail privacy@bancosardegna.it; internet www.bancosardegna.it; f. 1953; cap. 155.2m., res 1,021.5m., dep. 8,042.1m. (Dec. 2012); Chair. Prof. FRANCO ANTONIO FARINA; Gen. Man. Dott. ALESSANDRO VANDELLI; 392 brs.

Banco Popolare Società Cooperativa: Piazza Nogara 2, 37121 Verona; tel. (45) 8675111; e-mail ufficio.stampa@bancopopolare.it; internet www.bancopopolare.it; f. 2007 by merger of Banca Popolare Italiana and Banco Popolare di Verona e Novara; cap. 4,294.2m., res 3,414.3m., dep. 56,427.9m. (Dec. 2012); Chair., Supervisory Bd CARLO FRATTA PASINI; Chair., Management Bd VITTORIO CODA.

Cassa di Risparmio di Parma e Piacenza, SpA (Cariparma): Via Università 1, 43100 Parma; tel. (0521) 912111; fax (0521) 912976; e-mail crprpc@cariparma.it; internet www.cariparma.it; f. 1860; name changed as above in 1993; 75% stake owned by Crédit Agricole SA (France); cap. 876.8m., res 3,346.3m., dep. 26,395.2m. (Dec. 2012); CEO GIAMPIERO MAIOLI; 537 brs.

Cassa di Risparmio di Venezia, SpA: San Marco 4216, Venezia 30124; tel. (041) 5291111; fax (041) 5292336; internet www.carive.it; f. 1822; owned by Intesa Sanpaolo, SpA; cap. 284.5m., res 84.8m., dep. 3,673.1m. (Dec. 2011); Chair. GIOVANNI SAMMARTINI; Gen. Man. MASSIMO MAZZEGA.

Cassa di Risparmio in Bologna, SpA (CARISBO): Via Farini 22, 40124 Bologna; tel. (051) 6454111; fax (051) 6454366; internet www.carisbo.it; f. 1837; owned by Intesa Sanpaolo, SpA; cap. 696.7m., res 191.2m., dep. 8,413.8m. (Dec. 2011); Pres. and Chair. FILIPPO CAVAZUTTI; Gen. Man. GIUSEPPE FELIZIANI; 201 brs.

Credito Bergamasco, SpA: Largo Porta Nuova 2, 24122 Bergamo; tel. (035) 393111; fax (035) 393144; e-mail ufficio.estero@creberg.it; internet www.creberg.it; f. 1891 as Banca Piccolo Credito Bergamasco; name changed as above in 1969; 88.9% owned by Banco Popolare Società Cooperativa; cap. 185.2m., res 1,209.2m., dep. 8,309.5m. (Dec. 2012); Pres. CESARE ZONCA; 245 brs.

Credito Emiliano, SpA (CREDEM): Via Emilia S. Pietro 4, 42100 Reggio-Emilia; tel. (0522) 582111; fax (0522) 433969; internet www.credem.it; f. 1910; cap. 332.4m., res 1,531.1m., dep. 18,539.1m. (Dec. 2012); Pres. GIORGIO FERRARI; CEO ADOLFO BIZZOCCHI; 563 brs.

Credito Valtellinese Società Cooperativa: Piazza Quadrivio 8, 23100 Sondrio; tel. (0342) 522111; fax (0342) 522700; e-mail creval@creval.it; internet www.creval.it; f. 1908; present name adopted 2005; cap. 1,516.7m., res 787.6m., dep. 19,083.9m. (Dec. 2012); Chair. GIOVANNI DE CENSI; Man. Dir MIRO FIORDI; 107 brs.

Intesa Sanpaolo, SpA: Piazza San Carlo 156, 10121 Torino; tel. (011) 5551; fax (011) 5552989; e-mail investor.relations@intesasanpaolo.com; internet www.group.intesasanpaolo.com; f. 2007 by merger of Sanpaolo IMI, SpA with Banca Intesa, SpA; cap. 8,546m., res 39,462m., dep. 285,343m. (Dec. 2012); CEO CARLO MESSINA.

UniCredit, SpA: Piazza Cordusio, 20123 Milano; tel. (02) 88621; fax (02) 88623034; e-mail info@unicreditgroup.eu; internet www.unicreditgroup.eu; f. 2007 by merger of Capitalia, SpA and Unicredito Italiano, SpA; present name adopted 2008; cap. 19,647.9m., res 42,271.2m., dep. 442,029.8m. (Dec. 2012); Chair. GIUSEPPE VITA; CEO FEDERICO GHIZZONI; 3 brs.

Unione di Banche Italiane Scpa (UBI Banca): Piazza Vittorio Veneto 8, 24122 Bergamo; tel. (035) 392111; fax (02) 392390; internet www.ubibanca.it; f. 2003 as Banche Popolari Unite; present name adopted 2007, following merger with Banca Lombarda e Piemontese; cap. 2,254.4, res 4,141.4m., dep. 64,256.4m. (Dec. 2012); Chair. EMILIO ZANETTI; Gen. Man. GRAZIANO CALDIANI.

FINANCIAL INSTITUTIONS

Dexia Crediop, SpA: Via Venti Settembre 30, 00187 Roma; tel. (06) 47711; fax (06) 47715952; e-mail cm@dexia-crediop.it; internet www.dexia-crediop.it; f. 1919; incorporated 1996 as CREDIOP; name changed as above in 2001; cap. 450.2m., res 668.7m., dep. 18,425.6m. (Dec. 2012); Dir JEAN BOURRELLY; Man. Dir JEAN LE NAOUR.

GE Capital Interbanca, SpA: Corso Venezia 56, 20121 Milano; tel. (02) 77311; fax (02) 76014913; e-mail marketing@interbanca.it; internet www.gecapitalinterbanca.it; f. 1961; acquired by GE Capital (United Kingdom) in Jan. 2009; name changed as above in 2012; cap. 217.3m., res 636.9m., dep. 270.8m. (Dec. 2012); Chair. FRANCESCO CARRI; 11 brs.

ICCREA Banca (Istituto Centrale del Credito Cooperativo): Via Lucrezia Romana 41, 00178 Roma; tel. (06) 72071; fax (06) 72077706; e-mail info@iccrea.bcc.it; internet www.iccrea.it; f. 1963; cap. 216.9m., res 237.6m., dep. 22,173.3m. (Dec. 2012); Chair. VITO LORENZO AUGUSTO DELL'ERBA; Gen. Man. LUCIANO GIORGIO GORNATI; 6 brs.

Mediobanca—Banca di Credito Finanziario, SpA: Piazzetta Enrico Cuccia 1, 20121 Milano; tel. (02) 88291; fax (02) 8829367; e-mail info@mediobanca.it; internet www.mediobanca.it; f. 1946; cap. 430.6m., res 6,589.9m., dep. 25,673.6m. (June 2013); Chair. RENATO PAGLIARO; Gen. Man. ALBERTO NAGEL; 1 br.

BANKERS' ORGANIZATION

Associazione Bancaria Italiana: Palazzo Altieri, Piazza del Gesù 49, 00186 Roma; tel. (06) 67671; fax (06) 6767457; e-mail abi@abi.it; internet www.abi.it; f. 1919; advocates the common interests of the banking industry; Pres. ANTONIO PATUELLI; Dir-Gen. Dott. GIOVANNI SABATINI; membership (1,003 mems) is composed of the following institutions: banks authorized to gather savings from the general public and exercise credit business as well as to perform other financial activities; brs and representative offices of foreign banks; asscns of banks or financial intermediaries; financial intermediaries engaging in one or more of the activities subject to mutual recognition under the Second Banking Directive or other financial activities subject to public prudential supervision.

STOCK EXCHANGES

Commissione Nazionale per le Società e la Borsa (CONSOB) (Commission for Companies and the Stock Exchange): Via G. B. Martini 3, 00198 Roma; tel. (06) 84771; fax (06) 8417707; e-mail consob@consob.it; internet www.consob.it; f. 1974; regulatory control over cos quoted on stock exchanges, convertible bonds, unlisted securities, insider trading, all forms of public saving except bank deposits and mutual funds; Dir-Gen. ANTONIO ROSATI.

Borsa Italiana (Italian Stock Exchange): Piazza degli Affari 6, 20123 Milano; tel. (02) 724261; fax (02) 72004333; e-mail media.relations@borsaitaliana.it; internet www.borsaitalia.it; merged with London Stock Exchange in 2007; Chair. ANGELO TANTAZZI; Pres. and CEO MASSIMO CAPUANO; 331 listed cos (Feb. 2010).

INSURANCE

In December 2012 there were 235 insurance and reinsurance companies operating in Italy, of which 135 were Italian.

Alleanza Toro, SpA: Via Mazzini 53, 10123 Torino; tel. (011) 0029111; fax (011) 837554; internet www.alleanzatoro.it; f. 2009; by the merger of Alleanza Assicurazioni, SpA and Toro Assicurazioni, SpA; life and non-life; Pres. LUIGI DE PUPPI.

Allianz, SpA: Largo Ugo Irneri 1, 34123 Trieste; tel. (40) 7781111; fax (40) 7781311; e-mail info@allianz.it; internet www.allianz.it; f. 1838; cap. 403m. (2008); Chair. CARLO SALVATORI; CEO GEORGE SARTOREL.

Assicurazioni Generali, SpA: Piazza Duca degli Abruzzi 2, 34132 Trieste; tel. (040) 671111; fax (040) 671127; e-mail press@generali.com; internet www.generali.com; f. 1831; life and non-life; Chair. GABRIELE GALATERI DI GENOLA; Group CEO MARIO GRECO.

Atradius Credit Insurance, NV, Rappresentanza Generale per l'Italia: Via Crescenzio 12, 00193 Roma; tel. (06) 688121; fax (06) 6874418; e-mail info.it@atradius.com; internet www.atradius.com; Chair., Supervisory Bd IGNACIO ÁLVAREZ; CEO ISIDORO UNDA.

Axa Assicurazioni: Corso Como 17, 20154 Milano; tel. (02) 480841; fax (02) 48084331; e-mail infodanni@axa.it; internet www.axa.it; f. 1956; Group CEO HENRI DE CASTRIES.

AXA MPS Assicurazioni Vita, SpA: Via Aldo Fabrizi 9, 00128 Roma; tel. (06) 508701; fax (06) 50870295; e-mail info@axa-mpsvita.it; internet www.axa-mps.it; f. 1974; Chair. PAOLO MANZATO; CEO FRÉDÉRIC MARIE DE COURTOIS D'ARCOLLIÈRES.

Carige Assicurazioni: Viale Certosa 222, 20156 Milano; tel. (02) 30761; fax (02) 3086125; e-mail info@carigeassicurazioni.it; internet www.carigeassicurazioni.it; f. 1920; part of Banca Carige group; Pres. PIERO GUIDO.

Creditras Vita, SpA: Corso d'Italia 23, 20122 Milano; tel. (02) 72161; fax (02) 72164032; e-mail info@creditrasvita.it; internet www.creditrasvita.it; f. 1995; part of Allianz, SpA; life insurance; Pres. PIERO BOTTO.

FATA Assicurazioni, SpA (Fondo Assicurativo Tra Agricoltori): Via Urbana 169A, 00184 Roma; tel. (06) 47651; fax (06) 4871187; e-mail info@fata-assicurazioni.it; internet www.fata-assicurazioni.it; f. 1927; subsidiary of Gruppo Generali; CEO GIORGIO CAGNETTI.

Fondiaria—Sai, SpA: Corso Galileo Galilei 12, 10126 Torino; tel. (055) 6657111; fax (055) 6657685; e-mail fondiaria-sai@fondiaria-sai.it; internet www.fondiaria-sai.it; f. 1879; owned by Unipol Gruppo Finanziario; non-life; Pres. FABIO CERCHIAI; Dir-Gen. CARLO CIMBRI.

Groupama Assicurazioni, SpA: Via Cesare Pavese 385, 00144 Roma; tel. (06) 30181; fax (06) 80210831; e-mail info@groupama.it; internet www.groupama.it; f. 1929; fmrly known as Nuova Tirrena, SpA; name changed as above in 2009; part of Groupama; Pres. FRANÇOIS SCHMITT; Dir-Gen. and CEO CHRISTOPHE BUSO.

HDI Assicurazioni, SpA: Via Abruzzi 10, 00187 Roma; tel. (06) 421031; fax (06) 42103500; e-mail hdi.assicurazioni@hdia.it; internet www.hdia.it; f. 2001.

INA Assitalia, SpA: Via Leonida Bissolati 23, 00187 Roma; tel. (06) 84831; fax (06) 84833898; e-mail info@inaassitalia.it; internet www.inaassitalia.it; f. 1912; subsidiary of Gruppo Generali; Pres. SERGIO BALBINOT; Man. Dir FABIO BUSCARINI.

Intesa Sanpaolo Vita, SpA: Viale Stelvio 55-57, 20159 Milano; tel. (02) 30511; fax (02) 30518188; internet www.intesasanpaolovita.it; f. 2012; life insurance; Pres. Prof. SALVATORE MACCARONE; CEO Dr GIANEMILIO OSCULATI.

Italiana Assicurazioni, SpA: Via Traiano 18, 20149 Milano; tel. (02) 397161; fax (02) 3271270; internet www.italiana.it; f. 1889; part of Gruppo Reale Mutua; as Cooperativa Italiana Incendio; name changed as above in 1995; Pres. ITI MIHALICH; LUIGI LANA.

Mediolanum Vita, SpA: Palazzo Meucci, Via Francesco Sforza 15, 20080 Basiglio, Milano; tel. (02) 90491; e-mail info@mediolanum.it; internet www.mediolanumvita.it; f. 1972; life insurance; Pres. DANILO PELLEGRINO; CEO LUIGI DEL FABBRO, EDOARDO LOMBARDI.

Milano Assicurazioni (Compagnia di Assicurazioni di Milano, SpA): Via Senigallia 18/2, 20161 Milano; tel. (02) 64021; fax (02) 64025389; e-mail milass@milass.it; internet www.milass.it; f. 1825; owned by Gruppo Unipol; Pres. FABIO CERCHIAI; CEO CARLO CIMBRI.

Poste Vita: Piazzale Konrad Adenauer 3, 00144 Roma; tel. (06) 549241; internet www.postevita.it; f. 2000; subsidiary of Gruppo Poste Italiane; life insurance; Pres. ROBERTO COLOMBO.

SARA Assicurazioni, SpA: Via Po 20, 00198 Roma; tel. (06) 84751; fax (06) 8475223; internet www.sara.it; f. 1924; Chair. ROSARIO ALESSI; Gen. Man. Dr ALESSANDRO SANTOLIQUIDO.

Società Cattolica di Assicurazione—Società Cooperativa: Lungadige Cangrande 16, 37126 Verona; tel. (045) 8391111; fax (045) 8391112; e-mail cattolica@cattolicaassicurazioni.it; internet www.cattolicaassicurazioni.it; f. 1896; CEO Dott. GIOVANNI BATTISTA MAZZUCCHELLI.

Società Reale Mutua di Assicurazioni: Via Corte d'Appello 11, 10122 Torino; tel. (011) 4311111; fax (011) 4350966; e-mail buongiornoreale@realmutua.it; internet www.realemutua.it; f. 1828; net profit 15.71m. (2012); Chair. Dott. ITI MIHALICH; Gen. Man. LUIGI LANA.

Swiss Re Italia, SpA: Via dei Giuochi Istmici 40, 00194 Roma; tel. (06) 323931; fax (06) 3296572; e-mail srit-communicazione@swissre.com; internet www.swissre.com; f. 1922; Chair. WALTER B. KIELHOLZ; Man. Dir MAURIZIO VALSECCHI.

Unipol Assicurazioni, SpA: Via Stalingrado 45, 40128 Bologna; tel. (051) 5077111; fax (051) 375349; internet www.unipolassicurazioni.it; f. 1963; present name adopted in 2011; part of Grupo Unipol; non-life; Pres. VANES GALANTI; CEO CARLO CIMBRI.

Vittoria Assicurazioni, SpA: Via Ignazio Gardella 2, 20149 Milano; tel. (02) 482191; fax (02) 48203693; internet www.vittoriaassicurazioni.com; f. 1921; cap. 3,277.1m. (July 2008); Chair. Dott. GIORGIO ROBERTO COSTA; CEO ROBERTO GUARENA.

Zurich Insurance PLC: Via Benigno Crespi 23, 20159 Milano; tel. (02) 59661; fax (02) 59662603; e-mail informazioni@zurich.it; internet www.zurich.it; f. 1872; fmrly known as l'Unione delle assicurazioni; CEO CAMILLO CANDIA.

Regulatory Authority

Istituto per la Vigilanza sulle Assicurazioni (IVASS): Via del Quirinale 21, 00187 Roma; tel. (06) 421331; fax (06) 42133206; e-mail scrivi@ivass.it; internet www.ivass.it; f. 2013; supervises insurance cos; Pres. and Dir-Gen. SALVATORE ROSSI.

Insurance Association

Associazione Nazionale fra le Imprese Assicuratrici (ANIA): Via della Frezza 70, 00186 Roma; tel. (06) 326881; fax (06) 3227135; e-mail info@ania.it; internet www.ania.it; f. 1944; Pres. Dott. ALDO MINUCCI; Dir-Gen. Prof. DARIO FOCARELLI; 230 mems.

Trade and Industry

GOVERNMENT AGENCIES

Agenzia per la promozione all'estero e l'internazionalizzaizone delle imprese italiane (ICE) (National Institute for Foreign Trade): Via Liszt 21, 00144 Roma; tel. (06) 59929388; fax (06) 89280312; e-mail assistenza.export@ice.it; internet www.ice.gov.it; f. 1926; govt agency for the promotion of foreign trade; Pres. RICCARDO M. MONTI; Dir-Gen. ROBERTO LUONGO.

Autorità Garante della Concorrenza e del Mercato (AGCM) (Italian Competition Authority): Piazza G. Verdi 6A, 00198 Roma; tel. (06) 858211; fax (06) 85821256; e-mail antitrust@agcm.it; internet www.agcm.it; f. 1990; Chair. GIOVANNI PITRUZZELLA; Sec.-Gen. ROBERTO CHIEPPA.

Cassa depositi e prestiti SpA (CDP): Via Goito 4, 00185 Roma; tel. (06) 42211; fax (06) 42214026; internet www.cassaddpp.it; f. 1850; provides loans to public bodies and local govt; 70% owned by Ministry of the Economy and Finance, 30% by banking foundations; Chair. FRANCO BASSANINI; CEO GIOVANNI GORNO TEMPINI.

Società Italiana per le Imprese All'Estero, SpA (SIMEST) (Italian Company for Businesses Abroad): Corso Vittorio Emanuele II 323, 00186 Roma; tel. (06) 686351; fax (06) 68635220; e-mail info@simest.it; internet www.simest.it; f. 1990; 76% owned by Ministry of Economic Development; Pres. GIANCARLO LANNA.

CHAMBER OF COMMERCE

Unioncamere (Union of Chambers of Commerce, Industry, Crafts and Agriculture): Piazza Sallustio 21, 00187 Roma; tel. (06) 47041; fax (06) 4704240; e-mail segretaria.generale@unioncamere.it; internet www.unioncamere.it; f. 1901; fmrly Unione Italiana delle Camere di Commercio, Industria, Artigianato e Agricoltura (Italian Union of Chambers of Commerce, Industry, Crafts and Agriculture); Pres. FERRUCCIO DARDANELLO; Sec.-Gen. CLAUDIO GAGLIARDI.

INDUSTRIAL AND TRADE ASSOCIATIONS

Confederazione Generale dell'Industria Italiana (Confindustria) (General Confederation of Italian Industry): Viale dell'Astronomia 30, 00144 Roma; tel. (06) 59031; fax (06) 5919615; e-mail piei@confindustria.it; internet www.confindustria.it; f. 1910; re-established 1944; mems: 99 local asscns, 100 trade asscns, 18 regional confeds, 25 sectoral feds and 265 associated orgs, totalling 149,288 firms and 5.52m. employees; Pres. GIORGIO SQUINZI; Dir-Gen. MARCELLA PANUCCI.

Principal Organizations Affiliated to Confindustria

Associazione delle Imprese del Farmaco (FARMINDUSTRIA) (Pharmaceutical Industry): Largo del Nazareno 3/8, 00187 Roma; tel. (06) 675801; fax (06) 6786494; e-mail farmindustria@farmindustria.it; internet www.farmindustria.it; f. 1978; Pres. Dott. MASSIMO SCACCABAROZZI; 200 mem. firms.

Associazione delle Industrie del Dolce della Pasta Italiane (AIDEPI) (Pasta, Breakfast Cereals, Chocolate and Cocoa-based Products, Ice Creams, Sugar Confectionery and Biscuit Manufacturers): Via del Poggio Fiorito 61, 00144 Roma; tel. (06) 8091071; fax (06) 8073186; e-mail aidepi@aidepi.it; internet www.aidepi.it; Pres. PAOLO BARILLA; Dir-Gen. MARIO PICCIALUTI.

Associazione Industrie per l'Aerospazio, i Sistemi e la Difesa (AIAD) (Aerospace, Systems and Defence Industries): Via Nazionale 54, 00184 Roma; tel. (06) 4880247; fax (06) 4827476; e-mail aiad@aiad.it; internet www.aiad.it; f. 1947; Pres. REMO PERTICA; Sec.-Gen. CARLO FESTUCCI.

Associazione Italiana Tecnico Economica del Cemento (AITEC) (Cement): Piazza G. Marconi 25, 00144 Roma; tel. (06) 54210237; fax (06) 5915408; e-mail info@aitecweb.com; internet www.aitecweb.com; f. 1959; Pres. ALVISE XILLO; Man. Dir Dott. GIUSEPPE SCHLITZER.

Associazione Mineraria Italiana (ASSOMINERARIA) (Oil and Mining Industry): Via delle Tre Madonne 20, 00197 Roma; tel. (06) 8073045; fax (06) 8073385; e-mail info@assomineraria.org; internet www.assomineraria.org; f. 1917; Pres. Dott. CLAUDIO DESCALZI; Dir-Gen. Dott. ANDREA KETOFF; 148 mems.

Associazione Nazionale Costruttori Edili (ANCE) (Construction): Via Guattani 16, 00161 Roma; tel. (06) 845671; fax (06) 84567550; e-mail info@ance.it; internet www.ance.it; f. 1946; Pres. PAOLO BUZZETTI; Dir-Gen. CARLO FERRONI; mems: 20,000 firms in 102 provincial and 20 regional asscns.

Associazione Nazionale delle Imprese Elettriche (ASSOELETTRICA) (Electricity Generators and Distributors): Via Benozzo Gozzoli 24, 00142 Roma; tel. (06) 8537281; fax (06) 85356431; e-mail info@assoelettrica.it; internet www.assoelettrica.it; f. 2002; Pres. CHICCO TESTA; Dir-Gen. STEFANO PUPOLIN; 120 mem. cos.

Associazione Nazionale Filiera Industria Automobilistica (ANFIA) (Motor Vehicle Industries): Corso Galileo Ferraris 61, 10128 Torino; tel. (011) 5546511; fax (011) 545986; e-mail anfia@anfia.it; internet www.anfia.it; f. 1912; Pres. ROBERTO VAVASSORI; 232 mems.

Associazione Nazionale Italiana Industrie Grafiche, Cartotecniche e Trasformatrici (ASSOGRAFICI) (Printing and Paper-Processing Industries): Piazza Conciliazione 1, 20123 Milano; tel. (02) 4981051; fax (02) 4816947; e-mail assografici@assografici.it; internet www.assografici.it; f. 1946; Pres. GIOVANNI COLOMBO; Gen. Dir Dott. CLAUDIO COVINI; 1,200 mems.

Confindustria Servizi Innovativi e Tecnologici (FITA) (Online Media, Market Research, Information Technology, etc.): Via Barbarini 11, 00187 Roma; tel. (06) 421401; fax (06) 62201362; internet www.confindustriasi.it; Pres. ENNIO LUCARELLI; 51 associated orgs and 62 regional sections.

Federazione delle Associazioni Nazionali di Categorie Industriali Varie (FEDERVARIE) (Miscellaneous Industries): Via Petitti 16, 20149 Milano; tel. (02) 32672222; fax (02) 32672299; e-mail info@confindustriafedervarie.it; internet www.confindustriafedervarie.it; f. 1945; Pres. Dott. DINO FENZI; 24 mem. asscns.

Federazione delle Associazioni Nazionali dell'Industria Meccanica Varia ed Affine (ANIMA) (Mechanical and Engineering Industries): Via Scarsellini 13, 20161 Milano; tel. (02) 45418500; fax (02) 45418545; e-mail anima@anima-it.com; internet www.anima-it.com; f. 1914; Pres. SANDRO BONOMI; Dir-Gen. ANDREA ORLANDO; 1,500 mems.

Federazione delle Imprese delle Comunicazioni e dell'Informatica (FEDERCOMIN) (Information and Communications Technologies): Via Barberini 11, 00187 Roma; tel. (06) 421401; fax (06)

42140444; e-mail info@federcomin.it; Pres. ALBERTO TRIPI; Dir-Gen. PIETRO VARALDO.

Federazione Industrie Prodotti Impianti e Servizi per le Costruzioni (FINCO) (Construction Services and Systems): Via Brenta 13, 00198 Roma; tel. (06) 8555203; fax (06) 8559860; e-mail finco@fincoweb.org; internet www.fincoweb.org; f. 1994; Pres. CIRINO MENDOLA; Dir-Gen. Dott. ANGELO ARTALE.

Federazione Italiana dell'Accessorio Moda e Persona (FIAMP) (Personal and Fashion Accessories): Via Petitti 16, 20149 Milano; tel. (02) 32673673; fax (02) 324233; e-mail segreteria@fiamp.it; internet www.fiamp.it; f. 2004; Pres. CIRILLO MARCOLIN.

Federazione Italiana dell'Industria Alimentare (FEDERALIMENTARE) (Food Industry): Viale Pasteur 10, 00144 Roma; tel. (06) 5903380; fax (06) 5903342; e-mail direzione@federalimentare.it; internet www.federalimentare.it; Pres. GIAN FILIPPO FERRUA MAGLIANI; Dir-Gen. FILIPPO FERRUA MAGLIANI; 17 mem. asscns.

Federazione Italiana delle Industrie del Legno, del Sughero, del Mobile e dell'Arredamento (FEDERLEGNO-ARREDO) (Wood, Cork, Furniture and Interior Design): Foro Bonaparte 65, 20121 Milano; tel. (02) 806041; fax (02) 80604392; e-mail flaroma@federlegno.it; internet www.federlegno.it; f. 1945; Pres. ROBERTO SNAIDERO; Dir-Gen. GIOVANNI DE PONTI; 2,400 mems.

Federazione Italiana Industriali Produttori Esportatori e Importatori di Vini, Acquaviti, Liquori, Sciroppi, Aceti e Affini (FEDERVINI) (Producers, Importers and Exporters of Wines, Brandies, Liqueurs, Syrups, Vinegars, etc.): Via Mentana 2B, 00185 Roma; tel. (06) 4941630; fax (06) 4941566; e-mail federvini@federvini.it; internet www.federvini.it; f. 1917; Pres. Dott. LAMBERTO VALLARINO GANCIA; Dir-Gen. OTTAVIO CAGIANO DE AZEVEDO.

Federazione Nazionale delle Associazioni dei Produttori di Beni Strumentali destinati allo Svolgimento di Processi Manifatturieri dell'Industria e dell'Artigianato (FEDERMACCHINE) (Machine manufacture): Viale Fulvio Testi 128, 20092 Cinisello Balsamo; tel. (02) 26255201; fax (02) 26255881; e-mail federmacchine@federmacchine.it; internet www.federmacchine.it; Pres. GIANCARLO LOSMA; Sec.-Gen. Dott. ALFREDO MARIOTTI.

Federazione Nazionale Fonderie (ASSOFOND) (Foundries): Via Copernico 54, 20090 Trezzano Sul Naviglio (Milano); tel. (02) 48400967; fax (02) 48401267; e-mail info@assofond.it; internet www.assofond.it; f. 1948; Pres. ENRICO FRIGERIO; Dir PAOLO PONZINI.

Federazione Nazionale Imprese Elettrotecniche ed Elettroniche (ANIE) (Electric and Electronic Sectors): Via Lancetti 34, 20158 Milano; tel. (02) 32641; fax (02) 3264395; e-mail info@anie.it; internet www.anie.it; Pres. CLAUDIO ANDREA GEMME; Gen. Dir MARIA ANTONIETTA PORTALURI.

Federazione Nazionale dell'Industria Chimica (FEDERCHIMICA) (Chemical Industry): Via Giovanni da Procida 11, 20149 Milano; tel. (02) 345651; fax (02) 34565310; e-mail federchimica@federchimica.it; internet www.federchimica.it; f. 1945 as Aschimici; renamed as above in 1984; Pres. CESARE PUCCIONI; Dir-Gen. Dott. CLAUDIO BENEDETTI; 1,350 mem. cos.

Federazione Nazionale Industria dei Viaggi e del Turismo (FEDERTURISMO) (Tourism and Travel): Viale Pasteur 10, 00144 Roma; tel. (06) 5911758; fax (06) 5910390; e-mail federturismo@federturismo.it; internet www.federturismo.it; f. 1993; Pres. RENZO IORIO; Dir-Gen. ANTONIO BARRECA; 25 sectoral asscns, 57 local asscns.

Federazione Nazionale dei Sistemi e delle Modalità di Trasporto e delle Attività Connesse (FEDERTRASPORTO): Viale Luigi Pasteur 10, 00144 Roma; tel. (06) 5903972; fax (06) 5903987; e-mail federtrasporto@federtrasporto.it; internet www.federtrasporto.it; f. 1993; Pres. ALBERTO BRANDANI; Dir VALERIA BATTAGLIA; 11 mem. asscns.

Federazione Sindacale dell'Industria Metalmeccanica Italiana (FEDERMECCANICA) (Metalworking): Piazzale B. Juarez 14, 00144 Roma; tel. (06) 5925446; fax (06) 5911913; e-mail mail.roma@federmeccanica.it; internet www.federmeccanica.it; f. 1971; Pres. PIER LUIGI CECCARDI; Dir ROBERTO SANTARELLI; 103 mem. asscns.

Unione Nazionale dei Cantieri e delle Industrie Nautiche e Affini (UCINA) (Marine Industry): Piazzale Kennedy 1, 16129 Genova; tel. (010) 5769811; fax (010) 5531104; e-mail ucina@ucina.it; internet www.ucina.it; Pres. Dott. ANTON FRANCESCO ALBERTONI.

Unione Petrolifera (Petroleum Industries): Piazzale Luigi Sturzo 31, 00144 Roma; tel. (06) 5423651; fax (06) 59602925; e-mail info@unionepetrolifera.it; internet www.unionepetrolifera.it; f. 1948; Pres. ALESSANDRO GILOTTI; Dir-Gen. Dott. PIETRO DE SIMONE; 26 mem. cos.

Other Industrial and Trade Organizations

Associazione fra le Società Italiane per Azioni (ASSONIME) (Limited Cos): Piazza Venezia 11, 00187 Roma; tel. (06) 695291; fax (06) 6790487; e-mail assonime@assonime.it; internet www.assonime.it; f. 1910; Pres. Dott. LUIGI ABETE; Dir-Gen. Prof. STEFANO MICOSSI.

Confederazione Generale della Agricoltura Italiana (CONFAGRICOLTURA) (Agriculture): Corso Vittorio Emanuele II 101, 00186 Roma; tel. (06) 68521; fax (06) 68308578; e-mail info@confagricoltura.it; internet www.confagricoltura.it; f. 1945; Pres. MARIO GUIDI.

Confederazione Generale Italiana del Commercio, del Turismo, dei Servizi e delle Piccole e Medie Industrie (PMI) (CONFCOMMERCIO) (Commerce, Tourism, Services and Small and Medium-sized Industries): Piazza G. G. Belli 2, 00153 Roma; tel. (06) 58661; fax (06) 5809425; e-mail confcommercio@confcommercio.it; internet www.confcommercio.it; f. 1945; Pres. Dott. CARLO SANGALLI; Dir-Gen. FRANCESCO RIVOLTA; 770,000 mems.

Confederazione Italiana della Piccola e Media Industria Privata (CONFAPI) (Small and Medium-sized Private Industries): Via del Plebiscito 117, 00186 Roma; tel. (06) 690151; fax (06) 6791488; e-mail mail@confapi.org; internet www.confapi.org; f. 1947; Pres. MAURIZIO CASASCO; Dir-Gen. Dott. ARMANDO OCCHIPINTI; 120,000 mems.

Confederazione Italiana della Proprietà Edilizia (CONFEDILIZIA) (Real Estate): Via Borgognona 47, 00187 Roma; tel. (06) 6793489; fax (06) 6793447; e-mail roma@confedilizia.it; internet www.confedilizia.it; f. 1945; Pres. CORRADO SFORZA FOGLIANI; Sec.-Gen. GIORGIO SPAZIANI TESTA.

Federazione delle Associazioni Italiane Alberghi e Turismo (FEDERALBERGHI) (Hotels and Tourism): Via Toscana 1, 00187 Roma; tel. (06) 42034610; fax (06) 42034690; e-mail info@federalberghi.it; internet www.federalberghi.it; f. 1950; Pres. BERNABO BOCCA; Dir-Gen. ALESSANDRO MASSIMO NUCARA; 30,000 mems.

UTILITIES

Autorità per l'Energia Elettrica e il Gas (AEEG) (Electric Energy and Gas Authority): Piazza Cavour 5, 20121 Milano; tel. (02) 655651; fax (02) 65565266; e-mail segretariatogenerale@autorita.energia.it; internet www.autorita.energia.it; regulatory authority; f. 1996; Pres. GUIDO PIER PAOLO BORTONI.

Electricity

A2A, SpA: Via Lamarmora 230, 25124 Brescia; tel. (030) 35531; fax (030) 3553204; e-mail infobs@a2a.eu; internet www.a2a.eu; f. 2008 by merger of AEM, AMSA and ASM; electricity and gas manufacture and distribution; Chair., Management Bd GRAZIANO TARANTINI.

Acea, SpA: Piazzale Ostiense 2, 00154 Roma; tel. (06) 57991; fax (06) 5758095; e-mail info@aceaspa.it; internet www.aceaspa.it; f. 1909; produces and distributes electricity in Rome area; also engaged in water provision; 51% stake owned by Rome City Council; Chair. GIANCARLO CREMONESI; CEO MARCO STADERINI.

Edison, SpA: Foro Buonaparte 31, 20121 Milano; tel. (02) 62221; fax (02) 62227456; e-mail infoweb@edison.it; internet www.edison.it; f. 1884 as Società Generale Italiana di Elettricità Sistema Edison; electricity and natural gas; 60% owned by Transalpina di Energia Srl; Chair. HENRY PROGLIO; CEO BRUNO LESCOEUR.

Enel, SpA: Via le Regina Margherita 137, 00198 Roma; tel. (06) 85091; fax (06) 85092162; internet www.enel.it; f. 1962; 31.23% owned by the Ministry of the Economy and Finance; partially privatized; generates and distributes electricity and gas; Chair. PAOLO ANDREA COLOMBO; CEO FULVIO CONTI.

Gestore dei Servizi Energitici (GSE): Viale Maresciallo Pilsudski 92, 00197 Roma; tel. (06) 80111; fax (06) 80114392; e-mail info@gse.it; internet www.gse.it; f. 2000 as Gestore del Sistema Eletrico, SpA; name changed to present in 2009; owned by the Ministry of the Economy and Finance; manages electricity transmission and co-ordinates the power network; Chair. EMILIO CREMONA; CEO NANDO PASQUALI.

Terna, SpA—Rete Elettrica Nazionale: Via Egidio Galbani 70, 00156 Roma; tel. (06) 83138111; e-mail info@terna.it; internet www.terna.it; f. 1999; electricity transmission co; owns nearly 100% of electricity transmission grid; Pres. LUIGI ROTH; CEO FLAVIO CATTANEO.

Gas

See the section on Electricity for companies that are involved in the supply of both gas and electricity.

Eni, SpA: Piazzale Mattei 1, 00144 Roma; tel. (06) 59821; fax (06) 59822141; e-mail segreteriasocietaria.azionisti@eni.com; internet www.eni.it; f. 1953; fmrly Ente Nazionale Idrocarburi; natural gas exploration, oil and gas power; 30% owned by Italian Government; Pres. (vacant); CEO PAOLO SCARONI.

Eni Power: Piazza Vanoni 1, 20097 San Donato Milanese; tel. (02) 5201; fax (02) 5203180; internet www.enipower.eni.it; f. 1999; owned by Eni, SpA (q.v.); power generation and sale; Pres. and CEO GIOVANNI MILANI.

Gruppo Hera, SpA: Viale C. Berti Pichat 2–4, 40127 Bologna; tel. (051) 287111; fax (051) 287525; internet www.gruppohera.it; f. 2002; distributes gas; also engaged in water provision; Chair. TOMASO TOMMASI DI VIGNANO; Man. Dir MAURIZIO CHIARINI.

Italgas, SpA: Largo Regio Parco 9, 10153 Torino; tel. (01) 123941; fax (01) 12394499; internet www.italgas.it; gas distribution; Pres. MARCO REGGIANI; CEO PAOLO MOSA.

Linde Gas Italia Srl: Via Guido Rossa 3, 20010 Arluno, Milano; tel. (02) 903731; fax (02) 90373599; e-mail lgi@it.linde-gas.com; internet www.linde-gas.it; f. 1991; CEO FABRIZIO ELIA.

Plurigas: Corso di Porta Vittoria 4, 20122 Milano; tel. (02) 77203033; fax (02) 77203255; e-mail info@plurigas.it; internet www.plurigas.it; f. 2001; gas distribution; 70% owned by A2A, SpA; Chair. VALTER PALLANO; CEO ANNAMARIA ARCUDI.

Snam Rete Gas: Piazza Santa Barbara 7, 20097 San Donato Milanese; tel. (02) 37031; fax (02) 37039227; e-mail postmaster@snamretegas.it; internet www.snamretegas.it; f. 1941 as Società Nazionale Metanodotti (Snam); adopted current name 2001; transports natural gas; Chair. LORENZO BINI SMAGHI; CEO FRANCESCO IOVANE.

Water

Municipal administrations are responsible for water supply in Italy. Legislation promulgated in 1994 provided for the consolidation of water supply into 'single territorial units'. Since the mid-1990s many municipalities have formed limited companies to manage water supply, for example the supplier for Rome (Acea, SpA—see the section on Electricity) and the supplier for Milan (Amiaque, SpA). A small number of municipalities have contracted private companies to manage water supply.

TRADE UNIONS

The three main trade union federations are the Confederazione Generale Italiana del Lavoro (CGIL), the Confederazione Italiana Sindacati Lavoratori (CISL) and the Unione Italiana del Lavoro (UIL).

National Federations

Confederazione Autonoma Italiana del Lavoro (CONFAIL): Viale Abruzzi 38, 20131 Milano; tel. (02) 29404554; fax (02) 29525692; e-mail info@confail.org; internet www.confail.org; Gen. Sec. EVANGELISTA ZACCARIA.

Confederazione Autonoma Sindacati Artigiani (CASARTIGIANI): Via Flaminio Ponzio 2, 00153 Roma; tel. (06) 57300241; fax (06) 5755036; e-mail casartigiani@tiscalinet.it; internet www.casartigiani.org; f. 1958; fed. of artisans' unions and regional and provincial asscns; Pres. GIACOMO BASSO.

Confederazione Generale Italiana dell'Artigianato (CONFARTIGIANATO) (Artisans): Via di S. Giovanni in Laterano 152, 00184 Roma; tel. (06) 703741; fax (06) 70452188; e-mail confartigianato@confartigianato.it; internet www.confartigianato.it; f. 1946; independent; 20 regional feds, 120 provincial asscns; 700,000 associate enterprises; Pres. GIORGIO NATALINO GUERRINI; Sec.-Gen. CESARE FUMAGALLI.

Confederazione Generale Italiana del Lavoro (CGIL) (Italian General Confederation of Labour): Corso d'Italia 25, 00198 Roma; tel. (06) 84761; fax (06) 8845683; e-mail info@mail.cgil.it; internet www.cgil.it; f. 1906 as Confederazione Generale del Lavoro; refounded 1944; confederation of 13 feds; Sec.-Gen. SUSANNA CAMUSSO; 6m. mems.

Confederazione Italiana Dirigenti e Alte Professionalità—Manager e Alte Professionalità per l'italia (CIDA—MAPI): Via Barberini 36, 00187 Roma; tel. (06) 97605111; fax (06) 97605109; e-mail ufficio_stampa@cida.it; internet www.cida.it; fed. of 10 managers' unions; Pres. Dott. SILVESTRE BERTOLINI; Dir Dott. ALBERTO SARTONI.

Confederazione Italiana Sindacati Addetti ai Servizi (CISAS): Via Sapri 6, 00185 Roma; tel. (06) 4466618; fax (06) 4466617; e-mail info@cafcisas.it; internet www.cisas.it; Gen. Sec. ONOFRIO DANIELLO.

Confederazione Generale dei Sindacati Autonomi dei Lavoratori (CONFSAL): Viale Trasevere 60, 00153 Roma; tel. (06) 5852071; fax (06) 5818218; e-mail info@confsal.it; internet www.confsal.it; f. 1979; Sec.-Gen. Prof. MARCO PAOLO NIGI.

Confederazione Italiana Sindacati Lavoratori (CISL): Via Po 21, 00198 Roma; tel. (06) 84731; fax (06) 8546076; e-mail cisl@cisl.it; internet www.cisl.it; f. 1950; affiliated to the International Confederation of Free Trade Unions and the ETUC; fed. of 19 unions; publishes *Conquiste del Lavoro* (see Press); Sec.-Gen. RAFFAELE BONANNI; 4,400,000 mems.

Confederazione Nazionale dell'Artigianato e delle Piccole Imprese (CNA) (National Confederation of Italian SMEs and Handicrafts): Via G. A. Guattani 13, 00161 Roma; tel. (06) 441881; fax (06) 44249511; e-mail cna@cna.it; internet www.cna.it; f. 1946; provincial asscns; Pres. IVAN MALAVASI; Gen. Sec. Dott. SERGIO SILVESTRINI.

Confederazione Unitaria Quadri (CUQ): Via Assarotti 9, 10122 Torino; tel. (011) 5612042; fax (011) 5630987; e-mail confquadri@tin.it; f. 1995; Pres. MARIO VIGNA.

Confederazione Unitaria Sindacati Autonomi Lavoratori (CUSAL): Via di Campo Marzio 46, 00186 Roma; tel. (06) 6872508; fax (06) 6872509; Pres. DOMENICO MANNO; Gen. Sec. FRANCESCO BRUNETTI.

Sindacato Nazionale dei Funzionari Direttivi, Dirigenti e delle Alte Professionalità della Pubblica Amministrazione (DIRSTAT): Piazza Risorgimento 59, 00192 Roma; tel. (06) 3222097; fax (06) 3212690; e-mail dirstat@dirstat.it; internet www.dirstat.it; f. 1948; fed. of 33 unions and asscns of civil service executives and officers; Pres. FIORILLO ALESSIO; Sec.-Gen. Dott. SERGIO DI DONNA.

Unione Generale del Lavoro (UGL): Via Margutta 19, 00187 Roma; tel. (06) 324821; fax (06) 324820; e-mail segreteriaugl@ugl.it; internet www.ugl.it; f. 1950 as CISNAL; name changed as above 1995; upholds traditions of national syndicalism; fed. of 64 unions, 77 provincial unions; Gen. Sec. GIOVANNI CENTRELLA; 2,137,979 mems.

Unione Italiana del Lavoro (UIL): Via Lucullo 6, 00187 Roma; tel. (06) 47531; fax (06) 4753208; e-mail info@uil.it; internet www.uil.it; f. 1950; socialist, social democrat and republican; affiliated to the International Confederation of Free Trade Unions and European Trade Union Confederation; 18 nat. trade union feds and 108 provincial union councils; Gen. Sec. LUIGI ANGELETTI; 1,758,729 mems.

Co-operative Unions

Associazione Generale delle Cooperative Italiane (AGCI): Via A. Bargoni 78, 00153 Roma; tel. (06) 583271; fax (06) 58327210; e-mail info@agci.it; internet www.agci.it; f. 1952; Pres. ROSARIO ALTIERI.

Confederazione Cooperative Italiane (CONFCOOPERATIVE): Borgo S. Spirito 78, 00193 Roma; tel. (06) 680001; fax (06) 68134236; e-mail esteri@confcooperative.it; internet www.confcooperative.it; f. 1919; confederation of co-operative unions; Pres. MAURIZIO GARDINI; Sec.-Gen. VINCENZO MANNINO.

Lega Nazionale delle Cooperative e Mutue (National League of Co-operative and Friendly Societies): Via Guattani 9, 00161 Roma; tel. (06) 84439391; fax (06) 84439406; e-mail info@legacoop.coop; internet www.legacoop.it; f. 1886; 10 affiliated unions; Pres. GIULIANO POLETTI.

Unione Nazionale Cooperative Italiane (UNCI): Via San Sotero 32, 00165 Roma; tel. (06) 39366729; fax (06) 39375080; e-mail info@unci.eu; internet www.unci.eu; f. 1971; Pres. PAOLO GALLIGIONI.

Transport

RAILWAYS

The majority of Italian lines are controlled by an independent state-owned corporation, Ferrovie dello Stato, SpA. Its subsidiary Trenitalia operates a large number of train services in the country, and offers links to Spain, Slovenia, Hungary, Austria, Belgium and France. In 2011 the total length of the network was 16,726 km, of which 11,925 were electrified. Apart from the state railway system there are 24 local and municipal railway companies, many of whose lines are narrow gauge. A 182-km high-speed link connecting Bologna and Milan opened in 2008; an extension of the line, to Rome via Florence, and further extensions to Turin in the north-west, and to Naples and Salerno in the south, were completed in 2009. Work on a high-speed link to Lyon, France, from Turin, including a 58-km tunnel of which 12 km will be in Italy, was expected to be completed by 2023. There are metro systems in Rome, Catania, Genoa, Milan, Naples and Turin.

Ferrovie dello Stato, SpA (FS): Piazza della Croce Rossa 1, 00161 Roma; tel. (06) 44101; e-mail info_ferservizi@ferservizi.it; internet www.fsitaliane.it; controls 9 subsidiaries; Pres. LAMBERTO CARDIA; CEO (vacant).

ROADS

In 2009 there were 6,661 km of motorway, 19,375 km of major roads and 154,513 km of secondary roads in Italy. The length of the total road network was an estimated 487,700 km in 2005. All the autostrade (motorways) are toll roads except for that between Salerno and Reggio Calabria and those in Sicily. In March 2009 the Government announced that plans to construct a 3.3-km road and rail bridge over the Straits of Messina, between Calabria and Sicily were to be revived.

ANAS, SpA: Via Monzambano 10, 00185 Roma; tel. (06) 44461; fax (06) 4456224; e-mail 841148@stradeanas.it; internet www.stradeanas.it; f. 1928 as Azienda Autonoma Statale della Strada (AASS); jt-stock co in partnership with the Ministry of the Economy and Finance; responsible for the construction and administration of state roads and their improvement and extension; Dir Dott. PIETRO CIUCCI.

Autostrade per l'Italia, SpA: Via Alberto Bergamini 50, 00159 Roma; tel. (06) 43631; fax (06) 43634090; e-mail info@autostrade.it; internet www.autostrade.it; maintenance and management of motorway network; Pres. Dott. FABIO CERCHIAAI; CEO GIOVANNI CASTELLUCCI.

SHIPPING

In 2013 the Italian flag registered fleet (2,221 vessels) had a total displacement of 18.5m. grt, including 294 tankers, 220 passenger ships and 77 general cargo ships.

Genova
(Genoa)

Costa Crociere, SpA: Piazza Piccapietra 48, 16121 Genova; tel. (010) 54831; fax (010) 5483290; e-mail corporate@costa.it; internet www.costacrociere.it; f. 1854; passenger and cargo service; Mediterranean, Northern Europe, Central and South America; Caribbean cruises; Chair. PIER LUIGI FOSCHI; CEO MICHAEL THAMM.

Fratelli Cosulich, SpA: Ponte Morosini 41, 16126 Genova; tel. (010) 27151; fax (010) 2715390; e-mail info@cosulich.it; internet www.cosulich.it; f. 1854; shipowners and shipping agents; domestic network and cargo to Near East, Red Sea, Hong Kong, Singapore, New York and Zürich; office network in main ports worldwide; Man. Dir AUGUSTO COSULICH.

Grandi Navi Veloci SpA: Via Fieschi 17, 16121 Genova; tel. (010) 55091; fax (010) 5509333; internet www.gnv.it; f. 1991; passenger, cargo, containers and tramp to Europe; Pres. ROBERTO MARTINOLI; Dir-Gen. ARIODANTE VALERI.

Ignazio Messina & C., SpA: Via G. d'Annunzio 91, 16121 Genova; tel. (010) 53961; fax (010) 5396264; e-mail info@messinaline.it; internet www.messinaline.it; services to Arabian Gulf, India, Pakistan, Nigeria, North, East, South and West Africa, Libya and Near East, Red Sea, Malta, Europe; Chair. GIANFRANCO MESSINA.

Napoli
(Naples)

Tirrenia di Navigazione, SpA: Palazzo Sirignano, Rione Sirignano 2, 80121 Napoli; tel. (081) 7201111; fax (081) 7201441; internet www.tirrenia.it; f. 1963; ferry services to Sardinia, Sicily, North Africa; part of Gruppo Tirrenia di Navigazione.

Palermo

Grimaldi Compagnia di Navigazione: Via Emerico Amari 8, Palermo; internet www.grimaldi.napoli.it; cargo; Italy to North Europe, South, Central, North America, West Africa; Chair. GIANLUCA GRIMALDI; Man. Dirs EMANUELE GRIMALDI, DIEGO PACELLA.

Sicilia Regionale Marittima, SpA (SIREMAR): Calata Marinai d'Italia, Porto di Palermo, 90139 Palermo; tel. (091) 7493111; fax (091) 7493366; e-mail info@siremar.it; internet www.siremar.it; f. 1976; owned by Gruppo Tirrenia di Navigazione; ferry services; Pres. Dott. GIUSEPPE RAVERA; Man. Dir FRANCO PERASSO.

Roma
(Rome)

Fratelli D'Amico Armatori, SpA: Via Liguria 36, 00187 Roma; tel. (06) 46711; fax (06) 4871914; e-mail damiship@damicofratelli.it; internet www.damicofratelli.it; dry cargo and tankers; Pres. GIUSEPPE D'AMICO; Gen. Man. CARLO CAMELI.

Trieste

Italia Marittima, SpA: Palazzo della Marineria, Passeggio S. Andrea 4, 34123 Trieste; tel. (040) 3180111; fax (040) 3180388; e-mail headoffice@ts.lloydtriestino.it; internet www.lloydtriestino.it; f. 1836; cargo services by container to South Africa, Australasia and Far East, plus trans-Pacific and -Atlantic services; privatized 1998; renamed as above in 2006; Pres. PIER LUIGI MANESCHI; Vice-Pres. and Man. Dir REN-GUNG SHYU; Dir-Gen. MAURIZIO SALCE.

Navigazione Montanari, SpA: Via S. Ceccarini 36, 61032 Fano; tel. (0721) 8801; fax (0721) 830430; e-mail info@navmont.com; internet www.navmont.com; f. 1889; cargo services to Mediterranean, Northern Europe, USA and Far East.

Venezia
(Venice)

Adriatica di Navigazione, SpA: Zattere 1411, CP 705, 30123 Venezia; tel. (041) 781861; fax (041) 781818; e-mail adrnav@interbusiness.it; internet www.adriatica.it; f. 1937; owned by Gruppo Tirrenia di Navigazione; passenger services from Italy, Albania, Croatia and Montenegro; Pres. GIORGIO GROSSO; Man. Dir ANTONIO CACUCCI.

Shipping Association

Confederazione Italiana Armatori (CONFITARMA): Piazza SS. Apostoli 66, 00187 Roma; tel. (06) 674811; fax (06) 69783730; e-mail confitarma@confitarma.it; internet www.confitarma.it; f. 1901; shipowners' asscn; Pres. PAOLO D'AMICO; Dir-Gen. GENNARO FIORE; 230 mems.

CIVIL AVIATION

In 2010 there were 40 commercial airports in Italy.

Civil Aviation Authority

Ente Nazionale per l'Aviazione Civile (ENAC) (Italian Civil Aviation Authority): Viale del Castro Pretorio 118, 00185 Roma; tel. (06) 445961; fax (06) 44596493; e-mail comunicazione@enac.gov.it; internet www.enac.gov.it; f. 1997; Pres. VITO RIGGIO; Dir-Gen. ALESSIO QUARANTA.

Airlines

Air Dolomiti: Via Paolo Bembo 70, 37062 Frazione di Dossobuono; tel. (045) 8605211; fax (045) 8605229; e-mail customer-relations@airdolomiti.it; internet www.airdolomiti.it; f. 1989; operates domestic flights and services between Italy and Austria, France and Germany; subsidiary of Deutsche Lufthansa AG; Pres. and CEO MICHAEL KRAUS.

Air One: Piazza Almerico da Schio, Palazzo RPU, 00054 Fiumicino; internet www.flyairone.it; f. 1983 as Aliadriatica; present name adopted 1995; acquired by Compagnia Aerea Italiana (CAI) 2009 and merged with Alitalia; Air One brand relaunched as a low-cost carrier 2010; domestic and international flights to destinations in Europe and North Africa.

Alitalia—Compagnia Aerea Italiana, SpA: Piazza Almerico da Schio, Palazzo RPU, 00054 Fiumicino; tel. (06) 65631; fax (06) 7093065; e-mail ufficio.stampa@alitalia.it; internet www.alitalia.com; f. 2008 as successor to the defunct, state-owned Alitalia, SpA (f. 1946); majority shareholding owned by Compagnia Aerea Italiana (CAI); 25% stake owned by Air France-KLM; merged with Air One 2009; domestic and international services throughout Europe and to Africa, North and South America, the Middle East, the Far East and Australia; Chair. ROBERTO COLANINNO; CEO GABRIELE DEL TORCHIO.

Livingston, SpA: Via Giovanni XXIII 206, 21010 Cardano al Campo; tel. (331) 267321; fax (331) 267421; e-mail info@lauda.it; internet www.lauda.it; f. 2003; acquired routes and fleet of Lauda Air Italia in 2005; operates charter and scheduled flights to destinations worldwide; owned by 4 Fly, SpA; Chair. GORDON MCDOUGALL; CEO PELLEGRINO D'AQUINO.

Meridiana Fly, SpA: Aeroporto Costa Smerelda, Olbia, 07026 Sardinia; tel. (0789) 52600; fax (0789) 645177; e-mail info.olbia@meridiana.it; internet www.meridiana.it; f. 1963 as Alisarda, renamed 2010 following merger with Eurofly; scheduled and charter services throughout Italy and Europe, and on a limited number of intercontinental services; Chair. MARCO RIGOTTI; CEO ROBERTO SCARAMELLA.

Tourism

A great number of tourists are attracted to Italy by its Alpine and Mediterranean scenery, sunny climate, Roman archaeological remains, medieval and Baroque churches, Renaissance towns and palaces, paintings and sculpture and famous opera houses. Each of the 95 provinces has a Board of Tourism; there are also about 300 Aziende Autonome di Cura, Soggiorno e Turismo, with information about tourist accommodation and health treatment, and about 2,000 Pro Loco Associations concerned with local amenities. In 2011 there were 47 UNESCO World Heritage Sites in Italy. There were some 48.7m. tourist arrivals in Italy in 2012; tourism receipts totalled a provisional US $41,185m. in that year.

Dipartimento per lo Sviluppo e la Competitività del Turismo: Via della Ferratella in Laterano 51, 00184 Roma; tel. (06) 455325955; fax (06) 70497131; e-mail cittadino@governo.it; part of the Office of the Prime Minister; Head of Dept CATERINA CITTADINO.

Ente Nazionale Italiano per il Turismo (ENIT) (Italian State Tourist Board): Via Marghera 2, 00185 Roma; tel. (06) 49711; fax (06) 4463379; e-mail sedecentrale@enit.it; internet www.enit.it; f. 1919; Chair. PIER LUIGI CELLI; Dir-Gen. ANDREA BABBI.

Defence

Italy has been a member of the North Atlantic Treaty Organization (NATO) since 1949. As assessed at November 2013, it maintained armed forces totalling 176,000, comprising an army of 103,100, a navy of 31,000 and an air force of 41,900. There were also reserves of 18,300 and paramilitary forces numbering 183,500 (including 104,200 military police—Carabinieri). Conscription was phased out by December 2004, under legislation that was approved in 2000 and which also provided for the recruitment of women soldiers. In November 2004 the European Union (EU) ministers responsible for defence agreed to create a number of 'battlegroups' (each comprising about 1,500 men), which could be deployed at short notice to crisis areas around the world. The EU battlegroups, two of which were to be ready for deployment at any one time, following a rotational schedule, reached full operational capacity from 1 January 2007.

Defence Expenditure: Budget estimated at €17,900m. in 2014.

General Chief of Defence Staff: Adm. LUIGI BINELLI MANTELLI.

Army Chief of Staff: Gen. CLAUDIO GRAZIANO.

Navy Chief of Staff: Adm. GIUSEPPE DE GIORI.

Air Force Chief of Staff: Gen. PASQUALE PREZIOSA.

Chief Commander of the Carabinieri: Lt-Gen. LEONARDO GALLITELLI.

Education

Compulsory education is free for students between the ages of six and 16 years, comprising six years of primary education, four years of lower secondary education and two years of higher secondary education. Pre-primary education is free and non-compulsory for pupils between the ages of three and six years. The curricula of all Italian schools are standardized by the Ministry of Education, Universities and Research. After primary school (scuola primaria), for children aged six to 11 years, the pupil enters the first level of secondary school (scuola media inferiore). An examination at the end of three years leads to a lower secondary school certificate (Diploma di Licenza della Scuola Media), which gives access to higher secondary school (scuola media superiore), of which only the first year is compulsory. Pupils wishing to enter a classical lycée (liceo classico) must also pass an examination in Latin.

Higher secondary education is provided by classical, artistic, linguistic and scientific lycées, training schools for elementary teachers and technical and vocational institutes (industrial, commercial, nautical, etc.). After five years at a lycée, the student sits an examination for the higher secondary school certificate (Diploma di Esame di Stato), which allows automatic entry into any university or non-university institute of higher education. Special four-year courses are provided at the teachers' training schools and the diploma obtained permits entry to a special university faculty of education, the magistero, and a number of other faculties. The technical institutes provide practical courses that prepare students for a specialized university faculty.

In 2011/12 enrolment at primary schools included 97% of all children in the relevant age-group, while the comparable ratio for secondary enrolment was 92%.

In 2006/07 there were 1.8m. undergraduate students in higher education in Italy; the largest universities were La Sapienza in Rome, with around 170,000 students, and Bologna, with more than 100,000 students. In 2007/08 there were 74 institutes of higher education. Following the introduction of university reforms, courses last for a three-year cycle, followed by a two-year specialized cycle. Study allowances are awarded to students according to their means and merit; however, most parents pay fees. In 2010 government expenditure on education was €69,321m. In 2012 expenditure on education was equivalent to 3.9% of gross domestic product.

JAMAICA

Introductory Survey

LOCATION, CLIMATE, LANGUAGE, RELIGION, FLAG, CAPITAL

Jamaica is the third largest island in the Caribbean Sea, lying 145 km (90 miles) to the south of Cuba and 160 km (100 miles) to the south-west of Haiti. The climate varies with altitude, being tropical at sea-level and temperate in the mountain areas. The average annual temperature is 27°C (80°F) and mean annual rainfall is 198 cm (78 ins). The official language is English, although a local patois is widely spoken. The majority of the population belong to Christian denominations, the Church of God being the most numerous. The national flag (proportions 1 by 2) consists of a diagonal yellow cross on a background of black (hoist and fly) and green (above and below). The capital is Kingston.

CONTEMPORARY POLITICAL HISTORY

Historical Context

Jamaica, a British colony from 1655, was granted internal self-government in 1959, and full independence, within the Commonwealth, was achieved on 6 August 1962. Jamaica formed part of the West Indies Federation between 1958 and 1961, when it seceded, following a referendum. The Federation was dissolved in 1962. The two dominant political figures after the Second World War were Sir Alexander Bustamante, leader of the Jamaica Labour Party (JLP), who retired as Prime Minister in 1967, and Norman Manley, a former Premier and leader of the People's National Party (PNP), who died in 1969. The JLP won the elections of 1962 and 1967 but, under the premiership of Hugh Shearer, it lost the 1972 elections to the PNP, led by Michael Manley, the son of Norman. Manley advocated democratic socialism and his Government put great emphasis on social reform and economic independence.

Domestic Political Affairs

The early 1970s were marked by escalating violence and crime, with gang warfare rife in the deprived areas of Kingston. More than 160 people were killed in the first half of 1976, and in June the Government declared a state of emergency. Despite the unrest, high unemployment and severe economic stagnation, the PNP was returned to power in December with an increased majority. By January 1979, however, there was again widespread political unrest, and violent demonstrations signalled growing discontent with the Manley administration. In 1980, in the context of a worsening economic crisis, Manley rejected the stipulation of the IMF, as a condition of its making further loans to Jamaica, that economic austerity measures be undertaken. He called a general election to seek support for his economic policies and his decision to end dependence on the IMF. The electoral campaign was one of the most violent in Jamaica's history. In the October election the JLP won 51 of the 60 seats in the House of Representatives. Edward Seaga, the leader of the JLP, became Prime Minister; he supported closer political and economic links with the USA and the promotion of free enterprise. Negotiations on IMF assistance were resumed.

In November 1983 Seaga announced that an election would take place in mid-December. Only four days were allowed for the nomination of candidates, and the PNP refused to participate, declaring the elections void. The JLP, opposed in only six constituencies (by independent candidates), won all 60 seats in the House of Representatives and formed a one-party legislature.

Devaluations of the Jamaican dollar and the withdrawal of food subsidies provoked demonstrations and sporadic violence in 1984. Despite government attempts to offset the effects of these economic austerity measures, imposed at the instigation of the IMF, unemployment, together with illicit trading in drugs, contributed to a rise in the incidence of crime and violence, especially in Kingston. In 1985 another increase in fuel prices precipitated further violent demonstrations in the capital and industrial unrest.

After a brief, and relatively peaceful, campaign, a general election took place in February 1989, in which the PNP secured an absolute majority of legislative seats. Manley, who had developed a more moderate image during his years in opposition, again became Prime Minister. The Government conceded the necessity for a devaluation of the Jamaican dollar in October. The two main parties achieved a limited consensus on the pursuit of an economic policy of austerity, despite its unpopularity and there was also agreement that further action should be taken against the drugs trade.

Patterson in power

In December 1991 controversy surrounding the waiving of taxes worth some US $30m. owed to Jamaica by an international company, Shell, resulted in the resignation of Horace Clarke, the Minister of Mining and Energy, and Percival J. Patterson, the Deputy Prime Minister, amid opposition allegations of corruption. In March 1992 Manley resigned. Patterson was appointed Prime Minister at the end of the month.

At a general election in March 1993 Patterson's PNP secured 52 of the 60 seats in the House of Representatives. The scale of the PNP victory was widely attributed to the success of Patterson's populist overtures to the island's majority population of African origin, and a perceived shift in political influence away from the capital, traditionally a power base of the JLP. In April Patterson announced plans to reform and modernize the electoral system. However, allegations of electoral malpractice and demands by the JLP for an official inquiry into suspected procedural abuses were rejected by the PNP. By February 1994 attempts at electoral reform had been undermined by the resignation of the Chairman of the Electoral Advisory Committee (EAC), and by the failure of the EAC to appoint a new Director of Elections. Demands for constitutional and electoral reform continued. An electronic voter registration system was installed in 1996 and new electoral rolls were finally completed in late 1997.

A general election was held in December 1997, at which the PNP won a majority of seats in the House of Representatives. Patterson, who was subsequently sworn in again as Prime Minister, announced plans for Jamaica to become a republic within five years.

In 1998 and 1999 many public protests against a deepening economic crisis and police actions resulted in several riots. There was further unrest in April 1999 following the announcement of a proposed significant increase in the price of diesel. The JLP and National Democratic Movement (formed in 1995 by Bruce Golding), while initially helping to organize the protests, dissociated themselves from the subsequent violence. In July the authorities announced that army personnel were to be deployed on patrols in greater Kingston in an attempt to combat the high incidence of crime, the majority of which was reportedly related to drugs-trafficking. In October the British Government announced that it would grant £2.9m. in assistance towards the reform and modernization of the Jamaican police force. In the same month an investigation was begun into widespread allegations of police corruption.

Confrontations between the police and various sectors of the community continued in 2001. The human rights organization Amnesty International claimed that the Jamaican police force had one of the highest records for the execution of its own citizens. In 2000 the police had shot dead 140 suspected criminals. Furthermore, in July conflict broke out between police and rival PNP and JLP factions in Kingston. Following three days of fighting, in which 25 people were reported to have been killed, units of the Jamaica Defence Force were deployed to restore order.

A Commission of Inquiry into the July disturbances opened in September 2001, but the JLP refused to co-operate with the investigation. Meanwhile, sporadic outbreaks of violence in Kingston continued: in October the Government was forced to deploy army, air and coastguard units to suppress unrest. In January 2002 seven people were shot dead by as many as 30 gunmen in a suburb known to be a traditional stronghold of the PNP, leading to accusations that the killings were politically motivated. In July the Commission of Inquiry cleared the security forces of the use of excessive brutality.

The PNP's fourth successive term

In a general election held in October 1992, the PNP was re-elected for a fourth consecutive term, albeit with a reduced majority. At his inauguration, Patterson became the first Jamaican Prime Minister to swear allegiance to the people and Constitution of Jamaica, rather than to the British monarch, in accordance with new legislation introduced in August. His new Cabinet retained most of the members of the previous administration.

In December 2002 the armed forces and police began a joint offensive on crime. The Government also revived a previously debated proposal to extend capital punishment to drugs-related crimes and to replace the Privy Council in London, United Kingdom, with a Caribbean Court of Justice (CCJ, see below) as the final court of appeal, thereby removing the Privy Council's ability to commute death sentences to life imprisonment. More than 1,000 murders were reported in 2002, and extended use of capital punishment gained increasing popular support. However, the Crime Management Unit (CMU), established in 2000, had been repeatedly criticized for its excessive use of force. In 2003 the CMU was disbanded and replaced by an Organised Crime Investigation Division. In October the police force was further criticized after two elderly men were accidentally shot during a confrontation between police and an armed gang. The killings prompted a protest, involving some 2,000 people, against alleged police and army tactics. In the same month a report was published by the UN Special Rapporteur, which condemned the Government and state security forces for the misuse of force and for failing properly to investigate those accused of extra-judicial executions. In mid-2004 the Prime Minister announced the launch of a National Investigative Authority to pursue allegations against the police. In 2004 the number of murders reached a record 1,445, largely attributed to gang-related conflicts.

In July 2004 the Privy Council abolished Jamaica's mandatory death sentence for convicted murderers. Legislative amendments to this effect were approved by the Senate in November. However, at the same time, amendments were also passed increasing the minimum period a convicted murderer must serve before being granted parole from seven to 20 years. In October the armed forces and the police launched Operation Kingfish, an intelligence-based task force intended to reduce the ever-rising crime rate. The initiative was particularly targeted at dismantling the estimated 13 major criminal networks on the island, which were thought to be responsible for much of the crime. By October 2007 more than 2,000 operations had been mounted, leading to 567 arrests.

In February 2006 Patterson was succeeded as leader of the PNP by Portia Simpson Miller. Upon assuming office as Prime Minister in the following month, Simpson Miller pledged to eradicate violent crime, protect human rights and create employment.

The Senate commenced discussions in February 2007 on the proposed Proceeds of Crime Act, approved by the House of Representatives in the previous month. Reducing the rates of violent and drugs-related crime had become an increasingly urgent matter of the Government. The opposition had expressed concerns that provisions contained within the new Act—awarding courts greater power to order the surrender of assets and property in the absence of a criminal conviction—might impinge upon citizens' fundamental rights.

In January 2007 the Attorney-General, Arnold J. Nicholson, marked the bicentenary of the abolition of the trans-Atlantic slave trade by proposing several constitutional reforms that would transform Jamaica into a republic, with a Jamaican President replacing the British monarch as Head of State. This post would not be vested with legislative or executive powers, but would be designated an independent arbiter of selected state appointments. Furthermore, a new Charter of Rights, the subject of extensive deliberations, was to be instituted, and all constitutional amendments would be ratified through an act of the Jamaican legislature, subject to approval in a plebiscite.

Meanwhile, in November 2006 the Government commissioned a Jamaican Justice System Reform Task Force to conduct a comprehensive review of the country's judicial system, with the assistance of representatives from the Canadian Bar Association. The final report was presented in May 2007. The main problems identified were delays in the justice system, poor infrastructure, underfunding, and a lack of consistency in the enforcement of laws.

The return of the JLP

The general election of 2007, originally scheduled for 27 August, was postponed until 3 September owing to the widespread disruption caused by Hurricane Dean, in which three people were killed and much of the country's infrastructure damaged, leading Simpson Miller to impose a state of emergency. The JLP won a narrow victory, securing 32 legislative seats, while the PNP won the remaining 28 seats. Some 60.5% of the registered electorate participated in the ballot. According to reports, at least 17 people were killed in political violence during the election campaign, in which the JLP focused on the high levels of crime in the country and the large fiscal deficit. The JLP leader, Bruce Golding (who had rejoined the party in 2001), was sworn in as Prime Minister on 11 September. Included in the new Cabinet was Audley Shaw, who was appointed Minister of Finance and the Public Service, and Dorothy Lightbourne, who became the country's first female Attorney-General.

Golding stated that anti-corruption measures and justice system reform would be priorities of the new Government. In November 2007 the Cabinet approved the drafting of legislation to create an Office of the Special Prosecutor, which would investigate high-level acts of corruption in the public and private sectors, and an independent commission to examine allegations of excessive use of force and of abuse by members of the security forces. (By June 2013 more than 400 members of the police force had been dismissed.) Lightbourne announced in February 2008 that the recommendations of the Jamaican Justice System Reform Task Force would be incorporated into a national development plan, Vision 2030, which would include the building of new courthouses and the creation of a court agency service, in which the Chief Justice would be responsible for the administration of the courts.

The Government, struggling with a liquidity crisis, imposed an unpopular fuel tax in April 2009, precipitating protests throughout the island. Further taxes were announced in December, including a new levy on staple food items, which resulted in a more vociferous response from the opposition and the public, forcing the Government to rescind the food duty and replace it with a luxury goods tax and an increase in income tax for high earners.

A series of legal challenges launched by the PNP during 2008–11 against JLP members of Parliament accused of holding dual citizenship, which had in some cases led to deputies losing their seats and by-elections being staged, prompted demands for constitutional reform. The Constitution prohibited Jamaican nationals who also possessed citizenship of a non-Commonwealth country from being elected to the legislature, a stipulation that Golding, in January 2011, described as 'an absurdity'. In March Parliament approved the introduction of the long-awaited Charter of Rights, which would protect the rights and freedoms of Jamaicans; the constitutional amendment was approved by the Governor-General in April.

In May 2011 the Minister of Energy and Mining, James Robertson, resigned. His departure from the Cabinet came after his visa was revoked by the USA following allegations of corrupt practices made by a Jamaican national seeking asylum in the USA. At the end of the following month the Prime Minister executed a reallocation of cabinet portfolios. Dorothy Lightbourne was among those dismissed from Government. Lightbourne had been criticized over her handling of the Dudus affair in 2010 (see below). Among the proposals made by the Commission of Inquiry into the affair was the separation of the posts of justice minister and the Attorney-General. To this end, Delroy Chuck, hitherto Speaker of the House of Representatives, was appointed Minister of Justice, while the Attorney-General post remained vacant. Clive Mullings was given the energy and mining portfolio.

Prime Minister Golding announced his intention in late September 2011 to stand down as premier and leader of the JLP by November. He cited the criticism he had received over his involvement in the Dudus affair as one of the main reasons for his resignation. An election for his successor was scheduled to be held at the JLP's party conference in November; however, by mid-October Andrew Holness, the Minister of Education, had emerged as the clear frontrunner. Following Golding's formal resignation as head of government on 23 October, Holness was installed as his successor. His new Cabinet, installed two days later, contained many members of the previous administration; Holness indicated he would make more wide-ranging changes once he had secured a popular mandate to govern. Although elections were not constitutionally due until December 2012,

Holness indicated that a ballot would be held by the end of the year. The PNP criticized the handover of power, insisting that a general election should have been called as soon as Golding announced his intention to resign.

Violent crime

The high level of violent crime continued to be a significant matter of concern. In November 2008 the House of Representatives voted in favour of retaining the death penalty, a decision later approved by the Senate, while in mid-2009 the Government announced plans to enhance the professionalism and accountability of the police force. The Golding administration also revealed that the judicial system would be reformed and additional judges would be appointed to expedite the trials of violent criminals. The Commissioner of Police, Hardley Lewin, resigned in November, after the Prime Minister indicated that he had 'lost confidence' in him. Police patrols were expanded in 2010, and a programme to address corruption was introduced in January, with 149 officers dismissed throughout the year as a result. In June legislative approval was secured for a series of security measures, which included the extension of certain police powers, new restrictions on bail and parole, and additional controls on firearms. The Government's anti-crime strategy appeared to be having a positive impact: the number of murders declined from 1,683 in 2009 to 1,124 in 2011, and to 1,087 in 2012, a nine-year low. Despite this, the murder rate remained the highest in the Caribbean and the third highest worldwide (after El Salvador and Honduras). The new PNP Government (see below) adopted further anti-crime initiatives in 2012, which, *inter alia*, aimed to reduce the average murder rate from three per day to less than one by 2017. However, the murder rate rose in 2013, to some 1,200 in total. The US Government's International Narcotics Control Strategy Report in 2014 claimed that Jamaica was making 'slow but steady' progress in combating drugs-trafficking, corruption and organized crime. In December 2013 the Government announced its new crime prevention strategy, the aim of which was to engage local communities in crime prevention programmes. In March 2014 the Criminal Justice Bill was enacted, which provided for the disruption and suppression of criminal organizations. In the same month the Government approved plans to merge the Jamaica Constabulary Force and the Island Special Constabulary Force in order to improve crime rates.

The Dudus affair

In 2009 the USA appealed for the extradition of Christopher 'Dudus' Coke, the alleged head of a major criminal gang operating from Tivoli Gardens (a slum area of Kingston), accusing him of drugs-smuggling and arms-trading. The Government initially rejected this petition on the grounds that evidence against Coke had been acquired through illegal wire-tapping. However, it was suspected that Coke was a political ally of Prime Minister Golding (Coke had allegedly mobilized the residents of Tivoli Gardens—Golding's constituency—to vote for the JLP during elections). Evidence to support this theory emerged in March 2010, when it was revealed that Golding apparently had procured the services of a law firm in the USA to lobby the US Administration to abandon its extradition request. Under domestic and US pressure, the Jamaican authorities finally issued a warrant for the arrest of Coke in May. However, this decision provoked Coke's supporters to erect barricades in Tivoli Gardens, and several police stations in the capital were attacked, prompting Golding to declare a state of emergency in the Kingston area on 23 May (subsequently extended for a further month in late June). Military troops were deployed to bolster the police operation to capture Coke, which involved some 2,000 members of the security forces. Violent clashes ensued in Tivoli Gardens, resulting in approximately 4,000 arrests and the deaths of 76 people, the vast majority of whom were civilians. On 1 June, by a margin of just two votes, Golding's Government survived a vote of no confidence in the House of Representatives, proposed by the PNP in protest against the administration's perceived mishandling of the affair. Finally, on 22 June Coke surrendered to the authorities; he was extradited to the USA on 24 June. A Commission of Inquiry concluded in June 2011 that the Prime Minister had acted 'inappropriately', but not 'criminally', in his involvement in the extradition request. It was also critical of the JLP's behaviour in the affair, but stopped short of accusing any of those involved of misconduct, a decision that was condemned by the PNP. Coke was sentenced to 23 years' imprisonment in June 2012. In May 2013, following the release of an interim report into the conduct of security forces during the state of emergency, the Government agreed to appoint a further Commission of Inquiry to investigate alleged human rights abuses.

Recent developments: the PNP in power

As expected, a general election was held on 29 December 2011. The PNP won an overwhelming victory, gaining 42 of the 63 seats in the House of Representatives. The JLP's legislative representation was reduced to 21 seats. The resounding defeat of the JLP was largely attributed to continuing public dissatisfaction with the Government's handling of the Dudus extradition. The PNP leader, Portia Simpson Miller, was sworn into office on 5 January 2012. Her Cabinet contained a mixture of experience and youth. Arnold J. Nicholson was appointed Minister of Foreign Affairs and Foreign Trade, while responsibility for finance and planning was given to Peter Phillips, who had been in charge of the PNP's successful electoral campaign. Another senior PNP figure, Peter Bunting, was designated Minister of National Security and thus assumed responsibility for addressing the country's spiralling violent crime rate. The new Government made clear its intention to adopt the Caribbean Court of Justice (CCJ, see Regional Relations) as its final appellate court in place of the Privy Council. In a further indication of the administration's desire to loosen ties with the United Kingdom, one of Simpson Miller's first announcements in office was to declare her intention to replace the Queen as Head of State with an elected President.

However, the new Government's most pressing concern on taking office was the resumption of negotiations with the IMF towards a new funding facility. An earlier stand-by arrangement had been halted in early 2011 after the previous administration had failed to keep its promises on fiscal austerity (see Economic Affairs). The suspension of disbursements also meant Jamaica was unable to access much-needed aid from other multilateral agencies. Phillips, in February 2012, announced a J $21,600m. reduction in the budget. As well as the lack of international funding, Phillips blamed the cut on the JLP administration's decision to increase public sector wages by 7% in 2011, contrary to IMF recommendations. However, in the following month, the House of Representatives approved an $11,200m. increase in budgetary expenditure. In September it was announced that some 3,000 public sector workers were to be made redundant; a further 4,000 posts were to be cut in 2013–14.

Jamaica celebrated 50 years of independence from the United Kingdom in August 2012. The annual Throne Speech, delivered by the Governor-General on 10 May, included the proposal that Jamaica become a republic. Simpson Miller reiterated that her Government would also advance moves to end the jurisdiction of the Privy Council, in consultation with the opposition. Although the JLP supported the proposal, the party insisted that both matters should be put to a referendum. In November Minister of Justice Mark Golding reiterated that support by a two-thirds' majority in both houses of Parliament would be sufficient for the CCJ proposal to become law. While the PNP enjoyed such a majority in the House of Representatives, it could only count of the support of 13 of the 21 senators. Debate on the CCJ proposal began in December 2013.

On 1 May 2013 the IMF approved a new four-year Extended Fund Facility, which would result in a disbursement to Jamaica of US $510m. from both the World Bank and the Inter-American Development Bank, in return for the Government's commitment to a series of fiscal reforms (see Economic Affairs). In September former finance minister Audley Shaw announced that he would challenge Andrew Holness as leader of the JLP, citing disunity within the party; at the election in November, however, Holness comfortably retained his leadership. In September Richard Azan, a Minister of State in the Ministry of Transport, Works and Housing resigned following a report by the Contractor-General of alleged improprieties in the awarding of a government construction contract. The House of Representatives passed a new Defamation Act in early November, which, in addition to abolishing criminal libel, was to end the distinction between libel and slander and establish 'defamation' as a cause of action.

Foreign Affairs

Regional relations

In 1998 Jamaica withdrew from a UN treaty that allowed prisoners sentenced to death to appeal for a review by the UN Commission on Human Rights; later that year it also withdrew from the Inter-American Court of Human Rights (see p. 396) of the Organization of American States. In 2001 Jamaica was one of

11 Caribbean nations to establish a CCJ, to be based in Trinidad and Tobago. The Court was to replace the Privy Council in the United Kingdom as the final court of appeal, and would allow for the executions of convicted criminals. (The Privy Council generally commuted death sentences to life imprisonment on appeal.) Despite opposition from the JLP and from the Jamaica Bar Association, in 2004 Parliament approved legislation replacing the Privy Council with the CCJ. Opposition groupings appealed to the Privy Council itself that the legislation should be annulled because it had been passed without the approval of the electorate in a referendum. In February 2005 the Privy Council upheld the appeal. In total, the Privy Council annulled three such bills to confer trading and appellate jurisdiction on to the CCJ. Nevertheless, in April the House of Representatives ratified membership of the CCJ, but only as a court of original jurisdiction on trade matters.

In 2005 Jamaica became one of 13 Caribbean nations to sign the Petrocaribe accord, under which the country would be allowed to purchase petroleum from Venezuela at reduced prices. In September 2013 Jamaica received a commitment from Venezuela not to change the terms of the accord at least until the expiry of its four-year Extended Fund Facility with the IMF in 2017. Jamaica made its first shipment of clinker under the trade compensation mechanism option of the accord in December 2013.

Other external relations

Relations between Jamaica and the USA have been hampered by persistent demands by the USA for the eradication of Jamaica's marijuana crop and deteriorated further in 2010 after the JLP Government appeared to attempt to prevent the extradition to the USA of alleged drugs-trafficker Christopher 'Dudus' Coke (see above). The cancellation by US authorities of the Minister of Energy and Mining's visa in May 2011 placed further strain on bilateral links.

Jamaica has enjoyed good diplomatic relations with the People's Republic of China since 1972, which have been strengthened by numerous trade and investment agreements. In April 2013 it was announced that the China Harbour Engineering Company (CHEC) was to invest in the development of a port in Jamaica comprising transshipment facilities, a manufacturing zone and an electricity generation plant. Although the exact location of the terminal had yet to be decided, in September CHEC indicated that its preferred option was the Goat Islands; this was contingent, however, on the results of an environmental impact study of the area. The terms of an initial framework agreement for the investment, worth some US $2,000m., were passed in the House of Representatives in February 2014. In August 2013, during a visit to China by Simpson Miller, a $16m. grant was pledged for development projects in Jamaica, as well as a loan of $300m. to the country's Major Infrastructure Development Programme. During a subsequent address to the House of Representative, however, Simpson Miller cautioned those inclined to question China's motives in investing such amounts in Jamaica. In February 2014 it was announced that Chinese nationals would no longer require a visa to visit Jamaica for up to 30 days as tourists.

CONSTITUTION AND GOVERNMENT

The Constitution came into force at Jamaica's independence in August 1962. The Head of State is the British monarch, who is represented locally by the Governor-General, appointed on the recommendation of the Prime Minister in consultation with the Leader of the Opposition. The Governor-General acts, in almost all matters, on the advice of the Cabinet.

Legislative power is vested in the bicameral Parliament: the Senate, with 21 appointed members, and the House of Representatives, with 63 elected members. Thirteen members of the Senate are appointed by the Governor-General on the advice of the Prime Minister and eight on the advice of the Leader of the Opposition. Members of the House are elected by universal adult suffrage for five years (subject to dissolution). Executive power lies with the Cabinet. The Prime Minister is appointed from the House of Representatives by the Governor-General, and is the leader of the party that holds the majority of seats in the House of Representatives. The Cabinet is responsible to Parliament. Jamaica is divided into 13 parishes.

REGIONAL AND INTERNATIONAL CO-OPERATION

Jamaica is a founding member of the Caribbean Community and Common Market (CARICOM, see p. 223) and of the Inter-American Development Bank (IDB, see p. 331). Jamaica was also one of the six founder members of CARICOM's Caribbean Single Market and Economy (CSME), which was inaugurated on 1 January 2006. The CSME is intended to facilitate the free movement of goods, services and labour throughout the CARICOM region. The country is a member of the Association of Caribbean States (see p. 449), and of the Community of Latin American and Caribbean States (see p. 464), which was formally inaugurated in December 2011.

Jamaica became a member of the UN upon independence in 1962. The country acceded to the World Trade Organization (see p. 434) in 1995. Jamaica joined the Commonwealth (see p. 236) upon independence. Jamaica is a signatory of the Cotonou Agreement (see p. 324) with the European Union (see p. 273).

ECONOMIC AFFAIRS

In 2012, according to estimates by the World Bank, Jamaica's gross national income (GNI), measured at average 2010–12 prices, was US $13,929m., equivalent to US $5,140 per head. During 2003–12, it was estimated, the population increased at an average rate of 0.4% per year, while gross domestic product (GDP) per head increased at an average annual rate of 0.4% during 2002–11. According to official figures, overall GDP decreased, in real terms, at an average annual rate of 0.1% in 2007–12; the economy expanded by 1.7% in 2011, before contracting by 0.5% in 2012.

Agriculture (including forestry and fishing) contributed 6.4% of GDP in 2012 and engaged 18.3% of the economically active population in mid-2013. The principal cash crops are sugar cane (sugar accounted for an estimated 5.5% of total export earnings in 2012), coffee, citrus fruit, pimento and cocoa. Agricultural GDP increased at an annual average rate of 0.9% in 2003–12; the sector's GDP declined by 10.3% in 2011 and by 2.5% in 2012.

Industry (including mining, manufacturing, public utilities and construction) contributed 20.0% of GDP in 2012 and engaged 15.1% of the economically active population in mid-2013. Industrial GDP decreased at an average rate of 1.6% during 2003–12; the sector increased by 2.9% in 2011, but declined by 3.2% in 2012.

Mining and quarrying contributed an estimated 1.3% of GDP in 2012, and engaged only 0.5% of the active labour force in mid-2013. Mining is the principal productive sector of the economy, and in 2012 bauxite and its derivative, alumina (aluminium oxide), accounted for an estimated 37.3% of total export earnings. Bauxite, of which Jamaica is one of the world's leading producers, is the major mineral mined, but there are also reserves of marble, gypsum, limestone, silica and clay.

Manufacturing contributed an estimated 8.8% of GDP in 2012 and engaged some 6.2% of the active labour force in mid-2013. Much of the activity in the sector is dependent upon the processing of sugar and bauxite. Manufacturing GDP decreased at an average annual rate of 1.3% during 2003–12; the sector increased by 1.8% in 2011, but decreased by 1.0% in 2012.

Construction contributed an estimated 6.9% of GDP in 2012 and engaged some 7.7% of the active labour force in mid-2013. Construction GDP decreased at an average annual rate of 0.6% during 2003–12; the sector increased by 0.8% in 2011, but declined by 4.4% in 2012.

Energy is derived almost entirely from imported petroleum (91.8% in 2011). In 2012 imports of mineral fuels and lubricants accounted for 36.2% of the total value of merchandise imports. Following delays, in October 2013 the Government accepted Energy World of Hong Kong's bid to build a 360 MW natural gas-fired plant in Old Harbour Bay by 2016; the Government planned to increase installed capacity by 480 MW to meet growing energy demands.

The services sector contributed an estimated 73.6% of GDP in 2012 and engaged some 66.6% of the active labour force in mid-2013. Tourism is the principal source of foreign exchange earnings. In 2012 it was estimated that tourism contributed (directly and indirectly) 27.4% of GDP. Visitor arrivals (excluding cruise ship passengers) stood at a provisional 2.0m. in 2012. The largest proportion of tourists is from the USA (63.3% in 2012). In addition, there were a further 1.3m. cruise ship arrivals in 2012. Tourism revenue totalled US $2,046m. in 2012. The GDP of the services sector increased at an average annual rate of 0.6% in 2003–12; the sector decreased by 0.1% in 2012.

In 2012 Jamaica recorded a visible merchandise trade deficit of US $4,158.0m., and there was a surplus of US $1,904.8m. on the current account of the balance of payments. In 2012 the principal source of imports (35.7%) was the USA. Other major suppliers were Venezuela and Trinidad and Tobago. In the same year the USA was also the principal market for exports (48.1%). Canada, Slovenia and the Netherlands were among other important purchasers. The principal exports in 2012 were crude materials, foodstuffs (including sugar and bananas), chemicals, and mineral fuels and lubricants. The principal imports in 2012 were mineral fuels and lubricants, foodstuffs, chemicals, and machinery and transport equipment.

In the financial year ending 31 March 2013 Jamaica recorded a provisional budget deficit of J $54,610.4m., equivalent to 4.1% of GDP. Jamaica's general government gross debt was $1,952,518m. in 2012, equivalent to 146.1% of GDP. Total external debt at the end of 2011 was US $14,350.0m., of which US $7,766.0m. was public and publicly guaranteed debt. In that year, the cost of servicing long-term public and publicly guaranteed debt and repayments to the IMF was equivalent to 36.5% of the value of exports of goods, services and income (excluding workers' remittances). The average annual rate of inflation was 11.2% in 2003–12; consumer prices increased by an annual average of 8.0% in 2012. Some 15.4% of the labour force were unemployed in mid-2013.

The People's National Party administration, which took office in 2012, inherited a widening current account deficit and falling export revenues, as well as declining tourism receipts. The new Government was quick to reopen negotiations with the IMF, disbursements on a US $1,270m. stand-by arrangement having been suspended in 2011 owing to the slow pace of tax and pension reform and the previous Government's failure to freeze public sector salaries. On 1 May 2013, it secured an agreement on a new $932.3m. four-year Extended Fund Facility, a deal which would also release $510m. from both the World Bank and the Inter-American Development Bank. Among the conditions of the IMF loan were a reduction in the public sector wage bill from 11% to 9% of GDP by 2016, implementation of a debt-exchange programme with creditors, and an acceleration of the privatization programme. Wide-ranging fiscal reform was also to be implemented, including the enactment of legislation that would give Parliament greater responsibility in managing the country's fiscal affairs. Trade unions warned that the measures would lead to business closures and an increase in the already high rate of unemployment; however, the Government asserted that the agreement was necessary to reduce the unsustainable debt burden and bring about much-needed economic stability. In September the credit ratings agency Standard & Poor's upgraded Jamaica's rating, citing the country's progress in stabilizing its economy. In February 2014 the IMF announced that Jamaica's economic activity had been positive and broadly on target, although there were some shortfalls in tax revenues. The Ministry of Finance in early 2014 set out fiscal prudence, a fall in energy costs, and crime reduction as the three main challenges for the country in that year. The IMF estimated GDP growth of 0.4% in 2013 and 1.2% in 2014.

PUBLIC HOLIDAYS

2015: 1 January (New Year's Day), 18 February (Ash Wednesday), 3 April (Good Friday), 6 April (Easter Monday), 25 May (for Labour Day), 1 August (Emancipation Day), 6 August (Independence Day), 19 October (National Heroes' Day), 25 December (Christmas Day), 26 December (Boxing Day).

Statistical Survey

Sources (unless otherwise stated): Statistical Institute of Jamaica, 7 Cecelio Ave, Kingston 10; tel. 926-5311; fax 926-1138; e-mail info@statinja.com; internet www.statinja.gov.jm; Jamaica Information Service, 58A Half Way Tree Rd, POB 2222, Kingston 10; tel. 926-3740; fax 926-6715; e-mail jis@jis.gov.jm; internet www.jis.gov.jm; Bank of Jamaica, Nethersole Pl., POB 621, Kingston; tel. 922-0750; fax 922-0854; e-mail info@boj.org.jm; internet www.boj.org.jm.

Area and Population

AREA, POPULATION AND DENSITY

Area (sq km)	10,991*
Population (census results)	
10 September 2001	2,607,632
5 April 2011	
Males	1,334,533
Females	1,363,450
Total	2,697,983
Population (UN estimates at mid-year)†	
2012	2,768,942
2013	2,783,890
2014	2,798,835
Density (per sq km) at mid-2014	254.6

* 4,243.6 sq miles.

† Source: UN, *World Population Prospects: The 2012 Revision.*

POPULATION BY AGE AND SEX
(UN estimates at mid–2014)

	Males	Females	Total
0–14	376,750	365,443	742,193
15–64	899,322	933,824	1,833,146
65 and over	101,973	121,523	223,496
Total	1,378,045	1,420,790	2,798,835

Source: UN, *World Population Prospects: The 2012 Revision.*

PARISHES
(population at 2011 census)

	Area (sq km)	Population	Density (per sq km)
Clarendon	1,196	245,103	204.9
Hanover	450	69,533	154.5
Kingston and St Andrew	453*	662,426	1,462.3
Manchester	830	189,797	228.7
Portland	814	81,744	100.4
St Ann	1,213	172,362	142.1
St Catherine	1,192	516,218	433.1
St Elizabeth	1,212	150,205	123.9
St James	595	183,811	308.9
St Mary	611	113,615	185.9
St Thomas	743	93,902	126.4
Trelawny	875	75,164	85.9
Westmoreland	807	144,103	178.6
Total	10,991	2,697,983	245.5

* Kingston 22 sq km, St Andrew 431 sq km.

PRINCIPAL TOWNS
(population at 2011 census)

Kingston (capital)	584,627	Montego Bay	110,115
Portmore	182,153	May Pen	61,548
Spanish Town	147,152	Mandeville	49,695

BIRTHS, MARRIAGES AND DEATHS*

	Registered live births		Registered marriages		Registered deaths	
	Number	Rate (per 1,000)	Number	Rate (per 1,000)	Number	Rate (per 1,000)
2006	43,243	16.3	18,960	7.2	23,181	8.7
2007	43,385	16.3	20,550	7.7	20,250	7.6
2008	43,112	16.1	19,966	7.5	22,152	8.3
2009	42,782	16.0	18,855	7.0	21,692	8.1
2010	40,508	15.1	21,503	8.0	20,910	7.8
2011	39,673	14.7	16,926	6.3	20,685	7.6
2012	39,348†	14.5†	16,998†	6.3†	20,175	7.5

* Data are tabulated by year of registration rather than by year of occurrence.

† Provisional.

Life expectancy (years at birth): 73.1 (males 70.6; females 75.7) in 2011 (Source: World Bank, World Development Indicators database).

ECONOMICALLY ACTIVE POPULATION

('000 persons aged 14 years and over, July 2013)

	Males	Females	Total
Agriculture, forestry and fishing	160.8	41.9	202.7
Mining and quarrying	4.9	0.5	5.4
Manufacturing	45.2	23.0	68.2
Electricity, gas and water	6.6	2.1	8.7
Construction	83.1	1.7	84.8
Wholesale and retail, repair of motor vehicles and equipment	96.4	117.0	213.4
Hotels and restaurants	31.2	43.7	74.9
Transport, storage and communications	60.6	14.4	75.0
Financial intermediation	8.2	16.4	24.6
Real estate, renting and business activities	38.9	31.1	70.0
Public administration and defence; compulsory social security	32.7	28.3	61.0
Education	17.9	50.2	68.1
Health and social work	8.7	25.4	34.1
Community, social and personal services	25.6	34.3	59.9
Private households with employed persons	10.6	45.5	56.1
Sub-total	631.4	475.5	1,106.9
Activities not adequately defined	0.7	0.5	1.2
Total employed	632.1	476.0	1,108.1
Unemployed	83.6	118.0	201.6
Total labour force	715.7	594.0	1,309.7

Health and Welfare

KEY INDICATORS

Total fertility rate (children per woman, 2011)	2.3
Under-5 mortality rate (per 1,000 live births, 2011)	18
HIV/AIDS (% of persons aged 15–49, 2012)	1.7
Physicians (per 1,000 head, 2008)	0.4
Hospital beds (per 1,000 head, 2010)	1.9
Health expenditure (2010): US $ per head (PPP)	397
Health expenditure (2010): % of GDP	5.2
Health expenditure (2010): public (% of total)	55.5
Access to water (% of persons, 2011)	93
Access to sanitation (% of persons, 2011)	80
Total carbon dioxide emissions ('000 metric tons, 2010)	7,158.0
Carbon dioxide emissions per head (metric tons, 2010)	2.6
Human Development Index (2012): ranking	85
Human Development Index (2012): value	0.730

For sources and definitions, see explanatory note on p. vi.

Agriculture

PRINCIPAL CROPS

('000 metric tons)

	2010	2011	2012
Sweet potatoes	35	42	42
Yams	137	135	145
Sugar cane	1,390	1,518	1,475
Coconuts	290*	290*	315†
Cabbages and other brassicas	25	33	33
Tomatoes	19	27	27
Pumpkins, squash and gourds	41	49	52
Carrots and turnips	21	32	30
Bananas	54	47	47
Plantains	30	35	36
Oranges	108	100	92
Lemons and limes†	24	26	27
Grapefruit and pomelos	1	—	—
Pineapples	20	18	20

* Unofficial figure.

† FAO estimate(s).

Pimento, allspice ('000 metric tons): 10 in 2005.

Aggregate production ('000 metric tons, may include official, semi-official or estimated data): Total cereals 2.6 in 2010, 3.0 in 2011, 3.1 in 2012; Total roots and tubers 224.7 in 2010, 240.5 in 2011, 248.3 in 2012; Total vegetables (incl. melons) 202.7 in 2010, 267.7 in 2011, 273.5 in 2012; Total fruits (excl. melons) 287.6 in 2010, 280.5 in 2011, 277.1 in 2012.

Source: FAO.

LIVESTOCK

('000 head, year ending September, FAO estimates unless otherwise indicated)

	2010	2011	2012
Horses	4	4	4
Mules	10	10	10
Asses	23	23	23
Cattle	170	170	170
Pigs	197*	200	205
Sheep	1.6	1.4	1.4
Goats	490	500	520
Poultry	13,500	13,000	13,500

* Unofficial figure.

Source: FAO.

LIVESTOCK PRODUCTS

('000 metric tons)

	2010	2011	2012
Cattle meat	5.3	5.6	5.8
Goat meat	0.9	1.3	1.1
Pig meat	8.0	7.1	9.5
Chicken meat	100.6	101.5	102.2
Cows' milk	12.5	12.4	12.8
Hen eggs*	6.0	7.5	6.2
Honey*	0.7	0.8	0.8

* FAO estimates.

Source: FAO.

Forestry

ROUNDWOOD REMOVALS

('000 cubic metres, excl. bark, FAO estimates)

	2010	2011	2012
Sawlogs, veneer logs and logs for sleepers	4	1	1
Other industrial wood	151	151	151
Fuel wood	545	541	537
Total	700	693	689

Source: FAO.

SAWNWOOD PRODUCTION
('000 cubic metres, incl. railway sleepers)

	1996	1997	1998
Coniferous (softwood)	3	3	3
Broadleaved (hardwood)	61	62	63
Total	64	65	66

1999–2012: Annual production as in 1998 (FAO estimates).

Source: FAO.

Fishing

('000 metric tons, live weight)

	2009	2010	2011*
Capture	16.3	15.4	15.1
Marine fishes	12.5	11.4	11.4
Freshwater fishes	0.4	0.4	0.4
Aquaculture	5.2*	4.1*	1.2
Nile tilapia	5.0	3.9	1.1
Total catch*	21.5	19.5	16.3

* FAO estimate(s).

Source: FAO.

Mining

('000 metric tons)

	2010	2011	2012
Bauxite*	8,540	10,190	9,339
Alumina	1,591	1,960	1,758
Crude gypsum	230	96	100†
Lime	300†	300	n.a.
Salt	19.0†	n.a.	n.a.

* Dried equivalent of crude ore.
† Estimated figure.

Source: US Geological Survey.

Industry

SELECTED PRODUCTS

	2010	2011	2012
Sugar ('000 metric tons)	121.2	143.2	136.2
Rum ('000 litres)	21,039	17,627	24,508
Diesel and fuel oil (million litres)	951.0	987.8	982.8
Motor spirit (petrol, million litres)	168.7	194.3	181.2
Kerosene, turbo and jet fuel (million litres)	124.3	114.8	122.8
Cement ('000 metric tons)	649.3	717.3	760.3

Concrete ('000 cu m): 164,155 in 2007.

2008: Molasses (metric tons) 62,654; Beer and stout ('000 litres) 85,987; Auto diesel oil ('000 litres) 206,536.

Electrical energy (million kWh): 6,008 in 2008; 5,533 in 2009; 4,157 in 2010 (Source: UN Industrial Commodity Statistics Database).

Finance

CURRENCY AND EXCHANGE RATES

Monetary Units
100 cents = 1 Jamaican dollar (J $).

Sterling, US Dollar and Euro Equivalents (31 December 2013)
£1 sterling = J $174.638;
US $1 = J $106.047;
€1 = J $146.250;
J $1,000 = £5.73 = US $9.43 = €6.84.

Average Exchange Rate (J $ per US $)
2011 85.892
2012 88.751
2013 100.241

GOVERNMENT FINANCE
(budgetary central government, non-cash basis, J $ million, year ending 31 March)

Summary of Balances

	2009	2010	2011†
Revenue	294,347	309,231	318,592
Less Expense	406,965	375,703	376,900
Gross operating balance	−112,617	−66,472	−58,308
Less Net acquisition of non-financial assets	13,017	26,752	29,650
Net lending/borrowing	−125,634	−93,224	−87,958

Revenue

	2009	2010	2011†
Tax revenue	262,787	274,493	286,196
Taxes on income, profits and capital gains	130,763	116,954	121,427
Taxes on goods and services	102,980	124,799	129,990
Grants	4,184	9,669	11,013
Other revenue	27,376	25,069	21,383
Total	294,347	309,231	318,592

Expense/Outlays

Expense by economic type	2009	2010	2011†
Compensation of employees	57,374	59,231	61,369
Use of goods and services	16,251	20,312	20,894
Interest	188,716	128,355	120,704
Social benefits	14,726	16,762	21,941
Other expense	129,897	151,043	151,992
Total	406,964	375,703	376,900

Outlays by functions of government*	2009	2010	2011†
General public services	229,812	173,781	190,440
Defence	9,896	10,138	9,991
Public order and safety	32,136	34,805	38,597
Economic affairs	37,884	61,976	44,447
Environmental protection	614	712	858
Housing and community amenities	6,493	7,112	8,669
Health	30,244	34,627	34,961
Recreation, culture and religion	3,654	3,441	3,584
Education	73,028	71,288	71,957
Social protection	5,864	7,071	7,380
Statistical discrepancy	–9,642	–2,494	–4,333
Total	419,982	402,455	406,550

* Including net acquisition of non-financial assets.
† Preliminary.

Source: IMF, *Government Finance Statistics Yearbook*.

2011/12 (central government operations, J$ million): *Revenue:* Tax revenue 289,882.2; Non-tax revenue 17,016.7; Other revenue 1,524.5; Capital revenue 10,585.1; Grants 3,448.8; Total 322,457.3. *Expenditure:* Current expenditure 349,960.7 (Programmes 89,699.4, Wages and salaries 139,556.9, Interest 120,704.4); Capital expenditure (incl. net lending) 53,230.9; Total 403,191.6 (Source: Ministry of Finance, Kingston).

2012/13 (central government operations, J$ million, provisional figures): *Revenue:* Tax revenue 319,764.9; Non-tax revenue 18,783.6; Other revenue 1,163.7; Capital revenue 1,015.8; Grants 3,940.5; Total 344,668.5. *Expenditure:* Current expenditure 361,521.0 (Programmes 87,201.5, Wages and salaries 147,381.8, Interest 126,937.7); Capital expenditure (incl. net lending) 37,757.9; Total 399,278.9 (Source: Ministry of Finance, Kingston).

2013/14 (central government operations, J$ million, budget figures): *Revenue:* Tax revenue 335,625.1; Non-tax revenue 18,555.2; Other revenue 1,681.3; Capital revenue 1,008.9; Grants 4,412.0; Total 361,282.5. *Expenditure:* Current expenditure 374,765.0 (Programmes 92,160.7, Wages and salaries 146,070.4, Interest 136,533.8); Capital expenditure (incl. net lending) 39,493.0; Total 414,258.0 (Source: Ministry of Finance, Kingston).

INTERNATIONAL RESERVES

(excl. gold, US$ million at 31 December)

	2010	2011	2012
IMF special drawing rights	329.7	315.9	306.5
Foreign exchange	2,171.4	1,966.1	1,674.3
Total	2,501.1	2,281.9	1,980.8

Source: IMF, *International Financial Statistics*.

MONEY SUPPLY

(J $ million at 31 December)

	2010	2011	2012
Currency outside depository corporations	47,015	51,505	53,502
Transferable deposits	106,836	117,908	105,951
Other deposits	373,907	391,282	418,009
Securities other than shares	72,502	70,567	40,837
Broad money	600,260	631,262	618,299

Source: IMF, *International Financial Statistics*.

COST OF LIVING

(Consumer Price Index at December; base: December 2006 = 100)

	2010	2011	2012
Food (incl. non-alcoholic beverages)	188.6	198.9	227.4
Alcohol and tobacco	207.8	218.5	231.8
Clothing and footwear	159.1	172.9	193.1
Housing, utilities and fuel	176.3	197.9	208.4
Transport	156.2	161.7	165.8
All items (incl. others)	168.1	178.2	192.5

NATIONAL ACCOUNTS

(J$ million at current prices)

Expenditure on the Gross Domestic Product

	2010	2011	2012
Government final consumption expenditure	185,669	196,091	214,210
Private final consumption expenditure	945,552	1,064,716	1,133,785
Increase in stocks	3,429	5,535	3,069
Gross fixed capital formation	229,408	259,834	258,093
Total domestic expenditure	1,364,058	1,526,176	1,609,157
Exports of goods and services	361,227	376,784	399,555
Less Imports of goods and services	571,608	663,195	695,660
GDP in purchasers' values	1,153,678	1,239,766	1,313,052

Gross Domestic Product by Economic Activity

	2010	2011	2012
Agriculture, forestry and fishing	62,331	70,438	75,465
Mining and quarrying	12,720	15,487	14,811
Manufacturing	88,783	96,566	103,554
Electricity and water	33,374	35,867	35,236
Construction	72,532	77,921	80,330
Wholesale and retail trade; repairs and installation of machinery	186,511	201,491	214,156
Hotels and restaurants	44,402	45,481	48,175
Transport, storage and communication	100,782	104,330	101,388
Finance and insurance services	104,030	111,869	117,281
Real estate, renting and business services	123,194	130,771	138,684
Producers of government services	142,581	152,708	167,043
Other services	64,817	69,803	74,995
Sub-total	1,036,057	1,112,732	1,171,118
Less Financial intermediation services indirectly measured	45,029	45,755	47,792
Gross value added in basic prices	991,030	1,066,975	1,123,327
Taxes, less subsidies, on products	162,648	172,790	189,725
GDP in market prices	1,153,678	1,239,766	1,313,052

BALANCE OF PAYMENTS

(US$ million)

	2010	2011	2012
Exports of goods	1,370.4	1,666.1	1,746.7
Imports of goods	–4,629.4	–5,881.4	–5,904.7
Balance on goods	–3,259.0	–4,215.3	–4,158.0
Exports of services	2,634.0	2,620.2	2,673.8
Imports of services	–1,824.4	–1,946.0	–2,034.9
Balance on goods and services	–2,449.4	–3,541.2	–3,519.1
Primary income received	243.2	221.5	283.8
Primary income paid	–737.8	–739.9	–717.3
Balance on goods, services and primary income	–2,944.0	–4,059.6	–3,952.6
Secondary income received	2,292.9	2,284.0	2,337.6
Secondary income paid	–282.9	–287.6	–289.8
Current balance	–934.0	–2,063.2	1,904.8
Capital account (net)	–22.1	–9.1	–26.2
Direct investment assets	–16.3	–29.1	24.2
Direct investment liabilities	185.8	172.8	228.8
Portfolio investment assets	–352.2	–70.8	285.3
Portfolio investment liabilities	–61.1	240.5	–138.6
Other investment assets	–1,143.1	–274.4	–369.7
Other investment liabilities	1,824.2	1,270.8	245.8
Net errors and omissions	171.0	494.9	818.2
Reserves and related items	–348.1	–267.8	–839.3

Source: IMF, *International Financial Statistics*.

External Trade

PRINCIPAL COMMODITIES
(US $ million)

Imports c.i.f.	2010	2011	2012
Foods	812.9	938.4	959.2
Beverages and tobacco	76.0	77.5	81.1
Crude materials (excl. fuels)	60.8	63.2	47.5
Mineral fuels and lubricants	1,688.7	2,441.8	2,390.3
Animal and vegetable oils and fats	32.6	58.6	51.6
Chemicals	696.9	909.6	924.0
Manufactured goods	587.1	647.1	623.7
Machinery and transport equipment	793.4	939.7	919.4
Miscellaneous manufactured articles	483.0	470.5	480.0
Total (incl. others)	5,326.4	6,614.8	6,594.9

Exports f.o.b.	2010	2011	2012
Foods	207.0	231.8	274.0
Beverages and tobacco	103.9	113.3	104.3
Crude materials (excl. fuels)	555.7	769.4	665.4
Mineral fuels and lubricants	157.4	186.6	200.8
Chemicals	83.3	46.5	209.7
Machinery and transport equipment	16.1	50.8	22.8
Miscellaneous manufactured articles	28.4	19.1	18.5
Total (incl. others)	1,371.2	1,664.8	1,747.3

PRINCIPAL TRADING PARTNERS
(US $ million)

Imports c.i.f.	2010	2011	2012
Belgium	62.4	65.6	53.5
Brazil	203.2	323.7	241.9
Canada	91.7	117.7	101.3
China, People's Republic	242.9	282.3	310.5
Colombia	56.4	70.5	54.6
Costa Rica	52.8	54.7	56.9
Dominican Republic	54.8	66.5	47.7
Germany	47.8	64.1	70.5
Japan	121.0	148.7	208.4
Mexico	77.2	242.6	264.1
Trinidad and Tobago	721.0	831.3	699.0
United Kingdom	80.9	85.1	83.7
USA	1,875.1	2,163.3	2,349.2
Venezuela	732.8	958.8	1,013.9
Total (incl. others)	5,225.2	6,436.6	6,580.4

Exports f.o.b.	2010	2011	2012
Bahamas	3.3	2.1	21.8
Barbados	8.9	9.2	23.8
Bulgaria	0.0	0.0	18.3
Canada	163.4	263.7	121.6
China, People's Republic	1.8	21.4	11.4
France	16.1	7.0	16.5
Georgia	8.0	9.1	36.2
Iceland	18.3	7.8	27.2
Italy	1.0	1.2	37.9
Japan	15.8	13.7	10.6
Latvia	0.0	0.0	59.9
Netherlands	68.3	91.4	70.6
Norway	68.5	41.8	0.1
Poland	0.0	0.0	18.6
Russia	37.3	10.7	59.2
Slovenia	0.0	51.5	71.4
Trinidad and Tobago	19.1	21.0	18.3
Ukraine	13.5	0.0	0.0
United Arab Emirates	13.9	1.7	69.2
United Kingdom	83.9	111.6	44.9
USA	659.1	839.3	823.5
Total (incl. others)	1,327.6	1,622.9	1,711.8

Source: Trade Map-Trade Competitiveness Map, International Trade Centre, www.intracen.org/marketanalysis.

Transport

RAILWAYS
(traffic)

	1988	1989	1990
Passenger-km ('000)	36,146	37,995	n.a.
Freight ton-km ('000)	115,076	28,609	1,931

Source: Jamaica Railway Corporation.

ROAD TRAFFIC
(motor vehicles in use at 31 December)

	2005	2006	2008*
Passenger cars	357,810	373,742	224,520
Motorcycles	27,038	29,061	6,249

* Data for 2007 were not available.

2010: Passenger cars 388,449; Buses 115,221; Lorries 3,095; Motorcycles 12,253.

Source: IRF, *World Road Statistics*.

SHIPPING

Flag Registered Fleet
(at 31 December)

	2011	2012	2013
Number of vessels	29	27	40
Total displacement ('000 grt)	157.3	123.1	168.4

Source: Lloyd's List Intelligence (www.lloydslistintelligence.com).

International Sea-borne Freight Traffic
('000 metric tons, estimates)

	2010	2011	2012
Goods loaded	14,668	16,570	12,951
Goods unloaded	12,401	13,844	11,013

Source: Port Authority of Jamaica.

CIVIL AVIATION
(traffic on scheduled services)

	2007	2008	2009
Kilometres flown (million)	57	27	26
Passengers carried ('000)	1,618	1,500	1,380
Passenger-km (million)	3,959	3,027	2,839
Total ton-km (million)	380	315	295

Source: UN, *Statistical Yearbook*.

2010: Passengers carried ('000) 978 (Source: World Bank, World Development Indicators database).

Tourism

VISITOR ARRIVALS BY COUNTRY OF ORIGIN

	2010	2011	2012
Canada	325,191	378,938	403,200
United Kingdom	184,355	n.a.	n.a.
USA	1,242,943	1,225,565	1,257,669
Total (incl. others)	1,921,678	1,951,752	1,986,082

Tourism revenue (US $ million): 2,001.3 in 2010; 2,012.5 in 2011; 2,046.3 in 2012.

Communications Media

	2010	2011	2012
Telephones ('000 main lines in use)	263.1	272.1	264.5
Mobile cellular telephones ('000 subscribers)	3,182.0	2,974.7	2,665.7
Broadband subscribers ('000)	116.7	106.5	119.7

Internet subscribers: 114,600 in 2009.

Source: International Telecommunication Union.

Education

(2012/13 unless otherwise indicated)

	Institutions	Teachers	Students
Pre-primary	2,936	10,269	138,124
Primary	933	11,704	264,862
Secondary	387	13,914	236,002
Special schools	30	425	3,748
Tertiary	15	1,162	16,171
University*	2	1,049	26,295

* Figures for 2011/12.

Source: Ministry of Education, Kingston.

Pupil-teacher ratio (primary education, UNESCO estimate): 20.6 in 2009/10 (Source: UNESCO Institute for Statistics).

Adult literacy rate (UNESCO estimates): 87.0% (males 82.1%; females 91.8%) in 2011 (Source: UNESCO Institute for Statistics).

Directory

The Government

HEAD OF STATE

Queen: HM Queen ELIZABETH II.

Governor-General: Sir PATRICK LINTON ALLEN (took office 26 February 2009).

CABINET
(April 2014)

The Government is formed by the People's National Party.

Prime Minister and Minister of Defence, Development, Information and Sports: PORTIA SIMPSON MILLER.

Minister of Foreign Affairs and Foreign Trade: ARNOLD NICHOLSON.

Minister of Finance and Planning: Dr PETER PHILLIPS.

Minister of National Security: PETER BUNTING.

Minister of Education: Rev. RONALD THWAITES.

Minister of Water, Land, Environment and Climate Change: ROBERT PICKERSGILL.

Minister of Tourism and Entertainment: Dr WYKEHAM MCNEIL.

Minister of Justice: MARK GOLDING.

Minister of Industry, Commerce and Investment: ANTHONY HYLTON.

Minister of Agriculture and Fisheries: ROGER CLARKE.

Minister of Local Government and Community Development: NOEL ASCOTT.

Minister of Labour and Social Security: DERRICK KELLIER.

Minister of Health: Dr FENTON FERGUSON.

Minister of Youth and Culture: LISA HANNAH.

Minister of Transport, Works and Housing: Dr OMAR DAVIES.

Minister of Science, Technology, Energy and Mining: PHILLIP PAULWELL.

Minister without Portfolio in the Office of the Prime Minister with responsibility for Information: SANDREA FALCONER.

Minister without Portfolio in the Ministry of Finance and Planning with responsibility for the Public Service: HORACE DALLEY.

Minister without Portfolio in the Ministry of Transport, Works and Housing with responsibility for Housing: Dr MORAIS GUY.

Minister without Portfolio in the Office of the Prime Minister with responsibility for Sports: NATALIE NEITA-HEADLEY.

There are also eight Ministers of State.

MINISTRIES

Office of the Governor-General: King's House, Hope Rd, Kingston 6; tel. 927-6424; fax 927-4561; e-mail kingshouse@kingshouse.gov.jm; internet www.kingshousejamaica.gov.jm.

Office of the Prime Minister: Jamaica House, 1 Devon Rd, POB 272, Kingston 6; tel. 927-9941; fax 968-8229; e-mail pmo@opm.gov.jm; internet www.opm.gov.jm.

Ministry of Agriculture and Fisheries: Hope Gardens, POB 480, Kingston 6; tel. 927-1731; fax 927-1904; e-mail webmaster@moa.gov.jm; internet www.moa.gov.jm.

Ministry of Education: 2 National Heroes Circle, Kingston 4; tel. 922-1400; fax 967-1837; e-mail webmaster@moec.gov.jm; internet www.moec.gov.jm.

Ministry of Finance and Planning: 30 National Heroes Circle, Kingston 4; tel. 922-8600; fax 922-7097; e-mail info@mof.gov.jm; internet www.mof.gov.jm.

Ministry of Foreign Affairs and Foreign Trade: 21 Dominica Dr., POB 624, Kingston 5; tel. 926-4220; fax 929-5112; e-mail mfaftjam@cwjamaica.com; internet www.mfaft.gov.jm.

Ministry of Health: Oceana Hotel Complex, 2–4 King St, Kingston 10; tel. 967-1100; fax 967-1643; e-mail webmaster@moh.gov.jm; internet www.moh.gov.jm.

Ministry of Industry, Commerce and Investment (MITEC): 4 St Lucia Ave, Kingston 5; tel. 968-7116; fax 960-7422; e-mail communications@miic.gov.jm; internet www.miic.gov.jm.

Ministry of Justice: Mutual Life Bldg, NCB South Tower, 2 Oxford Rd, Kingston 5; tel. 906-4923; fax 906-1712; e-mail customerservice@moj.gov.jm; internet www.moj.gov.jm.

Ministry of Labour and Social Security: 1F North St, POB 10, Kingston; tel. 922-9500; fax 922-6902; e-mail mlss_perm_sect@yahoo.com; internet www.mlss.gov.jm.

Ministry of Local Government and Community Development: 85 Hagley Park Rd, Kingston 11; tel. 754-0992; fax 754-1000; e-mail communications@mlge.gov.jm; internet www.localgovjamaica.gov.jm.

Ministry of National Security: NCB North Tower, 2 Oxford Rd, Kingston 5; tel. 906-4908; fax 754-3601; e-mail information@mns.gov.jm; internet www.mns.gov.jm.

Ministry of Science, Technology, Energy and Mining: PCJ Bldg, 36 Trafalgar Rd, Kingston 10; tel. 929-8990; fax 960-1623; e-mail info@mem.gov.jm; internet www.mem.gov.jm.

Ministry of Tourism and Entertainment: 64 Knutsford Blvd, Kingston 5; tel. 929-9200; fax 929-9375; e-mail info@visitjamaica.com; internet www.tourismja.com.

Ministry of Transport, Works and Housing: 138H Maxfield Ave, Kingston 10; tel. 754-1900; fax 960-2886; e-mail ps@mtw.gov.jm; internet www.mtw.gov.jm.

Ministry of Water, Land, Environment and Climate Change: 25 Dominica Dr., Kingston 5; tel. 926-1690; fax 926-0543; e-mail info@mwh.gov.jm; internet www.mwh.gov.jm.

Ministry of Youth and Culture: 4–6 Trafalgar Rd, Kingston 5; tel. 978-7654; fax 968-4511; e-mail info@micys.gov.jm; internet www.micys.gov.jm.

Legislature

PARLIAMENT

Houses of Parliament: Gordon House, 81 Duke St, POB 636, Kingston; tel. 922-0202; fax 967-0064; e-mail clerk@japarliament.gov.jm; internet www.japarliament.gov.jm; Clerk HEATHER COOKE.

Senate

President: FLOYD MORRIS.

Deputy President: ANGELLA BROWN BURKE.

The Senate has a total of 21 members, including the President and Deputy President; 13 members are appointed on the advice of the Prime Minister and eight on the recommendation of the Leader of the Opposition.

House of Representatives

Speaker: MICHAEL PEART.

Deputy Speaker: LLOYD B. SMITH.

General Election, 29 December 2011

	Seats
People's National Party (PNP)	42
Jamaica Labour Party (JLP)	21
Total	63

Election Commission

Electoral Office of Jamaica (EOJ): 43 Duke St, Kingston; tel. 922-0425; fax 967-4058; e-mail eojinfo@eoj.com.jm; internet www.ecj.com.jm; f. 1943; Dir ORRETTE FISHER.

Political Organizations

Jamaica Alliance Movement (JAM): Flamingo Beach, Falmouth, Trelawny, Kingston; tel. 861-5233; e-mail nowjam@gmail.com; internet www.nowjam.org; f. 2001; Rastafarian; Pres. ASTOR BLACK.

Jamaica Labour Party (JLP): 20 Belmont Rd, Kingston 5; tel. 929-1183; e-mail join@jamaicalabourparty.com; internet www.jamaicalabourparty.com; f. 1943; supports free enterprise in a mixed economy and close co-operation with the USA; Leader ANDREW HOLNESS; Gen. Sec. HORACE CHANG.

National Democratic Movement (NDM): The Trade Centre, Unit 9, 30-32 Red Hills Rd, Kingston 10; tel. 906-8485; fax 922-7874; e-mail ndmjamaica@yahoo.com; internet www.ndmj.org; f. 1995; advocates a clear separation of powers between the central executive and elected representatives; supports private investment and a market economy; mem. of the New Jamaica Alliance; Chair. PETER TOWNSEND; Pres. EARL DELISSER.

People's National Party (PNP): 89 Old Hope Rd, Kingston 6; tel. 978-1337; fax 927-4389; e-mail information@pnpjamaica.com; internet www.pnpjamaica.com; f. 1938; socialist principles; affiliated with the National Workers' Union; Pres. PORTIA SIMPSON MILLER; Chair. ROBERT PICKERSGILL; Gen. Sec. PETER BUNTING.

Diplomatic Representation

EMBASSIES AND HIGH COMMISSIONS IN JAMAICA

Argentina: Dyoll Life Bldg, 6th Floor, 40 Knutsford Blvd, Kingston 5; tel. 926-5588; fax 926-0580; e-mail embargen@cwjamaica.com; Ambassador ARIEL FERNÁNDEZ.

Belgium: 6 St Lucia Ave, Kingston 5; tel. 754-7903; fax 906-5943; e-mail kingston@diplobel.fed.be; internet www.diplomatie.be/kingston; Ambassador GODELIEVE VAN DEN BERGH.

Brazil: 23 Millsborough Crescent, Kingston 6; tel. 946-9812; fax 927-5897; e-mail brasemb.kingston@itamaraty.gov.br; internet kingston.itamaraty.gov.br; Ambassador ANTÔNIO FRANCISCO DA COSTA E SILVA NETO.

Canada: 3 West Kings House Rd, POB 1500, Kingston 10; tel. 926-1500; fax 511-3493; e-mail kngtn@international.gc.ca; internet www.canadainternational.gc.ca/jamaica-jamaique; High Commissioner ROBERT READY.

Chile: Courtleigh Corporate Centre, 5th Floor, South Sixth St, Lucia Ave, Kingston 5; tel. 968-0260; fax 968-0265; e-mail echile.jamaica@minrel.gov.cl; internet chileabroad.gov.cl/jamaica; Ambassador EDUARDO BONILLA MENCHACA.

China, People's Republic: 8 Seaview Ave, POB 232, Kingston 10; tel. 927-3871; fax 927-6920; e-mail chinaemb_jm@mfa.gov.cn; internet jm.china-embassy.org; Ambassador DONG XIAOJUN.

Colombia: Victoria Mutual Bldg, 4th Floor, 53 Knutsford Blvd, Kingston 5; tel. 929-1701; fax 968-0577; e-mail ekingston@cancilleria.gov.co; internet www.embajadaenjamaica.gov.co; Ambassador LUÍS GUILLERMO MARTÍNEZ FERNÁNDEZ.

Costa Rica: 58 Hope Rd, Kingston 6; tel. 978-5210; e-mail embacostaricajamaica@gmail.com; Chargé d'affaires a.i. TANISHIA ELOÍSA ELLIS HAYLES.

Cuba: 9 Trafalgar Rd, Kingston 5; tel. 978-0931; fax 978-5372; e-mail embacubajam@cwjamaica.com; internet www.cubadiplomatica.cu/jamaica; Ambassador BERNARDO GUANCHE HERNÁNDEZ.

Dominican Republic: Townhouse, 12 Norbrook Views, 13 Norbrook Cres., Kingston 8; tel. 931-0044; fax 925-1057; e-mail domemb@cwjamaica.com; Ambassador Dr JOSÉ TOMÁS ARES GERMÁN.

France: 13 Hillcrest Ave, POB 93, Kingston 6; tel. 946-4000; fax 946-4020; e-mail frenchembassyjamaica@gmail.com; Ambassador GINETTE DE MATHA.

Germany: 10 Waterloo Rd, POB 444, Kingston 10; tel. 926-6728; fax 620-5457; e-mail germanembassa.kingston@gmail.com; internet www.kingston.diplo.de; Ambassador JOSEF BECK.

Haiti: 2 Munroe Rd, Kingston 6; tel. 927-7595; fax 978-7638; Chargé d'affaires a.i. MAX ALCE.

India: 27 Seymour Ave, POB 446, Kingston 6; tel. 927-4270; fax 978-2801; e-mail hicomindkin@cwjamaica.com; internet www.hcikingston.com; High Commissioner PRATAP SINGH.

Japan: NCB Towers, North Tower, 6th Floor, 2 Oxford Rd, POB 8104, Kingston 5; tel. 929-3338; fax 968-1373; internet www.jamaica.emb-japan.go.jp; Ambassador YASUO TAKASE.

Korea, Republic: 5 Oakridge, Kingston 8; tel. 924-2731; fax 924-7325; e-mail jamaica@mofat.go.kr; internet jam.mofat.go.kr; Chargé d'affaires a.i. KI-MO LIM.

Mexico: PCJ Bldg, 36 Trafalgar Rd, Kingston 10; tel. 926-4242; fax 929-7995; e-mail embamexj@cwjamaica.com; internet embamex.sre.gob.mx/jamaica; Ambassador GERARDO LOZANO ARREDONDO.

Nicaragua: 2 Ottawa Ave, Kingston 6; tel. 285-9200; fax 631-7357; e-mail rhooker@cancilleria.gob.ni; Ambassador DAVID SIDNEY MCFIELD.

Nigeria: 5 Waterloo Rd, POB 94, Kingston 10; tel. 968-3732; fax 968-7371; e-mail nhckingston@mail.infochan.com; High Commissioner OLATOKUNBO KAMSON.

Panama: 34 Annette Cres., Suite 103, Kingston 10; tel. 924-5236; fax 924-5235; e-mail panaemba@hotmail.com; Ambassador JORGE ENRIQUE CONSTANTINO GONZÁLEZ.

Peru: 23 Barbados Ave, POB 1818, Kingston 5; tel. 920-5027; fax 920-4360; e-mail embaperu-kingston@rree.gob.pe; Ambassador LUIS SÁNDIGA CABRERA.

Russia: 22 Norbrook Dr., Kingston 8; tel. 924-1048; fax 925-8290; e-mail rusembja@colis.com; internet en.rejamaica.ru; Ambassador VLADIMIR POLENOV.

Saint Christopher and Nevis: 11A Opal Ave, Golden Acres, Red Hills, St Andrew; tel. 944-3861; e-mail clrharper@yahoo.com; fax 945-0105; High Commissioner CEDRIC HARPER.

Senegal: Courtleigh Corporate Centre, 6–8 St Lucia Ave, Kingston 5; tel. 906-2919; fax 622-5758; e-mail senegalembassyjamaica@gmail.com; Ambassador Dr NAFISSATOU DIAGNE.

South Africa: 15 Hillcrest Ave, Kingston 6; tel. 620-4840; fax 978-0339; e-mail jamaicak@dirco.gov.za; High Commissioner MATHU JOYINI.

Spain: Courtleigh Corporate Centre, 6th Floor, 6–8 St Lucia Ave, Kingston 5; tel. 929-5555; fax 929-8965; e-mail emb.kingston@mae.es; Ambassador CELSA NUÑO.

Trinidad and Tobago: 25 Windsor Ave, Kingston 5; tel. 926-5730; fax 926-5801; e-mail kgnhctt@cwjamaica.com; internet www.kgnhctt.org; High Commissioner Dr IVA CAMILLE GLOUDON.

United Kingdom: 28 Trafalgar Rd, POB 575, Kingston 10; tel. 510-0700; fax 510-0737; e-mail PPA.Kingston@fco.gov.uk; internet ukinjamaica.fco.gov.uk; High Commissioner DAVID FITTON.

USA: 142 Old Hope Rd, Kingston 6; tel. 702-6000; e-mail kingstonirc@state.gov; internet kingston.usembassy.gov; Chargé d'affaires a.i. ELIZABETH LEE MARTINEZ.

Venezuela: PCJ Bldg, 3rd Floor, 36 Trafalgar Rd, POB 26, Kingston 10; tel. 926-5510; fax 926-7442; e-mail embavene@n5.com.jm; Ambassador MARÍA JACQUELINE MENDOZA ORTEGA.

Judicial System

The judicial system is based on English common law and practice. Final appeal is to the Judicial Committee of the Privy Council in the United Kingdom.

Justice is administered by the Privy Council, Court of Appeal, Supreme Court, Resident Magistrates' Court (which includes the Traffic Court), two Family Courts and the Courts of Petty Sessions. The Caribbean Court of Justice, based in Trinidad and Tobago, is the court with jurisdiction for trade disputes.

Judicial Service Commission: Office of the Services Commissions, 30 National Heroes Circle, Kingston 4; tel. 922-8600; fax 924-9764; e-mail communications@osc.gov.jm; internet www.osc.gov.jm; advises the Governor-General on judicial appointments, etc.; Chief Justice ZAILA ROWENA MCCALLA.

Supreme Court: Public Bldg E, 134 Tower St, POB 491, Kingston; tel. 922-8300; fax 967-0669; e-mail webmaster@sc.gov.jm; internet supremecourt.gov.jm; Chief Justice ZAILA MCCALLA.

Court of Appeal: Public Bldg West, King St, POB 629, Kingston; tel. 922-8300; fax 967-1843; e-mail info@courtofappeal.gov.jm; internet www.courtofappeal.gov.jm; Pres. SEYMOUR PANTON.

Attorney-General: PATRICK ATKINSON.

Religion

CHRISTIANITY

Jamaica Council of Churches: 14 South Ave, Kingston 10; tel. and fax 926-0974; e-mail jchurch@cwjamaica.com; internet jamaicacouncilofchurches.yolasite.com; f. 1941; 10 mem. churches and 3 agencies; Gen. Sec. GARY HARRIOT.

The Anglican Communion

Anglicans in Jamaica are adherents of the Church in the Province of the West Indies, comprising eight dioceses. The Archbishop of the Province is the Bishop of Barbados. The Bishop of Jamaica and the Cayman Islands is assisted by three suffragan Bishops (of Kingston, Mandeville and Montego Bay). According to the 2001 census, some 4% of the population are Anglicans.

Bishop of Jamaica and the Cayman Islands: Rt Rev. HOWARD KINGSLEY AINSWORTH GREGORY, Church House, 2 Caledonia Ave, Kingston 5; tel. 926-8925; fax 968-0618; e-mail info@anglicandiocese.com; internet anglicandiocese.dthost.com.

The Roman Catholic Church

Jamaica comprises the archdiocese of Kingston in Jamaica (which also includes the Cayman Islands), and the dioceses of Montego Bay and Mandeville. Some 3% of the population are Roman Catholics. The Archbishop and Bishops participate in the Antilles Episcopal Conference (currently based in Port of Spain, Trinidad and Tobago).

Archbishop of Kingston in Jamaica: Most Rev. CHARLES HENRY DUFOUR, Archbishop's Residence, 21 Hopefield Ave, POB 43, Kingston 6; tel. 927-9915; fax 927-4487; e-mail rcabkgn@cwjamaica.com; internet www.archdioceseofkingston.org.

Other Christian Churches

According to the 2001 census, the largest religious bodies are the Church of God (whose members represent 24% of the population), Seventh-day Adventists (11% of the population), Pentecostalists (10%) and Baptists (7%). Other denominations include Jehovah's Witnesses, the Methodist and Congregational Churches, United Church, the Church of the Brethren, the Ethiopian Orthodox Church, the Disciples of Christ, the Moravian Church, the Church of Latter-Day Saints (Mormons), the Salvation Army and the Religious Society of Friends (Quakers).

Baptist Union: 2B Washington Blvd, Kingston 20; tel. 969-2223; fax 924-6296; e-mail info@jbu.org.jm; internet www.jbu.org.jm; f. 1849; 40,000 mems in 330 churches; Pres. Rev. LUKE SHAW; Gen. Sec. Rev. KARL JOHNSON.

Jamaica Union Conference of Seventh-day Adventists: 125 Manchester Rd, Mandeville; tel. 962-2284; fax 962-3417; e-mail info@wiunion.org; internet jmunion.org; f. 1903; 205,000 mems.

Methodist Church (Jamaica District): 143 Constant Spring Rd, POB 892, Kingston 8; tel. 925-6768; fax 924-2560; e-mail jamaicamethodist@cwjamaica.com; internet www.jamaicamethodist.org; f. 1789; 15,820 mems; District Pres. Rev. EVERALD GALBRAITH.

Moravian Church in Jamaica and the Cayman Islands: 3 Hector St, POB 8369, Kingston 5; tel. 619-1148; e-mail moravianchurch@cwjamaica.com; internet www.jamaicamoravian.com; f. 1754; 30,000 mems.

United Church in Jamaica and the Cayman Islands: 12 Carlton Cres., POB 359, Kingston 10; tel. 926-6059; fax 929-0826; e-mail synod@ucjci.com; internet www.ucjci.com; f. 1965 by merger of the Congregational Union of Jamaica (f. 1877) and the Presbyterian Church of Jamaica and Grand Cayman to become United Church of Jamaica and Grand Cayman; merged with Disciples of Christ in Jamaica in 1992 when name changed as above; 20,000 mems; Moderator Rt. Rev. J. OLIVER DALEY; Gen. Sec. Rev. NORBERT STEPHENS.

RASTAFARIANISM

Rastafarianism is an important influence in Jamaican culture. The cult is derived from Christianity and a belief in the divinity of Ras (Prince) Tafari Makonnen (later Emperor Haile Selassie) of Ethiopia. It advocates racial equality and non-violence, but causes controversy in its use of 'ganja' (marijuana) as a sacrament. According to the 2001 census, 1% of the population are Rastafarians. Although the religion is largely unorganized, there are some denominations.

Haile Selassie Jahrastafari Royal Ethiopian Judah Coptic Church: 11 Welcome Ave, Kingston 11; tel. 461-2721; fax 639-4173; e-mail royalethiopian@gmail.com; internet www.nationofjahrastafari.org; f. 1966; not officially incorporated; Head Pres. Dr MATT O'NEIL MYRIE HAILE SELASSIE I.

BAHÁ'Í FAITH

National Spiritual Assembly: 208 Mountain View Ave, Kingston 6; tel. 927-7051; fax 978-2344; internet www.jm.bahai.org; incorporated in 1970.

ISLAM

According to the 2001 census, there are an estimated 5,000 Muslims (less than 1% of the population).

JUDAISM

According to the 2001 census, there are some 350 Jews (less than 1% of the population).

United Congregation of Israelites: K. K. Shaare Shalom Synagogue, 92 Duke St, Kingston 6; tel. and fax 922-5931; e-mail info@ucija.org; internet www.ucija.org; f. 1655; 250 mems; Rabbi DANA EVAN KAPLAN.

The Press

DAILIES

The Gleaner: 7 North St, POB 40, Kingston; tel. 922-3400; fax 922-6223; e-mail feedback@jamaica-gleaner.com; internet www.jamaica-gleaner.com; f. 1834; morning; independent; Chair. and Man. Dir CHRISTOPHER BARNES; Editor-in-Chief GARFIELD GRANDISON; circ. 50,000.

Jamaica Observer: 40–42 1/2 Beechwood Ave, Kingston 5; tel. 920-8136; fax 926-7655; e-mail editorial@jamaicaobserver.com; internet www.jamaicaobserver.com; f. 1993; Chair. GORDON 'BUTCH' STEWART.

The Jamaica Star: 7 North St, POB 40, Kingston; tel. 922-3400; fax 922-6223; e-mail star@gleanerjm.com; internet jamaica-star.com; f. 1951; evening; Editor-in-Chief GARFIELD GRANDISON; Editor DWAYNE GORDON; circ. 45,000.

PERIODICALS

All Woman: 40-42 1/2 Beechwood Ave, Kingston 5; tel. 920-8136; e-mail editorial@jamaicaobserver.com; internet www.jamaicaobserver.com/magazines/allwoman; beauty, health and wellness; published by the Jamaica Observer Ltd; other publs include *Sunday Observer* and *Western News*; Editor NOVIA MCDONALD-WHYTE.

The Anglican: 2 Caledonia Ave, Cross Roads, Kingston 5; tel. 920-2714; fax 968-0618; e-mail info@anglicandiocese.com; internet www.anglicandiocesejamaica.com; f. 2004 following cessation of *Jamaica Churchman*; quarterly; circ. 9,000.

Catholic Opinion: Roman Catholic Chancery Office, 21 Hopefield Ave, POB 43, Kingston 6; tel. 927-9915; fax 927-4487; e-mail rcabkgn@cwjamaica.com; internet www.archdioceseofkingston.org; 6 a year; religious; circulated in the *Sunday Gleaner*; Editor Mgr MICHAEL LEWIS; circ. 100,000.

Children's Own: 7 North St, POB 40, Kingston; tel. 922-3400; fax 922-6223; e-mail feedback@jamaica-gleaner.com; internet www.jamaica-gleaner.com; weekly during term-time; publ. by The Gleaner Co; other publs include *Sunday Gleaner* and *Weekend Star*; Editor-in-Chief GARFIELD GRANDISON; circ. 120,000.

HHG Magazine: 5–7 Dunrobin Ave, Kingston 10; tel. 924-4306; fax 924-4985; e-mail hhgmagazine@cwjamaica.com; internet www.hhgmagazine.com; f. 2001; published by Health, Home & Garden Promotions; 3 a year; Editor-in-Chief FAY WINT-SMITH.

Jamaica Journal: 10–16 East St, Kingston; tel. 922-0620; fax 922-1147; e-mail jamaicajournal@instituteofjamaica.org.jm; internet jj.instituteofjamaica.org.jm/ioj_wp; f. 1967; 2 a year; literary, historical and cultural review; publ. by Institute of Jamaica; Chair. of Editorial Cttee Dr KIM ROBINSON.

The Jamaican Magazine: POB 24, Kingston 7; tel. 977-3779; e-mail deeksdesigns@gmail.com; internet www

.thejamaicanmagazine.com; f. 1986; art, culture and design; Editor LORRAINE MURRAY.

Mandeville Weekly: 29 Ward Ave, Mandeville, Manchester; tel. 961-0118; fax 961-0119; e-mail mandevilleweekly@flowja.com; internet www.mandevilleweekly.com; f. 1993; Chair. and Editor-in-Chief ANTHONY FRECKLETON; Man. Dir WENDY FRECKLETON.

North Coast Times: 130 Main St, Ocho Rios; tel. and fax 974-9306; e-mail sales@northcoasttimesja.com; internet www.northcoasttimesja.com; f. 1995; weekly; Publr FRANKLIN MCKNIGHT.

Panache Jamaica: 22B Old Hope Rd, Kingston; e-mail editor@panachejamagazine.com; internet www.panachejamagazine.com; f. 2008; fashion and lifestyle; Editorial Dir TRICIA WILLIAMSON.

Tallawah: Kingston; e-mail tyronesreid@gmail.com; internet www.tallawahmagazine.com; celebrity and lifestyle; monthly; Editor TYRONE S. REID.

West Indian Medical Journal: Faculty of Medical Sciences, University of the West Indies, Mona, Kingston 7; tel. 927-1214; fax 927-1846; e-mail wimj@uwimona.edu.jm; internet myspot.mona.uwi.edu/fms/wimj; f. 1951; monthly; Editor-in-Chief EVERARD N. BARTON; circ. 2,000.

PRESS ASSOCIATION

The Press Association of Jamaica (PAJ): 5 East Ave, Kingston 8; tel. and fax 631-6390; internet pressassociationjamaica.org; f. 1943; Pres. JENNI CAMPBELL; Sec. INGRID BROWN.

Publishers

Jamaica Publishing House Ltd: 97B Church St, Kingston; tel. 967-3866; fax 922-5412; e-mail jph@cwjamaica.com; f. 1969; subsidiary of Jamaica Teachers' Asscn; English language and literature, mathematics, history, geography, social sciences, music; Chair. WOODBURN MILLER; Man. ELAINE R. STENNETT.

LMH Publishing Ltd: 7 Norman Rd, Suite 10–11, Sagicor Industrial Park, POB 8296, Kingston CSO; tel. 938-0005; fax 759-8752; e-mail lmhbookpublishing@cwjamaica.com; internet www.lmhpublishing.com; f. 1970; educational textbooks, general, travel, fiction; Chair. L. MICHAEL HENRY; Man. Dir DAWN CHAMBERS-HENRY.

Ian Randle Publishers (IRP): 11 Cunningham Ave, POB 686, Kingston 6; tel. 978-0745; fax 978-1156; e-mail clp@ianrandlepublishers.com; internet www.ianrandlepublishers.com; f. 1991; history, biography, politics, sociology, law, cooking and music; Chair. IAN RANDLE; Man. Dir CHRISTINE RANDLE.

University of the West Indies Press (UWI Press): 7A Gibraltar Hall Rd, Mona, Kingston 7; tel. 977-2659; fax 977-2660; internet www.uwipress.com; f. 1992; Caribbean history, culture and literature, gender studies, education and political science; Man. Editor SHIVAUN HEARNE; Gen. Man. LINDA SPETH.

Western Publishers Ltd: 4 Cottage Rd, POB 1258, Montego Bay; tel. 952-5253; fax 952-6513; e-mail westernmirror@mail.infochan.com; internet westernmirror.com; f. 1980; CEO and Editor-in-Chief LLOYD B. SMITH.

GOVERNMENT PUBLISHING HOUSE

Jamaica Printing Services: 77 1/2 Duke St, Kingston; tel. 967-2250; fax 967-2225; e-mail jps_1992@yahoo.com; internet jps1992.org; Gen. Man. BLONDELL WYNDHAM.

ASSOCIATION

Caribbean Publishers' Network (CAPNET): 11 Cunningham Ave, Kingston 6; e-mail info@capnetonline.net; internet www.capnetonline.net; non-profit regional asscn; Pres. NEYSHA SOODEEN.

Broadcasting and Communications

TELECOMMUNICATIONS

Anbell Telecommunications Ltd: 51 Knutsford Blvd, Kingston 5; tel. 906-8479; fax 906-8487; e-mail support@anbell.net; internet anbell.net/telecom.htm; internet service provider; Man. GARFIELD BOLT.

Columbus Communications Jamaica Ltd (Flow): 6–8 St Lucia Ave, Kingston 5; tel. 620-3000; e-mail mediainquires@flowjamaica.com; internet discoverflow.co/jamaica; f. 2006; cable, internet and telephone service provider; Pres. and COO MICHELLE ENGLISH.

Digicel Jamaica: 14 Ocean Blvd, Kingston 5; tel. 619-5000; fax 920-0948; e-mail customercare@digicelgroup.com; internet www.digiceljamaica.com; f. 2001; mobile cellular telephone operator; owned by Irish consortium, Mossel (Jamaica) Ltd; absorbed all operations and subscribers of Claro Jamaica in 2012; Chair. DENIS O'BRIEN; CEO (Caribbean and Central America) ANDY THORBURN.

LIME: 7 Cecilio Ave, Kingston 10; tel. 926-9700; fax 929-9530; e-mail customer.services@lime.com; internet www.lime.com/jm; f. 1989; name changed as above in 2008; 79% owned by Cable & Wireless (UK); landline, internet and mobile services; CEO TONY RICE; Man. Dir (Jamaica and the Cayman Islands) GARRY SINCLAIR.

Noble Wi-Fi: Montego; tel. 410-8532; e-mail Sales-WiFi@noblecoms.com; internet noblecoms.com; f. 2014; internet service provider in north Jamaica; Dir RYAN FERNANDEZ.

Regulatory Authority

The sector is regulated by the Office of Utilities Regulation (see Utilities).

BROADCASTING

Radio

Independent Radio: 6 Bradley Ave, Kingston 10; tel. 968-4880; fax 968-9165; commercial; broadcasts 24 hrs a day on FM; Man. Dir NEWTON JAMES.

Power 106: 6 Bradley Ave, Kingston 10; tel. 968-4880; fax 968-9165; e-mail power106@cwjamaica.com; internet www.go-jamaica.com/power; f. 1992; talk and sports programmes.

IRIE FM: 1B Coconut Grove, Ocho Rios, St Ann; tel. 968-5023; fax 968-8332; e-mail customerservice@iriefm.net; internet www.iriefm.net; f. 1990; owned by Grove Broadcasting Co; reggae music; Man. BRIAN SCHMIDT.

KLAS Sports FM 89: 17 Haining Rd, Kingston 5; tel. 929-1344; fax 960-0572; e-mail admin@klassportsradio.com; internet www.klassportsradio.com; f. 1991; sports broadcasting.

Kool 97 FM: 1 Braemar Ave, Kingston 10; tel. 978-4037; fax 978-3346; e-mail contact@kool97fm.com; internet www.kool97fm.com; f. 2001; music, news and tourism information.

Linkz 96 FM: 8 Beckford St, Savanna La Mar, Westmoreland; tel. 955-3686; fax 955-9523; e-mail linkz96fm@yahoo.com; internet www.linkzfm.com; f. 2004; Chair ROGER ALLEN.

Love FM: 81 Hagley Park Rd, Kingston 10; tel. 968-9596; e-mail webmaster@love101.org; internet www.lovefm.org; f. 1993; commercial radio station, religious programming on FM; owned by National Religious Media Ltd; Gen. Man. Rt Rev. HERRO BLAIR (acting).

Radio Jamaica Ltd (RJR): Broadcasting House, 32 Lyndhurst Rd, POB 23, Kingston 5; tel. 926-1100; fax 929-7467; e-mail rjr@radiojamaica.com; internet www.radiojamaica.com; f. 1947; commercial, public service; 3 channels; Man. Dir GARY ALLEN; Gen. Man. Radio Services FRANCOIS ST JUSTE.

FAME 95 FM: 32 Lyndhurst Rd, Kingston 5; tel. 18763567406 (mobile); internet www.fame95fm.com; e-mail famefm@rjrgroup.com; f. 1984; broadcasts on FM, island-wide 24 hrs a day; Gen. Man. FRANCOIS ST JUSTE.

Hitz 92 FM: internet www.radiohitz92fm.com; broadcasts on FM, island-wide 24 hrs a day; youth station.

RJR 94 FM: internet rjr94fm.com; broadcasts on AM and FM, island-wide 24 hrs a day; Exec. Producer NORMA BROWN-BELL.

Roots FM: Mustard Seed Communities, POB 267, Kingston 10; tel. 923-2165; fax 923-6000; e-mail roots.fm@mustardseed.com; internet www.mustardseed.com; Chair TREVOR GORDON-SOMERS.

Stylz FM: 4 Boundbrook Ave, Port Antonio, Portland; tel. 993-3358; fax 993-3814; e-mail hueljacks@hotmail.com; internet www.rudelikedat.com/stylzfm; CEO HUEL JACKSON.

TBC FM: 51 Molynes Rd, Kingston 10; tel. 754-5120; fax 968-9159; e-mail gcallam@tbcradio.org; internet www.tbcradio.org; Gen. Man. GARY CALLAM.

ZIP 103 FM: 1B Courtney Walsh Dr., Kingston 10, Jamaica; tel. 929-6233; fax 929-4691; e-mail zip103fm@cwjamaica.com; internet www.zipfm.net; f. 2002; commercial radio station; Dir D'ADRA WILLIAMS.

104.9 FM: Shop 10, R.T. Plaza, Off Port Henderson Rd, Portmore, St Catherine; tel. 740-5087; e-mail motherincrisis@yahoo.com; internet www.suncityradio.fm; CEO DOREEN BILLINGS.

Television

Creative TV (CTV): Caenwood Campus, 37 Arnold Rd, Kingston 5; tel. 967-4482; fax 924-9432; internet www.creativetvjamaica.com; operated by Creative Production & Training Centre Ltd (CPTC); local cable channel; regional cultural, educational and historical programming; CEO Dr HOPETON DUNN.

CVM Television: 69 Constant Sprint Rd, Kingston 10; tel. 931-9400; fax 931-9417; e-mail contact@cvmtv.com; internet www.cvmtv.com; Pres. and CEO DAVID MCBEAN.

Love Television: Kingston; internet www.love101.org; f. 1997; religious programming; owned by National Religious Media Ltd.

Television Jamaica Limited (TVJ): 32 Lyndhurst Rd, Kingston 5; tel. 926-1100; fax 929-1029; e-mail tvjadmin@cwjamaica.com; internet www.televisionjamaica.com; f. 1959 as Jamaica Broadcasting Corpn; privatized and adopted current name in 1997; subsidiary of RJR Communications Group; island-wide VHF transmission 24 hrs a day; Chair. MILTON SAMUDA; Gen. Man.Dir GARY ALLEN.

Regulatory Authorities

Broadcasting Commission of Jamaica: 5th Floor, Victoria Mutual Bldg, 53 Knutsford Blvd, Kingston 5; tel. 920-9537; fax 929-1997; e-mail info@broadcom.org; internet www.broadcastingcommission.org; f. 1986; Chair. Prof. HOPETON DUNN.

Spectrum Management Authority: 13–19 Harbour St, Kingston; tel. 967-7948; fax 922-4093; e-mail info@sma.gov.jm; internet www.sma.gov.jm; f. 2000; national regulator for radio frequency spectrum; govt-run; Man. Dir (vacant).

Finance

(cap. = capital; res = reserves; dep. = deposits; m. = million; brs = branches; amounts in Jamaican dollars)

REGULATORY AUTHORITY

Jamaica International Financial Services Authority: Kingston; f. 2011 following an Act of Parliament; Chair. ERIC CRAWFORD.

BANKING

Central Bank

Bank of Jamaica: Nethersole Pl., POB 621, Kingston; tel. 922-0750; fax 922-0854; e-mail info@boj.org.jm; internet www.boj.org.jm; f. 1960; cap. 4.0m., res 8,831.2m., dep. 198,440.4m. (Dec. 2009); Gov. and Chair. BRIAN HECTOR WYNTER.

Commercial Banks

Citibank, NA: 19 Hillcrest Ave, Kingston 6; tel. 926-3270; fax 978-8889; e-mail peter.moses@citi.com; internet www.citibank.com/jamaica; owned by Citifinance Ltd; cap. 25.7m., res 128.4m., dep. 87.2m. (Dec. 2003); Man. Dir PETER MOSES.

FirstCaribbean International Bank (Jamaica) Ltd: 78 Halfway Tree Rd, POB 762, Kingston 10; tel. 929-9310; fax 926-7751; internet www.firstcaribbeanbank.com; adopted present name in 2002 following merger of Caribbean operations of CIBC and Barclays Bank PLC; Barclays relinquished its stake in 2006; cap. 1,396.7m., res 5,671m., dep. 42,595.3m. (Oct. 2011); Exec. Chair. MICHAEL MANSOOR; CEO RIK PARKHILL; Country Man. NIGEL HOLNESS; 13 brs.

National Commercial Bank Jamaica Ltd: 'The Atrium', 32 Trafalgar Rd, POB 88, Kingston 10; tel. 929-9050; fax 929-8399; tel. ncbinfo@jncb.com; internet www.jncb.com; f. 1837; merged with Mutual Security Bank in 1996; cap. 6,465.7m., res 27,379.9m., dep. 164,734.4m. (Sept. 2012); Chair. MICHAEL LEE-CHIN; Man. Dir PATRICK HYLTON; 37 brs.

RBC Royal Bank (Jamaica) Limited: 17 Dominica Dr., Kingston 5; tel. 960-2340; fax 960-5120; e-mail rbtt@cwjamaica.com; internet www.rbtt.com/jm; f. 1993 as Jamaica Citizens Bank Ltd; acquired by Royal Bank of Trinidad and Tobago in 2001 and name changed to RBTT Bank Jamaica Ltd; present name adopted 2011; to be sold to Sagicor Ltd in 2014; cap. 8,167.8m., res 2,764.5m., dep. 40,986m. (Dec. 2010); Chair. SURESH SOOKOO; 23 brs.

Scotiabank Jamaica Ltd (Canada): Scotiabank Centre Bldg, cnr Duke and Port Royal Sts, POB 709, Kingston; tel. 922-1000; fax 924-9294; e-mail customercare-jam@scotiabank.com; internet www.scotiabank.com.jm; f. 1967; subsidiary of Bank of Nova Scotia (Canada); cap. 2,927.2m., res 18,264.3m., dep. 151,668.4m. (Oct. 2010); Chair. SYLVIA CHROMINSKA; Pres. and CEO JACQUELINE SHARP; 35 brs.

Development Banks

Development Bank of Jamaica Ltd: 11A–15 Oxford Rd, POB 466, Kingston 5; tel. 929-4000; fax 929-6055; e-mail mail@dbankjm.com; internet www.dbankjm.com; f. 2000 following merger of Agricultural Credit Bank of Jamaica and the National Devt Bank of Jamaica; provides funds for medium- and long-term devt-orientated projects; Chair. JOSEPH M. MATALON; Man. Dir MILVERTON REYNOLDS.

Jamaica Mortgage Bank: 33 Tobago Ave, POB 950, Kingston 5; tel. 929-6350; fax 968-5428; e-mail info@jmb.gov.jm; internet www.jmb.gov.jm; f. 1971 by the Jamaican Govt and the US Agency for Int. Devt; govt-owned statutory org. since 1973; functions primarily as a secondary market facility for home mortgages and to mobilize long-term funds for housing devts in Jamaica; also insures home mortgage loans made by approved financial institutions, thus transferring risk of default on a loan to the Govt; Chair. HOWARD MOLLISON; Gen. Man. PATRICK THELWALL.

Sagicor Investments Jamaica Ltd: 60 Knutsford Blvd, Kingston 5; tel. 929-5583; fax 926-4385; e-mail options@sagicor.com; internet www.sagicor.com; fmrly Trafalgar Devt Bank, name changed as Pan Caribbean Financial Services in Dec. 2002; present name adopted in 2012; Chair. RICHARD O. BYLES; Pres. and CEO DONOVAN H. PERKINS.

Other Banks

National Export-Import Bank of Jamaica Ltd: 11 Oxford Rd, Kingston 5; tel. 960-9690; fax 960-9115; e-mail info@eximbankja.com; internet www.eximbankja.com; f. 1986; govt-owned; replaced Jamaica Export Credit Insurance Corpn; finances import and export of goods and services; Chair. WILLIAM CLARKE; Man. Dir LISA BELL.

Banking Association

Jamaica Bankers' Association: PSOJ Bldg, 39 Hope Rd, POB 1079, Kingston 10; tel. 927-6238; fax 927-5137; e-mail jbainfo@jba.org.jm; internet www.jba.org.jm; f. 1973; Pres. BRUCE BOWEN.

STOCK EXCHANGE

Jamaica Stock Exchange Ltd: 40 Harbour St, POB 1084, Kingston; tel. 967-3271; fax 967-3277; internet www.jamstockex.com; f. 1968; 51 listed cos (2012); Chair. DONOVAN PERKINS; Gen. Man. MARLENE STREET FORREST.

INSURANCE

Financial Services Commission: 39–43 Barbados Ave, Kingston 5; tel. 906-3010; fax 906-3018; e-mail inquiry@fscjamaica.org; internet www.fscjamaica.org; f. 2001; succeeded the Office of the Superintendent of Insurance; regulatory body; Chair. COLIN BULLOCK; Exec. Dir JANICE P. HOLNESS.

Principal Companies

Advantage General Insurance Co Ltd: 4-6 Trafalgar Rd, Kingston 5; tel. 978-3690; fax 978-3718; internet www.advantagegeneral.com; f. 1964; general; Chair. DENNIS G. COHEN; Pres. and CEO MARK THOMPSON.

British Caribbean Insurance Co Ltd (BCIC): 36 Duke St, POB 170, Kingston; tel. 922-1260; fax 922-4475; e-mail dsales@bcic-jm.com; internet www.bcionline.com; f. 1962; affiliate of Victoria Mutual Insurance Co; general; Chair. JOSEPH M. MATALON; Man. Dir PETER LEVY.

General Accident Insurance Co Jamaica Ltd: 58 Half Way Tree Rd, Kingston 10; tel. 929-8451; fax 929-1074; e-mail info@genac.com; internet www.genac.com; f. 1981; general; Chair. PAUL B. SCOTT; Man. Dir SHARON DONALDSON.

Globe Insurance Co of Jamaica Ltd: 19 Dominica Dr., POB 401, Kingston 5; tel. 926-3720; fax 929-2727; e-mail info@globeins.com; internet www.globeins.com; f. 1963; fmr subsidiary of Lascelles deMercado, bought by Guardian Holdings Ltd in Sept. 2012; general; Man. Dir EVAN THWAITES.

Guardian General Insurance Jamaica Ltd: 19 Dominica Dr., Kingston 5; tel. 929-8080; fax 929-2727; e-mail insure@wia.com.jm; internet www.guardiangroup.com; f. 1969; subsidiary of Guardian Holdings Ltd (Trinidad and Tobago); general; Pres. KAREN BHOORASINGH.

Guardian Life: 12 Trafalgar Rd, Kingston 5; tel. 978-8815; fax 978-4225; e-mail guardian@ghl.com.jm; internet www.guardianlife.com.jm; subsidiary of Guardian Holdings Ltd (Trinidad and Tobago); pension and life policies; Pres. and CEO ERIC HOSIN.

Insurance Co of the West Indies Ltd (ICWI): 2 St Lucia Ave, POB 306, Kingston 5; tel. 926-9040; fax 929-6641; e-mail direct@icwi.net; internet icwi.com/jamaica; general; Chair. and CEO DENNIS LALOR.

Jamaica General Insurance Co Ltd: 19–21 Knutsford Blvd, New Kingston; tel. 926-3204; fax 968-1920; e-mail info@jiiconline.com; internet www.jiiconline.com; f. 1981; subsidiary of GraceKennedy Ltd; general; Chair. PETER MOSS-SOLOMON; Man. Dir GRACE BURNETT.

JN General Insurance Company Ltd (JNGI): NEM House, 9 King St, Kingston; tel. 922-1460; fax 922-4045; e-mail info@nemjam.com; internet www.nemjam.com; f. 1934; fmrly NEM Insurance, present name adopted 2012; subsidiary of Jamaica National Bldg Soc; general; Chair. OLIVER CLARKE; Gen. Man. CHRISTOPHER HIND.

NCB Insurance Co Ltd (NCBIC): 32 Trafalgar Rd, Kingston 10; tel. 935-2730; fax 929-7301; e-mail ncbic@jncb.com; internet www.ncbinsurance.com; f. 1989; fmrly OMNI Insurance Services Ltd; life; Chair. WAYNE CHEN; Gen. Man. VERNON JAMES.

Sagicor Life Jamaica Ltd: 28–48 Barbados Ave, Kingston 5; tel. 960-8920; fax 960-1927; internet www.sagicorjamaica.com; f. 1970; owned by Sagicor Group (Barbados); merged with Island Life

Insurance Co Ltd in 2001; renamed as above in 2009; life; Chair. R. DANNY WILLIAMS; Pres. and CEO RICHARD O. BYLES.

Scotia Jamaica Life Insurance Co Ltd (SJLIC): Duke and Port Royal Sts, Kingston; tel. 922-3765; e-mail sjlic.service@scotiabank.com; internet www.scotiabank.com; f. 1995; life; Pres. HUGH REID.

Association

Insurance Association of Jamaica (IAJ): 3–3A Richmond Ave, Kingston 10; tel. 929-8404; fax 906-1804; e-mail iaj@cwjamaica.com; internet www.iaj-online.com; f. 2005 by merger of the Jamaica Asscn of General Insurance Cos (JAGIC) and the Life Insurance Cos Asscn of Jamaica (LICA); Pres. HUGH REID; Exec. Dir ORVILLE JOHNSON.

Trade and Industry

GOVERNMENT AGENCY

Jamaica Information Service (JIS): 58A Half Way Tree Rd, POB 2222, Kingston 10; tel. 926-3740; fax 926-6715; e-mail jis@jis.gov.jm; internet www.jis.gov.jm; f. 1963; govt agency; CEO DONNA-MARIE ROWE.

DEVELOPMENT ORGANIZATIONS

Agro-Investment Corpn: Ministry of Agriculture and Fisheries, 188 Spanish Town Rd, Kingston 11; tel. 764-8071; fax 758-7160; e-mail agricultural@cwjamaica.com; internet www.assp.gov.jm; f. 2009; following the merger of Agricultural Devt Corp (ADC) and Agricultural Support Services Productive Projects Fund Ltd (ASSPPFL); agricultural devt, investment facilitation, promotion and management; Chair. DAVID LOWE; CEO HERSHELL BROWN.

JAMPRO Trade and Invest, Jamaica (JAMPRO): 18 Trafalgar Rd, Kingston 10; tel. 978-7755; fax 946-0090; e-mail info@jamprocorp.com; internet www.jamaicatradeandinvest.org; f. 1988 by merger of Jamaica Industrial Development Corpn, Jamaica National Export Corpn and Jamaica Investment Promotion Ltd; trade and investment promotion agency; Chair. MILTON SAMUDA; Pres. DIANE EDWARDS.

Planning Institute of Jamaica: 16 Oxford Rd, Kingston 5; tel. 960-9339; fax 906-5011; e-mail info@pioj.gov.jm; internet www.pioj.gov.jm; f. 1955 as the Central Planning Unit; adopted current name in 1984; formulates policy on and monitors performance in the fields of the economy and social, environmental and trade issues; publishing and analysis of social and economic performance data; Chair. and Dir-Gen. Dr GLADSTONE HUTCHINSON.

Urban Development Corpn: The Office Centre, 8th Floor, 12 Ocean Blvd, Kingston; tel. 922-8310; fax 922-9326; e-mail info@udcja.com; internet www.udcja.com; f. 1968; responsibility for urban renewal and devt within designated areas; Chair. WAYNE CHEN; Gen. Man. DESMOND YOUNG (acting).

CHAMBERS OF COMMERCE

American Chamber of Commerce of Jamaica: The Jamaica Pegasus, 81 Knutsford Blvd, Kingston 5; tel. 929-7866; fax 929-8597; e-mail amcham.ja@gmail.com; internet www.amchamjamaica.org; f. 1986; affiliated to the Chamber of Commerce of the USA; Pres. DERRICK NEMBHARD; Exec. Dir BECKY STOCKHAUSEN.

Jamaica Chamber of Commerce: UDC Office Centre, Suites 13–15, 12 Ocean Blvd, Kingston 10; tel. 922-0150; fax 924-9056; e-mail info@jamaicachamber.org.jm; internet www.jamaicachamber.org.jm; f. 1779; Pres. MILTON JEFFERSON SAMUDA; Gen. Man PATRICIA PEART; 450 mems.

INDUSTRIAL AND TRADE ASSOCIATIONS

Cocoa Industry Board: Marcus Garvey Dr., POB 1039, Kingston 15; tel. 923-6411; fax 923-5837; e-mail cocoajam@cwjamaica.com; f. 1957; has statutory powers to regulate and develop the industry; owns and operates 4 central fermentaries; Chair. FRANK PHIPPS; Man. and Sec. STEVE WATSON.

Coconut Industry Board: 18 Waterloo Rd, Kingston 10; tel. 926-1770; fax 968-1360; e-mail info@coconutindustryboard.org.jm; internet www.coconutindustryboard.org.jm; f. 1945; 9 mems; Chair. RICHARD A. JONES; Gen. Man. YVONNE BURNS.

Coffee Industry Board: 1 Willie Henry Dr., POB 508, Kingston 13; tel. 758-1259; fax 758-3907; e-mail datacoordinator@ciboj.org; internet www.ciboj.org; f. 1950; 9 mems; has wide statutory powers to regulate and develop the industry; Chair. HOWARD MITCHELL; Dir-Gen. CHRISTOPHER GENTLES.

Jamaica Bauxite Institute: Hope Gardens, POB 355, Kingston 6; tel. 927-2073; fax 927-1159; f. 1975; adviser to the Govt in the negotiation of agreements, consultancy services to clients in the bauxite/alumina and related industries, laboratory services for mineral and soil-related services, pilot plant services for materials and equipment-testing, research and devt; Chair. GARY PEART; Exec. Dir PARRIS LYEW-AYEE.

Jamaica Exporters' Association (JEA): 1 Winchester Rd, Kingston 10; tel. 960-4908; fax 960-9869; e-mail info@exportja.org; internet www.exportjamaica.org; f. 1966; promotes devt of export sector; Pres. VITUS EVANS; Gen. Man. JEAN SMITH.

Jamaica Manufacturers' Association Ltd (JMA): 85A Duke St, Kingston; tel. 922-8880; fax 922-9205; e-mail jma@cwjamaica.com; internet www.jma.com.jm; f. 1947; 340 mems; Pres. BRIAN PENGELLEY.

Sugar Industry Authority: 5 Trevennion Park Rd, POB 127, Kingston 5; tel. 926-5930; fax 926-6149; e-mail sia@cwjamaica.com; internet www.jamaicasugar.org; f. 1970; statutory body under portfolio of Min. of Agriculture and Fisheries; responsible for regulation and control of sugar industry and sugar-marketing; conducts research through Sugar Industry Research Institute; Exec. Chair. DERICK HEAVEN.

Trade Board Ltd: Air Jamaica Bldg, 10th Floor, 72 Harbour St, Kingston; tel. 967-0507; fax 948-5441; e-mail info@tradeboard.gov.jm; internet www.tradeboard.gov.jm; Trade Admin. DOUGLAS WEBSTER.

EMPLOYERS' ORGANIZATIONS

All-Island Banana Growers' Association Ltd: Banana Industry Bldg, 10 South Ave, Kingston 4; tel. 922-5497; fax 922-5497; e-mail aibga@cwjamaica.com; f. 1946; 1,500 mems (1997); Chair. GRETEL SESSING; Sec. I. CHANG.

Citrus Growers' Association Ltd: Bog Walk, St Catherine; tel. 708-2150; fax 708-2538; internet www.jcgja.com; f. 1944; 13,000 mems; Chair. JOHN THOMPSON; Gen. Man. DENNIS BOOTH.

Jamaica Association of Sugar Technologists: c/o Sugar Industry Research Institute, Kendal Rd, Mandeville; tel. 962-2241; fax 962-1288; e-mail jast@jamaicasugar.org; f. 1936; 275 mems; Chair. EARLE ROBERTS; Pres. IAN MAXWELL.

Jamaica Gasoline Retailers' Association (JGRA): Kings Plaza, POB 156, Kingston 10; tel. 929-2998; fax 929-8281; e-mail jgra@cwjamaica.com; internet jgrajm.org; f. 1951; Pres. DERRICK THOMPSON.

Jamaica Livestock Association: Newport East, POB 36, Kingston; tel. 922-7130; fax 922-8934; internet www.jlaltd.com; f. 1941; 7,584 mems; Man. Dir and CEO HENRY J. RAINFORD.

Jamaica Sugar Cane Growers' Association (JSCGA): 4 North Ave, Kingston Gardens, Kingston 4; tel. 922-3010; fax 922-2077; e-mail allcane@cwjamaica.com; f. 1941; registered cane farmers; 27,000 mems; fmrly All-Island Cane Farmers' Asscn; name changed as above in 2008; Pres. ALLAN RICKARDS; Gen. Man. KARL JAMES.

Private Sector Organization of Jamaica (PSOJ): The Carlton Alexander Bldg, 39 Hope Rd, POB 236, Kingston 10; tel. 927-6957; fax 927-5137; e-mail psojinfo@psoj.org; internet www.psoj.org; f. 1976; federative body of private business individuals, cos and asscns; Pres. CHRISTOPHER ZACCA; CEO SANDRA GLASGOW.

Small Businesses' Association of Jamaica (SBAJ): 2 Trafalgar Rd, Kingston 5; tel. 978-0168; fax 927-7071; e-mail sbaj1org@yahoo.com; internet sbaj.org.jm; f. 1974; Pres. Dr MEREDITH DERBY.

Sugar Manufacturing Corpn of Jamaica Ltd: 5 Trevennion Park Rd, Kingston 5; tel. 925-3650; fax 926-6746; est. to represent sugar mfrs in Jamaica; deals with all aspects of the sugar industry and its by-products; provides liaison between the Govt, the Sugar Industry Authority and the Jamaica Sugar Cane Growers' Asscn; 9 mems; Gen. Man. DERYCK T. BROWN.

UTILITIES

Regulatory Authority

Office of Utilities Regulation (OUR): PCJ Resource Centre, 3rd Floor, 36 Trafalgar Rd, Kingston 10; tel. 968-6053; fax 929-3635; e-mail consumer@our.org.jm; internet www.our.org.jm; f. 1997; regulates provision of services in the following sectors: water and sewerage, electricity, telecommunications, public passenger transportation; Dir-Gen. ALBERT GORDON.

Electricity

Jamaica Energy Partners (JEP): 10–16 Grenada Way, RKA Bldg, 3rd Floor, Kingston 5; tel. 920-1746; fax 920-1750; e-mail info@jamenergy.com; internet jamenergy.com; f. 1995; owned by Conduit Capital Partners (USA); owns and operates 2 power barges at Old Harbour Bay, St Catherine; sells electricity to JPSCo; Gen. Man. and CEO WAYNE MCKENZIE.

Jamaica Public Service Co (JPSCo): Dominion Life Bldg, 6 Knutsford Blvd, POB 54, Kingston 5; tel. 926-3190; fax 968-5341; e-mail calljps@jpsco.com; internet www.myjpsco.com; responsible for the generation and supply of electricity to the island; the JPSCo operating licence due to expire in 2027; Pres. and CEO KELLY TOMBLIN.

South Jamaica Power Co (SJPC): Kingston; jtly owned by Japan's Marubeni Corpn (40%), East West Power Korea (40%) and JPSCo (20%); Man. Dir VALENTINE FAGAN.

Water

National Water Commission: LOJ Centre, 5th Floor, 28–48 Barbados Ave, Kingston 5; tel. 929-5430; fax 926-1329; e-mail pr@nwc.com.jm; internet www.nwcjamaica.com; f. 1980; statutory body; provides potable water and waste water services; Chair. Dr LEARY MYERS.

Water Resources Authority: Hope Gardens, POB 91, Kingston 7; tel. 927-0077; fax 977-0179; e-mail info@wra.gov.jm; internet www.wra.gov.jm; f. 1996; manages, protects and controls allocation and use of water supplies; Man. Dir BASIL FERNANDEZ.

TRADE UNIONS

Caribbean Union of Teachers: 97 Church St, Kingston; tel. 922-1385; fax 922-3257; e-mail infor@caribbeanteachers.com; internet www.caribbeanteachers.com; f. 1935; umbrella org.; affiliates in 21 Caribbean countries; Pres. MARVIN ANDALL; Gen. Sec. Dr ADOLPH CAMERON.

Jamaica Confederation of Trade Unions (JCTU): 1A Hope Blvd, Kingston 6; tel. 927-2468; fax 977-4575; e-mail jctu@cwjamaica.com; Pres. LLOYD GOODLEIGH.

National Workers' Union of Jamaica (NWU): 130–132 East St, POB 344, Kingston 16; tel. 922-1150; fax 922-6608; e-mail nwyou@cwjamaica.com; f. 1952; affiliated to the International Trade Union Confederation; Pres. VINCENT MORRISON; Vice. Pres. HOWARD DUNCAN; 10,000 mems.

Transport

RAILWAYS

There are about 339 km of railway, all standard gauge, in Jamaica. Passenger services ceased in 1992. In 2008 the Government announced that the People's Republic of China was to provide assistance in the reconstruction of the railway system between Kingston and Montego Bay, and Spanish Town and Ewarton.

Jamaica Railway Corpn (JRC): 142 Barry St, POB 489, Kingston; tel. 922-6443; fax 922-4539; e-mail odcrooks@cwjamaica.com; internet www.mtw.gov.jm/dep_agencies/ja_rail.aspx; f. 1845 as Jamaica Railway Co, the earliest British colonial railway; transferred to JRC in 1960; govt-owned; autonomous, statutory corpn until 1990, when it was partly leased to Alcan Jamaica Co Ltd (subsequently West Indies Alumina Co); planned privatization announced 2012; 215 km of railway; Chair. JOSEPH A. MATALON; Gen. Man. OWEN CROOKS.

Jamalco (Alcoa Minerals of Jamaica): Clarendon Parish, Clarendon; tel. 986-2561; fax 986-9637; internet www.alcoa.com/jamaica/en/home.asp; 43 km of standard gauge railway; transport of bauxite; CEO KLAUS KLEINFELD.

ROADS

Jamaica has a good network of tar-surfaced and metalled motoring roads. In 2010 there were 22,121 km of roads in Jamaica. In 2004 the Export-Import Bank of China loaned US $340m. for the Jamaica Road Development Infrastructure Programme, a five-year project to rehabilitate more than 570 km of roads across the island. Development of a 66-km highway, the North–South Link, began in 2013. Work on the US $610m. project by the China Harbour Engineering Company was expected to be completed by December 2015.

Jamaica Urban Transit Company (JUTC): 1 Michael Manley Dr., Twickenham Park, Spanish Town, St Catherine; tel. 749-3192; fax 924-8158; e-mail marketing@jutc.com.jm; internet www.jutc.com; f. 1999; operates public transport in Kingston metropolitan region; Chair. Rev. GARNETT ROPER; Man. Dir Rear-Adm. HARDLEY LEWIN.

Transport Authority: 119 Maxfield Ave, Kingston 10; tel. 926-8912; fax 929-4178; e-mail customerservice@ta.org.jm; internet www.ta.org.jm; regulatory body; administers the licensing of public and commercial vehicles; Chair. NORTON HINDS; Man. Dir DANIEL DAWES.

SHIPPING

The principal ports are Kingston, Montego Bay and Port Antonio. The port at Kingston is a major transshipment terminal for the Caribbean area. In 2008 the fifth phase of an expansion project in Kingston was completed, doubling the port's handling capacity. Further plans for the expansion of Jamaica's port facilities, to include the construction of three additional berths and a second terminal at Montego Bay, were under way. A new cruise ship pier at Falmouth opened in 2011. At December 2013 the flag registered fleet comprised 40 vessels, totalling 168,417 grt.

Port Authority of Jamaica: 15–17 Duke St, Kingston; tel. 922-0290; fax 948-3575; e-mail paj@portjam.com; internet www.portjam.com; f. 1966; Govt's principal maritime agency; responsible for monitoring and regulating the navigation of all vessels berthing at Jamaican ports, for regulating the tariffs on public wharves, and for the devt of industrial free zones in Jamaica; Pres. and Chair. NOEL A. HYLTON.

Kingston Free Zone Co Ltd: 27 Shannon Dr., POB 1025, Kingston 15; tel. 923-6021; fax 923-6023; e-mail blee@portjam.com; internet www.pajfz.com; f. 1976; subsidiary of Port Authority of Jamaica; management and promotion of an export-orientated industrial free trade zone for cos from various countries; Gen. Man. KARLA HUIE.

Montego Bay Free Zone: POB 1377, Montego Bay; tel. 979-8696; fax 979-8088; e-mail gchenry@portjam.com; internet www.mbfz-jamaica.com; Vice-Pres. GLORIA HENRY.

Shipping Association of Jamaica: 4 Fourth Ave, Newport West, POB 1050, Kingston 13; tel. 923-3491; fax 923-3421; e-mail saj@jamports.com; internet www.jamports.com; f. 1939; 78 mems; regulates the supply and management of stevedoring labour in Kingston; represents mems in negotiations with govt and trade bodies; Pres. KIM CLARKE; Gen. Man. TREVOR RILEY.

Principal Shipping Company

Jamaica Freight and Shipping Co Ltd (JFS): 80–82 Second St, Newport West, Kingston 12; tel. 923-9271; fax 923-4091; e-mail jfs@jashipco.com; internet www.jashipco.com; f. 1976; liner and port agents, stevedoring services; Exec. Chair. CHARLES JOHNSTON.

CIVIL AVIATION

There are three international airports linking Jamaica with North America, Europe, and other Caribbean islands. The Norman Manley International Airport is situated 22.5 km outside Kingston. Sangster International Airport is 5 km from Montego Bay. A J $800m. programme to expand and improve the latter was completed in 2009. The Ian Fleming International Airport at Boscobel, 10 km from Ocho Rios, opened in 2011. In May the national airline, Air Jamaica, was taken over by the Trinidadian Caribbean Airlines.

Airports Authority of Jamaica: Norman Manley International Airport, Palisadoes; tel. 924-8452; fax 924-8419; e-mail aaj@aaj.com.jm; internet www.airportsauthorityjamaica.aero; Chair. MARK HART; Pres. EARL ANTHONY RICHARDS.

Civil Aviation Authority: 4 Winchester Rd, POB 8998, Kingston 10; tel. 960-3948; fax 920-0194; e-mail info@jcaa.gov.jm; internet www.jcaa.gov.jm; f. 1996; Dir-Gen. Lt Col OSCAR DERBY.

Air Jamaica Ltd: 72–76 Harbour St, Kingston; tel. 922-3460; fax 967-3125; internet www.airjamaica.com; f. 1968; privatized in 1994, reacquired by Govt in 2004; sold to Caribbean Airlines (Trinidad and Tobago) in 2011; Govt of Jamaica retained 16% share; services within the Caribbean and to Canada (in asscn with Air Canada), the USA and the United Kingdom; Chair. GEORGE M. NICHOLAS, III; CEO ROBERT CORBIE (acting).

Exec Direct Aviation (EDA): Bldg II, Suite 11, 1 Ripon Rd, Kingston 5; tel. 618-5884; fax 618-5888; internet www.flyexecdirect.com; f. 2011; cargo services to Caribbean, Central and South American destinations; COO KAMAL CLARKE.

Fly Jamaica Airways: 2 Holborn Rd, Kingston 10; tel. 632-7300; fax 908-3069; e-mail info@fly-jamaica.com; internet www.fly-jamaica.com; f. 2013; Chair. and CEO Capt. PAUL RONALD REECE; Sec. Capt. LLOYD TAI.

Jamaica Air Shuttle: Tinson Pen Aerodrome, Marcus Garvey Dr., Kingston 11; tel. 923-0371; fax 506-9071; e-mail reservations@jamaicaairshuttle.com; internet www.jamaicaairshuttle.com; f. 2005; domestic and regional charter services to the Cayman Islands, Cuba, Dominican Republic and Haiti; Chair. CHRISTOPHER READ.

TimAir Ltd: Sangster International Airport, Montego Bay; tel. 952-2516; fax 979-1113; e-mail timair@usa.net; internet www.timair.com; f. 1983; charter services; Pres. FRASER MCCONNELL; Man. COLLEEN MCCONNELL.

Tourism

Tourists, mainly from the USA, visit Jamaica for its beaches, mountains, historic buildings and cultural heritage. In 2012 there were 1,986,082 visitor arrivals. Tourism receipts totalled US $2,046m. in that year.

Jamaica Hotel and Tourist Association (JHTA): 2 Ardenne Rd, Kingston 10; tel. 926-3635-6; fax 929-1054; e-mail info@jhta.org; internet www.jhta.org; f. 1961; trade asscn for hoteliers and other cos involved in Jamaican tourism; Pres. EVELYN SMITH; Exec. Dir CAMILLE NEEDHAM.

Jamaica Tourist Board (JTB): 64 Knutsford Blvd, Kingston 5; tel. 929-9200; fax 929-9375; e-mail info@visitjamaica.com; internet www.visitjamaica.com; f. 1955; a statutory body set up by the Govt to promote all aspects of the tourism industry; Chair. DENNIS MORRISON; Dir of Tourism JOHN LYNCH.

Defence

As assessed at November 2013, the total strength of the Jamaican Defence Force was 2,830. This included an army of 2,500, a coastguard of 190 and an air wing of 140 members on active service. There were some 980 reservists.

Defence Budget: an estimated J $12,100m. (US $129m.) in 2013.

Chief of Defence Staff: Maj.-Gen. ANTONY BERTRAM ANDERSON.

Education

Primary education is compulsory in certain districts, and free education is ensured. The education system consists of a primary cycle of six years, followed by two secondary cycles of three and four years, respectively. In 2009/10 enrolment at primary schools included 82% of children in the relevant age-group. In the same year enrolment at secondary schools included 84% of children in the relevant age-group. Higher education was provided by four institutions, including the University of the West Indies, which has two campuses, at Mona and Montego Bay. Government spending on education in 2012/13 was budgeted at some J $73,829m.

JAPAN

Introductory Survey

LOCATION, CLIMATE, LANGUAGE, RELIGION, FLAG, CAPITAL

Japan lies in eastern Asia and comprises a curved chain of more than 3,000 islands. Four large islands, named (from north to south) Hokkaido, Honshu, Shikoku and Kyushu, account for about 98% of the land area. Hokkaido lies just to the south of Sakhalin, a large Russian island, and about 1,300 km (800 miles) east of Russia's mainland port of Vladivostok. Southern Japan is about 150 km (93 miles) east of the Republic of Korea (South Korea). Although summers are temperate everywhere, the climate in winter varies sharply from cold in the north to mild in the south. Temperatures in Tokyo range from −6°C (21°F) to 30°C (86°F). Typhoons and heavy rains are common in summer. The official language is Japanese. A small minority of indigenous Ainu speak a distinct language. The major religions are Shintoism and Buddhism, and there is a Christian minority. The national flag (proportions 7 by 10) is white, with a red disc (a sun without rays) in the centre. The capital is Tokyo.

CONTEMPORARY POLITICAL HISTORY

Historical Context

Following Japan's defeat in the Second World War, Japanese forces surrendered in August 1945. Japan signed an armistice in September, and the country was placed under US military occupation. A new democratic Constitution, which took effect in May 1947, renounced war and abandoned the doctrine of the Emperor's divinity. Following the peace treaty of September 1951, Japan regained its independence on 28 April 1952, although it was not until 1972 that the last of the US-administered outer islands, the remaining Ryukyu Islands (including Okinawa), were returned to Japanese sovereignty. The conservative Shigeru Yoshida served as Prime Minister in 1946–47 and again between 1948 and 1954, when he was succeeded by Ichiro Hatoyama.

Domestic Political Affairs

Liberal Democratic Party dominance, 1955–93

In November 1955 rival conservative groups merged to form the Liberal Democratic Party (LDP). Nobusuke Kishi, who became Prime Minister in February 1957, was succeeded by Hayato Ikeda in July 1960. Ikeda was replaced by Eisaku Sato in November 1964. Sato remained in office until July 1972, when he was succeeded by Kakuei Tanaka. Tanaka's premiership was beset by problems, leading to his replacement by Takeo Miki in December 1974. Tanaka was subsequently accused of accepting bribes from the Marubeni Corporation, and he was arrested in July 1976. The LDP lost its overall majority in the House of Representatives (the lower house of the Kokkai or Diet) at legislative elections held in December 1976. Miki resigned and was succeeded by Takeo Fukuda. However, Masayoshi Ohira defeated Fukuda in the LDP presidential election of November 1978, and replaced him as Prime Minister in December. Ohira was unable to win a majority in the lower house at elections in October 1979. In May 1980 the Government was defeated in a motion of no confidence, forcing the dissolution of the lower house. Ohira died before the elections in June, when the LDP won 284 of the 511 seats. In July Zenko Suzuki was elected President of the LDP, and subsequently appointed Prime Minister. The growing factionalism of the LDP and the worsening economic crisis prompted Suzuki's resignation as Prime Minister and LDP President in October 1982. He was succeeded by Yasuhiro Nakasone.

At elections in June 1983 for one-half of the seats in the House of Councillors (the upper house of the Diet), a new electoral system was used. Of the 126 contested seats, 50 were filled on the basis of proportional representation. Two small parties thus entered the House of Councillors for the first time. The LDP increased its strength from 134 to 137 members in the 252-seat chamber. This result was seen as an endorsement of Nakasone's policies of increased expenditure on defence, closer relations with the USA and greater Japanese involvement in international affairs.

In October 1983 former Prime Minister Tanaka was found guilty of having accepted bribes. However, Tanaka's refusal to relinquish his parliamentary seat prompted an opposition-led boycott of the Diet, forcing Nakasone to call premature legislative elections in December. The Komeito (Clean Government Party), the Democratic Socialist Party (DSP) and the Japan Socialist Party (JSP) gained seats, at the expense of the Communists and the New Liberal Club (NLC). The LDP, which had performed badly in the elections, formed a coalition with the NLC (which had split from the LDP over the Tanaka affair in 1976) and several independents. Nakasone called further early elections, held in July 1986, at which the LDP won 304 of the 512 seats. The record majority enabled the LDP to dispense with its coalition partner, the NLC (which disbanded in August and rejoined the LDP). In September the leaders of the LDP agreed to alter by-laws to allow party presidents one-year extensions beyond the normal limit of two terms of two years each. Nakasone was thus able to retain the posts of President of the LDP and Prime Minister until October 1987.

In July 1987 the Secretary-General of the LDP, Noboru Takeshita, left the Tanaka faction, with 113 other members, and announced the formation of a major new grouping within the ruling party. In the same month Tanaka's position was further weakened when the Tokyo High Court upheld his 1983 conviction for accepting bribes. In October 1987 Nakasone nominated Takeshita as his successor. The Diet was convened and Takeshita was formally elected as Prime Minister in November. In the new Cabinet Takeshita maintained a balance among the five major factions of the LDP, retaining only two members of Nakasone's previous Cabinet, but appointing four members of the Nakasone faction to senior ministerial posts (including Nakasone's ally, Sosuke Uno, as Minister of Foreign Affairs).

In January 1989 Emperor Hirohito, who had reigned since 1926, died after a long illness, thus ending the Showa era. He was succeeded by his son, Akihito, and the new era was named Heisei ('achievement of universal peace').

The Prime Minister and the LDP suffered a serious setback in June 1988 when several senior party members, including Nakasone, Kiichi Miyazawa and Takeshita himself, were alleged to have been indirectly involved in share-trading irregularities with the Recruit Cosmos Company. Three cabinet ministers and the Chairman of the DSP were subsequently forced to resign, owing to their alleged involvement in the Recruit affair. In April 1989, as the allegations against politicians widened to include charges of bribery and malpractice, Takeshita announced his resignation. He was subsequently found to have accepted donations worth more than 150m. yen from the Recruit organization. Takeshita nominated Sosuke Uno as his successor. Uno was elected Prime Minister by the Diet in June, and a new Cabinet was appointed. Uno was the first Japanese Prime Minister since the foundation of the LDP not to command his own political faction. Meanwhile, in May, following an investigation into the Recruit affair undertaken by an LDP special committee, public prosecutors indicted 13 people. Nakasone resigned from the LDP, assuming responsibility for the scandal, but did not relinquish his seat in the Diet.

Within days of Uno's assumption of office, a Japanese magazine published allegations of sexual impropriety involving the Prime Minister. As a result of the ensuing outcry and a considerable increase in support for the JSP, led by Chairwoman Takako Doi, in July 1989 the LDP lost its majority in the upper house for the first time in its history. Uno's offer to resign was accepted by the LDP, which in August chose the relatively unknown Toshiki Kaifu, a former Minister of Education, to be the party's President and the new Prime Minister. Although the House of Councillors' ballot rejected Kaifu as the new Prime Minister in favour of Takako Doi, the decision of the lower house was adopted, in accordance with stipulations embodied in the Constitution.

At legislative elections held in February 1990, the LDP was returned to power with an unexpectedly large measure of support, securing 275 of the 512 seats in the House of Representatives. In January 1991 the JSP changed its English name to the

Social Democratic Party of Japan (SDPJ) and Makato Tanabe later replaced Takako Doi as Chairman of the party. In September senior LDP officials forced Kaifu to abandon proposals for electoral reform, and the Takeshita faction of the LDP subsequently withdrew its support for the Prime Minister. With the backing of this faction, former Minister of Finance Kiichi Miyazawa was elected President of the LDP in October, and in November the Diet endorsed his appointment as Prime Minister. However, his position was undermined by new allegations of involvement in the Recruit affair, publicized by the SDPJ in December.

In early 1992 public disgust at official corruption was registered at two prefectural by-elections to the upper house, when the LDP lost seats that had previously been considered secure to Rengo-no-kai (the political arm of RENGO, the trade union confederation). However, the anti-Government alliance that had supported Rengo-no-kai disintegrated in May over the issue of the authorization of Japanese involvement in UN peacekeeping operations. Members of the SDPJ attempted to obstruct the vote in the lower house by submitting their resignations en masse. However, the Speaker ruled that these could not be accepted during the current Diet session. The successful passage through the Diet of the legislation on international peacekeeping improved the Government's standing, and in elections to the upper house in July the LDP won 69 of the 127 seats contested. The SDPJ, by contrast, lost 25 of its 46 seats; the Komeito increased its total strength from 20 to 24 seats, but Rengo-no-kai failed to win any seats, owing to the dissolution of the informal coalition it had facilitated between the SDPJ and the DSP. The Japan New Party (JNP), founded by LDP dissidents only two months prior to the elections, secured four seats. A formal split within the Takeshita faction took place in December 1992. The new faction was to be led nominally by Tsutomu Hata, the Minister of Finance, although it was widely recognized that Ichiro Ozawa, the former LDP Secretary-General, held effective power in the grouping.

Electoral reform was a major political issue in the first half of 1993. While the LDP favoured a single-member constituency system, the opposition parties proposed various forms of proportional representation. In June the lower house adopted a motion of no confidence against the Government, after the LDP refused to modify its reform proposals to meet opposition demands. Numerous LDP members opposed the Government or abstained from the vote. The Ozawa-Hata group, comprising 44 former LDP members, immediately established a new party, the Shinseito (Japan Renewal Party, JRP), in order to contest the forthcoming legislative elections. Another new party, the New Party Sakigake, was also formed by LDP Diet members. In the elections to the House of Representatives, held in July, the LDP won 223 of the 511 seats, thus falling 33 seats short of a majority. Miyazawa resigned as Prime Minister and a seven-party coalition Government was formed, excluding the LDP, which consequently became an opposition party for the first time since its formation. In August Morihiro Hosokawa, the leader of the JNP, was elected Prime Minister, defeating the new President of the LDP, Yohei Kono.

Successive Governments, 1994–2001

Hosokawa resigned as Prime Minister in April 1994. He was subsequently replaced by Tsutomu Hata, at the head of a minority Government which excluded the SDPJ and the New Party Sakigake. Hata was obliged to resign in June, however, owing to his continued failure to command a viable majority in the Diet, and a new coalition, composed of the SDPJ, the LDP and the New Party Sakigake, took office. The LDP thus ended its brief period in opposition. Tomiichi Murayama, the leader of the SDPJ, became Prime Minister, and Kono was appointed Deputy Prime Minister and Minister of Foreign Affairs.

In July 1994 Murayama recognized the constitutional right to the existence of Japan's Self-Defence Forces (SDF, the armed forces). In December nine opposition parties, including the JNP, the JRP, the DSP and the Komeito, amalgamated to form a new political party, the Shinshinto (New Frontier Party, NFP). A faction of the Komeito remained outside the new party and was renamed Komei. Kaifu was elected leader of the NFP; Ozawa was appointed Secretary-General. The creation of the NFP was widely perceived to be a response to the approval by the Diet in November 1994 of the electoral reform bills first proposed in 1993, which appeared to favour larger political parties. Under the terms of the new law, the House of Representatives was to be reduced to 500 seats, comprising 300 single-seat constituencies and 200 seats determined by proportional representation; the proportional-representation base was to be divided into 11 regions, and a party would qualify for a proportional-representation seat if it received a minimum of 2% of the vote.

In January 1995 a massive earthquake in the Kobe region caused thousands of deaths and serious infrastructural damage. The Government was severely criticized for the poor co-ordination of the relief operation. In March the poisonous gas sarin was released into the Tokyo underground railway system, killing 12 people and injuring more than 5,000. A religious sect, Aum Shinrikyo, was accused of perpetrating the attack. Following a further gas attack, in Yokohama in April, a number of sect members were detained by the authorities. In June Shoko Asahara, the leader of Aum Shinrikyo, was indicted on a charge of murder; his trial continued until February 2004, when he was sentenced to death for his role in the Tokyo attack. (However, at April 2014, owing to various procedural delays, Asahara had not yet been executed.)

Participation in the elections to the House of Councillors held in July 1995 was low. With one-half of the 252 seats being contested, the LDP won only 49 seats, the SDPJ 16 and the New Party Sakigake three, whereas the NFP, benefiting from the support of the Soka Gakkai religious organization, secured 40 seats. In September Ryutaro Hashimoto, the Minister of International Trade and Industry, was elected as the new leader of the LDP, after Yohei Kono announced that he would not seek re-election.

In December 1995 Kaifu was succeeded by Ozawa as leader of the NFP. In January 1996 Murayama resigned as Prime Minister; however, he was re-elected Chairman of the SDPJ. The LDP leader, Ryutaro Hashimoto, was elected Prime Minister. A coalition Cabinet, largely dominated by the LDP, was formed. In August Shoichi Ide and Hiroyuki Sonoda were elected Leader and Secretary-General, respectively, of the New Party Sakigake following the resignations of Masayoshi Takemura and Yukio Hatoyama. The latter left the party and founded the Democratic Party of Japan (DPJ), with other dissident members of the New Party Sakigake and individual members of the SDPJ and NFP.

At legislative elections held in October 1996 the LDP won 239 of the 500 seats in the House of Representatives, while the NFP secured 156, the DPJ 52, the Japanese Communist Party (JCP) 26, the SDPJ 15, and the New Party Sakigake two seats. In November Hashimoto was re-elected Prime Minister, and formed the first single-party Cabinet since 1993. Soon after the elections several government ministers and party leaders were implicated in various corruption scandals. In December 1996 former Prime Minister Hata left the NFP and established a new party, Taiyoto (Sun Party), together with 12 other dissident NFP members. Later that month Takako Doi was formally appointed Chairwoman of the SDPJ.

By September 1997 the LDP had regained its majority in the House of Representatives, following a series of defections by members of the NFP. In December a much-reduced NFP was dissolved. Six new parties were founded by former NFP members—Ozawa and his supporters forming the Liberal Party (LP)—and a significant political realignment thus took place. In January 1998 six opposition parties, including the DPJ, formed a parliamentary group, Minyuren, which constituted the largest opposition bloc in the Diet. In March the parties comprising Minyuren agreed on their integration into the DPJ, formally establishing a new DPJ, with Naoto Kan as its President, in the following month.

Meanwhile, during 1997 various circumstances contributed to the development of an economic crisis. The Government announced a series of measures designed to encourage economic growth, including a reduction in taxes and, in a major reversal of policy in response to the recent failure of several financial institutions, the use of public funds to support the banking system. In January 1998 two senior officials from the Ministry of Finance were arrested on suspicion of accepting bribes from banks. The Minister of Finance, Hiroshi Mitsuzuka, resigned, accepting responsibility for the affair. As more banks and other financial institutions became implicated in the scandal, the central bank initiated an internal investigation into its own operations. In March the Governor resigned after a senior bank executive was arrested, amid further allegations of bribery. Trials of those implicated in the scandals took place in 1998 and 1999. A number of financial deregulation measures took effect on 1 April 1998, as part of Japan's 'Big Bang' reform process. Hashimoto's administration was widely criticized for its slow reaction to the growing economic crisis. In June the SDPJ and the New Party Sakigake withdrew from their alliance with the ruling LDP.

The LDP performed poorly in elections for one-half of the seats in the House of Councillors in July 1998, retaining only 44 of its 61 seats contested, while the DPJ won 27 seats, increasing its representation to 47 seats, and the JCP became the third largest party in the upper house, taking 15 seats. Hashimoto resigned as Prime Minister and President of the LDP and was succeeded in both posts by Keizo Obuchi, hitherto Minister of Foreign Affairs. Although designated an 'economic reconstruction' Cabinet, doubts arose about the Obuchi Government's commitment to comprehensive reform. Kiichi Miyazawa, the former Prime Minister, was appointed Minister of Finance. Obuchi announced the establishment of an Economic Strategy Council and promised substantial tax reductions. The issue of banking reform dominated the following months, and in October the Diet approved banking legislation that included provisions for the nationalization of failing banks, as demanded by the opposition.

Komei merged with another party, Shinto Heiwa, in November 1998 to form New Komeito, which thus became the second largest opposition party. Also in that month Fukushiro Nukaga, the Director-General of the Defence Agency, resigned from the Government to assume responsibility for a procurement scandal. In mid-November the LDP and the LP reached a basic accord on the formation of a coalition, although this would still lack a majority in the upper house. The Government was reorganized in January 1999 to include the LP.

At local elections in April 1999, 11 of the 12 governorships contested were won by the incumbents, all standing as independents. At the gubernatorial election for Tokyo, the convincing victory of Shintaro Ishihara, an outspoken nationalist writer and a former Minister of Transport under the LDP (although now unaffiliated), was regarded as an embarrassment for the ruling party. In August the Diet voted to grant official legal status to the de facto national flag (*Hinomaru*) and anthem (*Kimigayo*), despite considerable opposition owing to their association with Japan's militaristic past. Meanwhile, in July New Komeito joined the ruling LDP-LP coalition, giving the Government a majority in the upper house and expanding its control in the lower house to more than 70% of the seats. However, negotiations on policy initiatives proved difficult, owing to differences over issues such as constitutional revision and New Komeito's opposition to a reduction in the number of seats in the lower house, as favoured by the LP. Obuchi was re-elected President of the LDP in September. Naoto Kan was replaced as President of the DPJ by Yukio Hatoyama, hitherto Secretary-General of the party. A new Cabinet was appointed in October. Notably, Michio Ochi was appointed Chairman of the Financial Reconstruction Commission. The LP and New Komeito each received one cabinet post. A basic accord on coalition policy included an agreement to seek a reduction in the number of seats in the House of Representatives, initially by 20 and subsequently by a further 30.

In December 1999 a political crisis was averted when the LP leader, Ichiro Ozawa, was persuaded not to withdraw his party from the ruling coalition, as he had threatened, over a delay in the proposal of legislation to reduce the number of seats in the lower house. Multi-party committees were established in both houses in January 2000, which were to review the Constitution over a period of five years. In February the Diet approved the controversial legislation on the reduction in seats, despite an opposition boycott. In the same month Michio Ochi was forced to resign from the Cabinet over remarks that suggested he would be lenient on banking reform.

Discord within the coalition increased, and in April 2000 the LP withdrew from the Government; 26 members of the LP formed the New Conservative Party—NCP (Hoshuto). In the same month Prime Minister Obuchi suffered a stroke and went into a coma, from which he never regained consciousness. The LDP elected Yoshiro Mori, the Secretary-General, as party President. Mori was subsequently elected Prime Minister by both Houses of the Diet; he immediately affirmed his commitment to the reform initiatives of his predecessor, and formed a coalition with New Komeito and the NCP. All ministers from the Obuchi administration were retained. In May Noboru Takeshita, the former Prime Minister, announced his retirement from politics and from the LDP; he died shortly afterwards. Former Prime Minister Ryutaro Hashimoto was appointed head of the Takeshita faction of the LDP, which had been led by Obuchi.

Following his appointment as Prime Minister, Mori made a number of controversial public statements, expressing imperialist views. Although forced to issue apologies, he did not retract his remarks. At the legislative elections held in June 2000 the number of seats in the House of Representatives was reduced from 500 to 480. The LDP won the largest number of seats, although its representation was reduced to 233. The DPJ increased its representation to 127 seats, New Komeito won 31 seats, the LP 22 seats, the NCP 20 seats and the SDPJ 19 seats. Despite numerous political gaffes and public errors of protocol, Mori was returned as Prime Minister and appointed a new Cabinet in July.

Corruption was a major issue throughout 2000, and various revelations of bribery resulted in several resignations. In November one LDP legislator resigned and another was arrested following the disclosure of a 'cash for questions' scandal involving an insurance company. In January 2001 Fukushiro Nukaga, the Minister of State for Economy, Industry and Information Technology, resigned, having admitted that he had accepted bribes from the company. In October 2000 Hidenao Nakagawa, Minister of State, Chief Cabinet Secretary, Director-General of the Okinawa Development Agency and Minister in Charge of Information Technology, resigned after it was alleged, *inter alia*, that he had links to a right-wing activist. In the following month former Minister of Construction Eiichi Nakao acknowledged in court that he had taken bribes in 1996 in exchange for the allocation of public works contracts.

The high incidence of corruption further undermined Mori, and during October 2000 the Prime Minister came under increasing pressure to resign after it was alleged in a magazine that some years previously he had been arrested for violation of an anti-prostitution law. Mori denied the allegation and sued the publication for libel. Mori's apparent suggestion that the Democratic People's Republic of Korea (North Korea) might release Japanese hostages (see Foreign Affairs) to a third country in order to avoid any admission of their existence led to harsh criticism. Nevertheless, in November the Prime Minister survived a motion of no confidence in the legislature.

Meanwhile, in November 2000 Fusako Shigenobu, the founder of the extremist left-wing Japanese Red Army, which had been responsible for a number of attacks during the 1970s, was arrested in Osaka. She was detained on suspicion of the seizure of the French embassy in the Netherlands in 1974 and subsequently indicted on various related charges. A number of other members had been repatriated from several countries since 1995 to be tried for terrorism. (Shigenobu was sentenced to 20 years' imprisonment in February 2006 for her involvement in the seizure of the embassy.)

A major government reorganization was announced in December 2000. The number of ministries was reduced from 23 to 13, mainly through mergers, and various state agencies were absorbed into the newly created Cabinet Office. Despite the publication in late 2000 of photographs apparently showing the Prime Minister in the company of an alleged gangster and convicted murderer, Mori won another vote of confidence in March 2001. In early April, however, he announced his intention to resign.

The administration of Junichiro Koizumi

In late April 2001 Junichiro Koizumi, a former Minister of Health and Welfare, unexpectedly defeated Ryutaro Hashimoto, the leader of the largest LDP faction, and one other candidate to secure the presidency of the ruling LDP and thus the premiership. Koizumi's victory was attributed to a change in party election rules that allowed a greater influence of local and ordinary party members in selecting the President. He subsequently reorganized the Cabinet, largely disregarding LDP factional politics, and appointed a number of reformists, including Makiko Tanaka, daughter of former Prime Minister Kakuei Tanaka, as Japan's first female Minister of Foreign Affairs, and Heizo Takenaka, an economics professor, as Minister of State for Economy, Industry and Information Technology. Koizumi also reorganized the LDP's senior leadership, appointing his ally Taku Yamasaki as Secretary-General, and Taro Aso as Chairman of the Policy Research Council. In addition to according priority to economic reform, Koizumi also sought to introduce direct elections for the post of prime minister and to upgrade the status of the SDF into that of a full army, which would involve an amendment to Article 9 of the Constitution, whereby Japan renounced the use of war.

In June 2001 the Government finally announced an economic reform programme, which included the privatization of special public institutions and a review of regulatory economic laws. However, veteran members of the LDP, particularly the Hashimoto faction, remained opposed to Koizumi's reforms. The Prime

Minister's popularity among the populace was a major factor in the LDP's gains in elections to the House of Councillors held in July. Koizumi aroused controversy later in that month when he made an official visit to the Yasukuni Shrine to honour Japan's war dead: the shrine includes memorials to officers who were convicted of serious war crimes. Koizumi made five further visits to the shrine during his term of office, incurring both domestic and international criticism.

In September 2001 the terrorist attacks on the USA by militants believed to be linked to the Islamist group al-Qa'ida again raised the subject of the role of Japan's military; Koizumi appeared to invoke the USA's subsequent war against the Taliban regime of Afghanistan as an argument to expand the role of the SDF. In October the Diet approved new legislation for the overseas deployment of the SDF in a non-combat support role, and in the following month Japan dispatched warships to the Indian Ocean, in the biggest such deployment since the Second World War (see Foreign Affairs). The Japanese people strongly supported logistical assistance to the USA, but there remained considerable public opposition to any amendment to Article 9 of the Constitution.

In December 2001 the Government agreed to abolish 17 public corporations and transfer 45 others (of a total of 163) to the private sector. However, Koizumi's major proposed reform, the privatization of the Postal Services Agency, was further delayed. Meanwhile, the opposition DPJ itself experienced divisions, between those who favoured co-operation with Koizumi and his reforms (including the President of the DPJ, Yukio Hatoyama) and those who favoured greater co-operation with other opposition parties. At the end of January 2002 Koizumi dismissed his Minister of Foreign Affairs, Makiko Tanaka, following months of disputes over reform within the ministry. The dismissal of the popular Tanaka was regarded as a victory for LDP veterans and as a setback for reform. The session of the Diet was extended until July in order to enable Koizumi to draft legislation for reforms to the postal services, as well as to the health service and defence and security sectors. These reforms were opposed by considerable elements within the LDP.

In September 2002 Koizumi implemented a long-expected cabinet reorganization, notably dismissing the Minister of State for the Financial Services Agency, Hakuo Yanagisawa, and appointing the Minister of State for Economic and Fiscal Policy, Heizo Takenaka, concurrently to hold that post. Plans to reform the banking sector created tensions between the LDP and its two coalition partners, New Komeito and the NCP. In October a tripartite committee of the ruling coalition published a banking reform plan that was far less radical than that sought by Takenaka, who had urged the nationalization of major banks to prevent their failure.

In December 2002 the opposition DPJ elected Naoto Kan as its President, replacing Yukio Hatoyama, who had been forced to resign from the post after the failure of secret attempts to merge the party with the smaller opposition LP. Kan had previously headed the DPJ during 1997–99. Four DPJ members of the Diet, led by former party Vice-President Hiroshi Kumagai, resigned from the party in December 2002 and joined the NCP; the President of that party, Takeshi Noda, resigned in favour of Kumagai.

In March 2003 the Governor of Tokyo, Shintaro Ishihara, announced that he would seek re-election, ending months of speculation that he might form a new political party in order to challenge Koizumi. At the local elections in April Ishihara was overwhelmingly re-elected, and pledged to use his position to campaign for reform in the country as a whole.

In April 2003 the LDP announced its intention to amend the Constitution explicitly to state the legitimacy of the SDF and to expand its role in international peacekeeping and collective self-defence. In May the House of Representatives approved new legislation granting the Government and the SDF greater powers to act in the event of an attack on Japan; the bill, which was supported by the DPJ as well as by the ruling coalition, was approved the following month by the House of Councillors. In July, despite vehement opposition, the House of Councillors approved proposals, recently endorsed by the lower chamber, to send peacekeeping forces to Iraq, thereby allowing the largest deployment of Japanese troops abroad since the Second World War. Although troops were to engage in humanitarian work only, critics argued that the deployment would violate the Constitution, as, in practice, troops would be unable to avoid conflict areas.

In September 2003 Koizumi was re-elected as leader of the LDP, defeating three rival candidates. Koizumi then announced a new Cabinet, which included the reappointment of Heizo Takenaka as Minister of State responsible for the Financial Services Agency, despite criticism of his banking reform policies (see above). Also in September, a merger agreement between the DPJ and the LP was signed, with the aim of creating an opposition movement capable of presenting a strong challenge to the LDP at the forthcoming legislative elections.

At the elections, held in November 2003, the LDP won 237 seats, thus losing 10 of its previous 247 seats in the House of Representatives. The party's strength increased to 245 following the recruitment of four independent candidates and the absorption of the NCP, one of the LDP's two coalition partners, which had won four seats. The LDP's other coalition partner, New Komeito, secured 34 seats. The DPJ (incorporating the former LP) won 177 seats, thereby increasing its representation by 40.

Plans for the SDF deployment to Iraq, following the approval of the requisite legislation in July 2003 (see above), were strongly criticized by the President of the DPJ, Naoto Kan. Popular protests against the Iraq mission took place, and opposition within Japan to the deployment was strengthened by the deaths of two Japanese diplomats in Iraq in November. In January 2004 the first Japanese troops departed for Iraq. In the same month it was announced that draft legislation on the reform of Japan's Constitution, including an amendment to Article 9, would be submitted in 2005.

In May 2004 a scandal over pension contributions prompted resignations by senior officials of the LDP and the opposition DPJ. The Chief Cabinet Secretary, Yasuo Fukuda of the LDP, resigned after admitting that he had not made the required payments to the compulsory state pension scheme. Naoto Kan resigned from the presidency of the DPJ shortly afterwards on similar grounds. Kan was replaced by Katsuya Okada, hitherto Secretary-General of the DPJ. In the same month a government proposal for pension reform, involving increased premiums and reduced benefits, was approved by the House of Representatives. The reform plan was approved by the House of Councillors in June, despite strong opposition from the DPJ. In July nationwide voting took place to elect one-half of the members of the House of Councillors. Of the 121 seats contested, the LDP won 49, while the DPJ secured 50 (thus increasing its overall representation in the chamber from 60 seats to 82). Although the LDP and its coalition partner New Komeito, with a combined total of 139 seats, retained a majority in the 242-member House, the outcome was generally interpreted as reflecting a decline in the popularity of Koizumi's administration. In September Koizumi effected a major reorganization of cabinet portfolios. Among notable new appointments was that of Nobutaka Machimura as Minister of Foreign Affairs. From October there were renewed protests against Japanese support for military operations in Iraq following the beheading of a Japanese tourist who had been taken hostage by a militant group there. None the less, in December the LDP announced that the term of the SDF mission in Iraq was to be extended by one year.

In August 2005 Koizumi's postal reform bill, which had been narrowly approved by the House of Representatives in the previous month, was defeated in the House of Councillors. A total of 37 LDP members from both houses rebelled against the party leadership and voted against the proposed legislation. Koizumi responded to the defeat by dissolving the House of Representatives and calling elections for 11 September. Prohibited from standing as party members, several LDP 'rebels' formed separate parties, including the People's New Party (Kokumin Shinto—PNP), led by Tamisuke Watanuki, and the New Party Nippon (Shinto Nippon), led by Yasuo Tanaka. Other dissidents chose to stand as independent candidates. In the event, the elections resulted in unequivocal victory for Koizumi and, by implication, an endorsement of his reform programme by the electorate. The LDP increased its representation in the House of Representatives to 296 of the 480 seats (its first overall majority since 1990 and the largest number of seats won by a single party since the end of the Second World War), thereby creating, with its ally New Komeito, a ruling coalition bloc of 327 seats and securing more than two-thirds of the chamber. The DPJ's share of seats, meanwhile, was reduced by 64 to 113, prompting the resignation of its President, Katsuya Okada. The subsequent DPJ leadership election was won by Seiji Maehara. In October Koizumi reorganized his Cabinet. Shinzo Abe was appointed Chief Cabinet Secretary, Taro Aso became Minister of Foreign Affairs and Sadakazu Tanigaki was retained as Minister of Finance. The postal reform bill was resubmitted to the legislature, and in mid-October was approved by both houses of the Diet.

In September 2006 Chief Cabinet Secretary Shinzo Abe, with the clear support of the Prime Minister, was elected to succeed Koizumi as LDP President. Having secured the support of both houses of the Diet, at the end of the month Abe formally took office as Prime Minister. Only one incumbent minister of the Koizumi administration, namely the Minister of Foreign Affairs, Taro Aso, retained his position in the new Cabinet.

The Governments of Abe, Fukuda and Aso

On assuming the premiership, Shinzo Abe swiftly arranged discussions with China and the Republic of Korea, relations with both of which had been strained by his predecessor's well-publicized visits to the Yasukuni Shrine (see Foreign Affairs). Abe envisaged the pursuit of an assertive foreign policy, stating that Japan should continue to seek a permanent seat on the UN Security Council and making clear his commitment to an uncompromising stance against North Korea. More controversially, he undertook to revise the country's pacifist Constitution to permit the Japanese military to perform a wider role abroad. In terms of economic strategy, Abe pledged to pursue the reformist policies of his predecessor.

The Prime Minister suffered his first political embarrassment in December 2006 when an official investigation found that during the tenure of his predecessor the Government had paid members of the public to ask specific questions of ministers at local meetings and that government officials had masqueraded as ordinary citizens. In the same month legislation to upgrade the Defence Agency was adopted by the Diet (the Defence Agency was officially upgraded to a full ministry in January 2007), but proposed legislation requiring schools to teach patriotism proved more contentious. Four groups, including the DPJ, filed a motion of no confidence against Abe in an attempt to halt the education bill, but the motion was rejected by the House of Representatives.

In April 2007 the DPJ performed well in local elections, while Governor Ishihara was re-elected in Tokyo for a third consecutive term, with the (unsolicited) support of the ruling coalition. Also in April the House of Representatives approved legislation setting out procedures for national referendums on constitutional reform. Although the 1947 Constitution stipulated that amendments required the approval of at least two-thirds of the members of both houses of the Diet, followed by endorsement in a national referendum, the legal framework for such a referendum had never been established. The new law provided for the participation of all citizens over the age of 18 (compared with a minimum voting age of 20 for elections), but failed to impose a minimum participation rate for the validity of the referendum. The House of Councillors adopted the legislation in May 2007.

It emerged in May 2007 that, in an apparent compromise designed to appease both his more nationalistic supporters and neighbouring countries, the Prime Minister had sent an offering to the Yasukuni Shrine in the previous month, but had refrained from visiting the shrine himself. Similarly, Abe chose not to visit the shrine on the anniversary of Japan's surrender in the Second World War in August, instead attending a commemoration ceremony in Tokyo.

The Minister of Agriculture, Forestry and Fisheries, Toshikatsu Matsuoka, committed suicide in May 2007, shortly before he was due to appear before a committee of the Diet that was investigating allegations that he had claimed false office expenses. Matsuoka had also been accused of accepting political donations from companies awarded contracts for public works projects by an agency affiliated to his ministry. By June public support for Abe had declined significantly, amid widespread anger over the loss of some 50m. pension records by the Social Insurance Agency. The Government suffered a further reverse in July when the Minister of Defence, Fumio Kyuma, was forced to resign after provoking an outcry with his suggestion that the US nuclear attacks on the Japanese cities of Hiroshima and Nagasaki in 1945, towards the end of the Second World War, had been inevitable. Yuriko Koike, hitherto Abe's special adviser on national security affairs, was appointed to replace Kyuma, becoming Japan's first female Minister of Defence.

The ruling LDP-New Komeito coalition lost its overall majority in the House of Councillors in the partial elections that were held on 29 July 2007. By contrast, the DPJ made significant gains, winning overall control of the house. The DPJ's Satsuki Eda subsequently became the first opposition politician to be elected Speaker of the upper house. Despite the ruling coalition's defeat in the elections, Abe remained in office, although Hidenao Nakagawa relinquished the post of Secretary-General of the LDP. At the beginning of August Norihiko Akagi, Matsuoka's successor as Minister of Agriculture, Forestry and Fisheries, was forced to resign from the Government over allegations that he, too, had submitted inaccurate claims for office expenses. The Minister of Justice, Jinen Nagase, was also accused of financial impropriety when it was revealed that he had accepted money from a company that he had advised on visa applications for its Chinese workers.

The Prime Minister reorganized the Cabinet in late August 2007 in an attempt to restore confidence in his administration. Several veteran members of the LDP were appointed to the Government, including faction leaders Nobutaka Machimura and Masahiko Koumura as Minister of Foreign Affairs and Minister of Defence, respectively, and Fukushiro Nukaga as Minister of Finance. Taro Aso became Secretary-General of the LDP. Only a week later, however, the new Minister of Agriculture, Forestry and Fisheries, Takehiko Endo, resigned, causing further embarrassment for Abe, after admitting that a private farming group of which he was Chairman had misappropriated state funds. In mid-September Abe himself resigned as Prime Minister and President of the LDP, acknowledging that he had lost the support and trust of the public.

Yasuo Fukuda, the son of a former Prime Minister and a moderate politician, who had served as Chief Cabinet Secretary under Koizumi, was elected as LDP President in late September 2007, and subsequently took office as Prime Minister, having secured the approval of a majority in the House of Representatives. Fukuda retained most of the ministers from his predecessor's Cabinet. Koumura, who became Minister of Foreign Affairs, was replaced at the Ministry of Defence by one of the few new appointees, Shigeru Ishiba (who had also held the defence portfolio in Koizumi's Government), while Machimura was appointed Chief Cabinet Secretary and Minister of State for the Abduction Issue. Aso was replaced as LDP Secretary-General by Bunmei Ibuki, hitherto Minister of Education, Culture, Sports, Science and Technology.

Fukuda advocated closer relations with neighbouring Asian countries (pledging not to visit the controversial Yasukuni Shrine), while maintaining a strong alliance with the USA, and promised to continue to pursue economic structural reforms. The new Prime Minister's first challenge was to secure approval for the extension of legislation enabling the Maritime Self-Defence Force to provide logistical support in the Indian Ocean to ships involved in US-led counter-terrorism operations in Afghanistan. The renewal of the legislation, which had first been adopted in 2001 and which was scheduled to expire at the beginning of November 2007, was opposed by the DPJ on the grounds that the US-led operations had not been sanctioned by the UN and that Japan's involvement violated its pacifist Constitution. Following the failure of efforts to reach a political consensus, in mid-October the Cabinet approved draft legislation that would extend the mission but, in a concession to its critics, would limit its role to supplying fuel and water to ships on anti-terrorism patrols rather than those involved in military operations. Yearly renewal of the proposed legislation would also be required. However, the Diet remained in deadlock over the issue at the end of October, leading to the suspension of the support mission.

In mid-November 2007 the House of Representatives approved the legislation to renew Japan's naval deployment in the Indian Ocean, shortly before Fukuda was due to visit the USA, which had been exerting strong pressure on Japan to resume its support for US counter-terrorism activities. The House of Councillors began debating the proposed resumption of the deployment in early December 2007, but the DPJ continued to refuse to approve the necessary legislation. In mid-January 2008 the Government forced through the passage of the bill, using its majority in the House of Representatives to supersede another vote against it by the House of Councillors (the first time this power had been used since 1951). Two Japanese vessels were dispatched to assist US forces in the Indian Ocean later that month.

In June 2008 the House of Representatives approved a resolution that for the first time formally recognized the minority Ainu as 'an indigenous people with a distinct language, religion and culture'. The resolution urged the establishment of a special panel to formulate government policy towards the Ainu people, who had long felt disadvantaged in the ethnically homogenous society of Japan and whose separate identity had been officially acknowledged only in 1997.

In August 2008 the Prime Minister effected an extensive cabinet reorganization, in which Bunmei Ibuki was appointed as Minister of Finance and Kaoru Yosano as Minister of State for Economic and Fiscal Policy. On the same day Taro Aso was appointed to replace Ibuki as Secretary-General of the LDP. In early September, however, the Prime Minister announced his resignation, citing the difficulties in reaching a consensus with the DPJ on the implementation of his legislative agenda. Shortly afterwards the Minister of Agriculture, Seiichi Ota, was also compelled to resign owing to the revelation of a scandal involving the import and distribution of contaminated rice.

Taro Aso was elected as the next President of the LDP, and in late September 2008 he was duly confirmed as Prime Minister by the House of Representatives. He immediately formed his Cabinet, appointing Shoichi Nakagawa as Minister of Finance, Hirofume Nakasone as Minister of Foreign Affairs and Yasukazu Hamada as Minister of Defence. Aso had been widely expected to call early elections for the House of Representatives, but he ultimately decided against this, preferring to focus immediately on economic policy in view of the developing global financial crisis.

In January 2009 Yoshimi Watanabe, a former Minister of State for Financial Services and Administrative Reform, who was opposed to the Government's fiscal stimulus programme and the additional budgetary expenditure involved, announced his departure from the LDP. (In August Watanabe formed a new political party, known as Your Party.) In February former Prime Minister Koizumi similarly criticized the Government's expenditure on the financial stimulus plans. Aso's plight worsened when the Minister of Finance, Shoichi Nakagawa, resigned, having apparently been intoxicated at a press conference held during a meeting of the Group of Seven (G7) leading industrialized nations in Italy.

In March 2009 the arrest of Takanori Okubo, the political secretary of Ichiro Ozawa, on suspicion of accepting illegal donations and falsifying party accounts, led to pressure on the leader of the opposition DPJ to resign. Okubo was formally indicted later in the month, and Ozawa, although denying any wrongdoing on his part, eventually responded to public opinion in May by resigning as President of the DPJ. He was replaced by the party's Deputy President, Yukio Hatoyama, who had been one of the original DPJ's founders in 1996 and had held the post of party President between 1999 and 2002.

The DPJ in power: 2009–12

In July 2009 diminishing support for the LDP was demonstrated when it was defeated by the DPJ in an election to the Tokyo Metropolitan Assembly (which the LDP had dominated for more than 40 years). As was widely predicted, at the legislative elections on 30 August the DPJ was overwhelmingly successful, securing 308 of the 480 seats in the House of Representatives, while the LDP won 119 seats and New Komeito 21. The LDP was thus removed from government for only the second time since 1955 (the first having been the 11-month period during which it had been out of office in 1993–94). Despite having secured an overall majority, the DPJ negotiated with the SDPJ and the PNP (which had won seven and three seats, respectively, in the House of Representatives) to form a coalition, in order to widen the Government's support, particularly in the House of Councillors, where the DPJ lacked an overall majority. Hatoyama took office as Prime Minister in mid-September 2009. He appointed Naoto Kan, a former President of the DPJ, as Deputy Prime Minister and Minister of State for National Policy, Economic and Fiscal Policy, and Science and Technology Policy: Kan was to preside over a new National Strategy Bureau, which was to formulate policy and supervise budgetary allocations, thereby reducing what was perceived by the DPJ as the excessive power of the civil service. Katsuya Okada, hitherto Secretary-General of the DPJ, became Minister of Foreign Affairs, and the new Minister of Finance was Hirohisa Fujii, who had held the same position during the period of non-LDP rule in 1993–94. The Chairman of the SDPJ, Mizuho Fukushima, and the leader of the PNP, Shizuka Kamei, both received ministerial posts.

In September 2009 Ozawa was appointed Secretary-General of the DPJ, despite the allegations of irregular funding that had caused his resignation as the party's President earlier in the year. Changes also took place within the parties that had been defeated in the August elections: Aso resigned as President of the LDP in early September and was succeeded by Sadakazu Tanigaki, the former Minister of Finance. The President of New Komeito, Akihiro Ota, and the party's Secretary-General, Kazuo Kitagawa, both of whom had lost their parliamentary seats in the elections, also resigned in early September. Ota was replaced by Natsuo Yamaguchi, hitherto the Chairman of the party's Policy Research Council.

Hatoyama's new Government announced its intention to impose stricter controls on expenditure by government departments. Although the Japanese economy was no longer technically in recession by September 2009, the new administration was confronted by considerable obstacles to economic recovery, in particular the very high level of government debt, the strength of the yen against the US dollar and the problem of persistent deflation. In January 2010, following the resignation of the Minister of Finance, Hirohisa Fujii, owing to ill health, Deputy Prime Minister Kan assumed additional responsibility for the finance portfolio.

In April 2010 two new political parties were established, composed mainly of dissatisfied former members of the LDP. The Sunrise Party of Japan was led by Takeo Hiranuma, an independent member of the House of Representatives and a former Minister of Economy, Trade and Industry; he was joined by some erstwhile senior members of the LDP, including Kaoru Yosano, the former Minister of Finance. The New Renaissance Party was established by Yoichi Masuzoe, hitherto an LDP member of the House of Councillors and a former Minister of Health, Labour and Welfare.

In May 2010 Hatoyama admitted that his party's electoral pledge to remove an unpopular US military air base from the southern island of Okinawa (see Foreign Affairs) could not realistically be fulfilled, and he proposed, instead, adhering to an agreement made with the USA in 2006, whereby the base would be transferred to an alternative site on the island. Later in May 2010 he dismissed the leader of the SDPJ, Mizuho Fukushima, from her ministerial post after she criticized the decision; the SDPJ then voted to leave the ruling coalition. Hatoyama also incurred criticism from within his own party, the DPJ, for his apparent vacillation over the Okinawa base. The controversy over Okinawa, together with the conviction in April of Hatoyama's former secretary for falsifying political funding reports, persistent allegations of financial irregularities on the part of Ozawa and the widespread perception that Ozawa wielded undue influence in policy-making all combined to reduce the popularity of the ruling party.

On 2 June 2010 Hatoyama announced his own resignation as Prime Minister and President of the DPJ, and that of Ozawa as Secretary-General of the party. The DPJ then elected Naoto Kan as its President, and he became Prime Minister (Japan's fifth in four years) on 8 June. Kan retained most of the principal ministers appointed by his predecessor: his own previous post as Minister of Finance was allocated to Yoshihiko Noda (hitherto the deputy minister), and Yoshito Sengoku was appointed Chief Cabinet Secretary. Yukio Edano was appointed Secretary-General of the DPJ. Kan declared that he would maintain the controversial policy on Okinawa that Hatoyama had been obliged to adopt, and identified the reduction of government debt as the most pressing problem confronting his administration. The PNP agreed to remain in coalition with the DPJ, and the PNP's leader, Kamei, initially retained his ministerial responsibility for postal reform and financial services, but he resigned within a few days, after the DPJ refused to extend the current session of the Diet in order to debate legislation, supported by Kamei, on reversing the 2007 privatization of Japan Post (as the Postal Services Agency had become in 2003). However, the PNP remained within the coalition, and Kamei's ministerial portfolio was assumed by Shozaburo Jimi, the party's Secretary-General.

At elections for one-half of the seats in the House of Councillors held in July 2010, the DPJ lost the small majority that it had commanded (with its coalition partners) in the upper house, winning 44 of the 121 seats contested, so that its total representation was reduced to 106 of the 242 seats. The LDP won 51 of the contested seats, bringing its total to 84, while the DPJ's coalition partner, the PNP, failed to win any seats. The DPJ's loss of support was widely attributed to Kan's emphasis, during the election campaign, on the possible introduction of an increase in consumption tax, in order to reduce the budgetary deficit.

Kan was re-elected as DPJ President in September 2010 (his election in June had been only for the remainder of Hatoyama's allotted term of office). Kan reappointed Katsuya Okada, hitherto Minister of Foreign Affairs, as Secretary-General of the DPJ; in the ensuing partial reorganization of the Cabinet, the foreign affairs portfolio was allocated to Seiji Maehara, hitherto responsible for land, infrastructure and transport, while Banri

Kaieda was appointed Minister of State for Economic and Fiscal Policy.

In December 2010 discussions took place on the possible establishment of a coalition between the DPJ and the Sunrise Party, but the latter refused to accept such an arrangement; however, one of the Sunrise Party's founding members, Kaoru Yosano, subsequently left the party, and in January 2011 he accepted the post of Minister of State for Economic and Fiscal Policy (a post that he had previously held, as a member of the LDP, in 2008–09). This appointment formed part of a cabinet reorganization, in which Yukio Edano replaced Yoshito Sengoku as Chief Cabinet Secretary, Akihiro Ohata replaced Sumio Mabuchi as Minister of Land, Infrastructure, Transport and Tourism, and Banri Kaieda replaced Ohata as Minister of Economy, Trade and Industry.

In January 2011 Ozawa was indicted for conspiring in the false reporting of political funds used in a purchase of land in 2004; three of his aides had been charged with the offence in February 2010. Ozawa denied the charge, claiming that he had no knowledge of his aides' actions, and refusing to relinquish his seat in the legislature or to accede to Kan's request that he temporarily leave the DPJ. The party's executive voted in February 2011 to suspend Ozawa's membership. Also in February, the trial of the three aides commenced; it concluded with their conviction in September. Ozawa's trial commenced the following month, and in April 2012 he was acquitted of the charges.

In early March 2011, meanwhile, Maehara resigned as Minister of Foreign Affairs, when it was revealed that he had illegally accepted a small political donation from a foreign national; he was replaced by the deputy minister, Takeaki Matsumoto.

On 11 March 2011 Japan was struck by a very severe earthquake, which had its epicentre in the Pacific Ocean off the north-east coast of Honshu island. The earthquake measured 9.0 in magnitude and caused a tsunami that devastated the adjoining coastal region, killing many thousands of people. Several nuclear power stations automatically shut down when the earthquake occurred, but one, at Fukushima, was seriously damaged, and its cooling systems were disabled. An evacuation was ordered within 20 km of the plant, while efforts were made to cool the nuclear reactors in order to prevent radioactive contamination. At the end of March the power station's operator, the Tokyo Electric Power Company (TEPCO), announced that four of the six nuclear reactors at Fukushima were to be decommissioned. As the critical situation at Fukushima continued, in April Japan's Nuclear and Industrial Safety Agency raised its evaluation of the crisis from Level 5 to Level 7, the highest level on the International Nuclear Event Scale, while confirmation emerged in early June that three of the reactors had experienced full meltdowns. Other nuclear power stations in Japan were closed down for safety inspections, while Kan began publicly to advocate the reduction of Japan's dependency on nuclear power and the investigation of renewable energy alternatives. In mid-December the Government announced that the Fukushima plant had reached a state of 'cold shutdown', but estimated that full decommissioning of the damaged reactors could take between 30 and 40 years. According to figures published by Japan's National Police Agency in March 2012, 15,848 people were known to have died in the disaster and 3,305 were unaccounted for; around 350,000 reportedly remained homeless. The Japanese economy was severely affected by the earthquake and its aftermath.

Sustained domestic and international criticism was directed at both the Government of Japan and TEPCO for their management of the Fukushima crisis, and the reliability of information regarding developments at the power plant was questioned. In particular, Kan came under personal attack for his handling of the tsunami and subsequent nuclear crisis. Critics argued that his decision to fly over the Fukushima site on the day after the earthquake delayed the operation to cool the reactors, and condemned his reluctance to extend the evacuation zone around the plant from 20 km to 30 km in radius. When a number of DPJ legislators, including Hatoyama and Ozawa, threatened to support a vote of no confidence initiated by the opposition in early June 2011, Kan pledged to resign once he had prepared a second emergency budget to finance reconstruction (the first such emergency budget having been approved in early May), and subsequently survived the vote. In late June Kan stated that his resignation would be conditional on the adoption of this second emergency budget, along with legislation concerning deficit bond issuance and the increased use of renewable energy. Kan also conducted a minor cabinet reshuffle in late June, appointing Goshi Hosono as Minister for the Restoration from and Prevention of Nuclear Accident, while Ryu Matsumoto became Minister for Reconstruction Measures from the Great East Japan Earthquake. However, Matsumoto resigned from his post in early July, after comments he made to regional governors in areas affected by the tsunami attracted widespread public disapproval; he was replaced by Tatsuo Hirano. In early August it was announced that three senior government officials involved in nuclear policy were to be dismissed, and a new nuclear safety watchdog was to be created under the auspices of the Ministry of the Environment. Both developments were widely interpreted as an attempt by the Government to distance itself from accusations of excessive intimacy with the nuclear industry.

On 26 August 2011, following the successful passage into law of the aforementioned legislative bills, Kan announced his resignation from the presidency of the DPJ and, consequently, from the post of Prime Minister. After a first round of voting in the DPJ's subsequent leadership election proved inconclusive, the second round was won on 29 August by Yoshihiko Noda, hitherto Minister of Finance, defeating Banri Kaieda. Noda was elected Prime Minister by the Diet on the following day, and then appointed a reordered Cabinet, in which Jun Azumi succeeded him as Minister of Finance, while Osamu Fujimura became Chief Cabinet Secretary and Koichiro Gemba assumed the foreign affairs portfolio. Yasuo Ichikawa became Minister of Defence, while Hosono, in addition to his existing nuclear accident portfolio, took on the post of Minister of the Environment. Yoshio Hachiro succeeded Kaieda as Minister of Economy, Trade and Industry, but resigned in early September after remarks he made on a visit to Fukushima were deemed offensive. He was replaced by Yukio Edano, who had served as Chief Cabinet Secretary in Kan's administration.

Noda, widely regarded as a fiscal conservative, sought to prioritize control of public debt and the rapidly appreciating yen. A third emergency reconstruction budget was approved in late November 2011, and in early December Noda instructed Azumi to draw up a fourth emergency budget to address reconstruction, a move unprecedented since the immediate post-war era. Meanwhile, a key proposal to increase sales tax from 5% to 10% by 2015, to finance rising welfare expenditures and reduce Japan's high levels of public debt, met with hostility from some DPJ members (notably Ozawa) as well as from the opposition and the public. A reorganization of the Government enacted by Noda in mid-January 2012 was widely interpreted as motivated by the desire to facilitate agreement on tax reform. The new post of Deputy Prime Minister was created and five cabinet ministers were replaced, including Minister of Defence Ichikawa (whose successor was Naoki Tanaka) and Minister for Consumer Affairs Kenji Yamaoka. Opposition parties had indicated that they would boycott further debates on tax reform unless Ichikawa and Yamaoka, who had both recently earned considerable opprobrium as a result of making what were considered to be highly inappropriate remarks in public, were dismissed. Katsuya Okada was appointed to the newly created post of Deputy Prime Minister, with responsibility for tax and social security reform. The Government submitted the necessary legislation for increasing sales tax to the Diet at the end of March 2012. Prime Minister Noda carried out another cabinet reorganization in early June in a renewed attempt to win opposition support for the proposed sales tax bill; among the changes was the replacement of Naoki Tanaka as Minister of Defence by Satoshi Morimoto. The approval of the sales tax legislation by the lower house later that month (and by the upper house in August) prompted the resignation of Ozawa and 48 other DPJ Diet members from the ruling party in early July. The dissidents then formed a new party, the People's Life First, under the leadership of Ozawa (the party merged into the newly formed Tomorrow Party of Japan in November). In mid-September Noda's Government suffered a further setback following the suspected suicide of the Minister of Postal Reform and Minister of State for Financial Services, Tadahiro Matsushita. Despite his recent political troubles (including the DPJ's apparent vacillation over the future of Japan's nuclear power sector), Noda was re-elected to the presidency of the DPJ later that month. A few days later former Prime Minister Shinzo Abe was elected to replace Sadakazu Tanigaki as President of the LDP. In an apparent attempt to revitalize his Government, public support for which was noticeably waning, Prime Minister Noda made a number of ministerial changes at the beginning of October, including the replacement of Azumi as Minister of Finance by Koriki Jojima. Three weeks later, however, the newly appointed Minister of Justice, Keishu Tanaka, resigned from his post on the grounds of ill health, amid allegations over irregular political funding and his connections with members of an organized crime group; he was replaced by Makoto Taki (who had held the justice portfolio prior to Tanaka's assumption of the role on 1 October). In late October the popular Governor of Tokyo, Shintaro Ishihara, stood down from his long-held post to form a new national political party, the Japan Restoration Party, which absorbed the Sunrise Party on its foundation the following month.

Recent developments: the LDP is returned to power

The loss of support for the DPJ was vividly illustrated by its resounding defeat at the hands of Shinzo Abe's LDP in the legislative elections held on 16 December 2012. In the poll, which attracted a turnout of only 59.3% of the electorate (the lowest ever recorded in the post-war period), the LDP secured an outright majority in the House of Representatives, taking 294 of the 480 seats, while the DPJ's representation plummeted from 230 seats to only 57 seats. Ishihara's Japan Restoration Party came in third place with 54 seats, New Komeito obtained 31 seats and Watanabe's Your Party won 18 seats. With the support of its ally New Komeito, the LDP accordingly controlled a two-thirds' majority in the lower house, thus giving it the power to over-rule the House of Councillors on stalled legislation. Following his party's overwhelming defeat, Noda resigned as President of the DPJ and was replaced by Banri Kaieda. Abe, whose electoral campaign had focused on restoring economic growth, reinstating nuclear energy and introducing a more assertive approach to foreign policy, assumed the premiership on 26 December at the head of a new Cabinet, which was almost exclusively composed of LDP members and which included former Prime Minister Taro Aso as Deputy Prime Minister and Minister of Finance, and Sadakazu Tanigaki as Minister of Justice. A few days later increasing tensions within the Tomorrow Party of Japan, which had performed poorly in the legislative elections, winning only nine seats in the House of Representatives, led to the defection from the party of Ozawa and most of its other Diet members to form the People's Life Party. Legislation was adopted in July 2013 reducing the number of seats in the House of Representatives by five, to 475, with effect from the next general election (scheduled to be conducted in 2016).

The LDP and New Komeito secured a majority in the Tokyo Metropolitan Assembly, deposing the incumbent DPJ, following an election in the capital in June 2013. More significantly, on 21 July the parties of the governing coalition also regained control of the House of Councillors after performing strongly in nationwide polls for one-half of the 242 seats in the upper chamber. The LDP increased its representation to 113 seats (compared with 84 following the 2010 elections) and New Komeito secured 20 seats (up from 19). Your Party, the JCP and the Japan Restoration Party also made modest gains. The standing of the DPJ (and its allies) in the upper house, however, deteriorated markedly, declining from 106 seats in 2010 to just 59. The rate of participation by the electorate was relatively low, at 52.6%. Goshi Hosono resigned as DPJ Secretary-General in the wake of the party's poor electoral showing; he was succeeded by Akihiro Ohata. In August 2013 Kenji Eda was replaced as Secretary-General of Your Party by Keiichiro Asao. Eda, along with several other Your Party dissidents, established the Unity Party in December.

Controversial state secrecy legislation, prescribing lengthy gaol terms for those convicted of leaking (or endeavouring to acquire) material that the authorities deemed to be sensitive, was passed by the Diet in December 2013. The new law attracted domestic and international criticism due to the apparent dearth of independent oversight, as well as concerns about the potential impact upon fundamental civil rights such as freedom of speech and freedom of the press. The Abe administration defended the legislation, citing the need to protect national security. Further controversy was generated in November when the Government, in an apparent attempt to exert control over NHK, the nation's public broadcasting network, orchestrated the replacement of several members of NHK's governing board with allies of the Prime Minister. In December the reconstituted board appointed a new President, Katsuto Momii, who intimated in the following month that the network would assume a pro-Government stance in its programming, prompting disquiet about the erosion of the broadcaster's independence. NHK was placed under renewed scrutiny in early 2014 after Momii and other recently installed network executives issued a series of contentious statements denying or downplaying Japanese atrocities during the Second World War, echoing similarly divisive comments made by some public officials during the previous year (see Relations with South Korea).

Yoichi Masuzoe—the President of the New Renaissance Party and a minister in Abe's first administration—was elected as Governor of Tokyo on 9 February 2014, comfortably defeating his main rivals, including former Prime Minister Hosokawa, who was supported by the DPJ. Hosokawa had directed most of his efforts during the pre-election period towards campaigning against nuclear power. Masuzoe, meanwhile, like Abe, had spoken out in support of resuming nuclear energy production, but had not made the issue a focal point of his campaign, preferring instead to present a broader policy platform. While some commentators (and, indeed, Hosokawa himself) had portrayed the gubernatorial election as a referendum on the nuclear question, the electorate was more concerned about economic matters and consequently found Masuzoe's wider-ranging manifesto more appealing than Hosokawa's narrow focus on energy, despite the fact that opinion polls continued to suggest widespread opposition to nuclear power.

In early December 2013 Abe established a National Security Council to oversee key security issues. Later in the month the Cabinet adopted the country's first National Security Strategy focusing on diplomatic and defence policy and providing for an increase in defence expenditure over the following five years. The document referred specifically to the expansion of China's maritime and air activities in relation to disputed territory with Japan and also to the threat posed by nuclear and missile development in North Korea. The strategy outlined Japan's plan to make a more 'proactive contribution to peace', notably with regard to the issue of collective self-defence as part of the Japan-US alliance, in line with Abe's stated aim to broaden the activities undertaken by the country's Self-Defense Forces, which were currently limited by the pacifist post-war Constitution. Abe was expected to seek cabinet approval later in the year for a reinterpretation of the Constitution to enable Japan to come to the defence of an ally, although he would need to secure the support of both his own party, the LDP, and its coalition partner New Komeito. In accordance with the National Security Strategy, restrictions on arms exports were relaxed at the beginning of April, allowing for exports in cases where it would promote peace and international co-operation or Japan's security.

Foreign Affairs

In the second half of the 20th century Japan, having renounced military activity in accordance with its 1947 Constitution, nevertheless gained international influence through its rapid economic growth: during the 1970s it became the world's second largest economy (after the USA) and retained this position until it was surpassed by China at the end of the first decade of the 21st century. Japan also became a major provider of overseas aid and investment. However, as a legacy of Japan's aggressive foreign policy during the first half of the 20th century, neighbouring countries remained suspicious of any sign of nationalist tendencies. Although Japan sought to increase its regional influence, its alliance with the USA remained the principal tenet of its foreign policy in the early 21st century.

Relations with the USA

Japan's bilateral security arrangements with the USA, concluded by treaty in 1951, granted the use of military bases in Japan to the USA, in return for a US commitment to provide military support to Japan in the event of external aggression. In May 1999 legislation was enacted on revised Guidelines for Japan-US Defense Co-operation (first compiled in 1978). These envisaged enhanced military co-operation between the USA and Japan, not only on Japanese territory but also in situations in unspecified areas around Japan, prompting criticism from China and Russia. The principal location for US bases in Japan was the island of Okinawa, in the far south of the country, which was returned from US administration to Japanese sovereignty only in 1972. The large US military presence caused resentment among many residents of Okinawa; in particular, the rape of a local schoolgirl by three US servicemen in 1995 led to considerable civil unrest on the island. Protracted negotiations with the US Government resulted in an agreement, concluded in May 2006, on the relocation of the principal US air base from Futenma, in a densely populated area of Okinawa, to a less populous area near the city of Nago, in the north of the island, while some 8,000 US military personnel (about one-third of those currently stationed on Okinawa) were to be relocated to the US Pacific Territory of Guam. However, many residents of the proposed site for the new air base opposed its construction.

The agreement was signed in February 2009 by Hillary Clinton, the US Secretary of State in the newly appointed Administration of President Barack Obama; however, after taking office in September of that year, the new Japanese Government (led by the DPJ, which had denounced the proposals while in opposition) undertook to review the agreement during 2010. In April 2010 about 100,000 residents of Okinawa attended a rally, demanding that the Futenma air base be removed from the island altogether. In May Prime Minister Yukio Hatoyama (reportedly after pressure from the US Government) declared that the complete removal of the base was not a feasible option, and stated that the Government would, after all, implement the 2006 agreement to relocate the air base within Okinawa. The Government's perceived indecisiveness over Okinawa was the principal reason for Hatoyama's resignation in June 2010. Under his successors, Naoto Kan and Yoshihiko Noda, the importance of the alliance with the USA was reaffirmed, but progress on implementing the 2006 agreement remained hampered by strong local opposition to the relocation of the base within the island. The 2014 deadline for relocation of the base and transfer of troops to Guam was abandoned in June 2011. At the end of April 2012, prior to a visit to the USA by Prime Minister Noda, agreement was reached on the transfer of 9,000 US marines from Okinawa to Guam and other US bases in the Pacific. It was, however, confirmed that plans to relocate the Futenma base to a less populated area, in accordance with the 2006 agreement, remained the only 'viable solution'. In April 2013 Japan and the USA reached agreement on the return of certain facilities and land on Okinawa to Japan and the relocation of the Futenma base after 2021. The Okinawa authorities formally sanctioned the Futenma relocation plan in December 2013, although local opposition—particularly in Nago, the proposed site of the new facility—remained widespread.

In September 2001, following the attacks on the USA by Islamist militants attributed to al-Qa'ida, Japan immediately pledged co-operation in the USA's 'war on terror', including military support within the limits imposed by Japan's Constitution. Koizumi announced that Japan would assist in the gathering of intelligence, and in the delivery of supplies and of medical and humanitarian relief. The requisite legislation was approved by the Diet, and in November Japan deployed several warships and 1,500 personnel to the Indian Ocean in this capacity, to support US military action in Afghanistan. Koizumi gave President George W. Bush his full support for the USA's military offensive against Iraq, which commenced in March 2003, despite strong opposition from the Japanese public. However, Japan refused to close the Iraqi embassy in Tokyo. Following the approval of legislation to permit the dispatch of Japanese troops to Iraq in a peacekeeping capacity, in early 2004 the first Japanese soldiers were deployed, numbering about 550 troops by April of that year. In December it was announced that the term of SDF involvement in Iraq would be extended by one year to aid the reconstruction of the country; however, following a further extension announced in December 2005, Japanese troops were withdrawn from Iraq in June and July 2006, with the exception of a small air support contingent.

In November 2007 the USA expressed disappointment at the withdrawal of Japan's Maritime Self-Defence Force from the Indian Ocean, where it had been supporting US-led counter-terrorism operations in Afghanistan since 2001 (see above), following the failure to secure approval for an extension of the mission in the Japanese Diet. Japan resumed its naval mission in support of US forces in the Indian Ocean in January 2008, after the Government forced the necessary legislation through the Diet. In October the House of Representatives voted to renew the naval mission. Upon taking office in September 2009, however, the new DPJ-led Government indicated that it would not support an extension of the mission in 2010, but would increase Japanese assistance for reconstruction in Afghanistan (see Other external relations). Accordingly, in January 2010 the Japanese naval mission was withdrawn from the Indian Ocean, despite US requests for its renewal.

Meanwhile, during the early 2000s disagreement persisted between Japan and the USA over President Bush's description of North Korea as part of an 'axis of evil'. Japan pursued a policy of engagement with North Korea (see below), while the USA adopted a more sceptical attitude to that country, particularly after North Korea allegedly admitted in October 2002 to pursuing a covert nuclear weapons programme. In December Japan and the USA held a meeting of ministers of defence and foreign affairs in Tokyo on outstanding security issues. As well as seeking an early resolution of the crisis over the North Korean nuclear weapons programme, the two countries moved closer to agreement on the deployment of a joint missile shield. In February 2003 the Japanese Government stated that the two countries would conduct joint training in ballistic missile interception off the coast of Hawaii for a period of two years, beginning in 2004, and in December 2003 the Japanese Government announced that it was to develop an anti-ballistic missile defence system in co-operation with the USA. The ship-based system was successfully tested for the first time in December 2007. In a bid to counter the growing ballistic missile threat from North Korea, in September 2012 Japan and the USA agreed to deploy a second joint missile defence system on Japanese territory; however, the exact location of the proposed system had not yet been determined.

Following talks in the USA in February 2013, Prime Minister Shinzo Abe and President Obama pledged to take a resolute stance on North Korea, which had recently conducted a nuclear test, and generally reaffirmed the Japanese-US security alliance. In early October, during a visit to Tokyo by US Secretary of State John Kerry and US Secretary of Defense Chuck Hagel, the two countries agreed to revise and broaden the Guidelines for Japan-US Defense Co-operation by the end of 2014, with the aim of giving Japan a greater role in protecting its own sovereignty. The two sides also agreed to boost bilateral regional military surveillance, including the installation of a second missile defence radar in Japan and the positioning of surveillance drones there for the first time. In April 2014 Obama confirmed that a group of uninhabited islands in the East China Sea, which were the focus of a territorial dispute with China (see below), were covered by Japan's mutual security treaty with the USA, although he emphasized that the dispute should be resolved peacefully.

Relations with China

Despite Japan's signing of a treaty of peace and friendship with the People's Republic of China in 1978, the historic enmity between the two countries continued to cause intermittent tension. Relations deteriorated in the late 1980s after China expressed concern at Japan's increased defence expenditure and at what China perceived as a more assertive military stance. Japanese aid to China was suspended in June 1989, following the Tiananmen Square massacre in the Chinese capital, Beijing, and was not resumed until November 1990. Relations between the two countries were strengthened by the visits to China by Emperor Akihito in October 1992, the first Japanese imperial visit to China, and by Prime Minister Hosokawa in March 1994. However, in August of that year Japan announced the suspension of economic aid to China, following renewed nuclear testing by the Chinese Government. The provision of economic aid was resumed in early 1997, following the declaration of a moratorium on Chinese nuclear testing.

In September 1997 China expressed concern at the revised US-Japanese security arrangements (see Relations with the USA), following a statement by a senior Japanese minister that the area around Taiwan might be covered under the new guidelines. In November 1998, during a six-day state visit by President Jiang Zemin, Obuchi and Jiang issued (but declined to sign) a joint declaration on friendship and co-operation, in which Japan expressed deep remorse for past aggression against China. However, China was reported to be displeased by the lack of a written apology. A subsequent US-Japanese agreement to initiate joint technical research on the development of a theatre missile defence system, followed by the Japanese Diet's approval, in May 1999, of legislation on the implementation of the revised US-Japanese defence guidelines, provoked severe criticism from China, despite Japan's insistence that military co-operation with the USA was purely defensive.

In April 2005 violent anti-Japanese protests took place across China, following Japan's approval of school textbooks that reportedly omitted any references to Japanese war crimes in China. The subsequent attacks on Japanese embassies and boycotts of Japanese products and companies were also thought to be partially motivated by Japan's ongoing campaign to acquire a permanent seat on the UN Security Council (see below), an ambition that China, a long-standing permanent member, vehemently opposed. A dispute between the two countries over the status of the Okinotori Shima coral reef chain, in the Pacific Ocean to the south of Japan, continued in 2005: Japan claimed that the chain constituted islands and thus, under international maritime law, Japanese sovereignty over them gave it the right to an exclusive economic zone in the surrounding waters, while

China insisted that Okinotori Shima merely constituted 'rocks', lacking the sustainable economic activity required to engender an exclusive zone. The two countries also made competing claims to potential petroleum fields in the East China Sea. In July the Chinese Government protested against the Japanese granting of drilling rights in disputed waters to Teikoku Oil Co, and in October Japanese officials asserted that their reconnaissance information showed that Chinese platforms were operating in a contested region. In May 2006 China and Japan agreed to accelerate negotiations on the development of disputed gas exploration in the East China Sea.

A periodic source of tension between the two countries is the Yasukuni Shrine (a Shinto memorial to Japan's war dead, including those convicted of war crimes). In August 2001 China criticized the first visit to the Yasukuni Shrine by Japanese Prime Minister Junichiro Koizumi and urged Japan to renounce its militaristic past. During a visit to China in October Koizumi apologized for Japan's past crimes in the country. However, he continued to arouse anger in China by making several more visits to the Yasukuni Shrine.

The appointment of Shinzo Abe as Prime Minister in September 2006, however, raised hopes of a significant improvement in Sino-Japanese relations. The new Prime Minister's visit to Beijing in October was the first meeting between Chinese and Japanese leaders for five years. President Hu Jintao described the visit as a turning point in Sino-Japanese relations and commended Abe for choosing China as the destination for his first official overseas trip as Prime Minister. During the visit the two nations pledged to expand relations in the areas of trade, investment and technology. Furthermore, Abe acknowledged that Japan had inflicted suffering on Asian people in the past, and, with regard to the issue of Taiwan, he confirmed that the Japanese Government would adhere firmly to its 'one China' policy. During a reciprocal visit by the Chinese Prime Minister, Wen Jiabao, in April 2007, he and Abe agreed to increase bilateral co-operation in a wide range of areas. In his address to the Japanese Diet, the first ever by a Chinese Prime Minister, Wen urged a spirit of reconciliation.

Meanwhile, however, in March 2007 Abe's questioning of the degree of compulsion used by Japan in engaging women for sexual purposes during the Second World War (see Relations with South Korea) had provoked much criticism in China and elsewhere, following which the Prime Minister was obliged to issue an apology for his remarks. In April the Japanese Supreme Court dismissed two appeals for compensation by Chinese nationals over their treatment by the Japanese during the war on the grounds that China had renounced all claims for reparation from Japan in a communiqué signed by the two countries in 1972. Subsequent similar appeals to the Court were also rejected.

It was anticipated that the improvement in Sino-Japanese relations experienced under Abe's premiership would continue under Yasuo Fukuda, who, upon taking office as Prime Minister in September 2007, expressed his intention to develop closer links with China and other neighbouring Asian countries. Fukuda and Wen held amicable talks in November while attending the annual summit meeting of the Association of Southeast Asian Nations (ASEAN, see p. 211), with both leaders emphasizing their commitment to strengthening bilateral relations. To this end, they agreed to accelerate efforts to resolve the ongoing dispute over exploration for hydrocarbons in the East China Sea. A goodwill visit to Japan by a Chinese warship later in that month (the first since 1934) was a further sign of improving relations, as was the first senior-level dialogue on closer economic co-operation, which was held in Beijing at the beginning of December. In June China and Japan agreed to establish a joint exploration project for natural gas in the East China Sea. In May 2012 Japanese Prime Minister Yoshihiko Noda attended a meeting in Beijing with President Hu Jintao and the South Korean President, Lee Myung-Bak, during which the three leaders agreed to initiate negotiations on the establishment of a trilateral free trade pact. (The negotiations duly commenced in March 2013 in the South Korean capital of Seoul.) Later in May 2012 the promotion of trade between Japan and China was given a major boost when it was announced that from June China would permit direct trading of the Chinese yuan and the Japanese yen rather than using the US dollar as an intermediary currency.

The Senkaku Islands (or Diaoyu Islands in Chinese), a group of uninhabited islands situated in the East China Sea, have proved a periodic source of conflict between Japan and China. The islands are controlled by Japan, but are also claimed by China and Taiwan. In April 2012 the populist Governor of Tokyo, Shintaro Ishihara, announced a plan for the Tokyo metropolitan government to buy the Senkaku Islands from their private Japanese owners. The proposal was condemned by the Chinese Government, which reasserted China's claim to sovereignty over the islands. Tension escalated in September as a result of the purchase of three of the islands from their private Japanese owner by the central Japanese Government (in order to avoid the potentially much more provocative purchase and development of the islands by the nationalistic Ishihara), and there was an intensification in violent incidents against Japanese citizens and businesses in China. The Chinese Government described Japan's purchase of three of the islands as 'completely illegal and invalid'. The subsequent dispatch by China and Taiwan of several marine surveillance vessels to patrol the area around the islands prompted Japan to lodge an official protest against territorial encroachment. In December Japan lodged a further protest against the alleged violation of its airspace near the disputed islands by a Chinese government aircraft; this was reportedly the first such intrusion by a Chinese aircraft since 1958. In February 2013 Japan again made a formal protest, accusing a Chinese naval frigate of directing weapon-targeting radar at a Japanese vessel and helicopter near the Senkaku Islands in the previous month; the Chinese Ministry of Defence rejected the allegations. China expressed opposition to an agreement signed by Japan and Taiwan in April, allowing vessels from Taiwan to fish within 19 km of the islands. Later that month Japanese Prime Minister Shinzo Abe warned China that he would authorize the use of military action if an attempt were made to seize the contested islands.

Bilateral relations deteriorated dramatically in November 2013 after China announced the establishment of an air defence identification zone encompassing large swathes of the East China Sea, including the waters surrounding the Senkaku Islands and certain expanses that Japan had previously declared to be within its own defence zone. Japan refused to recognize this edict and formally protested to the Chinese authorities. Later that month, in an apparent act of defiance, Japanese, South Korean and US military aircraft flew through the Chinese zone unannounced, although in December US Vice-President Joseph Biden toured the region in an effort to defuse the situation. Japan announced a number of security measures during December, including an increase in the defence budget, the adoption of a new, more expansive, military doctrine, the formation of a national security council, and the enactment of state secrecy legislation. China criticized Japan's new National Security Strategy, claiming it would increase regional tensions. In January 2014 the Abe administration produced new educational guidelines advocating that Japanese sovereignty over the Senkakus and other contested islands be emphasized during relevant school classes. New textbooks incorporating these changes were also to be published. China and South Korea castigated the Japanese authorities for this move.

Relations with North Korea

Attempts to establish full diplomatic relations with North Korea in early 1991 were hindered by North Korean demands for financial reparations for the Japanese colonization of the country during 1910–45 and by North Korea's refusal to allow International Atomic Energy Agency inspectors access to its nuclear facilities. Relations improved during 1995–96 after Japan provided emergency aid to North Korea when serious food shortages were reported. Concerns that North Korea had developed a missile capable of reaching Japanese territory resulted in the suspension of food aid in mid-1996, but, following bilateral negotiations in August 1997, at which it was agreed to reopen discussions aimed at establishing diplomatic relations, provision of food aid resumed in October. Agreement was also reached concerning the issue of visits to relatives in Japan by the estimated 1,800 Japanese nationals resident in North Korea; the first such visits took place in November. However, food aid and diplomatic normalization talks were again suspended in mid-1998, following the testing by North Korea of a suspected missile over Japanese territory. Tensions were further exacerbated in March 1999, when two suspected North Korean spy ships, which had infiltrated Japanese waters, were pursued and fired on by Japanese naval forces. Relations improved following North Korea's agreement with the USA, in September, to suspend its reported plans to test a new long-range missile. In October, following unofficial talks between Japanese and North Korean government officials in Singapore, Japan lifted a ban on charter flights to North Korea. In December the Japanese Government announced that it would resume the provision of food aid. Several rounds of negotiations on the establishment of diplomatic relations were held in 2000, despite an announcement by Japan in September that normal bilateral relations would not be instituted until the cases of 10 Japanese citizens allegedly abducted by North Korean agents had been solved. In December 2001 the Japanese coastguard sank a suspected North Korean spy vessel after it had been expelled from Japan's exclusive economic zone.

In an unexpected diplomatic initiative, in September 2002 Junichiro Koizumi became the first incumbent Japanese Prime Minister to visit the North Korean capital, Pyongyang. His one-day visit, during which he held discussions with the 'Supreme Leader', Kim Jong Il, was dominated by the latter's admission that North Korean agents had abducted 12 Japanese citizens in the 1970s and 1980s, of whom five were still alive. Kim apologized for the abductions, but attributed them to rogue elements within the security services. The admission led to a hardening of attitudes against North Korea among the Japanese public, with some sources indicating that the total number of Japanese abductees might be as high as 100. The surviving captives were temporarily allowed to return to Japan in October, although they had to leave behind any spouses or children. However, the Japanese authorities refused to allow them to return to North Korea.

Japan became alarmed in October 2002 after North Korean representatives allegedly admitted to visiting US officials that North Korea was pursuing a secret nuclear weapons programme. Koizumi announced that Japan would halt further economic co-operation with North Korea until the issues of the abducted Japanese citizens and the nuclear programme were resolved. North Korea's admission led to increased co-operation between Japan and the USA over how to resolve the crisis, with Japan moving closer to participating in a missile shield with the USA (see above). The North Korean Government warned Japan that it would abandon its moratorium on missile-testing if normalization talks failed to make any progress. In separate incidents in February and March 2003 North Korea test-launched two short-range ground-to-ship missiles in the Sea of Japan (also known as the East Sea), and in April tested a third missile in the Yellow Sea. However, it refrained from testing longer-range ballistic missiles, which Japan considered a threat to its security. Japan and North Korea were two of the six countries to participate in the talks on North Korea's nuclear programme hosted by China, the first round of which commenced in Beijing in August.

In January 2004 the House of Representatives approved legislation allowing Japan to impose economic sanctions on North Korea. In April the House of Councillors approved legislation requiring all ships entering Japanese ports from March 2005 to be insured against oil damage. This in effect amounted to a ban on entry by North Korean ships. Following a further visit by Koizumi to Pyongyang in May 2004, five children of the abductees who had returned to Japan in 2002 were permitted to fly to Tokyo. Their release had been secured in return for pledges of food aid and medical supplies. The Government of North Korea joined South Korea and China in condemning the approval in 2005 of a controversial history textbook for use in Japanese schools, as well as Prime Minister Koizumi's repeated visits to the controversial Yasukuni Shrine. The first round of diplomatic normalization talks between Japan and North Korea since 2002 was held in Beijing in February 2006.

The issue of abducted Japanese citizens came to the fore again in June 2006, when the Diet approved the North Korean Human Rights Act, which warned that economic sanctions would be imposed on North Korea unless it worked to resolve human rights issues, including the question of the abductees. Relations deteriorated further in the following month when North Korea conducted missile tests over the Sea of Japan, including the test of an intercontinental ballistic missile. Japan reacted immediately by banning a North Korean trading ferry from its ports and by imposing a moratorium on charter flights from Pyongyang. In September the Japanese Government announced the unilateral imposition of more comprehensive sanctions, which included freezing the assets of North Korean officials suspected of having links to their country's nuclear weapons programme.

Following Shinzo Abe's appointment as Prime Minister in September 2006, Japan adopted a more aggressive policy towards North Korea. Long known for his uncompromising stance on the North Korean issue, Abe appointed a special adviser on North Korean abductions, and established a cabinet panel to deal with the affair. North Korea's announcement in October that it had tested a nuclear device greatly increased tensions. Clearly alarmed by the possibility of a nuclear power within the immediate region, Japan not only gave strong support to the UN Security Council's sanctions but also imposed its own additional restrictions, including a ban on all North Korean imports and on the entry of North Korean ships into Japanese waters.

In February 2007 the six-party talks on the North Korean nuclear programme resulted in an agreement aimed at curbing nuclear activities in that country, beginning with the closure of the Yongbyon nuclear site in return for substantial amounts of fuel aid from the other five participating countries. However, Japan insisted that it would only provide aid once progress had been made on the question of the abducted Japanese nationals. As a result of the agreement, in March Japan and North Korea held their first diplomatic normalization talks for more than a year, although no apparent progress was made. After Yongbyon was officially declared closed in July, North Korea accused Japan of attempting to obstruct the normalization talks and to disrupt the six-party process with its refusal to provide energy aid and its insistence on the resolution of the abduction issue, which North Korea claimed had already been settled. A second round of bilateral negotiations was held in early September. Yasuo Fukuda, who took office as Japanese Prime Minister later that month, favoured a more conciliatory approach to North Korea than that of his predecessor. Nevertheless, in October Japan announced that it would not resume aid to North Korea and extended sanctions for a further six months, despite the latter's recent commitment to disabling fully its Yongbyon facilities and declaring details of all its nuclear programmes by the end of the year (a deadline that, in the event, was missed), citing a continued lack of progress in the dispute over the abductees. The sanctions were further renewed in April 2008.

In March 2009, following North Korea's announcement of its imminent launch of what was declared to be a communications satellite, Japan prepared its missile interceptors, in the country's first deployment of this advanced technology. The Japanese Government reiterated its warning that it would attempt to destroy any missile or debris that threatened Japanese territory. In April, in response to the launch of the North Korean rocket, the Japanese Government renewed its sanctions against North Korea for a further year, but decided against a ban on exports to the country. In May 2010, following the sinking of a South Korean naval vessel, apparently by a North Korean torpedo, the Japanese Government extended its sanctions against North Korea.

Japan condemned the failed launch by North Korea in April 2012 of a rocket-mounted satellite, which was widely believed to be the testing of a long-range missile. In August Japan and North Korea held their first direct official talks (in Beijing) for four years. Hopes of any amelioration in relations under the new 'Great Leader' Kim Jong Un were dashed, however, by an announcement by the North Korean state media in February 2013 that North Korea had conducted an underground nuclear weapons test (its third such test in seven years). In response, Prime Minister Shinzo Abe called an urgent meeting of the UN Security Council, at which North Korea's provocative action met with unanimous condemnation. Following a series of threats made by North Korea against South Korea, Japan and US bases in the region, in April Japan dispatched two warships to the Sea of Japan and deployed missile defence systems in three locations in Tokyo to protect against a potential missile launch from North Korea. Informal talks between Japanese and North Korean officials were conducted in China in March 2014, when the two sides agreed to resume official dialogue (suspended since December 2012 when North Korea launched a long-range rocket over Japan). North Korea launched two medium-range ballistic missiles into the sea in March 2014 to coincide with a trilateral meeting of the South Korean, Japanese and US leaders in The Hague, Netherlands, provoking a protest from Japan. However, the first formal negotiations between North Korea and Japan since Abe took office went ahead as planned at the end of the month in Beijing. Talks focused on the issues of North Korean abductions of Japanese citizens and nuclear weapons and missile programmes.

Relations with South Korea

Japan's relations with the Republic of Korea have intermittently been affected by the sensitive issue of Japanese colonial rule in 1910–45, and by territorial and fishing disputes. In February 1995 Prime Minister Murayama publicly acknowledged that

Japan was responsible, in part, for the post-war division of the Korean peninsula. However, he was forced to retract the statement, following bitter controversy in the Diet. During a state visit by the South Korean President, Kim Dae-Jung, to Japan in October 1998, a joint declaration was signed, in which Japan apologized for the suffering inflicted on the Korean people during Japanese colonial rule. Japan also pledged substantial aid to the Republic of Korea to stimulate economic recovery. In August 1999 Japan and the Republic of Korea held their first joint military exercises since the Second World War, in the Tsushima Straits. In October 2000 Koizumi visited Seoul and apologized for past crimes and suffering under Japanese rule. In November Japan and the Republic of Korea, along with China, agreed to establish regular contacts between their ministers of finance and foreign affairs. Relations were adversely affected in 2001 and 2005 by the approval by the Japanese authorities of textbooks considered misleading with regard to Japan's wartime aggression.

A long-standing dispute between Japan and the Republic of Korea concerns sovereignty over a group of islands, called Takeshima in Japanese or Dokdo in Korean, situated in the Sea of Japan. The South Korean Government claims that the islands are historically part of Korea, while the Japanese Government maintains that they were incorporated into Japan at the beginning of the 20th century. In May 2006 the South Korean Government provoked fury in Japan by announcing a five-year plan for the disputed islands, which included the development of island facilities and the exploration of marine and mineral resources. Following Japan's renewal of its claim to the Takeshima islands in July 2008, when they were defined as Japanese territory in new teaching materials, the South Korean ambassador was recalled from Tokyo. In June 2011 a Korean Air test flight flew over the islands, in response to which the Japanese Government banned its officials from travelling with the airline.

Meanwhile, Prime Minister Shinzo Abe provoked considerable anger in March 2007, particularly in China and South Korea, when he claimed that there was no evidence that coercion had been used to recruit 'comfort women' (women used for sexual purposes by the Japanese armed forces during the Second World War, a group of whom had been denied official compensation by a Japanese court in 2000). Abe apologized for his remarks before the Japanese House of Councillors later in March. Abe's successor as Prime Minister, Yasuo Fukuda, who took office in September, declared his intention to strengthen relations with the Republic of Korea and other neighbouring Asian countries, notably pledging not to visit the controversial Yasukuni Shrine. Repeated visits to the shrine by Prime Minister Koizumi had been strongly condemned by the Republic of Korea and had resulted in considerable tensions between the two countries.

In August 2010, the month of the centenary of Japan's annexation of the Korean peninsula, the recently appointed DPJ Prime Minister, Naoto Kan, again apologized for the suffering caused by colonial rule. In January 2011 the Japanese and South Korean defence ministers drew up agreements on the sharing of information and equipment, the first such military accords between the two countries since the end of Japanese imperial rule in 1945. In October 2011 Kan's successor, Yoshihiko Noda, visited Seoul for a meeting with the South Korean President Lee Myung-Bak, which focused on economic co-operation. Noda had previously indicated that, like his predecessor Kan, he would refrain from visiting the Yasukuni Shrine. Nevertheless, in a reciprocal visit to Japan in December, Lee raised once more the issue of compensation for Korean 'comfort women'. In June 2012, in response to persistent anti-Japanese sentiment, the South Korean Government postponed the official signing of the historic military pacts that had been agreed with Japan the previous year. Furthermore, Japan temporarily withdrew its ambassador from Seoul in August following a surprise visit to the disputed Takeshima islands by Lee Myung-Bak, the first by a South Korean President. None the less, negotiations on a trilateral free trade agreement, between Japan, South Korea and China, commenced in March 2013. However, in April South Korea cancelled a planned high-level meeting with Japan as a mark of protest against Deputy Prime Minister Taro Aso's visit to the Yasukuni Shrine earlier that month. Several other members of the Japanese Government visited the controversial shrine in August and October, prompting renewed criticism from South Korea and China, while Aso attracted additional regional censure in mid-2013 after making provocative comments about Nazi Germany. Japan's relations with its neighbours had been further undermined in May after Toru Hashimoto, the mayor of Osaka, publicly defended the recruitment of 'comfort women' during the Second World War. In December, moreover, Prime Minister Abe also made a trip to the Yasukuni Shrine, which unsurprisingly generated outrage in South Korea and China; later that month the South Korean Government suspended a number of defence co-operation initiatives with Japan. In a bid to ease tension between the two neighbouring countries, following intensive diplomatic manoeuvring, the USA engineered the holding of a trilateral meeting involving Obama, Abe and South Korean President Park Geun-Hye, on the sidelines of a nuclear security summit in The Hague, the Netherlands, in late March 2014. Abe and Park agreed to resume dialogue between the two countries.

Other regional relations

During the 1990s and 2000s Japan sought to strengthen economic and security relations with the member countries of ASEAN. Japan's influence in South-East Asia largely depended on its aid and investment programmes. In November 2002 Japan signed an agreement to develop a comprehensive economic partnership with ASEAN members within 10 years—including the possible formation of a Japan-ASEAN free trade area. Japan participated in the inaugural East Asia Summit meeting, convened in Malaysia in December 2005, which was attended by the 'ASEAN + 3' countries (the member nations of ASEAN, plus China, Japan and the Republic of Korea), along with Australia, New Zealand and India.

In May 2000 Singapore agreed to allow Japan to use its military bases for evacuating its citizens from crisis locations, and for regional peacekeeping missions, the first agreement of its kind between Japan and another country, and in October 2001 Japan reached a comprehensive free trade agreement with Singapore (which took effect in November 2002). In July 2006 a free trade agreement between Japan and Malaysia took effect, and a similar agreement with the Philippines was approved by the Japanese legislature in December. During 2007 free trade agreements were also concluded with Thailand and Brunei, and with Indonesia, which was to provide Japan with a stable supply of liquefied natural gas (LNG). Negotiations on a comprehensive free trade agreement between Japan and ASEAN were concluded in November. In January 2008 Prime Minister Yasuo Fukuda held a meeting in Tokyo with the ministers responsible for foreign affairs of Cambodia, Laos, Myanmar, Thailand and Viet Nam, offering increased economic aid to the five countries, while encouraging them to make more progress on human rights issues and democratization. Japan had provided substantial aid to Myanmar, but this was suspended in 2003 in protest against the detention of the country's opposition leader, Aung San Suu Kyi, although Japan continued to provide emergency and humanitarian aid.

As Japan continued its efforts to improve relations with South-East Asia, in March 2009 the Japanese Ministry of Defence hosted a meeting of senior security officials from member countries of ASEAN, the first such meeting ever held in Japan. In October 2010, against the backdrop of renewed diplomatic tension between Japan and China (see above), Japan and Viet Nam concluded an agreement on increasing the supply of rare earth minerals from Viet Nam (thus reducing Japan's dependence on imports of these minerals from China), and on co-operation in the development of nuclear power plants in Viet Nam. At a meeting held in Tokyo in April 2012 between President Thein Sein of Myanmar and Prime Minister Noda, the latter agreed to resume development aid to Myanmar and to write off more than US $3,700m. of that country's debt. As part of his policy to strengthen ties with South-East Asia (apparently to counter the growing dominance of China), the newly appointed Japanese Prime Minister, Shinzo Abe, visited all 10 ASEAN member states during 2013—Viet Nam, Thailand and Indonesia in January, Myanmar in May, Malaysia, Singapore and the Philippines in July, Brunei in October, and Cambodia and Laos in November. Abe also hosted a Japan-ASEAN summit meeting in December.

In November 2001 Japan announced plans to send 700 SDF members to East Timor as part of an international peacekeeping force, the UN Integrated Mission in East Timor (UNMIT). The first contingent of the force, which consisted mostly of engineers, arrived in March 2002. In March 2009, during a visit to Tokyo by the Timorese Prime Minister, Xanana Gusmão, it was announced that Japan was to provide assistance in the training of military personnel in Timor-Leste (as East Timor had been renamed upon its independence in 2002). The UNMIT troops left Timor-Leste when the mission's mandate expired in December 2012.

In March 2007 the Australian Prime Minister, John Howard, visited Tokyo for discussions with his Japanese counterpart. The two heads of government signed a new security agreement, to encompass peacekeeping and counter-terrorism operations, as well as issues of maritime and aviation security. The conclusion of this agreement, the first such bilateral accord since Japan's signing of the security treaty with the USA in 1951, was regarded as a clear manifestation of Japan's changing position with regard to international affairs. In April 2007 Japan and Australia commenced negotiations on a bilateral free trade agreement. One of the principal obstacles was Japan's reluctance to liberalize access to the Japanese market for Australian agricultural products. None the less, in March 2014 Australian Prime Minister Tony Abbott announced that the free trade agreement with Japan would be finalized within weeks.

In June 2010 the Australian Government filed a complaint against Japan at the International Court of Justice (ICJ), claiming that Japan, by hunting whales in the Southern Ocean, was in breach of international regulations on whaling. Public hearings were conducted at the ICJ in mid-2013, and a final judgment was delivered at the end of March 2014, when the ICJ ruled that Japan should halt its whaling programme in the Antarctic as it had not sufficiently justified that the quotas it set were necessary for the purposes of scientific research. Japan agreed to comply with the ruling. (see The whaling controversy). Meanwhile, in February 2011 Japan requested that the Australian and New Zealand Governments take action to prevent environmental groups from obstructing whaling ships. In February 2013 Australia made an official protest to Japan following the reported incursion of a Japanese whaling vessel into Australia's exclusive economic zone in the Southern Ocean. In February 2014 New Zealand also issued a formal protest to Japan after a similar incident occurred in New Zealand's exclusive economic zone.

Relations with Russia

Japan's relations with Russia have been dominated by the issue of the Northern Territories, known in Russia as the Southern Kurile (Kuril) Islands. These four small islands, situated close to Hokkaido, were annexed in 1945 by the USSR, and thousands of Japanese residents were subsequently deported. Both countries claimed sovereignty over the islands, and as a result no formal peace treaty ending the Second World War was concluded between them. After 1956, when Japan and the USSR resumed diplomatic relations, little progress was made with regard to resolving the dispute. A number of discussions took place during the 1990s, although relations between the two countries deteriorated following the disposal of nuclear waste in Japanese waters by Russian ships in November 1993, and Russia's decision, in August 1994, to open fire on Japanese vessels that were alleged to have been fishing in Russian waters. In November 1996 Japan indicated that it was prepared to resume the disbursement of aid, withheld since 1991, and in May 1997 the Japanese Government abandoned its opposition to Russia's proposed joining of the G7. Russian plans for joint development of the mineral and fishing resources of the disputed territory were followed, in July, by an outline agreement on the jurisdiction of the islands. Negotiations resulted in the conclusion of a framework fisheries agreement in December. Agreement was reached in November 1998 on the establishment of subcommissions to examine issues of border delimitation and joint economic activity on the disputed islands and in September 1999 on improved access to the disputed islands for former Japanese inhabitants. Despite the repudiation of Japan's claim to any of the islands by the Russian President, Vladimir Putin, during his first official visit to Tokyo in September, Russia subsequently offered to abide by a 1956 declaration that it would relinquish two of the islands after the signature of a peace treaty; however, Japan initially rejected this partial solution.

In January 2003 Prime Minister Koizumi visited Moscow for a summit meeting with Putin, during which the two agreed to engage North Korea. Koizumi also visited the Russian Far East, where he met regional leaders. Both Japan and Russia favoured the construction of a pipeline that would transport petroleum from Angarsk, in Siberia, to Nakhodka on Russia's Pacific coast, from where it could be shipped to Japan. The scheme would significantly reduce Japan's dependency on Middle Eastern supplies. The first stage of the pipeline, to Skorovodino in Amur oblast, was completed in December 2009, and linked by rail to the terminal at Koz'mino, near Nakhodka, which was inaugurated that same month. Japan began to receive petroleum from the East Siberian pipeline in February 2010. Meanwhile, Japan and Russia both attended the six-party talks in Beijing on the North Korean nuclear weapons programme between 2003 and 2007.

Tensions over the disputed islands were exacerbated in August 2006 when, in the first such incident for 50 years, a Japanese fisherman was shot dead by a Russian patrol boat near the Northern Territories; three other fishermen were temporarily detained. While the Russian coastguard insisted that the fishing vessel had defied orders to halt, the Japanese Government disputed this claim, accusing Russia of acting with excessive force. After the incident, Russia was reported to have intensified its patrols in the area, and in 2007 two more Japanese boats were seized.

In November 2010 the Russian President, Dmitrii Medvedev, paid a visit to one of the Northern Territories islands, the first Russian head of state to do so, and undertook to increase investment in the islands. The Japanese Prime Minister, Naoto Kan, initially described the visit as regrettable, and a formal protest was delivered to the Russian Government. In February 2011 the Russian Minister of Defence also visited the islands, and in the same month, addressing a rally on Japan's annual Northern Territories Day, Kan responded to nationalist sentiment by describing Medvedev's earlier visit as an 'unforgivable outrage'. The Russian Government then ordered a strengthening of the defences on the disputed islands. Later in February the Japanese Minister of Foreign Affairs visited Moscow to discuss the dispute, but no progress was reported. Japan was further angered by a second visit to the Northern Territories by Medvedev, in July 2012, and by the alleged violation of Japanese airspace by Russian military aircraft over the disputed islands in February 2013. Nevertheless, the new Japanese premier, Shinzo Abe, visited Russia in April and held productive discussions with President Putin. Both leaders agreed that negotiations on the territorial dispute would be resumed, while steps to enhance security and economic co-operation were to be taken. Talks on the islands recommenced in August, although no substantive progress had been reported by early 2014.

Despite the impasse regarding the Northern Territories, in late March 2014, at a meeting held in Tokyo, the Japanese defence and foreign affairs ministers conducted talks with their Russian counterparts on mutual security issues. As a result of these ground-breaking negotiations (the first of their kind), the two countries agreed that their armed forces would co-operate in their fight against terrorism and piracy, and that bilateral, high-level talks on security and defence matters, including cyber security, would be undertaken more frequently.

Other external relations

In September 1990 Japan contributed financially to the international effort to force an unconditional Iraqi withdrawal from Kuwait. A controversial LDP-sponsored Peace Co-operation Bill, which provided for the dispatch to the Persian (Arabian) Gulf area of some 2,000 non-combatant personnel, was withdrawn in November after it encountered substantial domestic political opposition. In January 1991, following repeated US demands for a greater financial commitment to the resolution of the Gulf crisis, the Japanese Government announced plans substantially to increase its contribution and to provide aircraft for the transport of refugees in the region. Opposition to the proposal was again vociferous. The Government secured the support of several centrist parties, by pledging that any financial aid from Japan would be employed in a 'non-lethal' capacity, and legislation to approve the new contribution was adopted by the Diet in March. In June 1992 controversial legislation to permit the SDF to participate in UN peacekeeping operations was approved. However, their role was to be confined to logistical and humanitarian tasks, unless a special dispensation from the Diet were granted. In September members of the SDF were dispatched to serve in the UN Transitional Authority in Cambodia (UNTAC). Japanese troops participated in further UN peacekeeping operations, in Mozambique in 1993, and, under Japanese command, on the Rwandan–Zairean border in 1994. Legislation was approved in November 1994 to enable Japanese forces to be deployed overseas if the Government believed the lives of Japanese citizens to be at risk.

In September 1994 Japan reiterated its desire to be a permanent member of the UN Security Council, particularly in view of its status as the world's largest donor of development aid and the second largest contributor (after the USA) to the UN budget. In the late 1990s and early 2000s the Japanese Government continued its campaign to obtain a permanent seat on the UN Security Council. In a speech to the UN General Assembly in September 2004 Koizumi stated that Japan's role in supporting reconstruction in Afghanistan and Iraq, as well as the Japanese contributions to negotiations with North Korea on its nuclear programme, entitled Japan to a permanent seat. Japan's bid was believed to have the support of the USA. However, the prospect of Japan gaining permanent representation in the UN's highest forum provoked strong objections from China and the Republic of Korea, as victims of past Japanese military aggression.

Following the commencement of US military action in Iraq in March 2003, the House of Councillors approved legislation to allow SDF forces to be dispatched to Iraq in a peacekeeping capacity. By mid-April 2004 there were some 550 Japanese troops stationed in Iraq. The withdrawal of these troops commenced at the end of June 2006 and was completed in July. A small contingent from the Japanese Air Self-Defence Force remained in a minor support role, transporting materials and personnel between Iraq and Kuwait; this mission was terminated in December 2008.

In March 2009, following several shooting incidents involving Japanese ships, the Government dispatched two naval destroyers to protect Japanese vessels and personnel from the increasing threat of piracy in the shipping lanes off the coast of Somalia. Proposals to widen the remit of the mission, to permit Japanese warships to provide protection for vessels of other nations if necessary, were approved by the House of Representatives in June.

In relations with South Asia, the Japanese Government criticized India and Pakistan for conducting nuclear tests in mid-1998 and suspended grants of non-humanitarian aid and loans to both countries. A series of missile tests carried out by India and Pakistan in April 1999 again provoked criticism from Japan. Following a visit to India by the Japanese Prime Minister in August 2000, differences over nuclear testing were set aside in favour of enhanced security, defence and research co-operation between Japan and India, which continued during 2001. The Indian Prime Minister, Atal Bihari Vajpayee, visited Japan in December, the first such visit since 1992. In addition to security issues, the two countries discussed closer co-operation in their software and computer industries. In December 2006 Indian Prime Minister Manmohan Singh visited Japan, where the two countries agreed to commence negotiations on a bilateral economic partnership agreement aimed at reducing the high tariffs hitherto imposed on Japanese automobiles and electronics. Prime Minister Singh returned to Tokyo in October 2008, when talks with his Japanese counterpart, Taro Aso, focused on the improvement of economic and military links. As a result of the discussions, the Japanese Government approved a low-interest loan for the construction of a new railway to carry freight between the Indian capital, New Delhi, and Mumbai; at US $4,500m., this was the largest loan ever extended by Japan to an overseas project. In October 2010 Singh and the Japanese Prime Minister, Naoto Kan, announced the completion of negotiations on the economic partnership agreement, which was to include a gradual elimination of most trade tariffs over a 10-year period. Kan's successor, Yoshihiko Noda, visited India in December 2011, where talks with Singh resulted in pledges of increased co-operation in maritime security, including the projected conduct of joint naval exercises in 2012, a development widely interpreted as a response to China's growing maritime assertiveness. Accordingly, Japan and India conducted their first joint naval exercise, off the coast of Tokyo, in June 2012. The new Japanese Prime Minister, Shinzo Abe, met Singh in the Japanese capital in May 2013, when the two leaders agreed to seek the early conclusion of a nuclear energy co-operation agreement. Emperor Akihito and Empress Michiko also met with the Indian Prime Minister during an unprecedented state visit by the Japanese royal couple to India in late 2013. Abe and Singh held further discussions in January 2014, during an official visit to India by the Japanese Prime Minister, after which they pledged to expand bilateral security ties.

The whaling controversy

Japan has a long tradition of whale-hunting by small fishing communities, but whaling only became a large-scale commercial activity after the Second World War. Concern over the increasing rarity of many whale species throughout the world, as well as unease at inhumane methods of killing, led to a moratorium on commercial whaling being adopted in 1982 by the International Whaling Commission (IWC, established in 1946 to conserve and regulate whale stocks: Japan became a member in 1951). The ban took effect in 1986, but Japan submitted a legal objection (as did Norway, Peru and the USSR), and continued commercial whaling until 1988, when it withdrew its objection to the ban (after the USA threatened to reduce the quota of fish catches allocated to Japan in US waters if it did not do so). However, by exploiting a provision of the IWC's founding convention, whereby governments might issue special permits to allow whaling for the purposes of scientific research, Japan continued to hunt whales, and whale meat remained legally on sale in Japan as a by-product of research. In 1994 the IWC banned whaling in the Southern Ocean, declaring the area a sanctuary for whales. Japan again submitted a legal objection to the ban, asserting that whale stocks in the area were sustainable, and continued to hunt whales in the Southern Ocean, still claiming to be doing so for the purposes of scientific research. By 2011 the IWC had 89 members, and it was widely suspected that Japan had recruited and offered aid to some developing countries in return for their support in opposing the IWC's ban on commercial whaling; Japan denied this, pointing out that it also provided aid for anti-whaling nations.

In recent years a number of conservation organizations have attempted to disrupt whaling in the Southern Ocean. In January 2010 a vessel of the US-based Sea Shepherd Conservation Society sank after colliding with a Japanese whaling ship, while in February a New Zealand activist, belonging to Sea Shepherd, was arrested by the Japanese coastguard after boarding a Japanese whaling vessel. In June the Australian Government initiated legal action against Japan at the ICJ, stating that Japan had breached its obligations under international law by continuing to hunt whales in the Southern Ocean sanctuary. In February 2011 Japan announced an early close to its Antarctic whaling season, after Sea Shepherd activists had obstructed whaling vessels. At the annual IWC conference in July, Japan and 22 other countries walked out of discussions on the formation of a South Atlantic whale sanctuary, disabling a vote on the proposal (which was, in the event, defeated at the annual conference in 2012). Although a resolution on 'Safety at Sea' tabled by Japan and directed primarily at Sea Shepherd was adopted at the 2011 conference, Sea Shepherd's activities were thought partially responsible for a reported catch of less than one-third of expected levels during Japan's Antarctic whaling season in early 2012.

Public hearings on the case before the ICJ commenced in June 2013. At the end of March 2014 the ICJ ruled that Japan should halt its whaling programme in the Antarctic as it had not sufficiently justified that the quotas it set were necessary for the purposes of scientific research. Japan agreed to comply with the ruling, cancelling the next scheduled hunt in the Antarctic, although it signalled its intention to submit a new research programme to the IWC later in the year, reflecting the criteria in the ICJ judgment. In April Japan proceeded with a planned whale hunt in the Pacific Ocean, but significantly reduced the quota of whales to be caught.

CONSTITUTION AND GOVERNMENT

Under the Constitution of 1947, the Emperor is head of state but has no governing power. Legislative power is vested in the bicameral Diet, comprising the House of Representatives (lower house), whose members are elected for a four-year term, and the House of Councillors (upper house), members of which are elected for six years, one-half being elected every three years. The House of Representatives comprises 480 seats—300 single-seat constituencies and 180 determined by proportional representation—and there are 242 seats in the House of Councillors. The number of seats in the House of Representatives was reduced from 500 for the 2000 elections; the reduction was in the number of seats determined by proportional representation. There is universal suffrage for all adults from 20 years of age. Executive power is vested in the Cabinet, which is responsible to the Diet. The Emperor appoints the Prime Minister (on designation by the Diet), who appoints the other Ministers in the Cabinet.

Japan has 47 prefectures, each administered by an elected Governor.

REGIONAL AND INTERNATIONAL CO-OPERATION

Japan is a member of the Asia-Pacific Economic Cooperation (APEC, see p. 201) forum, the Asian Development Bank (ADB, see p. 207), the UN's Economic and Social Commission for Asia and the Pacific (ESCAP, see p. 28) and the Colombo Plan (see p. 449). Japan is also an observer member of the South Asian Association for Regional Co-operation (SAARC, see p. 420) and the Arctic Council (see p. 448).

Japan became a member of the UN in 1956. As a contracting party to the General Agreement on Tariffs and Trade, Japan acceded to the World Trade Organization (WTO, see p. 434) upon its establishment in 1995. Japan is also a member of the Organisation for Economic Co-operation and Development (OECD, see p. 379). The country participates in the Group of Eight major industrialized nations (G8, see p. 465) and the Group of 20 major industrialized and systemically important emerging market nations (G20, see p. 456).

ECONOMIC AFFAIRS

In 2012, according to estimates by the World Bank, Japan's gross national income (GNI), measured at average 2010–12 prices, was US $6,105,798m., equivalent to $47,870 per head (or $36,290 per head on an international purchasing-power parity basis). During 2003–12, it was estimated, the population remained stagnant, while gross domestic product (GDP) per head increased, in real terms, by an average of 0.8% per year. According to official figures, overall GDP increased, in real terms, at an average annual rate of 0.9% in 2003–12. Real GDP, measured at constant prices, grew by 0.5% in 2011, but remained constant in 2012.

Agriculture (including forestry and fishing) contributed 1.2% of GDP and engaged 3.9% of the employed labour force in 2012. The principal crops are rice, sugar beets, cabbages, potatoes and citrus fruits. During 2003–12, according to official sources, agricultural GDP declined, in real terms, at an average rate of 0.7% annually; sectoral GDP increased by 0.4% in 2012.

Industry (including mining, manufacturing, construction and utilities) contributed 25.6% of GDP and engaged 25.3% of the employed labour force in 2012. During 2003–12, according to official sources, industrial GDP increased at an average annual rate of 0.6%; the sector's GDP grew by 15.2% in 2010, but decreased by 2.7% and 2.4% in 2011 and 2012, respectively.

Mining and quarrying contributed a mere 0.1% of GDP and engaged less than 0.1% of the employed labour force in 2012. While the domestic output of limestone and sulphur is sufficient to meet domestic demand, all of Japan's requirements of bauxite, crude petroleum and iron ore, and a high percentage of its requirements of copper ore and coking coal, are met by imports. During 2003–12, according to official sources, mining GDP declined at an average annual rate of 8.0%; however, the sector grew by 4.3% in 2011 and by 0.9% in 2012.

Manufacturing contributed 18.2% of GDP and engaged 16.6% of the employed labour force in 2012. The most important branches of manufacturing are machinery and transport equipment, electrical and electronic equipment, and iron and steel. Manufacturing GDP increased by an average of 1.7% per year in 2003–12, according to official figures; sectoral GDP increased by 20.8% in 2010, but decreased by 2.7% and 2.3% in 2011 and 2012, respectively.

Construction contributed 5.7% of GDP and engaged 8.1% of the employed labour force in 2012. Construction GDP decreased by an average of 2.2% per year in 2003–12, according to official figures; the GDP of the sector expanded by 1.1% in 2012.

Japan imports most of its energy requirements, with imports of crude and partly refined petroleum comprising 17.3% of the value of total imports in 2012, according to official figures. Natural gas accounted for 41.5% of electricity output in 2012, coal for 28.4%, petroleum for 11.5%, hydropower for 7.6% and nuclear power for only 1.1% (compared with 26.9% in 2010). By May 2012, in response to the accident at Fukushima nuclear power plant in March 2011, all Japanese nuclear reactors were offline, pending routine maintenance work and safety evaluations. Plans to phase out nuclear power in response to the accident were reversed by the Government of Shinzo Abe. In April 2014 the Cabinet approved a national energy policy, the Basic Energy Plan, which confirmed that nuclear power was to feature in the country's future energy composition, while the production of power by renewable sources was also to be promoted. The Plan provided for the eventual reactivation of nuclear reactors that complied with stringent regulatory standards.

The services sector contributed 73.2% of GDP and engaged 70.9% of the employed labour force in 2012. The GDP of the services sector increased by an average of 0.6% annually in 2003–12. The sector's GDP expanded by 2.1% in 2012. Tourism receipts, totalling US $14,576m. in 2012, according to provisional figures, are a significant source of revenue. The number of tourist arrivals decreased by 27.8% in 2011, to 6.2m, but recovered in 2012, rising by 34.6%, to 8.4m.

In 2012, according to IMF figures, Japan recorded a visible merchandise trade deficit of US $53,480m., while there was a surplus of $60,860m. on the current account of the balance of payments. In 2012 the People's Republic of China and the USA were the principal markets for Japanese exports, purchasing 18.1% and 17.6% of the total, respectively; other leading purchasers were the Republic of Korea, Taiwan, Thailand and Hong Kong. The principal source of imports in that year was China (which supplied 21.3% of imports); other major suppliers were the USA, Australia, Saudi Arabia and the United Arab Emirates. The principal exports in 2012 were machinery and transport equipment, manufactured goods and chemicals. The principal imports were mineral fuels and lubricants, electrical machinery, chemicals, food and live animals, and manufactured goods.

The budget for the financial year ending March 2014 projected expenditure of 95,882,000m. yen. The allocation for social security remained the largest single category of government expenditure. With tax revenue expected to reach 50,001,000m. yen in that year, the Government planned to issue bonds totalling 41,250,000m. yen. Japan's general government gross debt was 1,083,750,400m. yen in 2011, equivalent to 230.3% of GDP. Japan's external debt was estimated at the equivalent of 53.4% of GNI in 2012. The annual rate of deflation averaged 0.1% in 2003–12. Consumer prices declined by 0.3% in 2011, but remained constant in 2012. The average rate of unemployment was 4.3% in 2012.

In terms of GDP the Japanese economy was the world's second largest (after the USA) for four decades until 2010 when it was surpassed by China. Economic performance has been constrained by the strength of the Japanese currency and by the recurrent problem of deflation, which in turn has had a negative effect on consumer demand. Japan also faces the long-term demographic challenge of a shrinking and ageing population. Moreover, international demand for Japanese exports declined sharply as a result of the global financial crisis of 2008. The tsunami that struck Japan in March 2011, and the subsequent crisis at the Fukushima nuclear power plant, had a serious impact on the economy. Following the disaster, the Bank of Japan (BoJ) released large amounts of money into the banking system in an attempt to stabilize the Japanese financial markets. During 2011 and early 2012 the Japanese Diet approved four emergency budgets, providing a total of some 20,000,000m. yen for post-crisis reconstruction. The already strong yen rose to its highest point since 1945 in relation to the US dollar in the aftermath of the tsunami. The resultant decline in exports (exacerbated by the financial crisis in the eurozone), together with a significant increase in fuel imports, following the closure of nuclear power stations in the wake of the Fukushima disaster, contributed to a trade deficit being recorded for 2011, the first such annual deficit for Japan in over 30 years, and the rate of growth of real GDP decelerated to only 0.5%. As the economy continued to flag in 2012, the Government and the BoJ implemented various stimulus measures. None the less, the economy technically entered recession at the end of September, having recorded negative growth for two consecutive quarters, before stabilizing in the final quarter; overall, growth in that year remained stagnant. The raised cost of fuel imports (as a result of the continuing nuclear shutdown) contributed to a record high trade deficit in 2012. On assuming power in December, Prime Minister Shinzo Abe pledged to revive the ailing economy by increasing public expenditure, weakening the value of the yen and transforming deflation into inflation. In January 2013 the Government approved a US $116,000m. stimulus package, which focused on infrastructure spending, job creation and investment, and the BoJ extended its asset purchase programme; a further expansion of the asset purchase programme was announced in April and additional stimulus measures were specified in October and December. However, concerns remained about Japan's record levels of gross government debt, which stood at around 240% of GDP, the highest in the industrialized world. In an attempt to reduce public debt, legislation had been adopted in August 2012 to double sales tax from 5% to 10% by 2015; the first incremental rise (to 8%) came into effect in April 2014. The Abe administration's policies appeared to have a positive (albeit moderate) impact on the economy during 2013. According to government revised estimates, the fiscal stimulus supported real GDP growth of 0.7% in that year, while consumer prices finally began to increase from mid-2013 due to the depreciation of the yen. A decline in unemployment was also reported, although investment levels remained subdued and the trade deficit widened further (despite an upturn in exports). The final stage in the Prime Minister's 'Abenomics' plan was the implementation of major structural reforms to liberalize the economy, but no significant progress was made on this front during 2013. Meanwhile, in September Tokyo was awarded the right to stage the 2020 summer Olympic Games. Although the costs associated with hosting this event were projected to be very high, the Government hoped that the consequent increase in activity in the construction and tourism sectors would further reinvigorate the economy. The IMF forecast economic growth of 1.7% in 2014.

PUBLIC HOLIDAYS

2015: 1 January (New Year's Day), 12 January (Coming of Age Day), 11 February (National Foundation Day), 21 March (Vernal Equinox Day), 29 April (Showa Day), 3 May (Constitution Memorial Day), 4 May (Greenery Day), 5 May (Children's Day), 19 July (Marine Day), 21 September (Respect for the Aged Day), 23 September (Autumnal Equinox), 12 October (Sports Day), 3 November (Culture Day), 23 November (for Labour Thanksgiving Day), 23 December (Emperor's Birthday),

Statistical Survey

Source (unless otherwise stated): Statistics Bureau and Statistics Center, 2-1-2, Kasumigaseki, Chiyoda-ku, Tokyo 100-8926; tel. (3) 5253-5111; fax (3) 3504-0265; e-mail webmaster@stat.go.jp; internet www.stat.go.jp.

Area and Population

AREA, POPULATION AND DENSITY

Area (sq km)	377,944*
Hokkaido district	83,457
Honshu district	231,112
Shikoku district	18,792
Kyushu district	42,190
Okinawa district	2,276
Population (census results)†	
1 October 2005	127,767,994
1 October 2010	
Males	62,327,737
Females	65,729,615
Total	128,057,352
Population (official estimates at 1 October)	
2011	127,799,000
2012	127,515,000
Density (per sq km) at 1 October 2012	337.4

* 145,925 sq miles; total includes 118 sq km (45.6 sq miles) within Honshu and Shikoku districts yet to be demarcated fully.

† Excluding foreign military and diplomatic personnel and their dependants.

POPULATION BY AGE AND SEX

('000 persons, official estimates at 1 October 2012)

	Males	Females	Total
0–14	8,474	8,073	16,547
15–64	40,378	39,796	80,175
65 and over	13,177	17,616	30,793
Total	62,029	65,486	127,515

Note: Totals may not be equal to the sum of components, owing to rounding.

PREFECTURES

(official population estimates at 1 October 2012)

Prefecture	Area (sq km)	Population ('000)	Density (per sq km)
Aichi	5,165	7,427	1,437.9
Akita	11,612	1,063	91.5
Aomori	9,607	1,350	140.5
Chiba	5,157	6,195	1,201.3
Ehime	5,678	1,415	249.2
Fukui	4,190	799	190.7
Fukuoka	4,977	5,085	1,021.7
Fukushima	13,783	1,962	142.3
Gifu	10,621	2,061	194.0
Gumma	6,363	1,992	313.1
Hiroshima	8,479	2,848	335.9
Hokkaido	83,457	5,460	65.4
Hyogo	8,396	5,571	663.5
Ibaraki	6,096	2,943	482.8
Ishikawa	4,186	1,163	277.8
Iwate	15,279	1,303	85.3
Kagawa	1,877	989	526.9
Kagoshima	9,189	1,690	183.9
Kanagawa	2,416	9,067	3,752.9
Kochi	7,105	752	105.8
Kumamoto	7,406	1,807	244.0
Kyoto	4,613	2,625	569.0
Mie	5,777	1,840	318.5
Miyagi	7,286	2,325	319.1
Miyazaki	7,735	1,126	145.6
Nagano	13,562	2,132	157.2
Nagasaki	4,104	1,408	343.1
Nara	3,691	1,390	376.6
Niigata	12,583	2,347	186.5
Oita	6,340	1,185	186.9
Okayama	7,113	1,936	272.2
Okinawa	2,276	1,409	619.1
Osaka	1,898	8,856	4,666.0
Saga	2,440	843	345.5
Saitama	3,797	7,212	1,899.4
Shiga	4,017	1,415	352.3
Shimane	6,708	707	105.4
Shizuoka	7,780	3,735	480.1
Tochigi	6,408	1,992	310.9
Tokushima	4,147	776	187.1
Tokyo-to	2,188	13,230	6,046.6
Tottori	3,507	582	166.0
Toyama	4,248	1,082	254.7
Wakayama	4,726	988	209.1
Yamagata	9,323	1,152	123.6
Yamaguchi	6,114	1,431	234.1
Yamanashi	4,465	852	190.8
Total	377,944*	127,515	337.4

* Total includes 59 sq km of area straddling more than one prefecture or not fully demarcated.

Note: Totals may not be equal to the sum of components, owing to rounding.

PRINCIPAL CITIES

(census results at 1 October 2010)*

Tokyo (capital)†	8,945,695	Utsunomiya	467,666
Yokohama	3,688,773	Kanazawa	462,361
Osaka	2,665,314	Fukuyama	461,357
Nagoya	2,263,894	Amagasaki	453,748
Sapporo	1,913,545	Nagasaki	443,766
Kobe	1,544,200	Machida	426,987
Kyoto	1,474,015	Toyama	421,953
Fukuoka	1,463,743	Toyota	421,487
Kawasaki	1,425,512	Takamatsu	419,429
Saitama	1,222,434	Yokosuka	418,325
Hiroshima	1,173,843	Fujisawa	409,657
Sendai	1,045,986	Hirakata	407,978
Kitakyushu‡	976,846	Kashiwa	404,012
Chiba	961,749	Gifu	399,745
Sakai	841,966	Toyonaka	389,341
Niigata	811,901	Nagano	381,511
Hamamatsu	800,866	Toyohashi	376,665
Sagamihara	717,544	Wakayama	370,364
Shizuoka	716,197	Nara	366,591
Okayama	709,584	Okazaki	363,743
Kumamoto	676,103	Takatsuki	357,359
Funabashi	609,040	Suita	355,798
Kagoshima	605,846	Asahikawa	347,095

Hachioji	580,053	Kochi	343,393
Matsuyama	517,231	Kawagoe	342,670
Higashiosaka	509,533	Iwaki	342,249
Kawaguchi	500,598	Tokorozawa	341,924
Himeji	485,992	Maebashi	340,291
Matsudo	484,457	Koriyama	338,712
Nishinomiyai	482,640	Koshigaya	326,313
Kurashiki	475,513	Akita	323,600
Oita	474,094	Naha	315,954
Ichikawa	473,919	Aomori	299,520

* With the exception of Tokyo, the data for each city refer to an urban county (*shi*), an administrative division that may include some scattered or rural population as well as an urban centre.

† The figure refers to the 23 wards (*ku*) of the old city. The population of Tokyo-to (Tokyo Prefecture) was 13,159,388 at the census of 1 October 2010.

‡ Including Kokura, Moji, Tobata, Wakamatsu and Yahata (Yawata).

BIRTHS, MARRIAGES AND DEATHS*

	Registered live births		Registered marriages†		Registered deaths	
	Number	Rate (per 1,000)	Number	Rate (per 1,000)	Number	Rate (per 1,000)
2005	1,062,530	8.4	714,265	5.7	1,083,796	8.6
2006	1,092,674	8.7	730,971	5.8	1,084,450	8.6
2007	1,089,818	8.6	719,822	5.7	1,108,334	8.8
2008	1,091,156	8.7	726,106	5.8	1,142,407	9.1
2009	1,070,035	8.5	707,734	5.6	1,141,865	9.1
2010	1,071,304	8.5	700,214	5.5	1,197,012	9.5
2011	1,050,806	8.3	661,895	5.2	1,253,066	9.9
2012	1,037,101	8.2	668,788	5.3	1,256,254	10.0

* Figures relate only to Japanese nationals in Japan.

† Data are tabulated by year of registration rather than by year of occurrence.

Source: Ministry of Health, Labour and Welfare, Tokyo.

Life expectancy (years at birth): 82.6 (males 79.4; females 85.9) in 2011 (Source: World Bank, World Development Indicators database).

ECONOMICALLY ACTIVE POPULATION*
(annual averages, '000 persons aged 15 years and over)

	2010	2011	2012
Agriculture and forestry	2,340	2,070	2,240
Fishing and aquaculture	180	160	160
Mining and quarrying	30	30	30
Manufacturing	10,490	9,970	10,320
Electricity, gas and water	340	290	310
Construction	4,980	4,730	5,030
Wholesale and retail trade	10,570	10,060	10,420
Restaurants and hotels	3,870	3,650	3,760
Transport, information and communications	5,460	5,190	5,280
Financing, insurance, real estate and business services	2,730	2,630	2,750
Health and welfare	6,530	6,480	7,060
Education	2,880	2,800	2,950
Government	2,200	2,100	2,240
Other services and activities not elsewhere classified	9,360	9,050	9,530
Sub-total	61,960	59,210	62,060
Activities not adequately defined	610	560	640
Total employed	62,570	59,770	62,700
Unemployed	3,340	2,840	2,850
Total labour force	65,900	62,610	65,550
Males	38,220	36,290	37,890
Females	27,680	26,320	27,660

* Figures are rounded to the nearest 10,000 persons, and therefore totals may not be equal to the sum of components.

Health and Welfare

KEY INDICATORS

Total fertility rate (children per woman, 2011)	1.4
Under-5 mortality rate (per 1,000 live births, 2011)	3
HIV/AIDS (% of persons aged 15–49, 2011)	<0.1
Physicians (per 1,000 head, 2008)	2.1
Hospital beds (per 1,000 head, 2009)	13.7
Health expenditure (2010): US $ per head (PPP)	3,120
Health expenditure (2010): % of GDP	9.2
Health expenditure (2010): public (% of total)	80.3
Total carbon dioxide emissions ('000 metric tons, 2010)	1,170,715.4
Carbon dioxide emissions per head (metric tons,2010)	9.2
Human Development Index (2012): ranking	12
Human Development Index (2012): value	0.912

For sources and definitions, see explanatory note on p. vi.

Agriculture

PRINCIPAL CROPS
('000 metric tons)

	2010	2011	2012
Wheat	571.3	746.3	857.8
Rice, paddy	10,604.0	10,500.0	10,654.0
Barley	149.0	171.5	172.4
Potatoes	2,290.0	2,349.0	2,500.0
Sweet potatoes	863.6	885.9	875.9
Taro (Cocoyam)	167.6	171.3	180.0*
Yams	173.4	165.9	170.0*
Sugar cane	1,469.0	1,000.0	1,108.0
Sugar beet	3,090.0	3,547.0	3,758.0
Beans, dry	76.9	69.9	86.2
Soybeans (Soya beans)	222.5	218.8	235.9
Cabbages and other brassicas	1,360.0	2,272.4	2,300.0*
Lettuce and chicory	537.9	542.4	543.0*
Spinach	269.0	263.5	275.0*
Tomatoes	690.9	703.0	722.3
Cauliflowers and broccoli	151.7	152.4	154.0*
Pumpkins, squash and gourds	220.5	209.2	212.0*
Cucumbers and gherkins	587.8	584.6	586.5
Aubergines (Eggplants)	330.1	322.4	327.4
Chillies and peppers, green	137.3	141.8	145.0
Onions and shallots, green	541.3	549.5	550.0*
Onions, dry	1,042.0	1,070.0	1,097.0
Carrots and turnips	595.7	617.3	619.0*
Maize, green	234.7	240.3	245.0*
Mushrooms and truffles*	59.6	60.2	61.5
Watermelons	369.2	362.5	380.0*
Cantaloupes and other melons	188.1	180.4	190.0*
Grapes	184.8	172.6	198.3
Apples	786.5	655.3	793.8
Pears	284.9	312.8	299.0
Peaches and nectarines	136.7	139.8	135.2
Plums and sloes	20.9	22.5	22.3
Oranges*	52.7	54.1	53.0
Tangerines, mandarins, clementines and satsumas	786.0	928.2	846.3
Persimmons	189.4	207.5	253.8
Strawberries	177.5	177.3	185.0*
Tea	85.0	82.1	85.9
Tobacco, unmanufactured	29.3	23.6	19.7

* FAO estimate(s).

Aggregate production ('000 metric tons, may include official, semi-official or estimated data): Total cereals 11,366.5 in 2010, 11,450.4 in 2011, 11,729.5 in 2012; Total roots and tubers 3,555.0 in 2010, 3,675.5 in 2011, 3,781.9 in 2012; Total vegetables (incl. melons) 11,083.8 in 2010, 11,176.3 in 2011, 11,351.2 in 2012; Total fruits (excl. melons) 2,883.1 in 2010, 2,949.1 in 2011, 3,056.9 in 2012.

Source: FAO.

LIVESTOCK
('000 head at 30 September)

	2010	2011	2012
Horses*	17	16	16
Cattle	4,376	4,230	4,172
Pigs	9,800*	9,768	9,735
Sheep*	12	13	13
Goats*	15	16	16
Chickens	286,000*	175,917	174,949

* FAO estimate(s).

Source: FAO.

LIVESTOCK PRODUCTS
('000 metric tons)

	2010	2011	2012
Cattle meat	515.0	500.4	518.7
Pig meat	1,292.5	1,267.3	1,296.9
Chicken meat	1,416.9	1,378.0	1,444.6*
Cows' milk	7,720.5	7,474.3	7,630.4
Hen eggs	2,515.3	2,482.6	2,506.8

* Unofficial figure.

Source: FAO.

Forestry

ROUNDWOOD REMOVALS
('000 cubic metres, excl. bark)

	2010	2011	2012
Sawlogs, veneer logs and logs for sleepers	13,072	14,016	13,923
Pulpwood	4,121	4,274	4,556
Fuel wood*	88	84	80
Total*	17,281	18,374	18,559

* FAO estimates.

Source: FAO.

SAWNWOOD PRODUCTION
('000 cubic metres, incl. railway sleepers)

	2009	2010	2011
Coniferous (softwood)	9,134	9,277	9,294
Broadleaved (hardwood)	157	138	140
Total	9,291	9,415	9,434

2012: Production assumed to be unchanged from 2011 (FAO estimates).

Source: FAO.

Fishing

('000 metric tons, live weight)

	2009	2010	2011
Capture	4,091.3	4,069.1*	3,761.2*
Chum salmon (Keta or Dog salmon)	215.5	173.5	143.5
Alaska (Walleye) pollock	227.3	251.2	238.9
Pacific saury (Skipper)	310.7	207.5*	215.4*
Japanese jack mackerel	165.2	159.4	168.4*
Japanese anchovy	341.9	350.7	261.6*
Skipjack tuna (Oceanic skipjack)	267.8	317.3	257.9
Chub mackerel	470.9	491.8	392.5
Yesso scallop	319.6	327.1	303.0*
Japanese flying squid	218.7	199.8	242.3
Aquaculture*	786.9	718.3	556.8
Japanese amberjack	154.9	138.9	146.2
Pacific cupped oyster	210.2	200.3	165.9
Yesso scallop	256.7	219.6	118.4
Total catch*	4,878.2	4,787.4	4,317.9

* FAO estimate(s).

Note: Figures exclude aquatic plants ('000 metric tons): 560.5 (capture 104.1, aquaculture 456.4) in 2009; 530.0 (capture 97.2, aquaculture 432.8) in 2010; 437.5 (capture 87.8, aquaculture 349.7) in 2011 (FAO estimates). Also excluded are aquatic mammals (generally recorded by number rather than by weight), pearls, corals and sponges. The number of whales caught was: 1,478 in 2009; 1,023 in 2010; 770 in 2011. The number of dolphins and porpoises caught was: 10,846 in 2009; 6,467 in 2010; 3,082 in 2011. The catch of other aquatic mammals ('000 metric tons) was: 1.4 in 2009; 0.9 in 2010; 0.5 in 2011. For the remaining categories, catches (in metric tons) were: pearls 22.0 in 2009; 21.0 in 2010; 20.0 in 2011 (FAO estimate) and corals 5.0 in 2009; 5.3 in 2010; 5.2 in 2011 (FAO estimate).

Source: FAO.

Mining

('000 metric tons unless otherwise indicated)

	2009	2010	2011
Hard coal*	1,100	1,000	900
Quartzite stone	9,189	9,159	9,543
Limestone	132,350	133,974	134,176
Gold ore (kg)†	7,708	8,544	8,691
Crude petroleum ('000 barrels)	5,795	5,491	5,235
Natural gas (million cu m)‡	3,539	3,396	3,298

* Estimates.

† Figures refer to the metal content of ores.

‡ Includes output from gas wells and coal mines.

Source: US Geological Survey.

Industry

SELECTED PRODUCTS
('000 metric tons unless otherwise indicated)

	2010	2011	2012
Cotton yarn—pure and mixed*	45	43	38
Woven cotton fabrics—pure and mixed (million sq m)	124	128	124
Flax yarn	0.8	—	—
Woven silk fabrics—pure and mixed (million sq m)	3.6	3.2	2.9
Wool yarn—pure and mixed	9	10	10
Woven woollen fabrics—pure and mixed (million sq m)	32	30	28
Woven fabrics of cellulosic fibres—pure and mixed (million sq m)†	92	98	84
Woven fabrics of non-cellulosic fibres (million sq m)	730	867	839
Leather footwear ('000 pairs)	17,366	16,532	16,215
Newsprint	3,349	3,211	3,254
Other printing and writing paper	9,547	8,765	8,420

—*continued*	2010	2011	2012
Paperboard	10,977	11,163	10,890
Rubber products	1,458	1,470	1,415
Road motor vehicle tyres (million)	170	167	160
Sulphuric acid—100%	7,037	6,416	6,711
Caustic soda—Sodium hydroxide	4,217	3,960	3,566
Ammonia	1,178	1,211	1,055
Cement	51,526	51,291	54,737
Pig iron	82,283	81,028	81,405
Ferro-alloys‡	893	834	908
Crude steel	109,599	107,601	107,232
Aluminium—unwrought§	1,104	1,057	1,067
Refined copper—unwrought	1,549	1,328	1,516
Electrolytic, distilled and rectified zinc—unwrought	574	545	571
Air-conditioning machines ('000)	19,233	18,329	17,430
Calculating machines ('000)	15	—	—
Video cameras ('000)	3,856	1,905	1,200
Digital cameras ('000)	24,253	19,545	17,994
DVD players ('000)	1,843	1,135	315
Cellular telephones ('000)	23,907	19,794	17,235
Personal computers ('000)	7,511	6,156	6,655
Passenger motor cars ('000)	8,310	7,159	8,554
Lorries and trucks ('000)	1,209	1,136	1,266
Motorcycles, scooters and mopeds ('000)	663	639	595
Bicycles ('000)	1,057	1,102	1,012
Watches	367,961	391,015	357,706
Construction: new dwellings started ('000)	813	834	n.a.
Electric energy (million kWh)	1,156,888	1,107,829	n.a.

* Including condenser cotton yarn.

† Fabrics of continuous and discontinuous rayon and acetate fibres, including pile and chenille fabrics at loom stage.

‡ Including silico-chromium.

§ Including alloys.

2009 ('000 metric tons): Liquefied petroleum gas 4,524; Naphthas 15,767; Motor spirit—gasoline 42,188; Kerosene 16,479; Jet fuel 10,623; Distillate fuel oil 50,048; Petroleum bitumen—Asphalt 4,608; Coke-oven coke 39,157 (Source: UN Industrial Commodity Statistics Database).

2010 ('000 metric tons): Motor spirit—gasoline 42,957; Kerosene 15,971; Jet fuel 10,983; Petroleum bitumen—Asphalt 4,369; Coke-oven coke 43,681 (Source: UN Industrial Commodity Statistics Database).

Finance

CURRENCY AND EXCHANGE RATES

Monetary Units

100 sen = 1 yen.

Sterling, Dollar and Euro Equivalents (31 December 2013)

£1 sterling = 173.408 yen;
US $1 = 105.300 yen;
€1 = 145.219 yen;
1,000 yen = £5.77 = $9.50 = €6.89.

Average Exchange Rate (yen per US $)

2011	79.807
2012	79.790
2013	97.596

BUDGET

('000 million yen, year ending 31 March)*

Revenue	2010/11	2011/12†	2012/13‡
Tax and stamp revenues	37,396	42,346	43,096
Government bond issues	44,303	44,244	42,851
Total (incl. others)	92,299	90,334	92,612

Expenditure	2010/11	2011/12†	2012/13‡
Defence	4,790	4,714	4,754
Social security	27,269	26,390	29,122
Public works	5,773	4,573	5,285
Servicing of national debt§	20,649	21,944	22,242
Transfer of local allocation tax to local governments	17,477	16,594	16,393
Total (incl. others)	92,299	90,334	92,612

* Figures refer only to the operations of the General Account budget. Data exclude transactions of other accounts controlled by the central Government: two mutual aid associations and four special accounts (including other social security funds).

† Initial forecasts.

‡ Budget figures.

§ Including the repayment of debt principal and administrative costs.

2013/14 (budget figures): *Revenue:* Tax and stamp revenues 50,001; Government bond issues 41,250; Total revenue (incl. others) 95,882. *Expenditure:* Defence 4,885; Social security 30,518; Public works 5,969; Servicing of national debt 23,270; Transfer of local allocation tax to local governments 16,142; Total (incl. others) 95,882.

Source: Ministry of Finance, Tokyo.

INTERNATIONAL RESERVES

(US $ million at 31 December)

	2010	2011	2012
Gold (national valuation)	34,695	37,666	40,939
IMF special drawing rights	20,626	19,745	19,910
Reserve position in IMF	4,608	17,178	13,659
Foreign exchange	1,036,256	1,221,249	1,193,578
Total	1,096,185	1,295,838	1,268,086

Source: IMF, *International Financial Statistics*.

MONEY SUPPLY

('000 million yen at 31 December)

	2010	2011	2012
Currency outside depository corporations	78,400	79,971	83,067
Transferable deposits	435,500	461,743	477,797
Other deposits	577,995	582,057	586,276
Broad money	1,091,895	1,123,770	1,147,139

Source: IMF, *International Financial Statistics*.

COST OF LIVING

(Consumer Price Index; average of monthly figures; base: 2010 = 100)

	2011	2012
Food (incl. beverages)	99.6	99.7
Housing	99.8	99.5
Rent	99.8	99.4
Fuel, light and water charges	103.3	107.3
Clothing and footwear	99.7	99.7
Miscellaneous	103.8	103.5
All items	99.7	99.7

NATIONAL ACCOUNTS
('000 million yen at current prices, year ending 31 December)

National Income and Product

	2010	2011	2012
Compensation of employees	243,474.3	245,070.4	245,758.5
Operating surplus and mixed income	97,020.1	87,813.1	90,650.8
Domestic primary incomes	340,494.4	332,883.5	336,409.3
Consumption of fixed capital	103,779.0	101,796.3	100,589.6
Statistical discrepancy	1,356.3	–594.0	–631.9
Gross domestic product (GDP) at factor cost	445,629.7	434,085.8	436,367.0
Indirect taxes	39,864.4	40,219.8	40,314.9
Less Subsidies	3,109.7	2,994.8	2,904.7
GDP in purchasers' values	482,384.4	471,310.8	473,777.2
Primary incomes received from abroad	18,238.4	20,382.1	21,213.7
Less Primary incomes paid abroad	5,264.1	5,707.0	6,168.9
Gross national income (GNI)	495,358.7	485,985.9	488,822.0

Expenditure on the Gross Domestic Product

	2010	2011	2012
Government final consumption expenditure	95,128.6	96,116.6	96,940.4
Private final consumption expenditure	285,867.1	284,244.3	287,696.8
Changes in stocks	–805.5	–1,883.1	–1,546.0
Gross fixed capital formation	96,431.0	97,107.0	100,067.7
Total domestic expenditure	476,621.1	475,584.8	483,158.9
Exports of goods and services	73,182.5	71,297.8	69,774.8
Less Imports of goods and services	67,419.2	75,571.8	79,156.5
GDP in purchasers' values	482,384.4	471,310.8	473,777.2
GDP at constant 2005 prices	525,154.1	527,883.9	527,851.2

Gross Domestic Product by Economic Activity

	2010	2011	2012
Agriculture, hunting, forestry and fishing	5,655.6	5,425.7	5,730.1
Mining and quarrying	301.0	303.5	306.2
Manufacturing	94,333.1	87,283.9	85,637.3
Electricity, gas and water	11,007.8	8,550.9	8,083.8
Construction	26,197.7	26,461.1	26,653.1
Wholesale and retail trade	65,980.5	67,131.0	68,122.2
Transport, storage and communications	49,443.5	48,729.1	49,970.7
Finance and insurance	23,766.0	22,430.0	21,559.1
Real estate*	56,890.0	56,725.7	56,871.4
Public administration	29,566.1	29,665.6	29,464.9
Other government services	14,357.8	14,376.0	14,032.3
Other business, community, social and personal services	91,266.4	91,183.0	93,789.1
Private non-profit services to households	10,009.2	10,698.7	11,133.8
Sub-total	478,774.6	468,964.2	471,354.1
Import duties	4,846.5	5,550.2	5,702.5
Less Consumption taxes for gross capital formation	2,593.0	2,609.5	2,647.6
Statistical discrepancy	1,356.3	–594.0	–631.9
GDP in purchasers' values	482,384.4	471,310.8	473,777.2

* Including imputed rents of owner-occupied dwellings.

Source: Economic and Social Research Institute, Tokyo.

BALANCE OF PAYMENTS
(US $ million)*

	2010	2011	2012
Exports of goods	735,440	789,950	776,640
Imports of goods	–626,910	–794,420	–830,120
Balance on goods	108,520	–4,470	–53,480
Exports of services	131,220	137,350	134,190
Imports of services	–164,880	–175,780	–184,690
Balance on goods and services	74,860	–42,900	–103,990
Primary income received	181,840	227,310	235,360
Primary income paid	–40,390	–51,520	–56,170
Balance on goods, services and primary income	216,310	132,890	75,200
Secondary income received	10,090	13,110	14,900
Secondary income paid	–22,480	–26,940	–29,240
Current balance	203,920	119,060	60,860
Capital account (net)	–4,960	500	–1,020
Direct investment assets	–59,660	–110,590	–123,140
Direct investment liabilities	1,080	80	2,530
Portfolio investment assets	–262,640	–103,050	–151,330
Portfolio investment liabilities	111,640	264,100	109,390
Financial derivatives and employee stock options assets	403,460	407,490	235,660
Financial derivatives and employee stock options liabilities	–391,510	–390,410	–242,790
Other investment assets	–130,140	–92,680	–118,720
Other investment liabilities	132,180	43,870	186,220
Net errors and omissions	40,500	38,260	4,090
Reserves and related items	43,850	176,620	–38,260

* Figures are rounded to the nearest US $10m., and totals may not, therefore, be equal to the sum of components.

Source: IMF, *International Financial Statistics*.

JAPANESE DEVELOPMENT ASSISTANCE
(net disbursement basis, US $ million)

	2009	2010	2011
Official flows	17,706	14,683	13,736
Bilateral assistance	6,001	7,337	6,592
Grants	5,327	6,943	8,216
Grant assistance	2,209	3,464	4,682
Technical assistance	3,118	3,478	3,534
Loans	674	395	–1,624
Contributions to multilateral institutions	3,467	3,684	4,239
Other official flows	8,237	3,662	2,905
Export credits	–786	–1,039	–622
Direct investment finance, etc.	7,498	4,217	3,889
Transfers to multilateral institutions	1,525	485	–362
Private flows	27,217	32,837	47,594
Export credits	–1,220	2,767	1,853
Direct investment and others	19,440	21,650	40,315
Bilateral investment in securities, etc.	7,010	7,428	5,844
Transfers to multilateral institutions	1,987	992	–419
Grants from private voluntary agencies	533	692	497
Total	45,456	48,213	61,828

External Trade

PRINCIPAL COMMODITIES
('000 million yen)

Imports c.i.f.	2010	2011	2012
Food and live animals	5,199	5,854	5,852
Fish and fish preparations*	1,260	1,350	1,400
Crude materials (inedible) except fuels	4,766	5,270	4,768
Mineral fuels, lubricants, etc.	17,398	21,816	24,088
Crude and partly refined petroleum	9,406	11,415	12,247
Petroleum products	1,593	2,226	2,462
Liquefied natural gas	3,472	4,787	6,004
Coal	2,111	2,459	2,321
Chemicals	5,379	6,098	5,926
Manufactured goods	5,379	6,069	5,508
Non-electrical machinery	4,826	4,970	5,004
Electrical machinery	8,101	7,989	8,438
Semi-conductors, etc.	2,136	1,762	1,779
Telephonic and telegraphic equipment	1,253	1,576	2,149
Transport equipment	1,681	1,738	2,312
Other	8,036	8,307	8,793
Clothing and clothing accessories	2,328	2,598	2,680
Total (incl. others)†	60,765	68,111	70,689

Exports f.o.b.	2010	2011	2012
Chemicals	6,925	6,798	6,365
Manufactured goods	8,785	8,786	8,442
Iron and steel	3,675	3,709	3,496
Machinery and transport equipment	41,225	39,436	39,243
Non-electrical machinery	13,317	13,803	12,843
Power-generating machinery	2,327	2,317	2,261
Electrical machinery, apparatus, etc.	12,650	11,600	11,405
Thermionic valves, tubes, etc.	4,153	3,565	3,339
Transport equipment	15,258	14,033	14,995
Road motor vehicles	9,174	8,204	9,225
Road motor vehicle parts	2,893	2,997	3,205
Other	8,007	7,948	7,258
Scientific instruments and optical equipment	2,014	2,109	2,084
Total (incl. others)‡	67,400	65,546	63,748

* Including crustacea and molluscs.
† Including re-imports not classified according to kind.
‡ Including re-exports not classified according to kind.

PRINCIPAL TRADING PARTNERS
('000 million yen)*

Imports c.i.f.	2010	2011	2012
Australia	3,948	4,514	4,504
Brazil	859	1,009	952
Canada	958	1,032	1,012
Chile	678	782	744
China, People's Republic	13,413	14,642	15,039
France	901	944	1,024
Germany	1,689	1,856	1,972
Indonesia	2,476	2,716	2,576
Iran	980	1,027	634
Italy	595	691	765
Korea, Republic	2,504	3,170	3,234
Kuwait	901	1,044	1,218
Malaysia	1,987	2,426	2,621
Philippines	695	712	745
Qatar	1,904	2,395	n.a.
Russia	1,412	1,514	1,660
Saudi Arabia	3,149	4,026	4,376
Singapore	715	691	700
South Africa	636	675	511
Taiwan	2,025	1,852	1,921
Thailand	1,840	1,953	1,886
United Arab Emirates	2,569	3,413	3,510
USA	5,911	5,931	6,082
Viet Nam	716	920	1,203
Total (incl. others)	60,765	68,111	70,689

Exports f.o.b.	2010	2011	2012
Australia	1,392	1,418	1,471
Belgium	586	542	500
Canada	817	709	819
China, People's Republic	13,086	12,902	11,509
Germany	1,777	1,871	1,660
Hong Kong	3,705	3,420	3,276
India	792	882	845
Indonesia	1,394	1,412	1,619
Korea, Republic	5,460	5,269	4,911
Malaysia	1,545	1,496	1,413
Mexico	838	815	844
Netherlands	1,431	1,429	1,290
Panama	1,359	1,190	n.a.
Philippines	969	894	946
Russia	703	941	1,005
Saudi Arabia	568	517	657
Singapore	2,209	2,170	1,859
Taiwan	4,594	4,058	3,673
Thailand	2,994	2,989	3,489
United Arab Emirates	643	592	716
United Kingdom	1,241	1,304	1,065
USA	10,374	10,018	11,188
Viet Nam	716	764	857
Total (incl. others)	67,400	65,546	63,748

* Imports by country of production; exports by country of last consignment.

Transport

RAILWAYS
(traffic, year ending 31 March)

	2009/10	2010/11	2011/12
Japan Railways Group:			
Passengers (million)	8,818	8,837	8,963
Passenger-km (million)	244,593	246,937	253,788
Freight ('000 tons)	30,790	n.a.	n.a.
Freight ton-km (million)	20,228	n.a.	n.a.
Other private railways:			
Passengers (million)	13,851	13,795	14,079
Passenger-km (million)	148,874	148,130	150,606
Freight ('000 tons)	12,857	n.a.	n.a.
Freight ton-km (million)	171	n.a.	n.a.
Total:			
Passengers (million)	22,669	22,632	23,042
Passenger-km (million)	393,466	395,067	404,394
Freight ('000 tons)	43,647	39,886	42,340
Freight ton-km (million)	20,399	19,998	20,471

ROAD TRAFFIC
('000 motor vehicles owned, year ending 31 March)

	2010	2011	2012
Passenger cars	40,135	40,143	40,009
Buses and coaches	227	226	226
Trucks, incl. trailers	6,215	6,136	6,068
Special use vehicles	1,498	1,495	1,501
Light two-wheeled vehicles	1,535	1,543	1,566
Light motor vehicles	29,050	29,569	30,254
Total	78,661	79,113	79,625

SHIPPING

Flag Registered Fleet
(at 31 December)

	2011	2012	2013
Number of vessels	3,569	3,564	3,561
Total displacement ('000 grt)	17,270	18,554	19,921

Source: Lloyd's List Intelligence (www.lloydslistintelligence.com).

International Sea-borne Traffic
('000 metric tons)

	2009	2010	2011
Exports	44,963	44,758	51,863
Imports	457,996	465,898	535,977
Cross transport	320,892	308,419	378,857
Total	823,851	819,075	966,697

CIVIL AVIATION
(traffic on scheduled services)

	2009	2010	2011
Kilometres flown (million)	976	945	938
Passengers carried (million)	99,336	98,932	89,747
Passenger-km (million)	142,406	139,111	122,731
Total ton-km (million)	7,036	7,661	6,565

Tourism

FOREIGN VISITOR ARRIVALS
(excl. Japanese nationals resident abroad)

Country of nationality	2010	2011	2012
Australia	225,751	162,578	206,600
China, People's Republic	1,412,875	1,043,246	1,430,000
Germany	124,360	80,772	109,000
Hong Kong	508,691	364,865	481,800
Korea, Republic	2,439,816	1,658,073	2,044,300
Singapore	180,960	111,354	142,200
Taiwan	1,268,278	993,974	1,466,700
Thailand	214,881	144,969	260,800
United Kingdom	184,045	140,099	174,200
USA	727,234	565,887	717,300
Total (incl. others)	8,611,175	6,218,752	8,368,100

Note: Figures for 2012 are rounded to the nearest 100 persons.

Source: mainly Japan National Tourist Organization.

Receipts from tourism (US $ million, excl. passenger transport): 13,199 in 2010; 10,966 in 2011; 14,576 in 2012 (provisional) (Source: World Tourism Organization).

Communications Media

	2010	2011	2012
Telephones ('000 main lines in use)	65,619	64,669	64,273
Mobile telephones ('000 subscribers)	123,287	132,761	138,363
Broadband subscribers ('000)	34,016	34,866	35,296
Book production:			
titles	74,714	75,810	n.a.
copies (million)	702	700	n.a.
Daily newspapers:			
number of titles	120	119	118
circulation ('000 copies)	49,322	48,345	47,778

Internet users ('000, estimate): 116,295 in 2009.

2013: *Daily newspapers:* numbers of titles 117; circulation ('000 copies) 46,999.

Sources: The Japan Newspaper Publishers and Editors Association; Foreign Press Center, *Facts and Figures of Japan*; International Telecommunication Union.

Education

(2012)

	Institutions	Teachers*	Students
Kindergartens	13,170	110,836	1,604,225
Elementary schools	21,460	418,707	6,764,619
Lower secondary schools	10,699	253,753	3,552,663
Upper secondary schools	5,022	237,224	3,355,609
Schools for special needs	1,059	76,387	129,994
Colleges of technology	57	4,337	58,765
Junior colleges	372	8,916	141,970
Universities	783	177,570	2,876,134
Special training schools	3,249	40,424	650,501
Miscellaneous vocational schools	1,392	8,954	120,195

* Figures refer to full-time teachers only.

Pupil-teacher ratio (primary education, UNESCO estimate): 17.5 in 2010/11 (Source: UNESCO Institute for Statistics).

Directory

The Government

HEAD OF STATE

His Imperial Majesty AKIHITO, Emperor of Japan (succeeded to the throne 7 January 1989).

THE CABINET

(April 2014)

The Government comprises a coalition of the Liberal Democratic Party (LDP) and New Komeito.

Prime Minister: SHINZO ABE (LDP).

Deputy Prime Minister, Minister of Finance and for Overcoming Deflation and Countering Yen Appreciation, and Minister of State for Financial Services: TARO ASO (LDP).

Minister for Internal Affairs and Communications, for Regional Revitalization and for Regional Government (Doshu-Sei), and Minister of State for Decentralization Reform: YOSHITAKA SHINDO (LDP).

Minister of Justice: SADAKAZU TANIGAKI (LDP).

Minister for Foreign Affairs: FUMIO KISHIDA (LDP).

Minister of Education, Culture, Sports, Science and Technology and for Rebuilding Education, and Minister for Tokyo Olympic and Paralympic Games: HAKUBUN SHIMOMURA (LDP).

Minister of Health, Labour and Welfare: NORIHISA TAMURA (LDP).

Minister of Agriculture, Forestry and Fisheries: YOSHIMASA HAYASHI (LDP).

Minister of Economy, Trade and Industry, for Nuclear Damage Economic Countermeasures and for Industrial Competitiveness, and Minister of State for the Corporation in Support of Compensation for Nuclear Damage: TOSHIMITSU MOTEGI (LDP).

Minister of Land, Infrastructure, Transport and Tourism: AKIHIRO OTA (New Komeito).

Minister of the Environment and Minister of State for the Nuclear Emergency Preparedness: NOBUTERU ISHIHARA (LDP).

Minister of Defence: ITSUNORI ONODERA (LDP).

Chief Cabinet Secretary and Minister for Strengthening National Security: YOSHIHIDE SUGA (LDP).

Minister for Reconstruction and for Comprehensive Policy Co-ordination for Revival from the Nuclear Accident at Fukushima: TAKUMI NEMOTO (LDP).

Chairman of the National Public Safety Commission and Minister of State for Disaster Management, for the Abduction Issue and for the Nation's Infrastructure Resilience: KEIJI FURUYA (LDP).

Minister of State for Economic and Fiscal Policy, for Total Reform of Social Security and Tax and for Economic Revitalization: AKIRA AMARI (LDP).

Minister of State for Okinawa and Northern Territories' Affairs, for Science and Technology Policy, for Space Policy, for Information Technology Policy, and for Ocean Policy and Territorial Issues: ICHITA YAMAMOTO (LDP).

Minister for Measures for Declining Birthrate and Gender Equality and for Support for Women's Empowerment and Child Rearing, and Minister of State for Consumer Affairs and Food Safety: MASAKO MORI (LDP).

Minister for Economic Revitalization, for Total Reform of Social Security and Tax and Minister of State for Economic and Fiscal Policy: AKIRA AMARI (LDP).

Minister for Administrative Reform, for Civil Service Reform, for 'Cool Japan' Strategy, for 'Challenge Again' Initiative and Minister of State for Regulatory Reform: TAMOMI INADA (LDP).

MINISTRIES

Imperial Household Agency: 1-1, Chiyoda, Chiyoda-ku, Tokyo 100-8111; tel. (3) 3213-1111; fax (3) 3282-1407; e-mail information@kunaicho.go.jp; internet www.kunaicho.go.jp.

Prime Minister's Office: 1-6-1, Nagata-cho, Chiyoda-ku, Tokyo 100-8968; tel. (3) 3581-2361; fax (3) 3581-1910; internet www.kantei.go.jp.

Cabinet Office: 1-6-1, Nagata-cho, Chiyoda-ku, Tokyo 100-8968; tel. (3) 5253-2111; internet www.cao.go.jp.

Ministry of Agriculture, Forestry and Fisheries: 1-2-1, Kasumigaseki, Chiyoda-ku, Tokyo 100-8950; tel. (3) 3502-5517; fax (3) 3592-7697; internet www.maff.go.jp.

Ministry of Defence: 5-1, Ichigaya, Honmura-cho, Shinjuku-ku, Tokyo 162-8801; tel. (3) 3268-3111; fax (3) 5261-8018; e-mail infomod@mod.go.jp; internet www.mod.go.jp.

Ministry of Economy, Trade and Industry: 1-3-1, Kasumigaseki, Chiyoda-ku, Tokyo 100-8901; tel. (3) 3501-1511; fax (3) 3501-6942; e-mail webmail@meti.go.jp; internet www.meti.go.jp.

Ministry of Education, Culture, Sports, Science and Technology: 3-2-2, Kasumigaseki, Chiyoda-ku, Tokyo 100-8959; tel. (3) 5253-4111; fax (3) 3595-2017; internet www.mext.go.jp.

Ministry of the Environment: 5 Godochosha, 1-2-2, Kasumigaseki, Chiyoda-ku, Tokyo 100-8975; tel. (3) 3581-3351; fax (3) 3502-0308; internet www.env.go.jp.

Ministry of Finance: 3-1-1, Kasumigaseki, Chiyoda-ku, Tokyo 100-8940; tel. (3) 3581-4111; fax (3) 5251-2667; e-mail info@mof.go.jp; internet www.mof.go.jp.

Ministry of Foreign Affairs: 2-2-1, Kasumigaseki, Chiyoda-ku, Tokyo 100-8919; tel. (3) 3580-3311; fax (3) 3581-2667; e-mail webmaster@mofa.go.jp; internet www.mofa.go.jp.

Ministry of Health, Labour and Welfare: 1-2-2, Kasumigaseki, Chiyoda-ku, Tokyo 100-8916; tel. (3) 5253-1111; fax (3) 3501-2532; e-mail www-admin@mhlw.go.jp; internet www.mhlw.go.jp.

Ministry of Internal Affairs and Communications: 2-1-2, Kasumigaseki, Chiyoda-ku, Tokyo 100-8926; tel. (3) 5253-5111; fax (3) 3504-0265; internet www.soumu.go.jp.

Ministry of Justice: 1-1-1, Kasumigaseki, Chiyoda-ku, Tokyo 100-8977; tel. (3) 3580-4111; fax (3) 3592-7011; e-mail webmaster@moj.go.jp; internet www.moj.go.jp.

Ministry of Land, Infrastructure, Transport and Tourism: 2-1-3, Kasumigaseki, Chiyoda-ku, Tokyo 100-8918; tel. (3) 5253-8111; fax (3) 3580-7982; e-mail webmaster@mlit.go.jp; internet www.mlit.go.jp.

Financial Services Agency: 3-2-1, Kasumigaseki, Chiyoda-ku, Tokyo 100-8967; tel. (3) 3506-6000; internet www.fsa.go.jp.

National Public Safety Commission: 2-1-2, Kasumigaseki, Chiyoda-ku, Tokyo 100-8974; tel. (3) 3581-0141; internet www.npsc.go.jp.

Legislature

DIET
(Kokkai)

The Diet consists of two chambers: the House of Councillors (upper house) and the House of Representatives (lower house). The members of the House of Representatives are elected for a period of four years (subject to dissolution). The House of Representatives has 480 members: 300 single-seat constituencies and 180 seats determined by proportional representation. The 242 members of the House of Councillors serve a six-year term of office, with elections for one-half of the members (including 48 chosen by proportional representation) being held every three years.

House of Councillors

Speaker: MASAAKI YAMAZAKI.

	Seats after elections*	
Party	11 July 2010	21 July 2013
Liberal Democratic Party	84	113
Democratic Party of Japan and the Shin-Ryokufukai	106	59
New Komeito	19	20
Your Party	11	18
Japanese Communist Party	6	11
Japanese Restoration Party	—	9
Social Democratic Party of Japan	4	3
People's New Party	3	—
Sunrise Party of Japan	3	1
New Renaissance Party	2	1
New Party Nippon	1	—
People's Life Party	—	2
Independents and others	3	4
Total	242	242†

* One-half of the seats are renewable every three years.
† Including one vacancy.

House of Representatives

Speaker: BUNMEI IBUKI.

Election, 16 December 2012

Party	Seats
Liberal Democratic Party	294
Democratic Party of Japan	57
Japan Restoration Party	54
New Komeito	31
Your Party	18
Tomorrow Party of Japan*	9
Japanese Communist Party	8
Social Democratic Party of Japan	2
People's New Party	1
New Party Daichi	1
Independents	5
Total	480

* On 29 December 2012 eight of the nine Tomorrow Party of Japan members of the House of Representatives left to form the Life Party.

Election Commission

Central Election Management Council: 2nd Bldg of Central Common Government Office, 2-1-2, Kasumigaseki, Chiyoda-ku, Tokyo 100-8926; tel. (3) 5253-5111; fax (3) 5253-5575; mems nominated by Diet and approved by Cabinet; regulates proportional representation electoral elements for both legislative chambers; single-constituency elections for both chambers are supervised by an Election Control Cttee est. by each prefectural govt; Chair. AKIRA ISHIHARA.

Political Organizations

The Political Funds Regulation Law provides that any organization wishing to support a candidate for an elective public office must be registered as a political party. There are more than 10,000 registered parties in the country, mostly of local or regional significance.

Ainu Party: 80-27, Nibutani Biratori, Saru-gun, Hokkaido 055-0101; tel. (145) 74-6033; fax (145) 74-6035; e-mail info@ainu-org.jp; f. 2012; advocates equal rights for indigenous people; Pres. SHIRO KAYANO; Gen. Sec. HIROYUKI NOMOTO.

Democratic Party of Japan (DPJ): 1-11-1, Nagata-cho, Chiyoda-ku, Tokyo 100-0014; tel. (3) 3595-9988; fax (3) 3595-9961; e-mail dpjenews@dpj.or.jp; internet www.dpj.or.jp; f. 1998; est. by the integration into the original DPJ (f. 1996) of the Democratic Reform League, Minseito and Shinto Yuai; advocates a cabinet formed and controlled by the people; absorbed Party Sakigake in 2001; absorbed Liberal Party in 2003; Pres. BANRI KAIEDA; Sec.-Gen. AKIHIRO OHATA.

Japan Restoration Party (Nippon Ishin No Kai): c/o Osaka Restoration Asscn, Sanei Nagahori Bldg, 2/F, 1-17-16 Shimanouchi, Chuo-ku, Osaka 542-0082; tel. (6) 6120-5581; fax (6) 6120-5582; internet www.j-ishin.jp; f. 2012; advocates a reduced reliance on nuclear power, regulated economic growth, the right to collective self-defence and constitutional reform; absorbed the Sunrise Party in Nov. 2012; Pres. TAKEO HIRANUMA; Sec.-Gen. ICHIRO MATSUI.

Japanese Communist Party (JCP): 4-26-7, Sendagaya, Shibuya-ku, Tokyo 151-8586; tel. (3) 3403-6111; fax (3) 5474-8358; e-mail info@jcp.or.jp; internet www.jcp.or.jp; f. 1922; 400,000 mems (2010); Chair. of Exec. Cttee KAZUO SHII; Sec.-Gen. TADAYOSHI ICHIDA.

Liberal Democratic Party (LDP) (Jiyu-Minshuto): 1-11-23, Nagata-cho, Chiyoda-ku, Tokyo 100-8910; tel. (3) 3581-6211; fax (3) 5511-8855; e-mail koho@ldp.jimin.or.jp; internet www.jimin.jp; f. 1955; advocates establishment of a welfare state, promotion of industrial devt, improvement of educational and cultural facilities, and constitutional reform as needed; absorbed New Conservative Party in 2003; Pres. SHINZO ABE; Sec.-Gen. SHIGERU ISHIBA.

New Komeito: 17, Minami-Motomachi, Shinjuku-ku, Tokyo 160-0012; tel. (3) 3353-0111; fax (3) 3225-0207; internet www.komei.or.jp; f. 1964; est. as Komeito; renamed Komei in 1994 following defection of some mems to the New Frontier Party (Shinshinto, dissolved in 1997); absorbed Reimei Club in 1998; renamed as above in 1998 following merger of Komei and Shinto Heiwa; advocates political moderation, humanism and globalism; 400,000 mems (2003); Pres. NATSUO YAMAGUCHI; Sec.-Gen. YOSHIHISA INOUE.

New Party Daichi (Shinto Daichi): 2-9-6 Nagata-cho, Chiyoda-ku, Tokyo 100-0014; tel. (3) 3593-0171; fax (11) 3593-0276; internet www.muneo.gr.jp; f. 2005; regional grouping based in Hokkaido; Leader MUNEO SUZUKI.

New Party Nippon (Shinto Nippon): 1-7-11, Hirakawa-cho, Chiyoda-ku, Tokyo 102-0093; tel. (3) 5213-0333; fax (3) 5213-0888; internet www.nippon-dream.com; f. 2005; founding mems included LDP rebels opposed to postal reform proposals of Prime Minister Koizumi; Leader YASUO TANAKA.

New Renaissance Party (Shinto Kaikaku): 2-8-15, Akasaka, Minato-ku, Tokyo; internet shintokaikaku.jp; f. 2010; conservative grouping; Pres. YOICHI MASUZOE; Sec.-Gen. HIROYUKI ARAI.

New Socialist Party: Miyako Sakura Kosan Bldg, 3/F, 7-9, Nihonbashi Tomizawa-cho, Chuo-ku, Tokyo; tel. (3) 5643-6002; fax (3) 3639-0150; e-mail honbu@sinsyakai.or.jp; internet www.sinsyakai.or.jp; f. 1996; est. by left-wing defectors from SDPJ; opposed to US military bases on Okinawa and introduction in 1996 of new electoral system; seeks to establish an ecological socio-economic system; Pres. MATSUEDA YOSHIHIRO; Sec.-Gen. OSANAMI HIROKUNI.

People's Life Party (Seikatsu No To): SR Bldg, 3/F, 2-12-8, Nagata-cho, Chiyoda-ku, Tokyo 100-0014; tel. (3) 5501-2200; fax (3) 5501-2202; f. 2012 following a split in the Tomorrow Party of Japan; Leader ICHIRO OZAWA; Dep. Leader YUKO MORI.

People's New Party (PNP) (Kokumin Shinto): Kohase Bldg, 3/F, 2-14-7, Hirakawa-cho, Chiyoda-ku, Tokyo 102-0093; tel. (3) 3239-4545; fax (3) 5275-2675; e-mail info@kokumin.or.jp; internet www.kokumin.or.jp; f. 2005; est. by rebels from LDP opposed to postal reform proposals of Prime Minister Koizumi; Leader SHOZABURO JIMI; Sec.-Gen. MIKIO SHIMOJI.

Social Democratic Party of Japan (SDPJ) (Shakai Minshuto): 2-4-3, Nagata-cho, Chiyoda-ku, Tokyo 100-0014; tel. (3) 3580-1171; fax (3) 3580-0691; e-mail kokusai@sdp.or.jp; internet www.sdp.or.jp; f. 1945; est. as Japan Socialist Party (JSP); adopted present name in 1996; seeks the establishment of collective non-aggression and a mutual security system incl. Japan, the USA, the People's Republic of China and the Commonwealth of Independent States; Chair. YOSHIDA TADASHI SATOSHI; Sec.-Gen. SEIJI MATAICHI.

Tomorrow Party of Japan (Nippon Mirai No To): SR Bldg, 3/F, 2-12-8 Nagata-cho, Chiyoda-ku, Tokyo; fax (3) 6701-7018; e-mail info@nippon-mirai.jp; internet www.nippon-mirai.jp; f. 2012; advocates a 10-year plan for the complete elimination of nuclear power; Pres. TOMOKO ABE; Sec.-Gen. TETSUNARI IIDA.

Unity Party (Yui No To): 2-9-6 Nagata-cho, Chiyoda-ku, Tokyo 100-0014; tel. (3) 5532-4110; fax (3) 5532-4130; internet www.yuinotoh.jp; f. 2013; Pres. KENJI EDA; Sec.-Gen. JIRO ONO.

Your Party (Minna No To): Towa Hanzomon Corp. Bldg, Rm 606, 2-12, Hayabusa-cho, Chiyoda-ku, Tokyo 102-0092; tel. (3) 5216-3710; fax (3) 5216-3711; internet www.your-party.jp; f. 2009; est. by fmr mems of LDP and DPJ; advocates reform of bureaucracy; Pres. YOSHIMI WATANABE.

Diplomatic Representation

EMBASSIES IN JAPAN

Afghanistan: 2-2-1, Azabudai, Minato-ku, Tokyo 106-0041; tel. (3) 5574-7611; fax (3) 5574-0195; e-mail info@afghanembassyjp.org; internet www.afghanembassyjp.org; Ambassador SAYED M. AMIN FATIMIE.

Albania: Hokkoku Shimbun Bldg, 4/F, 6-4-8, Tsukiji, Chuo-ku, Tokyo 104-0045; tel. (3) 3543-6861; fax (3) 3543-6862; e-mail embassy.tokyo@mfa.gov.al; internet emb-al.jp; Ambassador BUJAR DIDA.

Algeria: 2-10-67, Mita, Meguro-ku, Tokyo 153-0062; tel. (3) 3711-2661; fax (3) 3710-6534; internet www.algerianembassy-japan.jp; Ambassador SID ALI KETRANDJI.

Angola: 2-10-24, Daizawa, Setagaya-ku, Tokyo 155-0032; tel. (3) 5430-7879; fax (3) 5712-7481; e-mail md-japan@angola.or.jp; internet www.angola.or.jp; Ambassador JOÃO MIGUEL VAHEKENI.

Argentina: 2-14-14, Moto-Azabu, Minato-ku, Tokyo 106-0046; tel. (3) 5420-7101; fax (3) 5420-7109; e-mail ejapo@mrecic.gov.ar; internet www.ejapo.mrecic.gov.ar; Ambassador RAÚL GUILLERMO DEJEAN RODRÍGUEZ.

Australia: 2-1-14, Mita, Minato-ku, Tokyo 108-8361; tel. (3) 5232-4111; fax (3) 5232-4149; internet www.australia.or.jp; Ambassador BRUCE MILLER.

Austria: 1-1-20, Moto-Azabu, Minato-ku, Tokyo 106-0046; tel. (3) 3451-8281; fax (3) 3451-8283; e-mail tokio-ob@bmeia.gv.at; internet www.bmeia.gv.at/tokio; Ambassador Dr BERNHARD ZIMBURG.

Azerbaijan: 1-19-15, Higashi-Gaoka, Meguro-ku, Tokyo 152-0021; tel. (3) 5486-4744; fax (3) 5486-7374; e-mail info@azembassy.jp; internet www.azembassy.jp; Ambassador GURSEL ISMAYILZADA.

Bahrain: Residence Viscountess 720 & 520, 1-11-36, Akasaka, Minato-ku, Tokyo 107-0052; tel. (3) 3584-8001; fax (3) 3584-8004; e-mail general@bahrain-embassy.or.jp; internet www.bahrain-embassy.or.jp; Ambassador Dr KHALIL HASSAN.

Bangladesh: 4-15-15, Meguro, Meguro-ku, Tokyo 153-0063; tel. (3) 5704-0216; fax (3) 5704-1696; e-mail bdembjp@yahoo.com; internet www.bdembassy.jp; Ambassador MASUD BIN MOMEN.

Belarus: Shirogane K House, 4-14-12, Shirogane, Minato-ku, Tokyo 108-0072; tel. (3) 3448-1623; fax (3) 3448-1624; e-mail japan@mfa.gov.by; internet japan.mfa.gov.by; Ambassador SYARHEY RAKHMANOV KIMOVICH.

Belgium: 5-4, Niban-cho, Chiyoda-ku, Tokyo 102-0084; tel. (3) 3262-0191; fax (3) 3262-0651; e-mail tokyo@diplobel.fed.be; internet countries.diplomatie.belgium.be/en/japan; Ambassador LUC LIEBAUT.

Benin: Asahi Bldg, 4/F, 1-2-2, Hirakawa-cho, Chiyoda-ku, Tokyo 102-0093; tel. (3) 5229-7232; fax (3) 5229-2838; e-mail abenintyo@beninembassy.jp; internet www.beninembassy.jp; Ambassador RUFIN ZOMAHOUN.

Bolivia: No. 38 Kowa Bldg, Rm 804, 4-12-24, Nishi-Azabu, Minato-ku, Tokyo 106-0031; tel. (3) 3499-5441; fax (3) 3499-5443; e-mail emboltk1@ad.il24.net; Chargé d'affaires. a.i. CARLOS MIGUYAN GIRONDA TELLEZ.

Bosnia and Herzegovina: 2–3/F, 5-3-29, Minami-Azabu, Minato-ku, Tokyo 106-0047; tel. (3) 5422-8231; fax (3) 5422-8232; e-mail bih8emb@gol.com; Ambassador ANESA KUNDUROVIĆ.

Botswana: Kearny Place, 6/F, 4-5-10, Shiba, Minato-ku, Tokyo 108-0014; tel. (3) 5440-5676; fax (3) 5765-7581; e-mail info@botswanaembassy.or.jp; internet www.botswanaembassy.or.jp; Chargé d'affaires a.i. PULE MPHOTHWE.

Brazil: 2-11-12, Kita-Aoyama, Minato-ku, Tokyo 107-8633; tel. (3) 3404-5211; fax (3) 3405-5846; e-mail webmaster@brasemb.or.jp; internet www.brasemb.or.jp; Ambassador ANDRÉ CORRÊA DO LAGO.

Brunei: 6-5-2, Kita-Shinagawa, Shinagawa-ku, Tokyo 141-0001; tel. (3) 3447-7997; fax (3) 3447-9260; e-mail contact@bruemb.jp; internet www.bruemb.jp; Ambassador Haji MAHAMUD Haji AHMAD.

Bulgaria: 5-36-3, Yoyogi, Shibuya-ku, Tokyo 151-0053; tel. (3) 3465-1021; fax (3) 3465-1031; e-mail Embassy.Tokyo@mfa.bg; internet www.mfa.bg/embassies/japan; Ambassador GEORGI VASSILEV.

Burkina Faso: 2-14-34, Moto Azabu, Minato-Ku, Tokyo 106-0046; tel. (3) 3444-2660; fax (3) 3444-2661; e-mail faso-amb@khaki.plala.or.jp; internet www.embassy-avenue.jp/burkina; Ambassador FRANÇOIS OUBIDA.

Cambodia: 8-6-9, Akasaka, Minato-ku, Tokyo 107-0052; tel. (3) 5412-8521; fax (3) 5412-8526; e-mail camembassyjp@gmail.com; internet www.cambodianembassy.jp; Ambassador HOR MONIRATH.

Cameroon: 3-27-16, Nozawa, Setagaya-ku, Tokyo 154-0003; tel. (3) 5430-4985; fax (3) 5430-6489; e-mail ambacamtokyo@gol.com; Ambassador Dr PIERRE NDZENGUE.

Canada: 7-3-38, Akasaka, Minato-ku, Tokyo 107-8503; tel. (3) 5412-6200; fax (3) 5412-6249; e-mail tokyo.admin@international.gc.ca; internet www.canadainternational.gc.ca/japan-japon; Ambassador MACKENZIE CLUGSTON.

Chile: Nihon Seimei Akabanebashi Bldg, 8/F, 3-1-14, Shiba, Minato-ku, Tokyo 105-0014; tel. (3) 3452-7561; fax (3) 3452-4457; e-mail echile.japon@minrel.gov.cl; internet chileabroad.gov.cl/japon; Ambassador PATRICIO TORRES.

China, People's Republic: 3-4-33, Moto-Azabu, Minato-ku, Tokyo 106-0046; tel. (3) 3403-3380; fax (3) 3403-3345; e-mail info@china-embassy.or.jp; internet www.china-embassy.or.jp; Ambassador CHENG YONGHUA.

Colombia: 3-10-53, Kami Osaki, Shinagawa-ku, Tokyo 141-0021; tel. (3) 3440-6451; fax (3) 3440-6724; e-mail embajada@emcoltokyo.or.jp; internet www.colombiaembassy.org; Ambassador PATRICIA CÁRDENAS.

Congo, Democratic Republic: 1–2/F, 5-8-5, Asakusabashi, Taito-ku, Tokyo 111-0053; tel. (3) 5820-1580; fax (3) 3423-3984; Chargé d'affaires a.i. RAPHAEL MWENDA BAMBINGANILA.

Costa Rica: No. 38 Kowa Bldg, Rm 901, 4-12-24, Nishi-Azabu, Minato-ku, Tokyo 106-0031; tel. (3) 3486-1812; fax (3) 3486-1813; Ambassador ÁLVARO ANTONIO CEDEÑO MOLINARI.

Côte d'Ivoire: 2-19-12, Uehara, Shibuya-ku, Tokyo 151-0064; tel. (3) 5454-1401; fax (3) 5454-1405; e-mail ambacijn@yahoo.fr; internet www.ahibo.com/ambaci-jp; Ambassador ÁLVARO ANTONIO CEDENO MOLINARI.

Croatia: 3-3-10, Hiroo, Shibuya-ku, Tokyo 150-0012; tel. (3) 5469-3014; fax (3) 5469-3015; e-mail croemb.tokyo@mvep.hr; internet www.cro-embassy.jp; Ambassador MIRA MARTINEC.

Cuba: 1-28-4, Higashi-Azabu, Minato-ku, Tokyo 106-0044; tel. (3) 5570-3182; fax (3) 5570-8566; e-mail embajada@ecujapon.jp; internet www.cubadiplomatica.cu/japon/EN/Mission/Embassy.aspx; Ambassador MARCOS RODRÍGUEZ COSTA.

Czech Republic: 2-16-14, Hiroo, Shibuya-ku, Tokyo 150-0012; tel. (3) 3400-8122; fax (3) 3400-8124; e-mail tokyo@embassy.mzv.cz; internet www.mzv.cz/tokyo; Ambassador KATEŘINA FIALKOVÁ.

Denmark: 29-6, Sarugaku-cho, Shibuya-ku, Tokyo 150-0033; tel. (3) 3496-3001; fax (3) 3496-3440; e-mail tyoamb@um.dk; internet japan.um.dk; Ambassador A. CARSTEN DAMSGAARD.

Djibouti: 5-18-10, Shimo Meguro, Meguro-ku, Tokyo 153-0064; tel. (3) 5704-0682; fax (3) 5725-8305; e-mail djibouti@fine.ocn.jp; internet www.djiboutiembassy.jp; Ambassador AHMED ARAITA ALI.

Dominican Republic: No. 38 Kowa Bldg, Rm 904, 4-12-24, Nishi-Azabu, Minato-ku, Tokyo 106-0031; tel. (3) 3499-6020; fax (3) 3499-2627; Ambassador HECTOR PAULINO DOMINGUEZ RODRIGUEZ.

Ecuador: No. 38 Kowa Bldg, Rm 806, 4-12-24, Nishi-Azabu, Minato-ku, Tokyo 106-0031; tel. (3) 3499-2800; fax (3) 3499-4400; e-mail info@ecuador-embassy.or.jp; internet www.ecuador-embassy.or.jp; Ambassador LEONARDO CARRIÓN EGUIGUREN.

Egypt: 1-5-4, Aobadai, Meguro-ku, Tokyo 153-0042; tel. (3) 3770-8022; fax (3) 3770-8021; e-mail egyptemb@leaf.ocn.ne.jp; internet www.mfa.gov.eg/Tokyo_Emb; Ambassador HESHAM AL-ZEMEITI.

El Salvador: No. 38 Kowa Bldg, 8/F, 4-12-24, Nishi-Azabu, Minato-ku, Tokyo 106-0031; tel. (3) 3499-4461; fax (3) 3486-7022; e-mail embesaltokio@gol.com; Ambassador MARTHA LIDIA ZELAYANDÍA CISNEROS.

Eritrea: Shirokanedai ST Bldg, Rm 401, 4-7-4, Shirokanedai, Minato-ku, Tokyo, 108-0071; tel. (3) 5791-1815; fax (3) 5791-1816; e-mail info@eritreaembassy-japan.org; internet www.eritreaembassy-japan.org; Ambassador ESTIFANOS AFEWORKI.

Estonia: 2-6-15, Jingu-mae, Shibuya-ku 150-0001; tel. (3) 5412-7281; fax (3) 5412-7282; e-mail embassy.tokyo@mfa.ee; internet www.estemb.or.jp; Ambassador TOIVO TASA.

Ethiopia: Takanawa Kaisei Bldg, 2/F, 3-4-1, Takanawa, Minato-ku, Tokyo 108-0074; tel. (3) 5420-6860; fax (3) 5420-6866; e-mail info@ethiopia-emb.or.jp; internet www.ethiopia-emb.or.jp; Ambassador MARKOS TEKLE RIKE.

Fiji: Noa Bldg, 14/F, 2-3-5, Azabudai, Minato-ku, Tokyo 106-0041; tel. (3) 3587-2038; fax (3) 3587-2563; e-mail info@fijiembassy.jp; internet www.fijiembassy.jp; Ambassador ISIKELI MATAITOGA.

Finland: 3-5-39, Minami-Azabu, Minato-ku, Tokyo 106-8561; tel. (3) 5447-6000; fax (3) 5447-6042; e-mail sanomat.tok@formin.fi; internet www.finland.or.jp; Ambassador MANU VIRTAMO.

France: 4-11-44, Minami-Azabu, Minato-ku, Tokyo 106-8514; tel. (3) 5798-6000; fax (3) 5798-6328; e-mail ambafrance.tokyo@diplomatie.fr; internet www.ambafrance-jp.org; Ambassador CHRISTIAN MASSET.

Gabon: 1-34-11, Higashi-Gaoka, Meguro-ku, Tokyo 152-0021; tel. (3) 5430-9171; fax (3) 5430-9175; e-mail info@gabonembassyjapan.org; internet www.gabonembassyjapan.org; Ambassador FRANÇOIS PENDJET BOMBILA.

Georgia: Residence Viscountess 220, 1-11-36, Akasaka, Minato-ku, Tokyo 107-0052; tel. (3) 5575-6091; fax (3) 5575-9133; e-mail tokio.emb@mfa.gov.ge; internet japan.mfa.gov.ge; Ambassador LEVAN TSINTSADZE.

Germany: 4-5-10, Minami-Azabu, Minato-ku, Tokyo 106-0047; tel. (3) 5791-7700; fax (3) 5791-7773; e-mail info@tokyo.diplo.de; internet www.tokyo.diplo.de; Ambassador STEFAN HERZBERG.

Ghana: 1-5-21, Nishi-Azabu, Minato-ku, Tokyo 106-0031; tel. (3) 5410-8631; fax (3) 5410-8635; e-mail mission@ghanaembassy.or.jp; internet www.ghanaembassy.or.jp; Ambassador EDMOND KOFI DEH.

Greece: 3-16-30, Nishi-Azabu, Minato-ku, Tokyo 106-0031; tel. (3) 3403-0871; fax (3) 3402-4642; e-mail gremb.tok@mfa.gr; internet www.mfa.gr/tokyo; Ambassador NIKOLAOS TSAMADOS.

Guatemala: No. 38 Kowa Bldg, Rm 905, 4-12-24, Nishi-Azabu, Minato-ku, Tokyo 106-0031; tel. (3) 3400-1830; fax (3) 3400-1820; e-mail embguate@minex.gob.gt; internet www.embassy-avenue.jp/guatemala; Ambassador BYRON RENE ESCOBEDO MENÉNDEZ.

Guinea: 12-9, Hachiyama-cho, Shibuya-ku, Tokyo 150-0035; tel. (3) 3770-4640; fax (3) 3770-4643; e-mail ambagui-tokyo@gol.com; Ambassador SENKOUN SYLLA.

Haiti: No. 38 Kowa Bldg, Rm 906, 4-12-24, Nishi-Azabu, Minato-ku, Tokyo 106-0031; tel. (3) 3486-7096; fax (3) 3486-7070; e-mail amb.japon@diplomatie.ht; Chargé d'affaires a.i. JUDITH EXAVIER.

Holy See: Apostolic Nunciature, 9-2, Sanban-cho, Chiyoda-ku, Tokyo 102-0075; tel. (3) 3263-6851; fax (3) 3263-6060; Apostolic Nuncio Most Rev. JOSEPH CHENNOTH (Titular Archbishop of Milevum).

Honduras: No. 38 Kowa Bldg, Rm 802, 4-12-24, Nishi-Azabu, Minato-ku, Tokyo 106-0031; tel. (3) 3409-1150; fax (3) 3409-0305; e-mail honduras@interlink.or.jp; Ambassador MARLENE VILLELA.

Hungary: 2-17-14, Mita, Minato-ku, Tokyo 108-0073; tel. (3) 3798-8801; fax (3) 3798-8812; e-mail mission.tio@mfa.gov.hu; internet www.mfa.gov.hu/kulkepviselet/JP/HU; Ambassador SZERDAHELYI ISTVÁN.

Iceland: 4-18-26, Takanawa, Minato-ku, Tokyo 108-0074; tel. (3) 3447-1944; fax (3) 3447-1945; e-mail icemb.tokyo@utn.stjr.is; internet www.iceland.is/jp; Ambassador ISTVAN SZERDAHELYI.

India: 2-2-11, Kudan-Minami, Chiyoda-ku, Tokyo 102-0074; tel. (3) 3262-2391; fax (3) 3234-4866; e-mail embassy@indembjp.org; internet www.embassyofindiajapan.org; Ambassador DEEPA GOPALAN WADHWA.

Indonesia: 5-2-9, Higashi-Gotanda, Shinagawa-ku, Tokyo 141-0022; tel. (3) 3441-4201; fax (3) 3447-1697; e-mail info@indonesianembassy.jp; internet kbritokyo.jp; Ambassador YUSRON IHZA MAHENDRA.

Iran: 3-13-9, Minami-Azabu, Minato-ku, Tokyo 106-0047; tel. (3) 3446-8011; fax (3) 3446-9002; e-mail info@iranembassyjp.org; internet www.tokyo.mfa.ir; Ambassador Dr REZA NAZARAHARI.

Iraq: 14-6 Kamiyama-cho, Shibuya-ku, Tokyo 150-0047; tel. (3) 5790-5311; fax (3) 5790-5315; e-mail embassy@iraqi-japan.com; internet www.iraqi-japan.com; Ambassador ALAA ABDUL MAJID AL-HASHIMY.

Ireland: Ireland House, 2-10-7, Kojimachi, Chiyoda-ku, Tokyo 102-0083; tel. (3) 3263-0695; fax (3) 3265-2275; e-mail tokyoembassy@dfa.ie; internet www.irishembassy.jp; Ambassador JOHN NEARY.

Israel: 3, Niban-cho, Chiyoda-ku, Tokyo 102-0084; tel. (3) 3264-0911; fax (3) 3264-0791; e-mail consular@tokyo.mfa.gov.il; internet tokyo.mfa.gov.il; Ambassador RUTH KAHANOFF.

Italy: 2-5-4, Mita, Minato-ku, Tokyo 108-8302; tel. (3) 3453-5291; fax (3) 3456-2319; e-mail ambasciata.tokyo@esteri.it; internet www.ambtokyo.esteri.it/ambasciata_tokyo; Ambassador DOMENICO GIORGI.

Jamaica: Toranomon Yatsuka Bldg, 2/F, 1-1-11, Atago, Minato-ku, Tokyo 105-0002; tel. (3) 3435-1861; fax (3) 3435-1864; e-mail mail@jamaicaemb.jp; internet www.jamaicaemb.jp; Ambassador RICARDO ALLICOCK.

Jordan: 39-8, Kamiyama-cho, Shibuya-ku, Tokyo 100-0014; tel. (3) 5478-7177; fax (3) 5478-0032; e-mail jor-emb@bird.ocn.ne.jp; Ambassador DEMIYE ZUHER HADDAD.

Kazakhstan: 1-8-14, Azabudai, Minato-ku, Tokyo 106-0041; tel. (3) 3589-1821; fax (3) 3589-1822; e-mail japan@mfa.kz; internet www.embkazjp.org; Ambassador AKYLBEK KAMALDINOV.

Kenya: 3-24-3, Yakumo, Meguro-ku, Tokyo 152-0023; tel. (3) 3723-4006; fax (3) 3723-4488; e-mail general@kenyarep-jp.com; internet www.kenyarep-jp.com; Ambassador BENSON H. O. OGUTU.

Korea, Republic: 4-4-10, Yotsuya, Shinjuku-ku, Tokyo 160-0004; tel. (3) 3452-7611; fax (3) 5232-6911; e-mail information_jp@mofat.go.kr; internet jpn-tokyo.mofat.go.kr; Ambassador LEE BYUNG-KEE.

Kosovo: M.G. Atago Bldg, 10/F, 3-13-7, Nishi-Shinbashi, Minato-ku, Tokyo 105-0003; tel. (3) 6809-2577; fax (3) 6809-2579; e-mail embassy.japan@rks-gov.net; internet www.ambasada-ks.net/jp; Ambassador AHMET SHALA.

Kuwait: 4-13-12, Mita, Minato-ku, Tokyo 108-0073; tel. (3) 3455-0361; fax (3) 3456-6290; e-mail consular@kuwait-embassy.or.jp; internet kuwait-embassy.or.jp; Ambassador Sheikh ABDUL RAHMAN AL-OTAIBI.

Kyrgyzstan: 5-6-16, Shimomeguro, Meguro-ku, Tokyo 153-0064; tel. (3) 3719-0828; fax (3) 3719-0868; e-mail office@kyrgyzemb.jp; Ambassador MOLDOGAZIEV RYSBEK TURGANBAEVICH.

Laos: 3-3-22, Nishi-Azabu, Minato-ku, Tokyo 106-0031; tel. (3) 5411-2291; fax (3) 5411-2293; Ambassador KHENTHONG NUANTHASING.

Latvia: 37-11, Kamiyama-cho, Shibuya-ku, Tokyo 150-0047; tel. (3) 3467-6888; fax (3) 3467-6897; e-mail embassy.japan@mfa.gov.lv; Ambassador NORMANS PENKE.

Lebanon: Residence Viscountess 410, 1-11-36, Akasaka, Minato-ku, Tokyo 107-0052; tel. (3) 5114-9950; fax (3) 5114-9952; Ambassador MOHAMMED EL-DIB.

Lesotho: U & M Akasaka Bldg, 3/F, 7-5-47, Akasaka, Minato-ku, Tokyo 107-0052; tel. (3) 3584-7455; fax (3) 3584-7456; e-mail bochabela@lesothotokyo.org; internet www.lesothotokyo.org; Ambassador RICHARD RAMOELETSI.

Liberia: Moto-Azabu Kokusai Mansion 201, 3-2-13, Moto-Azabu, Minato-ku, Tokyo 106-0046; tel. (3) 3479-9882; fax (3) 3479-9883; e-mail embassyofliberia@heart.ocn.ne.jp; internet www.liberianembassyjp.org; Ambassador YOUNGOR SEVELEE TELEWODA.

Libya: 10-14, Daikanyama-cho, Shibuya-ku, Tokyo 150-0034; tel. (3) 3477-0701; fax (3) 3464-0420; internet www.lytokyo.org; Ambassador AHMED ABDEL KARIM SALEM OWN.

Lithuania: 3-7-18, Moto-Azabu, Minato-ku, Tokyo 106-0046; tel. (3) 3408-5091; fax (3) 3408-5092; e-mail amb.jp@mfa.lt; internet jp.mfa.lt; Ambassador EGIDIJUS MEILUNAS.

Luxembourg: Luxembourg House, 1/F, 8–9, Yonban-cho, Chiyoda-ku, 102-0081; tel. (3) 3265-9621; fax (3) 3265-9624; e-mail infotokyo.amb@mae.etat.lu; internet tokyo.mae.lu; Ambassador MARC UNGEHEUER.

Madagascar: 2-3-23, Moto-Azabu, Minato-ku, Tokyo 106-0046; tel. (3) 3446-7252; fax (3) 3446-7078; e-mail ambtyo@r5.dion.ne.jp; internet www.madagascar-embassy.jp; Chargé d'affaires a.i. EUGÈNE MAHAONISON.

Malawi: Takanawa-Kaisei Bldg, 7/F, 3-4-1, Takanawa, Minato-ku, Tokyo 108-0074; tel. (3) 3449-3010; fax (3) 3449-3220; e-mail malawi@luck.ocn.ne.jp; internet www.malawiembassy.org; Ambassador RUEBEN NGWENYA.

Malaysia: 20-16, Nanpeidai-cho, Shibuya-ku, Tokyo 150-0036; tel. (3) 3476-3840; fax (3) 3476-4971; e-mail maltokyo@kln.gov.my; internet www.kln.gov.my/web/jpn_tokyo; Ambassador Dato' SHAHARUDDIN BIN MOHAMMED SOM.

Maldives: Iikura IT Bldg, 8/F, 1-9-10, Azabudai, Minato-ku, Tokyo 106-0041; tel. (3) 6234-4315; fax (3) 6234-4316; e-mail info@maldivesembassy.jp; internet www.maldivesembassy.jp; Ambassador AHMED KHALEEL.

Mali: 3-12-9, Kami-Osaki, Shinagawa-ku, Tokyo 141-0021; tel. (3) 5447-6881; fax (3) 5447-6882; e-mail info@ambamali-jp.org; internet www.ambamali-jp.org; Ambassador MAHAMANE BANIA TOURÉ.

Marshall Islands: Meiji Park Heights, 1/F, Rm 101, 9-9, Minami-Motomachi, Shinjuku-ku, Tokyo 106-0012; tel. (3) 5379-1701; fax (3) 5379-1810; e-mail alfred@rmiembassyjp.org; Ambassador TOM D. KIJINER.

Mauritania: 5-17-5, Kita-Shinagawa, Shinagawa-ku, Tokyo 141-0001; tel. (3) 3449-3810; fax (3) 3449-3822; e-mail ambarim@seagreen.ocn.ne.jp; internet www.amba-mauritania.jp; Ambassador YAHYA NGAM.

Mexico: 2-15-1, Nagata-cho, Chiyoda-ku, Tokyo 100-0014; tel. (3) 3581-1131; fax (3) 3581-4058; e-mail cheller@sre.gob.mx; internet www.sre.gob.mx/japon; Ambassador CLAUDE HELLER ROUASSANT.

Micronesia, Federated States: Reinanzaka Bldg, 2/F, 1-14-2, Akasaka, Minato-ku, Tokyo 107-0052; tel. (3) 3585-5456; fax (3) 3585-5348; e-mail fsmemb@fsmemb.or.jp; Ambassador JOHN FRITZ.

Mongolia: Pine Crest Mansion, 21-4, Kamiyama-cho, Shibuya-ku, Tokyo 150-0047; tel. (3) 3469-2088; fax (3) 3469-2216; e-mail embmong@gol.com; Ambassador SODOVJAMTSYN KHÜRELBAATAR.

Morocco: 5-4-30, Minami-Aoyama, Minato-ku, Tokyo 107-0062; tel. (3) 5485-7171; fax (3) 5485-7173; e-mail sifamato@circus.ocn.ne.jp; internet www.morocco-emba.jp; Ambassador Dr SAMIR ARROUR.

Mozambique: Shiba Amerex Bldg, 6/F, 3-12-17 Mita, Minato-ku, Tokyo 108-0073; tel. (3) 5419-0973; fax (3) 5442-0556; e-mail moz.tokyo@embamoc.jp; internet www.embamoc.jp; Ambassador BELMIRO JOSÉ MALATE.

Myanmar: 4-8-26, Kita-Shinagawa, Shinagawa-ku, Tokyo 140-0001; tel. (3) 3441-9291; fax (3) 3447-7394; e-mail contact@myanmar-embassy-tokyo.net; internet www.myanmar-embassy-tokyo.net; Ambassador KHIN MAUNG TING.

Namibia: AMEREX Bldg, 3-5-7, Azabudai, Minato-ku, Tokyo 106-0041; tel. (3) 6426-5460; fax (3) 6426-5461; Ambassador SOPHIA NANGOMBE (designate).

Nepal: Fukukawa House B, 6-20-28, Shimomeguro, Meguro-ku, Tokyo.153-0064; tel. (3) 3713-6241; e-mail nepembjp@big.or.jp; internet www.nepal-embassy.org; Ambassador Dr MADAN KUMAR BHATTARAI.

Netherlands: 3-6-3, Shiba Koen, Minato-ku, Tokyo 105-0011; tel. (3) 5776-5400; fax (3) 5776-5535; e-mail osa@minbuza.nl; internet japan.nlambassade.org; Ambassador RADINCK JAN VAN VOLLENHOVEN.

New Zealand: 20-40, Kamiyama-cho, Shibuya-ku, Tokyo 150-0047; tel. (3) 3467-2271; fax (3) 3467-2278; e-mail tky@mfat.govt.nz; internet www.nzembassy.com/japan; Ambassador MARK SINCLAIR.

Nicaragua: No. 38 Kowa Bldg, Rm 903, 4-12-24, Nishi-Azabu, Minato-ku, Tokyo 106-0031; tel. (3) 3499-0400; fax (3) 3710-2028; e-mail nicjapan@gol.com; Ambassador SAÚL ARANA CASTELLÓN.

Nigeria: 3-6-1 Toranomon, Minato-ku, Tokyo 105-0001; tel. (3) 5425-8011; fax (3) 5425-8016; e-mail info@nigeriaembassy.jp; internet www.nigeriaembassy.jp; Ambassador GODWIN NSUDE AGBO.

Norway: 5-12-2, Minami-Azabu, Minato-ku, Tokyo 106-0047; tel. (3) 6408-8100; fax (3) 6408-8199; e-mail emb.tokyo@mfa.no; internet www.norway.or.jp; Ambassador ARNE WALTHER.

Oman: 4-2-17, Hiroo, Shibuya-ku, Tokyo 150-0012; tel. (3) 5468-1088; e-mail info@omanembassy.jp; internet omanembassy.jp; Ambassador KHALID BIN HASHIL BIN MOHAMMED AL-MUSLAHI.

Pakistan: 4-6-17, Minami-Azabu, Minato-ku, Tokyo 106-0047; tel. (3) 5421-7741; fax (3) 5421-3610; e-mail info@pakistanembassyjapan.com; internet www.pakistanembassyjapan.com; Ambassador FARRUKH AMIL.

Palau: Rm 201, 1-1, Katamachi, Shinjuku-ku, Tokyo 160-0001; tel. (3) 3354-5500; Ambassador FRANCIS MATSUTARO.

Panama: No. 38 Kowa Bldg, Rm 902, 4-12-24, Nishi-Azabu, Minato-ku, Tokyo 106-0031; tel. (3) 3499-3741; fax (3) 5485-3548; e-mail panaemb@gol.com; internet www.embassyofpanamainjapan.org; Ambassador JORGE DEMETRIO KOSMAS SIFAKI.

Papua New Guinea: 5-32-20, Shimo Meguro, Meguro-ku, Tokyo 153-0064; tel. (3) 3454-7801; fax (3) 3454-7275; e-mail png-tyo@nifty.ne.jp; Ambassador GABRIEL DUSAVA.

Paraguay: Ichibancho TG Bldg 2, 7/F, 2-2, Ichiban-cho, Chiyoda-ku, Tokyo 102-0082; tel. (3) 3265-5271; fax (3) 3265-5273; e-mail embajada-consulado@embapar.jp; internet www.embapar.jp; Ambassador NAOYUKI TOYOTOSHI.

Peru: 2-3-1, Hiroo, Shibuya-ku, Tokyo 150-0012; tel. (3) 3406-4243; fax (3) 3409-7589; e-mail embperutokyo@embperujapan.org; internet www.embajadadelperuenjapon.org; Ambassador ELARD ALBERTO ESCALA SÁNCHEZ-BARRETO.

Philippines: 5-15-5, Roppongi, Minato-ku, Tokyo 106-8537; tel. (3) 5562-1600; fax (3) 5562-1603; e-mail info@philembassy.net; internet tokyo.philembassy.net; Ambassador MANUEL M. LOPEZ.

Poland: 2-13-5, Mita, Meguro-ku, Tokyo 153-0062; tel. (3) 5794-7020; fax (3) 5794-7024; e-mail tokio.amb.sekretariat@msz.gov.pl; internet www.tokio.polemb.net; Ambassador CYRYL KOZACZEWSKI.

Portugal: Kamiura-Kojimachi Bldg, 5/F, 3-10-3, Kojimachi, Chiyoda-ku, Tokyo 102-0083; tel. (3) 5212-7322; fax (3) 5226-0616; e-mail portugal@embportjp.org; internet www.embaixadadeportugal.jp; Ambassador JOSÉ FREITAS FERRAZ.

Qatar: 2-3-28, Moto-Azabu, Minato-ku, Tokyo 106-0046; tel. (3) 5475-0611; fax (3) 5475-0617; e-mail tokyo@mofa.gov.qa; Ambassador YOUSUF MOHAMED BILAL.

Romania: 3-16-19, Nishi-Azabu, Minato-ku, Tokyo 106-0031; tel. (3) 3479-0311; fax (3) 3479-0312; e-mail office@ambrom.jp; internet tokyo.mae.ro; Ambassador RADU SERBAN.

Russia: 2-1-1, Azabudai, Minato-ku, Tokyo 106-0041; tel. (3) 3583-4445; fax (3) 3505-0407; e-mail embassy@u01.gate01.com; internet www.russia-emb.jp; Ambassador EVGENY V. AFANASIEV.

Rwanda: Annex Fukazawa, 1-17-17, Fukazawa, Setagaya-ku, Tokyo 158-0081; tel. (3) 5752-4255; fax (3) 3703-0342; internet www.rwandaembassy-japan.org; Ambassador CHARLES MURIGANDE.

Samoa: Seiko Bldg, 3/F, 2-7-4, Irifune, Chuo-ku, Tokyo 104-0042; tel. (3) 6228-3692; Ambassador Leiataua Tuitolova'a Dr KILIFOTI ETEUATI.

San Marino: 3-5-1, Moto-Azabu, Minato-ku, Tokyo 106-0046; tel. (3) 5414-7745; fax (3) 3405-6789; e-mail sanmarinoemb@tiscali.it; Ambassador MANLIO CADELO.

Saudi Arabia: 1-8-4, Roppongi, Minato-ku, Tokyo 106-0032; tel. (3) 3589-5241; fax (3) 3589-5200; e-mail info@saudiembassy.or.jp; internet www.saudiembassy.or.jp; Ambassador ABDULAZIZ TURKISTANI.

Senegal: 1-3-4, Aobadai, Meguro-ku, Tokyo 153-0042; tel. (3) 3464-8451; fax (3) 3464-8452; e-mail senegal@senegal.jp; Ambassador BOUNA SÉMOU DIOUF.

Serbia: 4-7-24, Kita-Shinagawa, Shinagawa-ku, Tokyo 140-0001; tel. (3) 3447-3571; fax (3) 3447-3573; e-mail embassy@serbianembassy.jp; internet www.tokyo.mfa.gov.rs; Chargé d'affaires a.i. NENAD GLIŠIĆ.

Singapore: 5-12-3, Roppongi, Minato-ku, Tokyo 106-0032; tel. (3) 3586-9111; fax (3) 3582-1085; e-mail singemb_tyo@sgmfa.gov.sg; internet www.mfa.gov.sg/tokyo; Ambassador CHIN SIAT YOON.

Slovakia: 2-11-33, Moto-Azabu, Minato-ku, Tokyo 106-0046; tel. (3) 3451-2200; fax (3) 3451-2244; e-mail emb.tokyo@mzv.sk; internet www.tokyo.mfa.sk; Ambassador MICHAL KOTTMAN.

Slovenia: 7-14-12, Minami-Aoyama, Minato-ku, Tokyo 107-0062; tel. (3) 5468-6275; fax (3) 5468-1182; e-mail vto@gov.si; internet tokyo.embassy.si; Ambassador HELENA DRNOVŠEK ZORKO.

South Africa: Hanzoman First Bldg, 4/F, 1-4 Kozimachi, Chiyoda-ku, Tokyo 102-0083; tel. (3) 3265-3366; fax (3) 3265-3573; e-mail cronjet@dfa.gov.za; internet www.sajapan.org; Ambassador MOHAU N. PHEKO.

Spain: 1-3-29, Roppongi, Minato-ku, Tokyo 106-0032; tel. (3) 3583-8531; fax (3) 3582-8627; e-mail emb.tokio@maec.es; internet www.exteriores.gob.es/Embajadas/TOKIO/en; Ambassador MIGUEL ÁNGEL NAVARRO PORTERA.

Sri Lanka: 2-1-54, Takanawa, Minato-ku, Tokyo 108-0074; tel. (3) 3440-6911; fax (3) 3440-6914; e-mail tokyojp@lankaembassy.jp; internet www.lankaembassy.jp; Ambassador WASANTHA KARANNAGODA.

Sudan: 4-7-1, Yakumo, Meguro-ku, Tokyo 152-0023; tel. (3) 5729-6170; fax (3) 5729-6171; e-mail info@sudanembassy.jp; internet www.sudanembassy.jp; Ambassador ABDELWAHAB MOHAMED AL-HIJAZI.

Sweden: 1-10-3-100, Roppongi, Minato-ku, Tokyo 106-0032; tel. (3) 5562-5050; fax (3) 5562-9095; e-mail ambassaden.tokyo@foreign.ministry.se; internet www.sweden.or.jp; Ambassador LARS VARGÖ.

Switzerland: 5-9-12, Minami-Azabu, Minato-ku, Tokyo 106-8589; tel. (3) 5449-8400; fax (3) 3473-6090; e-mail tok.vertretung@eda.admin.ch; internet www.eda.admin.ch/tokyo; Ambassador URS BUCHER.

Syria: Homat Jade, 6-19-45, Akasaka, Minato-ku, Tokyo 107-0052; tel. (3) 3586-8977; fax (3) 3586-8979; Chargé d'affaires a.i WARIF HALABI.

Tajikistan: 3-5-22, Hiroo, Shibuya-ku, Tokyo.150-0012; tel. (3) 6427-2625; fax (3) 6427-2623; e-mail tajembjapan@yahoo.com; internet www.tajikistan.jp; Ambassador BOBOZODA GULOMJON JURA.

Tanzania: 4-21-9, Kami Yoga, Setagaya-ku, Tokyo 158-0098; tel. (3) 3425-4531; fax (3) 3425-7844; e-mail tzrepjp@tanzaniaembassy.or.jp; internet www.tanzaniaembassy.or.jp; Ambassador SALOME T. SIJAONA.

Thailand: 3-14-6, Kami-Osaki, Shinagawa-ku, Tokyo.141-0021; tel. (3) 3712-0950; fax (3) 3719-7507; e-mail infosect@thaiembassy.jp; internet www.thaiembassy.jp; Ambassador THANATIP UPATISING.

Timor-Leste: Rokuban-cho House, 1/F, 3-4, Rokuban-cho, Chiyoda-ku, Tokyo 102-0085; tel. (3) 3238-0210; Ambassador ISILIO COELHO DA SILVA.

Tunisia: 3-6-6, Kudan-Minami, Chiyoda-ku, Tokyo 102-0074; tel. (3) 3511-6622; fax (3) 3511-6600; e-mail mailbox@tunisia.or.jp; internet www.tunisia.or.jp; Ambassador ILYES AL-KOSRI.

Turkey: 2-33-6, Jingumae, Shibuya-ku, Tokyo 150-0001; tel. (3) 6439-5700; fax (3) 3470-5136; e-mail embassy.tokyo@mfa.gov.tr; internet tokyo.be.mfa.gov.tr; Ambassador SERDAR KILIÇ.

Turkmenistan: 2-6-14, Higashi, Shibuya-ku, Tokyo 150-0011; tel. (3) 5766-1150; Ambassador GURBANMAMET ELIASOV.

Uganda: 9-23, Hachiyama-cho, Shibuya-ku, Tokyo 150-0035; tel. (3) 3462-7107; fax (3) 3462-7108; e-mail ugabassy@hpo.net; internet www.uganda-embassy.jp; Ambassador BETTY GRACE AKECH OKULLO.

Ukraine: 3-15-31, Nishi-Azabu, Minato-ku, Tokyo 106-0031; tel. (3) 5474-9770; fax (3) 5474-9772; e-mail ukrcn@rose.ocn.ne.jp; internet japan.mfa.gov.ua; Ambassador IHOR KHARCHENKO.

United Arab Emirates: 9-10, Nanpeidai-cho, Shibuya-ku, Tokyo 150-0036; tel. (3) 5489-0804; fax (3) 5489-0813; Ambassador SAEED ALI AL-NOWAIS.

United Kingdom: 1, Ichiban-cho, Chiyoda-ku, Tokyo 102-8381; tel. (3) 5211-1100; fax (3) 5275-3164; e-mail consular.tokyo@fco.gov.uk; internet ukinjapan.fco.gov.uk; Ambassador TIMOTHY HITCHENS.

USA: 1-10-5, Akasaka, Minato-ku, Tokyo 107-8420; tel. (3) 3224-5000; fax (3) 3505-1862; internet tokyo.usembassy.gov; Ambassador CAROLINE KENNEDY.

Uruguay: No. 38 Kowa Bldg, Rm 908, 4-12-24, Nishi-Azabu, Minato-ku, Tokyo 106-0031; tel. (3) 3486-1888; fax (3) 3486-9872; e-mail urujap@luck.ocn.ne.jp; Ambassador EDUARDO BOUZOUT VIGNOLI.

Uzbekistan: 2-1-52, Takanawa, Minato-ku, Tokyo 108-0074; tel. (3) 6277-5625; fax (3) 3760-5950; Ambassador FARRUKH ISLOMDJONOVICH TURSUNOV.

Venezuela: No. 38 Kowa Bldg, Rm 703, 4-12-24, Nishi-Azabu, Minato-ku, Tokyo 106-0031; tel. (3) 3409-1501; fax (3) 3409-1505; e-mail embavene@interlink.or.jp; Ambassador SEIKO LUIS ISHIKAWA KOBAYASHI.

Viet Nam: 50-11, Moto-Yoyogi-cho, Shibuya-ku, Tokyo 151-0062; tel. (3) 3466-3313; fax (3) 3466-3391; e-mail vnembasy@blue.ocn.ne.jp; internet www.vietnamembassy-japan.org; Ambassador DOAN XUAN HUNG.

Yemen: No. 38 Kowa Bldg, Rm 807, 4-12-24, Nishi-Azabu, Minato-ku, Tokyo 106-0031; tel. (3) 3499-7151; fax (3) 3499-4577; e-mail info@yemen.jp; internet www.yemen.jp; Chargé d'affaires a.i. HATEM MOHAMED HUSSEIN.

Zambia: 1-10-2, Ebara, Shinagawa-ku, Tokyo 142-0063; tel. (3) 3491-0121; fax (3) 3491-0123; e-mail infoemb@zambia.or.jp; internet www.zambia.or.jp; Ambassador NG'ONA MWELWA CHIBESAKUNDA.

Zimbabwe: 5-9-10, Shiroganedai, Minato-ku, Tokyo 108-0071; tel. (3) 3280-0331; fax (3) 3280-0466; e-mail zimtokyo@chive.ocn.ne.jp; Ambassador STUART H. COMBERBACH.

Judicial System

The basic principles of the legal system are set forth in the Constitution, which lays down that judicial power is vested in the Supreme Court and in such inferior courts as are established by law, and enunciates the principle that no organ or agency of the Executive shall be given final judicial power. Judges are to be independent in the exercise of their conscience, and may not be removed except by public impeachment, unless judicially declared mentally or physically incompetent to perform official duties. The justices of the Supreme Court are appointed by the Cabinet, the sole exception being the Chief Justice, who is appointed by the Emperor after designation by the Cabinet.

The Court Organization Law, which came into force on 3 May 1947, decreed the constitution of the Supreme Court and the establishment of four types of lower court—High, District, Family (established 1 January 1949) and Summary Courts. The system of trial by jury, suspended since 1943, was reinstated in 2009. Jurors are selected at random from the electoral register.

SUPREME COURT

This court is the highest legal authority in the land, and consists of a Chief Justice and 14 associate justices. It has jurisdiction over Jokoku (Jokoku appeals) and Kokoku (Kokoku appeals), prescribed in codes of procedure. It conducts its hearings and renders decisions through a Grand Bench or three Petty Benches. Both are collegiate bodies, the former consisting of all justices of the Court, and the latter of five justices. A Supreme Court Rule prescribes which cases are to be handled by the respective Benches. It is, however, laid down by law that the Petty Bench cannot make decisions as to the constitutionality of a statute, ordinance, regulation, or disposition, or as to cases in which an opinion concerning the interpretation and application of the Constitution, or of any laws or ordinances, is at variance with a previous decision of the Supreme Court.

Supreme Court: 4-2, Hayabusa-cho, Chiyoda-ku, Tokyo 102-8651; tel. (3) 3264-8111; fax (3) 3221-8975; internet www.courts.go.jp; Chief Justice HIRONOBU TAKESAKI.

LOWER COURTS

High Court

There are High Courts in Tokyo, Osaka, Nagoya, Hiroshima, Fukuoka, Sendai, Sapporo and Takamatsu, with six branch offices. A High Court conducts its hearings and renders decisions through a collegiate body, consisting of three judges, though for cases of insurrection the number of judges must be five. The Court has jurisdiction over: Koso appeals from judgments in the first instance rendered by District Courts, from judgments rendered by Family Courts, and from judgments concerning criminal cases rendered by Summary Courts; and Kokoku appeals against rulings and orders rendered by District Courts and Family Courts, and against rulings and orders concerning criminal cases rendered by Summary Courts, except those coming within the jurisdiction of the Supreme Court. It also deals with Jokoku appeals from judgments in the second instance rendered by District Courts and from judgments rendered by Summary Courts, except those concerning criminal cases, and actions in the first instance relating to cases of insurrection.

District Court

A District Court is generally the court of first instance, except for matters specifically coming under the exclusive original jurisdiction of other types of court. It also has appellate jurisdiction over appeals in civil cases lodged against judgments of summary courts. The Court conducts hearings and renders decisions through a single judge or, for certain types of cases, through a collegiate body of three judges. Japan has 50 district courts, with 203 branches.

Family Court

A Family Court handles cases through a single judge in case of rendering judgments or decisions. However, in accordance with the provisions of other statutes, it conducts its hearings and renders decisions through a collegiate body of three judges. A conciliation is effected through a collegiate body consisting of a judge and two or more members of the conciliation committee selected from among citizens. Japan has 50 family courts, with 203 branches and 77 local offices.

The Court adjudicates on cases relating to family, juvenile and adult criminal cases according to the Law for Adjudgment of Domestic Relations, Juvenile Law and Labour Standard Law, respectively, and in accordance with other laws especially enacted for the protection of juveniles.

Summary Court

A Summary Court handles cases through a single judge, and has jurisdiction in the first instance over the following matters: claims where the value of the subject matter does not exceed 1.4m. yen; criminal cases of offences liable to a fine or lesser penalty; offences liable to a fine as an optional penalty; and certain specified offences such as theft and embezzlement. There are 438 summary courts in Japan.

A Summary Court cannot impose imprisonment or a graver penalty. When it deems proper the imposition of a sentence of imprisonment or a graver penalty, it must transfer such cases to a District Court, but it can impose imprisonment with labour not exceeding three years for certain specified offences.

Religion

The traditional religions of Japan are Shintoism and Buddhism. Neither is exclusive, and many Japanese subscribe at least nominally to both.

SHINTOISM

Shintoism is an indigenous religious system embracing the worship of ancestors and of nature. It is divided into two cults: national Shintoism, which is represented by the shrines; and sectarian Shintoism, which developed during the second half of the 19th century. In 1868 Shinto was designated a national religion and all Shinto shrines acquired the privileged status of a national institution. Complete freedom of religion was introduced in 1947.

BUDDHISM

World Buddhist Fellowship: Hozenji Buddhist Temple, 3-24-2, Akabane-dai, Kita-ku, Tokyo; Head Rev. FUJI NAKAYAMA.

CHRISTIANITY

National Christian Council in Japan: Japan Christian Center, 2-3-18-24, Nishi-Waseda, Shinjuku-ku, Tokyo 169-0051; tel. (3) 3203-0372; fax (3) 3204-9495; e-mail general@ncc-j.org; internet ncc-j.org; f. 1923; 14 mems (churches and other bodies), 18 assoc. mems; Chair. KOUICHI KOBASHI; Gen. Sec. SHOUKO AMINAKA.

The Anglican Communion

Anglican Church in Japan (Nippon Sei Ko Kai): 65, Yarai-cho, Shinjuku-ku, Tokyo 162-0805; tel. (3) 5228-3171; fax (3) 5228-3175; e-mail general-sec.po@nskk.org; internet www.nskk.org; f. 1887; 11 dioceses; Primate of Japan Most Rev. NATHANIEL MAKOTO UEMATSU (Bishop of Hokkaido); Gen. Sec. JOHN MAKITO AIZAWA; 54,898 mems (2007).

The Orthodox Church

Japanese Orthodox Church (Nippon Haristosu Seikyoukai): Holy Resurrection Cathedral (Nicolai-Do), 4-1-3, Kanda Surugadai, Chiyoda-ku, Tokyo 101; tel. (3) 3291-1885; fax (3) 3291-1886; e-mail info@orthodoxjapan.jp; internet www.orthodoxjapan.jp; 3 dioceses; Archbishop of Tokyo, Primate and Metropolitan of All Japan Most Rev. DANIEL NUSHIRO; 24,821 mems.

Protestant Church

United Church of Christ in Japan (Nihon Kirisuto Kyodan): 2-3-18, Nishi-Shinjuku, Shinjuku-ku, Tokyo 169-0051; tel. (3) 3202-0541; fax (3) 3207-3918; e-mail ecumeni-c@uccj.org; internet www.uccj.or.jp; f. 1941; union of 34 Congregational, Methodist, Presbyterian, Reformed and other Protestant denominations; Moderator Rev. HIDEO ISHIBASHI; Gen. Sec. Rev. AOBORA TAEMAE; 196,044 mems (2007).

The Roman Catholic Church

Japan comprises three archdioceses and 13 dioceses. There were an estimated 554,447 adherents at 31 December 2007.

Catholic Bishops' Conference of Japan (Chuo Kyogikai): 2-10-10, Shiomi, Koto-ku, Tokyo 135-8585; tel. (3) 5632-4411; fax (3) 5632-4453; e-mail info@cbcj.catholic.jp; internet www.cbcj.catholic.jp; Pres. Most Rev. LEO JUN IKENAGA (Bishop of Osaka).

Archbishop of Nagasaki: Most Rev. JOSEPH MITSUAKI TAKAMI, Catholic Centre, 10-34, Uenomachi, Nagasaki-shi 852-8113; tel. (95) 846-4246; fax (95) 848-8310; internet www.nagasaki.catholic.jp.

Archbishop of Osaka: Most Rev. LEO JUN IKENAGA, Archbishop's House, 2-24-22, Tamatsukuri, Chuo-ku, Osaka 540-0004; tel. (6) 6941-9700; fax (6) 6946-1345; internet www.osaka.catholic.jp.

Archbishop of Tokyo: Most Rev. PETER TAKEO OKADA, Archbishop's House, 3-16-15, Sekiguchi, Bunkyo-ku, Tokyo 112-0014; tel. (3) 3943-2301; fax (3) 3944-8511; e-mail diocese@tokyo.catholic.jp; internet www.tokyo.catholic.jp.

Other Christian Churches

Japan Baptist Convention: 1-2-4, Minami-Urawa, Minami-ku, Saitama-shi, Saitama 336-0017; tel. (48) 883-1091; fax (48) 883-1092; internet www.bapren.jp; f. 1947; Gen. Sec. Rev. MAKOTO KATO; 33,734 mems (March 2003).

Japan Baptist Union: 2-3-18, Nishi-Waseda, Shinjuku-ku, Tokyo 169-0051; tel. (3) 3202-0053; fax (3) 3202-0054; e-mail gs@jbu.or.jp; internet www.jbu.or.jp; f. 1958; Moderator TOMIJI YAMAMOTO; Gen. Sec. KAZUO OHYA; 3,900 mems.

Japan Evangelical Lutheran Church: 1-1, Sadohara-cho, Ichigaya-shi, Shinjuku-ku, Tokyo 162-0842; tel. (3) 3260-8631; fax (3) 3260-8641; e-mail contact@jelc.or.jp; internet www.jelc.or.jp; f. 1893; Pres. Rev. SUMIYUKI WATANABE; Exec. Dir Rev. YASUHIRO TATENO; 21,990 mems (2010).

Korean Christian Church in Japan: Japan Christian Center, Rm 52, 2-3-18, Nishi-Waseda, Shinjuku-ku, Tokyo 169-0051; tel. (3) 3202-5398; fax (3) 3202-4977; e-mail info@kccj.jp; internet kccj.jp; f. 1908; Moderator KIM MUSA; Gen. Sec. HONG SONG-WAN; 6,219 mems (2011).

West Japan Evangelical Lutheran Church: 2-2-11 Nakajimadori, Chuo-Ku, Kobe 651-0052; tel. (78) 242-0887; fax (78) 242-4166; e-mail office@wjelc.or.jp; internet www.wjelc.or.jp; 3,887 mems (2010).

Among other denominations active in Japan are the Christian Catholic Church, the German Evangelical Church and the Tokyo Union Church.

OTHER COMMUNITIES

Bahá'í Faith

The National Spiritual Assembly of the Bahá'ís of Japan: 7-2-13, Shinjuku, Shinjuku-ku, Tokyo 160-0022; tel. (3) 3209-7521; fax (3) 3204-0773; e-mail info@bahaijp.org; internet www.bahaijp.org; f. 1955; Mem. DARYOUSH YAZDANI.

Judaism

Jewish Community of Japan: 3-8-8, Hiroo, Shibuya-ku, Tokyo 150-0012; tel. (3) 3400-2559; fax (3) 3400-1827; e-mail office@jccjapan.or.jp; internet www.jccjapan.or.jp; f. 1953; Pres. JEROME ROSENBERG; Leader Rabbi ANTONIO DI GESÙ.

Islam

Islam has been active in Japan since the late 19th century. There is a small Muslim community, maintaining several mosques, including those at Kobe, Nagoya, Chiba and Isesaki, the Arabic Islamic Institute and the Islamic Center in Tokyo. The construction of Tokyo Central Mosque was completed in 2000.

Islamic Center, Japan: 1-16-11, Ohara, Setagaya-ku, Tokyo 156-0041; tel. (3) 3460-6169; fax (3) 3460-6105; e-mail info@islamcenter.or.jp; internet www.islamcenter.or.jp; f. 1965; Chair. Dr SALIH AL-SAMARRAI.

The New Religions

Many new religions (Shinko Shukyo) emerged in Japan after 1945, based on a fusion of Shinto, Buddhist, Daoist, Confucian and Christian beliefs. Among the most important of these are Tenrikyo, Omotokyo, Soka Gakkai, Rissho Kosei-kai, Kofuku-no-Kagaku and Agonshu.

Kofuku-no-Kagaku (Institute for Research in Human Happiness): 1-6-7, Shinagawa-ku, Tokyo 142-0041; tel. (3) 6384-3777; fax (3) 6384-3778; e-mail info@irhpress.co.jp; internet www.irhpress.co.jp; f. 1986; believes its founder to be reincarnation of Buddha; 8.25m. mems; Leader RYUHO OKAWA.

Rissho Kosei-kai: 5/F, Fumon Hall, 2-6-1, Wada, Suginami-ku, Tokyo 166-8537; tel. and fax (3) 5341-1124; e-mail info@rk-world.org; internet www.rk-world.org; f. 1938; Buddhist lay org. based on the teaching of the Lotus Sutra, active inter-faith co-operation towards peace; Pres. Rev. Dr NICHIKO NIWANO; 2.05m. mem. households with 245 brs worldwide (2009).

Soka Gakkai: 32, Shinano-machi, Shinjuku-ku, Tokyo 160-8583; tel. (3) 5360-9830; fax (3) 5360-9885; e-mail contact@sgi.org; internet www.sgi.org; f. 1930; society of lay practitioners of the Buddhism of Nichiren; membership of 8.27m. households (2005); group promotes activities in education, international cultural exchange and consensus-building towards peace, based on the humanist world view of Buddhism; Hon. Pres. DAISAKU IKEDA; Pres. MINORU HARADA.

The Press

In 2013 there were 127 daily newspapers in Japan. Their average circulation was among the highest in the world. The large number of weekly news journals is a notable feature of the Japanese press.

NATIONAL DAILIES

Asahi Shimbun: 5-3-2, Tsukiji, Chuo-ku, Tokyo 104-8011; tel. (3) 3545-0131; fax (3) 3545-0358; internet www.asahi.com; f. 1879; also publ. by Osaka, Seibu and Nagoya head offices and Hokkaido branch office; Editor-in-Chief TOSHIAKI MIURA; circ. morning 8.1m., evening 3.7m.

Mainichi Shimbun: 1-1-1, Hitotsubashi, Chiyoda-ku, Tokyo 100-8051; tel. (3) 3212-0321; fax (3) 3211-3598; internet www.mainichi.co.jp; f. 1882; also publ. by Osaka, Seibu and Chubu head offices, and Hokkaido branch office; Pres. MASATO KITAMURA; Editor-in-Chief TOSHIFUMI KAWANO; circ. morning 3.4m., evening 1.3m.

Nihon Keizai Shimbun: 1-3-7, Otemachi, Chiyoda-ku, Tokyo 1008066; tel. (3) 3270-0251; fax (3) 5255-2661; e-mail ecntct@nikkei.co.jp; internet www.nikkei.co.jp; f. 1876; also publ. by Osaka head office and Sapporo, Nagoya and Seibu branch offices; Pres. KEN KOYANAGI; Editor-in-Chief YUICHI TAKAHASHI; circ. morning 3.3m., evening 1.6m.

Sankei Shimbun: 1-7-2, Otemachi, Chiyoda-ku, Tokyo 100-8077; tel. (3) 3231-7111; internet sankei.jp; f. 1933; also publ. by Osaka head office; Pres. and CEO NAGAYOSHI SUMIDA; Editor-in-Chief MASAFUMI KATAYAMA; circ. morning 2.0m., evening 636,649.

Yomiuri Shimbun: 1-7-1, Otemachi, Chiyoda-ku, Tokyo 100-8055; tel. (3) 3242-1111; e-mail webmaster@yomiuri.co.jp; internet www.yomiuri.co.jp; f. 1874; also publ. by Osaka, Seibu and Chubu head offices, and Hokkaido and Hokuriku branch offices; Chair. and Editor-in-Chief TSUNEO WATANABE; circ. morning 10.0m., evening 4.0m.

PRINCIPAL LOCAL DAILIES

Tokyo

Daily Sports: 1-5-7, Hyogo Higashikawasaki-cho, Chuo-ku, Tokyo 650-0044; tel. (3) 5434-1752; e-mail dsmaster@daily.co.jp; internet www.daily.co.jp; f. 1948; morning; Pres. NOBUHIKO NUMATA; circ. 400,254.

The Daily Yomiuri: 1-7-1, Otemachi, Chiyoda-ku, Tokyo 100-8055; tel. (3) 3242-1111; internet www.yomiuri.co.jp; f. 1955; morning; English; Man. Editor SHIGEYUKI OKADA; circ. 33,743.

Dempa Shimbun: 1-11-15, Higashi-Gotanda, Shinagawa-ku, Tokyo 141-8790; tel. (3) 3445-6111; fax (3) 3444-7515; e-mail multim@dempa.co.jp; internet www.dempa.co.jp; f. 1950; morning; Pres. TETSUO HIRAYAMA; circ. 300,000.

The Japan Times: 4-5-4, Shibaura, Minato-ku, Tokyo 108-8071; tel. (3) 3453-5312; internet www.japantimes.co.jp; f. 1897; morning; English; Chair. and Publr TOSHIAKI OGASAWARA; Dir and Pres. TAKEHARU TSUTSUMI; circ. 105,000.

The Mainichi Daily News: 1-1-1, Hitotsubashi, Chiyoda-ku, Tokyo 100-8051; tel. (3) 3212-0321; internet mdn.mainichi.jp; f. 1922; morning; English; also publ. from Osaka; Man. Editor YUTAKA ASAHINA; combined circ. 55,000.

Nihon Kaiji Shimbun (Japan Maritime Daily): Mori Bldg, 5-19-2, Shimbashi, Minato-ku, Tokyo 105-0004; tel. (3) 3436-3221; fax (3) 3436-3247; e-mail webmaster@jmd.co.jp; internet www.jmd.co.jp; f. 1942; morning; Man. Editor OSAMI ENDO; circ. 55,000.

Nihon Nogyo Shimbun (Agriculture): 2-3, Akihabara, Taito-ku, Tokyo 110-8722; tel. (3) 5295-7411; fax (3) 3253-0980; internet www.agrinews.co.jp; f. 1928; morning; Man. Editor YASUNORI INOUE; circ. 423,840.

Nihon Sen-i Shimbun (Textiles and Fashion): 1-6-5, Nihonbashi Kobuna-cho, Chuo-ku, Tokyo 103-0012; tel. (3) 5649-8711; fax (3) 5469-8717; internet www.nissenmedia.com; f. 1943; morning; Man. Editor KIYOSHIGE SEIRYU; circ. 116,000.

Nikkan Kogyo Shimbun (Industrial Daily News): 14-1, Nihonbashi Koami-cho, Chuo-ku, Tokyo 103-8548; tel. (3) 5644-7000; fax (3) 5644-7100; internet www.nikkan.co.jp; f. 1915; morning; Pres. HARUHIRO IMIZU; circ. 533,145.

Nikkan Sports News: 3-5-10, Tsukiji, Chuo-ku, Tokyo 104-8055; tel. (3) 5550-8888; fax (3) 5550-8901; e-mail webmast@nikkansports.co.jp; internet www.nikkansports.com; f. 1946; morning; Pres. YOSHITAKA SUZUKI; circ. 1,965,000.

Sankei Sports: 1-7-2, Otemachi, Chiyoda-ku, Tokyo 100-8077; tel. (3) 3231-7111; internet www.sanspo.com; f. 1963; morning; Man. Editor YUKIO INADA; circ. 809,245.

Shipping and Trade News: Tokyo News Service Ltd, 1-1-2, Uchisaiwai-cho, Chiyoda-ku, Tokyo 100-0011; tel. (3) 5510-8961; fax (3) 3504-6039; e-mail editorial.a@tokyonews.co.jp; internet www.tokyonews.co.jp/marine; f. 1949; English; Man. Editor TAKASHI TAKEDA; circ. 15,000.

Sports Hochi: 4-6-49, Kohnan, Minato-ku, Tokyo 108-8485; tel. (3) 5479-1111; e-mail webmaster@hochi.yomiuri.co.jp; internet hochi.yomiuri.co.jp; f. 1872; fmrly *Hochi Shimbun*; morning; Pres. TADASHI HAYAKAWA; circ. 755,670.

Sports Nippon: 2-1-30, Etchujima, Koto-ku, Tokyo 135-8735; tel. (3) 3820-0700; e-mail customer@sponichi.co.jp; internet www.sponichi.co.jp; f. 1949; morning; Pres. MORITO YUKIO; circ. 929,421.

Suisan Keizai Shimbun (Fisheries): 6-8-19, Roppongi, Minato-ku, Tokyo 106-0032; tel. (3) 3404-6531; fax (3) 3404-0863; internet www.suikei.co.jp; f. 1948; morning; Man. Editor NAGIKO YASUNARI; circ. 61,000.

Tokyo Chunichi Sports: 1-4, Uchisaiwai-cho, Chiyoda-ku, Tokyo 100-8505; tel. (3) 6910-2211; internet www.chunichi.co.jp/chuspo; f. 1956; evening; Pres. OOSHIMA TORAO; circ. 676,972.

Tokyo Shimbun: 1-4, Uchisaiwai-cho, Chiyoda-ku, Tokyo 100-8505; tel. (3) 6910-2211; internet www.chunichi.co.jp; f. 1942; Pres. OOSHIMA TORAO; circ. morning 605,096, evening 336,010.

Tokyo Sports: 2-1-30, Etchujima, Koto-ku, Tokyo 135-8721; tel. (3) 3820-0801; internet www.tokyo-sports.co.jp; f. 1959; evening; Pres. TSUNEO TACHIKAWA; circ. 1,560,000.

Yukan Fuji: 1-7-2, Otemachi, Chiyoda-ku, Tokyo 100-8077; tel. (3) 3231-7111; fax (3) 3246-0377; e-mail desk@zakzak.co.jp; internet www.zakzak.co.jp; f. 1969; evening; Man. Editor MASAMI KATO; circ. 268,984.

Osaka District

The Mainichi Daily News: 3-4-5, Umeda, Kita-ku, Osaka 530-8251; tel. (6) 6345-1551; internet www.mainichi.co.jp; f. 1922; morning; English; Pres. YUTAKA ASAHINA.

Nikkan Sports: 3-14-24, Hanshin, Fukushima Ward, Osaka; tel. (6) 6229-7005; internet www.nikkansports.com; f. 1950; morning; Man. Editor SUSUMU MATSUMOTO; circ. 513,498.

Sankei Kansai: 2-1-57, Minato-cho, Naniwa-ku, Osaka 556-8660; tel. (6) 6633-1221; fax (6) 6633-9738; e-mail osaka-soukyoku@sankei.co.jp; internet www.sankei-kansai.com; f. 1922; evening; fmrly *Osaka Shimbun*, name changed as above 2004; Pres. SUMIDA NAGAYOSHI; circ. 88,887.

Sankei Sports: 2-1-57, Minato-cho, Naniwa-ku, Osaka 556-8660; tel. (3) 3231-7111; fax (3) 3275-8994; f. 1955; morning; Pres. SUMIDA NAGAYOSHI; circ. 552,519.

Sports Nippon: 3-4-5, Umeda, Kita-ku, Osaka 530-8278; tel. (6) 6346-8500; f. 1949; morning; Man. Editor HIDETOSHI ISHIHARA; circ. 477,300.

Kanto District

Chiba Nippo (Chiba Daily News): 4-14-10, Chuo, Chuo-ku, Chiba 260-0013; tel. (43) 222-9211; internet www.chibanippo.co.jp; f. 1957; morning; Man. Editor YASUHIDE AKADA; circ. 200,000.

Ibaraki Shimbun: 2-15, Kitami-cho, Mito 310-8686; tel. (29) 248-5500; fax (29) 248-7745; e-mail i-net@ibaraki-np.co.jp; internet www.ibaraki-np.co.jp; f. 1891; morning; Pres. TAKASHI KOTABE; circ. 117,240.

Jomo Shimbun: 1-50-21, Furuichi-machi, Maebashi 371-8666; tel. (27) 254-9911; internet www.raijin.com; f. 1887; morning; Man. Dir WATANABE SACHIO; circ. 311,534.

Joyo Shimbun: 2-7-6, Manabe, Tsuchiura 300-0051; tel. (298) 21-1780; e-mail info-02@joyo-net.com; internet www.joyo-net.com; f. 1948; morning; Pres. MINEO IWANAMI; Man. Editor AKIRA SAITO; circ. 88,700.

Kanagawa Shimbun: 2-23, Ota-cho, Kanagawa, Naka-ku, Yokohama 231-8445; tel. (45) 227-1111; e-mail soumu@kanagawa-np.co.jp; internet www.kanagawa-shimbun.jp; f. 1890; morning; Pres. JUNICHI SAITO; Man. Dir REN KATO; circ. 210,000.

Saitama Shimbun: 2-282-3, Yoshino, Kita-ku, Saitama; tel. (48) 795-9930; fax (48) 653-9020; e-mail desk@saitama-np.co.jp; internet www.saitama-np.co.jp; f. 1944; morning; Pres. HIDEKI OGAWA; circ. 162,071.

Shimotsuke Shimbun: 1-8-11, Showa, Utsunomiya 320-8686; tel. (286) 25-1111; internet www.shimotsuke.co.jp; f. 1884; morning; Pres. YOSHINORI KANDO; circ. 316,847.

Tohoku District
(North-east Honshu)

Akita Sakigake Shimpo: 1-1, San-no-rinkai-machi, Akita 010-8601; tel. (18) 888-1800; fax (18) 866-9285; internet www.sakigake.co.jp; f. 1874; Man. Editor NAOKI OGASAWARA; circ. 230,000.

Daily Tohoku: 1-3-12, Shiroshita, Hachinohe 031-8601; tel. (178) 44-5111; internet www.daily-tohoku.co.jp; f. 1945; morning; Pres. KIYOSHI ARASE; circ. 106,410.

Fukushima Minyu: 4-29, Yanagi-machi, Fukushima 960-8648; tel. (24) 523-1191; fax (24) 523-2605; internet www.minyu-net.com; f. 1895; Man. Editor SHUNSUKE KANDA; circ. morning 250,000, evening 7,000.

Hokuu Shimpo: 3-2, Nishi-Dori-machi, Noshiro 016-0891; tel. (185) 54-3150; internet www.hokuu.co.jp; f. 1895; morning; Chair. KOICHI YAMAKI; circ. 31,490.

Iwate Nichi-nichi Shimbun: 60, Minami-Shinmachi, Ichinoseki 021-8686; tel. (191) 26-5114; e-mail iwanichi@iwanichi.co.jp; internet www.iwanichi.co.jp; f. 1923; morning; Pres. MANABU YAMAGISHI; circ. 59,850.

Iwate Nippo: 3-7, Uchimaru, Morioka 020-8622; tel. (19) 653-4111; fax (19) 626-1882; e-mail center@iwate-np.co.jp; internet www.iwate-np.co.jp; f. 1876; Pres. MIURA HIROSHI; circ. morning 267,890, evening 225,678.

Kahoku Shimpo: 1-2-28, Itsutsubashi, Aoba-ku, Sendai 980-8660; tel. (22) 211-1127; fax (22) 211-1448; e-mail houdou@po.kahoku.co.jp; internet www.kahoku.co.jp; f. 1897; Exec. Dir and Man. Editor MASAHIKO ICHIRIKI; circ. morning 503,318, evening 133,855.

Mutsu Shimpo: 2-1, Shimo-shirogane-cho, Hirosaki 036-8356; tel. (172) 34-3111; fax (172) 32-3138; e-mail box@mutusinpou.co.jp; internet www.mutusinpou.co.jp; f. 1946; morning; Man. Editor YUJI SATO; circ. 53,500.

Shonai Nippo: 8-29, Baba-cho, Tsuruoka 997-8691; tel. (235) 22-1480; fax (235) 22-1427; internet www.shonai-nippo.co.jp; f. 1946; morning; Pres. and CEO MASAYUKI HASHIMOTO; circ. 20,000.

To-o Nippo: 3-1-89, Dainitonya-machi, Aomori 030-0180; tel. (17) 739-1111; fax (17) 739-1141; internet www.toonippo.co.jp; f. 1888; Exec. Dir YOSHIO WAJIMA; Man. Editor TAKAO SHIOKOSHI; circ. morning 262,532, evening 258,590.

Yamagata Shimbun: 2-5-12, Hatagomachi, Yamagata 990-8550; tel. (23) 622-5271; e-mail info@yamagata-np.jp; internet yamagata-np.jp; f. 1876; Exec. Chair. YOSUKE KUROSAWA; Pres. and CEO SAGAE KOJI; circ. morning 213,057, evening 213,008.

Yonezawa Shimbun: 3-3-7, Monto-cho, Yonezawa 992-0039; tel. (238) 22-4411; fax (238) 24-5554; e-mail info@www.yoneshin.com; internet www.yoneshin.com; f. 1879; morning; Man. Dir and Editor-in-Chief MASAO HOKARI; circ. 13,750.

Chubu District
(Central Honshu)

Chubu Keizai Shimbun: 4-4-38, Meieki, Nakamura-ku, Nagoya 450-8561; tel. (52) 561-5215; fax (52) 561-5229; internet www.chukei-news.co.jp; f. 1946; morning; Pres. and CEO NAGAI SEITAIRA; circ. 87,000.

Chunichi Shimbun: 1-6-1, San-no-maru, Naka-ku, Nagoya 460-8511; tel. (52) 201-8811; internet www.chunichi.co.jp; f. 1942; Chair. BUNGO SHIRAI; Pres. KOIDE NORIAKI; circ. 4.2m.

Chunichi Sports: 1-6-1, San-no-maru, Naka-ku, Nagoya 460-8511; tel. (52) 201-8811; internet www.chunichi.co.jp/chuspo; f. 1954; evening; Pres. OOSHIMA TARAO; circ. 4.2m.

Gifu Shimbun: 10, Imako-machi, Gifu 500-8577; tel. (58) 264-1151; internet www.gifu-np.co.jp; f. 1881; Exec. Dir and Man. Editor TADASHI TANAKA; circ. morning 170,176, evening 31,775.

Higashi-Aichi Shimbun: 62, Torinawate, Shinsakae-machi, Toyohashi 441-8666; tel. (532) 32-3111; fax (532) 32-3737; e-mail hensyu@higashiaichi.co.jp; internet www.higashiaichi.co.jp; f. 1957; morning; Pres. MASATO FUJIMURA; circ. 55,000.

Nagano Nippo: 3-1323-1, Takashima, Suwa 392-8611; tel. (266) 52-2000; fax (266) 58-8895; e-mail info@nagano-np.co.jp; internet www.nagano-np.co.jp; f. 1901; morning; Man. Editor HIDDYUKI SAKYIU; circ. 73,000.

Shinano Mainichi Shimbun: 657, Minami-Agatamachi, Nagano 380-8546; tel. (26) 236-3000; fax (26) 236-3098; internet www.shinmai.co.jp; f. 1873; Man. Editor SOTARO KOSAKA; circ. morning 500,000, evening 50,876.

Shizuoka Shimbun: 3-1-1, Toro, Suruga-ku, Shizuoka 422-8670; tel. (54) 284-8900; fax (54) 284-8994; e-mail webmaster@shizuokaonline.com; internet www.shizuokaonline.com; f. 1941; Man. Editor JUN MATSUI; circ. morning 730,746, evening 730,782.

Yamanashi Nichi-Nichi Shimbun: 2-6-10, Kita-Guchi, Kofu 400-8515; tel. (552) 31-3199; fax (552) 31-3161; e-mail info@sannichi.co.jp; internet www.sannichi.co.jp; f. 1872; morning; Man. Editor NOGUCHI EIICHI; circ. 200,000.

Hokuriku District
(North Coastal Honshu)

Fukui Shimbun: 56, Owada-cho, Fukui 910-8552; tel. (776) 57-5111; internet www.fukuishimbun.co.jp; f. 1899; morning; Man. Editor YOSHIDA MASATO; circ. 207,000.

Hokkoku Shimbun: 2-5-1, Korinbo, Kanazawa 920-8588; tel. (762) 60-3402; fax (762) 60-3403; e-mail admin@hokkoku.co.jp; internet www.hokkoku.co.jp; f. 1893; Pres. and Man. Editor HIDEKAZU TOBITA; circ. morning 335,826, evening 93,021.

Hokuriku Chunichi Shimbun: 2-12-30, Korinbo, Kanazawa 920-8573; tel. (76) 261-3111; internet www.chunichi.co.jp/hokuriku; f. 1960; Pres. OOSHIMA TORAO; circ. 4.2m.

Kita-Nippon Shimbun: 2-14, Azumi-cho, Toyama 930-8680; tel. (764) 45-3300; internet www.kitanippon.co.jp; f. 1884; Dir and Man. Editor HITOSHI ITAKURA; circ. morning 240,000.

Niigata Nippo: 772-2, Nishi-ku, Niigata 950-1189; tel. (25) 378-9111; internet www.niigata-nippo.co.jp; f. 1942; Dir and Man. Editor MICHIEI TAKAHASHI; circ. morning 499,545, evening 63,790.

Kinki District
(West Central Honshu)

Daily Sports: 1-5-7, Higashi-Kawasaki-cho, Chuo-ku, Kobe 650-0044; tel. (78) 362-7100; e-mail dsmaster@daily.co.jp; internet www.daily.co.jp; morning; Man. Editor TAKASHI HIRAI; circ. 584,448.

Ise Shimbun: 34-6, Honmachi, Tsu 514-0831; tel. (59) 224-0003; fax (59) 226-3554; internet www.isenp.co.jp; f. 1878; morning; Man. Editor SENZO KOBAYASHI; circ. 108,630.

Kii Minpo: 100, Akizu-cho, Tanabe 646-8660; tel. (739) 22-7171; fax (739) 26-0077; internet www.agara.co.jp; f. 1911; evening; Man. Editor YOHACHIRO KOYAMA; circ. 45,342.

Kobe Shimbun: 1-5-7, Higashi-Kawasaki-cho, Chuo-ku, Kobe 650-8571; tel. (78) 362-7100; fax (78) 360-5501; internet www.kobe-np.co.jp; f. 1898; Pres. MIZUO HASHIDA; circ. morning 563,717, evening 239,604.

Kyoto Shimbun: 239, Shoshoi-machi, Ebisugawa-agaru, Karasuma-dori, Nakagyo-ku, Kyoto 604-8577; tel. (75) 241-5430; fax (75) 252-5454; e-mail kpdesk@mb.kyoto-np.jp; internet www.kyoto-np.co.jp; f. 1879; Man. Editor SYOZO MASUDA; circ. morning 504,304, evening 319,015.

Nara Shimbun: 2-4, Sanjo-machi, Nara 630-8686; tel. (742) 32-1000; fax (742) 32-2770; e-mail info@nara-np.co.jp; internet www.nara-np.co.jp; f. 1946; morning; Dir and Man. Editor HARUO AMARI; circ. 120,000.

Chugoku District
(Western Honshu)

Chugoku Shimbun: 7-1, Dobashi-cho, Naka-ku, Hiroshima 730-8677; tel. (82) 236-2111; fax (82) 236-2456; e-mail denshi@hiroshima-cdas.or.jp; internet www.chugoku-np.co.jp; f. 1892; Pres. KAZUYUKI KAWAMOTO; circ. morning 723,981, evening 75,248.

Nihonkai Shimbun: 2-137, Tomiyasu, Tottori 680-8688; tel. (857) 21-2888; fax (857) 21-2891; e-mail info@nnn.co.jp; internet www.nnn.co.jp; f. 1976; morning; Pres. YOSHIOKA RIKATA; circ. 171,120.

San-In Chuo Shimpo: 383, Tono-machi, Matsue 690-8668; tel. (852) 32-3440; e-mail sanin@sanin-chuo.co.jp; internet www.sanin-chuo.co.jp; f. 1882; morning; Pres. TETSUO MORIWAKI; circ. 181,000.

Sanyo Shimbun: 2-1-1, Yanagi-machi, Okayama 700-8634; tel. (86) 803-8008; internet www.sanyo.oni.co.jp; f. 1879; Man. Dir and Man. Editor KOSHIMUNE TAKAMASA; circ. morning 500,000, evening 58,097.

Ube Jiho: 3-6-1, Kotobuki-cho, Ube 755-8557; tel. (836) 31-1511; internet www.ubenippo.co.jp; f. 1912; evening; Exec. Dir and Man. Editor KAZUYA WAKI; circ. 52,300.

Shikoku Island

Ehime Shimbun: 1-12-1, Otemachi, Matsuyama 790-8511; tel. (89) 935-2111; fax (89) 941-8108; e-mail webmaster@ehime-np.co.jp; internet www.ehime-np.co.jp; f. 1876; morning; Man. Editor HIDEO DOI; circ. 49,810,029.

Kochi Shimbun: 3-2-15, Honmachi, Kochi 780-8572; tel. (88) 822-2111; e-mail master@kochinews.co.jp; internet www.kochinews.co.jp; f. 1904; Pres. HAYAO MIYATA; circ. 230,000.

Tokushima Shimbun: 2-5-2, Naka-Tokushima-cho, Tokushima 770-8572; tel. (88) 655-7373; fax (86) 654-0165; e-mail jouhou@topics.or.jp; internet www.topics.or.jp; f. 1944; Dir and Man. Editor HIROSHI MATSUMURA; circ. 250,000.

Hokkaido Island

Doshin Sports: 3-6, Nishi-Odori, Chuo-ku, Sapporo 060-8711; tel. (11) 210-5573; fax (11) 210-5575; e-mail koe@hokkaido-np.co.jp; internet www.hokkaido-np.co.jp; f. 1982; morning; Pres. TOSHIKAZU MASTUDA; circ. 146,390.

Hokkaido Shimbun: 3-6, Nishi-Odori, Chuo-ku, Sapporo 060-8711; tel. (11) 210-5573; fax (11) 210-5575; internet www.hokkaido-np.co.jp; f. 1942; Man. Editor MASATOSHI MURATA; circ. morning 1.2m., evening 701,934.

Kushiro Shimbun: 7-3, Kurogane-cho, Kushiro 085-8650; tel. (154) 22-1111; fax (154) 22-0050; internet www.news-kushiro.jp; f. 1946; morning; Pres. and CEO KASUGAI SHIGERU; circ. 80,000.

Muroran Mimpo: 1-3-16, Hon-cho, Muroran 051-8550; tel. (143) 22-5121; fax (143) 24-1337; e-mail honsya@muromin.mnw.jp; internet www.muromin.mnw.jp; f. 1945; Man. Editor TSUTOMO KUDO; circ. morning 63,300, evening 52,630.

Nikkan Sports: 3-1-30, Higashi, Kita-3 jo, Chuo-ku, Sapporo 060-8521; tel. (11) 242-3900; fax (11) 272-1754; internet www.nikkansports.com; f. 1962; morning; Pres. YOSHITAKA SUZUKI; circ. 142,330.

Tokachi Mainichi Shimbun: 8-2, Minami, Higashi-Ichijo, Obihiro 080-8688; tel. (155) 22-2121; fax (155) 25-2700; e-mail info@kachimai.co.jp; internet www.tokachi.co.jp; f. 1919; evening; Editor-in-Chief MITSUSHIGE HAYASHI; circ. 85,160.

Tomakomai Mimpo: 3-1-8, Wakakusa-cho, Tomakomai 053-8611; tel. (144) 32-5311; fax (144) 32-6386; e-mail henshu@tomamin.co.jp; internet www.tomamin.co.jp; f. 1950; evening; Dir and Man. Editor RYUICHI KUDO; circ. 60,676.

Yomiuri Shimbun: 4-1, Nishi, Kita-4 jo, Chuo-ku, Sapporo 060-8656; tel. (11) 242-3111; internet www.yomiuri.co.jp; f. 1959; Chair. and Editor-in–Chief WATANABE TSUNEO; circ. morning 261,747, evening 81,283.

Kyushu Island

Kumamoto Nichi-Nichi Shimbun: 172, Yoyasu-machi, Kumamoto 860-8506; tel. (96) 361-3082; internet www.kumanichi.com; f. 1942; Man. Editor EIICHI IZU; circ. morning 385,784, evening 99,049.

Kyushu Sports: Fukuoka Tenjin Center Bldg, 2-14-8, Tenjin-cho, Chuo-ku, Fukuoka 810-0001; tel. (92) 781-7401; f. 1966; morning; Head Officer HIROSHI MITOMI; circ. 449,850.

Minami-Nippon Shimbun: 1-9-33, Yojirou, Kagoshima 890-8603; tel. (99) 813-5001; fax (99) 813-5016; e-mail webmaster@373news.com; internet www.373news.com; f. 1881; Man. Editor NAOSUMI SAKASEGAWA; circ. morning 405,795.

Miyazaki Nichi-Nichi Shimbun: 1-1-33, Takachihodori, Miyazaki 880-8570; tel. (985) 26-9315; fax (985) 20-7254; e-mail info@the-miyanichi.co.jp; internet www.the-miyanichi.co.jp; f. 1940; morning; Pres. YASUHISA MACHIKAWA; circ. 235,759.

Nagasaki Shimbun: 3-1, Mori-machi, Nagasaki 852-8601; tel. (95) 844-2111; e-mail houdou@nagasaki-np.co.jp; internet www.nagasaki-np.co.jp; f. 1889; Dir and Man. Editor TAKAHIRO MOTOMURA; circ. morning 200,000.

Nankai Nichi-Nichi Shimbun: 10-3, Nagahama-cho, Naze 894-8601; tel. (997) 53-2121; fax (997) 52-2354; e-mail nankainn@po.synapse.ne.jp; internet www.nankainn.com; f. 1946; morning; Man. Editor MICHIO MURAYAMA; circ. 20,345.

Nishi-Nippon Shimbun: 1-4-1, Tenjin, Chuo-ku, Fukuoka 810-8721; tel. (92) 711-5555; internet www.nishinippon.co.jp; f. 1877; Pres. TAKAO KAWASAKI; Man. Dir KOGA YASUSHI; circ. morning 850,779, evening 148,750.

Oita Godo Shimbun: 3-9-15, Funai-machi, Oita 870-8605; tel. (975) 36-2121; internet www.oita-press.co.jp; f. 1886; Dir and Man. Editor KEN NAGANO; circ. morning 250,300, evening 250,264.

Okinawa Times: 1-3-31, Omoro-machi, Naha 900-8678; tel. (98) 860-3000; fax (98) 860-3664; internet www.okinawatimes.co.jp; f. 1948; Pres. TOYOHIRA YOSHITAKA; circ. morning 205,624.

Ryukyu Shimpo: 905, Naha 900-8525; tel. (98) 865-5111; fax (98) 861-6444; internet www.ryukyushimpo.co.jp; f. 1893; Man. Editor TATSUHIRO HIGA; circ. 203,470.

Saga Shimbun: 3-2-23, Tenjin, Saga 840-8585; tel. (952) 28-2121; fax (952) 29-5760; internet www.saga-s.co.jp; f. 1884; morning; Man. Editor SEIICHIRO NAKAO; circ. 150,768.

Yaeyama Mainichi Shimbun: 614, Tonoshiro, Ishigaki 907-0004; tel. (9808) 2-2121; internet www.y-mainichi.co.jp; f. 1950; morning; Exec. Dir and Man. Editor KIYOTAKA NAKAMA; circ. 18,000.

WEEKLIES

An-An: Magazine House, 3-13-10, Ginza, Chuo-ku, Tokyo 104-8003; tel. (3) 3545-7050; fax (3) 3546-0034; internet magazineworld.jp/anan; f. 1970; fashion; Editor ISHI YAMAZAKI MENG; circ. 650,000.

Diamond Weekly: Diamond Bldg, 6-12-17, Jingumae, Shibuya-ku, Tokyo 150-8409; tel. (3) 5778-7200; e-mail info@diamond.co.jp; internet www.diamond.co.jp; f. 1913; economics; Editor LUGU FUMIAKI; Man. Dir KUME ISAO; circ. 81,000.

Hanako: Magazine House, 3-13-10, Ginza, Chuo-ku, Tokyo 104-8003; tel. (3) 3545-7070; fax (3) 3545-7281; internet magazineworld.jp/hanako; f. 1988; consumer guide; Editor ISHI YAMAZAKI MENG; circ. 350,000.

Nikkei Business: Nikkei Business Publications Inc, 1-17-3, Shirokane, Minato-ku, Tokyo 108-8646; tel. (3) 6811-8101; fax (3) 5421-9117; internet www.nikkeibp.co.jp; f. 1969; Pres. TAIRA HIROSHI NAGATA; circ. 330,000.

Shukan Bunshun: Bungei-Shunju Ltd, 3-23, Kioi-cho, Chiyoda-ku, Tokyo 102-8008; tel. (3) 3288-6123; fax (3) 3234-3964; e-mail kawabe@bunshun.co.jp; internet www.bunshun.co.jp; f. 1959; general interest; Editor MANABU SHINTANI; circ. 800,000.

Shukan Gendai: Kodan-Sha Co Ltd, 2-12-21, Otowa, Bunkyo-ku, Tokyo 112; tel. (3) 5395-3438; fax (3) 3943-7815; f. 1959; general; Editor-in-Chief TETSU SUZUKI; circ. 500,000.

Shukan Josei: Shufu-To-Seikatsu Sha Ltd, 3-5-7, Kyobashi, Chuo-ku, Tokyo 104; tel. (3) 3563-5130; fax (3) 3563-2073; f. 1957; women's interest; Editor HIDEO KIKUCHI; circ. 638,000.

Shukan Post: Shogakukan Publishing Co Ltd, 2-3-1, Hitotsubashi, Chiyoda-ku, Tokyo 101-01; tel. (3) 3230-5951; internet www.weeklypost.com; f. 1969; general; Editor NORIMICHI OKANARI; circ. 696,000.

Shukan SPA: Fuso-Sha Co, 1-15-1, Kaigan, Minato-ku, Tokyo 105; tel. (3) 5403-8875; f. 1952; general interest; Editor-in-Chief TOSHIHIKO SATO; circ. 400,000.

Shukan ST: Japan Times Ltd, 4-5-4, Shibaura, Minato-ku, Tokyo 108-8071; tel. (3) 3452-4077; fax (3) 3452-3303; e-mail shukanst@japantimes.co.jp; internet www.japantimes.co.jp/shukan-st; f. 1951; English and Japanese; Editor MITSURU TANAKA; circ. 150,000.

Sunday Mainichi: Mainichi Newspapers Publishing Dept, 1-1-1, Hitotsubashi, Chiyoda-ku, Tokyo 100-51; tel. (3) 3212-0321; fax (3) 3212-7580; f. 1922; general interest; Editor HIDEHIRO SATO; circ. 237,000.

Tenji Mainichi: Mainichi Newspapers Publishing Dept, 3-4-5, Umeda, Osaka; tel. (6) 6346-8386; fax (6) 6346-8385; f. 1922; in Japanese braille; Editor YUTAKA ASAHINA; circ. 14,000.

Weekly Economist: Mainichi Newspapers Publishing Dept, 1-1-1, Hitotsubashi, Chiyoda-ku, Tokyo 100-51; tel. (3) 3212-0321; f. 1923; Editorial Chief NOBUHIRO SHUDO; circ. 120,000.

Weekly Toyo Keizai: Toyo Keizai Inc, 1-2-1, Hongoku-cho, Nihonbashi, Chuo-ku, Tokyo 103-8345; tel. (3) 3246-5551; fax (3) 3270-0332; e-mail sub@toyokeizai.co.jp; internet www.toyokeizai.net; f. 1895; business, economics, finance, and corporate information; Editor TAKAHASHI HIROSHI; circ. 80,000.

PERIODICALS

Brutus: Magazine House, 3-13-10, Ginza, Chuo-ku, Tokyo 104-8003; tel. (3) 3545-7000; fax (3) 3546-0034; internet magazineworld.jp/

brutus; f. 1980; every 2 weeks; men's interest; Pres. ISHIZAKI TAKESHI; circ. 250,000.

Bungei-Shunju: Bungei-Shunju Ltd, 3-23, Kioi-cho, Chiyoda-ku, Tokyo 102-8008; tel. (3) 3265-1211; fax (3) 3221-6623; internet www.bunshun.co.jp; f. 1923; monthly; general; Pres. HIRAO TAKAHIRO; circ. 647,000.

Business Tokyo: Keizaikai Bldg, 2-13-18, Minami-Aoyama, Minato-ku, Tokyo 105; tel. (3) 3423-8500; fax (3) 3423-8505; f. 1987; Dir TAKUO IDA; Editor ANTHONY PAUL; circ. 125,000.

Chuokoron: Chuokoron-Shinsha Inc, 2-8-7, Kyobashi, Chuo-ku, Tokyo 104-8320; tel. (3) 3563-1866; fax (3) 3561-5929; e-mail hanbai@chuko.co.jp; internet www.chuko.co.jp; f. 1887; monthly; general interest; Chief Editor HIROSHI KOIZUMI; circ. 90,000.

Croissant: Magazine House, 3-13-10, Ginza, Chuo-ku, Tokyo 104-03; tel. (3) 3545-7111; fax (3) 3546-0034; f. 1977; every 2 weeks; home; Editor MASAAKI TAKEUCHI; circ. 600,000.

Fujinkoron: Chuokoron-Sha Inc, 2-8-7, Kyobashi, Chuo-ku, Tokyo 104; tel. (3) 3563-1866; fax (3) 3561-5920; internet www.fujinkoron.jp; f. 1916; monthly; women's literature; Editor YUKIKO YUKAWA; circ. 185,341.

Geijutsu Shincho: Shincho-Sha, 71, Yarai-cho, Shinjuku-ku, Tokyo 162-8711; tel. (3) 3266-5211; fax (3) 3266-5235; e-mail geishin@shinchosha.co.jp; f. 1950; monthly; fine arts, music, architecture, films, drama and design; Editor ICHIRO MOTOHASHI; circ. 50,000.

Ginza: Magazine House, 3-13-10, Ginza, Chuo-ku, Tokyo 104-8003; tel. (3) 3545-7040; fax (3) 3545-2133; internet magazineworld.jp/ginza; f. 1997; monthly; women's interest; Pres. ISHI YAMAZAKI MENG; circ. 250,000.

Ie-no-Hikari (Light of Home): Ie-no-Hikari Asscn, 11, Ichigaya Funagawaramachi, Shinjuku-ku, Tokyo 162-8448; tel. (3) 3266-9038; fax (3) 3266-9337; e-mail zugakon@ienohikari.or.jp; internet www.ienohikari.net; f. 1925; monthly; rural and general interest; Pres. SHUZO SUZUKI; circ. 928,000.

Japan Company Handbook: Toyo Keizai Inc, 1-2-1, Nihonbashi Hongoku-cho, Chuo-ku, Tokyo 103-8345; tel. (3) 3246-5551; fax (3) 3279-0332; e-mail info@toyokeizai.co.jp; internet www.toyokeizai.co.jp; f. 1974; quarterly; English; Editor EIICH FURUSHO; total circ. 16,000.

Junon: Shufu-To-Seikatsu Sha Ltd, 3-5-7, Kyobashi, Chuo-ku, Tokyo 104-8357; tel. (3) 3563-5120; fax (3) 5250-7081; e-mail webmaster@mb.shufu.co.jp; internet www.shufu.co.jp/junon; f. 1973; monthly; television and entertainment; circ. 560,000; Pres. KATSUTOSHI.

Keizaijin: Kansai Economic Federation, Nakanoshima Center Bldg, 6-2-27, Nakanoshima, Kita-ku, Osaka 530-6691; tel. (6) 6441-0104; fax (6) 6443-0443; e-mail kef_60_eng@kankeiren.or.jp; internet www.kankeiren.or.jp; f. 1947; monthly; economics; Editor M. YASUTAKE; circ. 2,600.

Lettuce Club: Toranomon Corpn, 2-2-5, Minatu-ku, Tokyo 105-8455; tel. (3) 5860-9820; fax (3) 5860-9829; e-mail info@sscom.co.jp; internet www.lettuceclub.net; f. 1987; every 2 weeks; cookery; Man. HIDEKI TAKAGAWA; circ. 800,000.

Money Japan: Toranomon Corpn, 2-2-5, Minato-ku, Tokyo 105-8455; tel. (3) 3560-8700; e-mail info@sscom.co.jp; internet www.moneyjapan-web.com; f. 1985; monthly; finance; Editor TOSHIO KOBAYASHI; circ. 500,000.

Popeye: Magazine House, 3-13-10, Ginza, Chuo-ku, Tokyo 104-8003; tel. (3) 3545-7160; fax (3) 3545-9026; internet magazineworld.jp/popeye; f. 1976; every 2 weeks; fashion, youth interest; Editor-in-Chief TAKAHIRO KINOSHITA; circ. 320,000.

President: President Inc, Hirakawacho Mori Tower, 13/F, 2-16-1, Hirakawa-cho, Chiyoda-ku, Tokyo 102-8641; tel. (3) 3237-3711; fax (3) 3237-3748; internet www.president.co.jp; f. 1963; monthly; business; Pres. YOSHIAKI NAGASAKA; circ. 263,308.

Ray: Shufunotomo Co Ltd, 2-9, Kanda Surugadai, Chiyoda-ku, Tokyo 101; tel. (3) 3294-1163; fax (3) 3291-5093; f. 1988; monthly; women's interest; Editor TATSURO NAKANISHI; circ. 244,000.

Ryoko Yomiuri: Yomiuri Travel Publishing Co Inc, 18-3, Nihonbashi, Chuo-ku, Tokyo 103-8545; tel. (3) 5847-8271; fax (3) 5847-8270; e-mail ad@ryokoyomiuri.co.jp; internet www.ryokoyomiuri.co.jp; f. 1966; monthly; travel; Pres. OGASAWARA SHINOBU; circ. 470,000.

Sekai: Iwanami Shoten Publishers, 2-5-5, Hitotsubashi, Chiyoda-ku, Tokyo 101-8002; tel. (3) 5210-4141; fax (3) 5210-4144; e-mail sekai@iwanami.co.jp; internet www.iwanami.co.jp/sekai; f. 1946; monthly; review of world and domestic affairs; Editor ATSUSHI OKAMOTO; circ. 120,000.

Shinkenchiku: Shinkenchiku-Sha Co Ltd, Kasumigaseki Bldg, 17/F, 3-2-5, Kasumigaseki, Chiyoda-ku, Tokyo 100-6017; tel. (3) 6205-4380; fax (3) 6205-4386; e-mail ja-business@japan-architect.co.jp; internet www.japlusu.com; f. 1925; monthly; architecture; Editor NOBUYUKI YOSHIDA; circ. 87,000.

Shiso (Thought): Iwanami Shoten Publishers, 2-5-5, Hitotsubashi, Chiyoda-ku, Tokyo 101-8002; tel. (3) 5210-4055; fax (3) 5210-4037; e-mail shiso@iwanami.co.jp; internet www.iwanami.co.jp/shiso; f. 1921; monthly; philosophy, social sciences and humanities; Editor TATSUO HAYASHI; circ. 20,000.

Shosetsu Shincho: Shincho-Sha, 71, Yarai-cho, Shinjuku-ku, Tokyo 162-8711; tel. (3) 3266-5241; fax (3) 3266-5412; f. 1947; monthly; literature; Editor-in-Chief TOSHIMASA FUKE; circ. 80,000.

Shufunotomo: Shufunotomo Co Ltd, 2-9, Kanda Surugadai, Chiyoda-ku, Tokyo 101; tel. (3) 5280-7531; fax (3) 5280-7431; e-mail international-info@shufunotomo.co.jp; internet www.shufunotomo.co.jp; f. 1917; monthly; home and lifestyle; Editor YOSHIYUKI OGINO; circ. 450,000.

Shukan Gendai: Kodan-Sha Ltd, 2-12-21, Otowa, Bunkyo-ku, Tokyo 112-8001; tel. (3) 5395-3637; fax (3) 5395-5791; f. 1966; monthly; cultural and political; Editor NOBUHIRO NAGASAKI.

So-en: Bunka Publishing Bureau, c/o Bunka Fashion College, 3-22-7, Yoyogi, Shibuya-ku, Tokyo 151-8524; tel. (3) 3299-2531; fax (3) 3370-3712; e-mail info-bpb@bunka.ac.jp; internet books.bunka.ac.jp; f. 1936; monthly; fashion; Editor KEIKO SASAKI; circ. 270,000.

NEWS AGENCIES

Jiji Tsushin (Jiji Press Ltd): 5-15-8, Ginza, Chuo-ku, Tokyo 104-8178; tel. (3) 6800-1111; e-mail info@jiji.co.jp; internet www.jiji.com; f. 1945; Pres. YUTAKA NISHIZAWA.

Kyodo Tsushin (Kyodo News): Shiodome Media Tower, 1-7-1, Higashi-Shimbashi, Minato-ku, Tokyo 105-7201; tel. (3) 6252-8301; fax (3) 6252-8795; e-mail kokusai@kyodonews.jp; internet www.english.kyodonews.jp; f. 1945; Pres. MASAKI FUKUYAMA; Man. Editor FUMIKZAU YOSHIDA.

Radiopress Inc: R-Bldg Shinjuku, 5F, 33-8, Wakamatsu-cho, Shinjuku-ku, Tokyo 162-0056; tel. (3) 5273-2171; fax (3) 5273-2180; e-mail rptokyo@oak.ocn.ne.jp; f. 1945; provides news from the People's Repub. of China, the former USSR, Democratic People's Repub. of Korea, Viet Nam and elsewhere to the press and govt offices; Pres. AKIO IJUIN.

PRESS ASSOCIATIONS

Foreign Correspondents' Club of Japan: Yaruku-cho Denki Kita Bldg, 20/F, 1-7-1, Yuraku-cho, Chiyoda-ku, Tokyo 100-0006; tel. (3) 3211-3161; fax (3) 3211-3168; e-mail nakamura@fccj.or.jp; internet www.fccj.or.jp; f. 1945; 193 cos; Pres. LUCY BIRMINGHAM; Sec. MICHAEL PENN.

Foreign Press Center: Nippon Press Center Bldg, 6/F, 2-2-1, Uchisaiwai-cho, Chiyoda-ku, Tokyo 100-0011; tel. (3) 3501-3401; fax (3) 3501-3622; e-mail rr@fpcjpn.or.jp; internet www.fpcj.jp; f. 1976; est. by The Japan Newspaper Publishers and Editors Asscn and the Japan Fed. of Economic Orgs; provides services to the foreign press; Pres. KIYOTAKA AKASAKA.

Nihon Shinbun Kyokai (The Japan Newspaper Publishers and Editors Asscn): Nippon Press Center Bldg, 2-2-1, Uchisaiwai-cho, Chiyoda-ku, Tokyo 100-8543; tel. (3) 3591-3462; fax (3) 3591-6149; e-mail nsk-intl@pressnet.or.jp; internet www.pressnet.or.jp; f. 1946; mems include 131 cos (104 daily newspapers, 4 news agencies and 23 radio and TV cos); Pres. KOJIRO SHIRAISHI; Man. Dir AKIRA KAWASHIMA.

Nihon Zasshi Kyokai (Japan Magazine Publishers Asscn): 1-7, Kanda Surugadai, Chiyoda-ku, Tokyo 101-0062; tel. (3) 3291-0775; fax (3) 3293-6239; f. 1956; 85 mems; Pres. HARUHIKO ISHIKAWA; Sec. GENYA INUI.

Publishers

Akane Shobo Co Ltd: 3-2-1, Nishi-Kanda, Chiyoda-ku, Tokyo 101-0065; tel. (3) 3263-0641; fax (3) 3263-5440; e-mail info@akaneshobo.co.jp; internet www.akaneshobo.co.jp; f. 1949; juvenile; Pres. MASAHARU OKAMOTO.

Akita Publishing Co Ltd: 2-10-8, Iidabashi, Chiyoda-ku, Tokyo 102-8101; tel. (3) 3264-7011; fax (3) 3265-5906; internet www.akitashoten.co.jp; f. 1948; social sciences, history, juvenile; Chair. SADAO AKITA; Pres. SADAMI AKITA.

ALC Press Inc: 2-54-12, Eifuku, Suginami-ku, Tokyo 168-8611; tel. (3) 3323-1101; fax (3) 3327-1022; e-mail info@alc.co.jp; internet www.alc.co.jp; f. 1969; linguistics, educational materials, dictionaries, juvenile; Pres. TERUMARO HIRAMOTO.

Asahi Shimbun Publications Division: 5-3-2, Tsukiji, Chuo-ku, Tokyo 104-8011; tel. (3) 5541-8757; fax (3) 3545-0311; e-mail doors@asahi.com; internet publications.asahi.com; f. 1879; general; Pres. KAZUMOTO URUMA.

Asakura Publishing Co Ltd: 6-29, Shin Ogawa-machi, Shinjuku-ku, Tokyo 162-8707; tel. (3) 3260-0141; fax (3) 3260-0180; e-mail edit@asakura.co.jp; internet www.asakura.co.jp; f. 1929; natural sciences, medicine, social sciences; Pres. KUNIZO ASAKURA.

Asuka Publishing Inc: 2-11-5, Suido, Bunkyo-ku, Tokyo 112-0005; tel. (3) 5395-7650; fax (3) 5395-7654; internet www.asuka-g.co.jp; f. 1973; sociology, law, economics, languages; Pres. EIICHI ISHINO.

Baifukan Co Ltd: 4-3-12, Kudan-Minami, Chiyoda-ku, Tokyo 102-0074; tel. (3) 3262-5256; fax (3) 3262-5276; e-mail bfkeigyo@mx7.mesh.ne.jp; internet www.baifukan.co.jp; f. 1924; engineering, natural and social sciences, psychology; Pres. ITARU YAMAMOTO.

Baseball Magazine-Sha: 3-10-10, Misaki-cho, Chiyoda-ku, Tokyo 101-8381; tel. (3) 3238-0081; fax (3) 3238-0106; internet www.bbm-japan.com; f. 1946; sports, physical education, recreation, travel; Pres. TETSUO IKEDA.

Bensey Publishing Inc: 2-20-6, Kanda Jimbo-cho, Chiyoda-ku, Tokyo 101-0051; tel. (3) 5215-9021; fax (3) 5215-9025; e-mail bensey@bensey.co.jp; internet www.bensey.co.jp; f. 1967; philosophy, religion, history, art, languages, literature; Pres. YOJI IKEJIMA.

Bijutsu Shuppan-Sha Ltd: Inaoka Kudan Bldg, 6/F, 2-38, Kanda Jimbo-cho, Chiyoda-ku, Tokyo 101-8417; tel. (3) 3234-2151; fax (3) 3234-9451; e-mail artmedia@bijutsu.co.jp; internet www.bijutsu.co.jp; f. 1905; fine arts, graphic design; Pres. KENTARO OSHITA.

Bonjinsha Co Ltd: 1-3-13, Hirakawa-cho, Chiyoda-ku, Tokyo 102-0093; tel. (3) 3263-3959; fax (3) 3263-3116; e-mail info@bonjinsha.com; internet www.bonjinsha.com; f. 1973; Japanese language teaching materials; Pres. HISAMITSU TANAKA.

Bun-eido Publishing Co Inc: 28, Kamitoba, Daimotsu-cho, Minami-ku, Kyoto 601-8691; tel. (75) 671-3161; fax (75) 671-3165; e-mail fujita@bun-eido.co.jp; internet www.bun-eido.co.jp; f. 1921; reference books, dictionaries, textbooks, juvenile, history; Pres. HIDEOHIRO MASUI.

Bungei Shunju Ltd: 3-23, Kioi-cho, Chiyoda-ku, Tokyo 102-8008; tel. (3) 3265-1211; fax (3) 3265-1363; internet www.bunshun.co.jp; f. 1923; fiction, general literature, recreation, economics, sociology; Dir TAKAHIRO HIRAO.

Bunri Co Ltd: 1-1-5, Sekiguchi, Bunkyo-ku, Tokyo 112-0014; tel. (3) 3268-4110; fax (3) 3268-1462; e-mail tezukatak@bnet.bunri.co.jp; internet www.bunri.co.jp; f. 1950; Pres. SHIRO HATA.

Chikuma Shobo: Chikumashobo Bldg, 2-5-3, Kuramae, Taito-ku, Tokyo 111-8755; tel. (3) 5687-2671; fax (3) 5687-1585; e-mail henshuinfo@chikumashobo.co.jp; internet www.chikumashobo.co.jp; f. 1940; general literature, fiction, history, juvenile, fine arts; Pres. AKIO KIKUCHI.

Child-Honsha Co Ltd: 5-24-21, Koishikawa, Bunkyo-ku, Tokyo 112-8512; tel. (3) 3813-3781; fax (3) 3813-3778; e-mail ehon@childbook.co.jp; internet www.childbook.co.jp; f. 1930; juvenile; Pres. SHUNJI ASAKA.

Chuo Hoki Publishing Co Ltd: 2-27-4, Yoyogi, Shibuya-ku, Tokyo 151-0053; tel. (3) 3379-3784; fax (3) 5351-7855; e-mail info@chuohoki.co.jp; internet www.chuohoki.co.jp; f. 1947; law, social sciences; Pres. AKIHIKO SHOMURA.

Chuo University Press: 742-1, Higashi-Nakano, Hachioji-shi, Tokyo 192-0393; tel. (426) 74-2351; fax (426) 74-2354; f. 1948; law, history, sociology, economics, science, literature; Pres. TAKEHIKO TAMATSUKURI.

Chuokoron-Shinsha Inc: 2-8-7, Kyobashi, Chuo-ku, Tokyo 104-8320; tel. (3) 3563-1261; fax (3) 3561-5920; internet www.chuko.co.jp; f. 1886; philosophy, history, sociology, general literature; Pres. TAMOTSU ASAMI.

Corona Publishing Co Ltd: 4-46-10, Sengoku, Bunkyo-ku, Tokyo 112-0011; tel. (3) 3941-3131; fax (3) 3941-3137; e-mail info@coronasha.co.jp; internet www.coronasha.co.jp; f. 1927; electronics, medical books, mechanical engineering, computer science; Pres. MASAYA GORAI.

Dempa Publications Inc: 1-11-15, Higashi-Gotanda, Shinagawa-ku, Tokyo 141-8715; tel. (3) 3445-6111; fax (3) 3444-7515; f. 1950; electronics, personal computer software, juvenile, trade newspapers, English and Japanese language publications; Pres. TETSUO HIRAYAMA.

Diamond Inc: 6-12-17, Jingumae, Shibuya-ku, Tokyo 150-8409; tel. (3) 5778-7233; fax (3) 5778-6618; e-mail info@diamond.co.jp; internet www.diamond.co.jp; f. 1913; business, management, economics, financial; Pres. FUMIAKI SHIKATANI.

Dohosha Ltd: TAS Bldg, 2-5-2, Nishi-Kanda, Chiyoda-ku, Tokyo 101-0065; tel. (3) 5276-0831; fax (3) 5276-0840; e-mail intl@dohosha.co.jp; f. 1997; general works, architecture, art, Buddhism, business, children's education, cooking, flower-arranging, gardening, medicine.

East Press Co Ltd: 1-19, Kanda Jimbo-cho, Chiyoda-ku, Tokyo 101-0051; tel. (3) 5259-7707; fax (3) 5259-7708; e-mail webmaster@eastpress.co.jp; internet www.eastpress.co.jp; f. 2005; literature, comics, business, self-help, parenting, health, sports, music; Chair. SHINGERU KOBAYASHI; Pres. OSAMU ASOSHINA.

Froebel-Kan Co Ltd: 6-14-9, Honkomagome, Bunkyo-ku, Tokyo 113-8611; tel. (3) 5395-6600; fax (3) 5395-6621; e-mail info-e@froebel-kan.co.jp; internet www.froebel-kan.co.jp; f. 1907; juvenile, educational; Pres. HIDEO MUTO.

Fukuinkan Shoten Publishers Inc: 6-6-3, Honkomagome, Bunkyo-ku, Tokyo 113-8686; tel. (3) 3942-2151; fax (3) 3942-1401; internet www.fukuinkan.co.jp; f. 1952; juvenile; Pres. NOBORU OGURA; Chair. KATSUMI SATO.

Fusosha Publishing Inc: 1-15-1, Kaigan, Minato-ku, Tokyo 105-8070; tel. (3) 5403-8851; fax (3) 3578-3078; e-mail gshoseki@fusosha.co.jp; internet www.fusosha.co.jp; f. 1984; social sciences, business, mystery, magazines, textbooks; Pres. EIICHI KUBOTA.

Futabasha Publishers Ltd: 3-28, Higashi-Goken-cho, Shinjuku-ku, Tokyo 162-8540; tel. (3) 5261-4832; fax (3) 5261-3480; e-mail general@futabasha.co.jp; internet www.futabasha.co.jp; f. 1948; fiction, non-fiction, comics, guide books; Pres. HIROSHI MOROZUMI.

Gakken Co Ltd: 4-40-5, Kamiikedai, Ota-ku, Tokyo 145-8502; tel. (3) 3726-8111; fax (3) 3493-3338; e-mail personnel@gakken.co.jp; internet www.gakken.co.jp; f. 1946; juvenile, educational, art, encyclopaedias, dictionaries; Pres. YOCHIRO ENDO.

Graphic-sha Publishing Co Ltd: 1-14-17 Kudan-Kita, Chiyoda-ku, Tokyo 102-0073; tel. (3) 3263-4318; fax (3) 3263-5297; e-mail info@graphicsha.co.jp; internet www.graphicsha.co.jp; f. 1962; art, design, architecture, manga techniques, hobbies; Pres. KUZE TOSHIRO.

Gyosei Corpn: 1-18-11, Shinkiba, Koto-ku, Tokyo 136-8575; tel. (3) 6892-6666; fax (3) 6892-6925; e-mail eigyo1@gyosei.co.jp; internet www.gyosei.co.jp; f. 1893; law, education, science, politics, business, art, language, literature, juvenile; Pres. YUJIRO SAWADA.

Hakusui-Sha Co Ltd: 3-24, Kanda Ogawa-machi, Chiyoda-ku, Tokyo 101-0052; tel. (3) 3291-7821; fax (3) 3291-7810; e-mail hpmaster@hakusuisha.co.jp; internet www.hakusuisha.co.jp; f. 1915; general literature, science and languages; Pres. NAOSHI OIKAWA.

Hayakawa Publishing Inc: 2-2, Kanda-Tacho, Chiyoda-ku, Tokyo 101-0046; tel. (3) 3252-3111; fax (3) 3258-0250; internet www.hayakawa-online.co.jp; f. 1945; wine books, children's books, coffee-table books, drama, comic books, monthly magazines; Pres. HIROSHI HAYAKAWA.

Heibonsha Ltd: 2-29-4 Hakusan, Bunkyo-ku, Tokyo 112-0001; tel. (3) 3818-0873; fax (3) 3818-0857; e-mail shop@heibonsha.co.jp; internet www.heibonsha.co.jp; f. 1914; encyclopaedias, art, history, geography, literature, science; Pres. NAOTO SHIMONAKA.

Hirokawa Publishing Co: 3-27-14, Hongo, Bunkyo-ku, Tokyo 113-0033; tel. (3) 3815-3651; fax (3) 5684-7030; f. 1925; natural sciences, medicine, pharmacy, nursing, chemistry; Pres. SETSUO HIROKAWA.

Hoikusha Publishing Co: 18-24, Hiroshi-bacho, Suita-shi, Osaka 564-0052; tel. (6) 6330-5680; fax (6) 6330-5681; e-mail matsui@hoikusha.co.jp; internet www.hoikusha.co.jp; f. 1947; natural sciences, juvenile, fine arts, geography; Pres. TAKAHIKO MATSUI.

Hokkaido University Press: Kita-9, Nishi-8, Kita-ku, Sapporo 060-0809; tel. (11) 747-2308; fax (11) 736-8605; e-mail hupress_2@hup.gr.jp; internet www.hup.gr.jp; f. 1970; social and natural sciences, technology, humanities; Pres. KATSUMI YOSHIDA.

Hokuryukan Co Ltd: 3-8-14, Takanawa, Minato-ku, Tokyo 108-0074; tel. (3) 5449-4591; fax (3) 5449-4950; e-mail hk-ns@hokuryukan-ns.co.jp; internet www.hokuryukan-ns.co.jp; f. 1891; natural sciences, medical science, juvenile, dictionaries; Pres. HISAKO FUKUDA.

The Hokuseido Press: Hayashi Bldg, 1-21-9, Sugamo, Toshima-ku, Tokyo 170-0002; tel. (3) 5940-0511; fax (3) 5940-0512; e-mail info@hokuseido.com; internet www.hokuseido.com; f. 1914; regional non-fiction, dictionaries, textbooks; Pres. KEISUKE YAMAMOTO.

Horitsubunka-sha: 71, Iwagakakiuchi-cho, Kamigamo, Kita-ku, Kyoto 603-8053; tel. (75) 791-7131; fax (75) 721-8400; e-mail henshu@hou-bun.co.jp; internet www.hou-bun.co.jp; f. 1947; law, politics, economics, sociology, philosophy; Pres. YASUSHI AKIYAMA.

Hosei University Press: 3-2-7, Kudan-Kita, Chiyoda-ku, Tokyo 102-0073; tel. (3) 5214-5540; fax (3) 5214-5542; e-mail mail@h-up.com; internet www.h-up.com; f. 1948; philosophy, history, economics, sociology, natural sciences, literature; Pres. TOSHIO MASUDA.

Ie-No-Hikari Association: 11, Funagawara-cho, Ichigaya, Shinjuku-ku, Tokyo 162-8448; tel. (3) 3266-9000; fax (3) 3266-9048; e-mail hikari@mxd.mesh.ne.jp; internet www.ienohikari.net; f. 1925; social sciences, agriculture, cooking; Pres. TOSHIHIRO SONODA.

Igaku-Shoin Ltd: 1-28-23, Hongo, Bunkyo-ku, Tokyo 113-8719; tel. (3) 3817-5610; fax (3) 3815-4114; e-mail info@igaku-shoin.co.jp; internet www.igaku-shoin.co.jp; f. 1944; medicine, nursing; Pres. YU KANEHARA.

Ikubundo Publishing Co Ltd: 5-30-21, Hongo, Bunkyo-ku, Tokyo 113-0033; tel. (3) 3814-5571; fax (3) 3814-5576; e-mail webmaster@

ikubundo.com; internet www.ikubundo.com; f. 1899; languages, dictionaries; Pres. TOSHIYUKI OI.

Institute for Financial Affairs Inc (KINZAI): 19, Minami-Motomachi, Shinjuku-ku, Tokyo 160-8519; tel. (3) 3358-1161; fax (3) 3359-7947; e-mail JDI04072@nifty.ne.jp; internet www.kinzai.or.jp; f. 1950; finance and economics, banking laws and regulations, accounting; Pres. MASATERU YOSHIDA.

Ishiyaku Publishers Inc: 1-7-10, Honkomagome, Bunkyo-ku, Tokyo 113-8612; tel. (3) 5395-7600; fax (3) 5395-7606; e-mail webmaster@ishiyaku.co.jp; internet www.ishiyaku.co.jp; f. 1921; medicine, dentistry, rehabilitation, nursing, nutrition and pharmaceutics; Pres. HIDEHO OHATA.

Iwanami Shoten, Publishers: 2-5-5, Hitotsubashi, Chiyoda-ku, Tokyo 101-8002; tel. (3) 5210-4000; fax (3) 5210-4039; e-mail rights@iwanami.co.jp; internet www.iwanami.co.jp; f. 1913; natural and social sciences, humanities, literature, fine arts, juvenile, dictionaries; Pres. ATSUSHI OKAMOTO.

Iwasaki Publishing Co Ltd: 1-9-2, Suido, Bunkyo-ku, Tokyo 112-0005; tel. (3) 3812-0151; fax (3) 3812-1381; e-mail ask@iwasakishoten.co.jp; internet www.iwasakishoten.co.jp; f. 1934; juvenile; Pres. HIROAKI IWASAKI.

Japan Broadcast Publishing Co Ltd: 41-1, Udagawa-cho, Shibuya-ku, Tokyo 150-8081; tel. (3) 3464-7311; fax (3) 3780-3394; e-mail kikaka@nhk-book.co.jp; internet www.nhk-book.co.jp; f. 1931; foreign language textbooks, gardening, home economics, sociology, education, art, juvenile; Pres. AKIHIDE MIZOGUCHI.

Japan External Trade Organization (JETRO): Ark Mori Bldg, 6/F, 1-12-32, Akasaka, Minato-ku, Tokyo 107-6006; tel. (3) 3582-5511; fax (3) 3587-2485; internet www.jetro.go.jp; f. 1958; trade, economics, investment; Chair. YASUO HAYASHI.

Japan Publications Trading Co Ltd: 1-2-1, Sarugaku-cho, Chiyoda-ku, Tokyo 101-0064; tel. (3) 3292-3751; fax (3) 3292-0410; e-mail jpt@jptco.co.jp; internet www.jptco.co.jp; f. 1942; general works, art, health, sports; Pres. HIROBUMI ANNOSHITA.

The Japan Times Ltd: 4-5-4, Shibaura, Minato-ku, Tokyo 108-8071; tel. (3) 3453-2013; fax (3) 3453-8023; e-mail jt-books@kt.rim.or.jp; internet bookclub.japantimes.co.jp; f. 1897; linguistics, culture, business; Pres. TOSHIAKI OGASAWARA.

Jikkyo Shuppan Co Ltd: 5, Goban-cho, Chiyoda-ku, Tokyo 102-8377; tel. (3) 3238-7700; fax (3) 3238-7719; internet www.jikkyo.co.jp; f. 1941; textbooks; Pres. YOJI TOTSUKA.

Jimbun Shoin: 9, Nishi-Uchihata-cho, Takeda, Fushimi-ku, Kyoto 612-8447; tel. (75) 603-1344; fax (75) 603-1814; e-mail jmsb@jimbunshoin.co.jp; internet www.jimbunshoin.co.jp; f. 1927; general literature, philosophy, fiction, social sciences, religion, fine arts; Pres. HIROSHI WATANABE.

Jitsugyo No Nihonsha Ltd: 1-3-9, Ginza, Chuo-ku, Tokyo 104-8233; tel. (3) 3562-1021; fax (3) 3562-2662; e-mail soumu@j-n.co.jp; internet www.j-n.co.jp; f. 1897; general, social sciences, juvenile, travel, business, comics; Pres. YOSHIKAZU MASUDA.

JTB Publishing (Japan Travel Bureau): Urban-net Ichigaya Bldg, 25-5, Haraikatamachi, Shinjuku-ku, Tokyo 162-8446; tel. (3) 6888-7811; fax (3) 6888-7809; e-mail jtbpublishing@rurubu.ne.jp; internet www.jtbpublishing.com; f. 2004; travel, geography, history, fine arts, languages; Pres. YUZURU TAKENAMI.

Kadokawa Group Publishing Inc: 2-13-3, Fujimi, Chiyoda-ku, Tokyo 102-8177; tel. (3) 3238-8715; fax (3) 3262-7734; e-mail k-master@kadokawa.co.jp; internet www.kadokawa.co.jp; f. 1945; literature, history, dictionaries, religion, fine arts, books on tape, compact discs, CD-ROMs, comics, animation, video cassettes, computer games; Pres. KOICHI SEKIYA.

Kaibundo Publishing Co Ltd: 2-5-4, Suido, Bunkyo-ku, Tokyo 112-0005; tel. (3) 5684-6289; fax (3) 3815-3953; e-mail okadayo@kaibundo.jp; internet www.kaibundo.jp; f. 1914; marine affairs, natural sciences, engineering, industry; Pres. SETSUO OKADA.

Kaiseisha Publishing Co Ltd: 3-5, Ichigaya Sadohara-cho, Shinjuku-ku, Tokyo 162-8450; tel. (3) 3260-3229; fax (3) 3260-3540; e-mail foreign@kaiseisha.co.jp; internet www.kaiseisha.net; f. 1936; juvenile; Pres. MASAKI IMAMURA.

Kanehara & Co Ltd: 2-31-14, Yushima, Bunkyo-ku, Tokyo 113-8687; tel. (3) 3811-7185; fax (3) 3813-0288; e-mail kanehara@abox5.so-net.ne.jp; internet www.kanehara-shuppan.co.jp; f. 1875; medical, agricultural, engineering and scientific; Pres. HIROMITSU KAWAI.

Keiso Shobo Publishing Co Ltd: 2-1-1, Suido, Bunkyo-ku, Tokyo 112-0005; tel. (3) 3814-6861; fax (3) 3814-6968; e-mail h-imura@keisoshobo.co.jp; internet www.keisoshobo.co.jp; f. 1948; law, economics, politics, literature, psychology, philosophy, sociology; Pres. HISATO IMURA.

Kenkyusha Ltd: 2-11-3, Fujimi, Chiyoda-ku, Tokyo 102-8152; tel. (3) 3288-7777; fax (3) 3288-7799; e-mail hanbai@kenkyusha.co.jp; internet www.kenkyusha.co.jp; f. 1907; bilingual dictionaries, books on languages; Pres. YUSUKE KOSAKAI.

Kinokuniya Co Ltd: 3-7-10, Shimomeguro, Meguro-ku, Tokyo 153-8504; tel. (3) 6910-0508; fax (3) 6420-1354; e-mail publish@kinokuniya.co.jp; internet www.kinokuniya.co.jp; f. 1927; humanities, social and natural sciences; Pres. MASASHI TAKAI.

KK Best Sellers Co Ltd: 2-29-7, Minami-Otsuka, Toshima-ku, Tokyo 170-8457; tel. (3) 5976-9121; fax (3) 5976-9237; e-mail muramatsu@bestsellers.co.jp; internet www.kk-bestsellers.com; f. 1967; non-fiction, general literature; Pres. MIKIO KURIHARA.

Kodansha Ltd: 2-12-21, Otowa, Bunkyo-ku, Tokyo 112-8001; tel. (3) 3946-6201; fax (3) 3944-9915; e-mail n-okazaki@kodansha.co.jp; internet www.kodansha.co.jp; f. 1909; fine arts, fiction, literature, juvenile, comics, dictionaries; Pres. YOSHINOBU NOMA.

Kosei Publishing Co Ltd: 2-7-1, Wada, Suginami-ku, Tokyo 166-8535; tel. (3) 5385-2319; fax (3) 5385-2331; e-mail kspub@kosei-shuppan.co.jp; internet www.kosei-shuppan.co.jp; f. 1966; general works, philosophy, religion, history, pedagogy, social science, art, juvenile; Pres. MORIYASU OKABE.

Kumon Publishing Co Ltd: Gobancho Grand Bldg, 3-1, Gobancho, Chiyoda-ku, Tokyo 102-8180; tel. (3) 3234-4004; fax (3) 3234-4483; e-mail international@kumonshuppan.com; internet www.kumonshuppan.com; f. 1988; juvenile, dictionaries, education; Pres. SHOICHI DOKAI.

Kwansei Gakuin University Press: 1-155, Uegahara Ichiban-cho, Nishi-Nomiya-shi, Hyogo 662-0891; tel. (798) 53-7002; fax (798) 53-9592; internet www.kwansei.ac.jp/press; f. 1997; natural and social sciences, philosophy, literature; Pres. KOJIRO MIYAHARA.

Kyoritsu Shuppan Co Ltd: 4-6-19, Kohinata, Bunkyo-ku, Tokyo 112-8700; tel. (3) 3947-2511; fax (3) 3947-2539; e-mail general@kyoritsu-pub.co.jp; internet www.kyoritsu-pub.co.jp; f. 1926; scientific and technical; Pres. MITSUAKI NANJO.

Kyoto University Press: Kyodai-Yoshida-Minami, 69, Yoshidakonoe-cho, Sakyo-ku, Kyoto 606-8315; tel. (75) 761-6182; fax (75) 761-6190; e-mail sales@kyoto-up.or.jp; internet www.kyoto-up.or.jp; f. 1989; history, literature, philology, anthropology, sociology, economics, area studies, ecology, architecture, psychology, philosophy, space physics, earth and planetary science; Rep. Prof. TAMEJIRO HIYAMA.

Kyushu University Press: 7-1-146, Hakozaki, Higashi-ku, Fukuoka 812-0053; tel. (92) 641-0515; fax (92) 641-0172; e-mail kup@mocha.ocn.ne.jp; internet www1.ocn.ne.jp/~kup; f. 1975; history, political science, law, economics, technology, linguistics, literature, psychology, medicine, agriculture; Chief Dir NAOYUKI ISOGAWA.

Maruzen Co Ltd: Shinagawa Bldg, 4-13-14, Higashi-Shinagawa, Shinagawa-ku, Tokyo 140-0002; tel. (3) 3272-0521; fax (3) 3272-0527; e-mail sitepub@maruzen.co.jp; internet pub.maruzen.co.jp; f. 1869; general works; Dir TAKEHIKO OGI.

Meisei University Press: 2-1-1, Hodokubo, Hino-shi, Tokyo 191-8506; tel. (42) 591-9979; fax (42) 593-0192; f. 1975; humanities, education, social and natural sciences; Pres. TETSUO OGAWA.

Minerva Shobo: 1, Tsutsumidani-cho, Hinooka, Yamashina-ku, Kyoto 607-8494; tel. (75) 581-5191; fax (75) 581-8379; e-mail info@minervashobo.co.jp; internet www.minervashobo.co.jp; f. 1948; general non-fiction and reference; Pres. KEIZO SUGITA.

Misuzu Shobo Ltd: 5-32-21, Hongo, Bunkyo-ku, Tokyo 113-0033; tel. (3) 3815-9181; fax (3) 3818-8497; e-mail info@msz.co.jp; internet www.msz.co.jp; f. 1947; general, philosophy, history, psychiatry, literature, science, art; Pres. HISAO MOCHITANI.

Morikita Shuppan Co Ltd: 1-4-11, Fujimi, Chiyoda-ku, Tokyo 102-0071; tel. (3) 3265-8341; fax (3) 3261-1349; e-mail hiro@morikita.co.jp; internet www.morikita.co.jp; f. 1950; natural sciences, engineering; Pres. HIROSHI MORIKITA.

Nagaoka Shoten Co Ltd: 1-7-14, Toyotama-Kami, Nerima-ku, Tokyo 176-8518; tel. (3) 3992-5155; fax (3) 3948-9161; e-mail info@nagaokashoten.co.jp; internet www.nagaokashoten.co.jp; f. 1963; dictionaries, home economics, sports, recreation, law; Pres. SHUICHI NAGAOKA.

Nakayama-Shoten Co Ltd: 1-25-14, Hakusan, Bunkyo-ku, Tokyo 113-8666; tel. (3) 3813-1100; fax (3) 3816-1015; e-mail kojima@nakayamashoten.co.jp; internet www.nakayamashoten.co.jp; f. 1948; medicine, biology, zoology; Pres. TADASHI HIRATA.

Nanzando Co Ltd: 4-1-11, Yushima, Bunkyo-ku, Tokyo; tel. (3) 5689-7868; fax (3) 5689-7869; e-mail nanzando-soumubu@nanzando.com; internet www.nanzando.com; f. 1901; medical reference, paperbacks; Pres. HAJIME SUZUKI.

Nigensha Publishing Co Ltd: 6-2-1, Honkomagome, Bunkyo-gu, Tokyo, 113-0021; tel. (3) 5395-2041; fax (3) 5395-2045; e-mail info@nigensha.jp; internet www.nigensha.co.jp; f. 1955; calligraphy, fine arts, art reproductions, cars, watches; Pres. YUKIKO KUROSU.

Nihon Vogue Co Ltd: 3-23, Ichigaya Honmura-cho, Shinjuku-ku, Tokyo 162-8705; tel. (3) 5261-5139; fax (3) 3269-8726; e-mail asai@tezukuritown.com; internet www.tezukuritown.com; f. 1954;

quilting, needlecraft, handicrafts, knitting, decorative painting, pressed flowers; Pres. NOBUAKI SETO.

Nihonbungeisha Co Ltd: 1-7, Kanda Jimbo-cho, Chiyoda-ku, Tokyo 101-0051; tel. (3) 3294-7771; fax (3) 3294-7780; e-mail mmac@nihonbungeisha.co.jp; internet www.nihonbungeisha.co.jp; f. 1959; home economics, sociology, fiction, technical books; Pres. SOUJI NISHIZAWA.

Nikkei Publishing Inc: Shin-Otemachi Bldg, 2-2-1, Otemachi, Chiyoda-ku, Tokyo 100-0004; tel. (3) 5255-2836; fax (3) 5255-2864; internet www.nikkeibook.com; f. 1876; economics, business, politics, fine arts, video cassettes, CD-ROMs; Pres. HISAO SAIDA.

Nippon Hyoronsha: 3-12-4, Minami-Otsuka, Toshima-ku, Tokyo 170-8474; tel. (3) 3987-8611; fax (3) 3987-8593; e-mail inform@nippyo.co.jp; internet www.nippyo.co.jp; f. 1918; jurisprudence, economics, science, mathematics, medicine, psychology, business; Pres. TOSHIMASA KURODA.

Nippon Jitsugyo Publishing Co Ltd: 3-2-12, Hongo, Bunkyo-ku, Tokyo 113-0033; tel. (3) 3814-5651; fax (3) 3818-2723; e-mail int@njg.co.jp; internet www.njg.co.jp; f. 1950; business, management, finance and accounting, sales and marketing; Chair. and CEO YOICHIRO NAKAMURA.

Nosan Gyoson Bunka Kyokai (Rural Culture Association): 7-6-1, Akasaka, Minato-ku, Tokyo 107-8668; tel. (3) 3585-1141; fax (3) 3589-1387; e-mail rural@mail.ruralnet.or.jp; internet www.ruralnet.or.jp; f. 1940; agriculture, food and health, education, economics, philosophy; Pres. YOSHIHIRO HAMAGUCHI.

NTT Publishing Co Ltd: JR Tokyu Meguro Bldg, 7/F, 3-1-1, Kami-Osaki, Shinagawa-ku, Tokyo 141-8654; tel. (3) 5434-1011; fax (3) 5434-1008; internet www.nttpub.co.jp; f. 1987; essays, biography, philosophy, sociology, history, management, economics, technology, telecommunications, picture books, computer game guides; Pres. SHINJI JIKUYA.

Obunsha Co Ltd: 55, Yokodera-cho, Shinjuku-ku, Tokyo 162-8680; tel. (3) 3266-6429; fax (3) 3266-6412; internet www.obunsha.co.jp; f. 1931; textbooks, reference, general science and fiction, magazines, encyclopaedias, dictionaries; software; audio-visual aids; CEO FUMIO AKAO.

Ohmsha Ltd: 3-1, Kanda Nishiki-cho, Chiyoda-ku, Tokyo 101-8460; tel. (3) 3233-0641; fax (3) 3233-2426; e-mail kaigaika@ohmsha.co.jp; internet www.ohmsha.co.jp; f. 1914; engineering, technical and scientific; Pres. OSAMI TAKEO.

Ongaku No Tomo Sha Corpn (ONT): 6-30, Kagurazaka, Shinjuku-ku, Tokyo 162-8716; tel. (3) 3235-2111; fax (3) 3235-2110; e-mail home_ontomo@ongakunotomo.co.jp; internet www.ongakunotomo.co.jp; f. 1941; compact discs, videograms, music magazines, music books, music data, music textbooks; Pres. KUMIO HORIUCHI.

Osaka University of Economics and Law: 6-10, Gakuonji, Yaoshi, Osaka 581-8511; tel. (729) 41-8211; fax (729) 41-9979; e-mail kondo-t@keiho-u.ac.jp; internet www.keiho-u.ac.jp/research/syuppan/index.html; f. 1987; economics, law, philosophy, history, natural science, languages, politics; Pres. SHUNKUO KANAZAWA.

Osaka University Press: 2-7, Yamadaoka, Suita-shi, Osaka 565-0871; tel. and fax (6) 6877-1614; e-mail info@osaka-up.or.jp; internet www.osaka-up.or.jp; f. 1993; economics, history, literature, medicine, philosophy, politics, science, sociology, technology; Pres. KIYOKAZU WASHIDA.

PHP Institute Inc: 11, Kita-Nouchi-cho, Nishi-Kujo, Minami-ku, Kyoto 601-8411; tel. (75) 681-3268; fax (75) 681-4560; internet www.php.co.jp; f. 1946; social sciences; Pres. MASAYUKI MATSUSHITA.

Poplar Publishing Co Ltd: 22-1, Daikyo-cho, Shinjuku-ku, Tokyo 160-8565; tel. (3) 3357-2216; fax (3) 3351-0736; e-mail info@poplar.co.jp; internet www.poplar.co.jp; f. 1947; general, children's, comics; CEO HIROYUKI SAKAI.

Sanrio Co Ltd: 1-6-1, Osaki, Shinagawa-ku, Tokyo 141-8603; tel. (3) 3779-8101; fax (3) 3779-8702; internet www.sanrio.co.jp; f. 1960; juvenile; Pres. SHINTARO TSUJI.

Sanseido Co Ltd: 2-22-14, Misaki-cho, Chiyoda-ku, Tokyo 101-8371; tel. (3) 3230-9411; fax (3) 3230-9547; e-mail ssd-s@sanseido-publ.co.jp; internet www.sanseido.co.jp; f. 1881; dictionaries, educational, languages, social and natural sciences; Pres. KATSUHIKO KITAGUCHI.

Sanshusha Publishing Co Ltd: Aoyama Kumano Jinja Bldg, 2-2-22, Jingu-mae, Shibuya-ku, Tokyo 150-0001; tel. (3) 3405-4511; fax (3) 3405-4522; e-mail webmaster@sanshusha.co.jp; internet www.sanshusha.co.jp; f. 1938; languages, dictionaries, philosophy, sociology, electronic publishing (CD-ROM); Pres. TOSHIHIDE MAEDA.

Seibido Shuppan Co Ltd: 1-7, Shinogawamachi, Shinjuku-ku, Tokyo 162-8445; tel. (3) 5206-8151; fax (3) 5206-8159; internet www.seibidoshuppan.co.jp; f. 1969; sports, recreation, travel guides, music, motor sports, cooking, novels, computer, childcare, picture books; Pres. ETSUJI FUKAMI.

Seibundo-Shinkosha Co Ltd: 3-3-11, Hongo, Bunkyo-ku, Tokyo 113-0033; tel. (3) 5800-5775; fax (3) 5800-5773; internet www.seibundo-shinkosha.net; f. 1912; scientific, gardening, electronics, graphic design; Pres. YUICHI OGAWA.

Seishun Publishing Co Ltd: 12-1, Wakamatsu-cho, Shinjuku-ku, Tokyo 162-0056; tel. (3) 3203-5121; fax (3) 3207-0982; e-mail info@seishun.co.jp; internet www.seishun.co.jp; f. 1955; science, education, history, sociology, philosophy, economics, literature; Pres. GENTARO OZAWA.

Seitoku University Press: 550, Iwase, Matsudo-shi, Chiba 271-8755; tel. (47) 365-1111; fax (47) 363-1401; e-mail shuppan@seitoku.ac.jp; f. 2002; human science, medicine, art; Pres. HIROAKI KAWAKAMI.

Seizando Shoten Publishing Co Ltd: 4-51, Minami-Motomachi, Shinjuku-ku, Tokyo 160-0012; tel. (3) 3357-5861; fax (3) 3357-5867; e-mail publisher@seizando.co.jp; internet www.seizando.co.jp; f. 1954; maritime affairs, aviation, engineering; Pres. NORIKO OGAWA.

Sekai Bunka Publishing Inc: 4-2-29, Kudan-Kita, Chiyoda-ku, Tokyo 102-8187; tel. (3) 3262-5111; fax (3) 3262-5750; e-mail y-muta@sekaibunka.co.jp; internet www.sekaibunka.com; f. 1946; history, natural sciences, geography, education, art, literature, juvenile; Pres. MINAKO SUZUKI.

Shincho-Sha Co Ltd: 71, Yarai-cho, Shinjuku-ku, Tokyo 162-8711; tel. (3) 3266-5250; fax (3) 3266-5432; e-mail shuppans@shinchosha.co.jp; internet www.shinchosha.co.jp; f. 1896; general literature, fiction, non-fiction, fine arts, philosophy; Pres. TAKANOBU SATO.

Shinkenchiku-Sha Co Ltd: 2-31-2, Yushima, Bunkyo-ku, Tokyo 113-8501; tel. (3) 3811-7101; fax (3) 3812-8229; e-mail ja-business@japan-architect.co.jp; internet www.japan-architect.co.jp; f. 1925; architecture; Pres. AKIHIKO OMORI.

Shinsei Publishing Co Ltd: 4-7-6, Taito, Taito-ku, Tokyo 110-0016; tel. (3) 3831-0743; fax (3) 3831-0758; internet www.shin-sei.co.jp; f. 1944; guidebooks, state examinations, personal computers; Pres. YASUHIRO TOMINAGA.

Shogakukan Inc: 2-3-1, Hitotsubashi, Chiyoda-ku, Tokyo 101-8001; tel. (3) 3230-5658; fax (3) 3230-9750; internet www.shogakukan.co.jp; f. 1922; juvenile, education, geography, history, encyclopaedias, dictionaries; Pres. MASAHIRO OHGA.

Shokabo Publishing Co Ltd: 8-1, Yomban-cho, Chiyoda-ku, Tokyo 102-0081; tel. (3) 3262-9166; fax (3) 3262-7257; e-mail info@shokabo.co.jp; internet www.shokabo.co.jp; f. 1716; natural sciences, engineering; Pres. KAZUHIRO YOSHINO.

Shokokusha Publishing Co Ltd: 25, Saka-machi, Shinjuku-ku, Tokyo 160-0002; tel. (3) 3359-3231; fax (3) 3357-3961; e-mail eigyo@shokokusha.co.jp; internet www.shokokusha.co.jp; f. 1932; architectural, technical and fine arts; Pres. TAKESHI GOTO.

Shueisha Inc: 2-5-10, Hitotsubashi, Chiyoda-ku, Tokyo 101-8050; tel. (3) 3230-6111; fax (3) 3262-1309; e-mail yoshizumi@shueisha.co.jp; internet www.shueisha.co.jp; f. 1925; literature, fine arts, language, juvenile, comics; Pres. and CEO HIDEKI YAMASHITA.

Shufunotomo Co Ltd: 2-9, Kanda Surugadai, Chiyoda-ku, Tokyo 101-8911; tel. (3) 5280-7567; fax (3) 5280-7568; e-mail international@shufunotomo.co.jp; internet www.shufunotomo.co.jp; f. 1916; domestic science, fine arts, gardening, handicraft, cookery and magazines; Pres. YOSHIYUKI OGINO.

Shufu-To-Seikatsusha Ltd: 3-5-7, Kyobashi, Chuo-ku, Tokyo 104-8357; tel. (3) 3563-5120; fax (3) 3563-2073; internet www.shufu.co.jp; f. 1935; home economics, recreation, fiction, medicine, comics, cooking, interiors, handicraft, fishing, fashion; Pres. KATSUHISA TAKANOU.

Shunju-Sha: 2-18-6, Soto-Kanda, Chiyoda-ku, Tokyo 101-0021; tel. (3) 3255-9611; fax (3) 3253-1384; e-mail main@shunjusha.co.jp; internet www.shunjusha.co.jp; f. 1918; philosophy, religion, literature, economics, music; Pres. AKIRA KANDA.

Sony Magazines Inc: Banchokaikan, 12-1, Goban-cho, Chiyoda-ku, Tokyo 102-8679; tel. (3) 3234-5811; fax (3) 3234-5842; internet www.sonymagazines.jp; f. 1979; music books, general literature; Pres. SHIGERU MURATA.

Taishukan Publishing Co Ltd: 2-1-1, Yushima, Bunkyo-ku, Tokyo 113-8541; tel. (3) 3868-2651; fax (3) 3868-2640; e-mail kimura@taishukan.co.jp; internet www.taishukan.co.jp; f. 1918; reference, Japanese and foreign languages, sports, dictionaries, audio-visual aids; Pres. KAZUYUKI SUZUKI.

Takahashi Shoten Co Ltd: 1-26-1, Otowa, Bunkyo-ku, Tokyo 112-0013; tel. (3) 3943-4525; fax (3) 3943-4288; e-mail ta_contact@takahashishoten.co.jp; internet www.takahashishoten.co.jp; f. 1952; business, food and drink, sport, dictionaries, education, juvenile; Pres. HIDEO TAKAHASHI.

Tamagawa University Press: 6-1-1, Tamagawa-Gakuen, Machida-shi, Tokyo 194-8610; tel. (42) 739-8933; fax (42) 739-8940; e-mail tup@tamagawa.ac.jp; internet www.tamagawa.jp/

introduction/press; f. 1929; education, philosophy, religion, arts, juvenile, area studies; Pres. YOSHIAKI OBARA.

Tankosha Publishing Co Ltd: 19-1, Miyanishi-cho Murasakino, Kita-ku, Kyoto 603-8691; tel. (75) 432-5151; fax (75) 432-5152; e-mail info@tankosha.co.jp; internet www.tankosha.co.jp; f. 1949; tea ceremony, fine arts, history; Pres. YOSHITO NAYA.

Teikoku-Shoin Co Ltd: 3-29, Kanda Jimbo-cho, Chiyoda-ku, Tokyo 101-0051; tel. (3) 3262-0834; fax (3) 3262-7770; e-mail kenkyu@teikokushoin.co.jp; internet www.teikokushoin.co.jp; f. 1926; geography, atlases, maps, textbooks, history, civil studies; Pres. MASAYOSHI SAITO.

Tohoku University Press, Sendai: 2-1-1, Katahira, Aoba-ku, Sendai 980-8577; tel. (22) 214-2777; fax (22) 214-2778; e-mail info@tups.jp; internet www.tups.jp; f. 1996; natural and social sciences, humanities, history, literature, psychology, philosophy, art, language; Chair. SHIGERU HISAMICHI.

Tokai University Press: 3-10-35, Minami-Yana, Hadano-shi, Kanagawa 257-0003; tel. (463) 79-3921; fax (463) 69-5087; e-mail webmaster@press.tokai.ac.jp; internet www.press.tokai.ac.jp; f. 1962; social sciences, cultural science, natural sciences, engineering, art; Pres. TATSURO MATSUMAE.

Tokuma Shoten Publishing Co Ltd: 2-2-1, Shiba-Daimon, Minato-ku, Tokyo 105-8055; tel. (3) 5403-4300; fax (3) 5403-4375; e-mail takeuti@shoten.tokuma.com; internet www.tokuma.jp; f. 1954; Japanese classics, history, fiction, juvenile; Pres. TORU IWABUCHI.

Tokyo News Service Ltd: Hamarikyu Park Side Place Bldg, 7-16-3, Tsukiji, Chuo-ku, Tokyo 104-8415; tel. (3) 6367-8000; fax (3) 3545-3628; internet www.tokyonews.co.jp; f. 1947; shipping, trade and television guides; Pres. T. OKUYAMA.

Tokyo Shoseki Co Ltd: 2-17-1, Horifune, Kita-ku, Tokyo 114-8524; tel. (3) 5390-7513; fax (3) 5390-7409; e-mail shoseki@tokyo-shoseki.co.jp; internet www.tokyo-shoseki.co.jp; f. 1909; textbooks, reference books, cultural and educational books; Pres. YASUNORI KAWABATA.

Tokyo Sogen-Sha Co Ltd: 1-5, Shin-Ogawa-machi, Shinjuku-ku, Tokyo 162-0814; tel. (3) 3268-8201; fax (3) 3268-8230; internet www.tsogen.co.jp; f. 1954; mystery and detective stories, science fiction, literature; Pres. SHINICHI HASEGAWA.

Toyo Keizai Inc: 1-2-1, Nihonbashi Hongoku-cho, Chuoku, Tokyo 103-8345; tel. (3) 3246-5551; fax (3) 3279-0332; e-mail info@toyokeizai.co.jp; internet toyokeizai.net; f. 1895; periodicals, economics, business, finance, corporation information; Pres. YUICHIRO YAMAGATA.

Tuttle Publishing Co Inc: Yaekari Bldg, 3/F, 5-4-12, Osaki Shinagawa-ku, Tokyo; tel. (3) 5437-0171; fax (3) 5437-0755; e-mail customer@tuttle.co.jp; internet www.tuttle.co.jp; f. 1948; Japanese and Asian religion, history, social sciences, arts, languages, literature, juvenile, cookery; Pres. ERIC OEY.

United Nations University Press: 5-53-70, Jingumae, Shibuya-ku, Tokyo 150-8925; tel. (3) 5467-1212; fax (3) 3499-2828; e-mail sales@hq.unu.edu; internet www.unu.edu; f. 1975; social sciences, humanities, pure and applied natural sciences; Head KONRAD OSTERWALDER.

University of Nagoya Press: 1, Furocho, Chikusa-ku, Nagoya 464-0814; tel. (52) 781-5027; fax (52) 781-0697; e-mail sogo@unp.nagoya-u.ac.jp; internet www.unp.or.jp; f. 1982; social sciences, humanities, natural sciences, medicine; Chair. MITSUKI ISHII.

University of Tokyo Press: 7-3-1, Hongo, Bunkyo-ku, Tokyo 113-8654; tel. (3) 3811-0964; fax (3) 3815-1426; e-mail info@utp.or.jp; internet www.utp.or.jp; f. 1951; natural and social sciences, humanities; Japanese and English; Chair. HIROSHI WATANABE.

Waseda University Press: 1-9-12-402, Shinjuku-ku, Tokyo 169-0071; tel. (3) 3203-1551; fax (3) 3207-0406; e-mail shuppanbu@list.waseda.jp; internet www.waseda-up.co.jp; f. 1886; politics, economics, law, sociology, philosophy, literature, education, business, drama, journalism; Pres. YOICHI SHIMADA.

Yama-Kei Publishers Co Ltd: Tokyo; tel. (3) 6744-1900; fax (3) 6234-1628; e-mail info@yamakei.co.jp; internet www.yamakei.co.jp; f. 1930; natural sciences, geography, mountaineering, outdoor activities; Pres. SEKIMOTO CHANGDA.

Yoshikawa Kobunkan: 7-2-8, Hongo, Bunkyo-ku, Tokyo 113-0033; tel. (3) 3813-9151; fax (3) 3812-3544; e-mail hongo@yoshikawa-k.co.jp; internet www.yoshikawa-k.co.jp; f. 1857; history, biography, art, languages, religion; Pres. MOTOYASU MAEDA.

Yuhikaku Publishing Co Ltd: 2-17, Kanda Jimbo-cho, Chiyoda-ku, Tokyo 101-0051; tel. (3) 3264-1312; fax (3) 3264-5030; e-mail shinsuke-ito@yuhikaku.co.jp; internet www.yuhikaku.co.jp; f. 1877; social sciences, law, economics; Pres. SADAHARU EGUSA.

Yuki Shobo: 3-7-9, Kudan-Minami, Chiyoda-ku, Tokyo 102-0074; tel. (3) 5275-8008; fax (3) 5275-8099; e-mail takeshi.nanri@yukishobo.co.jp; internet www.yukishobo.co.jp; f. 1957; home economics, juvenile, recreation, sociology, sports; Pres. MASAO OKAJIMA.

Yuzankaku Shuppan: 2-6-9, Fujimi, Chiyoda-ku, Tokyo 102-0071; tel. (3) 3262-3231; fax (3) 3262-6938; e-mail info@yuzankaku.co.jp; internet www.yuzankaku.co.jp; f. 1916; history, fine arts, religion, archaeology; Pres. TETSUO MIYATA.

Zen-on Music Co Ltd: 2-13-3, Kami-Ochiai, Shinjuku-ku, Tokyo 161-0034; tel. (3) 3227-6270; fax (3) 3227-6276; e-mail akira@zen-on.co.jp; internet www.zen-on.co.jp; f. 1931; classics, pop, books on music; Pres. NORIYUKI HONMA.

Zoshindo Juken Kenkyusha Co Ltd: 2-19-15, Shinmachi, Nishi-ku, Osaka 550-0013; tel. (6) 6532-1581; fax (6) 6532-1588; e-mail jzoshindo@ybb.ne.jp; internet www.zoshindo.co.jp; f. 1890; educational, juvenile; Pres. AKITAKA OKAMATO.

GOVERNMENT PUBLISHING HOUSE

Government Publications' Service Centre: 1-2-1, Kasumigaseki, Chiyoda-ku, Tokyo 100-0013; tel. (3) 3504-3885; fax (3) 3504-3889.

PUBLISHERS' ASSOCIATIONS

Japan Book Publishers Association: 6, Fukuro-machi, Shinjuku-ku, Tokyo 162-0828; tel. (3) 3268-1302; fax (3) 3268-1196; e-mail rd@jbpa.or.jp; internet www.jbpa.or.jp; f. 1957; 459 mems (2010); Pres. MASAHIRO OGA; Exec. Dir TADASHI YAMASHITA.

Publishers' Association for Cultural Exchange, Japan: 1-2-1, Sarugaku-cho, Chiyoda-ku, Tokyo 101-0064; tel. (3) 3291-5685; fax (3) 3233-3645; e-mail culturalexchange@pace.or.jp; internet www.pace.or.jp; f. 1953; 75 mems (2010); Pres. TADATAKA EGUSA; Man. Dir HARUHIKO ISHIKAWA.

Broadcasting and Communications

Telecommunications and broadcasting are regulated by the Ministry of Internal Affairs and Communications.

TELECOMMUNICATIONS

EMOBILE Ltd: Shin-Nikko Bldg, 2-10-1, Toranomon, Minato-ku, Tokyo; tel. (3) 3588-7682; fax (3) 3588-7201; internet www.emobile.jp; f. 2005; owned by eAccess Ltd; mobile voice and data services; Pres. ERIC GAN.

KDDI Corpn: Garden Air Tower, 3-10-10, Iidabashi, Chiyoda-ku, Tokyo 102-8460; tel. (3) 3347-0077; fax (3) 6678-0305; internet www.kddi.com; f. 1984; est. by merger of DDI Corpn, Kokusai Denshin Denwa Corpn (KDD) and Nippon Idou Tsuhin Corpn (IDO); major international telecommunications carrier; Pres. TADASHI ONODERA.

Livedoor Co Ltd: Roppongi Hills Mori Tower, 38/F, 6-10-1, Roppongi, Minato-ku, Tokyo; tel. (3) 5155-0121; fax (3) 5766-7221; e-mail info@livedoor.jp; internet www.livedoor.com; f. 1996; acquired by NHN Japan in 2010; internet portal; network operations and maintenance; Pres. TAKESHI IDEZAWA.

NEC Biglobe: 1-11-1, Osaki, Shinagawa-ku, Tokyo 141-0032; internet www.jpn.nec.com; f. 2006; provides internet and other information services; part of the NEC Group; Pres. YOSHIYUKI KOSEKI.

Nippon Telegraph and Telephone Corpn (NTT): 2-3-1, Otemachi, Chiyoda-ku, Tokyo 100-8116; tel. (3) 5205-5111; fax (3) 5205-5589; internet www.ntt.co.jp; f. 1985; operates local, long-distance and international services; largest telecommunications co in Japan; holding co for NTT East, NTT West, NTT Communications, NTT Data Corpn and NTT DOCOMO; Pres. and CEO SATOSHI MIURA.

NTT DOCOMO: 2-11-1, Nagatacho, Chiyoda-ku, Tokyo 100-6150; tel. (3) 5156-1111; fax (3) 5156-0271; internet www.nttdocomo.co.jp; f. 1991; operates mobile telephone network; Pres. and CEO RYUJI YAMADA.

SoftBank Telecom Corpn: 1-9-1, Higashi-Shimbashi, Minato-ku, Tokyo 105-7316; tel. 0088-41; e-mail tcsc@tm.softbank.co.jp; internet www.softbanktelecom.co.jp; fmrly Japan Telecom; fixed-line business acquired by Ripplewood Holdings in 2003; acquired by SoftBank Corpn in 2004; merged with International Digital Communications (IDC) in 2005; name changed as above in 2006; Chair. and CEO MASAYOSHI SON.

Digital Phone and Digital TU-KA also operate mobile telecommunication services in Japan.

BROADCASTING

NHK (Japan Broadcasting Corporation): 2-2-1, Jinnan, Shibuya-ku, Tokyo 150-8001; tel. (3) 3465-1111; fax (3) 3469-8110; e-mail webmaster@www.nhk.or.jp; internet www.nhk.or.jp; f. 1925; fmrly Nippon Hoso Kyokai (NHK—Japan Broadcasting Corpn); Japan's sole public broadcaster; operates 5 TV channels (incl. 2 terrestrial services—general TV and educational TV, and 3 satellite services—BS-1, BS-2 and digital Hi-Vision—HDTV), 3 radio channels, Radio 1,

Radio 2, and FM Radio, and 3 worldwide services, NHK World TV, NHK World Premium and NHK World Radio Japan; headquarters in Tokyo, regional headquarters in Osaka, Nagoya, Hiroshima, Fukuoka, Sendai, Sapporo and Matsuyama; Pres. KATSUTO MOMII; Exec. Dir-Gen. of Broadcasting HIDEMI HYUGA.

National Association of Commercial Broadcasters in Japan (NAB-J): 3-23, Kioi-cho, Chiyoda-ku, Tokyo 102-8577; tel. (3) 5213-7711; fax (3) 5213-7730; e-mail webmaster@nab.or.jp; internet www.nab.or.jp; f. 1951; includes 133 TV cos and 110 radio cos, of which 42 operate both radio and TV, with 664 radio stations and 8,315 TV stations (incl. relay stations); Pres. MICHISADA HIROSE; Exec. Dir TOSHIO FUKUDA.

Some of the most important companies are:

Asahi Hoso—Asahi Broadcasting Corpn: 1-1-30, Fukushima, Fukushima-ku, Osaka 553-8503; tel. (6) 6458-5321; internet www.asahi.co.jp; f. 1951; Pres. SATOSHI WAKISAKA.

Bunka Hoso—Nippon Cultural Broadcasting, Inc: 1-31, Hamamatsu-cho, Minato-ku, Tokyo 105-8002; tel. (3) 5403-1111; internet www.joqr.co.jp; f. 1952; Pres. MIKI AKIHIRO.

Chubu-Nippon Broadcasting Co Ltd: 1-2-8, Shinsakae, Naka-ku, Nagoya 460-8405; tel. (052) 241-8111; internet hicbc.com; f. 1950; Pres. YOICHI OISHI.

Fuji Television Network, Inc: 2-4-8, Daiba, Minato-ku, Tokyo 137-8088; tel. (3) 5500-8888; fax (3) 5500-8027; internet www.fujitv.co.jp; f. 1959; owns Nippon Broadcasting System, Inc; 12.75% stake in internet provider Livedoor; Chair. and CEO HISASHI HIEDA; Pres. KOU TOYODA.

Kansai TV Hoso (KTV)—Kansai Telecasting Corpn: 2-1-7, Ogimachi, Kita-ku, Osaka 530-8408; tel. (6) 6314-8888; internet www.ktv.co.jp; f. 1958; Pres. SUMIO FUKUI.

Mainichi Hoso (MBS)—Mainichi Broadcasting System, Inc: 17-1, Chayamachi, Kita-ku, Osaka 530-8304; tel. (6) 6359-1123; fax (6) 6359-3503; internet www.mbs.jp; f. 1950; Pres. MASAHIRO YAMAMOTO.

Nippon Hoso—Nippon Broadcasting System, Inc: 2-4-8, Daiba, Minato-ku, Tokyo 137-8686; tel. (3) 5500-1234; fax (3) 5500-3902; e-mail saiyo2013@jolf.jp; internet www.jolf.co.jp; f. 1954; 49.8% controlling stake acquired by Livedoor Co Ltd in 2005, but subsequently purchased by Fuji TV Network, Inc; Pres. AKINOBU KAMEBUCHI.

Nippon TV Hoso-MO (NTV)—Nippon Television Network Corpn: 1-6-1, Higashi-Shimbashi, Minato-ku, Tokyo 105-7444; tel. (3) 6215-1111; fax (3) 6215-3157; internet www.ntv.co.jp; f. 1953; Chair. NORITADA HOSOKAWA; Pres. YOSHIO OKUBO.

Okinawa TV Hoso (OTV)—Okinawa Television Broadcasting Co Ltd: 1-2-20, Kumoji, Naha 900-8588; tel. (988) 63-2111; fax (988) 61-0193; e-mail otvweb@otv.co.jp; internet www.otv.co.jp; f. 1959; Pres. BUNKI TOMA.

Radio Nikkei: 1-9-15, Akasaka, Minato-ku, Tokyo 107-8373; tel. (3) 3583-8151; fax (3) 3583-9062; internet www.radionikkei.jp; f. 1954; Pres. KENJI SUZUKI.

Ryukyu Hoso (RBC)—Ryukyu Broadcasting Co: 2-3-1, Kumoji, Naha 900-8711; tel. (98) 867-2151; fax (98) 864-5732; e-mail info@rbc.co.jp; internet www.rbc.co.jp; f. 1954.

Tokyo Hoso (TBS)—Tokyo Broadcasting System Holdings Inc: 5-3-6, Akasaka, Minato-ku, Tokyo 107-8006; tel. (3) 3746-1111; fax (3) 3588-6378; internet www.tbs.co.jp; f. 1951; Chair. HIROSHI INOUE; Pres. TOSHICHIKA ISHIHARA.

TV Asahi Corpn: 6-9-1, Roppongi, Minato-ku, Tokyo 106-8001; tel. (3) 6406-1111; fax (3) 3405-3714; internet www.tv-asahi.co.jp; f. 1957; Pres. HIROSHI HAYAKAWA.

TV Osaka (TVO)—Television Osaka, Inc: 1-2-18, Otemae, Chuo-ku, Osaka 540-8519; tel. (6) 6947-7777; fax (6) 6946-9796; e-mail takoru@tv-osaka.co.jp; internet www.tv-osaka.co.jp; f. 1982; Pres. MAKOTO FUKAGAWA.

TV Tokyo Corpn: 4-3-12, Toranomon, Minato-ku, Tokyo 105-8012; tel. (3) 5470-7777; fax (3) 5473-6393; internet www.tv-tokyo.co.jp; f. 1964; Pres. and CEO MASAYUKI SHIMADA.

Yomiuri TV Hoso (YTV)—Yomiuri Telecasting Corporation: 2-2-33, Shiromi, Chuo-ku, Osaka 540-8510; tel. (6) 6947-2111; e-mail licensing@ytv.co.jp; internet www.ytv.co.jp; f. 1958; 20 hrs broadcasting daily; Pres. KOJI TAKADA.

Satellite, Cable and Digital Television

In addition to the two broadcast satellite services that NHK introduced in 1989, a number of commercial satellite stations are in operation. Cable television is available in urban areas. Satellite digital television services first became available in 1996. Terrestrial digital broadcasting was launched in December 2003. The switch from analogue to digital services was completed in July 2011.

SKY Perfect JSAT Corp: 1-4-14, Akasaka, Minato-ku, Tokyo 107-0052; tel. (3) 5571-7800; internet www.sptvjsat.com; f. 1994; Chair. SHIGEKI NISHIYAMA; Pres. SHINJI TAKADA.

Finance

(cap. = capital; p.u. = paid up; res = reserves; dep. = deposits; m. = million; brs = branches; amounts in yen)

BANKING

Japan's central bank and bank of issue is the Bank of Japan. At March 2010 there were 201 banks in the country, including five major commercial banks, 16 trust banks and 64 regional banks.

An important financial role is played by co-operatives and by the many small enterprise institutions. There are also two types of private financial institutions for small business. At August 2005 there were 175 Credit Co-operatives and at March 2010 there were 271 Shinkin Banks (credit associations), which lend only to members. The latter also receive deposits.

The most popular form of savings is through the post office network. In October 2005 legislation was approved to permit the privatization of Japan Post. Following its transfer to a holding company, Japan Post was divided into four units (savings, insurance and postal services, along with personnel and property management). Having been established in September 2006, the Japan Post Bank (JPB) commenced operations on 1 October 2007. The JPB thus became the world's largest financial institution in terms of deposits; it is also the largest provider of life insurance.

Central Bank

Nippon Ginko (Bank of Japan): 2-1-1, Motoishi-cho, Nihonbashi, Chuo-ku, Tokyo 103-0021; tel. (3) 3279-1111; fax (3) 5200-2256; e-mail prdmail@boj.or.jp; internet www.boj.or.jp; f. 1882; cap. 100m., res 2,660,006m., dep. 38,168,703m. (March 2010); Gov. HARUHIKO KURODA; Dep. Govs HIROSHI NAKASO, KIKUO OWATA; 32 brs.

Principal Commercial Banks

Asahi Shinkin Bank: 2-1-2, Higashi-Kanda, Chiyoda-ku, Tokyo 101-0031; tel. (3) 3862-0321; fax (3) 5687-6867; internet www.asahi-shinkin.co.jp; f. 1923; est. as Shinyo Kumiai Tomin Kinko; name changed as above after merger in 2002; cap. 22,048m., res 32,805m., dep. 1,692,300m. (March 2012); Chair. KUNITAKE MORIWAKI; Pres. KAZUO KOBAYASHI; 62 brs.

Ashikaga Bank Ltd: 4-1-25, Sakura, Utsunomiya, Tochigi 320-8610; tel. (28) 622-0111; e-mail ashigin@ssctnet.or.jp; internet www.ashikagabank.co.jp; f. 1895; nationalized Nov. 2003 owing to insolvency; cap. 135,000m., res 13,067m., dep. 4,807,955m. (March 2012); CEO SATOSHI FUJISAWA; 150 brs.

Bank of Fukuoka Ltd: 2-13-1, Tenjin, Chuo-ku, Fukuoka 810-8727; tel. (92) 723-2442; fax (92) 711-1371; internet www.fukuokabank.co.jp; f. 1945; cap. 82,329m., res 137,125m., dep. 7,991,413m. (March 2011); Chair. and Pres. MASAAKI TANI; 166 brs.

Bank of Tokyo-Mitsubishi UFJ Ltd: 2-7-1, Marunouchi, Chiyoda-ku, Tokyo 100-8388; tel. (3) 3240-1111; fax (3) 3240-4197; internet www.bk.mufg.jp; f. 2006; est. through merger of Bank of Tokyo-Mitsubishi Ltd and UFJ Bank Ltd; specializes in international banking and financial business; subsidiary of Mitsubishi UFJ Financial Group (f. 2005 through merger of Mitsubishi Tokyo Financial Group and UFJ Holdings); cap. 1,711,958m., res 4,369,110m., dep. 116,239,242m. (March 2012); Pres. NOBUYUKI HIRANO; 841 brs (767 domestic, 74 overseas).

Bank of Yokohama Ltd: 3-1-1, Minatomirai, Nishi-ku, Yokohama, Kanagawa 220-8611; tel. (45) 225-1111; fax (45) 225-1160; e-mail iroffice@hamagin.co.jp; internet www.boy.co.jp; f. 1920; cap. 215,628m., res 227,524m., dep. 11,089,041m. (March 2012); Chair. TADASHI OGAWA; Pres. TATSUMARO TERAZAWA; 197 brs (196 domestic, 1 overseas).

Chiba Bank Ltd: 1-2, Chiba-minato, Chuo-ku, Chiba 260-8720; tel. (43) 245-1111; fax (43) 242-9121; e-mail int@chibabank.co.jp; internet www.chibabank.co.jp; f. 1943; cap. 145,069m., res 136,457m., dep. 9,639,615m. (March 2012); Pres. HIDETOSHI SAKUMA; 156 domestic brs, 3 overseas brs.

Chiba Kogyo Bank Ltd: 2-1-2, Saiwa-cho, Mihama-ku, Chiba; tel. (43) 243-2111; fax (43) 244-9203; internet www.chibakogyo-bank.co.jp; f. 1952; cap. 57,941m., res 33,400m., dep. 2,116,586m. (March 2012); Pres. and CEO SHUNICHI AOYAGI; 71 brs.

Hachijuni Bank: 178-8, Okada, Nagano-shi, Nagano 380-8682; tel. (26) 227-1182; fax (26) 226-5077; internet www.82bank.co.jp; f. 1931; cap. 52,243m., res 90,889m., dep. 5,725,089m. (March 2012); Chair. YOSHIYUKI YAMAURA; Pres. SHOICHI YUMOTO; 156 brs (155 domestic, 1 overseas).

Hokkaido Bank Ltd: 4-1, Nishi-Odori, Chuo-ku, Sapporo 060-8678, Hokkaido; tel. (11) 233-1093; fax (11) 231-3133; internet www.hokkaidobank.co.jp; f. 1951; cap. 93,524m., res 27,223m., dep. 4,155,748m. (March 2012); Pres. YOSHIHIRO SEKIHACHI; 139 brs.

Hokkoku Bank Ltd: 1 Shimotsutsumi-cho, Kanazawa 920-8670, Ishikawa; tel. (76) 263-1111; fax (76) 223-3362; internet www.hokkokubank.co.jp; f. 1943; cap. 26,673m., res 42,552m., dep. 3,096,757m. (March 2012); Pres. TATEKI ATAKA; 112 brs.

Hokuetsu Bank Ltd: 2-2-14, Otedori, Nagaoka 940-8650, Niigata; tel. (258) 353-111; fax (258) 375-113; internet www.hokuetsubank.co.jp; f. 1942; cap. 24,538m., res 29,329m., dep. 2,157,929m. (March 2012); Pres. SATORU ARAKI; 89 brs.

Hokuriku Bank Ltd: 1-2-26, Tsutsumichodori, Toyama 930-8637; tel. (76) 423-7111; fax (76) 491-5908; e-mail info@hokuhoku-fg.co.jp; internet www.hokugin.co.jp; f. 1877; cap. 140,409m., res 45,333m., dep. 5,545,101m. (March 2012); Pres. EISHIN IHORI; 188 brs.

Hokuto Bank Ltd: 3-1-41, Nakadori, Akita 010-0001; tel. (18) 833-4211; fax (18) 832-1942; e-mail hokutobank@hokutobank.co.jp; internet www.hokutobank.co.jp; f. 1895; est. as Masuda Bank Ltd, name changed as above after merger with Akita Akebono Bank in 1993; cap. 11,000m., res 23,085m., dep. 1,115,137m. (March 2012); Pres. TAKEO KAGAYA; 84 brs.

Japan Net Bank: 2-1-1, Nishi-Shinjuku, Shinjuku-ku, Tokyo 163-0406; tel. (3) 6739-5000; internet www.japannetbank.co.jp; f. 2000; Japan's first internet-only bank; cap. 37,250m., res 4,393m., dep. 494,419m. (March 2012); Pres. YOSHIYUKI MIYAI.

Joyo Bank Ltd: 2-5-5, Minami-Machi, Mito-shi, Ibaraki 310-0021; tel. (29) 231-2151; fax (29) 255-6522; e-mail joyointl@po.net-ibaraki.ne.jp; internet www.joyobank.co.jp; f. 1935; cap. 85,113m., res 83,703m., dep. 7,277,708m. (March 2012); Chair. KUNIO ONIZAWA; Pres. KAZUYOSHI TERAKADO; 172 brs.

Juroku Bank Ltd: 8-26, Kandamachi, Gifu 500-8516; tel. (582) 652-111; fax (582) 661-698; internet www.juroku.co.jp; f. 1877; cap. 36,839m., res 65,418m., dep. 4,889,423m. (March 2012); Pres. HAKUMI HORIE; 149 brs.

Kansai Urban Banking Corpn: 1-2-4, Nishi-Shinbashi, Chuo-ku, Osaka; tel. (6) 6834-4581; internet www.kansaiurban.co.jp; f. 1922; cap. 470,039m., res 64,400m., dep. 3,945,438m. (March 2012); Chair. and CEO AKIRA KITAMURA; Pres. KOJI KITA; 147 brs.

Kumamoto Family Bank Ltd: 6-29-20, Suizenji, Kumamoto 862-8601; tel. (96) 385-1111; fax (96) 385-4272; internet www.kf-bank.jp; f. 1992; cap. 33,847m., res 35,097m., dep. 1,095,663m. (March 2011); Pres. KENJI HAYASHI.

Miyazaki Bank Ltd: 4-3-5, Tachibanadori-Higashi, Miyazaki 880-0805; tel. (985) 273-131; fax (985) 225-952; e-mail kokusai@miyagin.co.jp; internet www.miyagin.co.jp; f. 1932; cap. 14,697m., res 20,238m., dep. 1,914,863m. (March 2012); Pres. KOICHI KOIKE; 97 brs.

Mizuho Bank Ltd: 1-3-3, Marunouchi, Chiyoda-ku, Tokyo 100-8210; tel. (3) 3596-1111; fax (3) 3596-2179; internet www.mizuhobank.co.jp; f. 1971 as Dai-Ichi Kangyo Bank; merged with Fuji Bank and Industrial Bank of Japan in 2002; merged with Mizuho Corporate Bank Ltd in July 2013; cap. 1,404,065m., res 1,225,839m., dep. 29,608,085m. (March 2012); Pres. and CEO YASUHIRO SATO; 334 domestic brs, 17 overseas brs.

North Pacific Bank (Hokuyo Bank): 3-7, Nishi-Odori, Chuo-ku, Sapporo 060-8661; tel. (11) 261-1416; fax (11) 232-6921; internet www.hokuyobank.co.jp; f. 1917; est. as Hokuyo Sogo Bank Ltd; adopted present name 1989; cap. 121,101m., res 131,934m., dep. 7,128,750m. (March 2012); Chair. RYUZO YOKOUCHI; Pres. JUNJI ISHII.

Resona Bank Ltd: 2-2-1, Bingo-machi, Chuo-ku, Osaka 540-8610; tel. (6) 6271-1221; internet www.resona-gr.co.jp; f. 1918; merged with Asahi Bank in 2002 and changed name as above; cap. 279,928m., res 633,189m., dep. 22,909,218m. (March 2013); Pres. KAZUHIRO HIGASHI; 339 brs.

Saitama Resona Bank Ltd: 7-4-1, Tokiwa, Urawa-ku, Saitama 330-9088; tel. (48) 824-2411; internet www.resona-gr.co.jp/saitamaresona; f. 2002; cap. 70,000m., res 129,350m., dep. 10,642,545m. (March 2012); Pres. MASAHITO KAMIJO.

San-in Godo Bank Ltd: 10, Uomachi, Matsue, Shimane 690-0062; tel. (852) 551-000; fax (852) 273-398; e-mail soki@gogin.co.jp; internet www.gogin.co.jp; f. 1941; cap. 20,705m., res 54,422m., dep. 3,585,898m. (March 2012); Pres. ICHIRO KUBOTA; Chair. MAKOTO FURUSE; 145 brs.

The Senshu Ikeda Bank Ltd: 18-14, Kita-ku, Osaka Chayamachi; tel. (6) 6375-1005; internet www.sihd-bk.jp; cap. 50,710m., res 82,038m., dep. 4,424,910m. (March 2012); Chair. KAZUYUKI KATAOKA; Pres. HIROHISA FUJITA.

Shiga Bank Ltd: 1-38, Hamamachi, Otsu 520-8686, Shiga; tel. (77) 521-2360; fax (77) 521-2892; internet www.shigagin.com; f. 1933; cap. 33,076m., res 77,403m., dep. 4,089,983m. (March 2012); Chair. KOICHI TAKATA; Pres. YOSHIO DAIDO; 134 domestic brs, 1 overseas.

Shikoku Bank Ltd: 1–1–1, Minami-Harimaya-cho, Kochi 780-8605; tel. (88) 823-2111; fax (88) 873-0322; internet www.shikokubank.co.jp; f. 1873; cap. 25,000m., res 26,178m., dep. 2,401,728m. (March 2012); Chair. AKIHIRO AOKI; Pres. TADASHI NOMURA; 112 brs.

Shimizu Bank: 2-1, Fujimi-cho, Shimizu-ku, Shozuoka-shi, Shizuoka 424-0941; tel. (543) 535-151; fax (543) 636-776; internet www.shimizubank.co.jp; f. 1928; cap. 8,670m., res 6,605m., dep. 1,305,199m. (March 2012); Chair. NORIJI YAMADA; Pres. KATSUICHIRO TOYOSHIMA; 77 brs.

Shizuoka Bank Ltd: 1-10, Gofuku-cho, Aoi-ku, Shizuoka 420-8761; tel. (54) 345-5700; fax (54) 349-5501; internet www.shizuokabank.co.jp; f. 1943; cap. 90,845m., res 116,717m., dep. 8,080,087m. (March 2012); Chair. SEIYA ITO; Pres. and CEO KATSUNORI NAKANISHI; 168 domestic brs, 3 overseas brs.

Toho Bank Ltd: 3-25, Ohmachi, Fukushima 960-8633; tel. (24) 523-3131; fax (24) 524-1583; internet www.tohobank.co.jp; f. 1941; cap. 23,519m., res 19,584m., dep. 4,033,235m. (March 2012); Chair. TOSHIO SEYA; Pres. SEISHI KITAMURA; 113 brs.

Tokyo Star Bank: 2-3-5 Akasaka, Minato-ku, Tokyo; tel. (3) 3586-3111; fax (3) 3586-5137; internet www.tokyostarbank.co.jp; f. 2001; est. as Nippon Finance Investment Ltd, name changed as above in May 2001; cap. 26,000m., res 27,570m., dep. 2,069,960m. (March 2012); Chair. YASUMINE SATAKE; Pres. MASARU IRIE; 31 brs.

Tokyo Tomin Bank Ltd: 2-3-11, Roppongi, Minato-ku, Tokyo 106-8525; tel. (3) 3582-8251; fax (3) 3582-1979; e-mail jdu02670@nifty.ne.jp; internet www.tominbank.co.jp; f. 1951; cap. 48,120m., res 17,805m., dep. 2,355,069m. (March 2013); Chair. TETSUYA SHIINA; Pres. ISAO KOBAYASHI; 72 brs.

Tomato Bank Ltd: 2-3-4, Bancho, Okayama 700-0811, Ehime; tel. (86) 221-1010; fax (86) 221-1040; internet www.tomatobank.co.jp; f. 1931; est. as Sanyo Sogo Bank; became a commercial bank in 1989, when present name was assumed; cap. 14,310m., res 14,389m., dep. 892,003m. (March 2012); Pres. TAKANOBU NAKAGAWA; 60 brs.

Tsukuba Bank Ltd: 2-11-7, Chuo-ku, Tsuchiura, Ibaraki 305-0032; tel. (29) 859-8111; internet www.tsukubabank.co.jp; f. 1952; cap. 48,868m., res 28,615m., dep. 2,001,931m. (March 2012); Chair. KOZO KIMURA; 147 brs.

Principal Trust Banks

Mitsubishi UFJ Trust and Banking Corporation: 1-4-5, Marunouchi, Chiyoda-ku, Tokyo 100-8212; tel. (3) 3212-1211; fax (3) 3514-6660; internet www.tr.mufg.jp; f. 2005; est. upon merger of Mitsubishi Tokyo Financial Group and UFJ Holdings to form Mitsubishi UFJ Financial Group, of which it is a subsidiary; cap. 324,279m., res 886,157m., dep. 17,243,293m. (March 2012); Chair. KINYA OKAUCHI; Pres. TATSUO WAKABAYASHI; 62 domestic brs, 5 overseas brs.

Mizuho Trust and Banking Co Ltd: 1-2-1, Yaesu, Chuo-ku, Tokyo 103-8670; tel. (3) 3278-8111; fax (3) 3274-4670; internet www.mizuho-tb.co.jp; f. 1925; fmrly Yasuda Trust and Banking Co Ltd; cap. 247,303m., res 30,403m., dep. 3,372,235m. (March 2011); Pres. and CEO TAKASHI NONAKA; 36 brs.

Sumitomo Mitsui Trust Bank Ltd: 1-4-1, Marunouchi, Chiyoda-ku, Tokyo 100-8233; internet www.smtb.jp; f. 1925; present name adopted following merger with Sakura Bank Ltd in 2001; wholly owned subsidiary of Sumitomo Mitsui Financial Group (SMFG—f. 2002); cap. 342,037m., res 300,102m., dep. 16,350,030m. (March 2012); Chair. KUNITARO KITAMURA; Pres. HITOSHI TSUNEKAGE; 118 domestic brs, 4 overseas brs.

Long-Term Credit Banks

Aozora Bank: 1-3-1, Kudan-Minami, Chiyoda-ku, Tokyo 102-8660; tel. (3) 3263-1111; fax (3) 3265-7024; e-mail sora@aozora.co.jp; internet www.aozorabank.co.jp; f. 1957; nationalized Dec. 1998, sold to consortium led by Softbank Corpn in Aug. 2000; fmrly The Nippon Credit Bank, name changed as above 2001; 62% owned by Cerberus Group; cap. 419,780m., res 13,505m., dep. 3,062,459m. (March 2012); Pres. and CEO SHINSUKE BABA; Chair. BRIAN PRINCE; 19 brs.

Shinsei Bank Ltd: 2-4-3, Nihonbashi-muromachi, Chuo-ku, Tokyo 103-8303; tel. (3) 6680-7000; internet www.shinseibank.com; f. 1952; est. as The Long-Term Credit Bank of Japan; nationalized Oct. 1998, sold to Ripplewood Holdings (USA), renamed as above June 2000; cap. 512,204m., res –5,287m., dep. 5,475,513m. (March 2012); Pres. and CEO SHIGEKI TOMA; 29 domestic brs, 1 overseas br.

Co-operative Bank

Shinkin Central Bank: 1-3-7, Yaesu, Chuo-ku, Tokyo 103-0028; tel. (3) 5202-7700; fax (3) 3278-7033; e-mail s1000551@facetoface.ne.jp; internet www.shinkin-central-bank.jp; f. 1950; cap. 490,998m., res 182,305m., dep. 22,592,928m. (March 2012); Chair. KOJI OMAE; Pres. and CEO MITSUO TANABE; 14 domestic brs, 4 overseas brs.

Principal Government Institutions

Development Bank of Japan: 1-9-6, Otemachi, Chiyoda-ku, Tokyo 100-8178; tel. (3) 3270-3211; fax (3) 3245-1938; e-mail safukas@dbj.go.jp; internet www.dbj.jp; f. 1951; est. as Japan Devt Bank; renamed Oct. 1999 following consolidation with Hokkaido and Tohoku Devt Finance Public Corpn; provides long-term loans; subscribes for corporate bonds; guarantees corporate obligations; invests in specific projects; borrows funds from Govt and abroad; issues external bonds and notes; provides market information and consulting services for prospective entrants to Japanese market; legislation providing for the bank's privatization (by 2015) approved in 2008; cap. 1,187,788m., res 1,107,342m., dep. 1,856,894m. (March 2012); Pres. and CEO TORU HASHIMOTO; 10 domestic brs, 6 overseas brs.

Japan Finance Corporation (JFC): 1-9-3, Otemachi, Chiyoda-ku, Tokyo 100-0004; internet www.jfc.go.jp; f. 2008; govt financial institution formed from merger of National Life Finance Corpn (NLFC), Agriculture, Forestry and Fisheries Finance Corpn (AFC), Japan Finance Corpn for Small and Medium Enterprise (JASME) and International Finance Operations (IFOs) of Japan Bank for International Cooperation (JBIC); cap. 3,075,700m., res 2,236,200m. (March 2012); Gov. and CEO SHOSAKU YASUI; 152 brs.

Japan Bank for International Cooperation (JBIC): 1-4-1, Otemachi, Chiyoda-ku, Tokyo 100-8144; tel. (3) 5218-3100; fax (3) 5218-3955; e-mail ir@jbic.go.jp; internet www.jbic.go.jp; f. 1999; est. by merger of The Export-Import Bank of Japan (f. 1950) and The Overseas Economic Co-operation Fund (f. 1961); governmental financial institution, responsible for Japan's external economic policy and co-operation activities; cap. 1,291,000m., res 951,272m. (March 2012); Gov. HIROSHI OKUDA.

Japan Post Bank Co Ltd (JPB): 1-3-2, Kasumigaseki, Chiyoda-ku, Tokyo 100-8798; tel. (3) 3504-4436; internet www.jp-bank.japanpost.jp; f. 2006; wholly owned by Japan Post Holdings Co Ltd; cap. 3,500,000m., res 5,167,567m., dep. 175,635,370m. (March 2012); Chair. SEIJIROU ADACHI; Pres. YOSHIYUKI IZAWA.

Norinchukin Bank (Central Co-operative Bank for Agriculture, Forestry and Fisheries): 1-13-2, Yuraku-cho, Chiyoda-ku, Tokyo 100-8420; tel. (3) 3279-0111; fax (3) 3218-5125; internet www.nochubank.or.jp; f. 1923; main banker to agricultural, forestry and fisheries co-operatives; receives deposits from individual co-operatives, federations and agricultural enterprises; extends loans to these and to local govt authorities and public corpns; adjusts excess and shortage of funds within co-operative system; issues debentures, invests funds and engages in other regular banking business; cap. 3,425,909m., res 382,150m., dep. 51,065,358m. (March 2012); Pres. and CEO YOSHIO KONO; 25 domestic brs, 5 overseas brs.

Shoko Chukin Bank (Central Co-operative Bank for Commerce and Industry): 2-10-17, Yaesu, Chuo-ku, Tokyo 104-0028; tel. (3) 3272-6111; fax (3) 3272-6169; e-mail JDK06560@nifty.ne.jp; internet www.shokochukin.co.jp; f. 1936; provides general banking services to facilitate finance for smaller enterprise co-operatives and other organizations formed mainly by small and medium-sized enterprises; issues debentures; began process of privatization in 2008; cap. 218,653m., res 559,102m., dep. 3,862,948m. (March 2012); Pres. TETSUO SEKI; 92 domestic brs, 1 overseas br.

Other government financial institutions include the Japan Finance Corpn for Municipal Enterprises, the Small Business Credit Insurance Corpn and the Okinawa Development Finance Corpn.

Foreign Banks

At March 2010 there were 56 foreign banks operating in Japan.

Bankers' Associations

Japanese Bankers Association: 1-3-1, Marunouchi, Chiyoda-ku, Tokyo 100-8216; tel. (3) 3216-3761; fax (3) 3201-5608; internet www.zenginkyo.or.jp; f. 1945; fmrly Fed. of Bankers Asscns of Japan; merged into Tokyo Bankers Asscn in 2011, new entity renamed as above; 122 full mems, 64 assoc. mems, 59 special mems, 3 bank holding co mems (April 2012); Chair. YASUHIRO SATO.

National Association of Labour Banks: 2-5-15, Kanda Surugadai, Chiyoda-ku, Tokyo 101-0062; tel. (3) 3295-6721; fax (3) 3295-6751; e-mail kikaku@ho.rokinbank.or.jp; internet all.rokin.or.jp; f. 1951; Pres. YASUHIKO OKADA.

Regional Banks Association of Japan: 3-1-2, Uchikanda, Chiyoda-ku, Tokyo 101-8509; tel. (3) 3252-5171; fax (3) 3254-8664; internet www.chiginkyo.or.jp; f. 1936; 64 mem. banks; Chair. HIDETOSHI SAKUMA.

Second Association of Regional Banks: 5, Sanban-cho, Chiyoda-ku, Tokyo 102-8356; tel. (3) 3262-2181; fax (3) 3262-2339; e-mail hp-master@dainichiginkyo.or.jp; internet www.dainichiginkyo.or.jp; f. 1989; fmrly Nat. Asscn of Sogo Banks; 42 commercial banks; Chair. NOBUO KOJIMA.

STOCK EXCHANGES

Nagoya Stock Exchange: 3-8-20, Sakae, Naka-ku, Nagoya 460-0008; tel. (52) 262-3172; fax (52) 241-1527; e-mail kikaku@nse.or.jp; internet www.nse.or.jp; f. 1949; Pres. NOBORU KUROYANAGI; Exec. Vice-Pres. MASAKI TAKEDA.

Osaka Securities Exchange (OSE): 1-8-16, Kitahama, Chuo-ku, Osaka 541-0041; tel. (6) 4706-0875; fax (6) 6231-2639; e-mail koho@ose.or.jp; internet www.ose.or.jp; f. 1949; 83 regular transaction partners, 5 transaction partners in futures and options trading, 2 IPO transaction partners; Pres. and CEO MICHIO YONEDA.

Jasdaq: 1-5-8, Nihonbashi Kayaba-cho, Chuo-ku, Tokyo 103-0025; tel. (3) 3669-5410; internet www.ose.or.jp/e/jasdaq; f. 1963; became wholly owned subsidiary of Osaka Securities Exchange 2009; resumed operations following merger of smaller markets, Jasdaq, Hercules and NEO in 2010; over 1,400 listed cos.

Sapporo Securities Exchange: 5-14-1, Nishi, Minami 1-jo, Chuo-ku, Sapporo 060-0061; tel. (11) 241-6171; fax (11) 251-0840; e-mail info@sse.or.jp; internet www.sse.or.jp; 75 listed cos; Pres. YOSHIRO ITOH.

SBI Japannext Co Ltd: 1-1-1, Hirakawacho Court, Hirakawacho, Chiyoda-ku, Tokyo, 102-0093; tel. (3) 4577-4040; fax (3) 3261-1702; e-mail ptsbiz@japannext.co.jp; internet en.japannext.co.jp; Co-CEOs CHUCK CHON, MASAMI HATAKEYAMA.

Tokyo Stock Exchange, Inc: 2-1, Nihonbashi Kabuto-cho, Chuo-ku, Tokyo 103-8224; tel. (3) 3665-1881; fax (3) 3662-0547; internet www.tse.or.jp; f. 1949; 97 general trading participants, 56 bond futures trading participants, 2 stock index futures trading participants; cap. 11,500m., issued shares 2,300,000 (June 2010); Chair. TAIZO NISHIMURO; Pres. and CEO ATSUSHI SAITO.

Supervisory Body

Securities and Exchange Surveillance Commission: 3-2-1, Kasumigaseki, Chiyoda-ku, Tokyo 100-8922; tel. (3) 3581-7868; fax (3) 5251-2151; internet www.fsa.go.jp/sesc; f. 1992; est. for the surveillance of securities and financial futures transactions; Chair. KENICHI SADO.

INSURANCE

Principal Life Companies

AIG Edison Life Insurance Co: Olinas Tower, 4-1-3, Sumida-ku, Tokyo 130-8625; tel. (3) 6658-6000; internet www.aigedison.co.jp; fmrly GE Edison Life Insurance Co, itself fmrly Toho Mutual Life Insurance Co; became subsidiary of Gibraltar Life Insurance in Feb. 2011; Pres. TORU MATSUZAWA.

AIG Star Life Insurance Co Ltd: 4-1-3, Sumida-ku, Tokyo 130-8625; internet www.aigstar-life.co.jp; fmrly Chiyoda Mutual Life Insurance Co, acquired by American International Group, Inc (AIG) in 2001; became subsidiary of Gibraltar Life Insurance in Feb. 2011; Pres. NORIO TOMONO.

Aioi Life Insurance Co Ltd: 3-1-6, Nihonbashi, Chuo-ku, Tokyo 103-0027; tel. (3) 3273-0101; internet www.ioi-life.co.jp; Pres. YOSHIHISA ISHII.

American Family Life Assurance Co of Columbus AFLAC Japan: Shinjuku Mitsui Bldg, 12/F, 2-1-1, Nishi-Shinjuku, Shinjuku-ku, Tokyo 163-0456; tel. (3) 3344-2701; fax (3) 0424-3001; internet www.aflac.co.jp; f. 1974; Chair. YOSHIKI OTAKE; Pres. HIDEFUMI MATSUI.

American Life Insurance Co (Japan): 4-1-3, Sumida-ku, Tokyo; tel. (3) 3284-4111; fax (3) 3284-3874; internet www.alico.co.jp; f. 1972; Pres. KAZUYUKI TAKAHASHI.

Asahi Mutual Life Insurance Co: 1-23, Tsurumaki, Tama-shi, Tokyo 206-8611; tel. (42) 338-3111; internet www.asahi-life.co.jp; f. 1888; Pres. MIKI SATO.

AXA Japan Holding Co Ltd: NBF Platinum Tower, 1-17-3, Minato-ku, Tokyo 150-8020; tel. (3) 3407-6210; internet www.axa.co.jp; Pres. and CEO JEAN-LOUIS LAURENT JOSI.

Cardif Assurance Vie: Infoss Tower, 9/F, 20-1, Sakuragaoka-cho, Shibuya-ku, Tokyo 150-0031; tel. (3) 6415-8275; internet www.cardif.co.jp/vie; f. 2000; Pres. ATSUSHI SAKAUCHI.

Dai-ichi Mutual Life Insurance Co: 1-13-1, Yuraku-cho, Chiyoda-ku, Tokyo 100-8411; tel. (3) 3216-1211; fax (3) 5221-8139; internet www.dai-ichi-life.co.jp; f. 1902; Chair. TOMIJIRO MORITA; Pres. KOICHIRO WATANABE.

Fuji Life Insurance Co Ltd: 1-18-17, Minami-Senba, Chuo-ku, Osaka-shi 542-0081; tel. (6) 6261-0284; fax (6) 6261-0113; internet www.fujiseimei.co.jp; f. 1996; Pres. YOSHIAKI YONEMURA.

Fukoku Mutual Life Insurance Co: 2-2-2, Uchisaiwai-cho, Chiyoda-ku, Tokyo 100-0011; tel. (3) 3508-1101; fax (3) 3591-6446; internet www.fukoku-life.co.jp; f. 1923; Chair. TOMOFUMI AKIYAMA; Pres. YOSHITERU YONEYAMA.

Gibraltar Life Insurance Co Ltd: 2-13-10, Tamati Hisashi, Tokyo 100-8953; tel. (3) 5501-6001; internet www.gib-life.co.jp; f. 1947; fmrly Kyoei Life Insurance Co Ltd, declared bankrupt Oct. 2000; resumed operations in 2001 as mem. of Prudential Financial, USA; Pres. MITSUO KURASHIGE.

Hartford Life Insurance K. K.: Shiodome Bldg, 15/F, 1-2-20, Kaigan, Minato-ku, Tokyo 105-0022; tel. (3) 6219-2111; internet www.hartfordlife.co.jp; f. 2000; Pres. and CEO JENNI SPARKS.

ING Life Insurance Co Ltd: New Otani Garden Court, 26/F, 4-1, Kioi-cho, Chiyoda-ku, Tokyo 102-0094; tel. (3) 5210-0300; fax (3) 5210-0430; internet www.ing-life.co.jp; f. 1985; Pres. EDDIE BERMAN.

Japan Post Insurance: 1-3-2, Kasumigaseki, Chiyoda-ku, Tokyo 100-8798; tel. (3) 3504-4411; internet www.jp-life.japanpost.jp; f. 2006; wholly owned by Japan Post Holdings Co Ltd; Chair. and CEO JOSUKE SHINDO; Pres. IZUMI YAMASHITA.

Kyoei Kasai Shinrai Life Insurance Co Ltd: 1-18-6, Shimbashi, Minato-ku, Tokyo 105-8604; tel. (3) 3504-0131; fax (3) 5372-7701; internet www.kyoeikasai.co.jp; f. 1996; Pres. KENZI SUGIYAMA.

Manulife Life Insurance Co: 4-34-1, Kokuryo-cho, Chofu-shi, Tokyo 182-8621; tel. (3) 2442-7120; fax (3) 2442-7977; e-mail craig_bromley@manulife.com; internet www.manulife.co.jp; f. 1999; fmrly Manulife Century Life Insurance Co; absorbed bankrupt Daihyaku Mutual Life Insurance Co in 2001; Pres. and CEO CRAIG BROMLEY.

MassMutual Life Insurance Co: 1-5-7, Ariake, Koto-ku, Tokyo 135-0063; internet www.massmutual.co.jp; Pres. MASANORI MIZOGUCHI.

Meiji Yasuda Life Insurance Co: 2-1-1, Marunouchi, Chiyoda-ku, Tokyo 100-0005; tel. (3) 3283-8111; fax (3) 3215-5219; internet www.meijiyasuda.co.jp; f. 2004; est. by merger of Meiji Life Insurance Co (f. 1881) and Yasuda Mutual Life Insurance Co (f. 1880); Chair. NORIKAJU SEKIGUTI; Pres. KENJI MATSUO.

Mitsui Life Insurance Co Ltd: 2-1-1, Otemachi, Chiyoda-ku, Tokyo 100-8123; tel. (3) 6831-8000; internet www.mitsui-seimei.co.jp; f. 1927; Chair. HIROSUMI TSUSUE; Pres. YUKITERU YAMAMOTO.

Nippon Life Insurance Co (Nissay): 3-5-12, Imabashi, Chuo-ku, Osaka 541-8501; tel. (6) 6209-5525; e-mail hosokawa15560@nissay.co.jp; internet www.nissay.co.jp; f. 1889; Chair. IKUO UNO; Pres. KUNIE OKAMOTO.

Nipponkoa Life Insurance Co Ltd: 4-2, Tsukiji, Chuo-ku, Tokyo 104-8407; tel. (3) 5565-8080; fax (3) 5565-8365; internet www.nipponkoa.co.jp/life; f. 1996; formed by merger of Nippon Fire and Marine Insurance and Koa Fire and Marine Insurance; Pres. KAZUO HASHIMOTO.

ORIX Life Insurance Corpn: Mita NN Bldg, 4-1-23, Shiba, Minato-ku, Tokyo 108-0014; tel. (3) 5419-5102; fax (3) 5419-5901; e-mail koho@orix.co.jp; internet www.orix.co.jp; f. 1991; Chair. and CEO YOSHIHIKO MIYAUCHI; Pres. MAKOTO INOUE.

Prudential Life Insurance Co Ltd: Prudential Tower, 2-13-10, Nagata-cho, Chiyoda-ku, Tokyo 100-0014; tel. (3) 5501-5500; fax (3) 3221-2305; internet www.prudential.co.jp; f. 1987; Chair. and CEO JOHN STRANGFELD; Pres. MITSUO KURASHIGE.

Sompo Japan DIY Life Insurance Co Ltd: 6-10-1, Shinjuku-Nishi, Shinjuku-ku, Tokyo 160-0023; tel. (3) 5345-7603; fax (3) 5345-7608; internet www.diy.co.jp; f. 1999; Pres. TATSUO SHIBUYA.

Sompo Japan Himawari Life Insurance Co Ltd: Shinjuku Mitsui Bldg, 35/F, 1-2-1, Nishi-Shinjuku, Shinjuku-ku, Tokyo; internet www.himawari-life.com; f. 2002; Pres. TOSHIO MATSUZAKI.

Sony Life Insurance Co Ltd: Shin-Aoyama Bldg, 3/F, 1-1-1, Minami-Aoyama, Minato-ku, Tokyo 107-8585; tel. (3) 3475-8811; fax (3) 3475-8914; internet www.sonylife.co.jp; Chair. KUNIKITA ANDO; Pres. TARO OKUDA.

Sumitomo Life Insurance Co: 7-18-24, Tsukiji, Chuo-ku, Tokyo 104-8430; tel. (3) 5550-1100; fax (3) 5550-1160; internet www.sumitomolife.co.jp; f. 1907; Pres. YOSHIO SATO.

T & D Holdings Inc: Shiodome Shiba-Rikyu Bldg, 1-2-3, Kaigan, Minato-ku, Tokyo 105-0022; tel. (3) 3434-9111; fax (3) 3434-9055; internet www.td-holdings.co.jp; f. 1895; fmrly Tokyo Mutual Life Insurance Co; T & D Financial Life Insurance Co Holdings company formed in April 2004 through merger of T & D Financial Life Insurance Co, Taiyo Mutual Life Insurance Co and Daido Life Insurance Co; Pres. NAOTERU MIYATO.

Tokio Marine & Nichido Life Insurance Co Ltd: 5-3-16, Ginza, Chuo-ku, Tokyo 106-0041; tel. (3) 5223-2111; fax (3) 5223-2165; internet www.tmn-anshin.co.jp; Pres. SUKEAKI OHTA.

Yamato Mutual Life Insurance Co: 1-1-7, Uchisaiwai-cho, Chiyoda-ku, Tokyo 100-0011; tel. (3) 3508-3111; fax (3) 3508-3118; internet www.yamato-life.co.jp; f. 1911; Pres. TAKEO NAKAZONO.

Zurich Life Insurance Co Ltd: Shinanomachi Rengakan, 35, Shinanomachi, Shinjuku-ku, Tokyo 160-0016; tel. (3) 5361-2700; fax (3) 5361-2705; internet www.zurichlife.co.jp; f. 1996; Pres. NAGANO TOSHIYUKI.

Principal Non-Life Companies

ACE Insurance: Arco Tower, 1-8-1, Shimomeguro, Meguro-ku, Tokyo 153-0064; tel. (3) 5740-0600; fax (3) 5740-0608; internet www.ace-insurance.co.jp; f. 1999; Chair. SHINIJI NOMOTO; Pres. TAKASHI IMAI.

Aioi Nissay Dowa Insurance Co Ltd: 1-28-1, Ebisu, Shibuya-ku, Tokyo 150-8488; tel. (3) 5424-0101; internet www.aioinissaydowa.co.jp; est. by merger of Aioi Insurance Co Ltd and Nissay Dowa General Insurance Co Ltd in 2010; Pres. KUNI SUZUKI.

Allianz Fire and Marine Insurance Japan Ltd: Anzen Bldg, 1-6-6, Moto-Akasaka, Minato-ku, Tokyo 107-0051; tel. (3) 4558-7500; e-mail netadmin@allianz.co.jp; internet www.allianz.co.jp; f. 1990; Chair. AXEL THEIS; Pres. MICHAEL MAICHER.

Asahi Fire and Marine Insurance Co Ltd: 2-6-2, Kaji-cho, Chiyoda-ku, Tokyo 101-8655; tel. (3) 3294-2211; fax (3) 3254-2296; e-mail asahifmi@blue.ocn.ne.jp; internet www.asahikasai.co.jp; f. 1951; Pres. KAZUHO OYA.

AXA Japan Holding Co Ltd: NBF Platinum Tower, 1-17-3, Minato-ku, Tokyo 150-8020; tel. (3) 3407-6210; internet www.axa.co.jp; f. 1998; Pres. JEAN-LOUIS LAURENT JOSI.

Daido Fire and Marine Insurance Co Ltd: 1-12-1, Kumoji, Naha-shi, Okinawa 900-8586; tel. (98) 867-1161; fax (98) 862-8362; internet www.daidokasai.co.jp; f. 1971; Pres. NAOTO MIRAYA.

Fuji Fire and Marine Insurance Co Ltd: 1-18-11, Minami-Senba, Chuo-ku, Osaka 542-8567; tel. (6) 6271-2741; fax (6) 6266-7115; internet www.fujikasai.co.jp; f. 1918; Pres. and CEO AKIRA KONDOH.

Japan Earthquake Reinsurance Co Ltd: Fuji Plaza, 4/F, 8-1, Nihonbashi Kobuna-cho, Chuo-ku, Tokyo 103-0024; tel. (3) 3664-6074; fax (3) 3664-6169; e-mail kanri@nihonjishin.co.jp; internet www.nihonjishin.co.jp; f. 1966; Chair. SHOZO WAKABAYASHI; Pres. HIDEO SUZUKI.

JI Accident & Fire Insurance Co Ltd: A1 Bldg, 20-5, Ichiban-cho, Chiyoda-ku, Tokyo 102-0082; tel. (3) 3237-2045; fax (3) 3237-2250; internet www.jihoken.co.jp; f. 1989; Pres. MITSUHITO MINAMISAWA.

Kyoei Mutual Fire and Marine Insurance Co: 1-18-6, Shimbashi, Minato-ku, Tokyo 105-8604; tel. (3) 3504-0131; fax (3) 3508-7680; e-mail reins.intl@kyoeikasai.co.jp; internet www.kyoeikasai.co.jp; f. 1942; Pres. KENJI SUGIYAMA.

Meiji Yasuda General Insurance Co Ltd: 2-11-1, Kanda Tsukasa-cho, Chiyoda-ku, Tokyo 101-0048; tel. (3) 3257-3111; fax (3) 3257-3295; internet www.meijiyasuda-sonpo.co.jp; f. 1996; Pres. SEIJI NISHI.

Mitsui Direct General Insurance Co Ltd: 1-5-3, Koraku, Bunkyou-ku, Tokyo 112-0004; tel. (3) 5804-7711; internet www.mitsui-direct.co.jp; f. 1996; Pres. TOSHIO KITAMURA.

Mitsui Sumitomo Insurance Co Ltd: 27-2-2, Shinkawa, Chuo-ku, Tokyo 104-8252; tel. (3) 3297-1111; internet www.ms-ins.com; f. 2001; formed by merger of Mitsui Marine and Fire Insurance and Sumitomo Marine and Fire Insurance; Chair. TOSHIAKI EGASHIRA; Pres. YASUYOSHI KARASAWA.

Nipponkoa Insurance Co Ltd: 3-7-3, Kasumigaseki, Chiyoda-ku, Tokyo 100-8965; tel. (3) 3593-3111; fax (3) 3593-5388; internet www.nipponkoa.co.jp; f. 1892; fmrly The Nippon Fire and Marine Insurance Co Ltd before merging with The Koa Fire and Marine Insurance Co Ltd; acquired Taiyo Fire and Marine Insurance Co Ltd in 2002; Pres. and CEO MAKOTO HYODO.

Nisshin Fire and Marine Insurance Co Ltd: 2-3, Kanda Surugadai, Chiyoda-ku, Tokyo 100-8329; tel. (3) 5282-5534; fax (3) 5282-5582; e-mail nisshin@mb.infoweb.ne.jp; internet www.nisshinfire.co.jp; f. 1908; Pres. HIROSHI MIYAJIMA.

Saison Automobile and Fire Insurance Co Ltd: Sunshine 60 Bldg, 3-1-1, Higashi-Ikebukuro, Toshima-ku, Tokyo 170-6068; tel. (3) 3988-2572; fax (3) 3980-7367; internet www.ins-saison.co.jp; f. 1982; Pres. KOSHIN MATUZAWA.

Secom General Insurance Co Ltd: 2-6-2, Hirakawa-cho, Chiyoda-ku, Tokyo 102-8645; tel. (3) 5216-6129; fax (3) 5216-6149; internet www.secom-sonpo.co.jp; Pres. ITIRO OJEKI.

Sompo Japan Insurance Inc: 26-1-1, Nishi-Shinjuku, Shinjuku-ku, Tokyo 160-8338; tel. (3) 3349-3111; fax (3) 3349-4697; internet www.sompo-japan.co.jp; f. 2002; est. by merger of Yasuda Fire and Marine Insurance (f. 1888) and Nissan Fire and Marine Insurance (f. 1911); Pres. MATATOSHI SATO.

Sonpo 24 Insurance Co Ltd: Sunshine 60 Bldg, 44/F, 3-1-1, Higashi-Ikebukuro, Toshima-ku, Tokyo 170-6044; tel. (3) 5957-0111; internet www.sonpo24.co.jp; Pres. ATSUSHI KUMANOMIDO.

Sony Assurance Inc: Aroma Sq., 11/F, 5-37-1, Kamata, Ota-ku, Tokyo 144-8721; tel. (3) 5744-0300; fax (3) 5744-0480; internet www.sonysonpo.co.jp; f. 1999; Pres. SHINICHI YAMAMOTO.

Toa Reinsurance Co Ltd: 3-6, Kanda Surugadai, Chiyoda-ku, Tokyo 101-8703; tel. (3) 3253-3171; fax (3) 3253-1208; internet www.toare.co.jp; f. 1940; Chair. TERUHIKO OHTANI; Pres. HIROSHI FUKUSHIMA.

Tokio Marine & Nichido Fire Insurance Co Ltd: 1-2-1, Marunouchi, Chiyoda-ku, Tokyo 100-8050; tel. (3) 3212-6211; internet www.tokiomarine-nichido.co.jp; f. 2004; Pres. SHUZO SUMI.

Insurance Associations

General Insurance Association of Japan (Nihon Songai Hoken Kyokai): General Insurance Bldg, 2-9, Kanda Awaji-cho, Chiyoda-ku, Tokyo 101-8335; tel. (3) 3255-1439; fax (3) 3255-1234; e-mail kokusai@sonpo.or.jp; internet www.sonpo.or.jp; f. 1946; 27 mems (Jan. 2014); Chair. MASAYA FUTAMIYA; Exec. Dir HIROMI ASANO.

General Insurance Rating Organization of Japan: 3-7-1, Nishi-Shinjuku, Shinjuku-ku, Tokyo 163-1029; e-mail service@nliro.or.jp; internet www.giroj.or.jp; f. 2002; 40 mems (July 2013); Chair. AKIO MORISHIMA; Exec. Dir HIROSHI AMEMIYA.

Life Insurance Association of Japan (Seimei Hoken Kyokai): Shin-Kokusai Bldg, 3/F, 3-4-1, Marunouchi, Chiyoda-ku, Tokyo 100-0005; tel. (3) 3286-2652; fax (3) 3286-2630; e-mail kokusai@seiho.or.jp; internet www.seiho.or.jp; f. 1908; 43 mem. cos (Jan. 2014); Chair. YOSHIO SATO.

Nippon Export and Investment Insurance: Chiyoda First Bldg, East Wing, 3/F, 3-8-1, Kanda Nishi, Chiyoda-ku, Tokyo; internet www.nexi.go.jp; f. 2001; Chair. and CEO TAKASHI SUZUKI.

Trade and Industry

CHAMBERS OF COMMERCE AND INDUSTRY

Japan Chamber of Commerce and Industry (Nihon Shoko Kaigi-sho): 3-2-2, Marunouchi, Chiyoda-ku, Tokyo 100-0005; tel. (3) 3283-7523; fax (3) 3216-6497; e-mail info@jcci.or.jp; internet www.jcci.or.jp; f. 1922; the central org. of all chambers of commerce and industry in Japan; mems: 514 local chambers of commerce and industry; Chair. TADASHI OKAMURA; Pres. TOSHIO NAKAMURA.

Principal chambers include:

Kobe Chamber of Commerce and Industry: 6-1, Minatojima-nakamachi, Chuo-ku, Kobe 650-8543; tel. (78) 303-5806; fax (78) 306-2348; e-mail kokusai-info@kobe-cci.or.jp; internet kobe-cci.weebly.com; f. 1878; 11,000 mems; Chair. TADAHARU OHASHI; Pres. YASUO MURATA.

Kyoto Chamber of Commerce and Industry: 240, Shoshoi-cho, Ebisugawa-agaru, Karasumadori, Nakakyo-ku, Kyoto 604-0862; tel. (75) 212-6420; fax (75) 251-0743; e-mail kokusai@kyo.or.jp; internet www.kyo.or.jp/kyoto; f. 1882; 11,500 mems; Chair. YOSHIO TATEISI; Pres. TUNEOKI OKUHARA.

Nagoya Chamber of Commerce and Industry: 2-10-19, Sakae, Naka-ku, Nagoya, Aichi 460-8422; tel. (52) 223-5722; fax (52) 232-5751; e-mail info@nagoya-cci.or.jp; internet www.nagoya-cci.or.jp; f. 1881; 17,000 mems; Chair. JIRO TAKAHASHI.

Naha Chamber of Commerce and Industry: 2-2-10, Kume Naha, Okinawa; tel. (98) 868-3758; fax (98) 866-9834; e-mail cci-naha@nahacci.or.jp; internet www.nahacci.or.jp; f. 1927; 4,874 mems; Chair. AKIRA SAKIMA; Pres. KOSEI YONEMURA.

Osaka Chamber of Commerce and Industry: 2-8, Hommachi-bashi, Chuo-ku, Osaka 540-0029; tel. (6) 6944-6400; fax (6) 6944-6293; e-mail intl@osaka.cci.or.jp; internet www.osaka.cci.or.jp; f. 1878; 28,500 mems; Chair. SHIGETAKA SATO; Pres. NADAMOTO MASAHIRO.

Tokyo Chamber of Commerce and Industry: 3-2-2, Marunouchi, Chiyoda-ku, Tokyo 100-0005; tel. (3) 3283-7523; fax (3) 3216-6497; e-mail kokusai@tokyo-cci.or.jp; internet www.tokyo-cci.or.jp; f. 1878; 77,247 mems (April 2010); Chair. TADASHI OKAMURA; Pres. TOSHIO NAKAMURA.

Yokohama Chamber of Commerce and Industry: Sangyo Boueki Center Bldg, 8/F, Yamashita-cho, Naka-ku, Yokohama 231-8524; tel. (45) 671-7400; fax (45) 671-7410; e-mail soumu@yokohama-cci.or.jp; internet www.yokohama-cci.or.jp; f. 1880; 14,965 mems; Chair. KENJI SASAKI; Pres. NAMIO OBA.

INDUSTRIAL AND TRADE ASSOCIATIONS

General

Association for the Promotion of International Trade, Japan (JAPIT): 1-9-13, Chiyoda-ku, Tokyo 101-0047; tel. (3) 6740-8261; fax (3) 6740-6160; internet www.japitcn.com; f. 1954 to promote trade with the People's Repub. of China; 700 mems; Chair. YOHEI KONO.

Industry Club of Japan: 1-4-6, Marunouchi, Chiyoda-ku, Tokyo; tel. (3) 3281-1711; fax (3) 3281-1797; e-mail soumu@kogyoclub.or.jp; internet www.kogyoclub.or.jp; f. 1917; est. to develop closer relations between industrialists at home and abroad and promote expansion of Japanese business activities; c. 1,600 mems; Pres. IMAI TAKASHI; Exec. Dir KOUICHIROU SHINNO.

Japan Commercial Arbitration Association: Hirose Bldg, 3/F, 3-17, Kanda Nishiki-cho, Chiyoda-ku, Tokyo 101-0054; tel. (3) 5280-5200; fax (3) 5280-5170; e-mail arbitration@jcaa.or.jp; internet www.jcaa.or.jp; f. 1950; 700 mems; provides facilities for mediation, conciliation and arbitration in international trade disputes; Pres. TADASHI OKAMURA.

Japan External Trade Organization (JETRO): Ark Mori Bldg, 6/F, 1-12-32, Akasaka-cho, Minato-ku, Tokyo 107-6006; tel. (3) 3582-5511; fax (3) 3582-5662; e-mail seh@jetro.go.jp; internet www.jetro.go.jp; f. 1958; information on international trade, investment, import promotion, exhibitions of foreign products; Chair. and CEO YASUO HAYASHI; Pres. TADASHI IZAWA.

Japan Federation of Smaller Enterprise Organizations (JFSEO) (Nippon Chusokigyo Dantai Renmei): 2-8-4, Nihonbashi, Kayaba-cho, Chuo-ku, Tokyo 103-0025; tel. (3) 3669-6862; f. 1948; 18 mems and c. 1,000 co-operative socs; Pres. MASATAKA TOYODA; Chair. of Int. Affairs SEIICHI ONO.

Japan General Merchandise Exporters' Association: 2-4-1, Hamamatsu-cho, Minato-ku, Tokyo; tel. (3) 3435-3471; fax (3) 3434-6739; f. 1953; 40 mems; Pres. TADAYOSHI NAKAZAWA.

Japan Productivity Center (JPC): 3-1-1, Shibuya, Shibuya-ku, Tokyo 150-8307; tel. (3) 3409-1112; fax (3) 3409-1986; internet www.jpc-net.jp; f. 1994; est. by merger between Japan Productivity Center and Social Economic Congress of Japan; fmrly Japan Productivity Center for Socio-Economic Development, renamed as above 2009; 10,000 mems; concerned with management problems and research into productivity; Chair. JIRO USHIO; Pres. TSUNEAKI TANIGUCHI.

Keizai Doyukai (Japan Association of Corporate Executives): 1-4-6, Marunouchi, Chiyoda-ku, Tokyo 100-0005; tel. (3) 3211-1271; fax (3) 3213-2946; e-mail kdcontact205@doyukai.or.jp; internet www.doyukai.or.jp; f. 1946; c.1,400 mems; corporate executives concerned with national and international economic and social policies; Chair. MASAMITSU SAKURAI.

Nihon Boeki-Kai (Japan Foreign Trade Council, Inc): World Trade Center Bldg, 6/F, 2-4-1, Hamamatsu-cho, Minato-ku, Tokyo 105-6106; tel. (3) 3435-5959; fax (3) 3435-5979; e-mail mail@jftc.or.jp; internet www.jftc.or.jp; f. 1947; 192 mems; Chair. SHOEI UTSUDA; Exec. Man. Dir MASAYOSHI AMANO.

Chemicals

Japan Chemical Industry Association: Sumitomo Fudosan Rokko Bldg, 1-4-1, Shinkawa, Chuo-ku, Tokyo 104-0033; tel. (3) 3297-2550; fax (3) 3297-2610; e-mail chemical@jcia-net.or.jp; internet www.nikkakyo.org; f. 1948; 266 mems; Chair. HIROMASA YONEKURA.

Japan Cosmetic Industry Association: 45 MT Bldg, 6/F, 5-1-5, Toranomon, Minato-ku, Tokyo 105-0001; tel. (3) 5472-2530; fax (3) 5472-2536; e-mail info@jcia.org; internet www.jcia.org; f. 1959; 687 mem. cos; Chair. REIJIRO KOBAYASHI.

Japan Perfumery and Flavouring Association: Saeki No. 3 Bldg, 3/F, 37, Kandakonya-cho, Chiyoda-ku, Tokyo 101-0035; tel. and fax (3) 3526-7855; f. 1947; Chair. YONEJIRO KORAYASHI.

Japan Pharmaceutical Manufacturers' Association: Torii Nihonbashi Bldg, 3-4-1, Nihonbashi Hon-cho, Chuo-ku, Tokyo 103-0023; tel. (3) 3241-0326; fax (3) 3242-1767; internet www.jpma.or.jp; 67 mems; Pres. YASUCHIKA HASEGAWA.

Photo-Sensitized Materials Manufacturers' Association: JCII Bldg, 25, Ichiban-cho, Chiyoda-ku, Tokyo 102-0082; tel. (3) 5276-3561; fax (3) 5276-3563; internet pmma.a.la9.jp; f. 1948; Pres. SHIGETAKA KOMORI.

Fishing and Pearl Cultivation

Japan Fisheries Association (Dainippon Suisankai): Sankaido Bldg, 1-9-13, Akasaka, Minato-ku, Tokyo 107-0052; tel. (3) 3585-6681; fax (3) 3582-2337; e-mail japan@suisankai.or.jp; internet www.suisankai.or.jp; Pres. TOSHIRO SHIRASU.

Japan Pearl Export and Processing Co-operative Association: 3-6-15, Kyobashi, Chuo-ko, Tokyo 104-0031; tel. (3) 3562-5011; f. 1951; 130 mems.

Japan Pearl Exporters' Association: 122, Higashi-Machi, Chuo-ku, Kobe 650-0031; tel. (78) 331-4031; fax (78) 331-4345; e-mail jpeakobe@lime.ocn.ne.jp; internet www.japan-pearl.com; f. 1954; 56 mems; Pres. YOSHIHIRO SHIMIZU.

Machinery and Precision Equipment

Camera and Imaging Products Association (CIPA) (Camera Eizo Kiki Kogyo-kai): JCII Bldg, 25, Ichiban-cho, Chiyoda-ku, Tokyo 102-0082; tel. (3) 5276-3891; fax (3) 5276-3893; internet www.cipa.jp; f. 1954; fmrly Japan Camera Industry Asscn, renamed as above 2002; 54 mems; Pres. TSUYOSHI KIKUKAWA.

Japan Clock and Watch Association: Kudan Sky Bldg, 1-12-11, Kudan-Kita, Chiyoda-ku, Tokyo 102-0073; tel. (3) 5276-3411; fax (3) 5276-3414; internet www.jcwa.or.jp; Chair. SHINJI HATTORI.

Japan Electric Association: Denki Bldg, 4/F, 1-7-1, Yuraku-cho, Chiyoda-ku, Tokyo 100-0006; tel. (3) 3216-0551; fax (3) 3214-6005; internet www.denki.or.jp; f. 1921; 4,610 mems; Pres. TATSUO KAWAI.

Japan Electric Measuring Instruments Manufacturers' Association (JEMIMA): Keisoku Kaikan Bldg, 2-15-12, Nihonbashi-Kakigara-cho, Chuo-ku, Tokyo 103-0014; tel. (3) 3662-8181; fax (3) 3662-8180; e-mail katsuta@jemima.or.jp; internet www.jemima.or.jp; 79 mems; Chair. SEIJI ONOKI.

Japan Electrical Manufacturers' Association: 17-4, Ichibancho, Chiyoda-ku, Tokyo 102-0082; tel. (3) 3556-5881; fax (3) 3556-5889; internet www.jema-net.or.jp; f. 1948; 262 mems; Chair. MICHIHIRO KITAZAWA; Pres. TOSHIMI HAYANO.

Japan Electronics and Information Technology Industries Association (JEITA): Ote Center Bldg, 1-1-3, Otemachi, Chiyoda-ku, Tokyo 100-0004; tel. (3) 5218-1050; fax (3) 5218-1070; internet www.jeita.or.jp; promotes manufacturing, international trade and consumption of electronics products and components; Chair. RYOJI CHUBACHI; Pres. TSUTOMU HANDA.

Japan Energy Association: Kawate Bldg, 1-5-8, Nishi-Shimbashi, Minato-ku, Tokyo 105-0003; tel. (3) 3502-1261; fax (3) 3502-2760; e-mail info@jea-wec.or.jp; internet www.jea-wec.or.jp; f. 1950; 133 mems; Chair. TERUAKI MASUMOTO; Exec. Dir HAJIME MURATA.

Japan Machine Tool Builders' Association: Kikai Shinko Bldg, 3-5-8, Shiba Koen, Minato-ku, Tokyo 105-0011; tel. (3) 3434-3961; fax (3) 3434-3763; e-mail intl@jmtba.or.jp; internet www.jmtba.or.jp; f. 1951; 112 mems; Chair. KENICHI NAKAMURA; Pres. TOSHIONI SHONO.

Japan Machine Tools Importers' Association: Toranomon Kogyo Bldg, 1-2-18, Toranomon, Minato-ku, Tokyo 105-0001; tel. (3) 3501-5030; fax (3) 3501-5040; e-mail info@jmtia.gr.jp; internet www.jmtia.gr.jp; f. 1955; 42 mems; Chair. YUZO CHIBA.

Japan Machinery Center for Trade and Investment (JMC): Kikai Shinko Bldg, 4/F, 3-5-8, Shiba Koen, Minato-ku, Tokyo 105-0011; tel. (3) 3431-9507; fax (3) 3436-6455; e-mail info@jmcti.or.jp; internet www.jmcti.org; f. 1952; 290 mem. cos; Pres. KENJI MIYAHARA.

The Japan Machinery Federation: Kikai Shinko Bldg, 3-5-8, Shiba Koen, Minato-ku, Tokyo 105-0011; tel. (3) 3434-5381; fax (3) 3434-2666; e-mail koho@jmf.or.jp; internet www.jmf.or.jp; f. 1952; Pres. MOTOTSUGU ITO; Exec. Dir KYOSHI ISHIZAKA.

Japan Microscope Manufacturers' Association: Kikai Shinko Bldg, 5-8-3, Shibakoen, Minato-ku, Tokyo 105-0011; tel. (3) 3432-5100; fax (3) 3432-5611; e-mail jmma@microscope.jp; internet www.microscope.jp; f. 1954; 27 mems; Chair. HIROYUKI SASA.

Japan Motion Picture Equipment Industrial Association: Kikai Shinko Bldg, 3-5-8, Shiba Koen, Minato-ku, Tokyo 105-0011; tel. (3) 3434-3911; fax (3) 3434-3912; Pres. MASAO SHIKATA; Gen. Sec. TERUHIRO KATO.

Japan Optical Industry Association: Kikai Shinko Bldg, 3-5-8, Shiba Koen, Minato-ku, Tokyo 105-0011; tel. (3) 3431-7073; f. 1946; 7 mems; Chair. MICHIO KARIYA; Exec. Sec. SHIRO IWAHASHI.

Japan Society of Industrial Machinery Manufacturers: Kikai Shinko Bldg, 3-5-8, Shiba Koen, Minato-ku, Tokyo 105-0011; tel. (3) 3434-6821; fax (3) 3434-4767; e-mail obd@jsim.or.jp; internet www.jsim.or.jp; f. 1948; 170 mems; Pres. YOSHIO HINOU.

Japan Textile Machinery Association: Kikai Shinko Bldg, Rm 101, 5-22, Shiba Koen, Minato-ku, Tokyo 105-0011; tel. (3) 3434-3821; fax (3) 3434-3043; e-mail am-jtma@jtma.or.jp; internet www.jtma.or.jp; f. 1951; Pres. TETSURO TOYODA.

Metals

Japan Aluminium Association (JAA): Tsukamoto-Sozan Bldg, 4-2-15, Ginza, Chuo-ku, Tokyo 104-0061; tel. (3) 3538-0221; fax (3) 3538-0233; internet www.aluminum.or.jp; f. 1999; est. by merger of Japan Aluminium Federation and Japan Light Metal Association; 146 mems; Chair. ISHIYAMA TAKASHI.

Japan Copper and Brass Association: Usagiya Bldg, 5/F, 1-10-10, Ueno, Taito-ku, Tokyo 110-0005; tel. (3) 3836-8801; fax (3) 3836-8808; e-mail jbmajwcc@copper-brass.gr.jp; internet www.copper-brass.gr.jp; f. 1948; 62 mems; Chair. TAKAO HASHIDA; Sec.-Gen. TOSHINOBU HIDAKA.

The Japan Iron and Steel Federation: Tekko Kaikan Bldg, 3-2-10, Nihonbashi Kayaba-cho, Chuo-ku, Tokyo 103-0025; tel. (3) 3669-4811; fax (3) 3664-1457; internet www.jisf.or.jp; f. 1948; mems: 61 mfrs, 61 dealers, 6 orgs; Chair. EIJI HAYASHIDA.

Japan Stainless Steel Association: TMM Bldg, 3/F, 1-10-5, Iwamoto-cho, Chiyoda-ku, Tokyo; tel. (3) 5687-7831; fax (3) 5687-8551; e-mail yabe@jssa.gr.jp; internet www.jssa.gr.jp; f. 1959; 80 mems; Chair. HIROSHI KINOSHITA.

Steel Castings and Forgings Association of Japan (JSCFA): Shikoku Bldg Bekkan, 8/F, 1-14-4, Uchikanda, Chiyoda-ku, Tokyo 101-0047; tel. (3) 5283-1611; fax (3) 5283-1613; e-mail cf@jscfa.gr.jp; internet www.jscfa.gr.jp; f. 1972; mems: 48 cos, 44 plants; Pres. YAMAGUCHI IKUHIRO.

Mining and Petroleum

Japan Coal Energy Center (JCOAL): Meiji Yasuda Seimei Mita Bldg, 9/F, 3-14-10, Mita, Minato-ku, Tokyo 108-0073; tel. (3) 6400-5191; fax (3) 6400-5206; e-mail jcoal-qa@jcoal.or.jp; internet www.jcoal.or.jp; f. 1997; est. by merger of Japan Coal Asscn, Coal Mining Research Centre, and the Japan Technical Cooperation Center for Coal Resources Devt; 111 mems; Pres. YOSHIHIKO NAGASAKI.

Japan Mining Industry Association: c/o Eiha Bldg, 17-11-3, Kanda Nishiki-cho, Chiyoda-ku, Tokyo 101-0054; tel. (3) 5280-2321; fax (3) 5280-7128; internet www.kogyo-kyokai.gr.jp; f. 1948; 52 mem. cos; Chair. SADAO SENDA; Pres. SHINICHI OZEKI.

Japan Petrochemical Industry Association: 1-4-1, Shinkawa, Chuo-ku, Tokyo 104-0033; tel. (3) 3297-2011; fax (3) 3297-2017; e-mail inquiries_hp@jpca.or.jp; internet www.jpca.or.jp; Chair. KYOHEI TAKAHASHI.

Japan Petroleum Development Association: Keidanren Bldg, 17/F, 1-3-2, Otemachi, Chiyoda-ku, Tokyo 100-0004; tel. (3) 3214-1701; fax (3) 3214-1703; e-mail jpda-sekkoren@sekkoren.jp; internet www.sekkoren.jp; f. 1961; Chair. NAOKI KURODA.

Paper and Printing

Japan Federation of Printing Industries: 1-16-8, Shintomi, Chuo-ku, Tokyo 104-0041; tel. (3) 3553-6051; fax (3) 3553-6079; internet www.jfpi.or.jp; f. 1985; 10 mems; Chair. SATOSHI SAWATARI.

Japan Paper Association: Kami Parupu Bldg, 3-9-11, Ginza, Chuo-ku, Tokyo 104-8139; tel. (3) 3248-4801; fax (3) 3248-4826; internet www.jpa.gr.jp; f. 1946; 54 mems; Chair. KAZUHISA SHINODA; Pres. MASATAKA HAYAMA.

Japan Paper Exporters' Association: Kami Parupu Bldg, 3-9-11, Ginza, Chuo-ku, Tokyo 104-8139; tel. (3) 3248-4831; fax (3) 3248-4834; e-mail info@jpeta.or.jp; internet www.jpeta.or.jp; f. 1952; 32 mems; Chair. SHINICHI SATO.

Japan Paper Importers' Association: Kami Parupu Bldg, 3-9-11, Ginza, Chuo-ku, Tokyo 104-8139; tel. (3) 3248-4831; fax (3) 3248-4834; e-mail info@jpeta.or.jp; internet jpeta.or.jp; f. 1981; 21 mems; Chair. YASUYUKI AMAKUSA.

Japan Paper Products Manufacturers' Association: 4-2-6, Kotobuki, Taito-ku, Tokyo; tel. (3) 3543-2411; f. 1949; Exec. Dir KIYOSHI SATOH.

Textiles

Central Raw Silk Association of Japan: 1-9-4, Yuraku-cho, Chiyoda-ku, Tokyo; tel. (3) 3214-5777; fax (3) 3214-5778.

Japan Chemical Fibers Association: Seni Kaikan, 7/F, 3-1-11, Nihonbashi-Honcho, Chuo-ku, Tokyo 103-0023; tel. (3) 3241-2311; fax (3) 3246-0823; internet www.jcfa.gr.jp; f. 1948; 17 mems, 1 assoc. mem, 20 supporting mems; Pres. AKIHIRO NIKKAKU; Dir-Gen. TSUNEHIRO OGARA.

Japan Cotton and Staple Fibre Weavers' Association: 1-8-7, Nishi-Azabu, Minato-ku, Tokyo; tel. (3) 3403-9671; internet www.jcwa-net.jp; 28 mems; Pres. OSAMU MAKOTO.

Japan Silk Spinners' Association: f. 1948; 95 mem. cos; Chair. ICHIJI OHTANI.

Japan Spinners' Association: Mengyo Kaikan Bldg, 6/F, 2-5-8, Bingomachi, Chuo-ku, Osaka 541-0051; tel. (6) 6231-8431; fax (6) 6229-1590; e-mail spinas@cotton.or.jp; internet www.jsa-jp.org; f. 1948; 16 mems; Head KOJIRO ABE.

Transport Machinery

Japan Association of Rolling Stock Industries: Awajicho Suny Bldg, 7/F, 1-2, Kanda Suda-cho, Chiyoda-ku, Tokyo 101-0041; tel. (3) 3257-1901; e-mail info@tetsushako.or.jp; internet www.tetsushako.or.jp; Chair. HIRAI MASAHARU.

Japan Auto Parts Industries Association: Jidosha Buhin Bldg, 5/F, 1-16-15, Takanawa, Minato-ku, Tokyo 108-0074; tel. (3) 3445-4211; fax (3) 3447-5372; e-mail info@japia.or.jp; internet www.japia.or.jp; f. 1948; 530 mem. cos; Chair. HISATAKA NOBUMOTO; Exec. Dir K. SHIBASAKI.

Japan Automobile Manufacturers Association, Inc (JAMA): Jidosha Kaikan, 1-1-30, Shiba Daimon, Minato-ku, Tokyo 105-0012; tel. (3) 5405-6126; fax (3) 5405-6136; e-mail kaigai_tky@mta.jama.or.jp; internet www.jama.or.jp; f. 1967; 14 mem. cos; Chair. TOSHIYUKI SHIGA; Pres. YOSHIYASU NAO.

Japan Bicycle Manufacturers' Association: 1-9-3, Akasaka, Minato-ku, Tokyo 107; tel. (3) 3583-3123; fax (3) 3589-3125; f. 1955.

Japan Ship Exporters' Association: Toranomon 30 Mori Bldg, 5/F, 3-2-2, Toranomon, Minato-ku, Tokyo 105-0001; tel. (3) 5425-9671;

fax (3) 5425-9674; e-mail postmaster@jsea.or.jp; internet www.jsea .or.jp; 32 mems; Pres. MASAMOTO TAZAKI.

Japanese Marine Equipment Association: Kaiyo Senpaku Bldg, 15-16, Toranomon, Minato-ku, Tokyo 105-0001; tel. (3) 3502-2041; fax (3) 3591-2206; e-mail info@jsmea.or.jp; internet www.jsmea.or .jp; f. 1956; 219 mems; Chair. ZENSHICHI ASASAKA.

Japanese Shipowners' Association: Kaiun Bldg, 2-6-4, Hirakawa-cho, Chiyoda-ku, Tokyo 102-8603; tel. (3) 3264-7171; fax (3) 3262-4760; internet www.jsanet.or.jp; Pres. KOJI MIYAHARA.

Shipbuilders' Association of Japan: 30 Mori Bldg, 5/F, 3-2-2, Toranomon, Minato-ku, Tokyo 105-0001; tel. (3) 5425-9527; fax (3) 5425-9533; internet www.sajn.or.jp; f. 1947; 21 mems; Chair. TAKAO MOTOYAMA.

Society of Japanese Aerospace Companies (SJAC): Toshin-Tameike Bldg, 2/F, 1-1-14, Akasaka, Minato-ku, Tokyo 107-0052; tel. (3) 3585-0511; fax (3) 3585-0541; e-mail itahara-hiroharu@sjac.or.jp; internet www.sjac.or.jp; f. 1952; reorg. 1974; 117 mems, 41 assoc. mems; Chair. KAZUO TSUKUDA; Pres. KOSUKE IMASHIMIZU.

Miscellaneous

Communications Industry Association of Japan (CIA-J): Shuwa Dai-ichi Hamamatsucho Bldg, 3/F, 2-2-12, Hamamatsu-cho, Minato-ku, Tokyo 105-0013; tel. (3) 5403-9363; fax (3) 5463-9360; e-mail admin@ciaj.or.jp; internet www.ciaj.or.jp; f. 1948; non-profit org. of telecommunications equipment mfrs; 236 mems; Chair. KAWAMURA TAKASHI; Pres. YOSHIYUKI SUKEMUNE.

Japan Canners' Association: Tokyo; tel. (3) 5256-4801; fax (3) 5256-4805; internet www.jca-can.or.jp; Pres. KEINOSUKE HISAI.

Japan Cement Association: Daiwa Nihonbashi-Honcho Bldg, 7/F, 1-9-4, Chuo-ku, Tokyo 103-0023; tel. (3) 5200-5057; fax (3) 5200-5062; e-mail international@jcassoc.or.jp; internet www.jcassoc.or.jp; f. 1948; 18 mem. cos; Chair. KEIJI TOKUUE.

Japan Lumber Importers' Association: Yushi Kogyo Bldg, 3-13-11, Nihonbashi, Chuo-ku, Tokyo 103-0027; tel. (3) 3271-0926; fax (3) 3271-0928; f. 1950; 130 mems; Pres. TAMBA TOSIKHITO.

Japan Plastics Industry Federation: 3-5-2 Nihonbashi-Kayabacho, Chuo-ku, Tokyo 103-0025; tel. (3) 6661-6811; fax (3) 6661-6810; e-mail info@jpif.gr.jp; internet www.jpif.gr.jp; f. 1950; 102 mems; Exec. Dir YASUHIKO MIZUNO.

Japan Plywood Manufacturers' Association: Meisan Bldg, 1-18-17, Nishi-Shimbashi, Minato-ku, Tokyo 105; tel. (3) 3591-9246; fax (3) 3591-9240; f. 1965; 92 mems; Pres. KOICHI MATAGA.

Japan Pottery Manufacturers' Federation: Toto Bldg, 1-1-28, Toranomon, Minato-ku, Tokyo; tel. (3) 3503-6761.

Japan Rubber Manufacturers' Association: Tobu Bldg, 2/F, 1-5-26, Moto-Akasaka, Minato-ku, Tokyo 107-0051; tel. (3) 3408-7101; fax (3) 3408-7106; e-mail soumu@jrma.gr.jp; internet www.jrma.gr .jp; f. 1950; 126 mems; Pres. MITSUAKI ASAI.

Japan Spirits and Liquors Makers' Association: Koura Dai-ichi Bldg, 7/F, 1-1-6, Nihonbashi-Kayaba-cho, Chuo-ku, Tokyo 103; tel. (3) 3668-4621.

Japan Sugar Refiners' Association: 5-7, Sanban-cho, Chiyoda-ku, Tokyo 102; tel. (3) 3288-1151; fax (3) 3288-3399; internet www .sugar.or.jp; f. 1949; 17 mems; Senior Man. Dir KATSUYUKI SUZUKI.

Japan Tea Exporters' Association: 17, Kitaban-cho, Aoiku, Shizuoka Prefecture 420-0005; tel. (54) 271-3428; fax (54) 271-2177; e-mail japantea1953@yahoo.co.jp; f. 1953; 76 mems; Pres. TOSHIAKI KIRISHIMA.

Japan Toy Association: 4-22-4, Higashi-Komagata, Sumida-ku, Tokyo 130; tel. (3) 3829-2513; fax (3) 3829-2510; e-mail otoiawase2009@toys.or.jp; internet www.toys.or.jp; 228 mems; Chair. TAKEO TAKASU.

Motion Picture Producers' Association of Japan, Inc: Nihonbashi Bldg, 2/F, 1-17-12, Nihonbashi, Chuo-ku, Tokyo 103-0027; tel. (3) 3243-9100; fax (3) 3243-9101; e-mail info@eiren.org; internet www.eiren.org; f. 1945; Pres. NOBUYOSHI OTANI.

EMPLOYERS' ORGANIZATION

Japan Business Federation (JBF) (Nippon Keidanren): Keidanren Kaikan, 1-3-2, Otemachi, Chiyoda-ku, Tokyo 100-8188; tel. (3) 6741-0171; fax (3) 6741-0301; e-mail webmaster@keidanren.or.jp; internet www.keidanren.or.jp; f. 2002; est. by merger of Keidanren (f. 1946) and Nikkeiren (f. 1948); 1,601 mems (June 2010); Chair. HIROMASA YONEKURA; Dir-Gen. YOSHIO NAKAMURA.

UTILITIES

Electricity

Chubu Electric Power Co Inc: 1, Higashi-Shin-cho, Higashi-ku, Nagoya 461-8680; tel. (52) 951-8211; fax (52) 962-4624; internet www .chuden.co.jp; f. 1951; Chair. TOSHIO MITA; Pres. and CEO AKIHISA MIZUNO.

Chugoku Electric Power Co Inc: 4-33, Komachi, Naka-ku, Hiroshima 730-8701; tel. (82) 241-0211; fax (82) 523-6185; e-mail angel@ inet.energia.co.jp; internet www.energia.co.jp; f. 1951; Chair. TAKASHI YAMASHITA; Pres. TOMOHIDE KARITA.

Electric Power Development Co Ltd (J-Power): 6-15-1, Ginza, Chuo-ku, Tokyo 104-8165; tel. (3) 3546-2211; fax (3) 3546-9532; e-mail webmaster@jpower.co.jp; internet www.jpower.co.jp; f. 1952; Chair. KIYOSHI SAWABE; Pres. MASAYOSHI KITAMURA.

Hokkaido Electric Power Co Inc: 1-2, Higashi-Odori, Chuo-ku, Sapporo, Hokkaido 060-8677; tel. (11) 251-1111; internet www.hepco .co.jp; f. 1951; Chair. YOSHITAKA SATO; Pres. KATSUHIKO KAWAI.

Hokuriku Electric Power Co Inc: 15-1, Ushijima-cho, Toyama-shi, Toyama 930-8686; e-mail pub-mast@rikuden.co.jp; internet www.rikuden.co.jp; f. 1951; Chair. ISAO NAGAHARA; Pres. SUSUMU KYUWA.

Kansai Electric Power Co Inc: 3-6-16, Nakanoshima, Kita-ku, Osaka 530-8270; tel. (6) 6441-8821; fax (6) 6441-8598; e-mail postmaster@kepco.co.jp; internet www.kepco.co.jp; Pres. MAKOTO YAGI.

Kyushu Electric Power Co Inc: 2-1-82, Watanabe-dori, Chuo-ku, Fukuoka 810-8726; tel. (92) 761-3031; fax (92) 731-8719; internet www.kyuden.co.jp; Chair. SHINGO MATSUO; Pres. TOSHIO MANABE.

Okinawa Electric Power Co Inc: 5-2-1, Makiminato, Urasoe, Okinawa 901-2602; tel. (98) 877-2341; fax (98) 877-6017; e-mail ir@ okiden.co.jp; internet www.okiden.co.jp; f. 1972; Chair. TSUGIYOSHI TOMA; Pres. DENICHIRO ISHIMINE.

Shikoku Electric Power Co Inc: 2-5, Marunouchi, Takamatsu 760-8573; tel. (878) 21-5061; fax (878) 26-1250; e-mail postmaster@ yonden.co.jp; internet www.yonden.co.jp; f. 1951; Chair. MOMOKI TOKIWA; Pres. AKIRA CHIBA.

Tohoku Electric Power Co Inc: 1-7-1, Hon-cho, Aoba-ku, Sendai 980-8550; tel. (22) 225-2111; fax (22) 225-2550; e-mail webmaster@ tohoku-epco.co.jp; internet www.tohoku-epco.co.jp; Chair. HIROAKI TAKAHASHI; Pres. MAKOTO KAIWA.

Tokyo Electric Power Co Inc: 1-2-2, Yuraku-cho, Chiyoda-ku, Tokyo 100-8560; tel. (3) 6373-1111; fax (3) 3596-8508; internet www .tepco.co.jp; Chair. KAZUHIKO SHIMOKOBE; Pres. TOSHIO NISHIZAWA.

Federation

Federation of Electric Power Companies of Japan (FEPC JAPAN): 1-3-2, Keidanren Kaikan, Ohte-machi, Chiyoda-ku, Tokyo 100-8118; tel. (3) 5221-1440; fax (3) 6361-9024; e-mail webadmin2@ fepc.or.jp; internet www.fepc.or.jp; f. 1952; Chair. MAKOTO YAGI.

Gas

Hokkaido Gas Co Ltd: 7-3-1, Nishi-Odori, Chuo-ku, Sapporo; tel. (11) 231-9511; internet www.hokkaido-gas.co.jp; Chair. SHIGERO KUSANO; CEO HIROSHI OHTSUKI.

Keiyo Gas Co Ltd: 2-8-8, Ichikawa-Minami, Ichikawa, Chiba 272-8580; tel. (47) 361-0211; fax (47) 325-1049; internet www.keiyogas.co .jp; f. 1927; Chair. TOMO KIKUCHI; Pres. HIDEKIYO GATAYAMA.

Osaka Gas Co Ltd: 4-1-2, Hiranomachi, Chuo-ku, Osaka 541-0046; tel. (6) 6205-4715; fax (6) 6222-5831; e-mail keiri@osakagas.co.jp; internet www.osakagas.co.jp; f. 1905; Pres. HIROSHI OZAKI.

Saibu Gas Co: 1-17-1, Chiyo, Hakata-ku, Fukuoka; tel. (92) 633-2345; internet www.saibugas.co.jp; f. 1930; Chair. HIROKI OGAWA; Pres. YUUJI TANAKA.

Toho Gas Co Ltd: 19-18, Sakurada-cho, Atsuta-ko, Nagoya 456-8511; tel. (52) 871-3511; internet www.tohogas.co.jp; f. 1922; Chair. TAKASHI SAEKI; Pres. KOICHI YASUI.

Tokyo Gas Co Inc: 1-5-20, Kaigan, Minato-ku, Tokyo 105; tel. (3) 3433-2111; fax (3) 5472-5385; internet www.tokyo-gas.co.jp; f. 1885; Chair. NORIO ICHINO; Pres. TSUYOSHI OKAMOTO.

Association

Japan Gas Association: 1-1-3, Nishi-Shinbashi, Minato-ku, Tokyo 105-0003; tel. (3) 3502-0116; fax (3) 3502-3676; internet www.gas.or .jp; f. 1947; comprises 209 city gas utilities and 275 assoc. mems; Chair. MITSUNORI TORIHARA.

Water

Nagoya City Waterworks & Sewerage Bureau: 3-1-1, Sannomaru, Naka-ku, Nagoya 460-8508; tel. (52) 972-3608; fax (52) 972-3710; e-mail mail@water.city.nagoya.jp; internet www.water.city .nagoya.jp.

Osaka City Waterworks Bureau: 2-1-10, Nanko-Kita, Suminoe-ku, Osaka 559-8558; tel. (6) 6458-1132; fax (6) 6458-2100; internet www.city.osaka.lg.jp.

Sapporo City Waterworks Bureau: 2-11, Higashi-Odori, Chuo-ku, Sapporo 060-0041; tel. (11) 211-7007; fax (11) 232-1740; e-mail su .somu@suido.city.sapporo.jp; internet www.city.sapporo.jp/suido.

Tokyo Bureau of Waterworks: Yotsuya Kumin Center, 3/F, 87 Naito-cho, Shinjuku-ku, Tokyo 160-8587; tel. (3) 5368-3055; fax (3) 3358-5900; internet www.waterworks.metro.tokyo.jp.

Yokohama Waterworks Bureau: 1-1, Minato-cho, Naka-ku, Yokohama; tel. (45) 671-3055; fax (45) 664-6774; e-mail su-somu@city.yokohama.jp; internet www.city.yokohama.jp/suidou.

Association

Japan Water Works Association (JWWA): 4-8-9, Kudan-Minami, Chiyoda-ku, Tokyo 102-0074; tel. (3) 3264-2281; fax (3) 3262-2244; e-mail kokusai@jwwa.or.jp; internet www.jwwa.or.jp; f. 1932; Exec. Dir MASARU OZAKU.

TRADE UNIONS

A feature of Japan's trade union movement is that the unions are usually based on single enterprises, embracing workers of different occupations in that enterprise. In June 2011 there were 55,148 unions; union membership stood at 9.96m. workers in that year.

Japanese Trade Union Confederation (JTUC–RENGO): 3-2-11, Kanda Surugadai, Chiyoda-ku, Tokyo 101-0062; tel. (3) 5295-0526; fax (3) 5295-0548; e-mail jtuc-kokusai@sv.rengo-net.or.jp; internet www.jtuc-rengo.org; f. 1989; 6.8m. mems; Pres. NOBUAKI KOGA.

Transport

RAILWAYS

Operated by the Japan Railways Group (see below), the high-speed Shinkansen rail network links major cities in Japan. The network consists of the Tokaido line from Tokyo to Shin-Osaka (552.6 km), the Sanyo line from Shin-Osaka to Hakata (623.3 km), the Tohoku line from Tokyo to Morioka (535.3 km) and the Joetsu line from Omiya to Niigata (303.6 km). The Yamagata Shinkansen from Fukushima to Yamagata (87 km) was converted in 1992 from a conventional railway line and is operated as a branch of the Tohoku Shinkansen with through trains from Tokyo. The network had a total route length of 27,182 km in 2012.

Japan Railways (JR) Group: 1-6-5, Marunouchi, Chiyoda-ku, Tokyo 100-0005; tel. (3) 3215-9649; fax (3) 3213-5291; fmrly the state-controlled Japanese National Railways (JNR); reorg. and transferred to private sector in 1987.

Central Japan Railway Co: JR Central Towers, 1-1-4, Meieki, Nakamura-ku, Nagoya 450-6101; tel. (3) 3274-9727; fax (3) 5255-6780; internet www.jr-central.co.jp; f. 1987; also operates travel agency services, etc.; Chair. YOSHIYUKI KASAI; Pres. YOSHIOMI YAMADA.

East Japan Railway Co: 2-2-2, Yoyogi, Shibuya-ku, Tokyo 151-8578; tel. (3) 5334-1151; fax (3) 5334-1110; internet www.jreast.co.jp; privatized in 1987; Chair. SATOSHI SEINO; Pres. and CEO TETSURO TOMITA.

Hokkaido Railway Co: 15-1-1, Kita-11-jo, Chuo-ku, Sapporo 060-8644; tel. (11) 700-5717; fax (11) 700-5719; e-mail keieki@jrhokkaido.co.jp; internet www.jrhokkaido.co.jp; Chair. HIROHIKO KAKINUMA; Pres. KOIKO AKIO.

Japan Freight Railway Co: 5-33-8, Sendagaya, Shibuya-ku, Tokyo 151-0051; internet www.jrfreight.co.jp; f. 1987; Chair. MASAAKI KOBAYASHI; Pres. SHUJI TAMURA.

Kyushu Railway Co: 3-25-21, Hakataekimae, Hakata-ku, Fukuoka 812-8566; tel. (92) 474-2501; fax (92) 474-9745; internet www.jrkyushu.co.jp; f. 1987; Chair. KOJI KARAIKE; Pres. SUSUMU ISHIHARA.

Shikoku Railway Co: 8-33, Hamano-cho, Takamatsu, Kagawa 760-8580; tel. (87) 825-1626; fax (87) 825-1623; internet www.jr-shikoku.co.jp; Chair. HIROSHI MATSUDA KIYOSHI; Pres. and CEO MASAFUMI IZUMI.

West Japan Railway Co: 2-4-24, Shibata, Kita-ku, Osaka 530-8341; tel. (6) 6375-8981; fax (6) 6375-8919; e-mail wjr01020@mxy.meshnet.or.jp; internet www.westjr.co.jp; fully privatized in 2004; Chair. TAKAYUKI SASAKI; Pres. SEIJI MANABE.

Other Principal Private Companies

Hankyu Hanshin Holdings Inc: 1-16-1, Shibata, Kita-ku, Osaka 530-0012; tel. (6) 6373-5001; fax (6) 6373-5042; e-mail web-info@hankyu-hanshin.co.jp; internet www.hankyu-hanshin.co.jp; f. 1907; links Osaka, Kyoto, Kobe and Takarazuka; Pres. KAZUO SUMI.

Keihan Electric Railway Co Ltd: 1-7-31, Otemae, Chuo-ku, Osaka; tel. (6) 6944-2521; fax (6) 6944-2501; internet www.keihan.co.jp; f. 1906; Chair. SHIGETAKA SATO; Pres. YOSHIFUMI KATO.

Keihin Express Electric Railway Co Ltd (Keikyu): 2-20-20, Takanawa, Minato-ku, Tokyo 108-8625; tel. (3) 3280-9120; fax (3) 3280-9199; internet www.keikyu.co.jp; f. 1899; Chair. AKIRA KOTANI; Pres. TSUNEO ISHIWATA.

Keio Electric Railway Co Ltd: 1-9-1, Sekido, Tama-shi, Tokyo 206-8052; tel. (42) 337-3106; fax (42) 374-9322; internet www.keio.co.jp; f. 1913; Chair. KAN KATO; Pres. TADASHI NAGATA.

Keisei Electric Railway Co Ltd: 1-10-3, Oshiage, Sumida-ku, Tokyo 131; tel. (3) 3621-2242; fax (3) 3621-2233; internet www.keisei.co.jp; f. 1909; Pres. NORIO SAIGUSA.

Kinki Nippon Railway Co Ltd (Kintetsu): 6-1-55, Uehommachi, Tennoji-ku, Osaka 543-8585; tel. (6) 6775-3444; fax (6) 6775-3468; internet www.kintetsu.co.jp; f. 1910; Chair. MASANORI YAMAGUCHI; Pres. TETSUYA KOBAYASHI.

Nagoya Railroad Co Ltd: 1-2-4, Meieki, Nakamura-ku, Nagoya-shi 450-8501; tel. (52) 588-0813; fax (52) 588-0815; e-mail info@meitetsu.co.jp; internet www.meitetsu.co.jp; Chair. HIDEO KONO; Pres. ADO YAMAMOTO.

Nankai Electric Railway Co Ltd: 5-1-60, Namba, Chuo-ku, Osaka 542; tel. (6) 6644-7121; internet www.nankai.co.jp; f. 1925; Chair. MAKOTO YAMANAKA; Pres. SHINJI WATARI.

Nishi-Nippon Railroad Co Ltd: 1-11-17, Tenjin-cho, Chuo-ku, Fukuoka 810; tel. (92) 761-6631; fax (92) 722-1405; e-mail www-admin@nnr.co.jp; internet www.nnr.co.jp; serves northern Kyushu; Chair. TSUGUO NAGAO; Pres. KAZAYUKI TAKESHIMA.

Odakyu Electric Railway Co Ltd: 1-8-3, Nishi-Shinjuku, Shinjuku-ku, Tokyo 160-8309; tel. (3) 3349-2526; fax (3) 3346-1899; e-mail ir@odakyu-dentetsu.co.jp; internet www.odakyu.jp; f. 1948; Chair. YORIHIKO OSUGA; Exec. Pres. TOSHIMITSU YAMAKI.

Sanyo Electric Railway Co Ltd: 3-1-1, Oyashiki-dori, Nagata-ku, Kobe 653; tel. (78) 653-0843; internet www.sanyo-railway.co.jp; Chair. FUMIHIRO AMANO; Pres. KAZUHIRO UEKADO.

Seibu Railway Co Ltd: 1-11-1, Kasunokidai, Tokorozawa-shi, Saitama 359; tel. (429) 26-2035; fax (429) 26-2237; internet www.seibu-group.co.jp/railways; f. 1894; Pres. TAKASHI GOTO.

Tobu Railway Co Ltd: 1-1-2, Oshiage, Sumida-ku, Tokyo 131-8522; tel. (3) 3621-5057; internet www.tobu.co.jp; f. 1897; Pres. YOSHIZUMI NEZU.

Tokyo Express Electric Railway (Tokyu) Co Ltd: 5-6, Nanpei-dai-cho, Shibuya-ku, Tokyo 150-8511; tel. (3) 3477-0109; fax (3) 3477-6109; e-mail public@tokyu.co.jp; internet www.tokyu.co.jp; f. 1922; Chair. TOSHIAKI KOSHIMURA; Pres. HIROFUMI NOMOTO.

Principal Subways, Monorails and Tunnels

Subway services operate in Tokyo, Osaka, Kobe, Nagoya, Sapporo, Yokohama, Kyoto, Sendai and Fukuoka. A subway was planned to begin operations in Kawasaki in 2018. Most subway lines operate reciprocal through-services with existing private railway lines which connect the cities with suburban areas.

The first commercial monorail system was introduced in 1964 with straddle-type cars between central Tokyo and Tokyo International Airport, a distance of 13 km. Monorails also operate in other cities, including Chiba, Hiroshima, Kitakyushu and Osaka.

In 1985 the 54-km Seikan Tunnel (the world's longest undersea tunnel), linking the islands of Honshu and Hokkaido, was completed. Electric rail services through the tunnel began operating in 1988.

Fukuoka City Subway: Fukuoka Municipal Transportation Bureau, 2-5-31, Daimyo, Chuo-ku, Fukuoka 810-0041; tel. (92) 732-4202; fax (92) 721-0754; internet subway.city.fukuoka.jp; 3 lines, of a combined 29.8 km open; Dir KENNICHIROU NISHI.

Kobe Rapid Transit Railway Co Ltd: 3-3-9 Tamondoori, Chuo-ku, Kobe; tel. (78) 351-0881; fax (78) 351-1607; internet www.kobe-kousoku.jp; 22.7 km open; Pres. and CEO KEIJI SHIMA.

Nagoya Subway: Transportation Bureau City of Nagoya, Nagoya City Hall, 3-1-1, Sannomaru, Naka-ku, Nagoya 460-8508; tel. (52) 972-3824; fax (52) 972-3938; e-mail goiken@tbcn.city.nagoya.lg.jp; internet www.kotsu.city.nagoya.jp; 87 km open; Dir-Gen. NOBUO YOSHII.

Osaka Monorail: 1-1-5, Higashi-Machi, Shin-Senri, Toyonakashi, Osaka 560-0082; tel. (6) 6871-8281; fax (6) 6871-8284; internet www.osaka-monorail.co.jp; 113.5 km open; Pres. AKIRA INOUE.

Osaka Underground Railway: Osaka Municipal Transportation Bureau, 1-12-62, Kujo-Minami, Nishi-ku, Osaka 550-8552; tel. (6) 6585-1400; fax (6) 6585-6466; internet www.kotsu.city.osaka.jp; f. 1933; 129.9 km; the 7.9 km computer-controlled 'New Tram' service began between Suminoekoen and Nakafuto in 1981; seventh line between Kyobashi and Tsurumi-ryokuchi opened in 1990; eighth line between Itakano and Imazato opened in 2006; Gen. Man. YOSHIHIDE KUSUMOTO.

Sapporo Transportation Bureau: 2-4-1, Oyachi-Higashi, Atsubetsu-ku, Sapporo 004-8555; tel. (11) 896-2708; fax (11) 232-2277; internet www.city.sapporo.jp/st; f. 1971; 3 lines of 48 km; Dir T. IKEGAMI.

Sendai City Subway: Sendai City Transportation Bureau, 1-4-15, Kimachidori, Aoba-ku, Sendai-shi, Miyagi-ken 980-0801; tel. (22) 224-5111; fax (22) 224-6839; internet www.kotsu.city.sendai.jp; 15.4 km open; Dir T. IWAMA.

Tokyo Metro Co Ltd: 3-19-6, Higashi-Ueno, Taito-ku, Tokyo 110-8614; tel. (3) 3837-7046; fax (3) 3837-7219; internet www.tokyometro.jp; f. 2004; operates 8 lines; 195.1 km open (2010); Pres. YOSHIMITSU OKU.

Tokyo Metropolitan Government (TOEI) Underground Railway: Bureau of Transportation, Tokyo Metropolitan Government, 2-8-1, Nishi-Shinjuku, Tokyo 163-8001; tel. (3) 5320-6026; internet www.kotsu.metro.tokyo.jp; operates 4 underground lines, totalling 105 km.

Yokohama Municipal Subway: Transportation Bureau, 6-145, Hanasaki-cho, Nishi-ku, Yokohama 220-0022; tel. (45) 664-2525; fax (45) 664-2828; internet www.city.yokohama.jp/me/koutuu; 40.4 km open; Dir-Gen. MICHINORI KISHIDA.

ROADS

In 2010 Japan's road network extended to an estimated 1,269,000 km, including approximately 55,000 km of highways, and in 2012 Japan had 8,325 km of motorways. In 1999 work was completed on a 29-year project to construct three routes, consisting of a total of 19 bridges, between the islands of Honshu and Shikoku across the Seto inland sea. There is a national bus service, 60 publicly operated services and 298 privately operated services.

In 2005 the major state-owned road authorities were transferred to the private sector. The Japan Highway Public Corpn was privatized and divided into three separate regional expressway companies, servicing central, eastern and western zones. The others were Metropolitan Expressway Public Corpn, Hanshin Expressway Public Corpn and Honshu-Shikoku Bridge Authority.

Central Nippon Expressway Co Ltd: Nagoya Sumimoto Bldg, 8/F, 2-18-19, Nishiki Naka-ku, Nagoya 460-0003; tel. (52) 222-1620; internet www.c-nexco.co.jp; f. 2005; Pres. and CEO TAKEKAZU KANEKO.

East Nippon Expressway Co Ltd: Kasumigaseki Bldg, 15/F, 3-2 Kasumigaseki, Chiyoda-ku, Tokyo 100-8979; tel. (3) 3506-0111; internet www.e-nexco.co.jp; f. 2005; Pres. and CEO. HIROSHI HIROSE.

West Nippon Expressway Co Ltd: 1-6-20, Dojima, Kita-ku, Osaka; tel. (6) 6344-4000; internet corp.w-nexco.co.jp; f. 2005; Pres. YOSHINARI ISHIZUKA.

SHIPPING

At 31 December 2013 the Japanese flag registered fleet comprised 3,561 vessels, with a total displacement of 19.9m. grt, including 675 general cargo carriers, 198 bulk carriers, 656 tankers and 173 gas tankers. The main ports are Tokyo, Yokohama, Nagoya and Osaka.

Principal Companies

Daiichi Chuo Kisen Kaisha: 2-14-4, Shintomi-cho, Chuo-ku, Tokyo 104-8544; tel. (3) 5540-1997; fax (3) 3523-8987; internet www.firstship.co.jp; f. 1960; liner and tramp services; Pres. MASAKAZU YAKUSHIJI.

Iino Kaiun Kaisha Ltd: Iino Bldg, 2-10-1, Uchisaiwai-cho, Chiyoda-ku, Tokyo 100-0011; tel. (3) 5408-0356; e-mail ikk_soumu2@ex.iino.co.jp; internet www.iino.co.jp; f. 1899; cargo and tanker services; Pres. TOMOYUKI SEKINE.

Kawasaki Kisen Kaisha Ltd (K Line): Iino Bldg, 2-1-1, Uchisaiwai-cho, Chiyoda-ku, Tokyo 100-8540; tel. (3) 3595-5000; fax (3) 3595-5001; e-mail otaki@email.kline.co.jp; internet www.kline.co.jp; f. 1919; containers, cars, LNG, LPG and oil tankers, bulk carriers; Chair. of Bd HIROYUKI MAEKAWA; Pres. JIRO ASAKURA.

Mitsui OSK Lines Ltd: Shosen Mitsui Bldg, 2-1-1, Toranomon, Minato-ku, Tokyo 105-8688; tel. (3) 3587-7092; fax (3) 3587-7734; internet www.mol.co.jp; f. 1942; merged with Navix Line Ltd in 1999; worldwide container, liner, tramp, and specialized carrier and tanker services; Chair. AKIMITSU ASHIDA; Pres. KOICHI MUTO.

Nippon Yusen Kaisha (NYK) Line: 2-3-2, Marunouchi, Chiyoda-ku, Tokyo 100-0005; tel. (3) 3284-5151; fax (3) 3284-6361; internet www.nyk.com; f. 1885; merged with Showa Line Ltd in 1998; worldwide container, cargo, pure car and truck carriers, tanker and bulk carrying services; Chair. KOJI MIYAHARA; Pres. YASUMI KUDO.

Nissho Shipping Co Ltd: Mori Bldg, 7/F, Rm 33, 3-8-21, Toranomon, Minato-ku, Tokyo 105-0001; tel. (3) 3438-3511; fax (3) 3438-3566; f. 1943; Pres. KENICHI YAMAGUCHI.

Ryukyu Kaiun KK: 1-24-11, Nishi-Machi, Naha, Okinawa 900-0036; tel. (98) 868-8161; fax (98) 868-8561; internet www.rkkline.co.jp; f. 1950; cargo and passenger services on domestic routes; Pres. YAMASHIRO HIROMI.

Taiheiyo Kaiun Co Ltd: Mitakokusai Bldg, 23/F, 1-4-28, Minato-ku, Tokyo 108-0073; tel. (3) 5445-5800; fax (3) 5445-5801; internet www.taiheiyokk.co.jp; f. 1951; cargo and tanker services; Pres. TAKESHI MATSUNAGA.

CIVIL AVIATION

Three international airports serve Tokyo: Narita, located in Chiba prefecture; Haneda; and Ibaraki, which opened in March 2010. A second runway was opened at Narita in 2002. A fourth runway at Haneda, along with a third terminal for international flights, opened in October 2010. In 1994 the world's first offshore international airport (Kansai International Airport) was opened in Osaka Bay, and a second runway was completed in 2007. Nearly 95 other airports handle regional and some international flights.

Air Do Co Ltd: 1-2-9, Kita Sanjo Nishi, Chuo-ku, Sapporo; tel. (11) 252-5533; fax (11) 252-5580; e-mail postbear@airdo.co.jp; internet www.airdo.co.jp; f. 1996, fmrly Hokkaido International Airlines Co Ltd, adopted trading name as above in 2012; domestic service between Tokyo and Sapporo; Pres. SAITO SADAO.

All Nippon Airways (ANA): Shiodome City Center, 1-5-2, Higashi-Shimbashi, Minato-ku, Tokyo 105-7133; tel. (3) 6735-1000; fax (3) 6735-1005; internet www.ana.co.jp; f. 1952; operates domestic passenger and freight services; scheduled international services to the Far East, the USA and Europe; charter services worldwide; Chair. YOJI OHASHI; Pres. and CEO SHINCHIRO ITO.

ANA Wings: 3-3-2, Haneda Airport, Ota-ku, Tokyo 144-8515; internet www.anawings.co.jp; f. 2010 from the merger of All Nippon Network, Air Next and Air Central; wholly owned subsidiary of All Nippon Airways; regional and domestic services; Pres. and CEO AKIHIKO HASEGAWA.

Hokkaido Air System: New Chitose Airport, Bibi Chitose City, Hokkaido 066-0055; tel. (123) 46-5533; fax (123) 46-5534; internet www.hac-air.co.jp; f. 1997; domestic services on Hokkaido; Pres. CHIHIRO TAMURA.

Ibex Airlines: 1-2-3, Shinsuna, Koto-ku, Tokyo 136-8640; internet www.ibexair.co.jp; f. 1999; operates domestic flights from Osaka and Narita International Airports; Chair. TAKAO ASAI; Pres. HATTORI HIROYUKI.

Japan Air Commuter: 787-4, Mizobe Humototyou, Kirishima, Kagoshima Prefecture; tel. (995) 582-151; fax (995) 582-673; e-mail info@jac.co.jp; internet www.jac.co.jp; f. 1983; subsidiary of JAL; domestic services; Chair. YOSHITOMI ONO; Pres. ARATA YASUJIMA.

Japan Airlines (JAL): 2-4-11, Higashi-Shinagawa, Shinagawa-ku, Tokyo 140-8605; tel. (3) 5769-6476; internet www.jal.com; f. 2002; Chair. KAZUO INAMORI; Pres. YOSHIHARU UEKI.

Japan Transocean Air Co Ltd: 3-24, Yamashita-cho, Naha-shi, Okinawa 900-0027; tel. (98) 857-2112; fax (98) 857-9396; internet www.jal.co.jp/jta; f. 1967; adopted present name 1993; subsidiary of JAL; domestic passenger services; Pres. MANABU SATO.

Skymark Airlines: 3-5-7, Haneda Airport, Ota-ku, Tokyo 144-0041; tel. (3) 5402-6767; fax (3) 5402-6770; e-mail info@skymark.co.jp; internet www.skymark.co.jp; f. 1997; domestic services; Chair. TAKASHI IDE; Pres. and CEO SHINICHI NISHIKUBO.

Tourism

The ancient capital of Kyoto, pagodas and temples, forests and mountains, traditional festivals and the classical Kabuki theatre are some of the many tourist attractions of Japan. Receipts from tourism (excluding passenger transport) in 2012 totalled an estimated US $14,576m. International arrivals declined by 27.8% in 2011, to 6.2m. This decrease, reportedly the largest since records began in 1950, was attributed to the impact of the earthquake, tsunami and nuclear disaster that occurred in March that year, as well as to the strength of the yen. In 2012, however, the number of arrivals recovered, rising by 34.6%, to 8.4m. The Republic of Korea, China and Taiwan are leading sources of visitors.

Japan National Tourism Organization (JNTO): Tokyo Kotsu Kaikan Bldg, 2-10-1, Yuraku-cho, Chiyoda-ku, Tokyo 100-0006; tel. (3) 3201-3331; fax (3) 3216-1846; internet www.jnto.go.jp; f. 1964; Pres. RYOICHI MATSUYAMA.

Japan Tourism Agency (JTA): General Affairs Division, National and Regional Planning Bureau, 2-1-3, Kasumigaseki, Chiyoda-ku, Tokyo 100-8918; tel. (3) 5253-8111; fax (3) 3580-7982; e-mail webmaster@mlit.go.jp; internet www.mlit.go.jp/kankocho; f. 2008; aims to promote Japan as a tourist destination and, in conjunction with JNTO, to achieve govt objectives; Commr NORIFUMI IDEE.

Defence

As assessed at November 2013, the total strength of the Japanese Self-Defence Forces was some 247,150: ground self-defence 151,050, maritime self-defence 45,500, air self-defence 47,100 and central staff 3,500. Paramilitary forces numbered 12,650, and reserve forces comprised an additional 56,100 personnel. Military service is voluntary. At November 2013 US forces stationed in Japan comprised 2,500 army, 12,500 air force and 6,750 navy personnel, together with 14,950 members of the US Marine Corps.

Defence Budget: 4,884,800m. yen for the financial year ending 31 March 2015.

Chief of the Joint Staff Council: Gen. SHIGERU IWASAKI.

Chief of Staff of Ground Self-Defence Force: Gen. EIJI KIMIZUKA.

Chief of Staff of Maritime Self-Defence Force: Adm. KATSUTOSHI KAWANO.

Chief of Staff of Air Self-Defence Force: Gen. HARUHIKO KATAOKA.

Education

Education is compulsory between the ages of six and 15. A kindergarten (*yochien*) system provides education for children aged between three and five years of age, although the majority of kindergartens are privately controlled. In 2012 there were 13,170 kindergartens, which were attended by 1.6m. children. All children between six and 15 are required to attend six-year elementary schools (*shogakko*) and three-year lower secondary schools (or middle schools—*chugakko*). In 2009/10 enrolment at pre-primary school included 88% of pupils in the relevant age-group, while enrolment at primary level in 2010/11 included 100% of pupils in the relevant age-group. Enrolment at secondary level included 99% of students in the relevant age-group in the same year. In 2012 there were 21,460 elementary schools, at which 6.8m. pupils were enrolled, and 10,699 lower secondary schools, at which 3.6m. pupils were enrolled. Upper secondary schools (or high schools— *kotogakko*) provide a three-year course in general topics, or a vocational course in subjects such as agriculture, commerce, fine art and technical studies. In 2012 there were 5,022 upper secondary schools, at which 3.4m. pupils were enrolled.

There are four types of institution for higher education. Universities (*daigaku*) offer degree and postgraduate courses. In 2012 there were 783 universities and graduate schools, at which 2.9m. students were enrolled. Junior colleges (*tanki-daigaku*) provide less specialized two- to three-year courses, credits for which can count towards a first degree. In 2012 there were 372 junior colleges in Japan. Both universities and junior colleges offer facilities for teacher training. Colleges of technology (*koto-senmon-gakko*), of which there were 57 in 2012, offer a five-year specialized training course. Since 1991 colleges of technology have been able to offer short-term advanced courses. A combined total of 200,735 students were enrolled at junior colleges and colleges of technology in 2012. Special training colleges (*senshu-gakko*) offer advanced courses in technical and vocational subjects, lasting for at least one year. In 2012 there were 3,249 special training colleges in Japan. The budget for the financial year ending 31 March 2015 allocated 5,442,100m. yen to education and science (equivalent to 5.7% of projected expenditure).

JORDAN

Introductory Survey

LOCATION, CLIMATE, LANGUAGE, RELIGION, FLAG, CAPITAL

The Hashemite Kingdom of Jordan is an almost landlocked state in western Asia. It is bordered by Israel and the Palestinian Territories to the west, by Syria to the north, by Iraq to the east and by Saudi Arabia to the south. The port of Aqaba, in the far south, gives Jordan a narrow outlet to the Red Sea. The climate is hot and dry. The average annual temperature is about 15°C (60°F), but there are wide diurnal variations. Temperatures in Amman are generally between −1°C (30°F) and 32°C (90°F). More extreme conditions are found in the valley of the River Jordan and on the shores of the Dead Sea (a lake on the Israeli–Jordanian frontier), where the temperature may exceed 50°C (122°F) in summer. The official language is Arabic. More than 90% of the population are Sunni Muslims, while there are small communities of Christians and Shi'a Muslims. The national flag (proportions 1 by 2) has three equal horizontal stripes, of black, white and green, with a red triangle, containing a seven-pointed white star, at the hoist. The capital is Amman.

CONTEMPORARY POLITICAL HISTORY

Historical Context

Palestine (including the present-day West Bank territory) and Transjordan (the East Bank) were formerly parts of Turkey's Ottoman Empire. During the First World War (1914–18), when Turkey was allied with Germany, the Arabs under Ottoman rule rebelled. British forces, with Arab support, occupied Palestine and Transjordan in 1917–18, when the Turks withdrew. British occupation continued after the war, when the Ottoman Empire was dissolved. In 1920 Palestine and Transjordan were formally placed under British administration by a League of Nations mandate. In 1921 Abdullah ibn Hussein, a member of the Hashimi (Hashemite) dynasty of Arabia, was proclaimed Amir (Emir) of Transjordan.

Under the British mandate Transjordan (formally separated from Palestine in 1923) gained increasing autonomy, and in 1928 the United Kingdom acknowledged its nominal independence, while retaining certain financial and military powers. Amir Abdullah followed a generally pro-British policy and supported the Allied cause in the Second World War (1939–45). The mandate was terminated on 22 March 1946, when Transjordan attained full independence. On 25 May Abdullah was proclaimed King, and a new Constitution took effect.

When the British Government terminated its mandate in Palestine in May 1948, Jewish leaders there proclaimed the State of Israel. Palestinian Arabs, however, with military support from Arab states, opposed Israeli claims, and hostilities continued until July. Transjordan's forces occupied about 5,900 sq km of Palestine, including East Jerusalem, and this was confirmed by the armistice with Israel in April 1949. In June the country was renamed Jordan, and in April 1950, following a referendum, King Abdullah formally annexed the West Bank territory, which contained many Arab refugees from Israeli-held areas.

Domestic Political Affairs

In July 1951 King Abdullah was assassinated in Jerusalem by a Palestinian belonging to an extremist Islamist organization. Abdullah was succeeded by his eldest son, Talal ibn Abdullah, hitherto Crown Prince. However, in August 1952, because of Talal's mental incapacity, the crown passed to his son, Hussein ibn Talal, then 16 years of age. King Hussein formally came to power in May 1953.

In March 1956, responding to Arab nationalist sentiment, King Hussein dismissed the British army officer who had been Chief of Staff of the British-equipped and -financed Arab Legion (the Jordanian armed forces) since 1939. Jordan's treaty relationship with the United Kingdom was ended in March 1957, and British troops completed their withdrawal from Jordan in July.

The refugee camps in the West Bank became the centre of Palestinian resistance to Israel, and during the 1950s there were numerous attacks on Israeli territory by groups of Palestinian *fedayeen* ('martyrs'). In September 1963 the creation of a unified 'Palestinian entity' was approved by the Council of the League of Arab States (the Arab League, see p. 362), and the first Palestinian congress was held in the Jordanian sector of Jerusalem in May–June 1964, at which it was agreed to form the Palestine Liberation Organization (PLO), which would be financed by the Arab League and would recruit military units to form a Palestine Liberation Army (PLA). The principal Palestinian guerrilla organization within the PLO was the Palestine National Liberation Movement, known as Fatah ('Conquest'), led from 1968 by Yasser Arafat. However, King Hussein regarded the establishment of the PLO as a threat to Jordanian sovereignty, and from the outset refused to allow the PLA to train in Jordan or the PLO to levy taxes from Palestinian refugees residing in his country.

In April 1965 Hussein nominated his brother Hassan ibn Talal to be Crown Prince. During the Six-Day War of June 1967 Israel made substantial military gains, including possession of the whole of Jerusalem (which was incorporated into Israel) and the West Bank; the latter became an Israeli 'administered territory'. The influx of Palestinian refugees into the East Bank bolstered the strength of the PLO, whose continued armed raids on the Israeli-administered territories challenged the personal authority of King Hussein and the sovereignty of the Jordanian Government. King Hussein responded by expelling the guerrilla groups, after a civil war that lasted from September 1970 to July 1971. Aid to Jordan from Kuwait and other wealthy Arab states, suspended after the expulsion of the Palestinian fighters, was only restored following Jordan's military support for Syria during the Arab–Israeli War of October 1973. At an Arab summit meeting in Rabat, Morocco, in October 1974 King Hussein supported a unanimous resolution recognizing the PLO as the 'sole legitimate representative of the Palestinian people' and granting the organization the right to establish an independent national authority on any piece of Palestinian land to be liberated.

In response to this resolution, in November 1974 both chambers of the Jordanian National Assembly (which had equal representation for the East and West Banks) approved constitutional amendments that empowered the King to dissolve the Assembly and to postpone elections for up to 12 months. The Assembly was dissolved later that month, although it was briefly reconvened in February 1976, when it approved a constitutional amendment giving the King power to postpone elections indefinitely and to convene the Assembly as required. A royal decree of April 1978 provided for the creation of a National Consultative Council, with 60 members appointed for a two-year term by the King, on the Prime Minister's recommendation, to debate proposed legislation.

Joint Palestinian-Jordanian peace initiatives

A proposal put forward by US President Ronald Reagan in September 1982 for an autonomous Palestinian authority on the West Bank, in association with Jordan, was rejected by Yasser Arafat following talks with King Hussein. In January 1984, however, the King responded by dissolving the National Consultative Council and recalling the National Assembly for the first time since 1967—in effect creating the kind of Palestinian forum envisaged by the Reagan initiative. Israel allowed the surviving West Bank deputies to attend the Assembly, which approved constitutional amendments enabling elections to be held in the East Bank, while West Bank deputies would be chosen by the Assembly itself. After discussions with the PLO leader in January 1984 on a joint Palestinian-Jordanian peace initiative, King Hussein's proposals for negotiations, based on UN Security Council Resolution 242 (the resolution, adopted in November 1967, sought to return the region's territorial boundaries to the pre-Six-Day War status, but incorporated implicit recognition of an Israeli state), met with a non-committal response from the Palestine National Council (PNC), which convened in Amman in November 1984. President Hosni Mubarak of Egypt gave his support to Hussein's proposals, following the resumption of diplomatic relations between the two countries in September. In February 1985 King Hussein and

Yasser Arafat announced the terms of a Jordanian-Palestinian agreement, proposing a confederated state of Jordan and Palestine to be reached through the convening of a conference of all concerned parties in the Middle East, including the PLO.

In July 1985 Israel rejected a list of seven Palestinians, five of whom were members of the PLO or had links with the PNC, whom King Hussein had presented to the USA as candidates for a joint Jordanian-Palestinian delegation to preliminary peace talks. Further progress was hindered by a series of terrorist incidents in which the PLO was implicated, and King Hussein came under increasing pressure to advance the peace process, if necessary without PLO participation. In September President Reagan revived his 1984 plan to sell military equipment to the value of some US $1,900m. to Jordan. The proposal was approved by the US Congress on the condition that Jordan enter into direct talks with Israel before 1 March 1986. However, such talks were obstructed by a gradual rapprochement between Jordan and Syria, both of which supported a Middle East peace settlement through an international conference.

Frustrated by the lack of co-operation from Yasser Arafat in advancing the aims of the Jordanian-PLO peace initiative, King Hussein publicly severed political links with the PLO on 19 February 1986. Arafat was subsequently ordered to close his main PLO offices in Jordan by 1 April. A number of Fatah officers loyal to Arafat were expelled, and in July the Jordanian authorities closed all 25 Fatah offices in Amman; only 12 bureaux belonging to the PLO remained.

Despite the termination of political co-ordination with the PLO, Jordan continued to reject Israeli requests for direct peace talks that excluded a form of PLO representation. However, Jordan's subsequent efforts to strengthen its influence in the Israeli-occupied territories (Occupied Territories), and to foster a Palestinian constituency there independent of Arafat's PLO, coincided with Israeli measures to grant limited autonomy to Palestinians in the West Bank. In March 1986 the Jordanian House of Representatives approved a draft law increasing the number of seats in the House from 60 to 142 (71 seats each for the East and West Banks), thereby providing for greater representation for West Bank Palestinians in the National Assembly. In August, with Israeli support, Jordan announced a five-year development plan, valued at US $1,300m., for the West Bank and Gaza Strip. Meanwhile, support for Arafat among Palestinians in the Occupied Territories, and in Jordan, was consolidated as he re-established himself at the head of a reunified PLO at the 18th session of the PNC in April 1987 (when the Jordanian-PLO accord of 1985 was formally abrogated).

In May 1987, following secret meetings with King Hussein, the Israeli Minister of Foreign Affairs, Shimon Peres, claimed to have made significant progress on the crucial issue of Palestinian representation at a Middle East peace conference. He reportedly had the consent of Egypt, Jordan and the USA to convene a conference involving the five permanent members of the UN Security Council and a delegation of Palestinians—including the PLO—who rejected terrorism and accepted Security Council Resolutions 242 and 338 (the latter defined the terms of immediate peace following the 1973 Arab–Israeli War) as the basis for negotiations. However, Israel's Prime Minister, Itzhak Shamir, reiterated his alternative proposal of direct regional talks excluding the PLO, and Peres failed to secure the support of a majority of the Israeli Cabinet for his proposals.

At the first full meeting of the Arab League for eight years, convened in Amman in November 1987, King Hussein pursued an agenda of greater Arab unity in support of Iraq in its war with Iran. Prior to the summit, Jordan restored full diplomatic relations with Libya (severed in 1984), which had modified its support for Iran. However, King Hussein's appeal for Egypt to be restored to membership of the League (suspended following the peace treaty with Israel in 1979) was resisted by Libya and Syria, although 11 Arab states subsequently re-established diplomatic relations. Jordan also announced the resumption of co-operation with the PLO.

These achievements were soon overshadowed by the Palestinian *intifada* (uprising), which erupted in the West Bank and Gaza Strip in December 1987, in protest against the continued Israeli occupation and the seemingly indifferent attitude of Arab League states to the Palestinians' plight. The *intifada*, and the increasingly violent Israeli response, boosted international support for the PLO and Palestinian national rights. At an extraordinary meeting of the Arab League held in the Algerian capital, Algiers, in June 1988, King Hussein gave the *intifada* his unconditional support and insisted that the PLO must represent the Palestinians at any future peace conference. Furthermore, in accordance with agreements reached at the meeting, on 31 July Jordan cancelled the West Bank development plan and severed its legal and administrative links with the territory.

On 15 November 1988 the PNC, meeting in Algiers, proclaimed the establishment of an independent State of Palestine and, for the first time, endorsed UN Security Council Resolution 242 as a basis for a Middle East peace settlement, thus implicitly recognizing Israel. Jordan and 60 other countries recognized the new state. Addressing a special session of the UN General Assembly in Geneva, Switzerland, in December, Arafat renounced violence on behalf of the PLO. The USA subsequently opened a dialogue with the organization.

In April 1989 there was rioting in several cities, after the Jordanian Government imposed sizeable price increases on basic goods and services. The riots led to the resignation of the Prime Minister, Zaid Rifai, and his Cabinet. Field Marshal Sharif Zaid ibn Shaker, a former Commander-in-Chief of the Jordanian Armed Forces, was appointed to head a new Government. King Hussein subsequently announced that a general election would be held for the first time since 1967. The election to the 80-seat House of Representatives, which proceeded in November 1989, was contested by 647 candidates, mostly independents, as the ban on political parties (in force since 1963) remained. However, the Muslim Brotherhood was able to present candidates for election, owing to its legal status as a charity; it won 20 seats, while as many as 14 seats were won by independent Islamist candidates who supported the Brotherhood. In December King Hussein appointed former premier Mudar Badran as Prime Minister. In January 1990 Badran pledged to abolish martial law (which had been suspended in December 1989) within four to six months, and to liberalize the judicial system; he also announced the abolition of the anti-communism law (in force since 1954). In April King Hussein appointed a 60-member commission to devise a national charter that would legalize political parties. The draft national charter was approved by the King in January 1991, and further endorsed by Hussein and leading political figures in June. Also in January the Cabinet was reorganized to include five members of the Muslim Brotherhood.

Iraq's invasion of Kuwait in August 1990, and the consequent imposition of economic sanctions by the UN against Iraq, had a profound impact on Jordan: Iraq was its principal trading partner, and Jordan relied on supplies of Iraqi petroleum. Although King Hussein condemned the Iraqi invasion, he was slow to do so, and advocated an 'Arab solution' to the crisis. There was considerable support for the Iraqi President, Saddam Hussain, among the Jordanian population, particularly among Palestinians. King Hussein was critical of the US-led deployment of multinational military forces in Saudi Arabia and the Persian (Arabian) Gulf, and in late 1990 he visited numerous Middle East and other capitals in an attempt to avert a war. Jordan's response to the Gulf crisis prompted the USA to review its military and economic assistance to the kingdom and led to a deterioration in Jordan's relations with Egypt and Saudi Arabia, both of which contributed to the US-led force. However, diplomatic relations between Jordan and Iran were re-established (having been severed in 1981).

Meanwhile, Jordan secured the approval of the USA by agreeing to join with a Palestinian delegation at the Middle East peace conference, which opened in Madrid, Spain, in October 1991. Subsequent talks in Washington, DC, USA, and Moscow, Russia, between the Israeli and the joint Jordanian-Palestinian delegations remained deadlocked with regard to substantive issues until September 1993, when Israel and the PLO agreed to a declaration of principles regarding Palestinian self-rule in the Occupied Territories. On the signing of the Declaration of Principles, which King Hussein welcomed, the Jordanian-Palestinian delegation was disbanded, and Jordan and Israel concluded an agreement that defined the agenda for subsequent bilateral negotiations within the context of the Middle East peace conference. The talks were to address the following issues: refugees and displaced persons; security; water resources; the demarcation of the border between Jordan and Israel; and future bilateral co-operation.

In 1991 Jordan and the PLO had agreed on the principle of confederation between Jordan and whatever Palestinian entity ultimately emerged from the Middle East peace process, and in July 1993 they undertook to form six committees to discuss relations between Jordan and the Occupied Territories during a period of transitional Palestinian self-rule. Jordan was formally excluded from discussion of some of the issues, however, following the signing of the Declaration of Principles. In January 1994 the PLO agreed to sign a comprehensive economic co-operation agreement with Jordan, and to establish a joint committee to co-ordinate financial policy in the Palestinian territories. In the same month Jordan signed a draft security accord with the PLO.

King Hussein concludes a peace treaty with Israel

On 25 July 1994 King Hussein and the Israeli Prime Minister, Itzhak Rabin, meeting in the US capital, signed the Washington Declaration, which formally ended the state of war that had existed between Jordan and Israel since 1948. In October 1994 the two countries signed a full peace treaty settling outstanding issues of contention between them and providing, *inter alia*, for the establishment of diplomatic relations and for talks on economic and security co-operation. The official normalization of relations between Jordan and Israel had been completed by 18 January 1996. In Jordan the peace treaty was opposed by Islamist militants, and it was also criticized by Syria. The PLO leadership complained that the treaty undermined Palestinian claims to sovereignty over Jerusalem. None the less, in January 1995 the PLO and Jordan signed an agreement regulating relations between Jordan and the Palestinian territories with regard to economic affairs, finance, banking, education, transport, telecommunications, information and administration. At the same time, the PLO acknowledged Jordan's custodianship of the Muslim holy places in Jerusalem for as long as Jordan recognized and supported Palestinian claims to sovereignty over East Jerusalem.

Meanwhile, in June 1991 Taher al-Masri was appointed to replace Badran as Prime Minister. However, in the period preceding the opening of the National Assembly in December, it became clear that al-Masri could not command majority support in the legislature; he was forced to resign in November, whereupon Sharif Zaid ibn Shaker again assumed the premiership. In July 1992 the House of Representatives adopted legislation whereby, subject to certain conditions, political parties were formally legalized. In May 1993 King Hussein appointed Abd al-Salam al-Majali, the head of the Jordanian delegation to the Middle East peace conference, to the premiership.

In August 1993 King Hussein unexpectedly dissolved the House of Representatives, and announced changes in voting procedures for subsequent general elections: voters were to be allowed to cast one vote only, rather than multiple votes equal to the number of candidates contesting a given constituency. Some 68% of the electorate were reported to have participated in Jordan's first multi-party general election, held on 8 November. By far the largest number of deputies returned to the House of Representatives were independent centrists loyal to the King. The Islamic Action Front (IAF, the political wing of the Muslim Brotherhood) emerged as the second largest party in the legislature. A new Senate (House of Notables) was appointed by the King on 18 November, and a new Cabinet, led by al-Majali, was announced in December. Al-Majali was dismissed in January 1995, whereupon ibn Shaker once again assumed the premiership.

King Hussein implemented a further extensive cabinet reorganization in February 1996, appointing Abd al-Karim al-Kabariti, the Minister of Foreign Affairs (a post he retained), as Prime Minister and Minister of Defence. In August rioting erupted in southern Jordan after the Government imposed a sharp increase on the price of bread. The unrest quickly spread to other parts of the country, including impoverished areas of the capital. King Hussein responded by suspending the legislature and deploying the army in order to suppress the worst disturbances. Prime Minister al-Kabariti was unexpectedly dismissed by Hussein in March 1997, reportedly as a result of disagreement over issues relating to Jordan's policies towards Israel. Al-Majali again assumed the premiership.

In July 1997 the IAF announced its intention to boycott the forthcoming parliamentary elections, in protest at what it regarded as the Government's overly concessionary policies towards Israel and at recent restrictive amendments to press legislation. Several other parties also boycotted the polls. At the general election, which took place on 4 November, 62 of the 80 seats in the new House of Representatives were won by pro-Government candidates; 10 seats were secured by nationalist and left-wing candidates, and eight by independent Islamists. A new Senate was appointed by the King on 22 November. In August 1998 Fayez al-Tarawneh was appointed Prime Minister, and a new Cabinet was subsequently named.

The accession of King Abdullah

Meanwhile, in July 1998 King Hussein began to undergo treatment for cancer in the USA. In August he issued a royal decree transferring responsibility for certain executive duties to his brother, Crown Prince Hassan. On King Hussein's return to Jordan in January 1999, he prompted renewed speculation about the royal succession by appointing Hassan as his 'deputy'. On 24 January King Hussein issued a royal decree naming his eldest son, Abdullah, as Crown Prince of Jordan. Although Hassan had been regent since 1965, King Hussein was said to have been dissatisfied with his brother's handling of Jordanian affairs during his absence, in particular his attempts to intervene in military matters. Two days later the King left Jordan for emergency treatment in the USA, following a rapid deterioration in his health. King Hussein returned to Amman on 5 February 1999 and was pronounced dead on 7 February. The Crown Prince was sworn in, as King Abdullah ibn al-Hussein, on the same day. Prince Hamzeh ibn al-Hussein, the late King's youngest son, became the new Crown Prince.

In March 1999 King Abdullah announced the formation of a new Cabinet, in which several ministers regarded as loyal to Prince Hassan were replaced. Abd al-Raouf al-Rawabdeh replaced al-Tarawneh as Prime Minister and Minister of Defence. Former premier al-Kabariti was appointed Chief of the Royal Court—an important post since the incumbent serves as the primary link between the King and the Government. King Abdullah charged al-Rawabdeh with implementing 'fundamental reforms', including a strengthening of the rule of law and further democratization, as well as economic reforms to address the serious problems of poverty and unemployment. Opposition groups expressed cautious loyalty to the new monarch. Although in March 1999 King Abdullah had, under a recent amnesty law, released almost 500 prisoners, in April the Arab Human Rights Organization in Jordan criticized the Government for an increase in human rights violations, including arrests of journalists and harsh treatment of prisoners held in detention centres. Nevertheless, censorship of the foreign press was revoked during that month, and in June the Government agreed to amend part of the controversial Press and Publications Law in order to ease certain restrictions on journalists.

In January 2000 al-Kabariti, a long-standing rival of al-Rawabdeh, resigned as Chief of the Royal Court for unspecified reasons. He was replaced by another former premier, Fayez al-Tarawneh. In June King Abdullah dismissed Prime Minister al-Rawabdeh, appointing Ali Abu al-Ragheb in his place; a new Cabinet was duly appointed.

In April 2001 King Abdullah extended the current term of the House of Representatives by two years. On 16 June the King ordered the dissolution of the House, which had been sitting in extraordinary session since April, and effected a cabinet reorganization. On 22 July he approved new electoral legislation, which provided for the redrawing of electoral boundaries (the number of constituencies was to rise from 21 to 44) in order to increase the number of seats in the House of Representatives from 80 to 104, and a reduction of the age of eligibility to vote from 19 years to 18. The Muslim Brotherhood threatened to boycott the forthcoming elections, in view of the Government's failure to meet its demand for the reintroduction of an 'electoral list' system. Critics of the amendments also complained that they failed to address the issue of under-representation in the legislature of Jordanians of Palestinian origin. Nevertheless, the new law did provide for the formation of special committees to monitor the electoral process. Shortly afterwards it was reported that the November elections were to be postponed until late 2002 for technical reasons. In August 2001 legislation was enacted imposing a ban on public gatherings and demonstrations. In October, following the suicide attacks on the USA (see Foreign Affairs), King Abdullah issued a royal decree amending Jordan's penal code in order to strengthen counter-terrorism measures; he also imposed tougher penalties on those found guilty of 'publication crimes'. In November the King appointed a new 40-member Senate upon the expiry of its term.

In January 2002 Prime Minister al-Ragheb submitted the resignation of his Government, but was asked by King Abdullah to form a new administration capable of initiating economic and social reforms prior to parliamentary elections. A new Cabinet was named shortly afterwards. In late January violent clashes, in which a policeman died, erupted between protesters and security forces in Ma'an, following the death of a local youth in police custody, who demonstrators alleged had been the victim of police brutality. The Government later announced that two investigations had been launched to determine the causes of both the adolescent's death and the subsequent riots. In November security forces in Ma'an carried out a large-scale operation aimed at detaining a local Islamist cleric, Muhammad Shalabi, and his supporters, who the Government claimed had played an important role in the unrest. Many observers believed that the security operation was linked to the recent assassination of a US diplomat (see Foreign Affairs). At least three civilians and two police officers were reportedly killed during the week-long campaign; however, Shalabi apparently evaded capture. Meanwhile, King Abdullah announced in August 2002 that legislative elections would be postponed until 2003, owing to the continuing instability in the region. In February of that year he approved amendments to draft electoral legislation that would—from the next general election—increase the number of seats in the House of Representatives from 104 to 110, in order to provide a quota of six seats for female legislators.

The 2003 legislative elections

At parliamentary elections held on 17 June 2003 tribal representatives and Hashemite loyalists won 80 of the 110 seats in the House of Representatives, while the IAF, the largest opposition party, won 17 seats. In late July a new Cabinet led by al-Ragheb was announced. However, the Prime Minister resigned in October, following considerable criticism of the Government over the slow pace of reform and accusations of corruption. Shortly thereafter, King Abdullah inaugurated a new Cabinet under the premiership of Faisal al-Fayez, who was also named as Minister of Defence. The appointment of three female ministers preceded that of an expanded 55-member Senate in November, in accordance with constitutional guidelines that membership of the Senate must be no larger than one-half that of the House of Representatives.

It was revealed in April 2004 that Jordanian security forces had made a number of arrests that had possibly averted a major terrorist attack in the kingdom. It was alleged that militant Islamists closely linked to the al-Qa'ida network had planted huge quantities of explosives in trucks, which they had planned to detonate against a number of targets, including the Prime Ministry and the Ministry of the Interior. One of the arrested militants reportedly confessed that the instigator of the plot was Abu Musab al-Zarqawi, the Jordanian national whom US officials believed was directing attacks against the US-led coalition, security forces and civilian targets in Iraq. In February 2006 a military court sentenced to death nine men, including al-Zarqawi (who, together with three other defendants, was charged *in absentia*), for their role in the terrorist plot.

In November 2004 King Abdullah removed the title of Crown Prince from his half-brother, Hamzeh ibn al-Hussein, citing the wish to give him more freedom to undertake tasks that this 'symbolic' position did not permit. The King accepted the resignation of al-Fayez's Government in April 2005 and appointed Adnan Badran as Prime Minister; two days later a new Government was sworn in. Among several changes to key portfolios, Dr Bassem Awadallah became Minister of Finance. Following Awadallah's resignation in June, however, Badran announced a reorganization of the Cabinet in the following month.

In November 2005 three Iraqi citizens carried out suicide bomb attacks in three hotels frequented by Western businessmen and diplomats in Amman, killing up to 60 people and injuring more than 100. Al-Zarqawi announced that he had instigated the blasts, most of the victims of which were Jordanians, as retaliation for the Government's support for the USA and other Western countries. Within two days over 120 people had been arrested in connection with the attacks, and thousands of Jordanians staged protests against the bombings and al-Zarqawi. Following Badran's resignation from the premiership later in the month, King Abdullah invited Marouf al-Bakhit, who had served as Jordan's ambassador to Israel until his appointment as national security adviser in the aftermath of the bombings, to form a new government. Abdullah appealed to al-Bakhit to increase security and combat the fundamentalist ideologies behind militant Islamism, as well as furthering the democratization process. The King inaugurated the new Cabinet in late November: al-Bakhit assumed additional responsibility for defence.

Details were published in January 2006 of a 10-year plan, the principal objectives of which were 'the creation of income-generating opportunities, the improvement of standards of living and the guarantee of social welfare'. As well as outlining plans for economic reform (see Economic Affairs), the National Agenda also included initiatives designed to: safeguard freedom of political activity and of the media; improve both the availability and quality of public services; and further empower women within Jordanian society. However, by 2014 the majority of the measures outlined in the plan had yet to be introduced.

In mid-2006 seven people were convicted (including six *in absentia*) and sentenced to death for their part in the November 2005 bombings in Amman. Meanwhile, in June 2006 al-Zarqawi was killed in a US air raid near the Iraqi town of Baquba.

The Prevention of Terrorism Act passed into law in November 2006, provoking censure from human rights organizations, including Amnesty International, which alleged that the new legislation could potentially be abused in order to suppress non-violent opponents of the Government. In June Amnesty International had claimed that the General Intelligence Department (GID)—the state agency responsible for internal security—routinely used torture as a tool with which to extract false confessions from political detainees, strongly implying that it did so on behalf of the US Administration. Furthermore, Jordan's State Security Court was accused of accepting confessions obtained by torture as admissible evidence, and of having based convictions on the grounds of such confessions alone.

The 2007 legislative elections

In early November 2007 one of the men convicted and sentenced to death *in absentia* for the 2002 murder of the US diplomat Laurence Foley (see Foreign Affairs) was also convicted of helping to plan the 2003 attack on the Jordanian embassy in Baghdad. Muammar al-Jaghbeer, who had been captured in Iraq and extradited to Jordan in 2005, was deemed to have acted on the orders of al-Zarqawi and was given a second death sentence. In late November 2007 al-Jaghbeer's death sentence for the murder of Foley was commuted to a 10-year term of imprisonment after a military court determined that he had had no intention to kill. In May 2008 the Supreme Court suspended al-Jaghbeer's 10-year sentence and ordered a new trial to take place at the State Security Court. Following the retrial, in July 2009 al-Jaghbeer was again convicted and sentenced to death for his role in Foley's murder. However, following an appeal hearing in November, this sentence was commuted to 15 years' imprisonment, with hard labour.

At legislative elections held on 20 November 2007 independents and tribal representatives loyal to King Abdullah secured 104 of the 110 seats in the House of Representatives. The IAF won the remaining six seats, down from 17 in the 2003 poll. The party subsequently accused the Government of vote-buying and other electoral fraud, pointing to its apparent failure to win a single seat in the two traditional IAF strongholds of Irbid and Zarqa, an impoverished city to the north-east of Amman. The Government insisted that, aside from a few isolated incidents of vote-buying, the proponents of which had been arrested, the polls had been conducted in a free and fair manner. However, in early November 2007 a coalition of non-governmental organizations had announced that, owing to new government restrictions, its members could no longer monitor the polls. On 22 November King Abdullah appointed Nader al-Dahabi as the new Prime Minister, in place of al-Bakhit. Al-Dahabi's new Cabinet was formally inaugurated on 25 November. Meanwhile, the King appointed Bassem Awadallah as Chief of the Royal Court.

In April 2008 24 out of Jordan's 36 registered political parties were dissolved after their failure to comply with the terms of a new political parties law, which came into force in April 2007 with the provision of a one-year deadline. The new law stipulated that parties must have a minimum of 500 founding members drawn from at least five different governorates, and compelled parties to grant the Government access to their accounts. Twelve parties, including the IAF, successfully validated their status. Meanwhile, a report released by the US-based organization Human Rights Watch alleged that the US Central Intelligence Agency (CIA) had transferred at least 14 suspected terrorists to Jordan for interrogation and torture between September 2001 and 2004. The allegations were denied by the Jordanian Government.

Awadallah tendered his resignation as Chief of the Royal Court in September 2008. Many observers believed that his strongly pro-reform approach had been opposed by conservative elements in the Jordanian establishment. In January 2009 Nasser Lozi, Chairman of Royal Jordanian Airline, was appointed as his replacement. In February King Abdullah approved a major reorganization of the Cabinet, which included the appointment of Nasser Judeh—formerly the Minister of State for Media Affairs and Communications—as the Minister of Foreign Affairs. A royal decree issued in July named Prince Hussein ibn al-Abdullah, the King's eldest son, as Crown Prince. The position had been vacant since King Abdullah relieved his half-brother, Prince Hamzeh, of the title in 2004.

The 2010 legislative elections

In late November 2009 King Abdullah issued royal decrees dissolving the House of Representatives, two years before the expiry of its term, and ordering the holding of early legislative elections. The dissolution was believed to be in response to widespread dissatisfaction with the parliament, which was viewed by many Jordanians as being hampered by tribal and partisan rivalries and ineffective in dealing with pressing economic, social and political issues. According to the Constitution, a new parliament was required to be formed within four months of dissolution. However, in a royal decree issued in early December, the King postponed legislative elections indefinitely pending the formulation of new electoral legislation.

Following this development, Prime Minister al-Dahabi submitted the resignation of his Government, and King Abdullah appointed Samir Rifai, son of former premier and incumbent Speaker of the Senate Zaid Rifai, as Prime Minister-designate. The King approved the formation of a new Cabinet led by Prime Minister Rifai on 14 December. Shortly afterwards Zaid Rifai submitted his resignation as Senate Speaker, thus averting concerns about the constitutionality of two close relatives heading both the upper house of the legislature and the Cabinet. On 17 December the King appointed a new Senate, with former Prime Minister Taher al-Masri as Speaker.

Following a significant rise in reports of inter-tribal violence and clashes between various tribes and the security forces, in early May 2010 the Government appointed a new Director of the Public Security Directorate (PSD), Maj.-Gen. Hussein Hazaa Majali, who was at the time serving as Jordan's ambassador to Bahrain, and was a former Commander of the Royal Guard. The Cabinet subsequently announced the establishment of a panel of inquiry to investigate the causes of the recent violence.

The revised electoral law, which was finally approved by royal decree in mid-May 2010, expanded the number of seats in the House of Representatives from 110 to 120; other changes included an increase in the number of seats reserved for female candidates from six to 12. However, the amended law retained the controversial 'one person, one vote' electoral system (in place since 1993), which was viewed by opposition groups as favouring tribal, rather than party, politics. Even after a reorganization of electoral districts, opponents of the legislation complained that it would increase representation from rural, tribal areas traditionally supportive of King Abdullah while lowering the number of seats from urban constituencies, where there was a higher proportion of Jordanians of Palestinian origin (who were considered more likely to vote for opposition Islamist candidates). In July 2010 the IAF declared that it was to boycott the legislative elections, stating that the authorities could not guarantee that they would be 'fair and transparent'.

At elections to the House of Representatives held on 9 November 2010, independents and tribal representatives loyal to the Hashemite monarchy secured all 120 of the seats in the newly enlarged legislature. A reported 17 of the elected independents were aligned with opposition groups, including one member of the IAF who had refused to join his party's boycott. According to the terms of the revised electoral law, 12 seats were allocated to the female candidates receiving the greatest number of votes. (A 13th woman was elected in Amman, independently of the quota system.) A reported 80 deputies were elected to parliament for the first time. Voter turnout was officially recorded at around 53%; however, the IAF claimed that the figure was in fact closer to 30%. During the polls, it was reported that one person had died in a series of violent clashes between opposing political factions; riots were also reported after the final results were announced.

Having on the previous day accepted the resignation of Prime Minister Samir Rifai, and asked him to form a new administration, on 24 November 2010 King Abdullah issued a royal decree endorsing a new Cabinet. On 25 November the King appointed a new Senate, which had been expanded from a membership of 55 to 60; al-Masri retained the post of Speaker. At the inauguration of the new National Assembly on 28 November, when Faisal al-Fayez was elected as Speaker of the House of Representatives, King Abdullah recommended that the temporary electoral legislation adopted in May be amended prior to it becoming a permanent law, to ensure that it advanced democratic reforms.

King Abdullah accelerates reforms after 2011 protests

During January 2011 anti-Government protests took place in cities across the country, including in Amman, by thousands of demonstrators angered by the high levels of unemployment and poverty, rapidly increasing prices for basic foodstuffs and perceived corruption among government officials. Many of the protesters, who included trade unionists, Islamists and leftist groups, demanded the resignation of the Prime Minister and a change in Jordan's political system to allow future Prime Ministers to be elected, rather than appointed by the King. Having first implemented new economic measures (see Economic Affairs), on 1 February King Abdullah dismissed Rifai and his administration, and designated Marouf al-Bakhit (premier during 2005–07) as Prime Minister. A new Government, which the King charged with swiftly implementing the necessary political reforms to modernize the kingdom and increase the level of democracy, was formed in early February 2011. This change of government appeared to be an attempt by the monarch to prevent a repeat of the large-scale street protests which in Tunisia and Egypt had recently led to the removal from office of both countries' Presidents. On 2 March Dr Khaled al-Karaki, hitherto a Deputy Prime Minister and the Minister of Education, was reappointed as Chief of the Royal Court (a position he had held in the early 1990s). On the following day al-Bakhit's new Government narrowly won a vote of confidence.

At the request of King Abdullah, on 14 March 2011 the Government established a National Dialogue Committee, to be chaired by Senate Speaker Taher al-Masri, which would, over a period of three to six months, enter into discussions with a number of groups—including political parties and trade unions, as well as youth and elders' representatives—concerning key political and social legislation, especially the electoral and political parties laws. The 'one person, one vote' system was reported to be one issue to be examined by the participants. However, calls by members of the opposition for a dissolution of parliament and fresh elections were rejected by the King. Many opposition politicians had questioned the appointment of the conservative al-Bakhit as premier and his ability to carry out genuine political and economic reforms. The Secretary-General of the IAF, Hamza Mansour, was said to have turned down an invitation for his movement to join the Government, and he declared that the IAF would not be involved in the work of the new committee owing to its composition and modest aims.

Meanwhile, largely small and peaceful demonstrations were staged by pro-democracy protesters in the kingdom throughout March 2011. The first fatality as a result of the protests was reported on 25 March, after a pro-reform rally near the Ministry of the Interior building in Amman turned into violent clashes between pro- and anti-Government protesters, leading to the intervention of the security forces; up to 160 people were wounded. The exact circumstances of the man's death were disputed by government and opposition sources. There were reports that some of the pro-Government loyalists had taken a nationalist stance, alleging that the demonstration had been instigated by Jordanians of Palestinian origin and thus posed a threat to the monarchy. On 27 March the Speaker of the House of Representatives, Faisal al-Fayez, read a statement declaring that the lower chamber rejected opposition demands immediately to reduce King Abdullah's constitutional powers. On 7 April a man was seriously wounded by setting fire to himself in front of the Prime Minister's office in Amman. Violence occurred again on 15 April, when a group of hardline Salafist Islamists who were demanding the release of Islamist prisoners allegedly attacked members of the police force in Zarqa; their assault apparently followed attacks on the Salafists by pro-regime supporters. More than 80 people were reportedly injured in the violence, including some 40 police officers, and dozens of Islamists were detained by the authorities (although many were subsequently released).

On 26 April 2011 King Abdullah established the Royal Committee on Constitutional Review, to be chaired by Ahmad Lozi (Prime Minister during 1971–73), which was to examine the recommendations of the National Dialogue Committee regarding possible amendments to the Constitution concerning political parties and the electoral system. On 4 June al-Masri presented the National Dialogue Committee's final report to the Prime Minister. However, opposition parties, including the IAF, expressed anger at what they considered to be the limited nature of the proposed reforms, particularly since they included the retention of the 'one person, one vote' system in the majority of parliamentary seats. During a significant televised speech on

12 June, the King announced that he would henceforth allow future cabinets to be formed on the basis of parliamentary majority and thus permit the Prime Minister to be appointed by parliament rather than by the monarch; however, the exact time-frame for the reform was unclear. Abdullah also outlined proposals to strengthen political parties and stated that, as part of the Government's national decentralization plan, municipal elections would take place by the end of 2011 under a new municipalities law.

The Minister of Justice, Hussein Mjalli, and the Minister of Health, Yassin Husban, both resigned in late May 2011 over their role in allowing a businessman, Khalid Shahin, who had been imprisoned in 2010 on corruption charges, to travel to the USA for medical treatment in February 2011; Shahin had not returned to Jordan. In late June the Minister of State for Media Affairs and Communications, Taher Odwan, also resigned in protest against what he deemed to be overly restrictive new legislation concerned with press and publications, the penal system and the fight against corruption. In a government reorganization effected by King Abdullah on 2 July, al-Bakhit retained the premiership. Notably, Mazen al-Saket replaced the unpopular Saad Hayel Srour as Minister of the Interior. (Srour had been accused of taking an excessively firm stance against those involved in the recent protests, and was also criticized over his role in allowing Shahin to leave the country.)

On 10 August 2011 the Prime Minister and his Cabinet were cleared of any wrongdoing by a parliamentary committee in relation to a case of alleged corruption that had occurred in 2007, when al-Bakhit had previously held the premiership. It had been alleged that he had personally authorized the construction of Jordan's first casino complex—which was to be used by tourists in the Dead Sea region—even though gambling is illegal under Jordanian law. After the Prime Minister was found not to have been fully informed of all the details of the proposed licence award (which was swiftly withdrawn), the former Minister of Tourism and Antiquities, Osama Dabbas, was the only government minister to remain implicated over the affair. However, Dabbas was cleared of all the charges against him by the Amman Criminal Court in May 2013.

The Royal Committee on Constitutional Review presented its findings to King Abdullah on 14 August 2011. Most notable among the 42 suggested amendments to the Constitution were the formation of an independent constitutional court in place of the Higher Council for the Interpretation of the Constitution; the establishment of an independent commission to monitor legislative and municipal elections; a reduction in the powers of the State Security Court; a lowering of the minimum age required to stand for election to the House of Representatives from 30 to 25; and new provisions that would improve freedom of the press, of expression and of scientific research. Although the proposed amendments were welcomed by many sections of Jordanian society, the IAF claimed that they did not go far enough, again insisting that future Prime Ministers should be elected and demanding a further reduction in the powers of the intelligence services. Both the House of Representatives and the Senate approved a total of 41 constitutional amendments during September. One crucial change had been the decision of parliament to retain the State Security Court, but to restrict its responsibilities to dealing with cases of terrorism, treason and espionage. The official endorsement of the constitutional amendments by King Abdullah at the end of September prompted further protests by opposition activists, who again demanded al-Bakhit's resignation. The Muslim Brotherhood urged more extensive reforms, such as dissolving the State Security Court and introducing an elected upper house. In early October it was announced that the municipal elections would be held in December. However, following the change of government in October 2011 (see below), the polls were subsequently postponed until early 2012 as the new administration planned to draft a new municipalities law. Despite the introduction of the revised legislation, which stated that the municipal elections should be held by September 2012, the polls did not in fact take place until August 2013 (see Recent developments).

Street demonstrations, albeit smaller in scale, were held throughout mid-2011 by protesters still frustrated by the lack of progress on political and economic reforms. By late September the demonstrators were increasingly focusing their attention on the Cabinet and parliament's perceived failure to reduce the high levels of corruption, and accusing them of protecting those involved in corrupt practices. On 16 October a reported 70 of the 120 deputies in the House of Representatives, which was in a period of recess, had asked the King to dismiss al-Bakhit owing to their dissatisfaction with the Prime Minister's performance. After al-Bakhit had been requested by King Abdullah to resign on 17 October, the King named Awn al-Khasawneh—a judge at the International Court of Justice who had previously served as chief of the royal court—as premier, and asked him to lead the country through an intense period of political reform (with reform of legislation concerning elections and political parties being a key component). On the same day Maj.-Gen. Faisal Jabril al-Shobaki was appointed as Director of the GID. A new Cabinet was inaugurated under Prime Minister al-Khasawneh on 24 October. The IAF Secretary-General, Hamza Mansour, declined an invitation for his party to join the new administration. On 25 October the King appointed Riyad Abu Karaki to become Chief of the Royal Court, in succession to Khaled al-Karaki. A new Senate was appointed on the same day, with al-Masri retaining the post of Speaker. On 26 October Abd al-Karim Dughmi was elected Speaker of the House of Representatives.

In February 2012 Muhammad al-Dahabi, the brother of former premier Nader al-Dahabi, was arrested on suspicion of money-laundering, embezzlement and the exploitation of public office, following allegations of corruption during his tenure as Director of the GID in 2005–09. Trial proceedings against Muhammad al-Dahabi began in Amman in mid-June 2012. In early November he was found guilty of the corruption charges and sentenced to 13 years' imprisonment, with hard labour; he was also required to pay a fine of US $29.6m. Meanwhile, in March 2012 the House of Representatives voted against recommendations by a committee investigating allegations of corruption involving the sale of a stake in the Jordan Phosphate Mines Co (JPMC) in 2006 to refer several former government ministers and senior officials, including former Prime Minister Marouf al-Bakhit, for further investigation. A report into the sale had concluded that the owners of KAMIL Holdings, which had purchased a 37% stake in JPMC, had provided false information and recommended that the sale be annulled.

A draft electoral law was approved by the Cabinet in early April 2012, and submitted to the House of Representatives for scrutiny. Among the changes proposed by the Government included the replacement of the 'one person, one vote' system with one under which voters would cast two ballots in favour of individual candidates for a particular governorate and a separate ballot for a national party. The number of seats in the House of Representatives would be increased from 120 to 138, 15 of which would be allocated to national political groups on a proportional basis. The quota for female legislators would also be increased from 12 to 15. The proposals were rejected by some opposition groups, notably the IAF. In late April al-Khasawneh tendered his resignation as Prime Minister, along with that of his Cabinet. Reports suggested that al-Khasawneh's Government was deemed to have been too slow in carrying out the requisite political reforms. Fayez al-Tarawneh (Prime Minister in 1998–99) was subsequently instructed by King Abdullah to form a new Government, which duly took office in early May 2012. The new Cabinet was asked by the King to administer the country for a 'limited transitional period' in order to adopt the necessary legislation to enable early parliamentary elections to be held in late 2012. However, street protests continued, as many demonstrators expressed frustration at King Abdullah's decision to install new ministers rather than implement the more far-reaching reforms being demanded by opposition groups. Nevertheless, a significant reform proposed by the Royal Committee on Constitutional Review was instituted later in May, when the members of the new Independent Election Commission (IEC) were sworn into office under the chairmanship of Abdelilah al-Khatib.

In mid-June 2012 the House of Representatives approved the new electoral law, which had been amended so that the number of seats in the legislature would be increased from 120 to 140, with 17 seats allocated to national political groups on a proportional basis. The number of seats allocated to female legislators would still be increased to 15. The legislation was endorsed by the Senate in late June and by King Abdullah in late July. In its final form, after an intervention by the monarch in a stated effort to encourage the participation of all political groups in the election process, the 2012 Elections Law raised the number of parliamentary seats set aside for political parties to 27; the House of Representatives would thus henceforth constitute 150 members. In mid-June members of the Muslim Brotherhood and left-wing activists had held demonstrations in protest against the electoral reforms, which they felt would unduly favour loyalists to the

King and independent candidates in future elections. Even after the introduction of a larger number of party-allocated seats, the political leadership of the Muslim Brotherhood voted in mid-July to boycott the forthcoming legislative polls. In September King Abdullah also angered many journalists by approving controversial amendments to the Press and Publications Law that would require online news websites to obtain a licence from the authorities and therefore render their content subject to official censorship. Government sources claimed to have prevented access to at least 300 such websites by June 2013, citing the failure of the sites' owners to register with the local authorities in time.

Recent developments: the 2013 legislative and municipal elections

On 4 October 2012 King Abdullah issued a decree dissolving the House of Representatives in order to allow for fresh parliamentary elections to be held; it was subsequently announced by the IEC that the polls would take place on 23 January 2013. Meanwhile, on 10 October 2012 the King appointed Abdullah Ensour, a reformist member of the Senate, as Prime Minister-designate. On the following day a new Cabinet under Ensour was inaugurated. During October the IAF repeated its pledge to boycott the next parliamentary elections, in protest at what the movement deemed to be unfair constituency sizes and the failure of the authorities to institute meaningful democratic reforms. One of the largest demonstrations held by Islamist opposition activists since the start of the protests in early 2011 was staged in Amman on 5 October 2012, when between 10,000 and 20,000 protesters demanded that the new electoral legislation be repealed.

Further street rallies were held in Amman and other cities in mid-November 2012 by Islamists, trade unionists and youth movements following the Government's decision to withdraw certain fuel subsidies, which had led to significant price rises (including a 53% rise in the price of cooking gas). Queues were reported at many petrol stations and sporadic acts of vandalism occurred. There were widespread calls for the Government under Prime Minister Ensour to resign, while some protesters were reported to have openly demanded an end to the Jordanian monarchy. Government officials insisted that the subsidies had been removed in an effort to resolve the country's 'very critical' financial situation (see Economic Affairs). Three people were reported to have died and more than 70 others were wounded (including many police officers) as several of the nationwide protests turned into violent clashes between demonstrators and the security forces.

At the elections to the newly expanded, 150-member House of Representatives, which took place on 23 January 2013, independents and tribal representatives loyal to King Abdullah were reported to have secured around 75% of the seats, with moderate Islamist and other candidates critical of the Government winning the remaining 25%; 37 of the newly elected deputies were said to come from the opposition. According to the IEC, voter turnout was 56.5%; however, the IAF dismissed this figure as being excessively high, and alleged that electoral fraud and vote-buying had occurred. The IEC Chairman, Abdelilah al-Khatib, admitted that instances of 'minor irregularities' had taken place, but affirmed that these had not affected the election's final outcome. Observers from the European Union also described the election process as 'transparent and credible', while also acknowledging that there had been instances of vote-buying. On 27 January Ensour submitted the resignation of his Cabinet to the King. On 5 March Ensour won a vote of confidence in the House of Representatives and four days later was asked by the King to remain as Prime Minister. On 30 March a new Cabinet was duly sworn into office. Among the notable appointees were a former Governor of the Central Bank, Umayya Touqan, as Minister of Finance, and a former Director of the PSD, Hussein Hazaa Majali, as Minister of the Interior and Municipal Affairs. Nasser Judeh retained the foreign affairs portfolio, although his title was amended to the Minister of Foreign and Expatriates Affairs. Excluding the Prime Minister, the Government included just 18 members, many of whom were allocated multiple portfolios, and none of whom were deputies in the House of Representatives. Meanwhile, at the inauguration of the new parliament on 11 February 2013 Saad Hayel Srour, the former Deputy Prime Minister and Minister of the Interior, was elected as Speaker of the House of Representatives.

Anti-Government protests continued in several cities in the aftermath of the poll, with some demonstrators increasingly demanding an end to King Abdullah's reign. During mid-2013 there was also a notable increase in the number of violent incidents being reported in southern Jordan, where tribal youths—many of whom were unemployed—protested against their poor living standards and the apparent failure of the Government to improve their economic situation. Four people died, and up to 30 were injured, after violence erupted at a university in Ma'an in April, and two others were killed following clashes at a university in Kerak in April and July. Many opposition activists accused the security forces of responding to the unrest with excessive force.

King Hussein effected an extensive reorganization of the Cabinet under Prime Minister Ensour in August 2013, in advance of municipal elections that were due to be held that month. The new Government—in which the number of ministers was increased from 19 to 27—included many technocrats, and was asked by the King to effect the necessary economic reforms, as required by the IMF, in order to reduce Jordan's huge budget deficit and stimulate growth. Although the key portfolios remained unchanged, the interior and municipal affairs portfolio was divided, with Majali remaining as Minister of the Interior and Walid al-Masri becoming Minister of Municipal Affairs.

At the municipal elections held on 27 August 2013, overall voter turnout was officially reported at 30% (compared with around 50% in 2007); however, in Amman the rate was estimated to be as low as 10%. The polls were again boycotted by the IAF and certain left-wing groups, which repeated their criticism that the Government had shown a failure to implement vital political reforms. Thus, the elections represented a success for tribal representatives loyal to the monarchy. There were several reports of election violations and some violent incidents occurred at polling stations; however, Ensour hailed the staging of the polls as having demonstrated a major achievement for his administration in view of Jordan's extremely difficult economic situation, the impact on the country of the massive inflow of Syrian refugees and the high level of insecurity felt across much of the Middle East region.

Foreign Affairs

Regional relations

Relations with Israel were severely undermined in September 1997 when the head of the political bureau of the Palestinian Islamic Resistance Movement (Hamas), Khalid Meshaal, survived an assassination attempt in Amman by agents of the Israeli intelligence service, Mossad. Intensive negotiations involving Crown Prince Hassan, Israeli Prime Minister Binyamin Netanyahu and US officials resulted in an agreement in October whereby Israel freed the Hamas spiritual leader, Sheikh Ahmad Yassin, in return for Jordan's release of two Mossad agents arrested in connection with the attack on Meshaal. A further 12 Mossad agents were expelled from Jordan following the release from Israeli custody of 23 Jordanian and 50 Palestinian detainees. Israel and Jordan signed several bilateral trade agreements in March 1998, and in October King Hussein's mediation at the US-brokered peace summit held between Israel and the Palestinian (National) Authority (PA) was crucial to the signing of the Wye Memorandum. In December Israel agreed to open its airspace to foreign airlines en route for Jordan.

Upon his accession in February 1999 King Abdullah assured Israel that he would pursue his father's commitment to the Middle East peace process. The King welcomed the reactivation of the stalled Wye Memorandum by the signing (to which he was a witness) of the Sharm el-Sheikh Memorandum (Wye Two—see the chapter on Israel) by the Israeli Prime Minister, Ehud Barak, and Yasser Arafat in September.

There was considerable speculation at the time of the Wye Two agreement that recent efforts to bring an end to Hamas's political activities in Jordan had been motivated by a consensus among the Jordanian, Palestinian, Israeli and US authorities on the need to contain potential Islamist opposition to a revival of the peace process. In August 1999 the Jordanian security forces closed down Hamas offices in Amman, on the grounds that these were being used by foreign groups for illegal political activities. The home of Khalid Meshaal was also raided, and in the following months numerous Hamas officials were arrested on various charges including involvement in illicit political activities and the illegal possession of firearms. In November it was reported that Hamas had rejected an offer by the Jordanian Government to release the detained activists provided that they agreed to cease all political activity and that their leaders left the country. Later in the month the Jordanian authorities released some 24 Hamas officials, including four leaders (among them Meshaal and spokesman Ibrahim Ghosheh) who were immediately flown to Qatar. In November 2000, during talks with Meshaal in Qatar, Jordan's Prime Minister, Ali Abu al-Ragheb, reportedly reiterated the conditions under which the Hamas leaders would be allowed to return to Jordan. The Jordanian authorities granted permission for Ghosheh to enter the country in June 2001, after he had agreed to end his involvement with Hamas.

In advance of the Israeli-Palestinian peace talks held at the US presidential retreat at Camp David, Maryland, in July 2000, Prime Minister al-Ragheb emphasized that the Jordanian Government would not accept any more Palestinian refugees and that it supported their right of return to their homeland. (Recent reports had implied that Jordan was being considered as a possible home for those displaced persons currently in refugee camps in Lebanon.) In June 2000 there were 1,570,192 Palestinian refugees in Jordan registered with the UN Relief and Works Agency for Palestine Refugees in the Near East (UNRWA, see p. 101). By July 2013 this figure had risen to 2,054,527. Meanwhile, in August 2000 King Abdullah reiterated that Jordan would not accept Israeli or international sovereignty over the Islamic holy sites in East Jerusalem, an issue that had been a major obstacle to progress at Camp David.

In October 2000 King Abdullah attended a US-brokered summit meeting between Barak and Arafat in Sharm el-Sheikh, Egypt. As violence between Palestinians and Israeli security forces escalated, Jordan came under growing pressure from other Arab states to sever diplomatic ties with Israel, while large-scale public demonstrations against Israeli and US policies towards the new Palestinian uprising (often termed the al-Aqsa *intifada*) were held in Amman and at Jordan's refugee camps. One 'anti-normalization' protest held in early October resulted in violent confrontations between protesters and police; the Government subsequently issued a ban on public demonstrations. Meanwhile, Jordan delayed the dispatch of its new ambassador to Israel, in response to the deteriorating situation in the West Bank and Gaza. In November the Israeli Vice-Consul in Amman was injured in a gun attack by militant Islamists; another Israeli diplomat was wounded in a similar attack in December.

The convening of a summit meeting of Arab League heads of state in Amman in March 2001 reflected Jordan's prominent role in diplomatic efforts to resolve the Israeli–Palestinian conflict. At the summit Arab leaders pledged to transfer funds to the PA as part of a US $1,000m. fund established in late 2000. Jordan and Egypt both refused to return their ambassadors to Israel in protest against Israeli military actions against the Palestinians, although they did not proceed to a formal suspension of diplomatic relations. The summit's final communiqué—the so-called Amman Declaration—repeated demands for Israel to withdraw its armed forces from all occupied territory. Further mass demonstrations were held in Jordanian cities and Palestinian refugee camps in March–April 2002, after Israel had reoccupied Palestinian-controlled towns in the West Bank. Jordanian anti-riot police responded forcefully to many unlicensed rallies.

On 4 June 2003 King Abdullah hosted a summit meeting between US President George W. Bush, Israeli premier Ariel Sharon and the newly appointed Palestinian Prime Minister, Mahmud Abbas. The aim of the summit was to begin the implementation of the 'roadmap' peace plan, an initiative that had been drawn up in late 2002 by the Quartet group (comprising the USA, the UN, Russia and the EU) and announced by President Bush in April 2003, following the US-led invasion of Iraq and the removal from power of Saddam Hussain.

In February 2004 a Jordanian delegation travelled to the International Court of Justice (ICJ) in The Hague, Netherlands, to present a 100-page document condemning Israel's construction of a 'security fence' in the West Bank (see the chapters on Israel and the Palestinian Territories). The ICJ had been asked by the UN General Assembly to rule on the legality of the barrier, and Jordan was one of 14 countries to present evidence against its construction. It was reported in March that King Abdullah and Ariel Sharon had held secret talks in southern Israel regarding the controversial barrier. In May, following sideline discussions at the World Economic Forum in Amman, Israel and Jordan agreed to upgrade their bilateral trade agreement, which had been signed months after the 1994 peace treaty. In February 2005 King Abdullah attended the summit meeting, held in Sharm el-Sheikh, between Sharon and Mahmud Abbas—recently elected as Executive President of the PA following the death of Arafat in November 2004—at which the two leaders issued verbal declarations that Israel and the PA would cease all acts of violence against each other. Later that month Jordan returned an ambassador to Tel-Aviv. However, at an Arab League summit in Algiers in March, King Abdullah failed to secure approval for a proposal for peace with Israel that would not oblige Israel to relinquish all the territories it had occupied in 1967.

Following the victory of Hamas in the Palestinian legislative elections of January 2006, King Abdullah argued that the election results should not prevent further peace negotiations from taking place between Israel and the PA. None the less, Jordan appeared increasingly supportive of US efforts to coerce the Hamas Cabinet into recognizing Israel through a process of isolation. In April the Government of Prime Minister al-Bakhit cancelled a planned official visit by Palestinian Minister of Foreign Affairs Mahmud Khalid al-Zahhar, after the apparent discovery of an arms and explosives cache which had allegedly been smuggled into Jordan by Hamas from Syria; Hamas officials denied the claim. In May Jordanian authorities announced that 20 Hamas members had been arrested on suspicion of plotting terrorist attacks in Jordan.

In May 2007 the ministers responsible for foreign affairs of Jordan, Israel and Egypt convened in the Egyptian capital, Cairo, to discuss an Arab League initiative for peace in the Middle East; the Arab proposal offered Israel peace and normalized relations with all Arab countries, in exchange for an Israeli withdrawal from those lands seized in 1967. However, the complete blockade of the Hamas-controlled Gaza Strip, imposed by the Israeli Government in January 2008, prompted forceful condemnation from King Abdullah, who insisted that meaningful peace negotiations could not be held while Israel persisted with such measures against the Palestinian people. Nevertheless, in April Israeli Prime Minister Ehud Olmert visited Amman for talks with the King, which largely focused on ways of advancing the objectives of the Annapolis Conference, the peace summit hosted by the USA in November 2007.

Israel's military offensive against Hamas targets in the Gaza Strip, launched on 27 December 2008, provoked a wave of protests throughout Jordan, with demonstrators demanding the severance of diplomatic ties with Israel. Two days later the same demand was made in a petition signed by 29 parliamentary deputies. The two countries' respective ambassadors were temporarily withdrawn from Amman and Tel-Aviv, and in early January 2009 Prime Minister al-Dahabi stated that relations with Israel were under review; however, no formal severance of diplomatic relations was announced. Throughout the crisis Jordan provided a vitally important route for humanitarian aid into the Gaza Strip. Following the Israeli declaration of a unilateral ceasefire on 18 January, King Abdullah attended a summit meeting on that day in Sharm el-Sheikh, jointly hosted by the Egyptian and French Presidents, Hosni Mubarak and Nicolas Sarkozy, which aimed to forge a unified European and Arab response to the crisis in Gaza. The Sharm el-Sheikh summit, which was also attended by PA President Abbas and the Secretaries-General of the UN and the Arab League, represented those parties committed to seeking solutions through the framework of the existing Middle East peace process.

In May 2009 Binyamin Netanyahu, who had been appointed Prime Minister of Israel in March, attended a summit in Jordan, during which the King reiterated the conditions of the Arab peace initiative. However, during the latter part of 2009 Jordan was critical of Israel's ongoing settlement construction in East Jerusalem, and tensions were exacerbated by allegations of Israeli encroachment on holy sites in Jerusalem, which led to sporadic outbreaks of civil unrest from September. By early 2010 it was reported that relations between King Abdullah and the Israeli premier were frozen. However, at the end of January the King held discussions on the stalled peace process with Israeli President Shimon Peres during the World Economic Forum in Davos, Switzerland. In late February the King strongly condemned Israel's decision to include two sites venerated by Jews, Muslims and Christians—Rachel's Tomb in Bethlehem and the Cave of the Patriarchs in Hebron—on a list of Israeli national heritage sites. In early April he described Jordan's relations with Israel as the worst they had been since 1994. The following week King Abdullah travelled to Washington, DC, where he was reported to have urged the US President, Barack Obama, to use his influence to persuade the Israeli Government to impose a permanent ban on Jewish settlement construction in the West Bank and to announce a clear time-frame for a resumption of Israeli-Palestinian 'proximity' talks, soon leading to formal, direct negotiations. Apparently in protest at the ongoing stalemate in the peace process, Jordan chose not to replace its ambassador to Tel-Aviv when, in July 2010, its current envoy was appointed to a ministerial post in Amman.

Direct negotiations between Netanyahu and Abbas—the first to take place between the leaders of Israel and the PA since December 2008—finally commenced in Washington, DC, in September 2010, chaired by US Secretary of State Hillary Clinton and attended by the US Special Envoy to the Middle East, George Mitchell. They followed meetings held on the previous day between President Obama and both Israeli and Palestinian leaders, as well as with King Abdullah of Jordan and Egypt's President Mubarak. However, the discussions ended without any substantial progress. In late November 2011 the King visited the West Bank for talks with President Abbas. This was his first visit to the territory since mid-2000, and was intended to demonstrate Jordan's continuing pursuit of a Middle East peace settlement and its solidarity with the Palestinians in their quest for statehood. (In September 2011 the PA leadership had submitted a formal application to the UN for full Palestinian membership.) The talks also came immediately prior to the summit between the rival Fatah and Hamas movements aimed at securing a lasting national unity agreement to end the division of the Palestinian enclaves.

Further direct negotiations finally took place between Israeli and Palestinian officials in Amman on 4 January 2012. However, after five 'exploratory' meetings in the period up to 25 January, with an emphasis being placed on the issues of borders and security, once again no breakthrough was reported. The PA continued to demand the complete cessation of Israeli settlement activity on the West Bank and an agreement from Israel to discuss the pre-1967 borders of a Palestinian state before agreeing to new peace talks. Both King Abdullah and the Minister of Foreign Affairs, Nasser Judeh, had participated in the meetings. At the end of September 2012—more than two years after Jordan had chosen not to replace its envoy to Israel—a new ambassador to Tel-Aviv was appointed; he formally assumed his post the following month. In December King Abdullah visited the West Bank town of Ramallah to hold talks with President Abbas, after the UN had, in the previous month, agreed to upgrade the status of the Palestinian territories to that of a 'non-member observer state'.

After several weeks of intensive diplomatic efforts by regional leaders, including King Abdullah, and the US Secretary of State, John F. Kerry, preliminary discussions regarding a final status agreement between Israel and the PA were held in Washington, DC, on 29–30 July 2013. Formal peace negotiations between the two sides began in Jerusalem on 14 August, and were attended by President Obama's Special Envoy for Israeli-Palestinian Negotiations, Martin Indyk. However, although the proposed deadline for a preliminary accord to be signed was 29 April 2014, no significant progress had been made by the end of March. The Israeli Government's pursuit of its controversial settlement-building programme in East Jerusalem and the West Bank continued to provoke both anger and frustration on the part of Palestinians, neighbouring Arab states and many in the wider international community, while Hamas militants continued to launch rocket attacks against Israeli targets.

In late February 2014 the Prime Minister and Minister of Defence, Abdullah Ensour, indicated that the Jordanian Government might reconsider its 1994 peace treaty with Israel, after members of the Knesset (parliament) debated legislation concerning an Israeli declaration of sovereignty over the Temple Mount/Haram al-Sharif compound in East Jerusalem, which is currently administered by Jordan. In response to the Knesset debate, Jordanian deputies in the House of Representatives voted unanimously to expel the Israeli ambassador from Amman and to recall Jordan's envoy to Tel-Aviv. However, the Ensour Government, which sought to ensure the continuation of Jordan's diplomatic relations with Israel, awaited the outcome of the Israeli debate before taking any possible action. Bilateral relations deteriorated further in early March 2014, after the reported shooting dead by Israeli soldiers of a Jordanian judge of Palestinian origin, Raed Zuaiter, on the West Bank side of the border at the King Hussein (or Allenby) Bridge crossing. The exact circumstances of the incident were disputed, with Israeli military sources claiming that the judge had attempted to seize one of the soldiers' weapons prior to being shot. The Ministry of Foreign and Expatriates Affairs responded by immediately summoning the Israeli chargé d'affaires in Amman to explain the Israelis' actions. The two countries subsequently agreed to hold a joint investigation into the affair, and the Israeli Government apologized for the judge's death following considerable pressure to do so from Jordan.

After August 1995, when Jordan granted political asylum to the two sons-in-law of the Iraqi President, Saddam Hussain, and their wives, King Hussein became more openly critical of the Iraqi regime; however, despite the political rupture, Jordan continued to provide Iraq with a crucial external economic link. In December 1997 Jordan recalled its chargé d'affaires from Baghdad and expelled a number of Iraqi diplomats from Jordan, in protest at the execution of four Jordanians by the Iraqi authorities. Later that month, however, the two countries signed an agreement whereby Iraq was to supply 4.8m. metric tons of crude petroleum and refined petroleum products to Jordan in 1998. In January of that year more than 50 Jordanian detainees were released by Iraq.

In response to critical confrontations between Iraq and the UN during 1998 over the issue of weapons inspections, Jordan indicated that it would not allow its territory or airspace to be used for air strikes against Iraq. King Hussein consistently advocated a diplomatic resolution of the crises, while urging Iraq to comply with all pertinent UN resolutions. This position allowed Jordan to improve its relations with some Arab states, notably Egypt. Jordan strongly condemned the air strikes carried out against Iraq by US and British forces in December, and in early 1999 the Jordanian National Assembly voted in favour of an end to the UN embargo against Iraq.

King Abdullah made attempts to improve Jordan's relations with Iraq following his accession in February 1999. In November 2000 Prime Minister al-Ragheb undertook an official visit to Iraq—the first visit by a Jordanian premier since 1991—and the two states agreed to increase the value of their trade agreement from US $300m. in 2000 to $450m. in 2001. By mid-2001 Jordan was increasingly concerned that the proposed imposition by the UN of so-called 'smart' sanctions against Iraq would result in the loss of its oil supply from Iraq, in addition to its main regional export market. At senior-level discussions held in Amman in January 2002, Iraq and Jordan renewed their oil protocol and also agreed to the creation of a free trade zone.

Following the ousting of Saddam Hussain's regime by the US-led coalition in April 2003, the establishment was announced in June of a joint Jordanian-Iraqi business council to facilitate relations between the two countries and to aid the recovery of the Iraqi economy. In early January 2005 Amman hosted a meeting of five of the six countries neighbouring Iraq to discuss the elections to a transitional Iraqi legislature scheduled to be held later that month. The Iranian Minister of Foreign Affairs, Kamal Kharrazi, boycotted the meeting after Jordanian officials accused largely Shi'a Iran of seeking to influence Iraqi voting in order to encourage the formation of a Shi'a-dominated government in the country. The conference emphasized the need to warn countries against external efforts to influence the outcome of the elections in Iraq. Following reports that a suicide bombing in the Iraqi town of Hillah in February (in which some 125 people died) had been perpetrated by a Jordanian militant, bilateral relations deteriorated and large anti-Jordanian protests took place in Baghdad. In the ensuing crisis, during which the Iraqi authorities alleged that Jordan was failing to prevent insurgents from crossing the border into Iraq, in March both countries temporarily withdrew diplomatic envoys from their respective capitals.

In September 2007 the UN High Commissioner for Refugees (UNHCR) estimated the number of displaced Iraqis living in Jordan at between 500,000 and 750,000 (some of whom had been displaced prior to the conflict in Iraq from 2003). In an attempt to stem the influx of refugees, Jordan had introduced new legislation in February 2007, rendering mandatory for all Iraqi refugees a recently introduced type of passport, issued only in Baghdad and, it was hoped, difficult to forge. Later that year the border with Iraq was effectively closed to all but exceptional cases. Despite the fact that Jordan, along with Syria, had absorbed more Iraqi refugees than any other countries, the kingdom was not a signatory to the Refugee Convention of 1951 and refused to accord the Iraqis official refugee status, preferring to describe them as 'guests' or 'temporary visitors'. In March 2008 the Government requested all Iraqi visitors to provide appropriate documents proving their entitlement to stay in Jordan, such as work contracts or evidence of investments in the kingdom. Those without the relevant qualifications (estimated to be some 80% of the total Iraqi population) were given two options: either to leave Jordan in return for exemption from overstay fines; or to pay one-half of their fines and receive a three-month temporary residency in which to rectify their status. However, the authorities stopped short of forceful deportations and concentrated on a policy of encouraging Iraqis to return home. By October it was reported that hundreds were returning to Iraq under an Iraqi government-sponsored scheme that gave financial assistance to families returning voluntarily after an absence of at least eight months. At December 2012 the Government estimated the number of Iraqi refugees living in Jordan at 450,500.

The official visit to Amman of Iraqi Prime Minister Nuri al-Maliki in June 2008 heralded new progress in bilateral relations, and in August King Abdullah made a surprise visit to Baghdad for further talks with al-Maliki. This was the first visit to Baghdad by an Arab head of state since the fall of the previous Iraqi regime in 2003. In September 2008 a new deal was announced governing the supply of subsidized Iraqi oil to Jordan. In October Nayef al-Zaidan took up his post as Jordan's new ambassador to Iraq—the first such appointment since the withdrawal of the previous ambassador following the bombing of the Jordanian embassy in August 2003. In January 2009 King Abdullah directed the Government to ease the restrictions on Iraqis entering and residing in the kingdom. Meanwhile, the volume of trade between the neighbouring countries had doubled in 2008 compared with the preceding year, and the signing of a free trade agreement in September 2009 led to a further increase in bilateral trade. At the same time, the Iraqi authorities expressed their intention to double the volume of crude oil exports to Jordan, although this was dependent on the completion of repairs on the Kirkuk–Banias oil pipeline; it was also hampered during 2010 by the extended delay in forming a new Iraqi Government after the legislative elections of March. In September 2011 a joint Iraqi-Jordanian committee pledged to implement additional measures to increase and enhance the efficiency of cross-border trade, and to extend railway and air transport links between the two countries.

King Abdullah decided not to attend the historic summit meeting of the Arab League held in Baghdad towards the end of March 2012, with Jordan instead being represented by Prime Minister Awn al-Khasawneh. Many Arab governments, notably those of the Gulf monarchies, had chosen to send lower-level delegations to the meeting in protest at the Iraqi Government's close relations with Iran and its apparently 'neutral' position on the Syrian crisis. Nevertheless, in early March 2013 the Iraqi and Jordanian authorities confirmed the launch of a joint project involving the construction of a 1,680-km double pipeline to transport crude petroleum and natural gas from Iraq's southern city of Basra to Aqaba. The project was expected to cost around US $18,000m. and to be completed in 2017. In January 2013 the respective Governments had pledged to expedite implementation of the free trade accord signed in 2009.

President Hafiz al-Assad of Syria led a high-level Syrian delegation at King Hussein's funeral in February 1999, following which Jordan's relations with Syria improved significantly. In August the first senior Syrian delegation for almost a decade visited Amman for a session of the Jordanian-Syrian Higher Committee; the meeting resulted in an accord that officials hoped might double the volume of bilateral trade. Later in the month Syria reportedly agreed to end the ban (imposed in 1994) on the free circulation of Jordanian newspapers and publications. King Abdullah attended the funeral of President Assad in June 2000, and acted swiftly to forge close relations with the new Syrian President, Bashar al-Assad. In November Syria confirmed that it had upgraded its diplomatic representation in Amman to ambassadorial status, and the Syrian state airline resumed regular flights to Amman after a hiatus of more than 20 years. The Syrian authorities declared in January 2001 that all Jordanian prisoners held in Syria would soon be released; in November Jordanian officials claimed that there were still hundreds of Jordanian nationals being held in Syrian prisons. In August 2002 the two countries signed an agreement under which Syria was to provide Jordan with water to ease the latter's water shortages. Despite relations being threatened in April 2006 by the discovery of an arms and explosives cache, allegedly smuggled into Jordan from Syria (see above), these were further consolidated in November 2007 by the King's first visit to Damascus for almost four years. Under the terms of a deal concluded between King Abdullah and President Assad in November, 18 Jordanian detainees were released by Syria. A multilateral free trade accord was signed by officials from Jordan, Syria, Lebanon and Turkey in August 2010, and in December the four countries established what was termed the Levant Business Forum, based in the Turkish city of İstanbul, to facilitate the further integration of their economies.

Relations between Jordan and Syria have been complicated by the military campaign being carried out by Syrian government forces in the wake of the protests which began in Syria's southern city of Dar'a, near the Jordanian border, in March 2011. Although the Jordanian authorities remain anxious about the consequences for their country's stability should the Syrian regime be ousted, in November King Abdullah became the first Arab leader to issue a public demand for President Assad to resign. His statement was followed by an attack on the Jordanian embassy in Damascus by supporters of Assad. In December some 3,000 Jordanians took part in a sit-in at the Syrian embassy in Amman against the Government's violent crackdown on protesters and other civilians, and demanded the expulsion of Syria's ambassador to Jordan.

According to UNHCR, by mid-2012 an estimated 26,000 Syrian refugees had registered with the agency in Jordan; however, the Government claimed that more than 140,000 Syrians had entered the kingdom since the start of the unrest. In early 2013, after hopes of a swift resolution to the conflict had diminished, the number of Syrians entering Jordan increased rapidly, adding further to the country's already grave economic problems and placing a severe strain on the Government's ability to provide basic services such as education, health care and utilities. King Abdullah requested urgent international assistance for those nations hosting Syrian refugees, in particular Jordan, Turkey and Lebanon. Some clashes were also reported in Amman between a minority of Jordanians who continued to support the Assad regime and those, including members of the IAF, who backed the Syrian opposition. Moreover, some defecting members of the Syrian regime had sought refuge in Jordan, and there were growing fears that the kingdom could eventually be drawn into the conflict. By July 2013, according to the UN, at least 100,000 Syrians had died in the violence and more than 4m. had been displaced (1.7m. of these abroad). In August UNHCR estimated the number of Syrian refugees resident in Jordan to be 515,000; around 140,000 Syrians were reported to be living in the Zaatari refugee camp near Mafraq, which had effectively become Jordan's fifth largest city.

On 22 May 2013 ministers responsible for the foreign affairs of Western and Arab countries represented at a Friends of the Syrian People (or Friends of Syria) conference, held in Amman, advocated a political solution to the Syrian crisis through the formation of a transitional government.

Upon his accession, King Abdullah sought to strengthen relations with other Arab states. His first major foreign visit, in March 1999, was for talks with President Mubarak in Egypt (with which Jordan had signed an agreement in December 1998 providing for the future establishment of a free trade zone). Meanwhile, following the restoration of full diplomatic relations with Kuwait (which had been severed at the start of the Gulf crisis in 1990), in March 1999 Jordan reopened its embassy in Kuwait City; in October Kuwait returned an ambassador to Amman. In May 2010 the Amir of Kuwait, Sheikh Sabah al-Ahmad al-Jaber al-Sabah, undertook the first visit to Jordan by a Kuwaiti leader since 1990. King Abdullah became the first Jordanian monarch to visit Lebanon for more than 30 years when, in September 1999, he held discussions with senior Lebanese officials regarding the Middle East peace process and bilateral issues (including a planned free trade agreement). However, despite signing an agreement on free trade and economic co-operation in October 2002, the two countries failed to ratify the agreement.

Pan-Arab relations were strained as a result of the US-led military campaign in Iraq in early 2003. Nevertheless, Jordan arranged to import oil from Saudi Arabia, Kuwait and the United Arab Emirates, reportedly at no cost, to circumvent shortages induced by the conflict in Iraq, and in May it was revealed that Jordan was conducting negotiations with the USA and the UN to seek a solution to the problem of interrupted oil supplies from Iraq. In November Minister of Foreign Affairs Marwan al-Muasher visited Iran, primarily to discuss the status of some 1,000 members of the dissident Iranian militant group, the Mujahidin-e-Khalq, who were formerly based in Iraq but who were now being held under Jordanian supervision in the border area between Iraq and Jordan.

In February 2004 Jordan signed a free trade agreement with Egypt, Morocco and Tunisia, which committed each party to removing trade tariffs between them and to intensifying economic co-operation, particularly with regard to legislation concerning customs procedures and standards; the so-called Agadir Agreement was ratified in 2006 and entered into force in 2007. Meanwhile, in January 2007 King Abdullah urged Iran to exercise its influence over its neighbours in a positive manner, imploring the Iranian Government to refrain from adding to existing regional instability, particularly within Iraq, the Palestinian territories and Lebanon. Relations between Jordan and Saudi Arabia have improved in recent years, and in December 2007 officials from the two countries signed a border pact on the demarcation of their shared marine border in the Gulf of Aqaba.

Turkish President Abdullah Gül made a three-day state visit to Jordan in December 2009, the first by a Turkish head of state in some nine years. During the visit, representatives of the two countries signed an agreement on the establishment of a free trade zone, which, it was hoped, would significantly boost bilateral trade, and provide Jordanian businesses with improved access to European markets. Agreements on the reduction of reciprocal visa fees and customs tariffs were also concluded. The free trade agreement entered into effect in March 2011. During a visit to the Turkish capital, Ankara, in March 2013, King Abdullah and President Gül held further discussions concerning bilateral trade and investment, as well as regional issues such as the conflict in Syria and the Middle East peace process.

Other external relations

Jordan's relations with the USA in the early 1990s were frequently strained by US allegations of Jordanian assistance to Iraq in circumventing the UN trade embargo, as well as Jordan's vocal criticism of US-led policies towards Iraq. However, in September 1993 US President Bill Clinton announced that some US $30m. in economic and military aid to Jordan was to be released in recognition of the country's enforcement of sanctions against Iraq and of its role in the Middle East peace process. In early 1994 renewed tensions emerged with the USA over the Jerusalem issue and the US-led naval blockade of Jordan's only port at Aqaba, imposed to enforce sanctions against Iraq. Following a sharp deterioration in Jordanian–Iraqi relations in August 1995, when King Hussein granted political asylum to four senior members of the Iraqi regime, Clinton promised to support Jordan in the event of any threat to its security; however, the USA failed to persuade Jordan to sever all economic links with Iraq. In January 1996 the USA offered Jordan $300m. in military assistance, and an expansion of bilateral military co-operation was announced in March. In June 1997 the USA pledged $100m. in economic aid to Jordan, reportedly in recognition of Jordan's contributions to the regional peace process; an assistance fund was established in August. In the same month Jordan signed a debt-rescheduling agreement with the USA, in accordance with a deal reached in May by members of the 'Paris Club' of Western official creditors to reschedule approximately $400m. of Jordanian debt.

In May 1999 King Abdullah began a three-week tour of the USA and several European capitals. Prior to the visit, the King had announced that, in anticipation of a summit of leaders of the Group of Eight (G8) industrialized countries, due to be held in Germany in June, he would be seeking US support for an agreement by Western countries to write off as much as 50% of Jordan's debt. He achieved some success when the 'Paris Club' agreed, in late May (two days after a meeting with President Clinton), to reschedule about US $800m. of Jordanian debt; in June the G8 leaders recommended debt-reduction arrangements for Jordan. During a visit by King Abdullah to Washington, DC, in October 2000, Jordan and the USA signed a free trade agreement involving the reciprocal removal of all customs duties by 2010. The deal was fully implemented in December 2001.

King Abdullah strongly condemned the September 2001 suicide attacks against New York and Washington, DC, for which the USA held Osama bin Laden's al-Qa'ida network principally responsible, and the King swiftly affirmed Jordan's commitment to the proposed US-led 'war on terror'. Jordanian armed forces joined US and European forces when, from early October, they launched military strikes against al-Qa'ida bases and the Sunni fundamentalist Taliban regime in Afghanistan (which was believed to be harbouring bin Laden). However, Abdullah emphasized that the international community must simultaneously renew efforts to resolve the Israeli–Palestinian conflict. He also warned that any extension of the US-led military action to target any Arab country, such as Iraq, would undermine the international campaign. In July 2002 King Abdullah asserted that Jordan would not allow its territory to be used by US troops to launch a military attack aimed at ousting the Iraqi regime of Saddam Hussain, and Jordanian officials denied reports in September that the Government had agreed to allow US forces to use Jordanian military bases in return for a guaranteed supply of cheap oil during a potential disruption to Iraq's oil supplies. In October the USA was said to have pledged a further US $85m. to Jordan, apparently in an effort to secure the country's support during a possible US-led military campaign in Iraq and to enable the Jordanian economy to withstand the consequences of a war.

At the end of October 2002 a senior US diplomat, Laurence Foley, was assassinated in Jordan. The Jordanian security forces detained a large number of suspected Islamist militants following the assassination, and in December two alleged members of al-Qa'ida—one Jordanian and the other Libyan—were arrested on suspicion of involvement in Foley's murder. The trial of 11 suspects charged with involvement in the murder began in July 2003, with six of the defendants, including Abu Musab al-Zarqawi, being tried *in absentia*. At the conclusion of the trial in April 2004, all but one of the defendants were convicted: al-Zarqawi and seven others were sentenced to death, and the remaining two were given terms of imprisonment. In February 2003, meanwhile, Jordanian officials confirmed that the USA was to provide the kingdom with an anti-missile defence system in the event of a conflict in Iraq; Jordan had received six F-16 fighter aircraft from the US military in January. King Abdullah visited the USA in April 2004, but a meeting with President Bush was cancelled in protest at US support for Israel, particularly following Israel's recent 'targeted killings' of Hamas leaders Sheikh Ahmad Yassin and Abd al-Aziz al-Rantisi, and at Bush's endorsement of Sharon's plan for an Israeli 'disengagement' from Gaza (see the chapter on Israel). The rescheduled meeting took place in May. In November 2006 the King hosted President Bush and Iraqi Prime Minister Nuri al-Maliki in Amman for talks that centred on the need to impose stability and security within Iraq; thousands of protesters amassed in the streets of Amman, rallying against US foreign policy, and three Jordanian men were arrested on suspicion of plotting to assassinate the US President during his visit.

In April 2009 King Abdullah was the first Arab head of state to visit the USA after the inauguration of President Barack Obama in January. The visit indicated that the King was likely to be a key intermediary in US-brokered efforts to forge a Middle East peace settlement. Abdullah conveyed to President Obama the resolutions of a recent Arab League summit in Doha, Qatar, during which member states had renewed their commitment to the Arab peace initiative. In March 2013 Obama made an official visit to Jordan, where he held talks with King Abdullah over the ongoing crisis in Syria and the process of political reforms in the kingdom. However, the visit was overshadowed somewhat by the publication of an article by a US news publication, in which negative remarks regarding several regional political leaders—including President Mursi of Egypt and President Assad of Syria—and the Muslim Brotherhood were attributed to Abdullah. In June it was revealed that 900 military personnel from the USA had been sent to Jordan to assist the Government in protecting its citizens from possible security risks arising from the Syrian civil war. The Obama Administration was also to send a consignment of F-16 fighter planes and *Patriot* missile-defence systems to the Jordanian authorities.

CONSTITUTION AND GOVERNMENT

A revised Constitution for the Hashemite Kingdom of Jordan was ratified in January 1952 by King Talal I. Two amendments were adopted in November 1974 giving the King the right to dissolve the Senate or to take away membership from any of its members, and to postpone general elections for a period not to exceed a year, if there are circumstances in which the Cabinet feels that it is impossible to hold elections. A further amendment in February 1976 enabled the King to postpone elections indefinitely. In January 1984 two amendments were adopted, allowing elections 'in any part of the country where it is possible to hold them' (effectively, only the East Bank) and empowering the National Assembly to elect deputies from the Israeli-held West Bank. (However, in July 1988 King Hussein dissolved the legislature, renouncing Jordan's administrative and legal ties to the West Bank.) Under the terms of a revised electoral law approved in July 2012, the number of seats in the House of Representatives reserved for women was increased from 12 to 15, while a further 27 seats were allocated to candidates from political parties.

Jordan is a constitutional monarchy. Legislative power is vested in a bicameral National Assembly: the Senate (House of Notables) has 60 members, appointed by the King for eight years (one-half of the members retiring every four years), while the House of Representatives (House of Deputies) has 150 members, elected by universal adult suffrage for four years. Executive power is vested in the King, who governs with the assistance of an appointed Cabinet, responsible to the Assembly. There are 12 administrative provinces.

REGIONAL AND INTERNATIONAL CO-OPERATION

Jordan was a founder member of the League of Arab States (the Arab League, see p. 362), and also participates in the Council of Arab Economic Unity (see p. 364) and the Arab Monetary Fund (see p. 199).

Jordan became a member of the UN in 1955, and joined the World Trade Organization (WTO, see p. 434) in 2000. The country is also a member of the Organization of Islamic Cooperation (OIC, see p. 403).

ECONOMIC AFFAIRS

In 2012, according to estimates by the World Bank, Jordan's gross national income (GNI), measured at average 2010–12 prices, was US $29,852m., equivalent to $4,720 per head (or $6,130 per head on an international purchasing-power parity basis). During 2003–12, it was estimated, the population increased at an average annual rate of 2.3%, while Jordan's gross domestic product (GDP) per head increased, in real terms, by an average of 3.6% per year. Overall GDP increased, in real terms, at an average annual rate of 5.9% in 2003–12; According to preliminary official figures, growth of 2.7% was recorded in 2012.

Agriculture (including hunting, forestry and fishing) contributed about 3.0% of Jordan's GDP in 2012, according to preliminary figures, and accounted for about 5.3% of the country's economically active population at mid-2014, according to FAO estimates. The principal cash crops are vegetables, fruit and nuts, and wheat production is also important; vegetables accounted for 6.0% of export earnings in 2012. In December 2013 Jordan, Israel and the Palestinian (National) Authority signed a water-sharing agreement whereby a 180-km pipeline would be constructed to transfer water from a desalination plant on the Gulf of Aqaba, which extends north from the Red Sea, to the Dead Sea, thereby reversing the latter's rapid loss of water supply as well as providing drinking water for the three territories. According to preliminary official figures, the sector's GDP increased at an average annual rate of 5.2% during 2003–12; GDP increased by an estimated 3.9% in 2011, but decreased by 9.4% in 2012.

Industry (including mining, manufacturing, construction and power) provided 28.5% of GDP in 2012, according to preliminary figures; about 25.6% of the country's active labour force were employed in the sector in 2011. According to preliminary official figures, during 2003–12 industrial GDP increased by an average of 5.8% per year; the sector's GDP increased by 0.8% in 2012.

Mining and quarrying contributed 3.6% of GDP in 2012, according to preliminary figures, and accounted for about 0.8% of the employed labour force in 2011. Mineral exports—of which phosphates and potash were the principal components—accounted for around 8.7% of total export earnings in 2012. In July 2009 parliamentary approval was granted for an agreement with Royal Dutch Shell of the Netherlands/United Kingdom to develop the kingdom's large reserves of oil-bearing shale. A concession agreement was signed with the Estonian company Eesti Energia in May 2010, and a similar agreement with the Saudi Arabian Corporation for Oil Shale was approved by the Government in March 2013. Meanwhile, the authorities concluded a deal with British Petroleum in October 2009 encompassing exploration rights and production at the Risha gasfield, near the border with Iraq. Preliminary official figures suggested that mining GDP decreased by an average rate of 0.6% per year during 2003–12; the sector's GDP increased by 17.7% in 2011, but decreased by 17.1% in 2012.

Manufacturing provided 17.8% of GDP in 2012, according to preliminary figures, and engaged some 18.4% of the employed labour force in 2011. The most important branches of manufacturing, measured by gross value of output, are food, beverages and tobacco, pharmaceutical and other chemical products, non-metallic mineral products, wearing apparel, refined petroleum products and metal products. According to preliminary official figures, manufacturing GDP increased by an average of 6.6% per year in 2003–12; the sector recorded growth of 2.3% in 2012.

The construction sector contributed 4.7% of GDP in 2012, according to preliminary figures; about 5.0% of the country's active labour force were employed in the sector in 2011. According to preliminary official figures, during 2003–12 construction GDP increased by an average of 5.4% per year; the sector's GDP contracted by 0.9% in 2012.

Energy has traditionally been derived principally from imported petroleum, but attempts are being made to develop alternative sources of power, including wind, solar and nuclear power. In 2003 petroleum provided 90.0% of total electricity production, but by 2009 this had declined to just 8.5%, increasing again to 72.5% in 2011; conversely, natural gas accounted for only 9.3% of total electricity production in 2003, but this increased to 91.0% in 2009, and decreased to 27.0% in 2011. This renewed reliance on petroleum as a source of power was largely attributed to the loss of supply from Egypt following the overthrow of that country's President, Hosni Mubarak, in February. The unreliable supply from Egypt led the Jordanian Government to increase fuel and electricity prices for some industrial consumers in May 2012 and to examine possible alternative sources of natural gas, such as Iraq and Qatar. Imports of mineral products comprised 32.1% of the total value of imports in 2012. Following the discovery of substantial reserves of uranium, the Government has instigated plans for the development of a nuclear power industry; several civil nuclear co-operation accords have been signed with other countries since 2008. In February 2012 the Jordan Atomic Energy Commission (JAEC) revealed that al-Mafraq governorate was its preferred location for the construction of the country's first nuclear power plant. In October 2013 the JAEC awarded a contract for the construction of two reactors to the Russian firm Rosatom; the plant was expected to begin production in 2021. In addition to boosting Jordan's domestic energy capacity, it is envisaged that the nuclear programme will facilitate the implementation of much-needed water desalination projects.

Services accounted for some 68.6% of Jordan's GDP in 2012, according to preliminary figures, and engaged an estimated 74.4% of the employed labour force in 2011. The tourism industry, which accounts for at least 14% of GDP, has suffered considerably since 2011 as a result of the ongoing political instability in neighbouring countries such as Egypt and Syria; the number of tourist arrivals declined from 8.2m. in 2010 to 6.8m. in 2011 and further, to 6.3m., in 2012. During 2003–12, according to preliminary official figures, the GDP of the sector increased by an average of 5.9% per year; sectoral growth increased by 4.8% in 2012.

In 2012 Jordan recorded a visible merchandise trade deficit of US $10,544.3m., and there was a deficit of $5,693.7m. on the current account of the balance of payments. In 2012 Saudi Arabia was the main source of imports (with 23.5% of the total); other major suppliers were the People's Republic of China and the USA. In that year Iraq was the principal market for exports (with 15.5% of the total); other significant purchasers were the USA, Saudi Arabia and India. The principal exports in 2012 were chemicals and related products, textiles, vegetable products, mineral products, machinery and mechanical appliances, and base metals and articles, while the principal imports were mineral fuels, oils and distillation products, machinery and mechanical appliances, chemicals and related products, base metals and articles, vegetable products, vehicles, aircraft and transport equipment, textiles, and prepared foodstuffs, beverages, spirits and tobacco products.

In 2013, according to budgeted official figures, a budget deficit of JD 1,309.7m. was envisaged (including external aid payments and revenues from the sale of land). Jordan's general government gross debt was JD 17,610m. in 2012, equivalent to 79.6% of GDP. Jordan's external debt totalled US $17,634m. at the end of 2011, of which $6,349m. was public and publicly guaranteed debt. In that year, the cost of servicing long-term public and publicly guaranteed debt and repayments to the IMF was equivalent to 6.7% of the value of exports of goods, services and income (excluding workers' remittances). According to official figures, the annual rate of inflation averaged 5.3% in 2006–12; consumer prices increased by an average of 4.6% in 2012. In the same year some 12.2% of the economically active population was unemployed.

By early 2014 the National Agenda, published by the Government in January 2006, had still not been effectively implemented by the authorities. This was an ambitious 10-year plan to improve the quality and effectiveness of public administration through the reduction of poverty and unemployment (by creating 600,000 jobs) and the achievement of annual real GDP growth of 7.2%. In early 2011, amid a series of anti-Government demonstrations being held in protest against increased prices for basic commodities, among other grievances, King Abdullah announced an additional US $125m. in subsidies for fuel and essential foodstuffs, as well as a wage increase for civil servants and a rise in pension payments. The country's fiscal situation worsened significantly during 2011–12, with the result that a new range of austerity measures were introduced in May 2012—including reduced spending on public institutions, an extension of the sales tax and a rise in electricity prices for industrial consumers—and some fuel subsidies were withdrawn in November to enable the authorities to secure IMF funding. Such policies led to greater levels of poverty among certain sections of the population and renewed public protests against the Government. Moreover, the profound instability arising from anti-government uprisings in many countries across the region had led to a decline in exports, foreign direct investment, tourism receipts and remittances from abroad, as well as higher energy costs. The continuing high levels of inflation and unemployment also remained a major concern. The rapid influx of refugees fleeing the conflict in neighbouring Syria during 2012–13 added considerably to the burden on Jordan's state finances, as the authorities struggled to provide sufficient housing, food and medical supplies. In August the IMF agreed a 36-month stand-by arrangement—worth an estimated $2,000m.—with the Government to assist it in achieving its fiscal and growth targets under the national economic programme for 2012–15. In early March 2013 the IMF commended the authorities for their 'strong commitment' to pursuing the recovery programme despite challenging external circumstances; the Fund released the second part of its stand-by arrangement, totalling some $385m. in April. GDP growth was 2.7% in 2012, and was projected by the Government to be 3.3% in 2013 and 3.5% in 2014. However, in March 2014 the IMF assessed that Jordan required a growth rate of at least 7% in order to create a sufficient number of jobs for the country's increasing population and to reduce poverty. Civil unrest continued into early 2014, as economic grievances were increasingly aggravated by the presence of around 600,000 Syrian refugees. In mid-2013 the Ministry of Labour reported that more than 160,000 Syrian refugees were now employed in Jordan. Despite aiming to reduce the fiscal deficit from 7.9% in 2012 to 5.4% in 2013 in its draft budget for 2013, the deficit was estimated to have increased to around 10% of GDP by the end of that year. The budget for 2014 anticipated a 12.8% increase in state spending in a further effort to stimulate growth.

PUBLIC HOLIDAYS

2015: 2 January* (Mouloud, Birth of Muhammad), 1 May (Labour Day), 25 May (Independence Day), 15 May* (Leilat al-Meiraj, Ascension of Muhammad), 17 July* (Id al-Fitr, end of Ramadan), 23 September* (Id al-Adha, Feast of the Sacrifice), 14 October* (Muharram, Islamic New Year), 23 December* (Mouloud, Birth of Muhammad).

* These holidays are dependent on the Islamic lunar calendar and may vary by one or two days from the dates given.

Statistical Survey

Source: Department of Statistics, POB 2015, Amman 11181; tel. (6) 5300700; fax (6) 5300710; e-mail stat@dos.gov.jo; internet www.dos.gov.jo.

Area and Population

AREA, POPULATION AND DENSITY

Area (sq km)	88,794*
Population (census results)	
10 December 1994	4,139,458
1 October 2004	
Males	2,626,287
Females	2,477,352
Total	5,103,639
Population (official estimates at 31 December)†	
2011	6,249,000
2012	6,388,000
2013	6,530,000
Density (per sq km) at 31 December 2013	73.5

* 34,284 sq miles.

† Figures exclude the refugee population, which, according to UNHCR estimates, totalled some 300,000 at the end of 2012 (including more than 60,000 from Iraq and almost 240,000 from Syria).

POPULATION BY AGE AND SEX
(estimated population at 31 December 2012)

	Males	Females	Total
0–14	1,223,055	1,159,270	2,382,325
15–64	1,962,900	1,831,475	3,794,375
65 and over	107,045	104,255	211,300
Total	3,293,000	3,095,000	6,388,000

Note: Figures are rounded to nearest five persons.

GOVERNORATES
(estimated population at 31 December 2012)

	Area (sq km)	Population	Density (per sq km)
Amman	7,579	2,473,400	326.3
Irbid	1,572	1,137,100	723.3
Al-Zarqa (Zarqa)	4,761	951,800	199.9
Al-Balqa	1,120	428,000	382.1
Al-Mafraq	26,551	300,300	11.3
Al-Karak (Kerak)	3,495	249,100	71.3
Jarash (Jerash)	410	191,700	467.6
Madaba	940	159,700	169.9
Ajloun	420	146,900	349.8
Al-Aqabah (Aqaba)	6,905	139,200	20.2
Ma'an	32,832	121,400	3.7
Al-Tafilah	2,209	89,400	40.5
Total	88,794	6,388,000	71.9

Note: Population figures are rounded to nearest 100 persons.

PRINCIPAL TOWNS
(population at 2004 census)

Amman (capital)	1,036,330	Wadi al-Sir	122,032
Al-Zarqa (Zarqa)	395,227	Tila' al-Ali (Tla' El-Ali)	113,197
Irbid	250,645	Khuraybat as-Suq (Khraibet Essoq)	84,975
Al-Rusayfah (Russeifa)	227,735	Al-Aqabah (Aqaba)	80,059
Al-Quwaysimah	135,500		

Mid-2011 (incl. suburbs, UN estimate): Amman 1,178,650 (Source: UN, *World Urbanization Prospects: The 2011 Revision*).

BIRTHS, MARRIAGES AND DEATHS*

	Registered live births		Registered marriages		Registered deaths	
	Number	Rate (per 1,000)	Number	Rate (per 1,000)	Number	Rate (per 1,000)
2005	152,276	27.8	56,418	10.3	17,883	3.3
2006	162,972	29.1	59,335	10.6	20,397	3.6
2007	185,011	32.3	60,548	10.6	20,924	3.7
2008	181,328	31.0	60,922	10.4	19,403	3.3
2009	179,872	30.1	63,389	10.6	20,251	3.4
2010	183,948	30.1	62,107	10.2	21,550	3.5
2011	178,435	28.6	64,665	10.3	21,730	3.5
2012	177,695	28.1	70,621	11.2	22,785	3.6

* Data are tabulated by year of registration rather than by year of occurrence. Registration of births and marriages is reported to be complete, but death registration is incomplete. Figures exclude foreigners, but include registered Palestinian refugees.

Life expectancy (years at birth): 73.6 (males 72.0; females 75.3) in 2011 (Source: World Bank, World Development Indicators database).

EMPLOYMENT
(economic survey at October, public and private sectors, excl. armed forces)

	2009	2010	2011
Mining and quarrying	8,626	8,520	8,600
Manufacturing	182,769	188,015	186,517
Electricity, gas and water	13,442	15,878	14,255
Construction	51,177	46,105	50,130
Wholesale and retail trade; repair of motor vehicles and motorcycles and personal and household goods	208,304	210,318	214,079
Hotels and restaurants	39,680	40,908	44,917
Transport, storage and communications	33,832	36,354	38,069
Financial intermediation	26,944	29,041	31,282
Real estate, renting and business activities	47,157	46,641	49,464
Public administration and compulsory social security	104,078	104,431	107,142
Education	165,294	170,384	181,940
Health and social work	55,682	57,879	59,647
Other community, social and personal service activities	25,288	23,241	26,055
Total employed	962,272	977,714	1,012,096
Males	742,631	752,121	779,466
Females	219,641	225,593	232,630

Note: Figures are assumed to exclude data for those engaged in agriculture and fishing—according to FAO estimates some 105,000 of a total economically active population of 1,965,000 were engaged in the sector at mid-2014. Figures include foreign nationals employed in Jordan, numbering 126,369 in 2009; 121,726 in 2010; 111,721 in 2011.

Health and Welfare

KEY INDICATORS

Total fertility rate (children per woman, 2011)	3.0
Under-5 mortality rate (per 1,000 live births, 2011)	21
HIV/AIDS (% of persons aged 15–49, 2007)	<0.2
Physicians (per 1,000 head, 2010)	2.6
Hospital beds (per 1,000 head, 2010)	1.8
Health expenditure (2010): US $ per head (PPP)	493
Health expenditure (2010): % of GDP	8.3
Health expenditure (2010): Public (% of total)	67.6
Access to water (% of persons, 2011)	96
Access to sanitation (% of persons, 2011)	98
Total carbon dioxide emissions ('000 metric tons, 2010)	20,821.2
Carbon dioxide emissions per head (metric tons, 2010)	3.4
Human Development Index (2012): ranking	100
Human Development Index (2012): value	0.700

For sources and definitions, see explanatory note on p. vi.

Agriculture

PRINCIPAL CROPS
('000 metric tons)

	2010	2011	2012
Wheat	22.1	19.8	19.2
Barley	10.7	29.3	32.1
Maize	29.0	16.5	14.4
Potatoes	174.9	216.5	141.6
Olives	171.7	131.8	155.6
Cabbages and other brassicas	20.3	22.1	39.5
Lettuce and chicory	48.2	40.4	39.5
Tomatoes	737.3	777.8	616.4
Cauliflowers and broccoli	54.7	62.5	35.7
Pumpkins, squash and gourds	69.7	93.1	69.0
Cucumbers and gherkins	176.2	227.6	155.9
Aubergines (Eggplants)	104.7	117.0	177.7
Chillies and peppers, green	55.1	63.7	70.5
Onions and shallots, green	3.5	1.1	3.0
Onions, dry	15.8	40.8	26.5
Beans, green	8.2	8.5	11.6
Okra	6.8	8.6	5.9
Watermelons	153.1	121.8	108.7
Cantaloupes and other melons	31.1	38.6	42.0
Bananas	43.8	48.3	38.9
Grapefruit and pomelos	8.4	7.6	8.1
Oranges	43.0	38.7	40.9
Tangerines, mandarins, clementines and satsumas	38.3	34.1	35.8
Lemons and limes	28.8	26.4	26.5
Apples	28.8	39.7	36.4
Peaches and nectarines	20.8	26.9	39.8
Grapes	29.7	38.4	35.7

Aggregate production ('000 metric tons, may include official, semi-official or estimated data): Total cereals 87.3 in 2010, 83.0 in 2011, 84.0 in 2012; Total roots and tubers 174.9 in 2010, 216.5 in 2011, 141.6 in 2012; Total vegetables (incl. melons) 1,609.7 in 2010, 1,749.6 in 2011, 1,518.3 in 2012; Total fruits (excl. melons) 289.6 in 2010, 319.7 in 2011, 321.5 in 2012.

Source: FAO.

LIVESTOCK
('000 head, year ending September)

	2010	2011	2012
Horses	2	2*	2*
Asses*	10	10	10
Mules*	1.5	1.5	1.5
Cattle	65.4	67.6	68.5
Camels	13†	12*	13*
Sheep	2,175.7	2,264.6	2,234
Goats	751.7	752.2	792.0
Chickens*	25,000	26,000	26,500

* FAO estimate(s).
† Unofficial figure.

Source: FAO.

LIVESTOCK PRODUCTS
('000 metric tons)

	2010	2011	2012
Cattle meat	12.3	17.8	19.6
Sheep meat	17.7	12.1	17.6
Goat meat	4.0	5.1	7.1
Chicken meat	187.5	190.5	190.3
Cows' milk	215.0	238.6	240.7
Sheep's milk	58.6*	57.9	59.8
Goats' milk	15.8	10.5	9.9
Hen eggs	69.3	69.3	43.3
Wool, greasy†	2.8	2.8	2.9

* Unofficial figure.
† FAO estimates.

Source: FAO.

Forestry

ROUNDWOOD REMOVALS
('000 cubic metres, excluding bark, FAO estimates)

	2010	2011	2012
Industrial wood	4	4	4
Fuel wood	302	310	318
Total	306	314	322

Source: FAO.

Fishing

(metric tons, live weight)

	2009	2010	2011
Capture	569	486	500
Freshwater fishes	350	350	350
Tunas	131	93	102
Aquaculture (Tilapias)	440	541	575
Common carp	230	259	404
Total catch	1,009	1,027	1,075

Source: FAO.

Mining

('000 metric tons unless otherwise indicated)

	2009	2010	2011
Crude petroleum ('000 barrels)	9.4	8.9	7.2
Phosphate rock	5,282	6,529	7,643
Potash salts*	1,120	2,141	2,259
Bromine	69	329	148
Gypsum	304	292	255

* Figures refer to the K_2O content.

Source: US Geological Survey.

Industry

SELECTED PRODUCTS
(42-gallon barrels unless otherwise indicated)

	2009	2010	2011
Asphalt	1,171	914	648
Phosphatic fertilizers ('000 metric tons)	721	812	824
Cement ('000 metric tons)	3,876	5,000	6,000
Liquefied petroleum gas	1,235	985	958
Motor spirit (petrol)	7,566	7,029	6,810
Kerosene	625	654	448
Jet fuels	2,444	2,717	2,721
Distillate fuel oils	8,750	6,739	7,684
Electric energy (million kWh)	14,272	14,777	14,647

2012 (million kWh): Electric energy 16,595.

Sources: mainly US Geological Survey.

Finance

CURRENCY AND EXCHANGE RATES

Monetary Units
1,000 fils = 1 Jordanian dinar (JD).

Sterling, Dollar and Euro Equivalents (31 December 2013)
£1 sterling = JD 1.169;
US $1 = 710 fils;
€1 = JD 0.979;
JD 10 = £8.55 = $14.08 = €10.21.

Exchange Rate: An official mid-point rate of US $1 = 709 fils (JD1 = $1.4104) has been maintained since October 1995.

BUDGET
(JD million)*

Revenue†	2011	2012	2013‡
Taxation	3,062.2	3,351.4	3,770.0
Taxes on income and profits	667.4	688.3	765.0
Corporations	519.6	556.5	613.0
Individuals	78.8	64.4	71.0
Taxes on domestic transactions	2,033.2	2,274.7	2,610.0
General sales tax	2,033.2	2,274.7	2,610.0
Taxes on foreign trade	287.0	285.6	285.0
Other revenue	1,116.0	1,351.2	1,502.0
Fees	599.5	682.4	806.9
Interest and profits	216.0	304.5	311.6
Repayment	43.8	28.6	40.0
Pensions	20.7	24.3	24.0
Total	4,198.8	4,726.9	5,296.0

Expenditure	2011	2012	2013‡
Current	5,739.5	6,202.8	6,210.1
Wages and salaries	950.2	1,109.0	1,201.7
Purchases of goods and services	265.4	235.5	256.1
Interest payments	429.5	582.9	800.0
Domestic	333.9	483.1	628.0
Foreign	95.6	99.9	172.0
Food and oil subsidies	796.5	892.7	225.0
Pensions	861.9	982.4	1,068.0
Defence and security	1,797.7	1,756.8	1,767.2
Capital	1,057.1	675.4	1,245.6
Total	6,796.6	6,878.2	7,455.7

* Figures represent a consolidation of the Current, Capital and Development Plan Budgets of the central Government. The data exclude the operations of the Health Security Fund and of other government agencies with individual budgets.
† Excluding foreign grants received (JD million): 1,215.0 in 2011; 327.3 in 2012 (preliminary); 850.0 in 2013 (budget figure).
‡ Budget figures.

Source: Ministry of Finance, Amman.

INTERNATIONAL RESERVES
(US $ million at 31 December)

	2010	2011	2012
Gold (national valuation)	589.3	637.7	739.9
IMF special drawing rights	225.8	224.8	220.3
Reserve position in the IMF	0.5	0.5	0.5
Foreign exchange	12,830.5	11,241.9	7,868.7
Total	13,646.1	12,105.0	8,829.4

Source: IMF, *International Financial Statistics*.

MONEY SUPPLY
(JD million at 31 December)

	2010	2011	2012
Currency outside banks	2,843.7	3,019.3	3,215.0
Demand deposits at commercial banks	3,657.2	4,206.3	3,934.5
Total money (incl. others)	6,504.4	7,228.0	7,152.1

Source: IMF, *International Financial Statistics*.

COST OF LIVING
(Consumer Price Index; base: 2006 = 100)

	2010	2011	2012
Food (incl. beverages)	137.7	143.4	150.0
Clothing (incl. footwear)	122.9	130.5	136.7
Housing	118.6	123.1	127.4
Other goods and services	114.4	120.2	127.0
All items	124.5	130.0	136.0

NATIONAL ACCOUNTS
(JD million at current prices)

Expenditure on the Gross Domestic Product

	2007	2008*	2009*
Government final consumption expenditure	2,499.4	3,363.6	3,699.5
Private final consumption expenditure	10,512.3	12,403.0	12,688.4
Changes in stocks	337.8	318.7	193.7
Gross fixed capital formation	3,334.1	4,342.9	4,254.2
Total domestic expenditure	16,683.6	20,428.2	20,835.8
Exports of goods and services	6,579.4	8,811.2	7,758.6
Less Imports of goods and services	11,131.6	13,646.0	11,682.2
GDP in purchasers' values	12,131.4	15,593.4	16,912.2
GDP in constant 1994 prices	8,629.0	9,252.1	9,759.9

* Preliminary.

GDP in constant 1994 prices (preliminary estimates): 9,985.5 in 2010; 10,243.8 in 2011; 10,515.3 in 2012.

Gross Domestic Product by Economic Activity
(preliminary estimates)

	2010	2011	2012
Agriculture, hunting, forestry and fishing	560.9	598.3	604.5
Mining and quarrying	621.8	803.5	723.5
Manufacturing	3,146.1	3,485.3	3,633.4
Electricity and water	380.0	417.5	482.8
Construction	896.2	888.0	961.7
Wholesale and retail trade, restaurants and hotels	1,723.9	1,845.3	2,055.8
Transport, storage and communications	2,285.2	2,426.1	2,637.4
Finance, insurance, real estate and business services	3,135.3	3,483.9	3,838.4
Public administration, defence, and social security	3,735.4	4,121.3	4,485.6
Other services	822.0	854.3	951.8
Sub-total	17,306.8	18,923.5	20,375.0
Less Imputed bank service charge	889.6	935.8	1,076.9
GDP in basic prices	16,417.2	17,987.7	19,298.2
Taxes on products (net)	2,344.8	2,488.9	2,667.3
GDP in purchasers' values	18,762.0	20,476.6	21,965.5

BALANCE OF PAYMENTS
(US $ million)

	2010	2011	2012
Exports of goods	7,028.3	8,006.3	7,886.6
Imports of goods	–13,822.4	–16,825.6	–18,430.9
Balance on goods	–6,794.1	–8,819.3	–10,544.3
Exports of services	5,600.0	5,140.3	5,685.8
Imports of services	–4,419.0	–4,475.5	–4,544.4
Balance on goods and services	–5,613.1	–8,154.5	–9,402.9
Primary income received	1,010.8	795.4	773.7
Primary income paid	–1,102.0	–975.1	–1,078.3
Balance on goods, services and primary income	–5,704.2	–8,334.2	–9,707.5
Secondary income received	4,372.5	5,365.5	4,646.5
Secondary income paid	–550.4	–499.7	–632.7

—continued	2010	2011	2012
Current balance	–1,882.1	–3,468.5	–5,693.7
Capital account (net)	2.3	2.3	2.3
Direct investment assets	–28.5	–30.8	–5.4
Direct investment liabilities	1,650.8	1,473.5	1,497.3
Portfolio investment assets	41.0	282.5	221.7
Portfolio investment liabilities	729.4	11.1	69.2
Other investment assets	–1,260.6	–498.2	–1,005.6
Other investment liabilities	1,375.4	390.0	752.8
Net errors and omissions	832.2	185.5	491.3
Reserves and related items	1,459.8	–1,652.6	–3,670.2

Source: IMF, *International Financial Statistics*.

External Trade

PRINCIPAL COMMODITIES
(distribution by HS, JD million)

Imports c.i.f.	2010	2011	2012
Live animals and animal products	426.3	496.1	599.0
Vegetable products	742.5	986.2	1,025.0
Cereals	422.7	604.5	621.7
Prepared foodstuffs; beverages, spirits and vinegar; tobacco and manufactured tobacco substitutes	665.9	738.5	815.8
Mineral products	2,503.7	3,979.3	4,725.9
Mineral fuels, oils, distillation products, etc.	2,441.3	3,921.4	4,692.8
Crude petroleum oils	1,357.1	1,856.3	1,958.2
Non-crude petroleum oils	680.1	1,588.5	2,286.1
Petroleum gases	338.2	253.0	301.7
Chemicals and related products	913.1	1,049.7	1,089.1
Plastics, rubbers, and articles thereof	449.9	536.5	617.7
Plastics and articles thereof	393.3	465.1	528.3
Textiles and textile articles	615.4	701.3	758.0
Base metals and articles thereof	951.8	1,037.9	1,093.4
Iron and steel	331.3	405.0	552.0
Machinery and mechanical appliances	1,577.1	1,624.0	1,565.9
Machinery, boilers, etc.	976.4	997.8	973.3
Electrical, electronic equipment	600.7	626.2	592.6
Vehicles, aircraft, vessels and associated transport equipment	929.0	795.2	850.8
Vehicles other than railway, tramway	841.9	708.1	748.4
Motor cars and other passenger vehicles	555.8	446.6	461.8
Total (incl. others)	11,050.1	13,440.2	14,733.7

Exports f.o.b.	2010	2011	2012
Live animals and animal products	152.3	168.8	192.1
Vegetable products	391.0	455.4	497.2
Edible vegetables, roots and tubers	312.1	340.3	334.5
Prepared foodstuffs; beverages, spirits and vinegar; tobacco and manufactured tobacco substitutes	247.0	257.1	272.7
Mineral products	330.6	512.1	488.4
Salt, sulphur, earth, stone, plaster, lime and cement	282.7	496.8	471.2
Natural calcium and aluminium phosphates, phosphatic chalk	265.0	446.1	426.0
Chemicals and related products	1,242.0	1,765.4	1,679.7
Inorganic chemicals	204.9	252.5	299.9
Pharmaceutical products	486.0	414.3	447.5
Medicaments put in doses	384.7	321.6	306.2
Fertilizers	763.3	889.9	723.0
Nitrogenous mineral or chemical fertilizers	218.6	256.1	204.1
Potassic mineral or chemical fertilizers	491.1	600.9	483.8
Plastics, rubbers, and articles thereof	135.7	171.9	229.1
Plastics and articles thereof	130.2	166.0	219.3
Textiles and textile articles	683.2	764.4	813.8
Articles of apparel and clothing accessories, knitted or crocheted	548.2	656.1	693.9
Pearls; precious or semi-precious stones; precious metals	233.5	273.0	182.3
Gold, unwrought, semi-manufactured or powdered	142.1	186.7	101.4
Base metals and articles thereof	338.4	363.2	287.3
Machinery and mechanical appliances	400.9	451.1	409.0
Machinery, boilers, etc.	182.2	203.4	185.6
Electrical, electronic equipment	219.4	247.7	223.4
Vehicles, aircraft, vessels and associated transport equipment	131.1	123.8	113.8
Total (incl. others)	4,990.1	5,684.6	5,599.5

PRINCIPAL TRADING PARTNERS
(countries of consignment, JD million)

Imports c.i.f.	2010	2011	2012
Argentina	117.4	173.7	233.3
Brazil	131.6	147.3	180.4
China, People's Republic	1,188.6	1,317.4	1,416.4
Egypt	492.9	535.0	560.5
France	246.6	264.2	265.7
Germany	729.0	607.5	575.2
India	275.3	360.2	506.8
Iraq	165.6	220.0	230.8
Italy	379.3	688.5	658.6
Japan	343.5	259.0	277.5
Korea, Republic	461.9	435.9	406.3
Malaysia	136.4	104.6	105.7
Netherlands	126.0	126.2	115.6
Romania	68.6	136.3	119.1
Russia	178.2	513.1	450.3
Saudi Arabia	2,164.4	2,968.7	3,469.7
Spain	85.1	163.5	137.0
Syria	267.2	268.4	171.3
Taiwan	127.7	178.5	194.4
Turkey	397.2	393.5	568.9
Ukraine	186.0	146.2	356.8
United Arab Emirates	286.0	504.9	418.8
United Kingdom	189.4	212.9	183.2
USA	615.6	861.4	977.5
Total (incl. others)	11,050.1	13,440.2	14,733.7

Exports f.o.b.	2010	2011	2012
Algeria	90.7	90.1	93.5
China, People's Republic	80.3	144.5	134.1
Egypt	101.9	89.2	93.6
Ethiopia	70.8	69.0	22.5
India	552.2	649.0	515.3
Indonesia	105.9	157.1	192.7
Iraq	800.8	862.2	868.3
Israel	74.8	80.5	89.0
Kuwait	64.0	102.0	74.9
Lebanon	164.2	238.3	208.6
Malaysia	50.7	80.0	46.7
Qatar	69.8	66.3	82.8
Saudi Arabia	475.4	482.9	547.9
Sudan	61.3	59.4	45.9
Switzerland	99.9	57.2	21.0
Syria	182.5	203.6	156.1
Turkey	43.2	69.7	93.9
United Arab Emirates	210.6	205.6	224.0
USA	659.2	738.7	799.0
Total (incl. others)	4,990.1	5,684.6	5,599.5

Transport

RAILWAYS
(traffic, million)

	2008	2009	2010
Passenger-km	0.4	0.9	1.3
Freight ton-km	448	439	344

Source: IRF, *World Road Statistics*.

ROAD TRAFFIC
(motor vehicles in use at 31 December)

	2008	2009	2010
Passenger cars	601,312	673,125	742,149
Buses	17,521	18,143	18,902
Lorries and vans	240,869	227,582	236,526
Motorcycles	3,845	3,489	4,079

Source: IRF, *World Road Statistics*.

2012 (licensed vehicles in use): Passenger cars 850,886; Buses 19,953; Vans and trucks 227,278; Tankers 7,552; Trailers 44,989, Others 63,224; *Total vehicles* 1,213,882.

SHIPPING

Flag Registered Fleet
(at 31 December)

	2011	2012	2013
Number of vessels	21	23	27
Displacement ('000 grt)	200.8	79.8	68.2

Source: Lloyd's List Intelligence (www.lloydslistintelligence.com).

International Sea-borne Freight Traffic
('000 metric tons)

	2010	2011	2012
Goods loaded	9,631	10,862	9,215
Goods unloaded	8,796	10,208	11,944

CIVIL AVIATION
(traffic on scheduled services)

	2010	2011
Kilometres flown (million)	69	72
Passengers carried ('000)	2,972	3,155
Passenger-km (million)	7,805	8,316
Total ton-km (million)	908	950

Source: UN, *Statistical Yearbook*.

2012 ('000): Passengers carried 3,339 (Source: World Bank, World Development Indicators database).

Tourism

ARRIVALS BY NATIONALITY
('000)*

	2010	2011	2012
Egypt	379.8	326.5	353.8
Iraq	254.3	292.1	373.1
Israel	244.3	211.9	203.7
Lebanon	186.1	108.6	65.9
Palestinian Territories	393.5	441.6	470.2
Saudi Arabia	1,337.4	1,074.2	1,144.1
Syria	2,382.6	1,903.7	1,190.2
Turkey	171.3	156.0	46.1
USA	181.7	156.6	159.4
Total (incl. others)	8,247.1	6,812.4	6,314.3

* Including pilgrims and excursionists (same-day visitors).

Source: Ministry of Tourism and Antiquities, Amman.

Tourism receipts (US $ million, excl. passenger transport): 3,585 in 2010; 3,000 in 2011; 3,460 in 2012 (provisional) (Source: World Tourism Organisation).

Communications Media

	2010	2011	2012
Telephones ('000 main lines in use)	485.5	465.4	434.4
Mobile cellular telephones ('000 subscribers)	6,620.0	7,482.6	8,984.3
Internet subscribers ('000)	248.3	208.1	n.a.
Broadband subscribers ('000)	195.8	199.9	193.6

Source: International Telecommunication Union.

Education

(2010/11 unless otherwise indicated)

	Schools	Teachers	Pupils
Pre-primary	1,248*	6,111	103,544
Primary	2,877*	39,441†	834,958
Secondary: general	1,002*	30,426†	694,344
Secondary: vocational	40*	2,759‡	25,076
Higher	22*	10,024§	252,446
of which universities‖	20	3,982	89,010

* 2003/04 figure.
† 2002/03 figure.
‡ 2007/08 figure.
§ 2009/10 figure.
‖ 1996/97 figures.

Source: partly UNESCO Institute for Statistics.

Pupil-teacher ratio (primary education, UNESCO estimate): 19.9 in 2002/03 (Source: UNESCO Institute for Statistics).

Adult literacy rate (UNESCO estimates): 95.9% (males 97.7%; females 93.9%) in 2011 (Source: UNESCO Institute for Statistics).

Directory

The Government

HEAD OF STATE

King: King ABDULLAH IBN AL-HUSSEIN (succeeded to the throne on 7 February 1999).

CABINET
(April 2014)

Prime Minister and Minister of Defence: ABDULLAH ENSOUR.

Minister of Higher Education and Scientific Research: Dr AMIN MAHMOUD.

Minister of Foreign and Expatriates Affairs: NASSER JUDEH.

Minister of the Interior: HUSSEIN HAZAA MAJALI.

Minister of Education: Dr MUHAMMAD THNEIBAT.

Minister of Industry, Trade and Supply: Dr HATEM HAFIZ AL-HALAWANI.

Minister of Water and Irrigation: Dr HAZEM AL-NASSER.

Minister of Agriculture: Dr AKIF AL-ZU'BI.

Minister of the Environment: TAHER AL-SHAKHSHIR.

Minister of Finance: Dr UMAYYA TOUQAN.

Minister of Public Sector Development: Dr KHLEIF AL-KHAWALDEH.

Minister of Awqaf (Religious Endowments) and Islamic Affairs: Dr HAYEL ABD AL-HAFIZ DAWOOD.

Minister of Labour and Minister of Tourism and Antiquities: NIDAL MARDI QATAMIN.

Minister of State for Prime Ministry Affairs: Dr AHMAD ZEYADAT.

Minister of Justice: Dr BASSAM SAMIR AL-TALHOUNI.

Minister of Municipal Affairs: WALID AL-MASRI.

Minister of Public Works and Housing: SAMI HALASEH.

Minister of Planning and International Co-operation: Dr IBRAHIM SAIF.

Minister of State for Media Affairs and Communications: Dr MUHAMMAD HUSSEIN MOMANI.

Minister of Social Development: REEM MAMDOUH ABU HASSAN.

Minister of State: SALAMEH AL-NEIMAT.

Minister of Health: Dr ALI AL-NAHLEH HIASAT.

Minister of Energy and Mineral Resources: Dr MUHAMMAD HAMAD.

Minister of Political and Parliamentary Affairs: KHALID AL-KALALDEH.

Minister of Culture: Dr LANA MAMKEGH.

Minister of Transport: Dr LINA SHABIB.

Minister of Information and Communications Technology: Dr AZZAM TALAL SLEIT.

Note: The Head of Intelligence and the Governor of the Central Bank also have full ministerial status.

MINISTRIES

The Prime Ministry of Jordan: POB 80, Amman 11180; tel. (6) 4641211; fax (6) 4642520; e-mail info@pm.gov.jo; internet www.pm.gov.jo.

Ministry of Agriculture: POB 2099, Amman; tel. (6) 5686151; fax (6) 5686310; e-mail moa.mail@moa.gov.jo; internet www.moa.gov.jo.

Ministry of Awqaf (Religious Endowments) and Islamic Affairs: POB 659, Amman; tel. (6) 5666141; fax (6) 5602254; e-mail awqaf@awqaf.gov.jo; internet www.awqaf.gov.jo.

Ministry of Culture: POB 6140, Amman; tel. (6) 5696218; fax (6) 5691640; e-mail info@culture.gov.jo; internet www.culture.gov.jo.

Ministry of Defence: POB 80, Amman; tel. (6) 4641211; fax (6) 4642520; e-mail info@jaf.mil.jo; internet www.jaf.mil.jo.

Ministry of Education: POB 1646, Amman 11118; tel. (6) 5607331; fax (6) 5666019; e-mail moe@moe.gov.jo; internet www.moe.gov.jo.

Ministry of Energy and Mineral Resources: POB 2310, Amman; tel. (6) 5803060; fax (6) 5865714; e-mail memr@memr.gov.jo; internet www.memr.gov.jo.

Ministry of the Environment: Amman; tel. (6) 5560113; fax (6) 5560288; e-mail info@moenv.gov.jo; internet www.moenv.gov.jo.

Ministry of Finance: POB 85, King Hussein St, Amman 11118; tel. (6) 4636321; fax (6) 4618527; e-mail info@mof.gov.jo; internet www.mof.gov.jo.

Ministry of Foreign and Expatriates Affairs: POB 35217, Amman 11180; tel. (6) 5735150; fax (6) 5735163; e-mail inquiry@mfa.gov.jo; internet www.mfa.gov.jo.

Ministry of Health: POB 86, Amman 11118; tel. (6) 5200230; fax (6) 5689177; e-mail info@moh.gov.jo; internet www.moh.gov.jo.

Ministry of Higher Education and Scientific Research: POB 35262, Amman 11180; tel. (6) 5347671; fax (6) 5349079; e-mail mohe@mohe.gov.jo; internet www.mohe.gov.jo.

Ministry of Industry, Trade and Supply: POB 2019, 11181 Amman; tel. (6) 5629030; fax (6) 5684692; e-mail info@mit.gov.jo; internet www.mit.gov.jo.

Ministry of Information and Communications Technology: POB 9903, Amman 11191; tel. (6) 5805700; fax (6) 5861059; e-mail moict@moict.gov.jo; internet www.moict.gov.jo.

Ministry of the Interior: POB 100, Amman; tel. (6) 5691141; fax (6) 5606908; e-mail info@moi.gov.jo; internet www.moi.gov.jo.

Ministry of Justice: POB 6040, Amman 11118; tel. (6) 4603630; fax (6) 4643197; e-mail feedback@moj.gov.jo; internet www.moj.gov.jo.

Ministry of Labour: POB 8160, Amman 11118; tel. (6) 5802666; fax (6) 5855072; e-mail info@mol.gov.jo; internet www.mol.gov.jo.

Ministry of Municipal Affairs: POB 1799, Amman 11118; tel. (6) 4641393; fax (6) 4640404; e-mail mma3@nic.net.jo; internet www.mma.gov.jo.

Ministry of Planning and International Co-operation: POB 555, Amman 11118; tel. (6) 4644466; fax (6) 4642247; e-mail mop@mop.gov.jo; internet www.mop.gov.jo.

Ministry of Political and Parliamentary Affairs: POB 841367, Amman 11180; tel. (6) 5695216; fax (6) 5686582; e-mail info@mopd.gov.jo; internet www.mopd.gov.jo.

Ministry of Public Sector Development: POB 3575, Amman 11821; tel. (6) 5695216; fax (6) 5686282; e-mail info@mopsd.gov.jo; internet www.mopsd.gov.jo.

Ministry of Public Works and Housing: POB 1220, Amman 11118; tel. (6) 5803838; fax (6) 5857590; e-mail mpwh@mpwh.gov.jo; internet www.mpwh.gov.jo.

Ministry of Social Development: POB 6720, Amman 11118; tel. (6) 5679327; fax (6) 5679961; e-mail contact@mosd.gov.jo; internet www.mosd.gov.jo.

Ministry of Tourism and Antiquities: POB 224, Amman 11118; tel. (6) 4603360; fax (6) 4648465; e-mail contacts@mota.gov.jo; internet www.mota.gov.jo.

Ministry of Transport: POB 35214, Amman 11180; tel. (6) 5518111; fax (6) 5527233; e-mail info@mot.gov.jo; internet www.mot.gov.jo.

Ministry of Water and Irrigation: POB 2412, Amman 11181; tel. (6) 5652265; fax (6) 5652287; e-mail admin@mwi.gov.jo; internet www.mwi.gov.jo.

Legislature

Majlis al-Umma (National Assembly)

Senate

POB 72, Amman 11101; tel. (6) 5664121; fax (6) 5689313; e-mail info@senate.jo; internet www.senate.jo.

The Senate (House of Notables) consists of 60 members, appointed by the King. The current Senate was appointed on 25 October 2011.

Speaker: TAHER AL-MASRI.

House of Representatives

POB 72, Amman 11118; tel. (6) 5635200; fax (6) 5685970; e-mail info@representatives.jo; internet www.representatives.jo.

Speaker: ATIF YOUSUF TARAWNEH.

General Election, 23 January 2013

Party/Group	Seats
Independents and tribal representatives	108
Islamic Centrist Party	3
Nation Party	2
National Current Party	2
National Union	2
Stronger Jordan	1
Other parties	17
Total	150*

* In accordance with the terms of electoral legislation approved in July 2012, 27 seats were allocated to political parties, while a further 15 seats were reserved for female candidates.

Election Commission

Independent Election Commission: POB 375, Tlaa al-Ali Area, Musa Saket Rd, Next to Chief Justice Bldg, Jordan 11953; tel. (6) 5607406; fax (6) 5607423; e-mail info@entikhabat.jo; internet www.entikhabat.jo; f. 2012; comprises Board of Commissioners and Executive apparatus; Chair. ABDELILAH AL-KHATIB.

Political Organizations

With the exception of the officially sanctioned Jordanian National Union (1971–76), political parties were effectively banned for most of the reign of King Hussein. However, in June 1991 a National Charter, one feature of which was the legalization of political parties, was formally endorsed. In August 1992 legislation allowing the formation of political parties was approved by royal decree, and by March 1993 nine parties had received official recognition. New amendments to the political parties law, approved by parliament in March 2007, required parties to have 500 founding members drawn from five different governorates with equal representation, and compelled parties to grant the Government access to their accounts; the reform also provided for public funding for political parties. Parties were given a period of one year to meet the new requirements or face dissolution. By April 2008 12 out of the 36 existing political parties had rectified their status; all other parties were dissolved, while two new parties were licensed. A number of parties were expected to launch lawsuits contesting their dissolution.

Arab Islamic Democratic Party (Dua'a): POB 104, Amman 11941; tel. and fax (6) 5514443; e-mail info@duaa-jo.com; f. 1993; moderate Islamist party; Founder YOUSUF ABU BAKR.

Higher Co-ordination Committee for Opposition Parties: Amman; opposition bloc currently consisting of 7 leftist, pan-Arab and Islamist parties: Baath Arab Progressive Party, Jordanian Arab Socialist Baath Party, Islamic Action Front, Jordanian Communist Party, Jordan People's Democratic Party (HASHD), National Movement for Direct Democracy and Jordanian Democratic Popular Unity Party (leftist).

Hizb-ut-Tahrir al-Islami (Party of Islamic Liberation): e-mail info@hizb-ut-tahrir.org; internet www.hizb-ut-tahrir.org; f. 1953; transnational org. prohibited in Jordan and many other countries; aims to establish Islamic caliphate throughout the world; denies claims that it is a militant group; Leader in Jordan RAMZI SAWALHAH.

Islamic Action Front (Jabhat al-Amal al-Islami—IAF): POB 925310, Abdali, Amman 11110; tel. (6) 5696985; fax (6) 5696987; e-mail info@jabha.net; internet www.jabha.net; f. 1992; seeks implementation of *Shari'a* (Islamic law) and preservation of the *Umma* (Islamic community); mem. of Higher Co-ordination Committee for Opposition Parties; Sec.-Gen. HAMZA MANSOUR.

Islamic Centrist Party (Hizb al-Wasat al-Islami): POB 2149, Haswa Bldg, 3rd Floor, Amman 11941; tel. and fax (6) 5353966; e-mail alwasaat@yahoo.com; internet www.wasatparty.org; f. 2001 by fmr mems of Islamic Action Front and Muslim Brotherhood; Sec.-Gen. Dr MUHAMMAD AHMAD AL-HAJ.

Jordan People's Democratic Party (Hizb al-Shaab al-Dimuqrati—HASHD): POB 9966, Amman 11191; tel. (6) 5691451; fax (6) 5686857; e-mail ahali@go.com.jo; internet www.hashd-ahali.org.jo; f. 1989; leftist party, which seeks to establish legal and institutional processes to protect the people, instigate economic, social, democratic and agricultural reform, and organize, unify and protect the working classes; supports the Palestinian cause; mem. of Higher Co-ordination Cttee for Opposition Parties; Sec.-Gen. ABLA ABU ULBAH.

Jordanian Arab Socialist Baath Party (Hizb al-Baath al-Arabi al-Ishtiraki al-Urduni): POB 8383, Amman; tel. (6) 4658618; fax (6) 4658617; f. 1993; promotes pan-Arabism; mem. of Higher Co-ordination Cttee for Opposition Parties; Sec.-Gen. AKRAM AL-HOMSI.

Jordanian Communist Party: POB 2349, Amman; tel. and fax (6) 4624939; e-mail jcp@nets.com.jo; internet www.jocp.org; f. 1951; merged with Communist Workers Party of Jordan 2008; Sec.-Gen. Dr MUNIR HAMARNEH.

Jordanian Democratic Popular Unity Party: POB 922110, Amman; tel. (6) 5692301; fax (6) 5692302; e-mail wihdaparty@gmail.com; internet www.wihda.org; f. 1990; publishes *Nida'a al-Watan* newspaper; Sec.-Gen. SAEED THIYAB.

National Constitutional Party (Al-Hizb al-Watani al-Dusturi—NCP): POB 1825237, Amman 11118; tel. (6) 5696256; fax (6) 5686248; f. 1997 by merger of 9 parties; Pres. ABD AL-HADI AL-MAJALI; Sec.-Gen. AHMAD SHUNNAQ.

National Current Party: Amman; f. 2009; seeks to promote the cause of national unity through the reform of political institutions; pro-monarchy; Sec.-Gen. ABDUL HADI MAJALI.

National Movement for Direct Democracy: POB 922478, Amman 11192; tel. (6) 5652125; fax (6) 5639925; f. 1997; Sec.-Gen. MUHAMMAD AL-QAQ.

Stronger Jordan (Urdun Aqwa): Amman; f. 2013; list formed to contest Jan. 2013 parliamentary elections; Leader ROLA AL-FARRA HROUB.

Other licensed parties include: Baath Arab Progressive Party, Al-Hayat, Jordan National Party, Mission Party (Hizb al-Risala) and the Unified Jordanian Front.

Diplomatic Representation

EMBASSIES IN JORDAN

Algeria: POB 830375, Amman 11183; tel. (6) 4641271; fax (6) 4616552; e-mail ambalg@go.com.jo; Ambassador MUHAMMAD QUWAR.

Australia: POB 35201, 41 Kayed al-Armouti St, Abdoun, Amman 11180; tel. (6) 5807000; fax (6) 5807001; e-mail amman.austremb@dfat.gov.au; internet www.jordan.embassy.gov.au; Ambassador HEIDI VENAMORE.

Austria: POB 830795, Jabal Amman, Amman 11183; tel. (6) 4601101; fax (6) 4612725; e-mail amman-ob@bmeia.gv.at; internet www.bmeia.gv.at/en/embassy/amman.html; Ambassador ASTRID HARZ.

Azerbaijan: POB 851894, 13 al-Awabed St, al-Kursi, Amman 11185; tel. (6) 5935525; fax (6) 5932826; e-mail amman@mission.mfa.gov.az; internet www.azembassyjo.org; Ambassador SABIR AGHABAYOV.

Bahrain: POB 5220, Faris al-Khoury St, Shmeisani, Amman 11183; tel. (6) 5664148; fax (6) 5664190; e-mail bahemb@maktoob.com; internet www.mofa.gov.bh/amman; Ambassador NASSER RASHID AL-KAABI.

Bangladesh: POB 5685, 10 Muzdalifa St, al-Rabieh, Amman 11183; tel. (6) 5529192; fax (6) 5529194; e-mail embangl@wanadoo.jo; internet www.bdembassyjordan.com; Ambassador MUHAMMAD ENAYET HUSSAIN.

Belgium: POB 942, 17 Sa'ad Jumah St, Jabal Amman, Amman 11118; tel. (6) 4655730; fax (6) 4655740; e-mail amman@diplobel.fed.be; internet www.diplomatie.be/amman; Ambassador THOMAS BAEKELANDT.

Bosnia and Herzegovina: POB 850836, 67 Said al-Mufti St, Amman 11185; tel. (6) 5856921; fax (6) 5856923; e-mail embjoamm@wanadoo.jo; Ambassador DARKO ZELENIKA.

Brazil: POB 5497, Amman 11183; tel. (6) 5923941; fax (6) 5931098; e-mail jorbrem@wanadoo.jo; Ambassador RENATE STILLE.

Brunei: POB 851752, Amman 11185; tel. (6) 5928021; fax (6) 5928024; e-mail amman.jordan@mfa.gov.bn; Chargé d'affaires a.i. MOHAMMAD SALIMIN BIN Haji MOHD DAUD.

Bulgaria: POB 950578, 7 al-Mousel St, Amman 11195; tel. (6) 5529392; fax (6) 5539393; e-mail embassy.amman@mfa.bg; internet www.mfa.bg/embassies/jordan; Ambassador VENELIN LAZAROV.

Canada: POB 815403, Amman 11180; tel. (6) 5901500; fax (6) 5901501; e-mail amman@international.gc.ca; internet www.canadainternational.gc.ca/jordan-jordanie; Ambassador BRUNO SACCOMANI.

Chile: POB 830663, 28 Hussein Abu Ragheb St, Abdoun, Amman 11183; tel. (6) 5923360; fax (6) 5924263; e-mail echile@orange.jo; internet chileabroad.gov.cl/jordania; Ambassador EDUARDO ESCOBAR MARÍN.

China, People's Republic: POB 7365, 9 Jakarta St, Amman 11118; tel. (6) 5516136; fax (6) 5518713; e-mail chinaemb_jo@hotmail.com; internet jo.china-embassy.org; Ambassador GAO YUSHENG.

Cyprus: POB 5525, Bldg 233, Wadi Sakra St, Amman 11183; tel. (6) 5657143; fax (6) 5657895; e-mail info@cyprusembassyamman.org; Ambassador CHARALAMBOS HADJISAVVAS.

Czech Republic: POB 2213, 34 Halab St, Abdoun, Amman 11181; tel. (6) 5927051; fax (6) 5927053; e-mail amman@embassy.mzv.cz; internet www.mzv.cz/amman; Ambassador PETR HLADÍK.

Egypt: POB 35178, 14 Riyad el-Mefleh St, Amman 11180; tel. (6) 5605202; fax (6) 5604082; e-mail eg.emb_amman@mfa.gov.eg; Ambassador KHALED THARWAT.

France: POB 5348, Amman 11183; tel. (6) 4641273; fax (6) 4659606; e-mail cad.amman-amba@diplomatie.fr; internet www.ambafrance-jo.org; Ambassador CAROLINE DUMAS.

Georgia: POB 851903, 31 Odeh Abu Tayeh, Shmeisani, Amman 11185; tel. (6) 5603793; fax (6) 5603819; e-mail geoemb@orange.jo; internet www.jordan.mfa.gov.ge; Ambassador ZURAB ERISTAVI.

Germany: POB 183, 25 Benghazi St, Jabal Amman 11118; tel. (6) 5901170; fax (6) 5901282; e-mail info@amman.diplo.de; internet www.amman.diplo.de; Ambassador RALPH TARRAF.

Greece: POB 35069, 7 Suleiman Youssef Sukkar St, Amman 11180; tel. (6) 5922724; fax (6) 5927622; e-mail gremb.amn@mfa.gr; internet www.mfa.gr/amman; Ambassador MARIA LUIZA MARINAKI.

Holy See: POB 142916, 14 Anton al-Naber St, Amman 11814; tel. (6) 5929934; fax (6) 5929931; e-mail nuntiusjordan@gmail.com; Apostolic Nuncio Most Rev. Archbishop GIORGIO LINGUA.

Hungary: POB 3441, 23 Yaqoub Ammari St, Abdoun, Amman 11181; tel. (6) 5925614; fax (6) 5930836; e-mail mission.amm@kum.hu; internet www.mfa.gov.hu/emb/amman; Ambassador Dr BÉLA JUNGBERT.

India: POB 2168, Amr bin Masadah St, Jabal Amman, 1st Circle, Amman 11181; tel. (6) 4622098; fax (6) 4659540; e-mail amb.amman@mea.gov.in; internet indembassy-amman.org; Ambassador RADHA RANJAN DASH.

Indonesia: POB 811784, 13 Ali Seedo al-Kurdi St, Sweifieh, Amman 11181; tel. (6) 5926908; fax (6) 5926796; e-mail amman96@go.com.jo; internet www.kemlu.go.id/amman; Ambassador TEGUH WARDOYO.

Iran: POB 173, Amman 11118; tel. (6) 4641281; fax (6) 4641383; e-mail pub-rel@iranembassyjordan.org; Ambassador MOSTAFA MOSLEH-ZADEH.

Iraq: POB 2025, Amman; tel. (6) 4623175; fax (6) 4619172; e-mail amaemb@mofaml.gov.iq; internet www.mofamission.gov.iq/amn; Ambassador Dr JAWAD HADI ABBAS.

Israel: POB 95866, 47 Maysaloon St, Dahiat al-Rabieh, Amman 11195; tel. (6) 5503500; fax (6) 5503579; e-mail embassy@amman.mfa.gov.il; internet amman.mfa.gov.il; Ambassador DANNY NEVO.

Italy: POB 9800, Jabal al-Weibdeh, 5 Hafiz Ibrahim St, Amman 11191; tel. (6) 4638185; fax (6) 4659730; e-mail info.amman@esteri.it; internet www.ambamman.esteri.it; Ambassador PATRIZIO FONDI.

Japan: POB 2835, Fa'eq Halazon St, Zahran, Abdun Shamali, Amman 11181; tel. (6) 5932005; fax (6) 5931006; e-mail mail@embjapan.org.jo; internet www.jordan.emb-japan.go.jp; Ambassador JUNICHI KOSUGE.

Kazakhstan: Abu Bakir al-Banany St, Amman; tel. (6) 5927953; fax (6) 5927952; e-mail kazemb@orange.jo; Ambassador BOLAT S. SARSENBAYEV.

Korea, Democratic People's Republic: POB 799, Amman; tel. (6) 4417614; fax (6) 4424735; e-mail dprk-embv@scs-net.org; Ambassador RI SI HONG.

Korea, Republic: POB 3060, Bahjat Homsi St, Amman 11181; tel. (6) 5930745; fax (6) 5930280; e-mail jordan@mofa.go.kr; internet jor.mofa.go.kr; Ambassador CHOI HONG-GHI.

Kuwait: POB 2107, Amman 11181; tel. (6) 5675135; fax (6) 5681971; e-mail q8@kuwaitembassyamman.org; Ambassador Dr HAMAD SALEH DUAIJ.

Lebanon: POB 811779, Amman 11181; tel. and fax (6) 5929111; Ambassador MICHELIN PAZ.

Libya: POB 2987, Amman; tel. (6) 5693101; fax (6) 5693404; Ambassador MUHAMMAD FIRANI.

Malaysia: POB 5351, Tayseer Na'nah St, off Umawiyyeen St, Abdoun, Amman 11183; tel. (6) 5902400; fax (6) 5934343; e-mail malamman@kln.gov.my; internet www.kln.gov.my/web/jor_amman; Ambassador Dato' ABDUL MALEK BIN ABDUL AZIZ.

Mauritania: POB 851594, Saleh Zakee St, Villa 19, Sweifiyeh, Amman 11185; tel. (6) 5855146; fax (6) 5855148; e-mail muritanyaembassy_amman1@hotmail.com; Ambassador ELY OULD AHMEDOU.

Morocco: POB 2175, Amman 11183; tel. (6) 5680591; fax (6) 5680253; e-mail ambmaroc@batelco.jo; Ambassador HASSAN ABD AL-KHALIQ.

Netherlands: POB 941361, 3 Abu Bakr Siraj al-Din St, Amman 11194; tel. (6) 5902200; fax (6) 5930161; e-mail amm-info@minbuza

.nl; internet jordan.nlembassy.org; Ambassador PAUL VAN DEN IJSSEL.

Norway: POB 830510, 25 Damascus St, Amman 11183; tel. (6) 5902450; fax (6) 5902479; e-mail emb.amman@mfa.no; internet www.norway.jo; Ambassador SISSEL BREIE.

Oman: POB 20192, Amman 11110; tel. (6) 5686155; fax (6) 5689404; e-mail amman@mofa.gov.om; Ambassador KHAMIS BIN MUHAMMAD BIN ABDULLAH AL-FARSI.

Pakistan: POB 1232, al-Akhtal St, Jabal al-Weibdeh, Amman 11118; tel. (6) 4622787; fax (6) 4611633; e-mail parepamman@gmail.com; internet www.embassyofpakistanjordan.com; Ambassador Lt-Gen. AHSAN AZHAR HAYAT.

Philippines: POB 925207, 5 Salem al-Batarseh St, Amman 11190; tel. (6) 5923748; fax (6) 5923744; e-mail ammanpe@dfa.gov.ph; internet www.philembassy-amman.net; Ambassador OLIVIA V. PALALA.

Poland: POB 942050, Amman 11194; tel. (6) 5512593; fax (6) 5512595; e-mail info@amman.polemb.net; internet www.amman.polemb.net; Ambassador KRZYSZTOF BOJKO.

Qatar: POB 5098, Bldg 38, Hajj Hassan St, Amman 11183; tel. (6) 5902300; fax (6) 5902301; e-mail amman@mofa.gov.qa; internet www.qatarembassy-jo.net; Ambassador ZAYED BIN SAEED AL-KHAYARIN.

Romania: POB 2869, 35 Madina Munawwara St, Amman 11181; tel. (6) 5813423; fax (6) 5812521; e-mail roemb@orange.jo; internet amman.mae.ro; Ambassador BOGDAN FILIP.

Russia: POB 2187, 22 Zahran St, 3rd Circle, Amman 11181; tel. (6) 4641158; fax (6) 4647448; e-mail rusembjo@mail.ru; internet www.jordan.mid.ru; Ambassador BORIS F. BOLOTIN.

Saudi Arabia: POB 2133, Zahrat al-Talhoni Bldg, Jabal Amman, Amman 11183; tel. (6) 5924154; fax (6) 5921154; e-mail joemb@mofa.gov.sa; Ambassador SAMI IBN ABDULLAH AL-SALIH.

South Africa: POB 851508, Sweifiyeh, Amman 11185; tel. (6) 5921194; fax (6) 5920080; e-mail saembjor@index.com.jo; Ambassador MOLEFE SAMUEL TSELE.

Spain: Zahran St, POB 454, Jabal Amman, Amman 11118; tel. (6) 4614166; fax (6) 4614173; e-mail emb.amman@maec.es; internet www.exteriores.gob.es/embajadas/amman; Ambassador SANTIAGO CABANAS ANSORENA.

Sri Lanka: POB 830731, al-Madina al-Munawara St, Amman 11183; tel. (6) 5820611; fax (6) 5820615; e-mail lankaembjo@orange.jo; Ambassador GAMINI RAJAPAKSE.

Sudan: POB 3305, Bayader Wadi al-Seer, 7th Circle, Musa Irsheed al-Taib St, Amman 11181; tel. (6) 5854500; fax (6) 5854501; e-mail sudani@nets.com.jo; Ambassador MUHAMMAD OSMAN MUHAMMAD SAEED.

Sweden: POB 830536, 20 Abd al-Majid al-Adwan St, Abdoun, Amman 11183; tel. (6) 5901300; fax (6) 5930179; e-mail ambassaden.amman@gov.se; internet www.swedenabroad.com/amman; Ambassador HELENA RIETZ.

Switzerland: POB 5341, 19 Ibrahim Ayoub St, 4th Circle, Amman 11183; tel. (6) 5931416; fax (6) 5930685; e-mail amm.vertretung@eda.admin.ch; internet www.eda.admin.ch/amman; Ambassador MICHAEL WINZAP.

Syria: POB 1733, Amman 11118; tel. (6) 5920684; fax (6) 5920635; Ambassador Gen. BAHJAT SULEIMAN.

Thailand: POB 144329, 33 al-Hashemeen St, Dirghabar-Abdoun, Amman 11814; tel. (6) 5903888; fax (6) 5903899; e-mail thaiamm@mfa.go.th; internet www.thaiembassy.org/amman; Ambassador PIRIYA KHEMPON.

Tunisia: POB 17185, Amman 11195; tel. (6) 5922743; fax (6) 5922769; e-mail atamman@go.com.jo; Ambassador AFIFAH MALLAH.

Turkey: POB 2062, 31 Abbas Mahmoud al-Aqqad St, Amman 11181; tel. (6) 5002325; fax (6) 4612353; e-mail embassy.amman@mfa.gov.tr; internet amman.emb.mfa.gov.tr; Ambassador SEDAT ÖNAL.

Ukraine: POB 5244, 6 al-Umouma St, al-Sahl, Amman; tel. (6) 5922402; fax (6) 5922408; e-mail emb_jo@mfa.gov.ua; internet www.mfa.gov.ua/jordan; Ambassador SERGIY PASKO.

United Arab Emirates: POB 2623, Bldg 65, 5th Circle, Boumedienne St, Amman 11181; tel. (6) 5934780; fax (6) 5932666; e-mail amman@mofa.gov.ae; internet www.uae-embassy.ae/embassies/jo; Ambassador Dr ABDULLAH NASIR SULTAN AL-AMERI.

United Kingdom: POB 87, Abdoun, Amman 11118; tel. (6) 5909200; fax (6) 5909279; e-mail amman.enquiries@fco.gov.uk; internet ukinjordan.fco.gov.uk; Ambassador PETER MILLETT.

USA: POB 354, Umawiyyeen St, Abdoun, Amman 11118; tel. (6) 5906000; fax (6) 5920133; e-mail webmasterjordan@state.gov; internet jordan.usembassy.gov; Ambassador STUART E. JONES.

Yemen: POB 3085, Prince Hashem bin Al-Hussain St, Amman 11181; tel. (6) 5923771; fax (6) 5923773; Ambassador SHAYA MOHSIN ZINDANI.

Judicial System

With the exception of matters of purely personal nature concerning members of non-Muslim communities, the law of Jordan was based on Islamic Law for both civil and criminal matters. During the days of the Ottoman Empire certain aspects of Continental law, especially French commercial law and civil and criminal procedure, were introduced. Owing to British occupation of Palestine and Transjordan from 1917 to 1948, the Palestine territory has adopted, either by statute or case law, much of the English common law. Since the annexation of the non-occupied part of Palestine and the formation of the Hashemite Kingdom of Jordan, there has been a continuous effort to unify the law. A Constitutional Court was formally inaugurated on 7 October 2012, to replace the Higher Council for the Interpretation of the Constitution.

Constitutional Court: f. 2012; The Constitutional Court, established by royal decree in October 2012, retains the authority to decide 'the constitutionality of laws and regulations in force and issue its judgements in the name of the King'. It also 'has the right to interpret the provisions of the Constitution if requested, either by virtue of a decision of the Council of Ministers or by a resolution taken by the Senate or the Chamber of Deputies passed by an absolute majority.' The court comprised nine members, including the President, appointed by the King; Pres. TAHER HIKMAT.

Court of Cassation (Supreme Court): The Court of Cassation consists of seven judges, who sit in full panel for exceptionally important cases. In most appeals, however, only five members sit to hear the case. All cases involving amounts of more than JD 100 may be reviewed by this Court, as well as cases involving lesser amounts and those that cannot be monetarily valued. However, for the latter types of cases, review is available only by leave of the Court of Appeal, or, upon refusal by the Court of Appeal, by leave of the President of the Court of Cassation. In addition to these functions as final and Supreme Court of Appeal, the Court of Cassation also sits as High Court of Justice to hear applications in the nature of habeas corpus, mandamus and certiorari dealing with complaints of a citizen against abuse of governmental authority; Pres. HISHAM TAL.

Courts of Appeal: There are three Courts of Appeal, each of which is composed of three judges, whether for hearing of appeals or for dealing with Magistrates Courts' judgments in chambers. Jurisdiction of the three Courts is geographical, with one each in Amman, Irbid and Ma'an. Appellate review of the Courts of Appeal extends to judgments rendered in the Courts of First Instance, the Magistrates' Courts and Religious Courts.

Courts of First Instance: The Courts of First Instance are courts of general jurisdiction in all matters civil and criminal except those specifically allocated to the Magistrates' Courts. Three judges sit in all felony trials, while only two judges sit for misdemeanour and civil cases. Each of the 11 Courts of First Instance also exercises appellate jurisdiction in cases involving judgments of less than JD 20 and fines of less than JD 10, rendered by the Magistrates' Courts.

Magistrates' Courts: There are 17 Magistrates' Courts, which exercise jurisdiction in civil cases involving no more than JD 250 and in criminal cases involving maximum fines of JD 100 or maximum imprisonment of one year.

Religious Courts: There are two types of religious court: the *Shari'a* Courts (Muslims); and the Ecclesiastical Courts (Eastern Orthodox, Greek Melkite, Roman Catholic and Protestant). Jurisdiction extends to personal (family) matters, such as marriage, divorce, alimony, inheritance, guardianship, wills, interdiction and, for the Muslim community, the constitution of *Awqaf* (Religious Endowments). When a dispute involves persons of different religious communities, the Civil Courts have jurisdiction in the matter unless the parties agree to submit to the jurisdiction of one or the other of the Religious Courts involved; Each *Shari'a* (Muslim) Court consists of one judge (*Qadi*), while most of the Ecclesiastical (Christian) Courts are normally composed of three judges, who are usually clerics. *Shari'a* Courts apply the doctrines of Islamic Law, based on the Koran and the *Hadith* (Precepts of Muhammad), while the Ecclesiastical Courts base their law on various aspects of Canon Law. In the event of conflict between any two Religious Courts or between a Religious Court and a Civil Court, a Special Tribunal of three judges is appointed by the President of the Court of Cassation, to decide which court shall have jurisdiction. Upon the advice of experts on the law of the various communities, this Special Tribunal decides on the venue for the case at hand; Chief of Islamic Justice AHMAD HILAYEL; Dir of *Shari'a* Courts Sheikh ISSAM ABD AL-RAZZAQ ARABIYYAT.

Religion

Over 90% of the population are Sunni Muslims, and the King can trace unbroken descent from the Prophet Muhammad. There is a Christian minority, living mainly in the towns, and there are smaller numbers of non-Sunni Muslims.

ISLAM

Chief of Islamic Justice and Imam of the Royal Court: AHMAD HILAYEL.

Grand Mufti of the Hashemite Kingdom of Jordan: Sheikh ABD AL-KARIM KHASAWNEH.

CHRISTIANITY

The Roman Catholic Church

Chaldean Rite

The Chaldean Patriarch of Babylon is resident in Baghdad, Iraq.

Chaldean Patriarchal Vicariate in Jordan: Jabal al-Wabdeh, POB 910833, Amman 11191; tel. and fax (6) 4629061; e-mail raymovicariate66@hotmail.com; internet www.chaldeanjordan.org; f. 2002; Patriarchal Exarch Rev. RAYMOND MOUSSALLI.

Latin Rite

Jordan forms part of the Patriarchate of Jerusalem (see the chapter on Israel).

Vicar-General for Transjordan: Most Rev. SELIM SAYEGH (Titular Bishop of Aquae in Proconsulari), Latin Vicariate, POB 851379, Sweifiyeh, Amman 11185; tel. (6) 5929546; fax (6) 5920548; e-mail regina-pacis2000@yahoo.com.

Maronite Rite

The Maronite community in Jordan is under the jurisdiction of the Maronite Patriarch of Antioch (resident in Lebanon).

Patriarchal Exarchate of Jordan: Mgr PAUL NABIL SAYAH, St Charbel's Parish, Amman; tel. (6) 4202558; fax (6) 4202559; e-mail stcharbelparish@yahoo.com.

Melkite Rite

Jordan forms part of the Greek-Melkite archdiocese of Petra (Wadi Musa) and Philadelphia (Amman).

Archbishop of Petra and Philadelphia: Most Rev. YASSER AYYACH, Archevêché Grec-Melkite Catholique, POB 2435, Jabal Amman 11181; tel. and fax (6) 5866673; e-mail fryaser@yahoo.com.

Syrian Rite

The Syrian Catholic Patriarch of Antioch is resident in Beirut, Lebanon.

Patriarchal Exarchate of Jerusalem (Palestine and Jordan): Mont Achrafieh, POB 510393, Rue Barto, Amman; e-mail st_thomas@bezeqint.net; Exarch Patriarchal Mgr GRÉGOIRE PIERRE MELKI (Titular Bishop of Batne of the Syrians).

The Anglican Communion

Within the Episcopal Church in Jerusalem and the Middle East, Jordan forms part of the diocese of Jerusalem. The President Bishop of the Church is the Bishop in Cyprus and the Gulf (see the chapter on Cyprus).

Other Christian Churches

The Coptic Orthodox Church, the Greek Orthodox Church (Patriarchate of Jerusalem) and the Evangelical Lutheran Church in Jordan are also active.

The Press

DAILIES

Al-Anbat: POB 962556, Amman 11192; tel. (6) 5200100; fax (6) 5200113; e-mail info@alanbat.net; internet www.alanbat.net; f. 2005; independent; Arabic; political; Man. Editor MAZEN AL-KHATIB.

Al-Arab al-Yawm (Arabs Today): POB 962198, Queen Rania St, Amman 11196; tel. (6) 5683333; fax (6) 5620552; e-mail mail@alarab-alyawm.com.jo; internet www.alarabalyawm.net; f. 1997; Arabic; Chief Editor FAHED AL-KHITAN.

Al-Diyar (The Homeland): Al-Fanar Complex, Queen Rania Al-Abdullah St, Amman; tel. (6) 5166588; f. 2004; Arabic; Chair. of Bd MAHMOUD KHARABSHEH.

Ad-Dustour (The Constitution): POB 591, Amman 11118; tel. (6) 5608000; fax (6) 5667170; e-mail dustour@addustour.com.jo; internet www.addustour.com; f. 1967; Arabic; publ. by the Jordan Press and Publishing Co Ltd; owns commercial printing facilities; Chair. KAMEL AL-SHARIF; Chief Editor MUHAMMAD HASSAN TAL; circ. 70,000.

Al-Ghad (Tomorrow): POB 3535, Amman 11821; tel. (6) 5544000; fax (6) 5544055; e-mail editorial@alghad.jo; internet www.alghad.jo; f. 2004; independent; Arabic; Editor-in-Chief MOUSA BARHOUMEH.

The Jordan Times: POB 6710, Queen Rania Al-Abdullah St, Amman 11118; tel. (6) 5600800; fax (6) 5696183; e-mail jotimes@jpf.com.jo; internet www.jordantimes.com; f. 1975; English; publ. by Jordan Press Foundation; Editor-in-Chief SAMIR BARHOUM; circ. 15,000.

Al-Rai (Opinion): POB 6710, Queen Rania Al-Abdullah St, Amman 11118; tel. (6) 5667171; fax (6) 5676581; e-mail info@jpf.com.jo; internet www.alrai.com; f. 1971; morning; independent; Arabic; publ. by Jordan Press Foundation; Chair. AHMAD ABD AL-FATTAH; Editor-in-Chief ABD AL-WAHAB ZGHEILAT; circ. 90,000.

Al-Sabeel (The Path): POB 213545, Amman 11121; tel. (6) 5692852; fax (6) 5692854; e-mail assabeel@assabeel.net; internet www.assabeel.net; f. 1993; fmrly weekly; became daily publ. 2009; Arabic; Islamist; Editor-in-Chief ATEF GOLANI.

WEEKLIES

Al-Ahali (The People): POB 9966, Amman 11191; tel. (6) 5691452; fax (6) 5686857; e-mail ahali@go.com.jo; internet www.hashd-ahali.org.jo; f. 1990; Arabic; publ. by the Jordan People's Democratic Party; Editor-in-Chief SALEM NAHHAS; circ. 5,000.

Akhbar al-Usbou (News of the Week): POB 605, Amman; tel. (6) 5677881; fax (6) 5677882; f. 1959; Arabic; economic, social, political; Chief Editor and Publr ABD AL-HAFIZ MUHAMMAD; circ. 50,000.

Al-Hadath: POB 961167, Amman 11196; tel. (6) 5160824; fax (6) 5160810; e-mail info@al-hadath.com; internet www.al-hadath.com; Arabic; general news; Man. Editor FATEH MANSOUR.

Al-Haqeqa al-Duwalia (Fact International): POB 712678, Amman 11171; tel. (6) 5828292; fax (6) 5816646; e-mail info@factjo.com; internet www.factjo.com; f. 1996; independent; Arabic and English; aims to promote moderate image of Islam and to counter conflicts within the faith; Editor-in-Chief HILMI AL-ASMAR.

Al-Liwa' (The Standard): POB 3067, 2nd Circle, Jabal Amman 11181; tel. (6) 5642770; fax (6) 5656324; e-mail info@al-liwa.com; internet www.al-liwa.com; f. 1972; Arabic; Editor-in-Chief HASSAN AL-TAL; circ. 15,000.

Al-Majd (The Glory): POB 926856, Amman 11190; tel. (6) 5530553; fax (6) 5530352; e-mail almajd@almajd.net; internet www.almajd.net; f. 1994; Arabic; political; Editor-in-Chief FAHID NIMER; circ. 8,000.

Shihan: POB 96-654, Amman; tel. (6) 5603585; fax (6) 5696183; Arabic; Editor-in-Chief (vacant); circ. 60,000.

The Star: POB 591, Queen Rania St, Amman 11118; tel. (6) 5653325; fax (6) 5697415; e-mail star@addustour.com.jo; internet www.star.com.jo; f. 1966; English; political, economic, social and cultural; publ. by the Jordan Press and Publishing Co; Editor-in-Chief MAHA AL-SHARIF; circ. 12,430.

PERIODICALS

Anty Magazine: POB 3024, Amman 11181; tel. (6) 5820058; fax (6) 5855892; e-mail chiefeditor@anty.jo; internet www.anty.jo; monthly; Arabic; publ. by Front Row Publishing and Media Services; fashion, culture and current affairs from a professional woman's perspective; Chief Editor SAHAR ALOUL; circ. 20,000.

Hatem: POB 6710, Queen Rania St, Amman 11118; tel. (6) 5600800; fax (6) 5676581; e-mail info@jpf.com.jo; children's; publ. by Jordan Press Foundation.

Huda El-Islam (The Right Way of Islam): POB 659, Amman; tel. (6) 5666141; f. 1956; monthly; Arabic; scientific and literary; publ. by the Ministry of Awqaf (Religious Endowments) and Islamic Affairs; Editor Dr AHMAD MUHAMMAD HULAYYEL.

Jordan: POB 224, Amman; e-mail webmaster@jordanembassyus.org; internet www.jordanembassyus.org/new/newsletter.shtml; f. 1969; quarterly; publ. by Jordan Information Bureau, Embassy of Jordan, Washington, DC, USA; 3 a year; Editor-in-Chief MERISSA KHURMA; circ. 100,000.

Jordan Business: POB 3024, Amman 11181; tel. (6) 5820058; fax (6) 5855892; e-mail info@frontrow.jo; internet www.jordan-business.net; monthly; English; publ. by Front Row Publishing and Media Services; circ. 10,000.

Jordan Today: Media Services International, POB 9313, Amman 11191; tel. (6) 652380; fax (6) 648298; e-mail star@arabia.com; internet www.jordantoday.com.jo; f. 1995; monthly; English; tourism, culture and entertainment; Editor-in-Chief ZEID NASSER; circ. 10,000.

Military Magazine: Army Headquarters, Amman; f. 1955; quarterly; dealing with military and literary subjects; publ. by Armed Forces.

Royal Wings: POB 3024, Amman 11181; tel. (6) 5820058; fax (6) 5855892; e-mail info@frontrow.jo; internet www.frontrow.jo; bi-monthly; Arabic and English; magazine for Royal Jordanian Airline; publ. by Front Row Publishing and Media Services; Man. Dir USAMA FARAJ; circ. 40,000.

Skin: POB 940166, ICCB Centre, Queen Rania Abdullah St, Amman 11194; tel. (6) 5163357; fax (6) 5163257; e-mail amer@neareastmedia.com; internet www.skin-online.com; f. 2006; quarterly; English; publ. by Near East Media Iraq; art, design, fashion, photography, film and music; Editor-in-Chief TARIQ AL-BITAR.

NEWS AGENCY

Jordan News Agency (PETRA): POB 6845, Amman 11118; tel. (6) 5609700; fax (6) 5682478; e-mail petra@petra.gov.jo; internet www.petra.gov.jo; f. 1965; independent entity since 2004; previously controlled by Ministry of Information prior to its disbandment in 2001; Chair. Dr MUHAMMAD HUSSEIN MOMANI (Minister of State for Media Affairs and Communications); Dir-Gen. RAMADAN AL-RAWASHDEH.

PRESS ASSOCIATION

Jordan Press Association (JPA): POB 8876, Abbas Mahmoud al-Aqqad St, Jabal Amman, 2nd Circle, Amman 18888; tel. (6) 5372005; fax (6) 5372003; e-mail info@jpa.jo; internet www.jpa.jo; f. 1953; Pres. ABD AL-WAHAB ZGHEILAT.

Publishers

Alfaris Publishing and Distribution Co: POB 9157, Amman 11191; tel. (6) 5605432; fax (6) 5685501; e-mail mkayyali@airpbooks.com; internet www.airpbooks.com; f. 1989; Dir MAHER SAID KAYYALI.

Aram Studies Publishing and Distribution House: POB 997, Amman 11941; tel. (6) 835015; fax (6) 835079; art, finance, health, management, science, business; Gen. Dir SALEH ABOUSBA.

Dar al-Manhal Publishers and Distributors: POB 926428, Amman 11190; tel. (6) 5698308; fax (6) 5639185; e-mail info@dmanhal.com; internet www.dmanhal.com; f. 1990; children's and educational publs; Exec. Man. KHALED BILBEISI.

Dar al-Nafa'es: POB 927511, al-Abdali, Amman 11190; tel. (6) 5693940; fax (6) 5693941; e-mail alnafaes@hotmail.com; internet www.al-nafaes.com; f. 1990; education, Islamic; CEO SUFYAN OMAR AL-ASHQR.

Dar al-Thaqafa: Amman 11118; tel. (6) 4646361; fax (6) 4610291; e-mail info@daralthaqafa.com; internet www.daralthaqafa.com; f. 1984; academic publr, specializes in law; Man. Editor KHALID MAHMOUD GABR.

Al Faridah for Specialized Publications: POB 1223, Amman 11821; tel. (6) 5630430; fax (6) 5630440; e-mail hakam@alfaridah.com.jo; internet www.alfaridah.com.jo; f. 2003; publr of magazines incl. *Layalina*, *Ahlan!*, *JO*, *Viva*, *Venture*; Editors-in-Chief RANIA OMEISH, SHIRENE RIFAI; Man. Dir QAIS ELIAS.

Front Row Publishing and Media Services: POB 3024, Muhammad Baseem Khammash St, Villa 3, Amman 11181; tel. (6) 5820058; fax (6) 5855892; e-mail info@frontrow.jo; internet www.frontrow.jo; f. 1997; publr of magazines incl. *Jordan Business*, *Living Well*, *Home*, *Royal Wings*; CEO IYAD SHEHADEH.

Jordan Book Centre Co Ltd: POB 301, al-Jubeiha, Amman 11941; tel. (6) 5151882; fax (6) 5152016; e-mail jbc@go.com.jo; internet www.JBC.com.jo; f. 1982; fiction, business, economics, computer science, medicine, engineering, general non-fiction; Man. Dir J. J. SHARBAIN.

Jordan Distribution Agency: POB 3371, Amman 11181; tel. (6) 5358855; fax (6) 5337733; e-mail jda@aramex.com; f. 1951; history; subsidiary of Aramex; Chair. FADI GHANDOUR; Gen. Man. WADIE SAYEGH.

Jordan House for Publication: POB 1121, Basman St, Amman; tel. (6) 24224; fax (6) 51062; f. 1952; medicine, nursing, dentistry; Man. Dir MURSI AL-ASHKAR.

Jordan Press and Publishing Co Ltd: POB 591, Amman 11118; tel. (6) 5608000; fax (6) 5667170; e-mail info@addustour.com.jo; internet www.addustour.com; f. 1967 by *Al-Manar* and *Falastin* dailies; publishes *Ad-Dustour* (daily), *Ad-Dustour Sport* (weekly) and *The Star* (English weekly); Chair. AMIN MASHAQBEH; Gen. Man. SAMER RAJOUB.

Jordan Press Foundation: POB 6710, Amman 11118; tel. (6) 5667171; fax (6) 5661242; e-mail info@jpf.com.jo; internet www.alrai.com; f. 1971; publishes *Al-Rai* (daily), *The Jordan Times* (daily) and *Hatem* (monthly); Chair. ALI AYED; Editor SAMIR HIYARI.

Al-Tanwir al-Ilmi (Scientific Enlightenment Publishing House): POB 4237, al-Mahatta, Amman 11131; tel. and fax (6) 4899619; e-mail taisir@yahoo.com; internet www.icieparis.net; f. 1990; affiliated with the Int. Centre for Innovation in Education; education, engineering, philosophy, science, sociology; Gen. Dir Prof. Dr TAISIR SUBHI YAMIN.

Broadcasting and Communications

TELECOMMUNICATIONS

Jordan Mobile Telephone Services Co (Zain Jordan): POB 940821, 8th Circle, King Abdullah II St, Amman 11194; tel. (7) 97900900 (mobile); fax (6) 5828200; e-mail info@jo.zain.com; internet www.jo.zain.com; f. 1994 as Jordan Mobile Telephone Services Co (JMTS—Fastlink); merged with Mobile Telecommunications Co (MTC—Kuwait) 2003, corpn renamed Zain Group 2007; Zain Jordan merged with PalTel (Palestinian Territories) in 2009; private co; has operated Jordan's first mobile telecommunications network since 1995; CEO, Levant Region and CEO, Jordan AHMAD AL-HANANDEH.

Jordan Telecom Group (Orange Jordan): POB 1689, Amman 11118; tel. (6) 5630090; fax (6) 5630098; e-mail webmaster@orange-jtg.jo; internet www.orange.jo; f. 1971; fmrly Jordan Telecommunications Corpn, Jordan Telecommunications Co and Jordan Telecom; current name adopted in Feb. 2006 following integration of the following cos' operations into a single management structure: Jordan Telecom, MobileCom (mobile cellular telecommunications services), Wanadoo (internet services) and e-Dimension (information technology); in 2007 Jordan Telecom, MobileCom and Wanadoo were all rebranded as Orange Jordan; 30.5% govt-owned, 69.5% privately owned: France Télécom SA, France, 51.0%; Social Security Corpn 12.4%; 6.1% of shares listed on Amman Stock Exchange; assets JD 664.8m., revenue JD 397.9m. (2007); CEO JEAN-FRANCOIS THOMAS.

Petra Jordanian Mobile Telecommunications: POB 941477, Amman 11194; tel. (6) 5630090; fax (6) 5630098; e-mail business@orange.jo; internet www.orange.jo; subsidiary of Jordan Telecom Group; CEO JEAN-FRANÇOIS THOMAS.

Umniah Mobile Company: POB 942481, Amman 11194; tel. (6) 5005000; fax (6) 5622772; e-mail contact@umniah.com; internet www.umniah.com; awarded contract for Jordan's third GSM licence in 2004; commenced operations in June 2005; first provider of wireless broadband internet services in Jordan; subsidiary of Alghanim Group (Kuwait); 96% owned by Bahrain Telecommunications Co (Batelco); 3m. mobile subscribers (2013); CEO IHAB HINNAWI.

Regulatory Authority

Telecommunications Regulatory Commission (TRC): POB 850967, Amman 11185; tel. (6) 5501120; fax (6) 5690830; e-mail trc@trc.gov.jo; internet www.trc.gov.jo; f. 1995; Chair. and CEO MUHAMMAD AL-TAANI.

BROADCASTING

A new Audio Visual Media Law, enacted in 2002, allowed for the establishment of private broadcasters in Jordan for the first time. By 2007 16 new radio licences had been awarded. Jordan's first licensed independent television channel, Al-Ghad TV (ATV), was officially launched in August 2007; however, the channel was taken off-air before it began broadcasting, owing to a dispute over the terms of its licence. In 2008 ATV was purchased by Arab Telemedia Group and plans were announced for the launch of a two-channel network. By early 2014 ATV had yet to begin broadcasting.

Regulatory Authority

Audio Visual Commission (AVC): POB 142515, Amman 11814; tel. (6) 5560378; fax (6) 5535093; e-mail avc.dg@nic.net.jo; internet www.avc.gov.jo; f. 2002; Dir-Gen. AMJAD AL-QADI.

Radio and Television

Jordan Radio and Television Corporation (JRTV): POB 1041, Amman; tel. (6) 773111; fax (6) 751503; e-mail general@jrtv.gov.jo; internet www.jrtv.jo; f. 1968; state broadcaster; operates 4 TV channels and 6 radio channels broadcasting programmes in Arabic, English and French; advertising accepted; Chair. Dr MUHAMMAD HUSSEIN MOMANI (Minister of State for Media Affairs and Communications); Dir-Gen. RAMADAN AL-RAWASHDEH; Dir of Radio Administration MAZEN AL-MAJALI; Dir of Television Administration AREF AL-FAYEZ.

Radio Al-Balad: POB 20513, Amman 11118; tel. (6) 4645486; fax (6) 4630238; e-mail info@ammannet.net; internet www.ammannet.net; f. 2000 as internet radio station AmmanNet; began broadcasting as an FM radio station 2005, renamed as above 2008; news, politics and community broadcasts; Gen. Man. DAOUD KUTTAB.

Sawt al-Madina (SAM): POB 1171, Amman 1953; tel. (6) 5500006; fax (6) 5500009; e-mail fateen@al-baddad.com; internet www.al-baddad.com; f. 2006; owned by Al-Baddad Media and Communications; radio station broadcasting news and politics programmes; Group Gen. Man. FATEEN H. AL-BADDAD.

Other independent radio stations include Mazaj FM, Amin FM, Al-Hayat FM, Rotana FM Jordan and Radio Fann FM.

Finance

(cap. = capital; p.u. = paid up; dep. = deposits; m. = million; res = reserves; br.(s) = branch(es); amounts in Jordanian dinars unless otherwise indicated)

BANKING

Central Bank

Central Bank of Jordan: POB 37, King Hussein St, Amman 11118; tel. (6) 4630301; fax (6) 4638889; e-mail redp@cbj.gov.jo; internet www.cbj.gov.jo; f. 1964; cap. 48.0m., res 742m., dep. 7,362m. (Dec. 2013); Gov. and Chair. ZIAD FARIZ; 2 brs.

National Banks

Arab Bank PLC: POB 950545, Shmeisani, Amman 11195; tel. (6) 5607231; fax (6) 5606793; e-mail corpcomm@arabbank.com.jo; internet www.arabbank.com; f. 1930; cap. US $776m., res $6,506m., dep. $36,722m. (Dec. 2012); Chair. SABIH AL-MASRI; CEO NEMEH SABBAGH; 84 brs in Jordan, 99 brs abroad.

Bank of Jordan PLC: POB 2140, Shmeisani, Amman 11181; tel. (6) 5696277; fax (6) 5696291; e-mail boj@bankofjordan.com.jo; internet www.bankofjordan.com; f. 1960; cap. 155m., res 77m., dep. 1,672m. (Dec. 2012); Chair. and Gen. Man. TAWFIK SHAKER FAKHOURI; 77 brs and offices.

Cairo Amman Bank: POB 950661, Cairo Amman Bank Bldg, Wadi Saqra St, Amman 11195; tel. (6) 5006000; fax (6) 5007100; e-mail info@cab.jo; internet www.cab.jo; f. 1960; cap. 100m., res 61m., dep. 1,541m. (Dec. 2012); Chair. YAZID ADNAN AL-MUFTI; Gen. Man. KAMAL GHARIB AL-BAKRI; 63 brs in Jordan, 18 brs in the West Bank.

Capital Bank of Jordan: POB 941283, Issam Ajlouni St, Amman 11194; tel. (6) 5100200; fax (6) 5692062; e-mail info@capitalbank.jo; internet www.capitalbank.jo; f. 1996 as Export and Finance Bank; name changed as above 2006; cap. 150m., res 25m., dep. 1,069m. (Dec. 2011); Chair. BASSEM KHALIL SALEM AL-SALEM; Gen. Man. HAYTHAM KAMHIYAH.

Jordan Ahli Bank: POB 3103, Queen Noor St, Shmeisani, Amman 11181; tel. (6) 5608730; fax (6) 5699867; e-mail info@ahlibank.com.jo; internet www.ahli.com; f. 1955 as Jordan Nat. Bank; name changed as above 2006; cap. 150m., res 91m., dep. 2,260m. (Dec. 2012); Chair. RAJAI MUASHER; CEO and Gen. Man. MARWAN AWAD; 46 brs in Jordan, 6 brs abroad.

Jordan Commercial Bank: POB 9989, Yakoub Sarrouf St, Shmeisani, Amman 11191; tel. (6) 5603931; fax (6) 5664110; e-mail jcb@jcbank.com.jo; internet www.jcbank.com.jo; f. 1977 as Jordan Gulf Bank; name changed as above 2004; cap. 93m., res 8m., dep. 714m. (Dec. 2012); Chair. MICHAELFAIQ IBRAHIM AL-SAYEGH; CEO and Gen. Man. ABDUL MAHDI ALAWI; 23 brs in Jordan, 3 brs in West Bank.

Jordan Islamic Bank: POB 926225, Shmeisani, Amman 11190; tel. (6) 5677377; fax (6) 5666326; e-mail jib@islamicbank.com.jo; internet www.jordanislamicbank.com; f. 1978; fmrly Jordan Islamic Bank for Finance and Investment; current name adopted Oct. 2009; cap. 125m., res 56m., dep. 2,726. (Dec. 2012); Chair. ADNAN AHMAD YOUSUF; Vice-Chair. and Gen. Man. MUSA ABD AL-AZIZ SHIHADEH; 59 brs.

Jordan Kuwait Bank: POB 9776, Abdali, Amman 11191; tel. (6) 5629400; fax (6) 5695604; e-mail info@jkbank.com.jo; internet www.jordan-kuwait-bank.com; f. 1976; cap. US $141m., res $252m., dep. $2,728m. (Dec. 2012); Chair. and CEO ABD AL-KARIM AL-KABARITI; Dir-Gen. MUHAMMAD YASSER M. AL-ASMAR; 43 brs.

Société Générale de Banque-Jordanie: POB 560, 30 Prince Shaker bin Zeid St, Shmeisani, Amman 11118; tel. (6) 500300; fax (6) 5693410; e-mail sgbj.webmaster@socgen.com; internet www.sgbj.com.jo; f. 1965 as Middle East Investment Bank; became part of the Société Générale Group (France) 2000; name changed as above 2003; cap. 100m., res 818,896, dep. 357m. (Dec. 2012); Chair. HASSAN MANGO; Gen. Man. NADIM ABAOUAT; 16 brs.

Specialized Credit Institutions

Agricultural Credit Corporation: POB 77, Amman 11118; tel. (6) 5661105; fax (6) 5668365; e-mail acc@go.com.jo; internet www.acc.gov.jo; f. 1959; cap. 24m., res 12.4m., total assets 125.1m. (Dec. 2000); Chair. Dr AKIF AL-ZU'BI (Minister of Agriculture); Vice-Chair. and Dir-Gen. MUHAMMAD AL-HAERI; 23 brs.

Arab Jordan Investment Bank: POB 8797, Arab Jordan Investment Bank Bldg, Shmeisani, Amman 11121; tel. (6) 5607126; fax (6) 5681482; e-mail info@ajib.com; internet www.ajib.com; f. 1978; cap. 100m., res 19m., dep. 859m. (Dec. 2012); Chair. ABD AL-KADER AL-QADI; CEO HANI AL-QADI; 8 brs in Jordan, 2 brs abroad.

Bank al Etihad: POB 35104, Prince Shaker Ben Zeid St, Shmeisani, Amman 11180; tel. (6) 5607011; fax (6) 5666149; e-mail info@bankaletihad.com; internet www.bankaletihad.com; f. 1978 as Arab Finance Corpn; name changed to Union Bank for Savings and Investment 1991; name changed as above 2011; cap. 100m., res 111m., dep. 1,493m. (Dec. 2012); Chair. ISAM SALFITI; Gen. Man. NADIA AL-SAEED; 22 brs.

Cities and Villages Development Bank (CVDB): POB 1572, Amman 11118; tel. (6) 5682691; fax (6) 5668153; e-mail cvdb100@hotmail.com; internet www.cvdb.gov.jo; f. 1979; 30% state-owned; cap. 50m. (Dec. 2002); Chair. ALI GHAZAWI; Gen. Man. WALID AL-MASRI; 10 brs.

Housing Bank for Trade and Finance (HBTF): POB 7693, Parliament St, Amman 11118; tel. (6) 5005555; fax (6) 5690207; e-mail info@hbtf.com.jo; internet www.hbtf.com; f. 1973; cap. 355m., res 1,476m., dep. 6,667m. (Dec. 2012); Chair. Dr MICHEL MARTO; Gen. Man. OMAR MALHAS; 116 brs.

INVESTBANK: Issam Ajlouni St, Shmeisani, Amman; tel. (6) 5001500; fax (6) 5681410; e-mail info@investbank.jo; internet www.investbank.jo; f. 1982 as Jordan Investment and Finance Corpn; name changed 2009; cap. 100m., res 20m., dep. 525m. (Dec. 2012); Chair. BISHER M. JARDANEH; CEO MUNTASER DAWWAS; 9 brs.

Jordan Dubai Islamic Bank: POB 1982, al-Kuliah al-Elmiah, Amman 11118; tel. (6) 4602200; fax (6) 4647821; e-mail idb@indevbank.com.jo; internet www.jdib.jo; f. 1965 as Industrial Devt Bank; current name adopted Jan. 2010; cap. 100m., res 21m., dep. 334m. (Dec. 2012); Chair. ISMAIL TAHBOUB; CEO SAMI HUSSAM AL-AFGHANI; 7 brs.

STOCK EXCHANGE

Amman Stock Exchange (ASE): POB 212466, Arjan, nr Ministry of the Interior, Amman 11121; tel. (6) 5664109; fax (6) 5664071; e-mail info@ase.com.jo; internet www.exchange.jo; f. 1978 as Amman Financial Market; name changed as above 1999; 240 listed cos (2013); Chair. MARWAN BATAYNEH; CEO NADER AZAR (acting).

INSURANCE

At the end of 2008 there were 29 companies operating in the insurance sector in Jordan.

Jordan Insurance Co Ltd (JIC): POB 279, Company's Bldg, 3rd Circle, Jabal Amman, Amman 11118; tel. (6) 4634161; fax (6) 4637905; e-mail allinsure@jicjo.com; internet www.jicjo.com; f. 1951; cap. 30m. (Dec. 2006); Chair. OTHMAN BDEIR; Man. Dir IMAD ABD AL-KHALEQ; 7 brs (3 in Jordan, 3 in the United Arab Emirates and 1 in Kuwait).

Middle East Insurance Co Ltd (MEICO): POB 1802, al-Kindi St, Um Uthanina, 5th Circle, Jabal Amman, Amman 11118; tel. (6) 5527100; fax (6) 5527801; e-mail info@meico.com.jo; internet www.meico.com.jo; f. 1962; cap. p.u. 18.0m., total assets 66,285.0m. (Dec. 2007); Chair. SAMIR KAWAR; Gen. Man. Dr RAJAI SWEIS; 13 brs.

National Insurance Co: POB 6156-2938, Sayed Qotub St, Shmeisani, Amman 11118; tel. (6) 5671169; fax (6) 5684900; e-mail natinsur@go.com.jo; f. 1965 as above; name changed to National Ahlia Insurance Co in 1986, following merger with Ahlia Insurance Co (f. 1975); reverted to original name July 2007; cap. 2m.; Chair. MUSTAFA ABU GOURA; Gen. Man. GHALEB ABU-GOURA.

Social Security Corporation: POB 926031, Amman 11110; tel. (6) 5501880; fax (6) 5501888; e-mail webmaster@ssc.gov.jo; internet www.ssc.gov.jo; f. 1978; regulates and implements a social security system, incl. the provision of health insurance, life insurance and unemployment benefit, funded by both voluntary and employer contributions; Dir-Gen. Dr MAEN NSOUR.

United Insurance Co Ltd: POB 7521, United Insurance Bldg, King Hussein St, Amman; tel. (6) 4648513; fax (6) 4629417; e-mail uic@united.com.jo; internet www.united.com.jo; f. 1972; all types of insurance; cap. p.u. 8m.; Chair. RAOUF ABU JABER; Gen. Man. IMAD AL-HAJI.

Insurance Federation

Jordan Insurance Federation (JOIF): POB 1990, Amman 11118; tel. (6) 5689266; fax (6) 5689510; internet www.joif.org; f. 1989 to replace the Jordan Asscn for Insurance Cos (f. 1956); regulatory and management authority; Chair. JAWAD HADID; Sec.-Gen. MAHER AL-HUSAIN.

Trade and Industry

GOVERNMENT AGENCIES

Jordan Atomic Energy Commission: POB 70, Amman 11934; tel. (6) 5230978; fax (6) 5231017; internet www.jaec.gov.jo; f. 2007; devt of civil nuclear energy programme; Chair. Dr KHALED TOUKAN.

Natural Resources Authority: POB 7, Amman 11118; tel. (6) 5504390; fax (6) 5811866; e-mail dirgen@nra.gov.jo; internet www.nra.gov.jo; f. 1965; supervision and devt of mineral and non-nuclear energy resources; Dir-Gen. Dr MAHER HIJAZIN.

DEVELOPMENT ORGANIZATIONS

Aqaba Development Corporation (ADC): POB 2680, Chamber of Commerce Bldg, Aqaba 77110; tel. (3) 2039100; fax (3) 2039110; e-mail info@adc.jo; internet www.adc.jo; f. 2004 by Aqaba Special Economic Zone Authority and Govt of Jordan; devt and strategic management of infrastructure, industry, trade, transport, real estate, tourism and education within Aqaba Special Economic Zone; CEO MUHAMMAD SALEM TURK.

Development Zones Commission (DZC): POB 141277, Amman 11814; tel. (6) 3001300; e-mail info@dzc.jo; internet www.dzc.jo; f. 2008; responsible for creating, developing and monitoring the 3 development zones within Jordan; Chief Commr BILAL BASHIR.

Jordan Enterprise Development Corporation (JEDCO): POB 7704, Amman 11118; tel. (6) 5603507; fax (6) 5684568; e-mail jedco@jedco.gov.jo; internet www.jedco.gov.jo; f. 2003 to replace Jordan Export Devt and Commercial Centres Corpn; devt and promotion of industry, trade and exports; Chair. HATEM HAFIZ AL-HALAWANI (Minister of Industry, Trade and Supply); CEO YARUB AL-QUDAH.

Jordan Investment Board (JIB): POB 893, Amman 11821; tel. (6) 5608400; fax (6) 5608416; e-mail info@jib.com.jo; internet www.jordaninvestment.com; f. 1995; CEO Dr MAEN NSOUR.

Jordan Valley Authority (JVA): POB 2769, Amman 11183; tel. (6) 5689400; fax (6) 5689916; e-mail jva_complain@mwi.gov.jo; internet www.jva.gov.jo; f. 1973 as Jordan Valley Comm.; renamed as above 1977; govt org. responsible for the integrated social and economic devt of the Jordan Valley, with particular emphasis on the utilization and management of water resources; responsible for construction of several major irrigation, hydroelectric and municipal water projects; other projects include housing, schools and rural roads, and the devt of tourism infrastructure; Sec.-Gen. MUSA AL-JAMA'ANI.

CHAMBERS OF COMMERCE AND INDUSTRY

Amman Chamber of Commerce: POB 287, Amman 11118; tel. (6) 5666151; fax 5666155; e-mail info@ammanchamber.org.jo; internet www.ammanchamber.org.jo; f. 1923; more than 45,000 regd mems (2013); Chair. ISSA MURAD; Dir-Gen. MUHANNAD ATTAR.

Amman Chamber of Industry: POB 1800, Amman 11118; tel. (6) 5643001; fax (6) 5647852; e-mail aci@aci.org.jo; internet www.aci.org.jo; f. 1962; approx. 7,500 regd industrial cos (2007); Chair. Dr HATEM H. HALAWANI.

Aqaba Chamber of Commerce: POB 12, Aqaba 77110; tel. (3) 2012229; fax (3) 2013070; e-mail info@aqabacc.com; internet www.aqabacc.com; f. 1965; Chair. NAEL AL-KABARITI; Sec.-Gen. MAHMOUD FRAIH.

Jordan Chamber of Commerce: POB 7029, Amman 11118; tel. (6) 5902040; fax (6) 5902051; e-mail info@jocc.org.jo; internet www.jocc.org.jo; f. 1955 as Fed. of the Jordanian Chambers of Commerce; renamed as above in 2003; intended to promote co-operation between the various chambers of commerce in Jordan, and to consolidate and co-ordinate the capabilities of each; Chair. NAEL AL-KABARITI; Sec.-Gen. SAEED SALEM BAZBAZ.

Jordan Chamber of Industry: POB 811986, Amman 11181; tel. (6) 4642649; fax (6) 4643719; e-mail jci@jci.org.jo; internet www.jci.org.jo; promotes competitiveness in the industrial sector and co-operation between the various chambers of industry in Jordan; Chair. Dr HATEM H. HALAWANI; Dir-Gen. ZAKI M. AYOUBI.

Professional Associations Council (PAC): Professional Associations Complex, Amman; rep. body for 14 professional asscns; Pres. TAHER SHAKHSHIR.

PETROLEUM AND GAS

Jordan Oil Shale Co: c/o Royal Dutch Shell plc, Carel van Bylandtlaan 30, 2596 HR The Hague, The Netherlands; e-mail webmaster@josco.jo; internet www.josco.jo; f. 2009; wholly owned subsidiary of Royal Dutch Shell plc (Netherlands/United Kingdom); exploration and exploitation of oil shale deposits.

Jordan Oil Shale Energy Co: POB 962497, Amman 11196; tel. (6) 5157064; fax (6) 5157046; e-mail info@joseco.com.jo; internet www.joseco.com.jo; f. 2007; state-owned; promotion and devt of oil shale projects; Chair. MAJED KHALIFA.

National Petroleum Co PLC: POB 3503, Amman 11821; tel. (6) 5548888; fax (6) 5536912; e-mail management@npc.com.jo; internet www.npc.com.jo; f. 1995; petroleum and natural gas exploration and production; signed partnership agreement with BP (United Kingdom) for devt of Risha gasfield 2009; Chair. Dr ABD AL-RAZZAQ AL NUSUR.

UTILITIES

Electricity

Electricity Regulatory Commission: POB 1865, Amman 11821; tel. (6) 5805000; fax (6) 5805003; e-mail abedalraheem.akayle@erc.gov.jo; internet www.erc.gov.jo; f. 2001; regulatory authority; Chief Commr and CEO Dr MUHAMMAD HAMAD (Minister of Energy and Mineral Resources).

Central Electricity Generating Company (CEGCO): POB 2564, Amman 11953; tel. (6) 5340008; fax (6) 5340800; e-mail cegco@cegco.com.jo; internet www.cegco.com.jo; part-privatized in Sept. 2007; 51% owned by ENARA Energy Arabia, 40% by Govt and 9% by Social Security Corpn; electricity generation; Chair. MUHAMMAD ABDULLAH RASHID ABUNAYYAN.

Electricity Distribution Company (EDCO): POB 2310, Orthodox St, 7th Circle, Jabal Amman, Amman; tel. (6) 5331330; fax (6) 5818336; e-mail info@edco.jo; internet www.edco.jo; f. 1999; privatized in Nov. 2007; wholly owned by Kingdom Electricity, a jt venture between Jordan, Kuwait and the United Arab Emirates; electricity distribution for southern, eastern and Jordan Valley regions; Dir-Gen. AHMAD ZINAT.

Irbid District Electricity Company (IDECO): POB 46, Amman; tel. (6) 7201500; fax (6) 7245495; e-mail ideco@ideco.com.jo; internet www.ideco.com.jo; f. 1957; 55.4% stake acquired by Kingdom Electricity (see EDCO) in Nov. 2007; electricity generation, transmission and distribution for northern regions; Chair. FAYEZ KHASAWNEH; Gen. Man. Eng. AHMAD THAINAT.

Jordanian Electric Power Company (JEPCO): POB 618, Amman 11118; tel. (6) 5503600; fax (6) 5503619; e-mail jepco@go.com.jo; internet www.jepco.com.jo; f. 1938; privately owned; electricity distribution for Amman, al-Salt, al-Zarqa and Madaba; Chair. ISSAM BDEIR; Gen. Man. MARWAN BUSHNAQ.

National Electric Power Company (NEPCO): POB 2310, Amman 11118; tel. (6) 5858615; fax (6) 5818336; e-mail info@nepco.com.jo; internet www.nepco.com.jo; f. 1996; fmrly Jordan Electricity Authority; electricity transmission; govt-owned; Chair. Eng. KHALDOUN QUTISHAT; Dir-Gen. Dr GHALEB AL-MAABRAH.

Samra Electric Power Co (SEPCO): POB 1885, Um Al-Sumaq, Zaal Abu Tayeh St, Amman 11821; tel. (6) 5506510; fax (6) 5506520; e-mail samra@sepco.com.jo; internet www.sepco.com.jo; f. 2004; electricity generation, gas turbines supply and installation and plant construction; Chair. Dr MAHIR MADADHAH; Dir-Gen. Eng. AMJAD AL-RAWASHDEH.

Water

Aqaba Water: POB 252, Aqaba 77110; tel. (3) 2014390; fax (3) 2015982; e-mail info@aw.jo; internet www.aqabawater.com; f. 2004; successor to the Water Authority in Aqaba; water supply and wastewater services; Pres. Eng. SAAD ABU HAMMOUR; CEO Eng. NAEM SALEH.

Jordan Water Company (Miyahuna): POB 922918, Amman 11192; tel. (6) 5666111; fax (6) 5682642; internet www.miyahuna.com.jo; f. 2007; owned by Water Authority of Jordan; operates as an independent commercial entity; management of water and sewage services in Amman; CEO Eng. MUNIR OWIES; Chair. Eng. ABD AL-RAHMAN AL-KHATIB.

Water Authority of Jordan (WAJ): POB 2412, Amman 11183; tel. (6) 5680100; fax (6) 5679143; e-mail info_waj@mwi.gov.jo; internet www.waj.gov.jo; f. 1984; govt-owned; scheduled for privatization; Sec.-Gen. Eng. TAWFIQ HABASHNEH.

TRADE UNION

The General Federation of Jordanian Trade Unions: POB 1065, Amman; tel. (6) 5675533; fax (6) 5687911; e-mail khyasat@rja.com.jo; f. 1954; 17 affiliated unions; 200,000 mems; mem. of Arab Trade Unions Confed; Pres. MAZEN MA'AYTEH.

Transport

RAILWAYS

The Hedjaz–Jordan Railway crosses the Syrian border and enters Jordanian territory south of Dar'a. It runs for approximately 366 km to Naqb Ishtar, passing through Zarqa, Amman, Qatrana and Ma'an. An express rail link between Amman and Damascus was inaugurated in 1999. In 2008 a feasibility study concerning the upgrade and revival of the entire Hedjaz Railway was launched by the Governments of Jordan, Saudi Arabia and Syria. Formerly a division of the Hedjaz–Jordan Railway, the Aqaba Railway was established as a separate entity in 1972; it retains close links with the Hedjaz, but there is no regular through traffic between Aqaba and Amman. It comprises 292 km of 1,050-mm gauge track and is used solely for the transportation of minerals from three phosphate mines to Aqaba port.

In 2008 the Government announced that it was seeking up to US $6,000m. in foreign investment in order to implement a major railway development plan. The proposals included a north–south line of more than 500 km linking the Red Sea port of Aqaba with

Amman, Zarqa and Irbid in the north, and would connect the network with systems in Syria, Iraq and Saudi Arabia. An international advisory team for the project was appointed in 2009. Plans to build and operate a 26-km light rail link between Amman and Zarqa were abandoned in 2011, owing to concerns over funding. In 2010 the total length of Jordanian railways was 294 route-km.

Aqaba Railways Corporation (ARC): POB 50, Ma'an; tel. (3) 2132114; fax (3) 2131861; e-mail arc@orange.jo; internet www.arc.gov.jo; f. 1975; length of track 292 km (1,050-mm gauge); privately owned; Dir-Gen. HUSSEIN KRISHAN.

Jordan Hedjaz Railways: POB 4448, Amman 11131; tel. (6) 4895414; fax (6) 4894117; e-mail mkhazaleh@jh-railway.com; internet www.jh-railway.com; f. 1952 as Hedjaz–Jordan Railway; administered by the Ministry of Transport; length of track 496 km (1,050-mm gauge); Chair. Dr LINA SHABIB (Minister of Transport); Dir-Gen. MAHMOUD KHAZALEH.

ROADS

Amman is linked by road with all parts of the kingdom and with neighbouring countries. All cities and most towns are connected by a two-lane, paved road system. In addition, several thousand kilometres of tracks make all villages accessible to motor transport. In 2010 there was a total road network of 7,100 km, of which 2,878 km were highways, main or national roads, 1,733 km were secondary or regional roads and 2,489 km were other roads.

Jordanian-Syrian Land Transport Co: POB 20686, Amman 11118; tel. (6) 4711545; fax (6) 4711517; e-mail josyco@josyco.com.jo; f. 1975; jt venture between Govts of Jordan and Syria; transports goods between ports in Jordan and Syria; operates 210 heavy-duty trailers; underwent restructuring in 2010; Dir-Gen. JAMIL ALI MUJAHID.

SHIPPING

The port of Aqaba, Jordan's only outlet to the sea, consists of a main port, container port (540 m in length) and industrial port, with 25 modern and specialized berths. It has 761,300 sq m of open and contained storage area. There is a ferry link between Aqaba and the Egyptian port of Nuweibeh. In 2008 the Government initiated a tendering process for a US $700m. project to relocate Aqaba's main port to the southern industrial zone. The new development, to be supervised by the Aqaba Development Corporation, was to significantly increase overall capacity, comprising a general cargo terminal with roll-on roll-off (ro-ro) facilities, a dedicated grain terminal and a new ferry terminal. Once vacated, the existing port site was to be redeveloped as a major new commercial, residential and tourism centre.

At 31 December 2013 Jordan's flag registered fleet totalled 27 vessels, with an aggregate displacement of 68,201 grt, of which one were general cargo ships.

Port Authorities

Aqaba Container Terminal (ACT): POB 1944, King Hussein bin Talal St, Aqaba 77110; tel. (3) 2091111; fax (3) 2039133; e-mail customerservice@act.com.jo; internet www.act.com.jo; CEO SOREN HANSEN.

Aqaba Ports Corporation: POB 115, Aqaba 77110; tel. (3) 2014031; fax (3) 2016204; e-mail info@aqabaports.gov.jo; internet www.aqabaports.com; f. 1952 as Aqaba Port Authority; name changed as above 1978; Dir-Gen. AWAD AL-MAAYTAH.

Principal Shipping Companies

Amman Shipping & Trading Co Ltd (ASTCO): POB 213083, 5th Floor, Blk A, Aqqad Bldg, Gardens St, Amman 11121; tel. (6) 5514620; fax (6) 5532324; e-mail sts@albitar.com; internet www.1stjordan.net/astco/index.html; f. 1990.

Arab Bridge Maritime Co: POB 989, Aqaba; tel. (3) 2092000; fax (3) 2092001; e-mail info@abmaritime.com.jo; internet www.abmaritime.com.jo; f. 1985; jt venture by Egypt, Iraq and Jordan; commercial shipping of passengers, vehicles and cargo between Aqaba and the Egyptian port of Nuweibeh; Man. Dir HUSSEIN AL-SOUOB.

T. Gargour & Fils (TGF): POB 419, 1st Floor, Bldg No. 233, Arar St, Wadi Saqra, Amman 11118; tel. (6) 4626611; fax (6) 4622425; e-mail tgf@tgf.com.jo; internet www.tgf.com.jo; f. 1928; shipping agents and owners; CEO Dr DUREID MAHASNEH.

Jordan National Shipping Lines Co Ltd (JNSL): POB 5406, Bldg No. 51, Wadi Saqra St, Amman 11183; POB 557, Aqaba; tel. (6) 5511500; fax (6) 5511501; e-mail jnslamman@jnslgroup.com; internet www.jnslgroup.com; f. 1976; 75% govt-owned; service from Antwerp (Netherlands), Bremen (Germany) and Tilbury (United Kingdom) to Aqaba; daily passenger ferry service to Egypt; land transportation to various regional destinations; Chair. AHMAD ARMOUSH.

Amin Kawar & Sons Co WLL: POB 222, 24 Abd al-Hamid Sharaf St, Shmeisani, Amman 11118; tel. (6) 5609500; fax (6) 5698322; e-mail kawar@kawar.com.jo; internet www.kawar.com; chartering, forwarding and shipping line agents; Chair. TAWFIQ KAWAR; CEO RUDAIN T. KAWAR; Pres. KARIM KAWAR.

Naouri Group: Um Uthaina, Saad Bin Abi Waqqas St, Bldg No. 30, Amman 11118; tel. (6) 5777901; fax (6) 5777911; e-mail info@naouri.com; internet www.naouri.com; f. 1994; operates several cos in shipping sector incl. Ammon Shipping and Transport, Salam Shipping and Forwarding, Kareem Logistics; Chair. IBRAHIM NAOURI.

Orient Shipping Co Ltd: Jordan Insurance Bldg, Bldg (A), 3rd Floor, POB 207, Amman 11118; tel. (6) 4641695; fax (6) 4651567; e-mail orship@orientshipping.jo; internet www.orientshipping.jo; f. 1965; shipping agency.

Petra Navigation and International Trading Co Ltd: POB 942502, Amman 11194; tel. (6) 5607021; fax (6) 5601362; e-mail info@petra.jo; internet www.petra.jo; f. 1977; general cargo, ro-ro and passenger ferries; Chair. AHMAD ARMOUSH; Man. Dir ANWAR SBEIH.

Red Sea Shipping Agency Co: POB 1248, 24 Sharif Abd al-Hamid Sharaf St, Shmeisani, Amman 11118; tel. (6) 5609501; fax (6) 5688241; e-mail rss@rssa.com.jo; internet www.redseashipping.com.jo; f. 1955.

Salam International Transport and Trading Co: POB 212955, Salam Trading Center, Arar St, Wadi Saqra, 11121; tel. (6) 5654510; fax (6) 5697014; e-mail tdajani@aagroup.jo; internet www.sittcogroup.com; f. 1996; publicly listed; diversified shipping, logistics, and oil and gas group; CEO TAREK DAJANI.

PIPELINES

Two oil pipelines cross Jordan. The former Iraq Petroleum Co pipeline, carrying petroleum from the oilfields in Iraq to Israel's Mediterranean port of Haifa, has not operated since 1967. The 1,717-km (1,067-mile) Trans-Arabian Pipeline (Tapline) carries petroleum from the oilfields of Dhahran in Saudi Arabia to Sidon on the Mediterranean seaboard in Lebanon. Tapline traverses Jordan for a distance of 177 km (110 miles) and has frequently been cut by hostile action. Confronted with the challenge of meeting rising oil demands, the Jordanian Government has been considering plans to rehabilitate disused sections of Tapline, at an estimated cost of US $200m.–$300m., since early 2005. In April 2013 the Governments of Jordan and Iraq signed an agreement for the construction of a US $18,000m., 1,700-km double pipeline to transport oil and natural gas from Basra province in Iraq to Aqaba.

CIVIL AVIATION

There are three international airports, two serving Amman and one in Aqaba. A 25-year concession to expand and operate Queen Alia International Airport at Zizya, 40 km south of Amman, including the construction of a new terminal building, was awarded to an international consortium, Airport International Group, in May 2007. The new terminal was officially opened in March 2013, increasing the airport's potential annual capacity to approximately 12m. passengers.

Jordan Civil Aviation Regulatory Commission (CARC): POB 7547, Amman 11110; tel. (6) 4892282; fax (6) 4891653; e-mail info@carc.gov.jo; internet www.carc.jo; f. 2007, to replace Civil Aviation Authority (f. 1950); Chief Commr and CEO Capt. MUHAMMAD AMIN AL-QURAN.

Aqaba Airports Co: POB 2662, King Hussein International Airport, Special Economic Zone, Aqaba 77110; tel. (3) 2034010; e-mail info@aac.jo; internet www.aac.jo; f. 2007; Dir MUNIR ASAD.

Jordan Aviation (JATE): POB 922358, Amman 11192; tel. (6) 5501760; fax (6) 5525761; e-mail info@jordanaviation.jo; internet www.jordanaviation.jo; f. 2000; first privately owned airline in Jordan; operates regional and international charter and scheduled flights; Chair. and CEO Capt. MUHAMMAD AL-KHASHMAN.

Royal Jordanian Airline: POB 302, Housing Bank Commercial Centre, Queen Noor St, Amman 11118; tel. (6) 5202000; fax (6) 5672527; e-mail AMMDDRJ@rj.com; internet www.rj.com; f. 1963; privatized in 2007; regional and international scheduled and charter services; Chair. NASSER A. LOZI; Pres. and CEO HUSSEIN H. DABBAS.

Royal Wings Co Ltd: POB 314018, Amman 11134; tel. (6) 5803340; fax (6) 5803344; e-mail info@royalwings.com.jo; internet www.royalwings.com.jo; f. 1996; subsidiary of Royal Jordanian Airline; operates regional and domestic scheduled and charter services; Man. Dir ABD AL-QADER KAILANI.

Tourism

The ancient cities of Jarash (Jerash) and Petra, and Jordan's proximity to biblical sites, have encouraged tourism. The development of

Jordan's Dead Sea coast is currently under way; owing to the Sea's mineral-rich waters, the growth of curative tourism is anticipated. The Red Sea port of Aqaba is also undergoing a major programme of development, with a view to becoming a centre for water sports, diving and beach holidays. Since the creation of the Wadi Rum Protected Area in 1998 tourism in this desert region is promoted on the basis of its unique ecosystem, landscape and the traditional culture of its Bedouin inhabitants. The National Tourism Strategy (NTS) 2004–10 set out ambitious targets that included doubling the figures for foreign visitors and tourism-related income and jobs. (By 2008 the sector appeared already to have achieved the goal of doubling income.) However, political turmoil in the Middle East and North Africa contributed to a decline in visitors and revenue in 2011. According to data from the Ministry of Tourism and Antiquities, the number of foreign visitors to Jordan declined by 17.2%, to 6.8m., while income from tourism also declined, to JD 2,130m. Visitor numbers declined further, to 6.3m., in 2012, although receipts increased slightly to JD 2,456m.

Ministry of Tourism and Antiquities: see Ministries; Sec.-Gen. FAROUK AL-HADIDI.

Jordan Tourism Board (JTB): POB 830688, Amman 11183; tel. (6) 5678444; fax (6) 5678295; e-mail info@visitjordan.com; internet www.visitjordan.com; f. 1997; Man. Dir NAYEF AL-FAYEZ.

Defence

Supreme Commander of the Armed Forces: King ABDULLAH IBN AL-HUSSEIN.

Chairman of the Joint Chiefs of Staff: Lt-Gen. MESHAAL MUHAMMAD AL-ZABIN.

Commander of the Royal Jordanian Navy: Maj.-Gen. DARI AL-ZABIN.

Commander of the Royal Jordanian Air Force: Maj.-Gen. MALEK AL-HABASHNEH.

Defence Budget (2013): JD 862m.

Total Armed Forces (as assessed at November 2013): 100,500: army 74,000; navy est. 500; special operations 14,000; air force 12,000. Reserves 65,000 (army 60,000, joint 5,000).

Paramilitary Forces (as assessed at November 2013): 15,000.

Education

Primary education, beginning at six years of age, is free and compulsory. This 10-year preparatory cycle is followed by a two-year secondary cycle. The UN Relief and Works Agency (UNRWA) provides educational facilities and services for Palestinian refugees. According to UNESCO estimates, in 2011 primary enrolment included 98% of children in the relevant age-group; in the same year secondary enrolment included 88% of children in the relevant age-group. There were 10,024 teachers and 246,928 students in higher education in 2009/10. Education in Jordan was provided at 5,167 schools and 22 institutions of higher education in 2003/04. The budget for central Government spending in 2012 allocated JD 738.5m. (11.1% of total current expenditure) to education.

INDEX OF INTERNATIONAL ORGANIZATIONS

(Main reference only)

B

C

O

P

Y

Z